THE OVERSTREET® Comic Book PRICE GUIDE

41st Edition

COMICS FROM THE 1500s–PRESENT INCLUDED
FULLY ILLUSTRATED CATALOGUE
& EVALUATION GUIDE

by ROBERT M. OVERSTREET

GEMSTONE PUBLISHING

J.C. Vaughn, Associate Publisher & Executive Editor
Mark Huesman, Creative Director & Production Coordinator
Heather Winter, Office Manager

SPECIAL CONTRIBUTORS TO THIS EDITION

Robert Beerbohm • Dr. Arnold T. Blumberg • Brady Bonney • Nicky Wheeler-Nicholson Brown
Michael Eury • Gene Gonzales • Rob Hughes • Charlie Novinskie • Richard D. Olson, Ph.D. • J.C. Vaughn

SPECIAL ADVISORS TO THIS EDITION

Grant Adey • Bill Alexander • David Alexander • Tyler Alexander • Lon Allen • Dave Anderson
David J. Anderson, DDS • Matt Ballesteros • Stephen Barrington • L.E. Becker • Robert L. Beerbohm
Jim Berry • Jon Bevans • Peter J. Bilelis • Steve Borock • Michael Browning • Brett Carreras
Gary Colabuono • Frank Cwiklik • Gary Dolgoff • Walter Durajlija • Ken Dyber • Bruce Ellsworth
Richard Evans • D'Arcy Farrell • Dan Fogel • Steven Gentner • Steve Geppi • Andy Greenham • Eric Groves
Jason Hamlin • Mark Haspel • Brian Ketterer • Dennis Keum • Phil Levine • Paul Litch • Tommy Maletta
Keith Marlow • Jon McClure • Todd McDevitt • Mike McKenzie • Steve Mortensen • Jamie Newbold
Terry O'Neill • Jim Pitts • Bill Ponseti • Mick Rabin • Jeff Rader • Yolanda Ramirez • Greg Reece
Rob Reynolds • Barry Sandoval • Buddy Saunders • Conan Saunders • Doug Simpson • Ben Smith
Mark Squirek • Tony Starks • Al Stoltz • Doug Sulipa • Chris Swartz • Michael Tierney • Frank Verzyl
John Verzyl • Rose Verzyl • Mike Wilbur • Harley Yee • Mark Zaid • Vincent Zurzolo, Jr.

See a full list of Overstreet Advisors on pages 1104-1107

NOTICE: Values for items pictured in this book are based on author's experience, consultations with a network of advisors including collectors specializing in various categories, and actual prices realized for specific items sold through private sales and auctions. The values offered in this book are approximations influences by many factors including condition, rarity and demand, and they should serve as only guidelines, presenting an average range of what one might expect to pay for the items. In the marketplace, knowledge and opinions held by both sellers and buyers determine prices asked and prices paid. This is not a price list of items for sale or items wanted by the author or publisher. The author and the publisher shall not be held responsible for losses that may occur in the purchase, sale or other transaction of property because of information contained herein. Efforts have been made to present accurate information, but the possibility of error exists. Readers who believe that have discovered an error are invited to mail corrective information to the author, Robert M. Overstreet at Gemstone Publishing, 1966 Greenspring Drive, Timonium, MD 21093. Verified corrections will be incorporated into future editions of this book.

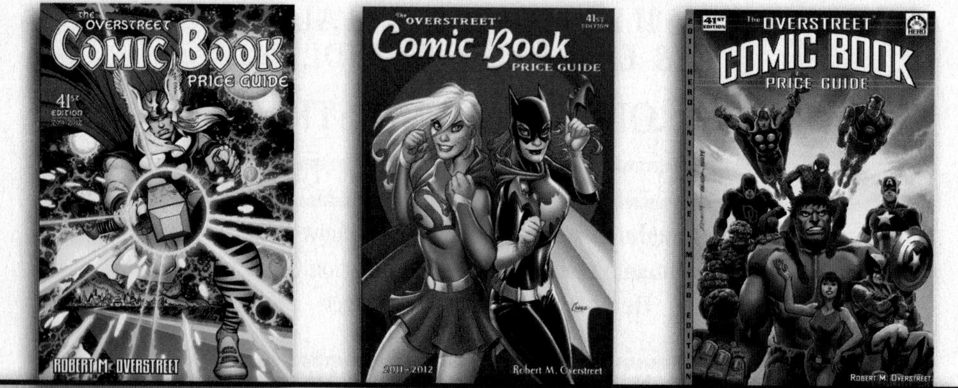

Thor Hardcover Edition ISBN: 978-1-60360-130-6
Thor Soft Cover Edition ISBN: 978-1-60360-131-3

Supergirl/Batgirl Hardcover Edition ISBN: 978-1-60360-132-0
Supergirl/Batgirl Soft Cover Edition ISBN: 978-1-60360-133-7

Marvel Heroes Hardcover Edition ISBN: 978-1-60360-134-4

Printed in the United States of America

10 9 8 7 6 5 4 3 2 1

Forty-First Edition: July 2011

TABLE OF CONTENTS

ACKNOWLEDGEMENTS

After last year's landmark 40th anniversary edition of *The Overstreet Comic Book Price Guide*, where could we go but onward into our fifth decade? As always, I would like to thank my wife, Caroline, for her support during this process.

For capturing the power and the energy of the character for our Thor cover, I don't think we could have done any better than definitive Thor artist Walter Simonson and color artist Laura Martin. Likewise, for the beauty, spirit and vitality of our Supergirl and Batgirl cover, artist Amanda Conner and color artist Paul Mounts were the perfect choices. Equally up to the task for our spectacular limited edition Marvel hardcover for The Hero Initiative were maestro John Romita, Sr., inker Tom Palmer, and color artist Dean White, who plied their crafts brilliantly for such a great cause. My personal and our collective thanks to all our cover artists, as well as to our "About This Book" artist Gene Gonzales.

Thanks as well go to our Mark Huesman and J.C. Vaughn, who this year not only produced the *Guide*, but also *The Overstreet Hall of Fame* special, an issue of *Comic Book Marketplace*, and *The Overstreet Guide To Collecting Comics* for Free Comic Book Day 2011 (and of course the weekly *Scoop* email newsletter).

Our new articles this year include contributions by Brady Bonney, Charlie Novinskie, Nicky Wheeler-Nicholson Brown, and Rob Hughes.

Special Thanks to the Overstreet Advisors who contributed to this edition, including Grant Adey, Bill Alexander, David Alexander, Tyler Alexander, Lon Allen, Dave Anderson, David J. Anderson, DDS, Matt Ballesteros, Stephen Barrington, L.E. Becker, Jim Berry, Jon Bevans, Peter J. Bilelis, Dr. Arnold T. Blumberg, Steve Borock, Michael Browning, Brett Carreras, Gary Colabuono, Jack Copley, Frank Cwiklik, Asher Densmore-Lynn, Peter Dixon, Gary Dolgoff, Walter Durajlija, Ken Dyber, Bruce Ellsworth, Richard Evans, D'Arcy Farrell, Dan Fogel, Steven Gentner, Steve Geppi, Andy Greenham, Eric Groves, Jim Halperin, Jason Hamlin, Mark Haspel, Ronnie Hayes, Brian Ketterer, Dennis Keum, Phil Levine, Paul Litch, Tommy Maletta, Keith Marlow, Jon McClure, Todd McDevitt, Mike McKenzie, Steve Mortensen, Jamie Newbold, Richard D. Olson, Ph.D., Terry O'Neill, Jim Pitts, Bill Ponseti, Mick Rabin, Jeff Rader, Yolanda Ramirez, Greg Reece, Rob Reynolds, Barry Sandoval, Buddy Saunders, Conan Saunders, Marc Sims, Doug Simpson, Ben Smith, Mark Squirek, Tony Starks, Al Stoltz, Doug Sulipa, Chris Swartz, Michael Tierney, Frank Verzyl, John Verzyl, Rose Verzyl, Eddie Wendt, Mike Wilbur, Harley Yee, Mark Zaid, Steve Zarelli and Vincent Zurzolo, Jr., as well as to our additional contributors, including Stephen Baer, Ron Ballard, Jonathan Calure, James Collet, Steven Dovas, Charles Herch, Ben Labonog, Jason Lohr, Rod Matlack, John Mlachnik, Bill Parker, James Pender and Dennis Petilli. Without their active participation, this project would not have been possible.

Additionally, I would like to personally extend my thanks to all of those who encouraged and supported first the creation of and then subsequently the expansion of the *Guide* over the past four decades. While it's impossible in this brief space to individually acknowledge every individual, mention is certainly due to Lon Allen (Golden Age data); Mark Arnold (Harvey data); Larry Bigman (Frazetta-Williamson data); Bill Blackbeard (Platinum Age cover photos); Steve Borock and Mark Haspel (Grading); Glenn Bray (Kurtzman data); Gary Carter (DC data); J. B. Clifford Jr. (EC data); Gary Coddington (Superman data); Gary Colabuono (Golden Age ashcan data); Wilt Conine (Fawcett data); Chris Cormier (Miracleman data); Dr. S. M. Davidson (Cupples & Leon data); Al Dellinges (Kubert data); Stephen Fishler (10-Point Grading system); Chris Friesen (Glossary additions); David Gerstein (Walt Disney Comics data); Gene Gonzales (introduction illustrations); Kevin Hancer (Tarzan data); Charles Heffelfinger and Jim Ivey (March of Comics listing); R. C. Holland and Ron Pussell (Seduction and Parade of Pleasure data); Grant Irwin (Quality data); Richard Kravitz (Kelly data); Phil Levine (giveaway data); Paul Litch (Copper & Modern Age data); Dan Malan & Charles Heffelfinger (Classic Comics data); Jon McClure (Whitman data); Fred Nardelli (Frazetta data); Michelle Nolan (Love comics); Mike Nolan (MLJ, Timely, Nedor data); George Olshevsky (Timely data); Dr. Richard Olson (Grading and Yellow Kid info); Chris Pedrin (DC War data); Scott Pell ('50s data); Greg Robertson (National data); Don Rosa (Late 1940s to 1950s data); Matt Schiffman (Bronze Age data); Frank Scigliano (Little Lulu data); Gene Seger (Buck Rogers data); Rick Sloane (Archie data); David R. Smith, Archivist, Walt Disney Productions (Disney data); Bill Spicer and Zetta DeVoe (Western Publishing Co. data); Tony Starks (Silver and Bronze Age data); Al Stoltz (Golden Age & Promo data); Doug Sulipa (Bronze Age data); Don and Maggie Thompson (Four Color listing); Mike Tiefenbacher & Jerry Sinkovec (Atlas and National data); Raymond True & Philip J. Gaudino (Classic Comics data); Jim Vadeboncoeur Jr. (Williamson and Atlas data); Richard Samuel West (Victorian Age and Platinum Age data); Kim Weston (Disney and Barks data); Cat Yronwode (Spirit data); Andrew Zerbe and Gary Behymer (M. E. data).

Finally, thanks, as always, to our advertisers, whose support makes this project possible, and to all of you who have purchased this edition.

my
comicshop.com

webuy
comics.com

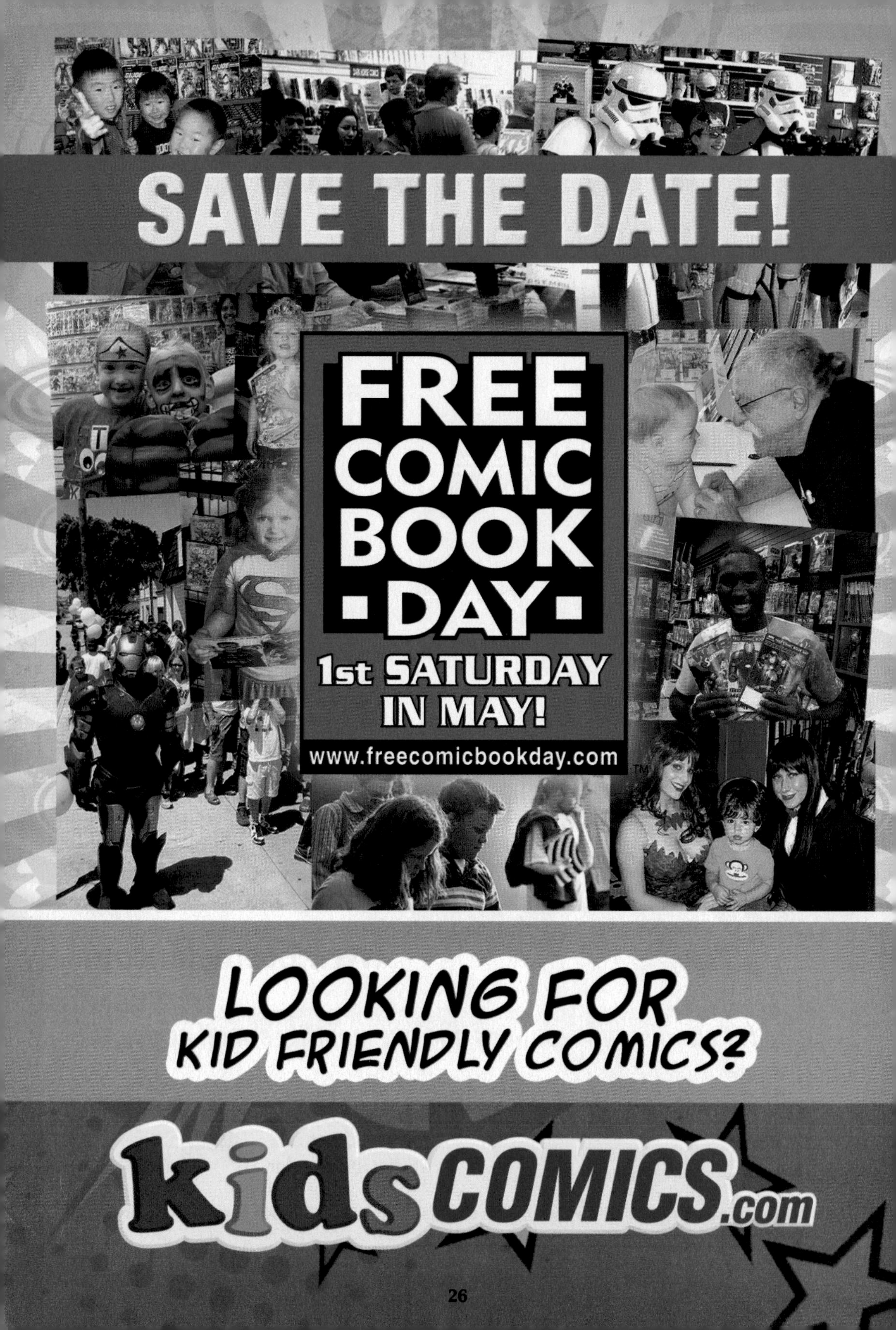

ROGER LANGRIDGE'S
SNARKED!
ALL NEW ORIGINAL STORY!
GET ISSUE #0 THIS AUGUST!
BUY ISSUE #1 THIS OCTOBER!
INTRODUCTORY #0 ISSUE
for ONLY $1
kaboom!
FROM THE MUPPET SHOW'S HARVEY AWARD WINNER ROGER LANGRIDGE
THE MOST ANTICIPATED SERIES OF 2011 IS HERE!

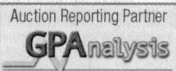

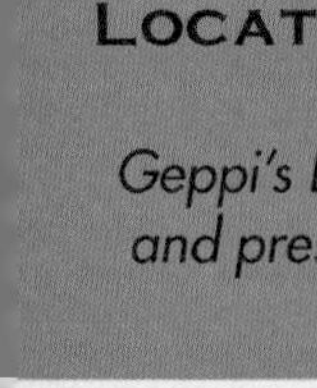

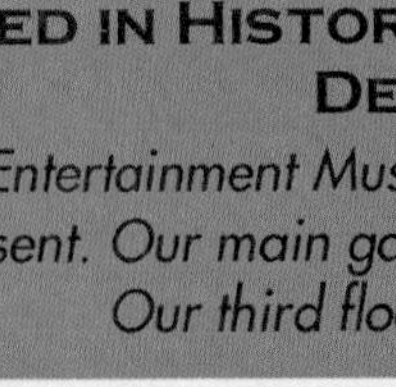

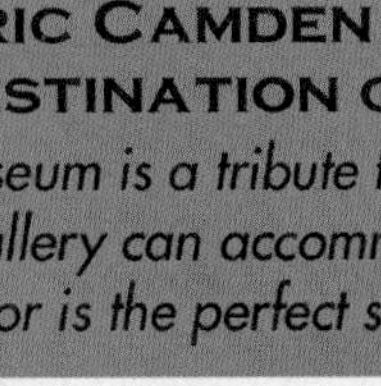

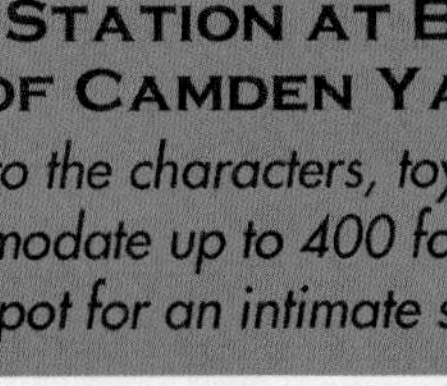

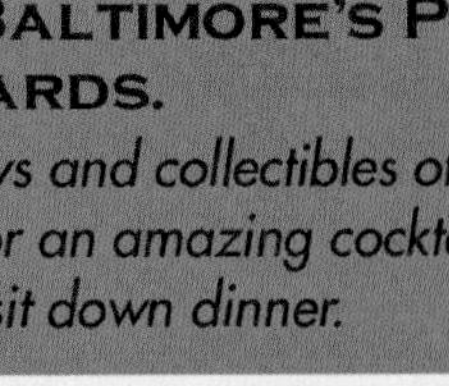

WORLDWIDE COMICS

The nation's largest dealer of vintage CGC comic books!

We focus our inventory on the rarest, most sought-after comic books in the marketplace today, including Silver and Bronze Age comics in 9.4 to 9.8, classic Golden Age covers and key issues, and pedigreed comics. Our tireless search brings you an endless supply of high quality material, listed in our "new arrivals" section of wwcomics.com almost every day.

Unlike auction houses that tend to favor the consignor, especially when bidders run prices up to nosebleed levels, we offer a set price for our comics. Consider us old school! We will also negotiate with you on the price of many comics listed on wwcomics.com for more than 30 days.

MATT NELSON AND STEPHEN RITTER, CO-OWNERS

Whether you're looking for Timelys in 9.4, Mile Highs, a solid Amazing Fantasy #15 for your collection, or a CGC 9.8 run of Iron Fist, wwcomics.com is the place to find it all.

972-345-2505 • 1440 Halsey Way, Suite #110 • Carrollton, TX 75007 • wwcomics.com

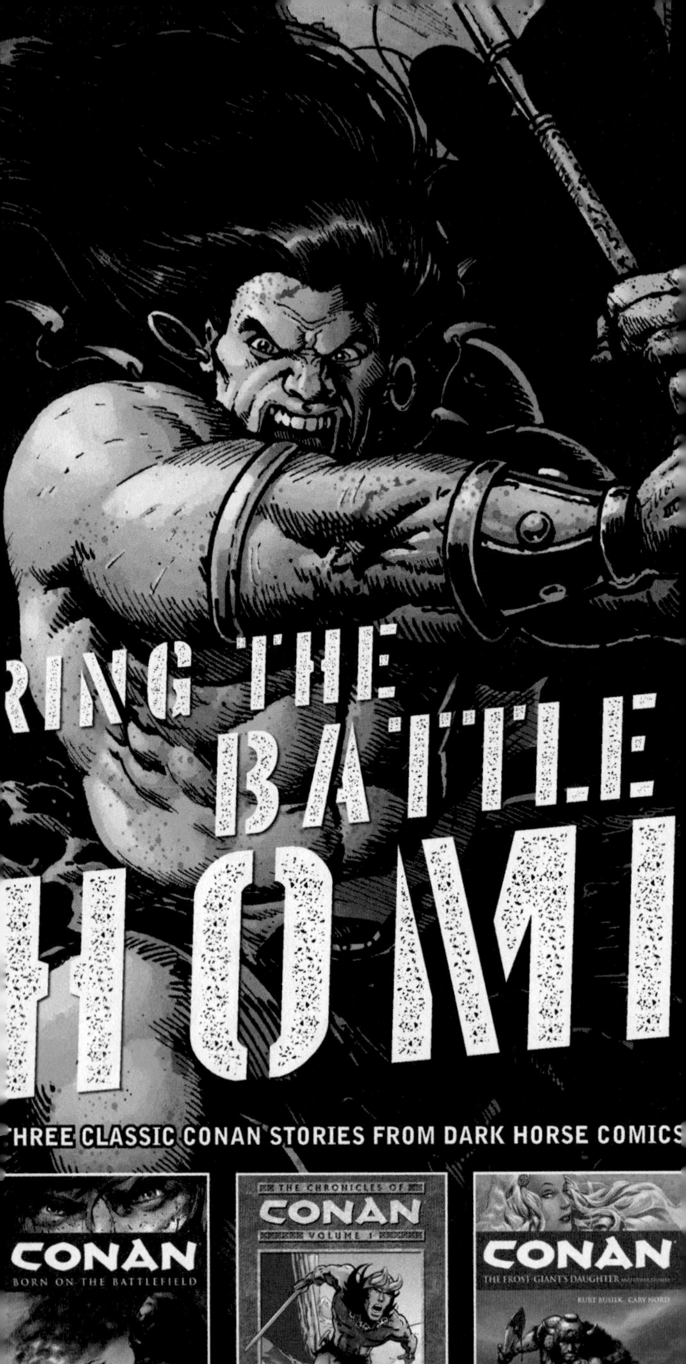

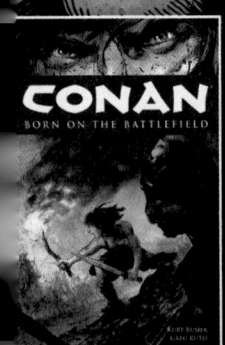

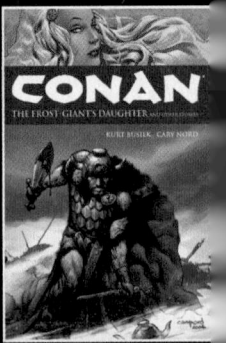

Love The Darkness comic you just read, but not sure where to get more or where to start? We've got you covered with this Guide to The Darkness trade paperback collections. ~Moo.

The Darkness: Origins

For the reader who wants to go back to the beginning!

•••••

The Darkness: Origins
Volume 1 trade paperback
Collects *The Darkness* issues #1-#6
$12.99, ISBN: 978-1-60706-097-0

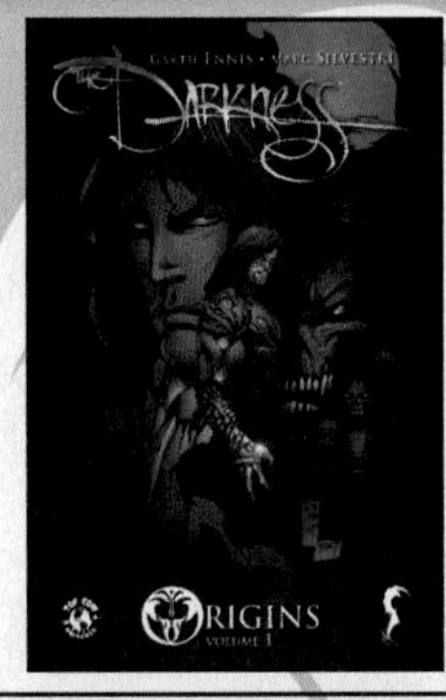

The Darkness: Origins Volume 2 trade paperback
Collects The Darkness issues #7-#10
plus Witchblade issues #18-#19
$14.99, ISBN: 978-1-60706-103-8

The Darkness: Origins Volume 3 trade paperback
Collects The Darkness issues #11-#18
$19.99, ISBN: 978-1-60706-208-0

More The Darkness: Origins trade paperback volumes on their way in 2011!

The Darkness: Accursed

For the gamer who's played The Darkness video game!

•••••

The Darkness: Accursed
Volume 1 trade paperback
Collects The Darkness issues #65-#70
$9.99, ISBN: 978-1-60706-958-0

The Darkness: Accursed Volume 2 trade paperback
Collects The Darkness issues #71-#75
$9.99, ISBN: 978-1-60706-044-4

The Darkness: Accursed Volume 3 trade paperback
Collects The Darkness issues #76-#79
plus The Darkness: Lodbrok's Hand
$12.99, ISBN: 978-1-60706-100-7

The Darkness: Accursed Volume 4 trade paperback
Collects The Darkness issues #80-#84
$14.99, ISBN: 978-1-60706-194-6

More The Darkness: Accursed trade paperback volumes on their way in 2011!

The Darkness: Compendium

For the collector who wants it all!

•••••

The Darkness: Compendium
Volume 1 soft cover
Collects The Darkness issues #1-#40
plus special bonus issues
$59.99, ISBN: 978-1-58240-643-5

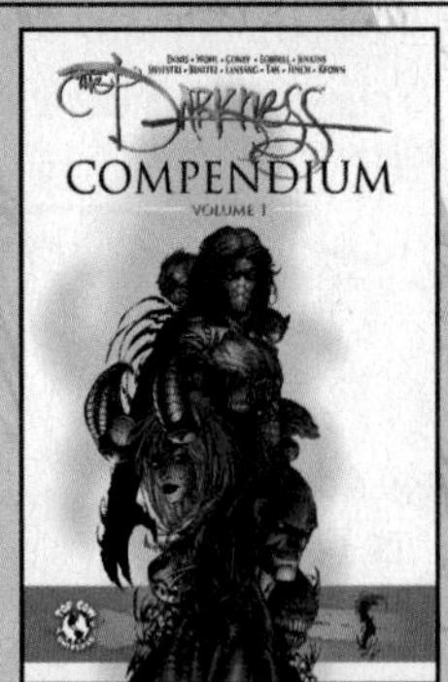

A new The Darkness Compendium soft cover will be released in 2011!!

CGC UNIVERSAL GRADE
9.2
12¢
the AMAZING SPIDER-MAN
2 GREAT FEATURE-LENGTH SPIDER-MAN THRILLERS!
THE FANTASTIC FOUR THINK I'M TRAPPED! BUT THEY DON'T SUSPECT MY REAL POWER!
EXTRA ADDED ATTRACTION: SPIDER-MAN MEETS THE FANTASTIC FOUR, AS
"the CHAMELEON STRIKES!"

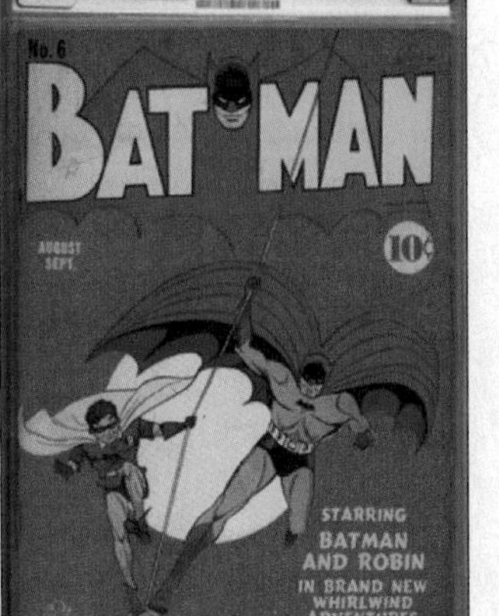
CGC UNIVERSAL GRADE
8.5
No. 6
BATMAN
AUGUST SEPT.
10¢
STARRING BATMAN AND ROBIN IN BRAND NEW WHIRLWIND ADVENTURES

now in TECHNICOLOR
WALT DISNEY'S
MICKEY MOUSE
Released thru UNITED ARTISTS

Overstreet Advisor
20 Years Experience
CGC Member Dealer
GREG REECE'S
RARE COMICS

the AMAZING SPIDER-MAN
the CHAMELEON STRIKES!
JOURNEY INTO MYSTERY
THOR
SHOWCASE
GREEN LANTERN
BATMAN
No. 1
SPRING ISSUE
10¢
ALL BRAND NEW ADVENTURES OF THE BATMAN AND ROBIN, THE BOY WONDER!
COMICS
SUPERMAN

NEW FOR 2011! TRIPWIRE #55

"Best mag of its kind I've ever seen." – Michael Moorcock, fantasy legend

"Tripwire is essential reading – one of the best on the market!" –Mark Verheiden, writer, BATTLESTAR GALACTICA, HEROES, FALLING SKIES

"I always read TRIPWIRE cover to cover!!" – Guillermo del Toro, director, HELLBOY and PAN'S LABYRINTH

TRIPWIRE might be the best franchise culture magazine going today." – STEVEN GRANT, comicbookresources

• Celebrate 50 years of Elric! TRIPWIRE interviews Michael Moorcock about the character and his return to comics with BOOM!

• It's the golden anniversary of the first family in comics! We talk Fantastic Four with some creators who helped shape FF history.

• DC's Green Lantern explodes onto the big screen and we delve into the character from the Golden Age to the present.

• Shaenon Garrity, creator of Narbonic and Skin Horse, explores webcomics from an insider's perspective.

• Bone hits 20 this year! So does Viz Entertainment! We look at both.

• TRIPWIRE's comic anthology STRIPWIRE returns with 20+ pages of strips and stories.

And there's so much more! 124 pages at $9.99 US ($10.95 CAN, £6.95 UK)

Now you can download our bi-monthly digital TRIPWIRE magazine for free! www.tripwire-magazine.com

HERITAGE
284 PAGES of ACTION!
HERITAGE
Comics & Comic Art Auction
February 25-27, 2010 | Dallas, Texas
10¢
CGC UNIVERSAL GRADE
Detective Comics #27
D.C. Comics, 5/39
8.0
OFF-WHITE TO WHITE Pages
0700757001
1st appearance of Batman (Bruce Wayne) and Commissioner James "Jim" Gordon.
MAY, 1939
64 PAGES OF ACTION!
No. 27
Detective COMICS
10¢
STARTING THIS ISSUE: THE AMAZING AND UNIQUE ADVENTURES OF THE BATMAN!
PR Newswire
MultiVu
Most valuable comic ever offered publicly, Feb. 25 at Heritage Auctions (HA.com)
www.prnewswire.com
Detective COMICS
europa cafe
at&t
SOLD FOR
$1,075,500
HIGHEST AUCTION PRICE EVER PAID FOR A COMIC BOOK!

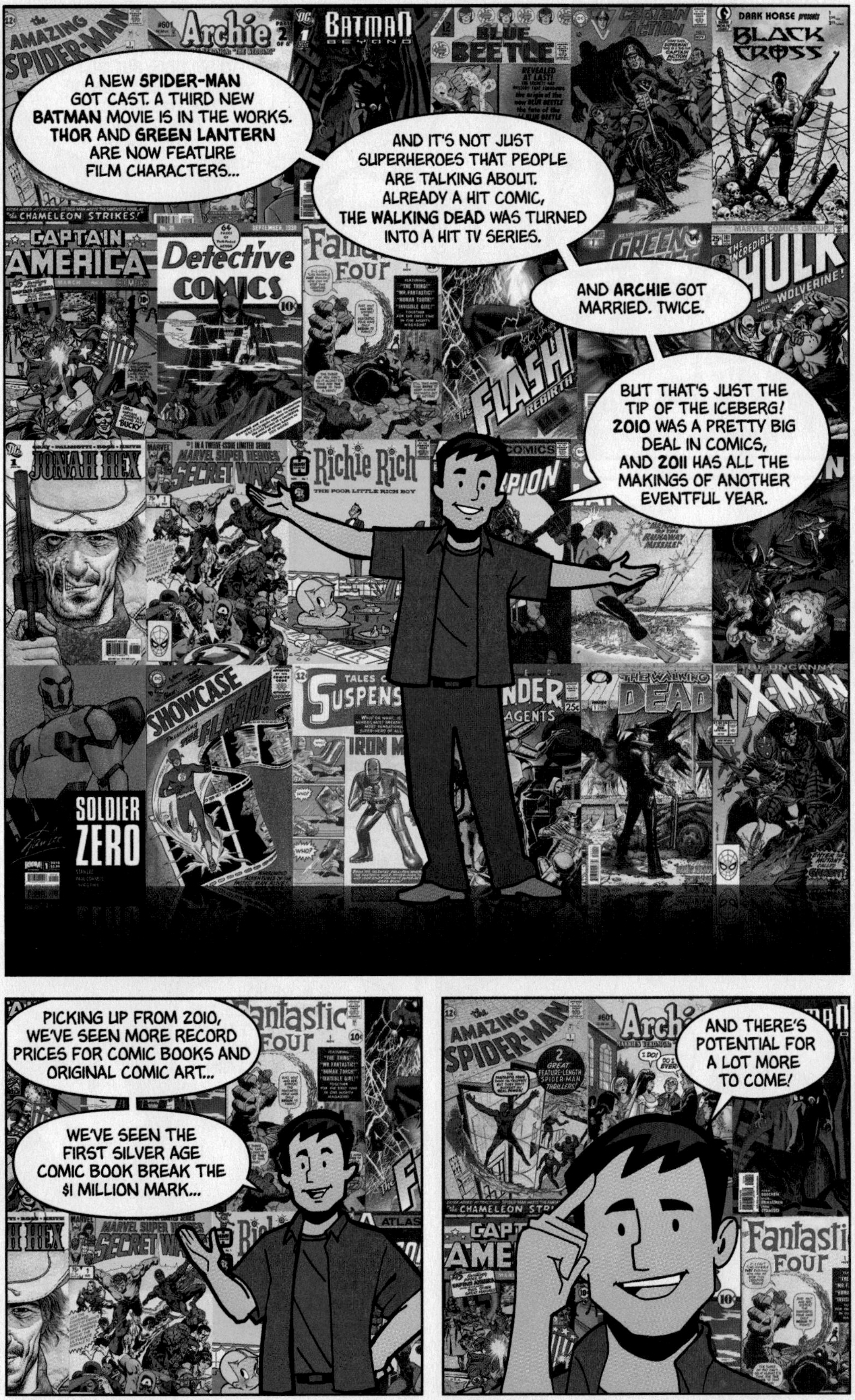

A NEW SPIDER-MAN GOT CAST. A THIRD NEW BATMAN MOVIE IS IN THE WORKS. THOR AND GREEN LANTERN ARE NOW FEATURE FILM CHARACTERS...

AND IT'S NOT JUST SUPERHEROES THAT PEOPLE ARE TALKING ABOUT. ALREADY A HIT COMIC, THE WALKING DEAD WAS TURNED INTO A HIT TV SERIES.

AND ARCHIE GOT MARRIED. TWICE.

BUT THAT'S JUST THE TIP OF THE ICEBERG! 2010 WAS A PRETTY BIG DEAL IN COMICS, AND 2011 HAS ALL THE MAKINGS OF ANOTHER EVENTFUL YEAR.

PICKING UP FROM 2010, WE'VE SEEN MORE RECORD PRICES FOR COMIC BOOKS AND ORIGINAL COMIC ART...
WE'VE SEEN THE FIRST SILVER AGE COMIC BOOK BREAK THE $1 MILLION MARK...

AND THERE'S POTENTIAL FOR A LOT MORE TO COME!

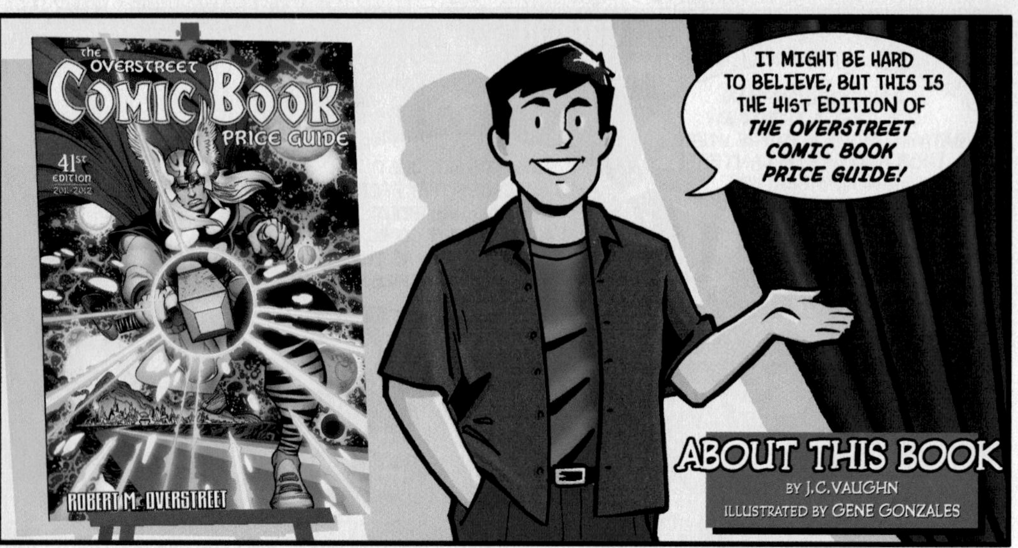
THE OVERSTREET
COMIC BOOK
PRICE GUIDE
41ST EDITION
2011-2012
ROBERT M. OVERSTREET
IT MIGHT BE HARD TO BELIEVE, BUT THIS IS THE 41ST EDITION OF *THE OVERSTREET COMIC BOOK PRICE GUIDE!*
ABOUT THIS BOOK
BY J.C. VAUGHN
ILLUSTRATED BY GENE GONZALES

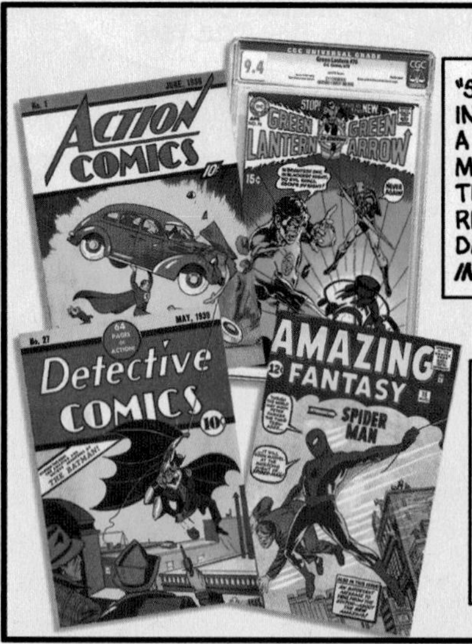
ACTION COMICS
GREEN LANTERN GREEN ARROW
DETECTIVE COMICS
AMAZING FANTASY
SPIDER MAN

"SINCE THE *GUIDE*'S DEBUT IN 1970, THERE HAVE BEEN A LOT OF CHANGES IN THE MARKETPLACE. FOR INSTANCE, THERE HAVE ALWAYS BEEN RECORD PRICES, BUT THESE DAYS THEY CAN MAKE ***INTERNATIONAL NEWS...***"

"WHEN YOU KEEP UP WITH ***RECORD PRICES***, WHAT'S ***SELLING***, WHAT'S ***NOT*** SELLING, AND WHAT'S SUDDENLY ***IN DEMAND***, IT HELPS YOU KNOW WHAT YOU SHOULD BE WILLING TO PAY OR WHEN TO SELL."

WOLVERINE
A MARVEL COMICS LIMITED SERIES
Buffy
THE TRANSFORMERS
Comico
Primer
GRENDEL

AND THERE HAVE BEEN LOTS OF OTHER CHANGES, TOO. WE'VE BEEN STUDYING THIS FOR ***FOUR DECADES*** NOW AND ONE THING IS REALLY CLEAR...

THE MORE YOU ***KNOW*** ABOUT COMICS, THE MORE YOU ***WANT*** TO KNOW. AND WE'VE BEEN HAPPY TO HELP PEOPLE LEARN FOR ***41 YEARS.***

ONE OF THE COOL THINGS ABOUT COMIC BOOKS IS THAT THERE ARE LOTS OF NEW ONES TO DISCOVER...

AND THERE ARE LITERALLY HUNDREDS OF THOUSANDS OF DIFFERENT BACK ISSUES, TOO!

BACK ISSUE COMICS RANGE FROM LESS THAN COVER PRICE TO *$1,500,000.*
A COMIC BOOK FOR *$1.5 MILLION?* HARD TO BELIEVE, HUH?

THE FIRST COMIC TO HIT $1 MILLION WAS *ACTION COMICS* #1, THE FIRST APPEARANCE OF *SUPERMAN.*
THE SECOND, JUST A FEW DAYS LATER, WAS *DETECTIVE COMICS* #27, THE FIRST APPEARANCE OF *BATMAN.*
ANOTHER ACTION #1 SOLD FOR *$1.5 MILLION* JUST A SHORT WHILE AFTER THAT.

MANY OTHERS HAVE SOLD FOR RECORD PRICES IN THE LAST YEAR OR SO, EVEN WITH THE TOUGH ECONOMY NATIONALLY.

THE GRADE AND SCARCITY OF THE ISSUES HAVE A LOT TO DO WITH THAT. WE'LL GET INTO THAT IN JUST A BIT...

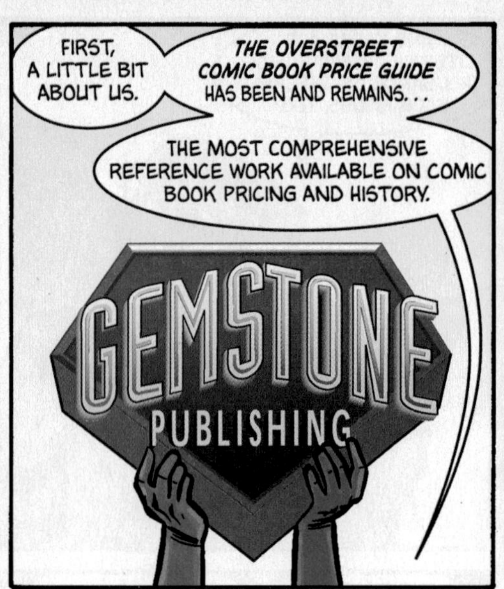

FIRST, A LITTLE BIT ABOUT US.
THE OVERSTREET COMIC BOOK PRICE GUIDE HAS BEEN AND REMAINS. . .
THE MOST COMPREHENSIVE REFERENCE WORK AVAILABLE ON COMIC BOOK PRICING AND HISTORY.
GEMSTONE
PUBLISHING

IT'S RESPECTED AND USED BY DEALERS AND COLLECTORS EVERYWHERE.
OVERSTREET PRICING AND GRADING STANDARDS ARE THE ACCEPTED FOUNDATIONS OF THE COMIC BOOK MARKETPLACE AROUND THE WORLD.
THROUGH HARD WORK, DILIGENCE AND CONSTANT CONTACT WITH THE MARKET FOR DECADES, OVERSTREET HAS BECOME THE MOST TRUSTED NAME IN COMICS.

OUR BOOK IS A DETAILED ALPHABETICAL LIST OF COMIC BOOKS AND THEIR MARKET VALUES.

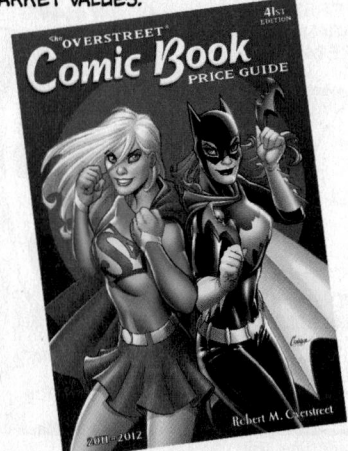

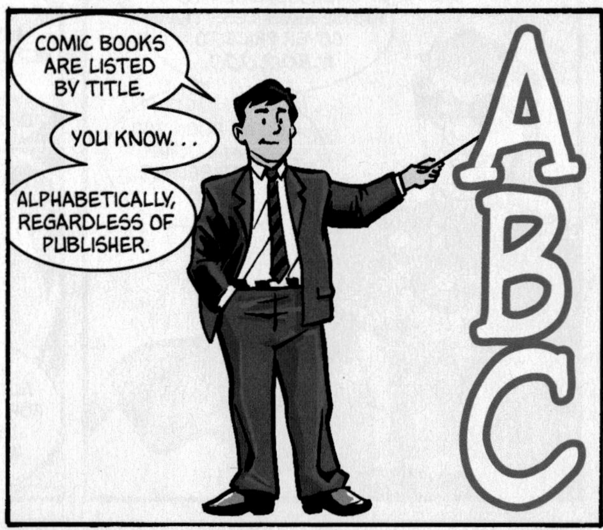

COMIC BOOKS ARE LISTED BY TITLE.
YOU KNOW. . .
ALPHABETICALLY, REGARDLESS OF PUBLISHER.
A
B
C

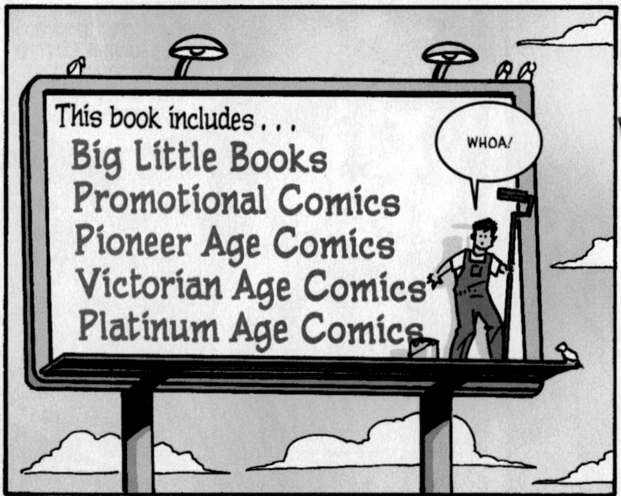

This book includes . . .
Big Little Books
Promotional Comics
Pioneer Age Comics
Victorian Age Comics
Platinum Age Comics
WHOA!

THE MAIN PRICING SECTION FEATURES COMICS FROM 1938 THROUGH THE PRESENT!

9.2
9.0
8.5
8.0
7.5
7.0
6.5
6.0
5.5
5.0
4.5
4.0
3.5
3.0
2.5
2.0

PRICES ARE LISTED IN SIX GRADES, RANGING FROM 2.0 TO 9.2 ON A 10.0 SCALE.

THERE ARE MORE GRADES THAN THE SIX WE HAVE LISTED, BUT THESE WILL GIVE YOU THE KEYS TO UNDERSTANDING THE MARKET.

WHILE PRICES BELOW 9.2 ARE FAIRLY STEADY, IT'S IMPORTANT TO NOTE THAT PRICES ABOVE 9.2 ARE FREQUENTLY CONSIDERED EXTREMELY VOLATILE.

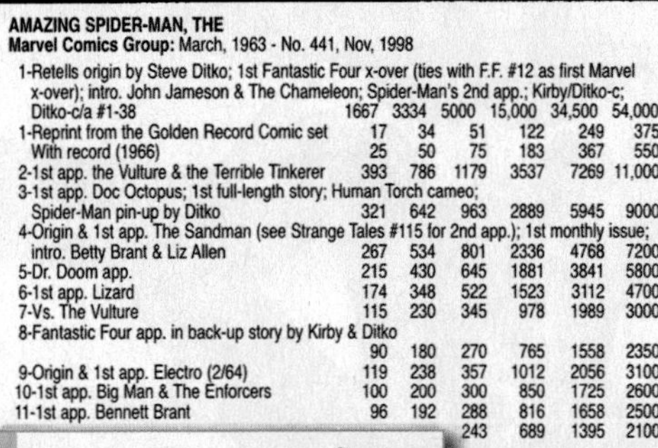

AMAZING SPIDER-MAN, THE
Marvel Comics Group: March, 1963 - No. 441, Nov, 1998

1-Retells origin by Steve Ditko; 1st Fantastic Four x-over (ties with F.F. #12 as first Marvel x-over); intro. John Jameson & The Chameleon; Spider-Man's 2nd app.; Kirby/Ditko-c; Ditko-c/a #1-38	1667	3334	5000	15,000	34,500	54,000
1-Reprint from the Golden Record Comic set	17	34	51	122	249	375
With record (1966)	25	50	75	183	367	550
2-1st app. the Vulture & the Terrible Tinkerer	393	786	1179	3537	7269	11,000
3-1st app. Doc Octopus; 1st full-length story; Human Torch cameo; Spider-Man pin-up by Ditko	321	642	963	2889	5945	9000
4-Origin & 1st app. The Sandman (see Strange Tales #115 for 2nd app.); 1st monthly issue; intro. Betty Brant & Liz Allen	267	534	801	2336	4768	7200
5-Dr. Doom app.	215	430	645	1881	3841	5800
6-1st app. Lizard	174	348	522	1523	3112	4700
7-Vs. The Vulture	115	230	345	978	1989	3000
8-Fantastic Four app. in back-up story by Kirby & Ditko	90	180	270	765	1558	2350
9-Origin & 1st app. Electro (2/64)	119	238	357	1012	2056	3100
10-1st app. Big Man & The Enforcers	100	200	300	850	1725	2600
11-1st app. Bennett Brant	96	192	288	816	1658	2500
			243	689	1395	2100

- Many of the comic books are listed in groups, such as 11-20, 21-30, 31-50 and so on.
- The prices listed along with such groupings represent the value of each issue in that group, not the group as a whole.
- It's difficult to overstate how much accurate grading plays into getting a good price for your sales or purchases.

THE DEFINITIVE GUIDE TO GRADING COMIC BOOKS!
OFFICIAL
OVERSTREET® COMIC BOOK GRADING GUIDE
THIRD EDITION
FEATURING THE 10 POINT GRADING SYSTEM
ROBERT M. OVERSTREET AND DR. ARNOLD T. BLUMBERG
HOUSE OF COLLECTIBLES
It's a good practice to develop relationships with dealers and other collectors who prove themselves trustworthy.
MANY PEOPLE HAVE STARTED USING INDEPENDENT, THIRD-PARTY GRADING SERVICES, SUCH AS CGC.
HEY, SOMEONE TOOK A BITE OUT OF THIS COMIC!

THE BEST PART IS THERE ARE MANY DIFFERENT WAYS TO COLLECT.

YOU CAN CHOOSE TO FOLLOW INDIVIDUAL PUBLISHERS, WRITERS, ARTISTS, CHARACTERS...

YOU CAN COLLECT SUPERHEROES, WAR COMICS, WESTERNS, ROMANCE OR WHATEVER YOU LIKE...

YOU CAN CHOOSE #1 ISSUES, FIRST APPEARANCES, CROSSOVERS, OR MANY OTHER VARIATIONS.

THE BEST THING TO COLLECT IS WHAT YOU LIKE, NOT WHAT SOMEONE ELSE LIKES.

WHETHER IT'S SPIDER-MAN OR EVERY COMIC THAT CAME OUT THE MONTH YOU WERE BORN, IT'S BEST TO DO IT WITH A PLAN.

THE BEST WAY TO HAVE A GOOD PLAN IS TO FIRST GET INFORMED.

THE BEST WAY TO GET INFORMED IS TO GO TO THE EXPERTS!
CAN'T I SAY "OR ELSE!" AFTER THAT?

LEARN THE INS AND OUTS OF COLLECTING, INCLUDING HOW TO TAKE CARE OF YOUR COLLECTION!

Learn how to grade your comics and why the grades make a difference!_

LEARN WHAT TO EXPECT AT CONVENTIONS OR WHEN BUYING AND SELLING COMICS.
AND MAYBE HOW TO FIGHT ZOMBIES...

IT'S ALSO IMPORTANT TO REMEMBER THAT THIS BOOK IS A GUIDE, NOT A DEALER'S PRICE LIST. THE MARKET SETS THE PRICES.

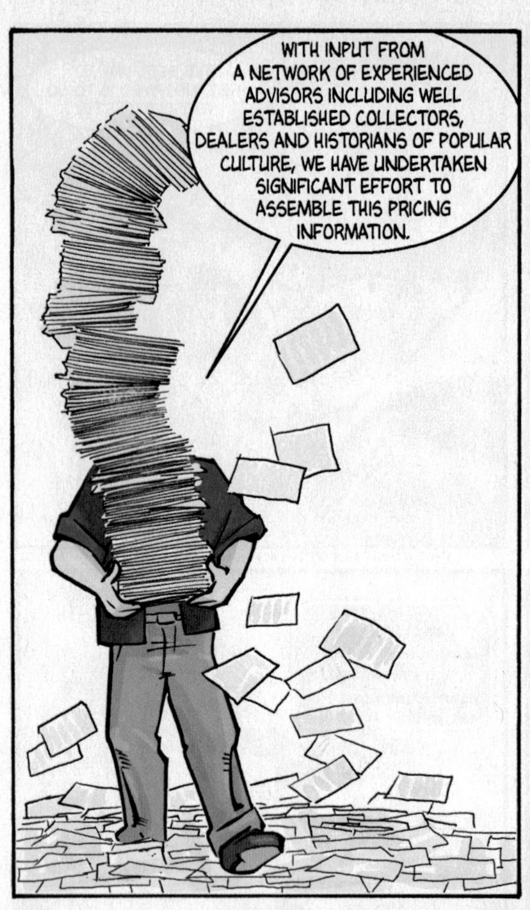
WITH INPUT FROM A NETWORK OF EXPERIENCED ADVISORS INCLUDING WELL ESTABLISHED COLLECTORS, DEALERS AND HISTORIANS OF POPULAR CULTURE, WE HAVE UNDERTAKEN SIGNIFICANT EFFORT TO ASSEMBLE THIS PRICING INFORMATION.

THE RESULTING LISTINGS COME THROUGH THE OBSERVATION AND DOCUMENTATION OF PRICES REALIZED THROUGH HOBBY AND TRADE SHOWS, CATALOG SALES, RETAIL SALES, AND INTERNET, LIVE AND MAIL-IN AUCTIONS. DOCUMENTED PERSONAL SALES MAY ALSO BE INCLUDED.

WE HAVE EARNED OUR REPUTATION FOR OUR CAUTIOUS, CONSERVATIVE APPROACH TO PRICING.

WE ACTIVELY ENCOURAGE READERS WHO BELIEVE THEY HAVE DISCOVERED AN ERROR TO MAIL RELATED INFORMATION TO THE AUTHOR.
WRITE TO: ROBERT M. OVERSTREET GEMSTONE PUBLISHING, INC. 1966 GREENSPRING DRIVE TIMONIUM, MD 21093
OR EMAIL FEEDBACK@GEMSTONEPUB.COM
VERIFIED CORRECTIONS WILL BE INCORPORATED INTO FUTURE EDITIONS OF THIS BOOK.
Editor's note: For more updates, visit *Scoop* at http://scoop.diamondgalleries.com.

OVERSTREET MARKET REPORT 2011

FOLLOWING RECENT RECORD-SETTING GOLDEN AGE SALES, IT WAS SILVER'S TURN TO SHINE

by Robert M. Overstreet

This CGC-certified 9.6 copy of ***Amazing Fantasy*** *#15 broke the $1 million barrier with a record-setting sale at $1,100,00. Also impressive were sales of this CGC-certified 9.4 copy of* ***Tales of Suspense*** *#39 for $147,500 and this CGC-certified 9.6 copy of* ***X-Men*** *#1 bringing $200,000.*

SILVER AGE KEYS SET RECORDS: The Silver Age saw its first $1 million comic when a CGC-certified 9.6 copy of *Amazing Fantasy* #15 sold for a record $1,100,000. A CGC 9.0 sold for $150,000; *Amazing Spider-Man* #1 in CGC 8.5 sold for $28,680; *Avengers* #1 in CGC 9.4 went for $100,000, #4 in CGC 9.4 brought $22,705; *Brave & the Bold* #28 in CGC 9.0 realized $31,700; *Fantastic Four* #1 in CGC 9.4 went for $300,000, and a CGC 8.0 copy sold for $47,800; *Green Lantern* #1 in CGC 9.2 went for $16,730. *Incredible Hulk* #181 in CGC 9.9 brought $150,000. *Iron Man* #1 in CC 9.6 brought $3,883.75. *Sgt. Fury* in CGC 9.0 went for $10,157.50; *Tales of Suspense* #39 in CGC 9.4 sold for $147,500 with a CGC 9.2 also selling for $49,750; and *X-Men* #1 in CGC 9.6 got $200,000.

While the demand for scarce, high grade copies of key comics shows no signs of ebbing, after the $1,000,000+ sales that occurred in the first quarter of 2010, record prices were also realized for lower grade copies of rare, vintage comic books.

A CGC-certified 5.0 copy of *Action Comics* #1 went for $436,000, while a CGC 3.0 sold for $300,000. *Action Comics* #7 in CGC 7.0 brought $175,000. *All Negro* #1 in CGC 3.0 brought $5,377.50. *Archie Comics* #1 in CGC 5.0 sold for $34,000, in CGC 8.5 sold for $167,300! *Batman* #1 in CGC 5.5 sold for $55,268.75; in CGC 3.0 brought $26,290, a #3 in CGC 9.4 sold for $32,265. *Detective Comics* #27 in CGC grade 7.5 sold for $657,250 and another copy in CGC 7.0 brought $492,937.50. Also a CGC 6.0 sold for $575,000 and a CGC 3.5 brought $240,000! A *Flash Comics* #2 in CGC 9.4 sold for $49,331.25, Mile High copy. *Looney Tunes* #1 in CGC 9.2 sold for $38,837.50. *Marvel Comics* #1 in CGC 6.0 sold for $71,700, in CGC 4.0 brought $38,837.50; a *Marvel Mystery* #9 in CGC 6.0, Larson pedigree, sold for $22,705, #46 in CGC 8.5 sold for $9,560. *More Fun* #52 in CGC 6.0 went for $28,680. A *Pep Comics* #22 in CGC 5.0 sold for $50,000. A *Superman* #1 in CGC 4.5 went for $90,000, #2 in CGC 9.2 sold for $85,000, #24 in CGC 9.4 sold for $41,825. *Suspense Comics* #3 in CGC 5.5 brought $15,535. *Terry-Toons* #1 in CGC 9.0 sold for $3585.

In looking back, the collapse of the U.S. housing bubble, which peaked in the fall of 2005, caused the stock market and other financial markets to plummet. The Dow Jones Industrial Average fell over a 17 month period from a high of 14,164 (reached on October 9th 2007) to a low of 6,469 (in March 2009).

Since that time, the stock market has recovered most of its losses passing 12,000 early this year. As unemployment remained around 9% officially (the real number is estimated by many to be double that) throughout 2010 into 2011, the economy stayed sluggish with businesses continuing to close or go bankrupt and housing continuing to lose value. However, during this same period, gold, silver, copper and other commodity prices boomed.

For the past three years, interest paid from CDs and other financial investments have been extremely low. With the declining value of the dollar, everyone's savings continue to shrink. However, among the best places to invest today are the collectibles fields including comic books. Comic book sales continued to show record prices paid for key rare, vintage issues in both the Golden Age and Silver Age periods resulting in numerous price increases in this edition. At the same time, second tier books continue to sell at and below *Guide* levels, and some cases prices had to be reduced to bring this edition more in line with the current market.

Even before their record-setting May 2011 sale of Frank Miller and Klaus Janson's Page 10 of *Batman: The Dark Knight Returns* #3 for $448,125 made everyone take notice, Heritage reported comic sales of $23,077,321 in 2010 with an additional $14,454,281 in comic illustrated art. This auction company has been very successful in marketing comic book investing to their large customer base which introduces comics to other markets they reach such as coins, art, fossils, minerals and Indian artifacts.

Metropolis reported 2010 as their best year in sales to date. Selling the two copies of *Action Comics* #1 through their sister company ComicConnect.com, for a $1 million and $1.5 million, brought them – and the industry as a whole – a lot of publicity (See their market report for other record sales of Gold and Silver keys). As Vincent Zurzolo, Jr. states "As evidenced by these sales, you can see that the vintage comic book market is strong. Key Golden and Silver Age comics are doing very well." and he also writes, "More common late Silver and Bronze Age issues have seen a reduction in price," adding "with more high grade issues coming into the market place, it will take some time for demand to catch up and prices to rebound."

Eric Groves in referring to the $1,500,000 dollar sale, wrote, "That sale, and others, verified the intrinsic value of the comic book as a genuine American artifact." He continues, "It also demonstrated that even in difficult economic times, the high end items still sell – to those who can afford them. In wrapping up, he states "Economists may say the recession is over, but high unemployment persists. Disposable income is down and to some extent, the Age of Frugality is upon us. There is a bright side for collectors in that bargains abound. It is a good time to buy." Not only did high grade copies of the Golden Age keys sell for record prices, they also brought record prices in low grade. A few examples to report are: An *Action* #7 in CGC 3.0 sold for $20,315, in CGC 1.8 brought $116,000 and in CGC 5.0 went for $465,000. A *Batman* #1 in CGC 2.0 auctioned off at $23,302 and a 1.0 brought $14,340! A *Detective* #27 in CGC 3.5 sold for $240,000. *Detective* #31 in CGC 2.5 sold for $14,340! A *Marvel Mystery* #9 in CGC 2.5 sold for $7767. A *Superman* #1 in CGC 1.8 for $28,000! As you can see, demand for these top key books in any grade couldn't be higher.

Buddy Saunders wrote, "I've been both surprised and pleased at the strength the comic market displayed in 2010. With so much of the economy down and unemployment high, comics held strong. Our stores enjoyed modest sales increases, and our website experienced its best year yet."

We have seen an upsurge in demand for many Silver Age books throughout 2010.

Harley Yee reported, "The 2010 market continued many trends from 2009 with high grade Marvels and Marvel keys being the top sellers." He continued, "Early Archie stuff has always been scarce, but recently has seen a surge in prices with early *Pep* issues setting record prices." And that's not even mentioning the six-figure sale of an *Archie* #1 in February 2011.

Dave Alexander wrote, "Silver Age has become the most popular time period for collecting," and added "The top Marvel titles are still the top Marvel titles and the high grade copies of *Amazing Spider-Man* that have sold in the six-figure range have provided additional

© DC

Original art also set records as Frank Miller and Klaus Janson's Page 10 from **Batman: The Dark Knight Returns #3** soared above pre-auction expectations with a final price of $448,125.

© DC

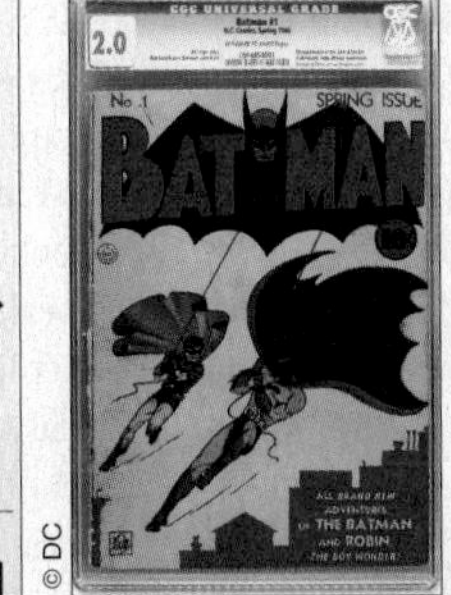

Low grade Golden Age enjoyed strong sales, as evidenced by a CGC-certified 3.0 copy of **Action Comics #7** selling for $20,315. A **Batman #1** with a CGC-certified grade of 2.0 brought $23,302.

positive publicity for the hobby."

For Golden Age books, he said, "Timely titles have hit high levels and are hard to find. Superman and Batman titles have the highest demand," and also said, "The big growth area is in Romance titles. We have located about 3,000 Romance issues in the last year. Many Romance books sell for huge multiples of *Guide* values. Certain icon covers go for 10-20x *Guide* prices."

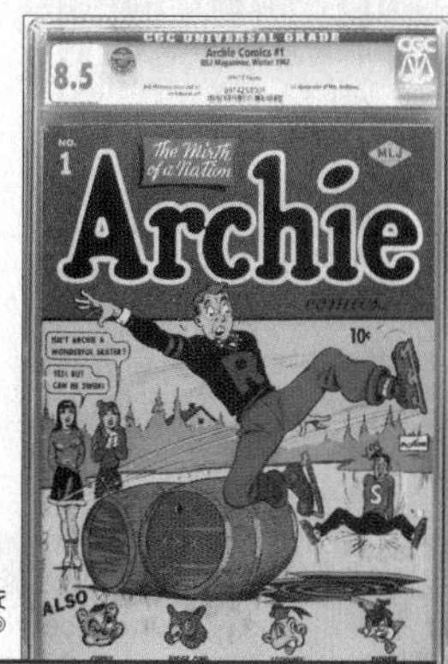

© AP

Archie Comics #1 leaped into six-figure territory. A CGC-certified 8.5 sold for $167,300.

Jason Hamlin of Brett's Comic Pile wrote "I can't count the number of people at conventions looking strictly for ultra-high grade keys. At every show we get asked multiple times a day, and a VF just won't do for many."

Jon McClure reported, "When it comes to the truly scarce, bad copies of key or variant issues bring good money from those who must have them. Mostly, the same books are on everyone's lists."

Dave Anderson, DDS, stated, "The really good material is stronger than ever and the prices realized reflect this." He continued, "It is currently difficult to get 50% of *Guide* values for more common, less desirable titles. However, this gap between high end and lower end material may eventually result in the lower end material looking more attractive due to the lower prices, so there is a good opportunity to purchase this material now while it is still possible to get it for well below *Guide* values."

As you can no doubt detect from the sampling of comments shared in this introduction, 2010 showed thousands of price changes, mostly positive, reflected in this edition. Please refer to individual listings which include these changes. Additionally, the following market reports were submitted from some of our many advisors and are published here for your information. While the opinions in these reports belong to each contributor and do not necessarily reflect the views of the publisher or the staff of *The Overstreet Comic Book Price Guide* or Gemstone Publishing, they will provide important insights into the thinking of many key players in the marketplace.

See you next year!

Bob

Robert M. Overstreet
Publisher

Overstreet Celebrates 40th Anniversary at Comic-Con

The celebration the *Guide's* 40th anniversary saw a major change for the release date, with a move to Preview Night at Comic-Con International: San Diego, which was July 21, 2010. As part of the celebration of the *Guide's* four decades of service to the comic book hobby and industry, Comic-Con International: San Diego invited Bob Overstreet to be one of the show's special guests.

"Remarkably, this was the first time Bob had ever allowed a show to pay his way to the convention. He's worked studiously over the years to avoid any conflict of interest, but we managed to twist his arm to allow fandom to honor his accomplishments," said J.C. Vaughn, Associate Publisher of Gemstone Publishing.

During the show, Bob had autograph stints at the Diamond Comic Distributors booth (joined at one point by *Guide* cover artist Mark Chiarello) and at an exclusive session at the Hard Rock Hotel suite of The Hero Initiative.

"The 40th anniversary received a great deal of attention, and both the fans and dealers seemed very happy about the new release date," Overstreet said. "On the day of its release, we got word that the Captain America hardcover of #40 had sold out. Many fans brought copies of the new editions to be signed, but I also autographed a lot of older ones, too. It was a great experience."

The Overstreet Comic Book Price Guide #40 also marked the first time a limited edition has been produced as a fundraiser. "The limited edition *Conan* #1 recreation cover for The Hero Initiative was a big hit last year and helped raise a lot of money for a great organization. John Romita, Jr. did the pencils on it, and this year John Romita, Sr. has done the pencils for our second Hero Initiative fund-raiser. I suspect it will be as well received as the first one, and I hope *Guide* #41 is received as an excellent kick-off to the *Guide's* next 40 years," Overstreet said.

PRICES: 1970 vs. TODAY

Action Comics #1

First appearance of Superman
1970 Mint Price: $300
2011 NM– Price: $1,400,000

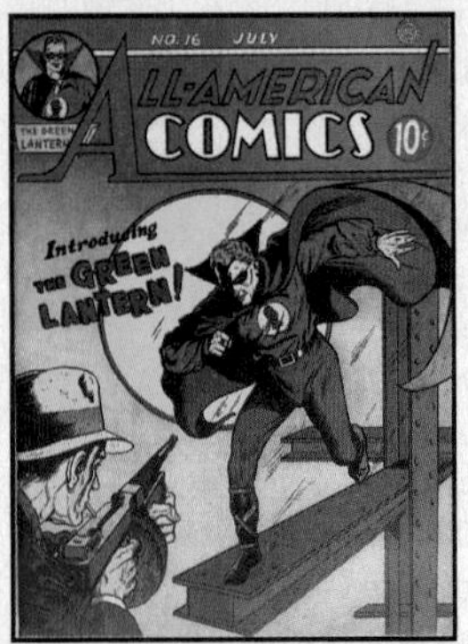

All-American Comics #16

First appearance of Green Lantern
1970 Mint Price: $50
2011 NM– Price: $400,000

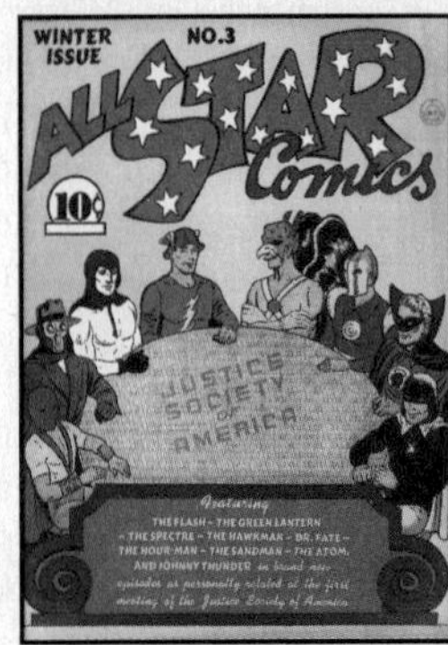

All Star Comics #3

First Justice Society of America
1970 Mint Price: $135
2011 NM– Price: $90,000

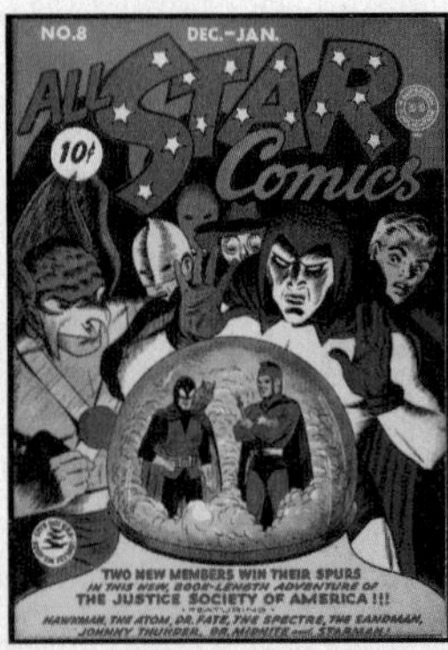

All Star Comics #8

First appearance of Womder Woman
1970 Mint Price: $45
2011 NM– Price: $75,000

Archie Comics #1

First Teen-Age comic
1970 Mint Price: $10
2011 NM– Price: $70,000

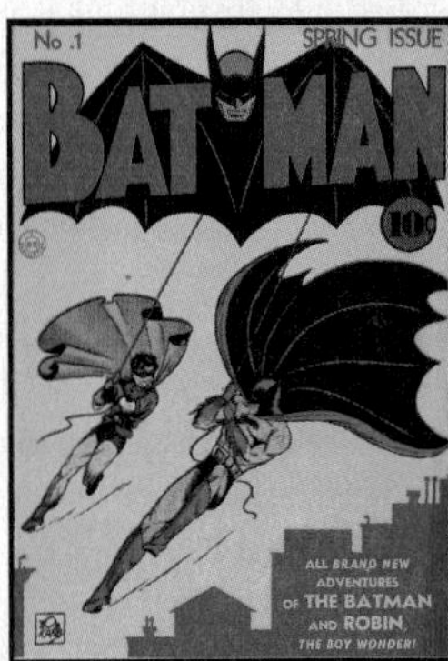

Batman #1

Debut of the Joker and Catwoman
1970 Mint Price: $175
2011 NM– Price: $285,000

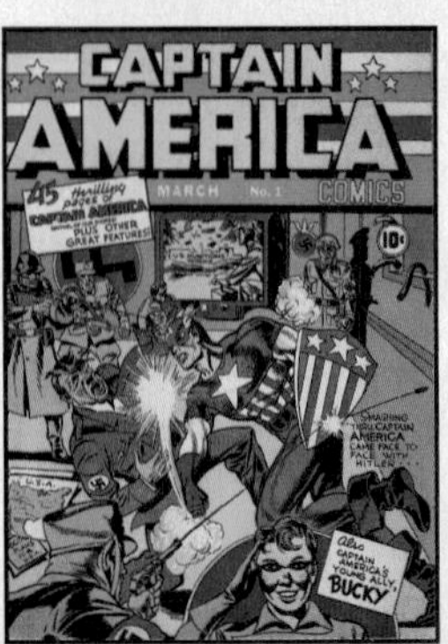

Captain America Comics #1

First appearance of Captain America
1970 Mint Price: $150
2011 NM– Price: $240,000

Crypt of Terror #17

First of the EC New Trend issues
1970 Mint Price: $30
2011 NM– Price: $5,200

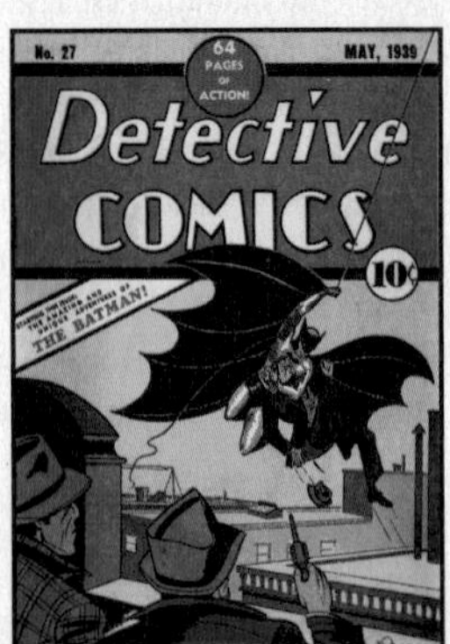

Detective Comics #27

First appearance of Batman
1970 Mint Price: $275
2011 NM– Price: $1,200,000

Detective Comics #38

First appearance of Robin
1970 Mint Price: $60
2011 NM– Price: $88,000

Flash Comics #1

Debut of the Flash and Hawkman
1970 Mint Price: $125
2011 NM– Price: $155,000

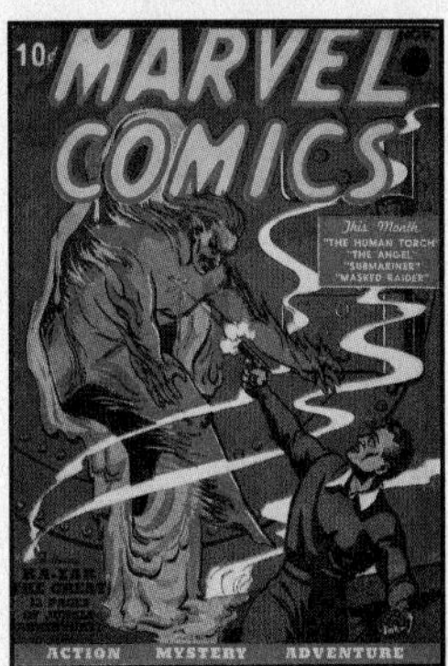

Marvel Comics #1

First Sub-Mariner and Human Torch
1970 Mint Price: $250
2011 NM– Price: $460,000

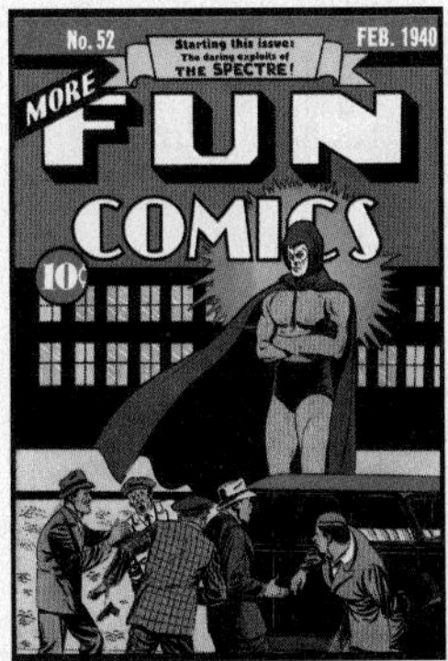

More Fun Comics #52

First appearance of The Spectre
1970 Mint Price: $100
2011 NM– Price: $145,000

More Fun Comics #56

First cover appearance of Dr. Fate
1970 Mint Price: $40
2011 NM– Price: $15,500

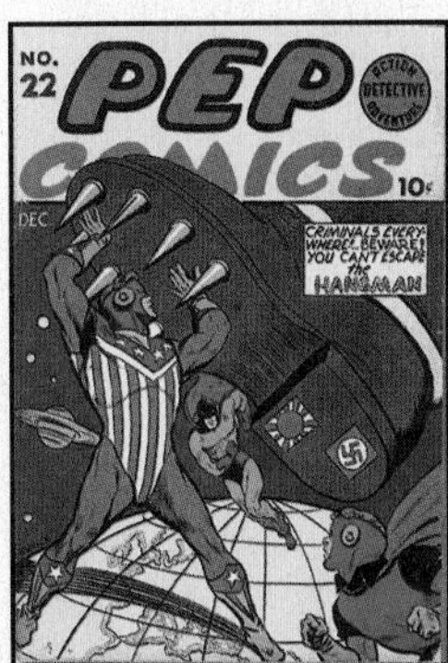

Pep Comics #22

First appearance of Archie
1970 Mint Price: $10
2011 NM– Price: $70,000

Superman #1

Superman's origin
1970 Mint Price: $250
2011 NM– Price: $560,000

Walt Disney's Comics & Stories #1

Donald Duck, Mickey Mouse reprints
1970 Mint Price: $115
2011 NM– Price: $42,000

Whiz Comics #2 (#1)

First appearance of Captain Marvel
1970 Mint Price: $235
2011 NM– Price: $100,000

PRICES: 1970 vs. TODAY

Amazing Fantasy #15

First appearance of Spider-Man
1970 Mint Price: $16
2011 NM– Price: $125,000

Amazing Spider-Man #1

Spider-Man's 2nd appearance
1970 Mint Price: $16
2011 NM– Price: $54,000

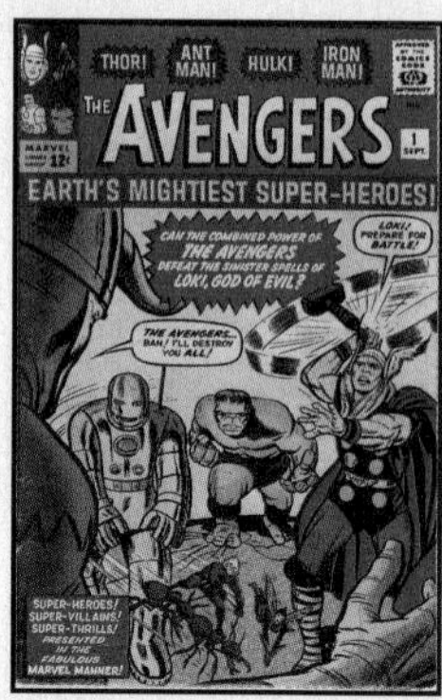

The Avengers #1

First appearance of the Avengers
1970 Mint Price: $6
2011 NM– Price: $15,000

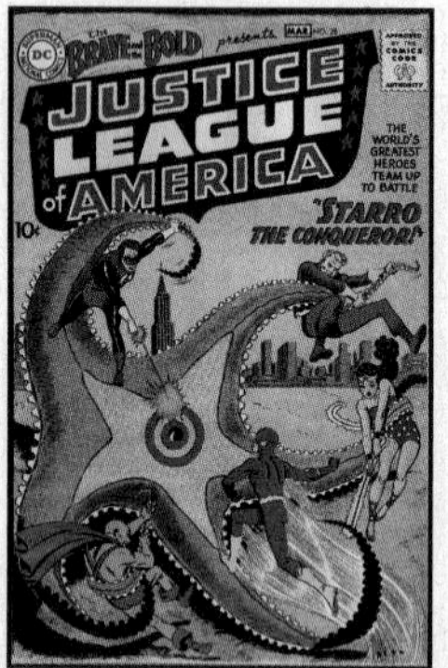

Brave and the Bold #28

First Justice League of America
1970 Mint Price: $5
2011 NM– Price: $20,000

Captain America #100

1st Silver Age Cap in his own title
1970 Mint Price: $1
2011 NM– Price: $650

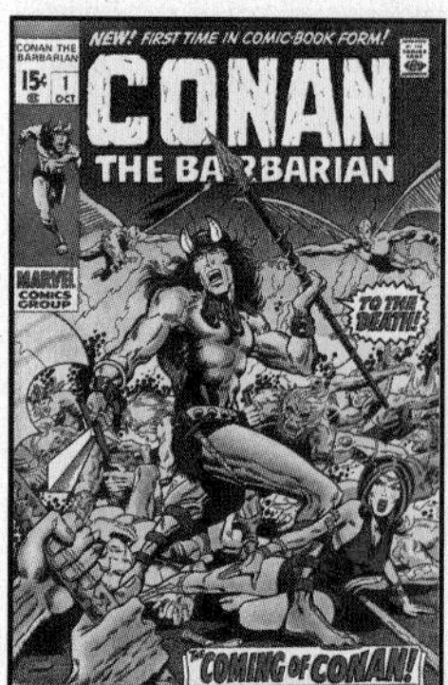

Conan the Barbarian #1

Comic book debut of Conan
1970 Mint Price: 15¢
2011 NM– Price: $475

Fantastic Four #1

First appearance of the Fantastic Four
1970 Mint Price: $12
2011 NM– Price: $80,000

Fantastic Four #48

Debuts of Silver Surfer & Galactus
1970 Mint Price: $1
2011 NM– Price: $1,500

Green Lantern #76

O'Neil/Adams issues begin
1970 Mint Price: 65¢
2011 NM– Price: $2,500

Incredible Hulk #1

First appearance of the Hulk
1970 Mint Price: $14
2011 NM– Price: $75,000

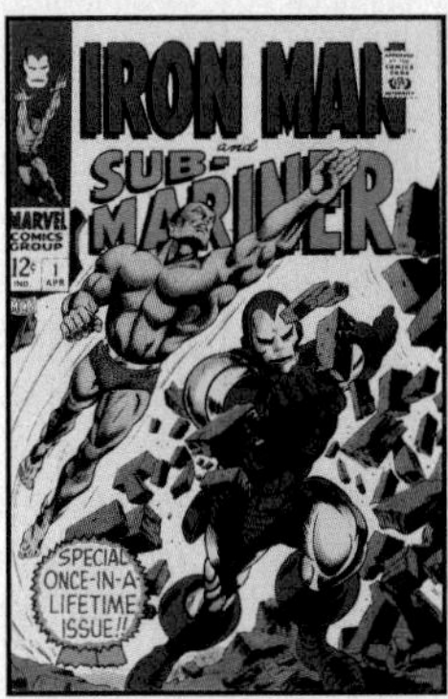

Iron Man & Sub-Mariner #1

Prelude to new #1 issues
1970 Mint Price: $1.15
2011 NM– Price: $320

Journey Into Mystery #83

First appearance of Thor
1970 Mint Price: $10
2011 NM– Price: $30,000

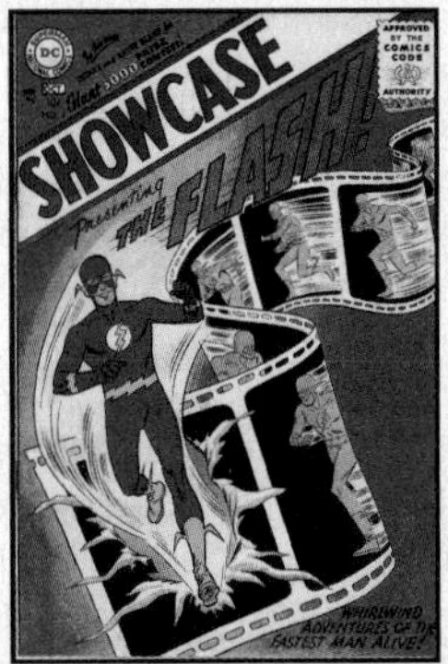

Showcase #4

First appearance of Silver Age Flash
1970 Mint Price: $12
2011 NM– Price: $56,000

Showcase #22

First Silver Age Green Lantern
1970 Mint Price: $6
2011 NM– Price: $16,000

Strange Tales #110

First appearance of Dr. Strange
1970 Mint Price: $3
2011 NM– Price: $3,800

Tales of Suspense #39

First appearance of Iron Man
1970 Mint Price: $6
2011 NM– Price: $25,000

Tales to Astonish #27

First appearance of Ant-Man
1970 Mint Price: $12
2011 NM– Price: $15,000

X-Men #1

First appearance of the X-Men
1970 Mint Price: $6
2011 NM– Price: $30,000

Grant Adey
Fats Comics Australia

Greetings from Australia, this is my second proud year as an advisor. In this report I'll discuss the trends in this neck of the woods. The books that are hot and sought after appear to be universal. Silver Age to Bronze Age keys sell quickly in VG or better, small bagged lots of 5 to 10 Silver Age comics are hot cakes when I'm able to do a good smash. Surprisingly more parents are becoming involved in their children reading, a very strong swing towards morality. I have split my dollar boxes for the first time in nine years. A special section for children which has Archies, Disney, Cartoon Network, Westerns, etc. is pushing the pile of ho hum dollar books out into the abyss. Super hero is still king, always was, always will be. Golden Age collectable comics are almost "all engines stop", appealing to mostly 50+ collectors these people seem to have other things on their priority list at the moment.

After nearly 10 years of trying to get Australians to embrace original comic book art there appears to be a little light on the horizon, I sold 2 Ray Moore *Phantom* strips for $2000usd each and a Wilson McCoy *Phantom* strip for $770. 6 Glenn Ford *Phantom* pages, 4 Glenn Ford painted covers for a little over $3500, all these prises were achieved by auction. An amazing result given this outruns what I've sold in the previous 8 years. Phantom reigns supreme in Australia outselling any other title. In later 2010 I was fortunate enough to buy a large lot of comics, books and items from the Lee Falk Estate. CGC noted "from the estate of Lee Falk" on the label of the 400 comics I had graded. Many thanks to CGC, without their foresight & recognition these books would have sadly been lost into my inventory. Vincent Zurzolo and the ComicConnect group took the Falk collection to market for me with absolute record breaking, I mean throw away the *Guide* blinder results, a staggering 52x *Guide* on a large chunk of the comics. I watched the New York auction on my laptop at the shop counter, I saw the bids and went "nah" "nah" and then to the roar of my regular customers "its kicked again" "extended time". I could only compare it to a bunch of guys gathered around a radio listening to the World Series. Every once in a while the stars align to give an outcome that can probably never be again. It's good to be there when the wheel goes around.

The last half of 2010 was turbulent business conditions and 2011 has started here like a train wreck. Brisbane was hit with disastrous floods which crippled the states economy for January and well into February and beyond. Fats Comics being the "last of the Mohicans" old school comic book store in Australia. All other comic book stores are new only, well, without these guys I would be doomed ... Special thanks goes to my Yankee buddies who keep pulling my leg out of never-ending bear traps: Jared Stern of Maryland, Jamie & Gino at Southern Cal. Comics. Bruce Ellsworth and Mike Clarke for their fantastic help throughout the year. From the furtherest outpost this is Slim signing off till 2012.

Bill Alexander
Collector

Greetings from Central California, where the recession of 2010 is still a happening reality. I collect and deal mainly in Bronze Age books and would first off like to say I observed a *Green Lantern #76* in CGC 9.8 grade sold for a record high Bronze Age sales price ($37,343.75) at auction in late 2010. I would also like to mention that a copy of *Archie's Mad House* #22 15c price variant, the "Holy Grail" of Archie 15c price variants, surfaced in July 2010. I was thrilled to actually see a scan of the book when an Archie enthusiast and collector I know was kind enough to send me a scan of it. In addition to this, another key Archie 15c price variant book, *Archie's Girls Betty and Veronica* #75 surfaced in 2010 as well, which I myself purchased in VG+ grade for $85.00, a bargain and steal of a price for that key book. Collector interest in Archie key books definately appears to be picking up at an incredibly fast rate, especially with Golden Age keys like *Pep Comics* #22 and *Archie Comics* #1 leading the way, with both books continuing to set record high sales at auction that land well over *Guide*.

The original owner of a copy of *Detective Comics* #27 was featured in a story in the local newspaper here in Central California. The owner purchased the book at a market in 1939 and 71 years later, when the book was placed up for auction, it sold in November 2010 in CGC 7.0 grade for a little less than a half million dollars, which is quite a profit on a dime investment!

Anyone out there ever seen an *Amazing Spider-Man* #122 or *Tomb of Dracula* #10 comic book in a 44-page format? The book definitely exists, as do other Marvel comics that were published with a cover date of 7/73 that contain the wrap-around four page Mennen sweepstakes Army ad insert on slick paper. It acts like a double cover on the books and precedes the comic stories inside them. These Variant Bronze Age Marvel books also contained a Mark Jewelers four page centerfold ad insert, making them 44 pagers and quite unique in format size. Only a very small percentage of the print run was printed thusly, intended for distribution in overseas U.S. military bases. These dual ad Marvel insert editions are seldom found in high grade and are uncommon in any grade!

Happy hunting and comic collecting to everyone out there.

© AP

Price variants like **Archie Comics Annual** #17 are a pretty sight for enthusiastic collectors.

David T. Alexander, Tyler Alexander and Eddie Wendt DTACollectibles.com

The key words for collecting in 2010 & 2011 have been price adjustments. For many items, we have seen wild swings in prices during the past 14 months. Many relatively obscure and modestly priced items in the *Guide* have absolutely blown through the roof. There are many comic books that do not sell very often and are not available at shows regularly. Think of it like this, when a dealer sells a $10.00 *Guide* item for $95.00, is he going to call the *Guide* publishers to share the information, or is he going to spend his time trying to find a few more copies before the word spreads? Other items, particularly those whose prices have become high but are commonly available, have had a downward trend. What many collectors overlook is that the information in this book is about a year old. In many instances the pricing information is outdated before the proofed copy has been sent to the printer. We applaud the efforts of everyone who has an active part in working on this guide. The effort to document a hobby like comic book collecting is monumental, and there is a huge value to be found in studying each edition of the *Guide*. In our opinion the most useful aspect of the *Guide* is to understand the relationship of values between books. When you can understand the relationships between the values you will be on your way to successful collecting. Those who have accumulated wealth from the hobby have mastered this concept.

Adventures of the Year: There were some wild experiences in the past year. We did not attend many conventions and instead confined most of our buying to larger original collections. This required a substantial amount of time on the road but resulted in a fantastic payoff. We deal in tons of paper collectibles in addition to comic books and this almost always insures that we will never leave any place empty handed. The best collection we scored had 14 boxes of various sizes full of Golden Age and Silver Age comic books and a large box of Radio Premiums. We had been aware of this collection for several years and even thought we had it pin-pointed in 2008 when we made a 1600 mile round trip only to find that the people had abandoned their residence about a month before we arrived. We had received the original tip from a distant relative of the family who was really interested in the finders' fee that we had offered him and we heard from him again in 2010. This time his info was up to date. WOW, what a score! There were only two Timely comics and only one had a cover. The DC and Fawcett issues were impressive. Lots of *Wonder Woman* and Captain Marvel titles were highlights of this group along with 1950s Atlas issues. There was even a blast of Quality issues highlighted by a long *Blackhawk* run. Oddly enough there were almost no pre-code horror comics except for the Atlas issues. Being able to sort through a large collection such as this is loads of fun and does provide a sociological perspective on individual collecting habits. Unfortunately we missed out on a lot of that fun as we took a zigzag route back to Florida and stopped to visit some of our top clients who bought over half of the collection. This collection came from an area that is jam packed with comic dealers and collectors and we are fortunate that the family did not attempt to contact any of the local stores or convention dealers.

We were able to buy out several struggling eBay dealers in 2010. Competition has become fierce on the internet and rising sales costs have caused many casual sellers to bail out. Our policy is to "buy everything" so we had loads of material pass through our hands. We generally do not deal in comic books published after 1975 so we had tons of material to pass on at low wholesale prices. This area had the largest price fluctuation of all. Sometimes lots of 5000 books would only bring 8 cents a book and other times we would get in the area of $1.50 a book. The quality of books did vary and our need to create space often had an impact on our price. We decided not to increase the size of our 5000 square foot warehouse this year so we were forced to move wholesale lots quicker.

The most harrowing deal of the year was the one we did not buy. We received a call from a fellow who said he had *Superman* #1 and about 100 other "old" books. (Maybe this is the time to insert that "old" is a relative term. We field calls weekly from people who offer us "old" comic books from as far back as 1998. These are not "old".) But, back to my story… He didn't seem to have a complete grasp of what he was selling but it seemed like an opportunity that should be investigated and it was less than 200 miles away. It was dark and damp when I arrived. The apartment was old, almost run down and in a seedy transient part of the city. That is not necessarily a bad thing; some of our best loads have come out of dives. Going up the stairs I noticed that there was paint splashed on the walls and steps, it looked strange. When I got inside his dimly lit abode I was overwhelmed by a grotesque odor, there were about 40 kitty litter trays; every surface seemed to have one. It appeared that when one filled up he did not bother to clean it out, he just bought another one. At least 20 cats were in the place, I couldn't count them, and they were jumping around like crazy. It was obvious that he had been drinking and among the mass of junk piled up everyplace, were overflowing ash trays and grocery bags full of fast food cartons and bottles. I saw a couple of beaten Silver Age comics on the coffee table covered with letters and newspapers. With blood shot eyes and slurred speech he explained that his wife was in jail and

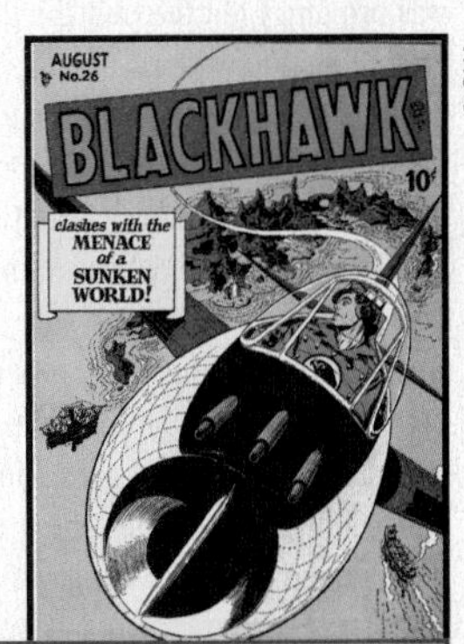

© QUA

*Gems like **Blackhawk** issues (#26 shown) are turning up in collections for sale.*

that they had had a "paint fight" in the stairway which led to the arrival of the police who hauled the old girl away after finding some outstanding warrants. He wanted to raise bail money with the books. Among the load of junk and animals in this dive one thing did stand out, I noticed a revolver on the kitchen counter. It is strange how your focus can suddenly be drawn in one direction. I was instantly aware that the cylinders had bullets, that thing was loaded! He had his friend, a swarthy looking individual, who did not speak fluent English, clear out a space and bring out two grocery bags that housed the comics. The first few were mundane Silver Age issues in average condition, then he pulled out his treasured piece. It was *Superman* Annual #1, not the original *Superman* issue from 1939. Have you ever tried to argue with alcohol? It does not work. Although he had a dog eared two year old price guide with a marker on the Superman page I was not able to explain the difference between the first issue and the Annual. He had dollar signs in those blood shot eyes and he had mentioned $10,000 more than once. My discussion was calm but he was heading towards getting heated and his intoxicated buddy was backing towards that kitchen counter. Fortunately he stumbled over a couple garbage bags and sprawled out on a rickety sofa. With that movement the old guy's attention was diverted and tension was broken. I did the only thing I could think of. I told him I did not deal in expensive books like he had but I would be happy to give him the names and numbers of a couple dealers who did handle "Valuable Books". I gave him a couple numbers and got out of there. I still haven't heard from the guys whose numbers I left with him.

Golden Age Books: As always our most popular sellers and largest sales volumes came from Golden Age titles. Timely titles have hit high price levels and are hard to find. We did not receive many Timely want lists last year. Superman and Batman titles have the highest demand and this trend has continued from 2009 into 2011. Superhero books are tops with Horror/Sci-fi, Jungle, newspaper reprint, War, Crime, and Romance genres being the next most popular in that order. The big growth area is in Romance titles. We have located about 3000 Romance issues in the last year and there is a real feeding frenzy for them. Many of these issues sell to non-traditional buyers who purchase no other types of comics and are not involved in the hobby or with price guides. This is the only area where we see an abundance of female collectors. Many bachelor collectors may want to look into getting into this area of comic collecting, if for no other reason than to connect with lady collectors who have similar interests. Many Romance books sell for huge multiples of *Guide* values. Certain icon covers go for 10-20x *Guide* prices. You might ask "What are the popular icon covers?" Look at a long run of any of these titles and certain issues will jump out at you when you have seen enough of them. We've been selling comic books full time for over 42 years. Some concepts took us over two decades to develop and understand. We can't share all our secrets here, but study the products and certain concepts will become more concrete to you. As we mentioned before, don't look at just the listed prices, but look for relative values. Detailed research can be done by examining the items on our website, DTAcollectibles.com. We still find that books from the 1947-1953 era are harder to locate than books from the WWII era. If we compare the books lost to the paper drives of WWII to the limited print runs and limited distribution areas of the 1950s era, it seems logical that fewer books were available after WWII. As a side note I can remember as a child that my parents often went to a neighborhood grocery store that carried comic books published only by Magazine Enterprises. That was OK with me as I was fascinated by the Ghost Rider, Tim Holt, and The Durango Kid who was a big B-Western movie hit. I also found Straight Arrow comics there and I was an avid follower of the radio series and I ate tons of Shredded Wheat to get the Straight Arrow premiums. Who distributed these comics and why only Magazine Enterprises has always been a mystery to me. To add to the mystery list, there was a small Mom & Pop grocery a few blocks from this store that only had a single comic rack that had only eight pockets to display eight titles. The only comics I ever saw in this store were Ajax/Farrell publications. This publisher did not print many books and to think that a distributor would exclusively carry their titles and no others is really a mystery to me. Maybe a grocery distributor had hooked up with Ajax. If anyone has any insight into this I would love to hear about it.

Pulps like **Argosy** with Tarzan covers were big movers.

Silver Age Comics: This has become the most popular time period for collecting. Actually many of these comics are really entertaining to read. The comic book movies have had a huge influence on the collecting hobby. The Marvel movies have often been true to the story line of the comic books and I think this has given the comic books more relevance to new collectors. The top Marvel titles are still the top Marvel titles and the high grade copies of *Amazing Spider-Man* that have sold in the six figure range have provided additional positive publicity for the hobby. The titles that are coming on strong now are *Tales to Astonish*, *Tales of Suspense* and *Strange Tales*. Watch out for *Strange Tales* if you have an investor mentality. *Strange Tales*, you heard it first right here.

Green Lantern has been the standard bearer for the DC line. The *Showcase* Green Lantern issues and #1-10 of the Silver Age series could be considered hot items. Try to find issue #7 which features the origin of Sinestro. Other DC titles that had positive movement in 2010 are *Mystery in Space*, all the War titles including late comer *Weird War*, *Hawkman*, *Brave and the Bold*, *Showcase*, all Romance titles and most of the 80 Page Giants.

Good Girl Art: Comics and other publications featuring girls have always been popular. GGA comics have been through various cycles of demand during the last 25 years. Their ups and downs have been related to price and not content. Recently we have seen new demand for these unique comic books.

Collectors who were new to our mailing list have been rapidly depleting our inventory of Fiction House and Fox titles. Not only do they devour our comic book inventory but they are also trying to deplete our inventory of *True Crime*, *Men's Adventure* and pulp magazines with Good Girl Art covers. The pulp titles from Fiction House have been in high demand. *Jungle Stories* and *Planet Stories* are just as popular as *Jungle Comics* and *Planet Comics*. We have two clients who buy doubles and triples of all GGA items. The hot artist in this area is now George Gross. His comic book work is limited but pulps and true crime magazines with his covers are extremely popular. *True Detective Cases*, *Women in Crime*, *Best True Fact Detective* and *Police Detective* are among the most popular. Try to find some of these. While you are at it, pick up some copies of *Rulah*, *All-Top*, *Phantom Lady*, *Sheena*, Jo-Jo and *Nyoka*. These comics are fun to read and to show your friends, the stories do not feel dated and the books are not stuck in a past time period.

Western Comics: The movie and TV related books were our top sellers in this area. Just like the recent Marvel and DC movies influence many comic buyers, those who appreciate the old Westerns seem to have current availability of old films and TV programs. Many old Westerns show up on cable TV and lots of films are available on DVD. The top of this list is Roy Rogers, the quintessential "good guy" whose screen life spanned over 20 years, and his name is still well known today. Many issues of his long running Dell series are easy to locate and some can be found at almost any comic book convention in the US. Try to complete the run of his comics. Roy Rogers appeared in the first photo cover Dell movie Western edition, *Four Color* #38, published in 1944. Try to find a nice copy of that one. Gene Autry, Hopalong Cassidy, Rocky Lane, Tim Holt, Lash Larue, Gabby Hayes, Rex Allen, Monte Hale and Tom Mix all had exciting film careers with their adventures appearing in comic books of the 1940s and 1950s. Many of these comics are available at most comic shows but each title has a few issues that are harder to locate. You probably will not get rich if you plan to invest in these titles but they are an important part of Americana and they do provide a lot of entertainment for the cost. Non-film related Westerns were steady sellers during 2010. The best Dell title of this group is clearly Turok, Son of Stone. I think this is the only 1950s Dell Western that was eventually turned into a video game. DC titles like *All-American Western* and *All Star Western* were very popular. *Tomahawk* was the most requested DC title but with over 130 issues it had the longest run of any of the DC Western series. The hottest non-film title was again *Red Ryder*. Whether it was the impressive Fred Harman art, the universal "good vs evil" theme or the Western background that continues to please collectors, we cannot determine what creates the most demand. We do know that we are always happy to see these comics when they are included in collections that we acquire. The few Fox Western titles usually sell quickly. Any issue with an Indian cover was a potential "hot" item. The Fiction House title *Indians* and the Dell series *Indian Chief* set world record prices for us.

Pre-Code Horror & Sci-Fi: These books had another banner sales year. Issues that were referenced in *Seduction of the Innocent* were very fast to sell. If you want some laughs, find the *Ladies Home Journal* issue from 1953 that has an article on comics and the *Seduction* book. Books with "Injury to the eye", snakes, skulls, torture, dismemberment, vampires, the occult, hangings, Rocket ship covers and extreme violence were most sought after. The copies that came our way in 2010 were all from collectors with changing tastes, not original owner Horror collections turning up, and believe me, we were looking for them.

Pulp Magazines: Again in 2010 Edgar Rice Burroughs pulps were our top volume mover. Burroughs' universally known character, Tarzan, was the first "bigger than life" superhero. Titles that featured Tarzan stories, such as *New Stories*, *Argosy*, *Amazing Stories*, and *Blue Book* were constant sellers. One strange phenomenon we have noticed is that other than the first *Tarzan* pulp in 1910, the *Tarzan* pulps generally sell for less than the equivalent hard back book edition which usually appeared after the pulp was on the stands. *John Carter Of Mars* issues had increased demand which was certainly enhanced by the announcement of the movie based on this famous *Mars* series.

The most popular hero pulp has been *The Shadow* but that position weakened with the economic collapse. We are not sure exactly what the relationship of these two events was but *The Spider* is now the most sought-after hero title followed closely by *Doc Savage*.

War and aviation pulps had increased demand. The concept of aviation was first popularized in the pulps of the early 1920s and those editions are very collectible today. *Wings*, *War Stories* by Dell, *Battle Birds*, *Dare-Devil Aces*, *G-8 and His Battle Aces* are some of the many titles that brought air adventure to the common man. These pulps are historic artifacts that would enhance any popular culture collection. Don't wait forever to obtain a few of these, the supply is not large.

Underground Comix: Still a fertile area for study and research. The recent Underground Price Guides have helped to identify and document many obscure editions. It has recently come to light that many limited edition, local publications have a commonality with the Undergrounds and there is lots of undocumented material to be researched. As in the past, Robert Crumb is the king here. Did anyone miss the film about his life or *American Splendor* about his friend, Harvey Pekar? These are both interesting parts of comic book history.

Magazines: The top seller here has been *Heavy Metal* which first appeared in the U.S. during early 1977. Moebius was one of the top artists to contribute material to this series. Now, almost 35 years after its first appearance, copies are highly sought after. For years issues seemed constantly available and now they have been absorbed into the population. Recently a CGC 9.8 copy of the first issue was sold in a private transaction for almost $1000. Mad Magazine issues pre-1964 have had a good turnover. Warren Publications are steady sellers; lots of collectors enjoy *Vampirella*, *Famous Monsters*, *Eerie* and *Creepy*. The sleeper this year has been *Sick* magazine. Joe Simon worked on the early issues and we have had multiple requests for copies of the first dozen issues.

Fanzines: We have been fortunate to have had one of the largest original fanzine collections to exist. The collection was originally amassed by the famous McGeehan brothers of California. It had virtually every comic book fanzine to be published prior to 1975. Many of these were very limited editions with print runs of 10 copies or less. These are really helpful in documenting the origins of organized comic book fandom. The earliest fanzines that were pivotal in generating an organized hobby appeared in 1960 through 1963. It is interesting to note that this was the also the beginning of the Marvel era. Obviously the dawn of Marvel's Silver Age set a stage that enhanced collector-to-collector communication which has led to the strong hobby that we enjoy today. Much of the collection was sold in 2010 and the remainder will be offered in 2011. Many of the titles were unknown to me prior to seeing the collection.

Original Art: We had nonstop interest all year from art collectors. Much Silver and Bronze Age art is being held tightly in private collections. Pieces that passed through our hands did exactly that...pass through our hands. Almost none of them were here long enough to receive an inventory number. We are happy to receive any comic book art, and even look forward to getting modern pieces. We did have a couple of Pulp magazine cover paintings that were here only temporarily early in the year. As we write this we have concluded a negotiation to acquire 47 pieces of art and really look forward to their arrival. As a general rule, covers dominate the value scale. Magazine, illustration and newspaper art also did very well during the year and we have leads on two collections that we hope to own shortly. We hope to hear from more art collectors in 2011.

Our Future: Considering some of the dismal forecasts for 2010, it was actually a really good year. Obviously many books had downturns in value but that is to be expected in any type of marketplace. We found out that comic books are not immune to economic market forces. The bright spot is that there is still rampant enthusiasm among collectors. I don't think any outside force will ever decrease the fun of collecting comic books. People love those comics, and so do I.

Dave Anderson, DDS
Collector

This year's market report is easy to write as there is a lot of consistency seen throughout all of the various collector markets. The really good material is stronger than ever and the prices realized reflect this. *Action Comics* #1 and *Detective Comics* #27 are truly scarce in high grade and the million dollar sales achieved will likely seem cheap in a short amount of time. However, it is currently difficult to get 50% of *Guide* values for more common, less desirable titles. Supply is plentiful and demand is low, so to extrapolate from the *Action* #1 and *Detective* #27 sales and compare these sales to the rest of the comic market as a whole is incorrect. However, this gap between high end and lower end material may evertially result in the lower end material looking more attractive due to the lower prices, so there is a good opportunity to purchase this material now while it is still possible to get it for well below *Guide* values.

Stephen Barrington
with Ronnie Hayes
Flea Market Comics

New comic sales were exceptional for the second straight year with DC's *Brightest Day* and *Batman: The Return Of Bruce Wayne* leading the way. Marvel sales are strong but the local fan base is getting a little annoyed with the constant re-launching of titles and more and more X-books.

The rest of the new comics sales are splintered with Dark Horse, Image, IDW and Zenescope filling out the spectrum. With the debut of *The Walking Dead* TV series, Image has seen a moderate increase in new and back issue sales. The first six issues, though, are hard to find. Zenescope's *Grimm Fairy Tales* line of comics sell well. Early issues of the flagship series have become too pricey for most collectors. Broadsword's *Tarot, Witch of the Black Rose*, are impossible to keep in stock.

Collectively, the Batman titles sell extremely well as do the Green Lantern titles. The Superman titles sales are up over the previous year. *Uncanny X-Men*, *X-Men Legacy*, *Wolverine* and all of the Avengers series are strong sellers. *Amazing Spider-Man* is still a steady seller despite the screwy storylines Marvel has foisted on its readership. And surprisingly enough, Archie Comics sales are up with recent back issues doing moderately.

Our shop continues to be the only one in a relatively large area along the Alabama, Florida and Mississippi Gulf Coast. You have to go to Biloxi, Miss., or Pensacola, Fla., to find another shop. And ours is only part-time.

Comic-collecting supplies sell very well as do special orders for action figures, statues and T-shirts.

Newer back-issue sales of *Spawn* are very strong, mainly because they're still cheap. X-titles (including *Wolverine*) have flooded our back-issue warehouse. Thousands have walked in the door with former collectors dumping them for little or nothing. We sell these from 25¢ to $1.00 each. With the exception of a couple of certain issues (*New Mutants* #98, *Uncanny X-Men* #266), we are drowning in X-issues.

Lower grade DC and Marvel comics from the 1960s and 1970s do well when not priced over $5.00. We have a special section for these.

DC back issues, with the exception of Batman titles, are very slow. Silver Age *Batman* and *Detective* are strong movers while *Amazing Spider-Man* is a distant second for Marvel. Low-grade early issues do a little better.

As usual, CGC comics are almost impossible to sell as well as any comic over the $200.00 mark. Mobile is a very tough market when trying to sell comics in this price range. Golden Age comics can take a while to move. Bronze Age sales are perking up for DC and Marvel, mainly because they are still cheap. There has been more interest in Gold Key's *Magnus, Robot Fighter* of the 1960s.

The Conan black and white magazines sell extremely well but only if they are not priced over $2.00 each. The EC horror and science fiction reprints still sell but are harder to come across.

Miscellaneous horror and science fiction comics from the 1950s (DC and Atlas) sell moderately but only if the price is right. Low-grade issues sell better because the pricing. *Classics Illustrated* still has an audience with us, regardless of the printing. The 1950s Dell Comics, even at more than 50-percent off, just gather dust and space.

We have abandoned trying to sell comics on eBay. Too many people have no idea how to grade or market comics. However, those who do, make it a great market for bargains on older issues. Heritage Sunday Night Auctions have been a gold mine this year with lots of groups being won well under *Guide* prices even with the buyer's premium and shipping.

Chicago Wizard-World: The Chicago Wizard-World convention was again fantastic with more dealers and bargains than we could count. Harley Yee (one of the best in the business) as usual, had a great selection of top Golden Age and Silver Age comics as did Metropolis Comics. Vincent Zurzolo and the gang had a great display. While there were a lot more celebrities this year, the selection of comics was terrific.

L.E. Becker
WARP 9

I once remember my father walking into my bedroom when I was 12 years old or so, asking what I was doing. "I just bought a perfect mint copy of *Incredible Hulk* #181 and I'm trying to find a mylar bag for it." My father, who didn't understand this hobby before (and still doesn't I guess) asked me what I paid for it. "$25.00 (this was 1983)"..."WHAT? $25.00 for ONE comic? Better you should put that $25.00 in the bank...in 20 years time, the interest accumulated would turn that into $500.00 at least." I tried to explain the significance of the book and the condition, and that in perhaps in 1 year's time I could at least double that investment. "No one except for you would pay that kind of money." Twenty plus years later, I retell that story to him and show him a CGC copy in 9.9 sells for an astonishing $20,000+. "I guess you showed me..."

So does that mean that comic books are solid investments? That you should clear out your bank account and take that extra $50,000 from your 2% annual savings account and put it into some *Hulk* #181s or *X-Men* #94s? Sell that lakefront property that's probably worth only half of what you paid for it 4 years ago, and try to purchase an *Action* #1? Sure...and while you're at it, see if you can get some of "them thar' magic beans" too. Maybe they can lead you to the goose that lays golden eggs. People who are making their money now within this hobby/industry are the ones who took a chance and bought that copy of *Flash Comics* #1 for $200.00 30 years ago and sold it for $400,000+. How long until that copy goes for $410,000? Five, ten years from now? And who's to say that prices won't fall? Hard to believe? *The Wall Street Journal* had an article on the rising collectible prices on comics. They placed it on par almost with the housing crisis.

I have people who come into my shop every day...EVERY DAY...asking for a comic that will make them money in a year or two. They are normally disappointed in my answer that the industry does not work like that, and they think I dont want to share my "secrets". Fine. Here is (one of) my secrets: don't invest in something that you have absolutely NO knowledge about. If you still persist, if you still want to make your "fortune" in the comic market, then for G-d's sake...DO YOUR RESEARCH!

OK...enough with the sermon. On to the market report...

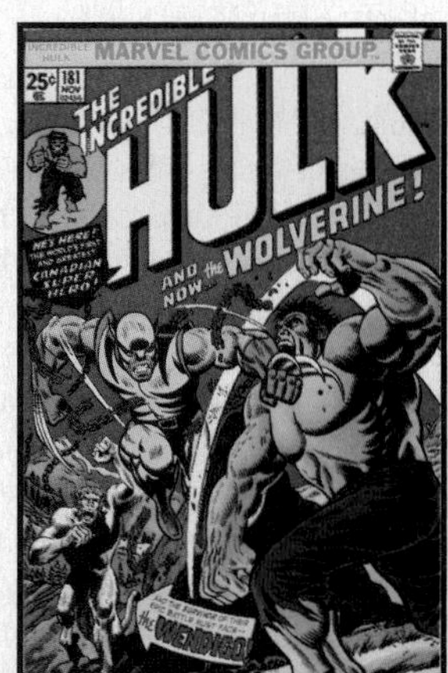

© MAR

Buying a mint copy of Incredible Hulk #181 in 1983 was a great investment.

New Comics: In general a very topsy turvey market. Comics that we used to order 100 copies of, now MAYBE 1/2. There are many Marvel & DC comics that we are down to ordering single digits of (ie: *Mighty Crusaders* 4 copies, *Thor: Mighty Avenger* 5 copies, etc). This is due in part to TWO problems. 1) TOO MANY comics being published. We only need ONE Thor title! We only need ONE Justice Society title! People are so confused by all of the spin off titles, many people drop the character altogether. Besides, with the economy getting worse (NOT better as the media states), more people are dropping books left and right due to too many titles and, of course, 2) EXPENSIVE COVER PRICE! $2.99 For a new comic seems to be an average acceptable limit. $3.25-3.50 kind of pushes the envelope...$3.99 makes it difficult to reach into the wallet. I have one customer who bought EVERY title on the rack. After the price jump he scaled back to maybe 1/2. I understand print cost is rising, but a full $1.00 (thats over a 30% price hike) does not seem like a viable option. DC just announced that they are lowering their cover prices back down to $2.99 (for their REGULAR titles), but is it too little, too late? Guess we'll see in a few months.

DC Comics: By far, Green Lantern has been leading the pack. Ever since Blackest Night, the popularity of the regular series, as well as *Green Lantern Corps* and *Emerald Warriors*, has been overwhelmingly popular. So too has the sequel *Brightest Day*. Many of the spin-offs to *Brightest Day* have been doing well also. Specificaly *Birds of Prey*, *Flash*, and *Justice League: Generation Lost*. All three titles have done exceedingly well.

Batman and Robin by Grant Morrison has also been doing very well sales wise, outselling the regular *Batman* series by 30%. Don't expect this to last however when Morrison is gone from the book...only to start the laughable *Batman, Inc.* ongoing series. Really? You are taking a character, shrouded in mystery, who is regarded, at best, an urban legend, and then you're going to GLOBALIZE him? On the positive side, there is a big buzz regarding David Finch's new *Dark Knight* series. I for one am looking very forward to it, as a regard Finch as one of my favorite modern day artists. On the opposite end, although Neal Adams is my all time favorite artist on Batman, I find *Batman: Odyssey* absolutely unreadable. Good thing that the artwork is so pretty. It sells better than most Batman mini series, but, in my opinion it would sell better if the story was better.

Superman and *Wonder Woman* both got shots in the arm as J. Michael Strazcinski (JMS) began his writing on each book. However, *Superman* has dropped in sales yet again (He's just going to walk the USA? Doesn't seem very "Super" to me), and *Wonder Woman*, although still very good in sales at the moment, is confusing not only many readers, but myself as well. Now it has been announced that JMS is leaving both titles to do more Graphic novel work for DC, specificaly a sequel to the hit *Superman: Earth One* original hardcover graphic novel. Earth One Superman was enjoyable, but is it really something that can be set to a sequel?

My sleeper pick this year is *THUNDER Agents*. This title will do well, not because of the history of the characters (which not many collectors know about), but because it is being written by comic's newest sensation, Nick Spencer, from Image's *Morning Glories*. The 1st issue was a complete sell out for us, and many people are really hot for the reorder. I can see this being a $10.00 comic soon IF the demand keeps up.

The Vertigo line needs a hit. *Fables*, although still a great book, has just about outstayed its welcome. Probably the best seller of this line (at least at our shop), it, by far, outsells ANY Vertigo title. *Scalped* and *Unwritten*, sell well, but NOTHING like previous comics such as *Preacher* or *Sandman* (although, as TPBs go, *Scalped* sells better than *Fables* trades ...go figure). Titles that were highly lauded as the "next big thing" have either languished in sales, or have been canceled. The approach of single one shot hardcovers have been accepted as a "ho-hum". Even *American Vampire*, which did well when Stephen King was one of the writers, dropped dramaticaly when King left the book (almost a 75% drop!!!). At least I will give credit to DC/Vertigo for trying something different. *How To Understand Israel In 60 Days Or Less* HC was a great example of how outside the box Vertigo can be...now if only we could sell more.

Marvel Comics: *Avengers* (the NEWER series...NOT to be confused with *New Avengers*) leads the pack for most ordered Marvel series for us. *Secret Avengers* is second (although a DISTANT second), and can anyone tell me why *New Avengers* is still being published? This title is an oxymoron, as there is ALREADY a NEW Avengers book. It doesn't make sense (except for a sales point explanation...it's still Bendis). *Captain America* (despite being a $3.99 book now), still has a steady readership, as does *Amazing Spider-Man*, *Thor*, and all of the core books. Any spin-off, mini series, or one-shot fodder are treated as such and can be found cluttering up the rack. For example, *Thor* sells a respectable 50-60 copies for us. The 2,678,087 mini series that follow, sell anywhere from a high of 20 copies (*For Asgard*) to a low of 5 (*Mighty Avenger*). The readers have spoken...they just want ONE title, with maybe ONE HIGH CALIBER mini or one shot per month.

Even the great Deadpool line has been taking a hit. Yes, I know he is Marvel's second most popular character right now (Wolverine is still first), but we do not need 2 Deadpool titles per week. It's overkill. Especially for a character who does not yet have his own film franchise...YET.

Marvel's ICON line is a semi-hit. Taking the once independent comics done by previous indy writers and making them Marvel titles...BRILLIANT! *Casanova* by Matt Fraction is enjoying a second life, however, David Mack's *Kabuki* just sits. Even the once-powerful, do-no-wrong Brian Bendis's comic *Powers* sells a small fraction of its previous run. However, *Scarlet* (Bendis's new series) is selling pre-Image power numbers (which is a good thing), and showcases Bendis's abilities as a cutting edge writer again. Mark Millar's *Kick Ass 2*, *Nemesis*, and *Superior* are ALL triple digit sellers...when they are on time. There should NOT be a

4 month gap between issues...EVER!

Marvel's MAX line has some decent books out also. *Deadpool Max* hit the ground running and seems poised to stay for awhile. *Punisher MAX*, by far my favorite comic is also selling well (Jason Aaron's rendition of this character and his cast is even better than Garth Ennis's rendition). The problem with this line, is that there are basically only a few titles under this imprint. This is one of the few exceptions where I think that there should be MORE titles from this line.

Image Comics: *The Walking Dead* still sells very high here. Even the TPBs, which are one of the few to sell in the double digits. The anticipation of the AMC TV series swelled up the demand even further. *Invincible* (by same writer Robert Kirkman) is a far distant second, selling maybe 1/3 the copies of *Walking Dead*. We sold a first print #1 back in April for an astonishing $300... and about 3 weeks later prices on-line were $400-500! *Chew* (which is poised to be a new TV series) has dropped slightly in readership, but the TPBs more than make up for it. Early back issues have been selling consistantly high, with a *Chew* #1 1st print going for $100.00!

Speaking of *Chew*, there has been a lot of mass speculation in many Image titles recently...almost like it was back in the early 1990s. *Morning Glories* and *Skull Kickers* have both been speculated on and high end back issues (*Morning Glories* #1) have been sold as high as $50.00. Even the one shot *Sea Bear & Grizzly Shark* (a drop dead funny comic) had been speculated on and sold as high as $30.00 (we sold it on eBay for that amount). So what is going on with all of the speculating with Image comics all of a sudden? Two trains of thought: 1) Quality of said titles are VERY high. Word of mouth on these new Image titles have got collectors wanting to try something out of the norm, and 2) Print runs of these books are exceptionaly LOW. *Skull Kickers* #1 had about a 3,000 1st print run. That's approximately ONE per shop on the average.

Green Lantern (#29 SDCC edition shown) is leading the pack of current DC titles.

Independents: IDW has come out with some unlikely hits. *The Last Unicorn* sold better than some Marvel and DC comics. The Star Trek and Angel titles have stayed steady, but the break out title from IDW is *True Blood*. We ordered very heavy on this title, and were NOT disappointed. Back issue sales of #1 have gone as high as $10.00 and is already into a 4th print. Hopefuly, IDW can get the license to other high profile cable series. *Dexter* would be a natural! At the same time, why isn't anyone doing any of the Adult Swim properties?

Dynamite Comics best selling title is *The Boys*. Constantly consistent in its readership and sales, and that also includes the TPBs The license for Green Hornet must be very expensive, because there are just WAY too many titles for this character. The only one that sells well is *Kevin Smith's Green Hornet* and, to a lesser extent, *Year One*. However, the rest just languish. *Warlord of Mars* has some promise as the first issue sold respectively well, but *Last Phantom* just sat. I also do not think it was a good idea to buy the Dabel Bros. properties out, as none of them are selling (and by none, I mean NONE).

BOOM! has renewed my faith in the comic companies again, as they have aggressively been touting their kids comics. Mostly all Disney properties, but as of now, parents have been coming in every Saturday to grab a few for their children. But with the good comes the bad. *Stan Lee's Weapon Zero* is aptly named. Lee might have wowed the comic community 50 years ago, but his ideas today seem trite and uninspired. Even with other people writing and fleshing out the characters, no one seems to care.

Jim Berry
Collector

It's my sincere pleasure to submit a report for *The Overstreet Comic Book Price Guide* this year. As this is my first report following a career of collecting and dealing on both coasts and spanning more than 25 years, I humbly add my comments and hope that I can add a few interesting observations. Though I don't own a storefront shop, I am active in buying and selling comics in the Northwest and I also spend a fair amount of time watching, buying and selling comics on ComicLink, ComicConnect, Heritage, and, especially, eBay.

As we enter 2011, we face a set of new challenges and innovations in our hobby, ranging from the advent of online comics to the continuing explosive growth of high-grade CGC keys, all coupled to an economy and political climate that is, at best, uncertain.

Online comics, without question, appear to be the wave of the future. I recently attended an art show featuring the private original comic art collection of Mike Richardson, the founder of Dark Horse Comics, in Milwaukee, Oregon where he repeatedly stressed the importance of finding a way to compete in the emerging market of online comics. My sense of online comics is that they will never be able to compete with the experience of reading a paper comic. But I'm also a 42 year-old guy who doesn't own a smart phone and can just

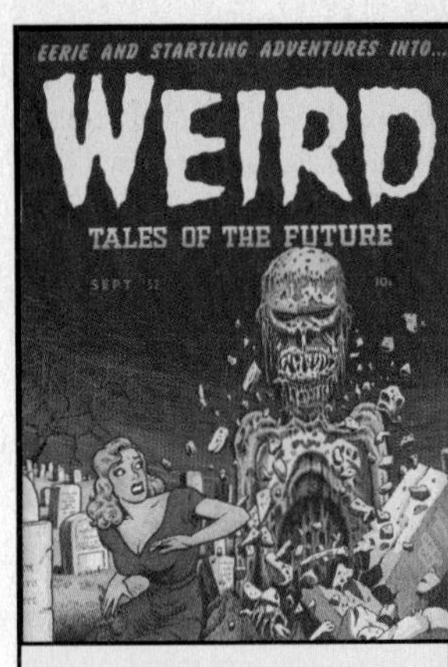

*Wolverton covers typically sell at multiples of Guide. (**Weird Tales of the Future** #3 shown)*

barely send a text message. It's hard to say, but I wouldn't be surprised if we see some big changes over the next few years in terms of a new readership emerging. How will it affect our hobby of collecting comics? Really, the important question here seems to be - Will there be another generation that falls in love with old paper? Will they take over the reigns and continue to drive sales and interest in our old, beautiful comic books? Only time will tell.

Clearly, for now, the interest in old comics is strong enough as they continue to sell at record prices. But the world of comic collecting now mirrors the population of our country as a whole. Here we have a fraction of collectors with money to spend on the eye-popping gems and the rest who have little surplus cash for comics. The good news here is that there are any number of ways for the have-nots to get their comic fix for little or no money. If you're just interested in reading, head on over to the library and take your pick of trade paperbacks. If you're interested in dealing, troll Craigslist. This free website has become a major source of comics over the past few years. For those willing to put in the time, Craiglist is a great source of cheap comics and a place where you can, occasionally, find a fantastic deal. Be prepared, however. Competition for comics via Craislist has recently increased to frenzied levels with so many people out of work and looking to turn a quick buck by being first at the sale so they can buy in bulk and flip them on eBay. What do I mean by "frenzied"? Here's a quick story: At one sale this past summer, I picked up a handful of '50s Dell Westerns from under a stack of *Life* magazines and started to flip through them, excited by what I might find. From across the room, a middle-aged woman yelped, "I'm buying all the old comics!" She came rushing over, plucked the books from my hands, and went to the register where the home-owner confirmed that he'd made a deal with her for every comic in the house. When I asked if I could just look at them, she said no then confirmed that she intended to sell the books on eBay and informed me that if I was interested in buying them from her, that's where I'd find them within a day or two.

Despite that example, the good news for comic buyers during this recession continues to be that you can find some fantastic deals on comics if you're willing to put the time in. Even with original owner '40s and '50s collections, sadly, becoming a thing of the past, there is no shortage of old comics available, especially on eBay which I consider to be the premier marketplace. Love it or hate it, eBay continues to define the market with its thousands of comic listings on any given day. It's a fun and mostly fair place to pursue collecting, and has become the true bellweather for the hobby.

Golden Age: '40s and '50s comics of every stripe are interesting to someone. It's simply an issue of supply and demand. So when it comes to Timely, DC, pre-code horror, WWII covers, good girl art, pedigree comics, artists like Frazetta, Wolverton, Baker and anything strange, rare, and high-grade, the *Guide* typically is just that - a guide. I've watched numerous un-slabbed books go for crazy multiples of *Guide* simply because those comics rarely make it to market and when they're presented as "attic-finds" with no reserve in what looks to be VG condition, all bets are off. Try winning an eBay auction for *Weird Mysteries* #5, *Mister Mystery* #12, or any *USA* Comic with a Schomburg cover in decent shape. In terms of selling Golden Age non-key comics, be prepared to take in around 30% of *Guide* or less on non-superhero material in mid to low grade. Things do sell, but it's an unpredictable market and definitely seems more tentative than years past.

The top Atom-Age horror comics, most issues of *Weird Mysteries*, *Weird Tales of the Future*, *Mister Mystery*, and Menace seem a little undervalued with the key covers by Wolverton and Baily (*Mister Mystery* #12, *Weird Mysteries* #3 and #5 and all the Wolverton covers from *Weird Tales of the Future* typically sell at multiples of *Guide*.) Same with early *Thing!* Ditko covers.

Silver Age: Spidey is still the king. So engrained in our culture is Spider-Man that he is one of the characters, along with Barney and Mickey Mouse, that my 2-year-old daughter recognizes and points out whenever she sees him. But if he is the king, his court includes all the usual suspects – Hulk, Iron Man, Thor, Daredevil, X-Men and The Avengers as well as the DC counterparts led by Batman and Green Lantern. Other DC comics, though incredibly cool and, actually, in many cases, harder to find, still haven't found the same sort of reliable fan-base as the big Marvel boys. I love those random copies of *Anthro* and *The Spectre*, and the tales of The Legion in *Adventure*, but sometimes, I have a hard time selling them.

By the time these words are in print, we'll be living in a whole new world of Super-Hero films including *Thor*, *Captain America*, and *Green Lantern*. Hopefully, the influence of these blockbusters will continue to generate interest in the characters but my feeling is that once the movies have come and gone, those titles will cool as people look to the next big thing.

Bronze Age: These are the books that I read as a kid growing up and they are still my favorites. Non-key high-grade Bronze sells reliably but, again, it's not unusual to see these books sell for considerably less than guide. As more and more '70s comics are discovered, I don't expect this trend to change. For the next generation of collectors, the quest for a nice copy of *Hulk* #181, *Green Lantern* #76, *X-Men* #94, and *House of Secrets* #92 is what I imagine when I think about the '80s and what it must have been like to try and find books like *Amazing Fantasy* #15 or *Brave and the Bold* #28. Anyone have a time machine I can borrow for a day or two?

The Northwest Convention Scene: The Portland Comic Show continues to be a fun one-day show and something to look forward to in the Spring and Fall with a focus on old comics and a ton of new-issue bargain hunters on the prowl for the gem lost in the 3-for-a-dollar box. The Emerald City Comicon, on the other hand, has become a huge destination show for collectors and dealers from all over the country. Thanks to Jim Demonakos, this show featured Stan Lee and Leonard Nimoy as guests in 2010 and, despite moving into a larger venue in Seattle's Convention Center, was so crowded at one point that you literally couldn't move in certain areas of the room. Dealers reported good sales and next year's show promises to be even better as it moves from 2 to 3 days. Thanks to Jim and his team for creating the premiere Northwest comic event.

Notable comics bought and sold this year include:

Amazing Fantasy #15 CGC 4.5 $7,600
Amazing Fantasy #15 CGC 5.5 $10,500
Avengers #1 CGC 4.5 Signature Series (Stan Lee) $1,430
Avengers #1 VG $735
Brave and the Bold #28 VG $535
Captain America Comics #14 VG $580
Captain America Comics #46 VG $2,800
Daredevil #1 CGC 7.5 Signature Series (Stan Lee) $2,600
Mister Mystery #12 VG+ $920
Showcase #22 VG+ $1,000
Thunda #1 GD/VG $170
Weird Tales of the Future #5 VG $356
Young Allies #9 FN- $349

I've noted in many closing reports that advisors often say, "Buy what you love," and while that is certainly true, I've also seen that CGC has, essentially, turned the high-end 9.2 and over category of key comics, into a financial market. I made two major purchases this year acting as, essentially, a broker for buyers who had no love for comics. In both situations, it was all about the investment. While I was happy to help, it just goes to show how our hobby has evolved from the days of Good, Fine or Mint to CGC 9.4 Signature Series.

So in closing, I will echo my fellows and say, definitely, buy what you love . . . but I'll add that, if you can afford it, it's probably not a bad idea to buy a CGC'd copy of *Amazing Fantasy* #15 either. Good luck in 2011.

Peter J. Bilelis, Esq.
Collector

The big news at the time of this writing is the continued (but slow) economic recovery and unprecedented change in Egypt. In the hobby, the big news was that individual comic book sales were reported to have topped $1 Million. And, a very positive trend is that comic book heroes are enjoying greater Silver Screen exposure. Over the next three years, more than a dozen such films are slated to be released, including another installment of both Superman and the Dark Knight, the Avengers, Captain America, Thor and Green Lantern. I think this is tremendously positive, as many of these heroes will be new to mainstream audiences, potentially drawing more people into the collecting aspect of our hobby. Finally, as a general statement, I think 2010 was a good year in the hobby, especially for the collector.

Availability: Overall, there was a lot of Golden Age material for sale. Very little of it, however, was comprised of the choice early issues from the more popular titles, although this wasn't readily obvious. What I mean is that at any given time you could have bought an *Action* #7, a *Detective* #31, a *Green Lantern* #1 or a *Marvel* #1, so it appeared that there were many of these books in the marketplace. But the fact is, the vast majority of these books, including *Action* #7 (CGC 2.0 – 4.0), *Detective* #29 (2.5 – 5.0), #31 (5.0 and 5.5) and #35 (2.5 – 4.0), *Green Lantern* #1 (9.0 and 7.0), *Young Allies* #1 (9.0) *Captain America* #1 and others (too many to name) that were for sale in 2010 were the exact same copies that had been cycling through the hobby over and over again for the past few years. Take those copies out of the picture, and there weren't very many other copies of these types of books around. Similarly, books that remained scarce in the marketplace included *More Fun* (except #54, 59 and 67), *Jackpot* (almost all), *Pep* #22 – 44, *Fantastic* (most) and many of the Raboy *Masters* (especially #24, 26-28, 31-35, 37 and 40 – which feature some of the very best WWII covers ever produced). And, unlike books from the Silver Age or Bronze Age, this scarcity statement about very early Golden Age is not qualified by availability in a given grade. With that said, most post-1941 Golden Age books were generally available. Finally, locating books in nice shape from the late 1940s – early 1950s also remained a challenge. Just try putting together a nice run of *Detectives* from this era or a run of *Perfect Crime* with an average grade above Fine.

Market Performance: I think it's fair to say that the hobby slightly resembled the villain Two-Face, in that it was primarily comprised of two overlapping, but mostly discrete personalities. And, market performance was somewhat dependent on "personality." On one side of the coin, there are the "blue chip" titles, comprised of books with characters that have mass appeal because they've transcended into Pop Culture. These titles consistently draw the most interest and are the best performers. On the other side of the coin, there are titles, many of which are very popular within the hobby and often do very well, but that don't, relatively speaking, command the same widespread interest level. The line between these two categories is not perfectly clear, as this second category comprises many keys (like *More Fun* #52 and 53, *Adventure* #40 and 73, etc.) and eye-candy books (like *Adventure* #79, *More Fun* #65, *All-Select* #1, *Mask* #1, etc.) that all do well. In terms of eye-candy books, I've found a growing interest in books with classic WWII covers. Even from a personal perspective, I've had more dealer requests this year than any other to sell (and at hefty prices) many of my WWII cover books (like *National* #7, most all *Masters* between #21 – 45, *Action* #19, 40, 43, *Adventure* #79, *More Fun* #72 and 75, *Daredevil Battles Hitler*, *Captain Marvel Jr.* #4 and 13, *Pep* #20 and 34, *Real Life* #3, etc.).

In terms of how Golden Age books sold in 2010, some set record high prices. In fact, when a collectible grade copy of any early *Action* with a Superman cover or any pre-Robin *Detective* with a Batman cover came to market, there was a "buzz." And that "buzz" often resulted in over-*Guide* prices being paid. As a general observation, however, there was a lot of price resistance and, except in rare cases, that "buzz" didn't necessarily equate to the same *Guide* multiples being paid as in the past. Furthermore, in many cases, quality books sold for less in 2010 than they did when these exact copies were sold some 3 – 6 years ago. At first blush, this would seem to defy the laws of supply and demand, given that many Golden Age books remained scarce. For instance, *Suspense Comics*, as a title, is quite scarce and virtually all issues feature a classic cover. Yet when several Edgar Church copies from this title were offered in 2009, each sold for far less than when last offered. This trend continued in 2010, as many titles, including *Wings*, *Star-Spangled*, *All-Select*, *All Star* (except for #3, 8, and 33) etc. performed similarly. I've also observed that, with ever-increasing prices, more people have curtailed collecting uber high-grade run books (even blue chips) as well as titles that feature forgotten characters.

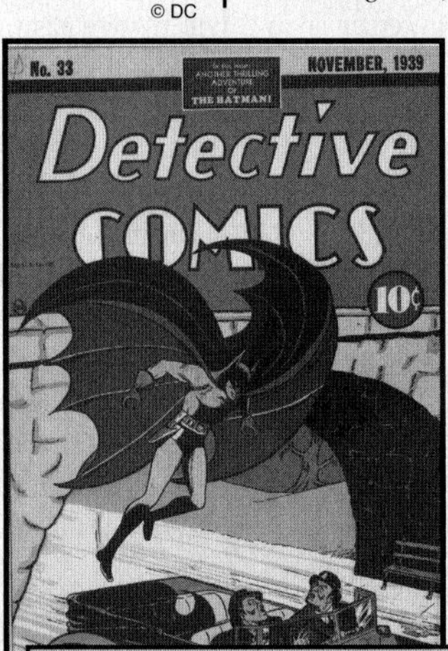

There's a buzz when pre-Robin **Detective Comics** issues (#33 shown) come to market.

I think this is a function of several factors – first, conservative spending in a tough economy. Second, prudent purchasing, as limited funds and ever-increasing prices mean people are forced to make tough decisions. Third, the sheer volume of Golden Age material flooding the market, especially by the various auction entities, has caused an over-saturation of material relative to available disposable income being allocated toward the hobby. This last factor has been present for some time, but coupled with a tough economy, its ramifications are now being felt. Given these factors, to conclude that scarcity of a given book should determine its price would misconstrue the laws of supply and demand, as the data would suggest something different – general availability of most material outpaced demand.

From a collector's perspective, this is opportunity knocking, as more has become affordable. I bought several books I've been hunting for years, including a very nice, white-paged copy of *Action* #12 for a very reasonable price. I even completed my Captain Marvel Jr. trilogy origin, by purchasing a *Whiz* #25, which is superior (and at a lower price) to another copy that a New York dealer has had for sale for years at a non-negotiable static pre-recession price. And, as indicated above, discriminating purchasing has not affected demand, especially for the cream, while lower grade Golden Age books were, once again, recession-proof. Indeed, blue chips keys were on-fire, almost regardless of grade (even single folios from key *Actions* and *Detectives* do well!). As such, I continue to believe that Golden Age is still a rock-solid segment and a prime area not only for collecting but also investing.

With respect to the Bronze Age, this era offers a ton of value for the collector. It showcases some of the finest talent – like Wrightson, Steranko, J. Buscema, Adams, Aparo, Romita and Byrne – and most any book from this era can be acquired, even if on a budget. And, unlike Golden Age, if you're a grade collector, you can locate virtually any book from this era in grade without much difficulty. For the Bronze Age high-grade collector, the challenge is in knowing what price to pay. I believe the guiding (general) principle is that there is nothing rare or unique. I reported 4 years ago that most highly collected books sold at "ridiculous" prices in any grade above 9.4, as many hobbyists thought books in 9.6 and 9.8 were uncommon or rare. This is no longer the case. The new standard for most Bronze Age books is 9.8. And, 9.8s are no longer unique, even for almost all keys (as of this writing, even the coveted *Green Lantern* #76 has 26 copies graded above 9.4). Given this dynamic, demand for "the best" likely will mean an increasing number of 9.8s and expect the number of 9.9s to increase, in turn redefining the *Guide* multiples at which books in 9.6 and 9.8 should be purchased.

So 2010 provided some interesting dynamics. The economic climate generally caused sale prices to flatten, yet sales volume (from $ - $$$$ books) confirmed a broad spectrum of interest, an indicator of continued stability and interest. With respect to Golden Age, some books proved to remain in extreme demand and continued to sell at record-setting prices, while those that were not moved quite well so long as priced right. Top-tier Bronze Age continued to excel. And, while dealers heavily discounted most Bronze Age in order to sell it, the lower prices for the more common material meant hobbyists could more easily quench their collecting thirst. Finally, I owe Malama Miller a big thank you for being my original partner in (collecting) crime, having introduced me to the world of comic books all those years ago. If you'd like to contact me to discuss comic books, I'd be happy to hear from you at pbilelis@yahoo.com. Good luck hunting in 2011.

Michael Browning Collector

This year, I decided to focus on a rather new aspect of our hobby: Trade paperbacks.

Trade paperbacks, or TPBs, as they are most commonly known, have been around for a long, long time, dating all the way back to the Fireside reprint volumes of Marvel and DC comics that started in the mid-1970s and ran up until around 1984's *X-Men: Dark Phoenix Saga*, which was published by Marvel, but still carried the listings for all the Fireside Marvels that had been published.

Dave Sim was one of the early TPB pioneers with his Swords of Cerebus collections and, later on, his phone book-format TPBs of the entire *Cerebus* run. Teenage Mutant Ninja Turtles collections from First Comics of the Mirage series were published, as well as a TMNT Collected volume (which is highly-sought-after now and costs anywhere from $250-$1,000).

From there, Marvel published a few trade paperback collections here and there, but it wasn't until DC's *Batman: The Dark Knight Returns* was published in two TPBs (and in hardcover) -- one a Warner bookstore edition and another for the new direct market -- that trade paperbacks really started to catch on. From that point, we got *Watchmen*, John Byrne's *Man of Steel*, *Batman: A Death in the Family*, *Justice League: A New Beginning* and many others.

Alan Moore's *Saga of the Swamp Thing* reprints in trade paperback started with his first arc on the series and then his second and it was just a few years before his entire run was collected. By that time, the full run of *Sandman* was being collected by DC.

Marvel published a lot of its more important stories in trade paperback, including *Thing: Project Pegasus*, *Hawkeye*, *Machine Man* by Barry Windsor-Smith, *Iron Man: Demon in a Bottle* (which was first called "The Power of Iron Man"), *New Mutants: Demon Bear* and others.

In the 1990s, reprinting stories in the trade paperback format became commonplace and both Marvel and DC started churning out the TPBs, as did Dark Horse, Malibu and Valiant and many of the independent companies also produced reprint tomes.

As the newsstand market diminished and the direct market took over by the late 1990s, comic book companies began to realize that there was a new market that was still untapped -- the bookstores. If comic companies could get their publications into bookstores, that would open up a whole new revenue stream. Comic writers and artists also liked the revenue from royalties, and getting their product into the hands of the bookstore crowd meant more money. So, most every writer started writing for the trade, which meant decompressed storytelling. Where a single story could have fit into a single issue of *Amazing Spider-Man*, now it was stretched out to fit a four-issue arc, which made for a really nice trade paperback. And that TPB was sold to bookstores as a "graphic novel," which, in more recent years, even got its own aisle in many of the larger bookseller chains like Books-A-Million and Borders. (I'm not even going to discuss Manga here, because that would take way too many pages).

As the bookstore market grew, companies like DC and Marvel decided to put nearly EVERYTHING into TPB.
But, not everything published as a TPB has a print run like *Watchmen*, which has been printed consistently since 1987 in TPB and hardcover and Absolute Editions and ...

We all know comic book collectors love rarities. We search out the *Gerber Photo Journals* for rare 8s and 9s and pay big money for 10s when we can find them. Now, we're paying big bucks for TPBs, too.

Some TPBs are very rare (Marvel's *Master of Kung Fu* Max TPB is extremely hard to find), while others are readily available whenever you want to click on eBay or any comic shop web site.

During the early 2000s, *Miracleman* became white hot. Single issues were selling for multiples of cover and the rarer, later issues were selling upwards of $100 for high-grade copies. The *Miracleman* Eclipse Comics trade paperbacks were also selling well. *Miracleman* TPB volumes 1-2 were selling for around $50-$75 for nice copies, while volume 3, *Olympus*, was selling for around $150. I bought my first copy -- a VG -- from S&G Collectibles in Sevierville, Tenn., in 2001 for $162 and tax because I wanted very badly to read the rest of the Alan Moore run and I knew the TPB was very hard to find at the time. From then on, I've kept a close eye on many of the rarer TPBs: Like Broadway Comics' *Fatale: Inherit the Earth*, which sells for around $50 in TPB and is almost never seen in hardcover. Like *Batman: Prodigy*, which sells regularly for around $35-$50, because of its Nightwing-centric storyline.
Like the *Thanos* TPBs by Jim Starlin and Keith Giffen, which all sell for upwards of $50 each or more if a bidding war ensues on eBay.

In early 2011, I was completely surprised by a sale on eBay of a trade paperback I had been buying regularly for under $20. A first print *Squadron Supreme*, which contains writer Mark Gruenwald's ashes in the ink, sold on eBay for $612 plus tax. Yes, you read that right -- $612 for a *Squadron Supreme* trade paperback! The entire 12-issue series sells as cheap as $10 in some places and the TPB sold for $612.

Many of today's TPBs are printed to order and don't have very high print runs, which leads to collectors seeking these out and paying high prices to own copies. One artist told me that the trade paperback of a series he drew was so rare the company publishing it didn't even send him a copy.

The rarity of some TPBs causes them to skyrocket in price, especially if its a TPB of one of the more popular characters, like the Kyle Rayner Green Lantern, whose trade paperbacks all sell for above cover price. *Green Lantern: The Power of Ion* is a $100 TPB when it pops up and many of the other Rayner GL trades sell for around $30 each.

The Wally West *Flash* trade paperbacks that reprint stories written by Geoff Johns all sell for $25-$50 each.

VALIANT trade paperbacks, such as the two *Magnus Robot Fighter* and two *Solar* TPBs are expensive, ranging from $35-$40 each and the *Solar* hardcover sells for over $100 when it pops up for sale.

Malibu's Ultraverse, which was sold to Marvel and hasn't been seen since, published three trade paperbacks of *Prime*, *The Strangers* and the Marvel crossover called *Godwheel*, and those are normally priced around $20 each. Not bad for companies that have been out of business since the 1990s!

Nowadays, almost as soon as TPBs go out of print, they go up in value, like the *Batgirl Rising* trade paperback that has cover price of $17.99, but sells for $35-$40. All because dealers can tag it as "OOP," which means it is out of print. The Marvel Omnibus line of oversized hardcover collections also has some rarities, like the Jack Kirby *Eternals* which sells for around $150 and Grant Morrison's *New X-Men*, which is an easy sale at $200. The Brian Michael Bendis *Daredevil Omnibus* HCs are in the $200-$250 range, as is the Garth Ennis *Punisher* and the *Tomb of Dracula* Volume 1. The Ed Brubaker *Daredevil* Vol. 1 sells for over $100 a copy, as copies of those TPBs that make up the Omnibus all sell for cover price or lower.

© MAR

Imagine the thrill of seeing the original art for *Amazing Fantasy* #15.

The *Gotham Central* HC line is reprinting the *Gotham Central* comic series, which was first reprinted as trade paperbacks. Volume 1 of the hardcover *Gotham Centrals* is an easy sale at $90, which is three times its cover price. Many of the *Nightwing* trade paperbacks are also high-dollar items, selling for around $30-$50 for the rare volumes.

This is an ever-growing corner of the comic collecting hobby. Many collectors dismiss TPBs and HCs as merely reprints. But, for those of us in the know, we are keeping our eyes on how much growth back issue sales of TPBs and hardcovers have made in the last few years and we understand that as collectors try to complete their collections, they will need these and will have to pay larger sums of cash to put these into their longboxes.

Comic Book Collecting Association
Steve Zarelli, CBCA President

It's hard to believe time has passed so quickly, but February marked the first anniversary of the Comic Book Collecting Association. While every other major collecting hobby such as coin collecting, autograph collecting and book collecting has at least one – and often several – collecting associations, the CBCA is the only such group representing comic book collectors, dealers and enthusiasts. Among our members are collectors of all genres, prominent dealers and industry pros.

Our mission is simple -- promote the comic book art form and hobby of comic book collecting by encouraging fellowship among comic book enthusiasts, providing information and education to the public, and helping to facilitate the buying, selling, and trading of comic books and related material in an environment of trustworthiness and integrity. Our growing numbers demonstrate that our message has resonated with many members of the hobby.

Staying true to our mission of Fellowship, Education and Ethics, we'd like to highlight some of our accomplishments and successes in year one:

• We published four editions of our newsletter, *The Comic Book Quarterly*
• We hosted a website and forum, which received over a quarter-million hits per month in 2010 (comiccollecting.org)
• The CBCA sponsored an Amateur Art Contest
• The group hosted a dinner at the New York Comic Con
• We sponsored a giveaway of one free year of GPAnalysis to a lucky member
• We coordinated a viewing of the *Amazing Fantasy* #15 art that was attended by members and industry pros
• We established a member discount to Collectibles Insurance Services as well as to Susan Cicconi's Restoration Lab
• The CBCA was sought by the media to comment on several high profile comic-related stories.

But, our work has just begun. Looking forward to 2011, our plans include:

• Offering an online grading guide
• Adding more educational content to our website
• Sponsoring a scientific laboratory study on the effects of pressing on paper
• Hosting member events, seminars, adding more member discounts and much more...

We can only do this with the support of the community and a robust membership. If you are not a member, we ask you to consider joining and becoming engaged in the association. As we always say in our emails and newsletters, your feedback and input is greatly appreciated and essential to our success.

Our hobby is evolving every day and we have great optimism for the art form we all love. Working together, we can all contribute toward a healthy and vibrant hobby that will continue to thrive for generations to come.

For additional information, please visit us at www.comiccollecting.org. Annual dues are merely $20.00.

Gary Dolgoff
Gary Dolgoff Comics

The World economy is still struggling… yet here, in this "Microcosm of Coolness" known as Comic Dealing and Collecting, our chosen hobby is alive and well. I, myself, have been buying (and selling) "with vigor" (to borrow an old J.F.K. expression).

Among our 2010 purchases by GDCOMICS are:

• Over $120,000 in 1960s Marvels (including comics from Fair/Poor to Very Fine, and better!

• Runs of 1950s – 1960s DCs (#1-up of *Superboy*, *Jimmy Olsen*, *Lois Lane*, *Showcase*, *Green Lantern*, *Justice League*, and many others…)

• Golden Age (early 1940s misc. publishers, #1s at 70% of *Guide*, runs of *Shadow* and *Green Hornet* at 60% of *Guide*, a wonderful collection of 1940s *Weird*, *Wonderworld*, etc… and much more!)

• Original Art: Everything from 1960s Marvel art to assorted 1980s DC and Marvel stuff and a stack of 1960s Millie the Model art!

• A *Classics Comics* collection

• 1,000+ Pre-Code, of every variety: Fiction House, Romance, Horror, Hero, War, etc!

Golden Age (1930s to 1955): I always enjoy buying these – from 'mainline to miscellaneous' – from Poor to Mint… truly, I do! I find that I've been fortunate to get in a few thousand of these "Goldy Oldies" this year, often paying 50%-70% *Guide* for them, even in lower grades. I was happy enough to get in *Captain America's (Weird Tales)* #73, paying near Guide for a GD/VG (3.0) copy. In fact, during the year, I've kept many Golden Age books for "meself" including: *Dead Who Walk*, *Haunt of Fear* #17 (with the three grisly ghouls on the cover), *Crime Suspense* #19 (Choking cover), *All-Negro* #1, *Action* #23 (1st Luthor with a beautiful, old-school Superman cover… timeless!), *Weird* #2-5 (low grade, but I love those "Weird" covers), several 1940s Timely superhero comics… and much, much more! Timelys are the best sellers, with *Captain America* leading the pack. Most go for over-*Guide*, and I pay for 'em accordingly, and quite happily.

Beautiful old-school Superman covers are irresistible. (Action Comics #23 shown)

DCs: It's been a while since I've had a run of *More Fun Comics* with The Spectre, and I'd love to get a set of 'em! (#52-107) Beautiful covers they are. Last year I bought a set of *Action* #89-299, plus about 40 earlier issues. These books sold well, and still do. In general, pre-code *All Stars* and titles with Batman, Superman, Flash, Green Lantern, and/or Wonder Woman still sell well enough and I always enjoy obtaining collections of those. Non-superhero Golden Age DCs (Western, Crime/Mystery, and especially Funny Animal) do not sell very well (though I'll buy them as part of a collection of oldies.)

Other Golden Age: In general, most late 1930s/early 1940s Superhero comics are decent sellers (although some titles, have lost some of their luster in recent years. Most Centaurs (*Amazing-Man*, *Amazing Mystery Funnies*, etc.) are still great sellers. *Hangman Comics* (MLJ Pub.), I haven't had in years, admittedly, because they're great books!

For Fiction House, *Planet*s sell well. *Jumbo Comics* sell fantastically from #1-10; #11-50 sell pretty well; #51-up sell OK. *Jungle Comics* sell, but not as well. Early Quality issues of all titles sell solidly and have great art, characters, etc. Middle and later 1940s Quality Comics sell fairly slowly, for the most part. MLJ are solid sellers for the most part, with great covers and "primitive art within". For Fox, *Mystery Men*, *Weird*, and *Wonderworld* are good sellers in all grades… and "cool to the eye". I love to buy misc. Golden Age; any size collection!

Silver Age: Early 1960s Marvels are the pillars of our industry in my experience - especially the #1 issues. They are, so-far, the best investment comics overall, with *Amazing Fantasy* #15, *Fantastic Four* #1, and *Incredible Hulk* #1 almost doubling in value in the *Guide* over the last two years (in Good, Very Good and Fine grades.

Marvels from mid-1960s to 1971: The main titles like *Avengers*, *Captain America*, *Daredevil* (to a certain extent), *Fantastic Four*, *Hulk*, *Iron Man*, and *X-Men* are solid sellers, and in our VG and better, sell quite well! *Thor* sells OK, and *Strange Tales*, *Tales of Suspense*, *Tales to Astonish* only sell well in nicer shape for us. *Sgt. Fury*, though a "fun-to-read" title, doesn't sell so well for us. But, I find that sellers are happier when I take "the good" AND the "not-so-good". Sets of 1960s Marvels (especially the better titles) sell well for me. I avidly buy them "a collection at a time".

1955 thru 1971 DCs (10¢ Cover Price): In our VG and better, Superhero 10¢ cover DCs sell quite well, especially the early *Showcase* and *Brave and the Bold*, and 10¢-c *Batman* comics. Also, the *Flash* #105 and *Green Lantern* #1 are solid sellers. In GD/VG and less, they sell "variably"… they can take quite a while to move (except for *Showcase* #4 and #24, which move well in all grades). Earlier *Mystery In Space* and *Strange Adventures* move well, as do *Our Army at War*.

DCs (12¢-15¢ Cover Price): If they are in our nice VG-/VG and better, I can usually move them pretty well, especially in "Sets-By-Title". I had several runs of VG-/VG and better DCs, ranging from *Green Lantern* to *Jimmy Olsen*… every one of those sets, sold! I buy these nicer DC collections avidly!

For GD/VG and lower grades, they mostly don't sell well, so I often discount them 20%-33% or more, and even then, "they ain't swift"! Batman issues sell better than most and *Green Lantern* #76 is an instant seller!

Archie, Harvey, Dell and Gold Key sell slowly for me (though I personally enjoy reading Archie comics to this day!)

1970s (Bronze-Age): Comics from this era have been under-valued for decades now. Price-wise, they are starting to have their day. I have sold over 10,000 "better 1970s" to happy comic dealers, both here and overseas, in the last year. Dealers and collectors especially like them in 'nice, clean shape', which is our VG and better. Some of the best 1970s comics are *Defenders* #1-10; *Marvel Team-Up* #1-10; *Ghost Rider* #1; *Tomb of Dracula* (a "great read with great art"); early 1970s *Batman* and *Detective*; *Amazing Spider-Man* #100-150; *X-Men* #94-142, plus *Giant-Size X-Men* #1; *Hulk* #121-182; *Iron Man* #60 and earlier; *Avengers* #100-150; and *Fantastic Four* #112.

1980s - 2000s: We at GDCOMICS have been paying more attention to this era. My able crew has been putting more and more of them in order. Generally speaking, our policy is to charge 75¢-$1.00 for most comics in nice shape that are $4 and less in NM- Overstreet.

For more expensive 1980s thru 2000s, we generally do all-right with 'em, as long as we charge about 25%-33% of NM- Overstreet for them. In general, we find that comics from the later 1990s thru the 2000s sell better because of their limited print run, and because of their cover price in relation to our 75¢-$1.00 whole price on them.

General Buying in Today's Market: I love buying old comics (in all grades!), Original Art, and Pulps. We have over 50,000 1940s-1971 comics, and approximately 200,000+ 1970s and early '80s comics, plus hundreds of thousands of 1980s-2000s comics, but I want to keep supplying myself for many lifetimes!

Finder's Fees: As a comic dealer, I find offering cash incentives to comic-collection-finders a great way to help the market thrive. Last year, we paid a fellow comic-dealer from down South approximately $10,500 in Finder's Fees in three months, for three collections that he sold to me. I take pride in always paying "the fee" for information leading to a deal (as long as I don't already know that the deal exists). Why not? As corny as it sounds, "just do the right thing".

eBay: We sell on eBay under GDCOMICS, and although eBay is very labor-intensive, we maintain a continuing, and substantial presence on the "bay-of-ee's" as I like to call it. The only problem is, eBay is so labor-intensive that we can only maintain 2,000+ oldies on there ('30s thru '60s comics, plus maybe a very few 1970s books). We also list on eBay a number of our "Sets for Sale" (1950s thru 2000s) and a lot of wholesale "Package Deals" ('50s thru 2000s). On eBay, we have a 100% satisfaction rating.

Website (www.gdcomics.com): We have a newly-revised website which serves the "Web-Goals" of: very secure, easy navigation, and easy Checkout! In addition, we've added vast amounts of comics 1940s thru the 2000s, plus we have a newly-expanded staff, that is "tres computer-savvy" with the goal of keeping the website "goin' and flowin".

For non-computer users, we will have a print catalog every once in a while. If you seriously collect and/or deal comics, just feel free to give us your contact info.

Have a GR-REAT! collecting and/or dealing year. - Gary D.

Walter Durajlija and Marc Sims
Big B Comics

For us the year 2010 started off slowly but as the year progressed so did our sales. Our back issue sales were down at the beginning of the year, I think largely in part to local collectors tightening their budgets. Many familiar faces from year's past have stopped coming around. I do not think this is an isolated issue. We exhibited at 2 Toronto Comic Cons in the spring and attendance at both was pretty abysmal. I swear I saw tumbleweeds blowing down the aisles of Wizard World Toronto.

For the first 6 months of the year, collections were few and far between. Luckily we did manage to find a nice little collection of Marvels just in time for the August Toronto Fan Expo (our big convention for the year). The collection cost us $8,000 and was nice because it was heavy on multiples of Marvel keys in affordable grades. It's nice going into a convention with multiple copies of *Iron Man* #1, *Captain America* #100, *Fantastic Four* #112, *Sub-Mariner* #8, 34, *Conan* #1, *Amazing Spider-Man* #121, 122, etc. A nice collection of about a dozen rarer Canadian Whites (AA and Maple Leaf) also came in just before the convention. We had a successful Fan Expo and we saw no evidence of a "market correction", at least not for the nice solid comic books being bought up by the collectors. Attendance was the polar opposite of the spring Toronto shows. The fire marshal was refusing entry as the building was over capacity and lines were stretching down several city blocks.

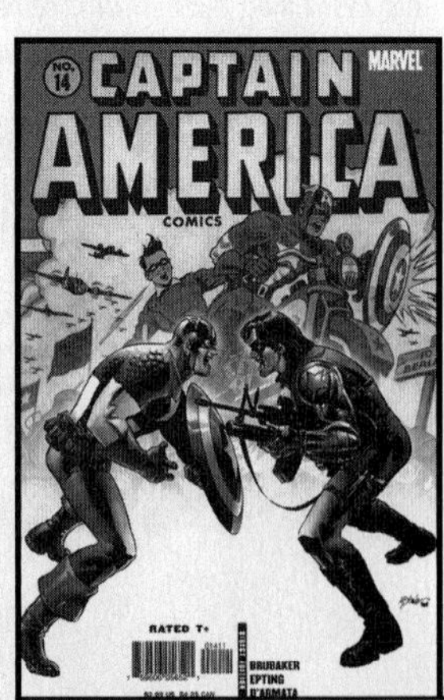

Ed Brubaker's **Captain America** is a great example of good story-telling. (#14 shown)

In October of 2010 we purchased a very large comic collection for $60,000. There were about 7000 books, all from the mid 1940s to the mid 1970s. Nice deep runs of the main Marvel and DC titles were present. Keys included a CGC 2.5 *Amazing Fantasy* #15, a raw *Amazing Spider-Man* #1 in GD/VG, a raw *Fantastic Four* #1 in GD+, a raw run of *X-Men* #1-10 in solid mid grades, 3 copies of

Fantastic Four #12, *Sgt. Fury* #1, *Tales to Astonish* #27, *Detective Comics* #58, *Justice League of America* #1, *Casper* #1 and on and on. The collection had a large run of early Harvey Comics and an excellent Dell run. It was nice to see a collection of this size surface and it was even nicer that we were able to pick it up. The only bad thing about a collection like this is that it meant that I, my price guide and the night lamp had to spend weeks together; we were almost inseparable. It's hard work and it really is an intricate dance looking at the comic book, going through the *Guide* and trying to figure out which books will bear *Guide*, get over *Guide*, or sell at a fraction of *Guide*. It was refreshing to note just how tied to the *Guide* we still are.

I think in recent years the Overstreet Comic Book Price Guide has become the most overlooked and undervalued tool in the hobby. While investors and speculators depend more on the real time results delivered by websites like GP Analysis, the *Overstreet* remains the backbone of the hobby. I'd say well over 90% of comic books trading above bargain bin prices are not tracked by any websites but many people treat those online sales as gospel. That 90% of sales happens in comic shops, comic book conventions, want ad posts and private sales. All these transactions are anchored by the *Overstreet Price Guide*. It has become evident that any comic book that is not one of the stars of an online auction is going to underperform in that auction. Take a quality early run book from Marvel in low to mid grade and post it on an auction. The result is usually a sale at a fraction of *Guide*. But this is just a very tiny segment of the market for these types of books. It is also a very limited selling window for a comic book surrounded by flashier comic books. I'll even venture to say that a good percentage of the buyers scooping up these bargains are dealers willing to keep inventory and wait out a higher price. Way more 4.0 copies of say *Amazing Spider-Man* #50 sell untracked than they do tracked. Because the tracked data is so limited these higher unreported prices actually make the data available online inaccurate. In actual fact the average prices realized for these books are much closer to the *Overstreet* values. Sure, the *Overstreet* is an annual printed price guide and by its nature cannot reflect quick market changes. But again these quick changes affect a very small percentage of comics and the speculators and investors represent a small fraction of collectors. For the vast majority of the comic books that we sell, a measure against the *Overstreet Price Guide* remains the main determinant of price.

On the retail side, 2010 was a year of challenges for many direct market comic book stores in North America. I know we had to work very hard just to stay at roughly the same sales level as 2009. Many other retailers that I speak with report sales being down anywhere from 10-30%. Very few of my retailing brethren reported any kind of positive gains in 2010. The biggest loser by far was new comic sales as a 33% line wide price increase and general consumer apathy towards much of Marvel's output resulted in a lot of customers cutting back on spending or falling out of comic collecting all together. The drop-off for DC was not as pronounced. Many pundits blame online piracy and/or legal digital downloads and though I'm sure this can account for some percentage of the drop in sales at the retail level, I am much more confident in putting the majority of the blame on bad stories and line saturation. When the big 2 produce good stories that people want to read, people come out to buy them. When they produce pap that is easily passed by, well, we are seeing the result. The sad thing is that genuinely good comics tend to get lost in the shuffle as many people are more apt to throw their hands up in frustration than to do the hard (and costly) work of searching out the good stuff. This just means that, more than ever, it's incumbent on retailers to do the work for them and point people in the right direction.

Let's get back to line saturation, because I really think this is a monumental problem in the industry. I see the mistakes of the early '90s being repeated all over again and it is frightening. As I do my weekly orders for new comic product I really have to scratch my head at 9 different Captain America comics or 11 different Thor comics, most priced at $3.99. Where exactly is the market for that? I place token orders or big fat zeros for many of them and no one amongst my customer base seems to be missing them. Marvel obviously wants to package as much material together in time to release graphic novels pre-movie, but I'm sure when it comes to ordering time I won't be ordering many of these graphic novels either. If the stories all look pretty much the same and there is little to no consumer interest, I just don't see the market for them. I would rather sell backlist products that I know are good stories that will get people into the shop looking for the next thing. Ed Brubaker's *Captain America* is a great example, but sadly Marvel has let many of these volumes go out of print while they churn out numerous mini-series without any identity whatsoever. I really just don't get it.

Sadly this looks to be a trend that will continue into 2011. The dearth of quality product shipping in the 1st quarter is going to really put a lot of stores into a bad spot. We have already seen large numbers of stores closing across North America in 2010. A 2010 census by Phil Boyle of Coliseum of Comics in Florida put the number of direct market comic book stores in the U.S. at roughly 1800. This was based on collecting hard data and actually contacting stores to verify their existence. The most commonly held number prior to this was 3000 stores in the U.S., but this was based solely on numbers of accounts with Diamond Comics Distributors. That is a pretty shocking difference and I think the worst is yet to come in 2011. There will be areas of the country that become drastically underserviced but at the same time there will be opportunities aplenty for smart and enterprising retailers to fill those voids.

It's not all doom and gloom though! 2010 had its fair share of hits as well. At the top of the list we have Bryan Lee O'Malley's *Scott Pilgrim*. This series of 6 graphic novels was a sales juggernaut for most of the calendar year and was important for the fact that it brought new faces into our stores. And, just as important, they were young faces! Robert Kirkman's *Walking Dead* was a similar smash success. This wonderful zombie apocalypse story was already one of our top sellers for several years. The added exposure of a hit TV series catapulted it to a whole new level. Both series prove that well done, engaging, and entertaining stories in comic book format can be extremely successful, and not just because of the added exposure in other media. *The Walking Dead* show aired just 6 episodes on a specialty cable channel not widely available in many markets. *Scott Pilgrim* the movie was a box office flop. But both series sell phenomenally well in comic book form because, as comics, they have mass appeal and are good. Period.

I think the next few years are really going to be telling for the comic book industry, particularly on the retail side. There are a lot of stores in cities across North America that opened in the late '70s and early '80s. Those stores that have had consistent ownership for the past 30 years will now have owners that are looking at retirement. Will they be able to sell their businesses? Are there buyers out there for them? If they close, will new stores come in to take their place? These are big questions and I don't know if we have the answers. Again, there are opportunities for well-run businesses to flourish in this market. Whether it be in collectible comics or whatever 2011 version of *Scott Pilgrim* is waiting out there for us all, here's to hoping that the collections come in big and fast and that Diamond is never out of stock.

Finally, Marc and I once again want to thank the staffs of Blue Beetle and Big B for their hard work and all of our great customers who continue to support us.

Ken Dyber
Cloud Nine Comics

Greetings, I've been buying and selling comics for over 25 years now, starting on the East coast in CT, and now on the West coast in Oregon. Feel free to visit Cloud 9 online at: www.cloudninecomics.com or email me: ken@cloudninecomics.com, you can always contact me as well for a private showing if you're coming to the Portland area. The website continues to evolve and improve with more 1 to 1 ratio cover scans, better design, and now direct links from GPAnalysis to our CGC slabbed books. Cloud 9 is also a CGC Authorized Dealer, so feel free to contact me if you have questions about CGC or would like to receive a discount on submitting your books to CGC. This year I was able to travel to the East coast and Midwest to shop, hitting about half a dozen stores in New England, and ones in Madison, Chicago, and Iowa City, which helped give me a sense of what was available across the country, and at what prices things were selling (or not selling).

The Year Overall: Other than the early record sales of *Action* #1 and *Detective* #27, which many advisors talked about in our 40th *Guide*, my overall feeling was 2010 was worse then 2009, and this is due to several reasons. First off, the economy! Unemployment is still around 10% nationwide, we're still at war, and the housing market is flat at best with interest rates at an all time low. Does this affect you folks out there who buy your couple books a week to read? Probably not, but for those of you that have a box at the local shop and normally bought 5-10 titles each week, you may now be buying 2-5. Oh yes, and that $4 cover price is ridiculous. Remember when cover prices, if they went up, went up $.10 or $.25, but to go right from $3 to $4? How about $3.25? Cheers to Vertigo for having a $1.00 cover price on some of their new first issues (even if it's only a few).

Other than economic related reasons, I saw less quality material come to the marketplace this past year. I feel this was not only locally in the Pacific Northwest, but nationally as well from my travels or weekly searches on the internet. On eBay, I'm also seeing more comics coming up for sale as "Buy It Now" only, instead of as auctions, which I feel takes away from the purpose of an auction site. There seemed to be very few interesting collections that came up for sale this year, most were Silver – Modern Age superhero. Where are the horror, Archie, jungle, or sci-fi collections? Locally I saw one large EC collection come in for the first time in almost a decade, and one superhero collection surfaced which another local dealer purchased, other than that, not much new in the Pacific Northwest.

After the economy and lack of quality material, I also saw some disturbing new trends arise in the value of some blue chips (even in high grade!). *Incredible Hulk* #181 in CGC 9.8 has consistently sold between $15,000-$25,000 for years now, with an average around $20,000. This year at present there have been 5 copies sold in this grade with 3 selling for $12,600, $13,351 & $11,950, that's 3 record low sales for the same book at its highest grade in the same year. Also, Silver Age Blue chips have finally stabilized for the first time in years almost across the board. *Tales of Suspense* #39 CGC 9.2 sold for $49,750, and in 2009 a 9.2 sold for $50,000, even *Amazing Fantasy* #15 has been flat in most grades this past year. So, demand is still there for this great investment books, but buying and flipping these books in a year or two, may not happen again for some years down the road. From what I've seen a book will get hot, sometimes doubling or even tripling in price, then cool off for 4-7 years, then get hot again, although who knows if the returns will be as large. In summary, now is a great time to buy, if you can find the right books to buy. When will that *Tales of Suspense* #39 CGC 9.2 will hit the $100,000 sales mark? 2012? 2015? 2020? You be the judge, but my bets are sooner than later.

Below are some thoughts about specific time periods, some books I've purchased, some books I've sold, and some basic thoughts on pricing in our beloved price guide.

Golden Age: It seems there is still steady demand for these great books, but I'm seeing increased resistance from buyers due to pricing. I'm not sure if the prices are right and people are just pinching their pockets, or if the *Guide* needs to remain flat for a year or two for inflation and interest to return to these books. I would like to know where are all of the Centaurs? Were 90% donated during the war paper drives? Try putting together a complete collection of this publisher! Finding copies of *The Arrow* on eBay in any grade is often difficult, and the asking price is usually double *Guide*. Female characters I think are still undervalued such as Wonder Woman, Sun Girl, Miss Fury, Blonde Phantom, Mary Marvel, or the first appearance of Star Sapphire in *All Flash* #32, (you know she'll be in one of these Green Lantern movies.)

At shows I've been finding more people asking for or collecting their favorite artists for this time period than putting together a run of a title or publisher. I think Nedors and Fiction House are way undervalued in general as they are much more difficult to find then Timelys or DCs. Try putting together a run of *Black Terror* or *Planet Comics* in Fine or better. It may not cost as much as a *Detective Comics* run, but it may be more difficult to find these books, forget about in grade. *Exciting Comics* #9 (1st Black Terror) & #39 (Nazis giving poison candy to kids) could skyrocket very soon, both sell way above *Guide*, and the highest graded CGC sale of #9 is only a 5.5, and there have only been two CGC sales of #39, so yes, very scarce. Buy what you love from this time period, as most books will cost one a decent bit, and there just aren't that many of them out there. Sales wise, I don't do much presently in this time period, but I did sell some *Blackhawk*, *Startling Terror Tales*, *Sensation Comics*, *Blue Bolt* and Archies.

Atomic Age: I'm buying more, selling more, and seeing more people ask for books from this period, which to me parallels the Bronze Age in diversity and affordability. EC horror books are regularly in demand, although usually at a small discount below *Guide*, war and Archie titles seem too cheap to me given their scarcity. There are quite a few cool crime/detective books from this period with some great artists doing just a few random issues. *Ken Shannon* issues seem quite reasonable with great artwork. Early 10¢ romance books were in high demand and selling at a good percent of *Guide* if I could keep them in stock. Pre-code Horror is always in demand, but pricing is a bit resistant, although I think it's more economic based than the *Guide* being too high. I'm seeing less and less Avon one shots in shops and at shows. Try collecting all these! Some titles I sold this year include: *Prize Comics Western*, *Mysterious Adventures*, *Tales From The Crypt*, *Strange Tales of the Unusual*, *I Love You*, and *Journey Into Fear*.

Silver Age: *Amazing Fantasy* #15 has finally cooled off after around a decade of insane increases. Still a great investment in all grades, but it may finally not be doubling every 3 years like it has been. My sales from this time period are about 70% superhero, 10% Archie, 10% Romance, and 10% Dell/Gold Key, however, over the years I've been buying mostly superhero, so I have a much larger stock. Starting this year I am actively going to search out less superhero comics, and more from other genres, as although their ticket prices are usually much lower, they seem to be much more liquid books for me when I get them in. *Amazing Spider-Man* interest was low for the 2nd year in a row, other than issues #1-10. *Incredible Hulk* #1-6 are still very much in demand, with #1 showing huge gains in all grades. *Fantastic Four* has picked up steam after a few cool years with more interest in #1-10, 25, 26, 48-50 & 52. *Avengers* #1 has cooled quite a bit, however issues #2-50 are selling regularly as people try and complete their runs on a still very affordable title. *X-Men*, other than #1 have just been collecting dust for several years now (the movies really weren't that bad!), and even this first issue has been basically flat price wise. *Captain America* has been hot for all issues, and #100 has been selling above *Guide* in all grades. *Thor* and *Journey Into Mystery* are selling fairly regularly, but not close to the *Avengers* volume wise. *Daredevil*, now this one is strange to me, as many of my dealer and collector friends save "*Daredevil*'s a soft book, or that books dead in the water, etc…", yet show after show, I sell more *Daredevil* keys or filler issues than other Marvel superheros typically (I have to include Bronze sales here with this title due to Bullseye & Elektra sales). *Sub-Mariner* to me is a soft book, however issue #8 sells quite well in all grades and is due for a large increase in *Guide*. *Iron Man* #1 is one of the most liquid books from this time period, and needs to go up in *Guide* in all grades by at least 25%.

© FH

Putting together a run of **Planet Comics** (#23 shown) can be difficult, but fun.

DC wise, *Green Lantern* #7 (1st Sinestro, which I talked about in the *Guide* last year) seems to now be more available since everyone has caught on about this book. It is still very tough to find, and needs a huge increase in *Guide* of about 300% in all grades as CGC 3.0-4.0's are selling for $300-$400 at present. Issues #14 & 16 (1st Sonar & S.A. Star Sapphire) seem way undervalued and are very hard to find about VF. The first issue is doing quite well in FN or higher, but lower grades copies still out-supply demand. *Teen Titans* books above FN seem quite hard to find, and #1 in high grade seems very affordable if you can find one, same for their first appearance in *Brave & the Bold*. *Showcase* #22 is currently one of the hottest books on the market if you can find one. *Flash* #105-110 still seem very undervalued to me, as he's probably one of the most well known characters of all time, and a huge player in the DC universe. *Wonder Woman*s are very affordable, and tough to find in any grade, especially FN or higher. *Adventure Comics* haven't been showing much demand other than a few people collecting the Legion run starting at #300. These are very hard to find in VF or higher, and have great story lines.

Archies sell almost as fast as I get them in, although usually at a discount off *Guide*. Another character to watch is Richie Rich, whose first appearance in *Little Dot* #1 seems very affordable, as do most of his titles. Romance titles are very much in demand with high grade selling at or above *Guide*, and low to mid-grade moving briskly, but slightly below *Guide*. In general, sales were slower this year for this time period as there is becoming resistance to pricing. Some titles/books I sold include: *Tales of Suspense* #39 CGC 3.0 for $1100, *Iron Man* #1 FN $120, *Journey Into Mystery* #121 VF $50, *Green Lantern* #7 CGC 5.5 $340, *Daredevil* #1 GD-/1.0 $120, *Batman* #171 VF- $115, *Avengers* #2 FN- $200, #9 VG $70, *Amazing Spider-Man* #14 CGC 7.5(rest.) $500.

Bronze Age: My best selling period for at least the 3rd year in a row. People are filling their runs for quite cheap, as many books are still available in VF/NM/9.0 or higher for quite affordable prices, and FN to VF copies can usually be found for $3-$5. I saw an increase in demand for DC horror this year (in grade), as many of these have some of the best covers of the decade. Keys that sell often with little price resistance include: *Green Lantern* #76 (which is now has the highest sale price from this time period with the only CGC 9.8 selling for $37,344!), *Hulk* #180-182, *Amazing Spider-Man* #121, 129 & 194, *Iron Man* #55, *Werewolf By Night* #32 (this one needs to go up about 100% in all grades in *Guide*!), *Fantastic Four* #112, *Daredevil* #131, 168, *Ghost Rider* #1, *Marvel Spotlight* #5 & 32 (1st Spider-Woman needs at least a 25% increase in all grades), *X-Men* #94 (interest returning after several slow years), *Giant-Size X-Men* #1, *Avengers* #94, 95 (Neal Adams), *Star Wars* #1 35¢ price variant, *Cerebus* #1, *Weird War Tales* #1, *Captain America* #117 (1st Falcon), and *Iron Fist* #14 (regular or variant).

One book I feel is a huge sleeper (and maybe it's because it's a DC) is *Superman's Pal Jimmy Olsen* #134 (1st Darkseid). He almost took over the universe a few years ago, and now he's the main villain on Smallville's last season. If only Superman will fight Doomsday or Darkseid in a movie!

House of Secrets #92 is still in demand, but showing price resistance. *Tomb of Dracula* #1 & 10, same thing. People want them, but aren't shelling out *Guide* for them at present. *Green Lantern* Neal Adams run is doing well, but the *X-Men* Byrne run has almost tanked in value for some odd reason. I love *Wonder Woman* 15¢ covers without costume, as they are harder to find, great covers, and showing great annual returns. Shorter run titles are showing demand like *Night Nurse*, *Beware The Cat*, *Black Panther*, *Black Goliath*, and *Champions*. *Conan* #1 is showing price resistance, and interest has been down on issues 23 & 24.

Gold Key/Whitman Funny Animal books sell quite well for 50¢ - $2, but not much more as it's usually parents buying these for their kids to read. Demand for Charltons has been up for cheap copies to fill runs, as well as high grade, as they are one of the most diverse publishers from this period.

Early Bronze Age has been showing substantial gains in *Guide* over the last 5 years or so, but the end of the Bronze Age has been virtually flat in *Guide*. This is also a great time period for people to invest in, as finding high grade NM-/9.2 books from this period in collections is becoming much more difficult than 3-5 years ago.

Some sales for me this past year include: *Amazing Spider-Man* #129 VF/NM $400, #121 VF $100 & VF- $75, *Daredevil* #168 VF $50, *Green Lantern* #76 CGC 5.5 $210, CGC 5.0 $155, *Hansi The Girl Who Loved the Swastika* nn FN- $38, *Hulk* #180 FN $45, #182 FN $25, *Weird War Tales* #1 VF $100, *Werewolf By Night* #32 FN+ $1075, and *Star Wars* #1 $.35 variant CGC 6.0 $1200!

Copper/Modern Age: Increased interest and sales in these periods continues in the 1980s and the late 1990s to the present. The most requested titles by far are *Deadpool*, *Walking Dead*, *G.I. Joe*, *Chew* and now *Morning Glories*. Image is the most dominant publisher in the last 5 years as far as collectability by a long shot. Marvel and DC seem interested in just re-launching their superheroes over and over with an occasional "World Ending" event to pull buyers in. I think it's time these two publishers hired some new writers with fresh ideas to bring to the table and do things that Image, Vertigo, Dynamite, Dark Horse and other smaller publishers are doing. I'm only reading a few current titles, as this isn't my main focus collecting wise, and these are *Buffy the Vampire Slayer* season 8 (story wandered a bit during the issues in the 20s, but the last half a year to year has been quite good again), the *House of Mystery* re-launch starring Fig which contains great stories within the overall story by guest writers and artists, *Mouse Guard*, and *Four Eyes*, although I have no clue what's going on here as it's been one issue in the last year I believe, which is too bad, as it's a great story about dragon fighting during the Great Depression. *Deadpool* is probably the most requested character for me at shows this past year, with copies from the '97 series selling almost as fast as I put them out. The entire series needs line listings with #1 at about $25, #2-10 in the $10-$15 range, and the last 20 issues or so when Marvel had their lower print runs in the $10-$35 range (#54 & 55 with the Punisher should be around $35 for NM- copies). *The Walking Dead* is possibly the most successful comic ever. CGC 9.8's are now regularly selling for $600 with a 9.9 selling for $1825 this year, although this 9.9 sale is down from a $2000 sale in '09), and 9.6 Sig. Series selling for an absurd $1500! The first issue in *Guide* should be around $200, with issue 2 at $100, 3-5 at $75, 6-10 at $50 and so forth. Never has a series gone up so fast so far, and not slowed down. *Chew* #1 is doing the same with CGC 9.8's now hitting $200 in just over a year, although I'm not sure if this one will have the same legs. Transformers have been slow for the last year or two, but still seem quite affordable to me and strong title overall. *New Mutants* #98 (1st Deadpool) has cooled off considerably with 9.8s now selling around $200-$250, which is probably due to it being fairly common. The *Moon Knight* 1980 series is one to keep an eye on, and due for price increase as it's quite hard to put a run together in VF/NM/9.0 range or higher. G.I. Joes are selling in all grades quite regularly, and the entire title deserves upward movement in *Guide*. *Cry For Dawn*, *Zelda*, *The Tick*, *Alien* (1st series), *Bone*, Grendel/*Primer* #2, *Albedo* (especially #2, which needs to be doubled in *Guide* in GD-FN), *THB*, and other low print run indies are great investments, and deserve upward movement in *Guide*. *Teenage Mutant Ninja Turtles* #1-10 are much harder to find than they used to be, and #1 deserves a line listing as sales are much more consistent than they once were. I would suggest a NM- price of $2000-2500 and a GD listing of $250. *New Teen Titans* #1 & 2 are selling regularly, and need a price increase, especially #1. *Amazing Spider-Man* #252, 300, 361, and 431 all sell consistently at *Guide* and deserve increases. *Amazing Spider-Man* #431 should have its own line listing of $12 and be one of the first breakthrough issues in this title from this period. *Amazing Spider-Man* #361 (first Carnage) will become a classic Copper Age cover, and most likely one of Spidey's most important villains. Vol. 2 issues #15-36 are still quite desirable and tough to find, and deserve line listings, with #36 having a top listing of $20. McFarlane's runs on *Spider-Man* and *Incredible Hulk* are consistently in demand and could move up. *X-Men* after the Byrne run seem quite affordable, as do issues #158, 201, 210-214, 222, 244, and 266, this last one due for a decent price increase as it's a classic cover from this time period and always in demand selling at or above *Guide*.

Cool miniseries are still in demand like *Ronin* by Frank Miller, as well as his *Wolverine* series, and *30 Days of Night*, *Batman: The Dark Knight*, *Origin*, *Crisis On Infinite Earths*, *300*, *Watchmen*, etc. *Miracleman* across the board is due for a price increase with focus on issues #1, 15, 20-24, especially issues 15, 23 & 24 which sell way above Guide in all grades. *Sweet Tooth* is a title to keep an eye on, as sales locally are consistent and the story idea is good. *DC Comics Presents* #26 (*New Teen Titans* preview) is a solid key.

Other books that sell regularly and need increases in Guide are: *Grimm Fairy Tales* #1, *Fables* #1, *Sandman* #1, *Preacher* #1 (early Vertigo #1's in general), and *Hellblazer* #1 (this whole series seems a great buy as it's one of the longest running Modern series). Another book to keep an eye on is *Superman: The Man of Steel* #18 (1st full Doomsday, and possibly a Copper Age classic cover). Superman doesn't have that many villains to fight, and this is arguably his most difficult, who I'm sure will make it to the big screen at some point. *NYX* #3 is also a book that is still performing well, and has started to get a second wind this past year, as this character continues to be developed by Marvel.

Valiant's... ah yes, so many produced, so many sold, so many available... or are there? *Harbinger*, *Solar*, *X-O Manowar*, *Rai* and *Shadowman* seem to be obtaining some demand/value. Gold variants still sell consistently. These books are now 15+ years old with some corners starting to get blunted, and a little stress on the spines. Buy these now for $.50-$2 if you can find them, as my thoughts are people have ignored these for so long or simply not cared enough to preserve them properly, that over the next 5-10 years, it will be much more difficult to find raw 9.6s or better. This is a great period to find keys that are available often in $1 boxes at shows or for only $3-$5, that in 5-10 years could very well be $25+ books. Some sales include: *John Byrne's Next Men* #23 NM $45, *Fables* #1 NM $45, *Sandman* #1 NM $45, *New Mutants* #1 NM $5, #98 NM- $62, *Amazing Spider-Man* #238 FN+ $30, #300 CGC 9.6 $210, CGC 9.4 $105, CGC 9.0 $80, #361 VF $6, Vol. 2 #1 NM+ $20, #36 NM $35, #529 NM $15, *Chew* #1 NM $30, *Deadpool* #1 NM $25, *G.I. Joe* #1 VF/NM $25, #21 VF/NM $30, *Kick-Ass* #1 CGC 9.6 $55, and *X-Men* #266 NM $60.

Suggestions For Pricing Spreads: Keep most of the *Guide* at current pricing. People are still collecting, but other than the richest 1% of our market, *Guide* prices are not being met for any time period, and often sale prices aren't even close to *Guide* (25-50% below for common issues of Silver-Bronze with line listings).

For key issues from Silver to Modern, Good pricing should go up, and in many instances considerably, such as books where their Good listing is in the $10-$40 range. *Albedo* #2 doesn't sell below $200 in any grade, so $32 for GD seems below the market by a ton, same is true for *Cerebus* #1, *TMNT* #1-4, *Iron Man* #1, *Incredible Hulk* #180-182 (181 should be at least $100 for GD, if not $125 as CGC 2.0s sell for $200 regularly), *Green Lantern* #76, *Werewolf By Night* #32, *Tomb of Dracula* #10, *Captain America* #100, etc... I don't think the tradition of VG being double of GD is valid, as people often will pay a good amount just to own a low grade copy, much more so then current *Guide*.

As for more common/filler issues, GD could go up, but VF and FN pricing could remain the same. VF and higher could go up, especially for Silver Age superhero, Archies, Romance, Horror, and other titles that are more collected/sold. NM- pricing is still low for most collected titles, and for the majority of key issues.

More consideration needs to be given towards Copper and Modern age books, as new keys like *Amazing Spider-Man* #431 are emerging, as well as titles like *Deadpool*, *Chew* and *The Walking Dead* where the entire title is in need of line listings, sometimes huge increases in guide are needed. *NYX* #3 has proved it is a Modern Age key, but $10 for NM- isn't close to what it sells for regularly getting $25 - $35. *New Mutants* #98 should go way up for maybe $50. *Walking Dead* #1 has proved it's not a flash in the pan, it should be around $200, with other issues following suit accordingly.

I hope Overstreet will consider expanding the number of new advisors that have a good amount of knowledge of Copper - Present books, as these are the largest percentage of books bought/sold in the marketplace, yet, least represented by advisor reports in the *Guide*. Not talking so much about new books that are selling off the racks each year, as store owners are reporting this info in the *Guide* well, but more so about titles and keys performing/selling well that need adjustment in the *Guide* on a more annual basis, as it seems we're covering this well in the Golden - Bronze Age pretty well, as most advisors have been contributing to the *Guide* for many years, and are older in age, and more knowledgeable in these time periods.

D'Arcy Farrell
Pendragon Comics

This past year has shown fantastic growth in TV and movie related sales. DVDs are flying off the shelves, morning cartoons are blistering with action, and the silver screen has lit up yet again.... all thanks to our medium, COMICS! Where would Hollywood be without us? Children yet again are talking about OUR heroes in the schoolyards and on Halloween. Birthday and Christmas gifts are once again Batmobiles, Spidey-cars, Iron Man rocket launchers and such! Bring back the underoos!

If you go into any decent DVD retailer, you will see *Batman: The Red Hood*, Iron Man cartoons, *Kick-Ass* and so much more filling the shelves. You wonder why Disney bought Marvel? It was to get in before it dominates everything.

Comics are where it is at. It has so many original storylines just waiting to be gobbled up and turned into a TV series like the amazing *Walking Dead*. Can you imagine a Vertigo title being done as well? How about an amazing story arc like *Crisis On Infinite Earths* or Old Man Logan? Or better yet, a one shot futuristic movie like *Batman: The Dark Knight Returns*? Now this has generated more new comic sales overall, nothing spectacular, but sales of trades and merchandise are climbing.

Since my last year review had decent feedback, I will maintain my format as in last year's 2010 Overstreet. Now on with more specifics in my review.

DC - New Comic Sales: The past year has been very big in sales. *Brightest Day* is a much bigger success than expected. I could hardly believe that issue #15 had bigger sales than issues #1-10 each. It just keeps increasing. Not that it is an amazing storyline, but after DC has gone through the Blackest Night storyline, everyone wants to see where it's going.

The Return of Bruce Wayne, of course everyone bought it, not sure if anyone liked it. I'm not quite sure how to say this, but only *All Star Batman* (especially issue #2) made me feel worse about reading a Batman story. I am glad it is over, whereas everything else Batman-related (like *Red Robin*) was great. *Batman: The Return* is a perfect one-shot for anyone to start up reading Batman at this point. DC is going in a good direction keeping Dick Grayson as Batman. I think we'll also see Babs swinging again. She did twinkle her toes after the Brainiac virus story 2-3 years back! Dick also proposed way back then as well!!

Green Lantern has had an amazing past few years. For a decade Hal was Parallax, nearly destroying the world, then in the end sacrificing himself to save it. Then he comes back in *GL Rebirth* (awesome, get the trade) which is a great starting point for new readers. By now, everyone knows the effects of Blackest Night. It brought back many dead heroes and villains into the DC universe and it has been crazy ever since. It has been a great GL ride, and timed with the new movie release is the "War of the Green Lanterns" storyline ending it once and for all (did I just say that?).

It seems long ago, but Blackest Night had only just begun! It was amazing in sales and the stories were well done. I especially liked the Golden Age Superman coming back in *Blackest Night: Superman* mini #1-3 and Dick Grayson's parents surprise appearance in *Blackest Night: Batman* #1-3. Wonder Woman becoming a Star Sapphire was cool as well. DC could do no wrong it seemed. A little bit too many one-shots from deceased titles, but you only had to buy those if you liked as it was not overly necessary like a typical crossover. *Green Lantern* #50 had Parallax come back to fight The Spectre in a huge battle. Awesome cover.

©DC

Death's appearance in Action Comics #894 brought in the Sandman fans too.

Here is a more detailed chronological review of 2010: Everyone loved all the GL rings! The Red Circle titles did poorly. Perhaps if done in the Wildstorm universe? It was decent in the 1960/70s but this was pale in comparison. Same with anything Milestone. It failed in the 1990s, and it will not do better now. *Batman & Robin* is awesome with Dick as Batman and Damian as Robin(the brat!). The constant bickering between Red Robin, Batgirl and Damian with Dick trying to keep it together is quite humerous. It has been a top 10 title from #1 on.

American Vampire sells very well and not just because of Stephen King's name. As mentioned already, *Brightest Day* came in May 2010 and I had not expected great things. The stories are OK, art is OK, and had followed great stories from *Blackest Night* and GL Sinestro Corps War and various Crisis stuff. I thought most DC customers would have tired of it. But to my suprise, the title kept selling out. I recall having to reorder 2-3 times every issue from #5-12 until I decided to just way overorder in future issues. It will segway into War of Green Lanterns, timed with the new movie. That may complete the whole storyline (I hope).

The anniversary issues *Batman* #700, *Superman* #700 and *Wonder Woman* #600 all sold very well. Supposedly, *Wonder Woman* #600 was controversial, and that is silly. It is a good story with good art and had increased sales that has continued since. *Green Arrow* #1 came out end of June 2010 and sold well, but only because of *Brightest Day* tie-in. It's not bad, but not good either. *Batman: Odyssey* by Neal Adams is doing well for sales. The art is a bit rough and the ink line is thick, but you can still see the genuis. *X-Files* and *30 Days of Night* is an example where two dying/dead titles can come together and sell. Seperately it would have bombed. Fan interest is so 1990s, like *Star Trek: The Next Generation* on these titles, even though *30 Days* is less than 10 years old, it has fallen to near death. *Superman: Earth One* HC was awesome! Reminiscent of the 1990s DC annuals that all had an Elseworlds theme. This sold exceedingly well everywhere. Go buy it! *GL Emerald Warriors* is a title that is not needed. It sells OK, but Brightest Day and GL stuff is covered already everywhere for 2+ years and I see no point to it. *Flash* with Barry Allen is selling well, but nowhere near the success as when Hal came back. I blame mostly the art on this one.

In September, DC came out with 5 War one-shots that were really nicely done. I would like DC to hire Ennis and Kubert (JOE!!!!) to do 2-3 War titles in a Vertigo banner for the mature reader. OK, it won't happen, but it's a nice thought. Perhaps if fans cared to write in to DC? *Action Comics* #894 with Death talking to Luthor was priceless. A funny single issue, it sold quite well mostly to Sandman fans. *Batman Inc.* #1 and *Batman: The Dark Knight* #1 both came out. Both sold very high. *Batman Inc.* not as well received, and we'll see in the new year if sales maintain or slide. I expect it to slide a bit and *Dark Knight* to hold. Batwoman is not really a new character, and will sell OK in this new age with up to date changes. I expect nothing special, and will hover mid-level in sales at most. *Superboy* with Connor Kent is a dead title. It might have been better at a different time, or maybe pop him into Legion. *THUNDER Agents* is also a bomb. Why does DC do this? Old 1960-70s titles from TOWER Comics and Red Circle Comics were like nicely done vintage independents. Why come back revived in this way? Stop it DC. Fling them in Vertigo with a twist. Or initiate them slowly with appearances! That would be cool! I remember in the title *Demon* in 1990s, the Haunted Tank and crew came back out of retirement for a 3 issue story arc, and that was such a nice story. That's the way to reintroduce old forgotten titles or heroes/villains. Not just give them a title to add to the lineup.

And finally, *Green Lantern: Larfleeze Christmas Special*! This was a well done Christmas issue. It even came with a cookie recipe with orange icing. This sold out, and I had to reorder it. When's the last time that happened for a holiday one-shot? Nice ending to an overall GREAT DC year!

Marvel - New Comic Sales: Well Spidey is practically back to normal. It was a rough couple of years, but we finally saw the effects of "One More Day" end with "One Moment In Time". Unfortuanetly, we also lost some good fans along the way. Hopefully Marvel doesn't do that again(they will). The story arc in *Amazing Spider-Man* "Grim Hunt" did quite well also. *Chaos War* did average, as did most Marvel books. It is nice to see *Kick-Ass* volume 2 arrive. Better sales than volume 1 thanks to the excellent movie. Too bad it is not coming monthly.

Marvel just keeps hammering titles out without any thought of direction or control. How many mini-series and relaunches do we need? Crossover after crossover as well! How many titles and specials do Wolverine and Deadpool deserve?

I'm beginning to see a bad trend at Marvel. It's hard enough for fans on a budget to buy all those *Amazing Spider-Man* monthly issues, but look at Marvel in Dec. 2010. Too many titles! *Wolverine*, *Wolverine The Best there Is*. *X-Men*, *Uncanny X-men*, *X-Men Legacy*. *Avengers*, *New Avengers*, *Secret Avengers*. These core titles would be fine BUT then look at all those minis and one-shots and secondary titles like *X-Men Forever*, *Wolverine First-Class*, *Deadpool XXXX* (he has too many to mention specifics). They are slowly making each group/hero a weekly showup on the comic shelf. Now some of it makes sense like *X-Men* and *Uncanny X-Men*.

And I'd rather see 2 issues of *Amazing Spider-Man* than 2 titles. DC does fine with *Action+Superman*, *GL+GL Corps*. And Batman rarely goes wrong even with 100+ titles (though *Return of Bruce Wayne* #1-6 is the exception, but it was needed, just badly done).

It reminds me of the late 1990s where Marvel saturated the shelves with 3-4 titles of every hero/group out there. Marvel please stop producing stories like Zombie XXX, you really haven't done it very well after the second *Marvel Zombies*. If you get an urge to do another Zombie story see *Walking Dead,* then go do one with the same class and quality. This is not personal opinion, most customers loved *Marvel Zombies 1* and *Marvel Zombies 2* and sales/commentary reflected that, but nothing after that. Hopefully the Zombies Squadron Supreme can revive it. I doubt it.

Here is a more detailed chronological review of 2010: At the beginning of 2010, see saw Spidey turn around with the story arc "The Gauntlet". Suddenly the art and story started to get better and some fans of Pete final felt relief that the bad writing and ideas were coming to an end. A worthwhile trade. Hulk on the otherhand was getting worse. Following the successful "Planet Hulk", Marvel continued with "World War Hulk" which was OK. After that, it just got worse. Especially when Marvel uses a tactic no one likes, and that is renaming a title trying to maintain its selling level, like *Incredible Hulk* to *Incredible Hercules* or from *Daredevil* to *Black Panther: The Man Without Fear*. These secondary heroes are not bad, but hardly deserve a title. At least Hudlin is not writing *Black Panther*. Arggh. Just give them a #1, then kill the title when sales slip, as you usually do(Marvel that is!).

The *What If?*s are very well done one-shots. Doing these once a year is a good move by Marvel(yes I said something nice about Marvel). It stays fresh! It also stays topical (up to date with current just-ended stories with the What If? twist).

Siege came out and ended fast, which made it even better. If you like Thor, you'll like this. It was well done, and didn't crossover everywhere. *Captain America: Reborn* concluded and sold highly. Whereas all the *Noir* titles busted, and most fans dislike them. I also hate digest-sized trades! For all ages, *Marvel Super Hero Squad* is perfect for young audiences! *X-Force* is a constant high level seller, especially drawing on the Messiah arc with Cable, great writing! Lets HOPE they don't overdo it(oops, they already did with *Generation Hope* late in 2010!). *Generation Hope* is really just passing time for when Marvel does some big grandeous crossover for the X-Universe where Hope either is going to destroy it then save it or something similar to Parallax/Hal Jordan or "Phoenix, Death of" storyline. It probably will be amazing, but prepared to be bored and buy lots of issues before it happens.

The *Kick-Ass* hardcover came out and sold beyond my expectations, through the roof! What exactly is the point of the Ultimate titles? They have an ending with Ultimatum, reboot, then let *Ultimate Spider-Man* go back to old numbering system? Now *Ultimate Spider-Man* is going to die in 2011?? At least *The Ultimates* is refreshing, volume 1.

X-Men major crossovers like 2nd Coming and X-Nation and X-Necrosha are not doing much for sales. As mentioned earlier, the Messiah War with Cable and X-Force was great in sales, art and story. Unfortunately, it seems to have fallen flat after that. *Uncanny X-Force* has been received very well and has continued the X-Force sales with no slippage whatsoever. All the X-titles with "*Forever*" are pointless in sales, nobody is buying this Marvel attempt at over-saturation of new releases. Millar is pumping out great minis and short series! He is by far Marvel's best superstar writer with *Kick-Ass*, *Nemesis*, Old Man Logan and *Superior*. The ICON imprint at Marvel cannot compare with DC's Vertigo, but its few titles, creator owned, are always well written and sell exceptionally well.

Avengers, *Secret Avengers* and *New Avengers* all started at #1 in May/June. They sold very well. Sales have maintained high levels, stories are OK, and will remain so as long as the upcoming big movies like *Thor*, *Cap*, *Iron Man 3*, and eventually, *The Avengers* have success and high profile. The younger collectors have the movies to connect with the comics, thus the high sales. I doubt the sales would be this high without the movies. The 1960/70s Western titles like *Rawhide Kid* were nice, well done though sales are limited due to audience ignorance. I grew up reading all those great Marvel Westerns, and can enjoy them...but the typical 20-30 year old collector has no clue. So yes it is nice to see, but sales will never be great. They could move these titles to a different imprint other than "Marvel Heroes", which mixes with Thor, Cap, Spidey and the likes. That could improve the sales. Placing these circa 1800s heroes of the West among 2010 Marvel Heroes banner does not help. If you make an effort, especially in writing, the sales will come. I think a movie like *Rawhide Kid* could work if done correctly, see *True Grit* or the amazing masterpiece *Unforgiven* and you can then imagine. Of course, it could be a flop like *Jonah Hex* by DC.

Shadowland! Great story and decent art throughout. Daredevil has been a high seller thoughout all his 100+ issues culminating with the Shadowland crossover. Well done, let's hope *Daredevil Reborn* is worthy to continue that streak. I'm uneasy with Black Panther taking over the numbering and "Hells Kitchen". This is a hero, like Silver Surfer, Marvel just can't maintain a title with. Surfer came close with Thanos stuff in the 1990s, but eventually faltered. So let's hope the writing is decent, and another *Incredible Hercules* doesn't happen. *X-Men* #1 vs. vampires started in July with high sales. It hasn't slipped, but that is typical for a main X-Title as those Marvel fans will buy anything that seems important (see Deadpool and his 100+ titles and minis and one-shots this year for proof!). I don't think much of it but Marvel is aiming for a one per week appearance of its main lineup. My advice? Refuse the trap, buy some ICON or Vertigo titles, and exercise your brain. Don't go down the Marvel or Image path of the late 1990s when the two companies battled for variant and quantity supremacy. *Scarlet* by Bendis came out in the summer as well, it was well done and good for sales. If you liked this, look out for Ennis book *Jennifer Blood* by Dynamite. Namor, first mutant? Really? Did we really want this out? Why not remake Defenders with him and Surfer, Strange et al?? That would be great. I know Marvel tried it already, but they made the mistake by having Larsen do it. Art and writing was lousy. Do that well and you'll find a place for the middle road heroes that have no titles. Perhaps make the Liberators (see *Avengers* #83) again! Wow! That would sell. Imagine a great female lineup with Black-Cat, Valkyrie, Hellcat, Tigra, or whoever. Such unused potential. The two Thor minis "For Asgard" and "First Thunder" sold well and stories were not bad. In September, Wolverine, Daken, and X-23 had their #1's for their ongoing series. Sure, of course we need Logan, but X-23 again? Just put her on a team. As per Daken, yes it sells, but the wrirting and art are not so good. People buy it only because of Logan. Again, Marvel trying for an every week presence of their top heroes. *Carnage* came out in October, and the art and story are great! The story makes you root for Carnage. Get the trade of this mini, it is a good read. It sold OK, but each week I suggest it, and the sales climb next issue, a good sign to buy it! *Chaos War* has come, sold mediocre, and no one talks much about it. This could've been done better, and the timing is wrong. Marvel fans need a break from the contant huge crossovers.

S.H.I.E.L.D. is a wonderful suprise! Hickman has done a great job, and my sales climb every month. Even the historical variants are great. A must read! Thank goodness Marvel is cutting a couple of Deadpool titles, but *Deadpool Team-Up* was kinda funny and not bad. I'm sure Marvel will create a couple more to replace them and we'll be at the same over saturation again. Still, overall, Marvel plugged out some good stuff, and the year was a success. With so much to chose from, CHOSE!! Don't buy it all. Spread out your reading. Expand to Vertigo, Batman, ICON, Radical, BOOM!, Avatar as my best picks for 2011 reading. Art lovers you are on your own. I can stomach bad art with great story, but the reverse?

Independent Overview:

Abstract: Terry Moore's *Echo* continues to be a very interesting tale on what happens when you bind with a living metal. Interesting doesn't do it justice, simple clean lines for the art and good character development. One of the better stories out there.

Archaia: What can I say ? *The Killer* is still a great story as the second arc continues. It is getting more complicated but that's what happens when politics are interjected into a simple assasination. *Days Missing*: Great covers but interior art detracted from the story. *Mouse Guard* continues to be popular. I'm not certain why but there it is.

Archie Comics: The dream marriage(s) story arc sold exceedingly high, as did the trades and well-priced slipcase hardcover. I haven't sold as much Archie combined in 25 years put together. Too bad it was a dream. Of course all the guys would pick Betty, but most of the buyers were girls. The *Life With Archie* mag sells only OK at most. It was not a work of art, nor was it smartly written, but it brought many newbies into stores continent wide. I probably won't see this success again forever from Archie.

Avatar: Continued its "in your face" horror. *Crossed* followed by *Crossed - Family Values* were definitely items you didn't leave around for the kiddies.Very enjoyable, which is a totally inappropriate description for the material. Unsettling and queasy would be more apt. There is probably a good movie waiting to be made out of this. Lucky for us, it appears that David Lapham has as many dark thoughts as Garth Ennis.

I think Alan Moore really wants to be master of the porno horror genre. He comes very close with *Neonomicon*. A welcome addition to the Lovecraft mythos. Other stories which were good but not quite as graphic were *Fevre Dream* which was interesting, but I was not impressed by the art. Covers were better than the interior. *Supergod* was excellent but I have a Warren Ellis bias and pick up anything by him. *Gravel* was a solid read and the last arc had a satisfactory ending, *The Chronicles of Wormwood* continued to be a superior story: The Anti-Christ and Jesus in a bar and a talking rabbit back at the apartment. What more do you want in a story?

Boom! Studios: Right at the top, I have to say Boom is doing great material for kids : *The Incredibles*, *Wall-E*, *Toy Story,* etc. Good introduction for future collectors. All have good art and simple stories. It gives the parents something to purchase without worrying about the content although I ALWAYS have the parent review any book they are getting for their child.

For the adults: *Codebreakers* had a good story and art. Positive feedback from customers. The same with *28 Days Later*. *Farscape* and *Do Androids Dream of Electric Sheep* were not received as positively.

The home run, which everyone knows, was *Irredeemable*. A great, great story which keeps getting better. Unfortunately, *Incorruptible* does not match it. Maybe because villans are always more interesting. The Stan Lee titles are a total waste, expected from us!

Dark Horse's restart of **Magnus, Robot Fighter** *focused attention on the classic character. (#1 shown)*

CBLDF: Get the Liberty Annual 2010 just because you should. And yes there are interesting bits in it. Yes I know its Image.

Dark Horse: The restarts of *Magnus Robot Fighter* and *Doctor Solar Man of The Atom* have been a welcome addition to the comic world; *Turok*, not so much. Nice touch including the original story in the first issues. Anything related to the Hellboy Universe has been good and customers were positive about The Storm, Buzzard and the Plague Ships etc. I must admit that I thought Hellboy in Mexico was a fun read. *Star Wars* comics still were popular, and any story which focused on Boba Fett or Darth Vader especially so.

Dynamite Entertainment: Of course Green Hornet was hot with the movie looming on the horizon. I liked the variation on the original story. Certainly the Kato change was interesting. There was definitely customer interest, at least at first but with so many Green Hornet titles at once it had diminishing returns.

Garth Ennis's *The Boys* still continues to be a welcome antidote to the normal men in tights stories. Good stories and just waiting to see how it pans out with Butcher and friends. ENNIS! *Jennifer Blood*!! Highly anticipated at our stores, this will sell well. You rarely can go wrong when you buy the E's and M's! E's are Ennis and Ellis. M's are Millar, Alan Moore, G. Morrison, F. Miller! For those of you who are tired of the superhero dribble, check out anything done by these writers, past, present and future. There are other writers unmentioned, but by far, these writers have a track record and skill that deserves mention every year. Customers seem to be getting the *Black Terror*, *Project SuperPowers* mainly due to the Alex Ross cover art. Any cover done by him is desirable.

IDW Entertainment: I know G.I. Joe, Transformers and Star Trek are the big guys for this company but take a look at *5 Days to Die*: A great story but not a happy one. Only 5 issues but a nice compact story and good art. *Kill Shakespeare*: Ok, remember all those guys that appear in the bard's plays? Well this is the true history. A good read. *Strange Science Fantasy*: A very odd and to use their words "bizarre landscapes and off the wall characters". Get it! *Yours Truly Jack The Ripper*. A faithful adaptation of Robert

Bloch's short story or at least this is how I remember it. Very well done. *John Byrne's Next Men*: Lets hope John doesn't give up and stop. First issue sold well, story decent, art not as grand of old.

Image Comics: Mostly excellent for the true independent offerings of this umbrella company. Although, for the main titles and originators of the company, I never see anything new or good, art or story. I wish all below would just go to Vertigo, Dark Horse, IDW, Radical, BOOM! Anyhow, below are my positive reviews (minus Haunt):

Walking Dead: There is no more to say than that. The best; period; full stop. *Chew*: A light-hearted look at a man with a very difficult job. If you don't know what I mean then get the trades at least. *Shuddertown:* Good gritty story about a female investigator in some fairly dark family business. Good read and positive feedback. *Cowboy Ninja Viking*: There are no words that will do this justice. You either love it or hate it. *Hack/Slash*: Customers like this take on killers, madmen and those that hunt them. *Haunt*: Sorry nothing special. First few issues sold well but I don't think it is moving much now.

© Robert Kirkman

The Walking Dead (#1 shown) is Image's best title; period.

Meta 4: Ted McKeever has created another intriguing story/character. Worth investing the time/money. *Sweets*: Another odd detective tale but again worth the time.

ONI Entertainment: What can I say about *Resurrection*? Anything that has Bill Clinton in it should be good and it is. Good post-alien invasion story. Very positive feedback on *The Sixth Gun*. Good combination of horror and western.

Scott Pilgrim: I know, I know it's old news but if I might cross sell for a moment: get the DVD. I have no financial interest but it is just a cool interpretation of a cool comic. And yes buy the comic. Movie bombed and did not deserve that fate. Bad timing for its release, which would fare better in mid-May than in summer. Teens' word of mouth is the best advertising.

Radical Publishing: From the customer's viewpoint, this is the best buy today for the price and page count. If those were the only reasons then it would be a "might buy", but the stories make it a must buy. Stories like *Time Bomb*, *After Dark*, *Driver for the Dead*, *Shrapnel*, and *Hot Wire* make for some of the best reading available. Hopefully the pending *Damaged* and *Hollow Point* will continue the trend. This company is cutting edge in all respects. High gloss prestige comics at $3.99-$4.99, excellent art (digital), and great stories. Even the $1 *Mata Hari* with the historic extra info at the back was an amazing buy.

Vertigo: Not an Indy but acts like one. Kudos to DC! Some of the best short and ongoing series appear under the Vertigo banner. *Fables*: Nothing else need to be said. The gold standard for Fairy tale/mundies stories. *American Vampire*: Another view of vampires and their interaction with mankind. Enjoyed the first story arc and it helped wash away the vileness of *Twilight* but that's another story. *Air*: I'm still not certain if I liked this but there was something compelling about it. I kept picking it up. *Daytripper*: I can't praise this enough and was sorry to see it end. Right now I would pick up anything done by Fabio Moon, The Daytripper stories went beyond just ordinary story telling. *House of Mystery*: Still good and enjoy seeing Cain once again even as a minor character. *Hellblazer*: At some point this will run out of steam but not yet. Customers still like Mr. Constantine. *Northlanders*: Lost me around issue #16 but customers still like it. *The Unwritten*: Sort of a whodunnit wrapped up in magic and books. Easier to read than explain but invest some time and catch up on the back issues. *iZombie*: OK, a ghost, a zombie and a wereterrier. I was hooked from issue one. Worthwhile investment of your time and money.

Zenescope: *Grimm Fairy Tales*, *Neverland* and *Tales from Wonderland* are still popular, but not as much as a year ago. Familiarity perhaps but the novelty may have worn off. And people who used to pick this up say it compares unfavourably to *Fables* which they prefer. Interestingly, these same people liked *Escape from Wonderland*. An up and coming company when *Grimm* first hit, has gone nowhere since. It needs new blood or stories or both!

<u>Trades To Buy!</u>

When you walk into your local comic book store, you are inundated with hundreds and thousands of trades, graphic novels and hardcovers. It is an excellent way for the infrequent reader to catch up on missed stories. It is also a great way to further your reading in genres and themes you had not done so before. So here I have made a list of stories in trade form that are worthy of your reading. I will attempt each year to add to this list.

Marvel Comics: *Wolverine: Old Man Logan* - another feat by Millar, by far the greatest seller of 2010. Excellent art, premise and story. Seeing Venom was a hoot!

Marvels - Alex Ross' 1994 masterpiece. Written by Busiek, story through eyes of a reporter from Marvel's 1960s beginning.

Kick-Ass - comic movie of the year 2010! Millar does it again. Excellent story on people trying to be heroes lacking powers, and getting really hurt.

Ultimate Wolverine vs Hulk - this book took forever to complete, but Lindelof and Yu made a great one time story.

Marvel Super Hero Secret Wars - OK, not the best story or art from this 1980s classic, but many adults grew up loving this maxi-series.Get the omnibus.

DC Comics: *Batman: Dark Knight Returns* - the best story written all-time! Frank Miller takes an aging Bruce out of retirement in this future timeline that lacks heroes.
Batman: Hush - get the complete trade with 13 issues. Jim Lee's art is spectacular. A mystery of sorts. This is your best starting point for Batman reading up to now.
Watchmen - Alan Moore phenom! Great movie, smart reading. Has it all. Only *DK Returns* compares. Trade is very affordable for all 12 issues.
Green Lantern: Rebirth - not just because of the movie, really well done, smartly written, and also good starting point for new GL readers.
Kingdom Come - the BEST Alex Ross art ever, and that is saying something. Futuristic Elseworlds. Just buy it!
Batman Vampire - a trilogy of trades in one affordable ($20) book. Batman vs Dracula! He has to synthesize vampirism to fight Draculas legions. Kelley Jones art to boot!
Batman: The Killing Joke HC - from 1980s, Joker long ago puts Babs in a wheelchair, creating Oracle. Alan Moore with Bolland. Awesome!
Independant Comic companies: *Maus* complete HC - tale of WWII, Nazis, holocaust of mice, just one of the best for a sad, smart read. Used in Universities and High Schools!
Irredeemable - by BOOM, story based on a great hero going bad, by Mark Waid who also wrote *Kingdom Come*!
The Walking Dead - need I say more? Buying the affordable Vol. 1 compendium for $60 gets you first 48 issues. Then trade volumes 9-up for the rest.
Bone - get the complete softcover, not the tons of trades. It is nice, well done, affordable, and Disney bought it for a good reason.
Time Bomb - by Radical, a simple 3-part story. Future soldiers go back to WWII in Germany! To me, anything Radical is worthy!
Crossed and *Crossed Family Values* - by Avatar. Really nasty stuff, great reading, NOT for kids or teens at all!
Vertigo by DC Comics: I could place everything in this section made by Vertigo, but I'll list the very best. Note, most Vertigo Vol. 1 trades go for around $9.99! A good test price.
Sandman - by Neil Gaiman, the grandaddy of all Vertigo. Not for everyone, very poetic and artsy, but amazing. Story based on the Endless, gods like Death!
Y, The Last Man - also a completed(now) tale, basis is that a virus wipes out all males on the planet, all but a guy and his monkey!
DMZ - ongoing, part of New York City is a DMZ, reporter goes in with Army on a photo-op and gets stuck there. Very political! "Can't trust the News" is its message.
Preacher - completed, by ENNIS! A young precher gets some god-like powers, starts travelling around U.S., amazing perfect run.
Fables - ongoing tale(s) of updated fairy tale characters brought to life in the city of Fabletown, where real life and crimes occur among New York citizens.

<u>Back Issue Sales</u>

Modern (1984-2009): Not much ever to say since it is a flatline in sales with few exceptions. The best in sales must be G.I. Joe and Transformers from the 1980s and anything Batman. I should mention *New Mutants* #86-100, especially #86,87,98 as these books are severly undervalued key books of the new age. *New Mutants* #98 listing at $25 for a NM- is a steal!
Copper Age - Late Bronze Age (1976-1984): The early 1980s low print DCs are a great investment and are going on 30 years! Actually most mainstream of any title is found quite low in cost here, readily available in high grade. And they are all verging on 30-40 years of age! Worthwhile unslabbed, especially anything DC like *Flash*, *GL*, *WW*, *JLA*!
Early Bronze Age (1970-1975): Near impossible to find high grade unslabbed copies, expect to pay premiums for anything key. I do not understand how a *Green Lantern* #76 can explode in price just like that where *Batman* #232,234, *Detective* #400 and *Avengers* #93 hover.
Yes *GL* #76 is an important issue with far reaching implications on society drawn by the amazing Neal Adams, but it seems too high. *Lois Lane* #106, *Jimmy Olsen* #134, *Iron Man* #55, *Avengers* #83,87,93-100, *JLA* #137,138 and ALL *Wonder Woman* #170-200 are all undervalued examples.
1960s Marvel: Always sells, always will, most copies fly in most grades. Name most anything, it sells. *Fantastic Four* #1-50 are my toughest requests to fill. Hottest book I'd say hands down is *Journey Into Mystery* #83 (scarce, low value comparitively) that is unattainable, *Avengers* #4 (abundant), *Amazing Fantasy* #15(hard to believe).
1960s DC: There are far less keys than in Marvels of the same time period, BUT......what keys there are like *Detective* #369 or *Wonder Woman* #159 or *Green Lantern* #40 are far more affordable. Many early Neal Adams are still under radar and CHEAP compared to *Green Lantern* #76. *JLA* is going to explode very very soon. Watch out for that. If the upcoming *Green Lantern* movie has even half the quality of the *Batman The Dark Knight*, *Brave and the Bold* #28-30 and *JLA* #1-10 will disappear everywhere.
1960s other: My best sales are all TV/MOVIE related, especially WESTERNS! Yes, I said Westerns! *Lone Ranger*, *Jace*, *Bonanza et al* sell here quite well, though mostly in high grade. I sold 2 sets, complete(Dell, GK) of *Wagon Train* alone! Ducks are slower this year, Classics better. Original Charltons do well, especially Ditko.
Golden Age - Atomic Age (1938-1955): Any main title sells, all early Ditko and Horror sells just as fast. What doesn't sell to well are ECs. I did move some *Batman*, *Detective*, *Superman*, and even *Mad* #1 & 2. I'd have sold *Action,* but I can never get those in quantity. The same goes for Timely. If a *Captain America* or *Human Torch* or *Marvel Mystery* shows up, next day it is gone.

From year-to-year, there were recorded HUGE sales for *Detective* #27, *Action* #1 and some others; bigger than normal. For those who are not CEOs or movie stars, don't fret. You can always pick up #2s and the like for far less. Sure it will not make the news, BUT record sales of #1s typically are like an earthquake....follow up tremors and shockwaves occur 1-2 years following. If you time it well, you can reap rewards on your investment. For example....if in the Silver Age if *Fantastic Four* #1, AF#15, JIM#83, TOS#39 all exploded in sales, I'd start looking for *Hulk* #1, *Daredevil* #1, *Tales to Astonish* #27 and the like.

Toronto Conventions 2010: The biggest in the Toronto area is Hobbystar in late August. It draws everyone, fan artist writer corporate and the like. It is a tough venue to visit so prepare ahead. I move everything at this show. High end to low grade books, trades, and new releases.

The Comicfan Appreciation event in April by the same company is smaller, but it concentrates mostly on comics and is very worth the effort to go. Wizard hosted a show early in 2010, and with low turnout and non-comic guests, it was a disappointment for the fans. Perhaps if they do a 2011 or 2012 it will fare better?

Conclusion: The comic industry is heading in the right direction. AMC's *Walking Dead* TV series was properly done and had huge ratings. Some effect in sales, which is nice, but the validation that comics(mostly, except the BOOM, Marvel, DC "all audiences" line) are not for kids anymore, comics are smart, comics can be mature and not naughty, is what I get from it. This is an audience that was passed up previous decades in a comic store. Now, with companies like IDW, Radical and BOOM, we can read intelligent thoughts with art and no tights! Movies are also being thought out well. Sure *Green Hornet* may flop, and who could ever out perform Heath Ledger, and other productions will miss the mark (*Scott Pilgrim* was well done but flogged!) or timing, but we will get those high points again. Most likely a *Kick-Ass 2* or *Batman 3* or *Avengers* or *JLA* movie will be awesome if not all! And as shown above on *Walking Dead*, the TV option (live not animated) for comics has just begun!

Have a great, safe investing, happy reading year!

Dan Fogel
Hippy Comix, Inc.

What, Me Recession? In this far-flung future world of 2011, I've now spent over 30 years as a dealer, 20 as a creator, and 10 as a publisher and distributor. We have now entered the era of 7-figure sales. The main effect of the economic downturn on our corner of the world has been a deluge of items offered for sale by hardcore collectors and fringe inheritors alike! I'm personally so swamped with collections offered for sale and consignment that I've teamed up with a few trusted fellow dealers to help me acquire and sell the constant influx of goodies, most notably Harvey Doss of Comic Man and Vince Dugar of The Golden Frog Curio and Emporium. A big shout-out to them both for their invaluable input for this market report!

Which Prices Should Go Up?: 3-D titles (all eras). Good through Fine prices for Platinum Age titles across the board and for DC, Quality, and Fiction House Golden Age books. Loose covers and pages of Golden Age keys and commons alike do well, as apparently there are still die-hards out there assembling their books the hard way! Increasingly hot are Atom and Silver Age Atlas/Marvel Pre-Code & Pre-Hero titles, especially *Journey Into Mystery*, *Tales Of Suspense*, and *Tales To Astonish*, including their Bronze and Modern Age reprints. All Marvels from 1962-1964 are increasing in demand. Silver Age *Green Lantern* & *Thor* keys (unless the movies tank!), especially *Green Lantern* #7 (1st Sinestro) & *Journey Into Mystery* #85 (1st Loki). Although already popular, the AMC series of *The Walking Dead* has made the title, like its antagonists, go "freakin' berserko"!

© MAR

Loki's debut in **Journey Into Mystery #85** makes this issue a key.

Which Prices Should Come Down?: 1980-2005 non-key books. Freeze Good though Very Fine for most late Silver though Copper Age books, as this market segment is soft, including (I kid you not!) X-Men and Spider-Man titles, which have leveled off except for *Amazing Spider-Man* #129 (1st Punisher) and *Incredible Hulk* #181 (1st Wolverine).

What are the Next Investment Frontiers?: Obviously, as the author and publisher of *Fogel's Underground Comix Price Guide* (2006) and *Fogel's Underground Comix Price Guide Supplement* (2010), I'm biased in the direction of this largely-untapped segment of the marketplace. What is indisputable is that "the big boys" have been stepping up selling and buying truly high-grade and rare, low print-run Underground comix for increasingly record amounts. The first printing (Plymell Edition) of *Zap Comix* #1 will probably have broken the $30K barrier for CGC-certified 9.4 or better by the time this sees print. No longer merely the "*Action Comics* #1 of the Undergrounds", this book is now the "UG *Amazing Fantasy* #15" now that it is poised to break out even as Silver Age Marvel, then DC, did 20 years ago! Look for *Zap Comix* #1 2nd print (Donahue Edition), and first prints of *Zap Comix* #0-4 to break out soon. Keep an eye on *Tales From The Ozone* #1 and the 1st prints of *The Fabulous Furry Freak Brothers* #1, *Bijou Funnies* #1, and *Feds 'N' Heads*. In general, you can't go wrong buying pre-1970 Robert Crumb, Gilbert Shelton, Art Spiegelman, Spain, Vaughn Bode, Robert Williams, Victor Moscoso, Rick Griffin, and S. Clay Wilson comix, portfolios, and posters!

In the near future I'll be delving deeper into 1930s-1970s comic book and science fiction fanzines, as well as 1960s Rock Posters. I recommend that you do the same!

Eternal thanx to my heroes/enablers, Bob Overstreet, Steve Geppi, J.C. Vaughn, and Mark Huesman of Gemstone

Publishing. And gratitude always to my customers, consigners, and fellow-travelers! Check me & my posse out at hippycomix.com and on eBay under the handles hippycomix, harvdoss, and graphxfan!

Stephen Gentner
Collector

Our comic book market continues to chug along! Prices realized for *Action* #1 and *Detective* #27 set new records at the absolute top of our hobby. I always felt that one day, the one million dollar mark would be reached for the first Superman or Batman. That the market achieved both over a million dollars in a down economy is stunning! Private transactions for ultra high grade Marvel Keys from the Silver Age also defy gravity! Books from all the Ages, Gold, Silver and Bronze in FN or less seem to be more problematic for prices realized. Motivated dealers seem to be willing to discount in these grades, and turn their money over. True VF or better books often end up being slabbed and put into online auctions for best returns. I have found that true VF or better condition books in desirable Gold, Silver, and to a lesser extent Bronze titles are harder to come by. Their prices reflect this.

As I am a collector and not a dealer, I thought I would share my "collecting direction" since the last *Guide* came out. I have been sleuthing the comic stores here in Portland, Oregon and found some interesting targets of opportunity to purchase, which were:

Golden Age: *Action Comics* #31 VG/FN $429; *Superman* #4 VG/FN $770; *Superman* #6 FN- $60.

Silver Age: *Brave and the Bold* #45-49, all in 9.0 $350 total; *Adventure Comics* #301 VF $86; #307 NM- $110; #308 VF- $52; #311 VF- $55; #346 VF/NM $100; #353 NM+ $200.

Bronze Age: Full runs of *The Shadow* and *Justice, Inc.*, all in high grade for a total of $210. *Doctor Strange* #170-183 in high grade for $250

My purchases were both for titles I'm chasing and also the aforementioned targets of opportunity. The *Supermans* and *Action* were nice paged and full color examples. All of these were from 1940 and are so charming in their content and art. How often does one get a chance to buy from a local "find" of Golden Age in nice shape? Not very!

Adventure Comics featuring the Legion of Super-Heroes continue to be difficult to find in high grade, but I am closing in on finishing them up. Those *Brave and the Bold* issues were the "Strange Sports Stories" run featuring Carmine Infantino art in his prime. I remember these being touted heavily in the house ads of the day with DC, and I think they are clever and fun stories! In Bronze, the Kaluta *Shadows* are always great to have, and Kirby laid hands on the *Justice* issues. These pulp homages were short lived, but good.

The sophistication, knowledge and market venues for comics today have increased noticeably. There is so much information available today online and in print, collectors and investors have a wealth of data to make informed decisions and purchases.

All of this helps translate healthy interest and continued strength for our hobby. A final word: I admit I am old school when it comes to comic collecting. That is, collecting an actual "book" to hold and enjoy. The upcoming digital comic product will appeal to many younger and computer-savvy readers, but as a collectable, tangible memory, I think digital comics are a "bird". Just saying...

Eric Groves
The Comic Art Foundation

The sale of *Action Comics* #1 in VF+ for $1,500,000 made news internationally this year. That sale, and others, verified the intrinsic value of the comic book as a genuine American artifact. It also demonstrated that even in difficult economic times, the high end items still sell – to those who can afford them. The general public may not know it, but below *Action* #1 are numerous other highly desirable comics which have held their value or appreciated in value over time. Comics are a good investment.

That said, the market in our neighborhood reflects only moderate sales and frequent discounts. Economists may say the recession is over, but high unemployment persists. Disposable income is down and to some extent, the Age of Frugality is upon us. There is a bright side for collectors in that bargains abound in just about every area except for the most sought after high grade, CGC graded books. Mid-grade Golden Age comics look pretty good at today's prices, as do many obscure titles published during the Atomic Age. It is a good time to buy.

Trends can be difficult to discern, but some are inescapable, especially for those of us who grew up in the Golden and Atomic Ages. Comics which are not generation-skipping ordinarily do not attract younger collectors new to the hobby. Sadly, this applies to older Westerns and many of the Dell titles. We also observe an oversupply of comics from the late Silver Age and early Bronze Age. Demand has yet to catch up with the many copies available. Here is the market as we see it.

© DC

Adventure Comics with the Legion are difficult to find in high grade. (#354 shown)

The Golden Age: Timelys remain highly desirable, as they usually are, but copies offered at multiples of *Guide* are a bit off-putting these days.

Captain America, *Human Torch* and *Marvel Mystery* are often out of range for the average collector. Some of the second team Timelys are not turning up that often, such as *Mystic*, *USA*, and *Young Allies*, and they sell briskly when available.

On the other hand, Golden Age DCs in GD, VG and FN are reasonably priced at this point. There is heavy demand for *Action* #1-125, *All-American* #16 on, *Detective* #27-38 and all issues of *Batman*, *Superman* and *Adventure* under #100. More than ever, collectors are gobbling up *Wonder Woman* and *Sensation*, with good reason. The lower numbers are beautiful, unique books. The same may be said of *Leading* and *More Fun*. But it is still all about pricing.

Fawcett titles are slow but steady. *Master Comics* with Raboy art are reliable sellers. So are low number *Whiz Comics*. *Captain Marvel*, *Captain Marvel Jr.* and *Marvel Family* plod along at very reasonable prices. Nedor comics, especially *Startling* and *Exciting* with Schomburg covers, are a good value. Fiction House books are also slower than before, but there is demand for *Wings* and *Planet*.

The Atomic Age: This era is perhaps the most mysterious and unpredictable of all, maybe because of the tremendous proliferation of titles after WWII. Every year we find Atlas titles to be the best sellers, but one never knows. We acquired a collection of *Comics on Parade*, *Fritzi Ritz* and *Nancy and Sluggo* (all relatively inexpensive) and off they went. Romance titles with great artists like Simon and Kirby are solid comics and they find new homes. ECs are slow to moderate, but by the same token, we can sell pre-trends like *Blackstone* and *Tiny Tots*.

In our view, the crime and war titles from this period are undervalued and perhaps underappreciated. They go to collectors of these genres at bargain prices. We are often surprised when we sell off-beat DC titles like *Leave It to Binky*, but we do. Some of the Harvey titles from this time are likewise good comics and trade hands at reasonable prices, lately *Green Hornet* in particular. Early *Archie* comics sell nicely, as do low numbers of *Jughead*, *Reggie* and *Betty and Veronica*.

Dell comics, regrettably, remain slow sellers. *Tarzan*, drawn by Jesse March, is actually excellent comic art, and sales have picked up somewhat, especially the lower numbers. Walt Disney comics, with the exception of high grade, early Carl Barks Ducks, are also slow, although they do better in foreign markets. Some Dell Westerns move with their photo covers, but not very quickly. It seems there were just too many of these "clean, wholesome" comics distributed back then. Today, there are not enough collectors to absorb them. Early *Little Lulu* does well, though.

The Silver Age: Marvel's dominance over the Silver Age has been met with reinvigorated collector interest in DCs. This is not to say that fandom's romance with Marvels is over, rather that some degree of balance has been restored.

For serious DC collectors, the tough issues are those from the early Silver Age (or late Atomic Age, depending on how you look at it). Issues published between, say, 1954 to 1959 are in somewhat short supply, especially in condition. It seems that some of these books were simply not well constructed to begin with, and they wore out more quickly. Included in this group are *Action*, *Adventure*, *Batman*, *Detective*, *Superman* and *World's Finest*. Demand for specific issues of *Showcase* and *Brave and the Bold* is palpable, but once again, the price tag is a huge factor in selling these comics. Many collectors are willing to settle for low to mid-grade copies at reasonable prices.

Second tier DC titles have not fared as well of late, although there is renewed interest in *Green Lantern*. Demand for *Atom*, *Aquaman*, *Hawkman*, *Challengers*, *Sea Devils* and the like has not been strong, but *Wonder Woman* is heating up nicely.

Later Silver Age DC issues, from 1962 to 1968, seem to be in abundant supply in all grades. Perhaps too many collections have been dumped on the market in recent times. They move slowly, with the exception of certain keys in high grade.

Marvels are still in demand, although lower numbers in condition generate some sticker shock. As in the past, *Amazing Spider-Man* and *Fantastic Four* lead the way, followed by *Incredible Hulk* #1 to 6. Early issues of *Tales of Suspense* are hot, for obvious reasons. *Avengers* and *Silver Surfer* are doing well. But as with DCs, higher numbers of these titles are so readily available that demand has yet to rise to absorb them.

The Convention Scene: In previous reports, we suggested that the San Diego convention has become an extension of the motion picture business. Comic books are a subsidiary interest. The Chicago Wizard convention suffers from an overdose of popular culture in general. We understand that former Illinois governor Rod Blagojevich was in attendance this year, signing autographs at $50 a pop. Comical maybe, but not a comic book. We do not set up at either show.

The Reed-produced C2E2 show in Chicago last spring was well managed and presented in a pleasant environment at the McCormick Center. However, only about one third of the space was devoted to the sale and display of back issue comics. There were not enough serious buyers and sales were slow. Time will tell with this one.

Meanwhile, local and regional shows tend to focus more on comics. The Oklahoma Alliance of Fandom ("OAF") is one of fandom's oldest non-profit comic book clubs. Led by master collectors Bart Bush and Robert Brown, OAF will present another down home convention at the Biltmore in Oklahoma City on November 12 and 13, 2011. If you want an old-fashioned comic book show with friendly dealers and reasonable prices, then come on down.

Conclusions: We think the market for back issue comics will improve gradually over the next few years, assuming the economy is restored to normal levels. Even so, those of us who influence pricing should be cautious and should avoid pushing prices upward too soon. We must always be mindful of the financial limitations on the average collector.

The purchasers of *Action* #1 and *Detective* #27 at astronomical prices have not revealed their identities. We may assume they are far more wealthy than most of the people who collect comics and who trust the *Guide* when they make their purchases. This is all the more reason why we should keep these recent sales in perspective. Comic collecting will live long and prosper only so long as the average fan is able to afford the books he wants.

Jason Hamlin and Brett Carreras
Brett's Comic Pile, LLC

2010 Market Report (by Jason Hamlin): First let me say what an honor it is to become an advisor to the *Guide* I have been reading/ studying/ memorizing since I got my first one in 1985! We feel truly honored to be in such esteemed company. 2010 was a challenging year for comics retailing to say the least. We did a number of national shows to varying degrees of success, the best of which for us were the New York Comicon, Wizard World Philadelphia, and Heroes Con in Charlotte. It's a shame the NYCC got moved to the fall from early spring. It's usually a nice jump start for the con season! The C2E2 in Chicago was a very well organized show, although sales were very slow for us, but I can see it becoming an excellent show in the future. The NYCC seems to have better attendance every year, and almost seemed almost too crowded for shoppers on Saturday! We took two vans to Charlotte and Philadelphia, where we had dozens of boxes of good runs of 1970s to present bagged, boarded and in order books for $1 each. They sold like hotcakes, people were filling in runs in huge stacks. It's always great to see people buying old comics just to read.

On the other hand, I can't count the number of people at conventions looking strictly for ultra-high grade keys. At every show we get asked multiple times a day, and a VF just won't do for many. It seems that many people want to invest in comics in these tough economic times and only the best will do. We just don't have enough of this stuff to go around! Considering the economic downturn, it's surprising how hard of a time we had restocking and finding collections to sell. I guess the competition in our area is getting tougher outside of the uber-high grade key crowd people who seemed to be buying less expensive books on the whole. Nice condition semi-key Bronze and Silver books moved very well this year if priced right.

Other Trends (by Brett Carreras): 2010 brought a TON of change for Brett's Comic Pile. We moved into a new warehouse in historic Richmond, we became the top seller on Comic Collector Live, we acquired our largest and most important single collection to date (2,000 Golden Age, 20,000 Silver Age, and 200,000 Bronze Age), operated the largest comic book convention EVER in Virginia, the VA Comicon on Nov 20-21, with Top Cow, Fangoria, Zenescope, Moonstone, Larry Hama and Ethan Van Sciver in attendance, we set up at over 20 national and regional shows, and two of our staff were invited to be Overstreet Advisors! Whew!

2010 had a frustratring convention schedule for us, as MANY of the shows we usually attend were moved on the calendar. Major shows were scheduled right on top of one another, and we had to wait almost a year and a half between New York Comicons. An exhausting show schedule in 2010 should hopefully be relieved a bit, as we spent that same year listing almost 200,000+ individually graded comics on ComicCollectorLive.com. Any collector who is not using this website is wasting his/her time and money. Imagine it as "eBay, but only for comic books, everything is fixed priced, and it has the easiest search function in the world." By the way, registration is FREE, and their electronic wantlist service is FREE! We have almost 20,000+ positive feedback on eBay, and CCL is STILL our absolutely BEST sales avenue. We have a single full-time lister on this site, who is averaging hundreds of new comic listings daily. We hope to have over 350,000 comics on the CCL system by the time you read this article, at our website BrettsComicPile.com. We will also be scaling back our convention schedule in 2011, focusing on shows that seem to consistently work for us. If you see us at a con please bring your wantlists, as we love to fill them for people!

Golden Age: We have tried testing the Golden Age market in the past, with varying success. Now we bring between 2-6 short boxes of *Guide*-priced Golden Age books to shows. Because of the cost of replacement on these books, we often try to replace from other dealers' inventory. Because of the scarcity of these comics, we purchase ONLY what we find to be interesting, including cool covers, or interesting artists, or even just the random off the wall book, as long as we can price them at or under $100. It has been a fun experiment so far, and we are looking forward to delving more into this market. We REALLY like the dynamic covers by L.B. Cole, especially affordable copies. I purchased a copy of *Mask Comics* #1 from my good friend Guy Rose, and within a month, sold it to a client for double *Guide*. One comic book we can NEVER find, and one that I think is TRULY rare is *Pep* #26. This is the first appearance of Veronica Lodge, who I believe may be the best-selling female comic book character of all time. When this book DOES come to market, it seems to fetch 3x *Guide* restored, and 6x *Guide* unrestored!

Silver Age: The hot DC books are *Green Lantern* #7 (always asked for...we haven't had this book in 2 years!), and *Detective Comics* #359. Neal Adams' Batman and GL/GA books are great sellers as always. 12¢-cover *Detective* and *Batman* comics priced AT *Guide*, for less than $20 zip out of our boxes, and low grade copies online FLY at $10 or less each! I think we could sell EVERY *Flash* #110-130 if they were low grade, priced AT *Guide*...IF we could find them! These early *Flash* books are awesome, but are an example of something that has actually been priced OUT of the range of your average collectors...even low grade copies are a stretch for most people this year. Other Silver DCs that sell are the war titles, *Green Lantern*, and truthfully not much else. GD to VG units of other titles move if discounted properly. Otherwise, DC is ice-cold. A Genuine rarity? A DC comic book published before 1963 in VF- or better. All non-key

Superman sales continue to slip, except for early Krypto and Supergirl appearances.

Marvel Silver Age books that sell well for us are Spidey (of course), *Fantastic Four* #52, *Daredevil* #16, *Avengers* #57, ALL Steranko issues, *Captain America* #100 and #117, *Amazing Spider-Man* #39 and #50, and *Strange Tales* #135, which seems to be asked for quite a lot lately. All 1964 and before issues, especially *Avengers* #1-9, *Journey* #83-100, *Hulk* #1-6, *Tales* #39-59, *Spidey* 1-20, *X-Men* #1-5, 12 and *Fantastic Four* #1-30. *Iron Man* #1s are very sellable in any grade. I wish I had them all…but these collections don't turn up very often. All Silver seems to go in two different directions for us….Low grade and CHEAP ($5-10), or High-Grade/important and IMPOSSIBLE to replace (over $100). Two different markets, but I wish they would figure out how to meet in the middle, and start looking at MID-GRADE books! It's very hard to move mid-grade books, even with STEEP discounting of non-key, non-*Amazing Spider-Man* Marvels.

Bronze Age: Leading into the Bronze Age, we had a new rarity rise to the top: *Fantastic Four* #110 Variant. This is MUCH more rare than most people imagine, as the ONLY copy that we had all year sold to a DEALER in GD+ for $50! The Usual Suspects sit at the top of the Marvel heap again this year: *Hulk* #181, *Spidey* #129, *Tomb of Dracula* #10, *Marvel Spotlight* #5, *Ghost Rider* #1, same as the last few years. *Defenders* #10 seemed to slow a bit, while *Iron Man* #128 and *Thor* #225 seemed to move very fast. *Iron Man* #55 used to sell at about the same as *Iron Man* #1 in GD to VG/FN, but has settled back into the $50 range for a VG.

Bronze Age African-American characters saw continued interest, with *Hero for Hire* #1 impossible to keep in stock in any grade better than VG, and #2-5 selling briskly. Black Panther appearances in *Jungle Action* sell through, with very attractive copies hard to find, and priced well at *Guide*. We have definitely noticed a trend over the last couple of years that lots of non-key VF or better Bronze books are being bought. Most of these books in nicer shape sell for $8-12. Good sellers of the 1970s include *Captain America* (which are surprisingly affordable, even in VERY nice shape!), *Black Panther*, *Thor*, *Avengers*, *Iron Man*, *Nova*, Hanna-Barbera titles, and of course *Spider-Man*. 20¢-cover titles seem to be impossible for us to find in nice condition, and are a steal when priced at *Guide* for nice copies, especially *Avengers*, and *Captain America*. Sadly, late 1970s *X-Men* have cooled quite a bit, with only the "Days of Future Past" run commanding *Guide* prices. With so many great titles during this time period pricing out at less than the cover price of a new book in low grades, the one slow ground seems to be Mid-grade non-key Bronze, which has to be priced like a GD/VG to move even if it is a FN.

DC Bronze sales are led by a single comic…*Green Lantern* #76. We have had three copies in the past year, and they all sold for 2-3x *Guide*, with the best copy coming in at FN. I think this is going to be another comic that most vendors can say "Whatever shape it is in, I can sell it" just like *Incredible Hulk* #181. No matter what the *Guide* says, if a vendor takes less than $200 for ANY copy of *Incredible Hulk* #181 (as long as it has the cover), they are missing out. I think *Green Lantern* #76 is a comic that should NEVER be sold for less than $100…and in a few short years, should be more. Bronze Batman sell well, as do all of the horror books, great bargains in VF or lower condition.

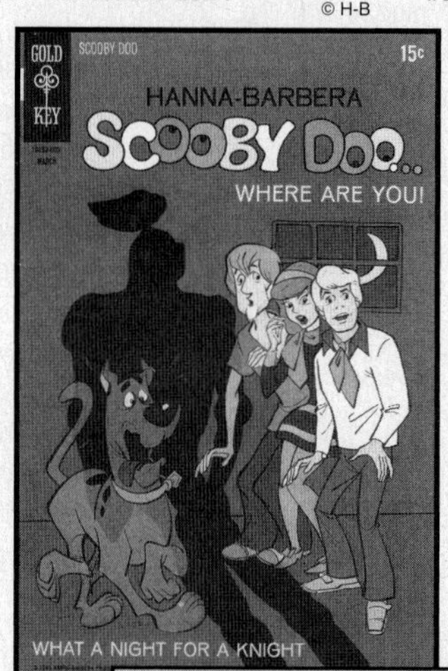

Gold Key's **Scooby Doo** *#1 is impossible to find.*

1980s to Present: We have expanded our reach of this market in the last 18 months. For many casual collectors, this is the time period that they remember, and grew up on. As much as I love Silver and Bronze books, we see this time period as being the EASIEST to sell, AND get collections. One thing to note for this time period, with VERY few exceptions, there are only two grades for this time period of importance: 1) VF/NM or better. 2) Everything else.

Here's something to consider from history. Pre-DC-Explosion Bronze are GREAT sellers, and are in demand, especially the late 1970s dollar books. DC 1970s and 1980s are much more in demand than 1960s DCs for us, even in the same titles. Pre-Crisis 1980s DCs are on the move, finally achieving *Guide* prices without hesitation (if $9 or below). DC titles include *Teen Titans*, *Batman* (moving VERY quickly for us), *Justice League of America* (from #150-200), *Flash*, and *Green Lantern*. *Green Lantern* is hot across the board, as issues from the last 5-10 years sell quickly as well. Investing for the future (or just want an AWESOME read for under $10)? Check out *Sgt. Rock*, or any ongoing DC horror book from 1981-1983. Low print runs, great artwork, and surprisingly hard to find in grade. Our late 1970s and early 1980s Batman section is almost gone!

Marvel best sellers include *Amazing Spider-Man*, *X-Men*, *G.I. Joe*, *Iron Man*, and *Daredevil*. Early '80s Marvels are very plentiful, but also great reads, and most of the major titles still hold up well today.

Strong post-1986 sellers for us include: *Spawn* #100 and up, *Invincible*, the last 20 or so *G.I. Joe* (Marvel) issues, Harley Quinn (ESPECIALLY her pre-solo-title appearances, *Mad Love* was fetching $40, now $30, and the one-shot with her first DCU appearance fetched $35-40), *Miracleman* #9 and up, and low print-run Archie and Image Turtles comics (from 1997 to 2002)! Many of these had GREAT covers by Mirage artists, and regularly sell through at the $4-8 range. Our two most requested books of the last year remain *Y: The*

Last Man and *Walking Dead* #1. *Y* sells for $100, and *Walking Dead* #1 seems to have settled at a whopping $275 online...When was the last time ANYTHING like this happened? *Harbinger* #1? *Turtles* #1? I expect *Walking Dead* #1 to hold its value now that the TV show has proven successful.

Deadpool has finally cooled down quite a bit. He has plenty of titles to keep his fans interested in current stories, though *New Mutants* #98 STILL moves at *Guide*. This could have been due to the overexposure Marvel gave him. Seems like he was on about 200 different covers last year. *G.I. Joe* #21 still sells quickly for $50-60 in VF/NM or better, but even beat up copies and second prints are easy to sell. *Simpsons*, *Futurama* and *Sonic* comics did VERY well for us this year. The *Futurama* #1 San Diego Variant sold at $25 in VF for us, with individual *Sonic* comics going for AT LEAST $6 and Giants (#50, 75, 100) at $10! We can't keep these in stock, as the print runs are pretty low, and a lot of them are sold to casual readers more so than traditional collectors. Another licensed comic we were THRILLED to find copies of is *Comic Smorgasbord* #1, a 1994 Transformers bot-con exclusive. Only 500 were made, and the shipment got lost at the con, so only a handful ever made it to the public. This is possibly the rarest recognized Transformers comic book ever made, and when we get them, we price them about the same as a Marvel *Transformers* #1, and our customers are eager for the opportunity to own this elusive comic!

Other Publishers: All Archies and Harveys sell quickly, especially pre-1964. Post-1969 issues sell if discounted, and rarely for more than $5 each. The Gold Key *Scooby Doo* #1 is impossible to find. When we get them, they sell for double *Guide*, UP to $100. 1970s on up is at a crawl, unless you can find high-grade, but even then it's a select market. Strangely, Phantom comics from ALL publishers sell at or above *Guide*, and we have sold through on *Tarzan* and *Godzilla* comics published after 1986. Dell and Gold Key *Tarzans* also sell well. We try to have a strong assortment of independent and interesting modern comics, and do quite well with them at shows. Top sellers for us in this category include: *Love and Rockets* (the Black and White self published #1 proto-issue is a steal at $100-125), *Eightball*, Chris Ware stuff, *THB*, and anything else by Paul Pope. One rarity from the West Coast we have had a few times is the Dark Horse *San Diego Comicon Comics* #2, featuring Hellboy. This one doesn't show up as often on the East Coast, and we predict it will crack $100 asking in perfect shape by the end of the year, as great copies are presently fetching $75 easily. Underground comix sales seemed to slow from the previous couple years, except for *Cherry*, which we sold completely out of this summer, and got asked for a few times per show. Another more risque book which sold well for us was the *Tarot Witch*: Website Edition of #1 which was a steady seller at $40.

Thank you again for inviting us to be Overstreet Advisors! Have a GREAT 2011!

Brian Ketterer
Collector

For the first time since I have been a comic book collector in the past 15 years, I would have to report that overall things were weaker in the vintage market than in the previous year. Auction results seemed slower for a great deal of the material, sales at shows seemed to be weaker and there were more discounts offered by many dealers to move more product than ever before. Naturally, the very top end of the market remained strong with top prices for truly rare pieces or unique ultra high grade.

I'm sure everyone reading this report is aware of the strong reported sales for the multiple *Action Comics* #1s sold by ComicConnect and the sales of *Detective Comics* #27s sold by Heritage. I think sales like this that are picked up by the media are excellent for our hobby and important for the market. With that said, the concern that was expressed throughout most of 2010 for the vintage market in other facets, mostly from late Silver Age (1966 forward) and on, is that the material sits and sits. There is just an overwhelming amount of 1970s Bronze age books and the market is flooded. In addition, the practice of pressing has ruined a good deal of the scarcity and fun of collecting the high end portion of that market because high grade copies are always available and if there isn't one in existence, one can be produced with a little effort through multiple attempts at pressing (there are notable exceptions like notoriously difficult books like *Avengers* #103 in 9.4 or better). Even late Silver Age is beginning to see a trend of falling prices due to supply become more readily available. With a widening gulf between top end prices and more common material, dealers who do not adjust to current pricing trends will begin to see their material continue to sit in their boxes, scratching their heads wondering why their VF and below books do not sell for *Guide* prices. The market is evolving and has been for some time. In a weaker economy, this is the segment that becomes exposed.

I attend many shows, both small and large, throughout the year, and I believe the above sentiment would have been even more pronounced but for this year's New York Comic Con put on by Reed Promotions. A first rate show (and it still has a few minor things to fix) with first rate talent and organization, Reed gave the New York comic book fans the show it deserved. Comic book fans responded in droves and the attendance figures I heard afterwards were in the neighborhood of 90,000 – 120,000 fans through the doors. In speaking with many of the vintage dealers who set up, almost all reported strong sales. This was a reverse in the trend of struggles and down sales that was the talk prior to New York. From expensive vintage books to dollar books, product seemed to be moving rapidly, and I witnessed many transactions of common books selling for strong prices. I'm not sure that New York can truly be said to be the "norm" for the current state of the market, but I can say that it is an indication that there is a whole segment of collectors who shop, buy vintage and are not doing extensive research on what a Fine book sells for in various sectors of the market. Instead, they see a book, they look at the price, they have some vague sense of its value, and decide whether to spend the money. These collectors are an entirely separate part of the vintage market, and probably the greater number than the experienced collector. While they probably spend less than $100 or $200 on books and are looking for quantity, they can easily be drawn in by discounts and accurate grading. Unfortunately, not enough dealers are following this trend to capture this business – yet.

As a side note, Wizard Productions ran a show in New York that was poorly attended the week before the Reed New York show. Like many people, I would have loved to have gone to that show and hope that they will move the show to another point in time away from the Reed show. I think it would benefit not only Wizard, but also it would really benefit the fans. Too many shows bunched too close together in both time and geography won't help anyone.

As part of my job, I have the opportunity to travel very frequently which gives me the opportunity to visit a number of comic book stores. Unfortunately, only a small number of them devote any space or effort to back issues and an even smaller number are able to provide accurate grading with an understanding of proper pricing. Those that do, I find, have a strong base following with customers who certainly have an appetite for vintage material. Again, pricing is key. Of course, I understand that new books and other products are truly the lifeblood of the comic book store and where they have to make their money.

One of the best examples of a store that knows how to grade, price and make an active continuous profit off of back issues and vintage material is Zapp Comics in Wayne, NJ owned by Ben Lichtenstein. For well over a decade, Ben has aggressively pursued collections, processes them quickly, but most importantly, grades accurately and prices fairly. New Jersey is also an extremely competitive area for vintage comics, and Ben does an excellent job obtaining fresh material. It's a first rate experience and if you are interested in vintage comics and in the New Jersey area, Zapp Comics is the cream of the crop.

Other first rate comic book stores I can highly recommend are: Bedrock City in Houston, TX owned by Richard Evans, Comic Universe in Folsom, PA owned by Frank Link, Collectors Corner in Parkville, MD owned by Randy Myers, Geoffrey's Comics in Los Angeles, CA, Main Street Comics in Milltown, NJ owned by Mike Pfiefer, Chicago Comics in Chicago, IL, and Eide's Entertainment in Pittsburgh, PA owned by Greg Eide.

I will throw out a topic that I think is going to bear watching over the next 5 or 10 years. Golden Age has always typically been thought of as the "top end" of our hobby. Books such as *Action* #1, *Detective Comics* #27 etc. will continue to remain the most important books. However, as time wears on the collectors who grew up with the Golden Age books get older, I predict that these books will become less and less significant to collectors as a whole. Will books such as *All-American* #16 and *All-Flash* #1 remain as desirable to many collectors to own? Will many minor titles like *Blue Bolt* or even later *All Star Comics* or many of the Fiction House books continue to have wide enough fan bases to maintain good long term stable prices? Will common run G.A. *Green Lanterns*, *All-American Comics* and even *Supermans* and *Batmans* still be as desirable at their current *Guide* prices? My wager is on "no". While Schomburg-covered Timelys and the core DC characters will maintain their popularity, I believe that many of the G.A. books will continue to decrease in popularity over time with many of them becoming harder and harder sellers with less and less interest at the prices currently listed. I'm sure there are many older collectors who may scoff at this notion, saying that G.A. will always be the hardest and rarest of all books to find and collect. It's possible that they're right. However, it is the Silver Age characters who are enjoying most of the focus and attention in the mainstream media, and I believe that many G.A. books will still be rare, but with fewer and fewer collectors actively seeking them out. Silver will become the new Gold.

Aside from the *Action* #1 and *Detective* #27 sales, Marvel keys remained incredibly strong overall. This is probably reflected by every other market report in this *Guide* and should come as no surprise to anyone. Pre-1965 Marvels and DCs from 1955-1962 also remained strong, most specifically in high grade. *Green Lantern* #76 saw its first CGC 9.8 grade given out with the book to be auctioned in an upcoming Heritage Auction. As it has continued to do for the past several years, *Green Lantern* #76 remained consistently strong in almost all grades. In addition, DC keys like *Showcase* #22 and *Brave and the Bold* #28 are seeing increased interest due to a variety of speculative factors. I believe this trend will continue as these characters gain in popularity and people discover how scarce DCs of this time period are in comparison to their Marvel counterparts. *Journey Into Mystery* #83, along with *Journey Into Mysterys* in general, have regained increased interest and attention. It is one of the tougher early Marvel runs to put together in high grade, with more collectors looking for them due to the *Thor* movie. Batman in Gold, Silver, and Bronze remain good sellers across the board. Neal Adams *Batman/Detective* books are almost routinely missing from dealers' inventories

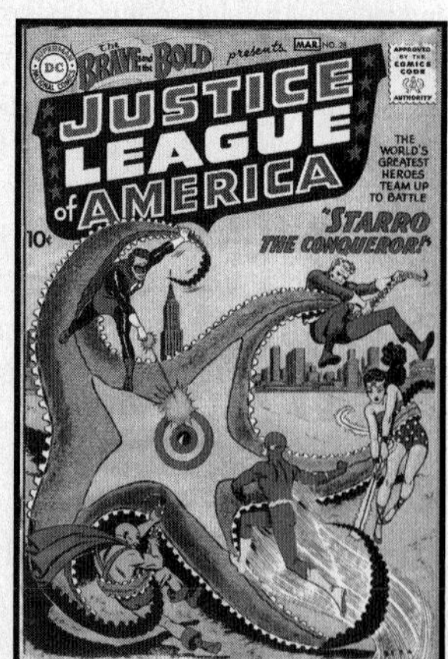

© DC

Speculators love *Brave and the Bold* #28.

in both stores and at shows. You should completely forget about finding nice runs of these in high grade as they are almost immediately snatched up. There is a much more narrow subset of books that I would buy universally when I see them, but Neal Adams drawn books require a much thinner margin to work on because of how rapidly I can move them. Frankly, I am offered so much quality material by a variety of outlets, aside from keys and early material, I am not enthusiastic about buying common Silver and Bronze Age unless at deep discounts.

The auction market is definitely becoming interesting to watch as each auction house has been settling into a role for some time now. For the most part, Heritage is the place to go for Golden Age and Original Art, ComicLink for high end Silver and Bronze Age, and ComicConnect stealing a bit of every facet from the other two. Surprisingly, ComicConnect has generated some very strong results in a short amount of time and has become a real force on the auction market. Still, the primary auction houses that remain strongest are Heritage and ComicLink. Pedigree Comics, owned by Doug Schmell, is also a site that runs comic auctions, but mostly focuses on high grade Marvels. While a definite presence, the auction market is generally controlled by the three houses mentioned above.

I would end my report with a similar sentiment to how I opened it. There is a tremendous amount of interest in the vintage market. I think there are plenty of collectors and interest in comics in general. However, I believe that there has been a slow correction over the past few years, and I believe that correction needs to continue. Sellers should expect that for the most part, they will need to adjust to offering deeper discounts on common material if they are interested in moving product on a rolling basis. While some shows like New York may provide for buyers interested in paying *Guide* prices even for common material, for the most part buyers are looking for discounts because there is clearly a perception that there are plenty of deals to be had if you are patient. More importantly, I think there should be a scale back in the overall prices for most common books from 1966 forward. Most are not rare and as dealers will tell you, they have warehouses full of the stuff. If there is a shift to moving product and not sitting on it, dealers, collectors and the market will all benefit because ultimately, more money will be infused back into the market.

Dennis Keum
Fantasy-Comics

Overall comic book sales remained steady for us throughout the year. Online sales continue to show gains in overall dollar volume based on quality and number of items listed. Fresh to the market and strictly graded books still continue to command *Guide* prices even in low to mid grades.

Many dealers report a weakening of sales prices when selling through venues such as eBay. Our sales show no softening of prices online. The fixed price format may take longer for an item to sell but a buyer will eventually come along that will pay *Guide* for nearly any book out there. We did offer some discounts of 10% to 20% on older inventory and noted that books sold at a brisk pace which means that there is some price sensitivity out there but there is also tremendous demand. The auction format is the right way to go for the truly unique ultra high grade and certified book where you can still consistently see multiples of *Guide*.

It is interesting to note the comic book market reflects structural trends that have been occurring in the overall U.S. economy as far as increasing wealth concentration of the very rich and escalating attention and compensation paid to superstar performers. In comics you can continue to see this trend as high end prices continue to escalate and overall prices on everything else remain relatively stagnant. What does this mean as far as investing in the comic book market goes? If you can afford it, buy important keys such as *Action* #1 and *Detective* #27. Silver Age books such as *Amazing Fantasy* #15 even in low grade are worth accumulating. Buy low to mid grade to read and enjoy and put together runs of your favorite titles but don't expect major price appreciation.

On the buying side we purchased four decent original owner collections during the year consisting of complete or near-complete runs of Silver and Bronze age Marvel and DC issues. While I have put in a twenty year career in banking and gave it up to pursue comics full time, if there is one reason that truly makes it worthwhile it is chasing down these collections. There is nothing quite like seeing old books in nice grades in its original state and learning how they were collected by the owner.

We did most of the major shows during the year primarily with an inventory of low to mid grade Silver and better Moderns. There seems to be an endless demand for low grade Silver. Just to note while many of the Silver and Bronze issues have been reprinted in Trade format, there is nothing like holding and reading the original comic book. Attendance at all the shows remain solid with an eager buying public. We met many important contacts and made valuable friends and look forward to the upcoming year.

Philip M. Levine and Jeff Rader
Paperpeddler Rare and Esoteric Comics and Collectibles

I'm Jeff Rader, and on behalf of myself and Phil Levine, let me give you a "Spoiler Alert". If you are in search of sales data on high grade Silver Marvels and DCs you will be sorely disappointed. If you are into the type of great items that fly under the radar of most, or are seeking a fun, different area of collecting, then we hope you will find something that catches your eye.

Phil has been in the comic dealing business since he started flipping back issues on the school yard in 1954. From there he graduated to making regular pilgrimages to the Passaic Book Center in the late '50s to stock up on the "good stuff". He began doing mail order in the late '60s, and started doing the convention scene in 1984. I have been an obsessive reader, researcher, indexer, and part-time dealer since being dragged to coin conventions by my Dad since I was 7 years old in '73. The only thing that caught my eye at the coin conventions were the stacks of old comics that many coin dealers had lying around. While I have been selling as Offbeat-Archives for the past decade or so I am much more of a reader and researcher and indexed for the APA-I, contributed marketplace reports to *Comic Book Marketplace*, and have been taking notes on every tiny nuance of every comic that has gone through my hands for nearly 4 decades.

Phil has been acquiring items, collections, and warehouses, for decades and we have finally decided that the time is right to go into high gear and start bringing to market the millions of items that Phil has been stocking up on forever.

Our areas of expertise are those that most others do not specialize in so we get the pleasure of reporting on items that are often overlooked by mainstream collectors. While the Million Dollar Babies, *Action Comics* #1, and *Detective Comics* #27, have brought our "little" hobby to the attention of the world there is a *lot* more to our pastime than the casual looker will ever know. The types of items we specialize in are pretty much the opposite of the headline-grabbers. We have a knack for digging up those that elude even the most knowledgeable collectors.

We primarily sell on eBay, and direct-to-collector dealings, but by the time this report sees print we will have three new specialty sites up and running, one devoted to collectibles that are *not* found everyplace else; the rare/esoteric/offbeat stuff that is still largely uncharted territory, along with a HUGE assortment of anything else imaginable. Since we do not deal in slabbed books, or specialize in whatever the current trend might be, we get a different view of the market than most. We have proven that once a reputation of solid, tight, grading is established raw books will still go for a nice price. Correctly graded, described, and reasonably priced books will almost always find a new home. The main thing we have found works out great with us that the BEST thing for business is a happy buyer. A large percentage of our customers come back for more, and often buying things that were not on their want lists in the first place.

I love reading through an *Amazing Fantasy* #15 just as much as the next fiend but most of these type books have skyrocketed out of the reach of collectors and into the realm of deep-pocketed investors. There are so many overlooked, un-researched, and outright ignored publishers, genres, and titles out there that I'll bet if any collector took a step out of their normal collecting parameters they would find something that they would love, and for a fraction of the price. Sample a few different types of books that you have not tried before and you may just find that you have been chasing the wrong "Grail" all this time. Odds are we may just have it.

Giveaways: One area of comic collecting that has something for everybody is Giveaways, and we just happen to have the largest collection of them ever amassed. Most of the upper-tier characters appeared in giveaways over the decades, Superman, Spider-Man, Batman, Captain Marvel, you name it and there's a good chance some company used them to promote their product, or further their cause. Genres that do not even exist in mainstream comics have a place in giveaways. How in the world would you classify *Doc Carter VD Comics* (or its unlisted follow-up), or a Charlie Brown with Sally comic entitled, "*Security is an Eye Patch*"? Collect Timelys? Give *The Adventures of Big Boy* a shot (and you might even get lucky enough to pick up an issue done by Human Torch artist, Bill Everett. Political/war comics? Go nab a Comic Cavalcade "*Tomorrow the World*". Religion? This genre is a goldmine with the Catechetical Guild and their *Blood is the Harvest* or *If the Devil Would Talk,* and we have them all. You EC collectors aren't left out either because they put out a few themselves; *Lucky Fights it Through*, *The K.O. Punch* (both fit right alongside Doc Carter since they also address VD), and a few others. *Thunda* is listed as being the "only comic done entirely by Frazetta". Nope, go take a look at *Li'l Abner and the Creatures from Drop-Outer Space*.

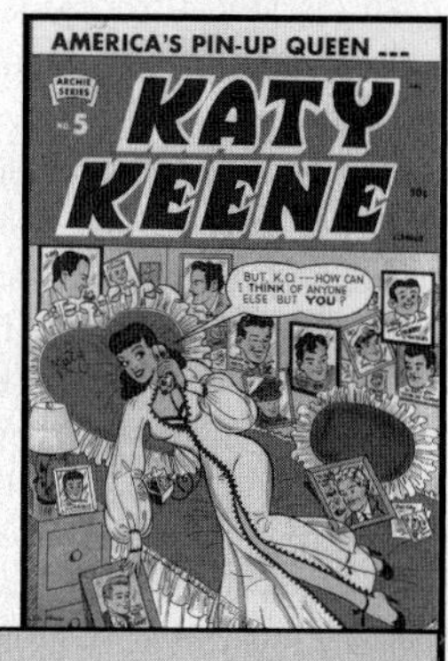

Katy Keene is a Good Girl Art collector's dream. (#5 shown)

Variant collectors could have a field day here. So many giveaways have variations ranging from minor to outright blatant. Are you one of those that loves truly rare books? You would not believe how many giveaways would qualify as Gerber 8s, 9s, and 10s...easily. Many titles are unique, and there are more out there waiting to be discovered. That is not even the tip of the *Red Iceberg* since the amount of giveaways listed is minuscule in comparison to how many have actually been published. While giveaways are one of the final uncharted frontiers of comics, keep your eyes peeled because soon there will be a major influx of information on this area of comics. We are in the midst of indexing the largest collection of giveaways ever amassed and in a short matter of time much of the unknown will become known. Very often "Unlisted" giveaways are listed as being "Very Rare", "Unique", and "Unknown"...not always the truth. Some "Unlisted" books are common as dirt, and others are absolutely unique. Soon the truth will be known.

Archie Comics: Archies have been put on quite a few more want lists than they were a couple years ago and the prices are jumping fast and HIGH! The problem here is that Archies were considered quarter box fodder for so long that putting runs together in any condition is a real chore, and a pricey one at that. Condition? Fuggedaboutit! The majority of Gold and Silver Archies out there are low grade, and page quality most often low. We recently sold a large collection of *Archie Comics*, from #20 - up, *Archie's Girls Betty and Veronica* #1 - up, *Archie's Pal Jughead* #1 - up, *Archie's Pals 'N' Gals* #1 - up, and many others titles. We were blessed with a collection in which most of the books had Off-White to Bone-White pages. Even the lower grade books brought on some voracious bidding due to the superior page quality. The funnest part about cataloging this collection was being able to see how much great stuff is buried in Archie titles that most will never see. Archies are rife with Good Girl Art, cameos (Elvis, The Beatles, Marilyn Monroe, etc.), innuendo covers and panels, cross-dressing, risqué shower/bath panels, lingerie galore, Universal monsters, UFOs & aliens, sexy pin-ups, cut-out paper doll pages, and much more. Katy Keene was in most of the early Archie titles and if GGA, lingerie, and sexy pin-ups are your thing Bill Woggon's Katy is a collector's dream.

For you superhero collectors that think Archies have nothing for you grab a copy of *Wilbur* #30 in which he tries his hand with The Green *Hairnet*. Or you can grab *Archie's Pals 'N' Gals* #13 for the story, "Superman Meets His Match" in which Archie gets decked out as Clark Kent. *The Mighty Crusaders*, *The Adventures of the Fly*, and Silver Age appearances of MLJ super-heroes like the Shield, and the Black Hood are often overlooked, and very affordable counterparts to DC and Marvel's Silver Age appearances of their Golden Age crime fighters.

There are countless sexy pin-ups, paper doll cut-out pages galore that have yet to be documented. Check out *Archie's Girls Betty and Veronica* #14. There is a panel in which Ronnie is taking a shower after a date at the beach. The panel clearly shows her tan unobscured by any telltale clothing marks, but also Archie's arm and handprint. The powers that were at MLJ/Archie knew how to put in just the right mix of goodies to have their comics flying off the racks and into the hands of both girls, *and* boys. Some sales include:

Archie Comics #20, VF- with White pages - $293
Archie Comics #50, VF-, Classic Betty Good Girl Art cover - $147
Archie's Girls Betty and Veronica #2, VG, Off-White - $180
Archie's Mechanics #1, VG, Off-White - $62
Archie's Pal Jughead #1, VF with White pages - $362
Archie's Pals 'N' Gals #1, VF/VF+ with White pages - $528
Archie's Pals 'N' Gals #1, with the rare original mailer – Qualified, structurally beautiful copy but it was printed when the red ink on the cover was running low - $132
Archie's Rival Reggie #1, VG, Cream to Off-White - $89
Pep Comics #59 , VF-, Off-White - $169

Charlton: Are you one of those that have scoffed at Charltons all these years? Well...I can't say I blame you, so did I at one point. As I am writing this report we are in the process of turning loose the largest collection of Charltons (over 5,000) ever seen on eBay. This has given us the opportunity to read, index, and catalog countless comics that have been overlooked for decades. Charlton was noted for putting out the cheapest product possible, and they managed to do just that by using an outdated cereal box press. Odds are they had no idea what the term "quality control" meant but that is often part of their appeal. Their output touched on every genre imaginable and when that wasn't enough they invented their own genres...*Zaza the Mystic*?! Violence? Good Girl Art? Drugs? Even after the Comics Code Authority kicked in Charlton still pushed the envelope as far as they could. Since they have been considered the neglected stepchild of comics for so long their titles are ripe for unlisted tidbits. Good Girl Art, by good and bad artists, abounds. Innuendos? Give *EH!* #4 a gander. Good luck finding a more blatant "headlights" cover, especially post-Code.

Charlton war books are chock full of unlisted Hitler covers and appearances, and there are even quite a few covers that rival some of the DC Big-5 masterpieces. Want to see what happens when Hitler gets a bit bent out of shape arguing with Mussolini, jams a Luger into his gut and pulls the trigger? Go grab a copy of *Army War Heroes* #29. Charlton was on the ball when it came to the Cuban Missile Crisis and Fidel Castro. There are a handful of Commie tyrant stories that could be nobody but the despot. Maurice Whitman, noted for his stunning Good Girl covers at Fiction House ended up at Charlton...but, ouch, no GGA here, not even Good Atomic Rabbit.

If you are a collector of Presidential/political appearances then Charlton is the place to poke around. They have snuck everybody in somehow, from "Ike" Eisenhower (saying, "I'm sorry, Atomic Mouse, but a trillion dollars is more than the government can spare..." deja vu?), Robert F. Kennedy, Ronald Reagan, Jacqueline Kennedy, to Richard Nixon, and even Mao Tse-tung. As for the non-political you can find parodies of Howard Cosell, Joe Namath, and even Peter Falk's Columbo. Another tidbit is that Hoppy the Marvel Bunny's last GA/SA appearance (***not** Atomic Mouse* #15), until his revival in the '80s, was purely accidental, and probably due in part to the colorist and editor having a too-long liquid lunch. Charlton, while notorious for their knock-offs of other publishers' successful characters, also had no qualms about doing outright swipes such as a Swamp Thing rip-off, and they had the foresight to have the first comic appearance of KISS, sort of, in a tale of a make-up laden heavy metal band singing, "Kiss me...Kiss me...". Don't think they left you Marvelites out in the cold. The absolute best swipe we have found so far, and we are nowhere near done looking, is the story Ditko did for

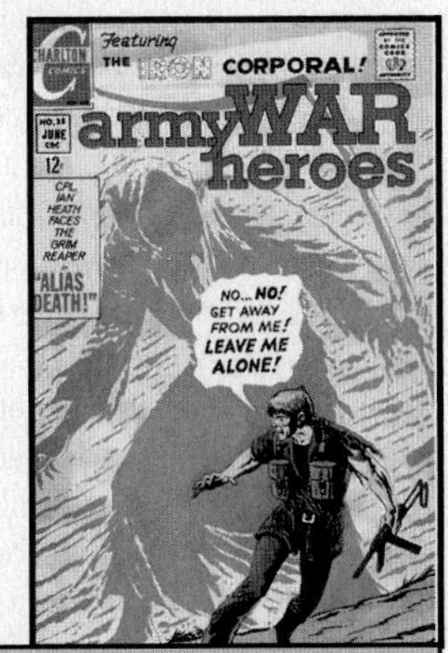

Charlton War comics have some memorable covers. (Army War Heroes #25 shown)

Ghostly Haunts #37. The green behemoth, with purple pants, is so undeniably the Incredible Hulk that it is almost as if Ditko was thumbing his nose at Marvel.

By the way...we all know that Marvel and DC had both direct and newsstand editions. Did you know that Charlton, possibly thinking (praying) they could become a big player in the game, also attempted the direct distribution trick. Take a closer look at some of your swan song age Charltons. Some of them have both variations with the UPC and the blank box. As Charlton made a few attempted comebacks their final shot in the game included some of their most horrendous printing, coloring, and artwork. This last shot also included some dismally LOW print runs. They are fun to collect in that train wreck kind of way and some of the last issues are elusive as heck. One sale of note: EH! #4, GD+/VG- , with Off-White pages for $132 (4.5x *Guide*).

Seduction of the Innocent/Parade of Pleasure/Censorship: Another of our areas of special interest is that of censorship in any form, but especially when it pertains to comic books. Aside from the *Seduction of the Innocent*, *Parade of Pleasure*, *and Love and Death*, there were numerous booklets ("Americana in Four Colors") including one from The Comics Code Authority ("*Facts About Comic Code Approved Comics*"), pamphlets, magazine articles going back to the early '40s, and the like, that denounced comic books, blamed them for everything from juvenile to delinquency to all but damaging the ozone layer (well, not really but close). There is a knowledgeable group of collectors that already specialize in this genre and they are a fervent group. We have anything and everything to do with censorship and the popularity of this area is rising fast.

Classic Comics/Classics Illustrated: We are noted experts in this area and with Phil having purchased the *Classics Illustrated*/Gilberton, and the Twin Circle warehouses we are stocked in depth with most issues, and also have many different rare peripheral items such as varying types of comic racks, editorial items, original artwork, rare foreign issues, and anything else you could possibly imagine. This is the one area of comics that can appeal to the basic collector, as a basic run from #1-169 is attainable, and on a relatively small budget. If you want to step it up a bit you can go for the run and seek out the different Highest Reorder Number issues, which is much more challenging, but makes for some fun searching. *Classics* are also THE area for variant and giveaway collectors. For the giveaway collector that thrives on the hunt go on the prowl for a "Shelter Thru the Ages", or better yet be the envy of all your friends when you nab a very rare "George Daynor" issue. If variants are your game you can give the *Classics* with the Coward Shoe ad a try. You'd have a better shot at completing a run of all the Marvel 30¢ and 35¢ variants than you would a set of Cowards, and there are still discoveries to be made. Sales: *Classics Illustrated - The United Nations '64* - Unread NM with White pages - $250, and a Cardboard 3-tiered comic stand - $100

Big Little Books: Big Little Books are a fun collecting area, and with all but a handful, it is possible to put together a nice run. They run the gamut from comics like Mickey Mouse, Dick Tracy, and Buck Rogers, to movies and television, with wonderful covers and interior artwork by some of the greats. We have a huge stock of issues and there are still quite a few collectors but we have found that there is some price resistance to the prices listed in the Guide. This is an area of early collectibles that if the pricing information were looked over, and corrected, there could be a resurgence in interest. When there is...you know where to come!

Platinum/Antediluvian: Platinum comics contain some of the funniest tales ever set to paper. Going back over a century we can get a glimpse into what made our grandparents laugh, a look into a more innocent era, and see what set the stages for the Golden Age of comic books. There are also unmentioned discoveries to be made in these books that have been around since the beginning of the last century. *Harold Teen* #1 is a cover-to-cover EARLY aviation comic that even features Charles Lindbergh. We have sold many and when priced correctly they find a happy new owner but this is another area that we think could use a review and some serious price corrections to reflect more of a reality in the market. Some sales include:

Bug Movies #1, Dell, 1931, VG for $100
Clancy the Cop, Dell, 1931, FN- for $100
Buster Brown On His Travels, 1910, Bright Fine for $250
Harold Teen #1, VG for $100
Mickey Mouse Comic #1, Dave McKay, 1931, Fair for $292

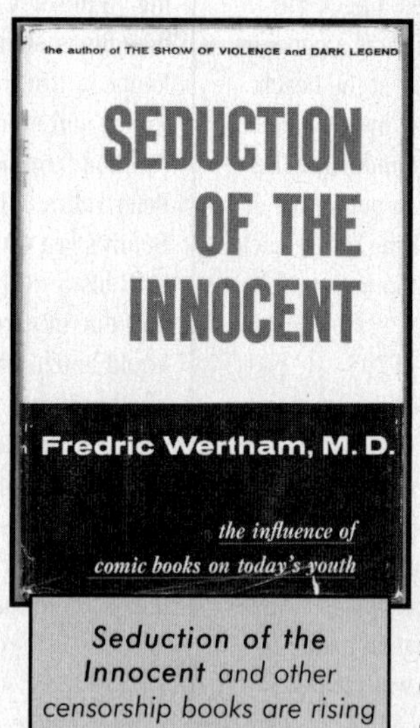

the author of THE SHOW OF VIOLENCE and DARK LEGEND
SEDUCTION OF THE INNOCENT
Fredric Wertham, M. D.
the influence of comic books on today's youth

Seduction of the Innocent and other censorship books are rising in popularity.

Unlisted in Guide: Our favorite area of research in the whole of comicdom is flipping through every single comic that goes through my hands to see what nobody else has noticed, or made public before. The list of unlisted items we have run across over the years fill page after page in notebooks. One thing that our many regulars know is that when they read our item descriptions there is a good chance that they are going to pick up a tidbit or two about something that they never realized before, and many end up being must-have books to them.

There are many Atomic Bomb cover/story/ mushroom cloud panel collectors that regularly come to us for issues they did not know belonged in their collections. Even Archie Comics snuck in the occasional Atomic bomb or mushroom cloud. Check out *Archie's Girls Betty and Veronica* #47 for Betty modeling her "Atomic Bonnet", or *Archie's Madhouse*

#3 for some more of the like. Charlton had a penchant for atomic bomb blasts also. Grab a *Blue Beetle* v2 #64, *Doomsday +1* #1 & #5, or even *The Flintstones* #38, yep, *The Flintstones*!

Unlisted innuendo and tantalizing near-nudity? Archie, Archie, ARCHIE! I could not even begin to list the number of times in which the stable of Archie artists (Bill Woggon reigns king of undressing and lingerie shots though) had some "innocuous" bath or shower panel showing one of the girls *barely* covering their tidbits. Two great ones though are *Laugh Comics* #25 in which Katy Keene is toweling off after a bath and that towel is poised just at the point of no return. *Archie's Rival Reggie* #9 has a story in which Laurie is in the bath on the phone and if she so much as twitched her arm it would have become an Underground.

Unlisted variants? We will never know for sure how many different variants exist out there but there are many that have escaped the notice of the masses. If it's price variants that you seek out just try to put together a run of the 15¢ cover price version of Dell's *Turok* #7-12. While most of the country got the standard 10¢ issues, Dell ran off a handful of each issue with an extra nickel tacked onto the cover price and gave them a trial run only in the San Francisco Bay Area. The price bump did not go over very well and after that failed test the cover price remained at a dime until issue #23 when they finally hit everybody with the price increase.

Original Artwork: This past year we sold a wide array of original artwork and it seems there is no shortage of avid collectors that love this area of the history of our hobby. In the beginning…original comic book artwork was trash, and I don't mean quality-wise. Pages were used as floor mats, thrown into the trash, and the lucky surviving pieces got tossed into closets or storage.

We sold a large stack of stories from Eastern Color's *Heroic Comics* that took us by surprise. Tales of battlefield bravery went to war collectors, stories about African-Americans went to collectors of African-American memorabilia, and even the tales of everyday heroes all found happy homes, with fervent bidding. One piece, about a genuine hero from WWII, Richard David DeWert USN, ended up being posted on a site with a tribute to his bravery, thrilling the men whose lives he gave his own life for all those years before. Heroic pages by H.G. Peter went to collectors that wanted excellent Golden Age examples of his work but did not want to pay "Wonder Woman" prices for them.

Many other Eastern Color/Famous Funnies pages, and stories, we sold were previously unpublished, including some great *Jingle Jangle Comics* stories that never made it into print, work destined for the never-finished *Famous Funnies* #219, and even *Club "16"* #6, which never even made it past issue #4. We also ran across a couple titles that never even made it past the planning stages. A few titles that we sold pages from that never made it to the stands were from *Let's Travel* #2, *Animated Comics* (maybe they were tossed aside after EC Comics nabbed the rights to the title?), and the high point of the group was *Toy Comics* #1, from the early '40s. We already knew that we had a winner with our publicly-unknown ashcan-type, editor's working copy of this comic (a mock-up issue comprised of stat copies of the stories, with an amazing cover by Larz Bourne) that never came to fruition, but after putting all the pieces together we realized that we also had the vast majority of all of the amazing artwork that was used in putting the comic together. Ever heard of Junkshop Jamboree? Fiorello Fennel (by Dave Tendlar)? The Burro of Brooklyn? The lisping Thammy Thimble? That's what I figured. Thankfully the unrealized project remained nearly intact and got slipped into a safe place for decades instead of being relegated to the trash heap. As things progress here on our end there will probably be a time when you can read a facsimile of this unpublished bit of hilarity, and fantastic artwork.

Another niche that has some of the most dedicated collectors around is *Classic Comics/Classics Illustrated*. While artwork was only a very small portion of what we sold this past year each and every piece we had found a new home, and usually after very fervent bidding. There are some bargains to be had in original art if you compare the price, rarity, and historicity of a page of artwork to the cost of a copy of the comic book itself. We sold countless *Classics Illustrated* pages for less than a high grade copy of the issue it appeared in would cost, including artwork by George Evans, and H.C. Kiefer. If that does not defy logic then I don't know what does. We also sold the painted cover, and artwork by Lou Cameron, to the complete book of *Classics Illustrated* #13 – Dr. Jekyll and Mr. Hyde to a very happy buyer for a bit over 5 figures.

For those that want a unique bit of publication history, for even less than original artwork, printer's proofs are the way to go. You can get a unique item for a fraction of what a newsstand copy of the same book will go for.

Discoveries: Though we have just begun going through Phil's collection we have already made a few discoveries worthy of mention. We ran across a few children's "block-book"-type puzzle books from 1949. The set includes 6 different books that were published with the inherent nature to be destroyed. The thick cardboard pages had die-cut puzzle pieces meant to be popped out by youngsters and inevitably lost. The kicker about this set is that 2 of the books were fully illustrated by Harvey Kurtzman, and his unique style is readily apparent, and reminiscent of his "Hey Look" work.

Our biggest comic history-changing find (so far, that is) was a copy of *Cheerio* #1, with a cover date of January 5, 1936. Noted comic collector, and researcher extraordinaire, Jon Berk, had previously turned up a registration copy of this over-sized comic magazine that was a sort of in-between stage printing submitted solely for copyright purposes by Harry "A" Chesler, Jr. At the time Mr. Berk announced his discovery it seemed that the story ended there publishing-wise since his copy contains mostly text, single panel gags, and blank filler pages, with all of the comic strips mentioned on the cover noticeably absent. We turned up a copy that also had the text and gags but…it had every single comic listed on the cover, and more, making it the first Chesler comic, knocking *Star Rangers* #1, from 1937 off of its pedestal. It also beats *The Comics Magazine*, which was absorbed by Centaur, by 5 months. It is definitely an evolutionary step in the formation of Centaur Publications seeing that most of the comic strips, all original, were later reprinted in other Chesler and Centaur comics where some became regularly occurring strips. Early comic detective, "Lucky Coyne", whose 1st appearance was previously recognized as being in *Funny Picture Stories*, actually made his debut here, and that is just one of many examples. Another first in comics that does deserve mention is that this comic contains the 1st actual nudity in a comic book, by artist Dick Ryan, in which a gal gets caught topless by a voyeuristic monkey. This unique copy, with the covers, and first two wraps completely split realized over $1,500, and the very pleased buyer was willing to go much higher to land this historic comic.

While going through items from the Harvey warehouse we found a detailed handwritten 166-page index of all Richie Rich stories from *Richie Rich* #1-#220, *Richie Rich Millions* #1-#113, and most other RR titles, and where all of the stories were subsequently reprinted. There were even listings for a few issues that were never published such as *Richie Rich Fortunes* #64, and *Richie Rich Dollars & Cents* #110, both originally slated for 12/82. Along with the Richie index was the Harvey check register from 01/76 to 07/76 which contains quite a bit of enlightening information as to where Harvey $$$ was going, including Joe Simon, Jerry Grandenetti, Bloomingdales and even a jewelry store. Some sales include: Set of 6 1949 puzzle books, with 2 by Kurtzman, NM for $404; Harvey Comics Richie Rich index for $787 and a Harvey check register for $100.

Since we are just getting started, our areas of contribution are slightly limited to certain areas but as time goes on we will be expanding our knowledge, and contributions to cover more publishers, genres, etc. By the time I sit down to type up our next Market Report we will have gone through, indexed, and sold a near-complete run of ACG comics, along with more Golden Age of all publishers and genres, *Classics Illustrated* items that fit the true definition of "RARE", *Seduction of the Innocent*-type items, and giveaways that others have not even dreamt of. Our long journey through the warehouses has just started, and there are many more discoveries to be made.

Remember, unless you actually pull back the cover and read a book or two you will never know what you might be missing. Thanks so much to all that have been a part of making our first year such a great one! Happy collecting!!!

Jon McClure
Collector

Disparity between the dollar values of ultra high-grade copies and low grade copies of key issues, or issues in general, continue to diverge. Despite the ongoing recession, killer examples continue to set records at auction because people pay big bucks for what the other guy can't find. When it comes to the truly scarce, bad copies of key or variant issues bring good money from those who must have them. Mostly the same books are on everyone's lists though, making it hard to say what something is truly worth. Just look at the listed value of *Action Comics* #1 until recently... it made big news, but only because outstanding copies rarely change hands, and *Guide* policy is generally to let the market speak with established sales. How does one value books like the Archie 15¢-cover variants that no one can find, let alone sell, especially variant keys like *Mad House* #22, vastly undervalued in the *Guide* already, that surfaced after my article came out last year? Another example is the 35¢-cover Marvel Price Variants; step right up and pick a Western, any Western. They are so rare that no copies are changing hands in any condition at any price, yet all of the books are confirmed to exist and have been for years.

I deal primarily in books that sell for $1000 and under. Last year's most notable sale was a raw copy of *All-Star Western* #10 VF/NM for $1000. I see a real future for this book in high grade as it is uncommon in any grade. *Weird Western Tales* #12 and *Weird War Tales* #1 sell over *Guide* with no resistance and continue to rise in price every year. Buy your nice copies now before they move past the triple digits! As for books in general, some very slight increase in Variants in general is there, but it is modest, possibly because the market, as I stated before, needs examples of actual sales for people to relate to, and you can't sell what isn't out there to find. Marvel's #1s sell well in all grades for Horror titles. *Conan* #1s sell well at 150-200% *Guide* for me, as do *Iron Man* #1s. War comics remain popular, particularly DC's big five, and Marvel's *War is Hell* sold out for me this year in all grades, especially #9. Ten to fifteen cent cover price Romance comics in the $5-7 range sold regardless of title, publisher, or issue number unless they were butt-ugly, awful copies. With more people than ever downsizing and selling off all or part of their collections, so-called "wholesale prices" dropped to new lows for lower grade books and relatively common books, making it possible for collectors to buy runs of even solid titles for a fraction of what they cost 2-3 years ago, and there's no end in sight. Most material will still sell if discounted sufficiently, although eBay results seem lower with each passing month.

Todd McDevitt
New Dimension Comics

I always think some background info on those writing these market reports is helpful, so here's a little about me. I started New Dimension Comics in 1986 while still in high school in my hometown. I have made comic books my life. 2011 marks my 25th anniversary in the business! NDC has grown to 4 stores surrounding the Pittsburgh, PA area. Many fortunate things have happened to me to get me this far. When I started, I thought I'd be 1 guy in my 1 store doing what I love and making enough money somedays to eat steak and others to get by with ramen noodles. I never expected to grow to this level. One of my rules has always been to buy everything I can. I think keeping a fresh and relentless flow of new material through my stores has been a huge component to my success. With the purchase of a giant warehouse, nothing holds me back from taking on loads of comics 100's of thousands at a time. So… I guess handling all these comics has brought me some insight to share here. So the good folks at Overstreet seem to think at least! They keep askin' me to come back!

Golden Age: I think with each year I report that "attic finds" still happen. I have seen a few things this past year, but nothing huge like the treasure troves that have blessed me in recent years. Most of my big book buys have been from collectors who have decided to "cash in" or dealers who also have tired of the business. And I can see why. Selling these types of books is a little tougher than before too. It seems the internet, auction houses, and CGC have made collectors not only more finicky, but more willing to wait to pull the trigger. Of course, there are exceptions. And no real surprise here it's the Marvels/Timelys. They are always the first to sell out of any batch I procure. Even so, I have just a handful that I have had in stock for a while now. This is probably the longest stretch that I can say that is true. The worst for me is that I'm digging these books more than ever personally. I end up paying for stuff that I WANT just to get those books for me!

Silver Age: Quality sells. I got an amazingly sweet collection in. Many could not have been read. No finger pock marks, nothing. I processed what I could and dragged it to a small show with low expectations. Who is gonna pay me $100 for NM *X-Men* #85? I recall joking about that exact book prior to the show opening with other dealers. Guess what I sold that day… That, plus an *Amazing Spider-Man* #101 in NM for $250 and a #108 in NM for $50. I always tell folks that I rarely use those "top prices in the right hand column in the *Price Guide*". But when I do, I ask one simple question to myself. : "How much nicer does it have to be?" I have also seen collectors salivate quicker when I tell them the books came from an original owner collection. There is something about the allure of comics right from a guy who had them when he was a kid that makes them even more appealing.

Another key note about Silver Age sales this year would be interest in prototype hero books. They are super cheap and FUN! Who wouldn't want to see a proto-Doctor Doom in action? I sold one for like $30 and of course the guy loved the price on what could be a major key book. Heck, some Golden Age books are worth extra due to the ads they have in them, like an ad for *Action* #1 in *Detective* #16. So why wouldn't pages of content that inspired a future icon be desired even more so?

On the low end, I maintain 2 Silver Age inventories that are just $1 and $3 each. I have never had more of them than I have right now. Where I have been lacking in buying Golden Age this year, I have more than made up for in volume on Silver Age. The $3 selection is my favorite to bring with me to conventions and it is hovering at about 10,000 comics now. Many are low grade, but many are just my 5th copy and that makes them overstock, so into the cheapies they go!

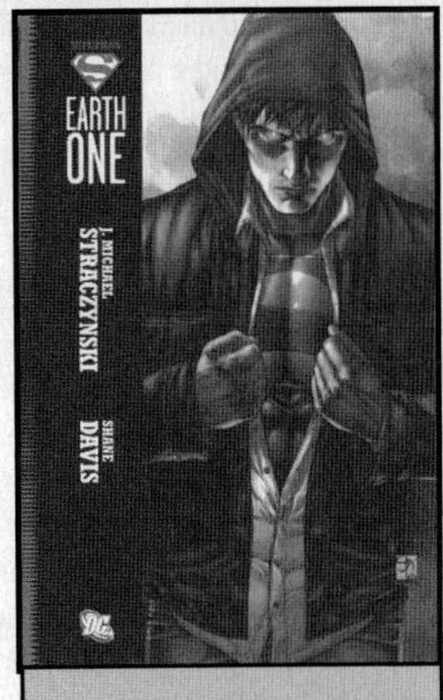

*Superman Earth One GN hit the top of the **NY Times** bestseller list.*

Modern Age: $3.99 comics! Every month! Really? Well… really. While lots of collectors whined about the rising costs, only few threw in the towel. Now Marvel and DC have both taken stances to run 2011 with no monthly $3.99s, but keep them at $2.99. While that sounds noble, I'm looking at my 4 stores and seeing the best year I've ever had. I'm not sure I want that formula messed with! Offhand, I can't say for sure that it is just $3.99 books that are making that magic happen. Chances are it's not. But, don't forget how rare some of those books become with all retail stores tightening their orders and with fewer stores in the country. This might explain why our back issue sales are still solid. In my region and on the road, I have a growing reputation for buying everything. I have a pretty big machine to feed and well, I can't say no! My wife likes jewelry, I like comics. But as much as it's an addiction, I am justified in the sales we have in that category. I do think a lot of it is that fans can't get everything they want elsewhere. No matter how on top of the new releases they are, there will always be a missed issue. Our niche is that we fight to have it in stock and when they come looking for it, we make them smile.

Trade paperbacks, collected editions, and graphic novels have continued to sell great. *Walking Dead* just keep flying out the door every week. I managed to sell an original *Walking Dead* #1 comic, in bad shape, for $60 twice in 2010. This AMC TV show is well received and fans the flames of an already super string buzz. We also saw *Superman Earth One* hit the top on the *New York Times* best seller list in 2010. Seems comics AREN'T just for kids anymore after all!

Variations - Old Variants: So many collectors have gotten their lists all crossed off that they are looking for something new. I ran across my first guy who was searching exclusively for *Spidey*'s with Mark Jewelers ad inserts in them. I bet I only see these maybe 5% of the time. It would be interesting to know the print runs on books like these. And how about the Direct Market? When the publishers first started selling non-returnables to comic specialty retailers, they changed the covers. Slightly, but it is a variation. I wonder how low the print runs were when that first happened? How hard would they be to find in nice shape? And at what point did the tide turn and the Direct Market was taking on the majority of comics? Another rarity for me to see—I'd say even less often than a Mark Jewelers ad book— are newsstand versions of Image books. Did you know that *Spawn*, *Gen 13*, *WildCATs*, and more had versions for the newsstand? They have a different cover stock and UPC codes before that was standard. Try finding these in nice condition!

There are more. Having handled comics for 25 years, I start to zen in on the little differences. I found *Action* #495 with 2 different colors on the DC logo. Not fading, not the printer running light on a pigment (the same color is fine on the rest of the book), not Whitman. How did this happen? Was there a shift change at the printing plant? Someone who likes green took over the nightshift? Maybe from a different printing plant altogether? More importantly, how many got out there like this? How many others are we missing? I just happened to buy a big stack of this issue or I may have never caught it. It makes me wonder how many more variations we would find if we start squinting at the INTERIORS too!

I guess my point is that as the hobby continues to polarize, the desires of collectors could easily swing the pendulum further than ever. Once you THINK you have all the *Amazing Spider-Man* comics, then you find out there are different inserts, covers, and maybe even a crazy printer operator to worry about too! What will be interesting to see is if premium prices will be paid for any of these if they are discovered to be rare.

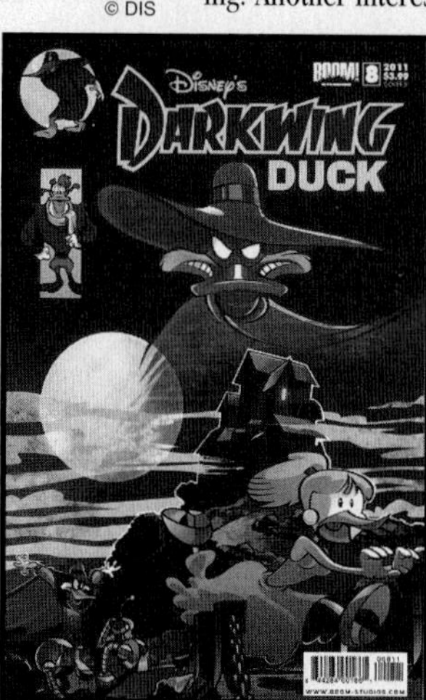

The popularity of the new **Darkwing Duck** series has surprised modern collectors. (#8 shown)

Steve Mortensen
Miracle Comics

2010 continued to be a good year for comics, especially the high end Golden, Silver and Bronze Age markets that reached new highs. We saw the first $1 million sale of any comic with the sale of *Action Comics* #1 and *Detective Comics* #27. On a personal note, in 2010 I launched a new business, Miracle Comics, specializing in Silver, Bronze and Modern Age CGC comics (many of you know me from my former business Colossus Comics). I continue to write for *Comic Buyer's Guide* and keep up with the trends of the current comic market, along with my day job as art director of a Silicon Valley biotech company. The modern CGC market continues to be a difficult place for investors, but deals can be had with variant covers and key books such as *Chew* #1, which has really taken off. *Walking Dead* #1 also is a great fan favorite and sells above $550 in CGC 9.8.

The Year in Review: In December 2009, the Image series *Chew* was hot. The #1s in CGC 9.9 were selling for $250+ and even a CGC 10.0 sold for $1,150 in November 2009. As of this writing, the series is still one of my favorites at issue #15. Also in Dec. 2009, *G.I. Joes* in CGC 9.8 were selling well and *Amazing Spider-Man* #583 Obama 1st print variants in CGC 9.8 dropped in price to $60 from a 2009 high of $375.

In January 2010, I had a chance to visit several Midwest comic stores and found that most of the back issue bins were empty of NM/MT comics. I realized that many dealers who were reluctant to embrace CGC in the past have begun sending in many of their prime candidates to CGC for grading. Another interesting thing is I saw very few CGC books for sale in the stores. Much of the high grade CGC market for Golden, Silver and Bronze Age books has almost completely moved to the web. Also, CGC celebrated their 10th anniversary in January 2010.

In February, a couple of titles caught my eye: *Green Lantern* back issues from the 1990s and *Marvel Comics Present* #74-84 (Barry Windsor-Smith covers). One particularly high demand modern comic is *Green Lantern* #47 (published 1993). It features Green Lantern and Green Arrow on the cover and sells for about $90 in CGC 9.8. On the Marvel side, the Barry Windsor-Smith covers from *Marvel Comics Present* are selling well in CGC 9.8. Many sell north of $50 and prices keep climbing due to the Weapon X storylines.

In March 2010, DC Comics began its saga of the Return of Bruce Wayne, which inspired many crossovers and produced loads of variant covers. As of this writing *Batman and Robin* #16 was just released – the issue in which Bruce Wayne confesses that he has been funding Batman all these years and that he will form a network of Batmen all over the world. Batman has been quite popular, especially in the Golden Age CGC buying circle. In February 2010 a *Detective Comics* #27 broke the record held by *Action Comics* #1 for the highest price paid for a comic of almost $1.1 million.

In April 2010, a copy of *Action Comics* #1 in CGC 8.5 sold for the record price of $1.5 million. To date, this is the highest price paid for any comic bypassing the sale of *Detective Comics* #27 CGC 8.0 in February. I wonder if in the next several years we'll see a "million-dollar club" with more rare books coming to market.

In May 2010, I noticed the drastic drop in prices of some CGC modern X-Men comics. *Uncanny X-Men* #207 in CGC 9.8 had a high of $304 in 2008 and in 2010 a copy sold for $52. Silver Age *X-Men* have taken a hit as well, while many collectors are flocking to the high grades. *X-Men* #50 in CGC 9.8 sells for $3,500+ while a CGC 8.0 sells for only $60. For the non-collector these two books would seem almost identical in condition.

In June 2010, I looked through some of my inventory to

find Frank Frazetta covers. Frazetta died in May 2010 and will be sorely missed by scores of fans. *Vampirella* #1 in CGC 9.2 sold for $1,673 in February 2010. Six copies exist in CGC 9.4 but no sales have been recorded. This is just one example of Frank's fine cover work and shows how hard it is to find his magazine covers in high grade.

In July 2010, I bought a collection of Harvey comics. Most were ungradable, but as a Bronze Age Horror fan I fell in love with the monster covers. Many Harvey File Copies have been graded and most are very affordable in 9.4 and 9.6 condition. The crown jewel of Harvey is probably the *Richie Rich* #1 from 1960. The highest graded copy is a CGC 9.6 and it sold for a high of $29,875 in 2006.

In August 2010, Marvel announced they would produce vampire variants of many of their titles. Many of these variants eventually sold for $10-15 each ungraded, which I think is a good buy considering dealers had to purchase $40-60 worth of inventory to get one. Both Marvel and DC are producing more variants making the regular covers less collectible, unfortunately.

In September 2010, *Darkwing Duck* surprised modern collectors with its popularity, and variant covers immediately began selling for $25 each. DC announced a new *Superboy* series by creator Jeff Lemire. His previous work, *Sweet Tooth*, has been sort-of a cult hit. Prices have been on the rise for *Sweet Tooth* #1 with CGC 9.8s selling for $50.

In October 2010, I noticed that *Fangoria Magazine* was coming out with its #300 issue. I remember as a teenager reading it and getting ideas for gruesome Halloween costumes. Issue #1 recently sold in September of 2010 for $323 in CGC 9.8 – a bargain as far as I'm concerned. I think these cult magazines in high grade are rare and I think will do well moving forward.

In November 2010, DC announced that they are coming out with a *Batman Beyond* ongoing series. There was a mini-series written by Adam Beechen that was produced earlier in the year and garnered great praise. Beechen is back for the ongoing series so it should be good. Perhaps the best investment buy however is *Superman/Batman* Annual #4, which features a future Batman and future Superman storyline. It has been selling online for $20 ungraded and I'm hoping that it increases in value with the new series coming out.

In conclusion, the high end comics market continues to be hot with collectors paying top dollar for the issues they want in high grade. Sadly, though, for Silver and Bronze owners with comics in the Fine to Very Fine category, they are lucky to get full *Guide* value even if the comic has been graded. The Modern market also continues to struggle in some areas but 1980s books are picking up in CGC 9.8 and are very affordable to the average collector in the $50-100 range for non-keys. With more movies coming down the pipeline like *Green Lantern*, *Thor* and another Batman film I'm sure the collectible back issue market will remain healthy in 2011.

Jamie Newbold
Southern California Comics

Hi Folks,

It's fire season in San Diego. Thankfully, the weather has been wet for awhile. We needed the break! It's also that time of the year where we generally note a decline in sales, manifested in the form of reduced new comic purchases. However, the sale of older comics has remained unfazed. In fact, that's been true for us since the beginning of the year. Even Comic-Con (which generated weak sales in 2009), finished in the plus column for us. 2010 has been a banner year for back-issue sales.

Store Sales: Our back issue sales were strong across the span of books from the 1940s to the 1970s. Comics from the 1980s to modern sell at bargain prices all the time. Nothing new there.

Walk-in and website sales remained consistent throughout the year, much more so than the previous, recessive years. Supply, convenience, price, and reputation drove sales in our direction. One more local store closed down and changed the buying habits of many. Those new customers discovered us, as well as our roundhouse of back issues and fueled our sales.

Yelp.com continued to spearhead sales at our store. I personally believe it is the number one internet proponent sending local, new customers our way. Their ads are expensive, but the free presence and generous information they promote online automatically is priceless. Otherwise, "googling" comic book stores in San Diego is the preeminent one-stop locator for new customers that eventually drop in at our store.

We poll most of the new faces that enter through our doors. The "why" they chose us and the "how" they found us are questions we ask. Their options to discover us are the phone book, the internet, word-of-mouth, and other advertising. The phone book is declining into antiquity - it seems to be a tool for hotel guests or shady characters looking to off-load anything for cash.

The internet, broken down into scattered search engines, reaches nearly all our customers. They type in "comic book stores San Diego" and run with the prompted selections. In contrast, the "Yellow Pages.com" site is seemingly impervious to inquiry. Rarely do we receive a customer that has utilized the phone book's on-line ad site. A few, well-informed comic book aficionados use the COMIC SHOP LOCATER site to search for stores in any area they are visiting. It's a service I pay for, so I'm relieved when the occasional customer announces their utilization of it.

We get plenty of feedback from people that were directed to us by friends and acquaintances. Perhaps twittering is the new word-of-mouth for this millennium.

With the influx of customers we've seen in the last ten months, we'd have expected to see increases in new comics sales. Sadly, the opposite is true.

Website/eBay/Internet Activity: Kind of a mushy area. No more and no less than previous years. Not surprising considering the proliferation of comic book conventions nationwide. Wow, they've re-surged like it was the 1970s all over again! Who needs to shop off of a website when eBay and a comic con are within everyone's reach?

Sales activity from eBay remained the same. We offered some better books for sale on ebay than we normally do. These comics consisted of better condition, low-numbered 1960s Marvels, DCs and various CGC books. They sold well during the brief period we offered them. But sales prices measured against GPAnalysis stats rarely matched up. That was disappointing. Our experiences still validate that store sales prices will often surpass internet sales. Just takes longer to move them sometimes.

One problem I have with my own website is the sheer consumption of time it takes to manage. I pay particular attention to details when we purchase a new collection at the store. Graded comics will end up on the site but it's a lengthy affair, loading hundreds of scans and lines of data. I find myself spending more time at home working on the site, uninterrupted by customers or phone calls, because I'm a poor, two-finger typist (can you tell?).

Potential customers frequently preface an inquiry about our site by asking if it is up to date. Their past experience has taught them that many comic book dealers infrequently update their sites. My employees built a Facebook page for our store, because I did not know what a Facebook was. We now use the website homepage and our Facebook page to announce significant events and encourage customer interaction. Our e-mail list also helps to fulfill our customer communication needs. All of these electronic mediums increase the consumption of time on computers and pulls me away from the paper and staple world. I do realize that these formats/venues are becoming market necessities to draw in customers. One really has to be dedicated to these forms of internet presence to make the chores worthwhile. I delegate what I can to my employees because I'd rather play with comic books. I also have a minor presence on the CGC Chat Boards but that also requires more time and typing than I can commit to. Frankly, I would rather talk to my customers than type to them.

New Comics: We continue to see a decline in the number of new copies sold each month. Customers come and go from San Diego with regularity (permanent departures rather than arrivals still seem to be the norm). Military deployments play havoc with an already wonky market.

Marvel attacked the market with its numerous and all-consuming crossover events. Civil War was replaced with Skrulls, which had their place taken by Siege, which was finally trumped with the Heroic Age. This proliferation of tie-in issues reduced reader interest. Fewer customers were interested in buying the crossovers and mini-series connected to each event. Meanwhile, DC captivated us with Blackest Night as well as its transitional series, *Brightest Day*, which started off with a bang. Blackest Night carried an edgy, DC-going-for-broke killer plot device. *Brightest Day* mellowed this feel out and lost a few readers long the way. The Batman story arcs maintained reader interest with a steady readership across all the Batman inclusive titles. The anticipation of Bruce Wayne's return to the present kept sales of the Batman titles at their highest.

The only constants this past year were the variety of variant covers produced for these books and the dollar increases that just about every company fell victim to. Variant cover sales were active in 2010. Marvel and DC continued to configure the selection of variants through our Diamond orders, which made it easy for buyers to locate these scarce copies when they ship. Marvel variants were consistently more desirable to our customers than other companies, DC included.

Despite the dreaded \$3.99 cover price increase across the board, DC and Marvel finally announced their revamped cover prices, which I am eagerly awaiting as I type this. Our customers have stated their uncertainty as to it altering their buying habits. I applaud the two companies for taking these bold, but necessary steps. What good are \$3.99 cover prices if I can't sell enough copies? Reduction to \$2.99 is helpful. It remains to be seen if smaller publishers will follow suit; if they can even afford to do so. I make less money at \$2.99. It is up to my customers to reciprocate by discovering more comic books to buy. Otherwise, Marvel and DC may have wasted their efforts. NOTE: If reduced story content or quality develops, then our customers will react.

Image started out strong with *Chew* and *Haunt* for 2009-2010. Both have lost ground late in 2010. Image brought out *Morning Glories* and *Skull-Kickers* with some fanfare, but not large sales numbers. *Walking Dead* sales grew with the advent of the TV show (which has proved a stellar hit). It really is that good! I hope its edginess and great storytelling deflates some of the sappy vampire stuff that currently saturates the market.

© MAR

Variant cover sales were active in 2010/2011. (**Avengers** #1 shown)

Dark Horse revamped the old Magnus and Dr. Solar titles. I like them and so do a few of my customers. Too early to tell if they will gain strength. Star Wars sales slipped a bit. *Conan* is still a wonderful title. I just don't understand where its audience has gone to. It should sell better than it does.

Incorruptible and *Irredeemable* from Boom Studios--read, read, read! Dynamite Entertainment fired off a full-volley spread of Green Hornet titles. I liked most of them. I was disappointed that many others did not. The movie has been panned by some of my customers for its casting even before its hit the theaters. Too bad. I thought casting Seth Rogen as the Green Hornet was risky and brilliant (if it works!). I expected Kevin Smith's involvement in the comic book to draw more readers than it did. IDW continued to scoot along with a wide range of titles. Transformers faltered but the G.I. Joe franchise continued with sales relatively unchanged. *Angel* and *Locke and Key* sold well. The *X-Files/30 Days of Night* title started strong and then quieted down. We particularly enjoyed the five-issue series written by Andy Schmidt, *Five Days to Die*. What a great little crime noir story.

We maintain a retail section for new, independent monthly titles. For years we've been trying to increase the sales of small press publications. Unfortunately, as in years past, they generally don't sell. For all the clamoring a small cadre of customers make, they still do not commit to purchasing these titles. We see new companies pop up in Diamond *Previews* and then disappear rapidly. Many independent titles are simply ignored. We read some of them at the store to expand our knowledge. Some are entertaining only if they complete the storyline. Others do not grab us, no matter how many months they exist. And still others suffer from a lack of punctuality.

Golden Age Sales: We purchased several Golden Age collections this year; some larger, some smaller. We kept most of the books raw, although some had already CGC'd. Our sales were nominal until we hit the 2010 San Diego Comic Con, where we blew through quite a bit of our Golden Age and did well.

One of the larger Golden Age collections consisted of over 350 comic books ranging from the mid-1930s to the very early 1940s. Early DCs, Centaurs, United Features and others. Near-complete runs of *King Comics*, *Feature Funnies* and *Ace Comics*. Low-numbered *More Fun Comics* and *New Adventure Comics*. We had an issue of *New Comics* #2, one of the earliest examples of comic books in existence. 25 of the more expensive and/or scarcest copies were submitted to CGC and then sent off to ComicLink. This collection was purchased from the son of the original owner.

The other Golden Age collection was more iconic. We were contacted by Nancy Maneely, daughter of famous Atlas artist Joe Maneely who had a large collection of his work. Nancy remains an avid fan of her father's prolific 1950s artwork for Atlas Comics. His death was an unfortunate accident that occurred in the late '50s. Nancy kept a vow to keep her father's name alive and did so by collecting examples of his work. Her collection spanned many decades and eventually resulted in duplicates, which she brought to us. We purchased the dupes consisting of around 300 1950s Atlas comics. Each contained some great examples of her father's artistry. He really was an exciting cover artist for Atlas and a quick one! Nancy was in the midst of creating and publishing her father's work in a pictorial biography. The wished-for release date is in 2011.

Silver Age Sales: TREE-MENDOUS! This was a good year for Silver Age. Sales were way up at this year's San Diego Comic-Con as well as our store. All titles, all issues, all grades. Discounts and sales priced items are still a must to gather all buyers together under one roof. But more of that stuff sold this year than last year.

We acquired numerous small Silver Age collections and one or two larger ones. High grade stuff was present but not in the quantity we needed to make a big sales splash. It was obvious that economic downturns dropped many of the collections into our laps. Only a few original owner collections of any substance surfaced. I was fortunate in one regard: I had to do less traveling to obtain these collections this past year. Most of these opportunities came to me at the store. I prefer it that way. Psychologically, I make a stronger case for myself in my own domain. Many of the collections that walked in remained with me after the owner left. Not always so lucky on the road, however.

One quick story: I had a gentleman, a little younger than me, bring in a small stack of Marvel Silver Age keys. Early books like *Amazing Spider-Man* #1 and *Avengers* #1. I pitched an offer and he declined. He quipped that he would just pass them onto his kids at the price I offered. My offer was not cheap and he understood. So before he left, I warned him that his teenage sons would never honor the value of these books as he did. He could pass them on but their positive response would be void...just a guess on my part! He returned one week later with the books and accepted my previous offer. He explained that he brought his two sons together to gift them his bounty...their response was; "So what?" End of story.

One other point of reference began at the 2010 SD Comic-Con. Among the better books we had to sell was an *Amazing Fantasy* #15 CGC 4.0 for $6,000. Now, my wife and I had been discussing buying it from the business for ourselves and purchasing other copies at this year's show (buying, as in investing- we'd be purchasing at full price, and then sitting on them for years.) So, I shopped and saw plenty of copies in the hands of friends and strangers alike. The prices were what I expected- high, as in no wiggle room for value advancement in five years. No big deal; it was only a thought. But I wondered why our copy hadn't sold when it was clearly priced close to *Overstreet* (we had it at $6,500). We had plenty of lookers and inquiries at our booth. A potential customer made an observation after shopping for a copy over the days that we were "the least overpriced dealers in the room"! A classic statement that I used later (and still use!), I love it!

Bronze Age Sales: Big ticket items moved a little slower than in the previous year, with the San Diego Comic-Con being the venue exception. Of course, we did not have the same Bronze Age inventory we had in 2009. That stuff can be expensive and time consuming to replace at wholesale prices. Our store saw an increase in *Sub-Mariner* back-issue sales. The timing was certainly beneficial since we had been sitting on a lot of copies for awhile. *Iron Man* and

Incredible Hulk still move, mostly at bargain prices for late Bronze. *X-Men* sold a little less while *Amazing Spider-Man* from the mid-to-late '70s just sits. Key books, notwithstanding.

DCs seem irrelevant. Even the Neal Adams *Green Lanterns* have slowed down - maybe just too expensive. However, Adams' Batman never go out of fashion. Archies, Disneys, Charltons and Gold Keys are rarely offered to us for resale. Those that we obtain often end up in bargain bins. Traditionally geared towards small children, these books are perused by adults (either for themselves or their children). We respect any adult that still believes comics are for kids.

CGC Sales: We submitted fewer books to CGC this past year than in previous years. We felt that many of the new, raw purchases would not net enough profit against the cost of submission. Although we scored quite a bit of high-grade stuff, the potential sales prices were not great enough to justify submission.

We purchased a large number of CGC books from collectors this year - more so than in most other years. The reasoning for these purchases is simple: we can make money off most CGC books at the prices we pay. The collectors could follow suit, but many of them over-extended themselves, paying out too much for the books and the accompanying CGC costs. We literally received a ground-swell of buying opportunities from people who owned CGC books and now needed a bailout. Selling them retail seemed to not be an option in most of these cases. The owners needed cash now and chose us for the negotiations.

We've always encouraged our customers to do their research before committing on any comic book purchase. We continually offer to do some research for them in the form of GPAnalysis, eBay, Heritage Auctions, and more. These purchases can be attributed to the state of the U.S. economy - most any bad financial news can. By the same token, we sold a lot of CGC books this year. Many of those sales went for less than market price and often for less than *Overstreet*.

Comic Conventions: This year, I attended the San Diego International Comic-Con, the summer Chicago show, and Terry O'Neill's show in Orange County, CA. The attendance at each show seemed larger than the buildings could contain. The crowds were impressive but quick tallies of sale successes among dealers were mixed, at least in the case of Chicago.

San Diego was a different story. We had the best show in recent years in terms of sales vs. the workload and general hassle of setting up. Other dealers also boasted of success in their sales. Security was noticeably increased and much more aggressive this year. Security supervisors acknowledged that theft is generally highest on the weekends. We witnessed plenty of random badge checks at the doors and within the Exhibitors' Hall. I'm glad the show will continue to operate in San Diego but I lament the cost increases for setting up. I wonder what the dollar amount might have become, had the show had moved to Anaheim…

There's a small, one-day con in San Diego, called the So Cal Comic Con, which premiered the weekend of Nov. 6th. Two local collector/dealers hosted the show continuing the lineage of comic book guys taking their hobby to the next level. We set up at the show and will continue to support their efforts in the future. We applaud the So Cal Comic Con guys for taking this financial risk in uncertain times. By the way; I attend few shows and may go down in history as the least "hardest" working dealer in comics" (Harley can keep his top spot!).

Prices Up or Down?: The recession may or may not be over. I can see from the lack of full-price sales on low-grade comics that the downward pricing trend has leveled off well-below *Price Guide* standards. We've acquired large quantities of that material from the 1950s to the '70s. If they ever go back up, I'll be waiting!

I don't know if there's anything left that could be expected to go up in value beyond the acknowledged copies we foresee rising. The market has not demonstrated a demand to justify the value increase for most of the comics produced after the Bronze Age. I don't see anything released on a monthly basis hitting a high mark in value and then staying there much longer than a month. I'd like to see the values increase in conjunction with *Overstreet* values on mid-grade '60s books. I think that their age justifies their value even if the demand is for lower prices. Many of us dealers have paid good money to acquire comic collections over the years at prices fair to the owners. It's a shame if we will never be able to realize most of the resale values that we supported through the years.

Terry O'Neill
Terry's Comics/CalComicCon

Sales from 2009 to 2010 have been steady, despite the continued economic slowdown. We have attended more conventions this year than any other year as a dealer. Most comic book conventions appeared to have good attendance, and again I had my best show ever in Chicago. Shows in other places have had mixed sales: Minnesota, New York and Denver were notable. San Diego, Charlotte and Philadelphia were down. Catalog orders have been steady, and repeat customers are the life blood of our mail order business. The few Internet auctions that we have tried, have been disappointing. This is because of all the shows we are doing we must continue to pay higher percentages on Marvel and DC keys to keep our display racks well stocked.

Golden Age: Sales of this material are still good. We are seeing many lower grade comics less than $100 moving at around 85% of *Guide*. While as always, higher grade Timely, DC, MLJ, Quality and Fawcett are selling well at or above *Guide*. Prize and Ace titles do well in middle to higher grades. also early Crime titles like *Crime Does Not Pay* are selling well around *Guide* or better depending on condition and cover. Early *Looney Tunes*, Early Four Colors and *Walt Disney Comics & Stories* are selling well at near *Guide* values. Some sales of note were: *Marvel Mystery* #18 FN@$950, *Namora* #2 VG- @$400, *Phantom Lady* #18 VG@$500, *Detective Comics* #66 FN (rest)@$740, *Detective Comics* #140 VG@$1200, *Keen Detective Funnies* V1#8 FR@$300, and *Marvel Tales* #95 VG-@$170.

Atom Age: We acquired a large collection last year with about 500 comics in higher grades from the late 1940s and early 1950s. These were mostly Crime, Western, War and Romance comics. We submitted about 90 of them for CGC grading and was pleased to get back many comics in the highest or near highest grade for that specific issue. Some highlights were a few *Two-Gun Kids*, with #1 coming in at CGC 9.4 and #3 CGC 9.4, #5 CGC 9.2 and #6 CGC 8.5. the #1 and #6 were the highest grades to date. We sold many of these comics quickly above *Guide* and it was great to see so many Atom Age comics in such high grades. Westerns are still going strong through mail order with *Roy Rogers* and *Gene Autry* our best two titles. Some sales of note were *Tex Morgan* #1 CGC 9.4@$775, *Venus* #18@VG/FN $450, *Turok* #3 VF/NM@$320, *Blue Beetle* (Fox) #51 FN/VF@$325, *Gangster and Gun Molls* #2 VF@$300, *Frankenstein* (Prize) #27 VF@ #180 , *Girls' Romance* #2 VF@$220, *John Wayne* #5 FN+@$220, and *Gangsters Can't Win* #2 VF+@$250.

Silver Age: Well, after many years of increasing prices, high-grade Silver has cooled a little. We did purchase a really nice original-owner collection of Marvel comics and did well selling high grade slabbed and un-slabbed comics. The prices that we were paid in 2010 were not high as in previous years for the same kind of material. Even *Amazing Spider-Man* has cooled a bit and is not our best selling Silver Age comic title any longer. This may be because it now *Guides* so high, relative to other titles. Many Marvel keys are still able to sell above *Guide* especially *Fantastic Four* #1, *Journey Into Mystery* #83, *Tales of Suspense* #39 and *Incredible Hulk* #1. *Iron Man* #1, *Silver Surfer* #1 and #4 are selling especially well.

Westerns like **Roy Rogers Comics #46** are showing strength through mail order sales.

DC Silver is still a strong seller in FN to VF grades. The higher grades, while much scarcer than Marvel, tend to move a little slower. There are a few titles that are moving like *Green Lantern*, *Action*, *Adventure* and *Detective*. This year was the 1st time since the middle 1990s that I felt I needed to discount my Silver Age down to half of *Guide* to move some of the more common titles in lower grades. This being said, I think it is time to cut guide prices for most lower grade Super-hero titles. I put a lot of lower priced comics in bargain bins and sold them for a flat price. This helped sales volumes at shows but caused me to re-evaluate how much I could pay for this material.

Most other genres (TV/Movie, Humor, Romance, Western) from the Silver Age are not selling as well as in previous years, and larger discounts are needed to sell many of these. The exceptions are Harvey titles like *Little Dot*, *Richie Rich* and *Sad Sack*, which I hardly ever get in quantity, but they sell well because they are already so affordable. *Magnus Robot Fighter* and *Doctor Solar* seem to be selling well if a good discount is offered.

Bronze Age: Many common titles of this era were selling at lower values, even in very high grades. Those truly rare gems, will be the comics, that after 10 years of grading, still are unique, or only two or three in grade. We purchased a *DC 100 Page Super Spectacular* #4 and it graded a CGC 9.6. To date, there are no others of the same or higher, and only two 9.4s. This is a scarce Bronze Age comic in grade. How many others like this can there be? Some of the better selling titles are *Avengers*, *Detective Comics*, *Eternals*, *Incredible Hulk*, *Master of Kung Fu* and *X-Men*. Anything from this era except a few keys are impossible to sell in less than VF unless priced at just a few dollars. Some sales of note were *Amazing Spider-Man* #129 VF+@ $550, *Giant-Size X-Men* #1 VF-@$350 and *X-Men* #94 FN/VF@$400.

Magazines: We picked up some nice magazines in a high grade Marvel collection. Some of the titles that sold very well were *Deadly Hands of Kung Fu*, *Rampaging Hulk* and *Savage Sword of Conan*. We hardly purchased any Warren or other magazines, so our sales were weak on those titles. Some sales of note were *Deadly Hands of Kung Fu* #26 NM+@$100, #31 NM+@$100 and *Foom* #1 NM@$200.

Modern Age & Independents: We usually only sell certain titles from this era, but with the purchase of an original owner collection from the 1960s - present, we have been willing to sell whole runs of many Marvel titles. *Wolverine* miniseries #1-4 are still selling, but at much lower prices. Otherwise high grade Marvel titles like *Avengers*, *Daredevil*, *Spider-Man* and *X-Men* are still selling at or above *Guide*. Some sales of note were *Amazing Spider-Man* #238 NM-@$75, *Wolverine* V1#1 CGC 9.8 @ $300, *Daredevil* #181 CGC 9.6 @$50 and *X-Men* #266 CGC 9.2@$50.

Graded books: I am still convinced that this is the best way to sell pre-1975 comics in very high grade. I believe it is the best way to keep really nice comics from getting damaged and to tell if any repairs or restoration has been done. As a hedge against inflation I recommend investing in comics, instead of (possibly overpriced) gold. The best investment comics are sure to be third party graded comics. Some sales of note were *Fantastic Four* #1 CGC 6.5 @$13,500, *Incredible Hulk* #1 CGC 1.8@ $1200, *Amazing Fantasy* #15 CGC 4.5 Trim@ $3600, and *Tales of Suspense* #39 CGC 2.5 @ $1300.

Internet Sales: Most of our internet sales have been through our eBay store, even though we have two websites with over 45,000 items listed. We have had steady sales of our graded comics through this venue. We usually sell only CGC graded comic books on eBay, but we list our entire inventory at www.Terryscomics.com and www.NationwideKomics.com .

In summary, despite the continuing recession of the past two years, we have still managed to maintain steady sales. I want to thank all the collectors out there that continue to keep collecting comics as a priority in their lives. I also want to thank all the investors that have used comics as tangible assets in their portfolios. Comics still seem to be a good place to spend our money.

Jim Pitts
Avalon Collectibles

While the economy has stayed in a holding pattern, many people have looked to comic books to keep their minds off unemployment, inflation, and wars overseas, so similar to a time our parents knew over half a century ago!

I was less active at shows this year due to a battle with cancer that kept me home for much of the Spring and early Summer, but let's take a gander at what was selling for me.

Pulps: Slowed down for me a bunch, and I bought several collections, other than "violence", "bondage", or "drug use" covers, which were snapped up quick, most sat in the boxes.

Big Little Books: I picked up a collection of low grade Mickey Mouse BLBs, most of which found new homes quickly in the $30 to $50 range. Crime and adventure titles didn't move to well for me.

© DIS

Mickey Mouse BLBs that are for sale find new homes quickly. (Mickey Mouse and the 7 Ghosts #1475 shown)

Golden Age: Since I was doing "smaller" shows to stay close to home for treatment this year I didn't sell much in the way of Golden Age. I preferred to acquire books from this era while the economy is slow. However a couple sales of note included *Superman* #2 FR $1,200, and *Batman* #18 (Hitler) VG $700.

Silver Age: While I was able to both buy and sell boxes full of Silver Age books over the past year, not many "keys" crossed my tables. With unemployment above the national average in California, people were out selling stuff in force at Flea Markets making it easy to get new material on a constant basis. While they were not in noteworthy condition, people were thrilled to buy from me over the last year over a dozen copies of *Fantastic Four* #48, 5 copies of *Silver Surfer* #1, 2 copies of *Hulk* #6, 4 copies of *Adventure* #300, 3 copies of *Batman* #200, and multiples of *Vampirella* #1, 2, and 3.

Bronze Age: An era I have more respect for all the time. While I don't deal in slabbed books this has become "bread and butter" for me. '70s DC War and Mystery books just don't stay in stock, and the people I'm selling to seem to prefer a copy they can pick up and read. Marvel titles from this era seem to be more condition driven as far as sales go, though key Spider-Man issues from this era will sell in most grades for me.

Modern Age: The key here is cheap since I don't sell slabbed items. But Deadpool, Swamp Thing, X-Men, and War books all have strong demand.

Undergrounds: As always my strongest area year in and out. Sales of Rick Griffin books stayed strong, I sold 5 copies of *Man From Utopia* at $80 to $100 each, 3 *Tales From The Tube* (comic size) at $60 to $75 each, *Tales From The Tube* (mag size) $50. Robert Crumb is, as always, the king. I sold a *Zap* #1 (Plymell) FR/GD $800, *Zap* #1 (Donahue) VF+ $800, *Zap* #2 GD/VG $150, *Zap* #3 NM $125, Alexander Galleries Crumb catalog NM $400. Other sales of note included *Freak Brothers* #1 (1st) FN $250 and *Bible of Filth* NM $300.

Rock Posters and Tickets: Always fairly strong for me, and this year was no different. Sales included 2 copies of BG-105 the Jimi Hendrix "Flying Eyeball" poster (second printings). A NM one went for $1,200 and I wholesaled a VG copy for $300. I also sold a complete set of "Eyeball" tickets for $500. Other Rick Griffin posters remain in high demand as well. Other sales of note included Big Brother and the Holding Co tickets to the Selland Arena in Fresno at $300 each and Cream tickets from the same venue at $500 each. Always make sure you know what printing you are getting when buying posters! I had several people bring me posters they bought thinking they were firsts that turned out to be seconds in terms of the printing.

So that was my year at large! Be safe, lets hope the economy turns around, and guys over 40 make sure you get a cancer screening! It saved my life!
See you all in the funny papers!

Bill Ponseti
Collector

Against all odds, the comic book market continued to be very strong at the high end of the spectrum. In spite of the continued negative economic conditions, comic books still sold for record prices in 2010. Last year I predicted that 2010 would bring our first $1,000,000 sale. Little did I know that it would happen more than once! Astonishing year to see the least.

Golden Age: Certainly high grade Golden Age comics still remain King of this sector of the hobby. So much so that the average collector has little to no chance of acquiring these issues for mainstream titles. Pre-Robin *Detectives* in any grade are now also out of reach for the rank and file collectors. Timely comics, at least *Captain America*, *USA Comics* (with Cap covers) and middle of the run *Marvel Mystery*

Comics in high grade sell for crazy money.

It's actually kind of depressing when a mid-run *Marvel Mystery* in high grade sells for more than an *All Star Comics* #3 in low or restored grade. However, bargains can be found in mainstream publishers' second tier titles and most of the non-Timely/non-DC publishers. If you are happy with lower grade copies like I am, there are still lots of fun books you can collect at an affordable price.

Silver Age: By and large, Silver Age comics prices have levelled off, and in many cases dropped in 2010. The notable exceptions are the big Marvel Key issues. *Fantastic Four* #1, *Amazing Spider-Man* #1, *Amazing Fantasy* #15, *Incredible Hulk* #1 and *Tales of Suspense* #39 all sell at very high prices in all grades. DC Keys have come back down to Earth. At the beginning of the year, *Showcase* #22 was selling for big dollars. By the end of the year, copies sat at those artificially inflated prices.

Bronze Age: If you aren't a *Hulk* #181, you can be had at a bargain! Still, the usual suspects sell when priced right.

Greg Reece
Greg Reece's Rare Comics

2010 continued the challenging times that began in 2009. Many common, very high grade pieces took absolute haircuts with many falling 50%. If history is any guide, 2009-2010 will have proven to be one of the great times to invest in the best. Keys, for the most part, escaped this debacle and even showed slight increases. Continuing trends from prior years, we simply cannot keep the following in stock, in any grade: *Giant-Size X-Men* #1, *X-Men* #94, *X-Men* #1, *Amazing Spider-Man* #1, *Amazing Spider-Man* #129, *Amazing Fantasy* #15, *Fantastic Four* #1, *Incredible Hulk* #181, *Brave And The Bold* #28, *Justice League of America* #1, *Showcase* #22 and *Flash* #105. A couple of keys that have slowed a little, at least for now, are *Avengers* #1 and *Iron Man* #1. On to the shows!

Pittsburgh: Our first stop of 2010. This is the smallest market we travel to on the trade circuit but it's close to home and we've developed some great customers out there. The chance to eat at Primanti Brothers (fries on the sandwich, sweet slaw) seals the deal. This was the first show we brought our full compliment of CGC books and it was well received.

Philadelphia: Jimmy and the guys at Wizard continue to bring in a nice crowd and the customers are ready to spend, despite being put directly behind the 40' t-shirt vendor. It would be great to see Marvel/DC and other big players attend to make the show feel more major league. Philadelphia fans deserve it.

Baltimore: What can you say here? Show gets better every year and if the devil is in the details, Mark Nathan and crew are at the top of the show promoter list. The show is very organized and well promoted with a great mix of artists/vendors while still maintaining the vibe of a pure comic book show. Take a 10 minute ride to G and M's for the best crab cake you will ever eat in your life.

New York: Wow, really hard to even start a report. The crowds were surreal. We sold it all, from low grade raw to CGC 9.8s and everything in between. Mark and the rest of the team at Reed have created an incredible show in just a few years. Far and away our best show for sales and buys.

Richmond: This show is up and coming. Brett really brought the people through the door, but the room may have been a little overwhelmed as there was plenty of better material available. It will be interesting to watch this show develop. Great eats at The Tobacco Company resturant in downtown Richmond.

We look forward to adding Chicago and Detroit to the 2011 schedule.

Internet: eBay becomes (thankfully) less and less of our business everyday. Launching our own website this year (gregreececomics.com) has been a nice punch to our customer base. We currently feature over 1,000 CGC slabs and will be adding our better raw inventory beginning in 2011.

Notable Sales: *Showcase* #22 CGC 2.0 $875, CGC 2.5 $975, 3.0 $1250, 5.0 $2800, *Avengers* #1 CGC 6.0 $3500, *Amazing Spider-Man* #1 CGC 4.0 $2800, *X-Men* #2 CGC 9.4 $10,000, *Batman* #62 CGC 8.0 $1900, *Tales From The Crypt* #32 CGC 9.4 $800, *Vampirella* #57 CGC 9.8 $400, *Batman* #193 CGC 9.8 $2200 + $500 in trade and *Captain America Comics* #4 CGC 8.0 $8300.

Investment Picks: If (when?) CGC starts grading Treasury Editions, these will explode in value. They are incredibly hard to store and to travel with, so most dealers, if they bother at all, bring them loose. If there was a NM/NM+ copy in their stock, it is eradicated quickly.

I still like *Brave and the Bold* #28, *JLA* #1, *Strange Tales* #115, *JIM* #83 (all picks from last year). Even though they moved up some, there is still room to the upside. I am especially high on *Strange Tales* #115.

White pages from the Golden Age - early Silver Age: when GPA (or someone), starts to officially track this, these will burn up the chart. They are incredibly difficult to find but if you're diligent, you can still find copies at little to no premium to their CR/OW counterparts. Do not expect this trend to continue so buy while you can.

Pedigrees are much like the white-paged copies mentioned above (in fact, many Pedigrees have white pages) in that they can, in many cases, be had for little to no premium over a similar, non-pedigreed copy. This is especially true of more recent pedigrees (Rocky Mountain, etc.) as a lot of collectors intially looked down their nose at these "newer" finds. They are still being auctioned off and are readily available for purchase. Once the market absorbs them and they only come up for resale, I believe pricing will move up.

Ice Cold: Westerns (except in very high grade), Funny Animals, lower-mid grade common Silver/Bronze. It sells but has to be discounted significantly.

In summary, I hope 2011 finds your friends and family healthy and that you find some great books for your collection. See you on the circuit!

Barry Sandoval
Heritage Auctions (HA.com)

As 2010 dawned, with the record auction price for a comic book standing at "only" $317,000, little did we know that within a year we would sell *three* comics for above that amount, and that all of them would be the same issue! It began with our well-documented auction sale of a VF 8.0 copy of *Detective Comics* #27 for $1,075,500. This book came to us from a savvy collector who had assembled his collection in the 1960s and 1970s, the days when an adult making a salary could afford all of key comics, if he or she could only find them for sale.

Later we offered a VF-minus 7.5 copy, bought by a college student in Hawaii in 1974 for $1,200, or 90% of the youngster's savings at the time. He ended up auctioning the comic in 2010 to help put his own son through college, and it's safe to say he accomplished that given the final price of $657,250.

Then we had the distinct pleasure of offering an original-owner copy of the book, believe it or not. The fellow who paid 10 cents for it in 1939, Robert Irwin of Sacramento, was in the auction room to see his FN/VF copy sell for $492,937.

The rarefied air of high six-figure books aside, we do have some other observations on the past year. One thing that's striking is that newcomers to the hobby do not let their collecting be defined by the tastes of earlier generations. Take Simon and Kirby. While geniuses in anyone's book, the prices of their comics were driven up by the old-school collector but seem to be cooling off these days. Not that *Captain America Comics* #1 has lost any ground, but look at *Adventure Comics* #73. Top of *Guide* was $25,000 last year, but collectors with that much to spend these days are spending it on something they can identify with, and the Manhunter is not that character.

Two books that many are looking for are *Detective Comics* #31 and #35: We think the *Overstreet* value is still too conservative on both of these Batman keys, and that they are among the 20 most valuable comics in the hobby. Issue #31 in particular is in very high demand in any grade. If you look at the *Guide* of 30 years ago, neither of these made the top 50 Golden Age books, but the likes of *Boy Explorers* #2, *Wow Comics* #1, *USA Comics* #1 and *Silver Streak* #6 did. We couldn't imagine someone preferring those books to a *Detective* #31 or #35 today.

Hot Covers: A few books that are hotly contested whenever we offer them are: *Exciting Comics* #39 (Nazis giving poisoned candy to kids), *Giant Comics Edition* #12 (Matt Baker prostitute cover), *Our Army At War* #112 (picturing all of Sgt. Rock's Easy Company; while superhero comics often show all the main characters together, war books rarely do), *Rangers Comics* #14 (a particularly eye-catching bondage cover) and *Weird Tales of the Future* #3 (a ghoulish Wolverton cover)

Significant and in demand: Despite what's noted above, significance is not dead, and here are some books that are hot for reasons other than the cover: *Peanuts* #1 (1953) and *Four Color* #878. It seems incredible that characters as popular as the Peanuts were previously a bit under the radar when it came to comic books, but that is the case. The 1953 *Peanuts* #1 had a "top of *Guide*" value of $210 last year, but we sold a FN/VF copy for $2,151. *Green Lantern* #7: Sinestro is getting his due as a great villain. *Daring Love* #1: Steve Ditko's first comic book work. *Gobbledygook* #1 and #2: Tricky because CGC won't authenticate them, but very sought-after if they have the right provenance (we sold #1 in VF+ for $11,352). A pre-Teenage Mutant Ninja Turtles Eastman and Laird publication, with the Turtles making their first printed appearance on the back cover. *House of Secrets* #81 and *House of Mystery* #174: The changeovers of these titles to horror/mystery format. Also *House of Mystery* #175 with the first appearance of Cain. Spirit section June 2, 1940: the first Spirit newspaper section.

Early *Action Comics*: We had the opportunity to auction an incredible bound volume set of *Action* #1-24. While #1 needs no introduction, and people have woken up to the demand for #7 (the second Superman cover), when we paged through this volume (carefully!) we realized that we had never previously seen high-grade copies of #5 (desert legionnaire cover), #8 (a redcoat fighting an Indian), or #10 or #13 (the third and fourth Superman covers). Very tough finds one and all.

© Nedor

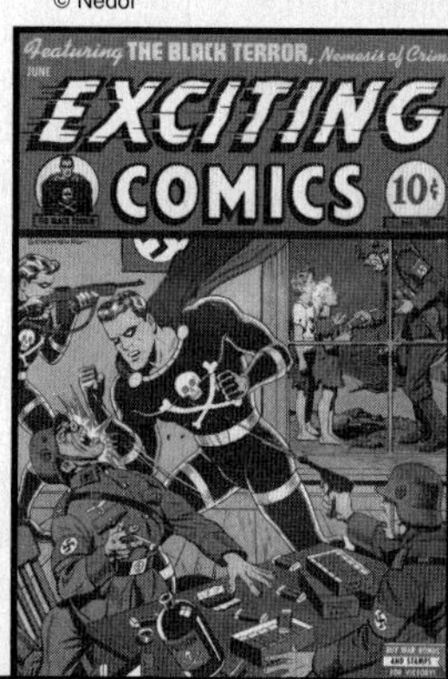

Exciting Comics #39 is one book that is hotly contested in every auction.

***Archie Comics* #1**: Some jaws dropped when a VF+ copy sold for $167,300 in our February 2011 auction. This may not have been thought of as a six-figure book in most quarters, but the winning bidder told us that he had been looking for a high-grade copy for four decades. In last year's market report we noted that issues #2-10 would also be in high demand, but no copies of those issues crossed our path in the ensuing year!

Savannah pedigree collection of high-grade DC: This collection has totaled $600,000 as we write this, with thousands of comics left to go. It was consigned to us by Shelton Drum of Heroes Aren't Hard to Find in North Carolina – it came from a collector who acquired his books directly from the distributor from the late 1950s through the 1970s, and it's particularly strong in DCs, especially non-superhero DCs.

This collection demonstrated once again that DC comics were preserved by fewer collectors than the Marvels of the same era, and are thus much tougher to find in top grades. While smash successes like *Showcase* #43 (Dr. No) fetching 4x *Guide* and *Showcase* #45 (Sgt. Rock) getting 8x *Guide* could be attributed to the popularity of James Bond or the fanatical following that DC War books have, how do you explain *Showcase* #25 featuring Rip Hunter fetching 5x *Guide*? Only by the fact that being the best copy ever offered counts for something, even for a lower-demand book.

A surprise even to us has been the performance of the 1960s-1970s DC romance comics from this same collection. Take *Secret Hearts* #121: not a key issue in anyone's book, reading copies are readily available for perhaps 5 dollars on eBay, and "top of *Guide*" is $32. The CGC 9.8 Savannah copy fetched $1,075! True Near Mint romance comics come along very seldom, and collectors realized the uniqueness of the opportunity

Twin Cities pedigree: The best Marvel Silver Age collection we've ever sold (and we've sold plenty) at $1 million plus, this came to us from the estate of Gary Dahlberg of Minneapolis, who tragically passed away at age 62 before he could enjoy the financial bonanza from his incredible collection. These incredible books put the lie to the often-heard lament "all the great collections have already been discovered." The initial auction totaled $1.3 million for just 407 comics!

Original Comic Art: Original art gets more expensive with each passing year, bad news for buyers but great news for our sellers with our comic art total hitting $9 million last year. A couple of new trends of note: Frank Miller's cover art for *Daredevil* #188 made some jaws drop by hitting $101,575, and a splash page from *Dark Knight Returns* #3 topped it to say the least by selling for $448,125, a new record sale (auction or otherwise) for a piece of American comic art. This goes to show that the generation that grew up in the 1980s now has serious money to spend – alas, the comics of that era are too plentiful in high grade for the most part to be particularly valuable, but original art is another story altogether.

Carl Barks Oil Paintings: When radio executive Kerby Confer decided to sell his collection of 40 Carl Barks paintings, it marked the first time in recent memory that top pieces by Barks came to market in a no-reserve auction. The fact that quite a few of them have topped $100,000 despite being sold with no reserve or minimum bid shows that demand for the "Good Duck Artist" is still robust.

My colleagues and I look forward to helping more collectors maximize the value of their four-color treasures in the coming year.

Buddy Saunders, Conan Saunders and Asher Densmore-Lynn MyComicShop.com

Overview by Buddy Saunders: This is my first year to serve as an Overstreet advisor, although I've been a comic collector since 1960 and a retailer since 1961. When I began collecting comics, Marvel was publishing the Lee/Kirby/Ayers big monster comics, and the switch to super heroes was still more than a year away. Those old monster issues of *Tales of Suspense*, *Tales to Astonish*, *Journey into Mystery*, and *Strange Tales* with the Lee/Ditko back-up stories remain among my favorite comics to this day.

Getting down to market trends, I've been both surprised and pleased at the strength the comic market displayed in 2010. With so much of the economy down and unemployment high, comics held strong. Our stores enjoyed modest sales increases, and our web site experienced its best year yet. In 2010, back issue and new comic sales experienced modest growth over the same months in 2009. The primary exception was the January/February period, when 2010 could not compete with the surge of interest in *Amazing Spider-Man* #583 and the Obama tie-ins of early 2009.

On the buying side of our operation, 2010 was an outstanding year. We bought almost 50% more back issues in 2010 than in the already-strong 2009. The economy-driven surge in the number of comics offered for sale through our online buying system appears to have kicked off in the summer of 2009, continued into 2010, and then jumped to new highs from February to August of 2010. Over the past year, we have frequently faced such a volume of comics being offered to us for sale that our monthly budget has been insufficient to buy everything sellers want to offer. Looking ahead, we plan to partially alleviate this supply pressure through a significant expansion of our consignment service.

As Overstreet advisors, we at mycomicshop.com plan to bring a data-driven perspective to the *Guide*, including coverage of the large number of comics at the lower end of the price spectrum to complement the Gold and Silver Age chartbusters that are already thoroughly tracked in these pages. We have over ten years worth of sales data from our web site and eBay store, covering 280,000 comics, graphic novels, and books, and encompassing 9 million data points. We hope to make this data, and especially all recent sales data, available to the *Overstreet Guide* as soon as the *Guide* is in a position to make use of it. We believe that reliable, automated delivery of such data from multiple retailers will help make the already reliable *Overstreet Guide* an even better resource for collectors.

Market Report by Conan Saunders:
2010 Top 20 Best-Selling New Comics
(listed from most sales to least)

Siege #2
Avengers #1
Blackest Night #7
Batman Return of Bruce Wayne #1
Blackest Night #8
Siege #3
Siege #1
Batman Return of Bruce Wayne #2
Batman #700
X-Force #26
X-Men Second Coming #1
Siege #4
Captain America Reborn #6
Brightest Day #0

Nemesis #1
X-Men #1
Ultimate X Ultimate Comics #1
Brightest Day #1
Batman and Robin #7
Secret Avengers #1

2010 Top 20 Best-Selling Graphic Novels and Trade Paperbacks - New Releases

Kick-Ass HC
Blackest Night HC
Superman Earth One HC
Walking Dead TPB Vol. 11
Blackest Night Green Lantern HC
Walking Dead TPB Vol. 12
Arkham Asylum Madness HC
Blackest Night Green Lantern Corps HC
Flash: Rebirth HC
Unwritten TPB Vol. 1
Blackest Night Black Lantern Corps HC
Green Lantern Secret Origin TPB
Batman and Robin HC Deluxe Edition Vol. 1
Chew TPB Vol. 2
Final Crisis TPB
Scott Pilgrim GN Vol. #6
Dark Tower Fall of Gilead HC
Serenity The Shepherd's Tale HC
Avengers/X-Men Utopia TPB
Walking Dead Hardcover Vol. 5

2010 Top 20 Best-Selling Graphic Novels and Trade Paperbacks - By Series

Walking Dead TPB
Scott Pilgrim GN
100 Bullets TPB
Y the Last Man TPB
Walking Dead HC
Kick-Ass HC
Ultimate X-Men TPB
Invincible TPB
Ultimate Spider-Man TPB
New Avengers TPB
Doc Savage SC Double Novel
Chronicles of Conan TPB
Fables TPB
JLA TPB
Shadow SC Double Novel
Buffy the Vampire Slayer TPB Season 8
Ex Machina TPB
Fantastic Four Visionaries John Byrne TPB
Irredeemable TPB
Preacher TPB

2010 Top 200 Best-Selling Comic Titles

The following table lists the top 200 comic titles sorted by the total quantity sold of both new and back issue comics. The first column is the rank for sales in 2010. The second and third columns show how the title's rank has changed relative to its rank in 2009 and 2000, respectively. A plus sign indicates that a title has moved up in the rankings, and minus that it has moved down. "New" indicates that a title is in the 2010 top 200 but had not yet been published and registered in the rankings for 2009 and/or 2000.

The column to the right of the title name shows the average percentage change in the price of issues belonging to that title. This represents an average across all issues of the title. It does not mean that all issues of the title moved by the same percentage. For example, 2010's 38th ranked title, *The Walking Dead*, reports an average price increase of 61%. Some issues of *TWD* increased by less than 61%, some even dropped in price, and some issues increased by substantially more than 61%. But, averaged together across all issues of the title, the average change was an increase of 61%. These percentages are calculated from over 60,000 actual sales in which an issue sold in a given grade in both 2009 and 2010.

2010 Rank	1 yr. change	10 yr. change	Title	Average % price change since 2009
1	0	0	Uncanny X-Men (1963)	13%
2	+1	+12	Batman (1940)	20%
3	-1	+35	Amazing Spider-Man (1998- 2nd Series)	-3%
4	+1	+18	Detective Comics (1937-)	20%
5	+1	+8	Action Comics (1938 DC)	32%
6	-2	-3	Amazing Spider-Man (1963-1998 1st Series)	34%
7	+6	+17	Superman (1987)	6%
8	0	-1	Avengers (1963-1996 1st Series)	25%
9	-2	-7	X-Men (1991-2008 1st Series)	17%
10	+11	0	Fantastic Four (1961-1996 1st Series)	-1%
11	+6	-6	Incredible Hulk (1962-1999 1st series)	28%
12	-2	+6	Adventures of Superman (1939)	36%
13	-4	-2	Spawn (1992)	24%
14	+4	+1	Thor (1962-1996 1st Series)	49%
15	0	-9	Daredevil (1964-1998 1st Series)	20%
16	+6	0	Iron Man (1968 1st Series)	25%
17	-1	-5	Captain America (1968 1st Series)	30%
18	-6	-9	Spectacular Spider-Man (1976 1st Series)	20%
19	-8	new	Green Lantern (2005- 3rd Series)	49%
20	-1	-16	Wolverine (1988 1st Series)	6%
21	+3	+23	Fantastic Four (1998 3rd Series)	25%
22	+6	+28	Flash (1987 2nd Series)	3%
23	+12	+6	Batman Legends of the Dark Knight (1989-2007)	9%
24	+24	new	Justice League of America (2006- 2nd Series)	-9%
25	+12	new	Superman Batman (2003)	10%
26	+76	new	Batman and Robin (2009)	14%
27	new	new	Brightest Day (2010)	
28	-5	+55	Daredevil (1998-2010 2nd Series)	6%
29	+10	-21	X-Factor (1986 1st Series)	4%
30	-3	+7	Thunderbolts (1997 Marvel)	17%
31	-5	new	Green Lantern Corps (2006)	26%
32	-18	new	New Avengers (2005 1st Series)	-7%
33	-1	+42	Robin (1993-2009)	21%
34	+19	0	Wonder Woman (1987-2006 2nd Series)	22%
35	-4	new	Captain America (2004 5th Series)	1%
36	+10	new	Invincible Iron Man (2008-)	28%
37	+33	new	X-Men Legacy (2008 Marvel)	-12%
38	+20	new	Walking Dead (2003 Image)	61%
39	-10	-3	Green Lantern (1990 2nd Series)	23%
40	+45	new	Buffy The Vampire Slayer (2007 Season 8)	-6%
41	+6	-21	New Mutants (1983 1st Series)	16%
42	+1	new	X-Force (2008 3rd Series)	23%

43	+41	new	Thor (2007 3rd Series)	-8%
44	+8	new	Supergirl (2005 4th Series)	31%
45	-20	new	Wolverine Origins (2006)	26%
46	+13	-29	X-Force (1991 1st Series)	-3%
47	+2	-21	Conan the Barbarian (1970 Marvel)	17%
48	+7	new	Hulk (2008 Marvel)	-21%
49	+27	new	Wonder Woman (2006 3rd Series)	3%
50	+11	new	Teen Titans (2003- 3rd Series)	2%
51	+5	-24	Spider-Man (1990)	-4%
52	+27	-21	JLA (1997)	12%
53	-17	-18	Justice League of America (1960 1st Series)	19%
54	-34	new	Wolverine (2003 2nd Series)	23%
55	-1	new	Justice Society of America (2006 3rd Series)	-8%
56	-18	+2	Hellblazer (1988)	15%
57	-24	+7	Nightwing (1996-2009)	12%
58	-13	+129	Savage Dragon (1993 2nd Series)	35%
59	-29	+22	Ultimate Spider-Man (2000)	-14%
60	+6	-20	Silver Surfer (1987 2nd Series)	12%
61	+14	new	Fables (2002)	5%
62	+24	-41	Excalibur (1988 1st Series)	16%
63	-21	-30	Web of Spider-Man (1985 1st Series)	0%
64	+3	new	X-Factor (2005 3rd Series)	13%
65	+22	-40	Avengers (1997 3rd Series)	10%
66	-1	-24	Witchblade (1995)	11%
67	+48	new	Blackest Night (2009)	-7%
68	+4	+27	Marvel Comics Presents (1988-1995 1st Series)	-6%
69	-35	new	Dark Avengers (2009 Marvel)	-2%
70	-30	-14	Marvel Team-Up (1972 1st Series)	57%
71	-27	+396	Ultimate X-Men (2001)	-8%
72	-21	-4	Green Lantern (1960 1st Series DC)	45%
73	+8	+12	Birds of Prey (1999-2009 1st Series)	17%
74	+15	-9	Superman The Man of Steel (1991)	23%
75	+139	new	New Mutants (2009- 3rd Series)	-8%
76	-26	new	Deadpool (2008 2nd Series)	50%
77	+39	-23	Avengers West Coast (1985)	20%
78	+137	new	Red Robin (2009-)	32%
79	+12	-6	Batman Shadow of the Bat (1992)	29%
80	-20	-39	Defenders (1972 1st Series)	44%
81	+2	-34	Alpha Flight (1983 1st Series)	15%
82	-25	-63	GI Joe (1982 Marvel)	27%
83	new	new	Batman Return of Bruce Wayne (2010)	
84	+9	new	Avengers Initiative (2007)	-20%
85	-11	new	Astonishing X-Men (2004- 3rd Series)	14%
86	+18	+7	Punisher (1987 2nd Series)	1%
87	-23	new	Mighty Avengers (2007)	-27%
88	+13	new	Boys (2006-)	-6%
89	new	new	Siege (2010 Marvel)	
90	+132	new	Adventure Comics (2009- 2nd Series)	0%
91	-28	-13	Incredible Hulk (1999 2nd Series)	21%
92	+20	new	52 (Weekly) (2006)	12%
93	-15	-40	Marvel Tales (1964 Marvel)	19%
94	-23	-15	Flash (1959 1st Series DC)	20%
95	+4	+23	Justice League America (1987)	5%
96	+10	+16	Green Arrow (1987 1st Series)	11%
97	-9	+14	Star Wars (1977 Marvel)	29%
98	new	new	Avengers (2010 4th Series)	
99	+154	new	Dark Wolverine (2009)	-22%
100	+197	new	Deadpool Merc with a Mouth (2009)	26%
101	-19	-38	Swamp Thing (1982 2nd Series)	7%
102	-10	+64	Adventure Comics (1938-1983 1st Series)	11%
103	+67	-13	Ghost Rider (1990 2nd Series)	5%
104	+283	new	Batgirl (2009 3rd Series)	18%
105	-9	-38	New Teen Titans (1984 2nd Series)	17%
106	+169	new	Incredible Hulk (2009 3rd Series)	-18%
107	-12	-84	Cable (1993-2002 1st Series)	16%
108	+39	-63	Iron Man (1998 3rd Series)	0%
109	+133	+131	Archie (1943)	57%
110	+115	new	Wizard the Comics Magazine (1991)	-29%
111	-31	new	Invincible (2003)	21%
112	+6	-18	Brave and the Bold (1955 1st Series)	23%
113	+67	new	Wolverine Weapon X (2009 Marvel)	-11%
114	-73	new	Ms. Marvel (2006-2010 2nd Series)	20%
115	+42	new	Green Arrow (2001 2nd Series)	20%
116	+4	-42	New Teen Titans (1980) (Tales of ...)	34%
117	-49	-14	Walt Disney's Comics and Stories	56%
118	+319	new	Ultimate Spider-Man (2009- 2nd Series)	-6%
119	new	new	Justice League Generation Lost (2010)	
120	-30	+49	Sonic the Hedgehog (1993- Ongoing Series)	48%
121	-24	+8	World's Finest (1941)	11%
122	+17	new	Secret Warriors (2009 Marvel)	-1%
123	new	new	Secret Avengers (2010 Marvel)	
124	-10	+252	Savage Sword of Conan (1974 Magazine)	13%
125	+12	+60	Simpsons Comics (1993)	42%
126	+163	new	Gotham City Sirens (2009)	45%
127	+50	+36	Punisher War Journal (1988 1st Series)	-9%
128	-34	new	Star Wars Legacy (2006)	20%
129	-8	new	Catwoman (2002-2008 3rd Series)	25%
130	-23	+6	Superboy (1949 1st Series DC)	6%
131	+35	new	Green Arrow Black Canary (2007)	-13%
132	+27	new	Secret Six (2008 3rd Series)	33%
133	+18	new	Titans (2008 2nd Series)	-8%
134	-9	new	Booster Gold (2007 DC 2nd Series)	37%
135	-9	-87	What If (1989 2nd Series)	-3%
136	-59	new	Cable (2008 2nd Series)	6%
137	-64	new	Punisher (2004 7th Series) Max	4%
138	+197	new	Batman Streets of Gotham (2009)	-22%
139	-29	new	Nova (2007 4th Series)	-10%
140	-35	new	Batman Confidential (2006)	15%
141	+49	new	Brave and the Bold (2007 3rd Series)	10%
142	-4	new	Backing Board: Current 100pk	-1%
143	new	new	Flash (2010 3rd Series DC)	
144	+25	-116	Generation X (1994)	5%
145	-34	-115	X-Men Classic (1986 Classic X-Men)	55%
146	+136	+171	Dark Horse Presents (1986)	-3%
147	-5	-50	Batgirl (2000 1st Series)	46%
148	+40	-88	Groo the Wanderer (1985 Marvel)	11%
149	+9	-8	Legion of Super Heroes (1989 4th Series)	30%
150	-4	-58	JSA (1999)	-13%
151	-18	-80	Marvel Two-in-One (1974-1983 1st Series)	44%
152	-8	-13	DC Comics Presents (1978 DC)	29%
153	+76	-5	Uncle Scrooge	-2%
154	-18	new	New X-Men (2004-2008)	29%
155	-42	-85	Catwoman (1993-2001 2nd Series)	40%
156	+108	new	Power Girl (2009 2nd Series)	22%
157	-4	-71	Wonder Woman (1942-1986 1st Series DC)	49%
158	+2	-43	Doctor Strange (1974-1987 2nd Series)	33%
159	+23	new	Countdown (to Final Crisis 2007 DC)	-15%
160	-60	new	Mad (Magazine #24 on)	56%
161	+3	-110	Gen 13 (1995 2nd Series)	10%
162	-14	-55	Legion of Super Heroes (1980 2nd Series)	15%
163	-39	new	Ultimate Fantastic Four (2004-2009)	-15%
164	-36	new	Jonah Hex (2005 2nd Series)	30%
165	new	new	X-Men (2010 2nd Series)	
166	+708	new	Haunt (2009 Image)	56%
167	-48	new	Incredible Hercules (2008-2010)	-23%
168	-38	-111	Thor (1998-2004 2nd Series)	22%
169	+23	-25	Azrael Agent of the Bat (1995)	14%
170	+39	+32	Spider-Man 2099 (1992)	30%
171	-44	-105	Transformers (1984 Marvel) 1st Printing	46%
172	-23	new	Captain America Reborn (2009 Marvel)	-25%

173	-70	new	Red Sonja (2005 Dynamite)	30%
174	-13	new	Exiles (2001-2008 1st Series Marvel)	20%
175	-66	new	Guardians of the Galaxy (2008 2nd Series)	-1%
176	-78	-100	Power Man and Iron Fist (1972)	46%
177	new	new	New Avengers (2010- 2nd Series)	
178	-46	-35	Batman Gotham Knights (2000)	26%
179	+27	-21	Doctor Strange (1988 3rd Series)	36%
180	-37	-28	Rom (1979)	37%
181	+30	-94	Ghost Rider (1973 1st Series)	53%
182	-51	+3128	Four Color (1942 Series 2)	18%
183	+16	-92	All Star Squadron (1981)	24%
184	-16	-152	X-Man (1995)	-4%
185	+13	new	Civil War (2006 Marvel)	-9%
186	+10	new	GI Joe (2008- IDW)	-19%
187	+51	+119	Marc Spector Moon Knight (1989)	26%
188	+33	new	X-Men Forever (2009 2nd Series)	-5%
189	new	new	Birds of Prey (2010 2nd Series)	
190	+38	-71	Superboy (1994 3rd Series)	24%
191	+42	+5	Nam (1986)	8%
192	+502	new	Chew (2009)	14%
193	-20	-31	Master of Kung Fu (1974)	39%
194	-18	new	She-Hulk (2005-2009 2nd Series)	-1%
195	+21	+49	Wildcats Covert Action Teams (1992)	8%
196	+23	new	Iron Man (2005- 4th Series)	-9%
197	+53	-95	Marvel Super Heroes Secret Wars (1984)	37%
198	-11	-114	Supergirl (1996 3rd Series)	9%
199	new	new	American Vampire (2010 Vertigo)	
200	new	new	Green Hornet (2010 Dynamite Entertainment)	

Grade Distribution Analysis by Asher Densmore-Lynn:
"I found a collection in my attic..."

Every dealer's heard this a thousand times. And every dealer's heard the next part of it the same thousand times. "They're in great shape -- for their age." Great shape "for their age"? Who knows what that means?

We've gotten pretty good at answering that question. We have a sophisticated collection-purchasing system that we've developed over several years while purchasing many, many books collected by people of all ages, all over America. And these are collections -- not multiple-lot transactions from dealers or "a list of books people sold on eBay," but the actual unfiltered contents of their collections, recorded no matter what grade we found the book in. The following chart shows the aggregate distribution of grades in the thousands of collections we've recorded.

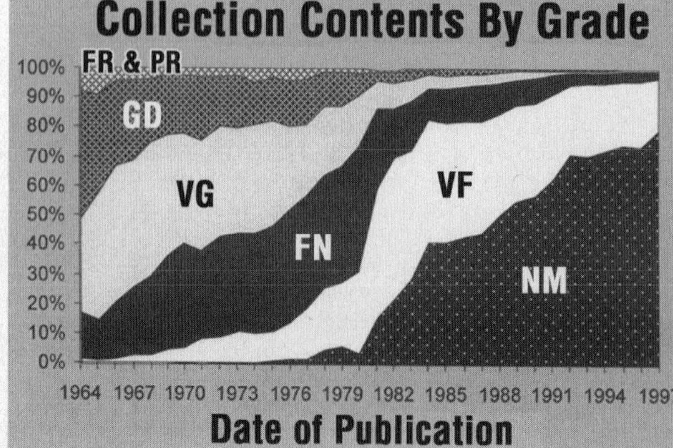

So if we decide that we've got a representative grading sample of every long box still lurking in American attics and closets and basements, what can we learn from it?

Little has changed in storage doctrine since the late 1990s.

This was a surprise, but from now all the way back to 1997, the graph for NM was essentially flat. No matter when it was purchased in the last 14 years, we expect to see four out of five copies of it in NM condition, with essentially no FNs. This is consistent with increased awareness of collectible value during and after the speculative bubble in the early 1990s.

As soon as they're purchased, 20% of all comics go down a grade.

Even for books published in 2010 -- books purchased, read once or twice, and almost immediately sent winging their way to us -- we find no more than 80% remain NM.

Modern Age books tend to Very Fine and Near Mint grades.

We grant that this isn't news to dealers and collectors, so take this instead as an example of how to read our results. 1990 is the first year FN copies make up ten percent of the sample, and 1985 is the first year that NM and VF appear with equal frequency. Even going back into the late Bronze Age around 1980, in the average collection you can still expect half of the books from that year to be VF or better.

Sight unseen, a Bronze Age collection that averages FN or VF isn't unreasonable.

Books graded GD or lower only make up fifteen to thirty percent of the sample in Bronze Age. Of books published in 1975, as many were found in FN as VG, and almost as many were VF as GD.

Few collections average below Very Good.

Even in the Silver Age, VG is where most books tend to settle. This is somewhat surprising; it takes more time and rough handling to push a book into GD territory than one might expect of a book this old. The middle of the Silver Age is over forty years ago, and yet we still expect a little better than two out every three books to be VG or better.

"No, your *Iron Man* #1 is probably not Near Mint."

1969 is the earliest we've ever recorded a NM book from a collection. It's not until 1973 that even 1% of recorded books come in at 9.2 or better. Most people with high-grade Bronze Age sell them individually, on eBay or through our own transaction system, long before they reach the point of selling their entire collection.

What about the comics already in circulation?

The previous analysis focused on groups of comics that could generally be considered original owner collections -- purchased, stored, and uncirculated among other collectors before being sold as a group. What do we know about the grade distribution of collectible back issues that have already been bought, sold, and traded by any number of collectors and dealers? Comics purchased from sellers using our online want list can help answer this question. Or second chart shows the grade distribution of comics sold to us through our online want list. Please note that this is not representative of all the comics out there in the marketplace. Lower grades of some books would be under-represented, because if we're already well-stocked in high grade copies, the lower grades won't be on our buying list and sellers will be unlikely or unable to submit them. On the flip side, high grade copies of older issues will generally be underrepresented because owners are more likely to sell them directly via consignment or auction.

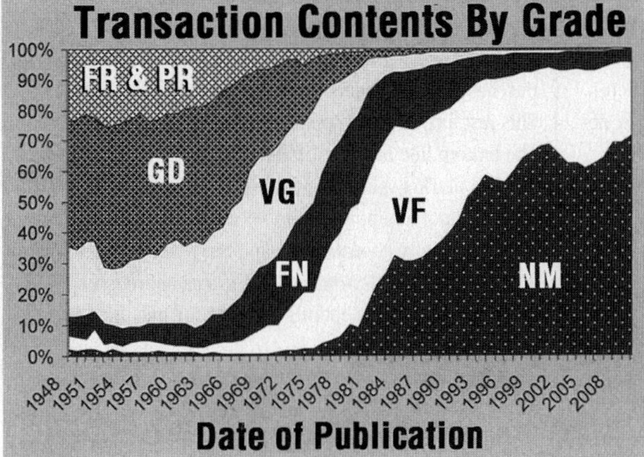

Grade Distribution of Comics Sold Using Mycomicshop's Online Want List

As we mentioned, in the broadest strokes much of this isn't news to anybody in the industry, but there's a difference between a generally understood trend and hard data, and as far as we know nothing like this has ever been published. We hope this will be useful, whether one is making a preliminary offer or trying to analyze scarcity and grade, and encourage anyone who'd like more information to contact us at webmaster@mycomicshop.com.

Doug Simpson
Paradise Comics

2010 has been a year of continuous growth for Paradise Comics. Despite all the issues involving retailers, our sales continued to show a modest growth at around 4%; thanks in no small part to our growing customer base. Our Internet sales also continued to grow and our website contributed to another increase by 5% in sales over last year.

The greatest area of growth in-store remains our sale of graphic novels. This format is definitely the direction the hobby is going and the major companies have started to take notice. Most of our new customers are coming to pick up graphic novels instead of regular monthly issues.

High Grade Key issues from the Silver and Bronze Age are selling consistently well and demand continues to be high. I simply couldn't keep up with the demand for high-grade Silver and Bronze Age books.

The usual suspects were in great demand: *Amazing Fantasy* #15, *Fantastic Four* #1, *Daredevil* #1, *Giant-Size X-Men* #1, *Incredible Hulk* #181, *X-Men* #94, *Incredible Hulk* #1, *Tales of Suspense* #39, and *Avengers* #4, were all highly requested along with a few other surprises: *Amazing Spider-Man* #50, *Silver Surfer* #3, *Green Lantern* #76 and *Cerebus* #1 are just a few examples.

Golden Age sales are still very sluggish and only Timely and early *Batman* and *Detective Comics* are a guaranteed sale. There is always a market for standard Golden Age hero comics, but never at *Guide*, and usually well below

Silver Age sales continued to be the bulk of our back issue market, with any high-grade copies selling out as fast as I can get them in.

For DC Silver Age, the greatest demand rests once again with the iconic characters Batman, Superman, Flash, and Green Lantern. Most other titles have been slow sellers. The one book that continued to be high on everyone's wish list was *Green Lantern* #76, the first Neal Adams work on the title.

Marvel Silver Age is selling very well, with *Amazing Spider-Man* and *X-Men* leading the way, and demand for secondary titles like *Avengers* and *Iron Man* is increasing. The Marvel Silver Age market is always strong and doesn't look to be slowing down anytime soon.

Bronze Age comic sales continued to rise but only for books in high grade, while demand for mid-grade copies has decreased sharply.

Marvel has the bulk of sales in this category, with John Byrne *X-Men* (#107-143) and all *Amazing Spider-Man* issues between #100 and #200 leading the way. These issues are on almost everyone's list and, if I had an entire box of each, they would be gone within a week. I have also noticed an increase in demand for *Avengers* and *Iron Man*. It goes without saying that *Incredible Hulk* #181 is the most in-demand Bronze Age book out there today.

DC titles, including *Batman*, *Justice League of America* and *Flash*, are always in high demand, and *Green Lantern* is still seeing incredible growth thanks to the Blackest Night and Brightest Day storylines.

Modern book sales have continued their fall in 2010, with the only bright spots being DC's Return of Bruce Wayne storyline and Marvel's Heroic Age reboot event.

Surprisingly, with all the controversy over the most recent *Amazing Spider-Man* stories, the sales continue to be high. I feel that the future of the medium is with the graphic novel and the increased output by all publishers will continue this trend.

CGC continues to be the ultimate standard in independent third-party grading. I would like to mention that CGC is still the exclusive grading company for Paradise Comics.

Some recent CGC sales include:

Amazing Spider-Man #6 CGC 7.0 $1,300
Amazing Spider-Man #10 CGC 9.2 $2500
Amazing Spider-Man #39 CGC 9.4 $4,200
Amazing Spider-Man #40 CGC 9.4 $3,200
Flash #105 CGC 6.0 $1700
Incredible Hulk #181 CGC 9.0 $1,375
X-Men #1 CGC 6.0 $4,000
X-Men #28 CGC 9.4 $1000
X-Men #94 CGC 9.2 $1050
Amazing Fantasy #15 CGC 2.0 (CGC Sig. Series) $4000
Amazing Spider-Man #1 4.5 (CGC Sig. Series) $4300
Amazing Spider-Man #129 9.2 (CGC Sig. Series) $1300

I also want to mention that 2010 was also the year that Wizard World made its Canadian debut with their inaugural Toronto Comic Con. Now a pop-culture focused event with guests from film and television as well as comics, the convention took place at the Direct Energy Centre, Exhibition Place 100 Princes' Blvd in downtown Toronto on March 26-28, 2010. This was our first year as predominantly a retail set up instead of promoter and the sales were tremendous. The March time frame is great for the Toronto market and I fully expect this show to be seriously large in the next couple of years.

Tony Starks
Comics Ina Flash!

This is my first market report for several years. My mother used to tell me if I couldn't say something nice to say nothing at all. So I have remained silent for the past several years – on the market report front anyway.

The market is very mixed. Every month brings reports of some new record sales on key books. Especially high grade key books. I'm not selling them so I'm not quoting the prices – let others brag about the $50,000 *Daredevil* #1 in NM+ (Silver Age) or the $50,000 *Amazing Fantasy* #15 in VF-. The ones selling have earned the bragging rights.

But do record prices on elite books – at best just a percent or two of the total books for sale - make for a healthy market? What about the other 98% of the market? It might be true that with million dollar books now established that there is more money flowing in the hobby than ever before. But is this a case – like the USA's economy in general – of the rich getting richer while the poor get poorer?

It seems only a handful of advisors are reporting the severely depressed state of more common books, while the rest don't mention it at all or just in passing note that common books in average condition are slow. Here is the situation. Market trends and online auctions have decimated the value of your VG run of *Amazing Spider-Man/FF/JLA/Flash* (add your own favorite), just as those same market trends and online auctions have greatly increased the value of your high grade keys. And I said HIGH GRADE keys. A lot of low grade keys have either not increased in value or have decreased as well. *JLA* #1 in high grade is a great book - a VF/NM will get you over the NM- *Guide* price. Less than VF copies can be had for no more than *Guide* and a VG for less than *Guide*.

All of this started six to eight years ago. eBay revealed that nice – but run - books were fairly common. Just a few examples of eBay sales: *Marvel Feature* #3 VF (3rd app. Defenders) $10.50/$45 in the *OPG*. *Werewolf By Night* #33 VF+ (second Moon Knight) $12.50/*OPG* $43. *Frankenstein* #1 VF $26/*OPG* $49. *Doctor Solar* #2 VF $12/*OPG* $63. *Amazing Spider-Man* #98 NM- (drug issue) $99/*OPG* $195. All these prices include the shipping costs. They are not exceptional bargains – they are representative of routine sale prices realized. So even "sort of special" issues in VF'ish shape are selling way below *Guide*. So imagine how VG copies of the run issues go. It is no better.

As the price for high grade keys goes up and up, a lot of collectors are selling their non-key issues to raise money to purchase the key books while they can still afford them. This just further depresses the value of those non-key issues. The bottom line is that for a lot of books, for MOST books, the true market value is one third to one-half the *Guide* price. It's not a blip, it's not the economy, it is the new market reality. So yes – *Action* #1 and *Detective* #27 are million dollar books. But *Action* and *Detectives* above issue #300 are mostly – with exceptions – selling for one third to one half of *Guide*.

Which brings us to *Overstreet Price Guide* itself: *The Guide* needs to reflect the market reality. As a dealer, I don't really care if *Batman* #172 in VG is worth $9.00 or $22 or if *Doctor Solar* #2 is $63 or $12. Both sales are way more than their cover price of 12 cents so I'm still selling collectibles. What matters is if I know what the market value is and I'm paying less than what I'm selling for. I can sell VG Silver and I can sell VF Bronze – just not at *Guide* prices.

The problem becomes purchasing stock. Those with comics to sell do not want to sell for 10-15% of *Guide*. They don't want to accept that the true market value of their books is actually only a third of the listed *OPG* price. Even when they are selling common books to fund their purchase of a nice CGC graded key in 9.4 on ComicLink, they don't want to accept that their *Action Comics* #405 in FN/VF is not worth the $15 the *Guide* says it is. They expected at least five bucks for the book, not a buck fifty. Many won't sell – and those that do are resentful. Even worse is explaining this to a non-collector who found a box of old comics in the attic and went out and bought a price guide. Your explanation and offer is considered outright thievery.

If this were a blip, I would be all for riding it out. But it's not. The *Guide*'s reason for existence is at stake here. I know dealers that don't even use the *Overstreet Comic Book Price Guide* now. Most stuff that comes in the door goes in the 50 cent/ $1 /$2 boxes. Nicer books they look up on the auction sites or GPA for recent sales.

Yet every cloud has a silver lining. If you are a collector that enjoys owning long runs of your favorite titles and characters – it's like you have found a time machine. You can purchase a lot of books now for the prices they were in the late '80s and early '90s. Consider this. A CGC graded 9.0 copy of *Avengers* #1 is a $25,000 book. A 6.5 is around $2600. Yet for about 1/10th of the price of 9.0 #1 or the same price as a #1 in 6.5, one could own the entire run of *Avengers* – all 500 + issues. IF you are willing to "settle" for 4.0 copies of *Avengers* #1 and #4, 4.0 to 5.0 for the rest up to issue #100 and 6.0-7.0 condition on issues to #100-200. After issue #200 mostly NM. It is now possible to make your collecting dollars go very far indeed.

Bargains abound – and that is the good news. Even "hot" books like *Amazing Spider-Man* #1 or *Green Lantern* #1 or *Avengers* #1 can be had for no more than *Guide* – often less – at VG or lesser conditions. Recent sales of such include Fair condition copies of *Amazing Spider-Man* #1 ($811) #2 ($120) and #3 ($106). Now Fair condition has always been a grade that the price varies according to the book. But the #1 sold for just over one-half of the Good price and issues #2 and #3 sold at one-third of the Good price.

A final observation or market forecast. The Marvel Keys have recorded the greatest price increases. Marvels have historically led the market. But DCs historically at some point play catch up. The key DCs appear to me to be overlooked and undervalued. In the past *Showcase* #4 and *Amazing Fantasy* #15 were close in value. Now *AF* #15 is dominating at 2.5x – 3.0x the price of *Showcase* #4. Spider-Man's first appearance is far more popular with fans than the Flash's reintroduction for certain. Spider-Man is an iconic hero, a hero for our times. But *Showcase* #4 is a far harder book to find and started the reintroduction of the Super Hero, began the Silver Age. Stan Lee and company would never have introduced the Fantastic Four, Spider-Man, Iron Man and the rest if DC had not been making money on the Flash, Green Lantern and the JLA for years. The major DCs all precede the major Marvels by years and are far more elusive in high grade. The DC keys could be poised for big leaps in the upcoming years, especially as DC ramps up their movie making business and moves outside the Batman and Superman franchises.

Al Stoltz
Basement Comics

What an amazingly strange year for selling comics! The show year started with Mega Con in Florida in February and people were desperate to buy something, anything from your Booth and either invest in it or add it to their collections. By November at the Virginia Comic Con you would need a rifle to even try to make someone spend a few dollars on quality material...what happened? The economy has seemed to have gotten better and people I know in and out of comic world are spending a few more dollars than normal. Did comics magically start to lose their luster as the year passed away? Yes and No!

From January to early August, show sales were steadily on the rise even after we failed to score any major collection to wow the crowd with for 2010. The usual suspects sold at all of those shows like *Hulk* #181, *Amazing Spider-Man* #129, *Giant-Size X-Men* and all the other issues along that vein. I guess what basically sold was High Grade (what a shock) and Key issues. We even again managed to sell huge runs of High Grade Dells such as *Little Lulu* and *Four Color* series. So I guess as long as it was glossy and shiny they wanted it.

Even hot books like **Amazing Spider-Man #1** can be affordable at VG or lesser grades.

It is however the average books that look like they are taking a turn in a new direction. From San Diego Comic-Con on the number of dealers both small an large were hanging signs that stated 40-90% off the table inventory. Silver Age that was Fine plus or less and just about all Bronze Age titles in even High Grade were being offered at a fraction of *Overstreet* values and the buyers had so many options that even then they did not sell out at blistering speeds. Is this a serious market correction that is long overdue or are dealers who are aging out just tired of carrying tons of boxes of inventory and just trying to cut back on what they are offering. If we go the way of baseball cards where cards are listed at a certain price then offered at a flat 50% off that right from the beginning then how can we ever expect the buyers to ever buy at retail prices at shows ever again? When I was a younger man, Mr. Steve Geppi when asked about having a sale at his store stated "How can you discount a collectible" and I have adhered to that since that day. We do not hang super discount signs but prefer to reward customers individually if they hit a certain spending level, and not at 50% off. How can you replace your inventory at these levels ?? I have heard that you just buy cheaper and sell cheaper.....great...but that cycle eventually leads to little or no value and everything from 1966 forward ending up in dollar bins. Will the massive discount movement continue in 2011? Will those who were bailing out due to slow economy in their areas just fold up their tents and leave show circuit anyway? Let's stay tuned and read next year's letter and see where the path has gone.

eBay sales were actually the pleasant surprise for 2011! The slow build from the crumbled economy had taken off this year. Only one month was the same as the year before and most months were up tremendously. All items offered were selling quickly and many being shipped out of the country. Strip reprints, Golden Age and Silver Age, Fanzines, Magazines and *Classics Illustrated*. Classics, as long as they were cheap were snapped up by I guess baby Boomers who wanted to go back and re-read these legendary comics. Love comics priced under $15.00 did very well as did Horror

Comics, that also had a ceiling of $30.00. Even the notoriously slow Summer months kept us busy packing and shipping items out in between traveling to Summer shows. All these steady and wonderful sales were generated out of our online eBay store, auctions were another story all together. Auctions all year have been a great way to DUMP items you no longer are in love with due to the fact that bidders will not run it up unless it is one of those magical key or rare issues that everyone wants. For example we listed a copy of *Zap Comics* #1 2nd print in Mint Condition and top closing bid was $11.55. CGC comics sell for far below GPAnalysis levels and with the exception of a few strange items we listed that surprised us with multiple bidders that paid crazy money for a comic we had little interest in.....who can tell these days! I can only hope that bidding stays active during the upcoming year and perhaps bargain hunters will just want anything to buy and read for the cold winter ahead!!

When the show schedule gets under way we all return to the fun old road warrior days of long drives and eating bad highway food until we get to our destination. This year started off with Mega Con in Orlando Florida and as usual it was run professionally and is a joy to set up at. I usually do okay at Mega Con but 2010 was really good and the huge crowds all seemed to want some comics. Sun, great food after show and made money...not a bad trip at all.

C2E2 had its first show in Chicago and to us it was a great experience. Load in was a little crazy and load out was a nightmare if you literally did not run and get your van like we did and get out right away. Buying was great at this show and collections walked in through the front door. The guys did a fantastic job and I am sure the show will build and become one of the shows to do each year.

We also returned to Heroes Con in Charlotte after at least a five year absence and it was also a lot of fun. If you are a comic person and want to spend time in a fantastic city, then this is it! Good crowd and we worked hard to make it a decent trip and well worth the six hour plus drive!

Wizard Philly was our June show and while it was only a little over an hour away and we feel we must set up at it, it is sliding down a path towards being less and less of a comic show. Our location was less than perfect and we blame ourselves for being the ones that picked it. We managed enough of buying and selling to make it an okay experience and will no doubt be back there yet again.

Chicago Wizard was as usual heavily attended but seemed to lose some of its steam compared to the year before. Wizard has lost the big comic publishers to fill the room but instead has loaded it with people to get autographs from...celebs and semi-celebs. My oldest son looks like Johnny Fair Play from Survivor and at least gets to yack with him once a year.

Baltimore Comic Con is my home town show! I live a whole thirty five minutes away from the show and have the best time at this show. While Marc Nathan never releases attendance totals, it is a well attended affair. Saturday was insane and Sunday a lot less, but added together it makes for a great show. If you are a comic collecting fan, then the Baltimore Comic Con is the show to attend! Lots of dealers and a crazy amount of comic artists and comic celebs! If you decide to attend due to this endorsement then please stop by my booths and offer to buy me lunch after you have had a great time here!!

NY Comic Con is going to be THE Monster Giant show either starting in 2011 or 2012! This show had at least 100,000 people in the building and this place rocked from opening bell to close of business on Sunday. Larry and Mark are super great to deal with and have always helped us out with any problem that has popped up. While New York City is not known for being my favorite city out there, I find I can relax and have fun at this show and do very well as an exhibitor. You like crowds? Huge San Diego like setups and live in East Coast? Come to this show and be ready to be wowed!

We will be celebrating twenty years as officially being known as Basement Comics in 2011. While I have done business far before that, we officially started as this business, and I threw my college degree away in 1991 and wanted to see if a living could be made out of this hobby. Two grown kids and living a decent life so far has proven that going out on my own was not a bad idea after all. I would like to thank all who read this and have spent even a dollar with me over the years. All the sales have contributed to the overall success and I greatly appreciate you keeping me in business and making sure I never became unhappy in an office somewhere looking out of a window wondering what else I should have done.

Thank You !!

Doug Sulipa
Doug Sulipa's Comic World

The worldwide recession continues and has affected sales on many back issues. Buyers have concentrated on four main continued avenues of collecting; (1) High Grade investment copies; (2) Low grade reading copies; (3) Key issues in ALL Grades, including #1s, Origins, top Artist issues, last issues and scarcer issues; (4) Below-*Guide* bargains while prices are depressed. Since the 1960s, downturns in the economy have not much affected sales of back issue collectible comics. However, this is not a normal recession, and it has many people running scared, thus buyers have been more careful and selective.

For the first time in nearly a decade, our percentage of high grade copies sales has started to decline. Investors no longer will pay high prices for just anything in high grade. They want popular titles (especially Marvel), older comics (especially pre-1975) and key issues. Our bestselling high grade comics were virtually all in the $5 to $50 each price range this year, mostly Bronze Age and including a lot of early to mid 1980s titles. Low grade reading copies of uncommon pre-1980 was the only area where sales were up this year. Sales on most 1955-1990 comics that were uncommon, scarce or rare in ANY grade were strong this year, many bringing 135-175%+ *Guide* prices.

By far the most requested Marvel and DC comics were all the major and minor Key issues, but many are getting hard to re-stock due to relentless demand, otherwise we would have sold a lot more. Strangely enough, for most 1975 & newer comics, the #1 issues are usually the most common issues, thus possibly not as good an investment as many expect. Meanwhile many LAST issues (especially on longer running titles) are in very low supply and high demand, with most remaining very undervalued. Many many KEY issue comics in GD-FN are now far too undervalued in *Guide* and near impossible to keep in stock (just try to find *Conan* #1 or *Iron Man* #1 in FN, or *Amazing Fantasy* #15 in FR/GD anywhere near *Guide*). Affordable KEY issues is a fast growing area for dealers. Most desirable books can easily bring anywhere from 125% to 200% *Guide* (thus many of the *Guide* prices are now wholesale).

As we have about 1,300,000 comics and related items in our warehouse, we have literally tons of overstock. We have continued our clearance sales by making up Overstock sets in groups of approx. 10, 25, 50 or 100 items, typically at 35-65% off *Guide* range. Clearance sets continue to be very popular, thus we hope to set up our efforts and offer hundreds to thousands more Clearance sets through the year 2011, ideally clearing out about 1/3 of our inventory over the next decade.

It needs to be noted that eBay auctions are often not a good indicator of value. A forced sale in a short period of time (typically 7 days) often causes skewed results. Imagine a typical antique shop putting everything in the store up for sale by auction in a 7-day period. Many good items would bring 5-20% of retail, but if the seller is patient, a lot of items can easily bring full retail. When I buy a collection, the percentage of retail I pay is based on estimated turnover time at full retail prices, broken down into 4 broad catagories; (1) Percentage that will sell in under 90 days; (2) 3-12 months; (3) 1-5 years; (4) 5-10 years or possibly never sell. I virtually never discount items in category 1. I am most likely to discount items in category 4. For items that fall into categories 2 or 3, I usually am patient and let them sit in my inventory until the right buyer comes along. When an eBay seller puts items in categories 2-4 up for auction, there could easily be no ready buyers that week, thus bad results. Ebay stores with fixed Buy-it-Now prices are a much better indicator of current values (although this still does not account for varied good to bad condition grading).

Archie Comics: Our Archie inventory is the world's biggest, with over 35,000+ Archie Comics (90% of 1958-2000 in stock; good selection of 1957 & older, 2001 & newer) and 10,000+ Digests in stock (95% of 1973-2005 issues in stock), thus we always do well with them. The great majority of our sales are items in the $2 to $20 each price ranges. But this year we had an above average number of advanced collectors filling in gaps in the collection in the $25-$100 each price range. Key issues and minor Key issues were in higher than usual demand. Key issue buyers typically wanted higher grades, but for most 1965-1985, even VF copies can be hard to find. Betty & Veronica were once again our strongest sellers, including all the Archie Giants and other related titles. All Golden Age 1941-1950 Archie titles are in demand (at 120%-150% *Guide* in any grade). Everything with Dan DeCarlo art is in demand (includes many non-Archie titles and his Adult Girlie magazine cartoons). All Archies from 1951-1964 are continued good sellers (most GD-FN copies we sell at 120-140% *Guide*). The circa 1960 Horror & Sci-Fi cover issues have about double the demand of other surrounding issues (at 120-135% *Guide*).

© AP

Cheryl Blossom's mini-series issues are up in demand. (**Cheryl Blossom #1** shown)

There was a lot of interest in 1982-1990 appearances of rich "bad girl" Cheryl Blossom. Interest in Cheryl Blossom exploded in 11/1994 because of the "Love Showdown" storyline where Archie picked Cheryl over Betty and Veronica. Since that time, she has been one of the most wanted characters by completionist fans. Her 1982-1983 appearances are in low supply due to Low Print runs and should continue to climb in value. The four 1995-1997 *Cheryl Blossom* mini-series and 1997-2001 on-going series are also well up in demand and a good long-term bet. It was a slower than average year for Katy Keene, probably as most are high valued and priced, but her Low Print 1983-1990 title and Digests continue to be in demand and short supply. Josie & the Pussycats has been a top seller for nearly a decade and this year was no different. Pre-Pussycats *Josie* #1-44 were up in demand, as were the 1960s appearances in *Laugh* #145-168 and *Pep*. Josie's first app in *Archie's Pals 'N' Gals* #23 is still very undervalued and now hard to find (sells at 150-200% *Guide*). Sabrina the Teen-Age Witch was not quite as popular this year, but still in steady demand. Early appearances of Little Sabrina (appearing in *Little Archie* #59-179) were selling decent, but later issues were slower titles.

The Red Circle/Archie Adventure Horror and superhero titles were titles often requested in VF or better, and they are in steady demand. The 1987-1992 Low Print Era Last Issues are in high demand as Minor-Key issues; *Archie and Me* #161 (2/87), *Archie at Riverdale High* #113 (2/87), *Archie Giant Series* #632 (7/92), *Archie's Girls Betty & Veronica* #347 (4/1987), *Archie's Pals 'N' Gals* #224 (9/1991), *Archie's TV Laughout* #105 (2/86), *Betty & Me* #200 (8/92), *Everything's Archie* #157 (9/91), *Jughead* #352

(6/87), *Laugh* #400 (4/87), *Life with Archie* #286 (9/91), *Pep* #411 (3/87); (at 150-200% *Guide*). The Archie brand *Teenage Mutant Ninja Turtles Adventures* are the comics of choice by the general public, as those are the ones they remember on the newsstands.

TMNT Adventures #1,19,50-72, *Special* #6-10, *Sourcebook* #1-2, Digests, and *Mighty Mutant Animals* #5-9, are Low Print items (sell at 200-400% *Guide*). Early *Sonic the Hedgehog* are in demand and are some of the most valuable comics of the 1990s, but later issues are slower sellers. The 1995-1997 era Hanna-Barbera titles are already hard to find, are in high demand, sold out with almost all dealers and very undervalued in the *Guide*, with #1-5 issues being uncommon (sell at 150% *Guide*) with most #6-up issues being scarce (sell at 200-400% *Guide*).

Archie Comics #1 is now one of the hottest comics of the entire Golden Age, with low to mid grade CGC copies selling in the 300-400% *Guide* range. All Golden Age Archie comics are top sellers in any grade. The 70th Anniversary of the Archie gang approaches, making them among the most enduring comic characters of all time, members of an elite club, as only a handful of characters have attained uninterrupted newsstand distribution for 7 decades. Most of the others are DC characters. Superhero collectors often underestimate the potential of Humor and Cartoon characters.

Atlas/Marvel: More and more Marvel collectors are looking backwards and discovering the Atlas titles. 90% of what we sell is in the FR/GD through VG range, which works out great, as these are the condition the majority of copies we locate fall into. The Horror and Sci-Fi titles were once again the most requested, especially the 1956-1962 Kirby and Ditko Era issues. We sold about 100 low grade issues (at 115-135% *Guide*). Fans in the US want the post-Code issues they remember in the 1970s Marvel Reprint titles; UK fans want originals of issues reprinted in their Alan Class titles. Next most requested were all the Western titles (old and newer at 120-135% *Guide*). *Millie the Model* #18-93 by Dan DeCarlo were impossible to keep in stock (GD-FN copies bring 150-200% *Guide*; VF-NM copies at 125-150% *Guide*). If I could locate a set of the DeCarlo *Millie*, they would likely prove to be the bestselling of all Atlas Marvels. The Humor, Cartoon and Parody, Romance and War Titles were moderate steady sellers (at 115-130% *Guide*).

ATLAS/Seaboard comics (1974-1975): When these first hit the market, they were among the first major top-selling comics among collectors (as opposed to just the general public). I pre-ordered and sold an average of 250-500 copies of each in my early comic shop years and remember them well. The IDs (independent distributors) did not want to give them shelf space, so they had above-average returns. For these and other reasons, the publisher folded before any one title could print more than 4 issues. For nearly 25 years these were dumped into bargain bins, causing the worldwide dealer inventories to virtually disappear, with remaining copies now mostly in the VG-FN Condition ranges (VF copies are now uncommon; strict VF/NM or better copies are scarcer).

Circa 1999, due to the internet and eBay, these were back in demand. For the last decade, we have had constant demand, especially from collectors/completionists who want the full set of all comics produced from this publisher. The biggest obstacle for the last decade has always been the scarce *Gothic Romances* #1 (sells at 200% *Guide*) and *My Secrets* #1 (B&W magazine; 2/1975; sells at 300-500% *Guide*); Many fans finally settle on collecting only all the color comics and skipping all the magazines (or just those 2 rare magazines).

Vicki #3 and 4 are scarce, bringing 200% *Guide* in ANY grade. All these mags are Uncommon to Scarce: *Devilina* #2, *Movie Monsters* #2-4, *Thrilling Adventures* #2 and *Weird Tales of the Macabre* #2 (sell at 125-150% Guide), *Movie Monsters* (#1 is Uncommon and sells for $30 in VF/NM; #2-4 are hard to keep in stock & bring $50 each in strict VF/NM).

Longtime fans love this publisher due to familiar creators including: Adams, Austin, Boyette, Buckler, Chaykin, Colan, Conway, Craig, Ditko, Fleisher, Heath, Marcos, McWilliams, Milgrom, Nostrand, Ploog, Sekowsky, Springer, Summers, Thorne, Toth, Wood and Wrightson.

With the return of new Atlas comics, demand for back issues is already up by almost 50%. Most of the 1974-1975 Atlas/Seaboard comics remain low-to-modesty priced in the *Guide*, all are undervalued, especially in strict VF/NM or better investment grades. Bigger demand for the vintage issues should continue as long as the new product continues to be released. If you have not yet sampled these back issues, now is a great time to give them a try.

Captain Canuck: 2010 was the 35th Anniversary for Captain Canuck, Canada's most famous comic title and superhero. *Captain Canuck* #4 (2/1978; 2nd print; 11" x 17" Treasury sized, with handwritten signed & numbered Certificate of Authenticity bound-in) is one of the rarest comics of the entire Bronze Age. It is also among our Top 10 Most Requested comics of the entire Bronze Age. I've only seen 3 copies on eBay in the last decade (a VF copy sold for $525 in 2005). I finally uncovered the first copy I have ever had in stock and sold it quickly in FN for $295.00. Current *Guide* value of $30 in Fine is absurdly low.

Among our Top 10 Most Requested comics of the entire Modern Age are *Captain Canuck Re-Born* #3(1993/1994, only 8,000 copies printed and amazingly Scarce; current VF/NM Value is $50+) and *Captain Canuck* #15 (8/2004; 150 copies printed; current VF/NM Value is $125+). Richard Comely has mentioned he might print a Limited 2nd Printing of both of these high demand comics. *Captain Canuck Legacy* #2 & 3 never got published and might also appear in a future Limited Edition. As a friend of Richard Comely for 35 years, you can be sure I will stock all these Limited Editions, if he ever gets around to publishing them.

The IDW hardcover collections of *Captain Canuck* have once again stirred up interest in the classic original back issues. Comely assembled 50 Limited Edition sets of the IDW HC Books #1 & 2 with autographs on front endpage of both books, and with a unique new Original Art sketch on the front endpage of the Book #1s. We sold all 5 sets we got within a week of receiving them at $85.00 per set.

Charlton Comics: We have the world's biggest selection of Charlton Comics, with 95% of 1960-1986 issues and about 50% of the 1940s-1959 issues in stock. Thus we are the destination for collectors to go to fill in missing numbers and complete their sets. The Horror and Sci-Fi Titles were the bestsellers in both Lower and High Grades, with all issues from 1966-1986 in High Demand. For 1965 & older, only the Ditko issues were in high demand. After the Horror titles, the Hanna Barbera comics were the next most consistent sellers. Third most requested are the better artist issues, including: Aparo, Boyette, Buscema, John Byrne, Ditko, Glanzman, Himes, Wayne Howard, Severin, Sanho Kim, Larson, Morisi, Don Newton, Staton, Tom Sutton, Wood, Williamson and Mike Zeck. Due to poor printing, Charlton comics are notoriously Scarce in strict VF or better. Most investors are happy with VF/NM or better copies, as there are very few CGC graded copies, and if they wait for better copies, they might never find them: (GD-FN = 120-140% *Guide*; VF-VF/NM = 110-120% *Guide*; raw NM- & 9.2 copies = 150% of 9.2 *Guide* prices; raw NM & 9.4 copies = 200% of 9.2 *Guide* prices).

The next most requested (moderate sellers) were all the Western, War and TV titles, mostly to fans that simply enjoy those genres. All the other many genres are solid steady sellers (at 115-125% *Guide*). Unlike the major publishers, Charlton has virtually nothing that does not eventually sell and because we have very little competition on these, we always do well with them.

DC Comics: DC comics continue to be the #2 bestselling back issue publisher (after Marvel), but many are gaining in popularity with back issue collectors. Key issues in ALL grades, including #1s, origins, top Artist issues, Last issues and Scarcer issues, were the strongest sellers. In this spirit, I have prepared the list to follow, of the fastest selling DC comics at full *Guide* or higher prices. Most of them sell in these ranges; (GD-FN = 110-140% *Guide*; FN/VF-VF+ = 100-120% *Guide*; VF/NM, 9.0 to NM-, 9.2 = 120-140% *Guide*). Notable exceptions are listed (I might have missed a few).

My list of the Top Silver-Copper Age DC Comics to own: *Action* #242,252-255,267,276,283-288,300,309,340,347, 360,373,425,432,440,484,583; *Adventure* #210,247-260, 267, 275,282,290,293,300-310,346,353,381,416,428, 431,440, 459-462,467,491-503; *Advs. of Bob Hope* #94,95,106-109; *Advs. of Jerry Lewis* #68,74,97,101-105, 112,117, *All American Men of War* #21,28,39,42,48, 57,63,64,67-69,82,89,112; *All New Collectors Edition* C-53-55, 58, C-56(Superman vs. Ali = Red Hot; 150-200% *Guide*); *All Star Comics* #58,69; *All-Star Western* #1,10,11; *Angel & the Ape* #1; *Aquaman* #1, 50-52; *Amazing World of DC* #1-4, 9,14-17; *Atari Force* (mini promo) #3-5(200% *Guide*); *Atom* #1,7,8,29; *Bat Lash* #1; *Batman* #105,121,129,139,155,169,171,179, 181,189,190,197,210, 219,227,232,234,237,238,243-245,251,254-262,332; *Batman Family* #1,10,18-20; *Beautiful Stories For Ugly Children* #26-30(200% *Guide*); *Best of DC Digest* #1,3,4,10,21 & the Low Print #41-71; *Beware the Creeper* #1; *Blackhawk* #108,118,133,141; *Blitzkrieg* #1-5; *Brave & the Bold* #1,25,28-30,34,50-63,79-87,93,182,197; *Capt. Action* #1; *Challengers of the Unknown* #1,74,82, *Dark Mansion* #1-4; *DC Comics Presents* #1,2,26,47,56,77,78, 85-88, 94,97 & *Annual* #1; *DC 100 Page Super-Spectacular* #4-14; *DC Special* #2-4,6,11,28,29; *DC Special Series* #1,3-13,15, 16,18-24,27; *DC Special Blue Ribbon Digest* #1,3,7,11,16, 20-24; *DC Superstars* #17; *Detective* #225,233,267,298, 311,318,325,327,328,359,362-364,369-372,377,385,387, 389,391,392, 394-424,437-445,471-474,478-483; *Doom Patrol* #86,99,100,121; *Doorway to Nightmare* #1; *1st Issue Special* #1,5,7-9,12,13; *Flash* #105-130,137,139,140,175,214,217-219,226,229,232,289, 300,306-313,350; *Flex Mentallo* #1-4; *Forever People* #1; *Fox & Crow* #1-10; *Freedom Fighters* #1,10-15; *Ghosts* #1-5,97-99; *GI Combat* #55-58, 66,67,68(1/59 = Red Hot 200% *Guide*), 83,87-100,108,114, 138,150,168,193,200-202; *Girls' Love* #150,161-170; *Girls' Romances* #109,134, 159,160; *Green Lantern* (1960-1986) #1,7,13,40,45,59, 61,76-90,100,112,116,123, 181,182,185, 188,194,195; *GL Corps* Annual #2,3(Alan Moore), *Hawk & Dove* #1, *Hawkman* #1,4, *Heart Throbs* #47,101,133-142, *Hot Wheels* #1-6, *House of Mystery* #174-195, 204,207,209, 213,215, 216, 218,221,224-229,231,236,251-256, 290,321, *House of Secrets* #61, 81-100,154, *In Days of the Mob* #1, *Joker* #1-9, *Jonah Hex* #1-10, 91-92 & Digest 1-3, *Justice League of America* #1-5,9,21,22, 29,30,37,38,46,47,55,56, 64,65, 71,74,94-102,107,108,110-116, 123,135-137,147, 148,159,160, 166-168,171,172,183-185,195-197,200,207-209,219, 220,231,232, 261; *Kamandi* #58,59; *Leave it to Binky* #61; *Legion* (1980) #259,290-294,300; *Legion*(1984-89) #37,38, *Limited Collectors' Edition* C#23-25,32-34,37, 39,41,43-46,48-52,57; *Men of War* #1,26; *Metal Men* #1, 21,27,45; *Metamorpho* #1; *Mr. Miracle* #1; *My Greatest Adv.* #80-85(Doom Patrol); *Mystery in Space* #53,75,87-90; *New Gods* #1; *New Teen Titans* #1,2; *New Titans* #130(last issue, 2/1996 = 400-600% *Guide*); *Our Army at War*

Forever People #1 is a top Bronze Age DC issue to own.

#51,61,67, 83(1st true app Sgt. Rock; 150-200% *Guide*), 84-128,130, 151-155,158,168,182,183,186,235-246,269,275; *Our Fighting Forces* #41,45, 123, 133-137; *Phantom Stranger* #1-14, 23,26,31,33,39-41; *Plastic Man* (1967) #1; *Plop* #1,5, 23(Lord of the Rings, Wood-a); *Preacher* #1; *Richard Dragon* #14; *Rima* #1; *Rip Hunter* #1; *Rudolph* 1950-1963; *Rudolph* #nn(1972; aka C-20 Treasury; GD-FN=300% *Guide*; VF-NM=200% *Guide*); *Sandman* (1989) #1,8,22; *Sea Devils* #1; *Secret Origins* #1(1961); *Secret Society of Super-Villains* #1,15; *Secrets of Haunted House* #1-5,44; *Sgt. Bilko* #1; *Sgt. Rock* #302-330; *Sgt Rock* #400-421(Low Print 150% *Guide*), 322(200% *Guide*); *Shazam!* #1,8,12-17, 25,28,34, 35; *Showcase* #1-10,13,14,17-20,22-24,30,34,37,43,45,53-55,57-62,64,70,73-77,79-81,83,84,97-99; *Sinister House* #1-4; *Spectre* #1-5,9; *Spirit World* #1; *Star Spangled War Stories* #45,62,64,67,84-90,92,94-100,134,138-155,181-183; *Strange Adventures* #117,124,180, 184,190,195,201, 205-217,222; *Super A/Super AA/Super B* (DC 1970s Magazines); *Superboy* #49,68,78, 80,83,86,89, 93,98,100,129, 138,147,185,197-200,202,205; *Super DC Giant* #S-13 thru S-26; *Super Friends* #1-10, *Supergirl* (1972) #1-10; *Superman* #100,123,127,129,146,147, 149,158,167,199,233,245, 249,252,254,272,278, 279,284,300,400,423, *Superman Family* #164; *Superman's GF Lois Lane* #1-10,14,29,33,47, 50,70,71,79,89, 93,105,106,111,113; *Superman's Pal Jimmy Olsen* #31,37,57,62,63,72,79,133; *Swamp Thing* (1972) #1, (1982) #20-30,37,171; *Swordquest* (mini promo) #3(200% Guide); *Tales of New Teen Titans* #42-44 & Annual #3; *Tarzan* #207; *Teen Beam* #2; *Teen Beat* #1, *Teen Titans* (1966) #1-5,20-23,46-53; *Tomahawk* #116-119,121,123-130(Adams covers); *TV Screen Funnies* (Scarce) #129-138; *Unexpected* #105,116,119,128,157-162; *Unknown Soldier* #205,219,265-268; *V for Vendetta*; *Watchmen*; *Warlord* #1; *Weird Mystery* #1,2,21; *Weird War* #1-5,8,64,68,93,94; *Weird Western* #12-20,29; Whitman Variants of DC Comics(150-200% *Guide*); *Witching Hour* #1-14; *Wonder Woman* (1942-86) #98-110,159,177-179,198-202,211, 214,267,268,281-283,287,291-293,329; *Wonder Woman* (1987-2006) #50,63,85-90; *World's Finest* #90,94,96-99, 129,142,144,156,169,173-178,198-200,223-228,244-252, 323; *Young Love* #39,69,73,78,79,88-96,107-114,121-126 and *Young Romance* #125,154,163,164,170-183,194-204.

Dell Comics: Dell Comics specialized in Popular Culture icons (licensing popular characters from other media, including cartoons (original, theater & TV), Golden Age of TV series, kids shows, movie classics, newspaper comic strips, novel & pulp series adaptations, radio stars and Westerns) and they featured more photo and painted covers than any other publisher in the history of comics. Because of this they have eternal worldwide appeal, as many of these TV shows are still in reruns all over the world, and on DVD, many with complete seasons. Many of the cartoon characters are so strong they have better worldwide recognition than almost all modern cartoon creations. Thus they have worldwide appeal in affordable grades and will sell forever when still in disposable income price ranges ($5 to $40 each), while slower in the pricey High Grade ranges ($50-$200+ each). The 1950s Dell sported some of the highest print runs in comics history, yet scores of them were well loved and read, and now residing in comics graveyards. But the upside is that almost all are still affordable in GD-FN, and most sets can be completed easier than perhaps any other publisher of the period. This adds to the desire to assemble complete sets. The majority of Dell sets have between 5 to 50 comics, certainly attainable goals. Even the long-running titles are mainly in the 100-250 copy range, and still no $1000 and up issues to worry about (as with Marvel, DC, etc).

We have one of the world's biggest selections with over 20,000 Dell comics in stock and thus they are usually our bestselling pre-1962 comics publisher. As usual, about 95% of what we sell falls into the range of FR/GD (reading copies) through FN (presentable, but still affordable). FN/VF and better copies were slower moving than usual this year. Most Dell comics in GD-FN are still undervalued in the *Guide*, while many VF-NM Dells are still overvalued in the *Guide*. The same Price-to-Condition spreads for Dell are far apart for Low Grades vs. High Grades, although this does not reflect real sales in the marketplace. The average VF is more than double the FN price in *Guide*, whereas VF copies should only list about 50% higher than FN copies. While most VF-NM- copies do not require a price drop, most GD-FN copies do need a price increase. These are especially popular with our international collectors around the world, and large amounts of back issues continue to disappear into permanent foreign collections each and every year.

Dell Variants (6/1956-1-2/1961 = 15 Cent variant; back cover variants with strips in place of ads; Giants with 30-35 cent cover prices) are up in demand since Jon McClure's article on Variants in *Overstreet* #40. The Dells that still have a demand in VF or better include: Key issues & First issues, *Tarzan*, *Turok*, Hanna-Barbera, popular TV shows, Carl Barks art comics and better Movie comics (John Wayne, Sci-Fi, etc).

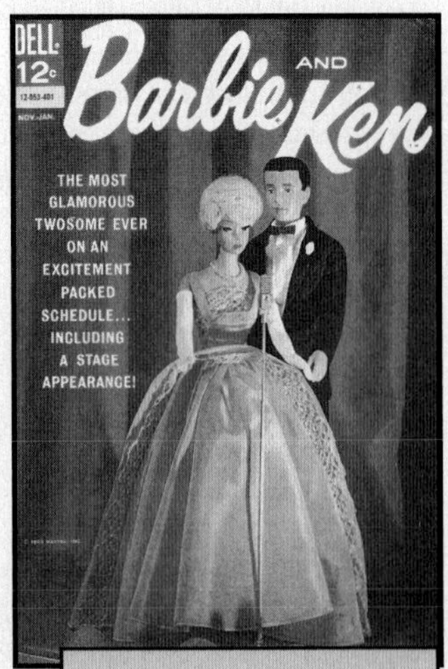

Dell's high print runs make completing a title run easy. (Barbie and Ken #5 shown)

Gold Key (see also Walt Disney comics): We have the world's biggest selection of Gold Key comics with over

35,000 in stock, with most in stock in GD-FN grades and a smaller selection in VF or better. We do our best to keep everything they published in stock at all times, including scores of Elusive to Scarce Cartoon titles. Thus we are now a major destination for many advanced and serious collectors who are looking to fill holes in their sets. In recent years I have run across more and more collectors completing large Gold Key collections (for example: all Hanna-Barbera, all Looney Tunes, all Cartoons, all Tarzan/Turok, all Horror titles, all Whitmans & Variants, all TV Titles, etc.) and a brave few that have attempted gathering the entire GK output. Collector Pat Simpson has a near complete GK set with all variants. His cataloged collection was of invaluable help to Jon McClure and me in our research for the *Overstreet* #40 Variant article. In addition, we are more than happy to help the constant flow of buyers that just want affordable reading copies.

Much like Dell comics, Gold Key continued their legacy and specialized in many Popular Culture icons, but added a lot of new original in-house titles. Because the price spreads for condition are much less extreme than with Dell, VF or better copies are decent sellers. Since most of these comics are sold to the general public and not to Collectors, even VF or higher graded copies can be a lot harder to find than one would expect. Putting together a VF to NM range set of Gold Key's *Doctor Solar*, *Magnus*, *Tarzan*, *Turok* or *Twilight Zone* (a few of the titles in demand in high grades) is actually a difficult task, but infinitely rewarding to those than manage to attain this lofty goal. These are beautiful comics, still very undervalued when compared to Marvel and DC comics of the same period.

As seen in the *Overstreet* #40 Variant article, Gold Key has a huge wealth of Variants from the pre-1988 vintage comics era, rivaling even Marvel and DC, thus they have become even more interesting to collectors of Scarce comics. Whitman Variants of the Gold Key comics (11/1971 thru 4/1980) continue to bring 125-200% of GK issue values to Variant collectors. Canadian Newsstand Variant cover price issues (4-8/1968 with 15 cent prices, 3/1972-4/1973 with 20 cent prices; 12/1977-3/1978 with reverse 30 Cent prices) sell at 125-150% *Guide* to Variant collectors. Whitman Variant 75 cent cover price issues (of 1984 Comics that are 60 cents in USA) are Rare and sell at 200%+ *Guide*.

As with Dell, most Gold Keys are currently undervalued in GD-FN condition ranges. All the uncommon to scarce issues tend to be sold out in virtually all dealer inventories worldwide. Many are so low that I am able to pay 75-100% *Guide* to restock Reading Copies. Many buyers will gladly pay 150-200% *Guide* in these grades. Most of our largest Gold Key orders (100-300+ comics for one one shipment) are for large groups of affordable reading copies.

Harvey Comics: We got in a nice collection of 400+ beautiful High Grade 1950s/1960s Harvey File Copies, most in the VF+, 8.5 through NM, 9.4 ranges. We sold a good number of the stronger characters (*Baby Huey*, *Casper*, *Harvey Hits*, *Hot Stuff*, *Little Audrey*, *Little Dot*, *Little Lotta*, *Playful Little Audrey*, *Sad Sack*, *Spooky*, *Wendy*, etc.). These strong titles were also our bestsellers in lower grades. The File copies of less popular characters and non-original Harvey characters had resistance (*Blondie*, *Family Funnies*, *Joe Palooka*, *Junior Funnies*, *Little Max*, *Mutt & Jeff*, *Warfront*, etc.), which surprises me, as many are undervalued and even scarcer than the mainstream titles. I sold them at these rates: 9.4 copies at 200% of 9.2 prices; 9.2 copies at 150% *Guide*; 9.0 copies at 9.2 prices; VF+ copies at 9.0 prices.

For Cartoon titles, late 1940s through 1962 were in high demand, 1963-1974 were in strong steady demand, 1976-1990 were in moderate demand and the Low Print 1991-1994 titles were in strong demand in any grade. The majority of our sales were books in the FR/GD through FN grade ranges. Many 1960s and 1970s titles are very undervalued in GD-FN grades and thus permanently sold out with almost all major dealers. We sell to them most GD-FN copies over *Guide* and thus have managed to keep nearly 90% of all titles in stock. We have 20,000 Richie Rich comics in stock and we have 10,000 other Harvey Comics in stock, easily the world's biggest selection. Most of them we sell in these price ranges: GD-FN = 125-150% *Guide*; FN/VF to VF/NM = 110-125% *Guide*.

A newly uncovered first app. is that of Fruitman in *Bunny* #3, thus now a superhero Key issue. Many fans always assumed the one-shot *Fruitman* #1 was the only appearance. He also appears in *Bunny* #6,8,9,10,12,13-17,19-21.

Marvel Comics: Marvel continues to be the bestselling back issue publisher. *Iron Man* was the title most up in demand this year (thanks to the movie sequel) and even though *Iron Man* #1 is one of the most common first issues of the 1960s, it was near impossible to keep in stock, selling at 125-200% of *Guide* everywhere. All 1970s Horror titles were in constant demand and many are getting harder to re-stock. Bronze Age comics were hands down the bestsellers (especially 1970-1974), followed by early 1961-1964 issues in any grades.

Key issues in ALL Grades, including #1s, Origins, top Artist issues, Last issues and Scarcer issues were far stronger sellers than any one title (often 3-10 times the demand of standard issues). In this spirit, I have prepared the list of the fastest selling Marvels at full *Guide* or higher prices. Most of them sell in these ranges: GD-FN = 135-200% *Guide*; FN/VF-VF+ = 110-135% *Guide*; VF/NM, 9.0 to NM-, 9.2 = 120-140% *Guide*. Notable exceptions are listed. I might have missed a few.

Here is my list of the top Marvel Comics to own: *Amazing Adventures* #11; *Amazing Spider-Man* #1-28, 50,96-98, 101,102,119-122,124,125,129,149,194,300, 441(Last issue 200-300% *Guide*), Annual #1,2; *Astonishing Tales* #12,25; *Avengers* #1-11,16,57,71,94-101,400-402(Last issues 200-300% *Guide*), Annual #1,7; *Brother Billy* #1; *Captain America* #100,109-113,117,153-155,241,247-255,332,454(Last issue 200-300% *Guide*), Annual #1; *Captain Britain* #1,2, 24; *Captain Marvel* #1,14,21,25-34; *Chamber of Chills* 4; *Champions* 1; *Chili*

1; *Conan* #1,3,23,24,271-274,275(Last issue 200-300% *Guide*); *Creatures on the Loose* #10,30; *Daredevil* #1-7,16-18,27,50-53,131,132,158,168,380(Last issue 200-300% *Guide*), Annual #1; *Dead of Night* 11; *Deadly Hands of Kung-Fu* #1,14,17,28; *Defenders* #1-3,8-11; *Dr. Strange*(1974) #1,14; *Dracula Lives* #1-3,11-13; *Electric Company* Mag (with Spider-Man) #1-50; *Fantastic Four* #1-38,48-50,52,53,55,73,110(Error ed = 200% *Guide*),112,121-123,155-157,166,167,416(Last issue 200-300% *Guide*); *Fear* 10,19,20; *Foom* #1-15, 22; *Film International* #1-4; *Frankenstein* #1; *Funtastic World of Hanna Barbera* #1-3; *Ghost Rider* (1973) #1,2,81; *Ghost Rider* (1990) #81-92,93(2/1998; Last issue 200-300% *Guide*); *Giant-Size Kid Colt* #1-3; *Giant-Size Spider-Man* #1-4; *Giant-Size X-Men* #1; *G.I. Joe* #21,93,150-155(all 150-200% *Guide*); *Gothic Tales of Love* #1-3(GD-FN= 300-500% *Guide*; VF-NM = 200-300% *Guide*); *Gunhawks* #1-7; *Gunslingers* #2,3; *Haunt of Horror* (Mag) #3-5(low print); *Hero For Hire* #1(150-200% *Guide*); *Homer the Happy Ghost* #1; *Incredible Hulk* (1962) #1-6, (1968) #102,118,122,126, 140,141,161,162,180,181,197,198, 200,250,314,330,331, 340,474(Last issue 200-300% *Guide*), Annual #1; *Invaders* #1,7-9,31-33; *Iron Fist* #1,14,15; *Iron Man* #1(GD-FN = 150-200% *Guide*),9,25,47,51-55,66,100,118,128(Alcoholic issue 150-300% *Guide*),150,169,282,284, 332(Last issue 200-300% *Guide*), Annual #1; *Journey into Mystery* #83-101,108,109,112, Annual #1; *Jungle Action* #5, 8; *Kull the Conqueror* (1971) #1, *Li'l Kids* #1-12; *Li'l Pals* #1-5; *Mad about Millie* #1; *Man-Thing* #1; *Marvel Chillers* #3,6; *Marvel Comics Super Special* #1,4,5; *Marvel Feature*(1971) #1-4,11,12; *Marvel Feature* (1975) #1; Marvel Novel (paperback series) #1-11; *Marvelmania* (mag); *Marvel Premiere* #1,3,15,28,50; *Marvel Preview* #1-3,7,8; *Marvel Presents* #3, *Marvel Spotlight* #2, 5(1st Ghost Rider; 1 50-250% *Guide*), 12, 28, 32; *Marvel Super Action* (mag) #1, *Marvel SuperHeroes* #1,12,14,18; *Marvel Super-Heroes Secret Wars* #8; *Marvel Tales* #1; *Marvel Team-Up* #1-4, 12,15, 53, John Byrne issues, 141, & Annual 1, *Marvel Treasury* #1-10; *Marvel Two-in-One* #1,8,46 & all Byrne, Perez, Miller art issues; *Master of Kung Fu* #15; *Masters of the Universe* #12-13; *Mighty Marvel Western* #1-5; *Millie the Model* #135,154,192; *Millie* Annual #1(150-200% *Guide*), 2,3; *Monsters on the Prowl* #9,16; *Monsters Unleashed* #1; *Moon Knight* #29,30; *Ms. Marvel* #16-18; *My Love* #1-39(GD-FN= 150% *Guide*); *New Mutants* #98(200% *Guide*); *Nick Fury* (1968) #1-5; *Night Nurse* #1-4; *Nostalgia Illustrated*; *Not Brand Echh* #1; *Our Love Story* #1-4,6-38(GD-FN= 150% *Guide*), #5(150-200% *Guide*); *Patsy & Hedy* Annual #1(150% *Guide*); *Peter the Little Pest* #1-4; *Pizzazz* #1; *Planet of the Apes* mag #21-28(150% *Guide*),29(200% *Guide*); *Power Man* #17,48-50, prototypes (Atlas/Marvel 1958-1961 era); *Punisher* (1986 Mini); *Pussycat* #1(GD-FN= 400% *Guide*; VF-NM- = 250% *Guide*); *Rampaging Hulk* #1-9, *Rawhide Kid* #17,22,23,31, 32,34,35,38,43,45,46,92,93; *Red Sonja* #1; *Red Wolf* #1; *Savage Sword* #221-235 (150-200% *Guide* and the scarce #235 at 400% *Guide*); *Savage Tales* #1; *Scooby Doo* #1; *Sensuous Streaker* #1(200-400% *Guide*); *Sgt. Fury* #1-10,13; *Shanna* #1; *Silver Surfer*(1968) #1,3,4,12; *Spectacular Spider-Man* #27,28,90,263; *Spidey Super Stories* #1-5; *Spider-Man Digest*; *Strange Tales* #89(Fin Fang Foom 150% *Guide*), #97(1st Aunt May & Uncle Ben 200% *Guide*), #101-115, 169-181, *Sub-Mariner* #1,8,14,34,35,50,59,69, Annual #1; *Superman vs. Spider-Man* #1; *Supernatural Thrillers* #5; *Super-Villain Team-Up* #1; *Tales of the Zombie* #1; *Tales of Suspense* #39-60,63,65,66,79,80; *Tales to Astonish* #27,35-52,57,59,60, 70,82,90-93,100; *Tex Dawson* #1; (1970s 30 cent Variants; 150-200% *Guide*); (1970s 35 cent Variants; 200-400% *Guide*); *Thor* #126-130,134,159,162,168,169, 180,181, 193,225,332,333,337,502(Last issue 200-300% *Guide*); *Tomb of Darkness* #9; *Tomb of Dracula* #1-5; 10,12,13,18; *Tommy the Movie*; *Transformers* #71-79 (150% *Guide*), #80(200% *Guide*); *Transformers Digest*; *Vampire Tales* #1,2,5,8,11; *War is Hell* #9; *Warlock* #1; *Werewolf by Night* #1-5,32,33; *Western Gunfighters* #1-5; *Western Kid* #1; *Western Team-Up* #1; *What If?* (1977) #1; *Wit & Wisdom of Watergate* #1(200% Guide); *X-Men* #1-15,28,35,50, 51,53,56-66,94-111,120,121; *You Don't Say* #1,2.

Variant Edition Comics: Jon McClure's Variant article in *Overstreet* #40 (on pages 1010-1038) has set the new and definitive standard, an absolute MUST HAVE for all Variant Collectors for the next decade. I was proud to have spent 40+ hours of labor assisting him with the monumental task. Since even most dealers and collectors are completely unfamiliar with this area of collecting, many noted to me it was 29 pages of dense and difficult reading, but usually easier to read the 2nd time through. Many of the newly uncovered Variants are not yet well known enough to have gained any premium values. But keep in mind, this is how the Marvel 30 & 35 cent cover price variants started, as they took several years to catch on, they are now some of the most sought after and hottest selling issues in the entire hobby. Because 90% of these Variants are NOT listed (and might never be listed) in the body of the main *Overstreet Guide*, it might take a while for momentum to build on these. There are probably 6000-9000 Canadian Cover Price Variants alone, and perhaps 3000-5000 UK Cover Price Variants.

The scarce 3/1962-4/1963 Archie Price Variants with 15 Cent Cover prices (approx 106 different estimated to exist) were noted in the article. We had several inquiries, but only had 4 in stock, and they sold instantly at 150% *Guide* (probably too low). These are some of the scarcest Test Variants and so far less than half have a single proven copy known to exist. Because of this, I think a reasonable starting point would be at 200% *Guide*. Eventually they could be worth 300-400% *Guide* values on regular issues.

We still have a good stock on many of the 35 Cent Variants of Archie and Harvey Square-bound Giants, as well as the 30 cent and 35 cent Dell Canadian Cover Price Variants. Only a few inquires so far, and they sold at 120-

135% *Guide*. As completionists learn of these, they will start to disappear from our inventory and only be replaced with increasing difficulty.

The early Marvel Direct Editions Variants (1977-1979) often mistakenly sold as "WHITMAN Variants of Marvel" comics are still in demand. These had print runs that vary from approx 2% to 10% of the quantities distributed as Newsstand editions. These Early Marvel Direct Editions (with Black Diamond on cover, with NO "cc" on cover, with NO UPC or obscured UPC Codes, or blank white UPC Codes) when correctly identified can sell at 120-150% *Guide* to Variant collectors. Whitman published Direct market White Logo printings from 2-6/1982 of many of their Gold Key/Whitman Cartoon titles, these sell at 150% *Guide* or more. The bestselling and by far the most requested Variants of the year for us were the Marvel and DC Canadian Newsstand Variant Cover Price editions, thus I have included a list of the most Desirable titles by these publishers. The scarcest titles as Canadian Variants are all the unpopular characters & all the Cartoon Series, but they are not included in the list for brevity purposes (We can email a free more complete list upon request)

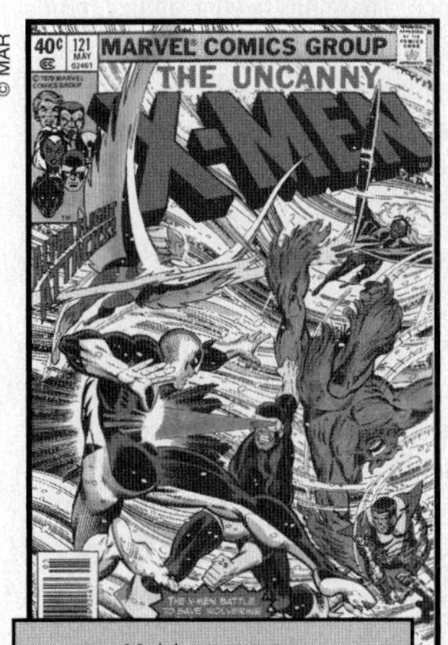

X-Men #121
is a top Bronze Age Marvel issue to own.

Marvel Canadian Newsstand Variant Cover Price editions (10/1982-08/1986 - Printed in USA) Higher Demand Variant Titles include; *Amazing Spider-Man* #233-279 & Annual #16-20, *Avengers* #224-270 & Annual #11-15, *Captain America* #274-320 & Annual #6-8, *Conan* #139-185 & Annual #7-11, *Conan* Annual #7-11, *Daredevil* #187-233, *Defenders* #112-151, *Dr. Strange* #55-81, *Ewoks* #1-5, *Fantastic Four* #247-293 & Annual #17-19, *Further Adventures of Indiana Jones* #1-33, *G.I. Joe* #4-50, *Ghost Rider* #73-81, *Iron Man* 163-209, Annual #5-8, *Incredible Hulk* #276-322 & Annual #11-14, *King Conan* #13-19, *Kitty Pryde and Wolverine* #1-6, *Machine Man* Mini Series #1-4 (Barry Smith-a), *Magik* #1-4(X-Men related), *Marvel Tales* #144-190, *Marvel Two in One* #92-100 & Annual #7, *Marvel Saga* #1-16, *Marvel Super Heroes Secret Wars* #1-12, *Marvel Team Up* #122-150 & Annual #5-7, *Master Of Kung Fu* #117-125, *Micronauts* #46-59, *New Mutants* #1-42, *Night Crawler* #1-4, *Power Man and Iron Fist* #86-125, *Power Pack* #1-19, *Red Sonja* #1-12, *Rom* #35-75 & Annual #1, *Secret Wars* II #1-9, *Spectacular Spider-Man* #71-117 & Annual #4-6, *Spider Woman* #46-50, *Star Wars Return of the Jedi* #1-4, *Star Wars* #64-103 & Annual #2-3, *Thing* #1-31, *Thor* #324-370 & Annual #10-13, *Transformers* #1-12, *Uncanny X-Men* #162-208 & Annual #6-10, *West Coast Avengers* (Mini) #1-4 & *West Coast Avengers* (on-going) #1-11 & Annual #1, *Web Of Spider-Man* #1-17 & Annual #1-2, *What If* #35-47, *Wolverine* Limited Series #2-4, *X-Factor* #1-7 (most sold at 150% *Guide*); These were again our bestselling variants of the year (most at 150% *Guide*). *X-Men* was the most requested title of the year. We sold 3 near-complete sets and 3 more partial sets, thus most of our variant X-Men inventory is already sold.

DC Comics; Canadian Newsstand VARIANT Cover Price editions (10/1982 thru 09/1988 - Printed in USA) Higher Demand Variant Titles include; *Action Comics* #536-599, *Adventures of Superman* #424-440, *All Star Squadron* #13-67, *America vs. the Justice Society* #1-4, *Aquaman* #1-4, *Batgirl Special* #1, *Batman* #337-423 & Annual 9-12 & Special 1, *Blackhawk* #251-273, *Blue Beetle* #1-24, *Brave and the Bold* #192-200, *Captain Atom* #1-9, *Captain Carrot* #1-20, *Cosmic Boy* #1-4, *Crisis on Infinite Earths* #1-12, *Daring New Adventures of Supergirl* #1-13, *DC Comics Presents* #50-97 & Annual #1-4, *Demon* #1-4, *Detective Comics* #519-590, *Doom Patrol* #1-12 & Annual #1, *Elvira's House of Mystery* #1-11 & Special #1, *Flash* #300-350, *Flash* (Volume-2) #1-18, *Fury of Firestorm* #5-64 & Annual 1-4, *Green Arrow* #1-4, *Green Lantern* #157-224 & Annual #1-3, *Hawkman* #1-17, *Hex* #1-18, *House of Mystery* #309-321, *Jonah Hex* #65-92, *Justice League* #1-16, *Justice League of America* #207-261 & Annual #1-3, *Last Days of the JSA* #1, *Legend of Wonder Woman* #1-4, *Legends* #1-6, *Legion of Super-Heroes* 282-313 & Annual #1-3, *Man of Steel* #1-6, *Masters of the Universe* #1-3, *Millenium* #1-8, *New Adventures of Superboy* #34-54, *New Teen Titans* #18-40 & Annual #2, *Power Girl* #1-4, *Secret Origins* #1-30, *Sgt. Rock* #422 & Annual 3,4, *Shazam* #1-4, *Star Trek* #1-54 & Annual #1-3, *Suicide Squad* #1-16, *Supergirl* #14-23, *Superman* #376-423 & Annual 9-12 & Special 1-3, *Superman* (Volume-2) #1-20 & Annual 1,2, *Super Powers* (Volume-1 #1-5; Volume-2 #1-6; Volume-3 #1-4), *Swamp Thing* #5-59 & Annual 2, *Sword of the Atom* #1-4 & Special 1-3, *Tales of the Legion of Super-Heroes* #314-354 & Annual 4-5, *Tales of the New Teen Titans* #1-4, *Tales of the Teen Titans* #41-91 & Annual #3, *Underworld* #1-4, *Unknown Soldier* #256-268, *V* #1-18, *Warlord* #62-131 & Annual #2-7, *The Weird* #1-4, *World of Krypton* #1-4, *World of Metropolis* #1-4, *World of Smallville* #1-4, *World's Finest* #284-323, *Wonder Woman* (Volume-1) #296-329, *Wonder Woman* (Volume-2) #1-18 (Most Sold at 150% *Guide*).

Canadian Newsstand Variant Print Runs are 10% or less of American issue quantities. Newsstand copies had lower survival rates than Direct editions, thus they are about 50-100 times scarcer than a USA Direct Edition printing, with perhaps an average of 2500 copies each still existing. Because newsstand copies were sold to non-collectors, perhaps 90%, they are in lower grades (GD thru FN). Only a handful of these Variants have even been graded by CGC.

Dates for Canadian Newsstand Cover Price Variants Existing include: Archie comics & Digests (Giant from late 1950s thru mid 60s; and 9/1982-4/1997 with Digest to 12/1997); Charlton (2/1983-8/1984), DC (all Newsstand comics, magazines and digests from 10/1982-9/1988); Dell (6/1956-1-2/1961 = 15 Cent variant; Back Cover variants with strips in place of ads; Giants with 30-35 cent cover prices); Gold Key/ Whitman (5-8/1968, 3/1972-4/1973, 12/1977-3/1978, 1-7/1984); Harvey (1959-3/1974 Giants with 35 Cent cover prices); MAD (some 1964 & 7/1978-7/1979); Marvel (all Newsstand comics, magazines & Digests from 10/1982-8/1986); and Warren (3/1977-3/1983).

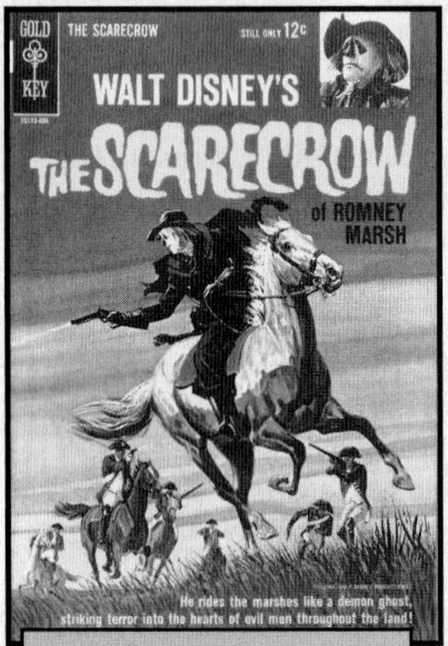

The Scarecrow of Romney Marsh (#1 shown) is one of the most requested of all Disney comics.

UK/British Pence cover price editions (1950s-1980s) of Dell, Marvel, DC, Gold Key and other publishers were published in the USA, but only sold in the UK. These are still being sold at discounted prices by UK dealers. Since these books are actually made in USA, Variants are 50-200+ times scarcer than the USA standard editions, so they should at least sell for the same as USA editions. Currently only the cheaper 1970s issues are bringing a small premium price in the USA. The high priced Silver Age issues are still being discounted and are a real bargain. Comics with the "MARVEL ALL-COLOUR COMICS" banner across the top of the front cover, mostly in the 1974-1980 Bronze Age era, sold at 120-150% *Guide*. The new UK on-line Price Guide by Duncan McAlpine was finally re-released in 10/2010, updating his 1997-98 guide. Duncan lists many "ND" (Not Distributed) periods in UK, where NO copies (USA Printings or UK Printings) were distributed and thus those issues are scarcer overseas.

Walt Disney: Walt Disney comics have been very popular worldwide for at least 60 years, especially the Cartoon titles. This is particularly true in Europe, where comics have less of a stigma and are more ingrained in the cultures of the lands. The Netherlands and Italy have reprinted most of the American comics, and due to their insatiable appetites for more, they have added thousands of new stories in their own original comics. Only a tiny portion of these European originals have seen print in the USA.

Carl Barks and Don Rosa have rock-star like status in certain circles. The childhoods of half the planet Earth were filled with the beloved memories of the Walt Disney movies, books, TV shows, merchandise, cartoons, theme parks and more. I have always been puzzled why the comics are not that popular among comic collectors. Certainly Carl Barks is widely considered one of the Top 10 creators in all of Comics History, with a huge cult following and some of the most valuable Original Art in our hobby. (Barks has always been my #1 favorite.)

This was a better than usual year for sales of Walt Disney comics. We have about 20,000 Walt Disney comics in stock from their many publishers (Dell, Gold Key, Whitman, Gladstone, Disney, March of Comics, Marvel, etc). Especially popular were all the Live Action TV Series and Movie Classic (both Cartoon & Live-Action) comics. Once again, *Scarecrow of Romney Marsh* #1-3 were the most requested of all Disney comics, undervalued in *Guide* and sold out with virtually all dealers. Even the reprint in *WD Showcase* #53 is hard to keep in stock. There has been a similar trend with Walt Disney movies, with Scarce/Rare titles (usually still on VHS, and out of print on DVD) inexplicably up in demand, selling for $25-100+ each on eBay, Amazon, Alibris & various websites (for example: *Almost Angels*, *Charley & the Angel*, *Diamonds on Wheels*, *Dr. Syn alias the Scarecrow**, *Emil and the Detectives**, *Fighting Prince of Donegal**, *Ghosts of Buxley Hall*, *Horsemasters**, *Light in the Forest**, *London Connection*, *Love Leads the Way*, *Scandalous John*, *Smith!*, *Tonka**, and *Westward Ho the Wagons**). Those seven marked with an asterix* have comic adaptations. These rare titles have fueled demand as an alternative source to experience these stories and this has lead non-comic-collectors to our website through Google searches. These buyers loved the comics and came back for many other items, thus we now have new collectors in our hobby. Affordable copies in the FR/GD through FN grades are typically what we have in stock and luckily are also the most popular grades. (VF or better copies are often too pricey & slower sellers).

The pre-1950 Golden Age Disney titles were in low supply and in good steady demand. The 1960s Gold Key titles were in higher demand than the (often more common) 1950s Dell titles. The Four Color one-shot titles were the most requested Dell comics (except for the the nature and science type series). Most notably popular were: *Annette Funicello*, *Brer Rabbit*, cartoon movie classics, Davy Crockett/Fess Parker, *Hardy Boys*, Hayley Mills, *Spin & Marty*, *Tinker Bell* & *Zorro*/ Guy Williams comics. (VF-VF/NM=110-120% *Guide*; GD-FN =120-140% *Guide*).

Warren, Skywald & Misc. Horror Comic Magazines: This year we had an endless stream of requests for affordable Reading Copies (FR/GD, GD and VG) for all the Horror Mag publishers (including Marvel) and had to actually seek out more Low Grade collections. Ten years ago we often had 10-25 copies each in VG or lower grades, but today we now have about 35% of the issues with nothing left under FN, and about 15% with nothing left under VF. The slowest sellers were FN through VF+ copies. There is still good demand for VF/NM or better investment copies (although somewhat diminished from 2007-2009 sales, due to the slow economy). Our stock of VF/NM or better copies has also dropped greatly in the last 4 years and they are getting harder to replace. (FR/GD-VG Reading Copies sold at 125-175% *Guide*. Mid-grade FN through VF+ copies sold at 110-120% *Guide*.) On average the High Grade copies brought these rates: VF/NM at 120-130% *Guide*; raw 9.2 copies at 150% *Guide*; raw 9.4 copies at 200% of 9.2 prices.

I got in a near-complete set of *Famous Monsters of Filmland* #1-130 (many #11-38 in VF to VF/NM, many #39-130 in VF/NM to 9.2) and was pleasantly surprised that we sold almost 50% of them in only 2 months for excellent prices.

Creepy, *Eerie* and *Vampirella* as usual made up 90% of our Warren sales. *Creepy* and *Eerie* are even sellers up to #80, but from #81-up, *Creepy* sells about 50% better than *Eerie*. Creepy stays more true to the one-shot Horror anthology stories; Eerie strays more towards an anthology of alternating on-going series of Sci-Fi, Fantasy, Sword & Sorcery characters. Due to the passing of Frank Frazetta in 2010, demand for everything Frazetta doubled (including calendars, comics, fanzines, mags, paperbacks, posters, portfolios and more). Thus all the Warrens with Frazetta covers were up in demand. *Vampirella* covers by Frazetta were up 100% in demand. Other Warrens with original covers by Frazetta were up 50% in demand. Warrens with reprint covers by Frazetta were up 25% in demand. All Rare and scarcer Warren titles were in constant demand as per usual (at 150-300% *Guide*).

Monster Magazines (*Famous Monster* imitators, film related) are always highly collected. Unfortunately these are not listed in *Overstreet* so they fall off the radar of comic collectors. These always worthwhile collecting and have steadily increased in value over the last 10-20 years. Some of the bestsellers include: *Castle of Frankenstein*, *Famous Monsters*, *Fangoria*, *Fantastic Monsters*, *For Monsters Only*, *Gorezone*, *Horror Monsters*, *Mad Monsters*, *Monsterscene*, *Monster Times*, *Monster World*, *Movie Monsters*, *Quasimodo's Monster Mag*, *Scream Queens*, and *World Famous Creatures*. The 1958-1975 issues are all scarce in strict VF or better (with 1976-1990 issues scarce in VF/NM or better). Prices vary widely from $5-$200+. Most are excellent sellers.

The miscellaneous Horror mags by Eerie Pub, Globe, Hamilton, Major, Modern Day, Stanley, Tempest Pub, and World Famous were in high demand in FR/GD to FN affordable Reading copies. There was resistance to FN/VF through VF+ copies. Investment copies in VF/NM or better, although scarce, were slower sellers this year.

Skywald published only 69 magazines total (*Crime Machine*, *Hell-Rider*, *King*, *Nightmare*, *Psycho* and *Scream*). Due to this small output, they consistently have the fastest turnover of all Horror Mag publishers. These sell great in any and all grades (at 125-150% *Guide*). Once sold, they are hard to re-stock.

Whitman Comics: It has been 9 years (2001) since I put up for eBay auction the rare *Uncle Scrooge* #179(a VG copy sold for $510, and a VF copy sold for $1200) when they still listed at $10 in NM in the *Guide*. In 2003, I auctioned a *Little Lulu* #260(VG, it sold for $710). In 2005, a 9.8 copy of *Lulu* #260 sold for $1827. This started the stampede to collect all the Pre-Pack-Only Whitman Comics (from 8-12/1980, 1983-1984). For about 4-5 years, collectors went wild buying GD-VF copies at 200% to 2000% of *Guide* (especially the scarcer 8-12/1980 issues).

In 2007, the Random House File Copies Archives got dumped on the market all at once. The Gold Key comics and more common Whitmans had 100 each or more on many issues. There was also a smaller selection of 8-12/1980 issues (smaller quantities of 0-25 copies each), with many issues still having ZERO copies among the File Copy collection. This all has stalled the market a while, but virtually all the scarcer issues have already been absorbed into the Marketplace. The number of CGC-Graded Pre-Pack Whitmans in 8.0 through 9.4 increased by 200%-300% over the last 3 years. Suddenly they stopped appearing, and there is once again a shortage of the Pre-Pack issues (especially 8-12/1980). It is now estimated that the 8-12/1980 Pre-Pack issues have an average of 100-250 copies each still existing, while the 1983-1984 issues have about 250-500 copies each existing. There are 47 different RARE 75¢ Canadian Variant cover price editions existing (U.S. copies were 60¢), all from 1984, with an estimated 75-150 copies each still existing. They sell fast at 200-300% of regular 60¢ edition prices. In the 1980's these issues were all thought to be Very Rare and were on everyone's want lists: *Buck Rogers* #10, *Popeye* #160,161, *Porky Pig* #99, *Woody Woodpecker* #192 (but by 2005 it was found that they were NOT printed and do NOT exist). Whitman printed at least 31 Direct Market White Logo Variants from 1981-82 (they sell for 150% of standard Yellow Logo regular editions). Nine 40¢ Whitman Reverse Variants exist of 50¢ Whitman comics (11/1980-1/1981) selling at around 200% of the standard 50¢ edition prices. Most Whitman variant collectors prefer raw, non-CGC copies (with the exception of the issues that *Guide* over $100).

About 69% of all Gold Key comics published from 11/1971 through 2/1980 are proven to exist as Whitman Variant Editions (5-50 times scarcer than regular GK printings). This has proven to be one of the toughest Variant sets to complete in its entirety and only a few are trying. A lot more Variant collectors are seeking to complete their favorite titles or genres. Adventure, Horror, SF and TV titles sell at 150-200% of GK issue values). Cartoon titles sell at 125-150% of GK issue values.

I present the Complete List of 67, now legendary Scarce to Rare 8-12/1980 Whitman Comics. I have added the current quantities so far graded by CGC, according to their 12/2010 Census: *Battle of the Planets* #7(10/1980; x32), #8(11/1980; x24), #9(12/1980; x28); *Beep Beep the Road Runner* #91(8/1980; x4), #92(9/1980; x4), #93(10/1980; x5); *Black Hole* #4(9/1980; x2); *Buck Rogers in the 25th Century* #8(11/1980; x2), #9(12/1980; x8); *Bugs Bunny*

#221(9/1980; x16), #222(11/1980; x4); *Chip 'N' Dale* #67(8/1980; x5), #68(11/1980; x7), #69(12/1980; x10); *Daffy Duck* #129(8/1980; x4), #130(1980; x8), #131(12/1980; x8); *Daisy and Donald* #45(8/1980; x3), #46(10/1980; x5), #47(12/1980; x16); *Donald Duck* #221(8/1980; x7), #222 (10/1980; x19), #223(11/1980; x15), #224(12/1980; x13); *Flash Gordon* #30(10/1980; x5); *Huey, Dewey and Louie Junior Woodchucks* #65(9/1980; x3), #66(11/1980; x7); *Little Lulu* #260(9/1980; x33), #261(11/1980; x23); *Looney Tunes* #33(8/1980; x7), #34(1980; x14), #35(1980; x11); *Mickey Mouse* #207 (8/1980; x7), #208(10/1980; x18), #209(12/1980; x4); *Pink Panther* #75(8/1980; x8), #76(101980; x16), #77(12/1980; x16); *Popeye* #158(9/1980; x7), #159(11/1980; x5); *Porky Pig* #97(9/1980; x11), #98(11/1980; x18); *Super Goof* #60(7/1980; x10), #61(9/1980; x16), #62(11/1980; x3); *Tom and Jerry* #330(8/1980; x3), #331(10/1980; x7), #332(12/1980; x12); *Tweety and Sylvester* #105(9/1980; x10), #106(10/1980; x5), #107(11/1980; x6); *Uncle Scrooge* #179(9/1980; x44), #180(11/1980; x11), #181(12/1980; x13); *Walt Disney's Comics and Stories* #479(8/1980; x4), #480(9/1980; x19), #481(10/1980; x5), #482(11/1980; x9), #483(12/1980; x7); *Winnie the Pooh* #20(8/1980; x2), #21(10/1980; x4), #22(1980; x10); *Woody Woodpecker* #190(10/1980; x13), #191(11/1980; x3); *Yosemite Sam* #68(9/1980; x7), #69(10/1980; x21), #70(12/1980; x5); Take note that there are still 20 different issues with 5 or less copies graded by CGC. The Big-4 (*Donald* #222, *Lulu* #260, *Scrooge* #179, *WDC&S* #480) have been well known tough-to-find issues for 30 years. They were the first to bring record prices on eBay, and thus now listing relatively high in the *Guide*. A disproportionate number of copies have been CGC graded, but they are still scarce and in huge demand in spite of what the skewed CGC quantities would indicate. *Battle of the Planets* #7-9 have more copies slabbed than other titles, as many dealers judge them as a "better" title and more worthwhile to slab. Sales on the 8-12/1980 issues were up by over 50% this year and we are once again starting to sell out on most issues. Lower grade copies are undervalued and in demand; (GD-FN = 150-200% *Guide*; VF-NM- = 125-150% *Guide*).

The above list gives an idea what is the most scarce in high grade (although I suspect a lot of VF or better copies valued at $30 or less in the *Guide* have not yet been submitted to CGC, as they are judged by dealers as not yet being worth the costs of certification.

Currently the 37 rarest 8-12/1980 Whitmans in ANY Condition are (in alphabetical order): *Beep Beep Roadrunner* #92,93, *Black Hole* #4, *Buck Rogers* #8, *Chip 'N' Dale* #67-69, *Daffy Duck* #130,131, *Daisy & Donald* #47, *Donald Duck* #221,222, *Huey Dewey Louie* #65,66, *Little Lulu* #260,261, *Looney Tunes* #33-35, *Mickey Mouse* #208,209, *Popeye* #158,159, *Super Goof* #62, *Tom & Jerry* #330,331, *Tweety & Sylvester* #105,107, *Uncle Scrooge* #179, *Walt Disney's Comics & Stories* #479,480, *Winnie the Pooh* #20-22, *Woody Woodpecker* #191 and *Yosemite Sam* #68,70. It's estimated that 100-150 copies each exist in the current marketplace.

Marvel Whitman Variants DO NOT exist. They are actually low print run early DIRECT Market variant editions from the 1977-1979 era (see page 1033 of Overstreet #40).

Whitman Variant editions of DC Comics are about 20-50 times scarcer than standard DC printings and are still in high demand among Variant collectors (at 150-200% *Guide*). Only a small quantity have so far been graded by CGC and they remain scarce in strict VF or better.

Chris Swartz
Collector

Now that 2010 is almost over we can reflect on the comic book market of the past year and talk about what a crappy movie *Jonah Hex* turned out to be, even with Megan Fox playing a hooker. 2010 had a lot of ups and downs in the comic book market. Record prices were realized for *Action Comics* #1 (CGC 8.5 $1,500,000) and *Detective Comics* #27 (CGC 8.0 $1,075,500) well above any previous prices for any comic book. However, the economy is still in the toilet, which has lead to the continued decline in comic prices for almost all non-key books and some keys, from all ages. The biggest areas to be affected have been high grade CGC graded books from the Modern to Bronze Age. People are no longer willing to spend outlandish prices to obtain a 9.4 or above on books like *Fantastic Four* #150. Many CGC graded books from the Bronze thru Modern Age sell for less than the cost of slabbing the books. Considering the majority of high grade books from the Bronze Age have been pressed, these high graded books are no longer elusive in high grades. Collectors are more often than not, opting to buy raw books in VF or above from these eras, for less than *Guide* value.

The only books from 2010 that I believe deserve a price increase are Golden and Silver Age keys in un-restored condition. All other books have been selling at or below *Guide* value. I think if the overall economic conditions continue in a downward spiral, this comic market trend will continue in 2011.

Golden Age - DC: The series with the most demand have remained the same for years: *Action Comics* #1-23, *Detective Comics* #27-40, 140, *Batman* #1-5, 11, *Superman* #1-14, *All-American* #16-20, 61, *Wonder Woman* #1-6, *All Star Comics* #3, 8, and *More Fun Comics* #52,55,73. They are selling well in all grades. Pre-Robin *Detectives* #28-37 and Superman *Action* covers (#7, 10, 13, 15, 23) always sell well above *Guide* value in any grade and condition. All of these *Detective* and *Action Comics* issues demand a price increase of at least 25% from last year's value. While numerous copies of issues such as *All-American Comics* #16 and *Adventure Comics* #40 have sold during 2010, most of them have been restored and have sold at a fraction of their un-restored counterparts.

Golden Age - Timely/Marvel: *Captain America Comics* #1-8, 16, 46 (Holocaust cover), 74 have sold very well during the past year. The hottest Timely comic of the past year was *Marvel Mystery Comics* #9. The copies sold within the past year have sold for multiple times *Guide* value. *Sub-Mariner Comics* #1 has had a huge increase in demand along with *All-Select Comics* #1. Supply for *Marvel Comics* #1 has exceeded demand and has decreased the value of this issue drastically. If you have ever wanted to own this book, now would be your best opportunity without having to work three jobs to afford it.

All Other Golden Age: Good Girl cover art books continue to sell without a problem with *Blue Beetle* #54 and *Phantom Lady* #17 leading the way. *Whiz Comics* #1 has sold for well less than *Guide* value during the past few years, so now would be the best time to pick up this issue for a reasonable price. If a *Shazam!* movie is ever given the green light, expect future prices to reflect the demand of this issue from collectors and investors.

© MAR

The upcoming Avengers movie has **Avengers #4** in strong demand.

Silver Age - Marvel: *Amazing Fantasy* #15 is still the most desirable Silver Age key, but prices have stabilized from recent years. *Incredible Hulk* #1 and *Journey Into Mystery* #83 are the other most demanded Marvel issues, selling above *Guide* value in all conditions, with lowered graded copies selling for a premium. *Amazing Spider-Man* #1, *Fantastic Four* #1, *X-Men* #1, and *Tales of Suspense* #39 have all sold around or below *Guide* value in all grades, except high grade (VF & above), which sell for well above *Guide* value. *Avengers* #1 and #4 have been in strong demand the past year with the *Avengers* movie on the horizon. The two Marvel keys that I think are the most undervalued are *Sgt. Fury and his Howling Commandos* #1 (1st Nick Fury) & *Strange Tales* #110 (1st Dr. Strange). The time to pick up these keys in high grade is now, before the market catches up with them.

Silver Age - DC: The two hottest DC books from this area are *Showcase* #4 (1st Silver Age Flash) and *Brave and the Bold* #28 (1st JLA). Both of these books are highly undervalued and are on the verge of exploding. Considering the importance of these DC keys and their value in relation to Marvel keys of the same era, these books are relative steals. *Green Lantern* #1, 7 and *Showcase* #22 have sold quite well, but have stabilized from the prices that were fetched last year.

Bronze Age - Marvel: Most keys such as *Incredible Hulk* #181, *Amazing Spider-Man* #129, and *Marvel Spotlight* #5 are easily obtainable and sell for around *Guide* value, except in high grade, which still sell for above *Guide*. Demand for these books in high grade is still strong, but with more issues being pressed and graded at 9.4 and above, the prices will start to drop. *Giant Size X-Men* #1 and *X-Men* #94 have sold well below *Guide* value in all grades with supply exceeding demand.

Bronze Age - DC: High grade copies of *Green Lantern* #76 (9.0 or above) have continued to sell above *Guide* value. Other DC keys in high demand include: *All-Star Western* #10 (even though the movie was horrible), *Batman* #227, 232, 234, and *Detective* #400.

San Diego Comic-Con: The 2010 Comic-Con was definitely better then 2009. Myself, along with my friend and fellow advisor Jamie Newbold (owner of Southern California Comics), were able to acquire a large *Detective Comics* run #32-80 that were part of Jerry Robinson's personal collection while working at DC. All of the books were signed by Mr. Robinson and CGC graded. While the amount of people that attend Comic-Con seems to increase, the amount of actual dealers that have booths at the show seems to dwindle each year. This is something that I would like to see change within the years to come. The San Diego Comic-Con originated from the gathering of back-issue comic book dealers into one place as a way for collectors to buy and talk about comics, and that, it seems, is something which with the Comic-Con has started to lose touch. I hope the city of San Diego and the Comic-Con administrators can come to a suitable agreement, because changing the venue from San Diego to another city would affect the total experience of attending Comic-Con, and not in a positive way.

Here are some notable books that I have sold or purchased within 2010:

Action Comics #15 CGC 3.5 $2,400
Detective Comics #30 CGC 5.5 $4,500
Detective Comics #32 CGC 2.0 (Signature Series Jerry Robinson) $1,100
Detective Comics #33 CGC 0.5 (complete, cover split and detached) $2,500
Detective Comics #34 CGC 1.8 $750
Detective Comics #37 CGC 1.0 $1,700
Detective Comics #39 CGC 2.0 $800
Detective Comics #39 CGC 1.0 (Signature Series Jerry Robinson) $400
Detective Comics #140 CGC 4.0 $1,500
Detective Comics #140 CGC 5.0 $2,000
Amazing Fantasy #15 CGC 1.8 (Signature Series Stan Lee) $2,700
X-Men #1 CGC 3.5 (Signature Series Stan Lee) $1,700
Captain America Comics #2 CGC 4.5 $3,500
Batman #55 CGC 5.5 $450
Batman #181 CGC 8.0 $260
Batman #232 CGC 9.2 $400
More Fun Comics #55 CGC 1.0 $1,200

Well, the best advice I can give to collectors is that if you are out of college and you still live in your parents' basement, maybe you should rethink your priorities, because you're giving the rest of us collectors a bad rap. Also, if you plan on attending any comic book show, please put on some deodorant as a common courtesy. Until next year, stay fanboys my friends.

Michael Tierney Collector's Edition & The Comic Book Store

While 2010 made big news with multiple Million Dollar book sales, in my market high ticket sales were the worst I've ever seen. But that doesn't mean that back issues weren't selling. This year ushered in a fundamental shift in what customers were buying. Back issue sales were no longer driven by collectors buying key issues, and became more driven by readers filling in the gaps of the story. Sales actually increased by nearly 20 percent over the year before for some months, but it was mostly Seventies and Eighties comics with price tags less than New Comic cover prices, which tells you that I sold a bunch of them! From the Dark Age of the Nineties, Marvel and DC were selling in that same price range, but nothing else moved from that period.

When I did sell a high dollar book, it didn't move until discounted during a sale. This is exemplified by the fact that my highest dollar back issue sale was a copy of *Brave & the Bold* #28, introducing the Justice League, in GD- because of a loose center page, for only $300. DC comics also had the next top sale with *Adventure Comics* #214, featuring the 2nd appearance of Krypto, in Fine+ for $190.

Disney Duck artist Carl Barks has always stayed in demand, with the sale of a couple of Donald Duck *Four Colors*, #408 and #422, both in Fine for $55 each. And early Jesse Marsh Dell *Tarzans* were moving. Sold #9 in VG- for $40, #25 in FN- for $42, #26 in FN- for $40, and *Tarzan's Jungle Annual* #1 in FN+ for $55.

My top Marvel back issue sale was a copy of *X-Men* #94 in VG+ for $80. While I did move some non-Super Hero Marvels, like *Patsy Walker* #26 in VG for $22.50. Marvel key sales have been trending downward for a while now, but this was a record low year.

The only real surprise was the reemergence of some interest for Western comics. Example sales were The Rebels (*Four Color* #1076) in VF for $25, Restless Gun (*Four Color* #1045) in VG for $20, and *Saddle Justice* #7 in GD+ for $17. It wasn't a lot of demand, but in a tough year it was a welcome surprise.

Thanks to a diversity of content, the old Dell *Four Color* comics kept moving, as you can tell by some of the key sales mentioned.

The economic woes of the local economy continued to get even worse this year, and put a lot of pressure on consumer buying not only in the area of old comics, but even more on new comics. New comics hit a record low in 2010, with at least one month where not a single comic had a print run of over 100,000. While this might make for some hot books in short supply in the future, it's rough to be a retailer right now.

In 2008, the #1 selling comic was the *Amazing Spider-Man* #583, thanks to the variants with the President Obama cover. This led to a number of other comics featuring Obama. But by 2010, things had changed, and I couldn't sell a single copy of 2008's hottest comic.

The industry did try repeating certain gimmicks to get interest percolating. In 2009 DC offered retailer incentives of Blackest Night giveaway rings, one for each color of lantern in the series; Green, Violet, Red, Blue, Indigo, Orange, Yellow, and Black. If a retailer qualified, customers got a specific ring with certain book purchases. The rings were hugely popular, as was Blackest Night.

In 2010, DC did another promotion by offering a Flash, White Lantern, and more Green Lantern rings for their sequel series; *Brightest Day*. These rings helped the series have a hugely successful launch and *Brightest Day* would remain a top seller throughout the year, but reader reactions were mostly disappointment. Spinoffs like *Birds of Prey* and *Green Arrow* were better received.

DC hit a home run with the original graphic novel, *Superman: Earth One*, where they skipped making periodicals and went straight for bookstore shelves.

© DC

Giveaway rings helped Brightest Day #0 have a huge launch.

While the *Iron Man 2* movie did well in theaters, it didn't provide any kind of bounce at all for the comics. The same was true for DC's *Jonah Hex* movie, which hexed the comic book.

Marvel's event books had their problems, as *Siege* experienced delay problems at the end, which caused a sharp sales falloff. The delays continued with the end of the Daredevil themed Shadowland event. And while the Fall of the Hulk's mystery of 'Who is the Red Hulk?' finally revealed the Red Hulk to be General Ross, and the Red She-Hulk to be his daughter Betty, no one cared. After teasing readers for a couple years, Marvel far exceeded the expiration of customer expectation.

But it wasn't all bad for Marvel. The *Avengers* relaunch was a strong seller, and *X-Men: Second Coming* was a hit.

Aside from the economy, the new comics industry encountered four core problems in 2010. Prices continuing to escalate across the line to $3.99 was the biggest problem, which publishers finally recognized by the end of the year and started scaling back to a $2.99 price point for 2011. Throughout the year I saw an incredible number of single copy sales, which had never happened before. Usually customers bought their comics in bunches. And even worse was when they'd slap down a credit card for that single copy, which meant that the credit card processors were the only ones making a profit. In my market, cash was scarce.

The number of titles shipping late seemed to get better, but it was still a sporadic problem. More endemic was uneven shipping, with light weeks at the start of the month, and an avalanche of product at the end. Customer's budgets couldn't handle this, and so they kept their spending habits from the light weeks, meaning that any new titles released in the latter part of the month was doomed. Marvel was the worst about this, until after their purchase by Disney. Then, later in the year, DC seemed to pick up where they left off.

Another problem was the late shipping caused by Monday holidays. You never disrupt your customer's shopping habits, and in a tough economy, the negative effects escalated. So many customers just skipped to the next week, and like with the product dumping at the end of the month, only spent that week's budget, once again meaning any new titles were doomed. Since the majority of comics are new titles, this made for real trouble. Fortunately, this problem was also recognized, and with 2011 changes were made to ensure that Wednesday is now New Comics Day each and every week, with no exceptions. That sound you hear in the distance is me clapping my approval.

The Fourth, and biggest, problem is the lack of a uniform Target Audience Guideline system for identifying content, like every other visual media already does. Marvel has one, but DC doesn't. The Independent publishers are a mixed bag, mostly going with 'either it's mature, or it's not.' The problem with this is that it was a huge missed opportunity, because in 2010 I saw huge numbers of new readers coming in, wanting to start the hobby of collecting comics. The ongoing wave of comic-related movies had a lot to do with this, as popular culture's embrace of comics grew ever stronger. There was even a TV reference where a character commented that saying he owned a comic book store was a sure fire way to pick up girls. Okay, the show was *Big Bang Theory*, and he was talking about ComicCon, but still...

Heavy media coverage of events like ComicCon was yet another source of new interest. It was a record year for new readers walking through the door. The catch was that all of the new readers were preteens being brought in by their parents, and all of mainstream comics are targeted at teen-agers or older. The only teen-agers buying comics are the ones who got hooked on the hobby as preteens. So, when the parents were trying to buy comics for their children, they ran into an information wall -- as in lack thereof. We did everything we could to guide these potential new shoppers, and the ones who returned were those who benefited most from our guidance. But many times the parents would be influenced more by what their children wanted than our suggestions, and when they later found those choices to be inappropriate, they weren't seen again. The lack of a Uniform Rating System is a huge missed opportunity for growing the sales of new comics. The interest is there, but the problem is that while comics have matured, we haven't matured in the packaging.

Kids today love comics just as much as they ever have. This year's Halloween on the Hill at my North Little Rock store was bigger than ever, as we gave away several thousand ashcan comics and 50 pounds of candy. The official crowd estimate was only 1200, but as always we kept getting hit two and three times again by the same Trick-or-Treaters. They just kept coming back for more -- which proves that comics are brain candy!

The industry addressed and made corrections in 2010 on three of the four biggest problems facing the sale of new comics. Hopefully the fourth and biggest problem of all will finally be up for correction. I've always said that new comic sales influence what sells old, and that was never more evident than this year.

Harley Yee
Harley Yee Rare Comics

The 2010 market continued many trends from 2009 with high grade Marvels and Marvel keys being the top sellers. With more movies coming in 2011 with many mainline heroes like Thor and Captain America, this will continue for 2011. Top sellers continue to be *Amazing Spider-Man*, *Thor* and *Iron Man*.

DC Golden Age remained steady in 2010 with top sellers *Batman*, *Action Comics* and *Wonder Woman*. DC Silver Age remains scarce and in high demand.

Timely prices have remained steady during 2010 with *Captain America Comics* and related titles being the top sellers.

Nedors have been strong for many years with War covers always selling out.

Early Archie stuff has always been scarce, but recently has seen a surge in prices with early *Pep* issues setting record prices.

Prices for mainline Horror and ECs have remained relatively inexpensive compared with other Golden Age, so demand has remained steady.

Fiction House has been steady with the early issues. Issues of *Fight Comics* and *Rangers Comics* are selling the quickest.

Fawcetts have remained relatively steady with *Master* and *Mary Marvel* issues the best sellers.

CGC books are continuing to grow in the overall marketplace as more books get graded. As the internet has become a more important part of the overall market, this will continue into 2011.

2011 should continue all these trends as the economy rebounds and the "baby boomers" become more active in the market.

Vincent Zurzolo, Frank Cwiklik & Rob Reynolds Metropolis/ComicConnect.com

Vincent Zurzolo - Metropolis Collectibles, Inc.

I love comic books. I have ever since I was a little kid. I still get excited when I open up a new or old comic book, waiting to see what is in store for me. Dynamic art, intriguing plots, compelling dialogue, twist endings… I just can't wait! Having passion in your life is so vitally important. I have been in the comic book business for over 24 years and it is still fun and exciting for me. I hope you feel the same way.

2010 has been a stellar year for me both on a personal and professional level. On May 29th, my fiancé Josephine and I were married at a beautiful Church in Midtown Manhattan. We moved into our new home in the city this past spring as well. And as of this writing, yes, we are still unpacking. Professionally speaking, business has never been better. We had our best year to date. I don't write this to sound boastful, as I realize how tough the economy has been the last few years. I am very grateful for the success we have had and I thank all who have patronized our business. To you all, a very sincere thank you. We will continue to strive to improve our business every day to meet your needs.

I believe, in part, one of the reasons Metropolis has had such a good year is due to the unparalleled level of publicity and marketing success we have had. Because of major sales, acquisitions and our general standing as an industry leader, we have appeared in newspapers, magazines, online articles, TV news programs, documentaries and even the TV show *Hollywood Treasures*. Through this barrage of publicity, people who have never purchased a comic book before are made aware of a new market for investment. They also want to know more about comics, collectors and their stories.

People love to tell their stories, whether they are buying or selling their comic books. Oftentimes, the story of the collector rivals the story inside the comic book itself. People's experiences with their collections have tremendous value. For example, take the Suscha News Pedigree Collection we found this past summer. It consisted of over 40 boxes of comic books, mostly Marvels, published between 1965-1977. What makes this collection so special to me is the story of the original owner. This man bought his books from a store called Suscha News in Sheboygan, Wisconsin. He made a deal with the store which enabled him to hand-pick all the books straight out of the distributor boxes before they ever made it to the newsstand. That is simply astounding and the first time I have ever heard of anything like this happening. Not only did he buy the best copies he could find, but then he held onto them for the next 45 years in virtually the same pristine condition until he was ready to sell. Throughout the decades, he made three major moves across country and dealt with countless challenges to keep the collection intact. So far, the reaction from comic collecting veterans and rookies alike who have seen the Suscha News Pedigree has been overwhelmingly positive.

The sale of this CGC-certified 9.4 copy of **Fantastic Four #1** for $300,000 was not too shabby.

Though our sister site ComicConnect.com grabs most of the attention with record breaking sales like the first comic to break a million dollars (*Action* #1 8.0) and our current world record of $1.5 million for the highest graded *Action Comics* #1 (8.5) the sales at Metropolis haven't been too shabby either. Here are some highlights: *Detective Comics* #27 CGC 6.0 $575,000, *Action Comics* #1 CGC 5.0 $465,000, *Fantastic Four* #1 CGC 9.4 $300,000, *Detective Comics* #27 CGC 3.5 $240,000, *Action Comics* #7 CGC 7.0 $175,000, *Amazing Fantasy* #15 CGC 9.0 $150,000, *Superman* #1 CGC 4.5 $90,000, *Superman* #2 CGC 9.2 $85,000, *Action Comics* #1 Ashcan CGC 9.0 $50,000, *Tales of Suspense* #39 CGC 9.2 $49,750, and *Detective Comics* #27 CGC 4.5 restored $44,500. Nobody gets better prices for key Golden and Silver Age comics than Metropolis and I think more record-breaking sales are just around the corner.

As evidenced by these sales, you can see that the vintage comic book market is strong. Key Golden and Silver Age comics are doing very well. But not all is rosy in the world of comic books. More common late Silver and Bronze Age issues have seen a reduction in price. With more high-grade issues coming into the market place, it will take some time for demand to catch up and prices to rebound. Based on past analysis I do believe that most of the prices will come back, so don't be too concerned. However, it may take some time, so remember, patience is a virtue.

As I mentioned above I really do love comic books. I read them as often as I can. If you are an investor putting your hard earned money into comics, it is still important to take time to read them. Recently, I read *Captain America Comics* #1-5 and *Fantastic Four* #1-10. The *Caps* hearken back to the early days of comics. Oftentimes the stories are basic "good guy beats up bad guy", but the art, WWII stories, Cap, Bucky and the Red Skull make it all worthwhile. *FF* #1-10 recapture a simpler time in comics. The stories are fun, and the originality of Kirby and Lee's creations ring as true today as they did then.

I've also had a chance to read the entire *Walking Dead Compendium*. This encompassed about five years of stories. I had a hard time putting it down. It was extremely graphic at times, but what else would you expect from a post apocalyptic zombie filled story? What really sets the series apart is the intense characterization, believable dialogue between people stuck in a horrible situation, and the observations Kirkman makes about human nature when people are put to the test.

Reading *Detective Comics* between issues #460 and #490 was very interesting for me as the stories seem as relevant today as they were almost 25 years ago. Stories about Islamic terrorists and illegal immigration could have been written just yesterday. It really made me think about how much and how little progress we have made over the last three decades.

In closing, yes Marvels are still hot, *Amazing Fantasy* #15 still sells really well and high grade DCs are tough to get. Let's see what's in store for us in 2011 when *Thor*, *Green Lantern*, *X-Men: First Class* and *Captain America* hit the movie theaters. Something is telling me 2011 will be a big year for comic books. Thanks for reading!

Frank Cwiklik - Metropolis Collectibles

It's been a tumultuous and hectic time for everyone these past few years, with changes coming almost daily, and the comic business has been no exception. However, many of these changes have allowed for new frontiers and new opportunities for comics dealers and collectors, and some of these changes have even allowed for some old methods and styles to come back into play. With the influx of new buyers, and the shift in interest from older collectors, previously moribund titles are now selling, and the sky seems to be the limit for hot key titles if you play your cards right. "May you live in interesting times", indeed!

While we are doing very well with top tier vintage comic books we're also returning to an old-school style of comic book retail. Many of our customers are completists looking for scarce books to finish their runs or new buyers who are building their collections with care and eagerness, looking for great deals and books that speak to them.

We've had quite a few customers come back into the fold, excited and energized by the action and heat generated by the record breaking prices in the vintage comic market. Plus, so many new books and collections come into our showroom that we're restocking our inventory to meet demand. With so many new collections coming in it's hard to keep up!

I've become the go-to guy for sorting new collections and separating out inventory selections from overstock. This puts me in a unique position to see the shift in customer interest, both from a sales perspective and from an inventory perspective. When I'm sorting through boxes and checking against our current stock, I'm surprised to see how many supposedly "dead" books need to be restocked because they are selling again. Off-grade Bronze Marvel, Silver Age DC, mid-grade pre-code Horror, all books that would have gathered dust years ago are selling well now, if priced a little below *Guide*. My client base has diversified dramatically and I'm now regularly talking to customers who are buying books simply for pleasure or on a budget. Collectors who would have been squeezed out of the market a few years ago are now happily shopping on our site as the bigger collectors and investors climb up to spend their time buying high grade books almost exclusively. This has helped our business as we are seeing an increase in interest in a broader spectrum of vintage comic books. New buyers are stepping into the marketplace as investment buyers move into specialized territory. It's exciting and refreshing, and a good sign for long-term growth in the market.

That's not to say we're not still selling keys and scarce high-ticket items. *Amazing Fantasy* #15 is still the unstoppable monster key, and we sold a really nice unrestored 9.0 CGC copy at this year's San Diego con for $150,000 -- nothing wrong with that! Mid-grade and lower-grade copies are still roaring along as well, with 5.0s selling in the $10K range, 6.0 copies selling at $17K, and a 6.5 CGC selling for $25,000 – healthy increases in value, all.

Also, my prediction about Wonder Woman holds true, as we sold not one, but two *Sensation Comics* #1s at San Diego this year, which is a great treat for a shameless Wonder Woman fanboy like me! San Diego also saw sales of the Rockford *Detective* #84 CGC 9.4 $3,650.00, the "D" Copy of *House of Mystery* #1 CGC 8.5 $2,000.00 and a *Fantastic Four* #48 CGC 9.6 $4,750.00 amongst others.

Convention sales in general this year were still not quite as intense as some past years, but certainly a step up from last year, and very strong in light of the slowly recovering economy. Reed's first C2E2 show in Chicago was a pleasure to work at, and while not quite at the sales level of San Diego or NYCC, it was still a very promising start, and I think hosting the show in Chicago proper is a great idea. The success of Wizard's venerable Chicago Comic Con in August proves that the Midwest can support 2 monster cons. I think between Reed's muscle and Wizard's expertise, we can bring the coastal convention magic to comic fans who can't make the trip to the other two big shows.

New York Comic Con is growing exponentially year by year. There's no getting around the fact that they put on a heck of a show. This year's show was busier than I have ever seen and shows the interest in comic books and pop culture is ever-increasing. I can't recommend the show enough to anyone who hasn't yet been, as it is, like NYC itself, a very unique phenomenon. Our sales were very healthy and we were nonstop busy. We sold *Captain America Comics* #46 CGC 8.5 for $11,700.00, the Rockford Pedigree *Detective* #38 CGC 6.5 for $10,000.00, a *Giant-Size X-Men* #1 CGC 9.6 for $3,000.00 and a *Sensation Comics* #1 CGC 5.0 for $7,000.00. Score another win for Wonder Woman!

The Wizard Big Apple Convention was strong. Filled with familiar faces and longtime clients stopping by to make purchases sales were healthy. It never ceases to amaze me that we meet brand new customers at the Big Apple Con. I'm also heartened to see at least one or two little tykes stopping at our booth and being able to identify the superheroes by name. A new generation of comic collectors is being born right before our very eyes.

The comic community is still taking its cues from Hollywood. With the upcoming *Green Lantern* and *Thor* movies making their way to cinemas soon, previously dead keys and issues of those series have become popular again. *Green Lantern* #7, the first appearance of Sinestro, which has always been a tough book in general has become increasingly popular. *Journey into Mystery* #83 has always been in demand, but is now on every speculator's must-watch list. And, with the upcoming *Avengers* and *Captain America* movies, *Avengers* #1, 4 and really any early *Avengers* in high grade are solid sellers.

Other than what I have mentioned already, it's challenging to list many specific books or trends to watch mostly because it's become such a varied and unusual market. What I can tell you is that I have a feeling the next trend is going to come out of nowhere as there's no single magic bullet anymore. New buyers and old are getting back into buying books that thrill them, please them and excite them. That is a good thing as that is what the hobby is all about anyway. While we've attracted more big time collectors who are hungrily devouring key books and setting record sales prices at auction, much of our day-to-day business is coming from clients buying stacks of Richie Rich keys for their Harvey fan friends; Katy Keene fans spending their money on reliving their childhoods with old issues of *Pep* or other Archie books; Batman fans building mid-grade runs of *Detective* and *Batman* Golden Age issues simply for the joy of reading them; and even newer collectors discovering the graphic, gory, glory of Biro crime books and snapping up group lots of *Crime Does Not Pay* for fun and entertainment. There's no obvious trend anymore, and I find that very energizing. While the glory and attention are being (understandably) paid to the big, top dollar sales, the underlying stability of the business can be seen with these smaller but still very committed collectors, who, in the midst of a recession are rediscovering the simple pleasures of the hobby and passing them on to other fans young and old.

I'm looking forward to hearing from more of them in the coming year, both on the phone and online, and meeting them all at convention time. Maybe that's you! Anyone who wants to know more, or would like our help in filling your want list, or building your collection, please feel free to contact me at orders@metropoliscomics.com or call 1-800-229-METRO (international 001-212-260-4147) – I'm always happy to help collectors old and new!

Rob Reynolds - ComicConnect.com

According to the *Guinness World Records* book, at 8 feet 11 inches, Robert Wadlow was the tallest man in medical history. Robert Hughes, tipping the scales at 1070 pounds, held the *Guinness* record for the world's heaviest man. In 2010, I, Robert Reynolds, had the pleasure of being on the team that sold the world's most expensive comic book for $1.5 Million. ComicConnect.com's achievement of landing squarely on the pages of the *Guinness World Records* book is the realization of a life-long dream.

This past year was indeed one for the record books at ComicConnect.com. In February, ComicConnect.com was the first to ever sell a comic book for 7 figures, with the $1 Million sale of *Action Comics* #1 CGC 8.0 VF. In the following month, ComicConnect.com made the record breaking sale of the *Action Comics* #1 CGC 8.5 VF+ for $1.5 Million. The phones rang night and day while my e-mail inbox went from orderly to much less so. Reporters from all over the world wanted interviews, and ComicConnect.com was offered Superman comics in a dozen different languages. Everyone wanted something, and surprisingly it was all amazingly positive.

With the worlds' economy in shambles, folks were losing their careers, their life-savings, and their homes. After sifting through thousands of phone calls and e-mails, the call we were waiting for came in. This call was about a comic, but it was a comic that came with a story that was told over family dinners, in diners, and at water coolers across the country and around the world. A family dealing with their house being foreclosed upon was packing up in the basement, and came across a box of Grandpa's old comics that had rested untouched for years. Inside, a copy of *Action Comics* #1 that was later certified 5.0 VG/FN by CGC. ComicConnect.com sold the comic at auction for $436,000, saving the family's home and leaving them with plenty of money left over.

Good ol' Archie Andrews was the surprise of the year for us when a copy of *Pep Comics* #22 CGC 5.0 VG/FN (Archie's first appearance) sold at auction. This was one of the few comics we auctioned where we really had no idea what the market would bear. And boy did it bear to the tune of $50,000. This sale of the *Pep* directly led to the sale of a copy of *Archie Comics* #1 CGC 5.0 VG/FN for $34,000 in our very next ComicConnect.com Event Auction. Buyers, by far, outstrip supply for these books and I highly recommend the purchase of any mid to high grade Archies that you can get your hands on.

With a total of six *Action Comics* #1 sales this year, totaling more than all other auction houses in the world combined, ComicConnect.com is truly the place for consignors and bidders to meet and trade the best of the best.

Noteworthy Golden Age comic sales:
Action Comics #1 CGC 8.5 VF+ $1,500,000
Action Comics #1 CGC 8.0 VF $1,000,000
Action Comics #1 CGC 5.0 VG/FN $436,000
Action Comics #1 CGC 3.0 G/VG $300,000
Action Comics #1 CGC 1.8 G- $116,000
Action Comics #1 Coverless $13,311
Action Comics #2 CGC 5.5 FN- Rockford Copy $19,200
All-Winners #19 CGC 8.5 VF+ $7,500
Archie Comics #1 CGC 5.0 VG/FN $34,000
Batman #1 CGC 1.5 FA/G $11,800
Batman #2 CGC 9.2 NM- $43,000
Batman #9 CGC 9.4 NM $15,000
Captain America Comics #2 CGC 8.5 VF+ $21,500
Detective Comics #27 CGC 7.5 VF-(R) $97,500
Detective Comics #28 CGC 7.5 VF- $35,000

Detective Comics #31 CGC 7.5 VF- $20,000
Detective Comics #33 CGC 8.0 VF $74,422
Detective Comics #38 CGC 8.0 VF $38,500
Famous Funnies #1 CGC 4.5 VG+ $20,628
More Fun Comics #101 CGC 9.0 VF/NM Double-c $16,200
Reform School Girl VF $10,000
Superman #1 CGC 1.8 $28,000
Superman #1 CGC 7.0 FN/VF (R) $19,000
Superman #2 CGC 9.0 VF/NM $47,000
Suspense Comics #3 CGC 7.0 FN/VF $25,525
Wonder Woman #1 CGC 7.5 VF- Rockford $16,200

In the Silver Age and later, major keys and unique high grade comics exceeded our expectations in auctions and in our fixed price marketplace. *Amazing Fantasy* #15, *Showcase* #22, *Fantastic Four* #1 and *Amazing Spider-Man* #1 performed admirably, while a comic like *Amazing Spider-Man* #54 that would sell for $30 or so in 5.0 VG/FN sold for a whopping $5,427 in CGC 9.8 NM/MT condition.

Transformers #1 CGC 9.9 Mint hit $1,550 while a Gem Mint copy of *Wolverine* #1 CGC 10.0 was snatched up for $14,000. These were the comics I collected as a boy back in Indiana and here, at ComicConnect.com, I get to sell them for small fortunes and I love every second of it.

©AP

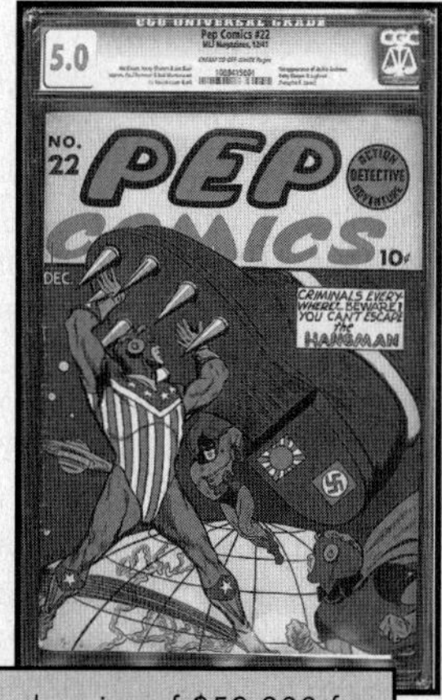

A sale price of $50,000 for this **Pep Comics #22** was the surprise of the year.

I see the first six issues of the *Incredible Hulk* as the next big run of books that will leap in value over the next couple of years (if only they could make a good movie!). But, if you are going to buy only one comic in 2011, I can't recommend *Amazing Fantasy* #15 enough, in any condition you can buy it.

ComicConnect.com debuted the newest comic book pedigree, the Suscha News Collection, in our last Event Auction of the season with a modest offering of just over 75 comics. With 40 short boxes to process, this is just the start of what we have to offer.

"This stunning collection was amassed by one of the most fastidious collectors I've ever met," said Vincent Zurzolo, my employer and co-owner of ComicConnect.com. "He made a deal with a comic book distributor that allowed him access to newly arrived comics before anyone else got their hands on them."

Besides low-distribution titles that many collectors just never saw, the original owner of the Suscha News Pedigree would carefully go through distributor boxes filled with the same issue of a book. He would get it down to around a dozen or so mint copies of a given book to try to find the MOST mint copies in the group. He was looking for books with the best centering, the shiniest staples, the flattest covers and the sharpest top and bottom of the spine. The collection dates back to the mid 1960s and ends in 1976, totaling almost 50 boxes of comic books.

Noteworthy Silver, Bronze, and Modern Age comic sales:
Amazing Fantasy #15 CGC 8.5 VF+ $108,000
Amazing Fantasy #15 CGC 8.0 VF $75,000
Amazing Spider-Man #1 CGC 7.5 VF- $9,500
Amazing Spider-Man #33 CGC 9.8 NM/MT $7,600
Amazing Spider-Man #101 CGC 9.8 NM/MT Suscha News $5,477
Avengers #4 CGC 9.4 NM $17,551
Fantastic Four #1 CGC 7.0 FN/VF $21,000
Fantastic Four #5 CGC 9.0 VF/NM $15,822
Fantastic Four #8 CGC 9.4 NM $14,300
Flash #123 CGC 9.2 NM- $5,500
Incredible Hulk #1 CGC 8.0 VF $33,000
Incredible Hulk #181 CGC 9.8 NM/MT $15,000
Journey into Mystery #83 CGC 7.5 VF- $10,207
Showcase #22 CGC 7.0 FN/VF $9,000
Tales of Suspense #39 CGC 8.5 VF+ $13,000
Wolverine #1 CGC 10.0 GEM $14,000
X-Men #94 CGC 9.8 NM/MT $26,500

ComicConnect.com's original comic art auctions hit their stride in 2010 with a large chunk coming from our representation of the L.B. Cole Estate Collection at auction. It was a memorable time going through all of the files and original art that the Golden Age legend had amassed over his career. The collection consisted of paintings, pencil work, recreations, and his files. Amazing.

Jack Kirby and Steve Ditko pages proved to be the gold standard for original art buyers and are always in demand. Collectors are willing to pay a premium for their work.

Noteworthy Original Art Sales:
Amazing Spider-Man #22 pg. 3 Steve Ditko $10,202
Fantastic Four #16 pg. 4 Jack Kirby $18,088
Ghost Rider #8 Cover Gil Kane $5,900
Peanuts Sunday Page Charles Schulz $39,000
Police Comics #2 pg. Paul Gustavson $6,498
Strange Tales #109 Five Page Story Steve Ditko $27,502
Tarzan Sunday Page Burne Hogarth $12,755
Warlord #39 Cover Mike Grell $4,400

Time flies when you are having fun and in 2010, I felt like I was in a rocket ship. I had an incredible trip to my first San Diego Comic-Con, where I helped sell an *Amazing Fantasy* #15 CGC 9.0 for $150,000 and I had a great time meeting so many of our customers. It was an amazing experience that I will always cherish.

I would like to extend my thanks and gratitude to all of our customers and consignors. Without so many passionate comic book fans, I wouldn't have the opportunity to work doing what I love. I'm always an e-mail (support@comicconnect.com) or a phone call (212.895.3999) away if I can ever be of service helping you buy or sell comics. I want to get back in the *Guinness* book with a new, amazing consignment to top our own world record.

THE WAR REPORT

by Matt Ballesteros

with Richard Evans, Andy Greenham, Keith Marlow and Mick Rabin & the War Correspondents

Welcome back! I am delighted to confirm that you are now reading the 3rd War Correspondent Report, a comprehensive dispatch on the War comic genre composed by devoted collectors and enthusiasts, and an annual account of the War comic book marketplace replete with insight and conjecture from renowned War book specialists from around the U.S. and Canada. Speaking of which, this year's War Correspondents consist of several returning and respected veterans of the field, such as Richard Evans, Keith Marlow and Mick Rabin. Further, hailing from the Great North, we are pleased to have our ranks bolstered by the venerable War comic expert Andy Greenham. Those of you who follow the genre should be all too familiar with the contributions each of these fine men has made to the pastime, and I want to thank them again here for their aid and significant role in developing this year's report.

As I have mentioned in the last two reports (and just about belabored to a nub), one of the original goals behind the creation of the War Correspondents was to develop a definitive ranking of the Top 10 to 20 War comics ever published. For the sanity of our return readers, I will not repeat all of the details regarding how we established our categorical methodology for ranking the books. For that, I recommend that you revisit our original reports in *Overstreet* #39 and #40, respectively. There you will find a blow-by-blow account of how we accomplished that feat. However, to give some point of reference, the key parameters that define the War comic book category are briefly summarized below.

This year's report will be much like last year's format, as our team felt that the overall structure and content delivered seemed to work well both from our point of view and from the feedback we received from our readers. We will share some thoughts on the market in general and will also dedicate a section of our report to providing opinions and musings on common queries as they relate to the War comic hobby. Of course, just as importantly, we will include the latest, most up-to-date war-comic rankings for the genre —which, interestingly, have had some noteworthy movement since our last publishing. So read on and enjoy.

Definition of a "War Book" revisited

Utilizing *Overstreet*, the web, and other publications, we developed a 2000+ catalog of war-related comic titles and then employed long-winded and complex processes to develop a refined list.

We narrowed the field by characterizing War comics as "stories centered on the military, which is involved in armed conflicts" and, as such, needed to be relegated to those wars which were categorized as "a major conflict". (I.e., no cold war, police actions, spy stories, etc.)

We eliminated war stories with super-heroes (by employing the notion that "any war story blended with a super-hero is by definition a 'fantasy' story and would not be a war story").

We defined and developed a classification for specific war themes. We selected "War Battle Tales" (I.e., stories that were predominantly centered on characters engulfed in battle). Therefore (for now) we purged classifications such as Military Life, War Adventure, War Propaganda, and Tragedy in Wartime, etc.

We categorized two main comic book ages:

- The Golden Age
- The Atom/Silver Age (which we will now, as of this year, officially expand to include the Bronze Age as one or two titles from that era keep making their way into the rankings)

As time progresses we may break the ages down a bit more, but these two categorizations seem to work quite well for now.

News from the Front - A Market Report

If you have been on the fence about getting into this niche of the comic collecting hobby, or you have been dabbling in periodic purchases but have not committed to the genre, it is our opinion that this year would be an opportune time to dive in. Let me share with you why: After three solid years of aggressive and heavy gains in the War book field, the market has ostensibly stabilized during the latter half of 2010 and into 2011. Except for some singular (yet significant) transactions, we witnessed radical price drops on low-grade books, meaningful price declines for mid-grade books and notable dips and steadied values for the sought after high grades. Candidly it is near impossible to predict how long the prices will remain at these relatively attainable levels. Thus, from an investment standpoint, we leave the value forecasting to you (although the War Correspondents are all looking to

© MAR

see if we can benefit from the slow-down by targeting more difficult to find and typically more expensive issues before they begin to increase in price). Speculation aside, whether you are one looking to complete your collection, a casual collector, a fan of the category, or simply someone who only recently gained interest in the genre for the sake of the art, stories or its overall mystique, then this is a fitting time to pick up copies of once nearly unattainable comics. But, before you go running to your comic shop or computer to snag great deals on War books, let me set your expectations based on one constant: you are not likely to find any form of affordable War book that is either listed as highest on census, a mid- to high- grade key, or known to be scarce in this segment of the hobby. These books are still commanding extremely high prices and (as we have mentioned before) in a lot of cases, summoning big dollar figures that are, by far, outdoing comparable superhero books of equivalent grade quality. However, what we ARE saying is that now is a good time to get some solid filler material that you will still be proud to own and show off. Mick Rabin had this to share about the topic:

"The 2010 auction results from Heritage and ComicLink suggest a bit of cooling down in terms of the record prices and hype that they'd received from the 2007-2009 period (roughly contemporaneous with Heritage's offering of Keith Marlow's unprecedented group of high grade War books until the Mound City auction in November of 2009). This doesn't mean that War comics are slow by any means, but it does mean that they typically can be acquired for prices anywhere from 15-40% cheaper than they were attaining before 2010."

So, why do we believe the prices stabilized? Contrary to what you are thinking, we strongly and emphatically believe that it has little to do with the economic downturn and a great deal to do with availability and supply. Thanks to Richard Evans' advocacy on that point, the War Correspondents spent significant time via conference-call debating the matter and reaching the same conclusion. Among other factors was the "War Comic Rush" that ignited in 2007 which drove buyers to shake out what were once considered nearly impossible books to find. And although high grade or key books are still very limited in number, supply has slowly been able to meet demand over these last four years, particularly for ardent collectors. Notwithstanding, these same collectors, even if small in numbers, would not hesitate to pay premiums for select scarce and high grade books at any given moment—so toss out the idea that a slow economy would hinder high dollar sales and new record prices being actualized (the recent Heritage auction featuring the Savannah pedigrees is a great example of that fact). Moreover, and probably the biggest factor, is that with all the attention this genre has received in recent years, the number of low to medium grade books have literally poured out into the market. Keith articulated a point that illustrates the phenomenon quite well. He noted that five years ago when hunting on eBay, you would only come across a couple thousand War comics at any given time, at whatever grade or abundance. Today, as of the date of this report, you can do an on-the-spot search for War comics on that same popular consumer portal and bring up literally ten thousand or more listings in the category. Not to mention the influence on the market by the escalated attention bestowed on the genre by auction sites like the aforementioned Heritage and ComicLink. In short, the above are all evidence that support our assertion that the possible price dips or leveling the market experienced in 2010 and part of 2011 have more to do with "greater amount of supply" versus potential "economic factors." We hope that you can use this information and our position on the specific matter to your benefit.

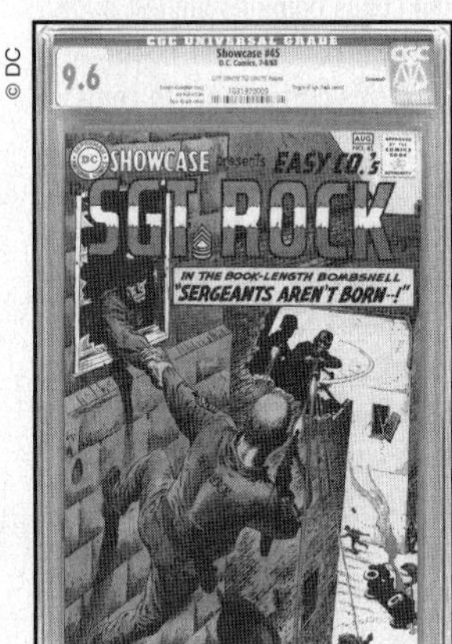

Prices in the War market are generally stabilizing, but high grade keys still command extremely high prices. (Showcase #45 shown)

Andy Greenham has had recent and firsthand experience with this fluctuating market deviation when he chose to sell his impressive and comprehensive War book collection through a series of ongoing auctions on Heritage during the latter half of 2010. He expressed the following with regard to his overall experience:

"I had been buying strongly for the past few years, putting two full collections of the Big Five together. I felt from doing this, I should have a pretty good grasp on what these books would sell for. I was wrong. The market is ever-changing. Books that I felt would sell for a lot, sometimes didn't and others that I felt would bring average results, did extremely well. To be honest, I wish I was a buyer in 2010 as it was definitely a buyer's market. Don't get me wrong, my sales were not all bad, in fact, I had a great deal of books that did very well for me. Even though it was very sad to see them go, overall, I was pleased with the final results."

Other Factors Influencing the War Comic Market

I hate to point out the obvious, but it would be negligent not to bring up the CGC Census (and third party grading in general). Its impact on our genre has been just as pervasive as it has on other comic niches. The prediction formula is straight forward: the highest census gets the highest prices. And although I am not intoning a fact that isn't already wholly known and accepted in the comic book industry, it is always good to note that, so far (except for a few odd cases), new, first time books recognized as "Single Highest on Census" continue to draw larger and larger dollar figures, underscoring the reality that regardless of the competition, there is always someone willing to pay exceedingly high prices for these new reigning books. Concurrently, unless the scarcity level of a War book keeps its value in place, books now relegated to 2nd or 3rd on census take an initial hit on the investment value. Blame easily pinned on the new king of a particular issue's census ranking, but it remains an important factor to consider as you think about purchasing or selling a cherished book.

Another noteworthy influencer is the highly debated and somewhat controversial practice of "pressing" books. Whether you are for it, against it, or remain generally neutral on the subject, you cannot ignore the impact that pressing has on the market—especially when its implementation allows a lower grade book on census to suddenly leap-frog the highest book on census. This circumstance has obviously affected pricing for War comics in ways that add another level of unpredictability and has played a role in driving prices up on high grade books. I won't dwell on this topic any further as there are far more astute experts on this subject matter, who most likely have already meticulously addressed the point. Nonetheless, it is worth mentioning.

Also to note, in our recent War Correspondent conference call, Mick perceptively emphasized the notion that online communities are playing a big role in the way collectors and buyers are acquiring War comics, specifically, the War comic community on the CGC Forum Boards. Although small in percentage, they seemingly represent what War book collectors are thinking overall in the market. In support of that axiomatic perception, Mick said: "War comics maintained a strong collector base (in 2010). The War comic threads on the CGC message boards remain abuzz with interest and a devoted group of enthusiasts."

And with the wealth of information shared daily on the boards, collectors abroad can easily refer to forums to get intelligence and insight on the genre, particular titles, writers, artists, and details on specific issues; thus arming them with the ability to make sounder acquisitions or sales. This is a factor that was non-existent prior to 2000, where most of us were buying, selling, and collecting with a learning curve and making decisions with only partial information. That is obviously not the case today. Not only are the boards insightful for the reader, but the threads are propagating an escalated interest from collectors. We highly recommend visiting (and contributing to) the boards for your own benefit.

Cover Fire

Due to a combination of aspects, such as the aforementioned third party grading and online communities, it is interesting to note that the overall buying psyche has changed over the last few years with respect to what drives a collector to buy a specific War book. Twenty years ago a significant influential factor to purchase a particular comic was highly subject to the contributing artists within the issue; for instance, the novelty that the "interior" was done by Heath or Kubert. And not surprisingly, yet indubitably, *Overstreet* gave and continues to bestow respect to the deserving creative scribes and artisans who had toiled on the interior pages of a comic book. However, with the advent of "slabbing", buyers and collectors are now judging books merely by their cover. A marked consequence of this trend has been the effect it is having on the price of some particular War comics. Coupled that with the fact that books are now being scanned and posted on boards, whereby multiparty admiration of books with "cool covers" thrive, thus creating a trend that has exponentially propelled prices on those specific issues. We suggest you not discount this important factor as there is a clear and evident frenzy and subsequent price boosts with regard to this latest cool cover craze. Andy had this to share about the point: "Another area within DC War that has been getting a lot of attention is classic, or cool, covers. Books that aren't specifically listed in *Overstreet*, but are known to the die-hard War collectors, are selling for very good prices, when found in nice grade. A little DC War classic cover cheat sheet needs to be created and perhaps we'll have that ready for our readers in next year's edition."

Something to Marvel At

Although its importance to the genre has not been lost on us, *Sgt. Fury* #1 has gained an enormous and surprising amount of momentum in 2010, and, candidly, with a force that has been stronger than we anticipated. Frankly, we have not been blind to the fact that this book is rather significant. In previous reports, even with the #10 spot on our list of top War comics, there was already rumbling among our ranks that the book would have to move up a slot or two in future listings. What we didn't anticipate was the amount of attention this book would receive in the last year! Whether you credit the recent movie mythos build-up with Samuel L. Jackson, or that the book was created by none other than the supreme Kirby and Lee, or the fact that for a Marvel Comic from only 1963 (unlike its superhero counterparts) there are very few high grade copies to be had, you cannot ignore that this book has garnered some concentrated interest. With only 200 or so books currently on Census, a 9.4 status being its highest book, and impending interest from non-War comic enthusiasts, you can expect some serious action on this core comic! In complete countenance, Andy offered: "In my opinion, the hottest War book of 2010 was not a DC War book; it was Marvel's *Sgt. Fury and His Howling Commandos* #1. My CGC 8.5 copy sold at Heritage for $5750. This book has taken the collecting community by storm, especially high grade copies of it. I believe one of the main reasons is that it is a Superhero/War comic. With it being borderline Superhero, there are masses of people that are looking for high grade copies of this book. I still consider *Sgt. Fury* to be a War book, but there is no denying the massive influx of interest in this particular title. My guess is many of the new buyers that are driving this price up are not war comic collectors."

Another Milestone

If you are a War comic fan of any station you are already aware that 2009 marked a 50th anniversary for the iconic character Sgt. Rock, and yes I have mentioned that in every report so far. It's just that the fifty year mark appears to be a key landmark for comic book characters in our industry when reflecting on their impact and relevance. It is apparent that when a key comic character reaches that particular milestone, there is a unified realization and veneration that exudes from the entire comic book marketplace over the character and the book in which he first appeared, and that reaction seemingly propels both into a comic collecting Hall of Fame. The most obvious example would be Superman and *Action* #1 reaching 50 in 1988 (by the way, any of you War comic cats have a copy of the 49 year old *Amazing Fantasy* #15?). And ok, while I may be comparing apples and oranges here in aligning Sgt. Rock with Superman, these half-century milestones are nevertheless worthy of acknowledgement for any comic book character or mythos. I am meandering, so let me get to the point. I mention all of this to bring to light the following: 2011 is the 50th year anniversary of *G.I. Combat* #87 and the introduction of the infamous Haunted Tank (and its loyal and revered crew) by the likes of respected war comic monolith's Kanigher and Heath. Don't underestimate this book and its significance to our genre!

Gaining Rank

Since our first report in *Overstreet* #39, we have been watchful of the market and its fluctuations and movements, providing a ranking of the top books in the War category. After developing the initial rank listing in 2008 we've been careful not to make any abrupt changes to the position of the books. Last year we barely modified the list, with only a few small changes in the teens. This year is another story. We have had ample time to watch the industry, test the market and receive feedback from all corners (thank you). As a result there have been some adjustments that we see as very befitting and necessary (including the committed inclusion of Bronze Age books). After careful deliberation we present the following war books ranked as:

GAINING RANK

TOP 35 ATOM / SILVER / BRONZE AGE WAR COMICS

ISSUE	2011 RANK	2010 RANK
Our Army at War #83	1	1
G.I. Combat #87	2	2
Our Army at War #81	3	4
G.I. Combat #68	4	3
Our Army at War #82	5	5
Sgt. Fury #1	6	10
Two Fisted Tales #18	7	7
Frontline Combat #1	8	8
Our Army at War #1	9	6
Our Army at War #90	10	9
G.I. Combat #44	11	11
Our Fighting Forces #1	12	13
Our Army at War #88	13	12
Star Spangled War Stories #131	14	16
All-American Men of War #127	15	17
Our Fighting Forces #45	14	14
Our Army at War #91	17	15
Our Army at War #151	18	19
Our Army at War #85	19	24
Star Spangled War Stories #84	20	20
All-American Men of War #28	20	18
Our Army at War #84	20	25
G.I. Combat #1	23	22
Our Army at War #112	24	23
Two-Fisted Tales Annual #1	25	21
Our Army at War #86	26	27
All-American Men of War #67	27	26
Star Spangled War Stories #90	27	-
Fightin' Marines #15 (#1)	29	29
Blazing Combat #1	30	28
All-American Men of War #82	31	30
G.I. Combat #91	32	-
Star Spangled War Stories #151	33	-
G.I. Combat #75	34	-
Our Army at War #100	35	-

Notable again: *Foxhole* #1 with the Classic Kirby cover. Perhaps as our ranking grows over time it will eventually brandish the Top 50 War books in the category, and we will see *Foxhole*, among other outstanding titles, make the list. Time will tell.

Mick also contributed the following with regard to our addition of *G.I. Combat* #75 to the Top 35 list: "*G.I. Combat* #75 began the legendary "perty-thirty" washtone run (ending with *G.I. Combat* #104). There has never been a run of washtones that lasted longer than *G.I. Combat* #75-104. Even the Sea Devils couldn't match that. In high grade, it is easily among the most difficult runs to assemble of ANY title from ANY run in the Silver/ Atomic age. And *G.I. Combat* #75 is the first of the uninterrupted run."

The titles and corresponding ranking for Golden Age War comics had very little movement since last year and hold steadfast in their original positions. They are as follows:

TOP 12 GOLDEN AGE WAR COMICS

ISSUE	2011 RANK	2010 RANK
Wings Comics #1	1	1
War Comics #1	2	2
Real Life Comics #3	3	3
Contact Comics #1	4	4
Real Life Comics #1	5	5
Bill Barnes Comics #1	6	6
Rangers Comics #8	7	8
Wings Comics #2	8	7
Remember Pearl Harbor nn	9	9
United States Marines nn	10	10
Don Winslow #1	11	-
American Library nn (#1)	12	-

TOP 5 ATLAS AND CHARLTON WAR COMICS

Last year we introduced the top five issues that from our point of view rank as the best Atlas and Charlton War books. This year, even after some scrutiny, the books remain at the ranks imparted on them last year. The only book that made any kind of upward move in our voting this year was Charlton's *Attack* #54, but it did not score enough voting points to claim a higher ranking than its original position.

TOP 5 ATLAS WAR BOOKS OF 2011

ISSUE	2011 RANK	2010 RANK
Combat #1	1	1
War Comics #1	2	2
War Action #1	3	3
Battleground #1	4	4
Navy Action #1	5	5

TOP 5 CHARLTON WAR BOOKS OF 2011

ISSUE	2011 RANK	2010 RANK
Fightin' Marines #15(#1)	1	1
Soldier & Marine Comics #1	2	2
Attack #54	3	3
U.S. Air Force Comics #1	4	4
Fightin' Air Force #3	5	5

Intel from the War Correspondents

Like last year, in this section of our report we wanted to supply whatever useful and helpful advice that might aid you in your continued pursuit of the War comic book collecting hobby. We consider key questions that we typically discuss amongst ourselves and then summarize our deliberations to share with you. Some of the information offered might even shed light on how certain titles or issues work their way up on to our top War lists. Following last year's framework, we broached many of the same subjects in an attempt to churn up new data from typical topics, and we even included some new subject matter posed by individuals who contacted us throughout the year (thanks – we like hearing from you and truly appreciate your feedback!)

Name some War books that are underrated or underappreciated and why:

G.I. Combat #88 - A scarce book and 2nd appearance of the Haunted Tank, a book which rarely shows up in Fine or better.

Our Fighting Forces #49 - 1st Pooch, very tough to find and very undervalued.

Our Army at War #218 First Glanzman USS Stevens – one of the best series ever written. Mick expounded with the following: "Glanzman deserves to have these ALL reprinted in *DC Archives* and *Showcase* formats. They are beautifully drawn and stunningly honest in their assessment of the war in the Pacific as Sam Glanzman himself witnessed it. To my knowledge, it is the longest running semiautobiographical works in DC Comics history. All of the original issues that featured Sam's USS Stevens stories are coveted by War comics collectors, but the first one is *Our Army at War* #218 and with a dark cover, it is tougher to get in high grade than many of the surrounding issues."

High Grade DC War Keys - OK, this may be stating the obvious, but to re-emphasize the fact that key high-grade DC War books are scarce, consider this: other than the single copies of *G.I. Combat* #68 in CGC 9.2 and *Our Army at War* #151 in CGC 9.2 (which are comparably low grades compared to other books of the same time period), there is not a single DC War book from our top 20 Rank that tops CGC 9.0 on the census. Stick that in your pipe and smoke it.

Name some War books to look out for in 2011:

Again, the keys: in short, the top 10 Books on any of our lists.

Classic covers and cool covers.

The issues that were tough in 2008 and 2009 remained tough in 2010. Mick added: "I certainly would have bought multiple copies of *Our Army at War* #100 and *G.I. Combat* #75-104 if they were available in grade."

Name War books that are perhaps overrated:

Although *Star Spangled War Stories* #90 made the "Overrated List" last year, we want to stress not to overlook it. Andy shared the following about the book: "It's not a favorite of mine, but it is still very sought after."

CGC 9.8 copies of Big-5 titles from mid-'70s to late '80s should not command any more of a premium than 9.4 copies since they tend to be relatively plentiful.

Our Army at War #218, the start of Sam Glanzman's USS Stevens series which deserves a wider following.

Name which War books have been easiest to find in 2010-2011:

Many 10 and 12 cent DC War books are readily available in GD to GD/VG, even VG. I feel they are overvalued with many dealers offering these for 50% of catalogue value.

All American Men of War #112 - a beautiful comic in every way, it comprises the 1st appearance and origin of Steve Savage - Balloon Buster with incredible interior and cover art by Russ Heath. However, multiple copies in 9.0 and above have met resistance to what would be considered reasonable prices on ComicLink and the CGC message boards.

Name War books that are currently overabundant:

Low grade War books. As reported in our Market Report throughout.

Low to mid-high grade copies of *Our Army at War* #151, *Sgt. Fury* #13, and *Showcase* #45 (as reported last year).

G.I. Combat #87 in 6.0 and below is relatively available right now if you want it.

The 9.6 copy of *Showcase* #45 attained a record price with the Savannah copy selling at Heritage this year, despite its more abundant availability in the 8.5 to 9.2 range.

Name which War books have been the hardest to find in 2011:

Our Fighting Forces #49

G.I. Combat #88

Star Spangled War Stories #6 (also listed as "extremely scarce" in Chris Pedrin's Big Five Information Guide).

All 10¢ War comics in high grade are tough.

Name featured key sales in 2011 and why they were important:

Not necessarily pedigree books, but with 500 CGC graded War books offered from the Andy Greenham collection, that in itself gave collectors much to choose from, in a market in short supply of quality War books.

Since the Mound City Auction, there have been numerous auctions – mainly Heritage – that prominently featured DC War comics. Though many have met with record prices, the vast majority of these War comics have sold for softer prices than before the Mound City Auction.

The release and auctioning of the Savannah Pedigrees will probably be the single most significant War books auction (for the first half of this year in the least, if not longer). The quality of the books themselves along with some of the highest grades seen for War books since the Mound City Auction, this was certainly an auction to note. See some of the record prices realized below. Could this be the beginning of the next upswing?

Showcase #45 in the Savannah Auction stands out because it's not just the War comic devotees who are vying for these issues. As with ANY DC Silver Age comic, but perhaps especially *Showcase* #45, 9.6 and better copies will routinely sell for record prices... And of course it did, realizing $6,600

Name key individual sales in 2011:

Sgt. Fury #1 CGC 9.0 $10,000 (A War book breaks the five figure barrier again! But take note, this was only a 9.0)

Sgt. Fury #1 CGC 8.5 $5750 (The hottest War book of 2010, *Sgt. Fury* #1 seems to be on fire with many long-time Marvel Collectors finally discovering how tough that book is to find in nice condition. It's met with a great deal of interest and record prices in recent auctions.)

Our Army At War #128 CGC 9.4 Savannah Pedigree $4500 (Key "Origin of Sgt Rock" book)

Our Army At War #118 CGC 9.6 Savannah Pedigree $3350 (Wow! Single highest by 3 slots, impossible to find in high grade, and only CGC 9.6 *Our Army At War* issue between issues #75 and #135)

G.I. Combat #100 CGC 9.4 $3,100 (Wow! That price was unexpected)

G.I. Combat #123 CGC 9.4 $2875 (Mlle. Marie app in Haunted Tank – big price for this book only underlines the growing interest in the one major female character in the DC War mythos!)

Our Army At War #120 CGC 9.4 Savannah Pedigree $2400 (highest previous book – a CGC 9.0)

Our Army At War #123 CGC 9.4 Savannah Pedigree $2300 (highest previous book – a CGC 9.2)

Our Army At War #116 CGC 9.4 Savannah Pedigree $2275 (surprisingly high price since there are two 9.4s on census, still, scarce book overall)

Our Army At War #117 CGC 9.4 Savannah Pedigree $2030 (same scenario as the *OAAW* #116)

Our Army At War #109 CGC 9.2 Savannah Pedigree $1675 (tale of Sgt. Rock's first battle – great price considering that the 9.0 went for twice that during the Mound City Auction)

Star Spangled War Stories #112 CGC 9.4 Savannah Pedigree $1675 (The Dino books are still getting plenty of love)

Our Army At War #83 CGC 6.0 $1600 (1st true Sgt. Rock appearance)

Our Army At War #107 CGC 9.4 Savannah Pedigree $1550 (only 8 books on census)

Star Spangled War Stories #118 CGC 9.4 Savannah Pedigree $1550 (Dinos attack!)

G.I. Combat #68 CGC 7.0 $1400 (Sgt. Rock prototype)

All-American Men Of War #94 $1300 (classic Russ Heath cover)

Our Army At War #60 CGC 9.0 $1300 (classic washtone cover)

G.I. Combat #87 CGC 6.5 $1100 (1st appearance of Haunted Tank)

Our Army At War #81 CGC 6.5 $1100 (last Sgt. Rock prototype)

Our Army At War #83 CGC 5.5 $1100 (1st true Sgt. Rock appearance)

Our Army At War #151 CGC 9.4 Savannah Pedigree $1000 (2nd highest on census that features the first appearance of Enemy Ace. A great deal

Sgt. Fury #1 was certainly the hottest War book of 2010.

for this book!)

Our Army At War #115 CGC 9.0 Savannah Pedigree $1000 (Mlle. Marie's 1st crossover is key, and $1000 for the 9.0 was a fair price for all parties)

Our Army At War #83 CGC 4.0 $900 ($900 for a 4.0? – this book is getting the attention it deserves!)

G.I. Combat #114 CGC 9.0 $850 (Origin of Haunted Tank)

G.I. Combat #87 CGC 6.0 $850 (1st appearance Haunted Tank)

Star Spangled War Stories #84 CGC 9.0 $775 (1st Mlle. Marie. Great price for the buyer!)

Our Fighting Forces #123 CGC 9.6 $750 (single highest for the first 1st Losers book – fair price)

Our Fighting Forces #27 CGC 9.0 $700 (great cover)

Our Fighting Forces #49 CGC 9.0 $550 (1st appearance of Pooch. Low price for a very undervalued book)

Last year, *Our Army At War* #100 was on the list as a book to look out for, and a CGC 7.0 copy of it sold for $425!

Our Army At War #1 CGC 6.0 $600 (good deal for the buyer)

Our Fighting Forces #45 CGC 7.5 $180 (1st Gunner and Sarge. What?! Previous sales were somewhere around $1100 for this one. Someone pulled off the perfect crime – nice one!)

Name a Copper thru Modern Age war book worth getting your hands on:

Andy contributed the following: "*Unknown Soldier* by Joshua Dysart and Alberto Ponticello has been a real joy for me to read. Even though it strays from the classic Unknown Soldier that we all know and love, the book has been the most enjoyable modern War book that I've read in the longest time. Unfortunately, the series has now ended with issue #25. However, with well written stories and superbly drawn artwork, it comes very highly recommended."

Name this year's choice for best DC War Cover:

Andy is planning on running his "Best Cover Contest" again this year on the CGC boards. With the intent of retiring the winners from the previous years, we look forward to seeing what gems surface to the top. However, candidates to consider in the future for best DC War Cover are:

- *Our Army At War* #112
- *Our Fighting Forces* #71
- *G.I. Combat* #78
- *G.I. Combat* #83
- *G.I. Combat* #87
- *Our Fighting Forces* #20

A Candidate to Consider for best NON-DC War Cover:

- *Foxhole* #1 (classic Jack Kirby cover)

In what issues can we find what you consider the finest War stories written?

Our Fighting Forces #40 "The Silent Ones" by Kubert.

Our Army at War #79 "What's the Price of a B-17" Kubert drawing in an almost Heathesque cross-hatching style. Intensely cool story.

Virtually EVERY one of Sam Glanzman's USS Stevens stories that began with *Our Army At War* #218 and ran from roughly 1970 until 1977 as a back-up feature in numerous issues of *Our Army At War*. The series is a triumph and Glanzman's work is amongst the best-kept secrets of all War collectors.

R. Ballard reminded us that one of the finest stories written in the early '70s was "Burma Sky" in *Our Fighting Forces* #146. Its engrossing tale of the Flying Tigers and a stoic hero amongst them—always leaves a lasting impression on the reader.

Name a key War comic or series that stands out in your mind that isn't a DC, Charlton or Atlas AND explain why you feel it is worth mentioning /collecting:

The obvious one here would be *Sgt. Fury and His Howling Commandos*. It's a long running series by Marvel Comics that literally every comic collector has heard of.

A much lesser known title would be *Combat* by Dell Publishing. The series ran 40 issues with the last 14 issues reprinting the first 14. The covers were beautifully painted, the stories were well-written and there's a whole lot of great Sam Glanzman artwork in there as well.

What information can you provide on variant issues:

There's not a lot of information on variants when it comes to War comics. For instance, with many of the later issues in *G.I. Combat* and *Sgt. Rock*, there were both newsstand and direct edition versions, usually identified by the UPC code or lack thereof. There are also pricing variants, such as Canadian, US, and British, at the very least. Whitman variants exist for *Sgt. Rock* #329 and many *Brave and the Bold* DC war books. Some books had Mark Jewellers inserts. Andy happily admits that: "Collecting these different versions of the same book have been fun to me and continue to prove to be a challenge."

Over and Out

OK, that's it for the Year 3 Report. As always, we hope you found this short editorial useful and entertaining. If you would like to hear more, would like us to cover a certain topic, would like to support or challenge our deliberations, OR would like to CONTRIBUTE to next year's report, please do not hesitate to contact the Overstreet Guide at *feedback@gemstonepub.com* or the War Correspondents themselves at *theboyz@warcomic.com* . The War Correspondents would like to thank the entire Overstreet crew: Bob Overstreet, J.C. Vaughn and Mark Huesman for allowing to us to pontificate without restraint.

I would like to close by thanking my comrades in arms, Richard Evans, Andy Greenham, Keith Marlow and Mick Rabin. Thanks guys, it's great to have you alongside in the trenches.

KEY SALES FROM 2010-2011

The following lists of sales were reported to Gemstone during the year and represent only a small portion of the total amount of important books that have sold.

PLATINUM AGE SALES

Bringing Up Father #1 VG/FN $53
Bringing Up Father #13 VG/FN $26
Buster Brown On His Travels FN $155.35
Comic Monthly #10 Foolish Questions VG/FN $131.45
Mickey Mouse Book (later printing) VG/FN $776.75
Mickey Mouse Book (later printing) VG/FN $657.25
Moon Mullins Series 6 VG/FN $34
Mutt and Jeff Book 7 VG $34
Mutt and Jeff Book 17 VG $47
Oh Skin-nay! $49
Toonerville Trolley #1 VG/FN $89.63
Yellow Kid in McFadden's Flats nn FN+ $6,572.50

GOLDEN AGE - ATOM AGE SALES

Action Comics #1 $13,311 (coverless)
Action Comics #31 VG/FN $429
Adventure Comics #82 VG $240
Adventure Comics #214 FN+ $190
Archie's Girls Betty & Veronica #10 GD- $22.50
Archie's Girls, B&V Annual #1 VF/NM $3,500
Batman #1 GD/VG $9,500
Batman #16 GD+ $400
Blackstone #1 VG $100
Captain America Comics #1 VG/FN $15,000
Captain America Comics #12 VG $950
Captain America Comics #46 VG $2,800
Champion Comics ashcan FN/VF $2,261.76
Custer's Last Stand VF $100
Detective Comics #38 VF $4,000 (restored)
Detective Comics #67 VG $300
Detective Comics #130 VG $136
Detective Comics #140 VG/FN $1,750
Dick Tracy Paint Book # VF/NM $250
Donald Duck Four Color #408 FN $55
Donald Duck Four Color #422 FN+ $55
Exciting #48 FN $180
Fight #60 VG/FN $55
Frankenstein (Prize) #27 VF $180
G.I. Joe (Ziff Davis) #18 VG $9
Gangster and Gun Molls #2 VF $300
Gangsters Can't Win #2 VF+ $250
Girls' Romance #2 VF $220
Haunt of Fear #26 VG $48
Human Torch #5 VG/FN $1,500
John Wayne #5 FN+ $220
Jungle Comics #74 VF $130
Keen Detective Funnies V1 ##8 FR $300
Kerry Drake #3 VG $32
Leading Comics #16 VG $100
Leave it to Binky #4 GD/VG $21
Mad #11 GD- $27.50
Mad Follies Magazine #7 FN $19
Marvel Mystery Comics #18 FN $950
Marvel Tales #95 VG- $170
Mickey Mouse Four Color #296 VG $30
Mister Mystery #12 VG+ $920
More Fun Comics #89 VG $285
Mr. District Attorney #53 VG- $14.75
Namora #2 VG- $400
Nancy & Sluggo #16 VG $18
National Comics #26 GD $45
Patsy Walker #26 VG $22.50
Peanuts #1 FN/VF $2,151
Phantom Lady #18 VG $500
Psychoanalysis #1 VG $30
Reform School Girl VF $10,000
Saddle Justice #7 GD+ $17
Sensation Comics #11 GD $100
Sensation Comics #24 GD $80
Sensation Comics #45 FN $160
Sensation Comics #50 VG/FN $130
Sensation Comics #76 VG $80
Smash Comics #40 VG $130
Space Detectives #1 VG $190
Superman #1 PGX 5.0 $13,000 (restored)
Superman #4 VG/FN $770
Superman #6 FN- $600
Tarzan (Dell) #9 VG- $40
Teen-Age Romances #77 FN $10
Thun'da #1 GD/VG $170
USA Comics #3 FN $1,688
USA Comics #4 FN+ $1,000
USA Comics #6 FR/GD $1,275
USA Comics #7 VG- $4,000

USA Comics #7 VG/FN $4,326 (restored)
Weird #17 FR $70
Weird Tales of the Future #5 VG $356
Wonder Woman #25 VG/FN $235
Young Allies #9 FN- $349
Young Romance Comics #1 VF $325

SILVER AGE SALES

Action Comics #252 GD $250
Action Comics #285 FN $55
Adventure Comics #301 VF $86
Adventure Comics #307 NM- $110
Adventure Comics #311 VF- $55
Adventure Comics #346 VF/NM $100
Adventure Comics #353 NM+ $200
All-American Men of War #94 VG $14
Amazing Fantasy #15 VG/FN $9,000
Amazing Spider-Man #1 VG $2,750
Amazing Spider-Man #1 FR $600
Amazing Spider-Man #2 GD $400
Amazing Spider-Man #3 GD/VG $300
Amazing Spider-Man #9 FR/GD $75
Amazing Spider-Man #19 VF- $200
Avengers #1 VG $735
Avengers #1 GD+ $450
Avengers #1 GD $400
Avengers #2 FN- $200
Avengers #3 FN $100
Avengers #9 GD- $35
Avengers #58 VG+ $14.50
Avengers #77 VF/NM $33
Avengers Annual #1 GD+ $13
Batman #139 GD+ $37
Batman #140 GD+ $25
Batman #171 VF- $115
Batman #193 VG+ $14.25
Brave & Bold #28-30 FN $2,800 set
Brave and the Bold #28 GD- $300
Brave and the Bold #28 VG $535
Brave and the Bold #51 FN+ $12
Captain America #100 FN $75
Captain America #109 NM $425
Captain America #110 NM $395
Captain America Annual #8 NM $22.50
Captain Atom #75 VG/FN $34
Detective Comics #181 VG $102
Fantastic Four #2 GD $250
Fantastic Four #3 VG $200
Fantastic Four #4 GD $175
Fantastic Four #5 GD $480
Fantastic Four #10 VG $185
Fantastic Four #11 VG- $172
Fantastic Four #12 FR/GD $250
Fantastic Four #19 VG- $60
Fantastic Four #25 GD/VG $95
Fantastic Four #25 GD/VG $33
Fantastic Four #47 NM $405
Fantastic Four #58 VG+ $19
Fantastic Four #83 NM+ $250
Fantastic Four #99 VF $18.50
Fantastic Four Annual #3 FN $40
Fantastic Four Annual #5 NM $325
Flash #145 VG+ $22
Green Lantern #1 GD- $150
Green Lantern #10 VG+ $65
Green Lantern #18 FN/VF $78
Green Lantern #19 FN $50
Green Lantern #21 FN/VF $60
Green Lantern #29 FN/VF $60
Green Lantern #41 NM+ $535
Green Lantern #61 VF $40
Iron Man #1 FN $120
Iron Man #1 GD $100 (signed by Stan Lee)
Journey Into Mystery #77 FN $30
Journey into Mystery #83 GD $1,000
Journey Into Mystery #101 VG $12
Journey Into Mystery #104 VG+ $17
Journey Into Mystery #114 FN+ $30
Journey Into Mystery #121 VF $50
Justice League of America #45 VF- $13.50
Masque of Red Death # FN $18
Mission Impossible #2 FN $18
Rebel (Four Color) #1076 VF $25
Restless Gun (Four Color) #1045 VG $20
Sgt. Fury #27 VG+ $12.50
Showcase #13 GD+ $495
Showcase #22 VG+ $1,000
Silver Surfer #10 VF/NM $85
Spectre #4 VG- $14.75
Strange Planets #12 VG- $12.50
Strange Tales #147 VG+ $12.50
Strange Tales Annual #1 FN $210
Sub-Mariner (v2) #2 FN- $28
Supercar #1 FN+ $85
Tales to Astonish #9 VG/FN $80
Thor #137 VF $20
Wonder Woman #105 GD $150
X-Men #1 VG- $1,100
X-Men #34 GD- $18.50
X-Men #63 GD- $13
X-Men #66 NM $425
X-Men #90 VG+ $19.50

BRONZE AGE TO MODERN AGE SALES

Bronze Age Sales:

Amazing Spider-Man #97 NM $300
Amazing Spider-Man #97 VG $17
Amazing Spider-Man #121 VF $100
Amazing Spider-Man #121 VF- $75
Amazing Spider-Man #122 FN+ $60
Amazing Spider-Man #129 VF/NM $550
Amazing Spider-Man #129 VF/NM $400
Amazing Spider-Man #137 VG $12.50
Captain America #193 VF+ $10.50
Cerebus #1 GD/VG $150
Conan the Barbarian #4 VG $10.50
Daredevil #168 VF $50
Deadly Hands of Kung Fu #26 NM+ $100
Deadly Hands of Kung Fu #31 NM+ $100
Detective Comics #400 FN/VF $150
Detective Comics #441 VF $21.75
Fantastic Four #123 NM+ $395
Foom #1 NM $200
Ghost Rider #1 VF/NM $195
Giant-Size X-Men #1 VF $450
Giant-Size X-Men #1 GD $50
Green Lantern #76 VF+ $1,250
Hansi The Girl Who Loved the Swastika FN- $38
House of Secrets #92 VF $300
Incredible Hulk #180 FN $45
Incredible Hulk #181 NM $2,400
Incredible Hulk #181 NM- $1,100
Incredible Hulk #181 VG+ $3,800
Incredible Hulk #181 GD $120 coupon cut out
Incredible Hulk #182 FN $25
Iron Fist #14 VF/NM $250
Ka-Zar (v1) #1 GD $12
Savage Tales (v1) #1 VG+ $34
Star Wars #7 VF/NM $10
Superman's Pal, Jimmy Olsen #134 VG $15
Tomb of Dracula #11 FN+ $15
Weird War Tales #1 VF $100
Werewolf By Night #32 FN+ $1,075
Wolverine #1 FN+ $18
X-Men #94 GD+ $70
X-Men #94 VG+ $80
Yogi Bear #1 FN $9

Copper Age Sales:

Amazing Spider-Man #238 NM- $75
Gobbledygook #1 VF+ $11,352
Gobbledygook #2 VF/NM $4,481.25
New Mutants #1 NM $5
Thundercats #1 VF/NM $12.75

Modern Age Sales:

Amazing Spider-Man #238 FN+ $30
Amazing Spider-Man #529 NM $20
Amazing Spider-Man #529 NM $15
Amazing Spider-Man Vol. 2 #1 NM+ $20
Amazing Spider-Man Vol. 2 #36 NM $35
Captain America (2005) #25 NM $15
Chew #1 NM $30
Crisis On Infinite Earths Absolute Slipcase Ed $100
Deadpool #1 NM $25
Fables #1 NM $45
GI Joe #1 VF/NM $25
GI Joe #21 VF/NM $30
JLA/Avengers HC #1 Oversized Slipcase Ed $100
John Byrne's Next Men #23 NM $45
New Mutants #98 NM- $62
Sandman #1 NM $45
Superman (v2) #75 NM $18
Transformers War Within #1 NM $12
X-Men #266 NM $60
X-Men (2nd) #25 NM $12

GOLDEN AGE - SALES OF CGC-CERTIFIED COMICS

Action Comics #1 VG/FN (5.0) $465,000
Action Comics #1 VG/FN (5.0) $436,000
Action Comics #1 GD- (1.8) $116,000
Action Comics #1 FR/GD (1.5) $63,000 (restored)
Action Comics #1 PR (0.5) $43,000 (restored)
Action Comics #2 FN- (5.5) $19,200 Rockford
Action Comics #7 FN/VF (7.0) $175,000
Action Comics #34 GD+ (2.5) $330
Action Comics #51 GD/VG (3.0) $304
Action Comics #96 FN/VF (7.0) $450
Action Comics (Ashcan) #1 VF/NM (9.0) $50,000
All-American Comics #16 FN (6.0) $10,200 (restored)
All Winners Comics #4 FR (1.0) $300
All-Winners Comics #19 VF+ (8.5) $7,500
Archie Comics #1 VF+ (8.5) $167,300
Archie Comics #1 FN/VF (7.0) $12,500
Archie Comics #1 VG/FN (5.0) $34,000
Batman #1 GD (2.0) $23,302.50
Batman #1 FR/GD (1.5) $11,800
Batman #1 FR/GD (1.5) $11,700
Batman #2 NM- (9.2) $43,000
Batman #5 FN/VF (7.0) $1,250

Batman #9 NM (9.4) $15,000
Batman #13 VG/FN (5.0) $560
Batman #31 VG/FN (5.0) $300
Batman #55 FN- (5.5) $450
Blue Beetle #51 FN/VF (7.0) $325
Blue Ribbon Comics #7 FN/VF (7.0) $300
Captain America Comics #1 GD/VG (3.0) $14,000
Captain America Comics #2 VF+ (8.5) $21,500
Captain America Comics #2 VG+ (4.5) $3,500
Captain America Comics #4 VF (8.0) $8,300
Captain America Comics #26 VG (4.0) $1,250
Captain America Comics #26 VG (4.0) $1,228
Captain America Comics #33 VG/FN (5.0) $1,700
Captain America Comics #46 VF+ (8.5) $11,700
Crime Does Not Pay #22 FN/VF (7.0) $4,800
Detective Comics #27 VF- (7.5) $657,250 Aloha
Detective Comics #27 VF- (7.5) $97,500 (restored)
Detective Comics #27 FN/VF (7.0) $492,937.50
Detective Comics #27 VG- (3.5) $240,000
Detective Comics #27 VG+ (4.5) $44,500 (restored)
Detective Comics #27 VG+ (4.5) $26,500
Detective Comics #28 VF- (7.5) $35,000
Detective Comics #29 VG/FN (5.0) $31,000
Detective Comics #29 VG- (3.5) $20,000
Detective Comics #30 FN- (5.5) $4,500
Detective Comics #31 VF- (7.5) $20,000
Detective Comics #32 GD (2.0) $1,100 (Sig. Series Jerry Robinson)
Detective Comics #33 VF (8.0) $74,422
Detective Comics #38 VF (8.0) $38,500
Detective Comics #38 FN+ (6.5) $10,000 Rockford
Detective Comics #39 FR (1.0) $400 (Sig. Series Jerry Robinson)
Detective Comics #139 FN/VF (7.0) $300
Detective Comics #140 VG/FN (5.0) $2,000
Famous Funnies #1 VG+ (4.5) $20,628
Flash Comics #4 NM (9.4) $17,925 Mile High
Flash Comics #12 NM/MT (9.8) $25,095 Mile High
Funny Pages Vol. 3 #7 VG- (3.5) $325
Green Lantern #3 NM (9.4) $33,460 Mile High
Green Lantern #10 NM (9.4) $10,157.50 Mile High
House of Mystery #1 VF+ (8.5) $2,000 "D" Copy
Human Torch Comics #2 (#1) VG/FN (5.0) $6,000
Human Torch Comics #7 GD/VG (3.0) $350 (restored)
Human Torch Comics #8 VG+ (4.5) $1,650
Human Torch Comics #17 VG (4.0) $460
Mad #1 NM/MT (9.8) $19,120 Gaines File
Mad #4 VF/NM (9.0) $870
Marvel Comics #1 FN (6.0) $71,700
Marvel Comics #1 VG (4.0) $38,838
Marvel Mystery #13 VF/NM (9.0) $7,133
Marvel Mystery Comics #17 PR (0.5) $375
Marvel Mystery Comics #22 GD+ (2.5) $450
Marvel Mystery Comics #28 VG/FN (5.0) $630
Marvel Mystery Comics #31 FR/GD (1.5) $300
Marvel Mystery Comics #45 VG (4.0) $405
Mary Marvel Comics #13 VF/NM (9.0) $320
Millie The Model #1 VG/FN (5.0) $350
More Fun Comics #55 FR (1.0) $1,200
More Fun Comics #101 VF/NM (9.0) $16,200 Double Cover
Namora #1 VG- (3.5) $600
Namora #2 FN- (5.5) $450
Nickel Comics #5 FN/VF (7.0) $375
Our Fighting Forces #1 VG/FN (5.0) $300
Pep Comics #22 VG/FN (5.0) $50,000
Pep Comics #43 VG- (3.5) $375
Phantom Detective #1 GD/VG (3.0) $300
Phantom Lady #19 VG (4.0) $390
Sensation Comics #1 VG/FN (5.0) $7,000
Star Spangled Comics #8 GD+ (2.5) $300
Strange Adventures #1 VF+ (8.5) $1,800
Sub-Mariner Comics #1 VG+ (4.5) $4,000
Sub-Mariner Comics #1 VG (4.0) $5,500
Sub-Mariner Comics #5 FR (1.0) $480
Sub-Mariner Comics #18 GD/VG (3.0) $315
Superman #1 VF+ (8.5) $44,812.50 (restored)
Superman #1 FN/VF (7.0) $19,000 (restored)
Superman #1 VG+ (4.5) $90,000
Superman #1 VG- (3.5) $50,050
Superman #1 GD- (1.8) $28,000
Superman #2 NM- (9.2) $85,000
Superman #2 VF/NM (9.0) $47,000
Superman #9 VF/NM (9.0) $6,775
Superman #76 VG+ (4.5) $649.50
Suspense Comics #3 FN/VF (7.0) $25,525
Suspense Comics #3 VG/FN (5.0) $6,300
Tales From the Crypt #32 NM (9.4) $800
Tex Morgan #1 NM (9.4) $775
This Magazine Is Haunted #3 GD+ (2.5) $315
USA Comics #7 GD+ (2.5) $2,750
USA Comics #6 GD/VG (3.0) $2,500
USA Comics #10 VG- (3.5) $2,400
Venus #18 VG/FN (5.0) $450
Walt Disney's Comics & Stories #32 FN (6.0) $540
War Against Crime #10 VG- (3.5) $334
Western Picture Stories #1 VG- (3.5) $400
Whiz Comics #2 (#1) FN/VF (8.0) $5,975 (restored)
Whiz Comics #2 (#1) FN/VF (7.0) $63,000
Wonder Woman #1 VF (8.0) $17,925
Wonder Woman #1 VF- (7.5) $16,200 Rockford
World's Finest Comics #5 FN/VF (7.0) $650
Young Allies Comics #4 FR (1.0) $300
Young Men #24 FN- (5.5) $1,000
Young Romance Comics #10 NM- (9.2) $300

Action Comics #252 VF/NM (9.0) $14,340 Twin Cities
Amazing Fantasy #15 NM+ (9.6) $1,100,000
Amazing Fantasy #15 VF/NM (9.0) $150,000
Amazing Fantasy #15 FN/VF (7.0) $33,460
Amazing Fantasy #15 FN+ (6.5) $21,510
Amazing Fantasy #15 FN (6.0) $19,120
Amazing Fantasy #15 FN- (5.5) $10,500
Amazing Fantasy #15 VG/FN (5.0) $8,700
Amazing Fantasy #15 VG/FN (5.0) $7,050
Amazing Fantasy #15 VG+ (4.5) $7,600
Amazing Fantasy #15 GD- (1.8) $2,700 (Sig. Series Stan Lee)
Amazing Spider-Man #1 VF+ (8.5) $29,875
Amazing Spider-Man #1 VG+ (4.5) $4,300 (Sig. Series)
Amazing Spider-Man #1 GD+ (2.5) $1,000
Amazing Spider-Man #2 NM+ (9.6) $65,725 Twin Cities
Amazing Spider-Man #2 GD (2.0) $350
Amazing Spider-Man #3 FN (6.0) $742
Amazing Spider-Man #3 GD/VG (3.0) $360
Amazing Spider-Man #4 NM+ (9.6) $77,675 Twin Cities
Amazing Spider-Man #4 VG/FN (5.0) $375
Amazing Spider-Man #5 GD/VG (3.0) $257
Amazing Spider-Man #6 FN/VF (7.0) $1,300
Amazing Spider-Man #6 GD/VG (3.0) $255
Amazing Spider-Man #7 VG (4.0) $218
Amazing Spider-Man #8 VF- (7.5) $700
Amazing Spider-Man #10 NM- (9.2) $2,500
Amazing Spider-Man #11 FN/VF (7.0) $600
Amazing Spider-Man #14 VF- (7.5) $500 (restored)
Amazing Spider-Man #15 FN/VF (7.0) $525
Amazing Spider-Man #17 VF (8.0) $700
Amazing Spider-Man #20 VG- (3.5) $100
Amazing Spider-Man #26 VF/NM (9.0) $600
Amazing Spider-Man #28 NM (9.4) $10,255
Amazing Spider-Man #33 NM/MT (9.8) $5,600
Amazing Spider-Man #34 NM+ (9.6) $4,100
Amazing Spider-Man #39 NM (9.4) $4,200
Amazing Spider-Man #40 NM/MT (9.8) $30,000
Amazing Spider-Man #40 NM (9.4) $3,200
Amazing Spider-Man #48 NM (9.4) $700
Amazing Spider-Man #50 FN+ (6.5) $245
Amazing Spider-Man #54 NM/MT (9.8) $5,427
Amazing Spider-Man #71 NM+ (9.6) $485
Amazing Spider-Man #75 VF/NM (9.0) $97
Atom #1 NM (9.4) $8,365 Twin Cities
Avengers #1 NM (9.4) $100,000
Avengers #1 VG/FN (5.0) $750
Avengers #1 VG+ (4.5) $1,430 (Sig. Series Stan Lee)
Avengers #2 NM- (9.2) $2,752
Avengers #2 FN- (5.5) $300
Avengers #4 NM+ (9.6) $91,501
Avengers #4 NM- (9.2) $6,600
Avengers #4 FN/VF (7.0) $1,000
Avengers #4 GD/VG (3.0) $325
Avengers #4 GD/VG (3.0) $300
Avengers #5 NM (9.4) $1,850
Avengers #12 NM+ (9.6) $9,088
Avengers #13 NM/MT (9.8) $8,375
Avengers #16 FN/VF (7.0) $100
Avengers #57 VF+ (8.5) $146
Batman #171 NM+ (9.6) $16,132.50 Twin Cities
Batman #181 VF (8.0) $260
Brave And The Bold #28 VF/NM (9.0) $31,070
Brave And The Bold #28 VF/NM (9.0) $21,510
Brave And The Bold #28 VF (8.0) $11,053 Savannah
Brave And The Bold #28 VG- (3.5) $1,000
Captain America #111 VF/NM (9.0) $100
Daredevil #1 VF- (7.5) $2,600 (Sig. Series Stan Lee)
Daredevil #1 VG- (3.5) $450
Daredevil #1 FR (1.0) $120
Daredevil #2 FN (6.0) $195
Daredevil #2 VG/FN (5.0) $160
Daredevil #3 VG (4.0) $82
Detective Comics #359 NM/MT (9.8) $13,127
Fantastic Four #1 NM (9.4) $300,000
Fantastic Four #1 FN+ (6.5) $13,500
Fantastic Four #1 FN (6.0) $9,212
Fantastic Four #1 VG (4.0) $4,000
Fantastic Four #1 GD+ (2.5) $2,000
Fantastic Four #1 GD (2.0) $1,700
Fantastic Four #1 FR/GD (1.5) $1,050
Fantastic Four #2 VG- (3.5) $639
Fantastic Four #3 VG (4.0) $450
Fantastic Four #4 FN (6.0) $1,100
Fantastic Four #4 VG/FN (5.0) $800
Fantastic Four #5 VF/NM (9.0) $15,822
Fantastic Four #11 GD/VG (3.0) $137
Fantastic Four #12 VG (4.0) $360
Fantastic Four #20 VG+ (4.5) $108
Fantastic Four #23 VF+ (8.5) $400
Fantastic Four #25 NM+ (9.6) $23,250
Fantastic Four #30 NM- (9.2) $650
Fantastic Four #42 NM- (9.2) $315
Fantastic Four #48 NM/MT (9.8) $13,145
Fantastic Four #48 NM+ (9.6) $4,750
Fantastic Four #48 FN (6.0) $300
Fantastic Four #49 VG/FN (5.0) $90
Fantastic Four #50 VG (4.0) $82
Fantastic Four #50 FN (6.0) $120
Fantastic Four #52 FN+ (6.5) $114

Fantastic Four #95 NM (9.4) $475
Flash #105 FN (6.0) $1,700
Flash #105 VF+ (8.5) $1,020 (restored)
Flash #123 GD (2.0) $140
Flash #151 VF (8.0) $95
Flash #175 VF (8.0) $125
Green Lantern #1 NM- (9.2) $16,730
Green Lantern #1 GD/VG (3.0) $400
Green Lantern #7 FN- (5.5) $340
Green Lantern #40 VF+ (8.5) $380
Green Lantern #40 VG+ (4.5) $97
Incredible Hulk #1 VF/NM (9.0) $74,000
Incredible Hulk #1 VF (8.0) $18,000
Incredible Hulk #1 FN- (5.5) $5,500
Incredible Hulk #1 GD- (1.8) $1,200
Incredible Hulk #2 NM (9.4) $23,255
Incredible Hulk #2 VF (8.0) $3,500
Incredible Hulk #2 VG+ (4.5) $400
Incredible Hulk #3 NM (9.4) $16,207
Incredible Hulk #5 VF/NM (9.0) $3,000
Incredible Hulk #6 NM+ (9.6) $18,000
Incredible Hulk #6 VG (4.0) $315
Incredible Hulk #105 NM/MT (9.8) $4,500
Journey Into Mystery #83 NM- (9.2) $82,800
Journey Into Mystery #83 VF/NM (9.0) $39,500
Journey Into Mystery #83 VF+ (8.5) $28,680 Twin Cities
Journey into Mystery #83 FN/VF (7.0) $6,000
Journey Into Mystery #83 GD+ (2.5) $1,200
Journey Into Mystery #85 NM- (9.2) $9,850
Journey Into Mystery #86 GD/VG (3.0) $95
Journey Into Mystery #90 VG/FN (5.0) $103
Journey Into Mystery #100 FN- (5.5) $83
Journey Into Mystery #112 VG+ (4.5) $110
Journey Into Mystery #120 VF (8.0) $89
Journey Into Mystery #124 NM+ (9.6) $475
Journey Into Mystery #124 VF (8.0) $97
Journey Into Mystery #125 NM+ (9.6) $1,275
Justice League Of America #1 VG+ (4.5) $700
Justice League Of America #1 VG (4.0) $650
Justice League Of America #1 GD+ (2.5) $420
Justice League Of America #22 VF/NM (9.0) $775
Metal Men #1 VF+ (8.5) $400
Richie Rich #1 NM+ (9.6) $23,900 File copy
Secret Hearts #121 NM/MT (9.8) $1,075
Sgt. Fury #1 FN (6.0) $500
Showcase #4 VG (4.0) $4,877
Showcase #6 VG/FN (5.0) $300 (restored)
Showcase #14 GD+ (2.5) $375
Showcase #22 VF (8.0) $23,900 Savannah
Showcase #22 FN (6.0) $8,000
Silver Surfer #1 VF+ (8.5) $675
Silver Surfer #1 VF+ (8.5) $650
Silver Surfer #1 VF+ (8.5) $552.50
Silver Surfer #3 VF (8.0) $111
Silver Surfer #4 VF/NM (9.0) $700
Silver Surfer #4 VF/NM (9.0) $550
Spectacular Spider-Man (Mag.) #1 NM+ (9.6) $500
Star Spangled War Stories #90 VG/FN (5.0) $370
Strange Tales #101 FN+ (6.5) $300
Strange Tales #110 NM (9.4) $22,107.50 Twin Cities
Strange Tales #114 VG (4.0) $100
Strange Tales Annual #1 VF- (7.5) $500
Tales Of Suspense #1 FN (6.0) $450
Tales Of Suspense #1 VG/FN (5.0) $400
Tales of Suspense #39 NM (9.4) $147,500
Tales Of Suspense #39 NM- (9.2) $56,762.50 Twin Cities
Tales of Suspense #39 NM- (9.2) $49,750
Tales of Suspense #39 VF/NM (9.0) $6,500 (restored)
Tales of Suspense #39 FN/VF (7.0) $3,805
Tales of Suspense #39 GD/VG (3.0) $1,100
Tales Of Suspense #39 VG- (3.5) $1,250
Tales Of Suspense #39 GD+ (2.5) $1,300
Tales Of Suspense #39 GD (2.0) $750
Tales Of Suspense #39 GD- (1.8) $300
Tales Of Suspense #40 FN- (5.5) $540
Tales of Suspense #40 GD- (1.8) $130
Tales of Suspense #42 VG+ (4.5) $113
Tales Of Suspense #48 FN/VF (7.0) $450
Tales of Suspense #49 VG (4.0) $108
Tales To Astonish #27 FN+ (6.5) $1,600
Tales To Astonish #27 VG (4.0) $600
Tales To Astonish #27 VG- (3.5) $765
Tales To Astonish #44 FN/VF (7.0) $320
Thor #127 NM+ (9.6) $1,350
Thor #137 NM/MT (9.8) $1,200
Thor #139 NM+ (9.6) $540
Thor #142 NM+ (9.6) $540
Turok Son Of Stone #3 VF/NM (9.0) $320
Turok Son Of Stone #7 NM- (9.2) $300
X-Men #1 NM+ (9.6) $200,000
X-Men #1 NM- (9.2) $60,000
X-Men #1 VF/NM (9.0) $28,680
X-Men #1 VF- (7.5) $300
X-Men #1 FN (6.0) $4,000
X-Men #1 FN (6.0) $2,200
X-Men #1 VG- (3.5) $1,700 (Sig. Series Stan Lee)
X-Men #2 NM (9.4) $10,000
X-Men #2 GD (2.0) $152
X-Men #5 FN/VF (7.0) $350
X-Men #6 VG (4.0) $100
X-Men #7 VF- (7.5) $450
X-Men #9 FN+ (6.5) $170
X-Men #28 NM (9.4) $1,000
X-Men #56 VF+ (8.5) $97

BRONZE AGE - SALES OF CGC-CERTIFIED COMICS

Amazing Adventures #13 NM/MT (9.8) $1,450
Amazing Spider-Man #101 NM/MT (9.8) $5,477
Amazing Spider-Man #129 NM- (9.2) $1,300
CGC Signature Series
Amazing Spider-Man #129 VF/NM (9.0) $585
Amazing Spider-Man #129 VF+ (8.5) $550
Amazing Spider-Man #252 NM- (9.2) $80
Avengers #96 NM/MT (9.8) $1,000
Batman #227 NM+ (9.6) $1,851
Batman #232 NM/MT (9.8) $1,971.75
Batman #232 NM- (9.2) $400
Cerebus The Aardvark #1 FN/VF (7.0) $1,015.75
Conan the Barbarian #1 NM+ (9.6) $1,912
Twin Cities
Daredevil #168 NM (9.4) $190
Daredevil #169 NM+ (9.6) $90
Detective Comics #400 NM+ (9.6) $1,673
Detective Comics #405 NM+ (9.6) $1,075.50
Ghost Rider #1 NM/MT (9.8) $2,629
Ghost Rider #1 VF/NM (9.0) $300
Giant-Size X-Men #1 NM+ (9.6) $3,000
Giant-Size X-Men #1 NM (9.4) $1,314.50
Giant-Size X-Men #1 NM- (9.2) $1,075.50
Giant Size X-Men #1 VF- (7.5) $350
Green Lantern #76 NM/MT (9.8) $37,343.75
Green Lantern #76 NM+ (9.6) $10,157.50
Green Lantern #76 NM+ (9.6) $8,365
Green Lantern #76 FN- (5.5) $210
Green Lantern #86 NM/MT (9.8) $1,400
House of Mystery #175 NM (9.4) $1,314.50 Savannah
House of Secrets #92 NM+ (9.6) $5,611
Howard the Duck #1 NM/MT (9.8) $1,011
Incredible Hulk #181 NM/MT (9.8) $15,001
Incredible Hulk #181 NM (9.4) $2,868
Incredible Hulk #181 VF/NM (9.0) $1,375
Incredible Hulk #181 VF+ (8.5) $1,200
Incredible Hulk #182 VF (8.0) $80
Iron Fist #14 NM/MT (9.8) $1,015.75
Iron Man #100 NM+ (9.6) $56
Marvel Comics Super Special #1 VF/NM (9.0) $150
Marvel Spotlight #5 NM (9.4) $375
Silver Surfer #14 NM+ (9.6) $1,792.50 Twin Cities
Star Wars #1 FN (6.0) $1,200 35¢-c variant
Superman's Pal Jimmy Olsen #140 NM (9.4) $90
Tomb of Dracula #10 NM/MT (9.8) $1,015.75
Transformers #1 MT (9.9) $1,550
Vampirella #57 NM/MT (9.8) $400
Weird Western Tales #14 NM- (9.2) $92
Wolverine #1 GM (10.0) $14,000
Wolverine #1 NM/MT (9.8) $300
Wonder Woman #201 NM+ (9.6) $262.90 Savannah
X-Men #94 NM/MT (9.8) $26,500
X-Men #94 NM/MT (9.8) $16,730
X-Men #94 NM/MT (9.8) $12,547.50
X-Men #94 NM- (9.2) $1,050
X-Men #94 FN/VF (7.0) $400
X-Men #99 VF/NM (9.0) $110
X-Men #102 VF/NM (9.0) $85
X-Men #141 NM (9.4) $80
X-Men (Uncanny) #142 NM (9.4) $100

COPPER AGE - SALES OF CGC-CERTIFIED COMICS

Amazing Spider-Man #300 NM/MT (9.8) $478
Amazing Spider-Man #300 NM+ (9.6) $210
Amazing Spider-Man #300 NM (9.4) $105
Batman: The Dark Knight Returns #1 NM+ (9.6) $100
Daredevil #181 NM+ (9.6) $50
Marvel Super Heroes Sectret Wars #8 GM (10.0) $5,676.25
Teenage Mutant Ninja Turtles #1 NM- (9.2) $3,107
X-Men #266 NM- (9.2) $50

MODERN AGE - SALES OF CGC-CERTIFIED COMICS

Blackest Night #1 NM/MT (9.8) $137.50
Sketch variant
Bone #1 NM+ (9.6) $1,742.99
Captain America #14 NM/MT (9.8) $80
Chew #1 NM/MT (9.8) $395 (Sig. Series)
Civil War #1 NM+ (9.6) $70 1:75 Sketch variant
Kick-Ass #1 NM+ (9.6) $55
Miracleman TPB #3 NM (9.4) $250
New Mutants #98 NM+ (9.6) $107.55
Siege #1 NM/MT (9.8) $112.50 Quesada variant
Spawn #1 NM/MT (9.8) $204.61 (Sig. Series)
Superman #75 Platinum NM (9.4) $130
Superman/Batman #1 RRP NM/MT (9.8) $555
Ultimate Spider-Man #1 NM/MT (9.8) $676
White variant
Walking Dead #3 NM/MT (9.8) $299.99 (Sig. Series)

TOP BOOKS

The following tables denote the rate of appreciation of the top Golden Age, Platinum Age, Silver Age and Bronze Age books, as well as selected genres over the past year. The retail value for a Near Mint- copy of each book (or VF where a Near Mint- copy is not known to exist) in 2011 is compared to its Near Mint- value in 2010. The rate of return for 2011 over 2010 is given. The place in rank is given for each comic by year, with its corresponding value in highest known grade. These tables can be very useful in forecasting trends in the market place. For instance, the investor might want to know which book is yielding the best dividend from one year to the next, or one might just be interested in seeing how the popularity of books changes from year to year. For instance, *Archie Comics* #1 was in 35th place in 2010 and has increased to 23rd place in 2011. Premium books are also included in these tables and are denoted with an asterisk(*).

The following tables are meant as a guide to the investor. However, it should be pointed out that trends may change at anytime and that some books can meet market resistance with a slowdown in price increases, while others can develop into real comers from a presently dormant state. In the long run, if the investor sticks to the books that are appreciating steadily each year, he shouldn't go very far wrong.

TOP 100 GOLDEN AGE BOOKS

TITLE/ISSUE#	2011 RANK	2011 NM- PRICE	2010 RANK	2010 NM- PRICE	$ INCR.	% INCR.
Action Comics #1	1	$1,400,000	1	$1,200,000	$200,000	17%
Detective Comics #27	2	$1,200,000	2	$1,050,000	$150,000	14%
Superman #1	3	$560,000	3	$500,000	$60,000	12%
Marvel Comics #1	4	$460,000	4	$450,000	$10,000	2%
All-American Comics #16	5	$400,000	5	$350,000	$50,000	14%
Batman #1	6	$285,000	6	$250,000	$35,000	14%
Captain America Comics #1	7	$240,000	7	$215,000	$25,000	12%
Flash Comics #1	8	$155,000	8	$145,000	$10,000	7%
More Fun Comics #52	9	$145,000	9	$135,000	$10,000	7%
Action Comics #7	10	$125,000	11	$100,000	$25,000	25%
Adventure Comics #40	11	$120,000	10	$115,000	$5,000	4%
Detective Comics #31	12	$100,000	14	$90,000	$10,000	11%
Detective Comics #33	12	$100,000	13	$92,000	$8,000	9%
Whiz Comics #2 (#1)	12	$100,000	12	$95,000	$5,000	5%
Action Comics #2	15	$95,000	17	$84,000	$11,000	13%
All Star Comics #3	16	$90,000	15	$85,000	$5,000	6%
Detective Comics #29	17	$88,000	18	$80,000	$8,000	10%
Detective Comics #38	17	$88,000	15	$85,000	$3,000	4%
Detective Comics #1	19	VF $84,000	19	VF $77,000	$7,000	9%
Marvel Mystery Comics #9	20	$80,000	20	$70,000	$10,000	14%
All Star Comics #8	21	$75,000	20	$70,000	$5,000	7%
More Fun Comics #53	21	$75,000	20	$70,000	$5,000	7%
Archie Comics #1	23	$70,000	35	$50,000	$20,000	40%
Pep Comics #22	23	$70,000	35	$50,000	$20,000	40%
Marvel Mystery Comics #2	25	$68,000	23	$65,000	$3,000	5%
Action Comics #10	26	$66,000	28	$55,000	$11,000	20%
Human Torch #2 (#1)	27	$65,000	24	$64,000	$1,000	2%
Sub-Mariner Comics #1	27	$65,000	24	$64,000	$1,000	2%
Green Lantern #1	29	$64,000	26	$62,000	$2,000	3%
Sensation Comics #1	30	$62,000	27	$60,000	$2,000	3%
Action Comics #3	31	$60,000	30	$54,000	$6,000	11%
Captain Marvel Adventures #1	32	$57,000	28	$55,000	$2,000	4%
Marvel Mystery Comics #5	32	$57,000	30	$54,000	$3,000	6%
Detective Comics #28	34	$56,000	35	$50,000	$6,000	12%
Wonder Woman #1	35	$55,000	32	$52,000	$3,000	6%
Adventure Comics #48	36	$54,000	32	$52,000	$2,000	4%
New Fun Comics #1	37	VF $52,000	34	VF $51,000	$1,000	2%
Suspense Comics #3	38	$50,000	38	$45,000	$5,000	11%
Detective Comics #35	39	$46,000	39	$40,000	$6,000	15%
Walt Disney's Comics & Stories #1	40	$42,000	39	$40,000	$2,000	5%

TITLE/ISSUE#	2011 RANK	2011 NM- PRICE	2010 RANK	2010 NM- PRICE	$ INCR.	% INCR.
All-American Comics #19	41	$39,000	43	$37,000	$2,000	5%
Captain America Comics #2	42	$38,000	46	$35,000	$3,000	9%
Daring Mystery Comics #1	42	$38,000	41	$38,000	$0	0%
Marvel Mystery Comics #3	42	$38,000	44	$36,000	$2,000	6%
*Marvel Mystery Comics 132 pg.	42	VF $38,000	44	VF $36,000	$2,000	6%
Superman #2	42	$38,000	46	$35,000	$3,000	9%
All Winners Comics #1	47	$35,000	41	$38,000	-$3,000	-8%
Batman #2	47	$35,000	49	$32,000	$3,000	9%
Captain America Comics 132 pg.	47	VF $35,000	48	VF $33,000	$2,000	6%
Action Comics #4	50	$34,000	52	$31,000	$3,000	10%
Action Comics #5	50	$34,000	52	$31,000	$3,000	10%
Action Comics #6	50	$34,000	52	$31,000	$3,000	10%
More Fun Comics #54	50	$34,000	49	$32,000	$2,000	6%
Marvel Mystery Comics #4	54	$33,000	59	$29,000	$4,000	14%
More Fun Comics #55	54	$33,000	52	$31,000	$2,000	6%
Motion Picture Funnies Wkly #1	54	$33,000	49	$32,000	$1,000	3%
Famous Funnies-Series 1 #1	57	VF $31,000	56	VF $30,000	$1,000	3%
More Fun Comics #73	57	$31,000	56	$30,000	$1,000	3%
Action Comics #13	59	$30,000	70	$25,000	$5,000	20%
All-Select Comics #1	59	$30,000	62	$28,000	$2,000	7%
Amazing Man Comics #5	59	$30,000	59	$29,000	$1,000	3%
Captain America Comics #3	59	$30,000	65	$27,000	$3,000	11%
New Book of Comics #1	59	VF $30,000	56	VF $30,000	$0	0%
New York World's Fair 1939	64	VF/NM $29,000	59	VF/NM $29,000	$0	0%
Mystic Comics #1	65	$28,000	65	$27,000	$1,000	4%
Wonder Comics #1	65	$28,000	63	$27,500	$500	2%
Marvel Mystery Comics #8	67	$27,000	70	$25,000	$2,000	8%
Wow Comics (FAW) #1	67	$27,000	65	$27,000	$0	0%
Silver Streak Comics #6	69	$26,500	68	$26,000	$500	2%
All-Flash #1	70	$26,000	63	$27,500	-$1,500	-5%
Young Allies Comics #1	70	$26,000	69	$25,500	$500	2%
Adventure Comics #73	72	$25,000	70	$25,000	$0	0%
Four Color Ser. 1 (Donald Duck) #4	72	$25,000	74	$24,000	$1,000	4%
Marvel Mystery Comics #10	72	$25,000	79	$23,000	$2,000	9%
World's Best Comics #1	72	$25,000	70	$25,000	$0	0%
New Fun Comics #6	76	VF $24,500	74	VF $24,000	$500	2%
Planet Comics #1	77	$24,500	74	$24,000	$500	2%
Adventure Comics #61	78	$24,000	74	$24,000	$0	0%
Detective Comics #2	78	VF $24,000	82	VF $22,000	$2,000	9%
Red Raven Comics #1	78	$24,000	78	$23,500	$500	2%
All Star Comics #1	81	$23,500	79	$23,000	$500	2%
Daredevil #1	81	$23,500	79	$23,000	$500	2%
All-American Comics #18	83	$23,000	82	$22,000	$1,000	5%
Famous Funnies #1	83	VF $23,000	81	VF $22,500	$500	2%
Green Giant Comics #1	83	$23,000	82	$22,000	$1,000	5%
Looney Tunes and Merrie Melodies #1	86	$22,500	82	$22,000	$500	2%
New Fun Comics #2	86	VF $22,500	82	VF $22,000	$500	2%
Action Comics #8	88	$22,000	89	$20,000	$2,000	10%
Action Comics #9	88	$22,000	89	$20,000	$2,000	10%
All-American Comics #17	88	$22,000	96	$19,000	$3,000	16%
All-American Comics #25	88	$22,000	88	$21,000	$1,000	5%
Superman #3	88	$22,000	89	$20,000	$2,000	10%
Jumbo Comics #1	93	VF $21,500	87	VF $21,500	$0	0%
Daring Mystery Comics #2	94	$21,000	89	$20,000	$1,000	5%
Dick Tracy-Feature Book nn (#1)	94	$21,000	96	$19,000	$2,000	11%
Double Action Comics #2	96	$20,500	89	$20,000	$500	3%
Batman #3	97	$20,000	-	$18,000	$2,000	11%
Comics Magazine #1	97	VF $20,000	96	VF $19,000	$1,000	5%
Exciting Comics #9	97	$20,000	96	$19,000	$1,000	5%
Four Color Ser. 2 (Donald Duck) #9	97	$20,000	96	$19,000	$1,000	5%
New Comics #1	97	VF $20,000	89	VF $20,000	$0	0%
USA Comics #1	97	$20,000	89	$20,000	$0	0%

TOP 20 SILVER AGE BOOKS

TITLE/ISSUE#	2011 RANK	2011 NM- PRICE	2010 RANK	2010 NM- PRICE	$ INCR.	% INCR.
Amazing Fantasy #15	1	$125,000	1	$100,000	$25,000	25%
Fantastic Four #1	2	$80,000	2	$70,000	$10,000	14%
Incredible Hulk #1	3	$75,000	3	$65,000	$10,000	15%
Showcase #4 (The Flash)	4	$56,000	4	$54,000	$2,000	4%
Amazing Spider-Man #1	5	$54,000	5	$50,000	$4,000	8%
Journey Into Mystery #83 (Thor)	6	$30,000	7	$24,000	$6,000	25%
X-Men #1	6	$30,000	6	$26,000	$4,000	15%
Tales of Suspense #39 (Iron Man)	8	$25,000	8	$20,000	$5,000	25%
Brave and the Bold #28	9	$20,000	10	$16,000	$4,000	25%
Showcase #8 (The Flash)	10	$18,500	9	$18,500	$0	0%
The Flash #105	11	$18,000	10	$16,000	$2,000	13%
Showcase #22 (Green Lantern)	12	$16,000	17	$12,500	$3,500	28%
Adventure Comics #247 (Legion)	13	$15,000	14	$13,500	$1,500	11%
Avengers #1	13	$15,000	17	$12,500	$2,500	20%
Justice League of America #1	13	$15,000	12	$14,000	$1,000	7%
Tales To Astonish #27 (Ant-Man)	13	$15,000	15	$13,000	$2,000	15%
Fantastic Four #5	17	$14,000	15	$13,000	$1,000	8%
Showcase #9 (Lois Lane)	17	$14,000	12	$14,000	$0	0%
Green Lantern #1	19	$12,500	19	$11,000	$1,500	14%
Amazing Spider-Man #2	20	$11,000	21	$10,000	$1,000	10%
Fantastic Four #2	20	$11,000	20	$10,500	$500	5%

TOP 10 BRONZE AGE BOOKS

TITLE/ISSUE#	2011 RANK	2011 NM- PRICE	2010 RANK	2010 NM- PRICE	$ INCR.	% INCR.
Star Wars #1 (35¢ price variant)	1	$3,000	1	$2,500	$500	20%
Green Lantern #76	2	$2,500	2	$2,000	$500	25%
Incredible Hulk #181	3	$1,700	3	$1,650	$50	3%
Iron Fist #14 (35¢ price variant)	4	$1,650	4	$1,600	$50	3%
Giant-Size X-Men #1	5	$1,300	5	$1,300	$0	0%
X-Men #94	6	$1,250	6	$1,200	$50	4%
Cerebus #1	7	$1,200	7	$1,100	$100	9%
DC 100 Page Super Spectacular #5	8	$1,150	9	$1,050	$100	10%
House of Secrets #92	8	$1,150	7	$1,100	$50	5%
Amazing Spider-Man #129	10	$925	10	$900	$25	3%

TOP 10 COPPER AGE BOOKS

TITLE/ISSUE#	2011 RANK	2011 NM- PRICE	2010 RANK	2010 NM- PRICE	$ INCR.	% INCR.
Gobbledygook #1	1	$5,000	2	$1,200	$3,800	317%
Gobbledygook #2	2	$2,000	4	$750	$1,250	167%
Miracleman #1 Gold Edition	3	$1,500	1	$1,500	$0	0%
Miracleman #1 Blue Edition	4	$800	3	$800	$0	0%
Albedo #2	5	$750	5	$700	$50	7%
Vampirella #113	6	$550	6	$535	$15	3%
Grendel #1	7	$190	7	$190	$0	0%
Primer #2	8	$160	8	$150	$10	7%
Spider-Man #1 (Platinum)	9	$130	9	$130	$0	0%
Spider-Man #1 (2nd pr. w/Gold UPC)	10	$120	10	$120	$0	0%

*Teenage Mutant Ninja Turtles #1 - Recent sales of this book include a CGC 9.6 for $11,500

TOP 20 BIG LITTLE BOOKS

BOOK #	TITLE	2011 RANK	2011 VF/NM PRICE	2010 RANK	2010 VF/NM PRICE	$ INCR.	% INCR.
731	Mickey Mouse the Mail Pilot (variant version of Mickey Mouse #717) (Fine copy sold at auction for $5,090)						
nn	Mickey Mouse and Minnie Mouse at Macy's	2	$3,500	2	$3,500	$0	0%
717	Mickey Mouse (skinny Mickey on-c)	3	$3,135	3	$3,135	$0	0%
W-707	Dick Tracy The Detective	4	$2,500	5	$2,310	$190	8%
nn	Mickey Mouse and Minnie March to Macy's	5	$2,400	4	$2,400	$0	0%
725	Big Little Mother Goose HC	5	$2,400	6	$2,200	$200	9%
717	Mickey Mouse (reg. Mickey on-c)	7	$1,750	7	$1,650	$100	6%
4063	Popeye Thimble Theater Starring... (2nd printing)	8	$1,620	8	$1,620	$0	0%
721	Big Little Paint Book (336 pg.)	9	$1,500	9	$1,500	$0	0%
725	Big Little Mother Goose SC	9	$1,500	9	$1,500	$0	0%
nn	Mickey Mouse the Mail Pilot (Great Big Midget Book)	9	$1,500	12	$1,400	$100	7%
nn	Mickey Mouse (Great Big Midget Book)	12	$1,485	12	$1,400	$85	6%
4062	Mickey Mouse and the Smugglers	13	$1,430	11	$1,430	$0	0%
4063	Popeye Thimble Theater Starring...(1st pr.)	14	$1,385	14	$1,385	$0	0%
nn	Buck Rogers	15	$1,320	15	$1,320	$0	0%
nn	Mickey Mouse Silly Symphonies	15	$1,320	15	$1,320	$0	0%
4062	Mickey Mouse, The Story of...	17	$1,210	17	$1,210	$0	0%
721	Big Little Paint Book (330 pg.)	18	$1,200	18	$1,200	$0	0%
nn	Mickey Mouse Sails For Treasure Island (Great Big Midget Book)	18	$1,200	18	$1,200	$0	0%
nn	Mickey Mouse and the Magic Carpet	20	$1,050	19	$1,050	$0	0%

TOP 10 PLATINUM AGE BOOKS

TITLE/ISSUE#	2011 RANK	2011 PRICE	2010 RANK	2010 PRICE	$ INCR.	% INCR.
Yellow Kid in McFadden Flats	1	FN $14,000	1	FN $14,000	$0	0%
Mickey Mouse Book (2nd printing)-variant	2	FN $12,000	2	FN $12,000	$0	0%
Mickey Mouse Book (1st printing)	2	VF $12,000	2	VF $12,000	$0	0%
Mickey Mouse Book (2nd printing)	4	VF $10,000	4	VF $10,000	$0	0%
Little Sammy Sneeze	5	FN $6,000	5	FN $6,000	$0	0%
Pore Li'l Mose	6	FN $5,775	6	FN $5,775	$0	0%
Buster Brown and His Resolutions 1903	7	FN $5,500	7	FN $5,500	$0	0%
Little Nemo 1906	8	FN $5,000	8	FN $5,000	$0	0%
Little Nemo 1909	9	FN $4,000	9	FN $4,000	$0	0%
Yellow Kid #1	10	FN $3,500	10	FN $3,500	$0	0%

TOP 10 CRIME BOOKS

TITLE/ISSUE#	2011 RANK	2011 NM- PRICE	2010 RANK	2010 NM- PRICE	$ INCR.	% INCR.
Crime Does Not Pay #22	1	$8,200	1	$7,500	$700	9%
Crime Does Not Pay #24	2	$5,200	2	$4,500	$700	16%
Crime Does Not Pay #23	3	$3,600	3	$3,000	$600	20%
True Crime Comics #2	4	$2,800	4	$2,500	$300	12%
The Killers #1	5	$2,000	6	$1,850	$150	8%
Crimes By Women #1	6	$1,950	5	$1,900	$50	3%
True Crime Comics #3	7	$1,900	7	$1,800	$100	6%
The Killers #2	8	$1,600	9	$1,500	$100	7%
True Crime Comics #4	9	$1,550	8	$1,525	$25	2%
Crime Does Not Pay, Best of ('44)	10	$1,400	-	$1,300	$100	8%
Crime Smashers #1	10	$1,400	-	$1,375	$25	2%
True Crime Comics V2 #1	10	$1,400	10	$1,400	$0	4%

TOP 10 HORROR BOOKS

TITLE/ISSUE#	2011 RANK	2011 NM- PRICE	2010 RANK	2010 NM- PRICE	$ INCR.	% INCR.
Vault of Horror #12	1	$8,700	1	$8,500	$200	2%
Eerie #1	2	$8,500	2	$8,200	$300	4%
Tales of Terror Annual #1	3	VF $6,600	3	VF $6,400	$200	3%
Journey into Mystery #1	4	$5,800	4	$5,500	$300	5%
Strange Tales #1	5	$5,500	5	$5,300	$200	4%
Crypt of Terror #17	6	$5,200	6	$5,100	$100	2%
Haunt of Fear #15	7	$5,100	6	$5,100	$0	0%
Crime Patrol #15	8	$4,700	8	$4,700	$0	0%
Tales to Astonish #1	9	$4,200	9	$4,000	$200	5%
House of Mystery #1	10	$3,900	10	$3,800	$100	3%

TOP 10 ROMANCE BOOKS

TITLE/ISSUE#	2011 RANK	2011 NM- PRICE	2010 RANK	2010 NM- PRICE	$ INCR.	% INCR.
Giant Comics Edition #12	1	$4,800	1	$4,000	$800	20%
Negro Romance #1	2	$2,200	2	$2,000	$200	10%
Negro Romance #2	3	$1,700	3	$1,600	$100	6%
Negro Romance #3	3	$1,700	3	$1,600	$100	6%
Intimate Confessions #1	5	$1,600	5	$1,400	$200	14%
Giant Comics Edition #9	6	$1,400	6	$1,250	$150	12%
Modern Love #1	7	$1,300	6	$1,250	$50	4%
A Moon, A Girl...Romance #9	8	$1,275	6	$1,250	$25	2%
A Moon, A Girl...Romance #12	8	$1,275	6	$1,250	$25	2%
Giant Comics Edition #9	10	$1,250	-	$1,100	$150	14%

TOP 10 SCI-FI BOOKS

TITLE/ISSUE#	2011 RANK	2011 NM- PRICE	2010 RANK	2010 NM- PRICE	$ INCR.	% INCR.
Mystery In Space #1	1	$6,400	1	$6,300	$100	2%
Strange Adventures #1	2	$5,900	2	$5,900	$0	0%
Showcase #17 (Adam Strange)	3	$5,200	3	$5,000	$200	4%
Weird Science-Fantasy Annual 1952	4	$4,300	4	$4,200	$100	2%
Showcase #15 (Space Ranger)	5	$4,200	5	$4,000	$200	5%
Journey Into Unknown Worlds #36	6	$4,100	5	$4,000	$100	3%
Fawcett Movie #15 (Man From Planet X)	7	$3,800	7	$3,800	$0	0%
Strange Adventures #9	8	$3,550	8	$3,550	$0	0%
Weird Fantasy #13 (#1)	9	$3,500	9	$3,500	$0	0%
Weird Science #12 (#1)	9	$3,500	9	$3,500	$0	0%

TOP 10 WESTERN BOOKS

TITLE/ISSUE#	2011 RANK	2011 NM- PRICE	2010 RANK	2010 NM- PRICE	$ INCR.	% INCR.
Gene Autry Comics #1	1	$10,000	1	$10,000	$0	0%
Hopalong Cassidy #1	2	$6,000	2	$7,500	-$1,500	-20%
*Lone Ranger Ice Cream 1939 2nd	2	VF $6,000	3	VF $6,000	$0	0%
*Lone Ranger Ice Cream 1939	4	VF $4,200	4	VF $4,200	$0	0%
Roy Rogers Four Color #38	5	$4,000	5	$4,000	$0	0%
Red Ryder Comics #1	6	$3,800	7	$3,800	$0	0%
*Tom Mix Ralston #1	7	$3,600	8	$3,600	$0	0%
*Red Ryder Victory Patrol '42	8	$3,500	5	$4,000	-$500	-13%
Western Picture Stories #1	9	$3,100	-	$3,000	$100	3%
*Red Ryder Victory Patrol '43	10	$3,000	9	$3,500	-$500	-14%
*Red Ryder Victory Patrol '44	10	$3,000	9	$3,500	-$500	-14%

GRADING DEFINITIONS

When grading a comic book, common sense must be employed. The overall eye appeal and beauty of the comic book must be taken into account along with its technical flaws to arrive at the appropriate grade.

10.0 GEM MINT (GM): This is an exceptional example of a given book - the best ever seen. The slightest bindery defects and/or printing flaws may be seen only upon very close inspection. The overall look is "as if it has never been handled or released for purchase." Only the slightest bindery or printing defects are allowed, and these would be imperceptible on first viewing. No bindery tears. Cover is flat with no surface wear. Inks are bright with high reflectivity. Well centered and firmly secured to interior pages. Corners are cut square and sharp. No creases. No dates or stamped markings allowed. No soiling, staining or other discoloration. Spine is tight and flat. No spine roll or split allowed. Staples must be original, centered and clean with no rust. No staple tears or stress lines. Paper is white, supple and fresh. No hint of acidity in the odor of the newsprint. No interior autographs or owner signatures. Centerfold is firmly secure. No interior tears.

9.9 MINT (MT): Near perfect in every way. Only subtle bindery or printing defects are allowed. No bindery tears. Cover is flat with no surface wear. Inks are bright with high reflectivity. Generally well centered and firmly secured to interior pages. Corners are cut square and sharp. No creases. Small, inconspicuous, lightly penciled, stamped or inked arrival dates are acceptable as long as they are in an unobtrusive location. No soiling, staining or other discoloration. Spine is tight and flat. No spine roll or split allowed. Staples must be original, generally centered and clean with no rust. No staple tears or stress lines. Paper is white, supple and fresh. No hint of acidity in the odor of the newsprint. Centerfold is firmly secure. No interior tears.

9.8 NEAR MINT/MINT (NM/MT): Nearly perfect in every way with only minor imperfections that keep it from the next higher grade. Only subtle bindery or printing defects are allowed. No bindery tears. Cover is flat with no surface wear. Inks are bright with high reflectivity. Generally well centered and firmly secured to interior pages. Corners are cut square and sharp. No creases. Small, inconspicuous, lightly penciled, stamped or inked arrival dates are acceptable as long as they are in an unobtrusive location. No soiling, staining or other discoloration. Spine is tight and flat. No spine roll or split allowed. Staples must be original, generally centered and clean with no rust. No staple tears or stress lines. Paper is off-white to white, supple and fresh. No hint of acidity in the odor of the newsprint. Centerfold is firmly secure. Only the slightest interior tears are allowed.

9.6 NEAR MINT+ (NM+): Nearly perfect with a minor additional virtue or virtues that raise it from Near Mint. The overall look is "as if it was just purchased and read once or twice." Only subtle bindery or printing defects are allowed. No bindery tears are allowed, although on Golden Age books bindery tears of up to 1/8" have been noted. Cover is flat with no surface wear. Inks are bright with high reflectivity. Well centered and firmly secured to interior pages. One corner may be almost imperceptibly blunted, but still almost sharp and cut square. Almost imperceptible indentations are permissible, but no creases, bends, or color break. Small, inconspicuous, lightly penciled, stamped or inked arrival dates are acceptable as long as they are in an unobtrusive location. No soiling, staining or other discoloration. Spine is tight and flat. No spine roll or split allowed. Staples must be original, generally centered, with only the slightest discoloration. No staple tears, stress lines, or rust migration. Paper is off-white, supple and fresh. No hint of acidity in the odor of the newsprint. Centerfold is firmly secure. Only the slightest interior tears are allowed.

9.4 NEAR MINT (NM): Nearly perfect with only minor imperfections that keep it from the next higher grade. Minor feathering that does not distract from the overall beauty of an otherwise higher grade copy is acceptable for this grade. The overall look is "as if it was just purchased and read once or twice." Subtle bindery defects are allowed. Bindery tears must be less than 1/16" on Silver Age and later books, although on Golden Age books bindery tears of up to 1/4" have been noted. Cover is flat with no surface wear. Inks are bright with high reflectivity. Generally well centered and secured to interior pages. Corners are cut square and sharp with ever-so-slight blunting permitted. A 1/16" bend is permitted with no color break. No creases. Small, inconspicuous, lightly penciled, stamped or inked arrival dates are acceptable as long as they are in an unobtrusive location. No soiling, staining or other discoloration apart from slight foxing. Spine is tight and flat. No spine roll or split allowed. Staples are generally centered; may have slight discoloration. No staple tears are allowed; almost no stress lines. No rust migration. In rare cases, a comic was not stapled at the bindery and therefore has a missing staple; this is not considered a defect. Any staple can be replaced on books up to Fine, but only vintage staples can be used on books from Very Fine to Near Mint. Mint books must have original staples. Paper is cream to off-white, supple and fresh. No hint of acidity in the odor of the newsprint. Centerfold is secure. Slight interior tears are allowed.

9.2 NEAR MINT– (NM–): Nearly perfect with only a minor additional defect or defects that keep it from Near Mint. A limited number of minor bindery defects are allowed. A light, barely noticeable water stain or minor foxing that does not distract from the beauty of the book is acceptable for this grade. Cover is flat with no surface wear. Inks are bright with only the slightest dimming of reflectivity. Generally well centered and secured to interior pages. Corners are cut square and sharp with ever-so-slight blunting permitted. A 1/16"-1/8" bend is permitted with no color break. No creases. Small, inconspicuous, lightly penciled, stamped or inked arrival dates are acceptable as long as they are in an unobtrusive location. No soiling, staining or other discoloration apart from slight foxing. Spine is tight and flat. No spine roll or split allowed. Staples may show some discoloration. No staple tears are allowed; almost no stress lines. No rust migration. In rare cases, a comic was not stapled at the bindery and therefore has a missing staple; this is not considered a defect. Any staple can be replaced on books up to Fine, but only vintage staples can be used on books from Very Fine to Near Mint. Mint books must have original staples. Paper is cream to off-white, supple and fresh. No hint of acidity in the odor of the newsprint. Centerfold is secure. Slight interior tears are allowed.

9.0 VERY FINE/NEAR MINT (VF/NM): Nearly perfect with outstanding eye appeal. A limited number of bindery defects are allowed. Almost flat cover with almost imperceptible wear. Inks are bright with slightly diminished reflectivity. An 1/8" bend is allowed if color is not broken. Corners are cut square and sharp with ever-so-slight blunting permitted but no creases. Several lightly penciled, stamped or inked arrival dates are acceptable. No obvious soiling, staining or other discoloration, except for very minor foxing. Spine is tight and flat. No spine roll or split allowed. Staples may show some discoloration. Only the slightest staple tears are allowed. A very minor accumulation of stress lines may be present if they are nearly imperceptible. No rust migration. In rare cases, a comic was not stapled at the bindery and therefore has a missing staple; this is not considered a defect. Any staple can be replaced on books up to Fine, but only vintage staples can be used on books from Very Fine to Near Mint. Mint books must have original staples. Paper is cream to off-white and supple. No hint of acidity in the odor of the newsprint. Centerfold is secure. Very minor interior tears may be present.

8.5 VERY FINE+ (VF+): Fits the criteria for Very Fine but with an additional virtue or small accumulation of virtues that improves the book's appearance by a perceptible amount.

8.0 VERY FINE (VF): An excellent copy with outstanding eye appeal. Sharp, bright and clean with supple pages. A comic book in this grade has the appearance of having been carefully handled. A limited accumulation of minor bindery defects is allowed. Cover is relatively flat with minimal surface wear beginning to show, possibly including some minute wear at corners. Inks are generally bright with moderate to high reflectivity. A 1/4" crease is acceptable if color is not broken. Stamped or inked arrival dates may be present. No obvious soiling, staining or other discoloration, except for minor foxing. Spine is almost flat with no roll. Possible minor color break allowed. Staples may show some discoloration. Very slight staple tears and a few almost very minor to minor stress lines may be present. No rust migration. In rare cases, a comic was not stapled at the bindery and therefore has a missing staple; this is not considered a defect. Any staple can be replaced on books up to Fine, but only vintage staples can be used on books from Very Fine to Near Mint. Mint books must have original staples. Paper is tan to cream and supple. No hint of acidity in the odor of the newsprint. Centerfold is mostly secure. Minor interior tears at the margin may be present.

7.5 VERY FINE– (VF–): Fits the criteria for Very Fine but with an additional defect or small accumulation of defects that detracts from the book's appearance by a perceptible amount.

7.0 FINE/VERY FINE (FN/VF): An above-average copy that shows minor wear but is still relatively flat and clean with outstanding eye appeal. A small accumulation of minor bindery defects is allowed. Minor cover wear beginning to show with interior yellowing or tanning allowed, possibly including minor creases. Corners may be blunted or abraded. Inks are generally bright with a moderate reduction in reflectivity. Stamped or inked arrival dates may be present. No obvious soiling, staining or other discoloration, except for minor foxing. The slightest spine roll may be present, as well as a possible moderate color break. Staples may show some discoloration. Slight staple tears and a slight accumulation of light stress lines may be present. Slight rust migration. In rare cases, a comic was not stapled at the bindery and therefore has a missing staple; this is not considered a defect. Any staple can be replaced on books up to Fine, but only vintage staples can be used on books from Very Fine to Near Mint. Mint books must have original staples. Paper is tan to cream, but not brown. No hint of acidity in the odor of the newsprint. Centerfold is mostly secure. Minor interior tears at the margin may be present.

6.5 FINE+ (FN+): Fits the criteria for Fine but with an additional virtue or small accumulation of virtues that improves the book's appearance by a perceptible amount.

6.0 FINE (FN): An above-average copy that shows minor wear but is still relatively flat and clean with no significant creasing or other serious defects. Eye appeal is somewhat reduced because of slight surface wear and the accumulation of small defects, especially on the spine and edges. A FINE condition comic book appears to have been read a few times and has been handled with moderate care. Some accumulation of minor bindery defects is allowed. Minor cover wear apparent, with minor to moderate creases. Inks show a major reduction in reflectivity. Blunted or abraded corners are more common, as is minor staining, soiling, discoloration, and/or foxing. Stamped or inked arrival dates may be present. A minor spine roll is allowed. There can also be a 1/4" spine split or severe color break. Staples show minor discoloration. Minor staple tears and an accumulation of stress lines may be present, as well as minor rust migration. In rare cases, a comic was not stapled at the bindery and therefore has a missing staple; this is not considered a defect. Any staple can be replaced on books up to Fine, but only vintage staples can be used on books from Very Fine to Near Mint. Mint books must have original staples. Paper is brown to tan and fairly supple with no signs of brittleness. No hint of acidity in the odor of the newsprint. Minor interior tears at the margin may be present. Centerfold may be loose but not detached.

5.5 FINE– (FN–): Fits the criteria for Fine but with an additional defect or small accumulation of defects that detracts from the book's appearance by a perceptible amount.

5.0 VERY GOOD/FINE (VG/FN): An above-average but well-used comic book. A comic in this grade shows some moderate wear; eye appeal is somewhat reduced because of the accumulation of defects. Still a desirable copy that has been handled with some care. An accumulation of bindery defects is allowed. Minor to moderate cover wear apparent, with minor to moderate creases and/or dimples. Inks have major to extreme reduction in reflectivity. Blunted or abraded corners are increasingly common, as is minor to moderate staining, discoloration, and/or foxing. Stamped or inked arrival dates may be present. A minor to moderate spine roll is allowed. A spine split of up to 1/2" may be present. Staples show minor discoloration. A slight accumulation of minor staple tears and an accumulation of minor stress lines may also be present, as well as minor rust migration. In rare cases, a comic was not stapled at the bindery and therefore has a missing staple; this is not considered a defect. Any staple can be replaced on books up to Fine, but only vintage staples can be used on books from Very Fine to Near Mint. Mint books must have original staples. Paper is brown to tan with no signs of brittleness. May have the faintest trace of an acidic odor. Centerfold may be loose but not detached. Minor tears may also be present.

4.5 VERY GOOD+ (VG+): Fits the criteria for Very Good but with an additional virtue or small accumulation of virtues that improves the book's appearance by a perceptible amount.

4.0 VERY GOOD (VG): The average used comic book. A comic in this grade shows some significant moderate wear, but still has not accumulated enough total defects to reduce eye appeal to the point that it is not a desirable copy. Cover shows moderate to significant wear, and may be loose but not completely detached. Moderate to extreme reduction in reflectivity. Can have an accumulation of creases or dimples. Corners may be blunted or abraded. Store stamps, name stamps, arrival dates, initials, etc. have no effect on this grade. Some discoloration, fading, foxing, and even minor soiling is allowed. As much as a 1/4" triangle can be missing out of the corner or edge; a missing 1/8" square is also acceptable. Only minor unobtrusive tape and other amateur repair allowed on otherwise high grade copies. Moderate spine roll may be present and/or a 1" spine split. Staples discolored. Minor to moderate staple tears and stress lines may be present, as well as some rust migration. Paper is brown but not brittle. A minor acidic odor can be detectable. Minor to moderate tears may be present. Centerfold may be loose or detached at one staple.

3.5 VERY GOOD– (VG–): Fits the criteria for Very Good but with an additional defect or small accumulation of defects that detracts from the book's appearance by a perceptible amount.

3.0 GOOD/VERY GOOD (GD/VG): A used comic book showing some substantial wear. Cover shows significant wear, and may be loose or even detached at one staple. Cover reflectivity is very low. Can have a book-length crease and/or dimples. Corners may be blunted or even rounded. Discoloration, fading, foxing, and even minor to moderate soiling is allowed. A triangle from 1/4" to 1/2" can be missing out of the corner or edge; a missing 1/8" to 1/4" square is also acceptable. Tape and other amateur repair may be present. Moderate spine roll likely. May have a spine split of anywhere from 1" to 1-1/2". Staples may be rusted or replaced. Minor to moderate staple tears and moderate stress lines may be present, as well as some rust migration. Paper is brown but not brittle. Centerfold may be loose or detached at one staple. Minor to moderate interior tears may be present.

2.5 GOOD+ (GD+): Fits the criteria for Good but with an additional virtue or small accumulation of virtues that improves the book's appearance by a perceptible amount.

2.0 GOOD (GD): Shows substantial wear; often considered a "reading copy." Cover shows significant wear and may even be detached. Cover reflectivity is low and in some cases completely absent. Book-length creases and dimples may be present. Rounded corners are more common. Moderate soiling, staining, discoloration and foxing may be present. The largest piece allowed missing from the front or back cover is usually a 1/2" triangle or a 1/4" square, although some Silver Age books such as 1960s Marvels have had the price corner box clipped from the top left front cover and may be considered Good if they would otherwise have graded higher. Tape and other forms of amateur repair are common in Silver Age and older books. Spine roll is likely. May have up to a 2" spine split. Staples may be degraded, replaced or missing. Moderate staple tears and stress lines may be present, as well as rust migration. Paper is brown but not brittle. Centerfold may be loose or detached. Moderate interior tears may be present.

1.8 GOOD– (GD–): Fits the criteria for Good but with an additional defect or small accumulation of defects that detracts from the book's appearance by a perceptible amount.

1.5 FAIR/GOOD (FR/GD): A comic showing substantial to heavy wear. A copy in this grade still has all pages and covers, although there may be pieces missing. Books in this grade are commonly creased, scuffed, abraded, soiled, and possibly unattractive, but still generally readable. Cover shows considerable wear and may be detached. Nearly no reflectivity to no reflectivity remaining. Store stamp, name stamp, arrival date and initials are permitted. Book-length creases, tears and folds may be present. Rounded corners are increasingly common. Soiling, staining, discoloration and foxing is generally present. Up to 1/10 of the back cover may be missing. Tape and other forms of amateur repair are increasingly common in Silver Age and older books. Spine roll is common. May have a spine split between 2" and 2/3 the length of the book. Staples may be degraded, replaced or missing. Staple tears and stress lines are common, as well as rust migration. Paper is brown and may show brittleness around the edges. Acidic odor may be present. Centerfold may be loose or detached. Interior tears are common.

1.0 FAIR (FR): A copy in this grade shows heavy wear. Some collectors consider this the lowest collectible grade because comic books in lesser condition are usually incomplete and/or brittle. Comics in this grade are usually soiled, faded, ragged and possibly unattractive. This is the last grade in which a comic remains generally readable. Cover may be detached, and inks have lost all reflectivity. Creases, tears and/or folds are prevalent. Corners are commonly rounded or absent. Soiling and staining is present. Books in this condition generally have all pages and most of the covers, although there may be up to 1/4 of the front cover missing or no back cover, but not both. Tape and other forms of amateur repair are more common. Spine roll is more common; spine split can extend up to 2/3 the length of the book. Staples may be missing or show rust and discoloration. An accumulation of staple tears and stress lines may be present, as well as rust migration. Paper is brown and may show brittleness around the edges but not in the central portion of the pages. Acidic odor may be present. Accumulation of interior tears. Chunks may be missing. The centerfold may be missing if readability is generally preserved (although there may be difficulty). Coupons may be cut.

0.5 POOR (PR): Most comic books in this grade have been sufficiently degraded to the point where there is little or no collector value; they are easily identified by a complete absence of eye appeal. Comics in this grade are brittle almost to the point of turning to dust with a touch, and are usually incomplete. Extreme cover fading may render the cover almost indiscernible. May have extremely severe stains, mildew or heavy cover abrasion to the point that some cover inks are indistinct/absent. Covers may be detached with large chunks missing. Can have extremely ragged edges and extensive creasing. Corners are rounded or virtually absent. Covers may have been defaced with paints, varnishes, glues, oil, indelible markers or dyes, and may have suffered heavy water damage. Can also have extensive amateur repairs such as laminated covers. Extreme spine roll present; can have extremely ragged spines or a complete, book-length split. Staples can be missing or show extreme rust and discoloration. Extensive staple tears and stress lines may be present, as well as extreme rust migration. Paper exhibits moderate to severe brittleness (where the comic book literally falls apart when examined). Extreme acidic odor may be present. Extensive interior tears. Multiple pages, including the centerfold, may be missing that affect readability. Coupons may be cut.

PUBLISHERS' CODES

The following abbreviations are used with cover reproductions throughout the book for copyright purposes:

ABC-America's Best Comics
AC-AC Comics
ACE-Ace Periodicals
ACG-American Comics Group
AJAX-Ajax-Farrell
AP-Archie Publications
BP-Better Publications
C & L-Cupples & Leon
CC-Charlton Comics
CEN-Centaur Publications
CCG-Columbia Comics Group
CG-Catechetical Guild
CHES-Harry 'A' Chesler
CLDS-Classic Det. Stories
CM-Comics Magazine
CN-Cartoon Network
CPI-Conan Properties Inc.
DC-DC Comics, Inc.
DELL-Dell Publishing Co.
DH-Dark Horse
DIS-Disney Enterprises, Inc.
DMP-David McKay Publishing
DS-D. S. Publishing Co.
EAS-Eastern Color Printing Co.
EC-E. C. Comics
ECL-Eclipse Comics
ENWIL-Enwil Associates
EP-Elliott Publications
ERB-Edgar Rice Burroughs
FAW-Fawcett Publications
FC-First Comics
FF-Famous Funnies
FH-Fiction House Magazines
FOX-Fox Features Syndicate
GIL-Gilberton
GK-Gold Key
GP-Great Publications
HARV-Harvey Publications
H-B-Hanna-Barbera
HILL-Hillman Periodicals
HOKE-Holyoke Publishing Co.
IM-Image Comics
KING-King Features Syndicate
LEV-Lev Gleason Publications
MAL-Malibu Comics
MAR-Marvel Characters, Inc.
ME-Magazine Enterprises
MLJ-MLJ Magazines
MS-Mirage Studios
NOVP-Novelty Press
NYNS-New York News Syndicate
PG-Premier Group
PINE-Pines
PMI-Parents' Magazine Institute
PRIZE-Prize Publications
QUA-Quality Comics Group
REAL-Realistic Comics
RH-Rural Home
S & S-Street and Smith Publishers
SKY-Skywald Publications
STAR-Star Publications
STD-Standard Comics
STJ-St. John Publishing Co.
SUPR-Superior Comics
TC-Tower Comics
TM-Trojan Magazines
TMP-Todd McFarlane Prods.
TOBY-Toby Press
TOPS-Tops Comics
UFS-United Features Syndicate
VAL-Valiant
VITL-Vital Publications
WB-Warner Brothers.
WEST-Western Publishing Co.
WHIT-Whitman Publishing Co.
WHW-William H. Wise
WMG-William M. Gaines (E. C.)
WP-Warren Publishing Co.
YM-Youthful Magazines
Z-D-Ziff-Davis Publishing Co.

OVERSTREET ADVISORS

Even before the first edition of *The Overstreet Comic Book Price Guide* was printed, author Robert M. Overstreet solicited pricing data, historical notations, and general information from a variety of sources. What was initially an informal group offering input quickly became an organized field of comic book collectors, dealers and historians whose opinions are actively solicited in advance of each edition of this book. Some of these Overstreet Advisors are specialists who deal in particular niches within the comic book world, while others are generalists who are interested in commenting on the broader marketplace. Each advisor provides information from their respective areas of interest and expertise, spanning the history of American comics.

While some choose to offer pricing and historical information in the form of annotated sales catalogs, auction catalogs, or documented private sales, assistance from others comes in the form of the market reports such as those beginning on page 72 in this book. In addition to those who have served as Overstreet Advisors almost since *The Guide*'s inception, each year new contributors are sought.

With that in mind, we are pleased to present our newest Overstreet Advisors:

THE CLASS OF 2011

JIM BERRY
Collector
Portland, OR

JON BEVANS
Diamond International Galleries
Timonium, MD

BRETT CARRERAS
Brett's Comic Pile
Richmond, VA

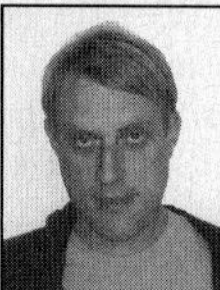

JASON HAMLIN
Brett's Comic Pile
Richmond, VA

JOHN HONE
Collector
Silver Spring, MD

TOMMY MALETTA
Best Comics International
New Hyde Park, NY

JEFF RADER
Paperpeddler Rare and Esoteric Comics and Collectibles
Lake Havasu, AZ

BUDDY SAUNDERS
Lone Star Comics
Arlington, TX

CONAN SAUNDERS
Lone Star Comics
Arlington, TX

DOUG SIMPSON
Paradise Comics
Toronto, ONT Canada

BEN SMITH
ComicConnect
New York, NY

A complete listing of our Overstreet Advisors can be found on our title page and beginning on page 1104.

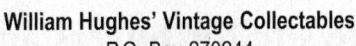

METROPOLIS IS BUYING!

METROPOLIS
COLLECTIBLES

www.metropoliscomics.com

THE NATION'S LARGEST COMIC DEALER

The following represents a sample of prices we will pay for your comic books. Other dealers say they pay top dollar, but when it comes down to it, they simply do not. If you have comics to sell, we invite you to contact every comic dealer in the country for offers. Then call us for your best offer. We can afford to pay the highest price for your vintage comics because that is all we sell. If you wish to sell us your comics, please ship us the books securely via FedEx with a track-number. If your collection is too large to ship, send us a detailed list and we'll travel to you. The prices below are for NM copies, but we are interested in all grades. Thank You.

Action #1	$3,500,000
Action #242	$18,000
Adventure #40	$100,000
Adventure #48	$70,000
Adventure #210	$22,000
All-American #16	$300,000
All-American #19	$40,000
All-Star #3	$145,000
Amazing Fantasy #15	$250,000
Amaz.Spiderman #1	$85,000
Amaz. Spiderman #129	$1,000
Avengers #1	$65,000
Avengers #4	$15,000
Batman #1	$300,000
Brave & the Bold #28	$65,000
Captain America #1	$170,000
Detective #1	$110,000
Detective #27	$2,500,000
Detective #38	$80,000
Detective #168	$16,000
Detective #225	$20,000
Donald Duck #9	$28,000
Fantastic Comics #3	$33,000
Fantastic Four #1	$260,000
Fantastic Four #5	$44,000
Flash Comics #1	$175,000
Green Lantern #1 (GA)	$50,000
Green Lantern #1 (SA)	$20,000
Human Torch #2 (#1)	$85,000
Incredible Hulk #1	$150,000
Incredible Hulk #181	$2,000
Journey Into Mystery #83	$85,000
Justice League #1	$35,000
Marvel Comics #1	$270,000
More Fun #52	$150,000
More Fun #54	$35,000
More Fun #55	$38,000
New Fun #6	$37,500
Pep Comics #22	$200,000
Showcase #4	$200,000
Showcase #22	$100,000
Superboy #1	$25,000
Superman #1	$1,000,000
Superman #14	$35,000
Suspense Comics #3	$60,000
Tales of Suspense #39	$85,000
Tales to Astonish #27	$40,000
Target Comics V1 #7	$12,000
Walt Disney C&S #1	$55,000
Whiz #2 (#1)	$150,000
Wonder Woman #1	$50,000
Young Allies #1	$30,000
X-Men #1	$90,000

Action Comics	#1-400
Adventure Comics	#32-400
Advs. Into Weird Worlds	all
All-American Comics	#1-102
All-Flash Quarterly	#1-32
All-Select	#1-11
All-Star Comics	#1-57
All-Winners	#1-21
Amazing Spiderman	#1-150
Amazing Man	#5-26
Amaz. Mystery Funnies	#1
Avengers	#1-100
Batman	#1-300
Blackhawk	#9-130
Boy Commandos	#1-32
Brave & the Bold	#1-100
Captain America	#1-78
Captain Marvel Advs.	#1-150
Challengers	#1-25
Classic Comics	#1-169
Comic Cavalcade	#1-63
Daredevil Comics	#1-60
Daring Mystery	#1-8
Detective Comics	#1-450
Donald Duck 4-Colors	#4-up
Fantastic Four	#1-100
Fight Comics	#1-86
Flash	#1-150
Fight Comics	#1-86
Flash	#105-150
Flash Comics	#1-104
Funny Pages	#6-42
Green Lantern (GA)	#1-38
Green Lantern (SA)	#1-90
Hit Comics	#1-65
Human Torch	#2(#1)-38
Incredible Hulk	#1-6
Jimmy Olsen	#1-150
Journey Into Mystery	#1-125
Jumbo Comics	#1-167
Jungle Comics	#1-163
Justice League	#1-110
Mad	#1-50
Marvel Mystery	#1-92
Military Comics	#1-43
More Fun Comics	#7-127
Mystery in Space	#1-75
Mystic Comics	#1-up
National Comics	#1-75
New Adventure	#12-31
New Comics	#1-11
New Fun Comics	#1-6
Our Army at War	#1-200
Our Fighting Forces	#1-180
Planet Comics	#1-73
Rangers Comics	#1-69
Reform School Girl	all
Sensation Comics	#1-116
Shadow Comics	all
Showcase	#1-100
Star-Spangled Comics	#1-130
Strange Tales	#1-145
Sub-Mariner	#1-42
Superboy	#1-110
Superman	#1-250
Tales From The Crypt	#20-46
Tales of Suspense	#1-80
Tales to Astonish	#1-80
Terrific Comics	all
Thing	#1-17
USA Comics	#1-17
Weird Comics	#1-20
Weird Mysteries	#1-12
Weird Tales From The Future	all
Wings Comics	#1-124
Whiz Comics	#1-155
Wonder Woman	#1-200
Wonderworld	#3-33
World s Finest	#1-200
X-Men	#1-30

METROPOLIS

METROPOLISCOMICS.COM, 873 BROADWAY SUITE 201, NEW YORK, NY 10003
PH: 212.260.4147 FX: 212.260.4304 BUYING@METROPOLISCOMICS.COM
TOLL-FREE 1.800.229.METRO (6387) INTERNATIONAL: 001.212.260.4147

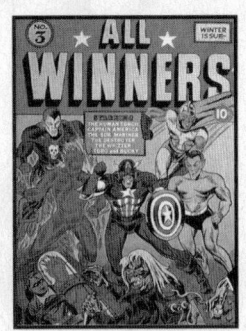

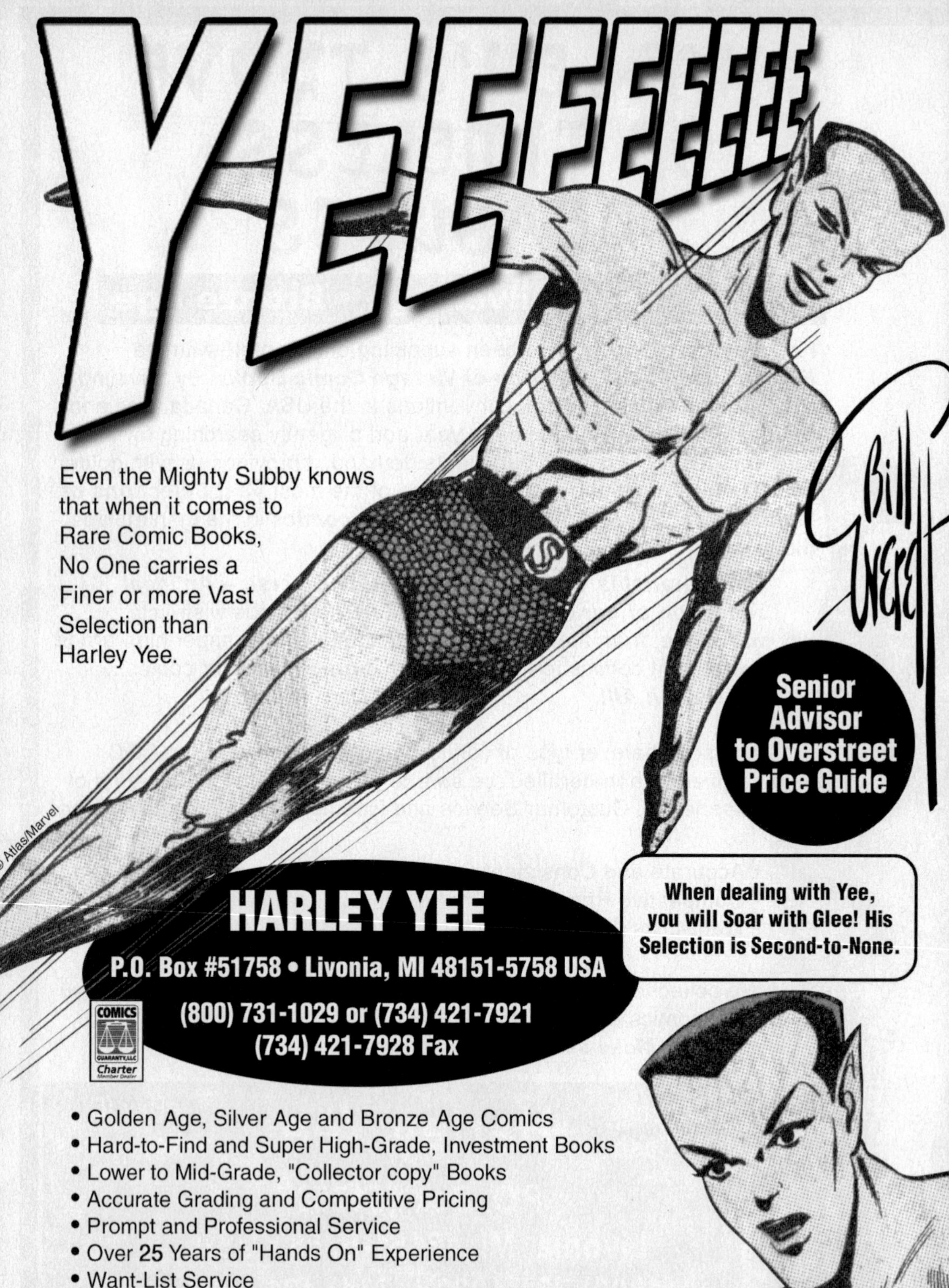
YEEEEEEEE
Even the Mighty Subby knows that when it comes to Rare Comic Books, No One carries a Finer or more Vast Selection than Harley Yee.
Bill Everett
Senior Advisor to Overstreet Price Guide
© Atlas/Marvel
When dealing with Yee, you will Soar with Glee! His Selection is Second-to-None.
HARLEY YEE
P.O. Box #51758 • Livonia, MI 48151-5758 USA
(800) 731-1029 or (734) 421-7921
(734) 421-7928 Fax
COMICS GUARANTY, LLC Charter Member Dealer
• Golden Age, Silver Age and Bronze Age Comics
• Hard-to-Find and Super High-Grade, Investment Books
• Lower to Mid-Grade, "Collector copy" Books
• Accurate Grading and Competitive Pricing
• Prompt and Professional Service
• Over 25 Years of "Hands On" Experience
• Want-List Service
• Setting Up at 30 or more Comic Conventions Every Year
HarleyYeeComics.com • HarleyComx@aol.com
eBay store: Harleycomics

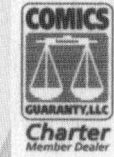

THE SELLER'S GUIDE

Yes, here are the pages you're looking for. These percentages will help you determine the sale value of your collection. If you do not find your title, call with any questions. We have purchased many of the major well-known collections. We are serious about buying your comics and paying you the most for them.

If you have comics or related items for sale call or send your list for a quote. No collection is too large or small. Immediate funds available of 500K and beyond.

These are some of the high prices we will pay. Percentages stated will be paid for any grade unless otherwise noted. All percentages based on this Overstreet Guide.

—JAMES PAYETTE

We are paying 100% of Guide for the following:

All Select	1-up
All Winners	6-up
America's Best	1-up
Black Terror	1-25
Captain Aero	3-25
Captain America	11-up
Catman	1-up
Dynamic	2-15
Exciting	3-50
Human Torch	6-35
Marvel Mystery	11-up
Pep	22-45
Prize	2-50
Reform School Girl	1
Speed	10-30
Startling	2-up
Sub-Mariner	3-32
Thrilling	2-52
U.S.A.	6-up
Wonder (Nedor)	1-up

We are paying 75% of Guide for the following:

Action 1-15
Adventure 247
All New 2-13
All Winners 1-5
Amazing Man all
Amazing Mystery Funnies all
Andy Devine
Arrow all
Captain America 1-10
Daredevil (2nd) 1
Detective 2-26
Detective Eye all
Detective Picture Stories all
Fantastic Four 1-2
Four Favorites 3-27
Funny Pages all
Funny Picture Stories all
Hangman all
Jumbo 1-10
Journey into Mystery 83
Keen Detective Funnies all
Marvel Mystery 1-10
Mystery Men all
Showcase 4
Spiderman 1-2
Superman 1
Superman's Pal 1
Tim McCoy all
Wonder (Fox)
Young Allies all

BUYING & SELLING GOLDEN & SILVER AGE COMICS SINCE 1975

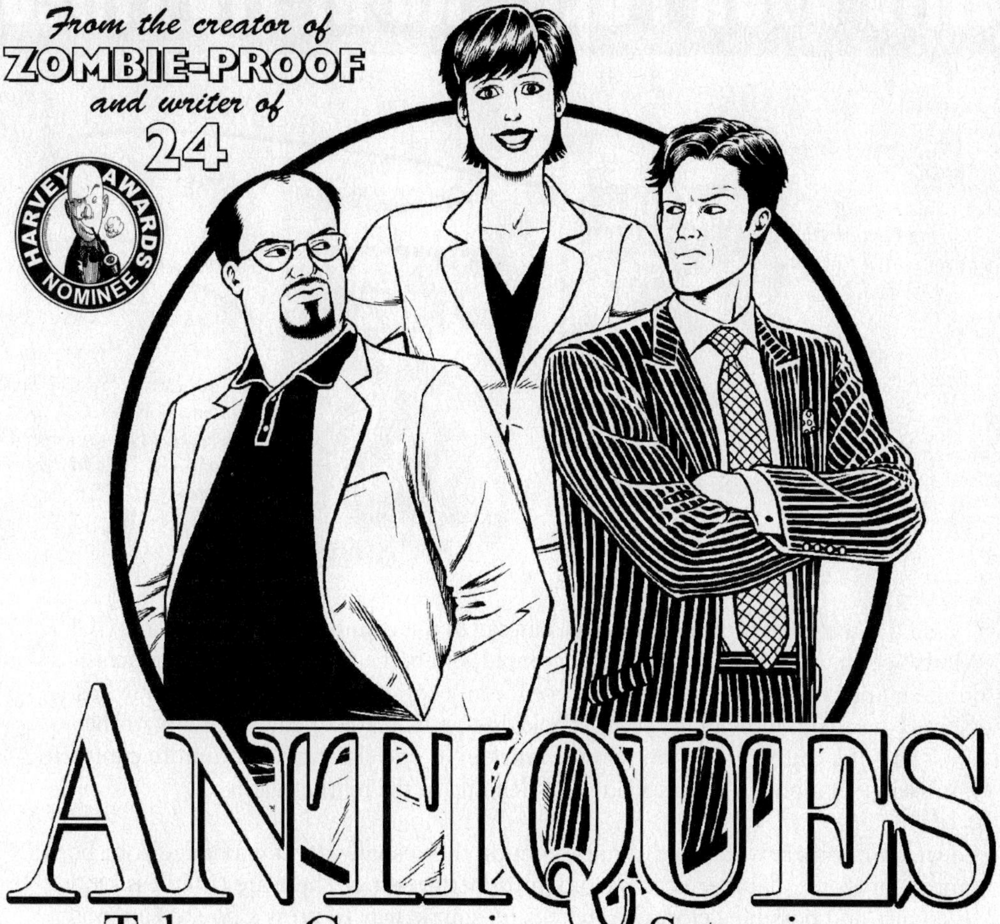

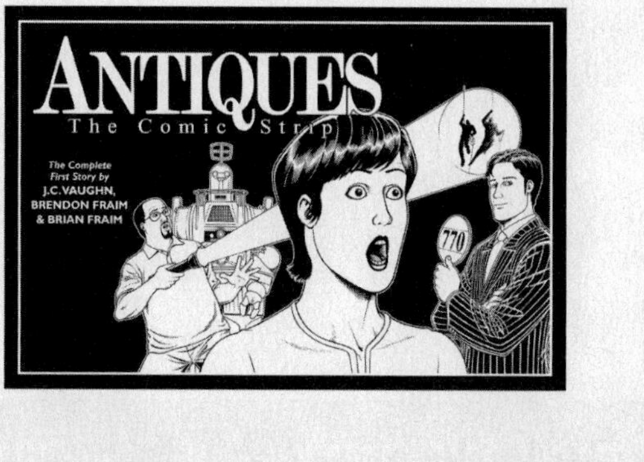

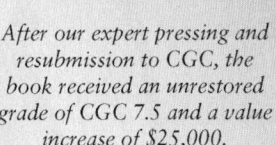

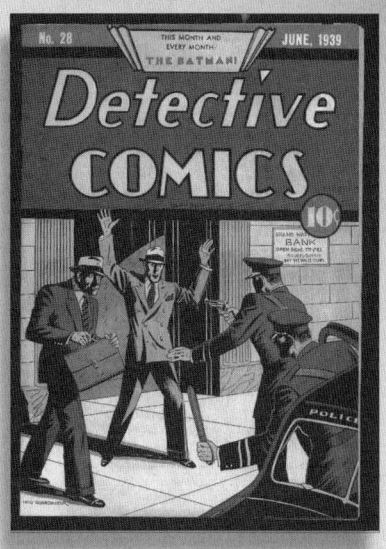

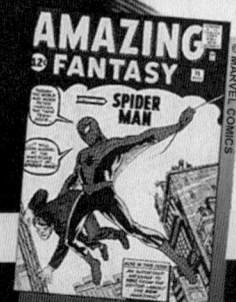

I BUY OLD COMICS
1930 to 1975

Any Title
Any Condition
Any Size Collection

Can Easily Travel to:

Atlanta
Chicago
Cincinnati
Dallas
Little Rock
Louisvillle
Memphis
St. Louis

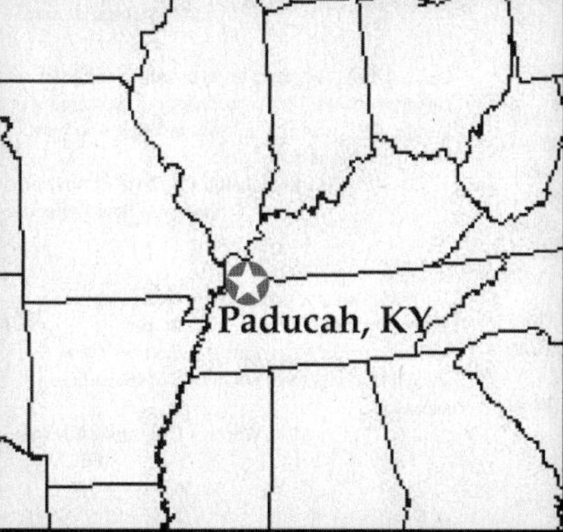

I want your comics:

Superhero
Western
Horror
Humor
Romance

Leroy Harper
PO BOX 212
WEST PADUCAH, KY 42086

PHONE 270-748-9364
EMAIL LHCOMICS@hotmail.com

Over 20 years of experience

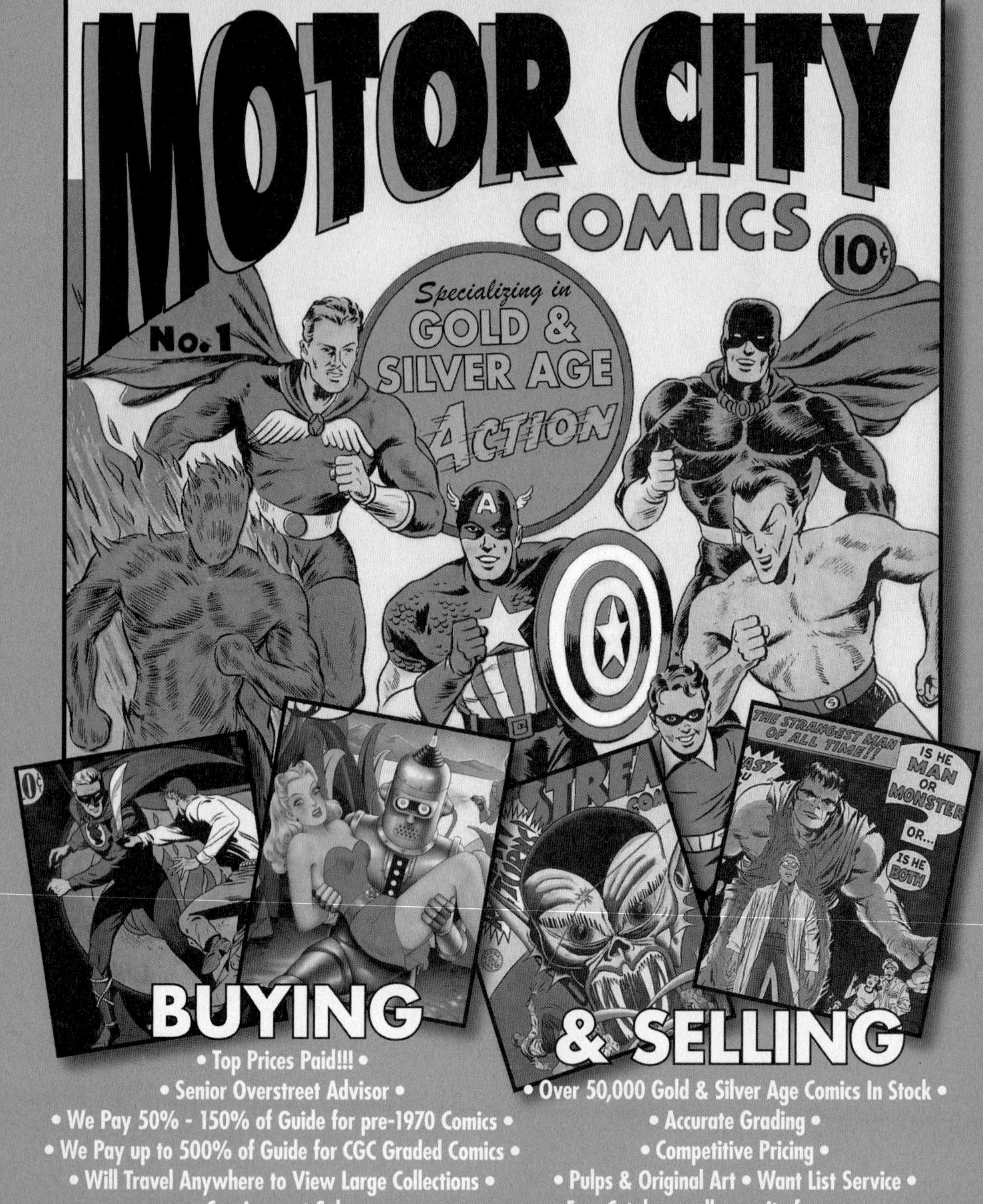
MOTOR CITY
COMICS
10¢
No. 1
Specializing in
GOLD &
SILVER AGE
ACTION
THE STRANGEST MAN OF ALL TIME!!
IS HE
MAN
OR
MONSTER
OR...
IS HE
BOTH
BUYING
& SELLING

IN
ILLINOIS

COMICS TO ASTONISH
WE SELL!
-COMICS OLD AND NEW!
-MAGIC THE GATHERING!
-WIZKIDS!
-NON SPORT CARDS!
-GRADED COMICS!
-STATUES!
-ACTION FIGURES!
-TPB'S!
-ORIGINAL ART!
-DC DIRECT!
-COMIC SUPPLIES!
9400 SNOWDEN RIVER PKWY
COLUMBIA, MD 21045
MONDAY-SATURDAY 12-8PM
SUNDAY 12-7PM
Check out our new website w/h tons of CGC books
CONTACT:
KEEGAN F. CONRAD
410-381-2732
COMICS2U@AOL.COM
VBBB
WE BUY!
-ALL COMICS 30'S TO 80'S!
-ENTIRE COLLECTIONS!
-BRONZE TO GOLDEN AGE!
-GRADED BOOKS!
WE HAVE OVER 80,000 BACK ISSUES!
WWW.COMICSTOASTONISH.COM

JOHN VERZYL AND DAUGHTER ROSE, "HARD AT WORK."

John Verzyl started collecting comic books in 1965, and within ten years he had amassed thousands of Golden and Silver Age comic books. In 1979, with his wife Nanette, he opened "COMIC HEAVEN," a retail store devoted entirely to the buying and selling of comic books.

Over the years, John Verzyl has come to be recognized as an authority in the field of comic books. He has served as a special advisor to the "Overstreet Comic Book Price Guide" for the last 25 years. Thousands of his "mint" comics were photographed for Ernst Gerber's "Photo-Journal Guide to Comic Books." His tables and displays at the annual San Diego Comic Convention and the Chicago Comic Convention draw customers from all over the country.

The first COMIC HEAVEN AUCTION was held in 1987, and today his Auction Catalogs are mailed out to more than ten thousand interested collectors and dealers.

Comic Heaven
John and Nanette Verzyl
P.O. Box 900
Big Sandy, TX 75755
www.comicheaven.net
1-903-636-5555

THESE DIDN'T HAPPEN WITHOUT YOUR HELP.

The Overstreet Comic Book Price Guide doesn't happen by magic. A network of advisors – made up of experienced dealers, collectors and comics historians – gives us input for every edition we publish. If you spot an error or omission in this edition or any of our publications, let us know!

Write to us at Gemstone Publishing Inc., 1966 Greenspring Dr., Timonium, MD 21093.
Or e-mail **feedback@gemstonepub.com**.

We want your help!

BIG LITTLE BOOKS

INTRODUCTION

In 1932, at the depths of the Great Depression, comic books were not selling despite their successes in the previous two decades. Desperate publishers had already reduced prices to 25¢, but this was still too much for many people to spend on entertainment.

Comic books quickly evolved into two newer formats, the comics magazine and the Big Little Book. Both types retailed for 10¢.

Big Little Books began by reprinting the art (and adapting the stories) from newspaper comics. As their success grew and publishers began commissioning original material, movie adaptations and other entertainment-derived stories became commonplace.

GRADING

Before a Big Little Book's value can be assessed, its condition or state of preservation must be determined. A book in **Near Mint** condition will bring many times the price of the same book in **Poor** condition. Many variables influence the grading of a Big Little Book and all must be considered in the final evaluation. Due to the way they are constructed, damage occurs with very little use - usually to the spine, book edges and binding. More important defects that affect grading are: Split spines, pages missing, page browning or brittleness, writing, crayoning, loose pages, color fading, chunks missing, and rolling or out of square. The following grading guide is given to aid the novice:

9.4 Near Mint: The overall look is as if it was just purchased and maybe opened once; only subtle defects are allowed; paper is cream to off-white, supple and fresh; cover is flat with no surface wear or creases; inks and colors are bright; small penciled or inked arrival dates are acceptable; very slight blunting of corners at top and bottom of spine are common; outside corners are cut square and sharp. Books in this grade could bring prices of guide and a half or more.

9.0 Very Fine/Near Mint: Limited number of defects; full cover gloss with only very slight wear on book corners and edges; very minor foxing; very minor tears allowed, binding still square and tight with no pages missing; paper quality still fresh from cream to off-white. Dates, stamps or initials allowed on cover or inside.

8.0 Very Fine: Most of the cover gloss retained with minor wear appearing at corners and around edges; spine tight with no pages missing; cream/tan paper allowed if still supple; up to 1/4" bend allowed on covers with no color break; cover relatively flat; minor tears allowed.

6.0 Fine: Slight wear beginning to show; cover gloss reduced but still clean, pages tan/brown but still supple (not brittle); up to 1/4" split or color break allowed; minor discoloration and/or foxing allowed.

4.0 Very Good: Obviously a read copy with original printing luster almost gone; some fading and discoloration, but not soiled; some signs of wear such as corner splits and spine rolling; paper can be brown but not brittle; a few pages can be loose but not missing; no chunks missing; blunted corners acceptable.

2.0 Good: An average used copy complete with only minor pieces missing from the spine, which may be partially split; slightly soiled or marked with spine rolling; color flaking and wear around edges, but perfectly sound and legible; could have minor tape repairs but otherwise complete.

1.0 Fair: Very heavily read and soiled with small chunks missing from cover; most or all of spine could be missing; multiple splits in spine and loose pages, but still sound and legible, bringing 50 to 70 percent of good price.

0.5 Poor: Damaged, heavily weathered, soiled or otherwise unsuited for collecting purposes.

IMPORTANT

Most BLBs on the market today will fall in the **Good** to **Fine** grade category. When **Very Fine** to **Near Mint** BLBs are offered for sale, they usually bring premium prices.

A WORD ON PRICING

The prices are given for **Good**, **Fine** and **Very Fine/ Near Mint** condition. A book in **Fair** would be 50-70% of the **Good** price. **Very Good** would be halfway between the **Good** and **Fine** price, and **Very Fine** would be halfway between the **Fine** and **Very Fine/**

Near Mint price. The prices listed were averaged from convention sales, dealers' lists, adzines, auctions, and by special contact with dealers and collectors from coast to coast. The prices and the spreads were determined from sales of copies in available condition or the highest grade known. Since most available copies are in the **Good** to **Fine** range, neither dealers nor collectors should let the **Very Fine/Near Mint** column influence the prices they are willing to charge or pay for books in less than near perfect condition.

The prices listed reflect a six times spread from **Good** to **Very Fine/ Near Mint** (1 - 3 - 6). We feel this spread accurately reflects the current market, especially when you consider the scarcity of books in **Very Fine/Near Mint** condition. When one or both end sheets are missing, the book's value would drop about a half grade.

Books with movie scenes are of double importance due to the high crossover demand by movie collectors.

Abbreviations: a-art; c-cover; nn-no number; p-pages; r-reprint.

Publisher Codes: BRP-Blue Ribbon Press; **ERB**-Edgar Rice Burroughs; **EVW**-Engel van Wiseman; **FAW**-Fawcett Publishing Co.; **Gold**-Goldsmith Publishing Co.; **Lynn**-Lynn Publishing Co.; **McKay**-David McKay Co.; **Whit**-Whitman Publishing Co.; **World**-World Syndicate Publishing Co.

Terminology: *All Pictures Comics*-no text, all drawings; *Fast-Action*-A special series of Dell books highly collected; *Flip Pictures*-upper right corner of interior pages contain drawings that are put into motion when rifled; *Movie Scenes*-book illustrated with scenes from the movie. *Soft Cover*-A thin single sheet of cardboard used in binding most of the giveaway versions.

"Big Little Book" and "Better Little Book" are registered trademarks of Whitman Publishing Co. "Little Big Book" is a registered trademark of the Saalfield Publishing Co.

"Pop-Up" is a registered trademark of Blue Ribbon Press. "Little Big Book" is a registered trademark of the Saalfield Co.

Top 20 Big Little Books and related size books*

Issue#	Rank	Title	Price
731	1	Mickey Mouse the Mail Pilot (variant version of Mickey Mouse #717) (Fine copy sold at auction for $5,090)	
nn	2	Mickey Mouse and Minnie Mouse at Macy's	$3,500
717	3	Mickey Mouse (skinny Mickey on-c)	$3,135
W-707	4	Dick Tracy The Detective	$2,500
nn	5	Mickey Mouse and Minnie March to Macy's	$2,400
725	5	Big Little Mother Goose HC	$2,400
717	7	Mickey Mouse (reg. Mickey on-c)	$1,750
4063	8	Popeye Thimble Theater Starring... (2nd printing)	$1,620
721	9	Big Little Paint Book (336 pg.)	$1,500
725	9	Big Little Mother Goose SC	$1,500
nn	9	Mickey Mouse Mail Pilot (Great Big Midget Book)	$1,500
nn	12	Mickey Mouse (Great Big Midget Book)	$1,485
4062	13	Mickey Mouse and the Smugglers	$1,430
4063	14	Popeye Thimble Theater Starring... (1st printing)	$1,385
nn	15	Buck Rogers	$1,320
nn	15	Mickey Mouse Silly Symphonies	$1,320
4062	17	Mickey Mouse, The Story of...	$1,210
721	18	Big Little Paint Book (320 pg.)	$1,200
nn	18	Mickey Mouse Sails For Treasure Island (Great Big Midget Book)	$1,200
nn	20	Mickey Mouse and the Magic Carpet	$1,050

*Includes only the various sized BLBs; no premiums, giveaways or other divergent forms are included.

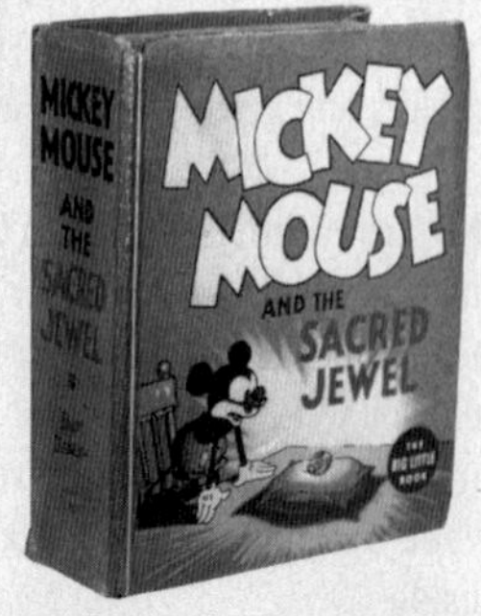

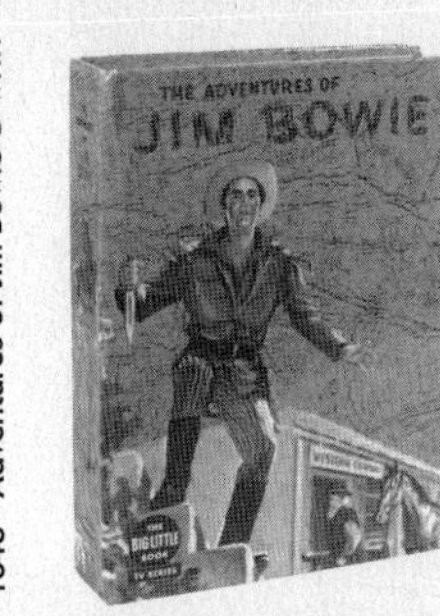

1648 - Adventures of Jim Bowie © WHIT

1497 - Bambi's Children © DIS

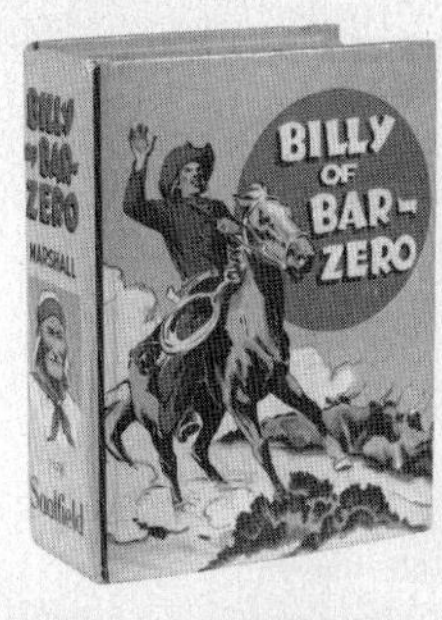

1178 - Billy of Bar-Zero © Saalfield

GD FN VF/NM

1175-0- Abbie an' Slats, 1940, Saalfield, 400 pgs. 12.00 30.00 80.00

1182- Abbie an' Slats-and Becky, 1940, Saalfield, 400 pgs. 12.00 30.00 80.00

1177- Ace Drummond, 1935, Whitman, 432 pgs. 12.00 30.00 85.00

Admiral Byrd (See Paramount Newsreel ...)

nn- Adventures of Charlie McCarthy and Edgar Bergen, The, 1938, Dell, 194 pgs., Fast-Action Story, soft-c 26.00 65.00 185.00

1422- Adventures of Huckleberry Finn, The, 1939, Whitman, 432 pgs., Henry E. Vallely-a 12.00 30.00 75.00

1648- Adventures of Jim Bowie (TV Series), 1958, Whitman, 280 pgs. 5.00 12.50 33.00

1056- Adventures of Krazy Kat and Ignatz Mouse in Koko Land, 1934, Saalfield, 160 pgs., oblong size, hard-c, Herriman-c/a 72.00 180.00 505.00

1306- Adventures of Krazy Kat and Ignatz Mouse in Koko Land, 1934, Saalfield, 164 pgs., oblong size, soft-c, Herriman-c/a 79.00 197.00 550.00

1082- Adventures of Pete the Tramp, The, 1935, Saalfield, hard-c, by C. D. Russell 12.00 30.00 75.00

1312- Adventures of Pete the Tramp, The, 1935, Saalfield, soft-c, by C. D. Russell 12.00 30.00 75.00

1053- Adventures of Tim Tyler, 1934, Saalfield, hard-c, oblong size, by Lyman Young 26.00 65.00 180.00

1303- Adventures of Tim Tyler, 1934, Saalfield, soft-c, oblong size, by Lyman Young 26.00 65.00 180.00

1058- Adventures of Tom Sawyer, The, 1934, Saalfield, 160 pgs., hard-c, Park Sumner-a 12.00 30.00 75.00

1308- Adventures of Tom Sawyer, The, 1934, Saalfield, 160 pgs., soft-c, Park Sumner-a 12.00 30.00 75.00

1448- Air Fighters of America, 1941, Whitman, 432 pgs., flip picture 12.00 30.00 85.00

Alexander Smart, ESQ. (See Top Line Comics)

759- Alice in Wonderland, 1933, Whitman, 160 pgs., hard-c, photo-c, movie scenes 46.00 115.00 325.00

1481- Allen Pike of the Parachute Squad U.S.A., 1941, Whitman, 432 pgs. 12.00 30.00 85.00

763- Alley Oop and Dinny, 1935, Whitman, 384 pgs., V. T. Hamlin-a 21.00 52.50 145.00

1473- Alley Oop and Dinny in the Jungles of Moo, 1938, Whitman, 432 pgs., V. T. Hamlin-a 21.00 52.50 145.00

nn- Alley Oop and the Missing King of Moo, 1938, Whitman, 36 pgs., 2 1/2" x 3 1/2", Penny Book 12.00 30.00 85.00

nn- Alley Oop in the Kingdom of Foo, 1938, Whitman, 68 pgs., 3 1/4" x 3 1/2", Pan-Am premium 29.00 73.00 200.00

nn- "Alley Oop the Invasion of Moo," 1935, Whitman, 260 pgs., Cocomalt premium, soft-c; V. T. Hamlin-a 22.00 52.50 155.00

Andy Burnette (See Walt Disney's...)

Andy Panda (Also see Walter Lantz ...)

531- Andy Panda, 1943, Whitman, 3 3/4x8 3/4", Tall Comic Book, All Pictures Comics 26.00 65.00 180.00

1425- Andy Panda and Tiny Tom, 1944, Whitman, All Pictures Comics 12.00 30.00 85.00

1431- Andy Panda and the Mad Dog Mystery, 1947, Whitman, 288 pgs., by Walter Lantz 12.00 30.00 80.00

1441- Andy Panda in the City of Ice, 1948, Whitman, All Picture Comics, by Walter Lantz 12.00 30.00 85.00

1459- Andy Panda and the Pirate Ghosts, 1949, Whitman, 88 pgs., by Walter Lantz 12.00 30.00 80.00

1485- Andy Panda's Vacation, 1946, Whitman, All Pictures Comics, by Walter Lantz 12.00 30.00 85.00

15- Andy Panda (The Adventures of), 1942, Dell, Fast-Action Story 26.00 65.00 180.00

707-10 - Andy Panda and Presto the Pup, 1949, Whitman 12.00 30.00 80.00

1130- Apple Mary and Dennie Foil the Swindlers, 1936, Whitman, 432 pgs. (Forerunner to Mary Worth) 12.00 30.00 80.00

1403- Apple Mary and Dennie's Lucky Apples, 1939, Whitman, 432 pgs. 12.00 30.00 80.00

2017- (#17)-Aquaman-Scourge of the Sea, 1968, Whitman, 260 pgs., 39 cents, hard-c, color illos 4.00 10.00 27.00

GD FN VF/NM

1192- Arizona Kid on the Bandit Trail, The, 1936, Whitman, 432 pgs. 11.00 27.50 70.00

1469- Bambi (Walt Disney's), 1942, Whitman, 432 pgs. 26.00 65.00 180.00

1497- Bambi's Children (Disney), 1943, Whitman, 432 pgs., Disney Studios-a 26.00 65.00 180.00

1138- Bandits at Bay, 1938, Saalfield, 400 pgs. 10.00 25.00 65.00

1459- Barney Baxter in the Air with the Eagle Squadron, 1938, Whitman, 432 pgs. 12.00 30.00 80.00

1083- Barney Google, 1935, Saalfield, hard-c 21.00 52.50 145.00

1313- Barney Google, 1935, Saalfield, soft-c 21.00 52.50 145.00

2031-(#31)- Batman and Robin in the Cheetah Caper, 1969, Whitman, 258 pgs. 4.00 10.00 27.00

5771- Batman and Robin in the Cheetah Caper, 1974, Whitman, 258 pgs., 49 cents 2.00 5.00 11.00

5771-1- Batman and Robin in the Cheetah Caper, 1974, Whitman, 258 pgs., 69 cents 2.00 5.00 11.00

5771-2- Batman and Robin in the Cheetah Caper, 1975?, Whitman, 258 pgs. 2.00 5.00 11.00

nn- Beauty and the Beast, nd (1930s), np (Whitman), 36 pgs., 3" x 3 1/2" Penny Book 4.00 10.00 27.00

760- Believe It or Not!, 1933, Whitman, 160 pgs., by Ripley (c. 1931) 12.00 30.00 80.00

Betty Bear's Lesson (See Wee Little Books)

1119- Betty Boop in Snow White, 1934, Whitman, 240 pgs., hard-c; adapted from Max Fleischer Paramount Talkartoon 86.00 215.00 600.00

1119- Betty Boop in Snow White, 1934, Whitman, 240 pgs., soft-c; same contents as hard-c (Rare) 128.00 320.00 900.00

1158- Betty Boop in "Miss Gullivers Travels," 1935, Whitman, 288 pgs., hard-c (Scarce) 100.00 250.00 700.00

2070- Big Big Paint Book, 1936, Whitman, 432 pgs., 8 1/2" x 11 3/8", B&W pages to color 25.00 62.00 175.00

1432- Big Chief Wahoo and the Lost Pioneers, 1942, Whitman, 432 pgs., Elmer Woggon-a 12.00 30.00 80.00

1443- Big Chief Wahoo and the Great Gusto, 1938, Whitman, 432 pgs., Elmer Woggon-a 12.00 30.00 80.00

1483- Big Chief Wahoo and the Magic Lamp, 1940, Whitman, 432 pgs., flip pictures, Woggon-c/a 12.00 30.00 80.00

725- Big Little Mother Goose, The, 1934, Whitman, 580 pgs. (Rare) Hardcover 300.00 750.00 2400.00

725- Big Little Mother Goose, The, 1934, Whitman, 580 pgs. (Rare) Softcover 188.00 470.00 1500.00

1005- Big Little Nickel Book, 1935, Whitman, 144 pgs., Blackie Bear stories and Donna the Donkey 11.00 27.50 70.00

1006- Big Little Nickel Book, 1935, Whitman, 144 pgs., Blackie Bear stories, folk tales in primer style 11.00 27.50 70.00

1007- Big Little Nickel Book, 1935, Whitman, 144 pgs., Peter Rabbit, etc. 11.00 27.50 70.00

1008- Big Little Nickel Book, 1935, Whitman, 144 pgs., Wee Wee Woman, etc. 11.00 27.50 70.00

721- Big Little Paint Book, The, 1933, Whitman, 320 pgs., 3 3/4" x 8 1/2", for crayoning; first printing has green page ends; second printing has purple page ends (both are rare) 150.00 375.00 1200.00

721- Big Little Paint Book, The, 1933, Whitman, 336 pgs., 3 3/4" x 8 1/2", for crayoning; first printing has green page ends; second printing has purple page ends (both are rare) 188.00 470.00 1500.00

1178- Billy of Bar-Zero, 1940, Saalfield, 400 pgs. 11.00 27.50 70.00

773- Billy the Kid, 1935, Whitman, 432 pgs., Hal Arbo-a 12.00 30.00 80.00

1159- Billy the Kid on Tall Butte, 1939, Saalfield, 400 pgs. 11.00 27.50 70.00

1174- Billy the Kid's Pledge, 1940, Saalfield, 400 pgs. 11.00 27.50 70.00

nn- Billy the Kid, Western Outlaw, 1935, Whitman, 260 pgs., Cocomalt premium, Hal Arbo-a, soft-c 12.00 30.00 85.00

1057- Black Beauty, 1934, Saalfield, hard-c 10.00 25.00 65.00

1307- Black Beauty, 1934, Saalfield, soft-c 10.00 25.00 65.00

1414- Black Silver and His Pirate Crew, 1937, Whitman, 300 pgs. 12.00 30.00 75.00

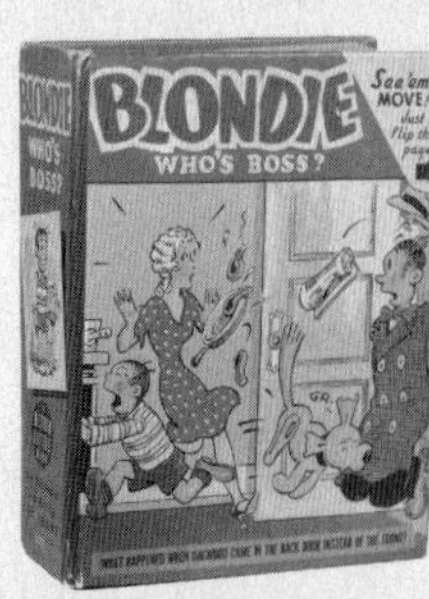

1423 - Blondie Who's Boss © WHIT

1181 - Broncho Bill © Saalfield

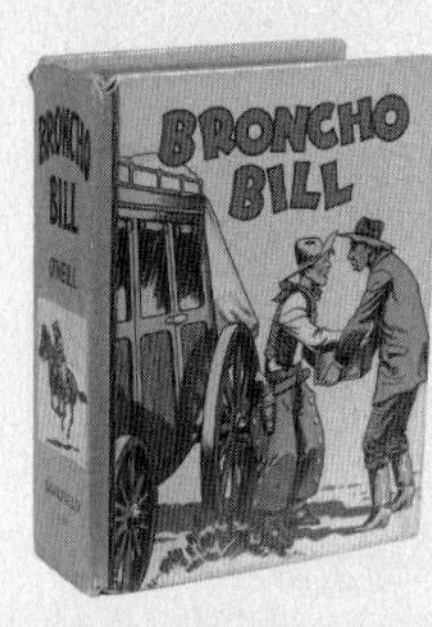

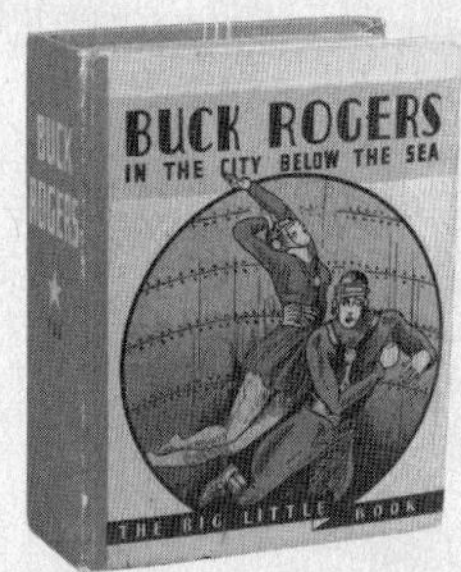

765 - Buck Rogers in the City Below the Sea © KING

GD FN VF/NM

1447- Blaze Brandon with the Foreign Legion, 1938, Whitman, 432 pgs. 12.00 30.00 75.00

1410- Blondie and Dagwood in Hot Water, 1946, Whitman, 352 pgs., by Chic Young 12.00 30.00 80.00

1415- Blondie and Baby Dumpling, 1937, Whitman, 432 pgs., by Chic Young 12.00 30.00 85.00

1419- Oh, Blondie the Bumsteads Carry On, 1941, Whitman, 432 pgs., flip pictures, by Chic Young 12.00 30.00 85.00

1423- Blondie Who's Boss?, 1942, Whitman, 432 pgs., flip pictures, by Chic Young 12.00 30.00 85.00

1429- Blondie with Baby Dumpling and Daisy, 1939, Whitman, 432 pgs., by Chic Young 12.00 30.00 85.00

1430- Blondie Count Cookie in Too!, 1947, Whitman, 288 pgs., by Chic Young 12.00 30.00 80.00

1438- Blondie and Dagwood Everybody's Happy, 1948, Whitman, 288 pgs., by Chic Young 12.00 30.00 80.00

1450- Blondie No Dull Moments, 1948, Whitman, 288 pgs., by Chic Young 12.00 30.00 80.00

1463- Blondie Fun For All, 1949, Whitman, 288 pgs., by Chic Young 12.00 30.00 80.00

1466- Blondie or Life Among the Bumsteads, 1944, Whitman, 352 pgs., by Chic Young 12.00 30.00 85.00

1476- Blondie and Bouncing Baby Dumpling, 1940, Whitman, 432 pgs., by Chic Young 12.00 30.00 85.00

1487- Blondie Baby Dumpling and All!, 1941, Whitman, 432 pgs. flip pictures, by Chic Young 12.00 30.00 85.00

1490- Blondie Papa Knows Best, 1945, Whitman, 352 pgs., by Chic Young 12.00 30.00 80.00

1491- Blondie-Cookie and Daisy's Pups, 1943, Whitman, 1st printing, 432 pgs. 12.00 30.00 85.00

1491- Blondie-Cookie and Daisy's Pups, 1943, Whitman,. 2nd printing with different back-c & 352 pgs. 12.00 30.00 75.00

703-10- Blondie and Dagwood Some Fun!, 1949, Whitman, by Chic Young 10.00 25.00 65.00

21- Blondie and Dagwood, 1936, Lynn, by Chic Young 21.00 52.50 145.00

1108- Bobby Benson on the H-Bar-O Ranch, 1934, Whitman, 300 pgs., based on radio serial 13.00 32.50 90.00

Bobby Thatcher and the Samarang Emerald (See Top-Line Comics)

1432- Bob Stone the Young Detective, 1937, Whitman, 240 pgs., movie scenes 12.00 30.00 85.00

2002- (#2)-Bonanza-The Bubble Gum Kid, 1967, Whitman, 260 pgs., 39 cents, hard-c, color illos 4.00 10.00 27.00

1139- Border Eagle, The, 1938, Saalfield, 400 pgs. 10.00 25.00 65.00

1153- Boss of the Chisholm Trail, 1939, Saalfield, 400 pgs. 10.00 25.00 65.00

1425- Brad Turner in Transatlantic Flight, 1939, Whitman, 432 pgs. 11.00 27.50 70.00

1058- Brave Little Tailor, The (Disney), 1939, Whitman, 5" x 5 1/2", 68 pgs., hard-c (Mickey Mouse) 16.00 40.00 115.00

1427- Brenda Starr and the Masked Impostor, 1943, Whitman, 352 pgs., Dale Messick-a 15.00 37.50 105.00

1426- Brer Rabbit (Walt Disney's ...), 1947, Whitman, All Picture Comics, from "Song Of The South" movie 22.00 52.50 155.00

704-10- Brer Rabbit, 1949, Whitman 19.00 47.50 135.00

1059- Brick Bradford in the City Beneath the Sea, 1934, Saalfield, hard-c, by William Ritt & Clarence Gray 18.00 45.00 125.00

1309- Brick Bradford in the City Beneath the Sea, 1934, Saalfield, soft-c, by Ritt & Gray 18.00 45.00 125.00

1468- Brick Bradford with Brocco the Modern Buccaneer, 1938, Whitman, 432 pgs., by Wm. Ritt & Clarence Gray 12.00 30.00 80.00

1133- Bringing Up Father, 1936, Whitman, 432 pgs., by George McManus 16.00 40.00 115.00

1100- Broadway Bill, 1935, Saalfield, photo-c, 4 1/2" x 5 1/4", movie scenes (Columbia Pictures, horse racing) 12.00 30.00 85.00

1580- Broadway Bill, 1935, Saalfield, soft-c, photo-c, movie scenes 12.00 30.00 85.00

1181- Broncho Bill, 1940, Saalfield, 400 pgs. 11.00 27.50 70.00

nn- Broncho Bill, 1935, Whitman, 148 pgs., 3 1/2" x 4", Tarzan Ice Cream cup lid premium 36.00 90.00 255.00

nn- Broncho Bill in Suicide Canyon (See Top-Line Comics)

1417- Bronc Peeler the Lone Cowboy, 1937, Whitman, 432 pgs., by Fred Harman, forerunner of Red Ryder (also see Red Death on the Range) 12.00 30.00 80.00

nn- Brownies' Merry Adventures, The, 1993, Barefoot Books, 202 pgs., reprints from Palmer Cox's late 1800s books 3.00 7.50 18.00

1470- Buccaneer, The, 1938, Whitman, 240 pgs., photo-c, movie scenes 13.00 32.50 90.00

1646- Buccaneers, The (TV Series), 1958, Whitman, 4 1/2" x 5 1/4", 280 pgs., Russ Manning-a 5.00 12.50 33.00

1104- Buck Jones in the Fighting Code, 1934, Whitman, 160 pgs., hard-c, movie scenes 19.00 47.50 135.00

1116- Buck Jones in Ride 'Em Cowboy (Universal Presents), 1935, Whitman, 240 pgs., photo-c, movie scenes 19.00 47.50 135.00

1174- Buck Jones in the Roaring West (Universal Presents), 1935, Whitman, 240 pgs., movie scenes 19.00 47.50 135.00

1188- Buck Jones in the Fighting Rangers (Universal Presents), 1936, Whitman, 240 pgs., photo-c, movie scenes 19.00 47.50 135.00

1404- Buck Jones and the Two-Gun Kid, 1937, Whitman, 432 pgs. 13.00 32.50 90.00

1451- Buck Jones and the Killers of Crooked Butte, 1940, Whitman, 432 pgs. 13.00 32.50 90.00

1461- Buck Jones and the Rock Creek Cattle War, 1938, Whitman, 432 pgs. 13.00 32.50 90.00

1486- Buck Jones and the Rough Riders in Forbidden Trails, 1943, Whitman, flip pictures, based on movie; Tim McCoy app. 18.00 45.00 125.00

3- Buck Jones in the Red Rider, 1934, EVW, 160 pgs., movie scenes 39.00 98.00 275.00

8- Buck Jones Cowboy Masquerade, 1938, Whitman, 132 pgs., soft-c, 3 3/4" x 3 1/2", Buddy Book premium 43.00 108.00 300.00

15- Buck Jones in Rocky Rhodes, 1935, EVW, 160 pgs., photo-c, movie scenes 57.00 142.00 400.00

4069- Buck Jones and the Night Riders, 1937, Whitman, 7" x 9", 320 pgs., Big Big Book 79.00 198.00 550.00

nn- Buck Jones on the Six-Gun Trail, 1939, Whitman, 36 pgs., 2 1/2" x 3 1/2", Penny Book 12.00 30.00 80.00

nn- Buck Jones Big Thrill Chewing Gum, 1934, Whitman, 8 pgs., 2 1/2" x 3 1/2" (6 diff.) each... 20.00 50.00 140.00

742- Buck Rogers in the 25th Century A.D., 1933, Whitman, 320 pgs., Dick Calkins-a 47.00 118.00 330.00

nn- Buck Rogers in the 25th Century A.D., 1933, Whitman, 204 pgs.,Cocomalt premium, Calkins-a 30.00 75.00 210.00

765- Buck Rogers in the City Below the Sea, 1934, Whitman, 320 pgs., Dick Calkins-a 36.00 90.00 255.00

765- Buck Rogers in the City Below the Sea, 1934, Whitman, 324 pgs., soft-c, Dick Calkins-c/a (Rare) 82.00 205.00 575.00

1143- Buck Rogers on the Moons of Saturn, 1934, Whitman, 320 pgs., Dick Calkins-a 38.00 95.00 255.00

nn- Buck Rogers on the Moons of Saturn, 1934, Whitman, 324 pgs., premium w/no ads, soft 3-color-c, Dick Calkins-a 64.00 160.00 450.00

1169- Buck Rogers and the Depth Men of Jupiter, 1935, Whitman, 432 pgs., Calkins-a 36.00 90.00 255.00

1178- Buck Rogers and the Doom Comet, 1935, Whitman, 432 pgs., Calkins-a 34.00 85.00 240.00

1197- Buck Rogers and the Planetoid Plot, 1936, Whitman, 432 pgs., Calkins-a 34.00 85.00 240.00

1409- Buck Rogers Vs. the Fiend of Space, 1940, Whitman, 432 pgs., Calkins-a 45.00 113.00 315.00

1437- Buck Rogers in the War with the Planet Venus, 1938, Whitman, 432 pgs., Calkins-a 34.00 85.00 240.00

1474- Buck Rogers and the Overturned World, 1941, Whitman, 432 pgs., flip pictures, Calkins-a 36.00 90.00 250.00

1490- Buck Rogers and the Super-Dwarf of Space, 1943, Whitman, 11 Pictures Comics, Calkins-a 34.00 85.00 240.00

4057- Buck Rogers, The Adventures of, 1934, Whitman, 7" x 9 1/2", 320 pgs., Big Big Book, "The Story of Buck Rogers on the Planet Eros," Calkins-c/a 130.00 327.00 1045.00

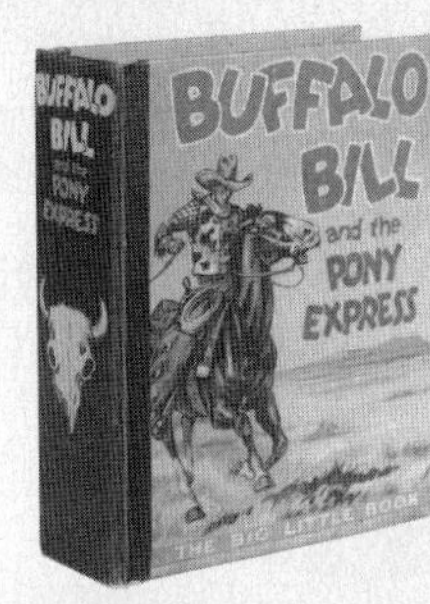
713 - Buffalo Bill and the Pony Express © WHIT

1488 - Captain Midnight and the Secret Squadron © FAW

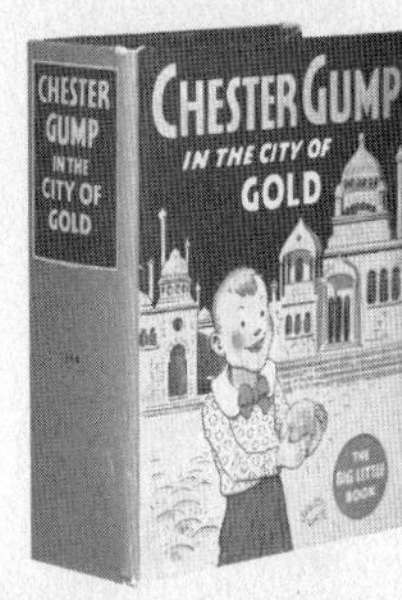
1146 - Chester Gump in the City of Gold © WHIT

GD FN VF/NM

nn- **Buck Rogers**, 1935, Whitman, 4" x 3 1/2", Tarzan Ice Cream cup premium (Rare) 165.00 412.00 1320.00

nn- **Buck Rogers in the City of Floating Globes,** 1935, Whitman, 258 pgs., Cocomalt premium, soft-c, Dick Calkins-a 115.00 287.00 810.00

nn- **Buck Rogers Big Thrill Chewing Gum**, 1934, Whitman, 8 pgs., 2 1/2" x 3 " (6 diff.) each... 29.00 73.00 200.00

1135- **Buckskin and Bullets**, 1938, Saalfield, 400 pgs. 11.00 27.50 70.00

Buffalo Bill (See Wild West Adventures of ...)

nn- **Buffalo Bill**, 1934, World Syndicate, All pictures, by J. Carroll Mansfield 11.00 27.50 70.00

713- **Buffalo Bill and the Pony Express**, 1934, Whitman, hard-c, 384 pgs., Hal Arbo-a 12.00 30.00 80.00

nn- **Buffalo Bill and the Pony Express**, 1934, Whitman, soft-c, 384 pgs., Hal Arbo-a; three-color premium (Rare) 71.00 178.00 500.00

1194- **Buffalo Bill Plays a Lone Hand**, 1936, Whitman, 432 pgs., Hal Arbo-a 11.00 27.50 70.00

530- **Bugs Bunny**, 1943, Whitman, All Pictures Comics, Tall Comic Book, 3 1/4" x 8 1/4", reprints/Looney Tunes 1 & 5 31.00 78.00 215.00

1403- **Bugs Bunny and the Pirate Loot**, 1947, Whitman, All Pictures Comics 12.00 30.00 80.00

1435- **Bugs Bunny**, 1944, Whitman, All Pictures Comics 12.00 30.00 85.00

1440- **Bugs Bunny in Risky Business**, 1948, Whitman, All Pictures & Comics 12.00 30.00 80.00

1455- **Bugs Bunny and Klondike Gold,** 1948, Whitman, 288 pgs. 12.00 30.00 80.00

1465- **Bugs Bunny The Masked Marvel**, 1949, Whitman, 288 pgs. 12.00 30.00 80.00

1496- **Bugs Bunny and His Pals,** 1945, Whitman, All Pictures Comics; r/Four Color Comics #33 12.00 30.00 80.00

13- **Bugs Bunny and the Secret of Storm Island**, 1942, Dell,194 pgs., Fast-Action Story 36.00 90.00 255.00

706-10- **Bugs Bunny and the Giant Brothers,** 1949, Whitman 11.00 27.50 70.00

2007- **(#7)-Bugs Bunny-Double Trouble on Diamond Island**, 1967, Whitman, 260 pgs., 39 cents, hard-c, color illos 5.00 12.50 33.00

2029-(#29)- **Bugs Bunny, Accidental Adventure,** 1969, Whitman, 256 pgs., hard-c, color illos. 4.00 10.00 22.00

2952- **Bugs Bunny's Mistake**, 1949, Whitman, 3 1/4" x 4", 24 pgs., Tiny Tales, full color (5 cents) (1030-5 on back-c) 11.00 27.50 70.00

5757-2- **Bugs Bunny in Double Trouble on Diamond Island**,1967, (1980-reprints #2007), Whitman, 260 pgs., soft-c, 79 cents, B&W 2.00 5.00 12.00

5758- **Bugs Bunny, Accidental Adventure**, 1973, Whitman, 256 pgs., soft-c, B&W illos. 2.00 5.00 12.00

5758-1- **Bugs Bunny, Accidental Adventure**, 1973, Whitman, 256 pgs., soft-c, B&W illos. 2.00 5.00 12.00

5772- **Bugs Bunny the Last Crusader**, 1975, Whitman, 49 cents, flip-it book 2.00 5.00 12.00

5772-2- **Bugs Bunny the Last Crusader**, 1975, Whitman, $1.50, flip-it book 1.00 2.50 6.00

1169- **Bullet Benton**, 1939, Saalfield, 400 pgs. 11.00 27.50 70.00

nn- **Bulletman and the Return of Mr. Murder**, 1941, Fawcett, 196 pgs., Dime Action Book 54.00 135.00 375.00

1142- **Bullets Across the Border** (A Billy The Kid story), 1938, Saalfield, 400 pgs. 11.00 27.50 70.00

Bunky (See Top-Line Comics)

837- **Bunty** (Punch and Judy), 1935, Whitman, 28 pgs., Magic-Action with 3 pop-ups 16.00 40.00 115.00

1091- **Burn 'Em Up Barnes**, 1935, Saalfield, hard-c, movie scenes 15.00 37.50 105.00

1321- **Burn 'Em Up Barnes**, 1935, Saalfield, soft-c, movie scenes 15.00 37.50 105.00

1415- **Buz Sawyer and Bomber 13**,1946, Whitman, 352 pgs., Roy Crane-a 15.00 37.50 105.00

1412- **Calling W-1-X-Y-Z, Jimmy Kean and the Radio Spies**, 1939, Whitman, 300 pgs. 12.00 30.00 80.00

GD FN VF/NM

Call of the Wild (See Jack London's...)

1107- **Camels are Coming**, 1935, Saalfield, movie scenes 12.00 30.00 75.00

1587- **Camels are Coming**, 1935, Saalfield, movie scenes 12.00 30.00 75.00

nn- **Captain and the Kids, Boys Vill Be Boys, The**, 1938, 68 pgs., Pan-Am Oil premium, soft-c 15.00 37.50 105.00

1128- **Captain Easy Soldier of Fortune**, 1934, Whitman, 432 pgs., Roy Crane-a 15.00 37.50 105.00

nn- **Captain Easy Soldier of Fortune**, 1934, Whitman, 436 pgs., Premium, no ads, soft 3-color-c, Roy Crane-a 26.00 65.00 180.00

1474- **Captain Easy Behind Enemy Lines**, 1943, Whitman, 352 pgs., Roy Crane-a 13.00 32.50 90.00

nn- **Captain Easy and Wash Tubbs**, 1935, 260 pgs., Cocomalt premium, Roy Crane-a 13.00 32.50 90.00

1444- **Captain Frank Hawks Air Ace and the League of Twelve**, 1938, Whitman, 432 pgs. 12.00 30.00 80.00

nn- **Captain Marvel**, 1941, Fawcett, 196 pgs., Dime Action Book 65.00 163.00 460.00

1402- **Captain Midnight and Sheik Jomak Khan**, 1946, Whitman, 352 pgs. 26.00 65.00 180.00

1452- **Captain Midnight and the Moon Woman**, 1943, Whitman, 352 pgs. 28.00 70.00 195.00

1458- **Captain Midnight Vs. The Terror of the Orient**, 1942, Whitman, 432 pgs., flip pictures, Hess-a 28.00 70.00 195.00

1488- **Captain Midnight and the Secret Squadron**, 1941, Whitman, 432 pgs. 28.00 70.00 195.00

Captain Robb of.. (See Dirigible ZR90 ...)

nn- **Cauliflower Catnip Pearls of Peril**, 1981, Teacup Tales, 290 pgs., Joe Wehrle Jr.-s/a; deliberately printed on aged-looking paper to look like an old BLB 4.00 10.00 27.00

20- **Ceiling Zero,** 1936, Lynn, 128 pgs., 7 1/2" x 5", hard-c, James Cagney, Pat O'Brien photos on-c, movie scenes, Warner Bros. Pictures 12.00 30.00 80.00

1093- **Chandu the Magician**, 1935, Saalfield, 5" x 5 1/4", 160 pgs., hard-c, Bela Lugosi photo-c, movie scenes 16.00 40.00 115.00

1323- **Chandu the Magician**, 1935, Saalfield, 5" x 5 1/4", 160 pgs., soft-c, Bela Lugosi photo-c 18.00 45.00 125.00

Charlie Chan (See Inspector ...)

1459- **Charlie Chan Solves a New Mystery** (See Inspector..), 1940, Whitman, 432 pgs., Alfred Andriola-a 16.00 40.00 110.00

1478- **Charlie Chan of the Honolulu Police, Inspector**, 1939, Whitman, 432 pgs., Andriola-a 16.00 40.00 110.00

Charlie McCarthy (See Story Of ...)

734- **Chester Gump at Silver Creek Ranch**, 1933, Whitman, 320 pgs., Sidney Smith-a 15.00 37.50 105.00

nn- **Chester Gump at Silver Creek Ranch**, 1933, Whitman, 204 pgs., Cocomalt premium, soft-c, Sidney Smith-a 18.00 45.00 125.00

nn- **Chester Gump at Silver Creek Ranch**, 1933, Whitman, 52 pgs., 4" x 5 1/2", premium-no ads, soft-c, Sidney Smith-a 26.00 65.00 180.00

766- **Chester Gump Finds the Hidden Treasure**, 1934, Whitman, 320 pgs., Sidney Smith-a 15.00 37.50 105.00

nn- **Chester Gump Finds the Hidden Treasure**, 1934, Whitman, 52 pgs., 3 1/2" x 5 3/4", premium-no ads, soft-c, Sidney Smith-a 26.00 65.00 180.00

nn- **Chester Gump Finds the Hidden Treasure**, 1934, Whitman, 52 pgs., 4" x 5 1/2", premium-no ads, Sidney Smith-a 26.00 65.00 180.00

1146- **Chester Gump in the City Of Gold**, 1935, Whitman, 432 pgs., Sidney Smith-a 15.00 37.50 105.00

nn- **Chester Gump in the City Of Gold**, 1935, Whitman, 436 pgs., premium-no ads, 3-color, soft-c, Sidney Smith-a 30.00 75.00 210.00

1402- **Chester Gump in the Pole to Pole Flight**, 1937, Whitman, 432 pgs. 13.00 32.50 90.00

5- **Chester Gump and His Friends,** 1934, Whitman, 132 pgs., 3 1/2" x 3 1/2", soft-c, Tarzan Ice Cream cup lid premium 29.00 73.00 200.00

nn- **Chester Gump at the North Pole**, 1938, Whitman, 68 pgs.

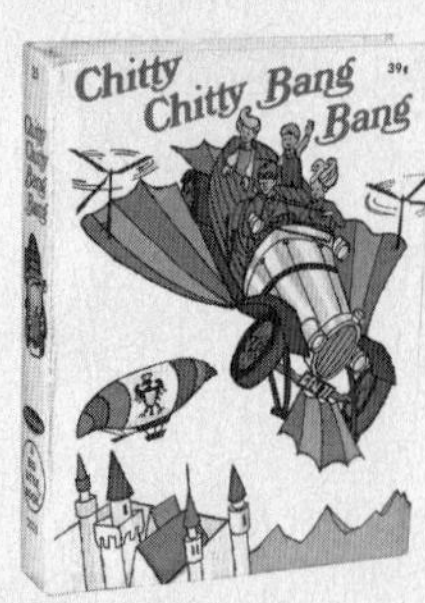

2025 - Chitty Chitty Bang Bang © DIS

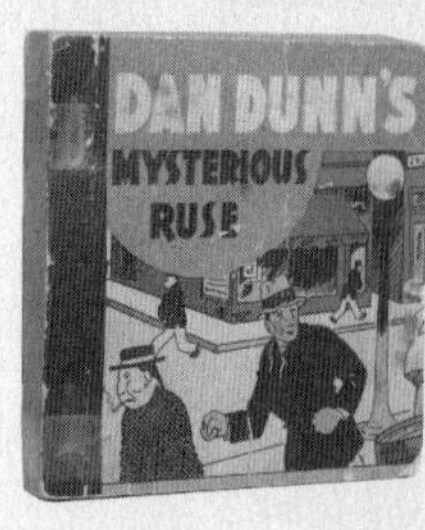

9 - Dan Dunn's Mysterious Ruse © WHIT

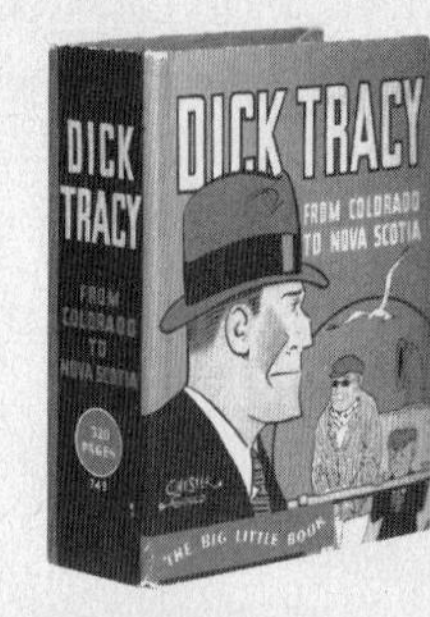

749 - Dick Tracy from Colorado to Nova Scotia © NYNS

GD FN VF/NM

soft-c, 3 3/4" x 3 1/2", Pan-Am giveaway 29.00 73.00 200.00

nn- **Chicken Greedy**, nd(1930s), np (Whitman), 36 pgs., 3" x 2 1/2", Penny Book 4.00 10.00 22.00

nn- **Chicken Licken**, nd (1930s), np (Whitman), 36 pgs., 3" x 2 1/2", Penny Book 4.00 10.00 22.00

1101- **Chief of the Rangers**, 1935, Saalfield, hard-c, Tom Mix photo-c, movie scenes from "The Miracle Rider" 21.00 52.50 145.00

1581- **Chief of the Rangers**, 1935, Saalfield, soft-c, Tom Mix photo-c, movie scenes 21.00 52.50 145.00

Child's Garden of Verses (See Wee Little Books)

L14- **Chip Collins' Adventures on Bat Island**, 1935, Lynn, 192 pgs. 12.00 30.00 85.00

2025- **Chitty Chitty Bang Bang**, 1968, Whitman, movie photos 4.00 10.00 27.00

Chubby Little Books, 1935, Whitman, 3" x 2 1/2", 200 pgs.

W803- **Golden Hours Story Book, The** 7.00 17.50 40.00

W803- **Story Hours Story Book, The** 7.00 17.50 40.00

W804- **Gay Book of Little Stories, The** 7.00 17.50 40.00

W804- **Glad Book of Little Stories, The** 7.00 17.50 40.00

W804- **Joy Book of Little Stories, The** 7.00 17.50 40.00

W804- **Sunny Book of Little Stories, The** 7.00 17.50 40.00

1453- **Chuck Malloy Railroad Detective on the Streamliner**,1938, Whitman, 300 pgs. 12.00 30.00 75.00

Cinderella (See Walt Disney's...)

Clyde Beatty (See The Steel Arena)

1410- **Clyde Beatty Daredevil Lion and Tiger Tamer**, 1939, Whitman, 300 pgs. 14.00 35.00 95.00

1480- **Coach Bernie Bierman's Brick Barton and the Winning Eleven**, 1938, 300 pgs. 11.00 27.50 70.00

1446- **Convoy Patrol** (A Thrilling U.S. Navy Story), 1942, Whitman, 432 pgs., flip pictures 11.00 27.50 70.00

1127- **Corley of the Wilderness Trail**, 1937, Saalfield, hard-c 11.00 27.50 70.00

1607- **Corley of the Wilderness Trail**, 1937, Saalfield, soft-c 11.00 27.50 70.00

1- **Count of Monte Cristo**, 1934, EVW, 160 pgs., (Five Star Library), movie scenes, hard-c (Rare) 43.00 108.00 300.00

1457- **Cowboy Lingo Boys' Book of Western Facts**, 1938, Whitman, 300 pgs., Fred Harman-a 12.00 30.00 75.00

1171- **Cowboy Malloy**, 1940, Saalfield, 400 pgs. 10.00 25.00 65.00

1106- **Cowboy Millionaire**, 1935, Saalfield, movie scenes with George O'Brien, photo-c, hard-c 15.00 37.50 105.00

1586- **Cowboy Millionaire**, 1935, Saalfield, movie scenes with George O'Brien, photo-c, soft-c 15.00 37.50 105.00

724- **Cowboy Stories**, 1933, Whitman, 300 pgs., Hal Arbo-a 12.00 30.00 85.00

nn- **Cowboy Stories**, 1933, Whitman, 52 pgs., soft-c, premium-no ads, 4" x 5 1/2" Hal Arbo-a 15.00 37.50 105.00

1161- **Crimson Cloak, The**, 1939, Saalfield, 400 pgs. 11.00 27.50 70.00

L19- **Curley Harper at Lakespur**, 1935, Lynn, 192 pgs. 11.00 27.50 70.00

5785-2- **Daffy Duck in Twice the Trouble**, 1980, Whitman, 260 pgs., 79 cents soft-c 1.00 2.50 6.00

2018-(#18)-**Daktari-Night of Terror**, 1968, Whitman, 260 pgs., 39 cents, hard-c, color illos 4.00 10.00 27.00

1010- **Dan Dunn And The Gangsters' Frame-Up**, 1937, Whitman, 7 1/4" x 5 1/2", 64 pgs., Nickel Book 45.00 114.00 320.00

1116- **Dan Dunn "Crime Never Pays,"** 1934, Whitman, 320 pgs., by Norman Marsh 14.00 35.00 95.00

1125- **Dan Dunn on the Trail of the Counterfeiters**, 1936, Whitman, 432 pgs., by Norman Marsh 14.00 35.00 95.00

1171- **Dan Dunn and the Crime Master**, 1937, Whitman, 432 pgs., by Norman Marsh 14.00 35.00 95.00

1417- **Dan Dunn and the Underworld Gorillas**, 1941, Whitman, All Pictures Comics, flip pictures, by Norman Marsh 14.00 35.00 95.00

1454- **Dan Dunn on the Trail of Wu Fang**, 1938, Whitman, 432 pgs., by Norman Marsh 16.00 40.00 115.00

1481- **Dan Dunn and the Border Smugglers**, 1938, Whitman, 432 pgs., by Norman Marsh 13.00 32.50 90.00

1492- **Dan Dunn and the Dope Ring**, 1940, Whitman, 432 pgs., by Norman Marsh 12.00 30.00 85.00

nn- **Dan Dunn and the Bank Hold-Up**, 1938, Whitman, 36 pgs., 2 1/2" x 3 1/2", Penny Book 11.00 27.50 70.00

nn- **Dan Dunn and the Zeppelin Of Doom**, 1938, Dell, 196 pgs., Fast-Action Story, soft-c 33.00 83.00 230.00

nn- **Dan Dunn Meets Chang Loo**, 1938, Whitman, 66 pgs., Pan-Am premium, by Norman Marsh 29.00 73.00 200.00

nn- **Dan Dunn Plays a Lone Hand**, 1938, Whitman, 36 pgs.,
2 1/2" x 3 1/2", Penny Book 11.00 27.50 70.00
3 3/4" x 3 1/2", Buddy book 39.00 98.00 275.00

6- **Dan Dunn Secret Operative 48 and the Counterfeiter Ring**, 1938, Whitman, 132 pgs., soft-c, 3 3/4" x 3 1/2", Buddy Book premium 39.00 98.00 275.00

9- **Dan Dunn's Mysterious Ruse**, 1936, Whitman, 132 pgs., soft-c, 3 1/2" x 3 1/2", Tarzan Ice Cream cup lid premium 39.00 98.00 275.00

1177- **Danger Trail North**, 1940, Saalfield, 400 pgs.11.00 27.50 70.00

1151- **Danger Trails in Africa**, 1935, Whitman, 432 pgs. 18.00 45.00 125.00

nn- **Daniel Boone**, 1934, World Syndicate, High Lights of History Series, hard-c, All in Pictures 11.00 27.50 70.00

1160- **Dan of the Lazy L**, 1939, Saalfield, 400 pgs. 11.00 27.50 70.00

1148- **David Copperfield**, 1934, Whitman, hard-c, 160 pgs., photo-c, movie scenes (W. C. Fields) 20.00 50.00 140.00

nn- **David Copperfield**, 1934, Whitman, soft-c, 164 pgs., movie scenes 20.00 50.00 140.00

1151- **Death by Short Wave**, 1938, Saalfield 12.00 30.00 75.00

1156- **Denny the Ace Detective**, 1938, Saalfield, 400 pgs. 10.00 25.00 65.00

1431- **Desert Eagle and the Hidden Fortress, The**, 1941, Whitman, 432 pgs., flip pictures 12.00 30.00 75.00

1458- **Desert Eagle Rides Again, The**, 1939, Whitman, 300 pgs. 12.00 30.00 75.00

1136- **Desert Justice**, 1938, Saalfield, 400 pgs. 10.00 25.00 65.00

1484- **Detective Higgins of the Racket Squad**, 1938, Whitman, 432 pgs. 12.00 30.00 75.00

1124- **Dickie Moore in the Little Red School House**, 1936, Whitman, 240 pgs., photo-c, movie scenes (Chesterfield Motion Picts. Corp) 13.00 32.50 90.00

W-707- **Dick Tracy the Detective, The Adventures of**, 1933, Whitman, 320 pgs. (The 1st Big Little Book), by Chester Gould (Scarce) 275.00 687.00 2500.00

nn- **Dick Tracy Detective, The Adventures of**, 1933, Whitman, 52 pgs., 4" x 5 1/2", premium-no ads, soft-c, by Chester Gould 100.00 250.00 695.00

nn- **Dick Tracy Detective, The Adventures of**, 1933, Whitman, 52 pgs., 4" x 5 1/2", inside back-c & back-c ads for Sundial Shoes, soft-c, by Chester Gould 107.00 268.00 750.00

710- **Dick Tracy and Dick Tracy, Jr.** (The Advs. of ...), 1933, Whitman, 320 pgs., by Chester Gould 79.00 198.00 550.00

nn- **Dick Tracy and Dick Tracy, Jr.** (The Advs. of ...), 1933, Whitman, 52 pgs., premium-no ads, soft-c, 4" x 5 1/2", by Chester Gould 79.00 198.00 550.00

nn- **Dick Tracy the Detective and Dick Tracy, Jr.**, 1933, Whitman, 52 pgs., premium-no ads, 3 1/2"x 5 1/4", soft-c, by Chester Gould 79.00 198.00 550.00

723- **Dick Tracy Out West**, 1933, Whitman, 300 pgs., by Chester Gould 49.00 122.00 345.00

749- **Dick Tracy from Colorado to Nova Scotia**, 1933, Whitman, 320 pgs., by Chester Gould 45.00 113.00 315.00

nn- **Dick Tracy from Colorado to Nova Scotia**, 1933, Whitman, 204 pgs., premium-no ads, soft-c, by Chester Gould 49.00 122.00 345.00

1105- **Dick Tracy and the Stolen Bonds**, 1934, Whitman, 320 pgs., by Chester Gould 26.00 65.00 185.00

1112- **Dick Tracy and the Racketeer Gang**, 1936, Whitman, 432 pgs., by Chester Gould 21.00 52.50 145.00

1137- **Dick Tracy Solves the Penfield Mystery**, 1934, Whitman, 320 pgs., by Chester Gould 26.00 65.00 185.00

1454 - Dick Tracy on the High Seas © NYNS

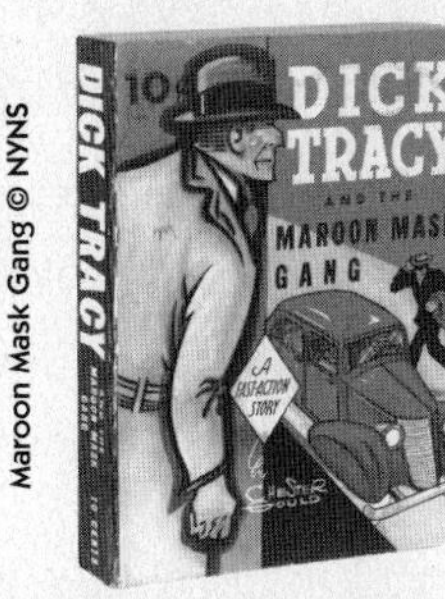

nn - Dick Tracy and the Maroon Mask Gang © NYNS

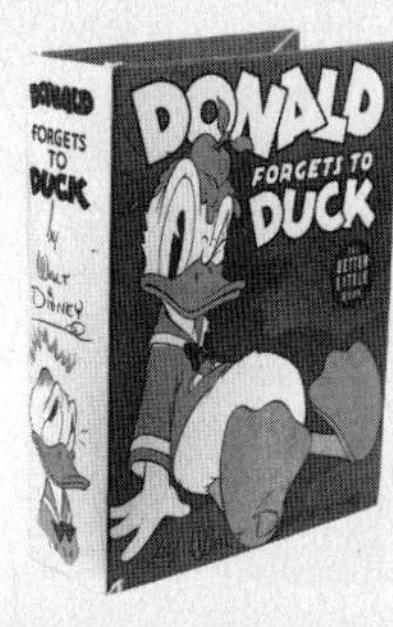

1434 - Donald Duck Forgets to Duck © DIS

GD FN VF/NM

nn- Dick Tracy Solves the Penfield Mystery, 1934, Whitman, 324 pgs., premium-no ads, 3-color, soft-c, by Chester Gould 64.00 160.00 450.00
1163- Dick Tracy and the Boris Arson Gang, 1935, Whitman, 432 pgs., by Chester Gould 24.00 60.00 165.00
1170- Dick Tracy on the Trail of Larceny Lu, 1935, Whitman, 432 pgs., by Chester Gould 21.00 52.50 145.00
1185- Dick Tracy in Chains of Crime, 1936, Whitman, 432 pgs., by Chester Gould 24.00 60.00 165.00
1412- Dick Tracy and Yogee Yamma, 1946, Whitman, 352 pgs., by Chester Gould 21.00 52.50 145.00
1420- Dick Tracy and the Hotel Murders, 1937, Whitman, 432 pgs., by Chester Gould 24.00 60.00 165.00
1434- Dick Tracy and the Phantom Ship, 1940, Whitman, 432 pgs., by Chester Gould 24.00 60.00 165.00
1436- Dick Tracy and the Mad Killer, 1947, Whitman, 288 pgs., by Chester Gould 18.00 45.00 125.00
1439- Dick Tracy and His G-Men, 1941, Whitman, 432 pgs., flip pictures, by Chester Gould 24.00 60.00 165.00
1445- Dick Tracy and the Bicycle Gang, 1948, Whitman, 288 pgs., by Chester Gould 18.00 45.00 125.00
1446- Detective Dick Tracy and the Spider Gang, 1937, Whitman, 240 pgs., movie scenes from "Adventures of Dick Tracy" (Republic serial) 29.00 73.00 200.00
1449- Dick Tracy Special F.B.I. Operative, 1943, Whitman, 432 pgs. by Chester Gould 24.00 60.00 165.00
1454- Dick Tracy on the High Seas, 1939, Whitman, 432 pgs., by Chester Gould 24.00 60.00 165.00
1460- Dick Tracy and the Tiger Lilly Gang, 1949, Whitman, 288 pgs., by Chester Gould 18.00 45.00 125.00
1478- Dick Tracy on Voodoo Island, 1944, Whitman, 352 pgs., by Chester Gould 18.00 45.00 125.00
1479- Detective Dick Tracy Vs. Crooks in Disguise, 1939, Whitman, 432 pgs., flip pictures, by Chester Gould 24.00 60.00 165.00
1482- Dick Tracy and the Wreath Kidnapping Case, 1945, Whitman, 352 pgs. 20.00 50.00 140.00
1488- Dick Tracy the Super-Detective, 1939, Whitman, 432 pgs., by Chester Gould 24.00 60.00 165.00
1491- Dick Tracy the Man with No Face, 1938, Whitman, 432 pgs. 24.00 60.00 165.00
1495- Dick Tracy Returns, 1939, Whitman, 432 pgs., based on Republic Motion Picture serial, Chester Gould-a 24.00 60.00 165.00
2001- (#1)-Dick Tracy-Encounters Facey, 1967, Whitman, 260 pgs., 39 cents, hard-c, color illos 4.00 10.00 27.00
4055- Dick Tracy, The Adventures of, 1934, Whitman, 7" x 9 1/2", 320 pgs., Big Big Book, by Chester Gould 107.00 268.00 750.00
4071- Dick Tracy and the Mystery of the Purple Cross, 1938, 7" x 9 1/2", 320 pgs., Big Big Book, by Chester Gould (Scarce) 130.00 327.00 1045.00
nn- Dick Tracy and the Invisible Man, 1939, Whitman, 3 1/4" x 3 3/4", 132 pgs., stapled, soft-c, Quaker Oats premium; NBC radio play script, Chester Gould-a 41.00 103.00 285.00
Vol. 2- Dick Tracy's Ghost Ship, 1939, Whitman, 3 1/2" x 3 1/2", 132 pgs., soft-c, stapled, Quaker Oats premium; NBC radio play script episode from actual radio show; Gould-a 41.00 103.00 285.00
3- Dick Tracy Meets a New Gang, 1934, Whitman, 3" x 3 1/2", 132 pgs., soft-c, Tarzan Ice Cream cup lid premium 70.00 175.00 490.00
11- Dick Tracy in Smashing the Famon Racket, 1938, Whitman, 3 3/4" x 3 1/2", Buddy Book-ice cream premium, by Chester Gould 70.00 175.00 490.00
nn- Dick Tracy Gets His Man, 1938, Whitman, 36 pgs., 2 1/2" x 3 1/2", Penny Book 12.00 30.00 75.00
nn- Dick Tracy the Detective, 1938, Whitman, 36 pgs., 2 1/2" x 3 1/2", Penny Book 12.00 30.00 75.00
9- Dick Tracy and the Frozen Bullet Murders, 1941, Dell, 196 pgs., Fast-Action Story, soft-c, by Gould 41.00 103.00 285.00
6833- Dick Tracy Detective and Federal Agent, 1936, Dell, 244 pgs., Cartoon Story Books, hard-c, by Gould 49.00 122.00 345.00
nn- Dick Tracy Detective and Federal Agent, 1936, Dell, 244 pgs., Fast-Action Story, soft-c, by Gould 46.00 115.00 320.00

GD FN VF/NM

nn- Dick Tracy and the Blackmailers, 1939, Dell, 196 pgs., Fast-Action Story, soft-c, by Gould 46.00 115.00 320.00
nn- Dick Tracy and the Chain of Evidence, Detective, 1938, Dell, 196 pgs., Fast-Action Story, soft-c, by Chester Gould 46.00 115.00 320.00
nn- Dick Tracy and the Crook Without a Face, 1938, Whitman, 68 pgs., 3 1/4" x 3 1/2", Pan-Am giveaway, Gould-c/a 49.00 122.00 345.00
nn- Dick Tracy and the Maroon Mask Gang, 1938, Dell, 196 pgs., Fast-Action Story, soft-c, by Gould 46.00 115.00 320.00
nn- Dick Tracy Cross-Country Race, 1934, Whitman, 8 pgs., 2 1/2" x 3", Big Thrill chewing gum premium (6 diff.) 18.00 45.00 125.00
nn- Dick Whittington and his Cat, nd(1930s), np(Whitman), 36 pgs., Penny Book 5.00 12.50 33.00
Dinglehoofer und His Dog Adolph (See Top-Line Comics)
Dinky (See Jackie Cooper in ...)
1464- Dirigible ZR90 and the Disappearing Zeppelin (Captain Robb of ...), 1941, Whitman, 300 pgs., Al Lewin-a 20.00 50.00 140.00
1167- Dixie Dugan Among the Cowboys, 1939, Saalfield, 400 pgs. 12.00 30.00 85.00
1188- Dixie Dugan and Cuddles, 1940, Saalfield, 400 pgs., by Striebel & McEvoy 12.00 30.00 85.00
Doctor Doom (See Foreign Spies... & International Spy...)
Dog of Flanders, A (See Frankie Thomas in ...)
1114- Dog Stars of Hollywood, 1936, Saalfield, photo-c, photo-illos 16.00 40.00 115.00
1594- Dog Stars of Hollywood, 1936, Saalfield, photo-c, soft-c, photo-illos 16.00 40.00 115.00
Donald Duck (See Silly Symphony... & Walt Disney's ...)
800- Donald Duck in Bringing Up the Boys, 1948, Whitman, hard-c, Story Hour series 12.00 30.00 85.00
1404- Donald Duck (Says Such a Life) (Disney), 1939, Whitman, 432 pgs., Taliaferro-a 31.00 78.00 220.00
1411- Donald Duck and Ghost Morgan's Treasure (Disney), 1946, Whitman, All Pictures Comics, Barks-a; reprints Four Color #9 38.00 95.00 255.00
1422- Donald Duck Sees Stars (Disney), 1941, Whitman, 432 pgs., flip pictures, Taliaferro-a 31.00 78.00 215.00
1424- Donald Duck Says Such Luck (Disney), 1941, Whitman, 432 pgs., flip pictures, Taliaferro-a 31.00 78.00 215.00
1430- Donald Duck Headed For Trouble (Disney), 1942, Whitman, 432 pgs., flip pictures, Taliaferro-a 31.00 78.00 215.00
1432- Donald Duck and the Green Serpent (Disney), 1947, Whitman, All Pictures Comics, Barks-a; reprints Four Color #108 34.00 85.00 240.00
1434- Donald Duck Forgets To Duck (Disney), 1939, Whitman, 432 pgs., Taliaferro-a 31.00 78.00 215.00
1438- Donald Duck Off the Beam (Disney), 1943, Whitman, 352 pgs., flip pictures, Taliaferro-a 31.00 78.00 215.00
1438- Donald Duck Off the Beam (Disney), 1943, Whitman, 432 pgs., flip pictures, Taliaferro-a 31.00 78.00 215.00
1449- Donald Duck Lays Down the Law, 1948, Whitman, 288 pgs., Barks-a 31.00 78.00 215.00
1457- Donald Duck in Volcano Valley (Disney), 1949, Whitman, 288 pgs., Barks-a 31.00 78.00 215.00
1462- Donald Duck Gets Fed Up (Disney), 1940, Whitman, 432 pgs.,Taliaferro-a 31.00 78.00 215.00
1478- Donald Duck-Hunting For Trouble (Disney), 1938, Whitman, 432 pgs., Taliaferro-a 31.00 78.00 215.00
1484- Donald Duck is Here Again!, 1944, Whitman, All Pictures Comics, Taliaferro-a 31.00 78.00 215.00
1486- Donald Duck Up in the Air (Disney), 1945, Whitman, 352 pgs., Barks-a 34.00 85.00 240.00
705-10- Donald Duck and the Mystery of the Double X, (Disney), 1949, Whitman, Barks-a 16.00 40.00 115.00
2033-(#33)- Donald Duck, Luck of the Ducks, 1969, Whitman, 256 pgs., hard-c, 39 cents, color illos. 4.00 10.00 22.00
2009-(#9)-Donald Duck-The Fabulous Diamond Fountain, (Walt Disney), 1967, Whitman, 260 pgs., 39 cents, hard-c, color illos 4.00 10.00 27.00
5756- Donald Duck-The Fabulous Diamond Fountain,

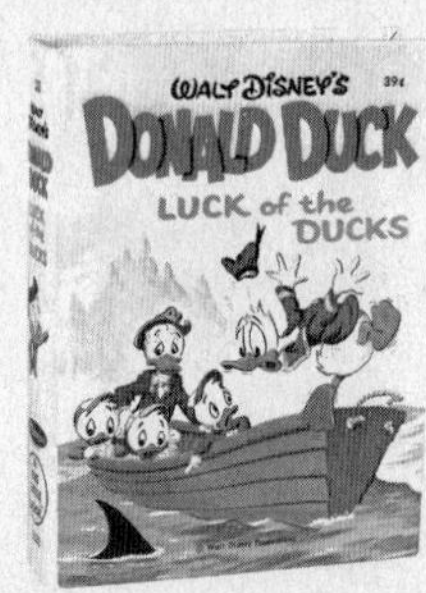

5764 - Donald Duck, Luck of the Ducks © DIS

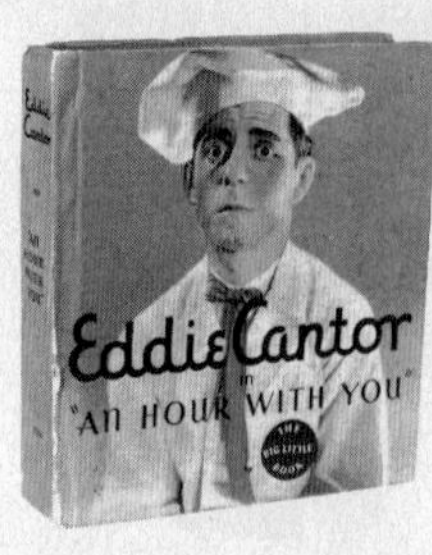

774 - Eddie Cantor in An Hour with You © WHIT

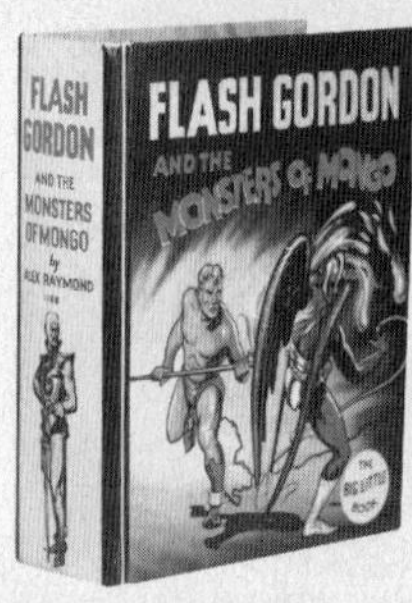

1166 - Flash Gordon and the Monsters of Mongo © KING

GD FN VF/NM

(Walt Disney), 1973, Whitman, 260 pgs., 79 cents, soft-c, color illos 3.00 7.50 20.00

5756-1- Donald Duck-The Fabulous Diamond Fountain, (Walt Disney), 1973, Whitman, 260 pgs., 79 cents, soft-c, color illos 3.00 7.50 20.00

5756-2- Donald Duck-The Fabulous Diamond Fountain, (Walt Disney), 1973, Whitman, 260 pgs., 79 cents, soft-c, color illos 3.00 7.50 20.00

5760- Donald Duck in Volcano Valley (Disney), 1973, Whitman, 39 cents, flip-it book 3.00 7.50 20.00

5760-2- Donald Duck in Volcano Valley (Disney), 1973, Whitman, 79 cents, flip-it book 2.00 5.00 14.00

5764- Donald Duck, Luck of the Ducks, 1969, Whitman, 256 pgs., soft-c, 49 cents, color illos. 3.00 7.50 20.00

5773- Donald Duck - The Lost Jungle City, 1975, Whitman, 49 cents, flip-it book; 6 printings through 1980 2.00 5.00 14.00

nn- Donald Duck and the Ducklings, 1938, Dell, 194 pgs., Fast-Action Story, soft-c, Taliaferro-a 58.00 146.00 410.00

nn- Donald Duck Out of Luck (Disney), 1940, Dell, 196 pgs., Fast-Action Story, has Four Color #4 on back-c, Taliaferro-a 58.00 146.00 410.00

8- Donald Duck Takes It on the Chin (Disney), 1941, Dell, 196 pgs., Fast-Action Story, soft-c, Taliaferro-a 58.00 146.00 410.00

L13- Donnie and the Pirates, 1935, Lynn, 192 pgs. 12.00 30.00 85.00

1438- Don O'Dare Finds War, 1940, Whitman, 432 pgs. 11.00 27.50 70.00

1107- Don Winslow, U.S.N., 1935, Whitman, 432 pgs. 20.00 50.00 140.00

nn- Don Winslow, U.S.N., 1935, Whitman, 436 pgs., premium-no ads, 3-color, soft-c 31.00 78.00 220.00

1408- Don Winslow and the Giant Girl Spy, 1946, Whitman, 352 pgs. 13.00 32.50 90.00

1418- Don Winslow Navy Intelligence Ace, 1942, Whitman, 432 pgs., flip pictures 18.00 45.00 125.00

1419- Don Winslow of the Navy Vs. the Scorpion Gang, 1938, Whitman, 432 pgs. 18.00 45.00 125.00

1453- Don Winslow of the Navy and the Secret Enemy Base, 1943, Whitman, 352 pgs. 18.00 45.00 125.00

1489- Don Winslow of the Navy and the Great War Plot, 1940, Whitman, 432 pgs. 18.00 45.00 125.00

nn- Don Winslow U.S. Navy and the Missing Admiral, 1938, Whitman, 36 pgs., 2 1/2" x 3 1/2", Penny Book 11.00 27.50 70.00

1137- Doomed To Die, 1938, Saalfield, 400 pgs. 11.00 27.50 70.00

1140- Down Cartridge Creek, 1938, Saalfield, 400 pgs. 11.00 27.50 70.00

1416- Draftie of the U.S. Army, 1943, Whitman, All Pictures Comics 12.00 30.00 75.00

1100B- Dreams (Your dreams & what they mean), 1938, Whitman, 36 pgs., 2 1/2" x 3 1/2", Penny Book 4.00 10.00 27.00

24- Dumb Dora and Bing Brown, 1936, Lynn 14.00 35.00 95.00

1400- Dumbo, of the Circus - Only His Ears Grew! (Disney), 1941, Whitman, 432 pgs., based on Disney movie 28.00 70.00 195.00

10- Dumbo the Flying Elephant (Disney), 1944, Dell, 194 pgs., Fast-Action Story, soft-c 46.00 115.00 320.00

nn- East O' the Sun and West O' the Moon, nd (1930s), np (Whitman), 36 pgs., 3" x 2 1/2", Penny Book 4.00 10.00 27.00

774- Eddie Cantor in An Hour with You, 1934, Whitman, 154 pgs., 4 1/4" x 5 1/4", photo-c, movie scenes 16.00 40.00 115.00

nn- Eddie Cantor in Laughland, 1934, Goldsmith, 132 pgs., soft-c, photo-c, Vallely-a 16.00 40.00 115.00

1106- Ella Cinders and the Mysterious House, 1934, Whitman, 432 pgs. 15.00 37.50 105.00

nn- Ella Cinders and the Mysterious House, 1934, Whitman, 52 pgs., premium-no ads, soft-c, 3 1/2" x 5 3/4" 22.00 52.50 155.00

nn- Ella Cinders, 1935, Whitman, 148 pgs., 3 1/4" x 4", Tarzan Ice Cream cup lid premium 36.00 90.00 255.00

nn- Ella Cinders Plays Duchess, 1938, Whitman, 68 pgs., 3 3/4" x 3 1/2", Pan-Am Oil premium 16.00 40.00 115.00

nn- Ella Cinders Solves a Mystery, 1938, Whitman, 68 pgs., Pan-Am Oil premium, soft-c 16.00 40.00 115.00

11- Ella Cinders' Exciting Experience, 1934, Whitman, 3 1/2" x 3 1/2", 132 pgs., Tarzan Ice Cream cup lid giveaway 36.00 90.00 255.00

1406- Ellery Queen the Adventure of the Last Man Club, 1940, Whitman, 432 pgs. 15.00 37.50 105.00

1472- Ellery Queen the Master Detective, 1942, Whitman, 432 pgs., flip pictures 15.00 37.50 105.00

1081- Elmer and his Dog Spot, 1935, Saalfield, hard-c 11.00 27.50 70.00

1311- Elmer and his Dog Spot, 1935, Saalfield, soft-c 11.00 27.50 70.00

722- Erik Noble and the Forty-Niners, 1934, Whitman, 384 pgs. 11.00 27.50 70.00

nn- Erik Noble and the Forty-Niners, 1934, Whitman, 386 pgs., 3-color, soft-c (Rare) 64.00 160.00 450.00

2019-(#19)- Fantastic Four in the House of Horrors, 1968, Whitman, 256 pgs., hard-c, color illos. 4.00 10.00 27.00

5775 - Fantastic Four in the House of Horrors, 1976, Whitman, 256 pgs., soft-c, color illos. 3.00 7.50 20.00

5775-1 - Fantastic Four in the House of Horrors, 1976, Whitman, 256 pgs., soft-c, color illos. 3.00 7.50 20.00

1058- Farmyard Symphony, The (Disney), 1939, 5" X 5 1/2", 68 pgs., hard-c 15.00 37.50 105.00

1129- Felix the Cat, 1936, Whitman, 432 pgs., Messmer-a 33.00 83.00 230.00

1439- Felix the Cat, 1943, Whitman, All Pictures Comics, Messmer-a 28.00 70.00 195.00

1465- Felix the Cat, 1945, Whitman, All Pictures Comics, Messmer-a 24.00 60.00 165.00

nn- Felix (Flip book), 1967, World Retrospective of Animation Cinema, 188 pgs., 2 1/2" x 4" by Otto Messmer 4.00 10.00 27.00

nn- Fighting Cowboy of Nugget Gulch, The, 1939, Whitman, 2 1/2" x 3 1/2", Penny Book 7.00 17.50 45.00

1401- Fighting Heroes Battle for Freedom, 1943, Whitman, All Pictures Comics, from "Heroes of Democracy" strip, by Stookie Allen 11.00 27.50 70.00

6- Fighting President, The, 1934, EVW (Five Star Library), 160 pgs., photo-c, photo ill., F. D. Roosevelt 12.00 30.00 85.00

nn- Fire Chief Ed Wynn and "His Old Fire Horse," 1934, Goldsmith, 132 pgs., H. Vallely-a, photo, soft-c 12.00 30.00 85.00

1464- Flame Boy and the Indians' Secret, 1938, Whitman, 300 pgs., Sekakuku-a (Hopi Indian) 11.00 27.50 70.00

22- Flaming Guns, 1935, EVW, with Tom Mix, movie scenes
Hardcover 78.00 195.00 550.00
(Scarce) Softcover 85.00 212.00 600.00

1110- Flash Gordon on the Planet Mongo, 1934, Whitman, 320 pgs., by Alex Raymond 49.00 122.00 345.00

1166- Flash Gordon and the Monsters of Mongo, 1935, Whitman, 432 pgs., by Alex Raymond 41.00 103.00 290.00

nn- Flash Gordon and the Monsters of Mongo, 1935, Whitman, 436 pgs., premium-no ads, 3-color, soft-c, by Raymond 61.00 153.00 430.00

1171- Flash Gordon and the Tournaments of Mongo, 1935, Whitman, 432 pgs., by Alex Raymond 43.00 108.00 300.00

1190- Flash Gordon and the Witch Queen of Mongo, 1936, Whitman, 432 pgs., by Alex Raymond 43.00 108.00 300.00

1407- Flash Gordon in the Water World of Mongo, 1937, Whitman, 432 pgs., by Alex Raymond 38.00 95.00 255.00

1423- Flash Gordon and the Perils of Mongo, 1940, Whitman, 432 pgs., by Alex Raymond 33.00 83.00 230.00

1424- Flash Gordon in the Jungles of Mongo, 1947, Whitman, 352 pgs., by Alex Raymond 24.00 60.00 170.00

1443- Flash Gordon in the Ice World of Mongo, 1942, Whitman, 432 pgs., flip pictures, by Alex Raymond 36.00 90.00 250.00

1447- Flash Gordon and the Fiery Desert of Mongo, 1948, Whitman, 288 pgs., Raymond-a 24.00 60.00 170.00

1469- Flash Gordon and the Power Men of Mongo, 1943, Whitman, 352 pgs., by Alex Raymond 36.00 90.00 250.00

1479- Flash Gordon and the Red Sword Invaders, 1945, Whitman, 352 pgs., by Alex Raymond 34.00 85.00 240.00

nn - Flintstones: It's About Time © H-B

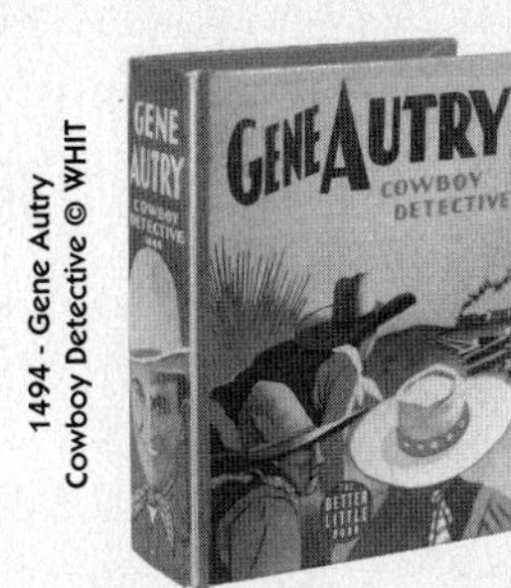

1494 - Gene Autry Cowboy Detective © WHIT

6833 - G-Man on Lightning Island © WHIT

GD FN VF/NM

1484- Flash Gordon and the Tyrant of Mongo, 1941, Whitman, 432 pgs., flip pictures, by Alex Raymond 36.00 90.00 250.00
1492- Flash Gordon in the Forest Kingdom of Mongo, 1938, Whitman, 432 pgs., by Alex Raymond 46.00 115.00 320.00
12- Flash Gordon and the Ape Men of Mor, 1942, Dell, 196 pgs., Fast-Action Story, by Alex Raymond 64.00 160.00 450.00
6833- Flash Gordon Vs. the Emperor of Mongo, 1936, Dell, 244 pgs., Cartoon Story Books, hard-c, Alex Raymond-c/a 79.00 198.00 550.00
nn- Flash Gordon Vs. the Emperor of Mongo, 1936, Dell, 244 pgs., Fast-Action Story, soft-c, Alex Raymond-c/a 62.00 155.00 440.00
1467- Flint Roper and the Six-Gun Showdown, 1941, Whitman, 300 pgs. 11.00 27.50 70.00
2014-(#14)- Flintstones-The Case of the Many Missing Things, 1968, Whitman, 260 pgs., 39 cents, hard-c, color illos 4.00 10.00 27.00
nn- Flintstones: A Friend From the Past, 1977, Modern Promotions, 244 pgs., 49 cents, soft-c, flip pictures 2.00 5.00 11.00
nn- Flintstones: It's About Time, 1977, Modern Promotions, 244 pgs., 49 cents, soft-c, flip pictures 2.00 5.00 11.00
nn- Flintstones: Pebbles & Bamm-Bamm Meet Santa Claus, 1977, Modern Promotions, 244 pgs., 49 cents, soft-c, flip pictures 2.00 5.00 11.00
nn- Flintstones: The Great Balloon Race, 1977, Modern Promotions, 244 pgs., 49 cents, soft-c, flip pictures 2.00 5.00 11.00
nn- Flintstones: The Mystery of the Many Missing Things, 1977, Modern Promotions, 244 pgs., 49 cents, soft-c, flip pictures 2.00 5.00 11.00
2003-(#3)- Flipper-Killer Whale Trouble, 1967, Whitman, 260 pgs., hard-c, 39 cents, color illos 3.00 7.50 20.00
2032-(#32)- Flipper, Deep-Sea Photographer, 1969, Whitman, 256 pgs., hard-c, color illos. 3.00 7.50 20.00
1108- Flying the Sky Clipper with Winsie Atkins, 1936, Whitman, 432 pgs. 11.00 27.50 70.00
1460- Foreign Spies Doctor Doom and the Ghost Submarine, 1939, Whitman, 432 pgs., Al McWilliams-a 13.00 32.50 90.00
1100B- Fortune Teller, 1938, Whitman, 36 pgs., 2 1/2" x 3 1/2", Penny Book 5.00 12.50 33.00
1175- Frank Buck Presents Ted Towers Animal Master, 1935, Whitman, 432 pgs. 12.00 30.00 80.00
2015-(#15)-Frankenstein, Jr. - The Menace of the Heartless Monster, 1968, Whitman, 260 pgs., 39 cents, hard-c, color illos. 4.00 10.00 27.00
16- Frankie Thomas in A Dog of Flanders, 1935, EVW, movie scenes 15.00 37.50 105.00
1121- Frank Merriwell at Yale, 1935, 432 pgs. 11.00 27.50 70.00
Freckles and His Friends in the North Woods (See Top-Line Comics)
nn- Freckles and His Friends Stage a Play, 1938, Whitman, 36 pgs., 2 1/2" x 3 1/2", Penny Book 11.00 27.50 70.00
1164- Freckles and the Lost Diamond Mine, 1937, Whitman, 432 pgs., Merrill Blosser-a 12.00 30.00 85.00
nn- Freckles and the Mystery Ship, 1935, Whitman, 66 pgs., Pan-Am premium 16.00 40.00 115.00
1100B- Fun, Puzzles, Riddles, 1938, Whitman, 36 pgs., 2 1/2" x 3 1/2", Penny Book 4.00 10.00 27.00
1433- Gang Busters Step In, 1939, Whitman, 432 pgs., Henry E. Vallely-a 13.00 32.50 90.00
1437- Gang Busters Smash Through, 1942, Whitman, 432 pgs. 13.00 32.50 90.00
1451- Gang Busters in Action!, 1938, Whitman, 432 pgs. 13.00 32.50 90.00
nn- Gang Busters and Guns of the Law, 1940, Dell, 4" x 5", 194 pgs., Fast-Action Story, soft-c 41.00 103.00 285.00
nn- Gang Busters and the Radio Clues, 1938, Whitman, 36 pgs., 2 1/2" x 3 1/2", Penny Book 11.00 27.50 70.00
1409- Gene Autry and Raiders of the Range, 1946, Whitman, 352 pgs. 15.00 37.50 105.00
1425- Gene Autry and the Mystery of Paint Rock Canyon, 1947, Whitman, 288 pgs. 15.00 37.50 105.00
1428- Gene Autry Special Ranger, 1941, Whitman, 432 pgs., Erwin Hess-a 20.00 50.00 140.00

GD FN VF/NM

1433- Gene Autry in Public Cowboy No. 1, 1938, Whitman, 240 pgs., photo-c, movie scenes (1st Autry BLB) 38.00 95.00 255.00
1434- Gene Autry and the Gun-Smoke Reckoning, 1943, Whitman, 352 pgs. 19.00 47.50 135.00
1439- Gene Autry and the Land Grab Mystery, 1948, Whitman, 290 pgs. 14.00 35.00 95.00
1456- Gene Autry in Special Ranger Rule, 1945, Whitman, 352 pgs., Henry E. Vallely-a 19.00 47.50 135.00
1461- Gene Autry and the Red Bandit's Ghost, 1949, Whitman, 288 pgs. 13.00 32.50 90.00
1483- Gene Autry in Law of the Range, 1939, Whitman, 432 pgs. 19.00 47.50 135.00
1493- Gene Autry and the Hawk of the Hills, 1942, Whitman, 428 pgs., flip pictures, Vallely-a 19.00 47.50 135.00
1494- Gene Autry Cowboy Detective, 1940, Whitman, 432 pgs., Erwin Hess-a 19.00 47.50 135.00
700-10- Gene Autry and the Bandits of Silver Tip, 1949, Whitman 12.00 30.00 80.00
714-10- Gene Autry and the Range War, 1950, Whitman 12.00 30.00 80.00
nn- Gene Autry in Gun-Smoke, 1938, Dell, 196 pgs., Fast-Action story, soft-c 46.00 115.00 320.00
2035-(#35)- Gentle Ben, Mystery of the Everglades, 1969, Whitman, 256 pgs., hard-c, color illos. 3.00 7.50 20.00
1176- Gentleman Joe Palooka, 1940, Saalfield, 400 pgs. 16.00 40.00 115.00
George O'Brien (See The Cowboy Millionaire)
1101- George O'Brien and the Arizona Badman, 1936?, Whitman 15.00 37.50 105.00
1418- George O'Brien in Gun Law, 1938, Whitman, 240 pgs., photo-c, movie scenes, RKO Radio Pictures 15.00 37.50 105.00
1457- George O'Brien and the Hooded Riders, 1940, Whitman, 432 pgs., Erwin Hess-a 11.00 27.50 70.00
nn- George O'Brien and the Arizona Bad Man, 1939, Whitman, 36 pgs., 2 1/2" x 3 1/2", Penny Book 11.00 27.50 70.00
1462- Ghost Avenger, 1943, Whitman, 432 pgs., flip pictures, Henry Vallely-a 11.00 27.50 70.00
nn- Ghost Gun Gang Meet Their Match, The, 1939. Whitman, 2 1/2" x 3 1/2", Penny Book 10.00 25.00 65.00
nn- Gingerbread Boy, The, nd(1930s), np(Whitman), 36 pgs., Penny Book 4.00 10.00 22.00
1118- G-Man on the Crime Trail, 1936, Whitman, 432 pgs. 12.00 30.00 80.00
1147- G-Man Vs. the Red X, 1936, Whitman, 432 pgs. 14.00 35.00 95.00
1162- G-Man Allen, 1939, Saalfield, 400 pgs. 11.00 27.50 70.00
1173- G-Man in Action, A, 1940, Saalfield, 400 pgs., J.R. White-a 11.00 27.50 70.00
1434- G-Man and the Radio Bank Robberies, 1937, Whitman, 432 pgs. 13.00 32.50 90.00
1469- G-Man and the Gun Runners, The, 1940, Whitman, 432 pgs. 13.00 32.50 90.00
1470- G-Man vs. the Fifth Column, 1941, Whitman, 432 pgs., flip pictures 13.00 32.50 90.00
1493- G-Man Breaking the Gambling Ring, 1938, Whitman, 432 pgs., James Gary-a 13.00 32.50 90.00
nn- G-Man on Lightning Island, 1936, Dell, 244 pgs., Fast-Action Story, soft-c, Henry E. Vallely-a 33.00 83.00 230.00
nn- G-Man, Underworld Chief, 1938, Whitman, Buddy Book premium, 50.00 125.00 350.00
6833- G-Man on Lightning Island, 1936, Dell, 244 pgs., Cartoon Story Book, hard-c, Henry E. Vallely-a 29.00 73.00 200.00
4- G-Men Foil the Kidnappers, 1936, Whitman, 132 pgs., 3 1/2" x 3 1/2", soft-c, Tarzan Ice Cream cup lid premium 36.00 90.00 255.00
1157- G-Men on the Trail, 1938, Saalfield, 400 pgs.11.00 27.50 70.00
1168- G Men on the Job, 1935, Whitman, 432 pgs.12.00 30.00 85.00
nn- G-Men on the Job Again, 1938, Whitman, 36 pgs., 2 1/2" x 3 1/2", Penny Book 11.00 27.50 70.00
nn- G-Men and Kidnap Justice, 1938, Whitman, 68 pgs., Pan-Am premium, soft-c 12.00 30.00 85.00

nn - The Gumps in Radio Land © L&F

nn - Huckleberry Hound Newspaper Reporter © H-B

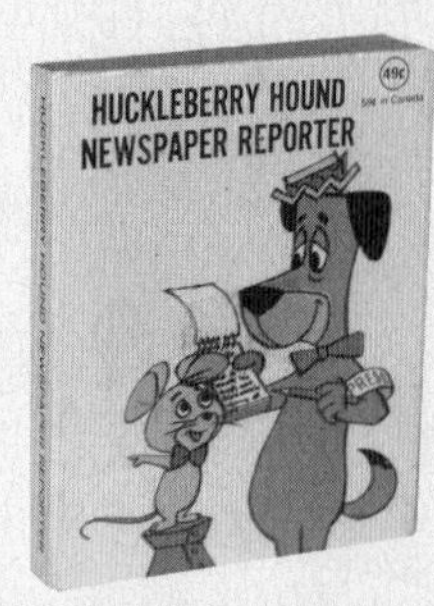

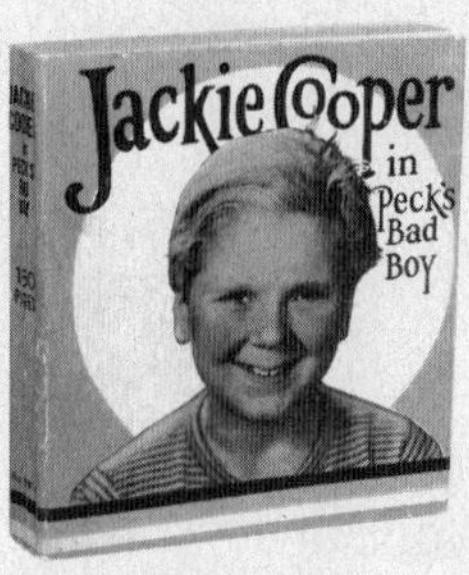

1314 - Jackie Cooper in Peck's Bad Boy © Saalfield

GD FN VF/NM

nn- G-Men and the Missing Clues, 1938, Whitman, 36 pgs., 2 1/2"x 3 1/2", Penny Book 11.00 27.50 70.00

1097- Go Into Your Dance, 1935, Saalfield, 160 pgs.. photo-c, movie scenes with Al Jolson & Ruby Keeler 15.00 37.50 105.00

1577- Go Into Your Dance, 1935, Saalfield, 160 pgs., photo-c, movie scenes, soft-c 15.00 37.50 105.00

2021- Goofy in Giant Trouble (Walt Disney's ...), 1968, Whitman, hard-c, 260 pgs., 39 cents, color illos. 3.00 7.50 20.00

5751- Goofy in Giant Trouble (Walt Disney's ...), 1968, Whitman, soft-c, 260 pgs., 39 cents, color illos. 3.00 7.50 20.00

5751-2- Goofy in Giant Trouble, 1968 (1980-reprint of '67 version), Whitman, soft-c, 260 pgs., 79 cents, B&W 1.00 2.50 6.00

8- Great Expectations, 1934, EVW, (Five Star Library), 160 pgs., photo-c, movie scenes 20.00 50.00 140.00

1453- Green Hornet Strikes!, The, 1940, Whitman, 432 pgs., Robert Weisman-a 49.00 122.00 345.00

1480- Green Hornet Cracks Down, The, 1942, Whitman, 432 pgs., flip pictures, Henry Vallely-a 46.00 115.00 320.00

1496- Green Hornet Returns, The, 1941, Whitman, 432 pgs., flip pictures 49.00 122.00 345.00

5778- Grimm's Ghost Stories, 1976, Whitman, 256 pgs., Laura French-s adapted from fairy tales; blue spine & back-c 2.00 5.00 13.00

5778-1- Grimm's Ghost Stories, 1976, Whitman, 256 pgs., reprint of #5778; yellow spine & back-c 2.00 5.00 13.00

1172- Gullivers' Travels, 1939, Saalfield, 320 pgs., adapted from Paramount Pict. Cartoons (Rare) Hardcover 50.00 125.00 350.00
(Scarce) Softcover 57.00 142.00 400.00

nn- Gumps In Radio Land, The (Andy Gump and the Chest of Gold), 1937, Lehn & Fink Prod. Corp., 100 pgs., 3 1/4" x 5 1/2", Pebeco Tooth Paste giveaway, by Gus Edson 24.00 60.00 165.00

nn- Gunmen of Rustlers' Gulch, The, 1939, Whitman, 36 pgs., 2 1/2" x 3 1/2", Penny Book 11.00 27.50 70.00

1426- Guns in the Roaring West, 1937, Whitman, 300 pgs. 11.00 27.50 70.00

1647- Gunsmoke (TV Series), 1958, Whitman, 280 pgs., 4 1/2" x 5 3/4" 7.00 17.50 44.00

1101- Hairbreath Harry in Department QT, 1935, Whitman, 384 pgs., by J. M. Alexander 12.00 30.00 85.00

1413- Hal Hardy in the Lost Land of Giants, 1938, Whitman, 300 pgs., "The World 1,000,000 Years Ago" 12.00 30.00 85.00

1159- Hall of Fame of the Air, 1936, Whitman, 432 pgs., by Capt. Eddie Rickenbacker 11.00 27.50 70.00

nn- Hansel and Grethel, The Story of, nd (1930s), no publ., 36 pgs., Penny Book 4.00 10.00 22.00

1145- Hap Lee's Selection of Movie Gags, 1935, Whitman, 160 pgs., photos of stars 15.00 37.50 105.00

Happy Prince, The (See Wee Little Books)

1111- Hard Rock Harrigan-A Story of Boulder Dam, 1935, Saalfield, hard-c, photo-c, photo illos. 11.00 27.50 70.00

1591- Hard Rock Harrigan-A Story of Boulder Dam, 1935, Saalfield, soft-c, photo-c, photo illos. 11.00 27.50 70.00

1418- Harold Teen Swinging at the Sugar Bowl, 1939, Whitman, 432 pgs., by Carl Ed 12.00 30.00 80.00

nn- Hercules - The Legendary Journeys, 1998, Chronicle Books, 310 pgs., based on TV series, 1-color (brown) illos 1.00 2.50 9.00

1100B- Hobbies, 1938, Whitman, 36 pgs., 2 1/2" x 3 1/2", Penny Book 4.00 10.00 22.00

1125- Hockey Spare, The, 1937, Saalfield, sports book 8.00 20.00 50.00

1605- Hockey Spare, The, 1937, Saalfield, soft-c 8.00 20.00 50.00

728- Homeless Homer, 1934, Whitman, by Dee Dobbin, for young kids 5.00 12.50 33.00

17- Hoosier Schoolmaster, The, 1935, EVW, movie scenes 15.00 37.50 105.00

715- Houdini's Big Little Book of Magic, 1927 (1933), 300 pgs. 16.00 40.00 115.00

nn- Houdini's Big Little Book of Magic, 1927 (1933), 196 pgs., American Oil Co. premium, soft-c 16.00 40.00 115.00

nn- Houdini's Big Little Book of Magic, 1927 (1933), 204 pgs., Cocomalt premium, soft-c 16.00 40.00 115.00

GD FN VF/NM

Huckleberry Finn (See The Adventures of...)

nn- Huckleberry Hound Newspaper Reporter, 1977, Modern Promotions, 244 pgs., 49 cents, soft-c, flip pictures 2.00 5.00 13.00

1644- Hugh O'Brian TV's Wyatt Earp (TV Series), 1958, Whitman, 280 pgs. 7.00 17.50 44.00

5782-2- Incredible Hulk Lost in Time, 1980, 260 pgs., 79¢-c, soft-c, B&W 2.00 5.00 10.00

1424- Inspector Charlie Chan Villainy on the High Seas, 1942, Whitman, 432 pgs., flip pictures 16.00 40.00 115.00

1186- Inspector Wade of Scotland Yard, 1940, Saalfield, 400 pgs. 11.00 27.50 70.00

1194- Inspector Wade and The Feathered Serpent, 1939, Saalfield, 400 pgs. 11.00 27.50 70.00

1448- Inspector Wade Solves the Mystery of the Red Aces, 1937, Whitman, 432 pgs. 11.00 27.50 70.00

1148- International Spy Doctor Doom Faces Death at Dawn, 1937, Whitman, 432 pgs., Arbo-a 12.00 30.00 85.00

1155- In the Name of the Law, 1937, Whitman, 432 pgs., Henry E. Vallely-a 11.00 27.50 70.00

2012-(#12)-Invaders, The-Alien Missile Threat (TV Series), 1967, Whitman, 260 pgs., hard-c, 39 cents, color illos. 4.00 10.00 27.00

1403- Invisible Scarlet O'Neil, 1942, Whitman, All Pictures Comics, flip pictures 12.00 30.00 85.00

1406- Invisible Scarlet O'Neil Versus the King of the Slums, 1946, Whitman, 352 pgs. 11.00 27.50 70.00

1098- It Happened One Night, 1935, Saalfield, 160 pgs., Little Big Book, Clark Gable, Claudette Colbert photo-c, movie scenes from Academy Award winner 21.00 52.50 145.00

1578- It Happened One Night, 1935, Saalfield, 160 pgs., soft-c 21.00 52.50 145.00

Jack and Jill (See Wee Little Books)

1432- Jack Armstrong and the Mystery of the Iron Key, 1939, Whitman, 432 pgs., Henry E. Vallely-a 12.00 30.00 85.00

1435- Jack Armstrong and the Ivory Treasure, 1937, Whitman, 432 pgs., Henry Vallely-a 12.00 30.00 85.00

Jackie Cooper (See Story Of..)

1084- Jackie Cooper in Peck's Bad Boy, 1934, Saalfield, 160 pgs., hard, photo-c, movie scenes 15.00 37.50 105.00

1314- Jackie Cooper in Peck's Bad Boy, 1934, Saalfield, 160 pgs., soft, photo-c, movie scenes 15.00 37.50 105.00

1402- Jackie Cooper in "Gangster's Boy," 1939, Whitman, 240 pgs., photo-c, movie scenes 15.00 37.50 105.00

13- Jackie Cooper in Dinky, 1935, EVW, 160 pgs., movie scenes 15.00 37.50 105.00

nn- Jack King of the Secret Service and the Counterfeiters, 1939, Whitman, 36 pgs., 2 1/2" x 3 1/2", Penny Book, by John G. Gray 11.00 27.50 70.00

L11- Jack London's Call of the Wild, 1935, Lynn, 20th Cent. Pic., movie scenes with Clark Gable 15.00 37.50 105.00

nn- Jack Pearl as Detective Baron Munchausen, 1934, Goldsmith, 132 pgs., soft-c 12.00 30.00 85.00

1102- Jack Swift and His Rocket Ship, 1934, Whitman, 320 pgs. 24.00 60.00 165.00

1498- Jane Arden the Vanished Princess, Whitman, 300 pgs. 11.00 27.50 70.00

1179- Jane Withers in This is the Life (20th Century-Fox Presents...), 1935, Whitman, 240 pgs., photo-c, movie scenes 15.00 37.50 105.00

1463- Jane Withers in Keep Smiling, 1938, Whitman, 240 pgs., photo-c, movie scenes 15.00 37.50 105.00

Jaragu of the Jungle (See Rex Beach's ...)

1447- Jerry Parker Police Reporter and the Candid Camera Clue, 1941, Whitman, 300 pgs. 11.00 27.50 70.00

Jim Bowie (See Adventures of ...)

nn- Jim Brant of the Highway Patrol and the Mysterious Accident, 1939, Whitman, 36 pgs., 2 1/2" x 3 1/2", Penny Book 10.00 25.00 65.00

1466- Jim Craig State Trooper and the Kidnapped Governor, 1938, Whitman, 432 pgs. 11.00 27.50 70.00

nn- Jim Doyle Private Detective and the Train Hold-Up, 1939, Whitman, 36 pgs., 2 1/2" x 3 1/2", Penny Book 12.00 30.00 75.00

1442 - Junior G-Men © WHIT

1133 - Kelly King at Yale Hall © Saalfield

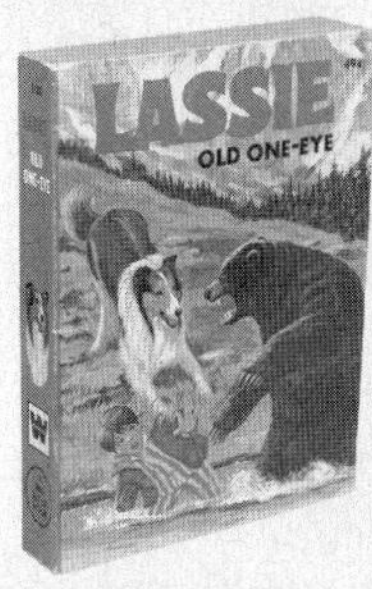

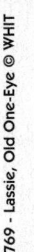

5769 - Lassie, Old One-Eye © WHIT

	GD	FN	VF/NM
1180- Jim Hardy Ace Reporter, 1940, Saalfield, 400 pgs., Dick Moores-a	12.00	30.00	75.00
1143- Jimmy Allen in the Air Mail Robbery, 1936, Whitman, 432 pgs.	12.00	30.00	75.00
27- Jimmy Allen in The Sky Parade, 1936, Lynn, 130 pgs., 5 x 7 1/2", Paramount Pictures, movie scenes	13.00	32.50	90.00
L15- Jimmy and the Tiger, 1935, Lynn, 192 pgs.	12.00	30.00	75.00
1428- Jim Starr of the Border Patrol, 1937, Whitman, 432 pgs.	12.00	30.00	75.00
Joan of Arc (See Wee Little Books)			
1105- Joe Louis the Brown Bomber, 1936, Whitman, 240 pgs., photo-c, photo-illos.	24.00	60.00	170.00
Joe Palooka (See Gentleman ...)			
1123- Joe Palooka the Heavyweight Boxing Champ, 1934, Whitman, 320 pgs., Ham Fisher-a	22.00	52.50	155.00
1168- Joe Palooka's Great Adventure, 1939, Saalfield	18.00	45.00	125.00
nn- Joe Penner's Duck Farm, 1935, Goldsmith, Henry Vallely-a	12.00	30.00	85.00
1402- John Carter of Mars, 1940, Whitman, 432 pgs., John Coleman Burroughs-a	86.00	215.00	600.00
nn- John Carter of Mars, 1940, Dell, 194 pgs., Fast-Action Story, soft-c	107.00	268.00	750.00
1164- Johnny Forty Five, 1938, Saalfield, 400 pgs.	11.00	27.50	70.00
John Wayne (See Westward Ho!)			
1100B- Jokes (A book of laughs galore), 1938, Whitman, 36 pgs., 2 1/2" x 3 1/2", Penny Book, laughing guy-c	4.00	10.00	22.00
1100B- Jokes (A book of side-splitting funny stories), 1938, Whitman, 36 pgs., 2 1/2" x 3 1/2", Penny Book, clowns on-c	4.00	10.00	22.00
2026-(#26)- Journey to the Center of the Earth, The Fiery Foe, 1968, Whitman	4.00	10.00	27.00
Jungle Jim (See Top-Line Comics)			
1138- Jungle Jim, 1936, Whitman, 432 pgs., Alex Raymond-a	22.00	52.50	155.00
1139- Jungle Jim and the Vampire Woman, 1937, Whitman, 432 pgs., Alex Raymond-a	22.00	52.50	155.00
1442- Junior G-Men, 1937, Whitman, 432 pgs., Henry E. Vallely-a	12.00	30.00	80.00
nn- Junior G-Men Solve a Crime, 1939, Whitman, 36 pgs., 2 1/2" x 3 1/2", Penny Book	12.00	30.00	80.00
1422- Junior Nebb on the Diamond Bar Ranch, 1938, Whitman, 300 pgs., by Sol Hess	12.00	30.00	80.00
1470- Junior Nebb Joins the Circus, 1939, Whitman, 300 pgs. by Sol Hess	12.00	30.00	80.00
nn- Junior Nebb Elephant Trainer, 1939, Whitman, 68 pgs., Pan-Am Oil premium, soft-c	15.00	37.50	105.00
1052- "Just Kids" (Adventures of ...), 1934, Saalfield, oblong size, by Ad Carter	22.00	52.50	155.00
1094- Just Kids and the Mysterious Stranger, 1935, Saalfield, 160 pgs., by Ad Carter	15.00	37.50	105.00
1184- Just Kids and Deep-Sea Dan, 1940, Saalfield, 400 pgs., by Ad Carter	12.00	30.00	85.00
1302- Just Kids, The Adventures of, 1934, Saalfield, oblong size, soft-c, by Ad Carter	22.00	52.50	155.00
1324- Just Kids and the Mysterious Stranger, 1935, Saalfield, 160 pgs., soft-c, by Ad Carter ,	15.00	37.50	105.00
1401- Just Kids, 1937, Whitman, 432 pgs., by Ad Carter	15.00	37.50	105.00
1055- Katzenjammer Kids in the Mountains, 1934, Saalfield, hard-c, oblong, H. H. Knerr-a	21.00	52.50	145.00
1305- Katzenjammer Kids in the Mountains, 1934, Saalfield, soft-c, oblong, H. H. Knerr-a	21.00	52.50	145.00
14- Katzenjammer Kids, The, 1942, Dell, 194 pgs., Fast-Action Story, H. H. Knerr-a	24.00	60.00	165.00
1411- Kay Darcy and the Mystery Hideout, 1937, Whitman, 300 pgs., Charles Mueller-a	13.00	32.50	90.00
1180- Kayo in the Land of Sunshine (With Moon Mullins), 1937, Whitman, 432 pgs., by Willard	15.00	37.50	105.00
1415- Kayo and Moon Mullins and the One Man Gang, 1939, Whitman, 432 pgs., by Frank Willard	12.00	30.00	85.00
7- Kayo and Moon Mullins 'Way Down South, 1938, Whitman, 132 pgs., 3 1/2" x 3 1/2", Buddy Book	31.00	78.00	220.00
1105- Kazan in Revenge of the North (James Oliver Curwood's...), 1937, Whitman, 432 pgs., Henry E. Vallely-a	11.00	27.50	70.00
1471- Kazan, King of the Pack (James Oliver Curwood's...), 1940, Whitman, 432 pgs.	10.00	25.00	65.00
1420- Keep 'Em Flying! U.S.A. for America's Defense, 1943, Whitman, 432 pgs., Henry E. Vallely-a, flip pictures	11.00	27.50	70.00
1133- Kelly King at Yale Hall, 1937, Saalfield	10.00	25.00	65.00
Ken Maynard (See Strawberry Roan & Western Frontier)			
5- Ken Maynard in "Wheels of Destiny," 1934, EVW, 160 pgs., movie scenes (scarce)	57.00	142.00	400.00
776- Ken Maynard in "Gun Justice," 1934, Whitman, 160 pgs., hard-c, movie scenes (Universal Pic.)	21.00	52.50	145.00
776- Ken Maynard in "Gun Justice," 1934, Whitman, 160 pgs., soft-c, movie scenes (Universal Pic.)	21.00	52.50	145.00
1430- Ken Maynard in Western Justice, 1938, Whitman, 432 pgs., Irwin Myers-a	12.00	30.00	85.00
1442- Ken Maynard and the Gun Wolves of the Gila, 1939, Whitman, 432 pgs.	12.00	30.00	85.00
nn- Ken Maynard in Six-Gun Law, 1938, Whitman, 36 pgs., 2 1/2" x 3 1/2", Penny Book	10.00	25.00	65.00
1134- King of Crime, 1938, Saalfield, 400 pgs.	11.00	27.50	70.00
King of the Royal Mounted (See Zane Grey)			
nn- Kit Carson, 1933, World Syndicate, by J. Carroll Mansfield, High Lights Of History Series, hard-c	11.00	27.50	70.00
nn- Kit Carson, 1933, World Syndicate, same as hard-c above but with a black cloth-c	11.00	27.50	70.00
1105- Kit Carson and the Mystery Riders, 1935, Saalfield, hard-c, Johnny Mack Brown photo-c, movie scenes	18.00	45.00	125.00
1585- Kit Carson and the Mystery Riders, 1935, Saalfield, soft-c, Johnny Mack Brown photo-c, movie scenes	18.00	45.00	125.00
Krazy Kat (See Adventures of...)			
2004- (#4)-Lassie-Adventure in Alaska (TV Series), 1967, Whitman, hard-c, 260 pgs., 39 cents, color illos	4.00	10.00	27.00
5754- Lassie-Adventure in Alaska (TV Series), 1973, Whitman, soft-c, 260 pgs., 49 cents, color illos	2.00	5.00	13.00
2027- Lassie and the Shabby Sheik (TV Series), 1968, Whitman, hard-c, 260 pgs., 39 cents	4.00	10.00	25.00
5762- Lassie and the Shabby Sheik (TV Series), 1972, Whitman, soft-c, 260 pgs., 39 cents	2.00	5.00	13.00
5769- Lassie, Old One-Eye (TV Series), 1975, Whitman, soft-c, 260 pgs., 49 cents, three printings	2.00	5.00	13.00
1132- Last Days of Pompeii, The, 1935, Whitman, 5 1/4" x 6 1/4", 260 pgs., photo-c, movie scenes	15.00	37.50	105.00
1128- Last Man Out (Baseball), 1937, Saalfield, hard-c	11.00	27.50	70.00
L30- Last of the Mohicans, The, 1936, Lynn, 192 pgs., movie scenes with Randolph Scott, United Artists Pictures	16.00	40.00	115.00
1126- Laughing Dragon of Oz, The, 1934, Whitman 432 pgs., by Frank Baum (scarce)	118.00	295.00	825.00
1086- Laurel and Hardy, 1934, Saalfield, 160 pgs., hard-c, photo-c, movie scenes	21.00	52.50	145.00
1316- Laurel and Hardy, 1934, Saalfield, 160 pgs. soft-c, photo-c, movie scenes	21.00	52.50	145.00
1092- Law of the Wild, The, 1935, Saalfield, 160 pgs., photo-c, movie scenes of Rex, The Wild Horse & Rin-Tin-Tin Jr.	12.00	30.00	85.00
1322- Law of the Wild, The, 1935, Saalfield, 160 pgs., photo-c, movie scenes, soft-c	12.00	30.00	85.00
1100B- Learn to be a Ventriloquist, 1938, Whitman, 36 pgs. 2 1/2" x 3 1/2", Penny Book	4.00	10.00	22.00
1149- Lee Brady Range Detective, 1938, Saalfield, 400 pgs.	10.00	25.00	65.00
L10- Les Miserables (Victor Hugo's ...), 1935, Lynn, 192 pgs., movie scenes	15.00	37.50	105.00
1441- Lightning Jim U.S. Marshal Brings Law to the West, 1940, Whitman, 432 pgs., based on radio program	12.00	30.00	85.00
nn- Lightning Jim Whipple U.S. Marshal in Indian Territory, 1939, Whitman, 36 pgs., 2 1/2" x 3 1/2", Penny Book	11.00	27.50	70.00
653- Lions and Tigers (With Clyde Beatty), 1934, Whitman, 160 pgs.,			

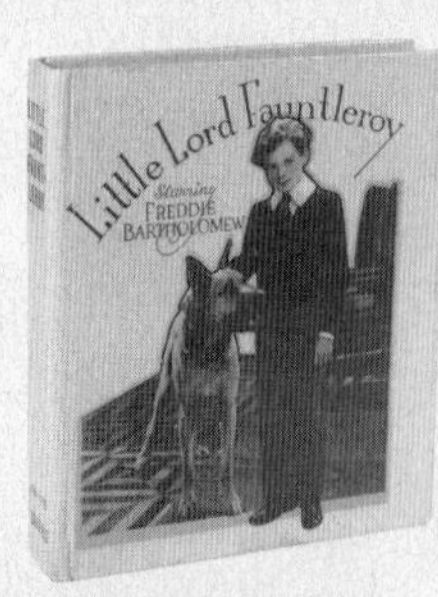
1118 - Little Lord Fauntleroy © Saalfield

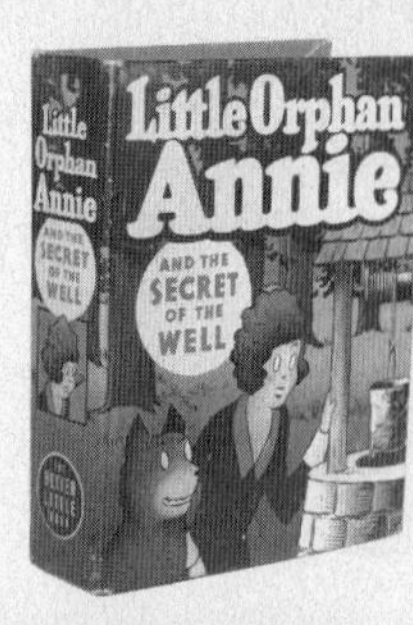

1417 - Little Orphan Annie and the Secret of the Well © WHIT

nn - Little Polly Flinders

GD FN VF/NM

photo-c movie scenes 15.00 37.50 105.00
1187- Li'l Abner and the Ratfields, 1940, Saalfield, 400 pgs., by Al Capp 19.00 47.50 135.00
1193- Li'l Abner and Sadie Hawkins Day, 1940, Saalfield, 400 pgs., by Al Capp 19.00 47.50 135.00
1198- Li'l Abner in New York, 1936, Whitman, 432 pgs., by Al Capp 21.00 52.50 145.00
1401- Li'l Abner Among the Millionaires, 1939, Whitman, 432 pgs., by Al Capp 21.00 52.50 145.00
1054- Little Annie Rooney, 1934, Saalfield, oblong - 4" x 8", All Pictures Comics, hard-c 20.00 50.00 140.00
1304- Little Annie Rooney, 1934, Saalfield, oblong - 4" x 8", All Pictures, soft-c 20.00 50.00 140.00
1117- Little Annie Rooney and the Orphan House, 1936, Whitman, 432 pgs. 12.00 30.00 80.00
1406- Little Annie Rooney on the Highway to Adventure, 1938, Whitman, 432 pgs. 12.00 30.00 80.00
1149- Little Big Shot (With Sybil Jason), 1935, Whitman, 240 pgs., photo-c, movie scenes 15.00 37.50 105.00
nn- Little Black Sambo, nd (1930s), np (Whitman), 36 pgs., 3" x 2 1/2", Penny Book 12.00 30.00 85.00
Little Bo-Peep (See Wee Little Books)
Little Colonel, The (See Shirley Temple)
1148- Little Green Door, The, 1938, Saalfield, 400 pgs. 11.00 27.50 70.00
1112- Little Hollywood Stars, 1935, Saalfield, movie scenes (Little Rascals, etc.), hard-c 15.00 37.50 105.00
1592- Little Hollywood Stars, 1935, Saalfield, movie scenes, soft-c 15.00 37.50 105.00
1087- Little Jimmy's Gold Hunt, 1935, Saalfield, 160 pgs., hard-c, Little Big Book, by Swinnerton 20.00 50.00 140.00
1317- Little Jimmy's Gold Hunt, 1935, Saalfield, 160 pgs., 4 1/4" x 5 3/4", soft-c, by Swinnerton 20.00 50.00 140.00
Little Joe and the City Gangsters (See Top-Line Comics)
Little Joe Otter's Slide (See Wee Little Books)
1118- Little Lord Fauntleroy, 1936, Saalfield, movie scenes, photo-c, 4 1/2" x 5 1/4", starring Mickey Rooney & Freddie Bartholomew, hard-c 12.00 30.00 85.00
1598- Little Lord Fauntleroy, 1936, Saalfield, photo-c, movie scenes, soft-c 12.00 30.00 85.00
1192- Little Mary Mixup and the Grocery Robberies, 1940, Saalfield 11.00 27.50 70.00
8- Little Mary Mixup Wins A Prize, 1936, Whitman, 132 pgs., 3 1/2" x 3 1/2", soft-c, Tarzan Ice Cream cup lid premium 36.00 90.00 255.00
1150- Little Men, 1934, Whitman, 4 3/4" x 5 1/4", movie scenes (Mascot Prod.), photo-c, hard-c 12.00 30.00 80.00
9- Little Minister, The,-Katharine Hepburn, 1935, 160 pgs., 4 1/4" x 5 1/2", EVW (Five Star Library), movie scenes (RKO) 16.00 40.00 115.00
1120- Little Miss Muffet, 1936, Whitman, 432 pgs., by Fanny Y. Cory 12.00 30.00 80.00
708- Little Orphan Annie, 1933, Whitman, 320 pgs., by Harold Gray, the 2nd Big Little Book 70.00 175.00 495.00
nn- Little Orphan Annie, 1928('33), Whitman, 52 pgs., 4" x 5 1/2", premium-no ads, soft-c, by Harold Gray 39.00 98.00 275.00
716- Little Orphan Annie and Sandy, 1933, Whitman, 320 pgs., by Harold Gray 33.00 83.00 230.00
716- Little Orphan Annie and Sandy, 1933, Whitman, 300 pgs., by Harold Gray 33.00 83.00 230.00
nn- Little Orphan Annie and Sandy, 1933, Whitman, 52 pgs., premium-no ads, 4" x 5 1/2", soft-c by Harold Gray 39.00 98.00 275.00
748- Little Orphan Annie and Chizzler, 1933, Whitman, 320 pgs., by Harold Gray 26.00 65.00 185.00
1010- Little Orphan Annie and the Big Town Gunmen, 1937, 7 1/4" x 5 1/2", 64 pgs., Nickel Book 15.00 37.50 105.00
nn- Little Orphan Annie with the Circus, 1934, Whitman, 320 pgs., same cover as L.O.A. 708 but with blue background, Ovaltine giveaway stamp inside front-c, by Harold Gray 58.00 146.00 410.00

GD FN VF/NM

1140- Little Orphan Annie and the Big Train Robbery, 1934, Whitman, 300 pgs., by Gray 20.00 50.00 140.00
1140- Little Orphan Annie and the Big Train Robbery, 1934, Whitman, 300 pgs., premium-no ads, soft-c, by Harold Gray 36.00 90.00 255.00
1154- Little Orphan Annie and the Ghost Gang, 1935, Whitman, 432 pgs. by Harold Gray 20.00 50.00 140.00
nn- Little Orphan Annie and the Ghost Gang, 1935, Whitman, 436 pgs., premium-no ads, 3-color, soft-c, by Harold Gray 36.00 90.00 255.00
1162- Little Orphan Annie and Punjab the Wizard, 1935, Whitman, 432 pgs., by Harold Gray 20.00 50.00 140.00
1186- Little Orphan Annie and the $1,000,000 Formula, 1936, Whitman, 432 pgs., by Gray 18.00 45.00 125.00
1414- Little Orphan Annie and the Ancient Treasure of Am, 1939, Whitman, 432 pgs., by Gray 16.00 40.00 115.00
1416- Little Orphan Annie in the Movies, 1937, Whitman, 432 pgs., by Harold Gray 16.00 40.00 115.00
1417- Little Orphan Annie and the Secret of the Well, 1947, Whitman, 352 pgs., by Gray 12.00 30.00 85.00
1435- Little Orphan Annie and the Gooneyville Mystery, 1947, Whitman, 288 pgs., by Gray 13.00 32.50 90.00
1446- Little Orphan Annie in the Thieves' Den, 1949, Whitman, 288 pgs., by Harold Gray 13.00 32.50 90.00
1449- Little Orphan Annie and the Mysterious Shoemaker, 1938, Whitman, 432 pgs., by Harold Gray 15.00 37.50 105.00
1457- Little Orphan Annie and Her Junior Commandos, 1943, Whitman, 352 pgs., by H. Gray 12.00 30.00 85.00
1461- Little Orphan Annie and the Underground Hide-Out, 1945, Whitman, 352 pgs., by Gray 12.00 30.00 85.00
1468- Little Orphan Annie and the Ancient Treasure of Am, 1949 (Misdated 1939), 288 pgs., by Gray 12.00 30.00 85.00
1482- Little Orphan Annie and the Haunted Mansion, 1941, Whitman, 432 pgs., flip pictures, by Harold Gray 16.00 40.00 115.00
3048- Little Orphan Annie and Her Big Little Kit, 1937, Whitman, 384 pgs., 4 1/2" x 6 1/2" box, includes miniature box of 4 crayons-red, yellow, blue and green 94.00 235.00 660.00
4054- Little Orphan Annie, The Story of, 1934, Whitman, 7" x 9 1/2", 320 pgs., Big Big Book, Harold Gray-c/a 102.00 255.00 715.00
nn- Little Orphan Annie Gets into Trouble, 1938, Whitman, 36 pgs., 2 1/2" x 3 1/2", Penny Book 11.00 27.50 70.00
nn- Little Orphan Annie in Hollywood, 1937, Whitman, 3 1/2" x 3 1/4", Pan-Am premium, soft-c 29.00 73.00 200.00
nn- Little Orphan Annie in Rags to Riches, 1939, Dell, 194 pgs., Fast-Action Story, soft-c 39.00 98.00 275.00
nn- Little Orphan Annie Saves Sandy, 1938, Whitman, 36 pgs., 2 1/2" x 3 1/2", Penny Book 11.00 27.50 70.00
nn- Little Orphan Annie Under the Big Top, 1938, Dell, 194 pgs., Fast-Action Story, soft-c 39.00 98.00 270.00
nn- Little Orphan Annie Wee Little Books (In open box) nn, 1934, Whitman, 44 pgs., by H. Gray

	GD	FN	VF/NM
L.O.A. And Daddy Warbucks	9.00	22.50	55.00
L.O.A. And Her Dog Sandy	9.00	22.50	55.00
L.O.A. And The Lucky Knife	9.00	22.50	55.00
L.O.A. And The Pinch-Pennys	9.00	22.50	55.00
L.O.A. At Happy Home	9.00	22.50	55.00
L.O.A. Finds Mickey	9.00	22.50	55.00
Complete set with box	57.00	143.00	400.00

nn- Little Polly Flinders, The Story of, nd (1930s), no publ., 36 pgs., 2 1/2" x 3", Penny Book 4.00 10.00 22.00
nn- Little Red Hen, The, nd(1930s), np(Whitman), 36 pgs., Penny Book 4.00 10.00 22.00
nn- Little Red Riding Hood, nd(1930s), np(Whitman), 36 pgs., 3" x 2 1/2", Penny Book 4.00 10.00 22.00
nn- Little Red Riding Hood and the Big Bad Wolf (Disney), 1934, McKay, 36 pgs., stiff-c, Disney Studio-a 33.00 83.00 230.00
757- Little Women, 1934, Whitman, 4 3/4" x 5 1/4", 160 pgs., photo-c, movie scenes, starring Katharine Hepburn 21.00 52.50 145.00

1405 - Lone Star Martin of the Texas Rangers © WHIT

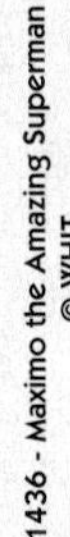

1436 - Maximo the Amazing Superman © WHIT

1153 - Mickey Mouse and the Bat Bandit © DIS

GD FN VF/NM

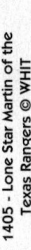

Littlest Rebel, The (See Shirley Temple)
1181- **Lone Ranger and his Horse Silver**, 1935, Whitman, 432 pgs., Hal Arbo-a 29.00 73.00 200.00
1196- **Lone Ranger and the Vanishing Herd**, 1936, Whitman, 432 pgs. 24.00 60.00 165.00
1407- **Lone Ranger and Dead Men's Mine, The**, 1939, Whitman, 432 pgs. 22.00 52.50 155.00
1421- **Lone Ranger on the Barbary Coast, The**, 1944, Whitman, 352 pgs., Henry Vallely-a 19.00 47.50 135.00
1428- **Lone Ranger and the Secret Weapon, The**, 1943, Whitman, 19.00 47.50 135.00
1431- **Lone Ranger and the Secret Killer, The**, 1937, Whitman 432 pgs., H. Anderson-a 24.00 60.00 165.00
1450- **Lone Ranger and the Black Shirt Highwayman, The**, 1939, Whitman, 432 pgs. 22.00 52.50 155.00
1465- **Lone Ranger and the Menace of Murder Valley, The**, 1938, Whitman, 432 pgs., Robert Wiseman-a 21.00 52.50 145.00
1468- **Lone Ranger Follows Through, The**, 1941, Whitman, 432 pgs., H.E. Vallely-a 21.00 52.50 145.00
1477- **Lone Ranger and the Great Western Span, The**, 1942, Whitman, 424 pgs., H. E. Vallely-a 19.00 47.50 135.00
1489- **Lone Ranger and the Red Renegades, The**, 1939, Whitman, 432 pgs. 24.00 60.00 165.00
1498- **Lone Ranger and the Silver Bullets**, 1946, Whitman, 352 pgs., Henry E. Vallely-a 19.00 47.50 135.00
712-10- **Lone Ranger and the Secret of Somber Cavern, The**, 1950, Whitman 12.00 30.00 80.00
2013- **(#13)-Lone Ranger Outwits Crazy Cougar, The**, 1968, Whitman, 260 pgs., 39 cents, hard-c, color illos 4.00 10.00 27.00
5774- **Lone Ranger Outwits Crazy Cougar, The**, 1976, Whitman, 260 pgs., 49 cents, soft-c, color illos 4.00 10.00 22.00
5774-1- **Lone Ranger Outwits Crazy Cougar, The**, 1979, Whitman, 260 pgs., 69 cents, soft-c, color illos 4.00 10.00 22.00
nn- **Lone Ranger and the Lost Valley, The**, 1938, Dell, 196 pgs., Fast-Action Story, soft-c 43.00 108.00 300.00
1405- **Lone Star Martin of the Texas Rangers**, 1939, Whitman, 432 pgs. 18.00 45.00 125.00
19- **Lost City, The**, 1935, EVW, movie scenes 16.00 40.00 115.00
1103- **Lost Jungle, The** (With Clyde Beatty), 1936, Saalfield, movie scenes, hard-c 16.00 40.00 115.00
1583- **Lost Jungle, The** (With Clyde Beatty), 1936, Saalfield, movie scenes, soft -c 13.00 32.50 90.00
753- **Lost Patrol, The**, 1934, Whitman, 160 pgs., photo-c, movie scenes with Boris Karloff 15.00 37.50 105.00
nn- **Lost World, The - Jurassic Park 2**, 1997, Chronicle Books, 312 pgs., adapts movie, 1-color (green) illos 3.00 7.50 20.00
1189- **Mac of the Marines in Africa**, 1936, Whitman, 432 pgs. 12.00 30.00 80.00
1400- **Mac of the Marines in China**, 1938, Whitman, 432 pgs. 12.00 30.00 80.00
1100B- **Magic Tricks** (With explanations), 1938, Whitman, 36 pgs., 2 1/2" x 3 1/2", Penny Book, rabbit in hat-c 4.00 10.00 22.00
1100B- **Magic Tricks** (How to do them), 1938, Whitman, 36 pgs., 2 1/2" x 3 1/2", Penny Book, genie-c 4.00 10.00 22.00
Major Hoople (See Our Boarding House)
2022-(#22)- **Major Matt Mason, Moon Mission**, 1968, Whitman, 256 pgs., hard-c, color illos. 4.00 10.00 27.00
1167- **Mandrake the Magician**, 1935, Whitman, 432 pgs., by Lee Falk & Phil Davis 24.00 60.00 170.00
1418- **Mandrake the Magician and the Flame Pearls**, 1946, Whitman, 352 pgs., by Lee Falk & Phil Davis 15.00 37.50 105.00
1431- **Mandrake the Magician and the Midnight Monster**, 1939, Whitman, 432 pgs., by Lee Falk & Phil Davis 16.00 40.00 115.00
1454- **Mandrake the Magician Mighty Solver of Mysteries**, 1941, Whitman, 432 pgs., by Lee Falk & Phil Davis, flip pictures 16.00 40.00 115.00
2011-(#11)-**Man From U.N.C.L.E., The**-The Calcutta Affair (TV Series), 1967, Whitman, 260 pgs., 39 cents, hard-c, color illos 4.00 10.00 27.00
1429- **Marge's Little Lulu Alvin and Tubby**, 1947, Whitman, All Pictures Comics, Stanley-a 31.00 78.00 215.00
1438- **Mary Lee and the Mystery of the Indian Beads**, 1937, Whitman, 300 pgs. 11.00 27.50 70.00
1165- **Masked Man of the Mesa, The**, 1939, Saalfield, 400 pgs. 10.00 25.00 65.00
nn- **Mask of Zorro, The**, 1998, Chronicle Books, 312 pgs., adapts movie, 1-color (yellow-green) illos 1.00 2.50 9.00
1436- **Maximo the Amazing Superman**, 1940, Whitman, 432 pgs., Henry E. Vallely-a 15.00 37.50 105.00
1444- **Maximo the Amazing Superman and the Crystals of Doom**, 1941, Whitman,432 pgs., Henry E. Vallely-a 15.00 37.50 105.00
1445- **Maximo the Amazing Superman and the Supermachine**, 1941, Whitman, 432 pgs. 15.00 37.50 105.00
755- **Men of the Mounted**, 1934, Whitman, 320 pgs. 15.00 37.50 105.00
nn- **Men of the Mounted**, 1933, Whitman, 52 pgs., 3 1/2" x 5 3/4", premium-no ads; other versions with Poll Parrot & Perkins ad; soft-c 21.00 52.50 145.00
nn- **Men of the Mounted**, 1934, Whitman, Cocomalt premium, soft-c, by Ted McCall 12.00 30.00 85.00
1475- **Men With Wings**, 1938, Whitman, 240 pgs., photo-c, movie scenes (Paramount Pics.) 12.00 30.00 85.00
1170- **Mickey Finn**, 1940, Saalfield, 400 pgs., by Frank Leonard 12.00 30.00 85.00
717- **Mickey Mouse** (Disney), (1st printing) 1933, Whitman, 320 pgs., Gottfredson-a, skinny Mickey on cover 392.00 980.00 3135.00
717- **Mickey Mouse** (Disney), (2nd printing)1933, Whitman, 320 pgs., Gottfredson-a, regular Mickey on cover 219.00 547.00 1750.00
nn- **Mickey Mouse** (Disney), 1933, Dean & Son, Great Big Midget Book, 320 pgs. 186.00 464.00 1485.00
731- **Mickey Mouse the Mail Pilot** (Disney), 1933, Whitman, (This is the same book as the 1st Mickey Mouse BLB #717(2nd printing) but with "The Mail Pilot" printed on the front. Lower left of back cover has a small box printed over the existing "No. 717." "No. 731" is printed next to it.) (sold at auction in 2001 in Fine condition for $5,090)
726- **Mickey Mouse in Blaggard Castle** (Disney), 1934, Whitman, 320 pgs., Gottfredson-a 47.00 118.00 330.00
731- **Mickey Mouse the Mail Pilot** (Disney), 1933, Whitman, 300 pgs., Gottfredson-a 47.00 118.00 330.00
731- **Mickey Mouse the Mail Pilot** (Disney), 1933, Whitman, 300 pgs., soft cover; Gottfredson-a (Rare) 85.00 212.00 600.00
nn- **Mickey Mouse the Mail Pilot** (Disney), 1933, Whitman, 292 pgs., American Oil Co. premium, soft-c, Gottfredson-a; another version 3 1/2" x 4 3/4" 47.00 118.00 330.00
nn- **Mickey Mouse the Mail Pilot** (Disney), 1933, Dean & Son, Great Big Midget Book (Rare) 187.00 467.00 1500.00
750- **Mickey Mouse Sails for Treasure Island** (Disney), 1933, Whitman, 320 pgs., Gottfredson-a 47.00 118.00 330.00
nn- **Mickey Mouse Sails for Treasure Island** (Disney), 1935, Whitman, 196 pgs., premium-no ads, soft-c, Gottfredson-a (Scarce) 56.00 140.00 395.00
nn- **Mickey Mouse Sails for Treasure Island** (Disney), 1935, Whitman, 196 pgs., Kolynos Dental Cream premium (Scarce) 56.00 140.00 395.00
nn- **Mickey Mouse Sails for Treasure Island** (Disney), 1933, Dean & Son, Great Big Midget Book, 320 pgs. 150.00 375.00 1200.00
756- **Mickey Mouse Presents a Walt Disney Silly Symphony** (Disney), 1934, Whitman, 240 pgs., Bucky Bug app. 43.00 108.00 300.00
801- **Mickey Mouse's Summer Vacation**, 1948, Whitman, hard-c, Story Hour series 12.00 30.00 85.00
1111- **Mickey Mouse Presents Walt Disney's Silly Symphonies Stories**, 1936, Whitman, 432 pgs., Donald Duck app. 43.00 108.00 300.00
1128- **Mickey Mouse and Pluto the Racer** (Disney), 1936, Whitman, 432 pgs., Gottfredson-a 38.00 95.00 255.00
1139- **Mickey Mouse the Detective** (Disney), 1934, Whitman, 300 pgs., Gottfredson-a 43.00 108.00 300.00
1139- **Mickey Mouse the Detective** (Disney), 1934, Whitman, 304 pgs., premium-no ads, soft-c, Gottfredson-a (Scarce) 64.00 160.00 450.00
1153- **Mickey Mouse and the Bat Bandit** (Disney), 1935,

1483 - Mickey Mouse Bell Boy Detective © DIS

nn - Minute-Man © FAW

1150 - Napoleon and Uncle Elby © Saalfield

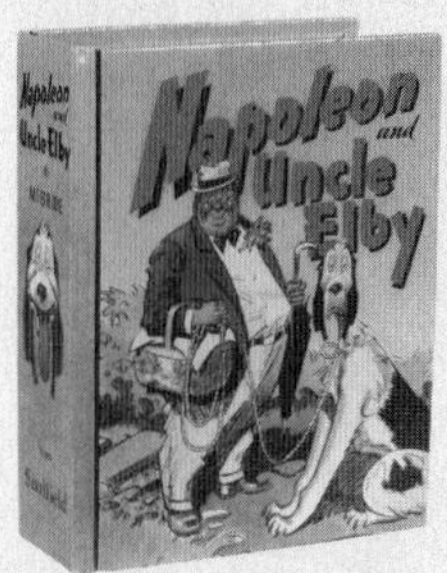

GD FN VF/NM

Whitman, 432 pgs., Gottfredson-a 39.00 98.00 275.00

nn- **Mickey Mouse and the Bat Bandit** (Disney), 1935, Whitman, 436 pgs., premium-no ads, 3-color, soft-c, Gottfredson-a (Scarce) 64.00 160.00 450.00

1160- **Mickey Mouse and Bobo the Elephant** (Disney), 1935, Whitman, 432 pgs., Gottfredson-a 39.00 98.00 275.00

1187- **Mickey Mouse and the Sacred Jewel** (Disney), 1936, Whitman, 432 pgs., Gottfredson-a 36.00 90.00 255.00

1401- **Mickey Mouse in the Treasure Hunt** (Disney), 1941, Whitman, 430 pgs., flip pictures of Pluto, Gottfredson-a 34.00 85.00 240.00

1409- **Mickey Mouse Runs His Own Newspaper** (Disney), 1937, Whitman, 432 pgs., Gottfredson-a 34.00 85.00 240.00

1413- **Mickey Mouse and the 'Lectro Box** (Disney), 1946, Whitman, 352 pgs., Gottfredson-a 24.00 60.00 165.00

1417- **Mickey Mouse on Sky Island** (Disney), 1941, Whitman, 432 pgs., flip pictures, Gottfredson-a; considered by Gottfredson to be his best Mickey story 34.00 85.00 240.00

1428- **Mickey Mouse in the Foreign Legion** (Disney), 1940, Whitman, 432 pgs., Gottfredson-a 34.00 85.00 240.00

1429- **Mickey Mouse and the Magic Lamp** (Disney), 1942, Whitman, 432 pgs., flip pictures 34.00 85.00 240.00

1433- **Mickey Mouse and the Lazy Daisy Mystery** (Disney), 1947, Whitman, 288 pgs. 24.00 60.00 165.00

1444- **Mickey Mouse in the World of Tomorrow** (Disney), 1948, Whitman, 288 pgs., Gottfredson-a 36.00 90.00 255.00

1451- **Mickey Mouse and the Desert Palace** (Disney), 1948, Whitman, 288 pgs. 24.00 60.00 165.00

1463- **Mickey Mouse and the Pirate Submarine** (Disney), 1939, Whitman, 432 pgs., Gottfredson-a 34.00 85.00 240.00

1464- **Mickey Mouse and the Stolen Jewels** (Disney), 1949, Whitman, 288 pgs. 33.00 83.00 230.00

1471- **Mickey Mouse and the Dude Ranch Bandit** (Disney), 1943, Whitman, 432 pgs., flip pictures 34.00 85.00 240.00

1475- **Mickey Mouse and the 7 Ghosts** (Disney), 1940, Whitman, 432 pgs., Gottfredson-a 34.00 85.00 240.00

1476- **Mickey Mouse in the Race for Riches** (Disney), 1938, Whitman, 432 pgs., Gottfredson-a 34.00 85.00 240.00

1483- **Mickey Mouse Bell Boy Detective** (Disney), 1945, Whitman, 352 pgs. 33.00 83.00 230.00

1499- **Mickey Mouse on the Cave-Man Island** (Disney), 1944, Whitman, 352 pgs. 33.00 83.00 230.00

2004- **Mickey Mouse, Here Comes** (Disney), 1936, Whitman, (Very Rare), 224 pgs., 12" x 8 1/4" box, with red, yellow and blue crayons, contains 224 loose pages to color, reprinted from early Mickey Mouse related movie and strip reprints 475.00 1187.00 3800.00

2020-(#20)- **Mickey Mouse, Adventure in Outer Space,** 1968, Whitman, 256 pgs.,hard-c, color illos. 4.00 10.00 27.00

5750- **Mickey Mouse, Adventure in Outer Space,** 1973, Whitman, 256 pgs.,soft-c, 39 cents, color illos. 2.00 5.00 13.00

3049- **Mickey Mouse and His Big Little Kit** (Disney), 1937, Whitman, 384 pgs., 4 1/2" x 6 1/2" box, includes miniature box of 4 crayons-red, yellow, blue and green 150.00 375.00 1210.00

3061- **Mickey Mouse to Draw and Color** (The Big Little Set), nd (early 1930s), Whitman, with crayons; box contains 320 loose pages to color, reprinted from early Mickey Mouse BLBs 123.00 308.00 880.00

4062- **Mickey Mouse, The Story Of**, 1935, Whitman, 7" x 9 1/2", 320 pgs., Big Big Book, Gottfredson-a 150.00 375.00 1210.00

4062- **Mickey Mouse and the Smugglers, The Story Of,** 1935, Whitman, (Scarce), 7" x 9 1/2", 320 pgs., Big Big Book, same contents as above version; Gottfredson-a 179.00 447.00 1430.00

708-10- **Mickey Mouse on the Haunted Island** (Disney), 1950, Whitman, Gottfredson-a 15.00 37.50 105.00

nn- **Mickey Mouse and Minnie at Macy's**, 1934 Whitman, 148 pgs., 3 1/4" x 3 1/2", soft-c, R. H. Macy & Co. Christmas giveaway (Rare, less than 20 known copies) 438.00 1095.00 3500.00

nn- **Mickey Mouse and Minnie March to Macy's**, 1935, Whitman, 148 pgs., 3 1/2" x 3 1/2", soft-c, R. H. Macy & Co. Christmas giveaway (scarce) 300.00 750.00 2400.00

GD FN VF/NM

nn- **Mickey Mouse and the Magic Carpet**, 1935, Whitman, 148 pgs., 3 1/2"x 4", soft-c, giveaway, Gottfredson-a, Donald Duck app. 131.00 328.00 1050.00

nn- **Mickey Mouse Silly Symphonies**, 1934, Dean & Son, Ltd (England), 48 pgs., with 4 pop-ups, Babes In The Woods, King Neptune
With dust jacket 165.00 412.00 1320.00
Without dust jacket 119.00 298.00 835.00

nn- **Mickey Mouse the Sheriff of Nugget Gulch** (Disney) 1938, Dell, 196 pgs., Fast-Action Story, soft-c, Gottfredson-a 56.00 140.00 395.00

nn- **Mickey Mouse Waddle Book**, 1934, BRP, 20 pgs., 7 1/2" x 10", forerunner of the Blue Ribbon Pop-Up books; with 4 removable articulated cardboard characters Book Only 100.00 200.00 500.00
(A complete copy in VG/FN w/VF dustjacket sold for $5676 in 2010)

nn- **Mickey Mouse with Goofy and Mickey's Nephews**, 1938, Dell, Fast-Action Story, Gottfredson-a 56.00 140.00 395.00

16- **Mickey Mouse and Pluto** (Disney), 1942, Dell, 196 pgs., Fast-Action story 56.00 140.00 395.00

512- **Mickey Mouse Wee Little Books** (In open box), nn, 1934, Whitman, 44 pgs., small size, soft-c
Mickey Mouse and Tanglefoot 13.00 32.50 90.00
Mickey Mouse at the Carnival 13.00 32.50 90.00
Mickey Mouse Will Not Quit! 13.00 32.50 90.00
Mickey Mouse Wins the Race! 13.00 32.50 90.00
Mickey Mouse's Misfortune 13.00 32.50 90.00
Mickey Mouse's Uphill Fight 13.00 32.50 90.00
Complete set with box 93.00 233.00 650.00

1493- **Mickey Rooney and Judy Garland and How They Got into the Movies**, 1941, Whitman, 432 pgs., photo-c 15.00 37.50 105.00

1427- **Mickey Rooney Himself**, 1939, Whitman, 240 pgs., photo-c, movie scenes, life story 15.00 37.50 105.00

532- **Mickey's Dog Pluto** (Disney), 1943, Whitman, All Picture Comics, A Tall Comic Book , 3 3/4" x 8 3/4" 41.00 103.00 285.00

284- **Midget Jumbo Coloring Book**, 1935, Saalfield 71.00 178.00 500.00

2113- **Midget Jumbo Coloring Book**, 1935, Saalfield, 240 pgs. 71.00 178.00 500.00

21- **Midsummer Night's Dream**, 1935, EVW, movie scenes 15.00 37.50 105.00

nn- **Minute-Man** (Mystery of the Spy Ring), 1941, Fawcett, Dime Action Book 57.00 143.00 400.00

710- **Moby Dick the Great White Whale, The Story of**, 1934, Whitman, 160 pgs., photo-c, movie scenes from "The Sea Beast" 15.00 37.50 105.00

746- **Moon Mullins and Kayo** (Kayo and Moon Mullins-inside), 1933, Whitman, 320 pgs., Frank Willard-c/a 16.00 40.00 115.00

nn- **Moon Mullins and Kayo**, 1933, Whitman, Cocomalt premium, soft-c, by Willard 16.00 40.00 115.00

1134- **Moon Mullins and the Plushbottom Twins**, 1935, Whitman, 432 pgs., Willard-c/a 16.00 40.00 115.00

nn- **Moon Mullins and the Plushbottom Twins**, 1935, Whitman, 436 pgs., premium-no ads, 3-color, soft-c, by Willard 29.00 73.00 200.00

1058- **Mother Pluto** (Disney), 1939, Whitman, 68 pgs., hard-c 13.00 32.50 90.00

1100B- **Movie Jokes** (From the talkies), 1938, Whitman, 36 pgs., 2 1/2" x 3 1/2", Penny Book 4.00 10.00 22.00

1408- **Mr. District Attorney on the Job**, 1941, Whitman, 432 pgs., flip pictures 12.00 30.00 75.00

nn- **Musicians of Bremen, The**, nd (1930s), np (Whitman), 36 pgs., 3" x 2 1/2", Penny Book 4.00 10.00 22.00

1113- **Mutt and Jeff**, 1936, Whitman, 300 pgs., by Bud Fisher 26.00 65.00 180.00

1116- **My Life and Times** (By Shirley Temple), 1936, Saalfield, Little Big Book, hard-c, photo-c/illos 16.00 40.00 115.00

1596- **My Life and Times** (By Shirley Temple), 1936, Saalfield, Little Big Book, soft-c, photo-c/illos 16.00 40.00 115.00

1497- **Myra North Special Nurse and Foreign Spies**, 1938, Whitman, 432 pgs. 12.00 30.00 85.00

1400- **Nancy and Sluggo**, 1946, Whitman, All Pictures Comics, Ernie Bushmiller-a 13.00 32.50 90.00

1487- **Nancy Has Fun**, 1946, Whitman, All Pictures Comics

1456 - Our Gang Adventures © WHIT

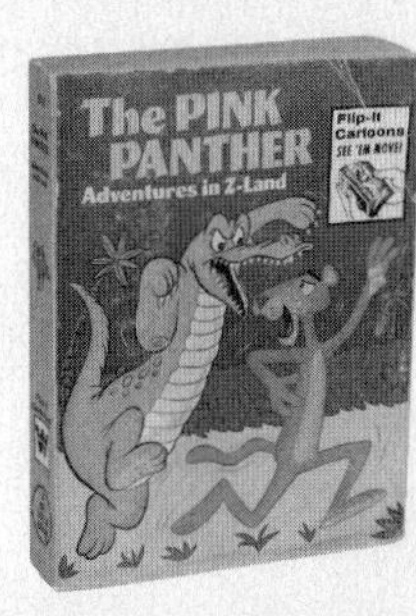

5776 - The Pink Panther Adventures in Z-Land © MGM

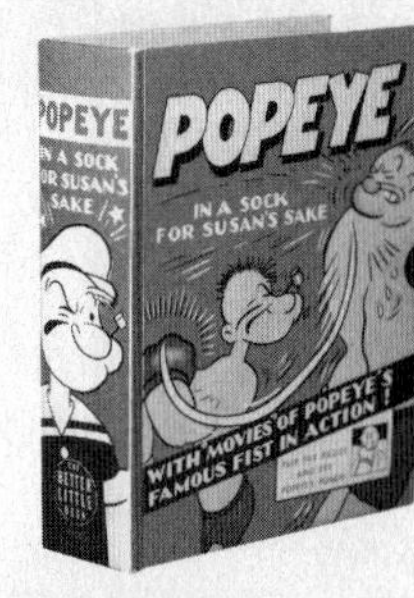

1485 - Popeye in A Sock For Susan's Sake © KING

GD FN VF/NM

13.00 32.50 90.00

1150- Napoleon and Uncle Elby, 1938, Saalfield, 400 pgs., by Clifford McBride 12.00 30.00 85.00

1166- Napoleon Uncle Elby And Little Mary, 1939, Saalfield, 400 pgs., by Clifford McBride 12.00 30.00 85.00

1179- Ned Brant Adventure Bound, 1940, Saalfield, 400 pgs. 11.00 27.50 70.00

1146- Nevada Rides The Danger Trail, 1938, Saalfield, 400 pgs., J.R. White-a 11.00 27.50 70.00

1147- Nevada Whalen, Avenger, 1938, Saalfield, 400 pgs. 11.00 27.50 70.00

Nicodemus O'Malley (See Top-Line Comics)

1115- Og Son of Fire, 1936, Whitman, 432 pgs. 16.00 40.00 115.00

1419- Oh, Blondie the Bumsteads (See Blondie)

11- Oliver Twist, 1935, EVW (Five Star Library), movie scenes, starring Dickie Moore (Monogram Pictures) 15.00 37.50 105.00

718- Once Upon a Time, 1933, Whitman, 364 pgs., soft-c 15.00 37.50 105.00

712- 100 Fairy Tales for Children, The, 1933, Whitman, 288 pgs., Circle Library 11.00 27.50 70.00

1099- One Night of Love, 1935, Saalfield, 160 pgs., hard-c, photo-c, movie scenes, Columbia Pictures, starring Grace Moore 15.00 37.50 105.00

1579- One Night of Love, 1935, Sat, 160 pgs., soft-c, photo-c, movie scenes, Columbia Pictures, starring Grace Moore 15.00 37.50 105.00

1155- $1000 Reward, 1938, Saalfield, 400 pgs. 11.00 27.50 70.00

Orphan Annie (See Little Orphan ...)

L17- O'Shaughnessy's Boy, 1935, Lynn, 192 pgs., movie scenes, w/Wallace Beery & Jackie Cooper (Metro-Goldwyn-Mayer) 12.00 30.00 85.00

1109- Oswald the Lucky Rabbit, 1934, Whitman, 288 pgs. 21.00 52.50 145.00

1403- Oswald Rabbit Plays G-Man, 1937, Whitman, 240 pgs., movie scenes by Walter Lantz 22.00 52.50 155.00

1190- Our Boarding House, Major Hoople and his Horse, 1940, Saalfield, 400 pgs. 12.00 30.00 85.00

1085- Our Gang, 1934, Saalfield, 160 pgs., photo-c, movie scenes, hard-c 15.00 37.50 105.00

1315- Our Gang, 1934, Saalfield, 160 pgs., photo-c, movie scenes, soft-c 15.00 37.50 105.00

1451- "Our Gang" on the March, 1942, Whitman, 432 pgs., flip pictures, Vallely-a 15.00 37.50 105.00

1456- Our Gang Adventures, 1948, Whitman, 288 pgs. 12.00 30.00 85.00

nn- Paramount Newsreel Men with Admiral Byrd in Little America, 1934, Whitman, 96 pgs., 6 1/4" x 6 1/4", photo-c, photo ill. 16.00 40.00 115.00

nn- Patch, nd (1930s), np (Whitman), 36 pgs., 3" x 2 1/2", Penny Book 4.00 10.00 22.00

1445- Pat Nelson Ace of Test Pilots, 1937, Whitman, 432 pgs. 11.00 27.50 70.00

1411- Peggy Brown and the Mystery Basket, 1941, Whitman, 432 pgs., flip pictures, Henry E. Vallely-a 12.00 30.00 75.00

1423- Peggy Brown and the Secret Treasure, 1947, Whitman, 288 pgs., Henry E. Vallely-a 12.00 30.00 75.00

1427- Peggy Brown and the Runaway Auto Trailer, 1937, Whitman, 300 pgs., Henry E. Vallely-a 12.00 30.00 75.00

1463- Peggy Brown and the Jewel of Fire, 1943, Whitman, 352 pgs., Henry E. Vallely-a 12.00 30.00 75.00

1491- Peggy Brown in the Big Haunted House, 1940, Whitman, 432 pgs., Vallely-a 12.00 30.00 75.00

1143- Peril Afloat, 1938, Saalfield, 400 pgs. 11.00 27.50 70.00

1199- Perry Winkle and the Rinkeydinks, 1937, Whitman, 432 pgs., by Martin Branner 15.00 37.50 105.00

1487- Perry Winkle and the Rinkeydinks get a Horse, 1938, Whitman, 432 pgs., by Martin Branner 15.00 37.50 105.00

Peter Pan (See Wee Little Books)

nn- Peter Rabbit, nd(1930s), np(Whitman), 36 pgs., Penny Book, 3" x 2 1/2" 5.00 12.50 33.00

Peter Rabbit's Carrots (See Wee Little Books)

GD FN VF/NM

1100- Phantom, The, 1936, Whitman, 432 pgs., by Lee Falk & Ray Moore 47.00 118.00 330.00

1416- Phantom and the Girl of Mystery, The, 1947, Whitman, 352 pgs. by Falk & Moore 21.00 52.50 145.00

1421- Phantom and Desert Justice, The, 1941, Whitman, 432 pgs., flip pictures, by Falk & Moore 28.00 70.00 195.00

1468- Phantom and the Sky Pirates, The, 1945, Whitman, 352 pgs., by Falk & Moore 24.00 60.00 170.00

1474- Phantom and the Sign of the Skull, The, 1939, Whitman, 432 pgs., by Falk & Moore 29.00 73.00 205.00

1489- Phantom, Return of the..., 1942, Whitman, 432 pgs., flip pictures, by Falk & Moore 28.00 70.00 195.00

1130- Phil Burton, Sleuth (Scout Book), 1937, Saalfield, hard-c 9.00 22.50 55.00

Pied Piper of Hamlin (See Wee Little Books)

1466- Pilot Pete Dive Bomber, 1941, Whitman, 432 pgs., flip pictures 11.00 27.50 70.00

5776- Pink Panther Adventures in Z-Land, The, 1976, Whitman, 260 pgs., soft-c, 49 cents, B&W 1.00 2.50 8.00

5776-2- Pink Panther Adventures in Z-Land, The, 1980, Whitman, 260 pgs., soft-c, 79 cents, B&W 1.00 2.50 8.00

5783-2- Pink Panther at Castle Kreep, The, 1980, Whitman, 260 pgs., soft-c, 79 cents, B&W 1.00 2.50 8.00

Pinocchio and Jiminy Cricket (See Walt Disney's ...)

nn- Pioneers of the Wild West (Blue-c), 1933, World Syndicate, High Lights of History Series 10.00 25.00 65.00
With dustjacket 57.00 142.00 400.00

nn- Pioneers of the Wild West (Red-c), 1933, World Syndicate, High Lights of History Series 10.00 25.00 65.00

1123- Plainsman, The, 1936, Whitman, 240 pgs., photo-c, movie scenes with Gary Cooper (Paramount Pics.) 26.00 65.00 180.00

Pluto (See Mickey's Dog ... & Walt Disney's ...)

2114- Pocket Coloring Book, 1935, Saalfield 39.00 98.00 270.00

1060- Polly and Her Pals on the Farm, 1934, Saalfield, 164 pgs., hard-c, by Cliff Sterrett 15.00 37.50 105.00

1310- Polly and Her Pals on the Farm, 1934, Saalfield, soft-c 15.00 37.50 105.00

1051- Popeye, Adventures of..., 1934, Saalfield, oblong-size, E.C. Segar-a, hard-c 58.00 146.00 410.00

1088- Popeye in Puddleburg, 1934, Saalfield, 160 pgs., hard-c, E. C. Segar-a 22.00 52.50 155.00

1113- Popeye Starring in Choose Your Weppins, 1936, Saalfield, 160 pgs., hard-c, Segar-a 46.00 115.00 320.00

1117- Popeye's Ark, 1936, Saalfield, 4 1/2" x 5 1/2", hard-c, Segar-a 24.00 60.00 165.00

1163- Popeye Sees the Sea, 1936, Whitman, 432 pgs., Segar-a 24.00 60.00 170.00

1301- Popeye, Adventures of..., 1934, Saalfield, oblong-size, Segar-a 58.00 146.00 410.00

1318- Popeye in Puddleburg, 1934, Saalfield, 160 pgs., soft-c, Segar-a 24.00 60.00 165.00

1405- Popeye and the Jeep, 1937, Whitman, 432 pgs., Segar-a 24.00 60.00 170.00

1406- Popeye the Super-Fighter, 1939, Whitman, All Pictures Comics, flip pictures, Segar-a 24.00 60.00 165.00

1422- Popeye the Sailor Man, 1947, Whitman, All Pictures Comics 16.00 40.00 115.00

1450- Popeye in Quest of His Poopdeck Pappy, 1937, Whitman, 432 pgs., Segar-c/a 24.00 60.00 170.00

1458- Popeye and Queen Olive Oyl, 1949, Whitman, 288 pgs., Sagendorf-a 16.00 40.00 115.00

1459- Popeye and the Quest for the Rainbird, 1943, Whitman, Winner & Zaboly-a 18.00 45.00 125.00

1480- Popeye the Spinach Eater, 1945, Whitman, All Pictures Comics 16.00 40.00 115.00

1485- Popeye in a Sock for Susan's Sake, 1940, Whitman, 432 pgs., flip pictures 18.00 45.00 125.00

1497- Popeye and Caster Oyl the Detective, 1941, Whitman, 432 pgs. flip pictures, Segar-a 21.00 52.50 145.00

1499- Popeye and the Deep Sea Mystery, 1939, Whitman, 432 pgs.,

2008 - Popeye-Ghost Ship To Treasure Island © KING

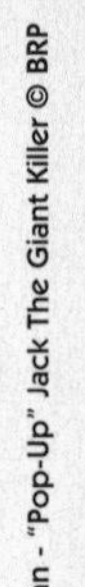

nn - "Pop-Up" Jack The Giant Killer © BRP

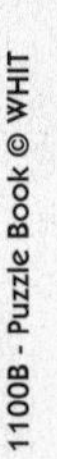

1100B - Puzzle Book © WHIT

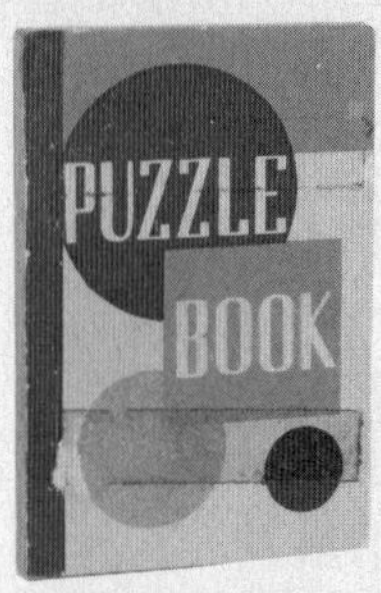

	GD	FN	VF/NM
Segar-c/a	21.00	52.50	145.00
1593- **Popeye Starring in Choose Your Weppins**, 1936, Saalfield, 160 pgs., soft-c, Segar-a	21.00	52.50	145.00
1597- **Popeye's Ark**, 1936, Saalfield, 4 1/2" x 5 1/2", soft-c, Segar-a	21.00	52.50	145.00
2008-(#8)- **Popeye-Ghost Ship to Treasure Island**, 1967, Whitman, 260 pgs., 39 cents, hard-c, color illos	4.00	10.00	27.00
5755- **Popeye-Ghost Ship to Treasure Island**, 1973, Whitman, 260 pgs., soft-c, color illos	2.00	5.00	11.00
2034-(#34)- **Popeye, Danger Ahoy!**, 1969, Whitman, 256 pgs., hard-c, color illos.	4.00	10.00	25.00
5768- **Popeye, Danger Ahoy!**, 1975, Whitman, 256 pgs., soft-c, color illos.	2.00	5.00	11.00
4063- **Popeye, Thimble Theatre Starring**, 1935, Whitman, 7" x 9 1/2", 320 pgs., Big Big Book, Segar-c/a; (Cactus cover w/yellow logo)	173.00	433.00	1385.00
4063- **Popeye, Thimble Theatre Starring**, 1935, Whitman, 7" x 9 1/2", 320 pgs., Big Big Book, Segar-c/a; (Big Balloon-c with red logo), (2nd printing w/same contents as above)	202.00	506.00	1620.00
5761- **Popeye and Queen Olive Oyl**, 1973, 260 pgs., B&W, soft-c	4.00	10.00	27.00
5761-2- **Popeye and Queen Olive Oyl**, 1973 (1980-reprint of 1973 version), 260 pgs., 79 cents, B&W, soft-c	2.00	5.00	11.00
103- **"Pop-Up" Buck Rogers in the Dangerous Mission** (with Pop-Up picture), 1934, BRP, 62 pgs., The Midget Pop-Up Book w/Pop-Up in center of book, Calkins-a	173.00	433.00	1385.00
206- **"Pop-Up" Buck Rogers - Strange Adventures in the Spider Ship, The**, 1935, BRP, 24 pgs., 8" x 9", 3 Pop-Ups, hard-c, by Dick Calkins	173.00	433.00	1385.00
nn- **"Pop-Up" Cinderella**, 1933, BRP, 7 1/2" x 9 3/4", 4 Pop-Ups, hard-c			
With dustjacket ($2.00)	118.00	295.00	825.00
Without dustjacket	90.00	225.00	630.00
207- **"Pop-Up" Dick Tracy-Capture of Boris Arson**, 1935, BRP, 24 pgs., 8" x 9", 3 Pop-Ups, hard-c, by Gould	116.00	290.00	810.00
210- **"Pop-Up" Flash Gordon Tournament of Death, The**, 1935, BRP, 24 pgs., 8" x 9", 3 Pop-Ups, hard-c, by Alex Raymond	173.00	433.00	1385.00
202- **"Pop-Up" Goldilocks and the Three Bears, The**, 1934, BRP, 24 pgs., 8" x 9", 3 Pop-Ups, hard-c	45.00	113.00	315.00
nn- **"Pop-Up" Jack and the Beanstalk**, 1933, BRP, hard-c (50 cents), 1 Pop-Up	45.00	113.00	315.00
nn- **"Pop-Up" Jack the Giant Killer**, 1933, BRP, hard-c (50 cents), 1 Pop-Up	45.00	113.00	315.00
nn- **"Pop-Up" Jack the Giant Killer**, 1933, BRP, 4 Pop-Ups, hard-c			
With dustjacket ($2.00)	118.00	295.00	825.00
Without dust jacket	90.00	225.00	630.00
nn- **"Pop-Up" Little Black Sambo**, (with Pop-Up picture), 1934, BRP, 62 pgs., The Midget Pop-Up Book, one Pop-Up in center of book	73.00	182.00	515.00
208- **"Pop-Up" Little Orphan Annie and Jumbo the Circus Elephant**, 1935, BRP, 24 pgs., 8" x 9 1/2", 3 Pop-Ups, hard-c, by H. Gray	119.00	298.00	835.00
nn- **"Pop-Up" Little Red Ridinghood**, 1933, BRP, hard-c (50 cents), 1 Pop-Up	57.00	143.00	400.00
nn- **"Pop-Up" Mickey Mouse, The**, 1933, BRP, 34 pgs., 6 1/2" x 9", 3,Pop-Ups, hard-c, Gottfredson-a (75 cents)	110.00	250.00	775.00
nn- **"Pop-Up" Mickey Mouse in King Arthur's Court, The**,1933, BRP, 56 pgs., 7 1/2" x 9 1/4", 4 Pop-Ups, hard-c, Gottfredson-a			
With dust jacket ($2.00)	302.00	756.00	2420.00
Without dustjacket	188.00	470.00	1500.00
101- **"Pop-Up" Mickey Mouse in "Ye Olden Days"** (with Pop-Up picture), 1934, 62 pgs., BRP, The Midget Pop-Up Book, one Pop-Up in center of book, Gottfredson-a	130.00	327.00	1045.00
nn- **"Pop-Up" Minnie Mouse, The**, 1933, BRP, 36 pgs., 6 1/2" x 9", 3 Pop-Ups, hard-c (75 cents), Gottfredson-a	110.00	275.00	775.00
203- **"Pop-Up" Mother Goose, The**, 1934, BRP, 24 pgs., 8" x 9 1/4", 3 Pop-Ups, hard-c	79.00	198.00	550.00
nn- **"Pop-Up" Mother Goose Rhymes, The**, 1933, BRP, 96 pgs., 7 1/2" x 9 1/4", 4 Pop-Ups, hard-c			
With dustjacket ($2.00)	107.00	268.00	750.00

	GD	FN	VF/NM
Without dustjacket	84.00	210.00	580.00
209- **"Pop-Up" New Adventures of Tarzan**, 1935, BRP, 24 pgs., 8" x 9", 3 Pop-Ups, hard-c	130.00	327.00	1045.00
104- **"Pop-Up" Peter Rabbit, The** (with Pop-Up picture), 1934, BRP, 62 pgs., The Midget Pop-Up Book, one Pop-Up in center of book	73.00	182.00	515.00
nn- **"Pop-Up" Pinocchio**, 1933, BRP, 7 1/2" x 9 3/4", 4 Pop-Ups, hard-c			
With dustjacket ($2.00)	118.00	295.00	825.00
Without dust jacket	90.00	225.00	630.00
102- **"Pop-Up" Popeye among the White Savages** (with Pop-Up picture), 1934, BRP, 62 pgs., The Midget Pop-Up Book, one Pop-Up in center of book, E. C. Segar-a	116.00	290.00	810.00
205- **"Pop-Up" Popeye with the Hag of the Seven Seas, The**, 1935, BRP, 24 pgs., 8" x 9", 3 Pop-Ups, hard-c, Segar-a	124.00	310.00	955.00
201- **"Pop-Up" Puss In Boots, The**, 1934, BRP, 24 pgs., 3 Pop-Ups, hard-c	46.00	115.00	320.00
nn- **"Pop-Up" Silly Symphonies, The** (Mickey Mouse Presents His ...), 1933, BRP, 56 pgs., 9 3/4" x 7 1/2", 4 Pop-Ups, hard-c			
With dust jacket ($2.00)	172.00	430.00	1375.00
Without dust jacket	121.00	304.00	865.00
nn- **"Pop-Up" Sleeping Beauty**, 1933, BRP, hard-c, (50 cents), 1 Pop-up	53.00	132.00	370.00
212- **"Pop-Up" Terry and the Pirates in Shipwrecked, The**, 1935, BRP, 24 pgs., 8" x 9", 3 Pop-Ups, hard-c	110.00	275.00	775.00
211- **"Pop-Up" Tim Tyler in the Jungle, The**, 1935, BRP, 24 pgs., 8" x 9", 3 Pop-Ups, hard-c	84.00	210.00	580.00
1404- **Porky Pig and His Gang**, 1946, Whitman, All Pictures Comics, Barks-a, reprints Four Color #48	24.00	60.00	165.00
1408- **Porky Pig and Petunia**, 1942, Whitman, All Pictures Comics, flip pictures, reprints Four Color #16 & Famous Gang Book of Comics	16.00	40.00	115.00
1176- **Powder Smoke Range**, 1935, Whitman, 240 pgs., photo-c, movie scenes, Hoot Gibson, Harey Carey app. (RKO Radio Pict.)	14.00	35.00	95.00
1058- **Practical Pig!, The** (Disney), 1939, Whitman, 68 pgs., 5" x 5 1/2", hard-c	12.00	30.00	85.00
758- **Prairie Bill and the Covered Wagon**, 1934, Whitman, 384 pgs., Hal Arbo-a	12.00	30.00	85.00
nn- **Prairie Bill and the Covered Wagon**, 1934, Whitman, 390 pgs., premium-no ads, 3-color, soft-c, Hal Arbo-a	18.00	45.00	125.00
1440- **Punch Davis of the U.S. Aircraft Carrier**, 1945, Whitman, 352 pgs.	10.00	25.00	65.00
nn- **Puss in Boots**, nd(1930s), np(Whitman), 36 pgs., Penny Book	4.00	10.00	22.00
1100B- **Puzzle Book**, 1938, Whitman, 36 pgs., 2 1/2" x 3 1/2", Penny Book	4.00	10.00	27.00
1100B- **Puzzles**, 1938, Whitman, 36 pgs., 2 1/2" x 3 1/2", Penny Book	4.00	10.00	27.00
1100B- **Quiz Book, The**, 1938, Whitman, 36 pgs., 2 1/2" x 3 1/2", Penny Book	4.00	10.00	27.00
1142- **Radio Patrol**, 1935, Whitman, 432 pgs., by Eddie Sullivan & Charlie Schmidt (#1)	12.00	30.00	85.00
1173- **Radio Patrol Trailing the Safeblowers**, 1937, Whitman, 432 pgs.	11.00	27.50	70.00
1496- **Radio Patrol Outwitting the Gang Chief**, 1939, Whitman, 432 pgs.	11.00	27.50	70.00
1498- **Radio Patrol and Big Dan's Mobsters**, 1937, Whitman, 432 pgs.	11.00	27.50	70.00
nn- **Raiders of the Lost Ark**, 1998, Chronicle Books, 304 pgs., adapts movie, 1-color (green) illos	4.00	10.00	22.00
1441- **Range Busters, The**, 1942, Whitman, 432 pgs., Henry E. Vallely-a	11.00	27.50	70.00
1163- **Ranger and the Cowboy, The**, 1939, Saalfield, 400 pgs.	11.00	27.50	70.00
1154- **Rangers on the Rio Grande**, 1938, Saalfield, 400 pgs.	11.00	27.50	70.00
1447- **Ray Land of the Tank Corps, U.S.A.**, 1942, Whitman, 432 pgs., flip pictures, Hess-a	11.00	27.50	70.00
1157- **Red Barry Ace-Detective**, 1935, Whitman, 432 pgs., by Will Gould	15.00	37.50	105.00

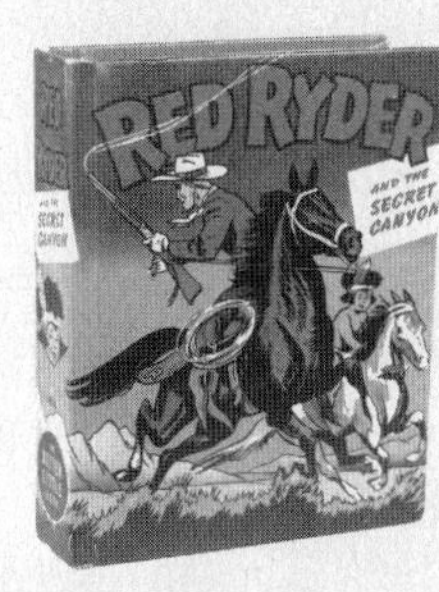

1454 - Red Ryder and the Secret Canyon © WHIT

1462 - Roy Rogers and the Mystery of the Lazy M © Roy Rogers

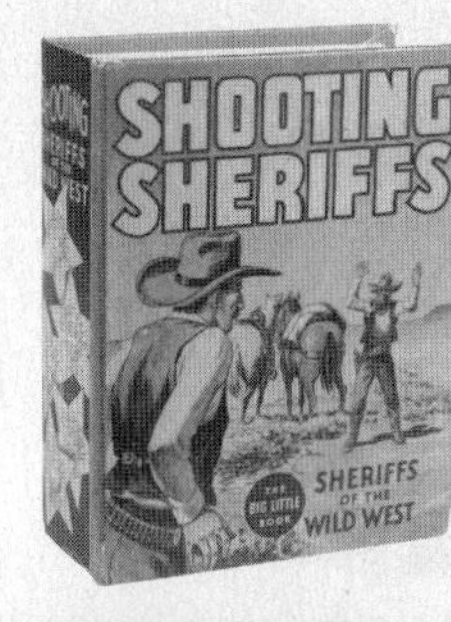

1195 - Shooting Sheriffs of the Wild West © WHIT

GD FN VF/NM

1426- Red Barry Undercover Man, 1939, Whitman, 432 pgs., by Will Gould 13.00 32.50 90.00

20- Red Davis, 1935, EVW, 160 pgs. 12.00 30.00 85.00

1449- Red Death on the Range, The, 1940, Whitman, 432 pgs., Fred Harman-a (Bronc Peeler) 12.00 30.00 85.00

nn- Red Falcon Adventures, The, 1937, Seal Right Ice Cream, 8 pgs., set of 50 books, circular in shape
Issue #1 87.00 218.00 605.00
Issue #2-5 60.00 150.00 420.00
Issue #6-10 49.00 122.00 345.00
Issue #11-50 31.00 78.00 220.00

nn- Red Hen and the Fox, The, nd(1930s), np(Whitman), 36 pgs., 3" x 2 1/2", Penny Book 4.00 10.00 22.00

1145- Red-Hot Holsters, 1938, Saalfield, 400 pgs. 11.00 27.50 70.00

1400- Red Ryder and Little Beaver on Hoofs of Thunder, 1939, Whitman, 432 pgs., Harman-c/a 20.00 50.00 140.00

1414- Red Ryder and the Squaw-Tooth Rustlers, 1946, Whitman, 352 pgs., Fred Harman-a 15.00 37.50 105.00

1427- Red Ryder and the Code of the West, 1941, Whitman, 432 pgs., flip pictures, by Harman 19.00 47.50 135.00

1440- Red Ryder the Fighting Westerner, 1940, Whitman, Harman-a 19.00 47.50 135.00

1443- Red Ryder and the Rimrock Killer, 1948, Whitman, 288 pgs., Harman-a 14.00 35.00 95.00

1450- Red Ryder and Western Border Guns, 1942, Whitman, 432 pgs., flip pictures, by Harman 19.00 47.50 135.00

1454- Red Ryder and the Secret Canyon, 1948, Whitman, 288 pgs., Harman-a 14.00 35.00 95.00

1466- Red Ryder and Circus Luck, 1947, Whitman, 288 pgs., by Fred Harman 14.00 35.00 95.00

1473- Red Ryder in War on the Range, 1945, Whitman, 352 pgs., by Fred Harman 15.00 37.50 105.00

1475- Red Ryder and the Outlaw of Painted Valley, 1943, Whitman, 352 pgs., by Harman 14.00 35.00 95.00

702-10- Red Ryder Acting Sheriff, 1949, Whitman, by Fred Hannan 12.00 30.00 85.00

nn- Red Ryder Brings Law to Devil's Hole, 1939, Dell, 196 pgs., Fast-Action Story, Harman-c/a 44.00 110.00 310.00

nn- Red Ryder and the Highway Robbers, 1938, Whitman, 36 pgs., 2 1/2" x 3 1/2", Penny Book 12.00 30.00 85.00

754- Reg'lar Fellers, 1933, Whitman, 320 pgs., by Gene Byrnes 13.00 32.50 90.00

nn- Reg'lar Fellers, 1933, Whitman, 202 pgs., Cocomalt premium, by Gene Byrnes 13.00 32.50 90.00

1424- Rex Beach's Jaragu of the Jungle, 1937, Whitman, 432 pgs. 11.00 27.50 70.00

12- Rex, King of Wild Horses in "Stampede," 1935, EVW, 160 pgs., movie scenes, Columbia Pictures 12.00 30.00 75.00

1100B- Riddles for Fun, 1938, Whitman, 36 pgs., 2 1/2" x 3 1/2", Penny Book 4.00 10.00 27.00

1100B- Riddles to Guess, 1938, Whitman, 36 pgs., 2 1/2" x 3 1/2", Penny Book 4.00 10.00 27.00

1425- Riders of Lone Trails, 1937, Whitman, 300 pgs. 12.00 30.00 75.00

1141- Rio Raiders (A Billy The Kid Story), 1938, Saalfield, 400 pgs. 12.00 30.00 75.00

2023-(#23)- The Road Runner, The Super Beep Catcher, 1968, Whitman, 256 pgs., hard-c, color illos. 1.00 2.50 9.00

5759- The Road Runner, The Super Beep Catcher, 1973, Whitman, 256 pgs., soft-c, 39 cents, B&W illos., and flip pictures 1.00 2.50 6.00

5767-2- Road Runner, The Lost Road Runner Mine, The, 1974 (1980), 260 pgs., 79 cents, B&W, soft-c 1.00 2.50 6.00

5784- The Road Runner and the Unidentified Coyote, 1974, Whitman, 260 pgs., soft-c, flip pictures 1.00 2.50 6.00

5784-2- The Road Runner and the Unidentified Coyote, 1980, Whitman, 260 pgs., soft-c, flip pictures 1.00 2.50 6.00

nn- Road To Perdition, 2002, Dreamworks, screenplay from movie, hard-c (Dreamworks and 20th Century Fox) 1.00 2.50 9.00

Robin Hood (See Wee Little Books)

10- Robin Hood, 1935, EVW, 160 pgs., movie scenes w/Douglas Fairbanks (United Artists), hard-c 18.00 45.00 125.00

719- Robinson Crusoe (The Story of...), nd (1933), Whitman, 364 pgs., soft-c 13.00 32.50 90.00

1421- Roy Rogers and the Dwarf-Cattle Ranch, 1947, Whitman, 352 pgs., Henry E. Vallely-a 18.00 45.00 125.00

1437- Roy Rogers and the Deadly Treasure, 1947, Whitman, 288 pgs. 18.00 45.00 125.00

1448- Roy Rogers and the Mystery of the Howling Mesa, 1948, Whitman, 288 pgs. 18.00 45.00 125.00

1452- Roy Rogers in Robbers' Roost, 1948, Whitman, 288 pgs. 18.00 45.00 125.00

1460- Roy Rogers Robinhood of the Range, 1942, Whitman, 432 pgs., Hess-a (1st) 21.00 52.50 145.00

1462- Roy Rogers and the Mystery of the Lazy M, 1949, Whitman 15.00 37.50 105.00

1476- Roy Rogers King of the Cowboys, 1943, Whitman, 352 pgs., Irwin Myers-a, based on movie 22.00 52.50 155.00

1494- Roy Rogers at Crossed Feathers Ranch, 1945, Whitman, 320 pgs., Erwin Hess-a , 3 1/4" x 5 1/2" 18.00 45.00 125.00

701-10- Roy Rogers and the Snowbound Outlaws, 1949, 3 1/4" x 5 1/2" 12.00 30.00 85.00

715-10- Roy Rogers Range Detective, 1950, Whitman, 2 1/2" x 5" 12.00 30.00 85.00

nn- Sandy Gregg Federal Agent on Special Assignment, 1939, Whitman, 36 pgs., 2 1/2" x 3 1/2", Penny Book 11.00 27.50 70.00

Sappo (See Top-Line Comics)

1122- Scrappy, 1934, Whitman, 288 pgs. 20.00 50.00 140.00

L12- Scrappy (The Adventures of...), 1935, Lynn, 192 pgs., movie scenes 20.00 50.00 140.00

1191- Secret Agent K-7,1940, Saalfield, 400 pgs., based on radio show 11.00 27.50 70.00

1144- Secret Agent X-9, 1936, Whitman, 432 pgs., Charles Flanders-a 15.00 37.50 105.00

1472- Secret Agent X-9 and the Mad Assassin, 1938, Whitman, 432 pgs., Charles Flanders-a 15.00 37.50 105.00

1161- Sequoia, 1935, Whitman, 160 pgs., photo-c, movie scenes 12.00 30.00 85.00

1430- Shadow and the Living Death, The, 1940, Whitman, 432 pgs., Erwin Hess-a 65.00 163.00 460.00

1443- Shadow and the Master of Evil, The, 1941, Whitman, 432 pgs., flip pictures, Hess-a 65.00 163.00 460.00

1495- Shadow and the Ghost Makers, The, 1942, Whitman, 432 pgs., John Coleman Burroughs-c 65.00 163.00 460.00

2024- Shazzan, The Glass Princess, 1968, Whitman, Hanna-Barbera 4.00 10.00 27.00

Shirley Temple (See My Life and Times & Story of..)

1095- Shirley Temple and Lionel Barrymore Starring In "The Little Colonel," 1935, Saalfield, photo hard-c, movie scenes 20.00 50.00 140.00

1115- Shirley Temple in "The Littlest Rebel," 1935, Saalfield, photo-c, movie scenes, hard-c 20.00 50.00 140.00

1575- Shirley Temple and Lionel Barrymore Starring In "The Little Colonel," 1935, Saalfield, photo soft-c, movie scenes 20.00 50.00 140.00

1595- Shirley Temple in "The Littlest Rebel," 1935, Saalfield, photo-c, movie scenes, soft-c 20.00 50.00 140.00

1195- Shooting Sheriffs of the Wild West, 1936, Whitman, 432 pgs. 11.00 27.50 70.00

1169- Silly Symphony Featuring Donald Duck (Disney), 1937, Whitman, 432 pgs., Taliaferro-a 38.00 95.00 255.00

1441- Silly Symphony Featuring Donald Duck and His (MIS) Adventures (Disney), 1937, Whitman, 432 pgs., Taliaferro-a 38.00 95.00 255.00

1155- Silver Streak, The, 1935, Whitman, 160 pgs., photo-c, movie scenes (RKO Radio Pict.) 12.00 30.00 75.00

Simple Simon (See Wee Little Books)

1649- Sir Lancelot (TV Series), 1958, Whitman, 280 pgs. 7.00 17.50 44.00

1112- Skeezix in Africa, 1934, Whitman, 300 pgs., Frank King-a 14.00 35.00 95.00

1408- Skeezix at the Military Academy, 1938, Whitman, 432 pgs., Frank King-a 14.00 35.00 95.00

1152 - Smilin' Jack and the Stratosphere Ascent © WHIT

1467 - Spike Kelly of the Commandos © WHIT

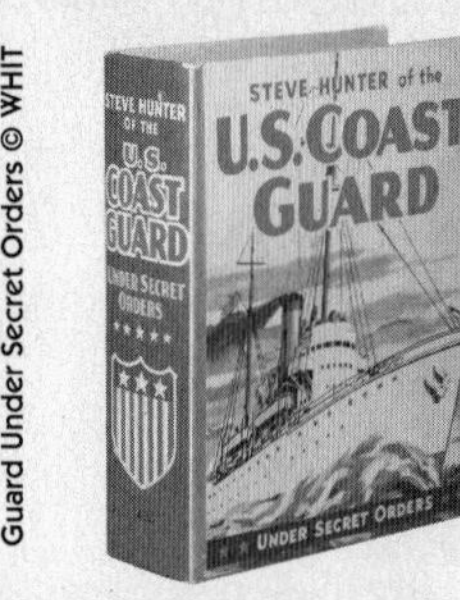

1426 - Steve Hunter of the U.S. Coast Guard Under Secret Orders © WHIT

	GD	FN	VF/NM
1414- Skeezix Goes to War, 1944, Whitman, 352 pgs., Frank King-a	14.00	35.00	95.00
1419- Skeezix on His Own in the Big City, 1941, Whitman, All Pictures Comics, flip pictures, Frank King-a	14.00	35.00	95.00
761- Skippy, 1934, Whitman, 320 pgs., by Percy Crosby	14.00	35.00	95.00
4056- Skippy, The Story of, 1934, Whitman, 320 pgs., 7" x 9 1/2", Big Big Book, Percy Crosby-a	70.00	175.00	490.00
nn- Skippy, The Story of, 1934, Whitman, Phillips Dental Magnesia premium, soft-c, by Percy Crosby	14.00	35.00	95.00
1439- Skyroads with Clipper Williams of the Flying Legion, 1938, Whitman, 432 pgs., by Lt. Dick Calkins, Russell Keaton-a	12.00	30.00	85.00
1127- Skyroads with Hurricane Hawk, 1936, Whitman, 432 pgs., by Lt. Dick Calkins, Russell Keaton-a	12.00	30.00	80.00
Smilin' Jack and his Flivver Plane (See Top-Line Comics)			
1152- Smilin' Jack and the Stratosphere Ascent, 1937, Whitman, 432 pgs., Zack Mosley-a	16.00	40.00	115.00
1412- Smilin' Jack Flying High with "Downwind," 1942, Whitman, 432 pgs., Zack Mosley-a	15.00	37.50	105.00
1416- Smilin' Jack in Wings over the Pacific, 1939, Whitman, 432 pgs., Zack Mosley-a	15.00	37.50	105.00
1419- Smilin' Jack and the Jungle Pipe Line, 1947, Whitman, 352 pgs., Zack Mosley-a	12.00	30.00	85.00
1445- Smilin' Jack and the Escape from Death Rock, 1943, Whitman, 352 pgs., Mosley-a	12.00	30.00	85.00
1464- Smilin' Jack and the Coral Princess, 1945, Whitman, 352 pgs., Zack Mosley-a	12.00	30.00	85.00
1473- Smilin' Jack Speed Pilot, 1941, Whitman, 432 pgs., Zack Mosley-a	16.00	40.00	115.00
2- Smilin' Jack and his Stratosphere Plane, 1938, Whitman, 132 pgs., Buddy Book, soft-c, Zack Mosley-a	39.00	98.00	275.00
nn- Smilin' Jack Grounded on a Tropical Shore, 1938, Whitman, 36 pgs., 2 1/2" x 3 1/2", Penny Book	11.00	27.50	70.00
11- Smilin' Jack and the Border Bandits, 1941, Dell, 196 pgs., Fast-Action Story, soft-c, Zack Mosley-a	36.00	90.00	255.00
745- Smitty Golden Gloves Tournament, 1934, Whitman, 320 pgs., Walter Berndt-a	15.00	37.50	105.00
nn- Smitty Golden Gloves Tournament, 1934, Whitman, 204 pgs., Cocomalt premium, soft-c, Walter Berndt-a	16.00	40.00	115.00
1404- Smitty and Herby Lost Among the Indians, 1941, Whitman, All Pictures Comics	11.00	27.50	70.00
1477- Smitty in Going Native, 1938, Whitman, 300 pgs., Walter Berndt-a	11.00	27.50	70.00
2- Smitty and Herby, 1936, Whitman, 132 pgs., 3 1/2" x 3 1/2", soft-c, Tarzan Ice Cream cup lid premium	36.00	90.00	255.00
9- Smitty's Brother Herby and the Police Horse, 1938, Whitman, 132 pgs., 3 1/4" x 3 1/2", Buddy Book-ice cream premium, by Walter Berndt	36.00	90.00	255.00
1010- Smokey Stover Firefighter of Foo, 1937, Whitman, 7 1/4" x 5 1/2", 64 pgs., Nickel Book, Bill Holman-a	16.00	40.00	115.00
1413- Smokey Stover, 1942, Whitman, All Pictures Comics, flip pictures, Bill Holman-a	14.00	35.00	95.00
1421- Smokey Stover the Foo Fighter, 1938, Whitman, 432 pgs., Bill Holman-a	14.00	35.00	95.00
1481- Smokey Stover the Foolish Foo Fighter, 1942, Whitman, All Pictures Comics	14.00	35.00	95.00
1- Smokey Stover the Fireman of Foo, 1938, Whitman, 3 3/4" x 3 1/2", 132 pgs., Buddy Book-ice cream premium, by Bill Holman	41.00	103.00	285.00
1100A- Smokey Stover, 1938, Whitman, 36 pgs., 2 1/2" x 3 1/2", Penny Book	12.00	30.00	80.00
nn- Smokey Stover and the Fire Chief of Foo, 1938, Whitman, 36 pgs., 2 1/2" x 3 1/2", Penny Book, yellow shirt on-c	12.00	30.00	80.00
nn- Smokey Stover and the Fire Chief of Foo, 1938, Whitman, 36 pgs., Penny Book, green shirt on-c	12.00	30.00	80.00
1460- Snow White and the Seven Dwarfs (The Story of Walt Disney's ...), 1938, Whitman, 288 pgs.	29.00	73.00	200.00
1136- Sombrero Pete, 1936, Whitman, 432 pgs.	11.00	27.50	70.00
1152- Son of Mystery, 1939, Saalfield, 400 pgs.	11.00	27.50	70.00
1191- SOS Coast Guard, 1936, Whitman, 432 pgs., Henry E. Vallely-a	12.00	30.00	75.00
2016-(#16)-Space Ghost-The Sorceress of Cyba-3 (TV Cartoon), 1968, Whitman, 260 pgs., 39¢-c, hard-c, color illos	10.00	25.00	60.00
1455- Speed Douglas and the Mole Gang-The Great Sabotage Plot, 1941, Whitman, 432 pgs., flip pictures	11.00	27.50	70.00
5779- Spider-Man Zaps Mr. Zodiac, 1976, 260 pgs., soft-c, B&W	1.00	2.50	9.00
5779-2- Spider-Man Zaps Mr. Zodiac, 1980, 260 pgs., 79¢-c, soft-c, B&W	1.00	2.50	6.00
1467- Spike Kelly of the Commandos, 1943, Whitman, 352 pgs.	11.00	27.50	70.00
1144- Spook Riders on the Overland, 1938, Saalfield, 400 pgs.	11.00	27.50	70.00
768- Spy, The, 1936, Whitman, 300 pgs.	13.00	32.50	90.00
nn- Spy Smasher and the Red Death, 1941, Fawcett, 4" x 5 1/2", Dime Action Book	58.00	146.00	410.00
1120- Stan Kent Freshman Fullback, 1936, Saalfield, 148 pgs., hard-c	9.00	22.50	55.00
1132- Stan Kent, Captain, 1937, Saalfield	9.00	22.50	55.00
1600- Stan Kent Freshman Fullback, 1936, Saalfield, 148 pgs., soft-c	9.00	22.50	55.00
1123- Stan Kent Varsity Man, 1936, Saalfield, 160 pgs., hard-c	9.00	22.50	55.00
1603- Stan Kent Varsity Man, 1936, Saalfield, 160 pgs., soft-c	9.00	22.50	55.00
nn- Star Wars - A New Hope, 1997, Chronicle Books, 320 pgs., adapts movie, 1-color (blue) illos	3.00	7.50	20.00
nn- Star Wars - Empire Strikes Back, The, 1997, Chronicle Books, 296 pgs., adapts movie, 1-color (blue) illos	3.00	7.50	20.00
nn- Star Wars - Episode 1 - The Phantom Menace, 1999, Chronicle Books, 344 pgs., adapts movie, 1-color (blue) illos	1.00	2.50	9.00
nn- Star Wars - Episode 2 - Attack of the Clones, 2002, Chronicle Books, 340 pgs., adapts movie, 1-color (blue) illos	1.00	2.50	9.00
nn- Star Wars - Return of the Jedi, 1997, Chronicle Books, 312 pgs., adapts movie, 1-color (blue) illos	3.00	7.50	20.00
1104- Steel Arena, The (With Clyde Beatty), 1936, Saalfield, hard-c, movie scenes adapted from "The Lost Jungle"	12.00	30.00	85.00
1584- Steel Arena, The (With Clyde Beatty), 1936, Saalfield, soft-c, movie scenes	12.00	30.00	85.00
1426- Steve Hunter of the U.S. Coast Guard Under Secret Orders, 1942, Whitman, 432 pgs.	11.00	27.50	70.00
1456- Story of Charlie McCarthy and Edgar Bergen, The, 1938, Whitman, 288 pgs.	15.00	37.50	105.00
Story of Daniel, The (See Wee Little Books)			
Story of David, The (See Wee Little Books)			
1110- Story of Freddie Bartholomew, The, 1935, Saalfield, 4 1/2" x 5 1/4", hard-c, movie scenes (MGM)	12.00	30.00	75.00
1590- Story of Freddie Bartholomew, The, 1935, Saalfield, 4 1/2" x 5 1/4", soft-c, movie scenes (MGM)	12.00	30.00	75.00
Story of Gideon, The (See Wee Little Books)			
W714- Story of Jackie Cooper, The, 1933, Whitman, 240 pgs., photo-c, movie scenes, "Skippy" & "Sooky" movie	15.00	37.50	105.00
Story of Joseph, The (See Wee Little Books)			
Story of Moses, The (See Wee Little Books)			
Story of Ruth and Naomi (See Wee Little Books)			
1089- Story of Shirley Temple, The, 1934, Saalfield, 160 pgs., hard-c, photo-c, movie scenes	13.00	32.50	90.00
1319- Story of Shirley Temple, The, 1934, Saalfield, 160 pgs., soft-c, photo-c, movie scenes	13.00	32.50	90.00
1090- Strawberry-Roan, 1934, Saalfield, 160 pgs., hard-c, Ken Maynard photo-c, movie scenes	13.00	32.50	90.00
1320- Strawberry-Roan, 1934, Saalfield, 160 pgs., soft-c, Ken Maynard photo-c, movie scenes	13.00	32.50	90.00
Streaky and the Football Signals (See Top-Line Comics)			
5780-2- Superman in the Phantom Zone Connection, 1980, 260 pgs., 79¢-c, soft-c, B&W	1.00	2.50	9.00
582- "Swap It" Book, The, 1949, Samuel Lowe Co., 260 pgs., 3 1/2" x 4 1/2"			
1. Little Tex in the Midst of Trouble	7.00	17.50	44.00
2. Little Tex's Escape	7.00	17.50	44.00

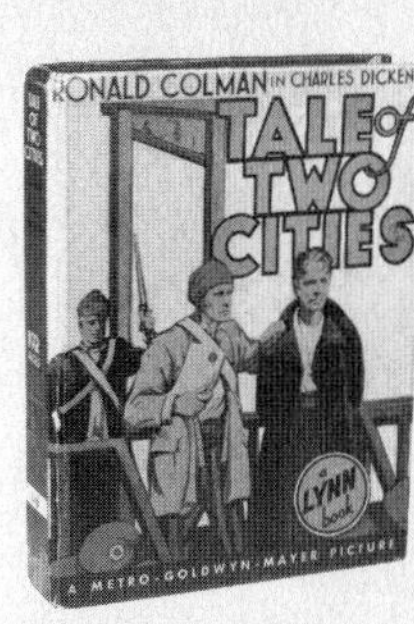

L16 - A Tale of Two Cities © LYNN

1442 - Tarzan and the Lost Empire © ERB

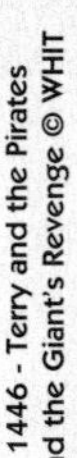

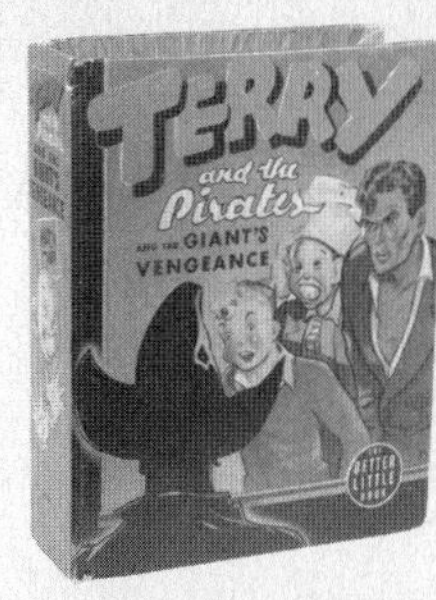

1446 - Terry and the Pirates and the Giant's Revenge © WHIT

	GD	FN	VF/NM
3. Little Tex Comes to the XY Ranch	7.00	17.50	44.00
4. Get Them Cowboy	7.00	17.50	44.00
5. The Mail Must Go Through! A Story of the Pony Express	7.00	17.50	44.00
6. Nevada Jones, Trouble Shooter	7.00	17.50	44.00
7. Danny Meets the Cowboys	7.00	17.50	44.00
8. Flint Adams and the Stage Coach	7.00	17.50	44.00
9. Bud Shinners and the Oregon Trail	7.00	17.50	44.00
10. The Outlaws' Last Ride	7.00	17.50	44.00
Sybil Jason (See Little Big Shot)			
747- **Tailspin Tommy in the Famous Pay-Roll Mystery**, 1933, Whitman, hard-c, 320 pgs., Hal Forrest-a (# 1)	15.00	37.50	105.00
747- **Tailspin Tommy in the Famous Pay-Roll Mystery**, 1933, Whitman, soft-c, 320 pgs., Hal Forrest-a (# 1)	15.00	37.50	105.00
nn- **Tailspin Tommy the Pay-Roll Mystery**, 1934, Whitman, 52 pgs., 3 1/2" x 5 1/4", premium-no ads, soft-c; another version with Perkins ad, Hal Forrest-a	26.00	65.00	185.00
1110- **Tailspin Tommy and the Island in the Sky,** 1936, Whitman, 432 pgs., Hal Forrest-a	13.00	32.50	90.00
1124- **Tailspin Tommy the Dirigible Flight to the North Pole**, 1934, Whitman, 432 pgs., H. Forrest-a	15.00	37.50	105.00
nn- **Tailspin Tommy the Dirigible Flight to the North Pole**, 1934, Whitman, 436 pgs., 3-color, soft-c, premium-no ads, Hal Forrest-a	36.00	90.00	255.00
1172- **Tailspin Tommy Hunting for Pirate Gold**, 1935, Whitman, 432 pgs., Hal Forrest-a	13.00	32.50	90.00
1183- **Tailspin Tommy Air Racer**, 1940, Saalfield, 400 pgs., hard-c	13.00	32.50	90.00
1184- **Tailspin Tommy in the Great Air Mystery**, 1936, Whitman, 240 pgs., photo-c, movie scenes	15.00	37.50	105.00
1410- **Tailspin Tommy the Weasel and His "Skywaymen,"** 1941, Whitman, All Pictures Comics, flip pictures	12.00	30.00	80.00
1413- **Tailspin Tommy and the Lost Transport**, 1940, Whitman, 432 pgs., Hal Forrest-a	12.00	30.00	80.00
1423- **Tailspin Tommy and the Hooded Flyer**, 1937, Whitman, 432 pgs., Hal Forrest-a	13.00	32.50	90.00
1494- **Tailspin Tommy and the Sky Bandits**, 1938, Whitman 432 pgs., Hal Forrest-a	13.00	32.50	90.00
nn- **Tailspin Tommy and the Airliner Mystery**, 1938, Dell, 196 pgs., Fast-Action Story, soft-c, Hal Forrest-a	47.00	118.00	330.00
nn- **Tailspin Tommy in Flying Aces**, 1938, Dell, 196 pgs., Fast-Action Story, soft-c, Hal Forrest-a	47.00	118.00	330.00
nn- **Tailspin Tommy in Wings Over the Arctic**, 1934, Whitman, Cocomalt premium, Forrest-a	20.00	50.00	140.00
nn- **Tailspin Tommy Big Thrill Chewing Gum**, 1934, Whitman, 8 pgs., 2 1/2" x 3 " (6 diff.) each..	13.00	32.50	90.00
3- **Tailspin Tommy on the Mountain of Human Sacrifice**, 1938, Whitman, soft-c, Buddy Book	43.00	108.00	300.00
7- **Tailspin Tommy's Perilous Adventure**, 1934, Whitman, 132 pgs., 3 1/2" x 3 1/2" soft-c, Tarzan Ice Cream cup premium	43.00	108.00	300.00
nn- **Tailspin Tommy**, 1935, Whitman, 148 pgs., 3 1/2" x 4", Tarzan Ice Cream cup premium	54.00	135.00	385.00
L16- **Tale of Two Cities, A**, 1935, Lynn, movie scenes	15.00	37.50	105.00
744- **Tarzan of the Apes**, 1933, Whitman, 320 pgs., by Edgar Rice Burroughs (1st)	46.00	115.00	325.00
nn- **Tarzan of the Apes**, 1935, Whitman, 52 pgs., 3 1/2" x 5 1/4", soft-c, stapled, premium, no ad; another version with a Perkins ad	58.00	146.00	410.00
769- **Tarzan the Fearless**, 1934, Whitman, 240 pgs., Buster Crabbe photo-c, movie scenes, ERB	33.00	83.00	230.00
770- **Tarzan Twins, The**, 1934, Whitman, 432 pgs., ERB	118.00	295.00	825.00
770- **Tarzan Twins, The**, 1935, Whitman, 432 pgs., ERB	58.00	146.00	410.00
nn- **Tarzan Twins, The**, 1935, Whitman, 52 pgs., 3 1/2" x 5 3/4", premium-no ads, soft-c, ERB	79.00	198.00	550.00
nn- **Tarzan Twins, The**, 1935, Whitman, 436 pgs., 3-color, soft-c, premium-no ads, ERB	84.00	210.00	580.00

	GD	FN	VF/NM
778- **Tarzan of the Screen** (The Story of Johnny Weissmuller), 1934, Whitman, 240 pgs., photo-c, movie scenes, ERB	34.00	85.00	240.00
1102- **Tarzan, The Return of**, 1936, Whitman, 432 pgs., Edgar Rice Burroughs	24.00	60.00	170.00
1180- **Tarzan, The New Adventures of**, 1935, Whitman, 160 pgs., Herman Brix photo-c, movie scenes, ERB	28.00	70.00	195.00
1182- **Tarzan Escapes**, 1936, Whitman, 240 pgs., Johnny Weissmuller photo-c, movie scenes, ERB	34.00	85.00	240.00
1407- **Tarzan Lord of the Jungle**, 1946, Whitman, 352 pgs., ERB	18.00	45.00	125.00
1410- **Tarzan, The Beasts of**, 1937, Whitman, 432 pgs., Edgar Rice Burroughs	21.00	52.50	145.00
1442- **Tarzan and the Lost Empire**, 1948, Whitman, 288 pgs., ERB	18.00	45.00	125.00
1444- **Tarzan and the Ant Men**, 1945, Whitman, 352 pgs., ERB	18.00	45.00	125.00
1448- **Tarzan and the Golden Lion**, 1943, Whitman, 432 pgs., ERB	22.00	52.50	155.00
1452- **Tarzan the Untamed**, 1941, Whitman, 432 pgs., flip pictures, ERB	22.00	52.50	155.00
1453- **Tarzan the Terrible**, 1942, Whitman, 432 pgs., flip pictures, ERB	22.00	52.50	155.00
1467- **Tarzan in the Land of the Giant Apes**, 1949, Whitman, ERB	18.00	45.00	125.00
1477- **Tarzan, The Son of**, 1939, Whitman, 432 pgs., ERB	22.00	52.50	155.00
1488- **Tarzan's Revenge**, 1938, Whitman, 432 pgs., ERB	22.00	52.50	155.00
1495- **Tarzan and the Jewels of Opar**, 1940, Whitman, 432 pgs.	22.00	52.50	155.00
4056- **Tarzan and the Tarzan Twins with Jad-Bal-Ja the Golden Lion**, 1936, Whitman, 7" x 9 1/2", 320 pgs., Big Big Book	115.00	288.00	810.00
709-10- **Tarzan and the Journey of Terror**, 1950, Whitman, 2 1/2" x 5", ERB, Marsh-a	12.00	30.00	75.00
2005- **(#5)-Tarzan: The Mark of the Red Hyena**, 1967, Whitman, 260 pgs., 39 cents, hard-c, color illos	4.00	10.00	27.00
nn- **Tarzan**, 1935, Whitman, 148 pgs., soft-c, 3 1/2" x 4", Tarzan Ice Cream cup premium, ERB (scarce)	130.00	327.00	1045.00
nn- **Tarzan and a Daring Rescue**, 1938, Whitman, 68 pgs., Pan-Am premium, soft-c, ERB (blank back-c version also exists)	71.00	178.00	500.00
nn- **Tarzan and his Jungle Friends**, 1936, Whitman, 132 pgs., soft-c, 3 1/2" x 3 1/2", Tarzan Ice Cream cup premium, ERB (scarce)	114.00	285.00	800.00
nn- **Tarzan in the Golden City**, 1938, Whitman, 68 pgs., Pan-Am premium, soft-c, ERB	71.00	178.00	500.00
nn- **Tarzan The Avenger**, 1939, Dell, 194 pgs., Fast-Action Story, ERB, soft-c	47.00	118.00	330.00
nn- **Tarzan with the Tarzan Twins in the Jungle**, 1938, Dell, 194 pgs., Fast-Action Story, ERB	47.00	118.00	330.00
1100B- **Tell Your Fortune**, 1938, Whitman, 36 pgs., 2 1/2" x 3 1/2", Penny Book	5.00	12.50	33.00
nn- **Terminator 2: Judgment Day**, 1998, Chronicle Books, 310 pgs., adapts movie, 1-color (blue-gray) illos	1.00	2.50	9.00
1156- **Terry and the Pirates**, 1935, Whitman, 432 pgs., Milton Caniff-a (#1)	18.00	45.00	125.00
nn- **Terry and the Pirates**, 1935, Whitman, 52 pgs., 3 1/2" x 5 1/4", soft-c, premium, Milton Caniff-a; 3 versions: No ad, Sears ad & Perkins ad	31.00	78.00	220.00
1412- **Terry and the Pirates Shipwrecked on a Desert Island**, 1938, Whitman, 432 pgs., Milton Caniff-a	15.00	37.50	105.00
1420- **Terry and War in the Jungle**, 1946, Whitman, 352 pgs., Milton Caniff-a	13.00	32.50	90.00
1436- **Terry and the Pirates The Plantation Mystery**, 1942, Whitman, 432 pgs., flip pictures, Milton Caniff-a	15.00	37.50	105.00
1446- **Terry and the Pirates and the Giant's Vengeance**, 1939, Whitman, 432 pgs., Caniff-a	15.00	37.50	105.00
1499- **Terry and the Pirates in the Mountain Stronghold**,			

nn - The Texas Ranger and The Rustler Gang © WHIT

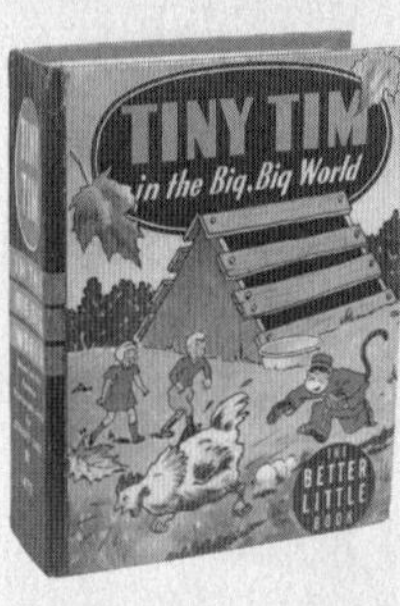

1472 - Tiny Tim in the Big, Big World © WHIT

nn - Tom Mix in The Fighting Cowboy © WHIT

GD FN VF/NM

1941, Whitman, 432 pgs., Caniff-a 15.00 37.50 105.00
4073- Terry and the Pirates, The Adventures of, 1938, Whitman, 7" x 9 1/2", 320 pgs., Big Big Book, Milton Caniff-a 87.00 218.00 605.00
4- Terry and the Pirates Ashore in Singapore, 1938, Whitman, 132 pgs., 3 1/2" x 3 3/4", soft-c, Buddy Book premium 38.00 95.00 255.00
10- Terry and the Pirates Meet Again, 1936, Whitman, 132 pgs., 3 1/2" x 3 1/2", soft-c, Tarzan Ice Cream cup lid premium 58.00 146.00 410.00
nn- Terry and the Pirates, Adventures of, 1938, 36 pgs., 2 1/2" x 3 1/2", Penny Book, Caniff-a 11.00 27.50 70.00
nn- Terry and the Pirates and the Island Rescue, 1938, Whitman, 68 pgs., 3 1/4" x 3 1/2", Pan-Am premium 29.00 73.00 200.00
nn- Terry and the Pirates on Their Travels, 1938, 36 pgs., 2 1/2" x 3 1/2", Penny Book, Caniff-a 11.00 27.50 70.00
nn- Terry and the Pirates and the Mystery Ship, 1938, Dell, 194 pgs., Fast-Action Story, soft-c 39.00 98.00 275.00
1492- Terry Lee Flight Officer U.S.A., 1944, Whitman, 352 pgs., Milton Caniff-a 12.00 30.00 85.00
7- Texas Bad Man, The (Tom Mix), 1934, EVW, 160 pgs., (Five Star Library), movie scenes 24.00 60.00 165.00
1429- Texas Kid, The, 1937, Whitman, 432 pgs. 11.00 27.50 70.00
1135- Texas Ranger, The, 1936, Whitman, 432 pgs., Hal Arbo-a 11.00 27.50 70.00
nn- Texas Ranger, The, 1935, Whitman, 260 pgs., Cocomalt premium, soft-c, Hal Arbo-a 12.00 30.00 85.00
nn- Texas Ranger and the Rustler Gang, The, 1936, Whitman, Pan-Am giveaway 29.00 73.00 200.00
nn- Texas Ranger in the West, The, 1938, Whitman, 36 pgs., 2 1/2" x 3 1/2", Penny Book 10.00 25.00 65.00
nn- Texas Ranger to the Rescue, The, 1938, Whitman, 36 pgs., 2 1/2" x 3 1/2", Penny Book 10.00 25.00 65.00
12- Texas Ranger in Rustler Strategy, The, 1936, Whitman, 132 pgs., 3 1/2" x 3 1/2", soft-c, Tarzan Ice Cream cup lid premium 36.00 90.00 255.00
Tex Thorne (See Zane Grey)
Thimble Theatre (See Popeye)
26- 13 Hours By Air, 1936, Lynn, 128 pgs., 5" x 7 1/2", photo-c, movie scenes (Paramount Pictures) 14.00 35.00 95.00
nn- Three Bears, The, nd (1930s), np (Whitman), 36 pgs., 3" x 2 1/2", Penny Book 4.00 10.00 22.00
1129- Three Finger Joe (Baseball), 1937, Saalfield, Robert A. Graef-a 10.00 25.00 65.00
nn- Three Little Pigs, The, nd (1930s), np (Whitman), 36 pgs., 3" x 2 1/2", Penny Book 4.00 10.00 22.00
1131- Three Musketeers, 1935, Whitman, 182 pgs., 5 1/4" x 6 1/4", photo-c, movie scenes 18.00 45.00 125.00
1409- Thumper and the Seven Dwarfs (Disney), 1944, Whitman, All Pictures Comics 24.00 60.00 165.00
1108- Tiger Lady, The (The life of Mabel Stark, animal trainer), 1935, Saalfield, photo-c, movie scenes, hard-c 11.00 27.50 70.00
1588- Tiger Lady, The, 1935, Saalfield, photo-c, movie scenes, soft-c 11.00 27.50 70.00
1442- Tillie the Toiler and the Wild Man of Desert Island, 1941, Whitman, 432 pgs., Russ Westover-a 12.00 30.00 85.00
1058- "Timid Elmer" (Disney), 1939, Whitman, 5" x 5 1/2", 68 pgs., hard-c 12.00 30.00 85.00
1152- Tim McCoy in the Prescott Kid, 1935, Whitman, 160 pgs., hard-c, photo-c, movie scenes 20.00 50.00 140.00
1193- Tim McCoy in the Westerner, 1936, Whitman, 240 pgs., photo-c, movie scenes 18.00 45.00 125.00
1436- Tim McCoy on the Tomahawk Trail, 1937, Whitman, 432 pgs., Robert Weisman-a 12.00 30.00 85.00
1490- Tim McCoy and the Sandy Gulch Stampede, 1939, Whitman, 424 pgs. 12.00 30.00 75.00
2- Tim McCoy in Beyond the Law, 1934, EVW, Five Star Library, photo-c, movie scenes (Columbia Pict.) Hardcover 21.00 52.00 145.00
(Rare) Softcover 54.00 135.00 375.00
10- Tim McCoy in Fighting the Redskins, 1938, Whitman, 130 pgs., Buddy Book, soft-c 34.00 85.00 240.00
14- Tim McCoy in Speedwings, 1935, EVW, Five Star Library, 160 pgs., photo-c, movie scenes (Columbia Pictures) 24.00 60.00 165.00
nn- Tim the Builder, nd (1930s), np (Whitman), 36 pgs., 3" x 2 1/2", Penny Book 4.00 10.00 22.00
Tim Tyler (Also see Adventures of ...)
1140- Tim Tyler's Luck Adventures in the Ivory Patrol, 1937, Whitman, 432 pgs., by Lyman Young 13.00 32.50 90.00
1479- Tim Tyler's Luck and the Plot of the Exiled King, 1939, Whitman, 432 pgs., by Lyman Young 12.00 30.00 80.00
767- Tiny Tim, The Adventures of, 1935, Whitman, 384 pgs., by Stanley Link 15.00 37.50 105.00
1172- Tiny Tim and the Mechanical Men, 1937, Whitman, 432 pgs., by Stanley Link 13.00 32.50 90.00
1472- Tiny Tim in the Big, Big World, 1945, Whitman, 352 pgs., by Stanley Link 13.00 32.50 90.00
2006- (#6)-Tom and Jerry Meet Mr. Fingers, 1967, Whitman, 39¢-c 260 pgs., hard-c, color illos. 4.00 10.00 27.00
5752- Tom and Jerry Meet Mr. Fingers, 1973, Whitman, 39¢-c 260 pgs., soft-c, color illos., 5 printings 2.00 5.00 11.00
2030-(#30)- Tom and Jerry, The Astro-Nots, 1969, Whitman, 256 pgs., hard-c, color illos. 3.00 7.50 20.00
5765- Tom and Jerry, The Astro-Nots, 1974, Whitman, 256 pgs., soft-c, color illos. 2.00 5.00 11.00
5787-2- Tom and Jerry Under the Big Top, 1980, Whitman, 79¢-c, 260 pgs., soft-c, B&W 2.00 5.00 11.00
723- Tom Beatty Ace of the Service, 1934, Whitman, 256 pgs., George Taylor-a 13.00 32.50 90.00
nn- Tom Beatty Ace of the Service, 1934, Whitman, 260 pgs., soft-c 13.00 32.50 90.00
1165- Tom Beatty Ace of the Service Scores Again, 1937, Whitman, 432 pgs., Weisman-a 12.00 30.00 80.00
1420- Tom Beatty Ace of the Service and the Big Brain Gang, 1939, Whitman, 432 pgs. 12.00 30.00 80.00
nn- Tom Beatty Ace Detective and the Gorgon Gang, 1938?, Whitman, 36 pgs., 2 1/2" x 3 1/2", Penny Book 11.00 27.50 70.00
nn- Tom Beatty Ace of the Service and the Kidnapers, 1938?, Whitman, 36 pgs., 2 1/2" x 3 1/2", Penny Book 11.00 27.50 70.00
1102- Tom Mason on Top, 1935, Saalfield, 160 pgs., Tom Mix photo-c, from Mascot serial "The Miracle Rider," movie scenes, hard-c 20.00 50.00 140.00
1582- Tom Mason on Top, 1935, Saalfield, 160 pgs., Tom Mix photo-c, movie scenes, soft-c 20.00 50.00 140.00
Tom Mix (See Chief of the Rangers, Flaming Guns & Texas Bad Man)
762- Tom Mix and Tony Jr. in "Terror Trail," 1934, Whitman, 160 pgs., movie scenes 20.00 50.00 140.00
1144- Tom Mix in the Fighting Cowboy, 1935, Whitman, 432 pgs., Hal Arbo-a 15.00 37.50 105.00
nn- Tom Mix in the Fighting Cowboy, 1935, Whitman, 436 pgs., premium-no ads, 3 color, soft-c, Hal Arbo-a 29.00 73.00 200.00
1166- Tom Mix in the Range War, 1937, Whitman, 432 pgs., Hal Arbo-a 12.00 30.00 85.00
1173- Tom Mix Plays a Lone Hand, 1935, Whitman, 288 pgs., hard-c, Hal Arbo-a 12.00 30.00 85.00
1183- Tom Mix and the Stranger from the South, 1936, Whitman, 432 pgs. 12.00 30.00 85.00
1462- Tom Mix and the Hoard of Montezuma, 1937, Whitman, H. E. Vallely-a 12.00 30.00 85.00
1482- Tom Mix and His Circus on the Barbary Coast, 1940, Whitman, 432 pgs., James Gary-a 12.00 30.00 85.00
3047- Tom Mix and His Big Little Kit, 1937, Whitman, 384 pgs., 4 1/2" x 6 1/2" box, includes miniature box of 4 crayons-red, yellow, blue and green 100.00 250.00 700.00
4068- Tom Mix and the Scourge of Paradise Valley, 1937, Whitman, 7" x 9 1/2", 320 pgs., Big Big Book, Vallely-a 70.00 175.00 490.00
6833- Tom Mix in the Riding Avenger, 1936, Dell, 244 pgs., Cartoon Story Book, hard-c 31.00 78.00 220.00
nn- Tom Mix Rides to the Rescue, 1939, 36 pgs., 2 1/2" x 3", Penny Book 11.00 27.50 70.00
nn- Tom Mix Avenges the Dry Gulched Range King, 1939, Dell, 196 pgs., Fast-Action Story, soft-c 33.00 83.00 230.00
nn- Tom Mix in the Riding Avenger, 1936, Dell, 244 pgs.,

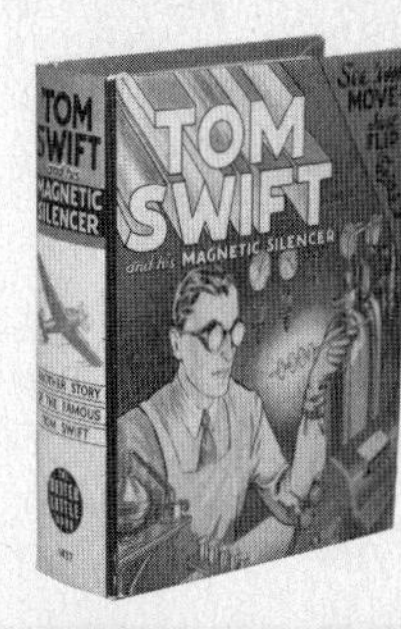

1437 - Tom Swift and His Magnetic Silencer © WHIT

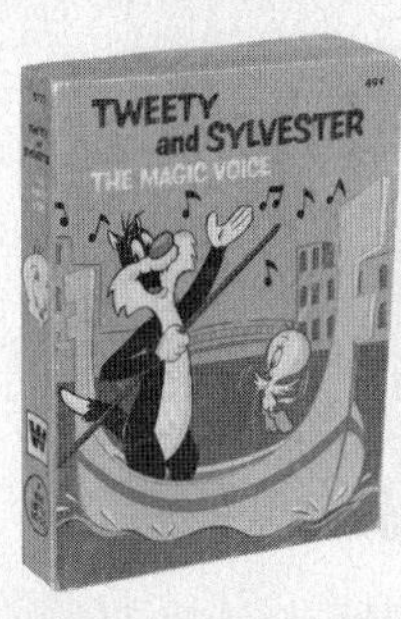

5777 - Tweety and Sylvester, The Magic Voice © WB

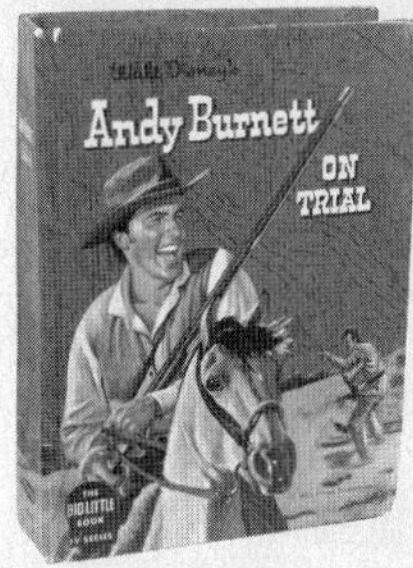

1645 - Walt Disney's Andy Burnett on the Trail © DIS

GD FN VF/NM

Fast-Action Story 33.00 83.00 230.00

nn- **Tom Mix the Trail of the Terrible 6**, 1935, Ralston Purina Co., 84 pgs., 3" x 3 1/2", premium 24.00 60.00 170.00

4- **Tom Mix and Tony in the Rider of Death Valley**, 1934, EVW, Five Star Library, 160 pgs., movie scenes (Universal Pictures), hard-c 24.00 60.00 165.00

4- **Tom Mix and Tony in the Rider of Death Valley**, 1934, EVW, Five Star Library, 160 pgs., movie scenes (Universal Pictures), soft-c (Rare) 57.00 142.00 400.00

7- **Tom Mix in the Texas Bad Man**, 1934, EVW, Five Star Library, 160 pgs., movie scenes, hard-c 24.00 60.00 165.00

7- **Tom Mix in the Texas Bad Man**, 1934, EVW, Five Star Library, 160 pgs., movie scenes; soft-c (Rare) 50.00 142.00 400.00

10- **Tom Mix in the Tepee Ranch Mystery**, 1938, Whitman, 132 pgs., Buddy Book, soft-c 34.00 85.00 240.00

1126- **Tommy of Troop Six** (Scout Book), 1937, Saalfield, hard-c 10.00 25.00 65.00

1606- **Tommy of Troop Six** (Scout Book), 1937, Saalfield, soft-c 10.00 25.00 65.00

Tom Sawyer (See Adventures of ...)

1437- **Tom Swift and His Magnetic Silencer**, 1941, Whitman, 432 pgs., flip pictures 50.00 125.00 350.00

1485- **Tom Swift and His Giant Telescope**, 1939, Whitman, 432 pgs., James Gary-a 36.00 90.00 250.00

540- **Top-Line Comics** (In Open Box), 1935, Whitman, 164 pgs., 3 1/2" x 3 1/2", 3 books in set, all soft-c:
- Bobby Thatcher and the Samarang Emerald 18.00 45.00 125.00
- Broncho Bill in Suicide Canyon 18.00 45.00 125.00
- Freckles and His Friends in the North Woods 18.00 45.00 125.00
- Complete set with box 62.00 155.00 440.00

541- **Top-Line Comics** (In Open Box), 1935, Whitman, 164 pgs., 3 1/2" x 3 1/2", 3 books in set; all soft-c:
- Little Joe and the City Gangsters 18.00 45.00 125.00
- Smilin' Jack and His Flivver Plane 18.00 45.00 125.00
- Streaky and the Football Signals 18.00 45.00 125.00
- Complete set with box 62.00 155.00 440.00

542- **Top-Line Comics** (In Open Box), 1935, Whitman, 164 pgs., 3 1/2" x 3 1/2", 3 books in set; all soft-c:
- Dinglehoofer Und His Dog Adolph by Knerr 18.00 45.00 125.00
- Jungle Jim by Alex Raymond 22.00 52.50 155.00
- Sappo by Segar 22.00 52.50 155.00
- Complete set with box 79.00 198.00 550.00

543- **Top-Line Comics** (In Open Box), 1935, Whitman, 164 pgs., 3 1/2" x 3 1/2", 3 books in set; all soft-c:
- Alexander Smart, ESQ by Winner 18.00 45.00 125.00
- Bunky by Billy de Beck 18.00 45.00 125.00
- Nicodemus O'Malley by Carter 18.00 45.00 125.00
- Complete set with box 62.00 155.00 440.00

1158- **Tracked by a G-Man**, 1939, Saalfield, 400 pgs. 10.00 25.00 65.00

25- **Trail of the Lonesome Pine, The**, 1936, Lynn, movie scenes 16.00 40.00 115.00

nn- **Trail of the Terrible 6** (See Tom Mix ...)

1185- **Trail to Squaw Gulch, The**, 1940, Saalfield, 400 pgs. 11.00 27.50 70.00

720- **Treasure Island**, 1933, Whitman, 362 pgs. 21.00 52.50 145.00

1141- **Treasure Island**, 1934, Whitman, 164 pgs., hard-c, 4 1/4" x 5 1/4", Jackie Cooper photo-c, movie scenes 16.00 40.00 115.00

1141- **Treasure Island**, 1934, Whitman, 164 pgs., soft-c, 4 1/4" x 5 1/4", Jackie Cooper photo-c, movie scenes 16.00 40.00 115.00

1018- **Trick and Puzzle Book**, 1939, Whitman, 100 pgs., soft-c 4.00 10.00 22.00

1100B- **Tricks Easy to Do** (Slight of hand & magic), 1938, Whitman, 36 pgs., 2 1/2" x 3 1/2", Penny Book 4.00 10.00 22.00

1100B- **Tricks You Can Do**, 1938, Whitman, 36 pgs., 2 1/2" x 3 1/2", Penny Book 4.00 10.00 22.00

5777- **Tweety and Sylvester, The Magic Voice**, 1976, Whitman, 260 pgs., soft-c, flip-it feature; 5 printings 2.00 5.00 11.00

1104- **Two-Gun Montana**, 1936, Whitman, 432 pgs., Henry E. Vallely-a 11.00 27.50 70.00

GD FN VF/NM

nn- **Two-Gun Montana Shoots it Out**, 1939, Whitman, 36 pgs., 2 1/2" x 3 1/2", Penny Book 11.00 27.50 70.00

1058- **Ugly Duckling, The** (Disney), 1939, Whitman, 68 pgs., 5" x 5 1/2", hard-c 14.00 35.00 95.00

nn- **Ugly Duckling, The**, nd (1930s), np (Whitman), 36 pgs., 3" x 2 1/2", Penny Book 4.00 10.00 22.00

Unc' Billy Gets Even (See Wee Little Books)

1114- **Uncle Don's Strange Adventures**, 1935, Whitman, 300 pgs., radio star-Uncle Don Carney 12.00 30.00 75.00

722- **Uncle Ray's Story of the United States,** 1934, Whitman, 300 pgs. 12.00 30.00 75.00

1461- **Uncle Sam's Sky Defenders**, 1941, Whitman, 432 pgs., flip pictures 11.00 27.50 70.00

1405- **Uncle Wiggily's Adventures**, 1946, Whitman, All Pictures Comics 16.00 40.00 115.00

1411- **Union Pacific**, 1939, Whitman, 240 pgs., photo-c, movie scenes 12.00 30.00 85.00
- With Union Pacific letter 57.00 142.00 400.00

1189- **Up Dead Horse Canyon**, 1940, Saalfield, 400 pgs. 10.00 25.00 65.00

1455- **Vic Sands of the U.S. Flying Fortress Bomber Squadron**, 1944, Whitman, 352 pgs. 12.00 30.00 85.00

1645- **Walt Disney's Andy Burnett on the Trail** (TV Series), 1958, Whitman, 280 pgs. 4.00 10.00 27.00

803- **Walt Disney's Bongo**, 1948, Whitman, hard-c, Story Hour Series 12.00 30.00 85.00

711-10-**Walt Disney's Cinderella and the Magic Wand**, 1950, Whitman, 2 1/2" x 5", based on Disney movie 12.00 30.00 75.00

845- **Walt Disney's Donald Duck and his Cat Troubles** (Disney), 1948, Whitman, 100 pgs., 5" x 5 1/2", hard-c 12.00 30.00 85.00

845- **Walt Disney's Donald Duck and the Boys**, 1948, Whitman, 100 pgs., 5" x 5 1/2", hard-c, Barks-a 28.00 70.00 195.00

2952- **Walt Disney's Donald Duck in the Great Kite Maker**, 1949, Whitman, 24 pgs., 3 1/4" x 4", Tiny Tales, full color (5 cents) 11.00 27.50 70.00

804- **Walt Disney's Mickey and the Beanstalk**, 1948, Whitman, hard-c, Story Hour Series 12.00 30.00 85.00

845- **Walt Disney's Mickey Mouse and the Boy Thursday**, 194 pgs., Whitman, 5" x 5 1/2", 100 pgs. 12.00 30.00 85.00

845- **Walt Disney's Mickey Mouse the Miracle Maker**, 1948, Whitman, 5" x 5 1/2", 100 pgs. 12.00 30.00 85.00

2952- **Walt Disney's Mickey Mouse and the Night Prowlers**, Whitman, 1949, 24 pgs., 3 1/4" x 4", Tiny Tales, full color (5 ¢) 11.00 27.50 70.00

5770- **Walt Disney's Mickey Mouse - Mystery at Disneyland**, Whitman, 1975, 260 pgs., four printings 2.00 5.00 13.00

5781-2- **Walt Disney's Mickey Mouse - Mystery at Dead Man's Cove**, Whitman, 1980, 260 pgs., two printings 2.00 5.00 11.00

845- **Walt Disney's Minnie Mouse and the Antique Chair**, 1948, Whitman, 5" x 5 1/2", 100 pgs. 12.00 30.00 85.00

1435- **Walt Disney's Pinocchio and Jiminy Cricket**, 1940, Whitman, 432 pgs. 21.00 52.50 145.00

845- **Walt Disney's Poor Pluto**, 1948, Whitman, 5" x 5 1/2", 100 pgs., hard-c 12.00 30.00 85.00

1467- **Walt Disney's Pluto the Pup** (Disney), 1938, Whitman, 432 pgs., Gottfredson-a 18.00 45.00 125.00

1066- **Walt Disney's Story of Clarabelle Cow** (Disney), 1938, Whitman, 100 pgs. 12.00 30.00 85.00

66- **Walt Disney's Story of Dippy the Goof** (Disney), 1938, Whitman, 100 pgs. 12.00 30.00 85.00

1066- **Walt Disney's Story of Donald Duck** (Disney), 1938, Whitman, 100 pgs., hard-c, Taliaferro-a 12.00 30.00 85.00

1066- **Walt Disney's Story of Mickey Mouse** (Disney), 1938, Whitman, 100 pgs., hard-c, Gottfredson-a, Donald Duck app. 12.00 30.00 85.00

1066- **Walt Disney's Story of Minnie Mouse** (Disney), 1938, Whitman, 100 pgs., hard-c 12.00 30.00 85.00

1066- **Walt Disney's Story of Pluto the Pup**, (Disney), 1938, Whitman, 100 pgs., hard-c 12.00 30.00 85.00

2952- **Walter Lantz Presents Andy Panda's Rescue**, 1949, Whitman, Tiny Tales, full color (5 cents) (1030-5 on back-c) 11.00 27.50 70.00

751- **Wash Tubbs in Pandemonia**, 1934, Whitman, 320 pgs., Roy Crane-a

L18 - Western Frontier © LYNN

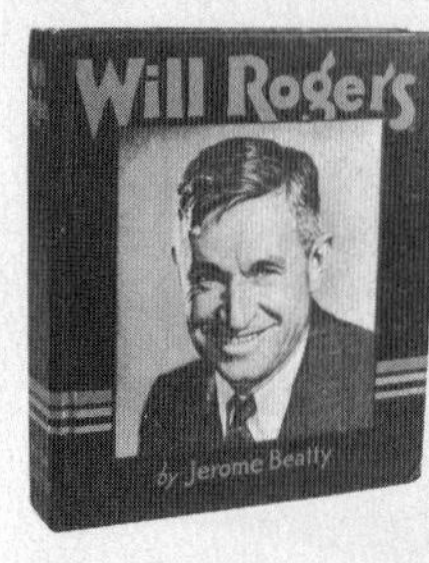

1096 - The Story of Will Rogers © Saalfield

1010 - Zane Grey's King of the Royal Mounted in Arctic Law © WHIT

GD FN VF/NM

12.00 30.00 85.00

nn- **Wash Tubbs in Pandemonia**, 1934, Whitman, 52 pgs., 4" x 5 1/2", premium-no ads, soft-c, Roy Crane-a 20.00 50.00 140.00

1455- **Wash Tubbs and Captain Easy Hunting For Whales**, 1938, Whitman, 432 pgs., Roy Crane-a 12.00 30.00 85.00

6- **Wash Tubbs in Foreign Travel**, 1934, Whitman, soft-c, 3 1/2" x 3 1/2", Tarzan Ice Cream cup premium 34.00 85.00 240.00

513- **Wee Little Books** (In Open Box), 1934, Whitman, 44 pgs., small size, 6 books in set
Child's Garden of Verses 5.00 12.50 30.00
The Happy Prince (The Story of) 5.00 12.50 30.00
Joan of Arc (The Story of) 5.00 12.50 30.00
Peter Pan (The Story of) 5.00 12.50 30.00
Pied Piper Of Hamlin 5.00 12.50 30.00
Robin Hood (A Story of...) 5.00 12.50 30.00
Complete set with box 31.00 78.00 220.00

514- **Wee Little Books** (In Open Box), 1934, Whitman, 44 pgs., small size, 6 books in set
Jack And Jill 5.00 12.50 30.00
Little Bo-Peep 5.00 12.50 30.00
Little Tommy Tucker 5.00 12.50 30.00
Mother Goose 5.00 12.50 30.00
Old King Cole 5.00 12.50 30.00
Simple Simon 5.00 12.50 30.00
Complete set with box 33.00 83.00 230.00

518- **Wee Little Books** (In Open Box), 1933, Whitman, 44 pgs., small size, 6 books in set, written by Thornton Burgess
Betty Bear's Lesson-1930 5.00 12.50 30.00
Jimmy Skunk's Justice-1933 5.00 12.50 30.00
Little Joe Otter's Slide-1929 5.00 12.50 30.00
Peter Rabbit's Carrots-1933 5.00 12.50 30.00
Unc' Billy Gets Even-1930 5.00 12.50 30.00
Whitefoot's Secret-1933 5.00 12.50 30.00
Complete set with box 33.00 83.00 230.00

519- **Wee Little Books** (In Open Box) (Bible Stories), 1934, Whitman, 44 pgs., small size, 6 books in set, Helen Janes-a
The Story of David 5.00 12.50 30.00
The Story of Gideon 5.00 12.50 30.00
The Story of Daniel 5.00 12.50 30.00
The Story of Joseph 5.00 12.50 30.00
The Story of Ruth and Naomi 5.00 12.50 30.00
The Story of Moses 5.00 12.50 30.00
Complete set with box 33.00 83.00 230.00

1471- **Wells Fargo**, 1938, Whitman, 240 pgs., photo-c, movie scenes 14.00 35.00 95.00

L18- **Western Frontier**, 1935, Lynn, 192 pgs., starring Ken Maynard, movie scenes 21.00 52.50 145.00

1121- **West Pointers on the Gridiron**, 1936, Saalfield, 148 pgs., hard-c, sports book 10.00 25.00 65.00

1601- **West Pointers on the Gridiron**, 1936, Saalfield, 148 pgs., soft-c, sports book 10.00 25.00 65.00

1124- **West Point Five, The**, 1937, Saalfield, 4 3/4" x 5 1/4", sports book, hard-c 10.00 25.00 65.00

1604- **West Point Five, The**, 1937, Saalfield, 4 1/4" x 5 1/4", sports book, soft-c 10.00 25.00 65.00

1164- **West Point of the Air**, 1935, Whitman, 160 pgs., photo-c, movie scenes 12.00 30.00 85.00

18- **Westward Ho!**, 1935, EVW, 160 pgs., movie scenes, starring John Wayne (Scarce) 71.00 178.00 500.00

1109- **We Three**, 1935, Saalfield, 160 pgs., photo-c, movie scenes, by John Barrymore, hard-c 11.00 27.50 70.00

1589- **We Three**, 1935, Saalfield, 160 pgs., photo-c, movie scenes, by John Barrymore, soft-c 11.00 27.50 70.00

Whitefoot's Secret (See Wee Little Books)

nn- **Who's Afraid of the Big Bad Wolf**, "Three Little Pigs" (Disney), 1933, McKay, 36 pgs., 6" x 8 1/2", stiff-c, Disney studio-a 39.00 98.00 275.00

nn- **Wild West Adventures of Buffalo Bill**, 1935, Whitman, 260 pgs., Cocomalt premium, soft-c, Hal Arbo-a 15.00 37.50 105.00

1096- **Will Rogers, The Story of**, 1935, Saalfield, photo-hard-c 12.00 30.00 75.00

GD FN VF/NM

1576- **Will Rogers, The Story of**, 1935, Saalfield, photo-soft-c 12.00 30.00 75.00

1458- **Wimpy the Hamburger Eater**, 1938, Whitman, 432 pgs., E.C. Segar-a 24.00 60.00 165.00

1433- **Windy Wayne and His Flying Wing**, 1942, Whitman, 432 pgs., flip pictures 11.00 27.50 70.00

1131- **Winged Four, The**, 1937, Saalfield, sports book, hard-c 11.00 27.50 70.00

1407- **Wings of the U.S.A.**, 1940, Whitman, 432 pgs., Thomas Hickey-a 11.00 27.50 70.00

nn- **Winning of the Old Northwest, The**, 1934, World Syndicate, High Lights of History Series, full color-c 11.00 27.50 70.00

nn- **Winning of the Old Northwest, The**, 1934, World Syndicate, High Lights of History Series; red & silver-c 11.00 27.50 70.00

1122- **Winning Point, The**, 1936, Saalfield, (Football), hard-c 9.00 22.50 58.00

1602- **Winning Point, The**, 1936, Saalfield, soft-c 9.00 22.50 58.00

nn- **Wizard of Oz Waddle Book**, 1934, BRP, 20 pgs., 7 1/2" x 10", forerunner of the Blue Ribbon Pop-Up books; with 6 removable articulated cardboard characters. Book only 54.00 135.00 375.00
Dust jacket only 61.00 153.00 490.00
Near Mint Complete - $12,500

710-10-**Woody Woodpecker Big Game Hunter**, 1950, Whitman, by Walter Lantz 10.00 25.00 65.00

2010-(#10)-**Woody Woodpecker-The Meteor Menace**, 1967, Whitman, 260 pgs., 39¢-c, hard-c, color illos. 4.00 10.00 27.00

5753- **Woody Woodpecker-The Meteor Menace**, 1973, Whitman, 260 pgs., no price, soft-c, color illos. 1.00 2.50 6.00

2028- **Woody Woodpecker-The Sinister Signal**, 1969, Whitman 4.00 10.00 22.00

5763- **Woody Woodpecker-The Sinister Signal**, 1974, Whitman, 1st printing-no price; 2nd printing-39¢-c 1.00 2.50 6.00

23- **World of Monsters, The**, 1935, EVW, Five Star Library, movie scenes 16.00 40.00 115.00

779- **World War in Photographs, The**, 1934, Whitman, photo-c, photo illus. 11.00 27.50 70.00

Wyatt Earp (See Hugh O'Brian ...)

nn- **Xena - Warrior Princess**, 1998, Chronicle Books, 310 pgs., based on TV series, 1-color (purple) illos 1.00 2.50 9.00

nn- **Yogi Bear Goes Country & Western**, 1977, Modern Promotions, 244 pgs., 49 cents, soft-c, flip pictures 2.00 5.00 13.00

nn- **Yogi Bear Saves Jellystone Park**, 1977, Modern Promotions, 244 pgs., 49 cents, soft-c, flip pictures 2.00 5.00 13.00

nn- **Zane Grey's Cowboys of the West**, 1935, Whitman, 148 pgs., 3 3/4" x 4", Tarzan Ice Cream Cup premium, soft-c, Arbo-a 39.00 98.00 275.00

Zane Grey's King of the Royal Mounted (See Men of the Mounted)

1010- **Zane Grey's King of the Royal Mounted in Arctic Law**, 1937, Whitman, 7 1/4" x 5 1/2", 64 pgs., Nickel Book 15.00 37.50 105.00

1103- **Zane Grey's King of the Royal Mounted,** 1936, Whitman, 432 pgs. 14.00 35.00 95.00

nn- **Zane Grey's King of the Royal Mounted**, 1935, Whitman, 260 pgs., Cocomalt premium, soft-c 18.00 45.00 125.00

1179- **Zane Grey's King of the Royal Mounted and the Northern Treasure**, 1937, Whitman, 432 pgs. 14.00 35.00 95.00

1405- **Zane Grey's King of the Royal Mounted the Long Arm of the Law**, 1942, Whitman, All Pictures Comics 14.00 35.00 95.00

1452- **Zane Grey's King of the Royal Mounted Gets His Man**, 1938, Whitman, 432 pgs. 14.00 35.00 95.00

1486- **Zane Grey's King of the Royal Mounted and the Great Jewel Mystery**, 1939, Whitman, 432 pgs. 14.00 35.00 95.00

5- **Zane Grey's King of the Royal Mounted in the Far North**, 1938, Whitman, 132 pgs., Buddy Book, soft-c (Rare) 50.00 125.00 350.00

nn- **Zane Grey's King of the Royal Mounted in Law of the North**, 1939, Whitman, 36 pgs., 2 1/2" x 3 1/2", Penny Book 9.00 22.50 58.00

nn- **Zane Grey's King of the Royal Mounted Policing the Frozen North**, 1938, Dell, 196 pgs., Fast-Action Story, soft-c 26.00 65.00 180.00

1440- **Zane Grey's Tex Thorne Comes Out of the West**, 1937, Whitman, 432 pgs. 11.00 27.50 70.00

1465- **Zip Saunders King of the Speedway**, 1939, 432 pgs., Weisman-a 11.00 27.50 70.00

PROMOTIONAL COMICS

THE MARKETING OF A MEDIUM

by Dr. Arnold T. Blumberg, DCD

with new material and additional research by Sol M. Davidson, PhD, and Robert L. Beerbohm

Everyone wants something for free. It's in our nature to look for the quick fix, the good deal, the complimentary gift. We long to hit the lottery and quit our job, to win the trip around the world, or find that pot of gold at the end of the proverbial rainbow. Collectors in particular are certainly built to appreciate the notion of the "free gift," since it not only means a new item to collect and enjoy, but no risk or obligation in order to acquire it.

Ah, but there's the rub. Because things are not always what they seem, and "free gifts" usually come with a price. As the saying goes, "there's no such thing as a free lunch," so if it seems too good to be true, it probably is. This is the case even in the world of comics, where premiums and giveaways have a familiar agenda hidden behind the bright colors and fanciful stories. But where did it all begin?

Some of the earliest characters that were used as successful tools in promotional comics were Palmer Cox's creation "The Brownies." The illustration shown here showcases them drinking and endorsing Seal Brand Coffee.

EXTRA EXTRA

As we learn more about the early history of the comic book industry through continual investigation and the publishing of articles like those regularly featured in this book, we gain a much greater understanding of the financial and creative forces at work in shaping the medium, but perhaps one of the most intriguing and least recognized factors that influenced the dawn of comics is the concept of the premium or giveaway. (Note: Some of the historical information referenced in this article is derived from material also presented in Robert L. Beerbohm's introductory articles to the Platinum Age and Modern Age sections.)

The birth of the comic book as we know it today is intimately connected with the development of the comic strip in American newspapers and their use as an advertising and marketing tool for staple products such as bread, milk, and cereal. From the very beginning, comic characters have played several roles in pop culture, entertaining the youth of the country while also (sometimes none too subtly) acting as hucksters for whatever corporation foots the bill. From important staples to frivolous material produced simply to make a buck, these products have utilized the comics medium to sell, sell, sell. And what better way to hook a prospective customer than to give them "something for nothing?"

Starting in the 1850s, comics were being used in free almanacs such as **Elton's**, **Hostetter's** and **Wright's** to lure readers for the little booklets to sell patent medicine, farm products, tobacco, shoe polish, etc. Most of these are exceedingly rare today, hence it is difficult to compile an accurate history. More mention of these early precursors can be found in the Victorian Comics Era essay following this one. But although comic characters themselves were already being aggressively merchandised all around the world by the mid-1890s--as with, for example, Palmer Cox's **The Brownies**--the real starting point for the success of comics as a giveaway marketing mechanism can be traced to the introduction of **The Yellow Kid**, Richard Outcault's now legendary newspaper strip.

Newspaper publishers had already recognized that comic strips could boost circulation as well as please sponsors and advertisers by drawing more eyes to the page, so Sunday "supplements" were introduced to entice fans. Outcault's creation cemented the theory with proof of comic characters' marketing and merchandising power.

This unused cover was designed as the second cover for "Motion Picture Funnies Weekly." While the concept for this promotional comic title never caught on, the inaugural issue did feature the origin and first printed appearance of the Sub-Mariner.

Soon after, Outcault (who had most likely been inspired by Cox's merchandising success with **The Brownies** in the first place) caught lightning in a bottle once more with **Buster Brown**, who has the distinction of being America's first nationally licensed comic strip character. Soon, comic strips proliferated throughout the nation's newspapers as tycoons like Hearst and Pulitzer recognized the drawing power of the new medium and fought circulation wars to capture the pennies of the nouveau readership. They paid exorbitant salaries to comic strip artists such as Rudolph Dirks (**Katzenjammer Kids**), and used the funnies as newspaper supplements and as premiums to attract readers. Corporations soon had the chance to license recognizable personas as their own personal pitchmen (or women or animals...). Comic character merchandise wasn't far behind, resulting in a boom of future collectibles now catalogued in volumes like **Hake's Price Guide to Character Toys**.

TWO BIRTHS FOR THE PRICE OF ONE

Comic books themselves were at the heart of this movement, and giveaway and premium collections of comic strips not only appealed to children and adults alike, but provided the impetus for the birth of the modern comic book format itself. It could be said that without the concept of the giveaway comic or the marketing push behind it, there would be no comic book industry as we have it today. Well-known now is the story of how in spring 1933 Harry Wildenberg of Eastern Color Printing Company convinced Proctor & Gamble to sponsor the first modern comic book, **Funnies on Parade**, as a premium. Its success led to the first continuing comic book, **Famous Funnies**, and the rest, as they say, is history.

In 1935, while working on the printing presses of Eastern Color developing how modern comic books get printed, Juliun J. Proskauer came up with an idea for printing "Comic-Books-For-Industry." In July 1936 he made his first sale through his newly formed William C. Popper & Co. to David M. Davies, then advertising manager for Seagram's Distillers Corp. for three million copies of **Seagram's Merrymakers** in time for the 1936-37 Christmas season. "Thus was a new industry born," wrote **Printing News** in August 1945.

Even a casual perusal of the listings in this section of the Guide will dazzle the reader with the endless variety of purposes that this medium has served. Yes, promos have been used to hawk products from athletic equipment to zithers and zip codes, but comics are too versatile an art form to be confined to a few uses. They've swayed elections in cities (**The O'Dwyer Story**, 1949), in states (**Giant for a Day**: Jacob Javits, 1946) and nationwide (**The Story of Harry Truman**, 1948); solicited for charities (**Donald Duck and the Red Feather**, 1948); addressed health issues (**Blondie**, 1949, mental hygiene); discouraged kids from smoking (**Captain America Meets the Asthma Monster**, 1987); coached youngsters in sports skills (**Circling the Bases**, 1947, A.G. Spaulding); explained scientific complexities (**Adventures in Science**, 1946-61, GE); pleaded for social justice (**Consumer Comics**, 1975); espoused religious causes (**Oral Roberts' True Stories**, 1950s); protected the environment (**Our Spaceship Earth**, 1947); encouraged tourism (**Wyoming, The Cowboy State**, 1954); conveyed a sense of history (**Louisiana Purchase**, 1953); taught about computers (**Superman Radio Shack Giveaway**, 1980); trained employees (**Dial Finance Dialogues**, 1961-70) and executives (**Beneficial Finance System, Managing New Employees**, 1950s); cautioned safety (**Willy Wing Flap**, 1944(?)); announced corporate annual results (**Motorola Annual Report**, 1952); defended free enterprise (**Steve Merritt**, 1949); hammered communism (**How Stalin Hopes to Destroy America**, 1951); fought discrimination (**Mammy Yokum & the Great Dogpatch Mystery**, 1956, B'nai Brith); aided young workers in job-hunting (**The Job Scene**, 1969); battled the scourge of sickle cell anemia (**Where's Herbie**, 1972, U.S. H.E.W.); inspired the overcoming of adversity (**Al Capp by Li'l Abner**, 1946); fostered reading (**Linus Gets a Library Card**, 1960); recruited for the armed forces (**Li'l Abner Joins the Navy**, 1950); beguiled readers into

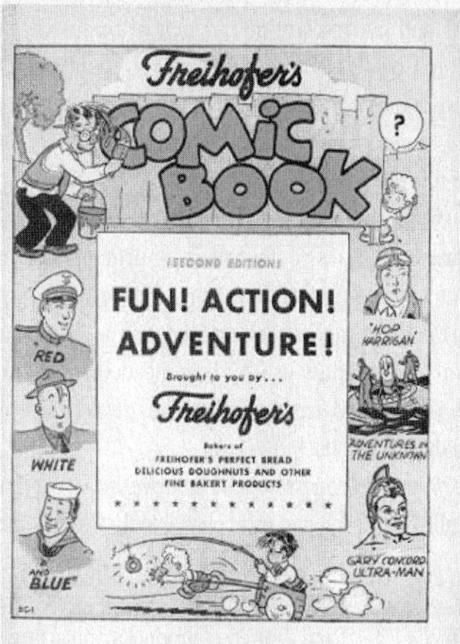

Every market and product has been on the promotional comic book bandwagon. Freihofer's Baking Company distributed a comic in the 1940s that featured reprinted pages from "All-American Comics."

learning languages (**Blondie**, 1949, Philadelphia public schools); and even instructed in such delicate matters as birth control (**Escape from Fear**, 1950 (revised 1959, etc.), for Planned Parenthood).

READ ALL ABOUT IT

The impact of this new approach to advertising was not lost on the business world. Contrary to modern belief, comic books were hardly discounted by the adults of the time...at least not those who had the marketing savvy to recognize an opportunity - or a threat - when they saw one. In the April 1933 issue of **Fortune** magazine, an article titled "The Funny Papers" trumpeted the arrival of comics as a force to be reckoned with in the world of advertising and business, and what's more, a force to fear as well. At first providing a brief survey of the newspaper comic strip business (which for many of the magazine's readers must have seemed a foreign topic for serious discussion), the article goes on to examine the incredible financial draw of comics and their characters:

"Between 70 and 75 per cent {sic} of the readers of any newspaper follow its comic sections regularly...Even the advertiser has succumbed to the comic, and in 1932 spent well over $1,000,000 for comic-paper space."

"**Comic Weekly** is the comic section of seventeen Hearst Sunday papers...Advertisers who market their wares through balloon-speaking manikins {sic} may enjoy the proximity of Jiggs, Maggie, Barney Google, and other funny Hearst headliners."

Although the article continues to cast the notion of relying on comic strip material to sell product in a negative light, actually suggesting that advertisers who utilize comics are violating unspoken rules of "advertising decorum" and bringing themselves "down to the level" of comics (and since when have advertisers been stalwart preservers of good taste and high moral standards), there is no doubt that they are viewing comics in a new light. The comic characters have arrived by 1933...and they're ready to help sell your merchandise too.

Fortune wasn't the only one to take notice as World War II came and went. In 1948, Louis P. Birk, the head of Brevity, Inc., an important promotional comics publisher said, "Comics are serious business." In an article in **Printers' Ink** magazine, he estimated that more than 80 different "comic booklets" had been produced and more than 45,000,000 million copies distributed in the five years before 1948. But of course, comics were serious business long before businessman/historian Birk noted the fact for posterity.

THE MARCH OF WAR AND BEYOND

Through the relentless currents of time, comic strips, books, and the characters that starred in them became more and more an intrinsic part of American culture. During the turmoil of the Great Depression and World War II, comic characters in print and celluloid form entertained while informing and selling at the same time, and premium and giveaway comics came well and truly into their own, pushing everything from loaves of bread to war bonds.

In the 1950s and '60s, there was a shift in focus as the power of giveaway and premium comics was applied to more altruistic endeavors than simply selling something. Comic book format pamphlets, fully illustrated and often inventively written, taught children about banking, money, the dangers of poison and other household products, and even chronicled moments in

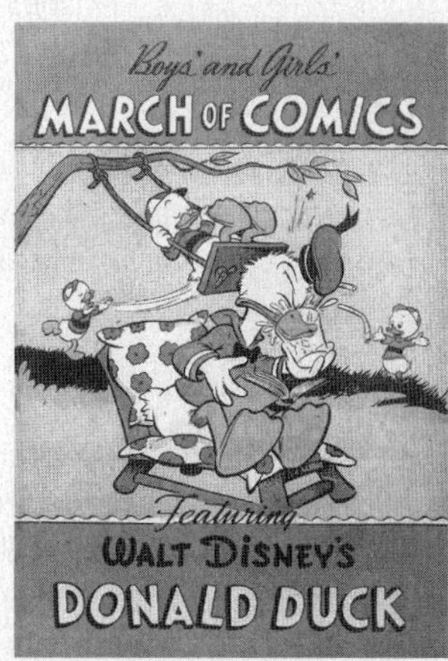

The promotional title "March of Comics" was a prolific comic that ran for 36 years and 488 issues featuring a variety of subjects and characters. (#20 shown)

American history. The comic book as giveaway was now not only a marketing gimmick--it was a tool for educating as well.

The 1970s and '80s saw another boom in premium and giveaway comics. Every product imaginable seemed to have a licensing deal with a comic book character, usually one of the prominent flag bearers of the Big Two, Marvel or DC. Spider-Man fought bravely against the Beetle for the benefit of All Detergent; Captain America allied himself with the Campbell Kids; and Superman helped a class of computer students beat a disaster-conjuring foe at his own game with the help of Radio Shack Tandy computers.

Newspapers rediscovered the power of comics, not just with enlarged strip supplements but with actual comic books. Spider-Man, the Hulk, and others turned up as giveaway comic extras in various American newspapers (including Chicago and Dallas publications), while a whole series of public information comics like those produced decades earlier used superheroes to caution children about the dangers of smoking, drugs, and child abuse.

Comics also turned up in a plethora of other toy products as the 1980s introduced kids to the joy of electronic games and action figures. Supplementary comics provided "free" with action figure and video game packages told the backstory about the product, adding depth to the play experience while providing an extra incentive to buy. Comics became an intrinsic part of the Atari line of video cartridges, for example, eventually spawning its own full-blown newsstand series as well.

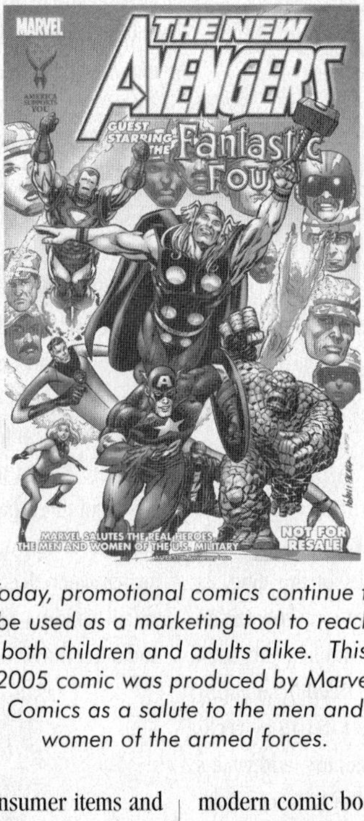

Today, promotional comics continue to be used as a marketing tool to reach both children and adults alike. This 2005 comic was produced by Marvel Comics as a salute to the men and women of the armed forces.

As the twentieth century gave way to the twenty-first, giveaway comics were still being produced for inclusion in action figure and video game packages, as well as in conjunction with countless consumer items and corporations. It seems that the medium still has a lot to offer for all those companies desperate to make the most of their market share.

A COMIC BY ANY OTHER NAME

One of the earliest names for promotional comics was "special purpose comics." In their pursuit of superheroes, collectors have allowed promotional comics to lie fallow - underappreciated and uncollected. Without a legitimate name, these products were given sundry other appellations - industrial comics, promos, giveaways, premiums, promics - each accurate but only for a small segment of the unorganized but lusty and lively medium. Perhaps no one name can cover all the variations and purposes of this branch of comic art, but for practical reasons if we accept the general premise that these comics were created to promote an idea, a product or a person, then "Promotional Comics" is probably as convenient a catch-all title as we can come up with.

We used the phrase "for practical reasons" because the word "practical" goes to the heart of promotional comics more than it does for any other comics product. What greater testimony is there to the medium's impact on American culture than to note their use by hard-headed, profit-minded business people and corporations? They invest their money and they expect results.

Today, premium comics continue to thrive and are still utilized as a valuable marketing and promotional tool. "Free" comics are still packaged with action figures and video games, and offered as mail-away premiums from a variety of product manufacturers. The comic industry itself has expanded its use of giveaway comics to self-promote as well, with "ashcan" and other giveaway editions turning up at conventions and comic shops to advertise upcoming series and special events. Many of these function as old-fashioned premiums, with a coupon or other response required from the reader to receive the comic.

As for the supplements and giveaways printed all those years ago, they have spawned a collectible fervor all their own, thanks to their atypical distribution and frequent rarity. For that and the desire to delve deeper into comics history, we hope that by focusing more directly on this genre, we can enhance our understanding of this vital component in the development and history of the modern comic book.

Whether you're a collector or not, we're all motivated by that desire to get something for nothing. For as long as consumers are enticed by the notion of the "free gift," promotional comics will remain a vital marketing component in many business models, but they will also continue to fight the stigma that has long been associated with the industry as a whole. "Respectable" sources like **Fortune** may have taken notice of the power of comic-related advertising 71 years ago, but after all this time comics still fight an uphill battle to establish some measure of dignity for the medium. Perhaps the higher visibility of promotional comics will eventually prove to be a deciding factor in that intellectual war.

See ya in the funny papers.

Action Comics #1 (USPS) © DC

Adventures of Big Boy #1 © Timely

Amazing Fantasy #15 (Spider-Man movie DVD) © MAR

	GD 2.0	VG 4.0	FN 6.0	VF 8.0	VF/NM 9.0	NM- 9.2

ACTION COMICS
DC Comics: 1947 - 1998 (Giveaway)

1 (1976) paper cover w/10¢ price, 16 pgs. in color; reprints complete Superman story from #1 ('38)	3	6	9	21	32	42
1 (1976) Safeguard Giveaway; paper cover w/"free", 16 pgs. in color; reprints complete Superman story from #1 ('38)	3	6	9	21	32	42
1 (1983) paper cover w/10¢ price, 16 pgs. in color; reprints complete Superman story from #1 ('38)	3	6	9	14	20	25
1 (1987 Nestle Quik; 1988, 50¢)	1	2	3	5	7	9
1 (1993)-Came w/Reign of Superman packs						4.00
1 (1998 U.S. Postal Service, $7.95) Reprints entire issue; extra outer half-cover contains First Day Issuance of 32¢ Superman stamp with Sept. 10, 1998 Cleveland, OH postmark	1	2	3	5	6	8
Theater (1947, 32 pgs., 5" x 7", nn)-Vigilante story based on Columbia Vigilante serial; no Superman-c or story	63	126	189	400	688	975

ACTION ZONE
CBS Television: 1994 (Promotes CBS Saturday morning cartoons)

1-WildC.A.T.s, T.M.N.Turtles, Skeleton Warriors stories; Jim Lee-c						4.00

ADVENTURE COMICS
IGA: No date (early 1940s) (Paper-c, 32 pgs.)

Two diff. issues; Super-Mystery-r from 1941	21	42	63	123	204	285

ADVENTURE IN DISNEYLAND
Walt Disney Productions (Dist. by Richfield Oil): May, 1955 (Giveaway, soft-c., 16 pgs)

nn	10	20	30	56	76	95

ADVENTURES @ EBAY
eBay: 2000 (6 3/4" x 4 1/2", 16 pgs.)

1-Judd Winick-a/Rucka & Van Meter-s; intro to eBay comic buying						2.50

ADVENTURES OF BIG BOY (Also titled Adventures of the Big Boy)
Timely Comics/Webs Adv. Corp./Illus. Features: 1956 - Present (Giveaway) (East & West editions of early issues)

1-Everett-c/a	106	212	318	673	1162	1650
2-Everett-c/a	37	74	111	222	361	500
3-5: 4-Robot-c	19	38	57	110	175	240
6-10: 6-Sci/fic issue	10	20	30	73	129	185
11-20: 11,13-DeCarlo-a	7	14	21	45	73	100
21-30	4	8	12	26	41	55
31-50	3	6	9	17	25	32
51-100	2	4	6	9	13	16
101-150	2	4	6	8	10	12
151-240	1	2	3	5	7	9
241-265,267-269,271-300:						6.00
266-Superman x-over	3	6	9	18	27	35
270-TV's Buck Rogers-c/s	3	6	9	14	20	25
301-400						4.00
401-500						3.00
1-(2nd series - '76-'84,Paragon Prod.) (...Shoney's Big Boy)	1	3	4	6	8	10
2-20						5.00
21-50						3.00
Summer, 1959 issue, large size	7	14	21	50	83	115

ADVENTURES OF G. I. JOE
1969 (3-1/4x7") (20 & 16 pgs.)

First Series: 1-Danger of the Depths. 2-Perilous Rescue. 3-Secret Mission to Spy Island. 4-Mysterious Explosion. 5-Fantastic Free Fall. 6-Eight Ropes of Danger. 7-Mouth of Doom. 8-Hidden Missile Discovery. 9-Space Walk Mystery. 10-Fight for Survival. 11-The Shark's Surprise.
Second Series: 2-Flying Space Adventure. 4-White Tiger Hunt. 7-Capture of the Pygmy Gorilla. 12-Secret of the Mummy's Tomb.
Third Series: Reprinted surviving titles of First Series. Fourth Series: 13-Adventure Team Headquarters. 14-Search For the Stolen Idol.

each....	3	6	9	18	27	35

ADVENTURES OF JELL-O MAN AND WOBBLY, THE
Welsh Publishing Group: 1991 ($1.25)

1						4.00

ADVENTURES OF KOOL-AID MAN
Marvel Comics: 1983 - No. 3, 1985 (Mail order giveaway)
Archie Comics: No. 4, 1987 - No. 8, 1989

1-8: 4-8-Dan DeCarlo-a/c	1	2	3	5	7	9

ADVENTURES OF MARGARET O'BRIEN, THE
Bambury Fashions (Clothes): 1947 (20 pgs. in color, slick-c, regular size) (Premium)

In "The Big City" movie adaptation (scarce)	20	40	60	117	189	260

	GD 2.0	VG 4.0	FN 6.0	VF 8.0	VF/NM 9.0	NM- 9.2

ADVENTURES OF QUIK BUNNY
Nestle's Quik: 1984 (Giveaway, 32 pgs.)

nn-Spider-Man app.	2	4	6	9	113	16

ADVENTURES OF STUBBY, SANTA'S SMALLEST REINDEER, THE
W. T. Grant Co.: nd (early 1940s) (Giveaway, 12 pgs.)

nn	7	14	21	37	46	55

ADVENTURES OF VOTEMAN, THE
Foundation For Citizen Education Inc.: 1968

nn	4	8	12	28	44	60

ADVENTURES WITH SANTA CLAUS
Promotional Publ. Co. (Murphy's Store): No date (early 50's) (9-3/4x 6-3/4", 24 pgs., giveaway, paper-c)

nn-Contains 8 pgs. ads	6	12	18	29	36	42
16 pg. version	6	12	18	33	41	48

AIR POWER (CBS TV & the U.S. Air Force Presents)
Prudential Insurance Co.: 1956 (5-1/4x7-1/4", 32 pgs., giveaway, soft-c)

nn-Toth-a? Based on 'You Are There' TV program by Walter Cronkite	10	20	30	56	76	95

ALASKA BUSH PILOT
Jan Enterprises: 1959 (Paper cover)

1-Promotes Bush Pilot Club (Value will be based on sale)
NOTE: *A CGC certified 9.9 Mint sold for $632.50 in 2005.*

ALICE IN BLUNDERLAND
Industrial Services: 1952 (Paper cover, 16 pgs. in color)

nn-Facts about government waste and inefficiency	14	28	42	76	108	140

ALICE IN WONDERLAND
Western Printing Company/Whitman Publ. Co.: 1965; 1969; 1982

Meets Santa Claus(1950s), nd, 16 pgs.	6	12	18	28	34	40
Rexall Giveaway(1965, 16 pgs., 5x7-1/4) Western Printing (TV, Hanna-Barbera)	3	6	9	16	23	30
Wonder Bakery Giveaway(1969, 16 pgs, color, nn, nd) (Continental Baking Company)	3	6	9	16	22	28

ALICE IN WONDERLAND MEETS SANTA
No publisher: nd (6-5/8x9-11/16", 16 pgs., giveaway, paper-c)

nn	9	18	27	50	65	80

ALL ABOARD, MR. LINCOLN
Assoc. of American Railroads: Jan, 1959 (16 pgs.)

nn-Abraham Lincoln and the Railroads	6	12	18	28	34	40

ALL NEW COMICS
Harvey Comics: Oct, 1993 (Giveaway, no cover price, 16 pgs.)(Hanna-Barbera)

1-Flintstones, Scooby Doo, Jetsons, Yogi Bear & Wacky Races previews for upcoming Harvey's new Hanna-Barbera line-up	1	2	3	4	5	7

NOTE: *Material previewed in Harvey giveaway was eventually published by Archie.*

AMAZING SPIDER-MAN, THE
Marvel Comics Group

Acme & Dingo Children's Boots (1980)-Spider-Woman app.	2	4	6	11	16	20
Adventures in Reading Starring... (1990,1991) Bogdanove & Romita-c/a						5.00
Aim Toothpaste Giveaway (36 pgs., reg. size)-1 pg. origin recap; Green Goblin-c/story	2	4	6	9	13	16
Aim Toothpaste Giveaway (16 pgs., reg. size)-Dr. Octopus app.	2	4	6	9	13	16
All Detergent Giveaway (1979, 36 pgs.), nn-Origin-r	2	4	6	9	13	16
Amazing Fantasy #15 (8/02) reprint included in Spider-Man DVD Collector's Gift Set						5.00
Amazing Fantasy #15 (2006) News America Marketing newspaper giveaway						4.00
Amazing Spider-Man nn (1990, 6-1/8x9", 28 pgs.)-Shan-Lon giveaway; retells origin of Spider-Man; Bagley-a/Saviuk-c	2	4	6	8	10	12
Amazing Spider-Man nn (1990, 6-1/8x9", 28 pgs.)-Shan-Lon giveaway; reprints Amazing Spider-Man #303 w/McFarlane-c/a	2	4	6	8	10	12
Amazing Spider-Man #1 Reprint (1990, 4-1/4x6-1/4", 28 pgs.)-Packaged with the book "Start Collecting Comic Books" from Running Press						4.00
Amazing Spider-Man #3 Reprint (2004)-Best Buy/Sony giveaway						2.50
Amazing Spider-Man #50 (Sony Pictures Edition) (8/04)-mini-comic included in Spider-Man 2 movie DVD Collector's Gift Set; r/#50 & various ASM covers with Dr. Octopus						2.50
Amazing Spider-Man #129 (Lion Gate Films) (6/04)-promotional comic given away at movie theaters on opening night for The Punisher						2.50
...& Power Pack (1984, nn)(Nat'l Committee for Prevention of Child Abuse) (two versions, mail offer & store giveaway)-Mooney-a; Byrne-c						
Mail offer	2	4	6	9	11	14
Store giveaway						5.00

Spidey and the Mini-Marvels © MAR

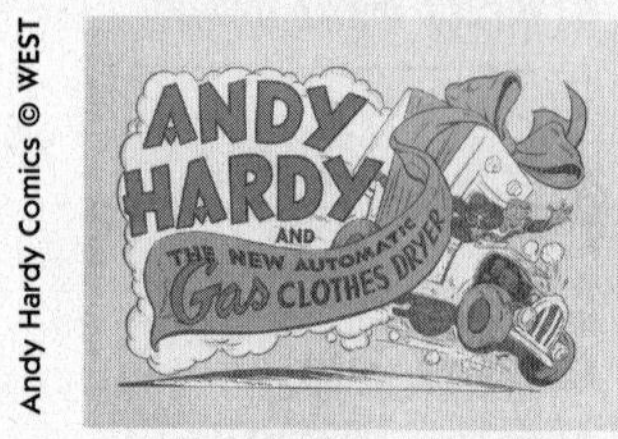

Andy Hardy Comics © WEST

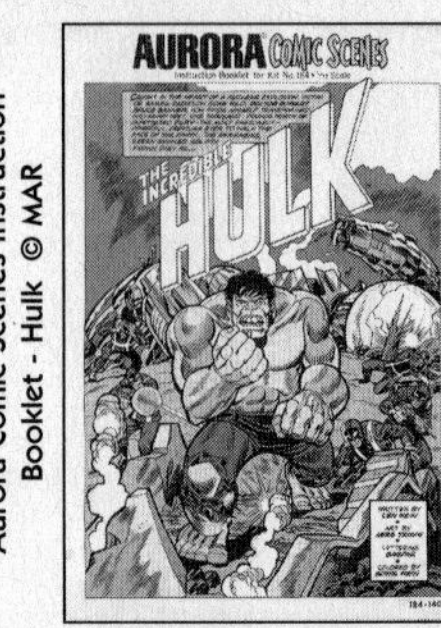

Aurora Comic Scenes Instruction Booklet - Hulk © MAR

GD VG FN VF VF/NM NM-
2.0 4.0 6.0 8.0 9.0 9.2

...& The Hulk (Special Edition)(6/8/80; 20 pgs.)-Supplement to Chicago Tribune
2 4 6 9 13 16
...& The Incredible Hulk (1981, 1982; 36 pgs.)-Sanger Harris or May D&F supplement to Dallas Times, Dallas Herald, Denver Post, Kansas City Star, Tulsa World; Foley's supplement to Houston Chronicle (1982, 16 pgs.)- "Great Rodeo Robbery"; The Jones Store-giveaway (1983, 16 pgs.) 2 4 6 13 18 22
...and the New Mutants Featuring Skids nn (National Committee for Prevention of Child Abuse/K-Mart giveaway)-Williams-c(i) 5.00
... Battles Ignorance (1992)(Sylvan Learning Systems) giveaway; Mad Thinker app. Kupperberg-a 1 2 3 5 7 9
...Captain America, The Incredible Hulk, & Spider-Woman (1981) (7-11 Stores giveaway; 36 pgs.) 2 4 6 10 14 18
...: Christmas in Dallas (1983) (Supplement to Dallas Times Herald) giveaway 2 4 6 10 14 18
...: Danger in Dallas (1983) (Supplement to Dallas Times Herald) giveaway 2 4 6 10 14 18
...: Danger in Denver (1983) (Supplement to Denver Post) giveaway for May D&F stores 2 4 6 10 14 18
..., Fire-Star, And Ice-Man at the Dallas Ballet Nutcracker (1983; supplement to Dallas Times Herald)-Mooney-p 2 4 6 10 14 18
Giveaway-Esquire Magazine (2/69)-Miniature-Still attached (scarce)
13 26 39 91 176 260
Giveaway-Eye Magazine (2/69)-Miniature-Still attached
10 20 30 68 119 170
...: Riot at Robotworld (1991; 16 pgs.)(National Action Council for Minorities in Engineering, Inc.) giveaway; Saviuk-c 1 2 3 5 6 8
..., Storm & Powerman (1982; 20 pgs.)(American Cancer Society) giveaway; also a 1991 2nd printing and a 1994 printing 1 2 3 5 6 8
...Vs. The Hulk (Special Edition; 1979, 20 pgs.)(Supplement to Columbus Dispatch)
2 4 6 13 18 22
...Vs. The Prodigy (Giveaway, 16 pgs. in color (1976, 5x6-1/2")-Sex education; (1 million printed; 35-50¢) 2 4 6 10 14 18
Spidey & The Mini-Marvels Halloween 2003 Ashcan (12/03, 8 1/2"x 5 1/2") Giarusso-s/a; Venom and Green Goblin app. 2.00

AMERICA MENACED!
Vital Publications: 1950 (Paper-c)

nn-Anti-communism 34 68 102 204 335 465

AMERICAN COMICS
Theatre Giveaways (Liberty Theatre, Grand Rapids, Mich. known): 1940's

Many possible combinations. "Golden Age" superhero comics with new cover added and given away at theaters. Following known: Superman #59, Capt. Marvel #20, Capt. Marvel Jr. #5, Action #33, Classics Comics #8, Whiz #39. Value would vary with book and should be 70-80 percent of the original.

ANDY HARDY COMICS
Western Printing Co.:

...& the New Automatic Gas Clothes Dryer (1952, 5x7-1/4", 16 pgs.) Bendix Giveaway (soft-c) 6 12 18 31 38 45

ANIMANIACS EMERGENCY WORLD
DC Comics: 1995

nn-American Red Cross 4.00

APACHE HUNTER
Creative Pictorials: 1954 (18 pgs. in color) (promo copy) (saddle stitched)

nn-Severin, Heath stories 15 30 45 85 130 175

AQUATEERS MEET THE SUPER FRIENDS
DC Comics: 1979

nn 2 4 6 10 14 18

ARCHIE AND HIS GANG (Zeta Beta Tau Presents...)
Archie Publications: Dec. 1950 (St. Louis National Convention giveaway)

nn-Contains new cover stapled over Archie Comics #47 (11-12/50) on inside; produced for Zeta Beta Tau 16 32 48 92 144 195

ARCHIE COMICS (Also see Sabrina)
Archie Publications

... And Friends and the Shield (10/02, 8 1/2"x 5 1/2") Diamond Comic Dist. 4.00
... And Friends - A Halloween Tale (10/98, 8 1/2"x 5 1/2") Diamond Comic Dist.; Sabrina and Sonic app.; Dan DeCarlo-a 4.00
... And Friends - A Timely Tale (10/01, 8 1/2"x 5 1/2") Diamond Comic Dist. 4.00
... And Friends Monster Bash 2003 (8 1/2"x 5 1/2") Diamond Comic Dist. Halloween 4.00
...And His Friends Help Raise Literacy Awareness In Mississippi nn (3/94)
1 2 3 5 6 8
...And His Friends Vs. The Household Toxic Wastes nn (1993, 16 pgs.) produced for the San Diego Regional Household Hazardous Materials Program
1 2 3 5 6 8
...And His Pals in the Peer Helping Program nn (2/91, 7"x4 1/2") produced by the FBI

GD VG FN VF VF/NM NM-
2.0 4.0 6.0 8.0 9.0 9.2

1 2 3 5 6 8
...And the History of Electronics nn (5/90, 36 pgs.)-Radio Shack giveaway; Bender-c/a
1 2 3 5 6 8
Fairmont Potato Chips Giveaway-Mini comics 1970 (6 issues-nn's.,6 7/8" x 2 1/4", 8 pgs. each)
3 6 9 19 29 38
Fairmont Potato Chips Giveaway-Mini comics 1971 (4 issues-nn's.,6 7/8" x 5", 8 pgs. each)
3 6 9 19 29 38
Little Archie, The House That Wouldn't Move ('07, 8-1/2" x 5-3/8" Halloween mini-comic) 2.00
Official Boy Scout Outfitter (1946, 9-1/2x6-1/2, 16 pgs.)-B. R. Baker Co. (Scarce) 48 96 144 302 514 725
...'s Ham Radio Adventure (1997) Morse code instruction; Goldberg-a 6.00
...'s Weird Mysteries (9/99, 8 1/2"x 5 1/2") Diamond Comic Dist. Halloween giveaway 3.00
Tales From Riverdale (2006, 8 1/2"x 5 1/2") Diamond Comic Dist. Halloween giveaway 3.00
...: The Dawn of Time ('10, 8-1/2" x 5-3/8" Halloween mini-comic) 3.00
...: The Mystery of the Museum Sleep-In ('08, 8-1/2" x 5-3/8" Halloween mini-comic) 3.00

ARCHIE SHOE-STORE GIVEAWAY
Archie Publications: 1944-50 (12-15 pgs. of games, puzzles, stories like Superman-Tim books, No nos. - came out monthly)

	GD	VG	FN	VF	VF/NM	NM-
(1944-47)-issues	18	36	54	105	165	225
2/48-Peggy Lee photo-c	18	36	54	105	165	225
3/48-Marylee Robb photo-c	15	30	45	90	140	190
4/48-Gloria De Haven photo-c	18	36	54	105	165	225
5/48,6/48,7/48	15	30	45	90	140	190
8/48-Story on Shirley Temple	19	38	57	109	172	235
10/48-Archie as Wolf on cover	16	32	48	94	147	200
5/49-Kathleen Hughes photo-c	15	30	45	84	127	170
7/49	14	28	42	82	121	160
8/49-Archie photo-c from radio show	21	42	63	122	199	275
10/49-Gloria Mann photo-c from radio show	16	32	48	94	147	200
11/49,12/49, 2/50, 3/50	15	30	45	83	124	165

ARCHIE'S JOKE BOOK MAGAZINE (See Joke Book ...)
Archie Publications

Drug Store Giveaway (No. 39 w/new-c) 7 14 21 35 43 50

ARCHIE'S TEN ISSUE COLLECTOR'S SET (Title inside of cover only)
Archie Publications: June, 1997 - No. 10, June, 1997 ($1.50, 20 pgs.)

1-10: 1,7-Archie. 2,8-Betty & Veronica. 3,9-Veronica. 4-Betty. 5-World of Archie. 6-Jughead. 10-Archie and Friends each... 5.00

ASTRO COMICS
American Airlines (Harvey): 1968 - 1979 (Giveaway)(Reprints of Harvey comics)

1968-Richie Rich, Hot Stuff, Casper, Wendy on-c only; Spooky and Nightmare app. inside
4 8 12 24 37 50
1970-Casper, Spooky, Hot Stuff, Stumbo the Giant, Little Audrey, Little Lotta, & Richie Rich reprints. Five different versions 3 6 9 20 30 40
1973,1975,1976: 1973-Three different versions 3 6 9 17 25 32
1977-r/Richie Rich & Casper #20. 1978-r/Richie Rich & Casper #25. 1979-r/Richie Rich & Casper #30 (scarce) 3 6 9 16 23 30

ATARI FORCE
DC Comics: 1982 - No. 5, 1983

1-3 (1982, 5X7", 52 pgs.)-Given away with Atari games
1 2 3 5 6 8
4,5 (1982-1983, 52 pgs.)-Given away with Atari games (scarcer)
2 4 6 9 12 15

AURORA COMIC SCENES INSTRUCTION BOOKLET (Included with superhero model kits)
Aurora Plastics Co.: 1974 (6-1/4x9-3/4," 8 pgs., slick paper)

181-140-Tarzan; Neal Adams-a 3 6 9 18 27 36
182-140-Spider-Man. 4 8 12 24 37 50
183-140-Tonto(Gil Kane art). 184-140-Hulk. 185-140-Superman. 186-140-Superboy. 187-140-Batman. 188-140-The Lone Ranger(1974-by Gil Kane). 192-140-Captain America(1975). 193-140-Robin 3 6 9 16 23 30

BACK TO THE FUTURE
Harvey Comics

Special nn (1991, 20 pgs.)-Brunner-c; given away at Universal Studios in Florida 6.00

BALTIMORE COLTS
American Visuals Corp.: 1950 (Giveaway)

nn-Eisner-c 43 86 129 271 461 650

BAMBI (Disney)
K. K. Publications (Giveaways): 1941, 1942

1941-Horlick's Malted Milk & various toy stores; text & pictures; most copies mailed out with store stickers on-c 42 84 126 265 445 625
1942-Same as 4-Color #12, but no price (Same as '41 issue?) (Scarce)
84 168 252 538 919 1300

Batman Onstar edition © DC

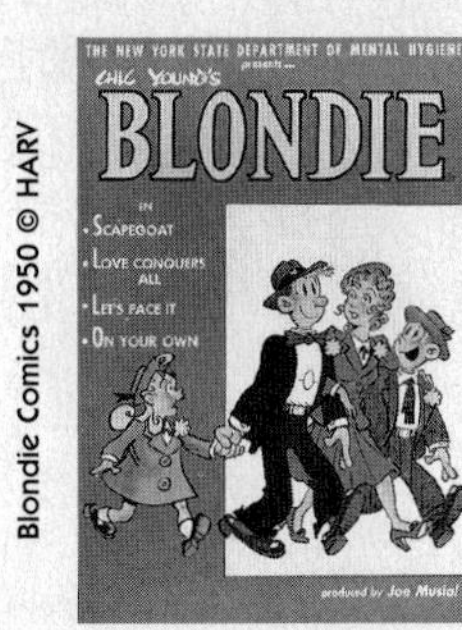

Blondie Comics 1950 © HARV

Bob & Betty & Santa's Wishing Whistle © Sears

GD VG FN VF VF/NM NM-
2.0 4.0 6.0 8.0 9.0 9.2

GD VG FN VF VF/NM NM-
2.0 4.0 6.0 8.0 9.0 9.2

BATMAN
DC Comics: 1966 - Present

Act II Popcorn mini-comic(1998) 4.00
Batman #121 Toys R Us edition (1997) r/1st Mr. Freeze 4.00
Batman #279 Mini-comic with Monogram Model kit (1995) 4.00
Batman #362 Mervyn's edition (1989) 5.00
Batman #608 New York Post edition (2002) 4.00
Batman Adventures #25 Best Western edition (1997) 4.00
Batman and Other DC Classics 1 (1989, giveaway)-DC Comics/Diamond Comic Distributors; Batman origin-r/Batman #47, Camelot 3000-r, Justice League-r('87), New Teen Titans-r 5.00
Batman and Robin movie preview (1997, 8 pgs.) Kellogg's Cereal promo 3.00
Batman Beyond Six Flags edition 1 2 3 5 6 8
Batman: Canadian Multiculturalism Custom (1992) 5.00
Batman Claritan edition (1999) 3.00
Kellogg's Poptarts comics (1966, Set of 6, 16 pgs.); All were folded and placed in Poptarts boxes. Infantino art on Catwoman and Joker issues.
"The Man in the Iron Mask", "The Penguin's Fowl Play", "The Joker's Happy Victims", "The Catwoman's Catnapping Caper", "The Mad Hatter's Hat Crimes", "The Case of the Batman II"
each.... 5 10 15 30 48 65
Mask of the Phantasm (1993) Mini-comic released w/video
1 2 3 5 7 9
Onstar - Auto Show Special Edition (OnStar Corp., 2001, 8 pgs.) Riddler app. 3.00
Pizza Hut giveaway (12/77)-exact-r of #122,123; Joker-c/story
2 4 6 9 12 15
Prell Shampoo giveaway (1966, 16 pgs.)- "The Joker's Practical Jokes" (6-7/8x3-3/8") 7 14 21 49 80 110
Revell in pack (1995) 4.00
...: The 10-Cent Adventure (3/02, 10¢) intro. to the "Bruce Wayne: Murderer" x-over; Rucka-s/ Burchett & Janson-a/Dave Johnson-c; these are alternate copies with special outer half-covers (at least 10 different) promoting comics, toys and games shops 3.00

BATMAN RECORD COMIC
National Periodical Publications: 1966 (one-shot)

1-With record (still sealed) 13 26 39 91 176 260
Comic only 8 16 24 58 97 135

BEETLE BAILEY
Charlton Comics: 1969-1970 (Giveaways)

Armed Forces ('69)-same as regular issue (#68) 2 4 6 10 14 18
Armed Forces ('70) 2 4 6 10 14 18
Bold Detergent ('69)-same as regular issue (#67) 2 4 6 10 14 18
Cerebral Palsy Assn. V2#71('69) - V2#73(#1,1/70) 4.00
Red Cross (1969, 5x7", 16 pgs., paper-c) 2 4 6 10 14 18

BELLAIRE BICYCLE CO.
Bellaire Bicycle Co.: 1940 (promotional comic)

nn-Contains Wonderworld #12 w/new-c. Contents can vary w/diff. 1940's books
25 50 75 150 245 340

BEST WESTERN GIVEAWAY
DC Comics: 1999

nn-Best Western hotels 2.50

BETTER LIFE FOR YOU, A
Harvey Publications Inc.: (16 pgs., paper cover)

nn-Better living through higher productivity 3 6 9 16 22 28

BEWARE THE BOOBY TRAP
Malcolm Alter: 1970 (5" x 7")

nn-Deals with drug abuse 4 8 12 24 37 50

B-FORCE (Milwaukee Brewers and Wisconsin Dental Asso.)
Dark Horse Comics: 2001 (School and stadium giveaway)

nn-Brewers players combat the evils of smokeless tobacco 3.00

BIG BOY (see Adventures of...)

BIG JIM'S P.A.C.K.
Mattel, Inc. (Marvel Comics): No date (1975) (16 pgs.)

nn-Giveaway with Big Jim doll; Buscema/Sinnott-c/a 4 8 12 24 37 50

"BILL AND TED'S EXCELLENT ADVENTURE" MOVIE ADAPTATION
DC Comics: 1989 (No cover price)

nn-Torres-a 4.00

BIONICLE (LEGO robot toys)
DC Comics: Jun, 2001 - No. 27, Nov, 2005 ($2.25/$3.25, 16 pages, available to LEGO club members)

1 1 2 3 5 6 8
2-5 6.00
6-13 4.00
14-27 3.00
The Legend of Bionicle (McDonald's Mini-comic, 4-1/4 x 7") 4.00
Special Edition #0 (Six Heroes...One Destiny) '03 San Diego Comic Con; Ashley Wood-c 6.00

BLACK GOLD
Esso Service Station (Giveaway): 1945? (8 pgs. in color)

nn-Reprints from True Comics 6 12 18 27 33 38

BLADE SINS OF THE FATHER
Marvel Comics: Aug, 1996 (24 pgs. with paper cover)

1-Theatrical preview; possibly limited to 2000 copies (Value will be based on sale)

BLAZING FOREST, THE (See Forest Fire and Smokey Bear)
Western Printing: 1962 (20 pgs., 5x7", slick-c)

nn-Smokey The Bear fire prevention 3 6 9 14 20 26

BLESSED PIUS X
Catechetical Guild (Giveaway): No date (Text/comics, 32 pgs., paper-c)

nn 6 12 18 33 41 48

BLIND JUSTICE (Also see Batman: Blind Justice)
DC Comics/Diamond Comic Distributors: 1989 (Giveaway, squarebound)

nn-Contains Detective #598-600 by Batman movie writer Sam Hamm, w/covers; published same time as originals? 6.00

BLONDIE COMICS
Harvey Publications: 1950-1964

1950 Giveaway 8 16 24 40 50 60
1962,1964 Giveaway 3 6 9 16 23 30
N. Y. State Dept. of Mental Hygiene Giveaway-(1950) Regular size; 16 pgs.; no # 4 8 12 24 37 50
N. Y. State Dept. of Mental Hygiene Giveaway-(1956) Regular size; 16 pgs.; no # 3 6 9 17 25 32
N. Y. State Dept. of Mental Hygiene Giveaway-(1961) Regular size; 16 pgs.; no # 3 6 9 16 22 28

BLOOD IS THE HARVEST
Catechetical Guild: 1950 (32 pgs., paper-c)

(Scarce)-Anti-communism (21 known copies) 181 362 543 1158 1979 2800
Black & white version (5 known copies), saddle stitched
90 180 270 576 988 1400
Untrimmed version (only one known copy); estimated value - $1000
NOTE: *In 1979 nine copies of the color version surfaced from the old Guild's files plus the five black & white copies.*

BLUE BIRD CHILDREN'S MAGAZINE, THE
Graphic Information Service: V1#2, 1957 - No. 10 1958 (16 pgs., soft-c, regular size)

V1#2-10: Pat, Pete & Blue Bird app. 2 4 6 8 11 14

BLUE BIRD COMICS
Various Shoe Stores/Charlton Comics: Late 1940's - 1964 (Giveaway)

nn(1947-50)(36 pgs.)-Several issues; Human Torch, Sub-Mariner app. in some
18 36 54 103 162 220
1959-Li'l Genius, Timmy the Timid Ghost, Wild Bill Hickok (All #1)
3 6 9 15 21 26
1959-(6 titles; all #2) Black Fury #1,4,5, Freddy #4, Li'l Genius, Timmy the Timid Ghost #4, Masked Raider #4, Wild Bill Hickok (Charlton) 3 6 9 14 20 25
1959-(#5) Masked Raider #21 3 6 9 16 22 28
1960-(6 titles)(All #4) Black Fury #6,8,9, Masked Raider #6, Freddy #8,9, Timmy the Timid Ghost #6,9, Li'l Genius #7,9 (Charlt.) 3 6 9 14 19 24
1961,1962-(All #10's) Atomic Mouse #12,13,16, Black Fury #11,12, Freddy, Li'l Genius, Masked Raider, Six Gun Heroes, Texas Rangers in Action, Timmy the Ghost, Wild Bill Hickok, Wyatt Earp #3,11-13,16-18 (Charlton) 2 4 6 13 18 22
1963-Texas Rangers #17 (Charlton) 2 4 6 9 13 16
1964-Mysteries of Unexplored Worlds #18, Teenage Hotrodders #18, War Heroes #18 (Charlton) 2 4 6 9 13 16
1965-War Heroes #18 2 4 6 8 10 12
NOTE: *More than one issue of each character could have been published each year. Numbering is sporadic.*

BOB & BETTY & SANTA'S WISHING WHISTLE
Sears Roebuck & Co.: 1941 (Christmas giveaway, 12 pgs.)

nn 14 28 42 78 112 145

BOBBY BENSON'S B-BAR-B RIDERS (Radio)
Magazine Enterprises/AC Comics

...in the Tunnel of Gold-(1936, 5-1/4x8"; 100 pgs.) Radio giveaway by Hecker-H.O. Company (H.O. Oats); contains 22 color pgs. of comics, rest in novel form
11 22 33 64 90 115
...And The Lost Herd-same as above 11 22 33 64 90 115

BOBBY SHELBY COMICS
Shelby Cycle Co./Harvey Publications: 1949

Bozo the Clown © DELL

Bulletman - Well Known Comics © FAW

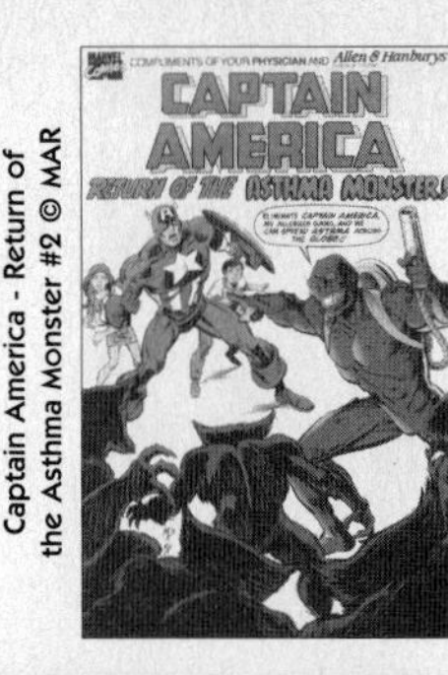

Captain America - Return of the Asthma Monster #2 © MAR

GD 2.0 | VG 4.0 | FN 6.0 | VF 8.0 | VF/NM 9.0 | NM- 9.2

nn 5 10 14 20 24 28

BONE
Cartoon Books: Halloween, 2008 (8-1/2" x 5-3/8" mini-comic giveaway)
nn-Jeff Smith-s/a 2.00

BOY SCOUT ADVENTURE
Boy Scouts of America: 1954 (16 pgs., paper cover)
nn 5 10 14 20 24 28

BOYS' RANCH
Harvey Publications: 1951
Shoe Store Giveaway #5,6 (Identical to regular issues except Simon & Kirby centerfold replaced with ad) 14 28 42 76 108 140

BOZO THE CLOWN (TV)
Dell Publishing Co.: 1961
Giveaway-1961, 16 pgs., 3-1/2x7-1/4", Apsco Products 5 10 15 32 51 70

BRER RABBIT IN "ICE CREAM FOR THE PARTY"
American Dairy Association: 1955 (5x7-1/4", 16 pgs., soft-c) (Walt Disney) (Premium)
nn-(Scarce) 37 74 111 222 361 500

BUCK ROGERS (In the 25th Century)
Kelloggs Corn Flakes Giveaway: 1933 (6x8", 36 pgs)
370A-By Phil Nowlan & Dick Calkins; 1st Buck Rogers radio premium & 1st app. in comics (tells origin) (Reissued in 1995) 80 160 240 600 - -
with envelope 100 200 300 750 - -

BUGS BUNNY (Puffed Rice Giveaway)
Quaker Cereals: 1949 (32 pgs. each, 3-1/8x6-7/8")
A1-Traps the Counterfeiters, A2-Aboard Mystery Submarine, A3- Rocket to the Moon, A4-Lion Tamer, A5-Rescues the Beautiful Princess, B1-Buried Treasure, B2-Outwits the Smugglers, B3-Joins the Marines, B4-Meets the Dwarf Ghost, B5-Finds Aladdin's Lamp, C1-Lost in the Frozen North, C2-Secret Agent, C3-Captured by Cannibals, C4-Fights the Man from Mars, C5-And the Haunted Cave
each.... 9 18 27 52 69 85
Mailing Envelope (has illo of Bugs on front)(Each envelope designates what set it contains, A,B or C on front) 9 18 27 52 69 85

BUGS BUNNY (3-D)
Cheerios Giveaway: 1953 (Pocket size) (15 titles)
each.... 11 22 33 62 86 110
Mailing Envelope (has Bugs drawn on front) 11 22 33 62 86 110

BUGS BUNNY
DC Comics: May, 1997 ($4.95, 24 pgs., comic-sized)
1-Numbered ed. of 100,000; "1st Day of Issue" stamp cancellation on-c 6.00

BUGS BUNNY POSTAL COMIC
DC Comics: 1997 (64 pgs., 7.5" x 5")
nn -Mail Fan; Daffy Duck app. 4.50

BULLETMAN
Fawcett Publications
Well Known Comics (1942)-Paper-c, glued binding; printed in red (Bestmaid/Samuel Lowe giveaway) 15 30 45 85 130 175

BULLS-EYE (Cody of The Pony Express No. 8 on)
Charlton: 1955
Great Scott Shoe Store giveaway-Reprints #2 with new cover 18 36 54 103 162 220

BUSTER BROWN COMICS (Radio)(Also see My Dog Tige in Promotional sec.)
Brown Shoe Co.: 1945 - No. 43, 1959 (No. 5: paper-c)
nn, nd (#1,scarce)-Featuring Smilin' Ed McConnell & the Buster Brown gang "Midnight" the cat, "Squeaky" the mouse & "Froggy" the Gremlin; covers mention diff. shoe stores. Contains adventure stories 60 120 180 381 653 925
2 19 38 57 111 178 245
3,5-10 13 26 39 74 105 135
4 (Rare)-Low print run due to paper shortage 17 34 51 98 154 210
11-20 9 18 27 47 61 75
21-24,26-28 6 12 18 31 38 45
25,33-37,40,41-Crandall-a in all 10 20 30 56 76 95
29-32-"Interplanetary Police Vs. the Space Siren" by Crandall (pencils only #29) 10 20 30 58 79 100
38,39,42,43 6 12 18 31 38 45

BUSTER BROWN COMICS (Radio)
Brown Shoe Co: 1950s
...Goes to Mars (2/58-Western Printing), slick-c, 20 pgs., reg. size 13 26 39 72 101 130
...In "Buster Makes the Team!" (1959-Custom Comics) 8 16 24 44 57 70
...In The Jet Age ('50s), slick-c, 20 pgs., 5x7-1/4" 10 20 30 58 79 100
...Of the Safety Patrol ('60-Custom Comics) 3 6 9 18 27 35
...Out of This World ('59-Custom Comics) 7 14 21 35 43 50
...Safety Coloring Book ('58, 16 pgs.)-Slick paper 7 14 21 35 43 50

GD 2.0 | VG 4.0 | FN 6.0 | VF 8.0 | VF/NM 9.0 | NM- 9.2

CALL FROM CHRIST
Catechetical Educational Society: 1952 (Giveaway, 36 pgs.)
nn 6 12 18 33 41 48

CANCELLED COMIC CAVALCADE
DC Comics, Inc.: Summer, 1978 - No. 2, Fall, 1978 (8-1/2x11", B&W)
(Xeroxed pgs. on one side only w/blue cover and taped spine)(Only 35 sets produced)
1-(412 pgs.) Contains xeroxed copies of art for: Black Lightning #12, cover to #13; Claw #13,14; The Deserter #1; Doorway to Nightmare #6; Firestorm #6; The Green Team #2,3.
2-(532 pgs.) Contains xeroxed copies of art for: Kamandi #60 (including Omac), #61; Prez #5; Shade #9 (including The Odd Man); Showcase #105 (Deadman), 106 (The Creeper); Secret Society of Super Villains #16 & 17; The Vixen #1; and covers to Army at War #2, Battle Classics #3, Demand Classics #1 & 2, Dynamic Classics #3, Mr. Miracle #26, Ragman #6, Weird Mystery #25 & 26, & Western Classics #1 & 2.
(A FN set of Number 1 & 2 was sold in 2005 for $3680; a VG set sold in 2007 for $2629)

NOTE: *In June, 1978, DC cancelled several of their titles. For copyright purposes, the unpublished original art for these titles was xeroxed, bound in the above books, published and distributed. Only 35 copies were made. Beware of bootleg copies.*

CAP'N CRUNCH COMICS (See Quaker Oats)
Quaker Oats Co.: 1963; 1965 (16 pgs.; miniature giveaways; 2-1/2x6-1/2")
(1963 titles)- "The Picture Pirates", "The Fountain of Youth", "I'm Dreaming of a Wide Isthmus". (1965 titles)- "Bewitched, Betwitched, & Betweaked", "Seadog Meets the Witch Doctor", "A Witch in Time" 5 10 15 34 55 75

CAPTAIN ACTION (Toy)
National Periodical Publications
...& Action Boy('67)-Ideal Toy Co. giveaway (1st app. Captain Action) 11 22 33 79 147 215

CAPTAIN AMERICA
Marvel Comics Group
...& The Campbell Kids (1980, 36pg. giveaway, Campbell's Soup/U.S. Dept. of Energy) 2 4 6 9 13 16
...Goes To War Against Drugs(1990, no #, giveaway)-Distributed to direct sales shops; 2nd printing exists 1 2 3 5 6 8
...Meets The Asthma Monster (1987, no #, giveaway, Your Physician and Glaxo, Inc.) 1 2 3 5 6 8
Return of The Asthma Monster Vol. 1 #2 (1992, giveaway, Your Physician & Allen & Hanbury's) 1 2 3 5 6 8
...Vs. Asthma Monster (1990, no #, giveaway, Your Physician & Allen & Hanbury's) 1 2 3 5 6 8

CAPTAIN AMERICA COMICS
Timely/Marvel Comics: 1954
Shoestore Giveaway #77 81 162 243 518 884 1250

CAPTAIN ATOM
Nationwide Publishers
...- Secret of the Columbian Jungle (16 pgs. in color, paper-c, 3-3/4x5-1/8")- Fireside Marshmallow giveaway 6 12 18 28 34 40

CAPTAIN BEN DIX
Bendix Aviation Corporation: 1943 (Small size)
nn 8 16 24 42 54 65

CAPTAIN BEN DIX IN ACTION WITH THE INVISIBLE CREW
Bendix Aviation Corp.: 1940s (nd), (20 pgs, 8-1/4"x11", heavy paper)
nn-WWII bomber-c; Japanese app. 7 14 21 35 43 50

CAPTAIN BEN DIX IN SECRETS OF THE INVISIBLE CREW
Bendix Aviation Corp.: 1940s (nd), (32 pgs, soft-c)
nn 6 12 18 31 38 45

CAPTAIN FORTUNE PRESENTS
Vital Publications: 1955 - 1959 (Giveaway, 3-1/4x6-7/8", 16 pgs.)
"Davy Crockett in Episodes of the Creek War", "Davy Crockett at the Alamo", "In Sherwood Forest Tells Strange Tales of Robin Hood" ('57), "Meets Bolivar the Liberator" ('59), "Tells How Buffalo Bill Fights the Dog Soldiers" ('57), "Young Davy Crockett" 4 7 9 14 17 20

CAPTAIN GALLANT (...of the Foreign Legion) (TV)
Charlton Comics
Heinz Foods Premium (#1?)(1955; regular size)-U.S. Pictorial; contains Buster Crabbe photos; Don Heck-a 1 3 4 6 8 10
Mailing Envelope 20.00

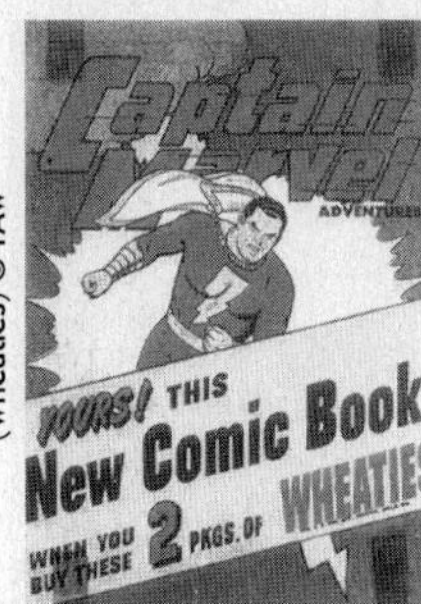

Captain Marvel Adventures (Wheaties) © FAW

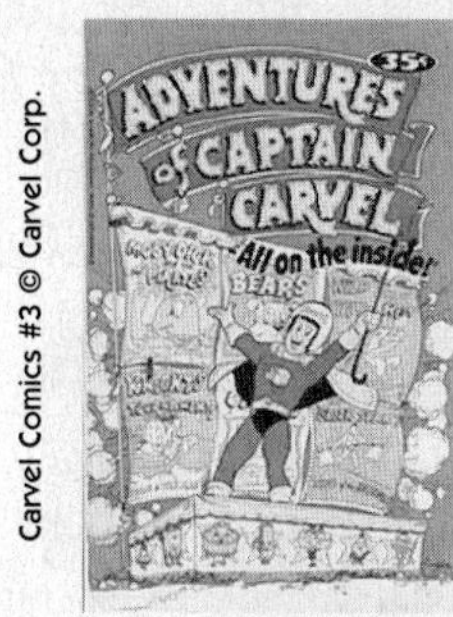

Carvel Comics #3 © Carvel Corp.

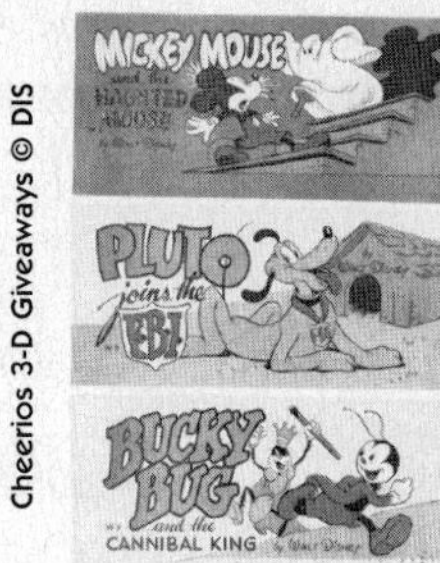

Cheerios 3-D Giveaways © DIS

	GD 2.0	VG 4.0	FN 6.0	VF 8.0	VF/NM 9.0	NM- 9.2

CAPTAIN JOLLY ADVENTURES
Johnston and Cushing: 1950's, nd (Post Corn Fetti cereal giveaway) (5-1/4" x 4-1/2")

	GD	VG	FN	VF	VF/NM	NM-
1-3: 1-Captain Jolly Advs. 2-Captain Jolly and His Pirate Crew in Off To Treasure Island. 3-C.J. & His Pirate Crew in The Terror Of The Deep	2	4	5	7	8	10

CAPTAIN MARVEL ADVENTURES
Fawcett Publications

	GD	VG	FN	VF	VF/NM	NM-
Bond Bread Giveaways-(24 pgs.; pocket size-7-1/4x3-1/2"; paper cover): "...& the Stolen City" ('48), "The Boy Who Never Heard of Capt. Marvel", "Meets the Weatherman" (1950) (reprint) each....	21	42	63	126	208	290
...Well Known Comics (1944; 12 pgs.; 8-1/2x10-1/2")-printed in red & in blue; soft-c; glued binding - (Bestmaid/Samuel Lowe Co. giveaway)	15	30	45	94	147	200

CAPTAIN MARVEL ADVENTURES (Also see Flash and Funny Stuff)
Fawcett Publications (Wheaties Giveaway): 1945 (6x8", full color, paper-c)

	GD	VG	FN	VF	VF/NM	NM-
nn- "Captain Marvel & the Threads of Life" plus 2 other stories (32 pgs.)	80	160	320	600	-	-

NOTE: *All copies were taped at each corner to a box of Wheaties and are never found in Fine or Mint condition. Prices listed for each grade include tape.*

CAPTAIN MARVEL AND THE LTS. OF SAFETY
Ebasco Services/Fawcett Publications: 1950 - 1951 (3 issues - no No.'s)

	GD	VG	FN	VF	VF/NM	NM-
nn (#1) "Danger Flies a Kite" ('50, scarce),	58	116	174	371	636	900
nn (#2)"Danger Takes to Climbing" ('50),	47	94	141	296	498	700
nn (#3)"Danger Smashes Street Lights" ('51)	47	94	141	296	498	700

CAPTAIN MARVEL, JR.
Fawcett Publications: (1944; 12 pgs.; 8-1/2x10-1/2")

	GD	VG	FN	VF	VF/NM	NM-
...Well Known Comics (Printed in blue; paper-c, glued binding)-Bestmaid/Samuel Lowe Co. giveaway	14	28	42	76	108	140

CARDINAL MINDSZENTY (The Truth Behind the Trial of...)
Catechetical Guild Education Society: 1949 (24 pgs., paper cover)

	GD	VG	FN	VF	VF/NM	NM-
nn-Anti-communism	11	22	33	60	83	105
Press Proof-(Very Rare)-(Full color, 7-1/2x11-3/4", untrimmed) Only two known copies						300.00
Preview Copy (B&W, stapled), 18 pgs.; contains first 13 pgs. of Cardinal Mindszenty and was sent out as an advance promotion. Only one known copy						300.00 - 400.00

NOTE: *Regular edition also printed in French. There was also a movie released in 1949 called "Guilty of Treason" which is a fact-based account of the trial and imprisonment of Cardinal Mindszenty by the Communist regime in Hungary.*

CARNIVAL OF COMICS
Fleet-Air Shoes: 1954 (Giveaway)

	GD	VG	FN	VF	VF/NM	NM-
nn-Contains a comic bound with new cover; several combinations possible; Charlton's Eh! known	5	10	15	24	30	35

CARTOON NETWORK
DC Comics: 1997 (Giveaway)

	GD	VG	FN	VF	VF/NM	NM-
nn-reprints Cow and Chicken, Scooby-Doo, & Flintstones stories						4.00

CARVEL COMICS (Amazing Advs. of Capt. Carvel)
Carvel Corp. (Ice Cream): 1975 - No. 5, 1976 (25¢; #3-5: 35¢) (#4,5: 3-1/4x5")

	GD	VG	FN	VF	VF/NM	NM-
1-3	1	2	3	5	6	8
4,5(1976)-Baseball theme	2	4	6	8	10	12

CASE OF THE WASTED WATER, THE
Rheem Water Heating: 1972? (Giveaway)

	GD	VG	FN	VF	VF/NM	NM-
nn-Neal Adams-a	4	8	12	28	44	60

CASPER SPECIAL
Target Stores (Harvey): nd (Dec, 1990) (Giveaway with $1.00 cover)

	GD	VG	FN	VF	VF/NM	NM-
Three issues-Given away with Casper video						6.00

CASPER, THE FRIENDLY GHOST (Paramount Picture Star...)(2nd Series)
Harvey Publications

	GD	VG	FN	VF	VF/NM	NM-
American Dental Association (Giveaways):						
...'s Dental Health Activity Book-1977	2	4	6	8	11	14
...Presents Space Age Dentistry-1972	2	4	6	9	13	16
..., His Den, & Their Dentist Fight the Tooth Demons-1974	2	4	6	9	13	16
Casper Rides the School Bus (1960, 7x3.5", 16 pgs.)	2	4	6	9	13	16

CELEBRATE THE CENTURY SUPERHEROES STAMP ALBUM
DC Comics: 1998 - No. 5, 2000 (32 pgs.)

	GD	VG	FN	VF	VF/NM	NM-
1-5: Historical stories hosted by DC heroes						4.00

CENTIPEDE
DC Comics: 1983

	GD	VG	FN	VF	VF/NM	NM-
1-Based on Atari video game	2	4	6	8	11	14

CENTURY OF COMICS
Eastern Color Printing Co.: 1933 (100 pgs.)
Bought by Wheatena, Malt-O-Milk, John Wanamaker, Kinney Shoe Stores, & others to be used as premiums and radio giveaways. No publisher listed.

	GD	VG	FN	VF	VF/NM	NM-
nn-Mutt & Jeff, Joe Palooka, etc. reprints	2350	4700	7050	18,000	-	-

CHEERIOS PREMIUMS (Disney)
Walt Disney Productions: 1947 (16 titles, pocket size, 32 pgs.)

	GD	VG	FN	VF	VF/NM	NM-
Mailing Envelope for each set "W,X,Y & Z" (has Mickey illo on front)(each envelope designates the set it contains on the front)	11	22	33	60	83	105
Set "W"						
W1-Donald Duck & the Pirates	11	22	33	60	83	105
W2-Bucky Bug & the Cannibal King	7	14	21	37	46	55
W3-Pluto Joins the F.B.I.	7	14	21	37	46	55
W4-Mickey Mouse & the Haunted House	8	16	24	42	54	65
Set "X"						
X1-Donald Duck, Counter Spy	11	22	33	60	83	105
X2-Goofy Lost in the Desert	7	14	21	37	46	55
X3-Br'er Rabbit Outwits Br'er Fox	7	14	21	37	46	55
X4-Mickey Mouse at the Rodeo	8	16	24	42	54	65
Set "Y"						
Y1-Donald Duck's Atom Bomb by Carl Barks. Disney has banned reprinting this book	76	152	228	483	829	1175
Y2-Br'er Rabbit's Secret	7	14	21	37	46	55
Y3-Dumbo & the Circus Mystery	7	14	21	37	46	55
Y4-Mickey Mouse Meets the Wizard	8	16	24	42	54	65
Set "Z"						
Z1-Donald Duck Pilots a Jet Plane (not by Barks)	11	22	33	60	83	105
Z2-Pluto Turns Sleuth Hound	7	14	21	37	46	55
Z3-The Seven Dwarfs & the Enchanted Mtn.	8	16	24	42	54	65
Z4-Mickey Mouse's Secret Room	8	16	24	42	54	65

CHEERIOS 3-D GIVEAWAYS (Disney)
Walt Disney Productions: 1954 (24 titles, pocket size) (Glasses came in envelopes)

	GD	VG	FN	VF	VF/NM	NM-
Glasses only...	8	16	24	40	50	60
Mailing Envelope (no art on front)	9	18	27	47	61	75
(Set 1)						
1-Donald Duck & Uncle Scrooge, the Firefighters	9	18	27	52	69	85
2-Mickey Mouse & Goofy, Pirate Plunder	9	18	27	47	61	75
3-Donald Duck's Nephews, the Fabulous Inventors	9	18	27	52	69	85
4-Mickey Mouse, Secret of the Ming Vase	9	18	27	47	61	75
5-Donald Duck with Huey, Dewey, & Louie; ...the Seafarers (title on 2nd page)	9	18	27	52	69	85
6-Mickey Mouse, Moaning Mountain	9	18	27	47	61	75
7-Donald Duck, Apache Gold	9	18	27	52	69	85
8-Mickey Mouse, Flight to Nowhere	9	18	27	47	61	75
(Set 2)						
1-Donald Duck, Treasure of Timbuktu	9	18	27	52	69	85
2-Mickey Mouse & Pluto, Operation China	9	18	27	47	61	75
3-Donald Duck and the Magic Cows	9	18	27	52	69	85
4-Mickey Mouse & Goofy, Kid Kokonut	9	18	27	47	61	75
5-Donald Duck, Mystery Ship	9	18	27	52	69	85
6-Mickey Mouse, Phantom Sheriff	9	18	27	47	61	75
7-Donald Duck, Circus Adventures	9	18	27	52	69	85
8-Mickey Mouse, Arctic Explorers	9	18	27	47	61	75
(Set 3)						
1-Donald Duck & Witch Hazel	9	18	27	52	69	85
2-Mickey Mouse in Darkest Africa	9	18	27	47	61	75
3-Donald Duck & Uncle Scrooge, Timber Trouble	9	18	27	52	69	85
4-Mickey Mouse, Rajah's Rescue	9	18	27	47	61	75
5-Donald Duck in Robot Reporter	9	18	27	52	69	85
6-Mickey Mouse, Slumbering Sleuth	9	18	27	47	61	75
7-Donald Duck in the Foreign Legion	9	18	27	52	69	85
8-Mickey Mouse, Airwalking Wonder	9	18	27	47	61	75

CHESTY AND COPTIE (Disney)
Los Angeles Community Chest: 1946 (Giveaway, 4pgs.)

	GD	VG	FN	VF	VF/NM	NM-
nn-(One known copy) by Floyd Gottfredson	77	154	231	489	845	1200

CHESTY AND HIS HELPERS (Disney)
Los Angeles War Chest: 1943 (Giveaway, 12 pgs., 5-1/2x7-1/4")

	GD	VG	FN	VF	VF/NM	NM-
nn-Chesty & Coptie	50	100	150	315	533	750

CHOCOLATE THE FLAVOR OF FRIENDSHIP AROUND THE WORLD
The Nestle Company: 1955

	GD	VG	FN	VF	VF/NM	NM-
nn	6	12	18	28	34	40

CHRISTMAS ADVENTURE, THE
S. Rose (H. L. Green Giveaway): 1963 (16 pgs.)

	GD	VG	FN	VF	VF/NM	NM-
nn	2	4	6	9	13	16

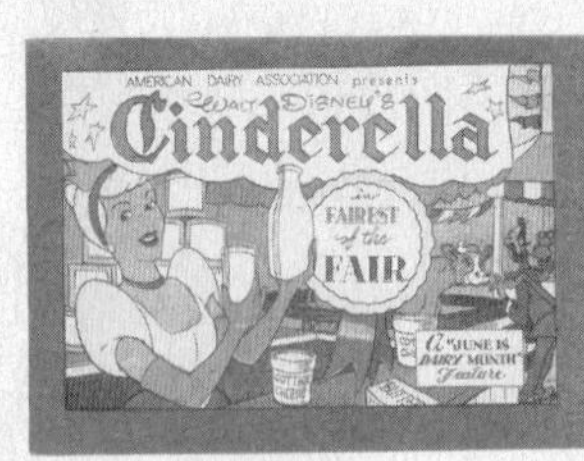

Cinderella in "Fairest of the Fair" © DIS

Cinema Comics Herald - Bedtime Story

Classics Giveaways - Saks 34th St. © Saks

	GD 2.0	VG 4.0	FN 6.0	VF 8.0	VF/NM 9.0	NM- 9.2

CHRISTMAS ADVENTURES WITH ELMER THE ELF
1949 (paper-c)
nn 4 7 10 14 17 20

CHRISTMAS AT THE ROTUNDA (Titled Ford Rotunda Christmas Book 1957 on) (Regular size)
Ford Motor Co. (Western Printing): 1954 - 1961 (Given away every Christmas at one location)
1954-56 issues (nn's) 7 14 21 37 46 55
1957-61 issues (nn's) 6 12 18 31 38 45

CHRISTMAS CAROL, A
Sears Roebuck & Co.: No date (1942-43) (Giveaway, 32 pgs., 8-1/4x10-3/4", paper cover)
nn-Comics & coloring book 18 36 54 105 165 225

CHRISTMAS CAROL, A
Sears Roebuck & Co.: 1940s ? (Christmas giveaway, 20 pgs.)
nn-Comic book & animated coloring book 17 34 51 100 158 215

CHRISTMAS CAROLS
Hot Shoppes Giveaway: 1959? (16 pgs.)
nn 4 8 11 16 19 22

CHRISTMAS COLORING FUN
H. Burnside: 1964 (20 pgs., slick-c, B&W)
nn 2 4 6 11 16 20

CHRISTMAS DREAM, A
Promotional Publishing Co.: 1950 (Kinney Shoe Store Giveaway, 16 pgs.)
nn 5 10 15 23 28 32

CHRISTMAS DREAM, A
J. J. Newberry Co.: 1952? (Giveaway, paper cover, 16 pgs.)
nn 4 8 12 18 22 25

CHRISTMAS DREAM, A
Promotional Publ. Co.: 1952 (Giveaway, 16 pgs., paper cover)
nn 4 8 12 18 22 25

CHRISTMAS FUN AROUND THE WORLD
No publisher: No date (early 50's) (16 pgs., paper cover)
nn 5 10 15 22 26 30

CHRISTMAS FUN BOOK
G. C. Murphy Co.: 1950 (Giveaway, paper cover)
nn-Contains paper dolls 6 12 18 28 34 40

CHRISTMAS IS COMING!
No publisher: No date (early 50's?) (Store giveaway, 16 pgs.)
nn 4 8 12 18 22 25

CHRISTMAS JOURNEY THROUGH SPACE
Promotional Publishing Co.: 1960
nn-Reprints 1954 issue Jolly Christmas Book with new slick cover
3 6 9 16 23 30

CHRISTMAS ON THE MOON
W. T. Grant Co.: 1958 (Giveaway, 20 pgs., slick cover)
nn 8 16 24 44 57 70

CHRISTMAS PLAY BOOK
Gould-Stoner Co.: 1946 (Giveaway, 16 pgs., paper cover)
nn 8 16 24 44 57 70

CHRISTMAS ROUNDUP
Promotional Publishing Co.: 1960
nn-Marv Levy-c/a 2 4 6 9 13 16

CHRISTMAS STORY CUT-OUT BOOK, THE
Catechetical Guild: No. 393, 1951 (15¢, 36 pgs.)
393-Half text & half comics 8 16 24 42 54 65

CHRISTMAS USA (Through 300 Years) (Also see Uncle Sam's...)
Promotional Publ. Co.: 1956 (Giveaway)
nn-Marv Levy-c/a 4 7 9 14 16 18

CHRISTMAS WITH SNOW WHITE AND THE SEVEN DWARFS
Kobackers Giftstore of Buffalo, N.Y.: 1953 (16 pgs., paper-c)
nn 8 16 24 42 54 65

CHRISTOPHERS, THE
Catechetical Guild: 1951 (Giveaway, 36 pgs.) (Some copies have 15¢ sticker)
nn-Stalin as Satan in Hell 21 42 63 121 201 280

CINDERELLA IN "FAIREST OF THE FAIR" (Walt Disney)
American Dairy Association (Premium): 1955 (5x7-1/4", 16 pgs., soft-c)
nn 10 20 30 56 76 95

CINEMA COMICS HERALD
Paramount Pictures/Universal/RKO/20th Century Fox/Republic:
1941 - 1943 (4-pg. movie "trailers", paper-c, 7-1/2x10-1/2")(Giveaway)
"Mr. Bug Goes to Town" (1941) 15 30 45 90 140 190
"Bedtime Story" 11 22 33 64 90 115
"Lady For A Night", John Wayne, Joan Blondell ('42) 18 36 54 107 169 230
"Reap The Wild Wind" (1942) 12 24 36 69 97 125
"Thunder Birds" (1942) 11 22 33 64 90 115
"They All Kissed the Bride" 11 22 33 64 90 115
"Arabian Nights" (nd) 12 24 36 69 97 125
"Bombardie" (1943) 11 22 33 64 90 115
"Crash Dive" (1943)-Tyrone Power 12 24 36 69 97 125
NOTE: *The 1941-42 issues contain line art with color photos. 1943 issues are line art.*

CLASSICS GIVEAWAYS (Classic Comics reprints)
12/41–Walter Theatre Enterprises (Huntington, WV) giveaway containing #2 (orig.) w/new generic-c (only 1 known copy) 84 168 252 533 917 1300
1942–Double Comics containing CC#1 (orig.) (diff. cover) (not actually a giveaway) (very rare) (also see Double Comics) (only one known copy)
148 296 444 940 1620 2300
12/42–Saks 34th St. Giveaway containing CC#7 (orig.) (diff. cover) (very rare; only 6 known copies) 300 600 900 2011 3506 5000
2/43–American Comics containing CC#8 (orig.) (Liberty Theatre giveaway) (different cover) (only one known copy) (see American Comics) 97 194 291 616 1058 1500
12/44–Robin Hood Flour Co. Giveaway - #7-CC(R) (diff. cover) (rare) (edition probably 5 [22]) 155 310 465 984 1692 2400
NOTE: How are above editions determined without CC covers? 1942 is dated 1942, and CC#1-first reprint did not come out until 5/43. 12/42 and 2/43 are determined by blue note at bottom of first text page only in original edition. 12/44 is estimated from page width each reprint edition had progressively slightly smaller page width.
1951–Shelter Thru the Ages (C.I. Educational Series) (actually Giveaway by the Ruberoid Co.) (16 pgs.) (contains original artwork by H. C. Kiefer) (there are 5 diff. back cover ad variations: "Ranch" house ad, "Igloo" ad, "Doll House" ad, "Tree House" ad & blank) (scarce) 52 104 156 330 565 800
1952–George Daynor Biography Giveaway (CC logo) (partly comic book/pictures/newspaper articles) (story of man who built Palace Depression out of junkyard swamp in NJ) (64 pgs.) (very rare; only 3 known copies, one missing back-c)
360 720 1080 2556 4428 6300
1953–Westinghouse/Dreams of a Man (C.I. Educational Series) (Westinghousebio./Westinghouse Co. giveaway) (contains original artwork by H. C. Kiefer) (16 pgs.) (also French/Spanish/Italian versions) (scarce) 47 94 141 296 498 700
NOTE: Reproductions of 1951, 1952, and 1953 exist with color photocopy covers and black & white photocopy interior ("W.C.N. Reprint") 2 4 5 7 8 10
1951-53–Coward Shoe Giveaways (all editions very rare); 2 variations of back-c ad exist:
With back-c photo ad: 5 (87), 12 (89), 22 (85), 32 (85), 49 (85), 69 (87), 72 (no HRN), 80 (0), 91 (0), 92 (0), 96 (0), 98 (0), 100 (0), 101 (0), 103-105 (all Os)
29 58 87 170 278 385
With back-c cartoon ad: 106-109 (all 0s), 110 (111), 112 (0)
31 62 93 184 302 420
1956–Ben Franklin 5-10 Store Giveaway (#65-PC with back cover ad) (scarce) 24 48 72 142 234 325
1956–Ben Franklin Insurance Co. Giveaway (#65-PC with diff. back cover ad) (very rare) 47 94 141 296 498 700
11/56–Sealtest Co. Edition - #4 (135) (identical to regular edition except for Sealtest logo printed, not stamped, on front cover) (only two copies known to exist)
28 56 84 165 270 375
1958–Get-Well Giveaway containing #15-CI (new cartoon-type cover) (Pressman Pharmacy) (only one copy known to exist) 27 54 81 162 266 370
1967-68–Twin Circle Giveaway Editions - all HRN 166, with back cover ad for National Catholic Press.
2(R68), 4(R67), 10(R68), 13(R68) 3 6 9 21 32 42
48(R67), 128(R68), 535(576-R68) 4 8 12 22 34 45
16(R68), 68(R67) 5 10 15 30 48 65
12/69–Christmas Giveaway ("A Christmas Adventure") (reprints Picture Parade #4-1953, new cover) (4 ad variations)
Stacey's Dept. Store 3 6 9 21 32 42
Anne & Hope Store 5 10 15 32 51 70
Gibson's Dept. Store (rare) 5 10 15 32 51 70
"Merry Christmas" & blank ad space 3 6 9 21 32 42

CLEAR THE TRACK!
Association of American Railroads: 1954 (paper-c, 16 pgs.)
nn 5 10 15 22 26 30

CLIFF MERRITT SETS THE RECORD STRAIGHT
Brotherhood of Railroad Trainsmen: Giveaway (2 different issues)
...and the Very Candid Candidate by Al Williamson 1 3 4 6 8 10

C-M-O Comics #2 © CEN

Crackajack Funnies © DELL

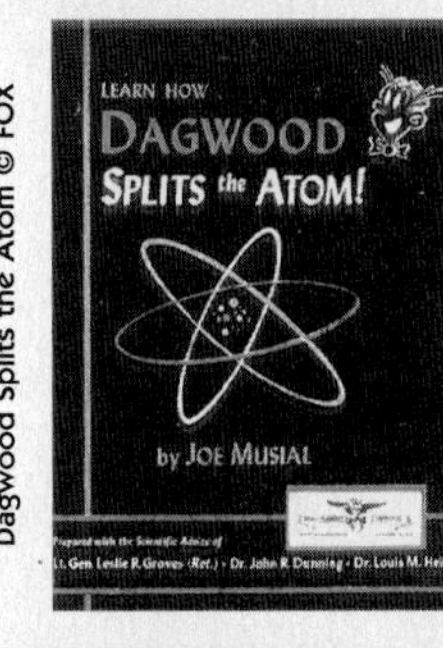

Dagwood Splits the Atom © FOX

	GD 2.0	VG 4.0	FN 6.0	VF 8.0	VF/NM 9.0	NM- 9.2
...Sets the Record Straight by Al Williamson (2 different-c: one by Williamson, the other by McWilliams)	1	3	4	6	8	10

CLYDE BEATTY COMICS (Also see Crackajack Funnies)
Commodore Productions & Artists, Inc.

...African Jungle Book('56)-Richfield Oil Co. 16 pg. giveaway, soft-c	10	20	30	54	72	90

C-M-O COMICS
Chicago Mail Order Co.(Centaur): 1942 - No. 2, 1942 (68 pgs., full color)

1-Invisible Terror, Super Ann, & Plymo the Rubber Man app. (all Centaur costume heroes)	89	178	267	565	970	1375
2-Invisible Terror, Super Ann app.	53	106	159	334	567	800

COCOMALT BIG BOOK OF COMICS
Harry 'A' Chesler (Cocomalt Premium): 1938 (Reg. size, full color, 52 pgs.)

1-(Scarce)-Biro-c/a; Little Nemo by Winsor McCay Jr., Dan Hastings; Jack Cole, Guardineer, Gustavson, Bob Wood-a	219	438	657	1402	2401	3400

COMIC BOOK (Also see Comics From Weatherbird)
American Juniors Shoe: 1954 (Giveaway)
Contains a comic rebound with new cover. Several combinations possible. Contents determine price.

COMIC BOOK MAGAZINE
Chicago Tribune & other newspapers: 1940 - 1943 (Similar to Spirit sections) (7-3/4x10-3/4"; full color; 16-24 pgs. ea.)

1940 issues	7	14	21	37	46	55
1941, 1942 issues	6	12	18	28	34	40
1943 issues	5	10	15	24	30	35

NOTE: *Published weekly. Texas Slim, Kit Carson, Spooky, Josie, Nuts & Jolts, Lew Loyal, Brenda Starr, Daniel Boone, Captain Storm, Rocky, Smokey Stover, Tiny Tim, Little Joe, Fu Manchu appear among others. Early issues had photo stories with pictures from the movies; later issues had comic art.*

COMIC BOOKS (Series 1)
Metropolitan Printing Co. (Giveaway): 1950 (16 pgs.; 5-1/4x8-1/2"; full color; bound at top; paper cover)

1-Boots and Saddles; intro The Masked Marshal	6	12	18	28	34	40
1-The Green Jet; Green Lama by Raboy	19	38	57	112	181	250
1-My Pal Dizzy (Teen-age)	4	8	12	18	22	25
1-New World; origin Atomaster (costumed hero)	9	18	27	52	69	85
1-Talullah (Teen-age)	4	8	12	18	22	25

COMIC CAVALCADE
All-American/National Periodical Publications

Giveaway (1944, 8 pgs., paper-c, in color)-One Hundred Years of Co-operation-r/Comic Cavalcade #9	47	94	141	296	498	700
Giveaway (1945, 16 pgs., paper-c, in color)-Movie "Tomorrow The World" (Nazi theme); r/Comic Cavalcade #10	61	122	183	390	670	950
Giveaway (c. 1944-45; 8 pgs, paper-c, in color)-The Twain Shall Meet-r/Comic Cavalcade #8	47	94	141	296	498	700

COMIC SELECTIONS (Shoe store giveaway)
Parents' Magazine Press: 1944-46 (Reprints from Calling All Girls, True Comics, True Aviation, & Real Heroes)

1	5	10	15	22	26	30
2-6	4	8	11	16	19	22

COMICS FROM WEATHER BIRD (Also see Comic Book, Edward's Shoes, Free Comics to You & Weather Bird)
Weather Bird Shoes: 1954 - 1957 (Giveaway)
Contains a comic bound with new cover. Many combinations possible. Contents would determine price. Some issues do not contain complete comics, but only parts of comics. Value equals 40 to 60 percent of contents.

COMICS READING LIBRARIES (Educational Series)
King Features (Charlton Publ.): 1973, 1977, 1979 (36 pgs. in color) (Giveaways)

R-01-Tiger, Quincy	2	4	6	8	11	14
R-02-Beetle Bailey, Blondie & Popeye	2	4	6	10	14	18
R-03-Blondie, Beetle Bailey	2	4	6	8	11	14
R-04-Tim Tyler's Luck, Felix the Cat	3	6	9	16	23	30
R-05-Quincy, Henry	2	4	6	8	11	14
R-06-The Phantom, Mandrake	3	6	9	16	23	30
1977 reprint(R-04)	2	4	6	9	13	16
R-07-Popeye, Little King	2	4	6	13	18	22
R-08-Prince Valiant (Foster), Flash Gordon	3	6	9	18	27	36
1977 reprint	2	4	6	11	16	20
R-09-Hagar the Horrible, Boner's Ark	2	4	6	10	14	18
R-10-Redeye, Tiger	2	4	6	8	11	14
R-11-Blondie, Hi & Lois	2	4	6	8	11	14
R-12-Popeye-Swee'pea, Brutus	2	4	6	13	18	22
R-13-Beetle Bailey, Little King	2	4	6	8	11	14
R-14-Quincy-Hamlet	2	4	6	8	11	14
R-15-The Phantom, The Genius	2	4	6	13	18	22
R-16-Flash Gordon, Mandrake	3	6	9	18	27	36
1977 reprint	2	4	6	10	14	18
Other 1977 editions....	2	4	6	8	10	12
1979 editions (68 pgs.)	2	4	6	8	10	12

NOTE: *Above giveaways available with purchase of $45.00 in merchandise. Used as a reading skills aid for small children.*

COMMANDMENTS OF GOD
Catechetical Guild: 1954, 1958

300-Same contents in both editions; diff-c	5	10	15	24	29	34

COMPLIMENTARY COMICS
Sales Promotion Publ.: No date (1950's) (Giveaway)

1-Strongman by Powell, 3 stories	8	16	24	40	50	60

CRACKAJACK FUNNIES (Giveaway)
Malto-Meal: 1937 (Full size, soft-c, full color, 32 pgs.)(Before No. 1?)

nn-Features Dan Dunn, G-Man, Speed Bolton, Buck Jones, The Nebbs, Clyde Beatty, Freckles, Major Hoople, Wash Tubbs	71	142	213	454	777	1100

CROSLEY'S HOUSE OF FUN (Also see Tee and Vee Crosley...)
Crosley Div. AVCO Mfg. Corp.: 1950 (Giveaway, paper cover, 32 pgs.)

nn-Strips revolve around Crosley appliances	5	10	15	22	26	30

DAGWOOD SPLITS THE ATOM (Also see Topix V8#4)
King Features Syndicate: 1949 (Science comic with King Features characters) (Giveaway)

nn-Half comic, half text; Popeye, Olive Oyl, Henry, Mandrake, Little King, Katzenjammer Kids app.	9	18	27	52	69	85

DAISY COMICS (Daisy Air Rifles)
Eastern Color Printing Co.: Dec, 1936 (5-1/4x7-1/2")

nn-Joe Palooka, Buck Rogers (2 pgs. from Famous Funnies No. 18, 1st full cover app.), Napoleon Flying to Fame, Butty & Fally	31	62	93	186	301	425

DAISY LOW OF THE GIRL SCOUTS
Girl Scouts of America: 1954, 1965 (16 pgs., paper-c)

1954-Story of Juliette Gordon Low	5	10	15	22	26	30
1965	2	4	6	9	12	15

DAN CURTIS GIVEAWAYS
Western Publishing Co.:1974 (3x6", 24 pgs., reprints)

1-Dark Shadows	3	6	9	16	23	30
2,6-Star Trek	3	6	9	16	23	30
3,4,7-9: 3-The Twilight Zone. 4-Ripley's Believe It or Not! 7-The Occult Files of Dr. Spektor. 8-Dagar the Invincible. 9-Grimm's Ghost Stories	2	4	6	11	16	20
5-Turok, Son of Stone (partial-r/Turok #78)	3	6	9	16	23	30

DANNY KAYE'S BAND FUN BOOK
H & A Selmer: 1959 (Giveaway)

nn	7	14	21	35	43	50

DAREDEVIL
Marvel Comics Group: 1993

...Vs. Vapora 1 (Engineering Show Giveaway, 16 pg.) - Intro Vapora						6.00

DAVY CROCKETT (TV)
Dell Publishing Co.

...Christmas Book (no date, 16 pgs., paper-c)-Sears giveaway	6	12	18	31	38	45
...Safety Trails (1955, 16pgs, 3-1/4x7")-Cities Service giveaway	8	16	24	40	50	60

DAVY CROCKETT
Charlton Comics

Hunting With... nn ('55, 16 pgs.)-Ben Franklin Store giveaway (Publ.-S. Rose)	5	10	15	24	30	35

DAVY CROCKETT
Walt Disney Prod.: (1955, 16 pgs., 5x7-1/4", slick, photo-c)

...In the Raid at Piney Creek-American Motors giveaway	8	16	24	40	50	60

DC SAMPLER
DC Comics: nn (#1) 1983 - No. 3, 1984 (36 pgs.; 6 1/2" x 10", giveaway)

nn(#1) -3: nn-Wraparound-c, previews upcoming issues. 3-Kirby-a	1	2	3	4	5	7

DC SPOTLIGHT
DC Comics: 1985 (50th anniversary special) (giveaway)

1-Includes profiles on Batman:The Dark Knight & Watchmen						6.00

DEATH JR. HALLOWEEN SPECIAL
Image Comics: Oct, 2006 (8-1/2"x 5-1/2", Halloween giveaway)

Dick Tracy Motorola Giveaway © NYNS

Donald and Mickey Merry Christmas 1944 © DIS

Escape From Fear 1962 © PPA

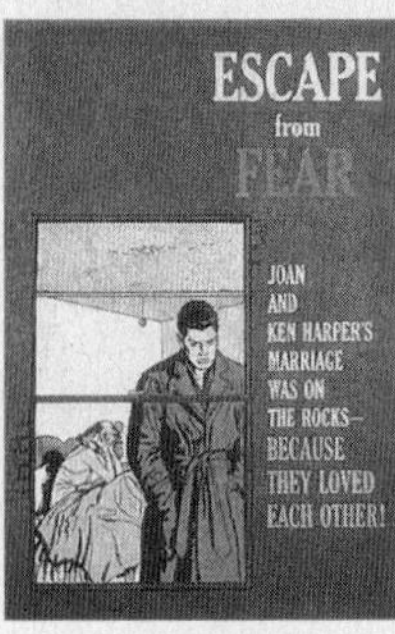

	GD 2.0	VG 4.0	FN 6.0	VF 8.0	VF/NM 9.0	NM- 9.2

nn-Guy Davis-a/Joe Morrisey-s; wraparound-c — 2.50

DENNIS THE MENACE
Hallden (Fawcett)

...& Dirt ('59)-Soil Conservation giveaway; r-# 36; Wiseman-c/a — 3 6 9 14 20 26
...& Dirt ('68)-reprints '59 edition — 2 4 6 8 11 14
...Away We Go('70)-Caladryl giveaway — 2 4 6 8 10 12
...Coping with Family Stress-giveaway — 2 4 6 8 10 12
...Takes a Poke at Poison('61)-Food & Drug Admin. giveaway; Wiseman-c/a — 2 4 6 8 10 12
...Takes a Poke at Poison-Revised 1/66, 11/70 — 1 2 3 5 6 8
...Takes a Poke at Poison-Revised 1972, 1974, 1977, 1981 — 1 2 3 4 5 7

DESERT DAWN
E.C./American Museum of Natural History: 1935 (paper-c)

nn-Johnny Jackrabbit stars. Three known copies: A Fair copy (brittle) sold for $657 in 2007. A GD+ copy (brittle) sold for $2300 in 2005. Another Fair copy (brittle) sold for $690 in 2004

DETECTIVE COMICS (Also see other Batman titles)
National Periodical Publications/DC Comics

27 (1984)-Oreo Cookies giveaway (32 pgs., paper-c) r-/Det. #27,#38 & Batman #1 (1st Joker) — 5 10 15 35 55 75
38 (1995) Blockbuster Video edition; reprints 1st Robin app. — 3.00
38 (1997) Toys R Us edition — 3.00
359 (1997) Toys R Us edition; reprints 1st Batgirl app. — 3.00
373 (1997, 6 1/4" x 4") Warner Brothers Home Video — 3.00

DICK TRACY GIVEAWAYS
1939 - 1958; 1990

Buster Brown Shoes Giveaway (1940s?, 36 pgs. in color); 1938-39-r by Gould — 29 58 87 170 278 385
Gillmore Giveaway (See Superbook)
...Hatful of Fun (No date, 1950-52, 32pgs.; 8-1/2x10")-Dick Tracy hat promotion; Dick Tracy games, magic tricks. Miller Bros. premium — 15 30 45 90 140 190
Motorola Giveaway (1953)-Reprints Harvey Comics Library #2; "The Case of the Sparkle Plenty TV Mystery" — 7 14 21 37 46 55
Original Dick Tracy by Chester Gould, The (Aug, 1990, 16 pgs., 5-1/2x8-1/2")-Gladstone Publ.; Bread Giveaway — 1 3 4 6 8 10
Popped Wheat Giveaway (1947, 16 pgs. in color)-1940-r; Sig Feuchtwanger Publ.; Gould-a — 4 8 12 18 22 25
...Presents the Family Fun Book; Tip Top Bread Giveaway, no date or number (1940, Fawcett Publ., 16 pgs. in color)-Spy Smasher, Ibis, Lance O'Casey app. — 43 86 129 271 461 650
Same as above but without app. of heroes & Dick Tracy on cover only — 14 28 42 82 121 160
Service Station Giveaway (1958, 16 pgs. in color)(regular size, slick cover)-Harvey Info. Press — 5 10 14 20 24 28
Shoe Store Giveaway (Weatherbird and Triangle Stores)(1939, 16 pgs.)-Gould-a — 14 28 42 76 108 140

DICK TRACY SHEDS LIGHT ON THE MOLE
Western Printing Co.: 1949 (16 pgs.) (Ray-O-Vac Flashlights giveaway)

nn-Not by Gould — 8 16 24 42 54 65

DICK WINGATE OF THE U.S. NAVY
Superior Publ./Toby Press: 1951; 1953 (no month)

nn-U.S. Navy giveaway — 5 10 15 24 30 35
1(1953, Toby)-Reprints nn issue? (same-c) — 5 10 14 20 24 28

DIG 'EM
Kellogg's Sugar Smacks Giveaway: 1973 (2-3/8x6", 16 pgs.)

nn-4 different issues — 1 3 4 6 8 10

DOC CARTER VD COMICS
Health Publications Institute, Raleigh, N. C. (Giveaway): 1949 (16 pgs. in color) (Paper-c)

nn — 19 38 57 110 175 250

DONALD AND MICKEY MERRY CHRISTMAS (Formerly Famous Gang Book Of Comics)
K. K. Publ./Firestone Tire & Rubber Co.: 1943 - 1949 (Giveaway, 20 pgs.)
Put out each Christmas; 1943 issue titled "Firestone Presents Comics" (Disney)

1943-Donald Duck-r/WDC&S #32 by Carl Barks — 71 142 213 451 776 1100
1944-Donald Duck-r/WDC&S #35 by Barks — 68 136 204 432 741 1050
1945- "Donald Duck's Best Christmas", 8 pgs. Carl Barks; intro. & 1st app. Grandma Duck in comic books — 100 200 300 635 1093 1550
1946-Donald Duck in "Santa's Stormy Visit", 8 pgs. Carl Barks — 69 138 207 438 757 1075
1947-Donald Duck in "Three Good Little Ducks", 8 pgs. Carl Barks — 69 138 207 438 757 1075
1948-Donald Duck in "Toyland", 8 pgs. Carl Barks — 69 138 207 438 757 1075
1949-Donald Duck in "New Toys", 8 pgs. Barks — 65 130 195 413 707 1000

DONALD DUCK
K. K. Publications: 1944 (Christmas giveaway, paper-c, 16 pgs.)(2 versions)

nn-Kelly cover reprint — 92 184 276 584 1005 1425

DONALD DUCK AND THE RED FEATHER
Red Feather Giveaway: 1948 (8-1/2x11", 4 pgs., B&W)

nn — 19 38 57 112 181 250

DONALD DUCK IN "THE LITTERBUG"
Keep America Beautiful: 1963 (5x7-1/4", 16 pgs., soft-c) (Disney giveaway)

nn — 5 10 15 34 55 75

DONALD DUCK "PLOTTING PICNICKERS" (See Frito-Lay Giveaway)

DONALD DUCK'S SURPRISE PARTY
Walt Disney Productions: 1948 (16 pgs.) (Giveaway for Icy Frost Twins Ice Cream Bars)

nn-(Rare)-Kelly-c/a — 219 438 657 1402 2401 3400

DOT AND DASH AND THE LUCKY JINGLE PIGGIE
Sears Roebuck Co.: 1942 (Christmas giveaway, 12 pgs.)

nn-Contains a war stamp album and a punch out Jingle Piggie bank — 12 24 36 67 94 120

DOUBLE TALK (Also see Two-Faces)
Feature Publications: No date (1962?) (32 pgs., full color, slick-c)
Christian Anti-Communism Crusade (Giveaway)

nn-Sickle with blood-c — 15 30 45 90 140 190

DRUMMER BOY AT GETTYSBURG
Eastern National Park & Monument Association: 1976

nn-Fred Ray-a — 3 6 9 14 20 25

DUMBO (Walt Disney's..., The Flying Elephant)
Weatherbird Shoes/Ernest Kern Co.(Detroit)/ Wieboldt's (Chicago): 1941
(K.K. Publ. Giveaway)

nn-16 pgs., 9x10" (Rare) — 42 84 126 265 445 625
nn-52 pgs., 5-1/2x8-1/2", slick cover in color; B&W interior; half text, half reprints 4-Color No. 17 (Dept. store) — 22 44 66 131 216 300

DUMBO WEEKLY
Walt Disney Prod.: 1942 (Premium supplied by Diamond D-X Gas Stations)

1 — 41 82 123 256 428 600
2-16 — 14 28 42 82 121 160
Binder only — 225
NOTE: *A cover and binder came separate at gas stations. Came with membership card.*

EAT RIGHT TO WORK AND WIN
Swift & Company: 1942 (16 pgs.) (Giveaway)

Blondie, Henry, Flash Gordon by Alex Raymond, Toots & Casper, Thimble Theatre(Popeye), Tillie the Toiler, The Phantom, The Little King, & Bringing up Father - original strips just for this book -(in daily strip form which shows what foods we should eat and why) — 30 60 90 177 289 400

EDWARD'S SHOES GIVEAWAY
Edward's Shoe Store: 1954 (Has clown on cover)

Contains comic with new cover. Many combinations possible. Contents determines price, 50-60 percent of original. (Similar to Comics From Weatherbird & Free Comics to You)

ELSIE THE COW
D. S. Publishing Co.

Borden's cheese comic picture bk ("40, giveaway) — 19 38 57 112 181 250
Borden Milk Giveaway-(16 pgs., nn) (3 ishs, 1957) — 14 28 42 81 118 155
Elsie's Fun Book(1950; Borden Milk) — 14 28 42 81 118 155
Everyday Birthday Fun With... (1957; 20 pgs.)(100th Anniversary); Kubert-a — 14 28 42 81 118 155

ESCAPE FROM FEAR
Planned Parenthood of America: 1956, 1962, 1969 (Giveaway, 8 pgs., color) (On birth control)

1956 edition — 11 22 33 60 83 105
1962 edition — 4 8 12 24 37 50
1969 edition — 3 6 9 14 20 25

EVEL KNIEVEL
Marvel Comics Group (Ideal Toy Corp.): 1974 (Giveaway, 20 pgs.)

nn-Contains photo on inside back-c — 4 8 12 28 44 60

FAMOUS COMICS (Also see Favorite Comics)
Zain-Eppy/United Features Syndicate: No date; Mid 1930's (24 pgs., paper-c)

nn-Reprinted from 1933 & 1934 newspaper strips in color; Joe Palooka, Hairbreadth Harry, Napoleon, The Nebbs, etc. (Many different versions known) — 61 122 183 387 669 950

Famous Gang Book of Comics © Firestone/WB

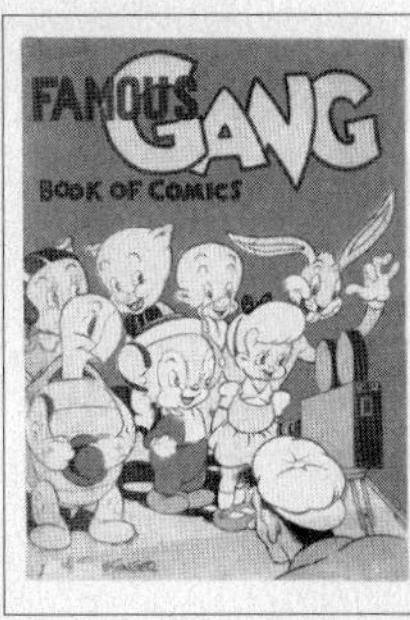

Fearless Fosdick © Capp Ent.

Flash Gordon Bread #1 © KING

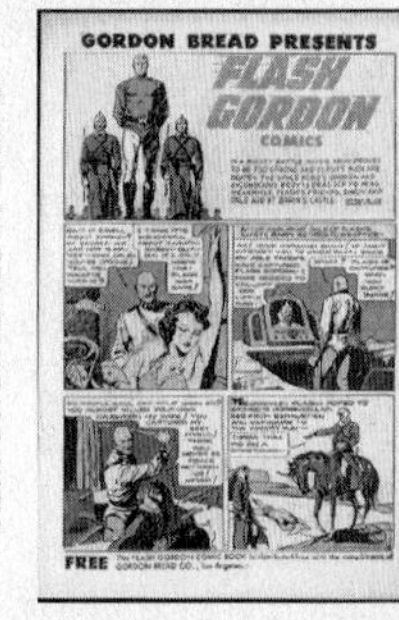

	GD 2.0	VG 4.0	FN 6.0	VF 8.0	VF/NM 9.0	NM- 9.2

FAMOUS FAIRY TALES
K. K. Publ. Co.: 1942; 1943 (32 pgs.); 1944 (16 pgs.) (Giveaway, soft-c)

1942-Kelly-a	39	78	117	236	388	540
1943-r-/Fairy Tale Parade No. 2,3; Kelly-a	25	50	75	150	245	340
1944-Kelly-a	22	44	66	131	216	300

FAMOUS FUNNIES -A CARNIVAL OF COMICS
Eastern Color: 1933
36 pgs., no date given, no publisher, no number; contains strip reprints of The Bungle Family, Dixie Dugan, Hairbreadth Harry, Joe Palooka, Keeping Up With the Jones, Mutt & Jeff, Reg'lar Fellers, S'Matter Pop, Strange As It Seems, and others. This book was sold by M. C. Gaines to Wheatena, Malt-O-Milk, John Wanamaker, Kinney Shoe Stores, & others to be given away as premiums and radio giveaways (1933). Originally came with a mailing envelope. 541 1082 1623 3950 6975 10,000

FAMOUS GANG BOOK OF COMICS (Becomes Donald & Mickey Merry Christmas 1943 on)
Firestone Tire & Rubber Co.: Dec, 1942 (Christmas giveaway, 32 pgs., paper-c)
nn-(Rare)-Porky Pig, Bugs Bunny, Mary Jane & Sniffles, Elmer Fudd; r/Looney Tunes 68 136 204 432 741 1050

FANTASTIC FOUR
Marvel Comics
nn (1981, 32 pgs.) Young Model Builders Club 2 4 6 9 12 15
Vol. 3 #60 Baltimore Comic Book Show (10/02, newspaper supplement) 200,000 copies were distributed to Baltimore Sun home subscribers to promote Baltimore Comic Con 4.00

FATHER OF CHARITY
Catechetical Guild Giveaway: No date (32 pgs.; paper cover)
nn 5 10 15 24 29 34

FAVORITE COMICS (Also see Famous Comics)
Grocery Store Giveaway (Diff. Corp.) (detergent): 1934 (36 pgs.)
Book 1-The Nebbs, Strange As It Seems, Napoleon, Joe Palooka, Dixie Dugan, S'Matter Pop, Hairbreadth Harry, etc. reprints 100 200 300 635 1093 1550
Book 2,3 61 122 183 387 664 940

FAWCETT MINIATURES (See Mighty Midget)
Fawcett Publications: 1946 (3-3/4x5", 12-24 pgs.) (Wheaties giveaways)
Captain Marvel "And the Horn of Plenty"; Bulletman story 16 32 48 94 147 200
Captain Marvel "& the Raiders From Space"; Golden Arrow story 16 32 48 94 147 200
Captain Marvel Jr. "The Case of the Poison Press!" Bulletman story 16 32 48 94 147 200
Delecta of the Planets; C. C. Beck art; B&W inside; 12 pgs.; 3 printing variations (coloring) exist 20 40 60 120 198 275

FEARLESS FOSDICK
Capp Enterprises Inc.: 1951
...& The Case of The Red Feather 6 12 18 27 33 38

FIGHT FOR FREEDOM
National Assoc. of Mfgrs./General Comics: 1949, 1951 (Giveaway, 16 pgs.)
nn-Dan Barry-c/a; used in **POP**, pg. 102 6 12 18 31 38 45

FIRE AND BLAST
National Fire Protection Assoc.: 1952 (Giveaway, 16 pgs., paper-c)
nn-Mart Baily A-Bomb-c; about fire prevention 15 30 45 85 130 175

FIRE CHIEF AND THE SAFE OL' FIREFLY, THE
National Board of Fire Underwriters: 1952 (16 pgs.) (Safety brochure given away at schools) (produced by American Visuals Corp.)(Eisner)
nn-(Rare) Eisner-c/a 40 80 120 252 426 600

FLASH, THE
DC Comics
nn-(1990) Brochure for CBS TV series 4.00
The Flash Comes to a Standstill (1981, General Foods giveaway, 8 pages, 3-1/2 x 6-3/4", oblong) 2 4 6 10 14 18

FLASH COMICS (Also see Captain Marvel and Funny Stuff)
National Periodical Publications: 1946 (6-1/2x8-1/4", 32 pgs.)(Wheaties Giveaway)
nn-Johnny Thunder, Ghost Patrol, The Flash & Kubert Hawkman app.; Irwin Hasen-c/a 190 380 900 - - -
NOTE: *All known copies were taped to Wheaties boxes and are never found in mint condition. Copies with light tape residue bring the listed prices in all grades*

FLASH FORCE 2000
DC Comics: 1984
1-5 6.00

FLASH GORDON
Dell Publishing Co.: 1943 (20 pgs.)
Macy's Giveaway-(Rare); not by Raymond 58 116 174 368 634 900

FLASH GORDON
Harvey Comics: 1951 (16 pgs. in color, regular size, paper-c) (Gordon Bread giveaway)
1,2: 1-r/strips 10/24/37 - 2/6/38. 2-r/strips 7/14/40 - 10/6/40; Reprints by Raymond each.... 2 4 6 10 14 18
NOTE: *Most copies have brittle edges.*

FLOOD RELIEF
Malibu Comics (Ultraverse): Jan, 1994 (36 pgs.)(Ordered thru mail w/$5.00 to Red Cross)
1-Hardcase, Prime & Prototype app. 6.00

FOREST FIRE (Also see The Blazing Forest and Smokey Bear)
American Forestry Assn.(Commerical Comics): 1949 (dated-1950) (16 pgs., paper-c)
nn-Intro/1st app. Smokey The Forest Fire Preventing Bear; created by Rudy Wendelein; Wendelein/Sparling-a; 'Carter Oil Co.' on back-c of original 18 36 54 103 162 220

FOREST RANGER HANDBOOK
Wrather Corp.: 1967 (5x7", 20 pgs., slick-c)
nn-With Corey Stuart & Lassie photo-c 2 4 6 13 18 22

FORGOTTEN STORY BEHIND NORTH BEACH, THE
Catechetical Guild: No date (8 pgs., paper-c)
nn 5 10 15 23 28 32

FORK IN THE ROAD
U.S. Army Recruiting Service: 1961 (16 pgs., paper-c)
nn 2 4 6 11 16 20

48 FAMOUS AMERICANS
J. C. Penney Co. (Cpr. Edwin H. Stroh): 1947 (Giveaway) (Half-size in color)
nn - Simon & Kirby-a 10 20 30 54 72 90

FOXHOLE ON YOUR LAWN
No Publisher: No date
nn-Charles Biro art 4 7 10 14 17 20

FRANKIE LUER'S SPACE ADVENTURES
Luer Packing Co.: 1955 (5x7", 36 pgs., slick-c)
nn - With Davey Rocket 4 8 12 17 21 24

FREDDY
Charlton Comics
Schiff's Shoes Presents... #1 (1959)-Giveaway 4 8 11 16 19 22

FREE COMIC BOOK DAY EDITIONS (Now listed in the regular section)

FREE COMICS TO YOU FROM... (name of shoe store) (Has clown on cover & another with a rabbit) (Like comics from Weather Bird & Edward's Shoes)
Shoe Store Giveaway: Circa 1956, 1960-61
Contains a comic bound with new cover - several combinations possible; some Harvey titles known. Contents determine price.

FREEDOM TRAIN
Street & Smith Publications: 1948 (Giveaway)
nn-Powell-c w/mailer 18 36 54 103 162 220

FREIHOFER'S COMIC BOOK
All-American Comics: 1940s (7 1/2 x 10 1/4")
2nd edition-(Scarce) Cover features All-American Comics characters Ultra-Man, Hop Harrigan, Red, White and Blue and others 57 114 171 362 619 875

FRIENDLY GHOST, CASPER, THE
Harvey Publications: 1967 (16 pgs.)
American Dental Assoc. giveaway-Small size 3 6 9 17 25 32

FRITO-LAY GIVEAWAY
Frito-Lay: 1962 (3-1/4x7", soft-c, 16 pgs.) (Disney)

nn-Donald Duck "Plotting Picnickers"	5	10	15	32	51	70
nn-Ludwig Von Drake "Fish Stampede"	3	6	9	20	30	40
nn- Mickey Mouse & Goofy "Bicep Bungle"	4	8	12	22	34	45

FRONTIER DAYS
Robin Hood Shoe Store (Brown Shoe): 1956 (Giveaway)
1 4 7 10 14 17 20

FRONTIERS OF FREEDOM
Institute of Life Insurance: 1950 (Giveaway, paper cover)
nn-Dan Barry-a 8 16 24 44 57 70

FUNNIES ON PARADE (Premium)(See Toy World Funnies)
Eastern Color Printing Co.: 1933 (36 pgs., slick cover)
No date or publisher listed
nn-Contains Sunday page reprints of Mutt & Jeff, Joe Palooka, Hairbreadth Harry, Reg'lar Fellers, Skippy, & others (10,000 print run). This book was printed for Proctor & Gamble to be given away & came out before

Future Cop: L.A.P.D. © EA

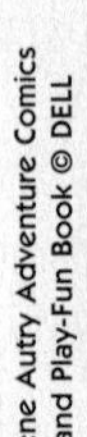

Gene Autry Adventure Comics and Play-Fun Book © DELL

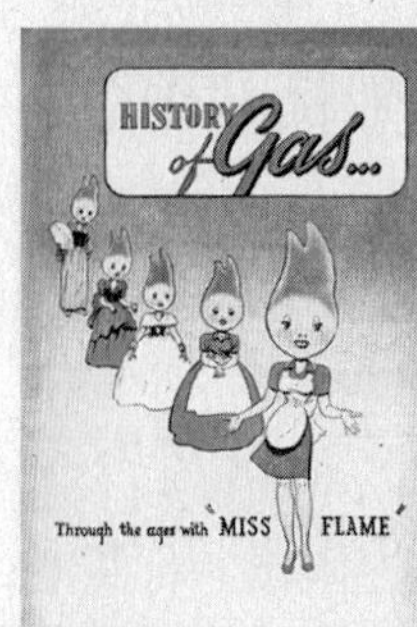

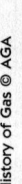

History of Gas © AGA

	GD 2.0	VG 4.0	FN 6.0	VF 8.0	VF/NM 9.0	NM- 9.2

Famous Funnies or Century of Comics. 1000 2000 3000 6000 10,500 15,000

FUNNY PICTURE STORIES
Comics Magazine Co./Centaur Publications: 1930s (Giveaway, 16-20 pgs., slick-c)

Promotes diff. laundries; has box on cover where "your Laundry Name" is printed 34 68 102 199 325 450

FUNNY STUFF (Also see Captain Marvel & Flash Comics)
National Periodical Publications (Wheaties Giveaway): 1946 (6-1/2x8-1/4")

nn-(Scarce)-Dodo & the Frog, Three Mouseketeers, etc.; came taped to Wheaties box; never found in better than fine 135 270 400 – – –

FUTURE COP: L.A.P.D. (Electronic Arts video game)
DC Comics (WildStorm): 1998

nn-Ron Lim-a/Dave Johnson-c 2.50

GABBY HAYES WESTERN (Movie star)
Fawcett Publications

Quaker Oats Giveaway nn's(#1-5, 1951, 2-1/2x7") (Kagran Corp.)-...In Tracks of Guilt, ...In the Fence Post Mystery, ...In the Accidental Sherlock, ...In the Frame-Up, ...In the Double Cross Brand known 10 20 30 54 72 90
Mailing Envelope (has illo of Gabby on front) 10 20 30 54 72 90

GARY GIBSON COMICS (Donut club membership)
National Dunking Association: 1950 (Included in donut box with pin and card)

1-Western soft-c, 16 pgs.; folded into the box 5 10 14 20 24 28

GENE AUTRY COMICS
Dell Publishing Co.

...Adventure Comics And Play-Fun Book ('47)-32 pgs., 8x6-1/2"; games, comics, magic (Pillsbury premium) 22 44 66 132 216 300
Quaker Oats Giveaway(1950)-2-1/2x6-3/4"; 5 different versions; "Death Card Gang", "Phantoms of the Cave", "Riddle of Laughing Mtn.", "Secret of Lost Valley", "Bond of the Broken Arrow" (came in wrapper) each... 10 20 30 58 79 100
Mailing Envelope (has illo. of Gene on front) 10 20 30 58 79 100
3-D Giveaway(1953)-Pocket-size; 5 different 10 20 30 58 79 100
Mailing Envelope (no art on front) 8 16 24 44 57 70

GENE AUTRY TIM (Formerly Tim) (Becomes Tim in Space)
Tim Stores: 1950 (Half-size) (B&W Giveaway)

nn-Several issues (All Scarce) 19 38 57 109 172 235

GENERAL FOODS SUPER-HEROES
DC Comics: 1979, 1980

1-4 (1979), 1-4 (1980) each... 12.00

G. I. COMICS (Also see Jeep & Overseas Comics)
Giveaways: 1945 - No. 73?, 1946 (Distributed to U. S. Armed Forces)

1-73-Contains Prince Valiant by Foster, Blondie, Smilin' Jack, Mickey Finn, Terry & the Pirates, Donald Duck, Alley Oop, Moon Mullins & Capt. Easy strip reprints (at least 73 issues known to exist) 8 16 24 42 54 65

GOLDEN ARROW
Fawcett Publications

...Well Known Comics (1944; 12 pgs.; 8-1/2x10-1/2"; paper-c; glued binding)- Bestmaid/Samuel Lowe giveaway; printed in green 10 20 30 54 72 90

GOLDILOCKS & THE THREE BEARS
K. K. Publications: 1943 (Giveaway)

nn 13 26 39 74 105 135

GREAT PEOPLE OF GENESIS, THE
David C. Cook Publ. Co.: No date (Religious giveaway, 64 pgs.)

nn-Reprint/Sunday Pix Weekly 5 10 15 23 28 32

GREAT SACRAMENT, THE
Catechetical Guild: 1953 (Giveaway, 36 pgs.)

nn 5 10 15 22 26 30

GREEN JET COMICS, THE (See Comic Books, Series 1)

GRENADA
Commercial Comics Co.: 1983 (Giveaway produced by the CIA)

1-Air dropped over Grenada during the 1983 invasion 30.00

GRIT (YOU'VE GOT TO HAVE...)
GRIT Publishing Co.: 1959

nn-GRIT newspaper sales recruitment comic; Schaffenberger-a. Later version has altered artwork 5 10 15 22 26 30

GROWING UP WITH JUDY
1952

nn-General Electric giveaway 4 7 10 14 17 20

GULF FUNNY WEEKLY (Gulf Comic Weekly No. 1-4)(See Standard Oil Comics)
Gulf Oil Company (Giveaway): 1933 - No. 422, 5/23/41 (in full color; 4 pgs.; tabloid size to 2/3/39; 2/10/39 on, regular comic book size)(early issues undated)

1 63 126 189 403 689 975
2-5 29 58 87 170 278 385
6-30 19 38 57 109 172 235
31-100 14 28 42 81 118 155
101-196 10 20 30 56 76 95
197-Wings Winfair begins(1/29/37); by Fred Meagher beginning in 1938 22 44 66 129 212 295
198-300 (Last tabloid size) 14 28 42 81 118 155
301-350 (Regular size) 9 18 27 52 69 85
351-422 8 16 24 42 54 65

GULLIVER'S TRAVELS
Macy's Department Store: 1939, small size

nn-Christmas giveaway 14 28 42 76 108 140

GUN THAT WON THE WEST, THE
Winchester-Western Division & Olin Mathieson Chemical Corp.: 1956 (Giveaway, 24 pgs.)

nn-Painted-c 5 10 15 24 30 35

HAPPINESS AND HEALING FOR YOU (Also see Oral Roberts'...)
Commercial Comics: 1955 (36 pgs., slick cover) (Oral Roberts Giveaway)

nn 9 18 27 52 69 85

NOTE: *The success of this book prompted Oral Roberts to go into the publishing business himself to produce his own material.*

HAPPY TOOTH
DC Comics: 1996

1 3.00

HARLEM YOUTH REPORT (Also see All-Negro Comics and Negro Romances)
Custom Comics, Inc.: 1964 (Giveaway)(No #1-4)

5-"Youth in the Ghetto" and "The Blueprint For Change"; distr. in Harlem only; has map of central Harlem on back-c (scarce) 103 206 309 659 1130 1600

HAWKMAN - THE SKY'S THE LIMIT
DC Comics: 1981 (General Foods giveaway, 8 pages, 3-1/2 x 6-3/4", oblong)

nn 2 4 6 10 14 18

HAWTHORN-MELODY FARMS DAIRY COMICS
Everybody's Publishing Co.: No date (1950's) (Giveaway)

nn-Cheerie Chick, Tuffy Turtle, Robin Koo Koo, Donald & Longhorn Legends 2 4 6 8 11 14

HENRY ALDRICH COMICS (TV)
Dell Publishing Co.

Giveaway (16 pgs., soft-c, 1951)-Capehart radio 3 6 9 17 25 32

HERE IS SANTA CLAUS
Goldsmith Publishing Co. (Kann's in Washington, D.C.): 1930s (16 pgs., 8 in color) (stiff paper covers)

nn 13 26 39 72 101 130

HERE'S HOW AMERICA'S CARTOONISTS HELP TO SELL U.S. SAVINGS BONDS
Harvey Comics: 1950? (16 pgs., giveaway, paper cover)

Contains: Joe Palooka, Donald Duck, Archie, Kerry Drake, Red Ryder, Blondie & Steve Canyon 19 38 57 112 181 250

HISTORY OF GAS
American Gas Assoc.: Mar, 1947 (Giveaway, 16 pgs.)

nn-Miss Flame narrates 6 12 18 29 36 42

HOME DEPOT, SAFETY HEROES
Marvel Comics.: Oct, 2005 (Giveaway)

nn-Spider-Man and the Fantastic Four on the cover; Olliffe-a/c; Roseman-s 2.50

HONEYBEE BIRDWHISTLE AND HER PET PEPI (Introducing...)
Newspaper Enterprise Assoc.: 1969 (Giveaway, 24 pgs., B&W, slick cover)

nn-Contains Freckles newspaper strips with a short biography of Henry Fornhals (artist) & Fred Fox (writer) of the strip 4 8 12 28 44 60

HOODS UP
Fram Corp.: 1953 (15¢, distributed to service station owners, 16 pgs.)

1-(Very Rare; only 2 known); Eisner-c/a in all (a CGC 9.0 copy sold for $1840 in 2006)
2-6-(Very Rare; only 1 known of #3, 2 known of #2,4) 48 96 144 302 514 725

NOTE: *Convertible Connie gives tips for service stations, selling Fram oil filters.*

HOOKED (Anti-drug comic distributed at NYC methadone clinics)
U.S. Dept. of Health: 1966 (giveaway, oblong)

nn-Distributed between May and July, 1966 3 6 9 20 30 40

Hoppy the Marvel Bunny (Well Known Comics) © FAW

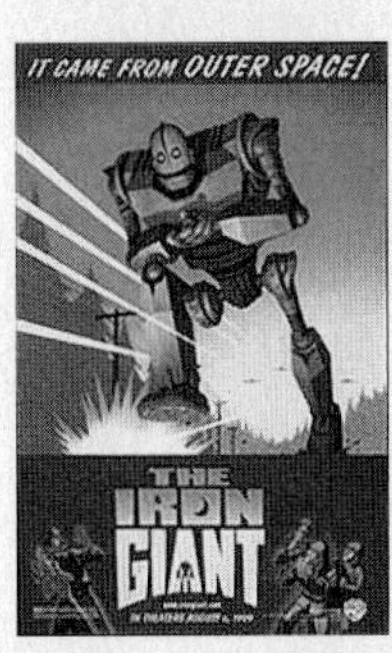

The Iron Giant #1 © WB

Joe the Genie 1950 © USSC

GD 2.0 | VG 4.0 | FN 6.0 | VF 8.0 | VF/NM 9.0 | NM- 9.2

HOPALONG CASSIDY
Fawcett Publications

Grape Nuts Flakes giveaway (1950,9x6") 14 28 42 78 112 145
...& the Mad Barber (1951 Bond Bread giveaway)-7x5"; used in **SOTI**, pgs. 308,309 18 36 54 103 162 220
...Meets the Brend Brothers Bandits (1951 Bond Bread giveaway, color, paper-c, 16 pgs., 3-1/2x7")- Fawcett Publ. 9 18 27 47 61 75
...Strange Legacy (1951 Bond Bread giveaway) 9 18 27 47 61 75
White Tower Giveaway (1946, 16pgs., paper-c) 9 18 27 52 69 85

HOPPY THE MARVEL BUNNY (WELL KNOWN COMICS)
Fawcett Publications: 1944 (8-1/2x10-1/2", paper-c)

Bestmaid/Samuel Lowe (printed in red or blue) 10 20 30 56 76 95

HOT STUFF, THE LITTLE DEVIL
Harvey Publications (Illustrated Humor):1963

Shoestore Giveaway 4 8 12 22 34 45

HOW KIDS ENJOY NEW YORK
American Airlines: 1966 (Giveaway, 40 pgs., 4x9")

nn-Includes 8 color pages by Bob Kane featuring a tour of New York and his studio (a VG copy sold for $180 and a FN+ sold for $250 in 2004)

HOW STALIN HOPES WE WILL DESTROY AMERICA
Joe Lowe Co. (Pictorial Media): 1951 (Giveaway, 16 pgs.)

nn 43 86 129 271 461 650

HURRICANE KIDS, THE (Also See Magic Morro, The Owl, Popular Comics #45)
R.S. Callender: 1941 (Giveaway, 7-1/2x5-1/4", soft-c)

nn-Will Ely-a. 8 16 24 44 57 70

IF THE DEVIL WOULD TALK
Roman Catholic Catechetical Guild/Impact Publ.: 1950; 1958 (32 pgs.; paper cover; in full color)

nn-(Scarce)-About secularism (20-30 copies known to exist); very low distribution 81 162 243 518 884 1250
1958 Edition-(Impact Publ.); art & script changed to meet church criticism of earlier edition; 80 plus copies known to exist 26 52 78 154 252 350
Black & White version of nn edition; small size; only 4 known copies exist 32 64 96 189 310 430

NOTE: *The original edition of this book was printed and killed by the Guild's board of directors. It is believed that a very limited number of copies were distributed. The 1958 version was a complete bomb with very limited, if any, circulation. In 1979, 11 original, 4 1958 reprints, and 4 B&W's surfaced from the Guild's old files in St. Paul, Minnesota.*

IN LOVE WITH JESUS
Catechetical Educational Society: 1952 (Giveaway, 36 pgs.)

nn 7 14 21 37 46 55

INTERSTATE THEATRES' FUN CLUB COMICS
Interstate Theatres: Mid 1940's (10¢ on cover) (B&W cover) (Premium)

Cover features MLJ characters looking at a copy of Top-Notch Comics, but contains an early Detective Comic on inside; many combinations possible 11 22 33 60 83 105

IN THE GOOD HANDS OF THE ROCKEFELLER TEAM
Country Art Studios: No date (paper cover, 8 pgs.)

nn-Joe Simon-a 8 16 24 42 54 65

IRON GIANT
DC Comics: 1999 (4 pages, theater giveaway)

1-Previews movie 3.00

IRON HORSE GOES TO WAR, THE
Association of American Railroads: 1960 (Giveaway, 16 pgs.)

nn-Civil War & railroads 3 6 9 14 20 25

IRON MAN
Marvel Comics

Marvel Halloween Ashcan 2007 (8-1/2" x 5-3/8") updated origin; Michael Golden-c 2.00

IS THIS TOMORROW?
Catechetical Guild: 1947 (One Shot) (3 editions) (52 pgs.)

1-Theme of communists taking over the USA; (no price on cover) Used in **POP**, pg. 102 22 44 66 131 216 300
1-(10¢ on cover) 26 52 78 154 252 350
1-Has blank circle with no price on cover 28 56 84 165 270 375
Black & White advance copy titled "Confidential" (52 pgs.)-Contains script and art edited out of the color edition, including one page of extreme violence showing mob nailing a Cardinal to a door; (only two known copies). A VF+ sold in 2/08 for $3346. A NM 9.6 sold in 1/07 for $5975

NOTE: *The original color version first sold for 10 cents. Since sales were good, it was later printed as a giveaway. Approximately four million in total were printed. The two black and white copies listed plus two other versions as well as a full color untrimmed version surfaced in 1979 from the Guild's old files in St. Paul, Minnesota.*

GD 2.0 | VG 4.0 | FN 6.0 | VF 8.0 | VF/NM 9.0 | NM- 9.2

IT'S FUN TO STAY ALIVE
National Automobile Dealers Association: 1948 (Giveaway, 16 pgs., heavy stock paper)

Featuring: Bugs Bunny, The Berrys, Dixie Dugan, Elmer, Henry, Tim Tyler, Bruce Gentry, Abbie & Slats, Joe Jinks, The Toodles, & Cokey; all art copyright 1946-48 drawn especially for this book 15 30 45 86 133 180

JACK & JILL VISIT TOYTOWN WITH ELMER THE ELF
Butler Brothers (Toytown Stores): 1949 (Giveaway, 16 pgs., paper cover)

nn 5 10 15 22 26 30

JACK ARMSTRONG (Radio)(See True Comics)
Parents' Institute: 1949

12-Premium version (distr. in Chicago only); Free printed on upper right-c; no price (Rare) 18 36 54 107 169 230

JACKIE JOYNER KERSEE IN HIGH HURDLES (Kellogg's Tony's Sports Comics)
DC Comics: 1992 (Sports Illustrated)

nn 5.00

JACKPOT OF FUN COMIC BOOK
DCA Food Ind.: 1957, giveaway

nn-Features Howdy Doody 11 22 33 64 90 115

JEDLICKA SHOES
DC Comics: 1961

nn-Contains Superman #14 9 18 27 60 100 140

JEEP COMICS
R. B. Leffingwell & Co.: 1945 - 1946

1-46 (Giveaways)-Strip reprints in all; Tarzan, Flash Gordon, Blondie, The Nebbs, Little Iodine, Red Ryder, Don Winslow, The Phantom, Johnny Hazard, Katzenjammer Kids; distr. to U.S. Armed Forces from 1945-1946 6 12 18 31 38 45

JINGLE BELLS CHRISTMAS BOOK
Montgomery Ward (Giveaway): 1971 (20 pgs., B&W inside, slick-c)

nn 6.00

JOAN OF ARC
Catechetical Guild (Topix) (Giveaway): No date (28 pgs., blank back-c)

nn-Ingrid Bergman photo-c; Addison Burbank-a 12 24 36 69 97 125

NOTE: *Unpublished version exists which came from the Guild's files.*

JOE PALOOKA (2nd Series)
Harvey Publications

...Body Building Instruction Book (1958 B&M Sports Toy giveaway, 16pgs., 5-1/4x7")-Origin 9 18 27 47 61 75
...Fights His Way Back (1945 Giveaway, 24 pgs.) Family Comics 15 30 45 85 130 175
...in Hi There! (1949 Red Cross giveaway, 12 pgs., 4-3/4x6") 9 18 27 50 65 80
...in It's All in the Family (1945 Red Cross giveaway, 16 pgs., regular size) 11 22 33 60 83 105

JOE THE GENIE OF STEEL
U.S. Steel Corp., Pittsburgh, PA: 1950 (16 pgs.)

nn 5 10 15 22 26 30

JOHNNY JINGLE'S LUCKY DAY
American Dairy Assoc.: 1956 (16 pgs.; 7-1/4x5-1/8") (Giveaway) (Disney)

nn 5 10 15 24 30 35

JO-JOY (The Adventures of...)
W. T. Grant Dept. Stores: 1945 - 1953 (Christmas gift comic, 16 pgs., 7-1/16x10-1/4")

1945-53 issues 7 14 21 35 43 50

JOLLY CHRISTMAS BOOK (See Christmas Journey Through Space)
Promotional Publ. Co.: 1951; 1954; 1955 (36 pgs.; 24 pgs.)

1951-(Woolworth giveaway)-slightly oversized; no slick cover; Marv Levy-c/a 7 14 21 37 46 55
1954-(Hot Shoppes giveaway)-regular size-reprints 1951 issue; slick cover added; 24 pgs.; no ads 6 12 18 31 38 45
1955-(J. M. McDonald Co. giveaway)-reg. size 6 12 18 28 34 40

JOURNEY OF DISCOVERY WITH MARK STEEL (See Mark Steel)

JUMPING JACKS PRESENTS THE WHIZ KIDS
Jumping Jacks Stores giveaway: 1978 (In 3-D) with glasses (4 pgs.)

nn 6.00

JUNGLE BOOK FUN BOOK, THE (Disney)
Baskin Robbins: 1978

nn-Ice Cream giveaway 2 4 6 9 12 15

JUSTICE LEAGUE OF AMERICA

Kite Book 1953 - Pinocchio © DIS

Kolynos Presents the White Guard © Whitehall Pharmacal

The Little Fir Tree © W.T. Grant

DC Comics: 1999 (included in Justice League of America Monopoly game)

	GD 2.0	VG 4.0	FN 6.0	VF 8.0	VF/NM 9.0	NM- 9.2
nn - Reprints 1st app. in Brave and the Bold #28						2.50

KASCO KOMICS
Kasko Grainfeed (Giveaway): 1945; No. 2, 1949 (Regular size, paper-c)

	GD 2.0	VG 4.0	FN 6.0	VF 8.0	VF/NM 9.0	NM- 9.2
1(1945)-Similar to Katy Keene; Bill Woggon-a; 28 pgs.; 6-7/8x9-7/8"	17	34	51	100	158	215
2(1949)-Woggon-c/a	13	26	39	74	105	135

KATY AND KEN VISIT SANTA WITH MISTER WISH
S. S. Kresge Co. : 1948 (Giveaway, 16 pgs., paper-c)

	GD 2.0	VG 4.0	FN 6.0	VF 8.0	VF/NM 9.0	NM- 9.2
nn	6	12	18	29	36	42

KELLOGG'S CINNAMON MINI-BUNS SUPER-HEROES
DC Comics: 1993 (4 1/4" x 2 3/4")

	GD 2.0	VG 4.0	FN 6.0	VF 8.0	VF/NM 9.0	NM- 9.2
4 editions: Flash, Justice League America, Superman, Wonder Woman and the Star Riders each.....						4.00

KERRY DRAKE DETECTIVE CASES
Publisher's Syndicate

	GD 2.0	VG 4.0	FN 6.0	VF 8.0	VF/NM 9.0	NM- 9.2
...in the Case of the Sleeping City-(1951)-16 pg. giveaway for armed forces; paper cover	6	12	18	29	36	42

KEY COMICS
Key Clothing Co./Peterson Clothing: 1951 - 1956 (32 pgs.) (Giveaway)

Contains a comic from different publishers bound with new cover. Cover changed each year. Many combinations possible. Distributed in Nebraska, Iowa, & Kansas. Contents would determine price, 40-60 percent of original.

KING JAMES "THE KING OF BASKETBALL"
DC Comics: 2004 (Promo comic for LeBron James and Powerade Flava23 sports drink)

	GD 2.0	VG 4.0	FN 6.0	VF 8.0	VF/NM 9.0	NM- 9.2
nn - Ten different covers by various artists; 4 covers for retail, 4 for mail-in, 1 for military commissaries, and 1 general market; Damion Scott-a/Gary Phillips-s						2.50

KIRBY'S SHOES COMICS
Kirby's Shoes: 1959 (8 pgs., soft-c)

	GD 2.0	VG 4.0	FN 6.0	VF 8.0	VF/NM 9.0	NM- 9.2
nn-Features Kirby the Golden Bear	3	5	7	10	12	14

KITE FUN BOOK
Pacific, Gas & Electric/Sou. California Edison/Florida Power & Light/ Missouri Public Service Co.: 1952 - 1998 (16 pgs, 5x7-1/4", soft-c)

	GD 2.0	VG 4.0	FN 6.0	VF 8.0	VF/NM 9.0	NM- 9.2
1952-Having Fun With Kites (P.G.&E.)	12	24	36	69	97	125
1953-Pinocchio Learns About Kites (Disney)	45	90	135	284	477	670
1954-Donald Duck Tells About Kites-Fla. Power, S.C.E. & version with label issues -Barks pencils-8 pgs.; inks-7 pgs. (Rare)	290	580	870	1856	3178	4500
1954-Donald Duck Tells About Kites-P.G.&E. issue -7th page redrawn changing middle 3 panels to show P.G.&E. in story line; (All Barks-a) Scarce	239	478	717	1530	2615	3700
1955-Brer Rabbit in "A Kite Tail" (Disney)	29	58	87	174	285	395
1956-Woody Woodpecker (Lantz)	14	28	42	80	115	150
1957-Ruff and Reddy (exist?)						
1958-Tom And Jerry (M.G.M.)	10	20	30	54	72	90
1959-Bugs Bunny (Warner Bros.)	5	10	15	30	48	65
1960-Porky Pig (Warner Bros.)	5	10	15	32	51	70
1960-Bugs Bunny (Warner Bros.)	5	10	15	32	51	70
1961-Huckleberry Hound (Hanna-Barbera)	6	12	18	37	59	80
1962-Yogi Bear (Hanna-Barbera)	4	8	12	28	44	60
1963-Rocky and Bullwinkle (TV)(Jay Ward)	7	14	21	45	73	100
1963-Top Cat (TV)(Hanna-Barbera)	4	8	12	22	34	45
1964-Magilla Gorilla (TV)(Hanna-Barbera)	3	6	9	20	30	40
1965-Jinks, Pixie and Dixie (TV)(Hanna-Barbera)	3	6	9	16	23	30
1965-Tweety and Sylvester (Warner); S.C.E. version with Reddy Kilowatt app.	2	4	6	10	14	18
1966-Secret Squirrel (Hanna-Barbera); S.C.E. version with Reddy Kilowatt app.	5	10	15	35	55	75
1967-Beep! Beep! The Road Runner (TV)(Warner)	2	4	6	13	18	22
1968-Bugs Bunny (Warner Bros.)	3	6	9	14	19	24
1969-Dastardly and Muttley (TV)(Hanna-Barbera)	4	8	12	22	34	45
1970-Rocky and Bullwinkle (TV)(Jay Ward)	5	10	15	30	48	65
1971-Beep! Beep! The Road Runner (TV)(Warner)	2	4	6	13	18	22
1972-The Pink Panther (TV)	2	4	6	11	16	20
1973-Lassie (TV)	3	6	9	16	23	30
1974-Underdog (TV)	2	4	6	13	18	22
1975-Ben Franklin	2	4	6	8	11	14
1976-The Brady Bunch (TV)	3	6	9	17	25	32
1977-Ben Franklin (exist?)	2	4	6	8	11	14
1977-Popeye	2	4	6	10	14	18
1978-Happy Days (TV)	2	4	6	13	18	22
1979-Eight is Enough (TV)	2	4	6	10	14	18
1980-The Waltons (TV, released in 1981)	2	4	6	10	14	18
1982-Tweety and Sylvester	2	4	6	9	13	16
1984-Smokey Bear	2	4	6	8	10	12
1986-Road Runner	1	3	4	6	8	10
1997-Thomas Edison						4.00
1998-Edison Field (Anaheim Stadium)						3.00

KNOW YOUR MASS
Catechetical Guild: No. 303, 1958 (35¢, 100 Pg. Giant) (Square binding)

	GD 2.0	VG 4.0	FN 6.0	VF 8.0	VF/NM 9.0	NM- 9.2
303-In color	7	14	21	35	43	50

KOLYNOS PRESENTS THE WHITE GUARD
Whitehall Pharmacal Co.: 1949 (paper cover, 8 pgs.)

	GD 2.0	VG 4.0	FN 6.0	VF 8.0	VF/NM 9.0	NM- 9.2
nn	6	12	18	27	33	38

K. O. PUNCH, THE (Also see Lucky Fights It Through & Sidewalk Romance)
E. C. Comics: 1948 (VD Educational giveaway)

	GD 2.0	VG 4.0	FN 6.0	VF 8.0	VF/NM 9.0	NM- 9.2
nn-Feldstein-splash; Kamen-a	84	168	252	538	919	1300

KOREA MY HOME (Also see Yalta to Korea)
Johnstone and Cushing: nd (1950s)

	GD 2.0	VG 4.0	FN 6.0	VF 8.0	VF/NM 9.0	NM- 9.2
nn-Anti-communist; Korean War	20	40	60	116	191	265

KRIM-KO KOMICS
Krim-ko Chocolate Drink: 5/18/35 - No. 6, 6/22/35; 1936 - 1939 (weekly)

	GD 2.0	VG 4.0	FN 6.0	VF 8.0	VF/NM 9.0	NM- 9.2
1-(16 pgs., soft-c, Dairy giveaways)-Tom, Mary & Sparky Advs. by Russell Keaton, Jim Hawkins by Dick Moores, Mystery Island! by Rick Yager begin	14	28	42	76	108	140
2-6 (6/22/35)	10	20	30	56	76	95
Lola, Secret Agent; 184 issues, 4 pg. giveaways - all original stories each....	7	14	21	37	46	55

LABOR IS A PARTNER
Catechetical Guild Educational Society: 1949 (32 pgs., paper-c)

	GD 2.0	VG 4.0	FN 6.0	VF 8.0	VF/NM 9.0	NM- 9.2
nn-Anti-communism	20	40	60	116	191	265
Confidential Preview-(8-1/2x11", B&W, saddle stitched)-only one known copy; text varies from color version, advertises next book on secularism (If the Devil Would Talk)	24	48	72	142	234	325

LADY AND THE TRAMP IN "BUTTER LATE THAN NEVER"
American Dairy Assoc. (Premium): 1955 (16 pgs., 5x7-1/4", soft-c) (Disney)

	GD 2.0	VG 4.0	FN 6.0	VF 8.0	VF/NM 9.0	NM- 9.2
nn	8	16	24	44	57	70

LASSIE (TV)
Dell Publ. Co

	GD 2.0	VG 4.0	FN 6.0	VF 8.0	VF/NM 9.0	NM- 9.2
The Adventures of... nn-(Red Heart Dog Food giveaway, 1949)-16 pgs, soft-c; 1st app. Lassie in comics	31	62	93	184	302	420

LIFE OF THE BLESSED VIRGIN
Catechetical Guild (Giveaway): 1950 (68pgs.) (square binding)

	GD 2.0	VG 4.0	FN 6.0	VF 8.0	VF/NM 9.0	NM- 9.2
nn-Contains "The Woman of the Promise" & "Mother of Us All" rebound	7	14	21	35	43	50

LIGHTNING RACERS
DC Comics: 1989

	GD 2.0	VG 4.0	FN 6.0	VF 8.0	VF/NM 9.0	NM- 9.2
1						4.50

LI'L ABNER (Al Capp's) (Also see Natural Disasters!)
Harvey Publ./Toby Press

	GD 2.0	VG 4.0	FN 6.0	VF 8.0	VF/NM 9.0	NM- 9.2
...& the Creatures from Drop-Outer Space-nn (Job Corps giveaway; 36 pgs., in color) (entire book by Frank Frazetta)	21	42	63	121	201	280
...Joins the Navy (1950) (Toby Press Premium)	11	22	33	62	86	110
Al Capp by Li'l Abner (Circa 1946, nd, giveaway) Al Capp bio and his life as an amputee	11	22	33	62	86	110

LITTLE ALONZO
Macy's Dept. Store: 1938 (B&W, 5-1/2x8-1/2")(Christmas giveaway)

	GD 2.0	VG 4.0	FN 6.0	VF 8.0	VF/NM 9.0	NM- 9.2
nn-By Ferdinand the Bull's Munro Leaf	9	18	27	50	65	80

LITTLE ARCHIE (See Archie Comics)

LITTLE DOT
Harvey Publications

	GD 2.0	VG 4.0	FN 6.0	VF 8.0	VF/NM 9.0	NM- 9.2
Shoe store giveaway 2	4	8	12	28	44	60

LITTLE FIR TREE, THE
W. T. Grant Co. : nd (1942) (8-1/2x11") (12 pgs. with cover, color & B&W, heavy paper) (Christmas giveaway)

	GD 2.0	VG 4.0	FN 6.0	VF 8.0	VF/NM 9.0	NM- 9.2
nn-Story by Hans Christian Anderson; 8 pg. Kelly-r/Santa Claus Funnies (not signed); X-Mas-c	87	174	261	552	951	1350

LITTLE KLINKER
Little Klinker Ventures: Nov, 1960 (20 pgs.) (slick cover) (Montgomery Ward Giveaway)

	GD 2.0	VG 4.0	FN 6.0	VF 8.0	VF/NM 9.0	NM- 9.2
nn	2	4	6	9	13	16

LITTLE MISS SUNBEAM COMICS

Little Miss Sunbeam 1957 © ME

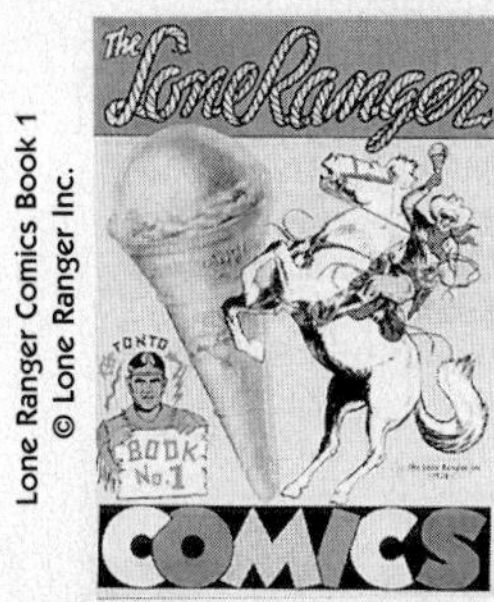

Lone Ranger Comics Book 1 © Lone Ranger Inc.

March of Comics #20 © DIS

GD VG FN VF VF/NM NM-
2.0 4.0 6.0 8.0 9.0 9.2

Magazine Enterprises/Quality Bakers of America

Bread Giveaway 1-4(Quality Bakers, 1949-50)-14 pgs. each 6 12 18 31 38 45

Bread Giveaway (1957,61; 16pgs, reg. size) 5 10 15 24 30 35

LITTLE ORPHAN ANNIE
David McKay Publ./Dell Publishing Co.

Junior Commandos Giveaway (same-c as 4-Color #18, K.K. Publ.)(Big Shoe Store); same back cover as '47 Popped Wheat giveaway; 16 pgs; flag-c; r/strips 9/7/42-10/10/42 26 52 78 154 252 350

Popped Wheat Giveaway ('47)-16 pgs. full color; reprints strips from 5/3/40 to 6/20/40 4 8 12 18 22 25

Quaker Sparkies Giveaway (1940) 18 36 54 103 162 220

Quaker Sparkies Giveaway (1941, full color, 20 pgs.); "LOA and the Rescue"; r/strips 4/13/39-6/21/39 & 7/6/39-7/17/39. "LOA and the Kidnappers"; r/strips 11/28/38-1/28/39 15 30 45 94 147 200

Quaker Sparkies Giveaway (1942, full color, 20 pgs.); "LOA and Mr. Gudge"; r/strips 2/13/38-3/21/38 & 4/18/37-5/30/37. "LOA and the Great Am" 15 30 45 88 137 185

LITTLE TREE THAT WASN'T WANTED, THE
W. T. Grant Co. (Giveaway): 1960, (Color, 28 pgs.)

nn-Christmas story, puzzles and games 4 8 12 22 34 45

LOADED (Also see Re-Loaded)
DC Comics: 1995 (Interplay Productions)

1-Garth Ennis-s; promotes video game 4.00

LONE RANGER, THE
Dell Publishing Co.

Cheerios Giveaways (1954, 16 pgs., 2-1/2x7", soft-c) #1- "The Lone Ranger, His Mask & How He Met Tonto". #2- "The Lone Ranger & the Story of Silver" each.... 15 30 45 85 130 175

Doll Giveaways (Gabriel Ind.)(1973, 3-1/4x5")- "The Story of The Lone Ranger," "The Carson City Bank Robbery" & "The Apache Buffalo Hunt" 2 4 6 12 16 20

How the Lone Ranger Captured Silver Book(1936)-Silvercup Bread giveaway 55 110 165 349 600 850

...In Milk for Big Mike (1955, Dairy Association giveaway), soft-c; 5x7-1/4", 16 pgs. 14 28 42 80 115 150

Legend of The Lone Ranger (1969, 16 pgs., giveaway)-Origin The Lone Ranger 4 8 12 22 34 45

Merita Bread giveaway (1954, 16 pgs., 5x7-1/4")- "How to Be a Lone Ranger Health & Safety Scout" 18 36 54 103 162 220

LONE RANGER COMICS, THE
Lone Ranger, Inc. : Book 1, 1939(inside) (shows 1938 on-c) (52 pgs. in color; regular size) (Ice cream mail order)

Book 1-(Scarce)-The first western comic devoted to a single character; not by Vallely 600 1200 1800 4200 - -

2nd version w/large full color promo poster pasted over centerfold & a smaller poster pasted over back cover; includes new additional premiums not originally offered (Rare) 857 1714 2571 6000 - -

LOONEY TUNES
DC Comics: 1991, 1998

Claritin promotional issue (1998) 3.00
Colgate mini-comic (1998) 3.00
Tyson's 1-10 (1991) 4.00

LUCKY FIGHTS IT THROUGH (Also see The K. O. Punch & Sidewalk Romance)
Educational Comics: 1949 (Giveaway, 16 pgs. in color, paper-c)

nn-(Very Rare)-1st Kurtzman work for E. C.; V.D. prevention 126 252 378 806 1378 1950

nn-Reprint in color (1977) 7.00

NOTE: *Subtitled "The Story of That Ignorant, Ignorant Cowboy". Prepared for Communications Materials Center, Columbia University.*

LUDWIG VON DRAKE (See Frito-Lay Giveaway)

MACO TOYS COMIC
Maco Toys/Charlton Comics: 1959 (Giveaway, 36 pgs.)

1-All military stories featuring Maco Toys 3 6 9 14 19 24

MAD MAGAZINE
DC Comics: 1997, 1999, 2008

Special Edition (1997, Tang giveaway) 3.00
Stocking Stuffer (1999) 3.00
San Diego Comic-Con Edition (2008) Watchmen parody with Fabry-a; Aragonés cartoons 3.00

MAGAZINELAND
DC Comics: 1977

nn-Kubert-c/a 3 6 9 16 22 28

MAGIC MORRO (Also see Super Comics #21, The Owl, & The Hurricane Kids)
K. K. Publications: 1941 (7-1/2 x 5-1/4", giveaway, soft-c)

nn-Ken Ernst-a. 10 20 30 54 72 90

MAGIC OF CHRISTMAS AT NEWBERRYS, THE
E. S. London: 1967 (Giveaway) (B&W, slick-c, 20 pgs.)

nn 1 3 4 6 8 10

MAJOR INAPAK THE SPACE ACE
Magazine Enterprises (Inapac Foods): 1951 (20 pgs.) (Giveaway)

1-Bob Powell-c/a 6.00

NOTE: *Many warehouse copies surfaced in 1973.*

MAMMY YOKUM & THE GREAT DOGPATCH MYSTERY
Toby Press: 1951 (Giveaway)

nn-Li'l Abner 15 30 45 88 137 185
nn-Reprint (1956) 5 10 15 22 26 30

MAN NAMED STEVENSON, A
Democratic National Committee: 1952 (20 pgs., 5 1/4 x 7")

nn 9 18 27 47 61 75

MAN OF PEACE, POPE PIUS XII
Catechetical Guild: 1950 (See Pope Pius XII... & To V2#8)

nn-All Powell-a 7 14 21 35 43 50

MAN OF STEEL BEST WESTERN
DC Comics: 1997 (Best Western hotels promo)

3-Reprints Superman's first post-Crisis meeting with Batman 4.00

MAN WHO RUNS INTERFERENCE
General Comics, Inc./Institute of Life Insurance: 1946 (Paper-c)

nn-Football premium 5 10 15 22 26 30

MAN WHO WOULDN'T QUIT, THE
Harvey Publications Inc.: 1952 (16 pgs., paper cover)

nn-The value of voting 4 8 12 18 22 25

MARCH OF COMICS (Boys' and Girls'...#3-353)
K. K. Publications/Western Publishing Co.: 1946 - No. 488, April, 1982 (#1-4 are not numbered) (K.K. Giveaway) (Founded by Sig Feuchtwanger)

Early issues were full size, 32 pages, and were printed with and without an extra cover of slick stock, just for the advertiser. The binding was stapled if the slick cover was added; otherwise, the pages were glued together at the spine. Most 1948 - 1951 issues were full size,24 pages, pulp covers. Starting in 1952 they were half-size (with a few exceptions) and 32 pages with slick covers.1959 and later issues had only 16 pages plus covers. 1952 -1959 issues read oblong; 1960 and later issues read upright. All have new stories except where noted.

nn (#1, 1946)-Goldilocks; Kelly back-c (16 pgs., stapled) 53 106 159 334 567 800
nn (#2, 1946)-How Santa Got His Red Suit; Kelly-a (11 pgs., r/4-Color #61 from 1944) (16pgs., stapled) 34 68 102 199 325 450
nn (#3, 1947)-Our Gang (Walt Kelly) 40 80 120 246 411 575
nn (#4)-Donald Duck by Carl Barks, "Maharajah Donald", 28 pgs.; Kelly-c? (Disney) 757 1514 2271 5602 9801 14,000
5-Andy Panda (Walter Lantz) 21 42 63 122 199 275
6-Popular Fairy Tales; Kelly-c; Noonan-a(2) 23 46 69 136 223 310
7-Oswald the Rabbit 21 42 63 126 206 285
8-Mickey Mouse, 32 pgs. (Disney) 50 100 150 315 533 750
9(nn)-The Story of the Gloomy Bunny 14 28 42 81 118 155
10-Out of Santa's Bag 14 28 42 78 112 145
11-Fun With Santa Claus 12 24 36 69 97 125
12-Santa's Toys 12 24 36 69 97 125
13-Santa's Surprise 12 24 36 69 97 125
14-Santa's Candy Kitchen 12 24 36 69 97 125
15-Hip-It-Ty Hop & the Big Bass Viol 11 22 33 64 90 115
16-Woody Woodpecker (1947)(Walter Lantz) 15 30 45 85 130 175
17-Roy Rogers (1948) 25 50 75 147 241 335
18-Popular Fairy Tales 14 28 42 80 115 150
19-Uncle Wiggily 13 26 39 72 101 130
20-Donald Duck by Carl Barks, "Darkest Africa", 22 pgs.; Kelly-c (Disney) 309 618 927 2194 3797 5400
21-Tom and Jerry 14 28 42 76 108 140
22-Andy Panda (Lantz) 12 24 36 67 94 120
23-Raggedy Ann & Andy; Kerr-a 14 28 42 82 121 160
24-Felix the Cat, 1932 daily strip reprints by Otto Messmer 20 40 60 118 194 270
25-Gene Autry 20 40 60 116 191 265
26-Our Gang; Walt Kelly 19 38 57 111 178 245
27-Mickey Mouse; r/in M. M. #240 (Disney) 35 70 105 207 339 470
28-Gene Autry 20 40 60 118 192 265

March of Comics #47 © Roy Rogers

March of Comics #70 © MGM

March of Comics #171 © Walter Lantz

	GD 2.0	VG 4.0	FN 6.0	VF 8.0	VF/NM 9.0	NM- 9.2
29-Easter Bonnet Shop	9	18	27	47	61	75
30-Here Comes Santa	8	16	24	44	57	70
31-Santa's Busy Corner	8	16	24	44	57	70
32-No book produced						
33-A Christmas Carol (12/48)	9	18	27	47	61	75
34-Woody Woodpecker	13	26	39	74	105	135
35-Roy Rogers (1948)	21	42	63	123	204	285
36-Felix the Cat(1949); by Messmer; '34 strip-r	18	36	54	105	165	225
37-Popeye	15	30	45	85	130	175
38-Oswald the Rabbit	10	20	30	58	79	100
39-Gene Autry	19	38	57	112	181	250
40-Andy and Woody	10	20	30	58	79	100
41-Donald Duck by Carl Barks, "Race to the South Seas", 22 pgs.; Kelly-c	300	600	900	2130	3665	5200
42-Porky Pig	11	22	33	60	83	105
43-Henry	10	20	30	56	76	95
44-Bugs Bunny	11	22	33	64	90	115
45-Mickey Mouse (Disney)	27	54	81	158	259	360
46-Tom and Jerry	11	22	33	64	90	115
47-Roy Rogers	19	38	57	110	175	240
48-Greetings from Santa	6	12	18	31	38	45
49-Santa Is Here	6	12	18	31	38	45
50-Santa Claus' Workshop (1949)	6	12	18	31	38	45
51-Felix the Cat (1950) by Messmer	15	30	45	94	147	200
52-Popeye	14	28	42	76	108	140
53-Oswald the Rabbit	10	20	30	54	72	90
54-Gene Autry	17	34	51	100	158	215
55-Andy and Woody	9	18	27	52	69	85
56-Donald Duck; not by Barks; Barks art on back-c (Disney)	28	56	84	165	270	375
57-Porky Pig	10	20	30	54	72	90
58-Henry	8	16	24	44	57	70
59-Bugs Bunny	10	20	30	58	79	100
60-Mickey Mouse (Disney)	25	50	75	150	245	340
61-Tom and Jerry	10	20	30	54	72	90
62-Roy Rogers	19	38	57	109	172	235
63-Welcome Santa (1/2-size, oblong)	6	12	18	31	38	45
64(nn)-Santa's Helpers (1/2-size, oblong)	6	12	18	31	38	45
65(nn)-Jingle Bells (1950) (1/2-size, oblong)	6	12	18	31	38	45
66-Popeye (1951)	12	24	36	69	97	125
67-Oswald the Rabbit	9	18	27	52	69	85
68-Roy Rogers	18	36	54	105	165	225
69-Donald Duck; Barks-a on back-c (Disney)	24	48	72	142	234	325
70-Tom and Jerry	9	18	27	50	65	80
71-Porky Pig	9	18	27	52	69	85
72-Krazy Kat	10	20	30	58	79	100
73-Roy Rogers	16	32	48	96	151	205
74-Mickey Mouse (1951)(Disney)	19	38	57	114	187	260
75-Bugs Bunny	9	18	27	52	69	85
76-Andy and Woody	9	18	27	50	65	80
77-Roy Rogers	15	30	45	90	140	190
78-Gene Autry (1951); last regular size issue	15	30	45	86	133	180
Note: All pre #79 issues came with or without a slick protective wrap-around cover over the regular cover which advertised Poll Parrot Shoes, Sears, etc. This outer cover protects the inside pages making them in nicer condition. Issues with the outer cover are worth 15-25% more						
79-Andy Panda (1952, 5x7" size)	7	14	21	35	43	50
80-Popeye	10	20	30	58	79	100
81-Oswald the Rabbit	6	12	18	29	36	42
82-Tarzan; Lex Barker photo-c	15	30	45	90	140	190
83-Bugs Bunny	7	14	21	37	46	55
84-Henry	6	12	18	29	36	42
85-Woody Woodpecker	6	12	18	29	36	42
86-Roy Rogers	14	28	42	76	108	140
87-Krazy Kat	8	16	24	44	57	70
88-Tom and Jerry	6	12	18	31	38	45
89-Porky Pig	6	12	18	29	36	42
90-Gene Autry	12	24	36	69	97	125
91-Roy Rogers & Santa	13	26	39	74	105	135
92-Christmas with Santa	5	10	15	24	30	35
93-Woody Woodpecker (1953)	5	10	15	23	28	32
94-Indian Chief	10	20	30	54	72	90
95-Oswald the Rabbit	5	10	15	23	28	32
96-Popeye	10	20	30	54	72	90
97-Bugs Bunny	7	14	21	35	43	50
98-Tarzan; Lex Barker photo-c	15	30	45	86	133	180
99-Porky Pig	5	10	15	23	28	32
100-Roy Rogers	11	22	33	62	86	110
101-Henry	5	10	15	22	26	30
102-Tom Corbett (TV)('53, early app).; painted-c	14	28	42	76	108	140
103-Tom and Jerry	5	10	15	23	28	32
104-Gene Autry	11	22	33	60	83	105
105-Roy Rogers	11	22	33	60	83	105
106-Santa's Helpers	5	10	15	24	30	35
107-Santa's Christmas Book - not published						
108-Fun with Santa (1953)	5	10	15	24	30	35
109-Woody Woodpecker (1954)	5	10	15	24	30	35
110-Indian Chief	6	12	18	31	38	45
111-Oswald the Rabbit	5	10	15	22	26	30
112-Henry	4	9	13	18	22	26
113-Porky Pig	5	10	15	22	26	30
114-Tarzan; Russ Manning-a	15	30	45	86	133	180
115-Bugs Bunny	6	12	18	27	33	38
116-Roy Rogers	11	22	33	60	83	105
117-Popeye	10	20	30	54	72	90
118-Flash Gordon; painted-c	12	24	36	67	94	120
119-Tom and Jerry	5	10	15	22	26	30
120-Gene Autry	11	22	33	60	83	105
121-Roy Rogers	11	22	33	60	83	105
122-Santa's Surprise (1954)	5	10	15	22	26	30
123-Santa's Christmas Book	5	10	15	22	26	30
124-Woody Woodpecker (1955)	4	9	13	18	22	26
125-Tarzan; Lex Barker photo-c	15	30	45	83	124	165
126-Oswald the Rabbit	4	9	13	18	22	26
127-Indian Chief	7	14	21	35	43	50
128-Tom and Jerry	4	9	13	18	22	26
129-Henry	4	8	12	17	21	24
130-Porky Pig	4	9	13	18	22	26
131-Roy Rogers	11	22	33	60	83	105
132-Bugs Bunny	5	10	15	23	28	32
133-Flash Gordon; painted-c	11	22	33	60	83	105
134-Popeye	8	16	24	42	54	65
135-Gene Autry	10	20	30	56	76	95
136-Roy Rogers	10	20	30	56	76	95
137-Gifts from Santa	4	7	10	14	17	20
138-Fun at Christmas (1955)	4	7	10	14	17	20
139-Woody Woodpecker (1956)	4	9	13	18	22	26
140-Indian Chief	7	14	21	35	43	50
141-Oswald the Rabbit	4	9	13	18	22	26
142-Flash Gordon	11	22	33	60	83	105
143-Porky Pig	4	9	13	18	22	26
144-Tarzan; Russ Manning-a; painted-c	14	28	42	80	115	150
145-Tom and Jerry	4	9	13	18	22	26
146-Roy Rogers; photo-c	10	20	30	56	76	95
147-Henry	4	8	11	16	19	22
148-Popeye	8	16	24	42	54	65
149-Bugs Bunny	5	10	15	22	26	30
150-Gene Autry	10	20	30	56	76	95
151-Roy Rogers	10	20	30	56	76	95
152-The Night Before Christmas	4	8	11	16	19	22
153-Merry Christmas (1956)	4	9	13	18	22	26
154-Tom and Jerry (1957)	4	9	13	18	22	26
155-Tarzan; photo-c	14	28	42	78	112	145
156-Oswald the Rabbit	4	9	13	18	22	26
157-Popeye	7	14	21	35	43	50
158-Woody Woodpecker	4	9	13	18	22	26
159-Indian Chief	7	14	21	35	43	50
160-Bugs Bunny	5	10	15	22	26	30
161-Roy Rogers	9	18	27	52	69	85
162-Henry	4	8	11	16	19	22
163-Rin Tin Tin (TV)	8	16	24	42	54	65
164-Porky Pig	4	9	13	18	22	26
165-The Lone Ranger	10	20	30	54	72	90
166-Santa and His Reindeer	4	7	10	14	17	20
167-Roy Rogers and Santa	9	18	27	52	69	85
168-Santa Claus' Workshop (1957, full size)	4	8	11	16	19	22
169-Popeye (1958)	7	14	21	35	43	50
170-Indian Chief	7	14	21	35	43	50
171-Oswald the Rabbit	4	8	12	17	21	24
172-Tarzan	11	22	33	64	90	115
173-Tom and Jerry	4	8	12	17	21	24
174-The Lone Ranger	10	20	30	54	72	90
175-Porky Pig	4	8	12	17	21	24
176-Roy Rogers	9	18	27	47	61	75

March of Comics #205 © Terry Toons

March of Comics #301 © WB

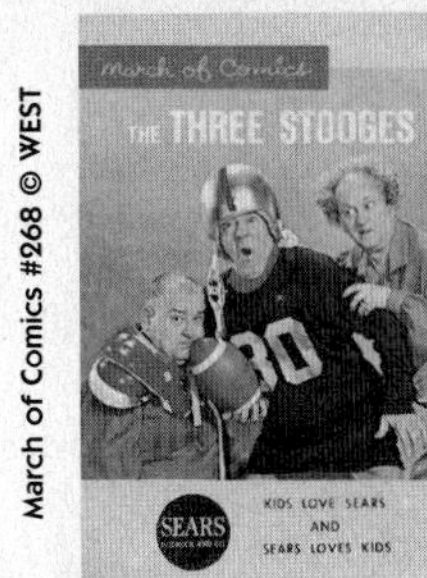

March of Comics #268 © WEST

	GD 2.0	VG 4.0	FN 6.0	VF 8.0	VF/NM 9.0	NM- 9.2
177-Woody Woodpecker	4	8	12	17	21	24
178-Henry	4	8	11	16	19	22
179-Bugs Bunny	4	8	12	17	21	24
180-Rin Tin Tin (TV)	7	14	21	37	46	55
181-Happy Holiday	4	7	9	14	16	18
182-Happi Tim	4	8	11	16	19	22
183-Welcome Santa (1958, full size)	4	7	9	14	16	18
184-Woody Woodpecker (1959)	4	8	11	16	19	22
185-Tarzan; photo-c	11	22	33	60	83	110
186-Oswald the Rabbit	4	8	11	16	19	22
187-Indian Chief	6	12	18	28	34	40
188-Bugs Bunny	4	8	11	16	19	22
189-Henry	4	7	10	14	17	20
190-Tom and Jerry	4	8	11	16	19	22
191-Roy Rogers	8	16	24	44	57	70
192-Porky Pig	4	8	11	16	19	22
193-The Lone Ranger	9	18	27	52	69	85
194-Popeye	6	12	18	31	38	45
195-Rin Tin Tin (TV)	7	14	21	35	43	50
196-Sears Special - not published						
197-Santa Is Coming	4	7	10	14	17	20
198-Santa's Helpers (1959)	4	7	10	14	17	20
199-Huckleberry Hound (TV)(1960, early app.)	8	16	24	42	54	65
200-Fury (TV)	6	12	18	28	34	40
201-Bugs Bunny	4	8	11	16	19	22
202-Space Explorer	8	16	24	42	54	65
203-Woody Woodpecker	4	7	10	14	17	20
204-Tarzan	9	18	27	52	69	85
205-Mighty Mouse	6	12	18	33	41	48
206-Roy Rogers; photo-c	8	16	24	42	54	65
207-Tom and Jerry	4	7	10	14	17	20
208-The Lone Ranger; Clayton Moore photo-c	11	22	33	62	86	110
209-Porky Pig	4	7	10	14	17	20
210-Lassie (TV)	6	12	18	33	41	48
211-Sears Special - not published						
212-Christmas Eve	4	7	10	14	17	20
213-Here Comes Santa (1960)	4	7	10	14	17	20
214-Huckleberry Hound (TV)(1961)	7	14	21	35	43	50
215-Hi Yo Silver	8	16	24	40	50	60
216-Rocky & His Friends (TV)(1961); predates Rocky and His Fiendish Friends #1 (see Four Color #1128)	10	20	30	58	79	100
217-Lassie (TV)	6	12	18	31	38	45
218-Porky Pig	4	7	10	14	17	20
219-Journey to the Sun	5	10	15	24	30	35
220-Bugs Bunny	4	8	11	16	19	22
221-Roy and Dale; photo-c	8	16	24	42	54	65
222-Woody Woodpecker	4	7	10	14	17	20
223-Tarzan	9	18	27	52	69	85
224-Tom and Jerry	4	7	10	14	17	20
225-The Lone Ranger	8	16	24	40	50	60
226-Christmas Treasury (1961)	4	7	10	14	17	20
227-Letters to Santa (1961)	4	7	10	14	17	20
228-Sears Special - not published?						
229-The Flintstones (TV)(1962); early app.; predates 1st Flintstones Gold Key issue (#7)	11	22	33	60	83	105
230-Lassie (TV)	6	12	18	27	33	38
231-Bugs Bunny	4	8	11	16	19	22
232-The Three Stooges	10	20	30	54	72	90
233-Bullwinkle (TV) (1962, very early app.)	10	20	30	58	79	100
234-Smokey the Bear	5	10	15	23	28	32
235-Huckleberry Hound (TV)	7	14	21	35	43	50
236-Roy and Dale	7	14	21	35	43	50
237-Mighty Mouse	6	12	18	27	33	38
238-The Lone Ranger	8	16	24	40	50	60
239-Woody Woodpecker	4	7	10	14	17	20
240-Tarzan	8	16	24	44	57	70
241-Santa Claus Around the World	4	7	9	14	16	18
242-Santa's Toyland (1962)	4	7	9	14	16	18
243-The Flintstones (TV)(1963)	8	16	24	44	57	70
244-Mister Ed (TV); early app.; photo-c	7	14	21	35	43	50
245-Bugs Bunny	4	8	11	16	19	22
246-Popeye	6	12	18	27	33	38
247-Mighty Mouse	6	12	18	27	33	38
248-The Three Stooges	10	20	30	54	72	90
249-Woody Woodpecker	4	7	10	14	17	20
250-Roy and Dale	7	14	21	35	43	50
251-Little Lulu & Witch Hazel	12	24	36	67	94	120

	GD 2.0	VG 4.0	FN 6.0	VF 8.0	VF/NM 9.0	NM- 9.2
252-Tarzan; painted-c	8	16	24	42	54	65
253-Yogi Bear (TV)	8	16	24	40	50	60
254-Lassie (TV)	6	12	18	27	33	38
255-Santa's Christmas List	4	7	10	14	17	20
256-Christmas Party (1963)	4	7	10	14	17	20
257-Mighty Mouse	6	12	18	27	33	38
258-The Sword in the Stone (Disney)	8	16	24	42	54	65
259-Bugs Bunny	4	8	11	16	19	22
260-Mister Ed (TV)	6	12	18	31	38	45
261-Woody Woodpecker	4	7	10	14	17	20
262-Tarzan	8	16	24	40	50	60
263-Donald Duck; not by Barks (Disney)	9	18	27	52	69	85
264-Popeye	6	12	18	27	33	38
265-Yogi Bear (TV)	6	12	18	31	38	45
266-Lassie (TV)	5	10	15	23	28	32
267-Little Lulu; Irving Tripp-a	10	20	30	56	76	95
268-The Three Stooges	9	18	27	47	61	75
269-A Jolly Christmas	3	6	8	12	14	16
270-Santa's Little Helpers	3	6	8	12	14	16
271-The Flintstones (TV)(1965)	8	16	24	44	57	70
272-Tarzan	8	16	24	40	50	60
273-Bugs Bunny	4	8	11	16	19	22
274-Popeye	6	12	18	27	33	38
275-Little Lulu; Irving Tripp-a	9	18	27	50	65	80
276-The Jetsons (TV)	14	28	42	76	108	140
277-Daffy Duck	4	8	11	16	19	22
278-Lassie (TV)	5	10	15	23	28	32
279-Yogi Bear (TV)	6	12	18	31	38	45
280-The Three Stooges; photo-c	9	18	27	47	61	75
281-Tom and Jerry	4	7	9	14	16	18
282-Mister Ed (TV)	6	12	18	31	38	45
283-Santa's Visit	4	7	9	14	16	18
284-Christmas Parade (1965)	4	7	9	14	16	18
285-Astro Boy (TV); 2nd app. Astro Boy	28	56	84	165	270	375
286-Tarzan	7	14	21	37	46	55
287-Bugs Bunny	4	8	11	16	19	22
288-Daffy Duck	4	7	10	14	17	20
289-The Flintstones (TV)	8	16	24	44	57	70
290-Mister Ed (TV); photo-c	5	10	15	24	30	35
291-Yogi Bear (TV)	6	12	18	27	33	38
292-The Three Stooges; photo-c	9	18	27	47	61	75
293-Little Lulu; Irving Tripp-a	8	16	24	42	54	65
294-Popeye	5	10	15	24	30	35
295-Tom and Jerry	4	7	9	14	16	18
296-Lassie (TV); photo-c	5	10	15	22	26	30
297-Christmas Bells	3	6	8	12	14	16
298-Santa's Sleigh (1966)	3	6	8	12	14	16
299-The Flintstones (TV)(1967)	8	16	24	44	57	70
300-Tarzan	7	14	21	37	46	55
301-Bugs Bunny	4	7	10	14	17	20
302-Laurel and Hardy (TV); photo-c	6	12	18	28	34	40
303-Daffy Duck	3	6	8	12	14	16
304-The Three Stooges; photo-c	8	16	24	44	57	70
305-Tom and Jerry	3	6	8	12	14	16
306-Daniel Boone (TV); Fess Parker photo-c	7	14	21	35	43	50
307-Little Lulu; Irving Tripp-a	7	14	21	37	46	55
308-Lassie (TV); photo-c	5	10	15	22	26	30
309-Yogi Bear (TV)	5	10	15	24	30	35
310-The Lone Ranger; Clayton Moore photo-c	11	22	33	62	86	110
311-Santa's Show	4	7	9	14	16	18
312-Christmas Album (1967)	4	7	9	14	16	18
313-Daffy Duck (1968)	3	6	8	12	14	16
314-Laurel and Hardy (TV)	6	12	18	27	33	38
315-Bugs Bunny	4	7	10	14	17	20
316-The Three Stooges	8	16	24	40	50	60
317-The Flintstones (TV)	8	16	24	42	54	65
318-Tarzan	7	14	21	35	43	50
319-Yogi Bear (TV)	5	10	15	24	30	35
320-Space Family Robinson (TV); Spiegle-a	12	24	36	69	97	125
321-Tom and Jerry	3	6	8	12	14	16
322-The Lone Ranger	7	14	21	37	46	55
323-Little Lulu; not by Stanley	5	10	15	24	30	35
324-Lassie (TV); photo-c	5	10	15	22	26	30
325-Fun with Santa	4	7	9	14	16	18
326-Christmas Story (1968)	4	7	9	14	16	18
327-The Flintstones (TV)(1969)	8	16	24	42	54	65
328-Space Family Robinson (TV); Spiegle-a	12	24	36	69	97	125

March of Comics #337 © H-B

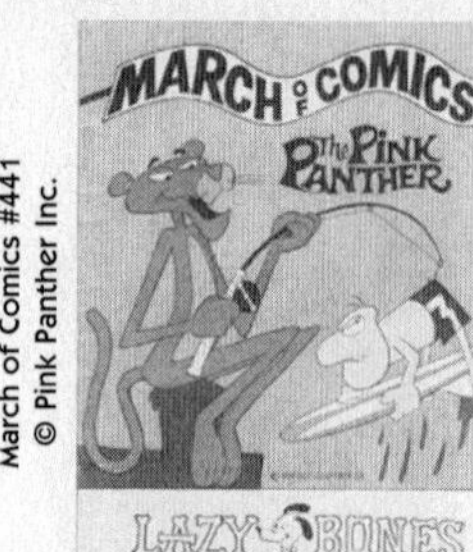

March of Comics #441 © Pink Panther Inc.

Martin Luther King and The Montgomery Story © Fellowship Reconciliation

	GD 2.0	VG 4.0	FN 6.0	VF 8.0	VF/NM 9.0	NM- 9.2
329-Bugs Bunny	4	7	10	14	17	20
330-The Jetsons (TV)	10	20	30	56	76	95
331-Daffy Duck	3	6	8	12	14	16
332-Tarzan	6	12	18	28	34	40
333-Tom and Jerry	3	6	8	12	14	16
334-Lassie (TV)	4	9	13	18	22	26
335-Little Lulu	5	10	15	24	30	35
336-The Three Stooges	8	16	24	40	50	60
337-Yogi Bear (TV)	5	10	15	24	30	35
338-The Lone Ranger	7	14	21	37	46	55
339-(Was not published)						
340-Here Comes Santa (1969)	3	6	8	12	14	16
341-The Flintstones (TV)	8	16	24	42	54	65
342-Tarzan	3	6	9	20	30	40
343-Bugs Bunny	2	4	6	10	14	18
344-Yogi Bear (TV)	3	6	9	16	23	30
345-Tom and Jerry	2	4	6	9	13	16
346-Lassie (TV)	3	6	9	15	21	26
347-Daffy Duck	2	4	6	9	13	16
348-The Jetsons (TV)	6	12	18	39	62	85
349-Little Lulu; not by Stanley	3	6	9	16	23	30
350-The Lone Ranger	3	6	9	18	27	35
351-Beep-Beep, the Road Runner (TV)	2	4	6	11	16	20
352-Space Family Robinson (TV); Spiegle-a	8	16	24	54	90	125
353-Beep-Beep, the Road Runner (1971) (TV)	2	4	6	11	16	20
354-Tarzan (1971)	3	6	9	18	27	35
355-Little Lulu; not by Stanley	3	6	9	16	23	30
356-Scooby Doo, Where Are You? (TV)	6	12	18	43	69	95
357-Daffy Duck & Porky Pig	2	4	6	8	11	14
358-Lassie (TV)	3	6	9	14	19	24
359-Baby Snoots	2	4	6	10	14	18
360-H. R. Pufnstuf (TV); photo-c	6	12	18	43	69	95
361-Tom and Jerry	2	4	6	8	11	14
362-Smokey Bear (TV)	2	4	6	8	11	14
363-Bugs Bunny & Yosemite Sam	2	4	6	9	13	16
364-The Banana Splits (TV); photo-c	6	12	18	37	59	80
365-Tom and Jerry (1972)	2	4	6	8	11	14
366-Tarzan	3	6	9	18	27	35
367-Bugs Bunny & Porky Pig	2	4	6	9	13	16
368-Scooby Doo (TV)(4/72)	6	12	18	37	59	80
369-Little Lulu; not by Stanley	3	6	9	14	19	24
370-Lassie (TV); photo-c	3	6	9	14	19	24
371-Baby Snoots	2	4	6	9	13	16
372-Smokey the Bear (TV)	2	4	6	8	11	14
373-The Three Stooges	4	8	12	24	37	50
374-Wacky Witch	2	4	6	8	11	14
375-Beep-Beep & Daffy Duck (TV)	2	4	6	8	11	14
376-The Pink Panther (1972) (TV)	2	4	6	10	14	18
377-Baby Snoots (1973)	2	4	6	9	13	16
378-Turok, Son of Stone; new-a	8	16	24	56	93	130
379-Heckle & Jeckle New Terrytoons (TV)	2	4	6	8	11	14
380-Bugs Bunny & Yosemite Sam	2	4	6	8	11	14
381-Lassie (TV)	2	4	6	11	16	20
382-Scooby Doo, Where Are You? (TV)	5	10	15	32	51	70
383-Smokey the Bear (TV)	2	4	6	8	11	14
384-Pink Panther (TV)	2	4	6	8	11	14
385-Little Lulu	2	4	6	13	18	22
386-Wacky Witch	2	4	6	8	11	14
387-Beep-Beep & Daffy Duck (TV)	2	4	6	8	11	14
388-Tom and Jerry (1973)	2	4	6	8	11	14
389-Little Lulu; not by Stanley	2	4	6	13	18	22
390-Pink Panther (TV)	2	4	6	8	11	14
391-Scooby Doo (TV)	4	8	12	26	41	55
392-Bugs Bunny & Yosemite Sam	2	4	6	8	10	12
393-New Terrytoons (Heckle & Jeckle) (TV)	2	4	6	8	10	12
394-Lassie (TV)	2	4	6	9	13	16
395-Woodsy Owl	2	4	6	8	10	12
396-Baby Snoots	2	4	6	8	11	14
397-Beep-Beep & Daffy Duck (TV)	2	4	6	8	10	12
398-Wacky Witch	2	4	6	8	10	12
399-Turok, Son of Stone; new-a	7	14	21	50	83	115
400-Tom and Jerry	2	4	6	8	10	12
401-Baby Snoots (1975) (r/#371)	2	4	6	8	11	14
402-Daffy Duck (r/#313)	1	3	4	6	8	10
403-Bugs Bunny (r/#343)	2	4	6	8	10	12
404-Space Family Robinson (TV)(r/#328)	6	12	18	41	66	90
405-Cracky	1	3	4	6	8	10

	GD 2.0	VG 4.0	FN 6.0	VF 8.0	VF/NM 9.0	NM- 9.2
406-Little Lulu (r/#355)	2	4	6	10	14	18
407-Smokey the Bear (TV)(r/#362)	2	4	6	8	10	12
408-Turok, Son of Stone; c-r/Turok #20 w/changes; new-a	6	12	18	39	62	85
409-Pink Panther (TV)	1	3	4	6	8	10
410-Wacky Witch	1	2	3	5	6	8
411-Lassie (TV)(r/#324)	2	4	6	9	13	16
412-New Terrytoons (1975) (TV)	1	2	3	5	6	8
413-Daffy Duck (1976)(r/#331)	1	2	3	5	6	8
414-Space Family Robinson (r/#328)	6	12	18	39	62	85
415-Bugs Bunny (r/#329)	1	2	3	5	6	8
416-Beep-Beep, the Road Runner (r/#353)(TV)	1	2	3	5	6	8
417-Little Lulu (r/#323)	2	4	6	10	14	18
418-Pink Panther (r/#384) (TV)	1	2	3	5	6	8
419-Baby Snoots (r/#377)	1	3	4	6	8	10
420-Woody Woodpecker	1	2	3	5	6	8
421-Tweety & Sylvester	1	2	3	5	6	8
422-Wacky Witch (r/#386)	1	2	3	5	6	8
423-Little Monsters	1	3	4	6	8	10
424-Cracky (12/76)	1	2	3	5	6	8
425-Daffy Duck	1	2	3	5	6	8
426-Underdog (TV)	4	8	12	22	34	45
427-Little Lulu (r/#335)	2	4	6	8	11	14
428-Bugs Bunny	1	2	3	4	5	7
429-The Pink Panther (TV)	1	2	3	4	5	7
430-Beep-Beep, the Road Runner (TV)	1	2	3	4	5	7
431-Baby Snoots	1	2	3	5	6	8
432-Lassie (TV)	2	4	6	8	10	12
433-437: 433-Tweety & Sylvester. 434-Wacky Witch. 435-New Terrytoons (TV). 436-Wacky Advs. of Cracky. 437-Daffy Duck	1	2	3	4	5	7
438-Underdog (TV)	3	6	9	20	30	40
439-Little Lulu (r/#349)	2	4	6	8	11	14
440-442,444-446: 440-Bugs Bunny. 441-The Pink Panther (TV). 442-Beep-Beep, the Road Runner (TV). 444-Tom and Jerry. 445-Tweety and Sylvester. 446-Wacky Witch	1	2	3	5	6	8
443-Baby Snoots	1	2	3	5	6	8
447-Mighty Mouse	2	4	6	8	10	12
448-455,457,458: 448-Cracky. 449-Pink Panther (TV). 450-Baby Snoots. 451-Tom and Jerry. 452-Bugs Bunny. 453-Popeye. 454-Woody Woodpecker. 455-Beep-Beep, the Road Runner (TV). 457-Tweety & Sylvester. 458-Wacky Witch	1	2	3	5	6	8
456-Little Lulu (r/#369)	2	4	6	8	10	12
459-Mighty Mouse	2	4	6	8	10	12
460-466: 460-Daffy Duck. 461-The Pink Panther (TV). 462-Baby Snoots. 463-Tom and Jerry. 464-Bugs Bunny. 465-Popeye. 466-Woody Woodpecker	1	2	3	5	6	8
467-Underdog (TV)	3	6	9	18	27	35
468-Little Lulu (r/#385)	1	2	3	5	6	8
469-Tweety & Sylvester	1	2	3	5	6	8
470-Wacky Witch	1	2	3	5	6	8
471-Mighty Mouse	1	3	4	6	8	10
472-474,476-478: 472-Heckle & Jeckle(12/80). 473-Pink Panther(1/81)(TV). 474-Baby Snoots. 476-Bugs Bunny. 477-Popeye. 478-Woody Woodpecker	1	2	3	5	6	8
475-Little Lulu (r/#323)	1	3	4	6	8	10
479-Underdog (TV)	3	6	9	16	23	30
480-482: 480-Tom and Jerry. 481-Tweety and Sylvester. 482-Wacky Witch	1	2	3	4	5	8
483-Mighty Mouse	1	3	4	6	8	10
484-487: 484-Heckle & Jeckle. 485-Baby Snoots. 486-The Pink Panther (TV). 487-Bugs Bunny	1	2	3	4	5	8
488-Little Lulu (4/82) (r/#335) (Last issue)	2	4	6	10	14	18

MARCH TO MARKET, THE
Swift & Co.: 1950 (Giveaway)

	GD 2.0	VG 4.0	FN 6.0	VF 8.0	VF/NM 9.0	NM- 9.2
nn-The story of meat	3	6	8	11	13	15

MARGARET O'BRIEN (See The Adventures of...)

MARK STEEL
American Iron & Steel Institute: 1967, 1968, 1972 (Giveaway) (24 pgs.)

	GD 2.0	VG 4.0	FN 6.0	VF 8.0	VF/NM 9.0	NM- 9.2
1967,1968- "Journey of Discovery with..."; Neal Adams art	4	8	12	26	41	55
1972- "...Fights Pollution"; N. Adams-a	2	4	6	11	16	20

MARTIN LUTHER KING AND THE MONTGOMERY STORY
Fellowship Reconciliation: 1956 (Giveaway, 16 pgs.) (A Spanish edition also exists)

nn-In color with paper-c (a CGC 9.2 copy sold for $350 and a FN+ sold for $200 in 2004)

MARVEL COLLECTOR'S EDITION: X-MEN
Marvel Comics: 1993 (3-3/4x6-1/2")

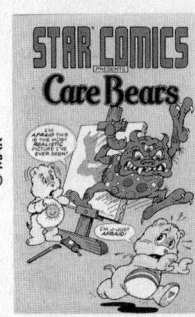

Marvel Comics Presents Care Bears © MAR

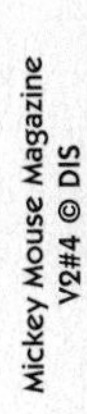
Mickey Mouse Magazine V2#4 © DIS

Military Courtesy © HARV

GD VG FN VF VF/NM NM-
2.0 4.0 6.0 8.0 9.0 9.2

1-4-Pizza Hut giveaways 5.00

MARVEL COMICS PRESENTS
Marvel Comics: 1987, 1988 (4 1/4 x 6 1/4, 20 pgs.)
...Mini Comic Giveaway
nn-(1988) Alf 1 2 3 5 6 8
nn-(1987) Captain America r/ #250 1 2 3 4 5 7
nn-(1987) Care Bears (Star Comics...) 1 2 3 4 5 7
nn-(1988) Flintstone Kids 1 2 3 5 6 8
nn-(1987) Heathcliffe (Star Comics...) 1 2 3 4 5 7
nn-(1987) Spider-Man-r/Spect. Spider-Man #21 1 2 3 4 5 7
nn-(1988) Spider-Man-r/Amazing Spider-Man #1 1 2 3 4 5 7
nn-(1988) X-Men-reprints X-Men #53; B. Smith-a 1 2 3 4 5 7

MARVEL GUIDE TO COLLECTING COMICS, THE
Marvel Comics: 1982 (16 pgs., newsprint pages and cover)
1-Simonson-c 1 2 3 4 5 7

MARVEL HALLOWEEN ASHCAN 2006
Marvel Comics: 2006 (8-1/2"x 5-1/2", Halloween giveaway)
nn-r/Marvel Adventures The Avengers #1 2.00

MARVEL MINI-BOOKS
Marvel Comics Group: 1966 (50 pgs., B&W; 5/8x7/8") (6 different issues) (Smallest comics ever published) (Marvel Mania Giveaways)
Captain America, Millie the Model, Sgt. Fury, Hulk, Thor
each... 2 4 6 11 16 20
Spider-Man 3 6 9 14 20 25
NOTE: *Each came from gum machines in six different color covers, usually one color: Pink, yellow, green, etc.*

MARVEL SUPER-HERO ISLAND ADVENTURES
Marvel Comics: 1999 (Sold at the park polybagged with Captain America V3 #19, one other comic, 5 trading cards and a cloisonne pin)
1-Promotes Universal Studios Islands of Adventures theme park 4.00

MARY'S GREATEST APOSTLE (St. Louis Grignion de Montfort)
Catechetical Guild (Topix) (Giveaway): No date (16 pgs.; paper cover)
nn 5 10 15 23 28 32

MASK
DC Comics: 1985
1-3 6.00

MASKED PILOT, THE (See Popular Comics #43)
R.S. Callender: 1939 (7-1/2x5-1/4", 16 pgs., premium, non-slick-c)
nn-Bob Jenney-a 8 16 24 44 57 70

MASTERS OF THE UNIVERSE (He-Man)
DC Comics: 1982 (giveaways with action figures, at least 35 different issues, unnumbered)
nn 2 4 6 8 10 12

MATRIX, THE (1999 movie)
Warner Brothers: 1999 (Recalled by Warner Bros. over questionable content)
nn-Paul Chadwick-s/a (16 pgs.); Geof Darrow-c 1 2 3 5 6 8

McCRORY'S CHRISTMAS BOOK
Western Printing Co: 1955 (36 pgs., slick-c) (McCrory Stores Corp. giveaway)
nn-Painted-c 4 8 12 18 22 25

McCRORY'S TOYLAND BRINGS YOU SANTA'S PRIVATE EYES
Promotional Publ. Co.: 1956 (16 pgs.) (Giveaway)
nn-Has 9 pg. story plus 7 pgs. toy ads 4 8 11 16 19 22

McCRORY'S WONDERFUL CHRISTMAS
Promotional Publ. Co.: 1954 (20 pgs., slick-c) (Giveaway)
nn 4 8 12 18 22 25

McDONALDS COMMANDRONS
DC Comics: 1985
nn-Four editions 5.00

MEDAL FOR BOWZER, A (Giveaway)
American Visuals Corp.: 1966 (8 pgs.)
nn-Eisner-c/script; Bowzer (a dog) survives untried pneumonia cure and earns his medal; (medical experimentation on animals) 26 52 78 154 252 350

MEET HIYA A FRIEND OF SANTA CLAUS
Julian J. Proskauer/Sundial Shoe Stores, etc.: 1949 (18 pgs.?, paper-c)(Giveaway)
nn 6 12 18 31 38 45

MEET THE NEW POST-GAZETTE SUNDAY FUNNIES
Pittsburgh Post Gazette: 3/12/49 (7-1/4x10-1/4", 16 pgs., paper-c)
Commercial Comics (insert in newspaper) (Rare)
Dick Tracy by Gould, Gasoline Alley, Terry & the Pirates, Brenda Starr, Buck Rogers by Yager, The Gumps, Peter Rabbit by Fago, Superman, Funnyman by Siegel & Shuster, The Saint, Archie, & others done especially for this book. A fine copy sold at auction in 1985 for $276.00.
260 520 780 1700 - -

MEN OF COURAGE
Catechetical Guild: 1949
Bound Topix comics-V7#2,4,6,8,10,16,18,20 6 12 18 31 38 45

MEN WHO MOVE THE NATION
Publisher unknown: (Giveaway) (B&W)
nn-Neal Adams-a 6 12 18 31 38 45

MERRY CHRISTMAS, A
K. K. Publications (Child Life Shoes): 1948 (Giveaway)
nn 7 14 21 35 43 50

MERRY CHRISTMAS
K. K. Publications (Blue Bird Shoes Giveaway): 1956 (7-1/4x5-1/4")
nn 4 8 12 18 22 25

MERRY CHRISTMAS FROM MICKEY MOUSE
K. K. Publications: 1939 (16 pgs.) (Color & B&W) (Shoe store giveaway)
nn-Donald Duck & Pluto app.; text with art (Rare); c-reprint/Mickey Mouse Mag. V3#3 (12/37)(Rare) 245 490 735 1556 2678 3800

MERRY CHRISTMAS FROM SEARS TOYLAND (See Santa's Christmas Comic)
Sears Roebuck Giveaway: 1939 (16 pgs.) (Color)
nn-Dick Tracy, Little Orphan Annie, The Gumps, Terry & the Pirates 103 206 309 654 1127 1600

MICKEY MOUSE (Also see Frito-Lay Giveaway)
Dell Publ. Co
...& Goofy Explore Business(1978) 2 4 6 8 10 12
...& Goofy Explore Energy(1976-1978, 36 pgs.); Exxon giveaway in color; regular size 2 4 6 8 10 12
...& Goofy Explore Energy Conservation(1976-1978)-Exxon 2 4 6 8 10 12
...& Goofy Explore The Universe of Energy(1985, 20 pgs.); Exxon giveaway in color; regular size 1 2 3 5 7 9
The Perils of Mickey nn (1993, 5-1/4x7-1/4", 16 pgs.)-Nabisco giveaway w/ games, Nabisco coupons & 6 pgs. of stories; Phantom Blot app. 6.00

MICKEY MOUSE MAGAZINE
Walt Disney Productions: V1#1, Jan, 1933 - V1#9, Sept, 1933 (5-1/4x7-1/4")
No. 1-3 published by Kamen-Blair (Kay Kamen, Inc.)
(Scarce)-Distributed by dairies and leading stores through their local theatres. First few issues had 5¢ listed on cover, later ones had no price.
V1#1 540 1080 2160 6500 - -
2-4 225 450 900 1750 - -
5-9 175 350 700 1350 - -

MICKEY MOUSE MAGAZINE
Walt Disney Productions: V1#1, 11/33 - V2#12, 10/35 (Mills giveaways issued by different dairies)
V1#1 129 258 387 826 1413 2000
2-12: 2-X-Mas issue 41 82 123 256 428 600
V2#1-4,6-12: 2-X-Mas issue. 4-St. Valentine-c 30 60 90 177 289 400
V2#5 (3/35) 1st app. Donald Duck in sailor outfit on-c 87 174 261 553 952 1350

MICKEY MOUSE MAGAZINE
K.K. Publications: V4#1, Oct, 1938 (Giveaway)
V4#1 40 80 120 252 426 600

MIGHTY ATOM, THE
Whitman
Giveaway (1959, '63, Whitman)-Evans-a 3 6 9 16 23 30
Giveaway ('64r, '65r, '66r, '67r, '68r)-Evans-r? 2 4 6 10 14 18
Giveaway ('73r, '76r) 2 4 6 8 11 14

MILES THE MONSTER (Initially sold only at the Dover Speedway track)
Dover International Speedway, Inc.: 2006 ($3.00)
1,2-Allan Gross & Mark Wheatley-s/Wheatley-a 3.00

MILITARY COURTESY
Harvey Publications: (16 pgs.)
nn-Regulations and saluting instructions 5 10 14 20 24 28

MINUTE MAN
Sovereign Service Station giveaway: No date (16 pgs., B&W, paper-c blue & red)
nn-American history 3 6 8 12 14 16

MINUTE MAN ANSWERS THE CALL, THE
By M. C. Gaines: 1942,1943,1944,1945 (4 pgs.) (Giveaway inserted in Jr. JSA Membership Kit)

Motion Picture Funnies Weekly #1 © FFI

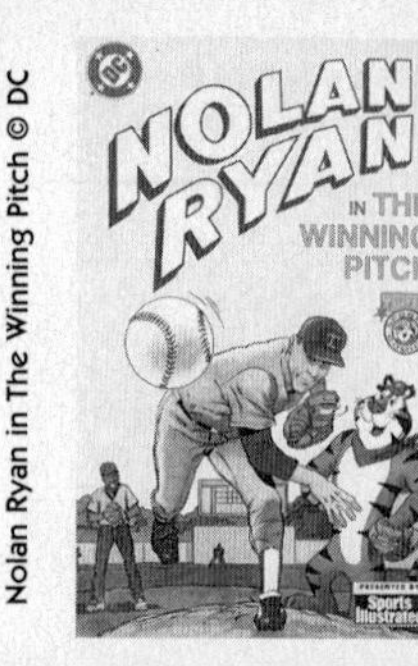

Nolan Ryan in The Winning Pitch © DC

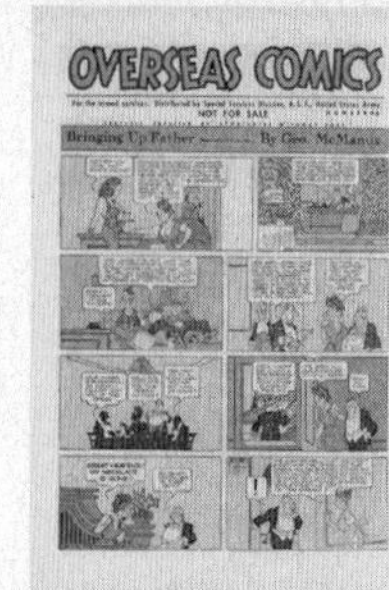

Overseas Comics

	GD 2.0	VG 4.0	FN 6.0	VF 8.0	VF/NM 9.0	NM- 9.2

nn-Sheldon Moldoff-a 21 42 63 121 201 280

MIRACLE ON BROADWAY
Broadway Comics: Dec, 1995 (Giveaway)

1-Ernie Colon-c/a; Jim Shooter & Co. story; 1st known digitally printed comic book; 1st app. Spire & Knights on Broadway (1150 print run) 20.00

NOTE: *Miracle on Broadway was a limited edition comic given to 1100 VIPs in the entertainment industry for the 1995 Holiday Season.*

MISS SUNBEAM (See Little Miss Sunbeam Comics)

MR. BUG GOES TO TOWN (See Cinema Comics Herald)
K.K. Publications: 1941 (Giveaway, 52 pgs.)

nn-Cartoon movie (scarce) 68 136 204 432 741 1050

MR. PEANUT, THE PERSONAL STORY OF
Planters Nut & Chocolate Co.: 1956

nn 4 8 12 22 34 45

MOTHER OF US ALL
Catechetical Guild Giveaway: 1950? (32 pgs.)

nn 5 10 15 23 28 32

MOTION PICTURE FUNNIES WEEKLY (Amazing Man #5 on?)
First Funnies, Inc.: 1939 (Giveaway)(B&W, 36 pgs.) No month given; last panel in Sub-Mariner story dated 4/39 (Also see Colossus, Green Giant & Invaders No. 20)

1-Origin & 1st printed app. Sub-Mariner by Bill Everett (8 pgs.); Fred Schwab-c; reprinted in Marvel Mystery #1 with color added over the craft tint which was used to shade the black & white version; Spy Ring, American Ace (reprinted in Marvel Mystery #3) app.
(Rare)-only eight known copies, one near mint with white pages, the rest with brown pages.
4600 9200 13,800 18,860 33,000 -

Covers only to #2-4 (set) 900

NOTE: Eight copies (plus one coverless) were discovered in 1974 in the estate of the deceased publisher. Covers only to issues No. 2-4 were also found which evidently were printed in advance along with #1. #1 was to be distributed only through motion picture movie houses. However, it is believed that only advanced copies were sent out and the motion picture houses not going for the idea. Possible distribution at local theaters in Boston suspected. The "pay" copy (graded at 9.0) was discovered after 1974, bringing the total known to nine. The last panel of Sub-Mariner contains a rectangular box with "Continued Next Week" printed in it. When reprinted in Marvel Mystery, the box was left in with lettering omitted.

MY DOG TIGE (Buster Brown's Dog)
Buster Brown Shoes: 1957 (Giveaway)

nn 5 10 15 24 30 35

MY GREATEST THRILLS IN BASEBALL
Mission of California: Date? (16 pg. Giveaway)

nn-By Mickey Mantle 53 106 159 337 581 825

MYSTERIOUS ADVENTURES WITH SANTA CLAUS
Lansburgh's: 1948 (paper cover)

nn 13 26 39 72 101 130

NAKED FORCE!
Commercial Comics: 1958 (Small size)

nn 3 6 8 11 13 15

NATURAL DISASTERS!
Graphic Information Service/ Civil Defense: 1956 (16 pgs., soft-c)

nn-Al Capp Li'l Abner-c; Li'l Abner cameo (1 panel); narrated by Mr. Civil Defense
10 20 30 54 72 90

NAVY: HISTORY & TRADITION
Stokes Walesby Co./Dept. of Navy: 1958 - 1961 (nn) (Giveaway)

1772-1778, 1778-1782, 1782-1817, 1817-1865, 1865-1936, 1940-1945:
1772-1778-16 pg. in color 5 10 15 22 26 30
1861: Naval Actions of the Civil War: 1865-36 pg. in color; flag-c
5 10 15 22 26 30

NEW ADVENTURE OF WALT DISNEY'S SNOW WHITE AND THE SEVEN DWARFS, A
(See Snow White Bendix Giveaway)

NEW ADVENTURES OF PETER PAN (Disney)
Western Publishing Co.: 1953 (5x7-1/4", 36 pgs.) (Admiral giveaway)

nn 14 28 42 76 108 140

NEW AVENGERS... (Giveaway for U.S Military personnel)
Marvel Comics: 2005 - Present (Distributed by Army & Air Force Exchange Service)

... Guest Starring the Fantastic Four (4/05) Bendis-s/Jurgens-a/c 4.00
...: Pot of Gold (AAFES 110th Anniversary Issue) (10/05) Jenkins-s/Nolan-a/c 4.00
(#3) ...: Avengers & X-Men Time Trouble (4/06) Kirkman-s 4.00
(#4) ...: Letters Home (12/06) Capt. America, Punisher, Silver Surfer, Ghost Rider on-c 4.00
5-The Spirit of America (10/05) Captain America app. 4.00
6-Fireline (8/08) Spider-Man, Iron Man & Hulk app. Richards-a/Dave Ross-c 4.00
7-An Army of One (2009) Frank Cho pin-up on back-c 4.00
8-The Promise (12/09) Captain America (Bucky) app. 4.00

	GD 2.0	VG 4.0	FN 6.0	VF 8.0	VF/NM 9.0	NM- 9.2

NEW FRONTIERS
Harvey Information Press (United States Steel Corp.) : 1958 (16 pgs., paper-c)

nn-History of barbed wire 3 6 9 14 19 24

NEW TEEN TITANS, THE
DC Comics: Nov. 1983

nn(11/83-Keebler Co. Giveaway)-In cooperation with "The President's Drug Awareness Campaign"; came in Presidential envelope w/letter from White House (Nancy Reagan)
1 2 3 4 5 7
nn-(re-issue of above on Mando paper for direct sales market); American Soft Drink Industry version; I.B.M. Corp. version 5.00

NOLAN RYAN IN THE WINNING PITCH (Kellogg's Tony's Sports Comics)
DC Comics: 1992 (Sports Illustrated)

nn 5.00

OLD GLORY COMICS
Chesapeake & Ohio Railway: 1944 (Giveaway)

nn-Capt. Fearless reprint 8 16 24 40 50 60

ON THE AIR
NBC Network Comic: 1947 (Giveaway, paper-c)

nn-(Rare) 18 36 54 105 165 225

OUT OF THE PAST A CLUE TO THE FUTURE
E. C. Comics (Public Affairs Comm.): 1946? (16 pgs.) (paper cover)

nn-Based on public affairs pamphlet "What Foreign Trade Means to You"
20 40 60 116 191 265

OUTSTANDING AMERICAN WAR HEROES
The Parents' Institute: 1944 (16 pgs., paper-c)

nn-Reprints from True Comics 5 10 15 22 26 30

OVERSEAS COMICS (Also see G.I. Comics & Jeep Comics)
Giveaway (Distributed to U.S. Armed Forces): 1944 - No. 105?, 1946 (7-1/4x10-1/4"; 16 pgs. in color)

23-105-Bringing Up Father (by McManus), Popeye, Joe Palooka, Dick Tracy, Superman, Gasoline Alley, Buz Sawyer, Li'l Abner, Blondie, Terry & the Pirates, Out Our Way
7 14 21 35 43 50

OWL, THE (See Crackajack Funnies #25 & Popular Comics #72)(Also see The Hurricane Kids & Magic Morro
Western Pub. Co./R.S. Callender: 1940 (Giveaway)(7-1/2x5-1/4")(Soft-c, color)

nn-Frank Thomas-a 15 30 45 86 133 180

OXYDOL-DREFT
Toby Press:1950 (Set of 6 pocket-size giveaways; distributed through the mail as a set) (Scarce)

1-3: 1-Li'l Abner. 2-Daisy Mae. 3-Shmoo 9 18 27 52 69 85
4-John Wayne; Williamson/Frazetta-c from John Wayne #3
13 26 39 72 101 130
5-Archie 12 24 36 67 94 120
6-Terrytoons Mighty Mouse 9 18 27 50 65 80
Mailing Envelope (has All Capp's Shmoo on front) 10 20 30 54 72 90

OZZIE SMITH IN THE KID WHO COULD (Kellogg's Tony's Sports Comics)
DC Comics: 1992 (Sports Illustrated)

nn-Ozzie Smith app. 5.00

PADRE OF THE POOR
Catechetical Guild: nd (Giveaway) (16 pgs., paper-c)

nn 5 10 15 24 30 35

PAUL TERRY'S HOW TO DRAW FUNNY CARTOONS
Terrytoons, Inc. (Giveaway): 1940's (14 pgs.) (Black & White)

nn-Heckle & Jeckle, Mighty Mouse, etc. 13 26 39 72 101 130

PEANUTS HALLOWEEN
Fantagraphics Books: Sept, 2008 (8-1/2" x 5-3/8" ashcan giveaway)

nn-Halloween themed reprints in color and B&W 2.00

PETER PAN (See New Adventures of Peter Pan)

PETER PENNY AND HIS MAGIC DOLLAR
American Bankers Association, N. Y. (Giveaway): 1947 (16 pgs.; paper-c; regular size)

nn-(Scarce)-Used in **SOTI**, pg. 310, 311 15 30 45 88 137 185
Diff. version (7-1/4x11")-redrawn, 16 pgs., paper-c 10 20 30 56 76 95

PETER WHEAT (The Adventures of...)
Bakers Associates Giveaway: 1948 - 1957? (16 pgs. in color) (paper covers)

nn(No.1)-States on last page, end of 1st Adventure of...; Kelly-a
26 52 78 154 252 350
nn(4 issues)-Kelly-a 14 28 42 82 121 160

The Plot to Steal the World © Work & Unity Group

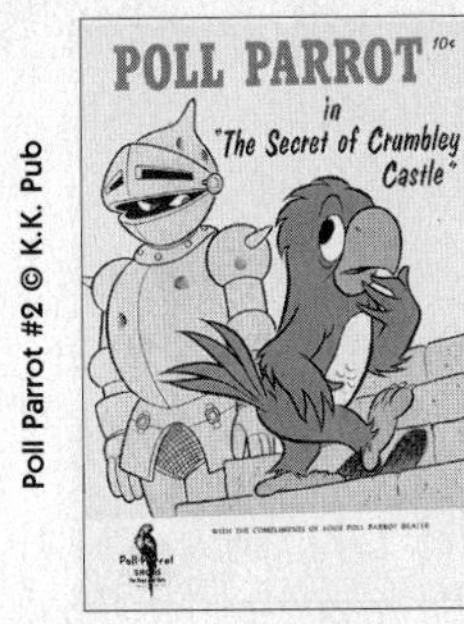

Poll Parrot #2 © K.K. Pub

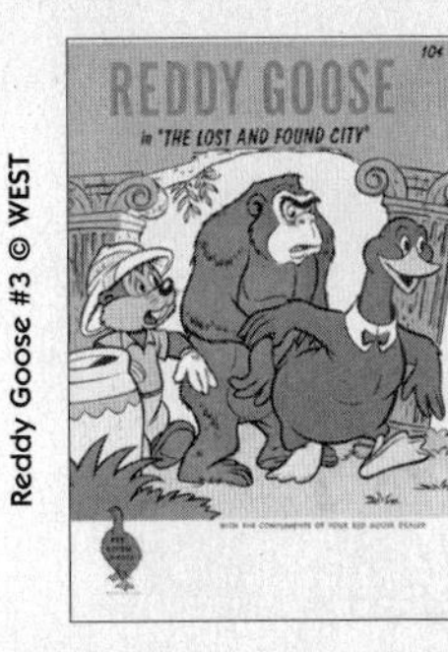

Reddy Goose #3 © WEST

	GD 2.0	VG 4.0	FN 6.0	VF 8.0	VF/NM 9.0	NM- 9.2
6-10-All Kelly-a	10	20	30	54	72	90
11-20-All Kelly-a	9	18	27	50	65	80
21-35-All Kelly-a	8	16	24	40	50	60
36-66	6	12	18	28	34	40
...Artist's Workbook ('54, digest size)	6	12	18	28	34	40
...Four-In-One Fun Pack (Vol. 2, '54), oblong, comics w/puzzles	7	14	21	35	43	50
...Fun Book ('52, 32 pgs., paper-c, B&W & color, 8-1/2x10-3/4")-Contains cut-outs, puzzles, games, magic & pages to color	8	16	24	44	57	70

NOTE: *Al Hubbard art #36 on; written by Del Connell.*

PETER WHEAT NEWS
Bakers Associates: 1948 - No. 30, 1950 (4 pgs. in color)

Vol. 1-All have 2 pgs. Peter Wheat by Kelly	21	42	63	123	204	285
2-10	13	26	39	72	101	130
11-20	8	16	24	40	50	60
21-30	6	12	18	28	34	40

NOTE: *Early issues have no date & **Kelly** art.*

PINOCCHIO
Cocomalt/Montgomery Ward Co.: 1940 (10 pgs.; giveaway, linen-like paper)

nn-Cocomalt edition	43	86	129	271	456	640
nn-store edition	36	72	108	215	350	485

PIUS XII MAN OF PEACE
Catechetical Guild: No date (12 pgs.; 5-1/2x8-1/2") (B&W)

nn-Catechetical Guild Giveaway	6	12	18	31	38	45

PLOT TO STEAL THE WORLD, THE
Work & Unity Group: 1948, 16pgs., paper-c

nn-Anti commumism	18	36	54	103	162	220

POCAHONTAS
Pocahontas Fuel Company (Coal): 1941 - No. 2, 1942

nn(#1), 2-Feat. life story of Indian princess Pocahontas & facts about Pocahontas coal, Pocahontas, VA.	15	30	45	85	130	175

POLL PARROT
Poll Parrot Shoe Store/International Shoe
K. K. Publications (Giveaway): 1950 - No. 4, 1951; No. 2, 1959 - No. 16, 1962

1 ('50)-Howdy Doody; small size	18	36	54	107	169	230
2-4('51)-Howdy Doody	15	30	45	88	137	185
2('59)-16('62): 2-The Secret of Crumbley Castle. 5-Bandit Busters. 7-The Make-Believe Mummy. 8-Mixed Up Mission('60). 10-The Frightful Flight. 11-Showdown at Sunup. 12-Maniac at Mubu Island. 13-...and the Runaway Genie. 14-Bully for You. 15-Trapped In Tall Timber. 16-...& the Rajah's Ruby('62)	3	6	9	16	23	30

POPEYE
Whitman

Bold Detergent giveaway (Same as regular issue #94)	2	4	6	9	13	16
Quaker Cereal premium (1989, 16pp, small size,4 diff.)(Popeye & the Time Machine, --On Safari, --& Big Foot, --vs. Bluto)	2	4	6	8	10	12

POPEYE
Charlton (King Features) (Giveaway): 1972 - 1974 (36 pgs. in color)

E-1 to E-15 (Educational comics)	2	4	6	9	13	16
nn-Popeye Gettin' Better Grades-4 pgs. used as intro. to above giveaways (in color)	2	4	6	9	13	16

POPSICLE PETE FUN BOOK (See All-American Comics #6)
Joe Lowe Corp.: 1947, 1948

nn-36 pgs. in color; Sammy 'n' Claras, The King Who Couldn't Sleep & Popsicle Pete stories, games, cut-outs	11	22	33	64	90	115
Adventure Book ('48)-Has Classics ad with checklist to HRN #343 (Great Expectations #43)	10	20	30	56	76	95

PORKY'S BOOK OF TRICKS
K. K. Publications (Giveaway): 1942 (8-1/2x5-1/2", 48 pgs.)

nn-7 pg. comic story, text stories, plus games & puzzles	47	94	141	296	498	700

POST GAZETTE (See Meet the New...)

PUNISHER: COUNTDOWN (Movie)
Marvel Comics: 2004 (7 1/4" X 4 3/4" mini-comic packaged with Punisher DVD)

nn-Prequel to 2004 movie; Ennis-s/Dillon-a/Bradstreet-c 2.50

PURE OIL COMICS (Also see Salerno Carnival of Comics, 24 Pages of Comics, & Vicks Comics)
Pure Oil Giveaway: Late 1930's (24 pgs., regular size, paper-c)

nn-Contains 1-2 pg. strips; i.e., Hairbreadth Harry, Skyroads, Buck Rogers by Calkins & Yager, Olly of the Movies, Napoleon, S'Matter Pop, etc. Also a 16 pg. 1938 giveaway with Buck Rogers	34	68	102	204	332	460

QUAKER OATS (Also see Cap'n Crunch)
Quaker Oats Co.: 1965 (Giveaway) (2-1/2x5-1/2") (16 pgs.)

	GD 2.0	VG 4.0	FN 6.0	VF 8.0	VF/NM 9.0	NM- 9.2
"Plenty of Glutton", starring Quake & Quisp;	3	6	9	14	19	24
"Lava Come-Back", "Kite Tale"	1	3	4	6	8	10

RAILROADS DELIVER THE GOODS!
Assoc. of American Railroads: Dec, 1954; Sept, 1957 (16 pgs., paper-c)

nn-The story of railway freight	5	10	15	24	30	35

RAILS ACROSS AMERICA!
Assoc. of American Railroads: nd (16 pgs.)

nn	5	10	15	24	30	35

REAL FUN OF DRIVING!!, THE
Chrysler Corp.: 1965, 1966, 1967 (Regular size, 16 pgs.)

nn-Schaffenberger-a (12 pgs.)	1	2	3	5	6	8

REAL HIT
Fox Features Publications: 1944 (Savings Bond premium)

1-Blue Beetle-r; Blue Beetle on-c	15	30	45	90	140	190

NOTE: *Two versions exist, with and without covers. The coverless version has the title, No. 1 and price printed at top of splash page.*

RED BALL COMIC BOOK
Parents' Magazine Institute: 1947 (Red Ball Shoes giveaway)

nn-Reprints from True Comics	4	8	11	16	19	22

REDDY GOOSE
International Shoe Co. (Western Printing): No number, 1958?; No. 2, Jan, 1959 - No. 16, July, 1962 (Giveaway)

nn (#1)	5	10	15	30	48	65
2-16	3	6	9	18	27	35

REDDY KILOWATT (5¢) (Also see Story of Edison)
Educational Comics (E. C.): 1946 - No. 2, 1947; 1956 - 1965 (no month) (16 pgs., paper-c)

nn-A Visit With Reddy (1948-1954?)	9	18	27	50	65	80
nn-Reddy Made Magic (1946, 5¢)	13	26	39	72	101	130
nn-Reddy Made Magic (1958)	9	18	27	50	65	80
2-Edison, the Man Who Changed the World (3/4" smaller than #1) (1947, 5¢)	13	26	39	72	101	130
...Comic Book 2 (1954)- "Light's Diamond Jubilee"	9	18	27	54	72	90
...Comic Book 2 (1956, 16 pgs.)- "Wizard of Light"	9	18	27	52	69	85
...Comic Book 2 (1958, 16 pgs.)- "Wizard of Light"	9	18	27	50	65	78
...Comic Book 2 (1965, 16 pgs.)- "Wizard of Light"	4	8	12	28	44	60
...Comic Book 3 (1956, 8 pgs.)- "The Space Kite"; Orlando story; regular size	9	18	27	47	61	75
...Comic Book 3 (1960, 8 pgs.)- "The Space Kite"; Orlando story; regular size	4	8	12	28	44	60

NOTE: *Several copies surfaced in 1979.*

REDDY MADE MAGIC
Educational Comics (E. C.): 1956, 1958 (16 pgs., paper-c)

1-Reddy Kilowatt-r (splash panel changed)	11	22	33	60	83	105
1 (1958 edition)	6	12	18	31	38	45

RED ICEBERG, THE
Impact Publ. (Catechetical Guild): 1960 (10¢, 16 pgs., Communist propaganda)

nn-(Rare)- "We The People" back-c	29	58	87	203	402	600
2nd version- "Impact Press" back-c	24	48	72	175	338	500
3rd version- "Explains comic" back-c	24	48	72	175	338	500
4th version- "Impact Press w/World Wide Secret Heart Program ad"	24	48	72	175	338	500
5th version- "Chicago Inter-Student Catholic Action" back-c	24	48	72	175	338	500

NOTE: *This book was the Guild's last anti-communist propaganda book and had very limited circulation. 3 - 4 copies surfaced in 1979 from the defunct publisher's files. Other copies do turn up.*

RED RYDER COMICS
Dell Publ. Co.

Buster Brown Shoes Giveaway (1941, color, soft-c, 32 pgs.)	20	40	60	114	182	250
Red Ryder Super Book of Comics (1944, paper-c, 32 pgs.; blank back-c) Magic Morro app.	21	42	63	122	199	275
Red Ryder Victory Patrol-nn(1942, 32 pgs.)(Langendorf bread; includes cut-out membership card and certificate, order blank and "Slide-Up" decoder, and a Super Book of Comics in color (same content as Super Book #4 w/diff. cover (Pan-Am)) (Rare)	226	452	678	1446	2473	3500
Red Ryder Victory Patrol-nn(1943, 32 pgs.)(Langendorf bread; includes cut-out "Rodeomatic" radio decoder, order coupon for "Magic V-Badge", cut-out membership card and certificate and a full color Super Book of comics comic book) (Rare)	194	388	582	1242	2121	3000

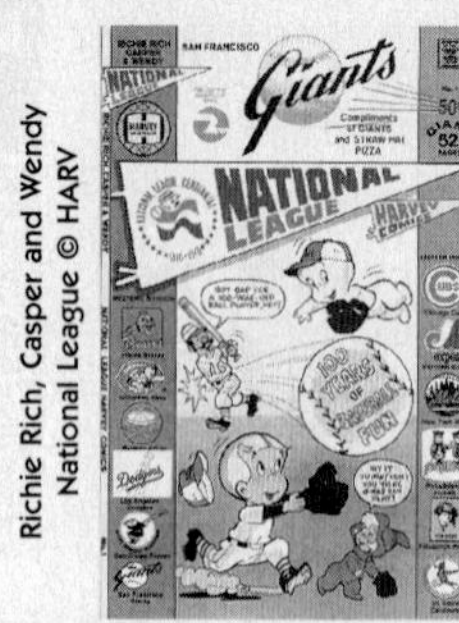

Richie Rich, Casper and Wendy National League © HARV

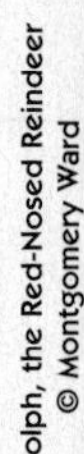
Rudolph, the Red-Nosed Reindeer © Montgomery Ward

Santa's Fun Book © Promo. Pub. Co.

	GD 2.0	VG 4.0	FN 6.0	VF 8.0	VF/NM 9.0	NM- 9.2
Red Ryder Victory Patrol-nn(1944, 32 pgs.)-r-/#43,44; comic has a paper-c & is stapled inside a triple cardboard fold-out-c; contains membership card, decoder, map of R.R. home range, etc. Herky app. (Langendorf Bread giveaway; sub-titled 'Super Book of Comics') (Rare)	194	388	582	1242	2121	3000
Wells Lamont Corp. giveaway (1950)-16 pgs. in color; regular size; paper-c; 1941-r	15	30	45	86	133	180
RICHIE RICH, CASPER & WENDY NATIONAL LEAGUE						
Harvey Publications: June, 1976 (52 pgs.) (newsstand edition also exists)						
1 (Released-3/76 with 6/76 date)	3	6	9	16	22	28
1 (6/76)-2nd version w/San Francisco Giants & KTVU 2 logos; has "Compliments of Giants and Straw Hat Pizza" on-c	3	6	9	16	22	28
1-Variants for other 11 NL teams, similar to Giants version but with different ad on inside front-c	3	6	9	16	22	28
RIDE THE HIGH IRON!						
Assoc. of American Railroads: Jan, 1957 (16 pgs.)						
nn-The Story of modern passenger trains	5	10	15	24	30	35
RIPLEY'S BELIEVE IT OR NOT!						
Harvey Publications						
J. C. Penney giveaway (1948)	9	18	27	50	65	80
ROBIN HOOD (New Adventures of...)						
Walt Disney Productions: 1952 (Flour giveaways, 5x7-1/4", 36 pgs.)						
"New Adventures of Robin Hood", "Ghosts of Waylea Castle", & "The Miller's Ransom" each....	5	10	15	22	26	30
ROBIN HOOD'S FRONTIER DAYS (...Western Tales, Adventures of... #1)						
Shoe Store Giveaway (Robin Hood Stores): 1956 (20 pgs., slick-c)(7 issues?)						
nn	5	10	15	25	31	36
nn-Issues with Crandall-a	8	16	24	40	50	60
ROCKETS AND RANGE RIDERS						
Richfield Oil Corp.: May, 1957 (Giveaway, 16 pgs., soft-c)						
nn-Toth-a	14	28	42	82	121	160
ROUND THE WORLD GIFT						
National War Fund (Giveaway): No date (mid 1940's) (4 pgs.)						
nn	11	22	33	64	90	115
ROY ROGERS COMICS						
Dell Publishing Co.						
...& the Man From Dodge City (Dodge giveaway, 16 pgs., 1954)-Frontier, Inc. (5x7-1/4")	12	24	36	69	97	125
Official Roy Rogers Riders Club Comics (1952; 16 pgs., reg. size, paper-c)	21	42	63	122	199	275
RUDOLPH, THE RED-NOSED REINDEER						
Montgomery Ward: 1939 (2,400,000 copies printed); Dec, 1951 (Giveaway)						
Paper cover-1st app. in print; written by Robert May; ill. by Denver Gillen	15	30	45	83	124	165
Hardcover version	19	38	57	109	172	235
1951 Edition (Has 1939 date)-36 pgs., slick-c printed in red & brown; pulp interior printed in four mixed-ink colors: red, green, blue & brown	11	22	33	62	86	110
1951 Edition with red-spiral promotional booklet printed on high quality stock, 8-1/2"x11", in red & brown, 25 pages composed of 4 fold outs, single sheets and the Rudolph comic book inserted (rare)	47	94	141	296	498	700
SABRINA THE TEENAGE WITCH						
Archie Comic Publications: (8 1/2"x 5 1/2", Diamond Comic Dist. Halloween giveaway)						
... And The Archies (2004)-Tania Del Rio-s/a; manga-style; Josie and the Pussycats app.						2.50
SAD CASE OF WAITING ROOM WILLIE, THE						
American Visuals Corp. (For Baltimore Medical Society): (nd, 1950?) (14 pgs. in color; paper covers; regular size)						
nn-By Will Eisner (Rare)	44	88	132	277	469	660
SAD SACK COMICS						
Harvey Publications: 1957-1962						
Armed Forces Complimentary copies, HD #1-40 (1957-1962)	3	6	9	16	22	28
SALERNO CARNIVAL OF COMICS (Also see Pure Oil Comics, 24 Pages of Comics, & Vicks Comics)						
Salerno Cookie Co.: Late 1930s (Giveaway, 16 pgs, paper-c)						
nn-Color reprints of Calkins' Buck Rogers & Skyroads, plus other strips from Famous Funnies	42	84	126	265	445	625
SALUTE TO THE BOY SCOUTS						
Association of American Railroads: 1960 (16 pgs.)						
nn-History of scouting and the railroad	3	6	9	14	19	24
SANTA AND POLLYANNA PLAY THE GLAD GAME						
Sales Promotion: Aug, 1960 (16 pgs.) (Disney giveaway)						
nn	2	4	6	13	18	22
SANTA & THE BUCCANEERS						
Promotional Publ. Co.: 1959 (Giveaway)						
nn-Reprints 1952 Santa & the Pirates	2	4	6	11	16	20
SANTA & THE CHRISTMAS CHICKADEE						
Murphy's: 1974 (Giveaway, 20 pgs.)						
nn	2	4	6	8	10	12
SANTA & THE PIRATES						
Promotional Publ. Co.: 1952 (Giveaway)						
nn-Marv Levy-c/a	4	8	11	16	19	22
SANTA CLAUS FUNNIES (Also see The Little Fir Tree)						
W. T. Grant Co./Whitman Publishing: nd; 1940 (Giveaway, 8x10"; 12 pgs., color & B&W, heavy paper)						
nn-(2 versions- no date and 1940)	14	28	42	76	108	140
SANTA IS HERE!						
Western Publ. (Giveaway): 1949 (oblong, slick-c)						
nn	6	12	18	31	58	45
SANTA ON THE JOLLY ROGER						
Promotional Publ. Co. (Giveaway): 1965						
nn-Marv Levy-c/a	2	4	6	8	10	12
SANTA! SANTA!						
R. Jackson: 1974 (20 pgs.) (Montgomery Ward giveaway)						
nn	1	3	4	6	8	10
SANTA'S BUNDLE OF FUN						
Gimbels: 1969 (Giveaway, B&W, 20 pgs.)						
nn-Coloring book & games	2	4	6	8	10	12
SANTA'S CHRISTMAS COMIC VARIETY SHOW (See Merry Christmas From Sears Toyland)						
Sears Roebuck & Co.: 1943 (24 pgs.)						
Contains puzzles & new comics of Dick Tracy, Little Orphan Annie, Moon Mullins, Terry & the Pirates, etc.	52	104	156	325	555	785
SANTA'S CHRISTMAS TIME STORIES						
Premium Sales, Inc.: nd (Late 1940s) (16 pgs., paper-c) (Giveaway)						
nn	6	12	18	31	38	45
SANTA'S CIRCUS						
Promotional Publ. Co.: 1964 (Giveaway, half-size)						
nn-Marv Levy-c/a	2	4	6	8	11	14
SANTA'S FUN BOOK						
Promotional Publ. Co.: 1951, 1952 (Regular size, 16 pgs., paper-c) (Murphy's giveaway)						
nn	5	10	15	23	28	32
SANTA'S GIFT BOOK						
No Publisher: No date (16 pgs.)						
nn-Puzzles, games only	4	8	11	16	19	22
SANTA'S NEW STORY BOOK						
Wallace Hamilton Campbell: 1949 (16 pgs., paper-c) (Giveaway)						
nn	6	12	18	31	38	45
SANTA'S REAL STORY BOOK						
Wallace Hamilton Campbell/W. W. Orris: 1948, 1952 (Giveaway, 16 pgs.)						
nn	6	12	18	31	38	45
SANTA'S RIDE						
W. T. Grant Co.: 1959 (Giveaway)						
nn	3	6	9	14	19	24
SANTA'S RODEO						
Promotional Publ. Co.: 1964 (Giveaway, half-size)						
nn-Marv Levy-a	2	4	6	8	11	14
SANTA'S SECRET CAVE						
W.T. Grant Co.: 1960 (Giveaway, half-size)						
nn	2	4	6	11	16	20
SANTA'S SECRETS						
Sam B. Anson Christmas giveaway: 1951, 1952? (16 pgs., paper-c)						
nn-Has games, stories & pictures to color	4	8	12	17	21	24
SANTA'S STORIES						
K. K. Publications (Klines Dept. Store): 1953 (Regular size, paper-c)						

Salute to the Boy Scouts © AAR

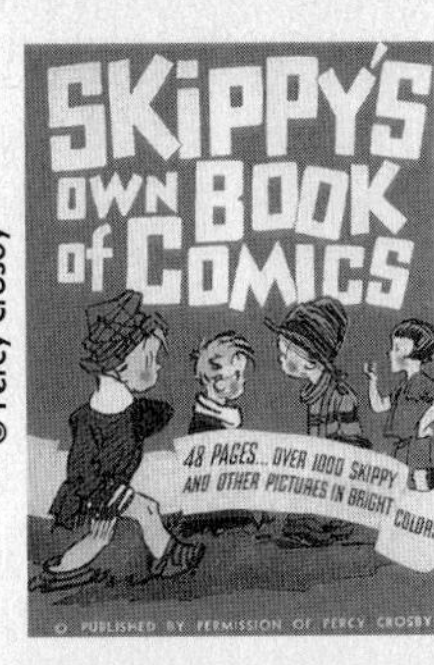

Skippy's Own Book of Comics © Percy Crosby

The Spirit 6/02/40 © Will Eisner

	GD 2.0	VG 4.0	FN 6.0	VF 8.0	VF/NM 9.0	NM- 9.2
nn-Kelly-a	15	30	45	88	137	185
nn-Another version (1953, glossy-c, half-size, 7-1/4x5-1/4")-Kelly-a	11	22	33	62	86	110
SANTA'S SURPRISE **K. K. Publications:** 1947 (Giveaway, 36 pgs., slick-c)						
nn	8	16	24	40	50	60
SANTA'S TOYTOWN FUN BOOK **Promotional Publ. Co.:** 1953 (Giveaway)						
nn-Marv Levy-c	4	8	11	16	19	22
SANTA TAKES A TRIP TO MARS **Bradshaw-Diehl Co., Huntington, W.VA.:** 1950s (nd) (Giveaway, 16 pgs.)						
nn	4	8	11	16	19	22
SCIENCE FAIR STORY OF ELECTRONICS **Radio Shack/Tandy Corp.:** 1975 - 1987 (Giveaway)						
11 different issues (approx. 1 per year) each....						3.00
SCOOBY-DOO! **DC Comics.:** 2002 (Burger King/Cartoon Network giveaway)						
1						2.50
SERGEANT PRESTON OF THE YUKON **Quaker Cereals:** 1956 (4 comic booklets) (Soft-c, 16 pgs., 7x2-1/2" & 5x2-1/2") Giveaways						
"How He Found Yukon King", "The Case That Made Him A Sergeant", "How Yukon King Saved Him From The Wolves", "How He Became A Mountie" each...	9	18	27	47	61	75
SHAZAM! (Visits Portland Oregon in 1943) **DC Comics:** 1989 (69¢ cover)						
nn-Promotes Super-Heroes exhibit at Oregon Museum of Science and Industry; reprints Golden Age Captain Marvel story	2	4	6	8	11	14
SHERIFF OF COCHISE, THE (TV) **Mobil:** 1957 (16 pgs.) Giveaway						
nn-Schaffenberger-a	4	9	13	18	22	26
SIDEWALK ROMANCE (Also see The K. O. Punch & Lucky Fights It Through) **Health Publications:** 1950						
nn-VD educational giveaway	32	64	96	188	307	425
SILLY PUTTY MAN **DC Comics:** 1978						
1	2	4	6	10	14	18
SKATING SKILLS **Custom Comics, Inc./Chicago Roller Skates:** 1957 (36 & 12 pgs.; 5x7", two versions) (10¢)						
nn-Resembles old ACG cover plus interior art	4	7	10	14	17	20
SKIPPY'S OWN BOOK OF COMICS (See Popular Comics) **No publisher listed:** 1934 (Giveaway, 52 pgs., strip reprints)						
nn-(Scarce)-By Percy Crosby	377	754	1131	2639	4620	6600
Published by Max C. Gaines for Phillip's Dental Magnesia to be advertised on the Skippy Radio Show and given away with the purchase of a tube of Phillip's Tooth Paste. This is the first four-color comic book of reprints about one character.						
SKY KING "RUNAWAY TRAIN" (TV) **National Biscuit Co.:** 1964 (Regular size, 16 pgs.)						
nn	6	12	18	41	66	90
SLAM BANG COMICS **Post Cereal Giveaway:** No. 9, No date						
9-Dynamic Man, Echo, Mr. E, Yankee Boy app.	9	18	27	50	65	80
SMILIN' JACK **Dell Publishing Co.**						
Popped Wheat Giveaway (1947)-1938 strip reprints; 16 pgs. in full color	2	4	6	8	11	14
Shoe Store Giveaway-1938 strip reprints; 16 pgs.	5	10	15	24	30	35
Sparked Wheat Giveaway (1942)-16 pgs. in full color	5	10	15	24	30	35
SMOKEY BEAR (See Forest Fire for 1st app.) **Dell Publ. Co.:** 1959,1960						
True Story of..., The -U.S. Forest Service giveaway-Publ. by Western Printing Co.; reprints 1st 16 pgs. of Four Color #932. Inside front-c differs slightly in 1959 & 1960 editions	6	12	18	28	34	40
1964,1969 reprints	3	6	9	14	19	24
SMOKEY STOVER **Dell Publishing Co.**						
General Motors giveaway (1953)	8	16	24	42	54	65

	GD 2.0	VG 4.0	FN 6.0	VF 8.0	VF/NM 9.0	NM- 9.2
National Fire Protection giveaway(1953 & 1954)-16 pgs., paper-c	8	16	24	42	54	65
SNOW FOR CHRISTMAS **W. T. Grant Co.:** 1957 (16 pgs.) (Giveaway)						
nn	4	8	12	18	22	25
SNOW WHITE AND THE SEVEN DWARFS **Bendix Washing Machines:** 1952 (32 pgs., 5x7-1/4", soft-c) (Disney)						
nn	11	22	33	62	86	110
SNOW WHITE AND THE SEVEN DWARFS **Promotional Publ. Co.:** 1957 (Small size)						
nn	6	12	18	28	34	40
SNOW WHITE AND THE SEVEN DWARFS **Western Printing Co.:** 1958 (16 pgs, 5x7-1/4", soft-c) (Disney premium)						
nn- "Mystery of the Missing Magic"	6	12	18	31	38	45
SNOW WHITE AND THE 7 DWARFS IN "MILKY WAY" **American Dairy Assoc.:** 1955 (16 pgs., soft-c, 5x7-1/4") (Disney premium)						
nn	7	14	21	35	43	50
SPACE GHOST COAST TO COAST **Cartoon Network:** Apr, 1994 (giveaway to Turner Broadcasting employees)						
1-(8 pgs.); origin of Space Ghost						6.00
SPACE PATROL (TV) **Ziff-Davis Publishing Co. (Approved Comics)**						
...'s Special Mission (8 pgs., B&W, Giveaway)	45	90	135	284	480	675
SPECIAL AGENT **Assoc. of American Railroads:** Oct, 1959 (16 pgs.)						
nn-The Story of the railroad police	6	12	18	28	34	40
SPECIAL DELIVERY **Post Hall Synd.:** 1951 (32 pgs.; B&W) (Giveaway)						
nn-Origin of Pogo, Swamp, etc.; 2 pg. biog. on Walt Kelly (One copy sold in 1980 for $150.00)						
SPECIAL EDITION (U. S. Navy Giveaways) **National Periodical Publications:** 1944 - 1945 (Regular comic format with wording simplified, 52 pgs.)						
1-Action (1944)-Reprints Action #80	54	108	162	343	574	825
2-Action (1944)-Reprints Action #81	54	108	162	343	574	825
3-Superman (1944)-Reprints Superman #33	54	108	162	343	574	825
4-Detective (1944)-Reprints Detective #97	54	108	162	343	574	825
5-Superman (1945)-Reprints Superman #34	54	108	162	343	574	825
6-Action (1945)-Reprints Action #84	54	108	162	343	574	825
NOTE: *Wayne Boring c-1, 2, 6. Dick Sprang c-4.*						
SPIDER-MAN (See Amazing Spider-Man, The)						
SPIRIT, THE (Weekly Comic Book) **Will Eisner:** 6/2/40 - 10/5/52 (16 pgs.; 8 pgs.) (no cover) (in color) (Distributed through various newspapers and other sources)						
NOTE: **Eisner** script, pencils/inks for the most part from 6/2/40-4/26/42; a few stories assisted by Jack Cole, Fine, Powell and Kotsky.						
6/2/40(#1)-Origin/1st app. The Spirit; reprinted in Police #11; Lady Luck (Brenda Banks) (1st app.) by Chuck Mazoujian & Mr. Mystic (1st. app.) by S. R. (Bob) Powell begin (rare)	194	388	582	1242	2121	3000
6/9/40(#2)	41	82	123	256	428	600
6/16/40(#3)-Black Queen app. in Spirit	30	60	90	177	289	400
6/23/40(#4)-Mr. Mystic receives magical necklace	22	44	66	132	216	300
6/30/40(#5)	22	44	66	132	216	300
7/7/40(#6)-1st app. Spirit carplane; Black Queen app. in Spirit	24	48	72	142	234	325
7/14/40(#7)-8/4/40(#10): 7/21/40-Spirit becomes fugitive wanted for murder	21	42	63	122	199	275
8/11/40-9/22/40	20	40	60	114	182	250
9/29/40-Ellen drops engagement with Homer Creep	18	36	54	107	169	230
10/6/40-11/3/40	18	36	54	107	169	230
11/10/40-The Black Queen app.	18	36	54	107	169	230
11/17/40, 11/24/40	18	36	54	107	169	230
12/1/40-Ellen spanking by Spirit on cover & inside; Eisner-1st 3 pgs., J. Cole rest	22	44	66	132	216	300
12/8/40-3/9/41	15	30	45	88	137	185
3/16/41-Intro. & 1st app. Silk Satin	20	40	60	114	182	250
3/23/41-6/1/41: 5/11/41-Last Lady Luck by Mazoujian; 5/18/41-Lady Luck by Nick Viscardi begins, ends 2/22/42	15	30	45	86	133	180
6/8/41-2nd app. Satin; Spirit learns Satin is also a British agent	17	34	51	98	154	210

The Spirit 4/03/49 © Will Eisner

The Spirit 5/07/50 © Will Eisner

Standard Oil Comics #5B © Standard Oil

	GD 2.0	VG 4.0	FN 6.0	VF 8.0	VF/NM 9.0	NM- 9.2
6/15/41-1st app. Twilight	16	32	48	94	147	200
6/22/41-Hitler app. in Spirit	16	32	48	94	147	200
6/29/41-1/25/42,2/8/42	14	28	42	81	118	155
2/1/42-1st app. Duchess	16	32	48	94	147	200
2/15/42-4/26/42-Lady Luck by Klaus Nordling begins 3/1/42	15	30	45	84	127	170
5/3/42-8/16/42-Eisner/Fine/Quality staff assists on Spirit	12	24	36	69	97	125
8/23/42-Satin cover splash; Spirit by Eisner/Fine although signed by Fine	17	34	51	98	154	210
8/30/42,9/27/42-10/11/42,10/25/42-11/8/42-Eisner/Fine/Quality staff assists on Spirit	12	24	36	67	94	120
9/6/42-9/20/42,10/18/42-Fine/Belfi art on Spirit; scripts by Manly Wade Wellman	9	18	27	50	65	80
11/15/42-12/6/42,12/20/42,12/27/42,1/17/43-4/18/43,5/9/43-8/8/43-Wellman/Woolfolk scripts, Fine pencils, Quality staff inks	9	18	27	50	65	80
12/13/42,1/3/43,1/10/43,4/25/43,5/2/43-Eisner scripts/layouts; Fine pencils, Quality staff inks	10	20	30	54	72	90
8/15/43-Eisner script/layout; pencils/inks by Quality staff; Jack Cole-a	8	16	24	44	57	70
8/22/43-12/12/43-Wellman/Woolfolk scripts, Fine pencils, Quality staff inks; Mr. Mystic by Guardineer-10/10/43-10/24/43	8	16	24	44	57	70
12/19/43-8/13/44-Wellman/Woolfolk/Jack Cole scripts; Cole, Fine & Robin King-a; Last Mr. Mystic-5/14/44	8	16	24	42	54	65
8/20/44-12/16/45-Wellman/Woolfolk scripts; Fine art with unknown staff assists	8	16	24	42	54	65

NOTE: *Scripts/layouts by Eisner, or Eisner/Nordling, Eisner/Mercer or Spranger/Eisner; inks by Eisner or Eisner/Spranger in issues 12/23/45-2/2/47.*

	GD 2.0	VG 4.0	FN 6.0	VF 8.0	VF/NM 9.0	NM- 9.2
12/23/45-1/6/46: 12/23/45-Christmas-c	9	18	27	52	69	85
1/13/46-Origin Spirit retold	13	26	39	72	101	130
1/20/46-1st postwar Satin app.	11	22	33	64	90	115
1/27/46-3/10/46: 3/3/46-Last Lady Luck by Nordling	9	18	27	52	69	85
3/17/46-Intro. & 1st app. Nylon	11	22	33	64	90	115
3/24/46,3/31/46,4/14/46	9	18	27	52	69	85
4/7/46-2nd app. Nylon	10	20	30	56	76	95
4/21/46-Intro. & 1st app. Mr. Carrion & His Pet Buzzard Julia	13	26	39	72	101	130
4/28/46-5/12/46,5/26/46-6/30/46: Lady Luck by Fred Schwab in issues 5/5/46-11/3/46	9	18	27	52	69	85
5/19/46-2nd app. Mr. Carrion	10	20	30	56	76	95
7/7/46-Intro. & 1st app. Dulcet Tone & Skinny	11	22	33	64	90	115
7/14/46-9/29/46	9	18	27	52	69	85
10/6/46-Intro. & 1st app. P'Gell	13	26	39	74	105	135
10/13/46-11/3/46,11/16/46-11/24/46	9	18	27	52	69	85
11/10/46-2nd app. P'Gell	11	22	33	62	86	110
12/1/46-3rd app. P'Gell	10	20	30	54	72	90
12/8/46-2/2/47	9	18	27	50	65	80

NOTE: *Scripts, pencils/inks by Eisner except where noted in issues 2/9/47-12/19/48.*

	GD 2.0	VG 4.0	FN 6.0	VF 8.0	VF/NM 9.0	NM- 9.2
2/9/47-7/6/47: 6/8/47-Eisner self satire	9	18	27	50	65	80
7/13/47- "Hansel & Gretel" fairy tales	11	22	33	64	90	115
7/20/47-Li'L Abner, Daddy Warbucks, Dick Tracy, Fearless Fosdick parody; A-Bomb blast-c	13	26	39	72	101	130
7/27/47-9/14/47	9	18	27	50	65	80
9/21/47-Pearl Harbor flashback	10	20	30	56	76	95
9/28/47-1st mention of Flying Saucers in comics-3 months after 1st sighting in Idaho on 6/25/47	17	34	51	98	154	210
10/5/47- "Cinderella" fairy tales	11	22	33	64	90	115
10/12/47-11/30/47	9	18	27	50	65	80
12/7/47-Intro. & 1st app. Powder Pouf	13	26	39	72	101	130
12/14/47-12/28/47	9	18	27	50	65	80
1/4/48-2nd app. Powder Pouf	10	20	30	54	72	90
1/11/48-1st app. Sparrow Fallon; Powder Pouf app.	10	20	30	54	72	90
1/18/48-He-Man ad cover; satire issue	10	20	30	54	72	90
1/25/48-Intro. & 1st app. Castanet	13	26	39	72	101	130
2/1/48-2nd app. Castanet	9	18	27	52	69	85
2/8/48-3/7/48	9	18	27	50	65	80
3/14/48-Only app. Kretchma	9	18	27	52	69	85
3/21/48,3/28/48,4/11/48-4/25/48	9	18	27	50	65	80
4/4/48-Only app. Wild Rice	9	18	27	52	69	85
5/2/48-2nd app. Sparrow	9	18	27	50	65	80
5/9/48-6/27/48,7/11/48,7/18/48: 6/13/48-TV issue	9	18	27	50	65	80
7/4/48-Spirit by Andre Le Blanc	8	16	24	42	54	65
7/25/48-Ambrose Bierce's "The Thing" adaptation classic by Eisner/Grandenetti	15	30	45	90	140	190
8/1/48-8/15/48,8/29/48-9/12/48	9	18	27	50	65	80
8/22/48-Poe's "Fall of the House of Usher" classic by Eisner/Grandenetti	15	30	45	90	140	190
9/19/48-Only app. Lorelei	10	20	30	54	72	90
9/26/48-10/31/48	9	18	27	50	65	80
11/7/48-Only app. Plaster of Paris	11	22	33	64	90	115
11/14/48-12/19/48	9	18	27	50	65	80

NOTE: *Scripts by Eisner or Feiffer or Eisner/Feiffer or Nordling. Art by Eisner with backgrounds by Eisner, Grandenetti, Le Blanc, Stallman, Nordling, Dixon and/or others in issues 12/26/48-4/1/51 except where noted.*

	GD 2.0	VG 4.0	FN 6.0	VF 8.0	VF/NM 9.0	NM- 9.2
12/26/48-Reprints some covers of 1948 with flashbacks	9	18	27	50	65	80
1/2/49-1/16/49	9	18	27	50	65	80
1/23/49,1/30/49-1st & 2nd app. Thorne	10	20	30	54	72	90
2/6/49-8/14/49	9	18	27	50	65	80
8/21/49,8/28/49-1st & 2nd app. Monica Veto	10	20	30	54	72	90
9/4/49,9/11/49	9	18	27	50	65	80
9/18/49-Love comic cover; has gag love comic ads on inside	10	20	30	54	72	90
9/25/49-Only app. Ice	9	18	27	52	69	85
10/2/49,10/9/49-Autumn News appears & dies in 10/9 issue	9	18	27	52	69	85
10/16/49-11/27/49,12/18/49,12/25/49	9	18	27	50	65	80
12/4/49,12/11/49-1st & 2nd app. Flaxen	9	18	27	52	69	85
1/1/50-Flashbacks to all of the Spirit girls-Thorne, Ellen, Satin, & Monica	4	28	42	76	108	140
1/8/50-Intro. & 1st app. Sand Saref	15	30	45	86	133	180
1/15/50-2nd app. Saref	13	26	39	72	101	130
1/22/50-2/5/50	9	18	27	50	65	80
2/12/50-Roller Derby issue	10	20	30	54	72	90
2/19/50-Half Dead Mr. Lox - Classic horror	11	22	33	64	90	115
2/26/50-4/23/50,5/14/50,5/28/50,7/23/50-9/3/50	9	18	27	50	65	80
4/30/50-Script/art by Le Blanc with Eisner framing	8	16	24	40	50	60
5/7/50,6/4/50-7/16/50-Abe Kanegson-a	8	16	24	40	50	60
5/21/50-Script by Feiffer/Eisner, art by Blaisdell, Eisner framing	8	16	24	40	50	60
9/10/50-P'Gell returns	10	20	30	54	72	90
9/17/50-1/7/51	9	18	27	50	65	80
1/14/51-Life Magazine cover; brief biography of Comm. Dolan, Sand Saref, Silk Satin, P'Gell, Sammy & Willum, Darling O'Shea, & Mr. Carrion & His Pet Buzzard Julia, with pin-ups by Eisner	11	22	33	64	90	115
1/21/51,2/4/51-4/1/51	9	18	27	50	65	80
1/28/51- "The Meanest Man in the World" by Eisner	11	22	33	64	90	115
4/8/51-7/29/51,8/12/51-Last Eisner issue	9	18	27	50	65	80
8/5/51,8/19/51-7/20/52-Not Eisner	8	16	24	40	50	60
7/27/52-(Rare)-Denny Colt in Outer Space by Wally Wood; 7 pg. S/F story of E.C. vintage	40	80	120	246	411	575
8/3/52-(Rare)- "Mission...The Moon" by Wood	40	80	120	246	411	575
8/10/52-(Rare)- "A DP On The Moon" by Wood	40	80	120	246	411	575
8/17/52-(Rare)- "Heart" by Wood/Eisner	37	74	111	222	361	500
8/24/52-(Rare)- "Rescue" by Wood	40	80	120	246	411	575
8/31/52-(Rare)- "The Last Man" by Wood	40	80	120	246	411	575
9/7/52-(Rare)- "The Man in The Moon" by Wood	40	80	120	246	411	575
9/14/52-(Rare)-Eisner/Wenzel-a	21	42	63	122	199	275
9/21/52-(Rare)- "Denny Colt, Alias The Spirit/Space Report" by Eisner/Wenzel	22	44	66	132	216	300
9/28/52-(Rare)- "Return From The Moon" by Wood	39	78	117	240	395	550
10/5/52-(Rare)- "The Last Story" by Eisner	20	40	60	114	182	250

Large Tabloid pages from 1946 on (Eisner) - Price 200 percent over listed prices.
NOTE: *Spirit sections came out in both large and small format. Some newspapers went to the 8-pg. format months before others. Some printed the pages so they cannot be folded into a small comic book section; these are worth less. (Also see Three Comics & Spiritman).*

SPY SMASHER
Fawcett Publications

	GD 2.0	VG 4.0	FN 6.0	VF 8.0	VF/NM 9.0	NM- 9.2
Well Known Comics (1944, 12 pgs., 8-1/2x10-1/2"), paper-c, glued binding, printed in green; Bestmaid/Samuel Lowe giveaway	15	30	45	83	124	165

STANDARD OIL COMICS (Also see Gulf Funny Weekly)
Standard Oil Co.: 1932-1934 (Giveaway, tabloid size, 4 pgs. in color)

	GD 2.0	VG 4.0	FN 6.0	VF 8.0	VF/NM 9.0	NM- 9.2
nn (Dec. 1932)	52	104	156	330	565	800
1-Series has original art	45	90	135	284	480	675
2-5	20	40	60	116	191	265
6-14: 14-Fred Opper strip, 1 pg.	14	28	42	76	108	140
1A (Jan 1933)	47	94	141	296	498	700
2A-14A (1933)	30	60	90	176	288	400
1B (1934)	37	74	111	222	361	500
2B-?B (1934)	30	60	90	176	288	400

NOTE: *Series A contains Frederick Opper's Si & Mirandi; Series B contains Goofus: He's From The Big City; McVittle by Walter O'Ehrle; interior strips include Pesty And His Pop & Smiling Slim by Sid Hicks.*

STAR TEAM
Marvel Comics Group: 1977 (6-1/2x5", 20 pgs.) (Ideal Toy Giveaway)

	GD 2.0	VG 4.0	FN 6.0	VF 8.0	VF/NM 9.0	NM- 9.2
nn	3	6	9	14	19	24

The Story of Harry S. Truman © DNC

Super Book of Comics #2 © WEST

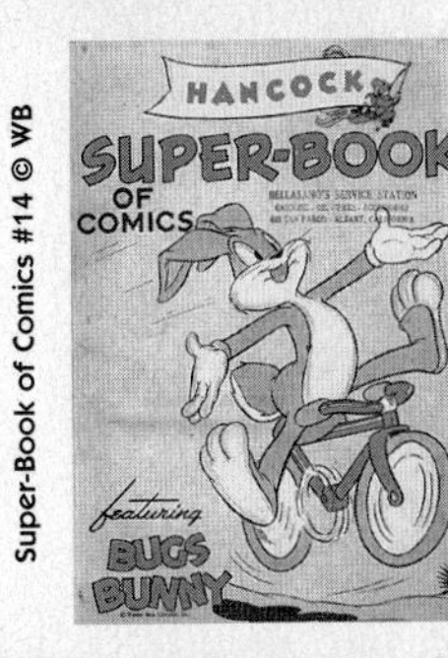

HANCOCK
SUPER-BOOK
OF
COMICS
featuring
BUGS
BUNNY

Super-Book of Comics #14 © WB

STEVE CANYON COMICS
Harvey Publications

	GD 2.0	VG 4.0	FN 6.0	VF 8.0	VF/NM 9.0	NM- 9.2
Dept. Store giveaway #3(6/48, 36pp)	10	20	30	54	72	90
...'s Secret Mission (1951, 16 pgs., Armed Forces giveaway); Caniff-a	9	18	27	47	61	75
Strictly for the Smart Birds (1951, 16 pgs.)-Information Comics Div. (Harvey) Premium	8	16	24	40	50	60

STORIES OF CHRISTMAS
K. K. Publications: 1942 (Giveaway, 32 pgs., paper cover)

	GD 2.0	VG 4.0	FN 6.0	VF 8.0	VF/NM 9.0	NM- 9.2
nn-Adaptation of "A Christmas Carol"; Kelly story "The Fir Tree"; Infinity-c	29	58	87	172	281	390

STORY HOUR SERIES (Disney)
Whitman Publ. Co.: 1948, 1949; 1951-1953 (36 pgs., paper-c) (4-3/4x6-1/2")
Given away with subscription to Walt Disney's Comics & Stories

	GD 2.0	VG 4.0	FN 6.0	VF 8.0	VF/NM 9.0	NM- 9.2
nn(1948)-Mickey Mouse and the Boy Thursday	12	24	36	67	94	120
nn(1948)-Mickey Mouse the Miracle Master	12	24	36	67	94	120
nn(1948)-Minnie Mouse and Antique Chair	12	24	36	67	94	120
nn(1949)-The Three Orphan Kittens(B&W & color)	9	18	27	47	61	75
nn(1949)-Danny-The Little Black Lamb	9	18	27	47	61	75
800(1948)-Donald Duck in "Bringing Up the Boys"	15	30	45	88	137	185
1953 edition	11	22	33	64	90	115
801(1948)-Mickey Mouse's Summer Vacation	10	20	30	56	76	95
1951, 1952 editions	7	14	21	35	43	50
802(1948)-Bugs Bunny's Adventures	9	18	27	50	65	80
803(1948)-Bongo	8	16	24	40	50	60
804(1948)-Mickey and the Beanstalk	9	18	27	47	61	75
805-15(1949)-Andy Panda and His Friends	8	16	24	40	50	60
806-15(1949)-Tom and Jerry	8	16	24	44	57	70
808-15(1949)-Johnny Appleseed	8	16	24	40	50	60

1948, 1949 Hard Cover Edition of each....30% - 40% more.

STOP AND GO, THE SAFETY TWINS
J.C. Penney: no date (giveaway)

	GD 2.0	VG 4.0	FN 6.0	VF 8.0	VF/NM 9.0	NM- 9.2
nn	5	10	15	24	30	35

STORY OF EDISON, THE
Educational Comics: 1956 (16 pgs.) (Reddy Killowatt)

	GD 2.0	VG 4.0	FN 6.0	VF 8.0	VF/NM 9.0	NM- 9.2
nn-Reprint of Reddy Kilowatt #2(1947)	7	14	21	35	43	50

STORY OF HARRY S. TRUMAN, THE
Democratic National Committee: 1948 (Giveaway, regular size, soft-c, 16 pg.)

	GD 2.0	VG 4.0	FN 6.0	VF 8.0	VF/NM 9.0	NM- 9.2
nn-Gives biography on career of Truman; used in **SOTI**, pg. 311	14	28	42	76	108	140

STORY OF THE BALLET, THE
Selva and Sons, Inc.: 1954 (16 pgs., paper cover)

	GD 2.0	VG 4.0	FN 6.0	VF 8.0	VF/NM 9.0	NM- 9.2
nn	4	8	11	16	19	22

STRANGE AS IT SEEMS
McNaught Syndicate: 1936 (B&W, 5" x 7", 24 pgs.)

	GD 2.0	VG 4.0	FN 6.0	VF 8.0	VF/NM 9.0	NM- 9.2
nn-Ex-Lax giveaway	8	16	24	44	57	70

STRAY
Dark Horse Comics: 2004 (8 1/2"x 5 1/2", Diamond Comic Dist. Halloween giveaway)

	GD 2.0	VG 4.0	FN 6.0	VF 8.0	VF/NM 9.0	NM- 9.2
nn-Reprint from The Dark Horse Book of Hauntings; Evan Dorkin-s/Jill Thompson-a						2.50

SUGAR BEAR
Post Cereal Giveaway: No date, circa 1975? (2 1/2" x 4 1/2", 16 pgs.)

	GD 2.0	VG 4.0	FN 6.0	VF 8.0	VF/NM 9.0	NM- 9.2
"The Almost Take Over of the Post Office", "The Race Across the Atlantic", "The Zoo Goes Wild" each...	1	2	3	5	6	8

SUNDAY WORLD'S EASTER EGG FULL OF EASTER MEAT FOR LITTLE PEOPLE
Supplement to the New York World: 3/27/1898 (soft-c, 16pg, 4"x8" approx., opens at top, color & B&W)(Giveaway)(shaped like an Easter egg)

	GD 2.0	VG 4.0	FN 6.0	VF 8.0	VF/NM 9.0	NM- 9.2
nn-By R.F. Outcault	18	36	54	103	162	220

SUPER BOOK OF COMICS
Western Publishing Co.: nd (1942-1943?) (Soft-c, 32 pgs.) (Pan-Am/Gilmore Oil/Kelloggs premiums)

	GD 2.0	VG 4.0	FN 6.0	VF 8.0	VF/NM 9.0	NM- 9.2
nn-Dick Tracy (Gilmore)-Magic Morro app. (2 versions: Dick Tracy Jr. on cover and a filing cabinet cover)	31	62	93	184	302	420
1-Dick Tracy & The Smuggling Ring; Stratosphere Jim app. (Rare) (Pan-Am)	31	62	93	184	302	420
1-Smilin' Jack, Magic Morro (Pan-Am)	13	26	39	74	105	135
2-Smilin' Jack, Stratosphere Jim (Pan-Am)	13	26	39	74	105	135
2-Smitty, Magic Morro (Pan-Am)	13	26	39	74	105	135
3-Captain Midnight, Magic Morro (Pan-Am)	22	44	66	131	216	300
3-Moon Mullins?	13	26	39	74	105	135
4-Red Ryder, Magic Morro (Pan-Am). Same content as Red Ryder Victory Patrol comic w/diff. cover	15	30	45	85	130	175
4-Smitty, Stratosphere Jim (Pan-Am)	13	26	39	74	105	135
5-Don Winslow, Magic Morro (Gilmore)	15	30	45	85	130	175
5-Don Winslow, Stratosphere Jim (Pan-Am)	15	30	45	85	130	175
5-Terry & the Pirates	17	34	51	98	154	210
6-Don Winslow, Stratosphere Jim (Pan-Am)-McWilliams-a	15	30	45	85	130	175
6-King of the Royal Mounted, Magic Morro (Pan-Am)	15	30	45	85	130	175
7-Dick Tracy, Magic Morro (Pan-Am)	19	38	57	111	178	245
7-Little Orphan Annie	11	22	33	64	90	115
8-Dick Tracy, Stratosphere Jim (Pan-Am)	17	34	51	98	154	210
8-Dan Dunn, Magic Morro (Pan-Am)	11	22	33	64	90	115
9-Terry & the Pirates, Magic Morro (Pan-Am)	17	34	51	98	154	210
10-Red Ryder, Magic Morro (Pan-Am)	15	30	45	85	130	175

SUPER-BOOK OF COMICS
Western Publishing Co.: (Omar Bread & Hancock Oil Co. giveaways) 1944 - No. 30, 1947 (Omar); 1947 - 1948 (Hancock) (16 pgs.)

NOTE: The Hancock issues are all exact reprints of the earlier Omar issues. The issue numbers were removed in some of the reprints.

	GD 2.0	VG 4.0	FN 6.0	VF 8.0	VF/NM 9.0	NM- 9.2
1-Dick Tracy (Omar, 1944)	15	30	45	94	147	200
1-Dick Tracy (Hancock, 1947)	14	28	42	78	112	145
2-Bugs Bunny (Omar, 1944)	8	16	24	40	50	60
2-Bugs Bunny (Hancock, 1947)	6	12	18	32	39	46
3-Terry & the Pirates (Omar, 1944)	11	22	33	60	83	105
3-Terry & the Pirates (Hancock, 1947)	10	20	30	54	72	90
4-Andy Panda (Omar, 1944)	8	16	24	40	50	60
4-Andy Panda (Hancock, 1947)	6	12	18	32	39	46
5-Smokey Stover (Omar, 1945)	6	12	18	32	39	46
5-Smokey Stover (Hancock, 1947)	5	10	15	24	30	35
6-Porky Pig (Omar, 1945)	8	16	24	40	50	60
6-Porky Pig (Hancock, 1947)	6	12	18	32	39	46
7-Smilin' Jack (Omar, 1945)	8	16	24	40	50	60
7-Smilin' Jack (Hancock, 1947)	6	12	18	32	39	46
8-Oswald the Rabbit (Omar, 1945)	6	12	18	32	39	46
8-Oswald the Rabbit (Hancock, 1947)	5	10	15	24	30	35
9-Alley Oop (Omar, 1945)	11	22	33	64	90	115
9-Alley Oop (Hancock, 1947)	11	22	33	60	83	105
10-Elmer Fudd (Omar, 1945)	6	12	18	32	39	46
10-Elmer Fudd (Hancock, 1947)	5	10	15	24	30	35
11-Little Orphan Annie (Omar, 1945)	8	16	24	42	53	64
11-Little Orphan Annie (Hancock, 1947)	7	14	21	36	45	54
12-Woody Woodpecker (Omar, 1945)	6	12	18	32	39	46
12-Woody Woodpecker (Hancock, 1947)	5	10	15	24	30	35
13-Dick Tracy (Omar, 1945)	11	22	33	64	90	115
13-Dick Tracy (Hancock, 1947)	11	22	33	60	83	105
14-Bugs Bunny (Omar, 1945)	6	12	18	32	39	46
14-Bugs Bunny (Hancock, 1947)	5	10	15	24	30	35
15-Andy Panda (Omar, 1945)	6	12	18	28	34	40
15-Andy Panda (Hancock, 1947)	5	10	15	24	30	35
16-Terry & the Pirates (Omar, 1945)	11	22	33	60	83	105
16-Terry & the Pirates (Hancock, 1947)	9	18	27	47	61	75
17-Smokey Stover (Omar, 1946)	6	12	18	32	39	46
17-Smokey Stover (Hancock, 1948?)	5	10	15	24	30	35
18-Porky Pig (Omar, 1946)	6	12	18	28	34	40
18-Porky Pig (Hancock, 1948?)	5	10	15	24	30	35
19-Smilin' Jack (Omar, 1946)	6	12	18	32	39	46
nn-Smilin' Jack (Hancock, 1948)	5	10	15	24	30	35
20-Oswald the Rabbit (Omar, 1946)	6	12	18	28	34	40
nn-Oswald the Rabbit (Hancock, 1948)	5	10	15	24	30	35
21-Gasoline Alley (Omar, 1946)	8	16	24	42	53	64
nn-Gasoline Alley (Hancock, 1948)	7	14	21	36	45	54
22-Elmer Fudd (Omar, 1946)	6	12	18	28	34	40
nn-Elmer Fudd (Hancock, 1948)	5	10	15	24	30	35
23-Little Orphan Annie (Omar, 1946)	8	16	24	40	50	60
nn-Little Orphan Annie (Hancock, 1948)	6	12	18	32	39	46
24-Woody Woodpecker (Omar, 1946)	6	12	18	28	34	40
nn-Woody Woodpecker (Hancock, 1948)	5	10	15	24	30	35
25-Dick Tracy (Omar, 1946)	11	22	33	60	83	105
nn-Dick Tracy (Hancock, 1948)	9	18	27	50	65	80
26-Bugs Bunny (Omar, 1946))	6	12	18	28	34	40
nn-Bugs Bunny (Hancock, 1948)	5	10	15	24	30	35
27-Andy Panda (Omar, 1946)	6	12	18	28	34	40
27-Andy Panda (Hancock, 1948)	5	10	15	24	30	35
28-Terry & the Pirates (Omar, 1946)	11	22	33	60	83	105
28-Terry & the Pirates (Hancock, 1948)	9	18	27	47	61	75

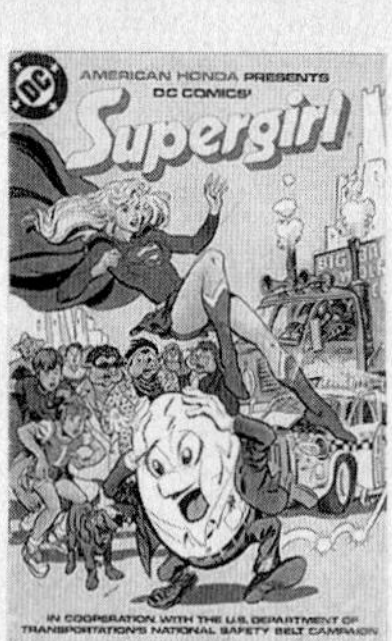

Supergirl (Honda) © DC

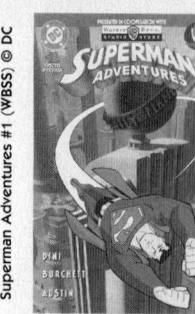

Superman Adventures #1 (WBSS) © DC

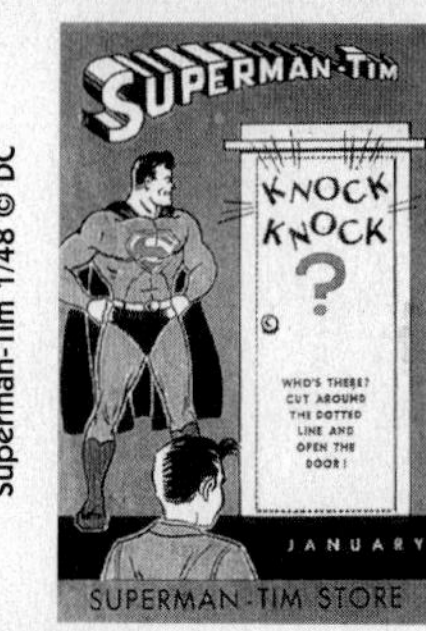

Superman-Tim 1/48 © DC

	GD 2.0	VG 4.0	FN 6.0	VF 8.0	VF/NM 9.0	NM- 9.2
29-Smokey Stover (Omar, 1947)	6	12	18	28	34	40
29-Smokey Stover (Hancock, 1948)	5	10	15	24	30	35
30-Porky Pig (Omar, 1947)	6	12	18	28	34	40
30-Porky Pig (Hancock, 1948)	5	10	15	24	30	35
nn-Bugs Bunny (Hancock, 1948)-Does not match any Omar book	6	12	18	28	34	40

SUPER CIRCUS (TV)
Cross Publishing Co.

1-(1951, Weather Bird Shoes giveaway)	8	16	24	40	50	60

SUPER FRIENDS
DC Comics: 1981 (Giveaway, no ads, no code or price)

...Special 1 -r/Super Friends #19 & 36	2	4	6	9	12	15

SUPERGEAR COMICS
Jacobs Corp.: 1976 (Giveaway, 4 pgs. in color, slick paper)

nn-(Rare)-Superman, Lois Lane; Steve Lombard app. (500 copies printed, over half destroyed?)	21	42	63	148	287	425

SUPERGIRL
DC Comics: 1984, 1986 (Giveaway, Baxter paper)

nn-(American Honda/U.S. Dept. Transportation) Torres-c/a	2	4	6	8	11	14

SUPER HEROES PUZZLES AND GAMES
General Mills Giveaway (Marvel Comics Group): 1979 (32 pgs., regular size)

nn-Four 2-pg. origin stories of Spider-Man, Captain America, The Hulk, & Spider-Woman	3	6	9	14	20	26

SUPERMAN
National Periodical Publ./DC Comics

72-Giveaway(9-10/51)-(Rare)-Price blackened out; came with banner wrapped around book; without banner	73	146	219	467	796	1125
72-Giveaway with banner	116	232	348	742	1271	1800
Bradman birthday custom (1988)(extremely limited distribution) - no reported sales for 2008						
... For the Animals (2000, Doris Day Animal Foundation, 30 pgs.) polybagged with Gotham Adventures #22, Hourman #12, Impulse #58, Looney Tunes #62, Stars and S.T.R.I.P.E. #8 and Superman Adventures #41						2.50
Kelloggs Giveaway-(2/3 normal size, 1954)-r-two stories/Superman #55	28	56	84	165	270	375
Kenner: Man of Steel (Doomsday is Coming) (1995, 16 pgs.) packaged with set of Superman and Doomsday action figures						4.00
...Meets the Quik Bunny (1987, Nestles Quik premium, 36 pgs.)	1	2	3	5	6	8
Pizza Hut Premiums (12/77)-Exact reprints of 1950s comics except for paid ads (set of 6 exist?); Vol. 1-r#97 (#113-r also known)	1	3	4	6	8	10
Radio Shack Giveaway-36 pgs. (7/80) "The Computers That Saved Metropolis", Starlin/Giordano-a; advertising insert in Action #509, New Advs. of Superboy #7, Legion of Super-Heroes #265, & House of Mystery #282. (All comics were 68 pgs.) Cover of inserts printed on newsprint. Giveaway contains 4 extra pgs. of Radio Shack advertising that inserts do not have	1	2	3	5	6	8
Radio Shack Giveaway-(7/81) "Victory by Computer"	1	2	3	5	6	8
Radio Shack Giveaway-(7/82) "Computer Masters of Metropolis"	1	2	3	5	6	8

SUPERMAN ADVENTURES, THE (TV)
DC Comics: 1996 (Based on animated series)

1-(1996) Preview issue distributed at Warner Bros. stores						4.00
Titus Game Edition (1998)						2.50

SUPERMAN AND THE GREAT CLEVELAND FIRE
National Periodical Publ.: 1948 (Giveaway, 4 pgs., no cover) (Hospital Fund)

nn-In full color	65	130	195	416	708	1000

SUPERMAN AT THE GILBERT HALL OF SCIENCE
National Periodical Publ.: 1948 (Giveaway) (Gilbert Chemistry Sets / A.C. Gilbert Co.)

nn	36	72	108	211	343	475

SUPERMAN (Miniature)
National Periodical Publ.: 1942; 1955 - 1956 (3 issues, no #'s, 32 pgs.)
The pages are numbered in the 1st issue: 1-32; 2nd: 1A-32A, and 3rd: 1B-32B

No date-Py-Co-Pay Tooth Powder giveaway (8 pgs.; circa 1942)	43	86	129	271	461	650
1-The Superman Time Capsule (Kellogg's Sugar Smacks)(1955)	24	48	72	142	234	325
1A-Duel in Space (1955)	22	44	66	131	216	300
1B-The Super Show of Metropolis (also #1-32, no B)(1955)	22	44	66	131	216	300

NOTE: *Numbering variations exist. Each title could have any combination-#1, 1A, or 1B.*

SUPERMAN RECORD COMIC
National Periodical Publications: 1966 (Golden Records)

(With record)-Record reads origin of Superman from comic; came with iron-on patch, decoder, membership card & button; comic-r/Superman #125,146	13	26	39	91	171	250
Comic only	7	14	21	45	73	100

SUPERMAN'S BUDDY (Costume Comic)
National Periodical Publications: 1954 (4 pgs., slick paper-c; one-shot)
(Came in box w/costume)

1-With box & costume	123	246	369	781	1341	1900
Comic only	55	110	165	349	600	850
1-(1958 edition)-Printed in 2 colors	17	34	51	98	154	210

SUPERMAN'S CHRISTMAS ADVENTURE
National Periodical Publications: 1940, 1944 (Giveaway, 16 pgs.)
Distributed by Nehi drinks, Bailey Store, Ivey-Keith Co., Kennedy's Boys Shop, Macy's Store, Boston Store

1(1940)-Burnley-a; F. Ray-c/r from Superman #6 (Scarce)-Superman saves Santa Claus. Santa makes real Superman Toys offered in 1940. 1st merchandising story; versions with Royal Crown Cola ad on front-c & Boston Store ad on front-c; cover art on each has the same layout but different art	360	720	1080	2520	4410	6300
nn(1944) w/Santa Claus & X-mas tree-c	97	194	291	616	1058	1500
nn(1944) w/Candy cane & Superman-c	90	180	270	572	986	1400

SUPERMAN-TIM (Becomes Tim)
Superman-Tim Stores/National Periodical Publ.: Aug, 1942 - May, 1950 (Half size)
(B&W Giveaway w/2 color covers) (Publ. monthly 2/43 on)

8/42 (#1)-All have Superman illos.	113	226	339	718	1234	1750
1/43 (#2)	39	78	117	234	380	525
2/43 (#3)	37	74	111	222	361	500
3/43 (#4)	37	74	111	222	361	500
4/43, 5/43, 6/43, 7/43, 8/43	33	66	99	198	324	450
9/43, 10/43, 11/43, 12/43	28	56	84	165	270	375
1/44-12/44	24	48	72	140	230	320
1/45-5/45, 10-12/45, 1/46-8/46	21	42	63	126	208	290
6/45-Classic Superman-c	23	46	69	138	227	315
7/45-Classic Superman flag-c	23	46	69	138	227	315
9/45-1st stamp album issue	48	96	114	302	509	715
9/46-2nd stamp album issue	40	80	120	252	426	600
10/46-1st Superman story	29	58	87	170	278	385
11/46, 12/46, 1/47-8/47 issues-Superman story in each; 2/47-Infinity-c. All 36 pgs.	29	58	87	170	278	385
9/47-Stamp album issue & Superman story	40	80	120	245	410	575
10/47, 11/47, 12/47-Superman stories (24 pgs.)	29	58	87	170	278	385
1/48-7/48,10/48, 11/48, 2/49, 4/49-11/49	23	46	69	138	227	315
8/48-Contains full page ad for Superman-Tim watch giveaway	23	46	69	138	227	315
9/48-Stamp album issue	31	62	93	186	301	425
1/49-Full page Superman bank cut-out	23	46	69	138	227	315
3/49-Full page Superman boxing game cut-out	23	46	69	138	227	315
12/49-3/50, 5/50-Superman stories	25	50	75	150	245	340
4/50-Superman story, baseball stories; photo-c without Superman	29	58	87	170	278	385

NOTE: *All issues have Superman illustrations throughout. The page count varies depending on whether a Superman-Tim comic story is inserted. If it is, the page count is either 36 or 24 pages. Otherwise all issues are 16 pages. Each issue has a special place for inserting a full color Superman stamp. The stamp album issues had spaces for the stamps given away the past year. The books were mailed as a subscription premium. The stamps were given away free (or when you made a purchase) only when you physically came into the store.*

SUPER SEAMAN SLOPPY
Allied Pristine Union Council, Buffalo, NY: 1940s, 8pg., reg. size (Soft-c)

nn	4	8	12	17	21	24

SWAMP FOX, THE
Walt Disney Productions: 1960 (14 pgs, small size) (Canada Dry Premiums)

Titles: (A)-Tory Masquerade, (B)-Turnabout Tactics, (C)-Rindau Rampage; each came in paper sleeve, books 1,2 & 3; Set with sleeves	5	10	15	34	55	75
Comic only	2	4	6	13	18	22

SWORDQUEST
DC Comics/Atari Pub.: 1982, 52pg., 5"x7" (Giveaway with video games)

1,2-Roy Thomas & Gerry Conway-s; George Pérez & Dick Giordano-c/a in all	2	4	6	10	14	18
3-Low print	3	6	9	16	22	28

SYNDICATE FEATURES (Sci/fi)
Harry A. Chesler Syndicate: V1#3, 11/15/37 (Tabloid size, 3 colors, 4 pgs.) (Editors premium) (Came folded)

V1#3-Dan Hastings daily strips-Guardineer-a	155	310	465	984	1692	2400

Tilly and Ted - Tinkertotland © W.T. Grant

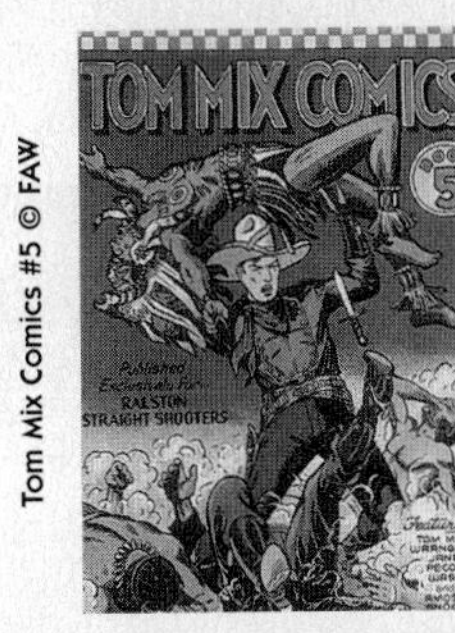

Tom Mix Comics #5 © FAW

Trapped © HARV

GD VG FN VF VF/NM NM-
2.0 4.0 6.0 8.0 9.0 9.2

TAKING A CHANCE
American Cancer Society: no date (giveaway)
nn-Anti-smoking 2 4 6 11 16 20

TASTEE-FREEZ COMICS (Also see Harvey Hits and Richie Rich)
Harvey Comics: 1957 (10¢, 36 pgs.)(6 different issues given away)
1-Little Dot on cover; Richie Rich "Ride 'Em Cowboy" story published one year prior to being printed in Harvey Hits #9. 18 36 54 129 252 375
2,4,5: 2-Rags Rabbit. 4-Sad Sack. 5-Mazie 4 8 12 26 41 55
3-Casper 5 10 15 34 55 75
6-Dick Tracy 5 10 15 34 55 75

TAYLOR'S CHRISTMAS TABLOID
Dept. Store Giveaway: Mid 1930s, Cleveland, Ohio (Tabloid size; in color)
nn-(Very Rare)-Among the earliest pro work of Siegel & Shuster; one full color page called "The Battle in the Stratosphere", with a pre-Superman look; Shuster art thoughout. (Only 1 known copy) Estimated value... 4000.00

TAZ'S 40TH BIRTHDAY BLOWOUT
DC Comics: 1994 (K-Mart giveaway, 16 pgs.)
nn-Six pg. story, games and puzzles 4.00

TEE AND VEE CROSLEY IN TELEVISION LAND COMICS (Also see Crosley's House of Fun)
Crosley Division, Avco Mfg. Corp. : 1951 (52 pgs.; 8x11"; paper cover; in color) (Giveaway)
Many stories, puzzles, cut-outs, games, etc. 7 14 21 35 43 50

TEEN-AGE BOOBY TRAP
Commercial Comics: 1970 (Small size)
nn 4 7 10 14 17 20

TENNESSEE JED (Radio)
Fox Syndicate? (Wm. C. Popper & Co.): nd (1945) (16 pgs.; paper-c; reg. size; giveaway)
nn 19 38 57 111 178 245

TENNIS (...For Speed, Stamina, Strength, Skill)
Tennis Educational Foundation: 1956 (16 pgs.; soft cover; 10¢)
Book 1-Endorsed by Gene Tunney, Ralph Kiner, etc. showing how tennis has helped them 6 12 18 28 34 40

TERRY AND THE PIRATES
Dell Publishing Co.: 1939 - 1953 (By Milton Caniff)
Buster Brown Shoes giveaway(1938)-32 pgs.; in color 19 38 57 112 181 250
Canada Dry Premiums-Books #1-3(1953, 36 pgs.; 2x5")-Harvey; #1-Hot Shot Charlie Flies Again; 2-In Forced Landing; 3-Dragon Lady in Distress) 14 28 42 78 112 145
Gambles Giveaway (1938, 16 pgs.) 9 18 27 50 65 80
Gillmore Giveaway (1938, 24 pgs.) 9 18 27 52 69 85
Popped Wheat Giveaway(1938)-Strip reprints in full color; Caniff-a 2 4 6 8 10 12
Shoe Store giveaway (Weatherbird & Poll-Parrot)(1938, 16 pgs., soft-c)(2-diff.) 9 18 27 52 69 85
Sparked Wheat Giveaway(1942, 16 pgs.)-In color 9 18 27 52 69 85

TERRY AND THE PIRATES
Libby's Radio Premium: 1941 (16 pgs.; reg. size)(shipped folded in the mail)
"Adventure of the Ruby of Genghis Khan" - Each pg. is a puzzle that must be completed to read the story 400 800 1200 2600 - -

THAT THE WORLD MAY BELIEVE
Catechetical Guild Giveaway: No date (16 pgs.) (Graymoor Friars distr.)
nn 4 8 12 18 22 25

3-D COLOR CLASSICS (Wendy's Kid's Club)
Wendy's Int'l Inc.: 1995 (5 1/2" x 8", comes with 3-D glasses)
The Elephant's Child, Gulliver's Travels, Peter Pan, The Time Machine, 20,000 Leagues Under the Sea: Neal Adams-a in all each.... 3.50

350 YEARS OF AMERICAN DAIRY FOODS
American Dairy Assoc.: 1957 (5x7", 16 pgs.)
nn-History of milk 3 6 8 12 14 16

THUMPER (Disney)
Grosset & Dunlap: 1942 (50¢, 32pgs., hardcover book, 7"x8-1/2" w/dust jacket)
nn-Given away (along with a copy of Bambi) for a $2.00, 2-year subscription to WDC&S in 1942. (Xmas offer). Book only 15 30 45 90 140 190
Dust jacket only 10 20 30 56 76 95

TILLY AND TED-TINKERTOTLAND
W. T. Grant Co.: 1945 (Giveaway, 20 pgs.)
nn-Christmas comic 7 14 21 37 46 55

TIM (Formerly Superman-Tim; becomes Gene Autry-Tim)
Tim Stores: June, 1950 - Oct, 1950 (B&W, half-size)
4 issues; 6/50, 9/50, 10/50 known 17 34 51 98 154 210

TIM AND SALLY'S ADVENTURES AT MARINELAND
Marineland Restaurant & Bar, Marineland, CA: 1957 (5x7", 16 pgs., soft-c)
nn-copyright Oceanarium, Inc. 2 4 6 8 11 14

TIME MACHINE, THE
DC Comics: 2002 (10 pgs.)
nn-Promotes the 2002 DreamWorks movie 6.00

TIME OF DECISION
Harvey Publications Inc.: (16 pgs., paper cover)
nn-ROTC recruitment 4 7 10 14 17 20

TIM IN SPACE (Formerly Gene Autry Tim; becomes Tim Tomorrow)
Tim Stores: 1950 (1/2 size giveaway) (B&W)
nn 14 28 42 78 112 145

TIM TOMORROW (Formerly Tim In Space)
Tim Stores: 8/51, 9/51, 10/51, Christmas, 1951 (5x7-3/4")
nn-Prof. Fumble & Captain Kit Comet in all 14 28 42 78 112 145

TITANS BEAT (Teen Titans)
DC Comics: Aug, 1996 (16 pgs., paper-c)
1-Intro./preview new Teen Titans members; Pérez-a 4.00

TOM MIX (...Commandos Comics #10-12)
Ralston-Purina Co.: Sept, 1940 - No. 12, Nov, 1942 (36 pgs.); 1983 (one-shot)
Given away for two Ralston box-tops; 1983 came in cereal box
1-Origin (life) Tom Mix; Fred Meagher-a 232 464 696 1473 2537 3600
2 52 104 156 330 565 800
3-9 40 80 120 252 426 600
10-12: 10-Origin Tom Mix Commando Unit; Speed O'Dare begins; Japanese sub-c. 12-Sci/fi-c 37 74 111 222 361 500
1983- "Taking of Grizzly Grebb", Toth-a; 16 pg. miniature 2 4 6 9 12 15

TOM SAWYER COMICS
Giveaway: 1951? (Paper cover)
nn-Contains a coverless Hopalong Cassidy from 1951; other combinations known 3 6 9 14 20 25

TOP-NOTCH COMICS
MLJ Magazines/Rex Theater: 1940s (theater giveaway)
1-Black Hood-c; content & covers can vary 41 82 123 256 428 600

TOPPS COMICS PRESENTS
Topps Comics: No. 0, 1993 (Giveaway, B&W, 36 pgs.)
0-Dracula vs. Zorro, Teenagents, Silver Star, & Bill the Galactic Hero 2.50

TOWN THAT FORGOT SANTA, THE
W. T. Grant Co.: 1961 (Giveaway, 24 pgs.)
nn 3 6 9 16 23 30

TOY LAND FUNNIES (See Funnies On Parade)
Eastern Color Printing Co.: 1934 (32 pgs., Hecht Co. store giveaway)
nn-Reprints Buck Rogers Sunday pages #199-201 from Famous Funnies #5. A rare variation of Funnies On Parade; same format, similar contents, same cover except for large Santa placed in center (value will be based on sale)

TOY WORLD FUNNIES (See Funnies On Parade)
Eastern Color Printing Co.: 1933 (36 pgs., slick cover, Golden Eagle and Wanamaker giveaway)
nn-Contains contents from Funnies On Parade/Century Of Comics. A rare variation of Funnies On Parade; same format, similar contents, same cover except for large Santa placed in center (value will be based on sale)

TRAPPED
Harvey Publications (Columbia Univ. Press): 1951 (Giveaway, soft-c, 16 pgs)
nn-Drug education comic (30,000 printed?) distributed to schools.; mentioned in **SOTI**, pgs. 256,350 2 4 6 8 10 12
NOTE: *Many copies surfaced in 1979 causing a setback in price; beware of trimmed edges, because many copies have a brittle edge.*

TRIPLE-A BASEBALL HEROES
Marvel Comics: 2007 (Minor league baseball stadium giveaway)
1-Special John Watson painted-c for Memphis, Durham and Buffalo; generic cover with team logos for each of the other 27 teams; Spider-Man, Iron Man, FF app. 3.00

TRIP TO OUTER SPACE WITH SANTA
Sales Promotions, Inc/Peoria Dry Goods: 1950s (paper-c)
nn-Comics, games & puzzles 5 10 15 22 26 30

Unkept Promise © Legion of Truth

Wheaties B-1 © DIS

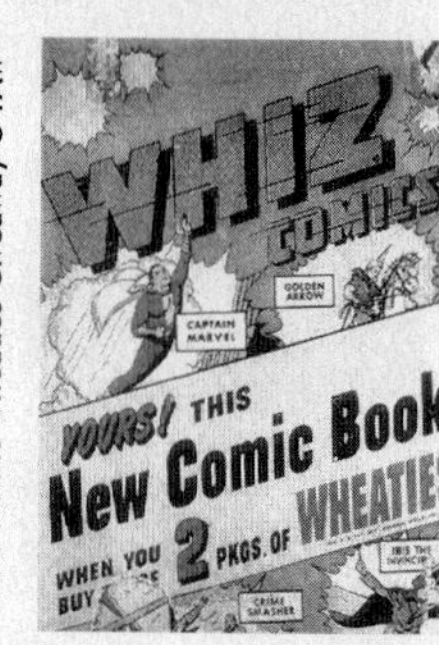

Whiz Comics Wheaties Giveaway © FAW

	GD 2.0	VG 4.0	FN 6.0	VF 8.0	VF/NM 9.0	NM- 9.2

TRIP WITH SANTA ON CHRISTMAS EVE, A
Rockford Dry Goods Co.: No date (Early 1950s) (Giveaway, 16 pgs., paper-c)
nn 5 10 15 22 26 30

TRUTH BEHIND THE TRIAL OF CARDINAL MINDSZENTY, THE (See Cardinal Mindszenty)

24 PAGES OF COMICS (No title) (Also see Pure Oil Comics, Salerno Carnival of Comics, & Vicks Comics)
Giveaway by various outlets including Sears: Late 1930s
nn-Contains strip reprints-Buck Rogers, Napoleon, Sky Roads, War on Crime 31 62 93 184 302 420

TWISTED METAL (Video game)
DC Comics: 1996
nn 3.00

TWO FACES OF COMMUNISM (Also see Double Talk)
Christian Anti-Communism Crusade, Houston, Texas: 1961 (Giveaway, paper-c, 36 pgs.)
nn 15 30 45 88 137 185

2001, A SPACE ODYSSEY (Movie)
Marvel Comics Group
Howard Johnson giveaway (1968, 8pp); 6 pg. movie adaptation, 2 pg. games, puzzles; McWilliams-a 2 4 6 9 12 15

UNCLE SAM'S CHRISTMAS STORY
Promotional Publ. Co.: 1958 (Giveaway)
nn-Reprints 1956 Christmas USA 2 4 6 10 13 16

UNCLE WIGGILY COMICS
Herberger's Clothing Store: 1942 (32 pgs., paper cover)
nn-Comic panels with 6 pages of puzzles 12 24 36 69 97 125

UNKEPT PROMISE
Legion of Truth: 1949 (Giveaway, 24 pgs.)
nn-Anti-alcohol 10 20 30 58 79 100

UNTOLD LEGEND OF THE BATMAN, THE
DC Comics: 1989 (28 pgs., 6X9", limited series of cereal premiums)
1-1st & 2nd printings known; Byrne-a 2 3 4 6 8 10
2,3: 1st & 2nd printings known 1 2 3 5 6 8

UNTOUCHABLES, THE (TV)
Leaf Brands, Inc.
Topps Bubblegum premiums produced by Leaf Brands, Inc.-2-1/2x4-1/2", 8 pgs. (3 diff. issues) "The Organization, Jamaica Ginger, The Otto Frick Story (drug), 3000 Suspects, The Antidote, Mexican Stakeout, Little Egypt, Purple Gang, Bugs Moran Story, & Lily Dallas Story" 3 6 9 16 23 30

VICKS COMICS (See Pure Oil Comics, Salerno Carnival of Comics & 24 Pages of Comics)
Eastern Color Printing Co. (Vicks Chemical Co.): nd (circa 1938) (Giveaway, 68 pgs. in color)
nn-Famous Funnies-r (before #40); contains 5 pgs. Buck Rogers (4 pgs. from F.F. #15, & 1 pg. from #16) Joe Palooka, Napoleon, etc. app. 54 108 162 343 592 840
nn-16 loose, untrimmed page giveaway; paper-c; r/Famous Funnies #14; Buck Rogers, Joe Palooka app. Has either "Vicks Comics" printed on cover or only a local store name as the logo. 22 44 66 131 216 300

WALT DISNEY'S COMICS & STORIES
K.K. Publications: 1942-1963 known (7-1/3"x10-1/4", 4 pgs. in color, slick paper) (folded horizontally once or twice as mailers) (Xmas subscription offer)
1942 mailer-r/Kelly cover to WDC&S 25; 2-year subscription + two Grosset & Dunlap hardcover books (32-pages each), of Bambi and of Thumper, offered for $2.00; came in an illustrated C&S envelope with an enclosed postage paid envelope
(Rare) Mailer only 21 42 63 123 204 285
with envelopes 27 54 81 158 259 360
1947,1948 mailer 17 34 51 98 154 210
1949 mailer-A rare Barks item: Same WDC&S cover as 1942 mailer, but with art changed so that nephew is handing teacher Donald a comic book rather than an apple, as originally drawn by Kelly. The tiny, 7/8"x1-1/4" cover shown was a rejected cover by Barks that was intended for C&S 110, but was redrawn by Kelly for C&S 111. The original art has been lost and this is its only app. (Rare) 39 78 117 233 377 520
1950 mailer-P.1 r/Kelly cover to Dell Xmas Parade 1 (without title); p.2 r/Kelly cover to C&S 101 (w/o title), but with the art altered to show Donald reading C&S 122 (by Kelly); hardcover book, "Donald Duck in Bringing Up the Boys" given with a $1.00 one-year subscription; P.4 r/full Kelly Xmas cover to C&S 99 (Rare) 17 34 51 98 154 210
1952 mailer-P1 r/cover WDC&S #88 14 28 42 80 115 150
1953 mailer-P.1 r/cover Dell Xmas Parade 4 (w/o title); insides offer "Donald Duck Full Speed Ahead," a 28-page, color, 5-5/8"x6-5/8" book, not of the Story Hour series; P.4 r/full Barks C&S 148 cover (Rare) 14 28 42 80 115 150
1963 mailer-Pgs. 1,2 & 4 r/GK Xmas art; P.3 r/a 1963 C&S cover (Scarce) 11 22 33 60 83 105
NOTE: *It is assumed a different mailer was printed each Xmas for at least twenty years.*

	GD 2.0	VG 4.0	FN 6.0	VF 8.0	VF/NM 9.0	NM- 9.2

WALT DISNEY'S COMICS & STORIES
Walt Disney Productions: 1943 (36 pgs.) (Dept. store Xmas giveaway)
nn-X-Mas-c with Donald & the Boys; Donald Duck by Jack Hannah; Thumper by Ken Hultgren 43 86 129 271 461 650

WALT DISNEY'S DONALD DUCK
Gemstone Publishing: 2006
nn-(8-1/2"x 5-1/2", Halloween giveaway) r/"A Prank Above" -Barks-s/a; Rosa-s/a 2.50
nn-(2008, 8-1/2"x 5-1/2", Halloween giveaway) "The Halloween Huckster"; Rota-s/a 2.50

WALT DISNEY'S UNCLE SCROOGE
Gemstone Publishing
nn-(2007, 8-1/2"x 5-1/2", Halloween giveaway) Hound of the Whiskevilles; Barks-s/a 2.50

WARLORD
DC Comics: (Remco Toy giveaway, 2-3/4x4")
nn 5.00

WATCH OUT FOR BIG TALK
Giveaway: 1950
nn-Dan Barry-a; about crooked politicians 7 14 21 37 46 55

WEATHER-BIRD (See Comics From..., Dick Tracy, Free Comics to You..., Super Circus & Terry and the Pirates)
International Shoe Co./Western Printing Co.: 1958 - No. 16, July, 1962 (Shoe store giveaway)
1 4 8 12 25 39 52
2-16 3 6 9 14 19 24
NOTE: *The numbers are located in the lower bottom panel, pg. 1. All feature a character called Weather-Bird.*

WEATHER BIRD COMICS (See Comics From Weather Bird)
Weather Bird Shoes: 1957 (Giveaway)
nn-Contains a comic bound with new cover. Several combinations possible; contents determine price (40 - 60 percent of contents).

WEEKLY COMIC MAGAZINE
Fox Publications: May 12, 1940 (16 pgs.) (Others exist w/o super-heroes)
(1st Version)-8 pg. Blue Beetle story, 7 pg. Patty O'Day story; two copies known to exist. (a VF copy sold in 5/07 for $1553)
(2nd Version)-7 two-pg. adventures of Blue Beetle, Patty O'Day, Yarko, Dr. Fung, Green Mask, Spark Stevens, & Rex Dexter (two known copies, a FN sold in 2007 for $1912, other is GD)
(3rd version)-Captain Valor (only one known copy, in VG+; it sold in 2005 for $480) -
Discovered with business papers, letters and exploitation material promoting **Weekly Comic Magazine** for use by newspapers in the same manner of **The Spirit** weeklies. Interesting note: these are dated three weeks before the first Spirit comic. Letters indicate that samples may have been sent to a few newspapers. These sections were actually 15-1/2x22" pages which will fold down to an approximate 8x10" comic booklet. Other various comic sections were found with the above, but were more like the Sunday comic sections in format.

WE HIT THE JACKPOT
General Comics, Inc./American Affairs: 1947 (Promotional comic)
nn 6 12 18 31 38 45

WHAT DO YOU KNOW ABOUT THIS COMICS SEAL OF APPROVAL?
No publisher listed (DC Comics Giveaway): nd (1955) (4 pgs., slick paper-c)
nn-(Rare) 77 154 231 489 845 1200

WHAT'S BEHIND THESE HEADLINES
William C. Popper Co.: 1948 (16 pgs.)
nn-Comic insert "The Plot to Steal the World" 6 12 18 31 38 45

WHAT'S IN IT FOR YOU?
Harvey Publications Inc.: (16 pgs., paper cover)
nn-National Guard recruitment 4 7 10 14 17 20

WHEATIES (Premiums)
Walt Disney Productions: 1950 & 1951 (32 titles, pocket-size, 32 pgs.)
Mailing Envelope (no art on front)(Designates sets A,B,C or D on front) 7 14 21 37 46 55

(Set A-1 to A-8, 1950)
A-1-Mickey Mouse & the Disappearing Island, A-5-Mickey Mouse, Roving Reporter each... 6 12 18 28 34 40
A-2-Grandma Duck, Homespun Detective, A-6-Li'l Bad Wolf, Forest Ranger, A-7-Goofy, Tightrope Acrobat, A-8-Pluto & the Bogus Money each... 5 10 15 24 30 35
A-3-Donald Duck & the Haunted Jewels, A-4-Donald Duck & the Giant Ape each... 8 16 24 42 54 65

(Set B-1 to B-8, 1950)
B-1-Mickey Mouse & the Pharoah's Curse, B-4-Mickey Mouse & the Mystery Sea Monster each... 6 12 18 31 38 45
B-2-Pluto, Canine Cowpoke, B-5-Li'l Bad Wolf in the Hollow Tree Hideout, B-7-Goofy & the Gangsters each... 5 10 15 24 30 35
B-3-Donald Duck & the Buccaneers, B-6-Donald Duck,Trail Blazer, B-8 Donald Duck, Klondike Kid each... 8 16 24 42 54 65

Wisco - Tex Farnum, Frontiersman © Vital

World's Finest Comics #176 (Best Western) © DC

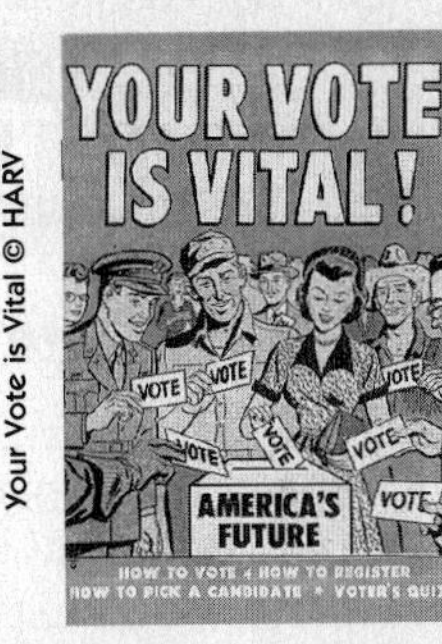

Your Vote is Vital © HARV

GD 2.0 | VG 4.0 | FN 6.0 | VF 8.0 | VF/NM 9.0 | NM- 9.2

(Set C-1 to C-8, 1951)
C-1-Donald Duck & the Inca Idol, C-5-Donald Duck in the Lost Lakes, C-8-Donald Duck Deep-Sea Diver each... 8 16 24 42 54 65
C-2-Mickey Mouse & the Magic Mountain, C-6-Mickey Mouse & the Stagecoach Bandits each... 6 12 18 31 38 45
C-3-Li'l Bad Wolf, Fire Fighter, C-4-Gus & Jaq Save the Ship, C-7-Goofy, Big Game Hunter each... 5 10 15 24 30 35
(Set D-1 to D-8, 1951)
D-1-Donald Duck in Indian Country, D-5-Donald Duck, Mighty Mystic each... 8 16 24 42 54 65
D-2-Mickey Mouse and the Abandoned Mine, D-6-Mickey Mouse & the Medicine Man each... 6 12 18 31 38 45
D-3-Pluto & the Mysterious Package, D-4-Bre'r Rabbit's Sunken Treasure, D-7-Li'l Bad Wolf and the Secret of the Woods, D-8-Minnie Mouse, Girl Explorer each... 5 10 15 24 30 35
NOTE: *Some copies lack the Wheaties ad.*

WHEEL OF PROGRESS, THE
Assoc. of American Railroads: Oct, 1957 (16 pgs.)
nn-Bill Bunce 6 12 18 28 34 40

WHIZ COMICS (Formerly Flash Comics & Thrill Comics #1)
Fawcett Publications
Wheaties Giveaway(1946, Miniature, 6-1/2x8-1/4", 32 pgs.); all copies were taped at each corner to a box of Wheaties and are never found in very fine or mint condition; "Capt. Marvel & the Water Thieves", plus Golden Arrow, Ibis, Crime Smasher stories 90 180 405 - - -

WILD KINGDOM (TV) (Mutual of Omaha's...)
Western Printing Co.: 1965, 1966 (Giveaway, regular size, slick-c, 16 pgs.)
nn-Front & back-c are different on 1966 edition 2 4 6 9 12 15

WISCO/KLARER COMIC BOOK (Miniature)
Marvel Comics/Vital Publ./Fawcett Publ.: 1948 - 1964 (3-1/2x6-3/4", 24 pgs.)
Given away by Wisco "99" Service Stations, Carnation Malted Milk, Klarer Health Wieners, Fleers Dubble Bubble Gum, Rodeo All-Meat Wieners, Perfect Potato Chips, & others; see ad in Tom Mix #21
Blackstone & the Gold Medal Mystery (1948) 8 16 24 42 54 65
Blackstone "Solves the Sealed Vault Mystery" (1950) 8 16 24 42 54 65
Blaze Carson in "The Sheriff Shoots It Out" (1950) 8 16 24 42 54 65
Captain Marvel & Billy's Big Game (r/Capt. Marvel Adv. #76) 24 48 72 145 238 330
(Prices vary widely on this book)
China Boy in "A Trip to the Zoo" #10 (1948) 5 10 15 24 30 35
Indoors-Outdoors Game Book 4 7 10 14 17 20
Jim Solar Space Sheriff in "Battle for Mars", "Between Two Worlds", "Conquers Outer Space", "The Creatures on the Comet", "Defeats the Moon Missile Men", "Encounter Creatures on Comet", "Meet the Jupiter Jumpers", "Meets the Man From Mars", "On Traffic Duty", "Outlaws of the Spaceways", "Pirates of the Planet X", "Protects Space Lanes", "Raiders From the Sun", "Ring Around Saturn", "Robots of Rhea", "The Sky Ruby", "Spacetts of the Sky", "Spidermen of Venus", "Trouble on Mercury" 7 14 21 35 43 50
Johnny Starboard & the Underseas Pirates (1948) 5 10 15 22 26 30
Kid Colt in "He Lived by His Guns" (1950) 8 16 24 44 57 70
Little Aspirin as the "Crook Catcher" #2 (1950) 4 7 10 14 17 20
Little Aspirin in "Naughty But Nice" #6 (1950) 4 7 10 14 17 20
Return of the Black Phantom (not M.E. character)(Roy Dare)(1948) 6 12 18 28 34 40
Secrets of Magic 4 8 11 16 19 22
Slim Morgan "Brings Justice to Mesa City" #3 4 8 11 16 19 22
Super Rabbit(1950)-Cuts Red Tape, Stops Crime Wave! 9 18 27 50 65 80
Tex Farnum, Frontiersman (1948) 5 10 15 22 26 30
Tex Taylor in "Draw or Die, Cowpoke!" (1950) 7 14 21 35 43 50
Tex Taylor in "An Exciting Adventure at the Gold Mine" (1950) 6 12 18 31 38 45
Wacky Quacky in "All-Aboard" 3 6 8 12 14 16
When School Is Out 3 6 8 12 14 16
Willie in a "Comic-Comic Book Fall" #1 4 8 11 16 19 22
Wonder Duck "An Adventure at the Rodeo of the Fearless Quacker!" (1950) 9 18 27 47 61 75
Rare uncut version of three; includes Capt. Marvel, Tex Farnum, Black Phantom Estimated value... 700.00
Rare uncut version of three; includes China Boy, Blackstone, Johnny Starboard & the Underseas Pirates Estimated value... 250.00
Rare uncut version of three; includes Willie in a "Comic-Comic Book Fall", Little Aspirin #2, Slim Morgan Brings Justice to Mesa City (a VF/FN copy sold for $54 in Nov. 2007)

WOLVERINE
Marvel Comics
145-(1999 Nabisco mail-in offer) Sienkiewicz-c 8 16 24 54 90 125
...Son of Canada (4/01, ed. of 65,000) Spider-Man & The Hulk app.; Lim-a 3.00

WOMAN OF THE PROMISE, THE
Catechetical Guild: 1950 (General Distr.) (Paper cover, 32 pgs.)
nn 6 12 18 28 34 40

WONDERFUL WORLD OF DUCKS (See Golden Picture Story Book)
Colgate Palmolive Co.: 1975
1-Mostly-r 1 3 4 6 8 10

WONDER WOMAN
DC Comics: 1977
Pizza Hut Giveaways (12/77)-Reprints #60,62 2 4 6 9 13 16
... - The Minotaur (1981, General Foods giveaway, 8 pages, 3-1/2 x 6-3/4", oblong) 2 4 6 13 18 22

WONDER WORKER OF PERU
Catechetical Guild: No date (5x7", 16 pgs., B&W, giveaway)
nn 5 10 15 27 33 38

WOODY WOODPECKER
Dell Publishing Co.
Clover Stamp-Newspaper Boy Contest('56)-9 pg. story-(Giveaway) 7 14 21 37 46 55
In Chevrolet Wonderland(1954-Giveaway)(Western Publ.)-20 pgs., full story line; Chilly Willy app. 18 36 54 103 162 220
...Meets Scotty MacTape(1953-Scotch Tape giveaway)-16 pgs., full size 18 36 54 103 162 220

WOOLWORTH'S CHRISTMAS STORY BOOK
Promotional Publ. Co.(Western Printing Co.): 1952 - 1954 (16 pgs., paper-c) (See Jolly Christmas Book)
nn: 1952 issue-Marv Levy c/a 6 12 18 33 41 48

WOOLWORTH'S HAPPY TIME CHRISTMAS BOOK
F. W. Woolworth Co. (Western Printing Co.): 1952 (Christmas giveaway)
nn-36 pgs. 6 12 18 31 38 45

WORLD'S FINEST COMICS
National Periodical Publ./DC Comics
Giveaway (c. 1944-45, 8 pgs., in color, paper-c)-Johnny Everyman-r/World's Finest 20 40 60 118 194 270
Giveaway (c. 1949, 8 pgs., in color, paper-c)- "Make Way For Youth" r/World's Finest; based on film of same name 18 36 54 107 169 230
#176, #179- Best Western reprint edition (1997) 3.00

WORLD'S GREATEST SUPER HEROES
DC Comics (Nutra Comics) (Child Vitamins, Inc.): 1977 (Giveaway, 3-3/4x3-3/4", 24 pgs.)
nn-Batman & Robin app.; health tips 2 4 6 9 13 16

WYOMING THE COWBOY STATE
1954 (Giveaway)
nn 5 10 15 22 26 30

XMAS FUNNIES
Kinney Shoes: No date (Giveaway, paper cover, 36 pgs.?)
Contains 1933 color strip-r; Mutt & Jeff, etc. 29 58 87 172 281 390

X-MEN THE MOVIE
Marvel Comics/Toys R' Us: 2000
Special Movie Prequel Edition 5.00

X2 PRESENTS THE ULTIMATE X-MEN #2
Marvel Comics/New York Post: July, 2003
Reprint distributed inside issue of the New York Post 2.50

YALTA TO KOREA (Also see Korea My Home)
M. Phillip Corp. (Republican National Committee): 1952 (Giveaway, paper-c)
nn-(8 pgs.)-Anti-communist propaganda book 18 36 54 103 162 220

YOGI BEAR (TV)
Dell Publishing Co.
Giveaway ('84, '86)-City of Los Angeles, "Creative First Aid" & "Earthquake Preparedness for Children" 1 2 3 4 5 7

YOUR TRIP TO NEWSPAPERLAND
Philadelphia Evening Bulletin (Printed by Harvey Press): June, 1955 (14x11-1/2", 12 pgs.)
nn-Joe Palooka takes kids on newspaper tour 5 10 15 24 30 35

YOUR VOTE IS VITAL!
Harvey Publications Inc.: 1952 (5" x 7", 16 pgs., paper cover)
nn-The importance of voting 4 8 12 18 22 25

THE PIONEER AGE

The American Comic Book: 1500s-1828

For the last few years, we have featured a tremendous article by noted historian and collector Eric C. Caren on the foundations of what we now call "The Pioneer Age" of comics. We look forward to a new article on this significant topic in *The Overstreet Comic Book Price Guide* #42. In the meantime, should you need it, Caren's article may be found in the 35th through 39th editions.

That said, even with the space constraints in this edition of the *Guide*, we could not possibly exclude reference to these incredible, formative works.

German broadsheet, dated 1569.

Why are these illustrations and sequences of illustrations important to the comic books of today?

The Murder of King Henry III (1589).

Quite frankly, because we can see in them the very building blocks of the comic art form.

The shooting of the Italian Concini (1617).

Over the course of just a few hundred years, we the evolution of narration, word balloons, panel-to-panel progression of story, and so much more. If these stories aren't developed first, how would be every have reached the point that that *The Adventures of Mr. Obadiah Oldbuck* could have come along in 1842?

As the investigation of comic book history has blown away the notion that comic books were a 20 century invention, it hasn't been easy to convince some, even with the clear, linear progression of the artful melding of illustration and words.

"Want to avoid an argument in social discourse? Steer clear of politics and religion. In the latter category, the most controversial subject is human evolution. Collectors can become just as squeamish when you start messing with the evolution of a particular collectible," Eric Caren wrote in his article. "In most cases, the origin of a particular comic character will be universally agreed upon, but try tackling the origin of printed comics and you are asking for trouble."

"The Bubblers Medley" (1720).

"Join, or Die" from the Pennsylvania Gazette, May 9, 1754.

"Amusement for John Bull..." from The European Magazine (1783).

But the evidence is there for any who choose to look. Before the original comics of the Golden Age, there were comic strip reprints collected in comic book form. The practice dated back decades earlier, of course, but coalesced into the current form when the realities of the Great Depression spawned the modern incarnation of the comic book and its immediate cousin, the Big Little Book.

Everything that came later, though, did so because the acceptance of the visual language had already been worked out. Before Spider-Man and the Hulk, before Superman and Batman, before the Yellow Kid, Little Nemo, and the Brownies, cartoonists and editorial illustrators were working out how to tell a story or simply convey their ideas in this new artform.

Without this sort of work, without these pioneers, we simply wouldn't be where we are today.

CONNECTICUT MIRROR.

Cartoons satirizing Napoleon on the front page of the Connecticut Mirror, dated January 7, 1811.

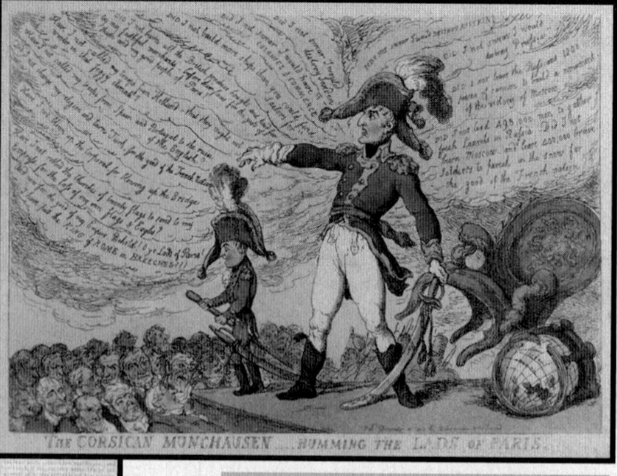

Another Napoleon cartoon, this time dubbing him "The Corsican Munchausen," from the London Strand, December 4, 1813.

"A Consultation at the Medical Board" from The Pasquin or General Satirist (1821).

THE NEW-HAMPSHIRE JOURNAL.

CONCORD, MONDAY, OCTOBER 20, 1828.

Monumental Inscriptions.

These Inscriptions, compiled from authentic sources, but principally from Official Documents, communicated by the Department of War to Congress, on the 25th of January, 1828, are, in this form, submitted to the serious consideration of the American People, under the firm conviction, that the facts embodied in them, ought to, and will, produce a cool and deliberate examination of the qualifications, from Nature and Education, of General ANDREW JACKSON, for the high Civil Station to which he aspires, and to attain which he electioneers with a boldness and pertinacity, unexampled in this Republic. If he shall be found guilty of having ILLEGALLY AND WANTONLY SHED THE BLOOD OF HIS COUNTRYMEN AND FELLOW SOLDIERS, ENTRUST NOT THE LIBERTY AND HAPPINESS OF THIS MOST FREE AND MOST HAPPY COUNTRY TO HIS KEEPING.

JACOB WEBB,

EDWARD LINDSEY,

HENRY LEWIS,

JOHN HARRIS,

David Morrow,

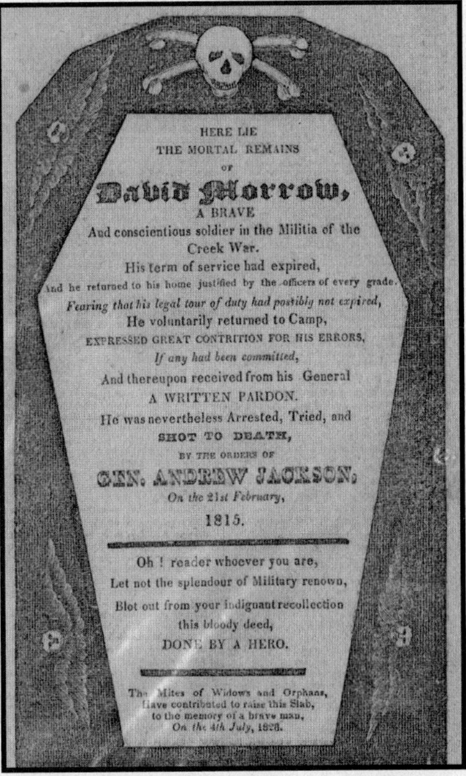

HERE LIE
THE MORTAL REMAINS
OF
David Morrow,
A BRAVE
And conscientious soldier in the Militia of the
Creek War.
His term of service had expired,
And he returned to his home justified by the officers of every grade.
Fearing that his legal tour of duty had possibly not expired,
He voluntarily returned to Camp,
EXPRESSED GREAT CONTRITION FOR HIS ERRORS,
If any had been committed,
And thereupon received from his General
A WRITTEN PARDON.
He was nevertheless Arrested, Tried, and
SHOT TO DEATH,
BY THE ORDERS OF
GEN. ANDREW JACKSON,
On the 21st February,
1815.

Oh! reader whoever you are,
Let not the splendour of Military renown,
Blot out from your indignant recollection
this bloody deed,
DONE BY A HERO.

The Mites of Widows and Orphans,
Have contributed to raise this Slab,
to the memory of a brave man,
On the 4th July, 1828.

Above left, the front page of The New Hampshire Journal, dated October 20, 1828, with multiple tombstone "panels." To the right is a detail of the bottom right tombstone.

THE VICTORIAN AGE

Comic Strips and Books: 1646-1900

A Concise History & Price Index Of The Field As Of 2008

ORIGINS OF EARLY AMERICAN COMIC STRIPS BEFORE THE YELLOW KID

by Robert Lee Beerbohm, Richard Samuel West & Richard D. Olson, PhD ©2009, 2011

(This article was originally created by Doug Wheeler, Robert Beerbohm and Richard D. Olson, PhD for CBPG #32 and continues to be revised annually by the current authors.) We welcome any and all corrections and additions. Special Thanks This Installment To Leonardo De Sa, Terrence Keegen, Gabriel Laderman and Joe Rainone.

Left: "The Burning of Mr. John Rogers," 1646 is the earliest-known North American cartoon printed on paper printed in the earliest children's primer in America.

"God's Revenge For Murder" By John Reynolds, unknown artist, 1656. Earliest-known sequential comic "panel" strip created in the English language.

Left: From his pamphlet Plain Truth 1747 containing Ben Franklin's earliest-known cartoon titled "Heaven Helps Only Those Who Help Themselves" depicting ancient "super hero" Hercules in the upper right corner. Middle: "A Warm Place - Hell", one of two images definitely known to be drawn and engraved by Paul Revere, 1768. Word balloons had wide-spread usage in many cartoons in the 1700s. Right: The Tables Turned by James Gillray, 1797 com-menting on an "invasion" of England by 1400 French convicts. The use of word balloons was wide spread in many parts of the world long before the Yellow Kid's parrot uttered a few words in 1896.

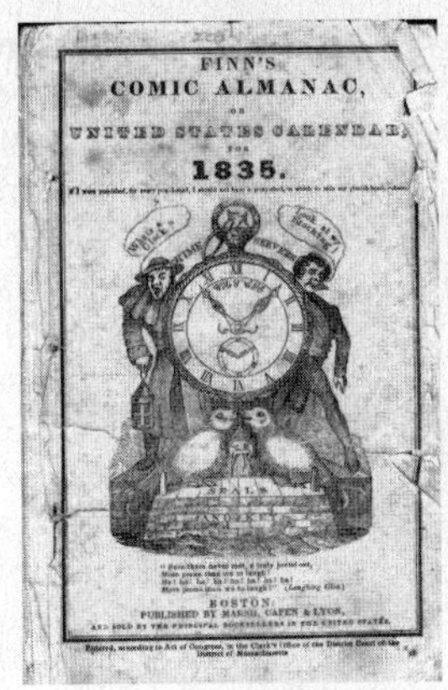

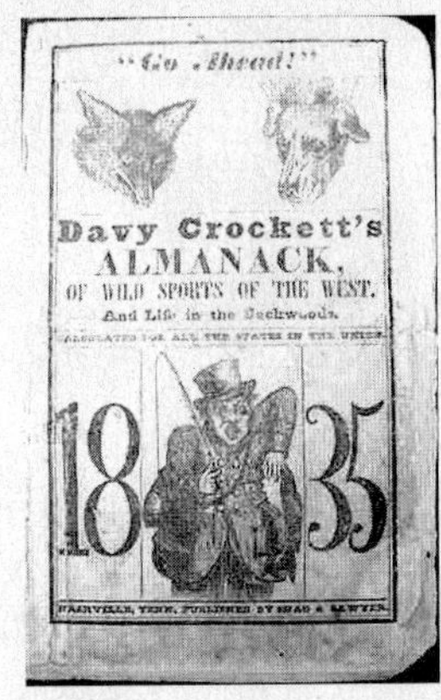

The Comic Almanac(k) debuted in America in 1831 with the earliest-known titles starting heavy with humor and sporting crude woodcut single panel cartoons. Ellm's American Comic Almanac was one of the first. By 1835 Davy Crockett, one of the nation's earliest national folk heroes, began issuing his own version. In the late 1840s the Comic Almanac(k)s began to offer tall-tale sequential comic strips which became somewhat commonplace in the 1850s, fueled by the advent of the California Gold Rush. They were instrumental in the development of the American comic strip and we will be reporting more new finds next year after more research into American folklore.

We have a lot of new discoveries to share with you again this year as amply evident in the price index which follows this year's history lesson. A quantum leap has finally been achieved in the area of introducing the comic book collecting world to *American Comic Almanac(k)s* as well as a huge multitude of American humor periodicals, many of which contained sequential comic strips.

This Victorian Era section is devoted to comic strips and books published during the years the United States expanded across the North American continent, fought a Civil War, shifted from an agrarian to an industrial society, "welcomed" waves of immigrants, and struggled over race, class, religion, temperance, and suffrage - and all of it depicted and satirized by generations of mostly now long-forgotten cartoonists. The social attitudes, beliefs, and conventions of 19th century America, the good as well as the bad, are to be found in abundance. Perhaps the first question to pop into most readers' minds will be, "What, beyond the happenstance of publication date, are Victorian Era comics?"

There has been a long slow-motion evolution of the comic strip which was not invented in America, contrary to many previous history books on the subject. One must examine many aspects of concurrent popular culture. The main aspect that we believe most distinguishes Victorian Era comic strips from those of later eras was the extremely rare use of word balloons within sequential (multi-picture) comic stories. When word balloons were used, it was nearly always within single-panel cartoons. On the occasions when they appeared inside a strip, with very few exceptions, the ballooned dialogue was inconsequential. Nineteenth-century comics tended to place both narration and dialogue beneath comic panels rather than within the panel's borders as they were thought by many to interfere with the art. Many of these comics are to the word balloon-strewn post-Yellow Kid comics of the 20th Century as silent movies are to the later "talkies." Just as sound changed how stories were structured on film, so too did comic strips change when the words were moved from beneath panels to inside them, and dialogue rather than narration drove the story in conjunction with the pictures.

The Victorian Era of actual comic strip books began on different dates in different nations, depending on when the first publication of a sequential comic book on their soil is known to have occurred. For the U.S. this happened when the American literary periodical *Brother Jonathan* printed the 40-page, 195-panel graphic novel *The Adventures of Mr. Obadiah Oldbuck* as a special extra dated September 14, 1842. Almost six decades later, America's Victorian comics came to their end, replaced by the onslaught of Platinum Age books reprinting newspaper strips from Bennett, Hearst, and Pulitzer Sunday comic sections, among many others.

There is considerable overlap between Victorian Era and Platinum Age comic books and strips. Those publications that continued from one century into the next, such as *Puck*, *Judge*, and *Life*, have their pre-1900 issues listed within the Victorian Age section, while their post-1899 issues can be found inside the Platinum Age. Some non-sequential (i.e., single-panel) American comic items existing prior to 1842 are also listed herein, going back to 1795. These belong to what could tentatively be called the Age of Caricature (1770s through 1830s). This was a fertile period for the art in England, when Gillray and Rowlandson, and, later, Cruikshank, Heath, and Seymour were that nation's top cartoonists. During the same period in the U.S., there were no artists who made their living as caricaturists, though William Charles, printer and engraver, did produce about two dozen spirited cartoon broadsides from 1805 to 1820, the most important ones concerning events of the War of 1812.

In addition, one can trace origins of American comic books to the humorous Comic Almanacs which began in earnest in the early 1830s.

The earliest known cartoon-like woodcut printed on paper in North America was in a Puritan children's book first published in 1646. Titled simply *The Burning of Mr. John*

The Comus Offering, 1830 sample page of single panel cartoons using word balloons in every panel. Very Rare.

Rogers, it showed in flaming graphic detail what happens to those who stray from the flock and have to be burned at the stake. Dr. Wertham would have had a field day with that one!

Cartoon broadsides and other single panel images, often using word balloons, appeared from pre-Revolution days through the end of the 19th Century. The earliest known attributed cartoon, designed by the ubiquitous Benjamin Franklin, was "Heaven Helps Only Those Who Help Themselves," which first appeared in his pamphlet *Plain Truth* in 1747.

The most popularly remembered 18th-Century American cartoons are likely Franklin's *"Join or Die"* in 1754, representing the American Colonies as severed snake parts, and *"The Bloody Massacre Perpetrated in King Street"* -- Paul Revere's 1770 depiction of the Boston Massacre, which he pirated from the earlier Henry Pelham broadsheet cartoon *"The Fruits of Arbitrary Power."*

In September 1826, John Warner Barber, New Haven, Ct. (1798-1885) designed and self-published the broadside *The Drunkard's Progress, Or The Direct Road to Poverty, Wretchedness and Ruin* showing in four stages sequentially "The Morning Dram" which is "The Beginning of Sorrow, " "The Grog Shop" with its "Bad Company," "The Confirmed Drunkard" in a state of "Beastly Intoxication," and the "Concluding Scene" with the family being driven off to the alms house. It is an interesting set of cuts, faintly reminiscent of Hogarth. Barber began his career in 1819, age 21, engraving on wood. He devoted most of his career to the multitude of art chores associated with book production. As late as 1870 he was issuing *Barber's Temperance Tracts,* which built upon his 1826 original plus four panels showing the positive effects of living without alcohol.

The first American whose fame was based primarily on his cartoons appears to be David Claypoole Johnston (1798-1865). Johnston provided illustrations for various almanacs, books, and periodicals, including the masthead for *Brother Jonathans.* Most notable of Johnston's comics work was his nine-issue series *Scraps*, which he self-published from 1828 to 1849. This series was highly influenced by George Cruikshank's series *Scraps and Sketches*, which first appeared in 1827. Because of the resemblance, Johnston became known in his day as "the American Cruikshank." Each issue of Johnston's *Scraps* consists of four large folio-sized pages, printed on one side, with nine to twelve single-panel cartoons per page, and each page often organized around a theme. Also popular was his comic album Outlines Illustrative of the Journal of F****** A*** K***** (1835), which parodied passages from the journal of recently published observations on America by British actress Fanny Kemble.

Johnston, himself a failed actor, had an interest in the theater his entire career. In addition to producing a number of prints depicting American actors in famous roles, he collaborated with actor Henry J. Finn to produce the 1831 *(American) Comic Annual*, with Finn as Editor and Johnston as artist, published by Richardson, Lord and Holbrook, Boston. It featured almost 30 full-page Johnston-designed copper engravings and woodcuts. Also that year, Finn solo produced *Finn's Comic Sketch Book*, a twelve-page album similar to Johnston's *Scraps* with upwards of half a dozen single-panel cartoons per page. It was published by Peabody and Co, of New York in business from 1831-1843. (Finn died tragically in a steamboat accident Jan. 13, 1840.)

Perhaps Johnston's most interesting contribution to the history of the comic strip in American came in 1837, when he produced the sequential comic broadside, *Illustrations of the Adventures & Achievements of the Renowned Don Quixote & his Doughty Squire Sancho Panza* (27.4 x 30.4 cm). This blank-reverse engraved print was an elaborate twelve-panel satire of the Andrew Jackson-Van Buren administration. It likely sold for 25 cents, seeing distribution in Boston, New York and Philadelphia. Much later, in 1863, Johnston drew another sequential comic broadside, *The House the Jeff Built* (27.5 x 36.7 cm), a bitter indictment of Jefferson Davis and the Southern slavocracy.

In July 1839, Wilson and Company, a newly formed New York printing firm, began publishing a mammoth newspaper by the name of *Brother Jonathan.* The publisher, J. Gregg Wilson had employed the newspaper format for *Brother Jonathan* to circumvent the higher postage rates imposed on magazines, but *Brother Jonathan* was a newspaper in format only -- it contained not a shred of news, instead specializing in serialized fiction, some of it written by Americans but most of it pirated from foreign sources. Despite the cost savings, the mammoth format had its limitations; when opened it measured a whopping three feet by four feet. So, once *Brother Jonathan* was an established success, Wilson and Day began in January 1841 the simultaneous publication of a magazine-sized quarto edition of *Brother Jonathan* that reprinted the contents of the mammoth edition.

Later that same year, to capitalize on the name recognition

of their successful twin publications, Wilson and Company started issuing book-length *Brother Jonathan Extras* in the same format as the quarto magazine. These reprints are counted among the earliest paperback books in America. Most of the *Extra* numbers were pirated European novels. For example their eighth extra was the first American printing of a Charles Dickens novel. But for their ninth *Extra*, they did something no American publisher had ever done before -- they pirated a graphic novel, Rodolphe Töpffer's *The Adventures of Mr. Obadiah Oldbuck*. By reformatting *Oldbuck* from its original small oblong strip design to fit *Brother Jonathan's* standard quarto format Wilson and Company inadvertently made this edition (alone) of *Obadiah Oldbuck* resemble a modern comic book. *Oldbuck's* arrival on the shores of the New World would directly inspire a wave of American imitators. [*This first Wilson printing of Oldbuck from 1842 was reprinted in same-size limited edition facsimile by the Naples Comicon in 2003. An English translation by Leonardo De Sá of Töpffer's original draft is at leonardo desa.interdinamica. net/comics/lds/]*

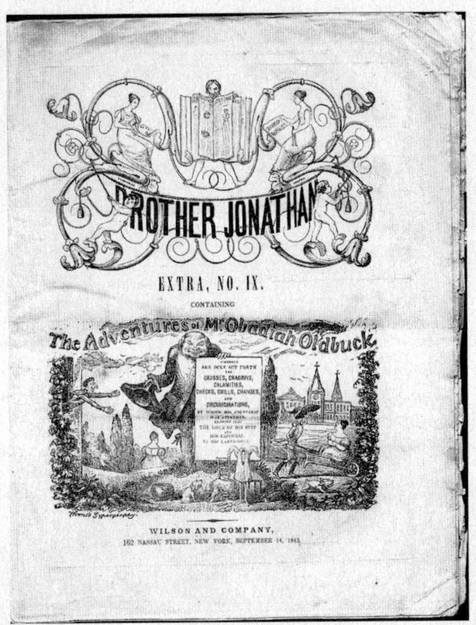

Cover to the subscriber version of the earliest-known sequential comic book published in America, The Adventures of Mr. Obadiah Oldbuck, Sept. 1842, Wilson & Co. New York, originally conceived in 1828 in Geneva Switzerland by creator Rodolphe Töpffer.

Even though in 1904 (in its September 3 edition), *The New York Times* accurately identified the *Brother Jonathan Extra* as the first American comic book as well as Wilson & Co. utilizing Tilt & Bougue's original printing plates as well as still being in print for sale in New York at such a late date, Töpffer has already been largely forgotten in the New World. It is high time Töpffer received credit long overdue as the inventor of the modern comic strip, laying previously long-held myths to rest.

Töpffer (1799-1846) was a playwright, novelist, artist, and teacher from Geneva, Switzerland, who in 1827 had begun producing what he called "picture novels," sharing them with his friends and students. His earliest editions were self-published via lithography on transfer paper as they use the word "autographie" in their imprints. The earliest printers were J. Freydig, Frutiger (1830s) and Schmidt (1840s). These first sequential comic books, scripted in Töpffer's native French language, found their way to Paris and became an instant hit. According to Gombrich in *Art and Illusion* (1960), "Töpffer recognized that he could rely on the reader to supplement from their own lives what was omitted between the panels. This is crucial in the development of the sequential comic strip."

The demand for his comic books soon outstripped the supply, and pirated editions, redrawn by others, were created by Parisian publisher Aubert to capitalize on this. In a world where international copyright conventions did not exist, this was perfectly legal, if morally questionable. Thus, in 1841, London publisher Tilt and Bogue commissioned George Cruikshank to create an English version of Töpffer's *Les Amours de M. Vieux Bois* by pirating Aubert's pirated edition of the Geneva original.

This English translation, co-financed by George Cruikshank himself, sported a new cover page by George's brother Robert, based on a montage of Töpffer's scenes. Confirmation of this fact came when George Cruikshank's personal copy surfaced in auction recently with the inscription "Copied from a French book by my Brother Robert" above the title page with the same scene. This is the translation that was reprinted by America's Wilson and Company as *The Adventures of Mr. Obadiah Oldbuck* utilizing the original Tilt and Bogue printing plates.

Tilt and Bogue followed up their success by translating into English two additional stories of Töpffer's seven published graphic novels: *Beau Ogleby*, circa 1843 (originally Histoire de M. Jabot), and *Bachelor Butterfly* two years later (from *Histoire de M. Cryptogame)*. David Bogue also published picture-story strip books by John Leighton using the pseudonym Luke Limner. He wrote and drew beautiful comic books titled *London Out of Town or The Adventures of the Browns At The Seaside; Comic Art-Manufactures; and The Ancient Story of the Old Dame and Her Pig* starting in 1847, but none of these seem to have ever been republished in America. They follow a definite Töpffer influence. This growing body of comic book production was made easier by the spreading understanding of transfer paper lithography, otherwise the panels would have had to have been drawn and lettered mirror reverse. Gombrich referred to Töpffer's comic books as "the innocent ancestors of today's manufactured dreams... everywhere in these countless episodes of almost surrealist inconsequence we find a mastery of physiognomic characterization which sets the standard for such influential humorous draftsmen in the 19th century as Wilhelm Busch in Germany."

A Register of The New York City Book Trades 1821-1842 by Sidney F. & Elizabeth Stege12, Huttner (The Bibliographical Society of America, NYC, 1993) mentions Benjamin H. Day bought into *Brother Jonathan*'s publisher,

Wilson and Company, in this year, becoming at some point an equal partner with owner J. Gregg Wilson. The Register lists them both as publishers of *Brother Jonathan* at the same address of 162 Nassau Street. Other historical artifacts state Day eventually became sole-owner and publisher. Exactly when has not yet been determined, though we have figured out with certainly before 1850 .

The Adventures of Obadiah Oldbuck, rare newly discovered 4th edition from mid 1850s. Says now "Published at Brother Jonathan Offices." Art & Story now accredited to the pseudonym "Timothy Crayon" - see Peter Piper ad previous page.

This is the same Benjamin H. Day who started the first successful penny newspaper in 1833, *The (New York) Sun*, transforming it in four short years into the largest circulation daily in the world at that time. He sold out his ownership of the Sun to his brother-in-law during the financial "panic" of 1837, a mistake he regretted the rest of his life. He re-emerged heavily involved in *Brother Jonathan* definitely by 1840 and as a partner by 1841. *Brother Jonathan's* offices were right next door to Tamany Hall. (See the first 20 minutes of the 2002 movie *Gangs of New York* to visualize the period atmosphere and their customer base.) According to *The Brothers Harper* by Eugene Exmen (Harper & Row, 1965), on page 125, "*Brother Jonathan...* offered in its weekly edition and also in special supplements very cheap reprints of English novels. In effect, it began a price-cutting war against the older established 'pirates' among the book publishers..." Day, it appears, had found the perfect project on which to build a new empire.

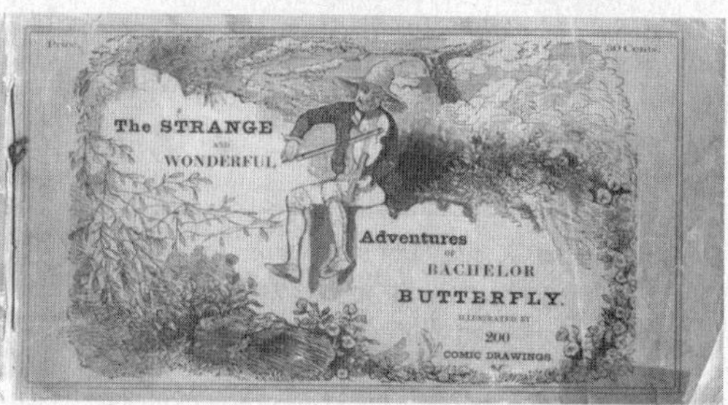

The Strange and Wonderful Adventures of Bachelor Butterfly *by Rodolphe Töpffer (New York, 1846) was America's 3rd comic book; Wilson & Company's second comic book, this time out staying with the original European format.*

Desirous of repeating the success they had with *Obadiah Oldbuck*, Wilson and Company published the first American edition of *Bachelor Butterfly* in 1846. Three years later, they reformatted *Obadiah Oldbuck* back into its original British shape using lithography, dropping a handful of comic panels and altering the text to hide these deletions. Soon thereafter, they published other comic books for a steadily growing market that they had helped to stimulate. In recognition of their significant role in the dissemination of sequential comics, Wilson and Company deserve to be remembered as the first comic book publisher in America.

Back in Europe, perhaps inspired by his involvement with Töpffer's *Obadiah Oldbuck*, George Cruikshank soon created several sequential comic books of his own. These too found their way to America. *The Bachelor's Own Book*, published first in Britain in 1844, became the second known U.S. published sequential comic book when it was reprinted by Burgess, Stringer and Company the following year. Next was Cruikshank's masterpiece *The Bottle*, the Hogarthian-style tale of a man whose addiction to alcohol brings himself and his family to ruin. After debuting in London in 1847, it was reprinted the same year in a British-American co-publication between David Bogue and Americans Wiley and Putnam. Both printings were in huge folio form, available in either black and white or professionally hand-tinted versions. In 1848, the story saw American print again, this time in smaller form, placed at the front of the otherwise prose volume *Temperance Tales; Or, Six Nights with the Washing-tonians*. It continued to be reprinted by a variety of publishers into the early 20th Century. *The Bottle* was even reproduced onto painted glass slides and then projected by magic lantern onto a screen for the moral edification of temperance audiences. *The Drunkard's Children, Cruikshank's sequel to The Bottle*, was issued July 1, 1848 as a British-American-Australian co-publishing venture, but was less successful, and had not nearly as many reprints.

The most clearly sequential, as well as fun, of George Cruikshank's comic books was *The Tooth-Ache*, first issued in London in 1849. It was reprinted in America later that same year by Philadelphia map maker J.L. Smith. An additional concurrent version was also issued from Boston.

When closed, this booklet appears an unassuming 5-1/4 inches tall by 3-1/4 inches wide. Its striking feature is that the book folds open accordion style, stretching the entire 43-panel story along one single strip of paper, which when fully extended is seven feet, three inches long! *The Tooth-Ache* was issued in both black and white and professionally hand-colored editions. Abridged editions of the story, printed in black and white and with a "normal" page-turning rather than foldout presentation, appeared inside promotional give-away comics issued by American companies in the 1880s.

Thanks to Töpffer, Cruikshank, and a handful of enterprising American publishers, the 1840s should be remembered as the decade when America first fell in love with the comics.

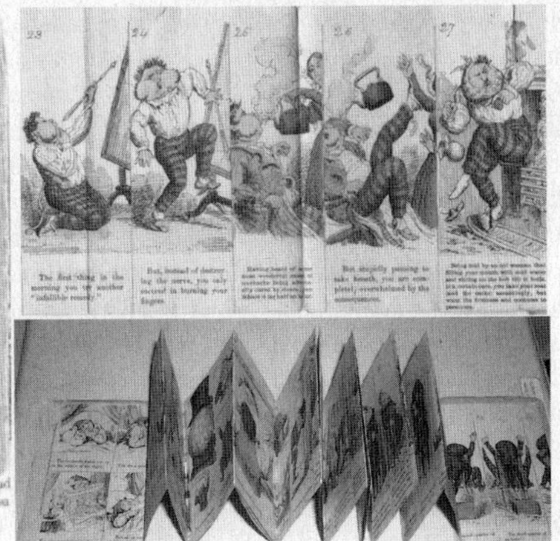

The Tooth-Ache by George Cruickshank 1849 © J. L. Smith, Philadelphia, PA. First American edition opens up accordian-like into a single continuous paper strip 7 feet, 3 inches long!

It had seen the U.S. publication of six sequential comic books, as well as the importation of other comics with foreign imprints. America's growing interest in graphic humor was further stimulated by the growth of two other fields: the cartoon broadside and the humor magazine.

As mentioned before, the cartoon broadside had been a part of the American scene since pre-Revolution days, but it did not flourish until stone lithography (introduced in 1818 and in wide use by the 1830s) made the reproduction of images relatively fast and cheap. From the early 1830s into the mid 1840s, the leading producer of cartoon broadsides in America was New York printer H. R. Robinson, who either drew his own cartoons or employed others, especially E. W. Clay, to do it. Clay is notable for having produced the first sequential comic broadside in America. Published in 1834 and entitled, "This Is the House that Jack Built" (50 x 32 cm), the nine-panel parody of the classic nursery rhyme was an attack on the Jackson Administration. The dominant theme of American cartoon broadsides was political, as befitted a nation where politics was the leading spectator sport. As the American electorate grew increasingly educated and prosperous, the demand for cartoon broadside also increased. During the 1840s, lithographers in New York, Boston, and Philadelphia, entered the field to satisfy that demand. The best known of these, Nathaniel Currier, later Currier and Ives, joined the fray in 1848. The firm employed many artists, but its chief political cartoonist was Louis Maurer and its chief comic artist was Thomas Worth.

Except for the three previously cited sequential cartoon broadsides, nearly all of the cartoon broadsides published in America from 1832 to 1876, its dominant era, were single panels. From the 1860s onward, broadside series on a single comic theme became common, the most famous being Thomas Worth's *Darktown* series. These can be loosely categorized as sequential comics since they employed the same characters and formed a story of sorts when hung together on a wall, as was the publisher's expectation. Sequential art or not, the cartoon broadsides nearly always employed the speech balloons that later became one of the defining characteristic of the American comic strip.

During the same decade that sequential comics and cartoon broadsides were growing in popularity, the illustrated American humor magazine made its debut. The British comic weekly *Punch*, founded in 1841, was an immediate success, both in England and the United States. It was a handsomely printed quarto, initially twelve pages and later sixteen, with a repeating cover design, backed by a page of small advertisements, humorous text interspersed with comic spot art, and a single panel full-page cartoon. A significant subset of *Punch*'s subscriber base was located in the U.S., to which thousands of copies were exported on an ongoing trans-Atlantic basis. Inevitably, enterprising American publishers attempted to repulse this invader with a home-grown comic weekly. The first, *Yankee Doodle*, came to town (New York, that is) on October 10, 1846, for one year. *Judy* (November 28, 1846 to February 20, 1847), *The John-Donkey* (January 1 to October 21, 1848), and *The Elephant* (January 22 to February 19, 1848) soon followed. None of them was successful, but all of them continued to feed the growing American interest in comic art.

By the late 1840s, comic art was flourishing in America. The conditions were right for the production of the earliest known American-created sequential comic book. Brothers James and Donald Read, who had worked for a time as cartoonists on *Yankee Doodle*, were the creators of *Journey to the Gold Diggins by Jeremiah Saddlebags*. This spirited send-up of the California gold rush craze was published in June 1849 by Stringer and Townsend, the late publishers of *Judy*, and, soon after, by U. P. James of Cincinnati. This Töpffer-influenced comic book chronicles the adventures of its hero *Jeremiah Saddlebags* in his get-rich-quick quest for gold in California. It is highly sought by collectors of Western Americana. Interestingly, the back cover of the Stringer and Townsend edition carries an advertisement for *Rose and Gertrude* - a Genevese Story, one of Rodolphe Töpffer's non-comics prose novels.

Stringer and Townsend was making something of a name for itself as a publisher of comic art. It will be remembered that it was one of the 1845 participants in the American publication of *The Bachelor's Own Book*. And, then, in 1846-47, it published *Judy*. Its decision to issue *Jeremiah Saddlebags* was all in due course.

The Gold Rush proved to be a gold mine for American comic artists. Aside from being a featured topic in the 1849 edition of David Claypool Johnston's *Scraps*, in comic almanacs, and in Currier cartoon prints, it was the subject of several other significant sequential series. The first, *The Adventures of Mr. Tom Plump* (a fat man who nearly starves to death in his failed attempt at California Gold riches), saw print in 1850. The second, *The Adventures of Jeremiah Old-Pot* (a twelve-part burlesque narrative of a New York businessman who attempts to get rich selling tin in price-inflated California), ran throughout 1852 in *Yankee Notions*. Though the narrative was distinctly American in its humor, the artwork was probably German in origin. *Yankee Notions'* Publisher, T. W. Strong, built his business on recycling old woodcuts with new captions attached. It should be noted that the *Old-Pot* series, borrowed or otherwise, was the first sequential art to appear in an American humor magazine. *Yankee Notions*, published from 1852 to 1875, also has the distinction of being the first comic monthly published in America.

"Moses Keyser the Bowery Bully's Trip to the California Gold Mines," was a 13-page comic story that appeared in *Elton's Californian Comic All-My-Nack* for 1850. It was reprinted at least twice in the circa 1850-51 booklet *The Clown, Or The Banquet of Wit* and later again in *Sam Slick's Comic Almanac* in 1857. *The Clown* is also notable as the earliest known anthology of sequential comics, with the bonus that each multi-panel story is by a different artist. Many of the artists are as yet unidentified, and how much of it is original American material versus that reprinted from Europe is presently unknown. But verified are cartoons by George Cruikshank, Elton (American), the Read brothers, Grandville (French), and Richard Doyle (British). The Doyle contribution reprints the comics story "Brown, Jones and Robinson and How They Went to a Ball," which originally saw print in the August 24, 1850 issue of *Punch*. This is the first known American appearance of these Doyle characters, and was almost certainly pirated.

Richard Doyle's *The Foreign Tour of Messrs. Brown, Jones, and Robinson* is basically a travelogue in illustrated form, told via humorous episodes, part sequential cartoon sequences, and part snapshots of moments jumping forward in time. This halfway sequential format was ideal for most 19th Century cartoonists, who, with rare exception, had not quite grasped how to maintain a single sequential story for much longer than two dozen successive panels. Doyle had simplified Töpffer's formula in a manner most artists could attempt to emulate. Episodes of "*Brown, Jones, and Robinson*" originally appeared in *Punch* in 1850, until a dispute between the Roman Catholic Doyle and Punch's editors over an anti-Papal joke ended with Doyle's resignation. Doyle redrew and expanded the story into a single album, first seeing print in 1854 from British publisher Bradbury and Evans.

New York Publisher D. Appleton brought the album to America, reprinting it in 1860, 1871, and 1877. Next, Dick and Fitzgerald of New York pirated Doyle's story sometime in the early 1870s. Doyle's format from *Foreign Tour* was emulated again and again. Examples include: the 1857 *Mr. Hardy Lee, His Yacht*, by Charles Stedman; the 1860s- 1870s G. W. Carleton-published *Our Artist In...* series, set in various Latin American countries; the Augustus Hoppin 1870s sketch novels *On the Nile, Crossing the Atlantic*, and *Ups and Downs on Land and Water*; and *Life* founder John Ames Mitchell's 1881 (pre-Life) *The Summer School of Philosophy at Mt. Desert*. D. Appleton, the official, authorized American publisher of *Foreign Tour*, even commissioned an American artist - Toby - to create a sequel comic album involving Doyle's characters visiting the U.S. and Canada, published in 1872 as *The American Tour of Messrs Brown, Jones and Robinson*. In terms of influencing the development of mid-19th Century American comics, Doyle's *Foreign Tour* ranks with the works of Töpffer, Cruikshank, and Busch.

Doyle was also the author of an equally popular earlier cartoon series for Punch, titled, *In Manners and Customs of Ye Englyshe, Mr. Pips Hys Diary*, which was reprinted in 1849. In this work, Doyle told his story using a deliberately primitive almost stick-figure art style, combined with the Hogarthian structure of large single panel cartoons leaping forward in time with each picture.

Manners and Customs of Ye Harvard Studente, which ran in the first year of the *Harvard Lampoon* (1876-current), shows the clearest influence. The series by then stu-

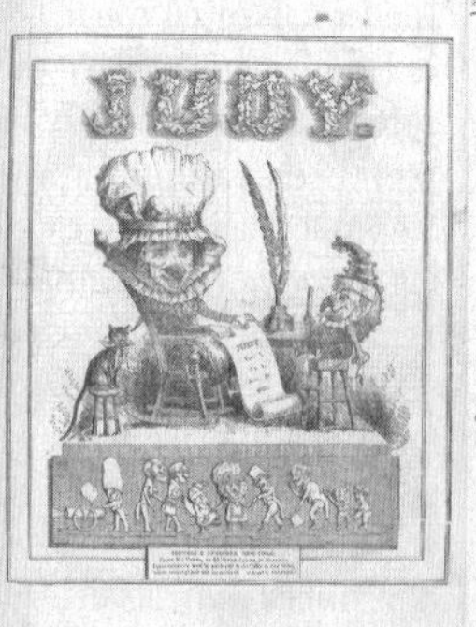

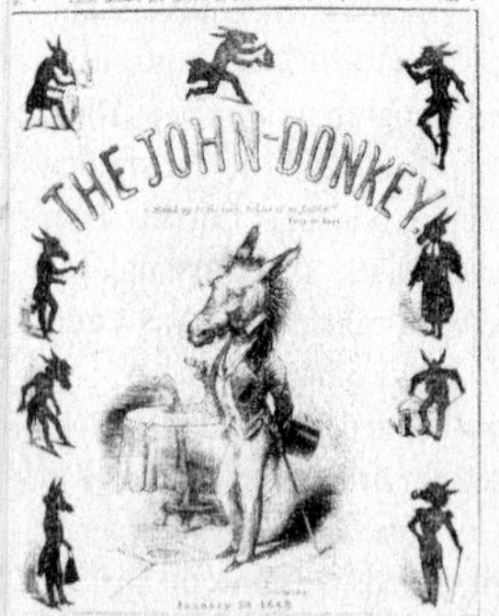

A few samples of the many humor magazines of the mid-1800s which ran cartoons. Wide-spread acceptance of the comic strip slowly evolved over the decades. Right: ***Yankee Doodle*** *#30, this title was the first American comic weekly which ran Oct 1846-Oct 1847; Second: Judy #1 ran Nov 28-Feb 20, 1847; Third:* ***The John-Donkey*** *#4 ran January-October 1848. Fourth:* ***The Lantern*** *#21, May 29, 1851 title ran Jan. 10, 1852-July 1853.*

dent Francis Gilbert Attwood was collected in 1877 by Houghton Mifflin. Attwood followed it up with *Manners and Customs of Ye Bostonians*, again in the pages of the *Harvard Lampoon*, but it is unknown whether that series was ever reprinted in book form. Attwood later became one of the regular artists in *Life*.

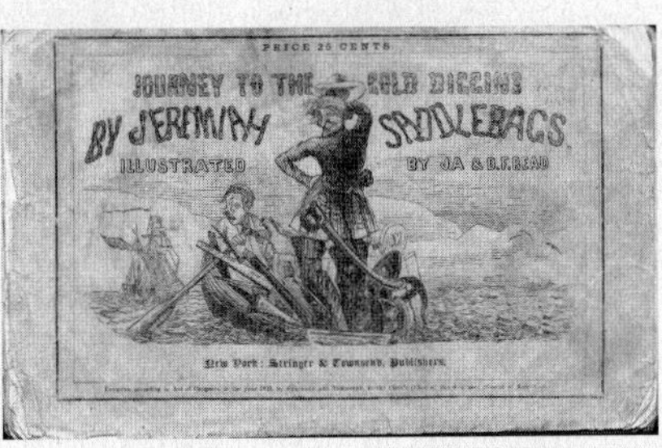

Journey to the Gold Diggins By Jeremiah Saddlebags, June 1849, so far the earliest known sequential comic book by American creators, J.A. and D.F. Read. Above: a couple sample pages. Note similarity to Töpffer's comics especially **Bachelor Butterfly**

The Extraordinary and Mirth-provoking Adventures by Sea and Land of Oscar Shanghai, inspired by Bachelor Butterfly, was issued May 1855 by Garrett and Company, Publishers, No. 18 Ann Street, New York. Oscar Shanghai has many misadventures including being swallowed by a whale, making a trip in a flying machine to Africa, where he is shot out of a huge bow by a "Black Prince" for refusing to marry a local princess of color. After more adventures, he makes it back home.

Oscar Shanghai's first publisher was confirmed in 2002 with the discovery of a very rare 36-page catalog from 1856 of books, pamphlets and prints handled by B.H. Day (successor to Wilson and Company) who was by this time publishing *Brother Jonathan* as a twice-a-year holiday pictorial only. The catalog has a few crossover advertisement pages from an associate publisher, Garrett and Company. This rediscovered treasure, which sold for $750 in 2002, contains within a sequential strip of one panel per page over 32 of those pages titled "*Peter Piper in Bengal,*" by John Tenniel, reprinted from four 1853 issues of *Punch*. In the narrative, Peter Piper tries his hand hunting all different kinds of wild game with many misadventures.

Amongst the many varied types of "Cheap Books" for sale in this rare catalog are the comic books *The Adventures of Obadiah Oldbuck, Bachelor Butterfly's Queer Love Adventures and Misfortunes*, and *The Fortunes of Ferdinand Flipper*, plus the aforementioned *Oscar Shanghai*. All were priced at "25¢ per copy, postage free, refunds paid out in stamps." There is also an advertisement for a comic book entitled *A Day's Sport - Or, Hunting Adventures of S. Winks Wattles, a Shopkeeper, Thomas Titt, a "legal gent," and Major Nicholas Noggin, a Jolly Good Fellow Generally* by Henry L. Stephens (1824-1882) of Philadelphia.

Stephens, later the political cartoonist for *Vanity Fair* (New York, 1859-1863) and a leading children's book illustrator, produced his first work, *Illustrations of the Poets: From Passages in the Life of Little Billy Vidkins*, a small wrappered album of 32 comic woodcuts, in 1849. It was first published by S. Robinson, of Philadelphia, and reprinted with variant titles several times in the 1850s including *Yankee Notions*. It is likely that Little *Billy Vidkins* was printed before *Jeremiah Saddlebags*, though more research is needed before making this claim.

Garrett and Company was also responsible for the 1856 publication of *The Sad Tale of the Courtship of Chevalier Slyfox-Wikof, Showing His Heart-Rending Astounding and Most Wonderful Love Adventures with Fanny Elssler and Miss Gambol*. This book parodied the very public relationship between the then-famous wealthy American aristocrat Henry Wikoff, and the even more famous European actress/ dancer Fanny Elssler. It is dated thusly because Wikoff's memoir is pictured in the comic book.

Apparently in late 1854 Garrett and Company formed a brief two-year partnership with Dick and Fitzgerald, officially becoming Garrett, Dick and Fitzgerald in November 1856, while continuing to operate out of the same 18 Ann Street address in New York. One month later they issued Richard Doyle's British published graphic novel *The Foreign Tour of Messrs. Brown, Jones, and Robinson*, reformatting it into the same oblong shape as Garrett's two prior comic books (which in turn were formatted in imitation of Töpffer's albums). This information came to light just this year. The interested scholar is encouraged to check out the new listings for Garrett's The Home Circle in the index.

In 1858, Garrett appears to have dropped out, leaving Dick and Fitzgerald alone with the former's book stock, his place of business, and most importantly, the printing plates for his comic books. For reasons unknown, Dick and Fitzgerald steered away from reprinting Garrett's comic books for more than a decade. But in the 1870s they resumed publication - not only of the three albums published by Garrett, but also of *Obadiah Oldbuck and Bachelor Butterfly* from Wilson and Company, and *Ferdinand Flipper* from *Brother Jonathan* - all of them also making use of the original printing plates. The inclusion of books from *Brother Jonathan*, Wilson and Company, and Garrett and Company all within the same promotional Peter Piper catalog from B.H. Day suggests that these early publishers of comic books had many over-lapping fields of interest,, and that Dick and Fitzgerald became the inheritor/acquirer of all of it. Dick and Fitzgerald also reprinted in the 1870s the earlier William T. Peter published *Ichabod Academicus* (how that title might have connected, if at all, with B.H. Day's business remains unclear). We can now say, though, that an evolving group of a handful of publishers was responsible, over a span of 46 years, beginning with the very first graphic novel published in America in 1842, for keeping in print in America a cluster of slightly over half a dozen graphic novels.

Yankee Notions #1, January, 1852. This title began the first sequential comic strips in an American humor magazine, The Adventures of Jerimiah Old-Pot.

Tebbel's *History of Book Publishing* in the US (vol. 1, pages 351-2) states that Burgess and Stringer was dissolved in late 1840s and became two firms, Stringer and Townsend, and Burgess and Garrett. Burgess retired in 1850 and his nephew William Brisbane Dick stepped into the partnership, whereupon the new company was renamed Garrett, Dick and Fitzgerald. Garrett retired in 1851 and the firm became Dick and Fitzgerald. The firm persisted under that name until 1917.

Collections reprinting cartoons from Punch saw print in the U.S., such as *Merry Pictures by the Comic Hands*, imported for the 1859 Christmas Season, plus various John Leech, George Du Maurier, and Phil May books which appeared from the 1850s through 1910s. Finally, many American weekly newspapers and weekly and monthly magazines, humorous and non-humorous, reprinted cartoons from Punch. Such inclusions often became a prelude to switching to original material by American artists, if that publication find's cartoon section find American cartoonists of sufficient talent.

Harper's Monthly, the leading American monthly, was a prime example. Soon after it commenced publication in November 1850, it began to carry a few pages of single panel cartoons reprinted from *Punch* at the rear of each issue. This evolved into reprinting sequential comic pages from the British periodical *Town Talk*, and then, starting December 1853, original sequential comics by the great Frank Bellew.

Bellew (1828-1888) should be regarded as the "Father of American Sequential Comics." Born in India, educated in France and England, he emigrated to America in 1850. His earliest work shows an influence from Doyle, but he rapidly developed his own unique art style. Bellew's comics, both sequential and single panel, graced nearly every American comic periodical published from the 1850s into the 1870s.

A month after the publication of the anonymous first installment of *Jeremiah Old-Pot* in *Yankee Notions*, Bellew began contributing his six-part, 18-panel comic series, *"Mr. Blobb in Search of a Physician"* to *The Lantern*, a New York comic weekly published from January 10, 1852 to July 2, 1853. The series ran in six of the nine issues published from January 31 through March 27, 1852. This was followed in April and May by the 16-panel, three-issue comic sequence *"Mr. Bulbear's Dream"*, which concluded with the main character awakened from his dream by falling out of bed, exactly like *Little Nemo* would do five decades later.

These two series were just the beginning for Bellew, who contributed a voluminous amount of work to the *New York Picayune* (1850-1860) (which he also edited for a time in 1857-58), *The Comic Monthly* (1859-1881), *Momus*, an 1860 comic daily, *The Phunniest of Awl* (1864-1867) (which he also edited), *Punchinello* (1870), and *Wild Oats* (1870-1881), to name the most prominent.

The Comic Monthly deserves special mention. Started in March 1859 and published by J. C. Haney and Company, of 119 Nassau Street, New York, *The Comic Monthly* was a profusely illustrated 16-page folio, the same size as *Harper's Weekly*. It focused its graphic satire on politics, the theater, and the comedy of everyday life. A preponderance of the purely comic satire took the form of sequential art. Here are random samplings of highlights from issues from 1860:

• February: "A Day of Humiliation, Fasting, Supplication, and Prayer (four panels, unsigned), "New Year Calls under the Influence of Hard Times" (twelve panels, unsigned), "Young Trouble-some; or, Master Jacky's Holidays" (nineteen panels covering three and half pages, unsigned);

• April: "Four Years After Marriage" (sixteen panels, unsigned), "Our Masked Ball" (twelve panel centerspread, Bellew), "Trials of a Witness" (eight panels, Bellew);

• May: "Precocities of Young Springles" (seven panels, unsigned), "The Fight for the Championship" (twenty-four panel centerspread, Bellew), "Steam Applied to Music" (three panels, unsigned), "The Course of True Love" (four panels, Bellew);

• June: "Further Particulars of the Fight" (nine panel cover, Bellew), "The Man Who Went to See the Fight" (twelve panels, unsigned);

• July: "Explaining American Politics to an Intelligent Foreigner" (twelve panels, unsigned), "The Meerschaum Mania" (two panels, Bellew), "The Art of Stump Speaking" (ten panels, unsigned), "Our Little Friend, Tom Noddy" (three panels, unsigned); "The Japanese in New York" (twelve panel centerspread, Bellew), "The Observant Child" (three panels, unsigned), "Mr. Dibbs Goes to Pike's Peak and Comes Back Again" (fourteen panel back cover, unsigned);

• September: "The Zouave Fever" (four panel cover, unsigned), "Mr. Lupell" (two panels, Bellew), "The Prince of Wales in America" (twenty-four panel centerspread, J. H. Howard), "D'ye Think It's True?" (three panels, Bellew);

• October: "The Duties of the Wide Awake" (four panels, Bellew), "Our Charley (two panels, unsigned), "The Three Young Friends" (eighteen panel back cover, unsigned);

• November: "The Hanlon's (sic) At Home" (nine panel

back cover, unsigned);

• December: "The Target Excursion" (seventeen panel centerspread, signed with an unidentifiable monogram); "The Sporting Critic" two panels, Bellew).

The Comic Monthly also published many multi-panel cartoons grouped under a single heading, which were not strictly sequential in nature. Bellew was the monthly's chief artist, assisted by Thomas Nast, A. R Waud, and others. Some of the unsigned art was certainly by Bellew, some by journeymen artists, and some of it pirated from European journals.

The Comic Monthly was not the first folio-sized humor magazine. Those laurels go to *The New York Picayune,* which began as a newspaper, switched to a folio in 1856, adopted *Punch's* format for thirty-five issues in 1857-58, and returned to a folio for the remainder of its run.

Frank Leslie's *Budget of Fun*, the greatest of the folio monthlies, began in January 1859 and was published until June 1878. Its star cartoonist during the sixties was William Newman (c. 1817-1870), one of the founding artists of Punch. As we have noted, *The Comic Monthly* began two months later.

Frank Leslie was born Henry Cart in Ipswich, England in 1821. He became a very skilled engraver before coming over to America in 1948. He first worked as manager for P.T. Barnum's *New York Illustrated News* for several years. in 1850 he legally had his name changed to Frank Leslie. He died in 1880 and his wife continued the numerous publications he was publishing. Many of Frank Leslie's periodicals had a lot of sequental comic art.

Quarto-sized monthlies to compete with the successful *Yankee Notions* were also proliferating. *Nick-Nax* was the first (May 1856 to December 1875), followed by *Phunny Phellow* (October 1859- 1876) and *Merryman's Comic Monthly* (January 1863 to December 1875), to name the most prominent.

Enterprising publishers continued to attempt an American comic weekly in the style of *Punch*. The most notable efforts, *Vanity Fair* (1859-1863), *Mrs. Grundy* (1865), and *Punchinello* (1870), were distinguished but unsuccessful.

Nearly all of them, weeklies and monthlies, to varying degrees, featured sequential comic art. By the time of the American Civil War, sequential comic art was a part of the American graphic landscape.

While Bellew stood out for his sequential comics, Thomas Nast (1840-1902) brought a new style to American political cartoons, of which he is regarded the father. Even though he created several sequential strips early in his career (especially for Nick-Nax in 1859), Nast made his name in the pages of the national news periodical, *Harper's Weekly*, for which he worked from 1862 until 1886. Nast was influenced more by the dark wood engravings of Franco-German illustrator Gustave Dore than by the cartoonists of *Punch*. His somber cartoons were a novelty in American cartooning. Nast in the pages of *Harper's Weekly* (and Newman in the pages of the *Budget of Fun*) popularized the extravagant double-page folio-sized cartoon, which had no precedent in European or American cartooning, save for the separately published cartoon broadsides. This format would come to full maturity after 1876 in the pages of *Puck* (1876-1918) and then *Judge* (1881-1947).

As Nast grew in prominence and success, American cartoonists increasingly emulated him. U.S. humor publications evolved towards an amalgamation of Nast and Punch, rather than sheer imitation of the latter. After the War, with Nast's style of cartoons more entrenched in American readers' minds, efforts to launch *Punch*-like American periodicals floundered quickly. *Mrs. Grundy*, ironically most famous for its cover design by Nast, died after a mere twelve issues (running July 8 to September 23, 1865). *Punchinello* (April 2 to December 24, 1870) struggled nine months before its backers gave up. *Punchinello* had been financed by Tammany Hall politicians Tweed and Sweeney, as counter-propaganda against Nast's ongoing assault upon their corruption. They attempted to buy and threaten Nast into silence, to no avail.

American comics continued their pull away from Anglo-Franco imitation with the infusion of a third major European influence – the German humor magazine. The German-American community swelled significantly after the failed revolution of 1848. These émigrés brought with them a culture of humor, expressed most flamboyantly in their native humor magazines, the most famous being *Kladderadatsch, Fliegende Blätter*, and *Münchener Bilderbogen*. As high in quality, as were the graphic artists who contributed to them, one German comic artist in particular excelled beyond the rest, his stories breaking out and crossing over into English language translations, the demand for which resulted in numerous printings. This artist, of course, was Heinrich Christian Wilhelm Busch (1832-1908).

Busch's work appeared in English in the 1860s in both British and American periodicals, often uncredited. For example, four of Busch's strips appeared in English in the pages of *Merryman's Monthly* in 1864, while in 1879 his graphic story "Fipps der Affe" was serialized across a 10-issue run of Puck as "Troddledums the Simian." The earliest known English language appearance of Busch in book form was *The Flying Dutchman, or The Wrath of Herr von Stoppelnoze*, in 1862, from New York publisher G. W. Carleton. Carleton not only pirated Busch's strip, but went so far as to credit the entire story to American

FRANK LESLIE'S
BUDGET OF FUN

Frank Leslie's Budget of Fun#19 June 1860 sports a comic strip on its front cover.

poet John G. Saxe, with Busch's cartoons mere illustrations accompanying Saxe's prose!

The next known English language Busch book was **A** *Bushel of Merry Thoughts*, an 1868 London-published anthology collecting various Busch strips. Some of these same stories later appeared in the U.S.-published *The Mischief Book* (1880), newly translated and with a few more Busch tales added. One of these additions was "Hans Huckebein," a tale of a mischievous pet raven who in the end gets drunk and accidentally hangs himself. It became, at least in the States, Busch's second most popular sequential comic story. The unrepentant bird was promoted to title character in two later collections: the rare *Hookeybeak the Raven and Other Tales* in 1878 and *Jack Huckaback, the Scapegrace Raven*, circa 1888. There were also at least three trade card series in the 1870s and 1880s that reprinted the ending sequence, as *Fritz Spindle-Shanks, The Raven Black.*

The most popular Busch tale, though, was easily Max und Moritz, which in the U.S. saw print as *Max and Maurice - A Juvenile History in Seven Tricks*. Published in Boston in 1871, this English language version saw at minimum of 60 reprintings by the century's end, plus countless more printings thereafter. A separate British translation debuted in 1874, under the title *Max and Moritz*. It is well known that the later Rudolph Dirks comic strip series, Katzenjammer Kids, beginning in late 1897, was based on *Max und Moritz*.

According to documents found by comics historian Alfredo Castelli, *Katzenjammer Kids* may not have been pirated as has been assumed but was licensed by William Randolph Hearst instead. Hearst's *New York Journal* was published in different language editions for New York City's immigrant communities. In the German edition, the strip was published under its original name, *Max und Moritz*. Numerous other translations of Busch were published in America - too many to name in this article. Several can be found in the Victorian Age Price Index.

The most significant humor magazine of the 1870s, prior to the founding of the German-language *Puck* in 1876, was *Wild Oats* (1870-1881), which for part of its run also published a German-language edition, *Schnedereddeng*. In terms of the quality of its cartoons and comics, this New York City publication was in 1872 at an artistic level *Puck* would not achieve until 1880. Published by Winchell and Small (later Collin and Small) and distributed through the New York News Company, *Wild Oats* carried a cross-section of old and new generation comic artists, from the more established W. M. Avery, Frank Beard, Frank Bellew, E.S. Bisbee, Michael Angelo Woolf, and Thomas Worth, to up-and-comers such as Livingston Hopkins,

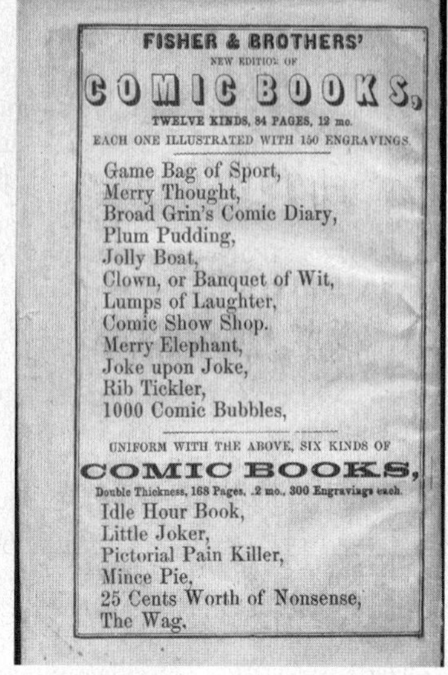
FISHER & BROTHERS'
NEW EDITION OF
COMIC BOOKS,
TWELVE KINDS, 84 PAGES, 12 mo.
EACH ONE ILLUSTRATED WITH 150 ENGRAVINGS.

Game Bag of Sport,
Merry Thought,
Broad Grin's Comic Diary,
Plum Pudding,
Jolly Boat,
Clown, or Banquet of Wit,
Lumps of Laughter,
Comic Show Shop.
Merry Elephant,
Joke upon Joke,
Rib Tickler,
1000 Comic Bubbles,

UNIFORM WITH THE ABOVE, SIX KINDS OF
COMIC BOOKS,
Double Thickness, 168 Pages, 12 mo., 300 Engravings each.

Idle Hour Book,
Little Joker,
Pictorial Pain Killer,
Mince Pie,
25 Cents Worth of Nonsense,
The Wag.

Earliest-known use of the description COMIC BOOKS dates from the early 1850s.

Frederick Burr Opper, Palmer Cox, and James A. Wales.

Wild Oats began carrying sequential comic strips as early as #26, dated March 14, 1872, with the Livingston Hopkins strip pictured on the next page (we do not know anything yet about the first 25 issues). The very next issue has a Worth double-page spread titled "The Political Humpty Dumpty... Horace Greeley" told in eleven panels plus the sequential fictional "Graphic Account of the Assassination of Queen Victoria" and "Love As the Angels Love." "The Doings of the Japanese Embassy At Washington" related in twelve panels by W. M. Avery follows up in #28 April 11, 1872. An unknown hand drew "The Physiology of Moving" in six panels in #30. Hopkins returns with a beautiful intense 28-panel double-page spread in #31 May 23. Hopkins and Worth alternated for many issues with sequential comic strips on baseball, horse racing and other pertinent subjects of the day. In #45 December 5, 1872, E.S. Bisbee contributed his first sequential in seventeen panels and Worth showed up in "Humor and Pathos of a New England Thanksgiving" in eleven panels. Issue 47 expands the concept with a twelve-panel job by Bisbee, twenty-panel effort on one page by Hopkins and a three-panel effort by Worth. And on it goes through 1873 as well - comic strip after comic strip. Issue 58 June 5, 1873, includes a particularly humorous nineteen-panel double-pager drawn by someone still unknown titled "The Terrible Adventures of Messrs. Buster and Stumps, with the Indians" which begins with two white men heading out west in an effort to exterminate Indians - and their misadventures of not quite getting the job done. It reads across both pages in a unique evolution similar to Popeye #2052 (found in the Platinum listings). Issue 65 contains two nine-panel Thomas Worth strips "Only a Mad Dog Scare - Another Lesson For Nervous People" and "Only a Cholera Scare - Something For Nervous People to Read and Ponder Over." Issue 66 Sept 18, 1873, has the very funny Hopkins twelve-panel strip as well as two more ten-panel Worth strips on the delights of Hunting and Fishing plus one by Hopkins titled "The Adventures of Mr Old Party with Jersey Mosquitoes" in twelve-panels. All told, four comic strips in this issue. They obviously liked what they were doing, judging from the exuberance of the work.

The next issue has Worth's nine-panel report on "The Adventures of Young Muttonhead among the Free Lovers" which was all about the "free sex" convention recently held in Chicago. Issue 68 has a nine-panel "An Adventure with a New Jersey Mosquito" which smacks of Winsor McCay in subject and even art style. Maybe McCay was inspired by this for his later animated cartoon as well as earlier Rarebit Fiend. We'll never know for sure. On through 1875, *Wild Oats* presented sequential comic strips issue after issue. With #148, October 27, 1875, Frederick Opper contributes his very first Wild Oats cover, a political cartoon on inflation then rampant in the US. He does covers through at least #161 before a short break and then comes back with many more. In #158, January 5, 1876, Palmer Cox - some five years before inventing The Brownies - begins a wonderful series of 24-panel double page spread comic strips, with a couple sample titles being "The Adventures of Mr. and Mrs. Sprowl And Their Christmas Turkey-A Crashing Chasing Tearful Tragedy But Happily Ending Well" and "Bachelor Broke and Widow Snuggi: A Pictorial Account of Their Sleigh Ride and What Became of It."

Even though he had been contributing many covers and interior single panel jobs to *Wild Oats* for years, Frank Bellew does not show up with his first comic strip until #190, August 16, 1876, with a nine-panel effort he titled, "Rodger's Patent Mosquito Armour." By this time America's "Father of the sequential comic strip" had inspired many other cartoonists to try their hand telling stories with words and pictures.

Another highly desirable American graphic novel, sought especially by collectors of Western lore, is *Quiddities of an Alaskan Trip* by William H. Bell which debuted in 1873. Bell was Timothy O'Sullivan's assistant photographer on the 1871-74 expeditions of Lt. George Wheeler, surveying and mapping the western territories for the U.S. government. The story panels are laid out within ornate frames like those of stereograph cards, such as Bell was involved in creating on the expedition. It involves a parody of a trip from Washington, D.C., to survey the newly purchased territory of Alaska, which at the time was derisively referred to as "Seward's Folly." Bell published *Quiddities* in Portland, Oregon, in 1873, meaning that he drew it while he was on just such an expedition.

The seemingly disparate influences of Thomas Nast and German comics came together in the work of Austrian immigrant Joseph Keppler (1838-1894). Like many cartoonists in America, Keppler desired to rival Nast. Unlike most, he possessed the talent and drive to accomplish it. Keppler, trained as an artist but working as an actor, began contributing comic art to *Kikeriki* (1861-1923) in his native Vienna. He emigrated to St. Louis in 1868, where he took his first stab at starting a comic weekly, the German language *Die Vehme* (Aug 28, 1869 - Aug. 20, 1870). Seven months later, still in St. Louis, he tried again, launching another German language humor periodical, titled *Puck*. This German *Puck* began on March 18, 1871, joined by an English language version one year later, but both ended on Aug. 24, 1872.

Keppler moved to New York City and began working for Frank Leslie. His cartoons appeared in *Frank Leslie's Illustrated Newspaper*, Frank Leslie's *Budget of Fun*, and the Leslie-owned *Jolly Joker* and *Day's Doings*. (To capitalize on the 1876 Centennial Exposition in Philadelphia, Leslie published in that year a paperback collection of Centennial-related humor, *Centennial Fun*, most of which was Keppler's work.) Four years after the first *Puck* died, Keppler was ready to try again. He re-launched the German language edition of *Puck* in New York City on September 27, 1876.

This *Puck* was both familiar and exotic. Its format of an extravagant centerspread cartoon sandwiched between front and back cover cartoons had by this time become something of a comic periodical standard, certainly for the monthlies. But *Puck* was different from what had come before. The cartoons were lithographed, not engraved, which lent to them a softer, more pleasing quality, and they were in color, something virtually without precedent in American comic periodical literature.

Initially, the magazine's cartoons were tinted in just one color, but *Puck* appeared, ambitiously, every week, and the coloring set it apart from anything else on American stands. The parallel English language edition of *Puck* was launched six months after the German version, on March 14, 1877. This English edition of *Puck* was a money-loser for several years, kept afloat by the German edition's profits and the determination of the English edition's literary editor, H.C. Bunner, not to give up. By 1880, *Puck* was a huge success. It became the new model for American humor publications. In time, Keppler hired other artists, most notably Frederick Burr Opper, Eugene Zimmerman ("Zim") and F. M. Howarth, and added black and white sequential comics to the magazine's interior and then, with increasing frequency in the early 1890s to the magazine's back cover. *Funny Folks* by F. M. Howarth, 1899, collected many early sequential comics from *Puck;* one of the titles many consider bridges the Victorian and Platinum Ages of comics. *Puck* was the model that inspired William Randolph Hearst to add a color comics section to his Sunday Journal in 1895.

With the first issue dated October 29, 1881, *Puck's* chief rival, *Judge*, was born. Founded by *Puck* artist James A. Wales, it also featured the work of Thomas Worth and Livingston Hopkins. *Judge* made several forays into *Puck*'s talent pool over the years. Its best capture was Eugene Zimmerman ("Zim"), who became for Judge the star artist that Frederick Burr Opper was for Puck.

Judge struggled financially for

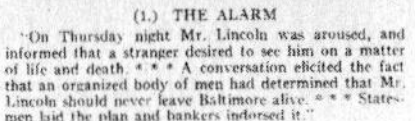

(1.) THE ALARM

"On Thursday night Mr. Lincoln was aroused, and informed that a stranger desired to see him on a matter of life and death. * * * A conversation elicited the fact that an organized body of men had determined that Mr. Lincoln should never leave Baltimore alive. * * * Statesmen laid the plan and bankers indorsed it."

(2.) THE COUNCIL

"Mr. Lincoln did not want to yield, and his friends cried with indignation. But they insisted, and he left."

(3.) THE SPECIAL TRAIN

"He wore a Scotch plaid cap and a very long military cloak, so that he was entirely unrecognizable."

(4.) THE OLD COMPLAINT

"Mr. Lincoln, accompanied by Mr. Seward, paid his respects to President Buchanan."

THE FLIGHT OF ABRAHAM

"The Flight of Abraham Lincoln," first appeared in ***Harper's Weekly****, March 9, 1861.*

several years, and likely would have ceased publication had it not been for Puck's powerful performance during the 1884 election. *Puck*'s success galvanized Republican powerbrokers into recognizing the importance of the political cartoon weekly. They financed newspaperman W. J. Arkell's purchase of *Judge* in 1886 to turn it into a reliable Republican house organ.

Numerous other Puck imitators emerged in the 1880s but quickly died. Note should be made of two that did not: the *Puck*-like *San Francisco Wasp*, which debuted August 5, 1876 (too early for it to be considered a *Puck* knockoff), and the black and white *Texas Siftings*, which debuted on May 9, 1881. Though neither was as successful as *Puck* or *Judge*, both cut their own paths, managing to survive as cartoon humor magazines into the 1890s.

Also worthy of mention is the New York City newspaper *The Daily Graphic* (March 4, 1873 to Sept 23, 1889), which claims the distinction of being the first regularly illustrated daily newspaper in the world, published every day except Sundays and holidays. The majority of its illustrations were portraits or depictions of news events, but nearly every issue contained some comic drawing, many of them gracing the front cover.

With so many pages to fill on a daily basis, *The Daily Graphic* became a rotating door for many young American cartoonists in the early stages of their careers (making one suspect that it was not the best paying gig in town). Within its pages, like needles to be found in the haystack of its more than 4800 issues, is early work by Livingston Hopkins (who mysteriously appears, vanishes, reappears, etc., for months to whole years at a time, right up to his 1884 departure to Australia), pre-*Life* work by Kemble, pre-*Harper*'s appearances by A.B. Frost and W.A. Rogers, pre-Puck and Judge Opper, C.J. Taylor, Hamilton, and Gillam. Old hats, too, appear at times, such as Michael Woolf and Frank Bellew, Sr.

Further, *The Daily Graphic* regularly plundered British periodicals for its back and sometimes center pages, not only perpetrating the usual swipes of single-panel *Punch* cartoons, but also stealing sequential strips from Punch's two main rival publications, *Judy* and *Fun*. This included occasionally reprinting (albeit at random) episodes of continuing British strips "The British Workman" by James Sullivan, and "McNab of that Ilk" by James Brown, though, strangely enough, not Marie Duval's *Ally Sloper*, despite the fact that *The Daily Graphic* did reprint some of Duval's non-"Sloper" strips. ("Ally Sloper" was a continuing sequential strip character who debuted in 1867, lasting into the 1920s, and had very successful solo British book collections of his strip appearances published as early as 1873, more than two decades prior to *Yellow Kid in McFadden*'s Flats).

Livingston Hopkins, whose art style changed like a chameleon from one year to the next, exhibited a definite Duval influence in his work within a year following the publication of the first *Ally Sloper* collection. Given that Hopkins worked for *The Daily Graphic* during the same period in which this newspaper was stealing cartoons from *Sloper*'s home publication, *Judy*, this can hardly be considered coincidental. Hopkins contributed a daily comic strip to *The Daily Graphic* in 1874-75, complete with word balloons. By the time Hopkins was preparing to emigrate to Australia to become lead cartoonist for the Sydney Bulletin, his art style was an imitation of Kemble's, who was also working at *The Daily Graphic*.

Life debuted on January 4, 1883, founded by J.A. Mitchell, and modeled after the Harvard Lampoon. It quickly rose to become the third main pillar of late 1800s American humor periodicals. Smaller in size, black and white, and priced the same as *Puck* and *Judge*, it nevertheless succeeded by appealing to a more genteel audience. Its earliest artists included Kemble and Palmer Cox, but its foremost artist was Charles Dana Gibson, becoming world renowned as the hand behind the graceful, aristocratic "Gibson Girls."

Unlike *Judge*, which had to become a low-brow imitation of *Life* to survive in the next century, and *Puck*, which attempted but failed to become an American version of the highbrow European humor magazines, Life transitioned into the 20th century virtually unaltered, and thrived. By the mid-1880s, with *Puck, Judge*, and *Life* all solidly in place, American comics and cartoon humor had come very much into their own, no longer looking first at Europe to take their cues.

Almanacs began to appear in America starting in 1639. Humor was introduced as early as 1647 by Samuel Danforth. A very important one was *Leed Almanac* beginning in 1687. John Tulley produced the first humorous almanac in 1688. James Franklin, brother of Ben, began the *Rhode Island Almanac* in 1728 using the name "Poor Robin" and his younger brother began *Poor Richard's Almanac* in 1732. Farmer's Almanac began in 1792 and used some humor.

The first comic almanac totally devoted to humor was published by Charles Ellm in Boston in 1831 and featured the artwork of D.C. Johnston. Perhaps the most famous comic almanacs (certainly the most valuable) are the *Davy Crockett* series (1835-1856) which began in Nashville, Tennessee. The comic periodicals all ended up issuing comic almanacs beginning with *Yankee Notions* in 1856 and continuing into the 1890s with a one-shot comic almanac published by *Judge* for the year 1894.

Beginning in the 1850s, a new breed of almanacs appeared. Usually created by medicine and farm product companies, they were distributed for free to promote the company's product. Competition amongst companies, whose goal was to get customers to read the almanacs and the advertisements contained therein again and again, meant that attention-getting humorous cartoons soon found their way back into these giveaway pamphlets. Initially their cartoons were done cheap, either poorly drawn or pirated from elsewhere, such as those found in the Hostetter's and Wright's almanac series. More elaborate promotional almanacs eventually did evolve, though, and amongst the best of these was *Barker's Illustrated Almanac*, first produced for the year 1878, and annually into the 1930s. Each *Barker's Almanac* contained ten to twelve full page cartoons, wonderful and bizarre in design, frequently racist, but also comically manic and crammed with details in a manner similar to Outcault's much later *Yellow Kid* pages. The cartoons in *Barker's Almanac* were so popular that in 1892, The Barker, Moore, and Mein Medicine Company published their first edition of *Barker's Komic Picture Souvenir*, reprinting nearly 150 pages of cartoons from their almanacs.

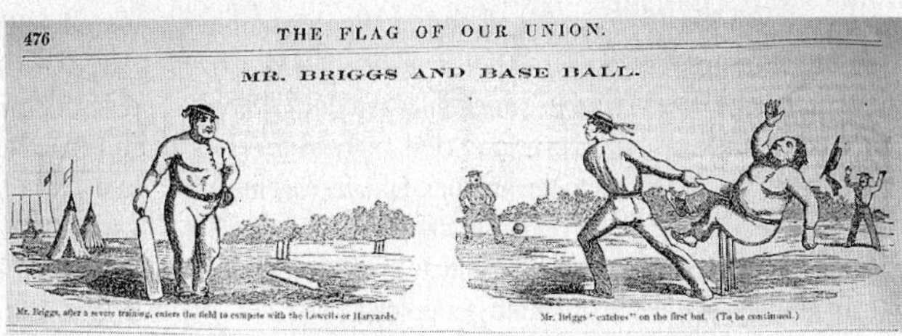

Flag of Our Union, July 23, 1870, sample panels from Pt 1 of a 3 part comic strip depicting early baseball game.

This first *Barker's Souvenir* features a wraparound color cover depicting people headed towards the Columbian World's Fair Exposition, which was to be held in Chicago the next year. It is the earliest confirmed "premium" comic book, sent to customers who mailed in a box label and outside wrapper from two different Barker's products. The *Souvenir* album was *Barker's* most in-demand premium. It was reprinted as a thick unnumbered booklet three more times in the 1890s, with the contents reorganized each time. Later, between 1901 and 1903, *Barker's* broke the album into three separate "Parts," each of which required still more box labels and wrappers to obtain. The 3-part series of reprint albums expanded to four parts circa 1906 or 1907. Both the 3 and 4-part album series had multiple printings.

Also very American in character were the country's promotional comics, which flourished throughout the latter half of the 19th century. They trace their beginnings to Comic Almanacs, which flourished in England and the United States since they first appeared in the 1830s. The first promotional comics which did not double as almanacs began to appear in the 1870s. They included the aforementioned reprints of Cruikshank and Busch strips, reprints of strips lifted from American sources (A.B. Frost's strip "The Bull Calf" was a particular favorite), and original material placing the product being promoted as the focus of the story. These original short cartoon dramas were in many ways similar in storyline to those found in modern television advertisements, except that the clothing is Victorian, and the claims, pre-F.D.A. and F.C.C., were unabashedly wild, over-the-top, and blunt. Chewing tobacco and snuff saved romances, calmed crying babies, and made the sick well. Stove polish that propelled you to wealth and power. Corsets that brought you a husband. The objective, of course, in an era before TV or radio, was to make each comic handout so entertaining that customers would want to keep and read the advertisement again and again.

The more wonderful graphics and outrageous claims tended to come from tobacco companies, who were using comic books and strips to sell their products more than a century before cries against "Joe Camel." The most elaborate of these were printed full color, and unfolded into a single long strip, just like Cruikshank's *The Tooth-Ache* from the 1840s, though usually limited to just the cover plus seven panels.

Examples are the Jackson Chewing Tobacco comics *How Adolphus Slim-Jim Used Jackson's Best and Ye Veracious Chronicle of Gruff and Pompey, and Durham Smoking Tobacco's Home Made Happy - A Romance for Married Men*. The artists of these comics are mostly unidentified, but their level of skill was equal to anything in *Puck* and *Judge*. *The Home Made Happy Comic*, in fact, was produced for Durham by The Graphic Company -- the publisher of *The Daily Graphic*, the aforementioned 1870s illustrated newspaper which included cartoons.

The earliest known anthology devoted to collecting the comic strips of a single American artist was A.B. Frost's *Stuff and Nonsense* in 1884. The next known American collection came in 1888, the very rare Frederick Burr Opper anthology, *Puck's Opper Book*. Both proved popular, so more Frost and Opper collections followed, to be joined within a few years by reprints collecting the cartoons and strips of Keppler, Kemble, Zim, Gibson, Mayer, Taylor, Frank Bellew's son "Chip," Howarth, Woolf, etc.

Puck, Judge, and *Texas Siftings* all began monthly Library series - 8-1/2" x 11" magazines, mostly black and white, which organized previously published material around one theme or one artist. For example, the first *Puck's Library* (July 1887) was titled "The National Game," and gathered beneath one cover *Puck* material poking fun at the game of baseball. The third (March 1888) and ninth (November 1889) issues of *Judge's Serial (later named Judge's Library)* were devoted entirely to the work of Zim.

Life tended more towards hardcover collections, such as its annual ten-issue series *The Good Things of Life* (1884-1893), which included cartoons and strips by Palmer Cox, T.S. Sullivant, Hy Mayer, and others. *The Good Things of Life* was published initially by the firm of White, Stokes, and Allen, but which by the fourth book, had become simply Frederick A. Stokes. Stokes published a number of other cartoon books in the 1880s and 1890s, the majority of them reprint collections. The experience he gained at this time with these reprint albums placed Stokes in the perfect position to pick up the wealth of material about to be created for the comics supplements of William R. Hearst's newspapers, making Stokes the first major publisher of the coming Platinum Age.

In 1892, Charles Scribner's Sons published A. B. Frost's *Bull Calf and Other Tales*. It contains sequential comic strip art on quite a few pages as well as single panel cartoons. By 1898, Charles Scribner's Sons also issued Kemble's *The Billy Goat and Other Comicalities* as a 112-page hardcover, which also has sequential comic strips.

In the early 1890s, the slum children cartoons of artist Michael Woolf (many of which were reprinted in the 1896 collection *99 Woolfs from Truth* and in the posthumous 1899 collection *Sketches of Lowly Life in a Great City*) were popular. *Truth* magazine, which followed Puck's format of color front cover, back cover and centerspread cartoons, but in style was more akin to the aristocratic Life, was initially unable to secure Woolf's services, creating an opportunity for the young cartoonist Richard F. Outcault, who desired to break into one of the weekly comic periodicals.

It was in his Woolf-inspired slum children cartoons for *Truth* that Outcault's prototype of the *Yellow Kid* first emerged. The bald, sack-clothed youngster made four appearances in *Truth*, starting with #372 on June 2, 1894, prior to his newspaper debut.

During the rise of Yellow Kid's popularity, he appeared in American comic magazines in parodies drawn by others, with politicians, even Hearst and Pulitzer, dressed up as the *Yellow Kid*. Such cartoons are known to have appeared in *Judge*, *Life*, *The Bee*, and *Vim* plus various newspapers across the country. More about the *Yellow Kid's* importance can be found in the Platinum Age section of this book.

While comics definitely have their roots in Europe, and the earliest American comic books either reprinted or emulated those of Europe, the direction of influence was by no means one way. By at least the 1870s, American cartoons were being published and seen in the Old World, as evidenced by the arrest in Spain of the on-the-lamb corrupt Tammany Hall politician Boss Tweed by Spanish police who recognized Tweed from a Nast cartoon.

European piracy of American cartoons was just as lucrative as the American piracy of Europeans. In the 1880s and '90s, the comics of Zim, Chip Bellew, and Charles Dana Gibson all saw reprint in Europe. In April 1899, *Pictorial Comedy*, a monthly magazine destined for a ten-year run, commenced publication in London. It was made up entirely of cartoons reprinted with permission from *Puck* and *Life*. F.M. Howarth's domestic comedies from *Puck* were favorites in France. American Hy Mayer was commissioned to create original comics work for *Black and White* (Britain), *Le Rire* (France), and *Fliegende Blätter*. Michael Woolf's slum children cartoons saw print in the British periodical *Pick-Me-Up*, during the same years that top British artist Phil May's first published work debuted in that publication. May later became famous for his Woolf-inspired street children cartoons as well as his influence on the development of comics in Australia.

As the 19th Century ended, American comics were coming to the fore worldwide, soon to explode into a position of dominance with the Platinum Age revolution brought about by the emergence of the color comic supplement in America's newspapers and the arrival of Richard F. Outcault's *Yellow Kid*.

Judge #791, Dec 12, 1896, depicting Tammany Hall politicians as RFO's Yellow Kid & Cox's Brownies. Art by Hamilton.

END NOTE: Victorian Era comics were issued in many relatively obscure formats compared to what most of us are used to today. The Victorian Era section can only grow as there are many more heretofore undiscovered comics from the 1800s which have fallen off the radar of history. Some may wonder why some of the earlier items listed contain as of yet no prices. The reason is simple. These books are part of a relatively "new" market which is still establishing itself.

High-grade copies are almost unheard of in almost all instances. Some books may truly have only a handful left in existence. We are sure there are some known to have been published which no (as of yet) known copies have survived the ravages of time and neglect.

Each year expect another quantum leap in our ever-expanding knowledge of the fascinating earliest origins of the comic strip as it relates to North America. Your input in helping this section of the Guide grow and mature is most welcome!

Robert Lee Beerbohm first sold comics through the legendary RBCC beginning in 1966, set up at his first comicon in 1967, helped found the northern California Comics & Comix chain of stores in August 1972, co-hosted Berkeleycon 1973, the first UG creator-owned comix con and operated comic book stores from 1972-1994. He now owns Robert Beerbohm Comic Art that specializes in buying and selling scarce comics and related material from the 1840s-1980s. He has been compiling a detailed history book of the business of the American comic book for some time now and hopes to complete it soon.

Contact Robert directly at www.BLBComics.com

Richard Olson is an Research Professor Emeritus at the University of New Orleans. He published the Richard Outcault Collector for years. Reach Richard directly at: rolsonredoak@bellsouth.net

Richard Samuel West is the author of Satire on Stone: The Political Cartoons of Joseph Keppler (University of Illinois, 1988) and The San Francisco Wasp: An Illustrate History (Periodyssey Press, 2004) and editor of several cartoon collections. He is the owner of Periodyssey, a business that specializes in buying and selling significant and unusual American magazines. Richard can be reached at: www.oldmagazines.com

All three are life-long collectors and students of all forms of the comics who welcome corrections and additions to this concise compilation of our earliest American comics heritage dating back almost two centuries. Happy Hunting!

The American Comic Almanac #5
1835 © Charles Ellms, NYC

The Strange and Wonderful Adventures
of Bachelor Butterfly by Rodolphe Töpffer
1870s © Dick & Fitzgerald, NYC

Barker's "Komic" Picture Souvenir, 3rd Edition
1894 © Barker, Moore & Klein Medicine Co.

COLLECTOR'S NOTE: Most of the books listed in this section were published well over a century before organized comics fandom began archiving and helping to preserve these fragile popular culture artifacts. With some of these comics now over 160 years old, they almost never surface in Fine+ or better shape. Be happy when you simply find a copy.

This year has seen price growth in quite a few comic books in this era. Since this section began growing almost a decade now, comic books from Wilson, Brother Jonathan, Huestis & Cozans, Garrett, Dick & Fitzgerald, Frank Leslie, Street & Smith and others continue to be recognized by the more savvy in this fine hobby as legitimate comic book collectors' items. We had been more concerned with simply establishing what is known to exist. For the most part, that work is now a *fait accompli* in this section compiled, revised, and expanded by Robert Beerbohm with special thanks this year to Terrance Keegan plus acknowledgment to Bill Blackbeard, Chris Brown, Alfredo Castelli, Darrell Coons, Leonardo De Sá, Scott Deschaine, Joe Evans, Ron Friggle, Tom Gordon III, Michel Kempeneers, Andy Konkykru, Don Kurtz, Richard Olson, Robert Quesinberry, Joseph Rainone, Steve Rowe, Randy Scott, John Snyder, Art Spiegelman, Steve Thompson, Richard Samuel West, Doug Wheeler and Richard Wright. Special kudos to long-time collector and scholar Gabriel Laderman.

The prices given for Fair, Good and Fine categories are for strictly graded editions. If you need help grading your item, we refer you to the grading section in this book or contact the authors of this essay. Items marked Scarce, Rare or Very Rare we are still trying to figure out how many copies might still be in existence. We welcome additions and corrections from any interested collectors and scholars at robert@BLBcomics.com

For ease ascertaining the contents of each item of this listing and the Platinum index list, we offer the following list of categories found immediately following most of the titles:

E - EUROPEAN ORIGINAL COMICS MATERIAL; Printed in Europe or reprinted in USA
G - GRAPHIC NOVEL (LONGER FORMAT COMIC TELLING A SINGLE STORY)
H - "HOW TO DRAW CARTOONS" BOOKS
I - ILLUSTRATED BOOKS NOTABLE FOR THE ARTIST, BUT NOT A COMIC.
M - MAGAZINE / PERIODICAL COMICS MATERIAL REPRINTS
N - NEWSPAPER COMICS MATERIAL REPRINTS
O - ORIGINAL COMIC MATERIAL NOT REPRINTED FROM ANOTHER SOURCE
P - PROMOTIONAL COMIC, EITHER GIVEN AWAY FOR FREE, OR A PREMIUM GIVEN IN CONJUNCTION WITH THE PURCHASE OF A PRODUCT.
S - SINGLE PANEL / NON-SEQUENTIAL CARTOONS

Measurements are in inches. The first dimension given is Height and the second is Width. Some original British editions are included in the section, so as to better explain and differentiate their American counterparts.

ACROBATIC ANIMALS
R.H. Russell: 1899 (9x11-7/8", 72 pgs, B&W, hard-c)
nn (Scarce) 150.00 300.00 600.00
NOTE: *Animal strips by Gustave Verbeck, presented 1 panel per page.*

ALMY'S SANTA CLAUS (P,E)
Edward C. Almy & Co., Providence, R.I.: nd (1880's) (5-3/4x4-5/8", 20 pgs, B&W, paper-c
nn - (Rare) 12.50 40.00 80.00
NOTE: *Department store Christmas giveaway containing an abbreviated 28-panel reprinting of George Cruikshank's **The Tooth-ache**. Santa Claus cover.*

AMERICAN COMIC ALMANAC, THE (OLD AMERICAN COMIC ALMANAC 1839-1846)
Charles Ellms: 1831-1846 (5x8, 52 pgs, B&W)
1 first American comic almanac ever prrinted 500.00 1000.00 2000.00
2-16 100.00 200.00 400.00
NOTE:#1 from 1831 is the First American Comic Almanac

AMERICAN PUNCH
American Punch Publishing Co: Jan 1879-March 1881, J.A. Cummings Engraving Co (last 3 issues) (Quarto Monthly)
Most issues 25.00 50.00 150.00

THE AMERICAN WIT
Richardson & Collins, NY: 1867-68 (18-1/2x13. 8 pgs, B&W)
2/3 Frank Bellew single panels 50.00 100.00 200.00

AMERICAN WIT AND HUMOR
Harper & Bros, NY: 1859 (
nn - numerous McLenan sequential comic strips 100.00 200.00 400.00

ATTWOOD'S PICTURES - AN ARTIST'S HISTORY OF THE LAST TEN YEARS OF THE NINETEENTH CENTURY (M,S)
Life Publishing Company, New York: 1900 (11-1/4x9-1/8", 156 pgs, B&W, gilted blue hard-c)
nn - By Attwood 40.00 80.00 160.00
NOTE: *Reprints monthly calendar cartoons which appeared in **LIFE**, for 1887 through 1899.*

BACHELOR BUTTERFLY, THE VERITABLE HISTORY OF MR. (E,G)
D. Bogue, London: 1845 (5-1/2x10-1/4", 74 pgs, B&W, gilted hardcover)
nn - By Rodolphe Töpffer (Scarce) 500.00 1250.00 2500.00
nn - Hand colored edition (Very Rare) (no known sales)
NOTE: *This is the British Edition, translated from the re-engraved by Cham serialization found in **L'Illustration** - a periodical from Paris publisher Dubochet. Predates the first French collected edition. Third Töpffer comic book published in English. The first story page is numbered Page 3. Page 17 shows Bachelor Butterfly being swallowed by a whale.*

BACHELOR BUTTERFLY, THE STRANGE ADVENTURES OF (E,G)
Wilson & Co., New York: 1846 (5-3/8x10-1/8", 68 pgs, B&W, soft-c)
nn - By Rodolphe Töpffer (Very Rare) 600.00 1500.00 3000.00
nn - At least one hand colored copy exists (Very Rare) (no known sales)
NOTE: *2nd Töpffer comic book printed in the U.S., 3rd earliest known sequential comic book in the USA. Reprinted from the British D. Bogue 1845 edition, itself from the earlier French language **Histoire de Mr. Cryptogame**. Released the same year as the French Dubochet edition. Two variations known, the earlier printing with Page number 17 placed on the inside (left) bottom corner in error, with slightly later printings corrected to place page number 17 on the outside (right) bottom corner of that page. Another first printing indicator is pages 17 and 20 are printed on the wrong side of the page. For both printings: the first story page is numbered 2. Page 17 shows Bachelor Butterfly already in the whale. In most panels with 3 lines of text, the third line is indented further than the second, which is in turn indented further than the first.*

BACHELOR BUTTERFLY, THE STRANGE ADVENTURES
Brother Jonathan Press, NY: 1854 (5-1/2x10-5/8", 68 pgs, paper-c, B&W) (Very Rare)
nn - By Rodolphe Töpffer 250.00 500.00 1000.00

BACHELOR BUTTERFLY,THE STRANGE & WONDERFUL ADVENTURES OF
Dick & Fitzgerald, New York: 1870s-1888 (various printings 30 Cent cover price, 68 pgs, B&W, paper cover) (all versions Rare) (E,G)
nn - Black print on blue cover (5-1/2x10-1/2"); string bound 112.00 225.00 450.00
nn - Black print on green cover (5-1/2x10-1/2"); string bound 100.00 200.00 400.00
NOTE: *Reprints the earlier Wilson & Co. edition. Page 2 is the first story page. Page 17 shows Bachelor Butterfly already in the whale. In most panels with 3 lines of text, the second and third lines are equally indented in from the first. Unknown which cover (blue or green) is earlier.*

BACHELOR'S OWN BOOK. BEING THE PROGRESS OF MR. LAMBKIN, (GENT.) IN THE PURSUIT OF PLEASURE AND AMUSEMENT (E,O,G)
(See also PROGRESS OF MR. LAMBKIN)
D. Bogue, London: August 1, 1844 (5x8-1/4", 28 pgs printed one side only, cardboard cover & interior) (all versions Rare)
nn - First printing hand colored 200.00 400.00 800.00
nn - First printing black & white 200.00 400.00 800.00
NOTE: *First printing has misspellings in the title. "PURSUIT" is spelled "PERSUIT", and "AMUSEMENT" is spelled "AMUSEMEMT".*
nn - Second printing hand colored 200.00 400.00 800.00
nn - Second printing black & white 200.00 400.00 800.00
NOTE: Second printing. The misspelling of "PURSUIT" has been corrected, but "AMUSEMEMT" error is still present.
nn - Third printing hand colored No misspellings 200.00 400.00 800.00
nn - Third printing black & white 200.00 400.00 800.00
NOTE: *By George Cruikshank. This is the British Edition. Issued both in black & white, and professionally hand-colored editions. Hand-colored editions have survived in higher quantities than uncolored. Originally made with thin paper sheets covering the plates.*

BACHELOR'S OWN BOOK; OR, THE PROGRESS OF MR. LAMBKIN, (GENT.), IN THE PURSUIT OF PLEASURE AND AMUSEMENT, AND ALSO IN SEARCH OF HEALTH AND HAPPINESS, THE (E,O,G)
David Bryce & Son: Glasgow: 1884 (one shilling; 7-5/8 x5-7/8", 62 pgs printed one side only, illustrated hardcover, page edges guilt
nn - Reprints the 1844 edition with altered title 17.50 35.00 70.00
nn - soft cover edition exists 15.00 30.00 60.00

BACHELOR'S OWN BOOK. BEIN-G TWENTY-FOUR PASSAGES IN THE LIFE OF MR. LAMBKIN, GENT. (E,G)
Burgess, Stringer & Co., New York on cover; Carey & Hart, Philadelphia on title page: 1845 (31-1/4 cents, 7-1/2x4-5/8", 52 pgs, B&W, paper cover)
nn - By George Cruikshank (Very Rare) (no known sales)
NOTE: *This is the second known sequential comic book story published in America. Reprints the earlier British edition. Pages printed on one side only. New cover art by an unknown artist.*

BAD BOY'S FIRST READER (O,S)
G.W. Carleton & Co.: 1881 (5-3/4 x 4-1/8", 44 pgs, B&W, paper cover)
nn - By Frank Bellew (Senior) 50.00 100.00 200.00
NOTE: *Parody of a children's ABC primer, one cartoon illustration plus text per page. Includes one panel of Boss Tweed. Frank Bellew is considered the "Father of the American Sequential Comics."*

BALL OF YARN OR, QUEER, QUIANT & QUIZZICAL STORIES, UNRAVELED WITH NEARLY 200 COMIC ENGRAVINGS OF FREAKS, FOLLIES & FOIBLES OF QUEER FOLKS BY THAT PRINCE OF COMICS, ELTON, THE (M)
Philip. J. Cozans, 116 Nassau St, NY: early 1850s (7-1/4x3-1/2", 76 pgs, yellow-wraps)
nn - sequential comic strips plus singles (no known sales)
NOTE: Mose Keyser-r, Jones, Smith & Robinson Goes To A Ball-r; The Adventures of Mr Goliah Starvemouse-r are all sequential comic strips printed in a number of sources

BARKER'S ILLUSTRATED ALMANAC (O,P,S)
Barker, Moore & Mein Medicine Co: 1878-1932+ (36 pgs, B&W, color paper-cr)
1878-1879 (Rare) 40.00 80.00 160.00
NOTE: *Not known yet what the cover art is.*
1880 Farmer Plowing Field-c 30.00 60.00 120.00
1881-1883 (Scarce,7-3/4x6-1/8") *4-mast ships & lighthouse-c* 30.00 60.00 120.00
1884-1889 (8x6-1/4") *Horse & Rider jumping picket fence-c* 20.00 40.00 80.00
1890-1897 (8-1/8x6-1/4") 20.00 40.00 80.00
1898-1899 (7-3/8x5-7/8") 20.00 40.00 80.00
1900+: see the Platinum Age Comics section (7x5-7/8")
NOTE: *Barker's Almanacs were actually issued in November of the year preceding the year which appears on the almanac. For example, the 1878 dated almanac was issued November 1877. They were given away to retailers of Barker's farm animal medicinal products, to in turn be given away to customers. Each Barker's Almanac contains 10 full page cartoons. These frequently included racist stereotypes of blacks. Each cartoon*

The Comical Adventures of Beau Ogleby
1843 © Tlit & Bogue, London

The Story of The Man of Humanity and The Bull Calf by A. B. Frost
1890 © C.H. Fargo & Co.

Buzz A Buzz Or The Bees By Wilhelm Busch
1873 © Henry Holt And Company, New York

contained advertisements for Barker's products. It is unknown whether the cartoons appeared only in the almanacs, or if they also ran as newspaper ads or flyers. Originally issued with a metal hook attached in the upper left hand corner, which could be used to hang the almanac.

BARKER'S "KOMIC" PICTURE SOUVENIR (P,S)
Barker, Moore & Mein Medicine Co: nd (1892-94) (color cardboard cover, B&W interior) (all unnumbered editions Very Rare)

nn - (1892) (1st edition, 6-7/8x10-1/2, 150 pgs) wraparound cover showing people headed towards Chicago for the 1893 World's Fair 150.00 300.00 650.00
nn - (1893) (2nd edition, ??? pgs) same cover as 1st edition 150.00 300.00 650.00
nn - (1894) (3rd edition, 180 pgs, 6-3/4x10-3/8") 150.00 300.00 650.00
NOTE: *New cover art showing crowd of people laughing with a copy of Barker's Almanac.The crowd picture is flanked on both sides by picture of a tall thin person.*
nn - (1894) (4th edition, 124 pgs, 6-3/8x9-3/8") same-c as 3rd edition 150.00 300.00 650.00
NOTE: *Essentially same-c as 3rd edition, except flanking picture on left edge is now gone. The 2nd through 4th editions state their printing on the first interior page, in the paragraph beneath the picture of the Barker's Building. These have been confirmed as premium comic books, predating the Buster Brown premiums. They reprint advertising cartoons from Barker's Illustrated Almanac. For the 50 page booklets by this same name, numbered as "Part"s, see the PLATINUM AGE SECTION. All "Editions in Parts", without exception, were published after 1900.*

BEAU OGLEBY, THE COMICAL ADVENTURES OF (E,G)
Tilt & Bogue: nd (c1843) (5-7/8x9-1/8", 72 pgs, printed one side only, green gilted hard-c, B&W)

nn - By Rodolphe Töpffer (Rare) 300.00 600.00 1500.00
nn - Hand coloured edition (Very Rare) (no known sales)
NOTE: *British Edition; no known American Edition. 2nd Töpffer comic book published in English. Translated from Paris publisher Aubert's unauthorized redrawn 1839 bootleg edition of Töpffer's **Histoire de Mr. Jabot**. The back most interior page is an advertisement for **Obadiah Oldbuck**, showing its comic book cover*

BEE, THE
Bee Publishing Co: May 16 1898-Aug 2 1898 (Chromolithographic Weekly)

most issues 50.00 100.00 200.00
8 June Yellow Kid Hearst cover issue 150.00 300.00 650.00

BEFORE AND AFTER. A LOCOFOCO CHRISTMAS PRESENT. (O, C)
D.C. Johnston, Boston: 1837 (4-3/4x3", 1 page, hand colored cardboard)

nn - (Very Rare) by David Claypoole Johnston (sold at auction for $400 in GD)
NOTE: *Pull-tab cartoon envelope, parodying the 1836 New York City mayoral election, picturing the candidate of the Locofoco Party smiling "Before the N.York election", then, when the tab is pulled, picturing him with an angry sneer "After the N.York election".*

BILLY GOAT AND OTHER COMICALITIES, THE (M)
Charles Scribner's Sons: 1898 (6-3/4x8-1/2", 116 pgs., B&W, Hardcover)

nn - By E. W. Kemble 125.00 250.00 600.00

BLACKBERRIES, THE (N,S) (see Coontown's 400)
R. H. Russell: 1897 (9"x12", 76 pgs, hard-c, every other page in color, every other page in one color sepia tone)

nn - By E. W. Kemble 162.00 325.00 1300.00
NOTE: *Tastefully done comics about Black Americana during the USA's Jim Crow days.*

BOOK OF BUBBLES, YE (S)
Endicott & Co., New York: March 1864 (6-1/4 x 9-7/8",160 pgs, guilt-illus. hard-c, B&W

nn - By unknown 150.00 300.00 600.00
NOTE: *Subtitle: A contribution to the New York Fair in aid of the Sanitary Commission; 68 single-sided pages of B&W cartoons, each with an accompanying limerick. A few are sequential.*

BOOK OF DRAWINGS BY FRED RICHARDSON (N,S)
Lakeside Press, Chicago: 1899 (13-5/8x10-1/2", 116 pgs, B&W, hard-c)

nn - 80.00 160.00 320.00
NOTE: *Reprinted from the **Chicago Daily News**. Mostly single panel. Includes one **Yellow Kid** parody, some Spanish-American War cartoons.*

BOTTLE, THE (E,O) (see also THE DRUNKARD'S CHILDREN, and TEA GARDEN TO TEA POT, and TEMPERANCE TALES; OR, SIX NIGHTS WITH THE WASHINGTONIANS)
D. Bogue, London, with others in later editions: nd (1846) (16-1/2x11-1/2", 16 pgs, printed one side only, paper cover)

D. Bogue, London (nd; 1846): first edition:
nn - Black & white (Scarce) 200.00 400.00 900.00
nn - Hand colored (Rare) (no known sales)
D. Bogue, London, and Wiley and Putnam, New York (nd; 1847) : second edition, misspells American publisher "Putnam" as "Putman":
nn - Black & white (Scarce) 150.00 300.00 600.00
nn - Hand colored (Rare) (no known sales)
D. Bogue, London, and Wiley and Putnam, New York (nd; 1847) : third edition has "Putnam" spelled correctly.
nn - Black & white (Scarce) 150.00 300.00 600.00
nn - Hand colored (Rare) (no known sales)
D. Bogue, London, Wiley and Putnam, New York, and J. Sands, Sydney, New South Wales: (nd; 1847) : fourth edition with no misspellings
nn - Black & white (Scarce) 150.00 300.00 600.00
nn - Hand colored (Rare) (no known sales)
NOTE: *By George Cruikshank. Temperance/anti-alcohol story. All editions are in precisely identical format. The only difference is to be found on the cover, where it lists who published it. Cover is text only - no cover art.*

FR1.0 GD2.0 FN6.0

BOTTLE, THE HISTORY OF THE
J.C. Becket, 22 Grea St James St, Montreal, Canada: 1851 (9-1/8x6", B&W)

nn - From Engravings by Cruikshank 150.00 300.00 650.00
NOTE: *As published in The Canada Temperance Advocate.*

BOTTLE, THE (E)
W. Tweedie, London: nd (1862) (11-1/2x17-1/3", 16 pgs, printed one side only, paper cover)

nn - Black & white; By George Cruikshank (Scarce) 100.00 200.00 400.00
nn - Hand colored (Scarce) (no known sales)

BOTTLE, THE (E)
Geo. Gebbie, Philadelphia: nd (c.1871) (11-3/8x17-1/8", 42 pgs, tinted interior, hard-c)

nn - By George Cruikshank 100.00 200.00 400.00
NOTE: *New cover art (cover not by Cruikshank).*

BOTTLE, THE (E)
National Temperance, London: nd (1881) (11-1/2x16-1/2", 16 pgs, printed one side only, paper-c, color)

nn - By George Cruikshank 100.00 200.00 400.00
NOTE: *See Platinum Age section for 1900s printings.*

BOTTLE, THE (E)
Marques, Pittsburgh, PA: 1884/85 (6x8", 8 plates, full color, illustrated envelope)
nn - art not by Cruickshank; New Art 50.00 100.00 200.00
NOTE: Says Presented by J.M. Gusky, Dealer in Boots and Shoes

BROAD GRINS OF THE LAUGHING PHILOSOPHER
Dick & Fitzgerald,NY: 1870s
nn - (4) panel sequential strip 25.00 50.00 150.00

BROTHER JONATHAN
Wilson & Co/Benj H Day, 48 Beekman, NYC: 1839-???

July 4 1846 - ads for Obadiah & Butterfly 50.00 100.00 200.00
July 4 1856 catalog list - front cover comic strip 100.00 200.00 400.00
Xmas/New Years 1856 75.00 150.00 300.00
average large size issues 25.00 50.00 100.00
NOTE: has full page advert for Fredinand Flipper comic book**116**

BULL CALF, THE (P,M)
Various: nd (c1890's) (3-7/8x4-1/8", 16 pgs, B&W, paper-c)

nn - By A.B. Frost Creme Oatmeal Toilet Soap 25.00 50.00 150.00
nn - By A.B. Frost Thompson & Taylor Spice Co, Chicago 25.00 50.00 150.00
NOTE: *Reprints the popular strip story by Frost, with the art modified to place a sign for Creme Oatmeal Soap within each panel. The back cover advertises the specific merchant who gave this booklet away - multiple variations exist.*

BULL CALF AND OTHER TALES, THE (M)
Charles Scribner's Sons: 1892 (120 pgs., 6-3/4x8-7/8", B&W, illus. hard cover)

nn - By Arthur Burdett Frost 50.00 150.00 500.00
NOTE: *Blue, grey, tan hard covers known to exist.*

BULL CALF, THE STORY OF THE MAN OF HUMANITY AND THE (P,M)
C.H. Fargo & Co.: 1890 (5-1/4x6-1/4", 24 pgs, B&W, color paper-c)

nn - By A.B. Frost 42.50 85.00 185.00
NOTE: *Fargo shoe company giveaway; pages alternate between shoe advertisements and the strip story.*

BUSHEL OF MERRY THOUGHTS, A (see Mischief Book, The) (E)
Sampson Low Son & Marsten: 1868 (68 pgs, handcolored hardcover, B&W)

nn - (6-1/4 x 9-7/8", 138 pgs) red binding, publisher's name on title page only 200.00 400.00 800.00
nn - (6-1/2 x 10", 134 pgs) green binding, publisher's name on cover & title page 200.00 400.00 800.00
NOTE: *Cover plus story title pages designed by Leighton Brothers, based on Busch art. Translated by Harry Rogers (who is credited instead of Busch). This is a British publication, notable as the earliest known English language anthology collection of Wilhelm Busch comic strips. Page 13 of second story missing from all editions (panel dropped). Unknown which of the two editions was published first. A modern reprint, by Dover in 1971.*

BUTTON BURSTER, THE (M) (says on cover "ten cents hard cash")
M.J. Ivers & Co., 86 Nassau St., New York: 1873 (11x8-1/8", soft paper, B&W)

By various cartoonists (Very Rare) 125.00 250.00 500.00
NOTE: *Reprints from various 1873 issues of Wild Oats; has (5) different sequential comic strips: (3) by Livingston Hopkins, (1) by Thomas Worth, other one creator presently unknown; Bellew, Sr. single panel cartoons.*

BUZZ A BUZZ OR THE BEES (E)
Griffith & Farran, London: September 1872 (8-1/2x5-1/2", 168 pgs, printed one side only, orange, black & white hardcover, B&W interior)

nn - By Wilhelm Busch (Scarce) 112.00 225.00 450.00
NOTE: *Reprint published by Phillipson & Golder, Chester; text written by English to accompany Busch art.*

BUZZ A BUZZ OR THE BEES (E)
Henry Holt & Company, New York: 1873 (9x6", 96 pgs, gilted hardcover, hand colored)

nn - By Wilhelm Busch (Scarce) 100.00 200.00 450.00
NOTE: *Completely different translation than the Griffith & Farran version. Also, contains 28 additional illustrations by Park Benjamin. The lower page count is because the Henry Holt edition prints on both sides of each page, and the Griffith & Farran edition is printed one side only.*

CALENDAR FOR THE MONTH; YE PICTORIAL LYSTE OF YE MATTERS OF

The Carpet Bag #14
1851 © Snow & Wilder

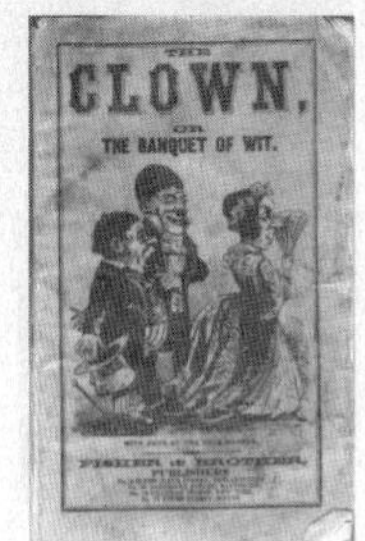
The Clown, or The Banquet of Wit
1851 © Fisher & Brother

Comic Monthly v2 #7
Sept. 1860 © J.C. Haney, NY

FR1.0 GD2.0 FN6.0

INTEREST FOR SUMMER READING (P,M)
S.E. Bridgman & Company, Northampton, Mass: nd (c. late 1880's-1890's) (5-5/8x7-1/4", 64 pgs, paper-c, B&W)

nn - (Very Rare) T.S. Sullivant-c/a 100.00 200.00 400.00
NOTE: *Book seller's catalog, with every other page reprinting cartoons and strips (from Life??). Art by: Chips Bellew, Gibson, Howarth, Kemble, Sullivant, Townsend, Woolf.*

CARICATURE AND OTHER COMIC ART
Harper & Brothers, NY: 1877 (9-5/16x7-1/8", 360 pgs, B&W, green hard-c)

nn - By James Parton (over 200 illustrations) 30.00 60.00 200.00
NOTE: *This is the earliest known serious history of comics & related genre from around the world produced by an American. Parton was a cousin of Thomas Nast's wife Sarah. A large portion of this book was first serialized in **Harper's Monthly** in 1875.*

CARPET BAG, THE
Snow & Wilder, later Wilder & Pickard, Boston: March 21 1851-March 26 1853

Each average issue 25.00 50.00 100.00
Samuel "Mark Twain" Clemmons issues (first app in print) 500.00 1000.00 2000.00
NOTE: *Many issues contain cartoons by DC Johnston, Frank Bellew, others; literature includes Artemus Ward's Miss Partington who had a mischevious little Katzenjammer Kids-like brat. Carpet Bag was not considered derogatory pre-Civil War.*

CARROT-POMADE (O,G)
James G. Gregory, Publisher, New York: 1864 (9x6-7/8", 36 pgs, B&W)

nn - By Augustus Hoppin 70.00 140.00 280.00
NOTE: *The story of a quack remedy for baldness, sequentially told in the format parodying ABC primers. Has protective tissue pages (not part of page count).*

CARTOONS BY HOMER C. DAVENPORT (M,N,S)
De Witt Publishing House: 1898 (16-1/8x12", 102 pgs, hard-c, B&W)

nn 100.00 200.00 400.00
NOTE: *Reprinted from Harper's Weekly and the New York Journal. Includes cartoons about the Spanish-American War. Title page reads "Davenport's Cartoons".*

CARTOONS BY WILL E. CHAPIN (P,N,S)
The Times-Mirror Printing and Binding House, Los Angeles: 1899 (15-1/4x12", 98 pgs, hard-c, B&W)

nn - scarce 100.00 200.00 400.00
NOTE: *Premium item for subscribing to the Los-Angeles Times-Mirror newspaper, from which these cartoons were reprinted. Includes cartoons about the Spanish-American War.*

CARTOONS OF OUR WAR WITH SPAIN (N,S)
Frederick A. Stokes Company: 1898 (11-1/2x10", 72 pgs, hardcover, B&W)

nn - By Charles Nelan (r-New York Herald) 40.00 100.00 200.00
nn - 2nd printing noted on copy right page 30.00 60.00 120.00

CARTOONS OF THE WAR OF 1898 (E,M,N,S)
Belford, Middlebrook & Co., Chicago: 1898 (7x10-3/8",190 pgs, B&W, hard-c)

nn 50.00 100.00 200.00
NOTE: *Reprints single panel editorial cartoons on the Spanish-American War, from American, Spanish, Latino, and European newspapers and magazines, at rate of 2 to 6 cartoons per page. Art by Bart, Berryman, Bowman, Bradley, Chapin, Gillam, Nelan, Tenniel, others.*

CENTENNIAL FUN (O,S) (Rare)
Frank Leslie, Philadelphia: (July) 1876 (25¢, 11x8", 32 pgs, paper cover, B&W)

nn - By Joseph Keppler-c/a;Thomas Worth-a 150.00 300.00 600.00
NOTE: *Issued for the 1876 Centennial Exposition in Philadelphia. Exists with both black & white, and orange, black & white covers. One copy of the latter had an embossed newstand label from Partland, Maine, implying that the orange cover version, at least, was distributed and sold outside of Philadelphia.*

CHAMPAIGNE
Frank Leslie: June-Dec 1871

1-7 scarce 150.00 225.00 350.00

CHIC
Chic Publishing Co: 1880-81 (Chromolithographic Weekly)

1-38 Livingston Hopkins, Charles Kendrick, CW Weldon 75.00 150.00 300.00

CHILDREN'S CHRISTMAS BOOK, THE
The New York Sunday World: 1897 (10-1/4x8-3/4", 16 pgs, full color)

Dec 12, 1897 - By George Luks, G.H. Grant, Will Crawford, others) (Rare) 50.00 100.00 280.00

CHIP'S DOGS (M)
R.H. Russell and Son Publishers: 1895 hardcover, B&W)

nn - By Frank P. W. "Chip" Bellew 25.00 50.00 100.00
Early printing 80 pgs, 8-7/8x11-7/8"; dark green border of hardcover surrounds all four sides of pasted on cover image; pages arranged in error -- see NOTE below. (more scarce)
nn - By Frank P. W. "Chip" Bellew 12.50 25.00 50.00
Later printing 72 pgs, 8-7/8x11-3/4";green border only on the binding side (one side) of the cover image.
NOTE: *Both are strip reprints from **LIFE**. The difference in page count is due to more blank pages in the first printing -- all printings have the same comics contents, but with the pages in the first printing arranged differently. This is noticeable particularly in the 2-page strip "Getting a Pointer", which appears on the 2nd & 3rd to last pages of the later printings, but in the early printing the first half of this strip is near the middle of the book, while the last half appears on the 2nd to last story page.*

CHIP'S OLD WOOD CUTS (M,S)
R.H. Russell & Son: 1895 (8-7/8x11-3/4", 72 pgs, hardcover, B&W)

nn - By Frank P. W. ("Chip") Bellew 25.00 50.00 100.00
nn - 1897 reprint 15.00 30.00 60.00

CHIP'S UN-NATURAL HISTORY (O,S)
Frederick A. Stokes & Brother: 1888 (7x5-1/4", 64 pgs, hardcover, B&W)

nn - By Frank P. W. ("Chip") Bellew 12.50 25.00 50.00
NOTE: *Title page lists publisher as "Successors to White, Stokes & Allen."*

CLOWN, OR THE BANQUET OF WIT, THE (E,M,O)
Fisher & Brother, Philadelphia, Baltimore, New York, Boston: nd (c.1851) (7-3/8x4-1/2", 88 pgs, paper cover, B&W)

nn - (Very Rare; 3 known copies) 400.00 800.00 1500.00
NOTE: *Earliest known multi-artist anthology of sequential comics; contains multiple sequential comics, plus numerous single panel cartoons. A mixture of reprinted and original material, involving both European and American artists. "Jones, Smith, and Robinson Goes to a Ball" by Richard Doyle (1st app. of Doyle's "Foreign Tour" in America, reprinted from PUNCH, August 24, 1850); "Moses Keyser The Bowery Bully's Trip to the Californian Gold Mines", by John H. Manning; "The Adventures of Mr. Gulp" (by the Read brothers?); more comics by artists unknown; cartoons by George Cruikshank, Grandville, Elton.*

COLD CUTS AND PICKLED EELS' FEET; DONE BROWN BY JOHN BROWN
P.J. Cozans, New York: nd (c1855-60) (B&W)

nn (Very Rare) 100.00 200.00 300.00
NOTE: *Mostly a children's book. But, pages 87 to 110, and 111 to 122, contain narrative sequential stories.*

COLLEGE SCENES (O,G)
N. Hayward, Boston: 1850 (5x6-3/4", 72 pgs, printed one side only, B&W lithography)

nn - (Rare) by Nathan Hayward 200.00 400.00 600.00
NOTE: *This is the 2nd such production for an American University; the first issued at Yale circa 1845, decent funny art of story about life of a Harvard student from his entrance thru graduation entirely in caricature. Has art on back cover as well.*

COLLEGE CUTS Chosen From The Columbia Spectator 1880-81-82 (S)
White & Stokes, NY: 1882 (8x9-5/8", 92 pgs, B&W)

By F. Benedict Herzog, H. McVickar, W. Bard McVickar, others 20.00 40.00 80.00
nn - 2nd edition reprint (1888) (8-1/4x10-3/8) 10.00 20.00 40.00

COMICAL COONS (M)
R.H. Russell: 1898 (8-7/8 x 11-7/8", 68 pgs, hardcover, B&W)

nn - By E. W. Kemble 300.00 600.00 1200.00
NOTE: *Black Americana collection of 2-panel stories.*

COMICAL ALMANAC
Anton Bicker, Cinncinati, OH: 1885 (9x6, 260 pgs, B&W, illustrated-c)

nn - two (12) page sequential Busch comic strips 50.00 100.00 200.00

COMIC ALMANAC, THE
John Berger. Baltimore: 1854-? (7-1/2x6-1/4, 36 pgs, B&W)

nn - 60.00 120.00 240.00

COMIC ANNUAL, AMERICAN (O,I)
Richardson, Lord, & Holbrook, Boston: 1831 (6-7/8x4-3/8", 268 pgs, B&W, hard-c)

nn - (Scarce) 150.00 300.00 600.00
NOTE: *Mostly text; front & back cover illustrations, 13 full page, and scattered smaller illustrations by David Claypoole Johnston; edited by Henry J. Finn.*

COMIC HISTORY OF THE UNITED STATES, (I)
Carleton & Co., NY: 1876 (6-7/8x5-1/8", 336 pgs, hardcover, B&W)

nn - By Livingston Hopkins. 12.50 25.00 50.00
2nd printing: Cassell, Petter, Galpin & Co.: 1880 (6-7/8x5-1/8", 336 pgs, hardcover, B&W)
nn - By Livingston Hopkins. 12.50 25.00 50.00
NOTE: *Text with many B&W illustrations; some are multi-panel comics. Not to beconfused with **Bill Nye's Comic History Of The U.S.** which contains Frederick Opper illustrations.*

COMIC MONTHLY, THE
J.C. Haney, N.Y.: March 1859-1880 (16 x 11-1/2", 30 pgs average, B&W)

Certain average issues with sequential comics 50.00 100.00 200.00
11 (Jan 1860) Bellew-c 25.00 50.00 100.00
v2#2 (Apr 1860) Bellew-c 25.00 50.00 100.00
v2#3 (May 1860) Bellew-c 25.00 50.00 100.00
v2#4 (June 1860) Comic Strip Cover 50.00 100.00 200.00
v2#5 (July 1860) Bellew-c; (12) panel Explaining American Politics To An Intelligent Foreigner; (10) panel The Art of Stump Speaking; (15) panel Mr. Dibbs Goes to Pike's Peak and Comes Back Again 100.00 200.00 400.00
v2#7 (Sept 1860) Comic Strip Cover; (24) panel double page spread The Prince of Wales In America 50.00 100.00 200.00
v2#8 (18) panel The Three Young Friends Sillouette Strip 25.00 50.00 100.00
v2#9 (Nov 1860) (9) panel sequential 25.00 50.00 100.00
v2#10 11 not indexed 25.00 50.00 100.00
v2#12 (Jan 1861) (12) panel double page spread 25.00 50.00 100.00

COMIC TOKEN FOR 1836, A COMPANION TO THE COMIC ALMANAC, THE
Charles Ellms, Boston: 1836 (8x5', 48 pgs, B&W)
nn - 50.00 100.00 200.00

COMIC WEEKLY, THE
???, NYC: 1881-???

issues with comic strips (Chips, etc) 60.00 125.00 250.00

The Comus Offering
1830-31 © B. Franklin Edmands

The Daily Graphic #158 Frank Bellew-c
Sept 4, 1873 © The Graphic Company, NY

Elton's Californian Comic All-My-Nack #17
1850 © Elton's, NY

FR1.0 GD2.0 FN6.0

COMIC WORLD
???: 1876-1879 (Quarto Monthly)

issues with comic strips 37.50 75.00 150.00

COMICS FROM SCRIBNER'S MAGAZINE (M)
Scribner's: nd (1891) (10 cents, 9-1/2x6-5/8", 24 pgs, paper cover, side stapled, B&W)

nn - (Rare) F.M.Howarth C&A 100.00 200.00 400.00
NOTE: *Advertised in SCRIBNER'S MAGAZINE in the June 1891 issue, page 793, as available by mail order for 10 cents. Collects together comics material which ran in the back pages of Scribner's Magazine. Art by Attwood, "Chip" Bellew, Dŏes, Frost, Gibson, Zim.*

COMUS OFFERING CONTAINING HUMOROUS SCRAPS OF DIVERTING COMICALITIES, THE (O, S)
B. Franklin Edmands, 25 Court St, Boston: c1830-31 (8-7/8x10-3/4", 16 pgs, thin brown paper-c, blank on backs,

nn - (William F Straton, Engraver, 15 Water St, Boston) (no known sales)
NOTE: All hand-colored single panel cartoons format definitely inspired by D.C. Johnston's Scraps with every panel character using well-defined word balloons. Might become a seminal step in the evolution of the American comic book. More research is needed.

CONTRASTS AND CONCEITS FOR CONTEMPLATION BY LUKE LIMNER (O)
Ackerman & Co, 96 Strand, London: c1848 (9-3/4x6-1/4, 48 pgs, B&W)
nn - By John Leighton 50.00 100.00 200.00

COONTOWN'S 400 (M) (see **Blackberries**) (M)
The Life (Magazine) Co.: 1899 (10-15/16x8-7/8, 68 pgs, cloth light-brown hard-c, B&W
nn - By E.W. Kemble (scarce) 250.00 500.00 1500.00
NOTE: *Tastefully drawn depictions of Black Americana over one hundred years ago during Jim Crow days.*

CROSSING THE ATLANTIC (O,G)
James R. Osgood & Co., Boston: 1872 (10-7/8x16", 68 pgs, hardcover, B&W);
Houghton, Osgood & Co., Boston: 1880

1st printing - by Augustus Hoppin 50.00 100.00 200.00
2nd printing (1880; 66 pgs; 8-1/8x11-1/8") 32.50 65.00 150.00

C.R. PITT'S COMIC ALMANAC
C.R. Pitt: 1880 (7-1/2x4-5/8", 28 pgs)

nn - contains (8) panel sequential 50.00 100.00 200.00

CRUIKSHANK'S OMNIBUS: A VEHICLE FOR FUN AND FROLIC (E,S)
E. Ferrett & Co., Philadelphia: 1845 (25 cents, 7-1/2" x 4-5/8", 96 pgs, B&W, paper-c)

nn - By George Cruikshank c/a (Very Rare) 150.00 300.00 600.00
NOTE: *Mostly prose, with 10 plates of cartoons printed on one-side (about half the plates with multiple cartoons), plus illustrated cover, all by George Cruikshank. First (perhaps only) American printing of Cruikshank's Omnibus, which was published first in Britain. It is only a partial reprinting.*

CYCLISTS' DICTIONARY (S)
Morgan & Wright, Chicago: 1894 (5 x3-3/4, 80 pgs, soft-c, B&W

nn - By Unknown 37.50 75.00 150.00

THE DAILY GRAPHIC
The Graphic Company, 39 Park Place, NY: 1873-Sept 23, 1889 (14x20-1/2, 8 pgs, B&W)

Average issues with comic strips 7.50 15.00 30.00
Average issues without comic strips 5.00 10.00 20.00
NOTE:

DAVY CROCKETT'S COMIC ALMANACK
???, Nashville, TN, then elsewhere: 1835-end (32 pages plus wraps)

1 500.00 1000.00 2000.00
2-13 15 end 250.00 500.00 1000.00
14 contains (17) panel Crocket comic strip bio 1848 1000.00 1500.00 3000.00

DAY'S DOINGS (was The Last Sensation) (Becomes New York Illustrated Times)
James Watts, NYC: #1 June 6 1868-early 1876 (11x16, 16 pgs, B&W)

average issue with comic strips 10.00 15.00 25.00
Paul Pry & Alley Sloper character issues 25.00 50.00 100.00
Aug 19 1871 - First Alley Sloper in America?? 50.00 100.00 200.00
NOTE: *James Watts was a shadow company for Frank Leslie; outright sold to Frank Leslie in 1873. There are a lot of issues with comic strips from 1868 up.*

DAY'S SPORT - OR, HUNTING ADVENTURES OF S. WINKS WATTLES, A SHOPKEEPER, THOMAS TITT, A "LEGAL GENT," AND MAJOR NICHOLAS NOGGIN, A JOLLY GOOD FELLOW GENERALLY, A (O)
Brother Jonathan, NY: c1850s (5-7/8x8-1/4, 44 pgs)

nn - By Henry L. Stephens, Philadelphia (Very Rare) (no known sales)

DEVIL'S COMICAL OLDMANICK WITH COMIC ENGRAVINGS OF THE PRINCIPAL EVENTS OF TEXAS, THE
Turner & Fisher, NY & Philadelphia: 1837 (7-7/8x5", 24 pgs)

nn- many single panel cartoons 100.00 200.00 400.00

DIE VEHME, ILLUSTRIRTES WOCHENBLATT FUR SCHERZ UND ERNEST (M,O)
Heinrich Binder, St. Louis: No.1 Aug 28, 1869 - No.?? Aug 20, 1870 (10 cents, 8 pgs, B&W, paper-c) (see also PUCK)

1-?? (Very Rare) by Joseph Keppler 100.00 200.00 400.00
NOTE: *Joseph Keppler's first attempt at a weekly American humor periodical. Entirely in German. The title translates into: **"The Star Chamber: An Illustrated Weekly Paper in Fun and Ernest"**.*

FR1.0 GD2.0 FN6.0

DOMESTIC MANNERS OF THE AMERICANS
The Imprint Society, Barre, Mass: 1969 (9-3/4 x 7-1/4", 390 pgs, hard-c in slipcase, B&W)

nn - 10.00 20.00 40.00
NOTE: *Reprints the 1832 edition of this book by Mrs. Trollope with an added insert. The 28-page insert is what is of primary interest to us -- it reproduces SCRAPS No. 4 (1833) by D.C. Johnston.*

DRUNKARD'S CHILDREN, THE (see also THE BOTTLE) (E,O)
David Bogue, London; John Wiley and G.P. Putnam, New York; J. Sands, Sydney, New South Wales: July 1, 1848 (16x11", 16 pgs, printed on one side only, paper-c)

nn - Black & white edition (Scarce) 300.00 600.00 950.00
nn - Hand colored edition (Rare) (no known sales)
NOTE: *Sequel story to THE BOTTLE, by George Cruikshank. Temperance/anti-alcohol story. British-American-Australian co-publication. Cover is text only - no cover art.*

DRUNKARD'S PROGRESS, OR THE DIRECT ROAD TO POVERTY, WRETCHEDNESS & RUIN, THE
J. W. Barber, New Haven, Conn.: Sept 1826 (single sheet)

nn - By John Warner Barber (Very Rare) (no known sales)
NOTE: *Broadside designed and printed by barber contains four large wood engravings showing "The Morning Dram" which is "The Beginning of Sorrow"; "The Grog Shop" with its "Bad Company"; "The Confirmed Drunkard" in a state of "Beastly Intoxication"; and the "Concluding Scene" with the family being drive off to the alms house. It is an interesting set of cuts, faintly reminiscent of Hogarth. Many modern reprints exist.*

DUEL FOR LOVE, A (O,P)
E.C. DeWitt & Co., Chicago: nd (c1880's) (3-3/8" x 2-5/8", 12 pgs, B&W, paper-c)

nn - Art by F.M. Howarth (Rare) 25.00 50.00 100.00
NOTE: *Advertising giveaway for DeWitt's Little Early Risers, featuring an 8-panel strip story, spread out 1 panel per page.*

DURHAM WHIFFS (O, P)
Blackwells Durham Tobacco Co: Jan 8 1878 (9x6.5", 8 pgs, color-c, B&W)

v1 #1 w/Trade Card Insert 37.50 75.00 150.00
NOTE: Sold in 2008 CGC 9.4 $1250

DYNALENE LAFLETS (P)
The Dynalene Company: nd (3 x 3-1/2", 16 pgs, B&W, paper cover)

nn - Dynalene Dyes promo (9) panel comic strip 25.00 50.00 75.00

ELEPHANT, THE
William H Graham, Tribune Building, NYC: Jan 22 1848-Feb 19 1848 (11x8.5", B&W)

1-5 Rare - single panel cartoons 150.00 300.00 600.00

ELTON'S COMIC ALL-MY-NACK (E,O.S)
Elton, Publisher, 18 Division & 98 Nassau St, NY: 1833-1852 (7-1/2x4-1/2", 36pgs, B&W

1-5 99% single panel cartoons 100.00 200.00 400.00
6 (1839) 100.00 200.00 400.00
NOTE: Two different covers & different interiors exist for this title and number
7-15 - 99% single panel cartoons 100.00 200.00 400.00
16 - contains 6 panel "A Tales of A Tayl-or" 1848-49 200.00 400.00 600.00
17 - contains "Moses Keyser, The Bowery Bully's Trip To the California Gold Mines" 1850 By John H. Manning, early comics creator, told in 15 panels 200.00 400.00 600.00
18-19 presently unknown contents 100.00 200.00 400.00
NOTE: *Contains both original American, and pirated European, cartoons. All single panel material, except where noted. Almanacs are published near the end of the year prior to that for which they are printed -- like calendars today. Thus, the 1833 No. 1 issue was really published in the last months of 1832. #17 has Elton's Californian Comic-All-My-Nack on the cover.*

ELTON'S COMIC ALMANAC (Publsiher change)
GW Cottrell & Co, Publishers & C Cornhill, Boston, Mass: 1853 (7-7/8x4-5/8,36pgs,B&W
20 - (2) sequential comic strips (9) panel "Jones, Smith and Robinson Goes To A Ball; (21) panel "The Adventures of Mr. Gulp" Rare 300.00 600.00 1200.00
NOTE: *Both strips appear in* The Clown, Or The Banquet of Wit

ELTON'S FUNNY ALMANACK (title change to Almanac)
Elton Publisher and Engraver, New York: 1846 (8x6-1/2", 36 pgs)

1 1846 50.00 100.00 200.00

ELTON'S FUNNY ALMANAC (#1 titled Almanack)
Elton & Co, New York: 1847-1853 (8x6-1/4, 36 pgs, B&W)
2 (1847) #3 (1848) 50.00 100.00 200.00
nn 1853 (8-1/8x4-7/8"; (5) panel comic strip "The Adventures of Mr. Goliah Starvemouse"

ELTON'S RIPSNORTER COMIC ALMANAC
Elton, 90 Nassau St, NY: 1850 (8x5, 24 pgs, B&W, paper-c)
nn - scarce 50.00 100.00 200.00

ENGLISH SOCIETY (S)
Harper & Brothers, Publishers, New York: 1897 (9-5/8x12-1/4", 206 pgs, B&W)

nn - by George Du Maurier 25.00 50.00 75.00

ENGLISH SOCIETY AT HOME (S)
James R. Osgood and Company: 1881 (10-7/8x8-5/8, 182 pgss, protective sheets on some pages - not included in pages count, hard-c, B&W 25.00 50.00 75.00

nn - by George Du Maurier

ENTER: THE COMICS (E,G)
University of Nebraska Press: 1965 (6-7/8x9-1/4", 120 pgs, hard-c)

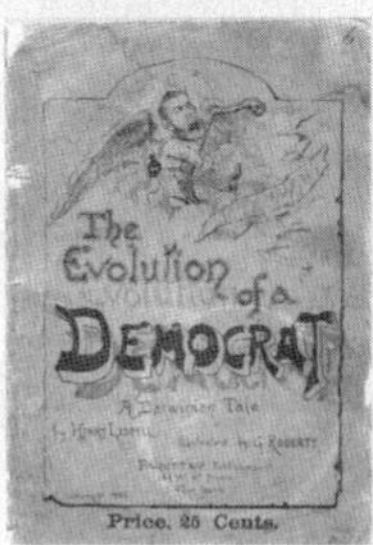

The Evolution Of A Democrat
1888 © Paquet & Co, NY

Flying Leaves
1880s © E.R. Herrick & Company, New York

Frank Leslie's Boys & Girls Sample Comic Strip Page
1870s © Frank Leslie

	FR1.0	GD2.0	FN6.0
nn - By Ellen Weisse	25.00	50.00	100.00

NOTE: *Contains overview of Töpffer's life and career plus only published English translation of Töpffer's Monsieur Crepin (1837); appears to have been re-drawn by Weisse in the days before xerox machines.*

ESQUIRE BROWN AND HIS MULE, STORY OF
A.C. Meyer, Baltimore, Maryland: 1880s (5x3/7/8", 28 pgs, B&W)

Booklet (9 panel story plus cough remedies catalog)	25.00	50.00	100.00
Fold-Out of Booklet (9 panel version)	25.00	50.00	100.00

"EVENTS OF THE WEEK" REPRINTED FROM THE CHICAGO TRIBUNE
Henry O. Shepard Co, Chicago: 1894 (5-3/8x15-7/8", 110 pg, B&W, hard-c)

First Series, Second Series - By HR Heaton	37.50	75.00	150.00

EVERYBODY'S COMICK ALMANACK
Turner & Fisher, NY & Philadelphia: 1837 (7-7/8x5", 36 pgs, B&W)

nn	50.00	100.00	200.00

EVOLUTION OF A DEMOCRAT - A DARWINIAN TALE, THE (O,G)
Paquet & Co., New York: 1888 (25 cents, 7-7/8x5-1/2", 100 pgs, printed one side only, orange paper cover, B&W) (Very Rare)

nn - Written by Henry Liddell, art by G. Roberty	300.00	600.00	1200.00

NOTE: *Political parody about the rise of an Irishman through Tammany Hall. Grover Cleveland appears as linked with Tammany. Ireland becomes the next state in the USA.*

FABLES FOR THE TIMES (S, I)
R.H. Russell & Son, New York: 1896 (9-1/8x12-1/8", 52 pgs, yellow hard-c)

nn - By H.W. Phillips and T.S. Sullivant Scarce	75.00	150.00	300.00

FERDINAND FLIPPER, ESQ., THE FORTUNES OF (O,G)
Brother Jonathan, Publisher, NY: nd (1851) (5-3/4 x 9-3/8", 84 pgs, B&W, printed both sides)

nn - By Various (Very Rare)	500.00	1000.00	2500.00

NOTE: *Extended title: "...Commencing With A Period of Four Months And Anterior To His Birth Going Thru The Various Stages of His Infancy, Childhood, Verdant Years, Manhood, Middle Life, and Green and Ripe Old Age, And Ending A Short Time Subsequent To His Sudden Decease With His Final Exit, Funeral And Burial." Extremely unique comic book, put together by gathering 145 independent single illustrations and cartoons, by various artists, and stringing them together into a sequential story. The majority of panels are by Grandville. Also included are at least 19 signed Charles Martin, reprinted from 1847 issues of Yankee Doodle, 5 panels from D.C. Johnston, plus other panels by F.O.C. Darley, T.H. Matheson, and others. The story also contains several panels of Gold Rush content . Printed by E.A. Alverds. The 1851 date is derived from an advertisement found in the Oct-Dec 1851 issue of the Brother Jonathan newspaper. It ispossible, however, that it actually came out even earlier.*

FERDINAND FLIPPER, ESQ., THE FORTUNES OF (G)
Dick & Fitzgerald, New York: nd (1870's to 1888) (30 Cents, 84 pgs, B&W, paper cover)

nn - (Very Rare reprint - several editions possible)	375.00	750.00	1500.00

FINN'S COMIC ALMANAC
Marsh, Capen, & Lyon; Boston: 1835-??? (4.5x7.5, 36 pgs, B&W)

nn	100.00	200.00	400.00

FINN'S COMIC SKETCHBOOK (S)
Peabody & Co., 223 Broadway, NY: 1831 (10-1/2x16", 12 pgs, B&W)

nn - By Henry J. Finn (Very Rare) (no known sales)

NOTE: *Designs on copper plates; etched by J. Harris, NY; should have tissue paper in front of each plate.*

50 GREAT CARTOONS (M,P,S)
Ram's Horn Press: 1899 (14x10-3/4, 112 pgs, hard-c)

nn - By Frank Beard	30.00	60.00	120.00

NOTE: *Premium in return for a subscription to **The Ram's Horn** magazine.*

FISHER'S COMIC ALMANAC
Ames Fisher and Brother, No 12 North Sixth St, Philadelphia , Charles Small in NYC, Also in Boston: 1841-1868 (4-1/2 x 7-1/4, 36 pgs, B&W)

1-7 (1841-1847)	100.00	200.00	400.00
12 reprints mermaid-c with word balloon (1868)	100.00	200.00	400.00

F**** A*** K*****, OUTLINES ILLUSTRATIVE OF THE JOURNAL OF** (O,S)
D.C. Johnston, Boston: 1835 (9-5/16 x 6", 12 pgs, printed one side only, blue paper cover, B&W interior) (see also **SCRAPS**)

nn - by David Claypoole Johnston (Scarce)	600.00	1000.00	1600.00

NOTE: *This is a series of 8 plates parodying passages from the Journal of Fanny (Frances) A. Kemble, a British woman who wrote a highly negative book about American Culture after returning from the U.S. Though remembered now for her campaign against slavery, she was prejudiced against most everything American culture, thus inspiring Johnston's satire. Contains 4 protective sheets (not part of page count.)*

FLYING DUTCHMAN; OR, THE WRATH OF HERR VONSTOPPELNOZE, THE (E)
Carleton Publishing, New York: 1862 (7-5/8x5-1/4", 84 pgs, printed on one side only, gilted hardcover, B&W)

nn - By Wilhelm Busch (Scarce)	35.00	70.00	160.00
nn - 1975 Scarce 100 copy-r 74 pgs Visual Studies Workshop	5.00	10.00	20.00

NOTE: *This is the earliest known English language book publication of a Wilhelm Busch work. The story is plagiarized by American poet John G. Saxe, who is credited with the text, while the uncredited Busch cartoons are described merely as accompanying illustrations.*

FLYING LEAVES (E)
E.R. Herrick & Company, New York: nd (c1889/1890's) (8-1/4" x 11-1/2", 76 pgs, B&W interior, orange, b&w hard-c)

nn- (Scarce)	85.00	175.00	260.00

NOTE: *Reprints strips and single panel cartoons from 1888 Fliegende Blatter issues, translated into English. Various artists, including Bechstein, Adolf Hengeler, Lothar Meggendorfer, Emil Reinicke.*

FOOLS PARADISE WITH THE MANY ADVENTURES THERE AS SEEN IN THE STRANGE SURPRISING PEEP SHOW OF PROFESSOR WOLLEY COBBLE, THE (E)
(see also THE COMICAL PEEP SHOW)
John Camden Hotten, London: Nov 1871 (1 crown, 9-7/8x7-3/8", 172 pgs, printed one side only, gilted green hardcover, hand colored interior)

	FR1.0	GD2.0	FN6.0
nn - By Wilhelm Busch (Rare)	400.00	800.00	1750.00

NOTE: *Title on cover is: **WALK IN! WALK IN!! JUST ABOUT TO BEGIN!!! the FOOLS PARADISE**; below the above title page. Anthology of Wilhelm Busch comics, translated into English.*

FOOLS PARADISE WITH THE MANY WONDERFUL SIGHTS AS SEEN IN THE STRANGE SURPRISING PEEP SHOW OF PROFESSOR WOLLEY COBBLE, FURTHER ADVENTURES IN (E)
Chatto & Windus, London: 1873 (10x7-3/8", 128 pgs, printed one side only, brown hardcover, hand colored interior)

nn - By Wilhelm Busch (Rare)	300.00	600.00	1320.00

NOTE: *Sequel to the 1871 **FOOLS PARADISE**, containing a completely different set of Busch stories, translated into English.*

FOOLS PARADISE MIRTH AND FUN FOR THE OLD & YOUNG (E)
Griffith & Farran, London: May 1883 (9-3/4x7-5/8", 78 pgs, color cover, color interior)

nn - By Wilhelm Busch (Rare)	100.00	200.00	420.00

NOTE: *Collection of selected stories reprinted from both the 1871 & 1873 **FOOLS PARADISE**.*

FOOLS PARADISE - MIRTH AND FUN FOR THE OLD & YOUNG (E)
E.P. Dutton and Co., NY: May 1883 (9-3/4x7-5/8", 78 pgs, color cover, color interior)

nn - By Wilhelm Busch (Rare)	100.00	200.00	420.00

NOTE: *Collection of selected stories reprinted from both the 1871 & 1873 **FOOLS PARADISE**.*

FOREIGN TOUR OFMESSRS. BROWN, JONES, AND ROBINSON, THE (see Messrs....)

FRANK LESLIE'S BOYS AND GIRLS
Frank Leslie, NYC: Oct 13 1866-#905 Feb 9 1884

average issue with comic strip	10.00	20.00	40.00

FRANK LESLIE'S BUDGET OF FUN
Frank Leslie, Ross & Tousey, 121 Nassau St, NYC: Jan 1859-1878 (newspaper size)

1-5 no comic strips	50.00	100.00	200.00
6 June 1859 (9) panel "The Wonderful Hunting Tour of Mr Borridge After the Deer"	75.00	150.00	300.00
7-9 no comic strips	25.00	50.00	100.00
10 Sept 1859 sequential comic strip	50.00	100.00	200.00
11 (8) panel sequential "Apropos of the Great Eastern"	50.00	100.00	200.00
12-14	25.00	50.00	100.00
15 Feb 1860 (12) panel "The Ballet Girl" strip	50.00	100.00	200.00
16-18	25.00	50.00	100.00
19 June 1860 comic strip front cover	100.00	200.00	300.00

NOTE: Cover is (11) panel "The Very Latest Fashionable Amusement..."; Back cover comic strip "Mr Jogg's Reasons For Preferring to Board to Keeping House" (7) panels using word balloons. Plus centerfold double page (18) panel spread "The New York May, Moving in General, and Mrs. Grundy's In Particular."

20 24 25 no comic strips	25.00	50.00	100.00
21 (7/15/60) (8) panel Mr Septimus Verdilater Visits the Baltimore Convention"	50.00	100.00	200.00
22 (8/1/60) (3) panel	25.00	50.00	100.00
23 (8/15/60) (12) panel "Superb Scheme For Perfecting of Dramatic Entertainment"	50.00	100.00	200.00
25 (9/15/60 (9) panel sequential	25.00	50.00	100.00
27 AbrahamLincoln Word Balloon cover	50.00	100.00	200.00
28 Wilhelm Busch sequential strip-r begin	50.00	100.00	200.00
29, 31-51 to be indexed next year	25.00	50.00	100.00
30 (12/15/60) (3) panel sequential strip	25.00	50.00	100.00
31 (Jan 1861) (12) panel The Boarding School Miss	25.00	50.00	100.00
32 (Feb 1861) (10) panel Telegraphic Horrors; Or, Mr Buchanan Undergoing A Series of Electric Shocks	50.00	100.00	200.00
35 (4/1/61) Abraham Lincoln Word Balloon cover	50.00	100.00	200.00
43 44 no sequential comic strips	25.00	50.00	100.00
45 (Nov 1861) (6) panel sequential; (11) panel The Budget Army and Infantry Tactics; First Bellew here? - Many Bellew full pagers begin	50.00	100.00	200.00
48 (Feb 1862) Bellew-c; (2) panel Bellew strip plus singles	50.00	100.00	200.00
49 (Mar 1862) Bellew-c; (16) panel Wilhelm Busch "The Fly Or The Disturbed Ducthman A Story without Words"	50.00	100.00	200.00
50 (April 1862) Bellew-c "Succession Bath" plus singles	25.00	50.00	100.00
51 (May 1862) Bellew-c; (25) panel Busch The Toothache (6) panel Definitions of the Day	50.00	100.00	200.00
52 (June 1862) Bellew-c; (9) panel A Cock & A Bull Expedition; (6) panel Bellew The First Campaign of the Home Guard	50.00	100.00	200.00

NOTE: Johnny Bull & Louis Napolean with Brother Jonathan

53-67 To Be Indexed in the Future	25.00	50.00	100.00
68 (11/18///63) (6) panel Bellew strip "Cuts On Cowards"	25.00	50.00	100.00

NOTE: contains (1) panel William Newman 1817-1870, mentor to Thomas Nast

71 (Feb 1864) Wiord Balloon Jefferson Davis-c	25.00	50.00	100.00
72 (Mar 1864) Word Balloon-c	25.00	50.00	100.00

Frank Tousey's Illustrated New York Monthly #9
June 1882 © Frank Tousey

Funny Fellow's Own Book
1852 © Philip Cozans

Funny Folk by F.M. Howarth
1899© E.P. Dutton

73 (April 1864) Word Balloon-c in (6) panels 25.00 50.00 100.00
74 (May 1864) Newman Word Balloon-c 25.00 50.00 100.00
75 77 78 no sequentials 25.00 50.00 100.00
76 (July 1864) Newman Word Balloon-c 25.00 50.00 100.00
79 (Oct 1864) Word Balloon-c 25.00 50.00 100.00
80 (Nov 1864) Robt E Lee & JeffDavis-c; no sequentials 25.00 50.00 100.00
81 (Dec 1864) Word Balloon "Abyss of War"-c 25.00 50.00 100.00
83 (2/18/65) Back-c (6) panel "Petroleum" 25.00 50.00 100.00
84 (Mar 1865) (6) panel sequential 25.00 50.00 100.00
85 (Apr 1865) Word Balloon-c 25.00 50.00 100.00
86 89 90 92 no sequentials 25.00 50.00 100.00
88 (7/6/65) (6) panel "Marriage" 25.00 50.00 100.00
91 (Oct 1865) (6) panel "Brief Confab At The Corner 25.00 50.00 100.00
93-98 yet to be indexed 25.00 50.00 100.00
99 (June 1866) (18) panel Mr Paul Peters Adventures
While Trout-Fishing In The Adirondacks 50.00 100.00 200.00
100 (July 1866) (4) panel sequential comic strip 25.00 50.00 100.00
102 (Sept 1866) (6) panel sequential comic strip 25.00 50.00 100.00
103 (Oct 1866) (9) panel strip; (12) pane;l back cover
Adventures of McTiffin At Long Branch 50.00 100.00 200.00
104 (Nov 1866) (4) panel; (23) panel "The Budget Rebuses; (2) panel
Glut On Treason Market;back-c; (6) sequential strip 25.00 50.00 100.00
105 (12/18/66) Word Balloon-c; (20) panel sequential back-c 37.50 65.00 130.00
NOTE: Artists include William Newman (1863-1868), William Henry Shelton, Joseph Keppler (1873-1876), James A. Wales (1876-1878), Frederick Burr Opper (1878)

FRANK LESLIE'S LADY'S MAGAZINE
Frank Leslie, NYC: Feb 1863-Dec 1882 (8.5x12", typically 152 pgs)
issues with comic strips 10.00 20.00 40.00

FRANK LESLIE'S PICTORIAL WEEKLY
Frank Leslie, Ross & Tousey, 121 Nassau St, NYC:
average issue (Very Rare) 50.00 100.00 200.00

FRANK TOUSEY'S NEW YORK COMIC MONTHLY
Frank Tousey, NYC: (no known sales)

FREAKS
???, Philadelphia: Jan 8, 1881-April? 1881 (Chromolithographic Weekly)
(Very Rare) 50.00 100.00 300.00

FREELANCE, THE
A.M. Soteldo Jr, Edito, 292 Broadway, NYC: 1874-75 (Folio Weekly)
(Rare) 25.00 50.00 100.00

FREE MASONRY EXPOSED
Winchell & Small, 113 Fulton, NY: 1871 (7-5/8x10-1/2", 36pgs, blue paper-c, B&W)
nn- Thomas Worth Scarce 100.00 200.00 400.00
NOTE: Scathing satircal look at Free Masons thru many cartoons, their power waning by the 1870s

FREETHINKERS' PICTORIAL TEXT-BOOK, THE (S,O)
The Truth Seeker Company, New York: 1890, 1896, 1898 (9x12, hard-c, B&W)
1 (1890 edition) - Scarce 382 pgs By Watson Heston 200.00 400.00 800.00
1 (1896 edition) - Scarce 378 pgs By Watson Heston (1890-r)100.00 200.00 450.00
2 (1898 edition) - Scarce 408 pgs By Watson Heston 125.00 250.00 450.00
NOTE: *Sought after by collectors of Freethought/Atheism material. There is also 200 copy Modern Reprint.*

FRITZ SPINDLE-SHANKS, THE RAVEN BLACK
Cosack & C o, Buffalo, NY: 1870/80s (4-3/8x2-3/4", color)
(10) card comic strip set by Wilhelm Busch 25.00 50.00 100.00

FUN BY RALL
Unknown: circa 1865 (11x7-7/8", 68 pgs, soft-c, B&W)
nn - By presently unknown (Very Rare) 100.00 200.00 350.00
NOTE: *Wraparound soft cover like modern comic book; yellow paper cover with red & black ink.*

FUN FOR THE FAMILY IN PICTURES
D. Lothrop and Company: 1886 (4 x 7", 48 pgs, Silver & Red stiff-c; interior pages have various single color inks)
nn - By unknown hand 50.00 100.00 200.00
NOTE: *Single panel cartoons and sequential stories.*

FUN FROM LIFE
Frederick A Stokes & Brother, New York: 1889 (9 1/8 by 7 1/8, 72 pages, hard-c)
nn - Mostly by Frank "Chips" Bellew Jr 62.50 125.00 250.00
NOTE: *Contains both single panel and many sequential comics reprints from Life.*

FUNNYEST OF AWL AND THE FUNNIEST SORT OF PHUN, THE
AT Bellew Or W. Jennings Demorest, 121 Nassau St, NY : 1865-67 (30 issues, 16x11 tabloid 16 pgs B&W Monthly, 1-8 © American News; 9-on © A.T. Bellews)
1 (April 1864) Bellew-c 50.00 100.00 200.00
4 (1865) Bellew-c 50.00 100.00 200.00
5 (1865) Busch (20) panel comic srtip The Toothache 75.00 150.00 300.00
7 (1865) Bellew-c 50.00 100.00 200.00
8 (1865) Special Petroleum oil issue - much cartoon art 100.00 200.00 400.00
9 (July 1865) Bellew Bullfrog-c; centerfold double page spread hanging
many Confederates; (6) panel strip hanging Jeff Davis 100.00 200.00 400.00
10 (Aug 1865) Bellew-c (13) panel Busch strip with two ducks, a frog
and a butcher who gets the ducks in the end 100.00 200.00 400.00
11 (Sept 1865) Bellew Bull Frog Anti-French-c 50.00 100.00 200.00
13 14 15 (12/65-1/66) Bellew-c no sequential comic strips 50.00 100.00 200.00
16 (March 1866) address change to 39 Park Ave 50.00 100.00 200.00
22 (Sept 1866) 133 Nassau St 50.00 100.00 200.00
34 (Oct 1867) 133 Nassau St (7) panel Baseball comic strip;
Last Known Issue - were there more? 100.00 200.00 400.00
NOTE: *Radical Republican politics distributed by Great American News Company; owned by Frank Bellew's wife as a front for her husband. When the Civil War ended, the brutal anti-Confederate comic strips and jokes switched to frogs and began attacking France. Funny thing, history says without France's help in the 1700s, there just might not have been a United States.*

FUNNY ALMANAC
Elton & Co., NY: 1853 (8-1/8x4-7/8, 36 pgs)
nn - sequential comic strip 50.00 100.00 200.00
NOTE: (5) panel strip "The Adventures of Mr. Goliah Starvemouse"

FUNNY FELLOWS OWN BOOK, A COMPANION FOR THE LOVERS OF FROLIC AND GLEE, THE (M,N)
Philip. J. Cozans, 116 Nassau ST, NY: 1852 (4-1/2x7-1/2", 196 pgs, burnt orange paper-c)
nn - contains many sequential comic strips (Very Rare) (no known sales)
NOTE: Collected from many different Comic Alamac(k)s including Mose Keyser (Calif Gold Rush); Jones, Smith and Robinson Goes To A Ball; Adventures of Mr. Gulp, Or the Effects of A Dinner Party; The Bowery Bully's Trip To The California Gold Mines plus lots more. This one is a sleeper so far.

FUNNY FOLK (M)
E. P. Dutton: 1899 (12x16-1/2", 90 pgs,14 strips in color-rest in b&w, hard-c)
nn - By Franklin Morris Howarth 162.50 325.00 1500.00
nn - London: J.M. Dent, 1899 embossed-c; same interior 200.00 450.00 900.00
NOTE: *Reprints many sequential strips & single panel cartoons from* ***Puck.*** *This is considered by many to be yet another "missing link" between Victorian & Platinum Age comic books. Most comic books 1900-1917 re-printing Sunday newspaper comic strips follow this size format, except using cardboard-c rather than hard-c.*

FUNNY SKETCHES...Also Embracing Comic Illustrations
Frank Harrison, New York: 1881 (6-5/8x5", 68 pgs, B&W, Color-c)
nn - contains (3) sequential comic strips; one strip is (6) pages long;
plus one (3) pages; one more (2) pager 75.00 150.00 300.00

GIBSON BOOK, THE (M,S)
Charles Scribner's Sons & R.H. Russell, New York: 1906 (11-3/8x17-5/8", gilted red hard-c, B&W)
Book I 50.00 100.00 200.00
NOTE: *Reprints in whole the books: Drawings, Pictures of People, London,Sketches and Cartoons, Education of Mr. Pipp, Americans. 414 pgs. 1907 2nd editions exist same value.*
Book II 50.00 100.00 200.00
NOTE: *Reprints in whole the books: A Widow and Her Friends, The Weaker Sex, Everyday People, Our Neighbors. 314 pgs 1907 second edition for both also exists. Same value.*

GIBSON'S PUBLISHED DRAWINGS, MR. (M,S) (see Plat index for later issues post 1900)
R.H. Russell, New York: No.1 1894 - No. 9 1904 (11x17-3/4", hard-c, B&W)
nn (No.1; 1894) Drawings 96 pgs 30.00 60.00 120.00
nn (No.2; 1896) Pictures of People 92 pgs 30.00 60.00 120.00
nn (No.3; 1898) Sketches and Cartoons 94 pgs 30.00 60.00 120.00
nn (No.4; 1899) The Education of Mr. Pipp 88 pgs 30.00 60.00 120.00
nn (No.5; 1900) Americans 30.00 60.00 120.00
NOTE: *By Charles Dana Gibson cartoons, reprinted from magazines, primarily* ***LIFE.*** *The Education of Mr. Pipp tells a story. Series continues how long after 1904? Each of these books originally came in a boxx and are worth more with the box.*

GIRL WHO WOULDN'T MIND GETTING MARRIED, THE (O)
Frederick Warne & Co., London & New York: nd (c1870's) (9-1/2x11-1/2", 28 pgs, printed 1 side, paper-c, B&W)
nn - By Harry Parkes 62.50 125.00 250.00
NOTE: *Published simultaneously with its companion volume,* ***The Man Who Would Like to Marry.***

GOBLIN SNOB, THE (O)
DeWitt & Davenport, New York: nd (c1853-56) (24 x 17 cm, 96 pgs, B&W, color hard-c)
nn - (Rare) by H.L. Stephens 250.00 500.00 1000.00

GOLDEN ARGOSY
Frank A. Munsey, 81 Warren St, NYC: 1880s (10-1/2x12, 16 pgs, B&W)
issues with full page comic strips by Chips and Bisbee 12.50 25.00 50.00

GOLDEN DAYS, THE
James Elverson, Publisher, NYC: March 6 1880-May 11 1907 weekly, 16 pgs
issues with comic strips 4.00 7.50 15.00
Horatio Alger issues 10.00 20.00 40.00
v10 #49-v11#1 1889 first Stratemeyer story 25.00 50.00 100.00

GOLDEN WEEKLY, THE
Frank Tousey, NYC: #1 Sept 25 1889-#145 Aug 18 1892 (10-3/4x14-1/2, 16 pgs, B&W)
average issue with comic striips 15.00 25.00 50.00

GREAT LOCOFOCO JUGGERNAUT, THE (S)
publisher unknown: Fall/Winter 1837 (7-5/8x3-1/4, handbill single page)

The Story of Han's The Swapper Cover & First Two Panels
1865 © L. Pranc & Co, Boston

Humpty Dumpty, The Adventures of...
© Gantz, Jones and Co.

Imagerie d'Epinal
1888 © Mumoristic Publishing Co.

FR1.0 GD2.0 FN6.0

nn - By David Claypoole Johnston (a VG copy sold for $2000 in 2005)
nn - **Imprint Society:** 1971 (reprint) 6.00 12.00 25.00

HALF A CENTURY OF ENGLISH HISTORY (S. M)
G.P. Putnam's Sons - The Knickerbocker Press, New York and London: 1884 (7-3/4 x 5-3/4", 316 pgs., illustrated hard-c)

nn - By Various 25.00 50.00 175.00
NOTE: *Subtitle: Pictorially Presented in a Series of Cartoons from the Collection of Mr. Punch. Comprising 150 plates by Doyle, Leech, Tenniel, and others, in which are portrayed the political careers of Peel, Palmerston, Russell, Cobden, Bright, Beaconsfield, Derby, Salisbury, Gladstone and other English statesmen.*

HAIL COLUMBIA! HISTORICAL, COMICAL, AND CENTENNIAL (O,S)
The Graphic Co., New York & Walter F. Brown, Providence, RI: 1876 (10x11-3/8", 60 pgs, red gilted hard-c, B&W)

nn - by Walter F. Brown (Scarce) 100.00 200.00 450.00

HANS HUCKEBEIN'S BATCH OF ODD STORIES ODDLY ILLUSTRATEDED
McLoughlin Bros., New York: 1880s (9-3/4x7-3/8, 36?? pg?

nn - By Wilhelm Busch (Rare) 75.00 150.00 300.00

HANS THE SWAPPER, THE STORY OF (O)
L. Pranc & Co., 159 Washington St, Boston: 1865 (33 inch long fold out in colors)

nn - unique fold out comic book on one long piece of paper 75.00 150.00 300.00

HARPER'S NEW MONTHLY MAGAZINE
Harper & Brothers, Franklin Square, NY: 1850-1870s (6-3/4x10, 140 pgs, paper-c, B&W)
1850s issues with comic strips in back advert section 10.00 20.00 40.00

HEALTH GUYED (I)
Frederick A. Stokes Company: 1890 (5-3/8 x 8-3/8, 56 pgs, hardcover, B&W)

nn - By Frank P.W. ("Chip") Bellew (Junior) 25.00 50.00 175.00
NOTE: *Text & cartoon illustration parody of a health guide.*

HEATHEN CHINEE, THE (O)
Western News Co.: 1870 (5-1/32x7-1/4, B&W, paper)
nn - 10 sheets printed on one side came in envelope 75.00 150.00 300.00

HITS AT POLITICS (M,S)
R.H. Russell, New York: 1899 (15" x 12", 156 pgs, B&W, hard-c)

nn - W.A. Rogers c/a 100.00 200.00 300.00
NOTE: *Collection of W.A. Rogers cartoons, all reprinted from Harper's Weekly. Includes Spanish-American War cartoons.*

THE HOME CIRCLE
Garrett & Co, NY: 1854-56 (26x19", 4 pgs, B&W)

1 (1/54) beautiful ad of Garrett Building 100.00 200.00 400.00
2/4 (4/66) Cover ad for Yale College Scraps 100.00 200.00 400.00
2/5 (5/55) First ad for Oscas Shanghai 75.00 150.00 300.00
2/6 (6/55) another ad forOscas Snanghai 75.00 150.00 300.00
2/8 (#20) (8/55) Oscar Shanghai comic book cover repro 200.00 400.00 800.00
3/1 (#25) (1/56) 200.00 400.00 800.00
NOTE: Garrett's 2nd comic book Courtship of Chavalier Slyfox-Wikoff
3/8 (#32) (8/56) 50.00 100.00 200.00
NOTE: First print ad for Foreign Tour of Messrs. Brown, Jones, and Robinson
35 (11/56) first official Garrett, Dick & Fitzgerald issue 50.00 100.00 200.00
37 (1/57) 100.00 200.00 400.00
NOTE: Front page comic strip repro ad for Messrs. Brown, Jones, and Robinson's Foreign Tour; Back cover full of short sequentials, singles panel

HOME MADE HAPPY. A ROMANCE FOR MARRIED MEN IN SEVEN CHAPTERS (O,P)
Genuine Durham Smoking Tobacco & The Graphic Co.: nd (c1870's) (5-1/4 tall x 3-3/8" wide folded, 27" wide unfolded, color cardboard)

nn - With all 8 panels attached (Scarce) 30.00 60.00 200.00
nn - Individual panels/cards 5.00 10.00 25.00
NOTE: *Consists of 8 attached cards, printed on one side, which unfold into a strip story of title card & 7 panels. Scrapbook hobbyists in the 19th Century tended to pull the panels apart to paste into their scrapbooks, making copies with all panels still attached scarce.*

HOME PICTURE BOOK FOR LITTLE CHILDREN (E,P)
Home Insurance Company, New York: July 1887 (8 x 6-1/8", 36 pgs, b&w, color paper-c)

nn (Scarce) 40.00 80.00 160.00
NOTE: *Contains an abbreviated 32-panel reprinting of "The Toothache" by George Cruikshank. Remainder of booklet does not contain comics. Some copies known to exist do not contain The Toothache - buyer beware!*

HOOD'S COMICALITIES. COMICAL PICTURES FROM HIS WORKS (E,S)
Porter & Coates: 1880 (8-1/2x10-3/8", 104 pgs, printed one side, hard-c, B&W)

nn 20.00 40.00 80.00
NOTE: *Reprints 4 cartoon illustrations per page from the British Hood's Comic Annuals, which were poetry books by Thomas Hood.*

HOOKEYBEAK THE RAVEN, AND OTHER TALES (see also JACK HUCKABACK, THE SCAPEGRACE RAVEN) (E)
George Routledge and Sons, London & New York: nd (1878) (7-1/4x5-5/8", 104 pgs, hardcover, B&W)

nn - By Wilhelm Busch (Rare) 100.00 200.00 400.00

HOW ADOLPHUS SLIM-JIM USED JACKSON'S BEST, AND WAS HAPPY. A LENGTHY TALE IN 7 ACTS. (O,P)

FR1.0 GD2.0 FN6.0

Jackson's Best Chewing Tobacco & Donaldson Brothers: nd(c1870's) (5-1/8 tall x 3-3/8" wide folded, 27" wide unfolded, color cardboard)

nn - With all 8 panels attached (Scarce) 30.00 60.00 200.00
nn - Individual panels/cards 5.00 10.00 25.00
NOTE: *Consists of 8 attached cards, printed on one side, which unfold into a strip story of title card & 7 panels. Scrapbook hobbyists in the 19th Century tended to pull the panels apart topaste into their scrapbooks, making copies with all panels still attached scarce.*

HOW DAYS' DURHAM STANDARD OF THE WORLD SMOKING TOBACCO MADE TWO PAIRS OF TWINS HAPPY (O,P)
J.R. Day & Bro. Standard Durham Smoking Tobacco, Durham, NC: nd (c late 1870's/early 1880's) (3-5/8" x 5-1/2", folded, 21-3/4" tall unfolded, color cardboard)

nn- With all 6 panels attached (Scarce) 120.00 240.00 480.00
nn- Individual panels/cards 20.00 40.00 60.00
NOTE: *Highly sought by both Black Americana and Tobacciana collectors. Recurring mid-19th Century story about two African-American twin brothers who romance and marry a pair of African-American twin sisters. Although the text is racist at points, the art is not. Consists of 6 attached cards, printed on one side, which unfold downwards into a strip story of title card & 5 panels. Scrapbook hobbyists in the 19th Century tended to pull the panels apart and paste into their scrapbooks, making copies with all panels attached scarce. Note, there are numerous cartoon tellings of this same story, including several card series versions (with different art, and story variations, each time). But, the above is the only version which unfolds as a strip of attached cards. The cards from all the unattached versions are smaller sized, and thus distinguishable.*

HUGGINIANA; OR, HUGGINS' FANTASY, BEING A COLLECTION OF THE MOST ESTEEMED MODERN LITERARY PRODUCTIONS (I,S,P)
H.C. Southwick, New York: 1808 (296 pgs, printed one side, B&W, hard-c)

nn - (Very Rare)) (no known sales)
NOTE: *The earliest known surviving collected promotional cartoons in America. This is a booklet collecting 7 folded plus 1 full page flyer advertisements for barber John Richard Desborus Huggins, who hired American artists Elkanah Tisdale and William S. Leney to modify previously published illustrations into cartoons referring to his barber shop.*

HUMOROUS MASTERPIECES - PICTURES BY JOHN LEECH (E,M)
Frederick A. Stokes: nd (late 1900's - early 1910's) No.1-2 (5-5/8x3-7/8", 68 pgs, cardboard covers, B&W)

1- John Leech (single panel cartoon-r from **Punch**) 17.50 35.00 70.00
2- John Leech (single panel cartoon-r from **Punch**) 17.50 35.00 70.00

HUMOURIST, THE (E,I,S)
C.V. Nickerson and Lucas and Deaver, Baltimore: No.1 Jan 1829 - No.12 Dec 1829 (5-3/4x3-1/2", B&W text w/hand colored cartoon pg.)

Bound volume No.1-12 (Very Rare; copies in libraries 270 pgs) (no known sales)
NOTE: *Earliest known American published periodical to contain a cartoon every issue. Surviving individual issues currently unknown -- all information comes from 1 surviving bound volume. Each issue is mostly text, with one full page hand-colored cartoon. Bound volume contains an additional hand-colored cartoons at front of each six month set (total of 14 cartoons in volume). Cartoons appear to be of British origin, possibly by George Cruikshank.*

HUMPTY DUMPTY, ADVENTURES OF...(I,P)
1877 (Promotional 4x3-1/2", 12 page chapbook from Gantz, Jones & Co, 10¢-c.)

nn-Promotes Gantz Sea Foam Baking Powder; early app. of a costumed character, dressed as Humpty Dumpty 50.00 100.00 350.00

HUSBAND AND WIFE, OR THE STORY OF A HAIR. (O,P)
Garland Stoves and Ranges, Michigan Stove Co.: 1883 (4-3/16 tall x 2-11/16" wide folded, 16" wide unfolded, color cardboard)

nn - With all 6 panels attached (Scarce) 25.00 50.00 125.00
nn - Individual panels/cards 5.00 10.00 25.00
NOTE: *Consists of 6 attached cards, printed on one side, which unfold into a strip story of title card & 5 panels. Scrapbook hobbyists in the 19th Century tended to pull the panels apart topaste into their scrapbooks, making copies with all panels still attached scarce.*

ICHABOD ACADEMICUS, THE COLLEGE EXPERIENCES OF (O,G)
William T. Peters, New Haven, CT: 1850 (5-1/2x9-3/4",108 pgs, B&W)

nn - By William T. Peters (Rare) 1000.00 2000.00 4000.00
NOTE: *Pages are not uniform in size. Also, a copy showed up on eBay with misspelled Academicus. Has "n" instead of "m" - not known yet which printing is earliest version.*

ICHABOD ACADEMICUS, THE COLLEGE EXPERIENCES OF (O,G)
Dick & Fitzgerald, New York: nd (1870s-1888) (paper-c, B&W)

nn - By William T. Peters (Very Rare) 250.00 500.00 1000.00
NOTE: *Pages are uniform in size.*

ILLUSTRATED SCRAP-BOOK OF HUMOR AND INTELLIGENCE (M)
John J. Dyer & Co.: nd (c1859-1860)

nn - Very Rare 200.00 400.00 800.00
NOTE: *A "printed scrapbook" of images culled from some unidentified periodical. About half of it is illustrations that would have accompanied prose pieces. There are pages of single panel cartoons (multiple per page). And there are roughly 8 to 12 pages of sequential comics (all different stories, but appears to all be by the same presently unidentified artist).*

THE ILLUSTRATED WEEKLY
Chars C Lucas & Co, 11 Dey St, NY: 1876 (15x18", 8pgs, 8¢ per issue)

2/8 (2/19/76) back-c all sequential comic strips 100.00 200.00 400.00
2/12 (3/18/76) full page of British-r sequentials 100.00 200.00 400.00
2/14 (4/1/76) April Fool Issue - (6) panel center; plus more 100.00 200.00 400.00
2/15 (4/8/76) (6) panel sequential 100.00 200.00 400.00
issues without comic strips 12.50 25.00 50.00

Jingo No. 3, Sept 24
1884 © Art Newspaper Co, Boston & NYC

Journey To The Gold Diggings By Jeremiah Saddlebags
1849 © Various - First Original USA Comic Book

The Lantern Dec 18
1852 © Stringer & Townsend

FR1.0 GD2.0 FN6.0

ILLUSTRATIONS OF THE POETS: FROM PASSAGES IN THE LIFE OF LITTLE BILLY VIDKINS (See A Day's Sport...)
S. Robinson, Philadelphia: May 1849 (14.7 cm x 11.3 cm, 32 pgs, B&W)

nn - by Henry Stephens (very rare) (no known sales)
NOTE: *Predates Journey to the Gold Diggins By Jeremiah Saddlebags by a few months and is an original American proto-comic strip book. More research needs to be done. A later edition brought $800 in G/VG 2007*

IMAGERIE d'EPINAL (untrimmed individual sheets) (E)
Pellerin for Humoristic Publishing Co, Kansas City, Mo.: nd (1888) No.1-60 (15-7/8x11-3/4",single sheets, hand colored) (All are Rare)

	FR1.0	GD2.0	FN6.0
1-14, 21, 22, 25-46, 49-60 - in the Album d'Images	17.50	35.00	70.00
15-20, 23,24, 47, 48 - not in the Album d'Images	30.00	60.00	120.00

NOTE: *Printed and hand colored in France expressly for the Humoristic Publishing Company . Printed on one side only. These are single sheets, sold separately. Reprints and translates the sheets from their original French.*

IMAGERIE d'EPINAL ALBUM d'IMAGES (E)
Pellerin for Humoristic Publishing Co., Kansas City. Mo: nd (1888) (15-1/2x11-1/2",108 pgs plus full color hard-c, hand colored interior)

	FR1.0	GD2.0	FN6.0
nn - Various French artists (Rare)	300.00	600.00	1800.00

NOTE: *Printed and hand colored in France expressly for the Humoristic Publishing Company . Printed on one side only. This is supposedly a collection of sixty broadsheets, originally sold separately. All copies known only have fifty of the sixty known of these broadsheets (slightly bigger, before binding, trimming the margins in the process, down to 15-1/4x11-3/8".). Three slightly different covers known to exist, with or without the indication in French "Textes en Anglais" ("Texts in Englishi), with or without the general title "Contes de FEes" ("Fairy Tales"). All known copies were collected with sheets 15-20, 23,24, 47, and 48 missing.*

IN LAUGHLAND (M)
R.H. Russell, New York: 1899 (14-9/16x12", 72 pgs, hard-c)

	FR1.0	GD2.0	FN6.0
nn - By Henry "Hy" Mayer (scarce)	150.00	300.00	600.00

NOTE: *Mostly strips plus single panel cartoon-r from various magazines. The majority are reprinted from Life, with the rest from: Truth, Dramatic Mirror, Black and White, Figaro Illustre, Le Rire, and Fliegende Blatter.*

IN THE "400" AND OUT (M,S) (see also **THE TAILOR-MADE GIRL**)
Keppler & Schwarzmann, New York: 1888 (8-1/4x12", 64 pgs, hardc, B&W)

	FR1.0	GD2.0	FN6.0
nn - By C.J. Taylor	42.50	85.00	170.00

NOTE: *Cartoons reprinted from **Puck**. The "400" is a reference to New York City's aristocratic elite.*

IN VANITY FAIR (M,S)
R.H.Russell & Son, New York: 1896 (11-7/8x17-7/8", 80 pgs, hard-c, B&W)

	FR1.0	GD2.0	FN6.0
nn - By A.B.Wenzell, r-LIFE and HARPER'S	45.00	90.00	180.00

JACK HUCKABACK, THE SCAPEGRACE RAVEN (see also HOOKEYBEAK THE RAVEN) (E)
Stroefer & Kirchner, New York: nd (c1877) (9-3/8x6-3/8", 56 pgs, printed one side only, hand colored hardcover, B&W interior)

	FR1.0	GD2.0	FN6.0
nn - By Wilhelm Busch (Rare)	75.00	150.00	350.00

NOTE: *The 1877 date is derived from a gift signature on one known copy. The publication date might in truth be earlier. There are also professionally hand colored copies known to exist which would be worth more.*

JEFF PETTICOATS
American News Company, NY: July 1865 (23 inches folded out; 6-1/4x8 folded,, B&W)
nn - Very Rare Frank Bellew (6) panel sequential foldout (10¢) (no known sales)
NOTE: printed also in **FUNNYEST OF AWL AND THE FUNNIEST SORT OF PHUN** #9 (July 1865) (6) panel strip hanging Jeff Davis; This sold hundreds of thousand of copies in its day

JINGO (M,O)
Art Newspaper Co., Boston & New York: No.1 Sept 10, 1884 - No.11 Nov 19, 1884 (10 cents, 13-7/8" x 10-1/4",16 pgs, color front/back-c and center, remainder B&W, paper-c)

	FR1.0	GD2.0	FN6.0
1-11(Rare)	50.00	100.00	200.00

NOTE: *Satirical Republican propaganda magazine, modeled after **Puck** and **Judge**, which was published during the last couple months of the 1884 Presidential Election campaign. The Republicans lost, **Jingo** ceased publication, and Republican backers soon after purchased **Judge** magazine.*

JOHN-DONKEY, THE (O, S)
George Dexter, Burgess, Stringer & Co., NYC: 1848 (10x7.5",16 pgs,B&W, 6¢

	FR1.0	GD2.0	FN6.0
1 Jan 1 1848	75.00	150.00	300.00
2-end (last issue Aug 12 1848)	50.00	100.00	200.00

JOLLY JOKER
Frank Leslie, NY: 1862-1878 (B&W, 10¢)

	FR1.0	GD2.0	FN6.0
20/6 (July 1877) (Bellew Opper cover & single panels	150.00	300.00	600.00

JOLLY JOKER, OR LAUGH ALL-ROUND
Dick & Fitzgerald, NY: 1870s? (8-1/4x4-7/8", 148, B&W, illustrated green cover)

	FR1.0	GD2.0	FN6.0
nn - cartoons on every page	100.00	200.00	400.00

JONATHAN'S WHITTLINGS OF THE WAR (O, S)
T.W. Strong, 98 Nassau St, NYC: April 1854-July 8 1854 (11.5x8.5", 16 pgs, B&W)

	FR1.0	GD2.0	FN6.0
1 April 1854	100.00	200.00	400.00

NOTE: *Begins Frank Bellew's sequential comic strip "Mr. Hookemcumsnivey, A Russian Gentleman, Hears That His Country Is In A State of War"*

	FR1.0	GD2.0	FN6.0
2-12 (July 8 1854) Many Bellew & Hopkins	100.00	200.00	400.00

JOURNAL CARRIER'S GREETING
???, Minn, Minn: 1897-98? (giveaway promo, 10-1/8x8-1/4, 36, B&W, paper-c)

	FR1.0	GD2.0	FN6.0
nn - rare	50.00	100.00	200.00

JOURNEY TO THE GOLD DIGGINS BY JEREMIAH SADDLEBAGS (O,G)
Various publishers: 1849 (25 cents, 5-5/8 x 8-3/4", 68 pgs, green & black paper cover, B&W interior)

	FR1.0	GD2.0	FN6.0
nn -- New York edition, Stringer & Townsend, Publishers (Very Rare) By J.A. and D.F. Read.	4500.00	7500.00	12000.00
nn -- Cincinnati, Ohio edition, published by U.P. James (Very Rare) By J.A. and D.F. Read.	4500.00	7500.00	12000.00
nn -- 1950 reprint, with introduction, published by William P. Wreden, Burlingame, California: 1950 (5-7/8 x 9", 92 pgs, hardcover, color interior) (390 copies printed) By J.A. and D.F. Read.	67.50	125.00	250.00

NOTE: *Earliest known original sequential comic book by an American creator; directly inspired by Töpffer's **Obadiah Oldbuck** and **Bachelor Butterfly** The New York and Cincinnati editions were both published in 1849, one soon after the other. Antiquarian Book sources have traditionally cited that the Cincinnati edition preceded the New York, but without referencing their evidence. Conflicting with this, the Cincinnati edition lists the New York publishers' 1849 copyright, while the New York edition makes no reference to the Cincinnati publishers. Such would indicate that the New York edition was first. Both are very rare, and until resolved both will be regarded as published simultaneously. A New York copy with missing back cover, detached front cover, and G/VG interior sold for $2000 in 2000. Two copies sold at auction in 2006 for $11,500 and 12,000. (Prices vary widely.)*

JUDGE (M,O)
Judge Publishing, New York: No.1 Oct 29, 1881 - No. 950, Dec ??, 1899 (10 cents, color front/back c and centerspread, remainder B&W, paper-c)

	FR1.0	GD2.0	FN6.0
1 (Scarce)	(no known sales)		
2-26 (Volume 1; Scarce)	20.00	40.00	80.00
27-790,792-950	12.50	25.00	50.00
791 (12/12/1896; Vol.31) - classic satirical-c depicting Tammany Hall politicians as the Yellow Kid & Cox's Brownies	50.00	150.00	350.00
Bound Volumes (six month, 26 issue run each):			
Vol. 1 (Scarce)	(no known sales)		
Vol. 2-30,32-37	140.00	280.00	600.00
Vol. 31 - includes issue 791 **YK/Brownies** parody	165.00	230.00	725.00

NOTE: *Rival publication to Puck. Purchased by Republican Party backers, following their loss in the 1884 Presidential Election, to become a Republican propaganda satire magazine.*

JUDGE, GOOD THINGS FROM
Judge Publishing Co., NY: 1887 (13-3/4x10.5", 68 pgs, color paper-c)

	FR1.0	GD2.0	FN6.0
1 first printing	50.00	100.00	200.00

NOTE: Zimmerman, Hamilton, Victor, Woolf, Beard, Ehrhart, De Meza, Howarth, Smith, Alfred Mitchell

JUDGE'S LIBRARY (M)
Judge Publishing, New York: No.1, April 1890 - No. 141, Dec 1899 (10 cents, 11x8-1/8", 36 pgs, color paper-c, B&W)

	FR1.0	GD2.0	FN6.0
1	10.00	20.00	40.00
2-141	10.00	20.00	40.00

151-??? (post-1900 issues; see Platinum Age section)
NOTE: ***Judge's Library** was a monthly magazine reprinting cartoons & prose from **Judge**, with each issue's material organized around the same subject. The cover art was often original. All issues were kept in print for the duration of the series, so later issues are more scarce than earlier ones.*

JUDGE'S QUARTERLY (M)
Judge Publishing Company/Arkell Publishing Company, New York: No.1 April 1892 - 31 Oct 1899 (25¢, 13-3/4x10-1/4", 64 pgs, color paper-c, B&W)

	FR1.0	GD2.0	FN6.0
1-11 13-31 contents presently unknown to us	15.00	30.00	60.00
12 ZIM Sketches From Judge Jan 1895	100.00	200.00	400.00

NOTE: *Similar to **Judge's Library**, except larger in size, and issued quarterly. All reprint material, except for the cover art.*

JUDGE'S SERIALS (M,S)
Judge Publishing, New York: March 1888 (10x7.5", 36 pgs)

	FR1.0	GD2.0	FN6.0
#3 - Eugene Zimmerman	100.00	200.00	400.00

NOTE: *A bit of sequential comic strips; mostly single panel cartoons. This series runs to at least #8.*

JUDY
Burgess, Stringer & Co., 17 Ann St, NYC: Nov 28 1846-Feb 20 47 (11x8.5",12 pgs,B&W)

	FR1.0	GD2.0	FN6.0
1 Nov 28 1846	67.50	125.00	250.00
2-13	50.00	100.00	200.00

JUVENILE GEM, THE (see also THE ADVENTURES OF MR. TOM PLUMP, and OLD MOTHER MITTEN) (O,I)
Huestis & Cozans: nd (1850-1852) (6x3-7/8", 64 pgs, hand colored paper-c, B&W) (all versions Very Rare)

nn - First printing(s) publisher's address is 104 Nassau Street (1850-1851) (1 copy sold for $800.00 in Fair)
nn - 2nd printing(s) publisher's address is 116 Nassau Street (1851-1852) (no known sales)
nn - 3rd printing(s) publisher's address is 107 Nassau Street (1852+) (no known sales)
NOTE: *The JUVENILE GEM is a gathering of multiple booklets under a single, hand colored cover (none of the interior booklets have the covers which they were given when sold separately). The publisher appears to have gathered whichever printings of each booklet were available when copies of THE JUVENILE GEM was assembled, so that the booklets within, and the conglomerate cover, may be from a mixture of printings. Contains two sequential comic booklets: THE ADVENTURES OF MR. TOM PLUMP, and OLD MOTHER MITTEN AND HER FUNNY KITTEN, plus five heavily illustrated children's booklets - **The Pretty Primer, The Funny Book, The Picture Book, The Two Sisters**, and **Story Of The Little Drummer**. Six of these -- including the two comic books -- were reprinted in the 1960's by Americana Review as a set of individual booklets, and included in a folder collectively titled "Six Children's Books of the 1850's".*

LANTERN, THE
Stringer & Townsend:1852-1853 (11x8-3/8", 12 pgs, soft paper, 6 ¢)

Leslie's Young America #1
1881 © Leslie & Company, NYC

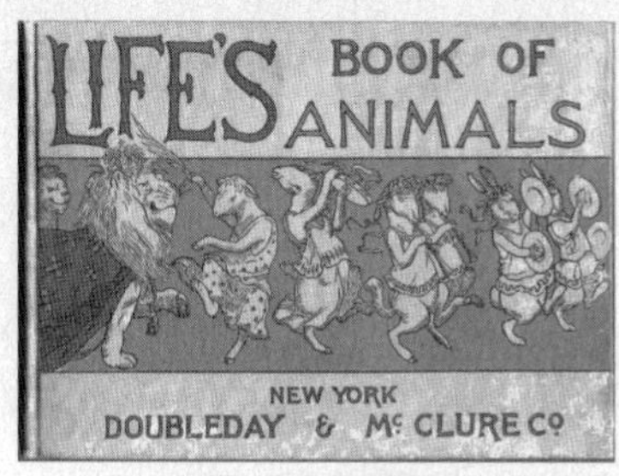

Life's Book of Animals
1888 © Doubleday & McClure Co.

Max and Maurice by Wilhelm Busch
1871 © Roberts Bros, Boston

FR1.0 GD2.0 FN6.0

1 Jan 10, 1852 37.50 75.00 150.00
2 25.00 50.00 100.00
3 First Frank Bellew cartoons onwards each issue 37.50 75.00 150.00
4 Bellew 's Mr Blobb begins 1/31/52 50.00 100.00 200.00
NOTE: *Bellew serial sequential comic strip "Mr Blobb In Search Of A Physician" becomes 2nd earliest known recurring character in American comic strips plus full page single panel Bellew cartoon "The Modern Frankenstein" take-off on Shelly's story.*
5 Hunsdale 2-panel "The Horrors of Slavery"; Mr Blobb 50.00 100.00 200.00
6 DF Read 15 panel "A Volley of Valentines"; Mr Blobb 50.00 100.00 200.00
7-8 10 Bellew's Mr Blobb continues 25.00 50.00 100.00
9 (4) panel "The Perils of Leap Year" MrBlobb 50.00 100.00 200.00
11 no Mr Blobb 20.00 40.00 80.00
12 Bellew's Mr Blobb continues 3/27/52 50.00 100.00 200.00
13 Bellew (10) panel sequential "Stump Speaking Studied" 50.00 100.00 200.00
14 no comic strips 20.00 40.00 80.00
15 Bellew's Mr Blobb ends (5) panel 4/17/52 50.00 100.00 200.00
16 Bellew begins new comic strip serial, "Mr. Bulbear, A Stockbroker, After having Supped at Delmonicos, Has A Dream", Part One, (6) panels 50.00 100.00 200.00
17 Bellew's Mr Bulbear continues 25.00 50.00 100.00
18 Bellew (8) panel "Trials of a Witness" 50.00 100.00 200.00
19 Bellew's Mr Bulbear's Dream continues 25.00 50.00 100.00
20-23 no comic strips 20.00 40.00 80.00
24 Bellew "Trials of a Publisher" (6) panel 50.00 100.00 200.00
25 comic strip "Travels of Jonathan Verdant"recurring character 25.00 50.00 100.00
26-49 contents to be indexed soon
50 (12/18/52) (2) panel Impertinent Smile 25.00 50.00 100.00
58 (2/12/53) (6) panel Trip to California 25.00 50.00 100.00
66 (4/9/53) (3) panel sequential strip 25.00 50.00 100.00

LAST SENSATION, THE (Becomes Day's Doings)
James Watts, NYC: Dec 27 1867-May 30 1868 (11x16 folio-size, 16 pgs, B&W)

issues with comic strips 50.00 100.00 200.00

LAUGH AND GROW FAT COMIC ALMANAC
Fisher & Brother, Philadelphia, New York & Boston: 1860-? (36 pgs)

nn 60.00 120.00 240.00

LEGEND OF SAM'L OF POSEN (O)
M.B. Curtis Company: 1884-85 (8x3-3/8", 44 pgs, Color-c, B&W interior)

nn - By M.B. Curtis 50.00 100.00 200.00
NOTE: Cover blurb says: From Early Days in Fatherland to affluence And Success in the Land of His Adoption, America

LESLIE'S YOUNG AMERICA (O. S)
Leslie & Co, 98 Chamber St, NY: 1881-82 (11-1/2x8", 5¢, B&W)

1 (7/9/81) back cover (6) panel strip 125.00 250.00 500.00
2 (7/16/81) back cover (9) panel strip 50.00 100.00 200.00
3 (7/23/81) back cover (16) panel Busch strip 67.50 125.00 250.00
9 (9/3/81) sequentials; Hopkins singles 50.00 100.00 200.00
15 (10/15/81) Zim or Frost? (6) panel strip 50.00 100.00 200.00
19 (11/12/81) (9) panel back-c strip 50.00 100.00 200.00
24 (4) panel strip 25 (2) panel back-c strip 50.00 100.00 200.00
26 27 (6) panel back-c strip 50.00 100.00 200.00
29 31 (12) panel strip 50.00 100.00 200.00
32 (2/11/82) (8) panel strip 50.00 100.00 200.00
issues without comic strips or Jules Verne 25.00 50.00 100.00
NOTE: Jules Verne stories begin with #1 and run thru at least #42

LIFE (M,O) (continues with Vol.35 No. 894+ in the Platinum Age section)
J.A.Mitchell: Vol.1 No.1 Jan. 4, 1883 - Vol.1 No.26 June 29, 1883 (10-1/4x8", 16 pgs, B&W, paper cover); J.A. Mitchell: Vol. 2 No. 27, July 5, 1883 - Vol. 6 No.148, Oct 29, 1885 (10-1/4x8-1/4", 16 pgs., B&W, paper cover); Mitchell & Miller: Vol.6 No.149, Nov. 5, 1885 - Vol. 31, No. 796, March 17, 1898 (10-3/8x8-3/8", 16 pgs., B&W, paper cover); Life Publishing Company: Vol. 31 No. 797, March 24, 1898 - Vol. 34 No. 893, Dec 28, 1899 (10-3/8 x 8-1/2", 20 pgs., B&W, paper cover)

1-26 (Scarce) (no known sales)
27-799 5.00 10.00 20.00
800 (4/7/1898) parody Yellow Kid / Spanish-American War cover (not by Outcault) 67.50 125.00 250.00
801-893 5.00 10.00 20.00
NOTE: *All covers for issues 1 - 26 are identical, apart from issue number & date.*
Hard bound collected volumes:
V. 1 (No.1-26) (Scarce) 67.50 125.00 250.00
V. 2-34 45.00 90.00 180.00
V. 31 YK #800 parody-c not by RFO 70.00 140.00 280.00
NOTE: *Because the covers of all issues in Volume 1 are identical, it was common practice to remove the covers before binding the issues together. This is not true of later volumes, though, in all volumes it was common to drop the advertising pages which appeared at the rear of each issue. Information on many more individual issues will expand next Guide.*

LIFE AND ADVENTURES OF JEFF DAVIS (I)
J.C. Haney & Co., NY: 1865 (10 cents, 7-1/2" x 4", 36 pgs, B&W, paper-c)

nn - By McArone (Scarce) 150.00 300.00 650.00

FR1.0 GD2.0 FN6.0

nn - 1974 Reprint (350) copies 6-3/4x4-3/8 50.00 10.00 20.00
nn - 1997 Reprint (7th Fla. Sutler, Clearwater, 6-3/4x4-1/4") – – 2.00
NOTE: *Humorous telling of the capture of Confederate President Jeff Davis in women's clothing, from the publisher of Merryman's Monthly. It contains an ad page for that publication; the material is perhaps reprinted from it. J.C. Haney licensed it to local printers, and so various publishers are found -- all printings currently regarded as simultaneous. (The Geo. H. Hees printing, Oswego, NY, contains an ad for the upcoming October 1865 issue of Merryman's Monthly, thus placing that printing in September 1865). Modern facsimile editions have been produced.*

LIFE IN PHILADELPHIA
W. Simpson, 66 Chestnut, Philadelphia; Siltart, No. 65 South Third St, Philadelphia: 1830 (7-3/4x6-7/8", 15 loose plates, hand colored copies exist, maybe B&W also)

nn - By Edward Williams Clay (1799-1857) (Very Rare) (no known sales)
NOTE: *First 13 plates etched, with many word balloons; scenes of exaggerated Black Americana in Philadelphia viewed one by one as broadsides. Had several publishers over the years. Was also eventually collected into a book of same name but only with the first 13 plates used; the last two not used in book. Collected book not yet viewed to share info.*

LIFE'S BOOK OF ANIMALS (M.S)
Doubleday & McClure Co.: 1898 (7-1/4x10-1/8", 88 pgs, color hardcover, B&W)

nn 25.00 50.00 100.00
NOTE: *Reprints funny animal single panel and strip cartoons reprinted from LIFE. Art by Blaisdell, Chip Bellew, Kemble, Hy Mayer, Sullivant, Woolf.*

LIFE'S COMEDY (M,S)
Charles Scribner's Sons: Series 1 1897 - Series 3 1898 (12x9-3/8", hardcover, B&W)

1 (142 pgs). 2, 3 (138 pgs) 60.00 120.00 240.00
NOTE: *Gibson a-1-3; c-3. Hy Mayer a-1-3. Rose O'Neill a-2-3. Stanlaws a-2-3. Sullivant a-1-2. Verbeek a-2. Wenzell a-1-3; c(painted)-2.*

LIFE, THE GOOD THINGS OF (M,S)
White, Stokes, & Allen, NY: 1884 - No.3 1886 ; Frederick A. Stokes, NY: No.4 1887; Frederick Stokes & Brother, NY: No.5 1888 - No.6 1889; Frederick A. Stokes Company, NY: No. 7 1890 - No.10 1893 (8-3/8x10-1/2", 74 pgs, gilted hardcover, B&W)

nn - 1884 (most common issue) 32.50 65.00 130.00
2 - 1885 32.50 65.00 130.00
3 - 1886 (76 pgs) 32.50 65.00 130.00
4 - 1887 (76 pgs) 32.50 65.00 130.00
5 - 1888 32.50 65.00 130.00
6 - 1889 32.50 65.00 130.00
7 - 1890 32.50 65.00 130.00
8 - 1891 (scarce) 50.00 100.00 200.00
9 - 1892 32.50 65.00 130.00
10 - 1893 32.50 65.00 130.00
NOTE: *Contains mostly single panel, and some sequential, comics reprinted from LIFE. Attwood a-1-4,10. Roswell Bacon a-5. Chip Bellew a-4-6. Frank Bellew a-4,6. Palmer Cox a-1. H. E. Dey a-5. C. D. Gibson a-4-10. F.M. Howarth a-5-6. Kemble a-1-3. Klapp a-5. Walt McDougall a-1-2. H. McVickar a-5; J. A. Mitchell a-5. Peter Newell a-2-3. Gray Parker a-4-5,7. J. Smith a-5. Albert E. Steiner a-5; T. S. Sullivant a-7-9. Wenzell a-8-10. Wilder a-3. Woolf a-3-6.)*

LIFE, THE SPICE OF (E,M,)
White and Allen: NY & London: 1888 (8-3/8x10-1/2",76 pgs, hard-c, B&W)

nn 50.00 100.00 200.00
NOTE: *Resembles **THE GOOD THINGS OF LIFE** in layout and format, and appears to be an attempt to compete with their former partner Frederick A. Stokes. However, the material is not from **LIFE**, but rather is reprinted and translated German sequential and single panel comics.*

LIFE'S PICTURE GALLERY (becomes LIFE'S PRINTS) (M,S,P)
Life Publishing Company, New York: nd (1898-1899) (paper cover, B&W) (all are scarce)

nn - (nd; 1898, 100 pgs, 5-1/4x8-1/2") Gibson-c of a woman with closed umbrella; 1st interior page announcing that after January 1, 1899 Gibson will draw exclusively for LIFE; the word "SPECIMEN" is printed in red, diagonally, across every print; a-Gibson, Rose O'Neill, Sullivant 37.50 75.00 150.00
nn - (nd; 1899, 128 pgs, 4-7/8x7-3/8") Gibson-c of a woman golfer; 1st interior page announcing that Gibson & Hanna, Jr. draw exclusively for LIFE; the word "SPECIMEN" is printed in red, horizontally, across every print. Includes prints from Gibson's **THE EDUCATION OF MR. PIPP**; a-Gibson, Sullivant 37.50 75.00 150.00
NOTE: *Catalog of prints reprinted from **LIFE** covers & centerspreads. The first catalog was given away free to anyone requesting it, but after many people got the catalog without ordering anything, subsequent catalogs were sold at 10 cents.*

LITTLE SICK BEAR, THE
Edwin W. Joy Co, San Francisco, CA: 1897 (6-1/4x5", 20 pgs, B&W, Scarce)
nn - By James Swinnerton one long sequential comic strip 200.00 400.00 800.00

LIGHT AND SHADE
William Drey Doppel Soap: 1892 (3-3/4x5-3/8", 20 pgs, B&W, color cover)

nn - By J.C. 50.00 100.00 200.00
NOTE: Contains (8) panel comic strip of black boy whose skin turns white using this soap.

LONDON OUT OF TOWN, OR THE ADVENTURES OF THE BROWNS AT THE SEA SIDE BY LUKE LIMNER, ESQ. (O)
David Bogue, 86 Fleet St, London: c1847 (5-1/2x4-1/4, 32 pgs, yellow paper hard-c, B&W

nn - By John Leighton 150.00 300.00 600.00
NOTE: one long sequential comic strip multiple-panel per page story; each page crammed with panels inspired by the Töpffer comic books Bogue began several years earlier.

LORGNETTE, THE (S)

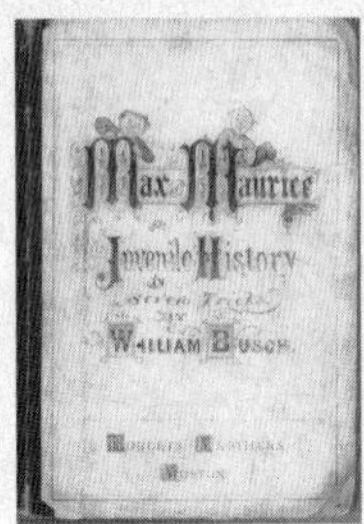

Max and Maurice by Wilhelm Busch
1871 © Roberts Brothers, Boston

Merryman's Monthly v3#5 with Bellew strip
May 1865 © J. C. Haney & Co., New York

Minneapolis Journal Cartoons Second Series
1895 © Minneapolis Journal

George J Coombes, New York: 1886 (6-1/2x8-3/4, 38 pgs, hard-c, B&W)

nn - By J.K. Bangs 50.00 100.00 200.00

LOVING BALLAD OF LORD BATEMAN, THE (E,I)
G.W. Carleton & Co., Publishers, Madison Square, NY: 1871 (9x5-7/8",16 pgs, soft-c, 6¢)

nn - By George Cruikshank 50.00 100.00 200.00

MADISON'S EXPOSITION OF THE AWFUL & TERRIFYING CEREMONIES OF THE ODD FELLOWS
T.E. Peterson & Brothers, 306 Chestnut St, Phila: 1870s? (5-3/4x9-1/4, 68 pgs, B&W)
nn - single panel cartoons 50.00 100.00 200.00

MANNERS AND CUSTOMS OF YE HARVARD STUDENTE (M,S)
Houghton Mifflin & Co., Boston & Moses King, Cambridge: 1877 (7-7/8x11", 72 pgs, printed one side, hardc, B&W)

nn - by F.G. Attwood 75.00 150.00 300.00
NOTE: *Collection of cartoons originally serialized in the **Harvard Lampoon**. Attwood later became a major cartoonist for **Life**.*

MAN WHO WOULD LIKE TO MARRY, THE (O)
Frederick Warne & Co., London & New York: nd (c 1880's) (9-1/2x11-1/2", 28 pgs, printed 1 side, paper-c, B&W)

nn - By Harry Parkes 62.50 125.00 250.00
NOTE: *Published simultaneously with its companion volume, **The Girl Who Wouldn't Mind Getting Married**.*

MAX AND MAURICE: A JUVENILE HISTORY IN SEVEN TRICKS (E)
(see also Teasing Tom and Naughty Ned)
Roberts Brothers, Boston: 1871 first edition (8-1/8 x 5-1/2", 76 pgs, hard & soft-c B&W)

nn - By Wilhelm Busch (green or brown cloth hardbound) 275.00 550.00 1000.00
nn - exactly the same, but soft paper cover 162.00 325.00 650.00
NOTE: *Page count includes 56 pgs of art, two blank endpapers at the front (one colored), 8 pgs of ads at the back, two blank endpapers at the end (one colored), and the covers. Green or brown illustrated hardcover. The name of the author is given on the title page as "William Busch." We assume this to be the 1st edition. Back side of title page states: Entered according to Act of Congress, in the year 1870, by Roberts Brothers, In the office of the Librarian of Congress at Washington.*

nn - By Wilhelm Busch (1872 edition) 225.00 470.00 900.00
nn - 1875 reprint 100.00 200.00 450.00
nn - 1882 reprint (76 pgs, hand colored- c/a, 75¢) 100.00 200.00 400.00
nn- 1889 reprint with new art on cover printed in full color 100.00 200.00 400.00
NOTE: *Each of the above contains 56 pages of art and text in a transitional format between a regular children's book and a comic book (the page count difference is ad pages in back). Seminal inspiration for William Randolph Hearst to acquire as a "new comic" (following the wild success of Outcault's Yellow Kid) to license M&M from Busch and hire Rudolph Dirks in late 1897 to create a New York American newspaper incarnation. In Hearst's English language newspapers it was called The Katzenjammer Kids and in his German language NYC newspaper it was titled Max & Moritz, Busch's original title. At least 50 other reprints versions are reputed to exist printed thru 1900. Translated from the 1865 German original. We are still sorting out the edition confusion.*

MAX AND MAURICE: A JUVENILE HISTORY IN SEVEN TRICKS (E)
(see also Teasing Tom and Naughty Ned)
Little, Brown, and Company, Boston: 1898-1902 (8-1/8 x 5-3/4", 72 pgs, hardcover, black ink on orange paper) (various early reprints)

nn - 1898 , 1899 By Wilhelm Busch 50.00 100.00 200.00
nn - 1902 (64 pages, B&W) 10.00 30.00 90.00

MERRY MAPLE LEAVES Or A Summer In The Country (S)
E.P. Dutton And Company, New York: 1872 (9-3/8x7-3/8", 90 and 86 pgs pgs, hard-c)

nn - By Abner Perk 25.00 50.00 150.00
NOTE: *Each drawing contained in a maple leaf motif by Livingston Hopkins and others.*

MERRYMAN'S MONTHLY A COMIC MAGAZINE FOR THE FAMILY (M,O,E)
J.C. Haney & Co, NY: 1863-1875 (10-7/8x7-13/16", 30 pgs average, B&W)

Certain issues with sequential comics 100.00 200.00 400.00
NOTE: *Sequential strips by Frank Bellew Sr, Wilhelm Busch found so far; others?*

MERRYTHOUGHT, OR LAUGHTER FROM YEAR TO YEAR, THE
Fisher & Brother, Phila, Baltimore: early 1850s (4-1/2x7", B&W)
nn - many singles, some sequential (Very Rare) (no known sales)
NOTE: See Vict article for back cover pic which is earliest known use of the term Comic Book

MESSRS. BROWN, JONES, AND ROBINSON, THE FOREIGN TOUR OF
(see also **THE CLOWN, OR THE BANQUET OF WIT**) (E,M,O,G)
Bradbury & Evans, London: 1854 (11-5/8x9-1/2", 196 pgs, gilted hard-c, B&W)

nn - By Richard Doyle 35.00 70.00 200.00
nn - Bradbury & Evans 1900 reprint 20.00 40.00 80.00
NOTE: *Protective sheets between each page (not part of page count). Expanded and redrawn sequential comics story from the serialized episodes originally published in PUNCH. Also comes in a 174 pg 8-3/4x11" version.*

MESSRS. BROWN, JONES, AND ROBINSON, THE LAUGHABLE ADVENTURES OF (E,M,G)
Garrett, Dick & Fitzgerald, NY: nd (1856 or 1857) (5-3/4x9-1/4", 100 pgs, printed one side only, paper-c, B&W)

nn - (Very Rare) by Richard Doyle c/a 300.00 500.00 1000.00
NOTE: *1st American reprinting of the "Foreign Tour"; reformatted into a small oblong format. Links the earlier Garrett & Co. to the later Dick & Fitzgerald. Back cover reprints full size the Garrett & Co. version cover for Oscar Shanghai. Interior front cover reprints full size the Garrett & Co. version cover for Slyfox-Wikof. Issued without a title page.*

MESSRS. BROWN, JONES, AND ROBINSON, THE FOREIGN TOUR OF (E,M,G)
D. Appleton & Co., New York: 1860 & 1877 (11-5/8x9-1/2", 196 pgs, gilted hard-c, B&W)

nn - (1860 printing) by Richard Doyle 30.00 60.00 200.00
nn - (1871 printing) by Richard Doyle 30.00 60.00 150.00
nn - (1877 printing) by Richard Doyle 30.00 60.00 150.00
NOTE: *Protective sheets between each page (not part of page count). Reprints the Bradbury & Evans edition.*

MESSRS BROWN JONES AND ROBINSON, THE AMERICAN TOUR OF (O,G)
D. Appleton & Co., New York: 1872 (11-5/8x9-1/2", 158 pgs, printed one side only, B&W, green gilted hard-c)

nn - By Toby 70.00 140.00 400.00
NOTE: *Original American graphic novel sequel to Richard Doyle's Foreign Tour of Brown, Jones, and Robinson, with the same characters visiting New York, Canada, and Cuba. Protective sheets between each page (not part of page count).*

MESSRS. BROWN, JONES, AND ROBINSON, THE LAUGHABLE ADVEN. OF (E,M,G)
Dick & Fitzgerald, NY: nd (late 1870's - 1888) (5-3/4x9-1/4", 100 pgs, printed one side only, green paper-c, B&W)

nn - (Scarce) by Richard Doyle 100.00 200.00 450.00
NOTE: *Reprints the Garrett, Dick & Fitzgerald printing, with the following changes: Takes what had been page 12 in the Garrett, D&F printing (art by M.H. Henry), and makes it a title page, which is numbered page 1. The first story page, "Go to the Races", is numbered 2 (whereas it is numbered 1 in the Garrett, Dick & Fitzgerald version). Numbering stays ahead of the G,D&F edition by 1 page up through page 12, after which the page numbering becomes identical.*

MINNEAPOLIS JOURNAL CARTOONS (N,S)
Minneapolis Journal: nn 1894 - No.2 1895 (7-3/4" x 10-7/8", 76 pgs, B&W, paper-c)

nn (1894) (Rare) 50.00 100.00 200.00
Second Series (1895) (Rare) 50.00 100.00 200.00
nn- "War Cartoons" Jan 1899 (9x8", 160 pgs, paperback, punched & string bound) (Scarce) 24.00 96.00 170.00
NOTE: *Reprints single panel cartoons from the prior year, by Charles "Bart" L. Bartholomew.*

MISCHIEF BOOK, THE (E)
R. Worthington, New York: 1880 (7-1/8 x 10-3/4", 176 pgs, hard-c, B&W)

nn - Green cloth binding; green on brown cover; cover art by R. Lewis based on Busch art by Wilhelm Busch 175.00 350.00 735.00
nn - Blue cloth binding; hand colored cover; completely different cover art based on Busch by Wilhelm Busch 175.00 350.00 735.00
NOTE: *Translated by Abby Langdon Alger. American published anthology collection of Wilhelm Busch comic strips. Includes two of the strips found in the British "Bushel of Merry-Thoughts" collection, translated better, and with the dropped panel restored. Unknown which cover version was first.*

MISSES BROWN, JONES AND ROBINSON, THE FOREIGN TOUR OF THE (E,O,G)
Bickers & Sons, London: nd (c1850's) (12-1/4" x 9-7/8", 108 pgs, printed on one side, B&W, hard-c)

nn- "by Miss Brown" (Rare) 100.00 200.00 400.00
NOTE: *A female take on Doyle's Foreign Tour, by an unknown woman artist, using the pseudonym "Miss Brown."*

MISS MILLY MILLEFLEUR'S CAREER (S)
Sheldon & Co., NY: 1869 (10-3/4x9-7/8", 74 pgs, purple hard-c)

nn - Artist unknown (Rare) 75.00 150.00 300.00

MR PODGER AT COUP'S GREATEST SHOW ON EARTH HIS HAPS AND MISHAPS, THE ADVENTURES OF (O,S)
W.C. Coup, New York: 1884 (5-5/8x4-1/4", 20 pgs, color-c, B&W)

nn - Circus Themes; Similar to Barker's Comic Almanacs 20.00 40.00 80.00

MR. TOODLES' GREAT ELEPHANT HUNT (See Peter Piper in Bengal)
Brother Jonathan, NYC: 1850s (4-1/4x7-7/8", page count presently unknown)

nn - catalog contains comic strip (Very Rare) (no known sales)

MR. TOODLES' TERRIFIC ELEPHANT HUNT
Dick & Fitzgerald, NYC: 1860s (5-3/4x9-1/4", 32 pgs, paper-c, B&W) (Very Rare)

nn - catalog reprint contains 28 panel comic strip 150.00 300.00 600.00

MRS GRUNDY
Mrs Grundy Publishing Co, NYC: July 8 1865-Sept 30 1865 (weekly)

1-13 Thomas Nast, Hoppin, Stephens, 50.00 100.00 200.00

MUSEUM OF WONDERS, A (O,I)
Routledge & Sons: 1894 (13x10", 64 pgs, color-c, color thru out)

nn - By Frederick Opper 100.00 200.00 450.00

MY FRIEND WRIGGLES, A (Laughter) Moving Panorama, of His Fortunes And Misfortunes, Illustrated With Over 200 Engravings, of Most Comic Catastrophes And Side-Splitting Merriment) (O,G)
Stearn & Co, 202 Williams St, NY: 1850s (5-7/8x9-3/4", 100 pgs, B&W)

nn - By S. P. Avery (also the engraver) (Very Rare) 200.00 400.00 800.00

MY SKETCHBOOK (E,S)
Dana Estes & Charles E. Lauriat, Boston; J. Sabins & Sons, New York: circa 1880s (9-3/8x12", brown hard-c)

nn - By George Cruikshank 25.00 50.00 150.00
NOTE: *Reprints British editions 1834-36; extensive usage of word balloons.*

Nasby's Life Of Andy Jonson
1866 © Jesse Haney Company

99 "Woolf's" from Truth
1896 © Truth Company

The Adventures of Obadiah Oldbuck 4th printing
mid-1850s © Brother Jonathan Offices, NY

FR1.0 GD2.0 FN6.0

NASBY'S LIFE OF ANDY JONSON (O, M)
Jesse Haney Co., Publishers No. 119 Nassau St, NY: 1866 (4-1/2x7-1/2, 48 pgs, B&W)
nn - President Andrew Johnson satire 100.00 200.00 450.00
NOTE: Blurb further reads: With a True Pictorial History of His STumping Tour Out West By Petroleum V. Nasby, A Dimmicrat of Thirty Years Standing, And Who Allus Tuk His Licker Straight. Front of book has long sequential comic strip satire on President Andrew Johnson, misspelling his name on the cover on purpose.

NAST'S ILLUSTRATED ALMANAC
Harper & Brothers, Franklin Square, NYC: 1872-1874 (8x5.5", 80 pgs, B&W, 35¢)
nn 60.00 120.00 240.00

NAST'S WEEKLY (O,S)
???: 1892-93 (Quarto Weekly)
all issues scarce 50.00 100.00 200.00

NATIONAL COMIC ALMANAC
An Association of Gentlemen, Boston: 1838-?? (8.25x4.75", 34 pgs, B&W)
nn 60.00 120.00 240.00

NEW AMERICAN COMIC ALL-IMAKE (ELTON'S BASKET OF COMICAL SCRAPS), THE
Elton, Publisher, New York: 1839 (7-1/2x4-5/8, 24 pgs)
1 100.00 200.00 400.00

NEW BOOK OF NONSENSE, THE: A Contribution To The Great Central Fair In Aid of the Sanitary Commission (O,S)
Ashmead & Evans, No. 724 Chestnut St, Philadelphia: June 1864 (red hard-c)
nn - Artists unknown (Scarce) 50.00 150.00 300.00

NEW YORK ILLUSTRATED NEWS
Frank Leslie, NYC: 10/14/76-June 1884
average issues with comic strips 10.00 20.00 40.00

NEW YORK PICAYUNE (see PHUN FOTOCRAFT)
Woodward & Hutchings: 1850-1855 newspaper-size weekly; 1856-1857 Folio Monthly 16x10.5; 1857-1858 Quarto Weekly; 1858-1860 Quarto Weekly
Average Issue With Comic Strips 50.00 100.00 200.00
Issues with Full Front Page Comic Strip 100.00 200.00 400.00
NOTE: *Many issues contain Frank Bellew sequential comic strips & single panel cartoons. Later issues published by Woodward, Levison & Robert Gun (1853-1857) ; Levison & Thompson (1857-1860)*

NICK-NAX
Levison & Haney, NY: 1857-1858? (11x7-3/4", 32 pgs, B&W, paper-c)
v2 #10 Feb 1858 has many single panel cartoons 50.00 100.00 200.00

99 "WOOLFS" FROM TRUTH (see Sketches of Lowly Life in a Great City, Truth)
Truth Company, NY: 1896 (9x5-1/2", 72 pgs, varnished paper-like cloth hard-c, 25 cents)
nn - By Michael Angelo Woolf (Rare) 150.00 300.00 600.00
NOTE: *Woolf's cartoons are regarded as a primary influence on R.F. Outcault in the later development of The Yellow Kid newspaper strip. Copy sold in 2002 on eBay for $800.00.*

NONSENSE OR, THE TREASURE BOX OF UNCONSIDERED TRIFLES
Fisher & Brother, 12 North Sixth St, Phila, PA, 64 Baltimore St, Baltimore, MD: early 1850s (4-1/2x7", 128 pgs, B&W)
nn - much Davy Crocket sequential story-telling comic strips 250.00 500.00 1000.00

OBADIAH OLDBUCK, THE ADVENTURES OF MR. (E,G)
Tilt & Bogue, London: nd (1840-41) (5-15/16x9-3/16", 176 pgs,B&W, gilted hard-c)
nn - By Rodolphe Töpffer 700.00 1200.00 2800.00
nn - Hand coloured edition (Very Rare) (no known sales)
NOTE: *This is the British edition, translating the unauthorized redrawn 1839 edition from Parisian publisher Aubert, adapted from Töpffer's "Les Amours de Mr. Vieux Bois" (aka "Histoire de Mr. Vieux Bois"), originally published in French in Switzerland, in 1837 (2nd ed. 1839). Early 19th century books are often found rebound, with original cover and/or title page gone. To distinguish editions having no cover or title page: the British oblong editions (published by Tilt & Bogue) use Roman Numerals to number pages. American oblong shaped editions use Arabic Numerals. British are printed on one side only. This is the earliest known English language sequential comic book. Has a new title page with art by Robert Cruikshank.*

OBADIAH OLDBUCK, THE ADVENTURES OF MR. (E,G)
Wilson and Company, New York: September 14, 1842 (11-3/4x9", 44 pgs, B&W, yellow paper-c on bookstand editions, hemp paper interior)
Brother Jonathan Extra No. IX - Rare bookstand edition 2500.00 5000.00 10000.00
Brother Jonathan Extra No. IX Very Rare subscriber/mailorder 2500.00 5000.00 10000.00
NOTE: *By Rodolphe Töpffer. Earliest known sequential American comic book, reprinting the 1841 British edition. Pages are numbered via Roman numerals. States "BROTHER JONATHAN EXTRA - ADVENTURES OF MR. OBADIAH OLDBUCK." at the top of each page. Prints 2 to 3 tiers of panels on both sides of each page. Copies could be had for ten cents according to adverts in* ***Brother Jonathan****. By Rodolphe Töpffer with cover masthead design by David Claypool Johnston, and cover art beneath the masthead reprinting Robert Cruikshank's title page art from the Tilt & Bogue edition. A special, additional cover was added for copies sold on stands (it was not issued with mail order or subscriber copies). Only 1 known copy possesses (partially) this very thin outer yellow cover. A decent (subscriber) copy sold on eBay in later October 2002 for over $3500.00. In 2005, a FR copy sold for $10,000; a G/VG for $20,000; and a VG for $20,000. A copy GVG sold in auction in 2007 for $9500. (Prices vary widely.)*

OBADIAH OLDBUCK, THE ADVENTURES OF MR. (E,G)
Wilson & Co, New York: nd (1849) (5-11/16x8-3/8", 84 pgs, B&W,paper-c)
nn - by Rodolphe Töpffer; title page by Robert Cruikshank (Very Rare) 500.00 1200.00 4000.00
NOTE: *2nd Wilson & Co printing, reformatted into a small oblong format, with nine panels edited out, and text modified to smooth out this removal. Results in four less printed tiers/strips. Pages are numbered via Arabic numerals. Every panel on Pages 11, 14, 19, 21, 24, 34, 35 has one line of text. Reformatted to conform with British first edition.*

OBADIAH OLDBUCK, THE ADVENTURES OF MR. (E,G)
Wilson & Co, 162 Nassau, NY: nd (early-1850s) (5-11/16x8-3/8", 84 pgs, B&W, yellow-c
nn - 3rd USA Printing by Rodolphe Töpffer; title page by Robert Cruikshank (Very Rare) Says By Timothy Crayon, an obvious pseudonym 800.00 1600.00 4500.00
NOTE: Front cover banner the giant is holding says "Done With Drawings By Timothy Crayon, Gypsographer, 188 Comic Etchings On Antimony" Title page changes address to No. 15 Spruce-Street. (Late 162 Nassau Street.)

OBADIAH OLDBUCK, THE ADVENTURES OF MR..
Brother Jonathan Offices: ND (mid-1850s) (5-11/16x8-3/8", 84 pages, B&W, oblong)
nn - 4th printing; Originally by Rodolphe Töpffer (Very Rare) 500.00 1200.00 4000.00
NOTE: *Cover States: "New York: Published at the Brother Jonathan Office". Front cover banner the giant is holding says "Done With Drawings By Timothy Crayon, Gypsographer, 188 Comic Designs On Antimony."*

OBADIAH OLDBUCK, THE ADVENTURES OF MR. (E,G)
Dick & Fitzgerald, New York: nd (various printings; est. 1870s to 1888) (Thirty Cents, 84 pgs, B&W, paper-c) (all versions scarce)
nn - Black print on green cover(5-11/16x8-15/16"); string bound 200.00 400.00 800.00
nn - Black print on blue cover; same format as green-c 200.00 400.00 800.00
nn - Black print on white cover(5-13/16x9-3/16"); staple bound beneath cover); this is a later printing than the blue or green-c 200.00 400.00 800.00
NOTE: *Reprints the abbreviated 1849 Wilson & Co. 2nd printing. Pages are numbered via Arabic numerals. Many of the panels on Pages 11, 14, 19, 21, 24, 34, 35 take two lines to print the same words found in the Wilson & Co version, which used only one text line for the same panels. Unknown whether the blue or green cover is earlier. White cover version has "thirty cents" line blackened out on the two copies known to exist. Robert Cruikshank's title page has been made the cover in the D&F editions.*

OLD FOGY'S COMIC ALMANAC
Philip J. Cozans, NY: 1858 (4-7/8x7-1/4, 48 pgs)
nn - sequential comic strip told one panel per page 50.00 100.00 200.00
NOTE: Contains (12) panel "Fourth of July in New York" sequential

OLD MOTHER MITTEN AND HER FUNNY KITTEN (see also **The Juvenile Gem**) (O)
Huestis & Cozans: nd(1850-1852) (6x3-7/8"12pgs, hand colored paper-c, B&W)
nn - first printing(s) publisher's address is 104 Nassau Street (1850-1851) (Very Rare) (no known sales)
NOTE: *A hand colored outer cover is highly rare, with only 1 recorded copy possessing it. Front cover image and text is repeated precisely on page 3 (albeit b&w), and only interior pages are numbered, together leading owners of coverless copies to believe they have the cover. The true back cover has ads for the publisher. Cover was issued only with copies which were sold separately - books which were bound together as part of THE JUVENILE GEM never had such covers.*

OLD MOTHER MITTEN AND HER FUNNY KITTEN (see JUVENILE GEM) (O)
Philip J. Cozans: nd (1850-1852) (6x3-7/8",12 pgs, hand colored paper-c, B&W)
nn - Second printing(s) publisher's address is 116 Nassau Street (1851-1852) (Very Rare) (no known sales)
nn - Third printing(s) publisher's address is 107 Nassau Street (1852+) (Very Rare) (no known sales)

OLD MOTHER MITTEN AND HER FUNNY KITTEN
Americana Review, Scotia, NY: nd (1960's) (6-1/4x4-1/8", 8 pgs, side-stapled, cardboard, B&W)
nn - Modern reprint 2.50 5.00 10.00
NOTE: *Issued within a folder titled SIX CHILDREN'S BOOKS OF THE 1850'S. States "Reprinted by American Review" at bottom of front cover. Reprints the 104 Nassau Street address.*

ON THE NILE (O,G)
James R. Osgood & Co., Boston: 1874 ; **Houghton, Osgood & Co., Boston:** 1880 (112 pgs, gilted green hardcover, B&W)
1st printing (1874; 10-3/4x16") - by Augustus Hoppin 45.00 90.00 180.00
2nd printing (1880; smaller sized) 32.50 65.00 130.00

OSCAR SHANGHAI, THE EXTRAORDINARY AND MIRTH-PROVKING ADVENTURES BY SEA & LAND OF (O, G)
Garrett & Co., Publishers, No. 18 Ann Street, New York: May 1855 (5-3/4x9-1/4", 100 pgs, printed one side only, paper-c, 25¢, B&W)
nn - Samuel Avery-c; interior by ALC Very Rare) 1000.00 2000.00 4000.00
NOTE: *Not much is known of this first edition as the data comes from a recently rediscovered* ***Brother Jonathan*** *catalog issued circa 1853-55. No original known yet to exist.*

OSCAR SHANGHAI, THE WONDERFUL AND AMUSING DOINGS BY SEA AND LAND OF (G)
Dick & Fitzgerald, 10 Ann St, NY: nd (1870s-1888) (25 ¢, 5-3/4x9-1/4", 100 pgs, printed one side only, green paper c, B&W)
nn - Cover by Samuel Avery; interior by ALC (Rare) 300.00 500.00 1000.00
NOTE: *Exact reprint of Garrett & Co original.*

OUR ARTIST IN CUBA (O)
Carleton, New York: 1865 (6-5/8x4-3/8", 120 pgs, printed one side only, gilted hard-c, B&W)
nn - By Geo. W. Carleton 37.50 75.00 150.00

OUR ARTIST IN CUBA, PERU, SPAIN, AND ALGIERS (O)
Carleton: 1877 (6-1/2x5-1/8", 156 pgs, hard-c, B&W)
nn - By Geo. W. Carleton 50.00 100.00 200.00
nn - By Geo. W. Carleton (wraps paper cover) (Rare) 45.00 90.00 180.00

The Wonderful and Amusing Doings by Sea & Land of Oscar Shanghai
1870s © Dick & Fitzgerald, New York

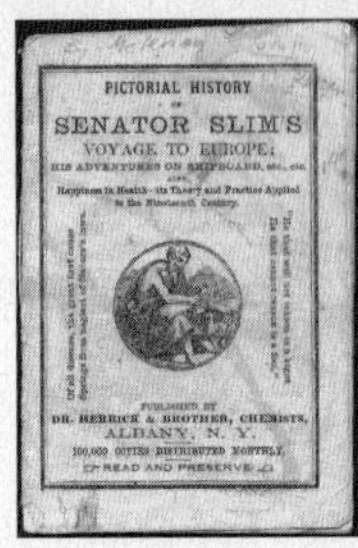

Pictorial History of Senator Slim's Voyage To Europe
1860 © Dr. Herrick & Brother, Albany, NY

Puck #1
1877 © Keppler & Schwarzman, NY

NOTE: *Reprints OUR ARTIST IN CUBA and OUR ARTIST IN PERU, then adds new section on Spain and Algiers.*

OUR ARTIST IN PERU (O)
Carleton, New York: 1866 (7-3/4x5-7/8", 68 pgs, gilted hardcover, B&W)
nn- By Geo. W. Carleton 37.50 75.00 150.00
NOTE: *Contains advertisement for the upcoming books* ***OUR ARTIST IN ITALY*** *and* ***OUR ARTIST IN FRANCE****, but no such publications have been found to date.*

PARSON SOURBALL'S EUROPEAN TOUR (O)
Duff and Ashmead: 1867 (6x7-1/2", 76 pgs, blue embossed title hard-c)
nn - By Horace Cope 100.00 200.00 400.00
NOTE: see **REV. MR. SOURBALL'S EUROPEAN TOUR, THE** for the soft paper cover version

PEN AND INK SKETCHES OF YALE NOTABLES (O,S)
Soule, Thomas and Winsor, St. Louis: 1872 (12-1/4x9-3/4", B&W)
By Squills 25.00 50.00 100.00
NOTE: *Printed by Steamlith Press, The R.P. Studley Company, St Louis.*

PETER PIPER IN BENGAL
Bengamin H Day.Publisher, Brother Jonathan Cheap Book Establishment, 48 Beekman, NY: 1953-55 (6-5/8x4-1/4, 36 pgs, yellow paper-c, B&W, 3 cents - two dollars per hundred) (Very Rare)
nn - By John Tenniel - 32 panel comic strip Punch-r 500.00 1000.00 2000.00
NOTE: *Actually also a catalog of inexpensive books, prints, maps and half a dozen comic books for sale on separate pages from publishers Day and Garrett - see full story of this brand new find in the Victorian Era essay. A complete copy with split spine sold in November 2002 for $750.00. Published date most likely 1855.*

THE PHILADELPHIA COMIC ALMANAC (S)
G. Strong, 44 Strawberry St, NYC: 1835 (8-1/2x5", 36 pgs)
nn - 100.00 200.00 600.00
NOTE: 77 engravings full of recurring cartoon characters but not sequential; early use of recurring characters.

PHIL MAY'S SKETCH BOOK (E,S,M)
R.H. Russell, New York: 1899 (14-5/8x10", 64 pgs, brown hard-c, B&W)
nn - By Phil May 32.50 65.00 130.00
NOTE: *American reprint of the British edition.*

PHUNNY PHELLOW, THE
Oakie, Dayton & Jones: Oct 1859-1876; **Street & Smith** 1876: (Folio Monthly)
average issue with Thomas Nast 50.00 100.00 200.00

PHUN FOTOCRAFT, KEWREUS KONSEETS KOMICALLY ILLUSTRATED BY A KWEER FELLER (N) (see **NEW YORK PICAYUNE**)
The New York Picayune, NY: 1850s (104 pgs)
nn - Mostly Frank Bellew, some John Leach 250.00 500.00 1000.00
NOTE: Many sequential comic strips as well as single cartoons all collected from The New York Picayune. Ross & Tousey, Agents, 121 Nassau St, NY. The Picayune ran many sequential comic strips in its decade.

PICTORIAL HISTORY OF SENATOR SLIM'S VOYAGE TO EUROPE
Dr. Herrick & Brother, Chemists, Albany, NY: 1860 (3-1/4x4-3/4", 32 pgs, B&W)
nn - By John McLenan Very Rare 150.00 300.00 600.00

PICTURES OF ENGLISH SOCIETY (Parchment-Paper Series, No.4) (M,S,E)
D. Appleton & Co., New York: 1884 (5-5/8x4-3/8", 108 pgs, paper-c, B&W)
4 - By George du Maurier; Punch-r 15.00 30.00 60.00
NOTE: *Every other page is a full page cartoon, with the opposite page containing the cartoon's caption.*

PICTURES OF LIFE AND CHARACTER (M,S,E)
Bradbury and Evans, London: No.1 1855 - No.5 c1864 (12-1/2x18", 100 pgs, illustrated hard-c, B&W)
nn (No.1) (1855) 32.50 65.00 130.00
2 (1858), 3 (1860) 32.50 65.00 130.00
4 (nd; c1862) 5 (nd; c1864) 32.50 65.00 130.00
nn (nd (late 1860's) 32.50 65.00 130.00
NOTE: 2-1/2x18-1/4", 494 pgs, green gilted-c) reprints 1-5 in one book
1-3 John Leech's... (nd; 12-3/8x10", ? pgs, red gilted-c). 25.00 50.00 100.00
NOTE: *Reprints John Leech cartoons from* ***Punch****, note that the Volume Number is mentioned only on the last page of these versions.*

PICTURES OF LIFE AND CHARACTER (E,M,S)
G.P. Putnam's Sons: 1880's (8-5/8x6-1/4", 218 pgs, hardcover, color-cr, B&W)
nn - John Leech (single panel **Punch** cartoon-r) 20.00 40.00 160.00
NOTE: *Leech reprints which extend back to the 1850s.*

PICTURES OF LIFE AND CHARACTER (Parchment-Paper Series) (E,M,S)
(see also Humerous Masterpieces)
D. Appleton & Co., NY: 1884 (30¢, 5-3/4 x 4-1/2", 104 pgs, paper-c, B&W)
nn - John Leech (single panel **Punch** cartoon-r) 20.00 40.00 160.00
NOTE: *An advertisment in the back refers to a cloth-bound edition for 50 cents.*

PIPPIN AMONG THE WIDE-AWAKES (O,S)
Werill & Chapin, 113 Nassau St, NYC, NY): 1860 (6x4-1/2", 36 pgs, 6 cents)
nn - Artist unknown (Very Rare) 100.00 200.00 400.00

PLISH AND PLUM (E.G)
Roberts Brothers, Boston: 1883 (8-1/8x5-3/4", 80 pgs, hardcover, B&W)
nn - By Wilhelm Busch 40.00 80.00 200.00
nn - Reprint (Roberts Brothers, 1895) 40.00 80.00 200.00
nn - Reprint (Little, Brown & Co., 1899) 40.00 80.00 200.00
NOTE: *The adventures of two dogs.*

POUNDS OF FUN
Frank Tousey, 34 North Moore St, NY: 1881 (6-1/2x9-1/2", 68pgs, B&W)
nn - Bellew, Worth, Woolf, Chips 40.00 80.00 200.00

PRESIDENTS MESSAGE, THE
G.P. Putnam's Sons, NY: 1887 (5-3/4x7-5/8, 44 pgs)
nn - (19) Thomas Nast single panel full page cartoons 40.00 80.00 200.00

PROTECT THE U.S. FROM JOHN BULL - PROTECTION PICTURES FROM JUDGE
Judge Publishing, New York: 1888 ((10 cents, 6-7/8x10-3/8", 36 pgs, paper-c, B&W)
nn - (Scarce) 25.00 50.00 100.00
NOTE: *Reprints both cartoons and commentary from* ***Puck****, concerning the issue of tariffs which were then being debated in Congress. Art by Gillam, Hamilton, Victor.*

PUCK (German language edition, St. Louis) (M,O) (see also Die Vehme)
Publisher unknown, St. Louis: No.1, March 18, 1871 - No. ??, Aug. 24, 1872 (B&W, paper-c)
1-?? (Very Rare) by Joseph Keppler (no known sales)
NOTE: *Joseph Keppler's second attempt at a weekly humor periodical, following* ***Die Vehme*** *one year earlier. This was his first attempt to launch using the title* ***Puck****. This German language version ran for a full year before being joined by an English language version.*

PUCK (English language edition, St. Louis) (M,O)
Publisher unknown, St. Louis: No.1, March ?? 1872 - No. ??, Aug. 24, 1872 (B&W, paper c)
1-?? (Very Rare) by Joseph Keppler (no known sales)
NOTE: *Same material as in the German language edition, but in English.*

PUCK, ILLUSTRIRTES HUMORISTISCHES WOCHENBLATT (German language edition, NYC) (M,O)
Keppler & Schwarzmann, New York: No.1 Sept (27) 1876 - 1164 Dec ?? 1899 (10 cents, color front/back-c and centerspread, remainder B&W, paper-c)
1-26 (Volume 1; Rare) by Joseph Keppler - these issues precede the English language version, and contain cartoons not found in them. Includes cartoons on the controversial Tilden-Hayes 1876 Presidential Election debacle. (no known sales)
27-52 (Volume 2; Rare) by Joseph Keppler - contains some cartoon material not found in the English language editions. Particularly in the earlier issues. (no known sales)
53-1164 7.50 15.00 30.00
Bound Volumes (six month, 26 issue run each):
Vol. 1 (Rare) (no known sales)
Vol. 2-4 (Rare) (no known sales)
Vol. 5-47 62.50 125.00 250.00
NOTE: *Joseph Keppler's second, and successful, attempt to launch* ***Puck****. In German. The first six months precede the launch of the English language edition. Soon after (but not immediately after) the launch of the English edition, both editions began sharing the same cartoons, but, their prose material always remained different. The German language edition ceased publication at the end of 1899, while the English language edition continued into the early 20th Century. First American periodical to feature printed color every issue.*

PUCK (English language edition, NYC) (M,O)
Keppler & Schwarzmann, New York: No.1 March (14) 1877 - 1190 Dec ?? 1899 (10 cents, color front/back-c and centerspread, remainder B&W, paper-c)
1 (Rare) by Joseph Keppler (no known sales)
2-26 (Rare) by Joseph Keppler (no known sales)
27-1190 12.50 25.00 50.00
(see Platinum Age section for year 1900+ issues)
Bound volumes (six month, 26 issue run each):
Vol. 1 (Rare) (one set sold on eBay for $2300.00)
Vol. 2 (Scarce) (one set sold on eBay for $1500.00)
Vol. 3-6 (pre-1880 issues) 175.00 375.00 750.00
Vol. 7-46 140.00 300.00 600.00
NOTE: *The English language editions began six months after the German editions, and so the English edition numbering is always one volume number, and 26 issue numbers, behind its parallel German language edition. Pre-1880 & post-1900 issues are more scarce than 1880's & 1890's.*

PUCK (miniature) (M,P,I)
Keppler & Schwarzmann, New York: nd (c1895) (7x5-1/8", 12 pgs, color front & back paper-c, B&W interior)
nn - Scarce 25.00 50.00 110.00
NOTE: *C.J.Taylor-c; F.M.Howarth-a; F.Opper-a; giveaway item promoting* ***Puck's*** *various publications. Mostly text, with art reprinted from* ***Puck****.*

PUCK, CARTOONS FROM (M,S)
Keppler & Schwarzmann, New York: 1893 (14-1/4x11-1/2", 244 pgs, hard-c, mostly B&W)
nn - by Joseph Keppler (Signed and Numbered) 100.00 200.00 400.00
NOTE: *Reprints Keppler cartoons from 1877 to 1893, mostly in B&W, though a few in color, with a text opposite each cartoon explaining the situation then being satirized. Issued only in an edition of 300 numbered issues, signed by Keppler. Only 1/4 of the pages are cartoons.*

PUCK'S LIBRARY (M)
Keppler & Schwarzmann, New York: No.1, July, 1887 - No. 174, Dec, 1899 (10 cents, 11-1/2x8-1/4", 36 pgs, color paper-c, B&W)
1- "The National Game" (Baseball) 50.00 100.00 200.00
2-149 10.00 20.00 40.00
NOTE: ***Puck's Library*** *was a monthly magazine reprinting cartoons & prose from* ***Puck****, with each issue's*

Rays of Light
1886 © Morse Bros., Canton, Mass.

Scraps, New Series #1 by D.C. Johnston
1849 © D.C. Johnston, Boston

Shakespeare Would Ride The Bicycle If Alive Today
1896 © Cleveland Bicycles, Toledo, OH.

material organized around the same subject. The cover art was often original. All issues were kept in print for the duration of the series, so later issues are more scarce than earlier ones.

PUCK, PICKINGS FROM (M)
Keppler & Schwarzmann, New York: No.1, Sept, 1891 - No. 34, Dec, 1899 (25 cents, 13-1/4x10-1/4", 68 pgs, color paper-c, B&W)

1-34 Scarce 15.00 30.00 60.00
NOTE: *Similar to **Puck's Library**, except larger in size, and issued quarterly. All reprint material, except for the cover art. There also exist variations with "RAILROAD EDITION 30 CENTS" printed on the cover in place of the standard 25 cent price.*

PUCK'S OPPER BOOK (M)
Keppler & Schwarzmann, New York: 1888 (11-3/4x13-7/8", color paper-c, 68 pgs,interior B&W, 30¢)

nn - (Very Rare) by F. Opper 225.00 450.00 750.00
NOTE: *Puck's first book collecting work by a single artist.; mostly sequential comic strips.*

PUCK'S PRINTING BOOK FOR CHILDREN (S,O.I)
Keppler & Schwarzman, Pubs, NY: 1891 (10-3/8x7-7/8", 52 pgs, color-c, B&W and color)

nn - Frederick B Opper (Very Rare) (no known sales)

NOTE: *Left side printed in color; Right side B&W to be colored in.*

PUCK PROOFS (M,P,S)
Keppler & Schwarzmann, New York: nd (1906-1909) (74 pgs, paper cover; B&W) (all are Scarce)

nn - (c.1906, no price, 4-1/8x5-1/4") B&W painted -c of couple kissing over a chess board; 1905 & 1906-r 25.00 50.00 100.00
nn- (c.1909, 10 cents, 4-3/8x5-3/8") plain green paper-c; 76 pgs 1905-1909-r 25.00 50.00 100.00
NOTE: *Catalog of prints available from **Puck**, reprinting mostly cover & centerspread art from **Puck**. There likely exist more as yet unreported **Puck Proofs** catalogs. Art by Rose O'Neill.*

PUCK, THE TARIFF ?, CARTOONS AND COMMENTS FROM (M,S)
Keppler & Schwarzmann, New York: 1888 (10 cents, 6-7/8x10-3/8", 36 pgs, paper-c, B&W)

nn - (Scarce) 37.50 75.00 200.00
NOTE: *Reprints both cartoons and commentary from **Puck**, concerning the issue of tariffs which were then being debated in Congress. Art by Gillam, Keppler, Opper, Taylor.*

PUCK, WORLD'S FAIR
Keppler & Schwarzmann, PUCK BUILDING, World's Fair Grounds, Chicago: No.1 May 1, 1893 - No.26 Oct 30, 1893 (10 cents, 11-1/4x8-3/4, 14 pgs, paper-c, color front/back/center pages, rest B&W)(All issues Scarce to Rare)

1-26 30.00 60.00 130.00
1-26 bound volume: 500.00 1100.00 2200.00
NOTE: *Art by Joseph Keppler, F. Opper, F.M. Howarth, C.J. Taylor, W.A. Rogers. This was a separate, parallel run of **Puck**, published during the 1893 Chicago World's Fair from within the fairgrounds, and containing all new and different material than the regular weekly **Puck**. Smaller sized and priced the same, this originally sold poorly, and had not as wide distribution as **Puck**, and so consequently issues are much more rare than regular **Puck** issues from the same period. Not to be confused with the larger sized regular **Puck** issues from 1893 which sometimes also contained World's Fair related material, and sometimes had the words "World's Fair" appear on the cover. Can also be distinguished by the fact that **Puck's** issue numbering was in the 800's in 1893, while these issue number 1 through 26.*

PUNCHINELLO
Punchinello Publishing Co, NYC: April 2-Dec 24 1870 (weekly)

1-39 Henry L. Stephens, Frank Bellew, Bowlend 12.50 25.00 50.00
NOTE: *Funded by the Tweed Ring, mild politics attacking Grant Admin & other NYC newspapers. Bound copies exist.*

QUIDDITIES OF AN ALASKAN TRIP (O,G)
G.A. Steel & Co., Portland, OR: 1873 (6-3/4x10-1/2", 80 pgs, gilted hard-c, Red-c and Blue-c exist, B&W)

nn - By William H. Bell (Scarce) 350.00 750.00 1500.00
NOTE: *Highly sought Western Americana collectors. Parody of a trip from Washington DC to Alaska, by a member of the team which went to survey Alaska, purchase commonly known then as "Seward's Folly".*

"RAG TAGS" AND THEIR ADVENTURES, THE (N,S)
A. M. Robertson, San Francisco: 1899 (10-1/4x13-7/8, 84 pgs, color hard-c, B&W inside)

nn - By Arthur M. Lewis (SF Chronicle newspaper-r) (Scarce) 60.00 120.00 240.00

RAYS OF LIGHT (O,P)
Morse Bros., Canton, Mass.: No.1 1886 (7-1/8x5-1/8", 8 pgs, color paper-c, B&W)

1- (Rare) 50.00 100.00 200.00
NOTE: *Giveaway pamphlet in guise of an educational publication, consisting entirely of a sequential story in which a teacher instructs her classroom of young girls in the use of Rising Sun Stove Polish. Color front & back covers.*

RELIC OF THE ITALIAN REVOLUTION OF 1849, A
Gabici's Music Stores, New Orleans: 1849 (10-1/8x12-3/4", 144 pgs, hardcover)

nn - By G. Daelli (Scarce) 100.00 200.00 400.00
NOTE: *From the title page: "Album of fifty line engravings, executed on copper, by the most eminent artists at Rome in 1849; secreted from the papal police after the 'Restoration of Order,' And just imported into America."*

REMARKS ON THE JACOBINIAD (I,S)
E.W. Weld & W. Greenough, Boston: 1795-98 (8-1/4x5-1/8", 72 pgs, a number of B&W plates with text)

nn - Written by Rev. James Sylvester Gardner,artist unknown (Rare) (no known sales)
NOTE: *Early comics-type characters. Not sequential comics, but uses word balloons. Satire directed against "The Jacobin Club," supporters of the French Revolution and Radical Republicans. Gardner came to America from England in 1783, was minister of Trinity Church, Boston. There appears to be some reprints of this done as late as 1798.*

REV. MR. SOURBALL'S EUROPEAN TOUR, THE RECREATION OF A CITY, THE
Duffield Ashmead, Philadelphia: 1867 (7-5/8x6-1/4", 72 pgs, turquoise blue soft wrappers)

By Horace Cope (Rare) 50.00 100.00 200.00
NOTE: see **PARSON SOURBALL'S EUROPEAN TOUR** for the hard cover version.

RHYMES OF NONSENSE TRUTH & FICTION (S)
G.W. Carleton & Co, Publishers, NY: 1874 (10x7-3/4", 44 pgs, hard-c, B&W) (Very Rare)

nn - By Chaucer Jones and Michael Angelo Raphael Smith 100.00 200.00 400.00
NOTE: *Creator names obviously pseudonyms; looks like weak A.B. Frost.*

ROMANCE OF A HAMMOCK, THE - AS RECITED BY MR. GUS WILLIAMS IN "ONE OF THE FINEST" (O,P)
Unknown: 1880s (5-1/2x3-5/8" folded, 7 attached cardboard cards which fold out into a strip, color)

nn - By presently unknown Scarce 75.00 150.00 300.00
NOTE: *12-panel story, which one begins reading on one side of the folded-out strip, then flip to the other side to continue -- unlike the vast majority of folded strips, which are printed on only one side. This was a promotional handout, for a play titled "One of the Finest". The story pictured comes from a poem read in the play by then famous New York stage actor Gus Williams, who is pictured on the "cover"/title card."*

SAD TALE OF THE COURTSHIP OF CHEVALIER SLYFOX-WIKOF, SHOWING HIS HEART-RENDING ASTOUNDING & MOST WONDERFUL LOVE ADVENTURES WITH FANNY ELSSLER AND MISS GAMBOL, THE (O,G)
Garrett & Co., NY: Jan 1856 (25 ¢, 5-3/4x9-1/4", 100 pages, paper-c, B&W)

nn - By T.C. Bond ?? (Very Rare) 500.00 1000.00 2000.00
NOTE: *No surviving copies yet reported -- known via ads in Home Circle published by Garrett. Cover art by John McLenan and Samuel Avery. Graphic novel parodying the real-life romance between European actress/dancer Fanny Elssler and American aristocrat Henry Wikoff. The entire graphic novel is reprinted in the 1976 book "Fanny Elssler in America."*

SAD TALE OF THE COURTSHIP OF CHEVALIER SLYFOX-WIKOF, SHOWING HIS HEART-RENDING ASTOUNDING & MOST WONDERFUL LOVE ADVENTURES WITH FANNY ELSSLER AND MISS GUMBEL, THE (G) (25 cents printed on cover)
Dick And Fitzgerald, NY: 1870s-1888 (5-3/4x9-1/4", ??? pages, soft paper-c, B&W)

nn - By T.C. Bond ?? (Very Rare) 250.00 500.00 1000.00
NOTE: *Reprint of Garrett original printing before G,D&F partnership begins.*

SALT RIVER GUIDE FOR DISAPPOINTED POLITICIANS
Winchell, Small & Co., 113 Fulton St, NY: 1870s (16 pgs, 10¢)

nn - single panel cartoons from WIld Oats (Rare) 75.00 150.00 300.00

SAM SLICK'S COMIC ALMANAC
Philip J. Cozans, NYC: 1857 (7.5x4.5, 48 pgs, B&W) 100.00 200.00 400.00
NOTE: *Contains reprint of* "Moses Keyser the Bowery Bully's Trip to the California Gold Mines" *from* Elton's Comic Almanac #17 1850.

SCRAPS (O,S) (see also **F****** A*** K*****)
D.C. Johnston, Boston: 1828 - No.8 1840; New Series No.1 1849 (12 pgs, printed one side only, paper-c, B&W)

1 - 1828 (9-1/4 x 11-3/4") (Very Rare) (no known sales)
2 - 1830 (9-3/4 x 12-3/4") (Very Rare) (no known sales)
3 - 1832 (10-7/8 x 13-1/8") (Very Rare) (no known sales)
4 - 1833 (11 x 13-5/8") (Very Rare) (no known sales)
5- 1834 (10-3/8 x 13-3/8") (Very Rare) (no known sales)
6 - 1835 (10-3/8 x 13-1/4") red lettering in title SCRAPS (Very Rare) 250.00 500.00 1000.00
6 - 1835 (10-3/8 x 13-1/4") no red lettering in title (Rare) 200.00 400.00 880.00
7 - 1837 (10-3/4 x 13-7/8") 1st Edition (Very Rare) 200.00 400.00 880.00
7 - 1837 (10-3/4 x 13-3/4") 2nd Edition (so stated) 100.00 175.00 375.00
NOTE: 20 pgs. of text (double-sided), 4 pgs. of art (single-sided), plus the covers. There are no protective sheets between the art pages.
8 - 1840 (10-1/2 x 13-7/8") (Rare) 200.00 400.00 880.00
New Series 1- 1849 (10-7/8 x 13-3/4") 125.00 250.00 475.00
NOTE: *By David Claypoole Johnston. All issues consist of four one-sided sheets with 9 to 12 single panel cartoons per sheet. The other pages are blank or text. With #1-5 the size of the pages can vary up to an inch. Contains 4 protective sheets (not part of page count) Only 1 3 4 and the 1849 New Series Number 1 has cover art along with 4 art pgs. (single sided) with 4 protective sheets and no text pages.New Series Number 1, as well as #6 with bo red lettering and the second printing of issue 7, have survived in higher numbers due to a 1940s warehouse discovery.*

THE SETTLEMENT OF RHODE ISLAND (O)
The Graphic Co. Photo-Lith 39 & 41, Park Place, New York: 1874 (11-3/8x10, 40 pgs, gilted blue hard-c

nn - Charles T. Miller & Walter F. Brown 50.00 100.00 250.00
NOTE: *This is also the Same Walter F. Brown that did "Hail Columbia".*

SHAKESPEARE WOULD RIDE THE BICYCLE IF ALIVE TODAY. "THE REASON WHY" (O,P,S)
Cleveland Bicycles H.A. Lozier & Co., Toledo, OH: 1896 (5-1/2x4",16 pgs, paper-c, color)

nn - By F. Opper (Rare) 70.00 140 .00 300.00
NOTE: *Original cartoons of Shakespearian characters riding bicycles; also popular amongst collectors of bicycle ephemera.*

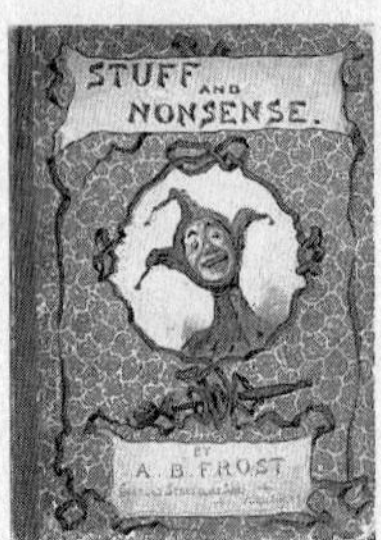

Stuff and Nonsense by A.B. Frost
1884 © Charles Scribner's Sons

Texas Siftings v6 #2 May 15
1886 ©Texas Siftings Publishing Co.

The Adventures Of Mr. Tom Plump
1851 © Huestis & Cozans, NY

FR1.0 GD2.0 FN6.0

SHAKINGS - ETCHINGS FROM THE NAVAL ACADEMY BY A MEMBER OF THE CLASS OF '67 (O,S)
Lee & Shepard, Boston: 1867 (7-7/8x10", 132 pages, blue hard-c)

	FR1.0	GD2.0	FN6.0
By: Park Benjamin	38.00	75.00	150.00

NOTE: *Park Benjamin later became editor of Harper's Bazaar magazine.*

SHOO FLY PICTORIAL (S)
John Stetson, Chestnut sT Theatre, Phila, PA: June 1870 (15-1/2x11-1/2", 8 pgs, B&W)

	FR1.0	GD2.0	FN6.0
1	67.50	125.00	250.00

SHYS AT SHAKSPEARE
J.P. and T.C.P., Philadelphia: 1869 (9-1/4x6", 52 pgs)

	FR1.0	GD2.0	FN6.0
nn - Artist unknown	75.00	150.00	300.00

SKETCHES OF LOWLY LIFE IN A GREAT CITY (M,S) (See 99 "Woolfs" From Truth)
G. P. Puntam's Sons: 1899 (8-5/8x11-1/4", 200 pgs, hard-c, B&W)
(reprints from Life and Judge of Woolf's cartoons of NYC slum children)

	FR1.0	GD2.0	FN6.0
nn - By Michael Angelo Woolf	75.00	150.00	350.00

NOTE: *Woolf's cartoons are regarded as a primary influence on R.F. Outcault in the later development of The Yellow Kid newspaper strip.*

SNAP (O,S)
Valentine & Townsend, Tribune Bldg, NYC: March 13,1885 (17x11, 8 pgs, B&W)

	FR1.0	GD2.0	FN6.0
1-Contains a sequential comic strip	50.00	100.00	150.00

SOCIETY PICTURES (M,S,E)
Charles H. Sergel Company, Chicago: 1895 (5-1/4x7-3/4", 168 pgs, printed 1 side, paper-c, B&W)

	FR1.0	GD2.0	FN6.0
nn - By George du Maurier; reprints from **Punch**.	12.50	25.00	50.00

SOLDIERS AND SAILORS HALF DIME TALES OF THE LATE REBELLION
Soldiers & Sailors Publishing Co: 1868 (5-1/4x7-7/8", 32 pgs)

	FR1.0	GD2.0	FN6.0
v1#1-#16 v2#1-#10	10.00	20.00	40.00
v2 #11 contains (5) page comic strip	20.00	40.00	80.00

NOTE: *Changes to Soldiers & Sailors Half Dime Magazine with v2 #1.*

SOUVENIR CONTAINING CARTOONS ISSUED BY THE PRESS BUREAU OF THE OHIO STATE REPUBLICAN EXECUTIVE COMMITTEE, A (S)
Ohio State Republican Executive Committee, Columbus, OH: 1899 (10-3/8x13-1/2, 248 pgs, Hard-c, B&W

	FR1.0	GD2.0	FN6.0
nn - By William L. Bloomer (Scarce)	100.00	200.00	400.00

SOUVENIR OF SOHMER CARTOONS FROM PUCK, JUDGE, AND FRANK LESLIE'S (M,S,P)
Sohmer Piano Co.: nd(c.1893) (6x4-3/4", 16 pgs, paper-c, B&W)

	FR1.0	GD2.0	FN6.0
nn	20.00	40.00	80.00

NOTE: *Reprints painted "cartoon" Sohmer Piano advertisements which appeared in the above publications. Artists include Keppler, Gillam, others.*

SPORTING NEW YORKER, THE
Ornum & Co, Beekman ST, NYC: 1870s

	FR1.0	GD2.0	FN6.0
issues with sequential comic strips (Rare)	50.00	100.00	200.00

STORY OF THE MAN OF HUMANITY AND THE BULL CALF, THE
(see Bull Calf, The Story of The Man Of Humanity And The)
NOTE: *Reprints of two of A. B. Frost's mostfamous sequential comic strips.*

STREET & SMITH'S LITERARY ALBUM
Street & Smith, NY: #1 Dec 23 1865-#225 Apr 9 1870 (11-3/4x16-3/4", 16 pgs, B&W)

	FR1.0	GD2.0	FN6.0
1 (23 Dec 1865)	10.00	30.00	50.00
2-129 131-225 (issues with short sequential strips)	7.50	15.00	30.00
130 (Steam Man satire parody)	100.00	200.00	300.00

STUFF AND NONSENSE (Harper's Monthly strip-r) (M)
Charles Scribner's Sons: 1884 (10-1/4x7-3/4", 100 pgs, hardcover, B&W)

	FR1.0	GD2.0	FN6.0
nn - By Arthur Burdett Frost	100.00	185.00	375.00
nn - By A.B. Frost (1888 reprint, 104 pgs)	40.00	80.00	180.00

NOTE: *Earliest known anthology devoted to collecting the comic strips of a single American artist. 1888 2nd printing has a different cover and is layed out somewhat differently inside with a new title page, 3 added pages of cartoons, and a couple more illustrations. For more Frost, the 2nd is worth checki ng out also.*

STUMPING IT (LAUGHING SERIES BRICKTOP STORIES #8) (O,S)
Collin & Small, NY: 1876 (6-5/8x9-1/4, 68 pgs, perfect bound, B&W)

	FR1.0	GD2.0	FN6.0
nn - Thomas Worth art abounds (some sequentials)	75.00	150.00	300.00

NOTE: Mainly single panel cartoons w/text; however, some sequential comic strips inside worth picking up

SUMMER SCHOOL OF PHILOSOPHY AT MT. DESERT, THE
Henry Holt & Co.: 1881 (10-3/8x8-5/8", 60 pgs, illus. gilt hard-c, B&W)

	FR1.0	GD2.0	FN6.0
nn - By J. A. Mitchell	60.00	120.00	240.00

NOTE: *J.A.Mitchell went on to found **LIFE** two years later in 1883. Also, the long-running mascot for **LIFE** was Cupid - which you see multitudes of Cupids flying around in this story.*

SURE WATER CURE, THE
Carey Grey & Hart, Phila, PA: c1841-43 (8-/2x5, 32 pgs, B&W

	FR1.0	GD2.0	FN6.0
nn - proto-comic-strip Very Rare	150.00	300.00	600.00

TAILOR-MADE GIRL, HER FRIENDS, HER FASHIONS, AND HER FOLLIES, THE
(see also IN THE "400" AND OUT) (M)

FR1.0 GD2.0 FN6.0

Charles Scribner's Sons, New York: 1888 (8-3/8x10-1/2", 68 pgs, hard-c, B&W)

	FR1.0	GD2.0	FN6.0
nn - Art by C.J. Taylor	17.50	35.00	70.00

NOTE: *Format is a full page cartoon on every other page, with a script style vignette, written by Philip H. Welch, on every page opposite the art.*

TALL STUDENT, THE
Roberts Brothers, Boston: 1873 (7x5", 48 pgs, printed one side only, gilted hard-c, B&W)

	FR1.0	GD2.0	FN6.0
nn - By Wilhelm Busch (Scarce)	37.50	75.00	150.00

TARIFF ?, CARTOONS AND COMMENTS FROM PUCK, THE (see Puck, The Tariff...)

TEASING TOM AND NAUGHTY NED WITH A SPOOL OF CLARK'S COTTON, THE ADVENTURES OF (O,P)
Clark's O.N.T. Spool Cotton: 1879 (4-1/4x3", 12 pgs, B&W, paper-c)

	FR1.0	GD2.0	FN6.0
nn	17.50	35.00	70.00

NOTE: *Knock-off of the "First Trick" in Wilhelm Busch's **Max and Maurice**, modified to involve Clark's Spool Cotton in the story, with similar but new art by an artist identified as "HB". The back cover advertises the specific merchant who gave this booklet away -- multiple variations of back cover suspected.*

TEMPERANCE TALES; OR, SIX NIGHTS WITH THE WASHINGTONIANS, VOL I & II
W.A. Leary & Co., Philadelphia: 1848 (50¢, 6-1/8x4", 328 pgs, B&W, hard-c)

	FR1.0	GD2.0	FN6.0
nn	100.00	200.00	400.00

NOTE: *Mostly text. This edition gathers Volume I & II together. The first 8 pages reprints George Cruikshank's **THE BOTTLE**, re-drawn & re-engraved by Phil A. Pilliner. Later editions of this book do not include **THE BOTTLE** reprint and are therefore of little interest to comics collectors.*

TEXAS SIFTINGS
Texas Siftings Publishing Co, Austin, Texas (1881-1887), **NYC** (1887-1897): 1881-1885 newspaper-size weekly; 1886-1897 folio weekly (15x10-3/4", 16 pgs, B&W 10¢

	FR1.0	GD2.0	FN6.0
1881-1885 issues	25.00	50.00	100.00
v6#1 (5/8/86) (8) panel strip Afterwhich He Emigrated; (16) panel The Tenor's Triumph Veni Vidi Vici	12.50	25.00	50.00
v6#2 (5/16/86 (5) panel sewuential	12.50	25.00	50.00
v6#3 no sequentials	12.50	25.00	50.00
v6#4 (5/29/86) Worth-c (4) panel Worth strip; (2) panel	12.50	25.00	50.00
v6#5 no sequentials	12.50	25.00	50.00
v6#6 (6/12/86) Comic Strip Cover (11) panels The Rise of a Great Artist (5) panel sequential	50.00	100.00	200.00
v6#7 (6/19/86) Worth-c (2) panel Wiorth; (10) panel Ha! Ha! The Honest Youth & the Lordly Villain	25.00	50.00	100.00
v6#8 (6/26/86) Worth-c; (15) panel The Kangaroo Hunter	25.00	50.00	100.00
v6#9 (7/3/86) Worth-c; Bellew (2) panel How Wives Get What They Want	12.50	25.00	50.00
v6#10 ((7/10/86) Baseball-c; (3) panel; (5) panel A Story Without Words from Fliegende Blätter	12.50	25.00	50.00
v6 #11 12 13 Worth-c no sequentials	12.50	25.00	50.00
v6#14 (8/7/86) Wiorth-c; (7) panel Mrs Cleveland Presents The President With A New Rocking Chair	12.50	25.00	50.00
v6#15 (8/14/86) Worth-c; (6) panel Worth strip	12.50	25.00	50.00
v6#16 (8/21/86) Worth-c Asleep At Post USA/Mexico Border (6) panel sequential	12.50	25.00	50.00
v6#17 no sequrntials	12.50	25.00	50.00
v6#18 (9/4/86) Worth-c; (3) panel from Fliegende	12.50	25.00	50.00
v6#19 (9/11/86) Worth Anarchist & Uncle Sam-c; (5) panel Duel of the Dudes	12.50	25.00	50.00
v6#20 (9/18/86) Worth-c (6) panel sequential	12.50	25.00	50.00
v6#21 (9/25/86) Worth-c; Verbeck single panel; (9) panel	12.50	25.00	50.00
v6#22 (10/2/86) Verbeck-c plus interiors	12.50	25.00	50.00
v6#23 (10/9/86) Worth-c Geronimo & Devil cover; Verbeck and Chips singles	25.00	50.00	100.00
v6#24 (10/16/86) Worth-c Verbeck strip "Evolution"	12.50	25.00	50.00
v6#25 no sequential strips	12.50	25.00	50.00
v6#26 (10/30/86) Worth-c; (6) panel Verbeck "A Warning To Smokers"	12.50	25.00	50.00

NOTE: *Many Thomas Worth sequential comic strips. Frank Bellew and Dan McCarthy appear. Wilhelm Busch-r from German Fligende Blaetter. Later issues in 1890s comics become sporadic*

THAT COMIC PRIMER (S)
G.W. Carleton & Co., Publishers: 1877 (6-5/8x5", 52 pgs, paper soft-c, B&W)

	FR1.0	GD2.0	FN6.0
nn - By Frank Bellew	75.00	150.00	300.00

NOTE: *Premium for the United States Life Insurance Company, New York.*

TIGER, THE LEFTENANT AND THE BOSUN, THE
Prudential Insurance Home Office, 878 & 880 Broad St, Newark, NJ: 1889 (4.5x3.25", 12 pgs) (Scarce)

	FR1.0	GD2.0	FN6.0
nn - 8 panel sequential story in color	50.00	100.00	200.00

TOM PLUMP, THE ADVENTURES OF MR. (see also The Juvenile Gem) (O)
Huestis & Cozans, New York: nd (c1850-1851) (6x3-7/8", 12 pgs, hand colored paper-c, B&W)

	FR1.0	GD2.0	FN6.0
nn- First printing(s) publisher's address is 104 Nassau Street (1850-1851) (Very Rare)	625.00	1250.00	2500.00

NOTE: *California Gold Rush story. The hand colored outer cover is highly rare, with only 1 recorded copy possessing it. The front cover image and text is repeated precisely on page 3 (albeit b&w), and only interior pages are numbered, together leading owners of coverless copies to believe they have the cover. The true back*

The Tooth-Ache by George Cruikshank
1849 © J. L. Smith, Philadelphia, PA

Uncle Josh's Trunk Full Of Fun
1870s © Dick & Fitzgerald

Wild Oats #115 March 10
1875 © Winchell & Small, NYC

FR1.0 GD2.0 FN6.0

cover contains ads for the publisher. The cover was issued only with copies which were sold separately - booklets which were bound together as part of ***THE JUVENILE GEM*** *never had such covers.*

TOM PLUMP, THE ADVENTURES OF MR. (see also The Juvenile Gem) (O)
Philip J. Cozans: nd (1851-1852) (6x3-7/8", 12 pgs,hand colored paper-c, B&W)

nn- Second printing(s) publisher's address is 116 Nassau Street (1851-1852)
(Very Rare) 400.00 800.00 1600.00
nn- Third printing(s) publisher's address is 107 Nassau Street (1852+)
(Very Rare) 400.00 800.00 1600.00

TOM PLUMP, THE ADVENTURES OF MR.
Americana Review, Scotia, NY: nd(1960's) (6-1/4x4-1/8", 8 pgs, side-stapled, cardboard-c, B&W)

nn - Modern reprint - 12.00 24.00
NOTE: *Issued within a folder titled SIX CHILDREN'S BOOKS OF THE 1850'S. States "Reprinted by American Review" at bottom of front cover. Reprints the 104 Nassau Street address.*)
nn - Modern reprint (Scarce 1980s) (5-1/2x4-1/4", 8 pgs,side-stapled) - 5.00 10.00
NOTE: *Photocopy reprint by a comix zine publisher, from an Americana Review cop; vailable by mail order*

TOOTH-ACHE, THE (E,O)
D. Bogue, London: 1849 (5-1/4x3-3/4)

nn - By Cruikshank, B&W (Very Rare) 250.00 500.00 1000.00
nn - By Cruikshank, hand colored (Rare) (no known sales)
NOTE: *Scripted by Horace Mayhew, art by George Cruikshank. This is the British edition. Price 1/6 b&w, 3 hand colored. In British editions, the panels are not numbered. Publisher's name appears on cover. Booklet's "pages" unfold into a single, long, strip.*

J.L. Smith, Philadelphia, PA: nd (1849) (5-1/8"x 3-3/4" folded, 86-7/8" wide unfolded, 26 pgs, cardboard-c, color, 15¢)

nn - By Cruikshank, hand colored (Very Rare) 400.00 800.00 1600.00
NOTE: *Reprints the D. Bogue edition. In American editions, the panels are numbered (43 panels, not counting front & back cover). Publisher's name stamped on inside front cover, plus printed along left-hand side of first interior page. Page 1 is pasted to inside back cover, and unfolds from there. Front cover not attached to back cover by design. Booklet's "pages" unfold into a single, long, strip (made from four individual strips pasted together on the blank back side). There is a fairly common1974 British Arts Council reprint.*

TRAMP, THE: His Tricks, Tallies, and Tell-Tales, with His Signs, Countersigns, Grips, Passwords and Villainies Exposed (O,S)
Dick & Fitzgerald, New York: 1878 (11-3/8x8, 36 pgs, paper-c, B&W, 25¢) (Rare)

1 Frank Bellew 150.00 300.00 600.00
NOTE: *Edited by Frank Bellew, A Bee And A Chip (Bellew's daughter and son Frank).*

TRUTH (See Platinum Age section for 1900-1906 issues)
Truth Company, NY: 1886-1906? (13-11/16x10-5/16", 16 pgs, process color-c & centerfolds, rest B&W)

1886-1887 issues 20.00 40.00 100.00
1888-1895 issues non Outcault issues 15.00 30.00 80.00
Mar 10 1894 - precursor Yellow Kid RFO 60.00 180.00 400.00
#372 June 2 1894 - first app Yellow Kid RFO 215.00 650.00 1300.00
June 23 1894 - precursor Yellow Kid R. F. Outcault 60.00 180.00 400.00
July 14 1894 -2nd app Yellow Kid RFO 110.00 330.00 700.00
Sept 15 1894 - (2) 3rd app YK RFO plus YK precursor 110.00 330.00 700.00
Feb 9 1895 - 4th app Yellow Kid RFO 110.00 330.00 700.00
1896-1899 issues 10.00 20.00 55.00
NOTE: *This magazine contains the earliest known appearances of* ***The Yellow Kid*** *by Richard Felton Outcault. Feb 9 1895 issue's YK cartoon was reprinted one week later in the* ***New York World*** *Feb 17 1895 edition. We are still sorting out further Outcault appearances. Truth also contained full color sequential strips by Hy Mayer on the back plus Woolf, Verbeek, etc.*

TRUTH, SELECTIONS FROM
Truth Company, NY: 1894-Spr 1897 (13-11/16x10-1/4, color-c, quarterly)

1-4 25.00 50.00 100.00
5-Outcault's early Yellow Kid 100.00 200.00 400.00
6-13 20.00 40.00 80.00
NOTE: *#5 reprints all early Outcault Yellow Kid appearances*

TURNER'S COMIC ALMANAC
Charles Strong, 298 Pearl St, NYC: ???-1843 (7.25x4.5", 36 pgs, B&W)

nn 60.00 120.00 240.00

TURNER'S COMICK ALMA-NACK
Turner & Fisher, NYC: 1844-?? (7.25x4.5", 36 pgs, B&W)

nn 60.00 120.00 240.00

TWO HUNDRED SKETCHES, HUMOROUS AND GROTESQUE, BY GUSTAVE DORE (E)
Frederick Warne & Co, London: 1867 (13-3/4x11-3/8, 94 pgs, hard-c, B&W)

nn - (1867) by Gustave Dore 100.00 200.00 500.00
nn - (Second Edition; 1871)- by Gustave Dore 50.00 100.00 240.00
nn - (Third Edition; 1870's)- by Gustave Dore 50.00 100.00 240.00
nn - (Fourth Edition; 1870's- by Gustave Dore 50.00 100.00 240.00
NOTE: *Contains sequential comics stories, single panel cartoons, and sketches. Reprints and translates material which originally appeared in the French publications "Le Journal pour Rire", circa 1848-49. Although dated 1867, it was likely published & available for the 1866 Christmas Season, as has been confirmed for the American edition. Printed by Dalziel. The American & first British editions were printed simultaneously, the American edition is not a reprint of the British.*

TWO HUNDRED SKETCHES, HUMOROUS AND GROTESQUE, BY GUSTAVE DORE (E)
Roberts Brothers, Boston: 1867 (13-3/4x11-3/8", 96 pgs, hard-c, B&W)

FR1.0 GD2.0 FN6.0

nn - By Gustave Dore 100.00 200.00 500.00
NOTE: *Although dated 1867, it was published & available for the 1866 Christmas Season. Printed by Dalziel, in England, and imported to the USA expressly for a USA publisher.*

UNCLE JOSH'S TRUNK-FUL OF FUN
Dick & Fitzgerald, 18 Ann St, NY: 1870s (5-3/4x9", 68 pgs, B&W & Red-c, B&W inside)

nn - Rare 75.00 125.00 200.00
NOTE: *Many single panel cartoons; (2) pages of early boxing sequential strip*

UNCLE SAM'S COMIC ALMANAC
M.J. Meyers, NY: 1879 (11x8", 32 pgs)

nn - 50.00 100.00200.00

UNDER THE GASLIGHT
Gaslight Publishing Co (Frank Tousey): Oct 13 1878-Apr 12 1879 (Folio, 16pgs)

1-27 75.00 125.00 200.00

UNITED STATES COMIC ALMANAC
King & Baird, Philadelphia: 1851-?? (7.5x4.5", 36 pgs, B&W)

nn 60.00 120.00 240.00

UPS AND DOWNS ON LAND AND WATER (O.G)
James R. Osgood & Co., Boston: 1871 ; **Houghton, Osgood & Co., Boston:** 1880 (108 pgs, gilted hard-c, B&W)

1st printing (1871; 10-3/4x16") - By Augustus Hoppin 45.00 90.00 180.00
2nd printing (1880; smaller sized) 32.50 65.00 130.00
NOTE: *Exists as blue or orange hard covers.*

VANITY FAIR
William A. Stephens (for Thompson & Camac): Dec 29 1859-July 4 1863 Quarto Weekly

average issues with comic strips 12.50 25.00 50.00

VERDICT, THE
Verdict Publishing Co: Dec 19 1898-Nov 12 1900 (Chromolithographic Weekly)

Average Issues 50.00 100.00 200.00
NOTE: *Artists included George B. Luks, Horace Taylor, MIRS. Striking anti-Republican weekly full o fsome of the most savage political cartoons of the era. The last brilliant burst of energy for the political cartoon weekly*

VERY VERY FUNNY (M,S)
Dick & Fitzgerald, New York: nd(c1880's) (10¢, 7-1/2x5", 68 pgs, paper-c, B&W)

nn - (Rare) 75.00 150.00 300.00
NOTE: *Unauthorized reprints of prose and cartoons extracted from Puck, Texas Siftings, and other publications. Includes art by Chips Bellew, Bisbee, Graetz, Opper, Wales, Zim.*

VIM
H. Wimmel, NYC: June 22-Aug 24 1898 (Chromolithographic Weekly)

average issue 50.00 100.00 200.00
Yellow Kid by Leon Barritt issues 75.00 150.00 300.00

WAR IN THE MIDST OF AMERICA. FROM A NEW POINT OF VIEW. (E,O,G)
Ackermann & Co., London: 1864 (4-3/8" x 5-7/8", folded, 36 feet wide unfolded, 80 pgs, hard-c, B&W)

nn- by Charles Dryden (rare) 375.00 750.00 1500.00
NOTE: *British graphic novel about the American Civil War, with a pro-Confederate bent. Adventures of a British artist who decides to visually summarize the American Civil War for his countrymen, from newspaper accounts. Reaching current events, he finds he can not finish the story until the War ends, and so he travels to America, to end it. Book unfolds into a single long strip (binding was issued split, to enable the unfolding).*

WASP, THE ILLUSTRATED SAN FRANCISCO
F. Korbel & Bros and Numerous Others: August 5 1876-April 25 1941 (Chromolithographic Weekly)

average 1800s issues with comic strips 50.00 100.00 200.00

WHAT I KNOW OF FARMING: Founded On The Experience of Horace Greeley (S)
The American News Company, New York: 1871 (7-1/4x4-1/2", paper-c, B&W)

nn - By Joseph Hull (Scarce) 35.00 70.00 140.00
NOTE: *Pay & Cox, Printers & Engravers, NY; political tract regarding Presidential elections.*

WILD FIRE
Wild Fire Co, NYC: Nov 30 1877-at least#16 Mar 1878 (Folio, 16 pgs)

1-16 12.50 25.00 50.00

WILD OATS, An Illustrated Weekly Journal of Fun, Satire, Burlesque, and Nits at Persons and Events of the Day (O)
Winchell & Small, 113 Fulton St /48 Ann St, NYC: Feb 1870-1881 (16-1/4x11", generally 16 pages, B&W, began as monthly, then bi-weekly, then weekly) All loose issues Very Rare (See *The Overstreet Price Guide* #35 2005 for a detailed index of single issue contents)

1-25 Very Rare - contents to be indexed next year 50.00 100.00 200.00
26-28 30 32 35 36 39 40 41 43-46 1872 (sequential strips) 50.00 100.00 200.00
29 33 37 42 no sequential strips 40.00 80.00 160.00
31 34 38 47 Hopkins sequential comic strips 50.00 100.00 200.00
48 (1/16/73) Worth 13 panel sequential; first Woolf-c 50.00 100.00 200.00
49 51 53 54 60 62 61 64 65 66 67 69 1873 sequential strips 50.00 100.00 200.00
50 52 56 59 63 71 no sequential strips 40.00 80.00 160.00
51 (Worth 18 panel double page spread, Woolf 9 panel 50.00 100.00 200.00
55 Hopkins 22 panel double page spread; Bellew-c 50.00 150.00 300.00
57 intense unknown 6 panel "Two Relics of Barbarism, or A Few Contrasted Pictures,

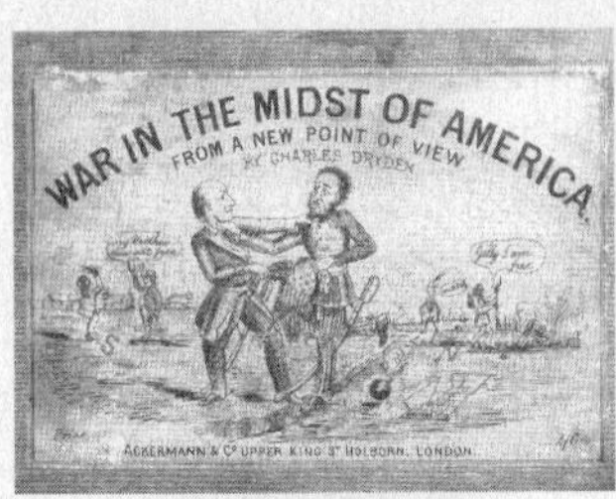

WAR IN THE MIDST OF AMERICA
FROM A NEW POINT OF VIEW
ACKERMANN & Co. UPPER KING St HOLBORN, LONDON.

War in the Midst of America
1864 © Ackerman & Co., London

Wild Oats #139 August 25
1875 © Winchell & Small, NY

Yankee Notions #7 (v2#1)
July 1852 © T.W. Strong, NY

	FR1.0	GD2.0	FN6.0
Showing the origin of the North American Indian	50.00	100.00	200.00
58 (6/5/73) unknown 19 panel double pager "The Terrible Adventures of Messrs Buster & Stumps, About Exterminating the Indians" reads across both pages like Popeye #2095 (1933); Woolf-c	100.00	200.00	400.00
68 (10/16/73) unknown 9 panel "Adv of New jersey Mosquito" looks like Winsor McCay type style: early inspiration for McCay's animated cartoon?	50.00	100.00	200.00
70 unknown 6 panel; Hopkins 6 panel "Hopkins novel: A Tale of True Love, with all the variations"; Bellew-c	50.00	100.00	200.00
72 (12/11/73) Worth 11 panel; Wales President Grant war-c	50.00	100.00	200.00
73 74 75 Hopkins sequential comic strip	75.00	150.00	300.00
76 77 sequential strips	50.00	100.00	200.00
78 Bellew 5 panel double pager	50.00	100.00	200.00
79-105 (March 1874-Dec 1874) contents presently unknown	50.00	100.00	200.00
106 107 111 no sequentials;Bellew-c #106 110;Wales-c #107	50.00	100.00	200.00
108 (1/20/75) Wales 12 panel double pg spread; Bellew-c	50.00	100.00	200.00
109 (1/27/75) unknown 6 panel; Wales-c	50.00	100.00	200.00
111 Busch 13 panel "The Conundrum of the Day - Is Lager Beer Intoxicating?"; Bellew-c	50.00	100.00	200.00
112 116 sequential comic strips	50.00	100.00	200.00
113 114 115 no sequentials Worth-c #114	40.00	80.00	160.00
117 intense Wales 6 panel "One of the Oppresions of the Civil Rights Laws"' Bellew-c	75.00	150.00	300.00
118-137 (3/31/75-8/4/75) no sequential comic strips	40.00	80.00	160.00
138 (8/18/75) Bellew Sr & Bellew "Chips" Jr singles appear	50.00	100.00	200.00
139-143 145-147 154-157 159 no sequentials	40.00	80.00	160.00
144 (9/29/75) Hopkins 8 panel sequential; Wales-c	50.00	100.00	200.00
148 (10/27/75) Opper's first cover; many Opper singles	75.00	150.00	300.00
149 150 151 152 153 all Opper-c and much interior work	50.00	100.00	200.00
158 (1/5/76) Palmer Cox 1rst comic strip 24 panel double page spread "The Adv of Mr & Mrs Sprowl And Their Christmas Turkey - A Crashing Chasing Tearful Tragedy But Happily Ending Well"; Opper-c	100.00	200.00	400.00
159 160 162 165 167 169-173 no sequentials	40.00	80.00	160.00
161 163 164 166 168 179 182 Palmer Cox sequential strips	100.00	200.00	400.00
174 (4/26/76) Cox 24 panel double pager "The Tramp's Progress; A Story of the West And the Union Pacific Railroad"	100.00	200.00	400.00
175-178 183-189 no sequentials	40.00	80.00	160.00
180 (6/7/76) Beard & Opper jam; Woolf, Bellew singles	50.00	100.00	200.00
181 more Mann two panel jobs; Opper-c	50.00	100.00	200.00
190 Bellew 9 panel "Rodger's Patent Mosquito Armour"	75.00	150.00	300.00
191-end contents to be indexed in the near future	40.00	80.00	160.00

NOTE: *There are very few lknown oose issues. All loose issues are Very Rare. Prices vary widely on this magazine. Issues with sequential comic strips would be in higher demand than issues with no comic strips. We present this index from the Library of Congress and New York Historical Society bound sets. We would love to hear from any one who turns up loose copies. This scarce humor bi-weekly contains easily a couple hundred original first-time published sequential comic strips found in most issues plus innumerable single panel cartoons in every issue*

WYMAN'S COMIC ALMANAC FOR THE TIMES
T.W.Strong, NY: 1854 (8x5", 24 pgs)

nn -	50.00	100.00	200.00

WOMAN IN SEARCH OF HER RIGHTS, THE ADVENTURES OF (G)
Lee & Shepard, Boston And New York: early 1870s (8-3/8x13", 40 pgs, hard-c)

By Florence Claxton (Very Rare)	400.00	800.00	1600.00

NOTE: *Earliest known original comic book sequential story by a woman; contains "nearly 100 original drawings by the author, which have been reproduced in fac-simile by the graphotype process of engraving." Tinted two color lithography; orange tint printed first, then printed 2nd time with black ink; early women's sufferage.*

WORLD OVER, THE (I)
G. W. Dillingham Company, New York: 1897 (192 pgs, hard-c)

nn - By Joe Kerr; 80 illustrations by R.F. Outcault (Rare)	250.00	500.00	1000.00

NOTE: soft cover editions also exist

WRECK-ELECTIONS OF BUSY LIFE (S)
Kellogg & Bulkeley: 1867 (9-1/4x11-3/4", ??? pages, soft-c)

nn - By J. Bowker (Rare)	100.00	200.00	400.00

NOTE: *Says "Sold by American News Company, New York" on cover.*

YANKEE DOODLE
W.H. Graham, Tribune Building, NYC: Oct 10 1846-Oct 2 1847 (Quarto weekly)

average issue	50.00	100.00	200.00

YANKEE NOTIONS, OR WHITTLINGS OF JONATHAN'S JACK-KNIFE
T.W. Strong, 98 Nassau St, NYC: Jan. 1852-1875 (11x8, 32 pgs, paper-c, 12.5¢, monthly)

1 Brother Jonathan character single panel cartoons	50.00	100.00	200.00

NOTE: *Begins continuing character sequential comic strip, "The Adventures of Jeremiah Oldpot" in "A Bird in the Hand Is Worth Two in The Bush"*

2-4	25.00	50.00	100.00
5 British X-Over	25.00	50.00	100.00

NOTE: *Single panel of John Bull & Brother Jonathan exchanging civilities (issues of Punch & Yankee Notions)*

6 end of Jeremiah Oldpot continued strip	25.00	50.00	100.00
v2#1 begin "Hoosier Bragg" sequential strip - six issue serial	25.00	50.00	100.00
v2#2 Feb 1853 two pg 12 panel sequential "Mr Vanity's Exploits, Arising Out Of A Valentine"	37.50	75.00	150.00
v2#3-v2#5 continues Hoosier Bragg	25.00	50.00	100.00
v2#6 Juen 1853 Lion Eats Hoosier Bragg, end of story	25.00	50.00	100.00
v3#1 begins referring to its cartoons as "Comic Art"	37.50	75.00	150.00
v4#1-V4#6 v5#1-v5#2 no sequential comic strips	20.00	40.00	80.00
v5#3 two sequential comic strips	37.50	75.00	150.00

NOTE: *Mr Take-A-Drop And The Maine Law (5) panels and The First Segar (7) panels (about smoking tobacco)*

v5#4 April 1856 begin Billy Vidkins	37.50	75.00	150.00

NOTE: *Begins reprinting "From Passages in the Life of Little Billy Vidkins, first issued as a stand alone proto-comic book in 1849 Illustrations of the Poets*

v5#5 The McBargem Guards (9) panel sequential; Vidkins	25.00	50.00	100.00
v5#6 v5 #9 no comics	20.00	40.00	80.00
v5#7 Billy Vidkins continues	25.00	50.00	100.00
v5#8 end of Vidkins By HL Stephens, Esq.	25.00	50.00	100.00
v5#10 (6) panel "How We Learn To Ride"; Timber is hero	25.00	50.00	100.00
v5#11 (7) panel "How Mr. Green Sparrowgrass Voted-A Warning For the Benefit of Quiet Citizens About To Excercize the Elective Franchise" plus Pt Two "How We Learn to Ride"	37.50	75.00	150.00
v5#12 (6) panel "How Mr Pipp Got Struck"; "The Eclipse" featuring Mr Phips; Pt 3 "How We Learn to Ride"	25.00	50.00	100.00
v6#1 (Jan 1857) (12) panel "A Tale of An Umbrella; (4) panel begins a serial "The Man Who Bought The Elephant; (8) panel How Our Young New Yorkers Celebrate New Years Day	25.00	50.00	100.00
v6#2 (Feb 1857) Pt 2 (4) panels The Man Who Bought the Elephant; (7) panel A Game of All Fours	25.00	50.00	100.00
v6#3 (Mar 1857) Pt 3 (4) panels The Man Who Bought the Elephant ending; (4) panel Ye Great Crinoline Monopoly	25.00	50.00	100.00
v6#4 no comic strips	25.00	50.00	100.00
v6#5 (May 1850) (3) panel A Short Trip to Mr Bumps, And How It Ended; (2) panel How mr Trembles Was Garrotted	25.00	50.00	100.00
v6#6 no comic strips	25.00	50.00	100.00
v6#7 (July 1857) (5) panel Alma Mater; (3) panel Three Tableaux In the Life of A Broadway Swell	25.00	50.00	100.00
v6 #8 9 no comic strips	25.00	50.00	100.00
v6#10 (Oct 1857) (3) panel Adv of Mr Near-Sight	25.00	50.00	100.00
v6#11 (Nov 1857) (11) panel Mrs Champignon's Dinner Party And the Way She Arranged Her Guests; (4) panel A Stroll in August	25.00	50.00	100.00
v6#12 (Dec 1857) (8) panel strip; (12) panel Young Fitz At A Blow Out in the Fifth Ave	25.00	50.00	100.00
v10#1 (Jan 1860) comic strip Bibbs at Central Park Skating Pond using word balloons	25.00	50.00	100.00

YE TRUE ACCOUNTE OF YE VISIT TO SPRINGFIELDE BY YE CONSTABEL HIS SPECIAL REPORTER
Frank Leslie: 1861 (5-1/8 x 5-1/4 or 93 inches when folded out, paper-c, B&W)

nn - Very Rare fold-out of 18 comic strip panels plus covers	-	-	

NOTE: *8 panels contain word balloons (Very Rare - only one copy known to exist.) First printed in Frank Leslie's Budget of Fun Jan 1 1861 issue. Abraham Lincoln Biography.*

YE VERACIOUS CHRONICLE OF GRUFF & POMPEY IN 7 TABLEAUX. (O,P)
Jackson's Best Chewing Tobacco & Donaldson Brothers: nd (c1870's) (5-1/8 tall x 3-3/8" wide folded, 27" wide unfolded, color cardboard)

nn - With all 8 panels attached (Scarce)	40.00	80.00	160.00
nn - Individual panels/cards	6.00	12.00	24.00

NOTE: *Black Americana interest. Consists of 8 attached cards, printed on one side, which unfold into a strip story of title card & 7 panels. Scrapbook hobbyists in the 19th Century tended to pull the panels apart and paste into their scrapbooks, making copies with all panels attached scarce.*

YOUNG AMERICA (continues as Yankee Doodle)
T.W. Strong, NYC: 1856

1-30 John McLennon	50.00	100.00	200.00

YOUNG AMERICA'S COMIC ALMANAC
T.W. Strong, NY: 1857 (7-1/2x5", 24 pgs)

nn	50.00	100.00	200.00

THE YOUNG MEN OF AMERICA (becomes Golden Weekly) (S)
Frank Tousey, NYC: 1887-88 (14x10-1/4", 16 pgs, B&W)

527 (10/13/87) Bellew strip "Story of A Black Eye"	25.00	50.00	100.00
530 (11/3/87) Thomas Worth (6) panel strip	125		
531 (11/10/87) Thomas Worth(3) panel strip			
537 (12/22/87) H.E. Patterson (3) panel strip			
544 (2/9/88) Caran s'Ache (6) panel strip-r	37.50	75.00	100.00
555 (4/26/88) Thomas Worth (3) panel strip			
556 (5/3/88) Thomas Worth (6) panel strip; Kit Carson-c	75.00	150.00	300.00
569 (8/21/88) Frank Bellew (2) panel strip			
570 (8/9/88) Kemble (2) panel strip			
571 (8/16/88) Kemble (2) panel strip; first Davy Crockett	75.00	150.00	300.00
Issues with just single panel cartoons	10.00	20.00	40.00

ZIM'S QUARTERLY (M)
(13-13/16x10-1/4", 60 pgs, color-c; most;y B&W, some interior color)

1 - Eugene Zimmerman	112.50	225.00	450.00

NOTE: *Approx. half sequential comic strips, other half single panel cartoons.*

For a free, lively e-mail discussion group of Victorian & Platinum Age comics collectors, fans, dealers, enthusiasts, and scholars you can join to look, listen, learn, and share at **PlatinumAgeComics@Yahoogroups.com/subscribe**.

Any addititions or corrections to this section are always welcome, very much encouraged and can be sent to **robert@BLBcomics.com** to be processed for next year's Guide.

THE PLATINUM AGE

The American Comic Book: 1883-1938

Further Concise History & Price Index Of The Field As Of 2008

NEWSPAPERS HARNESS COMICS POWER MYRIAD FORMATS COMPETE

by Robert Lee Beerbohm and Richard D. Olson, PhD ©2009, 2011

(This article was originally created by Robert L. Beerbohm and Richard D. Olson beginning in CBPG #27 1997 and is revised annually as new information comes to light.)

The story of the success of the modern comic strip as we know it today is tied closely to the companies who sponsored and bought licenses from the copyright holder for the purpose of advertising products. Platinum Age comic books have come back into their own after languishing mostly forgotten for a few decades. With this series of comics history research updates now marking its first decade, these historically important books are seem by many now as very collectible. Online sources such as eBay and bookfinder.com have demonstrate that many of these Platinum books are actually not scarce at all as previously thought, though they are in any type of higher-grade condition. Even so, most Platinum Age books are much rarer than so-called Golden Age comic books, yet despite this scarcity, *Mutt & Jeff*, *Bringing Up Father*, *The Katzenjammer Kids*, and many more were more popular than say Superman and Batman when they were introduced. Recent research has come up with some more amazing rediscoveries. There is much that can be learned and applied to today's comics market by a simple historical examination of the medium's evolution over more than 160 years.

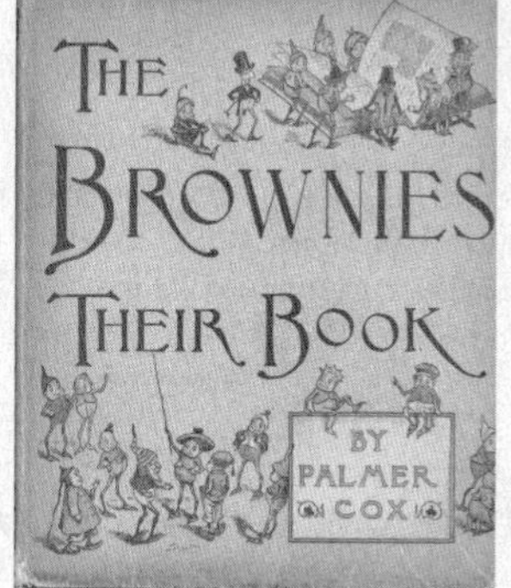

The Brownies' first book, 1887 by Palmer Cox, set a precedent for the Platinum Age, collecting and reprinting previously published material.

It should be noted that "ages" are applied to historical periods in the history of comics for convenience. In fact, ages typically overlap and there is no discrete beginning or ending for any given "age." This is the case with the Platinum Age, which clearly began with Palmer Cox's creation of *The Brownies* in 1883 even though it overlaps with the Victorian Age which ran through the end of the 19th Century. Cox introduced a qualitative change to the field, not an incremental quantitative change. Specifically, he produced art and verse for children in children's magazines and then merchandised those characters. He published work for children not only in books but in magazines and newspapers, and he merchandised his creations to an extent that had never been done previously.

The Brownies in the Philippines by Palmer Cox, Oct 1904 - scarce original art from the book. President Roosevelt is pictured within these multitudes of Brownie madness, a Cox "signature trademark." Cox's stories are comic strip-oriented in nature of time sequence as he boldly took his Brownies around the world.

Palmer Cox was born in 1840 near Granby, Quebec. He journeyed to Oakland, California in 1863, and began publishing cartoon, prose and poems in the local press and media outlets such as *The San Francisco Examiner* wherein by 1867 it has been reported he also began creating sequential comic strips, though none have yet surfaced.

His first book, *Squibs of California*, was published in 1874. He subsequently moved to New York in 1875 and almost immediately began working for the magazine *Wild Oats*, of which more is written about in the preceding Victorian Age history introduction as well as a sample of his sequential work. He drew dozens of sequential comic strips for *Wild Oats*, a humor magazine so scarce only one issue has been offered on eBay in the past six years.

Soon thereafter he became a major contributor to the Scribner publications, including *The St. Nicholas*, an illustrated magazine for young folk. His first cartoon for them was "The Wasp And The Bee," published in the March 1879 cover-date issue. While it is now clear that Cox used elves and brownie-like characters in his art for several different magazines as early as 1877 in *Harper's Young People* magazine as well as using Brownies-type characters beginning in the Feb

1881 issue of *Wide Awake*, the first true appearance of the Brownies in their own story using that title, a combination of art and verse was February, 1883, in *St. Nicholas*. Palmer Cox's *The Brownies* were the first North American comics-type characters to be internationally merchandised. Even though Cox was continuously doing sequential comic strips in magazines like *Wild Oats*, he left the popular medium of comics when he hit paydirt with *The Brownies*. For over a quarter of a century, Cox deftly combined the popular advertising motifs of animals and fairies into a wonderful, whimsical world of society at its best and worst.

The Inter Ocean Jr.

VOL. XXIII., SUNDAY MAY 27, 1894. NO. 64.

THE TING-LINGS LISTEN TO THE PHONOGRAPH.

Chicago Inter Ocean Jr., May 27, 1894 Cover of The Ting-Lings by Charles W. Saalburg, was inspired by Palmer Cox's The Brownies and later provided inspiration for Outcault's Yellow Kid.

The Brownies' first book was issued in 1887, titled *The Brownies: Their Book*; many more followed. Cox also added a run of his hugely popular characters in *Ladies Home Journal* from October 1891 through February 1895, as well as a special for December 1910. With the 1892-93 World's Fair, the merchandising exploded with a host of products, including pianos, paper dolls and other figurines, chairs, stoves, puzzles, cough drops, coffee, soap, boots, candy, and many more. *Brownies* material was being produced in Europe as well as the United States of America.

Cox tried out *The Brownies* as a newspaper strip in the *San Francisco Examiner* during 1898, where he had begun his newspaper career over 30 years before, and then in the *New York World* in 1900. It was then syndicated from 1903 through 1907. He seems to have retired from regularly drawing *The Brownies* with the January 1914 issue of *St. Nicholas* when he was 74. A wealthy man, he lived to the ripe old age of 84, spending his last decade in his home he affectionately called Brownie Castle, back in Granby, Quebec.

By the mid-1890s, while keeping careful track of steadily rising circulations of magazines with graphic humor such as *Harper's, Puck, St. Nicholas, Judge, Life* and *Truth*, New York based newspaper publishers began to recognize that illustrated humor would sell extra papers. This is what *The Yellow Kid* taught these publishers. Thus was born the Sunday "comic supplement." Most of the super star favorites were under contract with these magazines. However, there was an artist working for *Truth* who wasn't. Roy L McCardell, then a staffer at *Puck*, informed Morrill Goddard, Sunday Editor of *The New York World*, that he knew someone who could fit what was needed at the then-largest newspaper in America.

Richard F. Outcault (1863-1928) first introduced his street children strip in *Truth* #372, June 2, 1894, somewhat inspired by Michael Angelo Woolf's slum kids single panel cartoons in **Life** which had begun in the mid 1880s. The interested collector should seek out a copy of Woolf's *Sketches of Lowly Life In A Great City* (1899) listed in the *Guide* for comparison study. Edward Harrigan's play "O'Reilly and the Four Hundred," which had a song beginning with the words "Down in Hogan's Alley..." also likely provided direct inspiration.

It's also probable that Outcault's *Hogan's Alley* cast, including the *Yellow Kid*, was inspired by Charles W. Saalburg's *The Ting Lings*, which began in the *Chicago Inter Ocean Jr* supplement post-dated May 1, 1894 in the April 29, 1894 edition of Chicago Inter Ocean. That first episode is titled: "The Brownies Welcome The Ting-Lings."

There is also a definite similarity in Mickey Dugan's appearance and clothing style to Saalburg's creation which we will now examine in more detail thanks to welcome, on-going research by long time comics historian Allan Holtz supplemented by living comics history legend Bill Blackbeard .

Charles Saalzburg was an artist who was also the genius behind color printing in newspapers. He seems to have pioneered the concept from whom all others learned their craft.

On June 23, 1892 the *Chicago Inter Ocean* introduced a section with mostly editorial cartoons titled the *Illustrated Supplement*, commemorating the Democratic National Convention held in that city. Early regulars included Thomas Nast and Art Young. Starting June 26, the *Inter Ocean* began steadily issuing this weekly four page supplement, typically featuring full page editorial cartoons on its front and back covers. In May 1893 the supplement began coming out twice a week, and even greater frequency to daily during the *World Columbian Exposition* held in Chicago later that same year as it was used as a wrapper to attract sales from fair goers. Art Young did some of the color cover art and comic strips for the early Fair supplements, printing them right at the Fair to goggle-eyed fair tourists. Thomas Nast did some art as well during a visit he made to the Fair.

By September 10, 1893 the *Inter Ocean* introduced color, a multi-panel editorial comic strip by Charles Saalburg. The supplement used yellow ink, a further nail in the coffin of various Yellow Kid myths which had clouded serious comics scholarship in earlier decades before being proven wrong.

On October 1, Tom E. Powers introduced their first sequential non-political comic strip in color, a humorous pantomime.

As the Exposition ended in November, the contents were soon aimed more at children, enhanced with color added to the center as well by December 24, 1893, then changing its title to *Inter Ocean Jr* in January 1894. This was accomplished easily by folding the single four page sheet into eight pages.

In the January 1894 Saalburg began using Brownies-inspired characters in his color comic strips. The present theory is the *Ting-Ling* characters took over solo five months later in response to a presumed cease and desist letter which inevitably must have been issued from Palmer Cox to the *Inter Ocean*.

However, on July 8 1894, the *Inter Ocean Jr* stopped color and full page comics-type work in this supplement, devolving back to simple small spot art works. By mid-1894, color comics printing genius Saalburg had been lured to Pulitzer's New York World, becoming Art Director in charge of coloring for the new color printing press at the *New York World.* The color supplement was soon to be unleashed in the largest city in America.

By the November 18, 1894 issue of the *World*, Outcault was working for Goddard and Saalburg. Outcault produced a successful Sunday newspaper sequential comic strip in color with "The Origin of a New Species" on the back page in the World's first colored Sunday supplement. Long time pro Walt McDougall, a famous cartoonist reputed to have turned the 1884 Presidential race with a single cartoon that ran in the *World*, handled the cartoon art on the front page. Earlier, *The World* began running full page color single panels on May 21, 1893. McDougall did various other page panels during 1893, but it was Jan. 28, 1894 when the first sequence of comic pictures in a New York World newspaper appeared in panels in the same format as our comic strips today. It was a full page cut up into nine panels. This historic sequence was drawn entirely in pantomime, with no words, by Mark Fenderson.

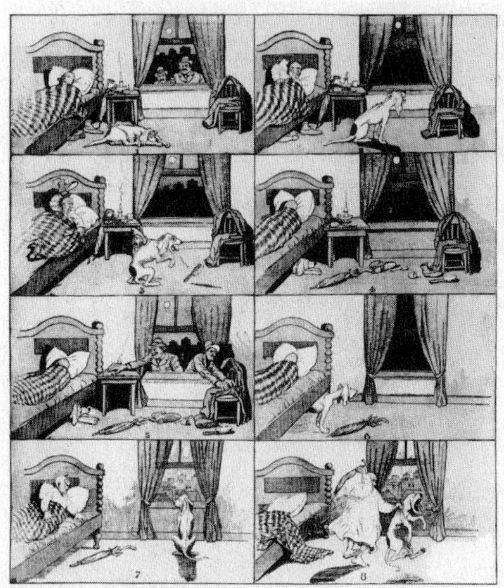

Walt McDougall & Mark Fenderson, the 2nd sequential comic strip in New York World, February 4, 1894, predates Yellow Kid in The World by over a year. Mark Fenderson drew the first NY World newspaper comic strip.

The second page to appear in panels was an eight panel strip from February 4, 1894, also lacking words except for the title. This page was a collaboration between Walt McDougall and Mark Fenderson titled "The Unfortunate Fate of a Well-Intentioned Dog." From then on, many full page color strips by McDougall and Fenderson appeared; they were the first cartoonists to draw for the Sunday newspaper comic section. It was Outcault, however, who soon became the most famous cartoonist featured. After first appearing in black and white in Pulitzer's *The New York World* on February 17, 1895 and again on March 10, 1895, *The Yellow Kid* was introduced to the public in color on May 5, 1895.

Some have erroneously reported in scholarly journals that perhaps it was Frank Ladendorf's "Uncle Reuben," first introduced May 26, 1895, which became the first regularly recurring comics character in newspapers. This is wrong, as even Outcault's "Yellow Kid" began in Pulitzer's paper a good three months before *Uncle Reuben*. Until firm evidence to the contrary comes to light, that honor will forever be enshrined with Jimmy Swinnerton's *Little Bears* cartoon characters, found all over inside Hearst's *San Francisco Examiner* beginning October 14, 1893 with the first one called "Baby Monarch. Though never actually a comic strip, they nonetheless were the earliest presently-known recurring comics-type characters in American newspapers. In June 1895, a semi-regular "Little Bears" feature began. On January 26, 1896, children were introduced, the title eventually changed to "Little Bears and Tykes," forever confusing some scholars decades later. There never was a strip titled *Little Bears and Tigers*, as the *Tigers* were strictly for New York consumption when Hearst ordered Swinnerton to move to the Big Apple to compete better in the brewing comic strip wars.

The Yellow Kid's importance is widely recognized today as the first newspaper comic strip to demonstrate without a doubt that the general public was ready for full color comics. *The Yellow Kid* was the first in the USA to show that comics could increase newspaper sales, and that comic characters could be merchandised. *The Yellow Kid* was the headlining spark of what was soon dubbed by Hearst as "eight pages of polychromatic effulgence that makes the rainbow look like a lead pipe."

Ongoing research suggests that Palmer Cox's fabulous success with *The Brownies* was a direct inspiration for Richard Outcault's future merchandising work. The ultimate proof lies in the fourth Yellow Kid cartoon, which appeared in the February 9, 1895 issue of *Truth*. It was reprinted in the *New York World* eight days later on February 17, 1895, becoming the first Yellow Kid cartoon in the newspapers. The caption read "FOURTH WARD BROWNIES. MICKEY, THE ARTIST (adding a finishing touch) Dere, Chimmy! If Palmer Cox wuz t' see yer, he'd git yer copyrighted in a minute." The Yellow Kid was widely licensed in the greater New York area for all kinds of products, including gum and cigarette cards, toys, pinbacks, cookies, postcards, tobacco products, and appliances. There was also a short-lived humor magazine from Street & Smith named *The Yellow Kid*, featuring exquisite Outcault covers, plus a 196-page comic book from Dillingham & Co. known as *The Yellow Kid in McFadden's Flats,* dated to early 1897. Check out the covers in "The Platinum Age" three-page comic strip elsewhere in this Guide. In addition, there were several Yellow Kid plays produced, spawning other collectibles like show posters, programs and illustrated sheet music. (For those interested in more information regarding the Yellow Kid, it is available on the Internet at www.neponset.com/yellowkid.)

"Fourth Ward Brownies," artwork by Richard F. Outcault, Feb. 17, 1895, the 4th Yellow Kid app. and 1st in Pulitzer's New York World. Note the Kid, second from left. This panel first saw print in Truth, Feb 9, 1895.

Mickey Dugan burned brightly for a few years as Outcault secured a copyright on the character with the United States Government by September 1896. By the time he completed the necessary paperwork, however, hundreds of business people nationwide had pirated the image of The Yellow Kid and plastered it all over every product imaginable; mothers were even dressing their newborns to look like Dugan. Outcault, however, kept regularly utilizing images of *The Yellow Kid* in his comics style advertising work confirmed as late as 1915. Outcault soon found himself in a maelstrom not of his choosing, which probably pushed him to eventually drop the character. Outcault's creation went back and forth between newspaper giants Pulitzer and Hearst until Bennett's New York Herald mercifully snatched the cartoonist away in 1900 to do what amounted to a few relatively short-run strips. Later, he did one particular strip for a year–a satire of rural Black America titled *Pore Li'l Mose His Letters to his Mammy*, and then his newer creation, *Buster Brown*, debuted May 4, 1902. *Mose* had a very rare comic book collection published in 1902 by Cupples & Leon, now highly sought after by today's savvy collectors. Outcault continued drawing him in the background of occasional *Buster Brown* strips for many years to come.

William Randolph Hearst loved the comic strip medium ever since he was a little boy growing up on *Max & Moritz* by Wilhelm Busch in American collected book editions translated from the original German (these collections were first published in book form in 1871, serving as the influence for *The Katzenjammer Kids*). One of the ways Hearst responded to losing Outcault in 1900 was by purchasing the highly successful 23-year-old humor magazine *Puck* from the heirs of founder Joseph Keppler. With *Puck* and its exclusive cartoonist contracts, he commanded, among others, the very popular F. M. Howarth and Frederick Burr Opper's undivided attention. Opper first burst upon the comics scene in America back in 1880. Within a year Hearst had expanded this *National Lampoon* of its day into the colored Sunday comics section, *Puck-The Comic Weekly*. At first featuring Rudolph Dirk's *The Katzenjammer Kids* (1897), *Happy Hooligan* and other fine strips by the wildly popular Opper and a few others including Rudolph's brother Gus Dirks, the Hearst comic section steadily added more strips. For decades to come, there wasn't anything else that could compete with *Puck*. Hearst hired the best of the best and transformed *Puck* into the most popular comics section anywhere.

Left: The Yellow Kid #1, March 20, 1897, Street & Smith as Howard Ainslee, NY.
Right: A rare full color "The Yellow Kid in McFadden's Flats" advertising sign promoting the first comic book featuring the Yellow Kid. The sign is from 1896 and measures 12x18".

The Adventures of Foxy Grandpa, late 1900, cover for the rare earliest known first edition of Carl "Bunny" Schultze's famous creation. He was one of the newspaper comics' first superstars.

Pore Li'l Mose by Richard Outcault, 1901. Bridges in between Yellow Kid and Buster Brown. Becoming scarce because many copies have been cut up.

Outcault, meanwhile, followed in Palmer Cox's footprints a decade later by using the nexus of a World's Fair as a jumping off venue. *Buster Brown* was an instant sensation when he debuted as the new merchandising mascot of the Brown Shoe Company at the 1904 St. Louis World's Fair in a special Buster Brown Shoes pavilion. The character has the honor of being the first nationally licensed comic strip character in America with this time Outcault in almost full control. Many hundreds of different *Buster Brown* premiums have been issued. Comic books by Frederick A. Stokes Company featuring *Buster Brown & His Dog Tige* began as early as 1903 with *Buster Brown and His Resolutions*, simultaneously published in several different languages throughout the world.

After a few years, Buster and Outcault returned to Hearst in late 1905, joining what soon became the flagship of the comics world. Buster's popularity quickly spread all over the United States and then the world as he single-handedly spawned the first great comic strip licensing dynasty. For years, there were little people traveling from town to town performing as *Buster Brown* and selling shoes while accompanied by small dogs named Tige. Many other highly competitive licensed strips would soon follow. We suggest getting *Hake's Price Guide to Character Toys* for info on several hundred *Buster Brown* competitors, as well as several pages of the more fascinating *Buster Brown* material.

Soon there were many comic strip syndicates not only offering hundreds of various comic strips but also offering to license the characters for any company interested in paying the fee. The history of the comic strip with wide popularity since *The Yellow Kid* has been intertwined with giveaway premiums and character-based, store-bought merchandise of all kinds. Since its infancy as a profitable art form unto itself with *The Yellow Kid*, the comic strip world has profited from selling all sorts of "stuff" to the public featuring their favorite character or strip as its motif. American business gladly responded to the desire for comic character memorabilia with thousands of fun items to enjoy and collect. Most of the early comics were not aimed specifically at kids, though children understandably enjoyed them as well.

Comic books have generally been associated with almost all of the licensed merchandise in this century. In the Platinum Age section beginning right after this essay, you will find a great many comic books in varied formats and sizes published before the advent of the first successful monthly newsstand comic magazine, *Famous Funnies*. What drove each of these evolutionary format changes was the need by their producers to make money so more books could be issued.

A very significant format was F. M. Howarth's *Funny Folks*, published in 1899 by E. P. Dutton and drawn from color as well as black and white pages of *Puck*. This rather large hardcover volume measured 16 1/2" wide by 12" tall. It contains numerous sequential comic strip pages as well as single gag illustrations. Howarth's art was a joy to behold and deserves wider recognition.

By Oct. 1900, Hearst had already caused Opper's *Folks In Funnyville* to be collected by publisher R. H. Russell, NY in a 12x9 hard cover format from his *New York Journal American Humorist* section. At the end of 1900, Carl Shultze had a first edition of *Vaudevilles and Other Things* published by Isaac H. Blanchard Co., NY. It measures 10 1/2" wide by 13" tall with 22 pages including covers. Each interior page is a 2 to 7 panel comic strip with lots of color.

There were also recently unearthed format variation second and third printings of *Vaudevilles* with the inscription "From the Originator of the 'Foxy Grandpa' Series" at the bottom of its front cover of the third printing. This note is lacking on the earlier first two editions, and it also switches format size to 11" tall by 13" wide. Discovered last year was a heretofore undocumented *The Adventures of Foxy Grandpa* - also issued in 1900 - new to the Platinum listings. The second number dated 1901 drops the words "The Adventures of..." from the title.

E. W. Kemble's *The Blackberries* had a color collection by 1901, also published by R. H. Russell, NY, as well as a few other comic-related volumes by Kemble still to be unearthed and properly identified. An earlier one was titled *Coontown's 400* (1899) newly listed this year. While the title is definitely not "PC" by today's standards, Kemble's drawings are excellent slices of African-American life in the USA with some humor

The Chicago Tribune introduced a straight super hero with obvious super strength called "Hugo Hercules" by the unknown artist J. Koerner. This Sunday strip ran September 7, 1902 through January 11, 1903 and ran only in this one paper. It is entirely possible a very young Chicago-resident named Philip Wylie read "Hugo" since that was the same name he gave his super-heroic main character in his much-later book The Gladiator (1930). Other appearances have Hugo running with almost super speed.

injected. Kemble did a good job documenting aspects of life.

Confirmed is the exact format of Hearst's 1902 *The Katzenjammer Kids and Happy Hooligan And His Brother Gloomy Gus*. They both measure 15 5/16" wide by 10" tall and contain 88 pages including covers. Confirmed also is the fact that there are two separate editions with different covers for the pictured 1902 first edition and a 1903 Frederick Stokes edition of *Katzenjammer Kids* and *Happy Hooligan* with differing contents. They both are two different books entirely, and what confuses many collectors is that they have identical indicia title pages, but so does an entirely different *KK* from 1905.

Settling on a popular size of 17" wide by 11" tall, comic books were soon available that featured Charles "Bunny" Schultze's *Foxy Grandpa*, Rudolph Dirk's *The Katzenjammer Kids*, Winsor McCay's *Little Sammy Sneeze, Rarebit Fiend* and *Little Nemo*, and Fred Opper's *Happy Hooligan* and *Maud*, in addition to dozens of *Buster Brown* comic books. For well over a decade, these large-size, full-color volumes were the norm, retailing for 60¢. These collections offered full-size Sunday comics with the back side blank per page.

Though not the first daily newspaper strip, the very rare *Brainy Bowers and Drowsy Dugan* by R. W. Taylor is now crowned the first collection of strip reprints from a daily newspaper published in America. There are now four different collections of Brainy Bower known to exist.

The Outbursts of Everett True by A. D. Condo and J. W. Raper was first published by Saalfield in 1907 in an 88-page hardcover collection. It qualifies as the second daily comic strip collection as it predates the first *Mutt & Jeff* collection from Ball by three years. Condo & Raper's creation began its regular run several times a week in 1905 daily newspapers and lasted until 1927, when Condo became too sick to continue. This same *Everett True* collection was later truncated a bit by Saalfield in 1921 to 56 strips in just 32 pages measuring the standard 10"x10" Cupples & Leon size.

By 1908 Stokes had a large backlist of full color comic books for sale at 60¢ each. Some of these titles date back to 1903 and were reprinted over and over as demand warranted. Note the number of titles in the advertisement pulled from the back of *The Three Fun Makers* shown below.

With the ever-increasing popularity of Bud Fisher's new daily strip sensation, *Mutt & Jeff,* a new format was created for reprinting daily strips in black and white, a hardcover book about 15" wide by 5" tall, published by Ball starting in 1910 for five volumes. In 1912, Ball also branched out with at least the

Left, The Outbursts of Everett True. 2nd daily strip collection, published 1907 Right: The earliest known comic book display ad, from in the back of1908 Stokes comic books, 27 titles then in print. Cover prices are 60¢.

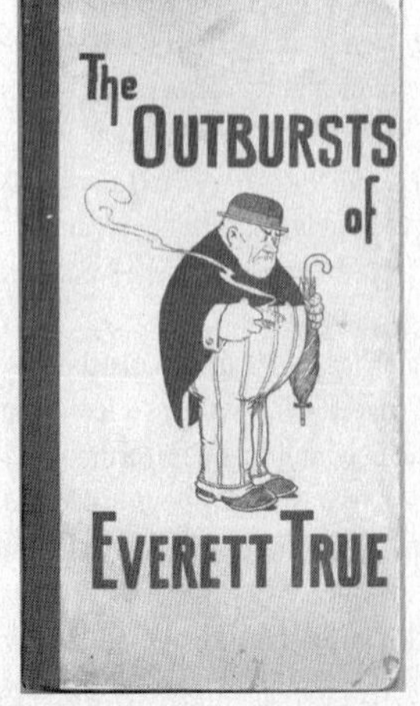

now-obscure *Doings of the Van Loons* by Fred I. Leipziger, a rare comic book in the same format as the *Mutt & Jeffs.*

Cartoons Magazine also began in 1912 and ran through 1921 before undergoing a radical format change. It is notable as a wonderful source for information on early comics and their creators. See also the Platinum index.

The next significant evolutionary change occurred in 1919, when Cupples & Leon began issuing their black and white daily strip reprint books in a new aforementioned format, about 10" wide by 10" tall, with four panels reprinted per page in a two by two matrix. These books were 52 pages for 25¢. The first ones featured *Bringing Up Father* and *Mutt & Jeff;* there were about 100 others.

By 1921, the last of the oblong (11"x15") color comic books were issued, with Cupples & Leon's *Jimmie Dugan* and *The Reg'lar Fellers* by Gene Byrne, and EmBee's *The Trouble Of Bringing Up Father* by self publisher George McManus. Of special historical interest, Embee issued the first 10¢ monthly comic book, *Comic Monthly,* with the first issue dated January 1922. A dozen 8-1/2"x9" issues were published, each featuring solo adventures of popular King Features strips. The monthly 10¢ comic book concept had finally arrived, though it would be more than a decade before it became truly successful.

Skippy by Percy Crosby debuted in the long-running humor magazine *Life* in the March 22, 1923 issue. By 1924 the first hard cover collection, *Life Presents Skippy*, was published. The newspaper comic strip debuted June 23, 1925 with the McClure syndicate. Hearst soon picked up a Sunday page a year later in mid-1926, then added a daily strip in 1929. By the 1930s it was red hot - think *Calvin & Hobbes or Peanuts* in popularity. In its day, it was one of the most popular comic strips ever created. Read the Modern era essay for more on *Skippy's* immense popularity.

In 1926, Cupples & Leon added a new 7" wide by 9" tall format with *Little Orphan Annie, Smitty,* and others. These were issued in both softcover and hardcover editions with dust jackets, and became extremely popular at 60¢ per copy.

Dell began publishing all original material in *The Funnies* in late 1929 in a larger tabloid format. At least three dozen issues were published before Delacorte threw in the towel. Even the extremely popular *Big Little Book*, introduced in 1932, can be viewed as a smaller version of the existing formats. The competition amongst publishers now included Dell, McKay, Sonnet, Saalfield and Whitman. The 1930s saw a definite shift in merchandising comic strip material from adults to children. This was the decade when Kellogg's placed *Buck Rogers* on the map, when Ovaltine issued tons of *Little Orphan Annie* material. Merchandising from such pioneers as Sam Gold and Kay Kamen spearheaded this next transformation of the comics biz beginning in the early 1930s.

Upwards of a thousand of these *Funnies On Parade* precursors, in all formats, were published through 1935 and were very popular. Towards the end of this era of once-popular comic book formats, beautiful collections of *Popeye, Mickey Mouse, Dick Tracy*, and many others were published which today command ever higher prices on the open market as they are rediscovered by the advanced collector who appreciates and enjoys truly great classic comics.

END NOTE: Each year we strive to add to the many 1930s variant formats. This Platinum Age section has grown as a result of advanced collectors who continue to report in with new finds. We encourage interested collectors and scholars to help with this section of the book, as each new data entry is very important for recovering our history. For corrections and additions to next year's next edition of *The Overstreet Guide* of some treasures you may have uncovered, please feel free to contact Gemstone Publishing at feedback@gemstonepub.com.

For further information on this era of American comic books, check out the previous evolving comics history essays in Guides #27,29-#40. Happy Hunting!

Comic Monthly #11 1922 (top), the first 10¢ monthly newsstand comic book title.

Banana Oil, a 1924 example of Cupples & Leon's then-revolutionary format from M.S. Publishers

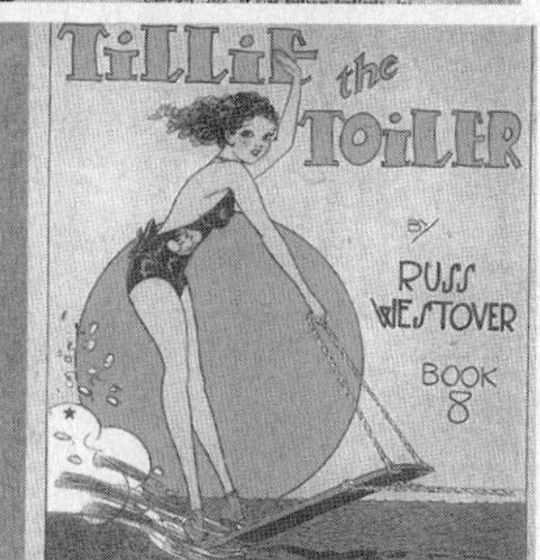

Tillie the Toiler #8 1933 from Cupples & Leon, another scarce number at the end of this once popular format.

David McKay published the last of the 10x10 comic books in 1935 as Famous Funnies grew in popularity.

The Platinum Age 1883–1938

by J.C. Vaughn & Gene Gonzales

OKAY, I'VE GOT A QUESTION FOR YOU.
WHY WOULD ANYONE IGNORE FACTS IN FAVOR OF OPINION?

WHY IN THE FACE OF OVERWHELMING EMPIRICAL EVIDENCE WOULD SOMEONE SAY THAT THE COMIC BOOKS OF *THE VICTORIAN AGE* AND *THE PLATINUM AGE* AREN'T COMIC BOOKS?
GOSH, I FEEL LIKE THE RIDDLER.

THE FIRST COLLECTION OF PREVIOUSLY PUBLISHED STRIPS FEATURING *THE BROWNIES* WAS PRINTED IN 1887.

THE BROWNIES BECAME THE ROAD MAP FOR SUCCESSFUL LICENSED CHARACTERS . . .

THE PATH THAT WAS LATER FOLLOWED BY THE *YELLOW KID*, *MICKEY MOUSE*, AND *SUPERMAN*.

THE YELLOW KID IN MCFADDEN'S FLATS WAS COLLECTED R.F. OUTCAULT'S SUCCESSFUL CHARACTER IN BOOK FORM.
LIKE MANY OTHERS IN THAT TIME, IT WAS A HUGE SUCCESS.
BUT NO ONE WOULD CALL THIS COLLECTION A COMIC BOOK, WOULD THEY?
50 Cents
THE YELLOW KID IN McFADDEN'S FLATS
BY E.W. TOWNSEND AUTHOR OF "CHIMMIE FADDEN"
AND R.F. OUTCAULT CREATOR OF THE "YELLOW KID"
DIS BOOK IS DE STORY OF ME SWEET YOUNG LIFE
G.W. DILLINGHAM Co. PUBLISHERS NEW YORK.
THIRTIETH THOUSAND.

THE MOST *POPULAR COMIC BOOKS* EVER PUBLISHED.
ARTEMUS WARD. HIS COMPLETE COMIC WRITINGS, WITH BIOGRAPHY AND ONE HUNDRED ILLUSTRATIONS. THE BIOGRAPHICAL SKETCH BY "ELI PERKINS." CLOTH BOUND, PRICE $1.50.
JOSH BILLINGS. HIS WORKS COMPLETE (FOUR VOLUMES IN ONE), WITH ONE HUNDRED ILLUSTRATIONS, BY THOMAS NAST, AND OTHERS. CLOTH BOUND, PRICE $2.00.
VERDANT GREEN. A RACY ENGLISH COLLEGE STORY, BY CUTHBERT BEDE. PROFUSELY ILLUSTRATED, AND CLOTH BOUND. PRICE $1.50.
SOLD EVERYWHERE, AND SENT BY MAIL, POSTAGE FREE, ON RECEIPT OF PRICE, BY G.W. DILLINGHAM CO., PUBLISHERS, 33 WEST 23D STREET, NEW YORK.
THE MOST
POPULAR COMIC BOOKS
EVER PUBLISHED.
ARTEMUS WARD.
JOSH BILLINGS.
VERDANT GREEN.
G. W. Dillingham Co., Publishers, 33 West 23d Street, New York.

SO, LET'S GET THIS STRAIGHT . . .
IN 1897 THESE GUYS KNEW IT WAS A COMIC BOOK, BUT THERE ARE STILL PEOPLE OUT THERE IN 2011 WHO DON'T?

WHO ELSE MIGHT HAVE BEEN DOING COMIC BOOKS?
I CREATED *LITTLE NEMO* IN 1905 AND SOON IT WAS BEING COLLECTED INTO COMIC BOOK REPRINTS.
LADIES AND GENTLEMEN, WINSOR McCAY.
LATER, *COMIC MONTHLY*, WHICH DEBUTED IN 1922, WAS THE FIRST MONTHLY NEWSSTAND COMIC BOOK.
DREAM OF THE RAREBIT FIEND
BANG!
Comic Monthly
PRICE 10¢
POLLY & HER PALS
BY CLIFF STERRETT.

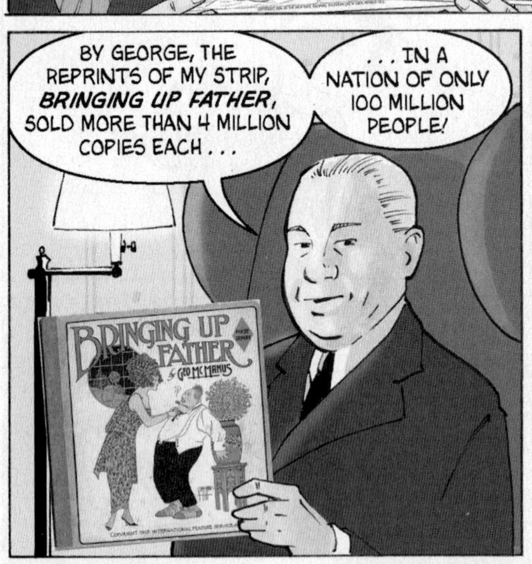
BY GEORGE, THE REPRINTS OF MY STRIP, *BRINGING UP FATHER*, SOLD MORE THAN 4 MILLION COPIES EACH . . .
. . . IN A NATION OF ONLY 100 MILLION PEOPLE!
BRINGING UP FATHER
by GEO McMANUS

FUNNIES ON PARADE, WHICH IS LITTLE MORE THAN AN INTERESTING FOOTNOTE IN COMICS HISTORY, WAS PUBLISHED IN 1933 . . .
IT WAS, OF COURSE, A COLLECTION OF REPRINTS . . .

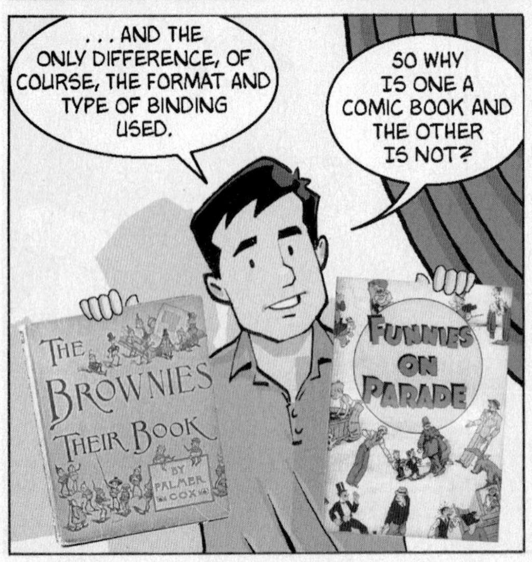
. . . AND THE ONLY DIFFERENCE, OF COURSE, THE FORMAT AND TYPE OF BINDING USED.
SO WHY IS ONE A COMIC BOOK AND THE OTHER IS NOT?
THE BROWNIES THEIR BOOK
BY PALMER COX
FUNNIES ON PARADE

IF YOU CAN FIGURE IT OUT, LET US KNOW.
IN THE MEANTIME, WE HOPE YOU ENJOY THIS YEAR'S LISTING OF PLATINUM AGE COMIC BOOKS.

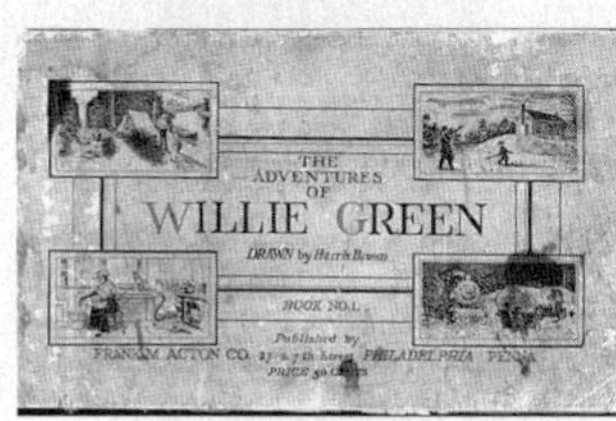

The Adventures of Willie Green
© Frank M. Acton

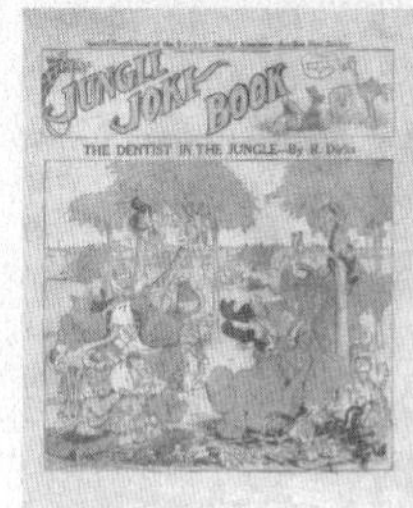

American-Journal-Examiner Joke Book
Special Supplement #12
1912 © New York American-Examiner

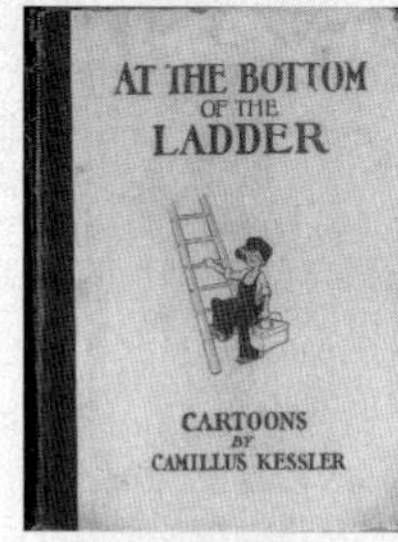

AT THE BOTTOM OF THE LADDER
CARTOONS BY CAMILLUS KESSLER

At The Bottom Of The Ladder
1926 © J.P. Lippincott Company

GD2.0 FN6.0 VF8.0

COLLECTOR'S NOTE: The books listed in this section were published many decades before organized comics fandom began archiving and helping to preserve these fragile popular culture artifacts. Consequently, copies of most all of these comics do not often surface in Fine+ or better shape. eBay has proven after more than a decade that many items once considered rare actually are not, though they almost always are in higher grades. For items marked scarce, we are trying to ascertain how many copies might still be in existence. Your input is always welcome.

Most Platinum Age comic books are in the Fair to VG range. If you want to collect these only in high grade, your collection will be extremely small. The prices given for Good, Fine and Very Fine categories are for strictly graded editions. If you need help grading your item, we refer you to the grading section in the front of this price guide or contact the authors of the Platinum essay. Most measurements are in inches. A few measurements are in centimeters. The first dimension given is Height and the second is Width.

For ease of ascertaining the contents of each item of this listing, there is a code letter or two following most titles we have been adding in over the years to aid you. A helpful list of categories pertaining to these codes can be found at the beginning of the Victorian Age pricing sections.This section created, revised, and expanded by Robert Beerbohm and Richard Olson with able assistance from Ray Agricola, Jon Berk, Bill Blackbeard, Roy Bonario, Ray Bottorff Jr., Chris Brown, Alfredo Castelli, Darrell Coons, Sol Davidson, Leonardo De Sá, Scott Deschaine, Mitchell Duval, Joe Evans, Tom Gordon III, Bruce Hamilton, Andy Konkykru, Don Kurtz, Gabriel Laderman, Bruce Mason, Donald Puff, Robert Quesinberry, Steve Rowe, Randy Scott, John Snyder, Art Spiegelman, Steve Thompson, Joan Crosby Tibbets, Richard Samuel West, Doug Wheeler, Richard Wright and Craig Yoe.

ADVENTURES OF EVA, PORA AND TED (M)
Evaporated Milk Association: 1932 (5x15", 16 pgs, B&W)

nn - By Steve 10.00 30.00 70.00
NOTE: *Appears to have had green, blue or white paper cover versions.*

ADVENTURES OF HAWKSHAW (N) (See Hawkshaw The Detective)
The Saalfield Publishing Co.: 1917 (9-3/4x13-1/2", 48 pgs., color & two-tone)

nn - By Gus Mager (only 24 pgs. of strips, reverse of each pg. is blank) 50.00 175.00 300.00
nn - 1927 Reprints 1917 issue 30.00 150.00 260.00
NOTE: *Started Feb 23, 1913-Sept 4, 1922, then begins again Dec 13, 1931-Feb 11, 1952.*

ADVENTURES OF SLIM AND SPUD, THE (M)
Prairie Farmer Publ. Co.: 1924 (3-3/4x 9-3/4", 104 pgs., B&W strip reprints)

nn 21.00 84.00 150.00
NOTE: *Illustrated mailing envelope exists postmarked out of Chicago, add 50%.*

ADVENTURES OF WILLIE WINTERS, THE (O,P)
Kelloggs Toasted Corn Flake Co.: 1912 (6-7/8x9-1/2", 20 pgs, full color)

nn - By Byron Williams & Dearborn Melvill 54.00 189.00 350.00

ADVENTURES OF WILLIE GREEN, THE (N) (see The Willie Green Comics)
Frank M. Acton Co.: 1915 (50¢, 52 pgs, 8-1/2X16", B&W, soft-c)

Book 1 - By Harris Brown; strip-r 54.00 189.00 350.00

A. E. F. IN CARTOONS BY WALLY, THE (N)
Don Sowers & Co.: 1933 (12x10-1/8", 88 pgs, hardcover B&W)

nn - By Wally Wallgren (WW One Stars & Stripes-r) 25.00 90.00 150.00

AFTER THE TOWN GOES DRY (I)
The Howell Publishing Co, Chicago: 1919 (48 pgs, 6-1/2x4", hardbound two color-c)

nn - By Henry C. Taylor; illus by Frank King 25.00 75.00 150.00

AIN'T IT A GRAND & GLORIOUS FEELING? (N) (Also see Mr. & Mrs.)
Whitman Publishing Co.: 1922 (9x9-3/4", 52 pgs., stiff cardboard-c)

nn - 1921 daily strip-r; B&W, color-c; Briggs-a 36.00 143.00 250.00
nn -(9x9-1/2", 28pgs., stiff cardboard-c)-Sunday strip-r in color (inside front-c says "More of the Married Life of Mr. & Mrs".) 36.00 143.00 250.00
NOTE: *Strip started in 1917; This is the 2nd Whitman comic book, after Brigg's MR. & MRS.*

ALL THE FUNNY FOLKS (I)
World Press Today, Inc.: 1926 (11-1/2x8-1/2", 112 pgs., color, hard-c)

nn-Barney Google, Spark Plug, Jiggs & Maggie, Tillie The Toiler, Happy Hooligan, Hans & Fritz, Toots & Casper, etc. 100.00 400.00 700.00
With Dust Jacket By Louis Biedermann 200.00 800.00 1600.00
NOTE: *Booklength race horse story masterfully enveloping all major King Features characters.*

ALPHONSE AND GASTON AND THEIR FRIEND LEON (N)
Hearst's New York American & Journal: 1902,1903 (10x15-1/4", Sunday strip reprints in color)

nn - (1902) - By Frederick Opper (scarce) 500.00 1800.00 –
nn - (1903) - By Frederick Opper (scarce) (72 pages) 500.00 1800.00 –
NOTE: *Strip ran Sept 22, 1901to at least July 17, 1904.*

ALWAYS BELITTLIN' (see Skippy; That Rookie From the 13th Squad; Between Shots)
Henry Holt & Co.: 1927 (6x8", hard-c with DJ,

nn -By Percy Crosby (text with cartoons) 43.00 172.00 300.00

ALWAYS BELITTLIN' (I) (see Skippy; That Rookie From the 13th Squad, Between Shots)
Percy Crosby, Publisher: 1933 (14 1/4 x 11", 72 pgs, hard-c, B&W)

GD2.0 FN6.0 VF8.0

nn - By Percy Crosby 43.00 172.00 300.00
NOTE: *Self-published; primarily political cartoons with text pages denouncing prohibition's gang warfare effects and cuts in the national defense budget as Crosby saw war looming in Europe and with Japan.*

AMERICAN-JOURNAL-EXAMINER JOKE BOOK SPECIAL SUPPLEMENT (O)
New York American: 1911-12 (12 x 9 3/4", 16 pgs) (known issues) (Very Rare)

1 Tom Powers Joke Book(12/10/11) 80.00 280.00 –
2 Mutt & Jeff Joke Book (Bud Fisher 12/17/11) 100.00 350.00 –
3 TAD's Joke Book (Thomas Dorgan 12/24/11) 80.00 300.00 –
4 F. Opper's Joke Book (Frederick Burr Opper 12/31/11) (contains Happy Hooligan) 100.00 350.00 –
5 not known to exist
6 Swinnerton's Joke Book (Jimmy Swinnerton 01/14/12) (contains Mr. Jack) 100.00 350.00 –
7 The Monkey's Joke Book (Gus Mager 01/21/12) (contains Sherlocko the Monk) 100.00 350.00 –
8 Joys And Glooms Joke Book (T. E. Powers 01/28/12) 80.00 280.00 –
9 The Dingbat Family's Joke Book (George Herriman 02/04/12) (contains early Krazy Kat & Ignatz) 200.00 700.00 –
10 Valentine Joke Book, A (Opper, Howarth, Mager, T. E. Powers 02/11/12) 80.00 280.00 –
11 Little Hatchet Joke Book (T. E. Powers 02/18/12) 80.00 280.00 –
12 Jungle Joke Book (Dirks, McCay 02/25/12) 100.00 400.00 –
13 The Hayseeds Joke Book (03/03/12) 80.00 280.00 –
14 Married Life Joke Book (T.E. Powers 03/10/12) 80.00 280.00 –
NOTE: *These were insert newspaper supplements similar to Eisner's later Spirit sections. A Valentine Joke Book recently surfaced from Hearst's Boston Sunday American proving that other cities besides New York City had these special supplements. Each issue also contains work by other cartoonists besides the cover featured creator and those already listed above such as Sidney Smith, Winsor McCay, Hy Mayer, Grace Weiderseim (later Drayton), others.*

AMERICA'S BLACK & WHITE BOOK 100 Pictured Reasons Why We Are At War (N,S)
Cupples & Leon: 1917 (10 3/4 x 8", 216 pgs)

nn - W. A. Rogers (New York Herald-r) 32.00 114.00 195.00

AMONG THE FOLKS IN HISTORY
Rand McNally Print Guild: 1935 (192 pgs, 8-1/2x9-1/2", hard-c, B&W)

nn - By Gaar Williams 21.00 84.00 150.00

AMONG THE FOLKS IN HISTORY
The Book and Print Guild: 1935 (200 pgs, 8-1/2x9-1/2:,

nn - By Gaar Williams 21.00 84.00 150.00
NOTE: *Both the above are evidently different editions and contain largely full-page, single panel cartoons similar to Briggs' work of that sort. 8 or 10 pages are broken into panels, usually with a this is how it was in the old days, this is how it is today theme.*

ANGELIC ANGELINA (N)
Cupples & Leon Company: 1909 (11-1/2x17", 56 pgs., 2 colors)

nn - By Munson Paddock 67.00 233.00 400.00
NOTE: *Strip ran March 22, 1908-Feb 7, 1909.*

ANDY GUMP, HIS LIFE STORY (I)
The Reilly & Lee Co, Chicago: 1924 (192 pgs, hardbound)

nn - By Sidney Smith (over 100 illustrations) 20.00 80.00 150.00

ANIMAL CIRCUS, THE (from Puggery Wee)
Rand McNally + Company: 1908 (48 pgs, 11x8-1/2", color-c, 3-color insides)

nn - By unknown 20.00 80.00 150.00
NOTE: *Illustrated verse, many pages with multiple illustrations.*

ANIMAL SERIALS
T. Y. Crowell: 1906 (9x6-7/8", 214 pgs, hard-c, B&W)

nn - By E Warde Blaisdell 20.00 80.00 150.00
NOTE: *Multi-page comic strip stories. Reprints of Sunday strip "Bunny Bright He's All-Right".*

A NOBODY'S SCRAP BOOK
Frederik A. Stokes Co., New York: 1900 (11" x 8-5/8", hard-c, color)

nn- (Scarce) 67.00 233.00 400.00
NOTE: *Designed in England, printed in Holland, on English paper -- which likely explains the mispelling of Frederick Stokes' name. Highly fragile paper. Strips and cartoons, all by the same unidentified artist, "A Nobody", almost certainly reprinted from somewhere, as they are very professional.*

AT THE BOTTOM OF THE LADDER (M)
J.P. Lippincott Company: 1926 (11x8-1/4", 296 pgs, hardcover, B&W)

nn - By Camillus Kessler 45.00 157.50 300.00
NOTE: *Hilarious single panel cartoons showing first jobs of then important "captains of industry."*

AUTO FUN, PICTURES AND COMMENTS FROM "LIFE"
Thomas Y. Crowell & Co.: 1905 (152 pgs, 9x7", hard-c, B&W)

nn -By various 45.00 157.00 300.00
NOTE: *The cover just has "Auto Fun" but the title page also has the subheading listed here. This is similar to other reprint books of Life cartoons printed in the guide. Largely single panel cartoons but also several sequential. One or more cartoons by Kemble, Levering, Dirks, Flagg, Sullivant. Sequential cartoons by Kemble, Levering, Sullivant, and the highpoint, a 2 pg 6 panel piece by Winsor McCay.*

BANANA OIL (N) (see also HE DONE HER WRONG)

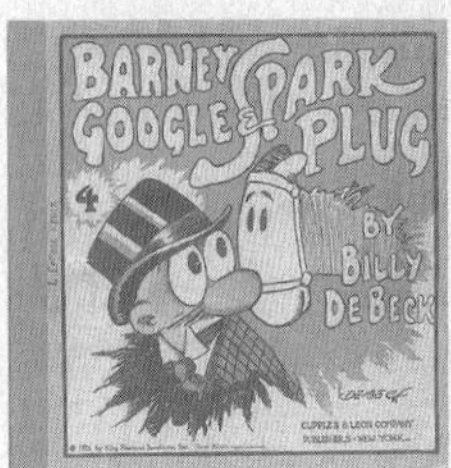

Barney Google and Spark Plug #4
1926 © Cupples & Leon

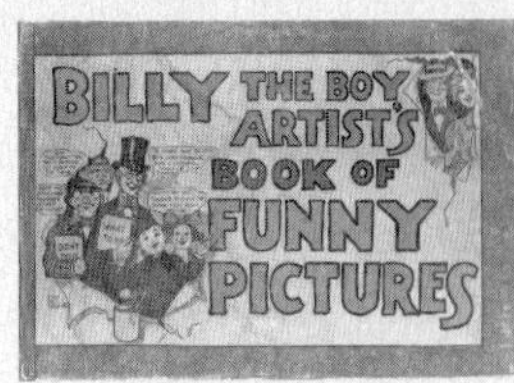

Bill the Boy Artist's Book by Ed Payne
1910 © C.M. Clark Publishing Co

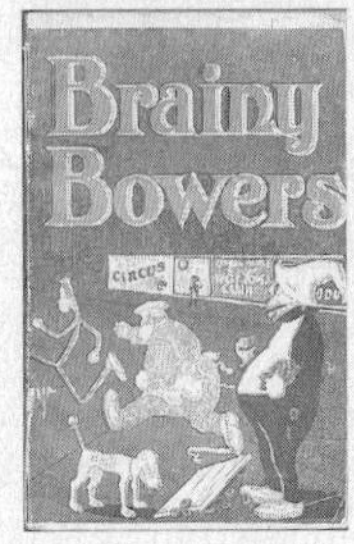

Brainy Bowers and Drowsy Duggan by R.W. Taylor
1905 © Star Publishing Co. - the first daily reprints

GD2.0 FN6.0 VF8.0

MS Publ. Co.: 1924 (9-7/8x10", 52 pgs., B&W)
nn - Milt Gross comic strips; not reprints 150.00 450.00 750.00

BARKER'S ILLUSTRATED ALMANAC (O,P,S) (See Barkers in Victorian Era section)
Barker, Moore & Mein Medicine Co: 1900-1932+ (36 pgs, B&W, color paper-c)
1900-1932+ (7x5-7/8") 20.00 70.00 125.00

BARKER'S "KOMIC" PICTURE SOUVENIR (P,S) (see Barker's in Victorian)
Barker, Moore & Mein Medicine Co: nd (Parts 1-3, 1901-1903; Parts 1-4, 1906+) (color cardboard-c, B&W interior, 50 pages)
Parts 1-3 (Rare, earliest printing, nd (1901)) 60.00 300.00 600.00
NOTE: *Same cover as 4th edition in Victorian Age Section, except has "Part 1", "Part 2", or "Part 3" printed in the blank space beneath the crate on which central figure is sitting. States "Edition in 3 Parts" on the first interior page, beneath the picture of the Barker's Building.*
Parts 1-3 (nd, c1901-1903) 40.00 200.00 400.00
NOTE: *New cover art on all Parts. States "Edition in 3 Parts" on the first interior page.*
Parts 1-4 (nd, c1906+) 25.00 100.00 300.00
NOTE: *States "Edition in 4 Parts" on the first interior page. Various printings known. These have been confirmed as premium comic books, predating the Buster Brown premiums. They reprint advertising cartoons from Barker's Illustrated Almanac. For the 50 page booklets by this same name, numbered as "Part"s, without exception, were published after 1900. Some editions are found to have 54 pages.*

BARNEY GOOGLE AND SPARK PLUG (N) (See **Comic Monthly**)
Cupples & Leon Co.: 1923 - No.6, 1928 (9-7/8x9-3/4"; 52 pgs., B&W, daily-r)
1 (nn)-By Billy DeBeck 60.00 240.00 450.00
2-4 (#5 & #6 do not exist) 46.00 186.00 350.00
NOTE: *Started June 17, 1919 as newspaper strip; Spark Plug introduced July 17, 1922; strip still running making it one of the oldest still in existence.*

BART'S CARTOONS FOR 1902 FROM THE MINNEAPOLIS JOURNAL (N,S)
Minneapolis Journal: 1903 (11x9", 102 pgs, paperback, B&W)
nn - By Charles L. Bartholomew 28.00 99.00 170.00

BELIEVE IT OR NOT! by Ripley (N,S)
Simon & Schuster: 1929 (8x 5-1/4", 68 pgs, red, B&W cover, B&W interior)
nn - By Robert Ripley (strip-r text & art) 40.00 120.00 240.00
NOTE: *1929 was the first printing of many reprintings . Strip began Dec 19, 1918 and is still running.*

BEN WEBSTER (N)
Standard Printing Company: 1928-1931 (13-3/4x4-7/16", 768 pgs, soft-c)
1 - "Bound to Win" 40.00 120.00 280.00
2 - "...in old Mexico 40.00 120.00 280.00
3 - "...At Wilderness Lake 40.00 120.00 280.00
4 - "...in the Oil Fields 40.00 120.00 280.00
NOTE: *Self Published by Edwin Alger, also contains fan's letter pages.*

BIG SMOKER
W.T. Blackwell & Co.: 1908 (16 pgs, 5-1/2x3-1/2", color-c & interior)
nn - By unknown 12.00 48.00 80.00
NOTE: *Stated reprint of 1878 version. no known copies yet of original printing.*

BILLY BOUNCE (I)
Donohue & Co.: 1906 (288 pgs, hardbound)
nn - By W.W. Denslow & Dudley Bragdon 150.00 525.00 900.00
NOTE: *Billy Bounce was created in 1901 as a comic strip by W. W. Denslow (strip ran from 1901 NOV 11 to 1905 DEC 3), but the series is best remembered in the C. W. Kahles version (from 1902 SEP 28). Denslow resumed his character in the above illustrated book.*

BILLY HON'S FAMOUS CARTOON BOOK (H)
Wasley Publishing Co.: 1927 (7-1/2x10", 68 pgs, softbound wraparound)
nn - By Billy Hon 12.00 48.00 80.00

BILLY THE BOY ARTIST'S BOOK OF FUNNY PICTURES (N)
C.M.Clark Publishing Co.: 1910 (9x12", hardcover-c, Boston Globe strip-r)
nn - By Ed Payne 125.00 400.00 750.00
NOTE: *This long lived strip ran in **The Boston Globe** from Nov 5 1899-Jan 7 1955; one of the longer run strips.*

BILLY THE BOY ARTIST'S PAINTING BOOK OF FUNNY PICTURES
(known to exist; more data required) - - -

BIRD CENTER CARTOONS: A Chronicle of Social Happenings (N,S)
A. C. McClurg & Co.: 1904 (12-3/8x9-1/2", 216 pgs, hardcover, B&W, single panels)
nn - By John McCutcheon 40.00 140.00 260.00
NOTE: *Strip began in **The Chicago Tribune** in 1903. Satirical cartoons and text concerning a mythical town.*

BLASTS FROM THE RAM'S HORN
The Rams Horn Company: 1902 (330 pgs, 7x9", B&W)
nn - By various 20.00 70.00 120.00
NOTE: *Cartoons reprinted from what was, apparently, a religious newspaper. Many cartoons by Frank Beard. Mostly single panel but occasionally sequential. Allegorical cartoons similar to the Christian Cartoons book. This book mixes cartoons and text sort of like the Caricature books. One or more cartoons on every page.*

BOBBY THATCHER & TREASURE CAVE (N)
Altemus Co.: 1932 (9x7", 86 pgs., B&W, hard-c)
nn - Reprints; Storm-a 54.00 189.00 400.00

BOBBY THATCHER'S ROMANCE (N)
The Bell Syndicate/Henry Altemus Co.: 1931 (8-3/4x7", color cover, B&W)
nn - By Storm 54.00 189.00 400.00

BOOK OF CARTOONS, A (M,S)
Edward T. Miller: 1903 (12-1/4x9-1/4", 120 pgs, hardcover, B&W)
nn - By Harry J. Westerman (Ohio State Journal-r) 20.00 70.00 120.00

BOOK OF DRAWINGS BY A.B. FROST, A (M,S)
P.F. Collier & Son: 1904 (15-3/8 x 11", 96 pgs, B&W)
nn - A.B. Frost 50.00 100.00 300.00
NOTE: *Pages alternate verses by Wallace Irwin and full-page plated by A.B.Frost. 39 plates.*

BOTTLE, THE (E) (see Victorian Age section for earlier printings)
Gowans & Gray, London & Glasgow: June 1905 (3-3/4x6", 72 pgs, printed one side only, paper cover, B&W)
nn - 1st printing (June 1905) 17.50 35.00 70.00
nn - 2nd printing (March 1906) 17.50 35.00 70.00
nn - 3rd printing (January 1911) 17.50 35.00 70.00
NOTE: *By George Cruikshank. Reprints both THE BOTTLE and THE DRUNKARD'S CHILDREN. Cover is text only - no cover art.*

BOTTLE, THE (E)
Frederick A. Stokes: nd (c1906) (3-3/4x6", 72 pgs, printed one side only, paper-c, B&W)
nn- by George Cruikshank 17.50 35.00 70.00
NOTE: *Reprint of the Gowans & Gray edition. Reprints both THE BOTTLE and THE DRUNKARD'S CHILDREN. Cover is text only - no cover art.*

BOYS AND FOLKS (N).
George H. Dornan Company: 1917 (10-1/4 x 8-1/4", 232 pgs. (single-sided), B&W strip-r.
nn - By Webster 21.00 64.00 150.00
NOTE: *Four sections: Life's Darkest Moments, Mostly About Folks, The Thrill That Comes Once in a Lifetime, and Our Boyhood Ambitions. Most are single-panel cartoons, but there are some sequential comic strips.*

BOY'S & GIRLS' BIG PAINTING BOOK OF INTERESTING COMIC PICTURES (N)
M. A. Donohue & Co.: 1914-16 (9x15, 70 pgs)
nn - By Carl "Bunny" Schultze (Foxy Grandpa-r) 81.00 284.00 -
#2 (1914) 81.00 284.00 -
#337 (1914) (sez "Big Painting & Drawing Book") 81.00 284.00 -
nn - (1916) (sez "Big Painting Book")(9-1/4x15") 81.00 284.00 -
NOTE: *These are all **Foxy Grandpa** items.*

BRAIN LEAKS: Dialogues of Mutt & Flea (N)
O. K. Printing Co. (Rochester Evening Times): 1911 (76 pgs, 6-5/8x4-5/8, hard-c, B&W)
nn - By Leo Edward O'Melia; newspaper strip-r 29.00 100.00 171.00

BRAINY BOWERS AND DROWSY DUGGAN (N)
Star Publishing: 1905 (7-1/4 x 4-9/16", 98 pgs., blue, brown & white color cover, B&W interior, 25¢) (daily strip-r 1902-04 Chicago Daily News)
#74 - By R. W. Taylor (Scarce) 500.00 1700.00 -
NOTE: *Part of a series of Atlantic Library Heart Series. Strip begins in 1901 and runs thru 1915. Taylor also created Yen the Janitor for the **New York World.***

BRAIN BOWERS AND DROWSY DUGAN (N)
Max Stein Pub. House, Chicago: 1905 (6-3/16x4-3/8", 64 pgs, B&W)
nn - By R.W. Taylor (Scarce) 500.00 1700.00 -
NOTE: *A coverless copy of this surfaced on eBay in 2002 selling for $700.00.;*

BRAINY BOWERS AND DROWSY DUGGAN GETTING ON IN THE WORLD WITH NO VISIBLE MEANS OF SUPPORT (STORIES TOLD IN PICTURES TO MAKE THEIR TELLING SHORT) (N)
Max Stein/Star Publishing: 1905 (7-3/8x5 1/8", 164 pgs, slick black, red & tan color cover, interior newsprint) (daily strip-r 1902-04 Chicago Daily News)
nn - By R. W. Taylor (Scarce) 500.00 1700.00 -
nn - Possible hard cover edition also? - - -
NOTE: *These Brainy Bowers editions are the earliest known daily newspaper strip reprint books.*

BRINGING UP FATHER (N)
Star Co. (King Features): 1917 (5-1/2x16-1/2", 100 pgs., B&W, cardboard-c)
nn - (Scarcer)-Daily strip- by George McManus 158.00 553.00 950.00

BRINGING UP FATHER (N)
Cupples & Leon Co.: 1919 - No. 26, 1934 (10x10", 52 pgs., B&W, stiff cardboard-c) (No. 22 is 9-1/4x9-1/2")
1-Daily strip-r by George McManus in all 25.00 100.00 260.00
2-10 25.00 100.00 250.00
11-20 40.00 200.00 375.00
21-26 (Scarcer) 60.00 300.00 550.00
The Big Book 1 (1926)-Thick book (hardcover, 142 pgs.) 127.00 508.00 1000.00
w/dust jacket (rare) 183.00 732.00 1325.00
The Big Book 2 (1929) 96.00 384.00 700.00
w/dust jacket (rare) 183.00 732.00 1325.00
NOTE: *The Big Books contain 3 regular issues rebound.* Strip began Jan 2 1913-May 28 2000

BRINGING UP FATHER, THE TROUBLE OF (N)
Embee Publ. Co.: 1921 (9-3/4x15-3/4", 46 pgs, Sunday-r in color)
nn - (Rare) 100.00 350.00 600.00
NOTE: *Ties with Mutt & Jeff (EmBee) and Jimmie Dugan And The Reg'lar Fellers (C&L) as the last of the*

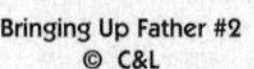
Bringing Up Father #2
© C&L

Brownie Clown of Brownie Town
© The Century Co.

Buster Brown His Dog Tige And Their Jolly Times
1906 © Cupples & Leon

GD2.0 FN6.0 VF8.0

oblong size era. This was self published by George McManus.

BRINGING UP FATHER (N) (see SAGARA'S ENGLISH CARTOONS
Publisher unknown (actually, unreadable), Tokyo: October 1924 (9-7/8" x 7-1/2", 90 pgs, color hard-c, B&W)

nn- (Scarce) by George McManus C&A (no known sales)
NOTE: *Published in Tokyo, Japan, with all strips in both English and Japanese, to facilitate learning English. Introduction by George McManus. Scarce in USA.*

BRONX BALLADS (I)
Simon & Schuster, NY: 1927 (9-1/2x7-1/4", hard-c, B&W)

nn - By Robert Simon and Harry Hershfield 36.00 143.00 250.00

BROWNIES, THE (not sequential comic strips)
The Century Co.: 1887 - 1914 (all came with dust jackets; add $100-150 to value if original dust jacket is included and intact)

Book 1 - The Brownies: Their Book (1887) 200.00 850.00 1320.00
Book 2 - Another Brownies Book (1890) 150.00 635.00 1000.00
Book 3 - The Brownies at Home (1893) 125.00 530.00 825.00
Book 4 - The Brownies Around the World (1894) 100.00 425.00 660.00
Book 5 - The Brownies Through the Union (1895) 100.00 425.00 660.00
Book 6 - The Brownies Abroad (1899) 100.00 425.00 660.00
Book 7 - The Brownies in the Philippines (1904) 100.00 425.00 660.00
Book 8 - The Brownies' Latest Adventures (1910) 100.00 425.00 660.00
Book 9 - The Brownies Many More Nights (1914) 100.00 425.00 660.00
...Raid on Kleinmaier Bros. (c. 1910, 16 pages) Kleinmaier Bros. Clothing, Marion, Ohio (no known sales)

BROWNIE CLOWN OF BROWNIE TOWN (N)
The Century Co.: 1908 (6-7/8 x 9-3/8", 112 pgs, color hardcover & interior)

nn - By Palmer Cox (rare; 1907 newspaper comic strip-r) 250.00 800.00 1400.00
NOTE: *The Brownies created 1883 in* ***St Nicholas Magazine.***

BUDDY TUCKER & HIS FRIENDS (N) (Also see **Buster Brown Nuggets**)
Cupples & Leon Co.: 1906 (11-5/8 x17", 58 pgs, color) (Scarce)

nn - 1905 Sunday strip-r by R. F. Outcault 500.00 1500.00 2500.00
NOTE: *Strip began Apr 30, 1905 thru at least Oct 1905.*

BUFFALO BILL'S PICTURE STORIES
Street & Smith Publications: 1909 (Soft cardboard cover)

nn - Very rare 67.00 233.00 400.00

BUGHOUSE FABLES (N) (see also **Comic Monthly**)
Embee Distributing Co. (King Features): 1921 (10¢, 4x4-1/2", 48 pgs.)

1-By Barney Google (Billy DeBeck) 46.00 186.00 350.00

BUG MOVIES (O) (Also see Clancy The Cop & Deadwood Gulch)
Dell Publishing Co.: 1931 (9-13/16x9-7/8", 52 pgs., B&W)

nn - Original material; Stookie Allen-a 150.00 300.00 500.00

BULL
Bull Publishing Company, New York: No.1, March, 1916 - No.12, Feb, 1917 (10 cents, 10-3/4x8-3/4", 24 pgs, color paper-c, B&W)

1-12 (Very Rare) – – –
NOTE: *Pro-German, Anti-British cartoon/humor monthly, whose goal was to keep the U.S. neutral and out of World War I. We know of no copies which have sold in the past few years.*

BUNNY'S BLUE BOOK (see also Foxy Grandpa) (N)
Frederick A. Stokes Co.: 1911 (10x15, 60¢)

nn - By Carl "Bunny" Schultze strip-r 100.00 350.00 –

BUNNY'S RED BOOK (see also Foxy Grandpa) (N)
Frederick A. Stokes Co.: 1912 (10-1/4x15-3/4", 64 pgs.)

nn - By Carl "Bunny" Schultze strip-r 100.00 350.00 –

BUNNY'S GREEN BOOK (see also Foxy Grandpa) (N)
Frederick A. Stokes Co.: 1913 (10x15")

nn - By Carl "Bunny" Schultze 100.00 350.00 –

BUSTER BROWN (C) (Also see Brown's Blue Ribbon Book of Jokes and Jingles & Buddy Tucker & His Friends)
Frederick A. Stokes Co.: 1903 - 1916 (Daily strip-r in color)

1903...& His Resolutions (11-1/4x16", 66 pgs.) by R. F. Outcault (Rare)-1st nationally distributed comic. Distr. through Sears & Roebuck 1600.00 5500.00 –
1904...His Dog Tige & Their Troubles (11-1/4x16-1/4", 66 pgs.)(Rare) 600.00 1875.00 –
1905...Pranks (11-1/4x16-3/8", 66 pgs.) 400.00 1450.00 –
1906...Antics (11x16-3/8", 66 pgs.) 400.00 1450.00 –
1906...And Company (11x16-1/2", 66 pgs.) 300.00 1050.00 –
1906...Mary Jane & Tige (11-1/4x16, 66 pgs.) 300.00 1050.00 –
NOTE: ***Yellow Kid*** *pictured on two pages.*
1908 Collection of Buster Brown Comics 250.00 835.00 –
1909 Outcault's Real Buster and The Only Mary Jane (11x16, 66 pgs, Stokes) 250.00 835.00 –

GD2.0 FN6.0 VF8.0

1910...Up to Date (10-1/8x15-3/4", 66 pgs.) 208.00 729.00 1315.00
1911...Fun And Nonsense (10-1/8x15-3/4", 66 pgs.) 183.00 642.00 1150.00
1912...The Fun Maker (10-1/8x15-3/4", 66 pgs.) -Yellow Kid (4 pgs.) 183.00 642.00 1150.00
1913...At Home (10-1/8x15-3/4", 56 pgs.) 167.00 583.00 1050.00
1914...And Tige Here Again (10x16, 62 pgs, Stokes) 153.00 535.00 1000.00
1915...And His Chum Tige (10x16, Stokes) 153.00 535.00 1000.00
1916...The Little Rogue (10-1/8x15-3/4", 62 pgs.) 162.00 567.00 1025.00
1917...And the Cat (5-1/2x 6-1/2, 26 pgs, Stokes) 115.00 402.00 750.00
1917...Disturbs the Family (5-1/2x 6 1/2, 26 pgs, Stokes
NOTE: *Story featuring statue of "the Chinese Yellow Kid"* 115.00 402.00 750.00
1917...The Real Buster Brown (5-1/2x 6 -/2, 26 pgs, Stokes 115.00 402.00 750.00

Frederick A. Stokes Co. Hard Cover Series (I)
...Abroad (1904, 10-1/4x8", 86 pgs., B&W, hard-c)-R. F. Outcault-a (Rare) 200.00 700.00 1260.00
...Abroad (1904, B&W, 67 pgs.)-R. F. Outcault-a 200.00 700.00 1260.00
NOTE: *Buster Brown Abroad is not an actual comic book, but prose with illustrations.*
..."Tige" His Story 1905 (10x8", 63 pgs., B&W) (63 illos.)
nn-By RF Outcault 143.00 500.00 –
...My Resolutions 1906 (10x8", B&W, 68 pgs.)-R.F. Outcault-a (Rare) 233.00 817.00 1475.00
...Autobiography 1907 (10x8", B&W, 71 pgs.) (16 color plates & 36 B&W illos) 67.00 233.00 440.00
...And Mary Jane's Painting Book 1907 (10x13-1/4", 60 pgs, both card & hardcover versions exist
nn-RFO (first printing blank on top of cover) 67.00 233.00 440.00
First Series- this is a reprint if it says First Series 67.00 233.00 440.00
Volume Two - By RFO 67.00 233.00 440.00
... My Resolutions by Buster Brown (1907, 68 pgs, small size, cardboard covers) scarce 43.00 150.00 285.00
NOTE: *Not actual comic book per se, but a compilation of the Resolutions panels found at the end of Outcault's Buster Brown newspaper strips.*

BUSTER BROWN (N)
Cupples & Leon Co./N. Y. Herald Co.: 1906 - 1917 (11x17", color, strip-r)
NOTE: *Early issues by R. F. Outcault; most C&L editions are not by Outcault.*

1906...His Dog Tige And Their Jolly Times (11-3/8x16-5/8", 68 pgs.) 300.00 1100.00 1900.00
1906...His Dog Tige & Their Jolly Times (11x16, 46 pgs.) 163.00 600.00 1025.00
1907...Latest Frolics (11-3/8x16-5/8", 66 pgs., r/'05-06 strips) 163.00 600.00 1025.00
1908...Amusing Capers (58 pgs.) 129.00 475.00 815.00
1909...The Busy Body (11-3/8x16-5/8", 62 pgs.) 129.00 475.00 815.00
1910...On His Travels (11x16", 58 pgs.) 115.00 402.00 750.00
1911...Happy Days (11-3/8x16-5/8", 58 pgs.) 115.00 402.00 750.00
1912...In Foreign Lands (10x16", 58 pgs) 115.00 402.00 750.00
1913...And His Pets (11x16", 58 pgs.) STOKES???? 115.00 402.00 750.00
1913...And His Pets (26 pg partial reprint) – – –
1914...Funny Tricks (11-3/8x16-5/8", 58 pgs.) 115.00 402.00 750.00
1916...At Play (10x16, 58 pgs) 115.00 402.00 750.00

BUSTER BROWN NUGGETS (N)
Cupples & Leon Co./N.Y.Herald Co.: 1907 (1905, 7-1/2x6-1/2", 36 pgs., color, strip-r, hard-c)(By R. F. Outcault) (NOTE: books are all unnumbered)

Buster Brown Goes Fishing, Goes Swimming, Plays Indian, Goes Shooting, Plays Cowboy, On Uncle Jack's Farm, Tige And the Bull, And Uncle Buster 39.00 137.00 275.00
Buddy Tucker Meets Alice in Wonderland 56.00 200.00 400.00
Buddy Tucker Visits The House That Jack Built 39.00 137.00 275.00

BUSTER BROWN MUSLIN SERIES (N)
Saalfield: 1907 (also contain copyright Cupples & Leon)

...Goes Fishing, Plays Indian, And the Donkey (1907, 6-7/8x6-1/8", 24 pgs., color)-r/1905 Sunday comics page by Outcault (Rare) 50.00 175.00 315.00
...Plays Cowboy (1907, 6-3/4x6", 10 pgs., color)-r/1905 Sunday comics page by Outcault (Rare) 50.00 175.00 315.00
NOTE: *These are muslin versions of the C&L BB Nugget series. Muslin books are all cloth books, made to be washable so as not easily stained/destroyed by very young children. The Muslin books contain one strip each (the title strip), to the more common NUGGET's three strips.*

BUSTER BROWN PREMIUMS (Advertising premium booklets)
Various Publishers: 1904 - 1912 (3x5" to 5x7"; sizes vary)

American Fruit Product Company, Rochester, NY
Buster Brown Duffy's 1842 Cider (1904, 7x5". 12 pgs, C.E. Sherin Co, NYC)
nn - By R. F. Outcault (scarce) 100.00 350.00 600.00

The Brown Shoe Company, St. Louis, USA
Set of five books (5x7", 16 pgs., color)
Brown's Blue Ribbon Book of Jokes and Jingles Book 1 (nn, 1904)-By R. F. Outcault; Buster Brown & Tige, Little Tommy Tucker, Jack & Jill, Little Boy Blue, Dainty Jane; The Yellow Kid app. on back-c (1st BB comic book premium) 300.00 1050.00 1900.00

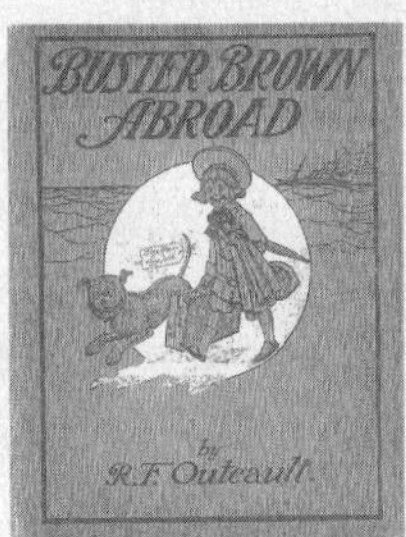

Buster Brown Abroad
1904 © Frederick A. Stokes Co.

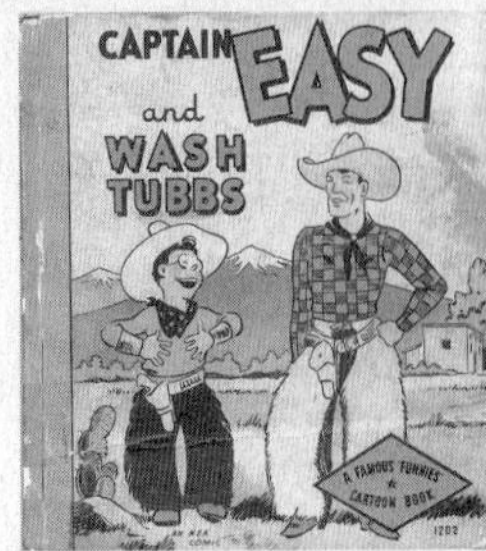

Captain Easy and Wash Tubbs by Roy Crane
1934 © Whitman Famous Comics Cartoon Book

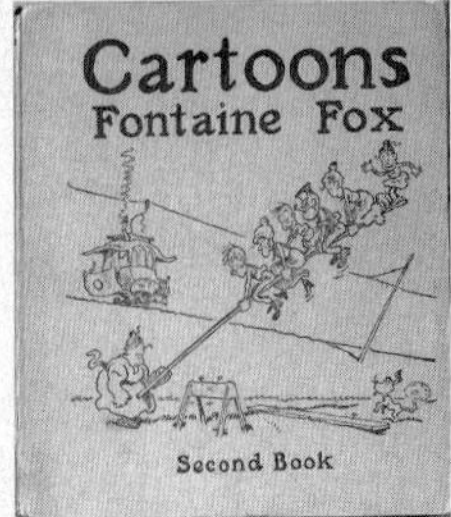

Cartoons Fontaine Fox Second Book
early 1920s © Harper & Bros, NY

GD2.0 FN6.0 VF8.0

Buster Brown's Blue Ribbon Book of Jokes and Jingles Book 2 (1905)-
Original color art by Outcault 200.00 600.00 1260.00
Buster's Book of Jokes & Jingles Book 3 (1909)
not by R.F. Outcault 150.00 400.00 840.00
NOTE: *Reprinted from the Blue Ribbon post cards with advert jingles added.*
Buster's Book of Instructive Jokes and Jingles Book 4 (1910)-Original color art
not by R.F. Outcault 150.00 585.00 1050.00
...Book of Travels nn (1912, 3x5")-Original color art not signed by Outcault
117.00 408.00 735.00
NOTE: *Estimated 5 or 6 known copies exist of books #1-4.*

The Buster Brown Bread Company

"Buster Brown" Bread Book of Rhymes, The (1904, 4x6", 12 pgs., half color, half B&W)- Original color art not signed by RFO 158.00 553.00 1000.00

Buster Brown's Hosiery Mills

"How Buster Brown Got The Pie" nn (nd, 7x5-1/4". 16 pgs, color paper cover and color interior By R.F. Outcault 83.00 292.00 525.00
"The Autobiography of Buster Brown" nn (nd,9x6-1/8", 36 pgs, text story & art by R.F. Outcault 83.00 292.00 525.00
NOTE: *Similar to, but a distinctly different item than "Buster Brown's Autobiography."*

The Buster Brown Stocking Company

Buster Brown Drawing Book, The nn (nd, 5x6", 20 pgs.)-B&W reproductions of 1903 R.F. Outcault art to trace 50.00 150.00 315.00
NOTE: *Reprints a comic strip from Burr McIntosh Magazine, which includes Buster, Yellow Kid, and Pore Li'l Mose (only known story involving all three.)*
Buster Brown Stocking Magazine nn (Jan. 1906, 7-3/4x5-3/8", 36 pgs.) R.F. Outcault
50.00 100.00 200.00
NOTE: *This was actually a store bought item selling for 5 cents per copy.*

Collins Baking Company

Buster Brown Drawing Book nn (1904, 5x3", 12 pgs.)-Original B&W art to trace, not signed by R.F. Outcault 50.00 150.00 315.00

C. H. Morton, St. Albans, VT

Merry Antics of Buster Brown, Buddy Tucker & Tige nn (nd, 3-1/2x5-1/2", 16 pgs.) -Original B&W art by R.F. Outcault 83.00 292.00 525.00

Ivan Frank & Company

Buster Brown nn (1904, 3x5", 12 pgs.)-B&W repros of R. F. Outcault Sunday pages (First premium to actually reproduce Sunday comic pages – may be first premium comic strip-r book?) 125.00 438.00 785.00
Buster Brown's Pranks (1904, 3-1/2x5-1/8", 12 pgs.)-reprints intro of Buddy Tucker into the BB newspaper strip before he was spun off into his own short lived newspaper strip
125.00 438.00 785.00

Kaufmann & Strauss

Buster Brown Drawing Book (1906, 28 pages, 5x3-1/2") Color Cover, B+W original story signed by Outcault, tracing paper inserted as alternate pages. Back cover imprinted for Nox' Em All Shoes 50.00 150.00 315.00

Pond's Extract

Buster Brown's Experiences With Pond's Extract nn (1904, 6-3/4x4-1/2", 28 pgs.) Original color art by R.F. Outcault (may be the first BB premium comic book with original art) 100.00 250.00 525.00

C. A. Cross & Co.

Red Cross Drawing Book nn (1906, 4-7/8x3-1/2", color paper -c, B&W interior, 12 pgs.)
50.00 150.00 315.00
NOTE: *This is for Red Cross coffee; not the health organization.*

Ringen Stove Company

Quick Meal Steel Ranges nn (nd, 5x3", 16 pgs.)-Original B&W art not signed by R.F. Outcault 50.00 150.00 315.00

Steinwender Stoffregen Coffee Co.

"Buster Brown Coffee" (1905, 4-7/8x3", color paper cover, B&W interior, 12 printed pages, plus 1 tracing paper page above each interior image (total of 8 sheets) (Very Rare)
83.00 292.00 525.00
NOTE: *Part of a BB drawing contest. If instructions had been followed, most copies would have ended up destroyed.*

U. S. Playing Card Company

Buster Brown - My Own Playing Cards (1906, 2-1/2x1-3/4", full color)
nn - By R. F. Outcault 42.00 147.00 250.00
NOTE: *Series of full color panels tell stories, average about 5 cards per story.*

Publisher Unknown

The Drawing Book nn (1906, 3-9/16x5", 8 pgs.)-Original B&W art to trace not by R.F. Outcault 50.00 150.00 300.00

BUTLER BOOK A Series of Clever Cartoons of Yale Undergraduate Life
Yale Record: June 16, 1913 (10-3/4 x 17", 34 pgs, paper cover B&W)
nn - By Alban Bernard Butler 21.00 73.00 130.00
NOTE: *Cartoons and strips reprinted from The Yale Record student newspaper.*

BUTTONS & FATTY IN THE FUNNIES
Whitman Publishing Co.: nd 1927 (10-1/4x15-1/2", 28pg., color)
W936 - Signed "M.E.B.", probably M.E. Brady; strips in color copyright The Brooklyn Daily Eagle; (very rare) 61.00 244.00 425.00

BY BRIGGS (M,N,P) (see also OLD GOLD THE SMOOTHER AND BETTER CIGARETTE)
Old Gold Cigarettes: nd (c1920's) (11" x 9-11/16", 44 pgs, cardboard-c, B&W)
nn- (Scarce) 20.00 70.00 130.00
NOTE: *Collection reprinting strip cartoons by Clare Briggs, advertising Old Gold Cigarettes. These strips originally appeared in various magazines, play program booklets, newspapers, etc. Some of the strips involve regular Briggs strip series. Contains all of the strips in the smaller, color "OLD GOLD" giveaways, plus more.*

GD2.0 FN6.0 VF8.0

CAMION CARTOONS
Marshall Jones Company: 1919 (7-1/2x5", 136 pgs, B&W)
nn - By Kirkland H. Day (W.W.One occupation) 20.00 70.00 120.00

CANYON COUNTRY KIDDIES (M)
Doubleday, Page & Co: 1923 (8x10-1/4", 88 pgs, hard-c, B&W)
nn - By James Swinnerton 39.00 137.00 260.00

CARLO (H)
Doubleday, Page & Co.: 1913 (8 x 9-5/8, 120 pgs, hardcover, B&W)
nn - By A.B. Frost 40.00 140.00 300.00
NOTE: *Original sequential strips about a dog. Became short lived newspaper comic strip in 1914. Originally published with a dust jacket which increases value 50%.*

CARTOON BOOK, THE
Bureau of Publicity, War Loan Organization, Treasury Department, Washington, D.C.: 1918 (6-1/2x4-7/8", 48 pgs, paper cover, B&W)
nn - By various artists 31.00 108.00 185.00
NOTE: *U.S. government issued booklet of WW I propaganda cartoons by 46 artists promoting the third sale of Liberty Loan bonds. The artists include: Berryman, Clare Briggs, Cesare, J. N. "Ding" Darling, Rube Goldberg, Kemble, McCutcheon, George McManus, F. Opper, T. E. Powers, Ripley, Satterfield, H. T. Webster, Gaar Williams.*

CARTOON CATALOGUE (S)
The Lockwood Art School, Kalamazoo, Mich.: 1919 (11-5/8x9, 52 pgs, B&W)
nn - Edited by Mr. Lockwood 20.00 60.00 140.00
NOTE: *Jammed with 100s of single panel cartoons and some sequential comics; Mr Lockwood began the very first cartoonist school back in 1892. Clare Briggs was one of his students.*

CARTOON COMICS
Lasco Publications, Detroit, Mich: #1, April 1930 - #2, May 1930 (8-3/6x5-1/5")
1, 2 - By Lu Harris 20.00 60.00 100.00
NOTE: *Contains recurring characters Hollywood Horace, Campus Charlie, Pair-A-Dice Alley and Jocko Monkey. Not much is presently known about the creator(s) or publisher.*

CARTOON HISTORY OF ROOSEVELT'S CAREER, A
The Review of Reviews Company: 1910 (276 pgs, 8-1/4x11",
nn - By various 43.00 129.00 325.00
NOTE: *Reprints editorial cartoons about Teddy Roosevelt from U.S. and international newspapers and cartoons from the humor magaines (Puck, Judge, etc.). A few cartoonists whose work is included are Dalrymple, Opper, McDougall, McCutcheon, Remington, Rogers, Kemble. Mostly single panel but 10 or so are sequential strips.*

CARTOON HUMOR
Collegian Press: 1938 (102 pgs, squarebound, B&W)
nn 20.00 70.00 120.00
NOTE: *Contains cartoons & strips by Otto Soglow, Syd Hoff, Peter Arno, Abner Dean, others.*

CARTOONIST'S PHILOSOPHY, A
Percy Crosby: 1931, HC, 252 pgs, 5-1/2x7-1/2", hard-c, celluloid dust wrapper
nn - By Percy Crosby (10 plates, 6 are of Skippy) 20.00 60.00 130.00
NOTE: *Crosby's partial autobiography regarding his return to France in 1929, and portrayals of Normandy, the "cliff dwellers" on Normandy cliffs (destroyed in WWII), his visit to London, comments on art, philosophy, several poems, and political dialogue. His description of his Cockney driver, " Harold" is amusing. Also describes his experience visiting Chicago to speak out against Capone, his concerns over the evils of Prohibition, and the economy prior to the 1929 crash. This book reveals he was aware of the dangers of his outspoken views, and is prophetic, re: his later years as political prisoner. Also reveals his religious beliefs.*

CARTOONS BY BRADLEY: CARTOONIST OF THE CHICAGO DAILY NEWS
Rand McNally & Company: 1917 (11-1/4x8-3/4", 112 pgs, hardcover, B&W)
nn - By Luther D. Bradley (editorial) 20.00 70.00 120.00

CARTOONS BY FONTAINE FOX (Toonerville Trolley) (S)
Harper & Brothers Publishers: nd early '20s (9x7-7/8",102 pgs., hard-c, B&W)
Second Book- By Fontaine Fox (Toonerville-r) 150.00 300.00 500.00

CARTOONS BY HALLADAY (N,S)
Providence Journal Co., Rhode Island: Dec 1914 (116 pgs, 10-1/2x 7-3/4", hard-c, B&W)
nn- (Scarce) 50.00 125.00 250.00
NOTE: *Cartoons on Rhode Island politics, plus some Teddy Roosevelt & WW I cartoons.*

CARTOONS BY McCUTCHEON (S)
A. C. McClurg & Co.: 1903 (12-3/8x9-3/4", 212 pgs., hardcover, B&W)
nn - By John McCutcheon 20.00 70.00 120.00

CARTOONS BY W. A. IRELAND (S)
The Columbus-Evening Dispatch: 1907 (13-3/4 x 10-1/2", 66 pgs, hardcover)
nn - By W. A. Ireland (strip-r) 20.00 70.00 120.00

CARTOONS MAGAZINE (I,N,S)
H. H. Windsor, Publisher: Jan 1912-June 1921; July 1921-1923; 1923-1924; 1924-1927 (1912-July 1913 issues 12x9-1/4", 68-76 pgs; 1913-1921 issues 10x7", average 112 to 188 pgs, color covers)
1912-Jan-Dec 30.00 75.00 125.00

Cartoons Magazine Sept, 1917
by various creators © H. H. Windsor, Chicago

Charlie Chaplin in the Movies by Segar
1917 © Essaney

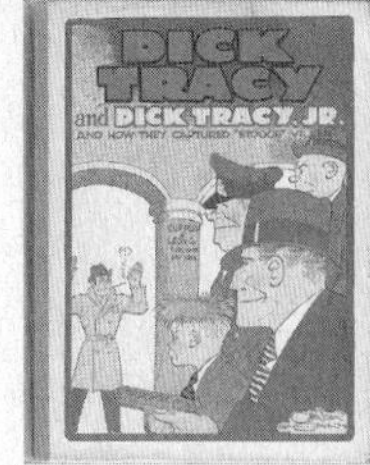

How Dick Tracy and Dick Tracy, Jr. And How They Captured Stooge Villar by Chester Gould
1933 © Cupples & Leon

	GD2.0	FN6.0	VF8.0
1913-1917	30.00	75.00	125.00
1917-(Apr) "How Comickers Regard Their Characters"	30.00	105.00	150.00
1917-(June) "A Genius of the Comic Page" - long article on George Herriman, Krazy Kat, etc with lots of Herriman art; "Cartoonists and Their Cars"	125.00	250.00	500.00
1918-1919	30.00	75.00	125.00
1920-June 1921	30.00	75.00	125.00
July 1921-1923 titled Wayside Tales & Cartoons Magazine	30.00	75.00	125.00
1923-1924 becomes Cartoons Magazine again	30.00	75.00	125.00
1924-1927 becomes Cartoons & Movie Magazine	30.00	75.00	125.00

NOTE: *Many issues contain a wealth of historical background on then current cartoonists of the day with an international slant; each issue profusely illustrated with many cartoons. We are unsure if this magazine continued after 1927.*

CARTOONS BY J. N. DARLING (S,N - some sequential strips)
The Register & Tribune Co., Des Moines, Iowa: 1909?-1920 (12x8-7/8",B&W)

	GD2.0	FN6.0	VF8.0
Book 1	15.00	51.00	90.00
Book 2 Education of Alonzo Applegate (1910)	15.00	51.00	90.00
2nd printing	10.00	30.00	90.00
Book 3 Cartoons From The Files (1911)	15.00	51.00	90.00
Book 4	15.00	51.00	90.00
Book 5 In Peace And War (1916)	15.00	51.00	90.00
Book 6 Aces & Kings War Cartoons (Dec 1, 1918)	15.00	51.00	90.00
Book 7 The Jazz Era (Dec 1920)	15.00	51.00	90.00
Book 8 Our Own Outlines of History (1922)	15.00	51.00	90.00

NOTE: *Some of the most inspired hard hitting cartoons ever printed. Are there more?*

CARTOONS THAT MADE PRINCE HENRY FAMOUS, THE (N,S)
The Chicago Record-Herald: Feb/March 1902 (12-1/8" x 9", 32 pgs, paper-c, B&W)

	GD2.0	FN6.0	VF8.0
nn- (Scarce) by McCutcheon	15.00	51.00	90.00

NOTE: *Cartoons about the visit of the British Prince Henry to the U.S.*

CAVALRY CARTOONS (O)
R. Montalboddi: nd (c1918) (14-1/4" x 11", 30 pgs, printed on one side, olive & black construction paper-c, B&W interior)

	GD2.0	FN6.0	VF8.0
nn - By R.Montalboddi	15.00	51.00	90.00

NOTE: *Comics about life in the U.S.Cavalry during World War I, by a soldier who was in the 1st Cavalry.*

CHARLIE CHAPLIN (N)
Essanay/M. A. Donohue & Co.: 1917 (9x16", B&W, large size soft-c)

	GD2.0	FN6.0	VF8.0
Series 1, #315-Comic Capers (9-3/4x15-3/4")-20 pgs. by Segar; Series 1, #316-In the Movies	165.00	525.00	1200.00
#317-Up in the Air (20 pgs), #318-In the Army	165.00	525.00	1400.00
Funny Stunts-(12-1/2x16-3/8",16 color pgs)	165.00	525.00	1400.00

NOTE: *All contain pre-Thimble Theatre Segar art. The thin paper used makes high grade copies very scarce.*

CHASING THE BLUES
Doubleday Page: 1912 (7-1/2x10", 108 pgs., B&W, hard-c)

	GD2.0	FN6.0	VF8.0
nn - By Rube Goldberg	150.00	525.00	900.00

NOTE: *Contains a dozen Foolish Questions, baseball, a few Goldberg poems and lots of sequential strips.*

CHRISTIAN CARTOONS (N,S)
The Sunday School Times Company: 1922 (7-1/4 x 6-1/8,104 pgs, brown hard-c, B&W)

	GD2.0	FN6.0	VF8.0
nn - E.J. Pace	15.00	51.00	90.00

NOTE: *Religious cartoons reprinted from The Sunday School Times.*

CLANCY THE COP (O))
Dell Publishing Co.: 1930 - No. 2, 1931 (10x10", 52 pgs., B&W, cardboard-c)
(Also see Bug Movies & Deadwood Gulch)

	GD2.0	FN6.0	VF8.0
1, 2-By VEP Victor Pazimino (original material; not reprints)	10000	250.00	500.00

CLIFFORD MCBRIDE'S IMMORTAL NAPOLEON & UNCLE ELBY (N)
The Castle Press: 1932 (12x17"; soft-c cartoon book)

	GD2.0	FN6.0	VF8.0
nn - Intro. by Don Herod	36.00	144.00	250.00

COLLECTED DRAWINGS OF BRUCE BAIRNSFATHER, THE
W. Colston Leigh: 1931 (11-1/4x8-1/4 ", 168 pages, hardcover, B&W)

	GD2.0	FN6.0	VF8.0
nn - By Bruce Bairnsfather	24.00	96.00	165.00

COMICAL PEEP SHOW
McLoughlin Bros: 1902 (36 pgs, B&W)

	GD2.0	FN6.0	VF8.0
nn	24.00	96.00	165.00

NOTE: *Comic stories of Wilhelm Busch redrawn; two versions with green or gold front cover logos; back covers different.*

COMIC ANIMALS (I)
Charles E. Graham & Co.: 1903 (9-3/4x7-1/4", 90 pgs, color cover)

	GD2.0	FN6.0	VF8.0
nn - By Walt McDougall (not comic strips)	43.00	150.00	260.00

COMIC CUTS (O)
H. L. Baker Co., Inc.: 5/19/34-7/28/34 (Tabloid size 10-1/2x15-1/2", 24 pgs., 5¢)
(full color, not reprints; published weekly; created for news stand sales)

	GD2.0	FN6.0	VF8.0
V1#1 - V1#7(6/30/34), V1#8(7/14/34), V1#9(7/28/34)-Idle Jack strips	200.00	400.00	800.00

NOTE: *According to a 1958 Lloyd Jacquet interview, this short-lived comics mag was the direct inspiration for Major Malcolm Wheeler-Nicholson's* ***New Fun Comics****, not* ***Famous Funnies****.*

COMIC MONTHLY (N)
Embee Dist. Co.: Jan, 1922 - No. 12, Dec, 1922 (10¢, 8-1/2"x9", 28 pgs., 2-color covers) (1st monthly newsstand comic publication) (Reprints 1921 B&W dailies)

	GD2.0	FN6.0	VF8.0
1-Polly & Her Pals by Cliff Sterrett	375.00	1125.00	2225.00
2-Mike & Ike by Rube Goldberg	140.00	490.00	1000.00
3-S'Matter, Pop?	140.00	490.00	1000.00
4-Barney Google by Billy DeBeck	140.00	490.00	1000.00
5-Tillie the Toiler by Russ Westover	140.00	490.00	1000.00
6-Indoor Sports by Tad Dorgan	140.00	490.00	1000.00

NOTE: *#6 contains more Judge Rummy than Indoor Sports.*

	GD2.0	FN6.0	VF8.0
7-Little Jimmy by James Swinnerton	140.00	490.00	1000.00
8-Toots and Casper b y Jimmy Murphy	140.00	490.00	1000.00
9-New Bughouse Fables by Barney Google	140.00	490.00	1000.00
10-Foolish Questions by Rube Goldberg	140.00	490.00	1000.00
11-Barney Google & Spark Plug by Billy DeBeck	140.00	490.00	1000.00
12-Polly & Her Pals by Cliff Sterrett	214.00	752.00	1500.00

NOTE: *This series was published by George McManus (Bringing Up Father) as Em & Rudolph Block, Jr., son of Hearst's cartoon editor for many years, as "Bee." One would have thought this series would have done very well considering the tremendous amount of talent assembled. All issues are extremely hard to find these days and rarely show up in any type of higher grade.*

COMIC PAINTING AND CRAYONING BOOK (H)
Saalfield Publ. Co.: 1917 (13-1/2x10", 32 pgs.) (No price on-c)

	GD2.0	FN6.0	VF8.0
nn - Tidy Teddy by F. M. Follett, Clarence the Cop, Mr. & Mrs. Butt-In; regular comic stories to read or color	50.00	175.00	300.00

COMPLETE TRIBUNE PRIMER, THE (I)
Mutual Book Company: 1901 (7 1/4 x 5", 152 pgs, red hard-c)

	GD2.0	FN6.0	VF8.0
nn - By Frederick Opper; has 75 Opper cartoons	25.00	88.00	150.00

COURTSHIP OF TAGS, THE (N)
McCormick Press: pre-1910 (9x4", 88 pgs, red & B&W-c, B&W interior)

	GD2.0	FN6.0	VF8.0
nn - By O. E. Wertz (strip-r Wichita Daily Beacon)	25.00	88.00	150.00

DAFFYDILS (N)
Cupples & Leon Co.: 1911 (5-3/4x7-7/8", 52 pgs., B&W, hard-c)

	GD2.0	FN6.0	VF8.0
nn - By "Tad" Dorgan	58.00	204.00	350.00

NOTE: *Also exists in self-published TAD edition: The T.A. Dorgan Company; unknown which is first printing.*

DAN DUNN SECRET OPERATIVE 48 (Also See Detective Dan) (N)
Whitman Publishing: 1937 ((5 1/2 x 7 1/4", 68pgs., color cardboard-c, B&W)

	GD2.0	FN6.0	VF8.0
1010 And The Gangsters' Frame-Up	50.00	150.00	300.00

NOTE: *There are two versions of the book the later printing has a 5 cent cover price. Dick Tracy look-alike character by Norman Marsh.*

DANGERS OF DOLLY DIMPLE, THE (N)
Penn Tobacco Co.: nd (1930's) (9-3/8x7-7/8", 28 pgs, red cardboard-c, B&W)

	GD2.0	FN6.0	VF8.0
nn - (Rare) by Walter Enright	25.00	88.00	150.00

NOTE: *Reprints newspaper comic strip advertisements, in which in every episode, Dolly Dimple's life is saved by Penn's Smoking Tobacco. - how very un-P.C. by today's standards.*

DEADWOOD GULCH (O) (See The Funnies 1929)(also see Bug Movies & Clancy The Cop)
Dell Publishing Co.: 1931 (10x10", 52 pgs., B&W, color covers, B&W interior)

	GD2.0	FN6.0	VF8.0
nn - By Charles "Boody" Rogers (original material)	150.00	300.00	600.00

DESTINY A Novel In Pictures (O)
Farrar & Rinehart: 1930 (8x7", 424 pgs, B&W, hard-c, dust jacket?)

	GD2.0	FN6.0	VF8.0
nn - By Otto Nuckel (original graphic novel)	25.00	100.00	175.00

DICK TRACY & DICK TRACY JR. CAUGHT THE RACKETEERS, HOW
Cupples & Leon Co.: 1933 (8-1/2x7", 88 pgs., hard-c) (See Treasure Box of Famous Comics) (N)

	GD2.0	FN6.0	VF8.0
2-(Numbered on pg. 84)-Continuation of Stooge Viller book (daily strip reprints from 8/3/33 thru 11/8/33)(Rarer than #1)	94.00	376.00	750.00
With dust jacket...	175.00	500.00	1000.00

DICK TRACY & DICK TRACY JR. AND HOW THEY CAPTURED "STOOGE" VILLER (N)
Cupples & Leon Co.: 1933 (8-1/2x7", 100 pgs., hard-c, one-shot)
Reprints 1932 & 1933 Dick Tracy daily strips

	GD2.0	FN6.0	VF8.0
nn(No.1)-1st app. of "Stooge" Viller	94.00	376.00	750.00
With dust jacket...	175.00	500.00	1000.00

DIMPLES By Grace Drayton (N) (See Dolly Dimples)
Hearst's International Library Co.: 1915 (6 1/4 x 5 1/4, 12 pgs) (5 known)

	GD2.0	FN6.0	VF8.0
nn-Puppy and Pussy; nn-She Goes For a Walk; nn-She Had A Sneeze; nn-She Has a Naughty Play Husband; nn-Wait Till Fido Comes Home	21.00	74.00	150.00

DOINGS OF THE DOO DADS, THE (N)
Detroit News (Universal Feat. & Specialty Co.): 1922 (50¢, 7-3/4x7-3/4", 34 pgs, B&W, red & white-c, square binding)

	GD2.0	FN6.0	VF8.0
nn-Reprints 1921 newspaper strip "Text & Pictures" given away as prize in the Detroit News Doo Dads contest; by Arch Dale	43.00	173.00	360.00

DOING THE GRAND CANYON
Fred Harvey: 1922 (7 x 4-3/4", 24 pgs, B&W, paper cover)

'Erbie And 'Is Playmates By F. Opper
1932 © Democratic National Committee

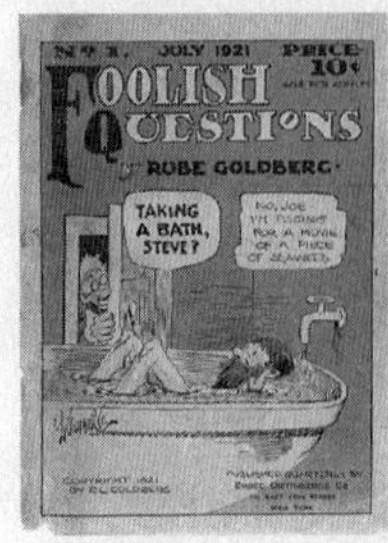

Foolish Questions by Rube Goldberg
1921 © EmBee Distributing Co., NY.

The Latest Adventures of Foxy Grandpa 1905
© Bunny Publ.

GD2.0 FN6.0 VF8.0

nn - John McCutcheon 20.00 40.00 100.00
NOTE: *Text & 8 cartoons about visiting the Grand Canyon.*

DOINGS OF THE VAN-LOONS (N) (from same company as Mutt & Jeff #1-#5)
Ball Publications: 1912 (5-3/4X15-1/2", 68pg., B&W, hard-c)
nn - By Fred I. Leipziger (scarce) 72.00 252.00 600.00

DOLLY DIMPLES & BOBBY BOUNCE (See Dimples)
Cupples & Leon Co.: 1933 (8-3/4x7", color hardcover, B&W)
nn - Grace Drayton-a 24.00 96.00 165.00

DOO DADS, THE (Sleepy Sam and Tiny the Elephant)
Universal Feature * Specialty Co: 1922 (5-1/4x14", 36 pgs.,B&W, R&W-c,square binding)
nn - By Arch Dale 35.00 125.00 250.00

DRAWINGS BY HOWARD CHANDLER CHRISTIE (S, M)
Moffat, Yard & Company, NY: 1905 (11-7/8x16-1/2", 68 pgs, hard-c, B&W)
nn - Howard C. Christie 30.00 60.00 120.00
NOTE: *Reprints1898-1905 from Haprer & Bros, Ch. Scribners Sons, Leslie's, MacMillians, McLurg, Russell.*

DREAMS OF THE RAREBIT FIEND (N)
Frederick A. Stokes Co.:1905 (10-1/4x7-1/2", 68 pgs, thin paper cover all B&W) newspaper reprints from the New York Evening Telegram printed on yellow paper
nn-By Winsor "Silas" McCay (Very Rare) (Five copies known to exist)
Estimated value.... 750.00 2500.00 –
NOTE: *A G/VG copy sold for $2,045 in May 2004. This item usually turns up with fragile paper.*

DRISCOLL'S BOOK OF PIRATES (O)
David McKay Publ.: 1934 (9x7", 124 pgs, B&W, hardcover)
nn - By Montford Amory ("Pieces of Eight strip-r) 21.00 64.00 150.00

DUCKY DADDLES
Frederick A. Stokes Co: July 1911 (15x10")
nn - By Grace Weiderseim (later Drayton) strip-r 50.00 175.00 300.00

DUMBUNNIES AND THEIR FRIENDS IN RABBITBORO, THE (O)
Albertine Randall Wheelan: 1931 (8-3/4x7-1/8", 82 pgs, color hardcover, B&W)
nn - By Albertine Randall Wheelan (self-pub) 34.00 103.00 240.00

EDISON - INSPIRATION TO YOUTH (N)(Also see Life of Thomas---)
Thomas A. Edison, Incorporated: 1939 (9-1/2 x 6-1/2, paper cover, B&W)
nn - Photo-c 46.00 138.00 275.00
NOTE: *Reprints strip material found in the 1928 Life of Thomas A. Edison in Word and Picture.*

'ERBIE AND 'IS PLAYMATES
Democratic National Committee: 1932 (8x9-1/2, 16 pgs, B&W)
nn - By Frederick Opper (Rare) 100.00 200.00 400.00
NOTE: *Anti-Hoover/Pro-Roosevelt political comics.*

EXPANSION BEING BART'S BEST CARTOONS FOR 1899
Minneapolis Journal: 1900 (10-1/4x8-1/4", 124 pgs, paperback, B&W)
v2#1 - By Charles L. Bartholomew 24.00 84.00 145.00

FAMOUS COMICS (N)
King Features Synd. (Whitman Pub. Co.): 1934 (100 pgs., daily newspaper-r) (3-1/2x8-1/2"; paper cover)(came in an illustrated box)
684 (#1) - Little Jimmy, Katz Kids & Barney Google 34.00 103.00 240.00
684 (#2) - Polly, Little Jimmy, Katzenjammer Kids 34.00 103.00 240.00
684 (#3) - Little Annie Rooney, Polly and Her Pals, Katzenjammer Kids
34.00 103.00 240.00
Box price... 75.00 150.00 375.00

FAMOUS COMICS CARTOON BOOKS (N)
Whitman Publishing Co.: 1934 (8x7-1/4", 72 pgs, B&W hard-c, daily strip-r)
1200-The Captain & the Kids; Dirks reprints credited to Bernard Dibble 29.00 86.00 200.00
1202-Captain Easy & Wash Tubbs by Roy Crane; 2 slightly different versions of cover exist 34.00 103.00 240.00
1203-Ella Cinders By Conselman & Plumb 28.00 84.00 195.00
1204-Freckles & His Friends 25.00 75.00 175.00
NOTE: *Called Famous Funnies Cartoon Books inside back area sales advertisement.*

FANTASIES IN HA-HA (M)
Meyer Bros & Co.: 1900 (14 x 11-7/8", 64 pgs, color cover hardcover, B&W)
nn - By Hy Mayer 50.00 150.00 300.00

FELIX (N)
Henry Altemus Company: 1931 (6-1/2"x8-1/4", 52 pgs., color, hard-c w/dust jacket)
1-3-Sunday strip reprints of Felix the Cat by Otto Messmer. Book No. 2 r/1931 Sunday panels mostly two to a page in a continuity format oddly arranged so each tier of panels reads across two pages, then drops to the next tier. (Books 1 & 3 have not been documented.)(Rare)
Each 104.00 416.00 900.00
With dust jacket 250.00 750.00 1200.00

FELIX THE CAT BOOK (N)
McLoughlin Bros.: 1927 (8"x15-3/4", 52 pgs, half in color-half in B&W)
nn - Reprints 23 Sunday strips by Otto Messmer from 1926 & 1927, every other one in color, two pages per strip. (Rare) 200.00 800.00 1550.00
260-Reissued (1931), reformatted to 9-1/2"x10-1/4" (same color plates, but one strip per every three pages), retitled ("Book" dropped from title) and abridged (only eight strips repeated from first issue, 28 pgs.).(Rare) 79.00 316.00 600.00

F. FOX'S FUNNY FOLK (see Toonerville Trolley; Cartoons by Fontaine Fox) (C)
George H. Doran Company: 1917 (10-1/4x8-1/4", 228 pgs, red, B&W cover, B&W interior, hardcover; dust jacket?)
nn - By Fontaine Fox (Toonerville Trolley strip-r) 150.00 450.00 750.00

52 CAREY CARTOONS (O,S)
Carey Cartoon Service, NY: 1915 (25 cents, 6-3/4" x 10-1/2", 118 pgs, printed on one side, color cardboard-c, B&W)
nn - (1915) War – – –
NOTE: *The Carey Cartoon Service supplied a weekly, hand-colored single panel cartoon broadsheet, on current news events, starting in 1906 or 1907, for window display in Carey Fountain Pen chain stores. These broadsheets were 22-1/2" x 33" in size. Starting circa 1915, Carey Fountain Pens began offering subscriptions for the broadsheets to other merchants, for window display in their stores as well. This collects, in B&W, the cartoons for 1915. An "Edition Deluxe" was also advertised, with all cartoons hand colored. It is currently unknown whether a reprint collection was only issued in 1915, or if other editions exist.*

52 LETTERS TO SALESMEN
Steven-Davis Company: 1927 (???)
nn - (Rare) 23.00 92.00 140.00
NOTE: *52 motivational letters to salesmen, with page of comics for each week, bound into embossed leather binder.*

FOLKS IN FUNNYVILLE (S)
R.H. Russell: 1900 (12"x9-1/4", 48 pgs.)(cardboard-c)
nn - By Frederick Opper 271.00 950.00 –
NOTE: *Reprinted from Hearst's NY Journal American Humorist supplements.*

FOOLISH QUESTIONS (S)
Small, Maynard & Co.: 1909 (6-7/8 x 5-1/2", 174 pgs, hardcover, B&W)
nn - By Rube Goldberg (first Goldberg item) 100.00 300.00 500.00
NOTE: *Comic strip began Oct 23, 1908 running thru 1941. Also drawn by George Frink in 1909.*

FOOLISH QUESTIONS THAT ARE ASKED BY ALL
Levi Strauss & Co./Small, Maynard & Co.: 1909 (5-1/2x5-3/4", 24 pgs, paper-c, B&W)
nn- (Rare) by Rube Goldberg 65.00 175.00 350.00

FOOLISH QUESTIONS (Boxed card set) (S)
Wallie Dorr Co., N.Y.: 1919 (5-1/4x3-3/4")(box & card backs are red)
nn - Boxed set w/52 B&W comics on cards; each a single panel gag complete set w/box
75.00 263.00 450.00
NOTE: *There are two diff sets put out simultaneously with the first set, by the same company. One set continues/picks up the numbering of the cards from the other set.*

FOOLISH QUESTIONS (S)
EmBee Distributing Co.: 1921 (10¢, 4x5 1/2; 52 pgs, 3 color covers; B&W)
1-By Rube Goldberg 46.00 160.00 300.00

FOXY GRANDPA
Foxy Grandpa Company, 33 Wall St, NY : 1900 (9x15", 84 pgs, full color, cardboard-c)
nn - By Carl Schultze (By Permission of New York Herald) 271.00 1200.00 –
NOTE: *This seminal comic strip began Jan 7, 1900 and was collected later that same year.*

FOXY GRANDPA (Also see The Funnies, 1st series) (N)
N. Y. Herald/Frederick A. Stokes Co./M. A. Donahue & Co./Bunny Publ. (L. R. Hammersly Co.): 1901 - 1916 (Strip-r in color, hard-c)
1901- 9x15" in color-N. Y. Herald 313.00 1100.00 –
1902- "Latest Larks of...", 32 pgs., 9-1/2x15-1/2" 164.00 575.00 –
1902- "The Many Advs. of...", 9x12", 148 pgs., Hammersly Co.
179.00 625.00 –
1903- "Latest Advs.", 9x15", 24 pgs., Hammersly Co. 164.00 575.00 –
1903- "...'s New Advs.", 11x15", 66 pgs., Stokes 164.00 575.00 –
1904- "Up to Date", 10x15", 66 pgs., Stokes 146.00 510.00 950.00
1904- "The Many Adventures of...", 9x15, 144pgs, Donohue 146.00 510.00 950.00
1905- "& Flip-Flaps", 9-1/2x15-1/2", 52 pgs. 146.00 510.00 950.00
1905- "The Latest Advs. of...", 9x15", 28, 52, & 68 pgs, M.A. Donohue Co.; re-issue of 1902 issue 104.00 365.00 700.00
1905- "Latest Larks of...", 9-1/2x15-1/2", 52 pgs., Donahue; re-issue of 1902 issue with more pages added 104.00 365.00 700.00
1905- "Latest Larks of...", 9-1/2x15-1/2", 24 pgs. edition, Donahue; re-issue of 1902 issue 104.00 365.00 700.00
1905- "Merry Pranks of...", 9-1/2x15-1/2", 28, 52 & 62 pgs., Donahue
104.00 365.00 700.00
1905-"...Surprises",10x15", color, 64 pg,Stokes, 60¢ 104.00 365.00 700.00
1906- "Frolics", 10x15", 30 pgs., Stokes 104.00 365.00 700.00
1907?-"...& His Boys",10x15", 64 color pgs, Stokes 104.00 365.00 700.00
1907- "Triumphs", 10x15", 62 pgs, Stokes 104.00 365.00 700.00
1908-"...Mother Goose", Stokes 104.00 365.00 700.00

Giggles
© Pratt Food Co.

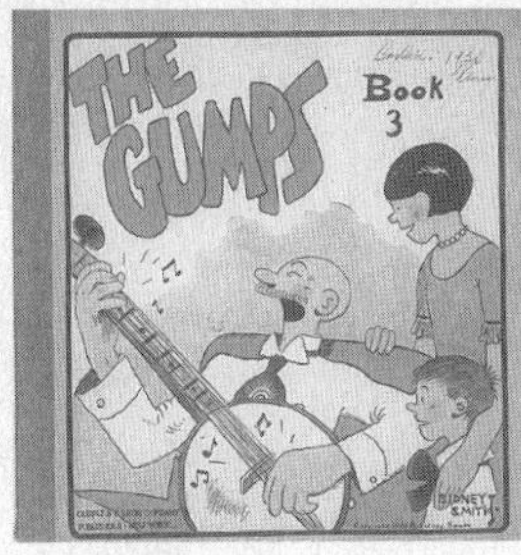

The Gumps #3 by Sidney Smith
1926 © Cupples & Leon

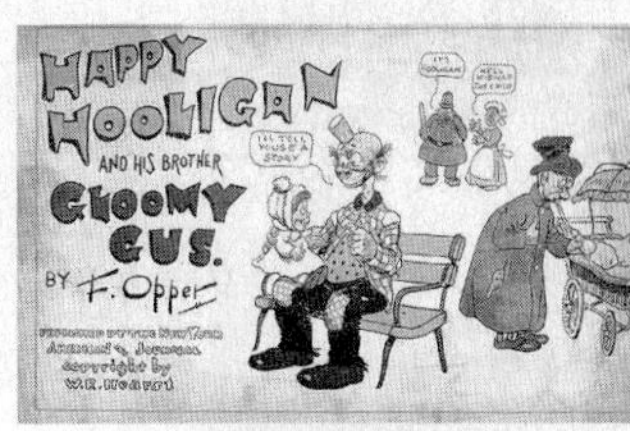

Happy Hooligan Book 1 1902
© Frederick A. Stokes

GD2.0 FN6.0 VF8.0

1909- "...& Little Brother", 10x15, 58 pgs, Stokes 104.00 365.00 700.00
1911- "Latest Tricks", r-1910,1911 Sundays-Stokes Co. 104.00 365.00 700.00
1914-(9-1/2x15-1/2", 24 pgs.)-6 color cartoons/page, Bunny Publ. Co. 88.00 306.00 575.00
1915 - ...Always Jolly (10x16, Stokes) 88.00 306.00 575.00
1916- "Merry Book", (10x15", 64 pgs, Stokes) 88.00 306.00 575.00
1917-"...Adventures (5 1/2 x 6 1/2, 26 pgs, Stokes) 57.00 200.00 400.00
1917-"...Frolics (5 1/2 x 6 1/2, 26 pgs, Stokes) 57.00 200.00 400.00
1917-"...Triumphs (5 1/2 x 6 1/2, 26 pgs, Stokes) 57.00 200.00 400.00

FOXY GRANDPA, FUNNY TRICKS OF (The Stump Books)
M.A. Donahue Co, Chicago: approx 1903 (1-7/8x6-3/8", 44 pgs, blue hardcover)
nn - By Carl Schultze 54.00 189.00 325.00
NOTE: *One of a series of ten "stump" books; the only comics one.*

FOXY GRANDPA'S MOTHER GOOSE (I)
Stokes: October 1903 (10-11/16x8-1/2", 86 pgs, hard-c)
nn - By Carl Schultze (not comics - illustrated book) 54.00 189.00 325.00

FOXY GRANDPA SPARKLETS SERIES (N)
M. A. Donahue & Co.: 1908 (7-3/4x6-1/2"; 24 pgs., color)
"... Rides the Goat", "...& His Boys", "...Playing Ball", "...Fun on the Farm", "...Fancy Shooting", "...Show His Boys Up-To-Date Sports", "...Plays Santa Claus"
each.... 88.00 306.00 525.00
900- "Playing Ball"; Bunny illos; 8 pgs., linen like pgs., no date 73.00 254.00 435.00

FOXY GRANDPA VISITS RICHMOND (O,P)
Dietz Printing Co., Richmond, VA / Hotel Rueger: nd (c1920's) (5-7/8" x 4-1/2", 16 pgs, paper-c, B&W)
nn - (Scarce) By Bunny 25.00 88.00 175.00
NOTE: *Promotional comic given away to its guests by the Hotel Rueger, about Foxy Grandpa visiting and enjoying the Hotel. Originally came in an envelope, with the words "Foxy Grandpa Visits Richmond -- and Rueger's" printed on it.*

FOXY GRANDPA VISITS WASHINGTON, D.C. (P)
Dietz Printing Co., Richmond, VA / Hamilton Hotel: nd (c1920's) (5-7/8" x 4-1/2", 16 pgs, paper-c, B&W)
nn - (Scarce) By Bunny 25.00 88.00 150.00
NOTE: *Mostly reprints "... Visits Richmond", changing all references to Hotel Rueger, to Hamilton Hotel instead. Also, changes depictions of a waiter and a cook from black to white, plus incompletely erases the cover art on a book Foxy Grandpa falls asleep with (the latter is how we know that the Richmond version was first).*

FRAGMENTS FROM FRANCE (S)
G. P. Putnam & Sons: 1917 (9x6-1/4", 168 pgs, hardcover, $1.75)
nn - By Bruce Bairnsfather 25.00 88.00 150.00
NOTE: *WW1 trench warfare cartoons; color dust jacket.*

FUNNIES, THE (H) (See Clancy the Cop, Deadwood Gulch, Bug Movies)
Dell Publishing Co.: 1929 - No. 36, 10/18/30 (10¢; 5¢ No. 22 on) (16 pgs.)
Full tabloid size in color; not reprints; published every Saturday
1-My Big Brudder, Jonathan, Jazzbo & Jim, Foxy Grandpa, Sniffy, Jimmy Jams & other strips begin; first four-color comic newsstand publication; also contains magic, puzzles & stories 200.00 700.00 1500.00
2-21 (1930, 10¢) 150.00 300.00 600.00
22(nn-7/12/30-5¢) 150.00 300.00 600.00
23(nn-7/19/30-5¢), 24(nn-7/26/30-5¢), 25(nn-8/2/30), 26(nn-8/9/30), 27(nn-8/16/30), 28(nn-8/23/30), 29(nn-8/30/30), 30(nn-9/6/30), 31(nn-9/13/30), 32(nn-9/20/30), 33(nn-9/27/30), 34(nn-10/4/30), 35(nn-10/11/30), 36(nn, no date-10/18/30)
each.... 150.00 300.00 600.00

GASOLINE ALLEY (Also see Popular Comics & Super Comics) (N)
Reilly & Lee Publishers: 1929 (8-3/4x7", B&W daily strip-r, hard-c)
nn - By King (96 pgs.) 125.00 300.00 600.00
with scarce Dust Wrapper 250.00 500.00 900.00
NOTE: *Of all the Frank King reprint books, this is the only one to reprint actual complete newspaper strips - all others are illustrated prose text stories.*

GIBSON'S PUBLISHED DRAWINGS, MR. (M,S) (see Victorian index for earlier issues)
R.H. Russell, New York: No.1 1894 - No. 9 1904 (11x17-3/4", hard-c, B&W)
nn (No.6; 1901) A Widow and her Friends (90 pgs.) 30.00 60.00 120.00
nn (No.7; 1902) The Social Ladder (88 pgs.) 30.00 60.00 120.00
8 - 1903 The Weaker Sex (88 pgs.) 30.00 60.00 120.00
9 - 1904 Everyday People (88 pgs.) 30.00 60.00 120.00
NOTE: *By Charles Dana Gibson cartoons, reprinted from magazines, primarily LIFE. The Education of Mr. Pipp tells a story. Series continues how long after 1904?*

GIGGLES
Pratt Food Co., Philadelphia, PA: 1908-09? (12x9", 8 pgs, color, 5 cents-c)
1-8: By Walt McDougall (#8 dated March 1909) 40.00 175.00 -
NOTE: *Appears to be monthly; almost tabloid size; yearly subscriptions was 25 cents.*

GOD'S MAN (H)
Jonathan Cape and Harrison Smith Inc.: 1929 (8-1/4x6", 298 pgs, B&W hardcover w/dust jacket) (original graphic novel in wood cuts)
nn - By Lynd Ward 43.00 171.00 300.00

GOLD DUST TWINS
N. K. Fairbank Co.: 1904 (4-5/8x6-3/4", 18 pgs, color and B&W)
nn - By E. W. Kemble (Rare) 30.00 60.00 130.00
NOTE: *Promo comic for Gold DustWashing Powder; includes page of watercolor paints.*

GOLF
Volland Co.: 1916 (9x12-3/4", 132 pgs, hard-c, B&W)
nn - By Clair Briggs 100.00 200.00 400.00

GUMPS, THE (N)
Landfield-Kupfer: No. 1, 1918 - No. 6, 1921; (B&W Daily strip-r)
Book No. 1(1918)(scarce)-cardboard-c, 5-1/4x13-1/3", 64 pgs., daily strip-r by Sidney Smith 75.00 250.00 500.00
Book No.2(1918)-(scarce); 5-1/4x13-1/3"; paper cover; 36 pgs. daily strip reprints by Sidney Smith 75.00 250.00 500.00
Book No. 3 100.00 350.00 700.00
Book No. 4 (1918) 5-3/8x13-7/8", 20 pgs. Color card-c 100.00 350.00 700.00
Book No. 5 10-1/4x13-1/2", 20 pgs. Color paper-c 100.00 350.00 700.00
Book No. 6 (Rare, 20 pgs, 8x13-3/8, strip-r 1920-21) 121.00 423.00 725.00

GUMPS, ANDY AND MIN, THE (N)
Landfield-Kupfer Printing Co., Chicago/Morrison Hotel: nd (1920s) (Giveaway, 5-1/2"x14", 20 pgs., B&W, soft-c)
nn - Strip-r by Sidney Smith; art & logo embossed on cover w/hotel restaurant menu on back-c or a hotel promo ad; 4 different contents of issues known 50.00 175.00 300.00

GUMPS, THE (N)
Cupples & Leon: 1924-1930 (10x10, 52 pgs, B&W)
1 - By Sidney Smith 61.00 244.00 450.00
2-7 39.00 154.00 300.00

THE GUMPS (P)
Cupples & Leon Company: 1924 (9 x 7-1/2", 28 pgs, paper cover)
nn (1924) 50.00 175.00 300.00
NOTE: *Promotional comic for Sunshine Andy Gump Biscuits. Daily strip-r from 1922-24.*

GUMP'S CARTOON BOOK, THE (N)
The National Arts Company: 1931 (13-7/8x10", 36 pgs, color covers, B&W)
nn - By Sidney Smith 57.00 228.00 450.00

GUMPS PAINTING BOOK, THE (N)
The National Arts Company: 1931 (11 x 15 1/4", 20 pgs, half in full color)
nn - By Sidney Smith 57.00 228.00 450.00

HALT FRIENDS! (see also **HELLO BUDDY**)
???: 1918? (4-3/8x5-3/4", 36 pgs, color-c, B&W, no cover price listed)
nn - Unknown 10.00 30.00 70.00
NOTE: *Says on front cover: "Comics of War Facts of Service Sold on its merits by Unemployed or Disabled Ex-Service Men. Credentials Shown On Request. Price - Pay What You Please." These are very common; contents vary widely.*

HAMBONE'S MEDITATIONS
Jahl & Co.: no date 1920 (6-1/8 x 7-1/2, 108 pgs, paper cover, B&W)
nn - By J. P. Alley 33.00 132.00 250.00
NOTE: *Reprint of racist single panel newspaper series, 2 cartoons per page.*

HAN OLA OG PER (N)
Anundsen Publishing Co, Decorah, Iowa: 1927 (10-3/8 x 15-3/4", 54 pgs, paper-c, B&W)
nn - American origin Norwegian language strips-r 33.00 131.00 230.00
NOTE: *1940s and modern reprints exist.*

HANS UND FRITZ (N)
The Saalfield Publishing Co.: 1917, 1927-29 (10x13-1/2", 28 pgs., B&W)
nn - By R. Dirks (1917, r-1916 strips) 96.00 335.00 600.00
nn - By R. Dirks (1923 edition- reprint of 1917 edition) 58.00 204.00 350.00
nn - By R. Dirks (1926 edition- reprint of 1917 edition) 58.00 204.00 350.00
The Funny Larks Of... By R. Dirks (©1917 outside cover; ©1916 inside indicia) 96.00 335.00 600.00
The Funny Larks Of... (1927) reprints 1917 edition of 1916 strips Halloween-c 58.00 204.00 350.00
The Funny Larks Of... 2 (1929) 58.00 204.00 350.00
193 - By R. Dirks; contains 1916 Sunday strip reprints of Katzenjammer Kids & Hawkshaw the Detective - reprint of 1917 nn edition (1929) this edition is not rare 58.00 204.00 350.00

HAPPY DAYS (S)
Coward-McCann Inc.: 1929 (12-1/2x9-5/8", 110 pgs, hardcover B&W)
nn - By Alban Butler (WW 1 cartoons) 20.00 60.00 120.00

HAPPY HOOLIGAN (See Alphonse...) (N)
Hearst's New York American & Journal: 1902,1903
Book 1-(1902)-"And His Brother Gloomy Gus", By Fred Opper; has 1901-02-r;

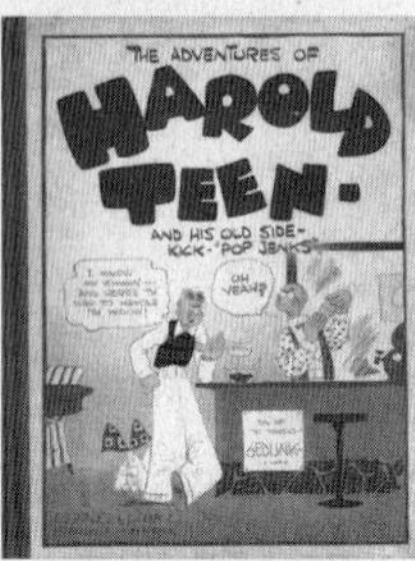

Harold Teen #2 by Carl Ed
1931 © Cupples & Leon

JIMMY
SWINNERTON
PUBLISHED by THE NEW YORK AMERICAN AND JOURNAL

Jimmy By Jimmy Swinnerton
1905 © Frederick A. Stokes

Joys & Glooms By T.E. Powers
1912 © Reilly & Britton Co.

	GD2.0	FN6.0	VF8.0
(yellow & black)(86 pgs.)(10x15-1/4")	600.00	1800.00	3000.00
New Edition, 1903 -10x15" 82 pgs. in color	350.00	1400.00	–

NOTE: *Strip ran March 26, 1900-Aug 14, 1932 and is widely recognized as setting the format standard for all newspaper comic strips which came after it. Opper (1857-1937) was going blind towards the end.*

HAPPY HOOLIGAN (N) (By Fredrick Opper)
Frederick A. Stokes Co.: 1906-08 (10-1/4x15-3/4", cardboard color-c)

	GD2.0	FN6.0	VF8.0
1906 - :Travels of...), 68 pgs,10-1/4x15-3/4", 1905-r	300.00	900.00	–
1907 - "--Home Again", 68 pgs., 10x15-3/4", 60¢; full color-c	300.00	900.00	–
1908 - "Handy--", 68 pgs, color	300.00	900.00	–

HAPPY HOOLIGAN, THE STORY OF (G)
McLoughlin Bros.: No. 281, 1932 (12x9-1/2", 20 pgs., soft-c)

281-Three-color text, pictures on heavy paper — 57.00 | 228.00 | 400.00
NOTE: *An homage to Opper's creation on its 30th Anniversary in 1932.*

HAROLD HARDHIKE'S REJUVENATION
O'Sullivan Rubber: 1917 (6-1/4x3-1/2, 16 pgs, B&W)

nn — 25.00 | 100.00 | 175.00
NOTE: *Comic book to promote rubber shoe heels.*

HAROLD TEEN (N)
Cupples & Leon Co.: 1929 (9-7/8x9-7/8", 52 pgs, cardboard covers)

	GD2.0	FN6.0	VF8.0
1 - By Carl Ed	50.00	200.00	500.00
nn - (1931, 8-11/16x6-7/8", 96 pgs, hardcover w/dj)	41.00	164.00	290.00

NOTE: *Title 2nd book:* ***HAROLD TEEN AND HIS OLD SIDE-KICK- POP JENKINS,*** *(Adv. of...). Precursor for Archie Andrews & crew; strip began May 4, 1919 running into 1959.*

HAROLD TEEN PAINT AND COLOR BOOK (N)
McLoughlin Bros Inc.: 1932 (13x9-3/4, 28 pgs, B&W and color)

#2054 — 25.00 | 100.00 | 175.00

HAWKSHAW THE DETECTIVE (See Advs. of..., Hans Und Fritz & Okay) (N)
The Saalfield Publishing Co.: 1917 (10-1/2x13-1/2", 24 pgs., B&W)

	GD2.0	FN6.0	VF8.0
nn - By Gus Mager (Sunday strip-r)	54.00	190.00	350.00
nn - By Gus Mayer (1923 reprint of 1917 edition)	25.00	100.00	175.00
nn - By Gus Mager (1926 reprint of 1917 edition)	25.00	100.00	175.00

NOTE: *Runs Feb 23, 1913-Sept 4, 1922, starts again from Dec 13, 1931-Feb 11, 1952; Sherlock Holmes spoof.*

HEALTH IN PICTURES
American Public Health Association, NYC: 1930 (6-1/2" x 5-3/16", 76 pgs, green & black paper-c, B&W interior)

nn - By various — 15.00 | 51.00 | 90.00
NOTE: *Collection of strips and cartoons put out by the Public Health Association, on topics ranging from boating and food safety, to small pox and typhoid prevention.*

HE DONE HER WRONG (O) (see also BANANA OIL)
Doubleday, Doran & Company: 1930 (8-1/4x 7-1/4", 276pgs, hard-c with dust jacket, B&W interiors)

nn - By Milt Gross — 75.00 | 225.00 | 400.00
NOTE: *A seminal original-material wordless graphic novel, not reprints. Several modern reprints.*

HELLO BUDDY (see also **HALT FRIENDS**)
???: 1919? (4-3/8x5-3/4", 36 pgs, color-c, B&W, 15¢)

nn - Unknown — 10.00 | 30.00 | 70.00
NOTE: *Says on front cover: "Comics of War Facts of Service Sold on its merits by Unemployed or Disabled Ex-Service Men." These are very common; contents vary widely.*

HENRY (N)
David McKay Co.: 1935 (25¢, soft-c)

Book 1 - By Carl Anderson — 57.00 | 200.00 | 400.00
NOTE: *Strip began March 19 1932; this book ties with Popeye (David McKay) and Little Annie Rooney (David McKay) as the last of the 10x10" Platinum Age comic books.*

HENRY (M)
Greenberg Publishers Inc.: 1935 (11-1/4x 8-5/8", 72 pgs, red & blue color hard-c, dust jacket, B&W interiors) (strip-r from Saturday Evening Post)

nn - By Carl Anderson — 57.00 | 200.00 | 400.00

HIGH KICKING KELLYS, THE (M)
Vaudeville News Corporation, NY: 1926 (5x11", B&W, two color soft-c)

nn - By Jack A. Ward (scarce) — 40.00 | 160.00 | 280.00

HIGHLIGHTS OF HISTORY (N)
World Syndicate Publishing Co.: 1933-34 (4-1/2x4", 288 pgs)

nn - 5 different unnumbered issues; daily strip-r — 10.00 | 40.00 | 70.00
NOTE: *Titles include Buffalo Bill, Daniel Boone, Kit Carson, Pioneers of the Old West, Winning of the Old Northwest. There are line drawing color covers and embossed hardcover versions. It is unknown which came out first.*

HOMER HOLCOMB AND MAY (N)
no publisher listed: 1920s (4 x 9-1/2", 40 pgs, paper cover, B&W)

nn - By Doc Bird Finch (strip-r) — 10.00 | 40.00 | 70.00

HOME, SWEET HOME (N)
M.S. Publishing Co.: 1925 (10-1/4x10")

nn - By Tuthill — 33.00 | 134.00 | 235.00

HOW THEY DRAW PROHIBITION (S)
Association Against Prohibition: 1930 (10x9", 100 pgs.)

nn - Single panel and multi-panel comics (rare) — 71.00 | 285.00 | 500.00
NOTE: *Contains art by J.N. "Ding" Darling, James Flagg, Rollin Kirby, Winsor McCay, T.E. Powers, H.T. Webster, others. Also comes with a loose sheet listing all the newspapers where the cartoons originally appeared.*

HOW TO BE A CARTOONIST (H)
Saalfield Pub. Co: 1936 (10-3/8x12-1/2", 16 pgs, color-c, B&W)

nn - By Chas. H. Kuhn — 10.00 | 40.00 | 70.00

HOW TO DRAW: A PRACTICAL BOOK OF INSTRUCTION (H)
Harper & Brothers: 1904 (9-1/4x12-3/8", 128 pgs, hardcover, B&W)

nn - Edited By Leon Barritt — 57.00 | 228.00 | 400.00
NOTE: *Strips reprinted include: "Buster Brown" by Outcault, "Foxy Grandpa" by Bunny, "Happy Hooligan" by Opper, "Katzenjammer Kids" by Dirks, "Lady Bountiful" by Gene Carr, "Mr. Jack" by Swinnerton, "Panhandle Pete" by George McManus, "Mr E.Z. Mark" by F.M. Howarth others; non-character strips by Hy Mayer, Winsor McCay, T.E. Powers, others; single panel cartoons by Davenport, Frost, McDougall, Nast, W.A. Rogers, Sullivant, others.*

HOW TO DRAW CARTOONS (H)
Garden City Publishing Co.: 1926, 1937 (10 1/4 x 7 1/2, 150 pgs)

	GD2.0	FN6.0	VF8.0
1926 first edition By Clare Briggs	25.00	75.00	150.00
1937 2nd edition By Clare Briggs	20.00	60.00	120.00

NOTE: *Seminal "how to" break into the comics syndicates with art by Briggs, Fisher, Goldberg, King, Webster, Opper, Tad, Hershfield, McCay, Ding, others. Came with Dust Jacket -add 50%.*

HOW TO DRAW FUNNY PICTURES: A Complete Course in Cartooning (H)
Frederick J. Drake & Co., Chicago: 1936 (10-3/8x6-7/8", 168 pgs, hardcover, B&W)

nn - By E.C. Matthews (200 illus by Eugene Zimmerman) — 20.00 | 60.00 | 120.00

HY MAYER (M)
Puck Publishing: 1915 (13-1/2 x 20-3/4", 52 pgs, hardcover cover, color & B&W interiors)

nn - By Hy Mayer(strip reprints from Puck) — 40.00 | 140.00 | 300.00

HYSTERICAL HISTORY OF THE CIVILIAN CONSERVATION CORPS
Peerless Engraving: 1934 (10-3/4x7-1/2", 104 pgs, soft-c, B&W)

nn - By various — 20.00 | 60.00 | 120.00
NOTE: *Comics about CCC life, includes two color insert postcards in back.*

INDOOR SPORTS (N,S)
National Specials Co., New York: nd circa 1912 (25 cents, 6 x 9", 68 pgs, B&W)

nn - Tad — 35.00 | 125.00 | 225.00
NOTE: *Cartoons reprinted from Hearst papers.*

IT HAPPENS IN THE BEST FAMILIES (N)
Powers Photo Engraving Co.: 1920 (52 pgs.)(9-1/2x10-3/4")

	GD2.0	FN6.0	VF8.0
nn - By Briggs; B&W Sunday strips-r	29.00	114.00	200.00
Special Railroad Edition (30¢)-r/strips from 1914-1920	26.00	103.00	180.00

JIMMIE DUGAN AND THE REG'LAR FELLERS (N)
Cupples & Leon: 1921, 46 pgs. (11"x16")

nn - By Gene Byrne — 71.00 | 284.00 | 500.00
NOTE: *Ties with EmBee's Mutt & Jeff and Trouble of Bringing Up Father as the last of this size.*

JIMMY (N) (see Little Jimmy Picture & Story Book)
N. Y. American & Journal: 1905 (10x15", 84 pgs., color)

nn - By Jimmy Swinnerton (scarce) — 300.00 | 800.00 | 1500.00
NOTE: *James Swinnerton was one of the original first pioneers of the American newspaper comic strip.*

JIMMY AND HIS SCRAPES (N)
Frederick A. Stokes: 1906, (10-1/4x15-1/4", 66 pgs, cardboard-c, color)

nn - By Jimmy Swinnerton (scarce) — 300.00 | 800.00 | 1500.00

JOE PALOOKA (N)
Cupples & Leon Co.: 1933 (9-13/16x10", 52 pgs., B&W daily strip-r)

nn - By Ham Fisher (scarce) — 114.00 | 456.00 | 800.00

JOHN, JONATHAN AND MR. OPPER BY F. OPPER (S,I,N)
Grant, Richards, 48 Leicester Square, W.C.: 1903 (9-5/8x8-3/8", 108 pgs, hard-c B&W)

nn - Opper (Scarce) — 50.00 | 200.00 | 380.00
NOTE: *British precursor-type companion to* WIllie And His Poppa *reprints from Hearst's* NY American & Journal *Opper cartoons interfacing* Uncle Sam *precursor* Brother Jonathan, John Bull. *Uses name* Happy Hooligan *in one cartoon, has* John Bull *smoking opium in another.*

JOLLY POLLY'S BOOK OF ENGLISH AND ETIQUETTE (S)
Jos. J. Frisch: 1931 (60 cents, 8 x 5-1/8, 88 pgs, paper-c, B&W)

nn - By Jos. J. Frisch — 20.00 | 60.00 | 120.00
NOTE: *Reprint of single panel newspaper series, 4 per page, of English and etiquette lessons taught by a flapper.*

JOYS AND GLOOMS (N)
Reilly & Britton Co.: 1912 (11x8", 72 pgs, hard-c, B&W interior)

nn - By T. E. Powers (newspaper strip-r) — 39.00 | 156.00 | 325.00

JUDGE - yet to be indexed

The Cruise of the Katzenjammer Kids
© NY American & Journal

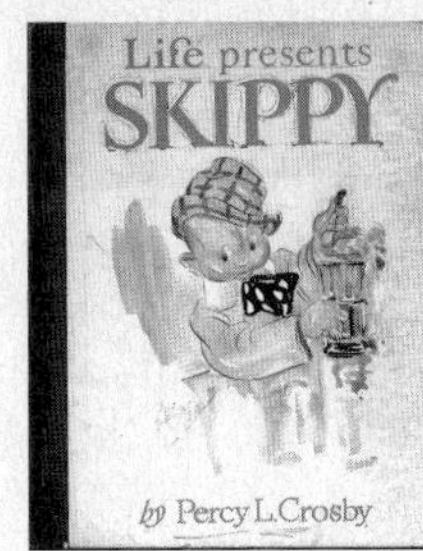

Life Presents Skippy by Percy L. Crosby
1924 © Life Publishing Company

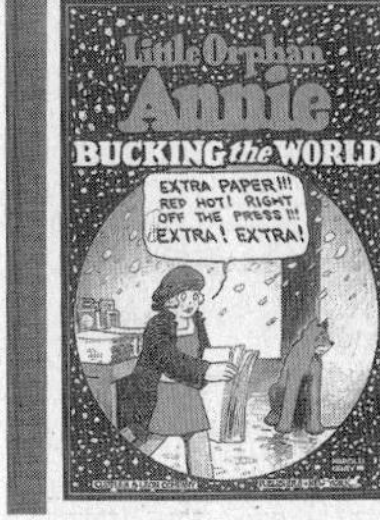

Little Orphan Annie by Harold Gray #2
1927 © Cupples & Leon

GD2.0 FN6.0 VF8.0

JUDGE'S LIBRARY - yet to be indexed

JUST KIDS COMICS FOR CRAYON COLORING
King Features. NYC: 1928 (11x8-1/2, 16 pgs, soft-c)

nn - By Ad Carter 33.00 100.00 200.00
NOTE: *Porous better grade paper; top pics printed in color; lower in b&w to color.*

JUST KIDS, THE STORY OF (I)
McLoughlin Bros.: 1932 (12x9-1/2", 20 pgs., paper-c)

283-Three-color text, pictures on heavy paper 39.00 156.00 275.00

KAPTIN KIDDO AND PUPPO (N)
Frederick A. Stokes Co.: 1910-1913 (11x16-1/2", 62 pgs)

1910-By Grace Wiederseim (later Drayton) 40.00 140.00 240.00
1910-Turr-ble Tales of... By Grace Wiederseim (Edward Stern & Co., 11x16-1/2", 64 pgs.) 40.00 140.00 240.00
1913- ...'Speriences By Grace Drayton 40.00 140.00 240.00
NOTE: *Strip ran approx. 1909-1912.*

KATZENJAMMER KIDS, THE (Also see Hans Und Fritz) (N)
New York American & Journal: 1902,1903 (10x15-1/4", 86 pgs., color)
(By Rudolph Dirks; strip first appeared in 1897) © W.R. Hearst
NOTE: *All KK books 1902-1905 all have the same exact title page with a 1902 copyright by W.R. Hearst; almost always look instead on the front cover.*

1902 (Rare) (red & black); has 1901-02 strips 1000.00 2400.00 -
1903- **A New Edition** (Rare), 86 pgs 750.00 2000.00 -
1904- 10x15", 84 pgs 250.00 900.00 -
1905?-The Cruise of the, 10x15", 60¢, in color 250.00 900.00 -
1905-A Series of Comic Pictures, 10x15", 84 pgs. in color, possible reprint of 1904 edition 250.00 800.00 -
1905-Tricks of... (10x15", 66 pgs, Stokes) 250.00 800.00 -
1906-Stokes (10x16", 32 pgs. in color) 186.00 800.00 -
1907- The Cruise of the, 10x15", 62 pgs 1905-r? 186.00 800.00 -
1910-The Komical...(10x15) 150.00 450.00 800.00
1921-Embee Dist. Co., 10x16", 20 pgs. in color 150.00 450.00 800.00

KATZENJAMMER KIDS MAGIC DRAWING AND COLORING BOOK (N)
Sam L Gabriel Sons And Company: 1931 (8 1/2 x 12", 36 pages, stiff-c

838-By Knerr 50.00 200.00 350.00

KEEPING UP WITH THE JONESES (N)
Cupples & Leon Co.: 1920 - No. 2, 1921 (9-1/4x9-1/4",52 pgs.,B&W daily strip-r)

1,2-By Pop Momand 39.00 154.00 270.00

KID KARTOONS (N,S)
The Century Co.: 1922 (232 pgs, printed 1 side, 9-3/4 x 7-3/4", hard-c, B&W)

nn - By Gene Carr (Metropolitan Movies strip-r) 60.00 240.00 -

KING OF THE ROYAL MOUNTED (Also See Dan Dunn) (N)
Whitman Publishing: 1937 (5 1/2 x 7 1/4", 68 pgs., color cardboard-c, B&W)

1010 36.00 144.00 250.00

LADY BOUNTIFUL (N)
Saalfield Publ. Co./Press Publ. Co.: 1917 (13-3/8x10", 36 pgs, color cardboard-c, B&W interiors)

nn - By Gene Carr; 2 panels per page 50.00 175.00 300.00
193S - 2nd printing (13-1/8x10",28 pgs color-c, B&W) 33.00 117.00 200.00

LAUGHS YOU MIGHT HAVE HAD From The Comic Pages of Six Week Day Issues of the Post-Dispatch (N)
St. Louis Post-Dispatch: 1921 (9 x 10 1/2", 28 pgs, B&W, red ink cover)

nn - Various comic strips 39.00 154.00 270.00

LIFE, DOGS FROM (M)
Doubleday, Page & Company: nn 1920 - No.2 1926 (130 pgs, 11-1/4 x 9", color painted-c, hard-c, B&W)

nn (No.1) 120.00 360.00 -
Second Litter 80.00 320.00 -
NOTE: *Reprints strips & cartoons featuring dogs, from Life Magazine. Editted by Thomas L. Masson. Highly sought by collectors of dog ephemera. Art in both books is mostly by Robert L. Dickey. Other art: Carl Anderson-1,2; Barbes-1; Chip Bellew-1; Lang Campbell-1,2; Percy Crosby-1,2; Edwina-2; Frueh-2; R.B. Fuller-1; Gibson-1,2; Don Herold-2; Gus Mager-2; Orr-1; J.R. Shaver-1,2; T.S. Sullivant-2; Russ Westover-1,2; Crawford Young-1.*

LIFE OF DAVY CROCKETT IN PICTURE AND STORY, THE
Cupples & Leon: 1935 (8-3/4x7", 64 pgs, B&W hard-c, dust jacket?)

nn - By C. Richard Schaare 29.00 116.00 200.00

LIFE OF THOMAS A. EDISON IN WORD AND PICTURE, THE (N)(Also see Edison...)
Thomas A. Edison Industries: 1928 (10x8", 56 pgs, paper cover, B&W)

nn - Photo-c 100.00 250.00 400.00
NOTE: *Reprints newspaper strip which ran August to November 1927.*

LIFE'S LITTLE JOKES (S)
M.S. Publ. Co.: No date (1924)(10-1/16x10", 52 pgs., B&W)

nn - By Rube Goldberg 64.00 257.00 525.00

LIFE, MINIATURE (see also LIFE (miniature reprint of of issue No. 1)) (M,P,S)
Life Publishing Co.: No. 1 - No. 4 1913, 1916, 1919 (5-3/4x4-5/8", 20 pgs, color paper-c

1- 3 (1913) 4 (1916) 5 (1919) (no known sales)
NOTE: *Giveaway item from Life, to promote subscriptions. All reprint material. No.2: James Montgomery Flagg-c; a-Chip Bellew, Gus Dirks, Gibson, F.M.Howarth, Art Young.*

LIFE'S PRINTS (was **LIFE'S PICTURE GALLERY** - See Victorian Age section) (M,S,P)
Life Publishing Company, New York: nd (c1907) (7x4-1/2", 132 pgs, paper cover, B&W)

nn - (nd; c1907) unillustrated black construction paper cover; reprints art from 1895-1907; art by J.M.Flagg, A.B.Frost, Gibson (Scarce) - - -
nn - (nd; c1908) b&w cardboard painted cover by Gibson, showing angel raising a champagne glass; reprints art from 1901-1908; art by J.M.Flagg, A.B.Frost, Gibson, Walt Kuhn, Art Young (Scarce) - - -
NOTE: *Catalog of prints reprinted from LIFE covers & centerspreads. There are likely more as yet unreported catalogs.*

LIFE, THE COMEDY OF LIFE
Life Publishing Company: 1907 (130 pgs, 11-3/4x9-1/4",embossed printed cloth covered board-c, B+W

nn - By various 20.00 80.00 120.00
NOTE: *Single cartoons and some sequential cartoons). Artists include Charles Dana Gibson, Harrison Cady, E.W. Kemble, James Montgomery Flagg.*

LILY OF THE ALLEY IN THE FUNNIES
Whitman Publishing Co.: No date (1927) (10-1/4x15-1/2"; 28 pgs., color)

W936 - By T. Burke (Rare) 57.00 228.00 400.00

LITTLE ANNIE ROONEY (N)
David McKay Co.: 1935 (25¢, soft-c)

Book 1 43.00 172.00 340.00
NOTE: *Ties with Henry & Popeye (David McKay) as the last of the 10x10" size Plat comic books.*

LITTLE ANNIE ROONEY WISHING BOOK (G) (See Happy Hooligan, Story of #281)
McLoughlin Bros.: 1932 (12x9-1/2", 16 pgs., soft-c, 3-color text, heavier paper)

282 - By Darrell McClure 41.00 144.00 250.00

LITTLE BIRD TOLD ME, A (E)
Life Publishing Co.: 1905? (96 pgs, hardbound)

nn - By Walt Kuhn (Life-r) 41.00 144.00 250.00

LITTLE FOLKS PAINTING BOOK (N)
The National Arts Company: 1931 (10-7/8 x 15-1/4", 20 pgs, half in full color)

nn - By "Tack" Knight (strip-r) 41.00 144.00 250.00

LITTLE JIMMY PICTURE AND STORY BOOK (I) (see Jimmy)
McLaughlin Bros., Inc.: 1932 (13-1/4 x 9-3/4", 20 pgs, cardstock color cover)

284 Text by Marion Kincaird; illus by Swinnerton 57.00 228.00 400.00

LITTLE JOHNNY & THE TEDDY BEARS (Judge-r) (M) (see Teddy Bear Books)
Reilly & Britton Co.: 1907 (10x14".; 68 pgs, green, red, black interior color)

nn - By J. R. Bray-a/Robert D. Towne-s 67.00 233.00 400.00

LITTLE JOURNEY TO THE HOME OF BRIGGS THE SKY-ROCKET, THE
Lockhart Art School: 1917 (10-3/4x7-7/8", 20 pgs, B&W) (I)

nn - About Clare Briggs (bio & lots of early art) 41.00 144.00 250.00

LITTLE KING, THE (see New Yorker Cartoon Albums for 1st appearance) (M)
Farrar & Reinhart, Inc: 1933 (10-1/4 x 8-3/4, 80 pgs, hardcover w/dust jacket

nn - By Otto Soglow (strip-r The New Yorker) 125.00 250.00 450.00
NOTE: *Copies with dust jacket are worth 50% more. Also exists in a 12x8-3/4 edition.*

LITTLE LULU BY MARGE (M)
Rand McNally & Company, Chicago: 1936 (6-9/16x6", 68 pgs, yellow hard-c, B&W)

nn - By Marjorie Henderson Buell 25.00 100.00 250.00
NOTE: *Begins reprinting single panel Little Lulu cartoons which began with Saturday Evening Post Feb. 23, 1935. This book was reprinted several times as late as 1940.*

LITTLE NAPOLEON
No publisher listed: 1924 , 50 pages, 10" by 10"; Color cardstock-c, B&W

nn - By Bud Counihan (Cupples &Leon format) 25.00 100.00 240.00

LITTLE NEMO (...in Slumberland) (N) (see also Little Sammy Sneeze, Dreams...Rarebit F)
Doffield & Co.(1906)/Cupples & Leon Co.(1909): 1906, 1909 (Sunday strip-r in color, cardboard covers)

1906-11x16-1/2" by Winsor McCay; 30 pgs. (scarce) 1500.00 5000.00 -
1909-10x14" by Winsor McCay (scarce) 1300.00 4000.00 -

LITTLE ORPHAN ANNIE (See Treasure Box of Famous Comics) (N)
Cupples & Leon Co.: 1926 - 1934 (8-3/4x7", 100 pgs., B&W daily strip-r, hard-c)

1 (1926)-Little Orphan Annie (softback see Treasure Box) 50.00 200.00 375.00
2 (1927)-In the Circus (softback see Wonder Box...) 36.00 144.00 275.00
3 (1928)-The Haunted House (softback see Wonder Box...) 36.00 144.00 275.00
4 (1929)-Bucking the World 36.00 144.00 275.00

The Trials of Lulu and Leander by Howarth
1906 © NY American & Journal

Maud the Mirthful Mule by Opper
1908 © Frederick A. Stokes

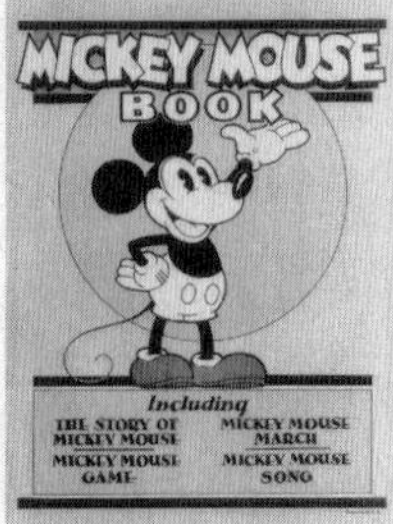

Mickey Mouse Book
1930 © Bibo & Lang

GD2.0 FN6.0 VF8.0

5 (1930)-Never Say Die 30.00 120.00 225.00
6 (1931)-Shipwrecked 30.00 120.00 225.00
7 (1932)-A Willing Helper 25.00 100.00 200.00
8 (1933)-In Cosmic City 25.00 100.00 200.00
9 (1934)-Uncle Dan (not rare) 25.00 100.00 200.00
NOTE: *Each book reprints dailies from the previous year. Each hardcover came with a dust jacket. Books with out dust jackets are worth 50% less. Many of copies of #9 Uncle Dan have been turning up on eBay recently.*

LITTLE ORPHAN ANNIE RUMMY CARDS (N)
Whitman Publishing Co., Racine: 1935 (box: 5 x 6 1/2" Cards: 3 1/2 x 2 1/4")
nn-Harold Gray 20.00 60.00 120.00
NOTE: *36 cards, including 1 instruction card, 5 character cards and 30 cards forming 5 sequential stories (6 cards each).*

LITTLE SAMMY SNEEZE (N) (see also Little Nemo, Dreams of A Rarebit Fiend)
New York Herald Co.: Dec 1905 (11x16-1/2", 72 pgs., color)
nn - By Winsor McCay (Very Rare) 2500.00 6000.00 –
NOTE: *Rarely found in fine to mint condition.*

LIVE AND LET LIVE
Travelers Insurance Co.: 1936 (5-3/4x7/3/4", 16 pgs. color and B&W)
nn - Bill Holman, Carl Anderson, etc 20.00 60.00 120.00

LULU AND LEANDER (N) (see also Funny Folk, 1899, in Victorian section)
New York American & Journal: 1904 (76 pgs); **William A Stokes & Co:** 1906
nn - By F.M. Howarth 300.00 750.00 1500.00
nn - The Trials of...(1906, 10x16", 68 pgs. in color) 300.00 750.00 1500.00
NOTE: *F. M. Howarth helped pioneer the American comic strip in the pages of PUCK magazine in the early 1890s before the Yellow Kid.*

MADMAN'S DRUM (O)
Jonathan Cape and Harrison Smith Inc.: 1930 (8-1/4x6", 274 pgs, B&W hardcover w/dust jacket) (original graphic novel in wood cuts)
nn - By Lynd Ward 50.00 175.00 300.00

MAMA'S ANGEL CHILD IN TOYLAND (I)
Rand McNally, Chicago: 1915 (128 pgs, hardbound)
nn - By M.T. "Penny" Ross & Marie C, Sadler 40.00 140.00 240.00
NOTE: *Mamma's Angel Child published as a comic strip by the "Chicago Tribune" 1908 Mar 1 to 1920 Oct 17.This novel dedicated to Esther Starring Richartz, "the original Mamma's Angel Kid."*

MAUD (N) (see also **Happy Hooligan**)
Frederick A. Stokes Co.: 1906 - 1908? (10x15-1/2", cardboard-c)
1906-By Fred Opper (Scarce), 66 pgs. color 400.00 1200.00 –
1907-The Matchless, 10x15" 70 pgs in color 300.00 900.00 –
1908-The Mirthful Mule, 10x15", 64 pgs in color 300.00 900.00 –
NOTE: *First run of strip began July 24, 1904 to at least Oct 6, 1907, spun out of* ***Happy Hooligan.***

MEMORIAL EDITION The Drawings of Clare Briggs (S)
Wm H. Wise & Company: 1930 (7-1/2x8-3/4", 284 pgs, pebbled false black leather, B&W) (posthumous boxed set of 7 books by Clare Briggs)
nn - The Days of Real Sport; nn-Golf; nn-Real Folks at Home; nn-Ain't it a Grand and Glorious Feeling?; nn-That Guiltiest Feeling; nn-Somebody's Always Taking the Joy Out of Life; nn-When a Feller Needs a Friend
Each book... 30.00 120.00 210.00
NOTE: *Also exists in a whitish cream colored paper back edition; first edition unknown presently.*

MENACE CARTOONS (M, S)
Menace Publishing Company, Aurora, Missouri: 1914 (10-3/8x8", 80 pgs, cardboard-c, B&W)
nn - (Rare) 50.00 150.00 450.00
NOTE: *Reprints anti-Catholic cartoons from K.K.K. related publication* ***The Menace.***

MEN OF DARING (N)
Cupples & Leon Co.: 1933 (8-3/4x7", 100 pgs)
nn - By Stookie Allen, intro by Lowell Thomas 30.00 90.00 200.00

MICKEY MOUSE BOOK
Bibo & Lang: 1930-1931 (12x9", stapled-c, 20 pgs., 4 printings)
nn - First Disney licensed publication (a magazine, not a book–see first book, Adventures of Mickey Mouse). Contains story of how Mickey met Walt and got his name; games, cartoons & song "Mickey Mouse (You Cute Little Feller)," written by Irving Bibo; Minnie, Clarabelle Cow, Horace Horsecollar & caricature of Walt shaking hands with Mickey. The changes made with the 2nd printing have been verified by billing affidavits in the Walt Disney Archives and include:Two Win Smith Mickey strips from 4/15/30 and 4/17/30 added to page 8 & back-c; "Printed in U.S.A." added to front cover; Bobette Bibo's age of 11 years added to title page; faulty type on the word "tail" corrected top of page 3; the word "start" added to bottom of page 7, removing the words "start 1 2 3 4" from the top of page 7; music and lyrics were rewritten on pages 12-14. A green ink border was added beginning with 2nd printing and some covers have inking variations. Art by Albert Barbelle, drawn in an Ub Iwerks style. Total circulation : 97,938 copies varying from 21,000 to 26,000 per printing.
1st printing. Contains the song lyrics **censored** in later printings, "When little Minnie's pursued by a big bad villain we feel so bad then we're glad when you up and kill him." Attached to the Nov. 15, 1930 issue of the Official Bulletin of the Mickey Mouse Club notes: "Attached to this Bulletin is a new Mickey Mouse Book that has just been published." This is thought to be the reason why a slightly disproportionate larger number of copies of the first printing still exist 1200.00 6000.00 12,000.00
2nd printing with a theater/advertising. Christmas greeting added to inside front cover (1 copy known with Dec. 27, 1930 date) – 12,000.00 –
2nd-4th printings 1050.00 5000.00 10,000.00
NOTE: *Theater/advertising copies do not qualify as separate printings. Most copies are missing pages 9 & 10 which had a puzzle to be cut out. Puzzle (pages 9 and 10) cut out or missing, subtract 60% to 75%.*

GD2.0 FN6.0 VF8.0

MICKEY MOUSE COLORING BOOK (S)
Saalfield Publishing Company:1931 (15-1/4x10-3/4", 32 pgs, color soft cover, half printed in full color interior, rest B&W
871 - By Ub Iwerks & Floyd Gottfredson (rare) 400.00 1200.00 2520.00
NOTE: *Contains reprints of first MM daily strip ever, including the "missing" speck the chicken is after found only on the original daily strip art by Iwerks plus other very early MM art. There were several other Saalfield Mickey Mouse coloring books manufactured around the same time.*

MICKEY MOUSE, THE ADVENTURES OF (I)
David McKay Co., Inc.: Book I, 1931 - Book II, 1932 (5-1/2"x8-1/2", 32 pgs.)
Book I-First Disney book, by strict definition (1st printing-50,000 copies)(see Mickey Mouse Book by Bibo & Lang). Illustrated text refers to Clarabelle Cow as "Carolyn" and Horace Horsecollar as "Henry". The name "Donald Duck" appears with a non-costumed generic duck on back cover & inside, not in the context of the character that later debuted in the Wise Little Hen.
Hardback w/characters on back-c 75.00 300.00 650.00
Softcover w/characters on back-c 38.00 151.00 350.00
Version without characters on back-c 45.00 180.00 400.00
Book II-Less common than Book I. Character development brought into conformity with the Mickey Mouse cartoon shorts and syndicated strips. Captain Church Mouse, Tanglefoot, Peg-Leg Pete and Pluto appear with Mickey & Minnie 46.00 186.00 400.00

MICKEY MOUSE COMIC (N)
David McKay Co.: 1931 - No. 4, 1934 (10"x9-3/4", 52 pgs., card board-c) (Later reprints exist)
1 (1931)-Reprints Floyd Gottfredson daily strips in black & white from 1930 & 1931, including the famous two week sequence in which Mickey tries to commit suicide 229.00 914.00 1680.00
2 (1932)-1st app. of Pluto reprinted from 7/8/31 daily. All pgs. from 1931 164.00 656.00 1200.00
3 (1933)-Reprints 1932 & 1933 Sunday pages in color, one strip per page, including the "Lair of Wolf Barker" continuity pencilled by Gottfredson and inked by Al Taliaferro & Ted Thwaites. First app. Mickey's nephews, Morty & Ferdie, one identified by name of Mortimer Fieldmouse, not to be confused with Uncle Mortimer Mouse who is introduced in the Wolf Barker story 214.00 856.00 1600.00
4 (1934)-1931 dailies, include the only known reprint of the infamous strip of 2/4/31 where the villainous Kat Nipp snips off the end of Mickey's tail with a pair of scissors 140.00 560.00 1050.00

MICKEY MOUSE (N)
Whitman Publishing Co.: 1933-34 (10x8-3/4", 34 pgs, cardboard-c)
948-1932 & 1933 Sunday strips in color, printed from the same plates as Mickey Mouse Book #3 by David McKay, but only pages 5-17 & 32-48 (including all of the "Wolf Barker" continuity) 157.00 629.00 1100.00
NOTE: *Some copies bound with back cover upside down. Variance doesn't affect value. Same art appears on front and back covers of all copies. Height of Whitman reissue trimmed 1/2 inch.*

MILITARY WILLIE
J. I. Austen Co.: 1907 (7x9-1/2", 12 pgs., every other page in color, stapled)
nn - By F. R. Morgan 70.00 245.00 400.00

MINNEAPOLIS TRIBUNE CARTOON BOOK (S)
Minneapolis Tribune: 1899-1903 (11-3/8x9-3/8", B&W, paper cover)
nn (#1) (1899) 28.00 99.00 170.00
nn (#2) (1900) 28.00 99.00 170.00
nn (#3) (1901) (published Jan 01, 1901) 28.00 99.00 170.00
nn (#4) (1902) (114 pgs) 28.00 99.00 170.00
nn (#5) (1903) (9x10-3/4",110 pgs, B&W; color-c) 28.00 99.00 170.00
NOTE: *All by Roland C. Bowman (editorial-r).*

MINUTE BIOGRAPHIES: INTIMATE GLIMPSES INTO THE LIVES OF 150 FAMOUS MEN AND WOMEN
Grossett & Dunlap: 1931, 1933 (10-1/4x7-3/4", 168 pgs, hardcover, B&W)
nn - By Nisenson (art) & Parker(text) 21.00 63.00 125.00
More.... (1933) 21.00 63.00 125.00

MISCHIEVOUS MONKS OF CROCODILE ISLE, THE (N)
J. I. Austen Co., Chicago: 1908 (8-1/2x11-1/2", 12 pgs., 4 pgs. in color)
nn - By F. R. Morgan; reads longwise 125.00 375.00 600.00

MR. & MRS. (Also see Ain't It A Grand and Glorious Feeling?) (N)
Whitman Publishing Co.: 1922 (9x9-1/2", 52 & 28 pgs., cardboard-c)
nn - By Briggs (B&W, 52 pgs.) 37.00 149.00 260.00
nn - 28 pgs.-(9x9-1/2")-Sunday strips-r in color 41.00 163.00 285.00

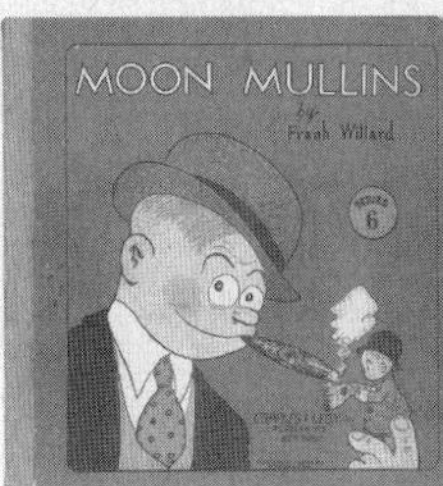

Moon Mullins #6 by Frank Willard
1932 @ Cupples & Leon

The Nebbs
© C&L

The Newlyweds by George McManus
1907 © Saalfield Publishing Co.

GD2.0 FN6.0 VF8.0

NOTE: *The earliest presently-known Whitman comic books*

MR. BLOCK (N)
Industrial Workers of the World (IWW): 1913, 1919

nn - By Ernest Riebe (C) 50.00 150.00 –
...And The Profiteers (original material) (H) 50.00 150.00 –
NOTE: *Mr Block was a daily strip published from 1912 NOV 7 to 1913 SEP ? by the socialist newspaper "Industrial Worker"; Mr Block was a "square" guy (his head was in fact a block) who enthusiastically supported the same system that exploited him. The noted Joe Hill wrote a song about him (Mr Block,1913, on the air of "It loooks me like a big time tonight") for the "Industrial Worker Songbook".*

MR. TWEE-DEEDLE (N)
Cupples & Leon: 1913, 1917 (11-3/8 x 16-3/4" color strips-r from NY Herald)

nn - By John B. Gruelle (later of Raggedy Ann fame) 350.00 900.00 1800.00
nn - "Further Adventures of..." By Gruelle 350.00 900.00 1800.00
NOTE: *Strip ran Feb 5, 1911-March 10, 1918.*

MONKEY SHINES OF MARSELEEN AND SOME OF HIS ADVENTURES (C)
McLaughlin Bros. New York: 1906 (10 x 12-3/8", 36 pgs, full color hardcover)

nn - By Norman E. Jennett strip-r NY Evening Telegram 100.00 250.00 450.00
NOTE: *Strip began in 1906 until at least March 13, 1910.*

MONKEY SHINES OF MARSELEEN (N)
Cupples & Leon Co.: 1909 (11-1/2 x 17", 58 pgs. in two colors)

nn - By Norman E. Jennett (strip-r New York Herald) 100.00 250.00 450.00

MOON MULLINS (N)
Cupples & Leon Co.: 1927 - 1933 (52 pgs., B&W daily strip-r)

Series 1 ('27)-By Willard 63.00 250.00 500.00
Series 2 ('28), Series 3 ('29), Series 4 ('30) 39.00 156.00 300.00
Series 5 ('31), 6 ('32), 7 ('33) 39.00 156.00 300.00
Big Book 1 ('30)-B&W (scarce) 100.00 400.00 750.00
w/dust jacket (rare) 183.00 732.00 1300.00

MOVING PICTURE FUNNIES
Saml Gabriel Sons & Company: 1918 (5-1/4 x 10-1/4", 52 pgs, B&W, illustrated hard-c)
nn 20.00 40.00 80.00
NOTE: *823 Comical illustrations that show a different scene when folded.*

MUTT & JEFF (...Cartoon, The) (N)
Ball Publications: 1911 - No. 5, 1916 (5-3/4 x 15-1/2", 72 pgs, B&W, hard-c)

1 (1910)(50¢) very common 71.00 286.00 500.00
2,3: 2 (1911)-Opium den panels; Jeff smokes opium (pipe dreams).
3 (1912) both very common 71.00 286.00 500.00
2-(1913) Reprint of 1911 edition with black ink cover 50.00 175.00 300.00
4 (1915) (50¢) (Scarce) 150.00 350.00 650.00
5 (1916) (Rare) -Photos of Fisher, 1st pg. (68 pages) 200.00 480.00 900.00
5-Scarce 84 page reprint edition 150.00 450.00 800.00
NOTE: *Mutt & Jeff first appeared in newspapers in 1907. Cover variations exist showing Mutt & Jeff reading various newspapers; i.e., The Oregon Journal, The American, and The Detroit News. Reprinting of each issue began soon after publication. No. 4 and 5 may not have been reprinted. Values listed include the reprints. Mutt & Jeff was the first successful American daily newspaper comic strip and as such remains one of the seminal strips of all time.*

MUTT & JEFF (N)
Cupples & Leon Co.: No. 6, 1919 - No. 22, 1934? (9-1/2x9-1/2", 52 pgs., B&W dailies, stiff-c)

6, 7 - By Bud Fisher (very common) 32.00 128.00 225.00
8-10 46.00 186.00 325.00
11-18 (Somewhat Scarcer) (#19-#22 do not exist) 60.00 å240.00 420.00
nn (1920) (Advs. of...) 11x16"; 44 pgs.; full color reprints of 1919 Sunday strips
93.00 372.00 650.00
Big Book nn (1926, 144 pgs., hardcovers) 114.00 456.00 800.00
w/dust jacket 193.00 772.00 1350.00
Big Book 1 (1928) - Thick book (hardcovers) 114.00 456.00 800.00
w/dust jacket (rare) 182.00 729.00 1275.00
Big Book 2 (1929) - Thick book (hardcovers) 114.00 456.00 800.00
w/dust jacket (rare) 182.00 729.00 1275.00
NOTE: *The Big Books contain three previous issues rebound.*

MUTT & JEFF (N)
Embee Publ. Co.: 1921 (9x15", color cardboard-c & interior)

nn - Sunday strips in color (Rare)- BY Bud Fisher 143.00 572.00 1000.00
NOTE: *Ties with The Trouble of Bringing Up Father (EmBee) and Jimmie Dugan & The Reg'lar Fellers (C&L) as the last of this size.*

MYSTERIOUS STRANGER AND OTHER CARTOONS, THE
McClure, Phillips & Co.: 1905 (12-3/8x9-3/4", 338 pgs, hardcover, B&W)

nn - By John McCutcheon 32.00 128.00 225.00

MY WAR - Szeged (Szuts)
Wm. Morrow Co.: 1932 (7x10-1/2", 210 pgs, hard-c, B&W)

nn - (All story panels, no words - powerful) 32.00 128.00 225.00

NAUGHTY ADVENTURES OF VIVACIOUS MR. JACK, THE
New York American & Journal: 1904 (15x10", color strips)

nn - By James Swinnerton; (Very Rare - 3 known copies) 800.00 1500.00 2000.00

GD2.0 FN6.0 VF8.0

NEBBS, THE (N)
Cupples & Leon Co.: 1928 (52 pgs., B&W daily strip-r)

nn - By Sol Hess; Carlson-a 40.00 160.00 280.00

NERVY NAT'S ADVENTURES (E)
Leslie-Judge Co.: 1911 (90 pgs, 85¢, 1903 strip reprints from **Judge**)

nn - By James Montgomery Flagg 75.00 263.00 450.00

THE NEWLYWEDS AND THEIR BABY (N)
Saalfield Publ. Co.: 1907 (13x10", 52 pgs., hardcover)

...& Their Baby' by McManus; daily strips 50% color 300.00 900.00 –
NOTE: *Strip ran Apr 10, 1904 thru Jan 14, 1906 and then May 19, 1907-Dec 5, 1916; was a huge success with Baby Snookums long before McManus invented Bringing Up Father; Snookums brought back as a topper strip over BUF Nov 19, 1944-Dec 30, 1956.*

THE NEWLYWEDS AND THEIR BABY'S COMIC PICTURES FOR PAINTING AND CRAYONING (N)
Saalfield Publishign Company: 1916 (10-1/4x14-3/4", 52 pgs. Cardboard-c)

nn - 44 B&W pages, covers, and one color wrap glued to B&W title page.
Color wrap: color title pg. & 3 pgs of color strips 83.00 290.00 500.00
nn - (1917, 10x14", 20 pgs, oblong, cardboard-c) partial reprint of 1916 edition
31.00 124.00 275.00

THE NEWLYWEDS AND THEIR BABY (N)
Saalfield Publishing Company: 1917 (10-1/8x13-9/16", 52 pgs, full color cardstock-c, some pages full color, others two color (orange, blue))

nn 83.00 290.00 500.00

NEW YORKER CARTOON ALBUM, THE (M)
Doubleday, Doran & Company Inc.: (1928-1931); **Harper & Brothers.:** (1931-1933); **Random House** (1935-1937), 12x9", various pg counts, hardcovers w/dust jackets)

1928: nn-114 pgs Arno, Held, Soglow, Williams, etc 20.00 60.00 120.00
1928: SECOND-114 pgs Arno, Bairnsfather, Gross, Held, Soglow, Williams
10.00 30.00 60.00
1930: THIRD-172 pgs Arno, Bairnsfather, Held, Soglow, Art Young
10.00 30.00 60.00
1931: FOURTH-154 pgs Arno, Held, Soglow, Steig, Thurber, Williams, Art Young, "Little King" by Soglow begins 10.00 30.00 60.00
1932: FIFTH-156 pgs Arno, Bairnsfather, Held, Hoff, Soglow, Steig, Thurber, Williams 10.00 30.00 60.00
1933: SIXTH-156 pgs same as above 10.00 30.00 60.00
1935: SEVENTH-164 pgs 10.00 30.00 60.00
1937: 168 pgs; Charles Addams plus same as above but no Little King, two page "Gone With The Wind" parody strip 10.00 30.00 60.00
NOTE: *Some sequential strips but mostly single panel cartoons.*

NIPPY'S POP (N)
The Saalfield Publishing Co.: 1917 (10-1/2x13-1/2", 36 pgs., B&W, Sunday strip-r)

nn - Charles M Payne (better known as S'Matter Pop) 43.00 152.00 260.00

OH, MAN (A Bully Collection of Those Inimitable Humor Cartoons) (S)
P.F. Volland & Co.: 1919 (8-1/2x13"; 136 pgs.)

nn - By Briggs 43.00 152.00 260.00
NOTE: *Originally came in illustrated box with Briggs art (box is Rare - worth 50% more with box).*

OH SKIN-NAY! (S)
P.F. Volland & Co.: 1913 (8-1/2x13", 136 pgs.)

nn - The Days Of Real Sport by Briggs 43.00 152.00 260.00
NOTE: *Originally came in illustrated box with Briggs art (box is Rare - worth 50% more with box).*

OLD GOLD THE SMOOTHER AND BETTER CIGARETTE...NOT A COUGH IN A CARLOAD (M,N,P) (see also BY BRIGGS)
Old Gold Cigarettes: nd (c1920's) (16 pgs, paper-c, color) (both Scarce)
nn- (4-1/4" x 3-7/8") cover strip is "Oh, Man!"; also contains: "Real Folks at Home", "Ain't It a Grand and Glorious Feelin?", "It Happens in the Best Regulated Families", and "Mr. and Mrs." (no known sales)
1440- (5-9/16" x 5-1/4") cover strip is "Frank and Ernest"; also contains: "That Guiltiest Feeling", "Real Folks at Home", "Oh, Man!", "When a Feller Needs a Friend". (no known sales)
NOTE: *Collection reprinting strip cartoons by Clare Briggs, advertising Old Gold Cigarettes. These strips originally appeared in various magazines, play program booklets, newspapers, etc. Some of the strips involve regular Briggs strip series. The two booklets contain a completely different set of comics.*

ON AND OFF MOUNT ARARAT (also see **Tigers**) (N)
Hearst's New York American & Journal: 1902, 86pgs. 10x15-1/4"

nn - Rare Noah's Ark satire by Jimmy Swinnerton (rare) 450.00 1500.00 –

ON THE LINKS (N)
Associated Feature Service: Dec, 1926 (9x10", 48 pgs.)

nn - Daily strip-r 25.00 100.00 175.00

ONE HUNDRED WAR CARTOONS (S)
Idaho Daily Statesman: 1918 (7-3/4x10", 102 pgs, paperback, B&W)

nn - By Villeneuve (WW I cartoons) 20.00 60.00 120.00

OUR ANTEDILUVIAN ANCESTORS (N,S)

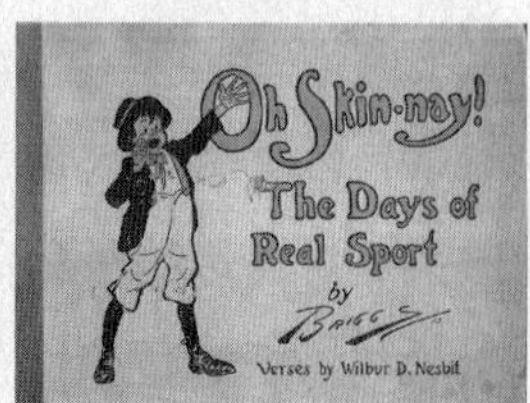

Oh Skin-nay! by Claire Briggs
1913 © P.F. Volland

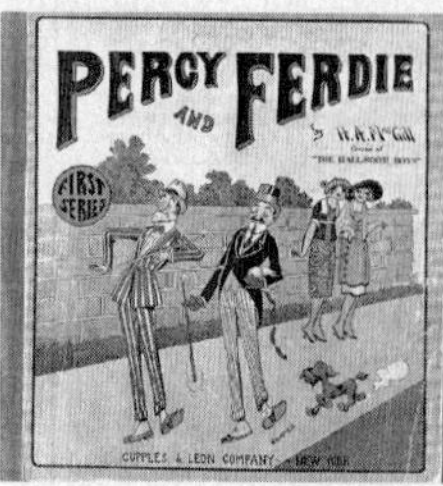

Percy and Ferdie
1921 © Cupples & Leon

Roger Bean, R.G. #4
© C&L

GD2.0 FN6.0 VF8.0

New York Evening Journal, NY: 1903 (11-3/8x8-7/8", hardcover)
nn - By F Opper 75.00 200.00 400.00
NOTE: *There is a simultaneously published British edition, identical size and contents, from C. Arthur Pearson Ltd, London. A collection of single panel cartoons about cavemen. Similar to an earlier British cartoon book "Prehistoric Peeps from Punch", by E.T. Reed.*

OUTBURSTS OF EVERETT TRUE, THE (N)
Saalfield Publ. Co.(Werner Co.): 1907 (92 pgs, 9-7/16x5-1/4")
1907 (2-4 panel strips-r)-By Condo & Raper 125.00 350.00 675.00
1921-Full color-c; reprints 56 of 88 cartoons from 1907 ed. (10x10", 32 pgs B&W) 125.00 225.00 350.00

OVER THERE COMEDY FROM FRANCE
Observer House Printing: nd (WW 1 era) (6x14", 60 pgs, paper cover)
nn - Artist(s) unknown 15.00 53.00 90.00

OWN YOUR OWN HOME (I)
Bobbs-Merrill Company, Indianapolis: 1919 (7-7/16x5-1/4")
nn - By Fontaine Fox – – –

PECKS BAD BOY (N)
Charles C. Thompson Co, Chicago (by Walt McDougal): 1906-1908 (strip-r)
The Adventures of... (1906) 11-1/2x16-1/4", 68 pgs 100.00 400.00 800.00
...& His Country Cousin Cynthia (1907) 12x16-1/2," 34 pgs In color 100.00 400.00 800.00
Advs. of...And His Country Cousins (1907) 5-1/2x10 1/2", 18 pgs In color 50.00 175.00 300.00
Advs. of...And His Country Cousins (1907) 11-1/2x16-1/4", 36 pgs 50.00 175.00 300.00
...& Their Advs With The Teddy Bear (1907) 5-1/2x10-1/2", 18 pgs in color 50.00 175.00 300.00
...& Their Balloon Trip To the Country (1907) 5-1/2x 10-1/2, 18 pgs in color 50.00 175.00 300.00
...With the Teddy Bear Show (1907) 5-1/2x 10-1/2 50.00 175.00 300.00
...With The Billy Whiskers Goats (1907) 5-1/2 x 10-1/2, 18 pgs in color 50.00 175.00 300.00
...& His Chums (1908) - 11x16-3/8", 36 pgs. Stanton & Van Vliet Co 100.00 400.00 750.00
...& His Chums (1908)-Hardcover; full color;16 pgs. 100.00 350.00 600.00
Advs. of...in Pictures (1908) (11x17, 36 pgs)-In color; Stanton & Van V. Liet Co. 100.00 400.00 700.00

PERCY & FERDIE (N)
Cupples & Leon Co.: 1921 (10x10", 52 pgs., B&W dailies, cardboard-c)
nn - By H. A. MacGill (Rare) 61.00 244.00 450.00

PETER RABBIT (N)
John H. Eggers Co. The House of Little Books Publishers: 1922 - 1923
B1-B4-(Rare)-(Set of 4 books which came in a cardboard box)-Each book reprints half of a Sunday page per page and contains 8 B&W and 2 color pages; by Harrison Cady (9-1/4x6-1/4", paper-c) each.... 43.00 172.00 300.00
Box only 57.00 228.00 400.00

PHILATELIC CARTOONS (M)
Essex Publishing Company, Lynn, Mass.: 1916 (8-11/16" x 5-7/8", 40 pgs, light blue construction paper-c, B&W interior)
nn - By Leroy S. Bartlett 25.00 75.00 175.00
NOTE: *Comics reprinted from The New England Philatelist.*

PICTORIAL HISTORY OF THE DEPARTMENT OF COMMERCE UNDER HERBERT HOOVER (see Picture Life of a Great American) (O)
Hoover-Curtis Campaign Committee of New York State: no date, 1928 (3-1/4 x 5-1/4, 32 pgs, paper cover, B&W)
nn - By Satterfield (scarce) 50.00 140.00 260.00
NOTE: *1928 Presidential Campaign giveaway. Original material, contents completely different from Picture Life of a Great American.*

PICTURE LIFE OF A GREAT AMERICAN (see Pictorial History of the Department of Commerce under Herbert Hoover) (O)
Hoover-Curtis Campaign Committee of New York State: no date, 1928 (paper cover, B&W)
nn - (8-3/4 x 7, 20 pgs) Text cover, 2 page text introduction, 18 pgs of comics (scarcer first print) 43.00 129.00 260.00
nn - (9 x 6-3/4,24 pgs) Illustrated cover,5 page text introduction, 18 pgs of comics (scarce) 43.00 129.00 260.00
NOTE: *1928 Presidential Campaign giveaway. Unknown which above version was published first. Both contain the same original comics material by Satterfield.*

PINK LAFFIN (I)
Whitman Publishing Co.: 1922 (9x12")(Strip-r; some of these actually text joke books)
...the Lighter Side of Life, ...He Tells 'Em, ...and His Family, ...Knockouts; Ray Gleason-a (All rare) each... 26.00 104.00 185.00

POLLY (AND HER PALS) - (N)
Newspaper Feature Service: 1916 (3x2-1/2", color)

GD2.0 FN6.0 VF8.0

Altogether: Three Rahs and a Tiger! by Cliff Sterrett 21.00 63.00 130.00
There Is A Limit To Pa's Patience by Cliff Sterrett 21.00 63.00 130.00
Pa's Lil Book Has Some Uncut Pages by Sterrett 21.00 63.00 130.00
NOTE: *Single newsprint sheet printed in full color on both sides, unfolds to show 12 panel story.*

POPEYE PAINT BOOK (N)
McLaughlin Bros, Inc., Springfield, Mass.: 1932 (9-7/8x13", 28 pgs, color-c)
2052 - By E. C. Segar 90.00 300.00 600.00
NOTE: *Contains a full color panel above and the exact same art in below panel n B&W which one was to color in; strip-r panels.*

POPEYE CARTOON BOOK (N)
The Saalfield Co.: 1934 (8-1/2x13", 40 pgs, cardboard-c)
2095-(scarce)-1933 strip reprints in color by Segar. Each page contains a vertical half of a Sunday strip, so the continuity reads row by row completely across each double page spread. If each page is read by itself, the continuity makes no sense. Each double page spread reprints one complete Sunday page from 1933 300.00 900.00 2700.00
12 Page Version 100.00 300.00 900.00

POPEYE (See **Thimble Theatre** for earlier Popeye-r from Sonnett) (N)
David McKay Publications: 1935 (25¢; 52 pgs, B&W) (By Segar)
1-Daily strip reprints- "The Gold Mine Thieves" 200.00 400.00 800.00
2-Daily strip-r (scarce) 200.00 400.00 900.00
NOTE: *Ties with Henry & Little Annie Rooney (David McKay) as the last of the 10x10" size books.*

PORE LI'L MOSE (N)
New York Herald Publ. by Grand Union Tea
Cupples & Leon Co.: 1902 (10-1/2x15", 78 pgs., color)
nn - By R. F. Outcault; Earliest known C&L comic book (scarce in high grade - very high demand) 1750.00 5775.00 –
NOTE: *Black Americana one page newspaper strips; falls in between Yellow Kid & Buster Brown. Complete copies have become scarce. Some have cut this book apart thinking that reselling individual pages will bring them more money.*

PRETTY PICTURES (M)
Farrar & Rinehart: 1931 (12 x 8-7/8", 104 pgs, color hardcover w/dust jacket, B&W; reprints from New Yorker, Judge, Life, Collier's Weekly)
nn - By Otto Soglow (contains "The Little King") 33.00 134.00 235.00

QUAINT OLD NEW ENGLAND (S)
Triton Syndicate: 1936 (5-1/4x6-1/4", 100 pgs, soft-c squarebound, B&W)
nn - By Jack Withycomb 36.00 144.00 250.00
NOTE: *Comics about weird doings in Old New England.*

RED CARTOONS (S)
Daily Worker Publishing Company: 1926 (12 x 9", 68 pgs,cardboard cover, B&W)
nn - By Various (scarce) 40.00 160.00 280.00
NOTE: *Reprint of American Communist Party editorial cartoons, from The Daily Worker, The Workers Monthly, and the Liberator. Art by Fred Ellis, William Gropper, Clive Weed, Art Young.*

REG'LAR FELLERS (See All-American Comics, Jimmie Dugan & The..., Popular Comics & Treasure Box of Famous Comics) (N)
Cupples & Leon Co./MS Publishing Co.: 1921-1929
1 (1921)-52 pgs. B&W dailies (Cupples & Leon, 10x10") 43.00 171.00 300.00
1925, 48 pgs. B&W dailies (MS Publ.) 39.00 157.00 275.00
Hardcover (1929, 8-3/4x7-1/2"; 96 pgs.)-B&W-r 54.00 214.00 375.00

REG'LAR FELLERS STORY PAINT BOOK
Whitman, Racine, Wisc.: 1932 (8-3/4x12-1/8", 132 pgs, red soft-c)
By Gene Byrnes 25.00 75.00 150.00

ROGER BEAN, R. G. (Regular Guy) (N)
The Indiana News Co, Distributers.: 1915 - No. 2, 1915 (5-3/8x17", 68 pgs., B&W, hardcovers); #3-#5 published by **Chas. B. Jackson:** 1916-1919
(No. 1 2 4 & 5 bound on side, No. 3 bound at top)
1-By Chas B. Jackson (68pgs.)(Scarce) 60.00 210.00 360.00
2- 5-5/8x17-1/8", 66 pgs (says 1913 inside - an obvious printing error) (red or green binding) 60.00 210.00 360.00
3-Along the Firing Line... (1916; 68 pgs, 6x17") 60.00 210.00 360.00
3-Along the Firing Line side-bound version 60.00 210.00 360.00
4-Into the Trenches and Out Again with... (1917, 68 pgs) 60.00 210.00 360.00
5 ...And The Reconstruction Period (1919, 5-3/8x15-1/2", 84 pgs) (Scarce) (has $1 printed on cover) 60.00 210.00 360.00
Baby Grand Editions 1-5 (10x10", cardboard-c) 60.00 210.00 360.00
NOTE: *No. 1 & 2 of the Twin Baby Grands (nd) 8-1/4x10-7/8", 52 pgs. #3 & #4 9x10-7/8" Cardboard cover. B&W strip reprints. Cover also says "Politics Pickles People Police."*
nn - 9x11, 68 pgs 60.00 210.00 360.00
NOTE: Has picture of Chic Jackson and a posthumous dedication from his three children. strip-r 1931-32

ROGER BEAN PHILOSOPHER
Schnull & Co: 1917 (5-1/2x17", 36 pgs., B&W, brown & black paper-c, square binding)
nn - By Chic Jackson (no known sales)

ROOKIE FROM THE 13TH SQUAD, THAT (N) (also Between Shots; Always Belittlin';Skippy)
Harper & Brothers Publishers: Feb. 1918 (8x9-1/4", 72 pgs, hardcover, B&W)
nn - By Lieut. P(ercy) L. Crosby 75.00 225.00 400.00

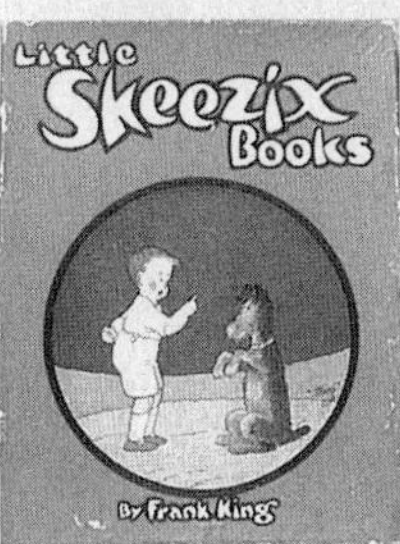

Little Skeezix Books by Frank King
1929 © Reilly & Lee

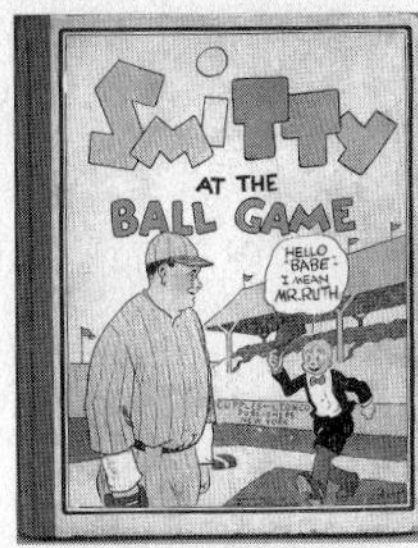

Smitty #2 By Walter Berndt
1929 © Cupples & Leon

Tailspin Tommy Story & Picture Book
By Hal Forest and Glenn Chappin
1932 © Cupples & Leon

NOTE: *Strip began in 1917 at an Army base during basic training.*

ROUND THE WORLD WITH THE DOO-DADS (see Doings of the Doo-Dads, Doo Dads)
Universal Feature And Specialty Co, Chicago: 1922 (12x10-1/2", 52 pgs, B&W, red & light blue-c, square binding)

nn - By Arch Dale newspaper strip-r 43.00 173.00 300.00
NOTE: *Intermixed single panel and sequential comic strips with scenes from Scotland, Ireland, England, Holland, Italy, Spain, Egypt, Africa, and Lions & Elephants along the Nile River, China, Australia & back home.*

RUBAIYKT OF THE EGG
The John C Winston Co, Philadelphia: 1905 (7x5/12", 64 pgs, purple-c, B&W)

nn - By Clare Victor Dwiggins 20.00 60.00 125.00
NOTE: *Book is printed & cut into the shape of an egg.*

RULING CLAWSS, THE (N,S)
The Daily Worker: 1935 (192 pgs, 10-1/4 x 7-3/8", hard-c, B&W)

nn - By Redfield 60.00 240.00 -
NOTE: *Reprints cartoons from the American Communist Party newspaper The Daily Worker.*

SAGARA'S ENGLISH CARTOONS AND CARTOON STORIES (N)
Bunkosha, Tokyo: nd (c1925) (6-5/8" x 4-1/4", 272 pgs, hard-c, B&W)

nn- (Scarce) - - -
NOTE: *Published in Tokyo, Japan, with all strips in both English and Japanese, to facilitate learning English. Majority of book is Bringing Up Father by George McManus. Also contains Japanese strip Father Takes it Easy, by T. Sagara, reprinted from the Kokusai News Agency.*

SAM AND HIS LAUGH (N)
Frederick A. Stokes: 1906 (10x15", cardboard-c, Sunday strip-r in color)

nn - By Jimmy Swinnerton (Extremely Rare) 600.00 1200.00 2400.00
NOTE: *Strip ran July 24, 1904-Dec 26 1906; its ethnic humor might be considered racist by today's standards.*

SCHOOL DAYS (N)
Harper & Bros.: 1919 (9x8", 104 pgs.)

nn - By Clare Victor Dwiggins 75.00 150.00 300.00

SEAMAN SI - A Book of Cartoons About the Funniest "Gob" in the Navy (N)
Pierce Publishing Co.: 1916 (4x8-1/2, 200 pgs, hardcover, B&W); 1918 (4-1/8x8-1/4, 104 pgs, hardcover, B&W)

nn - By Perce Pearce (1916) 50.00 150.00 300.00
nn - 1918 - (Reilly & Britton Co.) 30.00 125.00 200.00
NOTE: *There exists two different covers for the 1918 reprints. The earlier edition was self published by the artist. The newspaper strip is sometimes also known as "The American Sailor."*

SECRET AGENT X-9 (N)
David McKay Pbll.: 1934 (Book 1: 84 pgs; Book 2: 124 pgs.) (8x7-1/2")

Book 1-Contains reprints of the first 13 weeks of the strip by Dashiell Hammett & Alex Raymond, complete except for 2 dailies 100.00 300.00 750.00
Book 2-Contains reprints immediately following contents of Book 1, for 20 weeks by Dashiell Hammett & Alex Raymond; complete except for two dailies. Last 5 strips misdated from 6/34, continuity correct 100.00 300.00 750.00

SILK HAT HARRY'S DIVORCE SUIT (N)
M. A. Donoghue & Co.: 1912 (5-3/4x15-1/2", oblong, B&W)

nn - Newspaper-r by Tad (Thomas A. Dorgan) 33.00 117.00 400.00

SINBAD A DOG'S LIFE (M)
Coward - McCann, Inc.: 1930 (11x 8-3/4", 104 pgs., single-sided, illustrated hard-c, B&W

nn - By Edwina 11.00 33.00 100.00
Sinbad...Again (1932, 10-15/16x 8-9/16", 104 pgs.) 11.00 33.00 100.00
NOTE: *Wordless comic strips from LIFE.*

SIS HOPKINS OWN BOOK AND MAGAZINE OF FUN
Leslie-Judge Co.: 1899-July 1911 (36 pgs, color-c, B&W) (merged into Judge's Library, later titled Film Fun)

any issue - By various 11.00 33.00 100.00
NOTE: *Zim, Flagg, Young, Newell, Adams, etc.*

SKEEZIX (Also see Gasoline Alley & Little Skeezix Books listed below) (I)
Reilly & Lee Co.: 1925 - 1928 (Strip-r, soft covers) (pictures & text)

...and Uncle Walt (1924)-Origin 26.00 104.00 180.00
...and Pal (1925), ...at the Circus (1926) 21.00 84.00 160.00
...& Uncle Walt (1927) (does this actually exist? reprint? never seen one yet)
...Out West (1928) 30.00 100.00 200.00
Hardback Editions... 34.00 136.00 235.00

SKEEZIX BOOKS, LITTLE (Also see Skeezix, Gasoline Alley) (G)
Reilly & Lee Co.: No date (1928, 1929) (Boxed set of three Skeezix books)

nn - Box with 3 issues of Skeezix. Skeezix & Pal, Skeezix at the Circus, Skeezix & Uncle Walt known. 1928 Set... 60.00 180.00 360.00
nn - Box with 4 issues of (3) above Skeezix plus "Out West" 80.00 330.00 550.00

SKEEZIX COLOR BOOK (N)
McLaughlin Bros. Inc, Springfield, Mass: 1929 (9-1/2x10-1/4", 28 pgs, one third in full color, rest in B&W)

2023 - By Frank King; strip-r to color 20.00 75.00 135.00

SKIPPY (see also Life Presents Skippy, Always Belittlin', That Rookie From 13th Squad)
No publisher listed: Circa 1920s (10x8", 16 pgs., color/B&W cartoons)

nn - By Percy Crosby 20.00 84.00 150.00

SKIPPY, LIFE PRESENTS (M)
Life Publishing Company & Henry Holt, NY: nd 1924 (134 pgs, 10-13/16x8-3/4", color hard-c, B&W

nn - By Percy L Crosby 100.00 300.00 500.00
NOTE: *Many sequential & single panel reprints from Skippy's earliest appearances in Life Magazine.*

SKIPPY
Greenberg, Publisher, Inc, NY: 1925. (11-14x8-5/8, 72 pgs, hard-c, B&W and color

nn - By Percy L. Crosby 50.00 150.00 300.00

NOTE: *Some but not all of these comics were also in Life Presents Skippy; issued with dust wrapper.*

SKIPPY AND OTHER HUMOR
Greenberg: Publisher, NY: 1929 (11-1/4x8-1/2",72 pgs,tan hard-c, B&W and color)

nn - By Percy L. Crosby 25.00 75.00 150.00
NOTE: *Came with a dust jacket.*

SKIPPY (I)
Grossett & Dunlap: 1929 (7-3/8x6, 370 pgs, hardcover text with some art)

nn - By Percy Crosby (issued with a dust jacket) 23.00 92.00 160.00
NOTE: *This is worth very little without the dust wrapper; very common without athe dust jacket.*

SKIPPY
Greenberg Press: 1930 (soft cover, ca. 16 pp.,

nn - By Percy Crosby (scarce) 50.00 175.00 300.00
NOTE: *Reprints from LIFE cartoons, color, b/w. Crosby told Greenberg to withdraw from the market as it cheapened the hard cover prior editions. Greenberg then stopped publishing per agreement, and sent Crosby all the copper & zinc bookplates, which were in Crosby estate until 1996.*

SKIPPY CRAYON AND COLORING BOOK (N)
McLoughlin Bros, Inc., Springfield, MA: 1931 (13x9-3/4", 28 pgs, color-c, color & B&W)

2050 - By Percy Crosby 28.00 84.00 195.00
NOTE: *This item says on the front cover: "Licensed by Percy Crosby" because he owned his creation. About half the pages have one panel pre-printed in full color with same one b&w below for person to copy the colors.*

SKIPPY RAMBLES (I)
G.P. Putnam's Sons: 1932 (7 1/8 x 5 1/8, 202 pgs)

nn - By Percy Crosby 21.00 84.00 150.00
NOTE: *Issued with a dustjacket. Has Skippy plates by Crosby every 4 or 5 pages.*

SKUDDABUD STARRY STORY SERIES - FOLK FROM THE FUTURE (O,G)
no publisher listed: 1936 (9" x 11-7/8", 48 pgs, cardboard-c, B&W)

Book One (Rare) "Parachuting" 21.00 84.00 150.00
NOTE: *By Columba Krebs. Top half of each page is a continuing strip story, while bottom half are different stories, in prose, about the same characters -- a race of aliens who have migrated to Earth, from their dying world.*

S'MATTER POP? (N)
Saalfield Publ. Co.: 1917 (10x14", 44 pgs., B&W, cardboard-c,)

nn - By Charlie Payne; in full color; pages printed on one side 48.00 169.00 290.00

S'MATTER POP? (N) (25 ¢ cover price)
E.I. Company, New York: 1927 (8-15/16x7-1/8", 52 pgs, yellow soft-c perfect bound

nn - By C.M. Payne (scarce) 24.00 84.00 145.00
NOTE: *First comic book published by Hugo Gernsback, noted for inventing Amazing Stories among other memorable science fiction pulps. The World Science Fiction Convention Award, The Hugo, is named for him.*

SMITTY (See Treasure Box of Famous Comics) (N)
Cupples & Leon Co.: 1928 - 1933 (9x7", 96 pgs., B&W strip-r, hardcover)

1928-(96 pgs. 7x8-3/4") By Walter Berndt 43.00 172.00 300.00
1929-At the Ball Game (Babe Ruth on cover) 57.00 229.00 450.00
1930-The Flying Office Boy, 1931-The Jockey, 1932-In the North Woods each... 31.00 126.00 250.00
1933-At Military School 31.00 126.00 250.00
NOTE: *Each hardbound was published with a dust jacket; worth 50% more with dust jacket. The 1929 edition is very popular with baseball collectors. Strip debuted Nov 27, 1922.*

SMOKEY STOVER (See Dan Dunn & King of the Royal Mounted) (N)
Whitman Publishing: 1937 (5 1/2 x 7 1/4", 68pgs., color cardboard-c, B&W)

1010 36.00 144.00 250.00

SOCIAL COMEDY (M)
Life Publishing Company: 1902 (11-3/4 x 9-1/2", 128 pgs, B&W, illustrated hardcover)

nn - Artists include C.D. Gibson & Kemble. 20.00 70.00 120.00
NOTE: *Reprints cartoons and a few sequential comics from LIFE. Came in unmarked slipcase.*

SOCIAL HELL, THE (O)
Rich Hill: 1902

nn - By Ryan Walker 21.00 74.00 130.00
NOTE: *"The conditions of workers and the corruption of a political system beholden to corporate interests have been a major focus of human rights concerns since the 19th century. This early graphic novel depicts the social evils of unreformed capitalism. Ryan Walker was a syndicate cartoonist for many mainstream newspapers as well as for the communist Daily Worker." This description comes from http://www.lib.uconn.edu/DoddCenter/ascexh3.html, where you can find also a reproduction of the cover. I add that Ryan Walker was the editor of "The Saint Louis Republic" comic section since its inception in 1897; the supplement published "Alma and Oliver", George McManus's first series.*

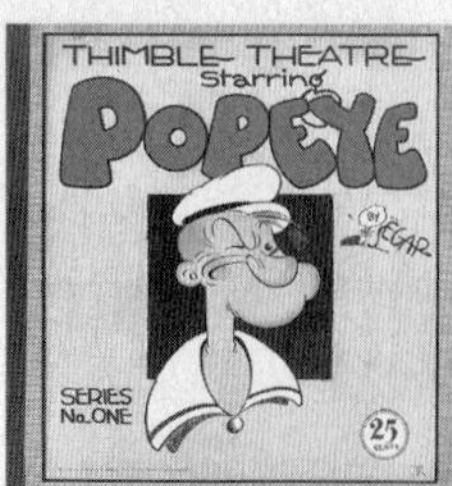

Thimble Theater #1 by E.C. Segar
1931 © Sonnet Publishing Co.

Tillie the Toiler #3 by Russ Westover
1927 © Cupples & Leon

Tim McCoy, Police Car 17
© Whitman Publ. Co.

GD2.0 FN6.0 VF8.0

SPORT AND THE KID (see The Umbrella Man) (N)
Lowman & Hanford Co.: 1913 (6-1/4x6-5/8",114 pgs, hardcover, B&W&orange)
nn - By J.R. "Dok" Hager 20.00 70.00 120.00

STORY OF CONNECTICUT (N)
The Hartford Times: Vol.1 1935 - Vol.3 1936 (10-1/2" x 7-3/8",304 pgs,color hard-c, B&W)
Vol.1 - 3 20.00 70.00 120.00
NOTE: *Collects a newspaper strip on Connecticut State history, which ran in the Hartford Times. Strip is in a similar format to "Texas History Movies". Also published in a plain, blue hardcover.*

STORY OF JAPAN IN CHINA, THE (N,S)
Trans-Pacific News Service, NYC: Vol. 3, No.1 March 10, 1938 (9" x 6", 36 pgs, construction paper-c, B&W)
Vol.3 No.1 21.00 64.00 150.00
NOTE: *Part of the "China Reference Series" of booklets, detailing the Japanese occupation and brutalization of China. Consists entirely of cartoons. The other booklets in the series have no cartoons. Art by: Ding, Fitzpatrick, Herblock, Herman, Rollin Kirby, Knox, Low, Manning, Orr, Shoemaker, Talburt.*

STRANGE AS IT SEEMS (S)
Blue-Star Publishing Co.: 1932 (64 pgs., B&W, square binding)
1-Newspaper-r (*Published with & without No. 1 and price on cover.*) 32.00 128.00 225.00
Ex-Lax giveaway (1936, B&W, 24 pgs., 5x7") - McNaught Synd. 13.00 52.00 90.00

SULLIVANT'S ABC ZOO (I)
The Old Wine Press: 1946 (11-3/4x9-3/8", hardcover)
nn - By T.S. Sullivant (Rare) – – –
NOTE: *Reprints Mitchell & Miller material 1895-1898 and Life Publishing 1898-1926.*

TAILSPIN TOMMY STORY & PICTURE BOOK (N)
McLoughlin Bros.: No. 266, 1931? (nd) (10x10-1/2", color strip-r)
266 - By Forrest 43.00 172.00 300.00

TAILSPIN TOMMY (Also see Famous Feature Stories & The Funnies)(N)
Cupples & Leon Co.: 1932 (100 pgs., hard-c) (B&W 1930 strip reprints)
nn - (Scarce)- by Hal Forrest & Glenn Chaffin 50.00 150.00 375.00

TALES OF DEMON DICK AND BUNKER BILL (O)
Whitman Publishing Co.: 1934 (5-1/4x10-1/2", 80 pgs, color hardcover, B&W)
793 - By Spencer 33.00 100.00 300.00

TARZAN BOOK (The Illustrated...) (N)
Grosset & Dunlap: 1929 (9x7", 80 pgs.)
1(Rare)-Contains 1st B&W Tarzan newspaper comics from 1929. By Hal Foster
Cloth reinforced spine & dust jacket (50¢); Foster-c
With dust jacket... 86.00 344.00 630.00
Without dust jacket... 43.00 172.00 315.00
2nd Printing(1934, 25¢, 76 pgs.)-4 Foster pgs. dropped; paper spine, circle in lower right cover with 25¢ price. The 25¢ is barely visible on some copies 34.00 136.00 250.00
1967-House of Greystoke reprint-7x10", using the complete 300 illustrations/text from the 1929 edition minus the original indicia, foreword, etc. Initial version bound in gold paper & sold for $5.00. Officially titled **Burroughs Bibliophile #2**. A very few additional copies were bound in heavier blue paper. Gold binding... 2.25 6.75 20.00
Blue binding... 2.50 7.50 27.00

TARZAN OF THE APES TO COLOR (N)
Saalfield Publishing Co.: No. 988, 1933 (15-1/4x10-3/4", 24 pgs)
(Coloring book)
988-(Very Rare)-Contains 1929 daily reprints with some new art by Hal Foster. Two panels blown up large on each page with one at the top of opposing pages on every other double-page spread. Believed to be the only time these panels appeared in color. Most color panels are reproduced a second time in B&W to be colored 271.00 1084.00 2000.00

TARZAN OF THE APES The Big Little Cartoon Book (N)
Whitman Publishing Company: 1933 (4-1/2x3 5/8", 320 pgs, color-c, B&W)
744 - By Hal Foster (comic strips on every page) 60.00 175.00 325.00

TECK HASKINS AT OHIO STATE (S)
Lea-Mar Press: 1908 (7-1/4x5-3/8", 84 pgs, B&W hardcover)
nn - By W.A. Ireland; football cartoons-r from Columbus Ohio Evening Dispatch 28.00 99.00 170.00
NOTE: *Small blue & white patch of cover art pasted atop a color cloth quilt patter; pasted patch can easily peel off some copies.*

TECK 1909 (S)
Lea-Mar Press: 1909 (8-5/8 x 8-1/8", 124 pgs., B&W hardcover, 25¢)
nn - By W.A. Ireland; Ohio State University baseball cartoons-r from Columbus Evening Dispatch 28.00 99.00 170.00

TEDDY BEAR BOOKS, THE (M) (see also LITTLE JOHNNY AND THE TEDDY BEARS)
Reilly & Britton Co., Chicago: 1907 (7-1/16" x 5-3/8", 24 pgs, hard-c, color
The Teddy Bears Come to Life, The Teddy Bears at the Circus, The Teddy Bears in a Smashup, The Teddy Bears on a Lark, The Teddy Bears on a Toboggan, The Teddy Bears at School, The Teddy Bears Go Fishing, The Teddy Bears in Hot Water
21.00 63.00 130.00
NOTE: *Books are all unnumbered. C & A by J.R. Bray; s-Robert D. Towne. Reprints "Little Johnny & the Teddy Bears" strips, from Judge Magazine. Similar in format to the Buster Brown Nuggets series. All eight books debuted simultaneously.*

TEDDY BEARS IN FUN AND FROLIC (M) (see LITTLE JOHNNY & THE TEDDY BEARS)
Reilly & Britton Co., Chicago: 1908 (8-3/4" x 8-3/4", 50 pgs, cardboard-c, color)
nn - (Rare) by J.R. Bray-a; Robert D. Towne-s 100.00 400.00 700.00
NOTE: *Reprints "Little Johnny & the Teddy Bears" strips, from Judge Magazine. Unknown if there were any other "Teddy Bear" titles published in this format.*

THE TEENIE WEENIES
Reilly & Britton, Chicago: 1916 (16-3/8x10-1/2", 52 pgs, cardboard-c, full color)
nn - By Wm. Donahey (Chicago Tribune-r) 200.00 550.00 900.00

TERROR OF THE TINY TADS (see also UPSIDE DOWNS OF LITTLE LADY LOVEKINS AND OLD MAN MUFFAROO)
Cupples & Leon: 1909 (11x17, 26 Sunday strips in Black & Red, Stiff cardboard-c)
nn - By Gustave Verbeek (Very Rare) (no known sales)

TEXAS HISTORY MOVIES (N)
Various editions, 1928 to 1986 (B&W)
Book I -1928 Southwest Press (7-1/4 x 5-3/8, 56 pgs, cardboard cover) for the Magnolia Petroleum Company 50.00 125.00 250.00
nn - 1928 Southwest Press (12-3/8 x 9-1/4, 232 pgs, HC) 75.00 200.00 400.00
nn - 1935 Magnolia Petroleum Company (6 x 9, 132 pgs, paper cover) 21.00 63.00 130.00
NOTE: *Exists with either Wagon Train or Texas Flag & Lafitte/pirate covers.*
nn - 1943 Magnolia Petroleum Company (132 pgs, paper cover) 16.00 48.00 100.00
nn - 1963 Graphic Ideas Inc (11 x 8-1/2, softcover) 12.00 37.00 75.00
NOTE: *Reprints daily newspaper strips from the Dallas News, on Texas history. 1935 editions onward distributed within the Texas Public School System. Prior to that they appear to be giveaway comic books for the Magnolia Petroleum Company. There are many more editions than the ones pointed out above.*

THAT SON-IN-LAW OF PA'S! (N)
Newspaper Feature Service: 1914 (2-1/2 by 3", color)
nn - *Imprinted on back for THE LESTER SHOE STORE.* 15.00 25.00 50.00
NOTE: *Single sheet printed in full color on both sides, unfolds to show 12 panel story.*

THIMBLE THEATRE STARRING POPEYE (See also Popeye) (N)
Sonnet Publishing Co.: 1931 - No. 2, 1932 (25¢, B&W, 52 pgs.)(Rare)
1-Daily strip serial-r in both by Segar 157.00 650.00 1300.00
2 136.00 544.00 1100.00
NOTE: *The very first Popeye reprint book. The first Thimble Theatre Sunday page appeared Dec 19, 1919. Popeye first entered Thimble Theatre on Jan 17, 1929.*

THREE FUN MAKERS, THE (N)
Stokes and Company: 1908 (10x15", 64 pgs., color) (1904-06 Sunday strip-r)
nn - Maud, Katzenjammer Kids, Happy Hooligan 800.00 2000.00 –
NOTE: *This is the first comic book to compile more than one newspaper strip together.*

TIGERS (Also see On and Off Mount Ararat) (N)
Hearst's New York American & Journal: 1902, 86 pgs. 10x15-1/4"
nn - Funny animal strip-r by Jimmy Swinnerton 600.00 1600.00 –
NOTE: *The strip began as The Journal Tigers in The New York Journal Dec 12, 1897-Sept 28 1903*

TILLIE THE TOILER (N)
Cupples & Leon Co.: 1925 - No. 8, 1933 (52 pgs., B&W, daily strip-r)
nn (#1) By Russ Westover 54.00 216.00 450.00
2-8 50.00 175.00 360.00
NOTE: *First newspaper strip appearance was in January, 1921.*

TILLIE THE TOILER MAGIC DRAWING AND COLORING BOOK
Sam L Gabriel Sons And Company: 1931 (8-1/2 x 12", 36 pages, stiff-c)
838-By Russ Westover 39.00 156.00 275.00

TIMID SOUL, THE (N)
Simon & Schuster: 1931 (12-1/4x9", 136 pgs, B&W hardcover, dust jacket?)
nn - By H. T. Webster (newspaper strip-r) 40.00 120.00 260.00

TIM McCOY, POLICE CAR 17 (O)
Whitman Publishing Co.: 1934 (14-3/4x11", 32 pgs, stiff color covers)
674-1933 original material 75.00 300.00 600.00
NOTE: *Historically important as first movie adaptation in comic books.*

TOAST BOOK
John C. Winston Co: 1905 (7-1/4 x 6,104 pgs, skull-shaped book, feltcover, B&W)
nn - By Clare Dwiggins 50.00 175.00 300.00
NOTE: *Cartoon illustrations accompanying toasts/poems, most involving alcohol.*

TOM SAWYER & HUCK FINN (N)
Stoll & Edwards Co.:1925 (10x10-3/4", 52 pgs, stiff covers)
nn - By "Dwig" Dwiggins; 1923, 1924-r color Sunday strips 5000 200.00 350.00
NOTE: *By Permission of the Estate of Samuel L. Clemons and the Mark Twain Company.*

TOONERVILLE TROLLEY AND OTHER CARTOONS (N) (See Cartoons by Fontaine Fox)
Cupples & Leon Co.: 1921 (10 x10", 52 pgs., B&W, daily strip-r)

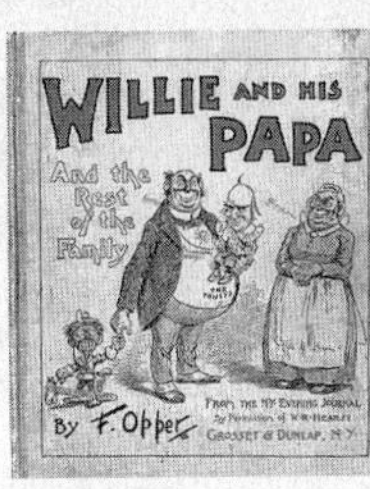

Willie and His Papa & the Rest of the Family by Opper
1901 © Grossett & Dunlap

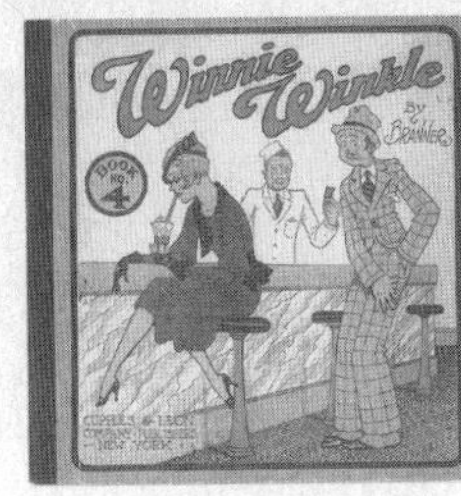

Winnie Winkle #4 by Branner
1933 © Cupples & Leon

The Yellow Kid #4 cover by Outcault
1897 © Howard Ainslee & Co.

GD2.0 FN6.0 VF8.0

1 - By Fontaine Fox 100.00 350.00 600.00

TRAINING FOR THE TRENCHES (M)
Palmer Publishing Company: 1917 (5-3/8 x 7", 20 pgs., paper-c, 10¢)
nn - By Lieut. Alban B. Butler, Jr. 21.00 84.00 150.00
NOTE: *Subtitle: "A book of humorous cartoons on a serious subject." Single-panels about military training.*

TREASURE BOX OF FAMOUS COMICS (N) (see Wonder Chest of Famous Comics)
Cupples & Leon Co.: 1934 8-1/2x(6-7/8", 36 pgs, soft covers) (Boxed set of 5 books)
Little Orphan Annie (1926) 21.00 84.00 165.00
Reg'lar Fellers (1928) 19.00 76.00 145.00
Smitty (1928) 19.00 76.00 145.00
Harold Teen (1931) 19.00 76.00 145.00
How Dick Tracy & Dick Tracy Jr. Caught The Racketeers (1933) 26.00 104.00 205.00
Softcover set of five books in box 160.00 640.00 1250.00
Box only 57.00 228.00 450.00
NOTE: *Dates shown are copyright dates; all books actually came out in 1934 or later. The softcovers are abbreviated versions of the hardcover editions listed under each character.*

T.R. IN CARTOONS (N)
A.C. McClurg & Co., Chicago: June 13, 1910 (10-5/8" x 8", 104? pgs, paper-c, B&W)
nn - By McCutcheon about Teddy Roosevelt - - -

TRUTH (See Victorian section for earlier issues including the first Yellow Kid appearances)
Truth Company, NY: 1886-1906? (13-11/16x10-5/16", 16 pgs, process color-c & center-folds, rest B&W)
1900-1906 issues 10.00 20.00 50.00

TRUTH SAVE IT FROM ABUSE & OVERWORK BEING THE EPISODE OF THE HIRED HAND & MRS. STIX PLASTER, CONCERTIST (N)
Radio Truth Society of WBAP: no date, 1924 (6-3/8 x 4-7/8, 40 pgs, paper cover, B&W)
nn - By V.T. Hamlin (Very Rare) 100.00 400.00 700.00
NOTE: *Radio station WBAP giveaway reprints strips from the Ft. Worth Texas Star-Telegram set at local radio station. 1st collected work by V.T. Hamlin, pre-Alley Oop.*

TWENTY FIVE YEARS AGO (see At The Bottom Of The Ladder) (M,S)
Coward-McCann: 1931 (5-3/4x8-1/4, 328 pgs, hardcover, B&W)
nn - By Camillus Kessler 32.00 128.00 225.00
NOTE: *Multi-image panel cartoons showing historical events for dates during the year.*

UMBRELLA MAN, THE (N) (See Sport And The Kid)
Lowman & Hanford Co.: 1911 (8-7/8x5-7/8",112 pgs, hard-c, B&W & orange)
nn - By J.R. "Dok" Hager (Seattle Times-r) 20.00 70.00 120.00

UNCLE REMUS AND BRER RABBIT (N)
Frederick A. Stokes Co.: 1907 (64 pgs, hardbound, color)
nn - By Joel C Harris & J.M. Conde 50.00 175.00 300.00

UPSIDE DOWNS OF LITTLE LADY LOVEKINS AND OLD MAN MUFFAROO
(see also TERROR OF THE TINY TADS)
New York Herald: 1905 (?) (N)
nn - By Gustav Verbeck 150.00 450.00 750.00

VAUDEVILLES AND OTHER THINGS (N)
Isaac H. Blandiard Co.: 1900 (13x10-1/2", 22 pgs., color) plus two reprints
nn - By Bunny (Scarce) 400.00 1200.00 -
nn - 2nd print "By the Creator of Foxy Grandpa" on-c but only has copyright info of 1900 (10-1/2x15 1/2, 28 pgs, color) 450.00 900.00 -
nn - 3rd print. "By the creator of Foxy Grandpa" on-c; has both 1900 and 1901 copyright info (11x13") 350.00 700.00 -

WALLY - HIS CARTOONS OF THE A.E.F. (N)
Stars & Stripes: 1917 (96 and 108 pgs, B&W)
nn - By Abian A "Wally" Wallgren (7x18; 96 pgs) 25.00 75.00 150.00
nn - another edition (108 pgs, 7x17-1/2) 25.00 75.00 150.00
NOTE: *World War One cartoons reprints from Stars & Stripes; sold to U.S. servicemen with profits to go to French War Orphans Fund. various editions from 1917-1920; there might be more than what we list here.*

WAR CARTOONS (S)
Dallas News: 1918 (11x9", 112 pgs, hardcover, B&W)
nn - By John Knott (WWOne cartoons) 20.00 70.00 125.00

WAR CARTOONS FROM THE CHICAGO DAILY NEWS (N,S)
Chicago Daily News: 1914 (10 cents, 7-3/4x10-3/4", 68 pgs, paper-c, B&W)
nn - By L.D. Bradley 20.00 70.00 125.00

WEBER & FIELD'S FUNNYISMS (S,M,O)
Arkell Comoany, NY: 1904 (10-7/8x8", 112 pgs, color-c, B&W)
1 - By various (only issue?) 20.00 70.00 150.00
NOTE: *Contains some sequential & many single panel strips by Outcault, George Luks, CA David, Houston, L Smith, Hy Mayer, Verbeck, Woolf, Sydney Adams, Frank "Chip" Bellew, Eugene "ZIM" Zimmerman, Phil May, FT Richards, Billy Marriner, Grosvenor and many others.*

WE'RE NOT HEROES (O,S)
E.C. Wells and J.W. Moss: 1933 (8-11/16" x 5-7/8", 52 pgs, B&W interior)
nn - By Eddie Wells; red & black paper-c 10.00 30.00 60.00
NOTE: *Amateurish cartoons about World War I vets in the Walter Reed Veteran's Hospital.*

GD2.0 FN6.0 VF8.0

WHEN A FELLER NEEDS A FRIEND (S)
P. F. Volland & Co.: 1914 (11-11/16x8-7/8)
nn - By Clare Briggs 37.00 131.00 225.00
NOTE: *Originally came in box with Briggs art (box is Rare); also numerous more modern reprints)*

WILD PILGRIMAGE (O)
Harrison Smith & Robert Haas: 1932 (9-7/8x7", 210 pgs, B&W hardcover w/dust jacket) (original wordless graphic novel in woodcuts)
nn - By Lynd Ward 50.00 175.00 300.00

WILLIE AND HIS PAPA AND THE REST OF THE FAMILY (I)
Grossett & Dunlap: 1901 (9-1/2x8", 200 pgs, hardcover from N.Y. Evening Journal by Permission of W. R. Hearst) (pictures & text)
nn - By Frederick Opper 100.00 260.00 450.00
NOTE: *Political satire series of single panel cartoons, involving whiny child Willie (President William McKinley), his rambunctious and uncontrollable cousin Teddy (Vice President Roosevelt), and Willie's Papa (trusts/monopolies) and their Maid (Senator) Hanna.*

WILLIE GREEN COMICS, THE (N) (see Adventures of Willie Green)
Frank M. Acton Co./Harris Brown: 1915 (8x15, 36 pgs); 1921 (6x10-1/8", 52 pgs, color paper cover, B&W interior, 25¢)
Book No. 1 By Harris Brown 45.00 158.00 270.00
Book 2 (*#2 sold via mail order directly from the artist)(very rare)* 45.00 172.00 300.00
NOTE: *Book No. 1 possible reprint of Adv. of Willie Green; definitely two different editions.*

WILLIE WESTINGHOUSE EDISON SMITH THE BOY INVENTOR (N)
William A. Stokes Co.: 1906 (10x16", 36 pgs. in color)
nn - By Frank Crane (Scarce) 350.00 850.00 1500.00
NOTE: *Comic strip began May 27, 1900 and ran thru 1914. Parody of inventors Westinghouse and Edison.*

WINNIE WINKLE (N)*Strip began as a daily Sept 20, 1920.*
Cupples & Leon Co.: 1930 - No. 4, 1933 (52 pgs., B&W daily strip-r)
1 43.00 172.00 400.00
2-4 29.00 116.00 300.00

WISDOM OF CHING CHOW, THE (see also The Gumps)
R. J. Jefferson Printing Co.: 1928 (4x3", 100 pgs, red & B&W cardboard cover) (newspaper strip-r The Chicago Tribune)
nn - By Sidney Smith (scarce) 30.00 90.00 150.00

WONDER CHEST OF FAMOUS COMICS (N) see Treasure Chest of Famous Comics)
Cupples & Leon Co.: 1935? 8-1/2x(6-7/8", 36 pgs, soft covers) (Boxed set of 5 books)
Little Orphan Annie #2 (1927) (Haunted House) 21.00 84.00 130.00
Little Orphan Annie #3 (1928) (in the Circus) 19.00 76.00 130.00
Smitty #2 (1929) (Babe Ruth app.) 19.00 76.00 130.00
Dolly Dimples and Bobby Bounce (1933) by Grace Drayton 19.00 76.00 130.00
How Dick Tracy & Dick Tracy Jr. Caught The Racketeers (1933) 26.00 104.00 185.00
Softcover set of five books in box 160.00 640.00 1125.00
Box only 57.00 228.00 400.00
NOTE: *Dates shown are original copyright dates of the first printings; all actually came out in 1934 or later. Extremely abbreviated versions of the hardcover editions listed under each character. It is suspected this came out the Christmas season following Teasure Chest of Famous Comics. which contains earlier editions.*

WORLD OF TROUBLE, A (S)
Minneapolis Journal: 1901 (10x8-3/4", 100 pgs, 40 pgs full color)
v3#1 - By Charles L. Bartholomew (editorial-r) 28.00 99.00 170.00

WRIGLEY'S "MOTHER GOOSE"
Wm. Wrigley Jr. Company, Chicago: 1915 (6" x 4", 28 pgs, full color)
nn - *Promotional comics for Wrigley's gum. Intro Wrigley's "Spearmen* 20.00 70.00 120.00
Book No. 2 20.00 70.00 120.00

YELLOW KID, THE (Magazine)(I) (becomes **The Yellow Book** #10 on)
Howard Ainslee & Co., N.Y.: Mar. 20, 1897 - #9, July 17, 1897
(5¢, B&W w/color covers, 52p., stapled) (not a comic book)
1-R.F. Outcault Yellow kid on-c only #1-6. The same Yellow Kid color ad app. on back-c #1-6 (advertising the New York Sunday Journal) 857.00 3500.00 -
2-6 (#2 4/3/97, #5 5/22/97, #6, 6/5/97) 743.00 2800.00 -
7-9 (Yellow Kid not on-c) 121.00 425.00 -
NOTE: *Richard Outcault's Yellow Kid from the Hearst New York American represents the very first successful newspaper comic strip in America. Listed here due to historical importance.*

YELLOW KID IN MCFADDEN'S FLATS, THE (N)
G. W. Dillingham Co., New York: 1897 (50¢, 7-1/2x5-1/2", 196 pgs., B&W, squarebound)
nn - The first "comic" book featuring The Yellow Kid; E. W. Townsend narrative w/R. F. Outcault Sunday comic page art-r & some original drawings 7000.00 14000.00 -
NOTE: *A Fair condition copy sold for $2,901 in August 2004.; restored app VF sold for $10,500 in 2005. A copy in Fine+ (spine intact) and loose bacl cover sold for $17,000 in 2006.*

YESTERDAYS (S)
The Reilly & Lee Co.: 1930 (8-3/4 x 7-1/2", 128 pgs, illustrated hard-c with dust jacket
nn - Text and cartoons about Victorian times by Frank Wing 20.00 40.00 80.00

Any addititions or corrections to this section are always welcome, very much encouraged and can be sent to **feedback@gemstonepub.com** to be processed for next year's Guide.

Golden Age & Beyond

The American Comic Book 1938–Present

by J.C. Vaughn & Gene Gonzales

EVERYTHING CHANGED IN JUNE 1938.
AT THE SAME TIME NOTHING CHANGED.

THE ERA OF THE SUPERHEROES ARRIVED, SO THE CONTENT OF COMICS DEFINITELY CHANGED . . .
. . . BUT NOTHING FUNDAMENTALLY CHANGED IN THE METHOD OF DELIVERING SEQUENTIAL STORYTELLING TO THE MASSES.

STILL, IT'S HARD TO IGNORE WHAT FOLLOWED.

AND IT'S HARD TO IGNORE THE VALUE ATTACHED TO SOME OF THE COMICS LISTED IN THIS SECTION.

FIRST, THOUGH, WE'LL TAKE A CLOSE-UP LOOK AT THE COMICS OF THE 1970S COURTESY OF BACK ISSUE EDITOR AND OVERSTREET ADVISOR MICHAEL EURY . . .
FOLLOWED BY OUR LARGEST PRICING SECTION.
TAKE IT AWAY, MICHAEL!

THE BRONZE AGE

GOING FOR THE BRONZE: LIFE AFTER THE SILVER AGE

by Michael Eury

It was 1970, and the Silver Age was over.

The Silver Age's innovations, the Julie Schwartz-edited revamps of Golden Age favorites and the Lee/Kirby/et al.-constructed House of Ideas, had grown familiar, and in some cases, stale. The bottom had dropped out of the TV *Batman* superhero boom and the Big Two and its competitors, reeling from declining sales, scratched their heads and pondered, "What do we try next?"

Their answer: *Try everything!* The 1970s *was* the decade of excess, after all, when there was no such thing as "too much" and nothing we, as a culture, wouldn't try. Hair got longer, music got louder, lapels got wider, bras got burned, movies got bloodier, drugs got mainstreamed . . . and Mom wore pantsuits while Dad sprouted muttonchops. Marvel and DC also got "with it," trying new genres, new ideas, and new formats, all in a hungry pursuit of the one thing there could *never* be too much of: money.

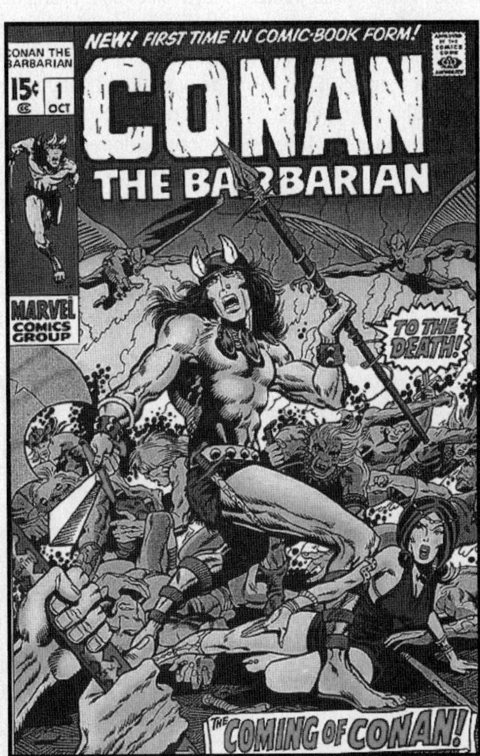

Today, Mom's pantsuits may have elastic waistlines and Dad's muttonchops-and hair-may be a distant memory, but the decade we now call the Bronze Age-1970–1979-was, arguably, the most influential of all of comics' landmark eras. It could have been comics' last dance, but instead it became a decade of renaissance, when through trial and error inroads were made that paved the way for the innovations of the 1980s, the 1990s, and the comic book industry we know today.

In their quest to find the next big thing, the first place publishers looked was *outside* of comics. For a mere $200 licensing fee ($50 beyond tight-fisted publisher Martin Goodman's budgeted $150), Marvel Comics writer/editor Roy Thomas landed the publication rights to Robert E. Howard's famed swordsman Conan. And while Marvel's *Conan the Barbarian* #1, written by Thomas, drawn by newcomer Barry (Windsor-) Smith, and cover-dated October 1970, didn't instantly ignite the comics world (*Conan* didn't look or read like the other material available, and early issues suffered from distribution challenges), before long the series developed a growing audience, and proved to publishers that they could sell material other than caped crusaders and lovesick all-American teens.

Sword-and-sorcery comics soon cut a swath through the stands, with licensed acquisitions Kull, Red Sonja, Thongor, and Solomon Kane joining Marvel's line, and DC countering with its acquisition of Fritz Leiber's Fafhrd and the Grey Mouser, in a 1973 series that made no attempt to hide the craze upon which it was capitalizing: *Sword and Sorcery* (original characters like the Warlord, Starfire, Stalker, Claw the Unconquered, IronJaw, and Wulf the Barbarian also premiered). Yet DC had already ventured into licensed terrain with its April 1972 cover–dated first issue of *Tarzan* (#207, continuing the numbering from previous publisher Gold Key). "[The estate of Tarzan creator Edgar Rice Burroughs] wanted their creative people on *Tarzan,*" Carmine Infantino, at the time DC's Editorial Director, revealed, a request to which he responded, "No, I want my guys on the book"—actually his "guy," Joe Kubert, whose heralded stint as writer/artist/editor produced some of, perhaps *the*, finest illustrated Tarzan stories ever.

Tomb of Dracula (*TOD*), first seen in (cover date) April 1972, was not a licensed property but might have been had Bram Stoker's 1897 vampire novel not fallen into public domain. *TOD* and *Werewolf by Night*, which preceded it into print by two months in

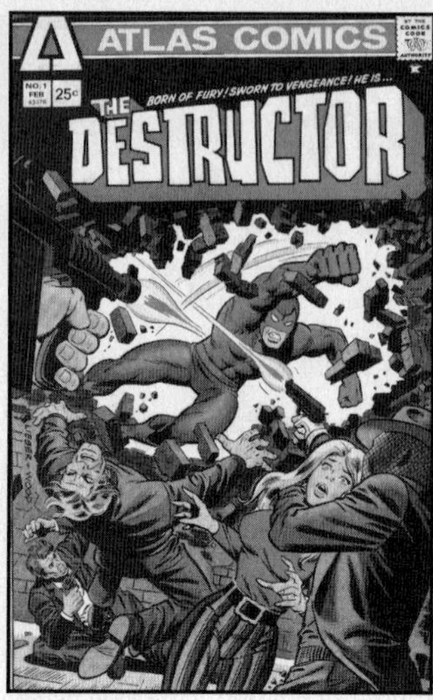

Marvel Spotlight #2, were Marvel's response to the 1971 lifting of the Comics Code Authority's prohibition against the depiction of vampires, werewolves, and the undead (although Morbius the Living Vampire, who debuted in October 1971's *Amazing Spider-Man* #101, was first out the gruesome gate), and spawned one of the decade's most popular trends. Frankenstein, Swamp Thing, Man-Thing, Bog Beast, Brother Voodoo, the Demon, and the Living Mummy were among the macabre protagonists in 1970s comics ("I pray that you will discontinue this corruption of impressionable young minds. . ." penned one concerned mother in response to Marvel's hellspawned super-hero, the Son of Satan). Some of them have resurfaced in the 2000s and have achieved acclaim beyond the four-color pages, including Ghost Rider, the star of a 2006 motion picture starring Nicolas Cage—who was weaned on Bronze Age comics (and chose his stage name from Marvel's own Hero for Hire, Luke Cage, another product of the 1970s).

Fu Manchu, the fictional "Yellow Peril" mastermind and subject of a series of novels by Sax Rohmer, brought his claw-fingered menace to comics in *Special Marvel Edition* #15 (December 1973), the first appearance of his created-for-comics son, Shang-Chi, better known as the Master of Kung Fu. Steve Englehart and Jim Starlin's response to the TV hit *Kung Fu* (1972–1975)—which itself was television's response to the trend of Hong Kong–born martial-arts movies and their patron saint, Bruce Lee—*Master of Kung Fu* became a long-running success for Marvel (most notably under Doug Moench and Paul Gulacy's tenure), and encouraged a gaggle of companions and imitators, including Sons of the Tiger, Iron Fist, Bronze Tiger, Lady Shiva, Karate Kid, and Richard Dragon, Kung Fu Fighter, as well as Seaboard/Atlas' 1975 copycat title *The Hands of the Dragon*.

Martial arts aside, Rohmer's Fu Manchu novels repre-

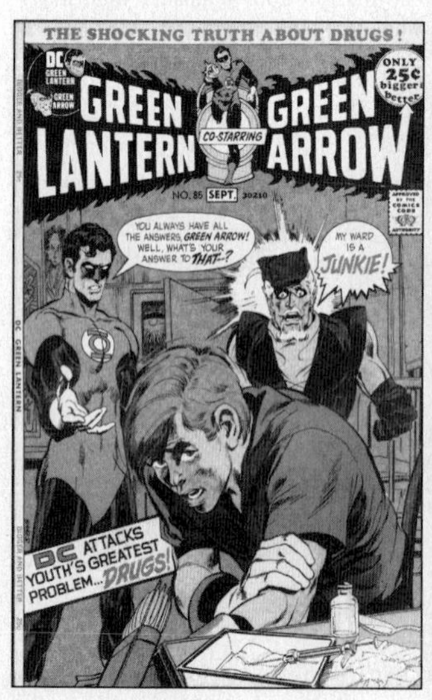

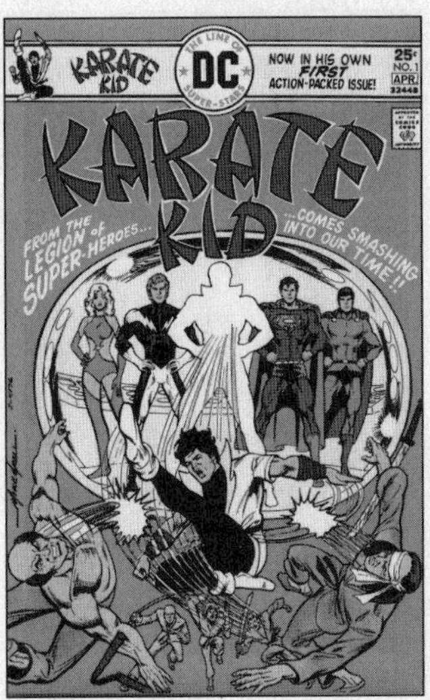

sented another 1970s' comics trend: pulp heroes. Doc Savage returned to spin racks in the form of a Marvel series in 1972. Dennis O'Neil and Michael Kaluta brought *The Shadow* to DC in 1973 (Jim Steranko, Alex Toth, and Bernie Wrightson were considered as the *Shadow* artist before then-newcomer Kaluta was signed). In 1975 DC also published four issues of *Justice, Inc.*, starring the chalk-skinned globetrotter the Avenger, and Howard Chaykin's mid-1970s' Dominic Fortune (for Marvel) and the Scorpion (for Seaboard) mined this pulp vein.

Beyond the world of pop literature, Marvel found mass media a ripe market for exploitation. Rock stars KISS became super-heroes, even fighting Dr. Doom (premiering in a magazine-formatted comic featuring the audacious stunt of mixing the band's *blood* with the printer's ink!), and comics based upon popular sci-fi films *Logan's Run*, *Planet of the Apes*, *Godzilla*, and *2001: A Space Odyssey* invaded the racks. DC was less ambitious in adapting cinematic properties, although its "DC TV Comic" line, including *Welcome Back, Kotter*, is noteworthy if for no other reason than the utter strangeness of it all.

No 1970s' screen property was more popular as a comic book than *Star Wars*, which premiered a few months before the May 25, 1977 release of the film, an anticipation-building maneuver brainstormed by Jedi master George Lucas. Roy Thomas was at the writing helm, and as he told *BACK ISSUE* in 2005, Lucas "had in mind the idea of Howard Chaykin as the artist." *Star Wars*' success title paved the way for other popular late-1970s' Marvel titles based upon sci-fi and toy properties, such as *Battlestar Galactica*, *The Micronauts*, and *Rom*.

Chaykin as Lucas' go-to artist illustrates another hallmark of 1970s' comics: the emergence of young talent. Comics publishing houses had been the exclusive domain of

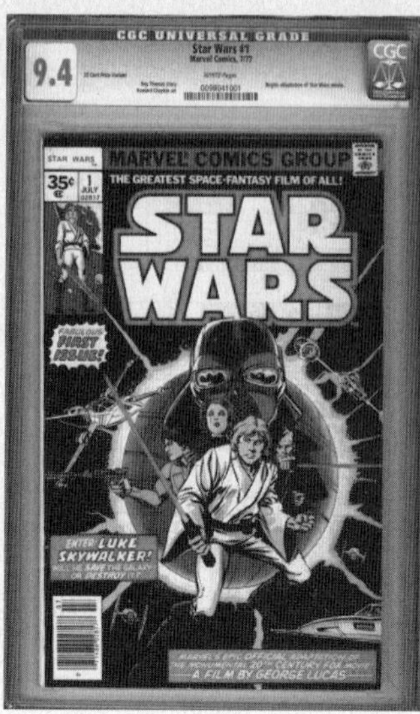

stuffed shirts in elbow-patched tweed jackets, but while looking outside of the field for new properties, the medium also looked *within* its fan base for the next talent wave. The transition, however, was not without its bumps in the road. As one of the "long-hairs" who broke the barrier, writer Denny O'Neil revealed, reflecting upon his visits to DC's headquarters, that "Steve Skeates and I were told by one of the functionaries not to walk past the Big Boss' office 'looking like that,' to take the long way around." "DC had been a closed shop," concurred Carmine Infantino, who "put aside a room for the freelance artists and writers, a place for them to go and discuss and enjoy each other's work." Another such site was Continuity Associates, the studio co-founded in 1971 by Neal Adams and Dick Giordano. Following the lead established in the late 1960s by visionaries Adams and his contemporary Steranko, who demonstrated that comics storytelling was not restricted to stodgy panel layouts or stereotypical dialogue, new artists and writers stormed the medium, daring to do things differently, Frank Brunner, John Byrne, Chris Claremont, Gerry Conway, Dave Cockrum, José Luis Garcia-Lopez, Steve Gerber, Michael Golden, Mike Grell, George Pérez, Mike Ploog, Frank Miller, Marshall Rogers, Bill Sienkiewicz, Walter Simonson, Len Wein, and Marv Wolfman, among their number.

Not to rest on their laurels, established talent became energized by this exciting new climate: John Buscema, Nick Cardy, Gene Colan, Gil Kane, Jack Kirby, Joe Kubert, Stan Lee, and John Romita, Sr. produced some of their best work in the 1970s, as did Curt Swan and Murphy Anderson with their "Swanderson" pairing on *Superman*. Marvel and DC took chances with traditional characters and with new characters existing within their universes. The coming of Kirby's Fourth World, *Green Lantern/Green Arrow*, Swamp Thing, Jonah Hex, the Punisher and Wolverine, Howard the Duck, Warlock, ethnic characters, and the new X-Men, plus the Joker's return to his homicidal roots and the deaths of Gwen

Stacy and the Green Goblin, suggest that the most significant innovation of the 1970s might have been a willingness to explore new directions with icons.

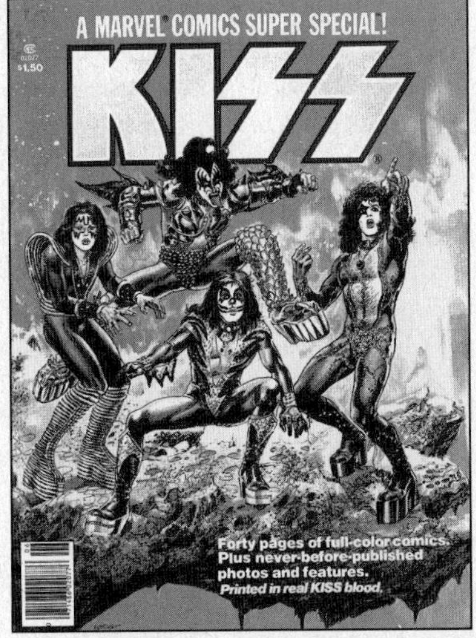

With new properties, new talent, and new characters bombarding the reader at a dizzying pace, little stability was to be found in the *shapes* of the comic books themselves. Publishers experimented with a variety of formats, in a move initially inspired by that perennial enemy of the long-time comic-book reader: the price increase.

Two years after jumping from a 12- to a 15-cent cover price, the 25-cent comic originated in the summer of 1971, as DC's titles, with their August cover dates, were now 48 pages (52 counting covers), hyped as "bigger and better" with roughly 22–25 new story pages backed up by 6–12 pages of Golden and Silver Age reprints. Marvel sucker-punched DC, delaying their price hike by one month (while blurbing their covers "Still 15¢"), then matching DC's price the next month, but trumping their original page count with 34–35 new story pages—and *then* undercutting their competitor by reverting to the standard 32-page format the following month, but at the cover price of 20 cents. DC, however, offered its readers something that Marvel's streamlined package could not: history. Newer readers sampled adventures of long-retired characters like Starman and Sandman, or more recently cancelled heroes including Deadman, keeping them alive in the fandom consciousness and inspiring budding writers and artists to, in later years, resuscitate them.

Is there any format that "says" the 1970s more than DC's 100-page Super Spectacular? In June and July 1971, DC published a trio of 100-pagers—*Weird Mystery Tales*, *Love Stories*, and *World's Greatest Super-Heroes*—each priced at 50 cents and reprinting material from the publisher's rich past. By 1973, 100-pagers returned as reprint specials, following in the footsteps of the Silver Age's beloved Annuals and 80-page giants. Before long several of DC's regular titles were converted to a bimonthly 100-page format, with new lead feature (or features) backed up by classics from yesteryear. (In December 1976 DC similarly converted some of its character-heavy titles like *Superman Family* into its new "Dollar Comic" format, featuring *all-new* stories in an 80-page [later a 64-page] package.)

Sharing the Super Spectacular's page count but at a much smaller size, the digest-sized comic (which began in the late 1960s at Gold Key) gained prominence in the 1970s in an attempt to broaden comics' availability. DC experimented with a 1972 *Tarzan* digest, announcing but never releasing a *Laurel and Hardy* digest (DC did, however, release a *Laurel and Hardy* one-shot comic). By decade's end, DC, Marvel, and Archie were publishing a host of reprint digests, aggressively fighting for rack space in supermarkets' highly visible checkouts. DC's and Marvel's digests were cancelled by the mid-1980s, but Archie's remain a durable fixture today, and the digest has morphed into a popular format for manga.

Comics reprints gained a bookstore presence throughout the 1970s, including Bonanza's trio of hardcovers, *Batman: From the 30's to the 70's*, *Superman: From the 30's to the 70's*, and *Shazam: From the 40's to the 70's*, the latter of which, not experiencing reprintings like the Batman and Superman editions, being quite scarce in today's collectibles market. Fireside's full-color trade paperback collections of Marvel and DC material were popular, particularly the Stan Lee–sanctioned line of super-hero trades beginning with *Origins of Marvel Comics* (1974). Near the end of the decade, Tempo Books' black-and-white paperback reprints of 1950s and 1960s DC material could be found in bookstores and K-Marts, as could Pocket Books' full-color line of reprints of early Marvels.

The *biggest* reprint format of the 1970s, bar none, was the tabloid, measuring approximately 10 1/4" x 13 1/4" and called "Treasury Editions" by Marvel and "Limited Collectors' Editions" by DC. Offering the added bonus of printing comics art close to full size (the standard dimensions of comics artboard of the day was 10" x 15"), these oversized comics soon housed all-new as well as classic material, and became the spotlight format for influential projects, including DC and Marvel's first super-hero team-up, *Superman vs. The Amazing Spider-Man* (1976).

Tabloids were envisioned as a doorway for comics to hop off the claustrophobic, kid-centric spin rack and be shelved alongside compatibly sized periodicals, but the black-and-white (B&W) comics magazine was most attrac-

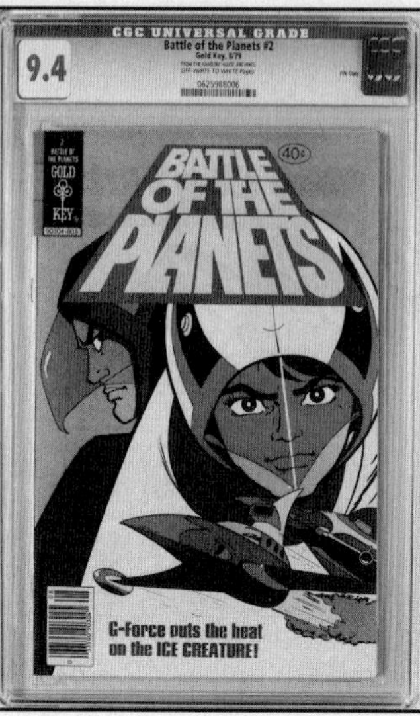

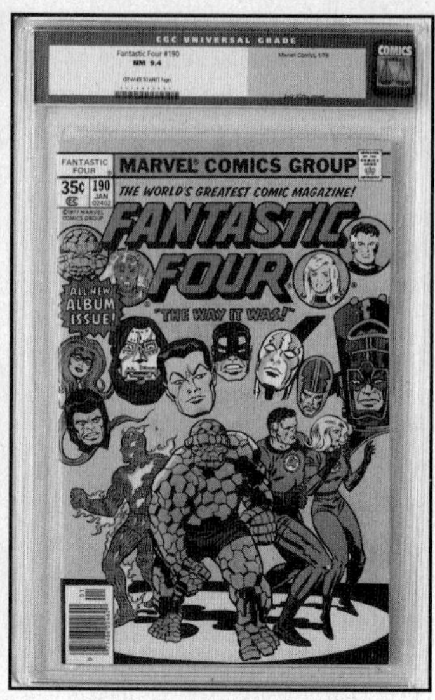

tive to publishers as a means of luring the older, more discerning reader to the comic-book art form. While the medium had previously dabbled in this arena, E.C.'s "Picto-Fiction" B&Ws of the 1950s being an early example, during the 1970s almost every comics house tried its hand at it, following the lead of publisher James Warren, the indisputable champ of black-and-whites since his 1964 launch of *Creepy*. Skywald's *Psycho*, Ross Andru and Mike Esposito's *Up Your Nose and Out Your Ear*, and Charlton's TV-licensed *The Six Million Dollar Man* were among 1970s' B&W comics magazine fare, but Marvel successfully milked this trend for several years, most notably with its long-running *Savage Sword of Conan*. A single issue each of Jack Kirby's ill-fated "Speak-Out" black-and-whites *In the Days of the Mob* and *Spirit World*, DC's 1971 attempt to stick an apprehensive toe in the B&W waters, was released under the banner of "Hampshire Distributor's Ltd." Always the trailblazer, Kirby had high hopes for finding a new audience with these magazines (he was developing two other titles, *True Divorce Cases* and *Soul Love*, but they were not produced), but spotty distribution of *Mob* and *Spirit* intimidated the publisher from releasing additional B&Ws.

The graphic novel was also born in the 1970s, thanks to Will Eisner's *A Contract with God* (1978). The biographical "comix" found in the undergrounds motivated Eisner to return to the fold after a hiatus, and at a time when he could have easily retired, Eisner essentially re-created the comics art form by producing this pioneering collection of intensely personal stories.

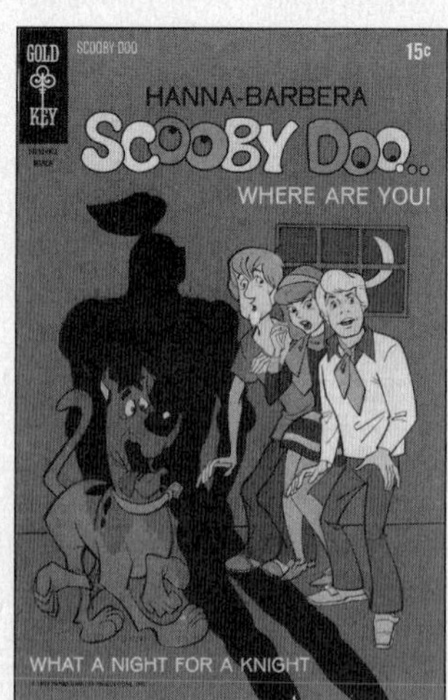

The final, but widest-reaching, breakthrough of the Bronze Age was merchandising. While popular comics stars had long been licensed for various products, comic-book characters became household names during the 1970s due to a ubiquitous barrage of Saturday-morning TV cartoons and primetime live-action dramas, action figures, records, coloring books, 7-11 Slurpee cups, lunchboxes, electric toothbrushes, Colorforms, clothing patches, View-Master reels, and Halloween costumes, culminating in *Superman: The Movie*'s elevation of the comic-book film to blockbuster status in 1978. While the innovations of 1970s publishing rebuilt the industry from within, the non-comics retailing of its characters cemented their statuses as cultural institutions.

Overstreet advisor Michael Eury is the Editor of TwoMorrows' *BACK ISSUE* magazine, the co-editor/co-author of *The Supervillain Book: The Ultimate Encyclopedia of Comic-Book and Hollywood Masterminds, Megalomaniacs, and Menaces* (Visible Ink Press, 2006), and the author of *The Justice League Companion* (2005), *Dick Giordano: Changing Comics, One Day at a Time* (2003), and *Captain Action: The Original Super-Hero Action Figure* (2002). A former editor for DC, Dark Horse, and Comico, Eury has written cartoons, comics, and copy for Nike, Toys R Us, Warner Bros., MSN, *Cracked*, and Bowen Designs. *Quotes for this article originally appeared in interviews in BACK ISSUE magazine and the book,* The Justice League Companion. *The author wishes to thank Dewey Cassell, Tom Field, Glenn Greenberg, Allan Harvey, Carmine Infantino, Dan Johnson, John Morrow, Dennis O'Neil, Diana Schutz, Tom Stewart, and Roy Thomas for their contributions.*

COMIC
CONNECT
www.comicconnect.com
WHERE THE ACTION IS!

ACTION COMICS

ACTION COMICS

Detective COMICS

ACTION COMICS

ACTION COMICS

ACTION COMICS

ACTION COMICS

AMAZING FANTASY
SPIDER MAN

ACTION COMICS

WALT DISNEY'S UNCLE SCROOGE

THE INCREDIBLE HULK

CAPTAIN AMERICA

HULK

Detective COMICS

AMAZING FANTASY
SPIDER MAN

SUPERMAN

MARVEL COMICS

SUSPENSE
IRON MAN

SHOWCASE
GREEN LANTERN

SHOWCASE

Abattoir #1 © Radical

Abbott and Costello #3 © STJ

Ace Comics #132 © DMP

	GD 2.0	VG 4.0	FN 6.0	VF 8.0	VF/NM 9.0	NM- 9.2

The correct title listing for each comic book can be determined by consulting the indicia (publication data) on the beginning interior pages of the comic. The official title is determined by those words of the title in capital letters only, and not by what is on the cover. Titles are listed in this book as if they were one word, ignoring spaces, hyphens, and apostrophes, to make finding titles easier. Exceptions are made in rare cases. Comic books listed should be assumed to be in color unless noted "B&W".

Comic publishers are invited to send us sample copies for possible inclusion in future guides.

PRICING IN THIS GUIDE: Prices for **GD 2.0** (Good), **VG 4.0** (Very Good), **FN 6.0** (Fine), **VF 8.0** (Very Fine), **VF/NM 9.0** (Very Fine/Near Mint),and **NM– 9.2** (Near Mint–) are listed in whole U.S. dollars except for prices below $7 which show dollars and cents. **The minimum price listed is $3.00**, the cover price for current new comics. Many books listed at this price can be found in $1.00 boxes at conventions and dealers stores.

A-1 (See A-One)

ABADAZAD
CrossGen (Code 6): Mar, 2004 - No. 3, May, 2004 ($2.95)

	GD	VG	FN	VF	VF/NM	NM-
1-3-Ploog-a/c; DeMatteis-s						3.00
1-2nd printing with new cover						3.00

ABATTOIR
Radical Comics: Oct, 2010 - No. 6 ($3.99/$3.50, limited series)

	GD	VG	FN	VF	VF/NM	NM-
1-($3.99) Cansino-a/Levin & Peteri-s						4.00
2-4-($3.50)						3.50

ABBIE AN' SLATS (...With Becky No. 1-4) (See Comics On Parade, Fight for Love, Giant Comics Edition 2, Giant Comics Editions #1, Sparkler Comics, Tip Topper, Treasury of Comics, & United Comics)
United Features Syndicate: 1940; March, 1948 - No. 4, Aug, 1948 (Reprints)

	GD	VG	FN	VF	VF/NM	NM-
Single Series 25 ('40)	39	78	117	236	388	540
Single Series 28	33	66	99	194	317	440
1 (1948)	17	34	51	98	154	210
2-4: 3-r/Sparkler #68-72	10	20	30	58	79	100

ABBOTT AND COSTELLO (...Comics)(See Giant Comics Editions #1 & Treasury of Comics)
St. John Publishing Co.: Feb, 1948 - No. 40, Sept, 1956 (Mort Drucker-a in most issues)

	GD	VG	FN	VF	VF/NM	NM-
1	62	124	186	394	677	960
2	36	72	108	214	347	480
3-9 (#8, 8/49; #9, 2/50)	24	48	72	140	230	320
10-Son of Sinbad story by Kubert (new)	28	56	84	165	270	375
11,13-20 (#11, 10/50; #13, 8/51; #15, 12/52)	17	34	51	98	154	210
12-Movie issue	18	36	54	105	165	225
21-30: 28-r/#8. 29,30-Painted-c	14	28	42	76	108	140
31-40: 33,38-Reprints	10	20	30	56	76	95
3-D #1 (11/53, 25¢)-Infinity-c	32	64	96	188	307	425

ABBOTT AND COSTELLO (TV)
Charlton Comics: Feb, 1968 - No. 22, Aug, 1971 (Hanna-Barbera)

	GD	VG	FN	VF	VF/NM	NM-
1	8	16	24	54	90	125
2	4	8	12	28	44	60
3-10	4	8	12	22	34	45
11-22	3	6	9	18	27	35

ABC (See America's Best TV Comics)

ABC: A-Z (one-shots)
America's Best Comics: Nov, 2005 - July, 2006 ($3.99, one-shots)

	GD	VG	FN	VF	VF/NM	NM-
... Greyshirt and Cobweb (1/06) character bios; Veitch-s/a; Gebbie-a; Dodson-c						4.00
... Terra Obscura and Splash Brannigan (3/06) character bios; Barta-a; Dodson-c						4.00
... Tom Strong and Jack B. Quick (11/05) character bios; Sprouse-a; Nowlan-a; Dodson-c						4.00
... Top Ten and Teams (7/06) character bios; Ha & Cannon-a; Veitch-a; Dodson-c						4.00

ABE SAPIEN... (Hellboy character)
Dark Horse Comics

	GD	VG	FN	VF	VF/NM	NM-
...: Drums of the Dead (3/98, $2.95) 1-Thompson-a. Hellboy back-up; Mignola-s/a/c						3.00
...: The Abyssal Plain (6/10 - No. 2, 7/10, $3.50) 1,2-Mignola & Arcudi-s/Snejbjerg-a						3.50
...: The Drowning (2/08 - No. 5, 6/08, $2.99) 1-5-Mignola-s/c; Alexander-a						3.00
...: The Haunted Boy (10/09, $3.50) 1-Mignola & Arcudi-s/Reynolds-a/Johnson-c						3.50

A. BIZARRO
DC Comics: Jul, 1999 - No. 4, Oct, 1999 (2.50, limited series)

	GD	VG	FN	VF	VF/NM	NM-
1-4-Gerber-s/Bright-a						3.00

ABOMINATIONS (See Hulk)
Marvel Comics: Dec, 1996 - No. 3, Feb, 1997 (1.50, limited series)

	GD	VG	FN	VF	VF/NM	NM-
1-3-Future Hulk storyline						3.00

ABRAHAM LINCOLN LIFE STORY (See Dell Giants)

ABRAHAM STONE
Marvel Comics (Epic): July, 1995 - No. 2, Aug, 1995 ($6.95, limited series)

	GD	VG	FN	VF	VF/NM	NM-
1,2-Joe Kubert-s/a						7.00

ABSENT-MINDED PROFESSOR, THE
Dell Publishing Co.: Apr, 1961 (Disney)

	GD	VG	FN	VF	VF/NM	NM-
Four Color #1199-Movie, photo-c; variant edition has a "Fabulous Formula" strip on back-c	8	16	24	56	93	130

ABSOLUTE VERTIGO
DC Comics (Vertigo): Winter, 1995 (99¢, mature)

	GD	VG	FN	VF	VF/NM	NM-
nn-1st app. Preacher. Previews upcoming titles including Jonah Hex: Riders of the Worm, The Invisibles (King Mob), The Eaters, Ghostdancing & Preacher	1	2	3	5	7	9

ABYSS, THE (Movie)
Dark Horse Comics: June, 1989 - No. 2, July, 1989 ($2.25, limited series)

	GD	VG	FN	VF	VF/NM	NM-
1,2-Adaptation of film; Kaluta & Moebius-a						3.00

ACCELERATE
DC Comics (Vertigo): Aug, 2000 - No. 4, Nov, 2000 ($2.95, limited series)

	GD	VG	FN	VF	VF/NM	NM-
1-4-Pander Bros.-a/Kadrey-s						3.00

ACCLAIM ADVENTURE ZONE
Acclaim Books: 1997 ($4.50, digest size)

	GD	VG	FN	VF	VF/NM	NM-
1-Short stories of Turok, Troublemakers, Ninjak and others						4.50

ACE COMICS
David McKay Publications: Apr, 1937 - No. 151, Oct-Nov, 1949 (All contain some newspaper strip reprints)

	GD	VG	FN	VF	VF/NM	NM-
1-Jungle Jim by Alex Raymond, Blondie, Ripley's Believe It Or Not, Krazy Kat begin (1st app. of each)	314	628	942	2198	3849	5500
2	92	184	276	538	982	1425
3-5	61	122	183	390	670	950
6-10	45	90	135	284	482	680
11-The Phantom begins (1st app., 2/38) (in brown costume)	82	164	246	528	902	1275
12-20	39	78	117	231	378	525
21-25,27-30	34	68	102	199	325	450
26-Origin & 1st app. Prince Valiant (5/39); begins series?	105	210	315	667	1146	1625
31-40: 37-Krazy Kat ends	24	48	72	142	234	325
41-60	19	38	57	109	172	235
61-64,66-76-(7/43; last 68 pgs.)	15	30	45	94	147	200
65-(8/42)-Flag-c	19	38	57	109	172	235
77-84 (3/44; all 60 pgs.)	14	28	42	80	115	150
85-99 (52 pgs.)	12	24	36	69	97	125
100 (7/45; last 52 pgs.)	14	28	42	80	115	150
101-134: 128-(11/47)-Brick Bradford begins. 134-Last Prince Valiant (all 36 pgs.)	10	20	30	56	76	95
135-151: 135-(6/48)-Lone Ranger begins	9	18	27	52	69	85

ACE KELLY (See Tops Comics & Tops In Humor)

ACE KING (See Adventures of Detective...)

ACES
Acme Press (Eclipse): Apr, 1988 - No. 5, Dec, 1988 ($2.95, B&W, magazine)

	GD	VG	FN	VF	VF/NM	NM-
1-5						3.00

ACES HIGH
E.C. Comics: Mar-Apr, 1955 - No. 5, Nov-Dec, 1955

	GD	VG	FN	VF	VF/NM	NM-
1-Not approved by code	23	46	69	184	292	400
2	13	26	39	104	167	230
3-5	12	24	36	96	153	210

NOTE: *All have stories by* ***Davis**, **Evans**, **Krigstein**, and **Wood**. **Evans** c-1-5.*

ACES HIGH
Gemstone Publishing: Apr, 1999 - No. 5, Aug, 1999 ($2.50)

	GD	VG	FN	VF	VF/NM	NM-
1-5-Reprints E.C. issues						3.00
Annual 1 ($13.50) r/#1-5						13.50

ACME NOVELTY LIBRARY, THE
Fantagraphics Books: Winter 1993-94 - Present (quarterly, various sizes)

	GD	VG	FN	VF	VF/NM	NM-
1-Introduces Jimmy Corrigan; Chris Ware-s/a in all	1	3	4	6	8	10
1-2nd and later printings						4.00

Action Adventure #3 © Gillmor

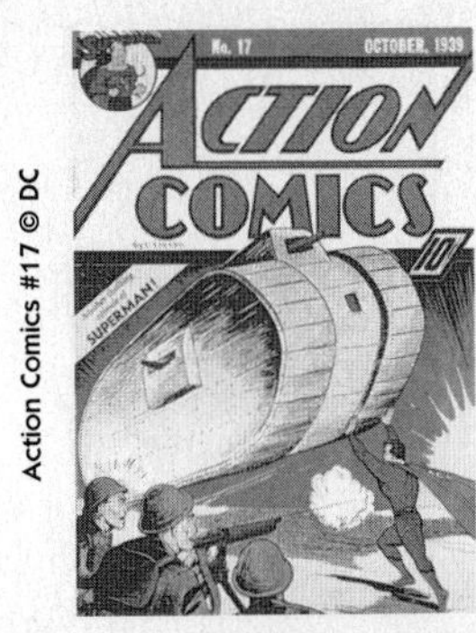

Action Comics #17 © DC

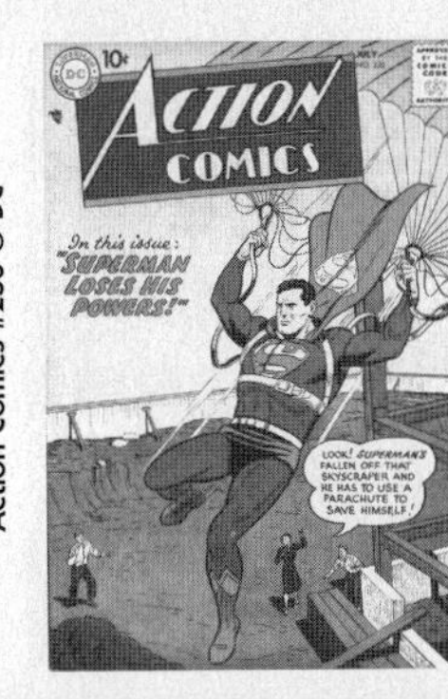

Action Comics #230 © DC

GD 2.0 VG 4.0 FN 6.0 VF 8.0 VF/NM 9.0 NM- 9.2

2,3: 2-Quimby 6.00
4-Sparky's Best Comics & Stories 1 2 3 4 5 7
5-12: Jimmy Corrigan in all 5.00
13,15-($10.95-c) 11.00
14-($12.95-c) Concludes Jimmy Corrigan saga 13.00
16,19-($15.95, hardcover) Rusty Brown 16.00
17-($16.95, hardcover) Rusty Brown 17.00
18-($17.95, hardcover) 18.00
Jimmy Corrigan, The Smartest Kid on Earth (2000, Pantheon Books, Hardcover, $27.50, 380 pgs.) Collects Jimmy Corrigan stories; folded dust jacket 27.50
Jimmy Corrigan, The Smartest Kid on Earth (2003, Softcover, $17.95) 18.00
NOTE: *Multiple printings exist for most issues.*

ACROSS THE UNIVERSE: THE DC UNIVERSE STORIES OF ALAN MOORE (Also see DC Universe: The Stories of Alan Moore)
DC Comics: 2003 ($19.95, TPB)

nn-Reprints selected Moore stories from '85-'87; Superman, Batman, Swamp Thing app. 20.00

ACTION ADVENTURE (War) (Formerly Real Adventure)
Gillmor Magazines: V1#2, June, 1955 - No. 4, Oct, 1955

V1#2-4 6 12 18 31 38 45

ACTION COMICS (...Weekly #601-642) (Also see The Comics Magazine #1, More Fun #14-17 & Special Edition) (Also see Promotional Comics section)
National Periodical Publ./Detective Comics/DC Comics: 6/38 - No. 583, 9/86; No. 584, 1/87 - Present

1-Origin & 1st app. Superman by Siegel & Shuster, Marco Polo, Tex Thompson, Pep Morgan, Chuck Dawson & Scoop Scanlon; 1st app. Zatara & Lois Lane; Superman story missing 4 pgs. which were included when reprinted in Superman #1; Clark Kent works for Daily Star; story continued in #2 90,000 180,000 270,000 700,000 1,050,000 1,400,000
1-Reprint, Oversize 13-1/2x10". **WARNING:** This comic is an exact reprint of the original except for its size. DC published it in 1974 with a second cover titling it as a Famous First Edition. There have been many reported cases of the outer cover being removed and the interior sold as the original edition. The reprint with the new outer cover removed is practically worthless. See Famous First Edition for value.

2-O'Mealia non-Superman covers thru #6 5588 11,176 16,764 41,910 68,455 95,000
3 (Scarce)-Superman apps. in costume in only one panel 3529 7058 10,587 26,468 43,234 60,000
4-6: 6-1st Jimmy Olsen (called office boy) 2000 4000 6000 15,000 24,500 34,000
7-2nd Superman cover 7353 14,706 22,059 55,148 90,074 125,000
8,9 1294 2588 3882 9705 15,853 22,000
10-3rd Superman cover by Shuster; splash panel used as cover art for Superman #1 3882 7764 11,646 29,115 47,558 66,000
11,14: 1st X-Ray Vision? 14-Clip Carson begins, ends #41; Zatara-c 735 1470 2205 5513 9007 12,500
12-Has 1 panel Batman ad for Det. #27 (5/39); Zatara sci-fi cover 824 1648 2472 6180 10,090 14,500
13-Shuster Superman-c; last Scoop Scanlon; centerspread has a 2-page ad for Superman #1 1765 3530 5295 13,238 21,619 30,000
15-Guardineer Superman-c; has ad mentioning Detective Comics and Batman; full page ad for New York World's Fair 1939 with 25¢-c 1118 2236 3354 8385 13,693 19,000
16-Has full page ad and 1 panel ad for New York World's Fair 1939 25¢ cover edition 518 1036 1554 3885 6343 8800
17-Superman cover; last Marco Polo; full page ad for New York World's Fair 1939 with 15¢-c 941 1882 2823 7058 11,529 16,000
18-Origin 3 Aces; has a 1 panel ad for New York World's Fair 1939 at the end of the Superman story (ad also in #16,17,19) 518 1036 1554 3885 6343 8800
19-Superman covers begin 853 1706 2559 6398 10,449 14,500
20-The 'S' left off Superman's chest; Clark Kent works at 'Daily Star' 824 1648 2472 6180 10,090 14,000
21-Has 2 ads for More Fun #52 (1st Spectre) 423 846 1269 3000 5250 7500
22,24,25: 24-Kent at Daily Planet. 25-Last app. Gargantua T. Potts, Tex Thompson's sidekick 423 846 1269 2938 5219 7400
23-1st app. Luthor (w/red hair) & Black Pirate; Black Pirate by Moldoff; 1st mention of The Daily Planet (4/40)-Has 1 panel ad for Spectre in More Fun 946 1892 2838 6906 12,203 17,500
26-28,30 366 732 1098 2562 4481 6400
29-1st Lois Lane-c (10/40) 400 800 1200 2800 4900 7000
31,32: 32-Intro/1st app. Krypto Ray Gun in Superman story by Burnley 258 516 774 1651 2826 4000
33-Origin Mr. America; Superman by Burnley; has half page ad for All Star Comics #3 265 530 795 1694 2897 4100
34,35,38,39 252 504 756 1613 2757 3900
36, 40: 36-Classic robot-c. 40-(9/41)-Intro/1st app. Star Spangled Kid & Stripesy; Jerry Siegel photo 258 516 774 1651 2826 4000
37-Origin Congo Bill 255 510 765 1619 2785 3950
41 219 438 657 1402 2401 3400

GD 2.0 VG 4.0 FN 6.0 VF 8.0 VF/NM 9.0 NM- 9.2

42-1st app./origin Vigilante; Bob Daley becomes Fat Man; origin Mr. America's magic flying carpet; The Queen Bee & Luthor app; Black Pirate ends; not in #41 245 490 735 1568 2684 3800
43-46,48-50: 44-Fat Man's i.d. revealed to Mr. America. 45-1st app. Stuff (Vigilante's oriental sidekick) 206 412 618 1318 2259 3200
47-1st Luthor cover in comics (4/42) 297 594 891 1301 3251 4600
51-1st app. The Prankster 213 426 639 1363 2332 3300
52-Fat Man & Mr. America become the Ameri-commandos; origin Vigilante retold; classic Superman and back-ups-c 239 478 717 1530 2615 3700
53-56,59,60: 56-Last Fat Man. 59-Kubert Vigilante begins?, ends #70. 60-First app. Lois Lane as Super-woman 161 322 483 1030 1765 2500
57-2nd Lois Lane-c in Action (3rd anywhere, 2/43) 181 362 543 1158 1979 2800
58-"Slap a Jap-c" 181 362 543 1158 1979 2800
61-Historic Atomic Radiation-c (6/43) 168 336 504 1075 1838 2600
62,63-Japan war-c: 63-Last 3 Aces 161 322 483 1030 1765 2500
64-Intro Toyman 168 336 504 1075 1838 2600
65-70 129 258 387 826 1413 2000
71-79: 74-Last Mr. America 103 206 309 659 1130 1600
80-2nd app. & 1st Mr. Mxyztplk-c (1/45) 132 264 396 838 1444 2050
81-88,90: 83-Intro Hocus & Pocus 97 194 291 621 1061 1500
89-Classic rainbow cover 100 200 300 635 1093 1550
91-99: 93-X-Mas-c. 99-1st small logo (8/46) 81 162 243 514 882 1250
100 116 232 348 742 1271 1800
101-Nuclear explosion-c (10/46) 155 310 465 992 1696 2400
102-107,109-120: 102-Mxyztplk-c. 105,117-X-Mas-c 74 148 222 470 810 1150
108-Classic molten metal-c 81 162 243 518 884 1250
121,122,124-126,128-140: 135,136,138-Zatara by Kubert 69 138 207 442 759 1075
123-(8/48) 1st time Superman flies, not leaps 70 140 210 445 765 1085
127-Vigilante by Kubert; Tommy Tomorrow begins (12/48, see Real Fact #6) 71 142 213 454 777 1100
141-157,159-161: 151-Luthor/Mr. Mxyztplk/Prankster team-up. 156-Lois as Super Woman. 161- Last 52 pgs. 68 136 204 435 743 1050
158-Origin Superman retold 135 270 405 864 1482 2100
162-180: 168,176-Used in **POP**, pg. 90. 173-Robot-c 66 132 198 419 722 1025
181-201: 191-Intro. Janu in Congo Bill. 198-Last Vigilante. 201-Last pre-code issue 63 126 189 403 689 975
202-220,232: 212-(1/56)-Includes 1956 Superman calendar that is part of story. 232-1st Curt Swan-c in Action 56 112 168 353 597 840
221-231,233-240: 221-1st S.A. issue. 224-1st Golden Gorilla story. 228-(5/57)-Kongorilla in Congo Bill story (Congorilla try-out) 47 94 141 296 498 700
241,243-251: 241-Batman x-over. 248-Origin/1st app. Congorilla; Congo Bill renamed Congorilla. 251-Last Tommy Tomorrow 40 80 120 246 411 575
242-Origin & 1st app. Brainiac (7/58); 1st mention of Shrunken City of Kandor 193 386 579 1689 3445 5200
252-Origin & 1st app. Supergirl (5/59); 1st app. Metallo 211 422 633 1846 3773 5700
253-2nd app. Supergirl 61 122 183 390 670 950
254-1st meeting of Bizarro & Superman-c/story; 3rd app. Supergirl 43 86 129 271 461 650
255-1st Bizarro Lois Lane-c/story & both Bizarros leave Earth to make Bizarro World; 4th app. Supergirl 39 78 117 240 395 550
256-260: 259-Red Kryptonite used 28 56 84 165 270 375
261-1st X-Kryptonite which gave Streaky his powers; last Congorilla in Action; origin & 1st app. Streaky The Super Cat 31 62 93 186 303 420
262,264-266,268-270 24 48 72 140 230 320
263-Origin Bizarro World (continues in #264) 31 62 93 182 296 410
267(8/60)-3rd Legion app; 1st app. Chameleon Boy, Colossal Boy, & Invisible Kid, 1st app. of Supergirl as Superwoman. 55 110 165 352 601 850
271-275,277-282: 274-Lois Lane as Superwoman. 280-Brief origin of Superman & Supergirl retold; Brainiac-c. 282-Last 10¢ issue 21 42 63 122 199 275
276(5/61)-6th Legion app; 1st app. Brainiac 5, Phantom Girl, Triplicate Girl, Bouncing Boy, Sun Boy, & Shrinking Violet; Supergirl joins Legion 39 78 117 231 378 525
283(12/61)-Legion of Super-Villains app. 1st 12¢ 14 28 42 95 188 280
284(1/62)-Mon-El app. 14 28 42 95 188 280
285(2/62)-12th Legion app; Brainiac 5 cameo; Supergirl's existence revealed to world; JFK & Jackie cameos 21 42 63 153 307 460
286-287,289-292,294-299: 286(3/62)-Legion of Super Villains app. 287(4/62)-15th Legion app. (cameo). 289(6/62)-16th Legion app. (Adult); Lightning Man & Saturn Woman's marriage 1st revealed. 290(7/62)-Legion app. (cameo); Phantom Girl app. 1st Supergirl emergency squad. 291-1st meeting Supergirl & Mr. Mxyzptlk. 292-2nd app. Superhorse (see Adv.#293). 297-Mon-El app. 298-Legion cameo 12 24 36 86 161 235
288-Mon-El app.; r-origin Supergirl 12 24 36 88 167 245

Action Comics #494 © DC

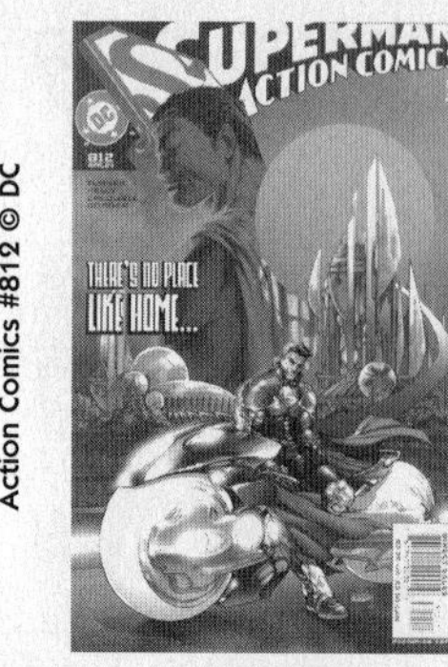

Action Comics #812 © DC

Action Comics Annual #11 © DC

	GD 2.0	VG 4.0	FN 6.0	VF 8.0	VF/NM 9.0	NM- 9.2
293-Origin Comet (Superhorse)	14	28	42	96	191	285
300-(5/63)	13	26	39	93	182	270
301-303,305,307,308,310-312,315-320: 307-Saturn Girl app. 317-Death of Nor-Kan of Kandor. 319-Shrinking Violet app.	9	18	27	64	110	155
304,306,313: 304-Origin/1st app. Black Flame (9/63). 306-Brainiac 5, Mon-El app. 313-Batman app.	9	18	27	65	113	160
309-(2/64)-Legion app.; Batman & Robin-c & cameo; JFK app. (he died 11/22/63; on stands last week of Dec, 1963)	10	20	30	68	119	170
314-Retells origin Supergirl; J.L.A. x-over	9	18	27	65	113	160
321-333,335-339: 336-Origin Akvar (Flamebird)	8	16	24	52	86	120
334-Giant G-20; origin Supergirl, Streaky, Superhorse & Legion (all-r)	11	22	33	77	144	210
340-Origin, 1st app. of the Parasite; 2 pg. pin-up	8	16	24	56	93	130
341,344,350,358: 341-Batman app. in Supergirl back-up story. 344-Batman x-over. 350-Batman, Green Arrow & Green Lantern app. in Supergirl back-up story. 358-Superboy meets Supergirl	7	14	21	45	73	100
342,343,345,346,348,349,351-357,359: 342-UFO story. 345-Allen Funt/Candid Camera story.	6	12	18	43	69	95
347,360-Giant Supergirl G-33,G-45; 347-Origin Comet-r plus Bizarro story. 360-Legion app.-r; r/origin Supergirl	9	18	27	60	100	140
361-364,367-372,374-378: 361-2nd app. Parasite. 362-366-Leper/Death story. 370-New facts about Superman's origin. 376-Last Supergirl in Action; last 12¢-c. 377-Legion begins (thru #392)	5	10	15	34	55	75
365,366: 365-JLA & Legion app. 366-JLA app.	6	12	18	37	59	80
373-Giant Supergirl G-57; Legion-r	8	16	24	56	93	130
379-399,401: 388-Sgt. Rock app. 392-Batman-c/app.; last Legion in Action; Saturn Girl gets new costume. 393-401-All Superman issues	3	6	9	20	30	40
400	4	8	12	23	36	48
402-Last 15¢ issue; Superman vs. Supergirl duel	3	6	9	20	30	40
403-413: All 52 pg. issues. 411-Origin Eclipso-(r). 413-Metamorpho begins, ends #418	3	6	9	20	30	40
414-424: 419-Intro. Human Target. 421-Intro Capt. Strong; Green Arrow begins. 422,423-Origin Human Target	2	4	6	9	13	16
425-Neal Adams-a(p); The Atom begins	3	6	9	14	19	24
426-431,433-436,438,439	2	4	6	8	10	12
432-1st Bronze Age Toyman app. (2/74)	2	4	6	13	18	22
437,443-(100 pg. Giants)	4	8	12	28	44	60
440-1st Grell-a on Green Arrow	2	4	6	9	13	16
441,442,444-448: 441-Grell-a on Green Arrow continues	1	3	4	6	8	10
449-(68 pgs.)	2	4	6	9	13	16
450-465,467-483,486,489-499: 454-Last Atom. 456-Grell Jaws-c. 458-Last Green Arrow.	1	2	3	4	5	7
466,485,487,488: 466-Batman, Flash app. 485-Adams-c. 487,488-(44 pgs.). 487-Origin & 1st app. Microwave Man; origin Atom retold	1	2	3	5	7	9
481-483,485-492,495-499,501-505,507,508-Whitman variants (low print run; none show issue # on cover)	1	3	4	6	8	10
484-Earth II Superman & Lois Lane wed; 40th anniversary issue(6/78)	2	4	6	8	10	12
484-Variant includes 3-D Superman punchout doll in cello. pack; 4 different inserts; Canadian promo?)	3	6	9	16	22	28
500-($1.00, 68 pgs.)-Infinity-c; Superman life story retold; shows Legion statues in museum	2	4	6	8	10	12
501-543,545,547-551: 511-514-Airwave II solo stories. 513-The Atom begins. 517-Aquaman begins; ends #541. 521-1st app. The Vixen. 532,536-New Teen Titans cameo. 535,536-Omega Men app. 551-Starfire becomes Red-Star						5.00
504,505,507,508-Whitman variants (no cover price)	1	3	4	6	8	10
544-(6/83, Mando paper, 68 pgs.)-45th Anniversary issue; origins new Luthor & Brainiac; Omega Men cameo; Shuster-a (pin-up); article by Siegel	1	2	3	4	5	7
546-J.L.A., New Teen Titans app.	1	2	3	5	6	8
552,553-Animal Man-c & app. (2/84 & 3/84)						6.00
554-582						3.00
583-Alan Moore scripts; last Earth 1 Superman story (cont'd from Superman #423)	2	4	6	8	10	12
584-Byrne-a begins; New Teen Titans app.						6.00
585-599: 586-Legends x-over. 596-Millennium x-over; Spectre app. 598-1st Checkmate						3.00
600-($2.50, 84 pgs., 5/88)						6.00
601-610,619-642: (#601-642 are weekly issues) ($1.50, 52 pgs.) 601-Re-intro The Secret Six; death of Katma Tui						3.00
611-618: 611-614-Catwoman stories (new costume in #611). 613-618-Nightwing stories						3.00
643-Superman & monthly issues begin again; Perez-c/a/scripts begin; swipes cover to Superman #1						4.00
644-649,651-661,663-673,675-683: 645-1st app. Maxima. 654-Part 3 of Batman storyline. 655-Free extra 8 pgs. 660-Death of Lex Luthor. 661-Begin $1.00-c. 667-($1.75, 52 pgs.). 675-Deathstroke cameo. 679-Last $1.00 issue. 683-Doomsday cameo						3.00
650-($1.50, 52 pgs.)-Lobo cameo (last panel)						4.00
662-Clark Kent reveals i.d. to Lois Lane; story cont'd in Superman #53						4.00
674-Supergirl logo & c/story (reintro)						6.00
683-685-2nd & 3rd printings						3.00
684-Doomsday battle issue						4.00
685,686-Funeral for a Friend issues; Supergirl app.						4.00
687-($1.95)-Collector's Ed.w/die-cut-c						3.50
687-($1.50)-Newsstand Edition with mini-poster						3.00
688-699,701-703-($1.50): 688-Guy Gardner-c/story. 697-Bizarro-c/story. 703-(9/94)-Zero Hour						3.00
695-($2.50)-Collector's Edition w/embossed foil-c						4.00
700-($2.95, 68 pgs.)-Fall of Metropolis Pt 1, Guice-a; Pete Ross marries Lana Lang and Smallville flashbacks with Curt Swan art & Murphy Anderson inks						4.00
700-Platinum						15.00
700-Gold						18.00
0(10/94), 704(11/94)-719,721-731: 710-Begin $1.95-c. 714-Joker app. 719-Batman-c/app. 721-Mr. Mxyzptlk app. 723-Dave Johnson-c. 727-Final Night x-over.						3.00
720-Lois breaks off engagement w/Clark						4.00
720-2nd print.						3.00
732-749,751-767: 732-New powers. 733-New costume, Ray app. 738-Immonen-s/a(p) begins. 741-Legion app. 744-Millennium Giants x-over. 745-747-70's-style Superman vs. Prankster. 753-JLA-c/app. 757-Hawkman-c. 760-1st Encantadora. 761-Wonder Woman app. 765-Joker & Harley-c/app. 766-Batman-c/app.						3.00
750-($2.95)						4.00
768,769,771-774: 768-Begin $2.25-c; Marvel Family-c/app. 771-Nightwing-c/app. 772,773-Ra's al Ghul app. 774-Martian Manhunter-c/app.						3.00
770-($3.50) Conclusion of Emperor Joker x-over						4.00
775-($3.75) Bradstreet-c; intro. The Elite						4.00
776-799: 776-Farewell to Krypton; Rivoche-c. 780-782-Our Worlds at War x-over. 781-Hippolyta and Major Lane killed. 782-War ends. 784-Joker: Last Laugh; Batman & Green Lantern app. 793-Return to Krypton. 795-The Elite app. 798-Van Fleet-c						3.00
800-(4/03, $3.95) Struzan painted-c; guest artists include Ross, Jim Lee, Jurgens, Sale						4.00
801-811: 801-Raney-a. 809-The Creeper app. 811-Mr. Majestic app.						3.00
812-Godfall part 1; Turner-c; Caldwell-a(p)						4.00
812-2nd printing; B&W sketch-c by Turner						3.00
813-Godfall pt. 4; Turner-c; Caldwell-a(p)						4.00
814-824, 826-828,830-836: 814-Reis-a/Art Adams-c; Darkseid app.; begin $2.50-c. 815,816-Teen Titans-c/app. 820-Doomsday app. 826-Capt. Marvel app. 827-Byrne-c/a begin. 831-Villains United tie-in. 835-Livewire app. 836-Infinite Crisis; revised origin						3.00
825-($2.99, 40 pgs.) Doomsday app.						4.00
829-Omac Project x-over Sacrifice pt. 2						5.00
829-(2nd printing) red tone cover						4.00
837-843-One Year Later; powers return after Infinite Crisis; Johns & Busiek-s						3.00
844-Donner & Johns-s/Adam Kubert-a/c begin; brown-toned cover						4.00
844-Andy Kubert variant-c						5.00
844-2nd printing with red-toned Adam Kubert cover						3.00
845-849,851-857: 845-Bizarro-c/app.; re-intro. General Zod, Ursa & Non. 846-Jax-Ur app. 847-849-No Kubert-a. 851-Kubert-a/c. 855-857-Bizarro app.; Powell-a/c						3.00
850-($3.99) Supergirl and LSH app., origin re-told; Guedes-a/c						4.00
858-($3.50) Legion of Super-Heroes app.; 1st meeting re-told; Johns-s/Frank-a/c						4.00
858-Variant-c (Superman & giant Brainiac robot) by Frank						5.00
858-Second printing with regular cover with red background instead of yellow						3.00
858-Special Edition (7/10, $1.00) r/#858 with "What's Next?" cover logo						1.00
859-878: 859-863-Legion of Super-Heroes app.; var-c on each (859-Andy Kubert. 860-Lightle. 861-Grell. 862-Giffen. 863-Frank) 864-Batman and Lightning Lad app. 866-Brainiac returns 869-"Soda Pop" cover edition, 870-Pa Kent dies. 871-New Krypton; Ross-c						3.00
869-Initial printing recalled because of beer bottles on cover						8.00
879-896: 879-($3.99) Back-up Capt. Atom feature begins. 890-Luthor stories begin. 894-Death (Sandman) app. 896-Secret Six app.						4.00
897,898-($2.99) 897-Joker app. 898-Larfleeze app.						3.00
#1,000,000 (11/98) Gene Ha-c; 853rd Century x-over						3.00
Annual 1 ('87, $2.95) Art Adams-c/a(p); Batman app.						5.00
Annual 2-6 ('89-'94, $2.95)-2-Pérez-c/a(i). 3-Armageddon 2001. 4-Eclipso vs. Shazam. 5-Bloodlines; 1st app. Loose Cannon. 6-Elseworlds story						4.00
Annual 7,9 ('95, '97, $3.95) 7-Year One story. 9-Pulp Heroes story						4.00
Annual 8 (1996, $2.95) Legends of the Dead Earth story						4.00
Annual 10 ('07, $3.99) Short stories by Johns & Donner and various incl. A. Adams, J. Kubert, Wight, Morales; origin of Phantom Zone, Mon-El; Metallo app.; Adam & Joe Kubert-c						4.00
Annual 11 (7/08, $4.99) Conclusion to General Zod story continued from #851; Kubert-a						5.00
Annual 12 (8/09, $4.99) Origin of Nightwing and Flamebird						5.00
Annual 13 (2/11, $4.99) 1st meeting of Luthor and Darkseid; Ra's al Ghul app.						5.00

NOTE: *Supergirl's origin in 262, 280, 285, 291, 305, 309.* ***N. Adams*** *c-356, 358, 359, 361-364, 366, 367, 370-374, 377-379i, 398-400, 402, 404,405, 419p, 466, 468, 469, 473i, 485.* ***Aparo*** *a-642.* ***Austin*** *c/a-682i.* ***Baily*** *a-24, 25.*

Adam-12 #2 © GK

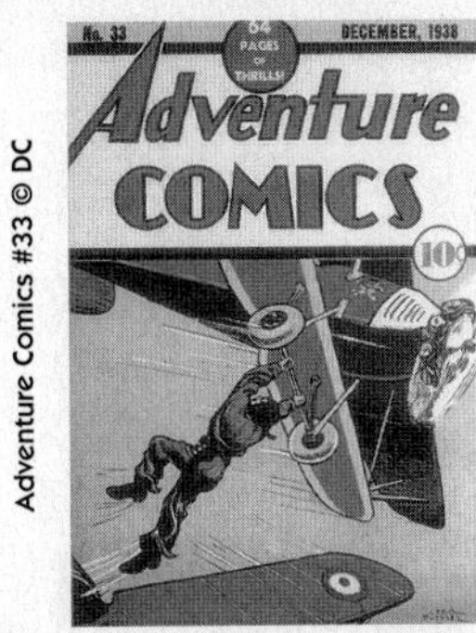

Adventure Comics #33 © DC

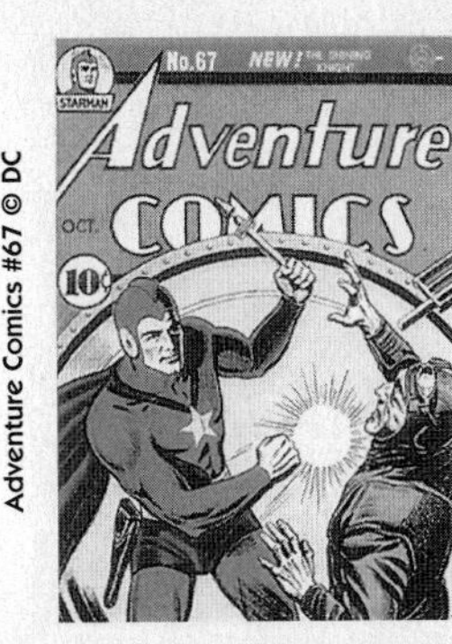

Adventure Comics #67 © DC

GD 2.0 | VG 4.0 | FN 6.0 | VF 8.0 | VF/NM 9.0 | NM- 9.2

__Boring__ a-164, 194, 211, 223, 233, 241, 250, 261, 266-268, 346, 348, 352, 356, 357. __Burnley__ a-28-33; c-48?, 53-55, 58, 59?, 60-63, 65, 66p, 67p, 70p, 71p, 79p, 82p, 84-86p, 90-92p, 93p?, 94p, 107p, 108p. __Byrne__ a-584-598p, 599i, 600p; c-584-591, 596-600. __Ditko__ a-642. __Giffen__ a-560, 563, 565, 577, 579; c-539, 560, 563, 565, 577, 579. __Grell__ a-440-442, 444-446, 450-452, 456-458; c-456. __Guardineer__ a-24, 25; c-8, 11, 12, 14-16, 18. 25. __Guice__ a(p)-676-681, 683-698, 700; c-683, 685, 686, 687(direct), 688-693i, 694-696, 697i, 698-700. __Infantino__ a-642. __Kaluta__ c-613. __Bob Kane's__ Clip Carson-14-41. __Gil Kane__ a-443r, 493r, 539-541, 544-546, 551-554, 601-605, 642; c-535p, 540, 541, 544p, 545-549, 551-554, 580, 627. __Kirby__ c-638. __Meskin__ a-42-121(most). __Mignola__ a-600, Annual 2; c-c-614. __Moldoff__ a-23-25, 443r. __Mooney__ a-667p. __Mortimer__ c-153, 154, 159-172, 174, 178-181, 184, 186-189, 191-193, 196, 200, 206. __Orlando__ a-617p; c-621. __Perez__ a-600i, 643-652p, Annual 2p; c-529p, 602, 643-651, Annual 2p. __Quesada__ c-Annual 4p. __Fred Ray__ c-34, 36-46, 50-52. __Siegel & Shuster__ a-1-27. __Paul Smith__ c-608. __Starlin__ a-509; c-631. __Leonard Starr__ a-597i(part), __Staton__ a-525p, 526p, 531p, 535p, 536p. __Swan/Moldoff__ c-281, 286, 287, 293, 298, 334. __Thibert__ c-676, 677p, 678-681, 684. __Toth__ a-406, 407, 413, 431; c-616. __Tuska__ a-486p, 550. __Williamson__ a-568i. __Zeck__ c-Annual 5

ACTION COMICS
DC Comics: (no date)

1-Ashcan comic, not distributed to newsstands, only for in-house use. Cover art is the rejected art to Detective Comics #2 and interior from Detective Comics #1. A CGC certified 9.0 copy sold for $17,825 in 2002 and for $29,000 in 2008.

ACTION FORCE (Also see G.I. Joe European Missions)
Marvel Comics Ltd. (British): Mar, 1987 - No. 50, 1988 ($1.00, weekly, magazine)

1,3: British G.I. Joe series. 3-w/poster insert 2 4 6 8 10 12
2,4 1 2 3 5 6 8
5-10 5.00
11-50 3.00
...Special 1 (7/87) Summer holiday special; Snake Eyes-c/app. 1 2 3 5 6 8
...Special 2 (10/87) Winter special; 5.00

ACTION FUNNIES
DC Comics: 1937/1938

nn - Ashcan comic, not distributed to newsstands, only for in house use. Cover art is Action Comics #3 and interior from Detective Comics #10. The Mallette/Brown copy in VG+ condition sold for $15,000 in 2005.

ACTION GIRL
Slave Labor Graphics: Oct, 1994 - No. 19 ($2.50/$2.75/$2.95, B&W)

1-19: 4-Begin $2.75-c. 19-Begin $2.95-c 3.00
1-6 ($2.75, 2nd printings): All read 2nd Print in indicia. 1-(2/96). 2-(10/95). 3-(2/96). 4-(7/96). 5-(2/97). 6-(9/97) 3.00
1-4 ($2.75, 3rd printings): All read 3rd Print in indicia. 3.00

ACTION PLANET COMICS
Action Planet: 1996 - No. 3, Sept, 1997 ($3.95, B&W, 44 pgs.)

1-3: 1-Intro Monster Man by Mike Manley & other stories 4.00
Giant Size Action Planet Halloween Special (1998, $5.95, oversized) 6.00

ACTUAL CONFESSIONS (Formerly Love Adventures)
Atlas Comics (MPI): No. 13, Oct, 1952 - No. 14, Dec, 1952

13,14 9 18 27 52 69 85

ACTUAL ROMANCES (Becomes True Secrets #3 on?)
Marvel Comics (IPS): Oct, 1949 - No. 2, Jan, 1950 (52 pgs.)

1 15 30 45 84 127 170
2-Photo-c 10 20 30 58 79 100

ADAM AND EVE
Spire Christian Comics (Fleming H. Revell Co.): 1975,1978 (35¢/39¢/49¢)

nn-By Al Hartley 2 4 6 9 13 16

ADAM: LEGEND OF THE BLUE MARVEL
Marvel Comics: Jan, 2009 - No. 5, May, 2009 ($3.99, limited series)

1-5-Grevioux-s/Broome-a; Avengers app. 4.00

ADAM STRANGE (Also see Green Lantern #132, Mystery In Space #53 & Showcase #17)
DC Comics: 1990 - No. 3, 1990 ($3.95, 52 pgs, limited series, squarebound)

Book One - Three: Andy & Adam Kubert-c/a 4.00
...: The Man of Two Worlds (2003, $19.95, TPB) r/#1-3; sketch pages by Andy Kubert 20.00

ADAM STRANGE (Leads into the Rann/Thanagar War mini-series)
DC Comics: Nov, 2004 - No. 8, June, 2005 ($2.95, limited series)

1-8-Andy Diggle-s/Pascal Ferry-a/c. 1-Superman app. 3.00
...: Planet Heist TPB (2005, $19.99) r/series; sketch pages 20.00
... Special (11/08, $3.50) Takes place durng Rann/Thanagar Holy War series; Starlin-s 4.00

ADAM-12 (TV)
Gold Key: Dec, 1973 - No. 10, Feb, 1976 (Photo-c)

1 6 12 18 43 69 95
2-10 4 8 12 22 34 45

GD 2.0 | VG 4.0 | FN 6.0 | VF 8.0 | VF/NM 9.0 | NM- 9.2

ADDAMS FAMILY (TV cartoon)
Gold Key: Oct, 1974 - No. 3, Apr, 1975 (Hanna-Barbera)

1 8 16 24 54 90 125
2,3 6 12 18 37 59 80

ADLAI STEVENSON
Dell Publishing Co.: Dec, 1966

12-007-612-Life story; photo-c 4 8 12 22 34 45

ADOLESCENT RADIOACTIVE BLACK BELT HAMSTERS (See Clint)
Comic Castle/Eclipse Comics: 1986 - No. 9, Jan, 1988 ($1.50, B&W)

1-9: 1st & 2nd printings exist 3.00
1-Limited Edition 6.00
1-In 3-D (7/86), 2-4 ($2.50) 3.00
Massacre The Japanese Invasion #1 (8/89, $2.00) 3.00

ADOLESCENT RADIOACTIVE BLACK BELT HAMSTERS
Dynamite Entertainment: 2008 - No. 4, 2008 ($3.50, limited series)

1-4-Tom Nguyen-a/Keith Champagne-s; 2 covers by Nguyen and Oeming 3.50

ADRENALYNN (See The Tenth)
Image Comics: Aug, 1999 - No. 4, Feb, 2000 ($2.50)

1-4-Tony Daniel-s/Marty Egeland-a; origin of Adrenalynn 3.00

ADULT TALES OF TERROR ILLUSTRATED (See Terror Illustrated)

ADVANCED DUNGEONS & DRAGONS (Also see TSR Worlds)
DC Comics: Dec, 1988 - No. 36, Dec, 1991 (Newsstand #1 is Holiday, 1988-89) ($1.25-$1.75)

1-Based on TSR role playing game 4.00
2-36: 25-$1.75-c begins 3.00
Annual 1 (1990, $3.95, 68 pgs.) 4.00

ADVENTURE BOUND
Dell Publishing Co.: Aug, 1949

Four Color #239 6 12 18 39 62 85

ADVENTURE COMICS (Formerly New Adventure)(...Presents Dial H For Hero #479-490)
National Periodical Publications/DC Comics: No. 32, 11/38 - No. 490, 2/82; No. 491, 9/82 - No. 503, 9/83

32-Anchors Aweigh (ends #52), Barry O'Neil (ends #60, not in #33), Captain Desmo (ends #47), Dale Daring (ends #47), Federal Men (ends #70), The Golden Dragon (ends #36), Rusty & His Pals (ends #52) by Bob Kane, Todd Hunter (ends #38) and Tom Brent (ends #39) begin 430 860 1290 2408 3504 4600
33-38: 37-Cover used on Double Action #2 210 420 630 1176 1713 2250
39(6/39)- Jack Wood begins, ends #42; early mention of Marijuana in comics 210 420 630 1176 1713 2250
40-(Rare, 7/39, on stands 6/10/39)-The Sandman begins by Bert Christman (who died in WWII); believed to be 1st conceived story (see N.Y. World's Fair for 1st published app.); Socko Strong begins, ends #54 6250 12,500 18,750 47,000 83,500 120,000
41-O'Mealia shark-c 595 1190 1785 4350 7675 11,000
42,44-Sandman-c by Flessel. 44-Opium story 757 1514 2271 5526 9763 14,000
43,45: 45-Full page ad for Flash Comics #1 354 708 1062 2478 4339 6200
46,47-Sandman covers by Flessel. 47-Steve Conrad Adventurer begins, ends #76 541 1082 1623 3950 6975 10,000
48-Intro & 1st app. The Hourman by Bernard Baily; Baily-c (Hourman c-48,50,52-59) 2700 5400 8100 20,000 37,000 54,000
49,50: 50-Cotton Carver by Jack Lehti begins, ends #64 290 580 870 1856 3178 4500
51,60-Sandman-c: 51-Sandman-c by Flessel. 366 732 1098 2562 4481 6400
52-59: 53-1st app. Jimmy "Minuteman" Martin & the Minutemen of America in Hourman; ends #78. 58-Paul Kirk Manhunter begins (1st app.), ends #72 258 516 774 1651 2826 4000
61-1st app. Starman by Jack Burnley (4/41); Starman c-61-72; Starman by Burnley in #61-80 1200 2400 3600 9000 16,500 24,000
62-65,67,68,70: 67-Origin & 1st app. The Mist; classic Burnley-c. 70-Last Federal Men 219 438 657 1402 2401 3400
66-Origin/1st app. Shining Knight (9/41) 265 530 795 1694 2897 4100
69-1st app. Sandy the Golden Boy (Sandman's sidekick) by Paul Norris (in a Bob Kane style); Sandman dons new costume 232 464 696 1485 2543 3600
71-Jimmy Martin becomes costumed aide to the Hourman; 1st app. Hourman's Miracle Ray machine 213 426 639 1363 2332 3300
72-1st Simon & Kirby Sandman (3/42, 1st DC work) 946 1892 2838 6906 12,203 17,500
73-Origin Manhunter by Simon & Kirby; begin new series; Manhunter-c (scarce) 1275 2550 3825 9550 17,275 25,000
74-78,80: 74-Thorndyke replaces Jimmy, Hourman's assistant; new Sandman-c begin by S&K. 75-Thor app. by Kirby; 1st Kirby Thor (see Tales of the Unexpected #16). 77-Origin

Adventure Comics #143 © DC

Adventure Comics #288 © DC

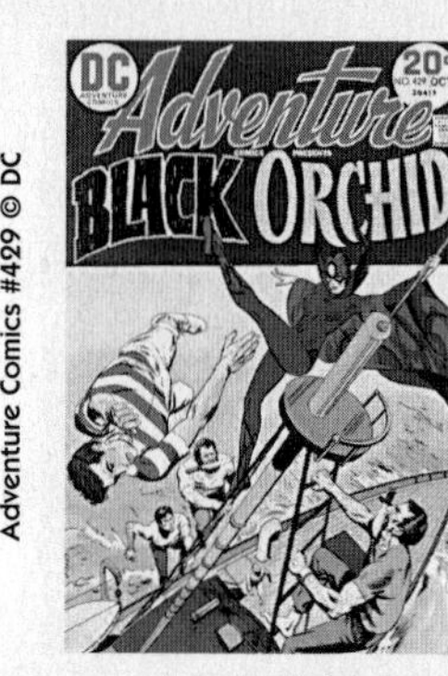

Adventure Comics #429 © DC

	GD 2.0	VG 4.0	FN 6.0	VF 8.0	VF/NM 9.0	NM- 9.2
Genius Jones; Mist story. 80-Last S&K Manhunter & Burnley Starman	194	388	582	1242	2121	3000
79-Classic Manhunter-c	271	542	813	1734	2967	4200
81-90: 83-Last Hourman. 84-Mike Gibbs begins, ends #102	123	246	369	787	1344	1900
91-Last Simon & Kirby Sandman	110	220	330	704	1202	1700
92-99,101,102: 92-Last Manhunter. 101-Shining Knight origin retold. 102-Last Starman, Sandman, & Genius Jones; most-S&K-c (Genius Jones cont'd in More Fun #108)	97	194	291	621	1061	1500
100-S&K-c	132	264	396	838	1444	2050
103-Aquaman, Green Arrow, Johnny Quick & Superboy all move over from More Fun Comics #107; 8th app. Superboy; Superboy-c begin; 1st small logo (4/46)	300	600	900	1950	3375	4800
104	110	220	330	704	1202	1700
105-110	77	154	231	493	847	1200
111-120: 113-X-Mas-c	69	138	207	442	759	1075
121,122-126,128-130: 128-1st meeting Superboy & Lois Lane	63	126	189	403	689	975
127-Brief origin Shining Knight retold	64	128	192	406	696	985
131-141,143-149: 132-Shining Knight 1st return to King Arthur time; origin aide Sir Butch	54	108	162	343	574	825
142-Origin Shining Knight & Johnny Quick retold	56	112	168	356	616	875
150,151,153,155,157,159,161,163-All have 6 pg. Shining Knight stories by Frank Frazetta. 159-Origin Johnny Quick. 161-1st Lana Lang app. in this title	68	136	204	435	743	1050
152,154,156,158,160,162,164-169: 166-Last Shining Knight. 168-Last 52 pg. issue	48	96	144	302	514	725
170-180	46	92	138	290	488	685
181-199: 189-B&W and color illo in **POP**	44	88	132	277	469	660
200 (5/54)	56	112	168	356	616	875
201-208: 207-Last Johnny Quick (not in 205)	41	82	123	256	428	600
209-Last pre-code issue; origin Speedy	42	84	126	265	445	625
210-1st app. Krypto (Superdog)-c/story (3/55)	330	660	990	2600	5000	7400
211-213,215-219	39	78	117	240	395	550
214-2nd app. Krypto	68	136	204	435	743	1050
220-Krypto-c/sty	43	86	129	271	461	650
221-246: 229-1st S.A. issue. 237-1st Intergalactic Vigilante Squadron (6/57). 239-Krypto-c	34	68	102	199	325	450
247(4/58)-1st Legion of Super Heroes app.; 1st app. Cosmic Boy, Saturn Girl & Lightning Boy (later Lightning Lad in #267) (origin)	550	1100	1650	5000	10,000	15,000
248-252,254,255-Green Arrow in all: 255-Intro. Red Kryptonite in Superboy (used in #252 but with no effect)	29	58	87	170	278	385
253-1st meeting of Superboy & Robin; Green Arrow by Kirby in #250-255 (also see World's Finest #96-99)	34	68	102	199	325	450
256-Origin Green Arrow by Kirby	68	136	204	435	743	1050
257-259: 258-Green Arrow x-over in Superboy	24	48	72	142	234	325
260-1st Silver-Age origin Aquaman (5/59)	76	152	228	486	831	1175
261-265,268,270: 262-Origin Speedy in Green Arrow. 270-Congorilla begins, ends #281,283	20	40	60	118	192	265
266-(11/59)-Origin & 1st app. Aquagirl (tryout, not same as later character)	21	42	63	122	199	275
267(12/59)-2nd Legion of Super Heroes; Lightning Boy now called Lightning Lad; new costumes for Legion	97	194	291	611	1256	1900
269-Intro. Aqualad (2/60); last Green Arrow (not in #206)	32	64	96	192	314	435
271-Origin Luthor retold	39	78	117	231	378	525
272-274,277-280: 279-Intro White Kryptonite in Superboy. 280-1st meeting Superboy & Lori Lemaris	19	38	57	111	176	240
275-Origin Superman-Batman team retold (see World's Finest #94)	25	50	75	147	241	335
276-(9/60) Robinson Crusoe-like story	20	40	60	114	182	250
281,284,287-289: 281-Last Congorilla. 284-Last Aquaman in Adv.; Mooney-a. 287,288-Intro Dev-Em, the Knave from Krypton. 287-1st Bizarro Perry White & Jimmy Olsen. 288-Bizarro-c. 289-Legion cameo (statues)	18	36	54	103	162	220
282(3/61)-5th Legion app; intro/origin Star Boy	37	74	111	222	361	500
283-Intro. The Phantom Zone	28	56	84	165	270	375
285-1st Tales of the Bizarro World-c/story (ends #299) in Adv. (see Action #255)	23	46	69	136	223	310
286-1st Bizarro Mxyzptlk; Bizarro-c	22	44	66	132	216	300
290(11/61)-9th Legion app; origin Sunboy in Legion (last 10¢ issue)	34	68	102	199	325	450
291,292,295-298: 291-1st 12¢ ish, (12/61). 292-1st Bizarro Lana Lang & Lucy Lane. 295-Bizarro-c; 1st Bizarro Titano	10	20	30	73	134	195
293(2/62)-13th Legion app; Mon-El & Legion of Super Pets (1st app./origin) app. (1st Superhorse). 1st Bizarro Luthor & Kandor	16	32	48	114	232	350
294-1st Bizarro Marilyn Monroe, Pres. Kennedy.	12	24	36	86	161	235
299-1st Gold Kryptonite (8/62)	11	22	33	75	138	200
300-Tales of the Legion of Super-Heroes series begins (9/62); Mon-El leaves Phantom Zone (temporarily), joins Legion	43	86	129	344	697	1050
301-Origin Bouncing Boy	14	28	42	99	200	300
302-305: 303-1st app. Matter-Eater Lad. 304-Death of Lightning Lad in Legion	12	24	36	86	161	235
306-310: 306-Intro. Legion of Substitute Heroes. 307-1st app. Element Lad in Legion. 308-1st app. Lightning Lass in Legion. 309-1st app. Legion of Super-Monsters	11	22	33	79	147	215
311-320: 312-Lightning Lad back in Legion. 315-Last new Superboy story; Colossal Boy app. 316-Origins & powers of Legion given. 317-Intro. Dream Girl in Legion; Lightning Lass becomes Light Lass; Hall of Fame series begins. 320-Dev-Em 2nd app.	10	20	30	68	119	170
321-Intro. Time Trapper	9	18	27	61	103	145
322-330: 327-Intro/1st app. Lone Wolf in Legion. 329-Intro The Bizarro Legionnaires; intro. Legion flight rings	8	16	24	56	93	130
331-340: 337-Chlorophyll Kid & Night Girl app. 340-Intro Computo in Legion	8	16	24	52	86	120
341-Triplicate Girl becomes Duo Damsel	7	14	21	47	76	105
342-345,347-351: 345-Last Hall of Fame; returns in 356,371. 348-Origin Sunboy; intro Dr. Regulus in Legion. 349-Intro Universo & Rond Vidar. 351-1st app. White Witch	7	14	21	45	73	100
346-1st app. Karate Kid, Princess Projectra, Ferro Lad, & Nemesis Kid.	9	18	27	63	107	150
352,354-360: 354,355-Superman meets the Adult Legion. 355-Insect Queen joins Legion (4/67)	6	12	18	41	66	90
353-Death of Ferro Lad in Legion	7	14	21	49	80	110
361-364,366,368-370: 369-Intro Mordru in Legion	6	12	18	37	59	80
365,367: 365-Intro Shadow Lass (memorial to Shadow Woman app. in #354's Adult Legion-s); lists origins & powers of L.S.H. 367-New Legion headquarters	6	12	18	39	62	85
371,372: 371-Intro. Chemical King (mentioned in #354's Adult Legion-s). 372-Timber Wolf & Chemical King join	6	12	18	39	62	85
373,374,376-380: 373-Intro. Tornado Twins (Barry Allen Flash descendants). 374-Article on comics fandom. 380-Last Legion in Adventure; last 12¢-c	5	10	15	35	55	75
375-Intro Quantum Queen & The Wanderers	6	12	18	39	62	85
381-Supergirl begins; 1st full length Supergirl story & her 1st solo book (6/69)	12	24	36	87	164	240
382-389	5	10	15	32	51	70
390-Giant Supergirl G-69	7	14	21	47	76	105
391-396,398	4	8	12	24	37	50
397-1st app. new Supergirl	5	10	15	32	51	70
399-Unpubbed G.A. Black Canary story	4	8	12	26	41	55
400-New costume for Supergirl (12/70)	5	10	15	32	51	70
401,402,404-408-(15¢-c)	3	6	9	18	27	35
403-68 pg. Giant G-81; Legion-r/#304,305,308,312	7	14	21	45	73	100
409-411,413-415,417-420-(52 pgs.): 413-Hawkman by Kubert r/B&B #44; G.A. Robotman-r/Det. #178; Zatanna by Morrow. 414-r-2nd Animal Man/Str. Advs. #184. 415-Animal Man-r/Str. Adv.#190 (origin recap). 417-Morrow Vigilante; Frazetta Shining Knight-r/Adv. #161; origin The Enchantress; no Zatanna. 418-Prev. unpub. Dr. Mid-Nite story from 1948; no Zatanna. 420-Animal Man-r/Str. Adv. #195	3	6	9	19	29	38
412-(52 pgs.) Reprints origin & 1st app. of Animal Man from Strange Adventures #180	3	6	9	19	29	38
416-Also listed as DC 100 Pg. Super Spectacular #10; Golden Age-r; r/1st app. Black Canary from Flash #86; no Zatanna (see DC 100 Pg. Super Spectacular #10 for price)						
421-424: 424-Last Supergirl in Adventure	3	6	9	14	20	25
425-New look, content change to adventure; Kaluta-c; Toth-a, origin Capt. Fear	3	6	9	16	23	30
426,427: 426-1st Adventurers Club. 427-Last Vigilante	2	4	6	9	12	15
428-Origin/1st app. Black Orchid (c/story, 6-7/73)	6	12	18	37	59	80
429,430-Black Orchid-c/stories	3	6	9	21	32	42
431-Spectre by Aparo begins, ends #440.	6	12	18	41	66	90
432-439-Spectre app. 433-437-Cover title is Weird Adventure Comics. 436-Last 20¢ issue	4	8	12	22	34	45
440-New Spectre origin.	4	8	12	28	44	60
441-458: 441-452-Aquaman app. 443-Fisherman app. 445-447-The Creeper app. 446-Flag-c. 449-451-Martian Manhunter app. 450-Weather Wizard app. in Aquaman story. 453-458-Superboy app. 453-Intro. Mighty Girl. 457,458-Eclipso app.	1	3	4	6	8	10
459,460 (68 pgs.): 459-New Gods/Darkseid storyline concludes from New Gods #19 (#459 is						

Adventure Comics (2009 series) #12 © DC

Adventure Is My Career © CN

Adventures Into Terror #31 © MAR

GD VG FN VF VF/NM NM-
2.0 4.0 6.0 8.0 9.0 9.2

dated 9-10/78) without missing a month. 459-Flash (ends #466), Deadman (ends #466), Wonder Woman (ends #464), Green Lantern (ends #460). 460-Aquaman (ends #478) 3 6 9 14 20 26
461,462 ($1.00, 68 pgs.): 461-Justice Society begins; ends 466.
461,462-Death Earth II Batman 4 8 12 26 41 55
463-466 ($1.00 size, 68 pgs.) 2 4 6 10 14 18
467-Starman by Ditko & Plastic Man begins; 1st app. Prince Gavyn (Starman). 2 4 6 8 11 14
468-490: 470-Origin Starman. 479-Dial 'H' For Hero begins, ends #490. 478-Last Starman & Plastic Man. 480-490: Dial 'H' For Hero 5.00
491-503: 491-100pg. Digest size begins; r/Legion of Super Heroes/Adv. #247, 267; Spectre, Aquaman, Superboy, S&K Sandman, Black Canary-r & new Shazam by Newton begin. 492,495,496,499-S&K Sandman-r/Adventure in all. 493-Challengers of the Unknown begins by Tuska w/brief origin. 493-495,497-499-G.A. Captain Marvel-r. 494-499-Spectre-r/Spectre 1-3, 5-7. 496-Capt. Marvel Jr. new-s, Cockrum-a. 498-Mary Marvel new-s; Plastic Man-r begin; origin Bouncing Boy-r/ #301. 500-Legion-r (Digest size, 148 pgs.).
501-503: G.A.-r 2 4 6 9 13 16
... 80 Page Giant (10/98, $4.95) Wonder Woman, Shazam, Superboy, Supergirl, Green Arrow, Legion, Bizarro World stories 5.00

NOTE: *Bizarro covers-285, 286, 288, 294, 295, 329. Vigilante app.-420, 426, 427.* ***N. Adams*** *a(r)-495i-498i; c-365-369, 371-373, 375-379, 381-383.* ***Aparo*** *a-431-433, 434i, 435, 436, 437i, 438i, 439-452, 503r; c-431-452.* ***Austin*** *a-449i 451i.* ***Bernard Baily*** *c-48, 50, 52-59.* ***Bolland*** *c-475.* ***Burnley*** *c-61-72, 116-120p.* ***Chaykin*** *a-438.* ***Ditko*** *a-467-478p; c-467p.* ***Creig Flessel*** *c-32, 33, 40, 42, 44, 46, 47, 51, 60.* ***Giffen*** *c-491p-494p, 500p.* ***Grell*** *a-435-437, 440.* ***Guardineer*** *c-34, 35, 45.* ***Infantino*** *a-416r.* ***Kaluta*** *c-425.* ***Bob Kane*** *a-38.* ***G. Kane*** *a-414r, 425; c-496-499, 537.* ***Kirby*** *a-250-256.* ***Kubert*** *a-413.* ***Meskin*** *a-81,127.* ***Moldoff*** *a-494i; c-49.* ***Morrow*** *a-413-415, 417, 422, 502r, 503r.* ***Netzer/Nasser*** *a-449-451.* ***Newton*** *a-459-461, 464-466, 491p, 492p.* ***Paul Norris*** *a-69.* ***Orlando*** *a-457p, 458p.* ***Perez*** *c-484-486, 490p.* ***Simon/Kirby*** *a-503r; c-73-97, 100-102.* ***Starlin*** *c-471.* ***Staton*** *a-445-447i, 456-458p, 459, 460, 461p-465p, 466,467p-478p, 502p(r); c-458, 461(back).* ***Toth*** *a-418, 419, 425, 431, 495p-497p.* ***Tuska*** *a-494p.*

ADVENTURE COMICS (Also see All Star Comics 1999 crossover titles)
DC Comics: May, 1999 ($1.99, one-shot)
1-Golden Age Starman and the Atom; Snejbjerg-a 3.00

ADVENTURE COMICS (See Final Crisis: Legion of Three Worlds)
DC Comics: No. 0, Apr, 2009 - No. 12, Aug, 2010; No. 516, Sept, 2010 - Present ($1.00/$3.99)
0-($1.00) R/Adventure Comics #247; new Luthor & Brainiac back-up-s; Lopresti-c 3.00
1-7-($3.99) Superboy stories; Johns-s/Manapul-a; Legion back-up-s. 5-7-Blackest Night 4.00
1-12-Variant 7-panel covers by various numbered with original #504-#515 5.00
8-12: 8-11-New Krypton x-over. 11-Mon-El leaves 21st century. 12-Legion; Levitz-s 4.00
516-521: 516-(9/10, resumes original numbering) flashback to Legion formation; Atom back-ups. 521-Adult Legion resumes; Mon-El joins Green Lanterns 4.00
522-524-($2.99) 523,524-Legion Academy; Jimenez-a/c 3.00

ADVENTURE COMICS SPECIAL (See New Krypton issues in 2009 Superman titles)
DC Comics: Jan, 2009 ($2.99, one-shot)
... Featuring the Guardian - James Robinson-s/Pere Pérez-a; origin re-told; intro. Gwen 3.00

ADVENTURE INTO MYSTERY
Atlas Comics (BFP No. 1/OPI No. 2-8): May, 1956 - No. 8, July, 1957
1-Powell s/f-a; Forte-a; Everett-c 39 78 117 240 395 550
2-Flying Saucer story 22 44 66 132 216 300
3,6-Everett-c 20 40 60 117 189 260
4,5,7: 4-Williamson-a, 4 pgs; Powell-a. 5-Everett-c/a, Orlando-a. 7-Torres-a; Everett-c 21 42 63 124 202 280
8-Moreira, Sale, Torres, Woodbridge-a, Severin-c 20 40 60 117 189 260

ADVENTURE IS MY CAREER
U.S. Coast Guard Academy/Street & Smith: 1945 (44 pgs.)
nn-Simon, Milt Gross-a 21 42 63 126 206 285

ADVENTURERS, THE
Aircel Comics/Adventure Publ.: Aug, 1986 - No. 10, 1987? ($1.50, B&W)
V2#1, 1987 - V2#9, 1988; V3#1, Oct, 1989 - V3#6, 1990
1-Peter Hsu-a 1 2 3 5 6 8
1-Cover variant, limited ed. 2 4 6 9 12 15
1-2nd print (1986); 1st app. Elf Warrior 3.00
2,3, 0 (#4, 12/86)-Origin, 5-10, Book II, reg. & Limited Ed. #1 3.50
Book II, #2,3,0,4-9 3.00
Book III, #1 (10/89, $2.25)-Reg. & limited-c, Book III, #2-6 3.00

ADVENTURES (No. 2 Spectacular... on cover)
St. John Publishing Co.: Nov, 1949 - No. 2, Feb, 1950 (No. 1 ...in Romance on cover) (Slightly larger size)
1(Scarce); Bolle, Starr-a(2) 27 54 81 158 259 360
2(Scarce)-Slave Girl; China Bombshell app.; Bolle, L. Starr-a 39 78 117 240 395 550

ADVENTURES FOR BOYS

GD VG FN VF VF/NM NM-
2.0 4.0 6.0 8.0 9.0 9.2

Bailey Enterprises: Dec, 1954
nn-Comics, text, & photos 8 16 24 40 50 60

ADVENTURES IN PARADISE (TV)
Dell Publishing Co.: Feb-Apr, 1962
Four Color #1301 6 12 18 39 62 85

ADVENTURES IN ROMANCE (See Adventures)

ADVENTURES IN SCIENCE (See Classics Illustrated Special Issue)

ADVENTURES IN THE DC UNIVERSE
DC Comics: Apr, 1997 - No. 19, Oct, 1998 ($1.75/$1.95/$1.99)
1-Animated style in all: JLA-c/app 5.00
2-11,13-17,19: 2-Flash app. 3-Wonder Woman. 4-Green Lantern. 6-Aquaman. 7-Shazam Family. 8-Blue Beetle & Booster Gold. 9-Flash. 10-Legion. 11-Green Lantern & Wonder Woman. 13-Impulse & Martian Manhunter. 14-Superboy/Flash race 3.50
12,18-JLA-c/app 3.50
Annual 1(1997, $3.95)-Dr. Fate, Impulse, Rose & Thorn, Superboy, Mister Miracle app. 4.50

ADVENTURES IN THE RIFLE BRIGADE
DC Comics (Vertigo): Oct, 2000 - No. 3, Dec, 2000 ($2.50, limited series)
1-3-Ennis-s/Ezquerra-a/Bolland-c 3.00
TPB (2004, $14.95) r/series and Operation Bollock series 15.00

ADVENTURES IN THE RIFLE BRIGADE: OPERATION BOLLOCK
DC Comics (Vertigo): Oct, 2001 - No. 3, Jan, 2002 ($2.50, limited series)
1-3-Ennis-s/Ezquerra-a/Fabry-c 3.00

ADVENTURES IN 3-D (With glasses)
Harvey Publications: Nov, 1953 - No. 2, Jan, 1954 (25¢)
1-Nostrand, Powell-a, 2-Powell-a 15 30 45 86 133 180

ADVENTURES INTO DARKNESS (See Seduction of the Innocent 3-D)
Better-Standard Publications/Visual Editions: No. 5, Aug, 1952- No. 14, 1954
5-Katz-c/a; Toth-a(p) 43 86 129 271 461 650
6-Tuska, Katz-a 32 64 96 188 307 425
7-9: 7-Katz-c/a. 8,9-Toth-a(p) 32 64 96 188 307 425
10-12: 10,11-Jack Katz-a. 12-Toth-a; lingerie panel 29 58 87 170 278 385
13-Toth-a(p); Cannibalism story cited by T. E. Murphy articles 37 74 111 222 361 500
14 21 42 63 122 199 275
NOTE: ***Fawcette*** *a-13.* ***Moreira*** *a-5.* ***Sekowsky*** *a-10, 11, 13(2).*

ADVENTURES INTO TERROR (Formerly Joker Comics)
Marvel/Atlas Comics (CDS): No. 43, Nov, 1950 - No. 31, May, 1954
43(#1) 71 142 213 454 777 1100
44(#2, 2/51)-Sol Brodsky-c 42 84 126 265 445 625
3(4/51), 4 32 64 96 188 307 425
5-Wolverton-c panel/Mystic #6; Rico-c panel also; Atom Bomb story 36 72 108 211 343 475
6,8: 8-Wolverton text illo r-/Marvel Tales #104; prototype of Spider-Man villain The Lizard 30 60 90 177 289 400
7-Wolverton-a "Where Monsters Dwell", 6 pgs.; Tuska-c; Maneely-c panels 61 122 183 390 670 950
9,10,12-Krigstein-a. 9-Decapitation panels 26 52 78 154 252 350
11,13-20 22 44 66 132 216 300
21-24,26-31 21 42 63 122 199 275
25-Matt Fox-a 26 52 78 154 252 350
NOTE: ***Ayers*** *a-21.* ***Colan*** *a-3, 5, 14, 21, 24, 25, 28, 29; c-27.* ***Colletta*** *a-30.* ***Everett*** *c-13, 21, 25.* ***Fass*** *a-28, 29.* ***Forte*** *a-28.* ***Heath*** *a-43, 44, 4-6, 22, 24, 26; c-43, 9, 11.* ***Lazarus*** *a-7.* ***Maneely*** *a-7(3 pg.), 10, 11, 21., 22 c-15, 29.* ***Don Rico*** *a-4, 5(3 pg.).* ***Sekowsky*** *a-43, 3, 4.* ***Sinnott*** *a-8, 9, 11, 28.* ***Tuska*** *a-14; c-7.*

ADVENTURES INTO THE UNKNOWN
American Comics Group: Fall, 1948 - No. 174, Aug, 1967 (No. 1-33: 52 pgs.)
(1st continuous series Supernatural comic; see Eerie #1)
1-Guardineer-a; adapt. of 'Castle of Otranto' by Horace Walpole 232 464 696 1485 2543 3600
2,3: 3-Feldstein-a (9 pgs) 81 162 243 518 884 1250
4,5: 5- 'Spirit Of Frankenstein' series begins, ends #12 (except #11) 42 84 126 265 445 625
6-10 36 72 108 211 343 475
11-16,18-20: 13-Starr-a 30 60 90 177 289 400
17-Story similar to movie 'The Thing' 34 68 102 204 335 465
21-26,28-30 26 52 78 154 252 350
27-Williamson/Krenkel-a (8 pgs.) 32 64 96 188 307 425
31-50: 38-Atom bomb panels 20 40 60 117 189 260
51-(1/54)-(3-D effect-c/story)-Only white cover 40 80 120 246 411 575

Adventures Into Weird Worlds #16 © MAR

Adventures of Bob Hope #3 © DC

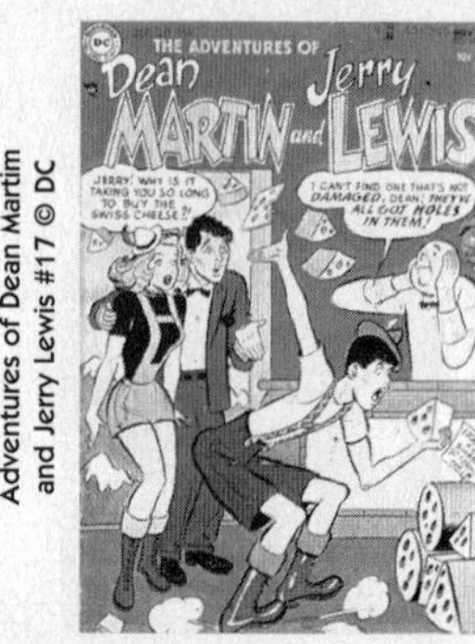

Adventures of Dean Martin and Jerry Lewis #17 © DC

	GD 2.0	VG 4.0	FN 6.0	VF 8.0	VF/NM 9.0	NM- 9.2
52-58: (3-D effect-c/stories with black covers). 52-E.C. swipe/Haunt Of Fear #14	39	78	117	231	378	525
59-3-D effect story only; new logo	30	60	90	177	289	400
60-Wood*esque*-a by Landau	15	30	45	88	137	185
61-Last pre-code issue (1-2/55)	15	30	45	88	137	185
62-70	8	16	24	54	90	125
71-90	6	12	18	43	69	95
91,96(#95 on inside),107,116-All have Williamson-a	7	14	21	47	76	105
92-95,97-99,101-106,108-115,117-128: 109-113,118-Whitney painted-c. 128-Williamson/Krenkel/Torres-a(r)/Forbidden Worlds #63; last 10¢ issue	5	10	15	34	55	75
100	6	12	18	39	62	85
129-153,157: 153,157-Magic Agent app.	4	8	12	24	37	50
154-Nemesis series begins (origin), ends #170	5	10	15	30	48	65
155,156,158-167,170-174	4	8	12	23	36	48
168-Ditko-a(p)	4	8	12	28	44	60
169-Nemesis battles Hitler	4	8	12	28	44	60
Nemesis Archives: Vol. One (Dark Horse Books, 9/08, $59.95) r/#154-170; creator bios						60.00

NOTE: *"Spirit of Frankenstein" series in 5, 6, 8-10, 12, 16.* ***Buscema*** *a-100, 106, 108-110, 158r, 165r.* ***Cameron*** *a-34.* ***Craig*** *a-152, 160.* ***Goode*** *a-45, 47, 60.* ***Landau*** *a-51, 59-63.* ***Lazarus*** *a-34, 48, 51, 52, 56, 58, 79, 87; c-31-56, 58.* ***Reinman*** *a-102, 111, 112, 115-118, 124, 130, 137, 141, 145, 164.* ***Whitney*** *c-12-30, 57, 59-on (most.)* ***Torres/Williamson*** *a-116.*

ADVENTURES INTO WEIRD WORLDS
Marvel/Atlas Comics (ACI): Jan, 1952 - No. 30, June, 1954

	GD 2.0	VG 4.0	FN 6.0	VF 8.0	VF/NM 9.0	NM- 9.2
1-Atom bomb panels	81	162	243	518	884	1250
2-Sci/fic stories (2); one by Maneely	40	80	120	246	411	575
3-10: 7-Tongue ripped out. 10-Krigstein, Everett-a	30	60	90	177	289	400
11-20	23	46	69	136	223	310
21-Hitler in Hell story	29	58	87	170	278	385
22-26: 24-Man holds hypo & splits in two	21	42	63	124	202	280
27-Matt Fox end of world story-a; severed head-c	40	80	120	246	411	575
28-Atom bomb story; decapitation panels	23	46	69	136	223	310
29,30	19	38	57	111	176	240

NOTE: ***Ayers*** *a-8, 26.* ***Everett*** *a-4, 5; c-6, 8, 10-13, 18, 19, 22, 24, 25; a-4, 25.* ***Fass*** *a-7.* ***Forte*** *a-21, 24.* ***Al Hartley*** *a-2.* ***Heath*** *a-1, 4, 17, 22; c-7, 9, 20.* ***Maneely*** *a-2, 3, 11, 20, 22, 23, 25; c-1, 3, 22, 25-27, 29.* ***Reinman*** *a-24, 28.* ***Rico*** *a-13.* ***Robinson*** *a-13.* ***Sinnott*** *a-25, 30.* ***Tuska*** *a-1, 2, 12, 15.* ***Whitney*** *a-7.* ***Wildey*** *a-28. Bondage c-22.*

ADVENTURES IN WONDERLAND (Also see Uncle Charlies Fables)
Lev Gleason Publications: April, 1955 - No. 5, Feb, 1956 (Jr. Readers Guild)

	GD 2.0	VG 4.0	FN 6.0	VF 8.0	VF/NM 9.0	NM- 9.2
1-Maurer-a	11	22	33	62	86	110
2-4	7	14	21	37	46	55
5-Christmas issue	8	16	24	40	50	60

ADVENTURES OF ALAN LADD, THE
National Periodical Publ.: Oct-Nov, 1949 - No. 9, Feb-Mar, 1951 (All 52 pgs.)

	GD 2.0	VG 4.0	FN 6.0	VF 8.0	VF/NM 9.0	NM- 9.2
1-Photo-c	68	136	204	435	743	1050
2-Photo-c	37	74	111	222	361	500
3-6: Last photo-c	30	60	90	177	289	400
7-9	24	48	72	140	230	320

NOTE: ***Dan Barry*** *a-1.* ***Moreira*** *a-3-7.*

ADVENTURES OF ALICE (Also see Alice in Wonderland & ...at Monkey Island)
Civil Service Publ./Pentagon Publishing Co.: 1945

	GD 2.0	VG 4.0	FN 6.0	VF 8.0	VF/NM 9.0	NM- 9.2
1	15	30	45	83	124	165
2-Through the Magic Looking Glass	11	22	33	62	86	110

ADVENTURES OF BARON MUNCHAUSEN, THE
Now Comics: July, 1989 - No. 4, Oct, 1989 ($1.75, limited series)

	GD 2.0	VG 4.0	FN 6.0	VF 8.0	VF/NM 9.0	NM- 9.2
1-4: Movie adaptation						3.00

ADVENTURES OF BARRY WEEN, BOY GENIUS, THE
Image Comics: Mar, 1999 - No. 3, May, 1999 ($2.95, B&W, limited series)

	GD 2.0	VG 4.0	FN 6.0	VF 8.0	VF/NM 9.0	NM- 9.2
1-3-Judd Winick-s/a						3.00
...: Secret Crisis Origin Files (Oni, 7/04, Free Comic Book Day giveaway - Winick-s/a						2.50
TPB (Oni Press, 11/99, $8.95) r/#1-3						9.00

ADVENTURES OF BARRY WEEN, BOY GENIUS 2.0, THE
Oni Press: Feb, 2000 - No. 3, Apr, 2000 ($2.95, B&W, limited series)

	GD 2.0	VG 4.0	FN 6.0	VF 8.0	VF/NM 9.0	NM- 9.2
1-3-Judd Winick-s/a						3.00
TPB (2000, $8.95)						9.00

ADVENTURES OF BARRY WEEN, BOY GENIUS 3, THE : MONKEY TALES
Oni Press: Feb, 2001 - No. 6, Feb, 2002 ($2.95, B&W, limited series)

	GD 2.0	VG 4.0	FN 6.0	VF 8.0	VF/NM 9.0	NM- 9.2
1-6-Judd Winick-s/a						3.00
TPB (2001, $8.95) r/#1-3; intro. by Peter David						9.00
...4 TPB (5/02, $8.95) r/#4-6						9.00

ADVENTURES OF BAYOU BILLY, THE (Based on video game)
Archie Comics: Sept, 1989 - No. 5, June, 1990 ($1.00)

	GD 2.0	VG 4.0	FN 6.0	VF 8.0	VF/NM 9.0	NM- 9.2
1-5: Esposito-c/a(i). 5-Kelley Jones-c						3.00

ADVENTURES OF BOB HOPE, THE (Also see True Comics #59)
National Per. Publ.: Feb-Mar, 1950 - No. 109, Feb-Mar, 1968 (#1-10: 52pgs.)

	GD 2.0	VG 4.0	FN 6.0	VF 8.0	VF/NM 9.0	NM- 9.2
1-Photo-c	206	412	618	1318	2259	3200
2-Photo-c	87	174	261	553	952	1350
3,4-Photo-c	54	108	162	343	574	825
5-10	40	80	120	246	411	575
11-20	28	56	84	165	270	375
21-31 (2-3/55; last precode)	20	40	60	114	182	250
32-40	10	20	30	69	122	175
41-50	9	18	27	61	103	145
51-70	7	14	21	50	83	115
71-93	6	12	18	37	59	80
94-Aquaman cameo	6	12	18	37	59	80
95-1st app. Super-Hip & 1st monster issue (11/65)	7	14	21	50	83	115
96-105: Super-Hip and monster stories in all. 103-Batman, Robin, Ringo Starr cameos	6	12	18	37	59	80
106-109-All monster-c/stories by N. Adams-c/a	8	16	24	52	86	120

NOTE: *Buzzy in #34. Kitty Karr of Hollywood in #15, 17-20, 23, 28. Liz in #26, 109. Miss Beverly Hills of Hollywood in #7, 8, 10, 13, 14. Miss Melody Lane of Broadway in #15. Rusty in #23, 25. Tommy in #24. No 2nd feature in #2-4, 6, 8, 11, 12, 28-108.*

ADVENTURES OF CAPTAIN AMERICA
Marvel Comics: Sept, 1991 - No. 4, Jan, 1992 ($4.95, 52 pgs., squarebound, limited series)

	GD 2.0	VG 4.0	FN 6.0	VF 8.0	VF/NM 9.0	NM- 9.2
1-4: 1-Origin in WW2; embossed-c; Nicieza scripts; Maguire-c/a(p) begins, ends #3. 2-4-Austin-c/a(i). 3,4-Red Skull app.						5.00

ADVENTURES OF CYCLOPS AND PHOENIX (Also See Askani'son & The Further Adventures of Cyclops And Phoenix)
Marvel Comics: May, 1994 - No. 4, Aug, 1994 ($2.95, limited series)

	GD 2.0	VG 4.0	FN 6.0	VF 8.0	VF/NM 9.0	NM- 9.2
1-4-Characters from X-Men; origin of Cable						4.00
Trade paperback ($14.95)-reprints #1-4						15.00

ADVENTURES OF DEAN MARTIN AND JERRY LEWIS, THE
(The Adventures of Jerry Lewis #41 on) (See Movie Love #12)
National Periodical Publications: July-Aug, 1952 - No. 40, Oct, 1957

	GD 2.0	VG 4.0	FN 6.0	VF 8.0	VF/NM 9.0	NM- 9.2
1	116	232	348	742	1271	1800
2-3 pg origin on how they became a team	53	106	159	334	567	800
3-10: 3- I Love Lucy text featurette	32	64	96	188	307	425
11-19: Last precode (2/55)	20	40	60	118	192	265
20-30	15	30	45	90	140	190
31-40	14	28	42	80	115	150

ADVENTURES OF DETECTIVE ACE KING, THE (Also see Bob Scully-- & Detective Dan)
Humor Publ. Corp.: No date (1933) (36 pgs., 9-1/2x12") (10¢, B&W, one-shot) (paper-c)

	GD 2.0	VG 4.0	FN 6.0	VF 8.0	VF/NM 9.0	NM- 9.2
Book 1-Along with Bob Scully & Detective Dan, the first comic w/original art & the first of a single theme.; Not reprints; Ace King by Martin Nadle (The American Sherlock Holmes). A Dick Tracy look-alike	400	800	1200	3200	-	-

ADVENTURES OF EVIL AND MALICE, THE
Image Comics: June, 1999 - No. 3, Nov, 1999 ($3.50/$3.95, limited series)

	GD 2.0	VG 4.0	FN 6.0	VF 8.0	VF/NM 9.0	NM- 9.2
1-3-Jimmie Robinson-s/a. 3-($3.95-c)						4.00

ADVENTURES OF FELIX THE CAT, THE
Harvey Comics: May, 1992 ($1.25)

	GD 2.0	VG 4.0	FN 6.0	VF 8.0	VF/NM 9.0	NM- 9.2
1-Messmer-r						5.00

ADVENTURES OF FORD FAIRLANE, THE
DC Comics: May, 1990 - No. 4, Aug, 1990 ($1.50, limited series, mature)

	GD 2.0	VG 4.0	FN 6.0	VF 8.0	VF/NM 9.0	NM- 9.2
1-4: Andrew Dice Clay movie tie-in; Don Heck inks						3.00

ADVENTURES OF HOMER COBB, THE
Say/Bart Prod. : Sept, 1947 (Oversized) (Published in the U.S., but printed in Canada)

	GD 2.0	VG 4.0	FN 6.0	VF 8.0	VF/NM 9.0	NM- 9.2
1-(Scarce)-Feldstein-c/a	34	68	102	199	325	450

ADVENTURES OF HOMER GHOST (See Homer The Happy Ghost)
Atlas Comics: June, 1957 - No. 2, Aug, 1957

	GD 2.0	VG 4.0	FN 6.0	VF 8.0	VF/NM 9.0	NM- 9.2
V1#1,2: 2-Robot-c	12	24	36	67	94	120

ADVENTURES OF JERRY LEWIS, THE (Adventures of Dean Martin & Jerry Lewis No. 1-40) (See Super DC Giant)
National Periodical Publ.: No. 41, Nov, 1957 - No. 124, May-June, 1971

	GD 2.0	VG 4.0	FN 6.0	VF 8.0	VF/NM 9.0	NM- 9.2
41	9	18	27	65	113	160
42-60	8	16	24	52	86	120
61-67,69-73,75-80	6	12	18	43	69	95
68,74-Photo-c (movie)	9	18	27	64	110	155

Adventures of Luther Arkwright #8 © DH

Adventures of Mighty Mouse #8 © STJ

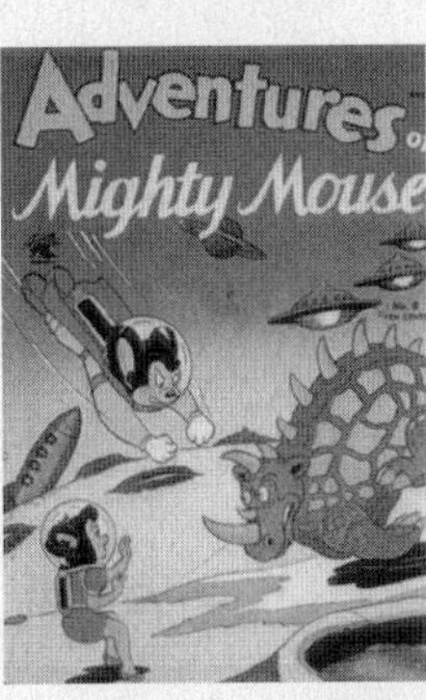

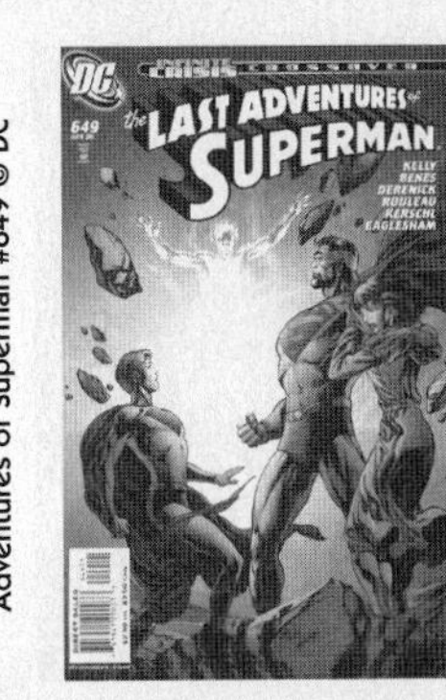

Adventures of Superman #649 © DC

	GD 2.0	VG 4.0	FN 6.0	VF 8.0	VF/NM 9.0	NM- 9.2
81,82,85-87,90,91,94,96,98,99	6	12	18	37	59	80
83,84,88: 83-1st Monsters-c/s. 84-Jerry as a Super-hero-c/s. 88-1st Witch, Miss Kraft	6	12	18	43	69	95
89-Bob Hope app.; Wizard of Oz & Alfred E. Neuman in MAD parody	7	14	21	47	76	105
92-Superman cameo	7	14	21	47	76	105
93-Beatles parody as babies	6	12	18	43	69	95
95-1st Uncle Hal Wack-A-Boy Camp-c/s	6	12	18	43	69	95
97-Batman/Robin/Joker-c/story; Riddler & Penguin app; Dick Sprang-c.	9	18	27	64	110	155
100	7	14	21	45	73	100
101,103,104-Neal Adams-c/a	8	16	24	52	86	120
102-Beatles app.; Neal Adams c/a	9	18	27	65	113	160
105-Superman x-over	7	14	21	47	76	105
106-111,113-116	4	8	12	28	44	60
112,117: 112-Flash x-over. 117-W. Woman x-over	7	14	21	45	73	100
118-124	4	8	12	26	41	55

NOTE: *Monster-c/s-90,93,96,98,101. Wack-A-Buy Camp-c/s-96,99,102,107,108.*

ADVENTURES OF JO-JOY, THE (See Jo-Joy)

ADVENTURES OF LASSIE, THE (See Lassie)

ADVENTURES OF LUTHER ARKWRIGHT, THE
Valkyrie Press/Dark Horse Comics: Oct, 1987 - No. 9, Jan, 1989 ($2.00, B&W) V2, #1, Mar, 1990 - V2#9, 1990 ($1.95, B&W)

1-9: 1-Alan Moore intro., V2#1-9 (Dark Horse): r-1st series; new-c	4.00
TPB (1997, $14.95) r/#1-9 w/Michael Moorcock intro.	15.00

ADVENTURES OF MIGHTY MOUSE (Mighty Mouse Adventures No. 1)
St. John Publishing Co.: No. 2, Jan, 1952 - No. 18, May, 1955

	GD 2.0	VG 4.0	FN 6.0	VF 8.0	VF/NM 9.0	NM- 9.2
2	25	50	75	150	245	340
3-5	15	30	45	84	127	170
6-18	11	22	33	62	86	110

ADVENTURES OF MIGHTY MOUSE (2nd Series) (Becomes Mighty Mouse #161 on)
(Two No. 144's; formerly Paul Terry's Comics; No. 129-137 have nn's)
St. John/Pines/Dell/Gold Key: No. 126, Aug, 1955 - No. 160, Oct, 1963

	GD 2.0	VG 4.0	FN 6.0	VF 8.0	VF/NM 9.0	NM- 9.2
126(8/55), 127(10/55), 128(11/55)-St. John	10	20	30	54	72	90
nn(129, 4/56)-144(8/59)-Pines	5	10	15	30	48	65
144(10-12/59)-155(7-9/62) Dell	4	8	12	28	44	60
156(10/62)-160(10/63) Gold Key	4	8	12	28	44	60

NOTE: *Early issues titled "Paul Terry's Adventures of ...."*

ADVENTURES OF MIGHTY MOUSE (Formerly Mighty Mouse)
Gold Key: No. 166, Mar, 1979 - No. 172, Jan, 1980

	GD 2.0	VG 4.0	FN 6.0	VF 8.0	VF/NM 9.0	NM- 9.2
166-172	1	2	3	5	6	8

ADVS. OF MR. FROG & MISS MOUSE (See Dell Junior Treasury No. 4)

ADVENTURES OF OZZIE & HARRIET, THE (See Ozzie & Harriet)

ADVENTURES OF PATORUZU
Green Publishing Co.: Aug, 1946 - Winter, 1946

	GD 2.0	VG 4.0	FN 6.0	VF 8.0	VF/NM 9.0	NM- 9.2
nn's-Contains Animal Crackers reprints	6	12	18	28	34	40

ADVENTURES OF PINKY LEE, THE (TV)
Atlas Comics: July, 1955 - No. 5, Dec, 1955

	GD 2.0	VG 4.0	FN 6.0	VF 8.0	VF/NM 9.0	NM- 9.2
1	24	48	72	140	230	320
2-5	15	30	45	86	133	180

ADVENTURES OF PIPSQUEAK, THE (Formerly Pat the Brat)
Archie Publications (Radio Comics): No. 34, Sept, 1959 - No. 39, July, 1960

	GD 2.0	VG 4.0	FN 6.0	VF 8.0	VF/NM 9.0	NM- 9.2
34	4	8	12	22	34	45
35-39	3	6	9	18	27	35

ADVENTURES OF QUAKE & QUISP, THE (See Quaker Oats "Plenty of Glutton")

ADVENTURES OF REX THE WONDER DOG, THE (Rex...No. 1)
National Periodical Publ.: Jan-Feb, 1952 - No. 45, May-June, 1959; No. 46, Nov-Dec, 1959

	GD 2.0	VG 4.0	FN 6.0	VF 8.0	VF/NM 9.0	NM- 9.2
1-(Scarce)-Toth-c/a	142	284	426	909	1555	2200
2-(Scarce)-Toth-c/a	63	126	189	403	689	975
3-(Scarce)-Toth-a	50	100	150	315	533	750
4,5	40	80	120	246	411	575
6-10	33	66	99	194	317	440
11-Atom bomb-c/story; dinosaur-c/sty	39	78	117	231	378	525
12-19: 19-Last precode (1-2/55)	21	42	63	122	199	275
20-46	15	30	45	88	137	185

NOTE: ***Infantino, Gil Kane** art in 5-19 (most)*

ADVENTURES OF ROBIN HOOD, THE (Formerly Robin Hood)
Magazine Enterprises (Sussex Publ. Co.): No. 7, 9/57 - No. 8, 11/57
(Based on Richard Greene TV Show)

	GD 2.0	VG 4.0	FN 6.0	VF 8.0	VF/NM 9.0	NM- 9.2
7,8-Richard Greene photo-c. 7-Powell-a	15	30	45	83	124	165

ADVENTURES OF ROBIN HOOD, THE
Gold Key: Mar, 1974 - No. 7, Jan, 1975 (Disney cartoon) (36 pgs.)

	GD 2.0	VG 4.0	FN 6.0	VF 8.0	VF/NM 9.0	NM- 9.2
1(90291-403)-Part-r of $1.50 editions	2	4	6	13	18	22
2-7: 1-7 are part-r	2	4	6	8	11	14

ADVENTURES OF SNAKE PLISSKEN
Marvel Comics: Jan, 1997 ($2.50, one-shot)

1-Based on Escape From L.A. movie; Brereton-c	4.00

ADVENTURES OF SPAWN, THE
Image Comics (Todd McFarlane Prods.): Jan, 2007; Nov, 2008 ($5.99)

1,2-Printed adaptation of the Spawn.com web comic; Khary Randolph-a	6.00

ADVENTURES OF SPIDER-MAN, THE (Based on animated TV series)
Marvel Comics: Apr, 1996 - No. 12, Mar, 1997 (99¢)

1-12: 1-Punisher app. 2-Venom cameo. 3-X-Men. 6-Fantastic Four	3.00

ADVENTURES OF SUPERBOY, THE (See Superboy, 2nd Series)

ADVENTURES OF SUPERMAN (Formerly Superman)
DC Comics: No. 424, Jan, 1987 - No. 499, Feb, 1993; No. 500, Early June, 1993 - No. 649, Apr, 2006 (This title's numbering continues with Superman #650, May, 2006)

424-Ordway-c/a/Wolfman-s begin following Byrne's Superman revamp	4.00
425-435,437-462: 426-Legends x-over. 432-1st app. Jose Delgado who becomes Gangbuster in #434. 437-Millennium x-over. 438-New Brainiac app. 440-Batman app. 449-Invasion	3.00
436-Byrne scripts begin; Millennium x-over	3.50
463-Superman/Flash race; cover swipe/Superman #199	5.00
464-Lobo-c & app. (pre-dates Lobo #1)	4.00
465-495: 467-Part 2 of Batman story. 473-Hal Jordan, Guy Gardner x-over. 477-Legion app. 491-Last $1.00-c. 480-($1.75, 52 pgs.). 495-Forever People-c/story; Darkseid app.	3.00
496,497: 496-Doomsday cameo. 497-Doomsday battle issue	4.00
496,497-2nd printings	3.00
498,499-Funeral for a Friend; Supergirl app.	4.00
498-2nd & 3rd printings	3.00
500-($2.95, 68 pgs.)-Collector's edition w/card	4.00
500-($2.50, 68 pgs.)-Regular edition w/different-c	3.00
500-Platinum edition	30.00
501-($1.95)-Collector's edition with die-cut-c	3.50
501-($1.50)-Regular edition w/mini-poster & diff.-c	3.00
502-516: 502-Supergirl-c/story. 508-Challengers of the Unknown app. 510-Bizarro-c/story. 516-(9/94)-Zero Hour	3.00
505-($2.50)-Holo-grafx foil-c edition	3.50
0,517-523: 0-(10/94). 517-(11/94)	3.00
524-549,551-580: 524-Begin $1.95-c. 527-Return of Alpha Centurion (Zero Hour). 533-Impulse-c/app. 535-Luthor-c/app. 536-Brainiac app. 537-Parasite app. 540-Final Night x-over. 541-Superboy-c/app.; Lois & Clark honeymoon. 545-New powers. 546-New costume. 555-Red & Blue Supermen battle. 557-Millennium Giants x-over. 558-560: Superman Silver Age-style story; Krypto app. 561-Begin $1.99-c. 565-JLA app.	3.00
550-($3.50)-Double sized	4.00
581-588: 581-Begin $2.25-c. 583-Emperor Joker. 588-Casey-s	3.00
589-595: 589-Return to Krypton; Rivoche-c. 591-Wolfman-s. 593-595-Our Worlds at War x-over. 593-New Suicide Squad formed. 594-Doomsday-c/app.	3.00
596-Aftermath of "War" x-over has panel showing damaged World Trade Center buildings; issue went on sale the day after the Sept. 11 attack	5.00
597-599,601-624: 597-Joker: Last Laugh. 604,605-Ultraman, Owlman, Superwoman app. 606-Return to Krypton. 612-616,619-623-Nowlan-c. 624-Mr. Majestic app.	3.00
600-($3.95) Wieringo-a; painted-c by Adel; pin-ups by various	4.00
625,626-Godfall parts 2,5; Turner-c; Caldwell-a(p)	4.00
627-641,643-648: 627-Begin $2.50-c, Rucka-s/Clark-a/Ha-c begin. 628-Wagner-c. 631-Bagged with Sky Captain CD; Lois shot. 634-Mxyzptlk visits DC offices. 639-Capt. Marvel & Eclipso app. 641-OMAC app. 643-Sacrifice aftermath; Batman & Wonder Woman app.	3.00
642-OMAC Project x-over Sacrifice pt. 3; JLA app.	5.00
642-(2nd printing) red tone cover	3.00
649-Last issue; Infinite Crisis x-over, Superman vs. Earth-2 Superman	4.00
#1,000,000 (11/98) Gene Ha-c; 853rd Century x-over	3.00
Annual 1 (1987, $1.25, 52 pgs.)-Starlin-c & scripts	4.00
Annual 2,3 (1990, 1991, $2.00, 68 pgs.): 2-Byrne-c/a(i); Legion '90 (Lobo) app. 3-Armageddon 2001 x-over	4.00
Annual 4-6 ('92-'94, $2.50, 68 pgs.): 4-Guy Gardner/Lobo-c/story; Eclipso storyline; Quesada-c(p). 5-Bloodlines storyline. 6-Elseworlds sty.	4.00
Annual 7,9('95, '97, $3.95)-7-Year One story. 9-Pulp Heroes sty	4.00
Annual 8 (1996, $2.95)-Legends of the Dead Earth story	4.00

Adventures on the Planet of the Apes #7 © MAR

Adventures With the DC SuperHeroes FCBD © DC

Agents of Atlas #9 © MAR

GD VG FN VF VF/NM NM-
2.0 4.0 6.0 8.0 9.0 9.2

GD VG FN VF VF/NM NM-
2.0 4.0 6.0 8.0 9.0 9.2

NOTE: ***Erik Larsen** a-431.*

ADVENTURES OF THE DOVER BOYS
Archie Comics (Close-up): September, 1950 - No. 2, 1950 (No month given)

1,2 9 18 27 52 69 85

ADVENTURES OF THE FLY (The Fly #1-6; Fly Man No. 32-39; See The Double Life of Private Strong, The Fly, Laugh Comics & Mighty Crusaders)
Archie Publications/Radio Comics: Aug, 1959 - No. 30, Oct, 1964; No. 31, May, 1965

1-Shield app.; origin The Fly; S&K-c/a 48 96 144 408 829 1250
2-Williamson, S&K-a 27 54 81 197 391 585
3-Origin retold; Davis, Powell-a 22 44 66 159 317 475
4-Neal Adams-a(p)(1 panel); S&K-c; Powell-a; 2 pg. Shield story
14 28 42 102 206 310
5,6,9,10: 9-Shield app. 9-1st app. Cat Girl. 10-Black Hood app.
11 22 33 77 144 210
7,8: 7-1st S.A. app. Black Hood (7/60). 8-1st S.A. app. Shield (9/60)
12 24 36 87 164 240
11-13,15-20: 13-1st app. Fly Girl w/o costume. 16-Last 10¢ issue. 20-Origin Fly Girl retold 8 16 24 56 93 130
14-Origin & 1st app. Fly Girl in costume 9 18 27 63 107 150
21-30: 23-Jaguar cameo. 27-29-Black Hood 1 pg. strips. 30-Comet x-over (1st S.A. app.) in Fly Girl 6 12 18 43 69 95
31-Black Hood, Shield, Comet app. 7 14 21 45 73 100
Vol. 1 TPB ('04, $12.95) r/#1-4 & Double Life of Private Strong #1,2; foreward by Joe Simon 13.00
NOTE: ***Simon** c-2-4. **Tuska** a-1. Cover title to #31 is Flyman; Advs. of the Fly inside.*

ADVENTURES OF THE JAGUAR, THE (See Blue Ribbon Comics, Laugh Comics & Mighty Crusaders)
Archie Publications (Radio Comics): Sept, 1961 - No. 15, Nov, 1963

1-Origin Jaguar (1st app?) by J. Rosenberger 21 42 63 150 300 450
2,3: 3-Last 10¢ issue 11 22 33 77 144 210
4-6-Catgirl app. (#4's-c is same as splash pg.) 9 18 27 63 107 150
7-10 8 16 24 52 86 120
11-15:13,14-Catgirl, Black Hood app. in both 7 14 21 45 73 100

ADVENTURES OF THE MASK (TV cartoon)
Dark Horse Comics: Jan, 1996 - No. 12, Dec, 1996 ($2.50)

1-12: Based on animated series 3.00

ADVENTURES OF THE NEW MEN (Formerly Newmen #1-21)
Maximum Press: No. 22, Nov, 1996; No. 23, March, 1997 ($2.50)

22,23-Sprouse-c/a 3.00

ADVENTURES OF THE OUTSIDERS, THE (Formerly Batman & The Outsiders; also see The Outsiders)
DC Comics: No. 33, May, 1986 - No. 46, June, 1987

33-46: 39-45-r/Outsiders #1-7 by Aparo 3.00

ADVENTURES OF THE SUPER MARIO BROTHERS (See Super Mario Bros.)
Valiant: 1990 - No. 9, Oct, 1991 ($1.50)

V2#1-9 6.00

ADVENTURES OF THE THING, THE (Also see The Thing)
Marvel Comics: Apr, 1992 - No. 4, July, 1992, ($1.25, limited series)

1-4: 1-r/Marvel Two-In-One #50 by Byrne; Kieth-c. 2-4-r/Marvel Two-In-One #80,51 & 77; 2-Ghost Rider-c/story; Quesada-c. 3-Miller-r/Quesada-c; new Perez-a (4 pgs.) 3.00

ADVENTURES OF THE X-MEN, THE (Based on animated TV series)
Marvel Comics: Apr, 1996 - No. 12, Mar, 1997 (99¢)

1-12: 1-Wolverine/Hulk battle. 3-Spider-Man-c. 5,6-Magneto-c/app. 3.00

ADVENTURES OF TINKER BELL (See Tinker Bell, 4-Color No. 896 & 982)

ADVENTURES OF TOM SAWYER (See Dell Junior Treasury No. 10)

ADVENTURES OF YOUNG DR. MASTERS, THE
Archie Comics (Radio Comics): Aug, 1964 - No. 2, Nov, 1964

1 4 8 12 22 34 45
2 3 6 9 16 22 28

ADVENTURES ON OTHER WORLDS (See Showcase #17 & 18)

ADVENTURES ON THE PLANET OF THE APES (Also see Planet of the Apes)
Marvel Comics Group: Oct, 1975 - No. 11, Dec, 1976

1-Planet of the Apes magazine-r in color; Starlin-c; adapts movie thru #6
3 6 9 18 27 35
2-5: 5-(25¢-c edition) 2 4 6 10 14 18
5-7-(30¢-c variants, limited distribution) 4 8 12 24 37 50
6-10: 6,7-(25¢-c edition). 7-Adapts 2nd movie (thru #11)
2 4 6 11 16 20
11-Last issue; concludes 2nd movie adaptation 3 6 9 14 20 26
NOTE: ***Alcala** a-6-11r. **Buckler** c-2p. **Nasser** c-7. **Ploog** a-1-9. **Starlin** c-6. **Tuska** a-1-5r.*

ADVENTURES WITH THE DC SUPER HEROES (Interior also inserted into some DC issues)
DC Comics/Geppi's Entertainment Museum: 2007 Free Comic Book Day giveaway

"The Batman and Cal Ripken, Jr. Hall of Fame Edition "A Rare Catch" " in indicia 2.25

AEON FLUX (Based on the 2005 movie which was based on the MTV animated series)
Dark Horse Comics: Oct, 2005 - No. 4, Jan, 2006 ($2.99, limited series)

1-4-Timothy Green II-a/Mike Kennedy-s 3.00
TPB (5/06, $12.95) r/series; cover gallery 13.00

AFRICA
Magazine Enterprises: 1955

1(A-1#137)-Cave Girl, Thun'da; Powell-c/a(4) 27 54 81 158 259 360

AFRICAN LION (Disney movie)
Dell Publishing Co.: Nov, 1955

Four Color #665 6 12 18 37 59 80

AFTER DARK
Sterling Comics: No. 6, May, 1955 - No. 8, Sept, 1955

6-8-Sekowsky-a in all 9 18 27 52 69 85

AFTER DARK (Co-created by Wesley Snipes)
Radical Comics: No. 0, Jun, 2010 - No. 3 ($1.00/$4.99, limited series)

0-($1.00) Milligan-s/Nentrup & Mattina-a 1.00
1-3-($4.99) Milligan-s/Manco-a 5.00

AFTER THE CAPE
Image Comics (Shadowline): Mar, 2007 - No. 3, May, 2007 ($2.99, B&W, limited series)

1-3-Jim Valentino-s/Marco Rudy-a 3.00
... Volume One TPB (9/07, $12.99) r/series; scripts, sketch pages, character profiles 13.00
...II (11/07 - No. 3, 1/08, $2.99) 1-3-Jim Valentino-s/Sergio Carrera-a 3.00

AGAINST BLACKSHARD 3-D (Also see SoulQuest)
Sirius Comics: August, 1986 ($2.25)

1 3.00

AGENCY, THE
Image Comics (Top Cow): August, 2001 - No. 6, Mar, 2002 ($2.50/$2.95/$4.95)

1-5: 1-Jenkins-s/Hotz-a; three covers by Hotz, Turner, Silvestri. 3-5-($2.95) 3.00
6-($4.95) Flip-c preview of Jeremiah TV series 5.00
Preview (2001, 16 pgs.) B&W pages, cover previews, sketch pages 3.00

AGENT LIBERTY SPECIAL (See Superman, 2nd Series)
DC Comics: 1992 ($2.00, 52 pgs, one-shot)

1-1st solo adventure; Guice-c/a(i) 3.00

AGENTS, THE
Image Comics: Apr, 2003 - No. 6, Sept, 2003 ($2.95, B&W)

1-5-Ben Dunn-c/a in all 3.00
6-Five pg. preview of The Walking Dead #1 2 4 6 11 16 20

AGENTS OF ATLAS
Marvel Comics: Oct, 2006 - No. 6, Mar, 2007 ($2.99, limited series)

1-6: 1-Golden Age heroes Marvel Boy & Venus app.; Kirk-a 3.00
... MGC 1 (7/10, $1.00) r/#1 with "Marvel's Greatest Comics" logo on cover 1.00
HC (2007, $24.99, dustjacket) r/#1-6, What If? #9, agents' debuts in '40s-'50s Atlas comics, creator interviews, character design art 25.00

AGENTS OF ATLAS (Dark Reign)
Marvel Comics: Apr, 2009 - Present ($3.99)

1-11: 1-Pagulayan-a; 2 covers by Art Adams and McGuinness; back-up with Wolverine app. 5-New Avengers app. 8-Hulk app. 4.00

AGENTS OF LAW (Also see Comic's Greatest World)
Dark Horse Comics: Mar, 1995 - No. 6, Sept, 1995 ($2.50)

1-6: 5-Predator app. 6-Predator app.; death of Law 3.00

AGENT X (Continued from Deadpool)
Marvel Comics: Sept. 2002 - No. 15, Dec, 2003 ($2.99/$2.25)

1-($2.99) Simone-s/Udon Studios-a; Taskmaster app. 3.50
2-9-($2.25) 2-Punisher app. 3.00
10-15-($2.99) 10,11-Evan Dorkin-s. 12-Hotz-a 3.00

AGE OF APOCALYPSE: THE CHOSEN
Marvel Comics: Apr, 1995 ($2.50, one-shot)

1-Wraparound-c 3.00

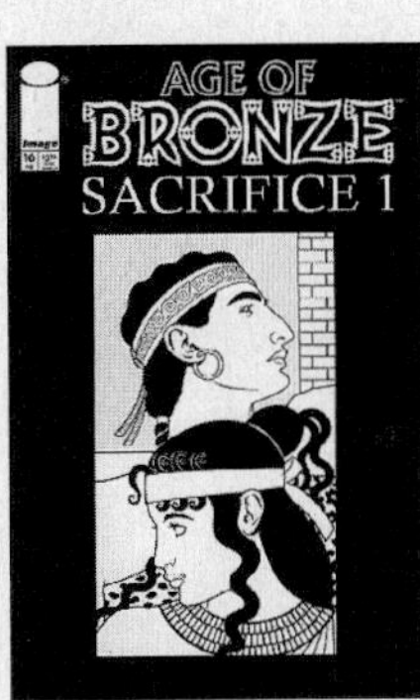
Age of Bronze #10 © Eric Shanower

Air #18 © Wilson & Perker

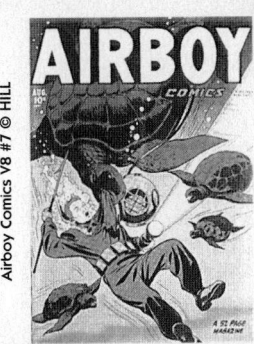

Airboy Comics V8 #7 © HILL

	GD 2.0	VG 4.0	FN 6.0	VF 8.0	VF/NM 9.0	NM- 9.2

AGE OF BRONZE
Image Comics: Nov, 1998 - Present ($2.95/$3.50, B&W)

1-6-Eric Shanower-c/s/a 3.50
7-31-($3.50) 3.50
...Behind the Scenes (5/02, $3.50) background info and creative process 3.50
Image Firsts: Age of Bronze #1 (4/10, $1.00) r/#1 with "Image Firsts" cover logo 1.00
...Special (6/99, $2.95) Story of Agamemnon and Menelaus 3.50
A Thousand Ships (7/01, $19.95, TPB) r/#1-9 20.00
Sacrifice (9/04, $19.95, TPB) r/#10-19 20.00

AGE OF HEROES, THE
Halloween Comics/Image Comics #3 on: 1996 - No. 5, 1999 ($2.95, B&W)

1-5: James Hudnall scripts; John Ridgway-c/a 3.00
...Special ($4.95) r/#1,2 5.00
...Special 2 ($6.95) r/#3,4 7.00
...Wex 1 ('98, $2.95) Hudnall-s/Angel Fernandez-a 3.00

AGE OF HEROES (The Heroic Age)
Marvel Comics: Jul, 2010 - No. 4, Oct, 2010 ($3.99, limited series)

1-4-Short stories of Avengers members by various. 4-Jae Lee-c 4.00

AGE OF INNOCENCE: THE REBIRTH OF IRON MAN
Marvel Comics: Feb, 1996 ($2.50, one-shot)

1-New origin of Tony Stark 3.00

AGE OF REPTILES
Dark Horse Comics: Nov, 1993 - No. 4, Feb, 1994 ($2.50, limited series)

1-4: Delgado-c/a/scripts in all 3.00
... The Hunt 1-5 (5/96 - No. 5, 9/96, $2.95) Delgado-c/a/scripts in all; wraparound-c 3.00
... The Journey 1-4 (11/09 - No. 4, 7/10 $3.50) Delgado-c/a/scripts in all; wraparound-c 3.50

AGE OF THE SENTRY, THE
Marvel Comics: Nov, 2008 - No. 6, Mar, 2010 ($2.99, limited series)

1-6-Silver Age style stories. 1-Origin retold; Bullock-c. 3-Coover-a 3.00

AGE OF X (X-Men titles crossover)
Marvel Comics: ($3.99, limited series)

... Alpha 1 (3/11, $3.99) Short stories by various; covers by Bachalo & Coipel 4.00
...: Universe 1 (5/11 - No. 2, $3.99) Pham-a; Bianchi-c; Avengers & Spider-Man app. 4.00

AGGIE MACK
Four Star Comics Corp./Superior Comics Ltd.: Jan, 1948 - No. 8, Aug, 1949

	GD	VG	FN	VF	VF/NM	NM-
1-Feldstein-a, "Johnny Prep"	40	80	120	251	418	585
2,3-Kamen-c	22	44	66	132	216	300
4-Feldstein "Johnny Prep"; Kamen-c	30	60	90	177	289	400
5-8-Kamen-c/a	24	48	72	142	234	325

AGGIE MACK
Dell Publishing Co.: Apr - Jun, 1962

	GD	VG	FN	VF	VF/NM	NM-
Four Color #1335	5	10	15	30	48	65

AIR
DC Comics (Vertigo): Oct, 2008 - No. 24, Oct, 2010 ($2.99)

1-6,8-24-G. Willow Wilson-s/M.K. Perker-a 3.00
7-($1.00) Includes story re-cap 3.00
... A History of the Future TPB (2011, $14.99) r/#18-24 15.00
... Flying Machine TPB (2009, $12.99) r/#6-10; Wilson intro. 13.00
... Letters From Lost Countries TPB (2009, $9.99) r/#1-5; character sketch pages 10.00
... Pure Land TPB (2010, $14.99) r/#11-17 15.00

AIR ACE (Formerly Bill Barnes No. 1-12)
Street & Smith Publications: V2#1, Jan, 1944 - V3#8(No. 20), Feb-Mar, 1947

	GD	VG	FN	VF	VF/NM	NM-
V2#1-Nazi concentration camp-c	45	90	135	284	480	675
V2#2-Classic-c	77	154	231	493	847	1200
V2#3-12: 7-Powell-a	16	32	48	94	147	200
V3#1-6: 2-Atomic explosion on-c	14	28	42	80	115	150
V3#7-Powell bondage-c/a; all atomic issue	23	46	69	136	223	310
V3#8 (V5#8 on-c)-Powell-c/a	15	30	45	84	127	170

AIRBOY (Also see Airmaidens, Skywolf, Target: Airboy & Valkyrie)
Eclipse Comics: July, 1986 - No. 50, Oct, 1989 (#1-8, 50¢, 20 pgs., bi-weekly; #9-on, 36 pgs.; #34-on monthly)

1-4: 2-1st Marisa; Skywolf gets new costume. 3-The Heap begins 4.00
5-Valkyrie returns; Dave Stevens-c 6.00
6-49: 9-Begin $1.25-c; Skywolf begins. 11-Origin of G.A. Airboy & his plane Birdie. 28-Mr. Monster vs. The Heap. 33-Begin $1.75-c. 38-40-The Heap by Infantino. 41-r/1st app. Valkyrie from Air Fighters. 42-Begin $1.95-c. 46,47-part-r/Air Fighters. 48-Black Angel-r/A.F 3.00
50 ($4.95, 52 pgs.)-Kubert-c 5.00

NOTE: *Evans* c-21. *Gulacy* c-7, 20. *Spiegle* a-34, 35, 37. *Ken Steacy* painted c-17, 33.

AIRBOY COMICS (Air Fighters Comics No. 1-22)
Hillman Periodicals: V2#11, Dec, 1945 - V10#4, May, 1953 (No V3#3)

	GD	VG	FN	VF	VF/NM	NM-
V2#11	74	148	222	470	810	1150
12-Valkyrie-c/app.	52	104	156	323	549	775
V3#1,2(no #3)	40	80	120	246	411	575
4-The Heap app. in Skywolf	37	74	111	222	361	500
5,7,8,10,11	33	66	99	194	317	440
6-Valkyrie-c/app.	36	72	108	216	351	485
9-Origin The Heap	37	74	111	222	361	500
12-Skywolf & Airboy x-over; Valkyrie-c/app.	39	78	117	240	395	550
V4#1-Iron Lady app.	33	66	99	194	317	440
2,3,12: 2-Rackman begins	25	50	75	147	241	335
4-Simon & Kirby-c	30	60	90	177	289	400
5-9,11-All S&K-a	28	56	84	165	270	375
10-Valkyrie-c/app.	31	62	93	182	296	410
V5#1-4,6-11: 4-Infantino Heap. 10-Origin The Heap	19	38	57	112	179	245
5-Skull-c.	21	42	63	126	206	285
12-Krigstein-a(p)	20	40	60	115	185	255
V6#1-3,5-12: 6,8-Origin The Heap	18	36	54	107	169	230
4-Origin retold	21	42	63	126	206	285
V7#1-12: 7,8,10-Origin The Heap	18	36	54	105	165	225
V8#1-3,5-12	16	32	48	96	151	205
4-Krigstein-a	17	34	51	100	158	215
V9#1,3,4,6-12: 7-One pg. Frazetta ad	15	30	45	84	127	170
2-Valkyrie app.	15	30	45	88	137	185
5(#100)	15	30	45	88	137	185
V10#1-4	14	28	42	81	118	155

NOTE: *Barry* a-V2#3, 7. *Bolle* a-V4#12. *McWilliams* a-V3#7, 9. *Powell* a-V7#2, 3, V8#1, 6. *Starr* a-V5#1, 12. *Dick Wood* a-V4#12. *Bondage-c* V5#8.

AIRBOY MEETS THE PROWLER
Eclipse Comics: Aug, 1987 ($1.95, one-shot)

1-John Snyder, III-c/a 3.00

AIRBOY-MR. MONSTER SPECIAL
Eclipse Comics: Aug, 1987 ($1.75, one-shot)

1 3.00

AIRBOY VERSUS THE AIR MAIDENS
Eclipse Comics: July, 1988 ($1.95)

1 3.00

AIR FIGHTERS CLASSICS
Eclipse Comics: Nov, 1987 - No. 6, May, 1989 ($3.95, 68 pgs., B&W)

1-6: Reprints G.A. Air Fighters #2-7. 1-Origin Airboy 4.00

AIR FIGHTERS COMICS (Airboy Comics #23 (V2#11) on)
Hillman Periodicals: Nov, 1941; No. 2, Nov, 1942 - V2#10, Fall, 1945

	GD	VG	FN	VF	VF/NM	NM-
V1#1-(Produced by Funnies, Inc.); No Airboy; Black Commander only app.	226	452	678	1446	2473	3500
2(11/42)-(Produced by Quality artists & Biro for Hillman); Origin & 1st app. Airboy & Iron Ace; Black Angel (1st app.), Flying Dutchman & Skywolf (1st app.) begin; Fuje-a; Biro-c/a	432	864	1296	3154	5577	8000
3-Origin/1st app. The Heap; origin Skywolf; 2nd Airboy app./c	194	388	582	1242	2121	3000
4-Japan war-c	161	322	483	1030	1765	2500
5-Japanese octopus War-c	129	258	387	826	1413	2000
6-Japanese soldiers as rats-c	168	336	504	1075	1838	2600
7-Classic Nazi swastika-c	165	330	495	1048	1799	2550
8-12: 8,10,11-War covers	87	174	261	553	952	1350
V2#1-Classic Nazi War-c	92	184	276	584	1005	1425
2-Skywolf by Giunta; Flying Dutchman by Fuje; 1st meeting Valkyrie & Airboy (she worked for the Nazis in beginning); 1st app. Valkyrie (11/43); Valkyrie-c	126	252	378	806	1378	1950
3,4,6,8,9	60	120	180	381	658	935
5,7: 5-Flag-c; Fuje-a. 7-Valkyrie app.	64	128	192	406	696	985
10-Origin The Heap & Skywolf	69	138	207	442	759	1075

NOTE: *Fuje* a-V1#2, 5, 7, V2#2, 3, 5, 7-9. *Giunta* a-V2#2, 3, 7, 9.

AIRFIGHTERS MEET SGT. STRIKE SPECIAL, THE
Eclipse Comics: Jan, 1988 ($1.95, one-shot, stiff-c)

1-Airboy, Valkyrie, Skywolf app. 3.00

AIR FORCES (See American Air Forces)

AIRMAIDENS SPECIAL

Akiko #29 © Crilley

Albedo Anthropomorphics #2 © TAI

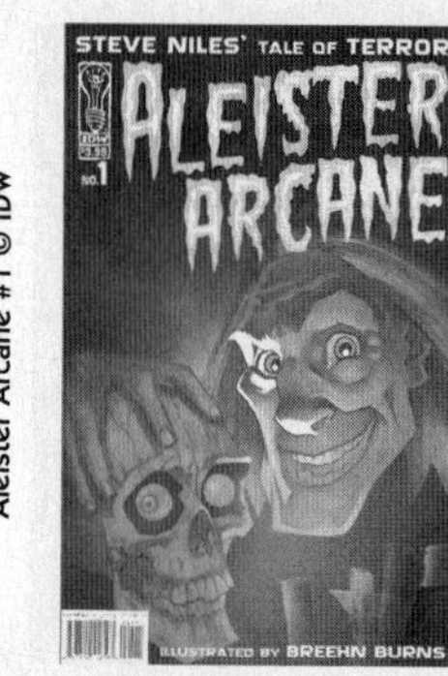

Aleister Arcane #1 © IDW

	GD 2.0	VG 4.0	FN 6.0	VF 8.0	VF/NM 9.0	NM- 9.2

Eclipse Comics: August, 1987 ($1.75, one-shot, Baxter paper)
1-Marisa becomes La Lupina (origin) 3.00

AIR RAIDERS
Marvel Comics (Star Comics)/Marvel #3 on: Nov, 1987- No. 5, Mar, 1988 ($1.00)
1,5: Kelley Jones-a in all 4.00
2-4: 2-Thunderhammer app. 3.00

AIRTIGHT GARAGE, THE (Also see Elsewhere Prince)
Marvel Comics (Epic Comics): July, 1993 - No. 4, Oct, 1993 ($2.50, lim. series, Baxter paper)
1-4: Moebius-c/a/scripts 5.00

AIR WAR STORIES
Dell Publishing Co.: Sept-Nov, 1964 - No. 8, Aug, 1966
1-Painted-c; Glanzman-c/a begins 4 8 12 28 44 60
2-8: 2,3-Painted-c 3 6 9 18 27 35

A.K.A. GOLDFISH
Caliber Comics: 1994 - 1995 (B&W, $3.50/$3.95)
...:Ace; ...:Jack; ...:Queen; ...:Joker; ...:King -Brian Michael Bendis-s/a 4.00
TPB (1996, $17.95) 20.00
Goldfish: The Definitive Collection (Image, 2001, $19.95) r/series plus promo art and new prose story; intro. by Matt Wagner 20.00
10th Anniversary HC (Image, 2002, $49.95) 50.00

AKIKO
Sirius: Mar, 1996 - Present ($2.50/$2.95, B&W)
1-Crilley-c/a/scripts in all 5.00
2 4.00
3-39: 25-($2.95, 32 pgs.)-w/Asala back-up pages 3.00
40-49,51,52: 40-Begin $2.95-c 3.00
50-($3.50) 3.50
Flights of Fancy TPB (5/02, $12.95) r/various features, pin-ups and gags 13.00
TPB Volume 1,4 ('97, 2/00, $14.95) 1-r/#1-7. 4-r/#19-25 15.00
TPB Volume 2,3 ('98, '99, $11.95) 2-r/#8-13. 3- r/#14-18 12.00
TPB Volume 5 (12/01, $12.95) r/#26-31 13.00
TPB Volume 6,7 (6/03, 4/04, $14.95) 6-r/#32-38. 7-r/#40-47 15.00

AKIKO ON THE PLANET SMOO
Sirius: Dec, 1995 ($3.95, B&W)
V1#1-($3.95)-Crilley-c/a/scripts; gatefold-c 5.00
Ashcan ('95, mail offer) 3.00
Hardcover V1#1 (12/95, $19.95, B&W, 40 pgs.) 20.00
The Color Edition(2/00,$4.95) 5.00

AKIRA
Marvel Comics (Epic): Sept, 1988 - No. 38, Dec, 1995 ($3.50/$3.95/$6.95, deluxe, 68 pgs.)
1-Manga by Katsuhiro Otomo 3 6 9 16 23 30
1,2-2nd printings (1989, $3.95) 5.00
2 2 4 6 9 12 15
3-5 2 4 6 8 10 12
6-16 1 2 3 5 7 9
17-33: 17-$3.95-c begins 6.00
34-37: 34-(1994)-$6.95-c begins. 35-37: 35-(1995). 37-Texeira back-up, Gibbons, Williams pin-ups 2 4 6 8 10 12
38-Moebius, Allred, Pratt, Toth, Romita, Van Fleet, O'Neill, Madureira pin-ups 2 4 6 8 11 14

ALADDIN & HIS WONDERFUL LAMP (See Dell Jr Treasury #2)

ALAN LADD (See The Adventures of...)

ALAN MOORE'S AWESOME UNIVERSE HANDBOOK (Also see Across the Universe:...)
Awesome Entertainment: Apr, 1999 ($2.95, B&W)
1-Alan Moore-text/ Alex Ross-sketch pages and 2 covers 5.00

ALAN MOORE...
DC Comics (WildStorm): TPB
...'s Complete WildC.A.T.S. (2007, $29.99) r/#21-34,50; ...Homecoming & ...Gang War 30.00
...: Wild Worlds (2007, $24.99) r/various WildStorm one-shots and limited series 25.00

ALARMING ADVENTURES
Harvey Publications: Oct, 1962 - No. 3, Feb, 1963
1-Crandall/Williamson-a 8 16 24 58 97 135
2-Williamson/Crandall-a 5 10 15 35 55 75
3-Torres-a 5 10 15 30 48 65
NOTE: *Bailey a-1, 3. Crandall a-1p, 2i. Powell a-2(2). Severin c-1-3. Torres a-2? Tuska a-1. Williamson a-1i, 2p.*

ALARMING TALES
Harvey Publications (Western Tales): Sept, 1957 - No. 6, Nov, 1958
1-Kirby-c/a(4); Kamandi prototype story by Kirby 30 60 90 177 289 400
2-Kirby-a(4) 20 40 60 118 192 265
3,4-Kirby-a. 4-Powell, Wildey-a 16 32 48 94 147 200
5-Kirby/Williamson-a; Wildey-a; Severin-c 17 34 51 100 158 215
6-Williamson-a?; Severin-c 14 28 42 80 115 150

ALBEDO
Thoughts And Images: Apr, 1985 - No. 14, Spring, 1989 (B&W)
Antarctic Press: (Vol. 2) Jun, 1991 - No. 10 ($2.50)
0-Yellow cover; 50 copies 14 28 42 99 200 300
0-White cover, 450 copies 8 16 24 54 90 125
0-Blue, 1st printing, 500 copies 7 14 21 49 80 110
0-Blue, 2nd printing, 1000 copies 4 8 12 26 41 55
0-3rd & 4th printing 3 6 9 14 19 24
1-Dark red - low print run 9 18 27 61 103 145
1-Bright red - low print run 6 12 18 39 62 85
2 -1st app. Usagi Yojimbo by Stan Sakai; 2000 copies - no 2nd printing 33 66 99 254 502 750
3 3 6 9 20 30 40
4-Usagi Yojimbo-c 4 8 12 24 37 50
5-14 1 2 3 5 7 9
(Vol. 2) 1-10, Color Special 4.00

ALBEDO ANTHROPOMORPHICS
Antarctic Press: (Vol. 3) Spring, 1994 - No. 4, Jan, 1996 ($2.95, color); (Vol. 4) Dec, 1999 - No. 2, Jan, 1999 ($2.95/$2.99, B&W)
V3#1-4-Steve Gallacci-c/a. V4#1,2 3.00

ALBERTO (See The Crusaders)

ALBERT THE ALLIGATOR & POGO POSSUM (See Pogo Possum)

ALBION (Inspired by 1960s IPC British comics characters)
DC Comics (WildStorm): Aug, 2005 - No. 6, Nov, 2006 ($2.99, limited series)
1-6-Alan Moore, Leah Moore & John Reppion-s/Shane Oakley-a; Dave Gibbons-c 3.00
TPB (2007, $19.99) r/series; intro by Neil Gaiman; reprints from 1960s British comics 20.00

ALBUM OF CRIME (See Fox Giants)

ALBUM OF LOVE (See Fox Giants)

AL CAPP'S DOGPATCH (Also see Mammy Yokum)
Toby Press: No. 71, June, 1949 - No. 4, Dec, 1949
71(#1)-Reprints from Tip Top #112-114 15 30 45 83 124 165
2-4: 4-Reprints from Li'l Abner #73 11 22 33 62 86 110

AL CAPP'S SHMOO (Also see Oxydol-Dreft & Washable Jones & Shmoo)
Toby Press: July, 1949 - No. 5, Apr, 1950 (None by Al Capp)
1-1st app. Super-Shmoo 28 56 84 165 270 375
2-5: 3-Sci-fi trip to moon. 4-X-Mas-c 20 40 60 114 182 250

AL CAPP'S WOLF GAL
Toby Press: 1951 - No. 2, 1952
1,2-Edited-r from Li'l Abner #63,64 17 34 51 98 154 210

ALEISTER ARCANE
IDW Publishing: Apr, 2004 - No. 3, June, 2004 ($3.99, limited series)
1-3-Steve Niles-s/Breehn Burns-a 4.00
TPB (10/04, $17.99) r/series; sketch pages 18.00

ALEXANDER THE GREAT (Movie)
Dell Publishing Co.: No. 688, May, 1956
Four Color 688-Buscema-a; photo-c 7 14 21 49 80 110

ALF (TV) (See Star Comics Digest)
Marvel Comics: Mar, 1988 - No. 50, Feb, 1992 ($1.00)
1-Photo-c 5.00
1-2nd printing 3.00
2-19: 6-Photo-c 3.00
20-22: 20-Conan parody. 21-Marx Brothers. 22-X-Men parody 3.50
23-30: 24-Rhonda-c/app. 29-3-D cover 3.00
31-43,46,47,49: 3.00
44,45: 44-X-Men parody. 45-Wolverine, Punisher, Capt. America-c 4.00
48-(12/91) Risqué Alf with seal cover 2 4 6 8 10 12
50-($1.75, 52 pgs.)-Final issue; photo-c 4.00
Annual 1-3: 1-Rocky & Bullwinkle app. 2-Sienkiewicz-c. 3-TMNT parody 4.00
...Comics Digest 1,2: 1-(1988)-Reprints Alf #1,2 1 3 4 6 8 10
Holiday Special 1,2 ('88, Wint. '89, 68 pgs.): 2-X-Men parody-c 4.00
Spring Special 1 (Spr/89, $1.75, 68 pgs.) Invisible Man parody 4.00

Alias #3 © MAR

Alien Legion #2 © MAR

Aliens Earth Angel #1 © 20th Cent. Fox

GD VG FN VF VF/NM NM-
2.0 4.0 6.0 8.0 9.0 9.2

TPB (68 pgs.) r/#1-3; photo-c 5.00

ALFRED HARVEY'S BLACK CAT
Lorne-Harvey Productions: 1995 ($3.50, B&W/color)

1-Origin by Mark Evanier & Murphy Anderson; contains history of Alfred Harvey & Harvey Publications; 5 pg. B&W Sad Sack story; Hildebrandts-c 6.00

ALGIE (LITTLE...)
Timor Publ. Co.: Dec, 1953 - No. 3, 1954

1-Teenage 8 16 24 40 50 60
1-Algie #1 cover w/Secret Mysteries #19 inside 9 18 27 50 65 80
2,3 5 10 15 24 30 35
Accepted Reprint #2(nd) 3 6 8 12 14 16
Super Reprint #15 2 4 6 8 11 14

ALIAS:
Now Comics: July, 1990 - No. 5, Nov, 1990 ($1.75)

1-5: 1-Sienkiewicz-c 3.00

ALIAS (Also see Jessica Jones apps. in New Avengers and The Pulse)
Marvel Comics (MAX Comics): Nov, 2001 - No. 28, Jan, 2004 ($2.99)

1-Bendis-s/Gaydos-a/Mack-c; intro Jessica Jones; Luke Cage app. 1 2 3 5 6 8
2-4 5.00
5-28: 7,8-Sienkiewicz-a (2 pgs.) 16-21-Spider-Woman app. 22,23-Jessica's origin. 24-28-Purple; Avengers app.; flashback-a by Bagley 3.00
... MGC 1 (6/10, $1.00) r/#1 with "Marvel's Greatest Comics" logo on cover 1.00
HC (2002, $29.99) r/#1-9; intro. by Jeph Loeb 30.00
Omnibus (2006, $69.99, hardcover with dustjacket) r/#1-28 and What If Jessica Jones Had Joined the Avengers?; original pitch, script and sketch pages 70.00
Vol. 1: TPB (2003, $19.99) r/#1-9 20.00
Vol. 2: Come Home TPB (2003, $13.99) r/#11-15 14.00
Vol. 3: The Underneath TPB (2003, $16.99) r/#10,16-21 17.00

ALICE (New Adventures in Wonderland)
Ziff-Davis Publ. Co.: No. 10, 7-8/51 - No. 11(#2), 11-12/51

10-Painted-c; Berg-a 26 52 78 154 252 350
11-(#2 on inside) Dave Berg-a 16 32 48 94 147 200

ALICE AT MONKEY ISLAND (See The Adventures of Alice)
Pentagon Publ. Co. (Civil Service): No. 3, 1946

3 10 20 30 54 72 90

ALICE IN WONDERLAND (Disney; see Advs. of Alice, Dell Jr. Treasury #1, The Dreamery, Movie Comics,Walt Disney Showcase #22, and World's Greatest Stories)
Dell Publishing Co.: No. 24, 1940; No. 331, 1951; No. 341, July, 1951

Single Series 24 (#1)(1940) 48 96 144 302 514 725
Four Color 331, 341-"Unbirthday Party w/..." 14 28 42 97 194 290
1-(Whitman, 3/84, pre-pack only)-r/4-Color #331 2 4 6 11 16 20

ALIEN ENCOUNTERS (Replaces Alien Worlds)
Eclipse Comics: June, 1985 - No. 14, Aug, 1987 ($1.75, Baxter paper, mature)

1-10: Nudity, strong language in all. 9-Snyder-a 4.00
11-14-Low print run 5.00

ALIEN LEGION (See Epic & Marvel Graphic Novel #25)
Marvel Comics (Epic Comics): Apr, 1984 - No. 20, Sept, 1987

nn-With bound-in trading card; Austin-i 4.00
2-20: 2-$1.50-c. 7,8-Portacio-i 3.00

ALIEN LEGION (2nd Series)
Marvel Comics (Epic): Aug, 1987(indicia)(10/87 on-c) - No. 18, Aug, 1990

V2#1-18-Stroman-a in all. 7-18-Farmer-i 3.00
...: Force Nomad TPB (Checker Book Pub. Group, 2001, $24.95) r/#1-11 25.00
...: Piecemaker TPB (Checker Book Pub. Group, 2002, $19.95) r/#12-18 20.00

ALIEN LEGION: (Series of titles; all Marvel/Epic Comics)
--BINARY DEEP, 1993 ($3.50, one-shot, 52 pgs.), nn-With bound-in trading card 3.50
--JUGGER GRIMROD, 8/92 ($5.95, one-shot, 52 pgs.) Book 1 6.00
--ONE PLANET AT A TIME, 5/93 - Book 3, 7/93 ($4.95, squarebound, 52 pgs.) Book 1-3: Hoang Nguyen-a 5.00
--ON THE EDGE (The... #2 & 3), 11/90 - No. 3, 1/91 ($4.50, 52 pgs.) 1-3-Stroman & Farmer-a 4.50
--TENANTS OF HELL, '91 - No. 2, '91 ($4.50, squarebound, 52 pgs.) Book 1,2-Stroman-c/a(p) 4.50

ALIEN NATION (Movie)
DC Comics: Dec, 1988 ($2.50; 68 pgs.)

GD VG FN VF VF/NM NM-
2.0 4.0 6.0 8.0 9.0 9.2

1-Adaptation of film; painted-c 4.00

ALIEN PIG FARM 3000
Image Comics (RAW Studios): Apr, 2007 - No. 4, July, 2007 ($2.99, limited series)

1-4-Steve Niles, Thomas Jane & Todd Farmer-s/Don Marquez-a 3.00

ALIEN RESURRECTION (Movie)
Dark Horse Comics: Oct, 1997 - No. 2, Nov, 1997 ($2.50; limited series)

1,2-Adaptation of film; Dave McKean-c 3.00

ALIENS, THE (Captain Johner and...)(Also see Magnus Robot Fighter...)
Gold Key: Sept-Dec, 1967; No. 2, May, 1982

1-Reprints from Magnus #1,3,4,6-10; Russ Manning-a in all 3 6 9 20 30 40
2-(Whitman) Same contents as #1 1 2 3 5 6 8

ALIENS (Movie) (See Alien: The Illustrated..., Dark Horse Comics & Dark Horse Presents #24)
Dark Horse Comics: May, 1988 - No. 6, July, 1989 ($1.95, B&W, limited series)

1-Based on movie sequel; 1st app. Aliens in comics 3 6 9 14 20 26
1-2nd - 6th printings; 4th w/new inside front-c 3.00
2 2 4 6 8 10 12
2-2nd & 3rd printing, 3-6-2nd printings 3.00
3 1 2 3 5 7 9
4-6 5.00
Mini Comic #1 (2/89, 4x6")-Was included with Aliens Portfolio 4.00
Collection 1 ($10.95,)-r/#1-6 plus Dark Horse Presents #24 plus new-a 12.00
Collection 1-2nd printing (1991, $11.95)-On higher quality paper than 1st print; Dorman painted-c 12.00
Hardcover ('90, $24.95, B&W)-r/1-6, DHP #24 30.00
... Omnibus Vol. 1 (7/07, $24.95, 9x6") r/1st & 2nd series and Aliens: Earth War 25.00
... Omnibus Vol. 2 (12/07, $24.95, 9x6") r/Genocide, Harvest and Colonial Marines series 25.00
... Omnibus Vol. 3 (3/08, $24.95, 9x6") r/Rogue, Salvation and Sacrifice, Labyrinth series 25.00
... Omnibus Vol. 4 (8/08, $24.95, 9x6") r/Music of the Spears, Stronghold, Berserker, Mondo Pest and Mondo Heat series and one-shots 25.00
... Omnibus Vol. 5 (11/08, $24.95, 9x6") r/Alchemy, Survival, Havoc series and various 25.00
... Omnibus Vol. 6 (2/09, $24.95, 9x6") r/Apocalypse GN, Xenogenesis & one-shots 25.00
... Outbreak (3rd printing, 8/96, $17.95)-Bolton-c 18.00
Platinum Edition - (See Dark Horse Presents: Aliens Platinum Edition) -

ALIENS
Dark Horse Comics: V2#1, Aug, 1989 - No. 4, 1990 ($2.25, limited series)

V2#1-Painted art by Denis Beauvais 5.00
1-2nd printing (1990), 2-4 3.00
...: Nightmare Asylum TPB (12/96, $16.95) r/series; Bolton-c 17.00

ALIENS
Dark Horse Comics: May, 2009 - No. 4, Nov, 2009 ($3.50, limited series)

1-4-John Arcudi-s/Zach Howard-a. 1,2-Howard-c. 3,4-Swanland-c 3.50

ALIENS: (Series of titles, all Dark Horse)
--ALCHEMY, 10/97 - No. 3, 11/97 ($2.95),1-3-Corben-c/a, Arcudi-s 3.00
--APOCALYPSE - THE DESTROYING ANGELS, 1/99 - No. 4, 4/99 ($2.95) 1-4-Doug Wheatly-a/Schultz-s 3.00
--BERSERKERS, 1/95 - No. 4, 4/95 ($2.50) 1-4 3.00
--COLONIAL MARINES, 1/93 - No. 10, 7/94 ($2.50) 1-10 3.00
--EARTH ANGEL, 8/94 ($2.95) 1-Byrne-a/story; wraparound-c 3.00
--EARTH WAR, 6/90 - No. 4, 10/90 ($2.50) 1-All have Sam Kieth-a & Bolton painted-c 5.00
1-2nd printing, 3,4 3.00
2 4.00
--GENOCIDE, 11/91 - No. 4, 2/92 ($2.50) 1-4-Suydam painted-c. 4-Wraparound-c, poster 3.00
--GLASS CORRIDOR, 6/98 ($2.95) 1-David Lloyd-s/a 3.00
--HARVEST (See Aliens: Hive)
--HAVOC, 6/97 - No. 2, 7/97 ($2.95) 1,2: Schultz-s, Kent Williams-c, 40 artists including Art Adams, Kelley Jones, Duncan Fegredo, Kevin Nowlan 3.00
--HIVE, 2/92 - No. 4,5/92 ($2.50) 1-4: Kelley Jones-c/a in all 3.00
...Harvest TPB ('98, $16.95) r/series; Bolton-c 17.00
--KIDNAPPED, 12/97 - No. 3, 2/98 ($2.50) 1-3 3.00
--LABYRINTH, 9/93 - No. 4, 1/94 ($2.50)1-4: 1-Painted-c 3.00
--LOVESICK, 12/96 ($2.95) 1 3.00
--MONDO HEAT, 2/96 ($2.50) nn-Sequel to Mondo Pest 3.00
--MONDO PEST, 4/95 ($2.95, 44 pgs.)nn-r/Dark Horse Comics #22-24 3.00

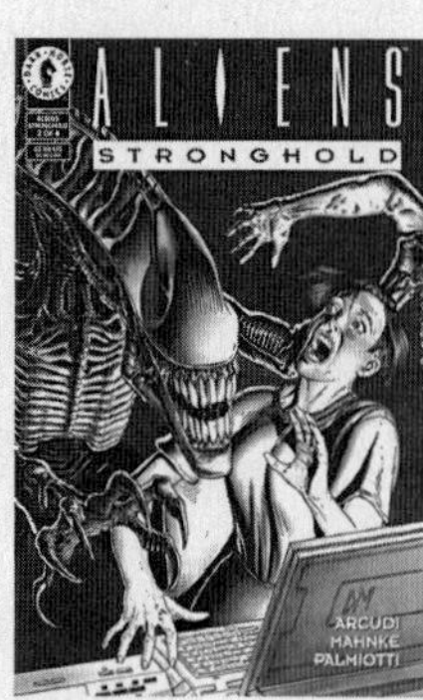

Aliens Stronghold #2 © 20th Cent. Fox

All-American Comics #16 © DC

All-American Comics #102 © DC

	GD 2.0	VG 4.0	FN 6.0	VF 8.0	VF/NM 9.0	NM- 9.2

--MUSIC OF THE SPEARS, 1/94 - No. 4, 4/94 ($2.50) 1-4 3.00
--NEWT'S TALE, 6/92 - No. 2, 7/92 ($4.95) 1,2-Bolton-c 5.00
--PIG, 3/97 ($2.95)1 3.00
--PREDATOR: THE DEADLIEST OF THE SPECIES, 7/93 - No. 12,8/95 ($2.50)
1-Bolton painted-c; Guice-a(p) 5.00
1-Embossed foil platinum edition 10.00
2-12: Bolton painted-c. 2,3-Guice-a(p) 3.00
--PURGE, 8/97 ($2.95) nn-Hester-a 3.00
--ROGUE, 4/93 - No. 4, 7/93 ($2.50)1-4: Painted-c 3.00
--SACRIFICE, 5/93 ($4.95, 52 pgs.) nn-P. Milligan scripts; painted-c/a 5.00
--SALVATION, 11/93 ($4.95, 52 pgs.) nn-Mignola-c/a(p); Gibbons script 5.00
--SPECIAL, 6/97 ($2.50) 1 3.00
--STALKER, 6/98 ($2.50)1-David Wenzel-s/a 3.00
--STRONGHOLD, 5/94 - No. 4, 9/94 ($2.50) 1-4 3.00
--SURVIVAL, 2/98 - No. 3, 4/98 ($2.95) 1-3-Tony Harris-c 3.00
--TRIBES, 1992 ($24.95, hardcover graphic novel) Bissette text-s with Dorman painted-a 25.00
...softcover ($9.95) 10.00

ALIENS VS. PREDATOR (See Dark Horse Presents #36)
Dark Horse Comics: June, 1990 - No. 4, Dec, 1990 ($2.50, limited series)

	GD	VG	FN	VF	VF/NM	NM-
1-Painted-c	1	2	3	5	6	8
1-2nd printing						3.00
0-(7/90, $1.95, B&W)-r/Dark Horse Pres. #34-36	1	2	3	5	7	9
2,3						5.00
4-Dave Dorman painted-c						4.00
Annual (7/99, $4.95) Jae Lee-c						5.00
... : Booty (1/96, $2.50) painted-c						3.00
... Omnibus Vol. 1 (5/07, $24.95, 9x6") r/#1-4 & Annual; ...: War; ...: Eternal						25.00
... Omnibus Vol. 2 (10/07, $24.95, 9x6") r/...: Xenogenesis #1-4; ...: Deadliest of the Species; ...: Booty and stories from ... Annual						25.00
...: One For One (8/10, $1.00) r/#1 with red cover frame						1.00
... : Thrill of the Hunt (9/04, $6.95, digest-size TPB) Based on 2004 movie						7.00
... Wraith 1 (7/98, $2.95) Jay Stephens-s						3.00

--VS. PREDATOR: DUEL, 3/95 - No. 2, 4/95 ($2.50) 1,2 3.00
--VS. PREDATOR: ETERNAL, 6/98 - No. 4, 9/98 ($2.50)1-4: Edginton-s/Maleev-a; Fabry-c 3.00
--VS. PREDATOR: THREE WORLD WAR, 1/10 - No. 6, 9/10 ($3.50) 1-6-Leonardi-a 3.50
--VS. PREDATOR VS. THE TERMINATOR, 4/00 - No. 4, 7/00 ($2.95) 1-4: Ripley app. 3.00
--VS. PREDATOR: WAR, No. 0, 5/95 - No. 4, 8/95 ($2.50) 0-4: Corben painted-c 3.00
--VS. PREDATOR: XENOGENESIS, 12/99 - No. 4, 3/00 ($2.95) 1-4: Watson-s/Mel Rubi-a 3.00
--XENOGENESIS, 8/99 - No. 4, 11/99 ($2.95) 1-4: T&M Bierbaum-s 3.00

ALIEN TERROR (See 3-D Alien Terror)

ALIEN: THE ILLUSTRATED STORY (Also see Aliens)
Heavy Metal Books: 1980 ($3.95, soft-c, 8x11")

	GD	VG	FN	VF	VF/NM	NM-
nn-Movie adaptation; Simonson-a	3	6	9	14	19	24

ALIEN^3 (Movie)
Dark Horse Comics: June, 1992 - No. 3, July, 1992 ($2.50, limited series)
1-3: Adapts 3rd movie; Suydam painted-c 3.00

ALIEN WORLDS (Also see Eclipse Graphic Album #22)
Pacific Comics/Eclipse: Dec, 1982 - No. 9, Jan, 1985

	GD	VG	FN	VF	VF/NM	NM-
1,2,4: 2,4-Dave Stevens-c/a						6.00
3,5-7						4.00
8,9	1	2	3	4	5	7
3-D No. 1-Art Adams 1st published art	1	2	3	4	5	7

ALISON DARE, LITTLE MISS ADVENTURES (Also see Return of ...)
Oni Press: Sept, 2000 ($4.50, B&W, one-shot)
1-J. Torres-s/J.Bone-c/a 4.50

ALISON DARE & THE HEART OF THE MAIDEN
Oni Press: Jan, 2002 - No. 2, Feb, 2002 ($2.95, B&W, limited series)
1,2-J. Torres-s/J.Bone-c/a 3.00

ALISTER THE SLAYER
Midnight Press: Oct, 1995 ($2.50)
1-Boris-c 3.00

ALL-AMERICAN COMICS (...Western #103-126, ...Men of War #127 on; also see The Big All-American Comic Book)
All-American/National Periodical Publ.: April, 1939 - No. 102, Oct, 1948

	GD	VG	FN	VF	VF/NM	NM-
1-Hop Harrigan (1st app.), Scribbly by Mayer (1st DC app.), Toonerville Folks, Ben Webster, Spot Savage, Mutt & Jeff, Red White & Blue (1st app.), Adventures in the Unknown, Tippie, Reg'lar Fellers, Skippy, Bobby Thatcher, Mystery Men of Mars, Daiseybelle, Wiley of West Point begin	575	1150	1725	4000	6400	8800
2-Ripley's Believe It or Not begins, ends #24	170	340	510	1100	1850	2600
3-5: 5-The American Way begins, ends #10	135	270	405	864	1482	2100
6,7: 6-Last Spot Savage; Popsicle Pete begins, ends #26, 28. 7-Last Bobby Thatcher	113	226	339	718	1234	1750
8-The Ultra Man begins & 1st-c app.	300	600	900	2010	3505	5000
9,10: 10-X-Mas-c	100	200	300	635	1093	1550
11,15: 11-Ultra Man-c. 15-Last Tippie & Reg'lar Fellars; Ultra Man-c	123	246	369	787	1344	1900
12-14: 12-Last Toonerville Folks	94	188	282	597	1024	1450
16-(Rare)-Origin/1st app. Green Lantern by Sheldon Moldoff (c/a)(7/40) & begin series; appears in costume on-c & only one panel inside; created by Martin Nodell. Inspired in 1940 by a switchman's green lantern that would give trains the go ahead to proceed	16,667	33,334	50,000	130,000	265,000	400,000
17-2nd Green Lantern	1100	2200	3300	8360	15,180	22,000
18-N.Y. World's Fair-c/story (scarce); The Atom app. in one panel announcing debut in next issue	1150	2300	3450	8740	15,870	23,000
19-Origin/1st app. The Atom (10/40); last Ultra Man	1950	3900	5850	14,600	26,800	39,000
20-Atom dons costume; Ma Hunkle becomes Red Tornado (1st app.)(1st DC costumed heroine, before Wonder Woman, 11/40); Rescue on Mars begins, ends #25; 1 pg. origin Green Lantern	541	1082	1623	3950	6975	10,000
21-Last Wiley of West Point & Skippy; classic Moldoff-c	459	918	1377	3350	5925	8500
22,23: 23-Last Daiseybelle; 3 Idiots begin, end #82	343	686	1029	2400	4200	6000
24-Sisty & Dinky become the Cyclone Kids; Ben Webster ends; origin Dr. Mid-Nite & Sargon, The Sorcerer in text with app.	360	720	1080	2520	4410	6300
25-Origin & 1st story app. Dr. Mid-Nite by Stan Asch; Hop Harrigan becomes Guardian Angel; last Adventure in the Unknown (scarce)	1100	2200	3300	8250	15,125	22,000
26-Origin/1st story app. Sargon, the Sorcerer	389	778	1167	2723	4762	6800
27: #27-32 are misnumbered in indicia with correct No. appearing on-c. Intro. Doiby Dickles, Green Lantern's sidekick	400	800	1200	2800	4900	7000
28-Hop Harrigan gives up costumed i.d.	206	412	618	1318	2259	3200
29,30	206	412	618	1318	2259	3200
31-40: 35-Doiby learns Green Lantern's i.d.	161	322	483	1030	1765	2500
41-50: 50-Sargon ends	129	258	387	828	1413	2000
51-60: 59-Scribbly & the Red Tornado ends	110	220	330	704	1202	1700
61-Origin/1st app. Solomon Grundy (11/44)	865	1730	2595	6315	11,158	16,000
62-70: 70-Kubert Sargon; intro Sargon's helper, Maximillian O'Leary	94	188	282	597	1024	1450
71-88: 71-Last Red White & Blue. 72-Black Pirate begins (not in #74-82); last Atom. 73-Winky, Blinky & Noddy begins, ends #82. 79,83-Mutt & Jeff-c. 85-1st Sportsmaster; Hasen "Derby" cover	74	148	222	470	810	1150
89-Origin & 1st app. Harlequin	129	258	387	826	1413	2000
90-99: 90-Origin/1st app. Icicle. 99-Last Hop Harrigan	126	252	378	806	1378	1950
100-1st app. Johnny Thunder by Alex Toth (8/48); western theme begins (Scarce)	206	412	618	1318	2259	3200
101-Last Mutt & Jeff (Scarce)	142	284	426	909	1555	2200
102-Last Green Lantern, Black Pirate & Dr. Mid-Nite (Scarce)	265	530	795	1694	2897	4100

NOTE: *No Atom in 47, 62-69.* **Kinstler** *Black Pirate-89.* **Stan Aschmeier** *a (Dr. Mid-Nite) 25-84; c-7.* **Mayer** *c-1, 2(part), 6, 10.* **Moldoff** *c-16-23.* **Nodell** *c-31.* **Paul Reinman** *a (Green Lantern)-53-55p, 56-84, 87; (Black Pirate)-83-88, 90; c-52, 55-76, 78, 80, 81, 87.* **Toth** *a-88, 92, 96, 98-102; c(p)-92, 96-102. Scribbly by* **Mayer** *in #1-59. Ultra Man by* **Mayer** *in #8-19.*

ALL AMERICAN COMICS
DC Comics: April 1939
nn - Ashcan comic, not distributed to newsstands, only for in house use. Cover art is Advenure Comics #33 and interior from Detective Comics #23 (no known sales)

ALL-AMERICAN COMICS (Also see All Star Comics 1999 crossover titles)
DC Comics: May, 1999 ($1.99, one-shot)
1-Golden Age Green Lantern and Johnny Thunder; Barreto-a 3.00

ALL-AMERICAN MEN OF WAR (Previously All-American Western)
National Periodical Publ.: No. 127, Aug-Sept, 1952 - No. 117, Sept-Oct, 1966

	GD	VG	FN	VF	VF/NM	NM-
127 (#1, 1952)	112	224	336	952	1926	2900
128 (1952)	54	108	162	459	930	1400
2(12-1/'52-53)-5	48	96	144	392	796	1200

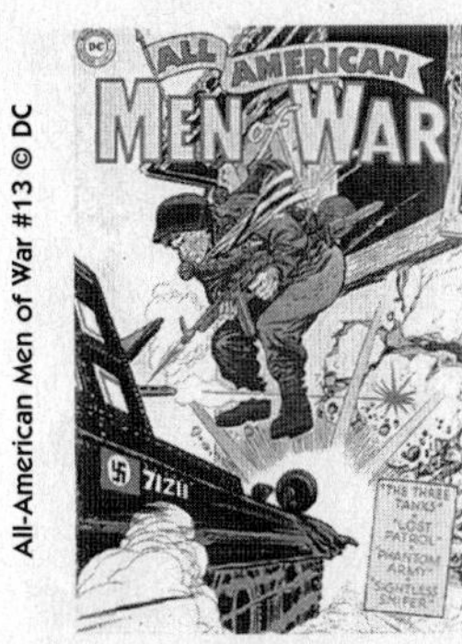

All-American Men of War #13 © DC

All-American Western #103 © DC

All-Flash #5 © DC

	GD 2.0	VG 4.0	FN 6.0	VF 8.0	VF/NM 9.0	NM- 9.2
6-Devil Dog story; Ghost Squadron story	38	76	114	304	602	900
7-10: 8-Sgt. Storm Cloud-s	38	76	114	304	602	900
11-16,18: 18-Last precode; 1st Kubert-c (2/55)	35	70	105	273	537	800
17-1st Frogman-s in this title	36	72	108	281	553	825
19,20,22-27	27	54	81	197	399	600
21-Easy Co. prototype	33	66	99	254	502	750
28 (12/55)-1st Sgt. Rock prototype; Kubert-a	47	94	141	376	763	1150
29,30,32-Wood-a	27	54	81	197	399	600
31,33,34,36-38,40: 34-Gunner prototype-s. 36-Little Sure Shot prototype-s. 38-1st S.A. issue	24	48	72	175	350	525
35-Greytone-c	27	54	81	197	399	600
39 (11/56)-2nd Sgt. Rock prototype; 1st Easy Co.?	35	70	105	273	537	800
41,43-47,49,50: 46-Tankbusters-c/s	21	42	63	150	300	450
42-Pre-Sgt. Rock Easy Co.-c/s	26	52	78	186	373	560
48-Easy Co.-c/s; Nick app.; Kubert-a	26	52	78	186	373	560
51-56,58-62,66: 61-Gunner-c/s	16	32	48	111	226	340
57(5/58),63,64 -Pre-Sgt. Rock Easy Co.-c/s	22	44	66	159	317	475
67-1st Gunner & Sarge by Andru & Esposito	41	82	123	328	664	1000
68,69: 68-2nd app. Gunner & Sarge. 69-1st Tank Killer-c/s	20	40	60	140	283	425
70	14	28	42	96	191	285
71-80: 71,72,76-Tank Killer-c/s. 74-Minute Commandos-c/s	12	24	36	86	161	235
81-Greytone-c	11	22	33	75	138	200
82-Johnny Cloud begins(1st app.), ends #117	20	40	60	140	283	425
83-2nd Johnny Cloud	13	26	39	91	176	260
84-88: 88-Last 10¢ issue	10	20	30	72	131	190
89-100: 89-Battle Aces of 3 Wars begins, ends #98	8	16	24	58	97	135
101-111,113-116: 111,114,115-Johnny Cloud	6	12	18	41	66	90
112-Balloon Buster series begins, ends #114,116	6	12	18	43	69	95
117-Johnny Cloud-c & 3-part story	6	12	18	43	69	95

NOTE: *Frogman stories in 17, 38, 44, 45, 50, 51, 53, 55-58, 63, 65, 66, 72, 76, 77.* ***Colan*** *a-112.* ***Drucker*** *a-47, 58, 61, 63, 65, 69, 71, 74, 77.* ***Grandenetti*** *c(p)-127, 128, 2-17(most).* ***Heath*** *a-14, 27, 32, 38, 41, 45, 47, 50, 51, 55-58, 62, 64, 71, 75, 76, 78, 95, 111-117; c-85, 91, 94-96, 100, 101, 110-112, others?* ***Infantino*** *a-8.* ***Kirby*** *a-29.* ***Krigstein*** *a-128('52), 2, 3, 5.* ***Kubert*** *a-22, 24, 28, 29, 33, 34, 36, 38, 39, 41-43, 47-50, 52, 53, 55, 56, 59, 60, 63-65, 69, 71-73, 76, 102, 103, 105, 106, 108, 114; c-41, 44, 52, 54, 55, 58, 64, 69, 76, 77, 79, 102-106, 108, 113-117, others? Tank Killer in 69, 71, 76 by* ***Kubert****.* ***P. Reinman*** *c-55, 57, 61, 62, 71, 72, 74-76, 80.* ***J. Severin*** *a-58.*

ALL AMERICAN MEN OF WAR
DC Comics: Aug/Sept. 1952

nn - Ashcan comic, not distributed to newsstands, only for in-house use. Cover art is All Star Western #58 and interior from Mr. District Attorney #21 (no known sales)

ALL-AMERICAN SPORTS
Charlton Comics: Oct, 1967

	GD 2.0	VG 4.0	FN 6.0	VF 8.0	VF/NM 9.0	NM- 9.2
1	3	6	9	20	30	40

ALL-AMERICAN WESTERN (Formerly All-American Comics; Becomes All-American Men of War)
National Periodical Publ.: No. 103, Nov, 1948 - No. 126, June-July, 1952 (103-121: 52 pgs.)

	GD 2.0	VG 4.0	FN 6.0	VF 8.0	VF/NM 9.0	NM- 9.2
103-Johnny Thunder & his horse Black Lightning continues by Toth, ends #126; Foley of The Fighting 5th, Minstrel Maverick, & Overland Coach begin; Captain Tootsie by Beck; mentioned in Love and Death	50	100	150	315	533	750
104-Kubert-a	36	72	108	216	351	485
105,107-Kubert-a	31	62	93	182	296	410
106,108-110,112: 112-Kurtzman's "Pot-Shot Pete" (1 pg.)	25	50	75	150	245	340
111,114-116-Kubert-a	26	52	78	156	256	355
113-Intro. Swift Deer, J. Thunder's new sidekick (4-5/50); classic Toth-c; Kubert-a	28	56	84	165	270	375
117-126: 121-Kubert-a; bondage-c	19	38	57	111	176	240

NOTE: ***G. Kane*** *c(p)-112, 119, 120, 123.* ***Kubert*** *a-103-105, 107, 111, 112(1 pg.), 113-116, 121.* ***Toth*** *a 103-125; c(p)-103-111,113-116, 121, 122, 124-126. Some copies of #125 have #12 on-c.*

ALL COMICS
Chicago Nite Life News: 1945

	GD 2.0	VG 4.0	FN 6.0	VF 8.0	VF/NM 9.0	NM- 9.2
1	15	30	45	83	124	165

ALLEGRA
Image Comics (WildStorm): Aug, 1996 - No. 4, Dec, 1996 ($2.50)

	GD 2.0	VG 4.0	FN 6.0	VF 8.0	VF/NM 9.0	NM- 9.2
1-4						3.00

ALLEY CAT (Alley Baggett)
Image Comics: July, 1999 - No. 6, Mar, 2000 ($2.50/$2.95)

	GD 2.0	VG 4.0	FN 6.0	VF 8.0	VF/NM 9.0	NM- 9.2
Preview Edition						6.00
Prelude						5.00
Prelude w/variant-c						6.00
1-Photo-c						3.00
1-Painted-c by Dorian						3.50
1-Another Universe Edition, 1-Wizard World Edition						7.00
2-4: 4-Twin towers on-c						3.00
5,6-($2.95)						3.00
Lingerie Edition (10/99, $4.95) Photos, pin-ups, cover gallery						5.00
...Vs. Lady Pendragon ('99, $3.00) Stinsman-c						3.00

ALLEY OOP (See The Comics, The Funnies, Red Ryder and Super Book #9)
Dell Publishing Co.: No. 3, 1942

	GD 2.0	VG 4.0	FN 6.0	VF 8.0	VF/NM 9.0	NM- 9.2
Four Color 3 (#1)	41	82	123	328	664	1000

ALLEY OOP
Argo Publ.: Nov, 1955 - No. 3, Mar, 1956 (Newspaper reprints)

	GD 2.0	VG 4.0	FN 6.0	VF 8.0	VF/NM 9.0	NM- 9.2
1	16	32	48	92	144	195
2,3	12	24	36	67	94	120

ALLEY OOP
Dell Publishing Co.: 12-2/62-63 - No. 2, 9-11/63

	GD 2.0	VG 4.0	FN 6.0	VF 8.0	VF/NM 9.0	NM- 9.2
1	6	12	18	41	66	90
2	5	10	15	34	55	75

ALLEY OOP
Standard Comics: No. 10, Sept, 1947 - No. 18, Oct, 1949

	GD 2.0	VG 4.0	FN 6.0	VF 8.0	VF/NM 9.0	NM- 9.2
10	24	48	72	140	230	320
11-18: 17,18-Schomburg-c	20	40	60	111	182	250

ALLEY OOP ADVENTURES
Antarctic Press: Aug, 1998 - No. 3, Dec, 1998 ($2.95)

	GD 2.0	VG 4.0	FN 6.0	VF 8.0	VF/NM 9.0	NM- 9.2
1-3-Jack Bender-s/a						3.00

ALLEY OOP ADVENTURES (Alley Oop Quarterly in indicia)
Antarctic Press: Sept, 1999 - No. 3, Mar, 2000 ($2.50/$2.99, B&W)

	GD 2.0	VG 4.0	FN 6.0	VF 8.0	VF/NM 9.0	NM- 9.2
1-3-Jack Bender-s/a						3.00

ALL-FAMOUS CRIME (2nd series - Formerly Law Against Crime #1-3; becomes All-Famous Police Cases #6 on)
Star Publications: No. 8, 5/51 - No. 10, 11/51; No. 4, 2/52 - No. 5, 5/52;

	GD 2.0	VG 4.0	FN 6.0	VF 8.0	VF/NM 9.0	NM- 9.2
8 (#1-1st series)	22	44	66	128	209	290
9 (#2)-Used in **SOTI**, illo- "The wish to hurt or kill couples in lovers' lanes is a not uncommon perversion;" L.B. Cole-c/a(r)/Law-Crime #3	37	74	111	222	361	500
10 (#3)	20	40	60	114	182	250
4 (#4-2nd series)-Formerly Law-Crime	19	38	57	109	172	235
5 (#5) Becomes All-Famous Police Cases #6	19	38	57	109	172	235

NOTE: *All have* ***L.B. Cole*** *covers.*

ALL FAMOUS CRIME STORIES (See Fox Giants)

ALL-FAMOUS POLICE CASES (Formerly All Famous Crime #5)
Star Publications: No. 6, Feb, 1952 - No. 16, Sept, 1954

	GD 2.0	VG 4.0	FN 6.0	VF 8.0	VF/NM 9.0	NM- 9.2
6	19	38	57	112	176	240
7,8: 7-Baker story. 8-Marijuana story	18	36	54	105	165	225
9-16	16	32	48	94	147	200

NOTE: ***L. B. Cole*** *c-all; a-15, 1pg.* ***Hollingsworth*** *a-15.*

ALL-FLASH (...Quarterly No. 1-5)
National Per. Publ./All-American: Summer, 1941 - No. 32, Dec-Jan, 1947-48

	GD 2.0	VG 4.0	FN 6.0	VF 8.0	VF/NM 9.0	NM- 9.2
1-Origin The Flash retold by E. E. Hibbard; Hibbard c-1-10,12-14,16,31p.	1400	2800	4200	10,500	18,250	26,000
2-Origin recap	314	628	942	2198	3849	5500
3,4	177	354	531	1124	1937	2750
5-Winky, Blinky & Noddy begins (1st app.), ends #32	129	258	387	826	1413	2000
6-10	106	212	318	673	1162	1650
11-13: 12-Origin/1st The Thinker. 13-The King app.	90	180	270	576	988	1400
14-Green Lantern cameo	106	212	318	673	1162	1650
15-20: 18-Mutt & Jeff begins, ends #22	81	162	243	518	884	1250
21-31	68	136	204	435	743	1050
32-Origin/1st app. The Fiddler; 1st Star Sapphire	135	270	405	864	1482	2100

NOTE: *Book length stories in 2-13, 16. Bondage c-31, 32.* ***Martin Nodell*** *c-15, 17-28.*

ALL FLASH (Leads into Flash [2nd series] #231)
DC Comics: Sept, 2007 ($2.99, one-shot)

	GD 2.0	VG 4.0	FN 6.0	VF 8.0	VF/NM 9.0	NM- 9.2
1-Wally West hunts down Bart's killers; Waid-s; two covers by Middleton & Sienkiewicz						3.00

ALL FOR LOVE (Young Love V3#5-on)
Prize Publications: Apr-May, 1957 - V3#4, Dec-Jan, 1959-60

	GD 2.0	VG 4.0	FN 6.0	VF 8.0	VF/NM 9.0	NM- 9.2
V1#1	8	16	24	58	97	135
2-6: 5-Orlando-c	5	10	15	32	51	70
V2#1-5(1/59), 5(3/59)	4	8	12	28	44	60
V3#1(5/59), 1(7/59)-4: 2-Powell-a	4	8	12	24	37	50

All Good nn © STJ

All-New Batman: Brave & the Bold #1 © DC

All-New Comics #8 © HARV

GD VG FN VF VF/NM NM-
2.0 4.0 6.0 8.0 9.0 9.2

ALL FUNNY COMICS
Tilsam Publ./National Periodical Publications (Detective): Winter, 1943-44 - No. 23, May-June, 1948

1-Genius Jones (1st app.), Buzzy (1st app., ends #4), Dover & Clover (see More Fun #93) begin; Bailey-a 47 94 141 296 498 700
2 22 44 66 132 216 300
3-10 15 30 45 83 124 165
11-13,15,18,19-Genius Jones app. 14 28 42 80 115 150
14,17,20-23 10 20 30 56 76 95
16-DC Super Heroes app. 31 62 93 182 296 410

ALL GOOD
St. John Publishing Co.: Oct, 1949 (50¢, 260 pgs.)

nn-(8 St. John comics bound together) 74 148 222 470 810 1150
NOTE: *Also see Li'l Audrey Yearbook & Treasury of Comics.*

ALL GOOD COMICS (See Fox Giants)
Fox Features Syndicate: No.1, Spring, 1946 (36 pgs.)

1-Joy Family, Dick Transom, Rick Evans, One Round Hogan 27 54 81 158 259 360

ALL GREAT
William H. Wise & Co.: nd (1945?) (132 pgs.)

nn-Capt. Jack Terry, Joan Mason, Girl Reporter, Baron Doomsday; Torture scenes 41 82 123 256 428 600

ALL GREAT COMICS (See Fox Giants)
Fox Feature Syndicate: 1946 (36 pgs.)

1-Crazy House, Bertie Benson Boy Detective, Gussie the Gob 27 54 81 158 259 360

ALL GREAT COMICS (Formerly Phantom Lady #13? Dagar, Desert Hawk No. 14 on)
Fox Features Syndicate: No. 14, Oct, 1947 - No. 13, Dec, 1947 (Newspaper strip reprints)

14(#12)-Brenda Starr & Texas Slim-r (Scarce) 57 114 171 362 621 880
13-Origin Dagar, Desert Hawk; Brenda Starr (all-r); Kamen-c; Dagar covers begin 65 130 195 416 708 1000

ALL-GREAT CONFESSIONS (See Fox Giants)

ALL GREAT CRIME STORIES (See Fox Giants)

ALL GREAT JUNGLE ADVENTURES (See Fox Giants)

ALL HALLOW'S EVE
Innovation Publishing: 1991 ($4.95, 52 pgs.)

1-Painted-c/a 1 2 3 4 5 7

ALL HERO COMICS
Fawcett Publications: Mar, 1943 (100 pgs., cardboard-c)

1-Capt. Marvel Jr., Capt. Midnight, Golden Arrow, Ibis the Invincible, Spy Smasher, Lance O'Casey; 1st Banshee O'Brien; Raboy-c 174 348 522 1114 1907 2700

ALL HUMOR COMICS
Quality Comics Group: Spring, 1946 - No. 17, December, 1949

1 21 42 63 122 199 275
2-Atomic Tot story; Gustavson-a 13 26 39 74 105 135
3-9: 3-Intro Kelly Poole who is cover feature #3 on. 5-1st app. Hickory? 8-Gustavson-a 9 18 27 47 61 75
10-17 8 16 24 42 54 65

ALLIANCE, THE
Image Comics (Shadowline Ink): Aug, 1995 - No. 3, Nov, 1995 ($2.50)

1-3: 2-(9/95) 3.00

ALL LOVE (...Romances No. 26)(Formerly Ernie Comics)
Ace Periodicals (Current Books): No. 26, May, 1949 - No. 32, May, 1950

26 (No. 1)-Ernie, Lily Belle app. 11 22 33 60 83 105
27-L. B. Cole-a 14 28 42 76 108 140
28-32 8 16 24 42 54 65

ALL-NEGRO COMICS
All-Negro Comics: June, 1947 (15¢)

1 (Rare) 1667 3334 5000 9000 11,750 14,500
NOTE: *Seldom found in fine or mint condition; many copies have brown pages.*

ALL-NEW ATOM, THE (See The Atom and DCU Brave New World)
DC Comics: Sept, 2006 - No. 25, Sept, 2008 ($2.99)

1-25: 1-18-Simone-s. 1-Intro Ryan Choi; Byrne-a thru #3. 4-11-Barrows-a. 12,13-Chronos app. 14,15-Countdown x-over. 17,18-Wonder Woman app. 3.00
...: Future/Past TPB (2007, $14.99) r/#7-11 15.00
...: My Life in Miniature TPB (2007, $14.99) r/#1-6 and app. in DCU Brave New World #1 15.00
...: Small Wonder TPB (2008, $17.99) r/#17,18,21-25 18.00
...: The Hunt For Ray Palmer TPB (2008, $14.99) r/#12-16 15.00

ALL-NEW BATMAN: BRAVE & THE BOLD (Based on the Cartoon Network series)
DC Comics: Jan, 2011 - Present ($2.99)

1-5: 1-Superman. 4-Wonder Woman app. 3.00

ALL-NEW COLLECTORS' EDITION (Formerly Limited Collectors' Edition: see for C-57, C-59)
DC Comics, Inc.: Jan, 1978 - Vol. 8, No. C-62, 1979 (No. 54-58: 76 pgs.)

C-53-Rudolph the Red-Nosed Reindeer 5 10 15 30 48 65
C-54-Superman Vs. Wonder Woman 4 8 12 26 41 55
C-55-Superboy & the Legion of Super-Heroes; Wedding of Lightning Lad & Saturn Girl; Grell-c/a 4 8 12 26 41 55
C-56-Superman Vs. Muhammad Ali: Wraparound Neal Adams-c/a; Adams & O'Neil-s (see "Superman Vs. Muhammad Ali" for reprint) 7 14 21 49 80 100
C-56-Superman Vs. Muhammad Ali (Whitman variant)-low print 9 18 27 63 107 150
C-57,C-59-(See Limited Collectors' Edition)
C-58-Superman Vs. Shazam; Buckler-c/a 4 8 12 26 41 55
C-60-Rudolph's Summer Fun(8/78) 4 8 12 26 41 55
C-61-(See Famous First Edition-Superman #1)
C-62-Superman the Movie (68 pgs.; 1979)-Photo-c from movie plus photos inside (also see DC Special Series #25) 3 6 9 16 22 28

ALL-NEW COMICS (...Short Story Comics No. 1-3)
Family Comics (Harvey Publications): Jan, 1943 - No. 14, Nov, 1946; No. 15, Mar-Apr, 1947 (10 x 13-1/2")

1-Steve Case, Crime Rover, Johnny Rebel, Kayo Kane, The Echo, Night Hawk, Ray O'Light, Detective Shane begin (all 1st app.?); Red Blazer on cover only; Sultan-a 300 600 900 1950 3375 4800
2-Origin Scarlet Phantom by Kubert 113 226 339 718 1234 1750
3-Nazi war-c 90 180 270 576 988 1400
4 74 148 222 470 810 1150
5-11: 5-Schomburg-c thru #11. 6-The Boy Heroes & Red Blazer (text story) begin, end #12; Black Cat app.; intro. Sparky in Red Blazer. 7-Kubert, Powell-a; Black Cat & Zebra app. 8,9: 8-Shock Gibson app.; Kubert, Powell-a; Schomburg-c. 9-Black Cat app.; Kubert-a. 10-The Zebra app. (from Green Hornet Comics); Kubert-a(3). 11-Girl Commandos, Man In Black app. 90 180 270 576 988 1400
12,13: 12-Kubert-a. 13-Stuntman by Simon & Kirby; Green Hornet, Joe Palooka, Flying Fool app.; Green Hornet-c 58 116 174 371 636 900
14-The Green Hornet & The Man in Black Called Fate by Powell, Joe Flying Fool app.; Flying Fool app.; J. Palooka-c by Ham Fisher 45 90 135 284 480 675
15-(Rare)-Small size (5-1/2x8-1/2"; B&W; 32 pgs.). Distributed to mail subscribers only. Black Cat and Joe Palooka app. 142 284 426 909 1555 2200
NOTE: *Also see Boy Explorers No. 2, Flash Gordon No. 5, and Stuntman No. 3.* **Powell** *a-11.* **Schomburg** *c-5-11. Captain Red Blazer & Spark on c-5-11 (w/Boy Heroes #12).*

ALL-NEW OFFICIAL HANDBOOK OF THE MARVEL UNIVERSE A TO Z
Marvel Comics: 2006 - No. 12, 2006 ($3.99, limited series)

1-12-Profile pages of Marvel characters not covered in 2004-2005 Official Handbooks 4.00
...: Update 1-4 (2007, $3.99) Profile pages 4.00

ALL-OUT WAR
DC Comics: Sept-Oct, 1979 - No. 6, Aug, 1980 ($1.00, 68 pgs.)

1-The Viking Commando(origin), Force Three(origin), & Black Eagle Squadron begin 2 4 6 11 16 20
2-6 2 4 6 8 10 12
NOTE: **Ayers** *a(p)-1-6.* **Elias** *r-2.* **Evans** *a-1-6.* **Kubert** *c-16.*

ALL PICTURE ADVENTURE MAGAZINE
St. John Publishing Co.: Oct, 1952 - No. 2, Nov, 1952 (100 pg. Giants, 25¢, squarebound)

1-War comics 34 68 102 204 332 460
2-Horror-crime comics 48 96 144 302 514 725
NOTE: *Above books contain three St. John comics rebound; variations possible.* **Baker** *art known in both.*

ALL PICTURE ALL TRUE LOVE STORY
St. John Publishing Co.: Oct., 1952 - No. 2, Nov., 1952 (100 pgs., 25¢)

1-Canteen Kate by Matt Baker 53 106 159 334 567 800
2-Baker-c/a 39 78 117 231 378 525

ALL-PICTURE COMEDY CARNIVAL
St. John Publishing Co.: October, 1952 (100 pgs., 25¢)(Contains 4 rebound comics)

1-Contents can vary; Baker-a 43 86 129 271 461 650

ALL REAL CONFESSION MAGAZINE (See Fox Giants)

ALL ROMANCES (Mr. Risk No. 7 on)
A. A. Wyn (Ace Periodicals): Aug, 1949 - No. 6, June, 1950

1 14 28 42 78 112 145

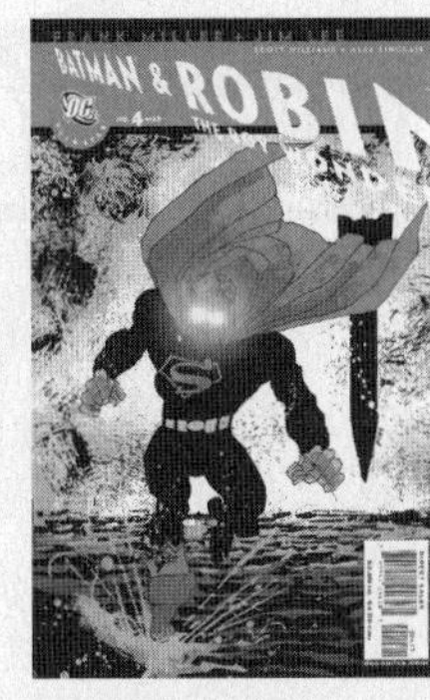

All Star Batman & Robin, The Boy Wonder #4 © DC

All Star Comics #22 © DC

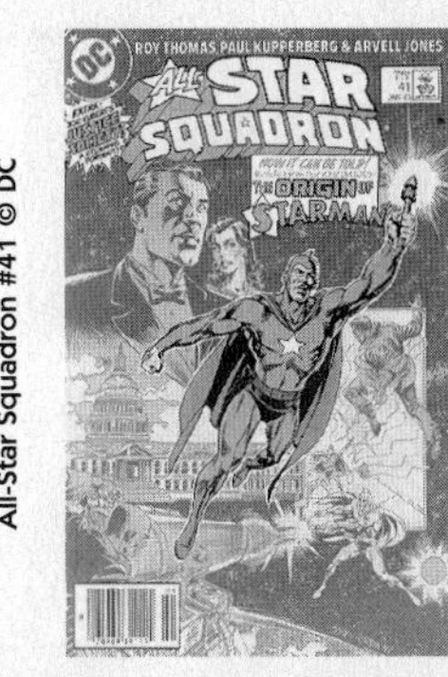

All-Star Squadron #41 © DC

GD VG FN VF VF/NM NM-
2.0 4.0 6.0 8.0 9.0 9.2

2 9 18 27 47 61 75
3-6 8 16 24 42 54 65

ALL-SELECT COMICS (Blonde Phantom No. 12 on)
Timely Comics (Daring Comics): Fall, 1943 - No. 11, Fall, 1946

1-Capt. America (by Rico #1), Human Torch, Sub-Mariner begin; Black Widow story (4 pgs.); Classic Schomburg-c 1567 3134 4700 11,000 20,500 30,000
2-Red Skull app. 486 972 1458 3550 6275 9000
3-The Whizzer begins 320 640 960 2240 3920 5600
4,5-Last Sub-Mariner 271 542 813 1734 2967 4200
6-9: 6-The Destroyer app. 8-No Whizzer 213 426 639 1363 2332 3300
10-The Destroyer & Sub-Mariner app.; last Capt. America & Human Torch issue 213 426 639 1363 2332 3300
11-1st app. Blonde Phantom; Miss America app.; all Blonde Phantom-c by Shores 277 554 831 1759 3030 4300

NOTE: ***Schomburg** c-1-10. **Sekowsky** a-7. #7 & 8 show 1944 in indicia, but should be 1945.*

ALL SELECT COMICS 70th ANNIVERARY SPECIAL
Marvel Comics: Sept, 2009 ($3.99, one-shot)

1-New stories of Blonde Phantom and Marvex the Super Robot; r/Marvex G.A. app. 4.00

ALL SPORTS COMICS (Formerly Real Sports Comics; becomes All Time Sports Comics No. 4 on)
Hillman Periodicals: No. 2, Dec-Jan, 1948-49; No. 3, Feb-Mar, 1949

2-Krigstein-a(p), Powell, Starr-a 34 68 102 199 325 450
3-Mort Lawrence-a 22 44 66 132 216 300

ALL STAR BATMAN & ROBIN, THE BOY WONDER
DC Comics: Sept, 2005 - No. 10, Aug, 2008 ($2.99)

1-Two covers; retelling of Robin's origin; Frank Miller-s/Jim Lee-a/c 3.00
1-Diamond Retailer Summit Edition (9/05) sketch-c 60.00
2-10: 2-7-Two covers by Lee and Miller. 3-Black Canary app. 4-Six pg. Batcave gatefold. 10-Edition without profanity 3.00
8-10: 8,9-Variant cover by Neal Adams. 10-Variant-c by Quitely 5.00
10-Recalled edition with insufficiently covered profanity inside; Jim Lee-c 20.00
10-Recalled edition with variant Quitely-c 40.00
... Special Edition (2/06, $3.99) r/#1 with Lee pencil pages and Miller script; new Miller-c 4.00
Vol. 1 HC (2008, $24.99, dustjacket) r/#1-9; cover gallery, sketch pages; Schreck intro. 25.00
Vol. 1 SC (2009, $19.99) r/#1-9; cover gallery, sketch pages; Schreck intro. 20.00

ALL STAR COMICS
DC Comics: Spring 1940

1-Ashcan comic, not distributed to newsstands, only for in-house use. Cover art is Flash Comics #1 and interior from Detective Comics #37. A CGC certified 7.0 copy sold for $15,600 in 2002.

ALL STAR COMICS (All Star Western No. 58 on)
National Periodical Publ./All-American/DC Comics: Sum, 1940 - No. 57, Feb-Mar, 1951; No. 58, Jan-Feb, 1976 - No. 74, Sept-Oct, 1978

1-The Flash (#1 by E.E. Hibbard), Hawkman (by Shelly), Hourman (by Bernard Baily), The Sandman (by Creig Flessel), The Spectre (by Baily), Biff Bronson, Red White & Blue (ends #2) begin; Ultra Man's only app. (#1-3 are quarterly; #4 begins bi-monthly issues) 1185 2370 3555 8900 16,200 23,500
2-Green Lantern (by Martin Nodell), Johnny Thunder begin; Green Lantern figure swipe from the cover of All-American Comics #16; Flash figure swipe from cover of Flash Comics #8; Moldoff/Bailey-c (cut & paste-c.) 508 1016 1524 3708 6554 9400
3-Origin & 1st app. The Justice Society of America (Win/40); Dr. Fate & The Atom begin, Red Tornado cameo 4500 9000 13,500 34,000 62,000 90,000
3-Reprint, Oversize 13-1/2x10". **WARNING:** This comic is an exact reprint of the original except for its size. DC published it in 1974 with a second cover titling it as a Famous First Edition. There have been many reported cases of the outer cover being removed and the interior sold as the original edition. The reprint with the new outer cover removed is practically worthless. See Famous First Edition for value.
4-1st adventure for J.S.A. 530 1060 1590 3869 6835 9800
5-1st app. Shiera Sanders as Hawkgirl (1st costumed super-heroine, 6-7/41) 459 918 1377 3350 5925 8500
6-Johnny Thunder joins JSA 300 600 900 1935 3343 4750
7-Batman, Superman, Flash cameo; last Hourman; Doiby Dickles app. 331 662 993 2317 4059 5800
8-Origin & 1st app. Wonder Woman (12-1/41-42)(added as 9 pgs. making book 76 pgs.; origin cont'd in Sensation #1; see W.W. #1 for more detailed origin); Dr. Fate dons new helmet; Hop Harrigan text stories & Starman begin; Shiera app.; Hop Harrigan JSA guest; Starman & Dr. Mid-Nite become members 3750 7500 11,250 28,000 51,500 75,000
9-11: 9-JSA's girlfriends cameo; Shiera app.; J. Edgar Hoover of FBI made associate member of JSA. 10-Flash, Green Lantern cameo; Sandman new costume. 11-Wonder Woman begins; Spectre cameo; Shiera app.; Moldoff Hawkman-c 300 600 900 1920 3310 4700
12-Wonder Woman becomes JSA Secretary 277 554 831 1773 3037 4300

GD VG FN VF VF/NM NM-
2.0 4.0 6.0 8.0 9.0 9.2

13,15: Sandman w/Sandy in #14 & 15. 15-Origin & 1st app. Brain Wave; Shiera app. 252 504 756 1613 2757 3900
14-(12/42) Junior JSA Club begins; w/membership offer & premiums 258 516 774 1651 2826 4000
16-20: 19-Sandman w/Sandy. 20-Dr. Fate & Sandman cameo 213 426 639 1363 2332 3300
21-23: 21-Spectre & Atom cameo; Dr. Fate by Kubert; Dr. Fate, Sandman end. 22-Last Hop Harrigan; Flag-c. 23-Origin/1st app. Psycho Pirate; last Spectre & Starman 168 336 504 1075 1838 2600
24-Flash & Green Lantern cameo; Mr. Terrific only app.; Wildcat, JSA guest; Kubert Hawkman begins; Hitler-c 168 336 504 1075 1838 2600
25-27: 25-Flash & Green Lantern start again. 26-Robot-c. 27-Wildcat, JSA guest (#24-26: only All-American imprint) 145 290 435 921 1586 2250
28-32 126 252 378 806 1378 1950
33-Solomon Grundy & Doiby Dickles app; classic Solomon Grundy cover & last G.A. app. 354 708 1062 2478 4339 6200
34,35-Johnny Thunder cameo in both 121 242 363 768 1322 1875
36-Batman & Superman JSA guests 284 568 852 1818 3109 4400
37-Johnny Thunder cameo; origin & 1st app. Injustice Society; last Kubert Hawkman 161 322 483 1030 1765 2500
38-Black Canary begins; JSA Death issue 226 452 678 1446 2473 3500
39,40: 39-Last Johnny Thunder 118 236 354 749 1287 1825
41-Black Canary joins JSA; Injustice Society app. (2nd app.?) 118 236 354 749 1287 1825
42-Atom & the Hawkman don new costumes 118 236 354 749 1287 1825
43-49,51-56: 43-New logo; Robot-c. 55-Sci/Fi story. 56-Robot-c 118 236 354 749 1287 1825
50-Frazetta art, 3 pgs. 126 252 378 806 1378 1950
57-Kubert-a, 6 pgs. (Scarce); last app. G.A. Green Lantern, Flash & Dr. Mid-Nite 171 342 513 1086 1868 2650
V12 #58-(1976) JSA (Flash, Hawkman, Dr. Mid-Nite, Wildcat, Dr. Fate, Green Lantern, Robin & Star Spangled Kid) app.; intro. Power Girl 6 12 18 41 66 90
V12 #59,60: 59-Estrada & Wood-a 3 6 9 18 27 35
V12 #61-68: 62-65-Superman app. 64,65-Wood-c/a; Vandal Savage app. 66-Injustice Society app. 68-Psycho Pirate app. 3 6 9 18 27 35
V12 #69-1st Earth-2 Huntress (Helena Wayne) 5 10 15 30 48 65
V12 #70-73: 70-Full intro. of Huntress 3 6 9 18 27 35
V12 #74-(44 pgs.) Last issue, story continues in Adventure Comics #461 & 462 (death of Earth-2 Batman; Staton-c/a 4 8 12 28 44 60
(See Justice Society Vol. 1 TPB for reprints of V12 revival)

NOTE: *No Atom-27, 36; no Dr. Fate-13; no Flash-8, 9, 11-23; no Green Lantern-8, 9,11-23; Hawkman in 1-57 (only one to app. in all 57 issues); no Johnny Thunder-5, 36; no Wonder Woman-9, 10, 23. Book length stories in 4-9, 11-14, 18-22, 25, 26, 29, 30, 32-36, 40, 42, 43. Johnny Peril in #42-46, 48, 49, 51, 52,54-57. **Baily** a-1-10, 12, 13, 14i, 15-20. **Burnley** Starman-8-13; c-12, 13. **Grell** c-58. **E.E. Hibbard** c-3, 4, 6-10. **Infantino** c-40. **Kubert** Hawkman-24-30, 33-37. **Lampert/Baily/Flessel** c-1, 2. **Moldoff** Hawkman-3-23; c-11. **Mart Nodell** c-25i, 26i, 27-32. **Purcell** c-5. **Simon & Kirby** Sandman 14-17, 19. **Staton** a-66-74p. c-74p. **Toth** a-37(2), 38(2), 40, 41; c-38, 41. **Wood** a-58i-63i, 64, 65; c-63i, 64, 65. Issues 1-7, 9-16 are 68 pgs.; #8 is 76 pgs.; #17-19 are 60 pgs.; #20-57 are 52 pgs.*

ALL STAR COMICS (Also see crossover 1999 editions of Adventure, All-American, National, Sensation, Smash, Star Spangled and Thrilling Comics)
DC Comics: May, 1999 - No. 2, May, 1999 ($2.95, bookends for JSA x-over)

1,2-Justice Society in World War 2; Robinson-s/Johnson-c 3.00
1-RRP Edition (price will be based on future sales)
...80-Page Giant (9/99, $4.95) Phantom Lady app. 5.00

ALL STAR INDEX, THE
Independent Comics Group (Eclipse): Feb, 1987 ($2.00, Baxter paper)

1 1 2 3 5 6 8

ALL-STAR SQUADRON (See Justice League of America #193)
DC Comics: Sept, 1981 - No. 67, Mar, 1987

1-Original Atom, Hawkman, Dr. Mid-Nite, Robotman (origin), Plastic Man, Johnny Quick, Liberty Belle, Shining Knight begin 1 2 3 5 7 9
2-10: 3-Solomon Grundy app. 4,7-Spectre app. 8-Re-intro Steel, the Indestructable Man 5.00
11-46,48,49: 12-Origin G.A. Hawkman retold. 23-Origin/1st app. The Amazing Man. 24-Batman app. 25-1st app. Infinity, Inc. (9/83), 26-Origin Infinity, Inc.(2nd app.); Robin app. 27-Dr. Fate vs. The Spectre. 30-35-Spectre app. 33-Origin Freedom Fighters of Earth-X. 36,37-Superman vs. Capt. Marvel; Ordway-c. 41-Origin Starman 4.00
47-Origin Dr. Fate; McFarlane-a (1st full story)/part-c (7/85) 2 4 6 9 12 15
50-Double size; Crisis x-over 1 2 3 5 6 8
51-66: 51-56-Crisis x-over. 61-Origin Liberty Belle. 62-Origin The Shining Knight. 63-Origin Robotman. 65-Origin Johnny Quick. 66-Origin Tarantula 6.00
67-Last issue; retells first case of the Justice Society 1 2 3 5 6 8
Annual 1-3: 1(11/82)-Retells origin of G.A. Atom, Guardian & Wildcat; Jerry Ordway's 1st pencils for DC. (1st work was inking Carmine Infantino in Mystery in Space #117).

All Star Superman #12 © DC

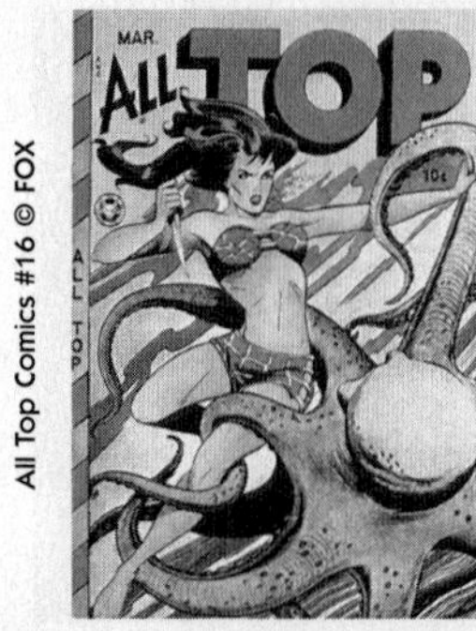

All Top Comics #16 © FOX

All Winners Comics #10 © MAR

GD VG FN VF VF/NM NM-
2.0 4.0 6.0 8.0 9.0 9.2

2(11/83)-Infinity, Inc. app. 3(9/84) 6.00
NOTE: *Buckler a-1-5; c-1, 3-5, 51. Kubert c-2, 7-18. JLA app. in 14, 15. JSA app. in 4, 14, 15, 19, 27, 28.*

ALL-STAR STORY OF THE DODGERS, THE
Stadium Communications: Apr, 1979 ($1.00)

1 2 4 6 9 13 16

ALL-STAR SUPERMAN (Also see FCBD edition in the Promotional Comics section)
DC Comics: Jan, 2006 - No. 12, Oct, 2008 ($2.99)

1-Grant Morrison-s/Frank Quitely-a/c 5.00
1-Variant-c by Neal Adams 20.00
1-Special Edition (2009, $1.00) r/#1 with "After Watchmen" cover logo frame 3.00
2-12: 3-Lois gets super powers. 7,8-Bizarro app. 3.00
Free Comic Book Day giveaway (6/08) reprints #1 2.00
Vol. 1 HC (2007, $19.99, dustjacket) r/#1-6; Bob Schreck intro. 20.00
Vol. 1 SC (2008, $12.99) r/#1-6; Schreck intro. 13.00
Vol. 2 HC (2009, $19.99, dustjacket) r/#7-12; Mark Waid intro. 20.00
Vol. 2 SC (2009, $12.99) r/#7-12; Mark Waid intro. 13.00

ALL STAR WESTERN (Formerly All Star Comics No. 1-57)
National Periodical Publ.: No. 58, Apr-May, 1951 - No. 119, June-July, 1961

58-Trigger Twins (ends #116), Strong Bow, The Roving Ranger & Don Caballero begin 45 90 135 284 480 675
59,60: Last 52 pgs. 27 54 81 158 259 360
61-66: 61-64-Toth-a 22 44 66 128 209 290
67-Johnny Thunder begins; Gil Kane-a 28 56 84 165 270 375
68-81: Last precode (2-3/55) 15 30 45 84 127 170
82-98: 97-1st S.A. issue 14 28 42 76 108 140
99-Frazetta-r/Jimmy Wakely #4 14 28 42 78 112 145
100 14 28 42 78 112 145
101-107,109-116,118,119 12 24 36 67 94 120
108-Origin J. Thunder; J. Thunder logo begins 22 44 66 128 209 290
117-Origin Super Chief 14 28 42 82 121 160
NOTE: *Gil Kane c(p)-58, 59, 61, 63, 64, 68, 69, 70-95(most), 97-199(most). Infantino art in most issues. Madame .44 app.- #117-119.*

ALL-STAR WESTERN (Weird Western Tales No. 12 on)
National Periodical Publications: Aug-Sept, 1970 - No. 11, Apr-May, 1972

1-Pow-Wow Smith-r; Infantino-a 5 10 15 34 55 75
2-Outlaw begins; El Diablo by Morrow begins; has cameos by Williamson, Torres, Kane, Giordano & Phil Seuling 5 10 15 32 51 70
3-Origin El Diablo 5 10 15 30 48 65
4-6: 5-Last Outlaw issue. 6-Billy the Kid begins, ends #8 3 6 9 21 32 42
7-9-(52 pgs.) 9-Frazetta-a, 3pgs.(r) 4 8 12 24 37 50
10-(52 pgs.) Jonah Hex begins (1st app., 2-3/72) 37 74 111 286 568 850
11-(52 pgs.) 2nd app. Jonah Hex; 1st cover 15 30 45 106 216 325
NOTE: *Neal Adams c-2-5; Aparo a-5. G. Kane a-3, 4, 6, 8. Kubert a-4r, 7-9r. Morrow a-2-4, 10, 11. No. 7-11 have 52 pgs.*

ALL SURPRISE (Becomes Jeanie #13 on) (Funny animal)
Timely/Marvel (CPC): Fall, 1943 - No. 12, Winter, 1946-47

1-Super Rabbit, Gandy & Sourpuss begin 39 78 117 240 395 550
2 20 40 60 114 182 250
3-10,12 15 30 45 88 137 185
11-Kurtzman "Pigtales" art 16 32 48 92 144 195

ALL TEEN (Formerly All Winners; All Winners & Teen Comics No. 21 on)
Marvel Comics (WFP): No. 20, January, 1947

20-Georgie, Mitzi, Patsy Walker, Willie app.; Syd Shores-c 18 36 54 103 162 220

ALL-TIME SPORTS COMICS (Formerly All Sports Comics)
Hillman Per.: V2, No. 4, Apr-May, 1949 - V2, No. 7, Oct-Nov, 1949 (All 52 pgs.)

V2#4 23 46 69 136 223 310
5-7: 5-(V1#5 inside)-Powell-a; Ty Cobb sty. 7-Krigstein-p; Walter Johnson & Knute Rockne sty 18 36 54 105 165 225

ALL TOP
William H. Wise Co.: 1944 (132 pgs.)

nn-Capt. V, Merciless the Sorceress, Red Robbins, One Round Hogan, Mike the M.P., Snooky, Pussy Katnip app. 34 68 102 199 325 450

ALL TOP COMICS (My Experience No. 19 on)
Fox Features Synd./Green Publ./Norlen Mag.: 1945; No. 2, Sum, 1946 - No. 18, Mar, 1949; 1957 - 1959

1-Cosmo Cat & Flash Rabbit begin (1st app.) 26 52 78 154 252 350
2 (#1-7 are funny animal) 14 28 42 80 115 150

GD VG FN VF VF/NM NM-
2.0 4.0 6.0 8.0 9.0 9.2

3-7: 7-Two diff. issues (7/47 & 9/47) 11 22 33 60 83 105
8-Blue Beetle, Phantom Lady, & Rulah, Jungle Goddess begin (11/47); Kamen-c 297 594 891 1901 3251 4600
9-Kamen-c 152 304 456 965 1658 2350
10-Kamen bondage-c 158 316 474 1003 1727 2450
11-13,15-17: 11,12-Rulah-c. 15-No Blue Beetle 123 246 369 787 1344 1900
14-No Blue Beetle; used in **SOTI**, illo- "Corpses of colored people strung up by their wrists" 181 362 543 1158 1979 2800
18-Dagar, Jo-Jo app; no Phantom Lady or Blue Beetle 77 154 231 493 847 1200
6(1957-Green Publ.)-Patoruzu the Indian; Cosmo Cat on cover only. 6(1958-Literary Ent.)-Muggy Doo; Cosmo Cat on cover only. 6(1959-Norlen)-Atomic Mouse; Cosmo Cat on-c only. 6(1959)-Little Eva. 6(Cornell)-Supermouse on-c 5 10 15 24 30 35
NOTE: *Jo-Jo by Kamen-12,18.*

ALL TRUE ALL PICTURE POLICE CASES
St. John Publishing Co.: Oct, 1952 - No. 2, Nov, 1952 (100 pgs.)

1-Three rebound St. John crime comics 45 90 135 284 480 675
2-Three comics rebound 34 68 102 199 325 450
NOTE: *Contents may vary.*

ALL-TRUE CRIME (...Cases No. 26-35; formerly Official True Crime Cases)
Marvel/Atlas Comics: No. 26, Feb, 1948 - No. 52, Sept, 1952
(OFI #26,27/CFI #28,29/LCC #30-46/LMC #47-52)

26(#1)-Syd Shores-c 34 68 102 199 325 450
27(4/48)-Electric chair-c 28 56 84 165 270 375
28-41,43-48,50-52: 35-37-Photo-c 14 28 42 78 112 145
42,49-Krigstein-a. 49-Used in **POP**, Pg 79 14 28 42 81 118 155
NOTE: *Colan a-46. Keller a-46. Robinson a-47, 50. Sale a-46. Shores c-26. Tuska a-48(3).*

ALL-TRUE DETECTIVE CASES (Kit Carson No. 5 on)
Avon Periodicals: #2, Apr-May, 1954 - No. 4, Aug-Sept, 1954

2(#1)-Wood-a 23 46 69 136 223 310
3-Kinstler-c 14 28 42 81 118 155
4-r/Gangsters And Gun Molls #2; Kamen-a 18 36 54 105 165 225
nn(100 pgs.)-7 pg. Kubert-a, Kinstler back-c 40 80 120 246 411 575

ALL TRUE ROMANCE (...Illustrated No. 3)
Artful Publ. #1-3/Harwell(Comic Media) #4-20?/Ajax-Farrell(Excellent Publ.) No. 22 on/Four Star Comic Corp.: 3/51 - No. 20, 12/54; No. 22, 3/55 - No. 30?, 7/57; No. 3(#31), 9/57;No. 4(#32), 11/57; No. 33, 2/58 - No. 34, 6/58

1 (3/51) 19 38 57 111 176 240
2 (10/51; 11/51 on-c) 12 24 36 67 94 120
3(12/51) - #5(5/52) 10 20 30 56 76 95
6-Wood-a, 9 pgs. (exceptional) 19 38 57 111 176 240
7-10 [two #7s: #7(11/52, 9/52 inside), #7(11/52, 11/52 inside)]. 10-Hollingsworth-c 9 18 27 52 69 85
11-13,16-19(9/54),20(12/54) (no #21): 11,13-Heck-a 8 16 24 42 54 65
14-Marijuana story 8 16 24 44 57 70
22: Last precode issue (1st Ajax, 3/55) 8 16 24 42 54 65
23-27,29,30(7/57): 29-Disbrow-a 7 14 21 37 46 55
28 (9/56)-L. B. Cole, Disbrow-a 11 22 33 64 90 115
3(#31, 9/57),4(#32, 11/57),33,34 (Farrell, '57- '58) 7 14 21 35 43 50

ALL WESTERN WINNERS (Formerly All Winners; becomes Western Winners with No. 5; see Two-Gun Kid No. 5)
Marvel Comics(CDS): No. 2, Winter, 1948-49 - No. 4, April, 1949

2-Black Rider (origin/1st app.) & his horse Satan, Kid Colt & his horse Steel, & Two-Gun Kid & his horse Cyclone begin; Shores c-2-4 74 148 222 470 810 1150
3-Anti-Wertham editorial 37 74 111 222 361 500
4-Black Rider i.d. revealed; Heath, Shores-a 37 74 111 222 361 500

ALL WINNERS COMICS (All Teen #20) (Also see Timely Presents: ...)
USA No. 1-7/WFP No. 10-19/YAI No. 21: Summer, 1941 - No. 19, Fall, 1946; No. 21, Winter, 1946-47; (No #20) (No. 21 continued from Young Allies No. 20)

1-The Angel & Black Marvel only app.; Capt. America by Simon & Kirby, Human Torch & Sub-Mariner begin (#1 was advertised as All Aces); 1st app. All-Winners Squad in text story by Stan Lee 1900 3800 5700 13,500 24,250 35,000
2-The Destroyer & The Whizzer begin; Simon & Kirby Captain America 514 1028 1542 3750 6625 9500
3 411 822 1233 2877 5039 7200
4-Classic War-c by Al Avison 423 822 1269 3067 5384 7700
5 300 600 900 1950 3375 4800
6-The Black Avenger only app.; no Whizzer story; Hitler, Hirohito & Mussolini-c 343 686 1029 2400 4200 6000
7-10 284 568 852 1818 3109 4400
11,13-18: 11-1st Atlas globe on-c (Winter, 1943-44; also see Human Torch #14).

Alpha Flight (3rd series) #1 © MAR

Altered Image #2 © Jim Valentino

Amazing Adult Fantasy #13 © MAR

	GD 2.0	VG 4.0	FN 6.0	VF 8.0	VF/NM 9.0	NM- 9.2
14-16-No Human Torch	187	374	561	1197	2049	2900
12-Red Skull story; last Destroyer; no Whizzer story	258	516	774	1651	2826	4000
19-(Scarce)-1st story app. & origin All Winners Squad (Capt. America & Bucky, Human Torch & Toro, Sub-Mariner, Whizzer, & Miss America; r-in Fantasy Masterpieces #10	757	1514	2271	5526	9763	14,000
21-(Scarce)-All Winners Squad; bondage-c	595	1190	1785	4350	7675	11,000

NOTE: *Everett Sub-Mariner-1, 3, 4; **Burgos** Torch-1, 3, 4. **Schomburg** c-1, 7-18. **Shores** c-19p, 21.*

(2nd Series - August, 1948, Marvel Comics (CDS))
(Becomes All Western Winners with No. 2)

	GD	VG	FN	VF	VF/NM	NM-
1-The Blonde Phantom, Capt. America, Human Torch, & Sub-Mariner app.	300	600	900	1950	3375	4800

ALL WINNERS COMICS 70th ANNIVERARY SPECIAL
Marvel Comics: Oct, 2009 ($3.99, one-shot)

1-New story of All Winners Squad; r/G.A. Capt Anerica app. from All Winners #12 4.00

ALL YOUR COMICS (See Fox Giants)
Fox Feature Syndicate (R. W. Voight): Spring, 1946 (36 pgs.)

	GD	VG	FN	VF	VF/NM	NM-
1-Red Robbins, Merciless the Sorceress app.	22	44	66	128	209	290

ALMANAC OF CRIME (See Fox Giants)

AL OF FBI (See Little Al of the FBI)

ALONE IN THE DARK (Based on video game)
Image Comics: Feb, 2003 ($4.95)

1-Matt Haley-c/a; Jean-Marc & Randy Lofficier-s 5.00

ALPHA AND OMEGA
Spire Christian Comics (Fleming H. Revell): 1978 (49¢)

	GD	VG	FN	VF	VF/NM	NM-
nn	2	4	6	8	11	14

ALPHA CENTURION (See Superman, 2nd Series & Zero Hour)
DC Comics: 1996 ($2.95, one-shot)

1 3.00

ALPHA FLIGHT (See X-Men #120,121 & X-Men/Alpha Flight)
Marvel Comics: Aug, 1983 - No. 130, Mar, 1994 (#52-on are direct sales only)

	NM-
1-(52 pgs.) Byrne-a begins (thru #28) -Wolverine & Nightcrawler cameo	5.00
2-28: 2-Vindicator becomes Guardian; origin Marrina & Alpha Flight. 3-Concludes origin Alpha Flight. 6-Origin Shaman. 7-Origin Snowbird. 10,11-Origin Sasquatch. 12-(52 pgs.)-Death of Guardian. 13-Wolverine app. 16,17-Wolverine cameo. 17-X-Men x-over (mostly r-/X-Men #109); 20-New headquarters. 25-Return of Guardian. 28-Last Byrne issue	3.50
29-32,35-49: 39-47,49-Portacio-a(i)	3.00
33,34-1st & 2nd app. Lady Deathstrike; Wolverine app. 34-Origin Wolverine	4.00
50-Double size; Portacio-a(i)	4.00
51-Jim Lee's 1st work at Marvel (10/87); Wolverine cameo; 1st Lee Wolverine; Portacio-a(i)	6.00
52,53-Wolverine app.; Lee-a on Wolverine; Portacio-a(i); 53-Lee/Portacio-a	4.00
54-73,76-86,91-99,101-105: 54,63,64-No Jim Lee-a. 54-Portacio-a(i). 55-62-Jim Lee-a(p). 71-Intro The Sorcerer (villain). 91-Dr. Doom app. 94-F.F. x-over. 99-Galactus, Avengers app. 102-Intro Weapon Omega	2.50
74,75,87-90,100: 74-Wolverine, Spider-Man & The Avengers app. 75-Double size ($1.95, 52 pgs.). 87-90-Wolverine. 4 part story w/Jim Lee-c. 89-Original Guardian returns. 100-($2.00, 52 pgs.)-Avengers & Galactus app.	4.00
106-Northstar revelation issue	3.50
106-2nd printing (direct sale only)	3.00
107-109,112-119,121-129: 107-X-Factor x-over. 112-Infinity War x-overs	3.00
110,111: Infinity War x-overs, Wolverine app. (brief). 111-Thanos cameo	3.00
120-($2.25)-Polybagged w/Paranormal Registration Act poster	3.00
130-($2.25, 52 pgs.)	4.00
Annual 1,2 (9/86, 12/87)	4.00
...Classics Vol. 1 TPB (2007, $24.99) r/#1-8; character profile pages; Byrne interview	25.00
Special V2#1(6/92, $2.50, 52 pgs.)-Wolverine-c/story	4.00

NOTE: ***Austin** c-1i, 2i, 53i. **Byrne** c-81, 82. **Guice** c-85, 91-99. **Jim Lee** a(p)-51, 53, 55-62, 64; c-53, 87-90. **Mignola** a-29-31p. **Whilce Portacio** a(i)-39-47, 49-54.*

ALPHA FLIGHT (2nd Series)
Marvel Comics: Aug, 1997 - No. 20, Mar, 1999 ($2.99/$1.99)

	NM-
1-($2.99)-Wraparound cover	6.00
2,3: 2-Variant-c	4.00
4-11: 8,9-Wolverine-c/app.	3.00
12-($2.99) Death of Sasquatch; wraparound-c	4.00
13-20	3.00
.../Inhumans '98 Annual ($3.50) Raney-a	3.50

ALPHA FLIGHT (3rd Series)
Marvel Comics: May, 2004 - No. 12, April, 2005 ($2.99)

	NM-
1-12: 1-6-Lobdell-s/Henry-c/a	3.00
... Vol. 1: You Gotta Be Kiddin' Me (2004, $14.99) r/#1-6	15.00

ALPHA FLIGHT: IN THE BEGINNING
Marvel Comics: July, 1997 ($1.95, one-shot)

(-1)-Flashback w/Wolverine 3.00

ALPHA FLIGHT SPECIAL
Marvel Comics: July, 1991 - No. 4, Oct, 1991 ($1.50, limited series)

1-4: 1-3-r-A. Flight #97-99 w/covers. 4-r-A.Flight #100 3.00

ALPHA KORPS
Diversity Comics: Sept, 1996 ($2.50)

1-Origin/1st app. Alpha Korps 3.00

ALTERED IMAGE
Image Comics: Apr, 1998 - No. 3, Sept, 1998 ($2.50, limited series)

1-3-Spawn, Witchblade, Savage Dragon; Valentino-s/a 3.00

ALTER EGO
First Comics: May, 1986 - No. 4, Nov, 1986 (Mini-series)

1-4 3.00

ALTER NATION
Image Comics: Feb, 2004 - No. 4, Jun, 2004 ($2.95, limited series)

1-4: 1-Two covers by Art Adams and Barberi; Barberi-a 3.00

ALVIN (TV) (See Four Color Comics No. 1042 or Three Chipmunks #1)
Dell Publishing Co.: Oct-Dec, 1962 - No. 28, Oct, 1973

	GD	VG	FN	VF	VF/NM	NM-
12-021-212 (#1)	9	18	27	60	100	140
2	5	10	15	35	55	75
3-10	5	10	15	30	48	65
11-"Chipmunks sing the Beatles' Hits"	5	10	15	34	55	75
12-28	4	8	12	24	37	50
Alvin For President (10/64)	5	10	15	30	48	65
...& His Pals in Merry Christmas with Clyde Crashcup & Leonardo 1 (02-120-402)-(12-2/64)	7	14	21	50	83	115
Reprinted in 1966 (12-023-604)	4	8	12	24	37	50

ALVIN & THE CHIPMUNKS
Harvey Comics: July, 1992 - No. 5, May, 1994

1-5: 1-Richie Rich app. 5.00

AMALGAM AGE OF COMICS, THE: THE DC COMICS COLLECTION
DC Comics: 1996 ($12.95, trade paperback)

nn-r/Amazon, Assassins, Doctor Strangefate, JLX, Legends of the Dark Claw, & Super Soldier 13.00

AMANDA AND GUNN
Image Comics: Apr, 1997 - No. 4, Oct, 1997 ($2.95, B&W, limited series)

1-4 3.00

AMAZING ADULT FANTASY (Formerly Amazing Adventures #1-6; becomes Amazing Fantasy #15) (See Amazing Fantasy for Omnibus HC reprint of #1-15)
Marvel Comics Group (AMI): No. 7, Dec, 1961 - No. 14, July, 1962

	GD	VG	FN	VF	VF/NM	NM-
7-Ditko-c/a begins, ends #14	44	88	132	352	714	1075
8-Last 10¢ issue	37	74	111	286	568	850
9-13: 12-1st app. Mailbag. 13-Anti-communist sty	36	72	108	281	553	825
13-2nd printing (1994)	2	4	6	8	10	12
14-Prototype issue (Professor X)	37	74	111	292	584	875

AMAZING ADVENTURE FUNNIES (Fantoman No. 2 on)
Centaur Publications: June, 1940 - No. 2, Sept. 1940

	GD	VG	FN	VF	VF/NM	NM-
1-The Fantom of the Fair by Gustavson (r/Amaz. Mystery Funnies V2#7,V2#8), The Arrow, Skyrocket Steele From the Year X by Everett (r/AMF #2); Burgos-a	174	348	522	1114	1907	2700
2-Reprints; Published after Fantoman #2	114	228	342	724	1242	1760

NOTE: ***Burgos** a-1(2). **Everett** a-1(3). **Gustavson** a-1(5), 2(3). **Pinajian** a-2.*

AMAZING ADVENTURES (Also see Boy Cowboy & Science Comics)
Ziff-Davis Publ. Co.: 1950; No. 1, Nov, 1950 - No. 6, Fall, 1952 (Painted covers)

	GD	VG	FN	VF	VF/NM	NM-
1950 (no month given) (8-1/2x11) (8 pgs.) Has the front & back cover plus Schomburg story used in Amazing Advs. #1 (Sent to subscribers of Z-D s/f magazines & ordered through mail for 10¢. Used to test market)	65	130	195	416	708	1000
1-Wood, Schomburg, Anderson, Whitney-a	84	168	252	538	919	1300
2-5: 2-Schomburg-a. 2,4,5-Anderson-a. 3,5-Starr-a	41	82	123	256	428	600
6-Krigstein-a	41	82	123	260	435	610

AMAZING ADVENTURES (Becomes Amazing Adult Fantasy #7 on) (See Amazing Fantasy for Omnibus HC reprint of #1-15)

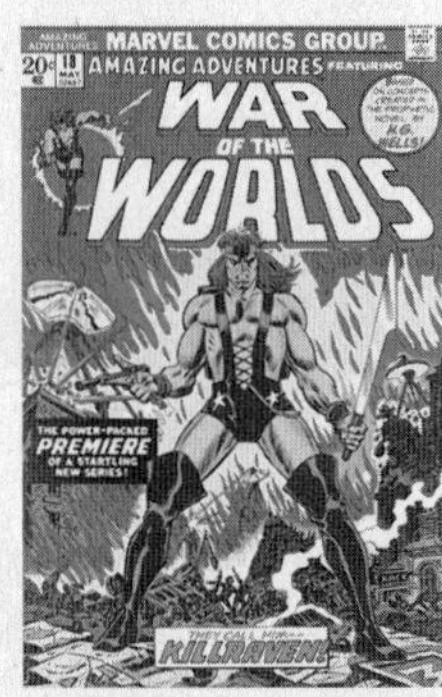

Amazing Adventures #18 © MAR

Amazing Fantasy (2004 series) #1 © MAR

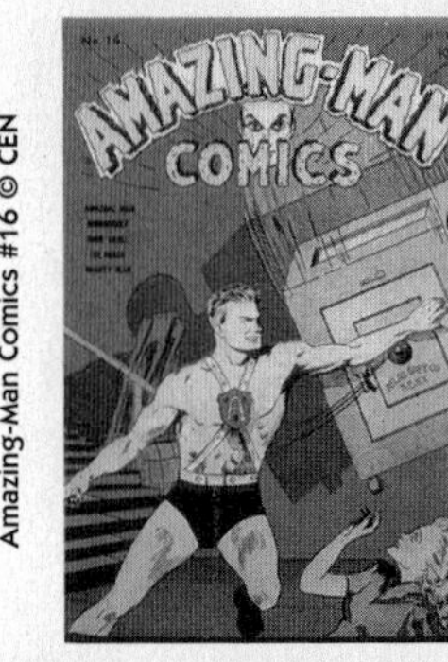

Amazing-Man Comics #16 © CEN

GD VG FN VF VF/NM NM-
2.0 4.0 6.0 8.0 9.0 9.2

GD VG FN VF VF/NM NM-
2.0 4.0 6.0 8.0 9.0 9.2

Atlas Comics (AMI)/Marvel Comics No. 3 on: June, 1961 - No. 6, Nov, 1961

1-Origin Dr. Droom (1st Marvel-Age Superhero) by Kirby; Kirby/Ditko-a (5 pgs.)
Ditko & Kirby-a in all; Kirby monster c-1-6 108 216 324 918 1854 2800
2 44 88 132 352 714 1075
3-6: 6-Last Dr. Droom 39 78 117 312 619 925

AMAZING ADVENTURES
Marvel Comics Group: Aug, 1970 - No. 39, Nov, 1976

1-Inhumans by Kirby(p) & Black Widow (1st app. in Tales of Suspense #52)
double feature begins 7 14 21 47 76 105
2-4: 2-F.F. brief app. 4-Last Inhumans by Kirby 4 8 12 22 34 45
5-8: Adams-a(p); 8-Last Black Widow; last 15¢-c 5 10 15 32 51 70
9,10: Magneto app. 10-Last Inhumans (origin-r by Kirby)
4 8 12 22 34 45
11-New Beast begins(1st app. in mutated form; origin in flashback); X-Men cameo in
flashback (#11-17 are X-Men tie-ins) 18 36 54 131 266 400
12-17: 12-Beast battles Iron Man. 13-Brotherhood of Evil Mutants x-over from X-Men.
15-X-Men app. 16-Rutland Vermont - Bald Mountain Halloween x-over; Juggernaut app.
17-Last Beast (origin); X-Men app. 8 16 24 56 93 130
18-War of the Worlds begins (5/73); 1st app. Killraven; Neal Adams-a(p)
3 6 9 20 30 40
19-35,38,39: 19-Chaykin-a. 25-Buckler-a. 35-Giffen's first published story (art),
along with Deadly Hands of Kung-Fu #22 (3/76) 1 3 4 6 8 10
36,37-(Regular 25¢ edition)(7-8/76) 1 3 4 6 8 10
36,37-(30¢-c variants, limited distribution) 6 12 18 37 59 80
NOTE: ***N. Adams** c-6-8. **Buscema** a-1p, 2p. **Colan** a-3-5p, 26p. **Ditko** a-24r. **Everett** a(i)3-5, 7-9. **Giffen** a-35i, 38p. **G. Kane** c-11, 25p, 29p. **Ploog** a-12i. **Russell** a-27-32, 34-37, 39; c-28, 30-32, 33i, 34, 35, 37, 39i. **Starliing** a-17. **Starlin** c-15p, 16, 17, 27. **Sutton** a-11-15p.*

AMAZING ADVENTURES
Marvel Comics Group: Dec, 1979 - No. 14, Jan, 1981

V2#1-Reprints story/X-Men #1 & 38 (origins) 1 3 4 6 8 10
2-14: 2-6-Early X-Men-r. 7,8-Origin Iceman 1 2 3 4 5 7
NOTE: ***Byrne** c-6p, 9p. **Kirby** a-1-14r; c-7, 9. **Steranko** a-12r. **Tuska** a-7-9.*

AMAZING ADVENTURES
Marvel Comics: July, 1988 ($4.95, squarebound, one-shot, 80 pgs.)

1-Anthology; Austin, Golden-a 5.00

AMAZING ADVENTURES OF CAPTAIN CARVEL AND HIS CARVEL CRUSADERS, THE
(See Carvel Comics in the Promotional Comics section)

AMAZING CHAN & THE CHAN CLAN, THE (TV)
Gold Key: May, 1973 - No. 4, Feb, 1974 (Hanna-Barbera)

1-Warren Tufts-a in all 4 8 12 22 34 45
2-4 3 6 9 16 23 30

AMAZING COMICS (Complete Comics No. 2)
Timely Comics (EPC): Fall, 1944

1-The Destroyer, The Whizzer, The Young Allies (by Sekowsky), Sergeant Dix;
Schomburg-c 265 530 795 1694 2897 4100

AMAZING DETECTIVE CASES (Formerly Suspense No. 2?)
Marvel/Atlas Comics (CCC): No. 3, Nov, 1950 - No. 14, Sept, 1952

3 30 60 90 177 289 400
4-6 18 36 54 103 162 220
7-10 16 32 48 92 144 195
11,12: 11-(3/52)-Horror format begins. 12-Krigstein-a 39 78 117 240 395 550
13-(Scarce)-Everett-a; electrocution-c/story 41 82 123 256 428 600
14 36 72 108 216 351 485
NOTE: ***Colan** a-9. **Maneely** c-13. **Sekowsky** a-12. **Sinnott** a-13. **Tuska** a-10.*

AMAZING FANTASY (Formerly Amazing Adult Fantasy #7-14)
Atlas Magazines/Marvel: #15, Aug, 1962 (Sept, 1962 shown in indicia); #16, Dec, 1995 - #18, Feb, 1996

15-Origin/1st app. of Spider-Man by Steve Ditko (11 pgs.); 1st app. Aunt May & Uncle Ben;
Kirby/Ditko-c 3500 7000 14,000 42,000 83,500 125,000
16-18 ('95-'96, $3.95): Kurt Busiek scripts; painted-c/a by Paul Lee 4.00
Amazing Fantasy Omnibus HC ("Amazing Adult Fantasy" on-c) (2007, $75.00, dustjacket)
r/Amazing Adventures #1-6, Amazing Adult Fantasy #7-14 and Amazing Fantasy #15 with
letter pages; foreword by Bissette; cover gallery from '70s reprint titles 75.00

AMAZING FANTASY (Continues from #6 in Araña: The Heart of the Spider)
Marvel Comics: Aug, 2004 - No. 20, June, 2006 ($2.99)

1-Intro. Anya Corazon; Fiona Avery-s/Mark Brooks-c/a 4.00
2-14,16-20: 3,4-Roger Cruz-a. 7-Intro. new Scorpion; Kirk-a. 10-Intro. Vampire By Night
13,14-Back-up Captain Universe stories. 16-20-Death's Head 3.00
15-($3.99) Spider-Man app.; intro 6 new characters incl. Mastermind Excello seen in World
War Hulk series; s/a by various 4.00
Death's Head 3.0: Unnatural Selection TPB (2006, $13.99) r/#16-20 14.00
Scorpion: Poison Tomorrow (2005, $7.99, digest) r/#7-13 8.00

AMAZING GHOST STORIES (Formerly Nightmare)
St. John Publishing Co.: No. 14, Oct, 1954 - No. 16, Feb, 1955

14-Pit & the Pendulum story by Kinstler; Baker-c 36 72 108 211 343 475
15-r/Weird Thrillers #5; Baker-c, Powell-a 26 52 78 152 249 345
16-Kubert reprints of Weird Thrillers #4; Baker-c; Roussos, Tuska-a;
Kinstler-a (1 pg.) 26 52 78 154 252 350

AMAZING HIGH ADVENTURE
Marvel Comics: 8/84; No. 2, 10/85; No. 3, 10/86 - No. 5, 1986 ($2.00)

1-5: Painted-c on all. 3,4-Baxter paper. 4-Bolton-c/a. 5-Bolton-a 4.00
NOTE: ***Bissette** a-4. **Severin** a-1, 3. **Sienkiewicz** a-1,2. **Paul Smith** a-2. **Williamson** a-2i.*

AMAZING JOY BUZZARDS
Image Comics: 2005 - No. 4, 2005 ($2.95, B&W with pink spot color in #1)

1-4-Mark Andrew Smith-s/Dan Hipp-a. 1-Mahfood back-c. 2-Morse back-c 3.00
Vol. 1 TPB (2005, $11.95) r/#1-4; bonus art and character design sketches 12.00
TPB (2008, $19.99) r/#1-4 and Vol. 2 #1-5 20.00

AMAZING JOY BUZZARDS (Volume 2)
Image Comics: Oct, 2005 - No. 5, Aug, 2006 ($2.99, B&W)

1-5: 1-Mark Andrew Smith-s/Dan Hipp-a. 4-Mahfood-a; Crosland-a. 5-Holgate-a 3.00
Vol. 2 TPB (2006, $12.99) r/#1-4; bonus art, pin-ups and character sketches 13.00

AMAZING-MAN COMICS (Formerly Motion Picture Funnies Weekly?)
(Also see Stars And Stripes Comics)
Centaur Publications: No. 5, Sept, 1939 - No. 26, Jan, 1942

5(#1)(Rare)-Origin/1st app. A-Man the Amazing Man by Bill Everett; The Cat-Man by Tarpe
Mills (also #8), Mighty Man by Filchock, Minimidget & sidekick Ritty, & The Iron Skull by
Burgos begins 1550 3100 4650 11,600 20,800 30,000
6-Origin The Amazing Man retold; The Shark begins; Ivy Menace by Tarpe Mills app.
343 686 1029 2400 4200 6000
7-Magician From Mars begins; ends #11 258 516 774 1651 2826 4000
8-Cat-Man dresses as woman 194 388 582 1242 2121 3000
9-Magician From Mars battles the 'Elemental Monster,' swiped into The Spectre in More Fun
#54 & 55. Ties w/Marvel Mystery #4 for 1st Nazi War-c on a comic (2/40)
206 412 618 1318 2259 3200
10,11: 11-Zardi, the Eternal Man begins; ends #16; Amazing Man dons costume;
last Everett issue 145 290 435 921 1586 2250
12,13 135 270 405 864 1482 2100
14-Reef Kinkaid, Rocke Wayburn (ends #20), & Dr. Hypno (ends #21) begin;
no Zardi or Chuck Hardy 110 220 330 704 1202 1700
15,17-20: 15-Zardi returns; no Rocke Wayburn. 17-Dr. Hypno returns; no Zardi
97 194 291 621 1061 1500
16-Mighty Man's powers of super strength & ability to shrink & grow explained; Rocke Wayburn
returns; no Dr. Hypno; Al Avison (a character) begins, ends #18 (a tribute to the famed
artist) 103 206 309 659 1130 1600
21-Origin Dash Dartwell (drug-use story); origin & only app. T.N.T.
113 226 339 718 1234 1750
22-Dash Dartwell, the Human Meteor & The Voice app; last Iron Skull & The Shark;
Silver Streak app. (classic-c) 226 452 678 1446 2473 3500
23-Two Amazing Man stories; intro/origin Tommy the Amazing Kid; The Marksman only app.
87 174 261 553 952 1350
24-King of Darkness, Nightshade, & Blue Lady begin; end #26; 1st app. Super-Ann
87 174 261 553 952 1350
25,26 (Scarce): Meteor Martin by Wolverton in both; 26-Electric Ray app.
142 284 426 909 1555 2200
NOTE: ***Everett** a-5-11; c-5-11. **Gilman** a-14-20. **Giunta/Mirando** a-7-10. **Sam Glanzman** a-14-16, 18-21, 23. **Louis Glanzman** a-6, 9-11, 14-21; c-13-19, 21. **Robert Golden** a-9. **Gustavson** a-6; c-22, 23. **Lubbers** a-14-21. **Simon** a-10. **Frank Thomas** a-6, 9-11, 14, 15, 17-21.*

AMAZING MYSTERIES (Formerly Sub-Mariner Comics No. 31)
Marvel Comics (CCC): No. 32, May, 1949 - No. 35, Jan, 1950 (1st Marvel Horror Comic)

32-The Witness app. 90 180 270 576 988 1400
33-Horror format 41 82 123 256 428 600
34,35: Changes to Crime. 34,35-Photo-c 21 42 63 126 206 285

AMAZING MYSTERY FUNNIES
Centaur Publications: Aug, 1938 - No. 24, Sept, 1940 (All 52 pgs.)

V1#1-Everett-c(1st); Dick Kent Adv. story; Skyrocket Steele in the Year X on cover only
377 754 1131 2639 4620 6600
2-Everett 1st-a (Skyrocket Steele) 200 400 600 1280 2190 3100
3 110 220 330 704 1202 1700
3(#4, 12/38)-nn on cover, #3 on inside; bondage-c

Amazing Spider-Girl #0 © MAR

Amazing Spider-Man #16 © MAR

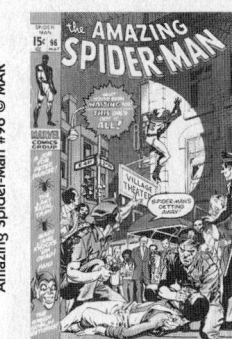

Amazing Spider-Man #96 © MAR

	GD 2.0	VG 4.0	FN 6.0	VF 8.0	VF/NM 9.0	NM- 9.2
	100	200	300	635	1093	1550
V2#1-4,6: 2-Drug use story. 3-Air-Sub DX begins by Burgos. 4-Dan Hastings, Sand Hog begins (ends #5). 6-Last Skyrocket Steele	84	168	252	538	919	1300
5-Classic Everett-c	187	374	561	1197	2049	2900
7 (Scarce)-Intro. The Fantom of the Fair & begins; Everett, Gustavson, Burgos-a	360	720	1080	2520	4410	6300
8-Origin & 1st app. Speed Centaur	148	296	444	947	1624	2300
9-11: 11-Self portrait and biog. of Everett; Jon Linton begins; early Robot cover (11/39)	84	168	252	538	919	1300
12 (Scarce)-1st Space Patrol; Wolverton-a (12/39); new costume Phantom of the Fair	200	400	600	1280	2190	3100
V3#1(#17, 1/40)-Intro. Bullet; Tippy Taylor serial begins, ends #24 (continued in The Arrow #2)	84	168	252	538	919	1300
18,20: 18-Fantom of the Fair by Gustavson	81	162	243	518	884	1250
19,21-24: Space Patrol by Wolverton in all	97	194	291	621	1061	1500

NOTE: ***Burgos** a-V2#3-9. **Eisner** a-V1#2, 3(2). **Everett** a-V1#2-4, V2#1, 3-6; c-V1#1-4,V2#3, 5, 18. **Filchock** a-V2#9. **Flessel** a-V2#6. **Guardineer** a-V1#4, V2#4-6; **Gustavson** a-V2#4, 5, 9-12, V3#1, 18, 19; c-V2#7, 9, 12, V3#1, 21, 22; **McWilliams** a-V2#9, 10. **TarpeMills** a-V2#2, 4-6, 9-12, V3#1. **Leo Morey**(Pulp artist) c-V2#10; text illo-V2#11. **FrankThomas** a-6-V2#11. **Webster** a-V2#4.*

AMAZING SAINTS
Logos International: 1974 (39¢)

nn-True story of Phil Saint	2	4	6	9	13	16

AMAZING SCARLET SPIDER
Marvel Comics: Nov, 1995 - No. 2, Dec, 1995 ($1.95, limited series)

1,2: Replaces "Amazing Spider-Man" for two issues. 1-Venom/Carnage cameos. 2-Green Goblin & Joystick-c/app. 3.00

AMAZING SCREW-ON HEAD, THE
Dark Horse Comics (Maverick): May, 2002 ($2.99, one-shot)

1-Mike Mignola-s/a/c 3.00

AMAZING SPIDER-GIRL (Also see Spider-Girl and What If...? (2nd series) #105)
Marvel Comics: No. 0, 2006; No. 1, Dec, 2006 - No. 30, May, 2009 ($2.99)

0-($1.99) Recap of the Spider-Girl series and character profiles; A.F. #15 cover swipe 2.50
1-14,16-24,26-($2.99) Frenz & Buscema-a. 9-Carnage returns. 19-Has #17 on cover 3.00
15,25,30-($3.99) 15-10th Anniversary issue. 25-Three covers 4.00
... Vol. 1: What Ever Happened to the Daughter of Spider-Man? TPB (2007, $14.99) r/#0-6 15.00
... Vol. 2: Comes the Carnage! TPB (2007, $13.99) r/#7-12 14.00
... Vol. 3: Mind Games TPB (2008, $13.99) r/#13-18 14.00

AMAZING SPIDER-MAN, THE (See All Detergent Comics, Amazing Fantasy, America's Best TV Comics, Aurora, Deadly Foes of..., Fireside Book Series, Friendly Neighborhood..., Giant-Size..., Giant Size Super-Heroes Featuring..., Marvel Age..., Marvel Collectors Item Classics, Marvel Fanfare, Marvel Graphic Novel, Marvel Knights..., Marvel Spec. Ed., Marvel Tales, Marvel Team-Up, Marvel Treasury Ed., New Avengers, Nothing Can Stop the Juggernaut, Official Marvel Index To..., Peter Parker..., Power Record Comics, Spectacular..., Spider-Man, Spider-Man Digest, Spider-Man Saga, Spider-Man 2099, Spider-Man Vs. Wolverine, Spidey Super Stories, Strange Tales Annual #2, Superman Vs. ..., Try-Out Winner Book, Ultimate Marvel Team-Up, Ultimate Spider-Man, Web of Spider- Man & Within Our Reach)

AMAZING SPIDER-MAN, THE
Marvel Comics Group: March, 1963 - No. 441, Nov, 1998

	GD 2.0	VG 4.0	FN 6.0	VF 8.0	VF/NM 9.0	NM- 9.2
1-Retells origin by Steve Ditko; 1st Fantastic Four x-over (ties with F.F. #12 as first Marvel x-over); intro. John Jameson & The Chameleon; Spider-Man's 2nd app.; Kirby/Ditko-c; Ditko-c/a #1-38	1667	3334	5000	15,000	34,500	54,000
1-Reprint from the Golden Record Comic set	17	34	51	122	249	375
With record (1966)	25	50	75	183	367	550
2-1st app. the Vulture & the Terrible Tinkerer	393	786	1179	3537	7269	11,000
3-1st app. Doc Octopus; 1st full-length story; Human Torch cameo; Spider-Man pin-up by Ditko	321	642	963	2889	5945	9000
4-Origin & 1st app. The Sandman (see Strange Tales #115 for 2nd app.); 1st monthly issue; intro. Betty Brant & Liz Allen	267	534	801	2336	4768	7200
5-Dr. Doom app.	215	430	645	1881	3841	5800
6-1st app. Lizard	174	348	522	1523	3112	4700
7-Vs. The Vulture	115	230	345	978	1989	3000
8-Fantastic Four app. in back-up story by Kirby & Ditko	90	180	270	765	1558	2350
9-Origin & 1st app. Electro (2/64)	119	238	357	1012	2056	3100
10-1st app. Big Man & The Enforcers	100	200	300	850	1725	2600
11-1st app. Bennett Brant	96	192	288	816	1658	2500
12-Doc Octopus unmasks Spider-Man-c/story	81	162	243	689	1395	2100
13-1st app. Mysterio	112	224	336	952	1926	2900
14-(7/64)-1st app. The Green Goblin (c/story)(Norman Osborn); Hulk x-over	170	340	510	1488	3044	4600
15-1st app. Kraven the Hunter; 1st mention of Mary Jane Watson (not shown)	85	170	255	723	1462	2200
16-Spider-Man battles Daredevil (1st x-over 9/64); still in old yellow costume	73	146	219	621	1261	1900
17-2nd app. Green Goblin (c/story); Human Torch x-over (also in #18 & #21)	81	162	243	689	1395	2100
18-1st app. Ned Leeds who later becomes Hobgoblin; Fantastic Four cameo; 3rd app. Sandman	48	96	144	400	813	1225
19-Sandman app.	38	76	114	304	602	900
20-Origin & 1st app. The Scorpion	65	130	195	553	1127	1700
21-2nd app. The Beetle (see Strange Tales #123)	39	78	117	312	619	925
22-1st app. Princess Python	38	76	114	304	602	900
23-3rd app. The Green Goblin-c/story; Norman Osborn app.; Marvel Masterwork pin-up by Ditko; fan letter by Jim Shooter	48	96	144	384	780	1175
24	36	72	108	281	553	825
25-(6/65)-1st brief app. Mary Jane Watson (face not shown); 1st app. Spencer Smythe; Norman Osborn app.	39	78	117	312	619	925
26-4th app. The Green Goblin-c/story; 1st app. Crime Master; dies in #27	40	80	120	320	635	950
27-5th app. The Green Goblin-c/story; Norman Osborn app.	39	78	117	312	619	925
28-Origin & 1st app. Molten Man (9/65, scarcer in high grade)	81	162	243	689	1395	2100
29,30	28	56	84	204	415	625
31-1st app. Harry Osborn who later becomes 2nd Green Goblin, Gwen Stacy & Prof. Warren.	32	64	96	246	486	725
32-38: 34-4th app. Kraven the Hunter. 36-1st app. Looter. 37-Intro. Norman Osborn. 38-(7/66)-2nd brief app. Mary Jane Watson (face not shown); last Ditko issue	23	46	69	168	334	500
39-The Green Goblin-c/story; Green Goblin's i.d. revealed as Norman Osborn; Romita-a begins (8/66; see Daredevil #16 for 1st Romita-a on Spider-Man)	34	68	102	267	526	785
40-1st told origin The Green Goblin-c/story	38	76	114	304	602	900
41-1st app. Rhino	34	68	102	262	519	775
42-(11/66)-3rd app. Mary Jane Watson (cameo in last 2 panels); 1st time face is shown	21	42	63	150	300	450
43-49: 44,45-2nd & 3rd app. The Lizard. 46-Intro. Shocker. 47-M. J. Watson & Peter Parker 1st date. 47-Green Goblin cameo; Harry & Norman Osborn app. 47,49-5th & 6th app. Kraven the Hunter	16	32	48	114	232	350
50-1st app. Kingpin (7/67)	58	116	174	493	997	1500
51-2nd app. Kingpin; Joe Robertson 1-panel cameo	22	44	66	159	317	475
52-58,60: 52-1st app. Joe Robertson & 3rd app. Kingpin. 56-1st app. Capt. George Stacy. 57,58-Ka-Zar app.	13	26	39	89	170	250
59-1st app. Brainwasher (alias Kingpin); 1st-c app. M. J. Watson	13	26	39	94	185	275
61-74: 61-1st Gwen Stacy cover app. 67-1st app. Randy Robertson. 69-Kingpin-c. 69,70-Kingpin app. 73-1st app. Silvermane. 74-Last 12¢ issue	10	20	30	71	128	185
75-83,87-89,91,92,95,99: 78,79-1st app. The Prowler. 83-1st app. Schemer & Vanessa (Kingpin's wife)	9	18	27	63	107	150
84-86,93: 84,85-Kingpin-c/story. 86-Re-intro & origin Black Widow in new costume. 93-1st app. Arthur Stacy	9	18	27	64	110	155
90-Death of Capt. Stacy	10	20	30	72	131	190
94-Origin retold	10	20	30	73	134	195
96-98-Green Goblin app. (97,98-Green Goblin-c); drug books not approved by CCA	11	22	33	75	138	200
100-Anniversary issue (9/71); Green Goblin cameo (2 pgs.)	14	28	42	99	200	300
101-1st app. Morbius the Living Vampire; Wizard cameo; last 15¢ issue (10/71)	17	34	51	122	249	375
101-Silver ink 2nd printing (9/92, $1.75)						3.00
102-Origin & 2nd app. Morbius (25¢, 52 pgs.)	12	24	36	87	164	240
103-118: 104,111-Kraven the Hunter-c/stories. 108-1st app. Sha-Shan. 109-Dr. Strange-c/story (6/72). 110-1st app. Gibbon. 113-1st app. Hammerhead. 116-118-reprints story from Spectacular Spider-Man Mag. in color with some changes	7	14	21	47	76	105
119,120-Spider-Man vs. Hulk (4 & 5/73)	9	18	27	65	113	160
121-Death of Gwen Stacy (6/73) (killed by Green Goblin) (reprinted in Marvel Tales #98 & 192)	20	40	60	140	283	425
122-Death of The Green Goblin-c/story (7/73) (reprinted in Marvel Tales #99 & 192)	20	40	60	144	290	435
123,126-128: 123-Cage app. 126-1st mention of Harry Osborn becoming Green Goblin	6	12	18	43	69	95
124-1st app. Man-Wolf (9/73)	7	14	21	49	80	110
125-Man-Wolf origin	7	14	21	45	73	100
129-1st app. The Punisher (2/74); 1st app. Jackal	39	78	117	312	619	925
130-133: 131-Last 20¢ issue	6	12	18	37	59	80

Amazing Spider-Man #243 © MAR

Amazing Spider-Man #368 © MAR

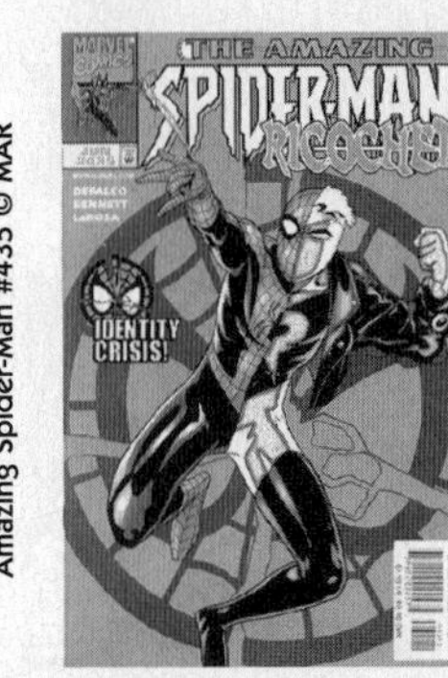

Amazing Spider-Man #435 © MAR

	GD 2.0	VG 4.0	FN 6.0	VF 8.0	VF/NM 9.0	NM- 9.2
134-(7/74); 1st app. Tarantula; Harry Osborn discovers Spider-Man's ID; Punisher cameo	6	12	18	41	66	90
135-2nd full Punisher app. (8/74)	9	18	27	63	107	150
136-1st app. Harry Osborn Green Goblin in costume	8	16	24	56	93	130
137-Green Goblin-c/story (2nd Harry Osborn Goblin)	6	12	18	43	69	95
138-141: 139-1st Grizzly. 140-1st app. Glory Grant	4	8	12	24	37	50
142,143-Gwen Stacy clone cameos: 143-1st app. Cyclone	4	8	12	24	37	50
144-147: 144-Full app. of Gwen Stacy clone. 145,146-Gwen Stacy clone storyline continues. 147-Spider-Man learns Gwen Stacy is clone	4	8	12	24	37	50
148-Jackal revealed	4	8	12	26	41	55
149-Spider-Man clone story begins, clone dies (?); origin of Jackal	7	14	21	47	76	105
150-Spider-Man decides he is not the clone	4	8	12	26	41	55
151-Spider-Man disposes of clone body	4	8	12	26	41	55
152-160-(Regular 25¢ editions). 159-Last 25¢ issue(8/76)	3	6	9	20	30	40
155-159-(30¢-c variants, limited distribution)	7	14	21	49	80	110
161-Nightcrawler app. from X-Men; Punisher cameo; Wolverine & Colossus app.	4	8	12	24	37	50
162-Punisher, Nightcrawler app.; 1st Jigsaw	4	8	12	24	37	50
163-168: 167-1st app. Will O' The Wisp	3	6	9	16	23	30
169-173-(Regular 30¢ edition). 169-Clone story recapped; Stan Lee cameo. 171-Nova app.	3	6	9	16	23	30
169-173-(35¢-c variants, limited dist.)(6-10/77)	14	28	42	95	188	280
174,175-Punisher app.	3	6	9	18	27	35
176-180-Green Goblin app.	3	6	9	19	29	38
181-188: 181-Origin retold; gives life history of Spidey; Punisher cameo in flashback (1 panel). 182-(7/78)-Peter's first proposal to Mary Jane, but she declines (in #183)	3	6	9	14	20	25
189,190-Byrne-a	3	6	9	16	23	30
191-193,196-199: 193-Peter & Mary Jane break up. 196-Faked death of Aunt May	2	4	6	11	16	20
NOTE: *Whitman 3-packs containing #192-194,196 exist.*						
194-1st app. Black Cat	5	10	15	32	51	70
195-2nd app. Black Cat	3	6	9	16	23	30
200-Giant origin issue (1/80)	4	8	12	22	34	45
201,202-Punisher app.	3	6	9	14	19	24
203-205,207,208,210-219: 203-3rd app. Dazzler (4/80). 210-1st app. Madame Web. 212-1st app. & origin of Hydro-Man	2	4	6	8	10	12
206-Byrne-a	2	4	6	9	12	15
209-Origin & 1st app. Calypso (10/80)	2	4	6	11	16	20
220-237: 225-(2/82)-Foolkiller-c/story. 226,227-Black Cat returns. 234-Free 16 pg. insert "Marvel Guide to Collecting Comics". 235-Origin Will-'O-The-Wisp. 236-Tarantula dies	1	3	4	6	8	10
238-(3/83)-1st app. Hobgoblin (Ned Leeds); came with skin "Tattooz" decal.						
NOTE: The same decal appears in the more common Fantastic Four #252 which is being removed & placed in this issue as incentive to increase value						
(Value listed is with or without tattooz)	8	16	24	54	90	125
239-2nd app. Hobgoblin & 1st battle w/Spidey	4	8	12	28	44	60
240-243,246-248: 241-Origin The Vulture. 242-Mary Jane Watson cameo (last panel). 243-Reintro Mary Jane after 4 year absence	1	3	4	6	8	10
244-3rd app. Hobgoblin (cameo)	2	4	6	9	12	15
245-(10/83)-4th app. Hobgoblin (cameo); Lefty Donovan gains powers of Hobgoblin & battles Spider-Man	2	4	6	9	12	15
249-251: 3 part Hobgoblin/Spider-Man battle. 249-Retells origin & death of 1st Green Goblin. 251-Last old costume	2	4	6	9	13	16
252-Spider-Man dons new black costume (5/84); ties with Marvel Team-Up #141 & Spectacular Spider-Man #90 for 1st new costume in regular title (See Marvel Super-Heroes Secret Wars #8 (12/84) for acquisition of costume)	5	10	15	30	48	65
253-1st app. The Rose	2	4	6	9	12	15
254-258: 256-1st app. Puma. 257-Hobgoblin cameo; 2nd app. Puma; M.J. Watson reveals she knows Spidey's i.d. 258-Hobgoblin app.	1	3	4	6	8	10
259-Full Hobgoblin app.; Spidey back to old costume; origin Mary Jane Watson	2	4	6	9	12	15
260-Hobgoblin app.	2	4	6	8	10	12
261-Hobgoblin-c/story; painted-c by Vess	2	4	6	9	11	14
262-Spider-Man unmasked; photo-c	1	3	4	6	8	10
263,264,266-274,277-280,282,283: 274-Zarathos (The Spirit of Vengeance) app. 277-Vess back-up art. 279-Jack O'Lantern-c/story. 282-X-Factor x-over	1	2	3	5	6	8
265-1st app. Silver Sable (6/85)	2	4	6	9	13	16
265-Silver ink 2nd printing ($1.25)						3.00
275-($1.25, 52 pgs.)-Hobgoblin-c/story; origin-r by Ditko	3	6	9	14	20	25

	GD 2.0	VG 4.0	FN 6.0	VF 8.0	VF/NM 9.0	NM- 9.2
276-Hobgoblin app.	1	3	4	6	8	10
281-Hobgoblin battles Jack O'Lantern	1	3	4	6	8	10
284,285: 284-Punisher cameo; Gang War story begins; Hobgoblin-c/story. 285-Punisher app.; minor Hobgoblin app.	1	3	4	6	8	10
286-288: 286-Hobgoblin-c & app. (minor). 287-Hobgoblin app. (minor). 288-Full Hobgoblin app.; last Gang War	1	3	4	6	8	10
289-(6/87, $1.25, 52 pgs.)-Hobgoblin's i.d. revealed as Ned Leeds; death of Ned Leeds; Macendale (Jack O'Lantern) becomes new Hobgoblin (1st app.)	3	6	9	14	20	25
290-292,295-297: 290-Peter proposes to Mary Jane. 292-She accepts; leads into wedding in Amazing Spider-Man Annual #21	1	2	3	5	6	8
293,294-Part 2 & 5 of Kraven story from Web of Spider-Man. 294-Death of Kraven	2	4	6	9	12	15
298-Todd McFarlane-c/a begins (3/88); 1st brief app. Eddie Brock who becomes Venom; (last pg.)	5	10	15	35	55	75
299-1st brief app. Venom with costume	4	8	12	22	34	45
300 ($1.50, 52 pgs.; 25th Anniversary)-1st full Venom app.; last black costume (5/88)	9	18	27	63	107	150
301-305: 301 ($1.00 issues begin). 304-1st bi-weekly issue	2	4	6	9	13	16
306-311,313,314: 306-Swipes-c from Action #1	2	4	6	8	11	14
312-Hobgoblin battles Green Goblin	2	4	6	11	16	20
315-317-Venom app.	3	6	9	14	19	24
318-323,325: 319-Bi-weekly begins again	1	2	3	5	7	9
324-Sabretooth app.; McFarlane cover only	1	2	3	5	7	9
326,327,329: 327-Cosmic Spidey continues from Spectacular Spider-Man (no McFarlane-c/a)						5.00
328-Hulk x-over; last McFarlane issue	1	3	4	6	8	10
330,331-Punisher app. 331-Minor Venom app.						5.00
332,333-Venom-c/story	1	3	4	6	8	10
334-336,338-343: 341-Tarantula app.						4.00
337-Hobgoblin app.						5.00
344-(2/91) 1st app. Cletus Kasady (Carnage)	2	4	6	9	12	15
345-1st full app. Cletus Kasady; Venom cameo on last pg.	2	4	6	9	12	15
346,347-Venom app.	1	3	4	6	8	10
348,349,351-359: 348-Avengers x-over. 351,352-Nova of New Warriors app. 353-Darkhawk app.; brief Punisher app. 354-Punisher cameo & Nova, Night Thrasher (New Warriors), Darkhawk & Moon Knight app. 357,358-Punisher, Darkhawk, Moon Knight, Night Thrasher, Nova x-over. 358-3 part gatefold-c; last $1.00-c. 360-Carnage cameo						3.00
350-($1.50, 52pgs.)-Origin retold; Spidey vs. Dr. Doom; pin-ups; Uncle Ben app.						5.00
360-Carnage cameo						4.00
361-(4/92) Intro Carnage (the Spawn of Venom); begin 3 part story; recap of how Spidey's alien costume became Venom	2	4	6	9	12	15
361-($1.25)-2nd printing; silver-c						3.00
362,363-Carnage & Venom-c/story	1	2	3	5	7	9
362-2nd printing						3.00
364,366-374,376-387: 364-The Shocker app. (old villain). 366-Peter's parents-c/story. 369-Harry Osborn back-up (Gr. Goblin II). 373-Venom back-up. 374-Venom-c/story. 376-Cardiac app. 378-Maximum Carnage part 3. 381,382-Hulk app. 383-The Jury app. 384-Venom/carnage app. 387-New costume Vulture						3.00
365-($3.95, 84 pgs.)-30th anniversary issue w/silver hologram on-c; Spidey/Venom/Carnage pull-out poster; contains 5 pg. preview of Spider-Man 2099 (1st app.); Spidey's origin retold; Lizard app.; reintro Peter's parents in Stan Lee 3 pg. text w/illo (story continues thru #370)						5.00
375-($3.95, 68 pgs.)-Holo-grafx foil-c; vs. Venom story; ties into Venom: Lethal Protector #1; Pat Olliffe-a.						5.00
388-($2.25, 68 pgs.)-Newsstand edition; Venom back-up & Cardiac & chance back-up						3.00
388-($2.95, 68 pgs.)-Collector's edition w/foil-c						3.50
389-396,398,399,401-420: 389-$1.50-c begins; bound-in trading card sheet; Green Goblin app. 394-Power & Responsibility Pt. 2. 396-Daredevil-c & app. 403-Carnage app. 406-1st New Doc Octopus. 407-Human Torch, Silver Sable, Sandman app. 409-Kaine, Rhino app. 410-Carnage app. 414-The Rose app. 415-Onslaught story; Spidey vs. Sentinels. 416-Epilogue to Onslaught; Garney-a(p); Williamson-a(i)						3.00
390-($2.95)-Collector's edition polybagged w/16 pg. insert of new animated Spidey TV show plus animation cel						3.50
394-($2.95, 48 pgs.)-Deluxe edition; flip book w/Birth of a Spider-Man Pt. 2; silver foil both-c; Power & Responsibility Pt. 2						4.00
397-($2.25)-Flip book w/Ultimate Spider-Man						3.00
400-($2.95)-Death of Aunt May						4.00
400-($3.95)-Death of Aunt May; embossed double-c						6.00
400-Collector's Edition; white-c	1	3	4	6	8	10
408-($2.95) Polybagged version with TV theme song cassette						8.00
421-424,426,428,429,432,433: 426-Begin $1.99-c. 432-Spiderhunt pt. 2						3.00

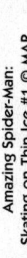

Amazing Spider-Man: Skating on Thin Ice #1 © MAR

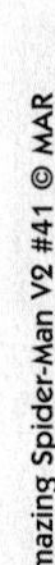
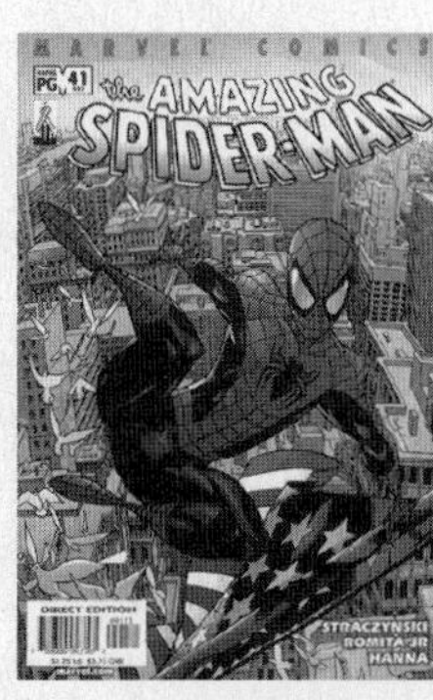

Amazing Spider-Man V2 #41 © MAR

Amazing Spider-Man #562 © MAR

GD 2.0 | VG 4.0 | FN 6.0 | VF 8.0 | VF/NM 9.0 | NM- 9.2

425-($2.99)-48 pgs., wraparound-c 4.00
427-($2.25) Return of Dr. Octopus; double gatefold-c 3.00
430,431-Carnage & Silver Surfer app. 4.00
434-440: 434-Double-c with "Amazing Ricochet #1". 438-Daredevil app. 439-Avengers-c/app. 440-Byrne-s 3.00
441-Final issue; Byrne-s 5.00
#500-up (See Amazing Spider-Man Vol. 2; series resumed original numbering after Vol. 2 #58)
#(-1) Flashback issue (7/97, $1.95-c) 3.00
Annual 1 (1964, 72 pgs.)-Origin Spider-Man; 1st app. Sinister Six (Dr. Octopus, Electro, Kraven the Hunter, Mysterio, Sandman, Vulture) (new 41 pg. story); plus gallery of Spidey foes; early X-Men app. 87 174 261 740 1495 2250
Annual 2 (1965, 25¢, 72 pgs.)-Reprints from #1,2,5 plus new Doctor Strange story 35 70 105 273 537 800
Special 3 (11/66, 25¢, 72 pgs.)-New Avengers story & Hulk x-over; Doctor Octopus-r from #11,12; Romita-a 16 32 48 117 239 360
Special 4 (11/67, 25¢, 68 pgs.)-Spidey battles Human Torch (new 41 pg. story) 14 28 42 96 191 285
Special 5 (11/68, 25¢, 68 pgs.)-New 40 pg. Red Skull story; 1st app. Peter Parker's parents; last annual with new-a 12 24 36 86 161 235
Special 5-2nd printing (1994) 2 4 6 8 10 12
Special 6 (11/69, 25¢, 68 pgs.)-Reprints 41 pg. Sinister Six story from annual #1 plus 2 Kirby/Ditko stories (r) 6 12 18 37 59 80
Special 7 (12/70, 25¢, 68 pgs.)-All-r(#1,2) new Vulture-c 6 12 18 37 59 80
Special 8 (12/71)-All-r 6 12 18 37 59 80
King Size 9 ('73)-Reprints Spectacular Spider-Man (mag.) #2; 40 pg. Green Goblin-c/story (re-edited from 58 pgs.) 6 12 18 37 59 80
Annual 10 (1976)-Origin Human Fly (vs. Spidey); new-a begins 3 6 9 16 22 28
Annual 11-13 ('77-'79):12-Spidey vs. Hulk-r/#119,120. 13-New Byrne/Austin-a; Dr. Octopus x-over w/Spectacular S-M Ann. #1 2 4 6 10 14 18
Annual 14 (1980)-Miller-c/a(p); Dr. Strange app. 3 6 9 14 20 25
Annual 15 (1981)-Miller-c/a(p); Punisher app. 3 6 9 18 27 35
Annual 16-20:16 ('82)-Origin/1st app. new Capt. Marvel (female heroine). 17 ('83)-Kingpin app. 18 ('84)-Scorpion app.; JJJ weds. 19 ('85). 20 ('86)-Origin Iron Man of 2020 1 2 3 4 5 7
Annual 21 (1987)-Special wedding issue; newsstand & direct sale versions exist & are worth same 2 4 6 8 10 12
Annual 22 (1988, $1.75, 68 pgs.)-1st app. Speedball; Evolutionary War x-over; Daredevil app. 6.00
Annual 23 (1989, $2.00, 68 pgs.)-Atlantis Attacks; origin Spider-Man retold; She-Hulk app.; Byrne-c; Liefeld-a(p), 23 pgs. 5.00
Annual 24 (1990, $2.00, 68 pgs.)-Ant-Man app. 4.00
Annual 25 (1991, $2.00, 68 pgs.)-3 pg. origin recap; Iron Man app.; 1st Venom solo story; Ditko-a (6 pgs.) 5.00
Annual 26 (1992, $2.25, 68 pgs.)-New Warriors-c/story; Venom solo story cont'd in Spectacular Spider-Man Annual #12 5.00
Annual 27,28 ('93, '94, $2.95, 68 pgs.)-27-Bagged w/card; 1st app. Annex. 28-Carnage-c/story; Rhino & Cloak and Dagger back-ups 4.00
'96 Special-($2.95, 64 pgs.)-"Blast From The Past" 4.00
'97 Special-($2.99)-Wraparound-c,Sundown app. 4.00
Marvel Graphic Novel - Parallel Lives (3/89, $8.95) 2 4 6 8 10 12
Marvel Graphic Novel - Spirits of the Earth (1990, $18.95, HC) 3 6 9 16 22 28
Super Special 1 (4/95, $3.95)-Flip Book 4.00
...: Skating on Thin Ice 1(1990, $1.25, Canadian)-McFarlane-c; anti-drug issue; Electro app. 1 2 3 5 7 9
...: Skating on Thin Ice 1 (2/93, $1.50, American) 4.00
...: Double Trouble 2 (1990, $1.25, Canadian) 6.00
...: Double Trouble 2 (2/93, $1.50, American) 3.00
...: Hit and Run 3 (1990, $1.25, Canadian)-Ghost Rider-c/story 1 2 3 5 7 9
...: Hit and Run 3 (2/93. $1.50, American) 3.00
... : Carnage (6/93, $6.95)-r/ASM #344,345,359-363 1 2 3 4 5 7
...: Chaos in Calgary 4 (Canadian; part of 5 part series)-Turbine,Night Rider, Frightful app. 2 4 6 8 11 14
...: Chaos in Calgary 4 (2/93, $1.50, American) 3.00
...: Deadball 5 (1993, $1.60, Canadian)-Green Goblin-c/story; features Montreal Expos 2 4 6 10 14 18
Note: Prices listed above are for English Canadian editions. French editions are worth double.
...: Soul of the Hunter nn (8/92, $5.95, 52 pgs.)-Zeck-c/a(p) 6.00
Wizard #1 Ace Edition ($13.99) r/#1 w/ new Ramos acetate-c 14.00
Wizard #129 Ace Edition ($13.99) r/#129 w/ new Ramos acetate-c 14.00
NOTE: ***Austin*** *a(i)-248, 335, 337, Annual 13; c(i)-188, 241, 242, 248, 331, 334, 343, Annual 25.* ***J. Buscema*** *a(p)-72, 73, 76-81, 84, 85.* ***Byrne*** *a-189p, 190p, 206p, Annual 3r, 6r, 7r, 13p; c-189p, 268, 296, Annual 12.* ***Ditko*** *a-1-38, Annual 1, Special 3(r), 2, 24(2); c-1i, 2-38.* ***Guice*** *c/a-Annual 18i.* ***Gil Kane*** *a(p)-89-105, 120-124, 150, Annual 10, 12i, 24p; c-90p, 96, 98, 99, 101-105p, 129p, 131p, 132p, 137-140p, 143p, 148p, 149p, 151p, 153p, 160p, 161p, Annual 10p, 24.* ***Kirby*** *a-8.* ***Erik Larsen*** *a-324, 327, 329-350; c-327, 329-350, 354i, Annual 25.* ***McFarlane*** *a-298p, 299p, 300-303, 304-323p, 325p, 328; c-298-325, 328.* ***Miller*** *c-218, 219.* ***Mooney*** *a-65i, 67-82i, 84-88i, 173i, 178i, 189i, 190i, 192i, 193i, 196-202i, 207i, 211-219i, 221i, 222i, 226i, 227i, 229-233i, Annual 11i, 17i.* ***Nasser*** *c-228p.* ***Nebres*** *a-Annual 24i.* ***Russell*** *c-357i.* ***Simonson*** *c-222, 337i.* ***Starlin*** *a-113i, 114i, 187p.* ***Williamson*** *a-365i.*

AMAZING SPIDER-MAN (Volume 2) (Some issues reprinted in "Spider-Man, Best Of" hardcovers)
Marvel Comics: Jan, 1999 - Present ($2.99/$1.99/$2.25)

1-($2.99)-Byrne-a 6.00
1-Sunburst variant-c 1 2 3 5 6 8
1-($6.95) Dynamic Forces variant-c by the Romitas 1 3 4 6 8 10
1-Marvel Matrix sketch variant-c 1 3 4 6 8 10
2-($1.99) Two covers -by John Byrne and Andy Kubert 4.00
3-11: 4-Fantastic Four app. 5-Spider-Woman-c 3.00
12-($2.99) Sinister Six return (cont. in Peter Parker #12) 4.00
13-17: 13-Mary Jane's plane explodes 3.00
18,19,21-24,26-28: 18-Begin $2.25-c. 19-Venom-c. 24-Maximum Security 3.00
20-($2.99, 100 pgs.) Spider-Slayer issue; new story and reprints 4.00
25-($2.99) Regular cover; Peter Parker becomes the Green Goblin 3.00
25-($3.99) Holo-foil enhanced cover 4.00
29-Peter is reunited with Mary Jane 3.00
30-Straczynski-s/Campbell-c begin; intro. Ezekiel 6.00
31-35: Battles Morlun 4.00
36-Black cover; aftermath of the Sept. 11 tragedy in New York 10.00
37-49: 39-'Nuff Said issue 42-Dr. Strange app. 43-45-Doctor Octopus app. 46-48-Cho-c 3.00
50-Peter and MJ reunite; Captain America & Dr. Doom app.; Campbell-c 4.00
51-58: 51,52-Campbell-c. 55,56-Avery scripts. 57,58-Avengers, FF, Cyclops app. 3.00
(After #58 [Nov, 2003] numbering reverts back to original Vol. 1 with #500, Dec, 2003)
500-($3.50) J. Scott Campbell-c; Romita Jr. & Sr.-a; Uncle Ben app. 4.00
501-524: 501-Harris-c. 503-504-Loki app. 506-508-Ezekiel app. 509-514-Sins Past; intro. Gabriel and Sarah Osborn; Deodato-a. 519-Moves into Avengers HQ. 521-Begin $2.50-c 524-Harris-c 3.00
525,526-Evolve or Die x-over. 525-David-s. 526-Hudlin-s; Spider-Man loses eye 4.00
525-528-2nd printings with variant-c. 525-Ben Reilly costume. 526-Six-Armed Spidey. 527-Spider-Man 2099. 528-Spider-Ham 5.00
527,528: Evolve or Die pt.9, 12 3.00
529-Debut of red and gold costume; Garney-a 10.00
529-2nd printing 5.00
529-3rd printing with Wieringo-c 3.00
530,531-Titanium Man app.; Kirkham-a. 531-Begin $2.99-c 6.00
532-538-Civil War tie-in. 538-Aunt May shot 5.00
539-543-Back in Black. 539-Peter wears the black costume 3.00
544-($3.99) "One More Day" pt. 1; Quesada-a/Straczynski-s 4.00
545-(12/08, $3.99) "One More Day" pt. 4; Quesada-a/Straczynski-s, Peter & MJ's marriage un-done; r/wedding from ASM Annual #21; 2 covers by Quesada and Djurdjevic 4.00
546-($3.99) Brand New Day begins; McNiven-a; Deodato, Winslade, Land, Romita Jr.-a; 1st app. Mr. Negative 5.00
546-Variant-c by Bryan Hitch 8.00
546-Second printing with new McNiven-c of Peter Parker 4.00
546-MGC (7/10, $1.00) r/#546 with "Marvel's Greatest Comics" logo on cover 1.00
: 547,548-McNiven-a. 549-551-Larroca-a. 550-Intro. Menace. 555-557-Bachalo-a. 559-Intro. Screwball. 560,561-MJ app. 565-New Kraven intro. 566,567-Spidey in Daredevil costume 3.00
568-($3.99) Romita Jr.-a begins; two covers by Romita Jr. and Alex Ross 6.00
568-Variant-c by John Romita Sr. 20.00
568-2nd printing with Romita Jr. Anti-Venom costume cover 4.00
569-Debut of Anti-Venom; Norman Osborn and Thunderbolts app.;Romita Jr.-c 3.00
569-Variant Venom-c by Granov 5.00
570-572-Two covers on each 3.00
573-($3.99) New Ways to Die conclusion; Spidey meets Stephen Colbert back-up; Ollife-a; two covers by Romita Jr. and Maguire 5.00
573-Variant cover with Stephen Colbert; cover swipe of AF #15 by Quesada 10.00
574-582: 577-Punisher app. 3.00
583-($3.99) Spidey meets Obama back-up story; regular Romita Sr. "Cougars" cover 8.00
583-($3.99) Obama variant-c with Spidey on left; Spidey meets Obama back-up story 40.00
583-($3.99) Second printing Obama variant-c with Spidey on right and yellow bkgrd 8.00
583-($3.99) 3rd-5th printings Obama variant-c: 3rd-Blue bkgrd w/flag. 4th-White bkgrd w/flag. 5th-Lincoln Memorial bkgrd 5.00
584-587, 589-599: 585-Menace ID revealed. 590,591-Fantastic Four app. 594-Aunt May engaged. 595-599-American Son; Osborn Avengers app. app. 3.00
588-($3.99) Conclusion to "Character Assassination"; Romita Jr.-a 4.00
600-(9/09, $4.99) Aunt May's wedding; Romita Jr.-a; Doc Octopus, FF app.; Mary Jane cameo; back-up story by Stan Lee; back-up with Doran-a; 2 covers by Romita Jr. & Ross 5.00
600-Variant covers by Romita Sr. and Quesada 10.00
601-604,606-611,613-616,618-621,623-627: 601-Back-up w/Quesada-a. 606,607-Black Cat

Amazing Spider-Man #641 © MAR

Amazing World of DC Comics #15 © DC

Ambush Bug: Year None #1 © DC

GD 2.0 | VG 4.0 | FN 6.0 | VF 8.0 | VF/NM 9.0 | NM- 9.2

GD 2.0 | VG 4.0 | FN 6.0 | VF 8.0 | VF/NM 9.0 | NM- 9.2

app.; Campbell-c. 611-Deadpool-c/app. 612-The Gauntlet begins; Waid-s.
615,616-Sandman app. 621-Black Cat app. 624-Peter Parker fired. 626-Gaydos-a 3.00
605,612,617,622,628-($3.99): 605-Mayhew-c. 613-Rhino back-up story. 617-New Rhino.
622-Bianchi-c; Morbius app. 628-Captain Universe app. 4.00
629-633-($2.99)-Bachalo-a; Lizard app. 3.00
634-641-($3.99) 634-637-Grim Hunt; Kaine app. 635-Kraven returns. 638-641-"One Moment in Time" wedding flashback/ret-con; Quesada-s 4.00
638-641-Variant covers by Quesada 10.00
642-646-($2.99) Waid-s/Azaceta-a; interlocking covers by Djurdjevic 3.00
647-($4.99) Short stories by various; Djurdjevic-c; cover gallery of Brand New Day issues 5.00
648-658-($3.99) 648-Big Time begins; Ramos-a; Hobgoblin app. 654-Flash Thompson becomes Venom; Marla Jameson killed. 655-Martin-a. 657,658-Fantastic Four app. 4.00
654.1-(4/11, $2.99) Flash Thompson as Venom; Ramos-a 3.00
1999, 2000 Annual (6/99, '00, $3.50) 1999-Buscema-a 4.00
2001 Annual ($2.99) Follows Peter Parker: S-M #29; last Mackie-s 4.00
Annual 1 (2008, $3.99) McKone-a; secret of Jackpot revealed; death of Jackpot 4.00
Annual 36 (9/09, $3.99) Debut of Raptor; Olliffe-a 4.00
Annual 37 (7/10, $3.99) Untold 1st meeting with Captain America; back-up w/Olliffe-a 4.00
Annual 38 (6/11, $3.99) Deadpool & Hulk app.; Garbett-a/McNiven-c 4.00
Collected Edition #30-32 ($3.95) reprints #30-32 w/cover #30 4.00
... 500 Covers HC (2004, $49.99) reprints covers for #1-500 & Annuals; yearly re-caps 50.00
Free Comic Book Day 2011 (Spider-Man) 1-Ramos-c/a; Spider-Woman & Shang-Chi app. 2.00
... Omnibus HC (2007, $99.99, dustjacket) r/Amazing Fantasy #15, Amazing Spider-Man #1-38, Annual #1,2, Strange Tales Annual #2 & Fantastic Four Annual #1; letter pages, bonus art, intro. by Stan Lee; bios, essays, Marvel Tales cover gallery 100.00
Spider-Man: Brand New Day - Extra!! #1 (9/08, $3.99) short stories; Bachalo,Olliffe-a 4.00
Spider-Man: Brand New Day Yearbook #1 (2008, $4.99) plot synopses; profile pages 5.00
...: Swing Shift (2007 FCBD Edition) Jimenez-c/a; Slott-s 2.25
...: Swing Shift Director's Cut (2008, $3.99) story from 2007 FCBD; Brand New Day info 4.00
The Many Loves of the Amazing Spider-Man (7/10, $3.99) short stories of Black Cat, Gwen & Carlie, and Mary Jane; s/a by various 4.00
...: The Short Halloween (7/09, $3.99) Bill Hader & Seth Meyers-s/Maguire-a 4.00
...Vol. 1: Coming Home (2001, $15.95) r/#30-35; J. Scott Campbell-c 16.00
...Vol. 2: Revelations (2002, $8.99) r/#36-39; Kaare Andrews-c 9.00
...Vol. 3: Until the Stars Turn Cold (2002, $12.99) r/#40-45; Romita Jr.-c 13.00
...Vol. 4: The Life and Death of Spiders (2003, $11.99) r/#46-50; Campbell-c 12.00
...Vol. 5: Unintended Consequences (2003, $12.99) r/#51-56; Dodson-c 13.00
...Vol. 6: Happy Birthday (2003, $12.99) r/#57,58,500-502 13.00
...Vol. 7: The Book of Ezekiel (2004, $12.99) r/#503-508; Romita Jr.-c 13.00
...Vol. 8: Sins Past (2005, $12.99) r/#509-514; cover sketch gallery 13.00
...Vol. 9: Skin Deep (2005, $9.99) r/#515-518 10.00
...Vol. 10: New Avengers (2005, $14.99) r/#519-524 15.00
Brand New Day #1-3 (11/08-1/09, $3.99) reprints #546-551 4.00
Civil War: Amazing Spider-Man TPB (2007, $17.99) r/#532-538; variant covers 18.00

AMAZING SPIDER-MAN EXTRA! (Continued from Spider-Man: Brand New Day - Extra!! #1)
Marvel Comics: No. 2, Mar, 2009 - No. 3, May, 2009 ($3.99)

2,3: 2-Anti-Venom app.; Bachalo-a. 3-Ana Kraven app.; Jimenez-a 4.00

AMAZING SPIDER-MAN FAMILY (Also see Spider-Man Family)
Marvel Comics: Oct, 2008 - No. 8, Sept, 2009 ($4.99, anthology)

1-8-New tales and reprints. 1-Includes r/ASM #300; Granov-c. 2-Deodato-c. 5-Spider-Girl new story. 6-Origin of Jackpot 5.00

AMAZING SPIDER-MAN PRESENTS: AMERICAN SON
Marvel Comics: Jul, 2010 - No. 4, Oct, 2010 ($3.99, limited series)

1-4-Reed-s/Briones-a/Djurdjevic-c; Gabriel Stacy app. 4.00

AMAZING SPIDER-MAN PRESENTS: ANTI-VENOM - NEW WAYS TO LIVE
Marvel Comics: Nov, 2009 - No. 3, Feb, 2010 ($3.99, limited series)

1-3-Wells-s/Siqueira-a; Punisher app. 4.00

AMAZING SPIDER-MAN PRESENTS: JACKPOT
Marvel Comics: Mar, 2010 - No. 3, Jun, 2010 ($3.99, limited series)

1-3-Guggenheim-s/Melo-a; Boomerang and White Rabbit app. 4.00

AMAZING WILLIE MAYS, THE
Famous Funnies Publ.: No date (Sept, 1954)

nn 81 162 243 518 884 1250

AMAZING WORLD OF DC COMICS
DC Comics: Jul, 1974 - No. 17, 1978 ($1.50, B&W, mail-order DC Pro-zine)

1-Kubert interview; unpublished Kirby-a; Infantino-c 7 14 21 50 83 115
2-4: 3-Julie Schwartz profile. 4-Batman; Robinson-c 5 10 15 35 55 75
5-Sheldon Mayer 5 10 15 30 48 65
6,8,13: 6-Joe Orlando; EC-r; Wrightson pin-up. 8-Infantino; Batman-r from Pop Tart giveaway. 13-Humor; Aragonés-c; Wood/Ditko-a; photos from serials of Superman, Batman, Captain Marvel 4 8 12 23 36 48
7,10-12: 7-Superman; r/1955 Pep comic giveaway. 10-Behind the scenes at DC; Showcase article. 11-Super-Villains; unpubl. Secret Society of S.V. story.
12-Legion; Grell-c/interview; 4 8 12 24 37 50
9-Legion of Super-Heroes; lengthy bios and history; Cockrum-c
7 14 21 50 83 115
14-Justice League 4 8 12 26 41 55
15-Wonder Woman; Nasser-c 5 10 15 32 51 70
16-Golden Age heroes 5 10 15 30 48 65
17-Shazam; G.A., 70s, TV and Fawcett heroes 4 8 12 26 41 55
Special 1 (Digest size) 3 6 9 21 32 42

AMAZING WORLD OF SUPERMAN (See Superman)

AMAZING X-MEN
Marvel Comics: Mar, 1995 - No. 4, July, 1995 ($1.95, limited series)

1-Age of Apocalypse; Andy Kubert-c/a 4.00
2-4 3.00

AMAZON
Comico: Mar, 1989 - No. 3, May, 1989 ($1.95, limited series)

1-3: Ecological theme; Steven Seagle-s/Tim Sale-a 3.00
1-3-(Dark Horse, 3/09 - No. 3, 5/09, $3.50) recolored reprint with creator interviews 3.50

AMAZON (Also see Marvel Versus DC #3 & DC Versus Marvel #4)
DC Comics (Amalgam): Apr, 1996 ($1.95, one-shot)

1-John Byrne-c/a/scripts 3.00

AMAZON ATTACK 3-D
The 3-D Zone: Sept, 1990 ($3.95, 28 pgs.)

1-Chaykin-a 6.00

AMAZONS ATTACK (See Wonder Woman #8 - 2006 series)
DC Comics: Jun, 2007 - No. 6, Late Oct, 2007 ($2.99, limited series)

1-6-Queen Hippolyta and Amazons attacks Wash., DC; Pfeifer-s/Woods-a 3.00

AMAZON WOMAN (1st Series)
FantaCo: Summer, 1994 - No. 2, Fall, 1994 ($2.95, B&W, limited series, mature)

1,2: Tom Simonton-c/a/scripts 3.00

AMAZON WOMAN (2nd Series)
FantaCo: Feb, 1996 - No. 4, May, 1996 ($2.95, B&W, limited series, mature)

1-4: Tom Simonton-a/scripts 3.00
...: Invaders of Terror ('96, $5.95) Simonton-a/s 6.00

AMBUSH (See Zane Grey, Four Color 314)

AMBUSH BUG (Also see Son of...)
DC Comics: June, 1985 - No. 4, Sept, 1985 (75¢, limited series)

1-4: Giffen-c/a in all 3.00
Nothing Special 1 (9/92, $2.50, 68pg.)-Giffen-c/a 3.00
Stocking Stuffer (2/86, $1.25)-Giffen-c/a 3.00

AMBUSH BUG: YEAR NONE
DC Comics: Sept, 2008 - No. 5, Jan, 2009; No. 7, Dec, 2009 ($2.99, limited series, no #6)

1-5,7-Giffen-s/a; Jonni DC app. 4-Conner-c. 7-Baltazar & Franco-a; Giffen-a 3.00

AMERICA AT WAR - THE BEST OF DC WAR COMICS (See Fireside Book Series)

AMERICA IN ACTION
Dell (Imp. Publ. Co.)/ Mayflower House Publ.: 1942; Winter, 1945 (36 pgs.)

1942-Dell-(68 pgs.) 17 34 51 98 154 210
1-(1945)-Has 3 adaptations from American history; Kiefer, Schrotter & Webb-a
14 28 42 76 108 140

AMERICAN, THE
Dark Horse Comics: July, 1987 - No. 8, 1989 ($1.50/$1.75, B&W)

1-8: ($1.50) 3.00
Collection ($5.95, B&W)-Reprints 6.00
Special 1 (1990, $2.25, B&W) 3.00

AMERICAN AIR FORCES, THE (See A-1 Comics)
William H. Wise(Flying Cadet Publ. Co./Hasan(No.1)/Life's Romances/ Magazine Ent. No. 5 on): Sept-Oct, 1944-No. 4, 1945; No. 5, 1951-No. 12, 1954

1-Article by Zack Mosley, creator of Smilin' Jack; German war-c
24 48 72 142 234 325
2-Classic-Japan war-c 47 94 141 296 498 700
3,4-Japan war-c 17 34 51 98 154 210
NOTE: *All part comic, part magazine. Art by* **Whitney, Chas. Quinlan, H. C. Kiefer,** *and* **Tony Dipreta.**
5(A-1 45)(Formerly Jet Powers), 6(A-1 54), 7(A-1 58), 8(A-1 65), 9(A-1 67), 10(A-1 74),

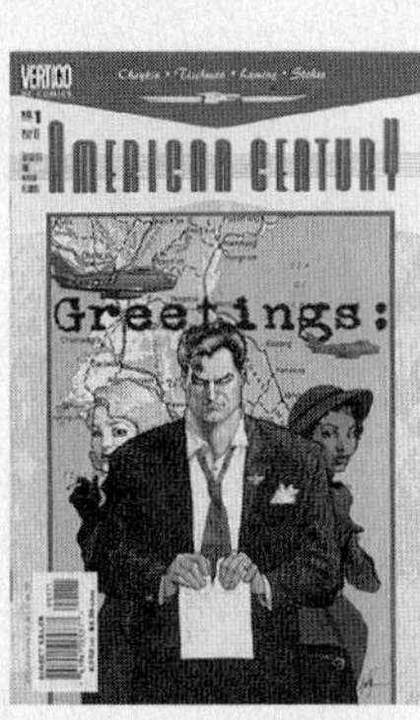

American Century #1 © Chaykin & DC

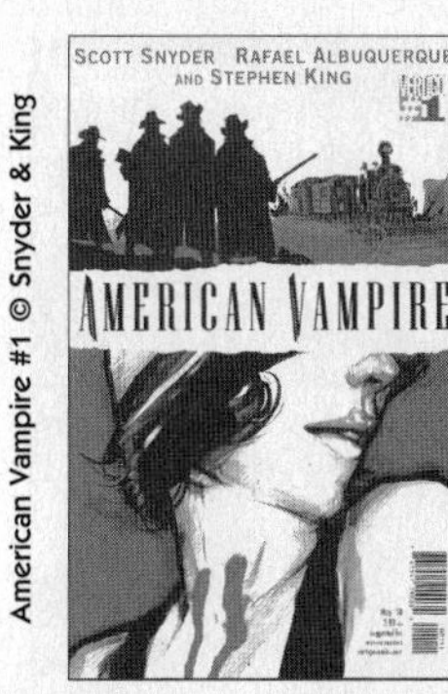

American Vampire #1 © Snyder & King

America's Best Comics #12 © NEDOR

11(A-1 79), 12(A-1 91) 9 18 27 52 69 85

NOTE: *Powell c/a-5-12.*

AMERICAN CENTURY
DC Comics (Vertigo): May, 2001 - No. 27, Oct, 2003 ($2.50/$2.75)

1-Chaykin-s/painted-c; Tischman-a 4.00
2-27: 5-New story arc begins. 10-16,22-27-Orbik-c. 17-21-Silke-c. 18-$2.75-c begins 3.00
Hollywood Babylon (2002, $12.95, TPB) r/#5-9; w/sketch-to-art pages 13.00
Scars & Stripes (2001, $8.95, TPB) r/#1-4; Tischman intro. 9.00

AMERICAN DREAM (From the M2 Avengers)
Marvel Comics: Jul, 2008 - No. 5, Sept, 2008 ($2.99, limited series)

1-5-DeFalco-s/Nauck-a 3.00

AMERICAN FLAGG! (See First Comics Graphic Novel 3,9,12,21 & Howard Chaykin's..)
First Comics: Oct, 1983 - No. 50, Mar, 1988

1,21-27: 1-Chaykin-c/a begins. 21-27-Alan Moore scripts 4.00
2-20,28-49: 31-Origin Bob Violence 3.00
50-Last issue 4.00
Special 1 (11/86)-Introduces Chaykin's Time² 4.00
...: Hard Times TPB (6/85, $11.95) r/#1-7; intro. by Michael Moorcock; bonus materials 12.00
...: Definitive Collection Volume 1 HC (2008, $49.99) r/#1-14 and material from the...: Hard Times TPB; intro by Michael Chabon; afterword by Jim Lee 50.00

AMERICAN FREAK: A TALE OF THE UN-MEN
DC Comics (Vertigo): Feb, 1994 - No. 5, Jun, 1994 ($1.95, mini-series, mature)

1-5 3.00

AMERICAN GRAPHICS
Henry Stewart: No. 1, 1954; No. 2, 1957 (25¢)

1-The Maid of the Mist, The Last of the Eries (Indian Legends of Niagara) (sold at Niagara Falls) 11 22 33 60 83 105
2-Victory at Niagara & Laura Secord (Heroine of the War of 1812) 8 16 24 40 50 60

AMERICAN INDIAN, THE (See Picture Progress)

AMERICAN LIBRARY
David McKay Publ.: 1943 - No. 6, 1944 (15¢, 68 pgs., B&W, text & pictures)

nn (#1)-Thirty Seconds Over Tokyo (movie) 39 78 117 231 378 525
nn (#2)-Guadalcanal Diary; painted-c (only 10¢) 28 56 84 165 270 375
3-6: 3-Look to the Mountain. 4-Case of the Crooked Candle (Perry Mason). 5-Duel in the Sun. 6-Wingate's Raiders 15 30 45 88 137 185

AMERICAN: LOST IN AMERICA, THE
Dark Horse Comics: July, 1992 - No. 4, Oct, 1992 ($2.50, limited series)

1-4: 1-Dorman painted-c. 2-Phillips painted-c. 3-Mignola-c. 4-Jim Lee-c 3.00

AMERICAN SPLENDOR: (Series of titles)
Dark Horse Comics: Aug, 1996 - Present (B&W, all one-shots)

--**COMIC-CON COMICS** (8/96) 1-H. Pekar script. --**MUSIC COMICS** (11/97) nn-H. Pekar-s/Sacco-a; r/Village Voice jazz strips. --**ODDS AND ENDS** (12/97) 1-Pekar-s. --**ON THE JOB** (5/97) 1-Pekar-s. --**A STEP OUT OF THE NEST** (8/94) 1-Pekar-s. --**TERMINAL** (9/99) 1-Pekar-s. --**TRANSATLANTIC** (7/98) 1-"American Splendour" on cover; Pekar-s 3.00
--**A PORTRAIT OF THE AUTHOR IN HIS DECLINING YEARS** (4/01, $3.99) 1-Photo-c. --**BEDTIME STORIES** (6/00, $3.95) 4.00

AMERICAN SPLENDOR
DC Comics: Nov, 2006 - No. 4, Feb, 2007 ($2.99, B&W)

1-4-Pekar-s/art by Haspiel and various. 1-Fabry-c 3.00
...: Another Day TPB (2007, $14.99) r/#1-4 15.00

AMERICAN SPLENDOR (Volume 2)
DC Comics (Vertigo): Jun, 2008 - No. 4, Sept, 2008 ($2.99, B&W)

1-4-Pekar-s/art by Haspiel and various. 1-Bond-c. 3-Cooke-c 3.00
...: Another Dollar TPB (2009, $14.99) r/#1-4 15.00

AMERICAN SPLENDOR: UNSUNG HERO
Dark Horse Comics: Aug, 2002 - No. 3, Oct, 2002 ($3.99, B&W, limited series)

1-3-Pekar script/Collier-a; biography of Robert McNeill 4.00
TPB (8/03, $11.95) r/#1-3 12.00

AMERICAN SPLENDOR: WINDFALL
Dark Horse Comics: Sept, 1995 - No. 2, Oct,1995 ($3.95, B&W, limited series)

1,2-Pekar script 4.00

AMERICAN TAIL: FIEVEL GOES WEST, AN
Marvel Comics: Early Jan, 1992 - No. 3, Early Feb, 1992 ($1.00, limited series)

1-3-Adapts Universal animated movie; Wildman-a 3.00

1-($2.95-c, 69 pgs.) Deluxe squarebound edition 5.00

AMERICAN VAMPIRE
DC Comics (Vertigo): May, 2010 - Present ($3.99)

1-10: 1-9-Snyder-s/Albuquerque-a. 1-5-Back-up story by Stephen King 4.00
1-5-Variant-c: 1-Jim Lee. 2-Berni Wrightson. 3-Andy Kubert. 5-Paul Pope 6.00
11,12-($2.99) 11-Santolouco-a. 12-Zezelj-a 3.00
HC (2010, $24.99, d.j.) r/#1-5; intro. by Stephen King; script pages and sketch art 25.00

AMERICAN VIRGIN
DC Comics (Vertigo): May, 2006 - No. 23, Mar, 2008 ($2.99)

1-23-Steven Seagle-s/Becky Cloonan-a in most. 1-3-Quitely-c. 4-14-Middleton-c 3.00
...: Head (2006, $9.99, TPB) r/#1-4; interviews with the creators and page development 10.00
...: Going Down (2007, $14.99, TPB) r/#5-9 15.00
...: Wet (2007, $12.99, TPB) r/#10-14 13.00
...: Around the World (Vol. 4) (2008, $17.99, TPB) r/#15-23 18.00

AMERICAN WAY, THE
DC Comics (WildStorm): Apr, 2006 - No. 8, Nov, 2006 ($2.99, limited series)

1-8-John Ridley-s/Georges Jeanty-a/c 3.00
TPB (2007, $19.99) r/series; covers; Jeanty sketch pages 20.00

AMERICA'S BEST COMICS
Nedor/Better/Standard Publications: Feb, 1942; No. 2, Sept, 1942 - No. 31, July, 1949 (New logo with #9)

1-The Woman in Red, Black Terror, Captain Future, Doc Strange, The Liberator, & Don Davis, Secret Ace begin 303 606 909 2121 3711 5300
2-Origin The American Eagle; The Woman in Red ends 116 232 348 742 1271 1800
3-Pyroman begins (11/42, 1st app.; also see Startling Comics #18, 12/42) 90 180 270 576 988 1400
4-6: 5-Last Capt. Future (not in #4); Lone Eagle app. 6-American Crusader app. 69 138 207 442 759 1075
7-Hitler, Mussolini & Hirohito-c 155 310 465 992 1696 2400
8-Last Liberator 68 136 204 435 743 1050
9-The Fighting Yank begins; The Ghost app. 74 148 222 470 810 1150
10-Flag-c 63 126 189 403 689 975
11-Hirohito & Tojo-c. (10/44) 87 174 261 553 952 1350
12-17,19-21: 14-American Eagle ends; Doc Strange vs. Hitler story. 21-Infinity-c 58 116 174 371 636 900
18-Classic-c 77 154 231 493 847 1200
22-Capt. Future app. 50 100 150 315 533 750
23-Miss Masque begins; last Doc Strange 58 116 174 371 636 900
24-Miss Masque bondage-c 56 112 168 356 608 860
25-Last Fighting Yank; Sea Eagle app. 42 84 126 265 445 625
26-31: 26-The Phantom Detective & The Silver Knight app.; Frazetta text illo & some panels in Miss Masque. 27,28-Commando Cubs. 27-Doc Strange. 28-Tuska Black Terror. 29-Last Pyroman 41 82 123 256 428 600

NOTE: *American Eagle not in 3, 8, 9, 13. Fighting Yank not in 10, 12. Liberator not in 2, 6, 7. Pyroman not in 9, 11, 14-16, 23, 25-27.* ***Schomburg (Xela)*** *c-5, 7-31. Bondage c-18, 24.*

AMERICA'S BEST COMICS
America's Best Comics: 1999 - 2008

... Preview (1999, Wizard magazine supplement) - Previews Tom Strong, Top Ten, Promethea, Tomorrow Stories 3.00
... Primer (2008, $4.99, TPB) r/Tom Strong #1, Tom Strong's Terrific Tales, Top Ten #1, Promethea #1, Tomorrow Stories #1,6 5.00
... Sketchbook (2002, $5.95, square-bound)-Design sketches by Sprouse, Ross, Adams, Nowlan, Ha and others 6.00
Special 1 (2/01, $6.95)-Short stories of Alan Moore's characters; art by various; Ross-c 7.00
TPB (2004, $17.95) Reprints short stories and sketch pages from ABC titles 18.00

AMERICA'S BEST TV COMICS (TV)
American Broadcasting Co. (Prod. by Marvel Comics): 1967 (25¢, 68 pgs.)

1-Spider-Man, Fantastic Four (by Kirby/Ayers), Casper, King Kong, George of the Jungle, Journey to the Center of the Earth stories (promotes new TV cartoon show) 12 24 36 85 155 225

AMERICA'S BIGGEST COMICS BOOK
William H. Wise: 1944 (196 pgs., one-shot)

1-The Grim Reaper, The Silver Knight, Zudo, the Jungle Boy, Commando Cubs, Thunderhoof app. 40 80 120 246 411 575

AMERICA'S FUNNIEST COMICS
William H. Wise: 1944 - No. 2, 1944 (15¢, 80 pgs.)

nn(#1), 2 32 64 96 188 307 425

AMERICA'S GREATEST COMICS

Amethyst, Princess of Gemworld #9 © DC

Andy Panda FC #409 © Walter Lantz

Angel #30 © 20th Cent. Fox

	GD	VG	FN	VF	VF/NM	NM-
	2.0	4.0	6.0	8.0	9.0	9.2

Fawcett Publications: May?, 1941 - No. 8, Summer, 1943 (15¢, 100 pgs., soft cardboard-c)

1-Bulletman, Spy Smasher, Capt. Marvel, Minute Man & Mr. Scarlet begin; Classic Mac Raboy-c. 1st time that Fawcett's major super-heroes appear together as a group on a cover. Fawcett's 1st squarebound comic 337 674 1011 2359 4130 5900
2 145 290 435 921 1586 2250
3 103 206 309 659 1130 1600
4,5: 4-Commando Yank begins; Golden Arrow, Ibis the Invincible & Spy Smasher cameo in Captain Marvel 76 152 228 486 831 1175
6,7: 7-Balbo the Boy Magician app.; Captain Marvel, Bulletman cameo in Mr. Scarlet 67 134 201 430 733 1035
8-Capt. Marvel Jr. & Golden Arrow app.; Spy Smasher x-over in Capt. Midnight; no Minute Man or Commando Yank 67 134 201 430 733 1035

AMERICA'S SWEETHEART SUNNY (See Sunny, ...)

AMERICA VS. THE JUSTICE SOCIETY
DC Comics: Jan, 1985 - No. 4, Apr, 1985 ($1.00, limited series)

1-Double size; Alcala-a(i) in all 2 4 6 8 10 12
2-4: 3,4-Spectre cameo 1 2 3 5 7 9

AMERICOMICS
Americomics: April, 1983 - No. 6, Mar, 1984 ($2.00, Baxter paper/slick paper)

1-Intro/origin The Shade; Intro. The Slayer, Captain Freedom and The Liberty Corps; Perez-c 5.00
1,2-2nd printings ($2.00) 3.00
2-6: 2-Messenger app. & 1st app. Tara on Jungle Island. 3-New & old Blue Beetle battle. 4-Origin Dragonfly & Shade. 5-Origin Commando D. 6-Origin the Scarlet Scorpion 3.00
Special 1 (8/83, $2.00)-Sentinels of Justice (Blue Beetle, Captain Atom, Nightshade & The Question) 4.50

AMETHYST
DC Comics: Jan, 1985 - No. 16, Aug, 1986 (75¢)

1-16: 8-Fire Jade's i.d. revealed 3.00
Special 1 (10/86, $1.25), 1-4 (11/87 - 2/88)(Limited series) 3.00

AMETHYST, PRINCESS OF GEMWORLD (See Legion of Super-Heroes #298)
DC Comics: May, 1983 - No. 12, Apr, 1984 (Maxi-series)

1-(60¢) 3.00
1,2-(75¢): tested in Austin & Kansas City 3 6 9 20 30 40
2-12, Annual 1(9/84): 5-11-Pérez-c(p) 3.00

AMORY WARS (Based on the Coheed and Cambria album The Second Stage Turbine Blade)
Image Comics: Jun, 2007 - No. 5, Jan, 2008 ($2.99, limited series)

1-5: 1-Claudio Sanchez-s/Gus Vasquez-a 3.00

AMORY WARS II
Image Comics: Jun, 2008 - No. 5, Oct, 2008 ($2.99, limited series)

1-5-Claudio Sanchez-s/Gabriel Guzman-a 3.00

AMORY WARS IN KEEPING SECRETS OF SILENT EARTH: 3
BOOM! Studios: May, 2010 - No. 12 ($3.99)

1-9: 1-Claudio Sanchez & Peter David-s/Chris Burnham-a. 1-Four covers 4.00

AMY RACECAR COLOR SPECIAL (See Stray Bullets)
El Capitán Books: July, 1997; Oct, 1999 ($2.95/$3.50)

1,2-David Lapham-a/scripts. 2-($3.50) 3.50

ANARCHO DICTATOR OF DEATH (See Comics Novel)

ANARKY (See Batman titles)
DC Comics: May, 1997 - No. 4, Aug, 1997 ($2.50, limited series)

1 3.50
2-4 3.00

ANARKY (See Batman titles)
DC Comics: May, 1999 - No. 8, Dec, 1999 ($2.50)

1-8: 1-JLA app.; Grant-s/Breyfogle-a. 3-Green Lantern app. 7-Day of Judgment; Haunted Tank app. 8-Joker-c/app. 3.00

ANCHORS ANDREWS (The Saltwater Daffy)
St. John Publishing Co.: Jan, 1953 - No. 4, July, 1953 (Anchors the Saltwater... No. 4)

1-Canteen Kate by Matt Baker (9 pgs.) 21 42 63 126 206 285
2-4 9 18 27 52 69 85

ANDY & WOODY (See March of Comics No. 40, 55, 76)

ANDY BURNETT (TV, Disney)
Dell Publishing Co.: Dec, 1957

Four Color 865-Photo-c 8 16 24 58 97 135

ANDY COMICS (Formerly Scream Comics; becomes Ernie Comics)
Current Publications (Ace Magazines): No. 20, June, 1948-No. 21, Aug, 1948

20,21: Archie-type comic 8 16 24 42 54 65

ANDY DEVINE WESTERN
Fawcett Publications: Dec, 1950 - No. 2, 1951

1 48 96 144 298 499 700
2 38 76 114 226 363 500

ANDY GRIFFITH SHOW, THE (TV)(1st show aired 10/3/60)
Dell Publishing Co.: #1252, Jan-Mar, 1962; #1341, Apr-Jun, 1962

Four Color 1252(#1) 34 68 102 262 519 775
Four Color 1341-Photo-c 32 64 96 246 486 725

ANDY HARDY COMICS (See Movie Comics #3 by Fiction House)
Dell Publishing Co.: April, 1952 - No. 6, Sept-Nov, 1954

Four Color 389(#1) 5 10 15 34 55 75
Four Color 447,480,515, #5,#6 4 8 12 26 41 55

ANDY PANDA (Also see Crackajack Funnies #39, The Funnies, New Funnies & Walter Lantz...)
Dell Publishing Co.: 1943 - No. 56, Nov-Jan, 1961-62 (Walter Lantz)

Four Color 25(#1, 1943) 48 96 144 392 796 1200
Four Color 54(1944) 27 54 81 197 399 600
Four Color 85(1945) 15 30 45 106 216 325
Four Color 130(1946),154,198 11 22 33 77 144 210
Four Color 216,240,258,280,297 8 16 24 58 97 135
Four Color 326,345,358 6 12 18 43 69 95
Four Color 383,409 5 10 15 34 55 75
16(11-1/52-53) - 30 4 8 12 28 44 60
31-56 4 8 12 22 34 45
(See March of Comics #5, 22, 79, & Super Book #4, 15, 27.)

A-NEXT (See Avengers)
Marvel Comics: Oct, 1998 - No. 12, Sept, 1999 ($1.99)

1-12: 1-Next generation of Avengers; Frenz-a. 2-Two covers. 3-Defenders app. 3.00
Spider-Girl Presents Avengers Next Vol. 1: Second Coming (2006, $7.99, digest) r/#1-6 8.00

ANGEL
Dell Publishing Co.: Aug, 1954 - No. 16, Nov-Jan, 1958-59

Four Color 576(#1, 8/54) 4 8 12 26 41 55
2(5-7/55) - 16 3 6 9 18 27 35

ANGEL (TV) (Also see Buffy the Vampire Slayer)
Dark Horse Comics: Nov, 1999 - No. 17, Apr, 2001 ($2.95/$2.99)

1-17: 1-3,5-7,10-14-Zanier-a. 1-4,7,10-Matsuda & photo-c. 16-Buffy-c/app. 3.00
...: Earthly Possessions TPB (4/01, $9.95) r/#5-7, photo-c 10.00
...: Surrogates TPB (12/00, $9.95) r/#1-3; photo-c 10.00

ANGEL (Buffy the Vampire Slayer)
Dark Horse Comics: Sept, 2001 - No. 4, May, 2002 ($2.99, limited series)

1-4-Joss Whedon & Matthews-s/Rubi-a; photo-c and Rubi-c on each 3.00

ANGEL (Buffy the Vampire Slayer) (Previously titled Angel: After the Fall)
IDW Publishing: No. 18, Feb, 2009 - Present ($3.99)

18-41: Multiple covers on all. 25-Juliet Landau-s 4.00

ANGEL (one-shots) (Buffy the Vampire Slayer)
IDW Publishing: ($3.99/$7.49)

...: Connor (8/06, $3.99) Jay Faerber-s/Bob Gill-a; 4 covers + 1 retailer cover 4.00
...: Doyle (7/06, $3.99) Jeff Mariotte-s/David Messina-a; 4 covers + 1 retailer cover 4.00
...: Gunn (5/06, $3.99) Dan Jolley-s/Mark Pennington-a; 4 covers + 2 retailer covers 4.00
...: Illyria (4/06, $3.99) Peter David-s/Nicola Scott-a; 4 covers + 2 retailer covers 4.00
...: Masks (10/06, $7.49) short stories of Angel, Illyria, Cordilia & Lindsay; puppet Angel app. 8.00
... Special • Lorne (3/10, $7.99) John Byrne-s/a; The Groosalugg app. 4.00
...: Vs. Frankenstein (10/09, $3.99) John Byrne-s/a/c 4.00
...: Vs. Frankenstein II (10/10, $3.99) John Byrne-s/a/c 4.00
...: Wesley (6/06, $3.99) Scott Tipton-s/Mike Norton-a; 4 covers + 1 retailer cover 4.00
Spotlight TPB (12/06, $19.99) r/Connor, Doyle, Gunn, Illyria & Wesley one-shots 20.00

ANGELA
Image Comics (Todd McFarlane Prod.): Dec, 1994 - No. 3, Feb, 1995 ($2.95, lim. series)

1-Gaiman scripts & Capullo-c/a in all; Spawn app. 1 2 3 5 6 8
2 6.00
3 5.00
Special Edition (1995)-Pirate Spawn-c 3 6 9 14 20 25
Special Edition (1995)-Angela-c 3 6 9 14 20 25
TPB ($9.95, 1995) reprints #1-3 & Special Ed. w/additional pin-ups 10.00

ANGEL: AFTER THE FALL (Buffy the Vampire Slayer) (Follows the last TV episode)

Angel and the Ape (2nd series) #1 © DC

Angelus #4 © TCOW

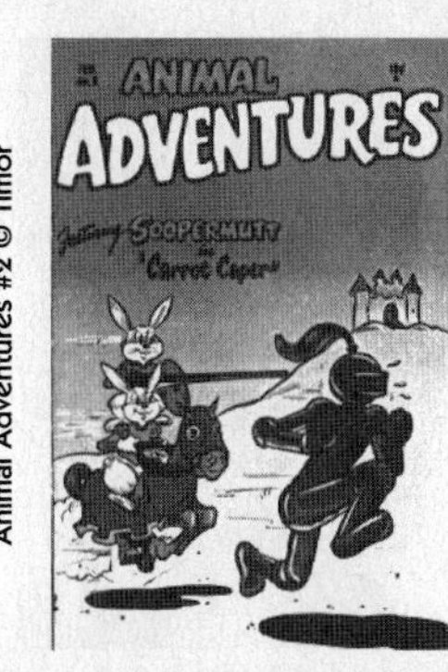

Animal Adventures #2 © Timor

	GD 2.0	VG 4.0	FN 6.0	VF 8.0	VF/NM 9.0	NM- 9.2

IDW Publishing: Nov, 2007 - No. 17, Feb, 2009 ($3.99)(Continues as Angel with #18)

1-Whedon & Lynch-s; multiple covers 5.00
2-17: Multiple covers on all 4.00

ANGELA/GLORY: RAGE OF ANGELS (See Glory/Angela: Rage of Angels)
Image Comics (Todd McFarlane Productions): Mar, 1996 ($2.50, one-shot)

1-Liefeld-c/Cruz-a(p); Darkchylde preview flip book 4.00
1-Variant-c 4.00

ANGEL: A HOLE IN THE WORLD (Adaptation of the 2-part TV episode)
IDW Publishing: Dec, 2009 - No. 5, Apr, 2010 ($3.99, limited series)

1-5-Fred becomes Illyria; Casagrande-a/c 4.00

ANGEL AND THE APE (Meet Angel No. 7) (See Limited Collector's Edition C-34 & Showcase No. 77)
National Periodical Publications: Nov-Dec, 1968 - No. 6, Sept-Oct, 1969

	GD	VG	FN	VF	VF/NM	NM-
1-(11-12/68)-Not Wood-a	5	10	15	30	48	65
2-5-Wood inks in all. 4-Last 12¢ issue	3	6	9	20	30	40
6-Wood inks	4	8	12	22	34	45

ANGEL AND THE APE (2nd Series)
DC Comics: Mar, 1991 - No. 4, June, 1991 ($1.00, limited series)

1-4 3.00

ANGEL AND THE APE (3rd Series)
DC Comics (Vertigo): Oct, 2001 - No. 4, Jan 2002 ($2.95, limited series)

1-4-Chaykin & Tischman-s/Bond-a/Art Adams-c 3.00

ANGEL: AULD LANG SYNE (Buffy the Vampire Slayer)
IDW Publishing: Nov, 2006 - No. 5, Mar, 2007 ($3.99, limited series)

1-5: 1-Three covers plus photo-c; Tipton-s/Messina-a 4.00

ANGEL: BARBARY COAST (Buffy the Vampire Slayer)
IDW Publishing: Apr, 2010 - No. 3, Jun, 2010 ($3.99, limited series)

1-3-Angel in 1906 San Francisco; Tischman-s/Urru-a; 2 covers on each 4.00

ANGEL: BLOOD & TRENCHES (Buffy the Vampire Slayer)
IDW Publishing: Mar, 2009 - No. 4, June, 2009 ($3.99, B&W&Red, limited series)

1-4-Angel in World War II Europe; John Byrne-s/a/c 4.00

ANGEL: ILLYRIA: HAUNTED (Buffy the Vampire Slayer)
IDW Publishing: Nov, 2010 - No. 4, Feb, 2011 ($3.99, limited series)

1-4-Tipton & Huehner-s/Casagrande-a; 2 covers 4.00

ANGEL LOVE
DC Comics: Aug, 1986 - No. 8, Mar, 1987 (75¢, limited series)

1-8, Special 1 (1987, $1.25, 52 pgs.) 3.00

ANGEL: NOT FADE AWAY (Buffy the Vampire Slayer)
IDW Publishing: May, 2009 - No. 3, July, 2009 ($3.99, limited series)

1-3-Adaptation of TV show's final episodes; Mooney-a 4.00

ANGEL OF LIGHT, THE (See The Crusaders)

ANGEL: OLD FRIENDS (Buffy the Vampire Slayer)
IDW Publishing: Nov, 2005 - No. 5, Mar, 2006 ($3.99, limited series)

1-5: Four covers plus photo-c on each; Mariotte-s/Messina-a; Gunn, Spike and Illyria app. 4.00
... Cover Gallery (6/06, $3.99) gallery of variant covers for the series 4.00
... Cover Gallery (12/06, $3.99) gallery of variant covers; preview of Angel: Auld Lang Syne 4.00
TPB (2006, $19.99) r/series; gallery of Messina covers 20.00

ANGEL: ONLY HUMAN (Buffy the Vampire Slayer)
IDW Publishing: Aug, 2009 - No. 5, Dec, 2009 ($3.99, limited series)

1-5-Lobdell-s/Messina-a; covers by Messina and Dave Dorman 4.00

ANGEL: REVELATIONS (X-Men character)
Marvel Comics: July, 2008 - No. 5, Nov, 2008 ($3.99, limited series)

1-5-Origin from childhood re-told; Adam Pollina-a/Aquirre-Sacasa-s 4.00

ANGEL: SMILE TIME (Buffy the Vampire Slayer)
IDW Publishing: Dec, 2008 - No. 3, Apr, 2009 ($3.99, limited series)

1-3-Adaptation of TV episode; Messina-a; Messina and photo covers for each 4.00

ANGEL: THE CURSE (Buffy the Vampire Slayer)
IDW Publishing: June, 2005 - No. 5, Oct, 2005 ($3.99, limited series)

1-5-Four covers on each; Mariotte-s/Messina-a 4.00
TPB (1/06, $19.99) r/#1-5; cover gallery of Messina covers 20.00

ANGELTOWN
DC Comics (Vertigo): Jan, 2005 - No. 5, May, 2005 ($2.95, limited series)

1-5-Gary Phillips-s/Shawn Martinbrough-a 3.00

ANGELUS
Image Comics (Top Cow): Dec, 2007; Dec, 2009 - Nov, 2010 ($2.99)

... Pilot Season 1-(12/07) Sejic-a/c; Edington-s; origin re-told 3.00
1-6-Marz-s/Sejic-a; multiple covers on each 3.00

ANGRY CHRIST COMIX (See Cry For Dawn)

ANIMA
DC Comics: Mar, 1994 - No. 15, July, 1995 ($1.75/$1.95/$2.25)

1-7,0,8-15: 7-(9/94)-Begin $1.95-c; Zero Hour x-over 3.00

ANIMAL ADVENTURES
Timor Publications/Accepted Publ. (reprints): Dec, 1953 - No. 3, May?, 1954

	GD	VG	FN	VF	VF/NM	NM-
1-Funny animal	8	16	24	40	50	60
2,3: 2-Featuring Soopermutt (2/54)	6	12	18	28	34	40
1-3 (reprints, nd)	3	6	8	11	13	15

ANIMAL ANTICS
DC Comics: Feb, 1946

nn - Ashcan comic, not distributed to newsstands, only for in-house use. Cover art is Star Spangled Comics #49 and interior is Boy Commandos #12 ; a cover sold for $1139 in 2010.

ANIMAL ANTICS (Movietown... No. 24 on)
National Periodical Publ: Mar-Apr, 1946 - No. 23, Nov-Dec, 1949 (All 52 pgs.?)

	GD	VG	FN	VF	VF/NM	NM-
1-Raccoon Kids begins by Otto Feuer; many-c by Grossman; Seaman Sy Wheeler by Kelly in some issues; Grossman-a in most issues	43	86	129	271	461	650
2	24	48	72	140	230	320
3-10: 10-Post-c/a	16	32	48	92	144	195
11-23: 14,15,18,19-Post-a	12	24	36	67	94	120

ANIMAL COMICS
Dell Publishing Co.: Dec-Jan, 1941-42 - No. 30, Dec-Jan, 1947-48

	GD	VG	FN	VF	VF/NM	NM-
1-1st Pogo app. by Walt Kelly (Dan Noonan art in most issues)	103	206	309	659	1130	1600
2-Uncle Wiggily begins	53	106	159	334	567	800
3,5	27	54	81	197	399	600
4,6,7-No Pogo	15	30	45	106	216	325
8-10	18	36	54	131	266	400
11-15	12	24	36	87	164	240
16-20	9	18	27	63	107	150
21-30: 24-30- "Jigger" by John Stanley	8	16	24	52	86	120

NOTE: *Dan Noonan a-18-30. **Gollub** art in most later issues; c-29, 30. **Kelly** c-7-26, part #27-30.*

ANIMAL CRACKERS (Also see Adventures of Patoruzu)
Green Publ. Co./Norlen/Fox Feat.(Hero Books): 1946; No. 31, July, 1950; No. 9, 1959

	GD	VG	FN	VF	VF/NM	NM-
1-Super Cat begins (1st app.)	19	38	57	111	176	240
2	10	20	30	58	79	100
31(Fox)-Formerly My Love Secret	8	16	24	42	54	65
9(1959-Norlen)-Infinity-c	5	10	14	20	24	28
nn, nd ('50s), no publ.; infinity-c	5	10	14	20	24	28

ANIMAL FABLES
E. C. Comics (Fables Publ. Co.): July-Aug, 1946 - No. 7, Nov-Dec, 1947

	GD	VG	FN	VF	VF/NM	NM-
1-Freddy Firefly (clone of Human Torch), Korky Kangaroo, Petey Pig, Danny Demon begin	53	106	159	334	567	800
2-Aesop Fables begin	34	68	102	199	325	450
3-6	28	56	84	165	270	375
7-Origin Moon Girl	69	138	207	442	759	1075

ANIMAL FAIR (Fawcett's...)
Fawcett Publications: Mar, 1946 - No. 11, Feb, 1947

	GD	VG	FN	VF	VF/NM	NM-
1	28	56	84	165	270	375
2	14	28	42	82	121	160
3-6	12	24	36	67	94	120
7-11	10	20	30	54	72	90

ANIMAL FUN
Premier Magazines: 1953 (25¢, came w/glasses)

	GD	VG	FN	VF	VF/NM	NM-
1-(3-D)-Ziggy Pig, Silly Seal, Billy & Buggy Bear	36	72	108	214	347	480

ANIMAL MAN (See Action Comics #552, 553, DC Comics Presents #77, 78, Last Days of Animal Man, Secret Origins #39, Strange Adventures #180 & Wonder Woman #267, 268)
DC Comics (Vertigo imprint #57 on): Sept, 1988 - No. 89, Nov, 1995 ($1.25/$1.50/$1.75/$1.95/$2.25, mature)

	GD	VG	FN	VF	VF/NM	NM-
1-Grant Morrison scripts begin, ends #26	2	4	6	8	10	12

2-10: 2-Superman cameo. 6-Invasion tie-in. 9-Manhunter-c/story. 10-Psycho Pirate app.

Animaniacs #23 © WB

Annie #1 © MAR

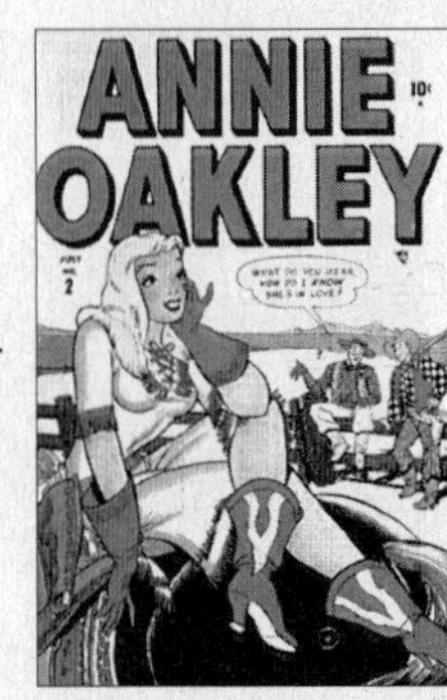

Annie Oakley #2 © MAR

GD 2.0 | VG 4.0 | FN 6.0 | VF 8.0 | VF/NM 9.0 | NM- 9.2

1 2 3 4 5 7
11-49,51-55,57-89: 23,24-Psycho Pirate app. 24-Arkham Asylum story; Bizarro Superman app. 25-Inferior Five app. 26-Morrison apps. in story; part photo-c (of Morrison?) 3.00
50-($2.95, 52 pgs.)-Last issue w/Veitch scripts 5.00
56-($3.50, 68 pgs.) 5.00
Annual 1 (1993, $3.95, 68 pgs.)-Bolland-c; Children's Crusade Pt. 3 6.00
...: Deus Ex Machina TPB (2003, $19.95) r/#18-26; Morrison-s; new Bolland-c 20.00
...: Origin of the Species TPB (2002, $19.95) r/#10-17 & Secret Origins #39 20.00
NOTE: *Bolland c-1-63. 71-Sutton-a(i)*

ANIMAL MYSTIC (See Dark One...)
Cry For Dawn/Sirius: 1993 - No. 4, 1995 ($2.95?/$3.50, B&W)
1 3 6 9 14 19 24
1-Alternate 4 8 12 22 34 45
1-2nd printing 5.00
2 2 4 6 10 14 18
2,3-2nd prints (Sirius) 3.50
3 ,4: 4-Color poster insert, Linsner-s 1 2 3 5 7 9
TPB ($14.95) r/series 18.00

ANIMAL MYSTIC WATER WARS
Sirius: 1996 - No. 6 ($2.95, limited series)
1-6-Dark One-c/a/scripts 5.00

ANIMAL WORLD, THE (Movie)
Dell Publishing Co.: No. 713, Aug, 1956
Four Color 713 4 8 12 26 41 55

ANIMANIACS (TV)
DC Comics: May, 1995 - No. 59, Apr, 2000 ($1.50/$1.75/$1.95/$1.99)
1 1 2 3 4 5 7
2-20: 13-Manga issue. 19-X-Files parody; Miran Kim-c; Adlard-a (4 pgs.) 4.00
21-59: 26-E.C. parody-c. 34-Xena parody. 43-Pinky & the Brain take over 3.00
A Christmas Special (12/94, $1.50, "1" on-c) 3.00

ANIMATED COMICS
E. C. Comics: No date given (Summer, 1947?)
1 (Rare) 84 168 252 538 919 1300

ANIMATED FUNNY COMIC TUNES (See Funny Tunes)

ANIMATED MOVIE-TUNES (Movie Tunes No. 3)
Margood Publishing Corp. (Timely): Fall, 1945 - No. 2, Sum, 1946
1,2-Super Rabbit, Ziggy Pig & Silly Seal 36 72 108 211 343 475

ANIMAX
Marvel Comics (Star Comics): Dec, 1986 - No. 4, June, 1987
1-4: Based on toys; Simonson-a 3.00

ANITA BLAKE (Circus of the Damned - The Charmer on cover)
Marvel Comics: July, 2010 - No. 5, Dec, 2010 ($3.99, limited series)
1-5-Laurell K. Hamilton & Jess Ruffner-s/Ron Lim-a/ Brett Booth-c 4.00
... - The Ingenue 1,2 (3/11 - No. 5, $3.99) Hamilton & Ruffner-s/Lim-a/Booth-c 4.00

ANITA BLAKE: VAMPIRE HUNTER GUILTY PLEASURES
Marvel Comics (Dabel Brothers): Dec, 2006 - No. 12, Aug, 2008 ($2.99)
1-Laurell K. Hamilton-s/Brett Booth-a; blue cover 6.00
1-Variant-c by Greg Horn 20.00
1-Sketch cover 25.00
1-2nd printing with red cover 3.00
2-Two covers 5.00
3-12 3.00
...: Handbook (2007, $3.99) profile pages of characters; glossary 4.00
... Volume One HC (6/07, $19.99, dust jacket) r/#1-6; cover gallery 20.00

ANITA BLAKE: VAMPIRE HUNTER THE FIRST DEATH, (LAURELL K. HAMILTON'S...)
Marvel Comics (Dabel Brothers): July, 2007 - No. 2, Dec, 2007 ($3.99)
1,2-Laurell K. Hamilton & Jonathon Green-s/Wellington Alves-a. 2-Marvel Zombie var-c 4.00
... HC (2008, $19.99, dust jacket) r/#1,2 & Guilty Pleasures Handbook 20.00

ANITA BLAKE, VAMPIRE HUNTER: THE LAUGHING CORPSE
Marvel Comics: Dec, 2008 - No. 5, Apr, 2009 ($3.99)
... - Book One (12/08 - No. 5, 4/09) 1-5-Laurell K. Hamilton-s/Ron Lim-a/c 4.00
... - Necromancer 1-5 (6/09 - No. 5, 11/09, $3.99) Lim-a/c 4.00
Anita Blake (Executioner on-c) #11-15 (12/09 - No. 15, 5/10) numbering continued; Lim-a 4.00

ANNE RICE'S INTERVIEW WITH THE VAMPIRE
Innovation Books: 1991 - No. 12, Jan, 1994 ($2.50, limited series)
1-12: Adapts novel; Moeller-a 3.00

GD 2.0 | VG 4.0 | FN 6.0 | VF 8.0 | VF/NM 9.0 | NM- 9.2

ANNE RICE'S THE MASTER OF RAMPLING GATE
Innovation Books: 1991 ($6.95, one-shot)
1-Bolton painted-c; Colleen Doran painted-a 7.00

ANNE RICE'S THE MUMMY OR RAMSES THE DAMNED
Millennium Publications: Oct, 1990 - No. 12, Feb, 1992 ($2.50, limited series)
1-12: Adapts novel; Mooney-p in all 3.00

ANNE RICE'S THE WITCHING HOUR
Millennium Publ./Comico: 1992 - No. 13, Jan, 1993 ($2.50, limited series)
1-13 3.00

ANNETTE (Disney, TV)
Dell Publishing Co.: No. 905, May, 1958; No. 1100, May, 1960
(Mickey Mouse Club)
Four Color 905-Annette Funicello photo-c 23 46 69 168 334 500
Four Color 1100-...'s Life Story (Movie); A. Funicello photo-c 18 36 54 131 266 400

ANNEX (See Amazing Spider-Man Annual #27 for 1st app.)
Marvel Comics: Aug, 1994 - No. 4, Nov, 1994 ($1.75)
1-4: 1,4-Spider-Man app. 2.50

ANNIE
Marvel Comics Group: Oct, 1982 - No. 2, Nov, 1982 (60¢)
1,2-Movie adaptation 4.00
Treasury Edition ($2.00, tabloid size) 3 6 9 18 27 35

ANNIE OAKLEY (See Tessie The Typist #19, Two-Gun Kid & Wild Western)
Marvel/Atlas Comics(MPI No. 1-4/CDS No. 5 on): Spring, 1948 - No. 4, 11/48; No. 5, 6/55 - No. 11, 6/56
1 (1st Series, 1948)-Hedy Devine app. 47 94 141 296 498 700
2 (7/48, 52 pgs.)-Kurtzman-a, "Hey Look", 1 pg; Intro. Lana; Hedy Devine app; Captain Tootsie by Beck 27 54 81 158 259 360
3,4 22 44 66 132 216 300
5 (2nd Series, 1955)-Reinman-a ; Maneely-c 17 34 51 98 154 210
6-9: 6,8-Woodbridge-a. 9-Williamson-a (4 pgs.) 14 28 42 80 115 150
10,11: 11-Severin-c 13 26 39 74 105 135

ANNIE OAKLEY AND TAGG (TV)
Dell Publishing Co./Gold Key: 1953 - No. 18, Jan-Mar, 1959; July, 1965 (Gail Davis photo-c #3 on)
Four Color 438 (#1) 13 26 39 92 179 265
Four Color 481,575 (#2,3) 9 18 27 64 110 155
4(7-9/55)-10 8 16 24 54 90 125
11-18(1-3/59) 7 14 21 45 73 100
1(7/65-Gold Key)-Photo-c (c-r/#6) 4 8 12 28 44 60
NOTE: *Manning a-13. Photo back c-4, 9, 11.*

ANNIHILATION
Marvel Comics: May, 2006 - No. 6, Mar, 2007 ($3.99/$2.99, limited x-over series)
Prologue (5/06, $3.99, one-shot) Nova, Thanos and Silver Surfer app. 4.00
1-6: 1-(10/06) Giffen-s/DiVito-a; Annihilus app. 3.00
...: Heralds of Galactus 1,2 (4/07-5/07, $3.99) 2-Silver Surfer app. 4.00
...: Nova 1-4 (6/06-9/06, $2.99) Abnett & Lanning-s/Walker-a/Dell'Otto-c. 2,3-Quasar app. 3.00
...: Ronan 1-4 (6/06-9/06, $2.99) Furman-s/Lucas-a/Dell'Otto-c 3.00
... Saga (2007, $1.99) re-cap of the series; DiVito-c 3.00
...: Silver Surfer 1-4 (6/06-9/06, $2.99) Giffen-s/Arlem-a/Dell'Otto-c 3.00
...: Super-Skrull 1-4 (6/06-9/06, $2.99) Grillo-Marxuach-s/Titus-a/Dell'Otto-c 3.00
...: The Nova Corps Files (2006, $3.99) profile pages of characters and alien races 4.00
Annihilation Book 1 HC (2007, $29.99, dustjacket) r/Drax the Destroyer #1-4, Annihilation Prologue and Annihilation: Nova #1-4; sketch and layout pages 30.00
Annihilation Book 1 SC (2007, $24.99) same content as HC 25.00
Annihilation Book 2 HC (2007, $29.99, dustjacket) r/Annihilation: Silver Surfer #1-4, ...: Super Skrull #1-4 and ...: Ronan #1-4; sketch and layout pages 30.00
Annihilation Book 2 SC (2007, $24.99) same content as HC 25.00
Annihilation Book 3 HC (2007, $29.99, dustjacket) r/Annihilation #1-6, Annihilation: Heralds of Galactus #1,2 and Annihilation: Nova Corps Files; sketch pages 30.00
Annihilation Book 3 SC (2007, $24.99) same content as HC 25.00

ANNIHILATION: CONQUEST (Also see Nova 2007 series)
Marvel Comics: Jan, 2008 - No. 6, Jun, 2008 ($3.99/$2.99, limited x-over series)
Prologue (8/07, $3.99, one-shot) the new Quasar, Moondragon app.; Perkins-a 4.00
1-5-Raney-a; Ultron app. 3-Moondragon dies 3.00
6-($3.99) 4.00
... - Quasar 1-4 (9/07-No. 4, 12/07, $2.99) Gage-s/Lilly-a. 1-Super-Adaptoid app. 3.00
... - Starlord 1-4 (9/07-No. 4, 12/07, $2.99) Giffen-s/Green-a 3.00

Ant-Man & Wasp #1 © MAR

A-1 Comics #27 © ME

A-1 Comics #64 © ME

	GD 2.0	VG 4.0	FN 6.0	VF 8.0	VF/NM 9.0	NM- 9.2

... - Wraith 1-4 (9/07-No. 4, 12/07, $2.99) Hotz-a/Grillo-Marxuach-s 3.00
Annihilation: Conquest Book 1 HC (2008, $29.99, dustjacket) r/Prologue; ...Quasar #1-4, ...Star-Lord #1-4; Annihilation Saga; design pages 30.00

ANNIHILATORS
Marvel Comics: May, 2011 - No. 4 ($4.99, limited series)
1,2: Quasar, Silver Surfer, Beta-Ray Bill, Ronan, Gladiator app.; Huat-a 5.00

ANOTHER WORLD (See Strange Stories From...)

ANT
Image Comics: Aug, 2005 - No. 11 ($2.99)
1-11: 1-Mario Gulley-s/a. 2-Savage Dragon & Spawn app. 3-Spawn-c/app. 3.00
Vol. 1: Reality Bites TPB (2006, $12.99) r/#1-4; sketch and concept art 13.00

ANTHRO (See Showcase #74)
National Periodical Publications: July-Aug, 1968 - No. 6, July-Aug, 1969

	GD	VG	FN	VF	VF/NM	NM-
1-(7-8/68)-Howie Post-a in all	6	12	18	37	59	80
2-5: 5-Last 12¢ issue	4	8	12	22	34	45
6-Wood-c/a (inks)	4	8	12	24	37	50

ANTI-HITLER COMICS
New England Comics Press: Summer, 1992 ($2.75, B&W, one-shot)
1-Reprints Hitler as Devil stories from wartime comics 6.00

ANT-MAN (See Irredeemable Ant-Man, The)

ANT-MAN & WASP
Marvel Comics: Jan, 2011 - No. 3, Mar, 2011 ($3.99, limited series)
1-3-Tim Seeley-s/a; Espin-c; Tigra app. 4.00

ANT-MAN'S BIG CHRISTMAS
Marvel Comics: Feb, 2000 ($5.95, square-bound, one-shot)
1-Bob Gale-s/Phil Winslade-a; Avengers app. 6.00

ANTONY AND CLEOPATRA (See Ideal, a Classical Comic)

ANYTHING GOES
Fantagraphics Books: Oct, 1986 - No. 6, 1987 ($2.00, #1-5 color & B&W/#6 B&W, lim. series)
1-6: 1-Flaming Carrot app. (1st in color?); G. Kane-c. 2-6: 2-Miller-c(p); Alan Moore scripts; Kirby-a; early Sam Kieth-a (2 pgs.). 3-Capt. Jack, Cerebus app.; Cerebus-c by N. Adams. 4-Perez-c. 5-3rd color Teenage Mutant Ninja Turtles app. 3.50

A-1
Marvel Comics (Epic Comics): 1992 - No. 4, 1993 ($5.95, limited series, mature)

	GD	VG	FN	VF	VF/NM	NM-
1-4: 1-Fabry-c/a, Russell-a, S. Hampton-a. 3-Bisley-c; Kent Williams-a. 4-McKean-a; Dorman-s/a	1	2	3	4	5	7

A-1 COMICS (A-1 appears on covers No. 1-17 only)(See individual title listings for #11-139) (1st two issues not numbered.)
Life's Romances Publ.-No. 1/Compix/Magazine Ent.: 1944 - No. 139, Sept-Oct, 1955 (No #2)
nn-(1944) (See Kerry Drake Detective Cases)

	GD	VG	FN	VF	VF/NM	NM-
1-Dotty Dripple (1 pg.), Mr. Ex, Bush Berry, Rocky, Lew Loyal (20 pgs.)	15	30	45	88	137	185
3-8,10: Texas Slim & Dirty Dalton, The Corsair, Teddy Rich, Dotty Dripple, Inca Dinca, Tommy Tinker, Little Mexico & Tugboat Tim, The Masquerader & others. 7-Corsair-c/s. 8-Intro Rodeo Ryan	10	20	30	56	76	95
9-All Texas Slim	10	20	30	58	79	100

(See Individual Alphabetical listings for prices)

11-Teena; Ogden Whitney-c
13-Guns of Fact & Fiction (1948). Used in **SOTI**, pg. 19; Ingels & Johnny Craig-a
17-Tim Holt #2; photo-c; last issue to carry A-1 on cover (9-10/48)
19-Tim Holt #3; photo-c
22-Dick Powell (1949)-Photo-c
23-Cowboys and Indians #6; Doc Holiday-c/story
25-Fibber McGee & Molly (1949) (Radio)
26-Trail Colt #2-Ingels-c
28-Christmas-(Koko & Kola #6) ('50)
30-Jet Powers #1-Powell-a
32-Jet Powers #2
33-Muggsy Mouse #1('51)
35-Jet Powers #3-Williamson/Evans-a
37-Ghost Rider #5-Frazetta-c (1951)
39-Muggsy Mouse #3
41-Cowboys 'N' Indians #7 (1951)
12,15-Teena
14-Tim Holt Western Adventures #1
16-Vacation Comics; The Pixies, Tom Tom, Flying Fredd, & Koko & Kola
18,20-Jimmy Durante; photo covers on both
21-Joan of Arc (1949)-Movie adaptation; Ingrid Bergman photo-covers & interior photos; Whitney-a
24-Trail Colt #1-Frazetta-r in-Manhunt #13; Ingels-c; L. B. Cole-a
27-Ghost Rider #1(1950)-Origin
29-Ghost Rider #2-Frazetta-c (1950)
31-Ghost Rider #3-Frazetta-c & origin ('51)
34-Ghost Rider #4-Frazetta-c (1951)
36-Muggsy Mouse #2; Racist-c
38-Jet Powers #4-Williamson/Wood-a
40-Dogface Dooley #1('51)
42-Best of the West #1-Powell-a
43-Dogface Dooley #2
45-American Air Forces #5-Powell-c/a
47-Thun'da, King of the Congo #1-Frazetta-c/a('52)
50-Danger Is Their Business #11 ('52)-Powell-a
53-Dogface Dooley #4
55-U.S. Marines #5-Powell-a
56-Thun'da #2-Powell-c/a
58-American Air Forces #7-Powell-a
60-The U.S. Marines #6-Powell-a
62-Starr Flagg, Undercover Girl #5 (#1) reprinted from A-1 #24
65-American Air Forces #8-Powell-a
67-American Air Forces #9-Powell-a
69-Ghost Rider #9(10/52)
71-Ghost Rider #10(12/52)-Vs. Frankenstein
74-American Air Forces #10-Powell-a
76-Best of the West #7
78-Thun'da #4-Powell-c/a
80-Ghost Rider #12(6/52)-One-eyed Devil-c
83-Thun'da #5-Powell-c/a
84-Ghost Rider #13(7-8/53)
86-Thun'da #6-Powell-c/a
88-Bobby Benson's B-Bar-B Riders #20
90-Red Hawk #11(1953)-Powell-c/a
91-American Air Forces #12-Powell-a
93-Great Western #8('54)-Origin The Ghost Rider; Powell-a
95-Muggsy Mouse #4
96-Cave Girl #12, with Thun'da; Powell-c/a
99-Muggsy Mouse #5
101-White Indian #12-Frazetta-a(r)
101-Dream Book of Romance #6 (4-6/54); Marlon Brando photo-c; Powell, Bolle, Guardineer-a
105-Great Western #9-Ghost Rider app.; Powell-a, 6 pgs.; Bolle-c
107-Hot Dog #1
108-Red Fox #15 (1954)-L.B. Cole-c/a; Powell-a
110-Dream Book of Romance #8 (10/54)-Movie photo-c
112-Ghost Rider #14 ('54)
114-Dream Book of Love #2- Guardineer, Bolle-a; Piper Laurie, Victor Mature photo-c
118-Undercover Girl #7-Powell-c
120-Badmen of the West #2
121-Mysteries of Scotland Yard #1; reprinted from Manhunt (5 stories)
124-Dream Book of Romance #8 (10-11/54)
126-I'm a Cop #2-Powell-a
128-I'm a Cop #3-Powell-a
130-Strongman #1-Powell-a (2-3/55)
132-Strongman #2
134-Strongman #3
136-Hot Dog #4
138-The Avenger #4-Powell-c/a
44-Ghost Rider #6
46-Best of the West #2
48-Cowboys 'N' Indians #8
49-Dogface Dooley #3
51-Ghost Rider #7 ('52)
52-Best of the West #3
54-American Air Forces #6(8/52)-Powell-a
57-Ghost Rider #8
59-Best of the West #4
61-Space Ace #5('53)-Guardineer-a
63-Manhunt #13-Frazetta
64-Dogface Dooley #5
66-Best of the West #5
68-U.S. Marines #7-Powell-a
70-Best of the West #6
72-U.S. Marines #8-Powell-a(3)
73-Thun'da #3-Powell-c/a
75-Ghost Rider #11(3/52)
77-Manhunt #14
79-American Air Forces #11-Powell-a
81-Best of the West #8
82-Cave Girl #11(1953)-Powell-c/a; origin (#1)
85-Best of the West #9
87-Best of the West #10(9-10/53)
89-Home Run #3-Powell-a; Stan Musial photo-c
92-Dream Book of Romance #5-Photo-c; Guardineer-a
94-White Indian #11-Frazetta-a(r); Powell-c
97-Best of the West #11
98-Undercover Girl #6-Powell-c
100-Badmen of the West #1-Meskin-a(?)
103-Best of the West #12-Powell-a
104-White Indian #13-Frazetta-a(r) ('54)
106-Dream Book of Love #1 (6-7/54) -Powell, Bolle-a; Montgomery Clift, Donna Reed photo-c
109-Dream Book of Romance #7 (7-8/54). Powell-a; movie photo-c
111-I'm a Cop #1 ('54); drug mention story; Powell-a
113-Great Western #10; Powell-a
115-Hot Dog #3
116-Cave Girl #13-Powell-c/a
117-White Indian #14
119-Straight Arrow's Fury #1 (origin); Fred Meagher-c/a
122-Black Phantom #1 (11/54)
123-Dream Book of Love #3 (10-11/54)-Movie photo-c
125-Cave Girl #14-Powell-c/a
127-Great Western #11('54)-Powell-a
129-The Avenger #1('55)-Powell-c
131-The Avenger #2('55)-Powell-c/a
133-The Avenger #3-Powell-c/a
135-White Indian #15
137-Africa #1-Powell-c/a(4)
139-Strongman #4-Powell-a

NOTE: ***Bolle*** *a-110. Photo-c-17-22, 89, 92, 101, 106, 109, 110, 114, 123, 124.*

APACHE
Fiction House Magazines: 1951

	GD	VG	FN	VF	VF/NM	NM-
1	22	44	66	132	216	300
I.W. Reprint No. 1-r/#1 above	3	6	9	18	27	35

APACHE KID (Formerly Reno Browne; Western Gunfighters #20 on)
(Also see Two-Gun Western & Wild Western)
Marvel/Atlas Comics(MPC No. 53-10/CPS No. 11 on): No. 53, 12/50 - No. 10, 1/52; No. 11, 12/54 - No. 19, 4/56
53(#1)-Apache Kid & his horse Nightwind (origin), Red Hawkins by Syd Shores begins

Approved Comics #11 © STJ

Aquaman #3 © DC

Aquaman (3rd series) #69 © DC

	GD 2.0	VG 4.0	FN 6.0	VF 8.0	VF/NM 9.0	NM- 9.2
	34	68	102	199	325	450
2(2/51)	17	34	51	98	154	210
3-5	13	26	39	72	101	130
6-10 (1951-52): 7-Russ Heath-a	11	22	33	60	83	105
11-19 (1954-56)	9	18	27	50	65	80

NOTE: ***Heath** a-7. c-11, 13. **Maneely** a-53; c-53(#1), 12, 14-16. **Powell** a-14. **Severin** c-17.*

APACHE MASSACRE (See Chief Victorio's...)

APACHE SKIES
Marvel Comics: Sept, 2002 - No. 4, Dec, 2002 ($2.99, limited series)

1-4-Apache Kid app.; Ostrander-s/Manco-c/a 3.00
TPB (2003, $12.99) r/#1-4 13.00

APACHE TRAIL
Steinway/America's Best: Sept, 1957 - No. 4, June, 1958

1	11	22	33	62	86	110
2-4: 2-Tuska-a	8	16	24	40	50	60

APE (Magazine)
Dell Publishing Co.: 1961 (52 pgs., B&W)

1-Comics and humor	4	8	12	26	41	55

APHRODITE IX
Image Comics (Top Cow): Sept, 2000 - No. 4, Mar, 2002 ($2.50)

1-3: 1-Four covers by Finch, Turner, Silvestri, Benitez 4.00
1-Tower Record Ed.; Finch-c 3.00
1-DF Chrome ($14.99) 15.00
4-($4.95) Double-sized issue; Finch-c 5.00
Convention Preview 10.00
...: Time Out of Mind TPB (6/04, $14.99) r/#1-4, & #0; cover gallery 15.00
Wizard #0 (4/00, bagged w/Tomb Raider magazine) Preview & sketchbook 5.00
#0-(6/01, $2.95) r/Wizard #0 with cover gallery 3.00

APOCALYPSE NERD
Dark Horse Comics: January, 2005 - No. 6, Oct, 2007 ($2.99, B&W)

1-6-Peter Bagge-s/a 3.00

APPARITION
Caliber Comics: 1995 ($3.95, 52 pgs., B&W)

1 ($3.95) 4.00
V2#1-6 ($2.95) 3.00
Visitations 4.00

APPLESEED
Eclipse Comics: Sept, 1988 - Book 4, Vol. 4, Aug, 1991 ($2.50/$2.75/$3.50, 52/68 pgs, B&W)

Book One, Vol. 1-5: 5-(1/89), Book Two, Vol. 1(2/89) -5(7/89): Art Adams-c, Book Three, Vol. 1(8/89) -4 ($2.75), Book Three, Vol. 5 ($3.50), Book Four, Vol. 1 (1/91) - 4 (8/91) ($3.50, 68 pgs.) 6.00

APPLESEED DATABOOK
Dark Horse Comics: Apr, 1994 - No. 2, May, 1994 ($3.50, B&W, limited series)

1,2: 1-Flip book format 3.50

APPROVED COMICS (Also see Blue Ribbon Comics)
St. John Publishing Co. (Most have no c-price): March, 1954 - No. 12, Aug, 1954 (Painted-c on #1-5,7,8,10)

1-The Hawk #5-r	10	20	30	56	76	95
2-Invisible Boy (3/54)-Origin; Saunders-c	16	32	48	92	144	195
3-Wild Boy of the Congo #11-r (4/54)	10	20	30	56	76	95
4,5: 4-Kid Cowboy-r. 5-Fly Boy-r	10	20	30	56	76	95
6-Daring Adv.-r (5/54); Krigstein-a(2); Baker-c	14	28	42	76	108	140
7-The Hawk #6-r	10	20	30	56	76	95
8-Crime on the Run (6/54); Powell-a; Saunders-c	10	20	30	56	76	95
9-Western Bandit Trails #3-r, with new-c; Baker-c/a	14	28	42	76	108	140
10-Dinky Duck (Terrytoons)	6	12	18	31	38	45
11-Fightin' Marines #3-r (8/54); Canteen Kate app; Baker-c/a	14	28	42	76	108	140
12-Northwest Mounties #4-r(8/54); new Baker-c	14	28	42	76	108	140

AQUAMAN (See Adventure Comics #260, Brave & the Bold, DC Comics Presents #5, DC Special #28, DC Special Series #1, DC Super Stars #7, Detective Comics, JLA, Justice League of America, More Fun #73, Showcase #30-33, Super DC Giant, Super Friends, and World's Finest Comics)

AQUAMAN (1st Series)
National Periodical Publications/DC Comics: Jan-Feb, 1962 - #56, Mar-Apr, 1971; #57, Aug-Sept,1977 - #63, Aug-Sept, 1978

GD 2.0 VG 4.0 FN 6.0 VF 8.0 VF/NM 9.0 NM- 9.2

	GD	VG	FN	VF	VF/NM	NM-
1-(1-2/62)-Intro. Quisp	92	184	276	782	1591	2400
2	33	66	99	254	502	750
3-5	20	40	60	140	283	425
6-10	13	26	39	93	182	270
11,18: 11-1st app. Mera. 18-Aquaman weds Mera; JLA cameo	11	22	33	77	144	210
12-17,19,20	11	22	33	75	138	200
21-32: 23-Birth of Aquababy. 26-Huntress app.(3-4/66). 29-1st app. Ocean Master, Aquaman's step-brother. 30-Batman & Superman-c & cameo	7	14	21	50	83	115
33-1st app. Aqua-Girl (see Adventure #266)	8	16	24	54	90	125
34-40: 35-1st app. Black Manta. 40-Jim Aparo's 1st DC work (8/68)	6	12	18	41	66	90
41-46,47,49: 45-Last 12¢-c	5	10	15	34	55	75
48-Origin reprinted	6	12	18	37	59	80
50-52-Deadman by Neal Adams	8	16	24	58	97	135
53-56('71): 56-1st app. Crusader; last 15¢-c	3	6	9	18	27	35
57('77)-63: 58-Origin retold	2	3	4	6	8	10

NOTE: ***Aparo** a-40-45, 46p, 47-59; c-58-63. **Nick Cardy** c-1-40. **Newton** a-60-63.*

AQUAMAN (1st limited series)
DC Comics: Feb, 1986 - No. 4, May, 1986 (75¢, limited series)

1-New costume; 1st app. Nuada of Thierna Na Oge	1	2	3	4	5	7

2-4: 3-Retelling of Aquaman & Ocean Master's origins. 5.00
Special 1 (1988, $1.50, 52 pgs.) 4.00
NOTE: ***Craig Hamilton** c/a-1-4p. **Russell** c-2-4i.*

AQUAMAN (2nd limited series)
DC Comics: June, 1989 - No. 5, Oct, 1989 ($1.00, limited series)

1-5: Giffen plots/breakdowns; Swan-a(p). 3.00
Special 1 (Legend of..., $2.00, 1989, 52 pgs.)-Giffen plots/breakdowns; Swan-a(p) 3.00

AQUAMAN (2nd Series)
DC Comics: Dec, 1991 - No. 13, Dec, 1992 ($1.00/$1.25)

1-5 2.50
6-13: 6-Begin $1.25-c. 9-Sea Devils app. 2.50

AQUAMAN (3rd Series)(Also see Atlantis Chronicles)
DC Comics: Aug, 1994 - No. 75, Jan, 2001 ($1.50/$1.75/$1.95/$1.99/$2.50)

1-(8/94)-Peter David scripts begin; reintro Dolphin 6.00
2-(9/94)-Aquaman loses hand 6.50
0-(10/94)-Aquaman replaces lost hand with hook. 6.50
3-8: 3-(11/94)-Superboy-c/app. 4-Lobo app. 6-Deep Six app. 3.50
9-69: 9-Begin $1.75-c. 10-Green Lantern app. 11-Reintro Mera. 15-Re-intro Kordax. 16-vs. JLA. 18-Reintro Ocean Master & Atlan (Aquaman's father). 19-Reintro Garth (Aqualad). 23-1st app. Deep Blue (Neptune Perkins & Tsunami's daughter). 23,24-Neptune Perkins, Nuada, Tsunami, Arion, Power Girl, & The Sea Devils app. 26-Final Night. 28-Martian Manhunter-c/app. 29-Black Manta-c/app. 32-Swamp Thing-c/app. 37-Genesis x-over. 41-Maxima-c/app. 43-Millennium Giants x-over; Superman-c/app. 44-G.A. Flash & Sentinel app. 50-Larsen-s begins. 53-Superman app. 60-Tempest marries Dolphin; Teen Titans app. 63-Kaluta covers begin. 66-JLA app. 3.00
70-75: 70-Begin $2.50-c. 71-73-Warlord-c/app. 75-Final issue 3.00
#1,000,000 (11/98) 853rd Century x-over 3.00
Annual 1 (1995, $3.50)-Year One story 4.00
Annual 2 (1996, $2.95)-Legends of the Dead Earth story 4.00
Annual 3 (1997, $3.95)-Pulp Heroes story 4.00
Annual 4,5 ('98, '99, $2.95)-4-Ghosts; Wrightson-c. 5-JLApe 4.00
...Secret Files 1 (12/98, $4.95) Origin-s and pin-ups 5.00
NOTE: ***Art Adams**-c, Annual 5. **Mignola** c-6. **Simonson** c-15.*

AQUAMAN (4th Series)(Titled Aquaman: Sword of Atlantis #40-on) (Also see JLA #69-75)
DC Comics: Feb, 2003 - No. 57, Dec, 2007 ($2.50/$2.99)

1-Veitch-s/Guichet-a/Maleev-c 4.00
2-14: 2-Martian Manhunter app. 8-11-Black Manta app. 3.00
15-39: 15-San Diego flooded; Pfeifer-s/Davis-c begin. 23,24-Sea Devils app. 33-Mera returns. 39-Black Manta app. 3.00
40-Sword of Atlantis; One Year Later begins ($2.99-c) Guice-a ; two covers 4.00
41-49,51-57: 41-Two covers. 42-Sea Devils app. 44-Ocean Master app. 3.00
50-($3.99) Tempest app.; McManus-a 4.00
...Secret Files 2003 (5/03, $4.95) background on Aquaman's new powers; pin-ups 5.00
...: Once and Future TPB (2006, $12.99) r/#40-45 13.00
...: The Waterbearer TPB (2003, $12.95) r/#1-4, stories from Aquaman Secret Files and JLA/JSA Secret Files #1; JG Jones-c 13.00

AQUAMAN: TIME & TIDE (3rd limited series) (Also see Atlantis Chronicles)
DC Comics: Dec, 1993 - No. 4, Mar, 1994 ($1.50, limited series)

1-4: Peter David scripts; origin retold. 3.00
Trade paperback ($9.95) 10.00

AQUANAUTS (TV)

Archard's Agents #1 © MAR

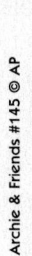

Archie & Friends #145 © AP

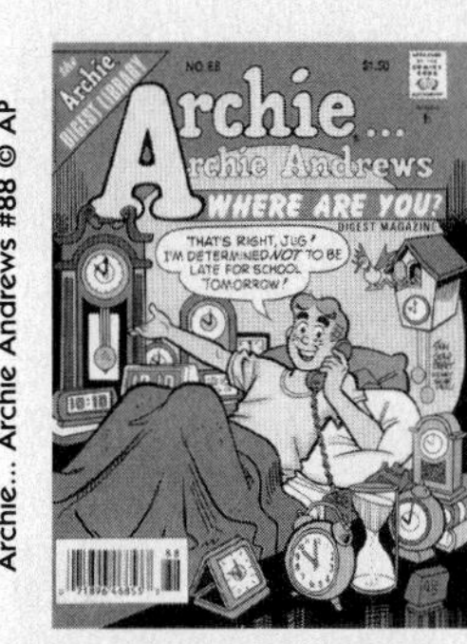

Archie... Archie Andrews #88 © AP

GD 2.0 | VG 4.0 | FN 6.0 | VF 8.0 | VF/NM 9.0 | NM- 9.2

Dell Publishing Co.: May - July, 1961
Four Color 1197-Photo-c 7 14 21 47 76 105

ARABIAN NIGHTS (See Cinema Comics Herald)

ARACHNOPHOBIA (Movie)
Hollywood Comics (Disney Comics): 1990 ($5.95, 68 pg. graphic novel)
nn-Adaptation of film; Spiegle-a 6.00
Comic edition ($2.95, 68 pgs.) 4.00

ARAK/SON OF THUNDER (See Warlord #48)
DC Comics: Sept, 1981 - No. 50, Nov, 1985
1,24,50: 1-1st app. Angelica, Princess of White Cathay. 24,50-(52 pgs.) 4.00
2-23,25-49: 3-Intro Valda. 12-Origin Valda. 20-Origin Angelica 3.00
Annual 1(10/84) 4.00

ARAÑA THE HEART OF THE SPIDER (See Amazing Fantasy (2004) #1-6)
Marvel Comics: March, 2005 - No. 12, Feb, 2006 ($2.99)
1-12: 1-Avery-s/Cruz-a. 4-Spider-Man-c/app. 3.00
Vol. 1: Heart of the Spider (2005, $7.99, digest) r/Amazing Fantasy (2004) #1-6 8.00
Vol. 2: In the Beginning (2005, $7.99, digest) r/#1-6 8.00
Vol. 3: Night of the Hunter (2006, $7.99, digest) r/#7-12 8.00

ARCANA (Also see Books of Magic limited & ongoing series and Mister E)
DC Comics (Vertigo): 1994 ($3.95, 68 pgs., annual)
1-Bolton painted-c; Children's Crusade/Tim Hunter story 4.00

ARCANUM
Image Comics (Top Cow Productions): Apr, 1997 - No. 8, Feb, 1998 ($2.50)
1/2 Gold Edition 12.00
1-Brandon Peterson-s/a(p), 1-Variant-c, 4-American Ent. Ed. 3.50
2-8 3.00
3-Variant-c 4.00
...: Millennium's End TPB (2005, $16.99) r/#1-8 & #1/2; cover gallery and sketch pages 17.00

ARCHANGEL (See Uncanny X-Men, X-Factor & X-Men)
Marvel Comics: Feb, 1996 ($2.50, B&W, one-shot)
1-Milligan story 3.00

ARCHARD'S AGENTS (See Ruse)
CrossGeneration Comics: Jan, 2003; Nov, 2003; Apr, 2004 ($2.95)
1-Dixon-s/Perkins-a 3.00
...: The Case of the Puzzled Pugilist (11/03) Dixon-s/Perkins-a 3.00
Vol. 3 - Deadly Dare (4/04) Dixon-s/McNiven-a; preview of Lady Death: The Wild Hunt 3.00

ARCHENEMIES
Dark Horse Comics: Apr, 2006 - No. 4, July, 2006 ($2.99, limited series)
1-4-Melbourne-s/Guichet-a 3.00

ARCHER & ARMSTRONG
Valiant: July (June inside), 1992 - No. 26, Oct, 1994 ($2.50)
0-(7/92)-B. Smith-c/a; Reese-i assists 4.00
0-(with Gold Valiant Logo) 2 4 6 8 10 12
1-7,9-26: 1-(8/92)-Origin & 1st app. Archer; Miller-c; B. Smith/Layton-a. 2-2nd app. Turok (c/story); Smith/Layton-a; Simonson-c. 3,4-Smith-c&a(p) & scripts. 10-2nd app. Ivar. 10,11-B. Smith-c. 21,22-Shadowman app. 22-w/bound-in trading card. 25-Eternal Warrior app. 26-Flip book w/Eternal Warrior #26 3.00
8-($4.50, 52 pgs.)-Combined with Eternal Warrior #8; B. Smith-c/a & scripts; 1st app. Ivar the Time Walker 4.50
...: First Impressions HC (2008, $24.95) recolored reprints #0-6; new "Formation of the Sect" story by Jim Shooter and Sal Velutto; Shooter commentary; new cover by Golden 25.00

ARCHIE (See Archie Comics) (Also see Christmas & Archie, Everything's..., Explorers of the Unknown, Jackpot, Little..., Oxydol-Dreft, Pep, Riverdale High, Teenage Mutant Ninja Turtles Adventures & To Riverdale and Back Again)

ARCHIE ALL CANADIAN DIGEST
Archie Publications: Aug, 1996 ($1.75, 96 pgs.)
1 1 2 3 5 6 8

ARCHIE AMERICANA SERIES, BEST OF THE FORTIES
Archie Publications: 1991,2002 ($10.95, trade paperback)
Vol. 1,2-r/early strips from 1940s 1-Intro. by Steven King. 2-Intro. by Paul Castiglia 11.00

ARCHIE AMERICANA SERIES, BEST OF THE FIFTIES
Archie Publications: 1991 ($8.95, trade paperback)
Vol. 2-r/strips from 1950's; 12.00
2nd printing (1998, $9.95) 12.00
Book 2 (2003, $10.95) 12.00

ARCHIE AMERICANA SERIES, BEST OF THE SIXTIES
Archie Publications: 1995 ($9.95, trade paperback)
Vol. 3-r/strips from 1960s; intro. by Frankie Avalon. 12.00

ARCHIE AMERICANA SERIES, BEST OF THE SEVENTIES
Archie Publications: 1997, 2008 ($9.95/$10.95, trade paperback)
Vol. 4 (1997, $9.95)-r/strips from 1970s 12.00
Vol. 8 Book 2 (2008, $10.95)-r/other strips from 1970s 12.00

ARCHIE AMERICANA SERIES, BEST OF THE EIGHTIES
Archie Publications: 2001 ($10.95, trade paperback)
Vol. 5-r/strips from 1980s; foreward by Steve Geppi 12.00

ARCHIE AMERICANA SERIES, BEST OF THE '90S
Archie Publications: 2008 ($11.95, trade paperback)
Vol. 9-r/strips from 1990s; new Lindsey cover 12.00

ARCHIE AND BIG ETHEL
Spire Christian Comics (Fleming H. Revell Co.): 1982 (69¢)
nn-(Low print run) 2 4 6 11 16 22

ARCHIE & FRIENDS
Archie Comics: Dec, 1992 - Present ($1.25-$2.99)
1 5.00
2,4,10-14,17,18,20-Sabrina app. 20-Archie's Band-c 4.00
3,5-9,16 3.00
15-Babewatch-s with Sabrina app. 6.00
19-Josie and the Pussycats app.; E.T. parody-c/s 5.00
21-46 3.00
47-All Josie and the Pussycats issue; movie and actress profiles/photos 3.50
48-142: 48-56,58,60,96-Josie and the Pussycats-c/s. 79-Cheryl Blossom returns. 100-The Veronicas-c/app. 101-Katy Keene begins. 129-Begin $2.50. 130,131-Josie and the Pussycats. 137-Cosmo, Super Duck, Pat the Brat and other old characters app. 2.50
143-154: 143-Begin $2.99-c. 145-Jersey Shore spoof. 146,147-Twilite. 154-Little Archie 3.00

ARCHIE & FRIENDS DOUBLE DIGEST MAGAZINE
Archie Comics: Feb, 2011 - Present ($3.99, digest-size)
1-5: 1-Staton-a 4.00

ARCHIE AND ME (See Archie Giant Series Mag. #578, 591, 603, 616, 626)
Archie Publications: Oct, 1964 - No. 161, Feb, 1987
1 14 28 42 99 200 300
2 9 18 27 63 107 150
3-5 6 12 18 43 69 95
6-10 4 8 12 28 44 60
11-20 3 6 9 20 30 40
21(6/68)-26,28-30: 21-UFO story. 26-X-Mas-c 3 6 9 16 23 30
27-Groovyman & Knowman superhero-s; UFO-sty 3 6 9 19 29 38
31-42: 37-Japan Expo '70-c/s 2 4 6 13 18 22
43-48,50-63-(All Giants): 43-(8/71) Mummy-s. 44-Mermaid-s. 62-Elvis cameo-c. 63-(2/74) 3 6 9 16 22 28
49-(Giant) Josie & the Pussycats-c/app. 3 6 9 20 30 40
64-66,68-99-(Regular size): 85-Bicentennial-s. 98-Collectors Comics 2 4 6 8 10 12
67-Sabrina app.(8/74) 2 4 6 10 14 18
100-(4/78) 2 4 6 8 11 14
101-120: 107-UFO-s 1 2 3 5 6 8
121(8/80)-159: 134-Riverdale 2001 6.00
160,161: 160-Origin Mr. Weatherbee. 161-Last issue 1 2 3 5 6 8

ARCHIE AND MR. WEATHERBEE
Spire Christian Comics (Fleming H. Revell Co.): 1980 (59¢)
nn - (Low print run) 2 4 6 11 16 20

ARCHIE...ARCHIE ANDREWS, WHERE ARE YOU? (...Comics Digest #9, 10; ...Comics Digest Mag. No. 11 on)
Archie Publications: Feb, 1977 - No. 114, May, 1998 (Digest size, 160-128 pgs., quarterly)
1 3 6 9 18 27 35
2,3,5,7-9-N. Adams-a; 8-r-/origin The Fly by S&K. 9-Steel Sterling-r 2 4 6 10 14 18
4,6,10 ($1.00/$1.50) 2 4 6 8 11 14
11-20: 17-Katy Keene story 2 3 4 6 8 10
21-50,100 1 2 3 5 6 8
51-70 4.00
71-99,101-114: 113-Begin $1.95-c 3.00

ARCHIE AS PUREHEART THE POWERFUL (Also see Archie Giant Series #142, Jughead as Captain Hero, Life With Archie & Little Archie)

Archie Comics #57 © AP

Archie Comics #616 © AP

Archie Comics - Little Archie FCBD 2007 © AP

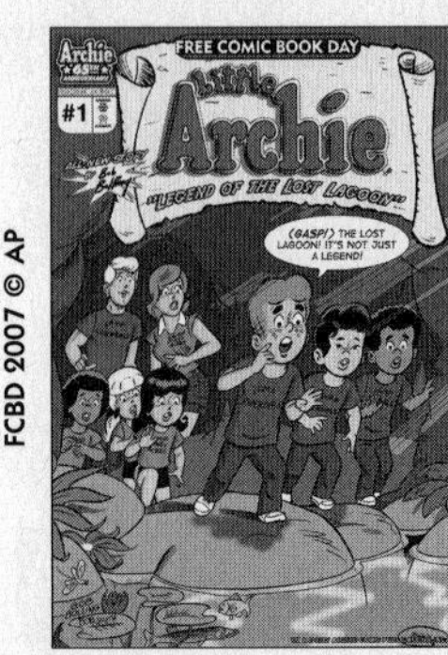

Archie Publications (Radio Comics): Sept, 1966 - No. 6, Nov, 1967

	GD 2.0	VG 4.0	FN 6.0	VF 8.0	VF/NM 9.0	NM- 9.2
1-Super hero parody	11	22	33	75	138	200
2	7	14	21	45	73	100
3-6	6	12	18	39	62	85

NOTE: *Evilheart cameos in all. Title: Archie As Pureheart the Powerful #1-3; ...As Capt. Pureheart-#4-6.*

ARCHIE AT RIVERDALE HIGH (See Archie Giant Series Magazine #573, 586, 604 & Riverdale High)
Archie Publications: Aug, 1972 - No. 113, Feb, 1987

	GD 2.0	VG 4.0	FN 6.0	VF 8.0	VF/NM 9.0	NM- 9.2
1	6	12	18	41	66	90
2	4	8	12	22	34	45
3-5	3	6	9	16	23	30
6-10	2	4	6	11	16	20
11-30	2	4	6	8	10	12
31(12/75)-46,48-50(12/77)	1	3	4	6	8	10
47-Archie in drag-s; Betty mud wrestling-s	2	4	6	9	13	16
51-80,100 (12/84)	1	2	3	5	6	8
81(8/81)-88, 91,93-95,98						6.00
89,90-Early Cheryl Blossom app. 90-Archies Band app.	3	6	9	14	19	24
92,96,97,99-Cheryl Blossom app. 96-Anti-smoking issue	2	4	6	10	14	18
101,102,104-109,111,112: 102-Ghost-c						6.00
103-Archie dates Cheryl Blossom-s	2	4	6	10	14	18
110,113: 110-Godzilla-s. 113-Last issue	1	2	3	5	6	8

ARCHIE COMICS (See Pep Comics #22 [12/41] for Archie's debut) (1st Teen-age comic; Radio show first aired 6/2/45 by NBC)
MLJ Magazines No. 1-19/Archie Publ. No. 20 on: Winter, 1942-43 - No. 19, 3-4/46; No. 20, 5-6/46 - Present

	GD 2.0	VG 4.0	FN 6.0	VF 8.0	VF/NM 9.0	NM- 9.2
1 (Scarce)-Jughead, Veronica app.; 1st app. Mrs. Andrews	4200	8400	12,600	32,000	51,000	70,000
2 (Scarce)	568	1136	1704	4146	7323	10,500
3 (60 pgs.)(scarce)	400	800	1200	2800	4900	7000
4,5: 4-Article about Archie radio series. 5-Halloween-c	271	542	813	1734	2967	4200
6,8-10: 6-X-Mas-c. 9-1st Miss Grundy cover	194	388	582	1242	2121	3000
7-1st definitive love triangle story	206	412	618	1318	2259	3200
11-20: 15,17,18-Dotty & Ditto by Woggon. 16,19-Woggon-a. 18-Halloween pumpkin-c.	119	238	357	762	1306	1850
21-30: 23-Betty & Veronica by Woggon. 25-Woggon-a. 30-Coach Piffle app., a Coach Kleats prototype. 34-Pre-Dilton try-out (named Dilbert)	74	148	222	470	810	1150
31-40	45	90	135	284	480	675
41-50	36	72	108	211	343	475
51-60	14	28	42	99	200	300
61-70 (1954): 65-70, Katy Keene app.	11	22	33	77	144	210
71-80: 72-74-Katy Keene app.	9	18	27	65	113	160
81-93,95-99	8	16	24	54	90	125
94-1st Coach Kleats in this title (see Pep #24)	9	18	27	61	103	145
100	9	18	27	64	110	155
101-122,126,128-130 (1962)	6	12	18	37	59	80
123-125,127-Horror/SF covers. 123-UFO-c/s	7	14	21	49	80	110
131,132,134-157,159,160: 137-1st Caveman Archie gang story	4	8	12	22	34	45
133 (12/62)-1st app. Cricket O'Dell	4	8	12	26	41	55
158-Archie in drag story	4	8	12	23	36	48
161(2/66)-184,186-188,190-195,197-199: 168-Superhero gag-c. 176,178-Twiggy-c 183-Caveman Archie gang story	3	6	9	16	23	32
185-1st "The Archies" Band story	4	8	12	24	37	50
189 (3/69)-Archie's band meets Don Kirshner who developed the Monkees	3	6	9	19	29	38
196 (12/69)-Early Cricket O'Dell app.	3	6	9	19	29	38
200 (6/70)	3	6	9	18	27	35
201-230(11/73): 213-Sabrina/Josie-c cameos. 229-Lost Child issue	2	4	6	10	14	18
231-260(3/77): 253-Tarzan parody	2	4	6	8	10	12
261-282, 284-299	1	2	3	5	7	9
283(8/79)-Cover/story plugs "International Children's Appeal" which was a fraudulent charity, according to TV's 20/20 news program broadcast July 20, 1979	1	3	4	6	8	10
300(1/81)-Anniversary issue	2	4	6	8	10	12
301-321,323-325,327-335,337-350: 323-Cheryl Blossom pin-up. 325-Cheryl Blossom app.						6.00
322-E.T. story	1	2	3	4	5	7
326-Early Cheryl Blossom story	2	4	6	9	13	16
336-Michael Jackson/Boy George parody	1	3	4	6	8	10
351-399: 356-Calgary Olympics Special. 393-Infinity-c; 1st comic book printed on recycled paper						5.00
400 (6/92)-Shows 1st meeting of Little Archie and Veronica						6.00
401-428						4.00
429-Love Showdown part 1						5.00
430-599: 467- "A Storm Over Uniforms" x-over parts 3,4. 538-Comic-Con issue						3.00
600-602: 600-(10/09) Archie proposes to Veronica. 601-Marries Veronica. 602-Twins born						3.00
603-606: 603-(1/10) Archie proposes to Betty. 604-Marries Betty. 605-Twins born						3.00
607-619: 609-Begin $2.99-c. 610-613-Man From RIVERDALE. 616,617-Obama & Palin app.; two covers on each						3.00
Annual 1 ('50)-116 pgs. (Scarce)	239	478	717	1530	2615	3700
Annual 2 ('51)	107	214	321	680	1165	1650
Annual 3 ('52)	61	122	183	390	670	950
Annual 4,5 (1953-54)	43	86	129	271	461	650
Annual 6-10 (1955-59): 8,9-(100 pgs.). 10-(84 pgs.) Elvis record on-c	15	30	45	106	216	325
Annual 11-15 (1960-65): 12,13-(84 pgs.) 14,15-(68 pgs.)	10	20	30	67	116	165
Annual 16-20 (1966-70)(all 68 pgs.): 20-Archie's band-c	6	12	18	41	66	90
Annual 21,22,24-26 (1971-75): 21,22-(68 pgs.). 22-Archie's band-s. 24-26-(52 pgs.). 25-Cavemen-s	4	8	12	22	34	45
Annual 23-Archie's band-c/s; Josie/Sabrina-c	5	10	15	30	48	65
Annual Digest 27 ('75)	4	8	12	24	37	50
...28-30	3	6	9	14	20	25
...31-34	2	4	6	9	13	16
...35-40 (...Magazine #35 on)	1	3	4	6	8	10
...41-65 ('94)						5.00
...66-69						3.00
...All-Star Specials (Winter '75, $1.25)-6 remaindered Archie comics rebound in each; titles: "The World of Giant Comics", "Giant Grab Bag of Comics", "Triple Giant Comics" & "Giant Spec. Comics	5	10	15	30	48	65

NOTE: *Archies Band-s-185, 188-192, 197, 198, 201, 204, 205, 208, 209, 215, 329, 330; Band-c-191, 330. Cavemen Archie Gang-s-183, 192, 197, 208, 210, 220, 223, 282, 333, 335, 338, 340.* ***Al Fagly*** *c-17-35.* ***Bob Montana*** *c-38, 41-50, 58, Annual 1-4.* ***Bill Woggon*** *c-53, 54.*

ARCHIE COMICS DIGEST (...Magazine No. 37-95)
Archie Publications: Aug, 1973 - No. 267, Nov, 2010 (Digest-size, 160-128 pgs.)

	GD 2.0	VG 4.0	FN 6.0	VF 8.0	VF/NM 9.0	NM- 9.2
1-1st Archie digest	9	18	27	63	107	150
2	5	10	15	32	51	70
3-5	4	8	12	24	37	50
6-10	3	6	9	16	23	30
11-33: 32,33-The Fly-r by S&K	2	4	6	10	14	18
34-60	1	3	4	6	8	10
61-80,100	1	2	3	5	6	8
81-99						5.00
101-140: 36-Katy Keene story						4.00
141-165						3.00
166-267: 194-Begin $2.39-c. 225-Begin $2.49-c. 236-65th Anniversary issue, r/1st app. in Pep #22 and entire Archie Comics #1 (1942)						3.00

NOTE: ***Neal Adams*** *a-1, 2, 4, 5, 19-21, 24, 25, 27, 29, 31, 33. X-mas c-88, 94, 100, 106.*

ARCHIE COMICS (Free Comic Book Day editions) (Also see Pep Comics)
Archie Publications: 2003 - Present

	GD 2.0	VG 4.0	FN 6.0	VF 8.0	VF/NM 9.0	NM- 9.2
... Free Comic Book Day Edition 1,2: 1-(7/03). 2-(9/04)						3.00
Little Archie "The Legend of the Lost Lagoon" FCBD Edition (5/07) Bolling-s/a						3.00
... Presents the Mighty Archie Art Players ('09) Free Comic Book Day giveaway						3.00
...'s 65th Anniversary Bash ('06) Free Comic Book Day giveaway						3.00
...'s Summer Splash FCBD Edition (5/10) Parent-a; Cheryl Blossom app.						3.00

ARCHIE COMICS PRESENTS: THE LOVE SHOWDOWN COLLECTION
Archie Publications: 1994 ($4.95, squarebound)

	GD 2.0	VG 4.0	FN 6.0	VF 8.0	VF/NM 9.0	NM- 9.2
nn-r/Archie #429, Betty #19, Betty & Veronica #82, & Veronica #39	1	2	3	5	6	8

ARCHIE GETS A JOB
Spire Christian Comics (Fleming H. Revell Co.): 1977

	GD 2.0	VG 4.0	FN 6.0	VF 8.0	VF/NM 9.0	NM- 9.2
nn	2	4	6	11	16	20

ARCHIE GIANT SERIES MAGAZINE
Archie Publications: 1954 - No. 632, July, 1992 (No #36-135, no #252-451)
(#1 not code approved) (#1-233 are Giants; #12-184 are 68 pgs.,#185-194,197-233 are 52 pgs.; #195,196 are 84 pgs.; #234-up are 36 pgs.)

	GD 2.0	VG 4.0	FN 6.0	VF 8.0	VF/NM 9.0	NM- 9.2
1-Archie's Christmas Stocking	148	296	444	947	1624	2300
2-Archie's Christmas Stocking('55)	77	154	231	493	847	1200
3-6-Archie's Christmas Stocking('56- '59)	53	106	159	334	567	800
7-10: 7-Katy Keene Holiday Fun(9/60); Bill Woggon-c. 8-Betty & Veronica Summer Fun						

Archie Giant Series Magazine #10 © AP

Archie Giant Series Magazine #140 © AP

Archie Giant Series Magazine #611 © AP

GD VG FN VF VF/NM NM-
2.0 4.0 6.0 8.0 9.0 9.2

(10/60); baseball story w/Babe Ruth & Lou Gehrig. 9-The World of Jughead (12/60); Neal Adams-a. 10-Archie's Christmas Stocking(1/61) 39 78 117 240 395 550

11,13,16,18: 11-Betty & Veronica Spectacular (6/61). 13-Betty & Veronica Summer Fun (10/61). 16-Betty & Veronica Spectacular (6/62). 18-Betty & Veronica Summer Fun (10/62) 25 50 75 150 245 340

12,14,15,17,19,20: 12-Katy Keene Holiday Fun (9/61). 14-The World of Jughead (12/61); Vampire-s. 15-Archie's Christmas Stocking (1/62). 17-Archie's Jokes (9/62); Katy Keene app. 19-The World of Jughead (12/62). 20-Archie's Christmas Stocking (1/63) 19 38 57 112 179 245

21,23,28: 21-Betty & Veronica Spectacular (6/63). 23-Betty & Veronica Summer Fun (10/63). 28-Betty & Veronica Summer Fun (9/64) 10 20 30 69 122 175

22,24,25,27,29,30: 22-Archie's Jokes (9/63). 24-The World of Jughead (12/63). 25-Archie's Christmas Stocking (1/64). 27-Archie's Jokes (8/64). 29-Around the World with Archie (10/64); Doris Day-s. 30-The World of Jughead (12/64) 9 18 27 63 107 150

26-Betty & Veronica Spectacular (6/64); all pin-ups; DeCarlo-c/a 10 20 30 70 125 180

31,33-35: 31-Archie's Christmas Stocking (1/65). 33-Archie's Jokes (8/65). 34-Betty & Veronica Summer Fun (9/65). 35-Around the World with Archie (10/65). 7 14 21 45 73 100

32-Betty & Veronica Spectacular (6/65); all pin-ups; DeCarlo-c/a 8 16 24 54 90 125

36-135-**Do not exist**

136-141: 136-The World of Jughead (12/65). 137-Archie's Christmas Stocking (1/66). 138-Betty & Veronica Spect. (6/66). 139-Archie's Jokes (6/66). 140-Betty & Veronica Summer Fun (8/66). 141-Around the World with Archie (9/66) 7 14 21 45 73 100

142-Archie's Super-Hero Special (10/66)-Origin Capt. Pureheart, Capt. Hero, and Evilheart 8 16 24 58 97 135

143-The World of Jughead (12/66); Capt. Hero-c/s; Man From R.I.V.E.R.D.A.L.E., Pureheart, Superteen app. 7 14 21 45 73 100

144-160: 144-Archie's Christmas Stocking (1/67). 145-Betty & Veronica Spectacular (6/67). 146-Archie's Jokes (6/67). 147-Betty & Veronica Summer Fun (8/67) 148-World of Archie (9/67). 149-World of Jughead (10/67). 150-Archie's Christmas Stocking (1/68). 151-World of Archie (2/68). 152-World of Jughead (2/68). 153-Betty & Veronica Spectacular (6/68). 154-Archie Jokes (6/68). 155-Betty & Veronica Summer Fun (8/68). 156-World of Archie (10/68). 157-World of Jughead (12/68). 158-Archie's Christmas Stocking (1/69). 159-Betty & Veronica Christmas Spectacular (1/69). 160-World of Archie (2/69); Frankenstein-s each... 4 8 12 24 37 50

161-World of Jughead (2/69); Super-Jughead-s; 11 pg.early Cricket O'Dell-s 4 8 12 26 41 55

162-183: 162-Betty & Veronica Spectacular (6/69). 163-Archie's Jokes(8/69). 164-Betty & Veronica Summer Fun (9/69). 165-World of Archie (9/69). 166-World of Jughead (9/69). 167-Archie's Christmas Stocking (1/70). 168-Betty & Veronica Christmas Spect. (1/70). 169-Archie's Christmas Love-In (1/70). 170-Jughead's Eat-Out Comic Book Mag. (12/69). 171-World of Archie (2/70). 172-World of Jughead (2/70). 173-Betty & Veronica Spectacular (6/70). 174-Archie's Jokes (8/70). 175-Betty & Veronica Summer Fun (9/70). 176-Li'l Jinx Giant Laugh-Out (8/70). 177-World of Archie (9/70). 178-World of Jughead (9/70). 179-Archie's Christmas Stocking(1/71). 180-Betty & Veronica Christmas Spect. (1/71). 181-Archie's Christmas Love-In (1/71). 182-World of Archie (2/71). 183-World of Jughead (2/71)-Last squarebound each... 3 6 9 18 27 35

184-189,193,194,197-199 (52 pgs.): 184-Betty & Veronica Spectacular (6/71). 185-Li'l Jinx Giant Laugh-Out (6/71). 186-Archie's Jokes (8/71). 187-Betty & Veronica Summer Fun (9/71). 188-World of Archie (9/71). 189-World of Jughead (9/71). 193-World of Archie (3/72).194-World of Jughead (4/72). 197-Betty & Veronica Spectacular (6/72). 198-Archie's Jokes (8/72). 199-Betty & Veronica Summer Fun (9/72) each... 3 6 9 16 22 28

190-Archie's Christmas Stocking (12/71); Sabrina-c 4 8 12 28 44 60

191-Betty & Veronica Christmas Spect.(2/72); Sabrina app. 4 8 12 24 37 50

192-Archie's Christmas Love-In (1/72); Archie Band-c/s 3 6 9 21 32 42

195-(84 pgs.)-Li'l Jinx Christmas Bag (1/72). 4 8 12 22 34 45

196-(84 pgs.)-Sabrina's Christmas Magic (1/72) 6 12 18 37 59 80

200-(52 pgs.)-World of Archie (10/72) 3 6 9 21 32 42

201-206,208-219,221-230,232,233 (All 52 pgs.): 201-Betty & Veronica Spectacular (10/72). 202-World of Jughead (11/72). 203-Archie's Christmas Stocking (12/72). 204-Betty & Veronica Christmas Spectacular (2/73). 205-Archie's Christmas Love-In (1/73). 206-Li'l Jinx Christmas Bag (12/72). 208-World of Archie (3/73). 209-World of Jughead (4/73). 210-Betty & Veronica Spectacular (6/73). 211-Archie's Jokes (8/73). 212-Betty & Veronica Summer Fun (9/73). 213-World of Archie (10/73). 214-Betty & Veronica Spectacular (10/73). 215-World of Jughead (11/73). 216-Archie's Christmas Stocking (12/73). 217-Betty & Veronica Christmas Spectacular (2/74). 218-Archie's Christmas Love-In (1/74). 219-Li'l Jinx Christmas Bag (12/73). 221-Betty & Veronica Spectacular (Advertised as World of Archie) (6/74). 222-Archie's Jokes (advertised as World of Jughead) (8/74). 223-Li'l Jinx (8/74). 224-Betty & Veronica Summer Fun (9/74). 225-World of Archie (9/74). 226-Betty & Veronica Spectacular (10/74). 227-World of Jughead (10/74). 228-Archie's Christmas Stocking (12/74). 229-Betty & Veronica Christmas Spectacular (12/74). 230-Archie's Christmas Love-In (1/75). 232-World of Archie (3/75). 233-World of Jughead (4/75) each... 2 4 6 11 16 20

207,220,231,243: Sabrina's Christmas Magic. 207-(12/72). 220-(12/73). 231-(1/75). 243-(1/76) each... 3 6 9 17 25 32

234-242,244-251 (36 pgs.): 234-Betty & Veronica Spectacular (6/75). 235-Archie's Jokes (8/75). 236-Betty & Veronica Summer Fun (9/75). 237-World of Archie (9/75) 238-Betty & Veronica Spectacular (10/75). 239-World of Jughead (10/75). 240-Archie's Christmas Stocking (12/75). 241-Betty & Veronica Christmas Spectacular (12/75). 242-Archie's Christmas Love-In (1/76). 244-World of Archie (3/76). 245-World of Jughead (4/76). 246-Betty & Veronica Spectacular (6/76). 247-Archie's Jokes (8/76). 248-Betty & Veronica Summer Fun (9/76). 249-World of Archie (9/76). 250-Betty & Veronica Spectacular (10/76). 251-World of Jughead each.... 2 4 6 9 12 15

252-451-**Do not exist**

452-454,456-466,468-478, 480-490,492-499: 452-Archie's Christmas Stocking (12/76). 453-Betty & Veronica Christmas Spectacular (12/76). 454-Archie's Christmas Love-In (1/77). 456-World of Archie (3/77). 457-World of Jughead (4/77). 458-Betty & Veronica Spectacular (6/77). 459-Archie's Jokes (8/77)-Shows 8/76 in error. 460-Betty & Veronica Summer Fun (9/77). 461-World of Archie (9/77). 462-Betty & Veronica Spectacular (10/77). 463-World of Jughead (10/77). 464-Archie's Christmas Stocking (12/77). 465-Betty & Veronica Christmas Spectacular (12/77). 466-Archie's Christmas Love-In (1/78). 468-World of Archie (2/78). 469-World of Jughead (2/78). 470-Betty & Veronica Spectacular(6/78). 471-Archie's Jokes (8/78). 472-Betty & Veronica Summer Fun (9/78). 473-World of Archie (9/78). 474-Betty & Veronica Spectacular (10/78). 475-World of Jughead (10/78). 476-Archie's Christmas Stocking (12/78). 477-Betty & Veronica Christmas Spectacular (12/78). 478-Archie's Christmas Love-In (1/79). 480-The World of Archie (3/79). 481-World of Jughead (4/79). 482-Betty & Veronica Spectacular (6/79). 483-Archie's Jokes (8/79). 484-Betty & Veronica Summer Fun(9/79). 485-The World of Archie (9/79). 486-Betty & Veronica Spectacular (10/79). 487-The World of Jughead (10/79). 488-Archie's Christmas Stocking (12/79). 489-Betty & Veronica Christmas Spectacular (1/80). 490-Archie's Christmas Love-in (1/80). 492-The World of Archie (2/80). 493-The World of Jughead (4/80). 494-Betty & Veronica Spectacular (6/80). 495-Archie's Jokes (8/80). 496-Betty & Veronica Summer Fun (9/80). 497-The World of Archie (9/80). 498-Betty & Veronica Spectacular (10/80). 499-The World of Jughead (10/80) each... 2 4 6 8 10 12

455,467,479,491,503-Sabrina's Christmas Magic: 455-(1/77). 467-(1/78). 479-(1/79) Dracula/Werewolf-s. 491-(1/80), 503(1/81) 2 4 6 11 16 20

500-Archie's Christmas Stocking (12/80) 2 4 6 8 11 14

501-514,516-527,529-532,534-539,541-543,545-550: 501-Betty & Veronica Christmas Spectacular (12/80). 502-Archie's Christmas Love-in (1/81). 504-The World of Archie (3/81). 505-The World of Jughead (4/81). 506-Betty & Veronica Spectacular (6/81). 507-Archie's Jokes (8/81). 508-Betty & Veronica Summer Fun (9/81). 509-The World of Archie (9/81). 510-Betty & Vernonica Spectacular (9/81). 511-The World of Jughead (10/81). 512-Archie's Christmas Stocking (12/81). 513-Betty & Veronica Christmas Spectacular (12/81). 514-Archie's Christmas Love-in (1/82). 516-The World of Archie(3/82). 517-The World of Jughead (4/82). 518-Betty & Veronica Spectacular (6/82). 519-Archie's Jokes (8/82). 520-Betty & Veronica Summer Fun (9/82). 521-The World of Archie (9/82). 522-Betty & Veronica Spectacular (10/82). 523-The World of Jughead (10/82).524-Archie's Christmas Stocking (1/83). 525-Betty and Veronica Christmas Spectacular (1/83). 526-Betty and Veronica Spectacular (5/83). 527-Little Archie (8/83). 529-Betty and Veronica Summer Fun (8/83). 530-Betty and Veronica Spectacular (9/83). 531-The World of Jughead (9/83). 532-The World of Archie (10/83). 534-Little Archie (1/84). 535-Archie's Christmas Stocking (1/84). 536-Betty and Veronica Christmas Spectacular (1/84). 537-Betty and Veronica Spectacular (6/84). 538-Little Archie (8/84). 539-Betty and Veronica Summer Fun (8/84). 541-Betty and Veronica Spectacular (9/84). 542-The World of Jughead (9/84). 543-The World of Archie (10/84). 545-Little Archie (12/84). 546-Archie's Christmas Stocking (12/84). 547-Betty and Veronica Christmas Spectacular (12/84). 548-?. 549-Little Archie. 550-Betty and Veronica Summer Fun each... 1 2 3 5 7 9

515,528,533,540,544: 515-Sabrina's Christmas Magic (1/82). 528-Josie and the Pussycats (8/83). 533-Sabrina; Space Pirates by Frank Bolling (10/83). 540-Josie and the Pussycats (8/84). 544-Sabrina the Teen-Age Witch (10/84). each... 2 4 6 10 14 18

551,562,571,584,597-Josie and the Pussycats 2 4 6 8 10 12

552-561,563-570,572-583,585-596,598-600: 552-Betty & Veronica Spectacular. 553-The World of Jughead. 554-The World of Archie. 555-Betty's Diary. 556-Little Archie (1/86). 557-Archie's Christmas Stocking (1/86). 558-Betty & Veronica Christmas Spectacular (1/86). 559-Betty & Veronica Spectacular. 560-Little Archie. 561-Betty & Veronica Summer Fun. 563-Betty & Veronica Spectacular. 564-World of Jughead. 565-World of Archie. 566-Little Archie. 567-Archie's Christmas Stocking. 568-Betty & Veronica Christmas Spectacular. 569-Betty & Veronica Spring Spectacular. 570-Little Archie. 571-Dracula-c/s. 572-Betty & Veronica Summer Fun. 573-Archie At Riverdale High. 574-World of Archie. 575-Betty & Veronica Spectacular. 576-Pep. 577-World of Jughead. 578-Archie And Me. 579-Archie's Christmas Stocking. 580-Betty and Veronica Christmas Spectacular. 581-Little Archie Christmas Special. 582-Betty & Veronica Spring Spectacular. 583-Little Archie. 585-Betty

Archie's Christmas Stocking #5 © AP

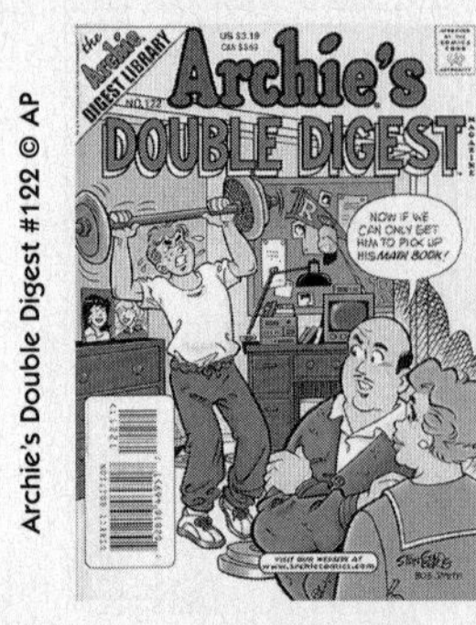

Archie's Double Digest #122 © AP

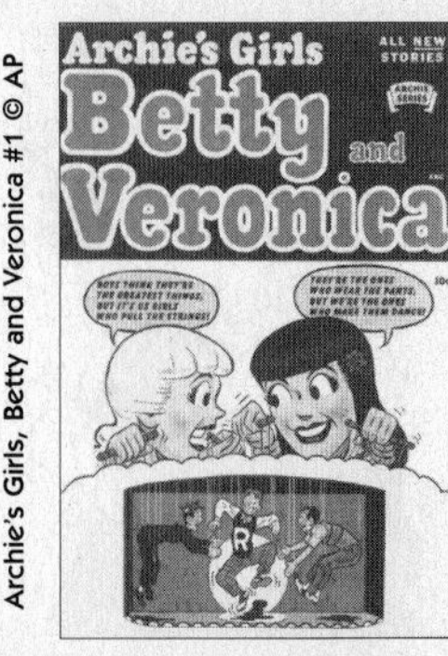

Archie's Girls, Betty and Veronica #1 © AP

GD VG FN VF VF/NM NM-
2.0 4.0 6.0 8.0 9.0 9.2

& Veronica Summer Fun. 586-Archie At Riverdale High. 587-The World of Archie (10/88); 1st app. Explorers of the Unknown. 588-Betty & Veronica Spectacular. 589-Pep (10/88). 590-The World of Jughead. 591-Archie & Me. 592-Archie's Christmas Stocking. 593-Betty & Veronica Christmas Spectacular. 594-Little Archie. 595-Betty & Veronica Spring Spectacular. 596-Little Archie. 598-Betty & Veronica Summer Fun. 599-The World of Archie (10/89); 2nd app. Explorers of the Unknown. 600-Betty and Veronica Spectacular
each.... 6.00
601,602,604-609,611-629: 601-Pep. 602-The World of Jughead. 604-Archie at Riverdale High. 605-Archie's Christmas Stocking. 606-Betty and Veronica Christmas Spectacular. 607-Little Archie. 608-Betty and Veronica Spectacular. 609-Little Archie. 611-Betty and Veronica Summer Fun. 612-The World of Archie. 613-Betty and Veronica Spectacular. 614-Pep (10/90). 615-Veronica's Summer Special. 616-Archie and Me. 617-Archie's Christmas Stocking. 618-Betty & Veronica Christmas Spectacular. 619-Little Archie. 620-Betty and Veronica Spectacular. 621-Betty and Veronica Summer Fun. 622-Josie & the Pussycats; not published. 623-Betty and Veronica Spectacular. 624-Pep Comics. 625-Veronica's Summer Special. 626-Archie and Me. 627-World of Archie. 628-Archie's Pals 'n' Gals Holiday Special. 629-Betty & Veronica Christmas Spectacular.
each.... 4.00
603-Archie and Me; Titanic app. 5.00
610-Josie and the Pussycats 1 2 3 4 5 7
630-631: 630-Archie's Christmas Stocking. 631-Archie's Pals 'n' Gals 4.00
632-Last issue; Betty & Veronica Spectacular 1 2 3 4 5 7
NOTE: *Archies Band-c-173,180,192; s-189,192. Archie Cavemen-165,225,232,244,249. Little Sabrina-527,534, 538,545,556,566. UFO-s-178,487,594.*

ARCHIE MEETS THE PUNISHER (Same contents as The Punisher Meets Archie)
Marvel Comics & Archie Comics Publ.: Aug, 1994 ($2.95, 52 pgs., one-shot)
1-Batton Lash story, John Buscema-a on Punisher, Stan Goldberg-a on Archie
1 2 3 4 5 7

ARCHIE'S ACTIVITY COMICS DIGEST MAGAZINE
Archie Enterprises: 1985 - No. 4 (Annual, 128 pgs., digest size)
1 (Most copies are marked) 2 4 6 9 13 16
2-4 1 2 3 5 7 9

ARCHIE'S CAR
Spire Christian Comics (Fleming H. Revell co.): 1979 (49¢)
nn 2 4 6 11 16 20

ARCHIE'S CHRISTMAS LOVE-IN (See Archie Giant Series Mag. No. 169, 181,192, 205, 218, 230, 242, 454, 466, 478, 490, 502, 514)

ARCHIE'S CHRISTMAS STOCKING (See Archie Giant Series Mag. No. 1-6,10, 15, 20, 25, 31, 137, 144, 150, 158, 167, 179, 190, 203, 216, 228, 240, 452, 464, 476, 488, 500, 512, 524, 535, 546, 557, 567, 579, 592, 605, 617, 630)

ARCHIE'S CHRISTMAS STOCKING
Archie Comics: 1993 - No. 7, 1999 ($2.00-$2.29, 52 pgs.)(Bound-in calendar poster in all)
1-Dan DeCarlo-c/a 5.00
2-5 4.00
6,7: 6-(1998, $2.25). 7-(1999, $2.29) 4.00

ARCHIE'S CIRCUS
Barbour Christian Comics: 1990 (69¢)
nn 2 4 6 10 14 18

ARCHIE'S CLASSIC CHRISTMAS STORIES
Archie Comics: 2002 ($10.95, TPB)
Volume 1 - Reprints stories from 1955-1964 Archie's Christmas Stocking issues 11.00

ARCHIE'S CLEAN SLATE
Spire Christian Comics (Fleming H. Revell Co.): 1973 (35/49¢)
1-(35¢-c edition)(Some issues have nn) 2 4 6 13 18 22
1-(49¢-c edition) 2 4 6 9 13 16

ARCHIE'S DATE BOOK
Spire Christian comics (Fleming H. Revell Co.): 1981
nn-(Low print) 2 4 6 11 16 20

ARCHIE'S DOUBLE DIGEST QUARTERLY MAGAZINE
Archie Comics: 1981 - Present ($1.95-$3.99, 256 pgs.) (Archie's Double Digest Magazine No. 10 on)
1 3 6 9 16 23 30
2-10; 6-Katy Keene story. 2 4 6 10 14 18
11-30: 29-Pureheart story 2 4 6 8 10 12
31-50 1 2 3 4 5 7
51-70,100 5.00
71-99 4.00
101-219: 115-Begin $3.19-c. 123-Begin $3.29-c. 170-Begin $3.69. 197-Begin $3.99-c. 4.00

GD VG FN VF VF/NM NM-
2.0 4.0 6.0 8.0 9.0 9.2

ARCHIE'S FAMILY ALBUM
Spire Christian Comics (Fleming H. Revell Co.): 1978 (39¢/49¢, 36 pgs.)
nn 2 4 6 11 16 20
nn (49¢-c edition) 2 4 6 8 11 14

ARCHIE'S FESTIVAL
Spire Christian Comics (Fleming H. Revell Co.): 1980 (49¢)
nn 2 4 6 11 16 20

ARCHIE'S GIRLS, BETTY AND VERONICA (Becomes Betty & Veronica)(Also see Veronica)
Archie Publications (Close-Up): 1950 - No. 347, Apr, 1987
1 290 580 870 1856 3178 4500
2 116 232 348 742 1271 1800
3-5: 3-Betty's 1st ponytail. 4-Dan DeCarlo's 1st Archie work
68 136 204 435 743 1050
6-10: 10-Katy Keene app. (2 pgs.) 53 106 159 334 567 800
11-20: 11,13,14,17-19-Katy Keene app. 17-Last pre-code issue (3/55). 20-Debbie's Diary (2 pgs.) 40 80 120 246 411 575
21-30: 27,30-Katy Keene app. 29-Tarzan 30 60 90 177 289 400
31-43,45-50: 41-Marilyn Monroe and Brigitte Bardot mentioned. 45-Fabian 1 pg. photo & bio. 46-Bobby Darin 1 pg. photo & bio 20 40 60 117 189 260
44-Elvis Presley 1 pg. photo & bio 22 44 66 132 216 300
51-55,57-74: 67-Jackie Kennedy homage. 73-Sci-fi-c 9 18 27 63 107 150
56-Elvis and Bobby Darin records parody 10 20 30 71 128 185
75-Betty & Veronica sell souls to Devil 16 32 48 114 232 350
76-99: 82-Bobby Rydell 1 pg. illustrated bio; Elvis mentioned on-c. 84-Connie Francis 1 pg. illustrated bio 6 12 18 43 69 95
100 7 14 21 49 80 110
101-104, 106-117,120 (12/65): 113-Monsters-s 5 10 15 30 48 65
105-Beatles wig parody (5 pg. story)(9/64) 5 10 15 32 51 70
118-(10/65) 1st app./origin Superteen (also see Betty & Me #3)
7 14 21 47 76 105
119-2nd app./last Superteen story 5 10 15 34 55 75
121,122,124-126,128-140 (8/67): 135,140-Mod-c. 136-Slave Girl-s
3 6 9 20 30 40
123-"Jingo"-Ringo parody-c 4 8 12 23 36 48
127-Beatles Fan Club-s 5 10 15 32 51 70
141-156,158-163,165-180 (12/70) 3 6 9 16 22 28
157,164-Archies Band 3 6 9 19 29 38
181-193,195-199 2 4 6 11 16 20
194-Sabrina-c/s 3 6 9 19 29 38
200-(8/72) 3 6 9 14 19 24
201-205,207,209,211-215,217-240 2 4 6 8 10 12
206,208,210, 216: 206,208,216-Sabrina c/app. 206-Josie-c. 210-Sabrina app.
3 6 9 16 22 28
241 (1/76)-270 (6/78) 1 3 4 6 8 10
271-299: 281-UFO-s 1 2 3 5 7 9
300 (12/80)-Anniversary issue 2 4 6 8 10 12
301-309 1 2 3 4 5 7
310-John Travolta parody story 1 3 4 6 8 10
311-319 6.00
320 (10/82)-Intro. of Cheryl Blossom on cover and inside story (she also appears, but not on the cover, in Jughead #325 with same 10/82 publication date)
8 16 24 56 93 130
321,322-Cheryl Blossom app. 322-Cheryl meets Archie for the 1st time
3 6 9 20 30 40
323,326,329,330,331,333-338: 333-Monsters-s 6.00
324,325-Crickett O'Dell app. 2 4 6 9 12 15
327,328-Cheryl Blossom app. 3 6 9 17 26 34
332,339: 332-Superhero costume party. 339-(12/85) Betty dressed as Madonna.
2 4 6 9 12 15
340-346 Low print 1 3 4 6 8 10
347 (4/87) Last issue; low print 2 4 6 8 10 12
Annual 1 (1953) 123 246 369 787 1344 1900
Annual 2 (1954) 48 96 144 302 514 725
Annual 3-5 (1955-1957) 39 78 117 236 388 540
Annual 6-8 (1958-1960) 27 54 81 158 259 360

ARCHIE'S HOLIDAY FUN DIGEST
Archie Comics: 1997 - Present ($1.75/$1.95/$1.99/$2.19/$2.39/$2.49, annual)
1-12-Christmas stories 2.50

ARCHIE'S JOKEBOOK COMICS DIGEST ANNUAL (See Jokebook...)

ARCHIE'S JOKE BOOK MAGAZINE (See Joke Book ...)
Archie Publ: 1953 - No. 3, Sum, 1954; No. 15, Fall, 1954 - No. 288, 11/82 (subtitled...Laugh-

Archie's Joke Book Magazine #15 © AP

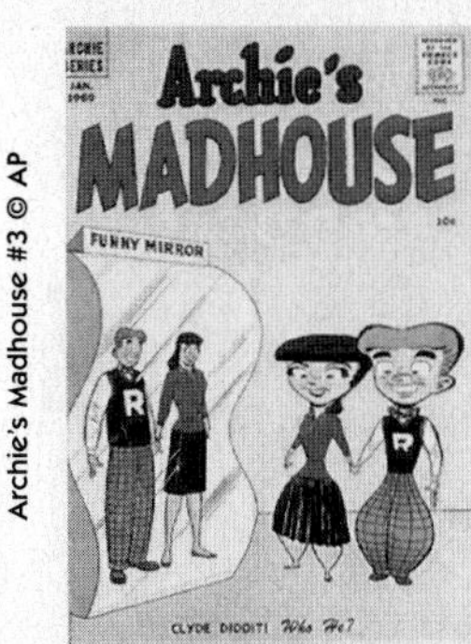

Archie's Madhouse #3 © AP

Archie's Pal Jughead Comics #100 © AP

	GD 2.0	VG 4.0	FN 6.0	VF 8.0	VF/NM 9.0	NM- 9.2
In #127-140; ...Laugh-Out #141-194)						
1953-One Shot (#1)	113	226	339	718	1234	1750
2	50	100	150	315	533	750
3 (no #4-14)	40	80	120	246	411	575
15-20: 15-Formerly Archie's Rival Reggie #14; last pre-code issue (Fall/54). 15-17-Katy Keene app.	25	50	75	150	245	340
21-30	16	32	48	94	147	200
31-43: 42-Bio of Ed "Kookie" Byrnes. 43-story about guitarist Duane Eddy	14	28	42	76	108	140
44-1st professional comic work by Neal Adams, 4 pgs.	31	62	93	186	303	420
45-47-N. Adams-a in all, 2-6 pgs.	18	36	54	103	162	230
48-Four pgs. N. Adams-a	18	36	54	103	162	230
49,50	6	12	18	41	66	90
51-56,60 (1962)	4	8	12	28	44	60
57-Elvis mentioned; Marilyn Monroe cameo	6	12	18	41	66	90
58,59-Horror/Sci-Fi-c	6	12	18	41	66	90
61-80 (8/64): 66-(12¢ cover). 76-Robot-c	3	6	9	18	27	35
66-(15¢ cover variant)	4	8	12	22	34	45
81-89,91,92,94-99	3	6	9	14	20	25
90,93: 90-Beatles gag. 93-Beatles cameo	3	6	9	17	25	32
100 (5/66)	3	6	9	16	23	30
101,103-117,119-123,127,129,131-140 (9/69): 105-Superhero gag-c. 108-110-Archies Archers Band-s. 116-Beatles/Monkees/Bob Dylan cameos (posters)	2	4	6	11	16	20
102 (7/66) Archie Band prototype-c; Elvis parody panel, Rolling Stones mention	3	6	9	18	27	35
118,124,125,126,128,130: 118-Archie Band-c; Veronica & Groovers band-s. 124-Archies Band-c/app. 125-Beatles cameo (poster). 126,130-Monkees cameo. 128-Veronica/Archies Band app.	3	6	9	16	23	30
141-173,175-181,183-199	2	4	6	8	11	14
174-Sabrina-c. 182-Sabrina cameo	2	4	6	9	13	16
200 (9/74)	2	4	6	9	13	16
201-230 (3/77)	1	2	3	5	6	8
231-239,241-287						6.00
240-Elvis record-c	2	3	4	6	8	10
288-Last issue	1	2	3	4	5	7

NOTE: *Archies Band-c-118,124,147,172; 1 pg.-s-127,128,138,140,143,147,167; 2 pg.-s-124,131, 155. Sabrina app.-247,248,252-259,261,262,264,266-270,274,277,284-286.*

ARCHIE'S JOKES (See Archie Giant Series Mag. No. 17, 22, 27, 33, 139, 146, 154, 163, 174, 186, 198, 211, 222, 235, 247, 459, 471, 483, 495, 519)

ARCHIE'S LOVE SCENE
Spire Christian Comics (Fleming H. Revell Co.): 1973 (35¢/39¢/49¢/no price)

	GD 2.0	VG 4.0	FN 6.0	VF 8.0	VF/NM 9.0	NM- 9.2
1-(35¢ Edition)	2	4	6	13	18	22
1-(39¢/49¢ Edition/no price) (Some copies have nn)	2	4	6	9	13	16

ARCHIE'S LOVE SHOWDOWN SPECIAL
Archie Publications: 1994 ($2.00, one-shot)

	GD 2.0	VG 4.0	FN 6.0	VF 8.0	VF/NM 9.0	NM- 9.2
1-Concludes x-over from Archie #429, Betty #19, B&V #82, Veronica #39						4.00

ARCHIE'S MADHOUSE (Madhouse Ma-ad No. 67 on)
Archie Publications: Sept, 1959 - No. 66, Feb, 1969

	GD 2.0	VG 4.0	FN 6.0	VF 8.0	VF/NM 9.0	NM- 9.2
1-Archie begins	22	44	66	159	317	475
2	12	24	36	86	161	235
3-5	9	18	27	63	107	150
6-10	7	14	21	47	76	105
11-17 (Last w/regular characters)	6	12	18	39	62	85
18-21,23,29: 18-New format begins. 23-No Sabrina	5	10	15	32	51	70
22-1st app. Sabrina, the Teen-age Witch (10/62)	25	50	75	183	367	550
24-2nd app.Sabrina a	11	22	33	77	144	210
25,26,28-Sabrina app. 25-1st app. Captain Sprocket (4/63); 3rd app. Sabrina; sci-fi/horror-c	9	18	27	63	107	150
27-Sabrina-c; no story	7	14	21	49	80	110
30,34,38-40: No Sabrina. 34-Bordered-c begin.	3	6	9	21	32	42
31,33,37-Sabrina app.	7	14	21	47	76	105
32-Sabrina app.?	3	6	9	21	32	42
35-Beatles cameo. No Sabrina	4	8	12	24	37	50
36-1st Salem the Cat w/Sabrina story	9	18	27	65	113	160
41-48,51-57,60-62,64-66; No Sabrina 43-Mighty Crusaders cameo. 44-Swipes Mad #4 (Super-Duperman) in "Bird Monsters From Outer Space"	3	6	9	18	27	35
49,50,58,59,63-Sabrina stories	5	10	15	35	55	75
Annual 1 (1962-63) no Sabrina	8	16	24	52	86	120
Annual 2 (1964) no Sabrina	5	10	15	35	55	75
Annual 3 (1965)-Origin Sabrina the Teen-Age Witch	10	20	30	71	128	185
Annual 4,5('66-68)(Becomes Madhouse Ma-ad Annual #7 on); no Sabrina	4	8	12	24	37	50
Annual 6 (1969)-Sabrina the Teen-Age Witch-sty	6	12	18	43	69	95

NOTE: *Cover title to #61-65 is "Madhouse" and to #66 is "Madhouse Ma-ad Jokes". Sci-Fi/Horror covers 6, 8, 11, 13, 15-26, 29, 35, 36, 38, 42, 43, 48, 51, 58, 60.*

ARCHIE'S MECHANICS
Archie Publications: Sept, 1954 - No. 3, 1955

	GD 2.0	VG 4.0	FN 6.0	VF 8.0	VF/NM 9.0	NM- 9.2
1-(15¢; 52 pgs.)	90	180	270	576	988	1400
2-(10¢)-Last pre-code issue	50	100	150	315	533	750
3-(10¢)	41	82	123	256	428	600

ARCHIE'S MYSTERIES (Continued from Archie's Weird Mysteries)
Archie Comics: No. 25, Feb, 2003 - No. 34, June, 2004 ($2.19)

	GD 2.0	VG 4.0	FN 6.0	VF 8.0	VF/NM 9.0	NM- 9.2
25-34- Archie and gang as "Teen Scene Investigators"						3.00

ARCHIE'S ONE WAY
Spire Christian Comics (Fleming H. Revell Co.): 1972 (35¢/39¢/49¢, 36 pgs.)

	GD 2.0	VG 4.0	FN 6.0	VF 8.0	VF/NM 9.0	NM- 9.2
nn-(35¢ Edition)	2	4	6	13	18	22
nn-(39¢, 49¢, no price editions)	2	4	6	9	13	16

ARCHIE'S PAL, JUGHEAD (Jughead No. 127 on)
Archie Publications: 1949 - No. 126, Nov, 1965

	GD 2.0	VG 4.0	FN 6.0	VF 8.0	VF/NM 9.0	NM- 9.2
1 (1949)-1st app. Moose (see Pep #33)	245	490	735	1568	2684	3800
2 (1950)	90	180	270	576	988	1400
3-5	53	106	159	334	567	800
6-10: 7-Suzie app.	37	74	111	222	361	500
11-20: 20-Jughead as Sherlock Holmes parody	24	48	72	142	234	325
21-30: 23-25,28-30-Katy Keene app. 23-Early Dilton-s. 28-Debbie's Diary app.	17	34	51	98	154	210
31-50: 49-Archies Rock 'N' Rollers band-c	8	16	24	52	86	120
51-57,59-70: 59- Bio of Will Hutchins of TV's Sugarfoot. 67-Betty seducing Jughead-c. 68-Early Archie Gang Cavemen-s	6	12	18	37	59	80
58-Neal Adams-a	7	14	21	45	73	100
71-76,83,84,89-99: 72-Jughead dates Betty & Veronica. 83 (4/62) 1st mention of Secret Society of Jughead Hating Girls. 84-1st app. Big Ethyl (5/62). 95-2nd app. Cricket O'Dell	4	8	12	26	41	55
77,78,80-82,85,86,88-Horror/Sci-Fi-c. 86(7/62) 1st app. The Brain	6	12	18	43	69	95
79-Creature From the Black Lagoon-c	7	14	21	50	83	115
87-2nd app. of Big Ethyl; UGAJ (United Girls Against Jughead)-s	5	10	15	32	51	70
100	5	10	15	30	48	65
101-Return of Big Ethyl	4	8	12	28	44	60
102-126	3	6	9	20	40	60
Annual 1 (1953, 25¢)	81	162	243	518	884	1250
Annual 2 (1954, 25¢)-Last pre-code issue	41	82	123	256	428	600
Annual 3-5 (1955-57, 25¢)	31	62	93	182	296	410
Annual 6-8 (1958-60, 25¢)	20	40	60	117	189	260

ARCHIE'S PAL JUGHEAD COMICS (Formerly Jughead #1-45)
Archie Comic Publ.: No. 46, June, 1993 - Present ($1.25-$2.50)

	GD 2.0	VG 4.0	FN 6.0	VF 8.0	VF/NM 9.0	NM- 9.2
46-204: 100-"A Storm Over Uniforms" x-over part 1,2. 166-Three Geeks cameo. 200-Tom Root-s; Sabrina cameo. 201-Begin $2.99-c						3.00

ARCHIE'S PALS 'N' GALS (Also see Archie Giant Series Magazine #628)
Archie Publ: 1952-53 - No. 6, 1957-58; No. 7, 1958 - No. 224, Sept, 1991
(...All News Stories on-c #49-59)

	GD 2.0	VG 4.0	FN 6.0	VF 8.0	VF/NM 9.0	NM- 9.2
1-(116 pgs., 25¢)	97	194	291	621	1061	1500
2(Annual)('54, 25¢)	46	92	138	290	488	685
3-5(Annual, '55-57, 25¢): 3-Last pre-code issue	34	68	102	204	332	460
6-10('58-'60)	21	42	63	122	199	275
11,13,14,16,17,20-(84 pgs.): 17-B&V paper dolls	14	28	42	76	108	140
12,15-(84 pgs.) Neal Adams-a. 12-Harry Belafonte 2 pg. photos & bio.	15	30	45	84	127	170
18-(84 pgs.) Horror/Sci-Fi-c	14	28	42	82	121	160
19-Marilyn Monroe app.	18	36	54	107	169	230
21,22,24-28,30 (68 pgs.)	7	14	21	45	73	100
23-(Wint./62) 6 pg. Josie-s with Pepper and Melody (1st app.) by DeCarlo; Betty in towel pin-up	16	32	48	114	232	350
29-Beatles satire (68 pgs.)	9	18	27	65	113	160
31(Wint. 64/65)-39 -(68 pgs.)	6	12	18	37	59	80
40-Early Superteen-s; with Pureheart	7	14	21	49	80	110
41(8/67)-43,45-50(2/69) (68 pgs.)	4	8	12	26	41	55
44-Archies Band-s; WEB cameo	5	10	15	30	48	65
51(4/69),52,55-64(6/71): 62-Last squarebound	3	6	9	19	29	38

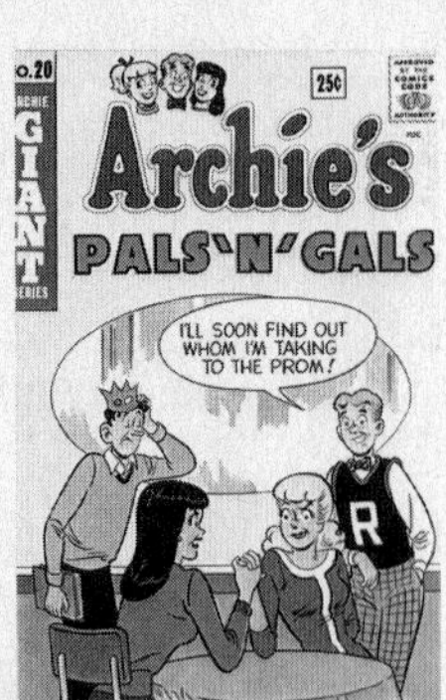

Archie's Pals 'n' Gals #20 © AP

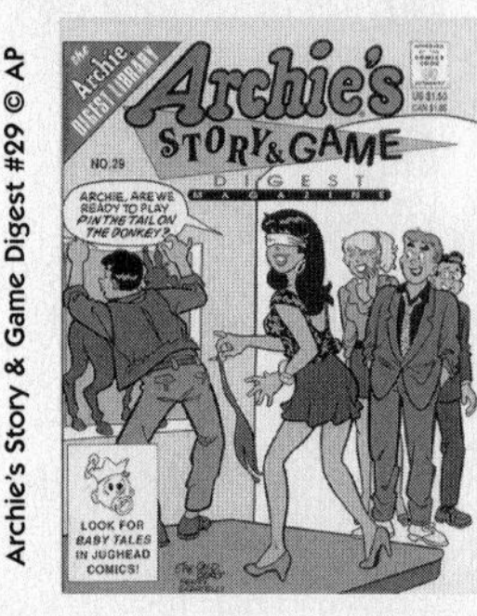

Archie's Story & Game Digest #29 © AP

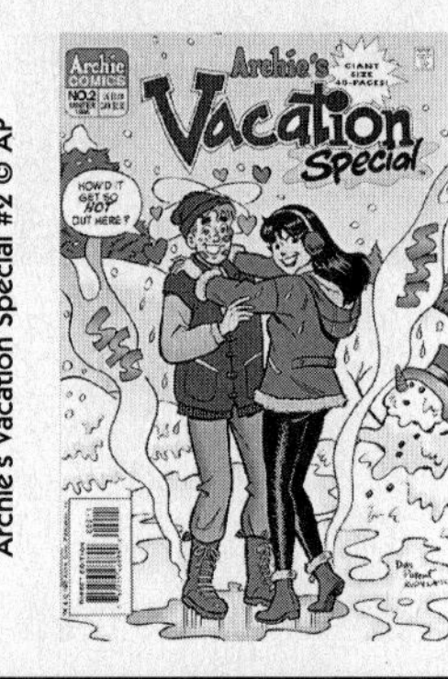

Archie's Vacation Special #2 © AP

	GD 2.0	VG 4.0	FN 6.0	VF 8.0	VF/NM 9.0	NM- 9.2
53-Archies Band-c/s	4	8	12	22	34	45
54-Satan meets Veronica-s	5	10	15	35	55	75
65(8/70),67-70,73,74,76-81,83(6/74) (52 pgs.)	3	6	9	14	20	25
66,82-Sabrina-c	3	6	9	21	32	42
71,72-Two part drug story (8/72,9/72)	3	6	9	21	32	42
75-Archies Band-s	3	6	9	17	25	32
84-99	2	4	6	8	10	12
100 (12/75)	2	4	6	9	13	16
101-130(3/79): 125,126-Riverdale 2001-s	1	2	3	5	6	8
131-160,162-170 (7/84)						6.00
161 (11/82) 3rd app./1st solo Cheryl Blossom-s and pin-up; 2nd Jason Blossom	4	8	12	22	34	45
171-173,175,177-197,199: 197-G. Colan-a						4.00
174,176,198: 174-New Archies Band-s. 176-Cyndi Lauper-c. 198-Archie gang on strike at Archie Ent. offices						6.00
200(9/88)-Illiteracy-s						6.00
201,203-223: Later issues $1.00 cover						3.00
202-Explains end of Archie's jalopy; Dezerland-c/s; James Dean cameo						6.00
224-Last issue						5.00

NOTE: *Archies Band-c-45,47,49,53,56; s-44,53,75,174. UFO-s-50,63,209,220.*

ARCHIE'S PALS 'N' GALS DOUBLE DIGEST MAGAZINE
Archie Comic Publications: Nov, 1992 - No. 146, Dec, 2010 ($2.50-$3.99)

	GD	VG	FN	VF	VF/NM	NM-
1-Capt. Hero story; Pureheart app.	2	4	6	8	10	12
2-10: 2-Superduck story; Little Jinx in all. 4-Begin $2.75-c	1	2	3	4	5	7
11-29						4.00
30-146: 40-Begin $2.99-c. 48-Begin $3.19-c. 56-Begin $3.29-c. 72-Begin $3.59-c. 100-Story uses screen captures from classic animated series. 102-Begin $3.69-c 125-128-"New Look" art; Moose and Midge break up. 130-Begin $3.99-c. 133-Reggie spotlight, also reprints early apps.						4.00

ARCHIE'S PARABLES
Spire Christian Comics (Fleming H. Revell Co.): 1973,1975 (39/49¢, 36 pgs.)

	GD	VG	FN	VF	VF/NM	NM-
nn-By Al Hartley; 39¢ Edition	2	4	6	13	18	22
49¢, no price editions	2	4	6	8	11	14

ARCHIE'S R/C RACERS (Radio controlled cars)
Archie Comics: Sept, 1989 - No. 10, Mar, 1991 (95¢/$1)

	GD	VG	FN	VF	VF/NM	NM-
1						6.00
2,5-7,10: 5-Elvis parody. 7-Supervillain-c/s. 10-UFO-c/s						4.00
3,4,8,9						3.00

ARCHIE'S RIVAL REGGIE (Reggie & Archie's Joke Book #15 on)
Archie Publications: 1949 - No. 14, Aug, 1954

	GD	VG	FN	VF	VF/NM	NM-
1-Reggie 1st app. in Jackpot Comics #5	90	180	270	576	988	1400
2	42	84	126	265	445	625
3-5	33	66	99	194	317	440
6-10	22	44	66	132	216	300
11-14: Katy Keene in No. 10-14, 1-2 pgs.	18	36	54	103	162	220

ARCHIE'S RIVERDALE HIGH (See Riverdale High)

ARCHIE'S ROLLER COASTER
Spire Christian Comics (Fleming H. Revell Co.): 1981 (69¢)

	GD	VG	FN	VF	VF/NM	NM-
nn-(Low print)	2	4	6	11	16	20

ARCHIE'S SOMETHING ELSE
Spire Christian Comics (Fleming H. Revell Co.): 1975 (39/49¢, 36 pgs.)

	GD	VG	FN	VF	VF/NM	NM-
nn-(39¢-c) Hell's Angels Biker on motorcycle-c	2	4	6	13	18	22
nn-(49¢-c)	2	4	6	9	13	16
Barbour Christian Comics Edition ('86, no price listed)	2	3	4	6	8	10

ARCHIE'S SONSHINE
Spire Christian Comics (Fleming H. Revell Co.): 1973, 1974 (39/49¢, 36 pgs.)

	GD	VG	FN	VF	VF/NM	NM-
39¢ Edition	2	4	6	13	18	22
49¢, no price editions	2	4	6	8	11	14

ARCHIE'S SPORTS SCENE
Spire Christian Comics (Fleming H. Revell Co.): 1983 (no cover price)

	GD	VG	FN	VF	VF/NM	NM-
nn-(Low print)	2	4	6	11	16	20

ARCHIE'S SPRING BREAK
Archie Comics: 1996 - Present ($2.00, 48 pgs., annual)

	GD	VG	FN	VF	VF/NM	NM-
1-4: 1,2-Dan DeCarlo-c						4.00

ARCHIE'S STORY & GAME COMICS DIGEST MAGAZINE
Archie Enterprises: Nov, 1986 - No. 39, Jan, 1998 ($1.25-$1.95, 128 pgs., digest-size)

	GD	VG	FN	VF	VF/NM	NM-
1: Marked-up copies are common	2	4	6	11	16	20
2-10	2	4	6	8	10	12
11-20	1	2	3	4	5	7
21-38						4.00
39-($1.95)						3.00

ARCHIE'S SUPER HERO SPECIAL (See Archie Giant Series Mag. No. 142)

ARCHIE'S SUPER HERO SPECIAL (...Comics Digest Mag. 2)
Archie Publications (Red Circle): Jan, 1979 - No. 2, Aug, 1979 (95¢, 148 pgs.)

	GD	VG	FN	VF	VF/NM	NM-
1-Simon & Kirby r-/Double Life of Pvt. Strong #1,2; Black Hood, The Fly, Jaguar, The Web app.	2	4	6	11	16	20
2-Contains contents to the never published Black Hood #1; origin Black Hood; N. Adams, Wood, McWilliams, Morrow, S&K-a(r); N. Adams-c. The Shield, The Fly, Jaguar, Hangman, Steel Sterling, The Web, The Fox-r	2	4	6	11	16	20

ARCHIE'S SUPER TEENS
Archie Comic Publications, Inc.: 1994 - No. 4, 1996 ($2.00, 52 pgs.)

	GD	VG	FN	VF	VF/NM	NM-
1-Staton/Esposito-c/a; pull-out poster						5.00
2-4: 2-Fred Hembeck script; Bret Blevins/Terry Austin-a						4.00

ARCHIE'S TV LAUGH-OUT ("...Starring Sabrina" on-c #1-50)
Archie Publications: Dec, 1969 - No. 105, Feb, 1986 (#1-7: 68 pgs.)

	GD	VG	FN	VF	VF/NM	NM-
1-Sabrina begins, thru #106	10	20	30	70	125	180
2 (68 pgs.)	6	12	18	41	66	90
3-6 (68 pgs.)	5	10	15	32	51	70
7-Josie begins, thru #105; Archie's & Josie's Bands cover logos begin	7	14	21	50	83	115
8-23 (52 pgs.): 10-1st Josie on-c. 12-1st Josie and Pussycats on-c. 14-Beatles cameo on poster	4	8	12	26	41	55
24-40: 37,39,40-Bicenntennial-c	3	6	9	14	20	25
41,47,56: 41-Alexandra rejoins J&P band. 47-Fonz cameo; voodoo-s. 56-Fonz parody; B&V with Farrah hair-c	3	6	9	16	22	28
42-46,48-55,57-60	2	4	6	9	12	15
61-68,70-80: 63-UFO-s. 79-Mummy-s	1	3	4	6	8	10
69-Sherlock Holmes parody	1	3	4	6	8	10
81-90,94,95,97-99: 84 Voodoo-s	1	2	3	5	6	8
91-Early Cheryl Blossom-s; Sabrina/Archies Band-c	3	6	9	14	20	26
92-A-Team parody	1	3	4	6	8	10
93-(2/84) Archie in drag-s; Hill Street Blues-s; Groucho Marx parody; cameo parody app. of Batman, Spider-Man, Wonder Woman and others	2	4	6	9	12	15
96-MASH parody-s; Jughead in drag; Archies Band-c	1	3	4	6	8	10
100-(4/85) Michael Jackson parody-c/s; J&P band and Archie band on-c	2	4	6	10	14	18
101-104-Lower print run. 104-Miami Vice parody-c	1	2	3	5	7	9
105-Wrestling/Hulk Hogan parody-c; J&P band-s	2	4	6	9	12	15

NOTE: ***Dan DeCarlo-a** 78-up(most), **c**-89-up(most). **Archies Band-s** 2,7,9-11,15,20,25,37,64,65,67,68,70,73,76,78,79,83,84,86,90,96,100,101; **Archies Band-c** 2,17,20,91,94,96,99-103. **Josie-s** 12,21,26,35,52,78,80,90. **Josie-c** 10,91,94. **Josie and the Pussycats (as a band in costume)-s** 7,9,10,37,38,41,42,66,84,99-101,105. **Josie w/Pussycats member Valerie &/or Melody-s** 17,20,22,25,27-29,31,33,36,39,40,43-51,53-65,67-77,79,81-83,85-89,92-94,102-104. **Josie w/Pussycats band-c** 12,14,17,18,22,24. **Sabrina-s** 1-9,11-86,88-106. **Sabrina-c** 1-18,21,23,27,49,91,94.*

ARCHIE'S VACATION SPECIAL
Archie Publications: Winter, 1994 - Present ($2.00/$2.25/$2.29/$2.49, annual)

	GD	VG	FN	VF	VF/NM	NM-
1						4.00
2-8: 8-(2000, $2.49)						3.00

ARCHIE'S WEIRD MYSTERIES (Continues as Archie's Mysteries)
Archie Comics: Feb, 2000 - No. 24, Dec, 2002 ($1.79/$1.99)

	GD	VG	FN	VF	VF/NM	NM-
1						3.50
2-24: 3-Mighty Crusaders app. 14-Super Teens-c/app.; Mighty Crusaders app.						3.00

ARCHIE'S WORLD
Spire Christian Comics (Fleming H. Revell Co.): 1973, 1976 (39/49¢)

	GD	VG	FN	VF	VF/NM	NM-
39¢ Edition	2	4	6	13	18	22
49¢ Edition, no price editions	2	4	6	8	11	14

ARCHIE 3000
Archie Comics: May, 1989 - No. 16, July, 1991 (75¢/95¢/$1.00)

	GD	VG	FN	VF	VF/NM	NM-
1,16: 16-Aliens-c/s						4.00
2-15: 6-Begin $1.00-c; X-Mas-c						3.00

ARCOMICS PREMIERE
Arcomics: July, 1993 ($2.95)

	GD	VG	FN	VF	VF/NM	NM-
1-1st lenticular-c on a comic (flicker-c)						3.00

AREA 52

Aria Preview © Haberlin & Holguin

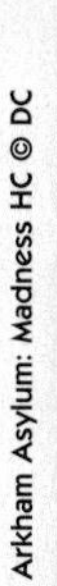
Arkham Asylum: Madness HC © DC

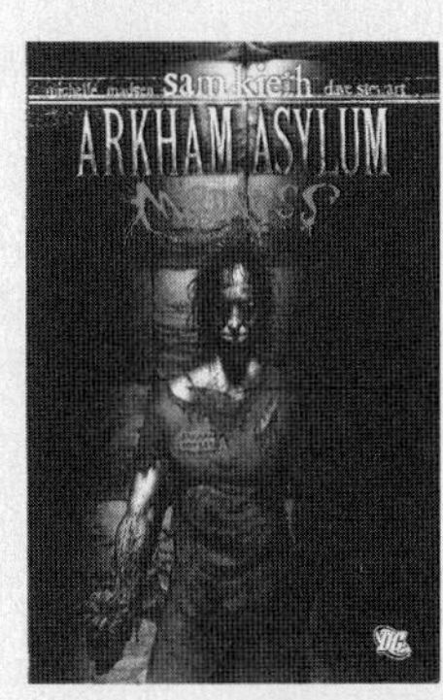

Armorines V2 #1 © Acclaim

GD 2.0 | VG 4.0 | FN 6.0 | VF 8.0 | VF/NM 9.0 | NM- 9.2

Image Comics: Jan, 2001 - No. 4, June, 2001 ($2.95)
1-4-Haberlin-s/Henry-a 3.00

ARES
Marvel Comics: Mar, 2006 - No. 5, July, 2006 ($2.99, limited series)
1-5-Oeming-s/Foreman-a 3.00
...: God of War TPB (2006, $13.99) r/series 14.00

ARGUS (See Flash, 2nd Series) (Also see Showcase '95 #1,2)
DC Comics: Apr, 1995 - No. 6, Oct, 1995 ($1.50, limited series)
1-6: 4-Begin $1.75-c 3.00

ARIA
Image Comics (Avalon Studios): Jan, 1999 - Present ($2.50)
Preview (11/98, $2.95) 5.00
1-Anacleto-c/a 1 2 3 5 6 8
1-Variant-c by Michael Turner 1 2 3 5 6 8
1-($10.00) Alternate-c by Turner 1 3 4 6 8 10
1,2-(Blanc & Noir) Black and white printing of pencil art 3.00
1-(Blanc & Noir) DF Edition 5.00
2-4: 2,4-Anacleto-c/a. 3-Martinez-a 3.00
4-($6.95) Glow in the Dark-c 1 3 4 6 8 10
Aria Angela 1 (2/00, $2.95) Anacleto-a; 4 covers by Anacleto, JG Jones, Portacio and Quesada 3.00
Aria Angela Blanc & Noir 1 (4/00, $2.95) Anacleto-c 3.00
Aria Angela European Ashcan 10.00
Aria Angela 2 (10/00, $2.95) Anacleto-a/c 3.00
...: A Midwinter's Dream 1 (1/02, $4.95, 7"x7") text-s w/Anacleto panels 5.00
...: The Enchanted Collection (5/04, $16.95) r/Summer's Spell & The Uses of Enchantment 17.00

ARIA: SUMMER'S SPELL
Image Comics (Avalon Studios): Mar, 2002 - No. 2, Jun, 2002 ($2.95)
1,2-Anacleto-c/Holguin-s/Pajarillo & Medina-a 3.00

ARIA: THE SOUL MARKET
Image Comics (Avalon Studios): Mar, 2001 - No. 6, Dec, 2001 ($2.95)
1-6-Anacleto-c/Holguin-s 3.00
HC (2002, $26.95, 8.25" x 12.25") oversized r/#1-6 27.00
SC (2004, $16.95, 8.25" x 12.25") oversized r/#1-6 17.00

ARIA: THE USES OF ENCHANTMENT
Image Comics (Avalon Studios): Feb, 2003 - No. 4, Sept, 2003 ($2.95)
1-4-Anacleto-c/Holguin-s/Medina-a 3.00

ARIANE AND BLUEBEARD (See Night Music #8)

ARIEL & SEBASTIAN (See Cartoon Tales & The Little Mermaid)

ARION, LORD OF ATLANTIS (Also see Warlord #55)
DC Comics: Nov, 1982 - No. 35, Sept, 1985
1-Story cont'd from Warlord #62 4.00
2-35, Special #1 (11/85) 3.000

ARION THE IMMORTAL (Also see Showcase '95 #7)
DC Comics: July, 1992 - No. 6, Dec, 1992 ($1.50, limited series)
1-6: 4-Gustovich-a(i) 3.00

ARISTOCATS (See Movie Comics & Walt Disney Showcase No. 16)

ARISTOKITTENS, THE (...Meet Jiminy Cricket No. 1)(Disney)
Gold Key: Oct, 1971 - No. 9, Oct, 1975
1 3 6 9 20 30 40
2-5,7-9 3 6 9 14 19 24
6-(52 pgs.) 3 6 9 16 22 28

ARIZONA KID, THE (Also see The Comics & Wild Western)
Marvel/Atlas Comics(CSI): Mar, 1951 - No. 6, Jan, 1952
1 22 44 66 128 209 290
2-4: 2-Heath-a(3) 12 24 36 69 97 125
5,6 10 20 30 56 76 95
NOTE: *Heath a-1-3; c-1-3.* ***Maneely*** *c-4-6.* ***Morisi*** *a-4-6.* ***Sinnott*** *a-6.*

ARK, THE (See The Crusaders)

ARKAGA
Image Comics: Sept, 1997 ($2.95, one-shot)
1-Jorgensen-s/a 3.00

ARKANIUM
Dreamwave Productions: Sept, 2002 - No. 5 ($2.95)
1-5: 1-Gatefold wraparound-c 3.00

GD 2.0 | VG 4.0 | FN 6.0 | VF 8.0 | VF/NM 9.0 | NM- 9.2

ARKHAM ASYLUM: LIVING HELL
DC Comics: July, 2003 - No. 6, Dec, 2003 ($2.50, limited series)
1-6-Ryan Sook-a; Batman app. 3-Batgirl-c/app. 3.00

ARKHAM ASYLUM: MADNESS
DC Comics: 2010 ($19.99, HC graphic novel, dustjacket)
HC-Sam Kieth-s/a/c; Joker, Two-Face, Harley and Ivy app. 20.00

ARKHAM REBORN
DC Comics: Dec, 2009 - No. 3, Feb, 2010 ($2.99, limited series)
1-3-David Hine-s/Jeremy Haun-a 3.00
Batman: Arkham Reborn TPB (2010, $12.99) r/#1-3, Detective Comics #864,865 and Batman: Battle For the Cowl: Arkham Asylum #1 13.00

ARMAGEDDON
Chaos! Comics: Oct, 1999 - No. 4, Jan, 2000 ($2.95, limited series)
Preview 5.00
1-4-Lady Death, Evil Ernie, Purgatori app. 3.00

ARMAGEDDON: ALIEN AGENDA
DC Comics: Nov, 1991 - No. 4, Feb, 1992 ($1.00, limited series)
1-4 3.00

ARMAGEDDON FACTOR, THE
AC Comics: 1987 - No. 2, 1987; No. 3, 1990 ($1.95)
1,2: Sentinels of Justice, Dragonfly, Femforce 3.00
3-($3.95, color)-Almost all AC characters app. 4.00

ARMAGEDDON: INFERNO
DC Comics: Apr, 1992 - No. 4, July, 1992 ($1.00, limited series)
1-4: Many DC heroes app. 3-A. Adams/Austin-a 3.00

ARMAGEDDON 2001
DC Comics: May, 1991 - No. 2, Oct, 1991 ($2.00, squarebound, 68 pgs.)
1-Features many DC heroes; intro Waverider 4.00
1-2nd & 3rd printings; 3rd has silver ink-c 3.00
2 3.00

ARMED & DANGEROUS
Acclaim Comics (Armada): Apr, 1996 - No.4, July, 1996 ($2.95, B&W)
1-4-Bob Hall-c/a & scripts 3.00
Special 1 (8/96, $2.95, B&W)-Hall-c/a & scripts. 3.00

ARMED & DANGEROUS HELL'S SLAUGHTERHOUSE
Acclaim Comics (Armada): Oct, 1996 - No. 4, Jan, 1997 ($2.95, B&W)
1-4: Hall-c/a/scripts. 3.00

ARMOR (AND THE SILVER STREAK) (Revengers Featuring... in indicia for #1-3)
Continuity Comics: Sept, 1985 - No.13, Apr, 1992 ($2.00)
1-13: 1-Intro/origin Armor & the Silver Streak; Neal Adams-c/a. 7-Origin Armor; Nebres-i 3.50

ARMOR (DEATHWATCH 2000)
Continuity Comics: Apr, 1993 - No. 6, Nov, 1993 ($2.50)
1-6: 1-3-Deathwatch 2000 x-over 3.00

ARMORINES (See X-O Manowar #25 for 16 pg. bound-in Armorines #0)
Valiant: June, 1994 - No. 12, June, 1995 ($2.25)
0-Stand-alone edition with cardstock-c 25.00
0-Gold 15.00
1-12: 7-Wraparound-c. 12-Byrne-c/swipe (X-Men, 1st Series #138) 3.00

ARMORINES (Volume 2)
Acclaim Comics: Oct, 1999 - No. 4 ($3.95/$2.50, limited series)
1-($3.95) Calafiore & P. Palmiotti-a 4.00
2,3-($2.50) 3.00

ARMOR X
Image Comics: March, 2005 - No. 4, June, 2005 ($2.95, limited series)
1-Keith Champagne-s/Andy Smith-a; flip covers on #2-4 3.00

ARMY AND NAVY COMICS (Supersnipe No. 6 on)
Street & Smith Publications: May, 1941 - No. 5, July, 1942
1-Cap Fury & Nick Carter 51 102 153 321 546 770
2-Cap Fury & Nick Carter 30 60 90 177 289 400
3,4: 4-Jack Farr-c/a 22 44 66 130 213 295
5-Supersnipe app.; see Shadow V2#3 for 1st app.; Story of Douglas MacArthur; George Marcoux-c/a 52 104 156 325 553 780

ARMY @ LOVE
DC Comics (Vertigo): May, 2007 - No. 12, Apr, 2008;

Army of Darkness #3 © Raimi

Artifacts #1 © TCOW

Ascension #5 © Banning & Finch

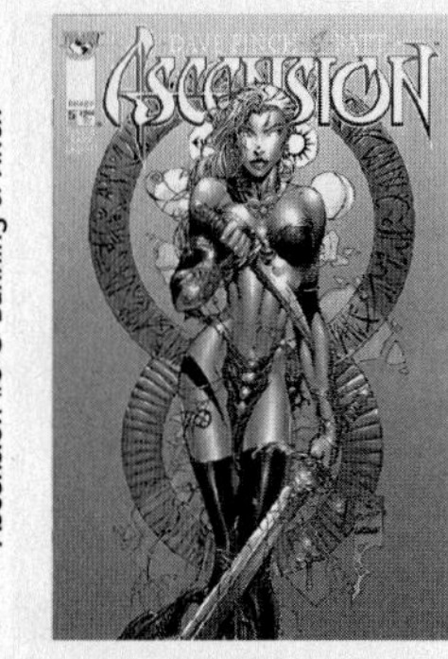

	GD 2.0	VG 4.0	FN 6.0	VF 8.0	VF/NM 9.0	NM- 9.2

V2 #1, Oct, 2008 - No. 6, Mar, 2009 ($2.99)

1-12-Rick Veitch-s/a(p); Gary Erskine-a(i) 3.00
(Vol. 2) 1-6-Veitch-s/a(p); Erskine-a(i) 3.00
...: Generation Pwned TPB (2008, $12.99) r/#6-12 13.00
...: The Hot Zone Club TPB (2007, $9.99) r/#1-5; intro. by Peter Kuper 10.00

ARMY ATTACK
Charlton Comics: July, 1964 - No. 4, Feb, 1965; V2#38, July, 1965 - No. 47, Feb, 1967

V1#1 5 10 15 30 48 65
2-4(2/65) 3 6 9 19 29 38
V2#38(7/65)-47 (formerly U.S. Air Force #1-37) 3 6 9 16 22 28
NOTE: *Glanzman a-1-3. Montes/Bache a-44.*

ARMY AT WAR (Also see Our Army at War & Cancelled Comic Cavalcade)
DC Comics: Oct-Nov, 1978

1-Kubert-c; all new story and art 2 4 6 11 16 20

ARMY OF DARKNESS (Movie)
Dark Horse Comics: Nov, 1992 - No. 2, Dec, 1992; No. 3, Oct, 1993 ($2.50, limited series)

1-3-Bolton painted-c/a 2 4 6 9 12 15
... Movie Adaptation TPB (2006, $14.99) r/#1-3; intro. by Busiek; Bruce Campbell interview 15.00

ARMY OF DARKNESS (Also see Marvel Zombies vs. Army of Darkness)
Dynamite Entertainment: 2005 - No. 13, 2007 ($2.99)

1-4 (Vs. Re-Animator):1,2-Four covers; Greene-a/Kuhoric-s. 3,4-Three covers 3.00
5-13: 5-7-Kuhoric-s/Sharpe-a; four covers. 8-11-Ash Vs. Dracula. 12,13-Death of Ash 3.00

ARMY OF DARKNESS: ...
Dynamite Entertainment: 2007 - No. 27, 2010 ($3.50/$3.99)

... From the Ashes 1-4-Kuhoric-s/Blanco-a; covers by Blanco & Suydam 3.50
5-8-(The Long Road Home); two covers on each 3.50
9-25: 9-12-(Home Sweet Hell), 13-King For a Day. 14-17-Hellbillies and Deadnecks 3.50
26,27-($3.99) Raicht-s/Cohn-a/c 4.00
...: Ash's Christmas Horror Special (2008, $4.99) Kuhoric-s/Simons-a; 2 covers 5.00

ARMY OF DARKNESS: ASHES 2 ASHES (Movie)
Devil's Due Publ.: July, 2004 - No. 4, 2004 ($2.99, limited series)

1-4-Four covers for each; Nick Bradshaw-a 3.00
1-Director's Cut (12/04, $4.99) r/#1, cover gallery, script and sketch pages 5.00
TPB (2005, $14.99) r/series; cover gallery; Bradshaw interview and sketch pages 15.00

ARMY OF DARKNESS: ASH SAVES OBAMA
Dynamite Entertainment: 2009 - No. 4, 2009 ($3.50, limited series)

1-4-Serrano-s/Padilla-a; covers by Parrillo and Nauck. 4-Obama app. 3.50

ARMY OF DARKNESS: SHOP TILL YOU DROP DEAD (Movie)
Devil's Due Publ.: Jan, 2005 - No. 4, July, 2005 ($2.99, limited series)

1-4:1-Five covers; Bradshaw-a/Kuhoric-s. 2-4: Two covers. 3-Greene-a 3.00

ARMY OF DARKNESS / XENA
Dynamite Entertainment: 2008 - No. 4, 2008 ($3.50, limited series)

1-4-Layman-s/Montenegro-a; two covers on each 3.50

ARMY SURPLUS KOMIKZ FEATURING CUTEY BUNNY
Army Surplus Komikz/Eclipse Comics: 1982 - No. 5, 1985 ($1.50, B&W)

1-Cutey Bunny begins 2 4 6 8 10 12
2-5: 5-(Eclipse)-JLA/X-Men/Batman parody 4.50

ARMY WAR HEROES (Also see Iron Corporal)
Charlton Comics: Dec, 1963 - No. 38, June, 1970

1 5 10 15 34 55 75
2-10 3 6 9 19 29 38
11-21,23-30: 24-Intro. Archer & Corp. Jack series 3 6 9 16 22 28
22-Origin/1st app. Iron Corporal series by Glanzman 4 8 12 24 37 50
31-38 2 4 6 10 14 18
Modern Comics Reprint 36 ('78) 4.00
NOTE: *Montes/Bache a-1, 16, 17, 21, 23-25, 27-30.*

AROUND THE BLOCK WITH DUNC & LOO (See Dunc and Loo)

AROUND THE WORLD IN 80 DAYS (Movie) (See A Golden Picture Classic)
Dell Publishing Co.: Feb, 1957

Four Color 784-Photo-c 7 14 21 50 83 115

AROUND THE WORLD UNDER THE SEA (See Movie Classics)

AROUND THE WORLD WITH ARCHIE (See Archie Giant Series Mag. #29, 35, 141)

AROUND THE WORLD WITH HUCKLEBERRY & HIS FRIENDS (See Dell Giant No. 44)

ARRGH! (Satire)
Marvel Comics Group: Dec, 1974 - No. 5, Sept, 1975 (25¢)

1-Dracula story; Sekowsky-a(p) 3 6 9 18 27 35
2-5: 2-Frankenstein. 3-Mummy. 4-Nightstalker(TV); Dracula-c/app., Hunchback. 5-Invisible Man, Dracula 2 4 6 13 18 22
NOTE *Alcala a-2; c-3. Everett a-1r, 2r. Grandenetti a-4. Maneely a-4r. Sutton a-1-3.*

ARROW (See Protectors)
Malibu Comics: Oct, 1992 ($1.95, one-shot)

1-Moder-a(p) 3.00

ARROW, THE (See Funny Pages)
Centaur Publications: Oct, 1940 - No. 2, Nov, 1940; No. 3, Oct, 1941

1-The Arrow begins(r/Funny Pages) 320 640 960 2240 3920 5600
2,3: 2-Tippy Taylor serial continues from Amazing Mystery Funnies #24. 3-Origin Dash Dartwell, the Human Meteor; origin The Rainbow-r; bondage-c 145 290 435 921 1586 2250
NOTE: *Gustavson a-1, 2; c-3.*

ARROWHEAD (See Black Rider and Wild Western)
Atlas Comics (CPS): April, 1954 - No. 4, Nov, 1954

1-Arrowhead & his horse Eagle begin 15 30 45 88 137 185
2-4: 4-Forte-a 10 20 30 54 72 90
NOTE: *Heath c-3. Jack Katz a-3. Maneely c-2. Pakula a-2. Sinnott a-1-4; c-1.*

ARROWSMITH (Also see Astro City/Arrowsmith flip book)
DC Comics (Cliffhanger): Sept, 2003 - No. 6, May, 2004 ($2.95)

1-6-Pacheco-a/Busiek-s 3.00
...: So Smart in Their Fine Uniforms TPB (2004, $14.95) r/#1-6 15.00

ARSENAL (Teen Titans' Speedy)
DC Comics: Oct, 1998 - No. 4, Jan, 1999 ($2.50, limited series)

1-4: Grayson-s. 1-Black Canary app. 2-Green Arrow app. 3.00

ARSENAL SPECIAL (See New Titans, Showcase '94 #7 & Showcase '95 #8)
DC Comics: 1996 ($2.95, one-shot)

1 3.00

ARTBABE
Fantagraphics Books: May, 1996 - Apr, 1999 ($2.50/$2.95/$3.50, B&W)

V1 #5, V2 #1-3 3.00
#4-($3.50) 3.50

ARTEMIS: REQUIEM (Also see Wonder Woman, 2nd Series #90)
DC Comics: June, 1996 - No. 6, Nov, 1996 ($1.75, limited series)

1-6: Messner-Loebs scripts & Benes-c/a in all. 1,2-Wonder Woman app. 3.00

ARTIFACTS
Image Comics (Top Cow): Jul, 2010 - No. 13 ($3.99, limited series)

0-(5/10, free) Free Comic Book Day edition; Sejic-a 1.00
1-6-Marz-s/Broussard-a. 1-Multiple covers; back-up origin of Witchblade 4.00

ART OF HOMAGE STUDIOS, THE
Image Comics: Dec, 1993 ($4.95, one-shot)

1-Short stories and pin-ups by Jim Lee, Silvestri, Williams, Portacio & Chiodo 5.00

ART OF ZEN INTERGALACTIC NINJA, THE
Entity Comics: 1994 - No. 2, 1994 ($2.95)

1,2 3.00

ARZACH (See Moebius...)
Dark Horse Comics: 1996 ($6.95, one-shot)

nn-Moebius-c/a/scripts 1 2 3 4 5 7

ASCENSION
Image Comics (Top Cow Productions): Oct, 1997 - No. 22, Mar, 2000 ($2.50)

Preview 5.00
Preview Gold Edition 8.00
Preview San Diego Edition 2 4 6 8 10 12
0 4.00
1/2 6.00
1-David Finch-s/a(p)/Batt-s/a(i) 4.00
1-Variant-c w/Image logo at lower right 6.00
2-22 3.00
... Collected Edition 1,2 (1998 - No. 2, $4.95, squarebound) 1-r/#1,2. 2-r/#3,4 5.00
Fan Club Edition 5.00

ASH
Event Comics: Nov, 1994 - No. 6, Dec, 1995; No. 0, May, 1996 ($2.50/$3.00)

0-Present & Future (Both 5/96, $3.00, foil logo-c)-w/pin-ups 3.00
0-Blue Foil logo-c (Present and Future) (1000 each) 4.00

Ash: Cinder and Smoke #2 © Q&P

Astonishing #15 © MAR

Astonishing Spider-Man & Wolverine #1 © MAR

GD 2.0 | VG 4.0 | FN 6.0 | VF 8.0 | VF/NM 9.0 | NM- 9.2

0-Silver Prism logo-c (Present and Future) (500 each) 10.00
0-Red Prism logo-c (Present and Future) (250 each) 20.00
0-Gold Hologram logo-c (Present and Future) (1000 each) 8.00
1-Quesada-p/story; Palmiotti-i/story: Barry Windsor-Smith pin-up
2 4 6 8 10 12
2-Mignola Hellboy pin-up 1 2 3 4 5 7
3,4: 3-Big Guy pin-up by Geoff Darrow. 4-Jim Lee pin-up 4.00
4-Fahrenheit Gold 7.00
4-6-Fahrenheit Red (5,6-1000) 8.00
4-6-Fahrenheit White 12.00
5, 6-Double-c w/Hildebrandt Bros.-a, Quesada & Palmiotti. 6-Texeira-c 3.00
5,6-Fahrenheit Gold (2000) 4.00
6-Fahrenheit White (500)-Texeira-c 12.00
Volume 1 (1996, $14.95, TPB)-r/#1-5, intro by James Robinson 15.00
Wizard Mini-Comic (1996, magazine supplement) 2.25
Wizard #1/2 (1997, mail order) 4.00

ASH: CINDER & SMOKE
Event Comics: May, 1997 - No. 6, Oct, 1997 ($2.95, limited series)
1-6: Ramos-a/Waid, Augustyn-s in all. 2-6-variant covers by Ramos and Quesada 3.00

ASH: FILES
Event Comics: Mar, 1997 ($2.95, one-shot)
1-Comics w/text 3.00

ASH: FIRE AND CROSSFIRE
Event Comics: Jan, 1999 - No. 5 ($2.95, limited series)
1,2-Robinson-s/Quesada & Palmiotti-c/a 3.00

ASH: FIRE WITHIN, THE
Event Comics: Sept, 1996 - No. 2, Jan, 1997 ($2.95, unfinished limited series)
1,2: Quesada & Palmiotti-c/s/a 3.00

ASH/ 22 BRIDES
Event Comics: Dec, 1996 - No. 2, Apr, 1997 ($2.95, limited series)
1,2: Nicieza-s/Ramos-c/a 3.00

ASKANI'SON (See Adventures of Cyclops & Phoenix limited series)
Marvel Comics: Jan, 1996 - No. 4, May, 1996 ($2.95, limited series)
1-4: Story cont'd from Advs. of Cyclops & Phoenix; Lobdell/Loeb story; Gene Ha-c/a(p) 3.00
TPB (1997, $12.99) r/#1-4; Gene Ha painted-c 13.00

ASPEN (MICHAEL TURNER PRESENTS:...) (Also see Fathom)
Aspen MLT, Inc.: July, 2003 - No. 3, Aug, 2003 ($2.99)
1-Fathom story; Turner-a/Johns-s; interviews w/Turner & Johns; two covers by Turner 3.00
2,3:2-Fathom story; Turner-a/Johns-s; two covers by Turner; pin-ups and interviews 3.00
... Seasons: Fall 2005 (12/05, $2.99) short stories by various; Turner-c 3.00
... Seasons: Spring 2005 (4/05, $2.99) short stories by various; Turner-c 3.00
... Seasons: Summer 2006 (10/06, $2.99) short stories by various; Turner-c 3.00
... Seasons: Winter 2009 (3/09, $2.99) short stories by various; Benitez-c 3.00
... Showcase: Aspen Matthews 1 (7/08, $2.99) Caldwell-a 3.00
... Showcase: Kiani 1 (10/09, $2.99) Scott Clark-a; covers by Clark and Caldwell 3.00
... Sketchbook 1 (2003, $2.99) sketch pages by Michael Turner and Talent Caldwell 3.00
... Splash: 2006 Swimsuit Spectacular 1 (3/06, $2.99) pin-up pages by various; Turner-c 3.00
... Splash: 2007 Swimsuit Spectacular 1 (8/07, $2.99) pin-up pages by various; Turner-c 3.00
... Splash: 2008 Swimsuit Spectacular 1 (7/08, $2.99) pin-up pages by various; Turner-c 3.00
... Splash: 2010 Swimsuit Spectacular 1 (8/10, $2.99) pin-up pages by various; 2 covers 3.00

ASPEN SHOWCASE
Aspen MLT: Oct, 2008 ($2.99)
...: Benoist 1 (10/08) - Krul-s/Gunnell-a; two covers by Gunnell & Manapul 3.00
...: Ember 1 (2/09) - Randy Green-a; two covers by Gunnell & Green 3.00

ASSASSINS
DC Comics (Amalgam): Apr, 1996 ($1.95)
1 3.00

ASSASSIN'S CREED: THE FALL (Based on the Ubisoft Entertainment videogame)
DC Comics: Jan, 2011 - No. 3, Mar, 2011 ($3.99, limited series)
1-3-Cam Stewart & Karl Kerschl-s/a 4.00

ASSAULT ON NEW OLYMPUS PROLOGUE
Marvel Comics: Jan, 2010 ($3.99, one-shot)
1-Spider-Man, Hercules, Amadeus Cho app.; Granov-c; leads into Inc. Hercules #138 4.00

ASTONISHING (Formerly Marvel Boy No. 1, 2)
Marvel/Atlas Comics(20CC): No. 3, Apr, 1951 - No. 63, Aug, 1957
3-Marvel Boy continues; 3-5-Marvel Boy-c 97 194 291 621 1061 1500
4-6-Last Marvel Boy; 4-Stan Lee app. 68 136 204 435 743 1050
7-10: 7-Maneely s/f story. 10-Sinnott s/f story 36 72 108 216 351 485
11,12,15,17,20 31 62 93 186 303 420
13,14,16,18,19-Krigstein-a. 18-Jack The Ripper sty
32 64 96 190 310 430
21,22,24 27 54 81 158 259 360
23-E.C. swipe "The Hole In The Wall" from Vault Of Horror #16
27 54 81 162 266 370
25,29: 25-Crandall-a. 29-Decapitation-c 25 50 75 147 241 335
26-28 23 46 69 136 223 310
30-Tentacled eyeball-c/story; classic-c 47 94 141 296 498 700
31-37-Last pre-code issue 20 40 60 120 195 270
38-43,46,48-52,56,58,59,61 17 34 51 98 154 210
44,45,47,53-55,57,60: 44-Crandall swipe/Weird Fantasy #22. 45,47-Krigstein-a. 53-Ditko-a.
54-Torres-a, 55-Crandall, Torres-a. 57-Williamson/Krenkel-a (4 pgs.).
60-Williamson/Mayo-a (4 pgs.) 18 36 54 105 165 225
62,63: 62-Torres, Powell-a. 63-Woodbridge-a 18 36 54 103 162 220

NOTE: ***Ayers** a-16, 49. **Berg** a-36, 53, 56. **Cameron** a-50. **Gene Colan** a-12, 20, 29, 56. **Ditko** a-53. **Drucker** a-41, 62. **Everett** a-3-6(3), 6, 10, 12, 37, 47, 48, 58; c-3-5, 13,15, 16, 18, 29, 47, 49, 51, 53-55, 57, 59-63. **Fass** a-11, 34. **Forte** a-26, 48, 53, 58, 60. **Fuje** a-11. **Heath** a-8, 29; c-8, 9, 19, 22, 25, 26. **Kirby** a-56. **Lawrence** a-28, 37, 38, 42. **Maneely** a-7(2), 19; c-7, 31, 33, 34, 56. **Moldoff** a-33. **Morisi** a-10, 60. **Morrow** a-52, 61. **Orlando** a-47, 58, 61. **Pakula** a-10. **Powell** a-43, 44, 48. **Ravielli** a-26, 28. **Reinman** a-32, 34, 38. **Robinson** a-20. **J. Romita** a-7, 18, 24, 43, 57,61. **Roussos** a-55. **Sale** a-28, 38, 59; c-32. **Sekowsky** a-13. **Severin** c-46. **Shores** a-16, 60. **Sinnott** a-11, 30, 31. **Whitney** a-13. **Ed Win** a-20. Canadian reprints exist.*

ASTONISHING SPIDER-MAN AND WOLVERINE
Marvel Comics: Jul, 2010 - No. 6 ($3.99, limited series)
1-5-Adam Kubert-a/Jason Aaron-s. 1-Bonus pin-up gallery; wraparound-c 4.00
1-Director's Cut (10/10, $4.99) r/#1 with full script & B&W art 5.00

ASTONISHING TALES (See Ka-Zar)
Marvel Comics Group: Aug, 1970 - No. 36, July, 1976 (#1-7: 15¢; #8: 25¢)
1-Ka-Zar (by Kirby(p) #1,2; by B. Smith #3-6) & Dr. Doom (by Wood #1-4; by Tuska #5,6; by Colan #7,8; 1st Marvel villain solo series) double feature begins; Kraven the Hunter-c/story; Nixon cameo 7 14 21 45 73 100
2-Kraven the Hunter-c/story; Kirby, Wood-a 4 8 12 22 34 45
3-6: B. Smith-p; Wood-a-#3,4. 5,6-Red Skull 2-part story
4 8 12 24 37 50
7-Last 15¢ issue; Black Panther app. 3 6 9 16 23 30
8-(25¢, 52 pgs.)-Last Dr. Doom of series 4 8 12 22 34 45
9-All Ka-Zar issues begin; Lorna-r/Lorna #14 2 4 6 11 16 20
10-B. Smith/Sal Buscema-a. 3 6 9 14 20 25
11-Origin Ka-Zar & Zabu; death of Ka-Zar's father 2 4 6 13 18 22
12-2nd app.Man-Thing; by Neal Adams (see Savage Tales #1 for 1st app.)
4 8 12 26 41 55
13-3rd app.Man-Thing 3 6 9 19 29 38
14-20: 14-Jann of the Jungle-r (1950s); reprints censored Ka-Zar-s from Savage Tales #1. 17-S.H.I.E.L.D. begins. 19-Starlin-a(p). 20-Last Ka-Zar (continues into 1974 Ka-Zar series)
1 3 4 6 8 10
21-(12/73)-It! the Living Colossus begins, ends #24 (see Supernatural Thrillers #1)
4 8 12 22 34 45
22-24: 23,24-IT vs. Fin Fang Foom 3 6 9 18 27 35
25-1st app. Deathlok the Demolisher; full length stories begin, end #36;
Perez's 1st work, 2 pgs. (8/74) 5 10 15 34 55 75
26-28,30 2 4 6 11 16 20
29-r/origin/1st app. Guardians of the Galaxy from Marvel Super-Heroes #18 plus-c w/4 pgs. omitted; no Deathlok story 1 3 4 6 8 10
31-34: 31-Watcher-r/Silver Surfer #3 2 4 6 9 12 15
35,36-(Regular 25¢ edition)(5,7/76) 2 4 6 9 12 15
35,36-(30¢-c, low distribution) 5 10 15 32 51 70

NOTE: ***Buckler** a-13i, 16p, 25, 26p, 27p, 28, 29p-36p; c-13, 25p, 26-30, 32-35p, 36. **John Buscema** a-9, 12p-14p, 16p; c-4-6p, 12p. **Colan** a-7p, 8p. **Ditko** a-21r. **Everett** a-6i. **G. Kane** a-11p, 15p; c-9, 10p, 11p, 14, 15p, 21p. **McWilliams** a-30i. **Starlin** a-19p; c-16p. **Sutton & Trimpe** a-8. **Tuska** a-5p, 6p, 8p. **Wood** a-1-4. **Wrightson** c-31i.*

ASTONISHING TALES (Anthology)
Marvel Comics: Apr, 2009 - No. 6, Sept, 2009 ($3.99, limited series)
1-6-Wolverine, Punisher, Iron Man and Iron Man 2020 app. 1-Wraparound-c 4.00

ASTONISHING THOR
Marvel Comics: Jan, 2011 - Present ($3.99)
1-3: 1-Robert Rodi-s/Mike Choi-a/Esad Ribic-c 4.00

ASTONISHING X-MEN
Marvel Comics: Mar, 1995 - No. 4, July, 1995 ($1.95, limited series)
1-Age of Apocalypse; Magneto-c 4.00
2-4 3.00

ASTONISHING X-MEN

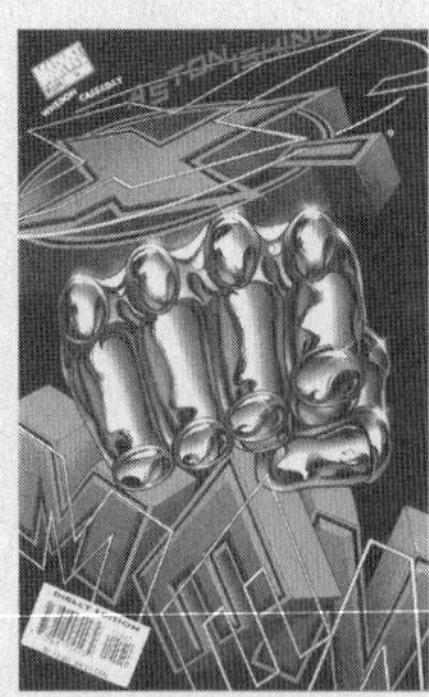
Astonishing X-Men #5 © MAR

Astounding Wolf-Man #7 © Kirkman & Howard

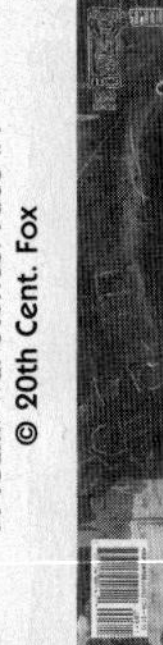
A-Team: War Stories: Face #1 © 20th Cent. Fox

GD	VG	FN	VF	VF/NM	NM-
2.0	4.0	6.0	8.0	9.0	9.2

Marvel Comics: Sept, 1999 - No.3, Nov, 1999 ($2.50, limited series)

1-3-New team, Cable & X-Man app.; Peterson-a 3.00
TPB (11/00, $15.95) r/#1-3, X-Men #92 & #95, Uncanny X-Men #375 16.00

ASTONISHING X-MEN (See Giant-Size Astonishing X-Men for story folllowing #24)
Marvel Comics: July, 2004 - No. 35, Oct, 2010 ($2.99)

1-Whedon-s/Cassaday-c/a; team of Cyclops, Beast, Wolverine, Emma Frost & Kitty Pryde 3.00
1-Director's Cut (2004, $3.99) different Cassaday partial sketch-c; cover gallery, sketch pages and script excerpt 4.00
1-Variant-c by Cassaday 10.00
1-Variant-c by Dell'Otto 5.00
2,3,5,6-X-Men battle Ord 3.00
4-Colossus returns 4.00
4-Variant Colossus cover by Cassaday 5.00
7-24: 7-Fantastic Four app. 9,10-X-Men vs. the Danger Room 3.00
7,9,10-12,19-24-Second printing variant covers 3.00
25-35: 25-Ellis-s/Bianchi-a begins; Bianchi wraparound-c. 31-Jimenez-a begins 3.00
36-($3.99) Pearson wraparound-c; Way-s/Pearson-a 4.00
.../Amazing Spider-Man: The Gauntlet Sketchbook ('09, giveaway) flip book preview 3.00
...: Ghost Boxes 1,2 (12/08-1/09, $3.99) Ellis-s/Davis & Granov-a; full Ellis script 4.00
... Saga (2006, $3.99) reprints highlights from #1-12; sketch pages and cover gallery 4.00
... Sketchbook Special ('08, $2.99) Costume sketches & blueprints by Bianchi & Larroca 3.00
...Vol. 1 HC (2006, $29.99, dust jacket) r/#1-12; interviews, sketch pages and covers 30.00
...Vol. 1: Gifted (2004, $14.99) r/#1-6; variant cover gallery 15.00
...Vol. 2: Dangerous (2005, $14.99) r/#7-12; variant cover gallery 15.00
...Vol. 3: Torn (2007, $14.99) r/#13-18; variant & sketch cover gallery 15.00

ASTONISHING X-MEN: XENOGENESIS
Marvel Comics: July, 2010 - No. 5, Apr, 2011 ($3.99, limited series)

1-5-Warren Ellis-s/Kaare Andrews-a/c. 1-Wraparound-c; script 4.00
1-Director's Cut (10/10, $4.99) r/#1 with full script & B&W art; cover sketches 5.00

ASTOUNDING SPACE THRILLS: THE COMIC BOOK
Image Comics: Apr, 2000 - No. 4, Dec, 2000 ($2.95, limited series)

1-4-Steve Conley-s/a. 2,3-Flip book w/Crater Kid 3.00
Galaxy-Sized Astounding Space Thrills 1 (10/01, $4.95) 5.00

ASTOUNDING WOLF-MAN
Image Comics: Jun, 2007 - No. 25, Nov, 2010 ($2.99)

1-Free Comic Boy Day issue; Kirkman-s/Howard-a; origin story 3.00
2-24: 11-Invincible x-over from Invincble #57 3.00
25-($4.99) Wraparound-c; Wolfcorps app. 5.00
Vol. 1 TPB (2008, $14.99) r/#1-7; sketch pages; Kirkman intro. 15.00

ASTRA
CPM Manga: 2001 - No. 8 ($2.95, B&W, limited series)

1-8: Created by Jerry Robinson; Tanaka-a. 1-Balent variant-c 3.00
TPB (2002, $15.95) r/#1-8; JH Williams III-c from #3 16.00

ASTRO BOY (TV) (See March of Comics #285 & The Original...)
Gold Key: August, 1965 (12¢)

1(10151-508)-Scarce; 1st app. Astro Boy in comics 26 52 78 186 373 560

ASTRO BOY THE MOVIE (Based on the 2009 CGI movie)
IDW Publishing: 2009 ($3.99, limited series)

...Official Movie Adaptation 1-4 (8/09 - No. 4, 9/09, $3.99) EJ Su-a 4.00
...Official Movie Prequel 1-4 (5/09 - No. 4, 8/09) Jourdan-a/c; Ashley Wood var-c on each 4.00

ASTRO CITY / ARROWSMITH (Flip book)
DC Comics (WildStorm Productions): Jun, 2004 ($2.95, one-shot flip book)

1-Intro. Black Badge; Ross-c; Arrowsmith a/c by Pacheco 3.00

ASTRO CITY (Also see Kurt Busiek's Astro City)
DC Comics (WildStorm Productions): Dec, 2004 - Dec, 2009 (one-shots)

...#1 Special Edition (8/10, $1.00) reprints first issue with "What's Next? cover logo 1.00
...: Astra Special 1,2 (11/09, 12/09, $3.99) Busiek-s/Anderson-a/Ross-c 4.00
... A Visitor's Guide (12/04, $5.95) short story, city guide and pin-ups by various; Ross-c 6.00
...: Beautie (4/08, $3.99) Busiek-s/Anderson-a/Ross-c; origin 4.00
...: Samaritan (9/06, $3.99) Busiek-s/Anderson-a/Ross-c; origin of Infidel 4.00
...: Silver Agent 1,2 (8,9/10, $3.99) Busiek-s/Anderson-a/Ross-c 4.00

ASTRO CITY: DARK AGE
DC Comics (WildStorm Productions): Aug, 2005 - No. 4, Dec, 2005 ($2.95, limited series)

Book One 1-4-Busiek-s/Anderson-a/Ross-c; Silver Agent and The Blue Knight app. 3.00
Book Two #1-4 (1/07-11/07, $2.99) Busiek-s/Anderson-a/Ross-c 3.00
Book Three #1-4 (7/09-10/09, $3.99) Busiek-s/Anderson-a/Ross-c 4.00
Book Four #1-4 (3/10-6/10, $3.99) Busiek-s/Anderson-a/Ross-c 4.00

GD	VG	FN	VF	VF/NM	NM-
2.0	4.0	6.0	8.0	9.0	9.2

... 1: Brothers and Other Strangers HC (2008, $29.99, d.j.) r/Book One #1-4, Book Two #1-4, and story from Astro City/Arrowsmith #1; Marc Guggenheim intro.; new Ross-c 30.00
... 1: Brothers and Other Strangers SC (2009, $19.99) same contents as HC 20.00
... 2: Brothers in Arms HC ('10, $29.99, d.j.) r/Book Three #1-4, Book Four #1-4, Ross-c 30.00

ASTRO CITY: LOCAL HEROES
DC Comics (WildStorm Productions): Apr, 2003 - No. 5, Feb, 2004 ($2.95, limited series)

1-5-Busiek-s/Anderson-a/Ross-c 3.00
HC (2005, $24.95) r/series; Kurt Busiek's Astro City V2 #21,22; stories from Astro City/Arrowsmith #1; and 9-11, The World's Finest... Vol. 2; Alex Ross sketch pages 25.00
SC (2005, $17.99) same contents as HC 18.00

ASYLUM
Millennium Publications: 1993 ($2.50)

1-3: 1-Bolton-c/a; Russell 2-pg. illos 3.00

ASYLUM
Maximum Press: Dec, 1995 - No. 11, Jan, 1997 ($2.95/$2.99, anthology)
(#1-6 are flip books)

1-11: 1-Warchild by Art Adams, Beanworld, Avengelyne, Battlestar Galactica. 2-Intro Mike Deodato's Deathkiss. 4-1st app.Christian; painted Battlestar Galactica story begins. 6-Intro Bionix (Six Million Dollar Man & the Bionic Woman). 7-Begin $2.99-c. 8-B&W-a. 9- Foot Soldiers & Kid Supreme. 10-Lady Supreme by Terry Moore-c/app. 4.00

ATARI FORCE (Also see Promotional comics section)
DC Comics: Jan, 1984 - No. 20, Aug, 1985 (Mando paper)

1-(1/84)-Intro Tempest, Packrat, Babe, Morphea, & Dart 4.00
2-20 3.00
Special 1 (4/86) 3.00
NOTE: ***Byrne*** *c-Special 1i.* ***Giffen*** *a-12p, 13i.* ***Rogers*** *a-18p, Special 1p.*

A-TEAM, THE (TV) (Also see Marvel Graphic Novel)
Marvel Comics Group: Mar, 1984 - No. 3, May, 1984 (limited series)

1-3 5.00
1,2-(Whitman bagged set) w/75¢-c 2 4 6 8 10 12
3-(Whitman, no bag) w/75¢-c 1 2 3 5 6 8

A-TEAM: SHOTGUN WEDDING (Based on the 2010 movie)
IDW Publishing: Mar, 2010 - No. 4, Apr, 2010 ($3.99, limited series)

1-4-Co-plotted by Joe Carnahan; Stephen Mooney-a; Snyder III-c 4.00

A-TEAM: WAR STORIES (Based on the 2010 movie)
IDW Publishing: Mar, 2010 - Apr, 2010 ($3.99, series of one-shots)

...: B.A. (3/10) Dixon & Burnham-s/Maloney-a/Gaydos & photo-c 4.00
...: Face (4/10) Dixon & Burnham-s/Muriel-a/Gaydos & photo-c 4.00
...: Hannibal (3/10) Dixon & Burnham-s/Petrus-a/Gaydos & photo-c 4.00
...: Murdock (4/10) Dixon & Burnham-s/Vilanova-a/Gaydos & photo-c 4.00

ATHENA INC. THE MANHUNTER PROJECT
Image Comics: Dec, 2001; Apr, 2002 - No. 6 ($2.95/$4.95/$5.95)

...The Beginning (12/01, $5.95) Anacleto-c/a; Haberlin-s 6.00
1-5: 1-(4/02, $2.95) two covers by Anacleto 3.00
6-($4.95) 5.00
...: Agents Roster #1 (11/02, $5.95, 8 1/2 x 11") bios and sketch pages by Anacleto 6.00
Vol. 1 TPB (4/03, $19.95) r/#1-6 & Agents Roster; cover gallery 20.00

ATHENA
Dynamite Entertainment: 2009 - No. 4, 2010 ($3.50)

1-4-Murray-s/Neves-a; multiple covers on each. 1-Obama flip cover 3.50

ATLANTIS CHRONICLES, THE (Also see Aquaman, 3rd Series & Aquaman: Time & Tide)
DC Comics: Mar, 1990 - No. 7, Sept, 1990 ($2.95, limited series, 52 pgs.)

1-7: 1-Peter David scripts. 7-True origin of Aquaman; nudity panels 3.25

ATLANTIS, THE LOST CONTINENT
Dell Publishing Co.: May, 1961

Four Color #1188-Movie, photo-c 10 20 30 68 119 170

ATLAS (See 1st Issue Special)

ATLAS
Dark Horse Comics: Feb, 1994 - No. 4, 1994 ($2.50, limited series)

1-4 3.00

ATLAS (Agents of Atlas)(The Heroic Age)
Marvel Comics: Jul, 2010 - No. 5, Nov, 2010 ($3.99/$2.99)

1-($3.99) Parker-s/Hardman-a/Dodson-c; 3-D Man app.; profile page 4.00
2-5-($2.99) 2,3,5-Pagulayan-c. 4-Jae Lee-c 3.00

ATMOSPHERICS

The Atom #4 © DC

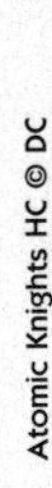
Atomic Knights HC © DC

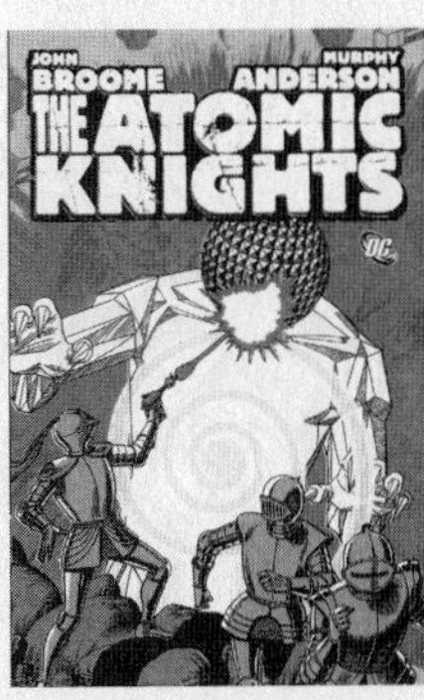

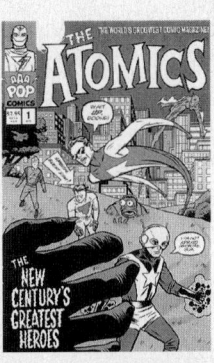

The Atomics #1 © Mike Allred

GD 2.0 | VG 4.0 | FN 6.0 | VF 8.0 | VF/NM 9.0 | NM- 9.2

Avatar Press: June, 2002 ($5.95, B&W, one-shot graphic novel)

1-Warren Ellis-s/Ken Meyer Jr.-painted-a/c 6.00

ATOM, THE (See Action #425, All-American #19, Brave & the Bold, D.C. Special Series #1, Detective Comics, Flash Comics #80, Hawkman, Identity Crisis, JLA, Power Of The Atom, Showcase #34 -36, Super Friends, Sword of The Atom, Teen Titans & World's Finest)

ATOM, THE (...& the Hawkman No. 39 on)
National Periodical Publ.: June-July, 1962 - No. 38, Aug-Sept, 1968

1-(6-7/62)-Intro Plant-Master; 1st app. Maya 92 184 276 782 1591 2400
2 33 66 99 254 502 750
3-1st Time Pool story; 1st app. Chronos (origin) 22 44 66 159 317 475
4,5: 4-Snapper Carr x-over 16 32 48 114 232 350
6,9,10 13 26 39 89 170 250
7-Hawkman x-over (6-7/63; 1st Atom & Hawkman team-up); 1st app. Hawkman since Brave & the Bold tryouts 27 54 81 197 399 600
8-Justice League, Dr. Light app. 13 26 39 91 176 260
11-15: 13-Chronos-c/story 10 20 30 70 125 180
16-20: 19-Zatanna x-over 8 16 24 54 90 125
21-28,30: 26-Two-page pin-up. 28-Chronos-c/story 7 14 21 49 80 110
29-1st solo Golden Age Atom x-over in S.A. 13 26 39 92 179 265
31-35,37,38: 31-Hawkman x-over. 37-Intro. Major Mynah; Hawkman cameo 6 12 18 41 66 90
36-G.A. Atom x-over 7 14 21 49 80 110

NOTE: ***Anderson** a-1-11i, 13i; c-inks-1-25, 31-35, 37. **Sid Greene** a-8i-37i. **Gil Kane** a-1p-37p; c-1p-28p, 29, 33p, 34; c-26i. **George Roussos** a-38i. **Mike Sekowsky** a-38p. Time Pool stories also in 6, 9,12, 17, 21, 27, 35.*

ATOM, THE (See All New Atom and Tangent Comics/ The Atom)

ATOM AGE (See Classics Illustrated Special Issue)

ATOM-AGE COMBAT
St. John Publishing Co.: June, 1952 - No. 5, Apr, 1953; Feb, 1958

1-Buck Vinson in all 50 100 150 315 533 750
2-Flying saucer story 31 62 93 182 296 410
3,5: 3-Mayo-a (6 pgs.). 5-Flying saucer-c/story 27 54 81 158 259 360
4 (Scarce) 31 62 93 182 296 410
1(2/58-St. John) 22 44 66 132 216 300

ATOM-AGE COMBAT
Fago Magazines: No. 2, Jan, 1959 - No. 3, Mar, 1959

2-A-Bomb explosion-c; 28 56 84 165 270 375
3 21 42 63 126 206 285

ATOMAN
Spark Publications: Feb, 1946 - No. 2, April, 1946

1-Origin & 1st app. Atoman; Robinson/Meskin-a; Kidcrusaders, Wild Bill Hickok, Marvin the Great app. 66 132 198 419 722 1025
2-Robinson/Meskin-a; Robinson c-1,2 41 82 123 256 428 600

ATOM & HAWKMAN, THE (Formerly The Atom)
National Periodical Publ: No. 39, Oct-Nov, 1968 - No. 45, Oct-Nov, 1969; No. 46, Mar, 2010

39-43: 40-41-Kubert/Anderson-a. 43-(7/69)-Last 12¢ issue; 1st S.A. app. Gentleman Ghost 6 12 18 39 62 85
44,45: 44-(9/69)-1st 15¢-c; origin Gentleman Ghost 6 12 18 39 62 85
46-(3/10, $2.99) Blackest Night crossover one-shot; Geoff Johns-s/Ryan Sook-a/c 3.00

NOTE: ***M. Anderson** a-39, 40i, 41i, 43, 44. **Sid Greene** a-40i-45i. **Kubert** a-40p, 41p; c-39-45.*

ATOM ANT (TV) (See Golden Comics Digest #2) (Hanna-Barbera)
Gold Key: January, 1966 (12¢)

1(10170-601)-1st app. Atom Ant, Precious Pup, and Hillbilly Bears 16 32 48 114 232 350

ATOM ANT & SECRET SQUIRREL (See Hanna-Barbera Presents)

ATOMIC AGE
Marvel Comics (Epic Comics): Nov, 1990 - No. 4, Feb, 1991 ($4.50, limited series, square-bound, 52 pgs.)

1-4: Williamson-a(i); sci-fi story set in 1957 4.50

ATOMIC ATTACK (True War Stories; formerly Attack, first series)
Youthful Magazines: No. 5, Jan, 1953 - No. 8, Oct, 1953 (1st story is sci/fi in all issues)

5-Atomic bomb-c; science fiction stories in all 39 78 117 242 401 560
6-8 26 52 78 154 252 350

ATOMIC BOMB
Jay Burtis Publications: 1945 (36 pgs.)

1-Airmale & Stampy (scarce) 71 142 213 454 777 1100

ATOMIC BUNNY (Formerly Atomic Rabbit)
Charlton Comics: No. 12, Aug, 1958 - No. 19, Dec, 1959

12 12 24 36 69 97 125
13-19 8 16 24 42 54 65

ATOMIC COMICS
Daniels Publications (Canadian): Jan, 1946 (Reprints, one-shot)

1-Rocketman, Yankee Boy, Master Key app. 39 78 117 242 401 560

ATOMIC COMICS
Green Publishing Co.: Jan, 1946 - No. 4, July-Aug, 1946 (#1-4 were printed w/o cover gloss)

1-Radio Squad by Siegel & Shuster; Barry O'Neal app.; Fang Gow cover-r/ Detective Comics (Classic-c) 81 162 243 518 884 1250
2-Inspector Dayton; Kid Kane by Matt Baker; Lucky Wings, Congo King, Prop Powers (only app.) begin 55 110 165 352 601 850
3,4: 3-Zero Ghost Detective app.; Baker-a(2) each; 4-Baker-c 39 78 117 242 401 560

ATOMIC KNIGHTS (See Strange Adventures #117)
DC Comics: 2010 ($39.99, HC with dustjacket)

HC-Reprints the original 1960-64 run from debut in Strange Adventures #117 to S.A. #160; new intro. by Murphy Anderson 40.00

ATOMIC MOUSE (TV, Movies) (See Blue Bird, Funny Animals, Giant Comics Edition & Wotalife Comics)
Capitol Stories/Charlton Comics: 3/53 - No. 54, 6/63; No. 1, 12/84; V2#10, 9/85 - No. 12, 1/86

1-Origin & 1st app.; Al Fago-c/a in most 33 66 99 194 317 440
2 15 30 45 84 127 170
3-10: 5-Timmy The Timid Ghost app.; see Zoo Funnies 10 20 30 58 79 100
11-13,16-25 8 16 24 40 50 60
14,15-Hoppy The Marvel Bunny app. 9 18 27 50 65 80
26-(68 pgs.) 12 24 36 67 94 120
27-40: 36,37-Atom The Cat app. 6 12 18 29 36 42
41-54 5 10 15 22 26 30
1 (1984)-Low print run; rep/#7-c w/diff. stories 2 4 6 8 10 12
V2#10 (9/85) -12(1/86)-Low print run 1 3 4 6 8 10

ATOMIC RABBIT (Atomic Bunny #12 on; see Giant Comics #3 & Wotalife)
Charlton Comics: Aug, 1955 - No. 11, Mar, 1958

1-Origin & 1st app.; Al Fago-c/a in all? 30 60 90 177 289 400
2 14 28 42 80 115 150
3-10 10 20 30 56 76 95
11-(68 pgs.) 14 28 42 80 115 150

ATOMICS, THE
AAA Pop Comics: Jan, 2000 - No. 15, Nov, 2001 ($2.95)

1-11-Mike Allred-s/a; 1-Madman-c/app. 3.00
12-15-($3.50): 13-15-Savage Dragon-c/app. 15-Afterword by Alex Ross; colored reprint of 1st Frank Einstein story 3.50
...King-Size Giant Spectacular: Jigsaw (2000, $10.00) r/#1-4 10.00
...King-Size Giant Spectacular: Lessons in Light, Lava, & Lasers (2000, $8.95) r/#5-8 9.00
...King-Size Giant Spectacular: Running With the Dragon ('02, $8.95) r/#13-15 and r/1st Frank Einstein app. in color 9.00
...King-Size Giant Spectacular: Worlds Within Worlds ('01, $8.95) r/#9-12 9.00
Madman and the Atomics, Vol. 1 TPB (2007, $24.99) r/#1-15, cover gallery, pin-ups, afterword by Alex Ross 25.00
...: Spaced Out & Grounded in Snap City TPB (10/03, $12.95) r/one-shots - It Girl, Mr. Gum, Spaceman and Crash Metro & the Star Squad; sketch pages 13.00

ATOMIC SPY CASES
Avon Periodicals: Mar-Apr, 1950 (Painted-c)

1-No Wood-a; A-bomb blast panels; Fass-a 36 72 108 214 347 480

ATOMIC THUNDERBOLT, THE
Regor Company: Feb, 1946 (one-shot) (scarce)

1-Intro. Atomic Thunderbolt & Mr. Murdo 63 126 189 403 689 975

ATOMIC TOYBOX
Image Comics: Dec, 1999 ($2.95)

1- Aaron Lopresti-c/s/a 3.00

ATOMIC WAR!
Ace Periodicals (Junior Books): Nov, 1952 - No. 4, Apr, 1953

1-Atomic bomb-c 123 246 369 787 1344 1900
2,3: 3-Atomic bomb-c 64 128 192 406 696 985
4-Used in **POP**, pg. 96 & illo. 64 128 192 406 696 985

ATOMIKA
Speakeasy Comics/Mercury Comics: Mar, 2005 - No. 6 ($2.99)

Attack #3 © YM

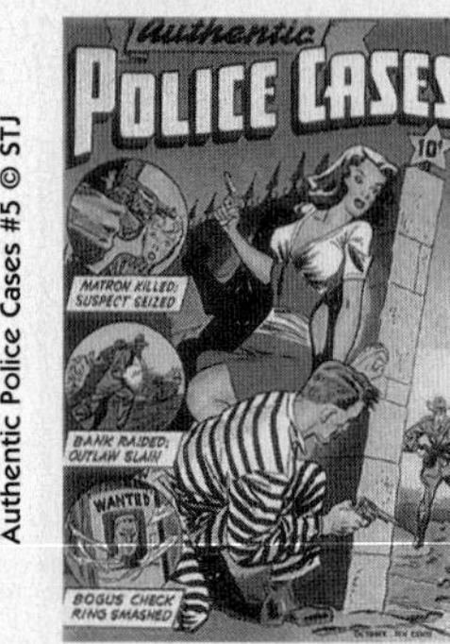

Authentic Police Cases #5 © STJ

The Authority V5 #22 © WSP

	GD	VG	FN	VF	VF/NM	NM-
	2.0	4.0	6.0	8.0	9.0	9.2

1-6: 1-Alex Ross-c/Sal Abbinanti-a/Dabb-s. 3-Fabry-c. 4-Four covers; Romita back-c 3.00
... God is Red TPB (5/06, $19.99) r/#1-6; cover gallery; Dabb foreword 20.00

ATOMIK ANGELS
Crusade Comics: May, 1996 - No. 4, Nov. 1996 ($2.50)

1-4: 1-Freefall from Gen 13 app. 3.00
1-Variant-c 4.00
Intrep-Edition (2/96, B&W, giveaway at launch party)-Previews Atomik Angels #1; includes Billy Tucci interview. 4.00

ATOM SPECIAL (See Atom & Justice League of America)
DC Comics: 1993/1995 ($2.50/$2.95)(68pgs.)

1,2: 1-Dillon-c/a. 2-McDonnell-a/Bolland-c/Peyer-s 3.00

ATOM THE CAT (Formerly Tom Cat; see Giant Comics #3)
Charlton Comics: No. 9, Oct, 1957 - No. 17, Aug, 1959

9 10 20 30 54 72 90
10,13-17 7 14 21 35 43 50
11,12: 11(64 pgs)-Atomic Mouse app. 12(100 pgs.) 11 22 33 62 86 110

ATTACK
Youthful Mag./Trojan No. 5 on: May, 1952 - No. 4, Nov, 1952; No. 5, Jan, 1953 - No. 5, Sept, 1953

1-(1st series)-Extreme violence 39 78 117 231 378 525
2,3-Both Harrison-c/a; bondage, whipping 21 42 63 122 199 275
4-Krenkel-a (7 pgs.); Harrison-a (becomes Atomic Attack #5 on)
21 42 63 122 199 275
5-(#1, Trojan, 2nd series) 15 30 45 86 133 180
6-8 (#2-4), 5 12 24 36 69 97 125

ATTACK
Charlton Comics: No. 54, 1958 - No. 60, Nov, 1959

54 (25¢, 100 pgs.) 12 24 36 69 97 125
55-60 7 14 21 35 43 50

ATTACK!
Charlton Comics: 1962 - No. 15, 3/75; No. 16, 8/79 - No. 48, 10/84

nn(#1)-('62) Special Edition 5 10 15 34 55 75
2('63), 3(Fall, '64) 3 6 9 21 32 42
V4#3(10/66), 4(10/67)-(Formerly Special War Series #2; becomes Attack At Sea V4#5):
3-Tokyo Rose story 3 6 9 17 25 32
1(9/71) 3 6 9 16 23 30
2-5: 2-Hitler app. 4-American Eagle app. 2 4 6 9 12 15
6-15(3/75): 8-Nixon app. 1 3 4 6 8 10
16(8/79) - 40 5.00
41-47 Low print run 7.00
48(10/84)-Wood-r; S&K-c (low print) 1 3 4 6 8 10
Modern Comics 13('78)-r 4.00
NOTE: *Sutton a-9,10,13.*

ATTACK!
Spire Christian Comics (Fleming H. Revell Co.): 1975 (39¢/49¢, 36 pgs.)

nn 2 4 6 9 13 16

ATTACK AT SEA (Formerly Attack!, 1967)
Charlton Comics: V4#5, Oct, 1968 (one-shot)

V4#5 3 6 9 17 25 32

ATTACK ON PLANET MARS (See Strange Worlds #18)
Avon Periodicals: 1951

nn-Infantino, Fawcette, Kubert & Wood-a; adaptation of Tarrano the Conqueror by Ray Cummings 84 168 252 538 919 1300

ATTITUDE LAD
Slave Labor Graphics: Apr, 1994 - No. 3, Nov, 1994 ($2.95, B&W)

1-3 3.00

AUDREY & MELVIN (Formerly Little...)(See Little Audrey & Melvin)
Harvey Publications: No. 62, Sept, 1974

62 2 4 6 9 13 16

AUGIE DOGGIE (TV) (See Hanna-Barbera Band Wagon, Quick-Draw McGraw, Spotlight #2, Top Cat & Whitman Comic Books)
Gold Key: October, 1963 (12¢)

1-Hanna-Barbera character 16 32 48 111 226 340

AUTHENTIC POLICE CASES
St. John Publishing Co.: 2/48 - No. 6, 11/48; No. 7, 5/50 - No. 38, 3/55

1-Hale the Magician by Tuska begins 47 94 141 296 498 700

	GD	VG	FN	VF	VF/NM	NM-
	2.0	4.0	6.0	8.0	9.0	9.2

2-Lady Satan, Johnny Rebel app. 29 58 87 170 278 385
3-Veiled Avenger app.; blood drainage story plus 2 Lucky Coyne stories; used in **SOTI**, illo. from Red Seal #16 50 100 150 315 533 750
4,5: 4-Masked Black Jack app. 5-Late 1930s Jack Cole-a(r); transvestism story
29 58 87 170 278 385
6-Matt Baker-c; used in **SOTI**, illo- "An invitation to learning", r-in Fugitives From Justice #3; Jack Cole-a; also used by the N.Y. Legis. Comm. 54 108 162 343 574 825
7,8,10-14: 7-Jack Cole-a; Matt Baker-a begins #8, ends #?; Vic Flint in #10-14.
10-12-Baker-a(2 each) 29 58 87 170 278 385
9-No Vic Flint 24 48 72 142 234 325
15-Drug-c/story; Vic Flint app.; Baker-c 30 60 90 177 289 400
16,17,19,22-Baker-c 23 46 69 136 223 310
18,20,21,23: Baker-a(i) 20 40 60 114 182 250
24-28 (All 100 pgs.): 26-Transvestism 39 78 117 231 378 525
29,31,32-Baker-c 18 36 54 105 165 225
30 15 30 45 85 130 175
33-38: 33-Baker-c. 34-Baker-c; r/#9. 35-Baker-c/a(2); r/#10. 36-r/#11; Vic Flint strip-r; Baker-c/a(2) unsigned. 37-Baker-c; r/#17. 38- Baker-c/a; r/#18
20 40 60 114 182 250
NOTE: ***Matt Baker** c-6-16, 17, 19, 22, 27, 29, 31-38; a-13, 16. Bondage c-1, 3.*

AUTHORITY, THE (See Stormwatch and Jenny Sparks: The Secret History of...)
DC Comics (WildStorm): May, 1999 - No. 29, Jul, 2002 ($2.50)

1-Wraparound-c; Warren Ellis-s/Bryan Hitch and Paul Neary-a
2 4 6 8 11 14
1-Special Edition (7/10, $1.00) r/#1 with "What's Next?" logo on cover 1.00
2-4 1 3 4 6 8 10
5-12: 12-Death of Jenny Sparks; last Ellis-s 1 2 3 5 6 8
13-Mark Millar-s/Frank Quitely-c/a begins 2 4 6 8 10 12
14-16-Authority vs. Marvel-esque villains 1 2 3 4 5 7
17-22: 17,18-Weston-a. 19,20,22-Quitely-a. 21-McCrea-a 5.00
23-29: 23-26-Peyer-s/Nguyen-a; new Authority. 24-Preview of "The Establishment." 25,26-Jenny Sparks app. 27,28-Millar-s/Adams-a/c 4.00
Annual 2000 ($3.50) Devil's Night x-over; Hamner-a/Bermejo-c
1 2 3 4 5 7
Absolute Authority Slipcased Hardcover (2002, $49.95) oversized r/#1-12 plus script pages by Ellis and sketch pages by Hitch 50.00
...: Earth Inferno and Other Stories TPB (2002, $14.95) r/#17-20, Annual 2000, and Wildstorm Summer Special; new Quitely-c 15.00
...: Human on the Inside HC (2004, $24.95, dust jacket) Ridley-s/Oliver-a/c 25.00
...: Human on the Inside SC (2004, $17.99) Ridley-s/Oliver-a/c 18.00
...: Kev (10/02, $4.95) Ennis-s/Fabry-c/a 5.00
...: Relentless TPB (2000, $17.95) r/#1-8 18.00
...: Scorched Earth (2/03, $4.95) Robbie Morrison-s/Frazer Irving-a/Ashley Wood-c 5.00
...: Transfer of Power TPB (2002, $17.95) r/#22-29 18.00
...: Under New Management TPB (2000, $17.95) r/#9-16; new Quitely-c 18.00

AUTHORITY, THE (See previews in Sleeper, Stormwatch: Team Achilles and Wildcats Version 3.0)
DC Comics (WildStorm): Jul, 2003 - No. 14, Oct, 2004 ($2.95)

1-14: 1-Robbie Morrison-s/Dwayne Turner-a. 5-Huat-a. 14-Portacio-a 3.00
#0 (10/03, $2.95) r/preview back-up-s listed above; Turner sketch pages 3.00
...: Fractured Worlds TPB (2005, $17.95) r/#6-14; cover gallery 18.00
...: Harsh Realities TPB (2004, $14.95) r/#0-5; cover gallery 15.00
.../Lobo: Jingle Hell (2/04, $4.95) Bisley-c/a; Giffen & Grant-s 5.00
.../Lobo: Spring Break Massacre (8/05, $4.99) Bisley-c/a; Giffen & Grant-s 5.00

AUTHORITY, THE (Volume 4) (The Lost Year)
DC Comics (WildStorm): Dec, 2006 - No. 2, May 2007; No. 3, Jan, 2010 - No. 12, Oct, 2010 ($2.99)

1,2-Grant Morrison-s/Gene Ha-a/c 3.00
1-Variant cover by Art Adams 5.00
3-12: 3-(1/10) Morrison & Giffen-s/Robertson-a. 3-12-Ha-c. 12-Ordway-a 3.00
...Reader: The Lost Year (1/10, $2.99) r/#1,2 3.00
... Book One (2010, $17.99) r/#1-7; cover sketch art 18.00

AUTHORITY, THE (Volume 5) (World's End)
DC Comics (WildStorm): Oct, 2008 - No. 29, Jan, 2011 ($2.99)

1-29: 1-5-Simon Coleby-a/c; Lynch back-up story w/Hairsine-a/Gage-s. 21-Simonson-c 3.00
...: Rule Britannia TPB (2010, $19.99) r/#8-17 20.00
...: World's End TPB (2009, $17.99) r/#1-7 18.00

AUTHORITY, THE: MORE KEV
DC Comics (WildStorm): Jul, 2004 - No. 4, Dec, 2004 ($2.95, limited series)

1-4-Garth Ennis-s/Glenn Fabry-c/a 3.00
...: Kev TPB (2005, $14.99) r/Authority: Kev one-shot and Authority: More Kev series 15.00

AUTHORITY, THE: PRIME

Automatic Kafka #7 © WSP

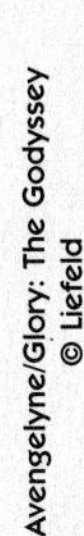
Avengelyne/Glory: The Godyssey © Liefeld

Avengers #42 © MAR

DC Comics (WildStorm): Dec, 2007 - No. 6, May, 2008 ($2.99, limited series)

	GD 2.0	VG 4.0	FN 6.0	VF 8.0	VF/NM 9.0	NM- 9.2
1-6-Gage-s/Robertson-c/a; Bendix app.						3.00
TPB (2008, $17.99) r/#1-6						18.00

AUTHORITY, THE: REVOLUTION
DC Comics (WildStorm): Dec, 2004 - No. 12, Dec, 2005 ($2.95/$2.99)

	GD 2.0	VG 4.0	FN 6.0	VF 8.0	VF/NM 9.0	NM- 9.2
1-12-Brubaker-s/Nguyen-a. 5-Henry Bendix returns. 7-Jenny Sparks app.						3.00
...: Book One TPB (2005, $14.99) r/#1-6; cover gallery and Nguyen sketch pages						15.00
...: Book Two TPB (2006, $14.99) r/#7-12; cover gallery and Nguyen sketch pages						15.00

AUTHORITY, THE: THE MAGNIFICENT KEV
DC Comics (WildStorm): Nov, 2005 - No. 5, Feb, 2006 ($2.99, limited series)

	GD 2.0	VG 4.0	FN 6.0	VF 8.0	VF/NM 9.0	NM- 9.2
1-5-Garth Ennis-s/Carlos Ezquerra-a/Glenn Fabry-c						3.00
TPB (2006, $14.99) r/#1-5						15.00

AUTOMATIC KAFKA
DC Comics (WildStorm): Sept, 2002 - No. 9, Jul, 2003 ($2.95)

	GD 2.0	VG 4.0	FN 6.0	VF 8.0	VF/NM 9.0	NM- 9.2
1-9-Ashley Wood-c/a; Joe Casey-s						3.00

AUTOMATON
Image Comics (Flypaper Press): Sept, 1998 - No. 3, 1998 ($2.95, lim. series)

	GD 2.0	VG 4.0	FN 6.0	VF 8.0	VF/NM 9.0	NM- 9.2
1-3-R.A. Jones-s/Peter Vale-a						3.00

AUTUMN
Caliber Comics: 1995 - No. 3, 1995 ($2.95, B&W)

	GD 2.0	VG 4.0	FN 6.0	VF 8.0	VF/NM 9.0	NM- 9.2
1-3						3.00

AUTUMN ADVENTURES (Walt Disney's...)
Disney Comics: Autumn, 1990; No. 2, Autumn, 1991 ($2.95, 68 pgs.)

	GD 2.0	VG 4.0	FN 6.0	VF 8.0	VF/NM 9.0	NM- 9.2
1-Donald Duck-r(2) by Barks, Pluto-r, & new-a						4.00
2-D. Duck-r by Barks; new Super Goof story						4.00

AVATAARS: COVENANT OF THE SHIELD
Marvel Comics: Sept, 2000 - No. 3, Nov, 2000 ($2.99, limited series)

	GD 2.0	VG 4.0	FN 6.0	VF 8.0	VF/NM 9.0	NM- 9.2
1-3-Kaminski-s/Oscar Jimenez-a						3.00

AVATAR
DC Comics: Feb, 1991 - No. 3, Apr, 1991 ($5.95, limited series, 100 pgs.)

	GD 2.0	VG 4.0	FN 6.0	VF 8.0	VF/NM 9.0	NM- 9.2
1-3: Based on TSR's Forgotten Realms						6.00

AVENGELYNE
Maximum Press: May, 1995 - No. 3, July, 1995 ($2.50/$3.50, limited series)

	GD 2.0	VG 4.0	FN 6.0	VF 8.0	VF/NM 9.0	NM- 9.2
1/2	2	4	6	8	10	12
1/2 Platinum						15.00
1-Newstand ($2.50)-Photo-c; poster insert						6.00
1-Direct Market ($3.50)-Chromium-c; poster	1	2	3	4	5	7
1-Glossy edition	2	4	6	12	16	20
1-Gold						12.00
2-3: 2-Polybagged w/card						3.00
3-Variant-c; Deodato pin-up						5.00
...Bible (10/96, $3.50)						4.00
.../Glory (9/95, $3.95) 2 covers						4.00
.../Glory Swimsuit Special (6/96, $2.95) photo and illos. covers						3.00
.../Glory: The Godyssey (9/96, $2.99) 2 covers (1 photo)						3.00
...Revelation One (Avatar, 1/01, $3.50) 3 covers by Haley, Rio, Shaw; Shaw-a						3.50
.../Shi (Avatar, 11/01, $3.50) Eight covers; Waller-a						3.50
...Swimsuit (8/95, $2.95)-Pin-ups/photos. 3-Variant-c exist (2 photo, 1 Liefeld-a)						4.00
...Swimsuit (1/96, $3.50, 2nd printing)-photo-c						4.00
Trade paperback (12/95, $9.95)						10.00
.../Warrior Nun Areala 1 (11/96, $2.99) also see Warrior Nun/Avengelyne						3.00

AVENGELYNE
Maximum Press: V2#1, Apr, 1996 - No. 14, Apr, 1997 ($2.95/$2.50)

	GD 2.0	VG 4.0	FN 6.0	VF 8.0	VF/NM 9.0	NM- 9.2
V2#1-Four covers exist (2 photo-c).						4.00
V2#2-Three covers exist (1 photo-c); flip book w/Darkchylde						5.00
V2#0, 3-14: 0-(10/96).3-Flip book w/Priest preview. 5-Flip book w/Blindside						3.00

AVENGELYNE (Volume 3)
Awesome Comics: Mar, 1999 ($2.50)

	GD 2.0	VG 4.0	FN 6.0	VF 8.0	VF/NM 9.0	NM- 9.2
1-Fraga & Liefeld-a						3.00

AVENGELYNE: ARMAGEDDON
Maximum Press: Dec, 1996 - No. 3, Feb, 1997 ($2.99, limited series)

	GD 2.0	VG 4.0	FN 6.0	VF 8.0	VF/NM 9.0	NM- 9.2
1-3-Scott Clark-a(p)						3.00

AVENGELYNE: DEADLY SINS
Maximum Press: Feb, 1996 - No. 2, Mar, 1996 ($2.95, limited series)

	GD 2.0	VG 4.0	FN 6.0	VF 8.0	VF/NM 9.0	NM- 9.2
1,2: 1-Two-c exist (1 photo, 1 Liefeld-a). 2-Liefeld-c; Pop Mhan-a(p)						3.00

AVENGELYNE/POWER
Maximum Press: Nov, 1995 - No.3, Jan, 1996 ($2.95, limited series)

	GD 2.0	VG 4.0	FN 6.0	VF 8.0	VF/NM 9.0	NM- 9.2
1-3: 1,2-Liefeld-c. 3-Three variant-c. exist (1 photo-c)						3.00

AVENGELYNE • PROPHET
Maximum Press: May, 1996; No. 2, Feb. 1997 ($2.95, unfinished lim. series)

	GD 2.0	VG 4.0	FN 6.0	VF 8.0	VF/NM 9.0	NM- 9.2
1,2-Liefeld-c/a(p)						3.00

AVENGER, THE (See A-1 Comics)
Magazine Enterprises: Feb-Mar, 1955 - No. 4, Aug-Sept, 1955

	GD 2.0	VG 4.0	FN 6.0	VF 8.0	VF/NM 9.0	NM- 9.2
1(A-1 #129)-Origin	39	78	117	240	395	550
2(A-1 #131), 3(A-1 #133) Robot-c, 4(A-1 #138)	27	54	81	158	259	360
IW Reprint #9('64)-Reprints #1 (new cover)	4	8	12	20	29	38

NOTE: *Powell a-2-4; c-1-4.*

AVENGERS, THE (TV)(Also see Steed and Mrs. Peel)
Gold Key: Nov, 1968 ("John Steed & Emma Peel" cover title) (15¢)

	GD 2.0	VG 4.0	FN 6.0	VF 8.0	VF/NM 9.0	NM- 9.2
1-Photo-c	14	28	42	99	200	300
1-(Variant with photo back-c)	18	36	54	131	266	400

AVENGERS, THE (See Essential..., Giant-Size..., JLA/..., Kree/Skrull War Starring..., Marvel Graphic Novel #27, Marvel Super Action, Marvel Super Heroes('66), Marvel Treasury Ed., Marvel Triple Action, New Avengers, Solo Avengers, Tales Of Suspense #49, West Coast Avengers & X-Men Vs....)

AVENGERS, THE (The Mighty Avengers on cover only #63-69)
Marvel Comics Group: Sept, 1963 - No. 402, Sept, 1996

	GD 2.0	VG 4.0	FN 6.0	VF 8.0	VF/NM 9.0	NM- 9.2
1-Origin & 1st app. The Avengers (Thor, Iron Man, Hulk, Ant-Man, Wasp); Loki app.	533	1066	1600	5000	10,000	15,000
2-Hulk leaves Avengers	104	208	312	884	1792	2700
3-2nd Sub-Mariner x-over outside the F.F. (see Strange Tales #107 for 1st); Sub-Mariner & Hulk team-up & battle Avengers; Spider-Man cameo (1/64)	69	138	207	587	1194	1800
4-Revival of Captain America who joins the Avengers; 1st Silver Age app. of Captain America & Bucky (3/64)	193	386	579	1689	3445	5200
4-Reprint from the Golden Record Comic set	13	26	39	91	176	260
With Record (1966)	18	36	54	127	259	390
5-Hulk app.	45	90	135	360	730	1100
6,8: 6-Intro/1st app. original Zemo & his Masters of Evil. 8-Intro Kang	35	70	105	273	537	800
7-Rick Jones app. in Bucky costume	37	74	111	294	585	875
9-Intro Wonder Man who dies in same story	48	96	144	392	796	1200
10-Intro/1st app. Immortus; early Hercules app. (11/64)	28	56	84	204	415	625
11-Spider-Man-c & x-over (12/64)	36	72	108	280	553	825
12-15: 15-Death of original Zemo	18	36	54	131	266	400
16-New Avengers line-up (Hawkeye, Quicksilver, Scarlet Witch join; Thor, Iron Man, Giant-Man, Wasp leave)	28	56	84	215	433	650
17,18	13	26	39	94	185	275
19-1st app. Swordsman; origin Hawkeye (8/65)	14	28	42	99	200	300
20-22: Wood inks	10	20	30	71	128	185
23-30: 23-Romita Sr. inks (1st Silver Age Marvel work). 25-Dr. Doom-c/story. 28-Giant-Man becomes Goliath (5/66)	9	18	27	65	113	160
31-40	8	16	24	56	93	130
41-46,49-52,54-56: 43-1st app. Red Guardian (dies in #44) . 46-Ant-Man returns (re-intro, 11/67). 52-Black Panther joins; 1st app. The Grim Reaper. 54-1st app. new Masters of Evil. 56-Zemo app; story explains how Capt. America became imprisoned in ice during WWII, only to be rescued in Avengers #4	7	14	21	49	80	110
47-Magneto-c/story	7	14	21	50	83	115
48-Origin/1st app. new Black Knight (1/68)	7	14	21	50	83	115
53-X-Men app.	10	20	30	67	116	165
57-1st app. S.A. Vision (10/68)	18	36	54	131	266	400
58-Origin The Vision	10	20	30	71	128	185
59-65: 59-Intro. Yellowjacket. 60-Wasp & Yellowjacket wed. 63-Goliath becomes Yellowjacket; Hawkeye becomes the new Goliath. 65-Last 12¢ issue	6	12	18	39	62	85
66,67-B. Smith-a	6	12	18	41	66	90
68-70: 69-Nighthawk cameo. 70-1st full app. Nighthawk	6	12	18	37	59	80
71-1st app. The Invaders (12/69); Black Knight joins	8	16	24	56	93	130
72-79,81,82,84-86,89-91: 82-Daredevil app	5	10	15	35	55	75
80-Intro. Red Wolf (9/70)	6	12	18	37	59	80
83-Intro. The Liberators (Wasp, Valkyrie, Scarlet Witch, Medusa & the Black Widow)	6	12	18	39	62	85
87-Origin The Black Panther	6	12	18	39	62	85
88-Written by Harlan Ellison	6	12	18	37	59	80
88-2nd printing (1994)	2	4	6	8	10	12

Avengers #186 © MAR

Avengers #378 © MAR

Avengers V3 #5 © MAR

	GD 2.0	VG 4.0	FN 6.0	VF 8.0	VF/NM 9.0	NM- 9.2
92-Last 15¢ issue; Neal Adams-c	6	12	18	43	69	95
93-(52 pgs.)-Neal Adams-c/a	13	26	39	91	176	260
94-96-Neal Adams-c/a	8	16	24	54	90	125
97-G.A. Capt. America, Sub-Mariner, Human Torch, Patriot, Vision, Blazing Skull, Fin, Angel, & new Capt. Marvel x-over	6	12	18	41	66	90
98,99: 98-Goliath becomes Hawkeye; Smith c/a(i). 99-Smith-c, Smith/Sutton-a	5	10	15	35	55	75
100-(6/72)-Smith-c/a; featuring everyone who was an Avenger	10	20	30	67	116	165
101-Harlan Ellison scripts	4	8	12	24	37	50
102-106,108,109	4	8	12	22	34	45
107-Starlin-a(p)	4	8	12	24	37	50
110,111-X-Men app.	6	12	18	39	62	85
112-1st app. Mantis	5	10	15	30	48	65
113-115,119-124,126-130: 123-Origin Mantis	3	6	9	19	29	38
116-118-Defenders/Silver Surfer app.	6	12	18	37	59	80
125-Thanos-c & brief app.	4	8	12	24	37	50
131-133,136-140: 136-Ploog-r/Amazing Advs. #12	3	6	9	16	22	28
134,135-Origin of the Vision revised (also see Avengers Forever mini-series)	4	8	12	22	34	45
141-143,145,152-163	2	4	6	9	12	15
144-Origin & 1st app. Hellcat	3	6	9	14	20	25
146-149-(Reg.25¢ editions)(4-7/76)	2	4	6	9	12	15
146-149-(30¢-c variants, limited distribution)	4	8	12	22	34	45
150-Kirby-a(r); new line-up: Capt. America, Scarlet Witch, Iron Man, Wasp, Yellowjacket, Vision & The Beast	2	4	6	10	14	18
150-(30¢-c variant, limited distribution)	4	8	12	26	41	55
151-Wonder Man returns w/new costume	2	4	6	10	14	18
160-164-(35¢-c variants, limited dist.)(6-10/77)	7	14	21	47	76	105
164-166: Byrne-a	2	4	6	10	14	18
167-180: 168-Guardians of the Galaxy app. 174-Thanos cameo. 176-Starhawk app.	1	2	3	5	6	8
181-191-Byrne-a: 181-New line-up: Capt. America, Scarlet Witch, Iron Man, Wasp, Vision, Beast & The Falcon. 183-Ms. Marvel joins. 185-Origin Quicksilver & Scarlet Witch	2	4	6	8	10	12
192-194,197-199						6.00
195,196: 195-1st Taskmaster cameo. 196-1st Taskmaster full app.	1	3	4	6	8	10
200-(10/80, 52 pgs.)-Ms. Marvel leaves.	1	3	4	6	8	10
201-213,217-238: 211-New line-up: Capt. America, Iron Man, Tigra, Thor, Wasp & Yellowjacket. 213-Yellowjacket leaves. 217-Yellowjacket & Wasp return. 221-Hawkeye & She-Hulk join. 227-Capt. Marvel (female) joins; origins of Ant-Man, Wasp, Giant-Man, Goliath, Yellowjacket, & Avengers. 230-Yellowjacket quits. 231-Iron Man leaves. 232-Starfox (Eros) joins. 234-Origin Quicksilver, Scarlet Witch. 238-Origin Blackout						4.50
214-Ghost Rider-c/story						6.00
215,216,239,240,250: 215,216-Silver Surfer app. 216-Tigra leaves. 239-(1/84) Avengers app. on David Letterman show. 240-Spider-Woman revived. 250-($1.00, 52 pgs.)						5.00
241-249, 251-262						3.50
263-(1/86) Return of Jean Grey, leading into X-Factor #1(story continues in FF #286)						6.00
264-299: 272-Alpha Flight app. 291-$1.00 issues begin. 297-Black Knight, She-Hulk & Thor resign. 298-Inferno tie-in						3.00
300 (2/89, $1.75, 68 pgs.)-Thor joins; Simonson-a						4.00
301-304,306-313,319-325,327,329-343: 302-Re-intro Quasar. 320-324-Alpha Flight app. (320-cameo). 327-2nd app. Rage. 341,342-New Warriors app. 343-Last $1.00-c						3.00
305,314-318: 305-Byrne scripts begin. 314-318-Spider-Man x-over						3.50
326-1st app. Rage (11/90)						4.00
328,344-349,351-359,361,362,364,365,367: 328-Origin Rage. 365-Contains coupon for Hunt for Magneto contest						3.00
350-($2.50, 68 pgs.)-Double gatefold-c showing-c to #1; r/#53 w/cover in flip book format; vs. The Starjammers						4.00
360-($2.95, 52 pgs.)-Embossed all-foil-c; 30th ann.						4.00
363-($2.95, 52 pgs.)-All silver foil-c						4.00
366-($3.95, 68 pgs.)-Embossed all gold foil-c						4.00
368,370-374,376-399: 368-Bloodties part 1; Avengers/X-Men x-over. 374-bound-in trading card sheet. 380-Deodato-a. 390,391-"The Crossing." 395-Death of "old" Tony Stark; wraparound-c.						3.00
369-($2.95)-Foil embossed-c; Bloodties part 5						4.00
375-($2.00, 52 pgs.)-Regular ed.; Thunderstrike returns; leads into Malibu Comics' Black September.						3.50
375-($2.50, 52 pgs.)-Collector's ed. w/bound-in poster; leads into Malibu Comics' Black September.						4.00
400-402: Waid-s; 402-Deodato breakdowns; cont'd in X-Men #56 & Onslaught: Marvel Universe.						4.00
#500-503 (See Avengers Vol. 3; series resumed original numbering after Vol. 3 #84)						

	GD 2.0	VG 4.0	FN 6.0	VF 8.0	VF/NM 9.0	NM- 9.2
Special 1 (9/67, 25¢, 68 pgs.)-New-a; original & new Avengers team-up	11	22	33	80	150	220
Special 2 (9/68, 25¢, 68 pgs.)-New-a; original vs. new Avengers	7	14	21	50	83	115
Special 3 (9/69, 25¢, 68 pgs.)-r/Avengers #4 plus 3 Capt. America stories by Kirby (art); origin Red Skull	5	10	15	30	48	65
Special 4 (1/71, 25¢, 68 pgs.)-Kirby-r/Avengers #5,6	3	6	9	20	30	40
Special 5 (1/72, 52 pgs.)-Spider-Man x-over	3	6	9	20	30	40
Annual 6 (11/76) Pérez-a; Kirby-c	2	4	6	11	16	20
Annual 7 (11/77)-Starlin-c/a; Warlock dies; Thanos app.	5	10	15	35	55	75
Annual 8 (1978)-Dr. Strange, Ms. Marvel app.	2	4	6	8	11	14
Annual 9 (1979)-Newton-a(p)	2	3	4	6	8	10
Annual 10 (1981)-Golden-p; X-Men cameo; 1st app. Rogue & Madelyne Pryor	5	10	15	35	55	75
Annual 11-13: 11(1982)-Vs. The Defenders. 12('83), 13('84)						4.00
Annual 14-18: 14('85),15('86),16('87),17('88)-Evolutionary War x-over, 18('89)-Atlantis Attacks						4.00
Annual 19-23 (90-'94, 68 pgs.). 22-Bagged/card						4.00
...: Galactic Storm Vol. 1 ('06, $29.99, TPB) r/Kree-Shi'ar war from Avengers #345-346, Capt. America #398-399, Avengers West Coast #80-81, Quasar #32-33, Wonder Man #7-8, Iron Man #278 and Thor #445; new Epting-c						30.00
...: Galactic Storm Vol. 2 ('06, $29.99, TPB) r/Kree-Shi'ar war from Avengers #347, Capt. America #400-401, Avengers West Coast #82, Quasar #34-36, Wonder Man #9, Iron Man #279, Thor #446 and What If #55-56						30.00
...: Kang - Time and Time Again ('05, $19.99, TPB) r/Avengers #69-71 & 267-269, Thor #140 and Incredible Hulk #135						20.00
...Kree-Skrull War ('00, $24.95, TPB) new Neal Adams-c						25.00
...: Legends Vol. 3: George Perez ('03, $16.99)-r/#161,162,194-196,201, Ann. #6 & 8						17.00
Marvel Double Feature...Avengers/Giant-Man #379 ($2.50, 52 pgs.)-Same as Avengers #379 w/Giant-Man flip book						3.00
Marvel Graphic Novel - Deathtrap: The Vault (1991, $9.95) Venom-c/app.	2	4	6	8	10	12
The Korvac Saga TPB (2003, $19.95)-r/#167,168,170-177; Perez-c						20.00
The Serpent Crown TPB (2005, $15.99)-r/#141-144,147-149; Hellcat app.						16.00
The Yesterday Quest ($6.95)-r/#181,182,185-187	1	2	3	4	5	7
Under Siege ('98, $16.95, TPB) r/#270,271,273-277						17.00
...: Vision and the Scarlet Witch TPB (2005, $15.99) r/wedding from Giant-Size Avengers #4 and "Vision and the Scarlet Witch" mini-series #1-4						16.00
...: Visionaries ('99, $16.95)-r/early George Perez art						17.00

NOTE: ***Austin*** *c(i)-157, 167, 168, 170-177, 181, 183-188, 198-201, Annual 8.* ***John Buscema*** *a-41-44p, 46p, 47p, 49, 50, 51-62p, 74-77, 79-85, 87-91, 97, 105p, 121p, 124p,125p, 152, 153p, 255-279p, 281-302p; c-41-66, 68-71, 73-91, 97-99, 178, 256-259p, 261-279p, 281-302p.* ***Byrne*** *a-164-166p, 181-191p, 233p, Annual 13i, 14p; c-186-190p, 233p, 260, 305p; scripts-305-312.* ***Colan*** *a(p)-63-65, 111, 206-208, 210, 211; c(p)-65, 206-208, 210, 211.* ***Ditko*** *a-Annual 13.* ***Guice*** *a-Annual 12p.* ***Don Heck*** *a-9-15, 17-40, 157.* ***Kane*** *c-37p, 159p.* ***Kane/Everett*** *c-97.* ***Kirby*** *a-1-8p, Special 3r, 4r(p); c-1-30, 148, 151-158; layouts-14-16.* ***Ron Lim*** *c(p)-335-341.* ***Miller*** *c-193p.* ***Mooney*** *a-86i, 179p, 180p.* ***Nebres*** *a-178i; c-179i.* ***Newton*** *a-204p, Annual 9p.* ***Perez*** *a(p)-141, 143, 144, 148, 150, 154, 155, 160, 161, 162, 167,168, 170, 171, 194-196, 198-202, Annual 6, 8; c(p)-160-162, 164-166, 170-174, 181,183-185, 191, 192, 194-201, 379-382, Annual 8.* ***Starlin*** *c-121, 135.* ***Staton*** *a-127-134i.* ***Tuska*** *a-47i,48i, 51i, 53i, 54i, 106p, 107p, 135p, 137-140p, 163p. Guardians of the Galaxy app. in #167, 168, 170, 173, 175, 181.*

AVENGERS, THE (Volume Two)
Marvel Comics: V2#1, Nov, 1996 - No. 13, Nov, 1997 ($2.95/$1.95/$1.99) (Produced by Extreme Studios)

	GD 2.0	VG 4.0	FN 6.0	VF 8.0	VF/NM 9.0	NM- 9.2
1-($2.95)-Heroes Reborn begins; intro new team (Captain America, Swordsman, Scarlet Witch, Vision, Thor, Hellcat & Hawkeye); 1st app. Avengers Island; Loki & Enchantress app.; Rob Liefeld-p & plot; Chap Yaep-p; Jim Valentino scripts; variant-c exists						5.00
1-($1.95)-Variant-c						6.00
2-13: 2,3-Jeph Loeb scripts begin, Kang app. 4-Hulk-c/app. 5-Thor/Hulk battle; 2 covers. 10,11,13-"World War 3"-pt. 2, x-over w/Image characters. 12-($2.99) "Heroes Reunited"-pt. 2						4.00
Heroes Reborn: Avengers (2006, $29.99, TPB) r/#1-12; pin-up and cover gallery						30.00

AVENGERS, THE (Volume Three)(See New Avengers for next series)
Marvel Comics: Feb, 1998 - No. 84, Aug, 2004; No. 500, Sept, 2004 - No. 503, Dec, 2004 ($2.99/$1.99/$2.25)

	GD 2.0	VG 4.0	FN 6.0	VF 8.0	VF/NM 9.0	NM- 9.2
1-($2.99, 48 pgs.) Busiek-s/Pérez-a/wraparound-c; Avengers reassemble after Heroes Return						5.00
1-Variant Heroes Return cover	1	2	3	4	5	7
1-Rough Cut-Features original script and pencil pages						3.00
2-($1.99)Pérez-c, 2-Lago painted-c						4.00
3,4: 3-Wonder Man-c/app. 4-Final roster chosen; Perez poster						3.50
5-11: 5,6-Squadron Supreme-c/app. 8-Triathlon-c/app.						3.00
12-($2.99) Thunderbolts app.						4.00
12-Alternate-c of Avengers w/white background; no logo						15.00
13-24,26,28: 13-New Warriors app. 16-18-Ordway-s/a. 19-Ultron returns. 26-Immonen-a						3.00
16-Variant-c with purple background						5.00

Avengers (2010 series) #1 © MAR

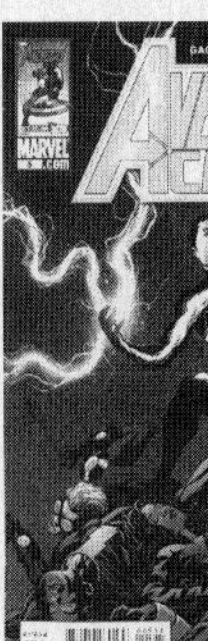

Avengers Academy #5 © MAR

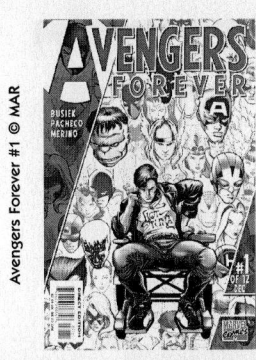

Avengers Forever #1 © MAR

GD VG FN VF VF/NM NM-
2.0 4.0 6.0 8.0 9.0 9.2

25,27-($2.99) 25-vs. the Exemplars; Spider-Man app. 27-100 pgs. 4.00
29-33,35-47: 29-Begin $2.25-c. 35-Maximum Security x-over; Romita Jr.-a. 36-Epting-a; poster by Alan Davis. 38-Davis-a begins ($1.99-c) 3.00
34-($2.99) Last Pérez-a; Thunderbirds app. 4.00
48-($3.50, 100 pgs.) new story w/Dwyer-a & r/#98-100 4.00
49,51-59: 49-'Nuff Said story. 51-Anderson-a. 52-Reis-a. 57-Johns-s begin 3.00
50,60-($3.50): 50 Dwyer-a; Quasar app. 4.00
61-84: 61,62-Frank-a; new line-up. 63-Davis-a. 64-Reis-a. 65-70-Coipel-a. 75-Hulk app. 76-Jack of Hearts dies; Jae Lee-c. 77-(50¢-c) Coipel-a/Cassaday-c. 78,80,81Coipel-a. 83,84-New Invaders app. 3.00

(After #84 [Aug, 2004], numbering reverted back to original Vol. 1 with #500, Sept, 2004)

500-($3.50) "Avengers Disassembled" begins; Bendis-s/Finch-a; Ant-Man (Scott Lang) killed, Vision destroyed 4.00
500-Director's Cut ($4.99) Cassaday foil variant-c plus interviews and galleries 5.00
501, 502-($2.25): 502-Hawkeye killed 3.00
503-($3.50) "Avengers Disassembled" ends; reprint pages from Avengers V1#16 4.00
#11/2 (12/99, $2.50) Timm-c/a/Stern-s; 1963-style issue 3.00
.../ Squadron Supreme '98 Annual ($2.99) 4.00
1999, 2000 Annual (7/99, '00, $3.50) 1999-Manco-a. 2000-Breyfogle-a 4.00
2001 Annual ($2.99) Reis-a; back-up-s art by Churchill 4.00
...: Above and Beyond TPB ('05, $24.99) r/#36-40,56, Annual 2001, & Avengers: The Ultron Imperative; Alan Davis-c 25.00
... Assemble HC ('04, $29.95, oversized) r/#1-11 & '98 Annual; Busiek intro.; Pérez pencil art and Busiek script from Avengers #1 30.00
... Assemble Vol. 2 HC ('05, $29.95, oversized) r/#12-22, #0 & Ann. 1999; Ordway intro. 30.00
... Assemble Vol. 3 HC ('06, $34.99, oversized) r/#23-34, #1 1/2 & Thunderbolts #42-44 35.00
... Assemble Vol. 4 HC ('07, $34.99, oversized) r/#35-40, Avengers 2000, Avengers 2001, Avengers: The Ultron Imperative, Maximum Security #1-3 & ...Dangerous Planet 35.00
... Assemble Vol. 5 HC ('07, $39.99, oversized) r/#41-56 and Avengers 2001 40.00
...: Clear and Present Dangers TPB ('01, $19.95) r/#8-15 20.00
...: Defenders War HC ('07, $19.99) r/#115-118 & Defenders #8-11; Englehart intro. 20.00
...: Disassembled HC ('06, $24.99) r/#500-503 & Avengers Finale; Director's Cut extras 25.00
...: Disassembled TPB ('05, $15.99) r/#500-503 & Avengers Finale; Director's Cut extras 16.00
...Finale 1 (1/05, $3.50) Epilogue to Avengers Disassembled; Neal Adams-c; art by various incl. Peréz, Maleev, Oeming, Powell, Mayhew, Mack, McNiven, Cheung, Frank 4.00
Free Comic Book Day (5/09, giveaway) New Avengers 1st battle vs. Dark Avengers 3.00
...: Living Legends TPB ('04, $19.99) r/#23-30; last Busiek/Pérez arc 20.00
...Supreme Justice TPB (4/01, $17.95) r/Squadron Supreme appearances in Avengers #5-7, '98 Annual, Iron Man #7, Capt. America #8, Quicksilver #10; Pérez-c 18.00
The Kang Dynasty TPB ('02, $29.99) r/#41-55 & 2001 Annual 30.00
The Morgan Conquest TPB ('00, $14.95) r/#1-4 15.00
.../Thunderbolts Vol. 1: The Nefaria Protocols (2004, $19.99) r/#31-34, 42-44 20.00
Ultron Unleashed TPB (8/99, $3.50) reprints early app. 4.00
Ultron Unlimited TPB (4/01, $14.95) r/#19-22 & #0 prelude 15.00
Wizard #0-Ultron Unlimited prelude 3.00
Vol. 1: World Trust TPB ('03, $14.99) r/#57-62 & Marvel Double-Shot #2 15.00
Vol. 2: Red Zone TPB ('04, $14.99) r/#64-70 15.00
Vol. 3: The Search For She-Hulk TPB ('04, $12.99) r/#71-76 13.00
Vol. 4: The Lionheart of Avalon TPB ('04, $11.99) r/#77-81 12.00
Vol. 5: Once an Invader TPB ('04, $14.99) r/#82-84, V1 #71; Invaders #0 & Ann #1 ('77) 15.00

AVENGERS (The Heroic Age)
Marvel Comics: July, 2010 - Present ($3.99)

1-New team assembled; Bendis-s/Romita Jr.-a; Kang app.; back-up text Avengers history 4.00
1-Variant-c by Land 6.00
1-Variant covers by Djurdjevic and John Romita Sr. 10.00
1-3-Second printings 4.00
2-12: 2-Wonder Man app. 4-6-Ultron app. 7-Red Hulk app. 12-Red Hulk joins 4.00
... Assemble 1 (7/10, $3.99) Handbook-style profiles of Avengers, enemies, allies 4.00
... Spotlight (7/10, $3.99) Creator interviews, previews, history of the team; trivia 4.00

AVENGERS ACADEMY (The Heroic Age)
Marvel Comics: Aug, 2010 - Present ($3.99/$2.99)

1-($3.99) Gage-s/McKone-a/c; Intro. team of Veil, Hazmat, Striker, Mettle, Finesse, Reptil 4.00
1-Variant-c by Djurdjevic 8.00
2-12-($2.99) 3,4-Juggernaut app. 5-Molina-a. 7-Absorbing Man app.; Raney-a 3.00

AVENGERS AND POWER PACK ASSEMBLE!
Marvel Comics: June, 2006 - No. 4, Sept, 2006 ($2.99, limited series)

1-4-GuriHiru-a/Sumerak-s. 1-Capt. America app. 2-Iron Man. 3-Spider-Man, Kang app. 3.00
TPB (2006, $6.99, digest-size) r/#1-4 7.00

AVENGERS AND THE INFINITY GAUNTLET
Marvel Comics: Oct, 2010 - No. 4, Jan, 2011 ($2.99, limited series)

1-Clevinger-s/Churilla-a; Dr. Doom and Thanos app. 1-Ramos-c. 2-Lim-c 3.00

GD VG FN VF VF/NM NM-
2.0 4.0 6.0 8.0 9.0 9.2

AVENGERS: CELESTIAL QUEST
Marvel Comics: Nov, 2001 - No. 8, June, 2002 ($2.50/$3.50, limited series)

1-7-Englehart-s/Santamaría-a; Thanos app. 3.00
8-($3.50) 4.00

AVENGERS: CLASSIC
Marvel Comics: Aug, 2007 - No. 12, Juy, 2008 ($3.99/$2.99)

1,12-($3.99) 1-Reprints Avengers #1 ('63) with new stories about that era; Art Adams-c 4.00
2-11-($2.99) R/#2-11 with back-up w/art by Oeming and others 3.00

AVENGERS COLLECTOR'S EDITION, THE
Marvel Comics: 1993 (Ordered through mail w/candy wrapper, 20 pgs.)

1-Contains 4 bound-in trading cards 5.00

AVENGERS: EARTH'S MIGHTIEST HEROES
Marvel Comics: Jan, 2005 - No. 8, Apr, 2005 ($3.50, limited series)

1-8-Retells origin; Casey-s/Kolins-a 3.50
HC (2005, $24.99, 7 1/2" x 11" with dustjacket) r/#1-8 25.00

AVENGERS: EARTH'S MIGHTIEST HEROES (Based on the Disney animated series)
Marvel Comics: Jan, 2011 - No. 4, Apr, 2011 ($3.99)

1-4-Yost-s/Wegener-a. 1-Hero profile pages. 2-Villain profile pages 4.00

AVENGERS: EARTH'S MIGHTIEST HEROES II
Marvel Comics: Jan, 2007 - No. 8, May, 2007 ($3.99, limited series)

1-8-Retells time when the Vision joined; Casey-s/Rosado-a. 6-Hank & Janet's wedding 4.00
HC (2007, $24.99, 7 1/2" x 11" with dustjacket) r/#1-8; cover sketches 25.00

AVENGERS FAIRY TALES
Marvel Comics: May, 2008 - No. 4, Dec, 2008 ($2.99, limited series)

1-4: 1-Peter Pan-style tale; Cebulski-a/Lemos-a. 2-The Vision. 3-Miyazawa-a 3.00

AVENGERS FOREVER
Marvel Comics: Dec, 1998 - No. 12, Feb, 2000 ($2.99)

1-Busiek-s/Pacheco-a in all 4.00
2-12: 4-Four covers. 6-Two covers. 8-Vision origin revised. 12-Rick Jones becomes Capt. Marvel 3.00
TPB (1/01, $24.95) r/#1-12; Busiek intro.; new Pacheco-c 25.00

AVENGERS INFINITY
Marvel Comics: Sept, 2000 - No. 4, Dec, 2000 ($2.99, limited series)

1-4-Stern-s/Chen-a 3.00

AVENGERS/ INVADERS
Marvel Comics: Jul, 2008 - No. 12, Aug, 2009 ($2.99, limited series)

1-Invaders journey to the present; Alex Ross-c/Sadowski-a; Thunderbolts app. 3.00
2-12: 2-New Avengers app.; Perkins variant-c. 3-12-Variant-c on each 3.00
... Sketchbook (2008, giveaway) Ross and Sadowski sketch art; Krueger commentary 3.00

AVENGERS/ JLA (See JLA/Avengers for #1 & #3)
DC Comics: No, 2, 2003; No. 4, 2003 ($5.95, limited series)

2-Busiek-s/Pérez-a; wraparound-c; Krona, Galactus app. 6.00
4-Busiek-s/Pérez-a; wraparound-c 6.00

AVENGERS LOG, THE
Marvel Comics: Feb, 1994 ($1.95)

1-Gives history of all members; Perez-c 3.00

AVENGERS NEXT (See A-Next and Spider-Girl)
Marvel Comics: Jan, 2007 - No. 5 ($2.99, limited series)

1-5-Lim-a/Wieringo-c; Spider-Girl app. 1-Avengers vs. zombies. 2-Thena app. 3.00
...: Rebirth TPB (2007, $13.99) r/#1-5 14.00

AVENGERS PRIME (The Heroic Age)
Marvel Comics: Aug, 2010 - No. 5, Mar, 2011 ($3.99, limited series)

1-5-Thor, Iron Man & Steve Rogers; Bendis-s/Davis-a; Enchantress app. 4.00
1-Variant-c by Djurdjevic 8.00

AVENGERS SPOTLIGHT (Formerly Solo Avengers #1-20)
Marvel Comics: No. 21, Aug, 1989 - No. 40, Jan, 1991 (75¢/$1.00)

21-Byrne-c/a 3.50
22-40: 26-Acts of Vengeance story. 31-34-U.S. Agent series. 36-Heck-i. 37-Mortimer-i. 40-The Black Knight app. 3.00

AVENGERS STRIKEFILE
Marvel Comics: Jan, 1994 ($1.75, one-shot)

1 3.00

AVENGERS: THE CHILDREN'S CRUSADE
Marvel Comics: Sept, 2010 - No. 9 ($3.99, limited series)

Avengers: The Initiative #20 © MAR

Avengers Unplugged #3 © MAR

Azrael (2nd series) #13 © DC

GD	VG	FN	VF	VF/NM	NM-
2.0	4.0	6.0	8.0	9.0	9.2

1-5-Young Avengers search for the Scarlet Witch; Heinberg-s/Cheung-a 4.00
1-4-Variant-c. 1-Jelena Djurdjevic. 2-Travis Charest. 3,4-Art Adams 6.00
... - Young Avengers (5/11, $3.99) Takes place between #4&5; Alan Davis-a/c

AVENGERS: THE CROSSING
Marvel Comics: July, 1995 ($4.95, one-shot)

1-Deodato-c/a; 1st app. Thor's new costume 5.00

AVENGERS: THE INITIATIVE (See Civil War and related titles)
Marvel Comics: Jun, 2007 - No. 35, Jun, 2010 ($2.99)

1-Caselli-a/Slott-s/Cheung-c; War Machine app. 4.00
2-35: 4,5-World War Hulk. 6-Uy-a. 14-19-Secret Invasion; 3-D Man app. 16-Skrull Kill Krew returns. 20-Tigra pregnancy revealed, 21-25-Ramos-a. 32-35-Siege 3.00
Annual 1 (1/08, $3.99) Secret Invasion tie-in; Cheung-c 4.00
... Featuring Reptil (5/09, $3.99) Gage-s/Uy-a 4.00
... Special 1 (1/09, $3.99) Slott & Gage-s/Uy-a 4.00
...: Vol. 1 - Basic Training HC (2007, $19.99, d.j.) r/#1-6 20.00
...: Vol. 1 - Basic Training SC (2008, $14.99) r/#1-6 15.00

AVENGERS: THE ORIGIN
Marvel Comics: Jun, 2010 - No. 5, Oct, 2010 ($3.99, limited series)

1-5-Casey-s/Noto-a/c; team origin (pre-Capt. America) re-told; Loki app. 4.00

AVENGERS: THE TERMINATRIX OBJECTIVE
Marvel Comics: Sept, 1993 - No. 4, Dec, 1993 ($1.25, limited series)

1 ($2.50)-Holo-grafx foil-c 3.50
2-4-Old vs. current Avengers 3.00

AVENGERS: THE ULTRON IMPERATIVE
Marvel Comics: Nov, 2001 ($5.99, one-shot)

1-Follow-up to the Ultron Unlimited ending in Avengers #42; BWS-c 6.00

AVENGERS, THOR & CAPTAIN AMERICA: OFFICIAL INDEX TO THE MARVEL UNIVERSE
Marvel Comics: Jun, 2010 - Present ($3.99)

1-12-Each issue has chronological synopsies, creator credits, character lists for 30-40 issues of Avengers, Captain America and Journey Into Mystery starting with debuts 4.00

AVENGERS/THUNDERBOLTS
Marvel Comics: May, 2004 - No. 6, Sept, 2004 ($2.99, limited series)

1-6: Busiek & Nicieza-s/Kitson-c. 1,2-Kitson-a. 3-6-Grummett-a 3.00
Vol. 2: Best Intentions (2004, $14.99) r/#1-6 15.00

AVENGERS: TIMESLIDE
Marvel Comics: Feb, 1996 ($4.95, one-shot)

1-Foil-c 5.00

AVENGERS TWO: WONDER MAN & BEAST
Marvel Comics: May, 2000 - No. 3, July, 2000 ($2.99, limited series)

1-3: Stern-s/Bagley-c/a 3.00

AVENGERS/ULTRAFORCE (See Ultraforce/Avengers)
Marvel Comics: Oct, 1995 ($3.95, one-shot)

1-Wraparound foil-c by Perez 4.00

AVENGERS UNITED THEY STAND
Marvel Comics: Nov, 1999 - No. 7, June, 2000 ($2.99/$1.99)

1-Based on the animated series 4.00
2-6-($1.99) 2-Avengers battle Hydra 3.00
7-($2.99) Devil Dinosaur-c/app.; reprints Avengers Action Figure Comic 4.00

AVENGERS UNIVERSE
Marvel Comics: Jun, 2000 - No. 3, Oct, 2000 ($3.99)

1-3-Reprints recent stories 4.00

AVENGERS UNPLUGGED
Marvel Comics: Oct, 1995 - No. 6, Aug, 1996 (99¢, bi-monthly)

1-6 3.00

AVENGERS VS. ATLAS (Leads into Atlas #1)
Marvel Comics: Mar, 2010 - No. 4, Jun, 2010 ($3.99, limited series)

1-4-Hardman-a; Ramos-c. 1-Back-up w/Miyazawa-a. 2-4-Original Avengers app. 4.00

AVENGERS VS. PET AVENGERS
Marvel Comics: Dec, 2010 - No. 4, Mar, 2011 ($2.99, limited series)

1-4-Eliopoulos-s/Guara-a; Fin Fang Foom app. 3.00

AVENGERS WEST COAST (Formerly West Coast Avengers)
Marvel Comics: No. 48, Sept, 1989 - No. 102, Jan, 1994 ($1.00/$1.25)

48,49: 48-Byrne-c/a & scripts continue thru #57 3.50
50-Re-intro original Human Torch 4.00
51-69,71-74,76-83,85,86,89-99: 54-Cover swipe/F.F. #1. 78-Last $1.00-c. 79-Dr. Strange x-over. 93-95-Darkhawk app. 3.00
70,75,84,87,88: 70-Spider-Woman app. 75 (52 pgs.)-Fantastic Four x-over. 84-Origin Spider-Woman retold; Spider-Man app. (also in #85,86). 87,88-Wolverine-c/story 3.50
100-($3.95, 68 pgs.)-Embossed all red foil-c 4.00
101,102: 101-X-Men x-over 5.00
Annual 5-8 ('90- '93, 68 pgs.)-5,6-West Coast Avengers in indicia. 7-Darkhawk app. 8-Polybagged w/card 4.00
...: Darker Than Scarlet TPB (2008, $24.99) r/#51-57,60-62; Byrne-s/a 25.00
...: Vision Quest TPB (2005, $24.99) r/#42-50; Byrne-s/a 25.00

AVIATION ADVENTURES AND MODEL BUILDING (True Aviation Advs. ...No. 15)
Parents' Magazine Institute: No. 16, Dec, 1946 - No. 17, Feb, 1947

16,17-Half comics and half pictures 8 16 24 42 54 65

AVIATION CADETS
Street & Smith Publications: 1943

nn 19 37 57 109 172 235

A-V IN 3-D
Aardvark-Vanaheim: Dec, 1984 ($2.00, 28 pgs. w/glasses)

1-Cerebus, Flaming Carrot, Normalman & Ms. Tree 4.00

AWAKENING, THE
Image Comics: Oct, 1997 - No. 4, Apr, 1998 ($2.95, B&W, limited series)

1-4-Stephen Blue-s/c/a 3.00

AWESOME ADVENTURES
Awesome Entertainment: Aug, 1999 ($2.50)

1-Alan Moore-s/ Steve Skroce-a; Youngblood story 3.00

AWESOME HOLIDAY SPECIAL
Awesome Entertainment: Dec, 1997 ($2.50, one-shot)

1-Flip book w/covers of Fighting American & Coven. Holiday stories also featuring Kaboom and Shaft by regular creators. 3.00
1-Gold Edition 5.00

AWFUL OSCAR (Formerly & becomes Oscar Comics with No. 13)
Marvel Comics: No. 11, June, 1949 - No. 12, Aug, 1949

11,12 14 28 42 80 115 150

AWKWARD UNIVERSE
Slave Labor Graphics: 12/95 ($9.95, graphic novel)

nn 10.00

AXA
Eclipse Comics: Apr, 1987 - No. 2, Aug, 1987 ($1.75)

1,2 3.00

AXEL PRESSBUTTON (Pressbutton No. 5; see Laser Eraser &...)
Eclipse Comics: Nov, 1984 - No. 6, July, 1985 ($1.50/$1.75, Baxter paper)

1-6: Reprints Warrior (British mag.). 1-Bolland-c; origin Laser Eraser & Pressbutton 3.00

AXIS ALPHA
Axis Comics: Feb, 1994 ($2.50, one-shot)

V1-Previews Axis titles including, Tribe, Dethgrip, B.E.A.S.T.I.E.S. & more; Pitt app. in Tribe story. 3.00

AZRAEL (...Agent of the Bat #47 on)(Also see Batman: Sword of Azrael)
DC Comics: Feb, 1995 - No. 100, May, 2003 ($1.95/$2.25/$2.50/$2.95)

1-Dennis O'Neil scripts begin 5.00
2,3 3.50
4-46,48-62: 5,6-Ras Al Ghul app. 13-Nightwing-c/app. 15-Contagion Pt. 5 (Pt. 4 on-c). 16-Contagion Pt. 10. 22-Batman-c/app. 23,27-Batman app. 27,28-Joker app. 35-Hitman app. 36-39-Batman, Bane app. 50-New costume. 53-Joker-c/app. 56,57,60-New Batgirl app. 3.00
47-($3.95) Flip book with Batman: Shadow of the Bat #80 4.00
63-74,76-92: 63-Huntress-c/app.; Azrael returns to old costume. 67-Begin $2.50-c. 70-79-Harris-c. 83-Joker x-over. 91-Bruce Wayne: Fugitive pt. 15 3.00
75-($3.95) New costume; Harris-c 4.00
93-100: 93-Begin $2.95-c. 95,96-Two-Face app. 100-Last issue; Zeck-c 3.00
#1,000,000 (11/98) Giarrano-a 3.00
Annual 1 (1995, $3.95)-Year One story 4.00
Annual 2 (1996, $2.95)-Legends of the Dead Earth story 4.00
Annual 3 (1997, $3.95)-Pulp Heroes story; Orbik-c 4.00
.../Ash (1997, $4.95) O'Neil-s/Quesada, Palmiotti-a 5.00
Plus (12/96, $2.95)-Question-c/app. 3.00

AZRAEL

Aztek: The Ultimate Man #10 © DC

Babe #7 © PRIZE

Baby Huey, The Baby Giant #4 © HARV

DC Comics: Dec, 2009 - No. 18, May, 2011 ($2.99)

	GD 2.0	VG 4.0	FN 6.0	VF 8.0	VF/NM 9.0	NM- 9.2
1-18: 1-9-Nicieza-s/Bachs-a. 1-Covers by Jock & Irving. 2,3-Jock-c. 5-Ragman app.						3.00
....: Angel in the Dark TPB (2010, $17.99) r/#1-6; cover gallery						18.00

AZRAEL: DEATH'S DARK KNIGHT
DC Comics: May, 2009 - No. 3, Jul, 2009 ($2.99, limited series)

	GD 2.0	VG 4.0	FN 6.0	VF 8.0	VF/NM 9.0	NM- 9.2
1-Battle For the Cowl tie-in; Nicieza-s/Irving-a/March-c						3.00
TPB (2010, $14.99) r/#1-3, Batman Annual #27 and Detecive Annual #11						15.00

AZTEC ACE
Eclipse Comics: Mar, 1984 - No. 15, Sept, 1985 ($2.25/$1.50/$1.75, Baxter paper)

	GD 2.0	VG 4.0	FN 6.0	VF 8.0	VF/NM 9.0	NM- 9.2
1-$2.25-c (52 pgs.)						4.00
2-15: 2-Begin 36 pgs.						3.00

NOTE: ***N. Redondo*** *a-1i-8i, 10i. c-6-8i.*

AZTEK: THE ULTIMATE MAN
DC Comics: Aug, 1996 - No. 10, May 1997 ($1.75)

	GD 2.0	VG 4.0	FN 6.0	VF 8.0	VF/NM 9.0	NM- 9.2
1-1st app. Aztek & Synth; Grant Morrison & Mark Millar scripts in all						6.00
2-9: 2-Green Lantern app. 3-1st app. Death-Doll. 4-Intro The Lizard King. 5-Origin. 6-Joker app.; Batman cameo. 7-Batman app. 8-Luthor app. 9-vs. Parasite-c/app.						4.00
10-JLA-c/app.	1	2	4	6	8	10
JLA Presents: Aztek the Ultimate Man TPB (2008, $19.99) r/#1-10						20.00

NOTE: ***Breyfogle*** *c-5p.* ***N. Steven Harris*** *a-1-5p.* ***Porter*** *c-1p.* ***Wieringo*** *c-2p.*

BABE (...Darling of the Hills, later issues)(See Big Shot and Sparky Watts)
Prize/Headline/Feature: June-July, 1948 - No. 11, Apr-May, 1950

	GD 2.0	VG 4.0	FN 6.0	VF 8.0	VF/NM 9.0	NM- 9.2
1-Boody Rogers-a	28	56	84	165	270	375
2-Boody Rogers-a	16	32	48	94	147	200
3-11-All by Boody Rogers	15	30	45	85	130	175

BABE
Dark Horse Comics (Legend): July, 1994 - No. 4, Jan, 1994 ($2.50, lim. series)

	GD 2.0	VG 4.0	FN 6.0	VF 8.0	VF/NM 9.0	NM- 9.2
1-4: John Byrne-c/a/scripts; ProtoTykes back-up story						3.00

BABE RUTH SPORTS COMICS (Becomes Rags Rabbit #11 on?)
Harvey Publications: April, 1949 - No. 11, Feb, 1951

	GD 2.0	VG 4.0	FN 6.0	VF 8.0	VF/NM 9.0	NM- 9.2
1-Powell-a	40	80	120	246	411	575
2-Powell-a	27	54	81	158	259	360
3-11: Powell-a in most	22	44	66	130	213	295

NOTE: *Baseball c-2-4, 9. Basketball c-1, 6. Football c-5. Yogi Berra c/story-8. Joe DiMaggio c/story-3. Bob Feller c/story-4. Stan Musial c-9.*

BABES IN TOYLAND (Disney, Movie) (See Golden Pix Story Book ST-3)
Dell Publishing Co.: No. 1282, Feb-Apr, 1962

	GD 2.0	VG 4.0	FN 6.0	VF 8.0	VF/NM 9.0	NM- 9.2
Four Color 1282-Annette Funicello photo-c	13	26	39	91	176	260

BABES OF BROADWAY
Broadway Comics: May, 1996 ($2.95, one-shot)

	GD 2.0	VG 4.0	FN 6.0	VF 8.0	VF/NM 9.0	NM- 9.2
1-Pin-ups of Broadway Comics' female characters; Alan Davis, Michael Kaluta, J. G. Jones, Alan Weiss, Guy Davis & others-a; Giordano-c.						3.00

BABE 2
Dark Horse Comics (Legend): Mar, 1995 - No. 2, May, 1995 ($2.50, lim. series)

	GD 2.0	VG 4.0	FN 6.0	VF 8.0	VF/NM 9.0	NM- 9.2
1,2: John Byrne-c/a/scripts						3.00

BABY HUEY
Harvey Comics: No. 1, Oct, 1991 - No. 9, June, 1994 ($1.00/$1.25/$1.50, quarterly)

	GD 2.0	VG 4.0	FN 6.0	VF 8.0	VF/NM 9.0	NM- 9.2
1 ($1.00): 1-Cover says "Big Baby Huey"						5.00
2-9 ($1.25-$1.50)						3.00

BABY HUEY AND PAPA (See Paramount Animated...)
Harvey Publications: May, 1962 - No. 33, Jan, 1968 (Also see Casper The Friendly Ghost)

	GD 2.0	VG 4.0	FN 6.0	VF 8.0	VF/NM 9.0	NM- 9.2
1	14	28	42	97	194	290
2	8	16	24	58	97	135
3-5	6	12	18	37	59	80
6-10	3	6	9	21	32	42
11-20	3	6	9	16	22	28
21-33	2	4	6	13	18	22

BABY HUEY DIGEST
Harvey Publications: June, 1992 (Digest-size, one-shot)

	GD 2.0	VG 4.0	FN 6.0	VF 8.0	VF/NM 9.0	NM- 9.2
1-Reprints	1	3	4	6	8	10

BABY HUEY DUCKLAND
Harvey Publications: Nov, 1962 - No. 15, Nov, 1966 (25¢ Giants, 68 pgs.)

	GD 2.0	VG 4.0	FN 6.0	VF 8.0	VF/NM 9.0	NM- 9.2
1	11	22	33	77	144	210
2-5	6	12	18	39	62	85
6-15	4	8	12	22	34	45

BABY HUEY, THE BABY GIANT (Also see Big Baby Huey, Casper, Harvey Hits #22, Harvey Comics Hits #60, & Paramount Animated Comics)
Harvey Publ: 9/56 - #97, 10/71; #98, 10/72; #99, 10/80; #100, 10/90; #101, 11/90

	GD 2.0	VG 4.0	FN 6.0	VF 8.0	VF/NM 9.0	NM- 9.2
1-Infinity-c	48	96	144	392	796	1200
2	23	46	69	163	324	485
3-Baby Huey takes anti-pep pills	14	28	42	99	200	300
4,5	10	20	30	71	128	185
6-10	7	14	21	47	76	105
11-20	5	10	15	35	55	75
21-40	4	8	12	24	37	50
41-60	3	6	9	16	23	30
61-79 (12/67)	2	4	6	13	18	22
80(12/68) - 95-All 68 pg. Giants	3	6	9	17	25	32
96,97-Both 52 pg. Giants	3	6	9	14	19	24
98-Regular size	2	4	6	9	12	15
99-Regular size	1	2	3	5	6	8
100,101 ($1.00)						4.00

BABYLON 5 (TV)
DC Comics: Jan, 1995 - No. 11, Dec, 1995 ($1.95/$2.50)

	GD 2.0	VG 4.0	FN 6.0	VF 8.0	VF/NM 9.0	NM- 9.2
1	2	4	6	8	11	14
2-5	1	2	3	5	7	9
6-11: 7-Begin $2.50-c	1	2	3	4	5	7
... The Price of Peace (1998, $9.95, TPB) r/#1-4,11						10.00

BABYLON 5: IN VALEN'S NAME
DC Comics: Mar, 1998 - No. 3, May, 1998 ($2.50, limited series)

	GD 2.0	VG 4.0	FN 6.0	VF 8.0	VF/NM 9.0	NM- 9.2
1-3						4.00

BABY SNOOTS (Also see March of Comics #359,371,396,401,419,431,443,450,462,474,485)
Gold Key: Aug, 1970 - No. 22, Nov, 1975

	GD 2.0	VG 4.0	FN 6.0	VF 8.0	VF/NM 9.0	NM- 9.2
1	3	6	9	20	30	40
2-11	2	4	6	11	16	20
12-22: 22-Titled Snoots, the Forgetful Elefink	2	4	6	8	10	12

BACCHUS (Also see Eddie Campbell's ...)
Harrier Comics (New Wave): 1988 - No. 2, Aug, 1988 ($1.95, B&W)

	GD 2.0	VG 4.0	FN 6.0	VF 8.0	VF/NM 9.0	NM- 9.2
1,2: Eddie Campbell-c/a/scripts.						3.00

BACHELOR FATHER (TV)
Dell Publishing Co.: No. 1332, 4-6/62 - No. 2, Sept.-Nov., 1962

	GD 2.0	VG 4.0	FN 6.0	VF 8.0	VF/NM 9.0	NM- 9.2
Four Color 1332 (#1), 2-Written by Stanley	7	14	21	50	83	115

BACHELOR'S DIARY
Avon Periodicals: 1949 (15¢)

	GD 2.0	VG 4.0	FN 6.0	VF 8.0	VF/NM 9.0	NM- 9.2
1(Scarce)-King Features panel cartoons & text-r; pin-up, girl wrestling photos; similar to Sideshow	77	154	231	493	847	1200

BACK DOWN THE LINE
Eclipse Books: 1991 (Mature adults, 8-1/2 x 11", 52 pgs.)

	GD 2.0	VG 4.0	FN 6.0	VF 8.0	VF/NM 9.0	NM- 9.2
nn (Soft-c, $8.95)-Bolton-c/a						9.00
nn (Limited Hard-c, $29.95)						30.00

BACKLASH (Also see The Kindred)
Image Comics (WildStorm Prod.): Nov,1994 - No. 32, May, 1997 ($1.95/$2.50)

	GD 2.0	VG 4.0	FN 6.0	VF 8.0	VF/NM 9.0	NM- 9.2
1-Double-c; variant-double-c						4.00
2-7,9-32: 5-Intro Mindscape; 2 pinups. 19-Fire From Heaven Pt 2. 20-Fire From Heaven Pt 10. 31-WildC.A.T.S app.						3.00
8-($1.95, newsstand)-Wildstorm Rising Pt. 8						3.00
8-($2.50, direct market)-Wildstorm Rising Pt. 8						3.00
25-($3.95)-Double-size						4.00
...& Taboo's African Holiday (9/99, $5.95) Booth-s/a(p)						6.00

BACKLASH/SPIDER-MAN
Image Comics (WildStorm Productions): Aug, 1996 - No. 2, Sept, 1996 ($2.50, lim. series)

	GD 2.0	VG 4.0	FN 6.0	VF 8.0	VF/NM 9.0	NM- 9.2
1,2: Pike (villain from WildC.A.T.S) & Venom app.						3.00

BACKPACK MARVELS (B&W backpack-sized reprint collections)
Marvel Comics: Nov, 2000 ($6.95, B&W, digest-size)

	GD 2.0	VG 4.0	FN 6.0	VF 8.0	VF/NM 9.0	NM- 9.2
Avengers 1 -r/Avengers #181-189; profile pages						7.00
Spider-Man 1-r/ASM #234-240						7.00
X-Men 1-r/Uncanny X-Men #167-173						7.00
X-Men 2-r/Uncanny X-Men #174-179; new painted-c by Greg Horn						7.00

BACK TO THE FUTURE (Movie, TV cartoon)
Harvey Comics: Nov, 1991 - No. 4, June, 1992 ($1.25)

	GD 2.0	VG 4.0	FN 6.0	VF 8.0	VF/NM 9.0	NM- 9.2
1-4: 1,2-Gil Kane-c; based on animated cartoon						3.00

BACK TO THE FUTURE: FORWARD TO THE FUTURE

Badger #10 © First Pub.

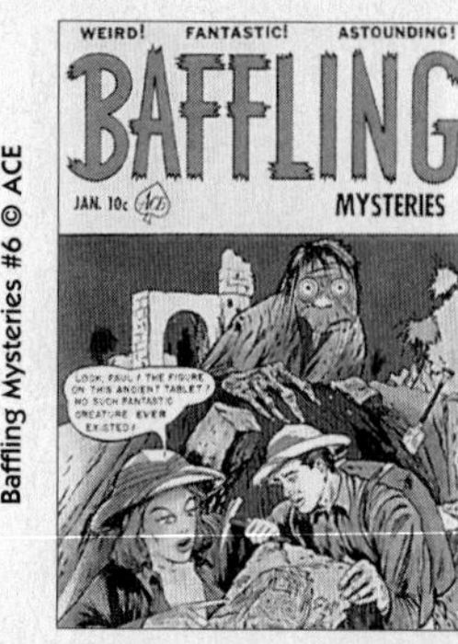

Baffling Mysteries #6 © ACE

Baltimore: The Plague Ships #2 © Mignola & Golden

	GD	VG	FN	VF	VF/NM	NM-
	2.0	4.0	6.0	8.0	9.0	9.2

GD VG FN VF VF/NM NM-
2.0 4.0 6.0 8.0 9.0 9.2

Harvey Comics: Oct, 1992 - No. 3, Feb, 1993 ($1.50, limited series)
1-3 — 3.00

BAD BOY
Oni Press: Dec, 1997 ($4.95, one-shot)
1-Frank Miller-s/Simon Bisley-a/painted-c — 5.00

BAD COMPANY
Quality Comics/Fleetway Quality #15 on: Aug, 1988 - No. 19?, 1990 ($1.50/$1.75, high quality paper)
1-19: 5,6-Guice-c — 3.00

BADGE OF JUSTICE (Formerly Crime And Justice #21)
Charlton Comics: No. 22, Jan, 1955; No. 2, Apr, 1955 - No. 4, Oct, 1955

	GD	VG	FN	VF	VF/NM	NM-
22(#1)-Giordano-c	10	20	30	58	79	100
2-4	7	14	21	35	43	50

BADGER, THE
Capital Comics(#1-4)/First Comics: Dec, 1983 - No. 70, Apr, 1991; V2#1, Spring, 1991
1 — 5.00
2-70: 52-54-Tim Vigil-c/a — 3.00
50-($3.95, 52 pgs.) — 4.00
V2#1 (Spring, 1991, $4.95) — 5.00

BADGER, THE
Image Comics: V3#78, May, 1997 - V3#88 ($2.95, B&W)
78-Cover lists #1, Baron-s — 3.00
79/#2, 80/#3, 81(indicia lists #80)/#4,82-88/#5-11 — 3.00

BADGER GOES BERSERK
First Comics: Sept, 1989 - No. 4, Dec, 1989 ($1.95, lim. series, Baxter paper)
1-4: 2-Paul Chadwick-c/a(2pgs.) — 3.00

BADGER: SHATTERED MIRROR
Dark Horse Comics: July, 1994 - No. Oct, 1994 ($2.50, limited series)
1-4 — 3.00

BADGER: ZEN POP FUNNY-ANIMAL VERSION
Dark Horse Comics: July, 1994 - No. 2, Aug, 1994 ($2.50, limited series)
1,2 — 3.00

BAD GIRLS
DC Comics: Oct, 2003 - No. 5, Feb, 2004 ($2.50, limited series)
1-5-Steve Vance-s/Jennifer Graves-a/Darwyn Cooke-c — 2.50
TPB (2009, $14.99) r/#1-5; Graves sketch pages — 15.00

BAD IDEAS
Image Comics: Apr, 2004 - No. 2, July, 2004 ($5.95, B&W, limited series)
1,2-Chinsang-s/Mahfood & Crosland-a — 6.00
..., Vol. 1: Collected! (2005, $12.99) r/#1,2 — 13.00

BADLANDS
Vortex Comics: May, 1990 ($3.00, glossy stock, mature)
1-Chaykin-c — 3.00

BADLANDS
Dark Horse Comics: July, 1991 - No. 6, Dec, 1991 ($2.25, B&W, limited series)
1-6: 1-John F. Kennedy-c; reprints Vortex Comics issue — 3.00

BADMEN OF THE WEST
Avon Periodicals: 1951 (Giant) (132 pgs., painted-c)

	GD	VG	FN	VF	VF/NM	NM-
1-Contains rebound copies of Jesse James, King of the Bad Men of Deadwood, Badmen of Tombstone; other combinations possible. Issues with Kubert-a...	40	80	120	243	402	560

BADMEN OF THE WEST! (See A-1 Comics)
Magazine Enterprises: 1953 - No. 3, 1954

	GD	VG	FN	VF	VF/NM	NM-
1 (A-1 100)-Meskin-a?	22	44	66	132	216	300
2 (A-1 120), 3: 2-Larsen-a	15	30	45	85	130	175

BADMEN OF TOMBSTONE
Avon Periodicals: 1950

	GD	VG	FN	VF	VF/NM	NM-
nn	15	30	45	94	147	200

BAD PLANET
Image Comics (Raw Studios): Dec, 2005 - No. 6, Nov, 2008 ($2.99)
1-6: 1-Thomas Jane & Steve Niles-s/Larosa & Bradstreet-a/c. 2-Wrightson-c. 3-3-D pages — 3.00

BADROCK (Also see Youngblood)
Image Comics (Extreme Studios): Mar, 1995 - No. 2, Jan, 1996 ($1.75/$2.50)
1-Variant-c (3) — 3.50
2-Liefeld-c/a & story; Savage Dragon app, flipbook w/Grifter/Badrock #2; variant-c exist — 3.00
Annual 1(1995,$2.95)-Arthur Adams-c — 3.00
Annual 1 Commemorative ($9.95)-3,000 printed — 10.00
.../Wolverine (6/96, $4.95, squarebound)-Sauron app; pin-ups; variant-c exists — 5.00
.../Wolverine (6/96)-Special Comicon Edition — 5.00

BADROCK AND COMPANY (Also see Youngblood)
Image Comics (Extreme Studios): Sept, 1994 - No.6, Feb, 1995 ($2.50)
1-6 : 6-Indicia reads "October 1994"; story cont'd in Shadowhawk #17 — 3.00

BAFFLING MYSTERIES (Formerly Indian Braves No. 1-4; Heroes of the Wild Frontier No. 26-on)
Periodical House (Ace Magazines): No. 5, Nov, 1951 - No. 26, Oct, 1955

	GD	VG	FN	VF	VF/NM	NM-
5	40	80	120	246	411	575
6-19,21-24: 8-Woodish-a by Cameron. 10-E.C. Crypt Keeper swipe on-c. 24-Last pre-code issue	26	52	78	154	252	350
20-Classic-c	34	68	102	204	332	460
25-Reprints; surrealistic-c	19	38	57	111	176	240
26-Reprints	17	34	51	100	158	215

NOTE: *Cameron a-8, 10, 16-18, 20-22. Colan a-5, 11, 25r/5. Sekowsky a-5, 6, 22. Bondage c-20, 23. Reprints in 18(1), 19(1), 24(3).*

BALBO (See Master Comics #33 & Mighty Midget Comics)

BALDER THE BRAVE
Marvel Comics Group: Nov, 1985 - No. 4, 1986 (Limited series)
1-4: Simonson-c/a; character from Thor — 3.00

BALLAD OF HALO JONES, THE
Quality Comics: Sept, 1987 - No. 12, Aug, 1988 ($1.25/$1.50)
1-12: Alan Moore scripts in all — 3.00

BALL AND CHAIN
DC Comics (Homage): Nov, 1999 - No. 4, Feb, 2000 ($2.50, limited series)
1-4-Lobdell-s/Garza-a — 3.00

BALLISTIC (Also See Cyberforce)
Image Comics (Top Cow Productions): Sept, 1995 - No. 3, Dec, 1995 ($2.50, limited series)
1-3: Wetworks app, Turner-c/a — 3.00
... Action (5/96, $2.95) Pin-ups of Top Cow characters participating in outdoor sports — 3.00
... Imagery (1/96, $2.50, anthology) Cyberforce app. — 3.00
.../ Wolverine (2/97, $2.95) Devil's Reign pt. 4; Witchblade cameo (1 page) — 4.00

BALOO & LITTLE BRITCHES (Disney)
Gold Key: Apr, 1968

	GD	VG	FN	VF	VF/NM	NM-
1-From the Jungle Book	4	8	12	24	37	50

BALTIMORE: THE PLAGUE SHIPS
Dark Horse Comics: Aug, 2010 - No. 5, Dec, 2010 ($3.50, limited series)
1-5-Mignola-s/c; Stenbeck-a; Lord Baltimore hunting vampires in 1916 Europe — 3.50

BAMBI (Disney) (See Movie Classics, Movie Comics, and Walt Disney Showcase No. 31)
Dell Publishing Co.: No. 12, 1942; No. 30, 1943; No. 186, Apr, 1948; 1984

	GD	VG	FN	VF	VF/NM	NM-
Four Color 12-Walt Disney's...	48	96	144	384	780	1175
Four Color 30-Bambi's Children (1943)	42	84	126	336	681	1025
Four Color 186-Walt Disney's...; reprinted as Movie Classic Bambi #3 (1956)	15	30	45	106	216	325
1-(Whitman, 1984; 60¢)-r/Four Color #186 (3-pack)	2	4	6	10	14	18

BAMBI (Disney)
Grosset & Dunlap: 1942 (50¢, 7"x8-1/2", 32pg, hard-c w/dust jacket)

	GD	VG	FN	VF	VF/NM	NM-
nn-Given away w/a copy of Thumper for a $2.00, 2-yr. subscription to WDC&S in 1942 (Xmas offer). Book only	22	44	66	132	216	300
w/dust jacket	39	78	117	240	395	550

BAMM BAMM & PEBBLES FLINTSTONE (TV)
Gold Key: Oct, 1964 (Hanna-Barbera)

	GD	VG	FN	VF	VF/NM	NM-
1	9	18	27	60	100	140

BANANA SPLITS, THE (TV) (See Golden Comics Digest & March of Comics No. 364)
Gold Key: June, 1969 - No. 8, Oct, 1971 (Hanna-Barbera)

	GD	VG	FN	VF	VF/NM	NM-
1-Photo-c on all	9	18	27	65	113	160
2-8	6	12	18	39	62	85

BANANA SUNDAY
Oni Press: July, 2005 - No. 4, Oct, 2005 ($2.99, B&W, limited series)
1-4-Root Nibot-s/Colleen Coover-a — 3.00
TPB (3/06, $11.95) r/#1-4; sketch gallery — 12.00

BAND WAGON (See Hanna-Barbera Band Wagon)

Barbie #9 © Mattel

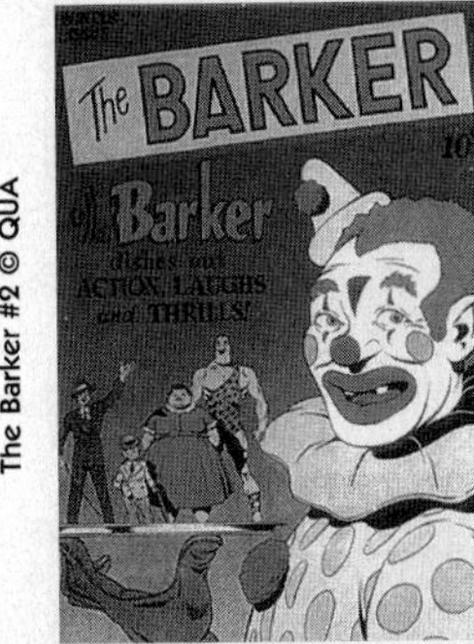

The Barker #2 © QUA

Bartman #5 © Bongo

GD 2.0 | VG 4.0 | FN 6.0 | VF 8.0 | VF/NM 9.0 | NM- 9.2

BANG! TANGO
DC Comics (Vertigo): Apr, 2009 - No. 6, Sept, 2009 ($2.99, limited series)
1-6-Kelly-s/Sibar-a/Chaykin-c 3.00

BANG-UP COMICS
Progressive Publishers: Dec, 1941 - No. 3, June, 1942
1-Cosmo Mann & Lady Fairplay begin; Buzz Balmer by Rick Yager in all (origin #1)
97 194 291 621 1061 1500
2,3 47 94 141 296 498 700

BANISHED KNIGHTS (See Warlands)
Image Comics: Dec, 2001 - No. 4, June, 2002 ($2.95)
1-4-Two covers (Alvin Lee, Pat Lee) 3.00

BANNER COMICS (Becomes Captain Courageous No. 6)
Ace Magazines: No. 3, Sept, 1941 - No. 5, Jan, 1942
3-Captain Courageous (1st app.) & Lone Warrior & Sidekick Dicky begin;
Jim Mooney-c 110 220 330 704 1202 1700
4,5: 4-Flag-c 68 136 204 435 743 1050

BARACK OBAMA (See Presidential Material: Barack Obama, Amazing Spider-Man #583, Savage Dragon #137)

BARACK THE BARBARIAN
Devil's Due Publishing: Jun, 2009 - No. 4, Oct, 2009 ($3.50/$3.99, limited series)
...Quest For The Treasure of Stimuli 1-3-($3.50) Conan spoof with Barack Obama; Hama-s 3.50
...Quest For The Treasure of Stimuli 4-($3.99) 4.00
...: The Red of Red Sarah 1 ($5.99, B&W) Sarah Palin satire; Hama-s 6.00

BARBARIANS, THE
Atlas Comics/Seaboard Periodicals: June, 1975
1-Origin, only app. Andrax; Iron Jaw app.; Marcos-a 2 4 6 10 14 18

BARBIE
Marvel Comics: Jan, 1991 - No. 63, Mar, 1996 ($1.00/$1.25/$1.50)
1-Polybagged w/doorknob hanger; Romita-c 2 4 6 9 12 15
2-49,51-62 1 2 3 5 7 9
50,63: 50-(Giant). 63-Last issue 2 4 6 8 10 12
... And Baby Sister Kelly (1995, 99¢-c, part of a Marvel 4-pack) scarce
3 6 9 14 20 25

BARBIE & KEN
Dell Publishing Co.: May-July, 1962 - No. 5, Nov-Jan, 1963-64
01-053-207(#1)-Based on Mattel toy dolls 36 72 108 281 553 825
2-4 28 56 84 204 415 625
5 (Rare) 28 56 84 215 433 650

BARBIE FASHION
Marvel Comics: Jan, 1991 - No. 53, May, 1995 ($1.00/$1.25/$1.50)
1-Polybagged w/Barbie Pink Card 2 4 6 9 12 15
2-49,51,52: 4-Contains preview to Sweet XVI 1 2 3 5 7 9
50,53: 50-(Giant). 53-Last issue 2 4 6 8 10 12

BARB WIRE (See Comics' Greatest World)
Dark Horse Comics: Apr, 1994 - No. 9, Feb, 1995 ($2.00/$2.50)
1-9: 1-Foil logo 3.00
Trade paperback (1996, $8.95)-r/#2,3,5,6 w/Pamela Anderson bio 9.00

BARB WIRE: ACE OF SPADES
Dark Horse Comics: May, 1996 - No. 4, Sept, 1996 ($2.95, limited series)
1-4: Chris Warner-c/a(p)/scripts; Tim Bradstreet-c/a(i) in all 3.00

BARB WIRE COMICS MAGAZINE SPECIAL
Dark Horse Comics: May, 1996 ($3.50, B&W, magazine, one-shot)
nn-Adaptation of film; photo-c; poster insert. 3.50

BARB WIRE MOVIE SPECIAL
Dark Horse Comics: May, 1996 ($3.95, one-shot)
nn-Adaptation of film; photo-c; 1st app. new look 4.00

BARKER, THE (Also see National Comics #42)
Quality Comics Group/Comic Magazine: Autumn, 1946 - No. 15, Dec, 1949
1 24 48 72 140 230 320
2 14 28 42 81 118 155
3-10 11 22 33 64 90 115
11-14 9 18 27 52 69 85
15-Jack Cole-a(p) 10 20 30 54 72 90
NOTE: ***Jack Cole** art in some issues.*

BARNABY
Civil Service Publications Inc.: 1945 (25¢,102 pgs., digest size)
V1#1-r/Crocket Johnson strips from 1942 5 10 14 20 24 28

BARNEY AND BETTY RUBBLE (TV) (Flintstones' Neighbors)
Charlton Comics: Jan, 1973 - No. 23, Dec, 1976 (Hanna-Barbera)
1 4 8 12 24 37 50
2-11: 11(2/75)-1st Mike Zeck-a (illos) 3 6 9 14 20 25
12-23: 17-Columbo parody 2 4 6 10 14 18
Digest Annual (1972, B&W, 100 pgs.) (scarce) 4 8 12 26 41 55

BARNEY BAXTER (Also see Magic Comics)
David McKay/Dell Publishing Co./Argo: 1938 - No. 2, 1956
Feature Books 15(McKay-1938) 40 80 120 246 411 575
Four Color 20(1942) 24 48 72 175 350 525
1,2 (1956-Argo) 9 18 27 50 65 80

BARNEY BEAR ...
Spire Christian Comics (Fleming H. Revell Co.): 1977-1982
...Home Plate nn-(1979, 49¢), ...In Toyland nn-(1982, 49¢),...Lost and Found nn-(1979, 49¢), Out of The Woods nn-(1980, 49¢), Sunday School Picnic nn-(1981, 69¢), The Swamp Gang!-(1977, 39¢) 2 4 6 9 12 15

BARNEY GOOGLE & SNUFFY SMITH
Dell Publishing Co./Gold Key: 1942 - 1943; April, 1964
Four Color 19(1942) 47 94 141 296 498 700
Four Color 40(1944) 20 40 60 140 283 425
Large Feature Comic 11(1943) 38 76 114 225 368 510
1(10113-404)-Gold Key (4/64) 4 8 12 26 41 55

BARNEY GOOGLE & SNUFFY SMITH
Toby Press: June, 1951 - No. 4, Feb, 1952 (Reprints)
1 14 28 42 76 108 140
2,3 8 16 24 44 57 70
4-Kurtzman-a "Pot Shot Pete", 5 pgs.; reprints John Wayne #5
12 24 36 69 97 125

BARNEY GOOGLE AND SNUFFY SMITH
Charlton Comics: Mar, 1970 - No. 6, Jan, 1971
1 3 6 9 17 25 32
2-6 2 4 6 11 16 20

BARNUM!
DC Comics (Vertigo): 2003; 2005 ($29.95, $19.95)
Hardcover (2003, $29.95, with dust jacket)-Chaykin & Tischman-s/Henrichon-a 30.00
Softcover (2005, $19.95)-Chaykin & Tischman-s/Henrichon-a 20.00

BARNYARD COMICS (Dizzy Duck No. 32 on)
Nedor/Polo Mag./Standard(Animated Cartoons): June, 1944 - No. 31, Sept, 1950; No. 10, 1957
1 (nn, 52 pgs.)-Funny animal 20 40 60 117 189 260
2 (52 pgs.) 13 26 39 72 101 130
3-5 10 20 30 54 72 90
6-12,16 9 18 27 47 61 75
13-15,17,21,23,26,27,29-All contain Frazetta text illos
10 20 30 56 76 95
18-20,22,24,25-All contain Frazetta-a & text illos 13 26 39 72 101 130
28,30,31 7 14 21 37 46 55
10 (1957)(Exist?) 4 7 10 14 17 20

BARRY M. GOLDWATER
Dell Publishing Co.: Mar, 1965 (Complete life story)
12-055-503-Photo-c 4 8 12 24 37 50

BARRY WINDSOR-SMITH: STORYTELLER
Dark Horse Comics: Oct, 1996 - No. 9, July, 1997 ($4.95, oversize)
1-9: 1-Intro Young Gods, Paradox Man & the Freebooters; Barry Smith-c/a/scripts 5.00
Preview 4.00

BAR SINISTER (Also see Shaman's Tears)
Acclaim Comics (Windjammer): Jun, 1995 - No. 4, Sept, 1995 ($2.50, lim. series)
1-4: Mike Grell-c/a/scripts 3.00

BARTMAN (Also see Simpson's Comics & Radioactive Man)
Bongo Comics: 1993 - No. 6, 1994 ($1.95/$2.25)
1-($2.95)-Foil-c; bound-in jumbo Bartman poster 6.00
2-6: 3-w/trading card 4.00

BART SIMPSON (See Simpsons Comics Presents Bart Simpson)

BASEBALL COMICS
Will Eisner Productions: Spring, 1949 (Reprinted later as a Spirit section)

Baseball's Greatest Heroes #2 © Magnum

Batgirl (2009 series) #12 © DC

Batman #2 © DC

GD VG FN VF VF/NM NM-
2.0 4.0 6.0 8.0 9.0 9.2

1-Will Eisner-c/a 69 138 207 442 759 1075

BASEBALL COMICS
Kitchen Sink Press: 1991 ($3.95, coated stock)
1-r/1949 ish. by Eisner; contains trading cards 6.00

BASEBALL HEROES
Fawcett Publications: 1952 (one-shot)
nn (Scarce)-Babe Ruth photo-c; baseball's Hall of Fame biographies
82 164 246 528 902 1275

BASEBALL'S GREATEST HEROES
Magnum Comics: Dec, 1991 - No. 2, May, 1992 ($1.75)
1-Mickey Mantle #1; photo-c; Sinnott-a(p) 5.00
2-Brooks Robinson #1; photo-c; Sinnott-a(i) 4.00

BASEBALL THRILLS
Ziff-Davis Publ. Co.: No. 10, Sum, 1951 - No. 3, Sum, 1952 (Saunders painted-c No.1,2)
10(#1)-Bob Feller, Musial, Newcombe & Boudreau stories
44 88 132 277 469 660
2-Powell-a(2)(Late Sum, '51); Feller, Berra & Mathewson stories
32 64 96 188 307 425
3-Kinstler-c/a; Joe DiMaggio story 32 64 96 188 307 425

BASEBALL THRILLS 3-D
The 3-D Zone: May, 1990 ($2.95, w/glasses)
1-New L.B. Cole-c; life stories of Ty Cobb & Ted Williams 6.00

BASICALLY STRANGE (Magazine)
John C. Comics (Archie Comics Group): Dec, 1982 ($1.95, B&W)
1-(21,000 printed; all but 1,000 destroyed; pgs. out of sequence)
3 6 9 16 23 30
1-Wood, Toth-a; Corben-c; reprints & new art 2 4 6 13 18 22

BASIC HISTORY OF AMERICA ILLUSTRATED
Pendulum Press: 1976 (B&W) (Soft-c $1.50; Hard-c $4.50)
07-1999-America Becomes a World Power 1890-1920. 07-2251-The Industrial Era 1865-1915. 07-226x-Before the Civil War 1830-1860. 07-2278-Americans Move Westward 1800-1850. 07-2286-The Civil War 1850-1876; Redondo-a. 07-2294-The Fight for Freedom 1750-1783. 07-2308-The New World 1500-1750. 07-2316-Problems of the New Nation 1800-1830. 07-2324-Roaring Twenties and the Great Depression 1920-1940. 07-2332-The United States Emerges 1783-1800. 07-2340-America Today 1945-1976. 07-2359-World War II 1940-1945
Softcover editions each 1 2 3 4 5 7
Hardcover editions each 14.00

BASIL (...the Royal Cat)
St. John Publishing Co.: Jan, 1953 - No. 4, Sept, 1953
1-Funny animal 7 14 21 37 46 55
2-4 5 10 15 22 26 30
I.W. Reprint 1 2 4 6 9 12 15

BASIL WOLVERTON'S FANTASTIC FABLES
Dark Horse Comics: Oct, 1993 - No. 2, Dec, 1993 ($2.50, B&W, limited series)
1,2-Wolverton-c/a(r) 6.00

BASIL WOLVERTON'S GATEWAY TO HORROR
Dark Horse Comics: June, 1988 ($1.75, B&W, one-shot)
1-Wolverton-r 6.00

BASIL WOLVERTON'S PLANET OF TERROR
Dark Horse Comics: Oct, 1987 ($1.75, B&W, one-shot)
1-Wolverton-r; Alan Moore-c 6.00

BASTARD SAMURAI
Image Comics: Apr, 2002 - No. 3, Aug, 2002 ($2.95)
1-3-Oeming & Gunter-s; Shannon-a/Oeming-i 3.00
TPB (2003, $12.95) r/#1-3; plus sketch pages and pin-ups 13.00

BATGIRL (See Batman: No Man's Land stories)
DC Comics: Apr, 2000 - No. 73, Apr, 2006 ($2.50)
1-Scott & Campanella-a 6.00
1-(2nd printing) 3.00
2-10: 8-Lady Shiva app. 4.50
11-24: 12-"Officer Down" x-over. 15-Joker-c/app. 24-Bruce Wayne: Murderer pt. 2. 4.00
25-($3.25) Batgirl vs Lady Shiva 4.50
26-29: 27- Bruce Wayne: Fugitive pt. 5; Noto-a. 29-B.W.:F. pt. 13 3.50
30-49,51-73: 30-32-Connor Hawke app. 39-Intro. Black Wind. 41-Superboy-c/app. 53-Robin (Spoiler) app. 54-Bagged with Sky Captain CD. 55-57-War Games. 63,64-Deathstroke app. 67-Birds of Prey app. 73-Lady Shiva origin; Sale-c 3.00
50-($3.25) Batgirl vs Batman 4.00

GD VG FN VF VF/NM NM-
2.0 4.0 6.0 8.0 9.0 9.2

Annual 1 ('00, $3.50) Planet DC; intro. Aruna 5.00
...: A Knight Alone (2001, $12.95, TPB) r/#7-11,13,14 13.00
...: Death Wish (2003, $14.95, TPB) r/#17-20,22,23,25 & Secret Files and Origins #1 15.00
...: Destruction's Daughter (2006, $19.99, TPB) r/#65-73 20.00
...: Fists of Fury (2004, $14.95, TPB) r/#15,16,21,26-28 15.00
...: Kicking Assassins (2005, $14.99, TPB) r/#60-64 15.00
... Secret Files and Origins (8/02, $4.95) origin-s Noto-a; profile pages and pin-ups 5.00
...: Silent Running (2001, $12.95, TPB) r/#1-6 13.00

BATGIRL (Cassandra Cain)
DC Comics: Sept, 2008 - No. 6, Feb, 2009 ($2.99)
1-6-Beechen-s/Calafiore-a 3.00

BATGIRL (Spoiler/Stephanie Brown)(Batman: Reborn)
DC Comics: Oct, 2009 - Present ($2.99)
1-19: 1-7-Garbett-a/Noto-c. 3-New costume. 8-Caldwell-a. 9-14-Lau-c. 14-Supergirl app. 3.00
1-Variant-c by Hamner 5.00
...: Batgirl Rising TPB (2010, $17.99) r/#1-7 20.00

BATGIRL ADVENTURES (See Batman Adventures, The)
DC Comics: Feb, 1998 ($2.95, one-shot) (Based on animated series)
1-Harley Quinn and Poison Ivy app.; Timm-c 5.00

BATGIRL SPECIAL
DC Comics: 1988 ($1.50, one-shot, 52 pgs)
1-Kitson-a/Mignola-c 1 2 3 5 7 9

BATGIRL: YEAR ONE
DC Comics: Feb, 2003 - No. 9, Oct, 2003 ($2.95, limited series)
1-9-Barbara Gordon becomes Batgirl; Killer Moth app.; Beatty & Dixon-s 3.00
TPB (2003, $17.95) r/#1-9 18.00

BAT LASH (See DC Special Series #16, Showcase #76, Weird Western Tales)
National Periodical Publications: Oct-Nov, 1968 - No. 7, Oct-Nov, 1969
(All 12¢ issues)
1-(10-11/68)-2nd app. Bat Lash; classic Nick Cardy-c/a in all
6 12 18 41 66 90
2-7 4 8 12 26 41 55

BAT LASH
DC Comics: Feb, 2008 - No. 6, Jul, 2008 ($2.99, limited series)
1-6-Aragonés & Brandvold-s/John Severin-a. 1-Two covers by Severin and Simonson 3.00
...: Guns and Roses TPB (2008, $17.99) r/#1-6 18.00

BATMAN (See All Star Batman & Robin, Anarky, Aurora [in Promo. Comics section], Azrael, The Best of DC #2, Blind Justice, The Brave & the Bold, Cosmic Odyssey, DC 100-Page Super Spec. #14,20, DC Special, DC Special Series, Detective, Dynamic Classics, 80-Page Giants, Gotham By Gaslight, Gotham Nights, Greatest Batman Stories Ever Told, Greatest Joker Stories Ever Told, Heroes Against Hunger, JLA,The Joker, Justice League of America, Justice League Int., Legends of the Dark Knight, Limited Coll. Ed., Man-Bat, Nightwing, Power Record Comics, Real Fact #5, Robin, Saga of Ra's Al Ghul, Shadow of the..., Star Spangled, Super Friends, 3-D Batman, Untold Legend of..., Wanted... & World's Finest Comics)

BATMAN
National Per. Publ./Detective Comics/DC Comics: Spring, 1940 - Present
(#1-5 were quarterly)
1-Origin The Batman reprinted (2 pgs.) from Det. #33 w/splash from #34 by Bob Kane; see Detective #33 for 1st origin; 1st app. Joker (2 stories intended for 2 separate issues of Det. Comics which would have been 1st & 2nd app.); splash pg. to 2nd Joker story is similar to cover of Det. #40 (story intended for #40); 1st app. The Cat (Catwoman) (1st villainess in comics); has Batman story (w/Hugo Strange) without Robin originally planned for Det. #38; mentions location (Manhattan) where Batman lives (see Det. #31). This book was created entirely from the inventory of Det. Comics; 1st Batman/Robin pin-up on back-c; has text piece & photo of Bob Kane
14,000 28,000 42,000 100,000 192,500 285,000
1-Reprint, oversize 13-1/2x10". **WARNING:** This comic is an exact duplicate reprint of the original except for its size. DC published it in 1974 with a second cover titling it as a Famous First Edition. There have been many reported cases of the outer cover being removed and the interior sold as the original edition. The reprint with the new outer cover removed is practically worthless. See Famous First Edition for value.
2-2nd app. The Joker; 2nd app. Catwoman (out of costume) in Joker story; 1st time called Catwoman (NOTE: A 15¢-c for Canadian distr. exists.)
1667 3334 5000 12,500 23,750 35,000
3-3rd app Catwoman (1st in costume & 1st costumed villainess); 1st Puppet Master app.; classic Kane & Robinson-c 1000 2000 3000 7600 13,800 20,000
4-4th app. The Joker (see Det. #45 for 3rd); 1st mention of Gotham City in a Batman comic (on newspaper)(Win/40) 811 1622 2433 5920 10,460 15,000
5-1st app. the Batmobile with its bat-head front 595 1190 1785 4350 7675 11,000
6,7: 7-Bullseye-c; Joker app. 514 1028 1542 3750 6625 9500
8-Infinity-c by Fred Ray; Joker app. 423 846 1269 3000 5250 7500
9-10:9-1st Batman x-mas story; Burnley-c. 10-Catwoman story (gets new costume)

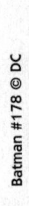

Batman #60 © DC

Batman #178 © DC

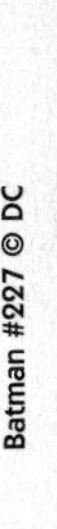
Batman #227 © DC

	GD 2.0	VG 4.0	FN 6.0	VF 8.0	VF/NM 9.0	NM- 9.2
	417	834	1251	2919	5110	7300
11-Classic Joker-c by Ray/Robinson (3rd Joker-c, 6-7/42); Joker & Penguin app.	811	1622	2433	5920	10,460	15,000
12,15: 12-Joker app. 15-New costume Catwoman	314	628	942	2198	3849	5500
13-Jerry Siegel (Superman's co-creator) appears in a Batman story.	320	640	960	2240	3920	5600
14-2nd Penguin-c; Penguin app. (12-1/42-43)	326	652	978	2282	3991	5700
16-Intro/origin Alfred (4-5/43); cover is a reverse of #9 cover by Burnley; 1st small logo	595	1190	1785	4350	7675	11,000
17,20: 17-Classic war-c; Penguin app. 20-1st Batmobile-c (12-1/43-44); Joker app.	290	580	870	1856	3178	4500
18-Hitler, Hirohito, Mussolini-c.	343	686	1029	2400	4200	6000
19-Joker app.	213	426	639	1363	2332	3300
21,22,24,26,28-30: 21-1st skinny Alfred in Batman (2-3/44). 21,30-Penguin app. 22-1st Alfred solo-c/story (Alfred solo stories in 22-32,36); Catwoman & The Cavalier app. 28-Joker story	161	322	483	1030	1765	2500
23-Joker-c/story; classic black-c	290	580	870	1856	3178	4500
25-Only Joker/Penguin team-up; 1st team-up between two major villains	258	516	774	1651	2826	4000
27-Classic Burnley Christmas-c; Penguin app.	216	432	648	1372	2361	3350
31,32,34-36,39: 32-Origin Robin retold; Joker app. 35-Catwoman story (in new costume w/o cat head mask). 36-Penguin app.	123	246	369	787	1344	1900
33-Christmas-c	145	290	435	921	1586	2250
37,40,44-Joker-c/stories	184	368	552	1168	2009	2850
38-Penguin-c/story	148	296	444	947	1624	2300
41,45,46: 41-1st Sci-fi cover/story in Batman; Penguin app.(6-7/47). 45-Christmas-c/story; Catwoman story. 46-Joker app.	92	184	276	584	1005	1425
42-2nd Catwoman-c (1st in Batman)(8-9/47); Catwoman story also.	174	348	522	1114	1907	2700
43-Penguin-c/story	129	258	387	826	1413	2000
47-1st detailed origin The Batman (6-7/48); 1st Bat-signal-c this title (see Detective #108); Batman tracks down his parent's killer and reveals i.d. to him	377	754	1131	2639	4620	6600
48-1000 Secrets of the Batcave; r-in #203; Penguin story	123	246	369	787	1344	1900
49-Joker-c/story; 1st app. Mad Hatter; 1st app. Vicki Vale	206	412	618	1318	2259	3200
50-Two-Face impostor app.	107	214	321	680	1165	1650
51,54,56,57,59,60: 57-Centerfold is a 1950 calendar; Joker app. 59-1st app. Deadshot; Batman in the future-c/story	92	184	276	584	1005	1425
52,55-Joker-c/stories	135	270	405	864	1482	2100
53-Joker story	95	190	285	603	1039	1475
58,61: 58-Penguin-c. 61-Origin Batman Plane II	103	206	309	659	1130	1600
62-Origin Catwoman; Catwoman-c	155	310	465	992	1696	2400
63,80-Joker stories. 63-1st app. Killer Moth; flying saucer story(2-3/51)	87	174	261	553	952	1350
64,70-72,74-77,79: 70-Robot-c. 72-Last 52 pg. issue. 74-Used in **POP**, Pg. 90. 76-Penguin story. 79-Vicki Vale in "The Bride of Batman"	74	148	222	470	810	1150
65,69-Catwoman-c/stories	113	226	339	718	1234	1750
66,73-Joker-c/stories. 66-Pre-2nd Batman & Robin team try-out. 73-Vicki Vale story	119	238	357	762	1306	1850
67-Joker story	87	174	261	553	952	1350
68,81-Two-Face-c/stories	92	184	276	584	1005	1425
78-(8-9/53)-Roh Kar, The Man Hunter from Mars story-the 1st lawman of Mars to come to Earth (green skinned)	89	178	267	565	970	1375
82,83,87-89: 89-Last pre-code issue	71	142	213	454	777	1100
84-Catwoman-c/story; Two-Face app.	107	214	321	680	1165	1650
85,86-Joker story. 86-Intro Batmarine (Batman's submarine)	73	146	219	467	796	1125
90,91,93-96,98,99: 99-(4/56)-Last G.A. Penguin app.	63	126	189	403	689	975
92-1st app. Bat-Hound-c/story	107	214	321	680	1165	1650
97-2nd app. Bat-Hound-c/story; Joker story	68	136	204	435	743	1050
100-(6/56)	290	580	870	1856	3178	4500
101-(8/56)-Clark Kent x-over who protects Batman's i.d. (3rd story)	64	128	192	406	696	985
102-104,106-109: 103-1st S.A. issue; 3rd Bat-Hound-c/story	58	116	174	371	636	900
105-1st Batwoman in Batman (2nd anywhere)	97	194	291	621	1061	1500
110-Joker story	60	120	180	381	653	925
111-120: 112-1st app. Signalman (super villain). 113-1st app. Fatman; Batman meets his counterpart on Planet X w/a chest plate similar to S.A. Batman's design (yellow oval w/black design inside).	50	100	150	315	533	750
121- Origin/1st app. of Mr. Zero (Mr. Freeze).	77	154	231	493	847	1200
122,124-126,128,130: 122,126-Batwoman-c/story. 124-2nd app. Signal Man. 128-Batwoman cameo. 130-Lex Luthor app.	41	82	123	256	428	600
123,127: 123-Joker story; Bat-Hound app. 127-(10/59)-Batman vs. Thor the Thunder God c/story; Joker story; Superman cameo	42	84	126	265	445	625
129-Origin Robin retold; bondage-c; Batwoman-c/story (reprinted in Batman Family #8)	52	104	156	328	552	775
131-135,137-139,141-143: 131-Intro 2nd Batman & Robin series (see #66; also in #135,145, 154,159,163). 133-1st Bat-Mite in Batman (3rd app. anywhere). 134-Origin The Dummy (not Vigilante's villain). 139-Intro 1st original Bat-Girl; only app. Signalman as the Blue Bowman. 141-2nd app. original Bat-Girl. 143-(10/61)-Last 10¢ issue	37	74	111	222	361	500
136-Joker-c/story	41	82	123	256	428	600
140-Joker story, Batwoman-c/s; Superman cameo	39	78	117	231	378	525
144-(12/61)-1st 12¢ issue; Joker story	23	46	69	170	340	510
145,148-Joker-c/stories	26	52	78	186	373	560
146,147,149,150	18	36	54	131	266	400
151-154,156-158,160-162,164-168,170: 152-Joker story. 156-Ant-Man/Robin team-up(6/63). 164-New Batmobile(6/64) new look & Mystery Analysts series begins	15	30	45	106	216	325
155-1st S.A. app. The Penguin (5/63)	32	64	96	246	486	725
159,163-Joker-c/stories. 159-Bat-Girl app. 163-Last Bat-Girl app. until Teen Titans #50	18	36	54	131	266	400
169-2nd SA Penguin app.	17	34	51	122	249	375
171-1st Riddler app.(5/65) since Dec. 1948	41	82	123	324	650	975
172-175,177,178,180,184	11	22	33	77	144	210
176-(80-Pg. Giant G-17); Joker-c/story; Penguin app. in strip-r; Catwoman reprint	13	26	39	91	176	260
179-2nd app. Silver Age Riddler	17	34	51	122	249	375
181-Batman & Robin poster insert; intro. Poison Ivy	25	50	75	183	367	550
182,187-(80 Pg. Giants G-24, G-30); Joker-c/stories	12	24	36	82	154	225
183-2nd app. Poison Ivy	14	28	42	99	200	300
185-(80 Pg. Giant G-27)	11	22	33	80	150	220
186-Joker-c/story	12	24	36	82	154	225
188,191,192,194-196,199	9	18	27	63	107	150
189-1st S.A. app. Scarecrow; retells origin of G.A. Scarecrow from World's Finest #3(1st app.)	16	32	48	114	232	350
190-Penguin-c/app.	11	22	33	80	150	220
193-(80-Pg. Giant G-37)	11	22	33	75	138	200
197-4th S.A. Catwoman app. cont'd from Det. #369; 1st new Batgirl app. in Batman (5th anywhere)	14	28	42	99	200	300
198-(80-Pg. Giant G-43); Joker-c/story-r/World's Finest #61; Catwoman-r/Det. #211; Penguin-r; origin-r/#47	11	22	33	77	144	210
200-(3/68)-Joker cameo; retells origin of Batman & Robin; 1st Neal Adams work this title (cover only)	13	26	39	91	176	260
201-Joker story	7	14	21	50	83	115
202,204-207,209-212: 210-Catwoman-c/app. 212-Last 12¢ issue	7	14	21	47	76	105
203-(80 Pg. Giant G-49); r/#48, 61, & Det. 185; Batcave Blueprints	9	18	27	61	103	145
208-(80 Pg. Giant G-55); New origin Batman by Gil Kane plus 3 G.A. Batman reprints w/Catwoman, Vicki Vale & Batwoman	9	18	27	61	103	145
213-(80-Pg. Giant G-61); 30th anniversary issue (7-8/69); origin Alfred (r/Batman #16), Joker(r/Det. #168), Clayface; new origin Robin with new facts	10	20	30	68	119	170
214-217: 214-Alfred given a new last name- "Pennyworth" (see Detective #96)	6	12	18	39	62	85
218-(80-Pg. Giant G-67)	7	14	21	50	83	115
219-Neal Adams-a	8	16	24	54	90	125
220,221,224-226,229-231	5	10	15	35	55	75
222-Beatles take-off; art lesson by Joe Kubert	7	14	21	47	76	105
223,228,233: 223,228-(80-Pg. Giants G-73,G-79). 233-G-85-(68 pgs., "64 pgs." on-c)	7	14	21	49	80	110
227-Neal Adams cover swipe of Detective #31	13	26	39	89	170	250
232-(6/71) Adams-a. Intro/1st app. Ra's al Ghul; origin Batman & Robin retold; last 15¢ issue (see Detective #411 (5/71) for Talia's debut)	16	32	48	114	232	350
234-(9/71)-1st modern app. of Harvey Dent/Two-Face; (see World's Finest #173 for Batman as Two-Face; only S.A. mention of character); N. Adams-a; 52 pg. issues begin, end #242	18	36	54	125	255	385
235,236,239-242: 239-XMas-c. 241-Reprint/#5	6	12	18	39	62	85
237-N. Adams-a. 1st Rutland Vermont - Bald Mountain Halloween x-over. G.A. Batman-r/ Det. #37; 1st app. The Reaper; Wrightson/Ellison plots	13	26	39	94	185	275
238-Also listed as DC 100 Page Super Spectacular #8; Batman, Legion, Aquaman-r; G.A.						

Batman #332 © DC

Batman #494 © DC

Batman #598 © DC

GD VG FN VF VF/NM NM-
2.0 4.0 6.0 8.0 9.0 9.2

Atom, Sargon (r/Sensation #57), Plastic Man (r/Police #14) stories; Doom Patrol origin-r; N. Adams wraparound-c
(see DC 100 Pg. Super Spectacular #8 for price)
243-245-Neal Adams-a 8 16 24 58 97 135
246-250,252,253: 246-Scarecrow app. 253-Shadow-c & app.
5 10 15 35 55 75
251-(9/73)-N. Adams-c/a; Joker-c/story 10 20 30 69 122 175
254,256-259,261-All 100 pg. editions; part-r: 254-(2/74)-Man-Bat-c & app. 256-Catwoman app. 257-Joker & Penguin app. 258-The Cavalier-r. 259-Shadow-c/app.
7 14 21 49 80 110
255-(100 pgs.)-N. Adams-c/a; tells of Bruce Wayne's father who wore bat costume & fought crime (r/Det. #235); r/story Batman #22 8 16 24 56 93 130
260-Joker-c/story (100 pgs.) 8 16 24 56 93 130
262 (68pgs.) 5 10 15 35 55 75
263,264,266-285,287-290,292,293,295-299: 266-Catwoman back to old costume
3 6 9 14 20 25
265-Wrightson-a(i) 3 6 9 16 22 28
286,291,294: 294-Joker-c/stories 3 6 9 18 27 35
300-Double-size 3 6 9 19 29 38
301-(7/78)-310,312-315,317-320,325-331,333-352: 304-(44 pgs.). 306-3rd app. Black Spider. 308-Mr. Freeze app. 310-1st modern app. The Gentleman Ghost in Batman; Kubert-c. 312,314,346-Two-Face-c/stories. 313-2nd app. Calendar Man. 318-Intro Firebug. 319-2nd modern age app. The Gentleman Ghost; Kubert-c. 344-Poison Ivy app. 345-1st app. new Dr. Death. 345,346,351-Catwoman back-ups 2 4 6 9 12 15
306-308,311-320,323,324,326-(Whitman variants; low print run; none show issue # on cover) 2 4 6 13 18 22
311,316,322-324: 311-Batgirl-c/story; Batgirl reteams w/Batman. 316-Robin returns. 322-324-Catwoman (Selina Kyle) app. 322,323-Cat-Man cameos (1st in Batman, 1 panel each). 323-1st meeting Catwoman & Cat-Man. 324-1st full app. Cat-Man this title
2 4 6 10 14 18
321,353,359-Joker-c/stories 3 6 9 14 20 25
332-Catwoman's 1st solo 2 4 6 11 16 20
354-356,358,360-365,369,370: 361-1st app Harvey Bullock
1 3 4 6 8 10
357-1st app. Jason Todd (3/83); see Det. #524; 1st brief app. Croc
2 4 6 9 13 16
366-Jason Todd 1st in Robin costume; Joker-c/story 2 4 6 13 18 22
367-Jason in red & green costume (not as Robin) 2 4 6 8 10 12
368-1st new Robin in costume (Jason Todd) 2 4 6 10 14 18
371-399,401-403: 371-Cat-Man-c/story; brief origin Cat-Man (cont'd in Det. #538). 386,387-Intro Black Mask (villain). 380-391-Catwoman app. 398-Catwoman & Two-Face app. 401-2nd app. Magpie (see Man of Steel #3 for 1st). 403-Joker cameo
1 2 3 5 6 8

NOTE: *Issues 397-399, 401-403, 408-416, 421-425, 430-432 all have 2nd printings in 1989; some with up to 8 printings. Some are not identified as reprints but have newer ads copyrighted after cover dates. All reprints have different back-c ads. All reprints are scarcer than 1st prints and have same value to variant collectors.*

400 ($1.50, 68pgs.)-Dark Knight special; intro by Stephen King; Art Adams/Austin-a
3 6 9 17 25 32
404-Miller scripts begin (end 407); Year 1; 1st modern app. Catwoman (2/87)
3 6 9 16 23 30
405-407: 407-Year 1 ends (See Detective Comics #575-578 for Year 2)
3 6 9 14 19 24
408-410: New Origin Jason Todd (Robin) 2 4 6 13 18 22
411-416,421-425: 411-Two-face app. 412-Origin/1st app. Mime. 414-Starlin scripts begin, end #429. 416-Nightwing-c/story. 423-McFarlane-c 6.00
417-420: "Ten Nights of the Beast" storyline 2 4 6 8 10 12
426-($1.50, 52 pgs.)- "A Death In The Family" storyline begins, ends #429
2 4 6 13 18 22
427- "A Death In The Family" part 2. 2 4 6 9 12 15
428-Death of Robin (Jason Todd) 2 4 6 13 18 22
429-Joker-c/story; Superman app. 2 4 6 8 10 12
430-432 4.00
433-435-Many Deaths of the Batman story by John Byrne-c/scripts 4.00
436-Year 3 begins (ends #439); origin original Robin retold by Nightwing (Dick Grayson); 1st app. Timothy Drake (8/89) 5.00
436-441: 436-2nd printing. 437-Origin Robin cont. 440,441: "A Lonely Place of Dying" Parts 1 & 3 4.00
442-1st app. Timothy Drake in Robin costume 5.00
443-456,458,459,462-464: 445-447-Batman goes to Russia. 448,449-The Penguin Affair Pts 1 & 3. 450-Origin Joker. 450,451-Joker-c/stories. 452-454-Dark Knight Dark City storyline; Riddler app. 455-Alan Grant scripts begin, ends #466, 470. 464-Last solo Batman story; free 16 pg. preview of Impact Comics line 4.00
457-Timothy Drake officially becomes Robin & dons new costume 6.00
457-Direct sale edition (has #000 in indicia) 6.00

GD VG FN VF VF/NM NM-
2.0 4.0 6.0 8.0 9.0 9.2

460,461,465-487: 460,461-Two part Catwoman story. 465-Robin returns to action with Batman. 470-War of the Gods x-over. 475-1st app. Renee Montoya. 475,476-Return of Scarface. 476-Last $1.00-c. 477,478-Photo-c 4.00
488-Cont'd from Batman: Sword of Azrael #4; Azrael-c & app.
1 2 3 5 6 8
489-Bane-c/story; 1st app. Azrael in Bat-costume 5.00
490-Riddler-c/story; Azrael & Bane app. 6.00
491,492: 491-Knightfall lead-in; Joker-c/story; Azrael & Bane app.; Kelley Jones-c begin. 492-Knightfall part 1; Bane app. 5.00
492-Platinum edition (promo copy) 10.00
493-496: 493-Knightfall Pt. 3. 494-Knightfall Pt. 5; Joker-c & app. 495-Knightfall Pt. 7; brief Bane & Joker apps. 496-Knightfall Pt. 9, Joker-c/story; Bane cameo 4.00
497-(Late 7/93)-Knightfall Pt. 11; Bane breaks Batman's back; B&W outer-c; Aparo-a(p); Giordano-a(i) 6.00
497-499: 497-2nd printing. 497-Newsstand edition w/o outer cover. 498-Knightfall part 15; Bane & Catwoman-c & app. (see Showcase 93 #7 & 8) 499-Knightfall Pt. 17; Bane app. 4.00
500-($2.50, 68 pgs.)-Knightfall Pt. 19; Azrael in new Bat-costume; Bane-c/story 4.00
500-($3.95, 68 pgs.)-Collector's Edition w/die-cut double-c w/foil by Joe Quesada & 2 bound-in post cards 6.00
501-508,510,511: 501-Begin $1.50-c. 501-508-Knightquest. 503,504-Catwoman app. 507-Ballistic app.; Jim Balent-a(p). 510-KnightsEnd Pt. 7. 511-(9/94)-Zero Hour; Batgirl-c/story 3.00
509-($2.50, 52 pgs.)-KnightsEnd Pt. 1 4.00
512-514,516-518: 512-(11/94)-Dick Grayson assumes Batman role 3.00
515-Special Ed.($2.50)-Kelley Jones-a begins; all black embossed-c; Troika Pt. 1 4.00
515-Regular Edition 3.00
519-534,536-549: 519-Begin $1.95-c. 521-Return of Alfred, 522-Swamp Thing app. 525-Mr. Freeze app. 527,528-Two Face app. 529-Contagion Pt. 6. 530-532-Deadman app. 533-Legacy prelude. 534-Legacy Pt. 5. 536-Final Night x-over; Man-Bat-c/app. 540,541-Spectre-c-app. 544-546-Joker & The Demon. 548,549-Penguin-c/app. 3.00
530-532 ($2.50)-Enhanced edition; glow-in-the-dark-c. 4.00
535-(10/96, $2.95)-1st app. The Ogre 3.00
535-(10/96, $3.95)-1st app. The Ogre; variant, cardboard, foldout-c 4.00
550-($3.50)-Collector's Ed., includes 4 collector cards; intro. Chase, return of Clayface; Kelley Jones-c 4.00
550-($2.95)-Standard Ed.; Williams & Gray-c 3.00
551,552,554-562: 551,552-Ragman c/app. 554-Cataclysm pt. 12. 3.00
553-Cataclysm pt.3 4.00
563-No Man's Land; Joker-c by Campbell; Bob Gale-s 5.00
564-574: 569-New Batgirl-c/app. 572-Joker and Harley app. 3.00
575-579: 575-New look Batman begins; McDaniel-a 3.00
580-598: 580-Begin $2.25-c. 587-Gordon shot. 591,592-Deadshot-c/app. 3.00
599-Bruce Wayne: Murderer pt. 7 3.50
600-($3.95) Bruce Wayne: Fugitive pt. 1; back-up homage stories in '50s, 60's, & 70s styles; by Aragonés, Gaudiano, Shanower and others 5.00
600-(2nd printing) 4.00
601-604, 606,607: 601,603-Bruce Wayne: Fugitive pt.3,13. 606,607-Deadshot-c/app. 3.00
605-($2.95) Conclusion to Bruce Wayne: Fugitive x-over; Noto-c 4.00
608-(12/02) Jim Lee-a/c & Jeph Loeb-s begin; Poison Ivy & Catwoman app. 8.00
608-2nd printing; has different cover with Batman standing on gargoyle 12.00
608-Special Edition; has different cover; 200 printed; used for promotional purposes (a CGC certified 9.2 copy sold for $700, and a CGC certified 9.8 copy sold for $2,100)
608-Special Edition (9/09, $1.00) printing has new "After Watchmen" logo cover frame 3.00
609-Huntress app. 9.00
610,611: 610-Killer Croc-c/app.; Batman & Catwoman kiss 8.00
612-Batman vs. Superman; 1st printing with full color cover 9.00
612-2nd printing with B&W sketch cover 15.00
613,614: 614-Joker-c/app. 7.00
615-617: 615-Reveals ID to Catwoman. 616-Ra's al Ghul app. 617-Scarecrow app. 5.00
618-Batman vs. "Jason Todd" 4.00
619-Newsstand cover; Hush story concludes; Riddler app. 5.00
619-Two variant tri-fold covers; one Heroes group, one Villains group 5.00
619-2nd printing with Riddler chess cover 5.00
620-Broken City pt. 1; Azzarello-s/Risso-a/c begin; Killer Croc app. 4.00
621-633: 621-625-Azzarello-s/Risso-a/c. 626-630-Winick-s/Nguyen-a/Wagner-c; Penguin & Scarecrow app. 631-633-War Games. 633-Conclusion to War Games x-over 3.00
634-638-Winick-s/Nguyen-a/Wagner-c; Red Hood app. 637-Amazo app. 638-Red Hood unmasked as Jason Todd 3.00
639-650: 640-Superman app. 641-Begin $2.50-c. 643,644-War Crimes; Joker app. 650-Infinite Crisis; Joker and Jason Todd app. 3.00
651-654-One Year Later; Bianchi-c 3.50
655-Begin Grant Morrison-s/Andy Kubert-a; Kubert-c w/red background 5.00
655-Variant cover by Adam Kubert, brown-toned image 15.00
656-665: 656-Intro. Damien, son of Talia and Batman (see Batman: Son of the Demon).

Batman #681 © DC

Batman #700 © DC

Batman Annual #16 © DC

	GD 2.0	VG 4.0	FN 6.0	VF 8.0	VF/NM 9.0	NM- 9.2
657-Damien in Robin costume. 659-662-Mandrake-a. 663-Van Fleet-a. 664-Bane app.						3.00
666-675: 666-Future story of adult Damien; Andy Kubert-a. 667-669-Williams III-a. 670,671-Resurrection of Ra's al Ghul; Daniel-a. 671-2nd printing						3.00
676-Batman R.I.P. begins; Morrison-s/Daniel-a/Alex Ross-c						4.00
676-Variant-c by Tony Daniel						12.00
676-Second (red-tinted Daniel-c) & third (B&W Daniel-c) printings						3.00
677-680,682-685: Batman R.I.P.; Alex Ross-c. 678-Bat-Mite app. 682-685-Last Rites						3.00
677-Variant-c with Red Hood by Tony Daniel						10.00
677-Second printing with B&W&red-tinted Daniel-c						3.00
681-($3.99) Batman R.I.P. conclusion						4.00
686-($3.99) Gaiman-s/Andy Kubert-a; continues in Detective #853; Kubert sketch pgs.; covers by Kubert and Ross; 2nd & 3rd printings exist						4.00
687-($3.99) Batman: Reborn begins; Dick Grayson becomes Batman; Winick-s/Benes-a						4.00
688-699: 688-691-Bagley-a. 692-697,699-Tony Daniel-s/a. 692-Catwoman app.						3.00
700-(8/10, $4.99) Morrison-s; art by Daniel, Quitely, Finch & Andy Kubert; Finch-c						5.00
700-Variant-c by Mignola						10.00
701-708: 701,702-Morrison-s; R.I.P story. 704-Batman Inc. begins; Daniel-s/a						3.00
#0 (10/94)-Zero Hour issue released between #511 & #512; Origin retold						3.00
#1,000,000 (11/98) 853rd Century x-over						3.00
Annual 1 (8-10/61)-Swan-c	56	112	168	476	963	1450
Annual 2	27	54	81	190	383	575
Annual 3 (Summer, '62)-Joker-c/story	27	54	81	192	389	585
Annual 4,5	14	28	42	96	191	285
Annual 6,7 (7/64, 25¢, 80 pgs.)	12	24	36	82	154	225
Annual V5#8 (1982)-Painted-c	1	3	4	6	8	10
Annual 9,10,12: 9(7/85). 10(1986). 12(1988, $1.50)	1	2	3	4	5	7
Annual 11 (1987, $1.25)-Penguin-c/story; Moore-s	1	2	3	5	7	9
Annual 13 (1989, $1.75, 68 pgs.)-Gives history of Bruce Wayne, Dick Grayson, Jason Todd, Alfred, Comm. Gordon, Barbara Gordon (Batgirl) & Vicki Vale; Morrow-i						6.00
Annual 14-17 ('90-'93, 68 pgs.)-14-Origin Two-Face. 15-Armageddon 2001 x-over; Joker app. 15 (2nd printing). 16-Joker-c/s; Kieth-c. 17 (1993, $2.50, 68 pgs.)-Azrael in Bat-costume; intro Ballistic						4.00
Annual 18 (1994, $2.95)						4.00
Annual 19 (1995, $3.95)-Year One story; retells Scarecrow's origin						4.00
Annual 20 (1996, $2.95)-Legends of the Dead Earth story; Giarrano-a						4.00
Annual 21 (1997, $3.95)-Pulp Heroes story						4.00
Annual 22,23 ('98, '99, $2.95)-22-Ghosts; Wrightson-c. 23-JLApe; Art Adams-c						4.00
Annual 24 ('00, $3.50) Planet DC; intro. The Boggart; Aparo-a						4.00
Annual 25 ('06, $4.99) Infinite Crisis-revised story of Jason Todd; unused Aparo page						6.00
Annual 26 ('07, $3.99) Origin of Ra's al Ghul; Damien app.						4.00
Annual 27 ('09, $4.99) Azrael app.; Calafiore-a; back-up story w/Kelley Jones-a						5.00
Annual 28 (2/11, $4.99) The Question, Nightrunner and Veil app.; Lau-c						5.00

NOTE: **Art Adams** *a-400p.* **Neal Adams** *c-200, 203, 210, 217, 219-222, 224-227, 229, 230, 232, 234, 236-241, 243-246, 251, 255, Annual 14.* **Aparo** *a-414-420, 426-435, 440-448, 450, 451, 480-483, 486-491, 494-500; c-414-416, 481, 482, 463i, 486, 487i.* **Bolland** *a-400; c-445-447.* **Burnley** *a-10, 12-18, 20, 22, 25, 27; c-9, 15, 16, 27, 28p, 40p, 42p.* **Byrne** *c-401, 433-435, 533-535, Annual 11.* **Travis Charest** *c-488-490p.* **Colan** *a-340p, 343-345p, 348-351p, 373p, 383p; c-343p, 345p, 350p.* **J. Cole** *a-238r.* **Cowan** *a-Annual 10p.* **Golden** *a-295p, 303p, 484, 485.* **Alan Grant** *scripts-455-466, 470, 474-476, 479, 480, Annual 16(part).* **Grell** *a-287, 288p, 289p, 290; c-287-290.* **Infantino/Anderson** *c-167, 173, 175, 181, 186, 191, 192, 194, 195, 198, 199.* **Infantino/Giella** *c-190.* **Kelley Jones** *a-513-519, 521-525, 527; c-491-499, 500(newsstand), 501-510, 513.* **Kaluta** *c-242, 248, 253, Annual 12.* **G. Kane/Anderson** *c-178-180.* **Bob Kane** *a-1, 2, 5; c-1-5, 7, 17.* **G. Kane** *a-(r)-254, 255, 259, 261, 353i.* **Kubert** *a-238r, 400; c-310, 319p, 327, 328, 344.* **McFarlane** *c-423.* **Mignola** *c-426-429, 452-454, Annual 18.* **Moldoff** *c-101-140.* **Moldoff/Giella** *a-164-175, 177-181, 183, 184, 186.* **Moldoff/Greene** *a-169, 172-174, 177-179, 181, 184.* **Mooney** *a-255r.* **Morrow** *a-Annual 13i.* **Newton** *a-305, 306, 328p, 331p, 332p, 337p, 338p, 346p, 352-357p, 360-372p, 374-378p; c-374p, 378p.* **Nino** *a-Annual 9.* **Irv Novick** *c-201, 202.* **Perez** *a-400; c-436-442.* **Fred Ray** *c-8, 10; w/***Robinson***-11.* **Robinson/Roussos** *a-12-17, 20, 22, 24, 25, 27, 28, 31, 33, 37.* **Robinson** *a-12, 14, 18, 22-32,34, 36, 37, 255r, 260r, 261r; c-6, 10, 12-14, 18, 21, 24, 26, 30, 37, 39.* **Simonson** *a-300p, 312p, 321p; c-300p, 312p, 366, 413i.* **P. Smith** *a-Annual 9.* **Dick Sprang** *c-19, 20, 22, 23, 25, 29, 31-36, 38, 51, 55, 66, 73, 76.* **Starlin** *c/a-402.* **Staton** *a-334.* **Sutton** *a-400.* **Wrightson** *a-265i, 400; c-320r. Bat-Hound app. in 92, 97, 103, 123, 125, 133, 156, 158. Bat-Mite app. in 133, 136, 144, 146, 158, 161. Batwoman app. in 105, 116, 122, 125, 128, 129, 131, 133, 139, 140, 141, 144, 145, 150, 151, 153, 154, 157, 159, 162, 163.* **Zeck** *c-417-420. Catwoman back-ups in 332, 345, 346, 348-351. Joker app. in 1, 2, 4, 5, 7-9, 11-13, 19, 20, 23, 25, 28, 32 & many more. Robin solo back-up stories in 337-339, 341-343.*

BATMAN (Hardcover books and trade paperbacks)

	NM- 9.2
...: ABSOLUTION (2002, $24.95)-Hard-c.; DeMatteis-s/Ashmore painted-a	25.00
...: ABSOLUTION (2003, $17.95)-Soft-c.; DeMatteis-s/Ashmore painted-a	18.00
...: A LONELY PLACE OF DYING (1990, $3.95, 132 pgs.)-r/Batman #440-442 & New Titans #60,61; Perez-c	4.00
...: ANARKY TPB (1999, $12.95) r/early appearances	13.00
...AND DRACULA: RED RAIN nn (1991, $24.95)-Hard-c.; Elseworlds storyline	32.00
...AND DRACULA: RED RAIN nn (1992, $9.95)-SC	12.00
...AND SON HC (2007, $24.99, dustjacket) r/Batman #655-658,663-666	25.00
...AND SON SC (2008, $14.99) r/Batman #655-658,663-666	15.00
...ANNUALS (See DC Comics Classics Library for reprints of early Annuals)	
ARKHAM ASYLUM Hard-c; Morrison-s/McKean-a (1989, $24.95)	30.00
ARKHAM ASYLUM Soft-c ($14.95)	15.00
ARKHAM ASYLUM 15TH ANNIVERSARY EDITION Hard-c (2004, $29.95) reprint with Morrison's script and annotations, original page layouts; Karen Berger afterword	30.00
ARKHAM ASYLUM 15TH ANNIVERSARY EDITION Soft-c (2005, $17.99)	18.00
...: AS THE CROW FLIES-(2004, $12.95) r/#626-630; Nguyen sketch pages	13.00
BIRTH OF THE DEMON Hard-c (1992, $24.95)-Origin of Ra's al Ghul	25.00
BIRTH OF THE DEMON Soft-c (1993, $12.95)	13.00
BLIND JUSTICE nn (1992, $7.50)-r/Det. #598-600	7.50
BLOODSTORM (1994, $24.95,HC) Kelley Jones-c/a	28.00
BRIDE OF THE DEMON Hard-c (1990, $19.95)	20.00
BRIDE OF THE DEMON Soft-c ($12.95)	13.00
...: BROKEN CITY HC-(2004, $24.95) r/#620-625; new Johnson-c; intro by Schreck	25.00
...: BROKEN CITY SC-(2004, $14.99) r/#620-625; new Johnson-c; intro by Schreck	15.00
...: BRUCE WAYNE: FUGITIVE Vol. 1 ('02, $12.95)-r/ story arc	13.00
...: BRUCE WAYNE: FUGITIVE Vol. 2 ('03, $12.95)-r/ story arc	13.00
...: BRUCE WAYNE: FUGITIVE Vol. 3 ('03, $12.95)-r/ story arc	13.00
...: BRUCE WAYNE-MURDERER? ('02, $19.95)-r/ story arc	20.00
...: CASTLE OF THE BAT ($5.95)-Elseworlds story	6.00
...: CATACLYSM ('99, $17.95)-r/ story arc	18.00
...: CHILD OF DREAMS (2003, $24.95, B&W, HC) Reprint of Japanese manga with Kia Asamiya-s/a/c; English adaptation by Max Allan Collins; Asamiya interview	25.00
...: CHILD OF DREAMS (2003, $19.95, B&W, SC)	20.00
...CHRONICLES VOL. 1 (2005, $14.99)-r/apps. in Detective Comics #27-38; Batman #1	15.00
...CHRONICLES VOL. 2 (2006, $14.99)-r/apps. in Detective Comics #39-45 and NY World's Fair 1940; Batman #2,3	15.00
...CHRONICLES VOL. 3 (2007, $14.99)-r/apps. in Detective Comics #46-50 and World's Best Comics #1; Batman #4,5	15.00
...CHRONICLES VOL. 4 (2007, $14.99)-r/apps. in Detective Comics #51-56 and World's Finest Comics #2,3; Batman #6,7	15.00
...CHRONICLES VOL. 5 (2008, $14.99)-r/apps. in Detective Comics #57-61 and World's Finest Comics #4; Batman #8,9	15.00
...CHRONICLES VOL. 6 (2008, $14.99)-r/apps. in Detective Comics #62-65 and World's Finest Comics #5,6; Batman #10,11	15.00
...CHRONICLES VOL. 7 (2009, $14.99)-r/apps. in Detective Comics #66-70 and World's Finest Comics #7; Batman #12,13	15.00
...CHRONICLES VOL. 8 (2009, $14.99)-r/apps. in Detective Comics #71-74 and World's Finest Comics #8,9; Batman #14,15	15.00
...CHRONICLES VOL. 9 (2010, $14.99)-r/apps. in Detective Comics #75-77 and World's Finest Comics #10; Batman #16,17	15.00
...CHRONICLES VOL. 10 (2010, $14.99)-r/apps. in Detective Comics #78-81 and World's Finest Comics #11; Batman #18,19	15.00
...: CITY OF CRIME (2006, $19.99) r/Detective Comics #800-808,811-814; Lapham-s	20.00
...: COLLECTED LEGENDS OF THE DARK KNIGHT nn (1994, $12.95)-r/Legends of the Dark Knight #32-34,38,42,43	13.00
...: CRIMSON MIST (1999, $24.95,HC)-Vampire Batman Elseworlds story Doug Moench-s/Kelley Jones-c/a	25.00
...: CRIMSON MIST (2001, $14.95,SC)	15.00
...: DARK JOKER-THE WILD (1993, $24.95,HC)-Elseworlds story; Moench-s/Jones-c/a	25.00
...: DARK JOKER-THE WILD (1993, $9.95,SC)	10.00
...DARK KNIGHT DYNASTY nn (1997, $24.95)-Hard-c.; 3 Elseworlds stories; Barr-s/ S. Hampton painted-a, Gary Frank, McDaniel-a(p)	25.00
...DARK KNIGHT DYNASTY Softcover (2000, $14.95) Hampton-c	15.00
...DEADMAN: DEATH AND GLORY nn (1996, $24.95)-Hard-c.; Robinson-s/ Estes-c/a	25.00
...DEADMAN: DEATH AND GLORY ($12.95)-SC	13.00
DEATH AND THE CITY (2007, $14.99, TPB)-r/Detective #827-834	15.00
DEATH IN THE FAMILY (1988, $3.95, trade paperback)-r/Batman #426-429 by Aparo	5.00
DEATH IN THE FAMILY: (2nd - 5th printings)	4.00
...: DETECTIVE (2007, $14.99, SC)-r/Detective Comics #821-826	15.00
...: DETECTIVE #27 HC (2003, $19.95)-Elseworlds; Uslan-s/Snejbjerg-a	20.00
...: DETECTIVE #27 SC (2004, $12.95)-Elseworlds; Uslan-s/Snejbjerg-a	13.00
DIGITAL JUSTICE nn (1990, $24.95, Hard-c.)-Computer generated art	25.00
... : EGO AND OTHER TALES HC (2007, $24.99)-r/Batman: Ego, Catwoman: Selina's Big Score, and stories from Batman Black and White and Solo; Darwyn Cooke-s/a	25.00
... : EGO AND OTHER TALES SC (2008, $17.99) same contents as HC	18.00
... :EVOLUTION (2001, $12.95, SC)-r/Detective Comics #743-750	13.00
... FACES (1995, $9.95, TPB) r/Legends of the Dark Knight #28-30	10.00
... FACES (2008, $12.99, TPB) Second printing	13.00
...: FACE THE FACE (2006, $14.99, TPB)-r/Batman #651-654, Detective #817-820	15.00
...: FALSE FACES HC (2008, $19.99)-r/Batman #588-590, Wonder Woman #160,161; Batman: Gotham City Secret Files #1 and Detective #787; Brian K. Vaughn intro.	20.00
...: FALSE FACES SC (2008, $14.99)-r/Batman #588-590, Wonder Woman #160,161; Batman: Gotham City Secret Files #1 and Detective #787; Brian K. Vaughn intro.	15.00
...: FORTUNATE SON HC (1999, $24.95) Gene Ha-a	25.00
...: FORTUNATE SON SC (2000, $14.95) Gene Ha-a	15.00
FOUR OF A KIND TPB (1998, $14.95)-r/1995 Year One Annuals featuring Poison Ivy, Riddler, Scarecrow, & Man-Bat	15.00

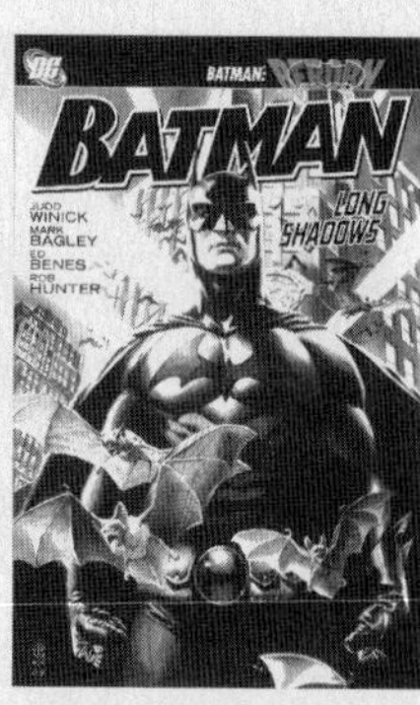

Batman: Long Shadows HC © DC

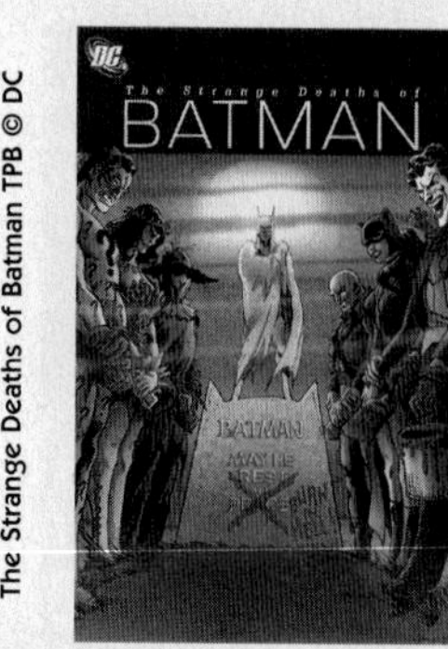

The Strange Deaths of Batman TPB © DC

Batman: Batgirl #1 © DC

GD 2.0 VG 4.0 FN 6.0 VF 8.0 VF/NM 9.0 NM- 9.2

GD 2.0 VG 4.0 FN 6.0 VF 8.0 VF/NM 9.0 NM- 9.2

... GOING SANE (2008, $14.95, TPB) r/Legends of the Dark Knight #65-68,200 15.00
...: GOTHAM BY GASLIGHT (2006, $12.99, TPB) r/Gotham By Gaslight & Master of the Future one-shots; Elseworlds Batman vs. Jack the Ripper 13.00
...GOTHIC (1992, $12.95, TPB)-r/Legends of the Dark Knight #6-10 13.00
...GOTHIC (2007, $14.99, TPB)-r/Legends of the Dark Knight #6-10 15.00
...: HARVEST BREED-(2000, $24.95) George Pratt-s/painted-a 25.00
...: HARVEST BREED-(2003, $17.95) George Pratt-s/painted-a 18.00
...: HAUNTED KNIGHT-(1997, $12.95) r/ Halloween specials 13.00
...: HEART OF HUSH HC-(2009, $19.99) r/#Detective #846-850; pin-ups 20.00
...: HEART OF HUSH SC-(2010, $14.99) r/#Detective #846-850; pin-ups 15.00
...: HONG KONG HC (2003, $24.95, with dustjacket) Doug Moench-s/Tony Wong-a 25.00
...: HONG KONG SC (2004, $17.95) Doug Moench-s/Tony Wong-a 18.00
...: HUSH SC-(2009, $24.99) r/#608-619; Wizard 0; variant cover gallery; Loeb intro 25.00
...: HUSH DOUBLE FEATURE-(2003, $3.95) r/#608,609(1st 2 Jim Lee-a issues) 4.00
...: HUSH VOLUME 1 HC-(2003, $19.95) r/#608-612; & new 2 pg. origin w/Lee-a 20.00
...: HUSH VOLUME 1 SC-(2004, $12.95) r/#608-612; includes CD of DC GN art 13.00
...: HUSH VOLUME 2 HC-(2003, $19.95) r/#613-619; Lee intro & sketchpages 20.00
...: HUSH VOLUME 2 SC-(2004, $12.95) r/#613-619; Lee intro & sketchpages 13.00
...: ILLUSTRATED BY NEAL ADAMS VOLUME 1 HC-(2003, $49.95) r/Batman, Brave and the Bold, and Detective Comics stories and covers 50.00
...: ILLUSTRATED BY NEAL ADAMS VOLUME 2 HC-(2004, $49.95) r/Adams' Batman art from 1969-71; intro. by Dick Giordano 50.00
...: ILLUSTRATED BY NEAL ADAMS VOLUME 3 HC-(2006, $49.99) r/Adams' Batman art from 1971-74; covers, pin-ups and design art; intro. by Denny O'Neil 50.00
... INTERNATIONAL TPB (2010, $17.99) R/Batman: Scottish Connection, Batman in Barcelona: Dragon's Knight and Batman: Legends of the DK #52,53; Jim Lee-c 18.00
... IN THE FORTIES TPB ($19.95) Intro. by Bill Schelly 20.00
... IN THE FIFTIES TPB ($19.95) Intro. by Michael Uslan 20.00
... IN THE SIXTIES TPB ($19.95) Intro. by Adam West 20.00
... IN THE SEVENTIES TPB ($19.95) Intro. by Dennis O'Neil 20.00
... IN THE EIGHTIES TPB ($19.95) Intro. by John Wells 20.00
.../ JUDGE DREDD FILES (2004, $14.95) reprints cross-overs 15.00
... :KING TUT'S TOMB TPB (2010, $14.99) r/Batman Confidential #26-28, Batman #353 and Brave and the Bold #164,171 15.00
... LEGACY-(1996, $17.95) reprints Legacy 18.00
...: LIFE AFTER DEATH HC-(2010, $19.99, dustjacket) r/#Batman #692-699 20.00
...: LONG SHADOWS HC-(2010, $19.99, dustjacket) r/#Batman #687-691 20.00
...: LOVERS & MADMEN-(See Batman Confidential)
...: MAD LOVE AND OTHER STORIES HC (2009, $19.99) r/Batman Adventures: Mad Love, Batman Advs. Holiday Special and other Dini/Timm collaborations; commentary 20.00
...: THE MANY DEATHS OF THE BATMAN (1992, $3.95, 84 pgs.)-r/Batman #433-435 w/new Byrne-c 4.00
...: MONSTERS (2009, $19.99, TPB)-r/Legends of the Dark Knight #71-73,83,84,89,90 20.00
...: THE MOVIES (1997, $19.95)-r/movie adaptations of Batman, Batman Returns, Batman Forever, Batman and Robin 20.00
...: NINE LIVES HC (2002, $24.95, sideways format) Motter-s/Lark-a 25.00
...: NINE LIVES SC (2003, $17.95, sideways format) Motter-s/Lark-a 18.00
...: OFFICER DOWN (2001, $12.95)-r/Commissioner shot x-over; Talon-c 13.00
...: PREY (1992, $12.95)-Gulacy/Austin-a 13.00
...: PRIVATE CASEBOOK HC (2008, $19.99)-r/Detective Comics #840-845 and story from DC Infinite Halloween Special #1 20.00
...: PRODIGAL (1997, $14.95)-Gulacy/Austin-a 15.00
...: R.I.P.: THE DELUXE EDITION HC (2009, $24.99)-r/Batman #676-683 and story from DC Universe #0 25.00
...: R.I.P.: SC (2010, $14.99)-r/Batman #676-683 and story from DC Universe #0 15.00
... SCARECROW TALES (2005, $19.99, TPB) r/Scarecrow stories & pin-ups from World's Finest #3 to present 20.00
...: SECRETS OF THE BATCAVE (2007, $17.99, TPB) r/Batcave stories 18.00
SHAMAN (1993, $12.95)-r/Legends/D.K. #1-5 13.00
...: SNOW (2007, $14.99, TPB)-r/Legends of the Dark Knight #192-196; Fisher-a 15.00
...: SON OF THE DEMON Hard-c (9/87, $14.95) (see Batman #655-658) 30.00
...: SON OF THE DEMON limited signed & numbered Hard-c (1,700) 45.00
...: SON OF THE DEMON Soft-c w/new-c ($8.95) 10.00
...: SON OF THE DEMON Soft-c (1989, $9.95, 2nd printing - 5th printing) 10.00
...: STRANGE APPARITIONS ($12.95) r/'77-'78 Englehart/Rogers stories from Detective #469-479; also Simonson-a 13.00
...: TALES OF THE DEMON (1991, $17.95, 212 pgs.)-Intro by Sam Hamm; reprints by Neal Adams(3) & Golden; contains Saga of Ra's al Ghul #1 18.00
TALES OF THE MULTIVERSE: BATMAN - VAMPIRE (2007, $19.99) r/Batman & Dracula: Red Rain, Batman: Bloodstorm and Batman: Crimson Mist; Van Lustbader foreword 20.00
...: TEN NIGHTS OF THE BEAST (1994, $5.95)-r/Batman #417-420 6.00
...: TERROR (2003, $12.95, TPB)-r/Legends of the Dark Knight #137-141; Gulacy-c 13.00
...: THE BLACK GLOVE (2009, $17.99, TPB) r/Batman #667-669,672-675 18.00
...: THE CHALICE (HC, '99, $24.95) Van Fleet painted-a 25.00
...: THE CHALICE (SC, '00, $14.95) Van Fleet painted-a 15.00
...: THE GREATEST STORIES EVER TOLD (2005, $19.99, TPB) Les Daniels intro. 20.00
...: THE GREATEST STORIES EVER TOLD VOLUME TWO (2007, $19.99, TPB) 20.00
...: THE JOKER'S LAST LAUGH ('08, $17.99) r/Joker's Last Laugh series #1-6 18.00
...: THE LAST ANGEL (1994, $12.95, TPB) Lustbader-s 13.00
...: THE RESURRECTION OF RA'S AL GHUL (2008, $29.99, HC w/DJ) r/x-over 30.00
...: THE RESURRECTION OF RA'S AL GHUL (2009, $19.99, SC) r/x-over 20.00
...: THE RING, THE ARROW AND THE BAT (2003, $19.95, TPB) r/Legends of the DCU #7-9 & Batman: Legends of the Dark Knight #127-131; Green Lantern & Green Arrow app. 20.00
...: THE STRANGE DEATHS OF BATMAN ('09, $19.99) r/Batman #291-294, Det. #347, World's Finest #184,269, Brave & the Bold #115, Nightwing #52; Aparo-c 20.00
...: THE WRATH ('09, $17.99) r/Batman Special #1 and Batman Confidential #13-16 18.00
...: THRILLKILLER (1998, $12.95, TPB)-r/series & Thrillkiller '62 13.00
...: TIME AND THE BATMAN HC ('11, $19.99) r/Batman #700-703; cover gallery 20.00
...: TWO-FACE AND SCARECROW YEAR ONE (2009, $19.99, TPB)-r/Year One: Batman Scarecrow #1,2 and Two Face: Year One #1,2 20.00
...: UNDER THE COWL (2010, $17.99, TPB)-r/app. Dick Grayson, Tim Drake, Damien Wayne, Jean Paul Valley and Terry McGinnis as Batman 18.00
...: UNDER THE HOOD (2005, $9.99, TPB)-r/Batman #635-641 10.00
...: UNDER THE HOOD Vol. 2 (2006, $9.99, TPB)-r/Batman #645-650 & Annual #25 10.00
...: VENOM (1993, $9.95, TPB)-r/Legends of the Dark Knight #16-20; embossed-c 10.00
... VS. TWO-FACE (2008, $19.99, TPB) r/initial (Det. #80) & classic battles; Bianchi-c 20.00
...: WAR CRIMES (2006, $12.99, TPB) r/x-over; James Jean-c 13.00
... WAR DRUMS (2004, $17.95) r/Detective #790-796 & Robin #126-128 18.00
...: WAR GAMES ACT 1,2,3 (2005, $14.95/$14.99, TPB) r/x-over; James Jean-c; each.. 15.00
...: WHATEVER HAPPENED TO THE CAPED CRUSADER? HC-(2009, $24.99, d.j.) r/Batman #686, Detective #853 and other Gaiman Batman stories; Gaiman intro.; Andy Kubert sketch pages; new Kubert cover 25.00
...: WHATEVER HAPPENED TO THE CAPED CRUSADER? SC-(2010, $14.99) 15.00
YEAR ONE Hard-c (1988, $12.95) r/Batman #404-407 18.00
YEAR ONE (1988, $9.95, TPB)-r/Batman #404-407 by Miller; intro by Miller 10.00
YEAR ONE (TPB, 2nd & 3rd printings) 10.00
YEAR ONE Deluxe HC (2005, $19.99, die-cut d.j.) new intro. by Miller and developmental material from Mazzucchelli; script pages and sketches 20.00
YEAR ONE (Deluxe) SC (2007, $14.99) r/story plus bonus material from 2005 HC 15.00
YEAR TWO (1990, $9.95, TPB)-r/Det. 575-578 by McFarlane; wraparound-c 10.00

BATMAN (one-shots)
... ABDUCTION, THE (1998, $5.95) 6.00
... ALLIES SECRET FILES AND ORIGINS 2005 (8/05, $4.99) stories/pin-ups by various 5.00
... & ROBIN (1997, $5.95)-Movie adaptation 6.00
...: ARKHAM ASYLUM - TALES OF MADNESS (5/98, $2.95) Cataclysm x-over pt. 16 3.00
... : BANE (1997, $4.95)-Dixon-s/Burchett-a; Stelfreeze-c; cover art interlocks w/Batman:(Batgirl, Mr. Freeze, Poison Ivy) 5.00
... : BATGIRL (1997, $4.95)-Puckett-s/Haley,Kesel-a; Stelfreeze-c; cover art interlocks w/Batman:(Bane, Mr. Freeze, Poison Ivy) 5.00
... : BATGIRL (6/98, $1.95)-Girlfrenzy; Balent-a 3.00
... : BLACKGATE (1/97, $3.95) Dixon-s 4.00
... : BLACKGATE - ISLE OF MEN (4/98, $2.95) Cataclysm x-over pt. 8; Moench-s/Aparo-a 3.00
... BOOK OF SHADOWS, THE (1999, $5.95) 6.00
BROTHERHOOD OF THE BAT (1995, $5.95)-Elseworlds-s 6.00
... BULLOCK'S LAW (8/99, $4.95) Dixon-s 5.00
.../CAPTAIN AMERICA (1996, $5.95, DC/Marvel) Elseworlds story; Byrne-c/s/a 6.00
... : CATWOMAN DEFIANT nn (1992, $4.95, prestige format)-Milligan scripts; cover art interlocks w/Batman: Penguin Triumphant; special foil logo 5.00
.../CATWOMAN: FOLLOW THE MONEY (1/11, $4.99) Chaykin-c/s/a 5.00
... /DANGER GIRL (2/05, $4.95)-Leinil Yu-a/c; Joker, Harley Quinn & Catwoman app. 5.00
... /DAREDEVIL (2000, $5.95)-Barreto-a 6.00
...: DARK ALLEGIANCES (1996, $5.95)-Elseworlds story, Chaykin-c/a 6.00
...: DARK KNIGHT GALLERY (1/96, $3.50)-Pin-ups by Pratt, Balent, & others 3.50
...:DAY OF JUDGMENT (11/99, $3.95) 4.00
...:DEATH OF INNOCENTS (12/96, $3.95)-O'Neil-s/ Staton-a(p) 4.00
.../DEMON (1996, $4.95)-Alan Grant scripts 5.00
.../DEMON: A TRAGEDY (2000, $5.95)-Grant-s/Murray painted-a 6.00
...:D.O.A. (1999, $6.95)-Bob Hall-s/a 7.00
...:/DOC SAVAGE SPECIAL (2010, $4.99)-Azzarello-s/Noto-a/covers by JG Jones & Morales; preview of First Wave line (Batman, Doc Savage, The Spirit, Blackhawks) 5.00
...:DREAMLAND (2000, $5.95)-Grant-s/Breyfogle-a 6.00
... : EGO (2000, $6.95)-Darwyn Cooke-s/a 7.00
... 80-PAGE GIANT (8/98, $4.95) Stelfreeze-c 6.00
... 80-PAGE GIANT 1 (2/10, $5.99) Andy Kubert-c; Catwoman, Poison Ivy app. 6.00
... 80-PAGE GIANT 2 (10/99, $4.95) Luck of the Draw 6.00
... 80-PAGE GIANT 3 (7/00, $5.95) Calendar Man 6.00
... 80-PAGE GIANT 2011 (2/11, $5.95) Nguyen-c; short stories of villains by various 6.00
... FOREVER (1995, $5.95, direct market) 6.00

Batman: Poison Ivy © DC

Batman Adventures (2nd series) #2 © DC

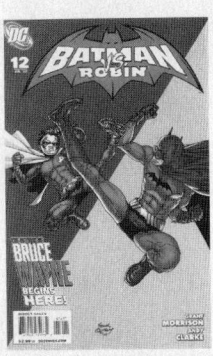

Batman and Robin #12 © DC

	GD 2.0	VG 4.0	FN 6.0	VF 8.0	VF/NM 9.0	NM- 9.2
... FOREVER (1995, $3.95, newsstand)						4.00
FULL CIRCLE nn (1991, $5.95, 68 pgs.)-Sequel to Batman: Year Two						6.00
...GALLERY, The 1 (1992, $2.95)-Pin-ups by Miller, N. Adams & others						3.00
...GOLDEN STREETS OF GOTHAM (2003, $6.95) Elseworlds in early 1900s						7.00
...GOTHAM BY GASLIGHT (1989, $3.95) Elseworlds; Mignola-a/Augustyn-s						4.00
...GOTHAM CITY SECRET FILES 1 (4/00, $4.95) Batgirl app.						5.00
...: GOTHAM NOIR (2001, $6.95)-Elseworlds; Brubaker-s/Phillips-c/a						7.00
.../GREEN ARROW: THE POISON TOMORROW nn (1992, $5.95, square-bound, 68 pgs.) Netzer-c/a						6.00
...: HIDDEN TREASURES 1 (12/10, $4.99) unpubl. story Wrightson-a; r/Swamp Thing #7						5.00
HOLY TERROR nn (1991, $4.95, 52 pgs.)-Elseworlds story						5.00
.../HOUDINI: THE DEVIL'S WORKSHOP (1993, $5.95)						6.00
... :HUNTRESS/SPOILER - BLUNT TRAUMA (5/98, $2.95) Cataclysm pt. 13; Dixon-s/Barreto & Sienkiewicz-a						3.00
...: I, JOKER nn (1998, $4.95)-Elseworlds story; Bob Hall-s/a						5.00
...: IN BARCELONA: DRAGON'S KNIGHT 1 (7/09, $3.99) Waid-s/Olmos-a/Jim Lee-c						4.00
...: IN DARKEST KNIGHT nn (1994, $4.95, 52 pgs.)-Elseworlds story; Batman w/Green Lantern's ring.						5.00
...:JOKER'S APPRENTICE (5/99, $3.95) Von Eeden-a						4.00
.../ JOKER: SWITCH (2003, $6.95)-Bolton-a/Grayson-s						7.00
...:JUDGE DREDD: JUDGEMENT ON GOTHAM nn (1991, $5.95, 68 pgs.) Simon Bisley-c/a; Grant/Wagner scripts						6.00
...:JUDGE DREDD: JUDGEMENT ON GOTHAM nn (2nd printing)						6.00
...:JUDGE DREDD: THE ULTIMATE RIDDLE (1995, $4.95)						5.00
...:JUDGE DREDD: VENDETTA IN GOTHAM (1993, $5.95)						6.00
...: KNIGHTGALLERY (1995, $3.50)-Elseworlds sketchbook.						3.50
.../ LOBO (2000, $5.95)-Elseworlds; Joker app.; Bisley-a						6.00
...: MASK OF THE PHANTASM (1994, $2.95)-Movie adapt.						3.00
...: MASK OF THE PHANTASM (1994, $4.95)-Movie adapt.						5.00
...: MASQUE (1997, $6.95)-Elseworlds; Grell-c/s/a						7.00
...: MASTER OF THE FUTURE nn (1991, $5.95, 68 pgs.)-Elseworlds; sequel to Gotham By Gaslight; Barreto-a; embossed-c						6.00
...: MITEFALL (1995, $4.95)-Alan Grant script, Kevin O'Neill-a						5.00
... : MR. FREEZE (1997, $4.95)-Dini-s/Buckingham-a; Stelfreeze-c; cover art interlocks w/Batman:(Bane, Batgirl, Poison Ivy)						5.00
... /NIGHTWING: BLOODBORNE (2002, $5.95) Cypress-a; McKeever-c						6.00
...: NOSFERATU (1999, $5.95) McKeever-a						6.00
...: OF ARKHAM (2000, $5.95)-Elseworlds; Grant-s/Alcatena-a						6.00
...: OUR WORLDS AT WAR (8/01, $2.95)-Jae Lee-c						3.00
...: PENGUIN TRIUMPHANT nn (1992, $4.95)-Staton-a(p); foil logo						5.00
...-PHANTOM STRANGER nn (1997, $4.95) nn-Grant-s/Ransom-a						5.00
... : PLUS (2/97, $2.95) Arsenal-c/app.						3.00
... : POISON IVY (1997, $4.95)-J.F. Moore-s/Apthorp-a; Stelfreeze-c; cover art interlocks w/Batman:(Bane, Batgirl, Mr. Freeze)						5.00
.../POISON IVY: CAST SHADOWS (2004, $6.95) Van Fleet-c/a; Nocenti-s						7.00
.../PUNISHER: LAKE OF FIRE (1994, $4.95, DC/Marvel)						5.00
... :REIGN OF TERROR ('99, $4.95) Elseworlds						5.00
...RETURNS MOVIE SPECIAL (1992, $3.95)						4.00
...RETURNS MOVIE PRESTIGE (1992, $5.95, squarebound)-Dorman painted-c						6.00
...:RIDDLER-THE RIDDLE FACTORY (1995, $4.95)-Wagner script						5.00
...: ROOM FULL OF STRANGERS (2004, $5.95) Scott Morse-s/c/a						6.00
...: SCARECROW 3-D (12/98, $3.95) w/glasses						4.00
.../ SCARFACE: A PSYCHODRAMA (2001, $5.95)-Adlard-a/Sienkiewicz-c						6.00
...: SCAR OF THE BAT nn (1996, $4.95)-Elseworlds; Max Allan Collins script; Barreto-a						5.00
... :SCOTTISH CONNECTION (1998, $5.95) Quitely-a						6.00
... :SEDUCTION OF THE GUN nn (1992, $2.50, 68 pgs.)						4.00
.../SPAWN: WAR DEVIL nn (1994, $4.95, 52 pgs.)						5.00
... SPECIAL 1 (4/84)-Mike W. Barr story; Golden-c/a	1	2	3	5	6	8
.../SPIDER-MAN (1997, $4.95) Dematteis-s/Nolan & Kesel-a						5.00
... : THE ABDUCTION ('98, $5.95)						6.00
...: THE BLUE, THE GREY, & THE BAT (1992, $5.95)-Weiss/Lopez-a						6.00
... :THE HILL (5/00, $2.95)-Priest-s/Martinbrough-a						3.00
... :THE KILLING JOKE (1988, deluxe 52 pgs., mature readers)-Bolland-c/a; Alan Moore scripts; Joker cripples Barbara Gordon	2	4	6	11	16	20
...: THE KILLING JOKE (2nd thru 11th printings)	2	4	6	8	10	12
...: THE KILLING JOKE : THE DELUXE EDITION (2008, $17.99, HC) re-colored version along with Bolland-s/a from Batman Black and White #4; sketch pages; Tim Sale intro.						18.00
...: THE MAN WHO LAUGHS (2005, $6.95)-Retells 1st meeting with the Joker; Mahnke-a						7.00
...: THE OFFICIAL COMIC ADAPTATION OF THE WARNER BROS. MOTION PICTURE (1989, $2.50, regular format, 68 pgs.)-Ordway-c						3.00
...: THE OFFICIAL COMIC ADAPTATION OF THE WARNER BROS. MOTION PICTURE (1989, $4.95, prestige format, 68 pgs.)-same interiors but different-c						5.00
...: THE ORDER OF BEASTS (2004, $5.95)-Elseworlds; Eddie Campbell-a						6.00
...: THE SPIRIT (1/07, $4.99)-Loeb-s/Cooke-a; P'Gell & Commissioner Dolan app.						5.00
...: THE 10-CENT ADVENTURE (3/02, 10¢) intro. to the "Bruce Wayne: Murderer" x-over; Rucka-s/Burchett & Janson-a/Dave Johnson-c						3.00

NOTE: (Also see Promotional Comics section for alternate copies with special outer half-covers promoting local comic shops)

	GD 2.0	VG 4.0	FN 6.0	VF 8.0	VF/NM 9.0	NM- 9.2
...: THE 12-CENT ADVENTURE (10/04, 12¢) intro. to the "War Games" x-over; Grayson-s/Bachs-a; Catwoman & Spoiler app.						3.00
...: TWO-FACE-CRIME AND PUNISHMENT-(1995, $4.95)-McDaniel-a						5.00
... : TWO FACES (11/98, $4.95) Elseworlds						5.00
...: VENGEANCE OF BANE SPECIAL 1 (1992, $2.50, 68 pgs.)-Origin & 1st app. Bane (see Batman #491)	2	4	6	8	10	12
...: VENGEANCE OF BANE SPECIAL 1 (2nd printing)						3.00
...:VENGEANCE OF BANE II nn (1995, $3.95)-sequel						4.00
...Vs. THE INCREDIBLE HULK (1995, $3.95)-r/DC Special Series #27						4.00
...: VILLAINS SECRET FILES (10/98, $4.95) Origin-s						5.00
... VILLAINS SECRET FILES AND ORIGINS 2005 (7/05, $4.99) Clayface origin w/ Mignola-a; Black Mask story, pin-up of villains by various; Barrionuevo-c						5.00

BATMAN ADVENTURES, THE (Based on animated series)
DC Comics: Oct, 1992 - No. 36, Oct, 1995 ($1.25/$1.50)

	GD 2.0	VG 4.0	FN 6.0	VF 8.0	VF/NM 9.0	NM- 9.2
1-Penguin-c/story						5.00
1 ($1.95, Silver Edition)-2nd printing						3.00
2-6,8-19: 2,12-Catwoman-c/story. 3-Joker-c/story. 5-Scarecrow-c/story. 10-Riddler-c/story. 11-Man-Bat-c/story. 12-Batgirl & Catwoman-c/story. 16-Joker-c/story; begin $1.50-c. 18-Batgirl-c/story. 19-Scarecrow-c/story.						3.50
7-Special edition polybagged with Man-Bat trading card						6.00
20-24,26-32: 26-Batgirl app.						3.00
25-($2.50, 52 pgs.)-Superman app.						4.00
33-36: 33-Begin $1.75-c						3.00
Annual 1,2 ('94, '95): 2-Demon-c/story; Ra's al Ghul app.						4.00
...: Dangerous Dames & Demons (2003, $14.95, TPB) r/Annual 1,2, Mad Love & Adventures in the DC Universe #3; Bruce Timm painted-c						30.00
Holiday Special 1 (1995, $2.95)						5.00
The Collected Adventures Vol. 1,2 ('93, '95, $5.95)						6.00
TPB ('98, $7.95) r/#1-6; painted wraparound-c						8.00

BATMAN ADVENTURES (Based on animated series)
DC Comics: Jun, 2003 - No. 17, Oct, 2004 ($2.25)

	GD 2.0	VG 4.0	FN 6.0	VF 8.0	VF/NM 9.0	NM- 9.2
1-Timm-c						3.00
1-Free Comic Book Day edition (6/03) Timm-c						3.00
2-17: 3,16-Joker-c/app. 4-Ra's al Ghul app. 6-8-Phantasm app. 14-Grey Ghost app.						3.00
Vol. 1: Rogues Gallery (2004, $6.95, digest size) r/#1-4 & Batman: Gotham Advs. #50						7.00
Vol. 2: Shadows & Masks (2004, $6.95, digest size) r/#5-9						7.00

BATMAN ADVENTURES, THE: MAD LOVE
DC Comics: Feb, 1994 ($3.95/$4.95)

	GD 2.0	VG 4.0	FN 6.0	VF 8.0	VF/NM 9.0	NM- 9.2
1-Origin of Harley Quinn; Dini-s/Timm-c/a	3	6	9	14	19	24
1-($4.95, Prestige format) new Timm painted-c	2	3	4	6	8	10

BATMAN ADVENTURES, THE: THE LOST YEARS (TV)
DC Comics: Jan, 1998 - No. 5, May, 1998 ($1.95) (Based on animated series)

	GD 2.0	VG 4.0	FN 6.0	VF 8.0	VF/NM 9.0	NM- 9.2
1-5-Leads into Fall '97's new animated episodes. 4-Tim Drake becomes Robin. 5-Dick becomes Nightwing						3.00
TPB-(1999, $9.95) r/series						10.00

BATMAN/ALIENS
DC Comics/Dark Horse: Mar, 1997 - No. 2, Apr, 1997 ($4.95, limited series)

	GD 2.0	VG 4.0	FN 6.0	VF 8.0	VF/NM 9.0	NM- 9.2
1,2: Wrightson-c/a.						5.00
TPB-(1997, $14.95) w/prequel from DHP #101,102						15.00

BATMAN/ALIENS II
DC Comics/Dark Horse: 2003 - No. 3, 2003 ($5.95, limited series)

	GD 2.0	VG 4.0	FN 6.0	VF 8.0	VF/NM 9.0	NM- 9.2
1-3-Edginton-s/Staz Johnson-a						6.00
TPB-(2003, $14.95) r/#1-3						15.00

BATMAN AND ROBIN (See Batman R.I.P. and Batman: Battle For The Cowl series)
DC Comics: Aug, 2009 - Present ($2.99)

	GD 2.0	VG 4.0	FN 6.0	VF 8.0	VF/NM 9.0	NM- 9.2
1-Grant Morrison-s/Frank Quitely-a/c; Dick Grayson & Damian Wayne team						5.00
1-Variant cover by J.G. Jones						20.00
1-Second thru Fourth printings - recolored Quitely covers						3.00
2-16-Quitely-c. 2-Three printings. 4-6-Tan-a. 7-9-Stewart-a; Batwoman & Squire app. 13-15-Joker app.; Irving-a. 16-Bruce Wayne returns; Batman Inc. announced						3.00
2-Variant-c by Adam Kubert						10.00
17-21: 17-McDaniel-a/March-c. 21-Gleason-a						3.00
... #1 Special Edition (6/10, $1.00) r/#1 with "What's Next?" cover logo						1.00
...: Batman Reborn - The Deluxe Edition HC (2010, $24.99) r/#1-6; design sketch art						25.00
...: Batman Reborn SC (2011, $14.99) r/#1-6; cover and character design sketch art						15.00
...: Batman vs. Robin - The Deluxe Edition HC (2010, $24.99) r/#7-12; cover sketch art						25.00

Batman Beyond (2010 series) #1 © DC

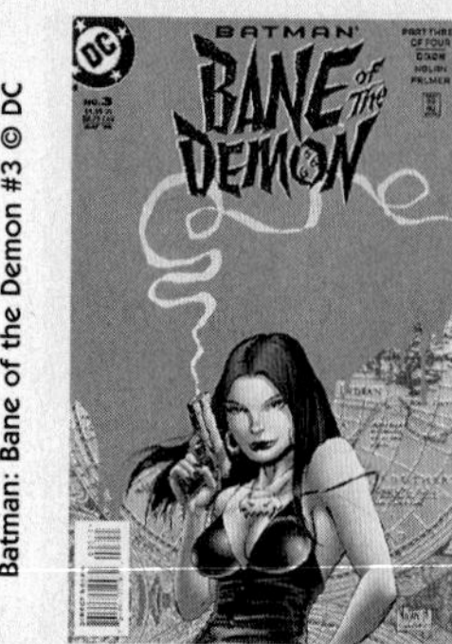

Batman: Bane of the Demon #3 © DC

Batman Confidential #31 © DC

GD VG FN VF VF/NM NM-
2.0 4.0 6.0 8.0 9.0 9.2

BATMAN AND ROBIN ADVENTURES (TV)
DC Comics: Nov, 1995 - No. 25, Dec, 1997 ($1.75) (Based on animated series)

1-Dini-s. 4.00
2-24: 2-4-Dini script. 4-Penguin-c/story. 5-Joker-c/story; Poison Ivy, Harley Quinn-c/app. 9-Batgirl & Talia-c/story. 10-Ra's al Ghul-c/story. 11-Man-Bat app. 12-Bane-c/app. 13-Scarecrow-c/app. 15 Deadman-c/app. 16-Catwoman-c/app. 18-Joker-c/app. 24-Poison Ivy app. 3.00
25-($2.95, 48 pgs.) 4.00
Annual 1,2 (11/96, 11/97): 1-Phantasm-c/app. 2-Zatara & Zatanna-c/app. 4.00
...: Sub-Zero(1998, $3.95) Adaptation of animated video 4.00

BATMAN AND SUPERMAN ADVENTURES: WORLD'S FINEST
DC Comics: 1997 ($6.95, square-bound, one-shot) (Based on animated series)

1-Adaptation of animated crossover episode; Dini-s/Timm-c. 7.00

BATMAN AND SUPERMAN: WORLD'S FINEST
DC Comics: Apr, 1999 - No. 10, Jan, 2000 ($4.95/$1.99, limited series)

1,10-($4.95, squarebound) Taylor-a 5.00
2-9-($1.99) 5-Batgirl app. 8-Catwoman-c/app. 3.00
TPB (2003, $19.95) r/#1-10 20.00

BATMAN AND THE OUTSIDERS (The Adventures of the Outsiders #33 on)
(Also see Brave & The Bold #200 & The Outsiders) (Replaces The Brave and the Bold)
DC Comics: Aug, 1983 - No. 32, Apr, 1986 (Mando paper #5 on)

1-Batman, Halo, Geo-Force, Katana, Metamorpho & Black Lightning begin 5.00
2-32: 5-New Teen Titans x-over. 9-Halo begins. 11,12-Origin Katana. 18-More info on Metamorpho's origin. 28-31-Lookers origin. 32-Team disbands 3.00
Annual 1,2 (9/84, 9/85): 2-Metamorpho & Sapphire Stagg wed 4.00
NOTE: ***Aparo** a-1-9, 11-13p, 16-20; c-1-4, 5i, 6-21, Annual 1, 2.* ***B. Kane** a-3r.* ***Layton** a-19i, 20i.* ***Lopez** a-3p.* ***Miller** c-Annual 1.* ***Perez** c-5p.* ***B. Willingham** a-14p.*

BATMAN AND THE OUTSIDERS (Resumes as The Outsiders with #15)
DC Comics: Dec, 2007 - No. 14, Feb, 2009 ($2.99)

1-14: 1-Batman, Catwoman, Martian Manhunter, Katana, Metamorpho, Thunder & Grace begin. 4-Batgirl joins. 11-13-Batman R.I.P. 3.00
... Special (3/09, $3.99) Alfred assembles a new team; Andy Kubert-a; two covers 4.00
...: The Chrysalis TPB (2008, $14.99) r/#1-5 15.00
...: The Snare TPB (2008, $14.99) r/#6-10 15.00

BATMAN: BANE OF THE DEMON
DC Comics: Mar, 1998 - No. 4, June, 1998 ($1.95, limited series)

1-4-Dixon-s/Nolan-a; prelude to Legacy x-over 3.00

BATMAN: BATTLE FOR THE COWL (Follows Batman R.I.P. storyline)
DC Comics: May, 2009 - No. 3, Jul, 2009 ($3.99, limited series)

1-3-Tony Daniel-s/a/c; 2 covers on each 4.00
...: Arkham Asylum (6/09, $2.99) Hine-s/Haun-a/Ladronn-c 3.00
...: Commissioner Gordon (5/09, $2.99) Mandrake-a/Ladronn-c; Mr. Freeze app. 3.00
...: Man-Bat (6/09, $2.99) Harris-s/Calafiore-a/Ladronn-c; Dr. Phosphorus app. 3.00
...: The Network (7/09, $2.99) Nicieza-s/Calafiore & Kramer-a/Ladronn-c 3.00
...: The Underground (6/09, $2.99) Yost-s/Raimondi-a/Ladronn-c 3.00
Companion SC (2009, $14.99) r/ five one-shots 15.00
HC (2009, $19.99) r/#1-3 & Gotham Gazette: Batman Dead & Gotham Gazette: Batman Alive; gallery of variant covers and sketch art 20.00
SC (2010, $14.99) same contents as HC 15.00

BATMAN BEYOND (Based on animated series)
DC Comics: Mar, 1999 - No. 6, Aug, 1999 ($1.99, limited series)

1-6: 1,2-Adaptation of pilot episode, Timm-c 3.00
TPB (1999, $9.95) r/#1-6 10.00

BATMAN BEYOND (Based on animated series)(Continuing series)
DC Comics: Nov, 1999 - No. 24, Oct, 2001 ($1.99)

1-24: 1-Rousseau-a; Batman vs. Batman. 14-Demon-c/app. 21,22-Justice League Unlimited-c/app. 3.00
...: Return of the Joker (2/01, $2.95) adaptation of video release 4.00

BATMAN BEYOND (Animated series)(See Superman/Batman Annual #4)
DC Comics: Aug, 2010 - No. 6, Jan, 2011 ($2.99, limited series)

1-6: 1-Benjamin-a; Nguyen-c; return of Hush 3.00
1-Variant-c by J.H. Williams III 6.00
...: Hush Beyond TPB (2011, $14.99) r/#1-6 15.00

BATMAN BEYOND
DC Comics: Mar, 2011 - Present ($2.99)

1-3-Justice League app.; Beechen-s/Benjamin-a/Nguyen-c 3.00
1-Variant-c by Darwyn Cooke 4.00

GD VG FN VF VF/NM NM-
2.0 4.0 6.0 8.0 9.0 9.2

BATMAN: BLACK & WHITE
DC Comics: June, 1996 - No. 4, Sept, 1996 ($2.95, B&W, limited series)

1-Stories by McKeever, Timm, Kubert, Chaykin, Goodwin; Jim Lee-c; Allred inside front-c; Moebius inside back-c 4.00
2-4: 2-Stories by Simonson, Corben, Bisley & Gaiman; Miller-c. 3-Stories by M. Wagner, Janson, Sienkiewicz, O'Neil & Kristiansen; B. Smith-c; Russell inside front-c; Silvestri inside back-c. 4-Stories by Bolland, Goodwin & Gianni, Strnad & Nowlan, O'Neil & Stelfreeze; Toth-c; pin-ups by Neal Adams & Alex Ross 3.00
Hardcover ('97, $39.95) r/series w/new art & cover plate 40.00
Softcover ('00, $19.95) r/series 20.00
Volume 2 HC ('02, $39.95, 7 3/4"x12") r/B&W back-up-s from Batman: Gotham Knights #1-16; stories and art by various incl. Ross, Buscema, Byrne, Ellison, Sale; Mignola-c 40.00
Volume 2 SC ('03, $19.95, 7 3/4"x12") same contents as HC 20.00
Volume 2 SC ('08, $19.99, reg. size) same contents as HC 20.00
Volume 3 HC ('07, $24.99, reg. size) r/B&W back-up-s from Batman: Gotham Knights #17-49; stories and art by various incl. Davis, DeCarlo, Morse, Schwartz, Thompson; Miller-c 25.00

BATMAN: BOOK OF THE DEAD
DC Comics: Jun, 1999 - No. 2, July, 1999 ($4.95, limited series, prestige format)

1,2-Elseworlds; Kitson-a 5.00

BATMAN CACOPHONY
DC Comics: Jan, 2009 - No. 3, Mar, 2009 ($3.99, limited series)

1-3-Kevin Smith-s/Walt Flanagan-a; Joker and Onomatoapoeia app.; Adam Kubert-c 4.00
1-3-Variant-c by Sienkiewicz 10.00
HC (2009, $19.99, d.j.) r/#1-3; Kevin Smith intro.; script for #3, cover gallery 20.00
SC (2010, $14.99) r/#1-3; Kevin Smith intro.; script for #3, cover gallery 15.00

BATMAN: CATWOMAN DEFIANT (See Batman one-shots)

BATMAN/ CATWOMAN: TRAIL OF THE GUN
DC Comics: 2004 - No. 2, 2004 ($5.95, limited series, prestige format)

1,2-Elseworlds; Van Sciver-a/Nocenti-s 6.00

BATMAN CHRONICLES, THE (See the Batman TPB listings for the Golden Age reprint series that shares this title)
DC Comics: Summer, 1995 - No. 23, Winter, 2001 ($2.95, quarterly)

1-3,5-19: 1-Dixon/Grant/Moench script. 3-Bolland-c. 5-Oracle Year One story, Richard Dragon app.,Chaykin-c. 6-Kaluta-c; Ra's al Ghul story. 7-Superman-c/app.11-Paul Pope-s/a. 12-Cataclysm pt. 10. 18-No Man's Land 3.50
4-Hitman story by Ennis, Contagion tie-in; Balent-c 2 4 6 8 10 12
20-23: 20-Catwoman and Relative Heroes-c/app. 21-Pander Bros.-a 3.00
...Gallery (3/97, $3.50) Pin-ups 3.50
...Gauntlet, The (1997, $4.95, one-shot) 5.00

BATMAN: CITY OF LIGHT
DC Comics: Dec, 2003 - No. 8, July, 2004 ($2.95, limited series)

1-8-Pander Brothers-a/s; Paniccia-s 3.00

BATMAN CONFIDENTIAL
DC Comics: Feb, 2007 - Present ($2.99)

1-49,51-54: 1-6-Diggle-s/Portacio-a/c. 7-12-Cowan-a; Joker's origin. 13-16-Morales-a. 17-21-Batgirl vs. Catwoman; Maguire-a. 22-25-McDaniel-a; Joker app. 26-28-King Tut app.; Garcia-Lopez-a. 40-43-Kieth-s/a. 44-48-Mandrake-a/c 3.00
50-($4.99) Bingham-a; back-up Silver Age-style JLA story 5.00
...: Dead to Rights SC (2010, $14.99) r/#22-25,29,30 15.00
...: Lovers and Madmen HC (2008, $24.99, dustjacket) r/#7-12; Brad Meltzer intro. 25.00
...: Lovers and Madmen SC (2009, $14.99) r/#7-12; Brad Meltzer intro. 15.00
...: Rules of Engagement HC (2007, $24.99, dustjacket) r/#1-6 25.00
...: The Bat and the Beast SC (2010, $12.99) r/#31-35 13.00
...: The Cat and the Bat SC (2009, $12.99) r/#17-21 13.00
...: Vs. The Undead SC (2010, $14.99) r/#44-48 15.00

BATMAN: DARK DETECTIVE
DC Comics: Early July, 2005 - No. 6, Late September, 2005 ($2.99, limited series)

1-6-Englehart-s/Rogers & Austin-a; Silver St. Cloud and The Joker app. 3.00

BATMAN: DARK KNIGHT OF THE ROUND TABLE
DC Comics: 1999 - No. 2, 1999 ($4.95, limited series, prestige format)

1,2-Elseworlds; Giordano-a 5.00

BATMAN: DARK VICTORY
DC Comics: 1999 - No. 13, 2000 ($4.95/$2.95, limited series)

Wizard #0 Preview 3.00
1-($4.95) Loeb-s/Sale-c/a 5.00
2-12-($2.95) 3.00
13-($4.95) 5.00
Hardcover (2001, $29.95) with dust jacket; r/#0,1-13 30.00

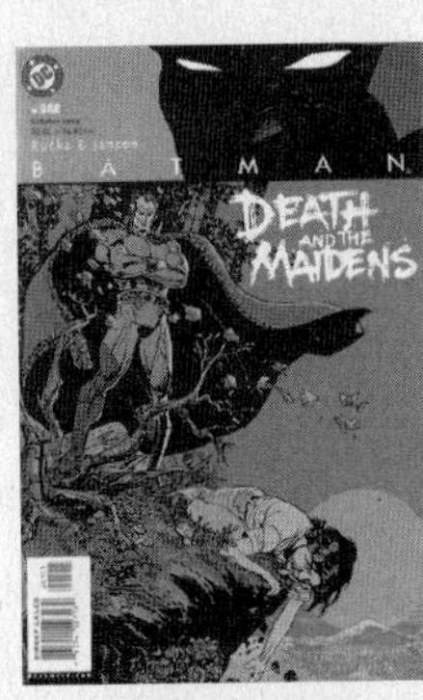

Batman: Death and the Maidens #1 © DC

Batman: Gotham Adventures #35 © DC

Batman, Inc. #1 © DC

GD 2.0 | VG 4.0 | FN 6.0 | VF 8.0 | VF/NM 9.0 | NM- 9.2

Softcover (2002, $19.95) r/#0,1-13 20.00

BATMAN: DEATH AND THE MAIDENS
DC Comics: Oct, 2003 - No. 9, Aug, 2004 ($2.95, limited series)

1-Ra's al Ghul app.; Rucka-s/Janson-a 4.00
2-9: 9-Ra's al Ghul dies 3.00
TPB (2004, $19.95) r/#1-9 & Detective #783 20.00

BATMAN/ DEATHBLOW: AFTER THE FIRE
DC Comics/WildStorm: 2002 - No. 3, 2002 ($5.95, limited series)

1-3-Azzarello-s/Bermejo & Bradstreet-a 6.00
TPB (2003, $12.95) r/#1-3; plus concept art 13.00

BATMAN: DEATH MASK
DC Comics/CMX: Jun, 2008 - No. 4, Sept, 2008 ($2.99, B&W, limited series, right-to-left manga style)

1-4-Yoshinori Natsume-s/a 3.00
TPB (2008, $9.99, digest size) r/#1-4; interview with Yoshinori Natsume 10.00

BATMAN FAMILY, THE
National Periodical Pub./DC Comics: Sept-Oct, 1975 - No. 20, Oct-Nov, 1978 (#1-4, 17-on: 68 pgs.) (Combined with Detective Comics with No. 481)

1-Origin/2nd app. Batgirl-Robin team-up (The Dynamite Duo); reprints plus one new story begins; N. Adams-a(r); r/1st app. Man-Bat from Det. #400
4 8 12 26 41 55
2-5: 2-r/Det. #369. 3-Batgirl & Robin learn each's i.d.; r/Batwoman app. from Batman #105. 4-r/1st Fatman app. from Batman #113. 5-r/1st Bat-Hound app. from Batman #92
3 6 9 16 23 30
6,9-Joker's daughter on cover (1st app?) 3 6 9 17 25 32
7,8,14-16: 8-r/Batwoman app.14-Batwoman app. 15-3rd app. Killer Moth. 16-Bat-Girl cameo (last app. in costume until New Teen Titans #47) 2 4 6 13 18 22
10-1st revival Batwoman; Cavalier app.; Killer Moth app.
3 6 9 19 29 38
11-13,17-20: 11-13-Rogers-a(p): 11-New stories begin; Man-Bat begins. 13-Batwoman cameo. 17-($1.00 size)-Batman, Huntress begin; Batwoman & Catwoman 1st meet. 18-20: Huntress by Staton in all. 20-Origin Ragman retold
3 6 9 18 27 35

NOTE: ***Aparo** a-17; c-11-16.* ***Austin** a-12i.* ***Chaykin** a-14p.* ***Michael Golden** a-15-17,18-20p.* ***Grell** a-1; c-1.* ***Gil Kane** a-2r.* ***Kaluta** c-17, 19.* ***Newton** a-13.* ***Robinson** a-1r, 3i(r), 9r.* ***Russell** a-18i, 19i.* ***Starlin** a-17; c-18, 20.*

BATMAN: FAMILY
DC Comics: Dec, 2002 - No. 8, Feb, 2003 ($2.95/$2.25, weekly limited series)

1,8-($2.95). John Francis Moore-s/Hoberg & Gaudiano-a 3.00
2-7-($2.25). 3-Orpheus & Black Canary app. 3.00

BATMAN: GCPD
DC Comics: Aug, 1996 - No. 4, Nov, 1996 ($2.25, limited series)

1-4: Features Jim Gordon; Aparo/Sienkiewicz-a 3.00

BATMAN: GORDON OF GOTHAM
DC Comics: June, 1998 - No. 4, Sept, 1998 ($1.95, limited series)

1-4: Gordon's early days in Chicago 3.00

BATMAN: GORDON'S LAW
DC Comics: Dec, 1996 - No. 4, Mar, 1997 ($1.95, limited series)

1-4: Dixon-s/Janson-c/a 3.00

BATMAN: GOTHAM ADVENTURES (TV)
DC Comics: June, 1998 - No. 60, May, 2003 ($2.95/$1.95/$1.99/$2.25)

1-($2.95) Based on Kids WB Batman animated series 4.00
2-3-($1.95): 2-Two-Face-c/app. 3.00
4-22: 4-Begin $1.99-c. 5-Deadman-c. 13-MAD #1 cover swipe 3.00
23-60: 31,60-Joker-c/app. 50-Catwoman-c/app. 53-Begin $2.25-c. 58-Creeper-c/app. 3.00
TPB (2000, $9.95) r/#1-6 10.00

BATMAN: GOTHAM AFTER MIDNIGHT
DC Comics: July, 2008 - No. 12, Jun, 2009 ($2.99, limited series)

1-12-Steve Niles-s/Kelley Jones-a/c. 1-Scarecrow app. 2-Man-Bat app. 5,6-Joker app. 3.00
TPB (2009, $19.99) r/#1-12; John Carpenter intro.; Jones sketch pages 20.00

BATMAN: GOTHAM COUNTY LINE
DC Comics: 2005 - No. 3, 2005 ($5.99, square-bound, limited series)

1-3-Steve Niles-s/Scott Hampton-a. 2,3-Deadman app. 6.00
TPB (2006, $17.99) r/#1-3 18.00

BATMAN: GOTHAM KNIGHTS
DC Comics: Mar, 2000 - No. 74, Apr, 2006 ($2.50/$2.75)

1-Grayson-s; B&W back-up by Warren Ellis & Jim Lee 4.00
2-10-Grayson-s; B&W back-ups by various 3.0

GD 2.0 | VG 4.0 | FN 6.0 | VF 8.0 | VF/NM 9.0 | NM- 9.2

11-($3.25) Bolland-c; Kyle Baker back-up story 3.25
12-24: 13-Officer Down x-over; Ellison back-up-s. 15-Colan back-up. 20-Superman-c/app. 3.00
25,26-Bruce Wayne: Murderer pt. 4,10 3.50
27-31: 28,30,31-Bruce Wayne: Fugitive pt. 7,14,17 3.00
32-49: 32-Begin $2.75-c; Kaluta-a back-up. 33,34-Bane-c/app. 35-Mahfood-a back-up. 38-Bolton-a back-up. 43-Jason Todd & Batgirl app. 44-Jason Todd flashback 3.00
50-54-Hush returns-Barrionuevo-a/Bermejo-c. 53,54-Green Arrow app. 4.00
55-($3.75) Batman vs. Hush; Joker & Riddler app. 4.00
56-74: 56-58-War Games; Jae Lee-c. 60-65-Hush app. 66-Villains United tie-in; Talia app. 3.00
Batman: Hush Returns TPB (2006, $12.99) r/#50-55,66; cover gallery 13.00

BATMAN: GOTHAM NIGHTS II (First series listed under Gotham Nights)
DC Comics: Mar, 1995 - No. 4, June, 1995 ($1.95, limited series)

1-4 3.00

BATMAN/GRENDEL (1st limited series)
DC Comics: 1993 - No. 2, 1993 ($4.95, limited series, squarebound; 52 pgs.)

1,2: Batman vs. Hunter Rose. 1-Devil's Riddle; Matt Wagner-c/a/scripts. 2-Devil's Masque; Matt Wagner-c/a/scripts 6.00

BATMAN/GRENDEL (2nd limited series)
DC Comics: June, 1996 - No. 2, July, 1996 ($4.95, limited series, squarebound)

1,2: Batman vs. Grendel Prime. 1-Devil's Bones. 2-Devil's Dance; Wagner-c/a/s 5.00

BATMAN: HARLEY & IVY
DC Comics: Jun, 2004 - No. 3, Aug, 2004 ($2.50, limited series)

1-3-Paul Dini-s/Bruce Timm-c/a 3.00
TPB (2007, $14.99) r/series; newly colored story from Batman: Gotham Knights #14 and Harley and Ivy: Love on the Lam series 15.00

BATMAN: HARLEY QUINN
DC Comics: 1999 ($5.95, prestige format)

1-Intro. of Harley Quinn into regular DC continuity; Dini-s/Alex Ross-c 9.00
1-(2nd printing) 6.00

BATMAN: HAUNTED GOTHAM
DC Comics: 2000 - No. 4, 2000 ($4.95, limited series, squarebound)

1-4-Doug Moench-s/Kelley Jones-c/a 5.00
TPB (2009, $19.99) r/#1-4 13.00

BATMAN/ HELLBOY/STARMAN
DC Comics/Dark Horse: Jan, 1999 - No. 2, Feb, 1999 ($2.50, limited series)

1,2: Robinson-s/Mignola-a. 2-Harris-c 3.00

BATMAN: HOLLYWOOD KNIGHT
DC Comics: Apr, 2001 - No. 3, Jun, 2001 ($2.50, limited series)

1-3-Elseworlds Batman as a 1940's movie star; Giordano-a/Layton-s 3.00

BATMAN/ HUNTRESS: CRY FOR BLOOD
DC Comics: Jun, 2000 - No. 6, Nov, 2000 ($2.50, limited series)

1-6: Rucka-s/Burchett-a; The Question app. 3.00
TPB (2002, $12.95) r/#1-6 13.00

BATMAN, INC.
DC Comics: Jan, 2011 - Present ($3.99/$2.99)

1-3-Morrison-s/Paquette-a; covers by Paquette & Williams 4.00
4-($2.99) Burnham-a, original Batwoman (Kathy Kane) app. 3.00

BATMAN: JEKYLL & HYDE
DC Comics: June, 2005 - No. 6, Nov, 2005 ($2.99, limited series)

1-6-Paul Jenkins-s; Two-Face app. 1-3-Jae Lee-a. 4-6-Sean Phillips-a 3.00
TPB (2008, $14.99) r/#1-6 15.00

BATMAN: JOKER TIME (...: It's Joker Time! on cover)
DC Comics: 2000 - No. 3 ($4.95, limited series, squarebound)

1-3-Bob Hall-s/a 5.00

BATMAN: JOURNEY INTO KNGHT
DC Comics: Oct, 2005 - No. 12, Nov, 2006 ($2.50/$2.99, limited series)

1-9-Andrew Helfer-s/Tan Eng Huat-a/Pat Lee-c 3.00
10-12-($2.99) Joker app. 3.00

BATMAN/ JUDGE DREDD "DIE LAUGHING"
DC Comics: 1998 - No. 2, 1999 ($4.95, limited series, squarebound)

1,2: 1-Fabry-c/a. 2-Jim Murray-c/a 5.00

BATMAN: KNIGHTGALLERY (See Batman one-shots)

BATMAN: LEAGUE OF BATMEN
DC Comics: 2001 - No. 2, 2001 ($5.95, limited series, squarebound)

Batman: Legends of the Dark Knight #121 © DC

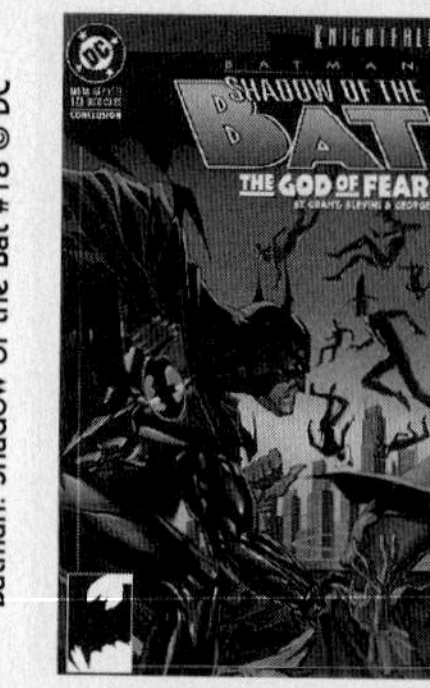

Batman: Shadow of the Bat #18 © DC

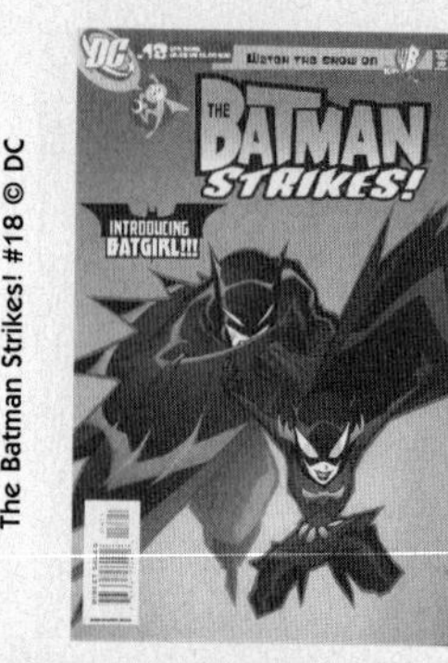

The Batman Strikes! #18 © DC

GD VG FN VF VF/NM NM-
2.0 4.0 6.0 8.0 9.0 9.2

1,2-Elseworlds; Moench-s/Bright & Tanghal-a/Van Fleet-c 6.00

BATMAN: LEGENDS OF THE DARK KNIGHT (Legends of the Dark...#1-36)
DC Comics: Nov, 1989 - No. 214, Mar, 2007 ($1.50/$1.75/$1.95/$1.99/$2.25/$2.50/$2.99)

1- "Shaman" begins, ends #5; outer cover has four different color variations, all worth same 4.00
2-10: 6-10- "Gothic" by Grant Morrison (scripts) 3.00
11-15: 11-15-Gulacy/Austin-a. 13-Catwoman app. 3.00
16-Intro drug Bane uses; begin Venom story 5.00
17-20 4.00
21-49,51-63: 38-Bat-Mite-c/story. 46-49-Catwoman app. w/Heath-c/a. 51-Ragman app.; Joe Kubert-c. 59,60,61-Knightquest x-over. 62,63-KnightsEnd Pt. 4 & 10 3.00
50-($3.95, 68 pgs.)-Bolland embossed gold foil-c; Joker-c/story; pin-ups by Chaykin, Simonson, Williamson, Kaluta, Russell, others 5.00
64-99: 64-(9/94)-Begin $1.95-c. 71-73-James Robinson-s,Watkiss-c/a. 74,75-McKeever-c/a/s. 76-78-Scott Hampton-c/a/s. 81-Card insert. 83,84-Ellis-s. 85-Robinson-s. 91-93-Ennis-s. 94-Michael T. Gilbert-s/a. 3.00
100-($3.95) Alex Ross painted-c; gallery by various 5.00
101-115: 101-Ezquerra-a. 102-104-Robinson-s 3.00
116-No Man's Land stories begin; Huntress-c 4.00
117-119,121-126: 122-Harris-c 3.00
120-ID of new Batgirl revealed 4.00
127-131: Return to Legends stories; Green Arrow app. 3.00
132-199, 201-204: 132-136 ($2.25-c) Archie Goodwin-s/Rogers-a. 137-141-Gulacy-a. 142-145-Joker and Ra's al Ghul app. 146-148-Kitson-a. 158-Begin $2.50-c 169-171-Tony Harris-c/a. 182-184-War Games. 182-Bagged with Sky Captain CD 3.00
200-($4.99) Joker-c/app. 5.00
205-214: 205-Begin $2.99-c. 207,208-Olivetti-a. 214-Deadshot app. 3.00
#0-(10/94)-Zero Hour; Quesada/Palmiotti-c; released between #64&65 3.00
Annual 1-7 ('91-'97, $3.50-$3.95, 68 pgs.): 1-Joker app. 2-Netzer-c/a. 3-New Batman (Azrael) app. 4-Elseworlds story. 5-Year One; Man-Bat app. 6-Legend of the Dead Earth story. 7-Pulp Heroes story 4.00
Halloween Special 1 (12/93, $6.95, 84 pgs.)-Embossed & foil stamped-c 1 2 3 4 5 7
Batman Madness-...Halloween Special (1994, $4.95) 5.00
Batman Ghosts-...Halloween Special (1995, $4.95) 5.00

NOTE: *Aparo a-Annual 1.* ***Chaykin*** *scripts-24-26.* ***Giffen*** *a-Annual 1.* ***Golden*** *a-Annual 1.* ***Alan Grant*** *scripts-38, 52, 53.* ***Gil Kane*** *c/a-24-26.* ***Mignola*** *a-54; c-54, 62.* ***Morrow*** *a-Annual 3i.* ***Quesada*** *a-Annual 1.* ***James Robinson*** *scripts- 71-73.* ***Russell*** *c/a-42, 43.* ***Sears*** *a-21, 23; c-21, 23.* ***Zeck*** *a-69, 70; c-69, 70.*

BATMAN-LEGENDS OF THE DARK KNIGHT: JAZZ
DC Comics: Apr, 1995 - No. 3, June, 1995 ($2.50, limited series)

1-3 3.00

BATMAN/LOBO
DC Comics: Oct, 2007 - No. 2, Nov, 2007 ($5.99, squarebound, limited series)

1,2-Sam Kieth-s/a 6.00

BATMAN: MANBAT
DC Comics: Oct, 1995 - No. 3, Dec, 1995 ($4.95, limited series)

1-3-Elseworlds-Delano-script; Bolton-a. 5.00
TPB-(1997, $14.95) r/#1-3 15.00

BATMAN: MITEFALL (See Batman one-shots)

BATMAN MINIATURE (See Batman Kellogg's)

BATMAN: NEVERMORE
DC Comics: June, 2003 - No. 5, Oct, 2003 ($2.50, limited series)

1-5-Elseworlds Batman & Edgar Allan Poe; Wrightson-c/Guy Davis-a/Len Wein-s 3.00

BATMAN: NO MAN'S LAND (Also see 1999 Batman titles)
DC Comics: (one shots)

nn (3/99, $2.95) Alex Ross-c; Bob Gale-s; begins year-long story arc 3.00
Collector's Ed. (3/99, $3.95) Ross lenticular-c 5.00
#0 (: Ground Zero on cover) (12/99, $4.95) Orbik-c 5.00
...: Gallery (7/99, $3.95) Jim Lee-c 4.00
...: Secret Files (12/99, $4.95) Maleev-c 5.00
TPB ('99, $12.95) r/early No Man's Land stories; new Batgirl early app. 13.00
No Law and a New Order TPB(1999, $5.95) Ross-c 6.00
Volume 2 ('00, $12.95) r/later No Man's Land stories; Batgirl(Huntress) app.; Deodato-c 13.00
Volume 3-5 ('00,'01 $12.95) 3-Intro. new Batgirl. 4-('00). 5-('01) Land-c 13.00

BATMAN: ODYSSEY
DC Comics: Sept, 2010 - No. 12 ($3.99, limited series)

1-6-Neal Adams-s/a/c. 1-Man-Bat app.; bonus sketch pages. 5,6-Joker app. 4.00
1-2-Variant B&W-version cover 5.00

BATMAN: ORPHANS
DC Comics: Early Feb, 2011 - No. 2, Late Feb, 2011 ($3.99, limited series)

1,2-Berganza-s/Barberi-a/c 4.00

BATMAN: ORPHEUS RISING
DC Comics: Oct, 2001 - No. 5, Feb, 2002 ($2.50, limited series)

1-5-Intro. Orpheus; Simmons-s/Turner & Miki-a 3.00

BATMAN: OUTLAWS
DC Comics: 2000 - No. 3, 2000 ($4.95, limited series)

1-3-Moench-s/Gulacy-a 5.00

BATMAN: PENGUIN TRIUMPHANT (See Batman one-shots)

BATMAN/PREDATOR III: BLOOD TIES
DC Comics/Dark Horse Comics: Nov, 1997 - No. 4, Feb, 1998 ($1.95, lim. series)

1-4: Dixon-s/Damaggio-c/a 3.00
TPB-(1998, $7.95) r/#1-4 8.00

BATMAN/RA'S AL GHUL (See Year One:...)

BATMAN RETURNS MOVIE SPECIAL (See Batman one-shots)

BATMAN: RIDDLER-THE RIDDLE FACTORY (See Batman one-shots)

BATMAN: RUN, RIDDLER, RUN
DC Comics: 1992 - Book 3, 1992 ($4.95, limited series)

Book 1-3: Mark Badger-a & plot 5.00

BATMAN SCARECROW (See Year One:...)

BATMAN: SECRET FILES
DC Comics: Oct, 1997 ($4.95)

1-New origin-s and profiles 5.00

BATMAN: SECRETS
DC Comics: May, 2006 - No. 5, Sept, 2006 ($2.99, limited series)

1-5-Sam Kieth-s/a/c; Joker app. 3.00
TPB (2007, $12.99) r/series 13.00

BATMAN: SHADOW OF THE BAT
DC Comics: June, 1992 - No. 94, Feb, 2000 ($1.50/$1.75/$1.95/$1.99)

1-The Last Arkham-c/story begins; Alan Grant scripts in all 4.00
1-($2.50)-Deluxe edition polybagged w/poster, pop-up & book mark 5.00
2-7: 4-The Last Arkham ends. 7-Last $1.50-c 3.00
8-28: 14,15-Staton-a(p). 16-18-Knightfall tie-ins. 19-28-Knightquest tie-ins w/Azrael as Batman. 25-Silver ink-c; anniversary issue 3.00
29-($2.95, 52 pgs.)-KnightsEnd Pt. 2 4.00
30-72: 30-KnightsEnd Pt. 8. 31-(9.94)-Begin $1.95-c; Zero Hour. 32-(11/94). 33-Robin-c. 35-Troika-Pt.2. 43,44-Cat-Man & Catwoman-c. 48-Contagion Pt. 1; card insert. 49-Contagion Pt.7. 56,57,58-Poison Ivy-c/app. 62-Two-Face app. 69,70-Fate app. 3.00
35-($2.95)-Variant embossed-c 4.00
73,74,76-78: Cataclysm x-over pts. 1,9. 76-78-Orbik-c 3.00
75-($2.95) Mr. Freeze & Clayface app.; Orbik-c 4.00
79,81,82: 79-Begin $1.99-c; Orbik-c 3.00
80-($3.95) Flip book with Azrael #47 4.00
83-No Man's Land; intro. new Batgirl (Huntress) 12.00
84,85-No Man's Land 4.00
86-94: 87-Deodato-a. 90-Harris-c. 92-Superman app. 93-Joker and Harley app. 94-No Man's Land ends 3.00
#0 (10/94) Zero Hour; released between #31&32 3.00
#1,000,000 (11/98) 853rd Century x-over; Orbik-c 3.00
Annual 1-5 ('93-'97 $2.95-$3.95, 68 pgs.): 3-Year One story; Poison Ivy app. 4-Legends of the Dead Earth story; Starman cameo. 5-Pulp Heroes story; Poison Ivy app. 4.00

BATMAN: SON OF THE DEMON (Also see Batman #655-658 and Batman Hardcovers)
DC Comics: 2006 ($5.99, reprints the 1987 HC in comic book format)

nn-Talia has Batman's son; Mike W. Barr-s/Jerry Bingham-a; new Andy Kubert-c 6.00

BATMAN-SPAWN: WAR DEVIL (See Batman one-shots)

BATMAN SPECTACULAR (See DC Special Series No. 15)

BATMAN: STREETS OF GOTHAM (Follows Batman: Battle For The Cowl series)
DC Comics: Aug, 2009 - Present ($3.99$2.99)

1-18: 1-Dini-s/Nguyen-a; back-up Manhunter feature; Jeanty-a. 10,11-Zsasz app. 4.00
19-21-($2.99) 19-Joker app. 3.00
...- Hush Money HC (2010, $19.99) r/#1-4, Detective #852 and Batman #685 20.00
...- Leviathan HC (2010, $19.99) r/#5-11 20.00

BATMAN STRIKES!, THE (Based on the 2004 animated series)
DC Comics: Nov, 2004 - No. 50, Dec, 2008 ($2.25)

1,2,4-50: 1,11-Penguin app. 2-Man-Bat app. 4-Bane app. 9-Joker app. 18-Batgirl debut.

Batman/Superman/Wonder Woman: Trinity HC © DC

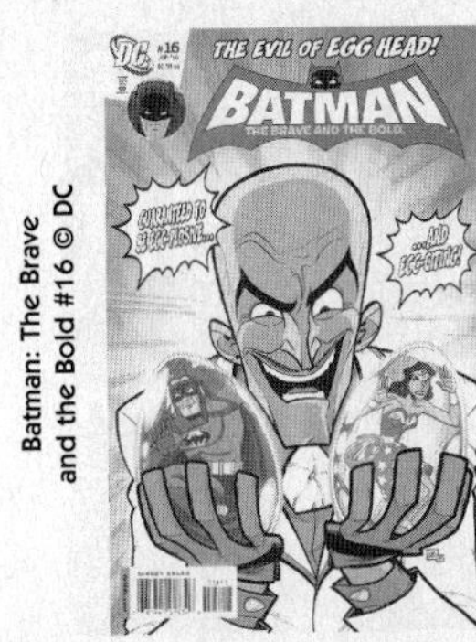

Batman: The Brave and the Bold #16 © DC

Batman: The Return of Bruce Wayne #1 © DC

	GD 2.0	VG 4.0	FN 6.0	VF 8.0	VF/NM 9.0	NM- 9.2

29-Robin debuts. 32,33-Cal Ripken 8-pg. insert. 44-Superman app. 3.00
1-Free Comic Book Day edition (6/05) Penguin app. 3.00
3-($2.95) Joker-c/app.; Catwoman & Wonder Woman-r from Advs. in the DCU 4.00
Jam Packed Action (2005, $7.99, digest) adaptations of two TV episodes 8.00
... Vol. 1: Crime Time (2005, $6.99, digest) r/#1-5 7.00
... Vol. 2: In Darkest Knight (2005, $6.99, digest) r/#6-10 7.00

BATMAN/ SUPERMAN/WONDER WOMAN: TRINITY
DC Comics: 2003 - No. 3, 2003 ($6.95, limited series, squarebound)
1-3-Matt Wagner-s/a/c. 1-Ra's al Ghul & Bizarro app. 7.00
HC (2004, $24.95, with dust-jacket) r/series; intro. by Brad Meltzer 30.00
SC (2004, $17.99) r/series; intro. by Brad Meltzer 18.00

BATMAN: SWORD OF AZRAEL (Also see Azrael & Batman #488,489)
DC Comics: Oct, 1992 - No. 4, Jan, 1993 ($1.75, limited series)
1-Wraparound gatefold-c; Quesada-c/a(p) in all; 1st app. Azrael 2 4 6 8 10 12
2-4: 4-Cont'd in Batman #488 1 2 3 5 6 8
Silver Edition 1-4 (1993, $1.95)-Reprints #1-4 3.00
Trade Paperback (1993, $9.95)-Reprints #1-4 10.00
Trade Paperback Gold Edition 15.00

BATMAN/ TARZAN: CLAWS OF THE CAT-WOMAN
Dark Horse Comics/DC Comics: Sept, 1999 - No. 4, Dec, 1999 ($2.95, limited series)
1-4: Marz-s/Kordey-a 3.00

BATMAN: TENSES
DC Comics: 2003 - No. 2, 2003 ($6.95, limited series)
1,2-Joe Casey-s/Cully Hamner-a; Bruce Wayne's first year back in Gotham 7.00

BATMAN: THE ANKH
DC Comics: 2002 - No. 2, 2002 ($5.95, limited series)
1,2-Dixon-s/Van Fleet-a 6.00

BATMAN: THE BRAVE AND THE BOLD (Based on the 2008 animated series)
DC Comics: Mar, 2009 - No. 22, Dec, 2010 ($2.50/$2.99)
1-18: 1-Power Girl app. 4-Sugar & Spike cameo. 7-Doom Patrol app. 9-Catman app. 3.00
19-22-($2.99) Cyborg Superman and the Green Lantern Corps app. 22-Aquaman app. 3.00
TPB (2009, $12.99) r/#1-6 13.00
...: The Fearsome Fangs Strike Again TPB (2010, $12.99) r/#7-12 13.00

BATMAN: THE CULT
DC Comics: 1988 - No. 4, Nov, 1988 ($3.50, deluxe limited series)
1-Wrightson-a/painted-c in all 6.00
2-4 5.00
Trade Paperback (1991, $14.95)-New Wrightson-c; Starlin intro. 15.00
Trade Paperback (2009, $19.99) 20.00

BATMAN: THE DARK KNIGHT
DC Comics: Jan, 2011 - Present ($3.99/$2.99)
1-David Finch-s/a; Penguin & Killer Croc app.; covers by Finch and Clarke 4.00
2-($2.99) Demon app. 3.00

BATMAN: THE DARK KNIGHT RETURNS (Also see Dark Knight Strikes Again)
DC Comics: Mar, 1986 - No. 4, 1986 ($2.95, squarebound, limited series)
1-Miller story & c/a(p); set in the future 5 10 15 30 48 65
1,2-2nd & 3rd printings, 3-2nd printing 6.00
2-Carrie Kelly becomes 1st female Robin 3 6 9 16 23 30
3-Death of Joker; Superman app. 3 6 9 14 20 25
4-Death of Alfred; Superman app. 2 4 6 11 16 20
Hardcover, signed & numbered edition ($40.00)(4000 copies) 250.00
Hardcover, trade edition 50.00
Softcover, trade edition (1st printing only) 2 4 6 9 12 15
Softcover, trade edition (2nd thru 8th printings) 1 2 3 4 5 7
10th Anniv. Slipcase set ('96, $100.00): Signed & numbered hard-c edition (10,000 copies), sketchbook, copy of script for #1, 2 color prints 100.00
10th Anniv. Hardcover ('96, $45.00) 45.00
10th Anniv. Softcover ('97, $14.95) 15.00
Hardcover 2nd printing ('02, $24.95) with 3 1/4" tall partial dustjacket 25.00
NOTE: The #2 second printings can be identified by matching the grey background colors on the inside front cover and facing page. The inside front cover of the second printing has a dark grey background which does not match the lighter grey of the facing page. On the true 1st printings, the backgrounds are both light grey. All other issues are clearly marked.

BATMAN: THE DOOM THAT CAME TO GOTHAM
DC Comics: 2000 - No. 3, 2001 ($4.95, limited series)
1-3-Elseworlds; Mignola-c/s; Nixey-a; Etrigan app. 5.00

BATMAN: THE KILLING JOKE (See Batman one-shots)

BATMAN: THE LONG HALLOWEEN
DC Comics: Oct, 1996 - No. 13, Oct, 1997 ($2.95/$4.95, limited series)
1-($4.95)-Loeb-s/Sale-c/a in all 1 2 3 5 6 8
2-5($2.95): 2-Solomon Grundy-c/app. 3-Joker-c/app., Catwoman, Poison Ivy app. 6.00
6-10: 6-Poison Ivy-c. 7-Riddler-c/app. 5.00
11,12 4.00
13-($4.95, 48 pgs.)-Killer revelations 5.00
Absolute Batman: The Long Halloween (2007, $75.00, oversized HC) r/series; interviews with the creators; Sale sketch pages; action figure line; unpubbed 4-page sequence 75.00
HC-($29.95) r/series 30.00
SC-($19.95) 20.00

BATMAN: THE MAD MONK ("Batman & the Mad Monk" on cover)
DC Comics: Oct, 2006 - No. 6, ($3.50, limited series)
1-5-Matt Wagner-s/a/c. 1-Catwoman app. 3.50
TPB (2007, $14.99) r/#1-6 15.00

BATMAN: THE MONSTER MEN ("Batman & the Monster Men" on cover)
DC Comics: Jan, 2006 - No. 6, June, 2006 ($2.99, limited series)
1-6-Matt Wagner-s/a/c 3.00
TPB (2006, $14.99) r/#1-6 15.00

BATMAN: THE OFFICIAL COMIC ADAPTATION OF THE WARNER BROS. MOTION PICTURE
(See Batman one-shots)

BATMAN: THE RETURN
DC Comics: Jan, 2011 ($4.99, one-shot)
1-Morrison-s/Finch-a; covers by Finch & Ha; costume design sketch art; script pages 5.00

BATMAN: THE RETURN OF BRUCE WAYNE (Follows Batman's "death" in Final Crisis #6)
DC Comics: Early Jul, 2010 - No. 6, Dec, 2010 ($3.99, limited series)
1-6-Bruce Wayne's time travels; Morrison-s/Andy Kubert-c. 1-Sprouse-a. 4-Jeanty-a 4.00
1-Second & third printings; 4.00
1-6-Variant covers: 1-Sprouse. 2-Irving. 3-Paquette. 4-Jeanty. 5-Sook. 6-Garbett 8.00
... - The Deluxe Edition HC (2011, $29.99) r/#1-6; sketch pages 30.00

BATMAN: THE ULTIMATE EVIL
DC Comics: 1995 ($5.95, limited series, prestige format)
1,2-Barrett, Jr. adaptation of Vachss novel. 6.00

BATMAN: THE WIDENING GYRE
DC Comics: Oct, 2009 - No. 6, Sept, 2010 ($3.99/$2.99/$4.99, limited series)
1-($3.99) Kevin Smith-s/Walt Flanagan-a; debut Baphomet; Demon app.; Sienkiewicz-c 4.00
1-5-Variant covers by Gene Ha 8.00
2-5-($2.99) 2-Silver St. Cloud returns. 5-Catwoman app. 3.00
6-($4.99) Joker, Deadshot & Catwoman app. 5.00
6-Variant cover by Gene Ha 10.00
HC (2010, $19.99, dj) r/#1-6; variant covers; afterword by Kevin Smith 20.00

BATMAN 3-D (Also see 3-D Batman)
DC Comics: 1990 ($9.95, w/glasses, 8-1/8x10-3/4")
nn-Byrne-a/scripts; Riddler, Joker, Penguin & Two-Face app. plus r/1953 3-D Batman; pin-ups by many artists 2 4 6 8 10 12

BATMAN: TOYMAN
DC Comics: Nov, 1998 - No. 4, Feb, 1999 ($2.25, limited series)
1-4-Hama-s 3.00

BATMAN: TURNING POINTS
DC Comics: Jan, 2001 - No. 5, Jan, 2001 ($2.50, weekly limited series)
1-5: 2-Giella-a. 3-Kubert-c/Giordano-a. 4-Chaykin-c/Brent Anderson-a. 5-Pope-c/a 3.00
TPB (2007, $14.99) r/#1-5 15.00

BATMAN: TWO-FACE-CRIME AND PUNISHMENT (See Batman one-shots)

BATMAN: TWO-FACE STRIKES TWICE
DC Comics: 1993 - No. 2, 1993 ($4.95, 52 pgs.)
1,2-Flip book format w/Staton-a (G.A. side) 5.00

BATMAN UNSEEN
DC Comics: Early Dec, 2009 - No. 5, Feb, 2010 ($2.99, limited series)
1-5-Doug Moench-s/Kelley Jones-a/c. Black Mask app. 3.00
SC (2010, $14.99) r/#1-5 15.00

BATMAN VERSUS PREDATOR
DC Comics/Dark Horse Comics: 1991 - No. 3, 1992 ($4.95/$1.95, limited series)
(1st DC/Dark Horse x-over)
1 (Prestige format, $4.95)-1 & 3 contain 8 Batman/Predator trading cards;

Battle #2 © MAR

Battle Action #3 © MAR

Battleaxes #4 © Terry LaBan

	GD 2.0	VG 4.0	FN 6.0	VF 8.0	VF/NM 9.0	NM- 9.2
Andy & Adam Kubert-a; Suydam painted-c						6.00
1-3 (Regular format, $1.95)-No trading cards						3.00
2,3-(Prestige)-2-Extra pin-ups inside; Suydam-c						5.00
TPB (1993, $5.95, 132 pgs.)-r/#1-3 w/new introductions & forward plus new wraparound-c by Dave Gibbons						6.00

BATMAN VERSUS PREDATOR II: BLOODMATCH
DC Comics: Late 1994 - No. 4, 1995 ($2.50, limited series)

	GD 2.0	VG 4.0	FN 6.0	VF 8.0	VF/NM 9.0	NM- 9.2
1-4-Huntress app.; Moench scripts; Gulacy-a						3.00
TPB (1995, $6.95)-r/#1-4						7.00

BATMAN VS. THE INCREDIBLE HULK (See DC Special Series No. 27)

BATMAN: WAR ON CRIME
DC Comics: Nov, 1999 ($9.95, treasury size, one-shot)

	GD 2.0	VG 4.0	FN 6.0	VF 8.0	VF/NM 9.0	NM- 9.2
nn-Painted art by Alex Ross; story by Alex Ross and Paul Dini						10.00

BATMAN/ WILDCAT
DC Comics: Apr, 1997 - No. 3, June, 1997 ($2.25, mini-series)

	GD 2.0	VG 4.0	FN 6.0	VF 8.0	VF/NM 9.0	NM- 9.2
1-3: Dixon/Smith-s: 1-Killer Croc app.						3.00

BATMAN: YEAR 100
DC Comics: 2006 - No. 4, 2006 ($5.99, squarebound, limited series)

	GD 2.0	VG 4.0	FN 6.0	VF 8.0	VF/NM 9.0	NM- 9.2
1-4-Paul Pope-s/a/c						6.00
TPB (2007, $19.99) r/series						20.00

BAT MASTERSON (TV) (Also see Tim Holt #28)
Dell Publishing Co.: Aug-Oct, 1959; Feb-Apr, 1960 - No. 9, Nov-Jan, 1961-62

	GD 2.0	VG 4.0	FN 6.0	VF 8.0	VF/NM 9.0	NM- 9.2
Four Color 1013 (#1) (8-10/59)	11	22	33	75	138	200
2-9: Gene Barry photo-c on all. 2,3,6-Two different back-c exist; variants have a comic strip on the back-c	7	14	21	45	73	100

BATS (See Tales Calculated to Drive You Bats)

BATS, CATS & CADILLACS
Now Comics: Oct, 1990 - No. 2, Nov, 1990 ($1.75)

	GD 2.0	VG 4.0	FN 6.0	VF 8.0	VF/NM 9.0	NM- 9.2
1,2: 1-Gustovich-a(i); Snyder-c						3.00

BAT-THING
DC Comics (Amalgam): June, 1997 ($1.95, one-shot)

	GD 2.0	VG 4.0	FN 6.0	VF 8.0	VF/NM 9.0	NM- 9.2
1-Hama-s/Damaggio & Sienkiewicz-a						3.00

BATTLE
Marvel/Atlas Comics(FPI #1-62/ Male #63 on): Mar, 1951 - No. 70, Jun, 1960

	GD 2.0	VG 4.0	FN 6.0	VF 8.0	VF/NM 9.0	NM- 9.2
1	36	72	108	211	343	475
2	19	38	57	109	172	235
3-10: 4-1st Buck Pvt. O'Toole. 10-Pakula-a	15	30	45	84	127	170
11-20: 11-Check-a	13	26	39	72	101	130
21,23-Krigstein-a	14	28	42	76	108	140
22,24-36: 32-Tuska-a. 36-Everett-a	11	22	33	62	86	110
37-Kubert-a (Last precode, 2/55)	12	24	36	67	94	120
38-40,42-48	10	20	30	58	79	100
41,49: 41-Kubert/Moskowitz-a. 49-Davis-a	11	22	33	62	86	110
50-54,56-58: 56-Colan-a; Ayers-a	10	20	30	56	76	95
55-Williamson-a (5 pgs.)	11	22	33	62	86	110
59-Torres-a	10	20	30	58	79	100
60-62: 60,62-Combat Kelly app. 61-Combat Casey app.	10	20	30	56	76	95
63-Ditko-a	15	30	45	85	130	175
64-66-Kirby-a. 66-Davis-a; has story of Fidel Castro in pre-Communism days (an admiring profile)	17	34	51	98	154	210
67,68: 67-Williamson/Crandall-a (4 pgs.); Kirby, Davis-a. 68-Kirby/Williamson-a (4 pgs.); Kirby/Ditko-a	17	34	51	100	158	215
69,70: 69-Kirby-a. 70-Kirby/Ditko-a	17	34	51	98	154	210

NOTE: ***Andru*** *a-37.* ***Berg*** *a-38, 14, 60-62.* ***Colan*** *a-19, 33, 55.* ***Everett*** *a-36, 50, 70; c-56, 57.* ***Heath*** *a-6, 9, 13, 31, 69; c-6, 9, 12, 26, 35, 37.* ***Kirby*** *c-64-69.* ***Maneely*** *a-4, 6, 31, 61; c-4, 22, 33, 48, 59, 61.* ***Orlando*** *a-47.* ***Powell*** *a-53, 55.* ***Reinman*** *a-4, 8-10, 14, 26, 32, 48.* ***Robinson*** *a-9, 39.* ***Romita*** *a-14, 26.* ***Severin*** *a-28, 32-34, 66-69; c-36, 50, 55.* ***Sinnott*** *a-33, 37, 63, 66.* ***Whitney*** *s-10.* ***Woodbridge*** *a-52, 55.*

BATTLE ACTION
Atlas Comics (NPI): Feb, 1952 - No. 12, 5/53; No. 13, 10/54 - No. 30, 8/57

	GD 2.0	VG 4.0	FN 6.0	VF 8.0	VF/NM 9.0	NM- 9.2
1-Pakula-a	28	56	84	165	270	375
2	15	30	45	88	137	185
3,4,6,7,9,10: 6-Robinson-c/a. 7-Partial nudity	11	22	33	64	90	115
5-Used in **POP**, pg. 93,94	12	24	36	67	94	120
8-Krigstein-a	12	24	36	69	97	125
11-15 (Last precode, 2/55)	11	22	33	62	86	110
16-30: 20-Romita-a. 22-Pakula-a. 27,30-Torres-a	10	20	30	56	76	95

NOTE: *Battle Brady app. 5-7, 10-12.* ***Berg*** *a-3.* ***Check*** *a-11.* ***Everett*** *a-7; c-13, 25.* ***Heath*** *a-3, 8, 18; c-3,15, 18, 21.* ***Maneely*** *a-1; c-5.* ***Reinman*** *a-1, 2, 20.* ***Robinson*** *a-6, 7; c-6.* ***Shores*** *a-7(2), 12, 20; c-11.* ***Sinnott*** *a-3, 27.* ***Woodbridge*** *a-28, 30.*

BATTLE ATTACK
Stanmor Publications: Oct, 1952 - No. 8, Dec, 1955

	GD 2.0	VG 4.0	FN 6.0	VF 8.0	VF/NM 9.0	NM- 9.2
1	14	28	42	80	115	150
2	9	18	27	47	61	75
3-8: 3-Hollingsworth-a	8	16	24	42	54	65

BATTLEAXES
DC Comics (Vertigo): May, 2000 - No. 4, Aug, 2000 ($2.50, limited series)

	GD 2.0	VG 4.0	FN 6.0	VF 8.0	VF/NM 9.0	NM- 9.2
1-4: Terry LaBan-s/Alex Horley-a						3.00

BATTLE BEASTS
Blackthorne Publishing: Feb, 1988 - No. 4, 1988 ($1.50/$1.75, B&W/color)

	GD 2.0	VG 4.0	FN 6.0	VF 8.0	VF/NM 9.0	NM- 9.2
1-4: 1-3- (B&W)-Based on Hasbro toys. 4-Color						3.00

BATTLE BRADY (Formerly Men in Action No. 1-9; see 3-D Action)
Atlas Comics (IPC): No. 10, Jan, 1953 - No. 14, June, 1953

	GD 2.0	VG 4.0	FN 6.0	VF 8.0	VF/NM 9.0	NM- 9.2
10: 10-12-Syd Shores-c	18	36	54	103	162	220
11-Used in **POP**, pg. 95 plus B&W & color illos	12	24	36	67	94	120
12-14	11	22	33	60	83	105

BATTLE CHASERS
Image Comics (Cliffhanger): Apr, 1998 - No. 4, Dec, 1998;
DC Comics (Cliffhanger): No. 5, May, 1999 - No. 8, May, 2001 ($2.50)
Image Comics: No. 9, Sept, 2001 ($3.50)

	GD 2.0	VG 4.0	FN 6.0	VF 8.0	VF/NM 9.0	NM- 9.2
Prelude (2/98)	1	3	4	6	8	10
Prelude Gold Ed.	1	3	4	6	8	10
1-Madureira & Sharrieff-s/Madureira-a(p)/Charest-c	1	2	3	5	7	9
1-American Ent. Ed. w/"racy" cover	1	3	4	6	8	10
1-Gold Edition						9.00
1-Chromium cover						40.00
1-2nd printing						3.00
2						5.00
2-Dynamic Forces BattleChrome cover	2	4	6	8	10	12
3-Red Monika cover by Madureira						4.00
4-8: 4-Four covers. 6-Back-up by Adam Warren-s/a. 7-Three covers (Madureira, Ramos, Campbell)						3.00
9-($3.50, Image) Flip cover/story by Adam Warren						3.50
...: A Gathering of Heroes HC ('99, $24.95) r/#1-5, Prelude, Frank Frazetta Fantasy Ill.; cover gallery						25.00
...: A Gathering of Heroes SC ('99, $14.95)						15.00
...Collected Edition 1,2 (11/98, 5/99, $5.95) 1-r/#1,2. 2-r/#3,4						6.00

BATTLE CLASSICS (See Cancelled Comic Cavalcade)
DC Comics: Sept-Oct, 1978 (44 pgs.)

	GD 2.0	VG 4.0	FN 6.0	VF 8.0	VF/NM 9.0	NM- 9.2
1-Kubert-r; new Kubert-c	2	4	6	8	10	12

BATTLE CRY
Stanmor Publications: 1952 (May) - No. 20, Sept, 1955

	GD 2.0	VG 4.0	FN 6.0	VF 8.0	VF/NM 9.0	NM- 9.2
1	16	32	48	94	147	200
2	10	20	30	58	79	100
3,5-10: 8-Pvt. Ike begins, ends #13,17	9	18	27	47	61	75
4-Classic E.C. swipe	10	20	30	54	72	90
11-20	8	16	24	42	54	65

NOTE: ***Hollingsworth*** *a-9; c-20.*

BATTLEFIELD (War Adventures on the...)
Atlas Comics (ACI): April, 1952 - No. 11, May, 1953

	GD 2.0	VG 4.0	FN 6.0	VF 8.0	VF/NM 9.0	NM- 9.2
1-Pakula, Reinman-a	22	44	66	132	216	300
2-5: 2-Heath, Maneely, Pakula, Reinman-a	14	28	42	80	115	150
6-11	11	22	33	60	83	105

NOTE: ***Colan*** *a-11.* ***Everett*** *a-8.* ***Heath*** *a-1, 2, 5p,7; c-2, 8, 9, 11.* ***Ravielli*** *a-11.*

BATTLEFIELD ACTION (Formerly Foreign Intrigues)
Charlton Comics: No. 16, Nov, 1957 - No. 62, 2-3/66; No. 63, 7/80 - No. 89, 11/84

	GD 2.0	VG 4.0	FN 6.0	VF 8.0	VF/NM 9.0	NM- 9.2
V2#16	8	16	24	44	57	70
17,20-30: 29-D-Day story	6	12	18	27	33	38
18,19-Check-a (2 stories in #18)	3	6	9	21	32	42
31-62(1966): 35-Hitler-c. 55,61-Hitler app.	3	6	9	16	22	28
63-80(1983-84)						5.00
81-83,85-89 (Low print run)	1	2	3	4	5	7
84-Kirby reprints; 3 stories	1	3	4	6	8	10

NOTE: ***Montes/Bache*** *a-43, 55, 62.* ***Glanzman*** *a-87r.*

BATTLEFIELDS
Dynamite Entertainment: 2008 - No. 9, 2010 ($3.50, limited series then numbered issues)

	GD 2.0	VG 4.0	FN 6.0	VF 8.0	VF/NM 9.0	NM- 9.2
...: Dear Billy 1-3 ('09 - No. 3, '09, $3.50) Ennis-s/Snejbjerg-a/Cassaday-c.1-Leach var-c						3.50

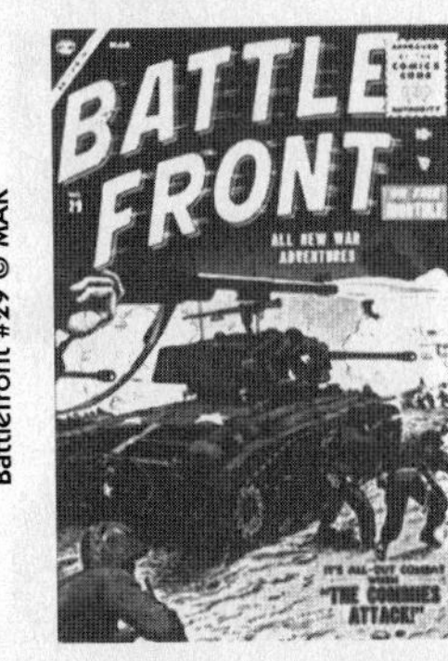

Battlefront #29 © MAR

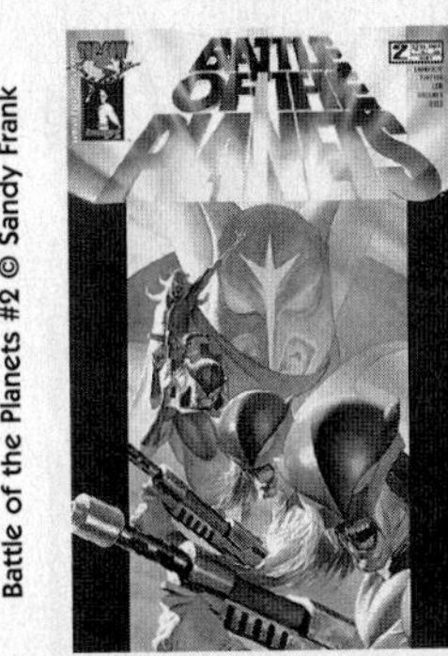

Battle of the Planets #2 © Sandy Frank

Battlestar Galactica #1 © Universal Studios

	GD 2.0	VG 4.0	FN 6.0	VF 8.0	VF/NM 9.0	NM- 9.2

...: Happy Valley 1-3 ('09 - No. 3, '09, $3.50) Ennis-s/Holden-a/Leach-c 3.50
...: The Night Witches 1-3 ('08 - No. 3, '09, $3.50) Ennis-s/Braun-a/Cassaday-c; Russian female pilots in WW2. 1-Leach var-c 3.50
...: The Tankies 1-3 ('09 - No. 3, '09, $3.50) Ennis-s/Ezquerra-a/Cassaday-c.1-Leach var-c 3.50
4-9: 4-6-Ezquerra-a/Leach-c. 7-9-Sequel to "The Night Witches"; Braun-a 3.50

BATTLE FIRE
Aragon Magazine/Stanmor Publications: Apr, 1955 - No. 7, 1955

	GD	VG	FN	VF	VF/NM	NM-
1	13	26	39	72	101	130
2	8	16	24	44	57	70
3-7	8	16	24	40	50	60

BATTLE FOR A THREE DIMENSIONAL WORLD
3D Cosmic Publications: May, 1983 (20 pgs., slick paper w/stiff-c, $3.00)

	GD	VG	FN	VF	VF/NM	NM-
nn-Kirby c/a in 3-D; shows history of 3-D	2	4	6	8	11	14

BATTLEFORCE
Blackthorne Publishing: Nov, 1987 - No. 2, 1988 ($1.75, color/B&W)

1,2: Based on game. 1-In color. 2-B&W 3.00

BATTLE FOR INDEPENDENTS, THE (Also See Cyblade/Shi & Shi/Cyblade: The Battle For Independents)
Image Comics (Top Cow Productions)/Crusade Comics: 1995 ($29.95)

	GD	VG	FN	VF	VF/NM	NM-
nn-boxed set of all editions of Shi/Cyblade & Cyblade/Shi plus new variant.	3	6	9	20	30	40

BATTLE FOR THE PLANET OF THE APES (See Power Record Comics)

BATTLEFRONT
Atlas Comics (PPI): June, 1952 - No. 48, Aug, 1957

	GD	VG	FN	VF	VF/NM	NM-
1-Heath-c	31	62	93	186	303	420
2-Robinson-a(4)	16	32	48	94	147	200
3-5-Robinson-a	14	28	42	82	121	160
6-10: Combat Kelly in No. 6-10. 6-Romita-a	13	26	39	72	101	130
11-22,24-28: 14,16-Battle Brady app. 22-Teddy Roosevelt & His Rough Riders story. 28-Last pre-code (2/55)	11	22	33	62	86	110
23,43-Check-a	11	22	33	64	90	115
29-39,41,44-47	10	20	30	56	76	95
40,42-Williamson-a	11	22	33	64	90	155
48-Crandall-a	11	22	33	60	83	105

NOTE: ***Ayers** a-19, 32, 35. **Berg** a-44. **Colan** a-21, 22, 32, 33, 35, 38, 40, 42. **Drucker** a-28, 29. **Everett** a-44. **Heath** c-23, 26, 27, 29, 32. **Maneely** a-22, 23, 26; c-2, 7, 13, 22, 34, 35, 41. **Morisi** a-42. **Morrow** a-41.**Orlando** a-47. **Powell** a-19, 21, 25, 29, 32, 40, 47. **Robinson** a-1-3, 4&5(4); c-4, 5. **Robert Sale** a-19. **Severin** a-32; c-40, 42, 45. **Sinnott** a-26; 48. **Woodbridge** a-45, 46.*

BATTLEFRONT
Standard Comics: No. 5, June, 1952

	GD	VG	FN	VF	VF/NM	NM-
5-Toth-a	15	30	45	83	124	165

BATTLE GODS: WARRIORS OF THE CHAAK
Dark Horse Comics: Apr, 2000 - No. 4, July, 2000 ($2.95)

1-4-Francisco Ruiz Velasco-s/a 3.00

BATTLE GROUND
Atlas Comics (OMC): Sept, 1954 - No. 20, Aug, 1957

	GD	VG	FN	VF	VF/NM	NM-
1	22	44	66	132	216	300
2-Jack Katz-a	14	28	42	80	115	150
3,4: 3-Jack Katz-a. 4-Last precode (3/55)	11	22	33	64	90	115
5-8,10	10	20	30	58	79	100
9,11,13,18: 9-Krigstein-a. 11,13,18-Williamson-a in each	12	24	36	67	94	120
12,15-17,19,20	10	20	30	54	72	90
14-Kirby-a	14	28	42	78	112	145

NOTE: ***Ayers** a-4, 13, 16. **Colan** a-3, 11, 13. **Drucker** a-7, 12, 13, 20. **Heath** c-2, 3, 5, 7, 13. **Maneely** a-3, 14, 19; c-1, 18, 19. **Orlando** a-17. **Pakula** a-11. **Reinman** a-2. **Severin** a-4, 5, 12, 19. c-20. **Sinnott** a-7, 16. **Tuska** a-11.*

BATTLE HEROES
Stanley Publications: Sept, 1966 - No. 2, Nov, 1966 (25¢, squarebound giants)

	GD	VG	FN	VF	VF/NM	NM-
1	4	8	12	23	36	48
2	3	6	9	17	25	32

BATTLE HYMN
Image Comics: Jan, 2005 - No. 5, Oct, 2005 ($2.95/$2.99, limited series)

1-5-WW2 super team; B. Clay Moore-s/Jeremy Haun-a; flip cover on #1-4 3.00

BATTLE OF THE BULGE (See Movie Classics)

BATTLE OF THE PLANETS (Based on syndicated cartoon by Sandy Frank)
Gold Key/Whitman No. 6 on: 6/79 - No. 10, 12/80

	GD	VG	FN	VF	VF/NM	NM-
1: Mortimer a-1-4,7-10	4	8	12	28	44	60
2-6,10	3	6	9	19	29	38
7-Low print run	5	10	15	35	55	75
8,9-Low print run: 8(11/80). 9-(3-pack only?)	5	10	15	30	48	65

BATTLE OF THE PLANETS (Also see Thundercats/...)
Image Comics (Top Cow): Aug, 2002 - No. 12, Sept, 2003 ($2.95/$2.99)

1-($2.95) Alex Ross-c & art director; Tortosa-a(p); re-intro. G-Force 3.00
1-($5.95) Holofoil-c by Ross 6.00
2-11-($2.99) Ross-c on all 3.00
12-($4.99) 5.00
#1/2 (7/03, $2.99) Benitez-c; Alex Ross sketch pages 3.00
... Battle Book 1 (5/03, $4.99) background info on characters, equipment, stories 5.00
... : Jason 1 (7/03, $4.99) Ross-c; Erwin David-a; preview of Tomb Raider: Epiphany 5.00
... : Mark 1 (5/03, $4.99) Ross-c; Erwin David-a; preview of BotP: Jason 5.00
.../Thundercats 1 (Image/WildStorm, 5/03, $4.99) 2 covers by Ross & Campbell 5.00
.../Witchblade 1 (2/03, $5.95) Ross-c; Christina and Jo Chen-a 6.00
Vol. 1: Trial By Fire (2003, $7.99) r/#1-3 8.00
Vol. 2: Blood Red Sky (9/03, $16.95) r/#4-9 17.00
Vol. 3: Destroy All Monsters (11/03, $19.95) r/#10-12, ...: Jason, ...: Mark, .../Witchblade 20.00
Vol. 1: Digest (1/04, $9.99, 7-3/8x5", B&W) r/#1-9 & ...: Mark 10.00
Vol. 2: Digest (8/04, $9.99, B&W) r/#10-12, ...: Jason, ...: Manga #1-3, .../Witchblade 10.00

BATTLE OF THE PLANETS: MANGA
Image Comics (Top Cow): Nov, 2003 - No. 3, Jan, 2004 ($2.99, B&W)

1-3-Edwin David-a/David Wohl-s; previews for Wanted & Tomb Raider #35 3.00

BATTLE OF THE PLANETS: PRINCESS
Image Comics (Top Cow): Nov, 2004 - No. 6, May, 2005 ($2.99, B&W, limited series)

1-6-Tortosa-a/Wohl-s. 1-Ross-c. 2-Tortosa-c 3.00

BATTLE POPE
Image Comics: June, 2005 - No. 14, Apr, 2007 ($2.99/$3.50, reprints 2000 B&W series in color)

1-5-Kirkman-s/Moore-a 3.00
6-10,12-14-($3.50) 14-Wedding 3.50
11-($4.99) Christmas issue 5.00
... Vol. 1: Genesis TPB (2006, $12.95) r/#1-4; sketch pages 13.00
... Vol. 2: Mayhem TPB (2006, $12.99) r/#5-8; sketch pages 13.00
... Vol. 3: Pillow Talk TPB (2007, $12.99) r/#9-11; sketch pages 13.00

BATTLER BRITTON (British comics character who debuted in 1956)
DC Comics (WildStorm): Sept, 2006 - No. 5, Jan, 2007 ($2.99, limited series)

1-5-WWII fighter pilots; Garth Ennis-s/Colin Wilson-a 3.00
TPB (2007, $19.99) r/#1-5; background of the character's British origins in the 1950s 20.00

BATTLE REPORT
Ajax/Farrell Publications: Aug, 1952 - No. 6, June, 1953

	GD	VG	FN	VF	VF/NM	NM-
1	12	24	36	67	94	120
2-6	8	16	24	40	50	60

BATTLE SQUADRON
Stanmor Publications: April, 1955 - No. 5, Dec, 1955

	GD	VG	FN	VF	VF/NM	NM-
1	11	22	33	62	86	110
2-5: 3-Iwo Jima & flag-c	7	14	21	37	46	55

BATTLESTAR GALACTICA (TV) (Also see Marvel Comics Super Special #8)
Marvel Comics Group: Mar, 1979 - No. 23, Jan, 1981

	GD	VG	FN	VF	VF/NM	NM-
1: 1-5 adapt TV episodes	2	4	6	9	12	15
2-23: 1-3-Partial-r	1	3	4	6	8	10

NOTE: ***Austin** c-9i, 10i. **Golden** c-18. **Simonson** a(p)-4, 5, 11-13, 15-20, 22, 23; c(p)-4, 5,11-17, 19, 20, 22, 23.*

BATTLESTAR GALACTICA (TV) (Also see Asylum)
Maximum Press: July, 1995 - No. 4, Nov, 1995 ($2.50, limited series)

1-4: Continuation of 1978 TV series 4.00
Trade paperback (12/95, $12.95)-reprints series 13.00

BATTLESTAR GALACTICA (1978 TV series)
Realm Press: Dec, 1997 - No. 5, July, 1998 ($2.99)

1-5-Chris Scalf-s/painted-a/c 3.00
...Search For Sanctuary (9/98, $2.99) Scalf & Kuhoric-s 3.00
...Search For Sanctuary Special (4/00, $3.99) Kuhoric-s/Scalf & Scott-a 4.00

BATTLESTAR GALACTICA (2003-2009 TV series)
Dynamite Entertainment: No. 0, 2006 - No. 12, 2007 (25¢/$2.99)

0-(25¢-c) Two covers; Pak-s/Raynor-a 3.00
1-($2.99) Covers by Turner, Tan, Raynor & photo-c; Pak-s/Raynor-a 3.00
2-12-Four covers on each 3.00
... Pegasus (2007, $4.99) story of Battlestar Pegasus & Admiral Cain; 2 covers 5.00
... Volume 1 HC (2007, $19.99) r/#0-4; cover gallery; Raynor sketch pages; commentary 20.00

Battletide #3 © MAR

Batwoman #0 © DC

Beany and Cecil FC #530 © DELL

	GD 2.0	VG 4.0	FN 6.0	VF 8.0	VF/NM 9.0	NM- 9.2

... Volume 1 TPB (2007, $14.99) r/#0-4; cover gallery; Raynor sketch pages; commentary 15.00
... Volume 2 HC (2007, $19.99) r/#5-8; cover gallery; Raynor sketch pages 20.00
... Volume 2 TPB (2007, $14.99) r/#5-8; cover gallery; Raynor sketch pages 15.00

BATTLESTAR GALACTICA, (Classic...) (1978 TV series characters)
Dynamite Entertainment: 2006 - Present ($2.99)
1-5: 1-Two covers by Dorman & Caldwell; Rafael-a. 2-Two covers 3.00

BATTLESTAR GALACTICA: APOLLO'S JOURNEY (1978 TV series)
Maximum Press: Apr, 1996 - No. 3, June, 1996 ($2.95, limited series)
1-3: Richard Hatch scripts 4.00

BATTLESTAR GALACTICA: CYLON APOCALYPSE (1978 TV series characters)
Dynamite Entertainment: 2007 - No. 4, 2007 ($2.99, limited series)
1-4-Carlos Rafael-a; 4 covers on each 3.00
TPB (2007, $14.99) r/series with cover gallery 15.00

BATTLESTAR GALACTICA: CYLON WAR (2003-2009 TV series)
Dynamite Entertainment: 2009 - No. 4, 2010 ($3.99, limited series)
1-3-First cylon war 40 years before the Caprica attack; Raynor-a; 2 covers 4.00

BATTLESTAR GALACTICA: GHOSTS (2003-2009 TV series)
Dynamite Entertainment: 2008 - No. 4, 2009 ($4.99, 40 pgs., limited series)
1-4-Intro. of the Ghost Squadron; Jerwa-s/Lau-a/Calero-c 5.00

BATTLESTAR GALACTICA: JOURNEY'S END (1978 TV series)
Maximum Press: Aug, 1996 - No. 4, Nov, 1996 ($2.99, limited series)
1-4-Continuation of the T.V. series 4.00

BATTLESTAR GALACTICA: ORIGINS (2003-2009 TV series)
Dynamite Entertainment: 2007 - No. 11, 2008 ($3.50)
1-11: 1-4-Baltar's origin; multiple covers. 5-8-Adama's origin. 9-11-Starbuck & Helo 3.50

BATTLESTAR GALACTICA: SEASON III
Realm Press: June/July, 1999 - No. 3, Sept, 1999 ($2.99)
1-3: 1-Kuhoric-s/Scalf & Scott-a; two covers by Scalf & Jae Lee. 2,3-Two covers 3.00
Gallery (4/00, $3.99) short story and pin-ups 4.00
1999 Tour Book (5/99, $2.99) 3.00
1999 Tour Book Convention Edition (6.99) 7.00
...Special: Centurion Prime (12/99, $3.99) Kuhoric-s 4.00

BATTLESTAR GALACTICA: SEASON ZERO (2003-2009 TV series)
Dynamite Entertainment: 2007 - No. 12, 2008 ($2.99)
1-12-Set 2 years before the Cylon attack; multiple covers 3.00
.../The Lone Ranger 2007 Free Comic Book Day Edition; flip book with Cassaday Lone Ranger-c 2.25

BATTLESTAR GALACTICA: SPECIAL EDITION (TV)
Maximum Press: Jan, 1997 ($2.99, one-shot)
1-Fully painted; Scalf-c/s/a; r/Asylum 3.00

BATTLESTAR GALACTICA: STARBUCK (TV)
Maximum Press: Dec, 1995 - No. 3, Mar, 1996 ($2.50, limited series)
1-3 4.00

BATTLESTAR GALACTICA: THE COMPENDIUM (TV)
Maximum Press: Feb, 1997 ($2.99, one-shot)
1 3.00

BATTLESTAR GALACTICA: THE ENEMY WITHIN (TV)
Maximum Press: Nov, 1995 - No. 3, Feb, 1996 ($2.50, limited series)
1-3: 3-Indicia reads Feb, 1995 in error. 4.00

BATTLESTAR GALACTICA: THE FINAL FIVE (2003 series)
Dynamite Entertainment: 2009 - No. 4, 2009 ($3.99, limited series)
1-4-Raynor-a; 2 covers on each 4.00

BATTLESTAR GALACTICA ZAREK (2003 series)
Dynamite Entertainment: 2007 - No. 4, 2007 ($3.50, limited series)
1-4-Origin story of political activist Tom Zarek; 2 covers on each 3.50

BATTLE STORIES (See XMas Comics)
Fawcett Publications: Jan, 1952 - No. 11, Sept, 1953

	GD	VG	FN	VF	VF/NM	NM-
1-Evans-a	16	32	48	92	144	195
2	10	20	30	56	76	95
3-11	9	18	27	47	61	75

BATTLE STORIES
Super Comics: 1963 - 1964
Reprints #10-13,15-18: 10-r/U.S Tank Commandos #? 11-r/? 11, 12,17-r/Monty Hall #?; 13-Kintsler-a (1pg).15-r/American Air Forces #7 by Powell; Bolle-r. 18-U.S. Fighting Air Force #? 2 4 6 9 13 16

BATTLETECH (See Blackthorne 3-D Series #41 for 3-D issue)
Blackthorne Publishing: Oct, 1987 - No. 6, 1988 ($1.75/$2.00)
1-6: Based on game. 1-Color. 2-Begin B&W 3.00
Annual 1 ($4.50, B&W) 5.00

BATTLETECH
Malibu Comics: Feb, 1995 ($2.95)
0 3.00

BATTLETECH FALLOUT
Malibu Comics: Dec, 1994 - No. 4, Mar, 1995 ($2.95)
1-4-Two edi. exist #1; normal logo 3.00
1-Gold version w/foil logo stamped "Gold Limited Edition 8.00
1-Full-c holographic limited edition 6.00

BATTLETIDE (Death's Head II & Killpower...)
Marvel Comics UK, Ltd.: Dec, 1992 - No. 4, Mar, 1993 ($1.75, mini-series)
1-4: Wolverine, Psylocke, Dark Angel app. 3.00

BATTLETIDE II (Death's Head II & Killpower...)
Marvel Comics UK, Ltd.: Aug, 1993 - No. 4, Nov, 1993 ($1.75, mini-series)
1-($2.95)-Foil embossed logo 4.00
2-4: 2-Hulk-c/story 3.00

BATWOMAN (See 52 #9 & 11 for debut and Detective Comics #854-860)
DC Comics: No. 0, Jan, 2011 - Present ($2.99)
0-Williams III-s; art by Williams III and Reeder; Williams III-c 3.00
0-Variant-c by Reeder 5.00
... Elegy The Deluxe Edition HC (2010, $24.99, d.j.) r/Detective #854-860; gallery of variant covers, sketch art and script pages; intro. by Rachel Maddow 25.00

BAY CITY JIVE
DC Comics (WildStorm): Jul, 2001 - No. 3, Sept, 2001 ($2.95, limited series)
1-3: Intro Sugah Rollins in 1970s San Francisco; Layman-s/Johnson-a 3.00

BAYWATCH COMIC STORIES (TV) (Magazine)
Acclaim Comics (Armada): May, 1996 - No. 4, 1997 ($4.95) (Photo-c on all)
1-4: Photo comics based on TV show 5.00

BEACH BLANKET BINGO (See Movie Classics)

BEAGLE BOYS, THE (Walt Disney)(See The Phantom Blot)
Gold Key: 11/64; No. 2, 11/65; No. 3, 8/66 - No. 47, 2/79 (See WDC&S #134)

	GD	VG	FN	VF	VF/NM	NM-
1	5	10	15	32	51	70
2-5	3	6	9	18	27	35
6-10	3	6	9	16	22	28
11-20: 11,14,19-r	2	4	6	11	16	20
21-30: 27-r	2	4	6	8	11	14
31-47	1	3	4	6	8	10

BEAGLE BOYS VERSUS UNCLE SCROOGE
Gold Key: Mar, 1979 - No. 12, Feb, 1980

	GD	VG	FN	VF	VF/NM	NM-
1	2	4	6	9	13	16
2-12: 9-r	1	2	3	5	6	8

BEANBAGS
Ziff-Davis Publ. Co. (Approved Comics): Winter, 1951 - No. 2, Spring, 1952

	GD	VG	FN	VF	VF/NM	NM-
1,2	12	24	36	69	97	125

BEANIE THE MEANIE
Fago Publications: No. 3, May, 1959

	GD	VG	FN	VF	VF/NM	NM-
3	5	10	15	24	30	35

BEANY AND CECIL (TV) (Bob Clampett's...)
Dell Publishing Co.: Jan, 1952 - 1955; July-Sept, 1962 - No. 5, July-Sept, 1963

	GD	VG	FN	VF	VF/NM	NM-
Four Color 368	22	44	66	159	317	475
Four Color 414,448,477,530,570,635(1/55)	13	26	39	94	185	275
01-057-209 (#1)	13	26	39	90	173	255
2-5	10	20	30	68	119	170

BEAR COUNTRY (Disney)
Dell Publishing Co.: No. 758, Dec, 1956

	GD	VG	FN	VF	VF/NM	NM-
Four Color 758-Movie	5	10	15	34	55	75

BEAST (See X-Men)
Marvel Comics: May, 1997 - No. 3, 1997 ($2.50, mini-series)
1-3-Giffen-s/Nocon-a 3.00

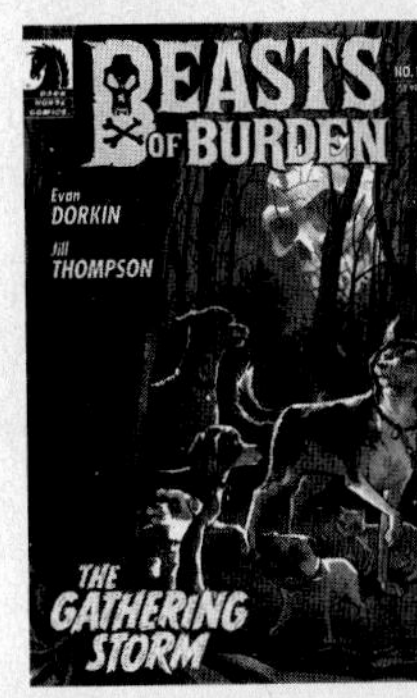

Beasts of Burden #1 © Dorkin & Thompson

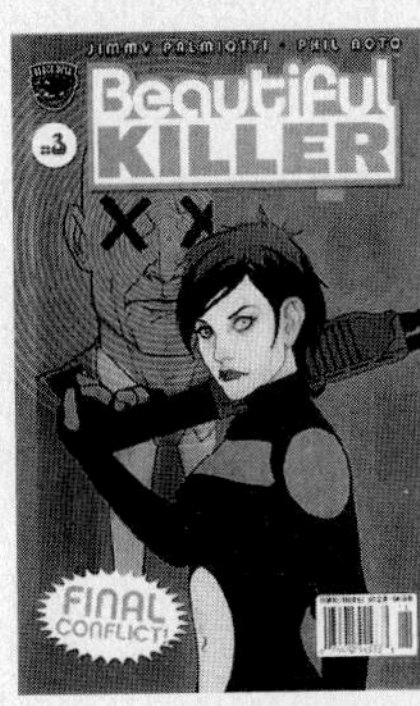

Beautiful Killer #3 © Black Bull

Beetlejuice #1 © Geffen

	GD 2.0	VG 4.0	FN 6.0	VF 8.0	VF/NM 9.0	NM- 9.2

BEAST BOY (See Titans)
DC Comics: Jan, 2000 - No. 4, Apr, 2000 ($2.95, mini-series)

1-4-Justiano-c/a; Raab & Johns-s 3.00

B.E.A.S.T.I.E.S. (Also see Axis Alpha)
Axis Comics: Apr, 1994 ($1.95)

1-Javier Saltares-c/a/scripts 3.00

BEASTS OF BURDEN (See Dark Horse Book of Hauntings, ...Monsters, ...The Dead, ...Witchcraft)
Dark Horse Comics: Sept, 2009 - No. 4, Dec, 2009 ($2.99, limited series)

1-4-Evan Dorkin-s/Jill Thompson-a/c 3.00
Volume 1: Animal Rites HC (6/10, $19.99) r/#1-4 & short stories from Dark Horse Books 20.00

BEATLES, THE (See Girls' Romances #109, Go-Go, Heart Throbs #101, Herbie #5, Howard the Duck Mag. #4, Laugh #166, Marvel Comics Super Special #4, My Little Margie #54, Not Brand Echh, Strange Tales #130, Summer Love, Superman's Pal Jimmy Olsen #79, Teen Confessions #37, Tippy's Friends & Tippy Teen)

BEATLES, THE (Life Story)
Dell Publishing Co.: Sept-Nov, 1964 (35¢)

1-(Scarce)-Stories with color photo pin-ups; Paul S. Newman-s
40 80 120 320 635 950

BEATLES EXPERIENCE, THE
Revolutionary Comics: Mar, 1991 - No. 8, 1991 ($2.50, B&W, limited series)

1-8: 1-Gold logo 5.00

BEATLES YELLOW SUBMARINE (See Movie Comics under Yellow...)

BEAUTIFUL KILLER
Black Bull Comics: Sept., 2002 - No. 3, Jan, 2003 ($2.99, limited series)

...Limited Preview Edition (5/02, $5.00) preview pgs. & creator interviews 5.00
1-Noto-a/Palmiotti-s; Hughes-c; intro Brigit Cole 3.00
2,3: 2-Jusko-c. 3-Noto-c 3.00
TPB (5/03, $9.99) r/#1-3; cover gallery and Adam Hughes sketch pages 10.00

BEAUTIFUL PEOPLE
Slave Labor Graphics: Apr, 1994 ($4.95, 8-1/2x11", one-shot)

nn 5.00

BEAUTIFUL STORIES FOR UGLY CHILDREN
DC Comics (Piranha Press): 1989 - No. 30, 1991 ($2.00/$2.50, B&W, mature)

Vol. 1-20: 12-$2.50-c begins 4.00
21-25 5.00
26-30-(Lower print run) 1 2 3 4 5 7
A Cotton Candy Autopsy ($12.95, B&W)-Reprints 1st two volumes 13.00

BEAUTY AND THE BEAST, THE
Marvel Comics Group: Jan, 1985 - No. 4, Apr, 1985 (limited series)

1-4: Dazzler & the Beast from X-Men; Sienkiewicz-c on all 3.00

BEAUTY AND THE BEAST (Graphic novel)(Also see Cartoon Tales & Disney's New Adventures of...)
Disney Comics: 1992

nn-($4.95, prestige edition)-Adapts animated film 7.00
nn-($2.50, newsstand edition) 3.00

BEAUTY AND THE BEAST
Disney Comics: Sept., 1992 - No. 2, 1992 ($1.50, limited series)

1,2 3.00

BEAUTY AND THE BEAST: PORTRAIT OF LOVE (TV)
First Comics: May, 1989 - No. 2, Mar, 1990 ($5.95, 60 pgs., squarebound)

1,2: 1-Based on TV show, Wendy Pini-a/scripts. 2-...: Night of Beauty; by Wendy Pini 6.00

BEAVER VALLEY (Movie)(Disney)
Dell Publishing Co.: No. 625, Apr, 1955

Four Color 625 6 12 18 41 66 90

BEAVIS AND BUTTHEAD (MTV's...)(TV cartoon)
Marvel Comics: Mar, 1994 - No. 28, June, 1996 ($1.95)

1-Silver ink-c. 1, 2-Punisher & Devil Dinosaur app. 5.00
1-2nd printing 3.00
2,3: 2-Wolverine app. 3-Man-Thing, Spider-Man, Venom, Carnage, Mary Jane & Stan Lee cameos; John Romita, Sr. art (2 pgs.) 3.00
4-28: 5-War Machine, Thor, Loki, Hulk, Captain America & Rhino cameos. 6-Psylocke, Polaris, Daredevil & Bullseye app. 7-Ghost Rider & Sub-Mariner app. 8-Quasar & Eon app. 9-Prowler & Nightwatch app. 11-Black Widow app. 12-Thunderstrike & Bloodaxe app. 13-Night Thrasher app. 14-Spider-Man 2099 app. 15-Warlock app. 16-X-Factor app. 25-Juggernaut app. 3.00

BECK & CAUL INVESTIGATIONS
Gauntlet Comics (Caliber): Jan, 1994 - No. 5, 1995? ($2.95, B&W)

1-5 3.00
Special 1 ($4.95) 5.00

BEDKNOBS AND BROOMSTICKS (See Walt Disney Showcase No. 6 & 50)

BEDLAM!
Eclipse Comics: Sept, 1985 - No. 2, Sept, 1985 (B&W-r in color)

1,2: Bissette-a 3.00

BEDTIME STORIES FOR IMPRESSIONABLE CHILDREN
Moonstone Books: Nov, 2010 ($3.99, B&W)

1-Short story anthology; Vaughn, Kuhoric & Tinnell-s; 3 covers 4.00

BEDTIME STORY (See Cinema Comics Herald)

BEELZELVIS
Slave Labor Graphics: Feb, 1994 ($2.95, B&W, one-shot)

1 3.00

BEEP BEEP, THE ROAD RUNNER (TV) (See Dell Giant Comics Bugs Bunny Vacation Funnies #8 for 1st app.) (Also see Daffy & Kite Fun Book)
Dell Publishing Co./Gold Key No. 1-88/Whitman No. 89 on: July, 1958 - No. 14, Aug-Oct, 1962; Oct, 1966 - No. 105, 1984

	GD	VG	FN	VF	VF/NM	NM-
Four Color 918 (#1, 7/58)	11	22	33	77	144	210
Four Color 1008,1046 (11-1/59-60)	7	14	21	47	76	105
4(2-4/60)-14(Dell)	6	12	18	43	69	95
1(10/66, Gold Key)	6	12	18	43	69	95
2-5	4	8	12	28	44	60
6-14	3	6	9	20	30	40
15-18,20-40	3	6	9	16	23	30
19-With pull-out poster	4	8	12	26	41	55
41-50	3	6	9	14	19	24
51-70	2	4	6	9	13	16
71-88	2	3	4	6	8	10
89,90,94-101: 100(3/82), 101(4/82)	2	4	6	8	10	12
91(8/80), 92(9/80), 93 (3-pack?) (low printing)	4	8	12	22	34	45
102-105 (All #90189 on-c; nd or date code; pre-pack) 102(6/83), 103(7/83), 104(5/84), 105(6/84)	3	6	9	16	22	28
#63-2970 (Now Age Books/Pendulum Pub. Comic Digest, 1971, 75¢, 100 pages, B&W) collection of one-page gags	4	8	12	28	44	60

NOTE: *See March of Comics #351, 353, 375, 387, 397, 416, 430, 442, 455. #5, 8-10, 35, 53, 59-62, 68-r; 96-102, 104 are 1/3-r.*

BEETLE BAILEY (See Giant Comic Album, Sarge Snorkel; also Comics Reading Libraries in the Promotional Comics section)
Dell Publishing Co./Gold Key #39-53/King #54-66/Charlton #67-119/Gold Key #120-131/ Whitman #132: #459, 5/53 - #38, 5-7/62; #39, 11/62 - #53, 5/66; #54, 8/66 - #65, 12/67;#67, 2/69 - #119, 11/76; #120, 4/78 - #132, 4/80

	GD	VG	FN	VF	VF/NM	NM-
Four Color 469 (#1)-By Mort Walker	11	22	33	75	138	200
Four Color 521,552,622	7	14	21	45	73	100
5(2-4/56)-10(5-7/57)	6	12	18	39	62	85
11-20(4-5/59)	4	8	12	28	44	60
21-38(5-7/62)	3	6	9	20	30	40
39-53(5/66)	3	6	9	17	25	32
54-65 (No. 66 publ. overseas only?)	3	6	9	16	22	28
67-69: 69-Last 12¢ issue	3	6	9	14	19	24
70-99	2	4	6	9	13	16
100	2	4	6	11	16	20
101-111,114-119	1	3	4	6	8	10
112,113-Byrne illos. (4 each)	2	4	6	9	12	18
120-132	1	2	3	4	5	7

BEETLE BAILEY
Harvey Comics: V2#1, Sept, 1992 - V2#9, Aug, 1994 ($1.25/$1.50)

V2#1 5.00
2-9-($1.50) 3.50
Big Book 1(11/92),2(5/93)(Both $1.95, 52 pgs.) 4.00
Giant Size V2#1(10/92),2(3/93)(Both $2.25,68 pgs.) 4.00

BEETLEJUICE (TV)
Harvey Comics: Oct, 1991 ($1.25)

1 3.50

BEETLEJUICE CRIMEBUSTERS ON THE HAUNT
Harvey Comics: Sept, 1992 - No. 3, Jan, 1993 ($1.50, limited series)

1-3 3.50

BEE 29, THE BOMBARDIER

Beowulf #1 © DC

Best Comics #2 © BP

The Best of DC #1 © DC

GD 2.0 | VG 4.0 | FN 6.0 | VF 8.0 | VF/NM 9.0 | NM- 9.2

Neal Publications: Feb, 1945
1-(Funny animal) 34 68 102 204 332 460

BEFORE THE FANTASTIC FOUR: BEN GRIMM AND LOGAN
Marvel Comics: July, 2000 - No. 3, Sept, 2000 ($2.99, limited series)
1-3-The Thing and Wolverine app.; Hama-s 3.00

BEFORE THE FANTASTIC FOUR: REED RICHARDS
Marvel Comics: Sept, 2000 - No. 3, Dec, 2000 ($2.99, limited series)
1-3-Peter David-s/Duncan Fegredo-c/a 3.00

BEFORE THE FANTASTIC FOUR: THE STORMS
Marvel Comics: Dec, 2000 - No. 3, Feb, 2001 ($2.99, limited series)
1-3-Adlard-a 3.00

BEHIND PRISON BARS
Realistic Comics (Avon): 1952
1-Kinstler-c 32 64 96 192 314 435

BEHOLD THE HANDMAID
George Pflaum: 1954 (Religious) (25¢ with a 20¢ sticker price)
nn 6 12 18 31 38 45

BELIEVE IT OR NOT (See Ripley's...)

BEN AND ME (Disney)
Dell Publishing Co.: No. 539, Mar, 1954
Four Color 539 4 8 12 26 41 55

BEN BOWIE AND HIS MOUNTAIN MEN
Dell Publishing Co.: 1952 - No. 17, Nov-Jan, 1958-59
Four Color 443 (#1) 9 18 27 60 100 140
Four Color 513,557,599,626,657 5 10 15 32 51 70
7(5-7/56)-11: 11-Intro/origin Yellow Hair 4 8 12 26 41 55
12-17 4 8 12 24 37 50

BEN CASEY (TV)
Dell Publishing Co.: June-July, 1962 - No. 10, June-Aug, 1965 (Photo-c)
12-063-207 (#1) 6 12 18 41 66 90
2(10/62),3,5-10 4 8 12 24 37 50
4-Marijuana & heroin use story 4 8 12 28 44 60

BEN CASEY FILM STORIES (TV)
Gold Key: Nov, 1962 (25¢) (Photo-c)
30009-211-All photos 7 14 21 45 73 100

BENEATH THE PLANET OF THE APES (See Movie Comics & Power Record Comics)

BEN FRANKLIN (See Kite Fun Book)

BEN HUR
Dell Publishing Co.: No. 1052, Nov, 1959
Four Color 1052-Movie, Manning-a 10 20 30 67 116 165

BEN ISRAEL
Logos International: 1974 (39¢)
nn-Christian religious 2 4 6 10 14 18

BEOWULF (Also see First Comics Graphic Novel #1)
National Periodical Publications: Apr-May, 1975 - No. 6, Feb-Mar, 1976
1 2 4 6 8 11 14
2,3,5,6: 5-Flying saucer-c/story 1 2 3 5 6 8
4-Dracula-c/s 1 2 3 5 7 9

BERNI WRIGHTSON, MASTER OF THE MACABRE
Pacific Comics/Eclipse Comics No. 5: July, 1983 - No. 5, Nov, 1984 ($1.50, Baxter paper)
1-5: Wrightson-c/a(r). 4-Jeff Jones-r (11 pgs.) 6.00

BERRYS, THE (Also see Funny World)
Argo Publ.: May, 1956
1-Reprints daily & Sunday strips & daily Animal Antics by Ed Nofziger
6 12 18 29 36 42

BERZERKER (Milo Ventimiglia Presents...)
Image Comics (Top Cow): No. 0, Feb, 2009 - No. 6, Jun, 2010 ($2.99/$3.99)
0-3-Jeremy Haun-a/Rick Loverd-s/Dale Keown-c. 0-Creator interviews 3.00
4-6-($3.99) Covers by Haun & Keown 4.00

BERZERKERS (See Youngblood V1#2)
Image Comics (Extreme Studios): Aug, 1995 - No. 3, Oct, 1995 ($2.50, limited series)
1-3: Beau Smith scripts, Fraga-a 3.00

BEST COMICS
Better Publications: Nov, 1939 - No. 4, Feb, 1940(10-11/16" wide x 8" tall, reads sideways)
1-(Scarce)-Red Mask begins(1st app.) & c/s-all 90 180 270 576 988 1400
2-4: 4-Cannibalism story 50 100 150 315 533 750

BEST FROM BOY'S LIFE, THE
Gilberton Company: Oct, 1957 - No. 5, Oct, 1958 (35¢)
1-Space Conquerors & Kam of the Ancient Ones begin, end #5; Bob Cousy photo/story
13 26 39 72 101 130
2,3,5 8 16 24 42 54 65
4-L.B. Cole-a 8 16 24 44 57 70

BEST LOVE (Formerly Sub-Mariner Comics No. 32)
Marvel Comics (MPI): No. 33, Aug, 1949 - No. 36, April, 1950 (Photo-c 33-36)
33-Kubert-a 14 28 42 81 118 155
34 10 20 30 54 72 90
35,36-Everett-a 11 22 33 60 83 105

BEST OF ARCHIE, THE
Perigee Books: 1980 ($7.95, softcover TPB)
nn-Intro by Michael Uslan & Jeffrey Mendel 6 12 18 39 62 85

BEST OF BUGS BUNNY, THE
Gold Key: Oct, 1966 - No. 2, Oct, 1968
1,2-Giants 4 8 12 28 44 60

BEST OF DC, THE (Blue Ribbon Digest) (See Limited Coll. Ed. C-52)
DC Comics: Sept-Oct, 1979 - No. 71, Apr, 1986 (100-148 pgs; mostly reprints)
1-Superman, w/"Death of Superman"-r 2 4 6 11 16 20
2,5-9: 2-Batman 40th Ann. Special. 5-Best of 1979. 6,8-Superman. 7-Superboy. 9-Batman, Creeper app. 2 4 6 8 10 12
3-Superfriends 2 4 6 9 12 15
4-Rudolph the Red Nosed Reindeer 2 4 6 9 13 16
10-Secret Origins of Super Villains; 1st ever Penguin origin-s
3 6 9 16 22 28
11-16,18-20: 11-The Year's Best Stories. 12-Superman Time and Space Stories.13-Best of DC Comics Presents. 14-New origin stories of Batman villains. 15-Superboy. 16-Superman Anniv. 18-Teen Titans new-s., Adams, Kane-a; Perez-c. 19-Superman. 20-World's Finest
1 2 3 5 7 9
17-Supergirl 2 4 6 8 10 12
21,22: 21-Justice Society. 22-Christmas; unpublished Sandman story w/Kirby-a
2 4 6 10 14 18
23-27: 23-(148 pgs.)-Best of 1981. 24 Legion, new story and 16 pgs. new costumes. 25-Superman. 26-Brave & Bold. 27-Superman vs. Luthor
2 4 6 9 12 15
28,29: 28-Binky, Sugar & Spike app. 29-Sugar & Spike, 3 new stories; new Stanley & his Monster story 2 4 6 9 13 16
30,32-36,38,40: 30-Detective Comics. 32-Superman. 33-Secret origins of Legion Heroes and Villains. 34-Metal Men; has #497 on-c from Adv. Comics. 35-The Year's Best Comics Stories (148 pgs.). 36-Superman vs. Kryptonite. 38-Superman. 40-World of Krypton
2 4 6 9 12 15
31-JLA 2 4 6 10 14 18
37,39: 37-"Funny Stuff", Mayer-a. 39-Binky 2 4 6 10 14 18
41,43,45,47,49,53,55,58,60,63,65,68,70: 41-Sugar & Spike new stories with Mayer-a. 43,49,55-Funny Stuff. 45,53,70-Binky. 47,65,68-Sugar & Spike. 58-Super Jrs. Holiday Special; Sugar & Spike. 60-Plop!; Wood-c(r) & Aragonés-r (5/85). 63-Plop!; Wrightson-a(r)
3 6 9 14 19 24
42,44,46,48,50-52,54,56,57,59,61,62,64,66,67,69,71: 42,56-Superman vs. Aliens. 44,57,67-Superboy & LSH. 46-Jimmy Olsen. 48-Superman Team-ups. 50-Year's best Superman. 51-Batman Family. 52 Best of 1984. 54,56,59-Superman. 61-(148 pgs.)Year's best. 62-Best of Batman 1985. 69-Year's best Team stories. 71-Year's best
2 4 6 10 14 18

NOTE: ***N. Adams** a-2r, 14r, 18r, 26, 51. **Aparo** a-9, 14, 26, 30; c-9, 14, 26. **Austin** a-51i. **Buckler** a-40p; c-16, 22. **Giffen** a-50, 52; c-33p. **Grell** a-33p. **Grossman** a-37. **Heath** a-26. **Infantino** a-10r, 18. **Kaluta** a-40. **G. Kane** a-10r, 18r; c-40, 44. **Kubert** a-10r, 21, 26. **Layton** a-21. **S. Mayer** c-29, 37, 41, 43, 47; a-28, 29, 37, 41, 43, 47, 58, 65, 68. **Moldoff** c-64p. **Morrow** a-40; c-40. **W. Mortimer** a-39p. **Newton** a-5, 51. **Perez** a-24, 50p; c-18, 21, 23. **Rogers** a-14, 51p. **Simonson** a-11r. **Spiegle** a-52. **Starlin** a-51. **Staton** a-5, 21. **Tuska** a-24. **Wolverton** a-60. **Wood** a-60, 63; c-60, 63. **Wrightson** a-60. New art in #14, 18, 24.*

BEST OF DENNIS THE MENACE, THE
Hallden/Fawcett Publications: Summer, 1959 - No. 5, Spring, 1961 (100 pgs.)
1-All reprints; Wiseman-a 7 14 21 45 73 100
2-5 4 8 12 28 44 60

BEST OF DONALD DUCK, THE
Gold Key: Nov, 1965 (12¢, 36 pgs.)(Lists 2nd printing in indicia)
1-Reprints Four Color #223 by Barks 8 16 24 54 90 125

Best of the Brave and the Bold #1 © DC

Betty #187 © AP

Betty and Veronica #92 © AP

GD VG FN VF VF/NM NM-
2.0 4.0 6.0 8.0 9.0 9.2

GD VG FN VF VF/NM NM-
2.0 4.0 6.0 8.0 9.0 9.2

BEST OF DONALD DUCK & UNCLE SCROOGE, THE
Gold Key: Nov, 1964 - No. 2, Sept, 1967 (25¢ Giants)
1(30022-411)('64)-Reprints 4-Color #189 & 408 by Carl Barks; cover of F.C. #189 redrawn by Barks 9 18 27 63 107 150
2(30022-709)('67)-Reprints 4-Color #256 & "Seven Cities of Cibola" & U.S. #8 by Barks 8 16 24 52 86 120

BEST OF HORROR AND SCIENCE FICTION COMICS
Bruce Webster: 1987 ($2.00)
1-Wolverton, Frazetta, Powell, Ditko-r 5.00

BEST OF JOSIE AND THE PUSSYCATS
Archie Comics: 2001 ($10.95, TPB)
1-Reprints 1st app. and noteworthy stories 12.00

BEST OF MARMADUKE, THE
Charlton Comics: 1960
1-Brad Anderson's strip reprints 3 6 9 20 30 40

BEST OF MS. TREE, THE
Pyramid Comics: 1987 - No. 4, 1988 ($2.00, B&W, limited series)
1-4 3.00

BEST OF RAY BRADBURY, THE
ibooks: 2003 ($18.95, TPB)
The Graphic Novel - Reprints from Ray Bradbury Comics; adaptations by various 19.00

BEST OF THE BRAVE AND THE BOLD, THE (See Super DC Giant)
DC Comics: Oct, 1988 - No. 6, Jan, 1989 ($2.50, limited series)
1-6: Neal Adams-r, Kubert-r & Heath-r in all 4.00

BEST OF THE SPIRIT, THE
DC Comics: 2005 ($14.99, TPB)
nn-Reprints 1st app. and noteworthy stories; intro by Neil Gaiman; Eisner bio. 15.00

BEST OF THE WEST (See A-1 Comics)
Magazine Enterprises: 1951 - No. 12, April-June, 1954
1(A-1 42)-Ghost Rider, Durango Kid, Straight Arrow, Bobby Benson begin 41 82 123 256 428 600
2(A-1 46) 22 44 66 128 209 290
3(A-1 52), 4(A-1 59), 5(A-1 66) 18 36 54 105 165 225
6(A-1 70), 7(A-1 76), 8(A-1 81), 9(A-1 85), 10(A-1 87), 11(A-1 97), 12(A-1 103) 15 30 45 84 127 170
NOTE: *Bolle a-9. Borth a-12. Guardineer a-5, 12. Powell a-1, 12.*

BEST OF UNCLE SCROOGE & DONALD DUCK, THE
Gold Key: Nov, 1966 (25¢)
1(30030-611)-Reprints part 4-Color #159 & 456 & Uncle Scrooge #6,7 by Carl Barks 8 16 24 52 86 120

BEST OF WALT DISNEY COMICS, THE
Western Publishing Co.: 1974 ($1.50, 52 pgs.) (Walt Disney)
(8-1/2x11" cardboard covers; 32,000 printed of each)
96170-Reprints 1st two stories less 1 pg. each from 4-Color #62 6 12 18 41 66 90
96171-Reprints Mickey Mouse and the Bat Bandit of Inferno Gulch from 1934 (strips) by Gottfredson 6 12 18 41 66 90
96172-r/Uncle Scrooge #386 & two other stories 6 12 18 41 66 90
96173-Reprints "Ghost of the Grotto" (from 4-Color #159) & "Christmas on Bear Mountain" (from 4-Color #178) 6 12 18 41 66 90

BEST ROMANCE
Standard Comics (Visual Editions): No. 5, Feb-Mar, 1952 - No. 7, Aug, 1952
5-Toth-a; photo-c 14 28 42 82 121 160
6,7-Photo-c 9 18 27 50 65 80

BEST SELLER COMICS (See Tailspin Tommy)

BEST WESTERN (Formerly Terry Toons? or Miss America Magazine
Marvel Comics (IPC): V7#24(#57)?; Western Outlaws & Sheriffs No. 60 on)
No. 58, June, 1949 - No. 59, Aug, 1949
58,59-Black Rider, Kid Colt, Two-Gun Kid app.; both have Syd Shores-c 20 40 60 115 185 255

BETA RAY BILL: GODHUNTER
Marvel Comics: Aug, 2009 - No. 3, Oct, 2009 ($3.99, limited series)
1-3-Kano-a; Thor and Galactus app.; reprints form Thor #337-339. 2,3-Silver Surfer app. 4.00

BETTIE PAGE COMICS
Dark Horse Comics: Mar, 1996 ($3.95)
1-Dave Stevens-c; Blevins & Heath-a; Jaime Hernandez pin-up 1 2 3 5 6 8

BETTIE PAGE COMICS: QUEEN OF THE NILE
Dark Horse Comics: Dec, 1999 - No. 3, Apr, 2000 ($2.95, limited series)
1-3-Silke-s/a; Stevens-c 4.00

BETTIE PAGE COMICS: SPICY ADVENTURE
Dark Horse Comics: Jan, 1997 ($2.95, one-shot, mature)
nn-Silke-c/s/a 5.00

BETTY (See Pep Comics #22 for 1st app.)
Archie Comics: Sept, 1992 - Present ($1.25-$2.99)
1 5.00
2-18,20-24: 20-1st Super Sleuther-s 3.00
19-Love Showdown part 2 5.00
25-Pin-up page of Betty as Marilyn Monroe, Madonna, Lady Di 5.00
26-50 3.00
51-192: 57- "A Storm Over Uniforms" x-over part 5,6. 186-Begin $2.99-c 3.00

BETTY AND HER STEADY (Going Steady with Betty No. 1)
Avon Periodicals: No. 2, Mar-Apr, 1950
2 10 20 30 56 76 95

BETTY AND ME
Archie Publications: Aug, 1965 - No. 200, Aug, 1992
1 10 20 30 70 125 180
2,3: 3-Origin Superteen 6 12 18 41 66 90
4-8: Superteen in new costume #4-7; dons new helmet in #5, ends #8. 5 10 15 30 48 65
9,10: Girl from R.I.V.E.R.D.A.L.E. 9-UFO-s 4 8 12 24 37 50
11-15,17-20(4/69) 3 6 9 19 29 38
16-Classic cover; w/risqué cover dialogue 5 10 15 30 48 65
21,24-35: 33-Paper doll page 3 6 9 16 23 30
22-Archies Band-s 3 6 9 17 25 32
23-I Dream of Jeannie parody 3 6 9 19 29 38
36(8/71),37,41-55 (52 pgs.): 42-Betty as vamp-s 3 6 9 16 23 30
38-Sabrina app. 4 8 12 23 36 48
39-Josie and Sabrina cover cameos 3 6 9 19 29 38
40-Archie & Betty share a cabin 3 6 9 17 25 32
56(4/71)-80(12/76): 79 Betty Cooper mysteries thru #86. 79-81-Drago the Vampire-s 2 4 6 9 13 16
81-99: 83-Harem-c. 84-Jekyll & Hyde-c/s 2 4 6 8 10 12
100(3/79) 2 4 6 9 12 15
101,118: 101-Elvis mentioned. 118-Tarzan mentioned 1 2 3 5 7 9
102-117,119-130(9/82): 103,104-Space-s. 124-DeCarlo-c begins 7.00
131-138,140,142-147,149-154,156-158: 135,136-Jason Blossom app. 136-Cheryl Blossom cameo. 137-Space-s. 138-Tarzan parody 5.00
139,141,148: 139-Katy Keene collecting-s; Archie in drag-s. 141-Tarzan parody-s. 148-Cyndi Lauper parody-s 6.00
155,159,160(8/87): 155-Archie in drag-s. 159-Superhero gag-c. 160-Wheel of Fortune parody 6.00
161-169,171-199 4.00
170,200: 170-New Archie Superhero-s 6.00

BETTY AND VERONICA (Also see Archie's Girls...)
Archie Enterprises: June, 1987 - Present (75¢-$2.99)
1 2 3 4 6 8 10
2-10 6.00
11-30 4.00
31-50 3.00
51-81 3.00
82-Love Showdown part 3 5.00
83-253: 242-Begin $2.50-c. 247-Begin $2.99-c 3.00
... Free Comic Book Day Edition #1 (6/05) Katy Keene-c/app.; Cheryl Blossom app. 2.50

BETTY & VERONICA ANNUAL DIGEST (...Digest Magazine #1-4, 44 on; ...Comics Digest Mag. #5-43)(Continues as Betty & Veronica Friends Double Digest #209-on)
Archie Publications: Nov, 1980 - No. 208, Nov, 2010 ($1.00/-$2.69, digest size)
1 3 6 9 16 22 28
2-10: 2(11/81-Katy Keene story), 3(8/82) 2 4 6 9 13 16
11-30 1 3 4 6 8 10
31-50 1 2 3 4 5 7
51-70 4.00
71-191: 110-Begin $2.19-c. 135-Begin $2.39-c. 165-Begin $2.49. 185-Includes reprint of Archie's Girls B&V #1 (1950) and new story where 1950 & 2008 B&V meet 3.00
192-208: 192-Begin $2.69-c 3.00

Beverly Hillbillies #7 © Filmway

Beware #16 (#4) © TM

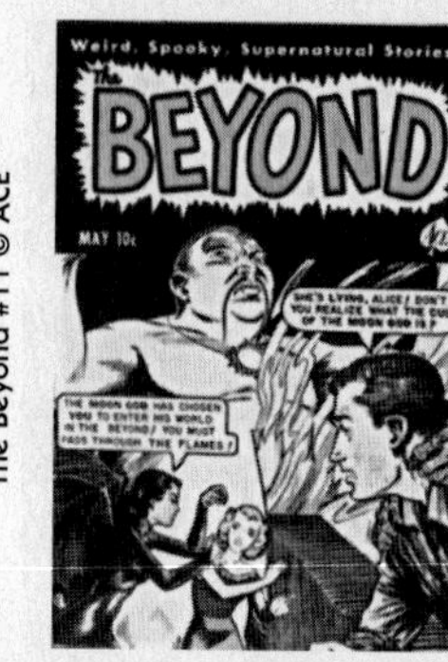

The Beyond #11 © ACE

GD VG FN VF VF/NM NM-
2.0 4.0 6.0 8.0 9.0 9.2

BETTY & VERONICA ANNUAL DIGEST MAGAZINE
Archie Comics: Sept, 1989 - No. 16, Aug, 1997 ($1.50/$1.75/$1.79, 128 pgs.)
1 1 2 3 5 7 9
2-10: 9-Neon ink logo 5.00
11-16: 16-Begin $1.79-c 3.00

BETTY & VERONICA CHRISTMAS SPECTACULAR (See Archie Giant Series Magazine #159, 168, 180, 191, 204, 217, 229, 241, 453, 465, 477, 489, 501, 513, 525, 536, 547, 558, 568, 580, 593, 606, 618)

BETTY & VERONICA DOUBLE DIGEST MAGAZINE
Archie Enterprises: 1987 - Present ($2.25-$3.99, digest size, 256 pgs.)(...Digest #12 on)
1 2 4 6 8 10 12
2-10 1 2 3 4 5 7
11-25: 5,17-Xmas-c. 16-Capt. Hero story 5.00
26-50 4.00
51-150: 87-Begin $3.19-c. 95-Begin $3.29-c. 114-Begin $3.59-c. 142-Begin $3.69-c 3.75
151-191: 151-(7/07)-Realistic style Betty & Veronica debuts (thru #154). 160-Cheryl Blossom spotlight. 170-173-Realistic style 4.00
Betty & Veronica: in Bad Boy Trouble Vol.1 TPB (2007, $7.49) r/new style from #151-154 8.00

BETTY & VERONICA FRIENDS DOUBLE DIGEST (Continues from B&V Digest Mag. #208)
Archie Publications: No. 209, Jan, 2011 - Present ($3.99, digest size)
209-214: 209-Cheryl Blossom app. 4.00

BETTY & VERONICA SPECTACULAR (See Archie Giant Series Mag. #11, 16, 21, 26, 32, 138, 145, 153, 162, 173, 184, 197, 201, 210, 214, 221, 226, 234, 238, 246, 250, 458, 462, 470, 482, 486, 494, 498, 506, 510, 518, 522, 526, 530, 537, 552, 559, 563, 569, 575, 582, 588, 600, 608, 613, 620, 623, and Betty & Veronica)

BETTY AND VERONICA SPECTACULAR
Archie Comics: Oct, 1992 - No. 90, Sept, 2009 ($1.25/$1.50/$1.75/$1.99/$2.19/$2.25/$2.50)
1-Dan DeCarlo-c/a 5.00
2-90: 48-Cheryl Blossom leaves Riverdale. 64-Cheryl Blossom returns 3.00

BETTY & VERONICA SPRING SPECTACULAR (See Archie Giant Series Magazine #569, 582, 595)

BETTY & VERONICA SUMMER FUN (See Archie Giant Series Mag. #8, 13, 18, 23, 28, 34, 140, 147, 155, 164, 175, 187, 199, 212, 224, 236, 248, 460, 484, 496, 508, 520, 529, 539, 550, 561, 572, 585, 598, 611, 621)
Archie Comics: 1994 - Present ($2.00/$2.25/$2.29)
1-($2.00, 52 pgs. plus poster) 4.00
2-6: 5-($2.25-c). 6-($2.29-c) 3.00
Vol. 1 (2003, $10.95) reprints stories from Archie Giant Series editions 12.00

BETTY BOOP'S BIG BREAK
First Publishing: 1990 ($5.95, 52 pgs.)
nn-By Joshua Quagmire; 60th anniversary ish. 6.00

BETTY PAGE 3-D COMICS
The 3-D Zone: 1991 ($3.95, "7-1/2x10-1/4," 28 pgs., no glasses)
1-Photo inside covers; back-c nudity 2 3 4 6 8 10

BETTY'S DIARY (See Archie Giant Series Magazine No. 555)
Archie Enterprises: April, 1986 - No. 40, Apr, 1991 (#1:65¢; 75¢/95¢)
1 1 2 3 4 5 7
2-10 4.00
11-40 3.00

BETTY'S DIGEST
Archie Enterprises: Nov, 1996 - No. 2 ($1.75/$1.79)
1,2 3.00

BEVERLY HILLBILLIES (TV)
Dell Publishing Co.: 4-6/63 - No. 18, 8/67; No. 19, 10/69; No. 20, 10/70; No. 21, Oct, 1971
1-Photo-c 14 28 42 95 188 280
2-Photo-c 9 18 27 60 100 140
3-9: All have photo covers 7 14 21 47 76 105
10: No photo cover 5 10 15 32 51 70
11-21: All have photo covers. 18-Last 12¢ issue. 19-21-Reprint #1-3 (covers and insides) 6 12 18 37 59 80
NOTE: *#1-9, 11-21 are photo covers.*

BEWARE (Formerly Fantastic; Chilling Tales No. 13 on)
Youthful Magazines: No. 10, June, 1952 - No. 12, Oct, 1952
10-E.A. Poe's Pit & the Pendulum adaptation by Wildey; Harrison/Bache-a; atom bomb and shrunken head-c 60 120 180 381 653 925
11-Harrison-a; Ambrose Bierce adapt. 39 78 117 240 395 550
12-Used in **SOTI**, pg. 388; Harrison-a 39 78 117 240 395 550

BEWARE
Trojan Magazines/Merit Publ. No. ?: No. 13, 1/53 - No. 16, 7/53; No. 5, 9/53 - No. 15, 5/55
13(#1)-Harrison-a 58 116 174 371 636 900
14(#2, 3/53)-Krenkel/Harrison-c; dismemberment, severed head panels 39 78 117 240 395 550
15,16(#3, 5/53; #4, 7/53)-Harrison-a 36 72 108 216 351 485
5,9,12,13 36 72 108 211 343 475
6-Ill. in **SOTI**- "Children are first shocked and then desensitized by all this brutality." Corpse on cover swipe/V.O.H. #26; girl on cover swipe/Advs. Into Darkness #10 64 128 192 406 696 985
7,8-Check-a 36 72 108 216 351 485
10-Frazetta/Check-c; Disbrow, Check-a 74 148 222 470 810 1150
11-Disbrow-a; heart torn out, blood drainage 39 78 117 240 395 550
14,15: 14-Myron Fass-c. 15-Harrison-a 30 60 90 177 289 400
NOTE: ***Fass** a-5, 6, 8; c-6, 11, 14. **Forte** a-8. **Hollingsworth** a-15(#3), 16(#4), 9; c-16(#4), 8, 9. **Kiefer** a-16(#4), 5, 6, 10.*

BEWARE (Becomes Tomb of Darkness No. 9 on)
Marvel Comics Group: Mar, 1973 - No. 8, May, 1974 (All reprints)
1-Everett-c; Kirby & Sinnott-r ('54) 3 6 9 18 27 35
2-8: 2-Forte, Colan-r. 6-Tuska-a. 7-Torres-r/Mystical Tales #7 2 4 6 13 18 22
NOTE: ***Infantino** a-4r. **Gil Kane** c-4. **Wildey** a-7r.*

BEWARE TERROR TALES
Fawcett Publications: May, 1952 - No. 8, July, 1953
1-E.C. art swipe/Haunt of Fear #5 & Vault of Horror #26 48 96 144 302 514 725
2 32 64 96 192 314 435
3-5,7 27 54 81 158 259 360
6-Classic skeleton-c 29 58 87 170 278 385
8-Tothish-a; people being cooked-c 32 64 96 192 314 435
NOTE: ***Andru** a-2. **Bernard Bailey** a-1; c-1-5. **Powell** a-1, 2, 8. **Sekowsky** a-2.*

BEWARE THE CREEPER (See Adventure, Best of the Brave & the Bold, Brave & the Bold, 1st Issue Special, Flash #318-323, Showcase #73, World's Finest Comics #249)
National Periodical Publications: May-June, 1968 - No. 6, Mar-Apr, 1969 (All 12¢ issues)
1-(5-6/68)-Classic Ditko-c; Ditko-a in all 9 18 27 63 107 150
2-6: 2-5-Ditko-c. 2-Intro. Proteus. 6-Gil Kane-c 5 10 15 34 55 75

BEWARE THE CREEPER
DC Comics (Vertigo): June, 2003 - No. 5, Oct, 2003 ($2.95, limited series)
1-5-Female vigilante in 1920s Paris; Jason Hall-s/Cliff Chiang-a 3.00

BEWITCHED (TV)
Dell Publishing Co.: 4-6/65 - No. 11, 10/67; No. 12, 10/68 - No. 13, 1/69; No. 14, 10/69
1-Photo-c 14 28 42 96 191 285
2-No photo-c 8 16 24 54 90 125
3-13-All have photo-c. 12-Rep. #1. 13-Last 12¢-c 7 14 21 47 76 105
14-No photo-c; reprints #2 5 10 15 34 55 75

BEYOND!
Marvel Comics: Sept, 2006 - No. 6, Feb, 2007 ($2.99, limited series)
1-6-McDuffie-s/Kolins-a; Spider-Man, Venom, Gravity, Wasp app. 6-Gravity dies 3.00
HC (2007, $19.99, dustjacket) r/series; cover sketches and sketch design pages 20.00
SC (2008, $14.99) r/series; cover sketches and sketch design pages 15.00

BEYOND, THE
Ace Magazines: Nov, 1950 - No. 30, Jan, 1955
1-Bakerish-a(p) 44 88 132 277 469 660
2-Bakerish-a(p) 29 58 87 170 278 385
3-10: 10-Woodish-a by Cameron 21 42 63 122 199 275
11-20: 18-Used in **POP**, pgs. 81,82 18 36 54 103 162 220
21-26,28-30 17 34 51 98 154 210
27-Used in **SOTI**, pg. 111 18 36 54 103 162 220
NOTE: ***Cameron** a-10, 11p, 12p, 15, 16, 21-27, 30; c-20. **Colan** a-6, 13, 17. **Sekowsky** a-2, 3, 5, 7, 11, 14, 27r. No. 1 was to appear as Challenge of the Unknown No. 7.*

BEYOND THE GRAVE
Charlton Comics: July, 1975 - No. 6, June, 1976; No. 7, Jan, 1983 - No. 17, Oct, 1984
1-Ditko-a (6 pgs.); Sutton painted-c 3 6 9 20 30 40
2-6: 2-5-Ditko-a; Ditko c-2,3,6 2 4 6 13 18 22
7-17: ('83-'84) Reprints. 8,11,16-Ditko-a. 11-Staton-a. 13-Aparo-c(r). 15-Sutton-c (low print run). 16-Palais-a 1 2 3 4 5 7
Modern Comics Reprint 2('78) 4.00
NOTE: ***Howard** a-4. **Kim** a-1. **Larson** a-4, 6.*

BIBLE, THE: EDEN
IDW Publishing: 2003 ($21.99, hardcover graphic novel)
HC-Scott Hampton painted-a; adaptation of Genesis by Dave Elliot and Keith Giffen 22.00

Big Bang Comics V2 #18 © Carlson

Big Chief Wahoo #1 © EAS

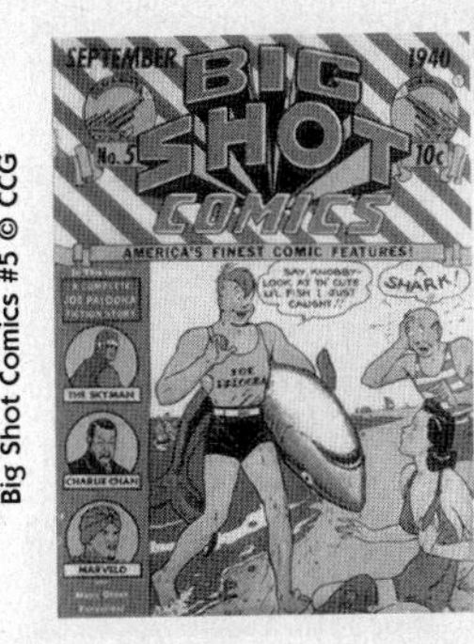

Big Shot Comics #5 © CCG

	GD 2.0	VG 4.0	FN 6.0	VF 8.0	VF/NM 9.0	NM- 9.2

BIBLE TALES FOR YOUNG FOLK (...Young People No. 3-5)
Atlas Comics (OMC): Aug, 1953 - No. 5, Mar, 1954

1	27	54	81	158	259	360
2-Everett, Krigstein-a; Robinson-c	18	36	54	105	165	225
3-5: 4,5-Robinson-c	15	30	45	88	137	185

BIG (Movie)
Hit Comics (Dark Horse Comics): Mar, 1989 ($2.00)

1-Adaptation of film; Paul Chadwick-c 3.00

BIG ALL-AMERICAN COMIC BOOK, THE (See All-American Comics)
All-American/National Per. Publ.: 1944 (132 pgs., one-shot) (Early DC Annual)

1-Wonder Woman, Green Lantern, Flash, The Atom, Wildcat, Scribbly, The Whip, Ghost Patrol, Hawkman by Kubert (1st on Hawkman), Hop Harrigan, Johnny Thunder, Little Boy Blue, Mr. Terrific, Mutt & Jeff app.; Sargon on cover only; cover by Kubert/Hibbard/Mayer and others 649 1298 1947 4738 8369 12,000

BIG BABY HUEY (See Baby Huey)

BIG BANG COMICS (Becomes Big Bang #4)
Caliber Press: Spring, 1994 - No. 4, Feb, 1995; No. 0, May, 1995 ($1.95, lim. series)

1-4-($1.95-c) 3.00
0-(5/95, $2.95) Alex Ross-c; color and B&W pages 3.00
Your Big Book of Big Bang Comics TPB ('98, $11.00) r/#0-2 11.00

BIG BANG COMICS (Volume 2)
Image Comics (Highbrow Ent.): V2#1, May, 1996 - No. 35, Jan, 2001 ($1.95-$3.95)

1-23,26: 1-Mighty Man app. 2-4-S.A. Shadowhawk app. 5-Begin $2.95-c. 6-Curt Swan/Murphy Anderson-c. 7-Begin B&W. 12-Savage Dragon-c/app. 16,17,21-Shadow Lady 3.00
24,25,27-35-($3.95): 35-Big Bang vs. Alan Moore's "1963" characters 4.00
...Presents the Ultiman Family (2/05, $3.50) 3.50
...Round Table of America (2/04, $3.95) Don Thomas-a 4.00
...Summer Special (8/03, $4.95) World's Nastiest Nazis app. 5.00

BIG BANG PRESENTS (Volume 3)
Big Bang Comics: July, 2006 - No. 5 ($2.95/$3.95, B&W)

1,2: 1-Protoplasman (Plastic Man homage) 3.00
3-5-($3.95) 3-Origin of Protoplasman. 4-Flip book 4.00

BIG BLACK KISS
Vortex Comics: Sep, 1989 - No, 3, Nov, 1989 ($3.75, B&W, lim. series, mature)

1-3-Chaykin-s/a 4.00

BIG BLOWN BABY (Also see Dark Horse Presents)
Dark Horse Comics: Aug, 1996 - No. 4, Nov, 1996 ($2.95, lim. series, mature)

1-4: Bill Wray-c/a/scripts 3.00

BIG BOOK OF ..., THE
DC Comics (Paradox Press): 1994 - 1999 (B&W)($12.95 - $14.95)

nn-...**BAD**,1998 ($14.95),...**CONSPIRACIES**, 1995 ($12.95), ...**DEATH**,1994 ($12.95), ...**FREAKS**, 1996 ($14.95), ...**GRIMM**, 1999 ($14.95), ...**HOAXES**, 1996 ($14.95), ...**LITTLE CRIMINALS**, 1996 ($14.95), ...**LOSERS**,1997 ($14.95), **MARTYRS**, 1997 ($14.95), ...**SCANDAL**,1997 ($14.95), ...**THE WEIRD WILD WEST**,1998 ($14.95), ...**THUGS**, 1997 ($14.95), ...**UNEXPLAINED**, 1997 ($14.95), ...**URBAN LEGENDS**, 1994 ($12.95), ...**VICE**, 1999 ($14.95), ...**WEIRDOS**, 1995 ($12.95) cover price

BIG BOOK OF FUN COMICS (See New Book of Comics)
National Periodical Publications: Spring, 1936 (Large size, 52 pgs.)
(1st comic book annual & DC annual)

1 (Very rare)-r/New Fun #1-5 2300 4600 6900 15,000 - -

BIG BOOK ROMANCES
Fawcett Publications: Feb, 1950 (no date given) (148 pgs.)

1-Contains remaindered Fawcett romance comics - several combinations possible 43 86 129 271 461 650

BIG CHIEF WAHOO
Eastern Color Printing/George Dougherty (distr. by Fawcett): July, 1942 - No. 7, Wint., 1943/44?(no year given)(Quarterly)

1-Newspaper-r (on sale 6/15/42)	42	84	126	265	445	625
2-Steve Roper app.	23	46	69	136	223	310
3-5: 4-Chief is holding a Katy Keene comic	18	36	54	105	165	225
6-7	14	28	42	82	121	160

NOTE: *Kerry Drake in some issues.*

BIG CIRCUS, THE (Movie)
Dell Publishing Co.: No. 1036, Sept-Nov, 1959

Four Color 1036-Photo-c 6 12 18 43 69 95

BIG COUNTRY, THE (Movie)
Dell Publishing Co.: No. 946, Oct, 1958

Four Color 946-Photo-c 7 14 21 47 76 105

BIG DADDY DANGER
DC Comics: Oct, 2002 - No. 9, June, 2003 ($2.95, limited series)

1-9-Adam Pollina-s/a/c 3.00

BIG DADDY ROTH (Magazine)
Millar Publications: Oct-Nov, 1964 - No. 4, Apr-May, 1965 (35¢)

1-Toth-a	16	32	48	114	232	350
2-4-Toth-a	11	22	33	79	147	215

BIGFOOT
IDW Publishing: Feb, 2005 - No. 4, May, 2005 ($3.99, limited series)

1-4-Steve Niles & Rob Zombie-s/Richard Corben-a/c 4.00

BIGG TIME
DC Comics (Vertigo): 2002 ($14.95, B&W, graphic novel)

nn-Ty Templeton-s/c/a 15.00

BIG GUY AND RUSTY THE BOY ROBOT, THE (Also See Madman Comics #6,7 & Martha Washington Stranded In Space)
Dark Horse (Legend): July, 1995 - No. 2, Aug, 1995 ($4.95, oversize, limited series)

1,2-Frank Miller scripts & Geoff Darrow-c/a 1 2 3 4 5 7
Trade paperback (10/96, $14.95)-r/1,2 w/cover gallery 15.00

BIG HAIR PRODUCTIONS
Image Comics: Feb, 2000 - No. 2, Mar, 2000 ($3.50, B&W)

1,2 3.50

BIG HERO ADVENTURES (See Jigsaw)

BIG HERO 6 (Also see Sunfire & Big Hero Six)
Marvel Comics: Nov, 2008 - No. 5, Mar, 2009 ($3.99, limited series)

1-5-Claremont-s/Nakayama-a; 1-Character design pages & Handbook entries 4.00

BIG JON & SPARKIE (Radio)(Formerly Sparkie, Radio Pixie)
Ziff-Davis Publ. Co.: No. 4, Sept-Oct, 1952 (Painted-c)

4-Based on children's radio program 18 36 54 107 169 230

BIG LAND, THE (Movie)
Dell Publishing Co.: No. 812, July, 1957

Four Color 812-Alan Ladd photo-c 9 18 27 60 100 140

BIG RED (See Movie Comics)

BIG SHOT COMICS
Columbia Comics Group: May, 1940 - No. 104, Aug, 1949

1-Intro. Skyman; The Face (1st app.; Tony Trent), The Cloak (Spy Master), Marvelo, Monarch of Magicians, Joe Palooka, Charlie Chan, Tom Kerry, Dixie Dugan, Rocky Ryan begin; Charlie Chan moves over from Feature Comics #31 (4/40)	265	530	795	1694	2897	4100
2	90	180	270	576	988	1400
3-The Cloak called Spy Chief; Skyman-c	81	162	243	518	884	1250
4,5	58	116	174	371	636	900
6-10: 8-Christmas-c	47	94	141	296	498	700
11-13	43	86	129	271	461	650
14-Origin & 1st app. Sparky Watts (6/41)	47	94	141	296	498	700
15-Origin The Cloak	50	100	150	315	533	750
16-20	37	74	111	222	361	500
21-23,26,27,29,30: 29-Intro. Capt. Yank; Bo (a dog) newspaper strip-r by Frank Beck begin, ends #104. 30-X-Mas-c	31	62	93	186	303	420
24-Classic Tojo-c.	65	130	195	416	708	1000
25-Hitler-c	53	106	159	334	567	800
28-Hitler, Tojo & Mussolini-c	71	142	213	454	777	1100
31,33-40	23	46	69	136	223	310
32-Vic Jordan newspaper strip reprints begin, ends #52; Hitler, Tojo & Mussolini-c	61	122	183	390	670	950
41,42,44,45,47-50: 42-No Skyman. 50-Origin The Face retold	20	40	60	117	189	260
43-Hitler-c	53	106	159	334	567	800
46-Hitler, Tojo-c (6/44)	52	104	156	323	549	775
51-Tojo Japanese war-c	26	52	78	154	252	350
52-56,58-60:	17	34	51	98	154	210
57-Hitler, Tojo Halloween mask-c	37	74	111	222	361	500
61-70: 63 on-Tony Trent, the Face	14	28	42	81	118	155
71-80: 73-The Face cameo. 74-(2/47)-Mickey Finn begins. 74,80-The Face app. in Tony Trent. 78-Last Charlie Chan strip-r	14	28	42	76	108	140

81-90: 85-Tony Trent marries Babs Walsh. 86-Valentines-c

Big Town #3 © DC

Billy and Buggy Bear #1 © MAR

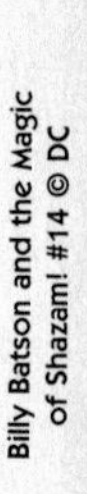

Billy Batson and the Magic of Shazam! #14 © DC

	GD 2.0	VG 4.0	FN 6.0	VF 8.0	VF/NM 9.0	NM- 9.2
	11	22	33	62	86	110
91-99,101-104: 69-94-Skyman in Outer Space. 96-Xmas-c	10	20	30	56	76	95
100	11	22	33	64	90	115

NOTE: ***Mart Bailey** art on "The Face" No. 1-104. **Guardineer** a-5. Sparky Watts by **Boody Rogers**-No. 14-42, 77-104, (by others No. 43-76). Others than Tony Trent wear "The Face" mask in No. 46-63, 93. Skyman by **Ogden Whitney**-No. 1, 2, 4, 12-37, 49, 70-101. Skyman covers-No. 1, 3, 7-12, 14, 16, 20, 27, 89, 95, 100.*

BIG SMASH BARGAIN COMICS
No publisher listed: Early 1950s (25¢, 160pgs., Canadian reprints)

1-4: Contains 4 comics from various companies bundled with new cover (scarce)	30	60	90	177	289	400

BIG TEX
Toby Press: June, 1953

1-Contains (3) John Wayne stories-r with name changed to Big Tex	10	20	30	58	79	100

BIG-3
Fox Features Syndicate: Fall, 1940 - No. 7, Jan, 1942

1-Blue Beetle, The Flame, & Samson begin	226	452	678	1446	2473	3500
2	84	168	252	538	919	1300
3-5	60	120	180	381	653	925
6,7: 6-Last Samson. 7-V-Man app.	45	90	135	284	480	675

BIG TOP COMICS, THE (TV's Great Circus Show)
Toby Press: 1951 - No. 2, 1951 (No month)

1	10	20	30	58	79	100
2	9	18	27	47	61	75

BIG TOWN (Radio/TV) (Also see Movie Comics, 1946)
National Periodical Publ: Jan, 1951 - No. 50, Mar-Apr, 1958 (No. 1-9: 52pgs.)

1-Dan Barry-a begins	68	136	204	435	743	1050
2	36	72	108	214	347	480
3-10	21	42	63	124	202	280
11-20	16	32	48	92	144	195
21-31: Last pre-code (1-2/55)	13	26	39	74	105	135
32-50: 46-Grey tone cover	10	20	30	56	76	95

BIG VALLEY, THE (TV)
Dell Publishing Co.: June, 1966 - No. 5, Oct, 1967; No. 6, Oct, 1969

1: Photo-c #1-5	5	10	15	34	55	75
2-6: 6-Reprints #1	4	8	12	22	34	45

BIKER MICE FROM MARS (TV)
Marvel Comics: Nov, 1993 - No. 3, Jan, 1994 ($1.50, limited series)

1-3: 1-Intro Vinnie, Modo & Throttle. 2-Origin						4.00

BILL & TED'S BOGUS JOURNEY
Marvel Comics: Sept, 1991 ($2.95, squarebound, 84 pgs.)

1-Adapts movie sequel						3.00

BILL & TED'S EXCELLENT COMIC BOOK (Movie)
Marvel Comics: Dec, 1991 - No. 12, 1992 ($1.00/$1.25)

1-12: 3-Begin $1.25-c						3.00

BILL BARNES COMICS (...America's Air Ace Comics No. 2 on) (Becomes Air Ace V2#1 on; also see Shadow Comics)
Street & Smith Publications: Oct, 1940(No. month given) - No. 12, Oct, 1943

1-23 pgs.-comics; Rocket Rooney begins	89	178	267	565	970	1375
2-Barnes as The Phantom Flyer app.; Tuska-a	44	88	132	277	469	660
3-5	40	80	120	242	401	560
6,8,10,12	34	68	102	204	332	460
7-(1942) Story about dropping atomic bomb on Japan	40	80	120	246	411	575
9-Classic WWII cover	41	82	123	256	428	600
11-Japanese WWII Gremlin cover	36	72	108	211	343	475

BILL BATTLE, THE ONE MAN ARMY (Also see Master Comics No. 133)
Fawcett Publications: Oct, 1952 - No. 4, Apr, 1953 (All photo-c)

1	14	28	42	76	108	140
2	8	16	24	44	57	70
3,4	8	16	24	40	50	60

BILL BLACK'S FUN COMICS
Paragon #1-3/Americomics #4: Dec, 1982 - No. 4, Mar, 1983 ($1.75/$2.00, Baxter paper) (1st AC comic)

1-(B&W fanzine; 7x8-1/2"; low print) Intro. Capt. Paragon, Phantom Lady & Commando D	2	4	6	13	18	22
2-4: 2,3-(B&W fanzines; 8-1/2x11"). 3-Kirby-c. 4-($2.00, color)-Origin Nightfall (formerly Phantom Lady); Nightveil app.; Kirby-a	1	3	4	6	8	10

BILL BOYD WESTERN (Movie star; see Hopalong Cassidy & Western Hero)
Fawcett Publ: Feb, 1950 - No. 23, June, 1952 (1-3,7,11,14-on: 36 pgs.)

1-Bill Boyd & his horse Midnite begin; photo front/back-c	36	72	108	214	347	480
2-Painted-c	19	38	57	111	176	240
3-Photo-c begin, end #23; last photo back-c	15	30	45	86	133	180
4-6(52 pgs.)	14	28	42	81	118	155
7,11(36 pgs.)	12	24	36	67	94	120
8-10,12,13(52 pgs.)	12	24	36	69	97	125
14-22	11	22	33	62	86	110
23-Last issue	12	24	36	67	94	120

BILL BUMLIN (See Treasury of Comics No. 3)

BILL ELLIOTT (See Wild Bill Elliott)

BILLI 99
Dark Horse Comics: Sept, 1991 - No. 4, 1991 ($3.50, B&W, lim. series, 52 pgs.)

1-4: Tim Sale-c/a						3.50

BILL STERN'S SPORTS BOOK
Ziff-Davis Publ. Co.(Approved Comics): Spring-Sum, 1951 - V2#2, Win, 1952

V1#10-(1951) Whitney painted-c	21	42	63	122	199	275
2-(Sum/52; reg. size)	16	32	48	94	147	200
V2#2-(1952, 96 pgs.)-Krigstein, Kinstler-a	21	42	63	126	206	285

BILL THE BULL: ONE SHOT, ONE BOURBON, ONE BEER
Boneyard Press: Dec, 1994 ($2.95, B&W, mature)

1						3.00

BILLY AND BUGGY BEAR (See Animal Fun)
I.W. Enterprises/Super: 1958; 1964

I.W. Reprint #1, #7('58)-All Surprise Comics #?(Same issue-r for both)	2	4	6	10	14	18
Super Reprint #10(1964)	2	4	6	8	11	14

BILLY BATSON AND THE MAGIC OF SHAZAM! (Follows Shazam: The Monster Society of Evil mini-series)
DC Comics: Sept, 2008 - No. 21, Dec, 2010 ($2.25/$2.50, all ages title)

1-17: 1-4-Mike Kunkel-s/a/c; Theo (Black) Adam app. 5-DeStefano-a. 13-16-Black Adam						3.00
1-Variant B&W sketch cover						3.50
18-21 ($2.99) 21-Justice League cameo						3.00
TPB (2010, $12.99) r/#1-6; cover and haracter sketches						13.00
...: Mr. Mind Over Matter TPB (2011, $12.99) r/#7-12						13.00

BILLY BUCKSKIN WESTERN (2-Gun Western No. 4)
Atlas Comics (IMC No. 1/MgPC No. 2,3): Nov, 1955 - No. 3, Mar, 1956

1-Mort Drucker-a; Maneely-c/a	16	32	48	88	137	185
2-Mort Drucker-a	10	20	30	56	76	95
3-Williamson, Drucker-a	12	24	36	67	94	120

BILLY BUNNY (Black Cobra No. 6 on)
Excellent Publications: Feb-Mar, 1954 - No. 5, Oct-Nov, 1954

1	9	18	27	50	65	80
2	6	12	18	28	34	40
3-5	5	10	15	24	30	35

BILLY BUNNY'S CHRISTMAS FROLICS
Farrell Publications: 1952 (25¢ Giant, 100 pgs.)

1	20	40	60	117	189	260

BILLY MAKE BELIEVE
United Features Syndicate: No. 14, 1939

Single Series 14	30	60	90	177	289	400

BILLY NGUYEN, PRIVATE EYE
Caliber Press: V2#1, 1990 ($2.50)

V2#1						3.00

BILLY THE KID (Formerly The Masked Raider; also see Doc Savage Comics & Return of the Outlaw)
Charlton Publ. Co.: No. 9, Nov, 1957 - No. 121, Dec, 1976; No. 122, Sept, 1977 - No. 123, Oct, 1977; No. 124, Feb, 1978 - No. 153, Mar, 1983

9	10	20	30	58	79	100
10,12,14,17-19: 12-2 pg Check-sty	8	16	24	40	50	60
11-(68 pgs.)-Origin & 1st app. The Ghost Train	9	18	27	50	65	80
13-Williamson/Torres-a	8	16	24	44	57	70

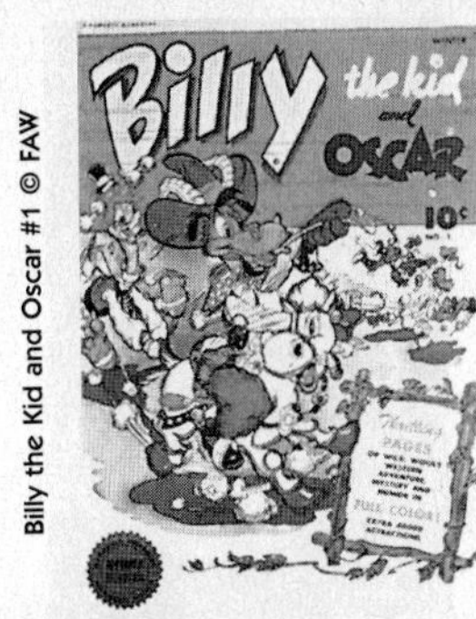

Billy the Kid and Oscar #1 © FAW

Birds of Prey (2nd series) #3 © DC

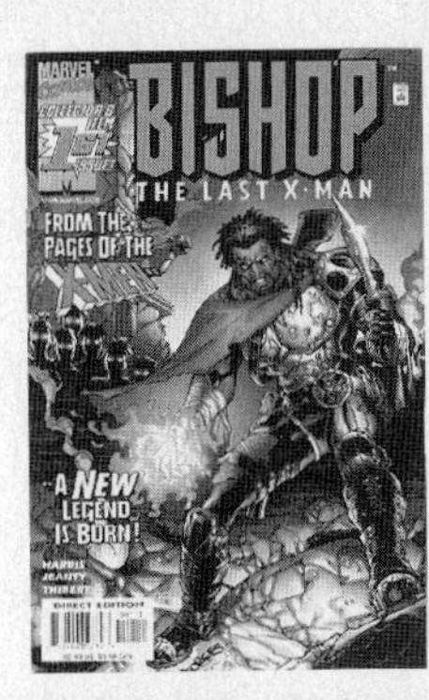

Bishop the Last X-Man #1 © MAR

	GD 2.0	VG 4.0	FN 6.0	VF 8.0	VF/NM 9.0	NM- 9.2
15-Origin; 2 pgs. Williamson-a	8	16	24	44	57	70
16-Williamson-a, 2 pgs.	8	16	24	42	54	65
20-26-Severin-a(3-4 each)	8	16	24	44	57	70
27-30: 30-Masked Rider app.	3	6	9	19	29	38
31-40	3	6	9	16	22	28
41-60	2	4	6	13	18	22
61-65	2	4	6	10	14	18
66-Bounty Hunter series begins.	3	6	9	14	20	25
67-80: Bounty Hunter series; not in #79,82,84-86	2	4	6	10	14	18
81-84,86-90: 87-Last Bounty Hunter. 88-1st app. Mr. Young of the Boothill Gazette	2	4	6	8	10	12
85-Early Kaluta-a (4 pgs.)	2	4	6	9	13	16
91-123: 110-Mr. Young of Boothill app. 111-Origin The Ghost Train. 117-Gunsmith & Co., The Cheyenne Kid app.	1	2	3	5	6	8
124(2/78)-153						6.00
Modern Comics 109 (1977 reprint)						4.00

NOTE: ***Boyette** a-88-110. **Kim** a-73. **Morsi** a-12,14. **Sattler** a-118-123. **Severin** a(r)-121-129, 134; c-23, 25. **Sutton** a-111.*

BILLY THE KID ADVENTURE MAGAZINE
Toby Press: Oct, 1950 - No. 29, 1955

	GD	VG	FN	VF	VF/NM	NM-
1-Williamson/Frazetta-a (2 pgs) r/from John Wayne Adventure Comics #2; photo-c	31	62	93	182	296	410
2-Photo-c	12	24	36	69	97	125
3-Williamson/Frazetta "The Claws of Death", 4 pgs. plus Williamson art	34	68	102	199	325	450
4,5,7,8,10: 4,7-Photo-c	9	18	27	52	69	85
6-Frazetta assist on "Nightmare"; photo-c	15	30	45	83	124	165
9-Kurtzman Pot-Shot Pete; photo-c	11	22	33	64	90	115
11,12,15-20: 11-Photo-c	8	16	24	42	54	65
13-Kurtzman-r/John Wayne #12 (Genius)	9	18	27	47	61	75
14-Williamson/Frazetta; r-of #1 (2 pgs.)	10	20	30	56	76	95
21,23-29	7	14	21	37	46	55
22-Williamson/Frazetta-r(1pg.)/#1; photo-c	8	16	24	42	54	65

BILLY THE KID AND OSCAR (Also see Fawcett's Funny Animals)
Fawcett Publications: Winter, 1945 - No. 3, Fall, 1946 (Funny animal)

	GD	VG	FN	VF	VF/NM	NM-
1	15	30	45	84	127	170
2,3	10	20	30	56	76	95

BILLY THE KID'S OLD TIMEY ODDITIES
Dark Horse Comics: Apr, 2005 - No. 4, July, 2005 ($2.99, limited series)

	GD	VG	FN	VF	VF/NM	NM-
1-4-Eric Powell-s/c; Kyle Hotz-a						3.00
TPB (2005, $13.95) r/series						14.00
... and the Ghostly Fiend of London (9/10 - No. 4, 12/10, $3.99) 1-3-Powell-s/c; Kyle Hotz-a; Goon back-up; Powell-s/a						4.00

BILLY WEST (Bill West No. 9,10)
Standard Comics (Visual Editions): 1949-No. 9, Feb, 1951; No. 10, Feb, 1952

	GD	VG	FN	VF	VF/NM	NM-
1	15	30	45	84	127	170
2	9	18	27	52	69	85
3-6,9,10	8	16	24	44	57	70
7,8-Schomburg-c	9	18	27	52	69	85

NOTE: ***Celardo** a-1-6, 9; c-1-3. **Moreira** a-3. **Roussos** a-2.*

BING CROSBY (See Feature Films)

BINGO (...Comics) (H. C. Blackerby)
Howard Publ.: 1945 (Reprints National material)

	GD	VG	FN	VF	VF/NM	NM-
1-L. B. Cole opium-c; blank back-c	36	72	108	211	343	475

BINGO, THE MONKEY DOODLE BOY
St. John Publishing Co.: Aug, 1951; Oct, 1953

	GD	VG	FN	VF	VF/NM	NM-
1(8/51)-By Eric Peters	8	16	24	42	54	65
1(10/53)	6	12	18	31	38	45

BINKY (Formerly Leave It to...)
National Periodical Publ./DC Comics: No. 72, 4-5/70 - No. 81, 10-11/71; No. 82, Summer/77

	GD	VG	FN	VF	VF/NM	NM-
72-76	4	8	12	24	37	50
77-79: (68 pgs.). 77-Bobby Sherman 1pg. story w/photo. 78-1 pg. sty on Barry Williams of Brady Bunch. 79-Osmonds 1pg. story	6	12	18	39	62	85
80,81 (52 pgs.)-Sweat Pain story	5	10	15	32	51	70
82 (1977, one-shot)	4	8	12	26	41	55

BINKY'S BUDDIES
National Periodical Publications: Jan-Feb, 1969 - No. 12, Nov-Dec, 1970

	GD	VG	FN	VF	VF/NM	NM-
1	7	14	21	49	80	110
2-12: 3-Last 12¢ issue	4	8	12	26	41	55

BIONIC WOMAN, THE (TV)
Charlton Publications: Oct, 1977 - No. 5, June, 1978

	GD	VG	FN	VF	VF/NM	NM-
1	4	8	12	22	34	45
2-5	3	6	9	16	23	30

BIRDS OF PREY (Also see Black Canary/Oracle: Birds of Prey)
DC Comics: Jan, 1999 - No. 127, Apr, 2009 ($1.99/$2.50/$2.99)

	GD	VG	FN	VF	VF/NM	NM-
1-Dixon-s/Land-c/a	1	3	4	6	8	10
2-4						6.00
5-7,9-15: 15-Guice-a begins.						4.00
8-Nightwing-c/app.; Barbara & Dick's circus date	2	4	6	9	12	15
16-38: 23-Grodd-c/app. 26-Bane app. 32-Noto-c begin						3.00
39,40-Bruce Wayne: Murderer pt. 5,12						3.50
41-Bruce Wayne: Fugitive pt. 2						4.00
42-46: 42-Fabry-a. 45-Deathstroke-c/app.						3.00
47-74,76-91: 47-49-Terry Moore-s/Conner & Palmiotti-a; Noto-c. 50-Gilbert Hernandez-s begin. 52,54-Metamorpho app. 56-Simone-s/Benes-a begin. 65,67,68,70-Land-c. 76-Debut of Black Alice (from Day of Vengeance). 86-Timm-a (7 pgs.)						3.00
75-($2.95) Pearson-c; back-up story of Lady Blackhawk						4.00
92-99,101-127: 92-One Year Later. 94-Begin $2.99-c; Prometheus app. 96,97-Black Alice app. 98,99-New Batgirl app. 99-Black Canary leaves the team. 104-107-Secret Six app.						3.00
100-($3.99) new team recruited; Black Canary origin re-told						4.00
TPB (1999, $17.95) r/ previous series and one-shots						18.00
...: Batgirl 1 (2/98, $2.95) Dixon-s/Frank-c						5.00
...: Batgirl/Catwoman 1 ('03, $5.95) Robertson-a; cont'd in BOP: Catwoman/Oracle 1						6.00
...: Between Dark & Dawn TPB (2006, $14.99) r/#69-75						15.00
...: Blood and Circuits TPB (2007, $17.99) r/#96-103						18.00
...: Catwoman/Oracle 1 ('03, $5.95) Cont'd from BOP: Batgirl/Catwoman 1; David Ross-a						6.00
...: Club Kids TPB (2008, $17.99) r/#109-112,118						18.00
...: Dead of Winter TPB (2008, $17.99) r/#104-108						18.00
...: Metropolis or Dust TPB (2008, $17.99) r/#113-117						18.00
...: Of Like Minds TPB (2004, $14.95) r/#55-61						15.00
...: Old Friends, New Enemies TPB (2003, $17.95) r/#1-6, ...: Batgirl, ...: Wolves						18.00
...: Perfect Pitch TPB (2007, $17.99) r/#86-90,92-95						18.00
...: Platinum Flats TPB (2009, $17.99) r/#119-124						18.00
...: Revolution 1 (1997, $2.95) Frank-c/Dixon-s						5.00
... Secret Files 2003 (8/03, $4.95) Short stories, pin-ups and profile pages; Noto-c						5.00
...: Sensei and Student TPB (2005, $17.95) r/#62-68						18.00
...: The Battle Within TPB (2006, $17.99) r/#76-85						18.00
...: The Ravens 1 (6/98, $1.95)-Dixon-s; Girlfrenzy issue						4.00
...: Wolves 1 (10/97, $2.95) Dixon-s/Giordano & Faucher-a						5.00

BIRDS OF PREY (Brightest Day)
DC Comics: Jul, 2010 - Present ($2.99)

	GD	VG	FN	VF	VF/NM	NM-
1-Simone-s/Benes-a/c; Hawk and Dove join team, Penguin app.						3.00
1-Variant cover by Chiang						5.00
2-10: 2-4-Penguin app. 7-10-"Death of Oracle". 8-March-a						3.00

BIRDS OF PREY: MANHUNT
DC Comics: Sept, 1996 - No. 4, Dec, 1996 ($1.95, limited series)

	GD	VG	FN	VF	VF/NM	NM-
1-Features Black Canary, Oracle, Huntress, & Catwoman; Chuck Dixon scripts; Gary Frank-c on all. 1-Catwoman cameo only	1	2	3	5	6	8
2-4						6.00

NOTE: ***Gary Frank** c-1-4. **Matt Haley** a-1-4p. **Wade Von Grawbadger** a-1i.*

BIRTH CAUL, THE
Eddie Campbell Comics: 1999 ($5.95, B&W, one-shot)

	GD	VG	FN	VF	VF/NM	NM-
1-Alan Moore-s/Eddie Campbell-a						6.00

BIRTH OF THE DEFIANT UNIVERSE, THE
Defiant Comics: May, 1993

	GD	VG	FN	VF	VF/NM	NM-
nn-Contains promotional artwork & text; limited print run of 1000 copies.	2	4	6	8	10	12

BISHOP (See Uncanny X-Men & X-Men)
Marvel Comics: Dec, 1994 - No.4, Mar, 1995 ($2.95, limited series)

	GD	VG	FN	VF	VF/NM	NM-
1-4: Foil-c; Shard & Mountjoy in all. 1-Storm app.						3.00

BISHOP THE LAST X-MAN
Marvel Comics: Oct, 1999 - No. 16, Jan, 2001 ($2.99/$1.99/$2.25)

	GD	VG	FN	VF	VF/NM	NM-
1-($2.99)-Jeanty-a						4.00
2-8-($1.99): 2-Two covers						3.00
9-11,13-16: 9-Begin $2.25-c. 15-Maximum Security x-over; Xavier app.						3.00
12-($2.99)						4.00

BISHOP: XAVIER SECURITY ENFORCER

Bite Club #1 © Chaykin, Tischman & DC

Black Cat #1 © MAR

Black Cat Mystery #45 © HARV

GD 2.0 | VG 4.0 | FN 6.0 | VF 8.0 | VF/NM 9.0 | NM- 9.2

Marvel Comics: Jan, 1998 - No.3, Mar, 1998 ($2.50, limited series)

1-3: Ostrander-s 3.00

BITE CLUB
DC Comics (Vertigo): Jun, 2004 - No. 6, Nov, 2004 ($2.95, limited series)

1-6-Chaykin-s/Tischman-a/Quitely-c 3.00
TPB Digest (2005, $9.99) r/#1-6; cover gallery 10.00
The Complete Bite Club TPB (2007, $19.99) r/#1-6 and ...: Vampire Crime Unit #1-5 20.00

BITE CLUB: VAMPIRE CRIME UNIT
DC Comics (Vertigo): Jun, 2006 - No. 5 ($2.99, limited series)

1-5:1-Chaykin & Tischman-s/Hahn-a/Quitely-c. 4-Chaykin-c 3.00

BIZARRE ADVENTURES (Formerly Marvel Preview)
Marvel Comics Group: No. 25, 3/81 - No. 34, 2/83 (#25-33: Magazine-$1.50)

25,26: 25-Lethal Ladies. 26-King Kull; Bolton-c/a 2 4 6 8 10 12
27,28: 27-Phoenix, Iceman & Nightcrawler app. 28-The Unlikely Heroes; Elektra by Miller; Neal Adams-a 2 4 6 10 14 18
29,30,32,33: 29-Stephen King's Lawnmower Man. 30-Tomorrow; 1st app. Silhouette. 32-Gods; Thor-c/s. 33-Horror; Dracula app.; photo-c 2 3 4 6 8 10
31-After The Violence Stops; new Hangman story; Miller-a 2 4 6 8 10 12
34 ($2.00, Baxter paper, comic size)-Son of Santa; Christmas special; Howard the Duck by Paul Smith 1 2 3 5 7 9

NOTE: ***Alcala** a-27i. **Austin** a-25i, 28i. **Bolton** a-26, 32. **J. Buscema** a-27p, 29, 30p; c-26. **Byrne** a-31 (2 pg.). **Golden** a-25p, 28p. **Perez** a-27p. **Rogers** a-25p. **Simonson** a-29; c-29. **Paul Smith** a-34.*

BIZARRO COMICS!
DC Comics: 2001 ($29.95, hardcover, one-shot)

HC-Short stories of DC heroes by various alternative cartoonists including Dorkin, Pope, Haspiel, Kidd, Kochalka, Millionaire, Stephens, Wray; includes "Superman's Babysitter" by Kyle Baker from Elseworlds 80-Page Giant recalled by DC; Groening-c 30.00
Softcover (2003, $19.95) 20.00

BIZARRO WORLD
DC Comics: 2005 ($29.95, hardcover, one-shot)

HC-Short stories by various alternative cartoonists including Bagge, Baker, Dorkin, Dunn, Kupperman, Morse, Oswalt, Pekar, Simpson, Stewart; Jaime Hernandez-c 30.00
Softcover (2006, $19.99) 20.00

BLACK ADAM (See 52 and Countdown)
DC Comics: Oct, 2007 - No. 6, Mar, 2008 ($2.99, limited series)

1-6: 1-Mahnke-a/c; Isis returns; Felix Faust app. 3.00
...: The Dark Age TPB (2008, $17.99) r/#1-6; Alex Ross-c 18.00

BLACK AND WHITE (See Large Feature Comic, Series I)

BLACK & WHITE (Also see Codename: Black & White)
Image Comics (Extreme): Oct, 1994 - No. 3, Jan, 1995 ($1.95, limited series)

1-3: Thibert-c/story 3.00

BLACK & WHITE MAGIC
Innovation Publishing: 1991 ($2.95, 98 pgs., B&W w/30 pgs. color, squarebound)

1-Contains rebound comics w/covers removed; contents may vary 3.00

BLACK AXE
Marvel Comics (UK): Apr, 1993 - No. 7, Oct, 1993 ($1.75)

1-4: 1-Romita Jr.-c. 2-Sunfire-c/s 3.00
5-7: 5-Janson-c; Black Panther app. 6,7-Black Panther-c/s 3.00

BLACKBALL COMICS
Blackball Comics: Mar, 1994 ($3.00)

1-Trencher-c/story by Giffen; John Pain by O'Neill 3.00

BLACKBEARD'S GHOST (See Movie Comics)

BLACK BEAUTY (See Son of Black Beauty)
Dell Publishing Co.: No. 440, Dec, 1952

Four Color 440 5 10 15 30 48 65

BLACKBURNE COVENANT, THE
Dark Horse Comics: Apr, 2003 - No. 4, July, 2003 ($2.99, limited series)

1-4-Nicieza-s/Raffaele-a 3.00
TPB (2003, $12.95) r/#1-4 13.00

BLACK CANARY (See All Star Comics #38, Flash Comics #86, Justice League of America #75 & World's Finest #244)
DC Comics: Nov, 1991 - No. 4, Feb, 1992 ($1.75, limited series)

1-4 3.00

BLACK CANARY

GD 2.0 | VG 4.0 | FN 6.0 | VF 8.0 | VF/NM 9.0 | NM- 9.2

DC Comics: Jan, 1993 - No. 12, Dec, 1993 ($1.75)

1-7 3.00
8-12: 8-The Ray-c/story. 9,10-Huntress-c/story 3.00

BLACK CANARY (Follows Oliver Queen's marriage proposal in Green Arrow #75)
DC Comics: Early Sept, 2007 - No. 4, Late Oct, 2007 ($2.99, bi-weekly limited series)

1-4-Bedard-s/Siqueira-a 3.00
... Wedding Planner 1 (11/07, $2.99) Roux-c/Ferguson & Norrie-a 3.00

BLACK CANARY/ORACLE: BIRDS OF PREY (Also see Showcase '96 #3)
DC Comics: 1996 ($3.95, one-shot)

1-Chuck Dixon scripts & Gary Frank-c/a. 1 2 3 5 7 9

BLACK CAT (AMAZING SPIDER-MAN PRESENTS...)
Marvel Comics: Aug, 2010 - No. 4, Dec, 2010 ($3.99, limited series)

1-4-Van Meter-s/Pulido-a/Conner-c; Spider-Man & Ana Kraven app. 4.00

BLACK CAT COMICS (...Western #16-19; ...Mystery #30 on)
(See All-New #7,9, The Original Black Cat, Pocket & Speed Comics)
Harvey Publications (Home Comics): June-July, 1946 - No. 29, June, 1951

1-Kubert-a; Joe Simon c-1,2 76 152 228 486 831 1175
2-Kubert-a 39 78 117 240 395 550
3,4: 4-The Red Demons begin (The Demon #4 & 5) 33 66 99 194 317 440
5,6,7: 5,6-The Scarlet Arrow app. in ea. by Powell; S&K-a in both. 6-Origin Red Demon. 7-Vagabond Prince by S&K plus 1 more story 39 78 117 240 395 550
8-S&K-a; Kerry Drake begins, ends #13 35 70 105 208 339 470
9-Origin Stuntman (r/Stuntman #1) 38 76 114 226 368 510
10-20: 14,15,17-Mary Worth app. plus Invisible Scarlet O'Neil-#15,20,24 26 52 78 154 252 350
21-26 21 42 63 124 202 280
27,28: 27-Used in **SOTI**, pg. 193; X-Mas-c; 2 pg. John Wayne story. 28-Intro. Kit, Black Cat's new sidekick 23 46 69 134 220 305
29-Black Cat bondage-c; Black Cat stories 22 44 66 128 209 290

BLACK CAT MYSTERY (Formerly Black Cat; ...Western Mystery #54; ...Western #55,56; ...Mystery #57; ...Mystic #58-62; Black Cat #63-65)
Harvey Publications: No. 30, Aug, 1951 - No. 65, Apr, 1963

30-Black Cat on cover and splash page only 32 64 96 190 310 430
31,32,34,37,38,40 26 52 78 156 256 355
33-Used in **POP**, pg. 89; electrocution-c 29 58 87 172 281 390
35-Atomic disaster cover/story 31 62 93 186 303 420
36,39-Used in **SOTI**: #36-Pgs. 270,271; #39-Pgs. 386-388 31 62 93 182 296 410
41-43 26 52 78 152 249 345
44-Eyes, ears, tongue cut out; Nostrand-a 27 54 81 162 266 370
45-Classic "Colorama" by Powell; Nostrand-a 43 86 129 271 461 650
46-49,51-Nostrand-a in all. 51-Story has blank panel covering censored art (post-Code) 26 52 78 156 256 355
50-Check-a; classic Warren Kremer-c showing a man's face & hands burning away 116 232 348 742 1271 1800
52,53 (r/#34 & 35) 17 34 51 98 154 210
54-Two Black Cat stories (2/55, last pre-code) 19 38 57 111 176 240
55,56-Black Cat app. 17 34 51 98 154 210
57(7/56)-Kirby-c 18 36 54 107 169 230
58-60-Kirby-a(4). 58,59-Kirby-c. 60,61-Simon-c 22 44 66 128 209 290
61-Nostrand-a; "Colorama" r/#45 19 38 57 112 179 245
62 (3/58)-E.C. story swipe 17 34 51 98 154 210
63-65: Giants(10/62,1/63, 4/63); Reprints; Black Cat app. 63-origin Black Kitten. 65-1 pg. Powell-a 20 40 60 115 185 255

NOTE: ***Kremer** a-37, 39, 43; c-36, 37, 47. **Meskin** a-51. **Palais** a-30, 31(2), 32(2), 33-35, 37-40. **Powell** a-32-35, 36(2), 40, 41, 43-53, 57. **Simon** c-63-65. **Sparling** a-44. Bondage c-32, 34, 43.*

BLACK COBRA (Bride's Diary No. 4 on) (See Captain Flight #8)
Ajax/Farrell Publications(Excellent Publ.): No. 1, 10-11/54; No. 6(No. 2), 12-1/54-55; No. 3, 2-3/55

1-Re-intro Black Cobra & The Cobra Kid (costumed heroes) 36 72 108 216 351 485
6(#2)-Formerly Billy Bunny 19 38 57 111 176 240
3-(Pre-code)-Torpedoman app. 18 36 54 105 165 225

BLACK CONDOR (Also see Crack Comics, Freedom Fighters & Showcase '94 #10,11)
DC Comics: June, 1992 - No. 12, May, 1993 ($1.25)

1-8-Heath-c 3.00
9-12: 9,10,12-Heath-c. 9,10-The Ray app. 12-Batman-c/app. 3.00

BLACK CROSS SPECIAL (See Dark Horse Presents)

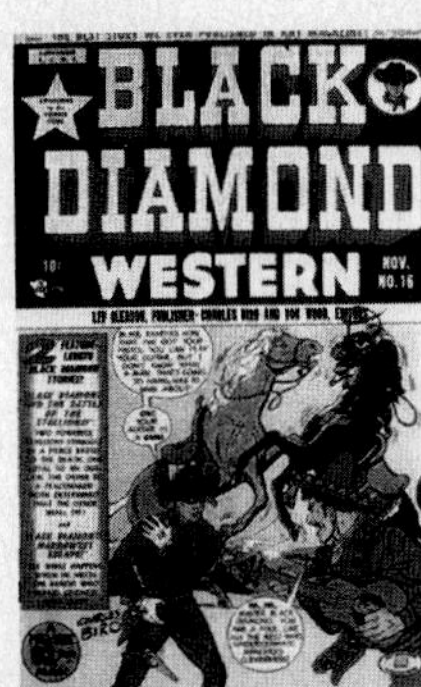

Black Diamond Western #16 © LEV

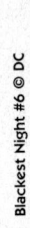

Blackest Night #6 © DC

Blackhawk #95 © QUA

GD 2.0 | VG 4.0 | FN 6.0 | VF 8.0 | VF/NM 9.0 | NM- 9.2

GD 2.0 | VG 4.0 | FN 6.0 | VF 8.0 | VF/NM 9.0 | NM- 9.2

Dark Horse Comics: Jan, 1988 ($1.75, B&W, one-shot)(Reprints & new-a)

1-1st printing 3.00
1-(2nd printing) has 2 pgs. new-a 3.00

BLACK CROSS: DIRTY WORK (See Dark Horse Presents)
Dark Horse Comics: Apr, 1997 ($2.95, one-shot)

1-Chris Warner-c/s/a 3.00

BLACK DIAMOND
Americomics: May, 1983 - No. 5, 1984 (no month)($2.00-$1.75, Baxter paper)

1-3-Movie adapt.; 1-Colt back-up begins 4.00
4,5 3.00

NOTE: ***Bill Black*** *a-1i; c-1.* ***Gulacy*** *c-2-5. Sybil Danning photo back-c-1.*

BLACK DIAMOND WESTERN (Formerly Desperado No. 1-8)
Lev Gleason Publ: No. 9, Mar, 1949 - No. 60, Feb, 1956 (No. 9-28: 52 pgs.)

	GD 2.0	VG 4.0	FN 6.0	VF 8.0	VF/NM 9.0	NM- 9.2
9-Black Diamond & his horse Reliapon begin; origin & 1st app. Black Diamond	21	42	63	122	199	275
10	12	24	36	69	97	125
11-15	10	20	30	54	72	90
16-28(11/49-11/51)-Wolverton's Bingbang Buster	14	28	42	76	108	140
29-40: 31-One pg. Frazetta anti-drug ad	9	18	27	47	61	75
41-50,53-59	8	16	24	40	50	60
51-3-D effect-c/story	15	30	45	85	130	175
52-3-D effect story	14	28	42	81	118	155
60-Last issue	8	16	24	44	57	70

NOTE: ***Biro*** *c-9-35?.* ***Cooper*** *a-12.* ***Myron Foss*** *a-54-58, c-54-56, 58.* ***Guardineer*** *a-9, 12, 15, 18.* ***Jack Keller*** *a-12.* ***Kida*** *a-9.* ***Maurer*** *a-10.* ***Ed Moore*** *a-16.* ***Morisi*** *a-55.* ***William Overgard*** *a-9-23.* ***Tuska*** *a-10, 48.* ***Bill Walton*** *a-57.*

BLACK DRAGON, THE
Marvel Comics (Epic Comics): 5/85 - No. 6, 10/85 (Baxter paper, mature)

1-6: 1-Chris Claremont story & John Bolton painted-c/a in all 3.00
TPB (Dark Horse, 4/96, $17.95, B&W, trade paperback) r/#1-6; intro by Anne McCaffrey 18.00

BLACKEST NIGHT (2009 Green Lantern & DC crossover) (Leads into Brightest Day series)
DC Comics: No. 0, Jun, 2009 - No. 8, May, 2010 ($3.99, limited series)

0-Free Comic Book Day edition; Johns-s/Reis-a; profile pages of different corps 3.00
1-8: 1-($3.99) Black Lantern Corps arises; Johns-s/Reis-c/a; Hawkman & Hawkgirl killed. 4-Nekron rises. 8-Dead heroes return 4.00
1-Variant cover by Van Sciver 15.00
1-3,5: 2nd-4th printings 4.00
2-8: 2-Cascioli variant-c. 3-Van Sciver variant-c. 4-7-Migliari variant-c. 8-Mahnke var-c 8.00
... Director's Cut (6/10, $5.99) Commentary with story panels; cover gallery, script pgs. 6.00
HC (2010, $29.99, d.j.) r/#0-8 & Blackest Night Director's Cut; variant cover gallery 30.00
...: Black Lantern Corps Vol. 1 HC (2010, $24.99, d.j.) r/BN: Batman, BN: Superman, and BN: Titans series; cover gallery and character sketch designs 25.00
...: Black Lantern Corps Vol. 2 HC (2010, $24.99, d.j.) r/BN: The Flash, BN: JSA, and BN: Wonder Woman series; cover gallery and character sketch designs 25.00
...: Rise of the Black Lanterns HC (2010, $24.99) r/one-shots Atom and Hawkman #46, Catwoman #83, Phantom Stranger #42, Power of Shazam #48, The Question #37, Starman #81, Weird Western Tales #71, Green Arrow #30 & Adventure Comics #7; sketch art 25.00

BLACKEST NIGHT: BATMAN (2009 Green Lantern & DC crossover)
DC Comics: Oct, 2009 - No. 3, Dec, 2009 ($2.99, limited series)

1-3: 1-Bat-parents rise as Black Lanterns; Deadman app.; Syaf-a/Andy Kubert-c; 2 printings. 3-Flying Graysons return 3.00
1-3-Variant-c by Sienkiewicz 5.00

BLACKEST NIGHT: JSA (2009 Green Lantern & DC crossover)
DC Comics: Feb, 2010 - No. 3, Apr, 2010 ($2.99, limited series)

1-3-Original Sandman, Dr. Midnite and Mr. Terrific rise; Barrows-a/c 3.00
1-3-Variant-c by Gene Ha 5.00

BLACKEST NIGHT: SUPERMAN (2009 Green Lantern & DC crossover)
DC Comics: Oct, 2009 - No. 3, Dec, 2009 ($2.99, limited series)

1-3-Earth-2 Superman and Lois become Black Lanterns; Barrows-a/c; 2 printings 3.00
1-3-Variant-c by Shane Davis 5.00

BLACKEST NIGHT: TALES OF THE CORPS (2009 Green Lantern & DC crossover)
DC Comics: Sept, 2009 - No. 3, Sept, 2009 ($3.99, weekly limited series)

1-3-Short stories by various; interlocking cover images. 3-Commentary on B.N. #0 4.00
HC (2010, $24.99) r/#1-3 & Adventure Comics #4,5 & Green Lantern #49; sketch art 25.00

BLACKEST NIGHT: THE FLASH (2009 Green Lantern & DC crossover)
DC Comics: Feb, 2010 - No. 3, Apr, 2010 ($2.99, limited series)

1-3-Rogues vs. Dead Rogues; Johns-s/Kolins-a 3.00
1-3-Variant-c by Manapul 5.00

BLACKEST NIGHT: TITANS (2009 Green Lantern & DC crossover)
DC Comics: Oct, 2009 - No. 3, Dec, 2009 ($2.99, limited series)

1-3-Terra and the original Hawk return; Benes-a/c 3.00
1-3-Variant-c by Brian Haberlin 5.00

BLACKEST NIGHT: WONDER WOMAN (2009 Green Lantern & DC crossover)
DC Comics: Feb, 2010 - No. 3, Apr, 2010 ($2.99, limited series)

1-3-Maxwell Lord returns; Rucka-s/Scott-a/Horn-c. 2,3-Mera app.; Star Sapphire 3.00
1-3-Variant-c by Ryan Sook 5.00

BLACK FLAG (See Asylum #5)
Maximum Press: Jan, 1995 - No.4, 1995; No. 0, July, 1995 ($2.50, B&W) (No. 0 in color)

Preview Edition (6/94, $1.95, B&W)-Fraga/McFarlane-c. 3.00
0-4: 0-(7/95)-Liefeld/Fraga-c. 1-(1/95). 3.00
1-Variant cover 5.00
2,4-Variant covers 3.00

NOTE: ***Fraga*** *a-0-4, Preview Edition; c-1-4.* ***Liefeld/Fraga*** *c-0.* ***McFarlane/Fraga*** *c-Preview Edition.*

BLACK FURY (Becomes Wild West No. 58) (See Blue Bird)
Charlton Comics Group: May, 1955 - No. 57, Mar-Apr, 1966 (Horse stories)

	GD 2.0	VG 4.0	FN 6.0	VF 8.0	VF/NM 9.0	NM- 9.2
1	12	24	36	67	94	120
2	7	14	21	37	46	55
3-10	6	12	18	28	34	40
11-15,19,20	4	8	10	18	22	25
16-18-Ditko-a	12	24	36	67	94	120
21-30	4	7	10	14	17	20
31-57	3	6	8	12	14	16

BLACK GOLIATH (See Avengers #32-35,41,54 and Civil War #4)
Marvel Comics Group: Feb, 1976 - No. 5, Nov, 1976

	GD 2.0	VG 4.0	FN 6.0	VF 8.0	VF/NM 9.0	NM- 9.2
1-Tuska-a(p) thru #3	3	6	9	14	20	25
2-5: 2-4-(Regular 25¢ editions). 4-Kirby-c/Buckler-a	2	4	6	9	13	16
2-4-(30¢-c variants, limited distribution)(4,6,8/76)	4	8	12	24	37	50

BLACKHAWK (Formerly Uncle Sam #1-8; see Military Comics & Modern Comics)
Comic Magazines(Quality)No. 9-107(12/56); National Periodical Publications No. 108 (1/57) -250; DC Comics No. 251 on: No. 9, Winter, 1944 - No. 243, 10-11/68; No. 244, 1-2/76 - No. 250, 1-2/77; No. 251, 10/82 - No. 273, 11/84

	GD 2.0	VG 4.0	FN 6.0	VF 8.0	VF/NM 9.0	NM- 9.2
9 (1944)	300	600	900	2070	3635	5200
10 (1946)	103	206	309	659	1130	1600
11-15: 14-Ward-a; 13,14-Fear app.	71	142	213	454	777	1100
16-19	61	122	183	390	670	950
20-Classic Crandall bondage-c; Ward Blackhawk	90	180	270	576	988	1400
21-30 (1950)	47	94	141	296	498	700
31-40: 31-Chop Chop by Jack Cole	39	78	117	231	378	525
41-49,51-60: 42-Robot-c	32	64	96	188	307	425
50-1st Killer Shark; origin in text	36	72	108	211	343	475
61,62: 61-Used in **POP**, pg. 91. 62-Used in **POP**, pg. 92 & color illo	28	56	84	168	274	380
63-70,72-80: 65-H-Bomb explosion panel. 66-B&W & color illos **POP**. 67-Hitler-s. 70-Return of Killer Shark; atomic explosion panel. 75-Intro. Blackie the Hawk	27	54	81	158	259	360
71-Origin retold; flying saucer-c; A-Bomb panels	31	62	93	182	296	410
81-86: Last precode (3/55)	24	48	72	140	230	320
87-92,94-99,101-107: 91-Robot-c. 105-1st S.A.	20	40	60	115	185	255
93-Origin in text	20	40	60	117	189	260
100	24	48	72	140	230	320
108-1st DC issue (1/57); re-intro. Blackie, the Hawk, their mascot; not in #115	37	74	111	294	585	875
109-117: 117-(10/57)-Mr. Freeze app.	14	28	42	98	197	295
118-(11/57)-Frazetta-r/Jimmy Wakely #4 (3 pgs.)	14	28	42	102	206	310
119-130 (11/58): 120-Robot-c	11	22	33	80	150	220
131-140 (9/59): 133-Intro. Lady Blackhawk	10	20	30	69	122	175
141-150,152-163,165,166: 141-Cat-Man returns-c/s. 143-Kurtzman-r/Jimmy Wakely #4. 150-(7/60)-King Condor returns. 166-Last 10¢ issue	8	16	24	56	93	130
151-Lady Blackhawk receives & loses super powers	9	18	27	60	100	140
164-Origin retold	9	18	27	60	100	140
167-180	6	12	18	41	66	90
181-190	5	10	15	35	55	75
191-196,199: 196-Combat Diary series begins	4	8	12	28	44	60
197,198,200: 197-New look for Blackhawks. 198-Origin retold	5	10	15	30	48	65
201,202,204-210	4	8	12	22	34	45
203-Origin Chop Chop (12/64)	4	8	12	26	41	55

211-227,229-243(1968): 230-Blackhawks become superheroes; JLA cameo

Black Hood #1 © AP

Black Knight #4 © MAR

Black Magic #1 © Headline

GD VG FN VF VF/NM NM-
2.0 4.0 6.0 8.0 9.0 9.2

242-Return to old costumes 3 6 9 18 27 35
228-Batman, Green Lantern, Superman, The Flash cameos.
3 6 9 20 30 40
244 ('76) -250: 250-Chuck dies 1 2 3 5 6 8
251-273: 251-Origin retold; Black Knights return. 252-Intro Domino. 253-Part origin Hendrickson. 258-Blackhawk's Island destroyed. 259-Part origin Chop-Chop. 265-273 (75¢ cover price) 4.00

NOTE: ***Chaykin*** *a-260; c-257-260, 262.* ***Crandall*** *a-10, 11, 13, 16?, 18-20, 22-26, 30-33, 35p, 36(2), 37, 38?, 39-44, 46-50, 52-58, 60, 63, 64, 66, 67; c-14-20, 22-63(most except #28-33, 36, 37, 39).* ***Evans*** *a-244, 245,246i, 248-250i.* ***G. Kane*** *c-263, 264.* ***Kubert*** *c-244, 245.* ***Newton*** *a-266p.* ***Severin*** *a-257.* ***Spiegle*** *a-261-267, 269-273; c-265-272.* ***Toth*** *a-260p.* ***Ward*** *a-16-27(Chop Chop, 8pgs. ea.); pencilled stories-No. 17-63(approx.).* ***Wildey*** *a-268. Chop Chop solo stories in #10-95?*

BLACKHAWK
DC Comics: Mar, 1988 - No. 3, May, 1988 ($2.95, limited series, mature)

1-3: Chaykin painted-c/a/scripts 4.00

BLACKHAWK (Also see Action Comics #601)
DC Comics: Mar, 1989 - No. 16, Aug, 1990 ($1.50, mature)

1 4.00
2-6,8-16: 16-Crandall-c swipe 3.00
7-($2.50, 52 pgs.)-Story-r/Military #1 4.00
Annual 1 (1989, $2.95, 68 pgs.)-Recaps origin of Blackhawk, Lady Blackhawk, and others 4.00
Special 1 (1992, $3.50, 68 pgs.)-Mature readers 4.00

BLACKHAWK INDIAN TOMAHAWK WAR, THE
Avon Periodicals: 1951 (Also see Fighting Indians of the Wild West)

nn-Kinstler-c; Kit West story 20 40 60 114 182 250

BLACK HEART ASSASSIN
Iguana Comics: Jan, 1994 ($2.95)

1 3.00

BLACK HOLE (See Walt Disney Showcase #54) (Disney, movie)
Whitman Publishing Co.: Mar, 1980 - No. 4, Sept, 1980

11295(#1) (1979, Golden, $1.50-c, 52 pgs., graphic novel; 8 1/2x11") Photo-c; Spiegle-a. 3 6 9 14 19 24
1-3: 1,2-Movie adaptation. 2,3-Spiegle-a. 3-McWilliams-a; photo-c. 3-New stories 2 4 6 9 12 15
4-Sold only in pre-packs; new story; Spiegle-a 8 16 24 52 86 120

BLACK HOOD, THE (See Blue Ribbon, Flyman & Mighty Comics)
Red Circle Comics (Archie): June, 1983 - No. 3, Oct, 1983 (Mandell paper)

1-Morrow, McWilliams, Wildey-a; Toth-c 6.00
2,3: The Fox by Toth-c/a; Boyette-a. 3-Morrow-a; Toth wraparound-c 4.00
(Also see Archie's Super-Hero Special Digest #2)

BLACK HOOD
DC Comics (Impact Comics): Dec, 1991 - No. 12, Dec, 1992 ($1.00)

1 4.00
2-12: 11-Intro The Fox. 12-Origin Black Hood 3.00
Annual 1 (1992, $2.50, 68 pgs.)-w/Trading card 4.00

BLACK HOOD COMICS (Formerly Hangman #2-8; Laugh Comics #20 on; also see Black Swan, Jackpot, Roly Poly & Top-Notch #9)
MLJ Magazines: No. 9, Wint., 1943-44 - No. 19, Sum., 1946 (on radio in 1943)

9-The Hangman & The Boy Buddies cont'd 113 226 339 718 1234 1750
10-Hangman & Dusty, the Boy Detective app. 64 128 192 406 696 985
11-Dusty app.; no Hangman 50 100 150 315 533 750
12-18: 14-Kinstler blood-c. 17-Hal Foster swipe from Prince Valiant; 1st issue with "An Archie Magazine" on-c 44 88 132 277 469 660
19-I.D. exposed; last issue 52 104 156 328 557 785

NOTE: *Hangman by* ***Fuje*** *in 9, 10.* ***Kinstler*** *a-15, c-14-16.*

BLACK JACK (Rocky Lane's...; formerly Jim Bowie)
Charlton Comics: No. 20, Nov, 1957 - No. 30, Nov, 1959

20 9 18 27 52 69 85
21,27,29,30 6 12 18 31 38 45
22,23: 22-(68 pgs.). 23-Williamson/Torres-a 8 16 24 42 54 65
24-26,28-Ditko-a 10 20 30 56 76 95

BLACK KNIGHT, THE
Toby Press: May, 1953; 1963

1-Bondage-c 30 60 90 177 289 400
Super Reprint No. 11 (1963)-Reprints 1953 issue 3 6 9 19 25 32

BLACK KNIGHT, THE
Atlas Comics (MgPC): May, 1955 - No. 5, April, 1956

1-Origin Crusader; Maneely-c/a 90 180 270 576 988 1400
2-Maneely-c/a(4) 61 122 183 390 670 950
3-5: 4-Maneely-c/a. 5-Maneely-c, Shores-a 48 96 144 301 511 720

BLACK KNIGHT (See The Avengers #48, Marvel Super Heroes & Tales To Astonish #52)
Marvel Comics: June, 1990 - No. 4, Sept, 1990 ($1.50, limited series)

1-4: 1-Original Black Knight returns. 3,4-Dr. Strange app. 3.00
... (MDCU) 1 (01/10, $3.99) Origin re-told; Frenz-a; originally from Marvel Digital Comics 4.00

NOTE: ***Buckler*** *c-1-4p*

BLACK KNIGHT: EXODUS
Marvel Comics: Dec, 1996 ($2.50, one-shot)

1-Raab-s; Apocalypse-c/app. 3.00

BLACK LAMB, THE
DC Comics (Helix): Nov, 1996 - No, 6, Apr, 1997 ($2.50, limited series)

1-6: Tim Truman-c/a/scripts 3.00

BLACKLIGHT (From ShadowHawk)
Image Comics: June, 2005 - Present ($2.99)

1,2-Toledo & Deering-a/Wherle-s 3.00

BLACK LIGHTNING (See The Brave & The Bold, Cancelled Comic Cavalcade, DC Comics Presents #16, Detective #490 and World's Finest #257)
National Periodical Publ./DC Comics: Apr, 1977 - No. 11, Sept-Oct, 1978

1-Origin Black Lightning 2 4 6 9 13 16
2,3,6-10 1 2 3 5 6 8
4,5-Superman-c/s. 4-Intro Cyclotronic Man 1 3 4 6 8 10
11-The Ray new solo story 2 4 6 8 10 12

NOTE: ***Buckler*** *c-1-3p, 6-11p. #11 is 44 pgs.*

BLACK LIGHTNING (2nd Series)
DC Comics: Feb, 1995 - No. 13, Feb, 1996 ($1.95/$2.25)

1-5-Tony Isabella scripts begin, ends #8 3.00
6-13: 6-Begin $2.25-c. 13-Batman-c/app. 3.00

BLACK LIGHTNING: YEAR ONE
DC Comics: Mar, 2009 - No. 6, May, 2009 ($2.99, bi-weekly limited series)

1-6-Van Meter-s/Hamner-a. 1-Two printings (white and yellow cover title logos) 3.00
TPB (2009, $17.99) r/#1-6 18.00

BLACK MAGIC (...Magazine) (Becomes Cool Cat V8#6 on)
Crestwood Publ. V1#1-4,V6#1-V7#5/Headline V1#5-V5#3,V7#6-V8#5: 10-11/50 - V4#1, 6-7/53: V4#2, 9-10/53 - V5#3, 11-12/54; V6#1, 9-10/57 - V7#2, 11-12/58: V7#3, 7-8/60 - V8#5, 11-12/61 (V1#1-5, 52pgs.; V1#6-V3#3, 44pgs.)

V1#1-S&K-a, 10 pgs.; Meskin-a(2) 148 296 444 947 1624 2300
2-S&K-a, 17 pgs.; Meskin-a 64 128 192 406 696 985
3-6(8-9/51)-S&K, Roussos, Meskin-a 54 108 162 346 591 835
V2#1(10-11/51),4,5,7(#13),9(#15),12(#18)-S&K-a 39 78 117 231 378 525
2,3,6,8,10,11(#17) 30 60 90 177 289 400
V3#1(#19, 12/52) - 6(#24, 5/53)-S&K-a 31 62 93 182 296 410
V4#1(#25, 6-7/53), 2(#26, 9-10/53)-S&K-a(3-4) 31 62 93 186 303 420
3(#27, 11-12/53)-S&K-a; Ditko-a (2nd published-a); also see Captain 3-D, Daring Love #1, Strange Fantasy #9, & Fantastic Fears #5 (Fant. Fears was 1st drawn, but not 1st publ.) 55 110 165 352 601 850
4(#28)-Eyes ripped out/story-S&K, Ditko-a 42 84 126 265 445 625
5(#29, 3-4/54)-S&K, Ditko-a 34 68 102 199 325 450
6(#30, 5-6/54)-S&K, Powell?-a 27 54 81 158 259 360
V5#1(#31, 7-8/54 - 3(#33, 11-12/54)-S&K-a 20 40 60 114 182 250
V6#1(#34, 9-10/57), 2(#35, 11-12/57) 12 24 36 67 94 120
3(1-2/58) - 6(7-8/58) 12 24 36 67 94 120
V7#1(9-10/58) - 3(7-8/60), 4(9-10/60) 10 20 30 56 76 95
5(11-12/60)-Hitler-c; Torres-a 15 30 45 88 137 185
6(1-2/61)-Powell-a(2) 10 20 30 56 76 95
V8#1(3-4/61)-Powell-c/a 10 20 30 56 76 95
2(5-6/61)-E.C. story swipe/W.F. #22; Ditko, Powell-a 11 22 33 60 83 105
3(7-8/61)-E.C. story swipe/W.F. #22; Powell-a(2) 11 22 33 60 83 105
4(9-10/61)-Powell-a(5) 10 20 30 56 76 95
5-E.C. story swipe/W.S.F. #28; Powell-a(3) 11 22 33 60 83 105

NOTE: ***Bernard Baily*** *a-V4#6?, V5#3(2).* ***Grandenetti*** *a-V2#3, 11.* ***Kirby*** *c-V1#1-6, V2#1-12, V3#1-6, V4#1, 2, 4-6, V5#1-3.* ***McWilliams*** *a-V3#2i.* ***Meskin*** *a-V1#1(2), 2, 3, 4(2), 5(2), 6, V2/1, 2, 3(2), 4(3), 5, 6(2), 7-9, 11, 12i, V3#1(2), 5, 6, V5#1(2), 2.* ***Orlando*** *a-V6#1, 4, V7#2; c-V6/1-6.* ***Powell*** *a-V5#1?.* ***Roussos*** *a-V1#3-5, 6(2), V2#3(2), 4, 5(2), 6, 8, 9, 10(2), 11, 12p, V3#1(2), 2i, 5, V5#2.* ***Simon*** *a-V2#12, V3#2, V7#5? c-V4#3?, V7#3?, 4, 5?, 6?, V8#1-5.* ***Simon & Kirby*** *a-V1#1, 2(2), 3-6, V2#1, 4, 5, 7, 9, 12, V3#1-6, V4#1(3), 2(4), 3(2), 4(2), 5, 6, V5#1-3; c-V2#1.* ***Leonard Starr*** *a-V1#1.* ***Tuska*** *a-V6#3, 4.* ***Woodbridge*** *a-V7#4.*

BLACK MAGIC
National Periodical Publications: Oct-Nov, 1973 - No. 9, Apr-May, 1975

1-S&K reprints 3 6 9 17 25 32

Black Orchid #10 © DC

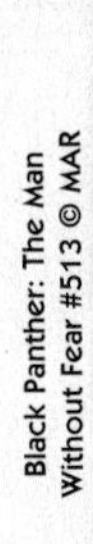
Black Panther: The Man Without Fear #513 © MAR

Black Pearl #3 © DH

	GD 2.0	VG 4.0	FN 6.0	VF 8.0	VF/NM 9.0	NM- 9.2

2-8-S&K reprints — 2 4 6 10 14 18
9-S&K reprints — 2 4 6 11 16 20

BLACKMAIL TERROR (See Harvey Comics Library)

BLACK MASK
DC Comics: 1993 - No. 3, 1994 ($4.95, limited series, 52 pgs.)

1-3 — 5.00

BLACK OPS
Image Comics (WildStorm): Jan, 1996 - No. 5, May, 1996 ($2.50, lim. series)

1-5 — 3.00

BLACK ORCHID (See Adventure Comics #428 & Phantom Stranger)
DC Comics: Holiday, 1988-89 - No. 3, 1989 ($3.50, lim. series, prestige format)

Book 1,3: Gaiman scripts & McKean painted-a in all — 6.00
Book 2-Arkham Asylum story; Batman app. — 1 2 3 5 6 8
TPB (1991, $19.95) r/#1-3; new McKean-c — 20.00

BLACK ORCHID
DC Comics: Sept, 1993 - No. 22, June, 1995 ($1.95/$2.25)

1-22: Dave McKean-c all issues — 3.00
1-Platinum Edition — 12.00
Annual 1 (1993, $3.95, 68 pgs.)-Children's Crusade — 4.00

BLACKOUTS (See Broadway Hollywood...)

BLACK PANTHER, THE (Also see Avengers #52, Fantastic Four #52, Jungle Action & Marvel Premiere #51-53)
Marvel Comics Group: Jan, 1977 - No. 15, May, 1979

1-Jack Kirby-s/a thru #12 — 4 8 12 22 34 45
2-13: 4,5-(Regular 30¢ editions). 8-Origin — 2 4 6 10 14 18
4,5-(35¢-c variants, limited dist.)(7,9/77) — 6 12 18 39 62 85
14,15-Avengers x-over. 14-Origin — 3 6 9 14 20 26
...By Jack Kirby Vol. 1 TPB (2005, $19.99) r/#1-7; unused covers and sketch pages — 20.00
...By Jack Kirby Vol. 2 TPB (2006, $19.99) r/#8-12 by Kirby and #13 non-Kirby — 20.00
NOTE: *J. Buscema c-15p. Layton c-13i.*

BLACK PANTHER
Marvel Comics Group: July, 1988 - No. 4, Oct, 1988 ($1.25)

1-4-Gillis-s/Cowan & Delarosa-a — 3.00

BLACK PANTHER (Marvel Knights)
Marvel Comics: Nov, 1998 - No. 62, Sept, 2003 ($2.50)

1-Texeira-a/c; Priest-s — 6.00
1-($6.95) DF edition w/Quesada & Palmiotti-c — 1 2 3 5 6 8
2-4: 2-Two covers by Texeira and Timm. 3-Fantastic Four app. — 4.00
5-35,37-40: 5-Evans-a. 6-8-Jusko-a. 8-Avengers-c/app. 15-Hulk app. 22-Moon Knight app. 23-Avengers app. 25-Maximum Security x-over. 26-Storm-c/app. 28-Magneto & Sub-Mariner-c/app. 29-WWII flashback meeting w/Captain America. 35-Defenders-c/app. 37-Luke Cage and Falcon-c/app. — 3.00
36-($3.50, 100 pgs.) 35th Anniversary issue incl. r/1st app. in FF #52 — 4.00
41-56: 41-44-Wolverine app. 47-Thor app. 48,49-Magneto app. — 3.00
57-62: 57-Begin $2.99-c. 59-Falcon app. — 3.00
...: The Client (6/01, $14.95, TPB) r/#1-5 — 15.00
... 2099 #1 (11/04, $2.99) Kirkman-s/Hotz-a/Pat Lee-c — 3.00

BLACK PANTHER (Marvel Knights)
Marvel Comics: Apr, 2005 - No. 41, Nov, 2008 ($2.99)

1-Reginald Hudlin-s/John Romita Jr. & Klaus Janson-a; covers by Romita & Ribic — 5.00
1-2nd printing; variant-c by Ribic — 3.00
2-7,9-15,17-20: 7-House of M; Hairsine-a. 10-14-Luke Cage app. 12,13-Blade app. 17-Linsner-c. 19-Doctor Doom app. — 3.00
8-Cho-c; X-Men app. — 4.00
8-2nd printing variant-c — 3.00
16-($3.99) Wedding of T'Challa and Storm; wraparound Cho-c; Hudlin-s/Eaton-a — 4.00
21-Civil War x-over; Namor app. — 8.00
21-2nd printing with new cover and Civil War logo — 3.00
22-25-Civil War: 23-25-Turner-c — 4.00
26-41: 26-30-T'Challa and Storm join the Fantastic Four. 27-30-Marvel Zombies app. 28-30-Suydam-c. 39-41-Secret Invasion — 3.00
Annual 1 (4/08, $3.99) Hudlin-s/Stroman & Lashley-a; alternate future; Uatu app. — 4.00
...: Bad Mutha TPB (2006, $10.99) r/#10-13 — 11.00
...: Civil War TPB (2007, $17.99) r/#19-25 — 18.00
...: Four the Hard Way TPB (2007, $13.99) r/#26-30; page layouts and character designs — 14.00
...: Little Green Men TPB (2008, $10.99) r/#31-34 — 11.00
...: The Bride TPB (2006, $14.99) r/#14-18; interview with the dress designer — 15.00
...: Who Is The Black Panther HC (2005, $21.99) r/#1-6; Hudlin afterword; cover gallery — 22.00
...: Who Is The Black Panther SC (2006, $14.99) r/#1-6; Hudlin afterword; cover gallery — 15.00

BLACK PANTHER
Marvel Comics: Apr, 2009 - No. 12, Mar, 2010 ($3.99/$2.99)

1-($3.99) Hudlin-s/Lashley-a; covers by Campbell & Lashley; Dr. Doom app. — 4.00
2-12-($2.99) 2-6-Campbell-c. 6-Shuri becomes female Black Panther — 3.00

BLACK PANTHER/CAPTAIN AMERICA: FLAGS OF OUR FATHERS
Marvel Comics: Jun, 2010 - No. 4, Sept, 2010 ($3.99, limited series)

1-4-Hudlin-s/Cowan-a; WW2 story; Howling Commandos & Red Skull app. — 4.00

BLACK PANTHER: PANTHER'S PREY
Marvel Comics: May, 1991 - No. 4, Oct, 1991 ($4.95, squarebound, lim. series, 52 pgs.)

1-4: McGregor-s/Turner-a — 5.00

BLACK PANTHER: THE MAN WITHOUT FEAR (Continues from Daredevil #512)
Marvel Comics: No. 513, Feb, 2011 - Present ($2.99)

513-517: 513-Aftermath of Shadowland; David Liss-s/Francavilla-a/Bianchi-c — 3.00
513-Variant-c by Francavilla — 5.00

BLACK PEARL, THE
Dark Horse Comics: Sept, 1996 - No. 5, Jan, 1997 ($2.95, limited series)

1-5: Mark Hamill scripts — 3.00

BLACK PHANTOM (See Tim Holt #25, 38)
Magazine Enterprises: Nov, 1954 (one-shot) (Female outlaw)

1 (A-1 #122)-The Ghost Rider story plus 3 Black Phantom stories; Headlight-c/a — 36 72 108 216 351 485

BLACK PHANTOM
AC Comics: 1989 - No. 3, 1990 ($2.50, B&W; #2 color)(Reprints & new-a)

1-3: 1-Ayers-r, Bolle-r/B.P. #1-3-Redmask-r — 3.00

BLACK PHANTOM, RETURN OF THE (See Wisco)

BLACK RIDER (Western Winners #1-7; Western Tales of Black Rider #28-31; Gunsmoke Western #32 on)(See All Western Winners, Best Western, Kid Colt, Outlaw Kid, Rex Hart, Two-Gun Kid, Two-Gun Western, Western Gunfighters, Western Winners, & Wild Western)
Marvel/Atlas Comics(CDS No. 8-17/CPS No. 19 on): No. 8, 3/50 - No. 18, 1/52; No. 19, 11/53 - No. 27, 3/55

8 (#1)-Black Rider & his horse Satan begin; 36 pgs; Stan Lee photo-c as Black Rider) — 42 84 126 265 445 625
9-52 pgs. begin, end #14 — 22 44 66 132 216 300
10-Origin Black Rider — 27 54 81 158 259 360
11-14: 14-Last 52pgs. — 17 34 51 98 154 210
15-19: 19-Two-Gun Kid app. — 15 30 45 85 130 175
20-Classic-c; Two-Gun Kid app. — 16 32 48 92 144 195
21-27: 21-23-Two-Gun Kid app. 24,25-Arrowhead app. 26-Kid Colt app. 27-Last issue; last precode. Kid Colt app. The Spider (a villain) burns to death — 14 28 42 81 118 155
NOTE: ***Ayers** c-22. **Jack Keller** a-15, 26, 27. **Maneely** a-14; c-16, 17, 25, 27. **Syd Shores** a-19, 21, 22, 23(3), 24(3), 25-27; c-19, 21, 23. **Sinnott** a-24, 25. **Tuska** a-12, 19-21.*

BLACK RIDER RIDES AGAIN!, THE
Atlas Comics (CPS): Sept, 1957

1-Kirby-a(3); Powell-a; Severin-c — 25 50 75 147 241 335

BLACK SEPTEMBER (Also see Avengers/Ultraforce, Ultraforce (1st series) #10 & Ultraforce/Avengers)
Malibu Comics (Ultraverse): 1995 ($1.50, one-shot)

Infinity-Intro to the new Ultraverse; variant-c exists. — 3.00

BLACKSTONE (See Super Magician Comics & Wisco Giveaways)

BLACKSTONE, MASTER MAGICIAN COMICS
Vital Publ./Street & Smith Publ.: Mar-Apr, 1946 - No. 3, July-Aug, 1946

1 — 34 68 102 199 325 450
2,3 — 20 40 60 114 182 250

BLACKSTONE, THE MAGICIAN (...Detective on cover only #3 & 4)
Marvel Comics (CnPC): No. 2, May, 1948 - No. 4, Sept, 1948 (No #1) (Cont'd from E.C. #1?)

2-The Blonde Phantom begins, ends #4 — 74 148 222 470 810 1150
3,4: 3-Blonde Phantom by Sekowsky — 43 86 129 271 461 650

BLACKSTONE, THE MAGICIAN DETECTIVE FIGHTS CRIME
E. C. Comics: Fall, 1947

1-1st app. Happy Houlihans — 53 106 159 334 567 800

BLACK SUN (X-Men Black Sun on cover)
Marvel Comics: Nov, 2000 - No. 5, Nov, 2000 ($2.99, weekly limited series)

1-(...: X-Men), 2-(...: Storm), 3-(...: Banshee and Sunfire), 4-(...: Colossus and Nightcrawler),

Black Terror #21 © Pub. Ent. Ltd.

Black Widow (2010 series) #7 © MAR

	GD 2.0	VG 4.0	FN 6.0	VF 8.0	VF/NM 9.0	NM- 9.2

5-(...: Wolverine and Thunderbird); Claremont-s in all; Evans interlocking painted covers; Magik returns 3.00

BLACK SUN
DC Comics (WildStorm): Nov, 2002 - No. 6, Jun, 2003 ($2.95, limited series)

1-6-Andreyko-s/Scott-a 3.00

BLACK SWAN COMICS
MLJ Magazines (Pershing Square Publ. Co.): 1945

	GD	VG	FN	VF	VF/NM	NM-
1-The Black Hood reprints from Black Hood No. 14; Bill Woggon-a; Suzie app. Caribbean Pirates-c	21	42	63	122	199	275

BLACK TARANTULA (See Feature Presentations No. 5)

BLACK TERROR (See America's Best Comics & Exciting Comics)
Better Publications/Standard: Winter, 1942-43 - No. 27, June, 1949

	GD	VG	FN	VF	VF/NM	NM-
1-Black Terror, Crime Crusader begin	314	628	942	2198	3849	5500
2	129	258	387	826	1413	2000
3	90	180	270	576	988	1400
4,5	74	148	222	470	810	1150
6-10: 7-The Ghost app.	63	126	189	403	689	975
11-20: 20-The Scarab app.	54	108	162	343	574	825
21-Miss Masque app.	55	110	165	352	601	850
22-Part Frazetta-a on one Black Terror story	53	106	159	334	567	800
23,25-27	47	94	141	296	498	700
24-Frazetta-a (1/4 pg.)	47	94	141	298	504	710

NOTE: ***Schomburg (Xela)** c-2-27; bondage c-2, 17, 24. **Meskin** a-27. **Moreira** a-27. **Robinson/Meskin** a-23, 24(3), 25, 26. **Roussos/Mayo** a-24. **Tuska** a-26, 27.*

BLACK TERROR, THE (Also see Total Eclipse)
Eclipse Comics: Oct, 1989 - No. 3, June, 1990 ($4.95, 52 pgs., squarebound, limited series)

1-3: Beau Smith & Chuck Dixon scripts; Dan Brereton painted-c/a 5.00

BLACK TERROR (Also see Project Superpowers)
Dynamite Entertainment: 2008 - No. 14, 2011 ($3.50/$3.99)

1-14-Golden Age hero. 1-Alex Ross-c/Mike Lilly-a; various variant-c exist 4.00

BLACKTHORNE 3-D SERIES
Blackthorne Publishing Co.: May, 1985 - No. 80, 1989 ($2.25/$2.50)

1-Sheena in 3-D #1. D. Stevens-c/retouched-a 1 2 3 5 6 8
2-10: 2-MerlinRealm in 3-D #1. 3-3-D Heroes #1. Goldyn in 3-D #1. 5-Bizarre 3-D Zone #1. 6-Salimba in 3-D #1. 7-Twisted Tales in 3-D #1. 8-Dick Tracy in 3-D #1. 9-Salimba in 3-D #2. 10-Gumby in 3-D #1 6.00
11-19: 11-Betty Boop in 3-D #1. 12-Hamster Vice in 3-D #1. 13-Little Nemo in 3-D #1. 14-Gumby in 3-D #2. 15-Hamster Vice #6 in 3-D. 16-Laffin' Gas #6 in 3-D. 17-Gumby in 3-D #3. 18-Bullwinkle and Rocky in 3-D #1. 19-The Flintstones in 3-D #1 6.00
20(#1),26(#2),35(#3),39(#4),52(#5),62,71(#6)-G.I. Joe in 3-D. 62-G.I. Joe Annual 2 4 6 8 11 14
21-24,27-28: 21-Gumby in 3-D #4. 22-The Flintstones in 3-D #2. 23-Laurel & Hardy in 3-D #1. 24-Bozo the Clown in 3-D #1. 27-Bravestarr in 3-D #1. 28- Gumby in 3-D #5 6.00
25,29,37-The Transformers in 3-D 2 4 6 10 14 18
30-Star Wars in 3-D #1 3 6 9 14 19 24
31-34,36,38,40: 31-The California Raisins in 3-D #1. 32-Richie Rich & Casper in 3-D #1. 33-Gumby in 3-D #6. 34-Laurel & Hardy in 3-D #2. 36-The Flintstones in 3-D #3. 38-Gumby in 3-D #7. 40-Bravestarr in 3-D #2 6.00
41-46,49,50: 41-Battletech in 3-D #1. 42-The Flintstones in 3-D #4. 43-Underdog in 3-D #1 44-The California Raisins in 3-D #2. 45-Red Heat in 3-D #1 (movie adapt.). 46-The California Raisins in 3-D #3. 49-Rambo in 3-D #1. 49-Sad Sack in 3-D #1. 50-Bullwinkle For President in 3-D #1 6.00
47,48-Star Wars in 3-D #2,3 2 4 6 9 13 16
51,53-60: 51-Kull in 3-D #1. 53-Red Sonja in 3-D #1. 54-Bozo in 3-D #2. 55-Waxwork in 3-D #1 (movie adapt.). 57-Casper in 3-D #1. 58-Baby Huey in 3-D #1. 59-Little Dot in 3-D #1. 60-Solomon Kane in 3-D #1 6.00
61,63-70,72-80: 61-Werewolf in 3-D #1. 63-The California Raisins in 3-D #4. 64-To Die For in 3-D #1. 65-Capt. Holo in 3-D #1. 66-Playful Little Audrey in 3-D #1. 67-Kull in 3-D #2. 69-The California Raisins in 3-D #5. 70-Wendy in 3-D #1. 72-Sports Hall of Shame #1. 74-The Noid in 3-D #1. 75-Moonwalker in 3-D #1 (Michael Jackson movie adapt.). 76-79. 80-The Noid in 3-D #2 1 2 3 4 5 7

BLACK WIDOW (Marvel Knights) (Also see Marvel Graphic Novel)
Marvel Comics: May, 1999 - No. 3, Aug, 1999 ($2.99, limited series)

1-(June on-c) Devin Grayson-s/J.G. Jones-c/a; Daredevil app. 5.00
1-Variant-c by J.G. Jones 6.00
2,3 4.00
...Web of Intrigue (6/99, $3.50) r/origin & early appearances 3.50
TPB (7/01, $15.95) r/Vol. 1 & 2; Jones-c 16.00

BLACK WIDOW (Marvel Knights) (Volume 2)
Marvel Comics: Jan, 2001 - No. 3, May, 2001 ($2.99, limited series)

1-3-Grayson & Rucka-s/Scott Hampton-c/a; Daredevil app. 3.00

BLACK WIDOW (Marvel Knights)
Marvel Comics: Nov, 2004 - No. 6, Apr, 2005 ($2.99, limited series)

1-6-Sienkiewicz-a/Land-c 3.00

BLACK WIDOW (Continues in Widowmaker #1)
Marvel Comics: Jun, 2010 - No. 8, Jan, 2011 ($3.99/$2.99)

1-($3.99) Liu-s/Acuña-a; Wolverine app.; back-up history text 4.00
1-Variant photo-c of Scarlett Johansson from Iron Man 2 movie 8.00
2-8-($2.99) 2-5-Acuña-a. 2,3-Elektra app. 3.00

BLACK WIDOW & THE MARVEL GIRLS
Marvel Comics: Feb, 2010 - No. 4, Apr, 2010 ($2.99, limited series)

1-4-Tobin-s. 1-Enchantress app. 2-Avengers app. 4-Storm app.; Miyazawa-a 3.00

BLACK WIDOW: DEADLY ORIGIN
Marvel Comics: Jan, 2010 - No. 4, Apr, 2010 ($3.99, limited series)

1-4-Granov-c; origin retold. 1-Wolverine and Bucky app. 3-Daredevil app. 4.00

BLACK WIDOW: PALE LITTLE SPIDER (Marvel Knights) (Volume 3)
Marvel Comics: Jun, 2002 - No. 3, Aug, 2002 ($2.99, limited series)

1-3-Rucka-s/Kordey-a/Horn-c 3.00

BLACK WIDOW 2 (THE THINGS THEY SAY ABOUT HER) (Marvel Knights)
Marvel Comics: Nov, 2005 - No. 6, Apr, 2006 ($2.99, limited series)

1-6-Phillips & Sienkiewicz-a/Morgan-s; Daredevil app. 3.00
TPB (2006, $15.99) r/#1-6 16.00

BLACKWULF
Marvel Comics: June, 1994 - No. 10, Mar, 1995 ($1.50)

1-($2.50)-Embossed-c; Angel Medina-a 3.50
2-10 3.00

BLADE (The Vampire Hunter)
Marvel Comics

1-(3/98, $3.50) Colan-a(p)/Christopher Golden-s 3.50
... Black & White TPB (2004, $15.99, B&W) reprints from magazines Vampire Tales #8,9; Marvel Preview #3,6; Crescent City Blues #1 and Marvel Shadow and Light #1 16.00
San Diego Con Promo (6/97) Wesley Snipes photo-c 3.00
...Sins of the Father (10/98, $5.99) Sears-a; movie adaption 6.00
Blade 2: Movie Adaptation (5/02, $5.95) Ponticelli-a/Bradstreet-c 6.00

BLADE (The Vampire Hunter)
Marvel Comics: Nov, 1998 - No. 3, Jan, 1999 ($3.50/$2.99)

1-($3.50) Contains Movie insider pages; McKean-a 3.50
2,3-($2.99): 2-Two covers 3.00

BLADE (Volume 2)
Marvel Comics (MAX): May, 2002 -No. 6, Oct, 2002 ($2.99)

1-6-Bradstreet-c/Hinz-s. 1-5-Pugh-a. 6-Homs-a 3.00

BLADE
Marvel Comics: Nov, 2006 - No. 12, Oct, 2007 ($2.99)

1-12: 1-Chaykin-a/Guggenheim-s; origin retold; Spider-Man app. 2-Dr. Doom-c/app. 5-Civil War tie-in; Wolverine app. 6-Blade loses a hand. 10-Spider-Man app. 3.00
...: Sins of the Father TPB (2007, $14.99) r/#7-12; afterword by Guggenheim 15.00
...: Undead Again TPB (2007, $14.99) r/#1-6; letters pages from #1&2 15.00

BLADE OF THE IMMORTAL (Manga)
Dark Horse Comics: June, 1996 - No. 131, Nov, 2007 ($2.95/$2.99/$3.95, B&W)

1-Hiroaki Samura-s/a in all 1 3 4 6 8 10
2-5: 2-#1 on cover in error 6.00
6-10 5.00
11,19,20,34-($3.95, 48 pgs.): 34-Food one-shot 4.00
12-18,21-33,35-41,43-105,107-131: 12-20-Dreamsong. 21-28-On Silent Wings. 29-33-Dark Shadow. 35-42-Heart of Darkness. 43-57-The Gathering 3.00
42-($3.50) Ends Heart of Darkness 3.50
106-($3.99) 4.00

BLADE RUNNER (Movie)
Marvel Comics Group: Oct, 1982 - No. 2, Nov, 1982

1,2-r/Marvel Super Special #22; 1-Williamson-c/a. 2-Williamson-a 3.50

BLADE: THE VAMPIRE-HUNTER
Marvel Comics: July, 1994 - No. 10, Apr, 1995 ($1.95)

1-($2.95)-Foil-c; Dracula returns; Wheatley-c/a 4.00
2-10: 2,3,10-Dracula-c/app. 8-Morbius app. 3.00

Blazing Comics #1 © Enwil

Blazing West #7 © ACG

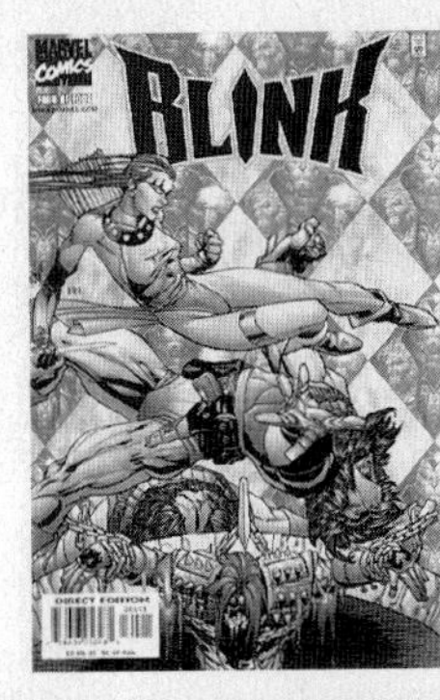

Blink #4 © MAR

GD VG FN VF VF/NM NM-
2.0 4.0 6.0 8.0 9.0 9.2

GD VG FN VF VF/NM NM-
2.0 4.0 6.0 8.0 9.0 9.2

BLADE: VAMPIRE-HUNTER
Marvel Comics: Dec, 1999 - No. 6, May, 2000 ($3.50/$2.50)

1-($3.50)-Bart Sears-s; Sears and Smith-a 3.50
2-6-($2.50): 2-Regular & Wesley Snipes photo-c 3.00

BLAIR WITCH CHRONICLES, THE
Oni Press: Mar, 2000 - No. 4, July, 2000 ($2.95, B&W, limited series)

1-4-Van Meter-s.1-Guy Davis-a. 2-Mireault-a 3.00
1-DF Alternate-c by John Estes 7.00
TPB (9/00, $15.95) r/#1-4 & Blair Witch Project one-shot 16.00

BLAIR WITCH: DARK TESTAMENTS
Image Comics: Oct, 2000 ($2.95, one-shot)

1-Edington-s/Adlard-a; story of murderer Rustin Parr 3.00

BLAIR WITCH PROJECT, THE (Movie companion, not adaptation)
Oni Press: July, 1999 ($2.95, B&W, one-shot)

1-(1st printing) History of the Blair Witch, art by Edwards, Mireault, and Davis; Van Meter-s; only the stick figure is red on the cover 12.00
1-(2nd printing) Stick figure and title lettering are red on cover 4.00
1-(3rd printing) Stick figure, title, and creator credits are red on cover 3.00
DF Glow in the Dark variant-c ($10.00) 10.00

BLAST (Satire Magazine)
G & D Publications: Feb, 1971 - No. 2, May, 1971

1-Wrightson & Kaluta-a/Everette-c 8 16 24 56 93 130
2-Kaluta-c/a 6 12 18 41 66 90

BLAST CORPS
Dark Horse Comics: Oct, 1998 ($2.50, one-shot, based on Nintendo game)

1-Reprints from Nintendo Power magazine; Mahn-a 3.00

BLASTERS SPECIAL
DC Comics: 1989 ($2.00, one-shot)

1-Peter David scripts; Invasion spin-off 3.00

BLAST-OFF (Three Rocketeers)
Harvey Publications (Fun Day Funnies): Oct, 1965 (12¢)

1-Kirby/Williamson-a(2); Williamson/Crandall-a; Williamson/Torres/Krenkel-a; Kirby/Simon-c 7 14 21 49 80 110

BLAZE
Marvel Comics: Aug, 1994 - No. 12, July, 1995 ($1.95)

1-($2.95)-Foil embossed-c 3.50
2-12: 2-Man-Thing-c/story. 11,12-Punisher app. 3.00

BLAZE CARSON (Rex Hart #6 on)(See Kid Colt, Tex Taylor, Wild Western, Wisco)
Marvel Comics (USA): Sept, 1948 - No. 5, June, 1949

1: 1,2-Shores-c 27 54 81 158 259 360
2,4,5: 4-Two-Gun Kid app. 5-Tex Taylor app. 18 36 54 105 165 225
3-Used by N.Y. State Legis. Comm. (injury to eye splash); Tex Morgan app. 19 38 57 111 176 240

BLAZE: LEGACY OF BLOOD (See Ghost Rider & Ghost Rider/Blaze)
Marvel Comics (Midnight Sons imprint): Dec, 1993 - No. 4, Mar, 1994 ($1.75, limited series)

1-4 3.00

BLAZE OF GLORY
Marvel Comics: Feb, 2000 - No. 4, Mar, 2000 ($2.99, limited series)

1-4-Ostrander-s/Manco-a; Two-Gun Kid, Rawhide Kid, Red Wolf and Ghost Rider app. 3.00
TPB (7/02, $9.99) r/#1-4 10.00

BLAZE THE WONDER COLLIE (Formerly Molly Manton's Romances #1?)
Marvel Comics(SePI): No. 2, Oct, 1949 - No. 3, Feb, 1950 (Both have photo-c)

2(#1), 3-(Scarce) 24 48 72 140 230 320

BLAZING BATTLE TALES
Seaboard Periodicals (Atlas): July, 1975

1-Intro. Sgt. Hawk & the Sky Demon; Severin, McWilliams, Sparling-a; Nazi-c by Thorne 2 4 6 10 14 18

BLAZING COMBAT (Magazine)
Warren Publishing Co.: Oct, 1965 - No. 4, July, 1966 (35¢, B&W)

1-Frazetta painted-c on all 25 50 75 183 367 550
2 8 16 24 54 90 125
3,4: 4-Frazetta half pg. ad 7 14 21 49 80 110
nn-Anthology (reprints from No. 1-4) (low print) 8 16 24 56 93 130

*NOTE: **Adkins** a-4. **Colan** a-3,4,nn. **Crandall** a-all. **Evans** a-1,4. **Heath** a-4,nn. **Morrow** a-1-3,nn. **Orlando** a-1-3,nn. **J. Severin** a-all. **Torres** a-1-4. **Toth** a-all. **Williamson** a-2. and **Wood** a-3,4,nn.*

BLAZING COMBAT: WORLD WAR I AND WORLD WAR II
Apple Press: Mar, 1994 ($3.75, B&W)

1,2: 1-r/Colan, Toth, Goodwin, Severin, Wood-a. 2-r/Crandall, Evans, Severin, Torres, Williamson-a 4.00

BLAZING COMICS (Also see Blue Circle Comics and Red Circle Comics)
Enwil Associates/Rural Home: 6/44 - #3, 9/44; #4, 2/45; #5, 3/45; #5(V2#2), 3/55 - #6(V2#3), 1955?

1-The Green Turtle, Red Hawk, Black Buccaneer begin; origin Jun-Gal; classic Japanese WWII splash 52 104 156 328 557 785
2-5: 3-Briefer-a. 5-(V2#2 inside) 36 72 108 211 343 475
5(3/55, V2#2-inside)-Black Buccaneer-c, 6(V2#3-inside, 1955)-Indian/Japanese-c; cover is from Apr. 1945 20 40 60 114 182 250

NOTE: No. 5 & 6 contain remaindered comics rebound and the contents can vary. Cloak & Daggar, Will Rogers, Superman 64, Star Spangled 130, Kaanga known. Value would be half of contents.

BLAZING SIXGUNS
Avon Periodicals: Dec, 1952

1-Kinstler-c/a; Larsen/Alascia-a(2), Tuska?-a; Jesse James, Kit Carson, Wild Bill Hickok app. 18 36 54 103 162 220

BLAZING SIXGUNS
I.W./Super Comics: 1964

I.W. Reprint #1,8,9: 1-r/Wild Bill Hickok #26, Western True Crime #? & Blazing Sixguns #1 by Avon; Kinstler-c. 8-r/Blazing Western #?; Kinstler-c. 9-r/Blazing Western #1; Ditko-r; Kintsler-c reprinted from Dalton Boys #1 2 4 6 10 14 18
Super Reprint #10,11,15-17: 10,11-r/The Rider #2,1. 15-r/Silver Kid Western #?. 16-r/Buffalo Bill #?; Wildey-r; Severin-c. 17(1964)-r/Western True Crime #? 2 4 6 10 14 18
12-Reprints Bullseye #3; S&K-a 4 8 12 19 29 38
18-r/Straight Arrow #? by Powell; Severin-c 2 4 6 10 14 18

BLAZING SIX-GUNS (Also see Sundance Kid)
Skywald Comics: Feb, 1971 - No. 2, Apr, 1971 (52 pgs.)

1-The Red Mask (3-D effect, not true 3-D), Sundance Kid begin (new-s), Avon's Geronimo reprint by Kinstler; Wyatt Earp app. 3 6 9 14 20 25
2-Wild Bill Hickok, Jesse James, Kit Carson-r plus M.E. Red Mask-r (3-D effect) 2 4 6 10 14 18

BLAZING WEST (The Hooded Horseman #21 on)
American Comics Group (B&I Publ./Michel Publ.): Fall, 1948 - No. 20, Nov-Dec, 1951

1-Origin & 1st app. Injun Jones, Tenderfoot & Buffalo Belle; Texas Tim & Ranger begins, ends #13 20 40 60 114 182 250
2,3 (1-2/49) 11 22 33 62 86 110
4-Origin & 1st app. Little Lobo; Starr-a (3-4/49) 10 20 30 56 76 95
5-10: 5-Starr-a 9 18 27 50 65 80
11-13 8 16 24 42 54 65
14(11-12/50)-Origin/1st app. The Hooded Horseman 13 26 39 74 105 135
15-20: 15,16,18,19-Starr-a 9 18 27 50 65 80

BLAZING WESTERN
Timor Publications: Jan, 1954 - No. 5, Sept, 1954

1-Ditko-a (1st Western-a?); text story by Bruce Hamilton 18 36 54 105 165 225
2-4 9 18 27 50 65 80
5-Disbrow-a 9 18 27 52 69 85

BLINDSIDE
Image Comics (Extreme Studios): Aug, 1996 ($2.50)

1-Variant-c exists 3.00

BLINK (See X-Men Age of Apocalypse storyline)
Marvel Comics: March, 2001 - No. 4, June, 2001 ($2.99, limited series)

1-4-Adam Kubert-c/Lobdell-s/Winick-script; leads into Exiles #1 3.00

BLIP
Marvel Comics Group: 2/1983 - 1983 (Video game mag. in comic format)

1-1st app. Donkey Kong & Mario Bros. in comics, 6pgs. comics; photo-c 2 3 4 6 8 10
2-Spider-Man photo-c; 6pgs. Spider-Man comics w/Green Goblin 2 4 6 8 10 12
3,4,6 6.00
5-E.T., Indiana Jones; Rocky-c 1 2 3 4 5 7
7-6pgs. Hulk comics; Pac-Man & Donkey Kong Jr. Hints 1 2 3 5 6 8

BLISS ALLEY
Image Comics: July, 1997 - No. 2, Sept, 1997 ($2.95, B&W)

1,2-Messner-Loebs-s/a 3.00

Blitzkrieg #4 © DC

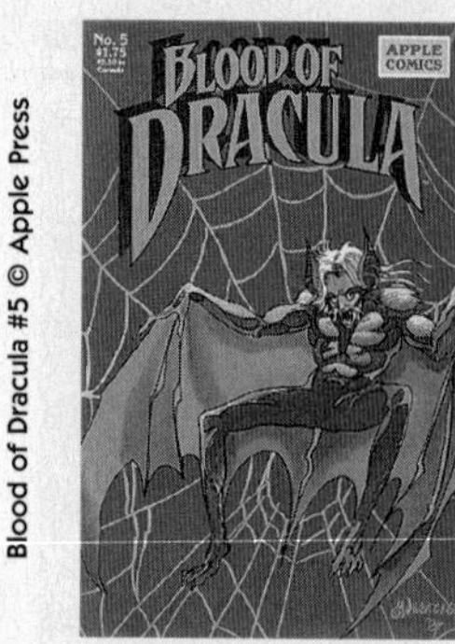

Blood of Dracula #5 © Apple Press

Bloodshot #5 © Voyager

BLITZKRIEG
National Periodical Publications: Jan-Feb, 1976 - No. 5, Sept-Oct, 1976

	GD 2.0	VG 4.0	FN 6.0	VF 8.0	VF/NM 9.0	NM- 9.2
1-Kubert-c on all	4	8	12	26	41	55
2-5	3	6	9	17	25	32

BLOCKBUSTERS OF THE MARVEL UNIVERSE
Marvel Comics: March, 2011 ($4.99, one-shot)

	GD 2.0	VG 4.0	FN 6.0	VF 8.0	VF/NM 9.0	NM- 9.2
1-Handbook-style summaries of Marvel crossover events like Civil War & Heroes Reborn						5.00

BLONDE PHANTOM (Formerly All-Select #1-11; Lovers #23 on)(Also see Blackstone, Marvel Mystery, Millie The Model #2, Sub-Mariner Comics #25 & Sun Girl)
Marvel Comics (MPC): No. 12, Winter, 1946-47 - No. 22, Mar, 1949

	GD 2.0	VG 4.0	FN 6.0	VF 8.0	VF/NM 9.0	NM- 9.2
12-Miss America begins, ends #14	177	354	531	1124	1937	2750
13-Sub-Mariner begins (not in #16)	103	206	309	659	1130	1600
14,15: 15-Kurtzman's "Hey Look"	97	194	291	621	1061	1500
16-Captain America with Bucky story by Rico(p), 6 pgs.; Kurtzman's "Hey Look" (1 pg.)	129	258	387	826	1413	2000
17-22: 22-Anti Wertham editorial	82	164	246	528	902	1275

NOTE: *Shores c-12-18.*

BLONDIE (See Ace Comics, Comics Reading Libraries (Promotional Comics section), Dagwood, Daisy & Her Pups, Eat Right to Work..., King & Magic Comics)
David McKay Publications: 1942 - 1946

	GD 2.0	VG 4.0	FN 6.0	VF 8.0	VF/NM 9.0	NM- 9.2
Feature Books 12 (Rare)	82	164	246	528	902	1275
Feature Books 27-29,31,34(1940)	21	42	63	122	199	275
Feature Books 36,38,40,42,43,45,47	20	40	60	114	182	250
...1944 (Hard-c, 1938, B&W, 128 pgs.)-1944 daily strip-r	16	32	48	94	147	200

BLONDIE & DAGWOOD FAMILY
Harvey Publ. (King Features Synd.): Oct, 1963 - No. 4, Dec, 1965 (68 pgs.)

	GD 2.0	VG 4.0	FN 6.0	VF 8.0	VF/NM 9.0	NM- 9.2
1	5	10	15	32	51	70
2-4	3	6	9	20	30	40

BLONDIE COMICS (...Monthly No. 16-141)
David McKay #1-15/Harvey #16-163/King #164-175/Charlton #177 on:
Spring, 1947 - No. 163, Nov, 1965; No. 164, Aug, 1966 - No. 175, Dec, 1967; No. 177, Feb, 1969 - No. 222, Nov, 1976

	GD 2.0	VG 4.0	FN 6.0	VF 8.0	VF/NM 9.0	NM- 9.2
1	34	68	102	199	325	450
2	17	34	51	100	158	215
3-5	15	30	45	83	124	165
6-10	13	26	39	74	105	135
11-15	10	20	30	54	72	90
16-(3/50; 1st Harvey issue)	11	22	33	62	86	110
17-20: 20-(3/51)-Becomes Daisy & Her Pups #21 & Chamber of Chills #21	6	12	18	39	62	85
21-30	5	10	15	35	55	75
31-50	4	8	12	28	44	60
51-80	4	8	12	24	37	50
81-99	4	8	12	22	34	45
100	4	8	12	26	41	55
101-124,126-130	3	6	9	18	27	35
125 (80 pgs.)	4	8	12	28	44	60
131-136,138,139	3	6	9	17	25	32
137,140-(80 pgs.)	4	8	12	26	41	55
141-147,149-154,156,160,164-167	3	6	9	16	23	30
148,155,157-159,161-163 are 68 pgs.	4	8	12	22	34	45
168-175	2	4	6	11	16	20
177-199 (no #176)-Moon landing-c/s	2	4	6	9	13	16
200-Anniversary issue; highlights of the Bumsteads	2	4	6	10	14	18
201-210,213-222	2	4	6	8	10	12
211,212-1st & 2nd app. Super Dagwood	2	4	6	9	13	16
Blondie, Dagwood & Daisy by Chic Young #1(Harvey, 1953, 100 pg. squarebound giant) new stories; Popeye (1 pg.) and Felix (1pg.) app.	30	60	90	177	289	400

BLOOD
Marvel Comics (Epic Comics): Feb, 1988 - No. 4, Apr, 1988 ($3.25, mature)

	GD 2.0	VG 4.0	FN 6.0	VF 8.0	VF/NM 9.0	NM- 9.2
1-4: DeMatteis scripts & Kent Williams-c/a						3.50

BLOOD AND GLORY (Punisher & Captain America)
Marvel Comics: Oct, 1992 - No. 3, Dec, 1992 ($5.95, limited series)

	GD 2.0	VG 4.0	FN 6.0	VF 8.0	VF/NM 9.0	NM- 9.2
1-3: 1-Embossed wraparound-c by Janson; Chichester & Clarke-s						6.00

BLOOD & ROSES: FUTURE PAST TENSE (Bob Hickey's...)
Sky Comics: Dec, 1993 ($2.25)

	GD 2.0	VG 4.0	FN 6.0	VF 8.0	VF/NM 9.0	NM- 9.2
1-Silver ink logo						3.00

BLOOD & ROSES: SEARCH FOR THE TIME-STONE (Bob Hickey's...)
Sky Comics: Apr, 1994 ($2.50)

	GD 2.0	VG 4.0	FN 6.0	VF 8.0	VF/NM 9.0	NM- 9.2
1						3.00

BLOOD AND SHADOWS
DC Comics (Vertigo): 1996 - Book 4, 1996 ($5.95, squarebound, mature)

	GD 2.0	VG 4.0	FN 6.0	VF 8.0	VF/NM 9.0	NM- 9.2
Books 1-4: Joe R. Lansdale scripts; Mark A. Nelson-c/a.						6.00

BLOOD AND WATER
DC Comics (Vertigo): May, 2003 - No. 5, Sept, 2003 ($2.95, limited series)

	GD 2.0	VG 4.0	FN 6.0	VF 8.0	VF/NM 9.0	NM- 9.2
1-5-Judd Winick-s/Tomm Coker-a/Brian Bolland-c						3.00
TPB (2009, $14.99) r/#1-5						15.00

BLOOD: A TALE
DC Comics (Vertigo): Nov, 1996 - No. 4, Feb, 1997 ($2.95, limited series)

	GD 2.0	VG 4.0	FN 6.0	VF 8.0	VF/NM 9.0	NM- 9.2
1-4: Reprints Epic series w/new-c; DeMatteis scripts; Kent Williams-c/a						3.00
TPB (2004, $19.95) r/#1-4						20.00

BLOODBATH
DC Comics: Early Dec, 1993 - No. 2, Late Dec, 1993 ($3.50, 68 pgs.)

	GD 2.0	VG 4.0	FN 6.0	VF 8.0	VF/NM 9.0	NM- 9.2
1-Neon ink-c; Superman app.; new Batman-c /app.						4.00
2-Hitman 2nd app.	1	2	3	4	5	7

BLOODHOUND
DC Comics: Sept, 2004 - No. 10, June, 2005 ($2.95)

	GD 2.0	VG 4.0	FN 6.0	VF 8.0	VF/NM 9.0	NM- 9.2
1-10: 1-Jolley-s/Kirk-a/Johnson-c. 5-Firestorm app. (cont. from Firestorm #7)						3.00

BLOOD LEGACY
Image Comics (Top Cow): May, 2000 - No. 4, Nov, 2000; Apr, 2003 ($2.50/$4.99)

	GD 2.0	VG 4.0	FN 6.0	VF 8.0	VF/NM 9.0	NM- 9.2
...: The Story of Ryan 1-4-Kerri Hawkins-s. 1-Andy Park-a(p); 3 covers						3.00
...: The Young Ones 1 (4/03, $4.99, one-shot) Basaldua-c/a						5.00
Preview Special ('00, $4.95) B&W flip-book w/The Magdalena Preview						5.00

BLOODLINES: A TALE FROM THE HEART OF AFRICA (See Tales From the Heart of Africa)
Marvel Comics (Epic Comics): 1992 ($5.95, 52 pgs.)

	GD 2.0	VG 4.0	FN 6.0	VF 8.0	VF/NM 9.0	NM- 9.2
1-Story cont'd from Tales From...						6.00

BLOOD OF DRACULA
Apple Comics: Nov, 1987 - No. 20?, 1990 ($1.75/$1.95, B&W)($2.25 #14,16 on)

	GD 2.0	VG 4.0	FN 6.0	VF 8.0	VF/NM 9.0	NM- 9.2
1-3,5-14,20: 1-10-Chadwick-c						4.00
4,16-19-Lost Frankenstein pgs. by Wrightson	1	2	3	4	5	7
15-Contains stereo flexidisc ($3.75)						5.00

BLOOD OF THE DEMON (Etrigan the Demon)
DC Comics: May, 2005 - No. 17, Sept, 2006 ($2.50/$2.99)

	GD 2.0	VG 4.0	FN 6.0	VF 8.0	VF/NM 9.0	NM- 9.2
1-14-Byrne-a(p) & plot/Pfeifer-script. 3,4-Batman app. 13-One Year Later						3.00
15-17-($2.99)						3.00

BLOOD OF THE INNOCENT (See Warp Graphics Annual)
WaRP Graphics: 1/7/86 - No. 4, 1/28/86 (Weekly mini-series, mature)

	GD 2.0	VG 4.0	FN 6.0	VF 8.0	VF/NM 9.0	NM- 9.2
1-4						3.00

BLOODPACK
DC Comics: Mar, 1995 - No. 4, June,1995 ($1.50, limited series)

	GD 2.0	VG 4.0	FN 6.0	VF 8.0	VF/NM 9.0	NM- 9.2
1-4						3.00

BLOODPOOL
Image Comics (Extreme): Aug, 1995 - No. 4, Nov, 1995 ($2.50, limited series)

	GD 2.0	VG 4.0	FN 6.0	VF 8.0	VF/NM 9.0	NM- 9.2
1-4: Jo Duffy scripts in all						3.00
Special (3/96, $2.50)-Jo Duffy scripts						3.00
Trade Paperback (1996, $12.95)-r/#1-4						13.00

BLOODSCENT
Comico: Oct, 1988 ($2.00, one-shot, Baxter paper)

	GD 2.0	VG 4.0	FN 6.0	VF 8.0	VF/NM 9.0	NM- 9.2
1-Colan-p						3.00

BLOODSEED
Marvel Comics (Frontier Comics): Oct, 1993 - No. 2, Nov, 1993 ($1.95)

	GD 2.0	VG 4.0	FN 6.0	VF 8.0	VF/NM 9.0	NM- 9.2
1,2: Sharp/Cam Smith-a						3.00

BLOODSHOT (See Eternal Warrior #4 & Rai #0)
Valiant/Acclaim Comics (Valiant): Feb, 1993 - No. 51, Aug, 1996 ($2.25/$2.50)

	GD 2.0	VG 4.0	FN 6.0	VF 8.0	VF/NM 9.0	NM- 9.2
0-(3/94, $3.50)-Wraparound chromium-c by Quesada(p); origin						4.00
0-Gold variant; no cover price						10.00

Note: There is a "Platinum variant" ; press run error of Gold ed. (25 copies exist) (A CGC certified 9.8 copy sold for $2,067 in 2004)

	GD 2.0	VG 4.0	FN 6.0	VF 8.0	VF/NM 9.0	NM- 9.2
1-($3.50)-Chromium embossed-c by B. Smith w/poster						4.00
2-5,8-14: 3-$2.25-c begins; cont'd in Hard Corps #5. 4-Eternal Warrior-c/story. 5-Rai & Eternal Warrior app. 14-(3/94)-Reese-c(i)						3.00

Bloody Mary #1 © Ennis & Ezquerra

Blue Beetle #48 © FOX

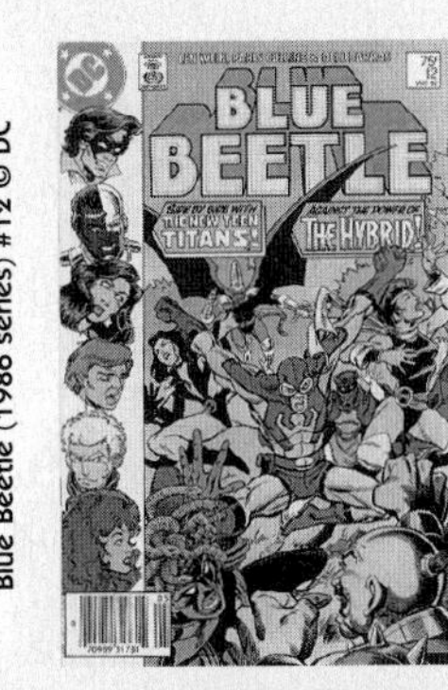

Blue Beetle (1986 series) #12 © DC

GD VG FN VF VF/NM NM-
2.0 4.0 6.0 8.0 9.0 9.2

6,7: 6-1st app. Ninjak (out of costume). 7-In costume 3.00
15(4/94)-51: 16-w/bound-in trading card. 51-Bloodshot dies? 3.00
Yearbook 1 (1994, $3.95) 4.00
Special 1 (3/94, $5.95)-Zeck-c/a(p); Last Stand 6.00

BLOODSHOT (Volume Two)
Acclaim Comics (Valiant): July, 1997 - No. 16, Oct, 1998 ($2.50)

1-16: 1-Two covers. 5-Copycat-c. X-O Manowar-c/app 2.50

BLOODSTONE
Marvel Comics: Dec, 2001 - No. 4, Mar, 2002 ($2.99)

1-4-Intro. Elsa Bloodstone; Abnett & Lanning-s/Lopez-a 3.00

BLOODSTREAM
Image Comics: Jan, 2004 - No. 4, Dec, 2004 ($2.95)

1-4-Adam Shaw painted-a 3.00

BLOODSTRIKE (See Supreme V2#3)
Image Comics (Extreme Studios): 1993 - No. 22, May, 1995; No. 25, May, 1994 ($1.95/$2.50)

1-22, 25: Liefeld layouts in early issues. 1-Blood Brothers prelude. 2-1st app. Lethal. 5-1st app. Noble. 9-Black and White part 6 by Art Thibert; Liefeld pin-up. 9,10-Have coupon #3 & 7 for Extreme Prejudice #0. 10-(4/94). 11-(7/94). 16:Platt-c; Prophet app. 17-19-polybagged w/card . 25-(5/94)-Liefeld/Fraga-c 3.00

NOTE: *Giffen story/layouts-4-6.* ***Jae Lee*** *c-7, 8.* ***Rob Liefeld*** *layouts-1-3.* ***Art Thibert*** *c-6i.*

BLOODSTRIKE ASSASSIN
Image Comics (Extreme Studios): June, 1995 - No. 3, Aug, 1995; No. 0, Oct, 1995 ($2.50, limited series)

0-3: 3-(8/95)-Quesada-c. 0-(10/95)-Battlestone app. 3.00

BLOOD SWORD, THE
Jademan Comics: Aug, 1988 - No. 53, Dec, 1992 ($1.50/$1.95, 68 pgs.)

1-53-Kung Fu stories in all 3.00

BLOOD SWORD DYNASTY
Jademan Comics: 1989 -No. 41, Jan, 1993 ($1.25, 36 pgs.)

1-Ties into Blood Sword 3.00
2-41: Ties into Blood Sword 3.00

BLOOD SYNDICATE
DC Comics (Milestone): Apr, 1993 - No. 35, Feb, 1996 ($1.50/-$3.50)

1-($2.95)-Collector's Edition; polybagged with poster, trading card, & acid-free backing board (direct sale only) 3.50
1-9,11-24,26,27,29,33-34: 8-Intro Kwai. 15-Byrne-c. 16-Worlds Collide Pt. 6; Superman-c/app. 17-Worlds Collide Pt. 13. 29-(99¢); Long Hot Summer x-over 3.00
10,28,30-32: 10-Simonson-c. 30-Long Hot Summer x-over 3.00
25-($2.95, 52 pgs.) 4.00
35-Kwai disappears; last issue 3.50

BLOODWULF
Image Comics (Extreme): Feb, 1995 - No. 4, May, 1995 ($2.50, limited series)

1-4: 1-Liefeld-c w/4 diferent captions & alternate-c. 3.00
Summer Special (8/95, $2.50)-Jeff Johnson-c/a; Supreme app; story takes place between Legend of Supreme #3 & Supreme #23. 3.00

BLOODY MARY
DC Comics (Helix): Oct, 1996 - No. 4, Jan, 1997 ($2.25, limited series)

1-4: Garth Ennis scripts; Ezquerra-c/a in all 3.50
TPB (2005, $19.99) r/#1-4 and Bloody Mary: Lady Liberty #1-4 20.00

BLOODY MARY: LADY LIBERTY
DC Comics (Helix): Sept, 1997 - No. 4, Dec, 1997 ($2.50, limited series)

1-4: Garth Ennis scripts; Ezquerra-c/a in all 3.00

BLUE
Image Comics (Action Toys): Aug, 1999 - No. 2, Apr, 2000 ($2.50)

1,2-Aronowitz-s/Struzan-c 3.00

BLUEBEARD
Slave Labor Graphics: Nov, 1993 - No. 3, Mar, 1994 ($2.95, B&W, lim. series)

1-3: James Robinson scripts. 2-(12/93) 3.00
Trade paperback (6/94, $9.95) 13.00
Trade paperback (2nd printing, 7/96, $12.95)-New-c 13.00

BLUE BEETLE, THE (Also see All Top, Big-3, Mystery Men & Weekly Comic Magazine)
Fox Publ. No. 1-11, 31-60; Holyoke No. 12-30: Winter, 1939-40 - No. 57, 7/48; No. 58, 4/50 - No. 60, 8/50

1-Reprints from Mystery Men #1-5; Blue Beetle origin; Yarko the Great-r/from Wonder Comics /Wonderworld #2-5 all by Eisner; Master Magician app.; (Blue Beetle in 4 different costumes) 459 918 1377 3350 5925 8500
2-K-51-r by Powell/Wonderworld #8,9 168 336 504 1075 1838 2600
3-Simon-c 123 246 369 787 1344 1900
4-Marijuana drug mention story 82 164 246 528 902 1275
5-Zanzibar The Magician by Tuska 71 142 213 454 777 1100
6-Dynamite Thor begins (1st); origin Blue Beetle 67 134 201 426 733 1040
7,8-Dynamo app. in both. 8-Last Thor 61 122 183 387 664 940
9-12: 9,10-The Blackbird & The Gorilla app. in both. 10-Bondage/hypo-c. 11(2/42)-The Gladiator app. 12(6/42)-The Black Fury app. 54 108 162 343 574 825
13-V-Man begins (1st app.), ends #19; Kubert-a; centerfold spread 63 126 189 403 689 975
14,15-Kubert-a in both. 14-Intro. side-kick (c/text only), Sparky (called Spunky #17-19); BB vs. The Red Robe (Red Skull swipe) 56 112 168 353 597 840
16-18: 17-Brodsky-c 46 92 138 290 488 685
19-Kubert-a 47 94 141 296 503 710
20-Origin/1st app. Tiger Squadron; Arabian Nights begin 50 100 150 315 533 750
21-26: 24-Intro. & only app. The Halo. 26-General Patton story & photo 39 78 117 236 388 540
27-Tamaa, Jungle Prince app. 37 74 111 222 361 500
28-30(2/44) 33 66 99 194 317 440
31(6/44), 33,34,36-40: 34-38-"The Threat from Saturn" serial. 30 60 90 177 289 400
32-Hitler-c 61 122 183 390 670 950
35-Extreme violence 36 72 108 216 351 485
41-45 (#43 exist?) 29 58 87 170 278 385
46-The Puppeteer app. 32 64 96 188 307 425
47-Kamen & Baker-a begin 148 296 444 947 1624 2300
48-50 110 220 330 704 1202 1700
51,53 94 188 282 597 1024 1450
52-Kamen bondage-c; true crime stories begin 139 278 417 883 1517 2150
54-Used in **SOTI**. Illo, "Children call these 'headlights' comics"; classic-c 258 516 774 1651 2826 4000
55-57: 56-Used in **SOTI**, pg. 145. 57(7/48)-Last Kamen issue; becomes Western Killers? 90 180 270 576 988 1400
58(4/50)-60-No Kamen-a 20 40 60 114 182 250

NOTE: ***Kamen*** *a-47-51, 53, 55-57; c-47, 49-52.* ***Powell*** *a-4(2). Bondage-c 9-12, 46, 52.*

BLUE BEETLE (Formerly The Thing; becomes Mr. Muscles No. 22 on) (See Charlton Bullseye & Space Adventures)
Charlton Comics: No. 18, Feb, 1955 - No. 21, Aug, 1955

18,19-(Pre-1944-r). 18-Last pre-code issue. 19-Bouncer, Rocket Kelly-r 20 40 60 120 195 270
20-Joan Mason by Kamen 26 52 78 152 249 345
21-New material 20 40 60 117 189 260

BLUE BEETLE (Unusual Tales #1-49; Ghostly Tales #55 on)(See Captain Atom #83 & Charlton Bullseye)
Charlton Comics: V2#1, June, 1964 - V2#5, Mar-Apr, 1965; V3#50, July, 1965 - V3#54, Feb-Mar, 1966; #1, June, 1967 - #5, Nov, 1968

V2#1-Origin/1st S.A. app. Dan Garrett-Blue Beetle 9 18 27 61 103 145
2-5: 5-Weiss illo; 1st published-a? 6 12 18 37 59 80
V3#50-54-Formerly Unusual Tales 5 10 15 34 55 75
1(1967)-Question series begins by Ditko 10 20 30 70 125 180
2-Origin Ted Kord-Blue Beetle (see Capt. Atom #83 for 1st Ted Kord Blue Beetle); Dan Garrett x-over 6 12 18 41 66 90
3-5 (All Ditko-c/a in #1-5) 6 12 18 37 59 80
1,3(Modern Comics-1977)-Reprints 1 2 3 5 6 8

NOTE: *#6 only appeared in the fanzine 'The Charlton Portfolio.'*

BLUE BEETLE (Also see Americomics, Crisis On Infinite Earths, Justice League & Showcase '94 #2-4)
DC Comics: June, 1986 - No. 24, May, 1988

1-Origin retold; intro. Firefist 4.00
2-10,15-19,21-24: 2-Origin Firefist. 5-7-The Question app. 21-Millennium tie-in 3.00
11-14-New Teen Titans x-over 3.50
20-Justice League app.; Millennium tie-in 3.50

BLUE BEETLE (See Infinite Crisis, Teen Titans, and Booster Gold #21)
DC Comics: May, 2006 - No. 36, Apr, 2009 ($2.99)

1-Hamner-a/Giffen & Rogers-s; Guy Gardner app. 4.00
1-2nd & 3rd printings 3.00
2-36: 2-2nd printing exists. 2-4-Oracle app. 5-Phantom Stranger app. 16-Eclipso app. 18,33-Teen Titans app. 20-Sinestro Corps. 21-Spectre app. 26-Spanish issue 3.00
...: Black and Blue TPB (2010, $17.99) r/#27,28,35,36 & Booster Gold #21-25,28,29 17.00
...: Boundaries TPB (2009, $14.99) r/#29-34 15.00

Blue Bolt #1 © NOVP

Blue Monday: Painted Moon #2 © Chynna Clugston

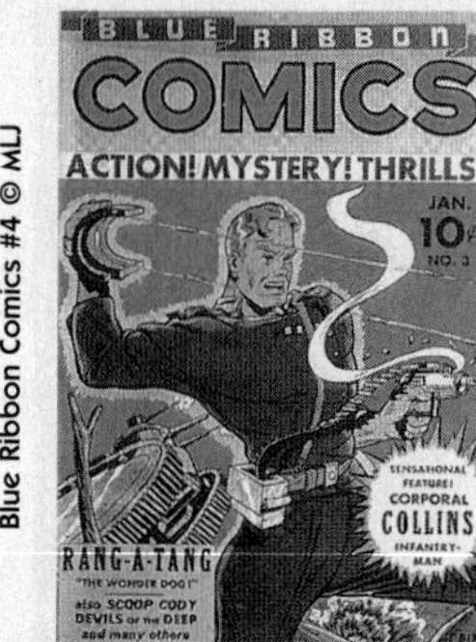

Blue Ribbon Comics #4 © MLJ

	GD 2.0	VG 4.0	FN 6.0	VF 8.0	VF/NM 9.0	NM- 9.2
...: End Game TPB (2008, $14.99) r/#20-26; English script for #26						15.00
...: Reach For the Stars TPB (2008, $14.99) r/#13-19						15.00
...: Road Trip TPB (2007, $12.99) r/#7-12						13.00
...: Shellshocked TPB (2006, $12.99) r/#1-6						13.00

BLUEBERRY (See Lt. Blueberry & Marshal Blueberry)
Marvel Comics (Epic Comics): 1989 - No. 5, 1990 ($12.95/$14.95, graphic novel)

	GD 2.0	VG 4.0	FN 6.0	VF 8.0	VF/NM 9.0	NM- 9.2
1,3,4,5-($12.95)-Moebius-a in all	3	6	9	14	19	24
2-($14.95)	3	6	9	14	20	26

BLUE BOLT
Funnies, Inc. No. 1/Novelty Press/Premium Group of Comics: June, 1940 - No. 101 (V10#2), Sept-Oct, 1949

	GD 2.0	VG 4.0	FN 6.0	VF 8.0	VF/NM 9.0	NM- 9.2
V1#1-Origin Blue Bolt by Joe Simon, Sub-Zero Man, White Rider & Super Horse, Dick Cole, Wonder Boy & Sgt. Spook (1st app. of each)	320	640	960	2240	3920	5600
2-Simon & Kirby's 1st art & 1st super-hero (Blue Bolt)	181	362	543	1158	1979	2800
3-1 pg. Space Hawk by Wolverton; 2nd S&K-a on Blue Bolt (same cover date as Red Raven #1); Simon-c	158	316	474	1003	1727	2450
4-S&K-a; classic Everett shark-c	155	310	465	992	1696	2400
5-S&K-a; Everett-a begins on Sub-Zero; 1st time S&K names app. in a comic	134	268	402	851	1463	2075
6,8-10-S&K-a	123	246	369	787	1344	1900
7-S&K-c/a	142	284	426	909	1555	2200
11,12: 11-Robot-c	116	232	348	742	1271	1800
V2#1-Origin Dick Cole & The Twister; Twister x-over in Dick Cole, Sub-Zero, & Blue Bolt; origin Simba Karno who battles Dick Cole thru V2#5 & becomes main supporting character V2#6 on; battle-c	41	82	123	249	417	585
2-Origin The Twister retold in text	34	68	102	204	332	460
3-5: 5-Intro. Freezum	30	60	90	177	289	400
6-Origin Sgt. Spook retold	26	52	78	154	252	350
7-12: 7-Lois Blake becomes Blue Bolt's costume aide; last Twister. 12-Text-sty by Mickey Spillaine	22	44	66	128	209	290
V3#1-3	18	36	54	107	169	230
4-12: 4-Blue Bolt abandons costume	15	30	45	86	133	180
V4#1-Hitler, Tojo, Mussolini-c	50	100	150	315	533	750
V4#2-12: 3-Shows V4#3 on-c, V4#4 inside (9-10/43). 5-Infinity-c. 8-Last Sub-Zero	13	26	39	72	101	130
V5#1-8, V6#1-3,5-10, V7#1-12	11	22	33	64	90	115
V6#4-Racist cover	21	42	63	122	199	275
V8#1-6,8-12, V9#1-4,7,8, V10#1(#100),V10#2(#101)-Last Dick Cole, Blue Bolt	10	20	30	56	76	95
V8#7,V9#6,9-L. B. Cole-c	22	44	66	128	209	290
V9#5-Classic fish in the face-c	22	44	66	128	209	290

NOTE: ***Everett*** *c-V1#4, 11, V2#1, 2.* ***Gustavson*** *a-V1#1-12, V2#1-7.* ***Kiefer*** *c-V3#1.* ***Rico*** *a-V6#10, V7#4. Blue Bolt not in V9#8.*

BLUE BOLT (Becomes Ghostly Weird Stories #120 on; continuation of Novelty Blue Bolt) (...Weird Tales of Terror #111,112,...Weird Tales #113-119)
Star Publications: No. 102, Nov-Dec, 1949 - No. 119, May-June, 1953

	GD 2.0	VG 4.0	FN 6.0	VF 8.0	VF/NM 9.0	NM- 9.2
102-The Chameleon, & Target app.	39	78	117	240	395	550
103,104-The Chameleon app. 104-Last Target	39	78	117	231	378	525
105-Origin Blue Bolt (from #1) retold by Simon; Chameleon & Target app.; opium den story	57	114	171	362	624	885
106-Blue Bolt by S&K begins; Spacehawk reprints from Target by Wolverton begin, ends #110; Sub-Zero begins; ends #109	54	108	162	346	591	835
107-110: 108-Last S&K Blue Bolt reprint. 109-Wolverton-c(r)/inside Spacehawk splash. 110-Target app.	54	108	162	338	574	810
111,112: 111-Red Rocket & The Mask-r; last Blue Bolt; 1pg. L. B. Cole-a. 112-Last Torpedo Man app.	50	100	150	315	533	750
113-Wolverton's Spacehawk-r/Target V3#7	52	104	156	328	552	775
114,116: 116-Jungle Jo-r	50	100	150	315	533	750
115-Sgt. Spook app.	52	104	156	328	552	775
117-Jo-Jo & Blue Bolt-r	51	102	153	320	543	765
118-"White Spirit" by Wood	52	104	156	328	552	775
119-Disbrow/Cole-c; Jungle Jo-r	51	102	153	320	543	765
Accepted Reprint #103(1957?, nd)	14	28	42	80	115	150

NOTE: ***L. B. Cole*** *c-102-108, 110 on.* ***Disbrow*** *a-112(2), 113(3), 114(2), 115(2), 116-118.* ***Hollingsworth*** *a-117.* ***Palais*** *a-112r. Sci/Fi c-105-110. Horror c-111.*

BLUE BULLETEER, THE (Also see Femforce Special)
AC Comics: 1989 ($2.25, B&W, one-shot)

	GD 2.0	VG 4.0	FN 6.0	VF 8.0	VF/NM 9.0	NM- 9.2
1-Origin by Bill Black; Bill Ward-a						4.00

BLUE BULLETEER (Also see Femforce Special)
AC Comics: 1996 ($5.95, B&W, one-shot)

	GD 2.0	VG 4.0	FN 6.0	VF 8.0	VF/NM 9.0	NM- 9.2
1-Photo-c						6.00

BLUE CIRCLE COMICS (Also see Red Circle Comics, Blazing Comics & Roly Poly Comic Book)
Enwil Associates/Rural Home: June, 1944 - No. 6, Apr, 1945

	GD 2.0	VG 4.0	FN 6.0	VF 8.0	VF/NM 9.0	NM- 9.2
1-The Blue Circle begins (1st app.); origin & 1st app. Steel Fist	34	68	102	199	325	450
2	20	40	60	117	189	260
3-Hitler parody-c	39	78	117	231	378	525
4-6: 5-Last Steel Fist.	19	38	57	109	172	235
6-(Dated 4/45, Vol. 2#3 inside)-Leftover covers to #6 were later restapled over early 1950's coverless comics; variations of the coverless comics exist. Colossal Features known.	19	38	57	109	172	235

BLUE DEVIL (See Fury of Firestorm #24, Underworld Unleashed, Starman (2nd) #38, Infinite Crisis and Shadowpact)
DC Comics: June, 1984 - No. 31, Dec, 1986 (75¢/$1.25)

	GD 2.0	VG 4.0	FN 6.0	VF 8.0	VF/NM 9.0	NM- 9.2
1						4.00
2-16,19-31: 4-Origin Nebiros. 7-Gil Kane-a. 8-Giffen-a						3.00
17,18-Crisis x-over						3.50
Annual 1 (11/85)-Team-ups w/Black Orchid, Creeper, Demon, Madame Xanadu, Man-Bat & Phantom Stranger						4.00

BLUE MONDAY: ... (one-shots)
Oni Press: Feb, 2002 - Present (B&W, Chynna Clugston-Major-s/a/c in all)

	GD 2.0	VG 4.0	FN 6.0	VF 8.0	VF/NM 9.0	NM- 9.2
Dead Man's Party (10/02, $2.95) Dan Brereton painted back-c						3.00
Inbetween Days (9/03, $9.95, 8" x 5-1/2") r/Dead Man's Party, Lovecats, & Nobody's Fool						10.00
Lovecats (2/02, $2.95) Valentine's Day themed						3.00
Nobody's Fool (2/03, $2.95) April Fool's Day themed						3.00

BLUE MONDAY: ABSOLUTE BEGINNERS
Oni Press: Feb, 2001 - No. 4, Sept, 2001 ($2.95, B&W, limited series)

	GD 2.0	VG 4.0	FN 6.0	VF 8.0	VF/NM 9.0	NM- 9.2
1-4-Chynna Clugston-Major-s/a/c						3.00
TPB (12/01, $11.95, 8" x 6") r/series						12.00

BLUE MONDAY: PAINTED MOON
Oni Press: Feb, 2004 - No. 4, Mar, 2005 ($2.99, B&W, limited series)

	GD 2.0	VG 4.0	FN 6.0	VF 8.0	VF/NM 9.0	NM- 9.2
1-4-Chynna Clugston-Major-s/a/c						3.00
TPB (4/05, $11.95, digest-sized) r/series; sketch pages						12.00

BLUE MONDAY: THE KIDS ARE ALRIGHT
Oni Press: Feb, 2000 - No. 3, May, 2000 ($2.95, B&W, limited series)

	GD 2.0	VG 4.0	FN 6.0	VF 8.0	VF/NM 9.0	NM- 9.2
1-3-Chynna Clugston-Major-s/a/c. 1-Variant-c by Warren. 2-Dorkin-c						3.00
3-Variant cover by J. Scott Campbell						4.00
TPB (12/00, $10.95, digest-sized) r/#1-3 & earlier short stories						11.00

BLUE MONDAY: THIEVES LIKE US
Oni Press: Dec, 2008 - No. 5 ($3.50, B&W, limited series)

	GD 2.0	VG 4.0	FN 6.0	VF 8.0	VF/NM 9.0	NM- 9.2
1-Chynna Clugston-s/a/c						3.50

BLUE PHANTOM, THE
Dell Publishing Co.: June-Aug, 1962

	GD 2.0	VG 4.0	FN 6.0	VF 8.0	VF/NM 9.0	NM- 9.2
1(01-066-208)-by Fred Fredericks	3	6	9	21	32	42

BLUE RIBBON COMICS (...Mystery Comics No. 9-18)
MLJ Magazines: Nov, 1939 - No. 22, Mar, 1942 (1st MLJ series)

	GD 2.0	VG 4.0	FN 6.0	VF 8.0	VF/NM 9.0	NM- 9.2
1-Dan Hastings, Richy the Amazing Boy, Rang-A-Tang the Wonder Dog begin (1st app. of each); Little Nemo app. (not by W. McCay); Jack Cole-a(3) (1st MLJ comic)	245	490	735	1568	2684	3800
2-Bob Phantom, Silver Fox (both in #3), Rang-A-Tang Club & Cpl. Collins begin (1st app. of each); Jack Cole-a	119	238	357	762	1306	1850
3-J. Cole-a	79	158	237	502	864	1225
4-Doc Strong, The Green Falcon, & Hercules begin (1st app. each); origin & 1st app. The Fox & Ty-Gor, Son of the Tiger	87	174	261	553	952	1350
5-8: 8-Last Hercules; 6,7-Biro, Meskin-a. 7-Fox app. on-c	64	128	192	406	696	985
9-(Scarce)-Origin & 1st app. Mr. Justice (2/41)	300	600	900	2040	3570	5100
10-13: 12-Last Doc Strong. 13-Inferno, the Flame Breather begins, ends #19; Devil-c	107	214	321	680	1165	1650
14,15,17,18: 15-Last Green Falcon	90	180	270	576	988	1400
16-Origin & 1st app. Captain Flag (9/41)	161	322	483	1030	1765	2500
19-22: 20-Last Ty-Gor. 22-Origin Mr. Justice retold	90	180	270	576	988	1400

NOTE: ***Biro*** *c-3-5; a-2 (Cpl. Collins & Scoop Cody).* ***S. Cooper*** *c-9-17. 20-22 contain "Tales From the Witch's Cauldron" (same strip as "Stories of the Black Witch" in Zip Comics). Mr. Justice c-9-18. Captain Flag c-16-18 (w/Mr. Justice), 19-22.*

BLUE RIBBON COMICS (Becomes Teen-Age Diary Secrets #4)
(Also see Approved Comics, Blue Ribbon Comics and Heckle & Jeckle)
Blue Ribbon (St. John): Feb, 1949 - No. 6, Aug, 1949

Bluntman and Chronic TPB © Miramax

Bob Colt #9 © FAW

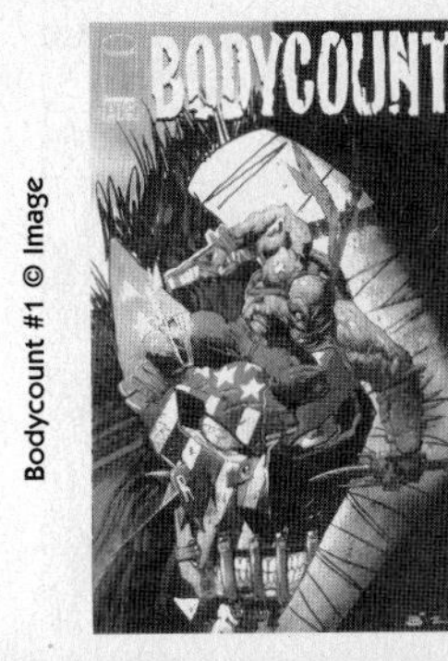

Bodycount #1 © Image

GD VG FN VF VF/NM NM-
2.0 4.0 6.0 8.0 9.0 9.2

1-Heckle & Jeckle (Terrytoons) 14 28 42 82 121 160
2(4/49)-Diary Secrets; Baker-c 37 74 111 222 361 500
3-Heckle & Jeckle (Terrytoons) 11 22 33 62 86 110
4(6/49)-Teen-Age Diary Secrets; Baker c/a(2) 37 74 111 222 361 500
5(8/49)-Teen-Age Diary Secrets; Oversize; photo-c; Baker-a(2)- Continues
as Teen-Age Diary Secrets 41 82 123 256 428 600
6-Dinky Duck(8/49)(Terrytoons) 8 16 24 42 54 65

BLUE RIBBON COMICS
Red Circle Prod./Archie Ent. No. 5 on: Nov, 1983 - No. 14, Dec, 1984
1-S&K-r/Advs. of the Fly #1,2; Williamson/Torres-r/Fly #2; Ditko-c
1 2 3 5 6 8
2-7,9,10: 3-Origin Steel Sterling. 5-S&K Shield-r; new Kirby-c. 6,7-The Fox app. 6.00
8-Toth centerspread; Black Hood app.; Neal Adams-a(r)
1 2 3 4 5 7
11,13,14: 11-Black Hood. 13-Thunder Bunny. 14-Web & Jaguar 6.00
12-Thunder Agents; Noman new Ditko-a 1 2 3 5 6 8
NOTE: ***N. Adams** a(r)-8. **Buckler** a-4i. **Nino** a-2i. **McWilliams** a-8. **Morrow** a-8.*

BLUE STREAK (See Holyoke One-Shot No. 8)

BLUNTMAN AND CHRONIC TPB(Also see Jay and Silent Bob, Clerks, and Oni Double Feature)
Image Comics: Dec, 2001 ($14.95, TPB)
nn-Tie-in for "Jay & Silent Bob Strike Back" movie; new Kevin Smith-s/Michael Oeming-a;
r/app. from Oni Double Feature #12 in color; Ben Affleck & Jason Lee afterwords 15.00

BLYTHE (Marge's)
Dell Publishing Co.: No. 1072, Jan-Mar, 1960
Four Color 1072 6 12 18 37 59 80

B-MAN (See Double-Dare Adventures)

BO (Tom Cat #4 on) (Also see Big Shot #29 & Dixie Dugan)
Charlton Comics Group: June, 1955 - No. 3, Oct, 1955 (A dog)
1-3: Newspaper reprints by Frank Beck 8 16 24 40 50 60

BOATNIKS, THE (See Walt Disney Showcase No. 1)

BOB BURDEN'S ORIGINAL MYSTERYMEN PRESENTS
Dark Horse Comics: 1999 - No. 4 ($2.95/$3.50)
1-3-Bob Burden-s/Sadowski-a(p) 3.50
4-($3.50) All Villain issue 3.50

BOBBY BENSON'S B-BAR-B RIDERS (Radio) (See Best of The West, The Lemonade Kid & Model Fun)
Magazine Enterprises/AC Comics: May-June, 1950 - No. 20, May-June, 1953
1-The Lemonade Kid begins; Powell-a (Scarce) 41 82 123 256 428 600
2 17 34 51 98 154 210
3-5: 4,5-Lemonade Kid-c (#4-Spider-c) 14 28 42 76 108 140
6-8,10 13 26 39 72 101 130
9,11,13-Frazetta-c; Ghost Rider in #13-15 by Ayers-a. 13-Ghost Rider-c
37 74 111 222 361 500
12,17-20: 20-(A-1 #88) 11 22 33 64 90 115
14-Decapitation/Bondage-c & story; classic horror-c 29 58 87 170 278 385
15-Ghost Rider-c 22 44 66 132 216 300
16-Photo-c 14 28 42 80 115 150
1 (1990, $2.75, B&W)-Reprints; photo-c & inside covers 3.00
NOTE: ***Ayers** a-13-15, 20. **Powell** a-1-12(4 ea.), 13(3), 14-16(Red Hawk only); c-1-8,1 0, 12. Lemonade Kid in most 1-13.*

BOBBY COMICS
Universal Phoenix Features: May, 1946
1-By S. M. Iger 9 18 27 47 61 75

BOBBY SHERMAN (TV)
Charlton Comics: Feb, 1972 - No. 7, Oct, 1972
1-Based on TV show "Getting Together" 6 12 18 37 59 80
2-7: Photo-c on all. 7-Bobby Sherman for President 4 8 12 24 37 50

BOB COLT (Movie star)(See XMas Comics)
Fawcett Publications: Nov, 1950 - No. 10, May, 1952
1-Bob Colt, his horse Buckskin & sidekick Pablo begin; photo front/back-c
begin 28 56 84 165 270 375
2 15 30 45 88 137 185
3-5 14 28 42 80 115 150
6-Flying Saucer story 12 24 36 69 97 125
7-10: 9-Last photo back-c 11 22 33 62 86 110

BOB HOPE (See Adventures of... & Calling All Boys #12)

BOB MARLEY, TALE OF THE TUFF GONG (Music star)

GD VG FN VF VF/NM NM-
2.0 4.0 6.0 8.0 9.0 9.2

Marvel Comics: Aug, 1994 - No, 3, Nov, 1994 ($5.95, limited series)
1-3 6.00

BOB POWELL'S TIMELESS TALES
Eclipse Comics: March, 1989 ($2.00, B&W)
1-Powell-r/Black Cat #5 (Scarlet Arrow), 9 & Race for the Moon #1 3.00

BOB SCULLY, THE TWO-FISTED HICK DETECTIVE (Also see Advs. of Detective Ace King and Detective Dan)
Humor Publ. Co.: No date (1933) (36 pgs., 9-1/2x11", B&W, paper-c; 10¢-c)
nn-By Howard Dell; not reprints; along with Advs. of Det. Ace King and Detective Dan,
the first comic w/original art & the first of a single theme; has a blue 2-tone cover
400 800 1200 3200 - -

BOB SON OF BATTLE
Dell Publishing Co.: No. 729, Nov, 1956
Four Color 729 4 8 12 24 37 50

BOB STEELE WESTERN (Movie star)
Fawcett Publications/AC Comics: Dec, 1950 - No. 10, June, 1952; 1990
1-Bob Steele & his horse Bullet begin; photo front/back-c begin
37 74 111 222 361 500
2 19 38 57 109 172 235
3-5: 4-Last photo back-c 14 28 42 82 121 160
6-10: 10-Last photo-c 13 26 39 72 101 130
1 (1990, $2.75, B&W)-Bob Steele & Rocky Lane reprints; photo-c & inside covers 3.00

BOB SWIFT (Boy Sportsman)
Fawcett Publications: May, 1951 - No. 5, Jan, 1952
1 10 20 30 58 79 100
2-5: Saunders painted-c #1-5 7 14 21 35 43 50

BOB, THE GALACTIC BUM
DC Comics: Feb, 1995 - No. 4, June, 1995 ($1.95, limited series)
1-4: 1-Lobo app. 3.00

BODY BAGS
Dark Horse Comics (Blanc Noir): Sept, 1996 - No. 4, Jan, 1997 ($2.95, mini-series, mature) (1st Blanc Noir series)
1-Jason Pearson-c/a/scripts in all. 1-Intro Clownface & Panda.
1 2 3 5 6 8
2 1 3 4 6 8 10
3,4 6.00
Body Bags 1 (Image Comics, 7/05, $5.99) r/#1&2 6.00
Body Bags 2 (Image Comics, 8/05, $5.99) r/#3&4 6.00
...: 3 The Hard Way (Image, 2/06, $5.99) new story & r/Dark Horse Presents Annual 1997
and Dark Horse Maverick 2000; Pearson-c 6.00
...: One Shot (Image, 11/08, $5.99) wraparound-c; Pearson-c/a/s 6.00

BODYCOUNT (Also see Casey Jones & Raphael)
Image Comics (Highbrow Entertainment): Mar, 1996 - No. 4, July, 1996 ($2.50, lim. series)
1-4: Kevin Eastman-a(p)/scripts; Simon Bisley-c/a(i); Turtles app. 3.00

BODY DOUBLES (See Resurrection Man)
DC Comics: Oct, 1999 - No. 4, Jan, 2000 ($2.50, limited series)
1-4-Lanning & Abnett-s. 2-Black Canary app. 4-Wonder Woman app. 3.00
...(Villains) (2/98, $1.95, one-shot) 1-Pearson-c; Deadshot app. 3.00

BOFFO LAFFS
Paragraphics: 1986 - No. 5 ($2.50/$1.95)
1-($2.50) First comic cover with hologram 3.50
2-5 3.00

BOLD ADVENTURES
Pacific Comics: Oct, 1983 - No. 3, June, 1984 ($1.50)
1-Time Force, Anaconda, & The Weirdling begin 3.00
2,3: 2-Soldiers of Fortune begins. 3-Spitfire 3.00
NOTE: ***Kaluta** c-3. **Nebres** a-1-3. **Nino** a-2, 3. **Severin** a-3.*

BOLD STORIES (Also see Candid Tales & It Rhymes With Lust)
Kirby Publishing Co.: Mar, 1950 - July, 1950 (Digest size, 144 pgs.)
March issue (Very Rare) - Contains "The Ogre of Paris" by Wood
174 348 522 1114 1907 2700
May issue (Very Rare) - Contains "The Cobra's Kiss" by Graham
Ingels (21 pgs.) 148 296 444 947 1624 2300
July issue (Very Rare) - Contains "The Ogre of Paris" by Wood
135 270 405 864 1482 2100

BOLT AND STAR FORCE SIX

Bomber Comics #3 © EP

Bone #45 © Jeff Smith

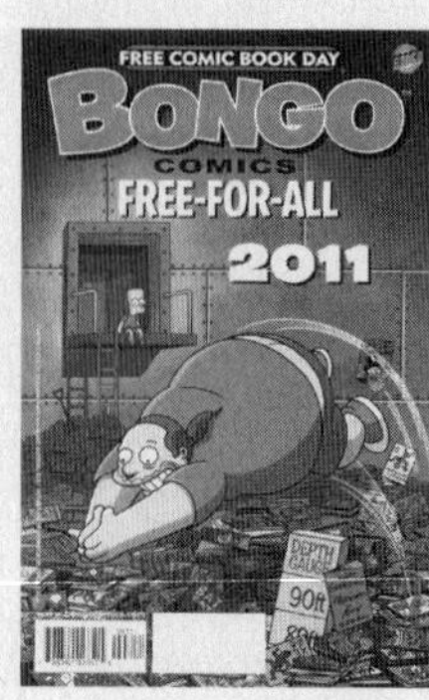

Bongo Comic Free-For-All 2011 © Bongo

	GD 2.0	VG 4.0	FN 6.0	VF 8.0	VF/NM 9.0	NM- 9.2

Americomics: 1984 ($1.75)

1-Origin Bolt & Star Force Six						3.00
Special 1 (1984, $2.00, 52pgs., B&W)						4.00

BOMBARDIER (See Bee 29, the Bombardier & Cinema Comics Herald)

BOMBAST
Topps Comics: 1993 ($2.95, one-shot) (Created by Jack Kirby)

1-Polybagged w/Kirbychrome trading card; Savage Dragon app.; Kirby-c; has coupon for Amberchrome Secret City Saga #0						3.00

BOMBA THE JUNGLE BOY (TV)
National Periodical Publ.: Sept-Oct, 1967 - No. 7, Sept-Oct, 1968 (12¢)

1-Intro. Bomba; Infantino/Anderson-c	4	8	12	24	37	50
2-7	3	6	9	16	23	30

BOMBER COMICS
Elliot Publ. Co./Melverne Herald/Farrell/Sunrise Times: Mar, 1944 - No. 4, Winter, 1944-45

1-Wonder Boy, & Kismet, Man of Fate begin	84	168	252	538	919	1300
2-Hitler-c and 8 pg. story	103	206	309	659	1130	1600
3: 2-4-Have Classics Comics ad to HRN 20	47	94	141	296	498	700
4-Hitler, Tojo & Mussolini-c; Sensation Comics #13-c/swipe; has Classics Comics ad to HRN 20.	97	194	291	621	1061	1500

BOMB QUEEN
Image Comics (Shadowline): Feb, 2006 - No. 4, May, 2006 ($3.50, mature)

1-4-Jimmie Robinson-s/a						3.50
... Vs. Blacklight One Shot #1 (8/06, $3.50) Robinson-a; Shadowhawk app.						3.50
..., Vol. 1: WMD: Woman of Mass Destruction TPB (7/06, $12.99) r/#1-4; bonus art						13.00

BOMB QUEEN II
Image Comics (Shadowline): Oct, 2006 - No. 3, Dec, 2006 ($3.50, mature)

1-3-Jimmie Robinson-s/a; intro. The Four Queens						3.50
..., Vol. 2: Dirty Bomb - Queen of Hearts TPB (7/07, $14.99) r/#1-3 & Blacklight One Shot; bonus art; Robinson interview						15.00

BOMB QUEEN III THE GOOD, THE BAD & THE LOVELY
Image Comics (Shadowline): Mar, 2007 - No. 4, Jun, 2007 ($3.50, mature)

1-4-Jimmie Robinson-a/Jim Valentino-s; Blacklight & Rebound app. 1-Linsner-c						3.50

BOMB QUEEN IV SUICIDE BOMBER
Image Comics (Shadowline): Aug, 2007 - No. 4, Dec, 2007 ($3.50, mature)

1-4-Jim Robinson-s/a. 3-She-Spawn app.						3.50

BOMB QUEEN (Volume 5)
Image Comics (Shadowline): May, 2008 - No. 6, Mar, 2009 ($3.50, mature)

Vol. 5 #1-6-Jim Robinson-s/a						3.50
Vol. 6 #1-4 (9/09, $3.50) Obama satire						3.50
... Presents: All Girl Comics (5/09, $3.50) Dee Rail, Blacklight, Rebound, Tempest app.						3.50
... vs. Hack/Slash (2/11, $3.50) Cassie and Vlad app.; Robinson-s/a						3.50

BONANZA (TV)
Dell/Gold Key: June-Aug, 1960 - No. 37, Aug, 1970 (All Photo-c)

Four Color 1110 (6-8/60)	29	58	87	223	449	675
Four Color 1221,1283, & #01070-207, 01070-210	16	32	48	111	226	340
1(12/62-Gold Key)	17	34	51	118	242	365
2	10	20	30	68	119	170
3-10	8	16	24	52	86	120
11-20	6	12	18	39	62	85
21-37: 29-Reprints	5	10	15	32	51	70

BONE
Cartoon Books #1-20, 28 on/Image Comics #21-27: Jul, 1991 - No. 55, Jun, 2004 ($2.95, B&W)

1-Jeff Smith-c/a in all	15	30	45	106	216	325
1-2nd printing	2	4	6	9	12	15
1-3rd thru 5th printings						4.00
2-1st printing	7	14	21	49	80	110
2-2nd & 3rd printings						4.00
3-1st printing	6	12	18	39	62	85
3-2nd thru 4th printings						4.00
4,5	4	8	12	26	41	55
6-10	2	4	6	13	18	22
11-20						6.00
13 1/2 (1/95, Wizard)	2	4	6	8	10	12
13 1/2 (Gold)	2	4	6	9	12	15
21-37: 21-1st Image issue						5.00
38-($4.95) Three covers by Miller, Ross, Smith	1	2	3	4	5	7
39-55-($2.95)						4.00
1-27-($2.95): 1-Image reprints begin w/new-c. 2-Allred pin-up.						3.00
... Holiday Special (1993, giveaway)	2	3	4	6	8	10
... Reader -($9.95) Behind the scenes info						10.00
... Sourcebook-San Diego Edition						3.00
...10th Anniversary Edition (8/01, $5.95) r/#1 in color; came with figure						6.00
Complete Bone Adventures Vol 1,2 ('93, '94, $12.95, r/#1-6 & #7-12)						13.00
...: One Volume Edition (2004, $39.95, 1300 pgs.) r/#1-54; extra material						40.00
Volume 1-($19.95, hard-c)-"Out From Boneville"						20.00
Volume 1-($12.95, soft-c)						13.00
Volume 2,5-($22.95, hard-c)-"The Great Cow Race" & "Rock Jaw"						23.00
Volume 2,5-($14.95, soft-c)						15.00
Volume 3,4-($24.95, hard-c)-"Eyes of the Storm" & "The Dragonslayer"						25.00
Volume 3,4,7-($16.95, soft-c)						17.00
Volume 6-($15.95, soft-c)-"Old Man's Cave"						16.00
Volume 7-($24.95, hard-c)-"Ghost Circles"						25.00
Volume 8-($23.95, hard-c)-"Treasure Hunters"						24.00

NOTE: *Printings not listed sell for cover price.*

BONGO (See Story Hour Series)

BONGO & LUMPJAW (Disney, see Walt Disney Showcase #3)
Dell Publishing Co.: No. 706, June, 1956; No. 886, Mar, 1958

Four Color 706 (#1)	6	12	18	37	59	80
Four Color 886	5	10	15	30	48	65

BONGO COMICS ...
Bongo Comics: 2005 - 2011 (Free Comic Book Day giveaways)

Gimme Gimme Giveaway! (2005) - Short stories from Simpsons Comics, Futurama Comics and Radioactive Man						2.50
Free-For-All! (2006, 2007, 2008, 2009,2010,2011) - Short stories in each						2.50

BONGO COMICS PRESENTS RADIOACTIVE MAN (See Radioactive Man)

BON VOYAGE (See Movie Classics)

BOOF
Image Comics (Todd McFarlane Prod.): July, 1994 - No. 6, Dec, 1994 ($1.95)

1-6						3.00

BOOF AND THE BRUISE CREW
Image Comics (Todd McFarlane Prod.): July, 1994 - No. 6, Dec, 1994 ($1.95)

1-6						3.00

BOOK AND RECORD SET (See Power Record Comics)

BOOK OF ALL COMICS
William H. Wise: 1945 (196 pgs.)(Inside f/c has Green Publ. blacked out)

nn-Green Mask, Puppeteer & The Bouncer	46	92	138	290	488	685

BOOK OF ANTS, THE
Artisan Entertainment: 1998 ($2.95, B&W)

1-Based on the movie Pi; Aronofsky-s						3.00

BOOK OF BALLADS AND SAGAS, THE
Green Man Press: Oct, 1995 - No. 4 ($2.95/$3.50/$3.25, B&W)

1-4: 1-Vess-c/a; Gaiman story.						3.50

BOOK OF COMICS, THE
William H. Wise: No date (1944) (25¢, 132 pgs.)

nn-Captain V app.	41	82	123	264	442	620

BOOK OF FATE, THE (See Fate)
DC Comics: Feb, 1997 - No. 12, Jan, 1998 ($2.25/$2.50)

1-12: 4-Two-Face-c/app. 6-Convergence. 11-Sentinel app.						3.00

BOOK OF LOST SOULS, THE
Marvel Comics (Icon): Dec, 2005 - No. 6, June, 2006 ($2.99)

1-6-Colleen Doran-a/c; J. Michael Straczynski-s						3.00
... Vol. 1: Introductions All Around (2006, $16.99, TPB) r/series						17.00

BOOK OF LOVE (See Fox Giants)

BOOK OF NIGHT, THE
Dark Horse Comics: July, 1987 - No. 3, 1987 ($1.75, B&W)

1-3: Reprints from Epic Illustrated; Vess-a						3.00
TPB-r/#1-3						15.00
Hardcover-Black-c with red crest						100.00
Hardcover w/slipcase (1991) signed and numbered						50.00

BOOK OF THE DEAD

Books of Faerie: Molly's Story #4 © DC

Books of Magic #8 © DC

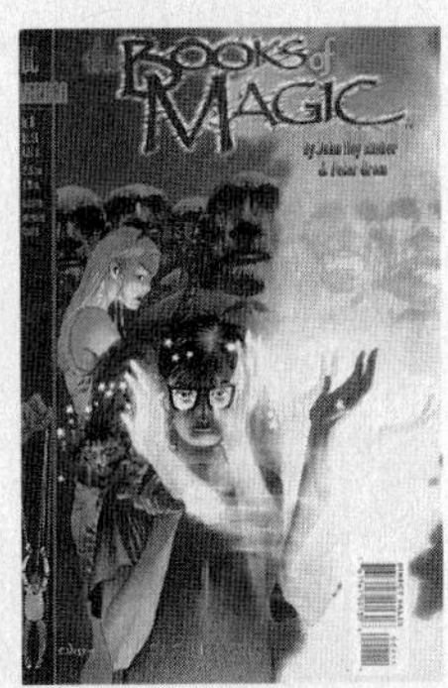

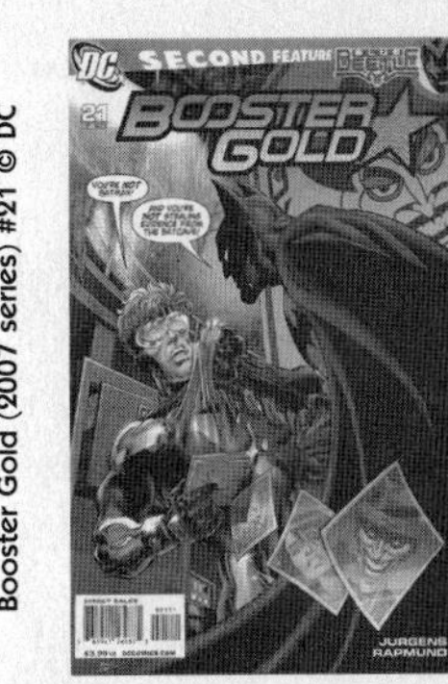

Booster Gold (2007 series) #21 © DC

GD VG FN VF VF/NM NM-
2.0 4.0 6.0 8.0 9.0 9.2

Marvel Comics: Dec, 1993 - No. 4, Mar, 1994 ($1.75, limited series, 52 pgs.)

1-4: 1-Ploog Frankenstein & Morrow Man-Thing-r begin; Wrightson-r/Chamber of Darkness #7. 2-Morrow new painted-c; Chaykin/Morrow Man-Thing; Krigstein-r/Uncanny Tales #54; r/Fear #10. 3-r/Astonishing Tales #10 & Starlin Man-Thing. 3,4-Painted-c 1 2 3 5 6 8

BOOKS OF DOOM (Dr. Doom from Fantastic Four)
Marvel Comics: Jan, 2006 - No. 6, June, 2006 ($2.99, limited series)

1-6-Life story/origin of Dr. Doom; Brubaker-s/Raimondi-a/Rivera-c 3.00
Fantastic Four: Books of Doom HC (2006, $19.99) r/#1-6 20.00
Fantastic Four: Books of Doom SC (2007, $14.99) r/#1-6 15.00

BOOKS OF FAERIE, THE
DC Comics (Vertigo): Mar, 1997 - No. 3, May, 1997 ($2.50, limited series)

1-3-Gross-a 3.00
TPB (1998, $14.95) r/#1-3 & Arcana Annual #1 15.00

BOOKS OF FAERIE, THE : AUBERON'S TALE
DC Comics (Vertigo): Aug, 1998 - No. 3, Oct, 1998 ($2.50, limited series)

1-3-Gross-a 3.00

BOOKS OF FAERIE, THE : MOLLY'S STORY
DC Comics (Vertigo): Sept, 1999 - No. 4, Dec, 1999 ($2.50, limited series)

1-4-Ney Rieber-s/Mejia-a 3.00

BOOKS OF MAGIC
DC Comics: 1990 - No. 4, 1991 ($3.95, 52 pgs., limited series, mature)

1-Bolton painted-c/a; Phantom Stranger app.; Gaiman scripts in all 1 3 4 6 8 10
2,3: 2-John Constantine, Dr. Fate, Spectre, Deadman app. 3-Dr. Occult app.; minor Sandman app. 1 2 3 4 5 7
4-Early Death-c/app. (early 1991) 1 2 3 5 6 8
Trade paperback-($19.95)-Reprints limited series 20.00

BOOKS OF MAGIC (Also see Hunter: The Age of Magic and Names of Magic)
DC Comics (Vertigo): May, 1994 - No. 75, Aug, 2000 ($1.95/$2.50, mature)

1-Charles Vess-c 2 4 6 8 10 12
1-Platinum 2 4 6 13 18 22
2-4: 4-Death app. 1 2 3 4 5 7
5-14; Charles Vess-c 4.00
15-75: 15-$2.50-c begins. 22-Kaluta-c. 25-Death-c/app; Bachalo-c. 51-Peter Gross-s/a begins. 55-Medley-a 3.00
Annual 1-3 (2/97, 2/98, '99, $3.95) 4.00
Bindings (1995, $12.95, TPB)-r/#1-4 13.00
Death After Death (2001, $19.95, TPB)-r/#42-50 20.00
Girl in the Box (1999, $14.95, TPB)-r/#26-32 15.00
Reckonings (1997, $12.95, TPB)-r/#14-20 13.00
Summonings (1996, $17.50, TPB)-r/#5-13, Vertigo Rave #1 17.50
The Burning Girl (2000, $17.95, TPB)-r/#33-41 18.00
Transformations (1998, $12.95, TPB)-r/#21-25 13.00

BOOKS OF MAGICK, THE : LIFE DURING WARTIME (See Books of Magic)
DC Comics (Vertigo): Sept, 2004 - No. 15, Dec, 2005 ($2.50/$2.75)

1-15: 1-Spencer-s/Ormston-a/Quitely-c; Constantine app. 2-Bagged with Sky Captain CD 6-Fegredo-a. 7-Constantine & Zatanna-c 3.00
... Book One TPB (2005, $9.95) r/#1-5 10.00

BOONDOCK SAINTS (Based on the movie)
12-Gauge Comics: May, 2010 - No. 2, Jun, 2010; Vol. 2, Oct, 2010 - No. 2, Nov, 2010 ($3.99)

...: In Nomine Patris 1,2-Troy Duffy-s/Guus Floor-a 4.00
...: In Nomine Patris Vol. 2: 1,2-Duffy-s/Floor-a 4.00

BOOSTER GOLD (See Justice League #4)
DC Comics: Feb, 1986 - No. 25, Feb, 1988 (75¢)

1-Dan Jurgens-s/a(p) 3.50
2-25: 4-Rose & Thorn app. 6-Origin. 6,7,23-Superman app. 8,9-LSH app. 22-JLI app. 24,25-Millennium tie-ins 3.00
NOTE: *Austin c-22i. Byrne c-23i.*

BOOSTER GOLD (See DC's weekly series 52)
DC Comics: Oct, 2007 - Present ($3.50/$2.99/$3.99)

1-Geoff Johns-s/Dan Jurgens-a(p); covers by Jurgens and Art Adams; Rip Hunter app. 5.00
2-20: 3-Jonah Hex app. 4-Barry Allen app. 5-Joker and Batgirl app. 8-Superman app. 3.00
21-29-($3.99) 21-Blue Beetle back-ups begin. 22-New Teen Titans app. 23-Photo-c. 26,27-Blackest Night; Ted Kord rises. 29-Cyborg Superman app. 4.00
30-42-($2.99): 32-34-Giffen & DeMatteis-s. 32-Emerald Empress app. 40-Origin retold 3.00
#0-(4/08) Blue Beetle (Ted Cord) returns; takes place between #6&7 3.00
#1,000,000-(9/08) Michelle Carter returns; takes place between #10&11 3.00
...: Blue and Gold (2008, $24.99, HC w/d.j.) r/#0,7-10,#1,000,000; cover sketches 25.00
...: Day of Death (2010, $14.99, SC) r/#20-25 and Brave and the Bold #23 15.00
...: 52 Pick-Up (2008, $24.99, HC w/d.j.) r/#1-6, original design sketches from Jurgens 25.00
...: Reality Lost (2009, $14.99, SC) r/#11,12,15-19 15.00
...: The Tomorrow Memory (2010, $17.99, SC) r/#26-31 18.00

BOOTS AND HER BUDDIES
Standard Comics/Visual Editions/Argo (NEA Service):
No. 5, 9/48 - No. 9, 9/49; 12/55 - No. 3, 1956

5-Strip-r 16 32 48 94 147 200
6,8 11 22 33 64 90 115
7-(Scarce) 14 28 42 80 115 150
9-(Scarce)-Frazetta-a (2 pgs.) 26 52 78 154 252 350
1-3(Argo-1955-56)-Reprints 6 12 18 31 38 45

BOOTS & SADDLES (TV)
Dell Publ. Co.: No. 919, July, 1958; No. 1029, Sept, 1959; No. 1116, Aug, 1960

Four Color 919 (#1)-Photo-c 7 14 21 50 83 115
Four Color 1029, 1116-Photo-c 5 10 15 34 55 75

BORDERLINE
Friction Press: June, 1992 ($2.25, B&W)

0-Ashcan edition; 1st app. of Cliff Broadway 3.00
1-Painted-c 3.00
1-Special Edition (bagged w/ photo, S&N) 4.00

BORDER PATROL
P. L. Publishing Co.: May-June, 1951 - No. 3, Sept-Oct, 1951

1 14 28 42 80 115 150
2,3 10 20 30 54 72 90

BORDER WORLDS (Also see Megaton Man)
Kitchen Sink Press: 7/86 - No. 7, 1987; V2#1, 1990 - No. 4, 1990 ($1.95-$2.00, B&W, mature)

1-7, V2#1-4: Donald Simpson-c/a/scripts 3.00

BORIS KARLOFF TALES OF MYSTERY (TV) (...Thriller No. 1,2)
Gold Key: No. 3, April, 1963 - No. 97, Feb, 1980

3-5-(Two #5's, 10/63,11/63): 5-(10/63)-11 pgs. Toth-a. 5 10 15 35 55 75
6-8,10: 10-Orlando-a 4 8 12 26 41 55
9-Wood-a 4 8 12 28 44 60
11-Williamson-a, 8 pgs.; Orlando-a, 5 pgs. 4 8 12 28 44 60
12-Torres, McWilliams-a; Orlando-a(2) 4 8 12 22 34 45
13,14,16-20 3 6 9 19 29 38
15-Crandall 3 6 9 20 30 40
21-Jeff Jones-a(3 pgs.) "The Screaming Skull" 3 6 9 20 30 40
22-Last 12¢ issue 3 6 9 16 23 30
23-30: 23-Reprint; photo-c 3 6 9 16 22 28
31-50: 36-Weiss-a 3 6 9 14 19 24
51-74: 74-Origin & 1st app. Taurus 2 4 6 10 14 18
75-79,87-97: 90-r/Torres, McWilliams-a/#12; Morrow-c 2 4 6 9 12 15
80-86-(52 pgs.) 2 4 6 10 14 18
Story Digest 1(7/70-Gold Key)-All text/illos.; 148 pp. 5 10 15 34 55 75
(See Mystery Comics Digest No. 2, 5, 8, 11, 14, 17, 20, 23, 26)
NOTE: ***Bolle** a-51-54, 56, 58, 59. **McWilliams** a-12, 14, 18, 19, 72, 80, 81, 93. **Orlando** a-11-15, 21. Reprints: 78, 81-86, 88, 90, 92, 95, 97.*

BORIS KARLOFF THRILLER (TV) (Becomes Boris Karloff Tales...)
Gold Key: Oct, 1962 - No. 2, Jan, 1963 (84 pgs.)

1-Photo-c 10 20 30 71 128 185
2 7 14 21 47 76 105

BORIS THE BEAR
Dark Horse Comics/Nicotat Comics #13 on: Aug, 1986 - No. 34, 1990 ($1.50/$1.75/$1.95, B&W)

1, 8, Annual 1 (1988, $2.50): 8-(44 pgs.) 4.00
1 (2nd printing),2,3,4A,4B,5-12, 14-34 3.00
13-1st Nicotat Comics issue 3.00

BORIS THE BEAR INSTANT COLOR CLASSICS
Dark Horse Comics: July, 1987 - No. 3, 1987 ($1.75/$1.95)

1-3 3.00

BORN
Marvel Comics: 2003 - No. 4, 2003 ($3.50, limited series)

1-4-Frank Castle (the Punisher) in 1971 Vietnam; Ennis-s/Robertson-a 3.50

The Bouncer #12 © FOX

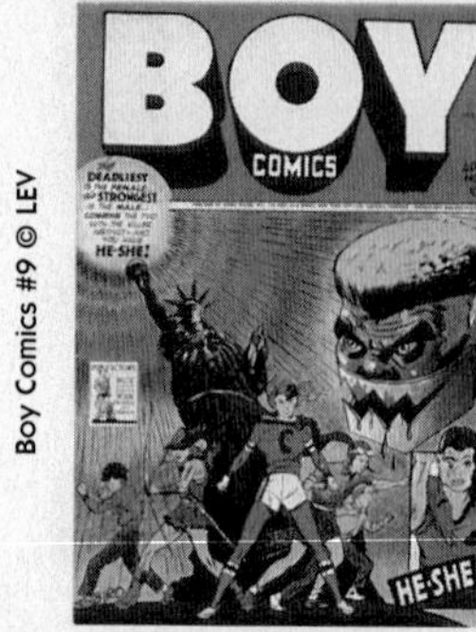

Boy Comics #9 © LEV

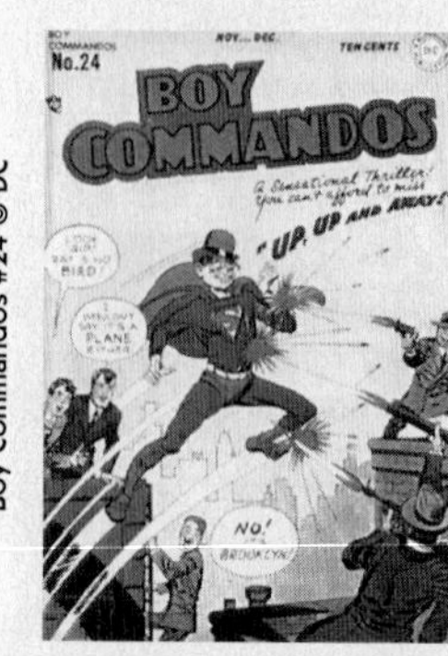

Boy Commandos #24 © DC

GD 2.0 VG 4.0 FN 6.0 VF 8.0 VF/NM 9.0 NM- 9.2

HC (2004, $17.99) oversized reprint of series; proposal, layout pages 18.00
Punisher: Born SC (2004, $13.99) r/series; proposal, layout pages 14.00

BORN AGAIN
Spire Christian Comics (Fleming H. Revell Co.): 1978 (39¢)
nn-Watergate, Nixon, etc. 2 4 6 11 16 20

BOUNCER, THE (Formerly Green Mask #9)
Fox Features Syndicate: 1944 - No. 14, Jan, 1945
nn(1944, #10?) 31 62 93 182 296 410
11 (9/44)-Origin; Rocket Kelly, One Round Hogan app.
23 46 69 136 223 310
12-14: 14-Reprints no # issue 19 38 57 111 176 240

BOUNTY GUNS (See Luke Short's..., Four Color 739)

BOX OFFICE POISON
Antarctic Press: 1996 - No. 21, Sept, 2000 ($2.95, B&W)
1-Alex Robinson-s/a in all 1 2 3 4 5 7
2-5 4.00
6-21, ...Kolor Karnival 1 (5/99, $2.99) 3.00
...Super Special 0 (5/97, $4.95) 5.00
Sherman's March: Collected BOP Vol. 1 (9/98, $14.95) r/#0-4 15.00
TPB (2002, $29.95, 608 pgs.) r/entire series 30.00

BOY AND HIS 'BOT, A
Now Comics: Jan, 1987 ($1.95)
1-A Holiday Special 3.00

BOY AND THE PIRATES, THE (Movie)
Dell Publishing Co.: No. 1117, Aug, 1960
Four Color 1117-Photo-c 6 12 18 43 69 95

BOY COMICS (Captain Battle No. 1 & 2; Boy Illustories No. 43-108) (Stories by Charles Biro) (Also see Squeeks)
Lev Gleason Publ. (Comic House): No. 3, Apr, 1942 - No. 119, Mar, 1956
3 (No.1)-1st app. & origin Crimebuster (ends #110), Bombshell (ends #8) Young Robin Hood (ends # 32), Yankee Longago (ends #28), Hero of the Month (ends #31), Case 1001-1005, 1006-1009 (ends #10); Swoop Storm begins (ends #32); Pepper Casey only app.; 1st app. Iron Jaw; Crimebuster's pet monkey Squeeks begins
320 640 960 2240 3920 5600
4-Hitler, Tojo Mussolini-c; Iron Jaw app. Little Wise Guys (prototype of later version) begins, ends #5 145 290 435 921 1586 2250
5-Japanese war-c 97 194 291 621 1061 1500
6-Origin Iron Jaw; origin & death of Iron Jaw's son killed by his father; Hitler app.; Little Dynamite begins, ends #39; 1st Iron Jaw-c 314 628 942 2198 3849 5500
7-Flag & Hitler, Tojo, Mussolini-c; Dickey Dean app. 110 220 330 704 1202 1700
8-Death of Iron Jaw; Iron Jaw-c & spash pg. 103 206 309 659 1130 1600
9,11-Iron Jaw sty/classic-c on ea. 97 194 291 621 1061 1500
10-Return of Iron Jaw; classic Biro Iron Jaw/Nazi-c 145 290 435 921 1586 2250
12,13: 12-Japanese torture-c. 13-Nazi firing squad-c 65 130 195 416 708 1000
14-Iron Jaw-c 74 148 222 470 810 1150
15-Death of Iron Jaw, killed by The Rodent 82 164 246 528 902 1275
16,18,20 (2/45) 43 86 129 271 461 650
17-(8/44)-Flag-c; The Moth app. 45 90 135 284 480 675
19-One of the greatest all-time stories 53 106 159 334 567 800
21-24: 24-Concentration camp story 32 64 96 188 307 425
25-Devil-c; hanging story (52 pgs.) 37 74 111 222 361 500
26-Bondage, torture-c/story (68 pgs.) 39 78 117 231 378 525
27-29,31,32-(All 68 pgs.). 28-Yankee Longago ends. 32-Swoop Storm & Young Robin Hood end 34 68 102 199 325 450
30-(10/46, 68 pgs.)-Origin Crimebuster retold from #3 w/Iron Jaw; Nazi work camp story
39 78 117 231 378 525
33-40: 34-Crimebuster story (2); suicide-c/story 22 44 66 132 216 300
41-50-41-Daredevil illus. text story 19 38 57 111 176 240
51-59: 57(9/50)-Dilly Duncan begins, ends #71 16 32 48 94 147 200
60-(12/50)-Iron Jaw returns c/sty 18 36 54 103 162 220
61-Origin Crimebuster & Iron Jaw retold c/sty 19 38 57 112 179 245
62-(2/51)-Death of Iron Jaw explained w/Iron Jaw-c 19 38 57 109 172 235
63-67,69-72: 63-McWilliams-a 14 28 42 76 108 140
68,73-Iron Jaw c/sty; 73-Frazetta 1 pg. ad 14 28 42 80 115 150
74,78,81-Iron Jaw c/sty (2-3) 12 24 36 67 94 120
75-77,84 11 22 33 62 86 110
79,80-Iron Jaw sty: 80(8/52)-1st app. Rocky X of the Rocketeers; becomes "Rocky X" #101; Iron Jaw, Sniffer & the Deadly Dozen in #80-118 11 22 33 64 90 115
82-Iron Jaw-c only 11 22 33 62 86 110
83,85-88-Iron Jaw c/sty. 87-The Deadly Dozen begins; becomes Iron Jaw #88 (4/53)
11 22 33 64 90 115
89(5/53)-92-The Claw serial app. in Rocky X (also see Silver Streak & Daredevil); on-c. 89-"Iron Jaw" becomes "Sniffrer & Iron Jaw" (ends #118); Iron Jaw c/story in all
12 24 36 67 94 120
93-Claw cameo & last app.; Woodesque-a on Rocky X by Sid Check; Iron Jaw-c/sty
11 22 33 64 90 115
94-97-Iron Jaw-c/sty in all 11 22 33 60 83 105
98,100:(4/54): 98-Rocky X by Sid Check 11 22 33 62 86 110
99,101-107,109,111,119: 101-Rocky X becomes spy strip. 106-Robin Hood app. 111-Crimebuster becomes Chuck Chandler, ends #119
10 20 30 54 72 90
108-(2/55)-Kubert & Ditko-a (Crimebuster, 8 pgs.) 11 22 33 62 86 110
110,112-118-Kubert-a 10 20 30 58 79 100
(See Giant Boy Book of Comics)
NOTE: *Boy Movies in 3-5,40,41. Iron Jaw app. 3,4,6,8,10,11,13-15; returns-60,62, 68, 69, 72-79, 81-118; c-60-62, 73, 74, 78, 81-83, 85-97.* ***Biro*** *c-all.* ***Jack Alderman*** *a-26.* ***Dan Barry*** *a-31,32, 35-38.* ***Al Borth*** *a- 51.* ***Dick Briefer*** *a-3-28, 124.* ***Sid Check*** a-93, 98. ***Ditko*** a-108. ***Bob Fujitani (Fuje)*** *a-55, 18pgs.* ***Jerry Gandenetti*** *a-52.* ***R. W. Hall*** *a-19-22.* ***Hubbell*** *a-30, 106, 108, 110, 111.* ***Joe Kubert*** *a-108, 110, 112-118.* ***Kenneth Landau*** *a-92.* ***George Mandel*** *a-3-30.* ***Norman Maurer*** *a-4-9, 12, 13, 31, 32, 35, 41, 43, 46, 51, 57, 61, 73, 74, 78-83.* ***Bob Montana*** *a-4, 16, 19.* ***Pete Morisi*** *a-111.* ***William Overgard*** *a-68, 71, 74, 86, 88.* ***Palais*** *a-14, 16, 17, 19, 20, 25, 26. among others.* ***Tuska*** *a-30.* ***Bob Wood*** *a-8-13.*

BOY COMMANDOS (See Detective #64 & World's Finest Comics #8)
National Periodical Publications: Winter, 1942-43 - No. 36, Nov-Dec, 1949
1-Origin Liberty Belle; The Sandman & The Newsboy Legion x-over in Boy Commandos; S&K-a, 48 pgs.; S&K cameo? (classic WWII-c) 400 800 1200 2800 4900 7000
2-Last Liberty Belle; Hitler-c; S&K-a, 46 pgs.; WWII-c
239 478 717 1530 2615 3700
3-S&K-a, 45 pgs.; WWII-c 135 270 405 864 1482 2100
4-6: All WWII-c. 6-S&K-a 84 168 252 538 919 1300
7-10: All WWII-c 53 106 159 334 567 800
11-13: All WWII-c. 11-Infinity-c 39 78 117 240 395 550
14,16,18-19-All have S&K-a. 18-2nd Crazy Quilt-c 32 64 96 188 307 425
15-1st app. Crazy Quilt, their arch nemesis 40 80 120 246 411 575
17,20-Sci/fi-c/stories 39 78 117 231 378 525
21,22,25: 22-3rd Crazy Quilt-c; Judy Canova x-over 25 50 75 150 245 340
23-S&K-c/a(all) 34 68 102 204 332 460
24-1st costumed superhero satire-c (11-12/47). 30 60 90 177 289 400
26-Flying Saucer story (3-4/48)-4th of this theme; see The Spirit 9/28/47(1st), Shadow Comics V7#10 (2nd, 1/48) & Captain Midnight #60 (3rd, 2/48)
31 62 93 182 296 410
27,28,30: 30-Cleveland Indians story 24 48 72 144 237 330
29-S&K story (1) 26 52 78 154 252 350
31-35: 32-Dale Evans app. on-c & in story. 33-Last Crazy Quilt-c. 34-Intro. Wolf, their mascot 22 44 66 128 209 290
36-Intro The Atomobile c/sci-fi story (Scarce) 40 80 120 246 411 575
The Boy Commandos by Joe Simon & Jack Kirby Volume One HC (2010, $49.99) reprints apps. in Detective #64-72, World's Finest #8,9 & Boy Commandos #1,2; Buhle intro. 50.00
NOTE: *Most issues signed by* ***Simon & Kirby*** *are not by them.* ***S&K*** *c-1-9, 13, 14, 17, 21, 23, 24, 30-32.* ***Feller*** *c-30.*

BOY COMMANDOS
National Per. Publ.: Sept-Oct, 1973 - No. 2, Nov-Dec, 1973 (G.A. S&K reprints)
1,2: 1-Reprints story from Boy Commandos #1 plus-c & Detective #66 by S&K. 2-Infantino/Orlando-c 2 4 6 10 14 18

BOY COMMANDOS COMICS
DC Comics: Sept/Oct. 1942
1-Ashcan comic, not distributed to newsstands, only for in-house use. Cover art is the splash page from the Boy Commandos story in Detective Comics #68 interior is from an unidentified issue of Detective Comics (no known sales)
nn - (9-10/42) Ashcan comic, not distributed to newsstands, only for in-house use. Cover art is the splash page from the Boy Commandos story in Detective Comics #68 interior is from Detective Comics #68 (no known sales)

BOY COWBOY (Also see Amazing Adventures & Science Comics)
Ziff-Davis Publ. Co.: 1950 (8 pgs. in color)
nn-Sent to subscribers of Ziff-Davis mags. & ordered through mail for 10¢; used to test market for Kid Cowboy 30 60 90 177 289 400

BOY DETECTIVE
Avon Periodicals: May-June, 1951 - No. 4, May, 1952
1 20 40 60 114 182 250
2-4: 3,4-Kinstler-c 14 28 42 80 115 150

BOY EXPLORERS COMICS (Terry and The Pirates No. 3 on)
Family Comics (Harvey Publ.): May-June, 1946 - No. 2, Sept-Oct, 1946
1-Intro The Explorers, Duke of Broadway, Calamity Jane & Danny Dixon...Cadet; S&K-c/a, 24 pgs. 71 142 213 454 777 1100

Boy Explorers Comics #1 © HARV

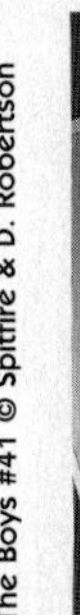

The Boys #41 © Spitfire & D. Robertson

B.P.R.D.: King of Fear #4 © Mike Mignola

	GD 2.0	VG 4.0	FN 6.0	VF 8.0	VF/NM 9.0	NM- 9.2
2-(Rare)-Small size (5-1/2x8-1/2"; B&W; 32 pgs.) Distributed to mail subscribers only; S&K-a	181	362	543	1158	1979	2800

(Also see All New No. 15, Flash Gordon No. 5, and Stuntman No. 3)

BOY ILLUSTORIES (See Boy Comics)

BOY LOVES GIRL (Boy Meets Girl No. 1-24)
Lev Gleason Publications: No. 25, July, 1952 - No. 57, June, 1956

	GD	VG	FN	VF	VF/NM	NM-
25(#1)	11	22	33	62	86	110
26,27,29-33: 30-33-Serial, 'Loves of My Life	8	16	24	44	57	70
34-42: 39-Lingerie panels	8	16	24	42	54	65
28-Drug propaganda story	8	16	24	44	57	70
43-Toth-a	9	18	27	47	61	75
44-50: 47-Toth-a? 50-Last pre-code (2/55)	8	16	24	40	50	60
51-57: 57-Ann Brewster-a	7	14	21	35	43	50

BOY MEETS GIRL (Boy Loves Girl No. 25 on)
Lev Gleason Publications: Feb, 1950 - No. 24, June, 1952 (No. 1-17: 52 pgs.)

	GD	VG	FN	VF	VF/NM	NM-
1-Guardineer-a	16	32	48	94	147	200
2	10	20	30	58	79	100
3-10	10	20	30	54	72	90
11-24	9	18	27	50	65	80

NOTE: *Briefer a-24. Fuje c-3,7. Painted-c 1-17. Photo-c 19-21, 23.*

BOYS, THE
DC Comics (WildStorm)/Dynamite Ent. #7 on: Oct, 2006 - Present ($2.99/$3.99, mature)

1-Garth Ennis-s/Darick Robertson-a 6.00
2-6 4.00
7-42-(Dynamite Ent.,). 19-Origin of the Homelander. 23-Variant-c by Cassaday 3.00
43-53-($3.99) Russ Braun-a 4.00
#1: Dynamite Edition (2009, $1.00) r/#1; flip book with Battlefields Night Witches 3.00
...: Herogasm 1-6 (2009 - No. 6, 2009, $2.99) Ennis-s/McCrea-a 3.00
... Volume 1: The Name of the Game TPB (2007, $14.99) r/#1-6; intro. by Simon Pegg 15.00
... Volume 2: Get Some TPB (2008, $19.99) r/#7-14 20.00
... Volume 3: Good For The Soul TPB (2008, $19.99) r/#15-22 20.00
... Volume 4: We Gotta Go Now TPB (2009, $19.99) r/#23-30; cover gallery 20.00

BOYS, THE: HIGHLAND LADDIE
Dynamite Entertainment: 2010 - No. 6, 2011 ($3.99, mature)

1-6-Garth Ennis-s/John McCrea-a 4.00

BOYS' AND GIRLS' MARCH OF COMICS (See March of Comics)

BOYS' RANCH (Also see Western Tales & Witches' Western Tales)
Harvey Publ.: Oct, 1950 - No. 6, Aug, 1951 (No.1-3, 52 pgs.; No. 4-6, 36 pgs.)

	GD	VG	FN	VF	VF/NM	NM-
1-S&K-c/a(3)	58	116	174	371	636	900
2-S&K-c/a(3)	40	80	120	246	411	575
3-S&K-c/a(2); Meskin-a	39	78	117	231	378	525
4-S&K-c/a, 5 pgs.	34	68	102	199	325	450
5,6-S&K-c, splashes & centerspread only; Meskin-a	20	40	60	114	182	250

BOZO (Larry Harmon's Bozo, the World's Most Famous Clown)
Innovation Publishing: 1992 ($6.95, 68 pgs.)

	GD	VG	FN	VF	VF/NM	NM-
1-Reprints Four Color #285(#1)	1	2	3	4	5	7

BOZO THE CLOWN (TV) (Bozo No. 7 on)
Dell Publishing Co.: July, 1950 - No. 4, Oct-Dec, 1963

	GD	VG	FN	VF	VF/NM	NM-
Four Color 285(#1)	17	34	51	122	249	375
2(7-9/51)-7(10-12/52)	10	20	30	73	134	195
Four Color 464,508,551,594(10/54)	10	20	30	67	116	165
1(nn, 5-7/62)	8	16	24	52	86	120
2 - 4(1963)	6	12	18	41	66	90

BOZZ CHRONICLES, THE
Marvel Comics (Epic Comics): Dec, 1985 - No. 6, 1986 (Lim. series, mature)

1-6-Logan/Wolverine look alike in 19th century. 1,3,5-Blevins-a 3.00

B.P.R.D. (Bureau of Paranormal Research and Defense) (Also see Hellboy titles)
Dark Horse Comics: (one-shots)

... Dark Waters (7/03, $2.99) Guy Davis-c/a; Augustyn-s 3.00
... Night Train (9/03, $2.99) Johns & Kolins-s; Kolins & Stewart-a 3.00
... The Ectoplasmic Man (6/08, $2.99) Stenbeck-a/Mignola-c; origin of Johann Kraus 3.00
... There's Something Under My Bed (11/03, $2.99) Pollina-a/c 3.00
... The Soul of Venice (5/03, $2.99) Oeming-a/c; Gunter & Oeming-s 3.00
... The Soul of Venice and Other Stories TPB (8/04, $17.95) r/one-shots & new story by Mignola and Cam Stewart; sketch pages by various 18.00
... War on Frogs (6/08,12/08, 6/09, 12/09, $2.99) 1-Trimpe-a/Mignola-c; Abe Sapien app. 2-Severin-a. 3-Moline-a. 4-Snejbjerg 3.00

B.P.R.D.: GARDEN OF SOULS
Dark Horse Comics: Mar, 2007 - No. 5, July, 2007 ($2.99, limited series)

1-5-Mignola & Arcudi-s/Guy Davis-a/Mignola-c 3.00

B.P.R.D.: HELL ON EARTH
Dark Horse Comics: ($3.50, limited series)

... Gods (1/11 - No. 3) 1-Mignola & Arcudi-s/Guy Davis-a; Ryan Sook-c 3.50
... New World (8/10 - No. 5, 12/10) 1-5-Mignola & Arcudi-s/Guy Davis-a/c 3.50

B.P.R.D.: HOLLOW EARTH (Mike Mignola's...)
Dark Horse Comics: Jan, 2002 - No. 3, June, 2002 ($2.99, limited series)

1-3-Mignola, Golden & Sniegoski-s/Sook-a/Mignola-c; Hellboy and Abe Sapien app. 3.00
... and Other Stories TPB (1/03; 7/04, $17.95) r/#1-3, Hellboy: Box Full of Evil, Abe Sapien: Drums of the Dead, and Dark Horse Extra; plus sketch pages 18.00

B.P.R.D.: KILLING GROUND
Dark Horse Comics: Aug, 2007 - No. 5, Dec, 2007 ($2.99, limited series)

1-5-Mignola & Arcudi-s/Guy Davis-a/c 3.00

B.P.R.D.: KING OF FEAR
Dark Horse Comics: Jan, 2010 - No. 5, May, 2010 ($2.99, limited series)

1,2-Mignola & Arcudi-s/Guy Davis-a; Mignola-c 3.00

B.P.R.D.: 1946
Dark Horse Comics: Jan, 2008 - No. 5, May, 2008 ($2.99, limited series)

1-5-Mignola & Dysart-s/Azaceta-a; Mignola/c 3.00

B.P.R.D.: 1947
Dark Horse Comics: Jul, 2009 - No. 5, Nov, 2009 ($2.99, limited series)

1-5-Mignola & Dysart-s/Bá & Moon-a; Mignola/c 3.00

B.P.R.D.: PLAGUE OF FROGS
Dark Horse Comics: Mar, 2004 - No. 5, July, 2004 ($2.99, limited series)

1-5-Mignola-s/Guy Davis-c/a 3.00
TPB (1/05, $17.95) r/series; sketchbook pages & afterword by Davis & Mignola 18.00

B.P.R.D.: THE BLACK FLAME
Dark Horse Comics: Sept, 2005 - No. 6, Jan, 2006 ($2.99, limited series)

1-6-Mignola & Arcudi-s/Guy Davis-a/ Mignola-c 3.00
TPB (7/06, $17.95) r/series; sketchbook pages & afterword by Davis & Mignola 18.00

B.P.R.D.: THE BLACK GODDESS
Dark Horse Comics: Jan, 2009 - No. 5, May, 2009 ($2.99, limited series)

1-5-Mignola & Arcudi-s/Guy Davis-a/Nowlan-c 3.00

B.P.R.D.: THE DEAD
Dark Horse Comics: Nov, 2004 - No. 5, Mar, 2005 ($2.99, limited series)

1-5-Mignola-s/Guy Davis-c/a 3.00

B.P.R.D.: THE UNIVERSAL MACHINE
Dark Horse Comics: Apr, 2006 - No. 5, Aug, 2006 ($2.99, limited series)

1-5-Mignola & Arcudi-s/Guy Davis-a/Mignola-c. 5-Mignola-a (5 pgs.) 3.00
TPB (1/07, $17.95) r/series; sketchbook pages by Davis; Mignola afterword 18.00

B.P.R.D.: THE WARNING
Dark Horse Comics: July, 2008 - No. 5, Nov, 2008 ($2.99, limited series)

1-5-Mignola & Arcudi-s/Guy Davis-c/a 3.00

BRADLEYS, THE (Also see Hate)
Fantagraphics Books: Apr, 1999 - No. 6, Jan, 2000 ($2.95, B&W, limited series)

1-6-Reprints Peter Bagge's-s/a 3.00

BRADY BUNCH, THE (TV)(See Kite Fun Book and Binky #78)
Dell Publishing Co.: Feb, 1970 - No. 2, May, 1970

	GD	VG	FN	VF	VF/NM	NM-
1	11	22	33	75	138	200
2	8	16	24	58	97	135

BRAIN, THE
Sussex Publ. Co./Magazine Enterprises: Sept, 1956 - No. 7, 1958

	GD	VG	FN	VF	VF/NM	NM-
1-Dan DeCarlo-a in all including reprints	12	24	36	69	97	125
2,3	8	16	24	42	54	65
4-7	4	8	12	24	37	50
I.W. Reprints #1-4,8-10('63),14: 2-Reprints Sussex #2 with new cover added	2	4	6	9	13	16
Super Reprint #17,18(nd)	2	4	6	9	13	16

BRAINBANX
DC Comics (Helix): Mar, 1997 - No. 6, Aug, 1997 ($2.50, limited series)

1-6: Elaine Lee-s/Temujin-a 3.00

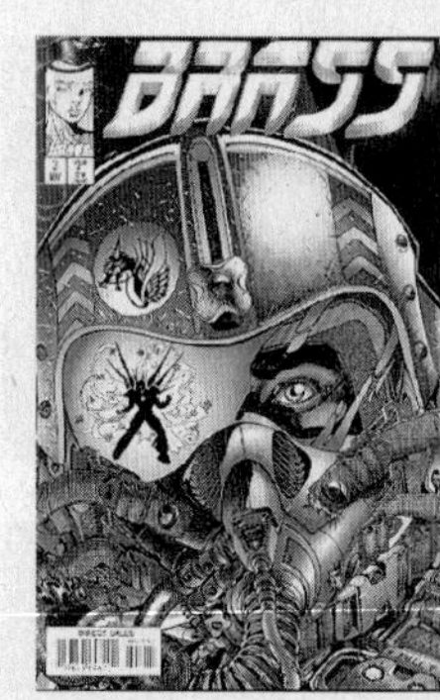

Brass #3 © WSP

Brave and the Bold #30 © DC

Brave and the Bold #72 © DC

	GD	VG	FN	VF	VF/NM	NM-
	2.0	4.0	6.0	8.0	9.0	9.2

BRAIN BOY
Dell Publishing Co.: Apr-June, 1962 - No. 6, Sept-Nov, 1963 (Painted c-#1-6)
Four Color 1330(#1)-Gil Kane-a; origin 11 22 33 75 138 200
2(7-9/62),3-6: 4-Origin retold 7 14 21 49 80 110

BRAM STOKER'S BURIAL OF THE RATS (Movie)
Roger Corman's Cosmic Comics: Apr, 1995 - No.3, June, 1995 ($2.50)
1-3: Adaptation of film; Jerry Prosser scripts 3.00

BRAM STOKER'S DRACULA (Movie)(Also see Dracula: Vlad the Impaler)
Topps Comics: Oct, 1992 - No. 4, Jan, 1993 ($2.95, limited series, polybagged)
1-(1st & 2nd printing)-Adaptation of film begins; Mignola-c/a in all; 4 trading cards & poster; photo scenes of movie 3.00
1-Crimson foil edition (limited to 500) 8.00
2-4: 2-Bound-in poster & cards. 4 trading cards in both. 3-Contains coupon to win 1 of 500 crimson foil-c edition of #1. 4-Contains coupon to win 1 of 500 uncut sheets of all 16 trading cards 3.00

BRAND ECHH (See Not Brand Echh)

BRAND OF EMPIRE (See Luke Short's...Four Color 771)

BRASS
Image Comics (WildStorm Productions): Aug, 1996 - No. 3, May, 1997 ($2.50, lim. series)
1-($4.50) Folio Ed.; oversized 4.50
1-3: Wiesenfeld-s/Bennett-a. 3-Grunge & Roxy(Gen 13) cameo 3.00

BRASS
DC Comics (WildStorm): Aug, 2000 - No. 6, Jan, 2001 ($2.50, limited series)
1-6-Arcudi-s 3.00

BRATH
CrossGeneration Comics: Feb, 2003 - No. 14, June, 2004 ($2.95)
Prequel-Dixon-s/Di Vito-a 3.00
1-14: 1-(3/03)-Dixon-s/Di Vito-a 3.00
Vol. 1: Hammer of Vengeance (2003, $9.95) Digest-sized reprint of Prequel & #1-6 10.00

BRATPACK/MAXIMORTAL SUPER SPECIAL
King Hell Press: 1996 ($2.95, B&W, limited series)
1,2: Veitch-s/a 3.00

BRATS BIZARRE
Marvel Comics (Epic/Heavy Hitters): 1994 - No. 4, 1994 ($2.50, limited series)
1-4: All w/bound-in trading cards 3.00

BRAVADOS, THE (See Wild Western Action)
Skywald Publ. Corp.: Aug, 1971 (52 pgs., one-shot)
1-Red Mask, The Durango Kid, Billy Nevada-r; Bolle-a; 3-D effect story 3 6 9 14 19 24

BRAVE AND THE BOLD, THE (See Best Of... & Super DC Giant) (Replaced by Batman & The Outsiders)
National Periodical Publ./DC Comics: Aug-Sept, 1955 - No. 200, July, 1983
1-Viking Prince by Kubert, Silent Knight, Golden Gladiator begin; part Kubert-c 296 592 888 2590 5295 8000
2 119 238 357 1012 2056 3100
3,4 64 128 192 544 1097 1650
5-Robin Hood begins (4-5/56, 1st DC app.), ends #15; see Robin Hood Tales #7 65 130 195 553 1127 1700
6-10: 6-Robin Hood by Kubert; last Golden Gladiator app.; Silent Knight; no Viking Prince. 8-1st S.A. issue 45 90 135 360 730 1100
11-22,24: 12,14-Robin Hood-c. 18,21-23-Grey tone-c. 22-Last Silent Knight. 24-Last Viking Prince by Kubert (2nd solo book) 37 74 111 286 568 850
23-Viking Prince origin by Kubert; 1st B&B single theme issue & 1st Viking Prince solo book 45 90 135 360 730 1100
25-1st app. Suicide Squad (8-9/59) 48 96 144 408 829 1250
26,27-Suicide Squad 28 56 84 215 433 650
28-(2-3/60)-Justice League intro./1st app.; origin/1st app. Snapper Carr 625 1250 1875 6200 13,100 20,000
29-Justice League (4-5/60)-2nd app. battle the Weapons Master; robot-c 207 414 621 1811 3706 5600
30-Justice League (6-7/60)-3rd app.; vs. Amazo 170 340 510 1488 3044 4600
31-1st app. Cave Carson (8-9/60); scarce in high grade; 1st try-out series 37 74 111 297 591 885
32,33-Cave Carson 22 44 66 162 324 485
34-Origin/1st app. Silver-Age Hawkman, Hawkgirl & Byth (2-3/61); Gardner Fox story, Kubert-c/a ; 1st S.A. Hawkman tryout series; 2nd in #42-44; both series predate Hawkman #1 (4-5/64) 178 356 534 1558 3179 4800

	GD	VG	FN	VF	VF/NM	NM-
	2.0	4.0	6.0	8.0	9.0	9.2

35-Hawkman by Kubert (4-5/61)-2nd app. 42 84 126 336 681 1025
36-Hawkman by Kubert; origin & 1st app. Shadow Thief (6-7/61)-3rd app. 37 74 111 295 585 875
37-Suicide Squad (2nd tryout series) 20 40 60 144 290 435
38,39-Suicide Squad. 38-Last 10¢ issue 17 34 51 122 249 375
40,41-Cave Carson Inside Earth (2nd try-out series). 40-Kubert-a. 41-Meskin-a 14 28 42 96 191 285
42-Hawkman by Kubert (2nd tryout series); Hawkman earns helmet wings; Byth app. 25 50 75 183 367 550
43-Hawkman by Kubert; more detailed origin 29 58 87 223 449 675
44-Hawkman by Kubert; grey-tone-c 24 48 72 175 350 525
45-49-Strange Sports Stories by Infantino 9 18 27 65 113 160
50-The Green Arrow & Manhunter From Mars (10-11/63); 1st Manhunter x-over outside of Detective Comics (pre-dates House of Mystery #143); team-ups begin 18 36 54 125 255 385
51-Aquaman & Hawkman (12-1/63-64); pre-dates Hawkman #1 20 40 60 140 283 425
52-(2-3/64)-3 Battle Stars; Sgt. Rock, Haunted Tank, Johnny Cloud, & Mlle. Marie team-up for 1st time by Kubert (c/a) 22 44 66 159 317 475
53-Atom & The Flash by Toth 10 20 30 69 122 175
54-Kid Flash, Robin & Aqualad; 1st app./origin Teen Titans (6-7/64) 33 66 99 254 502 750
55-Metal Men & The Atom 9 18 27 63 107 150
56-The Flash & Manhunter From Mars 9 18 27 63 107 150
57-Origin & 1st app. Metamorpho (12-1/64-65) 16 32 48 117 239 360
58-2nd app. Metamorpho by Fradon 10 20 30 70 125 180
59-Batman & Green Lantern; 1st Batman team-up in Brave and the Bold 12 24 36 87 164 240
60-Teen Titans (2nd app.)-1st app. new Wonder Girl (Donna Troy), who joins Titans (6-7/65) 16 32 48 114 232 350
61-Origin Starman & Black Canary by Anderson 12 24 36 87 164 240
62-Origin Starman & Black Canary cont'd. 62-1st S.A. app. Wildcat (10-11/65); 1st S.A. app. of G.A. Huntress (W.W. villain) 11 22 33 77 144 210
63-Supergirl & Wonder Woman 9 18 27 60 100 140
64-Batman Versus Eclipso (see H.O.S. #61) 8 16 24 58 97 135
65-Flash & Doom Patrol (4-5/66) 6 12 18 43 69 95
66-Metamorpho & Metal Men (6-7/66) 6 12 18 43 69 95
67-Batman & The Flash by Infantino; Batman team-ups begin, end #200 (8-9/66) 7 14 21 50 83 115
68-Batman/Metamorpho/Joker/Riddler/Penguin-c/story; Batman as Bat-Hulk (Hulk parody) 9 18 27 60 100 140
69-Batman & Green Lantern 7 14 21 45 73 100
70-Batman & Hawkman; Craig-a(p) 7 14 21 45 73 100
71-Batman & Green Arrow 7 14 21 45 73 100
72-Spectre & Flash (6-7/67); 4th app. The Spectre; predates Spectre #1 7 14 21 47 76 105
73-Aquaman & The Atom 6 12 18 43 69 95
74-Batman & Metal Men 6 12 18 43 69 95
75-Batman & The Spectre (12-1/67-68); 6th app. Spectre; came out between Spectre #1 & #2 7 14 21 45 73 100
76-Batman & Plastic Man (2-3/68); came out between Plastic Man #8 & #9 6 12 18 43 69 95
77-Batman & The Atom 6 12 18 43 69 95
78-Batman, Wonder Woman & Batgirl 6 12 18 43 69 95
79-Batman & Deadman by Neal Adams (8-9/68); early Deadman app. 9 18 27 65 113 160
80-Batman & Creeper (10-11/68); N. Adams-a; early app. The Creeper; came out between Creeper #3 & #4 8 16 24 58 97 135
81-Batman & Flash; N. Adams-a 8 16 24 58 97 135
82-Batman & Aquaman; N. Adams-a; origin Ocean Master retold (2-3/69) 8 16 24 58 97 135
83-Batman & Teen Titans; N. Adams-a (4-5/69) 8 16 24 58 97 135
84-Batman (G.A., 1st S.A. app.) & Sgt. Rock; N. Adams-a; last 12¢ issue (6-7/69) 8 16 24 58 97 135
85-Batman & Green Arrow; 1st new costume for Green Arrow by Neal Adams (8-9/69) 9 18 27 65 113 160
86-Batman & Deadman (10-11/69); N. Adams-a; story concludes from Strange Adventures #216 (1-2/69) 8 16 24 58 97 135
87-Batman & Wonder Woman 4 8 12 28 44 60
88-Batman & Wildcat 4 8 12 28 44 60
89-Batman & Phantom Stranger (4-5/70); early Phantom Stranger app. (came out between Phantom Stranger #6 & 7 4 8 12 26 41 55
90-Batman & Adam Strange 4 8 12 26 41 55
91-Batman & Black Canary (8-9/70) 4 8 12 26 41 55

Brave and the Bold #167 © DC

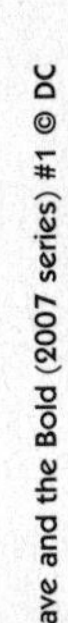
Brave and the Bold (2007 series) #1 © DC

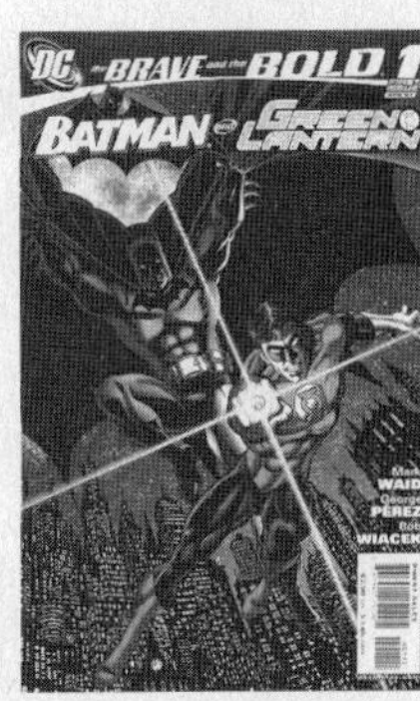

Breaking Into Comics The Marvel Way #1 © MAR

	GD 2.0	VG 4.0	FN 6.0	VF 8.0	VF/NM 9.0	NM- 9.2
92-Batman; intro the Bat Squad	4	8	12	26	41	55
93-Batman-House of Mystery; N. Adams-a	7	14	21	47	76	105
94-Batman-Teen Titans	4	8	12	23	36	48
95-Batman & Plastic Man	3	6	9	21	32	42
96-Batman & Sgt. Rock; last 15¢ issue	4	8	12	22	34	45
97-Batman & Wildcat; 52 pg. issues begin, end #102; reprints origin & 1st app. Deadman from Strange Advs. #205	4	8	12	22	34	45
98-Batman & Phantom Stranger; 1st Jim Aparo Batman-a?	4	8	12	22	34	45
99-Batman & Flash	4	8	12	22	34	45
100-(2-3/72, 25¢, 52 pgs.)-Batman-Green Lantern-Green Arrow-Black Canary-Robin; Deadman-r by Adams/Str. Advs. #210	6	12	18	41	66	90
101-Batman & Metamorpho; Kubert Viking Prince	3	6	9	21	32	42
102-Batman-Teen Titans; N. Adams-a(p)	5	10	15	32	51	70
103-107,109,110: Batman team-ups: 103-Metal Men. 104-Deadman. 105-Wonder Woman. 106-Green Arrow. 107-Black Canary. 109-Demon. 110-Wildcat	3	6	9	14	20	26
108-Sgt. Rock	3	6	9	16	22	28
111-Batman/Joker-c/story	3	6	9	19	29	38
112-117: All 100 pgs.; Batman team-ups: 112-Mr. Miracle. 113-Metal Men; reprints origin/1st Hawkman from Brave and the Bold #34; r/origin Multi-Man/Challengers #14. 114-Aquaman. 115-Atom; r/origin Viking Prince from #23; r/Dr. Fate/Hourman/Solomon Grundy/Green Lantern from Showcase #55. 116-Spectre. 117-Sgt. Rock; last 100 pg. issue	5	10	15	32	51	70
118-Batman/Wildcat/Joker-c/story	3	6	9	17	25	32
119,121-123,125-128,132-140: Batman team-ups: 119-Man-Bat. 121-Metal Men. 122-Swamp Thing. 123-Plastic Man/Metamorpho. 125-Flash. 126-Aquaman. 127-Wildcat. 128-Mr. Miracle. 132-Kung-Fu Fighter. 133-Deadman. 134-Green Lantern. 135-Metal Men. 136-Metal Men/Green Arrow. 137-Demon. 138-Mr. Miracle. 139-Hawkman. 140-Wonder Woman	2	4	6	8	10	12
120-Kamandi (68 pgs.)	3	6	9	14	19	24
124-Sgt. Rock	2	4	6	9	12	15
129,130-Batman/Green Arrow/Atom parts 1 & 2; Joker & Two Face-c/stories	2	4	6	13	18	22
131-Batman & Wonder Woman vs. Catwoman-c/sty	2	4	6	10	14	18
141-Batman/Black Canary vs. Joker-c/story	2	4	6	13	18	22
142-160: Batman team-ups: 142-Aquaman. 143-Creeper; origin Human Target (44 pgs.). 144-Green Arrow; origin Human Target part 2 (44 pgs.). 145-Phantom Stranger. 146-G.A. Batman/Unknown Soldier. 147-Supergirl. 148-Plastic Man; X-Mas-c. 149-Teen Titans. 150-Anniversary issue; Superman. 151-Flash. 152-Atom. 153-Red Tornado. 154-Metamorpho. 155-Green Lantern. 156-Dr. Fate. 157-Batman vs. Kamandi (ties into Kamandi #59). 158-Wonder Woman. 159-Ra's Al Ghul. 160-Supergirl.	1	3	4	6	8	10
145(11/79)-147,150-159,165(8/80)-(Whitman variants; low print run; none show issue # on cover)	2	4	6	9	13	16
161-181,183-190,192-195,198,199: Batman team-ups: 161-Adam Strange. 162-G.A. Batman/Sgt. Rock. 163-Black Lightning. 164-Hawkman. 165-Man-Bat. 166-Black Canary; Nemesis (intro) back-up story begins, ends #192; Penguin-c/story. 167-G.A. Batman/Blackhawk; origin Nemesis. 168-Green Arrow. 169-Zatanna. 170-Nemesis. 171-Scalphunter. 172-Firestorm. 173-Guardians of the Universe. 174-Green Lantern. 175-Lois Lane. 176-Swamp Thing. 177-Elongated Man. 178-Creeper. 179-Legion. 180-Spectre. 181-Hawk & Dove. 183-Riddler. 184-Huntress & Earth II Batman. 185-Green Arrow. 186-Hawkman. 187-Metal Men. 188,189-Rose & the Thorn. 190-Adam Strange. 192-Superboy vs. Mr. I.Q. 194-Flash. 195-I...Vampire. 198-Karate Kid. 199-Batman vs. The Spectre						6.00
182-G.A. Robin; G.A. Starman app.; 1st modern app. G.A. Batwoman	2	4	6	8	10	12
191-Batman/Joker-c/story; Nemesis app.	2	4	6	8	11	14
196-Ragman; origin Ragman retold.	1	2	3	5	6	8
197-Catwoman; Earth II Batman & Catwoman marry; 2nd modern app. of G.A. Batwoman; Scarecrow story in Golden Age style	2	4	6	11	16	20
200-Double-sized (64 pgs.); printed on Mando paper; Earth One & Earth Two Batman app. in separate stories; intro/1st app. Batman & The Outsiders	2	4	6	8	10	12

NOTE: ***Neal Adams** a-79-86, 93, 100r, 102; c-75, 76, 79-86, 88-90, 93, 95, 99, 100r. **M. Anderson** a-115r; c-72i, 96i. **Andru/Esposito** c-25-27. **Aparo** a-98, 100-102, 104-125, 126i, 127-136, 138-145, 147, 148i, 149-152, 154, 155, 157-162, 168-170, 173-178, 180-182, 184, 186i-189i, 191i-193i, 195, 196, 200; c-105-109, 111-136, 137i, 138-175, 177, 180-184, 186-200. **Austin** a-166i. **Bernard Baily** c-32, 33, 58. **Buckler** a-185, 186p; c-137, 178p, 185p, 186p. **Giordano** a-143, 144. **Infantino** a-67p, 72p, 97r, 98r, 115r, 172p, 183p, 190p, 194p; c-45-49, 67p, 69p, 70p, 72p, 96p, 98r. **Kaluta** c-176. **Kane** a-115r; c-59, 64. **Kubert** &/or **Heath** a-1-24; reprints-101, 113, 115, 117. **Kubert** a-99r; c-22-24, 34-36, 40, 42-44, 52. **Mooney** a-114r. **Mortimer** a-64, 69. **Newton** a-153p, 156p, 165p. **Irv Novick** c-1(part), 2-21. **Fred Ray** a-78r. **Roussos** a-50, 76i, 114r. **Staton** 148p. 52 pgs.-97, 100; 68 pgs.-120; 100 pgs.-112-117.*

BRAVE AND THE BOLD, THE
DC Comics: Dec, 1991 - No. 6, June, 1992 ($1.75, limited series)

1-6: Green Arrow, The Butcher, The Question in all; Grell scripts in all — 3.00

NOTE: *Grell c-3, 4-6.*

BRAVE AND THE BOLD, THE
DC Comics: Apr, 2007 - No. 35, Aug, 2010 ($2.99)

1-Batman & Green Lantern team-up; Roulette app.; Waid-s/Peréz-c/a; 2 covers — 4.00
2-35: 2-GL & Supergirl. 3-Batman & Blue Beetle vs. Fatal Five; Lobo app. 4-6-LSH app. 12-Megistus conclusion; Ordway-a. 14-Kolins-a. 16-Superman & Catwoman. 28-Blackhawks app. 29-Batman/Brother Power the Geek. 31-Atom/Joker — 3.00
...: Demons and Dragons HC (2009, $24.99, dustjacket) r/#13-16; Brave & the Bold V1 #181, Flash V3 #107 and Impulse #17; Mark Waid commentary — 25.00
...: Demons and Dragons SC (2010, $17.99) same contents as HC — 18.00
...: Milestone SC (2010, $17.99) r/#24-26 and Static #12, Hardware #16, Xombi #6 — 18.00
Team-ups of the Brave and the Bold HC (2010, $24.99) r/#27-33
...: The Book of Destiny HC (2008, $24.99, dustjacket) r/#7-12; Ordway sketch pages — 25.00
...: The Book of Destiny SC (2009, $17.99) r/#7-12; Ordway sketch pages — 18.00
...: The Lords of Luck HC (2007, $24.99, dustjacket) r/#1-6 with Waid intro & annotations — 25.00
...: The Lords of Luck SC (2008, $17.99) r/#1-6 with Waid intro & annotations — 18.00
...: Without Sin SC (2009, $17.99) r/#17-22 — 18.00

BRAVE AND THE BOLD ANNUAL NO. 1 1969 ISSUE, THE
DC Comics: 2001 ($5.95, one-shot)

1-Reprints silver age team-ups in 1960s-style 80 pg. Giant format — 6.00

BRAVE AND THE BOLD SPECIAL, THE (See DC Special Series No. 8)

BRAVE EAGLE (TV)
Dell Publishing Co.: No. 705, June, 1956 - No. 929, July, 1958

	GD	VG	FN	VF	VF/NM	NM-
Four Color 705 (#1)-Photo-c	6	12	18	43	69	95
Four Color 770, 816, 879 (2/58), 929-All photo-c	4	8	12	26	41	55

BRAVE NEW WORLD (See DCU Brave New World)

BRAVE OLD WORLD (V2K)
DC Comics (Vertigo): Feb, 2000 - No. 4, May, 2000 ($2.50, mini-series)

1-4-Messner-Loeb-s/Guy Davis & Phil Hester-a — 3.00

BRAVE ONE, THE (Movie)
Dell Publishing Co.: No. 773, Mar, 1957

	GD	VG	FN	VF	VF/NM	NM-
Four Color 773-Photo-c	5	10	15	34	55	75

BRAVURA
Malibu Comics (Bravura): 1995 (mail-in offer)

0-wraparound holographic-c; short stories and promo pin-ups of Chaykin's Power & Glory, Gil Kane's & Steven Grant's Edge, Starlin's Breed, & Simonson's Star Slammers — 5.00
1 1/2 — 7.00

BREACH
DC Comics: Mar, 2005 - No. 11, Jan, 2006 ($2.95/$2.50)

1-11: 1-Marcos Martin-a/Bob Harras-s; origin. 4-JLA-c/app. — 3.00

BREAKDOWN
Devil's Due Publ.: Oct, 2004 - No. 6, Apr, 2005 ($2.95)

1-6: 1-Two covers by Dave Ross and Leinil Yu; Dixon-s/Ross-a — 3.00

BREAKFAST AFTER NOON
Oni Press: May, 2000 - No. 6, Jan, 2001 ($2.95, B&W, limited series)

1-6-Andi Watson-s/a — 3.00
TPB (2001, $19.95) r/series — 20.00

BREAKING INTO COMICS THE MARVEL WAY
Marvel Comics: May, 2010 - No. 2, May, 2010 ($3.99, limited series)

1,2-Short stories by various newcomer artists; artist profiles — 4.00

BREAKNECK BLVD.
MotioN Comics/Slave Labor Graphics Vol. 2: No. 0, Feb, 1994 - No. 2, Nov, 1994; Vol. 2#1, Jul, 1995 - #6, Dec., 1996 ($2.50/$2.95, B&W)

0-2, V2#1-6: 0-Perez/Giordano-c — 3.00

BREAK-THRU (Also see Exiles V1#4)
Malibu Comics (Ultraverse): Dec, 1993 - No. 2, Jan, 1994 ($2.50, 44 pgs.)

1,2-Perez-c/a(p); has x-overs in Ultraverse titles — 2.50

BREATHTAKER
DC Comics: 1990 - No. 4, 1990 ($4.95, 52 pgs., prestige format, mature)

Book 1-4: Mark Wheatley-painted-c/a & scripts; Marc Hempel-a — 5.00
TPB (1994, $14.95) r/#1-4; intro by Neil Gaiman — 15.00

'BREED
Malibu Comics (Bravura): Jan, 1994 - No. 6, 1994 ($2.50, limited series)

1-(48 pgs.)-Origin/1st app. of 'Breed by Starlin; contains Bravura stamps; spot varnish-c — 4.00

Brenda Starr #9 © SUPR

Brigade #1 © Rob Liefeld

Brightest Day #5 © DC

	GD 2.0	VG 4.0	FN 6.0	VF 8.0	VF/NM 9.0	NM- 9.2

2-6: 2-5-contains Bravura stamps. 6-Death of Rachel 3.00
...:Book of Genesis (1994, $12.95)-reprints #1-6 13.00

'BREED II
Malibu Comics (Bravura): Nov, 1994 - No. 6, Apr, 1995 ($2.95, limited series)

1-6: Starlin-c/a/scripts in all. 1-Gold edition 3.00

BREEZE LAWSON, SKY SHERIFF (See Sky Sheriff)

BRENDA LEE'S LIFE STORY
Dell Publishing Co.: July-Sept., 1962

	GD	VG	FN	VF	VF/NM	NM-
01-078-209	8	16	24	52	86	120

BRENDA STARR (Also see All Great)
Four Star Comics Corp./Superior Comics Ltd.: No. 13, 9/47; No. 14, 3/48; V2#3, 6/48 - V2#12, 12/49

	GD	VG	FN	VF	VF/NM	NM-
V1#13-By Dale Messick	87	174	261	553	952	1350
14-Classic Kamen bondage-c	168	336	504	1075	1838	2600
V2#3-Baker-a?	69	138	207	442	759	1075
4-Used in **SOTI**, pg. 21; Kamen-c	84	168	252	538	919	1300
5-10	68	136	204	435	743	1050
11,12 (Scarce)	71	142	213	454	777	1100

NOTE: *Newspaper reprints plus original material through #6. All original #7 on.*

BRENDA STARR (...Reporter)(Young Lovers No. 16 on?)
Charlton Comics: No. 13, June, 1955 - No. 15, Oct, 1955

	GD	VG	FN	VF	VF/NM	NM-
13-15-Newspaper-r	32	64	96	188	307	425

BRENDA STARR REPORTER
Dell Publishing Co.: Oct, 1963

	GD	VG	FN	VF	VF/NM	NM-
1	11	22	33	80	150	220

BRER RABBIT (See Kite Fun Book, Walt Disney Showcase #28 and Wheaties)
Dell Publishing Co.: No. 129, 1946; No. 208, Jan, 1949; No. 693, 1956 (Disney)

	GD	VG	FN	VF	VF/NM	NM-
Four Color 129 (#1)-Adapted from Disney movie "Song of the South"	24	48	72	175	350	525
Four Color 208 (1/49)	11	22	33	75	138	200
Four Color 693-Part-r #129	8	16	24	56	93	130

BRIAN BOLLAND'S BLACK BOOK
Eclipse Comics: July, 1985 (one-shot)

1-British B&W-r in color 3.00

BRIAN PULIDO'S LADY DEATH... (See Lady Death)

BRICK BRADFORD (Also see Ace Comics & King Comics)
King Features Syndicate/Standard: No. 5, July, 1948 - No. 8, July, 1949 (Ritt & Grey reprints)

	GD	VG	FN	VF	VF/NM	NM-
5	19	38	57	112	176	240
6-Robot-c (by Schomburg?).	36	72	108	216	351	485
7-Schomburg-c. 8-Says #7 inside, #8 on-c	15	30	45	94	147	200

BRIDE'S DIARY (Formerly Black Cobra No. 3)
Ajax/Farrell Publ.: No. 4, May, 1955 - No. 10, Aug, 1956

	GD	VG	FN	VF	VF/NM	NM-
4 (#1)	10	20	30	54	72	90
5-8	7	14	21	37	46	55
9,10-Disbrow-a	9	18	27	47	61	75

BRIDES IN LOVE (Hollywood Romances & Summer Love No. 46 on)
Charlton Comics: Aug, 1956 - No. 45, Feb, 1965

	GD	VG	FN	VF	VF/NM	NM-
1	12	24	36	67	94	120
2	8	16	24	40	50	60
3-6,8-10	4	8	12	22	34	45
7-(68 pgs.)	4	8	12	28	44	60
11-20	3	6	9	16	23	30
21-45	2	4	6	11	16	20

BRIDES ROMANCES
Quality Comics Group: Nov, 1953 - No. 23, Dec, 1956

	GD	VG	FN	VF	VF/NM	NM-
1	15	30	45	90	140	190
2	10	20	30	54	72	90
3-10: Last precode (3/55)	9	18	27	50	65	80
11-17,19-22: 15-Baker-a(p)?; Colan-a	8	16	24	44	57	70
18-Baker-a	10	20	30	54	72	90
23-Baker-c/a	14	28	42	78	112	145

BRIDE'S SECRETS
Ajax/Farrell(Excellent Publ.)/Four-Star: Apr-May, 1954 - No. 19, May, 1958

	GD	VG	FN	VF	VF/NM	NM-
1	14	28	42	76	108	140
2	8	16	24	44	57	70
3-6: Last precode (3/55)	7	14	21	37	46	55
7-11,13-19: 18-Hollingsworth-a	7	14	21	35	43	50
12-Disbrow-a	8	16	24	40	50	60

BRIDE-TO-BE ROMANCES (See True...)

BRIGADE
Image Comics (Extreme Studios): Aug, 1992 - No. 4, 1993 ($1.95, lim. series)

1-Liefeld part plots/scripts in all, Liefeld-c(p); contains 2 Brigade trading cards 3.00
1-Gold foil stamped logo edition 8.00
2-Contains coupon for Image Comics #0 & 2 trading cards 3.00
2-With coupon missing 2.00
3,4: 3-Contains 2 trading cards; 1st Birds of Prey. 4-Flip book featuring Youngblood #5 3.00

BRIGADE
Image Comics (Extreme): V2#1, May, 1993 - V2#22, July, 1995, V2#25, May, 1996 ($1.95/$2.50)

V2#1-22,25: 1-Gatefold-c; Liefeld co-plots; Blood Brothers part 1; Bloodstrike app. 2-(6/93, V2#1 on inside)-Foil merricote-c (newsstand ed. w/out foil-c exists). 3-Perez-c(i); Liefeld scripts. 8,9-Coupons #2 & 6 for Extreme Prejudice #0 bound-in. 11-(8/94, $2.50) WildC.A.T.S app. 16-Polybagged w/ trading card. 22-"Supreme Apocalypse" Pt. 4; w/ trading card 3.00
0-(9/93)-Liefeld scripts; 1st app. Warcry; Youngblood & Wildcats app.; 3.00
20-Variant-c. by Quesada & Palmiotti 3.00
Sourcebook 1 (8/94, $2.95) 3.00
1-(Awesome Ent., 7/00, $2.99) Flip book w/Century preview 3.00
1-(6/10, $3.99) Liefeld-s/Mychaels-a; covers by Liefeld & Mychaels 4.00

BRIGAND, THE (See Fawcett Movie Comics No. 18)

BRIGHTEST DAY (Also see Blackest Night and Green Lantern)
DC Comics: No. 0, Jun, 2010 - No. 24 ($3.99/$2.99)

0-($3.99) Johns & Tomasi-s/Pasarin-a/Finch-c 4.00
0-Variant-c by Reis 8.00
1-22-($2.99) 1-Black Manta returns. 4-Intro. Jackson (new Aqualad) 16-Aqualad origin. 18-Hawkman & Hawkgirl killed. 20-Aquaman killed 3.00
1-22: Variant covers. 1-6,9-18,20-23-by Reis, 7,8 White Lantern by Sook. 19-by Frank 6.00
...: The Atom Special (9/10, $2.99) Lemire-s/Asrar-a/Frank-c 3.00
... Volume 1 HC (2010, $29.99) r/#0-7; cover gallery 30.00

BRING BACK THE BAD GUYS (Also see Fireside Book Series)
Marvel Comics: 1998 ($24.95, TPB)

1-Reprints stories of Marvel villains' secrets 25.00

BRINGING UP FATHER
Dell Publishing Co.: No. 9, 1942 - No. 37, 1944

	GD	VG	FN	VF	VF/NM	NM-
Large Feature Comic 9	30	60	90	177	289	400
Four Color 37	18	36	54	125	255	385

BRING ON THE BAD GUYS (See Fireside Book Series)

BRING THE THUNDER
Dynamite Entertainment: 2010 - No. 4, 2011 ($3.99)

1-3-Alex Ross-c/Ross & Nitz-s/Tortosa-a 4.00

BROADWAY HOLLYWOOD BLACKOUTS
Stanhall: Mar-Apr, 1954 - No. 3, July-Aug, 1954

	GD	VG	FN	VF	VF/NM	NM-
1	14	28	42	80	115	150
2,3	10	20	30	54	72	90

BROADWAY ROMANCES
Quality Comics Group: January, 1950 - No. 5, Sept, 1950

	GD	VG	FN	VF	VF/NM	NM-
1-Ward-c/a (9 pgs.); Gustavson-a	38	76	114	225	368	510
2-Ward-a (9 pgs.); photo-c	26	52	78	154	252	350
3-5: All-Photo-c	15	30	45	83	124	165

BROKEN ARROW (TV)
Dell Publishing Co.: No. 855, Oct, 1957 - No. 947, Nov, 1958

	GD	VG	FN	VF	VF/NM	NM-
Four Color 855 (#1)-Photo-c	6	12	18	37	59	80
Four Color 947-Photo-c	5	10	15	32	51	70

BROKEN CROSS, THE (See The Crusaders)

BROKEN TRINITY
Image Comics (Top Cow): July, 2008 - No. 3, Nov, 2008 ($2.99, limited series)

1-3-Witchblade, Darkness & Angelus app.; Marz-s/Sejic & Hester-a; two covers 3.00
...: Aftermath 1 (4/09, $2.99) Marz & Hill-s/Lucas & Kirkham-a 3.00
...: Angelus 1 (12/08, $2.99) Marz-s/Stelfreeze-a; two covers 3.00
...: Pandora's Box 1-6 (2/10 - No. 6, 4/11 $3.99) Tommy Lee Edwards-c 4.00
...: The Darkness 1 (8/08, $2.99) Hester-s/Lucas-a; two covers 3.00
...: Witchblade 1 (12/08, $2.99) Marz-s/Blake-a; two covers 3.00

BRONCHO BILL (See Comics On Parade, Sparkler & Tip Top Comics)

Brother Power, The Geek #1 © DC

Brute & Babe #2 © Ominous

Buck Duck #2 © MAR

	GD 2.0	VG 4.0	FN 6.0	VF 8.0	VF/NM 9.0	NM- 9.2

United Features Syndicate/Standard(Visual Editions) No. 5-on: 1939 - 1940; No. 5, 1?/48 - No. 16, 8?/50

Single Series 2 ('39)	52	104	156	328	552	775
Single Series 19 ('40)(#2 on cvr)	42	84	126	265	445	625
5	15	30	45	84	127	170
6(4/48)-10(4/49)	10	20	30	54	72	90
11(6/49)-16	9	18	27	47	61	75

NOTE: *Schomburg c-6, 7, 9-13, 15, 16.*

BROOKS ROBINSON (See Baseball's Greatest Heroes #2)

BROTHER BILLY THE PAIN FROM PLAINS
Marvel Comics Group: 1979 (68pgs.)

1-B&W comics, satire, Jimmy Carter-c & x-over w/Brother Billy peanut jokes. Joey Adams-a (scarce)	4	8	12	23	36	48

BROTHERHOOD, THE (Also see X-Men titles)
Marvel Comics: July, 2001 - No. 9, Mar, 2002 ($2.25)

1-Intro. Orwell & the Brotherhood; Ribic-a/X-s/Sienkiewicz-c 3.00
2-9: 2-Two covers (JG Jones & Sienkiewicz). 4-6-Fabry-c. 7-9-Phillips-c/a 3.00

BROTHER POWER, THE GEEK (See Saga of Swamp Thing Annual & Vertigo Visions)
National Periodical Publications: Sept-Oct, 1968 - No. 2, Nov-Dec, 1968

1-Origin; Simon-c(i?)	5	10	15	34	55	75
2	3	6	9	20	30	40

BROTHERS, HANG IN THERE, THE
Spire Christian Comics (Fleming H. Revell Co.): 1979 (49¢)

nn	2	4	6	10	14	18

BROTHERS IN ARMS (Based on the World War II military video game)
Dynamite Entertainment: 2008 - No. 4, 2008 ($3.99/$3.50)

1-($3.99) Fabbri-a; two covers by Fabbri & Sejic 4.00
2-4-($3.50) Two covers by Fabbri & Sejic on each 3.50

BROTHERS OF THE SPEAR (Also see Tarzan)
Gold Key/Whitman No. 18: June, 1972 - No. 17, Feb, 1976; No. 18, May, 1982

1	5	10	15	35	55	75
2-Painted-c begin, end #17	3	6	9	19	29	38
3-10	3	6	9	16	22	28
11-18: 12-Line drawn-c. 13-17-Spiegle-a. 18(5/82)-r/#2; Leopard Girl-r	2	4	6	11	16	20

BROTHERS, THE CULT ESCAPE, THE
Spire Christian Comics (Fleming H. Revell Co.): 1980 (49¢)

nn	2	4	6	11	16	20

BROWNIES (See New Funnies)
Dell Publishing Co.: No. 192, July, 1948 - No. 605, Dec, 1954

Four Color 192(#1)-Kelly-a	13	26	39	89	170	250
Four Color 244(9/49), 293 (9/50)-Last Kelly c/a	10	20	30	68	119	170
Four Color 337(7-8/51), 365(12-1/51-52), 398(5/52)	6	12	18	37	59	80
Four Color 436(11/52), 482(7/53), 522(12/53), 605	5	10	15	34	55	75

BRUCE GENTRY
Better/Standard/Four Star Publ./Superior No. 3: Jan, 1948 - No. 8, Jul, 1949

1-Ray Bailey strip reprints begin, end #3; E. C. emblem appears as a monogram on stationery in story; negligee panels	60	120	180	381	653	925
2,3	38	76	114	228	369	510
4-8	25	50	75	150	245	340

NOTE: *Kamenish a-2-7; c-1-8.*

BRUCE JONES' OUTER EDGE
Innovation: 1993 ($2.50, B&W, one-shot)

1-Bruce Jones-c/a/script 3.00

BRUCE LEE (Also see Deadly Hands of Kung Fu)
Malibu Comics: July, 1994 - No. 6, Dec, 1994 ($2.95, 36 pgs.)

1-6: 1-(44 pgs.)-Mortal Kombat prev., 1st app. in comics. 2,6-(36 pgs.) 5.00

BRUCE WAYNE: AGENT OF S.H.I.E.L.D. (Also see Marvel Vs. DC #3 & DC Vs. Marvel #4)
Marvel Comics (Amalgam): Apr, 1996 ($1.95, one-shot)

1-Chuck Dixon scripts & Cary Nord-c/a. 3.00

BRUCE WAYNE: THE ROAD HOME (See Batman: The Return of Bruce Wayne)
DC Comics: Dec, 2010 ($2.99, series of one-shots with interlocking covers)

...: Batgirl 1 - Bryan Miller-s/Pere Pérez-a 3.00
...: Batman and Robin 1 - Nicieza-s/Richards-a; Vicki Vale app. 3.00
...: Catwoman 1 - Fridolfs-s/Nguyen-a; Harley & Ivy app. 3.00
...: Commissioner Gordon 1 - Beechen-s/Kudranski-a; Penguin app. 3.00
...: Oracle 1 - Andreyko-s/Padilla-a; Man-Bat & Manhunter app. 3.00
...: Outsiders 1 - Barr-s/Saltares-a 3.00
...: Ra's al Ghul 1 - Nicieza-s/McDaniel-a 3.00
...: Red Robin 1 - Nicieza-s/Bachs-a; Ra's al Ghul app. 3.00

BRUISER
Anthem Publications: Feb, 1994 ($2.45)

1 3.00

BRUTE, THE
Seaboard Publ. (Atlas): Feb, 1975 - No. 3, July, 1975

1-Origin & 1st app; Sekowsky-a(p)	2	4	6	10	14	18
2-Sekowsky-a(p); Fleisher-s	2	4	6	8	10	12
3-Brunner/Starlin/Weiss-a(p)	2	4	6	9	12	15

BRUTE & BABE
Ominous Press: July, 1994 - No. 2, Aug, 1994

1-($3.95, 8 tablets plus-c)-"...It Begins..."; tablet format 4.00
2-($2.50, 36 pgs.)-"Mael's Rage", 2-(40 pgs.)-Stiff additional variant-c 3.00

BRUTE FORCE
Marvel Comics: Aug, 1990 - No. 4, Nov, 1990 ($1.00, limited series)

1-4: Animal super-heroes; Delbo & DeCarlo-a 3.00

B-SIDES (The Craptacular...)
Marvel Comics: Nov, 2002 - No. 3, Jan, 2003 ($2.99, limited series)

1-3-Kieth-c/Weldele-a. 2-Dorkin-a (1 pg.) 2-FF cameo. 3-FF app. 3.00

BUBBLEGUM CRISIS: GRAND MAL
Dark Horse Comics: Mar, 1994 - No. 4, June, 1994 ($2.50, limited series)

1-4-Japanese manga 3.00

BUCCANEER
I. W. Enterprises: No date (1963)

I.W. Reprint #1(r-/Quality #20), #8(r-/#23): Crandall-a in each	3	6	9	16	23	30

BUCCANEERS (Formerly Kid Eternity)
Quality Comics: No. 19, Jan, 1950 - No. 27, May, 1951 (No. 24-27: 52 pgs.)

19-Captain Daring, Black Roger, Eric Falcon & Spanish Main begin; Crandall-a	48	96	144	302	514	725
20,23-Crandall-a	36	72	108	215	350	485
21-Crandall-c/a	39	78	117	236	388	540
22-Bondage-c	28	56	84	165	270	375
24-26: 24-Adam Peril, U.S.N. begins. 25-Origin & 1st app. Corsair Queen. 26-last Spanish Main	24	48	72	142	234	325
27-Crandall-c/a	34	68	102	205	335	465
Super Reprint #12 (1964)-Crandall-r/#21	3	6	9	16	23	30

BUCCANEERS, THE (TV)
Dell Publishing Co.: No. 800, 1957

Four Color 800-Photo-c	7	14	21	47	76	105

BUCKAROO BANZAI (Movie)
Marvel Comics Group: Dec, 1984 - No. 2, Feb, 1985

1,2-Movie adaptation; r/Marvel Super Special #33; Texiera-c/a 3.00

BUCKAROO BANZAI: RETURN OF THE SCREW
Moonstone: 2006 - No. 3, 2006 ($3.50, limited series)

1-3: 1-Three covers by Haley, Stribling, Beck; Thompson-a 3.50
Preview (2006, 50¢) B&W preview; history of movie and spin-off projects 3.00

BUCK DUCK
Atlas Comics (ANC): June, 1953 - No. 4, Dec, 1953

1-Funny animal stories in all	15	30	45	90	140	190
2-4: 2-Ed Win-a(5)	10	20	30	56	76	95

BUCK JONES (Also see Crackajack Funnies, Famous Feature Stories, Master Comics #7 & Wow Comics #1, 1936)
Dell Publishing Co.: No. 299, Oct, 1950 - No. 850, Oct, 1957 (All Painted-c)

Four Color 299(#1)-Buck Jones & his horse Silver-B begin; painted back-c begins, ends #5	12	24	36	87	164	240
2(4-6/51)	8	16	24	52	86	120
3-8(10-12/52)	6	12	18	43	69	95
Four Color 460,500,546,589	6	12	18	41	66	90
Four Color 652,733,850	5	10	15	32	51	70

BUCK ROGERS (Also see Famous Funnies, Pure Oil Comics, Salerno Carnival of Comics,

Buck Rogers (2009 series) #11 © Dille Family

Buffalo Bill Picture Stories #2 © S&S

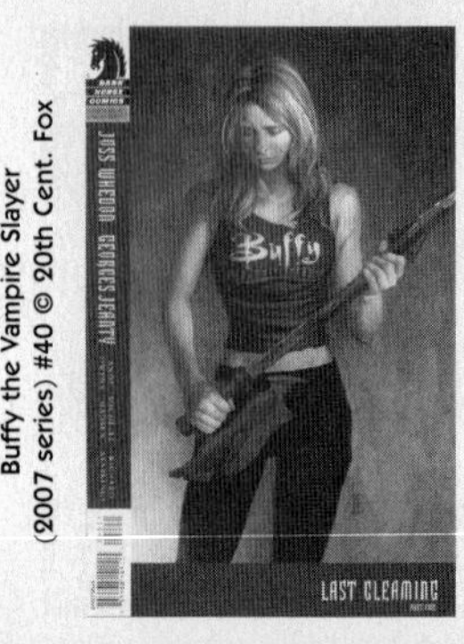

Buffy the Vampire Slayer (2007 series) #40 © 20th Cent. Fox

24 Pages of Comics, & Vicks Comics)
Famous Funnies: Winter, 1940-41 - No. 6, Sept, 1943
NOTE: Buck Rogers first appeared in the pulp magazine Amazing Stories Vol. 3 #5 in Aug, 1928.

	GD 2.0	VG 4.0	FN 6.0	VF 8.0	VF/NM 9.0	NM- 9.2
1-Sunday strip reprints by Rick Yager; begins with strip #190; Calkins-c	314	628	942	2198	3849	5500
2 (7/41)-Calkins-c	132	264	396	838	1444	2050
3 (12/41), 4 (7/42)	115	230	345	730	1253	1775
5,6: 5-Story continues with Famous Funnies No. 80; Buck Rogers, Sky Roads. 6-Reprints of 1939 dailies; contains B.R. story "Crater of Doom" (2 pgs.) by Calkins not-r from Famous Funnies	97	194	291	621	1061	1500

BUCK ROGERS
Toby Press: No. 100, Jan, 1951 - No. 9, May-June, 1951

	GD 2.0	VG 4.0	FN 6.0	VF 8.0	VF/NM 9.0	NM- 9.2
100(#7)-All strip-r begin	31	62	93	182	296	410
101(#8), 9-All Anderson-a(1947-49-r/dailies)	23	46	69	136	223	310

BUCK ROGERS (...in the 25th Century No. 5 on) (TV)
Gold Key/Whitman No. 7 on: Oct, 1964; No. 2, July, 1979 - No. 16, May, 1982 (No #10; story was written but never released. #17 exists only as a press proof without covers and was never published)

	GD 2.0	VG 4.0	FN 6.0	VF 8.0	VF/NM 9.0	NM- 9.2
1(10128-410, 12¢)-1st S.A. app. Buck Rogers & 1st new B. R. in comics since 1933 giveaway; painted-c; back-c pin-up	10	20	30	71	128	185
2(7/79)-6: 3,4,6-Movie adaptation; painted-c	2	4	6	9	12	15
7,11 (Whitman)	2	4	6	11	16	20
8,9 (prepack)(scarce)	3	6	9	18	27	35
12-16: 14(2/82), 15(3/82), 16(5/82)	2	4	6	8	10	12
Giant Movie Edition 11296(64pp, Whitman, $1.50), reprints GK #2-4 minus cover; tabloid size; photo-c (See Marvel Treasury)	3	6	9	18	27	35
Giant Movie Edition 02489(Western/Marvel, $1.50), reprints GK #2-4 minus cover	3	6	9	17	25	32

NOTE: *Bolle a-2p,3p, Movie Ed.(p).* ***McWilliams*** *a-2i,3i, 5-11, Movie Ed.(i). Painted c-1-9,11-13.*

BUCK ROGERS (Comics Module)
TSR, Inc.: 1990 - No. 10, 1991 ($2.95, 44 pgs.)

	GD 2.0	VG 4.0	FN 6.0	VF 8.0	VF/NM 9.0	NM- 9.2
1-10 (1990): 1-Begin origin in 3 parts. 2-Indicia says #1. 2,3-Black Barney back-up story. 4-All Black Barney issue; B. B.-c. 5-Indicia says #6; Black Barney-c & lead story; Buck Rogers back-up story. 10-Flip book (72pgs.)						4.00

BUCK ROGERS
Dynamite Entertainment: No. 0, 2009 - No. 12, 2010 (25¢/$3.50)

	GD 2.0	VG 4.0	FN 6.0	VF 8.0	VF/NM 9.0	NM- 9.2
0-(25¢) Beatty-s/Rafael-a/Cassaday-c						3.00
1-12: 1-($3.50) Three covers by Cassaday, Ross and Wagner; origin re-told						3.50
Annual 1 (2011, $4.99) Rafael-a; covers by Rafael & Sadowski						5.00

BUCKSKIN (TV)
Dell Publishing Co.: No. 1011, July, 1959 - No. 1107, June-Aug, 1960

	GD 2.0	VG 4.0	FN 6.0	VF 8.0	VF/NM 9.0	NM- 9.2
Four Color 1011 (#1)-Photo-c	7	14	21	47	76	105
Four Color 1107-Photo-c	6	12	18	43	69	95

BUCKY O'HARE (Funny Animal)
Continuity Comics: 1988 ($5.95, graphic novel)

	GD 2.0	VG 4.0	FN 6.0	VF 8.0	VF/NM 9.0	NM- 9.2
1-Golden-c/a(r); r/serial-Echo of Futurepast #1-6	1	2	3	4	5	7
Deluxe Hardcover ($40.00, 52 pg., 8 x 11")						40.00

BUCKY O'HARE
Continuity Comics: Jan, 1991 - No. 5, 1991 ($2.00)

	GD 2.0	VG 4.0	FN 6.0	VF 8.0	VF/NM 9.0	NM- 9.2
1-6: 1-Michael Golden-c/a						3.00

BUDDIES IN THE U.S. ARMY
Avon Periodicals: Nov, 1952 - No. 2, 1953

	GD 2.0	VG 4.0	FN 6.0	VF 8.0	VF/NM 9.0	NM- 9.2
1-Lawrence-c	14	28	42	80	115	150
2-Mort Lawrence-c/a	10	20	30	54	72	90

BUFFALO BEE (TV)
Dell Publishing Co.: No. 957, Nov, 1958 - No. 1061, Dec-Feb, 1959-60

	GD 2.0	VG 4.0	FN 6.0	VF 8.0	VF/NM 9.0	NM- 9.2
Four Color 957 (#1)	8	16	24	58	97	135
Four Color 1002 (8-10/59), 1061	7	14	21	45	73	100

BUFFALO BILL (See Frontier Fighters, Super Western Comics & Western Action Thrillers)
Youthful Magazines: No. 2, Oct, 1950 - No. 9, Dec, 1951

	GD 2.0	VG 4.0	FN 6.0	VF 8.0	VF/NM 9.0	NM- 9.2
2-Annie Oakley story	14	28	42	80	115	150
3-9: 2-4-Walter Johnson-c/a. 9-Wildey-a	10	20	30	54	72	90

BUFFALO BILL CODY (See Cody of the Pony Express)

BUFFALO BILL, JR. (TV) (See Western Roundup)
Dell/Gold Key: Jan, 1956 - No. 13, Aug-Oct, 1959; 1965 (All photo-c)

	GD 2.0	VG 4.0	FN 6.0	VF 8.0	VF/NM 9.0	NM- 9.2
Four Color 673 (#1)	9	18	27	60	100	140
Four Color 742,766,798,828,856(11/57)	6	12	18	39	62	85
7(2-4/58)-13	5	10	15	34	55	75
1(6/65, Gold Key)-Photo-c(r/F.C. #798); photo-b/c	4	8	12	24	37	50

BUFFALO BILL PICTURE STORIES
Street & Smith Publications: June-July, 1949 - No. 2, Aug-Sept, 1949

	GD 2.0	VG 4.0	FN 6.0	VF 8.0	VF/NM 9.0	NM- 9.2
1,2-Wildey, Powell-a in each	14	28	42	78	112	145

BUFFY THE VAMPIRE SLAYER (Based on the TV series)(Also see Tales of the Vampires)
Dark Horse Comics: 1998 - No. 63, Nov, 2003 ($2.95/$2.99)

	GD 2.0	VG 4.0	FN 6.0	VF 8.0	VF/NM 9.0	NM- 9.2
1-Bennett-a/Watson-s; Art Adams-c	1	2	3	5	7	9
1-Variant photo-c	1	2	3	5	7	9
1-Gold foil logo Art Adams-c						15.00
1-Gold foil logo photo-c						20.00
2-15-Regular and photo-c. 4-7-Gomez-a. 5,8-Green-c						5.00
16-48: 29,30-Angel x-over. 43-45-Death of Buffy. 47-Lobdell-s begin. 48-Pike returns						3.00
50-($3.50) Scooby gang battles Adam; back-up story by Watson						4.00
51-63: 51-54-Viva Las Buffy; pre-Sunnydale Buffy & Pike in Vegas						3.00
Annual '99 ($4.95)-Two stories and pin-ups	1	2	3	4	5	7
...: A Stake to the Heart TPB (3/04, $12.95) r/#60-63						13.00
...: Chaos Bleeds (6/03, $2.99) Based on the video game; photo & Campbell-c						3.00
...: Creatures of Habit (3/02, $17.95) text with Horton & Paul Lee-a						18.00
...: Jonathan 1 (1/01, $2.99) two covers; Richards-a						3.00
...: Lost and Found 1 (3/02, $2.99) aftermath of Buffy's death; Richards-a						3.00
... Lovers Walk (2/01, $2.99) short stories by various; Richards & photo-c						3.00
...: Note From the Underground (3/03, $12.95) r/#47-50						13.00
...: Omnibus Vol. 1 (7/07, $24.95, 9x6") r/Spike & Dru #3, Origin #1-3 and Buffy #51-59						25.00
...: Omnibus Vol. 2 (9/07, $24.95, 9x6") r/Buffy #60-63 and various one-shots & specials						25.00
...: Omnibus Vol. 3 (1/08, $24.95, 9x6") r/Buffy #1-8,12,16, Annual '99						25.00
...: Omnibus Vol. 4 (5/08, $24.95, 9x6") r/Buffy #9-11,13-15,17-20,50 and various						25.00
...: Omnibus Vol. 5 (9/08, $24.95, 9x6") r/Buffy #21-28 and various one-shots & specials						25.00
...: Omnibus Vol. 6 (2/09, $24.95, 9x6") r/Buffy #29-38 and various one-shots & specials						25.00
...: One For One (9/10, $1.00) r/#1 with red cover frame						1.00
...: Reunion (6/02, $3.50) Buffy & Angel's; Espenson-s; art by various						3.50
...: Slayer Interrupted TPB (2003, $14.95) r/#56-59						15.00
...: Tales of the Slayers (10/02, $3.50) art by Matsuda and Colan; art & photo-c						3.50
...: The Death of Buffy TPB (8/02, $15.95) r/#43-46						16.00
...: Viva Las Buffy TPB (7/03, $12.95) r/#51-54						13.00
Wizard #1/2	1	2	3	6	8	9

BUFFY THE VAMPIRE SLAYER ("Season Eight" of the TV series)
Dark Horse Comics: Mar, 2007 - No. 40, Jan, 2011 ($2.99)

	GD 2.0	VG 4.0	FN 6.0	VF 8.0	VF/NM 9.0	NM- 9.2
1-Joss Whedon-s/Georges Jeanty-a/Jo Chen-c						6.00
1-Variant cover by Jeanty						5.00
1-RRP with B&W Jeanty cover (edition of 1000)						70.00
1-4: 1-2nd thru 5th printings. 2-2nd-4th printings. 3,4-2nd & 3rd printings						3.00
2-5-Jeanty-a; covers by Chen & Jeanty						4.00
6-13,16-19-Two covers by Chen & Jeanty. 6-9-Faith app.; Vaughan-s. 10,11-Whedon-s. 12-15-Goddard-s; Dracula app. 16-19-Fray app.; Whedon-s/Moline-a						3.00
20-40: 20-28,31-40-Two covers by Chen and Jeanty. 20-Animation style flashback. 21,26-30-Espenson-s. 30-Hughes-c. 31-Whedon-s. 32-35-Meltzer-s. 36-40-Whedon-s						3.00
...: Riley (8/10, $3.50) Espensen-s/Moline-a; Riley Finn and Sam; Angel app.						3.50
... Tales of the Vampires (6/09, $2.99) Cloonan-s/Lolos-a; covers by Chen & Bá/Moon						3.00
...: Willow (12/09, $3.50) Whedon-s/Moline-a; Willow meets the Snake Guide						3.50
...: Volume One: The Long Way Home TPB (11/07, $15.95) r/#1-5 and variant covers						16.00
...: Volume Two: No Future for You TPB (6/08, $15.95) r/#6-10 and variant covers						16.00
...: Volume Three: Wolves at the Gate TPB (11/08, $15.95) r/#11-15 and variant covers						16.00
...: Volume Four: Time of Your Life TPB (5/09, $15.95) r/#16-20 and variant covers						16.00
...: Volume Five: Predators and Prey TPB (9/09, $15.95) r/#21-25 and variant covers						16.00
...: Volume Six: Retreat TPB (3/10, $15.99) r/#26-30 and stories from MySpace DHP						16.00

NOTE: *Later printings have Jo Chen cover art with different credit graphics.*

BUFFY THE VAMPIRE SLAYER: ANGEL
Dark Horse Comics: May, 1999 - No. 3, July, 1999 ($2.95, limited series)

	GD 2.0	VG 4.0	FN 6.0	VF 8.0	VF/NM 9.0	NM- 9.2
1-3-Gomez-a; Matsuda-c & photo-c for each						3.00

BUFFY THE VAMPIRE SLAYER: GILES
Dark Horse Comics: Oct, 2000 ($2.95, one-shot)

	GD 2.0	VG 4.0	FN 6.0	VF 8.0	VF/NM 9.0	NM- 9.2
1-Eric Powell-a; Powell & photo-c						3.00

BUFFY THE VAMPIRE SLAYER: HAUNTED
Dark Horse Comics: Dec, 2001 - No. 4, Mar, 2002 ($2.99, limited series)

	GD 2.0	VG 4.0	FN 6.0	VF 8.0	VF/NM 9.0	NM- 9.2
1-4-Faith and the Mayor app.; Espenson-s/Richards-a						3.00
TPB (9/02, $12.95) r/series; photo-c						13.00

BUFFY THE VAMPIRE SLAYER: OZ
Dark Horse Comics: July, 2001 - No. 3, Sept, 2001 ($2.99, limited series)

Bugs Bunny FC #355 © WB

Bulletproof Coffin #5 © Kane & Hine

Bulls-Eye #4 © PRIZE

GD VG FN VF VF/NM NM-
2.0 4.0 6.0 8.0 9.0 9.2

1-3-Totleben & photo-c; Golden-s 3.00

BUFFY THE VAMPIRE SLAYER: SPIKE AND DRU
Dark Horse Comics: Apr, 1999; No. 2, Oct, 1999; No. 3, Dec, 2000 ($2.95)
1-3: 1,2-Photo-c. 3-Two covers (photo & Sook) 3.00

BUFFY THE VAMPIRE SLAYER: THE ORIGIN (Adapts movie screenplay)
Dark Horse Comics: Jan, 1999 - No. 3, Mar, 1999 ($2.95, limited series)
1-3-Brereton-s/Bennett-a; reg & photo-c for each 3.00

BUFFY THE VAMPIRE SLAYER: WILLOW & TARA
Dark Horse Comics: Apr, 2001 ($2.99, one-shot)
1-Terry Moore-a/Chris Golden & Amber Benson-s; Moore-c & photo-c 3.00
TPB (4/03, $9.95) r/#1 & W&T - Wilderness; photo-c 10.00

BUFFY THE VAMPIRE SLAYER: WILLOW & TARA - WILDERNESS
Dark Horse Comics: Jul, 2002 - No. 2, Sept, 2002 ($2.99, limited series)
1,2-Chris Golden & Amber Benson-s; Jothikaumar-c & photo-c 3.00

BUG
Marvel Comics: Mar, 1997 ($2.99, one-shot)
1-Micronauts character 3.00

BUGALOOS (Sid & Marty Krofft TV show)
Charlton Comics: Sept, 1971 - No. 4, Feb, 1972
1 5 10 15 32 51 70
2-4 3 6 9 20 30 40
NOTE: *No. 3(1/72) went on sale late in 1972 (after No. 4) with the 1/73 issues.*

BUGHOUSE (Satire)
Ajax/Farrell (Excellent Publ.): Mar-Apr, 1954 - No. 4, Sept-Oct, 1954
V1#1 21 42 63 126 206 285
2-4 14 28 42 80 115 150

BUGS BUNNY (See The Best of..., Camp Comics, Comic Album #2, 6, 10, 14, Dell Giant #28, 32, 46, Dynabrite, Golden Comics Digest #1, 3, 5, 6, 8, 10, 14, 15, 17, 21, 26, 30, 34, 39, 42, 47, Kite Fun Book, Large Feature Comic #8, Looney Tunes and Merry Melodies, March of Comics #44, 59, 75, 83, 97, 115, 132, 149, 160, 179, 188, 201, 220, 231, 245, 259, 273, 287, 301, 315, 329, 343, 363, 367, 380, 392, 403, 415, 428, 440, 452, 464, 476, 487, Porky Pig, Puffed Wheat, Story Hour Series #802, Super Book #14, 26 and Whitman Comic Books)

BUGS BUNNY (See Dell Giants for annuals)
Dell Publishing Co./Gold Key No. 86-218/Whitman No. 219 on: 1942 - No. 245, April, 1984
Large Feature Comic 8(1942)-(Rarely found in fine-mint condition)
206 412 618 1318 2259 3200
Four Color 33 ('43) 96 192 288 816 1658 2500
Four Color 51 33 66 99 254 502 750
Four Color 88 22 44 66 159 317 475
Four Color 123('46),142,164 15 30 45 104 212 320
Four Color 187,200,217,233 12 24 36 82 154 225
Four Color 250-Used in **SOTI**, pg. 309 12 24 36 86 161 235
Four Color 266,274,281,289,298('50) 10 20 30 68 119 170
Four Color 307,317(#1),327(#2),338,347,355,366,376,393
9 18 27 60 100 140
Four Color 407,420,432(10/52) 7 14 21 50 83 115
Four Color 498(9/53),585(9/54), 647(9/55) 6 12 18 41 66 90
Four Color 724(9/56),838(9/57),1064(12/59) 5 10 15 34 55 75
28(12-1/52-53)-30 6 12 18 39 62 85
31-50 5 10 15 30 48 65
51-85(7-9/62) 4 8 12 24 37 50
86(10/62)-88-Bugs Bunny's Showtime-(25¢, 80pgs.) 6 12 18 41 66 90
89-99 3 6 9 17 25 32
100 3 6 9 18 27 35
101-118: 108-1st Honey Bunny. 118-Last 12¢ issue 3 6 9 14 19 24
119-140 2 4 6 11 16 20
141-170 2 4 6 9 12 15
171-218: 218-Publ. by Whitman only? 2 4 6 8 10 12
219,220,225-237(5/82): 229-Swipe of Barks story/WDC&S #223. 233(2/82)
2 4 6 8 10 12
221(9/80),222(11/80)-Pre-pack? (Scarce) 3 6 9 21 32 42
223 (1/81, 50¢-c), 224 (3/81)-Low distr. 2 4 6 11 16 20
223 (1/81, 40¢-c) Cover price error variant 3 6 9 16 22 28
238-245 (#90070 on-c, nd, nd code; pre-pack): 238(5/83), 239(6/83), 240(7/83), 241(7/83), 242(8/83), 243(8/83), 244(3/84), 245(4/84) 3 6 9 14 19 24
NOTE: *Reprints-100,102-104,110,115,123,143,144,147,167,173,175-177,179-185,187,190.*
nn (Xerox Pub. Comic Digest, 1971, 100 pages, B&W)
collection of one-page gags 4 8 12 24 37 50
...Comic-Go-Round 11196-(224 pgs.)($1.95)(Golden Press, 1979)
4 8 12 26 41 55
...Winter Fun 1(12/67-Gold Key)-Giant 5 10 15 32 51 70

BUGS BUNNY
DC Comics: June, 1990 - No. 3, Aug, 1990 ($1.00, limited series)
1-3: Daffy Duck, Elmer Fudd, others app. 4.00

BUGS BUNNY (...Monthly on-c)
DC Comics: 1993 - No. 3, 1994? ($1.95)
1-3-Bugs, Porky Pig, Daffy, Road Runner 3.50

BUGS BUNNY (Digest-size reprints from Looney Tunes)
DC Comics: 2005 - Present ($6.99, digest)
Vol. 1: What's Up Doc? - Reprints from Looney Tunes #37,41,43-45,48,52,55,57-59,63 7.00

BUGS BUNNY & PORKY PIG
Gold Key: Sept, 1965 (Paper-c, giant, 100 pgs.)
1(30025-509) 7 14 21 45 73 100

BUGS BUNNY'S ALBUM (See Bugs Bunny, Four Color No. 498,585,647,724)

BUGS BUNNY LIFE STORY ALBUM (See Bugs Bunny, Four Color No. 838)

BUGS BUNNY MERRY CHRISTMAS (See Bugs Bunny, Four Color No. 1064)

BUILDING, THE
Kitchen Sink Press: 1987; 2000 (8 1/2" x 11" sepia toned graphic novel)
nn-Will Eisner-s/c/a 10.00
nn-(DC Comics, 9/00, $9.95) reprints 1987 edition 10.00

BULLET CROW, FOWL OF FORTUNE
Eclipse Comics: Mar, 1987 - No. 2, Apr, 1987 ($2.00, B&W, limited series)
1,2-The Comic Reader-r & new-a 2.50

BULLETMAN (See Fawcett Miniatures, Master Comics, Mighty Midget Comics, Nickel Comics & XMas Comics)
Fawcett Publications: Sum, 1941 - #12, 2/12/43; #14, Spr, 1946 - #16, Fall, 1946 (No #13)
1-Silver metallic-c 383 766 1149 2681 4691 6700
2-Raboy-c 168 336 504 1075 1838 2600
3,5-Raboy-c each 135 270 405 864 1482 2100
4 97 194 291 621 1061 1500
6,8-10: 10-Intro. Bulletdog 81 162 243 518 884 1250
7-Ghost Stories told by night watchman of cemetery begins; Eisnerish-a; hidden message "Chic Stone is a jerk". 90 180 270 576 988 1400
11,12,14-16 (nn 13): 12-Robot-c 60 120 180 381 653 925
NOTE: ***Mac Raboy** c-1-3, 5, 6, 10. "Bulletman the Flying Detective" on cover #8 on.*

BULLET POINTS
Marvel Comics: Jan, 2007 - No. 5, May, 2007 ($2.99, limited series)
1-5: 1-Steve Rogers becomes Iron Man; Straczynski-s/Edwards-a. 4,5-Galactus app. 3.00
TPB (2007, $13.99) r/#1-5; layout pages by Edwards 14.00

BULLETPROOF COFFIN
Image Comics: Jun, 2010 - No. 6, Dec, 2010 ($3.99, limited series)
1-6-David Hine-s/Shaky Kane-a/c 4.00

BULLETPROOF MONK (Inspired the 2003 film)
Image Comics (Flypaper Press): 1998 - No. 3, 1999 ($2.95, limited series)
1-3-Oeming-a 3.00
...: Tales of the BPM (3/03, $2.95) Flip book; 2 covers by Sale; art by Sale, Oeming, Dave Johnson; Seann William Scott afterword 3.00
TPB (2002, $9.95) r/#1-3; foreword by John Woo 10.00

BULLETS AND BRACELETS (Also see Marvel Versus DC #3 & DC Versus Marvel #4)
Marvel Comics (Amalgam): Apr, 1996 ($1.95)
1-John Ostrander script & Gary Frank-c/a 3.00

BULLS-EYE (Cody of The Pony Express No. 8 on)
Mainline No. 1-5/Charlton No. 6,7: 7-8/54-No. 5, 3-4/55; No. 6, 6/55; No. 7, 8/55
1-S&K-c, 2 pgs.-a 61 122 183 390 670 950
2-S&K-c/a 50 100 150 315 533 750
3-5-S&K-c/a(2 each). 4-Last pre-code issue (1-2/55). 5-Censored issue with tomahawks removed in battle scene 41 82 123 256 428 600
6-S&K-c/a 37 74 111 222 361 500
7-S&K-c/a(3) 41 82 123 256 428 600

BULLS-EYE COMICS (Formerly Komik Pages #10; becomes Kayo #12)
Harry 'A' Chesler: No. 11, 1944
11-Origin K-9, Green Knight's sidekick, Lance; The Green Knight, Lady Satan, Yankee Doodle Jones app. 45 90 135 284 480 675

BULLSEYE: GREATEST HITS (Daredevil villain)

Buster Bear #1 © QUA

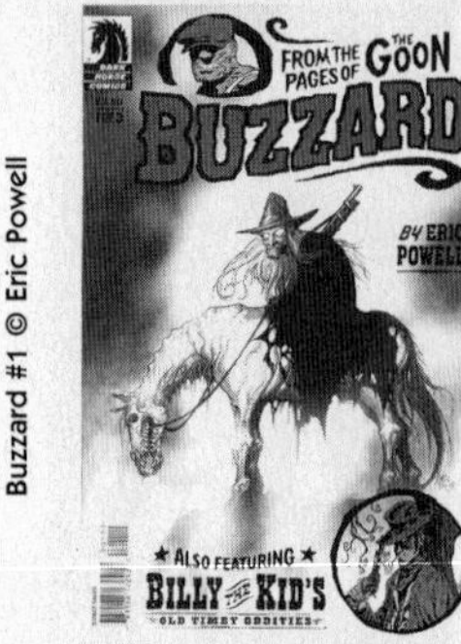

Buzzard #1 © Eric Powell

Buzzy #6 © DC

Marvel Comics: Nov, 2004 - No. 5, Mar, 2005 ($2.99, limted series)

	GD 2.0	VG 4.0	FN 6.0	VF 8.0	VF/NM 9.0	NM- 9.2
1-5-Origin of Bullseye; Steve Dillon-a/Deodato-c. 3-Punisher app.						3.00
TPB (2005, $13.99) r/#1-5						14.00

BULLSEYE: PERFECT GAME (Daredevil villain)
Marvel Comics: Jan, 2011 - No. 2, Feb, 2011 ($3.99, limited series)

	GD 2.0	VG 4.0	FN 6.0	VF 8.0	VF/NM 9.0	NM- 9.2
1,2-Huston-s/Martinbrough-a; Bullseye as baseball pitcher						4.00

BULLWHIP GRIFFIN (See Movie Comics)

BULLWINKLE (...and Rocky No. 22 on; See March of Comics #233 and Rocky & Bullwinkle) (TV) (Jay Ward)
Dell/Gold Key: 3-5/62 - #11, 4/74; #12, 6/76 - #19, 3/78; #20, 4/79 - #25, 2/80

	GD 2.0	VG 4.0	FN 6.0	VF 8.0	VF/NM 9.0	NM- 9.2
Four Color 1270 (3-5/62)	17	34	51	122	249	375
01-090-209 (Dell, 7-9/62)	14	28	42	97	194	290
1(11/62, Gold Key)	13	26	39	92	179	265
2(2/63)	9	18	27	63	107	150
3(4/72)-11(4/74-Gold Key)	5	10	15	34	55	75
12-14: 12(6/76)-Reprints. 13(9/76), 14-New stories	3	6	9	18	27	35
15-25	2	4	6	11	16	20
Mother Moose Nursery Pomes 01-530-207 (5-7/62, Dell)	16	32	48	111	226	340

NOTE: *Reprints: 6, 7, 20-24.*

BULLWINKLE AND ROCKY (TV)
Charlton Comics: July, 1970 - No. 7, July, 1971

	GD 2.0	VG 4.0	FN 6.0	VF 8.0	VF/NM 9.0	NM- 9.2
1-Has 1 pg. pin-up	7	14	21	47	76	105
2-7: 3-Snidely Whiplash app.	5	10	15	32	51	70

BULLWINKLE AND ROCKY
Star Comics/Marvel Comics No. 3 on: Nov, 1987 - No. 9, Mar, 1989

	GD 2.0	VG 4.0	FN 6.0	VF 8.0	VF/NM 9.0	NM- 9.2
1-9: Boris & Natasha in all. 3,5,8-Dudley Do-Right app. 4-Reagan-c						4.50
Marvel Moosterworks (1/92, $4.95)	2	4	6	8	10	12

BUMMER
Fantagraphics Books: June, 1995 ($3.50, B&W, mature)

	GD 2.0	VG 4.0	FN 6.0	VF 8.0	VF/NM 9.0	NM- 9.2
1						3.50

BUNNY (Also see Harvey Pop Comics and Fruitman Special)
Harvey Publications: Dec, 1966 - No. 20, Dec, 1971; No. 21, Nov, 1976

	GD 2.0	VG 4.0	FN 6.0	VF 8.0	VF/NM 9.0	NM- 9.2
1-68 pg. Giants begin	8	16	24	56	93	130
2-10: 2-1st app. Fruitman	5	10	15	30	48	65
11-18: 18-Last 68 pg. Giant	4	8	12	28	44	60
19-21-52 pg. Giants: 21-Fruitman app.	4	8	12	26	41	55

BURKE'S LAW (TV)
Dell Publ.: 1-3/64; No. 2, 5-7/64; No. 3, 3-5/65 (All have Gene Barry photo-c)

	GD 2.0	VG 4.0	FN 6.0	VF 8.0	VF/NM 9.0	NM- 9.2
1-Photo-c	5	10	15	34	55	75
2,3-Photo-c	4	8	12	24	37	50

BURNING ROMANCES (See Fox Giants)

BUSTER BEAR
Quality Comics Group (Arnold Publ.): Dec, 1953 - No. 10, June, 1955

	GD 2.0	VG 4.0	FN 6.0	VF 8.0	VF/NM 9.0	NM- 9.2
1-Funny animal	11	22	33	60	83	105
2	7	14	21	35	43	50
3-10	6	12	18	28	34	40
I.W. Reprint #9,10 (Super on inside)	2	4	6	9	13	16

BUSTER BROWN COMICS (See Promotional Comics section)

BUSTER BUNNY
Standard Comics(Animated Cartoons)/Pines: Nov, 1949 - No. 16, Oct, 1953

	GD 2.0	VG 4.0	FN 6.0	VF 8.0	VF/NM 9.0	NM- 9.2
1-Frazetta 1 pg. text illo.	11	22	33	60	83	105
2	7	14	21	35	43	50
3-14,16	6	12	18	28	34	40
15-Racist-c	10	20	30	54	72	90

BUSTER CRABBE (TV)
Famous Funnies Publ.: Nov, 1951 - No. 12, 1953

	GD 2.0	VG 4.0	FN 6.0	VF 8.0	VF/NM 9.0	NM- 9.2
1-1st app.(?) Frazetta anti-drug ad; text story about Buster Crabbe & Billy the Kid	39	78	117	231	378	525
2-Williamson/Evans-c; text story about Wild Bill Hickok & Pecos Bill	37	74	111	218	354	490
3-Williamson/Evans-c/a	39	78	117	231	378	525
4-Frazetta-c/a, 1pg.; bondage-c	47	94	141	296	498	700
5-Frazetta-c; Williamson/Krenkel/Orlando-a, 11pgs. (per Mr. Williamson)	123	246	369	787	1344	1900
6,8	19	38	57	109	172	235
7-Frazetta one pg. ad	19	38	57	111	176	240
9-One pg. Frazetta Boy Scouts ad (1st?)	15	30	45	94	147	200
10-12	12	24	36	69	97	125

NOTE: Eastern Color sold 3 dozen each NM file copies of #s 9-12 a few years ago.

BUSTER CRABBE (The Amazing Adventures of...)(Movie star)
Lev Gleason Publications: Dec, 1953 - No. 4, June, 1954

	GD 2.0	VG 4.0	FN 6.0	VF 8.0	VF/NM 9.0	NM- 9.2
1,4: 1-Photo-c. 4-Flash Gordon-c	21	42	63	122	199	275
2,3-Toth-a	19	38	57	111	176	240

BUTCH CASSIDY
Skywald Comics: June, 1971 - No. 3, Oct, 1971 (52 pgs.)

	GD 2.0	VG 4.0	FN 6.0	VF 8.0	VF/NM 9.0	NM- 9.2
1-Pre-code reprints and new material; Red Mask reprint, retitled Maverick; Bolle-a; Sutton-a	3	6	9	16	22	28
2,3: 2-Whip Wilson-r. 3-Dead Canyon Days reprint/Crack Western No. 63; Sundance Kid app.; Crandall-a	2	4	6	10	14	18

BUTCH CASSIDY (...& the Wild Bunch)
Avon Periodicals: 1951

	GD 2.0	VG 4.0	FN 6.0	VF 8.0	VF/NM 9.0	NM- 9.2
1-Kinstler-c/a	19	38	57	111	176	240

NOTE: ***Reinman** story; Issue number on inside spine.*

BUTCH CASSIDY (See Fun-In No. 11 & Western Adventure Comics)

BUTCHER, THE (Also see Brave and the Bold, 2nd Series)
DC Comics: May, 1990 - No. 5, Sept, 1990 ($1.50, mature)

	GD 2.0	VG 4.0	FN 6.0	VF 8.0	VF/NM 9.0	NM- 9.2
1-5: 1-No indicia inside						3.00

BUTCHER KNIGHT
Image Comics (Top Cow): Jan, 2001 - No. 4, June, 2001 ($2.95, limited series)

	GD 2.0	VG 4.0	FN 6.0	VF 8.0	VF/NM 9.0	NM- 9.2
Preview (B&W, 16 pgs.) Dwayne Turner-c/a						3.0
1-4-Dwayne Turner-c/a						3.00

BUZ SAWYER (Sweeney No. 4 on)
Standard Comics: June, 1948 - No. 3, 1949

	GD 2.0	VG 4.0	FN 6.0	VF 8.0	VF/NM 9.0	NM- 9.2
1-Roy Crane-a	28	56	84	165	270	375
2-Intro his pal Sweeney	15	30	45	88	137	185
3	12	24	36	69	97	125

BUZ SAWYER'S PAL, ROSCOE SWEENEY (See Sweeney)

BUZZ, THE (Also see Spider-Girl)
Marvel Comics: July, 2000 - No. 3, Sept, 2000 ($2.99, limited series)

	GD 2.0	VG 4.0	FN 6.0	VF 8.0	VF/NM 9.0	NM- 9.2
1-3-Buscema-a/DeFalco & Frenz-s						3.00

BUZZARD (See The Goon)
Dark Horse Comics: Jun, 2010 - No. 3, Aug, 2010 ($3.50, limited series)

	GD 2.0	VG 4.0	FN 6.0	VF 8.0	VF/NM 9.0	NM- 9.2
1-3-Eric Powell-c; Buzzard story w/Powell-s/a; Billy The Kid back-up; Powell-s/Hotz-a						3.50

BUZZ BUZZ COMICS MAGAZINE
Horse Press: May, 1996 ($4.95, B&W, over-sized magazine)

	GD 2.0	VG 4.0	FN 6.0	VF 8.0	VF/NM 9.0	NM- 9.2
1-Paul Pope-c/a/scripts; Moebius-a						5.00

BUZZY (See All Funny Comics)
National Periodical Publications/Detective Comics: Winter, 1944-45 - No. 75, 1-2/57; No. 76, 10/57; No. 77, 10/58

	GD 2.0	VG 4.0	FN 6.0	VF 8.0	VF/NM 9.0	NM- 9.2
1 (52 pgs. begin); "America's favorite teenster"	33	66	99	194	317	440
2 (Spr, 1945)	17	34	51	98	154	210
3-5	14	28	42	76	108	140
6-10	11	22	33	60	83	105
11-20	10	20	30	54	72	90
21-30	9	18	27	47	61	75
31,35-38	8	16	24	44	57	70
32-34,39-Last 52 pgs. Scribbly story by Mayer in each (these four stories were done for Scribbly #14 which was delayed for a year)	9	18	27	50	65	80
40-77: 62-Last precode (2/55)	8	16	24	42	54	65

BUZZY THE CROW (See Harvey Comics Hits #60 & 62, Harvey Hits #18 & Paramount Animated Comics #1)

BY BIZARRE HANDS
Dark Horse Comics: Apr, 1994 - No. 3, June, 1994 ($2.50, B&W, mature)

	GD 2.0	VG 4.0	FN 6.0	VF 8.0	VF/NM 9.0	NM- 9.2
1-3: Lansdale stories						3.00

CABBOT: BLOODHUNTER (Also see Bloodstrike & Bloodstrike: Assassin)
Maximum Press: Jan, 1997 ($2.50, one-shot)

	GD 2.0	VG 4.0	FN 6.0	VF 8.0	VF/NM 9.0	NM- 9.2
1-Rick Veitch-a/script; Platt-c; Thor, Chapel & Prophet cameos						3.00

CABLE (See Ghost Rider &..., & New Mutants #87) (Title becomes Soldier X)
Marvel Comics: May, 1993 - No. 107, Sept, 2002 ($3.50/$1.95/$1.50-$2.25)

	GD 2.0	VG 4.0	FN 6.0	VF 8.0	VF/NM 9.0	NM- 9.2
1-($3.50, 52 pgs.)-Gold foil & embossed-c; Thibert a-1-4p; c-1-3						5.00
2-15: 3-Extra 16 pg. X-Men/Avengers ann. preview. 4-Liefeld-a assist; last Thibert-a(p).						

Cable (2008 series) #23 © MAR

Cage #1 © MAR

Calling All Boys #8 © PMI

GD 2.0 | VG 4.0 | FN 6.0 | VF 8.0 | VF/NM 9.0 | NM- 9.2

6-8-Reveals that Baby Nathan is Cable; gives background on Stryfe. 9-Omega Red-c/story. 11-Bound-in trading card sheet 3.50
16-Newsstand edition 3.00
16-Enhanced edition 5.00
17-20-($1.95)-Deluxe edition, 20-w/bound in '95 Fleer Ultra cards 3.50
17-20-($1.50)-Standard edition 3.00
21-24, 26-44, -1(7/97): 21-Begin $1.95-c; return from Age of Apocalyse. 24-Grizzly dies. 28-vs. Sugarman; Mr. Sinister app. 30-X-Man-c/app.; Exodus app. 31-vs. X-Man. 32-Post app. 33-Post-c/app; Mandarin app (flashback); includes "Onslaught Update". 34-Onslaught x-over; Hulk-c/app; Apocalypse app. (cont'd in Hulk #444). 35-Onslaught x-over; Apocalypse vs. Cable. 36-w/card insert. 38-Weapon X-c/app; Psycho Man & Micronauts app. 40-Scott Clark-a(p). 41-Bishop-c/app. 3.00
25 ($3.95)-Foil gatefold-c 4.00
45-49,51-74: 45-Operation Zero Tolerance. 51-1st Casey-s. 54-Black Panther. 55-Domino-c/app. 62-Nick Fury-c/app.63-Stryfe-c/app. 67,68-Avengers-c/app. 71,73-Liefeld-a 3.00
50-($2.99) Double sized w/wraparound-c 4.00
75 -($2.99) Liefeld-c/a; Apocalypse: The Twelve x-over 4.00
76-79: 76-Apocalypse: The Twelve x-over 3.00
80-96: 80-Begin $2.25-c. 87-Mystique-c/app. 3.00
97-99,101-107: 97-Tischman-s/Kordey-a/c begin 3.00
100-($3.99) Dialogue-free 'Nuff Said back-up story 4.00
... Classic Vol. 1 TPB (2008, $29.99) r/#1-4, New Mutants #87, Cable: Blood & Metal #1,2 30.00
.../Machine Man '98 Annual ($2.99) Wraparound-c 3.00
.../X-Force '96 Annual ($2.95) Wraparound-c 3.00
...'99 Annual ($3.50) vs. Sinister; computer photo-c 3.50
...Second Genesis 1 (9/99, $3.99) r/New Mutants #99, 100 and X-Force #1; Liefeld-c 4.00
...: The End (2002, $14.99, TPB) r/#101-107 15.00

CABLE
Marvel Comics: May, 2008 - No. 25, Jun, 2010 ($2.99/$3.99)

1-23: 1-10-Olivetti-c/a. 1-Liefeld var-c. 2-Finch var-c. 3-Romita Jr. var-c. 4-Bishop app.; Djurdjevic var-c. 5-Silvestri var-c. 6-Liefeld var-c. 13-15-Messiah War x-over; Deadpool app. 16,17-Gulacy-a 3.00
24,25-($3.99) 24-Bishop app. 25-Deadpool app.; Medina-a 4.00

CABLE - BLOOD AND METAL (Also see New Mutants #87 & X-Force #8)
Marvel Comics: Oct, 1992 - No. 2, Nov, 1992 ($2.50, limited series, 52 pgs.)

1-Fabian Nicieza scripts; John Romita, Jr.-c/a in both; Cable vs. Stryfe; 2nd app. of The Wild Pack (becomes The Six Pack); wraparound-c 4.00
2-Prelude to X-Cutioner's Song 3.00

CABLE/DEADPOOL ("Cable & Deadpool" on cover)
Marvel Comics: May, 2004 - No. 50, Apr, 2008 ($2.99)

1-49: 1-Nicieza-s/Liefeld-c. 7-9-X-Men app. 17-House of M. 21-Heroes For Hire app. 30,31-Civil War. 30-Great Lakes Avengers app. 33-Liefeld-c. 43,44-Wolverine app. 3.00
50-($3.99) Final issue; Spider-Man and the Avengers app. 4.00
... Vol. 1: If Looks Could Kill TPB (2004, $14.99) r/#1-6 15.00
... Vol. 2: The Burnt Offering TPB (2005, $14.99) r/#7-12 15.00
... Vol. 3: The Human Race TPB (2005, $14.99) r/#13-18 15.00
... Vol. 4: Bosom Buddies TPB (2006, $14.99) r/#19-24 15.00
... Vol. 5: Living Legends TPB (2006, $13.99) r/#25-29 14.00
... Vol. 6: Paved With Good Intentions TPB (2007, $14.99) r/#30-35 15.00
... Vol. 7: Separation Anxiety TPB (2007, $17.99) r/#36-42; sketch pages 18.00
Deadpool Vs. The Marvel Universe TPB (2008, $24.99) r/#43-50 25.00

CADET GRAY OF WEST POINT (See Dell Giants)

CADILLACS & DINOSAURS (TV)
Marvel Comics (Epic Comics): Nov, 1990 - No. 6, Apr, 1991 ($2.50, limited series)

1-6: r/Xenozoic Tales in color w/new-c 3.00
...In 3-D #1 (7/92, $3.95, Kitchen Sink)-With glasses 6.00

CADILLACS AND DINOSAURS (TV)
Topps Comics: V2#1, Feb, 1994 - V2#9, 1995 ($2.50, limited series)

V2#1-($2.95)-Collector's edition w/Stout-c & bound-in poster; Buckler-a; foil stamped logo; Giordano-a in all 6.00
V2#1-9: 1-Newsstand edition w/Giordano-c. 2,3-Collector's editions w/Stout-c & posters. 2,3-Newsstand ed. w/Giordano-c; w/o posters. 4-6-Collectors & Newsstand editions; Kieth-c. 7-9-Linsner-c 3.00

CAGE (Also see Hero for Hire, Power Man & Punisher)
Marvel Comics: Apr, 1992 - No. 20, Nov, 1993 ($1.25)

1,3,10,12: 3-Punisher-c & minor app. 10-Rhino & Hulk-c/app. 12-(52 pgs.)-Iron Fist app. 4.00
2,4-9,11,13-20: 9-Rhino-c/story; Hulk cameo 3.00

CAGE (Volume 3)
Marvel Comics (MAX): Mar, 2002 - No. 5, Sept, 2002 ($2.99, mature)

1-5-Corben-c/a; Azzarello-s 3.00
HC (2002, $19.99, with dustjacket) r/#1-5; intro. by Darius James; sketch pages 20.00
SC (2003, $13.99) r/#1-5; intro. by Darius James 14.00

CAGED HEAT 3000 (Movie)
Roger Corman's Cosmic Comics: Nov, 1995 - No. 3, Jan, 1996 ($2.50)

1-3: Adaptation of film 3.00

CAGES
Tundra Publ.: 1991 - No. 10, May, 1996 ($3.50/$3.95/$4.95, limited series)

	GD	VG	FN	VF	VF/NM	NM-
1-Dave McKean-c/a in all	2	4	6	8	10	12
2-Misprint exists	1	2	3	5	6	8
3-9: 5-$3.95-c begins						4.00
10-($4.95)						5.00

CAIN'S HUNDRED (TV)
Dell Publishing Co.: May-July, 1962 - No. 2, Sept-Nov, 1962

	GD	VG	FN	VF	VF/NM	NM-
nn(01-094-207)	3	6	9	20	30	40
2	3	6	9	16	22	28

CAIN/VAMPIRELLA FLIP BOOK
Harris Comics: Oct, 1994 ($6.95, one-shot, squarebound)

	GD	VG	FN	VF	VF/NM	NM-
nn-contains Cain #3 & #4; flip book is r/Vampirella story from 1993 Creepy Fearbook	1	2	3	5	7	9

CALIBER PRESENTS
Caliber Press: Jan, 1989 - No. 24, 1991 ($1.95/$2.50, B&W, 52 pgs.)

	GD	VG	FN	VF	VF/NM	NM-
1-Anthology; 1st app. The Crow; Tim Vigil-c/a	6	12	18	41	66	90
2-Deadworld story; Tim Vigil-a	2	4	6	10	14	18
3-24: 15-24 ($3.50, 68 pgs.)						4.00

CALIBER PRESENTS: CINDERELLA ON FIRE
Caliber Press: 1994 ($2.95, B&W, mature)

1 3.00

CALIBER SPOTLIGHT
Caliber Press: May, 1995 ($2.95, B&W)

1-Kabuki app 3.50

CALIFORNIA GIRLS
Eclipse Comics: June, 1987 - No. 8, May, 1988 ($2.00, 40 pgs, B&W)

1-8: All contain color paper dolls 3.00

CALL, THE
Marvel Comics: June, 2003 - No. 4, Sept, 2003 ($2.25)

1-4-Austen-s/Olliffe-a 3.00

CALLING ALL BOYS (Tex Granger No. 18 on)
Parents' Magazine Institute: Jan, 1946 - No. 17, May, 1948 (Photo c-1-5,7,8)

	GD	VG	FN	VF	VF/NM	NM-
1	14	28	42	82	121	160
2-Contains Roy Rogers article	9	18	27	50	65	80
3-7,9,11,14-17: 6-Painted-c. 11-Rin Tin Tin photo on-c; Tex Granger begins. 14-J. Edgar Hoover photo on-c. 15-Tex Granger-c begin	7	14	21	37	46	55
8-Milton Caniff story	9	18	27	52	69	85
10-Gary Cooper photo on-c	9	18	27	52	69	85
12-Bob Hope photo on-c	14	28	42	80	115	150
13-Bing Crosby photo on-c	12	24	36	69	97	125

CALLING ALL GIRLS
Parents' Magazine Institute: Sept, 1941 - No. 89, Sept, 1949 (Part magazine, part comic)

	GD	VG	FN	VF	VF/NM	NM-
1	20	40	60	114	182	250
2-Photo-c	11	22	33	62	86	110
3-Shirley Temple photo-c	15	30	45	85	130	175
4-10: 4,5,7,9-Photo-c. 9-Flag-c	10	20	30	54	72	90
11-Tina Thayer photo-c; Mickey Rooney photo-b/c; B&W photo inside of Gary Cooper as Lou Gehrig in "Pride of Yankees"	11	22	33	64	90	115
12-20	8	16	24	44	57	70
21-39,41-43(10-11/45)-Last issue with comics	9	18	27	47	61	75
40-Liz Taylor photo-c	21	42	63	126	206	285
44-51(7/46)-Last comic book size issue	7	14	21	37	46	55
52-89	6	12	18	31	38	45

NOTE: *Jack Sparling art in many issues; becomes a girls' magazine "Senior Prom" with #90.*

CALLING ALL KIDS (Also see True Comics)
Parents' Magazine Institute: Dec-Jan, 1945-46 - No. 26, Aug, 1949

	GD	VG	FN	VF	VF/NM	NM-
1-Funny animal	14	28	42	82	121	160
2	9	18	27	47	61	75
3-10	7	14	21	37	46	55

Camp Candy #2 © DIC

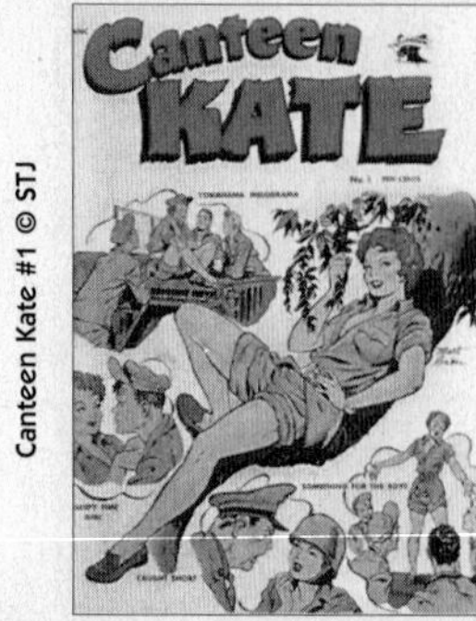

Canteen Kate #1 © STJ

Captain Action Season 2 #1 © CA Ent.

	GD 2.0	VG 4.0	FN 6.0	VF 8.0	VF/NM 9.0	NM- 9.2

11-26 7 14 21 35 43 50

CALL OF DUTY, THE : THE BROTHERHOOD
Marvel Comics: Aug, 2002 - No. 6, Jan, 2003 ($2.25)
1-Exploits of NYC Fire Dept.; Finch-c/a; Austen & Bruce Jones-s 4.00
2-6-Austen-s 3.00
...Vol 1: The Brotherhood & The Wagon TPB (2002, $14.99) r/#1-6 & ...The Wagon #1-4 15.00

CALL OF DUTY, THE : THE PRECINCT
Marvel Comics: Sept, 2002 - No. 5, Jan, 2003 ($2.25, limited series)
1-Exploits of NYC Police Dept.; Finch-c; Bruce Jones-s/Mandrake-a 3.00
2-4 3.00
...Vol 2: The Precinct TPB (2003, $9.99) r/#1-4 10.00

CALL OF DUTY, THE : THE WAGON
Marvel Comics: Oct, 2002 - No. 4, Jan, 2003 ($2.25, limited series)
1-4-Exploits of NYC EMS Dept.; Finch-c; Austen-s/Zelzej-a 3.00

CALVIN (See Li'l Kids)

CALVIN & THE COLONEL (TV)
Dell Publishing Co.: No. 1354, Apr-June, 1962 - No. 2, July-Sept, 1962
Four Color 1354(#1) 8 16 24 56 93 130
2 6 12 18 39 62 85

CAMELOT 3000
DC Comics: Dec, 1982 - No. 11, July, 1984; No. 12, Apr, 1985 (Direct sales, maxi series, Mando paper)
1-12: 1-Mike Barr scripts & Brian Bolland-c/a begin. 5-Intro Knights of New Camelot 4.00
TPB (1988, $12.95) r/#1-12 15.00
...: The Deluxe Edition (2008, $34.99, HC) r/#1-12; oversized & recolored; Barr intro.; design and promotional art; original proposal page 35.00
NOTE: *Austin a-7i-12i. Bolland a-1-12p; c-1-12.*

CAMERA COMICS
U.S. Camera Publishing Corp./ME: July, 1944 - No. 9, Summer, 1946
nn (7/44) 25 50 75 147 241 335
nn (9/44) 19 38 57 109 172 235
1(10/44)-The Grey Comet (slightly smaller page size than subsequent issues)
19 38 57 109 172 235
2-16 pgs. of photos with 32 pgs. of comics 14 28 42 82 121 160
3-Nazi WW II-c; photos 15 30 45 85 130 175
4-9: All 1/3 photos 13 26 39 74 105 135

CAMP CANDY (TV)
Marvel Comics: May, 1990 - No. 6, Oct, 1990 ($1.00, limited series)
1-6: Post-c/a(p); featuring John Candy 4.00

CAMP COMICS
Dell Publishing Co.: Feb, 1942 - No. 3, April, 1942 (All have photo-c)
1- "Seaman Sy Wheeler" by Kelly, 7 pgs.; Bugs Bunny app.; Mark Twain adaptation (scarce)
81 162 243 518 884 1250
2-Kelly-a, 12 pgs.; Bugs Bunny app.; classic-c 81 162 243 518 884 1250
3-(Scarce)-Dave Berg & Walt Kelly-a 61 122 183 390 670 950

CAMP RUNAMUCK (TV)
Dell Publishing Co.: Apr, 1966
1-Photo-c 4 8 12 22 34 45

CAMPUS LOVES
Quality Comics Group (Comic Magazines): Dec, 1949 - No. 5, Aug, 1950
1-Ward-c/a (9 pgs.) 35 70 105 208 339 470
2-Ward-c/a 26 52 78 154 252 350
3-5 15 30 45 83 124 165
NOTE: *Gustavson a-1-5. Photo c-3-5.*

CAMPUS ROMANCE (...Romances on cover)
Avon Periodicals/Realistic: Sept-Oct, 1949 - No. 3, Feb-Mar, 1950
1-Walter Johnson-a; c-/Avon paperback #348 30 60 90 177 289 400
2-Grandenetti-a; c-/Avon paperback #151 21 42 63 122 199 275
3-c-/Avon paperback #201 21 42 63 122 199 275
Realistic reprint 14 28 42 76 108 140

CANADA DRY PREMIUMS (See Swamp Fox, The & Terry & The Pirates in the Promotional Comics section)

CANCELLED COMIC CAVALCADE (See the Promotional Comics section)

CANDID TALES (Also see Bold Stories & It Rhymes With Lust)
Kirby Publ. Co.: April, 1950; June, 1950 (Digest size) (144 pgs.) (Full color)
nn-(Scarce) Contains Wood female pirate story, 15 pgs., and 14 pgs. in June issue; Powell-a
129 258 387 826 1413 2000
NOTE: *Another version exists with Dr. Kilmore by Wood; no female pirate story.*

CANDY (Teen-age)(Also see Police Comics #37)
Quality Comics Group (Comic Magazines): Autumn, 1947 - No. 64, Jul, 1956
1-Gustavson-a 24 48 72 140 230 320
2-Gustavson-a 14 28 42 82 121 160
3-10 10 20 30 56 76 95
11-30 8 16 24 42 54 65
31-64: 64-Ward-c(p)? 7 14 21 37 46 55
Super Reprint No. 2,10,12,16,17,18('63- '64):17-Candy #12
2 4 6 10 14 18
NOTE: *Jack Cole 1-2 pg. art in many issues.*

CANDY COMICS
William H. Wise & Co.: Fall, 1944 - No. 3, Spring, 1945
1-Two Scoop Scuttle stories by Wolverton 39 78 117 240 395 550
2,3-Scoop Scuttle by Wolverton, 2-4 pgs. 26 52 78 154 252 350

CANNON (See Heroes, Inc. Presents Cannon)

CANNON: DAWN OF WAR (Michael Turner's...)
Aspen MLT, Inc.: Nov, 2004 ($2.99)
1-Turnbull-a; two covers by Turnbull and Turner 3.00

CANNONBALL COMICS
Rural Home Publishing Co.: Feb, 1945 - No. 2, Mar, 1945
1-The Crash Kid, Thunderbrand, The Captive Prince & Crime Crusader begin; skull-c
103 206 309 659 1130 1600
2-Devil-c 77 154 231 493 847 1200

CANTEEN KATE (See All Picture All True Love Story & Fightin' Marines)
St. John Publishing Co.: June, 1952 - No. 3, Nov, 1952
1-Matt Baker-c/a 74 148 222 470 810 1150
2-Matt Baker-c/a 47 94 141 296 498 700
3-(Rare)-Used in **POP**, pg. 75; Baker-c/a 54 108 162 343 574 825

CAPE, THE
IDW Publishing: Dec, 2010 ($3.99)
1-Zach Howard-c/a; Jason Ciaramella-s 4.00

CAPER
DC Comics: Dec, 2003 - No. 12, Nov, 2004 ($2.95, limited series)
1-12: 1-4-Judd Winick-s/Farel Dalrymple-a. 5-8-John Severin-a. 9-12-Fowler-a 3.00

CAPES
Image Comics: Sept, 2003 - No. 3, Nov, 2003 ($3.50)
1-3-Robert Kirkman-s/Mark Englert-a/c 3.50

CAP'N QUICK & A FOOZLE (Also see Eclipse Mag. & Monthly)
Eclipse Comics: July, 1984 - No. 3, Nov, 1985 ($1.50, color, Baxter paper)
1-3-Rogers-c/a 3.00

CAPTAIN ACTION (Toy)
National Periodical Publications: Oct-Nov, 1968 - No. 5, June-July, 1969 (Based on Ideal toy)
1-Origin; Wood-a; Superman-c app. 7 14 21 45 73 100
2,3,5-Kane/Wood-a 5 10 15 34 55 75
4 4 8 12 28 44 60

CAPTAIN ACTION COMICS (Toy)
Moonstone: No. 0, 2008 - Present (Based on the Ideal toy)
0-($1.99) Origin re-told; Sparacio-a; three covers; character history by Michael Eury 3.00
1-5: 1-($3.99) Sparacio-a; intro. by Jim Shooter 4.00
... Comics Special 1 (2010, $5.99) 3 covers by Barreto, Ordway & Spiegle 6.00
...: First Mission, Last Day (2008, $3.99) origin story re-told; Nicieza-s/Procopio-a 4.00
... Season 2 (2010, $3.99) 1-3: 1-Covers by Allred & Texiera; Obama app. 4.00
... Winter Special (2011, $4.99) Green Hornet & Kato on-c & text story 5.00

CAPTAIN AERO COMICS (Samson No. 1-6; also see Veri Best Sure Fire & Veri Best Sure Shot Comics)
Holyoke Publishing Co.: V1#7(#1), Dec, 1941 - V2#4(#10), Jan, 1943; V3#9(#11), Sept, 1943 -V4#3(#17), Oct, 1944; #21, Dec, 1944 - #26, Aug, 1946 (No #18-20)
V1#7(#1)-Flag-Man & Solar, Master of Magic, Captain Aero, Cap Stone, Adventurer begin; Nazi WWII-c 187 374 561 1197 2049 2900
8,10: 8(#2)-Pals of Freedom app. 10(#4)-Origin The Gargoyle; Kubert-a
94 188 282 597 1024 1450
9(#3)-Hitler-sty; Catman back-c; Alias X begins; Pals of Freedom app.
106 212 318 673 1162 1650
11,12(#5,6)-Kubert-a; Miss Victory in #6 74 148 222 470 810 1150
V2#1,2(#7,8): 8-Origin The Red Cross; Miss Victory app.; Brodsky-c(i)

Captain America #100 © MAR

Captain America #225 © MAR

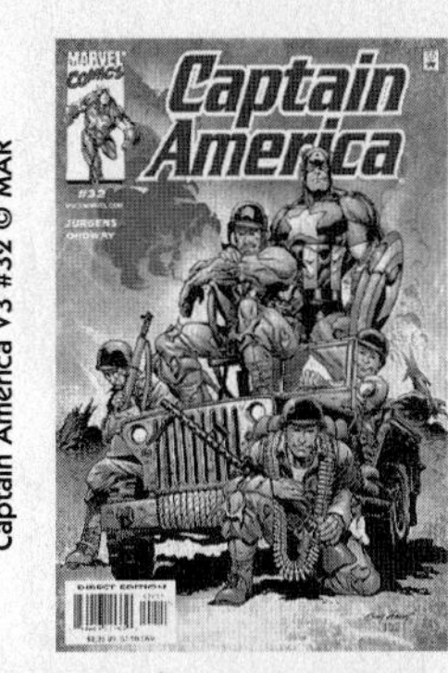

Captain America V3 #32 © MAR

GD 2.0 VG 4.0 FN 6.0 VF 8.0 VF/NM 9.0 NM- 9.2

45 90 135 284 480 675
3(#9)-Miss Victory app. 41 82 123 260 438 615
4(#10)-Miss Victory app.; Japanese WWII-c 39 78 117 231 378 525
V3#9 - V3#12(#11-14): All Quinlan Japanese WWII-c. 9-Miss Victory app.
31 62 93 182 296 410
V3#13(#15),V4#2(#16): Schomburg Japanese WWII-c. 13-Miss Victory app.
39 78 117 231 378 525
V4#3(#17), 21-24-L. B. Cole Japanese WWII covers. 22-Intro/origin Mighty Mite.
52 104 156 322 549 775
25-L. B. Cole SciFi-c 54 108 162 343 574 825
26-L. B. Cole SciFi-c; Palais-a(2) (scarce) 129 258 387 826 1413 2000
NOTE: ***L.B. Cole*** *c-17, 21-26.* ***Hollingsworth*** *a-23.* ***Infantino*** *a-23, 26.* ***Schomburg*** *c-15, 16.*

CAPTAIN AMERICA (See Adventures of..., All-Select, All Winners, Aurora, Avengers #4, Blood and Glory, Captain Britain 16-20, Giant-Size..., The Invaders, Marvel Double Feature, Marvel Fanfare, Marvel Mystery, Marvel Super-Action, Marvel Super Heroes V2#3, Marvel Team-Up, Marvel Treasury Special, Power Record Comics, Ultimates, USA Comics, Young Allies & Young Men)

CAPTAIN AMERICA (Formerly Tales of Suspense #1-99) (Captain America and the Falcon #134-223 & Steve Rogers: Captain America #444-454 appears on cover only)
Marvel Comics Group: No. 100, Apr, 1968 - No. 454, Aug, 1996

100-Flashback on Cap's revival with Avengers & Sub-Mariner; story continued
from Tales of Suspense #99; Kirby-c/a begins 28 56 84 215 433 650
101-The Sleeper-c/story; Red Skull app. 9 18 27 63 107 150
102-104: 102-Sleeper-c/s. 103,104-Red Skull-c/sty 7 14 21 49 80 110
105-108: 107-Red Skull & Hitler-c 6 12 18 41 66 90
109-Origin Capt. America retold in detail 8 16 24 58 97 135
109-2nd printing (1994) 2 4 6 8 10 12
110-Rick Jones dons Bucky's costume & becomes Cap's partner; Hulk x-over; Steranko-a
Classic Steranko-c 10 20 30 70 125 180
111,113-Classic Steranko-c/a: 111-Death of Steve Rogers. 113-Cap's funeral; Avengers app.
9 18 27 64 110 155
112-S.A. recovery retold; last Kirby-c/a 6 12 18 37 59 80
114-116,119,120: 115-Last 12¢ issue 4 8 12 26 41 55
117-1st app. The Falcon (9/69) 11 22 33 80 150 220
118-2nd app. The Falcon 6 12 18 39 62 85
121-136,139,140: 121-Retells origin. 133-The Falcon becomes Cap's partner; origin Modok.
140-Origin Grey Gargoyle retold 3 6 9 19 29 38
137,138-Spider-Man x-over 4 8 12 23 36 48
141,142: 142-Last 15¢ issue 3 6 9 16 23 30
143-(52 pgs). 3 6 9 19 29 38
144-153: 144-New costume Falcon. 153-1st brief app. Jack Monroe
2 4 6 13 18 22
154-1st full app. Jack Monroe (Nomad)(10/72) 3 6 9 14 19 24
155-Origin re-told; origin Jack Monroe 3 6 9 14 19 24
156-171,176-179: 155-158-Cap's strength increased. 160-1st app. Solarr. 164-1st app.
Nightshade. 176-End of Capt. America. 2 4 6 8 11 14
172-175: X-Men x-over 2 4 6 13 18 22
180-Intro/origin of Nomad (Steve Rogers) 3 6 9 14 19 24
181-Intro/origin new Cap. 2 4 6 11 16 20
182,184-192: 186-True origin The Falcon 2 3 4 6 8 10
183-Death of new Cap; Nomad becomes Cap 2 4 6 9 12 15
193-Kirby-c/a begins 2 4 6 13 18 22
194-199-(Regular 25¢ edition)(4-7/76) 2 4 6 10 14 18
196-199-(30¢-c variants, limited distribution) 5 10 15 32 51 70
200-(Regular 25¢ edition)(8/76) 2 4 6 11 16 20
200-(30¢-c variant, limited distribution) 6 12 18 37 59 80
201-214-Kirby-c/a 2 4 6 8 11 14
210-214-(35¢-c variants, limited dist.)(6-10/77) 7 14 21 45 73 100
215,216,218-229,231-234,236-240,242-246: 215-Retells Cap's origin. 216-r/story from Strange Tales #114. 229-Marvel Man app. 233-Death of Sharon Carter. 234-Daredevil x-over.
244,245-Miller-c 6.00
217,230,235: 217-1st app. Marvel Man (later Quasar). 230-Battles Hulk-c/story cont'd in
Hulk #232. 235-(7/79) Daredevil x-over; Miller-a(p)1 2 3 4 5 7
241-Punisher app.; Miller-c. 3 6 9 19 29 38
241-2nd print 3.00
247-255-Byrne-a. 255-Origin; Miller-c. 1 2 3 5 7 9
256-281,284,285,289-322,324-326,328-331: 264-Old X-Men cameo in flashback.
265,266-Nick Fury & Spider-Man app. 267-1st app. Everyman. 269-1st Team America.
279-(3/83)-Contains Tattooz skin decals. 281-1950s Bucky returns. 284-Patriot (Jack Mace)
app. 285-Death of Patriot. 298-Origin Red Skull. 328-Origin & 1st app. D-Man 3.00
282-Bucky becomes new Nomad (Jack Monroe) 5.00
282-Silver ink 2nd print ($1.75) w/original date (6/83) 3.00
283,327,333-340: 283-2nd app. Nomad. 327-Capt. Amer. battles Super Patriot. 333-Intro &
origin new Captain (Super Patriot). 339-Fall of the Mutants tie-in 4.00
286-288-Deathlok app. 4.00
323-1st app. new Super Patriot (see Nick Fury) 4.00
332-Old Cap resigns 1 2 3 5 6 8
341-343,345-349 3.00
344-($1.50, 52 pgs.)-Ronald Reagan cameo 4.00
350-($1.75, 68 pgs.)-Return of Steve Rogers (original Cap) to original costume 4.00
351-382,384-396: 351-Nick Fury app. 354-1st app. U.S. Agent (6/89, see Avengers West
Coast). 360-1st app. Crossbones. 375-Daredevil app. 386-U.S. Agent app. 387-389-Red
Skull back-up stories. 396-Last $1.00-c. 396,397-1st app. all new Jack O'Lantern 3.00
383-($2.00, 68 pgs.)-50th anniversary issue; Red Skull story; Jim Lee-c(i) 4.00
397-399,401-424,425: 402-Begin 6 part Man-Wolf story w/Wolverine in #403-407.
405-410-New Jack O'Lantern app. in back-up story. 406-Cable & Shatterstar cameo.
407-Capwolf vs. Cable-c/story. 408-Infinity War x-over; Falcon solo back-up.
423-Vs. Namor-c/story 3.00
400-($2.25, 84 pgs.)-Flip book format w/double gatefold-c; r/Avengers #4 plus-c; contains
cover pin-ups. 4.00
425-($2.95, 52 pgs.)-Embossed Foil-c ed.n; Fighting Chance Pt. 1 4.00
426-443,446,447,449-453: 427-Begin $1.50-c; bound-in trading card sheet. 449-Thor app.
450-"Man Without A Country" storyline begins, ends #453; Bill Clinton app; variant-c exists.
451-1st app.Cap's new costume. 453-Cap gets old costume back; Bill Clinton app. 3.00
444-Mark Waid scripts & Ron Garney-c/a(p) begins, ends #454; Avengers app. 5.00
445,454: 445-Sharon Carter & Red Skull return. 4.00
448-($2.95, double-sized issue)-Waid script & Garney-c/a; Red Skull "dies" 5.00
#600-up (See Captain America 2005 series, resumed original numbering after #50)
Special 1(1/71)-Origin retold 6 12 18 37 59 80
Special 2(1/72, 52 pgs.)-Colan-r/Not Brand Echh; all-r 4 8 12 22 34 45
Annual 3('76, 52 pgs.)-Kirby-c/a(new) 3 6 9 16 23 30
Annual 4('77, 34 pgs.)-Magneto-c/story 3 6 9 16 23 30
Annual 5-7: (52 pgs.)('81-'83) 5.00
Annual 8(9/86)-Wolverine-c/story 3 6 9 20 30 40
Annual 9-13('90-'94, 68 pgs.)-9-Nomad back-up. 10-Origin retold (2 pgs.). 11-Falcon solo story.
12-Bagged w/card. 13-Red Skull-c/story 4.00
...Ashcan Edition ('95, 75¢) 3.00
... and the Falcon: Madbomb TPB (2004, $16.99) r/#193-200; Kirby-s/a 17.00
... and the Falcon: Nomad TPB (2006, $24.99) r/#177-186; Cap becomes Nomad 25.00
... and the Falcon: Secret Empire TPB (2005, $19.99) r/#169-176 20.00
... and the Falcon: The Swine TPB (2006, $29.99) r/#206-214 & Annual #3,4 30.00
... By Jack Kirby: Bicentennial Battles TPB (2005, $19.99) r/#201-205 & Marvel Treasury
Special Featuring Captain America's Bicentennial Battles; Kirby-s/a 20.00
...: Deathlok Lives! nn(10/93, $4.95)-r/#286-288 5.00
...Drug War 1-(1994, $2.00, 52 pgs.)-New Warriors app. 4.00
...Man Without a Country(1998, $12.99, TPB)-r/#450-453 13.00
...Medusa Effect 1 (1994, $2.95, 68 pgs.)-Origin Baron Zemo 4.00
...Operation Rebirth (1996, $9.95)-r/#445-448 10.00
... 65th Anniversary Special (5/06, $3.99) WWII flashback with Bucky; Brubaker-s 4.00
...Streets of Poison ($15.95)-r/#372-378 16.00
...: The Movie Special nn (5/92, $3.50, 52 pgs.)-Adapts movie; printed on coated stock;
The Red Skull app. 4.00
NOTE: ***Austin*** *c-225i, 239i, 246i.* ***Buscema*** *a-115p, 217p; c-136p, 217, 297.* ***Byrne*** *c-223(part), 238, 239, 247p-254p, 290, 291, 313p; a-247-254p, 255, 313p, 350.* ***Colan*** *a(p)-116-137, 256, Annual 5; c(p)-116-123, 126, 129.* ***Everett*** *a-136i, 137i; c-126i.* ***Garney*** *a(p)-444-454.* ***Gil Kane*** *a-145p; c-147p, 149p, 150p, 170p, 172-174, 180, 181p, 183-190p, 215, 216, 220, 221.* ***Kirby*** *a(p)-100-109, 112, 193-214, 216, Special 1, 2(layouts), Annual 3, 4; c-100-109, 112, 126p, 193-214.* ***Ron Lim*** *a(p)-366, 368-378, 380-386; c-366p, 368-378p, 379, 380-393p.* ***Miller*** *c-241p, 244p, 245p, 255p, Annual 5.* ***Mooney*** *a-149i.* ***Morrow*** *a-144.* ***Perez*** *c-243p, 246p.* ***Robbins*** *c(p)-183-187, 189-192, 225.* ***Roussos*** *a-140i, 168i.* ***Shores*** *a-102i, 107i, 109i.* ***Starlin/Sinnott*** *c-162.* ***Sutton*** *a-244i.* ***Tuska*** *a-112i, 215p, Special 2.* ***Waid*** *scripts-444-454.* ***Williamson*** *a-313i.* ***Wood*** *a-127i.* ***Zeck*** *a-263-289; c-300.*

CAPTAIN AMERICA (Volume Two)
Marvel Comics: V2#1, Nov, 1996 - No. 13, Nov, 1997($2.95/$1.95/$1.99)
(Produced by Extreme Studios)

1-($2.95)-Heroes Reborn begins; Liefeld-c/a; Loeb scripts; reintro Nick Fury 6.00
1-($2.95)-(Variant-c)-Liefeld-c/a 6.00
1-(7/96, $2.95)-(Exclusive Comicon Ed.)-Liefeld-c/a. 1 2 3 5 6 8
2-11,13: 5-Two-c. 6-Cable-c/app. 13-"World War 3"-pt. 4, x-over w/Image 3.00
12-($2.99) "Heroes Reunited"-pt. 4 4.00
Heroes Reborn: Captain America (2006, $29.99, TPB) r/#1-12 & Heroes Reborn #1/2 30.00

CAPTAIN AMERICA (Vol. Three) (Also see Capt. America: Sentinel of Liberty)
Marvel Comics: Jan, 1998 - No. 50, Feb, 2002 ($2.99/$1.99/$2.25)

1-($2.99) Mark Waid-s/Ron Garney-a 4.00
1-Variant cover 6.00
2-($1.99): 2-Two covers 3.00
3-11: 3-Returns to old shield. 4-Hawkeye app. 5-Thor-c/app. 7-Andy Kubert-c/a begin.
9-New shield 3.00
12-($2.99) Battles Nightmare; Red Skull back-up story 4.00
13-17,19-Red Skull returns 3.00
18-($2.99) Cap vs. Korvac in the Future 4.00

Captain America V4 #4 © MAR

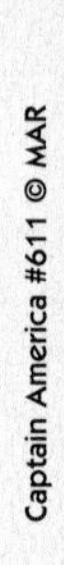

Captain America #611 © MAR

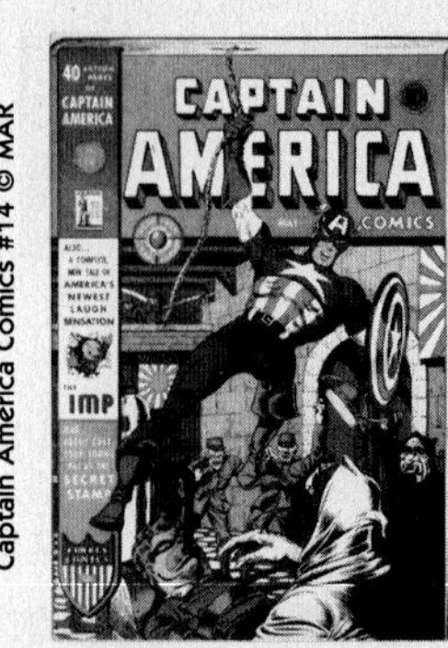

Captain America Comics #14 © MAR

GD 2.0 | VG 4.0 | FN 6.0 | VF 8.0 | VF/NM 9.0 | NM- 9.2

20-24,26-29: 20,21-Sgt. Fury back-up story painted by Evans 3.00
25-($2.99) Cap & Falcon vs. Hatemonger 4.00
30-49: 30-Begin $2.25-c. 32-Ordway-a. 33-Jurgens-s/a begins; U.S. Agent app. 36-Maximum Security x-over. 41,46-Red Skull app. 3.00
50-($5.95) Stories by various incl. Jurgens, Quitely, Immonen; Ha-c 6.00
.../Citizen V '98 Annual ($3.50) Busiek & Kesel-s 4.00
1999 Annual ($3.50) Flag Smasher app. 4.00
2000 Annual ($3.50) Continued from #35 vs. Protocide; Jurgens-s 4.00
2001 Annual ($2.99) Golden Age flashback; Invaders app. 4.00
...: To Serve and Protect TPB (2/02, $17.95) r/Vol. 3 #1-7 18.00

CAPTAIN AMERICA (Volume 4)
Marvel Comics: Jun, 2002 - No. 32, Dec, 2004 ($3.99/$2.99)

1-Ney Rieber-s/Cassaday-c/a 4.00
2-9-($2.99) 3-Cap reveals Steve Rogers ID. 7-9-Hairsine-a 3.00
10-32: 10-16-Jae Lee-a. 17-20-Gibbons-s/Weeks-a. 21-26-Bachalo-a. 26-Bucky flashback. 27,28-Eddie Campbell-a. 29-32-Red Skull app. 3.00
...Vol. 1: The New Deal HC (2003, $22.99) r/#1-6; foreward by Max Allan Collins 23.00
...Vol. 2: The Extremists TPB (2003, $13.99) r/#7-11; Cassaday-c 14.00
...Vol. 3: Ice TPB (2003, $12.99) r/#12-16; Jae Lee-a; Cassaday-c 13.00
...Vol. 4: Cap Lives TPB (2004, $12.99) r/#17-22 & Tales of Suspense #66 13.00
Avengers Disassembled: Captain America TPB (2004, $17.99) r/#29-32 and Captain America and the Falcon #5-7 18.00

CAPTAIN AMERICA
Marvel Comics: Jan, 2005 - Present ($2.99)

1-Brubaker-s/Epting-c/a; Red Skull app. 4.00
2-24: 10-House of M. 11-Origin of the Winter Soldier. 13-Iron Man app. 24-Civil War 3.00
6,8-Retailer variant covers 6.00
25-($3.99) Captain America shot dead; handcuffed red glove cover by Epting 10.00
25-($3.99) Variant edition with running Cap cover by McGuinness 12.00
25-($3.99) 2nd printing with "The Death of The Dream" cover by Epting 4.00
25 Director's Cut-($4.99) w/script with Brubaker commentary; pencil pages, variant and un-used covers gallery; article on media hype 5.00
26-33-Falcon & Winter Soldier app. 3.00
34-(3/08) Bucky becomes the new Captain America; Alex Ross-c 3.00
34-Variant-c by Steve Epting 3.00
34-($3.99) Director's Cut; includes script; pencil art, costume designs, cover gallery 4.00
34-DF Edition with Alex Ross portrait cover; signed by Ross 25.00
35-49-Bucky as Captain America. 43-45-Batroc app. 46,47-Sub-Mariner app. 3.00
50-(7/09, $3.99) Bucky's birthday flashbacks; Captain America's life synopsis; Martin-a 4.00

(After #50, numbering reverts to original with #600, Aug, 2009)

600-(8/09, $4.99) Covers by Ross and Epting; leads into Captain America: Reborn series; art by Guice, Chaykin, Ross, Eaglesham; commentary by Joe Simon; cover gallery 5.00
601-615-($3.99) 601-Gene Colan-a; 3 covers. 602-Nomad back-up feature begins. 606-Baron Zemo returns. 611-615-Trial of Captain America 4.00
615.1 (5/11, $2.99) Brubaker-s/Breitweiser-a/Acuña-c 3.00
616-(5/11, $4.99) 70th Anniversary Issue; short stories by Brubaker, Chaykin, Deodato, McGuinness, Grist and others, Charest-c 5.00
616-Variant-c by Epting 8.00
... and Batroc (5/11, $3.99) Gillen-s/Arlem-a; Bucky vs. Batroc in Paris 4.00
... and Crossbones (5/11, $3.99) Harms-s/Shalvey-a/Tocchini-c 4.00
... and Falcon (5/11, $3.99) Williams-s/Isaacs-a/Tocchini-c 4.00
... and the First Thirteen (5/11, $3.99) Peggy Carter in WWII France 1943 4.00
... and the Secret Avengers (5/11, $3.99) DeConnick-s/Tocchini-a/c; Black Widow app. 4.00
... By Ed Brubaker Omnibus Vol. 1 HC (2007, $74.99, dustjacket) r/#1-25; Capt. America 65th Anniv. Spec. and Winter Soldier: Winter Kills; Brubaker intro.; bonus material 75.00
Civil War: Captain America TPB (2007, $11.99) r/#22-24 & Winter Soldier: Winter Kills 12.00
...: Fighting Avenger (6/11, $4.99) 1st WWII mission; Gurihiru-a/c; Kitson var-c 5.00
...MGC #1 (5/10, $1.00) r/#1 with "Marvel's Greatest Comics" cover logo 1.00
...: Red Menace Vol. 1 SC (2006, $11.99) r/#15-17 and 65th Anniversary Special 12.00
...: Red Menace Vol. 2 SC (2006, $10.99) r/#18-21; Brubaker interview 11.00
... Theater of War: America First! (2/09, $3.99) 1950s era tale; Chaykin-s/a; reprints 4.00
... Theater of War: America the Beautiful (3/09, $4.99) WW2 tale; Jenkins-s/Erskine-a 5.00
... Theater of War: Operation Zero-Point (12/08, $3.99) WW2 tale; Breitweiser-a 4.00
...: The Death of Captain America Vol. 1 HC (2007, $19.99) r/#25-30; variant covers 20.00
...: The Death of Captan America Vol. 2 HC (2008, $19.99) r/#31-36; variant covers 20.00
...Vol. 1: Winter Soldier HC (2005, $21.99) r/#1-7; concept sketches 22.00
...Vol. 1: Winter Soldier SC (2006, $16.99) r/#1-7; concept sketches 17.00
...: Who Won't Wield the Shield (6/10, $3.99) Deadpool & Forbush Man app. 4.00
...: Winter Soldier Vol. 2 HC (2006, $19.99) r/#8,9,11-14 20.00
...: Winter Soldier Vol. 2 SC (2006, $14.99) r/#8,9,11-14 15.00

CAPTAIN AMERICA AND THE FALCON
Marvel Comics: May, 2004 - No. 14, June, 2005 ($2.99, limited series)

1-4-Priest-s/Sears-a 3.00
5-14: 5-8-Avengers Disassembled x-over. 6,7-Scarlet Witch app. 8-12-Modok app. 3.00
... Vol. 1: Two Americas (2005, $9.99) r/#1-4 10.00
... Vol. 2: Brothers and Keepers (2005, $17.99) r/#8-14 18.00

CAPTAIN AMERICA & THE KORVAC SAGA
Marvel Comics: Feb, 2011 - No. 4, May, 2011 ($2.99, limited series)

1-4-McCool-s/Rousseau-a/c. 4-Galactus app. 3.00

CAPTAIN AMERICA/BLACK PANTHER (See Black Panther/Captain America: Flags of Our Fathers)

CAPTAIN AMERICA COMICS
Timely/Marvel Comics (TCI 1-20/CmPS 21-68/MjMC 69-75/Atlas Comics (PrPI 76-78): Mar, 1941 - No. 75, Feb, 1950; No. 76, 5/54 - No. 78, 9/54
(No. 74 & 75 titled Capt. America's Weird Tales)

Issue	GD 2.0	VG 4.0	FN 6.0	VF 8.0	VF/NM 9.0	NM- 9.2
1-Origin & 1st app. Captain America & Bucky by S&K; Hurricane, Tuk the Caveboy begin by S&K; 1st app. Red Skull; Hitler-c (by Simon?); intro of the "Capt. America Sentinels of Liberty Club" (advertised on inside front-c.); indicia reads Vol. 2, Number 1	10,000	20,000	30,000	70,000	142,500	240,000
2-S&K Hurricane; Tuk by Avison (Kirby splash); classic Hitler-c	1850	3700	5550	13,690	25,845	38,000
3-Classic Red Skull-c & app; Stan Lee's 1st text (1st work for Marvel)	1460	2920	4380	10,804	20,402	30,000
4-Early use of full pg. panel in comic; back-c pin-up of Captain America and Bucky	919	1838	2757	6709	11,855	17,000
5	865	1730	2595	6315	11,158	16,000
6-Origin Father Time; Tuk the Caveboy ends	757	1514	2271	5526	9763	14,000
7-Red Skull app.; classic-c	838	1676	2514	6117	10,809	15,500
8-10-Last S&K issue, (S&K centerfold #6-10)	595	1190	1785	4350	7675	11,000
11-Last Hurricane, Headline Hunter; Al Avison Captain America begins, ends #20; Avison-c(p)	459	918	1377	3350	5925	8500
12-The Imp begins, ends #16; last Father Time	443	886	1329	3234	5667	8200
13-Origin The Secret Stamp; classic-c	541	1082	1623	3950	6975	10,000
14,15	443	886	1329	3234	5667	8200
16-Red Skull unmasks Cap; Red Skull-c	595	1190	1785	4350	7675	11,000
17-The Fighting Fool only app.	411	822	1233	2877	5039	7200
18-Classic-c	423	846	1269	3000	5250	7500
19-Human Torch begins #19	366	732	1098	2562	4481	6400
20-Sub-Mariner app.; no Human Torch	360	720	1080	2520	4410	6300
21-25: 25-Cap drinks liquid opium	343	686	1029	2400	4200	6000
26-30: 27-Last Secret Stamp; last 68 pg. issue. 28-60 pg. issues begin.	331	662	993	2317	4059	5800
31-35,38-40: 34-Centerfold poster of Cap	300	600	900	2010	3505	5000
36-Classic Hitler-c	400	800	1200	2800	4900	7000
37-Red Skull app.	343	686	1029	2400	4200	6000
41-45,47: 41-Last Japan War-c. 47-Last German War-c	258	516	774	1651	2826	4000
46-German Holocaust-c; classic	411	822	1233	2877	5039	7200
48-58,60	174	348	522	1114	1907	2700
59-Origin retold	320	640	960	2240	3920	5600
61-Red Skull-c/story	343	686	1029	2400	4200	6000
62,64,65: 65-Kurtzman's "Hey Look"	226	452	678	1446	2473	3500
63-Intro/origin Asbestos Lady	232	464	696	1485	2543	3600
66-Bucky is shot; Golden Girl teams up with Captain America & learns his i.d; origin Golden Girl	297	594	891	1901	3251	4600
67-69: 67-Captain America/Golden Girl team-up; Mxyztplk swipe; last Toro in Human Torch. 68-Sub-Mariner/Namora, and Captain America/Golden Girl team-up. 69-Human Torch/Sun Girl team-up.	290	580	870	1856	3178	4500
70-73: 70-Sub-Mariner/Namora, and Captain America/Golden Girl team-up. 70-SciFi-c/story. 71-Anti Wertham editorial; The Witness, Bucky app.	300	600	900	2010	3505	5000
74-(Scarce)(10/49)-Titled "Captain America's Weird Tales"; Red Skull-c & app.; classic-c	892	1784	2676	6512	11,506	16,500
75(2/50)-Titled "C.A.'s Weird Tales"; no C.A. app.; horror cover/stories	300	600	900	2010	3505	5000
76-78(1954): Human Torch/Toro stories; all have communist-c/stories	161	322	483	1030	1765	2500
132-Pg. Issue (B&W-1942)(Canadian)-Very rare. Has blank inside-c and back-c; contains Marvel Mystery #33 & Captain America #18 w/cover from Captain America #22; same contents as one version of the Marvel Mystery annuals	5833	11,667	17,500	35,000	-	-

NOTE: ***Crandall*** *a-2i, 3i, 9i, 10i.* ***Kirby*** *c-1, 2, 5-8p.* ***Rico*** *c-69-71.* ***Romita*** *c-77, 78.* ***Schomburg*** *c-3, 4, 26-29, 31, 33, 37-39, 41, 42, 45-54, 58.* ***Sekowsky*** *c-55, 56.* ***Shores*** *c-1i, 2i, 5-7i, 11i, 20-25, 30, 32, 34, 35, 40, 57, 59-67.* ***S&K*** *c-9, 10. Bondage c-3, 7, 15, 16, 34, 38.*

CAPTAIN AMERICA COMICS #1 70TH ANNIVERSARY EDITION
Marvel Comics: May, 2011 ($4.99, one-shot)

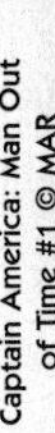
Captain America: Man Out of Time #1 © MAR

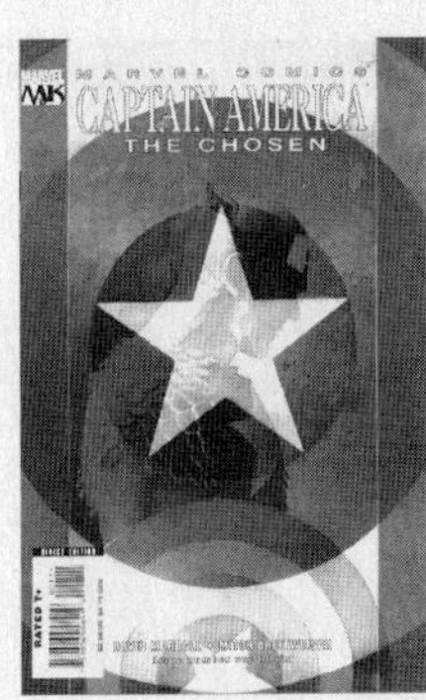

Captain America: The Chosen #1 © MAR

Captain Atom #5 © Nationwide

	GD 2.0	VG 4.0	FN 6.0	VF 8.0	VF/NM 9.0	NM- 9.2

1-Recolored reprint of entire 1941 issue including Hurricane & Tuk stories; Ching-c 5.00

CAPTAIN AMERICA COMICS 70TH ANNIVERSARY SPECIAL
Marvel Comics: June, 2009 ($3.99, one-shot)

1-WWII flashback; Marcos Martin-a; Marcos-2 covers; r/Capt. America Comics #7 4.00

CAPTAIN AMERICA: DEAD MEN RUNNING
Marvel Comics: Mar, 2002 - No. 3, May, 2002 ($2.99, limited series)

1-3-Macan-s/Zezelj-a 3.00

CAPTAIN AMERICA: FOREVER ALLIES
Marvel Comics: Oct, 2010 - No. 4, Jan, 2011 ($3.99, limited series)

1-4-Stern-s/Dragotta-a; Bucky in present & WW2 flashbacks; Young Allies app. 4.00

CAPTAIN AMERICA: HAIL HYDRA
Marvel Comics: Mar, 2011 - No. 5, Jul, 2011 ($2.99, limited series)

1-4-Cap vs. Hydra; Granov-c. 1-WWII flashback. 2-Kirby-style art by Scioli. 4-Hotz-a 3.00

CAPTAIN AMERICA: MAN OUT OF TIME
Marvel Comics: Jan, 2011 - No. 5, May, 2011 ($3.99, limited series)

1-5-Waid-s/Molina-a/Hitch-c; Cap's unfreezing in modern times re-told 4.00

CAPTAIN AMERICA/NICK FURY: BLOOD TRUCE
Marvel Comics: Feb, 1995 ($5.95, one-shot, squarebound)

nn-Chaykin story 6.00

CAPTAIN AMERICA/NICK FURY: THE OTHERWORLD WAR
Marvel Comics: Oct, 2001 ($6.95, one-shot, squarebound)

nn-Manco-a; Bucky and Red Skull app. 7.00

CAPTAIN AMERICA: PATRIOT
Marvel Comics: Nov, 2010 - No. 4, Feb, 2011 ($3.99, limited series)

1-4-Kesel-s/Breitweiser-a; 1-WW2 story; Patriot & the Liberty Legion app. 4.00

CAPTAIN AMERICA: REBORN (Titled Reborn in #1-3)
Marvel Comics: Sept, 2009 - No. 6, Mar, 2010 ($3.99, limited series)

1-6-Steve Rogers returns from the dead; Brubaker-s/Hitch & Guice-a. 1-Covers by Hitch, Ross & Quesada. 2-Origin re-told. 4-Joe Kubert var-c. 5-Cassaday var-c 4.00
1-4-Variant-c by Cassaday. 2-Variant-c by Sale. 5-Finch var-c 10.00
... MGC #1 (5/11, $1.00) r/#1 with "Marvel's Greatest Comics" logo on cover 1.00
...: Who Will Wield the Shield? (2/10, $3.99) Aftermath of series; Guice & Luke Ross-a 4.00

CAPTAIN AMERICA: RED, WHITE & BLUE
Marvel Comics: Sept, 2002 ($29.99, one-shot, hardcover with dustjacket)

nn-Reprints from Lee & Kirby, Steranko, Miller and others; and new short stories and pin-ups by various incl. Ross, Dini, Timm, Waid, Dorkin, Sienkiewicz, Miller, Bruce Jones, Collins, Piers-Rayner, Pope, Deodato, Quitely, Nino; Stelfreeze-c 30.00
TPB (2007, $19.99) 20.00

CAPTAIN AMERICA, SENTINEL OF LIBERTY (See Fireside Book Series)

CAPTAIN AMERICA: SENTINEL OF LIBERTY
Marvel Comics: Sept, 1998 - No. 12, Aug, 1999 ($1.99)

1-Waid-s/Garney-a 3.00
1-Rough Cut ($2.99) Features original script and pencil pages 3.00
2-5: 2-Two-c; Invaders WW2 story 2.50
6-($2.99) Iron Man-c/app. 3.00
7-11: 8-Falcon-c/app. 9-Falcon poses as Cap 3.00
12-($2.99) Final issue; Bucky-c/app. 4.00

CAPTAIN AMERICA SPECIAL EDITION
Marvel Comics Group: Feb, 1984 - No. 2, Mar, 1984 ($2.00, Baxter paper)

1-Steranko-c/a(r) in both; r/ Captain America #110,111 6.00

	GD	VG	FN	VF	VF/NM	NM-
2-Reprints the scarce Our Love Story #5, and C.A. #113	1	2	3	5	6	8

CAPTAIN AMERICA THEATER OF WAR
Marvel Comics: 2009 - 2010 ($3.99, series of one-shots)

...: A Brother in Arms (6/09) Jenkins-s/McCrea-a; WWII story 4.00
...: Ghosts of My Country (12/09) Jenkins-s/Bonetti-a/Guice-c 4.00
...: Prisoners of Duty (2/10) Higgins & Siegel-s/Padilla-a; WWII story 4.00
...: To Soldier On (10/09) Jenkins-s/Blanco-a/Noto-c; Captain America in Iraq 4.00

CAPTAIN AMERICA: THE CHOSEN
Marvel Comics: Nov, 2007 - No. 6, Mar, 2008 ($3.99, limited series)

1-6-Breitweiser-a/Morrell-s 4.00

CAPTAIN AMERICA: THE CLASSIC YEARS
Marvel Comics: Jun, 1998 -No. 2 (trade paperbacks)

1-($19.95) Reprints Captain America Comics #1-5 25.00
2-($24.95) Reprints Captain America Comics #6-10 25.00

CAPTAIN AMERICA: THE LEGEND
Marvel Comics: Sept, 1996 ($3.95, one-shot)

1-Tribute issue; wraparound-c 4.00

CAPTAIN AMERICA: THE 1940S NEWSPAPER STRIP
Marvel Comics: Aug, 2010 - No. 3, Oct, 2010 ($3.99, limited series)

1-3-Karl Kesel-s/a; new stories set in WW2, formatted like 1940s newspaper comics 4.00

CAPTAIN AMERICA: WHAT PRICE GLORY
Marvel Comics: May, 2003 - No. 4, May, 2003 ($2.99, weekly limited series)

1-4-Bruce Jones-s/Steve Rude & Mike Royer-a 3.00

CAPTAIN AMERICA: WHITE
Marvel Comics: No. 0, Sept, 2008 ($2.99, unfinished limited series)

0-Bucky's origin retold; Loeb-s/Sale-a; interviews with creators; Sale sketch art 3.00

CAPTAIN AND THE KIDS, THE (See Famous Comics Cartoon Books)

CAPTAIN AND THE KIDS, THE (See Comics on Parade, Katzenjammer Kids, Okay Comics & Sparkler Comics)
United Features Syndicate/Dell Publ. Co.: 1938 -12/39; Sum, 1947 - No. 32, 1955; Four Color No. 881, Feb, 1958

	GD	VG	FN	VF	VF/NM	NM-
Single Series 1(1938)	103	206	309	659	1130	1600
Single Series 1(Reprint)(12/39- "Reprint" on-c)	48	96	144	302	514	725
1(Summer, 1947-UFS)-Katzenjammer Kids	17	34	51	98	154	210
2	11	22	33	60	83	105
3-10	9	18	27	52	69	85
11-20	8	16	24	42	54	65
21-32 (1955)	8	16	24	40	50	60
50th Anniversary issue-(1948)-Contains a 2 pg. history of the strip, including an account of the famous Supreme Court decision allowing both Pulitzer & Hearst to run the same strip under different names	15	30	45	94	147	200
Special Summer issue, Fall issue (1948)	11	22	33	60	83	105
Four Color 881 (Dell)	4	8	12	28	44	60

CAPTAIN ATOM
Nationwide Publishers: 1950 - No. 7, 1951 (5¢, 5x7-1/4", 52 pgs.)

	GD	VG	FN	VF	VF/NM	NM-
1-Science fiction	42	84	126	265	445	625
2-7	23	46	69	136	223	310

CAPTAIN ATOM (Formerly Strange Suspense Stories #77)(Also see Space Adventures)
Charlton Comics: V2#78, Dec, 1965 - V2#89, Dec, 1967

	GD	VG	FN	VF	VF/NM	NM-
V2#78-Origin retold; Bache-a (3 pgs.)	8	16	24	56	93	130
79-82: 79-1st app. Dr. Spectro; 3 pg. Ditko cut & paste /Space Adventures #24. 82-Intro. Nightshade (9/66)	6	12	18	37	59	80
83-86: Ted Kord Blue Beetle in all. 83-(11/66)-1st app. Ted Kord. 84-1st app. new Captain Atom	5	10	15	32	51	70
87-89: Nightshade by Aparo in all	5	10	15	32	51	70
83-85(Modern Comics-1977)-reprints	1	2	3	4	5	7

NOTE: *Aparo a-87-89.* ***Ditko*** *c/a(p) 78-89. #90 only published in fanzine 'The Charlton Bullseye' #1, 2.*

CAPTAIN ATOM (Also see Americomics & Crisis On Infinite Earths)
DC Comics: Mar, 1987 - No. 57, Sept, 1991 (Direct sales only #35 on)

1-(44 pgs.)-Origin/1st app. with new costume 4.00
2-49: 5-Firestorm x-over. 6-Intro. new Dr. Spectro. 11-Millennium tie-in. 14-Nightshade app. 16-Justice League app. 17-$1.00-c begins; Swamp Thing app. 20-Blue Beetle x-over. 24,25-Invasion tie-in 3.00
51-57: 50-($2.00, 52 pgs.). 57-War of the Gods x-over 3.00
Annual 1,2 ('88, '89)-1-Intro Major Force 4.00

CAPTAIN ATOM: ARMAGEDDON (Restarts the WildStorm Universe)
DC Comics (WildStorm): Dec, 2005 - No. 9, Aug, 2006 ($2.99, limited series)

1-9-Captain Atom appears in WildStorm Universe; Pfeifer-s/Camuncoli-a. 1-Lee-c 3.00
TPB (2007, $19.99) r/series 20.00

CAPTAIN BATTLE (Boy Comics #3 on) (See Silver Streak Comics)
New Friday Publ./Comic House: Summer, 1941 - No. 2, Fall, 1941

	GD	VG	FN	VF	VF/NM	NM-
1-Origin Blackout by Rico; Captain Battle begins (1st appeared in Silver Streak #10, 5/41)	145	290	435	921	1586	2250
2	81	162	243	518	884	1250

CAPTAIN BATTLE (2nd Series)
Magazine Press/Picture Scoop No. 5: No. 3, Wint, 1942-43; No. 5, Sum, 1943 (No #4)

	GD	VG	FN	VF	VF/NM	NM-
3-Origin Silver Streak-r/SS#3; origin Lance Hale-r/Silver Streak; Simon-a(r) (52 pgs., nd)	71	142	213	454	777	1100
5-Origin Blackout retold (68 pgs.)	50	100	150	315	533	750

Captain Britain #2 © MAR

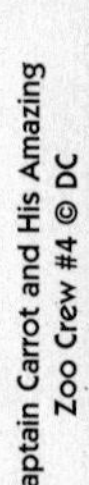
Captain Carrot and His Amazing Zoo Crew #4 © DC

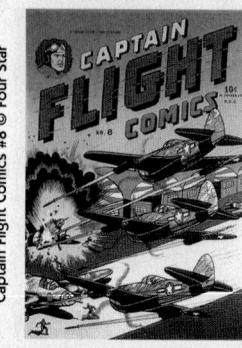

Captain Flight Comics #8 © Four Star

GD 2.0 | VG 4.0 | FN 6.0 | VF 8.0 | VF/NM 9.0 | NM- 9.2

CAPTAIN BATTLE, JR.
Comic House (Lev Gleason): Fall, 1943 - No. 2, Winter, 1943-44

1-Nazi WWII-c by Rico. Hitler/Claw sty; The Claw vs. The Ghost 135 270 405 864 1482 2100
2-Wolverton's Scoop Scuttle; Don Rico-c/a; The Green Claw story is reprinted from Silver Streak #6; bondage/torture-c 81 162 243 518 884 1250

CAPTAIN BEN DIX (See Promotional Comics section)

CAPTAIN BRITAIN (Also see Marvel Team-Up No. 65, 66)
Marvel Comics International: Oct. 13, 1976 - No. 39, July 6, 1977 (Weekly)

1-Origin; with Capt. Britain's face mask inside 2 4 6 13 18 22
2-Origin, part II; Capt. Britain's Boomerang inside 2 4 6 9 13 16
3-11: 3,8-Vs. Bank Robbers. 4-7-Vs. Hurricane. 9-11: Vs. Dr. Synne 1 2 3 5 6 8
12-23,25-27: (scarce)-12,13-Vs. Dr. Synne. 14,15-Vs. Mastermind. 16-23,25,26-With Captain America. 17-Misprinted & color section reprinted in #18. 27-Origin retold 2 4 6 10 14 18
24-With C.B.'s Jet Plane inside 3 6 9 14 19 24
28-32,36-39: 28-32-Vs. Lord Hawk. 37-39-Vs. Highwayman & Munipulator 5.00
33-35-More on origin 6.00
Annual (1978, Hardback, 64 pgs.)-Reprints #1-7 with pin-ups of Marvel characters 2 4 6 11 16 20
Summer Special (1980, 52 pgs.)-Reprints 1 2 3 4 5 7

NOTE: *No. 1, 2, & 24 are rarer in mint due to inserts. Distributed in Great Britain only. Nick Fury-r by* **Steranko** *in 1-20, 24-31, 35-37. Fantastic Four-r by* **J. Buscema** *in all. New* **Buscema**-*a in 24-30. Story from No. 39 continues in Super Spider-Man (British weekly) No. 231-247. Following cancellation of his series, new Captain Britain stories appeared in "Super Spider-Man" (British weekly) No. 231-247. Captain Britain stories which appear in Super-Spider-Man No 248-253 are reprints of Marvel Team-Up No. 65&66. Capt. Britain strips also appeared in Hulk Comic (weekly) 1, 3-30, 42-55, 57-60, in Marvel Superheroes (monthly) 377-388, in Daredevils (monthly) 1-11, Mighty World of Marvel (monthly) 7-16 & Captain Britain (monthly) 1-14. Issues 1-23 have B&W & color, paper-c, & are 32 pgs. Issues 24 on are all B&W w/glossy-c & are 36 pgs.*

CAPTAIN BRITAIN AND MI: 13 (Also see Secret Invasion x-over titles)
Marvel Comics: Jul, 2008 - No. 15, Sept, 2009 ($2.99)

1-Skrull invasion; Black Knight app.; Kirk-a 4.00
1-2nd printing with Kirk variant-c; 3rd printing with B&W cover 3.00
2-15: 5-Blade app. 9,10-Dracula app. 3.00
... Annual 1 (8/09, $3.99) Land-c; Meggan in Hell; Dr. Doom cameo; Collins-a 4.00

CAPTAIN CANUCK
Comely Comix (Canada)(All distr. in U. S.): 7/75 - No. 4, 7/77; No. 4, 7-8/79 - No. 14, 3-4/81

1-1st app. Bluefox 5.00
2,3(5-7/76)-2-1st app. Dr. Walker, Redcoat & Kebec. 3-1st app. Heather 4.00
4(1st printing-2/77)-10x14-1/2"; (5.00); B&W; 300 copies serially numbered and signed with one certificate of authenticity 7 14 21 50 83 115
4(2nd printing-7/77)-11x17", B&W; only 15 copies printed; signed by creator Richard Comely, serially #'d and two certificates of authenticity inserted; orange cardboard covers (Very Rare) 10 20 30 72 131 190
4-14: 4(7-8/79)-1st app. Tom Evans & Mr. Gold; origin The Catman. 5-Origin Capt. Canuck's powers; 1st app. Earth Patrol & Chaos Corps. 8-Jonn 'The Final Chapter'. 9-1st World Beyond. 11-1st 'Chariots of Fire' story 4.00
15-(8/04, $15.00) Limited edition of unpublished issue from 1981; serially #'d edition of 150; signed by creator Richard Comely 4 8 12 26 41 55
... Legacy 1 (9-10/06) Comely-s/a 3.00
... Legacy Special Edition ($7.95, 52 pgs., limited ed. of 1000) Comely-s/a 1 2 3 5 6 8
Special Collectors Pack (polybagged) 1 3 4 6 8 10
Summer Special 1(7-9/80, 95¢, 64 pgs.) 4.00

NOTE: *30,000 copies of No. 2 were destroyed in Winnipeg.*

CAPTAIN CANUCK: UNHOLY WAR
Comely Comix: Oct, 2004 - No. 3 ($2.50, limited series)

1-Riel Langlois-s/Drue Langlois-a 3.00

CAPTAIN CARROT AND HIS AMAZING ZOO CREW (Also see New Teen Titans & Oz-Wonderland War)
DC Comics: Mar, 1982 - No. 20, Nov, 1983

1-20: 1-Superman app. 3-Re-intro Dodo & The Frog. 9-Re-intro Three Mouseketeers, the Terrific Whatzit. 10,11-Pig Iron reverts back to Peter Porkchops. 20-Changeling app. 3.00

CAPTAIN CARROT AND THE FINAL ARK (DC Countdown tie-in)
DC Comics: Dec, 2007 - No. 3, Feb, 2008 ($2.99, limited series)

1-3-Bill Morrison-s/Scott Shaw!-a. 3-Batman, Red Arrow, Hawkgirl & Zatanna app. 3.00
TPB (2008, $19.99) r/#1-3; Captain Carrot and His Amazing Zoo Crew #1,14,15; New Teen Titans #16 and stories from Teen Titans (2003 series) #30,31; cover gallery 20.00

CAPTAIN CARVEL AND HIS CARVEL CRUSADERS (See Carvel Comics)

GD 2.0 | VG 4.0 | FN 6.0 | VF 8.0 | VF/NM 9.0 | NM- 9.2

CAPTAIN CONFEDERACY
Marvel Comics (Epic Comics): Nov, 1991 - No. 4, Feb, 1992 ($1.95)

1-4: All new stories 3.00

CAPTAIN COURAGEOUS COMICS (Banner #3-5; see Four Favorites #5)
Periodical House (Ace Magazines): No. 6, March, 1942

6-Origin & 1st app. The Sword; Lone Warrior, Capt. Courageous app.; Capt. moves to Four Favorites #5 in May 77 154 231 493 847 1200

CAPT'N CRUNCH COMICS (See Cap'n...)

CAPTAIN DAVY JONES
Dell Publishing Co.: No. 598, Nov, 1954

Four Color 598 5 10 15 30 48 65

CAPTAIN EASY (See The Funnies & Red Ryder #3-32)
Hawley/Dell Publ./Standard(Visual Editions)/Argo: 1939 - No. 17, Sept, 1949; April, 1956

nn-Hawley(1939)-Contains reprints from The Funnies & 1938 Sunday strips by Roy Crane 89 178 267 565 970 1375
Four Color 24 (1943) 50 100 150 315 533 750
Four Color 111(6/46) 13 26 39 89 170 250
10(Standard-10/47) 13 26 39 72 101 130
11,12,14,15,17: 11-17 all contain 1930s & '40s strip-r 10 20 30 54 72 90
13,16: Schomburg-c 11 22 33 62 86 110
Argo 1(4/56)-Reprints 7 14 21 37 46 55

CAPTAIN EASY & WASH TUBBS (See Famous Comics Cartoon Books)

CAPTAIN ELECTRON
Brick Computer Science Institute: Aug, 1986 ($2.25)

1-Disbrow-a 3.00

CAPTAIN EO 3-D (Michael Jackson Disney theme parks movie)
Eclipse Comics: July, 1987 (Eclipse 3-D Special #18, $3.50, Baxter)

1-Adapts 3-D movie; Michael Jackson-c/app. 6.00
1-2-D limited edition 2 4 6 9 12 15
1-Large size (11x17", 8/87)-Sold only at Disney Theme parks ($6.95) 3 6 9 14 20 25

CAPTAIN FEARLESS COMICS (Also see Holyoke One-Shot #6, Old Glory Comics & Silver Streak #1)
Helnit Publishing Co. (Holyoke Publ. Co.): Aug, 1941 - No. 2, Sept, 1941

1-Origin Mr. Miracle, Alias X, Captain Fearless, Citizen Smith Son of the Unknown Soldier; Miss Victory (1st app.) begins (1st patriotic heroine? before Wonder Woman) 84 168 252 538 919 1300
2-Grit Grady, Captain Stone app. 50 100 150 315 533 750

CAPTAIN FLAG (See Blue Ribbon Comics #16)

CAPTAIN FLASH
Sterling Comics: Nov, 1954 - No. 4, July, 1955

1-Origin; Sekowsky-a; Tomboy (female super hero) begins; only pre-code issue; atomic rocket-c 40 80 120 242 401 560
2-4: 4-Flying saucer invasion-c 22 44 66 130 213 295

CAPTAIN FLEET (Action Packed Tales of the Sea)
Ziff-Davis Publishing Co.: Fall, 1952

1-Painted-c 15 30 45 90 140 190

CAPTAIN FLIGHT COMICS
Four Star Publications: May, 1944 - No. 10, Dec, 1945; No. 11, Feb-Mar, 1947

nn-Captain Flight begins 45 90 135 284 480 675
2-4: 4-Rock Raymond begins, ends #7 26 52 78 154 252 350
5-Bondage, classic torture-c; Red Rocket begins; the Grenade app. (scarce) 119 238 357 762 1306 1850
6 24 48 72 144 237 330
7-10: 7-L. B. Cole covers begin, end #11. 8-Yankee Girl begins; intro. Black Cobra & Cobra Kid & begins. 9-Torpedoman app.; last Yankee Girl; Kinstler-a. 10-Deep Sea Dawson, Zoom of the Jungle, Rock Raymond, Red Rocket, & Black Cobra app; bondage-c 52 104 156 322 549 775
11-Torpedoman, Blue Flame (Human Torch clone) app.; last Black Cobra, Red Rocket; classic L. B. Cole sci-fi robot-c (scarce) 174 348 522 1114 1907 2700

CAPTAIN GALLANT (...of the Foreign Legion) (TV) (Texas Rangers in Action No. 5 on?)
Charlton Comics: 1955; No. 2, Jan, 1956 - No. 4, Sept, 1956

Non-Heinz version (#1)-Buster Crabbe photo on-c; full page Buster Crabbe photo inside front-c 8 16 24 44 57 70
(Heinz version is listed in the Promotional Comics section)
2-4: Buster Crabbe in all. 2-Crabbe photo back-c 6 12 18 31 38 45

Captain Hobby Comics #1 © Export

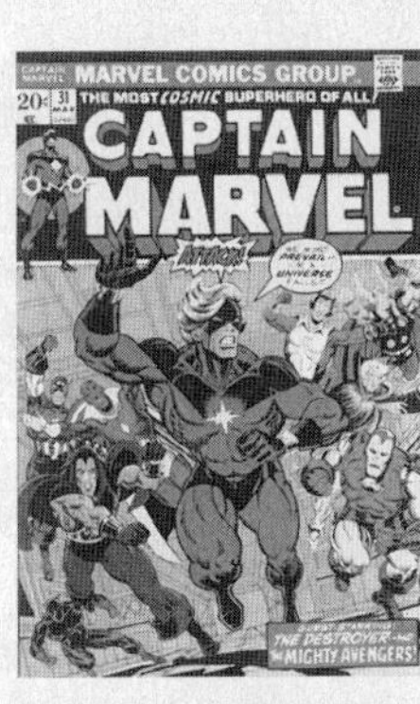

Captain Marvel #31 © MAR

Captain Marvel Adventures #17 © FAW

CAPTAIN GLORY
Topps Comics: Apr, 1993 ($2.95) (Created by Jack Kirby)

	GD 2.0	VG 4.0	FN 6.0	VF 8.0	VF/NM 9.0	NM- 9.2
1-Polybagged w/Kirbychrome trading card; Ditko-a & Kirby-c; has coupon for Amberchrome Secret City Saga #0						3.00

CAPTAIN HERO (See Jughead as...)

CAPTAIN HERO COMICS DIGEST MAGAZINE
Archie Publications: Sept, 1981

	GD 2.0	VG 4.0	FN 6.0	VF 8.0	VF/NM 9.0	NM- 9.2
1-Reprints of Jughead as Super-Guy	2	4	6	10	14	18

CAPTAIN HOBBY COMICS
Export Publication Ent. Ltd. (Dist. in U.S. by Kable News Co.): Feb, 1948 (Canadian)

	GD 2.0	VG 4.0	FN 6.0	VF 8.0	VF/NM 9.0	NM- 9.2
1	8	16	24	40	50	60

CAPT. HOLO IN 3-D (See Blackthorne 3-D Series #65)

CAPTAIN HOOK & PETER PAN (Movie)(Disney)
Dell Publishing Co.: No. 446, Jan, 1953

	GD 2.0	VG 4.0	FN 6.0	VF 8.0	VF/NM 9.0	NM- 9.2
Four Color 446	9	18	27	60	100	140

CAPTAIN JET (Fantastic Fears No. 7 on)
Four Star Publ./Farrell/Comic Media: May, 1952 - No. 5, Jan, 1953

	GD 2.0	VG 4.0	FN 6.0	VF 8.0	VF/NM 9.0	NM- 9.2
1-Bakerish-a	23	46	69	136	223	310
2	14	28	42	82	121	160
3-5,6(?)	12	24	36	69	97	125

CAPTAIN JOHNER & THE ALIENS
Valiant: May, 1995 - No. 2, May, 1995 ($2.95, shipped in same month)

	GD 2.0	VG 4.0	FN 6.0	VF 8.0	VF/NM 9.0	NM- 9.2
1,2: Reprints Magnus Robot Fighter 4000 A.D. back-up stories; new Paul Smith-c						3.00

CAPTAIN JUSTICE (TV)
Marvel Comics: Mar, 1988 - No. 2, Apr, 1988 (limited series)

	GD 2.0	VG 4.0	FN 6.0	VF 8.0	VF/NM 9.0	NM- 9.2
1,2-Based on the 1987 "Once a Hero" television series						3.00

CAPTAIN KANGAROO (TV)
Dell Publishing Co.: No. 721, Aug, 1956 - No. 872, Jan, 1958

	GD 2.0	VG 4.0	FN 6.0	VF 8.0	VF/NM 9.0	NM- 9.2
Four Color 721 (#1)-Photo-c	14	28	42	97	194	290
Four Color 780, 872-Photo-c	12	24	36	86	161	235

CAPTAIN KIDD (Formerly Dagar; My Secret Story #26 on)(Also see Comic Comics & Fantastic Comics)
Fox Feature Syndicate: No. 24, June, 1949 - No. 25, Aug, 1949

	GD 2.0	VG 4.0	FN 6.0	VF 8.0	VF/NM 9.0	NM- 9.2
24,25: 24-Features Blackbeard the Pirate	15	30	45	83	124	165

CAPTAIN MARVEL (See All Hero, All-New Collectors' Ed., America's Greatest, Fawcett Miniature, Gift, JSA, Kingdom Come, Legends, Limited Collectors' Ed., Marvel Family, Master No. 21, Mighty Midget Comics, Power of Shazam!, Shazam, Special Edition Comics, Whiz, Wisco (in Promotional Comics section), World's Finest #253 and XMas Comics)

CAPTAIN MARVEL (Becomes ...Presents the Terrible 5 No. 5)
M. F. Enterprises: April, 1966 - No. 4, Nov, 1966 (25¢ Giants)

	GD 2.0	VG 4.0	FN 6.0	VF 8.0	VF/NM 9.0	NM- 9.2
nn-(#1 on pg. 5)-Origin; created by Carl Burgos	5	10	15	32	51	70
2-4: 3-(#3 on pg. 4)-Fights the Bat	3	6	9	21	32	42

CAPTAIN MARVEL (Marvel's Space-Born Super-Hero! Captain Marvel #1-6; see Giant-Size..., Life Of..., Marvel Graphic Novel #1, Marvel Spotlight V2#1 & Marvel Super-Heroes #12)
Marvel Comics Group: May, 1968 - No. 19, Dec, 1969; No. 20, June, 1970 - No. 21, Aug, 1970; No. 22, Sept, 1972 - No. 62, May, 1979

	GD 2.0	VG 4.0	FN 6.0	VF 8.0	VF/NM 9.0	NM- 9.2
1	14	28	42	99	200	300
2-Super Skrull-c/story	8	16	24	54	90	125
3-5: 4-Captain Marvel battles Sub-Mariner	6	12	18	41	66	90
6-11: 11-Capt. Marvel given great power by Zo the Ruler; Smith/Trimpe-c; Death of Una	4	8	12	24	37	50
12,13,15-20: 16,17-New costume	3	6	9	16	23	30
14,21: 14-Capt. Marvel vs. Iron Man; last 12¢ issue. 21-Capt. Marvel battles Hulk; last 15¢ issue	4	8	12	24	37	50
22-24	3	6	9	14	20	26
25,26: 25-Starlin-c/a begins; Starlin's 1st Thanos saga begins (3/73), ends #34; Thanos cameo (5 panels). 26-Minor Thanos app. (see Iron Man #55); 1st Thanos-c	5	10	15	32	51	70
27,28-2nd & 3rd app. Thanos. 28-Thanos-c/s	4	8	12	26	41	55
29,30-Thanos cameos. 29-C.M. gains more powers	3	6	9	18	27	35
31,32: Thanos app. 31-Last 20¢ issue. 32-Thanos-c	3	6	9	19	29	38
33-Thanos-c & app.; Capt. Marvel battles Thanos; Thanos origin re-told	4	8	12	26	41	55
34-1st app. Nitro; C.M. contracts cancer which eventually kills him; last Starlin-c/a	3	6	9	18	27	35
35,37-40,42,46-48,50,53-56,58-62: 39-Origin Watcher. 58-Thanos cameo	2	4	6	8	10	12
36,41,43,49: 36-R-origin/1st app. Capt. Marvel from Marvel Super-Heroes #12. 41,43-Wrightson part inks; #43-c(i). 49-Starlin & Weiss-p assists	2	4	6	8	11	14
44,45-(Regular 25¢ editions)(5,7/76)	2	4	6	8	10	12
44,45-(30¢-c variants, limited distribution)	4	8	12	28	44	60
51,52-(Regular 30¢ editions)(7,9/77)	2	4	6	8	10	12
51,52-(35¢-c variants, limited distribution)	5	10	15	32	51	70
57-Thanos appears in flashback	2	4	6	9	12	15

NOTE: *Alcala a-35.* ***Austin*** *a-46i, 49-53i; c-52i.* ***Buscema*** *a-18p-21p.* ***Colan*** *a(p)-1-4; c(p)-1-4, 8, 9.* ***Heck*** *a-5-10p, 16p.* ***Gil Kane*** *a-17-21p; c-17-24p, 37p, 53.* ***Starlin*** *a-36.* ***McWilliams*** *a-40i. #25-34 were reprinted in The Life of Captain Marvel.*

CAPTAIN MARVEL
Marvel Comics: Nov, 1989 ($1.50, one-shot, 52 pgs.)

	GD 2.0	VG 4.0	FN 6.0	VF 8.0	VF/NM 9.0	NM- 9.2
1-Super-hero from Avengers; new powers						4.00

CAPTAIN MARVEL
Marvel Comics: Feb, 1994 ($1.75, 52 pgs.)

	GD 2.0	VG 4.0	FN 6.0	VF 8.0	VF/NM 9.0	NM- 9.2
1-(Indicia reads Vol 2 #2)-Minor Captain America app.						4.00

CAPTAIN MARVEL
Marvel Comics: Dec, 1995 - No. 6, May, 1996 ($2.95/$1.95)

	GD 2.0	VG 4.0	FN 6.0	VF 8.0	VF/NM 9.0	NM- 9.2
1 ($2.95)-Advs. of Mar-Vell's son begins; Fabian Nicieza scripts; foil-c						3.50
2-6: 2-Begin $1.95-c						3.00

CAPTAIN MARVEL (Vol. 3) (See Avengers Forever)
Marvel Comics: Jan, 2000 - No. 35, Oct, 2002 ($2.50)

	GD 2.0	VG 4.0	FN 6.0	VF 8.0	VF/NM 9.0	NM- 9.2
1-Peter David-s in all; two covers						4.00
2-10: 2-Two covers; Hulk app. 9-Silver Surfer app.						3.00
11-35: 12-Maximum Security x-over. 17,18-Starlin-a. 27-30-Spider-Man 2099 app.						3.00
Wizard #0-Preview and history of Rick Jones						4.00
...: First Contact (8/01, $16.95, TPB) r/#0,1-6						17.00

CAPTAIN MARVEL (Vol. 4) (See Avengers Forever)
Marvel Comics: Nov, 2002 - No. 25, Sept, 2004 ($2.25/$2.99)

	GD 2.0	VG 4.0	FN 6.0	VF 8.0	VF/NM 9.0	NM- 9.2
1-Peter David-s/Chriscross-a ; 3 covers by Ross, Jusko & Chriscross						4.00
2-7: 2,3-Punisher app. 3-Alex Ross-c; new costume debuts. 4-Noto-c. 7-Thor app.						3.00
3-Sketchbook Edition-($3.50) includes Ross' concept design pages for new costume						4.00
8-25: 8-Begin $2.99-c; Thor app.; Manco-c. 10-Spider-Man-c/app. 15-Neal Adams-c						3.00
Vol. 1: Nothing To Lose (2003, $14.99, TPB) r/#1-6						15.00
Vol. 2: Coven (2003, $14.99, TPB) r/#7-12						15.00
Vol. 3: Crazy Like a Fox (2004, $14.99, TPB) r/#13-18						15.00
Vol. 4: Odyssey (2004, $16.99, TPB) r/#19-25						17.00

CAPTAIN MARVEL (Vol. 5) (See Secret Invasion x-over titles)
Marvel Comics: Jan, 2008 - No. 5, Jun, 2008 ($2.99)

	GD 2.0	VG 4.0	FN 6.0	VF 8.0	VF/NM 9.0	NM- 9.2
1-5-Mar-Vell "from the past in the present"; McGuinness-c/Weeks-a						3.00
3,4-Skrull variant-c						4.00

CAPTAIN MARVEL ADVENTURES (See Special Edition Comics for pre #1)
Fawcett Publications: 1941 (March) - No. 150, Nov, 1953 (#1 on stands 1/16/41)

	GD 2.0	VG 4.0	FN 6.0	VF 8.0	VF/NM 9.0	NM- 9.2
nn(#1)-Captain Marvel & Sivana by Jack Kirby. The cover was printed on unstable paper stock and is rarely found in Fine or Mint condition; blank back inside-c	3000	6000	9000	22,500	39,750	57,000
2-(Advertised as #3, which was counting Special Edition Comics as the real #1); Tuska-a	423	846	1269	3067	5384	7700
3-Metallic silver-c	300	600	900	2010	3505	5000
4-Three Lt. Marvels app.	210	420	630	1334	2292	3250
5	165	330	495	1048	1799	2550
6-10: 9-1st Otto Binder scripts on Capt. Marvel	126	252	378	806	1378	1950
11-15: 12-Capt. Marvel joins the Army. 13-Two pg. Capt. Marvel pin-up. 15-Comic cards on back-c begin, end #26	103	206	309	659	1130	1600
16,17: 17-Painted-c	94	188	282	597	1024	1450
18-Origin & 1st app. Mary Marvel & Marvel Family (12/11/42); painted-c; Mary Marvel by Marcus Swayze	271	542	813	1734	2967	4200
19-Mary Marvel x-over; Christmas-c	79	158	237	502	864	1225
20,21,23-Attached to the cover, each has a miniature comic just like the Mighty Midget Comics #11, except that each has a full color promo ad on the back cover. Most copies were circulated without the miniature comic. These issues with miniatures attached are very rare, and should not be mistaken for copies with the similar Mighty Midget glued in its place. The Mighty Midgets had blank back covers except for a small victory stamp seal. Only the Capt. Marvel, Captain Marvel Jr. and Golden Arrow No. 11 miniatures have been positively documented as having been affixed to these covers. Each miniature was only partially glued by its back cover to the Captain Marvel comic making it easy to see if it's the genuine miniature rather than a Mighty Midget. with comic attached....	377	754	1131	2639	4620	6600
20,23-Without miniature	71	142	213	454	777	1100
21-Without miniature; Hitler-c	123	246	369	787	1344	1900
22-Mr. Mind serial begins; Mr. Mind first heard	97	194	291	621	1061	1500
24,25	68	136	204	432	746	1060

Captain Marvel Adventures #124 © FAW

Captain Marvel, Jr. #9 © FAW

Captain Midnight #33 © FAW

	GD 2.0	VG 4.0	FN 6.0	VF 8.0	VF/NM 9.0	NM- 9.2
26-28,30: 26-Flag-c; subtle Mr. Mind 2-panel cameo. 27-1st full Mr. Mind app. (his voice was only heard over the radio before now) (9/43)	57	114	171	362	619	875
29-1st Mr. Mind-c (11/43)	60	120	180	381	653	925
31-35: 35-Origin Radar (5/44, see Master #50)	51	102	153	318	539	760
36-40: 37-Mary Marvel x-over	47	94	141	296	498	700
41-46: 42-Christmas-c. 43-Capt. Marvel 1st meets Uncle Marvel; Mary Batson cameo. 46-Mr. Mind serial ends	39	78	117	240	395	550
47-50	37	74	111	222	361	500
51-53,55-60: 51-63-Bi-weekly issues. 52-Origin & 1st app. Sivana Jr.; Capt. Marvel Jr. x-over	33	66	99	194	317	440
54-Special oversize 68 pg. issue	34	68	102	199	325	450
61-The Cult of the Curse serial begins	36	72	108	211	343	475
62-65-Serial cont.; Mary Marvel x-over in #65	33	66	99	194	317	440
66-Serial ends; Atomic War-c	37	74	111	222	361	500
67-77,79: 69-Billy Batson's Christmas; Uncle Marvel, Mary Marvel, Capt. Marvel Jr. x-over. 71-Three Lt. Marvels app. 79-Origin Mr. Tawny	30	60	90	177	289	400
78-Origin Mr. Atom	33	66	99	194	317	440
80-Origin Capt. Marvel retold	68	136	204	435	743	1050
81-84,86-90: 81,90-Mr. Atom app. 82-Infinity-c. 82,86,88,90-Mr. Tawny app.	28	56	84	165	270	375
85-Freedom Train issue	32	64	96	192	314	435
91-99: 92-Mr. Tawny app. 96-Gets 1st name "Tawky"	27	54	81	160	263	365
100-Origin retold; silver metallic-c	47	94	141	296	498	700
101-115,117-120	27	54	81	158	259	360
116-Flying Saucer issue (1/51)	31	62	93	182	296	410
121-Origin retold	35	70	105	208	339	470
122-137,139,140	27	54	81	158	259	360
138-Flying Saucer issue (11/52)	31	62	93	182	296	410
141-Pre-code horror story "The Hideous Head-Hunter"	29	58	87	170	278	385
142-149: 142-used in **POP**, pgs. 92,96	28	56	84	165	270	375
150-(Low distribution)	50	100	150	315	533	750

NOTE: *Swayze a-12, 14, 15, 18, 19, 40; c-12, 15, 19.*

CAPTAIN MARVEL AND THE GOOD HUMOR MAN (Movie)
Fawcett Publications: 1950

	GD 2.0	VG 4.0	FN 6.0	VF 8.0	VF/NM 9.0	NM- 9.2
nn-Partial photo-c w/Jack Carson & the Captain Marvel Club Boys	47	94	141	296	498	700

CAPTAIN MARVEL COMIC STORY PAINT BOOK (See Comic Story...)

CAPTAIN MARVEL, JR. (See Fawcett Miniatures, Marvel Family, Master Comics, Mighty Midget Comics, Shazam & Whiz Comics)

CAPTAIN MARVEL, JR.
Fawcett Publications: Nov, 1942 - No. 119, June, 1953 (No #34)

	GD 2.0	VG 4.0	FN 6.0	VF 8.0	VF/NM 9.0	NM- 9.2
1-Origin Capt. Marvel Jr. retold (Whiz #25); Capt. Nazi app. Classic Raboy-c	568	1136	1704	4146	7323	10,500
2-Vs. Capt. Nazi; origin Capt. Nippon	203	406	609	1289	2220	3150
3	115	230	345	730	1253	1775
4-Classic Raboy-c	121	242	363	768	1322	1875
5-Vs. Capt. Nazi	97	194	291	621	1061	1500
6-8: 8-Vs. Capt. Nazi	81	162	243	518	884	1250
9-Classic flag-c	89	178	267	565	970	1375
10-Hitler-c	135	270	405	864	1482	2100
11,12,15-Capt. Nazi app.	68	136	204	435	743	1050
13-Classic Hitler, Tojo and Mussolini football-c	135	270	405	864	1482	2100
14,16-20: 14-X-Mas-c. 16-Capt. Marvel & Sivana x-over. 19-Capt. Nazi & Capt. Nippon app.	57	114	171	362	619	875
21-30: 25-Flag-c	45	90	135	284	480	675
31-33,36-40: 37-Infinity-c	33	66	99	194	317	440
35-#34 on inside; cover shows origin of Sivana Jr. which is not on inside. Evidently the cover to #35 was printed out of sequence and bound with contents to #34	33	66	99	194	317	440
41-70: 42-Robot-c. 53-Atomic Bomb-c/story	27	54	81	160	263	365
71-99,101-104: 87-Robot-c. 104-Used in **POP**, pg. 89	22	44	66	128	209	290
100	25	50	75	150	245	340
105-114,116-118: 116-Vampira, Queen of Terror app.	22	44	66	132	216	300
115-Classic injury to eye-c; Eyeball story w/injury-to-eye panels	65	130	195	416	708	1000
119-Electric chair-c (scarce)	61	122	183	390	670	950

NOTE: ***Mac Raboy** c-1-28, 30-32, 57, 59 among others.*

CAPTAIN MARVEL PRESENTS THE TERRIBLE FIVE
M. F. Enterprises: Aug, 1966; V2#5, Sept, 1967 (No #2-4) (25¢)

	GD 2.0	VG 4.0	FN 6.0	VF 8.0	VF/NM 9.0	NM- 9.2
1	5	10	15	30	48	65
V2#5-(Formerly Captain Marvel)	3	6	9	19	29	38

CAPTAIN MARVEL'S FUN BOOK
Samuel Lowe Co.: 1944 (1/2" thick) (cardboard covers)(25¢)

	GD 2.0	VG 4.0	FN 6.0	VF 8.0	VF/NM 9.0	NM- 9.2
nn-Puzzles, games, magic, etc.; infinity-c	37	74	111	222	361	500

CAPTAIN MARVEL SPECIAL EDITION (See Special Edition)

CAPTAIN MARVEL STORY BOOK
Fawcett Publications: Summer, 1946 - No. 4, Summer?, 1948

	GD 2.0	VG 4.0	FN 6.0	VF 8.0	VF/NM 9.0	NM- 9.2
1-Half text	53	106	159	334	567	800
2-4	39	78	117	231	378	525

CAPTAIN MARVEL THRILL BOOK (Large-Size)
Fawcett Publications: 1941 (B&W w/color-c)

	GD 2.0	VG 4.0	FN 6.0	VF 8.0	VF/NM 9.0	NM- 9.2
1-Reprints from Whiz #8,10, & Special Edition #1 (Rare)	310	620	930	3100	-	-

NOTE: *Rarely found in Fine or Mint condition.*

CAPTAIN MIDNIGHT (TV, radio, films) (See The Funnies, Popular Comics & Super Book of Comics)(Becomes Sweethearts No. 68 on)
Fawcett Publications: Sept, 1942 - No. 67, Fall, 1948 (#1-14: 68 pgs.)

	GD 2.0	VG 4.0	FN 6.0	VF 8.0	VF/NM 9.0	NM- 9.2
1-Origin Captain Midnight, star of radio and movies; Captain Marvel cameo on cover	300	600	900	2070	3635	5200
2-Smashes the Jap Juggarnaut	135	270	405	864	1482	2100
3-Classic Nazi war-c	129	258	387	826	1413	2000
4,5: 4-Grapples the Gremlins	107	214	321	680	1165	1650
6-8	65	130	195	416	708	1000
9-Raboy-c	67	134	201	426	731	1035
10-Raboy Flag-c	68	136	204	432	746	1060
11-20: 11,17,18-Raboy-c. 16 (1/44)	48	96	144	302	514	725
21-Classic WWII-c	53	106	159	334	567	800
22,25-30: 22-War savings stamp-c	40	80	120	246	411	575
23-WWII Concentration Camp-c	48	96	144	302	514	725
24-Japan flag sunburst-c	54	108	162	343	574	825
31-40	31	62	93	182	296	410
41-59,61-67: 50-Sci/fi theme begins?	23	46	69	136	223	310
60-Flying Saucer issue (2/48)-3rd of this theme; see The Spirit 9/28/47(1st), Shadow Comics V7#10 (2nd, 1/48) & Boy Commandos #26 (4th, 3-4/48)	34	68	102	199	325	450

CAPTAIN NICE (TV)
Gold Key: Nov, 1967 (one-shot)

	GD 2.0	VG 4.0	FN 6.0	VF 8.0	VF/NM 9.0	NM- 9.2
1(10211-711)-Photo-c	6	12	18	43	69	95

CAPTAIN N: THE GAME MASTER (TV)
Valiant Comics: 1990 - No. 6? ($1.95, thick stock, coated-c)

	GD 2.0	VG 4.0	FN 6.0	VF 8.0	VF/NM 9.0	NM- 9.2
1-6: 4-6-Layton-c						3.00

CAPTAIN PARAGON (See Bill Black's Fun Comics)
Americomics: Dec, 1983 - No. 4, 1985

	GD 2.0	VG 4.0	FN 6.0	VF 8.0	VF/NM 9.0	NM- 9.2
1-Intro/1st app. Ms. Victory						4.00
2-4						3.00

CAPTAIN PARAGON AND THE SENTINELS OF JUSTICE
AC Comics: April, 1985 - No. 6, 1986 ($1.75)

	GD 2.0	VG 4.0	FN 6.0	VF 8.0	VF/NM 9.0	NM- 9.2
1-6: 1-Capt. Paragon, Commando D., Nightveil, Scarlet Scorpion, Stardust & Atoman						3.00

CAPTAIN PLANET AND THE PLANETEERS (TV cartoon)
Marvel Comics: Oct, 1991 - No. 12, Oct, 1992 ($1.00/$1.25)

	GD 2.0	VG 4.0	FN 6.0	VF 8.0	VF/NM 9.0	NM- 9.2
1-N. Adams painted-c						4.00
2-12: 3-Romita-c						3.00

CAPTAIN POWER AND THE SOLDIERS OF THE FUTURE (TV)
Continuity Comics: Aug, 1988 - No. 2, 1988 ($2.00)

	GD 2.0	VG 4.0	FN 6.0	VF 8.0	VF/NM 9.0	NM- 9.2
1,2: 1-Neal Adams-c/layouts/inks; variant-c exists.						3.00

CAPTAIN PUREHEART (See Archie as...)

CAPTAIN ROCKET
P. L. Publ. (Canada): Nov, 1951

	GD 2.0	VG 4.0	FN 6.0	VF 8.0	VF/NM 9.0	NM- 9.2
1	45	90	135	284	480	675

CAPT. SAVAGE AND HIS LEATHERNECK RAIDERS (...And His Battlefield Raiders #9 on)
Marvel Comics Group (Animated Timely Features): Jan, 1968 - No. 19, Mar, 1970
(See Sgt. Fury No. 10)

	GD 2.0	VG 4.0	FN 6.0	VF 8.0	VF/NM 9.0	NM- 9.2
1-Sgt. Fury & Howlers cameo	5	10	15	35	55	75
2,7,11: 2,4-Origin Hydra. 7-Pre-"Thing" Ben Grimm story. 11-Sgt. Fury app.	3	6	9	18	27	35

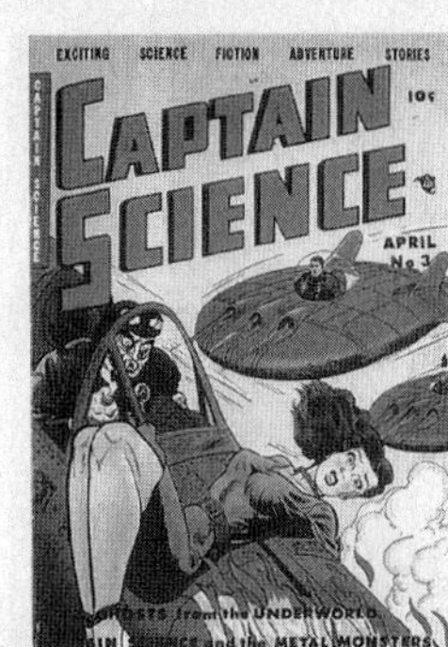

Captain Science #3 © YM

Captain Video #5 © FAW

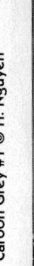

Carbon Grey #1 © H. Nguyen

GD 2.0 | VG 4.0 | FN 6.0 | VF 8.0 | VF/NM 9.0 | NM- 9.2

3-6,8-10,12-14: 14-Last 12¢ issue 3 6 9 16 23 30
15-19 3 6 9 14 19 24
NOTE: Ayres/Shores a-1-8,11. Ayres/Severin a-9,10,17-19. Heck/Shores a-12-15.

CAPTAIN SCIENCE (Fantastic No. 8 on)
Youthful Magazines: Nov, 1950; No. 2, Feb, 1951 - No. 7, Dec, 1951

1-Wood-a; origin; 2 pg. text w/ photos of George Pal's "Destination Moon." 90 180 270 576 988 1400
2-Flying saucer-c swipes Weird Science #13(#2)-c 50 100 150 315 533 750
3,6,7; 3,6-Bondage c-swipes/Wings #94,91 42 84 126 265 445 625
4,5-Wood/Orlando-c/a(2) each 82 164 246 528 902 1275
NOTE: Fass a-4. Bondage c-3, 6, 7.

CAPTAIN SILVER'S LOG OF SEA HOUND (See Sea Hound)

CAPTAIN SINBAD (Movie Adaptation) (See Fantastic Voyages of... & Movie Comics)

CAPTAIN STERNN: RUNNING OUT OF TIME
Kitchen Sink Press: Sept, 1993 - No. 5, 1994 ($4.95, limited series, coated stock, 52 pgs.)

1-5: Berni Wrightson-c/a/scripts 6.00
1-Gold ink variant 10.00

CAPTAIN STEVE SAVAGE (...& His Jet Fighters, No. 2-13)
Avon Periodicals: 1950 - No. 8, 1/53; No. 5, 9-10/54 - No. 13, 5-6/56

nn(1st series)-Harrison/Wood art, 22 pgs. (titled "...Over Korea") 40 80 120 242 401 560
1(4/51)-Reprints nn issue (Canadian) 18 36 54 105 165 225
2-Kamen-a 14 28 42 82 121 160
3-11 (#6, 11-12/54, last precode) 11 22 33 62 86 110
12-Wood-a (6 pgs.) 15 30 45 83 124 165
13-Check, Lawrence-a 11 22 33 64 90 115
NOTE: Kinstler c-2-5, 7-9, 11. Lawrence a-8. Ravielli a-5, 9.
5(9-10/54-2nd series)(Formerly Sensational Police Cases) 10 20 30 56 76 95
6-Reprints nn issue; Harrison/Wood-a 10 20 30 58 79 100
7-13: 9,10-Kinstler-c. 10-r/cover #2 (1st series). 13-r/cover #8 (1st series) 8 16 24 44 57 70

CAPTAIN STONE (See Holyoke One-Shot No. 10)

CAPT. STORM (Also see G. I. Combat #138)
National Periodical Publications: May-June, 1964 - No. 18, Mar-Apr, 1967

1-Origin 10 20 30 69 122 175
2-7,9-18: 3,6,13-Kubert-a. 4-Colan-a. 12-Kubert-c 7 14 21 45 73 100
8-Grey-tone-c 8 16 24 54 90 125

CAPTAIN 3-D (Super hero)
Harvey Publications: December, 1953 (25¢, came with 2 pairs of glasses)

1-Kirby/Ditko-a (Ditko's 3rd published work tied with Strange Fantasy #9, see also Daring Love #1 & Black Magic V4 #3); shows cover in 3-D on inside; Kirby/Meskin-c 12 24 36 69 97 125
NOTE: Half price without glasses

CAPTAIN THUNDER AND BLUE BOLT
Hero Comics: Sept, 1987 - No. 10, 1988 ($1.95)

1-10: 1-Origin Blue Bolt. 3-Origin Capt. Thunder. 6-1st app. Wicket. 8-Champions x-over 2.50

CAPTAIN TOOTSIE & THE SECRET LEGION (Advs. of...)(Also see Monte Hale #30,39 & Real Western Hero)
Toby Press: Oct, 1950 - No. 2, Dec, 1950

1-Not Beck-a; both have sci/fi covers 32 64 96 188 307 425
2-The Rocketeer Patrol app.; not Beck-a 20 40 60 114 182 250

CAPTAIN TRIUMPH (See Crack Comics #27)

CAPTAIN UNIVERSE... (5-part x-over)
Marvel Comics: 2005; Jan, 2006

.../ Daredevil 1 (1/06, $2.99) Part 2; Faerber-s/Santacruz-a 3.00
.../ Hulk 1 (1/06, $2.99) Part 1; Faerber-s/Magno-a 3.00
.../ Invisible Woman 1 (1/06, $2.99) Part 4; Faerber-s/Raiz-a; Gladiator app. 3.00
.../ Silver Surfer 1 (1/06, $2.99) Part 5; Faerber-s/Magno-a 3.00
.../ X-23 1 (1/06, $2.99) Part 3; Faerber-s/Portella-a; Scorpion app. 3.00
...: Power Unimaginable TPB (2005, $19.99)-Reprints from Marvel Spotlight #9-11, Incredible Hulk Ann. #10, Marvel Fanfare #25, Web of Spider-Man Ann. #5&6, Marvel Comics Presents #148, Cosmic Power Unlimited #5 20.00
...: Universal Heroes TPB (2005, $13.99) reprints .../Hulk, .../Daredevil, ...X-23 and back-up stories from Amazing Fantasy (2005) #13,14 14.00

CAPTAIN VENTURE & THE LAND BENEATH THE SEA (See Space Family Robinson)
Gold Key: Oct, 1968 - No. 2, Oct, 1969

1-r/Space Family Robinson serial; Spiegle-a 4 8 12 28 44 60
2-Spiegle-a 4 8 12 24 37 50

CAPTAIN VICTORY AND THE GALACTIC RANGERS
Pacific Comics: Nov, 1981 - No. 13, Jan, 1984 ($1.00, direct sales, 36-48 pgs.) (Created by Jack Kirby)

1-1st app. Mr. Mind 4.00
2-13: 3-N. Adams-a 3.00
Special 1-(10/83)-Kirby c/a(p) 4.00
NOTE: Conrad a-10, 11. Ditko a-6. Kirby a-1-3p; c-1-13.

CAPTAIN VICTORY AND THE GALACTIC RANGERS
Jack Kirby Comics: July, 2000 - No. 2, Sept, 2000 ($2.95, B&W)

1,2-New Jeremy Kirby-s with reprinted Jack Kirby-a; Liefeld pin-up art 3.00

CAPTAIN VIDEO (TV) (See XMas Comics)
Fawcett Publications: Feb, 1951 - No. 6, Dec, 1951 (No. 1,5,6-36pgs.; 2-4, 52 pgs.)

1-George Evans-a(2); 1st TV hero comic 100 200 300 635 1093 1550
2-Used in **SOTI**, pg. 382 65 130 195 416 708 1000
3-6-All Evans-a except #5 mostly Evans 54 108 162 343 574 825
NOTE: Minor Williamson assists on most issues. Photo c-1, 5, 6; painted c-2-4.

CAPTAIN WILLIE SCHULTZ (Also see Fightin' Army)
Charlton Comics: No. 76, Oct, 1985 - No. 77, Jan, 1986

76,77-Low print run 1 2 3 5 6 8

CAPTAIN WIZARD COMICS (See Meteor, Red Band & Three Ring Comics)
Rural Home: 1946

1-Capt. Wizard dons new costume; Impossible Man, Race Wilkins app. 35 70 105 208 339 470

CAPTAIN WONDER
Image Comics: Feb, 2011 ($4.99, 3-D comic with glasses)

1-Haberlin-s/Tan-a; sketch pages, crossword puzzle, paper dolls 5.00

CARBON GREY
Image Comics: Mar, 2011 - No. 3 ($2.99)

1-Khari Evans, Kinsun Loh & Hoang Nguyen-a; Nguyen-c 3.00

CARE BEARS (TV, Movie)(See Star Comics Magazine)
Star Comics/Marvel Comics No. 15 on: Nov, 1985 - No. 20, Jan, 1989

1-20: Post-a begins. 11-$1.00-c begins. 13-Madballs app. 5.00

CAREER GIRL ROMANCES (Formerly Three Nurses)
Charlton Comics: June, 1964 - No. 78, Dec, 1973

V4#24-31 3 6 9 14 20 25
32-Elvis Presley, Herman's Hermits, Johnny Rivers line drawn-c 10 20 30 69 122 175
33-37,39-50: 39-Tiffany Sinn app. 2 4 6 13 18 22
38-(2/67) 1st app. Tiffany Sinn, C.I.A. Sweetheart, Undercover Agent (also see Secret Agent #10; Dominguel-a 3 6 9 17 25 32
51-78: 54-Jonnie Love anti-drup PSA. 67-Susan Dey pin-up. 70-David Cassidy pin-up 2 4 6 10 14 18

CAR 54, WHERE ARE YOU? (TV)
Dell Publishing Co.: Mar-May, 1962 - No. 7, Sept-Nov, 1963; 1964 - 1965 (All photo-c)

Four Color 1257(#1, 3-5/62) 8 16 24 56 93 130
2(6-8/62)-7 5 10 15 32 51 70
2,3(10-12/64), 4(1-3/65)-Reprints #2,3,&4 of 1st series 3 6 9 20 30 40

CARL BARKS LIBRARY OF WALT DISNEY'S GYRO GEARLOOSE COMICS AND FILLERS IN COLOR, THE
Gladstone: 1993 ($7.95, 8-1/2x11", limited series, 52 pgs.)

1-6: Carl Barks reprints 1 3 4 6 8 10

CARL BARKS LIBRARY OF WALT DISNEY'S COMICS AND STORIES IN COLOR, THE
Gladstone: Jan, 1992 - No. 51, Mar, 1996 ($8.95, 8-1/2x11", 60 pgs.)

1,2,6,8-51: 1-Barks Donald Duck-r/WDC&S #31-35; 2-r/#36,38-41; 6-r/#57-61; 8-r/#67-71; 9-r/#72-76; 10-r/#77-81; 11-r/#82-86; 12-r/#87-91; 13-r/#92-96; 14-r/#97-101; 15-r/#102-106; 16-r/#107-111; 17-r/#112,114,117,124,125; 18-r/#126-130; 19-r/#131,132(2),133,134; 20-r/#135-139; 21-r/#140-144; 22-r/#145-149; 23-r/#150-154; 24-r/#155-159; 25-r/#160-164; 26-r/#165-169; 27-r/#170-174;28-r/#175-179; 29-r/#180-184; 30-r/#185-189; 31-r/#190-194; 32-r/#195-199;33-r/#200-204; 34-r/#205-209; 35-r/#210-214; 36-r/#215-219; 37-r/#220-224; 38-r/#225-229; 39-r/#230-234; 40-r/#235-239; 41-r/#240-244; 42r/#245-249; 43-r/#250-254; 44-50; All contain one Heroes & Villains trading card each 2 4 6 9 12 15
3,4,7: 3-r/#42-46. 4-r/#47-51. 7-r/#62-66. 2 4 6 11 16 20

Carnage (2010 series) #1 © MAR

Cars #2 © DIS/Pixar

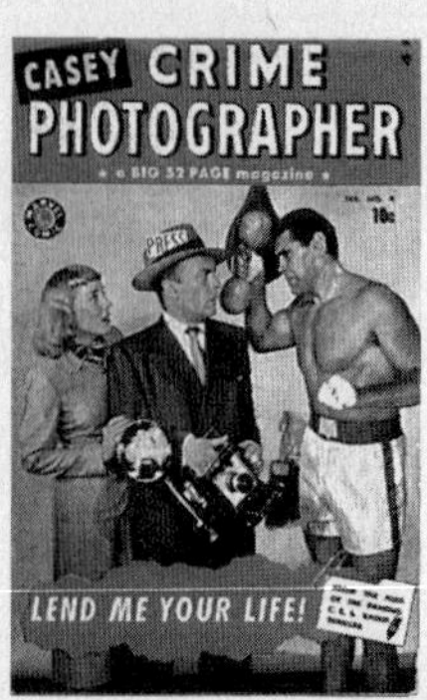

Casey-Crime Photographer #4 © MAR

	GD 2.0	VG 4.0	FN 6.0	VF 8.0	VF/NM 9.0	NM- 9.2
5-r/#52-56	3	6	9	16	23	30

CARL BARKS LIBRARY OF WALT DISNEY'S DONALD DUCK ADVENTURES IN COLOR, THE
Gladstone: Jan, 1994 - No. 25, Jan, 1996 ($7.95-$9.95, 44-68 pgs., 8-1/2"x11")
(all contain one Donald Duck trading card each)

	GD	VG	FN	VF	VF/NM	NM-
1-5,7-25-Carl Barks-r: 1-r/FC #9; 2-r/FC #29; 3-r/FC #62; 4-r/FC #108; 5-r/FC #147 & #79(Mickey Mouse); 7-r/FC #159. 8-r/FC #178 & 189. 9-r/FC #199 & 203; 10-r/FC 223 & 238; 11-r/Christmas Parade #1 & 2; 12-r/FC #296; 13-r/FC #263; 14-r/MOC #20 & 41; 15-r/FC 275 & 282; 16-r/FC #291&300; 17-r/FC #308 & 318; 18-r/Vac. Parade #1 & Summer Fun #2; 19-r/FC #328 & 367	2	4	6	9	12	15
6-r/MOC #4, Cheerios "Atom Bomb," D.D. Tells About Kites	3	6	9	14	20	25

CARL BARKS LIBRARY OF WALT DISNEY'S DONALD DUCK CHRISTMAS STORIES IN COLOR, THE
Gladstone: 1992 ($7.95, 44pgs., one-shot)

	GD	VG	FN	VF	VF/NM	NM-
nn-Reprints Firestone giveaways 1945-1949	2	4	6	10	14	18

CARL BARKS LIBRARY OF WALT DISNEY'S UNCLE SCROOGE COMICS ONE PAGERS IN COLOR, THE
Gladstone: 1992 - No. 2, 1993 ($8.95, limited series, 60 pgs., 8-1/2x11")

	GD	VG	FN	VF	VF/NM	NM-
1-Carl Barks one pg. reprints	3	6	9	16	23	30
2-Carl Barks one pg. reprints	2	4	6	10	14	18

CARNAGE
Marvel Comics: Dec, 2010 - No. 5 ($3.99, limited series)
1-4-Spider-Man & Iron Man app.; Clayton Crain-a/c; Wells-s 4.00
...: It's a Wonderful Life (10/96, $1.95) David Quinn scripts 3.00
...: Mind Bomb (2/96, $2.95) Warren Ellis script; Kyle Hotz-a 3.00

CARNATION MALTED MILK GIVEAWAYS (See Wisco)

CARNEYS, THE
Archie Comics: Summer, 1994 ($2.00, 52 pgs)
1-Bound-in pull-out poster 4.00

CARNIVAL COMICS (Formerly Kayo #12; becomes Red Seal Comics #14)
Harry 'A' Chesler/Pershing Square Publ. Co.: 1945

	GD	VG	FN	VF	VF/NM	NM-
nn (#13)-Guardineer-a	18	36	54	105	165	225

CAROLINE KENNEDY
Charlton Comics: 1961 (one-shot)

	GD	VG	FN	VF	VF/NM	NM-
nn-Interior photo covers of Kennedy family	9	18	27	61	103	145

CAROUSEL COMICS
F. E. Howard, Toronto: V1#8, April, 1948

	GD	VG	FN	VF	VF/NM	NM-
V1#8	8	16	24	42	54	65

CARS (Based on the 2006 Pixar movie)
Boom Entertainment: No. 0, Nov, 2009 - No. 7, Jun, 2010 ($2.99)
0-7: 0,1-Three covers on each. 2-7-Two covers on each 3.00
...: Adventures of Tow Mater 1-4 (7/10 - No. 4, 10/10, $2.99) 1-Two covers 3.00
...: Radiator Springs 1-4 (7/09 - No. 4, 10/09, $2.99) Two covers on each 3.00
...: The Rookie 1-4 (3/09 - No. 4, 6/09, $2.99) Origin of Lightning McQueen 3.00

CARS, WORLD OF (Free Comic Book Day giveaway)
BOOM Kids!: May, 2009
1-Based on the Disney/Pixar movie 2.50

CARTOON CARTOONS (Anthology)
DC Comics: Mar, 2001 - No. 33, Oct, 2004 ($1.99/$2.25)
1-33-Short stories of Cartoon Network characters. 3,6,10,13,15-Space Ghost. 13-Begin $2.25-c. 17-Dexter's Laboratory begins 3.00

CARTOON KIDS
Atlas Comics (CPS): 1957 (no month)

	GD	VG	FN	VF	VF/NM	NM-
1-Maneely-c/a; Dexter The Demon, Willie The Wise-Guy, Little Zelda app.	11	22	33	64	90	115

CARTOON NETWORK ACTION PACK (Anthology)
DC Comics: July, 2006 - Present ($2.25/$2.50/$2.99)
1-31-Short stories of Cartoon Network characters. 1,4,6-Rowdyruff Boys app. 3.00
32-57: 32-Begin $2.50-c. 50-Ben 10/Generator Rex team-up 3.00

CARTOON NETWORK BLOCK PARTY (Anthology)
DC Comics: Nov, 2004 - No. 59, Sept, 2009 ($2.25/$2.50)
1,2,4-51-Short stories of Cartoon Network characters 3.00
3-($2.95) Bonus pages 4.00
52-59: 52-Begin $2.50-c. 59-Last issue; Powerpuff Girls app. 3.00
Cartoon Network 2-in-1: Ben 10 Alien Force/The Secret Saturdays TPB (2010, $12.99) reprints stories from #26-42 13.00
Cartoon Network 2-in-1: Foster's Home For Imaginary Friends/Powerpuff Girls TPB (2010, $12.99) reprints stories from #19-21,23,25,26,28,30-32,34-38,41 13.00
... Vol. 1: Get Down! (2005, $6.99, digest) reprints from Dexter's Lab and Cartoon Cartoons 7.00
... Vol. 2: Read All About It! (2005, $6.99, digest) reprints 7.00
... Vol. 3: Can You Dig It?; ... Vol. 4: Blast Off! (2006, $6.99, digest) reprints 7.00

CARTOON NETWORK PRESENTS
DC Comics: Aug, 1997 - No. 24, Aug, 1999 ($1.75-$1.99, anthology)

	GD	VG	FN	VF	VF/NM	NM-
1-Dexter's Lab						5.00
1-Platinum Edition	1	2	3	5	7	9
2-10: 2-Space Ghost						3.50
11-24: 12-Bizarro World						3.00

CARTOON NETWORK PRESENTS SPACE GHOST
Archie Comics: Mar, 1997 ($1.50)
1-Scott Rosema-p 6.00

CARTOON NETWORK STARRING... (Anthology)
DC Comics: Sept, 1999 - No. 18, Feb, 2001 ($1.99)
1-Powerpuff Girls 5.00
2-18: 2,8,11,14,17-Johnny Bravo. 12,15,18-Space Ghost 3.00

CARTOON TALES (Disney's...)
W.D. Publications (Disney): nd, nn (1992) ($2.95, 6-5/8x9-1/2", 52 pgs.)
nn-Ariel & Sebastian-Serpent Teen; Beauty and the Beast; A Tale of Enchantment; Darkwing Duck - Just Us Justice Ducks; 101 Dalmatians - Canine Classics; Tale Spin - Surprise in the Skies; Uncle Scrooge - Blast to the Past 4.00

CARVERS
Image Comics (Flypaper Press): 1998 - No. 3, 1999 ($2.95)
1-3-Pander Bros.-a/Fleming-s 3.00

CAR WARRIORS
Marvel Comics (Epic): June, 1991 - No. 4, Sept, 1991 ($2.25, lim. series)
1-4: 1-Says April in indicia 3.00

CASANOVA
Image Comics: June, 2006 - No. 14, May, 2008 ($1.99, B&W& olive green or blue)
1-14: 1-7-Matt Fraction-s/Gabriel Bá-a/c. 8-14-Fabio Moon-a 3.00
...: Luxuria TPB (2008, $12.99) r/#1-7; sketch pages and cover gallery 13.00
1-4 (Marvel Comics, 10/10 - No. 4, 12/10, $3.99) Recolored reprints Image series #1-7 4.00
...: Gula (Marvel, 1/11 - No. 4, 4/11) r/Image series #8-14. 4-New story pages 4.00

CASE FILES: SAM & TWITCH (Also see the Spawn titles)
Image Comics: May, 2003 - No. 25, July, 2006 ($2.50/$2.95, color #1-6/B&W #7-on)
1-25: 1-5-Scott Morse-a/Marc Andreyko-s. 7-13-Paul Lee-a. 13-Niles-s 3.00

CASE OF THE SHOPLIFTER'S SHOE (See Perry Mason, Feature Book No.50)

CASE OF THE WINKING BUDDHA, THE
St. John Publ. Co.: 1950 (132 pgs.; 25¢; B&W; 5-1/2x7-5-1/2x8")

	GD	VG	FN	VF	VF/NM	NM-
nn-Charles Raab-a; reprinted in Authentic Police Cases No. 25	31	62	93	186	303	420

CASEY BLUE
DC Comics (WildStorm): Jul, 2008 - No. 6, Dec, 2008 ($2.99, limited series)
1-6-B. Clay Moore-s/Carlos Barberi-a 3.00
...: Beyond Tomorrow TPB (2009, $19.99) r/#1-6; Barberi sketch pages 20.00

CASEY-CRIME PHOTOGRAPHER (Two-Gun Western No. 5 on)(Radio)
Marvel Comics (BFP): Aug, 1949 - No. 4, Feb, 1950

	GD	VG	FN	VF	VF/NM	NM-
1-Photo-c; 52 pgs.	25	50	75	150	245	340
2-4: Photo-c	18	36	54	105	165	225

CASEY JONES (TV)
Dell Publishing Co.: No. 915, July, 1958

	GD	VG	FN	VF	VF/NM	NM-
Four Color 915-Alan Hale photo-c	5	10	15	34	55	75

CASEY JONES & RAPHAEL (See Bodycount)
Mirage Studios: Oct, 1994 ($2.75, unfinished limited series)
1-Bisley-c; Eastman story & pencils 3.00

CASEY JONES: NORTH BY DOWNEAST
Mirage Studios: May, 1994 - No. 2, July, 1994 ($2.75, limited series)
1,2-Rick Veitch script & pencils; Kevin Eastman story & inks 3.00

CASPER ADVENTURE DIGEST
Harvey Comics: V2#1, Oct, 1992 - V2#8, Apr, 1994 ($1.75/$1.95, digest-size)
V2#1: Casper, Richie Rich, Spooky, Wendy 5.00

Casper and the Ghostly Trio #4
© Paramount

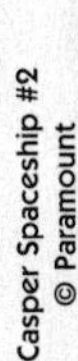

Casper Spaceship #2
© Paramount

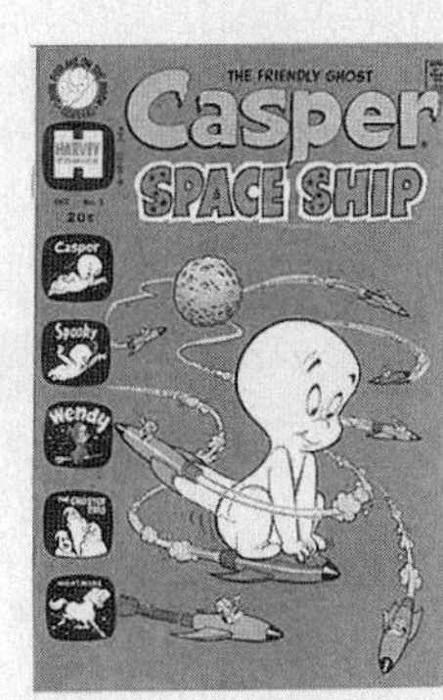

Casper, The Friendly Ghost #15
© Paramount

	GD 2.0	VG 4.0	FN 6.0	VF 8.0	VF/NM 9.0	NM- 9.2
2-8						3.50

CASPER AND...
Harvey Comics: Nov, 1987 - No. 12, June, 1990 (.75/$1.00, all reprints)

	GD 2.0	VG 4.0	FN 6.0	VF 8.0	VF/NM 9.0	NM- 9.2
1-Ghostly Trio						5.00
2-12: 2-Spooky; begin $1.00-c. 3-Wendy. 4-Nightmare. 5-Ghostly Trio. 6-Spooky. 7-Wendy. 8-Hot Stuff. 9-Baby Huey. 10-Wendy.11-Ghostly Trio. 12-Spooky						3.00

CASPER AND FRIENDS
Harvey Comics: Oct, 1991 - No. 5, July, 1992 ($1.00/$1.25)

	GD 2.0	VG 4.0	FN 6.0	VF 8.0	VF/NM 9.0	NM- 9.2
1-Nightmare, Ghostly Trio, Wendy, Spooky						4.00
2-5						3.00

CASPER AND FRIENDS MAGAZINE: Mar, 1997 - No. 3, July, 1997 ($3.99)

	GD 2.0	VG 4.0	FN 6.0	VF 8.0	VF/NM 9.0	NM- 9.2
1-3						4.00

CASPER AND NIGHTMARE (See Harvey Hits# 37, 45, 52, 56, 59, 62, 65, 68,71, 75)

CASPER AND NIGHTMARE (Nightmare & Casper No. 1-5)
Harvey Publications: No. 6, 11/64 - No. 44, 10/73; No. 45, 6/74 - No. 46, 8/74 (25¢)

	GD 2.0	VG 4.0	FN 6.0	VF 8.0	VF/NM 9.0	NM- 9.2
6: 68 pg. Giants begin, ends #32	5	10	15	34	55	75
7-10	4	8	12	22	34	45
11-20	3	6	9	18	27	35
21-37: 33-37-(52 pg. Giants)	3	6	9	14	20	26
38-46	2	4	6	10	14	18

NOTE: *Many issues contain reprints.*

CASPER AND SPOOKY (See Harvey Hits No. 20)
Harvey Publications: Oct, 1972 - No. 7, Oct, 1973

	GD 2.0	VG 4.0	FN 6.0	VF 8.0	VF/NM 9.0	NM- 9.2
1	3	6	9	18	27	35
2-7	2	4	6	10	14	18

CASPER AND THE GHOSTLY TRIO
Harvey Pub.: Nov, 1972 - No. 7, Nov, 1973; No. 8, Aug, 1990 - No. 10, Dec, 1990

	GD 2.0	VG 4.0	FN 6.0	VF 8.0	VF/NM 9.0	NM- 9.2
1	3	6	9	18	27	35
2-7	2	4	6	10	14	18
8-10						6.00

CASPER AND WENDY
Harvey Publications: Sept, 1972 - No. 8, Nov, 1973

	GD 2.0	VG 4.0	FN 6.0	VF 8.0	VF/NM 9.0	NM- 9.2
1: 52 pg. Giant	3	6	9	18	27	35
2-8	2	4	6	10	14	18

CASPER BIG BOOK
Harvey Comics: V2#1, Aug, 1992 - No. 3, May, 1993 ($1.95, 52 pgs.)

	GD 2.0	VG 4.0	FN 6.0	VF 8.0	VF/NM 9.0	NM- 9.2
V2#1-Spooky app.						4.00
2,3						3.00

CASPER CAT (See Dopey Duck)
I. W. Enterprises/Super: 1958; 1963

	GD 2.0	VG 4.0	FN 6.0	VF 8.0	VF/NM 9.0	NM- 9.2
1,7: 1-Wacky Duck #?.7-Reprint, Super No. 14('63)	2	4	6	9	13	16

CASPER DIGEST (...Magazine #?; ...Halloween Digest #8, 10)
Harvey Publications: Oct, 1986 - No. 18, Jan, 1991 ($1.25/$1.75, digest-size)

	GD 2.0	VG 4.0	FN 6.0	VF 8.0	VF/NM 9.0	NM- 9.2
1	1	3	4	6	8	10
2-18: 11-Valentine-c. 18-Halloween-c						6.00

CASPER DIGEST (...Magazine #? on)
Harvey Comics: V2#1, Sept, 1991 - V2#14, Nov, 1994 ($1.75/$1.95, digest-size)

	GD 2.0	VG 4.0	FN 6.0	VF 8.0	VF/NM 9.0	NM- 9.2
V2#1						5.00
2-14						3.50

CASPER DIGEST STORIES
Harvey Publications: Feb, 1980 - No. 4, Nov, 1980 (95¢, 132 pgs., digest size)

	GD 2.0	VG 4.0	FN 6.0	VF 8.0	VF/NM 9.0	NM- 9.2
1	2	4	6	9	13	16
2-4	1	2	3	5	7	9

CASPER DIGEST WINNERS
Harvey Publications: Apr, 1980 - No. 3, Sept, 1980 (95¢, 132 pgs., digest size)

	GD 2.0	VG 4.0	FN 6.0	VF 8.0	VF/NM 9.0	NM- 9.2
1	2	4	6	9	13	16
2,3	1	2	3	5	7	9

CASPER ENCHANTED TALES DIGEST
Harvey Comics: May, 1992 - No. 10, Oct, 1994 ($1.75, digest-size, 98 pgs.)

	GD 2.0	VG 4.0	FN 6.0	VF 8.0	VF/NM 9.0	NM- 9.2
1-Casper, Spooky, Wendy stories						5.00
2-10						4.00

CASPER GHOSTLAND
Harvey Comics: May, 1992 ($1.25)

	GD 2.0	VG 4.0	FN 6.0	VF 8.0	VF/NM 9.0	NM- 9.2
1						3.00

CASPER GIANT SIZE
Harvey Comics: Oct, 1992 - No. 4, Nov, 1993 ($2.25, 68 pgs.)

	GD 2.0	VG 4.0	FN 6.0	VF 8.0	VF/NM 9.0	NM- 9.2
V2#1-Casper, Wendy, Spooky stories						5.00
2-4						4.00

CASPER HALLOWEEN TRICK OR TREAT
Harvey Publications: Jan, 1976 (52 pgs.)

	GD 2.0	VG 4.0	FN 6.0	VF 8.0	VF/NM 9.0	NM- 9.2
1	3	6	9	18	27	35

CASPER IN SPACE (Formerly Casper Spaceship)
Harvey Publications: No. 6, June, 1973 - No. 8, Oct, 1973

	GD 2.0	VG 4.0	FN 6.0	VF 8.0	VF/NM 9.0	NM- 9.2
6-8	2	4	6	10	14	18

CASPER'S GHOSTLAND
Harvey Publications: Winter, 1958-59 - No. 97, 12/77; No. 98, 12/79 (25¢)

	GD 2.0	VG 4.0	FN 6.0	VF 8.0	VF/NM 9.0	NM- 9.2
1-84 pgs. begin, ends #10	17	34	51	122	249	375
2	10	20	30	69	122	175
3-10	8	16	24	52	86	120
11-20: 11-68 pgs. begin, ends #61. 13-X-Mas-c	6	12	18	41	65	90
21-40	5	10	15	30	48	65
41-61	3	6	9	17	25	32
62-77: 62-52 pgs. begin	2	4	6	9	13	16
78-98: 94-X-Mas-c	2	4	6	8	10	12

NOTE: *Most issues contain reprints w/new stories.*

CASPER SPACESHIP (Casper in Space No. 6 on)
Harvey Publications: Aug, 1972 - No. 5, April, 1973

	GD 2.0	VG 4.0	FN 6.0	VF 8.0	VF/NM 9.0	NM- 9.2
1: 52 pg. Giant	3	6	9	19	29	38
2-5	2	4	6	11	16	20

CASPER STRANGE GHOST STORIES
Harvey Publications: October, 1974 - No. 14, Jan, 1977 (All 52 pgs.)

	GD 2.0	VG 4.0	FN 6.0	VF 8.0	VF/NM 9.0	NM- 9.2
1	3	6	9	19	29	38
2-14	2	4	6	11	16	20

CASPER, THE FRIENDLY GHOST (See America's Best TV Comics, Famous TV Funday Funnies, The Friendly Ghost..., Nightmare &..., Richie Rich and..., Tastee-Freez, Treasury of Comics, Wendy the Good Little Witch & Wendy Witch World)

CASPER, THE FRIENDLY GHOST (Becomes Harvey Comics Hits No. 61 (No. 6), and then continued with Harvey issue No. 7)(1st Series)
St. John Publishing Co.: Sept, 1949 - No. 5, Aug, 1951

	GD 2.0	VG 4.0	FN 6.0	VF 8.0	VF/NM 9.0	NM- 9.2
1(1949)-Origin & 1st app. Baby Huey & Herman the Mouse (1st comic app. of Casper and the 1st time the name Casper app. in any media, even films)	300	600	900	1950	3375	4800
2,3 (2/50 & 8/50)	100	200	300	635	1093	1550
4,5 (3/51 & 8/51)	73	146	219	467	796	1125

CASPER, THE FRIENDLY GHOST (Paramount Picture Star...)(2nd Series)
Harvey Publications (Family Comics): No. 7, Dec, 1952 - No. 70, July, 1958
Note: No. 6 is Harvey Comics Hits No. 61 (10/52)

	GD 2.0	VG 4.0	FN 6.0	VF 8.0	VF/NM 9.0	NM- 9.2
7-Baby Huey begins, ends #9	32	64	96	246	491	735
8,9	20	40	60	140	283	425
10-Spooky begins (1st app., 6/53), ends #70?	26	52	78	190	383	575
11,12: 2nd & 3rd app. Spooky	14	28	42	96	191	285
13-18: Alfred Harvey app. in story	13	26	39	89	170	250
19-1st app. Nightmare (4/54)	21	42	63	153	307	460
20-Wendy the Witch begins (1st app., 5/54)	26	52	78	186	373	560
21-30: 24-Infinity-c	10	20	30	69	122	175
31-40: 38-Early Wendy app. 39-1st app. Samson Honeybun. 40-1st app. Dr. Brainstorm	8	16	24	54	90	125
41-1st Wendy app. on-c	9	18	27	61	103	145
42-50: 43-2nd Wendy-c. 46-1st app. Spooky's girl Pearl.	6	12	18	43	69	95
51-70 (Continues as Friendly Ghost... 8/58) 58-Early app. Bat Balfrey. 63-2nd app. Something the Baby Ghost. 66-1st app. Wildcat Witch	5	10	15	34	55	75
Harvey Comics Classics Vol. 1 TPB (Dark Horse Books, 6/07, $19.95) Reprints Casper's earliest appearances in this title, Little Audrey, and The Friendly Ghost Casper, mostly B&W with some color stories; history, early concept drawings and animation art						20.00

NOTE: *Baby Huey app. 7-9, 11, 121, 14, 16, 20. Buzzy app. 14, 16, 20. Nightmare app. 19, 27, 36, 37, 42, 46, 51, 53, 56, 70. Spooky app. 10-70. Wendy app. 20, 29-31, 35, 37, 38, 41-49, 51, 52, 54-58, 61, 64, 68.*

CASPER THE FRIENDLY GHOST (Formerly The Friendly Ghost...)(3rd Series)
Harvey Comics: No. 254, July, 1990 - No. 260, Jan, 1991 ($1.00)

	GD 2.0	VG 4.0	FN 6.0	VF 8.0	VF/NM 9.0	NM- 9.2
254-260						3.00

CASPER THE FRIENDLY GHOST (4th Series)
Harvey Comics: Mar, 1991 - No. 28, Nov, 1994 ($1.00/$1.25/$1.50)

Catholic Comics #7 © Catholic Publ.

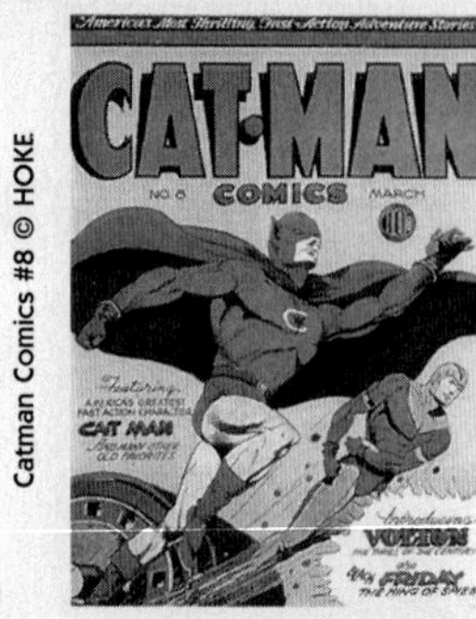

Catman Comics #8 © HOKE

Catwoman (2nd series) #70 © DC

GD VG FN VF VF/NM NM-
2.0 4.0 6.0 8.0 9.0 9.2

1-Casper becomes Mighty Ghost; Spooky & Wendy app. 5.00
2-28: 7,8-Post-a. 11-28-($1.50) 3.00

CASPER T.V. SHOWTIME
Harvey Comics: Jan, 1980 - No. 5, Oct, 1980

1 2 4 6 9 13 16
2-5 1 2 3 5 7 9

CASSETTE BOOKS (Classics Illustrated)
Cassette Book Co./I.P.S. Publ.: 1984 (48 pgs, b&w comic with cassette tape)
NOTE: *This series was illegal. The artwork was illegally obtained, and the Classics Illustrated copyright owner, Twin Circle Publ. sued to get an injunction to prevent the continued sale of this series. Many C.I. collectors obtained copies before the 1987 injunction, but now they are already scarce. Here again the market is just developing, but sealed mint copies of com ic and tape should be worth at least $25.*
1001 (CI#1-A2)New-PC 1002(CI#3-A2)CI-PC 1003(CI#13-A2)CI-PC
1004(CI#25)CI-LDC 1005(CI#10-A2)New-PC 1006(CI#64)CI-LDC

CASTILIAN (See Movie Classics)

CASTLEVANIA: THE BELMONT LEGACY
IDW Publishing: March 2005 - No. 5, July, 2005 ($3.99, limited series)

1-5-Marc Andreyko-s/E.J. Su-a 4.00

CASTLE WAITING
Olio: 1997 - No. 7, 1999 ($2.95, B&W)
Cartoon Books: Vol. 2, Aug, 2000 - No. 16 ($2.95/$3.95, B&W)
Fantagraphics Books: Vol. 3, 2006 - Present ($5.95/$3.95, B&W)

1-Linda Medley-s/a in all 1 2 3 5 6 8
2 4.00
3-7 3.00
The Lucky Road TPB r/#1-7 17.00
Hiatus Issue (1999) Crilley-c; short stories and previews 3.00
Vol. 2 #1-6,14-16 (#5&6 also have #12&13 on cover, for series numbering) 3.00
Vol. 3 #1 ($5.95) r/#15,16 and new story 6.00
Vol. 3 #2-15 ($3.95) 4.00

CASUAL HEROES
Image Comics (Motown Machineworks): Apr, 1996 ($2.25, unfinished lim. series)

1-Steve Rude-c 2.50

CAT, T.H.E. (TV) (See T.H.E. Cat)

CAT, THE (See Movie Classics)

CAT, THE (Female hero)
Marvel Comics Group: Nov, 1972 - No. 4, June, 1973

1-Origin & 1st app. The Cat (who later becomes Tigra); Mooney-a(i); Wood-c(i)/a(i)
4 8 12 24 37 50
2,3: 2-Marie Severin/Mooney-a. 3-Everett inks 3 6 9 14 20 25
4-Starlin/Weiss-a(p) 3 6 9 16 22 28

CATALYST: AGENTS OF CHANGE (Also see Comics' Greatest World)
Dark Horse Comics: Feb, 1994 - No.7, Nov, 1994 ($2.00, limited series)

1-7: 1-Foil stamped logo 3.00

CAT & MOUSE
EF Graphics (Silverline): Dec, 1988 ($1.75, color w/part B&W)

1-1st printing (12/88, 32 pgs.), 1-2nd printing (5/89, 36 pgs.) 3.00

CAT FROM OUTER SPACE (See Walt Disney Showcase #46)

CATHOLIC COMICS (See Heroes All Catholic...)
Catholic Publications: June, 1946 - V3#10, July, 1949

1 30 60 90 177 289 400
2 16 32 48 94 147 200
3-13(7/47): 11-Hollingsworth-a 14 28 42 82 121 160
V2#1-10 11 22 33 62 86 110
V3#1-10: Reprints 10-part Treasure Island serial from Target V2#2-11 (see Key Comics #5)
11 22 33 64 90 115
NOTE: ***Orlando** c-V2#10, V3#5, 6, 8.*

CATHOLIC PICTORIAL
Catholic Guild: 1947

1-Toth-a(2) (Rare) 39 78 117 240 395 550

CATMAN COMICS (Formerly Crash Comics No. 1-5)
Holyoke Publishing Co./Continental Magazines V2#12, 7/44 on:
5/41 - No. 17, 1/43; No. 18, 7/43 - No. 22, 12/43; No. 23, 3/44 - No. 26, 11/44; No. 27, 4/45 - No. 30, 12/45; No. 31, 6/46 - No. 32, 8/46

1(V1#6)-Origin The Deacon & Sidekick Mickey, Dr. Diamond & Rag-Man; The Black Widow app.; The Catman by Chas. Quinlan & Blaze Baylor begin
411 822 1233 2877 5039 7200

GD VG FN VF VF/NM NM-
2.0 4.0 6.0 8.0 9.0 9.2

2(V1#7) 177 354 531 1124 1937 2750
3(V1#8)-The Pied Piper begins; classic Hitler, Stalin & Mussolini-c
174 348 522 1114 1907 2700
4(V1#9) 113 226 339 718 1234 1750
5(V2#10)-1st app. Kitten; The Hood begins (c-redated), 6,7(V2#11,12)
100 200 300 635 1093 1550
8(V2#13,3/42)-Origin Little Leaders; Volton by Kubert begins (his 1st comic book work)
119 238 357 762 1306 1850
9,10(V2#14,15): 10-Origin Blackout; Phantom Falcon begins
87 174 261 553 952 1350
11 (V3#1)-Kubert-a 87 174 261 553 952 1350
12 (V3#2), 14, 15, 17. 12-Volton by Brodsky, not Kubert. 14-Brodsky-a
74 148 222 470 810 1150
13-(scarce) 129 258 387 826 1413 2000
16 (V3#5)-Hitler, Tojo, Mussolini, Goehring-c 129 258 387 826 1413 2000
18(V3#8, 7/43)-(scarce) 89 178 267 565 970 1375
19,20: 19 (V2#6)-Hitler, Tojo, Mussolini-c. 20 (V2#7): Classic Hitler-c
142 284 426 909 1555 2200
21-23 (V2#10, 3/44) 73 146 219 467 796 1125
nn(V3#13, 5/44)-Rico-a; Schomburg bondage-c 77 154 231 493 847 1200
nn(V2#12, 7/44, nn(V3#1, 9/44)-Origin The Golden Archer; Leatherface app.
66 132 198 419 722 1025
nn(V3#2, 11/44)-L. B. Cole-c 110 220 330 704 1202 1700
27-Origins Catman & Kitten retold; L. B. Cole Flag-c; Infantino-a
123 246 369 787 1344 1900
28-Dr. Macabre app.; L. B. Cole-c/a 142 284 426 909 1555 2200
29-32-L. B. Cole-c; bondage-#30 119 238 357 762 1306 1850
NOTE: ***Fuje** a-11, 27, 28(2), 29(3), 30. **Palais** a-11, 16, 27, 28, 29(2), 30(2), 32; c-25(7/44). **Rico** a-11(2), 23, 27, 28.*

CAT TALES (3-D)
Eternity Comics: Apr, 1989 ($2.95)

1-Felix the Cat-r in 3-D 5.00

CATWOMAN (Also see Action Comics Weekly #611, Batman #404-407, Detective Comics, & Superman's Girlfriend Lois Lane #70, 71)
DC Comics: Feb, 1989 - No. 4, May, 1989 ($1.50, limited series, mature)

1 1 3 4 6 8 10
2-4: 3-Batman cameo. 4-Batman app. 1 2 3 5 7 9
Her Sister's Keeper (1991, $9.95, trade paperback)-r/#1-4 10.00

CATWOMAN (Also see Showcase '93, Showcase '95 #4, & Batman #404-407)
DC Comics: Aug, 1993 - No. 94, Jul, 2001 ($1.50-$2.25)

0-(10/94)-Zero Hour; origin retold. Released between #14&15 3.00
1-($1.95)-Embossed-c; Bane app.; Balent c-1-10; a-1-10p 5.00
2-20: 3-Bane flashback cameo. 4-Brief Bane app. 6,7-Knightquest tie-ins; Batman (Azrael) app. 8-1st app. Zephyr. 12-KnightsEnd pt. 6. 13-new Knights End Aftermath.
14-(9/94)-Zero Hour 3.50
21-24, 26-30, 33-49: 21-$1.95-c begins. 28,29-Penguin cameo app. 36-Legacy pt. 2. 38-40-Year Two; Batman, Joker, Penguin & Two-Face app. 46-Two-Face app. 3.00
25,31,32: 25-($2.95)-Robin app. 31,32-Contagion pt. 4 (Reads pt. 5 on-c) & pt. 9. 4.00
50-($2.95, 48 pgs.)-New armored costume 4.00
50-($2.95, 48 pgs.)-Collector's Ed.w/metallic ink-c 4.00
51-77: 51-Huntress-c/app. 54-Grayson-s begins. 56-Cataclysm pt.6. 57-Poison Ivy-c/app. 63-65-Joker-c/app. 72-No Man's Land; Ostrander-s begins 3.00
78-82: 80-Catwoman goes to jail 3.00
83-94: 83-Begin $2.25-c. 83,84,89-Harley Quinn-c/app. 3.00
#1,000,000 (11/98) 853rd Century x-over 3.00
Annual 1 (1994, $2.95, 68 pgs.)-Elseworlds story; Batman app.; no Balent-a 4.00
Annual 2,4 ('95, '97, $3.95) 2-Year One story. 4-Pulp Heroes 4.00
Annual 3 (1996, $2.95)-Legends of the Dead Earth story 4.00
...Plus 1 (11/97, $2.95) Screamqueen (Scare Tactics) app. 4.00
TPB ($9.95) r/#15-19, Balent-c 10.00

CATWOMAN (Also see Detective Comics #759-762)
DC Comics: Jan, 2002 - No. 82, Oct, 2008; No. 83, Mar, 2010 ($2.50/$2.99)

1-Darwyn Cooke & Mike Allred-a; Ed Brubaker-s 6.00
2-4 3.00
5-54: 5-9-Rader-a/Paul Pope-c. 10-Morse-c. 16-JG Jones-c. 22-Batman-c/app. 34-36-War Games. 43-Killer Croc app. 44-Hughes-c begin. 50-Zatanna app. 52-Catwoman kills Black Mask. 53-One Year Later; Helena born 3.00
55-82: 55-Begin $2.99-c. 56-58-Wildcat app. 74-Zatanna app. 75-78-Salvation Run 3.00
83-(3/10, $2.99) Blackest Night one-shot; Black Mask app.; Hughes-c 3.00
...: Catwoman Dies TPB (2008, $14.99) r/#66-72; Hughes cover gallery 15.00
...: Crime Pays TPB (2008, $14.99) r/#73-77 15.00
...: Crooked Little Town TPB (2003, $14.95) r/#5-10 & Secret Files; Oeming-c 15.00

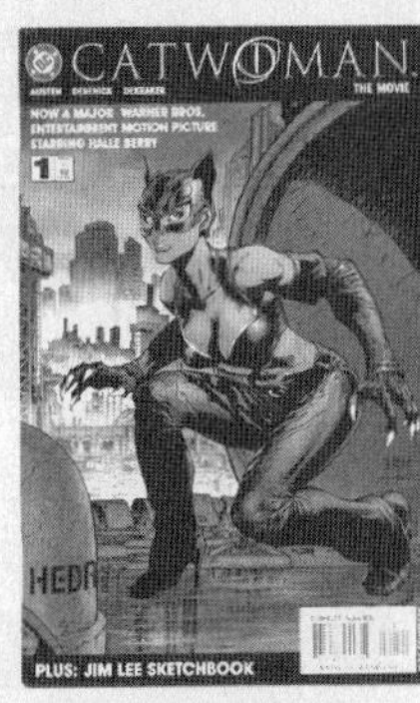

Catwoman: The Movie #1 © DC

Caught #4 © MAR

Cerebus #171 © Sim & Gerhard

GD VG FN VF VF/NM NM-
2.0 4.0 6.0 8.0 9.0 9.2

...: It's Only a Movie TPB (2007, $19.99) r/#59-65 20.00
...: Relentless TPB (2005, $19.95) r/#12-19 & Secret Files 20.00
... Secret Files and Origins (10/02, $4.95) origin-s Oeming-a; profiles and pin-ups 5.00
...Selina's Big Score HC (2002, $24.95) Cooke-s/a; pin-ups by various 25.00
...Selina's Big Score SC (2003, $17.95) Cooke-s/a; pin-ups by various 18.00
...: The Dark End of the Street TPB (2002, $12.95) r/#1-4 & Slam Bradley back-up stories from Detective Comics #759-762 13.00
...: The Long Road Home TPB (2009, $17.99) r/#78-82 18.00
...: The Replacements TPB (2007, $14.99) r/#53-58 15.00
...: Wild Ride TPB (2005, $14.99) r/#20-24 & Secret Files #1 15.00

CATWOMAN/ GUARDIAN OF GOTHAM
DC Comics: 1999 - No. 2, 1999 ($5.95, limited series)
1,2-Elseworlds; Moench-s/Balent-a 6.00

CATWOMAN: NINE LIVES OF A FELINE FATALE
DC Comics: 2004 ($14.95, TPB)
nn-Reprints notable stories from Batman #1 to the present; pin-ups by various; Bolland-c 15.00

CATWOMAN: THE MOVIE (2004 Halle Berry movie)
DC Comics: 2004 ($4.95/$9.95)
1-($4.95) Movie adaptation; Jim Lee-c and sketch pages; Derenick-a 5.00
... & Other Cat Tales TPB (2004, $9.95)-r/Movie adaptation; Jim Lee sketch pages, r/Catwoman #0, Catwoman (2nd series) #11 & 25; photo-c 10.00

CATWOMAN/VAMPIRELLA: THE FURIES
DC Comics/Harris Publ.: Feb, 1997 ($4.95, squarebound, 46 pgs.) (1st DC/Harris x-over)
nn-Reintro Pantha; Chuck Dixon scripts; Jim Balent-c/a 5.00

CATWOMAN: WHEN IN ROME
DC Comics: Nov, 2004 - No. 6, Aug, 2005 ($3.50, limited series)
1-6-Jeph Loeb-s/Tim Sale-a/c; Riddler app. 3.50
HC (2005, $19.99, dustjacket) r/series; intro by Mark Chiarello; sketch pages 20.00
SC (2007, $12.99) r/series; intro by Mark Chiarello; sketch pages 13.00

CATWOMAN/WILDCAT
DC Comics: Aug, 1998 - No. 4, Nov, 1998 ($2.50, limited series)
1-4-Chuck Dixon & Beau Smith-s; Stelfreeze-c 3.00

CAUGHT
Atlas Comics (VPI): Aug, 1956 - No. 5, Apr, 1957
1 22 44 66 132 216 300
2-4: 3-Maneely, Pakula, Torres-a. 4-Maneely-a 14 28 42 76 108 140
5-Crandall, Krigstein-a 14 28 42 80 115 150
NOTE: *Drucker a-2. Heck a-4. Severin c-1, 2, 4, 5. Shores a-4.*

CAVALIER COMICS
A. W. Nugent Publ. Co.: 1945; 1952 (Early DC reprints)
2(1945)-Speed Saunders, Fang Gow 20 40 60 117 189 260
2(1952) 12 24 36 67 94 120

CAVE GIRL (Also see Africa)
Magazine Enterprises: No. 11, 1953 - No. 14, 1954
11(A-1 82)-Origin; all Cave Girl stories 48 96 144 301 511 720
12(A-1 96), 13(A-1 116), 14(A-1 125)-Thunda by Powell in each 38 76 114 226 368 510
NOTE: *Powell c/a in all.*

CAVE GIRL
AC Comics: 1988 ($2.95, 44 pgs.) (16 pgs. of color, rest B&W)
1-Powell-r/Cave Girl #11; Nyoka photo back-c from movie; Powell/Bill Black-c; Special Limited Edition on-c 4.00

CAVE KIDS (TV) (See Comic Album #16)
Gold Key: Feb, 1963 - No. 16, Mar, 1967 (Hanna-Barbera)
1 7 14 21 45 73 100
2-5 4 8 12 24 37 50
6-16: 7,12-Pebbles & Bamm Bamm app. 16-1st Space Kidettes 3 6 9 20 30 40

CAVEWOMAN
Basement Comics: Jan, 1994 - No. 6, 1995 ($2.95)
1 3 6 9 16 23 30
2 2 4 6 9 12 15
3-6 1 2 3 5 6 8
...: Meets Explorers ('97, $2.95) 3.00
...: One-Shot Special (7/00, $2.95) Massey-s/a 3.00

CELESTINE (See Violator Vs. Badrock #1)

GD VG FN VF VF/NM NM-
2.0 4.0 6.0 8.0 9.0 9.2

Image Comics (Extreme): May, 1996 - No. 2, June, 1996 ($2.50, limited series)
1,2: Warren Ellis scripts 3.00

CENTURION OF ANCIENT ROME, THE
Zondervan Publishing House: 1958 (no month listed) (B&W, 36 pgs.)
(Rare) All by Jay Disbrow 77 154 231 493 847 1200

CENTURIONS (TV)
DC Comics: June, 1987 - No. 4, Sept, 1987 (75¢, limited series)
1-4 3.00

CENTURY: DISTANT SONS
Marvel Comics: Feb, 1996 ($2.95, one-shot)
1-Wraparound-c 3.00

CENTURY OF COMICS (See Promotional Comics section)

CEREBUS BI-WEEKLY
Aardvark-Vanaheim: Dec. 2, 1988 - No. 27, Nov. 24, 1989 ($1.25, B&W)
Reprints Cerebus The Aardvark #1-27
1-16, 18, 19, 21-27: 3.00
17-Hepcats app. 2 4 6 8 10 12
20-Milk & Cheese app. 2 4 6 10 12 15

CEREBUS: CHURCH & STATE
Aardvark-Vanaheim: Feb, 1991 - No. 30, Apr, 1992 ($2.00, B&W, bi-weekly)
1-30: r/Cerebus #51-80 3.00

CEREBUS: HIGH SOCIETY
Aardvark-Vanaheim: Feb, 1990 - No. 25, 1991 ($1.70, B&W)
1-25: r/Cerebus #26-50 3.00

CEREBUS JAM
Aardvark-Vanaheim: Apr, 1985
1-Eisner, Austin, Dave Sim-a (Cerebus vs. Spirit) 6.00

CEREBUS THE AARDVARK (See A-V in 3-D, Nucleus, Power Comics)
Aardvark-Vanaheim: Dec, 1977 - No. 300, March, 2004 ($1.70/$2.00/$2.25, B&W)
0 3.00
0-Gold 20.00
1-1st app. Cerebus; 2000 print run; most copies poorly printed 48 96 144 392 796 1200
Note: *There is a counterfeit version known to exist. It can be distinguished from the original in the following ways: inside cover is glossy instead of flat, black background on the front cover is blotted or spotty. Reports show that a counterfeit #2 also exists.*
2-Dave Sim art in all 13 26 39 94 185 275
3-Origin Red Sophia 11 22 33 80 150 220
4-Origin Elrod the Albino 10 20 30 67 116 165
5,6 8 16 24 56 93 130
7-10 6 12 18 43 69 95
11,12: 11-Origin The Cockroach 5 10 15 35 55 75
13-15: 14-Origin Lord Julius 5 10 15 30 48 65
16-20 4 8 12 22 34 45
21-B. Smith letter in letter column 6 12 18 41 66 90
22-Low distribution; no cover price 4 8 12 26 41 55
23-30: 23-Preview of Wandering Star by Teri S. Wood. 26-High Society begins, ends #50 3 6 9 16 23 30
31-Origin Moonroach 3 6 9 17 25 32
32-40, 53-Intro. Wolveroach (brief app.) 2 4 6 8 10 12
41-50,52: 52-Church & State begins, ends #111; Cutey Bunny app. 1 2 3 5 7 9
51,54: 51-Cutey Bunny app. 54-1st full Wolveroach story 2 4 6 8 11 14
55,56-Wolveroach app.; Normalman back-ups by Valentino 1 3 4 6 8 10
57-100: 61,62: Flaming Carrot app. 65-Gerhard begins 4.00
101-160: 104-Flaming Carrot app. 112/113-Double issue. 114-Jaka's Story begins, ends #136. 139-Melmoth begins, ends #150. 151-Mothers & Daughters begins, ends #200 3.00
161-Bone app. 1 3 4 6 8 10
162-231: 175-($2.25, 44 pgs). 186-Strangers in Paradise cameo. 201-Guys storyline begins; Eddie Campbell's Bacchus app. 220-231-Rick's Story 3.00
232-265-Going Home 3.00
266-288,291-299-Latter Days: 267-Five-Bar Gate. 276-Spore (Spawn spoof) 3.00
289&290 ($4.50) Two issues combined 5.00
300-Final issue 3.00
Free Cerebus (Giveaway, 1991-92?, 36 pgs.)-All-r 4.00

CHAIN GANG WAR

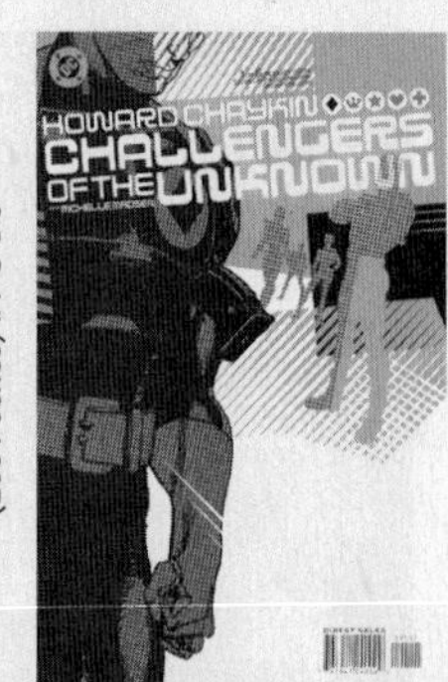

Challengers of the Unknown (2004 series) #1 © DC

Chamber of Chills #19 © HARV

The Champions #1 © MAR

DC Comics: July, 1993 - No. 12, June, 1994 ($1.75)

	GD 2.0	VG 4.0	FN 6.0	VF 8.0	VF/NM 9.0	NM- 9.2
1-($2.50)-Embossed silver foil-c, Dave Johnson-c/a						3.50
2-4,6-12: 3-Deathstroke app. 4-Brief Deathstroke app. 6-New Batman (Azrael) cameo. 11-New Batman-c/story. 12-New Batman app.						3.00
5-($2.50)-Foil-c; Deathstroke app; new Batman cameo (1 panel)						3.50

CHAINS OF CHAOS
Harris Comics: Nov, 1994 - No. 3, Jan, 1995 ($2.95, limited series)

	GD 2.0	VG 4.0	FN 6.0	VF 8.0	VF/NM 9.0	NM- 9.2
1-3-Re-Intro of The Rook w/ Vampirella						3.00

CHALLENGE OF THE UNKNOWN (Formerly Love Experiences)
Ace Magazines: No. 6, Sept, 1950 (See Web Of Mystery No. 19)

	GD 2.0	VG 4.0	FN 6.0	VF 8.0	VF/NM 9.0	NM- 9.2
6- "Villa of the Vampire" used in N.Y. Joint Legislative Comm. Publ; Sekowsky-a	39	78	117	231	378	525

CHALLENGER, THE
Interfaith Publications/T.C. Comics: 1945 - No. 4, Oct-Dec, 1946

	GD 2.0	VG 4.0	FN 6.0	VF 8.0	VF/NM 9.0	NM- 9.2
nn; nd; 32 pgs.; Origin the Challenger Club; Anti-Fascist with funny animal filler	55	110	165	352	601	850
2-4: Kubert-a; 4-Fuje-a	43	86	129	271	461	650

CHALLENGERS OF THE FANTASTIC
Marvel Comics (Amalgam): June 1997 ($1.95, one-shot)

	GD 2.0	VG 4.0	FN 6.0	VF 8.0	VF/NM 9.0	NM- 9.2
1-Karl Kesel-s/Tom Grummett-a						2.50

CHALLENGERS OF THE UNKNOWN (See Showcase #6, 7, 11, 12, Super DC Giant, and Super Team Family) (See Showcase Presents for B&W reprints)
National Per. Publ./DC Comics: 4-5/58 - No. 77, 12-1/70-71; No. 78, 2/73 - No. 80, 6-7/73; No. 81, 6-7/77 - No. 87, 6-7/78

	GD 2.0	VG 4.0	FN 6.0	VF 8.0	VF/NM 9.0	NM- 9.2
1-(4-5/58)-Kirby/Stein-a(2); Kirby-c	211	422	633	1846	3773	5700
2-Kirby/Stein-a(2)	65	130	195	553	1127	1700
3-Kirby/Stein-a(2); Rocky returns from space with powers similar to the Fantastic Four (9/58)	56	112	168	476	963	1450
4-8-Kirby/Wood-a plus cover to #8	43	86	129	344	697	1050
9,10	25	50	75	183	367	550
11-Grey tone-c	24	48	72	175	355	535
12-15: 14-Origin/1st app. Multi-Man (villain)	18	36	54	125	255	385
16-22: 18-Intro. Cosmo, the Challengers Spacepet. 22-Last 10¢ issue	13	26	39	91	176	260
23-30	9	18	27	63	107	150
31-Retells origin of the Challengers	9	18	27	64	110	155
32-40	7	14	21	47	76	105
41-47,49,50,52-60: 43-New look begins. 47-1st Sponge-Man. 49-Intro. Challenger Corps. 55-Death of Red Ryan. 60-Red Ryan returns	5	10	15	35	55	75
48,51: 48-Doom Patrol app. 51-Sea Devils app.	6	12	18	37	59	80
61-68: 64,65-Kirby origin-r, parts 1 & 2. 66-New logo. 68-Last 12¢ issue.	4	8	12	24	37	50
69-73,75-80: 69-1st app. Corinna. 77-Last 15¢ issue	3	6	9	16	23	30
74-Deadman by Tuska/Adams; 1 pg. Wrightson-a	6	12	18	41	66	90
81,83-87: 81-(6-7/77). 83-87-Swamp Thing app. 84-87-Deadman app.	2	4	6	8	10	12
82-Swamp Thing begins (thru #87, c/s	2	4	6	9	12	15

NOTE: ***N. Adams** c-67, 68, 70, 72, 74i, 81i. **Buckler** c-83-86p. **Giffen** a-83-87p. **Kirby** a-75-80r; c-75, 77, 78. **Kubert** c-64, 66, 69, 76, 79. **Nasser** c/a-81p, 82p. **Tuska** a-73. **Wood** r-76.*

CHALLENGERS OF THE UNKNOWN
DC Comics: Mar, 1991 - No. 8, Oct, 1991 ($1.75, limited series)

	GD 2.0	VG 4.0	FN 6.0	VF 8.0	VF/NM 9.0	NM- 9.2
1-Jeph Loeb scripts & Tim Sale-a in all (1st work together); Bolland-c						3.50
2-8: 2-Superman app. 3-Dr. Fate app. 6-G. Kane-c(p). 7-Steranko-c/swipe by Art Adams						3.00
... Must Die! (2004, $19.95, TPB) r/series; intro by Bendis; Sale sketch pages						20.00

NOTE: ***Art Adams** c-7. **Hempel** c-5. **Gil Kane** c-6p. **Sale** a-1-8; c-3, 8. **Wagner** c-4.*

CHALLENGERS OF THE UNKNOWN
DC Comics: Feb, 1997 - No. 18, July, 1998 ($2.25)

	GD 2.0	VG 4.0	FN 6.0	VF 8.0	VF/NM 9.0	NM- 9.2
1-18: 1-Intro new team; Leon-c/a(p) begins. 4-Origin of new team. 11,12-Batman app. 15-Millennium Giants x-over; Superman-c/app.						3.00

CHALLENGERS OF THE UNKNOWN
DC Comics: Aug, 2004 - No. 6, Jan, 2005 ($2.95, limited series)

	GD 2.0	VG 4.0	FN 6.0	VF 8.0	VF/NM 9.0	NM- 9.2
1-6-Intro. new team; Howard Chaykin-s/a						3.00

CHALLENGE TO THE WORLD
Catechetical Guild: 1951 (10¢, 36 pgs.)

	GD 2.0	VG 4.0	FN 6.0	VF 8.0	VF/NM 9.0	NM- 9.2
nn	6	12	18	31	38	45

CHAMBER (See Generation X and Uncanny X-Men)
Marvel Comics: Oct, 2002 - No. 4, Jan, 2003 ($2.99, limited series)

	GD 2.0	VG 4.0	FN 6.0	VF 8.0	VF/NM 9.0	NM- 9.2
1-4-Bachalo-c/Vaughan-s/Ferguson-a. 1-Cyclops app.						3.00

CHAMBER OF CHILLS (Formerly Blondie Comics #20; ...of Clues No. 27 on)
Harvey Publications/Witches Tales: No. 21, June, 1951 - No. 26, Dec, 1954

	GD 2.0	VG 4.0	FN 6.0	VF 8.0	VF/NM 9.0	NM- 9.2
21 (#1)	50	100	150	315	533	750
22,24 (#2,4)	37	74	111	222	361	500
23 (#3)-Excessive violence; eyes torn out	39	78	117	231	378	525
5(2/52)-Decapitation, acid in face scene	39	78	117	231	378	525
6-Woman melted alive	37	74	111	222	361	500
7-Used in **SOTI**, pg. 389; decapitation/severed head panels	36	72	108	211	343	475
8-10: 8-Decapitation panels	30	60	90	177	289	400
11,12,14: 14-Spider-Man precursor (11/52)	24	48	72	142	234	325
13,15-24-Nostrand-a in all. 13,21-Decapitation panels. 18-Atom bomb panels. 20-Nostrand-c	29	58	87	170	278	385
25,26	20	40	60	114	182	250

NOTE: *About half the issues contain bondage, torture, sadism, perversion, gore, cannabalism, eyes ripped out, acid in face, etc. **Elias** c-4-11, 14-19, 21-26. **Kremer** a-12, 17. **Palais** a-21(1), 23. **Nostrand/Powell** a-13, 15, 16. **Powell** a-21, 23, 24('51), 5-8, 11, 13, 18-21, 23-25. Bondage-c-21, 24('51), 7. 25-r/#5; 26-r/#9.*

CHAMBER OF CHILLS
Marvel Comics Group: Nov, 1972 - No. 25, Nov, 1976

	GD 2.0	VG 4.0	FN 6.0	VF 8.0	VF/NM 9.0	NM- 9.2
1-Harlan Ellison adaptation	4	8	12	24	37	50
2-5: 2-1st app. John Jakes' Brak the Barbarian	3	6	9	14	20	25
6-25: 22,23-(Regular 25¢ editions)	2	4	6	11	16	20
22,23-(30¢-c variants, limited distribution)(5,7/76)	4	8	12	24	37	50

NOTE: ***Adkins** a-1i, 2i. **Brunner** a-2-4; c-4. **Chaykin** a-4. **Ditko** r-14, 16, 19, 23, 24. **Everett** a-3i, 11r,21r. **Heath** a-1r. **Gil Kane** c-2p. **Kirby** r-11, 18, 19, 22. **Powell** a-13r. **Russell** a-1p, 2p. **Shores** a-5 . **Williamson/Mayo** a-13r. **Robert E. Howard** horror story adaptation-2, 3.*

CHAMBER OF CLUES (Formerly Chamber of Chills)
Harvey Publications: No. 27, Feb, 1955 - No. 28, April, 1955

	GD 2.0	VG 4.0	FN 6.0	VF 8.0	VF/NM 9.0	NM- 9.2
27-Kerry Drake-r/#19; Powell-a; last pre-code	7	14	21	35	43	50
28-Kerry Drake	6	12	18	28	34	40

CHAMBER OF DARKNESS (Monsters on the Prowl #9 on)
Marvel Comics Group: Oct, 1969 - No. 8, Dec, 1970

	GD 2.0	VG 4.0	FN 6.0	VF 8.0	VF/NM 9.0	NM- 9.2
1-Buscema-a(p)	8	16	24	56	93	130
2,3: 2-Neal Adams scripts. 3-Smith, Buscema-a	5	10	15	30	48	65
4-A Conan-esque tryout by Smith (4/70); reprinted in Conan #16; Marie Severin/Everett-c	9	18	27	65	113	160
5,8: 5-H.P. Lovecraft adaptation. 8-Wrightson-c	4	8	12	26	41	55
6	4	8	12	22	34	45
7-Wrightson-c/a, 7pgs. (his 1st work at Marvel); Wrightson draws himself in 1st & last panels; Kirby/Ditko-r; last 15¢-c	6	12	18	41	66	90
1-(1/72; 25¢ Special, 52 pgs.)	4	8	12	26	41	55

NOTE: ***Adkins/Everett** a-8. **Buscema** a-Special 1r. **Craig** a-5. **Ditko** a-6-8r. **Heck** a-1, 2, 8, Special 1r. **Kirby** a(p)-4, 5, 7r. **Kirby/Everett** c-5. **Severin/Everett** c-6. **Shores** a-2, 3i, Special 1r. **Sutton** a-1, 2i, 4, 7, Special 1r. **Wrightson** c-7, 8.*

CHAMP COMICS (Formerly Champion No. 1-10)
Worth Publ. Co./Champ Publ./Family Comics(Harvey Publ.): No. 11, Oct, 1940 - No. 24, Dec, 1942; No. 25, April, 1943

	GD 2.0	VG 4.0	FN 6.0	VF 8.0	VF/NM 9.0	NM- 9.2
11-Human Meteor cont'd. from Champion	95	190	285	603	1039	1475
12-17,20: 14,15-Crandall-c. 20-The Green Ghost app.	74	148	222	470	810	1150
18,19-Simon-c. 19-The Wasp app.	95	190	285	603	1039	1475
21-23,25: 22-The White Mask app. 23-Flag-c	54	108	162	343	574	825
24-Hitler, Tojo & Mussolini-c	77	154	231	493	847	1200

CHAMPION (See Gene Autry's...)

CHAMPION COMICS
Worth Publ. Co.: Oct, 1939 (ashcan)

nn-Ashcan comic, not distributed to newsstands, only for in house use. A FN/VF copy sold for $2,261.76 in 2010.

CHAMPION COMICS (Formerly Speed Comics #1?; Champ Comics No. 11 on)
Worth Publ. Co.(Harvey Publications): No. 2, Dec, 1939 - No. 10, Aug, 1940 (no No.1)

	GD 2.0	VG 4.0	FN 6.0	VF 8.0	VF/NM 9.0	NM- 9.2
2-The Champ, The Blazing Scarab, Neptina, Liberty Lads, Jungleman, Bill Handy, Swingtime Sweetie begin	155	310	465	992	1696	2400
3-7: 7-The Human Meteor begins?	79	158	237	502	864	1225
8-10: 8-Simon-c. 9-1st S&K-c (1st collaboration together). 10-Bondage-c by Kirby	174	348	522	1114	1907	2700

CHAMPIONS, THE
Marvel Comics Group: Oct, 1975 - No. 17, Jan, 1978

	GD 2.0	VG 4.0	FN 6.0	VF 8.0	VF/NM 9.0	NM- 9.2
1-Origin & 1st app. The Champions (The Angel, Black Widow, Ghost Rider, Hercules, Iceman); Venus x-over	4	8	12	24	37	50
2-4,8-10,16: 2,3-Venus x-over	2	4	6	11	16	20

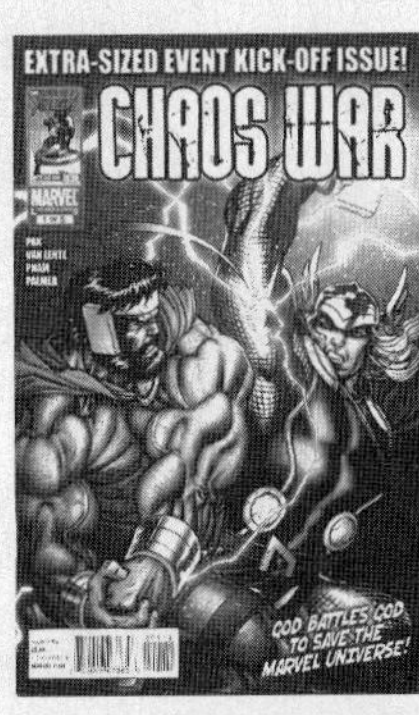

Chaos War #1 © MAR

Charismagic #0 © Aspen MLT

Charlton Bullseye #3 © CC

	GD	VG	FN	VF	VF/NM	NM-
	2.0	4.0	6.0	8.0	9.0	9.2

5-7-(Regular 25¢ edition)(4-8/76) 6-Kirby-c 2 4 6 11 16 20
5-7-(30¢-c variants, limited distribution) 5 10 15 30 48 65
11-14,17-Byrne-a. 14-(Regular 30¢ edition) 2 4 6 13 18 22
14,15-(35¢-c variant, limited distribution) 6 12 18 37 59 80
15-(Regular 30¢ edition)(9/77)-Byrne-a 2 4 6 13 18 22
... Classic Vol. 1 TPB (2006, $19.99) r/#1-11; unused cover to #7 20.00
... Classic Vol. 2 TPB (2007, $19.99) r/#12-17, Iron Man Ann. #4, Avengers #163, Super-Villain Team-Up #14 and Peter Parker, The Spectacular Spider-Man #17-18 20.00

NOTE: ***Buckler/Adkins** c-3. **Byrne** a-11-15, 17. **Kane/Adkins** c-1. **Kane/Layton** c-11. **Tuska** a-3p, 4p, 6p, 7p. Ghost Rider c-1-4, 7, 8, 10, 14, 16, 17 (4, 10, 14 are more prominent).*

CHAMPIONS (Game)
Eclipse Comics: June, 1986 - No. 6, Feb, 1987 (limited series)

1-6: 1-Intro Flare; based on game. 5-Origin Flare 3.00

CHAMPIONS (Also see The League of Champions)
Hero Comics: Sept, 1987 - No. 12, 1989 ($1.95)

1-12: 1-Intro The Marksman & The Rose. 14-Origin Malice 3.00
Annual 1(1988, $2.75, 52pgs.)-Origin of Giant 4.00

CHAMPION SPORTS
National Periodical Publications: Oct-Nov, 1973 - No. 3, Feb-Mar, 1974

1 3 6 9 16 23 30
2,3 2 4 6 9 12 15

CHANNEL ZERO
Image Comics: Feb, 1998 - No. 5 ($2.95, B&W, limited series)

1-5, ...Dupe (1/99) -Brian Wood-s/a 3.00

CHAOS (See The Crusaders)

CHAOS! BIBLE
Chaos! Comics: Nov, 1995 ($3.30, one-shot)

1-Profiles of characters & creators 3.50

CHAOS! CHRONICLES
Chaos! Comics: Feb, 2000 ($3.50, one-shot)

1-Profiles of characters, checklist of Chaos! comics and products 3.50

CHAOS EFFECT, THE
Valiant: 1994

Alpha (Giveaway w/trading card checklist) 3.00
Alpha-Gold variant, Alpha-Red variant, Omega-Gold variant 5.00
Omega (11/94, $2.25); Epilogue Pt. 1, 2 (12/94, 1/95; $2.95) 3.00

CHAOS! GALLERY
Chaos! Comics: Aug, 1997 ($2.95, one-shot)

1-Pin-ups of characters 3.00

CHAOS! QUARTERLY
Chaos! Comics: Oct, 1995 -No. 3, May, 1996 ($4.95, quarterly)

1-3: 1-anthology; Lady Death-c by Julie Bell. 2-Boris "Lady Demon"-c 5.00
1-Premium Edition (7,500) 25.00

CHAOS WAR
Marvel Comics: Dec, 2010 - No. 4, Mr, 2011 ($3.99, limited series)

1-5-Hercules, Thor and others vs. Chaos King; Pham-a. 3-5-Galactus app. 4.00
...: Alpha Flight 1 (1/11, $3.99) McCann-s/Brown-a 4.00
...: Ares 1 (2/11, $3.99) Oeming-s/Segovia-a 4.00
...: Chaos King 1 (1/11, $3.99) Kaluta-a/c; Monclair-s 4.00
...: Dead Avengers 1-3 (1/11 - No. 3, 3/11, $3.99) Grummett-a; Capt. Marvel app. 4.00
...: God Squad 1 (2/11, $3.99) Sumerak-s/Panosian-a 4.00
...: Thor 1,2 (1/11 - No. 2, 2/11, $3.99) DeMatteis-s/Ching-a 4.00
...: X-Men 1,2 (2/11 - No. 2, 3/11, $3.99) Braithwaite-a; Thunderbird, Banshee app. 4.00

CHAPEL (Also see Youngblood & Youngblood Strikefile #1-3)
Image Comics (Extreme Studios): No. 1 Feb, 1995 - No. 2, Mar, 1995 ($2.50, limited series)

1,2 3.00

CHAPEL (Also see Youngblood & Youngblood Strikefile #1-3)
Image Comics (Extreme Studios): V2 #1, Aug, 1995 - No. 7, Apr, 1996 ($2.50)

V2#1-7: 4-Babewatch x-over. 5-vs. Spawn. 7-Shadowhawk-c/app; Shadowhunt x-over 3.00
#1-Quesada & Palmiotti variant-c 3.00

CHAPEL (Also see Youngblood & Youngblood Strikefile #1-3)
Awesome Entertainment: Sept, 1997 ($2.99, one-shot)

1 (Reg. & alternate covers) 3.00

CHARISMAGIC
Aspen MLT: No. 0, Mar, 2011 - Present ($1.99/$2.99)

0-($1.99) Khary Randolph-a/ Vince Hernandez-s; 3 covers 2.00
1-($2.99) Four covers 3.00

CHARLEMAGNE (Also see War Dancer)
Defiant Comics: Mar, 1994 - No. 5, July, 1994 ($2.50)

1/2 (Hero Illustrated giveaway)-Adam Pollina-c/a.
1-(3/94, $3.50, 52 pgs.)-Adam Pollina-c/a. 4.00
2,3,5: Adam Pollina-c/a. 2-War Dancer app. 5-Pre-Schism issue. 3.00
4-($3.25, 52 pgs.) 4.00

CHARLIE CHAN (See Big Shot Comics, Columbia Comics, Feature Comics & The New Advs. of...)

CHARLIE CHAN (The Adventures of...) (Zaza The Mystic No. 10 on) (TV)
Crestwood(Prize) No. 1-5; Charlton No. 6(6/55) on: 6-7/48 - No. 5, 2-3/49; No.6, 6/55 - No. 9, 3/56

1-S&K-c, 2 pgs.; Infantino-a 87 174 261 553 952 1350
2-5-S&K-c: 3-S&K-c/a 50 100 150 315 533 750
6 (6/55-Charlton)-S&K-c/ 37 74 111 222 361 500
7-9 20 40 60 118 192 265

CHARLIE CHAN
Dell Publishing Co.: Oct-Dec, 1965 - No. 2, Mar, 1966

1-Springer-a/c 5 10 15 35 55 75
2 4 8 12 22 34 45

CHARLIE McCARTHY (See Edgar Bergen Presents...)
Dell Publishing Co.: No. 171, Nov, 1947 - No. 571, July, 1954 (See True Comics #14)

Four Color 171 23 46 69 168 334 500
Four Color 196-Part photo-c; photo back-c 14 28 42 99 200 300
1(3-5/49)-Part photo-c; photo back-c 13 26 39 93 182 270
2-9(7/52; #5,6-52 pgs.) 8 16 24 56 93 130
Four Color 445,478,527,571 6 12 18 39 62 85

CHARLTON ACTION: FEATURING "STATIC" (Also see Eclipse Monthly)
Charlton Comics: No, 11, Oct, 1985 - No. 12, Dec, 1985

11,12-Ditko-c/a; low print run 6.00

CHARLTON BULLSEYE
CPL/Gang Publications: 1975 - No. 5, 1976 ($1.50, B&W, bi-monthly, magazine format)

1: 1 & 2 are last Capt. Atom by Ditko/Byrne intended for the never published Capt. Atom #90; Nightshade app.; Jeff Jones-a 5 10 15 30 48 65
2-Part 2 Capt. Atom story by Ditko/Byrne 3 6 9 21 32 42
3-Wrong Country by Sanho Kim 2 4 6 13 18 22
4-Doomsday + 1 by John Byrne 3 6 9 17 25 32
5-Doomsday + 1 by Byrne, The Question by Toth; Neal Adams back-c; Toth-c 4 8 12 24 37 50

CHARLTON BULLSEYE
Charlton Publications: June, 1981 - No. 10, Dec, 1982; Nov, 1986

1-1st Blue Beetle app. since '74, 1st app. The Question since '75; 1st app. Rocket Rabbit; Neil The Horse shown on preview page 1 2 3 5 7 9
2-5: 2-Charlton debut of Neil The Horse; Rocket Rabbit app. 4-Vanguards 6.00
6-10: Low print run. 6-Origin & 1st app. Thunderbunny. 7-1st apps. of Captain Atom & Nightshade since '75. 9-1st app. Bludd. 1 2 3 5 7 9

NOTE: *Material intended for issue #11-up was published in **Scary Tales** #37-up.*

CHARLTON CLASSICS
Charlton Comics: Apr, 1980 - No. 9, Aug, 1981

1-Hercules-r by Glanzman in all 6.00
2-9 5.00

CHARLTON CLASSICS LIBRARY (1776)
Charlton Comics: V10 No.1, Mar, 1973 (one-shot)

1776 (title) - Adaptation of the film musical "1776"; given away at movie theatres; also a newsstand version 3 6 9 14 19 24

CHARLTON PREMIERE (Formerly Marine War Heroes)
Charlton Comics: V1#19, July, 1967; V2#1, Sept, 1967 - No. 4, May, 1968

V1#19, V2#1,2,4: V1#19-Marine War Heroes. V2#1-Trio; intro. Shape, Tyro Team & Spookman. 2-Children of Doom; Boyette classic-a. 4-Unlikely Tales; Aparo, Ditko-a 3 6 9 16 22 28
V2#3-Sinistro Boy Fiend; Blue Beetle & Peacemaker x-over 3 6 9 18 27 35

CHARLTON SPORT LIBRARY - PROFESSIONAL FOOTBALL
Charlton Comics: Winter, 1969-70 (Jan. on cover) (68 pgs.)

1 3 6 9 20 30 40

CHASE (See Batman #550 for 1st app.)

Chase #9 © DC

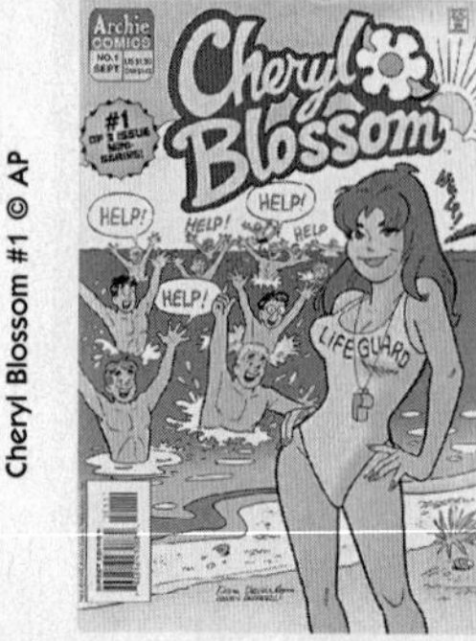

Cheryl Blossom #1 © AP

Chew #11 © John Layman

	GD 2.0	VG 4.0	FN 6.0	VF 8.0	VF/NM 9.0	NM- 9.2

DC Comics: Feb, 1998 - No. 9, Oct, 1998; #1,000,000 Nov, 1998 ($2.50)

1-9: Williams III & Gray-a. 1-Includes 4 Chase cards. 4-Teen Titans app. 7,8-Batman app. 9-GL Hal Jordan-c/app. 3.00
#1,000,000 (11/98) Final issue; 853rd Century x-over 3.00

CHASING DOGMA (See Jay and Silent Bob)

CHASSIS
Millenium Publications: 1996 - No. 3 ($2.95)

1-3: 1-Adam Hughes-c. 2-Conner var-c. 3.00

CHASSIS
Hurricane Entertainment: 1998 - No. 3 ($2.95)

0,1-3: 1-Adam Hughes-c. 0-Green var-c. 3.00

CHASSIS (Vol. 3)
Image Comics: Nov, 1999 - No. 4 ($2.95, limited series)

1-4: 1-Two covers by O'Neil and Green. 2-Busch var-c. 3.00
1-($6.95) DF Edition alternate-c by Wieringo 7.00

CHASTITY
Chaos! Comics: (one-shots)

#1/2 (1/01, $2.95) Batista-a 3.00
Heartbreaker (3/02, $2.99) Adrian-a/Molenaar-c 3.00
Love Bites (3/01, $2.99) Vale-a/Romano-c 3.00
Reign of Terror 1 (10/00, $2.95) Grant-s/Ross-a/Rio-c 3.00
Re-Imagined 1 (7/02, $2.99) Conner-c; Toledo-a 3.00

CHASTITY: CRAZYTOWN
Chaos! Comics: Apr, 2002 - No. 3, June, 2002 ($2.99, limited series)

1-3-Nicieza-s/Batista-c/a 3.00

CHASTITY: LUST FOR LIFE
Chaos! Comics: May, 1999 - No. 3, July, 1999 ($2.95, limited series)

1-3-Nutman-s/Benes-c/a 3.00

CHASTITY: ROCKED
Chaos! Comics: Nov, 1998 - No. 4, Feb, 1999 ($2.95, limited series)

1-4-Nutman-s/Justiniano-c/a 3.00

CHASTITY: SHATTERED
Chaos! Comics: Jun, 2001 - No. 3, Sept, 2001 ($2.99, limited series)

1-3-Kaminski & Pulido-s/Batista-c/a 3.00

CHASTITY: THEATER OF PAIN
Chaos! Comics: Feb, 1997 - No. 3, June, 1997 ($2.95, limited series)

1-3-Pulido-s/Justiniano-c/a 3.00
TPB (1997, $9.95) r/#1-3 10.00

CHECKMATE (TV)
Gold Key: Oct, 1962 - No. 2, Dec, 1962

	GD	VG	FN	VF	VF/NM	NM-
1-Photo-c on both	6	12	18	37	59	80
2	5	10	15	32	51	70

CHECKMATE! (See Action Comics #598 and The OMAC Project)
DC Comics: Apr, 1988 - No. 33, Jan, 1991 ($1.25)

1-33: 13: New format begins 3.00
NOTE: *Gil Kane c-2, 4, 7, 8, 10, 11, 15-19.*

CHECKMATE (See Infinite Crisis and The OMAC Project)
DC Comics: Jun, 2006 - No. 31, Dec, 2008 ($2.99)

1-Rucka-s/Saiz-a/Bermejo-c; Alan Scott, Mr. Terrific, Sasha Bordeaux app. 4.00
1-2nd printing with B&W cover 3.00
2-31: 2,3-Kobra, King Faraday, Amanda Waller, Fire app. 13-15-Outsiders app. 26-Chimera origin 3.00
...: A King's GameTPB (2007, $14.99) r/#1-7 15.00
...: Chimera TPB (2009, $17.99) r/#26-31 18.00
...: Fall of the Wall TPB (2008, $14.99) r/#16-22 15.00
...: Pawn Breaks TPB (2007, $14.99) r/#8-12 15.00

CHERYL BLOSSOM (See Archie's Girls, Betty and Veronica #320 for 1st app.)
Archie Publications: Sept, 1995 - No. 3, Nov, 1995 ($1.50, limited series)

	GD	VG	FN	VF	VF/NM	NM-
1-3	1	2	3	4	5	7
Special 1-4 ('95, '96, $2.00)	1	2	3	4	5	7

CHERYL BLOSSOM (Cheryl's Summer Job)
Archie Publications: July, 1996 - No. 3, Sept, 1996 ($1.50, limited series)

1-3 5.00

CHERYL BLOSSOM (...Goes Hollywood)

	GD 2.0	VG 4.0	FN 6.0	VF 8.0	VF/NM 9.0	NM- 9.2

Archie Publications: Dec, 1996 - No. 3, Feb, 1997 ($1.50, limited series)

1-3 5.00

CHERYL BLOSSOM
Archie Publications: Apr, 1997 - No. 37, Mar, 2001 ($1.50/$1.75/$1.79/$1.99)

	GD	VG	FN	VF	VF/NM	NM-
1-Dan DeCarlo-c/a	1	2	3	5	7	9

2-10: 2-7-Dan DeCarlo-c/a 5.00
11-37: 32-Begin $1.99-c. 34-Sabrina app. 3.00

CHESTY SANCHEZ
Antarctic Press: Nov, 1995 - No. 2, Mar, 1996 ($2.95, B&W)

1,2 3.00
...Super Special (2/99, $5.99) 6.00

CHEVAL NOIR
Dark Horse Comics: 1989 - No. 48, Nov, 1993 ($3.50, B&W, 68 pgs.)

1-8,10 ($3.50): 6-Moebius poster insert 4.00
9,11,13,15,17,20,22 ($4.50, 84 pgs.) 4.50
12,18,19,21,23 ($3.95): 12-Geary-a; Mignola-c 4.00
14 ($4.95, 76 pgs.)(7 pgs. color) 5.00
16,24 ($3.75): 16-19-Contain trading cards 4.00
25,26 ($3.95): 26-Moebius-a begins 4.00
27-48 ($2.95): 33-Snyder III-c 3.00
NOTE: ***Bolland** a-2, 6, 7, 13, 14. **Bolton** a-2, 4, 45; c-4, 20. **Chadwick** c-13. **Dorman** painted c-16. **Geary** a-13, 14. **Kelley Jones** c-27. **Kaluta** a-6; c-6, 18. **Moebius** c-5, 9, 26. **Dave Stevens** c-1, 7. **Sutton** painted c-36.*

CHEW
Image Comics: Jun, 2009 - Present ($2.99)

1-Layman-s/Guillory-a 20.00
1-2nd-4th printings 3.00
2-1st printing 5.00
2-(2nd printing) - 5: Multiple printings exist 3.00
6-18: 15-Gatefold wraparound-c 3.00
Image Firsts: Chew #1 (4/10, $1.00) r/#1 with "Image Firsts" cover logo 1.00

CHEYENNE (TV)
Dell Publishing Co.: No. 734, Oct, 1956 - No. 25, Dec-Jan, 1961-62

	GD	VG	FN	VF	VF/NM	NM-
Four Color 734(#1)-Clint Walker photo-c	14	28	42	96	191	285
Four Color 772,803: Clint Walker photo-c	9	18	27	60	100	140
4(8-10/57) - 20: 4-9,13-20-Clint Walker photo-c. 10-12-Ty Hardin photo-c	6	12	18	43	69	95
21-25-Clint Walker photo-c on all	7	14	21	45	73	100

CHEYENNE AUTUMN (See Movie Classics)

CHEYENNE KID (Formerly Wild Frontier No. 1-7)
Charlton Comics: No. 8, July, 1957 - No. 99, Nov, 1973

	GD	VG	FN	VF	VF/NM	NM-
8 (#1)	8	16	24	42	54	65
9,15-19	6	12	18	29	36	42
10-Williamson/Torres-a(3); Ditko-c	11	22	33	60	83	105
11-(68 pgs.)-Cheyenne Kid meets Geronimo	10	20	30	58	79	100
12-Williamson/Torres-a(2)	10	20	30	58	79	100
13-Williamson/Torres-a (5 pgs.)	8	16	24	44	57	70
14-Williamson-a (5 pgs.?)	8	16	24	42	54	65
20-22,24,25-Severin c/a(3) each	4	8	12	22	34	45
23,27-29	3	6	9	16	22	28
26,30-Severin-a	3	6	9	18	27	35
31-59	2	4	6	10	14	18
60-65,67-80	2	4	6	8	11	14
66-Wander by Aparo begins, ends #87	2	4	6	10	14	18
81-99: Apache Red begins #88, origin in #89	2	4	6	8	11	14

Modern Comics Reprint 87,89(1978) 4.00

CHIAROSCURO (THE PRIVATE LIVES OF LEONARDO DA VINCI)
DC Comics (Vertigo): July, 1995 - No. 10, Apr, 1996 ($2.50/$2.95, limited series, mature)

1-9: McGreal and Rawson-s/Truog & Kayanan-a 3.00
10-($2.95) 3.00
TPB (2005, $24.99) r/series; intro. by Alisa Kwitney, afterword by Pat McGreal 25.00

CHICAGO MAIL ORDER (See C-M-O Comics)

CHIEF, THE (Indian Chief No. 3 on)
Dell Publishing Co.: No. 290, Aug, 1950 - No. 2, Apr-June, 1951

	GD	VG	FN	VF	VF/NM	NM-
Four Color 290(#1)	8	16	24	52	86	120
2	6	12	18	41	66	90

CHIEF CRAZY HORSE (See Wild Bill Hickok #21)
Avon Periodicals: 1950 (Also see Fighting Indians of the Wild West!)

	GD	VG	FN	VF	VF/NM	NM-
nn-Fawcette-c	21	42	63	126	206	285

Chilling Tales #13 © YM

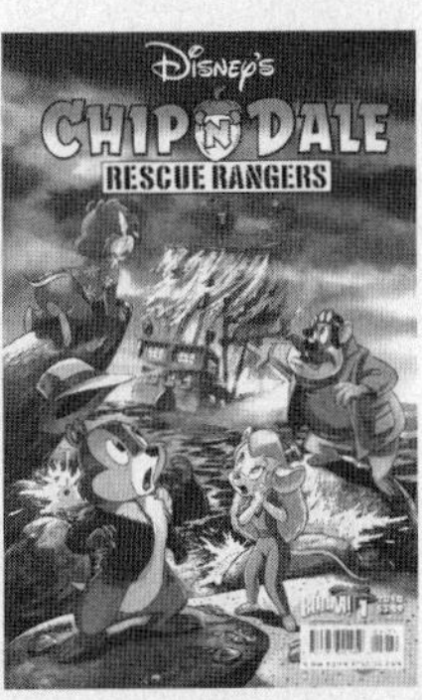
Chip 'n' Dale Rescue Rangers #1 © DIS

C.H.I.X. #1 © Studiosaurus

GD VG FN VF VF/NM NM-
2.0 4.0 6.0 8.0 9.0 9.2

CHIEF VICTORIO'S APACHE MASSACRE (See Fight Indians of/Wild West!)
Avon Periodicals: 1951
nn-Williamson/Frazetta-a (7 pgs.); Larsen-a; Kinstler-c
46 92 138 290 488 685

CHILDREN OF FIRE
Fantagor Press: Nov, 1987 - No. 3, 1988 ($2.00, limited series)
1-3: by Richard Corben 4.00

CHILDREN OF THE VOYAGER (See Marvel Frontier Comics Unlimited)
Marvel Frontier Comics: Sept, 1993 - No. 4, Dec, 1993 ($1.95, limited series)
1-($2.95)-Embossed glow-in-the-dark-c; Paul Johnson-c/a 4.00
2-4 3.00

CHILDREN'S BIG BOOK
Dorene Publ. Co.: 1945 (25¢, stiff-c, 68 pgs.)
nn-Comics & fairy tales; David Icove-a 14 28 42 82 121 160

CHILDREN'S CRUSADE, THE
DC Comics (Vertigo): Dec, 1993 - No. 2, Jan, 1994 ($3.95, limited series)
1,2-Gaiman scripts & Bachalo-a; framing issues for Children's Crusade x-over 4.00

CHILD'S PLAY: THE SERIES (Movie)
Innovation Publishing: May, 1991 - #3, 1991 ($2.50, 28pgs.)
1-3 3.00

CHILD'S PLAY 2 THE OFFICIAL MOVIE ADAPTATION (Movie)
Innovation Publishing: 1990 - No. 3, 1990 ($2.50, bi-weekly limited series)
1-3: Adapts movie sequel 3.00

CHILI (Millie's Rival)
Marvel Comics Group: 5/69 - No. 17, 9/70; No. 18, 8/72 - No. 26, 12/73
1 9 18 27 65 113 160
2,4,5 6 12 18 37 59 80
3-Millie & Chili visit Marvel and meet Stan Lee & Stan Goldberg (6 pgs.)
6 12 18 41 66 90
6-17 5 10 15 30 48 65
18-26 4 8 12 26 41 55
Special 1(12/71, 52 pgs.) 6 12 18 39 62 85

CHILLER
Marvel Comics (Epic): Nov, 1993 - No. 2, Dec, 1993 ($7.95, lim. series)
1,2-(68 pgs.) 1 2 3 5 6 8

CHILLING ADVENTURES IN SORCERY (...as Told by Sabrina #1, 2)
(Red Circle Sorcery No. 6 on)
Archie Publications (Red Circle Prods.): 9/72 - No. 2, 10/72; No. 3, 10/73 - No. 5, 2/74
1-Sabrina cameo as narrator 5 10 15 32 51 70
2-Sabrina cameo as narrator 3 6 9 18 27 35
3-5: Morrow-c/a, all. 4,5-Alcazar-a 2 4 6 11 16 20

CHILLING TALES (Formerly Beware)
Youthful Magazines: No. 13, Dec, 1952 - No. 17, Oct, 1953
13(No.1)-Harrison-a; Matt Fox-c/a 69 138 207 442 759 1075
14-Harrison-a 47 94 141 296 498 700
15-Has #14 on-c; Matt Fox-c; Harrison-a 54 108 162 343 574 825
16-Poe adapt.-'Metzengerstein'; Rudyard Kipling adapt.- 'Mark of the Beast,'
by Kiefer; bondage-c 41 82 123 256 428 600
17-Matt Fox-c; Sir Walter Scott & Poe adapt. 47 94 141 296 498 700

CHILLING TALES OF HORROR (Magazine)
Stanley Publications: V1#1, 6/69 - V1#7, 12/70; V2#2, 2/71 - V2#6, 10/71(50¢, B&W, 52 pgs.)
V1#1 8 16 24 52 86 120
2-4,(no #5),6,7: 7-Cameron-a 5 10 15 35 55 75
V2#2-6: 2-Two different #2 issues exist (2/71 & 4/71). 2-(2/71) Spirit of Frankenstein -r/Adventures into the Unknown #16. 4-(8/71) different from other V2#4(6/71)
5 10 15 32 51 70
V2#4-(6/71) r/9 pg. Feldstein-a from Adventures into the Unknown #3
5 10 15 35 55 75
NOTE: *Two issues of V2#2 exist, Feb, 1971 and April, 1971. Two issues of V2#4 exist, Jun, 1971 and Aug, 1971.*

CHILLY WILLY (Also see New Funnies #211)
Dell Publ. Co.: No. 740, Oct, 1956 - No. 1281, Apr-June, 1962 (Walter Lantz)
Four Color 740 (#1) 7 14 21 49 80 110
Four Color 852 (2/58),967 (2/59),1017 (9/59),1074 (2-4/60),1122 (8/60), 1177 (4-6/61), 1212 (7-9/61), 1281 5 10 15 30 48 65

CHIMERA
CrossGeneration Comics: Mar, 2003 - No. 4, July, 2003 ($2.95, limited series)
1-4-Marz-s/Peterson-c/a 3.00
Vol. 1 TPB (2003, $15.95) r/#1-4 plus sketch pages, 3-D models, how-to guides 16.00

CHIMICHANGA
Albatross Exploding Funny Books: 2010 ($3.00, B&W)
1-3-Eric Powell-s/a/c 3.00

CHINA BOY (See Wisco in the Promotional Comics section)

CHIP 'N' DALE (Walt Disney)(See Walt Disney's C&S #204)
Dell Publishing Co./Gold Key/Whitman No. 65 on: Nov, 1953 - No. 30, June-Aug, 1962; Sept, 1967 - No. 83, July, 1984
Four Color 517(#1) 11 22 33 75 138 200
Four Color 581,636 6 12 18 43 69 95
4(12/55-2/56)-10 6 12 18 37 59 80
11-30 5 10 15 30 48 65
1(Gold Key, 1967)-Reprints 3 6 9 20 30 40
2-10 2 4 6 13 18 22
11-20 2 4 6 9 12 15
21-40 2 4 6 8 10 12
41-64,70-77: 75(2/82), 76(2-3/82), 77(3/82) 1 2 3 5 7 9
65,66 (Whitman) 2 4 6 8 11 14
67-69 (3-pack? 1980): 67(8/80), 68(10/80) (scarce) 4 8 12 24 37 50
78-83 (All #90214; 3-pack, nd, nd code): 78(4/83), 79(5/83), 80(7/83), 81(8/83), 82(5/84), 83(7/84) 3 6 9 16 22 28
NOTE: *All Gold Key/Whitman issues have reprints except No. 32-35, 38-41, 45-47. No. 23-28, 30-42, 45-47, 49 have new covers.*

CHIP 'N DALE RESCUE RANGERS
Disney Comics: June, 1990 - No. 19, Dec, 1991 ($1.50)
1-New stories; origin begins 3.50
2-19: 2-Origin continued 3.00

CHIP 'N DALE RESCUE RANGERS
BOOM! Studios: Dec, 2010 - Present ($3.99)
1-5: 1-Brill-s/Castellani-a; 3 covers 4.00
... Free Comic Book Day Edition (5/11) Flip book with Darkwing Duck 2.00

CHITTY CHITTY BANG BANG (See Movie Comics)

C.H.I.X.
Image Comics (Studiosaurus): Jan, 1998 ($2.50)
1-Dodson, Haley, Lopresti, Randall, and Warren-s/c/a 3.00
1-($5.00) "X-Ray Variant" cover 5.00
C.H.I.X. That Time Forgot 1 (8/98, $2.95) 3.00

CHOICE COMICS
Great Publications: Dec, 1941 - No. 3, Feb, 1942
1-Origin Secret Circle; Atlas the Mighty app.; Zomba, Jungle Fight, Kangaroo Man, & Fire Eater begin 155 310 465 992 1696 2400
2 77 154 231 493 847 1200
3-Double feature; Features movie "The Lost City" (classic cover); continued from Great Comics #3 155 310 465 992 1696 2400

CHOLLY AND FLYTRAP (Arthur Suydam's...)
Image Comics: Nov, 2004 - No. 4, June, 2005 ($4.95/$5.95, limited series)
1-($4.95) Arthur Suydam-s/a/c 6.00
2-4-($5.95) 6.00

CHOO CHOO CHARLIE
Gold Key: Dec, 1969
1-John Stanley-a 8 16 24 52 86 120

CHOSEN
Dark Horse Comics: Jan, 2004 - No. 3, Aug, 2004 ($2.99, limited series)
1-Story of the second coming; Mark Millar-s/Peter Gross-a 4.00
2,3 3.00

CHRISTIAN (See Asylum)
Maximum Press: Jan, 1996 ($2.99, one-shot)
1-Pop Mhan-a 3.00

CHRISTIAN HEROES OF TODAY
David C. Cook: 1964 (36 pgs.)
nn 3 6 9 18 27 35

CHRISTMAS (Also see A-1 Comics)
Magazine Enterprises: No. 28, 1950
A-1 28 8 16 24 42 54 65

CHRISTMAS ADVENTURE, A (See Classics Comics Giveaways, 12/69)

Christmas Parade #1 © DIS

Chronos #6 © DC

Cinderella Love #25 © STJ

GD 2.0 | VG 4.0 | FN 6.0 | VF 8.0 | VF/NM 9.0 | NM- 9.2

CHRISTMAS ALBUM (See March of Comics No. 312)

CHRISTMAS ANNUAL
Golden Special: 1975 ($1.95, 100 pgs., stiff-c)
nn-Reprints Mother Goose stories with Walt Kelly-a 4 8 12 22 34 45

CHRISTMAS & ARCHIE
Archie Comics: Jan, 1975 ($1.00, 68 pgs., 10-1/4x13-1/4" treasury-sized)
1-(scarce) 6 12 18 39 62 85

CHRISTMAS BELLS (See March of Comics No. 297)

CHRISTMAS CARNIVAL
Ziff-Davis Publ. Co./St. John Publ. Co. No. 2: 1952 (25¢, one-shot, 100 pgs.)
nn 36 72 108 211 343 475
2-Reprints Ziff-Davis issue plus-c 17 34 51 98 154 210

CHRISTMAS CAROL, A (See March of Comics No. 33)

CHRISTMAS EVE, A (See March of Comics No. 212)

CHRISTMAS IN DISNEYLAND (See Dell Giants)

CHRISTMAS PARADE (See Dell Giant No. 26, Dell Giants, March of Comics No. 284, Walt Disney Christmas Parade & Walt Disney's...)

CHRISTMAS PARADE (Walt Disney's)
Gold Key: 1962 (no month listed) - No. 9, Jan, 1972 (#1,5: 80 pgs.; #2-4,7-9: 36 pgs.)
1 (30018-301)-Giant 9 18 27 60 100 140
2-6: 2-r/F.C. #367 by Barks. 3-r/F.C. #178 by Barks. 4-r/F.C. #203 by Barks. 5-r/Christmas Parade #1 (Dell) by Barks; giant. 6-r/Christmas Parade #2 (Dell) by Barks (64 pgs.); giant 6 12 18 41 66 90
7-Pull-out poster (half price w/o poster) 5 10 15 32 51 70
8-r/F.C. #367 by Barks; pull-out poster 6 12 18 41 66 90
9 4 8 12 26 41 55

CHRISTMAS PARTY (See March of Comics No. 256)

CHRISTMAS STORIES (See Little People No. 959, 1062)

CHRISTMAS STORY (See March of Comics No. 326 in the Promotional Comics section)

CHRISTMAS STORY BOOK (See Woolworth's Christmas Story Book)

CHRISTMAS TREASURY, A (See Dell Giants & March of Comics No. 227)

CHRISTMAS WITH ARCHIE
Spire Christian Comics (Fleming H. Revell Co.): 1973, 1974 (49¢, 52 pgs.)
nn-Low print run 2 4 6 13 18 22

CHRISTMAS WITH MOTHER GOOSE
Dell Publishing Co.: No. 90, Nov, 1945 - No. 253, Nov, 1949
Four Color 90 (#1)-Kelly-a 16 32 48 111 226 340
Four Color 126 ('46), 172 (11/47)-By Walt Kelly 13 26 39 89 170 250
Four Color 201 (10/48), 253-By Walt Kelly 11 22 33 75 138 200

CHRISTMAS WITH SANTA (See March of Comics No. 92)

CHRISTMAS WITH THE SUPER-HEROES (See Limited Collectors' Edition)
DC Comics: 1988; No. 2, 1989 ($2.95)
1,2: 1-(100 pgs.)-All reprints; N. Adams-r, Byrne-c; Batman, Superman, JLA, LSH Christmas stories; r-Miller's 1st Batman/DC Special Series #21. 2-(68 pgs.)-Superman by Chadwick; Batman, Wonder Woman, Deadman, Green Lantern, Flash app.; Morrow-a; Enemy Ace by Byrne; all new-a 5.00

CHROMA-TICK, THE (...Special Edition, #1,2) (Also see The Tick)
New England Comics Press: Feb, 1992 - No. 8, Nov, 1993 ($3.95/$3.50, 44 pgs.)
1,2-Includes serially numbered trading card set 5.00
3-8 ($3.50, 36 pgs.): 6-Bound-in card 4.00

CHROME
Hot Comics: 1986 - No. 3, 1986 ($1.50, limited series)
1-3 3.00

CHROMIUM MAN, THE
Triumphant Comics: Aug, 1993 - No.10, May, 1994 ($2.50)
1-1st app. Mr. Death; all serially numbered 3.00
2-10: 2-1st app. Prince Vandal. 3-1st app. Candi, Breaker & Coil. 4,5-Triumphant Unleashed x-over. 8,9-(3/94). 10-(5/94) 3.00
0-(4/94)-Four color-c, 0-All pink-c & all blue-c; no cover price 3.00

CHROMIUM MAN: VIOLENT PAST, THE
Triumphant Comics: Jan, 1994 - No. 2, Jan, 1994 ($2.50, limited series)
1,2-Serially numbered to 22,000 each 3.00

CHRONICLES OF CONAN, THE (See Conan the Barbarian)

GD 2.0 | VG 4.0 | FN 6.0 | VF 8.0 | VF/NM 9.0 | NM- 9.2

CHRONICLES OF CORUM, THE (Also see Corum...)
First Comics: Jan, 1987 - No. 12, Nov, 1988 ($1.75/$1.95, deluxe series)
1-12: Adapts Michael Moorcock's novel 3.00

CHRONOS
DC Comics: Mar, 1998 - No. 11, Feb. 1999 ($2.50)
1-11-J.F. Moore-s/Guinan-a 3.00
#1,000,000 (11/98) 853rd Century x-over 3.00

CHUCK (Based on the NBC TV series)
DC Comics (WildStorm): Aug, 2008 - No. 6, Jan, 2009 ($2.99, limited series)
1-6-Jeremy Haun-a/Kristian Donaldson-c; Noto back-up-a 3.00
TPB (2009, $19.99) r/#1-6; photo-c 20.00

CHUCKLE, THE GIGGLY BOOK OF COMIC ANIMALS
R. B. Leffingwell Co.: 1945 (132 pgs., one-shot)
1-Funny animal 22 44 66 132 216 300

CHUCK NORRIS (TV)
Marvel Comics (Star Comics): Jan, 1987 - No. 4, July, 1987
1-3: Ditko-a 3.50
4-No Ditko-a (low print run) 5.00

CHUCK WAGON (See Sheriff Bob Dixon's...)

CHUCKY (Based on the 1988 killer doll movie Child's Play)
Devil's Due Publishing: Apr, 2007 - No. 4, Nov, 2007 ($3.50/$5.50)
1-3-Pulido-s/Medors-a; art & photo covers 3.50
4-($5.50) 5.50
TPB (2007, $18.99) r/series; gallery of variant covers; 4 pages of script and sketch art 19.00

CHYNA (WWF Wrestling)
Chaos! Comics: Sept, 2000; July, 2001 ($2.95/$2.99, one-shots)
1-Grant-s/Barrows-a; photo-c 3.00
1-($9.95) Premium Edition; Cleavenger-c 10.00
II -(7/01, $2.99) Deodato-a; photo-c 3.00

CICERO'S CAT
Dell Publishing Co.: July-Aug, 1959 - No. 2, Sept-Oct, 1959
1-Cat from Mutt & Jeff 5 10 15 30 48 65
2 4 8 12 26 41 55

CIMARRON STRIP (TV)
Dell Publishing Co.: Jan, 1968
1-Stuart Whitman photo-c 4 8 12 24 37 50

CINDER AND ASHE
DC Comics: May, 1988 - No. 4, Aug, 1988 ($1.75, limited series)
1-4: Mature readers 3.00

CINDERELLA (Disney) (See Movie Comics)
Dell Publishing Co.: No. 272, Apr, 1950 - No. 786, Apr, 1957
Four Color 272 12 24 36 86 161 235
Four Color 786-Partial-r #272 7 14 21 45 73 100

CINDERELLA
Whitman Publishing Co.: Apr, 1982
nn-Reprints 4-Color #272 1 2 3 4 5 7

CINDERELLA: FABLES ARE FOREVER (See Fables)
DC Comics (Vertigo): Apr, 2011 - No. 6 ($2.99, limited series)
1,2-Roberson-s/McManus-a/Zullo-c; Dorothy Gale app. 3.00

CINDERELLA: FROM FABLETOWN WITH LOVE (See Fables)
DC Comics (Vertigo): Jan, 2010 - No. 6, Jun, 2010 ($2.99, limited series)
1-6: Roberson-s/McManus-a/Zullo-c 3.00
TPB (2010, $14.99) r/#1-6 15.00

CINDERELLA LOVE
Ziff-Davis/St. John Publ. Co. No. 12 on: No. 10, 1950; No. 11, 4-5/51; No. 12, 9/51; No. 4, 10-11/51 - No. 11, Fall, 1952; No. 12, 10/53 - No. 15, 8/54; No. 25, 12/54 - No. 29, 10/55 (No #16-24)
10(#1)(1st Series, 1950)-Painted-c 18 36 54 105 165 225
11(#2, 4-5/51)-Crandall-a; Saunders painted-c 13 26 39 72 101 130
12(#3, 9/51)-Photo-c 11 22 33 62 86 110
4-8: 4,6,7-Photo-c 10 20 30 58 79 100
9-Kinstler-a; photo-c 11 22 33 64 90 115
10,11(Fall/'52): 10,11-Photo-c 10 20 30 58 79 100
12(St. John-10/53)-#13:13-Painted-c. 10 20 30 56 76 95
14-Baker-a 12 24 36 69 97 125

Cisco Kid #4 © DELL

City of Heroes #1 © NCsoft

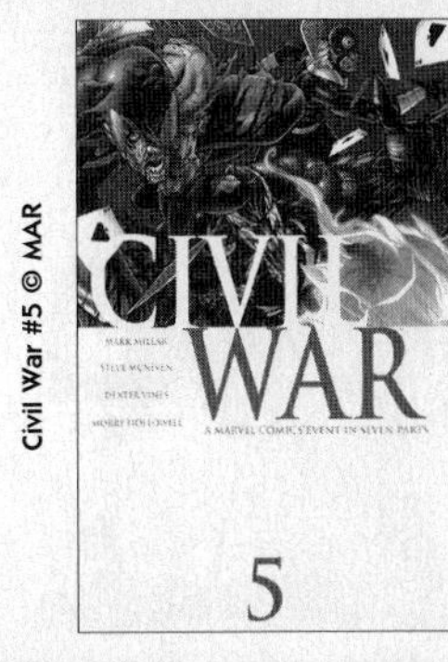

Civil War #5 © MAR

GD VG FN VF VF/NM NM-
2.0 4.0 6.0 8.0 9.0 9.2

15(8/54)-Matt Baker-c 14 28 42 82 121 160
25(2nd Series)(Formerly Romantic Marriage) Baker-c 14 28 42 82 121 160
26-Baker-c; last precode (2/55) 14 28 42 82 121 160
27,29: Both Matt Baker-c 14 28 42 82 121 160
28 9 18 27 52 69 85

CINDY COMICS (...Smith No. 39, 40; Crime Can't Win No. 41 on)(Formerly Krazy Komics) (See Junior Miss & Teen Comics)
Timely Comics: No. 27, Fall, 1947 - No. 40, July, 1950

27-Kurtzman-a, 3 pgs: Margie, Oscar begin 24 48 72 140 230 320
28-31-Kurtzman-a 15 30 45 85 130 175
32-40: 33-Georgie story; anti-Wertham editorial 12 24 36 69 97 125
NOTE: *Kurtzman's "Hey Look"-#27(3), 29(2), 30(2), 31; "Giggles 'n' Grins"-28.*

CINNAMON: EL CICLO
DC Comics: Oct, 2003 - No. 5, Feb, 2004 ($2.50, limited series)

1-5-Van Meter-s/Chaykin-c/Paronzini-a 3.00

CIRCUS (...the Comic Riot)
Globe Syndicate: June, 1938 - No. 3, Aug, 1938

1-(Scarce)-Spacehawks (2 pgs.), & Disk Eyes by Wolverton (2 pgs.), Pewee Throttle by Cole (2nd comic book work; see Star Comics V1#11), Beau Gus, Ken Craig & The Lords of Crillon, Jack Hinton by Eisner, Van Bragger by Kane 500 1000 1500 3600 6300 9000
2,3-(Scarce)-Eisner, Cole, Wolverton, Bob Kane-a in each 280 5560 840 1764 2982 4200

CIRCUS BOY (TV) (See Movie Classics)
Dell Publishing Co.: No. 759, Dec, 1956 - No. 813, July, 1957

Four Color 759 (#1)-The Monkees' Mickey Dolenz photo-c 12 24 36 82 154 225
Four Color 785 (4/57),813-Mickey Dolenz photo-c 10 20 30 69 122 175

CIRCUS COMICS
Farm Women's Pub. Co./D. S. Publ.: 1945 - No. 2, Jun, 1945; Wint., 1948-49

1-Funny animal 14 28 42 80 115 150
2 9 18 27 50 65 80
1(1948)-D.S. Publ.; 2 pgs. Frazetta 24 48 72 140 230 320

CIRCUS OF FUN COMICS
A. W. Nugent Publ. Co.: 1945 - No. 3, Dec, 1947 (A book of games & puzzles)

1 15 30 45 84 127 170
2,3 10 20 30 54 72 90

CISCO KID, THE (TV)
Dell Publishing Co.: July, 1950 - No. 41, Oct-Dec, 1958

Four Color 292(#1)-Cisco Kid, his horse Diablo, & sidekick Pancho & his horse Loco begin; painted-c begin 21 42 63 150 300 450
2(1/51) 11 22 33 75 138 200
3-5 10 20 30 69 122 175
6-10 9 18 27 60 100 140
11-20 8 16 24 52 86 120
21-36-Last painted-c 6 12 18 43 69 95
37-41: All photo-c 8 16 24 54 90 125
NOTE: ***Buscema*** *a-40.* ***Ernest Nordli*** *painted c-5-16, 20, 35.*

CISCO KID COMICS
Bernard Bailey/Swappers Quarterly: Winter, 1944 (one-shot)

1-Illustrated Stories of the Operas: Faust; Funnyman by Giunta; Cisco Kid (1st app.) & Superbaby begin; Giunta-c 43 86 129 271 461 650

CITIZEN SMITH (See Holyoke One-Shot No. 9)

CITIZEN V AND THE V-BATTALION (See Thunderbolts)
Marvel Comics: June, 2001 - No. 3, Aug, 2001 ($2.99, limited series)

1-3-Nicieza-a; Michael Ryan-c/a 3.00
...: The Everlasting 1-4 (3/02 - No. 4, 7/02) Nicieza-s/LaRosa-a(p) 3.00

CITY OF HEROES (Online game)
Dark Horse Comics/Blue King Studios: Sept, 2002; May, 2004 - No. 7 ($2.95)

1-(no cover price) Dakan-s/Zombo-a 3.00
1-7-($2.95) 3.00

CITY OF HEROES (Online game)
Image Comics: June, 2005 - No. 20, Aug, 2007 ($2.99)

1-20: 1-Waid-s; Pérez-c. 6-Flp-c with City of Villains. 7-9-Jurgens-s 3.00

CITY OF OTHERS
Dark Horse Comics: Apr, 2007 - No. 4, Aug, 2007 ($2.99, limited series)

1-4-Bernie Wrightson-a/c; Steve Niles & Wrightson-s 3.00

GD VG FN VF VF/NM NM-
2.0 4.0 6.0 8.0 9.0 9.2

TPB (2/08, $14.95) r/#1-4; Wrightson sketch pages 15.00

CITY OF SILENCE
Image Comics: May, 2000 - No. 3, July, 2000 ($2.50)

1-3-Ellis-s/Erskine-a 3.00
TPB (6/04, $9.95) r/#1-3; pin-up gallery 10.00

CITY OF THE LIVING DEAD (See Fantastic Tales No. 1)
Avon Periodicals: 1952

nn-Hollingsworth-c/a 50 100 150 315 533 750

CITY OF TOMORROW
DC Comics (WildStorm): June, 2005 - No. 6, Nov, 2005 ($2.99, limited series)

1-6-Howard Chaykin-s/a 3.00
TPB (2006, $19.99) r/#1-6 20.00

CITY PEOPLE NOTEBOOK
Kitchen Sink Press: 1989 ($9.95, B&W, magazine sized)

nn-Will Eisner-s/a 10.00
nn-(DC Comics, 2000) Reprint 10.00

CITY SURGEON (Blake Harper...)
Gold Key: August, 1963

1(10075-308)-Painted-c 4 8 12 24 37 50

CIVIL WAR (Also see Amazing Spider-Man for TPB)
Marvel Comics: July, 2006 - No. 7, Jan, 2007 ($3.99/$2.99, limited series)

1-($3.99) Millar-s/McNiven-a & wraparound-c 1 2 3 5 6 8
1-Variant cover by Michael Turner 2 4 6 9 12 15
1-Aspen Comics Variant cover by Turner 2 4 6 9 12 15
1-Director's Cut (2006, $4.99) r/#1 plus promo art, variant covers, sketches and script 5.00
2-($2.99) Spider-Man unmasks 1 2 3 4 5 7
2-Turner variant cover 5.00
2-B&W sketch variant cover 20.00
2-2nd printing 4.00
3-7: 3-Thor returns. 4-Goliath killed 4.00
3-7-Turner variant covers 5.00
3-7-B&W sketch variant covers 15.00
TPB (2007, $24.99) r/#1-7; gallery of variant covers 25.00
...: Battle Damage Report (2007, $3.99) Post-Civil War character profiles; McGuinness-c 4.00
...: Choosing Sides (2/07, $3.99) Colan-c; Howard the Duck app.; 2 covers by Yu & Colan 4.00
... Companion TPB (2007, $13.99) r/Civil War Files, ...:Battle Damage Report, Marvel Spotlight: Millar/McNiven, Marvel Spotlight: Civil War Aftermath and Daily Bugle CW 14.00
Daily Bugle Civil War Newspaper Special #1 (9/06, 50¢, newsprint) Daily Bugle "newspaper" overview of the crossover; Mayhew-a 2.50
...Files (2006, $3.99) profile pages of major Civil War characters; McNiven-c 4.00
...: Marvel Universe TPB (2007, $11.99) r/Civil War: Choosing Sides, CW: The Return, She-Hulk #8, CW: The Initiative; She-Hulk sketch page; variant cover gallery 12.00
...: MGC #1 (6/10, $1.00) r/#1 with "Marvel's Greatest Comics" cover logo 1.00
...: The Confession (5/07, $2.99) Maleev-c/a; Bendis-s 3.00
...: The Initiative (4/07, $4.99) Silvestri-c/a; previews of post-Civil War series 5.00
...: The Return (3/07, $2.99) Captain Marvel returns; The Sentry app.; Raney-a 3.00
...: The Road to Civil War TPB (2007, $14.99) r/New Avengers: Illuminati, Fantastic Four #536 & 537, Amazing Spider-Man #529-531; Spider-Man costume sketches by Bachalo 15.00
... War Crimes (2/07, $3.99) Kingpin in prison; Tieri-s/Staz Johnson-a 4.00
... War Crimes TPB (2007, $17.99) r/Civil War: War Crimes one-shot and Underworld #1-5 18.00
... X-Men Universe TPB (2007, $13.99) r/Cable & Deadpool #30-32; X-Factor #8,9 14.00

CIVIL WAR CHRONICLES (Reprints of Civil War and related Marvel issues)
Marvel Comics: Oct, 2007 - No. 12, Sept, 2008 ($4.99, limited series)

1-12: Reprints Civil War, Civil War: Frontline and x-over issues 5.00

CIVIL WAR: FRONTLINE (Tie-in to Civil War and related Marvel issues)
Marvel Comics: Aug, 2006 - No. 11, Apr, 2007 ($2.99, limited series)

1-Jenkins-s/Bachs-a/Watson-c; back-up stories by various 4.00
2-11: 3-Green Goblin app. 11-Aftermath of Civil War #7 3.00
... Book 1 TPB (2007, $14.99) r/#1-6 15.00
... Book 2 TPB (2007, $14.99) r/#7-11 15.00

CIVIL WAR: HOUSE OF M
Marvel Comics: Nov, 2008 - No. 5, Mar, 2009 ($2.99, limited series)

1-5-Gage-s/DiVito-a 3.00

CIVIL WAR MUSKET, THE (Kadets of America Handbook)
Custom Comics, Inc.: 1960 (25¢, half-size, 36 pgs.)

nn 3 6 9 16 22 28

CIVIL WAR: X-MEN (Tie-in to Civil War)

Claire Voyant #4 © STD

Clandestine #7 © MAR

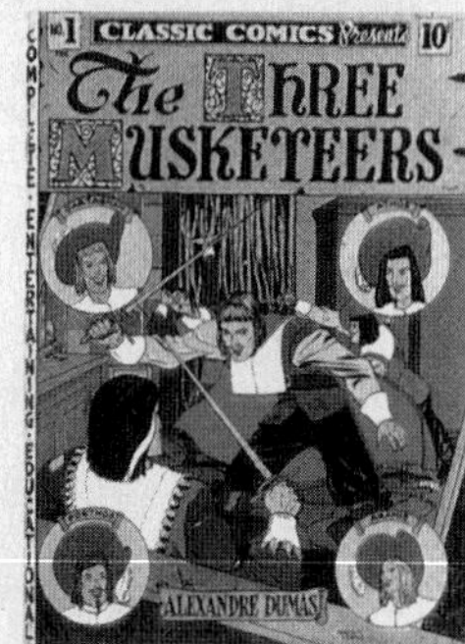

Classic Comics #1 © GIL

	GD 2.0	VG 4.0	FN 6.0	VF 8.0	VF/NM 9.0	NM- 9.2

Marvel Comics: Sept, 2006 - No. 4, Dec, 2006 ($2.99, limited series)

1-4-Paquette-a/Hine-s; Bishop app. 3.00
1-Variant cover by Michael Turner 10.00
TPB (2007, $11.99) r/#1-4, profile pages of minor characters 12.00

CIVIL WAR: YOUNG AVENGERS & RUNAWAYS (Tie-in to Civil War)
Marvel Comics: Sept, 2006 - No. 4, Dec, 2006 ($2.99, limited series)

1-4-Caselli-a/Wells-s/Cheung-c 3.00
TPB (2007, $11.99) r/#1-4, profile pages of characters 12.00

CLAIRE VOYANT (Also see Keen Teens)
Leader Publ./Standard/Pentagon Publ.: 1946 - No. 4, 1947 (Sparling strip reprints)

	GD 2.0	VG 4.0	FN 6.0	VF 8.0	VF/NM 9.0	NM- 9.2
nn	69	138	207	442	759	1075
2,4: 2-Kamen-c. 4-Kamen bondage-c	52	104	156	323	549	775
3-Kamen bridal-c; contents mentioned in Love and Death, a book by Gershom Legman(1949) referenced by Dr. Wertham in **SOTI**	63	126	189	403	689	975

CLANDESTINE (Also see Marvel Comics Presents & X-Men: ClanDestine)
Marvel Comics: Oct, 1994 - No.12, Sept, 1995 ($2.95/$2.50)

1-($2.95)-Alan Davis-c/a(p)/scripts & Mark Farmer-c/a(i) begin, ends #8; Modok app.; Silver Surfer cameo; gold foil-c 3.50
2-12: 2-Wraparound-c. 2,3-Silver Surfer app. 5-Origin of ClanDestine. 6-Capt. America, Hulk, Spider-Man, Thing & Thor-c; Spider-Man cameo. 7-Spider-Man-c/app; Punisher cameo. 8-Invaders & Dr. Strange app. 10-Captain Britain-c/app. 11-Sub-Mariner app. 3.00
Preview (10/94, $1.50) 3.00
... Classic HC (2008, $29.99, DJ) r/#1-8, Marvel Comics Presents #158, X-Men and Clandestine #1&2, sketch pages and cover gallery; Alan Davis afterword 30.00

CLANDESTINE
Marvel Comics: Apr, 2008 - No. 5, Aug, 2008 ($2.99, limited series)

1-5: 1-Alan Davis-c/a(p)/scripts & Mark Farmer-c/a(i). 2-5-Excalibur app. 3.00

CLASH
DC Comics: 1991 - No. 3, 1991 ($4.95, limited series, 52 pgs.)

Book One - Three: Adam Kubert-c/a 5.00

CLASSIC BATTLESTAR GALACTICA (See Battlestar Galactica, Classic...)

CLASSIC COMICS/ILLUSTRATED - INTRODUCTION
by Dan Malan

Since the first publication of this special introduction to the **Classics** section, a number of revisions have been made to further clarify the listings. **Classics** reprint editions prior to 1963 had either incorrect dates or no dates listed. Those reprint editions should be identified only by the highest number on the reorder list (HRN). Past *Guides* listed what were calculated to be approximately correct dates, but many people found it confusing for the *Guide* to list a date not listed in the comic itself.

We have also attempted to clear up confusion about edition variations, such as color, printer, etc. Such variations are identified by letters. Editions are determined by three categories. Original edition variations are designated as Edition 1A, 1B, etc. All reprint editions prior to 1963 are identified by HRN only. All reprint editions from 9/63 on are identified by the correct date listed in the comic.

Information is also included on four reprintings of **Classics**. From 1968-1976, Twin Circle, the Catholic newspaper, serialized over 100 **Classics** titles. That list can be found under non-series items at the end of this section. In 1972, twelve **Classics** were reissued as **Now Age Books Illustrated**. They are listed under **Pendulum Illustrated Classics**. In 1982, 20 **Classics** were reissued, adapted for teaching English as a second language. They are listed under **Regents Illustrated Classics**. Then in 1984, six **Classics** were reissued with cassette tapes. See the listing under **Cassette Books**.

UNDERSTANDING CLASSICS ILLUSTRATED
by Dan Malan

Since **Classics Illustrated** is the most complicated comic book series, with all its reprint editions and variations, changes in covers and artwork, a variety of means of identifying editions, and the most extensive worldwide distribution of any comic-book series, this introductory section is provided to assist you in gaining expertise about this series.

THE HISTORY OF CLASSICS

The **Classics** series was the brain child of Albert L. Kanter, who saw in the new comic-book medium a means of introducing children to the great classics of literature. In October of 1941 his Gilberton Co. began the **Classic Comics** series with **The Three Musketeers**, with 64 pages of storyline. In those early years, the struggling series saw irregular schedules and numerous printers, not to mention variable art quality and liberal story adaptations. With No.13 the page total was reduced to 56 (except for No. 33, originally scheduled to be No. 9), and with No. 15 the coming-next ad on the outside back cover moved inside. In 1945 the Jerry Iger Shop began producing all new CC titles, beginning with No. 23. In 1947 the search for a classier logo resulted in **Classics Illustrated**, beginning with No. 35, **Last Days of Pompeii**. With No. 45 the page total dropped again to 48, which was to become the standard.

Two new developments in 1951 had a profound effect upon the success of the series. One was the introduction of painted covers, instead of the old line drawn covers, beginning with No. 81, **The Odyssey**. The second was the switch to the major national distributor Curtis. They raised the cover price from 10 to 15 cents, making it the highest priced comic-book, but it did not slow the growth of the series, because they were marketed as books, not comics. Because of this higher quality image, **Classics** flourished during the fifties while other comic series were reeling from outside attacks. They diversified with their new **Juniors**, **Specials**, and **World Around Us** series.

Classics artwork can be divided into three distinct periods. The pre-Iger era (1941-44) was mentioned above for its variable art quality. The Iger era (1945-53) was a major improvement in art quality and adaptations. It came to be dominated by artists Henry Kiefer and Alex Blum, together accounting for some 50 titles. Their styles gave the first real personality to the series. The EC era (1954-62) resulted from the demise of the EC horror series, when many of their artists made the major switch to classical art.

But several factors brought the production of new CI titles to a complete halt in 1962. Gilberton lost its 2nd class mailing permit. External factors like television, cheap paperback books, and Cliff Notes were all eating away at their market. Production halted with No.167, **Faust**, even though many more titles were already in the works. Many of those found their way into foreign series, and are very desirable to collectors. In 1967, **Classics Illustrated** was sold to Patrick Frawley and his Catholic publication, Twin Circle. They issued two new titles in 1969 as part of an attempted revival, but succumbed to major distribution problems in 1971. In 1988, First Publishing acquired the rights to use the old CI series art, logo, and name from the Frawley Group, and released a short-lived series featuring contributions of modern creators. Acclaim Books and Twin Circles issued a series of **Classics** reprints from 1997-1998.

One of the unique aspects of the **Classics Illustrated** (CI) series was the proliferation of reprint variations. Some titles had as many as 25 editions. Reprinting began in 1943. Some **Classic Comics** (CC) reprints (r) had the logo format revised to a banner logo, and added a motto under the banner. In 1947 CC titles changed to the CI logo, but kept their line drawn covers (LDC). In 1948, Nos. 13, 18, 29 and 41 received second covers (LDC2), replacing covers considered too violent, and reprints of Nos. 13-44 had pages reduced to 48, except for No. 26, which had 48 pages to begin with.

Starting in the mid-1950s, 70 of the 80 LDC titles were reissued with new painted covers (PC). Thirty of them also received new interior artwork (A2). The new artwork was generally higher quality with larger art panels and more faithful but abbreviated storylines. Later on, there were 29 second painted covers (PC2), mostly by Twin Circle. Altogether there were 199 interior art variations (169 (O)s and 30 A2 editions) and 272 different covers (169 (O)s, four LDC2s, 70 new PCs of LDC (O)s, and 29 PC2s). It is mildly astounding to realize that there are nearly 1400 different editions in the U.S. CI series.

FOREIGN CLASSICS ILLUSTRATED

If U.S. Classics variations are mildly astounding, the veritable plethora of foreign CI variations will boggle your imagination. While we still anticipate additional discoveries, we presently know about series in 25 languages and 27 countries. There were 250 new CI titles in foreign series, and nearly 400 new foreign covers of U.S. titles. The 1400 U.S. CI editions pale in comparison to the 4000 plus foreign editions. The very nature of CI lent itself to flourishing as an international series. Worldwide, they published over one billion copies! The first foreign CI series consisted of six Canadian Classic Comic reprints in 1946.

The following chart shows when CI series first began in each country:
1946: Canada. 1947: Australia. 1948: Brazil/The Netherlands. 1950: Italy. 1951: Greece/Japan/Hong Kong(?)/England/Argentina/Mexico. 1952: West Germany. 1954: Norway. 1955: New Zealand/South Africa. 1956: Denmark/Sweden/Iceland. 1957: Finland/France. 1962: Singapore(?). 1964: India (8 languages). 1971: Ireland (Gaelic). 1973: Belgium(?) /Philippines(?) & Malaysia(?).

Significant among the early series were Brazil and Greece. In 1950, Brazil was the first country to begin doing its own new titles. They issued nearly 80 new CI titles by Brazilian authors. In Greece in 1951 they actually had debates in parliament about the effects of Classics Illustrated on Greek culture, leading to the inclusion of 88 new Greek History & Mythology titles in the CI series.

But by far the most important foreign CI development was the joint European series which began in 1956 in 10 countries simultaneously. By 1960, CI had the largest European distribution of any American publication, not just comics! So when all the problems came up with U.S. distribution, they literally moved the CI operation to Europe in 1962, and continued producing new titles in all four CI series. Many of them were adapted and drawn in the U.S., the most famous of which was the British CI #158A. Dr. No, drawn by Norman Nodel. Unfortunately, the British CI series ended in late 1963, which limited the European CI titles available in English to 15. Altogether there were 82 new CI art titles in the joint European series, which ran until 1976.

IDENTIFYING CLASSICS EDITIONS

HRN: This is the highest number on the reorder list. It should be listed in ( ) after the title number. It is crucial to understanding various CI editions.

ORIGINALS (O): This is the all-important First Edition. To determine (O)s,there is one pri-

Classic Comics #2 © GIL

Classic Comics #3 © GIL

Classic Comics #4 © GIL

GD	VG	FN	VF	VF/NM	NM-
2.0	4.0	6.0	8.0	9.0	9.2

mary rule and two secondary rules (with exceptions):

Rule No. 1: All (O)s and only (O)s have coming-next ads for the next number. **Exceptions**: No. 14(15) (reprint) has an ad on the last inside text page only. No. 14(0) also has a full-page outside back cover ad (also rule 2). Nos.55(75) and 57(75) have coming-next ads. (Rules 2 and 3 apply here). Nos. 168(0) and 169(0) do not have coming-next ads. No.168 was never reprinted; No. 169(0) has HRN (166). No. 169(169) is the only reprint.

Rule No. 2: On nos.1-80, all (O)s and only (O)s list 10c on the front cover. **Exceptions**: Reprint variations of Nos. 37(62), 39(71), and 46(62) list 10c on the front cover. (Rules 1 and 3 apply here.)

Rule No. 3: All (O)s have HRN close to that title No. **Exceptions**: Some reprints also have HRNs close to that title number: a few CC(r)s, 58(62), 60(62), 149(149), 152(149) 153(149), and title nos. in the 160's. (Rules 1 and 2 apply here.)

DATES: Many reprint editions list either an incorrect date or no date. Since Gilberton apparently kept track of CI editions by HRN, they often left the (O) date on reprints. Often, someone with a CI collection for sale will swear that all their copies are originals. That is why we are so detailed in pointing out how to identify original editions. Except for original editions, which should have a coming-next ad, etc., all CI dates prior to 1963 are incorrect! So you want to go by HRN only if it is (165) or below, and go by listed date if it is 1963 or later. There are a few (167) editions with incorrect dates. They could be listed either as (167) or (62/3), which is meant to indicate that they were issued sometime between late 1962 and early 1963.

COVERS: A change from CC to LDC indicates a logo change, not a cover change; while a change from LDC to LDC2, LDC to PC, or from PC to PC2 does indicate a new cover. New PCs can be identified by HRN, and PC2s can be identified by HRN and date. Several covers had color changes, particularly from purple to blue.

Notes: If you see 15 cents in Canada on a front cover, it does not necessarily indicate a Canadian edition. Editions with an HRN between 44 and 75, with 15 cents on the cover are Canadian. Check the publisher's address. An HRN listing two numbers with a / between them indicates that there are two different reorder lists in the front and back covers. Official Twin Circle editions have a full-page back cover ad for their TC magazine, with no CI reorder list. Any CI with just a Twin Circle sticker on the front is not an official TC edition.

TIPS ON LISTING CLASSICS FOR SALE

It may be easy to just list Edition 17, but Classics collectors keep track of CI editions in terms of HRN and/or date, (O) or (r), CC or LDC, PC or PC2, A1 or A2, soft or stiff cover, etc. Try to help them out. For originals, just list (0), unless there are variations such as color (Nos. 10 and 61), printer (Nos. 18-22), HRN (Nos. 95, 108, 160), etc. For reprints, just list HRN if it's (165) or below. Above that, list HRN and date. Also, please list type of logo/cover/art for the convenience of buyers. They will appreciate it.

CLASSIC COMICS (Also see Best from Boys Life, Cassette Books, Famous Stories, Fast Fiction, Golden Picture Classics, King Classics, Marvel Classics Comics, Pendulum Illustrated Classics, Picture Parade, Picture Progress, Regents Ill. Classics, Spitfire, Stories by Famous Authors, Superior Stories, and World Around Us.)

CLASSIC COMICS (Classics Illustrated No. 35 on)
Elliot Publishing #1-3 (1941-1942)/Gilberton Publications #4-167 (1942-1967) /Twin Circle Pub. (Frawley) #168-169 (1968-1971):
10/41 - No. 34, 2/47; No. 35, 3/47 - No. 169, Spring 1969
(Reprint Editions of almost all titles 5/43 - Spring 1971)
(Painted Covers (0)s No. 81 on, and (r)s of most Nos. 1-80)

Abbreviations:
A–Art; C or c–Cover; CC–Classic Comics; CI–Classics Ill.; Ed–Edition; LDC–Line Drawn Cover; PC–Painted Cover; r–Reprint

1. The Three Musketeers

Ed	HRN	Date	Details	A	C	GD	VG	FN	VF	VF/NM	NM-
1	–	10/41	Date listed-1941; Elliot Pub; 68 pgs.	1	1	454	908	1362	3314	5857	8400
2	10	–	10¢ price removed on all (r)s; Elliot Pub; CC-r	1	1	34	68	102	199	325	450
3	15	–	Long Isl. Ind. Ed.; CC-r	1	1	24	48	72	140	230	320
4	18/20	–	Sunrise Times Ed.; CC-r	1	1	18	36	54	105	165	225
5	21	–	Richmond Courier Ed.; CC-r	1	1	16	32	48	94	147	200
6	28	1946	CC-r	1	1	14	28	42	80	115	150
7	36	–	LDC-r	1	1	8	16	24	42	54	65
8	60	–	LDC-r	1	1	6	12	18	27	33	38
9	64	–	LDC-r	1	1	5	10	15	22	26	30
10	78	–	C-price 15¢;LDC-r	1	1	4	9	13	18	22	26
11	93	–	LDC-r	1	1	4	9	13	18	22	26
12	114	–	Last LDC-r	1	1	4	8	11	16	19	22
13	134	–	New-c; old-a; 64 pg. PC-r	1	2	3	6	9	19	29	38
14	143	–	Old-a; PC-r; 64 pg.	1	2	2	4	6	11	16	20
15	150	–	New-a; PC-r; Evans/Crandall-a	2	2	3	6	9	17	25	32
16	149	–	PC-r	2	2	2	4	6	8	11	14
17	167	–	PC-r	2	2	2	4	6	8	11	14
18	167	4/64	PC-r	2	2	2	4	6	8	11	14
19	167	1/65	PC-r	2	2	2	4	6	8	11	14
20	167	3/66	PC-r	2	2	2	4	6	8	11	14
21	166	11/67	PC-r	2	2	2	4	6	8	11	14
22	166	Spr/69	C-price 25¢ ; stiff-c; PC-r	2	2	2	4	6	8	11	14
23	169	Spr/71	PC-r; stiff-c	2	2	2	4	6	8	11	14

2. Ivanhoe

Ed	HRN	Date	Details	A	C	GD	VG	FN	VF	VF/NM	NM-
1	(O)	12/41?	Date listed-1941; Elliot Pub; 68 pgs.	1	1	232	464	696	1485	2543	3600
2	10	–	Price & 'Presents' removed; Elliot Pub; CC-r	1	1	31	62	93	182	296	410
3	15	–	Long Isl. Ind. ed.; CC-r	1	1	20	40	60	117	189	260
4	18/20	–	Sunrise Times ed.; CC-r	1	1	18	36	54	103	162	225
5	21	–	Richmond Courier ed.; CC-r	1	1	16	32	48	94	147	200
6	28	1946	Last 'Comics'-r	1	1	14	28	42	80	115	150
7	36	–	1st LDC-r	1	1	9	18	27	47	61	75
8	60	–	LDC-r	1	1	6	12	18	27	33	38
9	64	–	LDC-r	1	1	5	10	15	22	26	30
10	78	–	C-price 15¢; LDC-r	1	1	4	9	13	18	22	26
11	89	–	LDC-r	1	1	4	8	12	17	21	24
12	106	–	LDC-r	1	1	4	7	10	14	17	20
13	121	–	Last LDC-r	1	1	4	7	10	14	17	20
14	136	–	New-c&a; PC-r	2	2	5	10	15	25	31	36
15	142	–	PC-r	2	2	2	4	6	9	13	16
16	153	–	PC-r	2	2	2	4	6	9	13	16
17	149	–	PC-r	2	2	2	4	6	9	13	16
18	167	–	PC-r	2	2	2	4	6	8	11	14
19	167	5/64	PC-r	2	2	2	4	6	8	11	14
20	167	1/65	PC-r	2	2	2	4	6	8	11	14
21	167	3/66	PC-r	2	2	2	4	6	8	11	14
22A	166	9/67	PC-r	2	2	2	4	6	8	11	14
22B	166	–	Center ad for Children's Digest & Young Miss; rare; PC-r	2	2	7	14	21	47	76	105
23	166	R/68	C-Price 25¢; PC-r	2	2	2	4	6	8	11	14
24	169	Win/69	Stiff-c	2	2	2	4	6	8	11	14
25	169	Win/71	PC-r; stiff-c	2	2	2	4	6	8	11	14

3. The Count of Monte Cristo

Ed	HRN	Date	Details	A	C	GD	VG	FN	VF	VF/NM	NM-
1	(O)	3/42	Elliot Pub; 68 pgs.	1	1	148	296	444	947	1624	2300
2	10	–	Conray Prods; CC-r	1	1	26	52	78	154	252	350
3	15	–	Long Isl. Ind. ed.; CC-r	1	1	20	40	60	117	189	260
4	18/20	–	Sunrise Times ed.; CC-r	1	1	18	36	54	107	169	230
5	20	–	Sunrise Times ed.; CC-r	1	1	17	34	51	98	154	210
6	21	–	Richmond Courier ed.; CC-r	1	1	16	32	48	94	147	200
7	28	1946	CC-r; new Banner logo	1	1	14	28	42	80	115	150
8	36	–	1st LDC-r	1	1	9	18	27	47	61	75
9	60	–	LDC-r	1	1	6	12	18	27	33	38
10	62	–	LDC-r	1	1	6	12	18	29	36	42
11	71	–	LDC-r	1	1	5	10	14	20	24	28
12	87	–	C-price 15¢; LDC-r	1	1	4	9	13	18	22	26
13	113	–	LDC-r	1	1	4	7	10	14	17	20
14	135	–	New-c&a; PC-r; Cameron-a	2	2	3	6	9	18	27	35
15	143	–	PC-r	2	2	2	4	6	8	13	16
16	153	–	PC-r	2	2	2	4	6	8	13	16
17	161	–	PC-r	2	2	2	4	6	8	13	16

Classic Comics #5 © GIL

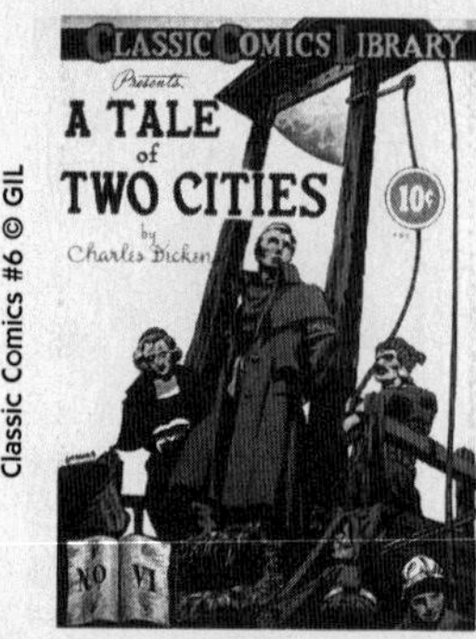

Classic Comics #6 © GIL

Classic Comics #8 © GIL

Ed	HRN	Date	Details	A	C	GD 2.0	VG 4.0	FN 6.0	VF 8.0	VF/NM 9.0	NM- 9.2
18	167	–	PC-r	2	2	2	4	6	8	11	14
19	167	7/64	PC-r	2	2	2	4	6	8	11	14
20	167	7/65	PC-r	2	2	2	4	6	8	11	14
21	167	7/66	PC-r	2	2	2	4	6	8	11	14
22	166	R/68	C-price 25¢; PC-r	2	2	2	4	6	8	11	14
23	169	–	Win/69 Stiff-c; PC-r	2	2	2	4	6	8	11	14

4. The Last of the Mohicans

Ed	HRN	Date	Details	A	C	GD 2.0	VG 4.0	FN 6.0	VF 8.0	VF/NM 9.0	NM- 9.2
1	(O)	8/42	Date listed-1942; Gilberton #4(0) on; 68 pgs.	1	1	126	252	378	806	1378	1950
2	12	–	Elliot Pub; CC-r	1	1	26	52	78	154	252	350
3	15	–	Long Isl. Ind. ed.; CC-r	1	1	20	40	60	117	189	260
4	20	–	Long Isl. Ind. ed.; CC-r; banner logo	1	1	18	36	54	105	165	225
5	21	–	Queens Home News ed.; CC-r	1	1	16	32	48	94	147	200
6	28	1946	Last CC-r; new	1	1	14	28	42	80	115	150
7	36	–	1st LDC-r	1	1	9	18	27	47	61	75
8	60	–	LDC-r	1	1	6	12	18	27	33	38
9	64	–	LDC-r	1	1	5	10	14	20	24	28
10	78	–	C-price 15¢; LDC-r	1	1	4	9	13	18	22	26
11	89	–	LDC-r	1	1	4	8	12	17	21	24
12	117	–	Last LDC-r	1	1	4	7	10	14	17	20
13	135	–	New-c; PC-r	1	2	5	10	15	24	30	35
14	141	–	PC-r	1	2	4	7	9	14	16	18
15	150	–	New-a; PC-r; Severin, L.B. Cole-a	2	2	6	12	18	27	33	38
16	161	–	PC-r	2	2	2	4	6	8	11	14
17	167	–	PC-r	2	2	2	4	6	8	11	14
18	167	6/64	PC-r	2	2	2	4	6	8	11	14
19	167	8/65	PC-r	2	2	2	4	6	8	11	14
20	167	8/66	PC-r	2	2	2	4	6	8	11	14
21	166	R/67	C-price 25¢; PC-r	2	2	2	4	6	8	11	14
22	169	Spr/69	Stiff-c; PC-r	2	2	2	4	6	8	11	14

5. Moby Dick

Ed	HRN	Date	Details	A	C	GD 2.0	VG 4.0	FN 6.0	VF 8.0	VF/NM 9.0	NM- 9.2
1A	(O)	9/42	Date listed-1942; Gilberton; 68 pgs.	1	1	152	304	456	965	1658	2350
1B			inside-c, rare free promo			232	464	696	1485	2543	3600
2	10	–	Conray Prods; Pg. 64 changed from 105 title list to letter from Editor; CC-r	1	1	27	54	81	158	259	360
3	15	–	Long Isl. Ind. ed.; Pg. 64 changed from Letter to the Editor to Ill. poem-Concord Hymn; CC-r	1	1	22	44	66	132	216	300
4	18/20	–	Sunrise Times ed.; CC-r	1	1	18	36	54	107	169	230
5	20	–	Sunrise Times ed.; CC-r	1	1	18	36	54	103	162	220
6	21	–	Sunrise Times ed.; CC-r	1	1	16	32	48	94	147	200
7	28	1946	CC-r; new banner logo	1	1	14	28	42	81	118	155
8	36	–	1st LDC-r	1	1	9	18	27	47	61	75
9	60	–	LDC-r	1	1	6	12	18	27	33	38
10	62	–	LDC-r	1	1	6	12	18	29	36	42
11	71	–	LDC-r	1	1	5	10	15	22	26	30
12	87	–	C-price 15¢; LDC-r	1	1	5	10	14	20	24	28
13	118	–	LDC-r	1	1	4	8	12	17	21	24
14	131	–	New c&a; PC-r	2	2	5	10	15	25	31	36
15	138	–	PC-r	2	2	2	4	6	9	12	16
16	148	–	PC-r	2	2	2	4	6	9	12	16
17	158	–	PC-r	2	2	2	4	6	9	12	16
18	167	–	PC-r	2	2	2	4	6	8	11	14
19	167	6/64	PC-r	2	2	2	4	6	8	11	14
20	167	7/65	PC-r	2	2	2	4	6	8	11	14
21	167	3/66	PC-r	2	2	2	4	6	8	11	14
22	166	9/67	PC-r	2	2	2	4	6	8	11	14
23	166	Win/69	New-c & c-price 25¢; Stiff-c; PC-r	2	3	3	6	9	16	23	30
24	169	Win/71	PC-r	2	3	3	6	9	14	19	24

6. A Tale of Two Cities

Ed	HRN	Date	Details	A	C	GD 2.0	VG 4.0	FN 6.0	VF 8.0	VF/NM 9.0	NM- 9.2
1	(O)	10/42	Date listed-1942; 68 pgs. Zeckerberg c/a	1	1	126	252	378	806	1378	1950
2	14	–	Elliot Pub; CC-r	1	1	24	48	72	142	234	325
3	18	–	Long Isl. Ind. ed.; CC-r	1	1	20	40	60	114	182	250
4	20	–	Sunrise Times ed.; CC-r	1	1	18	36	54	105	165	225
5	28	1946	Last CC-r; new banner logo	1	1	14	28	42	80	115	150
6	51	–	1st LDC-r	1	1	8	16	24	42	54	65
7	64	–	LDC-r	1	1	5	10	15	23	28	32
8	78	–	C-price 15¢; LDC-r	1	1	5	10	14	20	24	28
9	89	–	LDC-r	1	1	4	7	10	14	17	20
10	117	–	LDC-r	1	1	4	7	10	14	17	20
11	132	–	New-c&a; PC-r; Joe Orlando-a	2	2	5	10	15	25	31	36
12	140	–	PC-r	2	2	2	4	6	8	11	14
13	147	–	PC-r	2	2	2	4	6	8	11	14
14	152	–	PC-r; very rare	2	2	17	34	51	98	154	210
15	153	–	PC-r	2	2	2	4	6	9	13	16
16	149	–	PC-r	2	2	2	4	6	9	13	16
17	167	–	PC-r	2	2	2	4	6	8	11	14
18	167	6/64	PC-r	2	2	2	4	6	8	11	14
19	167	8/65	PC-r	2	2	2	4	6	8	11	14
20	166	5/67	PC-r	2	2	2	4	6	8	11	14
21	166	Fall/68	New-c & 25¢; PC-r	2	3	3	6	9	17	25	32
22	169	Sum/70	Stiff-c; PC-r	2	3	2	4	6	13	18	22

7. Robin Hood

Ed	HRN	Date	Details	A	C	GD 2.0	VG 4.0	FN 6.0	VF 8.0	VF/NM 9.0	NM- 9.2
1	(O)	12/42	Date listed-1942; first Gift Box ad-bc; 68 pgs.	1	1	94	188	282	597	1024	1450
2	12	–	Elliot Pub; CC-r	1	1	23	46	69	136	223	310
3	18	–	Long Isl. Ind. ed.; CC-r	1	1	19	38	57	111	176	240
4	20	–	Nassau Bulletin ed.; CC-r	1	1	18	36	54	103	162	220
5	22	–	Queens Cty. Times ed.; CC-r	1	1	16	32	48	94	147	200
6	28	–	CC-r	1	1	14	28	42	81	118	155
7	51	–	LDC-r	1	1	8	16	24	42	54	65
8	64	–	LDC-r	1	1	5	10	15	24	30	35
9	78	–	LDC-r	1	1	4	9	13	18	22	26
10	97	–	LDC-r	1	1	4	8	12	17	21	24
11	106	–	LDC-r	1	1	4	7	10	14	17	20
12	121	–	LDC-r	1	1	4	7	10	14	17	20
13	129	–	New-c; PC-r	1	2	5	10	15	25	31	36
14	136	–	New-a; PC-r	2	2	5	10	15	24	29	34
15	143	–	PC-r	2	2	2	4	6	9	13	16
16	153	–	PC-r	2	2	2	4	6	9	13	16
17	164	–	PC-r	2	2	2	4	6	8	11	14
18	167	–	PC-r	2	2	2	4	6	8	11	14
19	167	6/64	PC-r	2	2	2	4	6	8	11	14
20	167	5/65	PC-r	2	2	2	4	6	8	11	14
21	167	7/66	PC-r	2	2	2	4	6	8	11	14
22	166	12/67	PC-r	2	2	2	4	6	8	11	14
23	169	Sum/69	Stiff-c; c-price 25¢; PC-r	2	2	2	4	6	8	11	14

8. Arabian Nights

Ed	HRN	Date	Details	A	C	GD 2.0	VG 4.0	FN 6.0	VF 8.0	VF/NM 9.0	NM- 9.2
1	(O)	2/43	Original; 68 pgs. Lilian Chestney-c/a	1	1	150	300	450	953	1639	2325
2	17	–	Long Isl. ed.; pg. 64 changed from Gift Box ad to Letter from British Medical	1	1	52	104	156	323	549	775

Classic Comics #9 © GIL

Classic Comics #11 © GIL

Classic Comics #14 © GIL

Ed	HRN	Date	Details	A	C	GD 2.0	VG 4.0	FN 6.0	VF 8.0	VF/NM 9.0	NM- 9.2
			Worker; CC-r								
3	20	–	Nassau Bulletin; Pg. 64 changed from letter to article-Three Men Named Smith; CC-r	1	1	42	84	126	265	445	625
4A	28	1946	CC-r; new banner logo, slick-c	1	1	31	62	93	182	296	410
4B	28	1946	Same, but w/stiff-c	1	1	31	62	93	182	296	410
5	51	–	LDC-r	1	1	22	44	66	128	209	290
6	64	–	LDC-r	1	1	19	38	57	111	176	240
7	78	–	LDC-r	1	1	18	36	54	105	165	225
8	164	–	New-c&a; PC-r	2	2	15	30	45	90	140	190

9. Les Miserables

Ed	HRN	Date	Details	A	C	GD 2.0	VG 4.0	FN 6.0	VF 8.0	VF/NM 9.0	NM- 9.2
1A	(O)	3/43	Original; slick paper cover; 68 pgs.	1	1	94	188	282	597	1024	1450
1B	(O)	3/43	Original; rough, pulp type-c; 68 pgs.	1	1	110	220	330	704	1202	1700
2	14	–	Elliot Pub; CC-r	1	1	26	52	78	154	252	350
3	18	3/44	Nassau Bul. Pg. 64 changed from Gift Box ad to Bill of Rights article; CC-r	1	1	22	44	66	128	209	290
4	20	–	Richmond Courier ed.; CC-r	1	1	19	38	57	111	176	240
5	28	1946	Gilberton; pgs. 60-64 rearranged/ illos added; CC-r	1	1	14	28	42	81	118	155
6	51	–	LDC-r	1	1	9	18	27	47	61	75
7	71	–	LDC-r	1	1	6	12	18	29	36	42
8	87	–	C-price 15¢; LDC-r	1	1	6	12	18	27	33	38
9	161	–	New-c&a; PC-r	2	2	7	14	21	37	46	55
10	167	9/63	PC-r	2	2	2	4	6	11	16	20
11	167	12/65	PC-r	2	2	2	4	6	11	16	20
12	166	R/1968	New-c & price 25¢; PC-r	2	3	3	6	9	18	27	35

10. Robinson Crusoe (Used in **SOTI**, pg. 142)

Ed	HRN	Date	Details	A	C	GD 2.0	VG 4.0	FN 6.0	VF 8.0	VF/NM 9.0	NM- 9.2
1A	(O)	4/43	Original; Violet-c; 68 pgs; Zuckerberg c/a	1	1	84	168	252	538	919	1300
1B	(O)	4/43	Original; blue-grey-c, 68 pgs.	1	1	92	184	276	584	1005	1425
2A	14	–	Elliot Pub; violet-c; 68 pgs; CC-r	1	1	29	58	87	170	278	385
2B	14	–	Elliot Pub; blue-grey-c; CC-r	1	1	25	50	75	147	241	335
3	18	–	Nassau Bul. Pg. 64 changed from Gift Box ad to Bill of Rights article; CC-r	1	1	19	38	57	111	176	240
4	20	–	Queens Home News ed.; CC-r	1	1	16	32	48	94	147	200
5	28	1946	Gilberton; pg. 64 changes from Bill of Rights to WWII article-One Leg Shot Away; last CC-r	1	1	14	28	42	80	115	150
6	51	–	LDC-r	1	1	8	16	24	42	54	65
7	64	–	LDC-r	1	1	6	12	18	27	33	38
8	78	–	C-price 15¢; LDC-r	1	1	5	10	14	20	24	28
9	97	–	LDC-r	1	1	4	9	13	18	22	26
10	114	–	LDC-r	1	1	4	7	10	14	17	20
11	130	–	New-c; PC-r	1	2	5	10	15	25	31	36
12	140	–	New-a; PC-r	2	2	5	10	15	24	29	34
13	153	–	PC-r	2	2	2	4	6	8	11	14
14	164	–	PC-r	2	2	2	4	6	8	11	14
15	167	–	PC-r	2	2	2	4	6	8	11	14
16	167	7/64	PC-r	2	2	2	4	6	10	14	18
17	167	5/65	PC-r	2	2	2	4	6	10	14	18
18	167	6/66	PC-r	2	2	2	4	6	8	11	14
19	166	Fall/68	C-price 25¢; PC-r	2	2	2	4	6	8	11	14
20	166	R/68	(No Twin Circle ad)	2	2	2	4	6	9	13	16
21	169	Sm/70	Stiff-c; PC-r	2	2	2	4	6	9	13	16

11. Don Quixote

Ed	HRN	Date	Details	A	C	GD 2.0	VG 4.0	FN 6.0	VF 8.0	VF/NM 9.0	NM- 9.2
1	10	5/43	First (O) with HRN list; 68 pgs.	1	1	87	174	261	553	952	1350
2	18	–	Nassau Bulletin ed.; CC-r	1	1	23	46	69	136	223	310
3	21	–	Queens Home News ed.; CC-r	1	1	19	38	57	111	176	240
4	28	–	CC-r	1	1	14	28	42	81	118	155
5	110	–	New-PC; PC-r	1	2	7	14	21	35	43	50
6	156	–	Pgs. reduced 68 to 52; PC-r	1	2	4	7	10	14	17	20
7	165	–	PC-r	1	2	2	4	6	9	13	16
8	167	1/64	PC-r	1	2	2	4	6	9	13	16
9	167	11/65	PC-r	1	2	2	4	6	9	13	16
10	166	R/1968	New-c & price 25¢; PC-r	1	3	3	6	9	18	27	36

12. Rip Van Winkle and the Headless Horseman

Ed	HRN	Date	Details	A	C	GD 2.0	VG 4.0	FN 6.0	VF 8.0	VF/NM 9.0	NM- 9.2
1	11	6/43	Original; 68 pgs.	1	1	87	174	261	553	952	1350
2	15	–	Long Isl. Ind. ed.; CC-r	1	1	23	46	69	136	223	310
3	20	–	Long Isl. Ind. ed.;	1	1	19	38	57	111	176	240
4	22	–	Queens Cty. Times ed.; CC-r	1	1	16	32	48	94	147	200
5	28	–	CC-r	1	1	14	28	42	80	115	150
6	60	–	1st LDC-r	1	1	8	16	24	40	50	60
7	62	–	LDC-r	1	1	5	10	15	23	28	32
8	71	–	LDC-r	1	1	4	9	13	18	22	26
9	89	–	C-price 15¢; LDC-r	1	1	4	8	12	17	21	24
10	118	–	LDC-r	1	1	4	7	10	14	17	20
11	132	–	New-c; PC-r	1	2	5	10	15	25	31	36
12	150	–	New-a; PC-r	2	2	5	10	15	24	29	34
13	158	–	PC-r	2	2	2	4	6	9	13	16
14	167	–	PC-r	2	2	2	4	6	9	13	16
15	167	12/63	PC-r	2	2	2	4	6	8	11	14
16	167	4/65	PC-r	2	2	2	4	6	8	11	14
17	167	4/66	PC-r	2	2	2	4	6	8	11	14
18	166	R/1968	New-c&price 25¢; PC-r; stiff-c	2	3	3	6	9	14	20	26
19	169	Sm/70	PC-r; stiff-c	2	3	2	4	6	10	14	18

13. Dr. Jekyll and Mr. Hyde (Used in **SOTI**, pg. 143)(1st horror comic?)

Ed	HRN	Date	Details	A	C	GD 2.0	VG 4.0	FN 6.0	VF 8.0	VF/NM 9.0	NM- 9.2
1	12	8/43	Original 60 pgs.	1	1	135	270	405	864	1482	2100
2	15	–	Long Isl. Ind. ed.; CC-r	1	1	34	68	102	199	325	450
3	20	–	Long Isl. Ind. ed.; CC-r	1	1	23	46	69	136	223	310
4	28	–	No c-price; CC-r	1	1	18	36	54	105	165	225
5	60	–	New-c; Pgs. reduced from 60 to 52; H.C. Kiefer-c; LDC-r	1	2	9	18	27	47	61	75
6	62	–	LDC-r	1	2	6	12	18	28	34	40
7	71	–	LDC-r	1	2	5	10	15	23	28	32
8	87	–	Date returns (erroneous); LDC-r	1	2	5	10	15	22	26	30
9	112	–	New-c&a; PC-r; Cameron-a	2	3	7	14	21	35	43	50
10	153	–	PC-r	2	3	2	4	6	9	13	16
11	161	–	PC-r	2	3	2	4	6	9	13	16
12	167	–	PC-r	2	3	2	4	6	8	11	14
13	167	8/64	PC-r	2	3	2	4	6	8	11	14
14	167	11/65	PC-r	2	3	2	4	6	8	11	14
15	166	R/68	C-price 25¢; PC-r	2	3	2	4	6	8	11	14
16	169	Wn/69	PC-r; stiff-c	2	3	2	4	6	8	11	14

14. Westward Ho!

Ed	HRN	Date	Details	A	C	GD 2.0	VG 4.0	FN 6.0	VF 8.0	VF/NM 9.0	NM- 9.2
1	13	9/43	Original; last outside bc coming-next ad; 60 pgs.	1	1	194	388	582	1242	2121	3000
2	15	–	Long Isl. Ind. ed.; CC-r	1	1	57	114	171	362	624	885

Classic Comics #16 © GIL

Classic Comics #18 © GIL

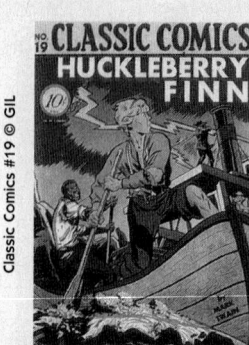

Classic Comics #19 © GIL

Ed	HRN	Date	Details	A	C	GD 2.0	VG 4.0	FN 6.0	VF 8.0	VF/NM 9.0	NM- 9.2
3	21	–	Queens Home News; Pg. 56 changed from coming-next ad to Three Men Named Smith; CC-r	1	1	45	90	135	284	480	675
4	28	1946	Gilberton; Pg. 56 changed again to WWII article- Speaking for America; last CC-r	1	1	39	78	117	240	395	550
5	53	–	Pgs. reduced from 60 to 52; LDC-r	1	1	36	72	108	211	343	475

15. Uncle Tom's Cabin (Used in **SOTI**, pgs. 102, 103)

Ed	HRN	Date	Details	A	C	GD 2.0	VG 4.0	FN 6.0	VF 8.0	VF/NM 9.0	NM- 9.2
1	14	11/43	Original; Outside-bc ad: 2 Gift Boxes; 60 pgs.; color var. on-c; green trunk,root on left & brown trunk, root on left	1	1	74	148	222	470	810	1150
2	15	–	Long Isl. Ind. listed- bottom inside-fc; also Gilberton listed bottom-pg. 1; CC-r; green root vs. brown root var. occurs again	1	1	25	50	75	147	241	335
3	21	–	Nassau Bulletin ed.; CC-r	1	1	20	40	60	114	182	250
4	28	–	No c-price; CC-r	1	1	14	28	42	81	118	155
5	53	–	Pgs. reduced 60 to 52; LDC-r	1	1	8	16	24	42	54	65
6	71	–	LDC-r	1	1	6	12	18	27	33	38
7	89	–	C-price 15¢; LDC-r	1	1	5	10	15	24	30	35
8	117	–	New-c/lettering changes; PC-r	1	2	5	10	15	25	31	36
9	128	–	'Picture Progress' promo; PC-r	1	2	2	4	6	10	14	18
10	137	–	PC-r	1	2	2	4	6	9	13	16
11	146	–	PC-r	1	2	2	4	6	9	13	16
12	154	–	PC-r	1	2	2	4	6	9	13	16
13	161	–	PC-r	1	2	2	4	6	8	11	14
14	167	–	PC-r	1	2	2	4	6	8	11	14
15	167	6/64	PC-r	1	2	2	4	6	8	11	14
16	167	5/65	PC-r	1	2	2	4	6	8	11	14
17	166	5/67	PC-r	1	2	2	4	6	8	11	14
18	166	Wn/69	New-stiff-c; PC-r	1	3	3	6	9	16	22	28
19	169	Sm/70	PC-r; stiff-c	1	3	2	4	6	10	14	18

16. Gullivers Travels

Ed	HRN	Date	Details	A	C	GD 2.0	VG 4.0	FN 6.0	VF 8.0	VF/NM 9.0	NM- 9.2
1	15	12/43	Original-Lilian Chestney c/a; 60 pgs.	1	1	76	152	228	486	831	1175
2	18/20	–	Price deleted; Queens Home News ed; CC-r	1	1	22	44	66	128	209	290
3	22	–	Queens Cty. Times ed.; CC-r	1	1	18	36	54	105	165	225
4	28	–	CC-r	1	1	14	28	42	80	115	150
5	60	–	Pgs. reduced to 48; LDC-r	1	1	6	12	18	31	38	45
6	62	–	LDC-r	1	1	5	10	15	23	28	32
7	78	–	C-price 15¢; LDC-r	1	1	5	10	14	20	24	28
8	89	–	LDC-r	1	1	4	8	12	17	21	24
9	155	–	New-c; PC-r	1	2	5	10	15	25	31	36
10	165	–	PC-r	1	2	2	4	6	8	11	14
11	167	5/64	PC-r	1	2	2	4	6	8	11	14
12	167	11/65	PC-r	1	2	2	4	6	8	11	14
13	166	R/1968	C-price 25¢; PC-r	1	2	2	4	6	8	11	14
14	169	Wn/69	PC-r; stiff-c	1	2	2	4	6	8	11	14

17. The Deerslayer

Ed	HRN	Date	Details	A	C	GD 2.0	VG 4.0	FN 6.0	VF 8.0	VF/NM 9.0	NM- 9.2
1	16	1/44	Original; Outside-bc ad: 3 Gift Boxes; 60 pgs.	1	1	64	128	192	406	696	985
2A	18	–	Queens Cty Times (inside-fc); CC-r	1	1	23	46	69	136	223	310
2B	18	–	Gilberton (bottom-pg. 1); CC-r; Scarce	1	1	33	66	99	194	317	440
3	22	–	Queens Cty. Times ed.; CC-r	1	1	19	38	57	109	172	235
4	28	–	CC-r	1	1	14	28	42	81	118	155
5	60	–	Pgs.reduced to 52; LDC-r	1	1	7	14	21	37	46	55
6	64	–	LDC-r	1	1	5	10	15	22	26	30
7	85	–	C-price 15¢; LDC-r	1	1	4	8	12	17	21	24
8	118	–	LDC-r	1	1	4	7	10	14	17	20
9	132	–	LDC-r	1	1	4	7	10	14	17	20
10	167	11/66	Last LDC-r	1	1	2	4	6	11	16	20
11	166	R/1968	New-c & price 25¢; PC-r	1	2	3	6	9	18	27	35
12	169	Spr/71	Stiff-c; letters from parents & educators; PC-r	1	2	2	4	6	10	14	18

18. The Hunchback of Notre Dame

Ed	HRN	Date	Details	A	C	GD 2.0	VG 4.0	FN 6.0	VF 8.0	VF/NM 9.0	NM- 9.2
1A	17	3/44	Orig.; Gilberton ed; 60 pgs.	1	1	87	174	261	553	952	1350
1B	17	3/44	Orig.; Island Pub. Ed.; 60 pgs.	1	1	77	154	231	493	847	1200
2	18/20	–	Queens Home News ed.; CC-r	1	1	24	48	72	142	234	325
3	22	–	Queens Cty. Times ed.; CC-r	1	1	19	38	57	111	176	240
4	28	–	CC-r	1	1	16	32	48	94	147	200
5	60	–	New-c; 8pgs. deleted; Kiefer-c; LDC-r	1	2	9	18	27	47	61	75
6	62	–	LDC-r	1	2	5	10	15	22	26	30
7	78	–	C-price 15¢; LDC-r	1	2	5	10	14	20	24	28
8A	89	–	H.C.Kiefer on bottom right-fc; LDC-r	1	2	4	9	13	18	22	26
8B	89	–	Name omitted; LDC-r	1	2	5	10	15	24	30	35
9	118	–	LDC-r	1	2	4	8	12	17	21	24
10	140	–	New-c; PC-r	1	3	7	14	21	35	43	50
11	146	–	PC-r	1	3	4	9	13	18	22	26
12	158	–	New-c&a; PC-r; Evans/Crandall-a	2	4	5	10	15	25	31	36
13	165	–	PC-r	2	4	2	4	6	9	13	16
14	167	9/63	PC-r	2	4	2	4	6	9	13	16
15	167	10/64	PC-r	2	4	2	4	6	9	13	16
16	167	4/66	PC-r	2	4	2	4	6	8	11	14
17	166	R/1968	New price 25¢; PC-r	2	4	2	4	6	8	11	14
18	169	Sp/70	Stiff-c; PC-r	2	4	2	4	6	8	11	14

19. Huckleberry Finn

Ed	HRN	Date	Details	A	C	GD 2.0	VG 4.0	FN 6.0	VF 8.0	VF/NM 9.0	NM- 9.2
1A	18	4/44	Orig.; Gilberton ed.; 60 pgs.	1	1	53	106	159	334	567	800
1B	18	4/44	Orig.; Island Pub.; 60 pgs.	1	1	55	110	165	352	601	850
2	18	–	Nassau Bulletin ed.; fc-price 15¢-Canada; no coming-next ad; CC-r	1	1	23	46	69	136	223	310
3	22	–	Queens City Times ed.; CC-r	1	1	19	38	57	111	176	240
4	28	–	CC-r	1	1	14	28	42	80	115	150
5	60	–	Pgs. reduced to 48; LDC-r	1	1	6	12	18	31	38	45
6	62	–	LDC-r	1	1	5	10	15	23	28	32
7	78	–	LDC-r	1	1	4	9	13	18	22	26
8	89	–	LDC-r	1	1	4	8	12	17	21	24
9	117	–	LDC-r	1	1	4	7	10	14	17	20
10	131	–	New-c&a; PC-r	2	2	5	10	15	24	30	35
11	140	–	PC-r	2	2	2	4	6	9	13	16
12	150	–	PC-r	2	2	2	4	6	9	13	16
13	158	–	PC-r	2	2	2	4	6	9	13	16
14	165	–	PC-r (scarce)	2	2	3	6	9	14	19	24
15	167	–	PC-r	2	2	2	4	6	8	11	14

Classic Comics #22 © GIL

Classic Comics #23 © GIL

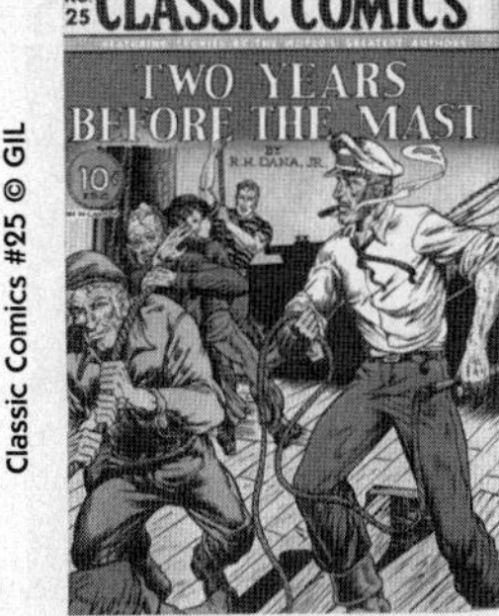

Classic Comics #25 © GIL

Ed	HRN	Date	Details	A	C	GD 2.0	VG 4.0	FN 6.0	VF 8.0	VF/NM 9.0	NM- 9.2
16	167	6/64	PC-r	2	2	2	4	6	8	11	14
17	167	6/65	PC-r	2	2	2	4	6	8	11	14
18	167	10/65	PC-r	2	2	2	4	6	8	11	14
19	166	9/67	PC-r	2	2	2	4	6	8	11	14
20	166	Win/69	C-price 25¢; PC-r; stiff-c	2	2	2	4	6	8	11	14
21	169	Sm/70	PC-r; stiff-c	2	2	2	4	6	8	11	14

20. The Corsican Brothers

Ed	HRN	Date	Details	A	C	GD 2.0	VG 4.0	FN 6.0	VF 8.0	VF/NM 9.0	NM- 9.2
1A	20	6/44	Orig.; Gilberton ed.; bc-ad: 4 Gift Boxes; 60 pgs.	1	1	47	94	141	296	498	700
1B	20	6/44	Orig.; Courier ed.; 60 pgs.	1	1	40	80	120	246	411	575
1C	20	6/44	Orig.; Long Island Ind. ed.; 60 pgs.	1	1	40	80	120	246	411	575
2	22	–	Queens Cty. Times ed.; white logo banner; CC-r	1	1	20	40	60	114	182	250
3	28	–	CC-r	1	1	19	38	57	109	172	235
4	60	–	Cl logo; no price; 48 pgs.; LDC-r	1	1	15	30	45	90	140	190
5A	62	–	LDC-r; Classics Ill. logo at top of pgs.	1	1	15	30	45	83	124	165
5B	62	–	w/o logo at top of pg. (scarcer)	1	1	15	30	45	86	133	180
6	78	–	C-price 15¢; LDC-r	1	1	14	28	42	81	118	155
7	97	–	LDC-r	1	1	14	28	42	78	112	145

21. 3 Famous Mysteries ("The Sign of the 4", "The Murders in the Rue Morgue", "The Flayed Hand")

Ed	HRN	Date	Details	A	C	GD 2.0	VG 4.0	FN 6.0	VF 8.0	VF/NM 9.0	NM- 9.2
1A	21	7/44	Orig.; Gilberton ed.; 60 pgs.	1	1	94	188	282	597	1024	1450
1B	21	7/44	Orig. Island Pub. Co.; 60 pgs.	1	1	97	194	291	621	1061	1500
1C	21	7/44	Original; Courier Ed.; 60 pgs.	1	1	84	168	252	538	919	1300
2	22	–	Nassau Bulletin ed.; CC-r	1	1	39	78	117	231	378	525
3	30	–	CC-r	1	1	28	56	84	165	270	375
4	62	–	LDC-r; 8 pgs. deleted; LDC-r	1	1	22	44	66	128	209	290
5	70	–	LDC-r	1	1	20	40	60	117	189	260
6	85	–	C-price 15¢; LDC-r	1	1	18	36	54	107	169	230
7	114	–	New-c; PC-r	1	2	18	36	54	107	169	230

22. The Pathfinder

Ed	HRN	Date	Details	A	C	GD 2.0	VG 4.0	FN 6.0	VF 8.0	VF/NM 9.0	NM- 9.2
1A	22	10/44	Orig.; No printer listed; ownership statement inside fc lists Gilberton & date; 60 pgs.	1	1	45	90	135	284	480	675
1B	22	10/44	Orig.; Island Pub. ed.; 60 pgs.	1	1	40	80	120	246	411	575
1C	22	10/44	Orig.; Queens Cty Times ed. 60 pgs.	1	1	40	80	120	246	411	575
2	30	–	C-price removed; CC-r	1	1	15	30	45	85	130	175
3	60	–	Pgs. reduced to 52; LDC-r	1	1	6	12	18	27	33	38
4	70	–	LDC-r	1	1	5	10	15	22	26	30
5	85	–	C-price 15¢; LDC-r	1	1	4	9	13	18	22	26
6	118	–	LDC-r	1	1	4	8	12	17	21	24
7	132	–	LDC-r	1	1	4	7	10	14	17	20
8	146	–	LDC-r	1	1	4	7	10	14	17	20
9	167	11/63	New-c; PC-r	1	2	4	8	12	24	37	50
10	167	12/65	PC-r	1	2	2	4	6	11	16	20
11	166	8/67	PC-r	1	2	2	4	6	11	16	20

23. Oliver Twist (1st Classic produced by the Iger Shop)

Ed	HRN	Date	Details	A	C	GD 2.0	VG 4.0	FN 6.0	VF 8.0	VF/NM 9.0	NM- 9.2
1	23	7/45	Original; 60 pgs.	1	1	45	90	135	284	480	675
2A	30	–	Printers Union logo on bottom left-fc same as 23(Orig.) (very rare); CC-r	1	1	30	60	90	177	289	400
2B	30	–	Union logo omitted; CC-r	1	1	15	30	45	84	127	170
3	60	–	Pgs. reduced to 48; LDC-r	1	1	6	12	18	29	36	42
4	62	–	LDC-r	1	1	5	10	15	23	28	32
5	71	–	LDC-r	1	1	5	10	14	20	24	28
6	85	–	C-price 15¢; LDC-r	1	1	4	9	13	18	22	26
7	94	–	LDC-r	1	1	4	7	10	14	17	20
8	118	–	LDC-r	1	1	4	7	10	14	17	20
9	136	–	New-PC, old-a; PC-r	1	2	5	10	15	24	30	35
10	150	–	Old-a; PC-r	1	2	4	7	10	14	17	20
11	164	–	Old-a; PC-r	1	2	4	8	11	16	19	22
12	164	–	New-a; PC-r; Evans/Crandall-a	2	2	4	8	12	24	37	50
13	167	–	PC-r	2	2	2	4	6	11	16	20
14	167	8/64	PC-r	2	2	2	4	6	8	11	14
15	167	12/65	PC-r	2	2	2	4	6	8	11	14
16	166	R/1968	New 25¢; PC-r	2	2	2	4	6	8	11	14
17	169	Win/69	Stiff-c; PC-r	2	2	2	4	6	8	11	14

24. A Connecticut Yankee in King Arthur's Court

Ed	HRN	Date	Details	A	C	GD 2.0	VG 4.0	FN 6.0	VF 8.0	VF/NM 9.0	NM- 9.2
1	–	9/45	Original	1	1	40	80	120	246	411	575
2	30	–	No price circle; CC-r	1	1	15	30	45	84	127	170
3	60	–	8 pgs. deleted; LDC-r	1	1	6	12	18	27	33	38
4	62	–	LDC-r	1	1	5	10	15	23	28	32
5	71	–	LDC-r	1	1	5	10	15	22	26	30
6	87	–	C-price 15¢; LDC-r	1	1	4	9	13	18	22	26
7	121	–	LDC-r	1	1	4	8	12	17	21	24
8	140	–	New-c&a; PC-r	2	2	5	10	15	25	31	36
9	153	–	PC-r	2	2	2	4	6	9	13	16
10	164	–	PC-r	2	2	2	4	6	8	11	14
11	167	–	PC-r	2	2	2	4	6	8	11	14
12	167	7/64	PC-r	2	2	2	4	6	8	11	14
13	167	6/66	PC-r	2	2	2	4	6	8	11	14
14	166	R/1968	C-price 25¢; PC-r	2	2	2	4	6	8	11	14
15	169	Spr/71	PC-r; stiff-c	2	2	2	4	6	8	11	14

25. Two Years Before the Mast

Ed	HRN	Date	Details	A	C	GD 2.0	VG 4.0	FN 6.0	VF 8.0	VF/NM 9.0	NM- 9.2
1	–	10/45	Original; Webb/Heames-a&c	1	1	40	80	120	246	411	575
2	30	–	Price circle blank; CC-r	1	1	15	30	45	84	127	170
3	60	–	8 pgs. deleted; LDC-r	1	1	6	12	18	27	33	38
4	62	–	LDC-r	1	1	5	10	15	23	28	32
5	71	–	LDC-r	1	1	4	9	13	18	22	26
6	85	–	C-price 15¢; LDC-r	1	1	4	8	12	17	21	24
7	114	–	LDC-r	1	1	4	7	10	14	17	20
8	156	–	3 pgs. replaced by fillers; new-c; PC-r	1	2	5	10	15	25	31	36
9	167	12/63	PC-r	1	2	2	4	6	8	11	14
10	167	12/65	PC-r	1	2	2	4	6	8	11	14
11	166	9/67	PC-r	1	2	2	4	6	8	11	14
12	169	Win/69	C-price 25¢; stiff-c PC-r	1	2	2	4	6	8	11	14

26. Frankenstein (2nd horror comic?)

Ed	HRN	Date	Details	A	C	GD 2.0	VG 4.0	FN 6.0	VF 8.0	VF/NM 9.0	NM- 9.2
1	26	12/45	Orig.; Webb/Brewster a&c; 52 pgs.	1	1	110	220	330	704	1202	1700
2A	30	–	Price circle blank; no indicia; CC-r	1	1	30	60	90	177	289	400
2B	30	–	With indicia; scarce; CC-r	1	1	34	68	102	204	332	460
3	60	–	LDC-r	1	1	16	32	48	94	147	200
4	62	–	LDC-r	1	1	15	30	45	85	130	175
5	71	–	LDC-r	1	1	8	16	24	40	50	60
6A	82	–	C-price 15¢; soft-c LDC-r	1	1	7	14	21	35	43	50

Classic Comics #28 © GIL

Classic Comics #31 © GIL

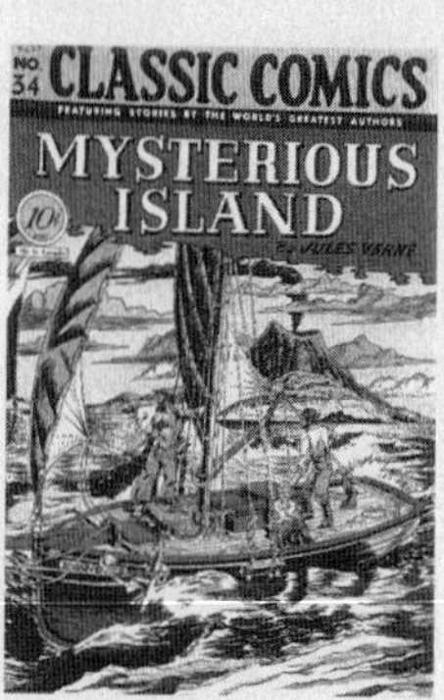

Classic Comics #34 © GIL

Ed	HRN	Date	Details	A	C	GD 2.0	VG 4.0	FN 6.0	VF 8.0	VF/NM 9.0	NM- 9.2
6B	82	–	Stiff-c; LDC-r	1	1	8	16	24	40	50	60
7	117	–	LDC-r	1	1	4	8	12	18	22	25
8	146	–	New Saunders-c; PC-r	1	2	6	12	18	29	36	42
9	152	–	Scarce; PC-r	1	2	8	16	24	40	50	60
10	153	–	PC-r	1	2	2	4	6	9	13	16
11	160	–	PC-r	1	2	2	4	6	9	13	16
12	165	–	PC-r	1	2	2	4	6	8	11	14
13	167	–	PC-r	1	2	2	4	6	8	11	14
14	167	6/64	PC-r	1	2	2	4	6	8	11	14
15	167	6/65	PC-r	1	2	2	4	6	8	11	14
16	167	10/65	PC-r	1	2	2	4	6	8	11	14
17	166	9/67	PC-r	1	2	2	4	6	8	11	14
18	169	Fall/69	C-price 25¢; stiff-c PC-r	1	2	2	4	6	8	11	14
19	169	Spr/71	PC-r; stiff-c	1	2	2	4	6	8	11	14

27. The Adventures of Marco Polo

Ed	HRN	Date	Details	A	C	GD 2.0	VG 4.0	FN 6.0	VF 8.0	VF/NM 9.0	NM- 9.2
1	–	4/46	Original	1	1	40	80	120	246	411	575
2	30	–	Last 'Comics' reprint; CC-r	1	1	15	30	45	84	127	170
3	70	–	8 pgs. deleted; no c-price; LDC-r	1	1	5	10	15	24	30	35
4	87	–	C-price 15¢; LDC-r	1	1	4	9	13	18	22	26
5	117	–	LDC-r	1	1	4	7	10	14	17	20
6	154	–	New-c; PC-r	1	2	5	10	15	24	30	35
7	165	–	PC-r	1	2	2	4	6	8	11	14
8	167	4/64	PC-r	1	2	2	4	6	8	11	14
9	167	6/66	PC-r	1	2	2	4	6	8	11	14
10	169	Spr/69	New price 25¢; stiff-c; PC-r	1	2	2	4	6	8	11	14

28. Michael Strogoff

Ed	HRN	Date	Details	A	C	GD 2.0	VG 4.0	FN 6.0	VF 8.0	VF/NM 9.0	NM- 9.2
1	–	6/46	Original	1	1	40	80	120	246	411	575
2	51	–	8 pgs. cut; LDC-r	1	1	15	30	45	84	127	170
3	115	–	New-c; PC-r	1	2	6	12	18	31	38	45
4	155	–	PC-r	1	2	4	7	10	14	17	20
5	167	11/63	PC-r	1	2	2	4	6	9	13	16
6	167	7/66	PC-r	1	2	2	4	6	9	13	16
7	169	Sm/69	C-price 25¢; stiff-c PC-r	1	3	3	6	9	15	21	26

29. The Prince and the Pauper

Ed	HRN	Date	Details	A	C	GD 2.0	VG 4.0	FN 6.0	VF 8.0	VF/NM 9.0	NM- 9.2
1	–	7/46	Orig.; "Horror"-c	1	1	57	114	171	362	619	875
2	60	–	8 pgs. cut; new-c by Kiefer; LDC-r	1	2	9	18	27	50	65	80
3	62	–	LDC-r	1	2	5	10	15	24	30	35
4	71	–	LDC-r	1	2	4	9	13	18	22	26
5	93	–	LDC-r	1	2	4	8	12	17	21	24
6	114	–	LDC-r	1	2	4	7	10	14	17	20
7	128	–	New-c; PC-r	1	3	5	10	15	24	30	35
8	138	–	PC-r	1	3	2	4	6	9	13	16
9	150	–	PC-r	1	3	2	4	6	9	13	16
10	164	–	PC-r	1	3	2	4	6	8	11	14
11	167	–	PC-r	1	3	2	4	6	8	11	14
12	167	7/64	PC-r	1	3	2	4	6	8	11	14
13	167	11/65	PC-r	1	3	2	4	6	8	11	14
14	166	R/68	C-price 25¢; PC-r	1	3	2	4	6	8	11	14
15	169	Sm/70	PC-r; stiff-c	1	3	2	4	6	8	11	14

30. The Moonstone

Ed	HRN	Date	Details	A	C	GD 2.0	VG 4.0	FN 6.0	VF 8.0	VF/NM 9.0	NM- 9.2
1	–	9/46	Original; Rico-c/a	1	1	40	80	120	246	411	575
2	60	–	LDC-r; 8pgs. cut	1	1	9	18	27	47	61	75
3	70	–	LDC-r	1	1	8	16	24	42	54	65
4	155	–	New L.B. Cole-c; PC-r	1	2	4	8	12	28	44	60
5	165	–	PC-r; L.B. Cole-c	1	2	3	6	9	16	23	30
6	167	1/64	PC-r; L.B. Cole-c	1	2	2	4	6	11	16	20
7	167	9/65	PC-r; L.B. Cole-c	1	2	2	4	6	10	14	18
8	166	R/1968	C-price 25¢; PC-r	1	2	2	4	6	9	13	16

31. The Black Arrow

Ed	HRN	Date	Details	A	C	GD 2.0	VG 4.0	FN 6.0	VF 8.0	VF/NM 9.0	NM- 9.2
1	30	10/46	Original	1	1	39	78	117	231	378	525
2	51	–	CI logo; LDC-r 8pgs. deleted	1	1	6	12	18	33	41	48
3	64	–	LDC-r	1	1	4	9	13	18	22	26
4	87	–	C-price 15¢; LDC-r	1	1	4	8	12	17	21	24
5	108	–	LDC-r	1	1	4	7	10	14	17	20
6	125	–	LDC-r	1	1	4	7	10	14	17	20
7	131	–	New-c; PC-r	1	2	5	10	15	24	30	35
8	140	–	PC-r	1	2	2	4	6	9	13	16
9	148	–	PC-r	1	2	2	4	6	9	13	16
10	161	–	PC-r	1	2	2	4	6	8	11	14
11	167	–	PC-r	1	2	2	4	6	8	11	14
12	167	7/64	PC-r	1	2	2	4	6	8	11	14
13	167	11/65	PC-r	1	2	2	4	6	8	11	14
14	166	R/1968	C-price 25¢; PC-r	1	2	2	4	6	8	11	14

32. Lorna Doone

Ed	HRN	Date	Details	A	C	GD 2.0	VG 4.0	FN 6.0	VF 8.0	VF/NM 9.0	NM- 9.2
1	–	12/46	Original; Matt Baker c&a	1	1	40	80	120	246	411	575
2	53/64	–	8 pgs. deleted; LDC-r	1	1	9	18	27	47	61	75
3	85	1951	C-price 15¢; LDC-r; Baker c&a	1	1	7	14	21	37	46	55
4	118	–	LDC-r	1	1	4	9	13	18	22	26
5	138	–	New-c; old-c becomes new title pg.; PC-r	1	2	6	12	18	28	34	40
6	150	–	PC-r	1	2	2	4	6	8	11	14
7	165	–	PC-r	1	2	2	4	6	8	11	14
8	167	1/64	PC-r	1	2	2	4	6	9	13	16
9	167	11/65	PC-r	1	2	2	4	6	9	13	16
10	166	R/1968	New-c; PC-r	1	3	3	6	9	17	25	32

33. The Adventures of Sherlock Holmes

Ed	HRN	Date	Details	A	C	GD 2.0	VG 4.0	FN 6.0	VF 8.0	VF/NM 9.0	NM- 9.2
1	33	1/47	Original; Kiefer-c; contains Study in Scarlet & Hound of the Baskervilles; 68 pgs.	1	1	123	246	369	787	1344	1900
2	53	–	"A Study in Scarlet" (17 pgs.) deleted; LDC-r	1	1	45	90	135	284	480	675
3	71	–	LDC-r	1	1	37	74	111	222	361	500
4A	89	–	C-price 15¢; LDC-r	1	1	29	58	87	170	278	385
4B	89	–	Kiefer's name omitted from-c	1	1	30	60	90	177	289	400

34. Mysterious Island (Last "Classic Comic")

Ed	HRN	Date	Details	A	C	GD 2.0	VG 4.0	FN 6.0	VF 8.0	VF/NM 9.0	NM- 9.2
1	35	2/47	Original; Webb/Heames-c/a	1	1	40	80	120	246	411	575
2	60	–	8 pgs. deleted; LDC-r	1	1	7	14	21	37	46	55
3	62	–	LDC-r	1	1	5	10	15	23	28	32
4	71	–	LDC-r	1	1	6	12	18	31	38	45
5	78	–	C-price 15¢ in circle; LDC-r	1	1	5	10	14	20	24	28
6	92	–	LDC-r	1	1	4	9	13	18	22	26
7	117	–	LDC-r	1	1	4	7	10	14	17	20
8	140	–	New-c; PC-r	1	2	5	10	15	24	30	35
9	156	–	PC-r	1	2	2	4	6	9	13	16
10	167	10/63	PC-r	1	2	2	4	6	8	11	14
11	167	5/64	PC-r	1	2	2	4	6	8	11	14
12	167	6/66	PC-r	1	2	2	4	6	8	11	14
13	166	R/1968	C-price 25¢; PC-r	1	2	2	4	6	8	11	14

35. Last Days of Pompeii (First "Classics Illustrated")

Ed	HRN	Date	Details	A	C	GD 2.0	VG 4.0	FN 6.0	VF 8.0	VF/NM 9.0	NM- 9.2
1	35	3/47	Original; LDC; Kiefer-c/a	1	1	40	80	120	246	411	575
2	161	–	New c&a; 15¢; PC-r; Kirby/Ayers-a	2	2	5	10	15	32	51	70
3	167	1/64	PC-r	2	2	3	6	9	16	22	28
4	167	7/66	PC-r	2	2	3	6	9	16	22	28
5	169	Spr/70	New price 25¢; stiff-c; PC-r	2	2	3	6	9	16	22	28

Classics Illustrated #37 © GIL

Classics Illustrated #40 © GIL

Classics Illustrated #45 © GIL

36. Typee

Ed	HRN	Date	Details	A	C	GD 2.0	VG 4.0	FN 6.0	VF 8.0	VF/NM 9.0	NM- 9.2
1	36	4/47	Original	1	1	26	52	78	154	252	350
2	64	–	No c-price; 8 pg. ed.; LDC-r	1	1	7	14	21	37	46	55
3	155	–	New-c; PC-r	1	2	5	10	15	24	30	35
4	167	9/63	PC-r	1	2	2	4	6	9	13	16
5	167	7/65	PC-r	1	2	2	4	6	9	13	16
6	169	Sm/69	C-price 25¢; stiff-c PC-r	1	2	2	4	6	9	13	16

37. The Pioneers

Ed	HRN	Date	Details	A	C	GD 2.0	VG 4.0	FN 6.0	VF 8.0	VF/NM 9.0	NM- 9.2
1	37	5/47	Original; Palais-c/a	1	1	24	48	72	142	234	325
2A	62	–	8 pgs. cut; LDC-r; price circle blank	1	1	6	12	18	28	34	40
2B	62	–	10¢; LDC-r;	1	1	26	52	78	154	252	350
3	70	–	LDC-r	1	1	4	8	12	17	21	24
4	92	–	15¢; LDC-r	1	1	4	8	11	16	19	22
5	118	–	LDC-r	1	1	4	7	10	14	17	20
6	131	–	LDC-r	1	1	4	7	10	14	17	20
7	132	–	LDC-r	1	1	4	7	10	14	17	20
8	153	–	LDC-r	1	1	4	7	10	14	17	20
9	167	5/64	LDC-r	1	1	2	4	6	9	13	16
10	167	6/66	LDC-r	1	1	2	4	6	9	13	16
11	166	R/1968	New-c; 25¢; PC-r	1	2	3	6	9	18	27	36

38. Adventures of Cellini

Ed	HRN	Date	Details	A	C	GD 2.0	VG 4.0	FN 6.0	VF 8.0	VF/NM 9.0	NM- 9.2
1	–	6/47	Original; Froehlich c/a	1	1	32	64	96	188	307	425
2	164	–	New-c&a; PC-r	2	2	3	6	9	18	27	36
3	167	12/63	PC-r	2	2	2	4	6	10	14	18
4	167	7/66	PC-r	2	2	2	4	6	10	14	18
5	169	Spr/70	Stiff-c; new price 25¢; PC-r	2	2	2	4	6	11	16	20

39. Jane Eyre

Ed	HRN	Date	Details	A	C	GD 2.0	VG 4.0	FN 6.0	VF 8.0	VF/NM 9.0	NM- 9.2
1	–	7/47	Original	1	1	31	62	93	182	296	410
2	60	–	No c-price; 8 pgs. cut; LDC-r	1	1	6	12	18	31	38	45
3	62	–	LDC-r	1	1	5	10	15	24	30	35
4	71	–	LDC-r; c-price 10¢	1	1	5	10	15	22	26	30
5	92	–	C-price 15¢; LDC-r	1	1	4	9	13	18	22	26
6	118	–	LDC-r	1	1	4	8	12	17	21	24
7	142	–	New-c; old-a; PC-r	1	2	6	12	18	28	34	40
8	154	–	Old-a; PC-r	1	2	4	8	12	17	21	24
9	165	–	New-a; PC-r	2	2	3	6	9	18	27	35
10	167	12/63	PC-r	2	2	3	6	9	14	19	24
11	167	4/65	PC-r	2	2	2	4	6	13	18	22
12	167	8/66	PC-r	2	2	2	4	6	13	18	22
13	166	R/1968	New-c; PC-r	2	3	5	10	15	34	55	75

40. Mysteries ("The Pit and the Pendulum", "The Advs. of Hans Pfall" & "The Fall of the House of Usher")

Ed	HRN	Date	Details	A	C	GD 2.0	VG 4.0	FN 6.0	VF 8.0	VF/NM 9.0	NM- 9.2
1	40	8/47	Original; Kiefer-c/a, Froehlich, Griffiths-a	1	1	58	116	174	371	636	900
2	62	–	LDC-r; 8pgs. cut	1	1	22	44	66	132	216	300
3	75	–	LDC-r	1	1	19	38	57	109	172	235
4	92	–	C-price 15¢; LDC-r	1	1	15	30	45	94	147	200

41. Twenty Years After

Ed	HRN	Date	Details	A	C	GD 2.0	VG 4.0	FN 6.0	VF 8.0	VF/NM 9.0	NM- 9.2
1	–	9/47	Original; 'horror'-c	1	1	39	78	117	231	378	525
2	62	–	New-c; no c-price 8 pgs. cut; LDC-r; Kiefer-c	1	2	7	14	21	37	46	55
3	78	–	C-price 15¢; LDC-r	1	2	5	10	15	23	28	32
4	156	–	New-c; PC-r	1	3	5	10	15	24	30	35
5	167	12/63	PC-r	1	3	2	4	6	8	11	14
6	167	11/66	PC-r	1	3	2	4	6	8	11	14
7	169	Spr/70	New price 25¢; stiff-c; PC-r	1	3	2	4	6	8	11	14

42. Swiss Family Robinson

Ed	HRN	Date	Details	A	C	GD 2.0	VG 4.0	FN 6.0	VF 8.0	VF/NM 9.0	NM- 9.2
1	42	10/47	Orig.; Kiefer-c&a;	1	1	23	46	69	136	223	310
2A	62	–	8 pgs. cut; outside bc: Gift Box ad; LDC-r	1	1	6	12	18	31	38	45
2B	62	–	8 pgs. cut; outside-bc: Reorder list; scarce; LDC-r	1	1	10	20	30	58	79	100
3	75	–	LDC-r	1	1	5	10	14	20	24	28
4	93	–	LDC-r	1	1	5	10	14	20	24	28
5	117	–	LDC-r	1	1	3	6	9	14	19	24
6	131	–	New-c; old-a; PC-r	1	2	3	6	9	15	21	26
7	137	–	Old-a; PC-r	1	2	2	4	6	10	14	18
8	141	–	Old-a; PC-r	1	2	2	4	6	10	14	18
9	152	–	New-a; PC-r	2	2	3	6	9	16	23	30
10	158	–	PC-r	2	2	2	4	6	8	11	14
11	165	–	PC-r	2	2	3	6	9	17	25	32
12	167	12/63	PC-r	2	2	2	4	6	8	11	14
13	167	4/65	PC-r	2	2	2	4	6	8	11	14
14	167	5/66	PC-r	2	2	2	4	6	8	11	14
15	166	11/67	PC-r	2	2	2	4	6	8	11	14
16	169	Spr/69	PC-r; stiff-c	2	2	2	4	6	8	11	14

43. Great Expectations (Used in **SOTI**, pg. 311)

Ed	HRN	Date	Details	A	C	GD 2.0	VG 4.0	FN 6.0	VF 8.0	VF/NM 9.0	NM- 9.2
1	43	11/47	Original; Kiefer-a/c	1	1	89	178	267	565	970	1375
2	62	–	No c-price; 8 pgs. cut; LDC-r	1	1	57	114	171	362	624	885

44. Mysteries of Paris (Used in **SOTI**, pg. 323)

Ed	HRN	Date	Details	A	C	GD 2.0	VG 4.0	FN 6.0	VF 8.0	VF/NM 9.0	NM- 9.2
1A	44	12/47	Original; 56 pgs.; Kiefer-c/a	1	1	64	128	192	406	696	985
1B	44	12/47	Orig.; printed on white/heavier paper; (rare)	1	1	75	150	225	476	818	1160
2A	62	–	8 pgs. cut; outside-bc: Gift Box ad; LDC-r	1	1	30	60	90	177	289	400
2B	62	–	8 pgs. cut; outside-bc: reorder list; LDC-r	1	1	30	60	90	177	289	400
3	78	–	C-price 15¢; LDC-r	1	1	25	50	75	147	241	335

45. Tom Brown's School Days

Ed	HRN	Date	Details	A	C	GD 2.0	VG 4.0	FN 6.0	VF 8.0	VF/NM 9.0	NM- 9.2
1	44	1/48	Original; 1st 48pg. issue	1	1	18	36	54	105	165	225
2	64	–	No c-price; LDC-r	1	1	7	14	21	35	43	50
3	161	–	New-c&a; PC-r	2	2	3	6	9	17	25	32
4	167	2/64	PC-r	2	2	2	4	6	9	13	16
5	167	8/66	PC-r	2	2	2	4	6	9	13	16
6	166	R/1968	C-price 25¢; PC-r	2	2	2	4	6	9	13	16

46. Kidnapped

Ed	HRN	Date	Details	A	C	GD 2.0	VG 4.0	FN 6.0	VF 8.0	VF/NM 9.0	NM- 9.2
1	47	4/48	Original; Webb-c/a	1	1	18	36	54	105	165	225
2A	62	–	Price circle blank; LDC-r	1	1	7	14	21	35	43	50
2B	62	–	C-price 10¢; rare; LDC-r	1	1	30	60	90	177	289	400
3	78	–	C-price 15¢; LDC-r	1	1	5	10	14	20	24	28
4	87	–	LDC-r	1	1	4	9	13	18	22	26
5	118	–	LDC-r	1	1	4	7	10	14	17	20
6	131	–	New-c; PC-r	1	2	5	10	15	23	28	32
7	140	–	PC-r	1	2	2	4	6	9	13	16
8	150	–	PC-r	1	2	2	4	6	9	13	16
9	164	–	Reduced pg.width; PC-r	1	2	2	4	6	8	11	14
10	167	–	PC-r	1	2	2	4	6	8	11	14
11	167	3/64	PC-r	1	2	2	4	6	8	11	14
12	167	6/65	PC-r	1	2	2	4	6	8	11	14
13	167	12/65	PC-r	1	2	2	4	6	8	11	14
14	166	9/67	PC-r	1	2	2	4	6	8	11	14
15	166	Win/69	New price 25¢; PC-r; stiff-c	1	2	2	4	6	8	11	14
16	169	Sm/70	PC-r; stiff-c	1	2	2	4	6	8	11	14

Classics Illustrated #48 © GIL

Classics Illustrated #51 © GIL

Classics Illustrated #53 © GIL

47. Twenty Thousand Leagues Under the Sea

Ed	HRN	Date	Details	A	C	GD 2.0	VG 4.0	FN 6.0	VF 8.0	VF/NM 9.0	NM- 9.2
1	47	5/48	Orig.; Kiefer-a&c;	1	1	19	38	57	111	176	240
2	64	–	No c-price; LDC-r	1	1	6	12	18	27	33	38
3	78	–	C-price 15¢; LDC-r	1	1	4	9	13	18	22	26
4	94	–	LDC-r	1	1	4	8	12	17	21	24
5	118	–	LDC-r	1	1	4	7	10	14	17	20
6	128	–	New-c; PC-r	1	2	5	10	15	24	30	35
7	133	–	PC-r	1	2	2	4	6	10	14	18
8	140	–	PC-r	1	2	2	4	6	9	13	16
9	148	–	PC-r	1	2	2	4	6	9	13	16
10	156	–	PC-r	1	2	2	4	6	9	13	16
11	165	–	PC-r	1	2	2	4	6	9	13	16
12	167	–	PC-r	1	2	2	4	6	9	13	16
13	167	3/64	PC-r	1	2	2	4	6	9	13	16
14	167	8/65	PC-r	1	2	2	4	6	9	13	16
15	167	10/66	PC-r	1	2	2	4	6	9	13	16
16	166	R/1968	C-price 25¢; new-c PC-r	1	3	3	6	9	16	22	28
17	169	Spr/70	Stiff-c; PC-r	1	3	2	4	6	13	18	22

48. David Copperfield

Ed	HRN	Date	Details	A	C	GD 2.0	VG 4.0	FN 6.0	VF 8.0	VF/NM 9.0	NM- 9.2
1	47	6/48	Original; Kiefer-c/a	1	1	18	36	54	105	165	225
2	64	–	Price circle replaced by motif of boy reading; LDC-r	1	1	6	12	18	27	33	38
3	87	–	C-price 15¢; LDC-r	1	1	4	8	12	17	21	24
4	121	–	New-c; PC-r	1	2	5	10	15	22	26	30
5	130	–	PC-r	1	2	2	4	6	9	13	16
6	140	–	PC-r	1	2	2	4	6	9	13	16
7	148	–	PC-r	1	2	2	4	6	9	13	16
8	156	–	PC-r	1	2	2	4	6	9	13	16
9	167	–	PC-r	1	2	2	4	6	8	11	14
10	167	4/64	PC-r	1	2	2	4	6	8	11	14
11	167	6/65	PC-r	1	2	2	4	6	8	11	14
12	166	5/67	PC-r	1	2	2	4	6	8	11	14
13	166	R/67	PC-r; C-price 25¢	1	2	2	4	6	10	14	18
14	166	Spr/69	C-price 25¢; stiff-c PC-r	1	2	2	4	6	8	11	14
15	169	Win/69	Stiff-c; PC-r	1	2	2	4	6	8	11	14

49. Alice in Wonderland

Ed	HRN	Date	Details	A	C	GD 2.0	VG 4.0	FN 6.0	VF 8.0	VF/NM 9.0	NM- 9.2
1	47	7/48	Original; 1st Blum a & c	1	1	21	42	63	124	202	280
2	64	–	No c-price; LDC-r	1	1	8	16	24	42	54	65
3A	85	–	C-price 15¢; soft-c LDC-r	1	1	7	14	21	37	46	55
3B	85	–	Stiff-c; LDC-r	1	1	8	16	24	40	50	60
4	155	–	New PC, similar to orig.; PC-r	1	2	4	8	12	26	41	55
5	165	–	PC-r	1	2	3	6	9	18	27	35
6	167	3/64	PC-r	1	2	3	6	9	16	23	30
7	167	6/66	PC-r	1	2	3	6	9	16	23	60
8A	166	Fall/68	New-c; soft-c; 25¢ c-price; PC-r	1	3	4	8	12	26	41	55
8B	166	Fall/68	New-c; stiff-c; 25¢ c-price; PC-r	1	3	7	14	21	45	73	100

50. Adventures of Tom Sawyer (Used in **SOTI**, pg. 37)

Ed	HRN	Date	Details	A	C	GD 2.0	VG 4.0	FN 6.0	VF 8.0	VF/NM 9.0	NM- 9.2
1A	51	8/48	Orig.; Aldo Rubano a&c	1	1	18	36	54	105	165	225
1B	51	9/48	Orig.; Rubano c&a	1	1	18	36	54	105	165	225
1C	51	9/48	Orig.; outside-bc: blue & yellow only; rare	1	1	23	46	69	136	223	310
2	64	–	No c-price; LDC-r	1	1	5	10	15	23	28	32
3	78	–	C-price 15¢; LDC-r	1	1	4	8	12	17	21	24
4	94	–	LDC-r	1	1	4	7	10	14	17	20
5	117	–	LDC-r	1	1	2	4	6	10	14	18
6	132	–	LDC-r	1	1	2	4	6	10	14	18
7	140	–	New-c; PC-r	1	2	3	6	9	18	27	35
8	150	–	PC-r	1	2	2	4	6	9	13	16
9	164	–	New-a; PC-r	2	2	3	6	9	18	27	35
10	167	–	PC-r	2	2	2	4	6	9	13	16
11	167	1/65	PC-r	2	2	2	4	6	8	11	14
12	167	5/66	PC-r	2	2	2	4	6	8	11	14
13	166	12/67	PC-r	2	2	2	4	6	8	11	14
14	169	Fall/69	C-price 25¢; stiff-c; PC-r	2	2	2	4	6	8	11	14
15	169	Win/71	PC-r	2	2	2	4	6	8	11	14

51. The Spy

Ed	HRN	Date	Details	A	C	GD 2.0	VG 4.0	FN 6.0	VF 8.0	VF/NM 9.0	NM- 9.2
1A	51	9/48	Original; inside-bc illo: Christmas Carol	1	1	17	34	51	100	158	215
1B	51	9/48	Original; inside-bc illo: Man in Iron Mask	1	1	17	34	51	100	158	215
1C	51	8/48	Original; outside-bc: full color	1	1	17	34	51	100	158	215
1D	51	8/48	Original; outside-bc: blue & yellow only; scarce	1	1	19	38	57	109	172	235
2	89	–	C-price 15¢; LDC-r	1	1	5	10	14	20	24	28
3	121	–	LDC-r	1	1	4	8	12	17	21	24
4	139	–	New-c; PC-r	1	2	3	6	9	18	27	35
5	156	–	PC-r	1	2	2	4	6	9	13	16
6	167	11/63	PC-r	1	2	2	4	6	8	11	14
7	167	7/66	PC-r	1	2	2	4	6	8	11	14
8A	166	Win/69	C-price 25¢; soft-c; scarce; PC-r	1	2	3	6	9	15	21	26
8B	166	Win/69	C-price 25¢; stiff-c; PC-r	1	2	2	4	6	8	11	14

52. The House of the Seven Gables

Ed	HRN	Date	Details	A	C	GD 2.0	VG 4.0	FN 6.0	VF 8.0	VF/NM 9.0	NM- 9.2
1	53	10/48	Orig.; Griffiths a&c	1	1	17	34	51	100	158	215
2	89	–	C-price 15¢; LDC-r	1	1	5	10	14	20	24	28
3	121	–	LDC-r	1	1	4	8	12	17	21	24
4	142	–	New-c&a; PC-r; Woodbridge-a	2	2	5	10	15	25	31	36
5	156	–	PC-r	2	2	2	4	6	9	13	16
6	165	–	PC-r	2	2	2	4	6	8	11	14
7	167	5/64	PC-r	2	2	2	4	6	9	13	16
8	167	3/66	PC-r	2	2	2	4	6	8	11	14
9	166	R/1968	C-price 25¢; PC-r	2	2	2	4	6	8	11	14
10	169	Spr/70	Stiff-c; PC-r	2	2	2	4	6	8	11	14

53. A Christmas Carol

Ed	HRN	Date	Details	A	C	GD 2.0	VG 4.0	FN 6.0	VF 8.0	VF/NM 9.0	NM- 9.2
1	53	11/48	Original & only ed; Kiefer-c/a	1	1	24	48	72	140	230	320

54. Man in the Iron Mask

Ed	HRN	Date	Details	A	C	GD 2.0	VG 4.0	FN 6.0	VF 8.0	VF/NM 9.0	NM- 9.2
1	55	12/48	Original; Froehlich-a, Kiefer-c	1	1	17	34	51	100	158	215
2	93	–	C-price 15¢; LDC-r	1	1	5	10	15	23	28	32
3A	111	–	(O) logo lettering; scarce; LDC-r	1	1	6	12	18	31	38	45
3B	111	–	New logo as PC; LDC-r	1	1	5	10	15	23	28	32
4	142	–	New-c&a; PC-r	2	2	5	10	15	24	30	35
5	154	–	PC-r	2	2	2	4	6	9	13	16
6	165	–	PC-r	2	2	2	4	6	8	11	14
7	167	5/64	PC-r	2	2	2	4	6	8	11	14
8	167	4/66	PC-r	2	2	2	4	6	8	11	14
9A	166	Win/69	C-price 25¢; soft-c PC-r	2	2	3	6	9	15	21	26
9B	166	Win/69	Stiff-c	2	2	2	4	6	8	11	14

55. Silas Marner (Used in **SOTI**, pgs. 311, 312)

Ed	HRN	Date	Details	A	C	GD 2.0	VG 4.0	FN 6.0	VF 8.0	VF/NM 9.0	NM- 9.2
1	55	1/49	Original-Kiefer-c	1	1	17	34	51	100	158	215
2	75	–	Price circle blank; 'Coming Next' ad; LDC-r	1	1	5	10	15	24	30	35
3	97	–	LDC-r	1	1	3	6	9	14	19	24
4	121	–	New-c; PC-r	1	2	3	6	9	18	27	35
5	130	–	PC-r	1	2	2	4	6	9	13	16
6	140	–	PC-r	1	2	2	4	6	9	13	16

Classics Illustrated #57 © GIL

Classics Illustrated #62 © GIL

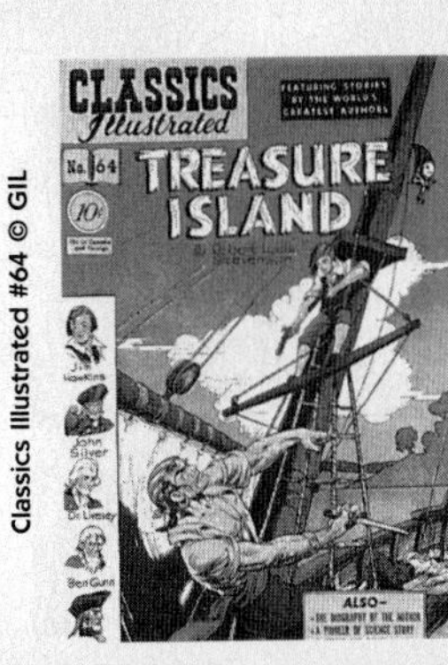

Classics Illustrated #64 © GIL

Ed	HRN	Date	Details	A	C	GD 2.0	VG 4.0	FN 6.0	VF 8.0	VF/NM 9.0	NM- 9.2
7	154	–	PC-r	1	2	2	4	6	9	13	16
8	165	–	PC-r	1	2	2	4	6	8	11	14
9	167	2/64	PC-r	1	2	2	4	6	8	11	14
10	167	6/65	PC-r	1	2	2	4	6	8	11	14
11	166	5/67	PC-r	1	2	2	4	6	8	11	14
12A	166	Win/69	C-price 25¢; soft-c PC-r	1	2	3	6	9	15	21	26
12B	166	Win/69	C-price 25¢; stiff-c PC-r	1	2	2	4	6	8	11	14

56. The Toilers of the Sea

Ed	HRN	Date	Details	A	C	GD 2.0	VG 4.0	FN 6.0	VF 8.0	VF/NM 9.0	NM- 9.2
1	55	2/49	Original; A.M. Froehlich-c/a	1	1	24	48	72	140	230	320
2	165	–	New-c&a; PC-r; Angelo Torres-a	2	2	8	16	24	40	50	60
3	167	3/64	PC-r	2	2	3	6	9	16	23	30
4	167	10/66	PC-r	2	2	3	6	9	16	23	30

57. The Song of Hiawatha

Ed	HRN	Date	Details	A	C	GD 2.0	VG 4.0	FN 6.0	VF 8.0	VF/NM 9.0	NM- 9.2
1	55	3/49	Original; Alex Blum-c/a	1	1	16	32	48	94	147	200
2	75	–	No c-price w/15¢ sticker; 'Coming Next' ad; LDC-r	1	1	5	10	15	24	30	35
3	94	–	C-price 15¢; LDC-r	1	1	5	10	14	20	24	28
4	118	–	LDC-r	1	1	3	6	9	14	19	24
5	134	–	New-c; PC-r	1	2	3	6	9	18	27	35
6	139	–	PC-r	1	2	2	4	6	9	13	16
7	154	–	PC-r	1	2	2	4	6	9	13	16
8	167	–	Has orig.date; PC-r	1	2	2	4	6	8	11	14
9	167	9/64	PC-r	1	2	2	4	6	8	11	14
10	167	10/65	PC-r	1	2	2	4	6	8	11	14
11	166	F/1968	C-price 25¢; PC-r	1	2	2	4	6	8	11	14

58. The Prairie

Ed	HRN	Date	Details	A	C	GD 2.0	VG 4.0	FN 6.0	VF 8.0	VF/NM 9.0	NM- 9.2
1	60	4/49	Original; Palais c/a	1	1	16	32	48	94	147	200
2A	62	–	No c-price; no coming-next ad; LDC-r	1	1	9	18	27	47	61	75
2B	62		10¢ (rare)	1	1	18	36	54	105	165	225
3	78	–	C-price 15¢ in dbl. circle; LDC-r	1	1	5	10	15	22	26	30
4	114	–	LDC-r	1	1	4	8	12	17	21	24
5	131	–	LDC-r	1	1	4	7	10	14	17	20
6	132	–	LDC-r	1	1	4	7	10	14	17	20
7	146	–	New-c; PC-r	1	2	5	10	15	23	28	32
8	155	–	PC-r	1	2	2	4	6	9	13	16
9	167	5/64	PC-r	1	2	2	4	6	8	11	14
10	167	4/66	PC-r	1	2	2	4	6	8	11	14
11	169	Sm/69	New price 25¢; stiff-c; PC-r	1	2	2	4	6	8	11	14

59. Wuthering Heights

Ed	HRN	Date	Details	A	C	GD 2.0	VG 4.0	FN 6.0	VF 8.0	VF/NM 9.0	NM- 9.2
1	60	5/49	Original; Kiefer-c/a	1	1	17	34	51	100	158	215
2	85	–	C-price 15¢; LDC-r	1	1	6	12	18	28	34	40
3	156	–	New-c; PC-r	1	2	5	10	15	25	31	36
4	167	1/64	PC-r	1	2	2	4	6	9	13	16
5	167	10/66	PC-r	1	2	2	4	6	9	13	16
6	169	Sm/69	C-price 25¢; stiff-c; PC-r	1	2	2	4	6	9	13	16

60. Black Beauty

Ed	HRN	Date	Details	A	C	GD 2.0	VG 4.0	FN 6.0	VF 8.0	VF/NM 9.0	NM- 9.2
1	62	6/49	Original; Froehlich-c/a	1	1	16	32	48	94	147	200
2	62	–	No c-price; no coming-next ad; LDC-r (rare)	1	1	18	36	54	107	169	230
3	85	–	C-price 15¢; LDC-r	1	1	5	10	15	23	28	32
4	158	–	New L.B. Cole-c/a; PC-r	2	2	7	14	21	35	43	50
5	167	2/64	PC-r	2	2	2	4	6	11	16	20
6	167	3/66	PC-r	2	2	2	4	6	11	16	20
7	166	R/1968	New-c&price, 25¢; PC-r	2	3	5	10	15	32	51	70

61. The Woman in White

Ed	HRN	Date	Details	A	C	GD 2.0	VG 4.0	FN 6.0	VF 8.0	VF/NM 9.0	NM- 9.2
1A	62	7/49	Original; Blum-c/a fc-purple; bc: top illos light blue	1	1	17	34	51	100	158	215
1B	62	7/49	Original; Blum-c/a fc-pink; bc: top illos light violet	1	1	17	34	51	100	158	215
2	156	–	New-c; PC-r	1	2	6	12	18	28	34	40
3	167	1/64	PC-r	1	2	2	4	6	11	16	20
4	166	R/1968	C-price 25¢; PC-r	1	2	2	4	6	11	16	20

62. Western Stories ("The Luck of Roaring Camp" and "The Outcasts of Poker Flat")

Ed	HRN	Date	Details	A	C	GD 2.0	VG 4.0	FN 6.0	VF 8.0	VF/NM 9.0	NM- 9.2
1	62	8/49	Original; Kiefer-c/a	1	1	15	30	45	90	140	190
2	89	–	C-price 15¢; LDC-r	1	1	5	10	15	23	28	32
3	121	–	LDC-r	1	1	3	6	9	15	21	26
4	137	–	New-c; PC-r	1	2	3	6	9	18	27	35
5	152	–	PC-r	1	2	2	4	6	8	11	14
6	167	10/63	PC-r	1	2	2	4	6	8	11	14
7	167	6/64	PC-r	1	2	2	4	6	8	11	14
8	167	11/66	PC-r	1	2	2	4	6	8	11	14
9	166	R/1968	New-c&price 25¢; PC-r	1	3	3	6	9	17	25	32

63. The Man Without a Country

Ed	HRN	Date	Details	A	C	GD 2.0	VG 4.0	FN 6.0	VF 8.0	VF/NM 9.0	NM- 9.2
1	62	9/49	Original; Kiefer-c/a	1	1	16	32	48	94	147	200
2	78	–	C-price 15¢ in double circle; LDC-r	1	1	5	10	15	23	28	32
3	156	–	New-c, old-a; PC-r	1	2	6	12	18	28	34	40
4	165	–	New-a & text pgs.; PC-r; A. Torres-a	2	2	5	10	15	23	28	32
5	167	3/64	PC-r	2	2	2	4	6	8	11	14
6	167	8/66	PC-r	2	2	2	4	6	8	11	14
7	169	Sm/69	New price 25¢; stiff-c; PC-r	2	2	2	4	6	8	11	14

64. Treasure Island

Ed	HRN	Date	Details	A	C	GD 2.0	VG 4.0	FN 6.0	VF 8.0	VF/NM 9.0	NM- 9.2
1	62	10/49	Original; Blum-c/a	1	1	17	34	51	100	158	215
2A	82	–	C-price 15¢; soft-c LDC-r	1	1	5	10	15	22	26	30
2B	82	–	Stiff-c; LDC-r	1	1	5	10	15	23	28	32
3	117	–	LDC-r	1	1	3	6	9	15	21	26
4	131	–	New-c; PC-r	1	2	3	6	9	18	27	35
5	138	–	PC-r	1	2	2	4	6	9	13	16
6	146	–	PC-r	1	2	2	4	6	9	13	16
7	158	–	PC-r	1	2	2	4	6	9	13	16
8	165	–	PC-r	1	2	2	4	6	8	11	14
9	167	–	PC-r	1	2	2	4	6	8	11	14
10	167	6/64	PC-r	1	2	2	4	6	8	11	14
11	167	12/65	PC-r	1	2	2	4	6	8	11	14
12A	166	10/67	PC-r	1	2	2	4	6	8	11	14
12B	166	10/67	w/Grit ad stapled in book	1	2	10	20	30	69	122	175
13	169	Spr/69	New price 25¢; stiff-c; PC-r	1	2	2	4	6	9	13	16
14	–	1989	Long John Silver's Seafood Shoppes; $1.95, First/Berkley Publ.; Blum-r	1	2						5.00

65. Benjamin Franklin

Ed	HRN	Date	Details	A	C	GD 2.0	VG 4.0	FN 6.0	VF 8.0	VF/NM 9.0	NM- 9.2
1	64	11/49	Original; Kiefer-c; Iger Shop-a	1	1	16	32	48	94	147	200
2	131	–	New-c; PC-r	1	2	5	10	15	24	30	35
3	154	–	PC-r	1	2	2	4	6	9	13	16
4	167	2/64	PC-r	1	2	2	4	6	9	13	16
5	167	4/66	PC-r	1	2	2	4	6	9	13	16
6	169	Fall/69	New price 25¢; stiff-c; PC-r	1	2	2	4	6	9	13	16

66. The Cloister and the Hearth

Classics Illustrated #68 © GIL

Classics Illustrated #71 © GIL

Classics Illustrated #78 © GIL

Ed	HRN	Date	Details	A	C	GD 2.0	VG 4.0	FN 6.0	VF 8.0	VF/NM 9.0	NM- 9.2
1	67	12/49	Original & only ed; Kiefer-a & c	1	1	31	62	93	186	303	420

67. The Scottish Chiefs

Ed	HRN	Date	Details	A	C	GD 2.0	VG 4.0	FN 6.0	VF 8.0	VF/NM 9.0	NM- 9.2
1	67	1/50	Original; Blum-a&c	1	1	15	30	45	85	130	175
2	85	–	C-price 15¢; LDC-r	1	1	5	10	15	23	28	32
3	118	–	LDC-r	1	1	3	6	9	15	21	26
4	136	–	New-c; PC-r	1	2	3	6	9	18	27	36
5	154	–	PC-r	1	2	2	4	6	9	13	16
6	167	11/63	PC-r	1	2	2	4	6	10	14	18
7	167	8/65	PC-r	1	2	2	4	6	9	13	16

68. Julius Caesar (Used in **SOTI**, pgs. 36, 37)

Ed	HRN	Date	Details	A	C	GD 2.0	VG 4.0	FN 6.0	VF 8.0	VF/NM 9.0	NM- 9.2
1	70	2/50	Original; Kiefer-c/a	1	1	15	30	45	85	130	175
2	85	–	C-price 15¢; LDC-r	1	1	5	10	15	22	26	30
3	108	–	LDC-r	1	1	4	9	13	18	22	26
4	156	–	New L.B. Cole-c; PC-r	1	2	6	12	18	28	34	40
5	165	–	New-a by Evans, Crandall; PC-r	2	2	5	10	15	24	30	35
6	167	2/64	PC-r	2	2	2	4	6	8	11	14
7	167	10/65	Tarzan books inside cover; PC-r	2	2	2	4	6	8	11	14
8	166	R/1967	PC-r	2	2	2	4	6	8	11	14
9	169	Win/69	PC-r; stiff-c	2	2	2	4	6	8	11	14

69. Around the World in 80 Days

Ed	HRN	Date	Details	A	C	GD 2.0	VG 4.0	FN 6.0	VF 8.0	VF/NM 9.0	NM- 9.2
1	70	3/50	Original; Kiefer-c/a	1	1	15	30	45	85	130	175
2	87	–	C-price 15¢; LDC-r	1	1	5	10	15	22	26	30
3	125	–	LDC-r	1	1	4	9	13	18	22	26
4	136	–	New-c; PC-r	1	2	5	10	15	25	31	36
5	146	–	PC-r	1	2	2	4	6	9	13	16
6	152	–	PC-r	1	2	2	4	6	9	13	16
7	164	–	PC-r	1	2	2	4	6	8	11	14
8	167	–	PC-r	1	2	2	4	6	8	11	14
9	167	7/64	PC-r	1	2	2	4	6	8	11	14
10	167	11/65	PC-r	1	2	2	4	6	8	11	14
11	166	7/67	PC-r	1	2	2	4	6	8	11	14
12	169	Spr/69	C-price 25¢; stiff-c; PC-r	1	2	2	4	6	8	11	14

70. The Pilot

Ed	HRN	Date	Details	A	C	GD 2.0	VG 4.0	FN 6.0	VF 8.0	VF/NM 9.0	NM- 9.2
1	71	4/50	Original; Blum-c/a	1	1	14	28	42	76	108	140
2	92	–	C-price 15¢; LDC-r	1	1	5	10	15	23	28	32
3	125	–	LDC-r	1	1	4	9	13	18	22	26
4	156	–	New-c; PC-r	1	2	6	12	18	28	34	40
5	167	2/64	PC-r	1	2	2	4	6	11	16	20
6	167	5/66	PC-r	1	2	2	4	6	9	13	16

71. The Man Who Laughs

Ed	HRN	Date	Details	A	C	GD 2.0	VG 4.0	FN 6.0	VF 8.0	VF/NM 9.0	NM- 9.2
1	71	5/50	Original; Blum-c/a	1	1	19	38	57	111	176	240
2	165	–	New-c&a; PC-r	2	2	14	28	42	80	115	155
3	167	4/64	PC-r	2	2	11	22	33	62	86	115

72. The Oregon Trail

Ed	HRN	Date	Details	A	C	GD 2.0	VG 4.0	FN 6.0	VF 8.0	VF/NM 9.0	NM- 9.2
1	73	6/50	Original; Kiefer-c/a	1	1	14	28	42	81	118	140
2	89	–	C-price 15¢; LDC-r	1	1	5	10	15	23	28	32
3	121	–	LDC-r	1	1	4	9	13	18	22	26
4	131	–	New-c; PC-r	1	2	5	10	15	25	31	36
5	140	–	PC-r	1	2	2	4	6	9	13	16
6	150	–	PC-r	1	2	2	4	6	9	13	16
7	164	–	PC-r	1	2	2	4	6	8	11	14
8	167	–	PC-r	1	2	2	4	6	8	11	14
9	167	8/64	PC-r	1	2	2	4	6	8	11	14
10	167	10/65	PC-r	1	2	2	4	6	8	11	14
11	166	R/1968	C-price 25¢; PC-r	1	2	2	4	6	8	11	14

73. The Black Tulip

Ed	HRN	Date	Details	A	C	GD 2.0	VG 4.0	FN 6.0	VF 8.0	VF/NM 9.0	NM- 9.2
1	75	7/50	1st & only ed.; Alex Blum-c/a	1	1	36	72	108	214	347	480

74. Mr. Midshipman Easy

Ed	HRN	Date	Details	A	C	GD 2.0	VG 4.0	FN 6.0	VF 8.0	VF/NM 9.0	NM- 9.2
1	75	8/50	1st & only edition	1	1	36	72	108	214	347	480

75. The Lady of the Lake

Ed	HRN	Date	Details	A	C	GD 2.0	VG 4.0	FN 6.0	VF 8.0	VF/NM 9.0	NM- 9.2
1	75	9/50	Original; Kiefer-c/a	1	1	14	28	42	76	108	140
2	85	–	C-price 15¢; LDC-r	1	1	5	10	15	24	30	35
3	118	–	LDC-r	1	1	5	10	14	20	24	28
4	139	–	New-c; PC-r	1	2	5	10	15	25	31	36
5	154	–	PC-r	1	2	2	4	6	9	13	16
6	165	–	PC-r	1	2	2	4	6	8	11	14
7	167	4/64	PC-r	1	2	2	4	6	8	11	14
8	167	5/66	PC-r	1	2	2	4	6	8	11	14
9	169	Spr/69	New price 25¢; stiff-c; PC-r	1	2	2	4	6	8	11	14

76. The Prisoner of Zenda

Ed	HRN	Date	Details	A	C	GD 2.0	VG 4.0	FN 6.0	VF 8.0	VF/NM 9.0	NM- 9.2
1	75	10/50	Original; Kiefer-c/a	1	1	14	28	42	76	108	140
2	85	–	C-price 15¢; LDC-r	1	1	5	10	15	23	28	32
3	111	–	LDC-r	1	1	3	6	9	16	21	26
4	128	–	New-c; PC-r	1	2	3	6	9	18	27	35
5	152	–	PC-r	1	2	2	4	6	9	13	16
6	165	–	PC-r	1	2	2	4	6	8	11	14
7	167	4/64	PC-r	1	2	2	4	6	8	11	14
8	167	9/66	PC-r	1	2	2	4	6	8	11	14
9	169	Fall/69	New price 25¢; stiff-c; PC-r	1	2	2	4	6	8	11	14

77. The Iliad

Ed	HRN	Date	Details	A	C	GD 2.0	VG 4.0	FN 6.0	VF 8.0	VF/NM 9.0	NM- 9.2
1	78	11/50	Original; Blum-c/a	1	1	14	28	42	76	108	140
2	87	–	C-price 15¢; LDC-r	1	1	5	10	15	24	30	35
3	121	–	LDC-r	1	1	3	6	9	15	21	26
4	139	–	New-c; PC-r	1	2	3	6	9	17	25	32
5	150	–	PC-r	1	2	2	4	6	9	13	16
6	165	–	PC-r	1	2	2	4	6	8	11	14
7	167	10/63	PC-r	1	2	2	4	6	8	11	14
8	167	7/64	PC-r	1	2	2	4	6	8	11	14
9	167	5/66	PC-r	1	2	2	4	6	8	11	14
10	166	R/1968	C-price 25¢; PC-r	1	2	2	4	6	8	11	14

78. Joan of Arc

Ed	HRN	Date	Details	A	C	GD 2.0	VG 4.0	FN 6.0	VF 8.0	VF/NM 9.0	NM- 9.2
1	78	12/50	Original; Kiefer-c/a	1	1	14	28	42	76	108	140
2	87	–	C-price 15¢; LDC-r	1	1	5	10	15	23	28	32
3	113	–	LDC-r	1	1	3	6	9	15	21	26
4	128	–	New-c; PC-r	1	2	3	6	9	18	27	35
5	140	–	PC-r	1	2	2	4	6	9	13	16
6	150	–	PC-r	1	2	2	4	6	9	13	16
7	159	–	PC-r	1	2	2	4	6	9	13	16
8	167	–	PC-r	1	2	2	4	6	8	11	14
9	167	12/63	PC-r	1	2	2	4	6	8	11	14
10	167	6/65	PC-r	1	2	2	4	6	8	11	14
11	166	6/67	PC-r	1	2	2	4	6	8	11	14
12	166	Win/69	New-c&price, 25¢; PC-r; stiff-c	1	3	3	6	9	17	25	32

79. Cyrano de Bergerac

Ed	HRN	Date	Details	A	C	GD 2.0	VG 4.0	FN 6.0	VF 8.0	VF/NM 9.0	NM- 9.2
1	78	1/51	Orig.; movie promo inside front-c; Blum-c/a	1	1	14	28	42	76	108	140
2	85	–	C-price 15¢; LDC-r	1	1	5	10	15	23	28	32
3	118	–	LDC-r	1	1	3	6	9	17	23	28
4	133	–	New-c; PC-r	1	2	3	6	9	17	25	32
5	156	–	PC-r	1	2	2	4	6	11	16	20
6	167	8/64	PC-r	1	2	2	4	6	11	16	20

80. White Fang (Last line drawn cover)

Ed	HRN	Date	Details	A	C	GD 2.0	VG 4.0	FN 6.0	VF 8.0	VF/NM 9.0	NM- 9.2
1	79	2/51	Orig.; Blum-c/a	1	1	14	28	42	76	108	140
2	87	–	C-price 15¢; LDC-r	1	1	5	10	15	24	30	35
3	125	–	LDC-r	1	1	3	6	9	15	21	26
4	132	–	New-c; PC-r	1	2	3	6	9	17	25	32
5	140	–	PC-r	1	2	2	4	6	9	13	16
6	153	–	PC-r	1	2	2	4	6	9	13	16
7	167	–	PC-r	1	2	2	4	6	8	11	14

Classics Illustrated #81 © GIL

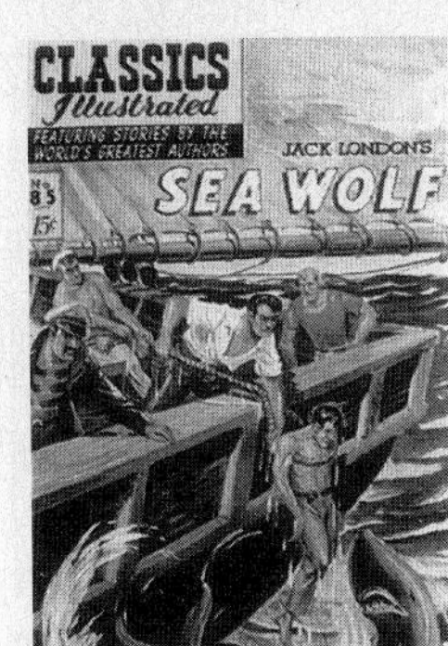

Classics Illustrated #85 © GIL

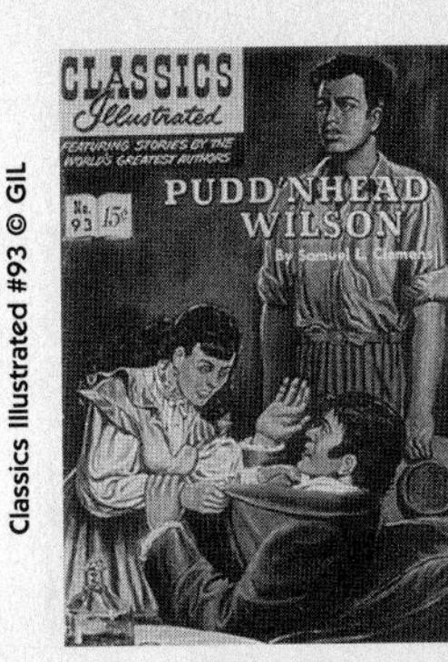

Classics Illustrated #93 © GIL

Ed	HRN	Date	Details	A	C	GD 2.0	VG 4.0	FN 6.0	VF 8.0	VF/NM 9.0	NM- 9.2
8	167	9/64	PC-r	1	2	2	4	6	8	11	14
9	167	7/65	PC-r	1	2	2	4	6	8	11	14
10	166	6/67	PC-r	1	2	2	4	6	8	11	14
11	169	Fall/69	New price 25¢; PC-r; stiff-c	1	2	2	4	6	8	11	14

81. The Odyssey (1st painted cover)

Ed	HRN	Date	Details	A	C	GD 2.0	VG 4.0	FN 6.0	VF 8.0	VF/NM 9.0	NM- 9.2
1	82	3/51	First 15¢ Original; Blum-c	1	1	14	28	42	76	108	140
2	167	8/64	PC-r	1	1	2	4	6	11	16	20
3	167	10/66	PC-r	1	1	2	4	6	11	16	20
4	169	Spr/69	New, stiff-c; PC-r	1	2	3	6	9	18	27	36

82. The Master of Ballantrae

Ed	HRN	Date	Details	A	C	GD 2.0	VG 4.0	FN 6.0	VF 8.0	VF/NM 9.0	NM- 9.2
1	82	4/51	Original; Blum-c	1	1	11	22	33	64	90	115
2	167	8/64	PC-r	1	1	3	6	9	14	19	24
3	166	Fall/68	New, stiff-c; PC-r	1	2	3	6	9	18	27	36

83. The Jungle Book

Ed	HRN	Date	Details	A	C	GD 2.0	VG 4.0	FN 6.0	VF 8.0	VF/NM 9.0	NM- 9.2
1	85	5/51	Original; Blum-c Bossert/Blum-a	1	1	11	22	33	64	90	115
2	110	–	PC-r	1	1	2	4	6	10	14	18
3	125	–	PC-r	1	1	2	4	6	9	13	16
4	134	–	PC-r	1	1	2	4	6	9	13	16
5	142	–	PC-r	1	1	2	4	6	9	13	16
6	150	–	PC-r	1	1	2	4	6	9	13	16
7	159	–	PC-r	1	1	2	4	6	9	13	16
8	167	–	PC-r	1	1	2	4	6	8	11	14
9	167	3/65	PC-r	1	1	2	4	6	8	11	14
10	167	11/65	PC-r	1	1	2	4	6	8	11	14
11	167	5/66	PC-r	1	1	2	4	6	8	11	14
12	166	R/1968	New c&a; stiff-c; PC-r	2	2	3	6	9	19	29	38

84. The Gold Bug and Other Stories ("The Gold Bug", "The Tell-Tale Heart", "The Cask of Amontillado")

Ed	HRN	Date	Details	A	C	GD 2.0	VG 4.0	FN 6.0	VF 8.0	VF/NM 9.0	NM- 9.2
1	85	6/51	Original; Blum-c/a; Palais, Laverly-a	1	1	15	30	45	83	124	165
2	167	7/64	PC-r	1	1	11	22	33	62	86	110

85. The Sea Wolf

Ed	HRN	Date	Details	A	C	GD 2.0	VG 4.0	FN 6.0	VF 8.0	VF/NM 9.0	NM- 9.2
1	85	7/51	Original; Blum-c/a	1	1	11	22	33	60	83	105
2	121	–	PC-r	1	1	2	4	6	9	13	16
3	132	–	PC-r	1	1	2	4	6	9	13	16
4	141	–	PC-r	1	1	2	4	6	9	13	16
5	161	–	PC-r	1	1	2	4	6	8	11	14
6	167	2/64	PC-r	1	1	2	4	6	8	11	14
7	167	11/65	PC-r	1	1	2	4	6	8	11	14
8	169	Fall/69	New price 25¢; stiff-c; PC-r	1	1	2	4	6	8	11	14

86. Under Two Flags

Ed	HRN	Date	Details	A	C	GD 2.0	VG 4.0	FN 6.0	VF 8.0	VF/NM 9.0	NM- 9.2
1	87	8/51	Original; first delBourgo-a	1	1	11	22	33	60	83	105
2	117	–	PC-r	1	1	2	4	6	10	14	18
3	139	–	PC-r	1	1	2	4	6	9	13	16
4	158	–	PC-r	1	1	2	4	6	9	13	16
5	167	2/64	PC-r	1	1	2	4	6	8	11	14
6	167	8/66	PC-r	1	1	2	4	6	8	11	14
7	169	Sm/69	New price 25¢; stiff-c; PC-r	1	1	2	4	6	8	11	14

87. A Midsummer Nights Dream

Ed	HRN	Date	Details	A	C	GD 2.0	VG 4.0	FN 6.0	VF 8.0	VF/NM 9.0	NM- 9.2
1	87	9/51	Original; Blum c/a	1	1	11	22	33	60	83	105
2	161	–	PC-r	1	1	2	4	6	9	13	16
3	167	4/64	PC-r	1	1	2	4	6	8	11	14
4	167	5/66	PC-r	1	1	2	4	6	8	11	14
5	169	Sm/69	New price 25¢; stiff-c; PC-r	1	1	2	4	6	8	11	14

88. Men of Iron

Ed	HRN	Date	Details	A	C	GD 2.0	VG 4.0	FN 6.0	VF 8.0	VF/NM 9.0	NM- 9.2
1	89	10/51	Original	1	1	11	22	33	60	83	105
2	154	–	PC-r	1	1	2	4	6	9	13	16
3	167	1/64	PC-r	1	1	2	4	6	8	11	14
4	166	R/1968	C-price 25¢; PC-r	1	1	2	4	6	8	11	14

89. Crime and Punishment (Cover illo. in **POP**)

Ed	HRN	Date	Details	A	C	GD 2.0	VG 4.0	FN 6.0	VF 8.0	VF/NM 9.0	NM- 9.2
1	89	11/51	Original; Palais-a	1	1	11	22	33	60	83	105
2	152	–	PC-r	1	1	2	4	6	9	13	16
3	167	4/64	PC-r	1	1	2	4	6	8	11	14
4	167	5/66	PC-r	1	1	2	4	6	8	11	14
5	169	Fall/69	New price 25¢ stiff-c; PC-r	1	1	2	4	6	8	11	14

90. Green Mansions

Ed	HRN	Date	Details	A	C	GD 2.0	VG 4.0	FN 6.0	VF 8.0	VF/NM 9.0	NM- 9.2
1	89	12/51	Original; Blum-c/a	1	1	11	22	33	60	83	105
2	148	–	New L.B. Cole-c; PC-r	1	2	5	10	15	22	26	30
3	165	–	PC-r	1	2	2	4	6	8	11	14
4	167	4/64	PC-r	1	2	2	4	6	8	11	14
5	167	9/66	PC-r	1	2	2	4	6	8	11	14
6	169	Sm/69	New price 25¢; stiff-c; PC-r	1	2	2	4	6	8	11	14

91. The Call of the Wild

Ed	HRN	Date	Details	A	C	GD 2.0	VG 4.0	FN 6.0	VF 8.0	VF/NM 9.0	NM- 9.2
1	92	1/52	Orig.; delBourgo-a	1	1	11	22	33	60	83	105
2	112	–	PC-r	1	1	2	4	6	9	13	16
3	125	–	'Picture Progress' on back-c; PC-r	1	1	2	4	6	9	13	16
4	134	–	PC-r	1	1	2	4	6	9	13	16
5	143	–	PC-r	1	1	2	4	6	9	13	16
6	165	–	PC-r	1	1	2	4	6	9	13	16
7	167	–	PC-r	1	1	2	4	6	8	11	14
8	167	4/65	PC-r	1	1	2	4	6	8	11	14
9	167	3/66	PC-r	1	1	2	4	6	8	11	14
10	166	11/67	PC-r	1	1	2	4	6	8	11	14
11	169	Spr/70	New price 25¢; stiff-c; PC-r	1	1	2	4	6	8	11	14

92. The Courtship of Miles Standish

Ed	HRN	Date	Details	A	C	GD 2.0	VG 4.0	FN 6.0	VF 8.0	VF/NM 9.0	NM- 9.2
1	92	2/52	Original; Blum-c/a	1	1	11	22	33	60	83	105
2	165	–	PC-r	1	1	2	4	6	9	13	16
3	167	3/64	PC-r	1	1	2	4	6	9	13	16
4	166	5/67	PC-r	1	1	2	4	6	9	13	16
5	169	Win/69	New price 25¢ stiff-c; PC-r	1	1	2	4	6	9	13	16

93. Pudd'nhead Wilson

Ed	HRN	Date	Details	A	C	GD 2.0	VG 4.0	FN 6.0	VF 8.0	VF/NM 9.0	NM- 9.2
1	94	3/52	Orig.; Kiefer-c/a;	1	1	11	22	33	60	83	105
2	165	–	New-c; PC-r	1	2	2	4	6	11	16	25
3	167	3/64	PC-r	1	2	2	4	6	9	13	16
4	166	R/1968	New price 25¢; soft-c; PC-r	1	2	2	4	6	9	13	16

94. David Balfour

Ed	HRN	Date	Details	A	C	GD 2.0	VG 4.0	FN 6.0	VF 8.0	VF/NM 9.0	NM- 9.2
1	94	4/52	Original; Palais-a	1	1	11	22	33	60	83	105
2	167	5/64	PC-r	1	1	2	4	6	11	16	20
3	166	R/1968	C-price 25¢; PC-r	1	1	2	4	6	13	18	22

95. All Quiet on the Western Front

Ed	HRN	Date	Details	A	C	GD 2.0	VG 4.0	FN 6.0	VF 8.0	VF/NM 9.0	NM- 9.2
1A	96	5/52	Orig.; del Bourgo-a	1	1	14	28	42	80	115	150
1B	99	5/52	Orig.; del Bourgo-a	1	1	12	24	36	69	97	125
2	167	10/64	PC-r	1	1	3	6	9	16	22	28
3	167	11/66	PC-r	1	1	3	6	9	16	22	28

96. Daniel Boone

Ed	HRN	Date	Details	A	C	GD 2.0	VG 4.0	FN 6.0	VF 8.0	VF/NM 9.0	NM- 9.2
1	97	6/52	Original; Blum-a	1	1	10	20	30	58	79	100
2	117	–	PC-r	1	1	2	4	6	9	13	16
3	128	–	PC-r	1	1	2	4	6	9	13	16
4	132	–	PC-r	1	1	2	4	6	9	13	16
5	134	–	"Story of Jesus" on back-c; PC-r	1	1	2	4	6	9	13	16
6	158	–	PC-r	1	1	2	4	6	9	13	16
7	167	1/64	PC-r	1	1	2	4	6	8	11	14

Classics Illustrated #97 © GIL

Classics Illustrated #100 © GIL

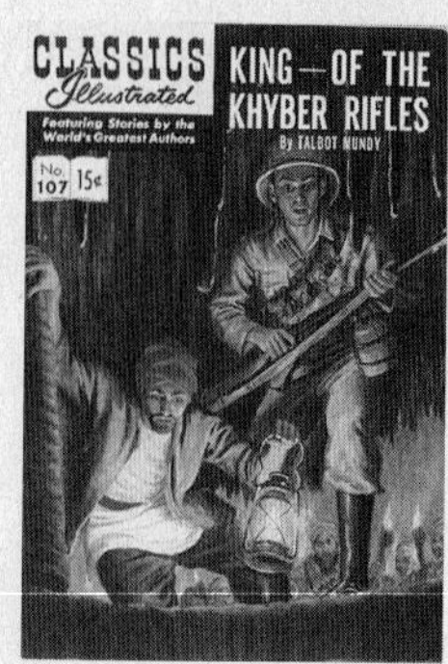

Classics Illustrated #107 © GIL

Ed	HRN	Date	Details	A	C	GD 2.0	VG 4.0	FN 6.0	VF 8.0	VF/NM 9.0	NM- 9.2
8	167	5/65	PC-r	1	1	2	4	6	8	11	14
9	167	11/66	PC-r	1	1	2	4	6	8	11	14
10	166	Win/69	New-c; price 25¢; PC-r; stiff-c	1	2	3	6	9	16	22	28

97. King Solomon's Mines

Ed	HRN	Date	Details	A	C	GD 2.0	VG 4.0	FN 6.0	VF 8.0	VF/NM 9.0	NM- 9.2
1	96	7/52	Orig.; Kiefer-a	1	1	10	20	30	58	79	100
2	118	–	PC-r	1	1	2	4	6	9	13	16
3	131	–	PC-r	1	1	2	4	6	9	13	16
4	141	–	PC-r	1	1	2	4	6	9	13	16
5	158	–	PC-r	1	1	2	4	6	9	13	16
6	167	2/64	PC-r	1	1	2	4	6	8	11	14
7	167	9/65	PC-r	1	1	2	4	6	8	11	14
8	169	Sm/69	New price 25¢; stiff-c; PC-r	1	1	2	4	6	8	11	14

98. The Red Badge of Courage

Ed	HRN	Date	Details	A	C	GD 2.0	VG 4.0	FN 6.0	VF 8.0	VF/NM 9.0	NM- 9.2
1	98	8/52	Original	1	1	10	20	30	58	79	100
2	118	–	PC-r	1	1	2	4	6	9	13	16
3	132	–	PC-r	1	1	2	4	6	9	13	16
4	142	–	PC-r	1	1	2	4	6	9	13	16
5	152	–	PC-r	1	1	2	4	6	9	13	16
6	161	–	PC-r	1	1	2	4	6	9	13	16
7	167	–	Has orig.date; PC-r	1	1	2	4	6	9	13	16
8	167	9/64	PC-r	1	1	2	4	6	9	13	16
9	167	10/65	PC-r	1	1	2	4	6	9	13	16
10	166	R/1968	New-c&price 25¢; PC-r; stiff-c	1	2	3	6	9	16	23	30

99. Hamlet (Used in **POP**, pg. 102)

Ed	HRN	Date	Details	A	C	GD 2.0	VG 4.0	FN 6.0	VF 8.0	VF/NM 9.0	NM- 9.2
1	98	9/52	Original; Blum-a	1	1	11	22	33	60	83	105
2	121	–	PC-r	1	1	2	4	6	9	13	16
3	141	–	PC-r	1	1	2	4	6	9	13	16
4	158	–	PC-r	1	1	2	4	6	9	13	16
5	167	–	Has orig.date; PC-r	1	1	2	4	6	8	11	14
6	167	7/65	PC-r	1	1	2	4	6	8	11	14
7	166	4/67	PC-r	1	1	2	4	6	8	11	14
8	169	Spr/69	New-c&price 25¢; PC-r; stiff-c	1	2	3	6	9	16	23	30

100. Mutiny on the Bounty

Ed	HRN	Date	Details	A	C	GD 2.0	VG 4.0	FN 6.0	VF 8.0	VF/NM 9.0	NM- 9.2
1	100	10/52	Original	1	1	10	20	30	58	79	100
2	117	–	PC-r	1	1	2	4	6	9	13	16
3	132	–	PC-r	1	1	2	4	6	9	13	16
4	142	–	PC-r	1	1	2	4	6	9	13	16
5	155	–	PC-r	1	1	2	4	6	9	13	16
6	167	–	Has orig. date;PC-r	1	1	2	4	6	8	11	14
7	167	5/64	PC-r	1	1	2	4	6	8	11	14
8	167	3/66	PC-r	1	1	2	4	6	8	11	14
9	169	Spr/70	PC-r; stiff-c	1	1	2	4	6	8	11	14

101. William Tell

Ed	HRN	Date	Details	A	C	GD 2.0	VG 4.0	FN 6.0	VF 8.0	VF/NM 9.0	NM- 9.2
1	101	11/52	Original; Kiefer-c delBourgo-a	1	1	10	20	30	58	79	100
2	118	–	PC-r	1	1	2	4	6	9	13	16
3	141	–	PC-r	1	1	2	4	6	9	13	16
4	158	–	PC-r	1	1	2	4	6	9	13	16
5	167	–	Has orig.date; PC-r	1	1	2	4	6	8	11	14
6	167	11/64	PC-r	1	1	2	4	6	8	11	14
7	166	4/67	PC-r	1	1	2	4	6	8	11	14
8	169	Win/69	New price 25¢; stiff-c; PC-r	1	1	2	4	6	8	11	14

102. The White Company

Ed	HRN	Date	Details	A	C	GD 2.0	VG 4.0	FN 6.0	VF 8.0	VF/NM 9.0	NM- 9.2
1	101	12/52	Original; Blum-a	1	1	13	26	39	74	105	135
2	165	–	PC-r	1	1	3	6	9	16	23	30
3	167	4/64	PC-r	1	1	3	6	9	16	23	30

103. Men Against the Sea

Ed	HRN	Date	Details	A	C	GD 2.0	VG 4.0	FN 6.0	VF 8.0	VF/NM 9.0	NM- 9.2
1	104	1/53	Original; Kiefer-c; Palais-a	1	1	11	22	33	60	83	105
2	114	–	PC-r	1	1	4	8	11	16	19	22
3	131	–	New-c; PC-r	1	2	5	10	15	24	30	35
4	158	–	PC-r	1	2	4	7	10	14	17	20
5	149	–	White reorder list; came after HRN-158; PC-r	1	2	5	10	15	22	26	30
6	167	3/64	PC-r	1	2	2	4	6	9	13	16

104. Bring 'Em Back Alive

Ed	HRN	Date	Details	A	C	GD 2.0	VG 4.0	FN 6.0	VF 8.0	VF/NM 9.0	NM- 9.2
1	105	2/53	Original; Kiefer-c/a	1	1	10	20	30	58	79	100
2	118	–	PC-r	1	1	2	4	6	9	13	16
3	133	–	PC-r	1	1	2	4	6	9	13	16
4	150	–	PC-r	1	1	2	4	6	9	13	16
5	158	–	PC-r	1	1	2	4	6	9	13	16
6	167	10/63	PC-r	1	1	2	4	6	8	11	14
7	167	9/65	PC-r	1	1	2	4	6	8	11	14
8	169	Win/69	New price 25¢; stiff-c; PC-r	1	1	2	4	6	8	11	14

105. From the Earth to the Moon

Ed	HRN	Date	Details	A	C	GD 2.0	VG 4.0	FN 6.0	VF 8.0	VF/NM 9.0	NM- 9.2
1	106	3/53	Original; Blum-a	1	1	10	20	30	58	79	100
2	118	–	PC-r	1	1	2	4	6	9	13	16
3	132	–	PC-r	1	1	2	4	6	9	13	16
4	141	–	PC-r	1	1	2	4	6	9	13	16
5	146	–	PC-r	1	1	2	4	6	9	13	16
6	156	–	PC-r	1	1	2	4	6	9	13	16
7	167	–	Has orig. date; PC-r	1	1	2	4	6	8	11	14
8	167	5/64	PC-r	1	1	2	4	6	8	11	14
9	167	5/65	PC-r	1	1	2	4	6	8	11	14
10A	166	10/67	PC-r	1	1	2	4	6	8	11	14
10B	166	10/67	w/Grit ad stapled in book	1	1	9	18	27	60	100	140
11	169	Sm/69	New price 25¢; stiff-c; PC-r	1	1	2	4	6	8	11	14
12	169	Spr/71	PC-r	1	1	2	4	6	8	11	14

106. Buffalo Bill

Ed	HRN	Date	Details	A	C	GD 2.0	VG 4.0	FN 6.0	VF 8.0	VF/NM 9.0	NM- 9.2
1	107	4/53	Orig.; delBourgo-a	1	1	10	20	30	56	76	95
2	118	–	PC-r	1	1	2	4	6	9	13	16
3	132	–	PC-r	1	1	2	4	6	9	13	16
4	142	–	PC-r	1	1	2	4	6	9	13	16
5	161	–	PC-r	1	1	2	4	6	8	11	14
6	167	3/64	PC-r	1	1	2	4	6	8	11	14
7	166	7/67	PC-r	1	1	2	4	6	8	11	14
8	169	Fall/69	PC-r; stiff-c	1	1	2	4	6	8	11	14

107. King of the Khyber Rifles

Ed	HRN	Date	Details	A	C	GD 2.0	VG 4.0	FN 6.0	VF 8.0	VF/NM 9.0	NM- 9.2
1	108	5/53	Original	1	1	10	20	30	56	76	95
2	118	–	PC-r	1	1	2	4	6	9	13	16
3	146	–	PC-r	1	1	2	4	6	9	13	16
4	158	–	PC-r	1	1	2	4	6	9	13	16
5	167	–	Has orig.date; PC-r	1	1	2	4	6	8	11	14
6	167	–	PC-r	1	1	2	4	6	8	11	14
7	167	10/66	PC-r	1	1	2	4	6	8	11	14

108. Knights of the Round Table

Ed	HRN	Date	Details	A	C	GD 2.0	VG 4.0	FN 6.0	VF 8.0	VF/NM 9.0	NM- 9.2
1A	108	6/53	Original; Blum-a	1	1	11	22	33	60	83	105
1B	109	6/53	Original; scarce	1	1	11	22	33	62	86	110
2	117	–	PC-r	1	1	2	4	6	9	13	16
3	165	–	PC-r	1	1	2	4	6	8	11	14
4	167	4/64	PC-r	1	1	2	4	6	8	11	14
5	166	4/67	PC-r	1	1	2	4	6	8	11	14
6	169	Sm/69	New price 25¢; stiff-c; PC-r	1	1	2	4	6	8	11	14

109. Pitcairn's Island

Ed	HRN	Date	Details	A	C	GD 2.0	VG 4.0	FN 6.0	VF 8.0	VF/NM 9.0	NM- 9.2
1	110	7/53	Original; Palais-a	1	1	11	22	33	60	83	105
2	165	–	PC-r	1	1	2	4	6	9	13	16
3	167	3/64	PC-r	1	1	2	4	6	9	13	16
4	166	6/67	PC-r	1	1	2	4	6	9	13	16

110. A Study in Scarlet

Classics Illustrated #114 © GIL

Classics Illustrated #122 © GIL

Classics Illustrated #128 © GIL

Ed	HRN	Date	Details	A	C	GD 2.0	VG 4.0	FN 6.0	VF 8.0	VF/NM 9.0	NM- 9.2
1	111	8/53	Original	1	1	15	30	45	83	124	165
2	165	–	PC-r	1	1	11	22	33	62	86	110

111. The Talisman

Ed	HRN	Date	Details	A	C	GD 2.0	VG 4.0	FN 6.0	VF 8.0	VF/NM 9.0	NM- 9.2
1	112	9/53	Original; last H.C. Kiefer-a	1	1	11	22	33	60	83	105
2	165	–	PC-r	1	1	2	4	6	9	13	16
3	167	5/64	PC-r	1	1	2	4	6	9	13	16
4	166	Fall/68	C-price 25¢; PC-r	1	1	2	4	6	9	13	16

112. Adventures of Kit Carson

Ed	HRN	Date	Details	A	C	GD 2.0	VG 4.0	FN 6.0	VF 8.0	VF/NM 9.0	NM- 9.2
1	113	10/53	Original; Palais-a	1	1	10	20	30	58	79	100
2	129	–	PC-r	1	1	2	4	6	9	13	16
3	141	–	PC-r	1	1	2	4	6	9	13	16
4	152	–	PC-r	1	1	2	4	6	9	13	16
5	161	–	PC-r	1	1	2	4	6	8	11	14
6	167	–	PC-r	1	1	2	4	6	8	11	14
7	167	2/65	PC-r	1	1	2	4	6	8	11	14
8	167	5/66	PC-r	1	1	2	4	6	8	11	14
9	166	Win/69	New-c&price 25¢; PC-r; stiff-c	1	2	3	6	9	14	20	25

113. The Forty-Five Guardsmen

Ed	HRN	Date	Details	A	C	GD 2.0	VG 4.0	FN 6.0	VF 8.0	VF/NM 9.0	NM- 9.2
1	114	11/53	Orig.; delBourgo-a	1	1	13	26	39	72	101	130
2	166	7/67	PC-r	1	1	4	8	12	22	34	45

114. The Red Rover

Ed	HRN	Date	Details	A	C	GD 2.0	VG 4.0	FN 6.0	VF 8.0	VF/NM 9.0	NM- 9.2
1	115	12/53	Original	1	1	13	26	39	72	101	130
2	166	7/67	PC-r	1	1	4	8	12	22	23	45

115. How I Found Livingstone

Ed	HRN	Date	Details	A	C	GD 2.0	VG 4.0	FN 6.0	VF 8.0	VF/NM 9.0	NM- 9.2
1	116	1/54	Original	1	1	14	28	42	76	108	140
2	167	1/67	PC-r	1	1	4	8	12	28	44	60

116. The Bottle Imp

Ed	HRN	Date	Details	A	C	GD 2.0	VG 4.0	FN 6.0	VF 8.0	VF/NM 9.0	NM- 9.2
1	117	2/54	Orig.; Cameron-a	1	1	14	28	42	76	108	140
2	167	1/67	PC-r	1	1	4	8	12	28	44	60

117. Captains Courageous

Ed	HRN	Date	Details	A	C	GD 2.0	VG 4.0	FN 6.0	VF 8.0	VF/NM 9.0	NM- 9.2
1	118	3/54	Orig.; Costanza-a	1	1	12	24	36	69	97	125
2	167	2/67	PC-r	1	1	3	6	9	14	20	26
3	169	Fall/69	New price 25¢; stiff-c; PC-r	1	1	3	6	9	14	20	26

118. Rob Roy

Ed	HRN	Date	Details	A	C	GD 2.0	VG 4.0	FN 6.0	VF 8.0	VF/NM 9.0	NM- 9.2
1	119	4/54	Original; Rudy & Walter Palais-a	1	1	14	28	42	76	108	140
2	167	2/67	PC-r	1	1	4	8	12	28	44	60

119. Soldiers of Fortune

Ed	HRN	Date	Details	A	C	GD 2.0	VG 4.0	FN 6.0	VF 8.0	VF/NM 9.0	NM- 9.2
1	120	5/54	Schaffenberger-a	1	1	12	24	36	67	94	120
2	166	3/67	PC-r	1	1	3	6	9	14	20	26
3	169	Spr/70	New price 25¢; stiff-c; PC-r	1	1	3	6	9	14	20	26

120. The Hurricane

Ed	HRN	Date	Details	A	C	GD 2.0	VG 4.0	FN 6.0	VF 8.0	VF/NM 9.0	NM- 9.2
1	121	6/54	Orig.; Cameron-a	1	1	12	24	36	67	94	120
2	166	3/67	PC-r	1	1	4	8	12	22	34	45

121. Wild Bill Hickok

Ed	HRN	Date	Details	A	C	GD 2.0	VG 4.0	FN 6.0	VF 8.0	VF/NM 9.0	NM- 9.2
1	122	7/54	Original	1	1	10	20	30	56	76	95
2	132	–	PC-r	1	1	2	4	6	9	13	16
3	141	–	PC-r	1	1	2	4	6	9	13	16
4	154	–	PC-r	1	1	2	4	6	9	13	16
5	167	–	PC-r	1	1	2	4	6	8	11	14
6	167	8/64	PC-r	1	1	2	4	6	8	11	14
7	166	4/67	PC-r	1	1	2	4	6	8	11	14
8	169	Win/69	PC-r; stiff-c	1	1	2	4	6	8	11	14

122. The Mutineers

GD VG FN VF VF/NM NM- 2.0 4.0 6.0 8.0 9.0 9.2

Ed	HRN	Date	Details	A	C	GD 2.0	VG 4.0	FN 6.0	VF 8.0	VF/NM 9.0	NM- 9.2
1	123	9/54	Original	1	1	11	22	33	60	83	105
2	136	–	PC-r	1	1	2	4	6	9	13	16
3	146	–	PC-r	1	1	2	4	6	9	13	16
4	158	–	PC-r	1	1	2	4	6	9	13	16
5	167	11/63	PC-r	1	1	2	4	6	8	11	14
6	167	3/65	PC-r	1	1	2	4	6	8	11	14
7	166	8/67	PC-r	1	1	2	4	6	8	11	14

123. Fang and Claw

Ed	HRN	Date	Details	A	C	GD 2.0	VG 4.0	FN 6.0	VF 8.0	VF/NM 9.0	NM- 9.2
1	124	11/54	Original	1	1	11	22	33	60	83	105
2	133	–	PC-r	1	1	2	4	6	9	13	16
3	143	–	PC-r	1	1	2	4	6	9	13	16
4	154	–	PC-r	1	1	2	4	6	9	13	16
5	167	–	Has orig.date; PC-r	1	1	2	4	6	8	11	14
6	167	9/65	PC-r	1	1	2	4	6	8	11	14

124. The War of the Worlds

Ed	HRN	Date	Details	A	C	GD 2.0	VG 4.0	FN 6.0	VF 8.0	VF/NM 9.0	NM- 9.2
1	125	1/55	Original; Cameron-c/a	1	1	14	28	42	76	108	140
2	131	–	PC-r	1	1	2	4	6	10	14	18
3	141	–	PC-r	1	1	2	4	6	10	14	18
4	148	–	PC-r	1	1	2	4	6	10	14	18
5	156	–	PC-r	1	1	2	4	6	10	14	18
6	165	–	PC-r	1	1	2	4	6	13	18	22
7	167	–	PC-r	1	1	2	4	6	9	13	16
8	167	11/64	PC-r	1	1	2	4	6	10	14	18
9	167	11/65	PC-r	1	1	2	4	6	9	13	16
10	166	R/1968	C-price 25¢; PC-r	1	1	2	4	6	9	13	16
11	169	Sm/70	PC-r; stiff-c	1	1	2	4	6	9	13	16

125. The Ox Bow Incident

Ed	HRN	Date	Details	A	C	GD 2.0	VG 4.0	FN 6.0	VF 8.0	VF/NM 9.0	NM- 9.2
1	–	3/55	Original; Picture Progress replaces reorder list	1	1	10	20	30	56	76	95
2	143	–	PC-r	1	1	2	4	6	9	13	16
3	152	–	PC-r	1	1	2	4	6	9	13	16
4	149	–	PC-r	1	1	2	4	6	9	13	16
5	167	–	PC-r	1	1	2	4	6	8	11	14
6	167	11/64	PC-r	1	1	2	4	6	8	11	14
7	166	4/67	PC-r	1	1	2	4	6	8	11	14
8	169	Win/69	New price 25¢; stiff-c; PC-r	1	1	2	4	6	8	11	14

126. The Downfall

Ed	HRN	Date	Details	A	C	GD 2.0	VG 4.0	FN 6.0	VF 8.0	VF/NM 9.0	NM- 9.2
1	5/55	–	Orig.; 'Picture Progress' replaces reorder list; Cameron-c/a	1	1	11	22	33	60	83	105
2	167	8/64	PC-r	1	1	2	4	6	13	18	22
3	166	R/1968	C-price 25¢; PC-r	1	1	2	4	6	13	18	22

127. The King of the Mountains

Ed	HRN	Date	Details	A	C	GD 2.0	VG 4.0	FN 6.0	VF 8.0	VF/NM 9.0	NM- 9.2
1	128	7/55	Original	1	1	11	22	33	60	83	105
2	167	6/64	PC-r	1	1	2	4	6	11	16	20
3	166	F/1968	C-price 25¢; PC-r	1	1	2	4	6	11	16	20

128. Macbeth (Used in **POP**, pg. 102)

Ed	HRN	Date	Details	A	C	GD 2.0	VG 4.0	FN 6.0	VF 8.0	VF/NM 9.0	NM- 9.2
1	128	9/55	Orig.; last Blum-a	1	1	11	22	33	60	83	105
2	143	–	PC-r	1	1	2	4	6	9	13	16
3	158	–	PC-r	1	1	2	4	6	9	13	16
4	167	–	PC-r	1	1	2	4	6	8	11	14
5	167	6/64	PC-r	1	1	2	4	6	8	11	14
6	166	4/67	PC-r	1	1	2	4	6	8	11	14
7	166	R/1968	C-Price 25¢; PC-r	1	1	2	4	6	8	11	14
8	169	Spr/70	Stiff-c; PC-r	1	1	2	4	6	8	11	14

129. Davy Crockett

Ed	HRN	Date	Details	A	C	GD 2.0	VG 4.0	FN 6.0	VF 8.0	VF/NM 9.0	NM- 9.2
1	129	11/55	Orig.; Cameron-a	1	1	14	28	42	81	118	155
2	167	9/66	PC-r	1	1	11	22	33	62	86	110

130. Caesar's Conquests

Ed HRN Date Details A C

Classics Illustrated #133 © GIL

Classics Illustrated #138 © GIL

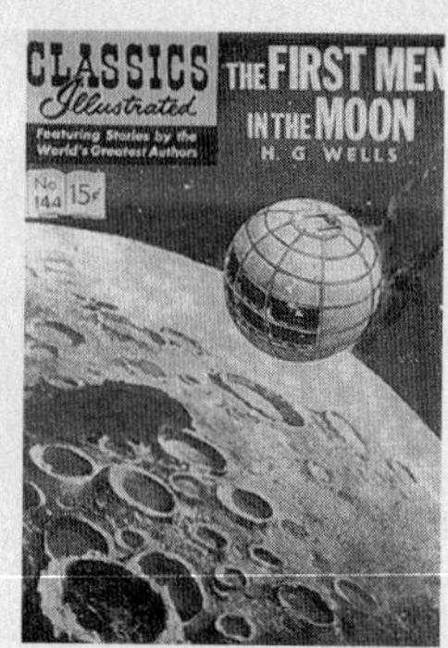

Classics Illustrated #144 © GIL

Ed	HRN	Date	Details	A	C	GD 2.0	VG 4.0	FN 6.0	VF 8.0	VF/NM 9.0	NM- 9.2
1	130	1/56	Original; Orlando-a	1	1	11	22	33	60	83	105
2	142	–	PC-r	1	1	2	4	6	9	13	16
3	152	–	PC-r	1	1	2	4	6	9	13	16
4	149	–	PC-r	1	1	2	4	6	9	13	16
5	167	–	PC-r	1	1	2	4	6	8	11	14
6	167	10/64	PC-r	1	1	2	4	6	8	11	14
7	167	4/66	PC-r	1	1	2	4	6	8	11	14

131. The Covered Wagon

Ed	HRN	Date	Details	A	C	GD 2.0	VG 4.0	FN 6.0	VF 8.0	VF/NM 9.0	NM- 9.2
1	131	3/56	Original	1	1	6	12	18	43	69	95
2	143	–	PC-r	1	1	2	4	6	9	13	16
3	152	–	PC-r	1	1	2	4	6	9	13	16
4	158	–	PC-r	1	1	2	4	6	9	13	16
5	167	–	PC-r	1	1	2	4	6	8	11	14
6	167	11/64	PC-r	1	1	2	4	6	8	11	14
7	167	4/66	PC-r	1	1	2	4	6	8	11	14
8	169	Win/69	New price 25¢; stiff-c; PC-r	1	1	2	4	6	8	11	14

132. The Dark Frigate

Ed	HRN	Date	Details	A	C	GD 2.0	VG 4.0	FN 6.0	VF 8.0	VF/NM 9.0	NM- 9.2
1	132	5/56	Original	1	1	11	22	33	60	83	105
2	150	–	PC-r	1	1	2	4	6	9	13	16
3	167	1/64	PC-r	1	1	2	4	6	9	13	16
4	166	5/67	PC-r	1	1	2	4	6	9	13	16

133. The Time Machine

Ed	HRN	Date	Details	A	C	GD 2.0	VG 4.0	FN 6.0	VF 8.0	VF/NM 9.0	NM- 9.2
1	132	7/56	Orig.; Cameron-a	1	1	7	14	21	50	83	115
2	142	–	PC-r	1	1	2	4	6	10	14	18
3	152	–	PC-r	1	1	2	4	6	10	14	18
4	158	–	PC-r	1	1	2	4	6	9	13	16
5	167	–	PC-r	1	1	2	4	6	9	13	16
6	167	6/64	PC-r	1	1	2	4	6	10	14	18
7	167	3/66	PC-r	1	1	2	4	6	9	13	16
8	166	12/67	PC-r	1	1	2	4	6	9	13	16
9	169	Win/71	New price 25¢; stiff-c; PC-r	1	1	2	4	6	9	13	16

134. Romeo and Juliet

Ed	HRN	Date	Details	A	C	GD 2.0	VG 4.0	FN 6.0	VF 8.0	VF/NM 9.0	NM- 9.2
1	134	9/56	Original; Evans-a	1	1	7	14	21	47	76	105
2	161	–	PC-r	1	1	2	4	6	9	13	16
3	167	9/63	PC-r	1	1	2	4	6	8	11	14
4	167	5/65	PC-r	1	1	2	4	6	8	11	14
5	166	6/67	PC-r	1	1	2	4	6	8	11	14
6	166	Win/69	New c&price 25¢; stiff-c; PC-r	1	2	3	6	9	17	25	32

135. Waterloo

Ed	HRN	Date	Details	A	C	GD 2.0	VG 4.0	FN 6.0	VF 8.0	VF/NM 9.0	NM- 9.2
1	135	11/56	Orig.; G. Ingels-a	1	1	7	14	21	47	76	105
2	153	–	PC-r	1	1	2	4	6	9	13	16
3	167	–	PC-r	1	1	2	4	6	8	11	14
4	167	9/64	PC-r	1	1	2	4	6	8	11	14
5	166	R/1968	C-price 25¢; PC-r	1	1	2	4	6	8	11	14

136. Lord Jim

Ed	HRN	Date	Details	A	C	GD 2.0	VG 4.0	FN 6.0	VF 8.0	VF/NM 9.0	NM- 9.2
1	136	1/57	Original; Evans-a	1	1	7	14	21	47	76	105
2	165	–	PC-r	1	1	2	4	6	8	11	14
3	167	3/64	PC-r	1	1	2	4	6	8	11	14
4	167	9/66	PC-r	1	1	2	4	6	8	11	14
5	169	Sm/69	New price 25 ¢; stiff-c; PC-r	1	1	2	4	6	8	11	14

137. The Little Savage

Ed	HRN	Date	Details	A	C	GD 2.0	VG 4.0	FN 6.0	VF 8.0	VF/NM 9.0	NM- 9.2
1	136	3/57	Original; Evans-a	1	1	7	14	21	47	76	105
2	148	–	PC-r	1	1	2	4	6	9	13	16
3	156	–	PC-r	1	1	2	4	6	9	13	16
4	167	–	PC-r	1	1	2	4	6	8	11	14
5	167	10/64	PC-r	1	1	2	4	6	8	11	14
6	166	8/67	PC-r	1	1	2	4	6	8	11	14
7	169	Spr/70	New price 25¢; stiff-c; PC-r	1	1	2	4	6	8	11	14

138. A Journey to the Center of the Earth

Ed	HRN	Date	Details	A	C	GD 2.0	VG 4.0	FN 6.0	VF 8.0	VF/NM 9.0	NM- 9.2
1	136	5/57	Original	1	1	8	16	24	56	93	130
2	146	–	PC-r	1	1	2	4	6	11	16	20
3	156	–	PC-r	1	1	2	4	6	11	16	20
4	158	–	PC-r	1	1	2	4	6	9	13	16
5	167	–	PC-r	1	1	2	4	6	8	11	14
6	167	6/64	PC-r	1	1	2	4	6	13	18	22
7	167	4/66	PC-r	1	1	2	4	6	13	18	22
8	166	R/68	C-price 25¢; PC-r	1	1	2	4	6	10	14	18

139. In the Reign of Terror

Ed	HRN	Date	Details	A	C	GD 2.0	VG 4.0	FN 6.0	VF 8.0	VF/NM 9.0	NM- 9.2
1	139	7/57	Original; Evans-a	1	1	6	12	18	43	69	95
2	154	–	PC-r	1	1	2	4	6	9	13	16
3	167	–	Has orig.date; PC-r	1	1	2	4	6	8	11	14
4	167	7/64	PC-r	1	1	2	4	6	8	11	14
5	166	R/1968	C-price 25¢; PC-r	1	1	2	4	6	8	11	14

140. On Jungle Trails

Ed	HRN	Date	Details	A	C	GD 2.0	VG 4.0	FN 6.0	VF 8.0	VF/NM 9.0	NM- 9.2
1	140	9/57	Original	1	1	6	12	18	43	69	95
2	150	–	PC-r	1	1	2	4	6	9	13	16
3	160	–	PC-r	1	1	2	4	6	9	13	16
4	167	9/63	PC-r	1	1	2	4	6	8	11	14
5	167	9/65	PC-r	1	1	2	4	6	8	11	14

141. Castle Dangerous

Ed	HRN	Date	Details	A	C	GD 2.0	VG 4.0	FN 6.0	VF 8.0	VF/NM 9.0	NM- 9.2
1	141	11/57	Original	1	1	7	14	21	49	80	110
2	152	–	PC-r	1	1	2	4	6	9	13	16
3	167	–	PC-r	1	1	2	4	6	9	13	16
4	166	7/67	PC-r	1	1	2	4	6	9	13	16

142. Abraham Lincoln

Ed	HRN	Date	Details	A	C	GD 2.0	VG 4.0	FN 6.0	VF 8.0	VF/NM 9.0	NM- 9.2
1	142	1/58	Original	1	1	7	14	21	47	76	105
2	154	–	PC-r	1	1	2	4	6	9	13	16
3	158	–	PC-r	1	1	2	4	6	9	13	16
4	167	10/63	PC-r	1	1	2	4	6	8	11	14
5	167	7/65	PC-r	1	1	2	4	6	8	11	14
6	166	11/67	PC-r	1	1	2	4	6	8	11	14
7	169	Fall/69	New price 25¢; stiff-c; PC-r	1	1	2	4	6	8	11	14

143. Kim

Ed	HRN	Date	Details	A	C	GD 2.0	VG 4.0	FN 6.0	VF 8.0	VF/NM 9.0	NM- 9.2
1	143	3/58	Original; Orlando-a	1	1	6	12	18	43	69	95
2	165	–	PC-r	1	1	2	4	6	8	11	14
3	167	11/63	PC-r	1	1	2	4	6	8	11	14
4	167	8/65	PC-r	1	1	2	4	6	8	11	14
5	169	Win/69	New price 25¢; stiff-c; PC-r	1	1	2	4	6	8	11	14

144. The First Men in the Moon

Ed	HRN	Date	Details	A	C	GD 2.0	VG 4.0	FN 6.0	VF 8.0	VF/NM 9.0	NM- 9.2
1	143	5/58	Original; Woodbridge/Williamson/Torres-a	1	1	7	14	21	50	83	115
2	152	–	(Rare)-PC-r	1	1	8	16	24	56	93	130
3	153	–	PC-r	1	1	2	4	6	9	13	16
4	161	–	PC-r	1	1	2	4	6	8	11	14
5	167	–	PC-r	1	1	2	4	6	8	11	14
6	167	12/65	PC-r	1	1	2	4	6	8	11	14
7	166	Fall/68	New-c&price 25¢; PC-r; stiff-c	1	2	3	6	9	16	23	30
8	169	Win/69	Stiff-c; PC-r	1	2	2	4	6	10	16	20

145. The Crisis

Ed	HRN	Date	Details	A	C	GD 2.0	VG 4.0	FN 6.0	VF 8.0	VF/NM 9.0	NM- 9.2
1	143	7/58	Original; Evans-a	1	1	7	14	21	47	76	105
2	156	–	PC-r	1	1	2	4	6	9	13	16
3	167	10/63	PC-r	1	1	2	4	6	8	11	14
4	167	3/65	PC-r	1	1	2	4	6	8	11	14
5	166	R/68	C-price 25¢; PC-r	1	1	2	4	6	8	11	14

146. With Fire and Sword

Ed	HRN	Date	Details	A	C	GD 2.0	VG 4.0	FN 6.0	VF 8.0	VF/NM 9.0	NM- 9.2
1	143	9/58	Original; Woodbridge-a	1	1	7	14	21	47	76	105
2	156	–	PC-r	1	1	2	4	6	10	14	18
3	167	11/63	PC-r	1	1	2	4	6	9	13	16

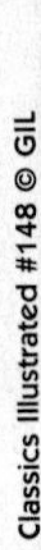
Classics Illustrated #148 © GIL

Classics Illustrated #152 © GIL

Classics Illustrated #162 © GIL

Ed	HRN	Date	Details	A	C	GD 2.0	VG 4.0	FN 6.0	VF 8.0	VF/NM 9.0	NM- 9.2
4	167	3/65	PC-r	1	1	2	4	6	9	13	16

147. Ben-Hur

Ed	HRN	Date	Details	A	C	GD 2.0	VG 4.0	FN 6.0	VF 8.0	VF/NM 9.0	NM- 9.2
1	147	11/58	Original; Orlando-a	1	1	7	14	21	45	73	100
2	152	–	Scarce; PC-r	1	1	7	14	21	47	76	105
3	153	–	PC-r	1	1	2	4	6	9	13	16
4	158	–	PC-r	1	1	2	4	6	9	13	16
5	167	–	Orig.date; but PC-r	1	1	2	4	6	8	11	14
6	167	2/65	PC-r	1	1	2	4	6	8	11	14
7	167	9/66	PC-r	1	1	2	4	6	8	11	14
8A	166	Fall/68	New-c&price 25¢; PC-r; soft-c	1	2	3	6	9	17	25	32
8B	166	Fall/68	New-c&price 25¢; PC-r; stiff-c; scarce	1	2	4	8	12	22	34	45

148. The Buccaneer

Ed	HRN	Date	Details	A	C	GD 2.0	VG 4.0	FN 6.0	VF 8.0	VF/NM 9.0	NM- 9.2
1	148	1/59	Orig.; Evans/Jenny-a; Saunders-c	1	1	6	12	18	43	69	95
2	568	–	Juniors list only PC-r	1	1	2	4	6	9	13	16
3	167	–	PC-r	1	1	2	4	6	8	11	14
4	167	9/65	PC-r	1	1	2	4	6	8	11	14
5	169	Sm/69	New price 25¢; PC-r; stiff-c	1	1	2	4	6	8	11	14

149. Off on a Comet

Ed	HRN	Date	Details	A	C	GD 2.0	VG 4.0	FN 6.0	VF 8.0	VF/NM 9.0	NM- 9.2
1	149	3/59	Orig.;G.McCann-a; blue reorder list	1	1	7	14	21	47	76	105
2	155	–	PC-r	1	1	2	4	6	9	13	16
3	149	–	PC-r; white reorder list; no coming-next ad	1	1	2	4	6	9	13	16
4	167	12/63	PC-r	1	1	2	4	6	8	11	14
5	167	2/65	PC-r	1	1	2	4	6	8	11	14
6	167	10/66	PC-r	1	1	2	4	6	8	11	14
7	166	Fall/68	New-c & price 25¢; PC-r	1	2	3	6	9	16	23	30

150. The Virginian

Ed	HRN	Date	Details	A	C	GD 2.0	VG 4.0	FN 6.0	VF 8.0	VF/NM 9.0	NM- 9.2
1	150	5/59	Original	1	1	7	14	21	49	80	110
2	164	–	PC-r	1	1	2	4	6	11	16	20
3	167	10/63	PC-r	1	1	3	6	9	15	21	26
4	167	12/65	PC-r	1	1	2	4	6	11	16	20

151. Won By the Sword

Ed	HRN	Date	Details	A	C	GD 2.0	VG 4.0	FN 6.0	VF 8.0	VF/NM 9.0	NM- 9.2
1	150	7/59	Original	1	1	7	14	21	47	76	105
2	164	–	PC-r	1	1	2	4	6	10	14	18
3	167	10/63	PC-r	1	1	2	4	6	10	14	18
4	166	7/67	PC-r	1	1	2	4	6	10	14	18

152. Wild Animals I Have Known

Ed	HRN	Date	Details	A	C	GD 2.0	VG 4.0	FN 6.0	VF 8.0	VF/NM 9.0	NM- 9.2
1	152	9/59	Orig.; L.B. Cole c/a	1	1	7	14	21	50	83	115
2A	149	–	PC-r; white reorder list; no coming-next ad; IBC: Jr. list #572	1	1	2	4	6	9	13	16
2B	149	–	PC-r; inside-bc: Jr. list to #555	1	1	2	4	6	9	13	16
2C	149	–	PC-r; inside-bc: has World Around Us ad; scarce	1	1	3	6	9	15	21	26
3	167	9/63	PC-r	1	1	2	4	6	8	11	14
4	167	8/65	PC-r	1	1	2	4	6	8	11	14
5	169	Fall/69	New price 25¢; stiff-c; PC-r	1	1	2	4	6	8	11	14

153. The Invisible Man

Ed	HRN	Date	Details	A	C	GD 2.0	VG 4.0	FN 6.0	VF 8.0	VF/NM 9.0	NM- 9.2
1	153	11/59	Original	1	1	8	16	24	54	90	125
2A	149	–	PC-r; white reorder list; no coming-next ad; inside-bc: Jr. list to #572	1	1	2	4	6	11	16	20
2B	149	–	PC-r; inside-bc: Jr. list to #555	1	1	2	4	6	13	18	22
3	167	–	PC-r	1	1	2	4	6	9	13	16
4	167	2/65	PC-r	1	1	2	4	6	9	13	16
5	167	9/66	PC-r	1	1	2	4	6	9	13	16
6	166	Win/69	New price 25¢; PC-r; stiff-c	1	1	2	4	6	9	13	16
7	169	Spr/71	Stiff-c; letters spelling 'Invisible Man' are 'solid' not 'invisible;' PC-r	1	1	2	4	6	9	13	16

154. The Conspiracy of Pontiac

Ed	HRN	Date	Details	A	C	GD 2.0	VG 4.0	FN 6.0	VF 8.0	VF/NM 9.0	NM- 9.2
1	154	1/60	Original	1	1	7	14	21	49	80	110
2	167	11/63	PC-r	1	1	2	4	6	13	18	22
3	167	7/64	PC-r	1	1	2	4	6	13	18	22
4	166	12/67	PC-r	1	1	2	4	6	13	18	22

155. The Lion of the North

Ed	HRN	Date	Details	A	C	GD 2.0	VG 4.0	FN 6.0	VF 8.0	VF/NM 9.0	NM- 9.2
1	154	3/60	Original	1	1	7	14	21	47	76	105
2	167	1/64	PC-r	1	1	2	4	6	11	16	20
3	166	R/1967	C-price 25¢; PC-r	1	1	2	4	6	10	14	18

156. The Conquest of Mexico

Ed	HRN	Date	Details	A	C	GD 2.0	VG 4.0	FN 6.0	VF 8.0	VF/NM 9.0	NM- 9.2
1	156	5/60	Orig.; Bruno Premiani-c/a	1	1	7	14	21	47	76	105
2	167	1/64	PC-r	1	1	2	4	6	10	14	18
3	166	8/67	PC-r	1	1	2	4	6	10	14	18
4	169	Spr/70	New price 25¢; stiff-c; PC-r	1	1	2	4	6	9	13	16

157. Lives of the Hunted

Ed	HRN	Date	Details	A	C	GD 2.0	VG 4.0	FN 6.0	VF 8.0	VF/NM 9.0	NM- 9.2
1	156	7/60	Orig.; L.B. Cole-c	1	1	7	14	21	49	80	110
2	167	2/64	PC-r	1	1	2	4	6	13	18	22
3	166	10/67	PC-r	1	1	2	4	6	13	18	22

158. The Conspirators

Ed	HRN	Date	Details	A	C	GD 2.0	VG 4.0	FN 6.0	VF 8.0	VF/NM 9.0	NM- 9.2
1	156	9/60	Original	1	1	7	14	21	49	80	110
2	167	7/64	PC-r	1	1	2	4	6	13	18	22
3	166	10/67	PC-r	1	1	2	4	6	13	18	22

159. The Octopus

Ed	HRN	Date	Details	A	C	GD 2.0	VG 4.0	FN 6.0	VF 8.0	VF/NM 9.0	NM- 9.2
1	159	11/60	Orig.; Gray Morrow-a; L.B. Cole-c	1	1	7	14	21	49	80	110
2	167	2/64	PC-r	1	1	2	4	6	13	18	22
3	166	R/1967	C-price 25¢; PC-r	1	1	2	4	6	13	18	22

160. The Food of the Gods

Ed	HRN	Date	Details	A	C	GD 2.0	VG 4.0	FN 6.0	VF 8.0	VF/NM 9.0	NM- 9.2
1A	159	1/61	Original	1	1	7	14	21	50	83	115
1B	160	1/61	Original; same, except for HRN	1	1	7	14	21	49	80	110
2	167	1/64	PC-r	1	1	2	4	6	13	18	22
3	166	6/67	PC-r	1	1	2	4	6	13	18	22

161. Cleopatra

Ed	HRN	Date	Details	A	C	GD 2.0	VG 4.0	FN 6.0	VF 8.0	VF/NM 9.0	NM- 9.2
1	161	3/61	Original	1	1	7	14	21	49	80	110
2	167	1/64	PC-r	1	1	3	6	9	14	19	24
3	166	8/67	PC-r	1	1	3	6	9	14	19	24

162. Robur the Conqueror

Ed	HRN	Date	Details	A	C	GD 2.0	VG 4.0	FN 6.0	VF 8.0	VF/NM 9.0	NM- 9.2
1	162	5/61	Original	1	1	7	14	21	49	80	110
2	167	7/64	PC-r	1	1	3	6	9	14	19	24
3	166	8/67	PC-r	1	1	3	6	9	14	19	24

163. Master of the World

Ed	HRN	Date	Details	A	C	GD 2.0	VG 4.0	FN 6.0	VF 8.0	VF/NM 9.0	NM- 9.2
1	163	7/61	Original; Gray Morrow-a	1	1	7	14	21	49	80	110
2	167	1/65	PC-r	1	1	2	4	6	13	18	22
3	166	R/1968	C-price 25¢; PC-r	1	1	2	4	6	13	18	22

164. The Cossack Chief

Ed	HRN	Date	Details	A	C

Classics Illustrated #168 © GIL

Classic Red Sonja #2 © Red Sonja LLC

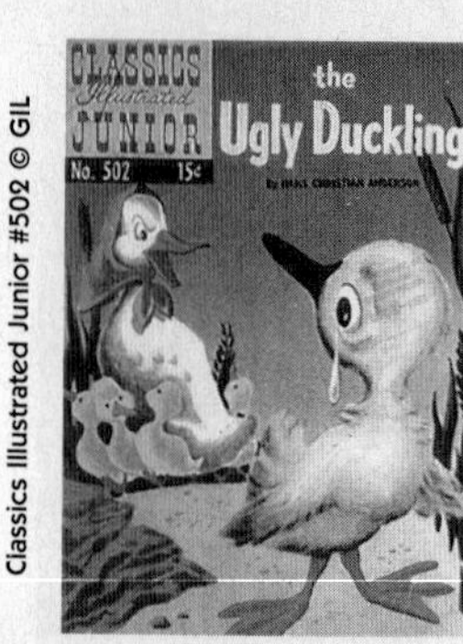

Classics Illustrated Junior #502 © GIL

Ed	HRN	Date	Details	A	C	GD 2.0	VG 4.0	FN 6.0	VF 8.0	VF/NM 9.0	NM- 9.2
1	164	(1961)	Orig.; nd(10/61?)	1	1	7	14	21	45	73	100
2	167	4/65	PC-r	1	1	2	4	6	13	18	22
3	166	Fall/68	C-price 25¢; PC-r	1	1	2	4	6	13	18	22

165. The Queen's Necklace

Ed	HRN	Date	Details	A	C	GD	VG	FN	VF	VF/NM	NM-
1	164	1/62	Original; Morrow-a	1	1	7	14	21	49	80	110
2	167	4/65	PC-r	1	1	2	4	6	13	18	22
3	166	Fall/68	C-price 25¢; PC-r	1	1	2	4	6	13	18	22

166. Tigers and Traitors

Ed	HRN	Date	Details	A	C	GD	VG	FN	VF	VF/NM	NM-
1	165	5/62	Original	1	1	9	18	27	63	107	150
2	167	2/64	PC-r	1	1	4	8	12	22	34	45
3	167	11/66	PC-r	1	1	4	8	12	22	34	45

167. Faust

Ed	HRN	Date	Details	A	C	GD	VG	FN	VF	VF/NM	NM-
1	165	8/62	Original	1	1	13	26	39	90	165	240
2	167	2/64	PC-r	1	1	6	12	18	39	62	85
3	166	6/67	PC-r	1	1	6	12	18	39	62	85

168. In Freedom's Cause

Ed	HRN	Date	Details	A	C	GD	VG	FN	VF	VF/NM	NM-
1	169	Win/69	Original; Evans/ Crandall-a; stiff-c; 25¢; no coming-next ad;	1	1	14	28	42	96	191	285

169. Negro Americans The Early Years

Ed	HRN	Date	Details	A	C	GD	VG	FN	VF	VF/NM	NM-
1	166	Spr/69	Orig. & last issue; 25¢; Stiff-c; no coming-next ad; other sources indicate publication date of 5/69	1	1	13	26	39	91	176	260
2	169	Spr/69	Stiff-c	1	1	8	16	24	52	86	120

NOTE: *Many other titles were prepared or planned but were only issued in British/European series.*

CLASSIC PUNISHER (Also see Punisher)
Marvel Comics: Dec, 1989 ($4.95, B&W, deluxe format, 68 pgs.)

1-Reprints Marvel Super Action #1 & Marvel Preview #2 plus new story 5.00

CLASSIC RED SONJA
Dynamite Entertainment: 2010 - No. 4, 2010 ($3.99)

1-4-Newly colored reprints of stories from Savage Sword of Conan magazine 4.00

CLASSICS ILLUSTRATED
First Publishing/Berkley Publishing: Feb, 1990 - No. 27, July, 1991 ($3.75/$3.95, 52 pgs.)

1-27: 1-Gahan Wilson-c/a. 4-Sienkiewicz painted-c/a. 6-Russell scripts/layouts. 7-Spiegle-a. 9-Ploog-c/a. 16-Staton-a. 18-Gahan Wilson-c/a; 20-Geary-a. 26-Aesop's Fables (6/91). 26,27-Direct sale only 5.00

CLASSICS ILLUSTRATED
Acclaim Books/Twin Circle PublishingCo.: Feb, 1997 - Present ($4.99, digest-size) (Each book contains study notes)

A Christmas Carol-(12/97), A Connecticut Yankee in King Arthur's Court-(5/97), All Quiet on the Western Front-(1/98), A Midsummer's Night Dream-(4/97) Around the World in 80 Days-(1/98), A Tale of Two Cities-(2/97)Joe Orlando-r, Captains Courageous-(11/97), Crime and Punishment-(3/97), Dr. Jekyll and Mr. Hyde-(10/97), Don Quixote-(12/97), Frankenstein-(10/97), Great Expectations-(4/97), Hamlet-(3/97), Huckleberry Finn-(3/97), Jane Eyre-(2/97), Kidnapped-(1/98), Les Miserables-(5/97), Lord Jim-(9/97),Macbeth-(5/97), Moby Dick-(4/97), Oliver Twist-(5/97), Robinson Crusoe-(9/97), Romeo & Juliet-(2/97), Silas Marner-(11/97), The Call of the Wild-(9/97), The Count of Monte Cristo-(1/98), The House of the Seven Gables-(9/97), The Iliad-(12/97), The Invisible Man-(10/97), The Last of the Mohicans-(12/97), The Master of Ballantrae-(11/97), The Odyssey-(3/97), The Prince and the Pauper-(4/97), The Red Badge Of Courage-(9/97), Tom Sawyer-(2/97) Wuthering Heights-(11/97) 5.00

NOTE: *Stories reprinted from the original Gilberton Classic Comics and Classics Illustrated.*

CLASSICS ILLUSTRATED GIANTS
Gilberton Publications: Oct, 1949 (One-Shots - "OS")

These Giant Editions, all with new front and back covers, were advertised from 10/49 to 2/52. They were 50¢ on the newsstand and 60¢ by mail. They are actually four Classics in one volume. All the stories are reprints of the Classics Illustrated Series.

NOTE: There were also British hardback Adventure & Indian Giants in 1952, with the same covers but different contents: Adventure - 2, 7, 10; Indian - 17, 22, 37, 58. They are also rare.

	GD	VG	FN	VF	VF/NM	NM-
"An Illustrated Library of Great Adventure Stories" - reprints of No. 6,7,8,10 (Rare); Kiefer-c	152	304	456	965	1658	2350
"An Illustrated Library of Exciting Mystery Stories" - reprints of No. 30,21,40, 13 (Rare); Blum-c	161	322	483	1030	1765	2500
"An Illustrated Library of Great Indian Stories" - reprints of No. 4,17,22,37 (Rare); Blum-c	152	304	456	965	1658	2350

INTRODUCTION TO CLASSICS ILLUSTRATED JUNIOR

Collectors of Juniors can be put into one of two categories: those who want any copy of each title, and those who want all the originals. Those seeking every original and reprint edition are a limited group, primarily because Juniors have no changes in art or covers to spark interest, and because reprints are so low in value it is difficult to get dealers to look for specific reprint editions.

In recent years it has become apparent that most serious Classics collectors seek Junior originals. Those seeking reprints seek them for low cost. This has made the previous note about the comparative market value of reprints inadequate. Three particular reprint editions are worth even more. For the 535-Twin Circle edition, see Giveaways. There are also reprint editions of 501 and 503 which have a full-page bc ad for the very rare Junior record. Those may sell as high as $10-$15 in mint. Original editions of 557 and 558 also have that ad.

There are no reprint editions of 577. The only edition, from 1969, is a 25 cent stiff-cover edition with no ad for the next issue. All other original editions have coming-next ad. But 577, like C.I. #168, was prepared in 1962 but not issued. Copies of 577 can be found in 1963 British/European series, which then continued with dozens of additional new Junior titles.

PRICES LISTED BELOW ARE FOR ORIGINAL EDITIONS, WHICH HAVE AN AD FOR THE NEXT ISSUE.

NOTE: *Non HRN 576 copies- many are written on or colored . Reprints with 576 HRN are worth about 1/3 original prices. All other HRN #'s are 1/2 original price*

CLASSICS ILLUSTRATED JUNIOR
Famous Authors Ltd. (Gilberton Publications): Oct, 1953 - Spring, 1971

	GD	VG	FN	VF	VF/NM	NM-
501-Snow White & the Seven Dwarfs; Alex Blum-a	12	24	36	69	97	125
502-The Ugly Duckling	9	18	27	47	61	75
503-Cinderella	8	16	24	40	50	60
504-512: 504-The Pied Piper. 505-The Sleeping Beauty. 506-The Three Little Pigs. 507-Jack & the Beanstalk. 508-Goldilocks & the Three Bears. 509-Beauty and the Beast. 510-Little Red Riding Hood. 511-Puss-N Boots. 512-Rumpelstiltskin	6	12	18	27	33	38
513-Pinocchio	7	14	21	37	46	55
514-The Steadfast Tin Soldier	8	16	24	44	57	70
515-Johnny Appleseed	6	12	18	27	33	38
516-Aladdin and His Lamp	6	12	18	29	36	42
517-519: 517-The Emperor's New Clothes. 518-The Golden Goose. 519-Paul Bunyan	6	12	18	27	33	38
520-Thumbelina	6	12	18	29	36	42
521-King of the Golden River	6	12	18	27	33	38
522,523,530: 522-The Nightingale. 523-The Gallant Tailor. 530-The Golden Bird	5	10	15	24	30	35
524-The Wild Swans	6	12	18	29	36	42
525,526: 525-The Little Mermaid. 526-The Frog Prince	6	12	18	29	36	42
527-The Golden-Haired Giant	6	12	18	27	33	38
528-The Penny Prince	6	12	18	27	33	38
529-The Magic Servants	6	12	18	27	33	38
531-Rapunzel	6	12	18	27	33	38
532-534: 532-The Dancing Princesses. 533-The Magic Fountain. 534-The Golden Touch	5	10	15	23	28	32
535-The Wizard of Oz	8	16	24	44	57	70
536-The Chimney Sweep	6	12	18	27	33	38
537-The Three Fairies	6	12	18	28	34	40
538-Silly Hans	5	10	15	23	28	32
539-The Enchanted Fish	6	12	18	31	38	45
540-The Tinder-Box	6	12	18	31	38	45
541-Snow White & Rose Red	5	10	15	24	30	35
542-The Donkey's Tale	5	10	15	24	30	35
543-The House in the Woods	6	12	18	27	33	38
544-The Golden Fleece	6	12	18	31	38	45
545-The Glass Mountain	5	10	15	24	30	35
546-The Elves & the Shoemaker	5	10	15	24	30	35
547-The Wishing Table	6	12	18	27	33	38
548-551: 548-The Magic Pitcher. 549-Simple Kate. 550-The Singing Donkey. 551-The Queen Bee	5	10	15	23	28	32
552-The Three Little Dwarfs	6	12	18	27	33	38
553,556: 553-King Thrushbeard. 556-The Elf Mound	5	10	15	23	28	32
554-The Enchanted Deer	6	12	18	29	36	42
555-The Three Golden Apples	5	10	15	24	30	35
557-Silly Willy	6	12	18	28	34	40
558-The Magic Dish; L.B. Cole-c; soft and stiff-c exist on original	7	14	21	35	43	50

559-The Japanese Lantern; 1 pg. Ingels-a; L.B. Cole-c

Classics Illustrated Special Issue #165A © GIL

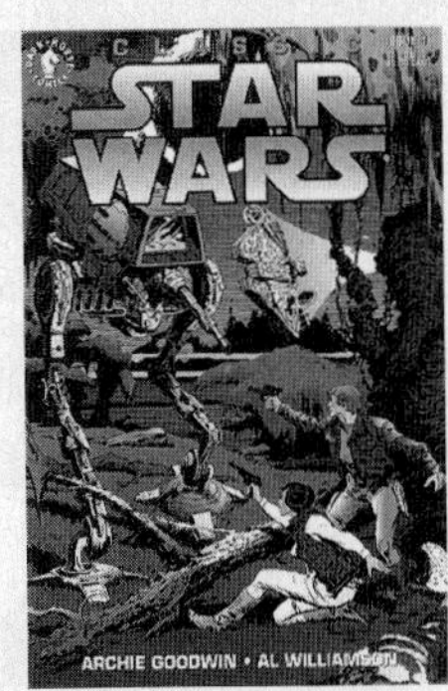

Classic Star Wars #1 © LucasFilm

Climax! #1 © Gilmore

GD 2.0 | VG 4.0 | FN 6.0 | VF 8.0 | VF/NM 9.0 | NM- 9.2

7 14 21 35 43 50
560-The Doll Princess; L.B. Cole-c 7 14 21 35 43 50
561-Hans Humdrum; L.B. Cole-c 6 12 18 29 36 42
562-The Enchanted Pony; L.B. Cole-c 7 14 21 35 43 50
563,565-568,570: 563-The Wishing Well; L.B. Cole-c. 565-The Silly Princess; L.B. Cole-c. 566-Clumsy Hans; L.B. Cole-c. 567-The Bearskin Soldier; L.B. Cole-c. 570-The Pearl Princess 6 12 18 27 33 38
564-The Salt Mountain; L.B.Cole-c. 568-The Happy Hedgehog; L.B. Cole-c. 6 12 18 28 34 40
569,573: 569-The Three Giants.573-The Crystal Ball 5 10 15 23 28 32
571,572: 571-How Fire Came to the Indians. 572-The Drummer Boy 6 12 18 29 36 42
574-Brightboots 5 10 15 24 30 35
575-The Fearless Prince 6 12 18 28 34 40
576-The Princess Who Saw Everything 7 14 21 35 43 50
577-The Runaway Dumpling 8 16 24 44 57 70
NOTE: *Prices are for original editions. Last reprint - Spring, 1971.* ***Costanza*** *&* ***Schaffenberger*** *art in many issues.*

CLASSICS ILLUSTRATED SPECIAL ISSUE
Gilberton Co.: (Came out semi-annually) Dec, 1955 - Jul, 1962 (35¢, 100 pgs.)
129-The Story of Jesus (titled ...Special Edition) "Jesus on Mountain" cover 15 30 45 85 130 175
"Three Camels" cover (12/58) 15 30 45 90 140 190
"Mountain" cover (no date)-Has checklist on inside b/c to HRN #161 & different testimonial on back-c 12 24 36 69 97 125
"Mountain" cover (1968 re-issue; has white 50¢ circle) 9 18 27 52 69 85
132A-The Story of America (6/56); Cameron-a 11 22 33 64 90 115
135A-The Ten Commandments(12/56) 11 22 33 62 86 110
138A-Adventures in Science(6/57); HRN to 137 10 20 30 58 79 100
138A-(6/57)-2nd version w/HRN to 149 7 14 21 35 43 50
138A-(12/61)-3rd version w/HRN to 149 7 14 21 35 43 50
141A-The Rough Rider (Teddy Roosevelt)(12/57); Evans-a 11 22 33 60 83 105
144A-Blazing the Trails West(6/58)- 73 pgs. of Crandall/Evans plus Severin-a 11 22 33 62 86 110
147A-Crossing the Rockies(12/58)-Crandall/Evans-a 11 22 33 60 83 105
150A-Royal Canadian Police(6/59)-Ingels, Sid Check-a 11 22 33 60 83 105
153A-Men, Guns & Cattle(12/59)-Evans-a (26 pgs.); Kinstler-a 11 22 33 60 83 105
156A-The Atomic Age(6/60)-Crandall/Evans, Torres-a 11 22 33 60 83 105
159A-Rockets, Jets and Missiles(12/60)-Evans, Morrow-a 11 22 33 60 83 105
162A-War Between the States(6/61)-Kirby & Crandall/Evans-a; Ingels-a 16 32 48 94 147 200
165A-To the Stars(12/61)-Torres, Crandall/Evans, Kirby-a 12 24 36 69 97 125
166A-World War II('62)-Torres, Crandall/Evans, Kirby-a 14 28 42 80 115 150
167A-Prehistoric World(7/62)-Torres & Crandall/Evans-a; two versions exist (HRN to 165 & HRN to 167) 14 28 42 76 108 140
nn Special Issue-The United Nations (1964; 50¢; scarce); this is actually part of the European Special Series, which cont'd on after the U.S. series stopped issuing new titles in 1962. This English edition was prepared specifically for sale at the U.N. It was printed in Norway 50 100 150 315 533 750
NOTE: *There was another U.S. Special Issue prepared in 1962 with artwork by* ***Torres*** *entitled World War I. Unfortunately, it was never issued in any English-language edition. It was issued in 1964 in West Germany, The Netherlands, and some Scandanavian countries, with another edition in 1974 with a new cover.*

CLASSICS LIBRARY (See King Classics)

CLASSIC STAR WARS (Also see Star Wars)
Dark Horse Comics: Aug, 1992 - No. 20, June, 1994 ($2.50)
1-Begin Star Wars strip-r by Williamson; Williamson redrew portions of the panels to fit comic book format 6.00
2-10: 8-Polybagged w/Star Wars Galaxy trading card. 8-M. Schultz-c 4.00
11-19: 13-Yeates-c. 17-M. Schultz-c. 19-Evans-c 3.00
20-($3.50, 52 pgs.)-Polybagged w/trading card 4.00
Escape To Hoth TPB ($16.95) r/#15-20 17.00
The Rebel Storm TPB - r/#8-14 17.00
Trade paperback ($29.95, slip-cased)-Reprints all movie adaptations 30.00
NOTE: *Williamson c-1-5,7,9,10,14,15,20.*

CLASSIC STAR WARS: (Title series). **Dark Horse Comics**
--A NEW HOPE, 6/94 - No. 2, 7/94 ($3.95)
1,2: 1-r/Star Wars #1-3, 7-9 publ; 2-r/Star Wars #4-6, 10-12 publ. by Marvel Comics 4.00
--DEVILWORLDS, 8/96 - No.2, 9/96 ($2.50s)1,2: r/Alan Moore-s 3.00
--HAN SOLO AT STARS' END, 3/97 - No. 3, 5/97 ($2.95)
1-3: r/strips by Alfredo Alcala 3.00
--RETURN OF THE JEDI, 10/94 - No.2, 11/94 ($3.50)
1,2: 1-r/1983-84 Marvel series; polybagged with w/trading card 3.50
--THE EARLY ADVENTURES, 8/94 - No. 9, 4/95 ($2.50)1-9 3.00
--THE EMPIRE STRIKES BACK, 8/94 - No. 2, 9/94 ($3.95)
1-r/Star Wars #39-44 published by Marvel Comics 4.00

CLASSIC X-MEN (Becomes X-Men Classic #46 on)
Marvel Comics Group: Sept, 1986 - No. 45, Mar, 1990
1-Begins-r of New X-Men 5.00
2-10: 10-Sabretooth app. 4.00
11-45: 11-1st origin of Magneto in back-up story. 17-Wolverine-c. 27-r/X-Men #121. 26-r/X-Men #120; Wolverine-c/app. 35-r/X-Men #129. 39-New Jim Lee back-up story (2nd-a on X-Men). 43-Byrne-c/a(r); $1.75, double-size 3.00
NOTE: ***Art Adams*** *c(p)-1-10, 12-16, 18-23.* ***Austin*** *c-10,15-21,24-28i.* ***Bolton*** *back up stories in 1-28,30-35.* ***Williamson*** *c-12-14i.*

CLAW (See Capt. Battle, Jr., Daredevil Comics & Silver Streak Comics)

CLAWS
Marvel Comics: Oct, 2006 - No. 3, Dec, 2006 ($3.99, limited series)
1-3-Wolverine and Black Cat team-up; Linsner-a/c 4.00
Wolverine & Black Cat: Claws HC (2007, $17.99, dustjacket) r/#1-3 & bonus Linsner art 18.00

CLAW THE UNCONQUERED (See Cancelled Comic Cavalcade)
National Periodical Publications/DC Comics: 5-6/75 - No. 9, 9-10/76; No. 10, 4-5/78 - No. 12, 8-9/78
1-1st app. Claw 2 4 6 8 10 12
2-12: 3-Nudity panel. 9-Origin 1 2 3 4 5 7
NOTE: ***Giffen*** *a-8-12p.* ***Kubert*** *c-10-12.* ***Layton*** *a-9i, 12i.*

CLAW THE UNCONQUERED (See Red Sonja/Claw: The Devil's Hands)
DC Comics: Aug, 2006 - No. 6, Jan, 2007 ($2.99)
1-6: 1,2-Chuck Dixon-s/Andy Smith; two covers by Smith & Van Sciver 3.00
TPB (2007, $17.99) r/#1-6; cover gallery 18.00

CLAY CODY, GUNSLINGER
Pines Comics: Fall, 1957
1-Painted-c 6 12 18 31 38 45

CLEAN FUN, STARRING "SHOOGAFOOTS JONES"
Specialty Book Co.: 1944 (10¢, B&W, oversized covers, 24 pgs.)
nn-Humorous situations involving Negroes in the Deep South
White cover issue... 18 36 54 105 165 225
Dark grey cover issue... 19 38 57 109 172 235

CLEMENTINA THE FLYING PIG (See Dell Jr. Treasury)

CLEOPATRA (See Ideal, a Classical Comic No. 1)

CLERKS: THE COMIC BOOK (Also see Tales From the Clerks and Oni Double Feature #1)
Oni Press: Feb, 1998 ($2.95, B&W, one-shot)
1-Kevin Smith-s 2 4 6 8 10 12
1-Second printing 4.00
...Holiday Special (12/98, $2.95) Smith-s 5.00
...The Lost Scene (12/99, $2.95) Smith-s/Hester-a 5.00

CLIFFHANGER (See Battle Chasers, Crimson, and Danger Girl)
WildStorm Prod./Wizard Press: 1997 (Wizard supplement)
0-Sketchbook preview of Cliffhanger titles 6.00

CLIMAX! (Mystery)
Gillmor Magazines: July, 1955 - No. 2, Sept, 1955
1 16 32 48 94 147 200
2 14 28 42 76 108 140

CLINT (Also see Adolescent Radioactive Black Belt Hamsters)
Eclipse Comics: Sept, 1986 - No. 2, Jan, 1987 ($1.50, B&W)
1,2 3.00

CLINT & MAC (TV, Disney)
Dell Publishing Co.: No. 889, Mar, 1958
Four Color 889-Alex Toth-a, photo-c 11 22 33 75 138 200

CLIVE BARKER'S BOOK OF THE DAMNED: A HELLRAISER COMPANION
Marvel Comics (Epic): Oct, 1991 - No. 3, Nov, 1992 ($4.95, semi-annual)
Volume 1-3-(52 pgs.): 1-Simon Bisley-c. 2-(4/92). 3-(11/92)-McKean-a (1 pg.) 5.00

Clive Barker's Hellraiser #1 © BOOM! Studios & Clive Barker

Cloak and Dagger #1 © MAR

Codename: Stryke Force #8 © TCOW

GD VG FN VF VF/NM NM-
2.0 4.0 6.0 8.0 9.0 9.2

CLIVE BARKER'S HELLRAISER (Also see Epic, Hellraiser Nightbreed –Jihad, Revelations, Son of Celluloid, Tapping the Vein & Weaveworld)
Marvel Comics (Epic Comics): 1989 - No. 20, 1993 ($4.50-6.95, mature, quarterly, 68 pgs.)

Book 1-4,10-16,18,19: Based on Hellraiser & Hellbound movies; Bolton-c/a; Spiegle & Wrightson-a (graphic album). 10-Foil-c. 12-Sam Kieth-a 6.00
Book 5-9 ($5.95): 7-Bolton-a. 8-Morrow-a 6.00
Book 17-Alex Ross-a, 34 pgs. 2 4 6 8 10 12
Book 20-By Gaiman/McKean 1 2 3 5 6 8
...Collected Best (Checker Books, '02, $21.95)-r/by various incl. Ross, Gaiman, Mignola 22.00
...Collected Best II ('03, $19.95)-r/by various incl. Bolton, L. Wachowski, Dorman 20.00
...Collected Best III ('04, $26.95)-r/by various incl. Bolton, L. Wachowski, Wrightson 27.00
...Dark Holiday Special ('92, $4.95)-Conrad-a 6.00
...Spring Slaughter 1 ('94, $6.95, 52 pgs.)-Painted-c 7.00
...Summer Special 1 ('92, $5.95, 68 pgs.) 6.00

CLIVE BARKER'S HELLRAISER
BOOM! Studios: Mar, 2011 - Present ($3.99)

1-Barker & Monfette-s/Manco-a; preview of Hellraiser Masterpieces; 3 covers 4.00

CLIVE BARKER'S NIGHTBREED (Also see Epic)
Marvel Comics (Epic Comics): Apr, 1990 - No. 25, Mar, 1993 ($1.95/$2.25/$2.50, mature readers)

1-25: 1-4-Adapt horror movie. 5-New stories; Guice-a(p) 3.00

CLIVE BARKER'S THE HARROWERS
Marvel Comics (Epic Comics): Dec, 1993 - No. 6, May, 1994 ($2.50)

1-($2.95)-Glow-in-the-dark-c; Colan-c/a in all 3.50
2-6 3.00
NOTE: ***Colan** a(p)-1-6; c-1-3, 4p, 5p. **Williamson** a(i)-2, 4, 5(part).*

CLOAK AND DAGGER
Ziff-Davis Publishing Co.: Fall, 1952

1-Saunders painted-c 29 58 87 170 278 385

CLOAK AND DAGGER (Also see Marvel Fanfare)
Marvel Comics Group: Oct, 1983 - No. 4, Jan, 1984 (Mini-series)
(See Spectacular Spider-Man #64)

1-4-Austin-c/a(i) in all. 4-Origin 3.00

CLOAK AND DAGGER (2nd Series)(Also see Marvel Graphic Novel #34 & Strange Tales)
Marvel Comics Group: July, 1985 - No. 11, Jan, 1987

1-11: 9-Art Adams-p 3.00
...And Power Pack (1990, $7.95, 68 pgs.) 8.00
NOTE: ***Mignola** c-7, 8.*

CLOAK AND DAGGER (3rd Series listed as Mutant Misadventures Of...)

CLOAK AND DAGGER
Marvel Comics: May, 2010 ($3.99, one-shot)

1-Stuart Moore-s/Mark Brooks-a; X-Men app. 4.00

CLOBBERIN' TIME
Marvel Comics: Sept, 1995 ($1.95) (Based on card game)

nn-Overpower game guide; Ben Grimm story 3.00

CLOCK MAKER, THE
Image Comics: Jan, 2003 - No. 4, May, 2003 ($2.50, comic unfolds to 10"x13" pages)

1-4-Krueger-s 3.00
... Act Two (4/04, $4.95, standard format) Krueger-s/Matt Smith-c 5.00

CLONEZONE SPECIAL
Dark Horse Comics/First Comics: 1989 ($2.00, B&W)

1-Back-up series from Badger & Nexus 3.00

CLOSE ENCOUNTERS (See Marvel Comics Super Special & Marvel Special Edition)

CLOSE SHAVES OF PAULINE PERIL, THE (TV cartoon)
Gold Key: June, 1970 - No. 4, March, 1971

1 4 8 12 22 34 45
2-4 3 6 9 16 23 30

CLOWN COMICS (No. 1 titled Clown Comic Book)
Clown Comics/Home Comics/Harvey Publ.: 1945 - No. 3, Win, 1946

nn (#1) 13 26 39 74 105 135
2,3 9 18 27 47 61 75

CLOUDBURST
Image Comics: June, 2004 ($7.95, squarebound)

1-Gray & Palmiotti-s/Shy & Gouveia-a 8.00

CLOUDFALL
Image Comics: Nov, 2003 ($4.95, B&W, squarebound)

1-Kirkman-s/Su-a/c 5.00

CLOWNS, THE (I Pagliacci)
Dark Horse Comics: 1998 ($2.95, B&W, one-shot)

1-Adaption of the opera; P. Craig Russell-script 3.00

CLUBHOUSE RASCALS (#1 titled ...Presents?) (Also see Three Rascals)
Sussex Publ. Co. (Magazine Enterprises): June, 1956 - No. 2, Oct, 1956

1-The Brain app. in both; DeCarlo-a 8 16 24 44 57 70
2 7 14 21 35 43 50

CLUB "16"
Famous Funnies: June, 1948 - No. 4, Dec, 1948

1-Teen-age humor 14 28 42 76 108 140
2-4 8 16 24 44 57 70

CLUE COMICS (Real Clue Crime V2#4 on)
Hillman Periodicals: Jan, 1943 - No. 15(V2#3), May, 1947

1-Origin The Boy King, Nightmare, Micro-Face, Twilight, & Zippo 181 362 543 1158 1979 2800
2 (scarce) 84 168 252 538 919 1300
3-5 (9/43) 45 90 135 284 480 675
6,8,9: 8-Palais-c/a(2) 34 68 102 206 336 465
7-Classic concentration camp torture-c (3/44) 71 142 213 454 777 1100
10-Origin/1st app. The Gun Master & begin series; content changes to crime (10/46) 36 72 108 216 351 486
11(12/46) 25 50 75 150 245 340
12-Origin Rackman; McWilliams-a, Guardineer-a(2) 31 62 93 182 296 410
V2#1-Nightmare new origin; Iron Lady app.; Simon & Kirby-a (3/47) 54 108 162 343 574 825
V2#2-S&K-a(2)-Bondage/torture-c; man attacks & kills people with electric iron. Infantino-a 70 140 210 445 765 1085
V2#3-S&K-a(3) 55 110 165 352 601 850

CLUELESS SPRING SPECIAL (TV)
Marvel Comics: May, 1997 ($3.99, magazine sized, one-shot)

1-Photo-c from TV show 4.00

CLUTCHING HAND, THE
American Comics Group: July-Aug, 1954

1 40 80 120 243 402 560

CLYDE BEATTY COMICS (Also see Crackajack Funnies)
Commodore Productions & Artists, Inc.: October, 1953 (84 pgs.)

1-Photo front/back-c; movie scenes and comics 22 44 66 132 216 300

CLYDE CRASHCUP (TV)
Dell Publishing Co.: Aug-Oct, 1963 - No. 5, Sept-Nov, 1964

1-All written by John Stanley 8 16 24 54 90 125
2-5 6 12 18 41 66 90

COBALT BLUE (Also see Power Comics)
Innovation Publishing: Sept, 1989 - No. 2, Oct, 1989 ($1.95, 28 pgs.)

1,2-Gustovich-c/a/scripts 3.00
The Graphic Novel ($6.95, color, 52 pgs.)-r/1,2 7.00

COBB
IDW Publishing: May, 2006 - No. 3, July, 2007 ($3.99, B&W)

1-3-Beau Smith-s/Eduardo Barreto-a/c; regular and retailer incentive covers 4.00

CODE NAME: ASSASSIN (See 1st Issue Special)

CODENAME: DANGER
Lodestone Publishing: Aug, 1985 - No. 4, May, 1986 ($1.50)

1-4 3.00

CODENAME: FIREARM (Also see Firearm)
Malibu Comics (Ultraverse): June, 1995 - No. 5, Sept, 1995 ($2.95, bimonthly limited series)

0-5: 0-2-Alec Swan back-up story by James Robinson 3.00
NOTE: ***Perez** c-0.*

CODENAME: GENETIX
Marvel Comics UK: Jan, 1993 - No. 4, May, 1993 ($1.75, limited series)

1-4: Wolverine in all 3.00

CODENAME: KNOCKOUT
DC Comics (Vertigo): No. 0, Jun, 2001 - No. 23, June, 2003 ($2.50/$2.75)

0-15: Rodi-s in all. 0-5-Small Jr. -a. 1-Two covers by Chiodo & Cho. 7,8,10,11,12-Paquette-a.

Code of Honor #4 © MAR

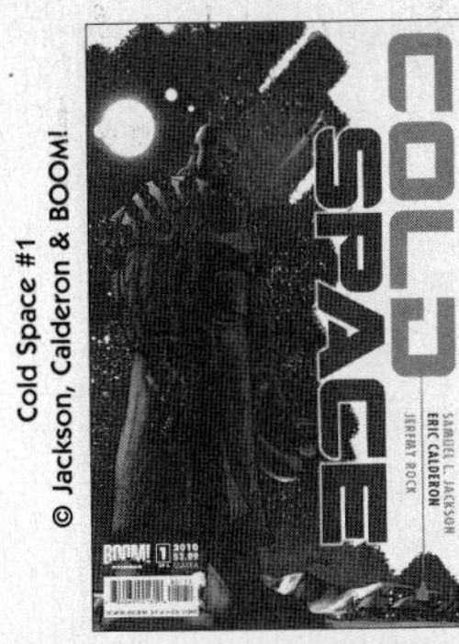

Cold Space #1 © Jackson, Calderon & BOOM!

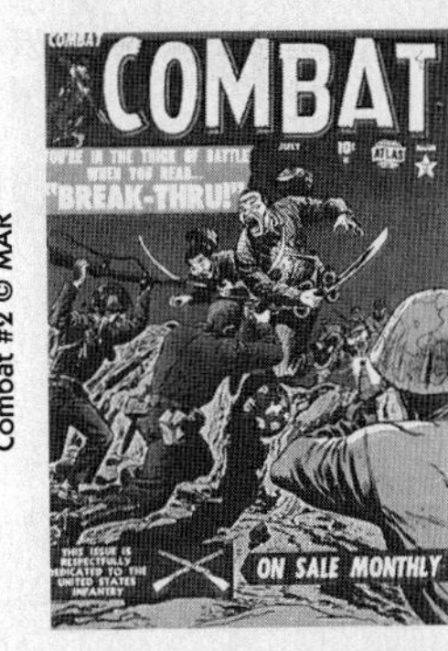

Combat #2 © MAR

GD 2.0 | VG 4.0 | FN 6.0 | VF 8.0 | VF/NM 9.0 | NM- 9.2

6,9,13,14-Conner-a 3.00
16-23: 16-Begin $2.75-c. 23-Last issue; JG Jones-c 3.00
...: The Devil You Say TPB (2010, $19.99) r/#0-6; intro. by Rodi 20.00

CODENAME SPITFIRE (Formerly Spitfire And The Troubleshooters)
Marvel Comics Group: No. 10, July, 1987 - No. 13, Oct, 1987

10-13: 10-Rogers-c/a (low printing) 3.50

CODENAME: STRYKE FORCE (Also See Cyberforce V1#4 & Cyberforce/Stryke Force: Opposing Forces
Image Comics (Top Cow Productions): Jan, 1994 - No. 14, Sept, 1995 ($1.95-$2.25)

0,1-14: 1-12-Silvestri stories, Peterson-a. 4-Stormwatch app. 14-Story continues in Cyberforce/Stryke Force: Opposing Forces; Turner-a 3.00
1-Gold, 1-Blue 4.00

CODE NAME: TOMAHAWK
Fantasy General Comics: Sept, 1986 ($1.75, high quality paper)

1-Sci/fi 3.00

CODE OF HONOR
Marvel Comics: Feb, 1997 - No. 4, May, 1997 ($5.95, limited series)

1-4-Fully painted by various; Dixon-s 6.00

CODY OF THE PONY EXPRESS (See Colossal Features Magazine)
Fox Features Syndicate: Sept, 1950 (See Women Outlaws)(One shot)

1-Painted-c 14 28 42 82 121 160

CODY OF THE PONY EXPRESS (Buffalo Bill...) (Outlaws of the West #11 on; Formerly Bullseye)
Charlton Comics: No. 8, Oct, 1955; No. 9, Jan, 1956; No. 10, June, 1956

8-Bullseye on splash pg; not S&K-a 8 16 24 44 57 70
9,10: Buffalo Bill app. in all 6 12 18 29 36 42

CODY STARBUCK (1st app. in Star Reach #1)
Star Reach Productions: July, 1978

nn-Howard Chaykin-c/a 3 6 9 14 20 25
2nd printing 2 4 6 8 10 12
NOTE: *Both printings say First Printing. True first printing is on lower-grade paper, somewhat off-register, and snow in snow sequence has green tint.*

CO-ED ROMANCES
P. L. Publishing Co.: November, 1951

1 9 18 27 50 65 80

COFFEE WORLD
World Comics: Oct, 1995 ($1.50, B&W, anthology)

1-Shannon Wheeler's Too Much Coffee Man story 3.00

COFFIN, THE
Oni Press: Sept, 2000 - No. 4, May, 2001 ($2.95, B&W, limited series)

1-4-Hester-s/Huddleston-a 3.00
TPB (8/01, $11.95, TPB) r/#1-4 12.00

COLD SPACE
Boom! Studios: Apr, 2010 - No. 4 ($3.99, limited series)

1-Samuel L. Jackson & Eric Calderon-s/Jeremy Rock-a 4.00

COLLECTORS DRACULA, THE
Millennium Publications: 1994 - No. 2, 1994 ($3.95, color/B&W, 52 pgs., limited series)

1,2-Bolton-a (7 pgs.) 4.00

COLLECTORS ITEM CLASSICS (See Marvel Collectors Item Classics)

COLORS IN BLACK
Dark Horse Comics: Mar, 1995 - No. 4, June, 1995 ($2.95, limited series)

1-4 3.00

COLOSSAL FEATURES MAGAZINE (Formerly I Loved) (See Cody of the Pony Express)
Fox Features Syndicate: No. 33, 5/50 - No. 34, 7/50; No. 3, 9/50 (Based on Columbia serial)

33,34: Cody of the Pony Express begins. 33-Painted-c. 34-Photo-c 14 28 42 81 118 155
3-Authentic criminal cases 14 28 42 81 118 155

COLOSSAL SHOW, THE (TV cartoon)
Gold Key: Oct, 1969

1 5 10 15 32 51 70

COLOSSUS (See X-Men)
Marvel Comics: Oct, 1997 ($2.99, 48 pgs., one-shot)

1-Raab-s/Hitch & Neary-a, wraparound-c 4.00

COLOSSUS COMICS (See Green Giant & Motion Picture Funnies Weekly)
Sun Publications (Funnies, Inc.?): March, 1940

1-(Scarce)-Tulpa of Tsang(hero); Colossus app. 757 1514 2271 5526 9763 14,000
NOTE: *Cover by artist that drew Colossus in Green Giant Comics.*

COLOUR OF MAGIC, THE (Terry Pratchett's...)
Innovation Publishing: 1991 - No. 4, 1991 ($2.50, limited series)

1-4: Adapts 1st novel of the Discworld series 3.00

COLT .45 (TV)
Dell Publishing Co.: No. 924, 8/58 - No. 1058, 11-1/59-60; No. 4, 2-4/60 - No. 9, 5-7/61

Four Color 924(#1)-Wayde Preston photo-c on all 10 20 30 69 122 175
Four Color 1004,1058, #4,5,7-9: 1004-Photo-b/c 8 16 24 56 93 130
6-Toth-a 9 18 27 60 100 140

COLUMBIA COMICS
William H. Wise Co.: 1943

1-Joe Palooka, Charlie Chan, Capt. Yank, Sparky Watts, Dixie Dugan app. 27 54 81 158 259 360

COMANCHE
Dell Publishing Co.: No. 1350, Apr-Jun, 1962

Four Color 1350-Disney movie; reprints FC #966 with title change from "Tonka" to "Comanche"; Sal Mineo photo-c 5 10 15 35 55 75

COMANCHEROS, THE
Dell Publishing Co.: No. 1300, Mar-May, 1962

Four Color 1300-Movie, John Wayne photo-c 14 28 42 95 188 280

COMBAT
Atlas Comics (ANC): June, 1952 - No. 11, April, 1953

1 27 54 81 158 259 360
2-Heath-c/a 15 30 45 86 133 180
3,5-9,11: 3-Romita-a. 6-Robinson-c; Romita-a 12 24 36 69 97 125
4-Krigstein-a 13 26 39 72 101 130
10-B&W and color illos. in **POP**; Sale-a, Forte-a 13 26 39 74 105 135
NOTE: *Combat Casey in 7-11.* ***Heath*** *a-2, 3; c-1, 2, 5, 9.* ***Maneely*** *a-1; c-3, 10.* ***Pakula*** *a-1.* ***Reinman*** *a-1.*

COMBAT
Dell Publishing Co.: Oct-Nov, 1961 - No. 40, Oct, 1973 (No #9)

1 7 14 21 45 73 100
2,3,5 4 8 12 26 41 55
4-John F. Kennedy c/story (P.T. 109) 5 10 15 34 55 75
6,7,8(4-6/63), 8(7-9/63) 4 8 12 24 37 50
10-26: 26-Last 12¢ issue 3 6 9 20 30 40
27-40(reprints #1-14). 30-r/#4 3 6 9 14 19 24

COMBAT CASEY (Formerly War Combat)
Atlas Comics (SAI): No. 6, Jan, 1953 - No. 34, July, 1957

6 (Indicia shows 1/52 in error) 18 36 54 107 169 230
7-R.Q. Sale-a 11 22 33 64 90 115
8-Used in **POP**, pg. 94 11 22 33 60 83 105
9,10,13-19-Violent art by R.Q. Sale; Battle Brady x-over #10 14 28 42 78 112 145
11,12,20-Last Precode (2/55) 10 20 30 54 72 90
21-34: 22,25-R.Q. Sale-a 9 18 27 50 65 80
NOTE: ***Everett*** *a-6.* ***Heath*** *c-10, 17, 19, 23, 30.* ***Maneely*** *c-6, 8, 15.* ***Powell*** *a-29(5), 30(5), 34.* ***Severin*** *c-26, 33, 34.*

COMBAT KELLY
Atlas Comics (SPI): Nov, 1951 - No. 44, Aug, 1957

1-1st app. Combat Kelly; Heath-a 31 62 93 186 303 420
2 16 32 48 94 147 200
3-10 14 28 42 78 112 145
11-Used in **POP**, pgs. 94,95 plus color illo. 14 28 42 76 108 140
12-Color illo. in **POP** 13 26 39 72 101 130
13-16 11 22 33 60 83 105
17-Violent art by R. Q. Sale; Combat Casey app. 14 28 42 81 118 155
18-20,22-44: 18-Battle Brady app. 28-Last precode (1/55). 38-Green Berets story (8/56) 10 20 30 54 72 90
21-Transvestism-c 10 20 30 56 76 95
NOTE: ***Berg*** *a-8, 12-14, 15-17, 19-23, 25, 26, 28, 31-37, 39, 41-44; c-2.* ***Colan*** *a-42.* ***Heath*** *a-4, 18; c-31.* ***Lawrence*** *a-23.* ***Maneely*** *a-4(2), 6, 7(3), 8; c-4, 5, 7, 8, 10, 25, 29, 39.* ***R.Q. Sale*** *a-17, 25.* ***Severin*** *c-41, 42.* ***Whitney*** *a-5.*

COMBAT KELLY (...and the Deadly Dozen)
Marvel Comics Group: June, 1972 - No. 9, Oct, 1973

1-Intro & origin new Combat Kelly; Ayers/Mooney-a; Severin-c (20¢) 3 6 9 20 30 40
2,5-8 2 4 6 11 16 20

Comedy Comics #15 © MAR

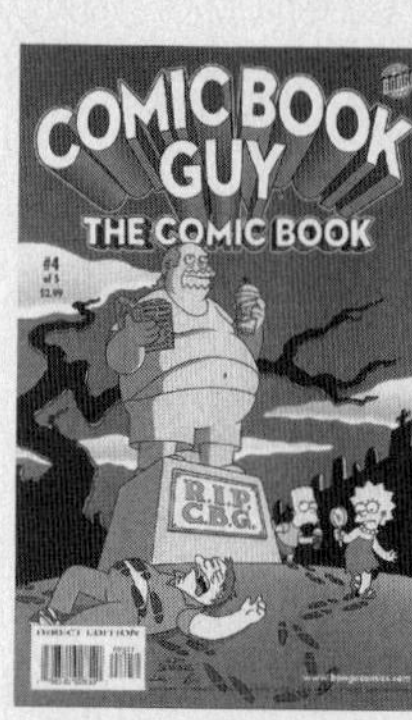

Comic Book Guy: The Comic Book #4 © Bongo

Comic Cavalcade #8 © DC

GD VG FN VF VF/NM NM-
2.0 4.0 6.0 8.0 9.0 9.2

3,4: 3-Origin. 4-Sgt. Fury-c/s 3 6 9 14 19 24
9-Death of the Deadly Dozen 3 6 9 16 23 30

COMBAT ZONE: TRUE TALES OF GIS IN IRAQ
Marvel Comics: 2005 ($19.99, squarebound)
Vol. 1-Karl Zinsmeister scripts adapted from his non-fiction books; Dan Jurgens-a 20.00

COMBINED OPERATIONS (See The Story of the Commandos)

COMEBACK (See Zane Grey 4-Color 357)

COMEDY CARNIVAL
St. John Publishing Co.: no date (1950's) (100 pgs.)
nn-Contains rebound St. John comics 36 72 108 211 343 475

COMEDY COMICS (1st Series) (Daring Mystery #1-8) (Becomes Margie Comics #35 on)
Timely Comics (TCI 9,10): No. 9, April, 1942 - No. 34, Fall, 1946
9-(Scarce)-The Fin by Everett, Capt. Dash, Citizen V, & The Silver Scorpion app.; Wolverton-a; 1st app. Comedy Kid; satire on Hitler & Stalin; The Fin, Citizen V & Silver Scorpion cont. from Daring Mystery 300 600 900 1950 3375 4800
10-(Scarce)-Origin The Fourth Musketeer, Victory Boys; Monstro, the Mighty app. 213 426 639 1363 2332 3300
11-Vagabond, Stuporman app. 54 108 162 343 574 825
12,13 19 38 57 111 176 240
14-Origin/1st app. Super Rabbit (3/43) plus-c 58 116 174 371 636 900
15-19 18 36 54 105 165 225
20-Hitler parody-c 26 52 78 154 252 350
21-Tojo-c 19 38 57 111 176 240
22-Hitler parody-c 22 44 66 132 216 300
23-32 14 28 42 80 115 150
33-Kurtzman-a (5 pgs.) 15 30 45 85 130 175
34-Intro Margie; Wolverton-a (5 pgs.) 24 48 72 142 234 325

COMEDY COMICS (2nd Series)
Marvel Comics (ACI): May, 1948 - No. 10, Jan, 1950
1-Hedy, Tessie, Millie begin; Kurtzman's "Hey Look" (he draws himself) 39 78 117 240 395 550
2 18 36 54 105 165 225
3,4-Kurtzman's "Hey Look" (?&3) 19 38 57 109 172 235
5-10 13 26 39 72 101 130

COMET, THE (See The Mighty Crusaders & Pep Comics #1)
Red Circle Comics (Archie): Oct, 1983 - No. 2, Dec, 1983
1-Re-intro & origin The Comet; The American Shield begins. Nino & Infantino art in both. Hangman in both 6.00
2-Origin continues. 5.00

COMET, THE
DC Comics (Impact Comics): July, 1991 - No. 18, Dec, 1992 ($1.00/$1.25)
1 4.00
2-18: 4-Black Hood app. 6-Re-intro Hangman. 8-Web x-over. 10-Contains Crusaders trading card. 4-Origin. Netzer(Nasser) c(p)-11,14-17 3.00
Annual 1 (1992, $2.50, 68 pgs.)-Contains Impact trading card; Shield back-up story 4.00

COMET MAN, THE (Movie)
Marvel Comics Group: Feb, 1987 - No. 6, July, 1987 (limited series)
1-6: 3-Hulk app. 4-She-Hulk shower scene-c/s. Fantastic 4 app. 5-Fantastic 4 app. 3.00
NOTE: ***Kelley Jones** a-1-6p.*

COMIC ALBUM (Also see Disney Comic Album)
Dell Publishing Co.: Mar-May, 1958 - No. 18, June-Aug, 1962
1-Donald Duck 9 18 27 60 100 140
2-Bugs Bunny 5 10 15 32 51 70
3-Donald Duck 7 14 21 47 76 105
4-6,8-10: 4-Tom & Jerry. 5-Woody Woodpecker. 6,10-Bugs Bunny. 8-Tom & Jerry. 9-Woody Woodpecker 4 8 12 28 44 60
7,11,15: Popeye. 11-(9-11/60) 6 12 18 33 49 65
12-14: 12-Tom & Jerry. 13-Woody Woodpecker. 14-Bugs Bunny 5 10 15 30 48 60
16-Flintstones (12-2/61-62)-3rd app. Early Cave Kids app. 8 16 24 54 90 125
17-Space Mouse (3rd app.) 5 10 15 32 51 70
18-Three Stooges; photo-c 8 16 24 54 90 125

COMIC BOOK
Marvel Comics-#1/Dark Horse Comics-#2: 1995 ($5.95, oversize)
1-Spumco characters by John K. 1 2 3 4 5 7
2-(Dark Horse) 6.00

GD VG FN VF VF/NM NM-
2.0 4.0 6.0 8.0 9.0 9.2

COMIC BOOK GUY: THE COMIC BOOK (BONGO COMICS PRESENTS...) (Simpsons)
Bongo Comics: 2010 - No. 5, 2010 ($3.99/$2.99, limited series)
1-($3.99) Four-layer cover w/classic swipes incl. FF#1; intro Graphic Novel Kid 4.00
2-($2.99) 2-Stan Lee cameo. 3-Includes Little Lulu spoof. 4-CBG origin 3.00

COMIC CAPERS
Red Circle Mag./Marvel Comics: Fall, 1944 - No. 6, Summer, 1946
1-Super Rabbit, The Creeper, Silly Seal, Ziggy Pig, Sharpy Fox begin 31 62 93 186 303 420
2 17 34 51 98 154 210
3-6 15 30 45 83 124 165

COMIC CAVALCADE
All-American/National Periodical Publications: Winter, 1942-43 - No. 63, June-July, 1954 (Contents change with No. 30, Dec-Jan, 1948-49 on)
1-The Flash, Green Lantern, Wonder Woman, Wildcat, The Black Pirate by Moldoff (also #2), Ghost Patrol, and Red White & Blue begin; Scribbly app.; Minute Movie 865 1730 2595 6315 11,158 16,000
2-Mutt & Jeff begin; last Ghost Patrol & Black Pirate; Minute Movies 245 490 735 1568 2684 3800
3-Hop Harrigan & Sargon, the Sorcerer begin; The King app. 161 322 483 1030 1765 2500
4,5: 4-The Gay Ghost, The King, Scribbly, & Red Tornado app. 5-Christmas-c. 5-Prints ad for Jr. JSA membership kit that includes "The Minute Man Answers The Call" 145 290 435 921 1586 2250
6-10: 7-Red Tornado & Black Pirate app.; last Scribbly. 9-Fat & Slat app.; X-Mas-c 116 232 348 742 1271 1800
11,12,14: 12-Last Red White & Blue 97 194 291 621 1061 1500
13-Solomon Grundy app.; X-Mas-c 181 362 543 1158 1979 2800
15-Just a Story begins 98 196 294 622 1074 1525
16-20: 19-Christmas-c 90 180 270 576 988 1400
21-23: 22-Johnny Peril begins. 23-Harry Lampert-c (Toth swipes) 86 172 258 546 936 1325
24-Solomon Grundy x-over in Green Lantern 116 232 348 742 1271 1800
25-28: 25-Black Canary app.; X-Mas-c. 26-28-Johnny Peril app. 28-Last Mutt & Jeff 77 154 231 493 847 1200
29-(10-11/48)-Last Flash, Wonder Woman, Green Lantern & Johnny Peril; Wonder Woman invents "Thinking Machine"; 2nd computer in comics (after Flash Comics #52); Leave It to Binky story (early app.) 90 180 270 576 988 1400
30-(12-1/48-49)-The Fox & the Crow, Dodo & the Frog & Nutsy Squirrel begin 41 82 123 256 428 600
31-35 23 46 69 136 223 310
36-49: 41-Last squarebound issue 17 34 51 100 158 215
50-62(Scarce) 21 42 63 122 199 275
63(Rare) 34 68 102 204 332 460
NOTE: ***Grossman** a-30-63. **E.E. Hibbard** c-(Flash only)-1-4, 7-14, 16-19, 21. **Sheldon Mayer** a(2-3)-40-63. **Moulson** c(G.L.)-7, 15. **Nodell** c(G.L.)-9. **H.G. Peter** c(W. Woman only)-1, 3-21, 24. **Post** a-31, 36. **Purcell** c(G.L.)-2-5, 10. **Reinman** a(Green Lantern)-4-6, 8, 9, 13, 15-21; c(Gr. Lantern)-6, 8, 19. **Toth** a(Green Lantern)-26-28; c-27. Atom app.-22, 23.*

COMIC COMICS
Fawcett Publications: Apr, 1946 - No. 10, Feb, 1947
1-Captain Kid; Nutty Comics #1 in indicia 15 30 45 85 130 175
2-10-Wolverton-a, 4 pgs. each. 5-Captain Kidd app. Mystic Moot by Wolverton in #2-10? 15 30 45 84 127 170

COMIC LAND
Fact and Fiction Publ.: March, 1946
1-Sandusky & the Senator, Sam Stupor, Sleuth, Marvin the Great, Sir Passer, Phineas Gruff app.; Irv Tirman & Perry Williams art 15 30 45 85 130 175

COMICO CHRISTMAS SPECIAL
Comico: Dec, 1988 ($2.50, 44 pgs.)
1-Rude/Williamson-a; Dave Stevens-c 4.00

COMICO COLLECTION (Also see Grendel)
Comico: 1987 ($9.95, slipcased collection)
nn-Contains exclusive Grendel: Devil's Vagary, 9 random Comico comics, a poster and newsletter in black slipcase w/silver ink 25.00

COMICO PRIMER (See Primer)

COMIC PAGES (Formerly Funny Picture Stories)
Centaur Publications: V3#4, July, 1939 - V3#6, Dec, 1939
V3#4-Bob Wood-a 54 108 162 343 574 825
5,6: 6-Schwab-c 47 94 141 296 498 700

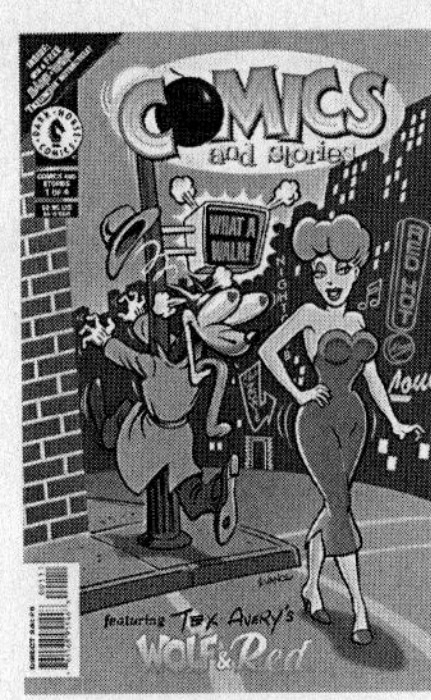

Comics and Stories #1 © DH

Comics On Parade #13 © UFS

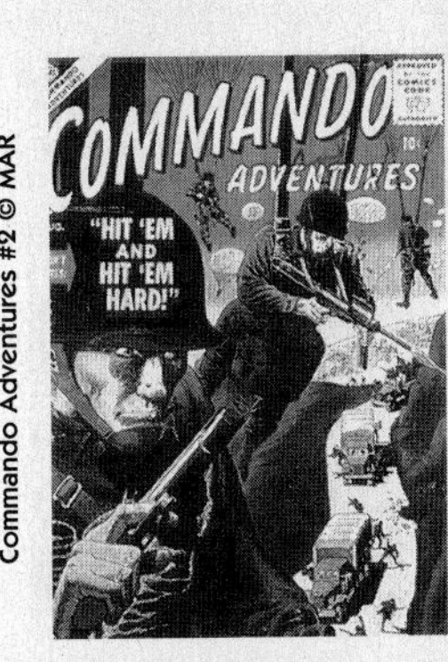

Commando Adventures #2 © MAR

	GD 2.0	VG 4.0	FN 6.0	VF 8.0	VF/NM 9.0	NM- 9.2

COMICS (See All Good)

COMICS, THE
Dell Publ. Co.: Mar, 1937 - No. 11, Nov, 1938 (Newspaper strip-r; bi-monthly)

1-1st app. Tom Mix in comics; Wash Tubbs, Tom Beatty, Myra North, Arizona Kid, Erik Noble & International Spy w/Doctor Doom begin 187 374 561 1197 2049 2900
2 82 164 246 528 902 1275
3-11: 3-Alley Oop begins 66 132 198 419 722 1025

COMICS AND STORIES (See Walt Disney's Comics and Stories)

COMICS & STORIES (Also see Wolf & Red)
Dark Horse Comics: Apr, 1996 - No. 4, July, 1996 ($2.95, lim. series) (Created by Tex Avery)

1-4: Wolf & Red app; reads Comics and Stories on-c. 1-Terry Moore-a. 2-Reed Waller-a 3.00

COMICS CALENDAR, THE (The 1946...)
True Comics Press (ordered through the mail): 1946 (25¢, 116 pgs.) (Stapled at top)

nn-(Rare) Has a "strip" story for every day of the year in color 40 80 120 242 401 560

COMICS DIGEST (Pocket size)
Parents' Magazine Institute: Winter, 1942-43 (B&W, 100 pgs)

1-Reprints from True Comics (non-fiction World War II stories) 10 20 30 54 72 90

COMICS EXPRESS
Eclipse Comics: Nov, 1989 - No. 2, Jan, 1990 ($2.95, B&W, 68pgs.)

1,2: Collection of strip-r; 2(12/89-c, 1/90 inside) 3.00

COMICS FOR KIDS
London Publ. Co./Timely: 1945 (no month); No. 2, Sum, 1945 (Funny animal)

1,2-Puffy Pig, Sharpy Fox 18 36 54 107 169 230

COMICS' GREATEST WORLD
Dark Horse Comics: Jun, 1993 - V4#4, Sept, 1993 ($1.00, weekly, lim. series)

Arcadia (Wk 1): V1#1,2,4: 1-X: Frank Miller-c. 2-Pit Bulls. 4-Monster. 3.00
1-B&W Press Proof Edition (1500 copies) 1 3 4 6 8 10
1-Silver-c; distr. retailer bonus w/print & cards 1 2 3 5 6 8
3-Ghost, Dorman-c; Hughes-a 4.00
Retailer's Prem. Emb. Silver Foil Logo-r/V1#1-4 1 3 4 6 8 10
Golden City (Wk 2: V2#1-4: 1-Rebel; Ordway-c. 2-Mecha; Dave Johnson-c.
3-Titan; Walt Simonson-c. 4-Catalyst; Perez-c. 3.00
1-Gold-c; distr. retailer bonus w/print & cards. 6.00
Retailer's Prem. Embos. Gold Foil Logo-r/V2#1-4 1 2 3 5 6 8
Steel Harbor (Week 3): V3#1-Barb Wire; Dorman-c; Gulacy-a(p) 4.00
2-4: 2-The Machine. 3-Wolfgang. 4-Motorhead 3.00
1-Silver-c; distr. retailer bonus w/print & cards 1 2 3 5 6 8
Retailer's Prem. Emb. Red Foil Logo-r/V3#1-4. 1 3 4 6 8 10
Vortex (Week 4): V4#1-4: 1-Division 13; Dorman-c. 2-Hero Zero; Art Adams-c.
3-King Tiger; Chadwick-a(p); Darrow-c. 4-Vortex; Miller-c. 3.00
1-Gold-c; distr. retailer bonus w/print & cards. 6.00
Retailer's Prem. Emb. Blue Foil Logo-r/V4#1-4. 1 2 3 5 6 8

COMICS' GREATEST WORLD: OUT OF THE VORTEX (See Out of The Vortex)

COMICS HITS (See Harvey Comics Hits)

COMICS MAGAZINE, THE (...Funny Pages #3)(Funny Pages #6 on)
Comics Magazine Co. (1st Comics Mag./Centaur Publ.): May, 1936 - No. 5, Sept, 1936 (Paper covers)

1-1st app. Dr. Mystic (a.k.a. Dr. Occult) by Siegel & Shuster (the 1st app. of a Superman prototype in comics). Dr. Mystic is not in costume but later appears in costume as a more pronounced prototype in More Fun #14-17. (1st episode of "The Koth and the Seven"; continues in More Fun #14; originally scheduled for publication at DC). 1 pg. Kelly-a; Sheldon Mayer-a 3500 7000 10,500 20,000 - -
2-Federal Agent (a.k.a. Federal Men) by Siegel & Shuster; 1 pg. Kelly-a 370 740 1110 2220 2960 3700
3-5 320 640 960 1920 2560 3200

COMICS NOVEL (Anarcho, Dictator of Death)
Fawcett Publications: 1947

1-All Radar; 51 pg anti-fascism story 32 64 96 192 314 435

COMICS ON PARADE (No. 30 on are a continuation of Single Series)
United Features Syndicate: Apr, 1938 - No. 104, Feb, 1955

1-Tarzan by Foster; Captain & the Kids, Little Mary Mixup, Abbie & Slats, Ella Cinders, Broncho Bill, Li'l Abner begin 366 732 1098 2562 4481 6400
2 (Tarzan & others app. on-c of #1-3,17) 129 258 387 826 1413 2000
3 97 194 291 621 1061 1500
4,5 77 154 231 493 847 1200
6-10 53 106 159 334 567 800
11-16,18-20 42 84 126 265 445 625
17-Tarzan-c 50 100 150 315 533 750
21-29: 22-Son of Tarzan begins. 22,24,28-Tailspin Tommy-c. 29-Last Tarzan issue 36 72 108 216 351 485
30-Li'l Abner 20 40 60 114 182 250
31-The Captain & the Kids 15 30 45 85 130 175
32-Nancy & Fritzi Ritz 14 28 42 78 112 145
33,36,39,42-Li'l Abner 16 32 48 94 147 200
34,37,40-The Captain & the Kids (10/41,6/42,3/43) 15 30 45 83 124 165
35,38-Nancy & Fritzi Ritz. 38-Infinity-c 14 28 42 76 108 140
41-Nancy & Fritzi Ritz 11 22 33 60 83 105
43-The Captain & the Kids 15 30 45 83 124 165
44 (3/44),47,50: Nancy & Fritzi Ritz 11 22 33 60 83 105
45-Li'l Abner 15 30 45 84 127 170
46,49-The Captain & the Kids 13 26 39 74 105 135
48-Li'l Abner (3/45) 15 30 45 84 127 170
51,54-Li'l Abner 14 28 42 76 108 140
52-The Captain & the Kids (3/46) 10 20 30 56 76 95
53,55,57-Nancy & Fritzi Ritz 10 20 30 56 76 95
56-The Captain & the Kids (r/Sparkler) 10 20 30 56 76 95
58-Li'l Abner; continues as Li'l Abner #61? 14 28 42 76 108 140
59-The Captain & the Kids 9 18 27 47 61 75
60-70-Nancy & Fritzi Ritz 8 16 24 44 57 70
71-99,101-104-Nancy & Sluggo: 71-76-Nancy only 8 16 24 42 54 65
100-Nancy & Sluggo 14 28 42 76 108 140
Special Issue, 7/46; Summer, 1948 - The Captain & the Kids app. 14 28 42 76 108 140

NOTE: Bound Volume (Very Rare) includes No. 1-12; bound by publisher in pictorial comic boards & distributed at the 1939 World's Fair and through mail order from ads in comic books (also see Tip Top) 297 594 891 1901 3251 4600

NOTE: *Li'l Abner reprinted from Tip Top.*

COMICS READING LIBRARIES (See the Promotional Comics section)

COMICS REVUE
St. John Publ. Co. (United Features Synd.): June, 1947 - No. 5, Jan, 1948

1-Ella Cinders & Blackie 12 24 36 67 94 120
2,4: 2-Hap Hopper (7/47). 4-Ella Cinders (9/47) 9 18 27 47 61 75
3,5: 3-Iron Vic (8/47). 5-Gordo No. 1 (1/48) 8 16 24 44 57 70

COMIC STORY PAINT BOOK
Samuel Lowe Co.: 1943 (Large size, 68 pgs.)

1055-Captain Marvel & a Captain Marvel Jr. story to read & color; 3 panels in color per pg. (reprints) 77 154 231 493 847 1200

COMIX BOOK
Marvel Comics Group/Krupp Comics Works No. 4,5: 1974 - No. 5, 1976 ($1.00, B&W, magazine) (#1-3 newsstand; #4,5 were direct distribution only)

1-Underground comic artists; 2 pgs. Wolverton-a 3 6 9 16 22 28
2,3: 2-Wolverton-a (1 pg.) 3 6 9 14 19 24
4(2/76), 4(5/76), 5 (Low distribution) 3 6 9 16 23 30

NOTE: *Print run No. 1-3: 200-250M; No. 4&5: 10M each.*

COMIX INTERNATIONAL
Warren Magazines: Jul, 1974 - No. 5, Spring, 1977 (Full color, stiff-c, mail only)

1-Low distribution; all Corben story remainders from Warren; Corben-c on all 9 18 27 65 113 160
2,4: 2-Two Dracula stories; Wood, Wrightson-r; Crandall-a; Maroto-a.
4-Printing w/ 3 Corben sty 6 12 18 37 59 80
3-5: 3-Dax story. 4-(printing without Corben story). 4-Crandall-a. 4,5-Vampirella stories.
5-Spirit story; Eisner-a 5 10 15 30 48 65

NOTE: *No. 4 had two printings with extra* ***Corben*** *story in one. No. 3 may also have a variation. No. 3 has two Jeff Jones reprints from Vampirella.*

COMMANDER BATTLE AND THE ATOMIC SUB
Amer. Comics Group (Titan Publ. Co.): Jul-Aug, 1954 - No. 7, Aug-Sep, 1955

1 (3-D effect)-Moldoff flying saucer-c 48 96 114 302 514 725
2,4-7: 2-Moldoff-c. 4-(1-2/55)-Last pre-code; Landau-a. 5-3-D effect story (2 pgs.). 6,7-Landau-a. 7-Flying saucer-c 31 62 93 186 303 420
3-H-Bomb-c; Atomic Sub becomes Atomic Spaceship 32 64 96 192 314 435

COMMANDO ADVENTURES
Atlas Comics (MMC): June, 1957 - No. 2, Aug, 1957

1-Severin-c 14 28 42 76 108 140
2-Severin-c; Reinman & Romita-a; Drucker-a? 10 20 30 54 72 90

COMMANDOS

Common Grounds #1 © TCOW

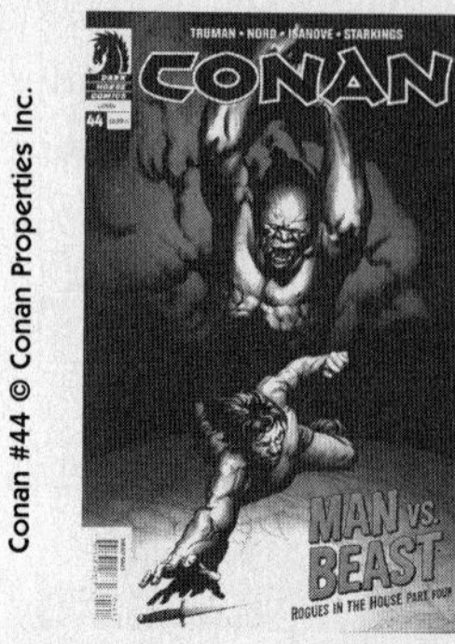

Conan #44 © Conan Properties Inc.

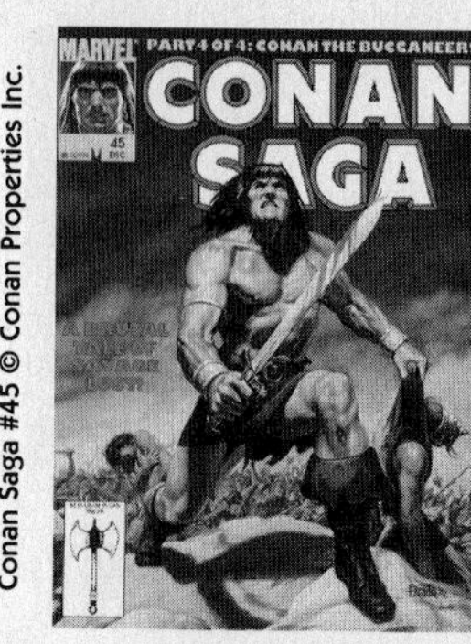

Conan Saga #45 © Conan Properties Inc.

GD VG FN VF VF/NM NM-
2.0 4.0 6.0 8.0 9.0 9.2

DC Comics: Oct. 1942
1-Ashcan comic, not distributed to newsstands, only for in-house use. Cover art is Boy Commandos #1 with interior being a Boy Commandos story from an unidentified issue of Detective Comics (no known sales)

COMMANDO YANK (See The Mighty Midget Comics & Wow Comics)

COMMON GROUNDS
Image Comics (Top Cow): Feb, 2004 - No. 6, July, 2004 ($2.99)
1-6: 1-Two covers; art by Jurgens and Oeming. 3-Bachalo, Jurgens-a. 4-Peréz-a 3.00
...: Baker's Dozen TPB (12/04, $14.99) r/#1-6; cover gallery; Holey Crullers pages 15.00

COMPLETE ALICE IN WONDERLAND (Adaptation of Carroll's original story)
Dynamite Entertainment: 2009 - Present ($4.99, limited series)
1-4-Leah Moore & John Reppion-s/Erica Awano-a/John Cassaday-c 5.00

COMPLETE BOOK OF COMICS AND FUNNIES
William H. Wise & Co.: 1944 (25¢, one-shot, 196 pgs.)
1-Origin Brad Spencer, Wonderman; The Magnet, The Silver Knight by Kinstler, & Zudo the Jungle Boy app. 45 90 135 284 480 675

COMPLETE BOOK OF TRUE CRIME COMICS
William H. Wise & Co.: No date (Mid 1940's) (25¢, 132 pgs.)
nn-Contains Crime Does Not Pay rebound (includes #22) 142 284 426 909 1555 2200

COMPLETE COMICS (Formerly Amazing Comics No. 1)
Timely Comics (EPC): No. 2, Winter, 1944-45
2-The Destroyer, The Whizzer, The Young Allies & Sergeant Dix; Schomburg-c 168 336 504 1075 1838 2600

COMPLETE DRACULA (Adaptation of Stoker's original story)
Dynamite Entertainment: 2009 - No. 5, 2009 ($4.99, limited series)
1-5-Leah Moore & John Reppion-s/Colton Worley-a/John Cassaday-c 5.00

COMPLETE FRANK MILLER BATMAN, THE
Longmeadow Press: 1989 ($29.95, hardcover, silver gilded pages)
HC-Reprints Batman: Year One, Wanted: Santa Claus--Dead or Alive, and The Dark Knight Returns 30.00

COMPLETE GUIDE TO THE DEADLY ARTS OF KUNG FU AND KARATE
Marvel Comics: 1974 (68 pgs., B&W magazine)
V1#1-Bruce Lee-c and 5 pg. story (scarce) 6 12 18 43 69 95

COMPLETE LOVE MAGAZINE (Formerly a pulp with same title)
Ace Periodicals (Periodical House): V26#2, May-June, 1951 - V32#4(#191), Sept, 1956
V26#2-Painted-c (52 pgs.) 11 22 33 62 86 110
V26#3-6(2/52), V27#1(4/52)-6(1/53) 9 18 27 50 65 80
V28#1(3/53), V28#2(5/53), V29#3(7/53)-6(12/53) 9 18 27 47 61 75
V30#1(2/54), V30#1(#176, 4/54),2,4-6(#181, 1/55) 9 18 27 47 61 75
V30#3(#178)-Rock Hudson photo-c 9 18 27 50 65 80
V31#1(#182, 3/55)-Last precode 8 16 24 44 57 70
V31#2(5/55)-6(#187, 1/56) 8 16 24 42 54 65
V32#1(#188, 3/56)-4(#191, 9/56) 8 16 24 42 54 65
NOTE: *(34 total issues). Photo-c V27#5-on. Painted-c V26#3.*

COMPLETE MYSTERY (True Complete Mystery No. 5 on)
Marvel Comics (PrPl): Aug, 1948 - No. 4, Feb, 1949 (Full length stories)
1-Seven Dead Men 45 90 135 284 480 675
2-4: 2-Jigsaw of Doom!; Shores-a. 3-Fear in the Night; Burgos-c/a (28 pgs.). 4-A Squealer Dies Fast 39 78 117 231 378 525

COMPLETE ROMANCE
Avon Periodicals: 1949
1-(Scarce)-Reprinted as Women to Love 42 84 126 265 445 625

CONAN (See Chamber of Darkness #4, Giant-Size..., Handbook of..., King Conan, Marvel Graphic Novel #19, 28, Marvel Treasury Ed., Power Record Comics, Robert E. Howard's.., Savage Sword of Conan, and Savage Tales)

CONAN
Dark Horse Comics: Feb, 2004 - No. 50, May, 2008 ($2.99)
0-(11/03, 25¢-c) Busiek-s/Nord-a 3.00
1-($2.99) Linsner-c/Busiek-s/Nord-a 5.00
1-(2nd printing) J. Scott Campell-c 3.00
1-(3rd printing) Nord-c 3.00
2-49: 18-Severin & Timm-a. 22-Kaluta-a (6 pgs.) 24-Harris-c. 29-31-Mignola-s 3.00
24-Variant-c with nude woman (also see Conan and the Demons of Khitai #3 for ad) 20.00
50-($4.99) Harris-c; new story and reprint from Conan the Barbarian #30 5.00
... and the Daughters of Midora (10/04, $4.99) Texiera-a/c 5.00

GD VG FN VF VF/NM NM-
2.0 4.0 6.0 8.0 9.0 9.2

...: Born on the Battlefield TPB (6/08, $17.95) r/#0,8,15,23,32,45,46; Ruth sketch pages 18.00
...: FCBD 2006 Special (5/06) Paul Lee-a; flip book with Star Wars FCBD 2006 Special 2.50
...: One For One (8/10, $1.00) r/#1 with red cover frame 1.00
...: The Blood-Stained Crown and Other Stories TPB (1/08, $14.95) r/#18,26-28,39 15.00
...: The Weight of the Crown (1/10, $3.50) Darick Robertson-s/a; 2 covers by Robertson 3.50
HC Vol. 1: The Frost Giant's Daughter and Other Stories (2005, $24.95) r/#1-6, partial #7; signed by Busiek; Nord sketch pages 25.00
Vol. 1: The Frost Giant's Daughter and Other Stories (2005, $15.95) r/#1-6, partial #7 16.00
Vol. 2: The God in the Bowl and Other Stories HC (2005, $24.95) r/#9-14 25.00
Vol. 2: The God in the Bowl and Other Stories SC (2006, $15.95) r/#9-14 16.00
Vol. 3: The Tower of the Elephant and Other Stories HC (5/06, $24.95) r/#0,16,17,19-22 25.00
Vol. 3: The Tower of the Elephant and Other Stories SC (6/06, $15.95) r/#0,16,17,19-22 16.00
Vol. 4: The Hall of the Dead and Other Stories HC (5/07, $24.95) r/#0,24,25,29-31,33,34 25.00
Vol. 4: The Hall of the Dead and Other Stories SC (6/07, $17.95) r/#0,24,25,29-31,33,34 18.00
Vol. 5: Rogues in the House and Other Stories SC (3/08, $17.95) r/#0,37,38,41-44 18.00
Vol. 6: The Hand of Nergal HC (10/08, $24.95) r/#0,47-50; sketch pages 25.00

CONAN AND THE DEMONS OF KHITAI
Dark Horse Comics: Oct, 2005 - No. 4, Jan, 2006 ($2.99, limited series)
1,2,4-Paul Lee-a/Akira Yoshida-s/Pat Lee-c 3.00
3-1st printing with red cover logo; letters page has image of Conan #24 nude variant-c 5.00
3-2nd printing with black cover logo; letters page has image of Conan #24 regular-c 3.00
TPB (7/06, $12.95) r/series 13.00

CONAN AND THE JEWELS OF GWAHLUR
Dark Horse Comics: Apr, 2005 - No. 3, June, 2005 ($2.99, limited series)
1-3-P. Craig Russell-s/a/c 3.00
HC (12/05, $13.95) r/series; P. Craig Russell interview and sketch pages 14.00

CONAN AND THE MIDNIGHT GOD
Dark Horse Comics: Dec, 2006 - No. 5, May, 2007 ($2.99, limited series)
1-5-Dysart-s/Conrad-a/Alexander-c 3.00
TPB (10/07, $14.95) r/#1-5 and Age of Conan: Hyborian Adventures one-shot 15.00

CONAN AND THE SONGS OF THE DEAD
Dark Horse Comics: July, 2006 - No. 5, Nov, 2006 ($2.99, limited series)
1-5-Timothy Truman-a/c; Joe Lansdale-s 3.00
TPB (4/07, $14.95) r/series; Truman sketch pages 15.00

CONAN: (Title Series): Marvel Comics
CONAN, 8/95 - No. 11, 6/96 ($2.95), 1-11: 4-Malibu Comic's Rune app. 3.00
...CLASSIC, 6/94 - No. 11, 4/95 ($1.50), 1-11: 1-r/Conan #1 by B. Smith, r/covers w/changes. 2-11-r/Conan #2-11 by Smith. 2-Bound w/cover to Conan The Adventurer #2 by mistake 2.50
...DEATH COVERED IN GOLD, 9/99 - No. 3, 11/99 ($2.99), 1-3-Roy Thomas-s/ John Buscema-a 3.00
...FLAME AND THE FIEND, 8/00 - No. 3, 10/00 ($2.99), 1-3-Thomas-s 3.00
...RETURN OF STYRM, 9/98 - No. 3, 11/98 ($2.99), 1-3-Parente & Soresina-a; painted-c 3.00
...RIVER OF BLOOD, 6/98 - No. 3, 8/98 ($2.50), 1-3 2.50
...SCARLET SWORD, 12/98 - No. 3, 2/99 ($2.99), 1-3-Thomas-s/Raffaele-a 3.00

CONAN: ROAD OF KINGS
Dark Horse Comics: Dec, 2010 - Present ($3.50)
1-Roy Thomas-s/Mike Hawthorne-a; covers by Wheatley & Keown 3.50

CONAN SAGA, THE
Marvel Comics: June, 1987 - No. 97, Apr, 1995 ($2.00/$2.25, B&W, magazine)
1-Barry Smith-r; new Smith-c 1 2 3 5 6 8
2-27: 2-9,11-new Barry Smith-c. 13,15-Boris-c. 17-Adams-r.18,25-Chaykin-r. 22-r/Giant-Size Conan 1,2 4.00
28-90: 28-Begin $2.25-c. 31-Red Sonja-r by N. Adams/SSOC #1; 1 pg. Jeff Jones-r. 32-Newspaper strip-r begin by Buscema. 33-Smith/Conrad-a. 39-r/Kull #1('71) by Andru & Wood. 44-Swipes-c/Savage Tales #1. 57-Brunner-r/SSOC #30. 66-r/Conan Annual #2 by Buscema. 79-r/Conan #43-45 w/Red Sonja. 85-Based on Conan #57-63 3.00
91-96 4.50
97-Last issue 1 2 3 4 5 7
NOTE: ***J. Buscema** r-32-on; c-86. **Chaykin** r-34. **Chiodo** painted c-63, 65, 66, 82. **G. Colan** a-47p. **Jusko** painted c-64, 83. **Kaluta** c-84. **Nino** a-37. **Ploog** a-50. **N. Redondo** painted c-48, 50, 51, 53, 57, 62. **Simonson** r-50-54, 56. **B. Smith** r-51. **Starlin** c-34. **Williamson** r-50i.*

CONAN THE ADVENTURER
Marvel Comics: June, 1994 - No. 14, July, 1995 ($1.50)
1-($2.50)-Embossed foil-c; Kayaran-a 3.50
2-14 3.00
2-Contents are Conan Classics #2 by mistake 3.00

Conan the Barbarian #9 © Conan Properties Inc.

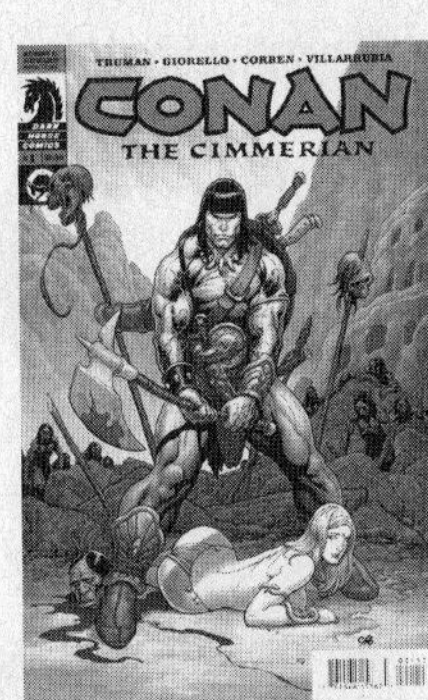

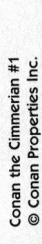

Conan the Cimmerian #1 © Conan Properties Inc.

Conan the King #21 © Conan Properties Inc.

GD 2.0 | VG 4.0 | FN 6.0 | VF 8.0 | VF/NM 9.0 | NM- 9.2

CONAN THE BARBARIAN
Marvel Comics: Oct, 1970 - No. 275, Dec, 1993

1-Origin/1st app. Conan (in comics) by Barry Smith; 1st brief app. Kull; #1-9 are 15¢ issues 22 44 66 159 317 475
2 10 20 30 67 116 165
3-(Low distribution in some areas) 14 28 42 96 191 285
4,5 8 16 24 58 97 135
6-9: 8-Hidden panel message, pg. 14. 9-Last 15¢-c 6 12 18 43 69 95
10,11 (25¢ 52 pg. giants): 10-Black Knight-r; Kull story by Severin 7 14 21 50 83 115
12,13: 12-Wrightson-c(i) 6 12 18 39 62 85
14,15-Elric app. 7 14 21 45 73 100
16,19,20: 16-Conan-r/Savage Tales #1 6 12 18 37 59 80
17,18-No Barry Smith-a 4 8 12 28 44 60
21,22: 22-Has reprint from #1 5 10 15 30 48 65
23-1st app. Red Sonja (2/73) 7 14 21 45 73 100
24-1st full Red Sonja story; last Smith-a 6 12 18 46 69 95
25-John Buscema-c/a begins 3 6 9 16 23 30
26-30 2 4 6 13 18 22
31-36,38-40 2 4 6 9 12 15
37-Neal Adams-c/a; last 20¢ issue; contains pull-out subscription form 3 6 9 17 25 32
41-43,46-50: 48-Origin retold 2 4 6 8 10 12
44,45-N. Adams-i(Crusty Bunkers). 45-Adams-c 2 4 6 9 12 15
51-57,59,60: 59-Origin Belit 1 2 3 5 6 8
58-2nd Belit app. (see Giant-Size Conan #1) 2 4 6 8 11 14
61-65-(Regular 25¢ editions)(4-8/76) 1 2 3 4 5 7
61-65-(30¢-c variants, limited distribution) 5 10 15 32 51 70
66-99: 68-Red Sonja story cont'd from Marvel Feature #7. 75-79-(Reg. 30¢-c). 84-Intro. Zula. 85-Origin Zula. 87-r/Savage Sword of Conan #3 in color 6.00
75-79-(35¢-c variants, limited distribution) 4 8 12 28 44 60
100-(52 pg. Giant)-Death of Belit 1 3 4 6 8 10
101-114 4.00
115-Double size 5.00
116-199,201-231,233-249: 116-r/Power Record Comic PR31. 244-Zula returns 4.00
200,232: 200-(52 pgs.). 232-Young Conan storyline begins; Conan is born 5.00
250-(60 pgs.) 5.00
251-270: 262-Adapted from R.E. Howard story 4.00
271-274 6.00
275-($2.50, 68 pgs.)-Final issue; painted-c (low print) 2 4 6 11 16 20
King Size 1(1973, 35¢)-Smith-r/#2,4; Smith-c 3 6 9 20 30 40
Annual 2(1976, 50¢)-New full length story 2 4 6 10 14 18
Annual 3,4: 3('78)-Chaykin/N. Adams-r/SSOC #2. 4('78)-New full length story 2 4 6 8 10 12
Annual 5,6: 5(1979)-New full length Buscema story & part-c, 6(1981)-Kane-c/a 6.00
Annual 7-12: 7('82)-Based on novel "Conan of the Isles" (new-a). 8(1984). 9(1984). 10(1986). 11(1986). 12(1987) 4.00
Special Edition 1 (Red Nails) 4.00
The Chronicles of Conan Vol. 1: Tower of the Elephant and Other Stories (Dark Horse, 2003, $15.95) r/#1-8; afterword by Roy Thomas 16.00
The Chronicles of Conan Vol. 2: Rogues in the House and Other Stories (Dark Horse, 2003, $15.95) r/#9-13,16; afterword by Roy Thomas 16.00
The Chronicles of Conan Vol. 3: The Monster of the Monoliths and Other Stories (Dark Horse, 2003, $15.95) r/#14,15,17-21; afterword by Roy Thomas 16.00
The Chronicles of Conan Vol. 4: The Song of Red Sonja and Other Stories (Dark Horse, 2004, $15.95) r/#23-26 & "Red Nails" from Savage Tales; afterword by Roy Thomas 16.00
The Chronicles of Conan Vol. 5: The Shadow in the Tomb and Other Stories (Dark Horse, 2004, $15.95) r/#27-34; afterword by Roy Thomas 16.00
The Chronicles of Conan Vol. 6: The Curse of the Skull and Other Stories (Dark Horse, 2004, $15.95) r/#35-42; afterword by Roy Thomas 16.00
The Chronicles of Conan Vol. 7: The Dweller in the Pool and Other Stories (Dark Horse, 2005, $15.95) r/#43-51; afterword by Roy Thomas 16.00
The Chronicles of Conan Vol. 8: Brothers of the Blade and Other Stories (Dark Horse, 2005, $16.95) r/#52-59; afterword by Roy Thomas 17.00
The Chronicles of Conan Vol. 9: Riders of the River-Dragons and Other Stories (Dark Horse, 11/05, $16.95) r/#60-63,65,69-71; afterword by Roy Thomas 17.00
The Chronicles of Conan Vol. 10: When Giants Walk the Earth and Other Stories (Dark Horse, 3/06, $16.95) r/#72-77,79-82; afterword by Roy Thomas 17.00
The Chronicles of Conan Vol. 11: The Dance of the Skull and Other Stories (Dark Horse, 2/07, $16.95) r/#82-86,88-90; afterword by Roy Thomas 17.00
The Chronicles of Conan Vol. 12: The King Beast of Abombi and Other Stories (Dark Horse, 7/07, $16.95) r/#91,93-100; afterword by Roy Thomas 17.00
The Chronicles of Conan Vol. 13: Whispering Shadows and Other Stories (Dark Horse, 12/07, $16.95) r/#92,100-107; afterword by Roy Thomas 17.00
The Chronicles of Conan Vol. 14: Shadow of the Beast and Other Stories (Dark Horse, 3/08, $16.95) r/#92,108-115; afterword by Roy Thomas 17.00
The Chronicles of Conan Vol. 15: The Corridor of Mullah-Kajar and Other Stories (Dark Horse, 7/08, $16.95) r/#116-121 & Annual #2; afterword by Roy Thomas 17.00

NOTE: ***Arthur Adams*** *c-248, 249.* ***Neal Adams*** *a-116r(i); c-49i.* ***Austin*** *a-125, 126; c-125i, 126i.* ***Brunner*** *c-17i. c-40.* ***Buscema*** *a-25-36p, 38, 39, 41-56p, 58-63p, 65-67p, 68, 70-78p, 84-86p, 88-91p, 93-126p, 136p, 140, 141-144p, 146-158p, 159, 161, 162, 163p, 165-185p, 187-190p, Annual 2(3pgs.). 3-5p, 7p; c(p)-26, 36, 44, 46, 52, 56, 58, 59, 64, 65, 72, 78-80, 83-91, 93-103, 105-126, 136-151, 155-159, 161, 162, 168, 169, 171, 172, 174, 175, 178-185, 188, 189, Annual 4, 5, 7.* ***Chaykin*** *a-79-83.* ***Golden*** *c-152.* ***Kaluta*** *c-167.* ***Gil Kane*** *a-12p, 17p, 18p, 127-130, 131-134p; c-12p, 17p, 18p, 23, 25, 27-32, 34, 35, 38, 39, 41-43, 45-51, 53-55, 57, 60-63, 65-71, 73p, 76p, 127-134.* ***Jim Lee*** *c-242.* ***McFarlane*** *c-241p.* ***Ploog*** *a-57.* ***Russell*** *a-21; c-251i.* ***Simonson*** *c-135.* ***B. Smith*** *a-1-11p, 12, 13-15p, 16, 19-21, 23, 24; c-1-11, 13-16, 19-24p.* ***Starlin*** *a-64.* ***Wood*** *a-47r. Issue Nos. 3-5, 7-9, 11, 16-18, 21, 23, 25, 27-30, 35, 37, 38, 42, 45, 52, 57, 58, 65, 69-71, 73, 79-83, 99, 100, 104, 114, Annual 2 have original Robert E. Howard stories adapted. Issues #32-34 adapted from Norvell Page's novel* ***Flame Winds****.*

CONAN THE BARBARIAN (Volume 2)
Marvel Comics: July, 1997 - No. 3, Oct, 1997 ($2.50, limited series)

1-3-Castellini-a 3.00

CONAN THE BARBARIAN MOVIE SPECIAL (Movie)
Marvel Comics Group: Oct, 1982 - No. 2, Nov, 1982

1,2-Movie adaptation; Buscema-a 3.50

CONAN THE BARBARIAN: THE USURPER
Marvel Comics: Dec, 1997 - No. 3, Feb, 1998 ($2.50, limited series)

1-3-Dixon-s 3.00

CONAN: THE BOOK OF THOTH
Dark Horse Comics: Mar, 2006 - No. 4, June, 2006 ($4.99, limited series)

1-4-Origin of Thoth-amon; Len Wein & Kurt Busiek-s/Kelley Jones-a/c 5.00
TPB (12/06, $17.95) r/#1-4 18.00

CONAN THE CIMMERIAN
Dark Horse Comics: No. 0, Jun, 2008 - No. 25, Nov, 2010 (99¢/$2.99)

0-Follows Conan #50; Truman-s/Giorello-a/c 3.00
1-(7/08, $2.99) Two covers by Joe Kubert and Cho; Giorello & Corben-a 3.00
2-25: 2-7-Cho-c; Giorello & Corben-a. 8-18-Linsner-c. 14-Joe Kubert-a (7 pgs.) 3.00

CONAN THE DESTROYER (Movie)
Marvel Comics Group: Jan, 1985 - No. 2, Mar, 1985

1,2-r/Marvel Super Special 3.00

CONAN THE FRAZETTA COVER SERIES
Dark Horse Comics: Dec, 2007 - No. 8 ($3.50/$5.99/$6.99)

1-($3.50) Reprints from Dark Horse series with Frazetta covers 3.50
2,3-($5.99) 6.00
4-6-($6.99) 7.00

CONAN THE KING (Formerly King Conan)
Marvel Comics Group: No. 20, Jan, 1984 - No. 55, Nov, 1989

20-49 4.00
50-54 5.00
55-Last issue 1 2 3 5 6 8

NOTE: ***Kaluta*** *c-20-23, 24i, 26, 27, 30, 50, 52.* ***Williamson*** *a-37i; c-37i, 38i.*

CONAN: THE LEGEND (See Conan 2004 series)

CONAN: THE LORD OF THE SPIDERS
Marvel Comics: Mar, 1998 - No. 3, May, 1998 ($2.50, limited series)

1-3-Roy Thomas-s/Raffaele-a 3.00

CONAN THE SAVAGE
Marvel Comics: Aug, 1995 - No. 10, May, 1996 ($2.95, B&W, Magazine)

1-10: 1-Bisley-c. 4-vs. Malibu Comics' Rune. 5,10-Brereton-c 4.00

CONAN VS. RUNE (Also See Conan #4)
Marvel Comics: Nov, 1995 ($2.95, one-shot)

1-Barry Smith-c/a/scripts 4.00

CONCRETE (Also see Dark Horse Presents & Within Our Reach)
Dark Horse Comics: March, 1987 - No. 10, Nov, 1988 ($1.50, B&W)

1-Paul Chadwick-c/a in all 1 3 4 6 8 10
1-2nd print 3.00
2 6.00
3-Origin 5.00
4-10 4.00
A New Life 1 (1989, $2.95, B&W)-r/#3,4 plus new-a (11 pgs.) 3.00
Celebrates Earth Day 1990 ($3.50, 52 pgs.) 6.00
Color Special 1 (2/89, $2.95, 44 pgs.)-r/1st two Concrete apps. from Dark Horse Presents #1,2 plus new-a 6.00
Depths TPB (7/05, $12.95)-r/#1-5, stories from DHP #1,8,10,150; other short stories 13.00

Concrete: Killer Smile #1 © Paul Chadwick

Congorilla #1 © DC

Conjurors #1 © DC

	GD	VG	FN	VF	VF/NM	NM-
	2.0	4.0	6.0	8.0	9.0	9.2

Land And Sea 1 (2/89, $2.95, B&W)-r/#1,2 — 6.00
Odd Jobs 1 (7/90, $3.50)-r/5,6 plus new-a — 3.50
...Vol. 1: Depths ('05, $12.95, 9"x6") r/#1-5 & short stories — 13.00
...Vol. 2: Heights ('05, $12.95, 9"x6") r/#6-10 & short stories — 13.00
...Vol. 3: Fragile Creatures (1/06, $12.95, 9"x6") r/mini-series & short stories from DHP — 13.00
...Vol. 4: Killer Smile (3/06, $12.95, 9"x6") r/mini-series & short stories from various — 13.00
...Vol. 5: Think Like a Mountain (5/06, $12.95, 9"x6") r/mini-series & short stories — 13.00
...Vol. 6: Strange Armor (7/06, $12.95, 9"x6") r/mini-series & short stories — 13.00
...Vol. 7: The Human Dilemma (4/06, $12.95, 9"x6") r/mini-series — 13.00

CONCRETE: (Title series), **Dark Horse Comics**
--ECLECTICA, 4/93 - No. 2, 5/93 ($2.95) 1,2 — 3.00
--FRAGILE CREATURE, 6/91 - No. 4, 2/92 ($2.50) 1-4 — 3.00
--KILLER SMILE, (Legend), 7/94 - No. 4, 10/94 ($2.95) 1-4 — 3.00
--STRANGE ARMOR, 12/97 - No. 5, 5/98 ($2.95, color) 1-5-Chadwick-s/c/a; retells origin — 3.00
--THE HUMAN DILEMMA, 12/04 - No. 6, 5/05 ($3.50)
1-6: Chadwick-a/c & scripts; Concrete has a child — 3.50
--THINK LIKE A MOUNTAIN, (Legend), 3/96 - No. 6, 8/96 ($2.95)
1-6: Chadwick-a/scripts & Darrow-c in all — 3.00

CONDORMAN (Walt Disney)
Whitman Publishing: Oct, 1981 - No. 3, Jan, 1982
1-3: 1,2-Movie adaptation; photo-c — 1 3 4 6 8 10

CONEHEADS
Marvel Comics: June, 1994 - No. 4, 1994 ($1.75, limited series)
1-4 — 3.00

CONFESSIONS ILLUSTRATED (Magazine)
E. C. Comics: Jan-Feb, 1956 - No. 2, Spring, 1956
1-Craig, Kamen, Wood, Orlando-a — 29 58 87 172 281 390
2-Craig, Crandall, Kamen, Orlando-a — 21 42 63 126 206 285

CONFESSIONS OF LOVE
Artful Publ.: Apr, 1950 - No. 2, July, 1950 (25¢, 7-1/4x5-1/4", 132 pgs.)
1-Bakerish-a — 34 68 102 199 325 450
2-Art & text; Bakerish-a — 21 42 63 122 199 275

CONFESSIONS OF LOVE (Formerly Startling Terror Tales #10; becomes Confessions of Romance No. 7 on)
Star Publications: No. 11, 7/52 - No. 14, 1/53; No. 4, 3/53- No. 6, 8/53
11-13: 12,13-Disbrow-a — 15 30 45 90 140 190
14,5,6 — 14 28 42 78 112 145
4-Disbrow-a — 14 28 42 81 118 155
NOTE: *All have* **L. B. Cole** *covers.*

CONFESSIONS OF ROMANCE (Formerly Confessions of Love)
Star Publications: No. 7, Nov, 1953 - No. 11, Nov, 1954
7 — 15 30 45 90 140 190
8 — 14 28 42 78 112 145
9-Wood-a — 15 30 45 84 127 170
10,11-Disbrow-a — 14 28 42 81 118 155
NOTE: *All have* **L. B. Cole** *covers.*

CONFESSIONS OF THE LOVELORN (Formerly Lovelorn)
American Comics Group (Regis Publ./Best Synd. Features): No. 52, Aug, 1954 - No. 114, June-July, 1960
52 (3-D effect) — 30 60 90 177 289 400
53,55 — 12 24 36 67 94 120
54 (3-D effect) — 30 60 90 177 289 400
56-Anti-communist propaganda story, 10 pgs; last pre-code (2/55) — 15 30 45 84 127 170
57-90,100 — 9 18 27 50 65 80
91-Williamson-a — 10 20 30 56 76 95
92-99,101-114 — 8 16 24 40 50 60
NOTE: **Whitney** *a-most issues; c-52, 53. Painted c-106, 107.*

CONFIDENTIAL DIARY (Formerly High School Confidential Diary; Three Nurses #18 on)
Charlton Comics: No. 12, May, 1962 - No. 17, Mar, 1963
12-17 — 3 6 9 15 21 26

CONGO BILL (See Action Comics & More Fun Comics #56)
National Periodical Publication: Aug-Sept, 1954 - No. 7, Aug-Sept, 1955
1 (Scarce) — 200 400 600 1600 - -
2,7 (Scarce) — 125 250 375 1000 - -
3-6 (Scarce). 4-Last pre-code issue — 100 200 300 800 - -

	GD	VG	FN	VF	VF/NM	NM-
	2.0	4.0	6.0	8.0	9.0	9.2

NOTE: *(Rarely found in fine to mint condition.)* ***Nick Cardy*** *c-1-7.*

CONGO BILL
DC Comics (Vertigo): Oct, 1999 - No. 4, Jan, 2000 ($2.95, limited series)
1-4-Corben-c — 3.00

CONGORILLA (Also see Actions Comics #224)
DC Comics: Nov, 1992 - No. 4, Feb, 1993 ($1.75, limited series)
1-4: 1,2-Brian Bolland-c — 3.00

CONJURORS
DC Comics: Apr, 1999 - No. 3, Jun, 1999 ($2.95, limited series)
1-3-Elseworlds; Phantom Stranger app.; Barreto-c/a — 3.00

CONNECTICUT YANKEE, A (See King Classics)

CONNOR HAWKE: DRAGON'S BLOOD (Also see Green Arrow titles)
DC Comics: Jan, 2007 - No. 6, Jun, 2007 ($2.99, limited series)
1-6-Chuck Dixon-s/Derec Donovan-a/c — 3.00
SC (2008, $19.99) r/#1-6 — 20.00

CONQUEROR, THE
Dell Publishing Co.: No., 690, Mar, 1956
Four Color 690-Movie, John Wayne photo-c — 14 28 42 99 200 300

CONQUEROR COMICS
Albrecht Publishing Co.: Winter, 1945
nn — 21 42 63 126 206 285

CONQUEROR OF THE BARREN EARTH (See The Warlord #63)
DC Comics: Feb, 1985 - No. 4, May, 1985 (Limited series)
1-4: Back-up series from Warlord — 3.00

CONQUEST
Store Comics: 1953 (6¢)
1-Richard the Lion Hearted, Beowulf, Swamp Fox — 7 14 21 35 43 50

CONQUEST
Famous Funnies: Spring, 1955
1-Crandall-a, 1 pg.; contains contents of 1953 ish. — 5 10 15 22 26 30

CONSPIRACY
Marvel Comics: Feb, 1998 - No. 2, Mar, 1998 ($2.99, limited series)
1,2-Painted art by Korday/Abnett-s — 3.00

CONSTANTINE (Also see Hellblazer)
DC Comics (Vertigo): 2005 (Based on the 2005 Keanu Reeves movie)
...: The Hellblazer Collection (2005, $14.95) Movie adaptation and r/#1, 27, 41; photo-c — 15.00
...: The Official Movie Adaptation (2005, $6.95) Seagle-s/Randall-a/photo-c — 7.00

CONSTRUCT
Caliber (New Worlds): 1996 - No. 6, 1997 ($2.95, B&W, limited series)
1-6: Paul Jenkins scripts — 3.00

CONSUMED
Platinum Studios: July, 2007 - No. 4, Oct, 2007 ($2.99, limited series)
1-4-Linsner-c/Budd-a/Shumskas-Tait-s — 3.00

CONTACT COMICS
Aviation Press: July, 1944 - No. 12, May, 1946
nn-Black Venus, Flamingo, Golden Eagle, Tommy Tomahawk begin — 54 108 162 343 574 825
2-5: 3-Last Flamingo. 3,4-Black Venus by L. B. Cole. 5-The Phantom Flyer app. — 40 80 120 243 402 560
6,11-Kurtzman's Black Venus; 11-Last Golden Eagle, last Tommy Tomahawk; Feldstein-a — 47 94 141 296 498 700
7-10 — 39 78 117 240 395 550
12-Sky Rangers, Air Kids, Ace Diamond app.; L.B. Cole sci-fi cover — 123 246 369 787 1344 1900
NOTE: **L. B. Cole** *a-3, 9; c-1-12.* **Giunta** *a-3.* **Hollingsworth** *a-5, 7, 10.* **Palais** *a-11, 12.*

CONTEMPORARY MOTIVATORS
Pendelum Press: 1977 - 1978 ($1.45, 5-3/8x8", 31 pgs., B&W)
14-3002 The Caine Mutiny; 14-3010 Banner in the Sky; 14-3029 God Is My Co-Pilot; 14-3037 Guadalcanal Diary; 14-3045 Hiroshima; 14-3053 Hot Rod; 14-3061 Just Dial a Number; 14-3088 The Diary of Anne Frank; 14-3096 Lost Horizon — 2 4 6 8 10 12
NOTE: *Also see Pendulum Illustrated Classics. Above may have been distributed the same.*

CONTEST OF CHAMPIONS (See Marvel Super-Hero...)

CONTEST OF CHAMPIONS II

Coo Coo Comics #42 © STD

"Cookie" #12 © ACG

Cosmo Cat #4 © FOX

	GD 2.0	VG 4.0	FN 6.0	VF 8.0	VF/NM 9.0	NM- 9.2

Marvel Comics: Sept, 1999 - No. 5 ($2.50, limited series)

1-5-Claremont-s/Jimenez-a 3.00

CONTRACTORS
Eclipse Comics: June, 1987 ($2.00, B&W, one-shot)

1-Funny animal 3.00

CONTRACT WITH GOD, A
Baronet Publishing Co./Kitchen Sink Press: 1978 ($4.95/$7.95, B&W, graphic novel)

	GD	VG	FN	VF	VF/NM	NM-
nn-Will Eisner-s/a	3	6	9	14	20	25
Reprint (DC Comics, 2000, $12.95)						13.00

CONVOCATIONS: A MAGIC THE GATHERING GALLERY
Acclaim Comics (Armada): Jan, 1996 ($2.50, one-shot)

1-pin-ups by various artists including Kaluta, Vess, and Dringenberg 3.00

COO COO COMICS (...the Bird Brain No. 57 on)
Nedor Publ. Co./Standard (Animated Cartoons): Oct, 1942 - No. 62, Apr, 1952

	GD	VG	FN	VF	VF/NM	NM-
1-Origin/1st app. Super Mouse & begin series (cloned from Superman); the first funny animal super hero series (see Looney Tunes #5 for 1st funny animal super hero)	31	62	93	186	303	420
2	15	30	45	88	137	185
3-10: 10-(3/44)	11	22	33	62	86	110
11-33: 33-1 pg. Ingels-a	9	18	27	52	69	85
34-40,43-46,48-Text illos by Frazetta in all. 36-Super Mouse covers begin	12	24	36	67	94	120
41-Frazetta-a (6-pg. story & 3 text illos)	22	44	66	128	209	290
42,47-Frazetta-a & text illos.	15	30	45	88	137	185
49-(1/50)-3-D effect story; Frazetta text illo	14	28	42	80	115	150
50,51-3-D effect-c only. 50-Frazetta text illo	13	26	39	74	105	135
52-62: 56-58,61-Super Mouse app.	8	16	24	44	57	70

"COOKIE" (Also see Topsy-Turvy)
Michel Publ./American Comics Group(Regis Publ.): Apr, 1946 - No. 55, Aug-Sept, 1955

	GD	VG	FN	VF	VF/NM	NM-
1-Teen-age humor	26	52	78	154	252	350
2	15	30	45	84	127	170
3-10	12	24	36	69	97	125
11-20	11	22	33	60	83	105
21-23,26,28-30	9	18	27	50	65	80
24,25,27-Starlett O'Hara stories	9	18	27	52	69	85
31-34,37-48,50,52-55	8	16	24	42	54	65
35,36-Starlett O'Hara stories	9	18	27	47	61	75
49,51: 49-(6-7/54)-3-D effect-c/s. 51-(10-11/54) 8pg. TrueVision 3-D effect story	13	26	39	74	105	135

COOL CAT (Formerly Black Magic)
Prize Publications: V8#6, Mar-Apr, 1962 - V9#2, July-Aug, 1962

	GD	VG	FN	VF	VF/NM	NM-
V8#6, nn(V9#1, 5-6/62), V9#2	3	6	9	18	27	35

COOL WORLD (Movie by Ralph Bakshi)
DC Comics: Apr, 1992 - No. 4, Sept, 1992 ($1.75, limited series)

1-4: Prequel to animated/live action movie. 1-Bakshi-c. Bill Wray inks in all 3.00
Movie Adaptation nn ('92, $3.50, 68pg.)-Bakshi-c 4.00

COPPER CANYON (See Fawcett Movie Comics)

COPS (TV)
DC Comics: Aug, 1988 - No. 15, Aug, 1989 ($1.00)

1 ($1.50, 52 pgs.)-Based on Hasbro Toys 4.00
2-15: 14-Orlando-c(p) 3.00

COPS: THE JOB
Marvel Comics: June, 1992 - No. 4, Sept, 1992 ($1.25, limited series)

1-4: All have Jusko scripts & Golden-c 3.00

CORBEN SPECIAL, A
Pacific Comics: May, 1984 (one-shot)

1-Corben-c/a; E.A. Poe adaptation 5.00

CORE, THE
Image Comics: July, 2008 ($3.99)

Pilot Season - Hickman-s/Rocafort-a 4.00

CORKY & WHITE SHADOW (Disney, TV)
Dell Publishing Co.: No. 707, May, 1956 (Mickey Mouse Club)

	GD	VG	FN	VF	VF/NM	NM-
Four Color 707-Photo-c	7	14	21	47	76	105

CORLISS ARCHER (See Meet Corliss Archer)

CORMAC MAC ART (Robert E. Howard's...)
Dark Horse Comics: 1990 - No. 4, 1990 ($1.95, B&W, mini-series)

1-4: All have Bolton painted-c; Howard adapts. 3.00

CORNY'S FETISH
Dark Horse Comics: Apr, 1998 ($4.95, B&W, one-shot)

1-Renée French-s/a; Bolland-c 5.00

CORPORAL RUSTY DUGAN (See Holyoke One-Shot #2)

CORPSES OF DR. SACOTTI, THE (See Ideal a Classical Comic)

CORSAIR, THE (See A-1 Comics No. 5, 7, 10 under Texas Slim)

CORTEZ AND THE FALL OF THE AZTECS
Tome Press: 1993 ($2.95, B&W, limited series)

1,2 3.00

CORUM: THE BULL AND THE SPEAR (See Chronicles Of Corum)
First Comics: Jan, 1989 - No. 4, July, 1989 ($1.95)

1-4: Adapts Michael Moorcock's novel 3.00

COSMIC BOOK, THE
Ace Comics: Dec, 1986 - No. 1, 1987 ($1.95)

1,2: 1-(44pgs.)-Wood, Toth-a. 2-(B&W) 3.00

COSMIC BOY (Also see The Legion of Super-Heroes)
DC Comics: Dec, 1986 - No. 4, Mar, 1987 (limited series)

1-4: Legends tie-ins all issues 3.00

COSMIC GUARD
Devil's Due Publ.: Aug, 2004 - No. 6, Dec, 2005 ($2.99)

1-6-Jim Starlin-s/a 3.00

COSMIC HEROES
Eternity/Malibu Graphics: Oct, 1988 - No. 11, Dec, 1989 ($1.95, B&W)

1-11: Reprints 1934-1936's Buck Rogers newspaper strips #1-728 3.00

COSMIC ODYSSEY
DC Comics: 1988 - No. 4, 1988 ($3.50, limited series, squarebound)

1-4: Reintro. New Gods into DC continuity; Superman, Batman, Green Lantern (John Stewart) app; Starlin scripts, Mignola-c/a in all. 2-Darkseid merges Demon & Jason Blood (separated in Demon limited series #4) 5.00
TPB (1992,2009, $19.99) r/#1-4; Robert Greenberger intro. 20.00

COSMIC POWERS
Marvel Comics: Mar, 1994 - No. 6, Aug, 1994 ($2.50, limited series)

1-6: 1-Ron Lim-c/a(p). 1,2-Thanos app. 2-Terrax. 3-Ganymede & Jack of Hearts app. 2.50

COSMIC POWERS UNLIMITED
Marvel Comics: May, 1995 - No. 5, May, 1996 ($3.95, quarterly)

1-5 4.00

COSMIC RAY
Image Comics: June, 1999 - No. 2 ($2.95, B&W)

1,2-Steven Blue-s/a 3.00

COSMIC SLAM
Ultimate Sports Entertainment: 1999 ($3.95, one-shot)

1-McGwire, Sosa, Bagwell, Justice battle aliens; Sienkiewicz-c 4.00

COSMO CAT (Becomes Sunny #11 on; also see All Top & Wotalife Comics)
Fox Publications/Green Publ. Co./Norlen Mag.: July-Aug, 1946 - No. 10, Oct, 1947; 1957; 1959

	GD	VG	FN	VF	VF/NM	NM-
1	26	52	78	152	249	345
2	15	30	45	84	127	170
3-Origin (11-12/46)	18	36	54	107	169	230
4-Robot-c	14	28	42	76	108	140
5-10	11	22	33	60	83	105
2-4(1957-Green Publ. Co.)	6	12	18	27	33	38
2-4(1959-Norlen Mag.)	5	10	15	23	28	32
I.W. Reprint #1	2	4	6	11	16	20

COSMO THE MERRY MARTIAN
Archie Publications (Radio Comics): Sept, 1958 - No. 6, Oct, 1959

	GD	VG	FN	VF	VF/NM	NM-
1-Bob White-a in all	15	30	45	85	130	175
2-6	11	22	33	60	83	105

COTTON WOODS
Dell Publishing Co.: No. 837, Sept, 1957

	GD	VG	FN	VF	VF/NM	NM-
Four Color 837	4	8	12	24	37	50

COUGAR, THE (Cougar No. 2)

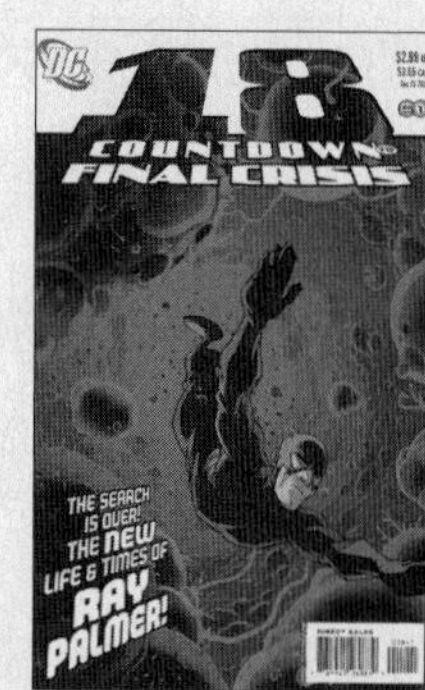

Countdown #18 © DC

Coup D'Etat: StormWatch #2 © WSP

Courtney Crumrin and the Night Things FCBD Edition © Ted Naifeh

GD VG FN VF VF/NM NM-
2.0 4.0 6.0 8.0 9.0 9.2

Seaboard Periodicals (Atlas): April, 1975 - No. 2, July, 1975
1,2: 1-Vampire; Adkins-a(p). 2-Cougar origin; werewolf-s; Buckler-c(p) 2 4 6 8 11 14

COUNTDOWN (See Movie Classics)

COUNTDOWN
DC Comics (WildStorm): June, 2000 - No. 8, Jan, 2001 ($2.95)
1-8-Mariotte-s/Lopresti-a 3.00

COUNTDOWN (Continued from 52 weekly series)
DC Comics: No. 51, July, 2007 - No. 1, June, 2008 ($2.99, weekly, limited series) (issue #s go in reverse)
51-Gatefold wraparound-c by Andy Kubert; Duela Dent killed; the Monitors app. 3.00
50-1: 50-Joker-c. 48-Lightray dies. 47-Mary Marvel gains Black Adam's powers. 46-intro. Forerunner. 43-Funeral for Bart Allen. 39-Karate Kid-c 3.00
Countdown to Final Crisis Vol. 1 TPB (2008, $19.99) r/#51-39 20.00
Countdown to Final Crisis Vol. 2 TPB (2008, $19.99) r/#38-26 20.00
Countdown to Final Crisis Vol. 3 TPB (2008, $19.99) r/#25-13 20.00
Countdown to Final Crisis Vol. 4 TPB (2008, $19.99) r/#12-1 20.00

COUNTDOWN: ARENA (Takes place during Countdown #21-18)
DC Comics: Feb, 2008 - No. 4, Feb, 2008 ($3.99, weekly, limited series)
1-4-Battles between alternate Earth heroes; McDaniel-a; Andy Kubert variant-c on each 4.00
TPB (2008, $17.99) r/#1-4; variant covers 18.00

COUNTDOWN PRESENTS: LORD HAVOK & THE EXTREMISTS
DC Comics: Dec, 2007 - No. 8 ($2.99, limited series)
1-6: 1-Tieri-s/Sharp-a/c; Challengers From Beyond app. 3.00
TPB (2008, $17.99) r/#1-6 18.00

COUNTDOWN PRESENTS THE SEARCH FOR RAY PALMER (Leads into Countdown #18)
DC Comics: Nov, 2007 - Feb, 2008 ($2.99, series of one-shots)
...: Wildstorm (11/07) Part 1; The Authority app.; Art Adams-c/Unzueta-a 3.00
...: Crime Society (12/07) Earth-3 Owlman & Jokester app.; Igle-a 3.00
...: Red Rain (1/08) Vampire Batman app.; Kelley Jones-c; Jones, Battle & Unzueta-a 3.00
...: Gotham By Gaslight (1/08) Victorian Batman app.; Tocchini-a/Nguyen-c 3.00
...: Red Son (2/08) Soviet Superman app.; Foreman-a 3.00
...: Superwoman/Batwoman (2/08) Conclusion; gender-reversed heroes; Sook-c 3.00
TPB (2008, $17.99) r/one-shots 18.00

COUNTDOWN SPECIAL
DC Comics: Dec, 2007 - Jun, 2008 ($4.99, collection of reprints related to Countdown)
...: Eclipso (5/08) r/Eclipso #10 & Spectre #17,18 (1994); Sook-c 5.00
...: Jimmy Olsen (1/08) r/Superman's Pal, Jimmy Olsen #136,147,148; Kirby-s/a; Sook-c 5.00
...: Kamandi (6/08) r/Kamandi: The Last Boy on Earth #1,10,29; Kirby-s/a; Sook-c 5.00
...: New Gods (3/08) r/Forever People #1, Mr. Miracle #1, New Gods #7; Kirby-s/a; Sook-c 5.00
...: Omac (4/08) r/Omac (1974) #1, Warlord #37-39, DC Comics Presents #61; Sook-c 5.00
...: The Atom 1,2 (2/08) r/stories from Super-Team Family #11-14; Sook-c on both 5.00
...: The Flash (12/07) r/Rogues Gallery in Flash (1st series) #106,113,155,174; Sook-c 5.00

COUNTDOWN TO ADVENTURE
DC Comics: Oct, 2007 - No. 8, May, 2008 ($3.99, limited series)
1-8: 1-Adam Strange, Animal Man and Starfire app.; origin of Forerunner 4.00
TPB (2008, $17.99) r/#1-8 18.00

COUNTDOWN TO INFINITE CRISIS (See DC Countdown)

COUNTDOWN TO MYSTERY (See Eclipso: The Music of the Spheres TPB for reprint)
DC Comics: Nov, 2007 - No. 8, Jun, 2008 ($3.99, limited series)
1-8: 1-Doctor Fate, Eclipso, The Spectre and Plastic Man app. 4.00
TPB (2008, $17.99) r/#1-8 18.00

COUNT DUCKULA (TV)
Marvel Comics: Nov, 1988 - No. 15, Jan, 1991 ($1.00)
1,8: 1-Dangermouse back-up. 8-Geraldo Rivera photo-c/& app.; Sienkiewicz-a(i) 5.00
2-7,9-15: Dangermouse back-ups in all 4.00

COUNT OF MONTE CRISTO, THE
Dell Publishing Co.: No. 794, May, 1957
Four Color 794-Movie, Buscema-a 8 16 24 56 93 130

COUP D'ETAT (Oneshots)
DC Comics (WildStorm): April, 2004 ($2.95, weekly limited series)
...: Sleeper 1 (part 1 of 4) Jim Lee-a; 2 covers by Lee and Bermejo 3.00
...: Stormwatch 1 (part 2 of 4) D'Anda-a; 2 covers by D'Anda and Bermejo 3.00
...: Wildcats Version 3.0 1 (part 3 of 4) Garza-a; 2 covers by Garza and Bermejo 3.00
...: The Authority 1 (part 4 of 4) Portacio-a; 2 covers by Portacio and Bermejo 3.00
...: Afterword 1 (5/04) Profile pages and prelude stories for Sleeper & Wetworks 3.00

GD VG FN VF VF/NM NM-
2.0 4.0 6.0 8.0 9.0 9.2

TPB (2004, $12.95) r/series and profile pages from Afterword 13.00

COURAGE COMICS
J. Edward Slavin: 1945
1,2,77 14 28 42 82 121 160

COURTNEY CRUMRIN...
Oni Press: July, 2005; July 2007; Dec, 2008 ($5.95, B&W, series of one-shots)
... And The Fire Thief's Tale (7/07) Naifeh-s/a 6.00
... And The Prince of Nowhere (12/08) Naifeh-s/a 6.00
... Tales Portrait of the Warlock as a Young Man (7/05) origin Uncle Aloysius; Naifeh-s/a 6.00

COURTNEY CRUMRIN & THE COVEN OF MYSTICS
Oni Press: Dec, 2002 - No. 4, March, 2003 ($2.95, B&W, limited series)
1-4-Ted Naifeh-s/a 3.00
TPB (9/03, $11.95, 8" x 5-1/2") r/#1-4 12.00

COURTNEY CRUMRIN & THE NIGHT THINGS
Oni Press: Mar, 2002 - No. 4, June, 2002 ($2.95, B&W, limited series)
1-4-Ted Naifeh-s/a 3.00
Free Comic Book Day Edition (5/03) Naifeh-s/a 2.50
TPB (12/02, $11.95) r/#1-4 12.00

COURTNEY CRUMRIN IN THE TWILIGHT KINGDOM
Oni Press: Dec, 2003 - No. 4, May, 2004 ($2.99, B&W, limited series)
1-4-Ted Naifeh-s/a 3.00
TPB (9/04, $11.95, digest-size) r/#1-4 12.00

COURTSHIP OF EDDIE'S FATHER (TV)
Dell Publishing Co.: Jan, 1970 - No. 2, May, 1970
1-Bill Bixby photo-c on both 6 12 18 37 59 80
2 4 8 12 24 37 50

COVEN
Awesome Entertainment: Aug, 1997 - No. 5, Mar, 1998 ($2.50)
Preview 1 2 3 5 6 8
1-Loeb-s/Churchill-a; three covers by Churchill, Liefeld, Pollina 1 2 3 5 6 8
1-Fan Appreciation Ed.(3/98); new Churchill-c 3.00
1+ :Includes B&W art from Kaboom 1 3 4 6 8 10
2-Regular-c w/leaping Fantom 6.00
2-Variant-c w/circle of candles 1 2 3 5 6 8
3-6-Contains flip book preview of ReGex 3.00
3-White variant-c 1 2 3 4 5 7
3,4: 3-Halloween wraparound-c. 4-Purple variant-c 3.00
...Black & White (9/98) Short stories 3.00
...Fantom Special (2/98) w/sketch pages 5.00

COVEN
Awesome Entertainment: Jan, 1999 - No. 3, June, 1999 ($2.50)
1-3: 1-Loeb-s/Churchill-a; 6 covers by various. 2-Supreme-c/app. 3-Flip book w/Kaboom preview 3.00
... Dark Origins (7/99, 2.50) w/Lionheart gallery 3.00

COVENANT, THE
Image Comics (Top Cow): 2005 ($9.99, squarebound, one-shot)
nn-Tone Rodriguez-a/Aron Coleite-s 10.00

COVERED WAGONS, HO (Disney, TV)
Dell Publishing Co.: No. 814, June, 1957 (Donald Duck)
Four Color 814-Mickey Mouse app. 5 10 15 34 55 75

COWBOY ACTION (Formerly Western Thrillers No. 1-4; Becomes Quick-Trigger Western No. 12 on)
Atlas Comics (ACI): No. 5, March, 1955 - No. 11, March, 1956
5 14 28 42 76 108 140
6-10: 6-8-Heath-c 10 20 30 54 72 90
11-Williamson-a (4 pgs.); Baker-a 11 22 33 62 86 110
NOTE: ***Ayers** a-8. **Drucker** a-6. **Maneely** c/a-5, 6. **Severin** c-10. **Shores** a-7.*

COWBOY COMICS (Star Ranger #12, Stories #14)(Star Ranger Funnies #15)
Centaur Publishing Co.: No. 13, July, 1938 - No. 14, Aug, 1938
13-(Rare)-Ace and Deuce, Lyin Lou, Air Patrol, Aces High, Lee Trent, Trouble Hunters begin 135 270 405 864 1482 2100
14-Filchock-c 90 180 270 576 988 1400
NOTE: ***Guardineer** a-13, 14. **Gustavson** a-13, 14.*

COWBOY IN AFRICA (TV)
Gold Key: Mar, 1968

Cowboy Love #6 © FAW

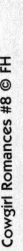

Cowgirl Romances #8 © FH

Crackajack Funnies #24 © DELL

GD 2.0 | VG 4.0 | FN 6.0 | VF 8.0 | VF/NM 9.0 | NM- 9.2

1(10219-803)-Chuck Connors photo-c 4 8 12 26 41 55

COWBOY LOVE (Becomes Range Busters?)
Fawcett Publications/Charlton Comics No. 28 on: 7/49 - V2#10, 6/50; No. 11, 1951; No. 28, 2/55 - No. 31, 8/55

V1#1-Rocky Lane photo back-c 15 30 45 88 137 185
2 8 16 24 44 57 70
V1#3,4,6 (12/49) 8 16 24 40 50 60
5-Bill Boyd photo back-c (11/49) 9 18 27 47 61 75
V2#7-Williamson/Evans-a 10 20 30 54 72 90
V2#8-11 7 14 21 35 43 50
V1#28 (Charlton)-Last precode (2/55) (Formerly Romantic Story?)
6 12 18 31 38 45
V1#29-31 (Charlton; becomes Sweetheart Diary #32 on)
6 12 18 28 34 40

NOTE: **Powell** a-10. **Marcus Swayze** a-2, 3. Photo c-1-11. No. 1-3, 5-7, 9, 10 are 52 pgs.

COWBOY ROMANCES (Young Men No. 4 on)
Marvel Comics (IPC): Oct, 1949 - No. 3, Mar, 1950 (All photo-c & 52 pgs.)

1-Photo-c 22 44 66 132 216 300
2-William Holden, Mona Freeman "Streets of Laredo" photo-c
16 32 48 94 147 200
3-Photo-c 15 30 45 84 127 170

COWBOYS 'N' INJUNS (...and Indians No. 6 on)
Compix No. 1-5/Magazine Enterprises No. 6 on: 1946 - No. 5, 1947; No. 6, 1949 - No. 8, 1952

1-Funny animal western 14 28 42 82 121 160
2-5-All funny animal western 10 20 30 54 72 90
6(A-1 23)-Half violent, half funny; Ayers-a 14 28 42 76 108 140
7(A-1 41, 1950), 8(A-1 48)-All funny 9 18 27 47 61 75
I.W. Reprint No. 1,7,10 (Reprinted in Canada by Superior, No. 7), 10('63)
2 4 6 11 16 20

COWBOY WESTERN COMICS (TV)(Formerly Jack In The Box; Becomes Space Western No. 40-45 & Wild Bill Hickok & Jingles No. 68 on; title:Cowboy Western Heroes No. 47 & 48; Cowboy Western No. 49 on)
Charlton (Capitol Stories): No. 17, 7/48 - No. 39, 8/52; No. 46, 10/53; No. 47, 12/53; No. 48, Spr, '54; No. 49, 5-6/54 - No. 67, 3/58 (nn 40-45)

17-Jesse James, Annie Oakley, Wild Bill Hickok begin; Texas Rangers app.
16 32 48 94 147 200
18,19-Orlando-c/a. 18-Paul Bunyan begins. 19-Wyatt Earp story
10 20 30 58 79 100
20-25: 21-Buffalo Bill story. 22-Texas Rangers-c/story. 24-Joel McCrea photo-c & adaptation from movie "Three Faces West". 25-James Craig photo-c & adaptation from movie "Northwest Stampede" 9 18 27 52 69 85
26-George Montgomery photo-c and adaptation from movie "Indian Scout"; 1 pg. bio on Will Rogers 10 20 30 58 79 100
27-Sunset Carson photo-c & adapts movie "Sunset Carson Rides Again" plus 1 other Sunset Carson story 39 78 117 240 395 550
28-Sunset Carson line drawn-c; adapts movies "Battling Marshal" & "Fighting Mustangs" starring Sunset Carson 20 40 60 114 182 250
29-Sunset Carson line drawn-c; adapts movies "Rio Grande" with Sunset Carson & "Winchester '73" w/James Stewart plus 5 pg. life history of Sunset Carson featuring Tom Mix 20 40 60 114 182 250
30-Sunset Carson photo-c; adapts movie "Deadline" starring Sunset Carson plus 1 other Sunset Carson story 39 78 117 240 395 550
31-34,38,39,47-50 (no #40-45): 50-Golden Arrow, Rocky Lane & Blackjack (r?) stories
9 18 27 47 61 75
35,36-Sunset Carson-c/stories (2 in each). 35-Inside front-c photo of Sunset Carson plus photo on-c 20 40 60 120 195 270
37-Sunset Carson stories (2) 15 30 45 94 147 200
46-(Formerly Space Western)-Space western story 15 30 45 94 147 200
51-57,59-66: 51-Golden Arrow(r?) & Monte Hale-r renamed Rusty Hall. 53,54-Tom Mix-r. 55-Monte Hale story(r?). 66-Young Eagle story. 67-Wild Bill Hickok and Jingles-c/story
7 14 21 35 43 50
58-(1/56, 15¢, 68 pgs.)-Wild Bill Hickok, Annie Oakley & Jesse James stories; Forgione-a
8 16 24 44 57 70
67-(15¢, 68 pgs.)-Williamson/Torres-a, 5 pgs. 9 18 27 50 65 80

NOTE: Many issues trimmed 1" shorter. **Maneely** a-67(5). Inside front/back photo c-29.

COWGIRL ROMANCES
Marvel Comics (CCC): No. 28, Jan, 1950 (52 pgs.)

28(#1)-Photo-c 21 42 63 126 206 285

COWGIRL ROMANCES
Fiction House Magazines: 1950 - No. 12, Winter, 1952-53 (No. 1-3: 52 pgs.)

1-Kamen-a 41 82 123 256 428 600
2 21 42 63 126 206 285
3-5: 5-12-Whitman-c (most) 19 38 57 112 179 245
6-9,11,12 19 38 57 109 172 235
10-Frazetta?/Williamson?-a; Kamen?/Baker-a; r/Mitzi story from Movie Comics #4 w/all new dialogue 31 62 93 186 303 420

COW PUNCHER (...Comics)
Avon Periodicals: Jan, 1947; No. 2, Sept, 1947 - No. 7, 1949

1-Clint Cortland, Texas Ranger, Kit West, Pioneer Queen begin; Kubert-a; Alabam stories begin 45 90 135 284 480 675
2-Kubert, Kamen/Feldstein-a; Kamen-c 39 78 117 231 378 525
3-5,7: 3-Kiefer story 28 56 84 165 270 375
6-Opium drug mention story; bondage, headlight-c; Reinman-a
37 74 111 222 361 500

COWPUNCHER
Realistic Publications: 1953 (nn) (Reprints Avon's No. 2)

nn-Kubert-a 12 24 36 69 97 125

COWSILLS, THE (See Harvey Pop Comics)

COW SPECIAL, THE
Image Comics (Top Cow): Spring-Summer 2000; 2001 ($2.95)

1-Previews upcoming Top Cow projects; Yancy Butler photo-c 3.00
Vol. 2 #1-Witchblade-c; previews and interviews 3.00

COYOTE
Marvel Comics (Epic Comics): June, 1983 - No. 16, Mar, 1986

1-10,15: 7-10-Ditko-a 3.00
11-1st McFarlane-a. 1 2 3 4 5 7
12-14,16: 12-14-McFarlane-a. 14-Badger x-over. 16-Reagan c/app. 5.00
Coyote Collection Vol. 1 (2005, $14.99) reprints from Coyote #1-7 & Scorpio Rose #1,2 plus Rogers layout pages for unpublished #3; Englehart intro. 15.00
Coyote Collection Vol. 2 (2005, $12.99) reprints from Coyote #1-4 13.00
Coyote Collection Vol. 3 (2006, $12.99) reprints from Coyote #5-8 13.00
Coyote Collection Vol. 4 (2007, $14.99) reprints from Coyote #9-12 15.00
Coyote Collection Vol. 5 (2007, $12.99) reprints from Coyote #13-16 13.00

CRACKAJACK FUNNIES (Also see The Owl)
Dell Publishing Co.: June, 1938 - No. 43, Jan, 1942

1-Dan Dunn, Freckles, Myra North, Wash Tubbs, Apple Mary, The Nebbs, Don Winslow, Tom Mix, Buck Jones, Major Hoople, Clyde Beatty, Boots begin
181 362 543 1158 1979 2800
2 71 142 213 454 777 1100
3 53 106 159 334 567 800
4 42 84 126 265 445 625
5-Nude woman on cover 43 86 129 271 461 650
6-8,10: 8-Speed Bolton begins (1st app.) 39 78 117 231 378 525
9-(3/39)-Red Ryder strip-r begin by Harman; 1st app. in comics & 1st cover app.
161 322 483 1030 1765 2500
11-14 34 68 102 199 325 450
15-Tarzan text feature begins by Burroughs (9/39); not in #26,35
37 74 111 222 361 500
16-24: 18-Stratosphere Jim begins (1st app., 12/39). 23-Ellery Queen begins plus-c (1st comic book app., 5/40) 27 54 81 158 259 360
25-The Owl begins (1st app., 7/40); in new costume #26 by Frank Thomas (also see Popular Comics #72) 71 142 213 454 777 1100
26-30: 28-Part Owl-c 48 96 144 302 509 715
31-Owl covers begin, end #42 48 96 144 302 514 725
32-Origin Owl Girl 54 108 162 343 574 825
33-38: 36-Last Tarzan issue. 37-Cyclone & Midge begin (1st app.)
47 94 141 296 503 710
39-Andy Panda begins (intro/1st app., 9/41) 57 114 171 362 619 875
40-42: 42-Last Owl-c. 37 74 111 222 361 500
43-Terry & the Pirates-r 22 44 66 132 216 300

NOTE: **McWilliams** art in most issues.

CRACK COMICS (Crack Western No. 63 on)
Quality Comics Group: May, 1940 - No. 62, Sept, 1949

1-Origin & 1st app. The Black Condor by Lou Fine, Madame Fatal, Red Torpedo, Rock Bradden & The Space Legion; The Clock, Alias the Spider (by Gustavson), Wizard Wells, & Ned Brant begin; Powell-a; Note: Madame Fatal is a man dressed as a woman
465 930 1395 3395 5998 8600
2 219 438 657 1402 2401 3400
3 152 304 456 965 1658 2350
4 123 246 369 787 1344 1900

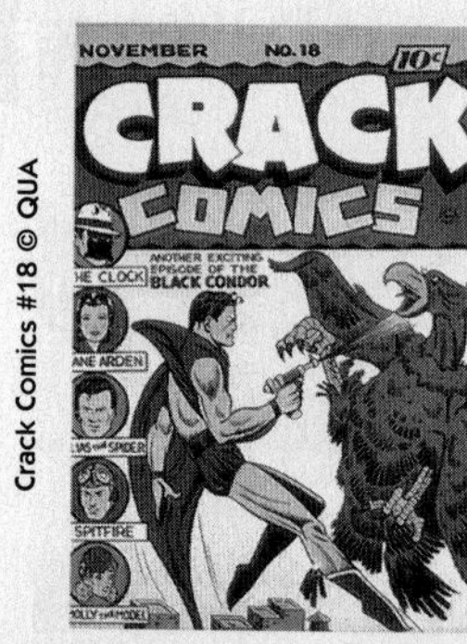

Crack Comics #18 © QUA

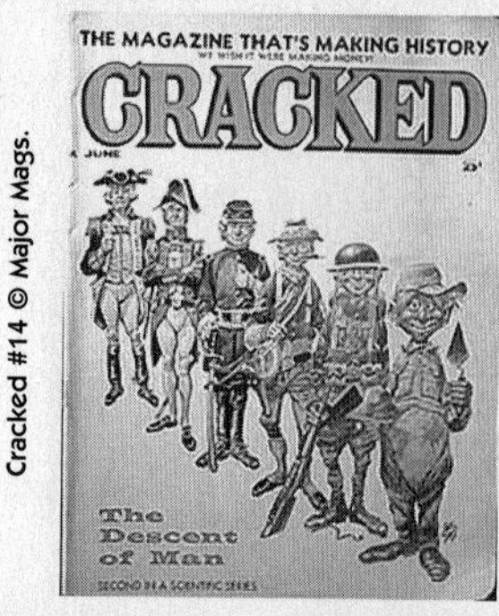

Cracked #14 © Major Mags.

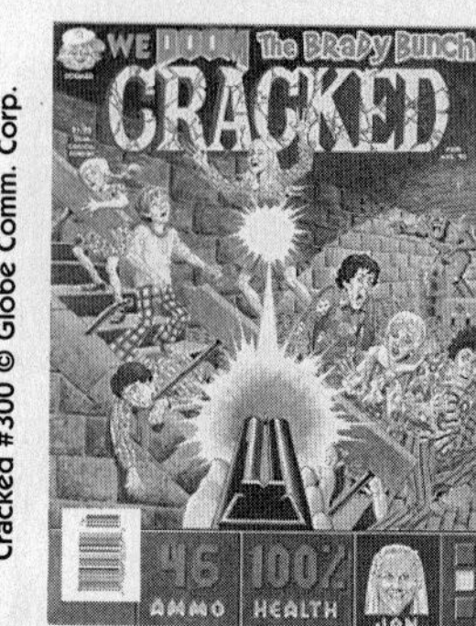

Cracked #300 © Globe Comm. Corp.

GD 2.0 VG 4.0 FN 6.0 VF 8.0 VF/NM 9.0 NM- 9.2

5-10: 5-Molly The Model begins. 10-Tor, the Magic Master begins
92 184 276 584 1005 1425
11-20: 13-1 pg. J. Cole-a. 15-1st app. Spitfire 81 162 243 514 887 1260
21-24: 23-Pen Miller begins; continued from National Comics #22. 24-Last Fine Black Condor
64 128 192 406 696 985
25,26: 26-Flag-c 48 96 144 302 514 725
27-(1/43)-Intro & origin Captain Triumph by Alfred Andriola (Kerry Drake artist)
& begin series 90 180 270 576 988 1400
28-30 41 82 123 256 428 600
31-39: 31-Last Black Condor 24 48 72 142 234 325
40-46 17 34 51 100 158 215
47-57,59,60-Capt. Triumph by Crandall 18 36 54 107 169 230
58,61,62-Last Captain Triumph 15 30 45 85 130 175

NOTE: *Black Condor by* **Fine**: *No. 1, 2, 5, 6, 8, 10-24; by* **Sultan**: *No. 3, 7; by* **Fugitani**: *No. 9.* **Cole** *a-34.* **Crandall** *a-61(unsigned); c-48, 49, 51-61.* **Guardineer** *a-17.* **Gustavson** *a-1, 2, 4, 7, 13, 17, 23.* **McWilliams** *a-15-27. Black Condor c-2, 4, 6, 8, 10, 12, 14, 16, 18, 20-26. Capt. Triumph c-27-62. The Clock c-1, 3, 5, 7, 9, 11, 13, 15, 17, 19.*

CRACK COMICS
Quality Comics: May 1940

1-Ashcan comic, not distributed to newsstands, only for in-house use. Cover art is the same as published version of Crack Comics #1with exception of text panel on bottom left of cover. A CGC certified 4.0 copy sold for $1,495 in 2005.

CRACKED (Magazine) (Satire) (Also see The 3-D Zone #19)
Major Magazines(#1-212)/Globe Communications(#213-346/American Media #347 on):
Feb-Mar, 1958 - No. 365, Nov, 2004

1-One pg. Williamson-a; Everett-c; Gunsmoke-s 16 32 48 117 239 360
2-1st Shut-Ups & Bonus Cut-Outs; Superman parody-c by Severin (his 1st cover on the title)
Frankenstein-s 10 20 30 68 119 170
3-5 8 16 24 52 86 120
6-10: 7-Reprints 1st 6 covers on-c. 8-Frankenstein-c. 10-Wolverton-a
6 12 18 41 66 90
11-12, 13(nn,3/60), 5 10 15 34 55 75
14-Kirby-a 6 12 18 41 66 90
15-17, 18(nn,2/61), 19,20 5 10 15 32 51 70
21-27(11/62), 27(No.28, 2/63; mis-#d), 29(5/63) 4 8 12 28 44 60
30-40(11/64): 37-Beatles and Superman cameos 4 8 12 24 37 50
41-45,47-56,59,60: 47,49,52-Munsters. 51-Beatles inside-c. 59-Laurel and Hardy photos
3 6 9 20 30 40
46,57,58: 46,58-Man From U.N.C.L.E. 46-Beatles. 57-Rolling Stones
4 8 12 22 34 45
61-80: 62-Beatles cameo. 69-Batman, Superman app. 70-(8/68) Elvis cameo.
71-Garrison's Gorillas; W.C. Fields photos 3 6 9 16 22 28
81-99: 99-Alfred E. Neuman on-c 3 6 9 14 19 24
100 3 6 9 18 27 35
101-119: 104-Godfather-c/s. 108-Archie Bunker-s. 112,119-Kung Fu (TV). 113-Tarzan-s.
115-MASH. 117-Cannon. 118-The Sting-c/s 2 4 6 10 14 18
120(12/74) Six Million Dollar Man-c/s; Ward-a 2 4 6 13 18 22
121,122,124-126,128-133,136-140: 121-American Graffiti. 122-Korak-c/s.
124,131-Godfather-c/s. 128-Capone-c. 129,131-Jaws. 132-Baretta-c/s. 133-Space 1999.
136-Laverne and Shirley/Fonz-c. 137-Travolta/Kotter-c/s. 138-Travolta/Laverne and Shirley/
Fonz-c. 139-Barney Miller-c/s. 140-King Kong-c/s; Fonz-s
2 4 6 10 14 18
123-Planet of the Apes-c/s; Six Million Dollar Man 2 4 6 13 18 22
127,134,135: 127-Star Trek-c/s; Ward-a. 134-Fonz-c/s; Starsky and Hutch. 135-Bionic Woman-
c/s; Ward-a 2 4 6 11 16 20
141,151-Charlie's Angels-c/s. 151-Frankenstein 2 4 6 11 16 20
142,143,150,152-155,157: 142-MASH-c/s. 143-Rocky-c/s; King Kong-s. 150-(5/78) Close
Encounters-c/s. 152-Close Enc./Star Wars-c/s. 153-Close Enc./Fonz-c/s. 154-Jaws II-c/s;
Star Wars-s. 155-Star Wars/Fonz-c 2 4 6 9 13 16
144,149,156,158-160: 144-Fonz/Happy Days-c. 149-Star Wars/Six Mil.$ Man-c/s.
156-Grease/Travolta-c. 158-Mork & Mindy. 159-Battlestar Galactica-c/s; MASH-s.
160-Superman-c/s 2 4 6 11 16 20
145,147-Both have insert postcards: 145-Fonz/Rocky/L&S-c/s. 147-Star Wars-s;
Farrah photo page (missing postcards-1/2 price) 3 6 9 14 20 26
146,148: 46-Star Wars-c/s with stickers insert (missing stickers-1/2 price). 148-Star Wars-c/s
with inside-c color poster 3 6 9 16 23 30
161,170-Ward-a: 161-Mork & Mindy-c/s. 170-Dukes of Hazzard-c/s
2 4 6 8 11 14
162,165-168,171,172,175-178,180-Ward-a: 162-Sherlock Holmes-s. 165-Dracula-c/s.
167-Mork-c/s. 168,175-MASH-c/s. 168-Mork-s. 172-Dukes of Hazzard/CHiPs-c/s.
176-Barney Miller-c/s 2 4 6 8 10 12
163,179:163-Postcard insert; Mork & Mindy-c/s. 179-Insult cards insert; Popeye,
Dukes of Hazzard-c/s 3 6 9 14 19 24
164,169,173,174: 164-Alien movie-c/s; Mork & Mindy-s. 169-Star Trek. 173,174-Star Wars-
Empire Strikes Back. 173-SW poster 2 4 6 9 13 16

GD 2.0 VG 4.0 FN 6.0 VF 8.0 VF/NM 9.0 NM- 9.2

181,182,185-191,193,194,196-198-most Ward-a: 182-MASH-c/s. 185-Dukes of Hazzard-c/s;
Jefferson-s. 187-Love Boat. 188-Fall Guy-s. 189-Fonz/Happy Days-c. 190,194-MASH-c/s.
191-Magnum P.I./Rocky-c; Magnum-s. 193-Knight Rider-s. 196-Dukes of Hazzard/Knight
Rider-c/s. 198-Jaws III-c/s; Fall Guy-s 1 2 3 5 7 9
183,184,192,195,199,200-Ward-a in all: 183-Superman-c/s. 184-Star Trek-c/s. 192-E.T.-c/s;
Rocky-s. 195-E.T.-c/s. 199-Jabba-c; Star Wars-s. 200-(12/83)
1 3 4 6 8 10
201,203,210-A-Team-c/s 6.00
202,204-206,211-224,226,227,230-233: 202-Knight Rider-s. 204-Magnum P.I.; A-Team-s.
206-Michael Jackson/Mr. T-c/s. 212-Prince-s; Cosby-s. 213-Monsters issue-c/s. 215-Hulk
Hogan/Mr. T-c/s. 216-Miami Vice-s; James Bond-s. 217-Rambo-s; Cosby-s; A-Team-s.
218-Rocky-c/s. 219-Arnold/Commando-c/s; Rocky-s; Godzilla. 220-Rocky-c/s.
221-Stephen King app. 223-Miami Vice-s. 224-Cosby-s. 226-29th Anniv.; Tarzan-s; Aliens-s;
Family Ties-s. 227-Cosby, Family Ties, Miami Vice-s. 230-Monkees-c/s; Elvis on-c;
232-Alf, Cheers, StarTrek-s. 233-Superman/James Bond-c/s; Robocop, Predator-s 5.00
207-209,225,234: 207-Michael Jackson-c/s. 208-Indiana Jones-c/s. 209-MichaelJackson/
Gremlins-c/s; Star Trek III-s. 225-Schwarzenegger/Stallone/G.I. Joe-c/s. 234-Don Martin-a
begins; Batman/Robocop/Clint Eastwood-c/s 6.00
228,229: 228-Star Trek-c/s; Alf, Pee Wee Herman-s. 229-Monsters issue-c/s; centerfold
with many superheroes 6.00
235,239,243,249: 235-1st Martin-c; Star Trek:TNG-s; Alf-s. 239-Beetlejuice-c/s; Mike Tyson-s.
243-X-Men and other heroes app. 249-Batman/Indiana Jones/Ghostbusters-c/s 6.00
236,244,245,248: 236-Madonna/Stallone-c/s; Twilight Zone-s. 244-Elvis-c/s; Martin-c.
245-Roger Rabbit-c/s. 248-Batman issue 6.00
237,238,240-242,246,247,250: 237-Robocop-s. 238-Rambo-c/s; Star Trek-s. 242-Dirty Harry-s,
Ward-a. 246-Alf-s; Star Trek-s., Ward-a. 247-Star Trek-s. 250-Batman/Ghostbusters-s 4.00
251-253,255,256,259,261-265,275-278,281,284,286-297,299: 252-Star Trek-s. 253-Back to
the Future-c/s. 255-TMNT-c/s. 256-TMNT-c/s; Batman, Bart Simpson on-c. 259-Die Hard II,
Robocop-s. 261-TMNT, Twin Peaks-s. 262-Rocky-c/s; Rocky Horror-s. 265-TMNT-s.
276-Aliens III, Batman-s. 277-Clinton-c. 284-Bart Simpson-c; 90210-s. 297-Van Damme-
s/photo-c. 299-Dumb & Dumber-c/s 4.00
254,257,266,267,272,280,282,285,298,300: 254-Back to the Future, Punisher-s; Wolverton-a,
Batman-s, Ward-a. 257-Batman, Simpsons-s; Spider-Man and other heroes app.
266-Terminator-c/s. 267-Toons-c/s. 272-Star Trek VI-s. 280-Swimsuit issue. 282-Cheers-c/s.
285-Jurassic Park-c/s. 298-Swimsuit issue; Martin-c. 300-(8/95) Brady Bunch-c/s 5.00
258,260,274,279,283: 258-Simpsons-c/s; Back to the Future-s. 260-Spider-Man-c/s;
Simpsons-s. 274-Batman-c/s. 279-Madonna-c/s. 283-Jurassic Park-c/s;
Wolverine app. inside back-c 5.00
301-305,307-365: 365-Freas-c 3.00
306-Toy Story-c/s 4.00
Biggest... (Winter, 1977) 2 4 6 13 18 22
Biggest, Greatest... nn('65) 5 10 15 30 48 65
Biggest, Greatest... 2('66/67) - #5('69/70) 3 6 9 20 30 40
Biggest, Greatest... 6('70) - #12(Wint. '77) 3 6 9 14 19 24
Biggest, Greatest...13(Fall '78) - #21(Fall/Wint. '86) 2 4 6 8 11 14
...Blockbuster 1(Sum '87), 2('88), 3(Sum. '89) 1 3 4 6 8 10
...Blockbuster 4 - 6(Sum. '92) 6.00
...Collectors' Edition 4 ('73; formerly ...Special) 2 4 6 13 18 22
5-9,10(10/75) 2 4 6 11 16 20
11-19,20(11/17) 2 4 6 8 11 14
21,22,23(5/78): 23-Ward-a 2 4 6 8 11 14
(#24-62,64 not numbered)
1978 (nn; July, Sept, Nov, Dec) (#24-27) 2 4 6 8 11 14
1979 (nn; May, July, Sept, Nov, Dec) (#28-33) 2 4 6 8 11 14
1980 (nn; Feb, May, July, Sept, Nov, Dec) (#34-39) 1 3 4 6 8 10
1981 (nn; Feb, May, July, Sept, Nov, Dec) (#40-45) 1 3 4 6 8 10
1982 (nn; Feb, May, July, Sept, Nov, Dec) (#46-51) 1 3 4 6 8 10
1983 (nn; Feb, May, Sept, Nov, Dec) (#52-56) 1 3 4 6 8 10
1984 (nn; Feb, May, July, Nov) (#57-60) 1 2 3 4 5 7
1985 (nn; Feb) (#61) 1 2 3 4 5 7
62(9/85), nn(#63,11/85), 64(12/85), 65-69, 70(4/87) 1 2 3 4 5 7
71,72,73(100 pgs., 1/88), 74-79, 80(9/89) 5.00
81-96, 97(two diff. issues), 98-115: 83-Elvis, Batman parodies 5.00
116('98)-Last issue? 6.00
...Digest 1(Fall, '86, 148 pgs.), 2(1/87) 1 2 3 6 8 10
...Digest 3-5 1 2 3 4 5 7
...Party Pack 1,2('88) - 4('90) 4.00
...Shut-Ups 1(2/72) 3 6 9 18 27 35
...Shut-Ups 2('72) becomes Cracked Spec. #3 3 6 9 14 19 24
...Special 3('73; formerly Cracked Shut-Ups; ...Collectors' Edition#4 on)
2 4 6 13 18 22
... Summer Special 1(Sum. '91), 2(Sum. '92)-Don Martin-a 4.00
... Summer Special 3(Sum. '93) - 8(Sum. '98) 3.00

Crack Western #69 © QUA

Crash Comics #1 © Tem Pub.

Crazy #3 © MAR

GD 2.0 | VG 4.0 | FN 6.0 | VF 8.0 | VF/NM 9.0 | NM- 9.2

... Super (Vol. 2, formerly Super Cracked) 5(Wint. '91/92) - 14(Wint.'97/98) 3.00
Extra Special... 1(Spr. '76) 2 4 6 11 16 20
Extra Special... 2(Spr./Sum. '77) 2 4 6 10 14 18
Extra Special... 3(Wint. '79) - 9(Wint. '86) 1 2 3 4 5 7
Giant... nn('65) 6 12 18 37 59 80
Giant... 2('66) - 5('69) 4 8 12 22 34 45
Giant...6('70) - 12('76) 3 6 9 17 25 32
Giant...nn(9/77, #13), nn(1/78, #14), nn(3/78, #15), nn(5/78, #16), nn(7/78, #17), nn(11/78, #18), nn(3/79, #19), nn(7/79, #20), nn(10/79, #21), nn(12/79, #22), nn(3/80, #23), nn(7/80, #24) 2 4 6 11 16 20
Giant...nn(10/80, #25), nn(12/80, #26), nn(3/81, #27), nn(7/81, #28), nn(10/81, #29), nn(12/81, #30), nn(7/82, #31), nn(10/82, #32), nn(12/82, #33), nn(7/83, #34), 2 4 6 8 11 14
Giant...nn(10/83, #35), nn(12/83, #36), nn(3/84, #37), nn(7/84, #38), nn(10/84, #39), nn(3/85, #40), nn(7/85, #41), nn(10/85, #42) 1 2 3 5 7 9
Giant...43(3/86) - 46(1/87), 47(Wint. '88), 48(Wint. '89) 1 2 3 4 5 7
King Sized... 1('67) 4 8 12 26 41 55
King Sized... 2('68) - 5('71) 3 6 9 18 27 35
King Sized... 6('72) - 11('77) 3 6 9 14 20 26
King Sized... 12(Fall '78) - 17(Sum. '83) 2 4 6 8 11 14
King Sized... 18-20 (Sum/'86) (#21,22 exist?) 1 3 4 6 8 10
Spaced Out... 1-4 ('93 - '94) 5.00
Super... 1('68) 4 8 12 26 41 55
Super... 2('69) - 6('73) 3 6 9 20 30 40
Super... 7('74), 8(Spr. '75) - 10(Spr. '77) 3 6 9 16 22 28
Super... 11(Sum. '78) - 16(Fall '81) 2 4 6 11 16 20
Super... 17(Spr. '82) - 22(Fall '83) 2 4 6 8 11 14
Super... 23(Sum. '84, mis-numbered as #24) 2 4 6 8 11 14
Super... 24(Fall '84, correctly numbered) 2 4 6 8 11 14
Super... 25(Wint. '85) - 32(Fall '86) 2 4 6 8 10 12
Super... (Vol. 2) 1('87, 100 pgs.)-Severin & Elder-a 1 3 4 6 8 10
Super... (Vol. 2) 2(Sum. '88), 3(Wint. '89), 4(exist?)(Becomes Cracked Super) 6.00

NOTE: ***Burgos*** *a-1-10.* ***Colan*** *a-257.* ***Davis*** *a-5, 11-17, 24, 40, 80; c-12-14, 16.* ***Elder*** *a-5, 6, 10-13; c-10.* ***Everett*** *a-1-10, 23-25, 61; c-1.* ***Heath*** *a-1-3, 6, 13, 14, 17, 110; c-6.* ***Jaffee*** *a-5, 6.* ***Don Martin*** *c-235, 244, 247, 259, 261, 264.* ***Morrow*** *a-8-10.* ***Reinman*** *a-1-4.* ***Severin*** *c/a-in most all issues.* ***Shores*** *a-3-7.* ***Torres*** *a-7-10.* ***Ward*** *a-22-24, 27, 35, 40, 120-193, 195, 197-205, 242, 244, 246, 247, 250, 252-257.* ***Williamson*** *a-1 (1 pg.).* ***Wolverton*** *a-10 (2 pgs.), Giant nn('65).* ***Wood*** *a-27, 35, 40. Alfred E. Neuman c-177, 200, 202. Batman c-234, 248, 249, 256, 274. Captain America c-256. Christmas c-234, 243. Spider-Man c-260. Star Trek c-127, 169, 207, 228. Star Wars c-145, 146, 148, 149, 152, 155, 173, 174, 199. Superman c-183, 233. #144, 146 have free full-color pre-glued stickers. #145, 147, 155, 163 have free full-color postcards. #123, 137, 154, 157 have free iron-ons.*

CRACKED MONSTER PARTY
Globe Communications: July, 1988 - No. 27, Wint. 1999/2000

1 2 4 6 10 14 18
2-10 2 4 6 8 10 12
11-26 1 2 3 4 5 7
27-Interview with a Vampire-c/s 2 4 6 8 10 12

CRACKED'S FOR MONSTERS ONLY
Major Magazines: Sept, 1969 - No. 9, Sept, 1969; June, 1972

1 5 10 15 30 48 65
2-9, nn(6/72) 3 6 9 20 30 40

CRACK WESTERN (Formerly Crack Comics; Jonesy No. 85 on)
Quality Comics Group: No. 63, Nov, 1949 - No. 84, May, 1953 (36 pgs., 63-68,74-on)

63(#1)-Ward-c; Two-Gun Lil (origin & 1st app.)(ends #84), Arizona Ames, his horse Thunder (with sidekick Spurs & his horse Calico), Frontier Marshal (ends #70), & Dead Canyon Days (ends #69) begin; Crandall-a 18 36 54 107 169 230
64,65: 64-Ward-c. Crandall-a in both. 15 30 45 83 124 165
66,68-Photo-c. 66-Arizona Ames becomes A. Raines (ends #84) 13 26 39 72 101 130
67-Randolph Scott photo-c; Crandall-a 14 28 42 80 115 150
69(52pgs.)-Crandall-a 13 26 39 72 101 130
70(52pgs.)-The Whip (origin & 1st app.) & his horse Diablo begin (ends #84); Crandall-a 13 26 39 72 101 130
71(52pgs.)-Frontier Marshal becomes Bob Allen F. Marshal (ends #84); Crandall-c/a 14 28 42 80 115 150
72(52pgs.)-Tim Holt photo-c 12 24 36 67 94 120
73(52pgs.)-Photo-c 10 20 30 58 79 100
74-76,78,79,81,83-Crandall-c. 83-Crandall-a(p) 11 22 33 62 86 110
77,80,82 8 16 24 44 57 70
84-Crandall-c/a 12 24 36 67 94 120

NOTE: ***Crandall*** *c-71p, 74-81, 83p(w/****Cuidera****-i).*

CRASH COMICS (Catman Comics No. 6 on)
Tem Publishing Co.: May, 1940 - No. 5, Nov, 1940

1-The Blue Streak, Strongman (origin), The Perfect Human, Shangra begin (1st app. of each); Kirby-a 326 652 978 2282 3991 5700
2-Simon & Kirby-a 168 336 504 1075 1838 2600
3,5-Simon & Kirby-a 142 284 426 909 1555 2200
4-Origin & 1st app. The Catman; S&K-a 343 686 1029 2400 4200 6000

NOTE: *Solar Legion by* ***Kirby*** *No. 1-5 (5 pgs. each). Strongman c-1-4. Catman c-5.*

CRASH DIVE (See Cinema Comics Herald)

CRASH METRO AND THE STAR SQUAD
Oni Press: May, 1999 ($2.95, B&W, one-shot)

1-Allred-s/Ontiveros-a 3.00

CRASH RYAN (Also see Dark Horse Presents #44)
Marvel Comics (Epic): Oct, 1984 - No. 4, Jan, 1985 (Baxter paper, lim. series)

1-4 3.00

CRAZY (Also see This Magazine is Crazy)
Atlas Comics (CSI): Dec, 1953 - No. 7, July, 1954

1-Everett-c/a 31 62 93 186 303 420
2 21 42 63 122 199 275
3-7: 4-I Love Lucy satire. 5-Satire on censorship 18 36 54 105 165 225

NOTE: ***Ayers*** *a-5.* ***Berg*** *a-1, 2.* ***Burgos*** *c-5, 6.* ***Drucker*** *a-6.* ***Everett*** *a-1-4.* ***Al Hartley*** *a-4.* ***Heath*** *a-3, 7; c-7.* ***Maneely*** *a-1-7, c-3, 4.* ***Post*** *a-3-6. Funny monster c-1-4.*

CRAZY (Satire)
Marvel Comics Group: Feb, 1973 - No. 3, June, 1973

1-Not Brand Echh-r; Beatles cameo (r) 3 6 9 16 23 30
2,3-Not Brand Echh-r; Kirby-a 2 4 6 10 16 20

CRAZY MAGAZINE (Satire)
Oct, 1973 - No. 94, Apr, 1983 (40-90¢, B&W magazine)
Marvel Comics: (#1, 44 pgs; #2-90, reg. issues, 52 pgs; #92-95, 68 pgs)'

1-Wolverton(1 pg.), Bode-a; 3 pg. photo story of Neal Adams & Dick Giordano; Harlan Ellison story; TV Kung Fu sty. 5 10 15 30 48 65
2-"Live & Let Die" c/s; 8pgs; Adams/Buscema-a; McCloud w5 pgs. Adams-a; Kurtzman's "Hey Look" 2 pg.-r 3 6 9 20 30 40
3-5: 3-"High Plains Drifter" w/Clint Eastwood c/s; Waltons app; Drucker, Reese-a. 4-Shaft-c/s; Ploog-a; Nixon 3 pg. app; Freas-a. 5-Michael Crichton's "Westworld" c/s; Nixon app. 3 6 9 17 25 32
6,7,18: 6-Exorcist c/s; Nixon app. 7-TV's Kung Fu c/s; Nixon app.; Ploog & Freas-a. 18-Six Million Dollar Man/Bionic Woman c/s; Welcome Back Kotter story 3 6 9 16 22 28
8-10: 8-Serpico c/s; Casper parody; TV's Police Story. 9-Joker cameo; Chinatown story; Eisner s/a begins; Has 1st 8 covers on-c. 10-Playboy Bunny-c; M. Severin-a; Lee Marrs-a begins; "Deathwish" story 3 6 9 14 20 26
11-17,19: 11-Towering Inferno. 12-Rhoda. 13-"Tommy" the Who Rock Opera. 14-Mandingo. 15-Jaws story. 16-Santa/Xmas-c; "Good Times" TV story; Jaws. 17-Bicentennial issue; Baretta; Woody Allen. 19-King Kong c/s; Reagan, J. Carter, Howard the Duck cameos, "Laverne & Shirley" 2 4 6 11 16 20
20,24,27: 20-Bicentennial-c; Space 1999 sty; Superheroes song sheet, 4pgs. 24-Charlie's Angels. 27-Charlie's Angels/Travolta/Fonz-c; Bionic Woman sty 3 6 9 14 19 24
21-23,25,26,28-30: 21-Starsky & Hutch. 22-Mount Rushmore/J. Carter-c; TV's Barney Miller; Superheroes spoof. 23-Santa/Xmas-c; "Happy Days" sty; "Omen" sty. 25-J. Carter-c/s; Grandenetti-a begins; TV's Alice; Logan's Run. 26-TV Stars-c; Mary Hartman, King Kong. 28-Donny & Marie Osmond-c/s; Marathon Man. 29-Travolta/Kotter-c; "One Day at a Time", Gong Show. 30-1977, 84 pgs. w/bonus; Jaws, Baretta, King Kong, Happy Days 2 4 6 9 12 15
31,33-35,38,40: 31-"Rocky"-c/s; TV game shows. 33-Peter Benchley's "Deep". 34-J. Carter-c; TV's "Fish". 35-Xmas-c with Fonz/Six Million Dollar Man/Wonder Woman/Darth Vader/ Travolta, TV's "Mash" & "Family Matters". 38-Close Encounters of the Third Kind-c/s. 40-"Three's Company-c/s 1 3 4 6 8 11
32-Star Wars/Darth Vader-c/s; "Black Sunday" 3 6 9 14 19 24
36,42,47,49: 36-Farrah Fawcett/Six Million Dollar Man-c; TV's Nancy Drew & Hardy Boys; 1st app. Howard The Duck in Crazy, 2 pgs. 42-84 pgs. w/bonus; TV Hulk/Spider-Man-c; Mash, Gong Show, One Day at a Time, Disco, Alice. 47-Battlestar Galactica xmas-c; movie "Foul Play". 49-1979, 84 pgs. w/bonus; Mork & Mindy-c; Jaws, Saturday Night Fever, Three's Company 2 4 6 9 12 15
37-1978, 84 pgs. w/bonus. Darth Vader-c; Barney Miller, Laverne & Shirley, Good Times, Rocky, Donny & Marie Osmond, Bionic Woman 2 4 6 13 18 22
39,44: 39-Saturday Night Fever-c/s. 44-"Grease"-c w/Travolta/O. Newton-John 2 4 6 11 16 20
41-Kiss-c & 1pg. photos; Disaster movies, TV's "Family", Annie Hall 4 8 12 28 44 60
43,45,46,48,51: 43-Jaws-c; Saturday Night Fever. 43-E.C. swipe from Mad #131. 45-Travolta/O. Newton-John/J. Carter-c; Eight is Enough. 46-TV Hulk-c/s; Punk Rock. 48-"Wiz"-c, Battlestar Galactica-s. 51-Grease/Mork & Mindy/D&M Osmond-c, Mork &

Crazy #54 © MAR

Crazyman #3 © Continuity

The Creeper by Steve Ditko HC © DC

GD 2.0 | VG 4.0 | FN 6.0 | VF 8.0 | VF/NM 9.0 | NM- 9.2

Mindy-sty. "Boys from Brazil" 1 3 4 6 8 11

50,58: 50-Superman movie-c/sty, Playboy Mag., TV Hulk, Fonz; Howard the Duck, 1 pg. 58-1980, 84 pgs. w/32 pg. color comic bonus insert-Full reprint of Crazy Comic #1, Battlestar Galactica, Charlie's Angels, Starsky & Hutch 2 4 6 11 16 20

52,59,60,64: 52-1979, 84 pgs. w/bonus. Marlon Brando-c; TV Hulk, Grease. Kiss, 1 pg. photos. 59-Santa Ptd-c by Larkin; "Alien", "Moonraker", Rocky-2, Howard the Duck, 1 pg. 60-Star Trek w/Muppets-c; Star Trek sty; 1st app/origin Teen Hulk; Severin-a. 64-84 pgs. w/bonus Monopoly game satire. "Empire Strikes Back", 8 pgs., One Day at a Time 2 4 6 11 16 20

53,54,65,67-70: 53-"Animal House"-c/sty; TV's "Vegas", Howard the Duck, 1 pg. 54-Love at First Bite-c/sty, Fantasy Island sty, Howard the Duck 1 pg. 65-(Has #66 on-c, Aug/'80). "Black Hole" w/Janson-a; Kirby,Wood/Severin-a(r), 5 pgs. Howard the Duck, 3 pgs.; Broderick-a; Buck Rogers, Mr. Rogers. 67-84 pgs. w/bonus; TV's Kung Fu, Exorcist; Ploog-a(r). 68-American Gigolo, Dukes of Hazzard, Teen Hulk; Howard the Duck, 3 pgs. Broderick-a; Monster sty/5 pg. Ditko-a(r). 69-Obnoxio the Clown-c/sty; Stephen King's "Shining", Teen Hulk, Richie Rich, Howard the Duck, 3pgs; Broderick-a. 70-84 pgs. Towering Inferno, Daytime TV; Trina Robbins-a 1 3 4 6 8 10

55-57,61,63: 55-84 pgs. w/bonus; Love Boat, Mork & Mindy, Fonz, TV Hulk. 56-Mork/Rocky/ J. Carter-c; China Syndrome. 57-TV Hulk with Miss Piggy-c, Dracula, Taxi, Muppets. 61-1980, 84 pgs. Adams-a(r), McCloud, Pro wrestling, Casper, TV's Police Story. 63-Apocalypse Now-Coppola's cult movie; 3rd app. Teen Hulk, Howard the Duck, 3 pgs. 2 4 6 8 11 14

62-Kiss-c & 2 pg. app; Quincy, 2nd app. Teen Hulk 4 8 12 24 37 50

66-Sept/'80, Empire Strikes Back-c/sty; Teen Hulk by Severin, Howard the Duck, 3pgs. by Broderick 2 4 6 10 14 18

71,72,75-77,79: 71-Blues Brothers parody, Teen Hulk, Superheroes parody, WKRP in Cincinnati, Howard the Duck, 3pgs. by Broderick. 72-Jackie Gleason/Smokey & the Bandit II-c/sty, Shogun, Teen Hulk. Howard the Duck, 3pgs. by Broderick. 75-Flash Gordon movie c/sty; Teen Hulk, Cat in the Hat, Howard the Duck 3pgs. by Broderick. 76-84 pgs. w/bonus; Monster-sty w/ Crandall-a(r), Monster-stys(2) w/Kirby-a(r), 5pgs. ea; Mash, TV Hulk, Chinatown. 77-Popeye movie/R. Williams-c/sty; Teen Hulk, Love Boat, Howard the Duck 3 pgs. 79-84 pgs. w/bonus color stickers; has new material; "9 to 5" w/Dolly Parton, Teen Hulk, Magnum P.I., Monster-sty w/5pgs, Ditko-a(r), "Rat" w/Sutton-a(r), Everett-a, 4 pgs.(r) 1 3 4 6 8 10

73,74,78,80: 73-84 pgs. w/bonus Hulk/Spiderman Finger Puppets-c & bonus; "Live & Let Die, Jaws, Fantasy Island. 74-Dallas/"Who Shot J.R."-c/sty; Elephant Man, Howard the Duck 3pgs. by Broderick. 78-Clint Eastwood-c/sty; Teen Hulk, Superheroes parody, Lou Grant. 80-Star Wars, 2 pg. app; "Howling", TV's "Greatest American Hero" 2 4 6 8 11 14

81,84,86,87,89: 81-.Superman Movie II-c/sty; Wolverine cameo, Mash, Teen Hulk. 84-American Werewolf in London, Johnny Carson app; Teen Hulk. 86-Time Bandits-c/sty; Private Benjamin. 87-Rubix Cube-c; Hill Street Blues, "Ragtime", Origin Obnoxio the Clown; Teen Hulk. 89-Burt Reynolds "Sharkey's Machine", Teen Hulk 1 3 4 6 8 10

82-X-Men-c w/new Byrne-a, 84 pgs. w/new material; Fantasy Island, Teen Hulk, "For Your Eyes Only", Spiderman/Human Torch-r by Kirby/Ditko; Sutton-a(r); Rogers-a; Hunchback of Notre Dame, 5 pgs. 2 4 6 11 16 20

83-Raiders of the Lost Ark-c/sty; Hart to Hart; Reese-a; Teen Hulk 2 4 6 9 13 20

85,88: 85-84 pgs; Escape from New York, Teen Hulk; Kirby-a(r), 5 pgs, Poseidon Adventure, Flintstones, Sesame Street. 88-84 pgs. w/bonus Dr. Strange Game; some new material; Jeffersons, X-Men/Wolverine, 10 pgs.; Byrne-a; Apocalypse Now, Teen Hulk 1 3 4 6 8 11

90-94: 90-Conan-c/sty; M. Severin-a; Teen Hulk. 91-84 pgs, some new material; Bladerunner-c/sty, "Deathwish-II, Teen Hulk, Black Knight, 10 pgs.-'50s-r w/Maneely-a. 92-Wrath of Khan Star Trek-c/sty; Joanie & Chachi, Teen Hulk. 93-"E.T."-c/sty, Teen Hulk, Archie Bunkers Place, Dr. Doom Game. 94-Poltergeist, Smurfs, Teen Hulk, Casper, Avengers parody-8pgs. Adams-a 2 4 6 10 14 18

Crazy Summer Special #1 (Sum, '75, 100 pgs.)-Nixon, TV Kung Fu, Babe Ruth, Joe Namath, Waltons, McCloud, Chariots of the Gods 3 6 9 14 19 24

NOTE: ***N. Adams*** *a-2, 61r, 94p.* ***Austin*** *a-82i.* ***Buscema*** *a-2, 82.* ***Byrne*** *c-82p.* ***Nick Cardy*** *c-7, 8, 10, 12-16, Super Special 1.* ***Crandall*** *a-76r.* ***Ditko*** *a-68r, 79r, 82r.* ***Drucker*** *a-3.* ***Eisner*** *a-9-16.* ***Kelly Freas*** *c-1-6, 9, 11; a-7.* ***Kirby/Wood*** *a-66r.* ***Ploog*** *a-1, 4, 7, 67r, 73r.* ***Rogers*** *a-82.* ***Sparling*** *a-92.* ***Wood*** *a-65r. Howard the Duck in 36, 50, 51, 53, 54, 59, 63, 65, 66, 68, 69, 71, 72, 74, 75, 77. Hulk in 46, c-42, 46, 57, 73. Star Wars in 32, 66; c-37.*

CRAZYMAN
Continuity Comics: Apr, 1992 - No. 3, 1992 ($2.50, high quality paper)

1-($3.95, 52 pgs.)-Embossed-c; N. Adams part-i 4.00
2,3 ($2.50): 2-N. Adams/Bolland-c 3.00

CRAZYMAN
Continuity Comics: V2#1, 5/93 - No. 4, 1/94 ($2.50, high quality paper)

V2#1-4: 1-Entire book is die-cut. 2-(12/93)-Adams-c(p) & part scripts. 3-(12/93). 4-Indicia says #3, Jan. 1993 3.00

GD 2.0 | VG 4.0 | FN 6.0 | VF 8.0 | VF/NM 9.0 | NM- 9.2

CRAZY, MAN, CRAZY (Magazine) (Becomes This Magazine is...?)
(Formerly From Here to Insanity)
Humor Magazines (Charlton): V2#1, Dec, 1955 - V2#2, June, 1956

V2#1,V2#2-Satire; Wolverton-a, 3 pgs. 15 30 45 85 130 175

CREATURE, THE (See Movie Classics)

CREATURE COMMANDOS (See Weird War Tales #93 for 1st app.)
DC Comics: May, 2000 - No. 8, Dec, 2000 ($2.50, limited series)

1-8: Truman-s/Eaton-a 3.00

CREATURES OF THE ID
Caliber Press: 1990 ($2.95, B&W)

1-Frank Einstein (Madman) app.; Allred-a 3 6 9 16 23 30

CREATURES OF THE NIGHT
Dark Horse Books: Nov, 2004 ($12.95, hardcover graphic novel)

HC-Neil Gaiman-s/Michael Zulli-a/c 13.00

CREATURES ON THE LOOSE (Formerly Tower of Shadows No. 1-9)(See Kull)
Marvel Comics: No. 10, March, 1971 - No. 37, Sept, 1975 (New-a & reprints)

10-(15¢)-1st full app. King Kull; see Kull the Conqueror; Wrightson-a 8 16 24 52 86 120
11-15: 13-Last 15¢ issue 3 6 9 18 27 35
16-Origin Warrior of Mars (begins, ends #21) 3 6 9 14 19 24
17-20 2 4 6 9 13 16
21-Steranko-c 3 6 9 16 23 30
22-Steranko-c; Thongor stories begin 3 6 9 17 25 32
23-29-Thongor-c/stories 1 3 4 6 8 10
30-Manwolf begins 3 6 9 18 27 35
31-33 2 4 6 9 13 16
34-37 2 4 6 8 10 12

NOTE: ***Crandall*** *a-13.* ***Ditko*** *r-15, 17, 18, 20, 22, 24, 27, 28.* ***Everett*** *a-16i(new).* ***Matt Fox*** *r-21i.* ***Howard*** *a-26i.* ***Gil Kane*** *a-16p, 17p, 19i; c-16, 17, 19, 20, 25, 29, 33p, 35p, 36p.* ***Kirby*** *a-10-15r, 16(2)r, 17r, 19r.* ***Morrow*** *a-20, 21.* ***Perez*** *a-33-37; c-34p.* ***Shores a-11. innott*** *r-21.* ***Sutton*** *c-10.* ***Tuska*** *a-30-32p.*

CREECH, THE
Image Comics: Oct, 1997 - No. 3, Dec, 1997 ($1.95/$2.50, limited series)

1-3: 1-Capullo-s/c/a(p) 3.00
TPB (1999, $9.95) r/#1-3, McFarlane intro. 10.00
Out for Blood 1-3 (7/01 - No. 3, 11/01; $4.95) Capullo-s/c/a 5.00

CREED
Hall of Heroes Comics: Dec, 1994 - No. 2, Jan, 1995 ($2.50, B&W)

1 2 4 6 9 12 15
2 2 4 6 8 10 12

CREED
Lightning Comics: June, 1995 - No. 3 ($2.75/$3.00, B&W/color)

1-($2.75) 4.00
1-($3.00, color) 5.00
1-($9.95)-Commemorative Edition 10.00
1-TwinVariant Edition (1250? print run) 10.00
1-Special Edition; polybagged w/certificate 4.00
1 Gold Collectors Edition; polybagged w/certificate 3.00
2,3-($3.00, color)-Butt Naked Edition & regular-c 3.00
3-($9.95)-Commemorative Edition; polybagged w/certificate & card 10.00

CREED: CRANIAL DISORDER
Lightning Comics: Oct, 1996 ($3.00, limited series)

1-3-Two covers 3.00
1-($5.95)-Platinum Edition 6.00
2,3-($9.95)Ltd.l Edition 10.00

CREED/TEENAGE MUTANT NINJA TURTLES
Lightning Comics: May, 1996 ($3.00, one-shot)

1-Kaniuga-a(p)/scripts; Laird-c; variant-c exists 3.00
1-($9.95)-Platinum Edition 10.00
1-Special Edition; polybagged w/certificate 5.00

CREEPER BY STEVE DITKO, THE
DC Comics: 2010 ($39.99, hardcover with dustjacket)

HC-Reprints Showcase #73, Beware the Creeper #1-6, First Issue Special #7 and apps. in World's Finest #249-255 and Cancelled Comic Cavalcade #2; intro. by Steve Niles 40.00

CREEPER, THE (See Beware... , Showcase #73 & 1st Issue Special #7)
DC Comics: Dec, 1997 - No. 11; #1,000,000 Nov, 1998 ($2.50)

1-11-Kaminski-s/Martinbrough-a(p). 7,8-Joker-c/app. 3.00
#1,000,000 (11/98) 853rd Century x-over 3.00

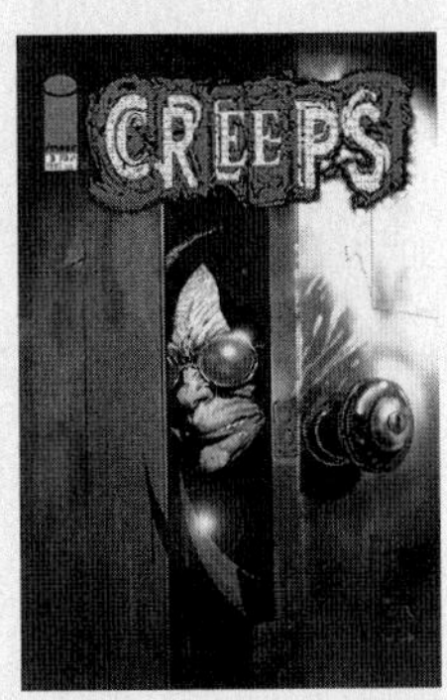

Creeps #3 © Mishkin & Mandrake

Creepy #120 © WP

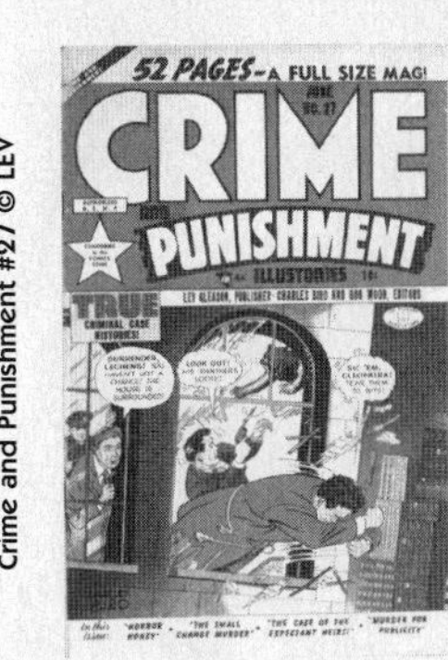

Crime and Punishment #27 © LEV

GD 2.0 | VG 4.0 | FN 6.0 | VF 8.0 | VF/NM 9.0 | NM- 9.2

CREEPER, THE (See DCU Brave New World)
DC Comics: Oct, 2006 - No. 6, Mar, 2007 ($2.99, limited series)

1-6-Niles-s/Justiniano-a/c; Jack Ryder becomes the Creeper. 2-6-Batman app. 3.00
... - Welcome to Creepsville TPB ('07, $19.99) r/#1-6 & story from DCU Brave New World 20.00

CREEPS
Image Comics: Oct, 2001 - No. 4, May, 2002 ($2.95)

1-4-Mandrake-a/Mishkin-s 3.00

CREEPSHOW
Plume/New American Library Pub.: July, 1982 (softcover graphic novel)

1st edition-nn-(68 pgs.) Kamen-c/Wrightson-a; screenplay by Stephen King for the George Romero movie 4 8 12 28 44 60
2nd-7th printings 3 6 9 18 27 35

CREEPSVILLE
Laughing Reindeer Press: V2#1, Winter, 1995 ($4.95)

V2#1-Comics w/text 5.00

CREEPY (See Warren Presents)
Warren Publishing Co./Harris Publ. #146: 1964 - No. 145, Feb, 1983; No. 146, 1985 (B&W, magazine)

1-Frazetta-a (his last story in comics?); Jack Davis-c; 1st Warren all comics magazine; 1st app. Uncle Creepy 12 24 36 84 157 230
2-Frazetta-c & 1 pg. strip 8 16 24 52 86 120
3-8,11-13,15-17: 3-7,9-11,15-17-Frazetta-c. 7-Frazetta 1 pg. strip. 15,16-Adams-a. 16-Jeff Jones-a 5 10 15 35 55 75
9-Creepy fan club sketch by Wrightson (1st published-a); has 1/2 pg. anti-smoking strip by Frazetta; Frazetta-c; 1st Wood and Ditko art on this title; Toth-a (low print) 7 14 21 50 83 115
10-Brunner fan club sketch (1st published work) 6 12 18 37 59 80
14-Neal Adams 1st Warren work 6 12 18 37 59 80
18-28,30,31: 27-Frazetta-c 4 8 12 26 41 55
29,34: 29-Jones-a 4 8 12 28 44 60
32-(scarce) Frazetta-c; Harlan Ellison sty 6 12 18 43 69 95
33,35,37,39,40,42-47,49: 35-Hitler/Nazi-s. 39-1st Uncle Creepy solo-s, Cousin Eerie app.; early Brunner-a. 42-1st San Julian-c. 44-1st Ploog-a. 46-Corben-a 4 8 12 22 34 45
36-(11/70)1st Corben art at Warren 4 8 12 28 44 60
38,41-(scarce): 38-1st Kelly-c. 41-Corben-a 5 10 15 32 51 70
48,55,65-(1972, 1973, 1974 Annuals) #55 & 65 contain an 8 pg. slick comic insert. 48-(84 pgs.). 55-Color poster bonus (1/2 price if missing). 65-(100 pgs.) Summer Giant 4 8 12 28 44 60
50-Vampirella/Eerie/Creepy-c 5 10 15 32 51 70
51,54,56-61,64: All contain an 8 pg. slick comic insert in middle. 59-Xmas horror. 54,64-Chaykin-a 4 8 12 24 37 50
52,53,66,71,72,75,76,78-80: 71-All Bermejo-a; Space & Time issue. 72-Gual-a. 78-Fantasy issue. 79,80-Monsters issue 3 6 9 18 27 35
62,63-1st & 2nd full Wrightson story art; Corben-a; 8 pg. color comic insert 4 8 12 24 37 50
67,68,73 3 6 9 20 30 40
69,70-Edgar Allan Poe issues; Corben-a 3 6 9 19 29 38
74,77: 74-All Crandell-a. 77-Xmas Horror issue; Corben-a,Wrightson-a 4 8 12 22 34 45
81,84,85,88-90,92-94,96-99,102,104-112,114-118,120,122-130: 84,93-Sports issue. 85,97,102-Monster issue. 89-All war issue; Nino-a. 94-Weird Children issue. 96,109-Aliens issue. 99-Disasters. 103-Corben-a. 104-Robots issue. 106-Sword & Sorcery.107-Sci-fi. 116-End of Man. 125-Xmas Horror 2 4 6 9 13 16
82,100,101: 82-All Maroto issue. 100-(8/78) Anniversary. 101-Corben-a 3 6 9 14 19 24
83,95-Wrightson-a. 83-Corben-a. 95-Gorilla/Apes. 2 4 6 11 16 20
86,87,91,103-Wrightson-a. 86-Xmas Horror 2 4 6 11 16 20
113-All Wrightson-r issue 3 6 9 18 27 35
119,121: 119-All Nino issue.121-All Severin-r issue 2 4 6 11 16 20
131,133-136,138,140: 135-Xmas issue 2 4 6 11 16 20
132,137,139: 132-Corben. 137-All Williamson-r issue. 139-All Toth-r issue 3 6 9 14 19 24
141,143,144 (low dist.): 144-Giant, $2.25; Frazetta-c 3 6 9 16 22 28
142,145 (low dist.): 142-(10/82, 100 pgs.) All Torres issue. 145-(2/83) last Warren issue 3 6 9 17 25 32
146 ($2.95)-1st from Harris; resurrection issue 6 12 18 43 69 95
Year Book '68-'70: '70-Neal Adams, Ditko-a(r) 5 10 15 32 51 70
Annual 1971,1972 5 10 15 30 48 65
1993 Fearbook ($3.95)-Harris Publ.; Brereton-c; Vampirella by Busiek-s/Art Adams-a; David-s; Paquette-a 4 8 12 24 37 50
... Archives - Volume One HC (Dark Horse, 8/08, $49.95) r/#1-5; Jon B. Cooke intro. 50.00
... Archives - Volume Two HC (Dark Horse, 12/08, $49.95) r/#6-10; Roy Thomas intro. 50.00
... Archives - Volume Three HC (Dark Horse, 6/09, $49.95) r/#11-15 50.00
...:The Classic Years TPB (Harris/Dark Horse, '91, $12.95) Kaluta-c; art by Frazetta,Torres, Crandall, Ditko, Morrow, Williamson, Wrightson 25.00

NOTE: *All issues contain many good artists works:* ***Neal Adams, Brunner, Corben, Craig (Taycee), Crandall, Ditko, Evans, Frazetta, Heath, Jeff Jones, Krenkel, McWilliams, Morrow, Nino, Orlando, Ploog, Severin, Torres, Toth, Williamson, Wood, & Wrightson****; covers by* ***Crandall, Davis, Frazetta, Morrow, San Julian, Todd/Bode****; Otto Binder's "Adam Link" stories in No. 2, 4, 6, 8, 9, 12, 13, 15 with* ***Orlando*** *art.* ***Frazetta*** *c-2-7, 9-11, 15-17, 27, 32, 83r, 89r, 91r.* ***E.A. Poe*** *adaptations in 66, 69, 70.*

CREEPY (Mini-series)
Harris Comics/Dark Horse: 1992 - Book 4, 1992 (48 pgs, B&W, squarebound)

Book 1-4: Brereton painted-c on all. Stories and art by various incl. David (all), Busiek(2), Infantino(2), Guice(3), Colan(1) 2 4 6 8 10 12

CREEPY
Dark Horse Comics: July, 2009 - Present ($4.99, 48 pgs, B&W, quarterly)

1-3: 1-Powell-c; art by Wrightson, Toth, Alexander 5.00

CREEPY THINGS
Charlton Comics: July, 1975 - No. 6, June, 1976

1-Sutton-c/a 2 4 6 13 18 22
2-6: Ditko-a in 3,5. Sutton c-3,4. 6-Zeck-c 2 4 6 8 10 12
Modern Comics Reprint 2-6(1977) 4.00

NOTE: ***Larson*** *a-2,6.* ***Sutton*** *a-1,2,4,6.* ***Zeck*** *a-2.*

CREW, THE
Marvel Comics: July, 2003 - No. 7, Jan, 2004 ($2.50)

1-7-Priest-s/Bennett-a; James Rhodes (War Machine) app. 3.00

CRIME AND JUSTICE (Badge Of Justice #22 on; Rookie Cop? No. 27 on)
Capitol Stories/Charlton Comics: March, 1951 - No. 21, Nov, 1954; No. 23, Mar, 1955 - No. 26, Sept, 1955 (No #22)

1 36 72 108 211 343 475
2 15 30 45 90 140 190
3-8,10-13: 6-Negligee panels 14 28 42 82 121 160
9-Classic story "Comics Vs. Crime" 27 54 81 158 259 360
14-Color illos in **POP**; gory story of man who beheads women 22 44 66 132 216 300
15-17,19-21,23,24: 15-Negligee panels. 23-Rookie Cop (1st app.) 11 22 33 62 86 110
18-Ditko-a 26 52 78 154 252 350
25,26: (scarce) 15 30 45 88 137 185

NOTE: ***Alascia*** *c-20.* ***Ayers*** *a-17.* ***Shuster*** *a-19-21; c-19. Bondage c-11, 12.*

CRIME AND PUNISHMENT (Title inspired by 1935 film)
Lev Gleason Publications: April, 1948 - No. 74, Aug, 1955

1-Mr. Crime app. on-c 39 78 117 231 378 525
2-Narrator, Officer Common Sense (a ghost) begins, ends #27? (see Crime Does Not Pay #41) 20 40 60 114 182 252
3-(6/48)-Used in **SOTI**, pg. 112; contains Biro & Gleason self censorship code of 12 listed restrictions 21 42 63 126 206 285
4,5 15 30 45 90 140 190
6-10 14 28 42 80 115 150
11-20 12 24 36 69 97 125
21-30 11 22 33 60 83 105
31-38,40-44,46: 46-One pg. Frazetta-a 10 20 30 54 72 90
39-Drug mention story "The Five Dopes" 15 30 45 83 124 165
45- "Hophead Killer" drug story 15 30 45 83 124 165
47-57,60-65,70-74: 9 18 27 52 69 85
58-Used in **POP**, pg. 79 10 20 30 58 79 100
59-Used in **SOTI**, illo "What comic-book America stands for" 34 68 102 199 325 450
66-Toth-c/a(4); 3-D effect issue (3/54); 1st "Deep Dimension" process 40 80 120 246 411 575
67- "Monkey on His Back" heroin story; 3-D effect issue 39 78 117 231 378 525
68-3-D effect issue; Toth-c (7/54) 32 64 96 188 307 425
69- "The Hot Rod Gang" dope crazy kids 15 30 45 83 124 165

NOTE: ***Belfi*** *a- 2, 3, 5.* ***Biro*** *c-most.* ***Al Borth*** *a-9, 35.* ***Cooper*** *a-9.* ***Joe Certa*** *a-8.* ***Tony Dipreta*** *a-3, 5, 15, 34.* ***Everett*** *a-31.* ***Bob Fujitani (Fuje)*** *a-2-20, 26, 27.* ***Joseph Gaguardi*** *a-15, 18, 20.* ***Fred Guardineer*** *a-2-5, 10-12, 14, 15, 17, 18, 20, 26-28, 32, 34, 35, 38-44, 51, 54.* ***Jack Keller*** *a-18.* ***Kinstler*** *c-69.* ***Martinott*** *a-13.* ***Al McWilliams*** *a-36, 41, 48, 49.* ***William Overgard*** *a-36.* ***Dick Rockwell*** *a-35, 51.* ***Robert Q. Sale*** *a-43.* ***George Tuska*** *a-28, 30, 51, 64, 70. Painted-c-31.*

CRIME AND PUNISHMENT: MARSHALL LAW TAKES MANHATTAN
Marvel Comics (Epic Comics): 1989 ($4.95, 52 pgs., direct sales only, mature)

nn-Graphic album featuring Marshall Law 5.00

Crime Clinic #5 © Z-D

Crime Detective Comics #6 © HILL

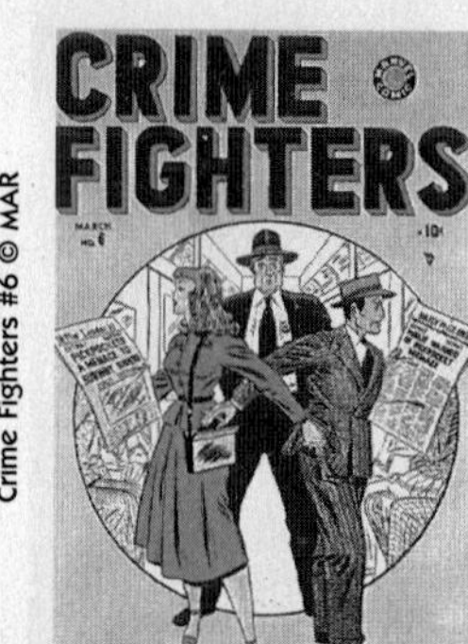

Crime Fighters #6 © MAR

CRIME BIBLE: THE FIVE LESSONS (Aftermath of DC's 52 series)
DC Comics: Dec, 2007 - No. 5, Apr, 2008 ($2.99, limited series)

	GD 2.0	VG 4.0	FN 6.0	VF 8.0	VF/NM 9.0	NM- 9.2
1-5-Rucka-s; The Question (Renee Montoya) app. 3-Batwoman app.						3.00
The Question: The Five Books of Blood HC (2008, $19.99) r/#1-5						20.00
The Question: The Five Books of Blood SC (2009, $14.99) r/#1-5						15.00

CRIME CAN'T WIN (Formerly Cindy Smith)
Marvel/Atlas Comics (TCI 41/CCC 42,43,4-12): No. 41, 9/50 - No. 43, 2/51; No. 4, 4/51 - No. 12, 9/53

	GD 2.0	VG 4.0	FN 6.0	VF 8.0	VF/NM 9.0	NM- 9.2
41(#1)	26	52	78	154	252	350
42(#2)	15	30	45	86	133	180
43(#3)-Horror story	18	36	54	107	169	230
4(4/51),5-12: 10-Possible use in **SOTI**, pg. 161	14	28	42	78	112	145

NOTE: *Robinson a-9-11. Tuska a-43.*

CRIME CASES COMICS (Formerly Willie Comics)
Marvel/Atlas Comics(CnPC No.24-8/MJMC No.9-12): No. 24, 8/50 - No. 27, 3/51; No. 5, 5/51 - No. 12, 7/52

	GD 2.0	VG 4.0	FN 6.0	VF 8.0	VF/NM 9.0	NM- 9.2
24 (#1, 52 pgs.)-True police cases	19	38	57	111	176	240
25-27(#2-4): 27-Morisi-a	14	28	42	82	121	160
5-12: 11-Robinson-a. 12-Tuska-a	13	26	39	74	105	135

CRIME CLINIC
Ziff-Davis Publishing Co.: No. 10, July-Aug, 1951 - No. 5, Summer, 1952

	GD 2.0	VG 4.0	FN 6.0	VF 8.0	VF/NM 9.0	NM- 9.2
10(#1)-Painted-c; origin Dr. Tom Rogers	28	56	84	165	270	375
11(#2),4,5: 4,5-Painted-c	19	38	57	111	176	240
3-Used in **SOTI**, pg. 18	20	40	60	114	182	250

NOTE: *All have painted covers by* ***Saunders***. ***Starr*** *a-10.*

CRIME CLINIC
Slave Labor Graphics: May, 1995 - No. 2, Oct, 1995 ($2.95, B&W, limited series)

	GD 2.0	VG 4.0	FN 6.0	VF 8.0	VF/NM 9.0	NM- 9.2
1,2						3.00

CRIME DETECTIVE COMICS
Hillman Periodicals: Mar-Apr, 1948 - V3#8, May-June, 1953

	GD 2.0	VG 4.0	FN 6.0	VF 8.0	VF/NM 9.0	NM- 9.2
V1#1-The Invisible 6, costumed villains app; Fuje-c/a, 15 pgs.	30	60	90	177	289	400
2,5: 5-Krigstein-a	15	30	45	85	130	175
3,4,6,7,10-12: 6-McWilliams-a	14	28	42	76	108	140
8-Kirbyish-a by McCann	13	26	39	76	108	140
9-Used in **SOTI**, pg. 16 & "Caricature of the author in a position comic book publishers wish he were in permanently" illo.	39	78	117	231	378	525
V2#1,4,7-Krigstein-a: 1-Tuska-a	13	26	39	72	101	130
2,3,5,6,8-12 (1-2/52)	11	22	33	60	83	105
V3#1-Drug use-c	11	22	33	62	86	110
2-8	9	18	27	50	65	80

NOTE: ***Briefer*** *a-11, V3#1.* ***Kinstlerish****-a by* ***McCann****-V2#7, V3#2.* ***Powell*** *a-10, 11.* ***Starr*** *a-10.*

CRIME DETECTOR
Timor Publications: Jan, 1954 - No. 5, Sept, 1954

	GD 2.0	VG 4.0	FN 6.0	VF 8.0	VF/NM 9.0	NM- 9.2
1	21	42	63	126	206	285
2	14	28	42	76	108	140
3,4	11	22	33	64	90	115
5-Disbrow-a (classic)	22	44	66	132	216	300

CRIME DOES NOT PAY (Formerly Silver Streak Comics No. 1-21)
Comic House/Lev Gleason/Golfing: No. 22, June, 1942 - No. 147, July, 1955
(1st crime comic)(Title inspired by film)

	GD 2.0	VG 4.0	FN 6.0	VF 8.0	VF/NM 9.0	NM- 9.2
22 (23 on cover, 22 on indicia)-Origin The War Eagle & only app.; Chip Gardner begins; #22 was rebound in Complete Book of True Crime (Scarce)	443	886	1329	3234	5717	8200
23-(7/42) (Scarce)	232	464	696	1485	2543	3600
24-(11/42) Intro. & 1st app. Mr. Crime; classic Biro-c showing woman's head on fire being pushed onto hot stovetop burner	300	600	900	2070	3635	5200
25-(1/43) 2nd app. Mr. Crime; classic '40s crime-c	103	206	309	659	1130	1600
26-(3/43) 3rd app. Mr. Crime	84	168	252	538	919	1300
27-Classic Biro-c pushing man into hot oven	97	194	291	621	1061	1500
28-30: 30-Wood and Biro app.	71	142	213	454	777	1100
31,32,34-40	41	82	123	256	428	600
33-(5/44) Classic Biro hanging & hatchet-c	90	180	270	576	988	1400
41-(9/45) Origin & 1st app. Officer Common Sense	36	72	108	211	343	475
42-(11/45) Classic electrocution-c	47	94	141	296	498	700
43-46,48-50: 44-50 are 68 pg. issues. 44-"Legs" Diamond story. 50-(3/47)-1st issue to advertise 5 million readers on front-c. 58-(12/47)-shows 6 million readers (these ads believed to have influenced the crime comic wave of 1948)	24	48	72	142	234	325
47-(9/46)-Electric chair-c	39	78	117	240	395	550
51-70: 58(12/47)-Thomas Dun, killer of thousands (1565) story. 63,64-Possible use in **SOTI**, pg. 306. 63-Contains Biro & Gleason self censorship code of 12 listed restrictions (5/48)	19	38	57	111	176	240
71-99: 87-Chip Gardner begins, ends #100	15	30	45	88	137	185
100	17	34	51	98	154	210
101-104,107-110: 102-Chip Gardner app	14	28	42	76	108	140
105-Used in **POP**, pg. 84	14	28	42	82	121	160
106,114-Frazetta-a, 1 pg.	14	28	42	78	112	145
111-Used in **POP**, pgs. 80 & 81; injury-to-eye sty illo	15	30	45	85	130	175
112,113,115-130	11	22	33	60	83	105
131-140	10	20	30	54	72	90
141,142-Last pre-code issue; Kubert-a(1)	11	22	33	62	86	110
143-Kubert-a in one story	11	22	33	62	86	110
144-146	10	20	30	54	72	90
147-Last issue (scarce); Kubert-a	15	30	45	88	137	185
1(Golfing-1945)	9	18	27	50	65	80
The Best of...(1944, 128 pgs.)-Series contains 4 rebound issues	90	180	270	576	988	1400
...1945 issue	65	130	195	416	708	1000
...1946-48 issues	48	96	144	302	514	725
...1949-50 issues	41	82	123	256	428	600
...1951-53 issues	37	74	111	218	354	490

NOTE: *Many issues contain violent covers and stories. Who Dunit by* ***Guardineer****-39-42, 44-105, 108-110; Chip Gardner by* ***Bob Jujitani (Fuge)****-88-103.* ***Alderman*** *a-29, 41-44, 49.* ***Dan Barry*** *a-67, 75.* ***Charles Biro*** *c-1-76, 122, 142.* ***Dick Briefer*** *a-29(2), 30, 31, 33, 37, 39.* ***G. Colan*** *a-105.* ***Tony Dipreta*** *a-79, 90, 92.* ***Fuje*** *c-88, 89, 91-94, 96, 98, 99, 102, 103.* ***Fred Guardineer*** *a-51, 57, 58(2), 66-68, 71, 74, 79, 81, 90, 92.* ***Joe Kubert*** *c-143.* ***Landau*** *a-118.* ***Al Mandell*** *a-37.* ***Norman Maurer*** *a-29, 39, 41, 42.* ***McWilliams*** *a-91, 93, 95, 100-103.* ***Rudy Palais*** *a-30, 33,* ***Bob Powell*** *a-146, 147.* ***George Tuska*** *a-48-50(2ea.), 51, 52 56, 57(2), 58, 60-64, 66-68, 71, 74, 81. Painted c-87-103. Bondage c-43, 62, 98.*

CRIME EXPOSED
Marvel Comics (PPI)/Marvel Atlas Comics (PrPI): June, 1948; Dec, 1950 - No. 14, June, 1952

	GD 2.0	VG 4.0	FN 6.0	VF 8.0	VF/NM 9.0	NM- 9.2
1(6/48)	34	68	102	199	325	450
1(12/50)	21	42	63	122	199	275
2	15	30	45	83	124	165
3-9,11,14	13	26	39	74	105	135
10-Used in **POP**, pg. 81	14	28	42	78	112	145
12-Krigstein & Robinson-a	14	28	42	78	112	145
13-Used in **POP**, pg. 81; Krigstein-a	14	28	42	80	115	150

NOTE: ***Keller*** *a-8, 10.* ***Maneely*** *c-8.* ***Robinson*** *a-11, 12.* ***Sale*** *a-4.* ***Tuska*** *a-3, 4.*

CRIMEFIGHTERS
Marvel Comics (CmPS 1-3/CCC 4-10): Apr, 1948 - No. 10, Nov, 1949

	GD 2.0	VG 4.0	FN 6.0	VF 8.0	VF/NM 9.0	NM- 9.2
1-Some copies are undated & could be reprints	25	50	75	150	245	340
2,3: 3-Morphine addict story	15	30	45	84	127	170
4-10: 4-Early John Buscema-a. 6-Anti-Wertham editorial. 9,10-Photo-c	14	28	42	76	108	140

CRIME FIGHTERS (...Always Win)
Atlas Comics (CnPC): No. 11, Sept, 1954 - No. 13, Jan, 1955

	GD 2.0	VG 4.0	FN 6.0	VF 8.0	VF/NM 9.0	NM- 9.2
11-13: 11-Maneely-a,13-Pakula, Reinman, Severin-a	12	24	36	69	97	125

CRIME-FIGHTING DETECTIVE (Shock Detective Cases No. 20 on; formerly Criminals on the Run)
Star Publications: No. 11, Apr-May, 1950 - No. 19, June, 1952 (Based on true crime cases)

	GD 2.0	VG 4.0	FN 6.0	VF 8.0	VF/NM 9.0	NM- 9.2
11-L. B. Cole-c/a (2 pgs.); L. B. Cole-c on all	18	36	54	107	169	230
12,13,15-19: 17-Young King Cole & Dr. Doom app.	15	30	45	83	124	165
14-L. B. Cole-c/a, r/Law-Crime #2	15	30	45	90	140	190

CRIME FILES
Standard Comics: No. 5, Sept, 1952 - No. 6, Nov, 1952

	GD 2.0	VG 4.0	FN 6.0	VF 8.0	VF/NM 9.0	NM- 9.2
5-1pg. Alex Toth-a; used in **SOTI**, pg. 4 (text)	23	46	69	136	223	310
6-Sekowsky-a	14	28	42	80	115	150

CRIME ILLUSTRATED (Magazine)
E. C. Comics: Nov-Dec, 1955 - No. 2, Spring, 1956 (25¢, Adult Suspense Stories on-c)

	GD 2.0	VG 4.0	FN 6.0	VF 8.0	VF/NM 9.0	NM- 9.2
1-Ingels & Crandall-a	18	36	54	105	165	225
2-Ingels & Crandall-a	14	28	42	82	121	160

NOTE: ***Craig*** *a-2.* ***Crandall*** *a-1, 2; c-2.* ***Evans*** *a-1.* ***Davis*** *a-2.* ***Ingels*** *a-1, 2.* ***Krigstein/Crandall*** *a-1.* ***Orlando*** *a-1, 2; c-1.*

CRIME INCORPORATED (Formerly Crimes Incorporated)
Fox Features Syndicate: No. 2, Aug, 1950; No. 3, Aug, 1951

	GD 2.0	VG 4.0	FN 6.0	VF 8.0	VF/NM 9.0	NM- 9.2
2	26	52	78	154	252	350
3(1951)-Hollingsworth-a	18	36	54	105	165	225

CRIME MACHINE (Magazine reprints pre-code crime and gangster comics)

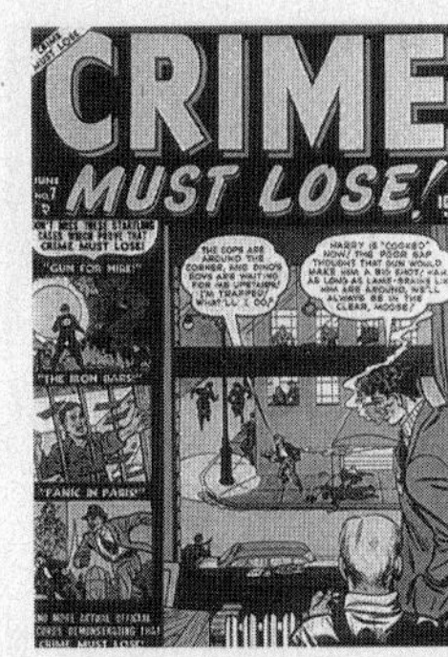

Crime Must Lose! #7 © MAR

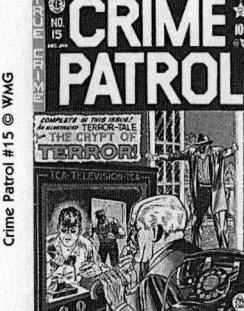

Crime Patrol #15 © WMG

Crime SuspenStories #1 © WMG

GD VG FN VF VF/NM NM-
2.0 4.0 6.0 8.0 9.0 9.2

Skywald Publications: Feb, 1971 - No. 2, May, 1971 (B&W, 68 pgs., roundbound)
1-Kubert-a(2)(r)(Avon); bikini girl in cake-c 6 12 18 41 66 90
2-Torres, Wildey-a; violent-c/a 4 8 12 28 44 60

CRIME MUST LOSE! (Formerly Sports Action?)
Sports Action (Atlas Comics): No. 4, Oct, 1950 - No. 12, April, 1952
4-Ann Brewster-a in all; c-used in N.Y. Legis. Comm. documents
19 38 57 111 176 240
5-12: 9-Robinson-a. 11-Used in **POP**, pg. 89 14 28 42 80 115 150

CRIME MUST PAY THE PENALTY (Formerly Four Favorites; Penalty #47, 48)
Ace Magazines (Current Books): No. 33, Feb, 1948; No. 2, Jun, 1948 - No. 48, Jan, 1956
33(#1, 2/48)-Becomes Four Teeners #34? 39 78 117 231 378 525
2(6/48)-Extreme violence; Palais-a? 24 48 72 142 234 325
3,4,8: 3- "Frisco Mary" story used in Senate Investigation report, pg. 7. 4,8-Transvestism stories 19 38 57 111 176 240
5-7,9,10 14 28 42 82 121 160
11-19 14 28 42 78 112 145
20-Drug story "Dealers in White Death" 20 40 60 114 182 250
21-32,34-40,42-48: 44-Last pre-code 11 22 33 62 86 110
33(7/53)- "Dell Fabry-Junk King" drug story; mentioned in Love and Death
15 30 45 90 140 190
41-reprints "Dealers in White Death" 12 24 36 67 94 120
NOTE: ***Cameron** a-29-31, 34, 35, 39-41. **Colan** a-20, 31. **Kremer** a-3, 37r. **Larsen** a-32. **Palais** a-5?,37.*

CRIME MUST STOP
Hillman Periodicals: October, 1952 (52 pgs.)
V1#1(Scarce)-Similar to Monster Crime; Mort Lawrence, Krigstein-a
97 194 291 621 1061 1500

CRIME MYSTERIES (Secret Mysteries #16 on; combined with Crime Smashers #7 on)
Ribage Publ. Corp. (Trojan Magazines): May, 1952 - No. 15, Sept, 1954
1-Transvestism story; crime & terror stories begin 61 122 183 390 670 950
2-Marijuana story (7/52) 41 82 123 256 428 600
3-One pg. Frazetta-a 39 78 117 231 378 525
4-Cover shows girl in bondage having her blood drained; 1 pg. Frazetta-a
63 126 189 403 689 975
5-10 34 68 102 199 325 450
11,12,14 31 62 93 186 303 420
13-(5/54)-Angelo Torres 1st comic work (inks over Check's pencils); Check-a
37 74 111 222 361 500
15-Acid in face-c 47 94 141 296 498 700
NOTE: ***Fass** a-13; c-4, 6, 10. **Hollingsworth** a-10-13, 15; c-2, 12, 13, 15. **Kiefer** a-4. **Woodbridge** a-13? Bondage-c-1, 8, 12.*

CRIME ON THE RUN (See Approved Comics #8)

CRIME ON THE WATERFRONT (Formerly Famous Gangsters)
Realistic Publications: No. 4, May, 1952 (Painted cover)
4 28 56 84 165 270 375

CRIME PATROL (Formerly International #1-5; International Crime Patrol #6; becomes Crypt of Terror #17 on)
E. C. Comics: No. 7, Summer, 1948 - No. 16, Feb-Mar, 1950
7-Intro. Captain Crime 76 152 228 486 831 1175
8-14: 12-Ingels-a 68 136 204 435 743 1050
15-Intro. of Crypt Keeper (inspired by Witches Tales radio show) & Crypt of Terror (see Tales From the Crypt #33 for origin); used by N.Y. Legis. Comm.; last pg. Feldstein-a
269 538 807 2152 3426 4700
16-2nd Crypt Keeper app.; Roussos-a 171 342 513 1368 2184 3000
NOTE: ***Craig** c/a in most issues. **Feldstein** a-9-16. **Kiefer** a-8, 10, 11. **Moldoff** a-7.*

CRIME PATROL
Gemstone Publishing: Apr, 2000 - No. 10, Jan, 2001 ($2.50)
1-10: E.C. reprints 3.00
Volume 1,2 (2000, $13.50) 1-r/#1-5. 2-r/#6-10 14.00

CRIME PHOTOGRAPHER (See Casey...)

CRIME REPORTER
St. John Publ. Co.: Aug, 1948 - No. 3, Dec, 1948 (Indicia shows Oct.)
1-Drug club story 58 116 174 371 636 900
2-Used in **SOTI**: illo- "Children told me what the man was going to do with the red-hot poker;" r/Dynamic #17 with editing; Baker-c; Tuska-a 87 174 261 553 952 1350
3-Baker-c; Tuska-a 45 90 135 284 480 675

CRIMES BY WOMEN
Fox Features Syndicate: June, 1948 - No. 15, Aug, 1951; 1954 (True crime cases)
1-True story of Bonnie Parker 126 252 378 806 1378 1950

GD VG FN VF VF/NM NM-
2.0 4.0 6.0 8.0 9.0 9.2

2,3: 3-Used in **SOTI**, pg. 234 65 130 195 416 708 1000
4,5,7-9,11-15: 8-Used in **POP**. 14-Bondage-c 60 120 180 381 653 925
6-Classic girl fight-c; acid-in-face panel 69 138 207 442 759 1075
10-Used in **SOTI**, pg. 72; girl fight-c 63 126 189 403 689 975
54(M.S. Publ.-'54)-Reprint; (formerly My Love Secret)
24 48 72 140 230 320

CRIMES INCORPORATED (Formerly My Past)
Fox Features Syndicate: No. 12, June, 1950 (Crime Incorporated No. 2 on)
12 24 48 72 142 234 325

CRIMES INCORPORATED (See Fox Giants)

CRIME SMASHER (See Whiz #76)
Fawcett Publications: Summer, 1948 (one-shot)
1-Formerly Spy Smasher 41 82 123 256 428 600

CRIME SMASHERS (Becomes Secret Mysteries No. 16 on)
Ribage Publishing Corp.(Trojan Magazines): Oct, 1950 - No. 15, Mar, 1953
1-Used in **SOTI**, pg. 19,20, & illo "A girl raped and murdered;" Sally the Sleuth begins
90 180 270 576 988 1400
2-Kubert-c 48 96 144 302 514 725
3,4 39 78 117 240 395 550
5-Wood-a 47 94 141 296 498 700
6,8-11: 8-Lingerie panel 32 64 96 188 307 425
7-Female heroin junkie story 36 72 108 211 343 475
12-Injury to eye panel; 1 pg. Frazetta-a 34 68 102 204 332 460
13-Used in **POP**, pgs. 79,80; 1 pg. Frazetta-a 34 68 102 204 332 460
14,15 26 52 78 154 252 350
NOTE: ***Hollingsworth** a-14. **Kiefer** a-15. Bondage c-7, 9.*

CRIME SUSPENSTORIES (Formerly Vault of Horror No. 12-14)
E. C. Comics: No. 15, Oct-Nov, 1950 - No. 27, Feb-Mar, 1955
15-Identical to #1 in content; #1 printed on outside front cover. #15 (formerly "The Vault of Horror") printed and blackened out on inside front cover with Vol. 1, No. 1 printed over it. Evidently, several of No. 15 were printed before a decision was made not to drop the Vault of Horror and Haunt of Fear series. The print run was stopped on No. 15 and continued on No. 1. All of the No. 15 issues were changed as described above.
160 320 480 1280 2040 2800
1 126 252 378 1008 1604 2200
2 64 128 192 512 819 1125
3-5: 3-Poe adaptation. 3-Old Witch stories begin 44 88 132 352 564 775
6-10: 9-Craig bio. 39 78 117 312 494 675
11,12,14,15: 15-The Old Witch guest stars 30 60 90 240 383 525
13,16-Williamson-a 32 64 96 256 411 565
17-Williamson/Frazetta-a (6 pgs.) Williamson bio. 39 78 117 312 499 685
18,19: 19-Used in **SOTI**, pg. 235 27 54 81 216 341 465
20-Cover used in **SOTI**, illo "Cover of a children's comic book"
36 72 108 288 457 625
21,24-26: 24- "Food For Thought" similar to "Cave In" in Amazing Detective Cases #13 (1952)
19 38 57 152 246 340
22-Used in Senate investigation on juvenile delinquency; Ax decapitation-c
80 160 240 640 1020 1400
23-Used in Senate investigation on juvenile delinquency
27 54 81 216 341 465
27-Last issue (Low distribution) 24 48 72 192 309 425
NOTE: ***Craig** a-1-21; c-1-18, 20-22. **Crandall** a-18-26. **Davis** a-4, 5, 7, 9-12, 20. **Elder** a-17,18. **Evans** a-15, 19, 21, 23, 25, 27; c-23, 24. **Feldstein** c-19. **Ingels** a-1-12, 14, 15, 27. **Kamen** a-2, 4-18, 20-27; c-25-27. **Krigstein** a-22, 24, 25, 27. **Kurtzman** a-1, 3. **Orlando** a-16, 22, 24, 26. **Wood** a-1, 3. Issues No. 1-3 were printed in Canada as "Weird Suspenstories." Issues No. 11-15 have E. C. "quickie" stories. No. 25 contains the famous "Are You a Red Dupe?" editorial. Ray Bradbury adaptations-15, 17.*

CRIME SUSPENSTORIES
Russ Cochran/Gemstone Publ.: Nov, 1992 - No. 27, May, 1999 ($1.50/$2.00/$2.50)
1-27: Reprints Crime SuspenStories series 3.00

CRIMINAL (Also see Criminal: The Sinners)
Marvel Comics (Icon): Oct, 2006 - No. 10, Oct, 2007 ($2.99)
Volume 2: Feb, 2008 - No. 7, Nov, 2008 ($3.50)
1-10-Ed Brubaker-s/Sean Phillips-a/c 3.00
Volume 2: 1-7-Brubaker-s/Phillips-a 3.50
... Vol. 1: Coward TPB (2007, $14.99) r/#1-5; intro. by Tom Fontana 15.00
... Vol. 2: Lawless TPB (2007, $14.99) r/#6-10; intro. by Frank Miller 15.00
... Vol. 3: The Dead and the Dying TPB (2008, $11.99) r/V2#1-4; intro. by John Singleton 12.00

CRIMINAL MACABRE: A CAL MCDONALD MYSTERY (Also see Last Train to Deadsville)
Dark Horse Comics: May, 2003 - No. 5, Sept, 2003 ($2.99)
1-5-Niles-s/Templesmith-a 3.00

CRIMINAL MACABRE: (limited series and one-shots)

Crimson: Scarlet X Blood on the Moon #1 © H. Ramos

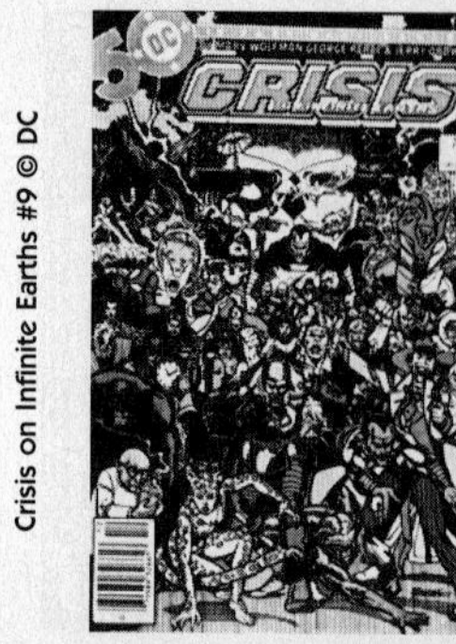

Crisis on Infinite Earths #9 © DC

Cross #4 © Andrew Vachss

	GD	VG	FN	VF	VF/NM	NM-
	2.0	4.0	6.0	8.0	9.0	9.2

Dark Horse Comics: ($2.99)
...: Cellblock 666 (9/08 - No. 4, 5/09)(#25-28 in series) 1-4-Niles-s/Stakal-a/Bradstreet-c 3.00
... :Feat of Clay (6/06, $2.99) Niles-s/Hotz-a/c 3.00
Free Comic Book Day: Criminal Macabre - Call Me Monster (5/11) flip book w/Baltimore 2.00
...: My Demon Baby (9/07 - No. 4, 4/08)(#21-24 in the series) 1-4-Niles-s/Stakal-a 3.00
...: Two Red Eyes (12/06 - No. 4, 3/07) 1-4-Niles-s/Hotz-a/Bradstreet-c 3.00

CRIMINALS ON THE RUN (Formerly Young King Cole) (Crime Fighting Detective No. 11 on)
Premium Group (Novelty Press): V4#1, Aug-Sep, 1948-#10, Dec-Jan, 1949-50

	GD	VG	FN	VF	VF/NM	NM-
V4#1-Young King Cole continues	26	52	78	154	252	350
2-6: 6-Dr. Doom app.	22	44	66	132	216	300
7-Classic "Fish in the Face" c by L. B. Cole	52	104	156	322	549	775
V5#1,2 (#8,9),10: 9,10-L. B. Cole-c	20	40	60	118	192	265

NOTE: *Most issues have* ***L. B. Cole*** *covers.* ***McWilliams*** *a-V4#6, 7, V5#2; c-V4#5.*

CRIMINAL: THE SINNERS
Marvel Comics (Icon): Sept, 2009 - No. 5, Mar, 2010 ($3.50)
1-5-Ed Brubaker-s/Sean Phillips-a/c 3.50

CRIMSON (Also see Cliffhanger #0)
Image Comics (Cliffhanger Productions): May, 1998 - No. 7, Dec, 1998;
DC Comics (Cliffhanger Prod.): No. 8, Mar, 1999 - No. 24, Apr, 2001 ($2.50)
1-Humberto Ramos-a/Augustyn-s 5.00
1-Variant-c by Warren 8.00
1-Chromium-c 20.00
2-Ramos-c with street crowd, 2-Variant-c by Art Adams 4.00
2-Dynamic Forces CrimsonChrome cover 15.00
3-7: 3-Ramos Moon background-c. 7-Three covers by Ramos, Madureira, & Campbell 3.50
8-23: 8-First DC issue 3.00
24-($3.50) Final issue; wraparound-c 4.00
DF Premiere Ed. 1998 ($6.95) covers by Ramos and Jae Lee 7.00
Crimson: Scarlet X Blood on the Moon (10/99, $3.95) 4.00
Crimson Sourcebook (11/99, $2.95) Pin-ups and info 3.00
Earth Angel TPB (2001, $14.95) r/#13-18 15.00
Heaven and Earth TPB (1/00, $14.95) r/#7-12 15.00
Loyalty and Loss TPB ('99, $12.95) r/#1-6 13.00
Redemption TPB ('01, $14.95) r/#19-24 15.00

CRIMSON AVENGER, THE (See Detective Comics #20 for 1st app.)(Also see Leading Comics #1 & World's Best/Finest Comics)
DC Comics: June, 1988 - No. 4, Sept, 1988 ($1.00, limited series)
1-4 3.00

CRIMSON DYNAMO
Marvel Comics (Epic): Oct, 2003 - No. 6, Apr, 2004 ($2.50/$2.99)
1-4,6: 1-John Jackson Miller-s/Steve Ellis-a/c 3.00
5-($2.99) Iron Man-c/app. 4.00

CRIMSON PLAGUE
Event Comics: June, 1997 ($2.95, unfinished mini-series)
1-George Perez-a 3.00

CRIMSON PLAGUE (George Pérez's...)
Image Comics (Gorilla): June, 2000 - No. 2, Aug, 2000 ($2.95, mini-series)
1-George Perez-a; reprints 6/97 issue with 16 new pages 3.00
2-($2.50) 3.00

CRISIS AFTERMATH: THE BATTLE FOR BLUDHAVEN (Also see Infinite Crisis)
DC Comics: Jun, 2006 - No. 6, Sept, 2006 ($2.99, limited series)
1-Atomic Knights return; Teen Titans app.; Jurgens-a/Acuna-c 4.00
1-2nd printing with pencil cover 3.00
2-6: 2-Intro S.H.A.D.E. (new Freedom Fighters) 3.00
TPB (2007, $12.99) r/#1-6 13.00

CRISIS AFTERMATH: THE SPECTRE (Also see Infinite Crisis, Gotham Central and Tales of the Unexpected)
DC Comics: Jul, 2006 - No. 3, Sept, 2006 ($2.99, limited series)
1-3-Crispus Allen becomes the Spectre; Pfeifer-s/Chiang-a/c 3.00
TPB (2007, $12.99) r/#1-3 and Tales of the Unexpected #1-3 13.00

CRISIS ON INFINITE EARTHS (Also see Official... Index and Legends of the DC Universe)
DC Comics: Apr, 1985 - No. 12, Mar, 1986 (maxi-series)

	GD	VG	FN	VF	VF/NM	NM-
1-1st DC app. Blue Beetle & Detective Karp from Charlton; Pérez-c on all	2	4	6	9	13	16
2-6: 6-Intro Charlton's Capt. Atom, Nightshade, Question, Judomaster, Peacemaker & Thunderbolt into DC Universe	1	3	4	6	8	10
7-Double size; death of Supergirl	2	4	6	13	16	22
8-Death of the Flash (Barry Allen)	2	4	6	11	16	20
9-11: 9-Intro. Charlton's Ghost into DC Universe. 10-Intro. Charlton's Banshee, Dr. Spectro, Image, Punch & Jewellee into DC Universe; Starman (Prince Gavyn) dies	1	3	4	6	8	10
12-(52 pgs.)-Deaths of Dove, Kole, Lori Lemaris, Sunburst, G.A. Robin & Huntress; Kid Flash becomes new Flash; 3rd & final DC app. of the 3 Lt. Marvels; Green Fury gets new look (becomes Green Flame in Infinity, Inc. #32)	2	4	6	8	11	14

Slipcased Hardcover (1998, $99.95) Wraparound dust-jacket cover by Pérez and Alex Ross; sketch pages by Pérez; intro by Wolfman 125.00
TPB (2000, $29.95) Wraparound-c by Pérez and Ross 30.00
NOTE: *Crossover issues: All Star Squadron 50-56,60; Amethyst 13; Blue Devil 17,18; DC Comics Presents 78,86-88,95; Detective Comics 558; Fury of Firestorm 41,42; G.I. Combat 274; Green Lantern 194-196,198; Infinity, Inc. 18-25 & Annual 1, Justice League of America 244,245 & Annual 3; Legion of Super-Heroes 16,18; Losers Special 1; New Teen Titans 13,14; Omega Men 31,33; Superman 413-415; Swamp Thing 44,46; Wonder Woman 327-329.*

CRISIS ON MULTIPLE EARTHS
DC Comics: 2002, 2003, 2004 ($14.95, trade paperbacks)
TPB-(2003) Reprints 1st 4 Silver Age JLA/JSA crossovers from J.L.ofA. #21,22; 29,30; 37,38; 46,47; new painted-c by Alex Ross; intro. by Mark Waid 15.00
Volume 2 (2003, $14.95) r/J.L.ofA. #55,56; 64,65; 73,74; 82,83; new Ordway-c 15.00
Volume 3 (2004, $14.95) r/J.L.ofA. #91,92; 100-102; 107,108; 113; Wein intro., Ross-c 15.00
Volume 4 (2006, $14.99) r/J.L.ofA. #123-124 (Earth-Prime),135-137 (Fawcett's Shazam characters), 147-148 (Legion of Super-Heroes); Ross-c 15.00
Volume 5 (2010, $19.99) r/J.L.ofA. #159-160 (Jonah Hex, Enemy Ace),171-172 (Murder of Mr. Terrific), 183-185 (New Gods & Darkseid); Pérez-c 20.00
... The Team-Ups Volume 1 (2005, $14.99) r/Flash #123,129,137,151; Showcase #55,56; Green Lantern #40, Brave and the Bold #61 and Spectre #7; new Ordway-c 15.00

CRITICAL MASS (See A Shadowline Saga: Critical Mass)

CRITTERS (Also see Usagi Yojimbo Summer Special)
Fantagraphics Books: 1986 - No. 50, 1990 ($1.70/$2.00, B&W)

	GD	VG	FN	VF	VF/NM	NM-
1-Cutey Bunny, Usagi Yojimbo app.	1	3	4	6	8	10
2,4,5,8,9						6.00
3,6,7,10-Usagi Yojimbo app.	1	2	3	4	5	7
11,14-Usagi Yojimbo app. 11-Christmas Special (68 pgs.)						4.00
12,13,15-22,24-37,39,40: 22-Watchmen parody; two diff. covers exist						3.00
23-With Alan Moore Flexi-disc ($3.95)						5.00
38-($2.75-c) Usagi Yojimbo app.						4.00
41-49						4.00
50 ($4.95, 84 pgs.)-Neil the Horse, Capt. Jack, Sam & Max & Usagi Yojimbo app.; Quagmire, Shaw-a	1	2	3	4	5	7
Special 1 (1/88, $2.00)						3.00

CROSS
Dark Horse Comics: No. 0, Oct, 1995 - No. 6, Apr, 1995 ($2.95, limited series, mature)
0-6: Darrow-c & Vachss scripts in all 3.00

CROSS AND THE SWITCHBLADE, THE
Spire Christian Comics (Fleming H. Revell Co.): 1972 (35-49¢)

	GD	VG	FN	VF	VF/NM	NM-
1-Some issues have nn	2	4	6	13	18	22

CROSS BRONX, THE
Image Comics: Sept, 2006 - No. 4, Dec, 2006 ($2.99, limited series)
1-4: 1-Oeming-a/c; Oeming & Brandon-s; Ribic var-c. 2-Johnson var-c. 4-Mack var-c 3.00

CROSSFIRE
Spire Christian Comics (Fleming H. Revell Co.): 1973 (39/49¢)

	GD	VG	FN	VF	VF/NM	NM-
nn	2	4	6	10	14	18

CROSSFIRE (Also see DNAgents)
Eclipse Comics: 5/84 - No. 17, 3/86; No. 18, 1/87 - No. 26, 2/88 ($1.50, Baxter paper) (#18-26 are B&W)

	GD	VG	FN	VF	VF/NM	NM-
1-11,14-26: 1-DNAgents x-over; Spiegle-c/a begins						3.00
12-Death of Marilyn Monroe; Dave Stevens-c	1	2	3	4	5	7
13-Death of Marilyn Monroe						5.00

CROSSFIRE AND RAINBOW (Also see DNAgents)
Eclipse Comics: June, 1986 - No. 4, Sept, 1986 ($1.25, deluxe format)
1-3: Spiegle-a. 4-Dave Stevens-c 2.50

CROSSGEN...
CrossGeneration Comics
CrossGenesis (1/00) Previews CrossGen universe; cover gallery 3.00
...Primer (1/00) Wizard supplement; intro. to the CrossGen universe 3.00
...Sampler (2/00) Retailer preview book 3.00

CROSSGEN CHRONICLES
CrossGeneration Comics: June, 2000 - No. 8 ($3.95)

The Crow #1 © Crowvision

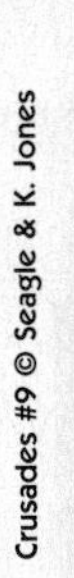
Crusades #9 © Seagle & K. Jones

Crux #18 © CRO

GD 2.0 | VG 4.0 | FN 6.0 | VF 8.0 | VF/NM 9.0 | NM- 9.2

1-Intro. to CrossGen characters & company 4.00
1-(no cover price) same contents, customer preview 4.00
2-8: 2-(3/01) George Pérez-c/a. 3-5-Pérez-a/Waid-s. 6,7-Nebres-c/a 4.00

CROSSING MIDNIGHT
DC Comics (Vertigo): Jan, 2007 - No. 19, Jul, 2008 ($2.99)
1-19: 1-Carey-s/Fern-a/Williams III-c. 10-12-Nguyen-a 3.00
...: Cut Here TPB (2007, $9.99) r/#1-5 10.00
...: A Map of Midnight TPB (2008, $14.99) r/#6-12; afterword by Carey 15.00
...: The Sword in the Soul TPB (2008, $14.99) r/#13-19 15.00

CROSSING THE ROCKIES (See Classics Illustrated Special Issue)

CROSSOVERS, THE
CrossGeneration Comics: Feb, 2003 - No. 12 ($2.95)
1-12-Robert Rodi-s. 1-6-Mauricet & Ernie Colon-a. 7-Staton-a begins 3.00
Vol. 1: Cross Currents (2003, $9.95) digest-sized reprints #1-6 10.00

CROW, THE (Also see Caliber Presents)
Caliber Press: Feb, 1989 - No. 4, 1989 ($1.95, B&W, limited series)
1-James O'Barr-c/a/scripts 6 12 18 37 59 80
1-3-2nd printing 6.00
2-4 4 8 12 22 34 45
2-3rd printing 4.00

CROW, THE
Tundra Publishing, Ltd.: Jan, 1992 - No. 3, 1992 ($4.95, B&W, 68 pgs.)
1-3: 1-r/#1,2 of Caliber series. 2-r/#3 of Caliber series w/new material. 3-All new material 1 2 3 5 6 8

CROW, THE
Kitchen Sink Press: 1/96 - No. 3, 3/96 ($2.95, B&W)
1-3: James O'Barr-c/scripts 5.00
#0-A Cycle of Shattered Lives (12/98, $3.50) new story by O'Barr 4.00

CROW, THE
Image Comics (Todd McFarlane Prod.): Feb, 1999 - No. 10, Nov, 1999 ($2.50)
1-10: 1-Two covers by McFarlane and Kent Williams; Muth-s in all. 2-6,10-Paul Lee-a 3.00
Book 1 - Vengeance (2000, $10.95, TPB) r/#1-3,5,6 11.00
Book 2 - Evil Beyond Reach (2000, $10.95, TPB) r/#4,7-10 11.00
Todd McFarlane Presents The Crow Magazine 1 (3/00, $4.95) 5.00

CROW, THE: CITY OF ANGELS (Movie)
Kitchen Sink Press: July, 1996 - No. 3, Sept, 1996 ($2.95, limited series)
1-3: Adaptation of film; two-c (photo & illos.). 1-Vincent Perez interview 3.00

CROW, THE: FLESH AND BLOOD
Kitchen Sink Press: May, 1996 - No. 3, July, 1996 ($2.95, limited series)
1-3: O'Barr-c 3.00

CROW, THE: RAZOR - KILL THE PAIN
London Night Studios: Apr, 1998 - No. 3, July, 1998 ($2.95, B&W, lim. series)
1-3-Hartsoe-s/O'Barr-painted-c 3.00
0(10/98) Dorien painted-c, Finale (2/99) 3.00
The Lost Chapter (2/99, $4.95), Tour Book-(12/97) pin-ups; 4 diff.-c 5.00

CROW, THE: WAKING NIGHTMARES
Kitchen Sink Press: Jan, 1997 - No. 4, 1998 ($2.95, B&W, limited series)
1-4-Miran Kim-c 5.00

CROW, THE: WILD JUSTICE
Kitchen Sink Press: Oct, 1996 - No. 3, Dec, 1996 ($2.95, B&W, limited series)
1-3-Prosser-s/Adlard-a 3.00

CROWN COMICS (Also see Vooda)
Golfing/McCombs Publ.: Wint, 1944-45; No. 2, Sum, 1945 - No. 19, July, 1949
1- "The Oblong Box" E.A. Poe adaptation 43 86 129 271 461 650
2,3-Baker-a; 3-Voodah by Baker 32 64 96 188 307 425
4-6-Baker-c/a; Voodah app. #4,5 34 68 102 199 325 450
7-Feldstein, Baker, Kamen-a; Baker-c 36 72 108 211 343 475
8-Baker-a; Voodah app. 27 54 81 158 259 360
9-11,13-19: Voodah in #10-19. 13-New logo 18 36 54 107 169 230
12-Master Marvin by Feldstein, Starr-a; Voodah-c 19 38 57 111 176 240
NOTE: *Bolle a-11, 13-16, 18, 19; c-11p, 15. Powell a-19. Starr a-11-13; c-11i.*

CRUCIBLE
DC Comics (Impact): Feb, 1993 - No. 6, July, 1993 ($1.25, limited series)
1-6: 1-(99¢)-Neon ink-c. 1,2-Quesada-c(p). 1-4-Quesada layouts 3.00

CRUEL AND UNUSUAL
DC Comics (Vertigo): June, 1999 - No. 4, Sept, 1999 ($2.95, limited series)
1-4-Delano & Peyer-s/McCrea-c/a 3.00

CRUSADER FROM MARS (See Tops in Adventure)
Ziff-Davis Publ. Co.: Jan-Mar, 1952 - No. 2, Fall, 1952 (Painted-c)
1-Cover is dated Spring 76 152 228 486 831 1175
2-Bondage-c 53 106 159 334 567 800

CRUSADER RABBIT (TV)
Dell Publishing Co.: No. 735, Oct, 1956 - No. 805, May, 1957
Four Color 735 (#1) 23 46 69 168 334 500
Four Color 805 17 34 51 124 252 380

CRUSADERS, THE (Religious)
Chick Publications: 1974 - Vol. 17, 1988 (39/69¢, 36 pgs.)
Vol.1-Operation Bucharest ('74). Vol.2-The Broken Cross ('74). Vol.3-Scarface ('74). Vol.4-Exorcists ('75). Vol.5-Chaos ('75) 3 6 9 14 20 25
Vol.6-Primal Man? ('76)-(Disputes evolution theory). Vol.7-The Ark-(claims proof of existence, destroyed by Bolsheviks). Vol.8-The Gift-(Life story of Christ). Vol.9-Angel of Light-(Story of the Devil). Vol.10-Spellbound?-(Tells how rock music is Satanic & produced by witches). 11-Sabotage?. 12-Alberto. 13-Double Cross. 14-The Godfathers. (No. 6-14 low in distribution; loaded with religious propaganda.). 15-The Force. 16-The Four Horsemen 3 6 9 14 20 25
Vol. 17-The Prophet (low print run) 3 6 9 16 23 30

CRUSADERS (Southern Knights No. 2 on)
Guild Publications: 1982 (B&W, magazine size)
1-1st app. Southern Knights 2 4 6 9 12 16

CRUSADERS, THE (Also see Black Hood, The Jaguar, The Comet, The Fly, Legend of the Shield, The Mighty... & The Web)
DC Comics (Impact): May, 1992 - No. 8, Dec, 1992 ($1.00/$1.25)
1-8-Contains 3 Impact trading cards 3.00

CRUSADES, THE
DC Comics (Vertigo): 2001 - No. 20, Dec, 2002 ($3.95/$2.50)
...: Urban Decree ('01, $3.95) Intro. the Knight; Seagle-s/Kelley Jones-c/a 4.00
1-(5/01, $2.50) Sienkiewicz-c 3.00
2-20: 2-Moeller-c. 18-Begin $2.95-c 3.00

CRUSH
Dark Horse Comics: Oct, 2003 - No. 4, Jan, 2004 ($2.99, limited series)
1-4-Jason Hall-s/Sean Murphy-a 3.00

CRUSH, THE
Image Comics (Motown Machineworks): Jan, 1996 - No. 5, July, 1996 ($2.25, limited series)
1-5: Baron scripts 3.00

CRUX
CrossGeneration Comics: May, 2001 - No. 33, Feb, 2004 ($2.95)
1-33: 1-Waid-s/Epting & Magyar-a/c. 6-Pelletier-a. 13-Dixon-s begin. 25-Cover has fake creases and other aging 3.00
Atlantis Rising Vol. 1 TPB (2002, $15.95) r/#1-6 16.00
Test of Time Vol. 2 TPB (12/02, $15.95) r/#7-12 16.00
Vol. 3: Strangers in Atlantis (2003, $15.95) r/#13-18 16.00
Vol. 4: Chaos Reborn (2003, $15.95) r/#19-24 16.00

CRY FOR DAWN
Cry For Dawn Pub.: 1989 - No. 9 ($2.25, B&W, mature)
1 8 16 24 52 86 120
1-2nd printing 3 6 9 18 27 35
1-3rd printing 3 6 9 14 20 25
2 5 10 15 32 51 70
2-2nd printing 2 4 6 11 16 20
3 4 8 12 24 37 50
3a-HorrorCon Edition (1990, less than 400 printed, signed inside-c) 200.00
4-6 3 6 9 14 19 24
5-2nd printing 1 2 3 5 6 8
7-9 2 4 6 10 14 18
4-9-Signed & numbered editions 3 6 9 14 20 25
Angry Christ Comix HC (4/03, $29.99) reprints various stories; and 30 pgs. new material 30.00
...Calendar (1993) 35.00

CRYIN' LION COMICS
William H. Wise Co.: Fall, 1944 - No. 3, Spring, 1945
1-Funny animal 15 30 45 83 124 165
2-Hitler and Tojo app. 13 26 39 74 105 135

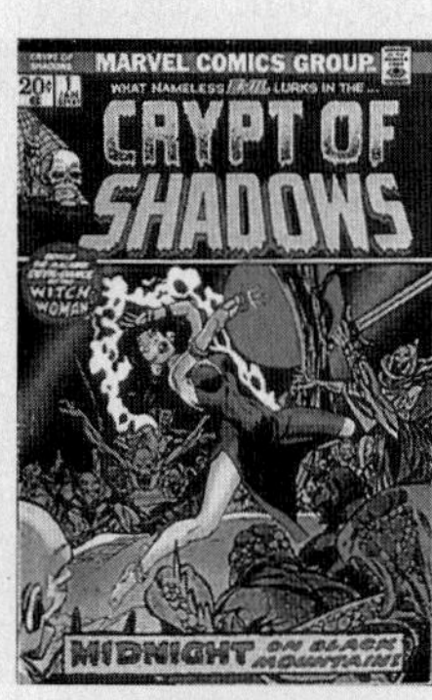

Crypt of Shadows #1 © MAR

CSI: Crime Scene Investigation #1 © CBS Worldwide

Curse of the Spawn #12 © TMP

	GD 2.0	VG 4.0	FN 6.0	VF 8.0	VF/NM 9.0	NM- 9.2
3	10	20	30	56	76	95

CRYPT
Image Comics (Extreme): Aug, 1995 - No.2, Oct. 1995 ($2.50, limited series)
1,2-Prophet app. 3.00

CRYPTIC WRITINGS OF MEGADETH
Chaos! Comics: Sept, 1997 - No. 4, Jun, 1998 ($2.95, quarterly)
1-4-Stories based on song lyrics by Dave Mustaine 3.00

CRYPT OF DAWN (see Dawn)
Sirius: 1996 ($2.95, B&W, limited series)
1-Linsner-c/s; anthology. 5.00
2, 3 (2/98) 4.00
4,5: 4- (6/98), 5-(11/98) 3.00
Ltd. Edition 20.00

CRYPT OF SHADOWS
Marvel Comics Group: Jan, 1973 - No. 21, Nov, 1975 (#1-9 are 20¢)

	GD	VG	FN	VF	VF/NM	NM-
1-Wolverton-r/Advs. Into Terror #7	3	6	9	20	30	40
2-10: 2-Starlin/Everett-c	3	6	9	14	19	24
11-21: 18,20-Kirby-a	2	4	6	11	16	20

NOTE: ***Briefer*** *a-2r.* ***Ditko*** *a-13r, 18-20r.* ***Everett*** *a-6, 14r; c-2i.* ***Heath*** *a-1r.* ***Gil Kane*** *c-1, 6.* ***Mort Lawrence*** *a-1r, 8r.* ***Maneely*** *a-2r.* ***Moldoff*** *a-8.* ***Powell*** *a-12r, 14r.* ***Tuska*** *a-2r.*

CRYPT OF TERROR (Formerly Crime Patrol; Tales From the Crypt No. 20 on)
(Also see EC Archives • Tales From the Crypt)
E. C. Comics: No. 17, Apr-May, 1950 - No. 19, Aug-Sept, 1950

	GD	VG	FN	VF	VF/NM	NM-
17-1st New Trend to hit stands	297	594	891	2376	3788	5200
18,19	166	332	498	1328	2114	2900

NOTE: ***Craig*** *c/a-17-19.* ***Feldstein*** *a-17-19.* ***Ingels*** *a-19.* ***Kurtzman*** *a-18.* ***Wood*** *a-18. Canadian reprints known; see Table of Contents.*

CSI: CRIME SCENE INVESTIGATION (Based on TV series)
IDW Publishing: Jan, 2003 - No. 5, May, 2003 ($3.99, limited series)
1-Two covers (photo & Ashley Wood); Max Allan Collins-s 4.00
2-5 4.00
Free Comic Book Day edition (7/04) Previews CSI: Bad Rap; The Shield: Spotlight; 24: One Shot; and 30 Days of Night 2.50
...: Case Files Vol. 1 TPB (8/06, $19.99) B&W rep/Serial TPB, CSI - Bad Rap and CSI - Demon House limited series 20.00
...: Serial TPB (2003, $19.99) r/#1-5; bonus short story by Collins/Wood 20.00
...: Thicker Than Blood (7/03, $6.99) Mariotte-s/Rodriguez-a 7.00

CSI: CRIME SCENE INVESTIGATION - BAD RAP
IDW Publishing: Aug, 2003 - No. 5, Dec, 2003 ($3.99, limited series)
1-5-Two photo covers; Max Allan Collins-s/Rodriguez-a 4.00
TPB (3/04, $19.99) r/#1-5 20.00

CSI: CRIME SCENE INVESTIGATION - DEMON HOUSE
IDW Publishing: Feb, 2004 - No. 5, Jun, 2004 ($3.99, limited series)
1-5-Photo covers on all; Max Allan Collins-s/Rodriguez-a 4.00
TPB (10/04, $19.99) r/#1-5 20.00

CSI: CRIME SCENE INVESTIGATION - DOMINOS
IDW Publishing: Aug, 2004 - No. 5, Dec, 2004 ($3.99, limited series)
1-5-Photo covers on all; Oprisko-s/Rodriguez-a 4.00

CSI: CRIME SCENE INVESTIGATION - DYING IN THE GUTTERS
IDW Publishing: Aug, 2006 - No. 5, Dec, 2006 ($3.99, limited series)
1-5-"Rich Johnston" murdered; comic creators (Quesada, Rucka, David, Brubaker, Silvestri and others) appear as suspects; Stephen Mooney-a; photo-c 4.00

CSI: CRIME SCENE INVESTIGATION - SECRET IDENTITY
IDW Publishing: Feb, 2005 - No. 5, Jun, 2005 ($3.99, limited series)
1-5-Photo covers on all; Steven Grant-s/Gabriel Rodriguez-a 4.00

CSI: MIAMI
IDW Publishing: Oct, 2003; Apr, 2004 ($6.99, one-shots)
... - Blood Money (9/04)-Oprisko-s/Guedes & Perkins-a 7.00
... - Smoking Gun (10/03)-Mariotte-s/Avilés & Wood-a 7.00
... - Thou Shalt Not... (4/04)-Oprisko-s/Guedes & Wood-a 7.00
TPB (2/05, $19.99) reprints one-shots 20.00

CSI: NY - BLOODY MURDER
IDW Publishing: July, 2005 - No. 5, Nov, 2005 ($3.99, limited series)
1-5-Photo covers on all; Collins-s/Woodward-a 4.00

C-23 (Jim Lee's...) (Based on Wizards of the Coast card game)
Image Comics: Apr, 1998 - No. 8, Nov, 1998 ($2.50)
1-8: 1,2-Choi & Mariotte-s/ Charest-c. 2-Variant-c by Jim Lee. 4-Ryan Benjamin-c. 5,8-Corben var-c. 6-Flip book with Planetary preview; Corben-c 3.00

CUD
Fantagraphics Books: 8/92 - No. 8, 12/94 ($2.25-$2.75, B&W, mature)
1-8: Terry LaBan scripts & art in all. 6-1st Eno & Plum 3.00

CUD COMICS
Dark Horse Comics: Jan, 1995 - No. 8, Sept, 1997 ($2.95, B&W)
1-8: Terry LaBan-c/a/scripts. 5-Nudity; marijuana story 3.00
Eno and Plum TPB (1997, $12.95) r/#1-4, DHP #93-95 13.00

CUPID
Marvel Comics (U.S.A.): Dec, 1949 - No. 2, Mar, 1950

	GD	VG	FN	VF	VF/NM	NM-
1-Photo-c	18	36	54	105	165	225
2-Bettie Page ('50s pin-up queen) photo-c; Powell-a (see My Love #4)	50	100	150	315	533	750

CURIO
Harry 'A' Chesler: 1930's(?) (Tabloid size, 16-20 pgs.)

	GD	VG	FN	VF	VF/NM	NM-
nn	18	36	54	107	169	230

CURLY KAYOE COMICS (Boxing)
United Features Syndicate/Dell Publ. Co.: 1946 - No. 8, 1950; Jan, 1958

	GD	VG	FN	VF	VF/NM	NM-
1 (1946)-Strip-r (Fritzi Ritz); biography of Sam Leff, Kayoe's artist	18	36	54	103	162	220
2	11	22	33	62	86	110
3-8	10	20	30	54	72	90
United Presents...(Fall, 1948)	10	20	30	54	72	90
Four Color 871 (Dell, 1/58)	4	8	12	24	37	50

CURSED
Image Comics (Top Cow): Oct, 2003 - No. 4, Feb, 2004 ($2.99)
1-4-Avery & Blevins-s/Molenaar-a 3.00

CURSE OF DRACULA, THE
Dark Horse Comics: July, 1998 - No. 3, Sept, 1998 ($2.95, limited series)
1-3-Marv Wolfman-s/Gene Colan-a 3.00
TPB (2005, $9.95) r/series; intro. by Marv Wolfman 10.00

CURSE OF DREADWOLF
Lightning Comics: Sept, 1994 ($2.75, B&W)
1 3.00

CURSE OF RUNE (Becomes Rune, 2nd Series)
Malibu Comics (Ultraverse): May, 1995 - No. 4, Aug, 1995 ($2.50, lim. series)
1-4: 1-Two covers form one image 3.00

CURSE OF THE SPAWN
Image Comics (Todd McFarlane Prod.): Sept, 1996 - No. 29, Mar, 1999 ($1.95)

	GD	VG	FN	VF	VF/NM	NM-
1-Dwayne Turner-a(p)						6.00
1-B&W Edition	2	4	6	9	13	16
2-3						4.00
4-29: 12-Movie photo-c of Melinda Clarke (Priest)						3.00
Blood and Sutures ('99, $9.95, TPB) r/#5-8						10.00
Lost Values ('00, $10.95, TPB) r/#12-14,22; Ashley Wood-c						11.00
Sacrifice of the Soul ('99, $9.95, TPB) r/#1-4						10.00
Shades of Gray ('00, $9.95, TPB) r/#9-11,29						10.00
The Best of the Curse of the Spawn (6/06, $16.99, TPB) B&W r/#1-8,12-16,20-29						17.00

CURSE OF THE WEIRD
Marvel Comics: Dec, 1993 - No. 4, Mar, 1994 ($1.25, limited series)
(Pre-code horror-r)

	GD	VG	FN	VF	VF/NM	NM-
1-4: 1,3,4-Wolverton-r(1-Eye of Doom; 3-Where Monsters Dwell; 4-The End of the World). 2-Orlando-r. 4-Zombie-r by Everett; painted-c	1	2	3	5	6	8

NOTE: ***Briefer*** *r-2.* ***Davis*** *a-4r.* ***Ditko*** *a-1r, 2r, 4r; c-1r.* ***Everett*** *r-1.* ***Heath*** *r-1-3.* ***Kubert*** *r-3.* ***Wolverton*** *a-1r, 3r, 4r.*

CUSTER'S LAST FIGHT
Avon Periodicals: 1950

	GD	VG	FN	VF	VF/NM	NM-
nn-Partial reprint of Cowpuncher #1	15	30	45	88	137	185

CUTEY BUNNY (See Army Surplus Komikz Featuring...)

CUTIE PIE
Junior Reader's Guild (Lev Gleason): May, 1955 - No. 3, Dec, 1955; No. 4, Feb, 1956; No. 5, Aug, 1956

	GD	VG	FN	VF	VF/NM	NM-
1	8	16	24	44	57	70
2-5: 4-Misdated 2/55	6	12	18	29	36	42

CUTTING EDGE

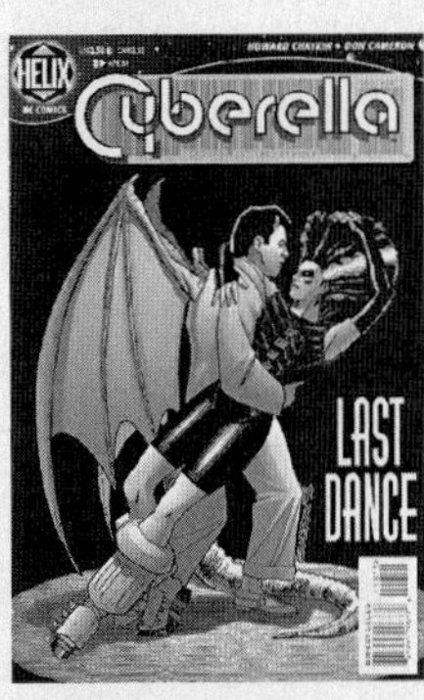

Cyberella #8 © Chaykin & Cameron

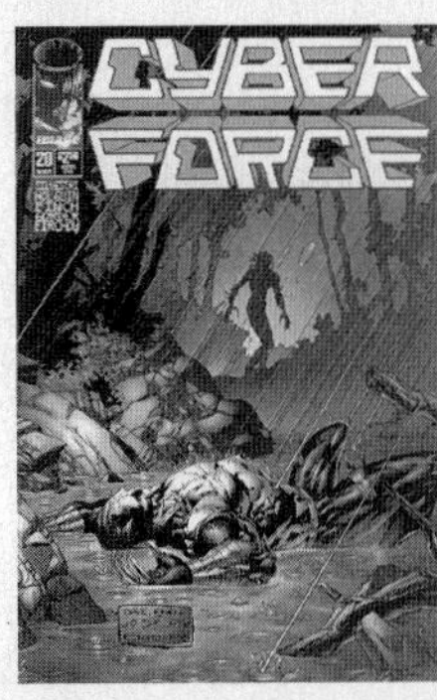

Cyberforce V2 #20 © TCOW

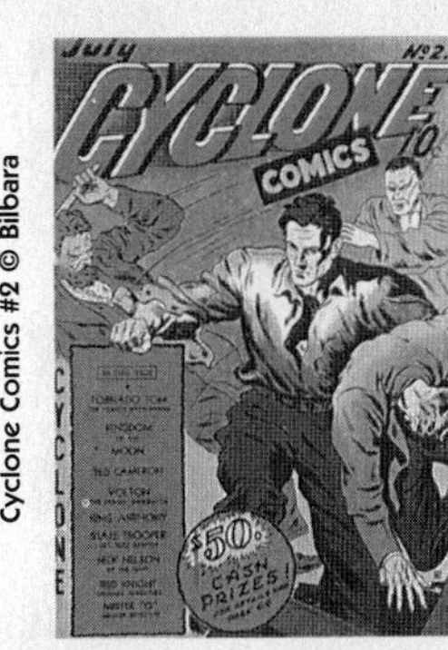

Cyclone Comics #2 © Bilbara

Marvel Comics: Dec, 1995 ($2.95)
1-Hulk-c/story; Messner-Loebs scripts 3.00

CVO: COVERT VAMPIRIC OPERATIONS
IDW Publishing: June, 2003 ($5.99, one-shot)
1-Alex Garner-s/Mindy Lee-a(p) 6.00
... - Human Touch 1 (8/04, $3.99, one-shot) Hernandez & Garner-a 4.00
TPB (9/04, $19.99) r/#1 and ... - Artifact #1-3; intro. by Garner 20.00

CVO: COVERT VAMPIRIC OPERATIONS - AFRICAN BLOOD
IDW Publishing: Sept, 2006 - No. 4, May, 2007 ($3.99, limited series)
1-4-El Torres-s/Luis Czerniawski-a 4.00

CVO: COVERT VAMPIRIC OPERATIONS - ARTIFACT
IDW Publishing: Oct, 2003 - No. 3, Dec, 2003 ($3.99, limited series)
1-3-Jeff Mariotte-s/Gabriel Hernandez-a/Alex Garner-c 4.00

CVO: COVERT VAMPIRIC OPERATIONS - ROGUE STATE
IDW Publishing: Nov, 2004 - No. 5, Mar, 2005 ($3.99, limited series)
1-5-Jeff Mariotte-s/Vazquez-a 4.00
TPB (7/05, $19.99) r/#1-5; cover gallery 20.00

CYBERELLA
DC Comics (Helix): Sept, 1996 - No. 12, Aug, 1997 ($2.25/$2.50)(1st Helix series)
1-12: 1-5-Chaykin & Cameron-a. 1,2-Chaykin-c. 3-5-Cameron-c 3.00

CYBERFORCE
Image Comics (Top Cow Productions): Oct, 1992 - No. 4, 1993; No. 0, Sept, 1993 ($1.95, limited series)
1-Silvestri-c/a in all; coupon for Image Comics #0; 1st Top Cow Productions title 6.00
1-With coupon missing 2.50
2-4,0: 2-(3/93). 3-Pitt-c/story. 4-Codename: Stryke Force back-up (1st app.); foil-c. 0-(9/93)-Walt Simonson-c/a/scripts 3.00

CYBERFORCE
Image Comics (Top Cow Productions)/Top Cow Comics No. 28 on:
V2#1, Nov, 1993 - No. 35, Sept. 1997 ($1.95)
V2#1-24: 1-7-Marc Silvestri/Keith Williams-c/a. 8-McFarlane-c/a. 10-Painted variant-c exists. 18-Variant-c exists. 23-Velocity-c. 3.00
1-3: 1-Gold Logo-c. 2-Silver embossed-c. 3-Gold embossed-c 10.00
1-(99¢, 3/96, 2nd printing) 3.00
25-($3.95)-Wraparound, foil-c 4.00
26-35: 28-(11/96)-1st Top Cow Comics iss. Quesada & Palmiotti's Gabriel app. 27-Quesada & Palmiotti's Ash app. 3.00
Annual 1,2 (3/95, 8/96, $2.50, $2.95) 3.00
NOTE: *Annuals read Volume One in the indica.*

CYBERFORCE (Volume 2)
Image Comics (Top Cow): Apr, 2006 - No. 6, Nov, 2006 ($2.99)
1-6: 1-Pat Lee-a/Ron Marz-s; three covers by Pat Lee, Marc Silvestri and Dave Finch 3.00
#0-(6/06, $2.99) reprints origin story from Image Comics Hardcover Vol. 1 3.00
.../X-Men 1 (1/07, $3.99) Pat Lee-a/Ron Marz-s; 2 covers by Lee and Silvestri 4.00
Vol. 1 TPB (12/06, $14.99) r/#1-6, #0 & story from The Cow Quarterly; cover gallery 15.00

CYBERFORCE/HUNTER-KILLER
Image Comics (Top Cow Productions): July, 2009 - No. 5, Mar, 2010 ($2.99)
1-5-Waid-s/Rocafort-a; multiple covers on each 3.00

CYBERFORCE ORIGINS
Image Comics (Top Cow Productions): Jan, 1995 - No. 3, Nov, 1995 ($2.50)
1-Cyblade (1/95) 5.00
1-Cyblade (3/96, 99¢, 2nd printing) 3.00
1A-Exclusive Ed.; Tucci-c 4.00
2,3: 2-Stryker (2/95)-1st Mike Turner-a. 3-Impact 3.00
(#4) Misery (12/95, $2.95) 3.00

CYBERFORCE/STRYKEFORCE: OPPOSING FORCES (See Codename: Stryke Force #15)
Image Comics (Top Cow Productions): Sept, 1995 - No. 2, Oct, 1995 ($2.50, limited series)
1,2: 2-Stryker disbands Strykeforce. 3.00

CYBERFORCE UNIVERSE SOURCEBOOK
Image Comics (Top Cow Productions): Aug, 1994/Feb, 1995 ($2.50)
1,2-Silvestri-c 3.00

CYBERFROG
Hall of Heroes: June, 1994 - No. 2, Dec, 1994 ($2.50, B&W, limited series)
1,2 3.00

CYBERFROG
Harris Comics: Feb, 1996 - No. 3, Apr, 1996 ($2.95)
0-3: Van Sciver-c/a/scripts. 2-Variant-c exists 5.00

CYBERFROG: (Title series), **Harris Comics**
--RESERVOIR FROG, 9/96 - No. 2, 10/96 ($2.95) 1,2: Van Sciver-c/a/scripts; wraparound-c 3.00
--3RD ANNIVERSARY SPECIAL, 1/97 - #2, ($2.50, B&W) 1,2 3.00
--VS. CREED, 7/97 ($2.95, B&W)1 3.00

CYBERNARY (See Deathblow #1)
Image Comics (WildStorm Productions): Nov, 1995 - No.5, Mar, 1996 ($2.50)
1-5 3.00

CYBERNARY 2.0
DC Comics (WildStorm): Sept, 2001 - No. 6, Apr, 2002 ($2.95, limited series)
1-6: Joe Harris-s/Eric Canete-a. 6-The Authority app. 3.00

CYBERPUNK
Innovation Publishing: Sept, 1989 - No. 2, Oct, 1989 ($1.95, 28 pgs.) Book 2, #1, May, 1990 - No. 2, 1990 ($2.25, 28 pgs.)
1,2, Book 2 #1,2:1,2-Ken Steacy painted-covers (Adults) 3.00

CYBERPUNK: THE SERAPHIM FILES
Innovation Publishing: Nov, 1990 - No. 2, Dec, 1990 ($2.50, 28 pgs., mature)
1,2: 1-Painted-c; story cont'd from Seraphim 3.00

CYBERPUNX
Image Comics (Extreme Studios): Mar, 1996 ($2.50)
1 3.00

CYBERRAD
Continuity Comics: 1991 - No. 7, 1992 ($2.00)(Direct sale & newsstand-c variations) V2#1, 1993 ($2.50)
1-7: 5-Glow-in-the-dark-c by N. Adams (direct sale only). 6-Contains 4 pg. fold-out poster; N. Adams layouts 3.00
V2#1-($2.95, direct sale ed.)-Die-cut-c w/B&W hologram on-c; Neal Adams sketches 4.00
V2#1-($2.50, newsstand ed.)-Without sketches 3.00

CYBERRAD DEATHWATCH 2000 (Becomes CyberRad w/#2, 7/93)
Continuity Comics: Apr, 1993 - No. 2, 1993 ($2.50)
1,2: 1-Bagged w/2 cards; Adams-c & layouts & plots. 2-Bagged w/card; Adams scripts 3.00

CYBER 7
Eclipse Comics: Mar, 1989 - #7, Sept, 1989; V2#1, Oct, 1989 - #10, 1990 ($2.00, B&W)
1-7, Book 2 #1-10: Stories translated from Japanese 3.00

CYBLADE
Image Comics (Top Cow Productions): Oct, 2008 - No. 4, Mar, 2009 ($2.99)
1-4: 1,2-Mays-a/Fialkov-s. 1-Two covers. 3,4-Ferguson-a 3.00
.../ Ghost Rider 1 (Marvel/Top Cow, 1/97, $2.95) Devil's Reign pt. 2 4.00
...: Pilot Season 1 (9/07, $2.99) Rick Mays-a 3.00

CYBLADE/SHI (Also see Battle For The Independents & Shi/Cyblade: The Battle For The Independents)
Image Comics (Top Cow Productions): 1995 ($2.95, one-shot)

	GD 2.0	VG 4.0	FN 6.0	VF 8.0	VF/NM 9.0	NM- 9.2
San Diego Preview	3	6	9	16	20	25
1-($2.95)-1st app. Witchblade	2	4	6	12	16	20
1-($2.95)-variant-c; Tucci-a	2	4	6	10	12	15

CYBRID
Maximum Press: July, 1995; No. 0, Jan, 1997 ($2.95/$3.50)
1-(7/95) 3.50
0-(1/97)-Liefeld-a/script; story cont'd in Avengelyne #4 3.50

CYCLONE COMICS (Also see Whirlwind Comics)
Bilbara Publishing Co.: June, 1940 - No. 5, Nov, 1940

	GD 2.0	VG 4.0	FN 6.0	VF 8.0	VF/NM 9.0	NM- 9.2
1-Origin Tornado Tom; Volton (the human generator), Tornado Tom, Kingdom of the Moon, Mister Q begin (1st app. of each)	90	180	270	576	988	1400
2	47	94	141	296	498	700
3-Classic-c (scarce)	103	206	309	659	1130	1600
4	47	94	141	296	498	700
5-(Scarce)	65	130	195	416	708	1000

Ashcan - (5/40) Not distributed to newsstands, only for in house use. Cover produced on green stock paper. A CGC certified FN (6.0) copy sold for $2,000 in 2006.

CYCLOPS (X-Men)
Marvel Comics: Oct, 2001 - No. 4, Jan, 2002 ($2.50, limited series)
1-4-Texeira-c/a. 1,2-Black Tom and Juggernaut app. 3.00

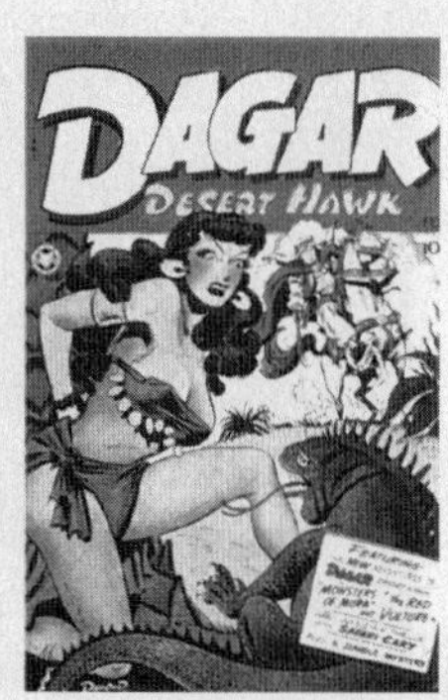

Dagar, Desert Hawk #14 © FOX

Daisy and Her Pups #22 © KING

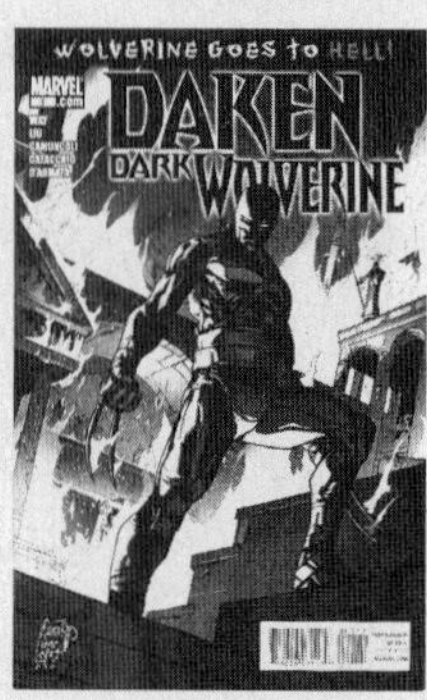

Daken: Dark Wolverine #1 © MAR

GD VG FN VF VF/NM NM-
2.0 4.0 6.0 8.0 9.0 9.2

1-(5/11, $2.99, one-shot) Haspiel-a; Batroc and the Circus of Crime app. 3.00

CYCLOPS: RETRIBUTION
Marvel Comics: 1994 ($5.95, trade paperback)
nn-r/Marvel Comics Presents #17-24 6.00

CY-GOR (See Spawn #38 for 1st app.)
Image Comics (Todd McFarlane Prod.): July, 1999 - No. 6, Dec, 1999 ($2.50)
1-6-Veitch-s 3.00

CYNTHIA DOYLE, NURSE IN LOVE (Formerly Sweetheart Diary)
Charlton Publications: No. 66, Oct, 1962 - No. 74, Feb, 1964
66-74 3 6 9 14 19 24

DAFFODIL
Marvel Comics (Soleil): 2010 - No. 3, 2010 ($5.99, limited series)
1-3-English version of French comic; Brrémaud-s/Rigano-a 6.00

DAFFY (Daffy Duck No. 18 on)(See Looney Tunes)
Dell Publishing Co./Gold Key No. 31-127/Whitman No. 128 on: #457, 3/53 - #30, 7-9/62; #31, 10-12/62 - #145, 6/84 (No #132,133)
Four Color 457(#1)-Elmer Fudd x-overs begin 10 20 30 72 131 190
Four Color 536,615('55) 6 12 18 43 69 95
4(1-3/56)-11('57) 5 10 15 35 55 75
12-19(1958-59) 4 8 12 28 44 60
20-40(1960-64) 3 6 9 20 30 40
41-60(1964-68) 3 6 9 16 23 30
61-90(1969-74)-Road Runner in most. 76-82-"Daffy Duck and the Road Runner" on-c
2 4 6 11 16 20
91-110 2 4 6 8 11 14
111-127 1 3 4 6 8 10
128,134-141: 139(2/82), 140(2-3/82), 141(4/82) 2 4 6 8 10 12
129(8/80),130,131 (pre-pack?) (scarce). 129-Sherlock Holmes parody-s
4 8 12 22 34 45
142-145(#90029 on-c; nd, nd code, pre-pack): 142(6/83), 143(8/83), 144(3/84), 145(6/84) 3 6 9 16 23 30
Mini-Comic 1 (1976; 3-1/4x6-1/2") 1 3 4 6 8 10
NOTE: *Reprint issues-No.41-46, 48, 50, 53-55, 58, 59, 65, 67, 69, 73, 81, 96, 103-108; 136-142, 144, 145(1/3-2/3-r). (See March of Comics No. 277, 288, 303, 313, 331, 347, 357,375, 387, 397, 402, 413, 425, 437, 460).*

DAFFY DUCK (Digest-size reprints from Looney Tunes)
DC Comics: 2005 ($6.99, digest)
Vol. 1: You're Despicable! - Reprints from Looney Tunes #38,43,45,47,51,53,54,58,61,62,66,70 7.00

DAFFY TUNES COMICS
Four-Star Publications: June, 1947; No. 12, Aug, 1947
nn 10 20 30 54 72 90
12-Al Fago-c/a; funny animal 9 18 27 50 65 80

DAGAR, DESERT HAWK (Captain Kidd No. 24 on; formerly All Great)
Fox Features Syndicate: No. 14, Feb, 1948 - No. 23, Apr, 1949 (No #17,18)
14-Tangi & Safari Cary begin; Good bondage-c/a 90 180 270 576 988 1400
15,16-E. Good-a; 15-Bondage-c 53 106 159 334 567 800
19,20,22: 19-Used in **SOTI**, pg. 180 (Tangi) 48 96 144 302 514 725
21,23: 21-Bondage-c; "Bombs & Bums Away" panel in "Flood of Death" story used in **SOTI**. 23-Bondage-c 52 104 156 328 552 775
NOTE: *Tangi by* ***Kamen****-14-16, 19, 20; c-20, 21.*

DAGAR THE INVINCIBLE (Tales of Sword & Sorcery...) (Also see Dan Curtis Giveaways & Gold Key Spotlight)
Gold Key: Oct, 1972 - No. 18, Dec, 1976; No. 19, Apr, 1982
1-Origin; intro. Villains Olstellon & Scor 4 8 12 24 37 50
2-5: 3-Intro. Graylin, Dagar's woman; Jarn x-over 3 6 9 14 19 24
6-1st Dark Gods story 2 4 6 9 13 16
7-10: 9-Intro. Torgus. 10-1st Three Witches story 2 4 6 9 13 16
11-18: 13-Durak & Torgus x-over; story continues in Dr. Spektor #15. 14-Dagar's origin retold. 18-Origin retold 2 4 6 8 10 12
19(4/82)-Origin-r/#18 6.00
NOTE: *Durak app. in 7, 12, 13. Tragg app. in 5, 11.*

DAGWOOD (Chic Young's) (Also see Blondie Comics)
Harvey Publications: Sept, 1950 - No. 140, Nov, 1965
1 14 28 42 99 200 300
2 9 18 27 63 107 150
3-10 8 16 24 52 86 120
11-20 6 12 18 41 66 90
21-30 5 10 15 34 55 75
31-50 5 10 15 30 48 65

GD VG FN VF VF/NM NM-
2.0 4.0 6.0 8.0 9.0 9.2

51-70 4 8 12 22 34 45
71-100 3 6 9 18 27 35
101-121,123-128,130,135 3 6 9 16 23 30
122,129,131-134,136-140-All are 68-pg. issues 4 8 12 22 34 45
NOTE: *Popeye and other one page strips appeared in early issues.*

DAI KAMIKAZE!
Now Comics: June, 1987 - No. 12, Aug, 1988 ($1.75)
1-1st app. Speed Racer; 2nd print exists 5.00
2-12 3.00

DAILY BUGLE (See Spider-Man)
Marvel Comics: Dec, 1996 - No. 3, Feb, 1997 ($2.50, B&W, limited series)
1-3-Paul Grist-s 3.00

DAISY AND DONALD (See Walt Disney Showcase No. 8)
Gold Key/Whitman No. 42 on: May, 1973 - No. 59, July, 1984 (no No. 48)
1-Barks-r/WDC&S #280,308 3 6 9 20 30 40
2-5: 4-Barks-r/WDC&S #224 2 4 6 11 16 20
6-10 2 4 6 9 12 15
11-20 1 3 4 6 8 10
21-41: 32-r/WDC&S #308 1 2 3 5 6 8
42-44 (Whitman) 2 4 6 8 11 14
45 (8/80),46-(pre-pack?)(scarce) 4 8 12 22 34 45
47-(12/80)-Only distr. in Whitman 3-pack (scarce) 5 10 15 35 55 75
48(3/81)-50(8/81): 50-r/#3 2 4 6 10 14 18
51-54: 51-Barks-r/4-Color #1150. 52-r/#2. 53(2/82), 54(4/82)
2 4 6 9 13 16
55-59-(all #90284 on-c, nd, nd code, pre-pack): 55(5/83), 56(7/83), 57(8/83), 58(8/83), 59(7/84) 3 6 9 14 19 24

DAISY & HER PUPS (Dagwood & Blondie's Dogs)(Formerly Blondie Comics #20)
Harvey Publications: No. 21, 7/51 - No. 27, 7/52; No. 8, 9/52 - No. 18, 5/54
21 (#1)-Blondie's dog Daisy and her 5 pups led by Elmer begin. Rags Rabbit app.
6 12 18 41 66 90
22-27 (#2-7): 26 has No. 6 on cover but No. 26 on inside. 23,25-The Little King app. 24-Bringing Up Father by McManus app. 25-27-Rags Rabbit app.
4 8 12 28 44 60
8-18: 8,9-Rags Rabbit app. 8,17-The Little King app. 11-The Flop Family Swan begins. 22-Cookie app. 11-Felix The Cat app. by 17,18-Popeye app.
4 8 12 26 41 55

DAISY DUCK & UNCLE SCROOGE PICNIC TIME (See Dell Giant #33)

DAISY DUCK & UNCLE SCROOGE SHOW BOAT (See Dell Giant #55)

DAISY DUCK'S DIARY (See Dynabrite Comics, & Walt Disney's C&S #298)
Dell Publishing Co.: No. 600, Nov, 1954 - No. 1247, Dec-Fef, 1961-62 (Disney)
Four Color 600 (#1) 7 14 21 47 76 105
Four Color 659, 743 (11/56) 6 12 18 37 59 80
Four Color 858 (11/57), 948 (11/58), 1247 (12-2/61-62)
5 10 15 32 51 70
Four Color 1055 (11-1/59-60), 1150 (12-1/60-61)-By Carl Barks)
9 18 27 60 100 140

DAISY HANDBOOK
Daisy Manufacturing Co.: 1946; No. 2, 1948 (10¢, pocket-size, 132 pgs.)
1-Buck Rogers, Red Ryder; Wolverton-a (2 pgs.) 21 42 63 122 199 275
2-Captain Marvel & Ibis the Invincible, Red Ryder, Boy Commandos & Robotman; Wolverton-a (2 pgs.); contains 8 pg. color catalog 21 42 63 122 199 275

DAISY MAE (See Oxydol-Dreft)

DAISY'S RED RYDER GUN BOOK
Daisy Manufacturing Co.: 1955 (25¢, pocket-size, 132 pgs.)
nn-Boy Commandos, Red Ryder; 1pg. Wolverton-a 15 30 45 85 130 175

DAKEN: DARK WOLVERINE
Marvel Comics: Nov, 2010 - Present ($3.99/$2.99)
1-Camuncoli-a/c; Way & Liu-s; back-up history of the character 4.00
2-8-($2.99) 3,4-Fantastic Four app. 7,8-Crossover with X-23 #8,9 3.00

DAKKON BLACKBLADE ON THE WORLD OF MAGIC: THE GATHERING
Acclaim Comics (Armada): June, 1996 ($5.95, one-shot)
1-Jerry Prosser scripts; Rags Morales-c/a. 6.00

DAKOTA LIL (See Fawcett Movie Comics)

DAKTARI (Ivan Tors) (TV)
Dell Publishing Co.: July, 1967 - No. 3, Oct, 1968; No. 4, Oct, 1969

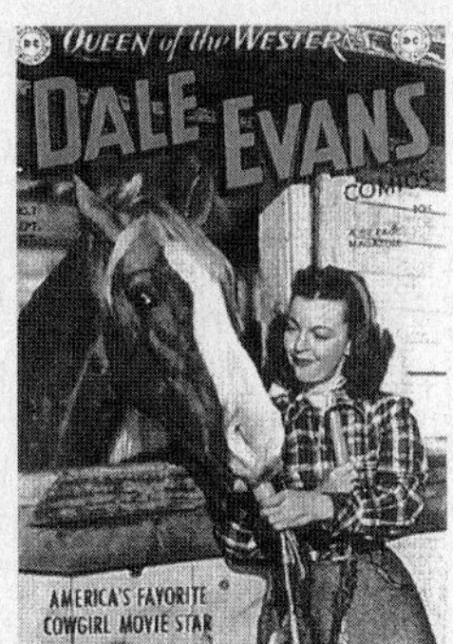

Dale Evans Comics #7 © DC

Danger #3 © Comic Media

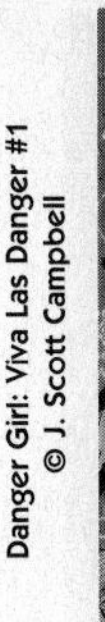
Danger Girl: Viva Las Danger #1 © J. Scott Campbell

	GD 2.0	VG 4.0	FN 6.0	VF 8.0	VF/NM 9.0	NM- 9.2
1-Marshall Thompson photo-c on all	4	8	12	24	37	50
2-4	3	6	9	18	27	35

DALE EVANS COMICS (Also see Queen of the West...)(See Boy Commandos #32)
National Periodical Publications: Sept-Oct, 1948 - No. 24, Jul-Aug, 1952 (No. 1-19: 52 pgs.)

	GD 2.0	VG 4.0	FN 6.0	VF 8.0	VF/NM 9.0	NM- 9.2
1-Dale Evans & her horse Buttermilk begin; Sierra Smith begins by Alex Toth	58	116	174	371	636	900
2-Alex Toth-a	30	60	90	177	289	400
3-11-Alex Toth-a	20	40	60	114	182	250
12-20: 12-Target-c	14	28	42	80	115	150
21-24	14	28	42	82	121	160

NOTE: *Photo-c-1, 2, 4-14.*

DALGODA
Fantagraphics Books: Aug, 1984 - No. 8, Feb, 1986 (High quality paper)

	GD 2.0	VG 4.0	FN 6.0	VF 8.0	VF/NM 9.0	NM- 9.2
1,8: 1- Fujitake-c/a in all. 8-Alan Moore story						4.00
2-7: 2,3-Debut Grimwood's Daughter.						3.00

DALTON BOYS, THE
Avon Periodicals: 1951

	GD 2.0	VG 4.0	FN 6.0	VF 8.0	VF/NM 9.0	NM- 9.2
1-(Number on spine)-Kinstler-c	17	34	51	100	158	215

DAMAGE
DC Comics: Apr, 1994 - No. 20, Jan, 1996 ($1.75/$1.95/$2.25)

	GD 2.0	VG 4.0	FN 6.0	VF 8.0	VF/NM 9.0	NM- 9.2
1-20: 6-(9/94)-Zero Hour. 0-(10/94). 7-(11/94). 14-Ray app.						3.00

DAMAGE CONTROL (See Marvel Comics Presents #19)
Marvel Comics: 5/89 - No. 4, 8/89; V2#1, 12/89 - No. 4, 2/90 ($1.00)
V3#1, 6/91 - No. 4, 9/91 ($1.25, all are limited series)

	GD 2.0	VG 4.0	FN 6.0	VF 8.0	VF/NM 9.0	NM- 9.2
V1#1-4,V2#1-4,V3#1-4: V1#4-Wolverine app. V2#2,4-Punisher app. 1-Spider-Man app. 2-New Warriors app. 3,4-Silver Surfer app. 4-Infinity Gauntlet parody						3.00

DAMNED
Image Comics (Homage Comics): June, 1997 - No. 4, Sept, 1997 ($2.50, limited series)

	GD 2.0	VG 4.0	FN 6.0	VF 8.0	VF/NM 9.0	NM- 9.2
1-4-Steven Grant-s/Mike Zeck-c/a in all						3.00

DAMN NATION
Dark Horse Comics: Feb, 2005 - No. 3, Apr, 2005 ($2.99, limited series)

	GD 2.0	VG 4.0	FN 6.0	VF 8.0	VF/NM 9.0	NM- 9.2
1-3-J. Alexander-a/Andrew Cosby-s						3.00

DANCES WITH DEMONS (See Marvel Frontier Comics Unlimited)
Marvel Frontier Comics: Sept, 1993 - No. 4, Dec, 1993 ($1.95, limited series)

	GD 2.0	VG 4.0	FN 6.0	VF 8.0	VF/NM 9.0	NM- 9.2
1-($2.95)-Foil embossed-c; Charlie Adlard & Rod Ramos-a						4.00
2-4						3.00

DAN DARE
Virgin Comics: Nov, 2007 - No. 7, July, 2008 ($2.99/$5.99)

	GD 2.0	VG 4.0	FN 6.0	VF 8.0	VF/NM 9.0	NM- 9.2
1-6-Ennis-s/Erskine-a. 1-Two covers by Talbot and Horn. 2-6-Two covers on each						3.00
7-($5.99) Double sized finale with wraparound Erskine-c; Gibbons variant-c						6.00

DANDEE: Four Star Publications: 1947 (Advertised, not published)

DAN DUNN (See Crackajack Funnies, Detective Dan, Famous Feature Stories & Red Ryder)

DANDY COMICS (Also see Happy Jack Howard)
E. C. Comics: Spring, 1947 - No. 7, Spring, 1948

	GD 2.0	VG 4.0	FN 6.0	VF 8.0	VF/NM 9.0	NM- 9.2
1-Funny animal; Vince Fago-a in all; Dandy in all	40	80	120	246	411	575
2	28	56	84	165	270	375
3-7: 3-Intro Handy Andy who is c-feature #3 on	22	44	66	132	216	300

DANGER
Comic Media/Allen Hardy Assoc.: Jan, 1953 - No. 11, Aug, 1954

	GD 2.0	VG 4.0	FN 6.0	VF 8.0	VF/NM 9.0	NM- 9.2
1-Heck-c/a	30	60	90	177	289	400
2,3,5,7,9-11:	16	32	48	94	147	200
4-Marijuana cover/story	20	40	60	114	182	250
6- "Narcotics" story; begin spy theme	18	36	54	105	165	225
8-Bondage/torture/headlights panels	20	40	60	118	192	265

NOTE: *Morisi a-2, 5, 6(3), 10; c-2. Contains some reprints from Danger & Dynamite.*

DANGER (Formerly Comic Media title)
Charlton Comics Group: No. 12, June, 1955 - No. 14, Oct, 1955

	GD 2.0	VG 4.0	FN 6.0	VF 8.0	VF/NM 9.0	NM- 9.2
12(#1)	14	28	42	76	108	140
13,14: 14-r/#12	11	22	33	60	83	105

DANGER
Super Comics: 1964

	GD 2.0	VG 4.0	FN 6.0	VF 8.0	VF/NM 9.0	NM- 9.2
Super Reprint #10-12 (Black Dwarf; #10-r/Great Comics #1 by Novack. #11-r/Johnny Danger #1. #12-r/Red Seal #14), #15-r/Spy Cases #26. #16-Unpublished Chesler material (Yankee Girl), #17-r/Scoop #8 (Capt. Courage & Enchanted Dagger), #18(nd)-r/Guns Against Gangsters #5 (Gun-Master, Annie Oakley, The Chameleon; L.B. Cole-r)	2	4	6	11	16	20

DANGER AND ADVENTURE (Formerly This Magazine Is Haunted; Robin Hood and His Merry Men No. 28 on)
Charlton Comics: No. 22, Feb, 1955 - No. 27, Feb, 1956

	GD 2.0	VG 4.0	FN 6.0	VF 8.0	VF/NM 9.0	NM- 9.2
22-Ibis the Invincible-c/story; Nyoka app.; last pre-code issue	11	22	33	62	86	110
23-Lance O'Casey-c/sty; Nyoka app.; Ditko-a thru #27	13	26	39	72	101	130
24-27: 24-Mike Danger & Johnny Adventure begin	9	18	27	50	65	80

DANGER GIRL (Also see Cliffhanger #0)
Image Comics (Cliffhanger Productions): Mar, 1998 - No. 4, Dec, 1998;
DC Comics (Cliffhanger Prod.): No. 5, July, 1999 - No. 7, Feb, 2001

	GD 2.0	VG 4.0	FN 6.0	VF 8.0	VF/NM 9.0	NM- 9.2
Preview-Bagged in DV8 #14 Voyager Pack						4.00
Preview Gold Edition						8.00
1-($2.95) Hartnell & Campbell-s/Campbell/Garner-a	1	2	3	5	6	8
1-($4.95) Chromium cover						45.00
1-American Entertainment Ed.						8.00
1-American Entertainment Gold Ed., 1-Tourbook edition						10.00
1-"Danger-sized" ed.; over-sized format	3	6	9	16	23	30
2-($2.50)						4.00
2-Smoking Gun variant cover, 2-Platinum Ed., 2-Dynamic Forces Omnichrome variant-c	2	4	6	9	13	16
2-Gold foil cover						9.00
2-Ruby red foil cover						90.00
3,4: 3-c by Campbell, Charest and Adam Hughes. 4-Big knife variant-c						3.00
3,5: 3-Gold foil cover. 5-DF Bikini variant-c						5.00
4-6						3.00
7-($5.95) Wraparound gatefold-c; Last issue						6.00
...: Hawaiian Punch (5/03, $4.95) Campbell-c; Phil Noto-a						5.00
...: Odd Jobs TPB (2004, $14.95) r/one-shots Hawaiian Punch, Viva Las Danger & Special; Campbell-c						15.00
San Diego Preview (8/98, B&W) flip book w/Wildcats preview						5.00
Sketchbook (2001, $6.95) Campbell-a; sketches for comics, toys, games						7.00
...Special (2/00, $3.50) art by Campbell, Chiodo, and Art Adams						3.50
... 3-D #1 (4/03, $4.95, bagged with 3-D glasses) r/ Preview & #1 in 3-D						5.00
...: Viva Las Danger (1/04, $4.95) Noto-a/Campbell-c						5.00
... :The Dangerous Collection nn(8/98; r-#1)						6.00
... :The Dangerous Collection 2,3: 2-(11/98, $5.95) r/#2,3. 3-('99) r/#4,5						6.00
... :The Dangerous Collection nn, 2-($10.00) Gold foil logo						10.00
... :The Ultimate Collection HC ($29.95) r/#1-7; intro by Bruce Campbell						30.00
... :The Ultimate Collection SC ($19.95) r/#1-7; intro by Bruce Campbell						20.00

DANGER GIRL: BACK IN BLACK
DC Comics (Cliffhanger): Jan, 2006 - No. 4, Apr, 2006 ($2.99, limited series)

	GD 2.0	VG 4.0	FN 6.0	VF 8.0	VF/NM 9.0	NM- 9.2
1-4-Hartnell-s/Bradshaw-a. 1-Campbell-c						3.00
TPB (2007, $12.99) r/series & covers						13.00

DANGER GIRL: BODY SHOTS
DC Comics (WildStorm): Jun, 2007 - No. 4, Sept, 2007 ($2.99, limited series)

	GD 2.0	VG 4.0	FN 6.0	VF 8.0	VF/NM 9.0	NM- 9.2
1-4-Hartnell-s/Bradshaw-a						3.00
TPB (2007, $12.99) r/series & covers						13.00

DANGER GIRL KAMIKAZE
DC Comics (Cliffhanger): Nov, 2001 - No. 2, Dec., 2001 ($2.95, lim. series)

	GD 2.0	VG 4.0	FN 6.0	VF 8.0	VF/NM 9.0	NM- 9.2
1,2-Tommy Yune-s/a						3.00

DANGER IS OUR BUSINESS!
Toby Press: 1953(Dec.) - No. 10, June, 1955

	GD 2.0	VG 4.0	FN 6.0	VF 8.0	VF/NM 9.0	NM- 9.2
1-Captain Comet by Williamson/Frazetta-a, 6 pgs. (science fiction)	45	90	135	284	480	675
2	14	28	42	80	115	150
3-10	12	24	36	67	94	120
I.W. Reprint #9('64)-Williamson/Frazetta-r/#1; Kinstler-c	8	16	24	52	86	120

DANGER IS THEIR BUSINESS (Also see A-1 Comic)
Magazine Enterprises: No. 50, 1952

	GD 2.0	VG 4.0	FN 6.0	VF 8.0	VF/NM 9.0	NM- 9.2
A-1 50-Powell-a	14	28	42	80	115	150

DANGER MAN (TV)
Dell Publishing Co.: No. 1231, Sept-Nov, 1961

	GD 2.0	VG 4.0	FN 6.0	VF 8.0	VF/NM 9.0	NM- 9.2
Four Color 1231-Patrick McGoohan photo-c	10	20	30	70	125	180

DANGER TRAIL (Also see Showcase #50, 51)
National Periodical Publ.: July-Aug, 1950 - No. 5, Mar-Apr, 1951 (52 pgs.)

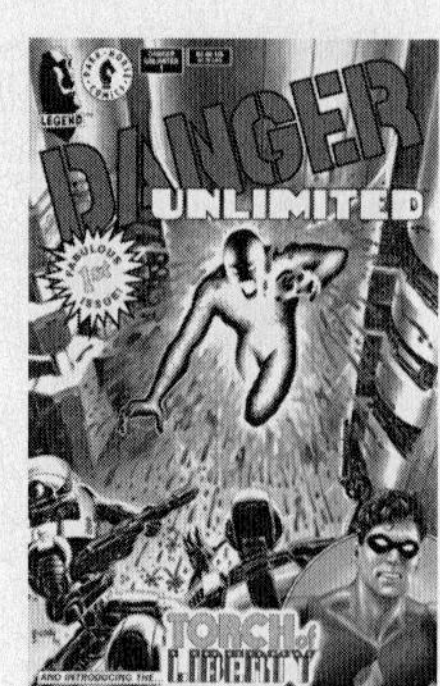

Danger Unlimited #1 © DH

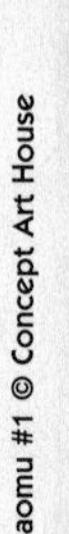

Daomu #1 © Concept Art House

Daredevil #17 © LEV

	GD 2.0	VG 4.0	FN 6.0	VF 8.0	VF/NM 9.0	NM- 9.2
1-King Faraday begins, ends #4; Toth-a in all	129	258	387	826	1413	2000
2	89	178	267	565	970	1375
3-(Rare) one of the rarest early '50s DCs	135	270	405	864	1482	2100
4,5: 5-Johnny Peril-c/story (moves to Sensation Comics #107); new logo (also see Comic Cavalcade #15-29)	68	136	204	432	746	1060

DANGER TRAIL
DC Comics: Apr, 1993 - No. 4, July, 1993 ($1.50, limited series)

	GD 2.0	VG 4.0	FN 6.0	VF 8.0	VF/NM 9.0	NM- 9.2
1-4: Gulacy-c on all						3.00

DANGER UNLIMITED (See San Diego Comic Con Comics #2 & Torch of Liberty Special)
Dark Horse (Legend): Feb, 1994 - No. 4, May, 1994 ($2.00, limited series)

	GD 2.0	VG 4.0	FN 6.0	VF 8.0	VF/NM 9.0	NM- 9.2
1-4: Byrne-c/a/scripts in all; origin stories of both original team (Doc Danger, Thermal, Miss Mirage, & Hunk) & future team (Thermal, Belebet, & Caucus). 1-Intro Torch of Liberty & Golgotha (cameo) in back-up story. 4-Hellboy & Torch of Liberty cameo in lead story						3.00
TPB (1995, $14.95)-r/#1-4; includes last pg. originally cut from #4						15.00

DAN HASTINGS (See Syndicate Features)

DANIEL BOONE (See The Exploits of..., Fighting... Frontier Scout...,The Legends of... & March of Comics No. 306)
Dell Publishing Co.: No. 1163, Mar-May, 1961

	GD 2.0	VG 4.0	FN 6.0	VF 8.0	VF/NM 9.0	NM- 9.2
Four Color 1163-Marsh-a	5	10	15	35	55	75

DANIEL BOONE (TV) (See March of Comics No. 306)
Gold Key: Jan, 1965 - No. 15, Apr, 1969 (All have Fess Parker photo-c)

	GD 2.0	VG 4.0	FN 6.0	VF 8.0	VF/NM 9.0	NM- 9.2
1-Back-c and last eight pages fold in half to form "Official Handbook Fess Parker as Daniel Boone Trail Blazers Club"	8	16	24	56	93	130
2-Back-c pin-up	5	10	15	32	51	70
3-5-Back-c pin-ups	4	8	12	26	41	55
6-15: 7,8-Back-c pin-up	3	6	9	20	30	40

DAN'L BOONE
Sussex Publ. Co.: Sept, 1955 - No. 8, Sept, 1957

	GD 2.0	VG 4.0	FN 6.0	VF 8.0	VF/NM 9.0	NM- 9.2
1	14	28	42	80	115	150
2	10	20	30	54	72	90
3-8	8	16	24	40	50	60

DANNY BLAZE (...Firefighter) (Nature Boy No. 3 on)
Charlton Comics: Aug, 1955 - No. 2, Oct, 1955

	GD 2.0	VG 4.0	FN 6.0	VF 8.0	VF/NM 9.0	NM- 9.2
1-Authentic stories of fire fighting	13	26	39	74	105	135
2	9	18	27	50	65	80

DANNY DINGLE (See Sparkler Comics)
United Features Syndicate: No. 17, 1940

	GD 2.0	VG 4.0	FN 6.0	VF 8.0	VF/NM 9.0	NM- 9.2
Single Series 17	26	52	78	154	252	350

DANNY THOMAS SHOW, THE (TV)
Dell Publishing Co.: No. 1180, Apr-June, 1961 - No. 1249, Dec-Feb, 1961-62

	GD 2.0	VG 4.0	FN 6.0	VF 8.0	VF/NM 9.0	NM- 9.2
Four Color 1180-Toth-a, photo-c	14	28	42	96	191	285
Four Color 1249-Manning-a, photo-c	13	26	39	91	176	260

DANTE'S INFERNO (Based on the video game)
DC Comics (WildStorm): Feb, 2010 - No. 6, Jul, 2010 ($3.99, limited series)

	GD 2.0	VG 4.0	FN 6.0	VF 8.0	VF/NM 9.0	NM- 9.2
1-6-Christos Gage-s/Diego Latorre-a						4.00
TPB (2010, $19.99) r/#1-6						20.00

DAOMU (Based on a novel series from China)
Image Comics: Feb, 2011 - Present ($2.99)

	GD 2.0	VG 4.0	FN 6.0	VF 8.0	VF/NM 9.0	NM- 9.2
1-3-Kennedy Xu-s/Ken Chou-a						3.00

DARBY O'GILL & THE LITTLE PEOPLE (Movie)(See Movie Comics)
Dell Publishing Co.: 1959 (Disney)

	GD 2.0	VG 4.0	FN 6.0	VF 8.0	VF/NM 9.0	NM- 9.2
Four Color 1024-Toth-a; photo-c.	9	18	27	65	113	160

DAREDEVIL ("Daredevil Comics" on cover of #2) (See Silver Streak Comics)
Lev Gleason Publications (Funnies, Inc. No. 1): July, 1941 - No. 134, Sept, 1956
(52 pgs. #52-80; 64 pgs. #35-41)(Charles Biro stories)

	GD 2.0	VG 4.0	FN 6.0	VF 8.0	VF/NM 9.0	NM- 9.2
1-No. 1 titled "Dardedevil Battles Hitler," Classic battle issue as Daredevil teams up in each strip - The Silver Streak, Lance Hale, Cloud Curtis, Dickey Dean & Pirate Prince to battle Hitler; The Claw unites with Hitler and Japanese and battles Daredevil; Origin of Hitler feature story "The Man of Hate." Classic Hitler photo app. on-c	1275	2550	3825	9500	16,500	23,500
2-London (by Jerry Robinson), Pat Patriot (by Reed Crandall), Nightro, Real American No. 1 (by Briefer #2-11), Dash Dillon, Whirlwind begin; Dickie Dean, Pirate Prince end; intro. & only app. Pioneer, Champion of America & Times Square. The Claw continues #2-4	331	662	993	2317	4059	5800
3-Intro./origin of 13. Newspaper editor has name "Roussos." Daredevil battles the Claw ill. text story	245	490	735	1568	2684	3800
4-The Claw captured and taken to New York Central Park Zoo. Whirlwind, the Blond Bomber begins, ends #6	187	374	561	1197	2049	2900
5-Ghost vs. Claw begins by Bob Wood, ends #20; 13 & Jinx begin; origin 13 retold in text; intro./origin Jinx, 13's sidekick; intro. Sniffer in Daredevil	139	278	417	883	1517	2150
6-(12/41)-Daredevil battles wolf with human brain. Dash Dillon ends	119	238	357	762	1306	1850
7,9: 7-(2/42), shows #6 on cover; delayed one month due to Pearl Harbor attack. 9-Daredevil vs. Daredevil-c; Sniffer strip begins, ends #69	97	194	291	621	1061	1500
8-Nazi WWII war-c. Nightro ends. Sniffer/Daredevil fight Nazi insurgents;	103	206	309	659	1130	1600
10-(5-42), "Remember Pearl Harbor" Japanese WWII-c; classic splash page w/American flag. Daredevil joins Air Corps. to fight Japanese. Ghost Battles Claw & Japanese. Last Whirlwind	110	220	330	704	1202	1700
11-Classic Quasimodo (hunchback of Notre Dame) bondage/torture-c/sty. London, Pat Patriot, Real America #1 end	300	600	900	2000	3000	4000
12-Origin of The Claw; Scoop Scuttle by Wolverton begins (2-4 pgs.), ends #22, not in #21. Charles Biro biography. Dickey Dean, Pirate Prince return (both end #32)	139	278	417	883	1517	2150
13-Intro of Little Wise Guys (10/42)(also see Boy #4); Daredevil fights Nazi hooded cult; Ghost battles Claw, Hitler & Nazis in Britain; Bob Wood biography	107	214	321	680	1165	1650
14-Classic Daredevil facial portrait-c; Hitler app.; "Slap the Jap" game included	71	142	213	454	777	1100
15-Death of Meatball	94	188	282	597	1024	1450
16,17: 16-WWII-c w/freighter hit by German torpedo. Meatball is buried & Curly joins Little Wise Guys team. 17-Japanese WWII-c	65	130	195	416	708	1000
18-New origin of Daredevil (not same as Silver Streak #6). Hitler, Mussolini Tojo and Mickey Mouse app. on-c at carnival	118	236	354	749	1287	1825
19,20: Last Ghost vs. Claw	60	120	180	381	653	925
21-Reprints cover of Silver Streak #6 (on inside) plus intro. of The Claw from Silver Streak #1. The Claw strip begins by Bob Q. Siege, ends #31	84	168	252	538	919	1300
22,23: 22-Daredevil fights the Tramp. 23-Dickie Dean by Bob Montana	43	86	129	271	461	650
24-Bloody puppet show-c	50	100	150	315	533	750
25-1st Little Wise Guys-c without Daredevil	34	68	102	199	325	450
26,28-30	41	82	123	256	428	600
27-Bondage/torture-c	55	110	165	352	601	850
31-Death of The Claw	81	162	243	518	884	1250
32-34: 32,33-Egbert app. 33-Roger Wilco begins, ends #35	33	66	99	194	317	440
35-37,39-41: 35-Two Daredevil stories begin, end #68; Chauncey app. 37-39-Go Along Gallagher app. (#35-41 are 64 pgs.); 41-Dickie Dean ends	34	68	102	204	332	460
38-Origin Daredevil retold from #18	45	90	135	284	480	675
42-Intro. Kilroy in Daredevil who unveils Daredevil's I.D.-c/sty	29	58	87	170	278	385
43-45,47,48-All Daredevil-c. 43-Daredevil in costume on-c & 1 panel only inside; 44-DD back in costume; i.d. revealed on-c.	27	54	81	158	259	360
46,50: DD not on-c	22	44	66	132	216	300
49-Wise Guys fight secret hooded group c/sty. DD not on-c	27	54	81	158	259	360
51,52,56-60,63-66,68,69-Last Daredevil & Sniffer (12/50). 56-Wise Guys start their own circus. DD not on-c	19	38	57	111	176	240
53-Daredevil/Wise Guys find lost palace of Zanzarah, an underground Egyptian tomb w/mummy & treasure; classic c/story. DD-c	20	40	60	120	195	270
54,55-Daredevil-c	20	40	60	117	189	260
61-Daredevil & Wise Guys in haunted house classic c/story. Daredevil/Wise Guys fly rocket into stratosphere. DD not on-c	20	40	60	120	195	270
62-Wise Guys in medieval times, a dream by Peewee locked in a medieval museum; classic c/story. DD not on-c	20	40	60	120	195	270
67-Last Daredevil-c	20	40	60	117	189	260
70-Little Wise Guys take over book without Daredevil. Daredevil removed from-c & logo; Air Devils w/Hot Rock Flanagan begins, ends #80	13	26	39	74	105	135
71-78,81: 81-Dilly Duncan begins, ends #134	10	20	30	56	76	95
79,80: 79-(10/51)-Daredevil returns; Wise Guys go to Africa. 80-Daredevil & Wise Guys blast into space & land on Mars; last Daredevil app. in title	11	22	33	60	83	105
82,90: One pg. Frazetta ad in both	10	20	30	56	76	95
83-89,91-99,101-134	9	18	27	52	69	85
100-(7/53)	11	22	33	60	83	105

NOTE: *Biro a-1-22, 38; c-1-134; script-1-134.* ***Dan Barry*** *a(Daredevil) 40-48;* ***Roy Belft****-a (Daredevil) 49-55.* ***Bolle*** *a-125.* ***Al Borth****-a(Daredevil) #57-59.* ***Briefer*** *a-1-11 (Real American #1); Pirate Prince-#1, 2, 12-31.* ***Tony***

Daredevil #10 © MAR

Daredevil #200 © MAR

Daredevil #248 © MAR

GD 2.0 | VG 4.0 | FN 6.0 | VF 8.0 | VF/NM 9.0 | NM- 9.2

*Dipreta-a(Wise Guys) #108-110, 112-134. **R.W. Hall** a-22. **Carl Hubbell** a-9-21, 23-26, 27(Daredevil), 28-32. **Al Mandel** a-13. **Hy Mankin**-a(Wise Guys)-#80, 81. **Maurer**-a(Daredevil)-23, 31, 37, 38, 41, 43-51, 53-67, 69; (Little Wise Guys)-70-89. **McWilliams** a-70, 73-80. **Bob Montana** a-12, 23, 27, 28, 31-33. **Wm. Overgard**-a(Daredevil) #67, (Wise Guys) 74-79, 83-85, 87. **Jerry Robinson** a(London) #2-8. **Roussos** a(Nightro)-2-8. **Bob Q. Siege**-a(Claw) 27-31; (Daredevil)-#35. **Wolverton** a-12-22. **Bob Wood**-a(The Claw)-1-20; (The Ghost)-5-20. **Dick Wood** sty-2-10, 13-22, 27-32. **Daredevil** not on-c #46,49-52,56-66,68-134.*

DAREDEVIL (...& the Black Widow #92-107 on-c only; see Giant-Size...,Marvel Advs., Marvel Graphic Novel #24, Marvel Super Heroes, '66 & Spider-Man &...)
Marvel Comics Group: Apr, 1964 - No. 380, Oct, 1998

1-Origin/1st app. Daredevil; intro Foggy Nelson & Karen Page; death of Battling Murdock; Bill Everett-c/a; reprinted in Marvel Super Heroes #1 (1966) 304 608 912 2645 5423 8200
2-Fantastic Four cameo; 2nd app. Electro (Spidey villain); Thing guest star 65 130 198 553 1127 1700
3-Origin & 1st app. The Owl (villain) 41 82 123 328 664 1000
4-Origin & 1st app. The Purple Man 35 70 105 273 537 800
5-Minor costume change; Wood-a begins 26 52 78 190 383 575
6-Mr. Fear app. 18 36 54 131 266 400
7-Daredevil battles Sub-Mariner & dons red costume for 1st time (4/65) 64 128 192 544 1097 1650
8-10: 8-Origin/1st app. Stilt-Man 14 28 42 102 206 310
11-15: 12-1st app. Plunderer; Ka-Zar app. 13-Facts about Ka-Zar's origin; Kirby-a 11 22 33 77 144 210
16,17-Spider-Man x-over. 16-1st Romita-a on Spider-Man (5/66) 17 34 51 122 249 375
18-Origin & 1st app. Gladiator 11 22 33 75 138 200
19,20 9 18 27 63 107 150
21-26,28-30: 24-Ka-Zar app. 7 14 21 47 76 105
27-Spider-Man x-over 8 16 24 52 86 120
31-40: 38-Fantastic Four x-over; cont'd in F.F. #73. 39-1st Exterminator (later becomes Death-Stalker) 6 12 18 41 66 90
41,42,44-49: 41-Death Mike Murdock. 42-1st app. Jester. 45-Statue of Liberty photo-c 6 12 18 37 59 80
43-Daredevil battles Captain America; origin partially retold 7 14 21 47 76 105
50-53: 50-52-B. Smith-a. 53-Origin retold; last 12¢ issue 6 12 18 39 62 85
54-56,58-60: 54-Spider-Man cameo. 56-1st app. Death's Head (9/69); story cont'd in #57 (not same as new Death's Head) 4 8 12 26 41 55
57-Reveals i.d. to Karen Page; Death's Head app. 5 10 15 30 48 65
61-76,78-80: 79-Stan Lee cameo. 80-Last 15¢ issue 4 8 12 22 34 45
77-Spider-Man x-over 4 8 12 28 44 60
81-(52 pgs.) Black Widow begins (11/71). 5 10 15 32 51 70
82,84-99: 87-Electro-c/story 3 6 9 18 27 35
83-B. Smith layouts/Weiss-p 3 6 9 20 30 40
100-Origin retold 4 8 12 26 41 55
101-104,106-120: 107-Starlin-c; Thanos cameo. 113-1st brief app. Deathstalker. 114-1st full app. Deathstalker 3 6 9 16 23 30
105-Origin Moondragon by Starlin (12/73); Thanos cameo in flashback (early app.) 3 6 9 18 27 35
121-130,137: 124-1st app. Copperhead; Black Widow leaves. 126-1st new Torpedo 3 6 9 14 20 25
131-Origin/1st app. new Bullseye (see Nick Fury #15) 9 18 27 63 107 150
132-2nd app. new Bullseye (Regular 25¢ edition) 6 12 18 37 59 80
132-(30¢-c variant, limited distribution)(4/76) 9 18 27 65 113 160
133-136-(Regular 25¢ editions). 133-Uri Geller app. 3 6 9 14 20 25
133-136-(30¢-c variants, limited distribution)(5-8/76) 4 8 12 24 37 50
138-Ghost Rider-c/story; Death's Head is reincarnated; Byrne-a 3 6 9 20 30 40
139,140,142-145,147-157: 142-Nova cameo. 147,148-(Reg. 30¢-c). 150-1st app. Paladin. 151-Reveals i.d. to Heather Glenn. 155-Black Widow returns. 156-The '60s Daredevil app. 2 4 6 13 18 22
141,146-Bullseye app. 4 8 12 22 34 45
146-(35¢-c variant, limited distribution) 7 14 21 45 73 100
147,148-(35¢-c variants, limited distribution) 5 10 15 32 51 70
158-Frank Miller art begins (5/79); origin/death of Deathstalker (see Captain America #235 & Spectacular Spider-Man #27 9 18 27 61 103 145
159 5 10 15 32 51 70
160,161-Bullseye app. 4 8 12 26 41 55
162-Ditko-a; no Miller-a 3 6 9 14 20 25
163,164: 163-Hulk cameo. 164-Origin retold 3 6 9 19 29 38
165-167,170 3 6 9 17 25 32
168-Origin/1st app. Elektra; 1st Miller scripts 11 22 33 75 138 200
169-2nd Elektra app. 5 10 15 35 55 75
171-173 3 6 9 16 23 30
174,175-Elektra app. 3 6 9 18 27 35
176-180-Elektra app. 178-Cage app. 179-Anti-smoking issue mentioned in the Congressional Record 3 6 9 17 25 32
181-(52 pgs.)-Death of Elektra; Punisher cameo out of costume 4 8 12 26 41 55
182-184-Punisher app. by Miller (drug issues) 3 6 9 14 20 26
185-191: 187-New Black Widow. 189-Death of Stick. 190-($1.00, 52 pgs.)-Elektra returns, part origin. 191-Last Miller Daredevil 2 4 6 8 10 12
192-195,198,199,201-207,209-218,220-226,234-237: 226-Frank Miller plots begin 4.00
196-Wolverine-c/app. 2 4 6 9 13 16
197-Bullseye-c/app.; 1st app. Yuriko Oyama (who becomes Lady Deathstrike) 5.00
200,238: 200-Bullseye app. 238-Mutant Massacre; Sabretooth app. 6.00
208,219,228-233: 208-Harlan Ellison scripts borrowed from Avengers TV episode "House that Jack Built". 219-Miller-c/script. 228-233-Last Miller scripts 5.00
227-Miller scripts begin 6.00
239,240,242-247 3.00
241-Todd McFarlane-a(p) 5.00
248,249-Wolverine app. 6.00
250,251,253,258: 250-1st app. Bullet. 258-Intro The Bengal (a villain) 3.00
252,260 (52 pgs.): 252-Fall of the Mutants. 260-Typhoid Mary app. 5.00
254-Origin & 1st app. Typhoid Mary (5/88) 1 2 3 4 5 8
255,256,258: 255,256-2nd/3rd app. Typhoid Mary. 259-Typhoid Mary app. 5.00
257-Punisher app. (x-over w/Punisher #10) 1 3 4 6 8 10
261-281,283-294,296-299,301-304,307-318: 270-1st app. Black Heart. 272-Intro Shotgun (villain). 281-Silver Surfer cameo. 283-Capt. America app. 297-Typhoid Mary app.; Kingpin storyline begins. 292-D.G. Chichester scripts begin. 293-Punisher app. 303-Re-intro the Owl. 304-Garney-c/a. 309-Punisher-c.; Terror app. 310-Calypso-c 3.00
282,295,300,305,306: 282-Silver Surfer app. 295-Ghost Rider app. 300-($2.00, 52 pgs.) Kingpin story ends. 305,306-Spider-Man-c 3.50
319-Prologue to Fall From Grace; Elektra returns 6.00
319-2nd printing w/black-c 3.00
320-Fall From Grace Pt 1 5.00
321-Fall From Grace regular ed.; Pt 2; new costume; Venom app. 3.00
321-($2.00)-Wraparound Glow-in-the-dark-c ed. 5.00
322-Fall From Grace Pt 3; Eddie Brock app. 4.00
323,324-Fall From Grace Pt. 4 & 5: 323-Vs. Venom-c/story. 324-Morbius-c/story 4.00
325-($2.50, 52 pgs.)-Fall From Grace ends; contains bound-in poster 4.00
326-349,351-353: 326-New logo. 328-Bound-in trading card sheet. 330-Gambit app. 348-1st Cary Nord art in DD (1/96);"Dec" on-c. 353-Karl Kesel scripts; Nord-c/a begins; Mr. Hyde-c/app. 3.00
350-($2.95)-Double-sized 4.00
350-($3.50)-Double-sized; gold ink-c 5.00
354-374,376-379: Kesel scripts, Nord-c/a in all. 354-$1.50-c begins. 355-Larry Hama layouts; Pyro app. 358-Mysterio-c/app. 359-Absorbing Man cameo. 360-Absorbing Man-c/app. 361-Black Widow-c/app. 363,366-370-Gene Colan-a(p). 368-Omega Red-c/app. 372-Ghost Rider-c/app. 376-379-"Flying Blind", DD goes undercover for S.H.I.E.L.D. 3.00
375-($2.99) Wraparound-c; Mr. Fear-c/app. 4.00
380-($2.99) Final issue; flashback story 5.00
Special 1(9/67, 25¢, 68 pgs.)-New art/story 7 14 21 47 76 105
Special 2,3: 2(2/71, 25¢, 52 pgs.)-Entire book has Powell/Wood-r; Wood-c. 3(1/72, 52 pgs.)-Reprints 3 6 9 19 29 38
Annual 4(10/76) 2 4 6 10 14 18
Annual 4(#5)-10: ('89-94 68 pgs.)-5-Atlantis Attacks. 6-Sutton-a. 7-Guice-a (7 pgs.). 8-Deathlok-c/story. 9-Polybagged w/card 4.00
... :Born Again TPB ($17.95)-r/#227-233; Miller-s/Mazzucchelli-a & new-c 20.00
... By Frank Miller and Klaus Janson Omnibus HC (2007, $99.99, dustjacket) r/#158-161, 163-191 and What If...? #28; intros by Miller and Janson; interviews, bonus art 100.00
... By Frank Miller and Klaus Janson Omnibus Companion HC (2007, $59.99, die-cut d.j.) r/#219,226-233, Daredevil: The Man Without Fear #1-5, Daredevil: Love and War, and Peter Parker, the Spect. Spider-Man #27-28; bonus materials 60.00
.../Deadpool- (Annual '97, $2.99)-Wraparound-c 4.00
....:Fall From Grace TPB ($19.95)-r/#319-325 20.00
... :Gang War TPB ($15.95)-r/#169-172,180; Miller-s/a(p) 16.00
...Legends: (Vol. 4) Typhoid Mary TPB (2003, $19.95) r/#254-257,259-263 20.00
... :Love's Labors Lost TPB ($19.99)-r/#215-217,219-222,225,226; Mazzucchelli-c 20.00
.../Punisher TPB (1988, $4.95)-r/D.D. #182-184 (all printings) 5.00
...Visionaries: Frank Miller Vol. 1 TPB ($17.95) r/#158-161,163-167 18.00
...Visionaries: Frank Miller Vol. 2 TPB ($24.95) r/#168-182; new Miller-c 25.00
...Visionaries: Frank Miller Vol. 3 TPB ($24.95) r/#183-191, What If? #28,35 & Bizarre Adventures #28; new Miller-c 25.00
... Vs. Bullseye Vol. 1 TPB (2004, $15.99) r/#131-132,146,169,181,191 16.00
Wizard Ace Edition: Daredevil (Vol. 1) #1 (4/03, $13.99) Acetate Campbell-c 14.00

NOTE: ***Art Adams** c-238p, 239. **Austin** a-191i; c-151i, 200i. **John Buscema** a-136, 137p, 234p, 235p; c-86p, 136i, 137p, 142, 219. **Byrne** c-200p, 201, 203, 223. **Capullo** a-286p. **Colan** a(p)-20-49, 53-82, 84-98, 100, 110, 112, 124, 153, 154, 156, 157, 363, 366-370, Spec. 1p; c(p)-20-42, 44-49, 53-60, 71, 92, 98, 138, 153, 154, 156, 157, Annual*

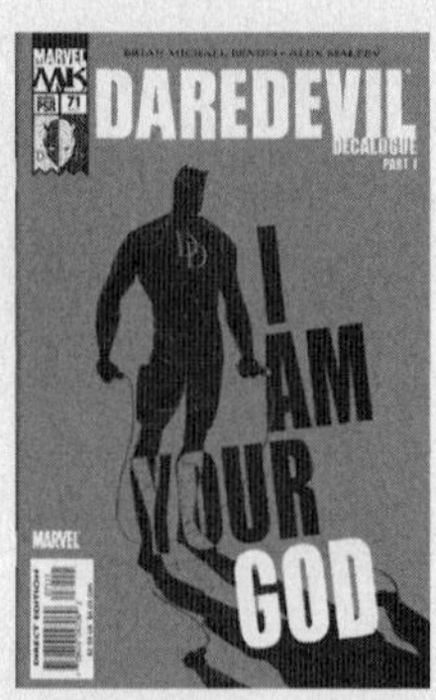

Daredevil V2 #71 © MAR

Daredevil #508 © MAR

Daredevil Reborn #2 © MAR

GD 2.0 | VG 4.0 | FN 6.0 | VF 8.0 | VF/NM 9.0 | NM- 9.2

*1. **Craig** a-50i, 52i. **Ditko** a-162, 234p, 235p, 264p; c-162. **Everett** c/a-1; inks-21, 83. **Garney** c/a-304. **Gil Kane** a-141p, 146-148p, 151p; c(p)-85, 90, 91, 93, 94, 115, 116, 119, 120, 125-128, 133, 139, 147, 152. **Kirby** c-2-4, 5p, 12p, 13p, 43, 136p. **Layton** c-202. **Miller** scripts-168-182, 183(part), 184-191, 219, 227-233; a-158-161p, 163-184p, 191p; c-158-161p, 163-184p, 185-189, 190p, 191. **Orlando** a-2-4p. **Powell** a-9p, 11p, Special 1r, 2r. **Simonson** c-199, 236p. **B. Smith** a-236p; c-51p, 52p, 217. **Starlin** a-105p. **Steranko** c-44i. **Tuska** a-39i, 145p. **Williamson** a(i)-237, 239, 240, 243, 248-257, 259-282, 283(part), 284, 285, 287, 288(part), 289(part), 293-300; c(i)-237, 243, 244, 248-257, 259-263, 265-278, 280-289, Annual 8. **Wood** a-5-8, 9i, 10, 11i, Spec. 2i; c-5i, 6-11, 164i.*

DAREDEVIL (Volume 2)(Marvel Knights)(Becomes Black Panther: The Man Without Fear #513)
Marvel Comics: Nov, 1998 - No. 512, Feb, 2011 ($2.50/$2.99)

1-Kevin Smith-s/Quesada & Palmiotti-a 12.00
1-($6.95) DF Edition w/Quesada & Palmiotti var.-c 15.00
1-($6.00) DF Sketch Ed. w/B&W-c 10.00
2-Two covers by Campbell and Quesada/Palmiotti 9.00
3-8: 4,5-Bullseye app. 5-Variant-c exists. 8-Spider-Man-c/app.; last Smith-s 6.00
9-15: 9-11-David Mack-s; intro Echo. 12-Begin $2.99-c; Haynes-a. 13,14-Quesada-a 4.00
16-19-Direct editions; Bendis-s/Mack-c/painted-a 4.00
18,19,21,22-Newsstand editions with variant cover logo "Marvel Unlimited Featuring... 4.00
20-($3.50) Gale-s/Winslade-a; back-up by Stan Lee-s/Colan-a; Mack-c 5.00
21-40: 21-25-Gale-s. 26-38-Bendis-s/Maleev-a. 32-Daredevil's ID revealed. 35-Spider-Man-c/app. 38-Iron Fist & Luke Cage app. 40-Dodson-a 3.50
41-(25¢-c) Begins "Lowlife" arc; Maleev-a; intro Milla Donovan 3.00
41-(Newsstand edition with 2.99¢-c) 3.00
42-45-"Lowlife" arc; Maleev-a 3.00
46-50-($2.99). 46-Typhoid Mary returns. 49-Bullseye app. 50-Art panels by various incl. Romita, Colan, Mack, Janson, Oeming, Quesada 3.00
51-64,66-74,76-81: 51-55-Mack-s/a; Echo app. 54-Wolverine-c/app. 61-64-Black Widow app. 71-Decalogue begins. 76-81-The Murdock Papers. 81-Last Bendis-s/Maleev-a 3.00
65-($3.99) 40th Anniversary issue; Land-c; art by Maleev, Horn, Bachalo and others 4.00
75-($3.99) Decalogue ends; Jester app. 4.00
82-99,101-119: 82-Brubaker-s/Lark-a begin; Foggy "killed". 84-86-Punisher app. 87-Other Daredevil ID revealed. 94-Romita-c. 111-Lady Bullseye debut 3.00
82-Variant-c by McNiven 4.00
100-($3.99) Three covers (Djurdjevic, Bermejo and Turner); art by Romita Sr., Colan, Lark, Sienkiewicz, Maleev, Bermejo & Djurdjevic; sketch art gallery; r/Daredevil #90 (1972) 4.00

(After Vol. 2 #119, Aug, 2009, numbering reverts to original Vol. 1 with #500)

500-(10/09, $4.99) Kingpin, Lady Bullseye app.; back-up stories, pin-up & cover galleries; r/#191; five covers by Djurdjevic, Darrow, Dell'Otto, Ross and Zircher 5.00
501-512: 501-Daredevil takes over The Hand; Diggle-s begins; Ribic-c. 508-Shadowland begins. 512-Black Panther app. 3.00
Annual #1 (12/07, $3.99) Brubaker-s/Fernandez-a/Djurdjevic-c; Black Tarantula app. 4.00
... & Captain America: Dead on Arrival (2008, $4.99) English version of Italian story 5.00
... Black & White 1 (10/10, $3.99) B&W short stories by various; Aja-c 4.00
... Blood of the Tarantula (6/08, $3.99) Parks & Brubaker-s/Samnee-a/Djurdjevic-c 4.00
... By Brian Michael Bendis Omnibus Vol. 1 HC (2008, $99.99) oversized r/#16-19,26-50, and 56-60 100.00
... By Ed Brubaker Saga (2008, giveaway) synopsis of issues #82-110, preview of #111 3.00
... Cage Match 1 (7/10, $2.99) flashback early Luke Cage team-up; Chen-a 3.00
... MGC #26 (8/10, $1.00) r/#26 with "Marvel's Greatest Comics" logo on cover 1.00
...2099 #1 (11/04, $2.99) Kirkman-s/Moline-a 3.00
TPB ($9.95) r/#1-3 10.00
...Vol. 1 HC (2001, $29.99, with dustjacket) r/#1-11,13-15 30.00
...Vol. 1 HC (2003, $29.99, with dustjacket) r/#1-11,13-15; larger page size 30.00
...Vol. 2 HC (2002, $29.99, with dustjacket) r/#26-37; afterword by Bendis 30.00
...Vol. 3 HC (2004, $29.99, with dustjacket) r/#38-50; Maleev sketch pages 30.00
...Vol. 4 HC (2005, $29.99, with dustjacket) r/#56-65; Vol. 1 #81 (1971) Black Widow 30.00
...Vol. 5 HC (2006, $29.99, with dustjacket) r/#66-75 30.00
...Vol. 6 HC (2006, $34.99, with dustjacket) r/#76-81 & What If Karen Page Had Lived? 35.00
(Vol. 1) Visionaries TPB ($19.95) r/#1-8; Ben Affleck intro. 20.00
(Vol. 2) Parts of a Hole TPB (1/02, $17.95) r/#9-15; David Mack intro. 18.00
(Vol. 3) Wake Up TPB (7/02, $9.99) r/#16-19 10.00
...Vol. 4: Underboss TPB (8/02, $14.99) r/#26-31 15.00
...Vol. 5: Out TPB (2003, $19.99) r/#32-40 20.00
...Vol. 6: Lowlife TPB (2003, $13.99) r/#41-45 14.00
...Vol. 7: Hardcore TPB (2003, $13.99) r/#46-50 14.00
...Vol. 8: Echo - Vision Quest TPB (2004, $13.99) r/#51-55; David Mack-s/a 14.00
...Vol. 9: King of Hell's Kitchen TPB (2004, $13.99) r/#56-60 14.00
...Vol. 10: The Widow TPB (2004, $16.99) r/#61-65 & Vol. 1 #81 17.00
...Vol. 11: Golden Age TPB (2005, $13.99) r/#66-70 14.00
...Vol. 12: Decalogue TPB (2005, $14.99) r/#71-75 15.00
...Vol. 13: The Murdock Papers TPB (2006, $14.99) r/#76-81 15.00
...: The Devil Inside and Out Vol. 1 (2006, $14.99) r/#82-87; Brubaker & Lark interview 15.00
...: The Devil Inside and Out Vol. 2 (2007, $14.99) r/#88-93; Bermejo cover sketches 15.00
...: Hell To Pay Vol. 1 TPB (2007, $14.99) r/#94-99; Djurdjevic cover sketches 15.00
...: Hell To Pay Vol. 2 TPB (2008, $15.99) r/#100-105 16.00

GD 2.0 | VG 4.0 | FN 6.0 | VF 8.0 | VF/NM 9.0 | NM- 9.2

DAREDEVIL/ BATMAN (Also see Batman/Daredevil)
Marvel Comics/ DC Comics: 1997 ($5.99, one-shot)

nn-McDaniel-c/a 6.00

DAREDEVIL BATTLES HITLER (See Daredevil #1[1941 series])

DAREDEVIL: BATTLIN' JACK MURDOCK
Marvel Comics: Aug, 2007 - No. 4, Nov, 2007 ($3.99, limited series)

1-4-Wells-s/DiGiandomenico-a; flashback to the fixed fight 4.00
TPB (2007, $12.99) r/#1-4; page layouts and cover inks 13.00

DAREDEVIL COMICS (Golden Age title) (See Daredevil)

DAREDEVIL/ ELEKTRA: LOVE AND WAR
Marvel Comics: 2003 ($29.99, hardcover with dust jacket)

HC-Larger-size reprints of Daredevil: Love and War (Marvel Graphic Novel #24) & Elektra: Assassin; Frank Miller-s; Bill Sienkiewicz-a 30.00

DAREDEVIL: FATHER
Marvel Comics: June, 2004 - No. 6, Feb, 2007 ($3.50/$2.99, limited series)

1-Quesada-s/a; Isanove-painted color 3.50
1-Director's Cut ($2.99) cover and page development art; partial sketch-c 3.00
2-6: 2-($2.99,10/05). 3-Santerians app. 3.00
HC (2006, $24.99) r/series; Lindelof intro.; sketch pages, cover pencils and bonus art 25.00

DAREDEVIL: NINJA
Marvel Comics: Dec, 2000 - No. 3, Feb, 2001 ($2.99, limited series)

1-3: Bendis-s/Haynes-a 3.00
1-Dynamic Forces foil-c 10.00
TPB (7/01, $12.95) r/#1-3 with cover and sketch gallery 13.00

DAREDEVIL NOIR
Marvel Comics: June, 2009 - No. 4, Sept, 2009 ($3.99, limited series)

1-4-Irvine-s/Coker-a; covers by Coker and Calero 4.00

DAREDEVIL: REBORN (Follows Shadowland x-over)
Marvel Comics: Mar, 2011 - No. 4 ($3.99, limited series)

1-3-Diggle-s/Gianfelice-a 4.00

DAREDEVIL: REDEMPTION
Marvel Comics: Apr, 2005 - No. 6, Aug, 2005 ($2.99, limited series)

1-6-Hine-s/Gaydos-a/Sienkiewicz-c 3.00
TPB (2005, $14.99) r/#1-6 15.00

DAREDEVIL/ SHI (See Shi/ Daredevil)
Marvel Comics/ Crusade Comics: Feb,1997 ($2.95, one-shot)

1 3.00

DAREDEVIL/ SPIDER-MAN
Marvel Comics: Jan, 2001 - No. 4, Apr, 2001 ($2.99, limited series)

1-4-Jenkins-s/Winslade-a/Alex Ross-c; Stilt Man app. 3.00
TPB (8/01, $12.95) r/#1-4; Ross-c 13.00

DAREDEVIL THE MAN WITHOUT FEAR
Marvel Comics: Oct, 1993 - No. 5, Feb, 1994 ($2.95, limited series) (foil embossed covers)

1-Miller scripts; Romita, Jr./Williamson-c/a 6.00
2-5 5.00
Hardcover 100.00
Trade paperback 20.00

DAREDEVIL: THE MOVIE (2003 movie adaptation)
Marvel Comics: March, 2003 ($3.50/$12.95, one-shot)

1-Photo-c of Ben Affleck; Bruce Jones-s/Manuel Garcia-a 3.50
TPB ($12.95) r/movie adaptation; Daredevil #32; Ultimate Daredevil & Elektra #1 and Spider-Man's Tangled Web #4; photo-c of Ben Affleck 13.00

DAREDEVIL: THE TARGET (Daredevil Bullseye on cover)
Marvel Comics: Jan, 2003 ($3.50, unfinished limited series)

1-Kevin Smith-s/Glenn Fabry-c/a 3.50

DAREDEVIL VS. PUNISHER
Marvel Comics: Sept, 2005 - No. 6, Jan, 2006 ($2.99, limited series)

1-5-David Lapham-s/a 3.00
TPB (2005, $15.99) r/#1-6 16.00

DAREDEVIL: YELLOW
Marvel Comics: Aug, 2001 - No. 6, Jan, 2002 ($3.50, limited series)

1-6-Jeph Loeb-s/Tim Sale-a/c; origin & yellow costume days retold 3.50
HC (5/02, $29.95) r/#1-6 with dustjacket; intro by Stan Lee; sketch pages 30.00
Daredevil Legends Vol. 1: Daredevil Yellow (2002, $14.99, TPB) r/#1-6 15.00

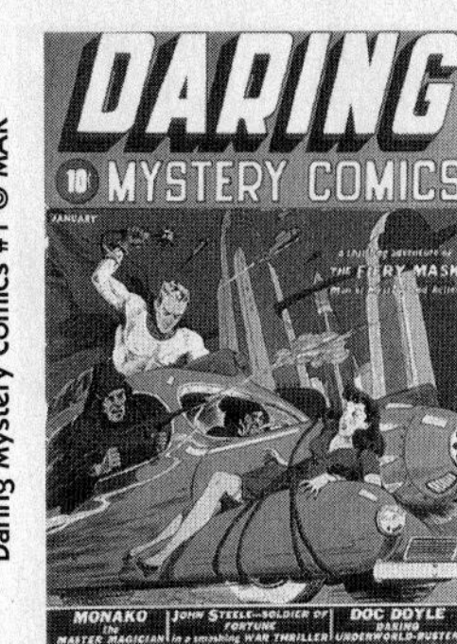

Daring Mystery Comics #1 © MAR

Dark Angel #14 © MAR

Darkchylde #4 © Randy Queen

	GD 2.0	VG 4.0	FN 6.0	VF 8.0	VF/NM 9.0	NM- 9.2

DARING ADVENTURES (Also see Approved Comics)
St. John Publishing Co.: Nov, 1953 (25¢, 3-D, came w/glasses)

1 (3-D)-Reprints lead story from Son of Sinbad #1 by Kubert 26 52 78 154 252 350

DARING ADVENTURES
I.W. Enterprises/Super Comics: 1963 - 1964

I. W. Reprint #8-r/Fight Comics #53; Matt Baker-a 5 10 15 30 48 65
I.W. Reprint #9-r/Blue Bolt #115; Disbrow-a(3) 5 10 15 32 51 70
Super Reprint #10,11('63)-r/Dynamic #24,16; 11-Marijuana story; Yankee Boy app.; Mac Raboy-a 4 8 12 22 34 45
Super Reprint #12('64)-Phantom Lady from Fox (r/#14 only? w/splash pg. omitted); Matt Baker-a 10 20 30 67 116 165
Super Reprint #15('64)-r/Hooded Menace #1 6 12 18 43 69 95
Super Reprint #16('64)-r/Dynamic #12 3 6 9 20 30 40
Super Reprint #17('64)-r/Green Lama #3 by Raboy 4 8 12 26 41 55
Super Reprint #18-Origin Atlas from unpublished Atlas Comics #1 4 8 12 24 37 50

DARING COMICS (Formerly Daring Mystery) (Jeanie Comics No. 13 on)
Timely Comics (HPC): No. 9, Fall, 1944 - No. 12, Fall, 1945

9-Human Torch, Toro & Sub-Mariner begin 139 278 417 883 1517 2150
10-12: 10-The Angel only app. 11,12-The Destroyer app. 113 226 339 718 1234 1750

NOTE: ***Schomburg** c-9-11. **Sekowsky** c-12? Human Torch, Toro & Sub-Mariner c-9-12.*

DARING CONFESSIONS (Formerly Youthful Hearts)
Youthful Magazines: No. 4, 11/52 - No. 7, 5/53; No. 8, 10/53

4-Doug Wildey-a; Tony Curtis story 17 34 51 98 154 210
5-8: 5-Ray Anthony photo on-c. 6,8-Wildey-a 14 28 42 76 108 140

DARING ESCAPES
Image Comics: Sept, 1998 - No. 4, Mar, 1999 ($2.95/$2.50, mini-series)

1-Houdini; following app. in Spawn #19,20 3.00
2-4-($2.50) 3.00

DARING LOVE (Radiant Love No. 2 on)
Gilmor Magazines: Sept-Oct, 1953

1–Steve Ditko's 1st published work (1st drawn was Fantastic Fears #5)(Also see Black Magic #27)(scarce) 97 194 291 621 1061 1500

DARING LOVE (Formerly Youthful Romances)
Ribage/Pix: No. 15, 12/52; No. 16, 2/53-c, 4/53-Indicia; No. 17-4/53-c & indicia

15 13 26 39 74 105 135
16,17: 17-Photo-c 11 22 33 64 90 115

NOTE: ***Colletta** a-15. **Wildey** a-17.*

DARING LOVE STORIES (See Fox Giants)

DARING MYSTERY COMICS (Comedy Comics No. 9 on; title changed to Daring Comics with No. 9)
Timely Comics (TPI 1-6/TCI 7,8): 1/40 - No. 5, 6/40; No. 6, 9/40; No. 7, 4/41 - No. 8, 1/42

1-Origin The Fiery Mask (1st app.) by Joe Simon; Monako, Prince of Magic (1st app.), John Steele, Soldier of Fortune (1st app.), Doc Denton (1st app.) begin; Flash Foster & Barney Mullen, Sea Rover only app; bondage-c 1950 3900 5850 14,625 26,312 38,000
2-(Rare)-Origin The Phantom Bullet (1st & only app.); The Laughing Mask & Mr. E only app.; Trojak the Tiger Man begins, ends #6; Zephyr Jones & K-4 & His Sky Devils app., also #4 1050 2100 3150 8000 14,500 21,000
3-The Phantom Reporter, Dale of FBI, Captain Strong only app.; Breeze Barton, Marvex the Super-Robot, The Purple Mask begin 514 1028 1542 3750 6625 9500
4,5: 4-Last Purple Mask; Whirlwind Carter begins; Dan Gorman, G-Man app. 5-The Falcon begins (1st app.); The Fiery Mask, Little Hercules app. by Sagendorf in the Segar style; bondage-c 371 742 1113 2600 4550 6500
6-Origin & only app. Marvel Boy by S&K; Flying Flame, Dynaman, & Stuporman only app.; The Fiery Mask by S&K; S&K-c 459 918 1377 3350 5925 8500
7-Origin and 1st app. The Blue Diamond, Captain Daring by S&K, The Fin by Everett, The Challenger, The Silver Scorpion & The Thunderer by Burgos; Mr. Millions app 371 742 1113 2600 4550 6500
8-Origin Citizen V; Last Fin, Silver Scorpion, Capt. Daring by Borth, Blue Diamond & The Thunderer; Kirby & part solo Simon-c; Rudy the Robot only app.; Citizen V, Fin & Silver Scorpion continue in Comedy #9 300 600 900 2070 3635 5200

NOTE: ***Schomburg** c-1-4, 7. **Simon** a-2, 3, 5. Cover features: 1-Fiery Mask; 2-Phantom Bullet; 3-Purple Mask; 4-G-Man; 5-The Falcon; 6-Marvel Boy; 7, 8-Multiple characters.*

DARING MYSTERY COMICS 70th ANNIVERARY SPECIAL
Marvel Comics: Nov, 2009 ($3.99, one-shot)

1-New story of The Phantom Reporter; r/app. in Daring Mystery #3 (1940); 2 covers 4.00

DARING NEW ADVENTURES OF SUPERGIRL, THE
DC Comics: Nov, 1982 - No. 13, Nov, 1983 (Supergirl No. 14 on)

1-Origin retold; Lois Lane back-ups in #2-12 1 2 3 5 6 8
2-13: 8,9-Doom Patrol app. 13-New costume; flag-c 4.00

NOTE: ***Buckler** c-1p, 2p. **Giffen** c-3p, 4p. **Gil Kane** c-6,8, 9, 11-13.*

DARK, THE
Continum Comics: Nov, 1990 - No. 4, Feb, 1993; V2#1, May, 1993 - V2#7, Apr?, 1994 ($1.95)

1-4: 1-Bright-p; Panosian, Hanna-i; Stroman-c. 2-(1/92)-Stroman-c/a(p). 4-Perez-c & part-i 3.00
V2#1,V2#2-6: V2#1-Red foil Bart Sears-c. V2#1-Red non-foil variant-c. V2#1-2nd printing w/blue foil Bart Sears-c. V2#2-Stroman/Bryant-a. 3-Perez-c(i). 3-6-Foil-c. 4-Perez-c & part-i; bound-in trading cards. 5,6-(2,3/94)-Perez-c(i). 7-(B&W)-Perez-c(i) 3.00
Convention Book 1 ,2(Fall/94, 10/94)-Perez-c 3.00

DARK ANGEL (Formerly Hell's Angel)
Marvel Comics UK, Ltd.: No. 6, Dec, 1992 - No. 16, Dec, 1993 ($1.75)

6-8,13-16: 6-Excalibur-c/story. 8-Psylocke app. 3.00
9-12-Wolverine/X-Men app. 3.50

DARK ANGEL: PHOENIX RESURRECTION (Kia Asamiya's...)
Image Comics: May, 2000 - No. 4, Oct, 2001 ($2.95)

1-4-Kia Asamiya-s/a. 3-Van Fleet variant-c 3.00

DARK AVENGERS (See Secret Invasion and Dark Reign titles)
Marvel Comics: Mar, 2009 - No. 16, Jul, 2010 ($3.99)

1-Norman Osborn assembles his Avengers; Bendis-s/Deodato-a/c 4.00
1-Variant Iron Patriot armor cover by Djurdjevic 8.00
2-16: 2-6-Bendis-s/Deodato-a/c. 2-4 Dr. Doom app. 7,8-Utopia x-over; X-Men app. 9-Nick Fury app. 11,12-Deodato & Horn-a. 13-16-Siege. 13-Sentry origin 4.00
Annual 1 (2/10, $4.99) Bendis-s/Bachalo-a; Marvel Boy new costume; Siege preview 5.00
,,,/ Uncanny X-Men: Exodus (11/09, $3.99) Conclusion of x-over; Deodato & Dodson-a 4.00
,,,/ Uncanny X-Men: Utopia (8/09, $3.99) Part 1 of x-over w/Uncanny X-Men #513,514 4.00

DARK AVENGERS: ARES
Marvel Comics: Dec, 2009 - No. 3, Feb, 2010 ($3.99, limited series)

1-3-Garcia-a/Gillen-s. 1-Nord-c. 2-Tan-c. 3-McGuinness-c 4.00

DARKCHYLDE (Also see Dreams of the Darkchylde)
Maximum Press #1-3/ Image Comics #4 on: June, 1996 - No. 5, Sept, 1997 ($2.95/ $2.50)

1-Randy Queen-c/a/scripts; "Roses" cover 6.00
1-American Entertainment Edition-wraparound-c 6.00
1-"Fashion magazine-style" variant-c 1 2 3 4 5 7
1-Special Comicon Edition (contents of #1) Winged devil variant-c 5.00
1-($2.50)-Remastered Ed.-wraparound-c 4.00
2(Reg-c),2-Spiderweb and Moon variant-c 6.00
3(Reg-c),3-"Kalvin Clein" variant-c by Drew 4.00
4,5(Reg-c), 4-Variant-c 4.00
5-B&W Edition, 5-Dynamic Forces Gold Ed. 8.00
0-(3/98, $2.50) 3.00
0-Remastered (1/01, $2.95) includes Darkchylde: Redemption preview 3.00
1/2-WIzard offer 4.00
1/2 Variant-c 6.00
... The Descent TPB ('98, $19.95) r/#1-5; bagged with Darkchylde The Legacy Preview Special 1998; listed price is for TPB only 20.00

DARKCHYLDE LAST ISSUE SPECIAL
Darkchylde Entertainment: June, 2002 ($3.95)

1-Wraparound-c; cover gallery 4.00

DARKCHYLDE REDEMPTION
Darkchylde Entertainment: Feb, 2001 - No. 2, Dec, 2001 ($2.95)

1,2: 1-Wraparound-c 3.00
1-Dynamic Forces alternate-c 6.00
1-Dynamic Forces chrome-c 16.00

DARKCHYLDE SKETCH BOOK
Image Comics (Dynamic Forces): 1998

1-Regular-c 8.00
1-DarkChrome cover 16.00

DARKCHYLDE SUMMER SWIMSUIT SPECTACULAR
DC Comics (WildStorm): Aug, 1999 ($3.95, one-shot)

1-Pin-up art by various 4.00

DARKCHYLDE SWIMSUIT ILLUSTRATED
Image Comics: 1998 ($2.50, one-shot)

1-Pin-up art by various 3.00

Dark Days #1 © Niles & Templesmith

Darkhawk #1 © MAR

Dark Horse Presents #50 © DH

	GD 2.0	VG 4.0	FN 6.0	VF 8.0	VF/NM 9.0	NM- 9.2

1-(6.95) Variant cover 7.00
1-Chromium cover 15.00

DARKCHYLDE THE DIARY
Image Comics: June, 1997 ($2.50, one-shot)
1-Queen-c/s/ art by various 3.00
1-Variant-c 5.00
1-Holochrome variant-c 8.00

DARKCHYLDE THE LEGACY
Image Comics/DC (WildStorm) #3 on: Aug, 1998 - No. 3, June, 1999 ($2.50)
1-3: 1-Queen-c. 2-Two covers by Queen and Art Adams 3.00

DARK CLAW ADVENTURES
DC Comics (Amalgam): June, 1997 ($1.95, one-shot)
1-Templeton-c/s/a & Burchett-a 3.00

DARK CROSSINGS: DARK CLOUDS RISING
Image Comics (Top Cow): June, 2000; Oct, 2000 ($5.95, limited series)
1-Witchblade, Darkness, Tomb Raider crossover; Dwayne Turner-a 6.00
1-(Dark Clouds Overhead) 6.00

DARK CRYSTAL, THE (Movie)
Marvel Comics Group: April, 1983 - No. 2, May, 1983
1,2-Adaptation of film 3.00

DARK DAYS (See 30 Days of Night)
IDW Publishing: June, 2003 - No. 6, Dec, 2003 ($3.99, limited series)
1-6-Sequel to 30 Days of Night; Niles-s/Templesmith-a 4.00
1-Retailer variant (Diamond/Alliance Fort Wayne 5/03 summit) 15.00
TPB (2004, $19.99) r/#1-6; cover gallery; intro. by Eric Red 20.00

DARKDEVIL (See Spider-Girl)
Marvel Comics: Nov, 2000 - No. 3, Jan, 2001 ($2.99, limited series)
1-3: 1-Origin of Darkdevil; Kingpin-c/app. 3.00

DARK DOMINION
Defiant: Oct, 1993 - No. 10, July, 1994 ($2.50)
1-10-Len Wein scripts begin. 4-Free extra 16 pgs. 7-9-J.G. Jones-c/a. 10-Pre-Schism issue; Shooter/Wein script; John Ridgway-a 3.00

DARKER IMAGE (Also see Deathblow, The Maxx, & Bloodwulf)
Image Comics: Mar, 1993 ($1.95, one-shot)
1-The Maxx by Sam Keith begins; Bloodwulf by Rob Liefeld & Deathblow by Jim Lee begin (both 1st app.); polybagged w/1 of 3 cards by Kieth, Lee or Liefeld 3.00
1-B&W interior pgs. w/silver foil logo 6.00

DARKEWOOD
Aircel Publishing: 1987 - No. 5, 1988 ($2.00, 28pgs, limited series)
1-5 3.00

DARK FANTASIES
Dark Fantasy: 1994 - No. 8, 1995 ($2.95)
1-Test print Run (3,000)-Linsner-c 1 2 3 5 6 8
1-Linsner-c 5.00
2-8: 2-4 (Deluxe), 2-4 (Regular), 5-8 (Deluxe; $3.95) 4.00
5-8 (Regular; $3.50) 3.50

DARK GUARD
Marvel Comics UK: Oct, 1993 - No. 4, Jan, 1994 ($1.75)
1-($2.95)-Foil stamped-c 3.50
2-4 3.00

DARKHAWK (Also see War of Kings)
Marvel Comics: Mar, 1991 - No. 50, Apr, 1995 ($1.00/$1.25/$1.50)
1-Origin/1st app. Darkhawk; Hobgoblin cameo 4.00
2,3,13,14: 2-Spider-Man & Hobgoblin app. 3-Spider-Man & Hobgoblin app. 13,14-Venom-c/story 3.50
4-12,15-24,26-49: 6-Capt. America & Daredevil x-over. 9-Punisher app. 11,12-Tombstone app. 19-Spider-Man & Brotherhood of Evil Mutants-c/story. 20-Spider-Man app. 22-Ghost Rider-c/story. 23-Origin begins, ends #25. 27-New Warriors-c/story. 35-Begin 3 part Venom story. 39-Bound-in trading card sheet 3.00
25,50: (52 pgs.)-Red holo-grafx foil-c w/double gatefold poster; origin of Darkhawk armor 4.00
Annual 1-3 ('92-'94,68 pgs.)-1-Vs. Iron Man. 2 -Polybagged w/card 4.00

DARKHOLD: PAGES FROM THE BOOK OF SINS (See Midnight Sons Unlimited)
Marvel Comics (Midnight Sons imprint #15 on): Oct, 1992 - No. 16, Jan, 1994
1-($2.75, 52 pgs.)-Polybagged w/poster by Andy & Adam Kubert; part 4 of Rise of the Midnight Sons storyline 4.00
2-10,12-16: 3-Reintro Modred the Mystic (see Marvel Chillers #1). 4-Sabertooth-c/sty. 5-Punisher & Ghost Rider app. 15-Spot varnish-c. 15,16-Siege of Darkness pt. 4&12 3.00
11-($2.25)-Outer-c is a Darkhold envelope made of black parchment w/gold ink 3.00

DARK HORSE BOOK OF... , THE
Dark Horse Comics: Aug, 2003 - Nov, 2006 ($14.95/$15.95, HC, 9 1/4" x 6 1/4")
... Hauntings (8/03, $14.95)-Short stories by various incl. Mignola (Hellboy), Thompson, Dorkin, Russell; Gianni-c 15.00
... Monsters (11/06, $15.95)-Short-s by Mignola, Thompson, Dorkin, Giffen, Busiek; Gianni-c 16.00
... The Dead (6/05, $14.95)-Short-s by Mignola, Thompson, Dorkin, Powell; Gianni-c 15.00
... Witchcraft (6/04, $14.95)-Short-s by Mignola, Thompson, Dorkin, Millionaire; Gianni-c 15.00

DARK HORSE CLASSICS (Title series), **Dark Horse Comics**
1992 ($3.95, B&W, 52 pgs. nn's): The Last of the Mohicans. 20,000 Leagues Under the Sea 4.00

DARK HORSE CLASSICS, 5/96 ($2.95) 1-r/Predator: Jungle Tales 3.00
--ALIENS VERSUS PREDATOR, 2/97 - No. 6, 7/97 ($2.95,) 1-6: r/Aliens Versus Predator 3.00
--GODZILLA: KING OF THE MONSTERS, 4/98 ($2.95) 1-6: 1-r/Godzilla: Color Special; Art Adams-a 3.00
--STAR WARS: DARK EMPIRE, 3/97 - No. 6, 8/97 ($2.95) 1-6: r/Star Wars: Dark Empire 3.00
--TERROR OF GODZILLA, 8/98 - No. 6, 1/99 ($2.95) 1-6-r/manga Godzilla in color; Art Adams-c 3.00

DARK HORSE COMICS
Dark Horse Comics: Aug, 1992 - No. 25, Sept, 1994 ($2.50)
1-Dorman double gategold painted-c; Predator, Robocop, Timecop (3-part) & Renegade stories begin 4.00
2-6,11-25: 2-Mignola-c. 3-Begin 3-part Aliens story; Aliens-c. 4-Predator-c. 6-Begin 4 part Robocop story. 12-Begin 2-part Aliens & 3-part Predator stories. 13-Thing From Another World begins w/Nino-a(i). 15-Begin 2-part Aliens: Cargo story. 16-Begin 3-part Predator story. 17-Begin 3-part StarWars: Droids story & 3-part Aliens: Alien story; Droids-c. 19-Begin 2-part X story; X cover 3.00
7-Begin Star Wars: Tales of the Jedi 3-part story 1 2 3 4 5 7
8-1st app. X and begins; begin 4-part James Bond 6.00
9,10: 9-Star Wars ends. 10-X ends; Begin 3-part Predator & Godzilla stories 4.00
NOTE: *Art Adams c-11.*

DARK HORSE DOWN UNDER
Dark Horse Comics: June, 1994 - No. 3, Oct, 1994 ($2.50, B&W, limited series)
1-3 3.00

DARK HORSE MAVERICK
Dark Horse Comics: July, 2000; July, 2001; Sept, 2002 (B&W, annual)
2000-($3.95) Short stories by Miller, Chadwick, Sakai, Pearson 4.00
2001-($4.99) Short stories by Sakai, Wagner and others; Miller-c 5.00
...: Happy Endings (9/02, $9.95) Short stories by Bendis, Oeming, Mahfood, Mignola, Miller, Kieth and others; Miller-c 10.00

DARK HORSE MONSTERS
Dark Horse Comics: Feb, 1997 ($2.95, one-shot)
1-reprints 3.00

DARK HORSE PRESENTS
Dark Horse Comics: July, 1986 - No. 157, Sept, 2000 ($1.50-$2.95, B&W)
1-1st app. Concrete by Paul Chadwick 2 4 6 8 11 14
1-2nd printing (1988, $1.50) 3.00
1-Silver ink 3rd printing (1992, $2.25)-Says 2nd printing inside 3.00
2-9: 2-6,9-Concrete app. 6.00
10-1st app. The Mask; Concrete app. 2 4 6 9 12 15
11-19,21-23: 11-19,21-Mask stories. 12,14,16,18,22-Concrete app. 15(2/88). 17-All Roachmill issue 6.00
20-(68 pgs.)-Concrete, Flaming Carrot, Mask 1 3 4 6 8 10
24-Origin Aliens-c/story (11/88); Mr. Monster app. 2 4 6 10 14 18
25-27,29-31,37-39,41,44,45,47-49: 38-Concrete. 44-Crash Ryan. 48,49-Contain 2 trading cards 3.00
28,33,40: 28-(52 pgs.)-Concrete app.; Mr. Monster story (homage to Graham Ingels). 33-(44 pgs.). 40-(52 pgs.)-1st Argosy story 4.00
32,34,35: 32-(68 pgs.)-Annual; Concrete, American. 34-Aliens-c/story. 35-Predator-c/app. 4.00
36-1st Aliens Vs. Predator story; painted-c, 36-Variant line drawn-c 5.00
42,43,46: 42,43-Aliens-c/stories. 46-Prequel to new Predator II mini-series 3.00
50-S/F story by Perez; contains 2 trading cards 4.00
51-53-Sin City by Frank Miller, parts 2-4; 51,53-Miller-c (see D.H.P. Fifth Anniversary Special for pt. 1) 1 2 3 4 6 8
54-61: 54-(9/91) The Next Men begins (1st app.) by Byrne; Miller-a/Morrow-c. Homocide by Morrow (also in #55). 55-2nd app. The Next Men; parts 5 & 6 of Sin City by Miller; Miller-c.

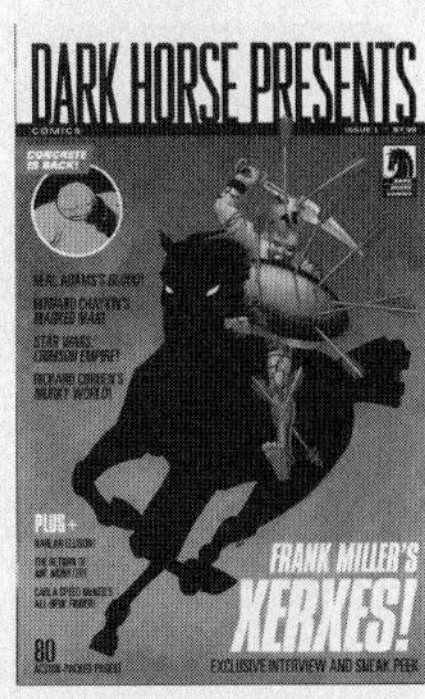

Dark Horse Presents (2011 series) #1 © DH

Dark Knight Strikes Again #3 © DC

Dark Mysteries #10 © Merit

	GD 2.0	VG 4.0	FN 6.0	VF 8.0	VF/NM 9.0	NM- 9.2

56-(68 pg. annual)-part 7 of Sin City by Miller; part prologue to Aliens: Genocide; Next Men by Byrne. 57-(52 pgs.)-Part 8 of Sin City by Miller; Next Men by Byrne; Byrne & Miller-c; Alien Fire story; swipes cover to Daredevil #1. 58,59-Alien Fire stories. 58-61- Part 9-12 Sin City by Miller 5.00
62-Last Sin City (entire book by Miller, c/a; 52 pgs.) 1 3 4 6 8 10
63-66,68-79,81-84-($2.25): 64-Dr. Giggles begins (1st app.), ends #66; Boris the Bear story. 66-New Concrete-c/story by Chadwick. 71-Begin 3 part Dominque story by Jim Balent; Balent-c. 72-(3/93)-Begin 3-part Eudaemon (1st app.) story by Nelson 3.00
67-($3.95, 68 pgs.)-Begin 3-part prelude to Predator: Race War mini-series; Oscar Wilde adapt. by Russell 4.00
80-Art Adams-c/a (Monkeyman & O'Brien) 4.00
85-87,92-99: 85-Begin $2.50-c. 92, 93, 95-Too Much Coffee Man 3.00
88-91-Hellboy by Mignola. 6.00
NOTE: *There are 5 different Dark Horse Presents #100 issues*
100-1-Intro Lance Blastoff by Miller; Milk & Cheese by Evan Dorkin 4.00
100-2-Hellboy-c by Wrightson; Hellboy story by Mignola; includes Roberta Gregory & Paul Pope stories 6.00
100-3-100-5: 100-3-Darrow-c, Concrete by Chadwick; Pekar story. 100-4-Gibbons-c: Miller story, Geary story/a. 100-5-Allred-c, Adams, Dorkin, Pope 3.00
101-125: 101-Aliens c/a by Wrightson, story by Pope. 103-Kirby gatefold-c. 106-Big Blown Baby by Bill Wray. 107-Mignola-c/a. 109-Begin $2.95-c; Paul Pope-c. 110-Ed Brubaker-a/s. 114-Flip books begin; Lance Blastoff by Miller; Star Slammers by Simonson. 115-Miller-c. 117-Aliens-c/app. 118-Evan Dorkin-c/a. 119-Monkeyman & O'Brien. 124-Predator. 125-Nocturnals 3.00
126-($3.95, 48 pgs.)-Flip book: Nocturnals, Starship Troopers 4.00
127-134,136-140: 127-Nocturnals. 129-The Hammer. 132-134-Warren-a 3.00
135-($3.50) The Mark 3.50
141-All Buffy the Vampire Slayer issue 4.00
142-149: 142-Mignola-c. 143-Tarzan. 146,147-Aliens vs. Predator. 148-Xena 3.00
150-($4.50) Buffy-c by Green; Buffy, Concrete, Fish Police app. 4.50
151-157: 151-Hellboy-c/app. 153-155-Angel flip-c. 156,157-Witch's Son 3.00
Annual 1997 ($4.95, 64 pgs.)-Flip book; Body Bags, Aliens. Pearson-c; stories by Allred & Stephens, Pope, Smith & Morrow 1 2 3 5 6 8
Annual 1998 ($4.95, 64 pgs.) 1st Buffy the Vampire Slayer comic app.; Hellboy story and cover by Mignola 1 2 3 4 5 7
Annual 1999 (7/99, $4.95) Stories of Xena, Hellboy, Ghost, Luke Skywalker, Groo, Concrete, the Mask and Usagi Yojimbo in their youth. 5.00
Annual 2000 ($4.95) Girl sidekicks; Chiodo-c and flip photo Buffy-c 5.00
...Aliens Platinum Edition (1992)-r/DHP #24,43,43,56 & Special 11.00
...Fifth Anniversary Special nn (4/91, $9.95)-Part 1 of Sin City by Frank Miller (c/a); Aliens, Aliens vs. Predator, Concrete, Roachmill, Give Me Liberty & The American stories 25.00
The One Trick Rip-off (1997, $12.95, TPB)-r/stories from #101-112 13.00
NOTE: ***Geary** a-59, 60. **Miller** a-Special, 51-53, 55-62; c-59-62, 100-1; c-51, 53, 55, 59-62, 100-1. **Moebius** a-63; c-63, 70. **Vess** a-78; c-75, 78.*

DARK HORSE PRESENTS
Dark Horse Comics: Apr, 2011 - Present ($7.99)

1-Frank Miller-c & Xerxes preview; Concrete by Chadwick; Neal Adams-s/a; Chaykin-s/a 8.00

DARK HORSE TWENTY YEARS
Dark Horse Comics: 2006 (25¢, one-shot)

nn-Pin-ups by Dark Horse artists of other artists' Dark Horse characters; Mignola-c 3.00

DARK IVORY
Image Comics: Mar, 2008 - No. 4, Jan, 2009 ($2.99, limited series)

1-4-Eva Hopkins & Joseph Michael Linsner-s/Linsner-a/c 3.00

DARK KNIGHT (See Batman: The Dark Knight Returns & Legends of the...)

DARK KNIGHT STRIKES AGAIN, THE (Also see Batman: The Dark Knight Returns)
DC Comics: 2001 - No. 3, 2002 ($7.95, prestige format, limited series)

1-Frank Miller-s/a/c; sequel set 3 years after Dark Knight Returns; 2 covers 8.00
2,3 8.00
HC (2002, $29.95) intro. by Miller; sketch pages and exclusive artwork; cover has 3 1/4" tall partial dustjacket 30.00
SC (2002, $19.95) intro. by Miller; sketch pages 20.00

DARKLON THE MYSTIC (Also see Eerie Magazine #79,80)
Pacific Comics: Oct, 1983 (one-shot)

1-Starlin-c/a(r) 4.00

DARKMAN (Movie)
Marvel Comics: Sept, 1990; Oct, 1990 - No. 3, Dec, 1990 ($1.50)

1 (9/90, $2.25, B&W mag., 68 pgs.)-Adaptation of film 4.00
1-3: Reprints B&W magazine 3.00

DARKMAN
Marvel Comics: V2#1, Apr, 1993 -No. 6, Sept, 1993 ($2.95, limited series)

V2#1 ($3.95, 52 pgs.) 4.00
2-6 3.00

DARKMAN VS. THE ARMY OF DARKNESS (Movie crossover)
Dynamite Entertainment: 2006 - No. 4, 2007 ($3.50)

1-4: 1-Busiek & Stern-s/Fry-a; photo-c and Perez and Bradshaw covers 3.50

DARK MANSION OF FORBIDDEN LOVE, THE (Becomes Forbidden Tales of Dark Mansion No. 5 on)
National Periodical Publ.: Sept-Oct, 1971 - No. 4, Mar-Apr, 1972 (52 pgs.)

1 18 36 54 131 266 400
2-4: 2-Adams-c. 3-Jeff Jones-c 10 20 30 69 122 175

DARKMINDS
Image Comics (Dreamwave Prod.): July, 1998 - No. 8, Apr, 1999 ($2.50)

1-Manga; Pat Lee-s/a; 2 covers 1 3 4 6 8 10
1-2nd printing 3.00
2, 0-(1/99, $5.00) Story and sketch pages 5.00
3-8, 1/2-(5/99, $2.50) Story and sketch pages 3.00
... Collected 1,2 (1/99,3/99; $7.95) 1-r/#1-3. 2-r/#4-6 8.00
... Collected 3 (5/99; $5.95) r/#7,8 6.00

DARKMINDS (Volume 2)
Image Comics (Dreamwave Prod.): Feb, 2000 - No. 10, Apr, 2001 ($2.50)

1-10-Pat Lee-c 3.00
0-(7/00) Origin of Mai Murasaki; sketchbook 3.00

DARKMINDS: MACROPOLIS
Image Comics (Dreamwave Prod.): Jan, 2002 - No. 4, Dec, 2002 ($2.95)

Preview (8/01) Flip book w/Banished Knights preview 3.00
1-4-Jo Chen-a 3.00

DARKMINDS: MACROPOLIS (Volume 2)
Dreamwave Prod.: Sept, 2003 - No. 4, Jul, 2004 ($2.95)

1-4-Chris Sarracini-s/Kwang Mook Lim-a 3.00

DARKMINDS / WITCHBLADE (Also see Witchblade/Dark Minds)
Image Comics (Top Cow/Dreamwave Prod.): Aug, 2000 ($5.95, one-shot)

1-Wohl-s/Pat Lee-a; two covers by Silvestri and Lee 6.00

DARK MYSTERIES (Thrilling Tales of Horror & Suspense)
"Master" - "Merit" Publications: June-July, 1951 - No. 24, July, 1955

1-Wood-c/a (8 pgs.) 135 270 405 864 1482 2100
2-Classic skull-c; Wood/Harrison-c/a (8 pgs.) 90 180 270 576 988 1400
3-9: 7-Dismemberment, hypo blood drainage stys 48 96 144 302 514 725
10-Cannibalism story; witch burning-c 53 106 159 334 567 800
11-13,15-18: 11-Severed head panels. 13-Dismemberment-c/story. 17-The Old Gravedigger host 42 84 126 265 445 625
14-Several E.C. Craig swipes 42 84 126 267 451 635
19-Injury-to-eye panel; E.C. swipe; torture-c 53 106 159 334 567 800
20-Female bondage, blood drainage story 47 94 141 296 498 700
21,22: 21-Devil-c. 22-Last pre-code issue, misdated 3/54 instead of 3/55 34 68 102 199 325 450
23,24 22 44 66 132 216 300
NOTE: ***Cameron** a-1, 2. **Myron Fass** c/a-21. **Harrison** a-3, 7; c-3. **Hollingsworth** a-7-17, 20, 21, 23. **Wildey** a-5. Woodish art by **Fleishman**-9; c-10, 14-17. Bondage c-10, 18, 19.*

DARK NEMESIS (VILLAINS) (See Teen Titans)
DC Comics: Feb, 1998 ($1.95, one-shot)

1-Jurgens-s/Pearson-c 3.00

DARKNESS, THE (See Witchblade #10)
Image Comics (Top Cow Productions): Dec, 1996 - No. 40, Aug, 2001 ($2.50)

Special Preview Edition-(7/96, B&W)-Ennis script; Silvestri-a(p) 2 4 6 9 13 16
0 2 4 6 8 10 12
0-Gold Edition 16.00
1/2 1 3 4 6 8 10
1/2-Christmas-c 3 6 9 14 19 24
1/2-(3/01, $2.95) r/#1/2 w/new 6 pg. story & Silvestri-c 3.00
1-Ennis-s/Silvestri-a, 1-Black variant-c 2 4 6 9 12 15
1-Platinum variant-c 20.00
1-DF Green variant-c 12.00
1,2: 1-Fan Club Ed. 1 3 4 6 8 10
3-5 6.00
6-10: 9,10-Witchblade "Family Ties" x-over pt. 2,3 4.00
7-Variant-c w/concubine 1 2 3 5 7 9
8-American Entertainment 6.00

Darkness #84 © TCOW

Dark Reign: The Cabal #1 © MAR

Darkseid (Villains) #1 © DC

	GD 2.0	VG 4.0	FN 6.0	VF 8.0	VF/NM 9.0	NM- 9.2
8-10-American Entertainment Gold Ed.						7.00
11-Regular Ed.; Ennis-s/Silvestri & D-Tron-c						3.00
11-Nine (non-chromium) variant-c (Benitez, Cabrera, the Hildebrandts, Finch, Keown, Peterson, Portacio, Tan, Turner						4.50
11-Chromium-c by Silvestri & Batt						20.00
12-19: 13-Begin Benitez-a(p)						3.00
20-24,26-40: 34-Ripclaw app.						3.00
25-($3.99) Two covers (Benitez, Silvestri)						4.00
25-Chromium-c variant by Silvestri						8.00
.../ Batman (8/99, $5.95) Silvestri, Finch, Lansing-a(p)						6.00
...Collected Editions #1-4 ($4.95,TPB) 1-r/#1,2. 2-r/#3,4. 3- r/#5,6. 4- r/#7,8						6.00
...Collected Editions #5,6 ($5.95, TPB)5- r/#11,12. 6-r/#13,14						6.00
Deluxe Collected Editions #1 (12/98, $14.95, TPB) r/#1-6 & Preview						15.00
...: Heart of Darkness (2001, $14.95, TPB) r/ #7,8, 11-14						15.00
Holiday Pin-up-American Entertainment						5.00
Holiday Pin-up Gold Ed.-American Entertainment						7.00
Image Firsts: Darkness #1 (9/10, $1.00) r/#1 with "Image Firsts" logo on cover						1.00
Infinity #1 (8/99, $3.50) Lobdell-s						3.50
Prelude-American Entertainment						4.00
Prelude Gold Ed.-American Entertainment						9.00
Volume 1 Compendium (2006, $59.99) r/#1-40, V2 #1, Tales of the Darkness #1-4; #1/2, Darkness/Witchblade #1/2, Darkness: Wanted Dead; cover and sketch gallery						60.00
...: Wanted Dead 1 (8/03, $2.99) Texiera-a/Tieri-s						3.00
Wizard ACE Ed.- Reprints #1	2	4	6	8	10	12

DARKNESS (Volume 2)
Image Comics (Top Cow Productions): Dec, 2002 - No. 24, Oct, 2004 ($2.99)

1-24: 1-6-Jenkins-s/Keown-a. 17-20-Lapham-s. 23,24-Magdalena app.						3.00
... Black Sails (3/05, $2.99) Marz-s/Cha-a; Hunter-Killer preview						3.00
... and Tomb Raider (4/05, $2.99) r/Darkness Prelude & Tomb Raider/Darkness Special						3.00
...: Resurrection TPB (2/04, $16.99) r/#1-6 & Vol. 1 #40						17.00
.../ The Incredible Hulk (7/04, $2.99) Keown-a/Jenkins-s						3.00
.../ Vampirella (7/05, $2.99) Terry Moore-s; two covers by Basaldua and Moore						3.00
... Vol. 5 TPB (2006, $19.99) r/#7-16 & The Darkness: Wanted Dead #1; cover gallery						20.00
... vs. Mr Hyde Monster War 2005 (9/05, $2.99) x-over w/Witchblade, Tomb Raider and Magdalena; two covers						3.00
.../ Wolverine (2006, $2.99) Kirkham-a/Tieri-s						3.00

DARKNESS (Volume 3) (Numbering jumps from #10 to #75)
Image Comics (Top Cow Productions): Dec, 2007 - Present ($2.99)

1-10: 1-Hester-s/Broussard-a. 1-Three covers. 7-9-Lucas-a. 8-Aphrodite IV app.						3.00
75 (2/09, $4.99) Four covers; Hester-s/art by various						5.00
76-90-($2.99) Multiple covers on each						3.00
...: Butcher (4/08, $3.99) Story of Butcher Joyce; Levin-s/Broussard-a/c						4.00
... / Darkchylde: Kingdom Pain 1 (5/10, $4.99) Randy Queen-s/a						5.00
... First Look (11/07, 99¢) Previews series; sketch pages						3.00
...: Lodbrok's Hand (12/08, $2.99) Hester-s/Oeming-a/c; variant-c by Carnevale						3.00
...: Shadows and Flame 1 (1/10, $2.99) Lucas-c/a						3.00

DARKNESS: FOUR HORSEMEN
Image Comics (Top Cow): Aug, 2010 - No. 4 ($3.99, limited series)

1-3-Hine-s/Wamester-a — 4.00

DARKNESS: LEVEL...
Image Comics (Top Cow): No. 0, Dec, 2006 - No. 5, Aug, 2007 ($2.99, limited series)

0-5: 0-Origin of The Darkness in WW1; Jenkins-s. 1-Jackie's origin retold; Sejic-a — 3.00

DARKNESS/ PITT
Image Comics (Top Cow): Dec, 2006; Aug, 2009 - No. 3, Nov, 2009 ($2.99)

...: First Look (12/06) Jenkins script pages with Keown B&W and color art — 3.00
1-3: 1-(8/09) Jenkins-s/Keown-a; covers by Keown and Sejic. 2,3-Two covers — 3.00

DARKNESS/ SUPERMAN
Image Comics (Top Cow Productions): Jan, 2005 - No. 2, Feb, 2005 ($2.99, limited series)

1,2-Marz-s/Kirkham & Banning-a/Silvestri-c — 3.00

DARKNESS VS. EVA: DAUGHTER OF DRACULA
Dynamite Entertainment: 2008 - No. 4, 2008 ($3.50, limited series)

1-4-Leah Moore & John Reppion-s/Salazar-a; three covers on each — 3.50

DARK REIGN (Follows Secret Invasion crossover)
Marvel Comics: 2009 ($3.99/$4.99, one-shots)

...: Files 1 (2009, $4.99) profile pages of villains tied in to Dark Reign x-over						5.00
...: Made Men 1 (11/09, $3.99) short stories by various incl. Pham, Leon, Oliver						4.00
...: New Nation 1 (2/09, $3.99) previews of various series tied in to Dark Reign x-over						4.00
...: The Cabal 1 (6/09, $3.99) Cabal members stories by various incl. Granov, Acuña						4.00
...: The Goblin Legacy 1 (2009, $3.99) r/ASM #39,40; Osborn history; Mayhew-a						4.00

DARK REIGN: ELEKTRA
Marvel Comics: May, 2009 - No. 5, Oct, 2009 ($3.99, limited series)

1-5-Mann-a/Bermejo-c; Elektra after the Skrull replacement. 2,3-Bullseye app. — 4.00

DARK REIGN: FANTASTIC FOUR
Marvel Comics: May, 2009 - No. 5, Sept, 2009 ($2.99, limited series)

1-5-Chen-a — 3.00

DARK REIGN: HAWKEYE
Marvel Comics: June, 2009 - No. 5, Mar, 2010 ($3.99, limited series)

1-5-Bullseye in the Dark Avengers; Raney-a/Langley-c. 5-Guinaldo-a — 4.00

DARK REIGN: LETHAL LEGION
Marvel Comics: Aug, 2009 - No. 3, Nov, 2009 ($3.99, limited series)

1-3-Santolouco-a/Edwards-c; Grim Reaper and Wonder Man app. — 4.00

DARK REIGN: MR. NEGATIVE (Also see Amazing Spider-Man #546)
Marvel Comics: Aug, 2009 - No. 3, Oct, 2009 ($3.99, limited series)

1-3-Jae Lee-c/Gugliotta-a; Spider-Man app. — 4.00

DARK REIGN: SINISTER SPIDER-MAN
Marvel Comics: Aug, 2009 - No. 4, Nov, 2009 ($3.99, limited series)

1-4-Bachalo-c/a; Venom/Scorpion as Dark Avenger Spider-Man — 4.00

DARK REIGN: THE HOOD
Marvel Comics: Jul, 2009 - No. 5, Nov, 2009 ($3.99, limited series)

1-5-Hotz-a/Djurdjevic-c — 4.00

DARK REIGN: THE LIST
Marvel Comics: 2009 - 2010 ($3.99, one-shots)

... - Amazing Spider-Man (1/10, $3.99) Adam Kubert-c/a; back-up r/Pulse #5						4.00
... - Avengers (11/09, $3.99) Bendis-s/Djurdjevic-c/a; Ronin (Hawkeye) app.						4.00
... - Daredevil (11/09, $3.99) Diggle-s/Tan-c/a; Bullseye app.; leads into Daredevil #501						4.00
... - Hulk (12/09, $3.99) Pak-s/Oliver-a; Skaar app.; back-up r/Amaz. Spider-Man #14						4.00
... - Punisher (12/09, $3.99) Romita Jr.-a/c; Castle killed by Daken; preview of Franken-Castle in Punisher #11						6.00
... - Secret Warriors (12/09, $3.99) McGuinness-a/c; Nick Fury; back-up r/Steranko-a						4.00
... - Wolverine (12/09, $3.99) Ribic-a/c; Marvel Boy and Fantomex app.						4.00
... - X-Men (11/09, $3.99) Alan Davis-a/c; Namor app.; back-up r/Kieth-a						4.00

DARK REIGN: YOUNG AVENGERS
Marvel Comics: Jul, 2009 - No. 5, Dec, 2009 ($3.99, limited series)

1-5-Brooks-a; Osborn's Young Avengers vs. original Young Avengers — 4.00

DARK REIGN: ZODIAC
Marvel Comics: Aug, 2009 - No. 3, Nov, 2009 ($3.99, limited series)

1-3-Casey-s/Fox-a. 1-Human Torch app. — 4.00

DARKSEID (VILLAINS) (See Jack Kirby's New Gods and New Gods)
DC Comics: Feb, 1998 ($1.95, one-shot)

1-Byrne-s/Pearson-c — 3.00

DARKSEID VS. GALACTUS: THE HUNGER
DC Comics: 1995 ($4.95, one-shot) (1st DC/Marvel x-over by John Byrne)

nn-John Byrne-c/a/script — 5.00

DARK SHADOWS
Steinway Comic Publ. (Ajax)(America's Best): Oct, 1957 - No. 3, May, 1958

	GD 2.0	VG 4.0	FN 6.0	VF 8.0	VF/NM 9.0	NM- 9.2
1	28	56	84	165	270	375
2,3	20	40	60	114	182	250

DARK SHADOWS (TV) (See Dan Curtis Giveaways)
Gold Key: Mar, 1969 - No. 35, Feb, 1976 (Photo-c: 1-7)

	GD 2.0	VG 4.0	FN 6.0	VF 8.0	VF/NM 9.0	NM- 9.2
1(30039-903)-With pull-out poster (25¢)	21	42	63	150	300	450
1-With poster missing	8	16	24	56	93	130
2	9	18	27	63	107	150
3-With pull-out poster	10	20	30	70	125	180
3-With poster missing	6	12	18	41	66	90
4-7: 7-Last photo-c	7	14	21	45	73	100
8-10	5	10	15	32	51	70
11-20	4	8	12	28	44	60
21-35: 30-Last painted-c	4	8	12	24	37	50
Story Digest 1 (6/70, 148pp.)-Photo-c (low print)	8	16	24	54	90	125

DARK SHADOWS (TV) (See Nightmare on Elm Street)
Innovation Publishing: June, 1992 - No. 4, Spring, 1993 ($2.50, limited series, coated stock)

1-Based on 1991 NBC TV mini-series; painted-c — 5.00
2-4 — 4.00

Darkstar and the Winter Guard #1 © MAR

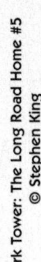

Dark Tower: The Long Road Home #5 © Stephen King

Darkwing Duck (2010 series) #6 © DIS

DARK SHADOWS: BOOK TWO
Innovation Publishing: 1993 - No. 4, July, 1993 ($2.50, limited series)

1-4-Painted-c. 4-Maggie Thompson scripts 4.00

DARK SHADOWS: BOOK THREE
Innovation Publishing: Nov, 1993 ($2.50)

1-(Whole #9) 4.00

DARKSTAR AND THE WINTER GUARD
Marvel Comics: Aug, 2010 - No. 3, Oct, 2010 ($3.99, limited series)

1-3-Gallaher-s/Ellis-a/Henry-c; back-up reprint from X-Men Unlimited #28 4.00

DARKSTARS, THE
DC Comics: Oct, 1992 - No. 38, Jan, 1996 ($1.75/$1.95)

1-1st app. The Darkstars 3.00
2-24,0,25-38: 5-Hawkman & Hawkwoman app. 18-20-Flash app. 24-(9/94)-Zero Hour. 0-(10/94). 25-(11/94). 30-Green Lantern app. 31-...vs. Darkseid. 32-Green Lantern app. 3.00
NOTE: ***Travis Charest** a(p)-4-7; c(p)-2-5; c-6-11. **Stroman** a-1-3; c-1.*

DARK TOWER: THE BATTLE OF JERICHO HILL (Based on Stephen King's Dark Tower)
Marvel Comics: Feb, 2010 - No. 5, Jun, 2010 ($3.99, limited series)

1-5-Peter David & Robin Furth-s/Jae Lee & Richard Isanove-a/c; variant-c for each 4.00

DARK TOWER: THE FALL OF GILEAD (Based on Stephen King's Dark Tower)
Marvel Comics: July, 2009 - No. 6, Jan, 2010 ($3.99, limited series)

1-6-Peter David & Robin Furth-s/Richard Isanove-a/Jae Lee-c; variant-c for each 4.00
Dark Tower: Guide to Gilead (2009, $3.99) profile pages of people and places 4.00

DARK TOWER: THE GUNSLINGER BORN (Based on Stephen King's Dark Tower series)
Marvel Comics: Apr, 2007 - No. 7, Oct, 2007 ($3.99, limited series)

1-Peter David & Robin Furth-s/Jae Lee & Richard Isanove-a; boyhood of Roland Deschain; afterword by Ralph Macchio; map of New Canaan 6.00
1-Variant cover by Quesada 8.00
1-Second printing with variant-c by Quesada 5.00
1-Sketch cover variant by Jae Lee 40.00
2-6-Jae Lee-c 4.00
2-Second printing with variant-c by Immonen 4.00
2-7-Variant covers. 2-Finch-c. 3-Yu-c. 4-McNiven-c. 5-Land-c. 6-Campbell. 7-Coipel 6.00
2-7-B&W sketch-c by Jae Lee 20.00
... MGC #1 (5/11, $1.00) r/#1 with "Marvel's Greatest Comics" logo on cover 1.00
... Sketchbook (2006, no cover price) pencil art and designs by Lee; coloring process 5.00
Dark Tower: Gunslinger's Guidebook (2007, $3.99) profile pages with Jae Lee-a 4.00
HC (2007, $24.99) r/#1-7; variant covers and sketch pages; Macchio intro. 25.00

DARK TOWER: THE GUNSLINGER - THE JOURNEY BEGINS (Stephen King's Dark Tower)
Marvel Comics: Jul, 2010 - No. 5, Nov, 2010 ($3.99, limited series)

1-Peter David & Robin Furth-s/Sean Phillips-a/c 4.00
1-Variant cover by Jae Lee 5.00

DARK TOWER: THE GUNSLINGER - THE LITTLE SISTERS OF ELURIA (Stephen King)
Marvel Comics: Feb, 2011 - No. 5, Jun, 2011 ($3.99, limited series)

1-Peter David & Robin Furth-s/Luke Ross-a/c 4.00

DARK TOWER: THE LONG ROAD HOME (Based on Stephen King's Dark Tower series)
Marvel Comics: May, 2008 - No. 5, Sept, 2008 ($3.99, limited series)

1-Peter David & Robin Furth-s/Jae Lee & Richard Isanove-a 4.00
1-Variant cover by Deodato 6.00
1-Sketch cover variant by Jae Lee 40.00
2-5-Jae Lee-c 4.00
2-5: 2-Variant-c by Quesada. 3-Djurdjevic var-c. 4-Garney var-c. 5-Bermejo var-c 6.00
2-5-B&W sketch-c by Jae Lee 20.00
2-Second printing with variant-c by Lee 4.00
Dark Tower: End-World Almanac (2008, $3.99) guide to locations and inhabitants 4.00

DARK TOWER: THE SORCEROR (Based on Stephen King's Dark Tower)
Marvel Comics: June, 2009 ($3.99, one-shot)

1-Robin Furth-s/Richard Isanove-a/c; the story of Marten Broadcloak 4.00

DARK TOWER: TREACHERY (Based on Stephen King's Dark Tower series)
Marvel Comics: Nov, 2008 - No. 6, Apr, 2009 ($3.99, limited series)

1-6-Peter David & Robin Furth-s/Jae Lee & Richard Isanove-a 4.00
1-Variant cover by Dell'otto 10.00

DARKWING DUCK (TV cartoon) (Also see Cartoon Tales)
Disney Comics: Nov, 1991 - No. 4, Feb, 1992 ($1.50, limited series)

1-4: Adapts hour-long premiere TV episode 3.00

DARKWING DUCK (TV cartoon)
BOOM! Studios (KABOOM!): Jun, 2010 - Present ($3.99)

1-Brill-s/Silvani-a; Launchpad McQuack app.; 3 covers 5.00
2-11: Multiple covers on all. 7-Batman #1 cover swipe. 8-Detective #31 cover swipe 4.00
Annual 1 (3/11, $4.99) Three covers; Quackerjack app. 5.00
... Free Comic Book Day Edition (5/11) Flip book with Chip 'N' Dale Rescue Rangers 2.00

DARK WOLVERINE (See Wolverine 2003 series)

DARK X-MEN (See Dark Avengers and the Dark Reign mini-series)
Marvel Comics: Jan, 2010 - No. 5, May, 2010 ($3.99, limited series)

1-5-Cornell-s/Kirk-a. 1-3-Bianchi-c. 1-Nate Grey returns 4.00
...: The Confession (11/09, $3.99) Cansino-a; Paquette-c 4.00

DARK X-MEN: THE BEGINNING (See Dark Avengers and the Dark Reign mini-series)
Marvel Comics: Sept, 2009 - No. 3, Oct, 2009 ($3.99, limited series)

1-3: 1-Cornell-s/Kirk-a; Jae Lee-c on all. 2-Daken app. 3-Mystique app.; Jock-a 4.00

DARLING LOVE
Close Up/Archie Publ. (A Darling Magazine): Oct-Nov, 1949 - No. 11, 1952 (no month) (52 pgs.)(Most photo-c)

	GD 2.0	VG 4.0	FN 6.0	VF 8.0	VF/NM 9.0	NM- 9.2
1-Photo-c	21	42	63	122	199	275
2-Photo-c	13	26	39	74	105	135
3-8,10,11: 3-6-photo-c	11	22	33	60	83	105
9-Krigstein-a	11	22	33	64	90	115

DARLING ROMANCE
Close Up (MLJ Publications): Sept-Oct, 1949 - No. 7, 1951 (All photo-c)

	GD 2.0	VG 4.0	FN 6.0	VF 8.0	VF/NM 9.0	NM- 9.2
1-(52 pgs.)-Photo-c	22	44	66	132	216	300
2	13	26	39	74	105	135
3-7	11	22	33	60	83	105

DARQUE PASSAGES (See Master Darque)
Acclaim (Valiant): April, 1998 ($2.50)

1-Christina Z.-s/Manco-c/a 2.50

DART (Also see Freak Force & Savage Dragon)
Image Comics (Highbrow Entertainment): Feb, 1996 - No. 3, May, 1996 ($2.50, lim. series)

1-3 3.00

DASTARDLY & MUTTLEY (See Fun-In No. 1-4, 6 and Kite Fun Book)

DATE WITH DANGER
Standard Comics: No. 5, Dec, 1952 - No. 6, Feb, 1953

	GD 2.0	VG 4.0	FN 6.0	VF 8.0	VF/NM 9.0	NM- 9.2
5,6-Secret agent stories: 6-Atom bomb story	9	18	27	52	69	85

DATE WITH DEBBI (Also see Debbi's Dates)
National Periodical Publ.: Jan-Feb, 1969 - No. 17, Sept-Oct, 1971; No. 18, Oct-Nov, 1972

	GD 2.0	VG 4.0	FN 6.0	VF 8.0	VF/NM 9.0	NM- 9.2
1-Teenage	6	12	18	41	66	90
2-5,17-(52 pgs) James Taylor sty.	4	8	12	22	34	45
6-12,18-Last issue	3	6	9	20	30	40
13-16-(68 pgs.): 14-1 pg. story on Jack Wild. 15-Marlo Thomas/"That Girl" story	4	8	12	24	37	50

DATE WITH JUDY, A (Radio/TV, and 1948 movie)
National Periodical Publications: Oct-Nov, 1947 - No. 79, Oct-Nov, 1960 (No. 1-25: 52 pgs.)

	GD 2.0	VG 4.0	FN 6.0	VF 8.0	VF/NM 9.0	NM- 9.2
1-Teenage	29	58	87	172	281	390
2	15	30	45	84	127	170
3-10	13	26	39	72	101	130
11-20	10	20	30	54	72	90
21-40	9	18	27	50	65	80
41-45: 45-Last pre-code (2-3/55)	8	16	24	44	57	70
46-79: 79-Drucker-c/a	8	16	24	42	54	65

DATE WITH MILLIE, A (Life With Millie No. 8 on)(Teenage)
Atlas/Marvel Comics (MPC): Oct, 1956 - No. 7, Aug, 1957; Oct, 1959 - No. 7, Oct, 1960

	GD 2.0	VG 4.0	FN 6.0	VF 8.0	VF/NM 9.0	NM- 9.2
1(10/56)-(1st Series)-Dan DeCarlo-a in #1-7	29	58	87	170	278	385
2	15	30	45	90	140	190
3-7	14	28	42	76	108	140
1(10/59)-(2nd Series)	15	30	45	90	140	190
2-7	11	22	33	62	86	110

DATE WITH PATSY, A (Also see Patsy Walker)
Atlas Comics: Sept, 1957 (One-shot)

	GD 2.0	VG 4.0	FN 6.0	VF 8.0	VF/NM 9.0	NM- 9.2
1-Starring Patsy Walker	13	26	39	74	105	135

DAUGHTERS OF THE DRAGON (See Heroes For Hire)
Marvel Comics: 2005; Mar, 2006 - No. 6, Aug, 2006 ($2.99, limited series)

1-6-Palmiotti & Gray-s/Evans-a. 1-Rhino app. 5,6-Iron Fist app. 3.00
... Deadly Hands Special (2005, $3.99) reprints app. from Deadly Hands of Kung Fu #32,33 & Bizarre Adventures #25; Claremont-s/Rogers-a; new Rogers-c & interview 4.00

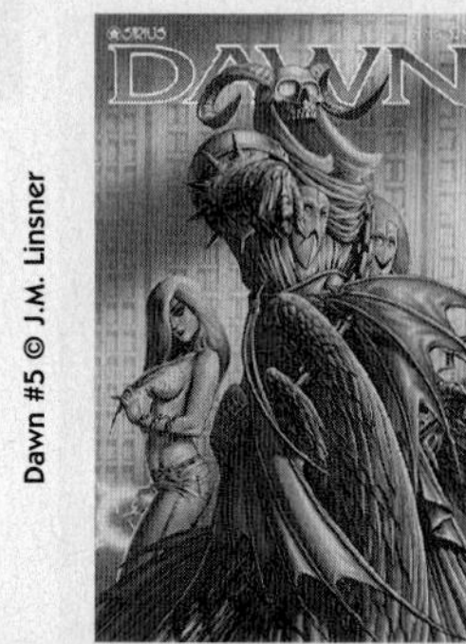

Dawn #5 © J.M. Linsner

Daytripper #5 © Ba & Moon

DC Comics Presents #32 © DC

GD VG FN VF VF/NM NM-
2.0 4.0 6.0 8.0 9.0 9.2

...: Samurai Bullets TPB (2006, $15.99) r/#1-6 16.00

DAVID AND GOLIATH (Movie)
Dell Publishing Co.: No. 1205, July, 1961

Four Color 1205-Photo-c 6 12 18 43 69 95

DAVID BORING (See Eightball)
Pantheon Books: 2000 ($24.95, hardcover w/dust jacket)

Hardcover - reprints David Boring stories from Eightball; Clowes-s/a 25.00

DAVID CASSIDY (TV)(See Partridge Family, Swing With Scooter #33 & Time For Love #30)
Charlton Comics: Feb, 1972 - No. 14, Sept, 1973

1-Most have photo covers 7 14 21 45 73 100
2-5 4 8 12 26 41 55
6-14 4 8 12 24 37 50

DAVID LADD'S LIFE STORY (See Movie Classics)

DAVY CROCKETT (See Dell Giants, Fightin..., Frontier Fighters, It's Game Time, Power Record Comics, Western Tales & Wild Frontier)

DAVY CROCKETT (Frontier Fighter...)
Avon Periodicals: 1951

nn-Tuska?, Reinman-a; Fawcette-c 18 36 54 105 165 225

DAVY CROCKETT (...King of the Wild Frontier No. 1,2)(TV)
Dell Publishing Co./Gold Key: 5/55 - No. 671, 12/55; No. 1, 12/63; No. 2, 11/69 (Walt Disney)

Four Color 631(#1)-Fess Parker photo-c 15 30 45 106 216 325
Four Color 639-Photo-c 13 26 39 91 176 260
Four Color 664,671(Marsh-a)-Photo-c 12 24 36 88 167 245
1(12/63-Gold Key)-Fess Parker photo-c; reprints 8 16 24 54 90 125
2(11/69)-Fess Parker photo-c; reprints 4 8 12 28 44 60

DAVY CROCKETT (...Frontier Fighter #1,2; Kid Montana #9 on)
Charlton Comics: Aug, 1955 - No. 8, Jan, 1957

1 10 20 30 58 79 100
2 7 14 21 37 46 55
3-8 6 12 18 28 34 40

DAWN
Sirius Entertainment/Image Comics: June, 1995 - No. 6, 1996 ($2.95)

1/2-w/certificate 1 2 3 5 6 8
1/2-Variant-c 2 4 6 10 14 18
1-Linsner-c/a 1 2 3 5 6 8
1-Black Light Edition 2 4 6 9 13 16
1-White Trash Edition 3 6 9 16 23 30
1-Look Sharp Edition 3 6 9 19 29 38
2-4: Linsner-c/a 4.50
2-Variant-c, 3-Limited Edition 2 4 6 13 18 22
4-6-Vibrato-c 3.50
4, 5-Limited Edition 2 4 6 8 10 12
6-Limited Edition 2 4 6 8 10 12
...Convention Sketchbook (Image Comics, 2002, $2.95) pin-ups 3.00
...2003 Convention Sketchbook (Image Comics, 3/03, $2.95) pin-ups 3.00
...2004 Convention Sketchbook (Image Comics, 4/04, $2.95) pin-ups 3.00
...2005 Convention Sketchbook (Image Comics, 5/05, $2.95) pin-ups 3.00
Genesis Edition ('99, Wizard supplement) previews Return of the Goddess 3.00
Lucifer's Halo TPB (11/97, $19.95) r/Drama, Dawn #1-6 plus 12 pages of new artwork 20.00
...: Not to Touch The Earth (9/10, $5.99) Linsner-s/c/a; pin-ups by various incl. Turner 6.00
...: Tenth Anniversary Special (9/99, $2.95) Interviews 3.00
The Portable Dawn ($9.95, 5"x4", 64 pgs.) Pocket-sized cover gallery 10.00

DAWN OF THE DEAD (George A. Romaro's...)
IDW Publishing: Apr, 2004 - No. 3, Jun, 2004 ($3.99, limited series)

1-3-Adaptation of the 2004 movie; Niles-s 4.00
TPB (9/04, $17.99) r/#1-3; intro. by George A. Romero 18.00

DAWN: THE RETURN OF THE GODDESS
Sirius Entertainment: Apr, 1999 - No. 4, July, 2000 ($2.95, limited series)

1-4-Linsner-s/a 3.00
TPB (4/02, $12.95) r/#1-4; intro. by Linsner 13.00

DAWN: THREE TIERS
Image Comics: Jun, 2003 - No. 6, Aug, 2005 ($2.95, limited series)

1-6-Linsner-s/a. 2-Preview of Vampire's Christmas 3.00

DAYDREAMERS (See Generation X)
Marvel Comics: Aug, 1997 - No. 3, Oct, 1997 ($2.50, limited series)

GD VG FN VF VF/NM NM-
2.0 4.0 6.0 8.0 9.0 9.2

1-3-Franklin Richards, Howard the Duck, Man-Thing app. 3.00

DAY OF JUDGMENT
DC Comics: Nov, 1999 - No. 5, Nov, 1999 ($2.95/$2.50, limited series)

1-($2.95) Spectre possessed; Matt Smith-a 3.00
2-5: Parallax returns. 5-Hal Jordan becomes the Spectre 3.00
...Secret Files 1 (11/99, $4.95) Harris-c 5.00

DAY OF VENGEANCE (Prelude to Infinite Crisis)(Also see Birds of Prey #76 for 1st app. of Black Alice)
DC Comics: June, 2005 - No. 6, Nov, 2005 ($2.50, limited series)

1-6: 1-Jean Loring becomes Eclipso; Spectre, Ragman, Enchantress, Detective Chimp, Shazam app.; Justiniano-a. 2,3-Capt. Marvel app. 4-6-Black Alice app. 3.00
...: Infinite Crisis Special 1 (3/06, $4.99) Justiniano-a/Simonson-c 5.00
TPB (2005, $12.99) r/series & Action #826, Advs. of Superman #639, Superman #216 13.00

DAYS OF THE DEFENDERS (See Defenders, The)
Marvel Comics: Mar, 2001 ($3.50, one-shot)

1-Reprints early team-ups of members, incl. Marvel Feature #1; Larsen-c 3.50

DAYS OF THE MOB (See In the Days of the Mob)

DAYTRIPPER
DC Comics (Vertigo): Feb, 2010 - No. 10, Nov, 2010 ($2.99, limited series)

1-10-Gabriel Bá & Fábio Moon-s/a 3.00
TPB (2010, $19.99) r/#1-10; sketch art pages 20.00

DAZEY'S DIARY
Dell Publishing Co.: June-Aug, 1962

01-174-208: Bill Woggon-c/a 4 8 12 28 44 60

DAZZLER, THE (Also see Marvel Graphic Novel & X-Men #130)
Marvel Comics Group: Mar, 1981 - No. 42, Mar, 1986

1,21,22,24,27,28,38,42: 1-X-Men app. 21-Double size; photo-c. 22 (12/82)-vs. Rogue Battle-c/sty. 24-Full app. Rogue w/Powerman (Iron Fist). 27-Rogue app. 28-Full app. Rogue; Mystique app. 38-Wolverine-c/app.; X-Men app. 42-Beast-c/app. 4.00
2-20,23,25,26,29-32,34-37,39-41: 2-X-Men app. 10,11-Galactus app. 23-Rogue/Mystique 1 pg. app. 26-Jusko-c. 40-Secret Wars II 3.00
33-Michael Jackson "Thriller" swipe-c/sty 3.00
One-shot (7/10, $3.99) Andrasofszky-a/c; Arcade app. 4.00
NOTE: *No. 1 distributed only through comic shops.* ***Alcala*** *a-1i, 2i.* ***Chadwick*** *a-38-42p; c(p)-39, 41, 42.* ***Guice*** *a-38i, 42i; c-38, 40.*

DC CHALLENGE (Most DC superheroes appear)
DC Comics: Nov, 1985 - No. 12, Oct, 1986 ($1.25/$2.00, maxi-series)

1-11: 1-Colan-a. 2,8-Batman-c/app. 4-Gil Kane-c/a 3.00
12-($2.00-c) Giant; low print 4.00
NOTE: *Batman app. in 1-4, 6-12. Joker app. in 7.* ***Infantino*** *a-3.* ***Ordway*** *c-12.* ***Swan/Austin*** *c-10.*

DC COMICS CLASSICS LIBRARY (Hardcover collections of classic DC stories)
DC Comics: 2009 - Present ($39.99, hardcover with dustjacket)

Batman: A Death in the Family ('09)- r/Batman #426-429, 440-442, New Titans #60,61 40.00
Batman Annuals ('09)- r/Batman Annual #1-3; afterword by Richard Bruning 40.00
Batman Annuals Volume 2 ('10)- r/Batman Annual #4-7; intro. by Michael Uslan 40.00
Flash of Two Worlds ('09)- r/Flash #123,129,137,151,170&173 team-ups with G.A. Flash 40.00
Justice League of America by George Pérez ('09) r/J.L.of A. #184-186, 192-194 40.00
Justice League of America by George Pérez Vol. 2 ('10) r/J.L.of A. #195-197,200 40.00
Legion of Super-Heroes: The Life and Death of Ferro Lad ('09) - r/Adventure Comics # 346, 347,352-355,357; intro. by Paul Levitz; afterword by Jim Shooter 40.00
Roots of the Swamp Thing ('09)- r/House of Secrets #92 & Swamp Thing #1-13; Wein intro. 40.00
Superman: Kryptonite Nevermore ('09)- r/Superman #233-238,240-242; afterword by Denny O'Neil 40.00

DC COMICS MEGA SAMPLER
DC Comics: 2009; Jul, 2010 (6-1/4" x 9-1/2", FCBD giveaways)

1, 2010- Short stories of kid-friendly titles; Tiny Titans, Billy Batson, Super Friends app. 2.50

DC COMICS PRESENTS
DC Comics: July-Aug, 1978 - No. 97, Sept, 1986 (Superman team-ups in all)

1-4th Superman/Flash race 4 8 12 26 41 55
1-(Whitman variant) 5 10 15 30 48 65
2-Part 2 of Superman/Flash race 3 6 9 14 20 25
2-4,9-12,14-16,19,21,22-(Whitman variants, low print run, none have issue # on cover) 3 6 9 14 20 25
3-10: 4-Metal Men. 6-Green Lantern. 8-Swamp Thing. 9-Wonder Woman 2 4 6 8 10 12
11-25,27-40: 13-Legion of Super-Heroes. 19-Batgirl. 31-Robin. 35-Man-Bat 6.00
26-(10/80)-Green Lantern; intro Cyborg, Starfire, Raven (1st app. New Teen Titans in 16 pg. preview); Starlin-c/a; Sargon the Sorcerer back-up 5 10 15 35 55 75

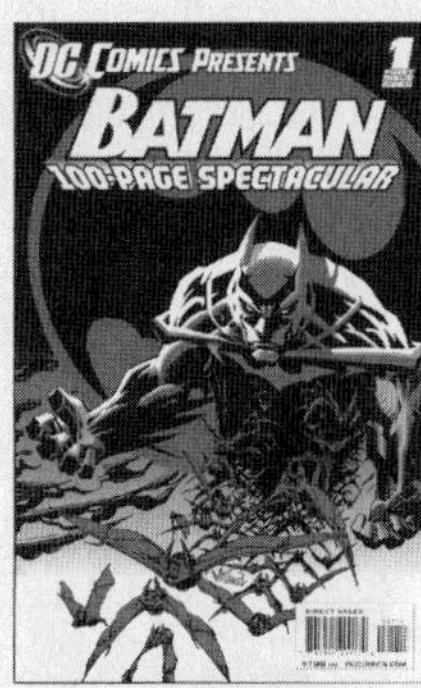

DC Comics Presents: Batman #1 © DC

DC First: Batgirl/Joker #1 © DC

DC Kids Mega Sampler #1 © DC

GD VG FN VF VF/NM NM-
2.0 4.0 6.0 8.0 9.0 9.2

GD VG FN VF VF/NM NM-
2.0 4.0 6.0 8.0 9.0 9.2

41,72,77,78,97: 41-Superman/Joker-c/story. 72-Joker/Phantom Stranger-c/story. 77,78-Animal Man app. (77-c also). 97-Phantom Zone 6.00
42-46,48-50,52-71,73-76,79-83: 42-Sandman. 43,80-Legion of Super-Heroes. 52-Doom Patrol; 1st app. Ambush Bug. 58-Robin. 82-Adam Strange. 83-Batman & Outsiders 4.00
47-He-Man-c/s (1st app. in comics) 2 4 6 11 16 20
51-Preview insert (16 pgs.) of He-Man (2nd app.) 1 3 4 6 8 10
84-Challengers of the Unknown; Kirby-c/s. 6.00
85-Swamp Thing; Alan Moore scripts 6.00
86,88-96: 86-88-Crisis x-over. 88-Creeper 4.00
87-Origin/1st app. Superboy of Earth Prime 1 3 4 6 8 10
Annual 1,4: 1(9/82)-G.A. Superman; 1st app. Alexander Luthor. 4(10/85)-Superwoman 4.00
Annual 2,3: 2(7/83)-Intro/origin Superwoman. 3(9/84)-Shazam 4.00
NOTE: ***Adkins** a-2, 54; c-2. **Buckler** a-33, 34; c-30, 33, 34. **Giffen** a-39; c-59. **Gil Kane** a-28, 35, Annual 3; c-48p, 56, 58, 60, 62, 64, 68, Annual 2, 3. **Kirby** c/a-84. **Kubert** c/a-66. **Morrow** c/a-65. **Newton** c/a-54p. **Orlando** c-53i. **Perez** a-26p, 61p; c-38, 61, 94. **Starlin** a-26-29p, 36p, 37p; c-26-29, 36, 37, 93. **Toth** a-84. **Williamson** i-79, 85, 87.*

DC COMICS PRESENTS: ...(Julie Schwartz tribute series of one-shots based on classic covers)
DC Comics: Sept, 2004 - Oct, 2004 ($2.50)

The Atom -(Based on cover of Atom #10) Gibbons-s/Oliffe-a; Waid-s/Jurgens-a; Bolland-c 3.00
Batman -(Batman #183) Johns-s/Infantino-a; Wein-s/Kuhn-a; Hughes-c 3.00
The Flash -(Flash #163) Loeb-s/McGuinness-a; O'Neil-s/Mahnke-a; Ross-c 3.00
Green Lantern -(Green Lantern #31) Azzarello-s/Breyfogle-a; Pasko-s/McDaniel-a; Bolland-c 3.00
Hawkman -(Hawkman #6) Bates-s/Byrne-a; Busiek-s/Simonson-a; Garcia-Lopez-c 3.00
Justice League of America -(J.L. of A. #53) Ellison & David-s/Giella-a; Wolfman-s/Nguyen-a; Garcia-Lopez-c 3.00
Mystery in Space -(M.I.S. #82) Maggin-s/Williams-a; Morrison-s/Ordway-a; Ross-c 3.00
Superman -(Superman #264) Stan Lee-s/Cooke-a; Levitz-s/Giffen-a; Hughes-c 3.00

DC COMICS PRESENTS: ...
DC Comics: Dec, 2010 - Present ($7.99, squarebound, one-shot reprints)

Batman 1 (12/10) r/Batman #582-585,600 8.00
Batman 2 (1/11) r/Batman #591-594 8.00
Batman 3 (2/11) r/Batman #595-598 8.00
Batman Beyond 1 (2/11) r/Batman Beyond #13,14,21,22 8.00
Batman/Catwoman 1 (12/10) r/Batman and Catwoman: Trail of the Gun 8.00
Brightest Day 1 (12/10) r/Strange Advs. #205, Hawkman #27,34,36, Solo #8, DC Hol. '09 8.00
Brightest Day 2 (1/11) r/Firestorm #11-13 & Martian Manhuner #11,24 8.00
Brightest Day 3 (2/11) r/Legends of the DC Univ. #25-27 & Teen Titans #27,28 8.00
Chase 1 (1/11) r/ Chase #1,6-8 8.00
Flash/Green Lantern: Faster Friends (1/11) r/G.L./Flash: Faster Friends & Flash/G.L. : FF 8.00
Green Lantern 1 (12/10) r/Green Lantern #137-140 (2001) 8.00
JLA 1 (2/11) r/JLA #90-93 8.00
Lobo 1 (3/11) r/Lobo #63,64 & DC First: Superman/Lobo #1 8.00
Superman 1 (12/10) r/Superman: The Man of Steel #121 & Superman #179,180,185 8.00
Superman 2 (1/11) r/Action #798, Superman: The Man of Steel #133, Superman #189 & Advs. of Superman #611 8.00
Superman 3 (2/11) r/Superman #177,178,181,182 8.00
T.H.U.N.D.E.R. Agents 1 (2/11) r/T.H.U.N.D.E.R. Agents #1,2,7 (1966) 8.00
Young Justice 1 (12/10) r/JLA World Without Grownups #1,2 8.00
Young Justice 2 (1/11) r/Y.J: The Secret, Y.J. Secret Files #1, Y.J. In No Man's Land 8.00
Young Justice 3 (2/11) r/Young Justice #7 & Y.J Secret Origins 80-Page Giant #1 8.00

DC COUNTDOWN (To Infinite Crisis)
DC Comics: May, 2005 ($1.00, 80 pages, one-shot)

1-Death of Blue Beetle; prelude to OMAC Project, Day of Vengeance, Rann/Thanagar War and Villains United mini-series; s/a by various; Jim Lee/Alex Ross-c 4.00

DC FIRST: ...(series of one-shots)
DC Comics: July, 2002 ($3.50)

Batgirl/Joker 1-Sienkiewicz & Terry Moore-a; Nowlan-c 3.50
Green Lantern/Green Lantern 1-Alan Scott & Hal Jordan vs. Krona 3.50
Flash/Superman 1-Superman races Jay Garrick; Abra Kadabra app. 3.50
Superman/Lobo 1-Giffen-s; Nowlan-c 3.50

DC GOES APE
DC Comics: 2008 ($19.99, trade paperback)

Vol. 1 - Reprints app. of Grodd, Beppo, Titano and other monkey tales; Art Adams-c 20.00

DC GRAPHIC NOVEL (Also see DC Science Fiction...)
DC Comics: Nov, 1983 - No. 7, 1986 ($5.95, 68 pgs.)

1-3,5,7: 1-Star Raiders. 2-Warlords; not from regular Warlord series. 3-The Medusa Chain; Ernie Colon story/a. 5-Me and Joe Priest; Chaykin-c. 7-Space Clusters; Nino-c/a 2 4 6 9 12 15
4-The Hunger Dogs by Kirby; Darkseid kills Himon from Mister Miracle & destroys New Genesis 5 10 15 34 55 75
6-Metalzoic; Sienkiewicz-c ($6.95) 2 4 6 9 12 15

DC HOLIDAY SPECIAL '09
DC Comics: Feb, 2010 ($5.99, one-shot)

1-Christmas short stories by various incl. Dragotta, Tucci, Chaykin; Dustin Nguyen-c 6.00

DC INFINITE HALLOWEEN SPECIAL
DC Comics: Dec, 2007 ($5.99, one-shot)

1-Halloween short stories by various incl. Dini, Waid, Hairsine, Kelley Jones; Gene Ha-c 6.00

DC KIDS MEGA SAMPLER
DC Comics: June, 2009 (Free Comic Book Day giveaway, one-shot)

1-Tiny Titans, Batman: The Brave and the Bold, Billy Batson/Shazam short stories 3.00

DC/MARVEL: ALL ACCESS (Also see DC Versus Marvel & Marvel Versus DC)
DC Comics: 1996 - No. 4, 1997 ($2.95, limited series)

1-4: 1-Superman & Spider-Man app. 2-Robin & Jubilee app. 3-Dr. Strange & Batman-c/app., X-Men, JLA app. 4-X-Men vs. JLA-c/app. rebirth of Amalgam 3.00

DC/MARVEL: CROSSOVER CLASSICS
DC Comics: 1998; 2003 ($14.95, TPB)

Vol. II-Reprints Batman/Punisher: Lake of Fire, Punisher/Batman: Deadly Knights, Silver Surfer/Superman, Batman & Capt. America 15.00
Vol. 4 (2003, $14.95) Reprints Green Lantern/Silver Surfer: Unholy Alliances, Darkseid/ Galactus: The Hunger, Batman & Spider-Man, and Superman/Fantastic Four 15.00

DC 100 PAGE SUPER SPECTACULAR
(Title is 100 Page... No. 14 on)(Square bound) (Reprints, 50¢)
National Periodical Publications: No. 4, Summer, 1971 - No. 13, 6/72; No. 14, 2/73 - No. 22, 11/73 (No #1-3)

4-Weird Mystery Tales; Johnny Peril & Phantom Stranger; cover & splashes by Wrightson; origin Jungle Boy of Jupiter 18 36 54 131 266 400
5-Love Stories; Wood inks (7 pgs.)(scarcer) 47 94 141 376 763 1150
6- "World's Greatest Super-Heroes"; JLA, JSA, Spectre, Johnny Quick, Vigilante & Hawkman; contains unpublished Wildcat story; N. Adams wrap-around-c; r/JLA #21,22 18 36 54 131 266 400
6-Replica Edition (2004, $6.95) complete reprint w/wraparound-c 7.00
7-(Also listed as Superman #245) Air Wave, Kid Eternity, Hawkman-r; Atom-r/Atom #3 10 20 30 68 119 170
8-(Also listed as Batman #238) Batman, Legion, Aquaman-r; G.A. Atom, Sargon (r/Sensation #57), Plastic Man (r/Police #14) stories; Doom Patrol origin-r; Neal Adams wraparound-c 12 24 36 87 164 240
9-(Also listed as Our Army at War #242) Kubert-c 10 20 30 68 119 170
10-(Also listed as Adventure Comics #416) Golden Age-reprints; r/1st app. Black Canary from Flash #86; no Zatanna 11 22 33 77 144 210
11-(Also listed as Flash #214) origin Metal Men-r/Showcase #37; never before published G.A. Flash story. 9 18 27 63 107 150
12,14: 12-(Also listed as Superboy #185) Legion-c/story; Teen Titans, Kid Eternity (r/Hit #46), Star Spangled Kid-r(S.S. #55). 14-Batman-r/Detective #31,32,156; Atom-r/Showcase #34 8 16 24 54 90 125
13-(Also listed as Superman #252) Ray(r/Smash #17), Black Condor, (r/Crack #18), Hawkman(r/Flash #24); Starman-r/Adv. #67; Dr. Fate & Spectre-r/More Fun #57; Neal Adams-c 11 22 33 77 144 210
15,16,18,19,21,22: 15-r/2nd Boy Commandos/Det. #64. 21-Superboy; r/Brave & the Bold #54. 22-r/All-Flash #13. 6 12 18 43 69 95
17,20: 17-JSA-r/All Star #37 (10-11/47, 38 pgs.), Sandman-r/Adv. #65 (8/41), JLA #23 (11/63) & JLA #43 (3/66). 20-Batman-r/Det. #66,68, Spectre; origin Two-Face 7 14 21 45 73 100
... : Love Stories Replica Edition (2000, $6.95) reprints #5 7.00
NOTE: ***Anderson** r-11, 14, 18i, 22. **B. Baily** r-18, 20. **Burnley** r-18, 20. **Crandall** r-14p, 20. **Drucker** r-4. **Grandenetti** a-22(2)r. **Heath** a-22r. **Infantino** r-17, 20, 22. **G. Kane** r-18. **Kirby** r-15. **Kubert** r-6, 7, 16, 17; c-16, 19. **Manning** a-19r. **Meskin** r-4, 22. **Mooney** r-15, 21. **Toth** r-17, 20.*

DC ONE MILLION (Also see crossover #1,000,000 issues and JLA One Million TPB)
DC Comics: Nov, 1998 - No. 4, Nov, 1998 ($2.95/$1.99, weekly lim. series)

1-($2.95) JLA travels to the 853rd century; Morrison-s 4.00
2-4-($1.99) 3.00
... Eighty-Page Giant (8/99, $4.95) 5.00
TPB ('99, $14.95) r/#1-4 and several x-over stories 15.00

DC SCIENCE FICTION GRAPHIC NOVEL
DC Comics: 1985 - No. 7, 1987 ($5.95)

SF1-SF7: SF1-Hell on Earth by Robert Bloch; Giffen-p. SF2-Nightwings by Robert Silverberg; G. Colan-p. SF3-Frost & Fire by Bradbury. SF4-Merchants of Venus. SF5-Demon With A Glass Hand by Ellison; M. Rogers-a. SF6-The Magic Goes Away by Niven. SF7-Sandkings by George R.R. Martin 2 4 6 8 11 14

DC SILVER AGE CLASSICS
DC Comics: 1992 ($1.00, all reprints)

DC Special #1 © DC

DC Super-Stars #4 © DC

DC: The New Frontier #1 © DC

GD VG FN VF VF/NM NM-
2.0 4.0 6.0 8.0 9.0 9.2

GD VG FN VF VF/NM NM-
2.0 4.0 6.0 8.0 9.0 9.2

...Action Comics #252-r/1st Supergirl. Adventure Comics #247-r/1st Legion of Super-Heroes. The Brave and the Bold #28-r/1st JLA. Detective Comics #225-r/1st Martian Manhunter. Detective Comics #327-r/1st new look Batman. Green Lantern #76-r/1st Green Lantern/ Green Arrow. House of Secrets #92-r/1st Swamp Thing. Showcase #4-r/1st S.A. Flash. Showcase #22-r/1st S.A. Green Lantern 3.00
...Sugar and Spike #99; includes 2 unpublished stories 4.00

DC SPECIAL (Also see Super DC Giant)
National Per. Publ.: 10-12/68 - No. 15, 11-12/71; No. 16, Spr/75 - No. 29, 8-9/77

1-All Infantino issue; Flash, Batman, Adam Strange-r; begin 68 pg. issues, end #21 9 18 27 63 107 150
2-Teen humor; Binky, Buzzy, Harvey app. 10 20 30 72 131 190
3-All-Girl issue; unpubl. GA Wonder Woman story 9 18 27 65 113 160
4,11: 4-Horror (1st Abel, brief). 11-Monsters 6 12 18 37 59 80
5-10,12-15: 5-All Kubert issue; Viking Prince, Sgt. Rock-r. 6-Western. 7,9,13-Strangest Sports. 12-Viking Prince; Kubert-c/a (r/B&B almost entirely). 15-G.A. Plastic Man origin-r/Police #1; origin Woozy by Cole; 14,15-(52 pgs.) 4 8 12 28 44 60
16-27: 16-Super Heroes Battle Super Gorillas; r/Capt. Storm #1, 1st Johnny Cloud/All-Amer. Men of War #82. 17-Early S.A. Green Lantern-r. 22-Origin Robin Hood. 26-Enemy Ace. 27-Captain Comet story 3 6 9 16 23 30
28-Earth Shattering Disaster Stories; Legion of Super-Heroes story 3 6 9 17 25 32
29-New "The Untold Origin of the Justice Society"; Staton-a/Neal Adams-c; Hitler app. in story and on cover 5 10 15 35 55 75

NOTE: ***N. Adams*** *c-3, 4, 6, 11, 29.* ***Grell*** *a-20; c-17, 20.* ***Heath*** *a-12r.* ***G. Kane*** *a-6p, 13r, 17r, 19-21r.* ***Kirby*** *a-4,11.* ***Kubert*** *a-6r, 12r, 22.* ***Meskin*** *a-10.* ***Moreira*** *a-10.* ***Staton*** *a-29p.* ***Toth*** *a-13, 20r. #1-15: 25¢; 16-27: 50¢; 28, 29: 60¢. #1-13, 16-21: 68 pgs.; 14, 15: 52 pgs.; 25-27: oversized.*

DC SPECIAL BLUE RIBBON DIGEST
DC Comics: Mar-Apr, 1980 - No. 24, Aug, 1982

1,2,4,5: 1-Legion reprints. 2-Flash. 4-Green Lantern. 5-Secret Origins; new Zatara and Zatanna 2 4 6 8 11 14
3-Justice Society 2 4 6 10 14 18
6,8-10: 6-Ghosts. 8-Legion. 9-Secret Origins. 10-Warlord-"The Deimos Saga"-Grell-s/c/a 2 4 6 8 11 14
7-Sgt. Rock's Prize Battle Tales 2 4 6 13 18 22
11,16: 11-Justice League. 16-Green Lantern/Green Arrow-r; all Adams-a 2 4 6 11 16 20
12-Haunted Tank; reprints 1st app. 2 4 6 13 18 22
13-15,17-19: 13-Strange Sports Stories. 14-UFO Invaders; Adam Strange app. 15-Secret Origins of Super Villains; JLA app. 17-Ghosts. 18-Sgt. Rock; Kubert front & back-c. 19-Doom Patrol; new Perez-c 2 4 6 9 13 16
20-Dark Mansion of Forbidden Love (scarce) 5 10 15 30 48 65
21-Our Army at War 3 6 9 16 22 28
22-24: 22-Secret Origins. 23-Green Arrow, w/new 7 pg. story. 24-House of Mystery; new Kubert wraparound-c 2 4 6 13 18 22

NOTE: ***N. Adams*** *a-16(6)r, 17r, 23r; c-16.* ***Aparo*** *a-6r, 24r; c-23.* ***Grell*** *a-8, 10; c-10.* ***Heath*** *a-14.* ***Infantino*** *a-15r.* ***Kaluta*** *a-17r.* ***Gil Kane*** *a-15r, 22r.* ***Kirby*** *a-5, 9, 23r.* ***Kubert*** *a-3, 18r, 21r; c-7, 12, 14, 17, 18, 21, 24.* ***Morrow*** *a-24r.* ***Orlando*** *a-17r, 22r; c-1, 20.* ***Toth*** *a-21r, 24r.* ***Wood*** *a-3, 17r, 24r.* ***Wrightson*** *a-16r, 17r, 24r.*

DC SPECIAL: CYBORG (From Teen Titans) (See Teen Titans 2003 series for TPB collection)
DC Comics: Jul, 2008 - No. 6, Dec, 2008 ($2.99, limited series)

1-6: 1-Sable-s/Lashley-a; origin re-told. 3-6-Magno-a 3.00

DC SPECIAL: RAVEN (From Teen Titans) (See Teen Titans 2003 series for TPB collection)
DC Comics: May, 2008 - No. 5, Sept, 2008 ($2.99, limited series)

1-5-Marv Wolfman-s/Damion Scott-a 3.00

DC SPECIAL SERIES
National Periodical Publications/DC Comics: 9/77 - No. 16, Fall, 1978; No. 17, 8/79 - No. 27, Fall, 1981 (No. 18, 19, 23, 24 - digest size, 100 pgs.; No. 25-27 - Treasury sized)

1-"5-Star Super-Hero Spectacular 1977"; Batman, Atom, Flash, Green Lantern, Aquaman, in solo stories, Kobra app.; N. Adams-c 4 8 12 26 41 55
2(#1)-"The Original Swamp Thing Saga 1977"-r/Swamp Thing #1&2 by Wrightson; new Wrightson wraparound-c. 2 4 6 11 16 20
3,4,6-8: 3-Sgt Rock. 4-Unexpected. 6-Secret Society of Super Villains, Jones-a. 7-Ghosts Special. 8-Brave and Bold w/ new Batman, Deadman & Sgt Rock team-up 2 4 6 13 18 22
5-"Superman Spectacular 1977"-(84 pg, $1.00)-Superman vs. Brainiac & Lex Luthor, new 63 pg. story 3 6 9 16 22 28
9-Wonder Woman; Ditko-a (11 pgs.) 3 6 9 16 22 28
10-"Secret Origins of Superheroes Special 1978"-(52 pgs.)-Dr. Fate, Lightray & Black Canary on-c/new origin stories; Staton, Newton-a 3 6 9 14 20 26
11-"Flash Spectacular 1978"-(84 pgs.) Flash, Kid Flash, GA Flash & Johnny Quick vs. Grodd; Wood-i on Kid Flash chapter 2 4 6 13 18 22
12-"Secrets of Haunted House Special Spring 1978" 2 4 6 13 18 22
13-"Sgt. Rock Special Spring 1978", 50 pg new story 3 6 9 14 19 24
14,17,20-"Original Swamp Thing Saga", Wrightson-a: 14-Sum '78, r/#3,4. 17-Sum '79 r/#5-7. 20-Jan/Feb '80, r/#8-10 2 4 6 9 13 16
15-"Batman Spectacular Summer 1978", Ra's Al Ghul-app.; Golden-a. Rogers-a/front & back-c 3 6 9 21 32 42
16-"Jonah Hex Spectacular Fall 1978"; death of Jonah Hex, Heath-a; Bat Lash and Scalphunter stories 6 12 18 43 69 95
18,19-Digest size: 18-"Sgt. Rock's Prize Battle Tales Fall 1979". 19-"Secret Origins of Super-Heroes Fall 1979"; origins Wonder Woman (new-a),r/Robin, Batman-Superman team, Aquaman, Hawkman and others 2 4 6 13 18 22
21-"Super-Star Holiday Special Spring 1980", Frank Miller-a in "Batman--Wanted Dead or Alive" (1st Batman story); Jonah Hex, Sgt. Rock, Superboy & LSH and House of Mystery/ Witching Hour-c/stories 4 8 12 26 41 55
22-"G.I. Combat Sept. 1980", Kubert-c. Haunted Tank-s 3 6 9 14 19 24
23,24-Digest size: 23-World's Finest-r. 24-Flash 2 4 6 11 16 20
V5#25-($2.95)-"Superman II, the Adventure Continues Summer 1981"; photos from movie & photo-c (see All-New Coll. Ed. C-62) 3 6 9 14 19 24
26-($2.50)-"Superman and His Incredible Fortress of Solitude Summer 1981" 3 6 9 14 19 24
27-($2.50)-"Batman vs. The Incredible Hulk Fall 1981" 4 8 12 24 37 50

NOTE: ***Aparo*** *c-8.* ***Heath*** *a-12i, 16.* ***Infantino*** *a-19r.* ***Kirby*** *a-23, 19r.* ***Kubert*** *c-13, 19r.* ***Nasser/Netzer*** *a-1, 10i, 15.* ***Newton*** *a-10.* ***Nino*** *a-4, 7.* ***Starlin*** *c-12.* ***Staton*** *a-1.* ***Tuska*** *a-19r. #25 & 26. were advertised as All-New Collectors' Edition C-63, C-64. #26 was originally planned as All-New Collectors' Ed. C-30?; has C-630 & A.N.C.E. on cover.*

DC SPECIAL: THE RETURN OF DONNA TROY
DC Comics: Aug, 2005 - No. 4, Late Oct, 2005 ($2.99, limited series)

1-4-Jimenez-s/Garcia-Lopez-a(p)/Pérez-i 3.00

DC SUPER-STARS
National Periodical Publications/DC Comics: March, 1976 - No. 18, Winter, 1978 (No. 3-18: 52 pgs.)

1-(68 pgs.)-Re-intro Teen Titans (predates T. T. #44 (11/76); tryout iss.) plus r/Teen Titans; W.W. as girl was original Wonder Girl 3 6 9 20 30 40
2-7,9,11,12,16: 2,4,6,8-Adam Strange; 2-(68 pgs.)-r/1st Adam Strange/Hawkman team-up from Mystery in Space #90 plus Atomic Knights origin-r. 3-Legion issue. 4-r/Tales/Unexpected #45 2 4 6 8 11 14
8-r/1st Space Ranger from Showcase #15, Adam Strange-r/Mystery in Space #89 & Star Rovers-r/M.I.S. #80 2 4 6 9 13 16
10-Strange Sports Stories; Batman/Joker-c/story 2 4 6 10 14 18
13-Sergio Aragonés Special 3 6 9 16 22 28
14,15,18: 15-Sgt. Rock 2 4 6 9 13 16
17-Secret Origins of Super-Heroes (origin of The Huntress); origin Green Arrow by Grell; Legion app.; Earth II Batman & Catwoman marry (1st revealed; also see B&B #197 & Superman Family #211) 5 10 15 35 55 75

NOTE: ***M. Anderson*** *r-2, 4, 6.* ***Aparo*** *c-7, 14, 18.* ***Austin*** *a-11i.* ***Buckler*** *a-14p; c-10.* ***Grell*** *a-17.* ***G. Kane*** *a-1r, 10r.* ***Kubert*** *c-15.* ***Layton*** *c/a-16i, 17i.* ***Mooney*** *a-4r, 6r.* ***Morrow*** *c/a-11r.* ***Nasser*** *a-11.* ***Newton*** *c/a-16p.* ***Staton*** *a-17; c-17. No. 10, 12-18 contain all new material; the rest are reprints. #1 contains new and reprint material.*

DC: THE NEW FRONTIER (Also see Justice League: The New Frontier Special)
DC Comics: Mar, 2004 - No. 6, Nov, 2004 ($6.95, limited series)

1-6-DCU in the 1940s-60s; Darwyn Cooke-c/s/a in all. 1-Hal Jordan and The Losers app. 2-Origin Martian Manhunter; Barry Allen app. 3-Challengers of the Unknown 7.00
...Volume One (2004, $19.95, TPB) r/#1-3; cover gallery & intro. by Paul Levitz 20.00
...Volume Two (2005, $19.99, TPB) r/#4-6; cover gallery & afterword by Cooke 20.00

DC TOP COW CROSSOVERS
DC Comics/Top Cow Productions: 2007 ($14.99, TPB)

SC-r/The Darkness/Batman; JLA/Witchblade; The Darkness/Superman; JLA/Cyberforce 15.00

DC 2000
DC Comics: 2000 - No. 2, 2000 ($6.95, limited series)

1,2-JLA visit 1941 JSA; Semeiks-a 7.00

DCU BRAVE NEW WORLD (See Infinite Crisis and tie-ins)
DC Comics: Aug, 2006 ($1.00, 80 pgs., one-shot)

1-Previews 2006 series Martian Manhunter, OMAC, The Creeper, The All-New Atom, The Trials of Shazam, and Uncle Sam and the Freedom Fighters; the Monitor app. 4.00

DCU (Halloween and Christmas one-shot anthologies)
DC Comics

... Halloween Special '09 (12/09, $5.99) Ha-c; art from Bagley, Tucci, K. Jones, Nguyen 6.00
... Halloween Special 2010 (12/10, $4.99) Ha-c; art from Tucci, Garbett; I...Vampire app. 5.00
... Holiday Special (2/09, $5.99) Christmas by various incl. Dini, Maguire, Reis; Quitely-c 6.00
... Holiday Special 2010 (2/11, $4.99) Jonah Hex, Spectre, Legion of S.H., Anthro app. 5.00
... Infinite Halloween Special (12/08, $5.99) Ralph & Sue Dibny app.; Gene Ha-c 6.00
... Infinite Holiday Special (2/07, $4.99) by various; Batwoman app.; Porter-c 5.00

DCU HEROES SECRET FILES

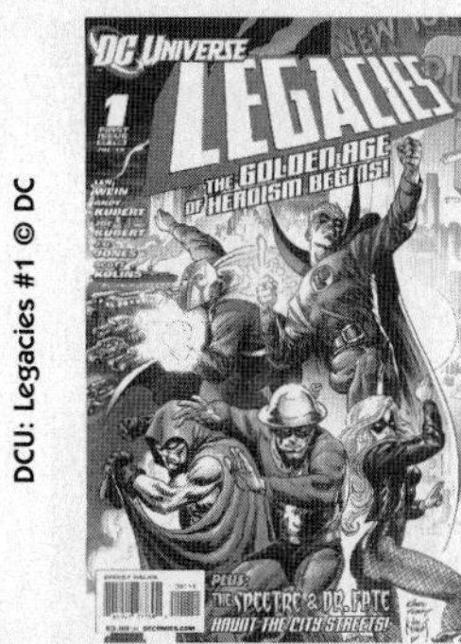

DCU: Legacies #1 © DC

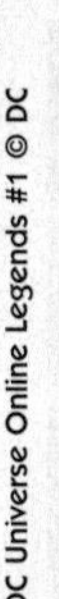

DC Universe Online Legends #1 © DC

Deadline #2 © MAR

	GD 2.0	VG 4.0	FN 6.0	VF 8.0	VF/NM 9.0	NM- 9.2

DC Comics: Feb, 1999 ($4.95, one-shot)

1-Origin-s and pin-ups; new Star Spangled Kid app. 5.00

DCU: LEGACIES
DC Comics: Jul, 2010 - No. 10, Apr, 2011 ($3.99, limited series)

1-10: 1,2-Andy Kubert-c; JSA app.; two covers on each. 3-JLA app.; Garcia-Lopez-a. 4-Sgt. Rock back-up; Joe Kubert-a. 5-Pérez-a. 8-Back-up Quitely-a 4.00

DC UNIVERSE CHRISTMAS, A
DC Comics: 2000 ($19.95)

TPB-Reprints DC Christmas stories by various 20.00

DC UNIVERSE: DECISIONS
DC Comics: Early Nov, 2008 - No. 4, Late Dec, 2008 ($2.99, limited series)

1-4-Assassination plot in the Presidential election; Winick & Willingham-s/Porter-a 3.00

DC UNIVERSE HOLIDAY BASH
DC Comics: 1997- 1999 ($3.95)

I,II-(X-mas '96,'97) Christmas stories by various 5.00
III (1999, for Christmas '98, $4.95) 5.00

DC UNIVERSE ILLUSTRATED BY NEAL ADAMS (Also see Batman Illustrated by Neal Adams HC Vol. 1-3)
DC Comics: 2008 ($39.99, hardcover with dustjacket)

Vol. 1 - Reprints Adams' non-Batman/non-Green Lantern work from 1967-1972; incl. Teen Titans, DC war, Enemy Ace, Superman and PSAs; promo art; Levitz foreword 40.00

DC UNIVERSE: LAST WILL AND TESTAMENT
DC Comics: Oct, 2008 ($3.99, one-shot)

1-Geo-Force vs. Deathstroke; DC heroes prepare for Final Crisis; Brad Meltzer-s; Adam Kubert & Joe Kubert-a; two covers 4.00

DC UNIVERSE ONLINE LEGENDS (Based on the online game)
DC Comics: Early Apr. 2011 - Present ($2.99)

1-4: 1-Wolfman & Bedard-s/Porter-a; DC heroes & Luthor vs. Brainiac. 1-Wraparound-c 3.00

DC UNIVERSE: ORIGINS
DC Comics: 2009 ($14.99, TPB)

nn-Reprints 2-page origins of DC characters from back-ups in 52, Countdown and Justice League: Cry For Justice #1-3; s/a by various; Alex Ross-c 15.00

DC UNIVERSE SPECIAL
DC Comics: July, 2008 - Aug, 2008 ($4.99, collection of reprints related to Final Crisis)

...: Justice League of America (7/08) r/J.L. of A. #111,166-168 & Detective #274; Sook-c 5.00
...: Reign in Hell (8/08) r/Blaze/Satanus War x-over; Sook-c 5.00
...: Superman (7/08) r/Mongul app. in Superman #32, Showcase '95 #7,8, Flash #102 5.00

DC UNIVERSE: THE STORIES OF ALAN MOORE (Also see Across the Universe:...)
DC Comics: 2006 ($19.99)

TPB-Reprints Batman: The Killing Joke, "Whatever Happened to the Man of Tomorrow", "For The Man Who Has Everything, and other classic Moore DC stories; Bolland-c 20.00

DC UNIVERSE: TRINITY
DC Comics: Aug, 1993 - No. 2, Sept, 1993 ($2.95, 52 pgs, limited series)

1,2-Foil-c; Green Lantern, Darkstars, Legion app. 4.00

DCU VILLAINS SECRET FILES
DC Comics: Apr, 1999 ($4.95, one-shot)

1-Origin-s and profile pages 5.00

DC VERSUS MARVEL (See Marvel Versus DC) (Also see Amazon, Assassins, Bruce Wayne: Agent of S.H.I. E. L.D., Bullets & Bracelets, Doctor Strangefate, JLX, Legend of the Dark Claw, Magneto & The Magnetic Men, Speed Demon, Spider-Boy, Super Soldier, X-Patrol)
DC Comics: No. 1, 1996, No. 4, 1996 ($3.95, limited series)

1,4: 1-Marz script, Jurgens-a(p); 1st app. of Access. 4.00
.../Marvel Versus DC ($12.95, trade paperback) r/1-4 13.00

DC/WILDSTORM DREAMWAR
DC Comics: Jun, 2008 - No. 6, Nov, 2008 ($2.99, limited series)

1-6-Giffen-s; Silver Age JLA, Teen Titans, JSA, Legion app. on WildStorm Earth 3.00
1-Variant-c of Superman & Midnighter by Garbett 6.00
TPB (2009, $19.99) r/series 20.00

DC: WORLD WAR III (See 52/WWIII)

D-DAY (Also see Special War Series)
Charlton Comics (no No. 3): Sum/63; No. 2, Fall/64; No. 4, 9/66; No. 5, 10/67; No. 6, 11/68

	GD	VG	FN	VF	VF/NM	NM-
1,2: 1(1963)-Montes/Bache-c. 2(Fall '64)-Wood-a(4)	4	8	12	22	34	45
4-6('66-'68)-Montes/Bache-a #5	3	6	9	14	20	25

DEAD AIR
Slave Labor Graphics: July, 1989 ($5.95, graphic novel)

nn-Mike Allred's 1st published work 6.00

DEAD CORPSE
DC Comics (Helix): Sept, 1998 - No. 4, Dec, 1998 ($2.50, limited series)

1-4-Pugh-a/Hinz-s 3.00

DEAD END CRIME STORIES
Kirby Publishing Co.: April, 1949 (52 pgs.)

	GD	VG	FN	VF	VF/NM	NM-
nn-(Scarce)-Powell, Roussos-a; painted-c	52	104	156	322	549	775

DEAD ENDERS
DC Comics (Vertigo): Mar, 2000 - No. 16, June, 2001 ($2.50)

1-16-Brubaker-s/Pleece & Case-a 3.00
Stealing the Sun (2000, $9.95, TPB) r/#1-4, Vertigo Winter's Edge #3 10.00

DEAD-EYE WESTERN COMICS
Hillman Periodicals: Nov-Dec, 1948 - V3#1, Apr-May, 1953

	GD	VG	FN	VF	VF/NM	NM-
V1#1-(52 pgs.)-Krigstein, Roussos-a	20	40	60	114	182	250
V1#2,3-(52 pgs.)	12	24	36	69	97	125
V1#4-12-(52 pgs.)	9	18	27	47	61	75
V2#1,2,5-8,10-12: 1-7-(52 pgs.)	8	16	24	40	50	60
3,4-Krigstein-a	8	16	24	44	57	70
9-One pg. Frazetta ad	8	16	24	40	50	60
V3#1	8	16	24	40	50	60

NOTE: ***Briefer** a-V1#8. Kinstleresque stories by **McCann**-12, V2#1, 2, V3#1. **McWilliams** a-V1#5. **Ed Moore** a-V1#4.*

DEADFACE: DOING THE ISLANDS WITH BACCHUS
Dark Horse Comics: July, 1991 - No. 3, Sept, 1991 ($2.95, B&W, lim. series)

1-3: By Eddie Campbell 3.00

DEADFACE: EARTH, WATER, AIR, AND FIRE
Dark Horse Comics: July, 1992 - No. 4, Oct, 1992 ($2.50, B&W, limited series; British-r)

1-4: By Eddie Campbell 3.00

DEAD IN THE WEST
Dark Horse Comics: Oct, 1993 - No. 2, Mar, 1994 ($3.95, B&W, 52 pgs.)

1,2-Timothy Truman-c 4.00

DEAD IRONS
Dynamite Entertainment: 2009 - No. 4, 2009 ($3.99)

1-4-Kuhoric-s/Alexander-a/Jae Lee-c 4.00

DEADLANDER (Becomes Dead Rider for #2)
Dark Horse Comics: Oct, 2007 - No. 4, ($2.99, limited series)

1-2-Kevin Ferrara-s/a 3.00

DEADLIEST HEROES OF KUNG FU (Magazine)
Marvel Comics Group: Summer, 1975 (B&W)(76 pgs.)

	GD	VG	FN	VF	VF/NM	NM-
1-Bruce Lee vs. Carradine painted-c; TV Kung Fu, 4pgs. photos/article; Enter the Dragon, 24 pgs. photos/article w/ Bruce Lee; Bruce Lee photo pinup	4	8	12	28	44	60

DEADLINE
Marvel Comics: June, 2002 - No. 4, Sept, 2002 ($2.99, limited series)

1-4: 1-Intro. Kat Farrell; Bill Rosemann-s/Guy Davis-a; Horn painted-c 3.00
TPB (2002. $9.99) r/#1-4 10.00

DEADLY DUO, THE
Image Comics (Highbrow Entertainment): Nov, 1994 - No. 3, Jan, 1995 ($2.50, lim. series)

1-3: 1-1st app. of Kill Cat 3.00

DEADLY DUO, THE
Image Comics (Highbrow Entertainment): June, 1995 - No. 4, Oct, 1995 ($2.50, lim. series)

1-4: 1-Spawn app. 2-Savage Dragon app. 3-Gen 13 app. 3.00

DEADLY FOES OF SPIDER-MAN (See Lethal Foes of...)
Marvel Comics: May, 1991 - No. 4, Aug, 1991 ($1.00, limited series)

1-4: 1-Punisher, Kingpin, Rhino app. 3.00

DEADLY HANDS OF KUNG FU, THE (See Master of Kung Fu)
Marvel Comics Group: April, 1974 - No. 33, Feb, 1977 (75¢) (B&W, magazine)

	GD	VG	FN	VF	VF/NM	NM-
1(V1#4 listed in error)-Origin Sons of the Tiger; Shang-Chi, Master of Kung Fu begins (ties w/Master of Kung Fu #17 as 3rd app. Shang-Chi); Bruce Lee painted-c by Neal Adams; 2pg. memorial photo pinup w/8 pgs. photos/articles; TV Kung Fu, 9 pgs. photos/articles; 15 pgs. Starlin-a	6	12	18	37	59	80

2-Adams painted-c; 1st time origin of Shang-Chi, 34 pgs. by Starlin. TV Kung Fu, 6 pgs.

Deadly Hands of Kung Fu #1 © MAR

Deadman: Dead Again #5 © DC

Deadpool (2008 series) #23 © MAR

GD VG FN VF VF/NM NM-
2.0 4.0 6.0 8.0 9.0 9.2

GD VG FN VF VF/NM NM-
2.0 4.0 6.0 8.0 9.0 9.2

photos & article w/2 pg. pinup. Bruce Lee, 11 pgs. ph/a 4 8 12 28 44 60
3,4,7,10: 3-Adams painted-c; Gulacy-a. Enter the Dragon, photos/articles, 8 pgs. 4-TV Kung Fu painted-c by Neal Adams; TV Kung Fu 7 pg. article/art; Fu Manchu; Enter the Dragon, 10 pg. photos/article w/Bruce Lee. 7-Bruce Lee painted-c & 9 pgs. photos/articles-Return of Dragon plus 1 pg. photo pinup. 10-(3/75)-Iron Fist painted-c & 34 pg. sty-Early app. 3 6 9 20 30 40
5,6: 5-1st app. Manchurian, 6 pgs. Gulacy-a. TV Kung Fu, 4 pg. article; reprints books w/Barry Smith-a. Capt. America-sty, 10 pgs. Kirby-a(r). 6-Bruce Lee photos/article, 6 pgs.; 15 pgs. early Perez-a 3 6 9 19 29 38
8,9,11: 9-Iron Fist, 2 pg. Preview pinup; Nebres-a. 11-Billy Jack painted-c by Adams; 17 pgs. photos/article 3 6 9 18 27 35
12,13: 12-James Bond painted-c by Adams; 14 pg. photos/article. 13-16 pgs. early Perez-a; Piers Anthony, 7 pgs. photos/article 3 6 9 17 25 32
14-Classic Bruce Lee painted-c by Adams. Lee pinup by Chaykin. Lee 16 pg. photos/article w/2 pgs. Green Hornet TV 6 12 18 43 69 95
15,19: 15-Sum, '75 Giant Annual #1. 20pgs. Starlin-a. Bruce Lee photo pinup & 3 pg. photos/ article re book; Man-Thing app. Iron Fist-c/sty; Gulacy-a 18pgs. 19-Iron Fist painted-c & series begins; 1st White Tiger 3 6 9 18 27 35
16,18,20: 16-1st app. Corpse Rider, a Samurai w/Sanho Kim-a. 20-Chuck Norris painted-c & 16 pgs. interview w/photos/article; Bruce Lee vs. C. Norris pinup by Ken Barr. Origin The White Tiger, Perez-a 3 6 9 16 23 30
17-Bruce Lee painted-c by Adams; interview w/R. Clouse, director Enter Dragon 7 pgs. w/B. Lee app. 1st Giffen-a (1pg. 11/75) 4 8 12 28 44 60
21-Bruce Lee 1pg. photos/article 3 6 9 16 23 30
22,30-32: 22-1st brief app. Jack of Hearts. 1st Giffen sty-a (along w/Amazing Adv. #35, 3/76). 30-Swordquest-c/sty & conclusion; Jack of Hearts app. 31-Jack of Hearts app; Staton-a. 32-1st Daughters of the Dragon-c/sty, 21 pgs. M. Rogers-a/Claremont-sty; Iron Fist pinup 3 6 9 16 22 28
23-26,29: 23-1st full app. Jack of Hearts. 24-Iron Fist-c & centerfold pinup. early Zeck-a; Shang Chi pinup; 6 pgs. Piers Anthony text sty w/Perez/Austin-a; Jack of Hearts app. early Giffen-a. 25-1st app. Shimuru, "Samurai", 20 pgs. Mantlo-sty/Broderick-a; "Swordquest"-c & begins 17 pg. sty by Sanho Kim; 11 pg. photos/article; partly Bruce Lee. 26-Bruce Lee painted-c & pinup; 16 pgs. interviews w/Kwon & Clouse; talk about Bruce Lee re-filming of Lee legend. 29-Ironfist vs. Shang Chi battle-c/sty; Jack of Hearts app. 3 6 9 18 27 35
27 3 6 9 14 20 26
28-All Bruce Lee Special Issue; (1st time in comics). Bruce Lee painted-c by Ken Barr & pinup. 36 pgs. comics chronicaling Bruce Lee's life; 15 pgs. B. Lee photos/article (Rare in high grade) 8 16 24 52 86 120
33-Shang Chi-c/sty; Classic Daughters of the Dragon, 21 pgs. M. Rogers-a/Claremont-story with nudity; Bob Wall interview, photos/article, 14 pgs. 3 6 9 20 30 40
...Special Album Edition 1(Summer, '74)-Iron Fist-c/story (early app., 3rd?); 10 pgs. Adams-i; Shang Chi/Fu Manchu, 10 pgs.; Sons of Tiger, 11 pgs.; TV Kung Fu, 6 pgs. photos/article 4 8 12 22 34 45

NOTE: ***Bruce Lee:** 1-7, 14, 15, 17, 25, 26, 28. **Kung Fu (TV):** 1, 2, 4. **Jack of Hearts:** 22, 23, 29-33. **Shang Chi Master of Kung Fu:** 1-9, 11-18, 29, 31, 33. **Sons of Tiger:** 1, 3, 4, 6-14, 16-19. **Swordquest:** 25-27, 29-33. **White Tiger:** 19-24, 26, 27, 29-33. **N. Adams** a-1i(part), 27i; c-1, 2-4, 11, 12, 14, 17. **Giffen** a-22p, 24p. **G. Kane** a-23p. **Kirby** a-5r. **Nasser** a-27p, 28. **Perez** a(p)-6-14, 16, 17, 19, 21. **Rogers** a-26, 32, 33. **Starlin** a-1, 2r, 15r. **Staton** a-28p, 31, 32.*

DEADMAN (See The Brave and the Bold & Phantom Stranger #39)
DC Comics: May, 1985 - No. 7, Nov, 1985 ($1.75, Baxter paper)
1-7: 1-Deadman-r by Infantino, N. Adams in all. 5-Batman-c/story-r/Strange Adventures. 7-Batman-r 3.00

DEADMAN
DC Comics: Mar, 1986 - No. 4, June, 1986 (75¢, limited series)
1-4: Lopez-c/a. 4-Byrne-c(p) 3.00

DEADMAN
DC Comics: Feb, 2002 - No. 9, Oct, 2002 ($2.50)
1-9: 1-4-Vance-s/Beroy-a. 3,4-Mignola-c. 5,6-Garcia-Lopez-a 3.00

DEADMAN
DC Comics (Vertigo): Oct, 2006 - No. 13, Oct, 2007 ($2.99)
1-13: 1-Bruce Jones-s/John Watkiss-a/c; intro Brandon Cayce 3.00
...: Deadman Walking TPB (2007, $9.99) r/#1-5 10.00

DEADMAN: DEAD AGAIN (Leads into 2002 series)
DC Comics: Oct, 2001 - No. 5, Oct, 2001 ($2.50, weekly limited series)
1-5: Deadman at the deaths of the Flash, Robin, Superman, Hal Jordan 3.00

DEADMAN: EXORCISM
DC Comics: 1992 - No. 2, 1992 ($4.95, limited series, 52 pgs.)
1,2: Kelley Jones-c/a in both 5.00

DEADMAN: LOVE AFTER DEATH
DC Comics: 1989 - No. 2, 1990 ($3.95, 52 pgs., limited series, mature)
Book One, Two: Kelley Jones-c/a in both. 1-contains nudity 4.00

DEAD OF NIGHT
Marvel Comics Group: Dec, 1973 - No. 11, Aug, 1975
1-Horror reprints 3 6 9 18 27 35
2-10: 10-Kirby-a. 6-Jack the Ripper-c/s 2 4 6 13 18 22
11-Intro Scarecrow; Kane/Wrightson-c 4 8 12 22 34 45
NOTE: *Ditko r-7, 10. Everett c-2. Sinnott r-1.*

DEAD OF NIGHT FEATURING DEVIL-SLAYER
Marvel Comics (MAX): Nov, 2008 - No. 4, Feb, 2009 ($3.99, limited series)
1-4-Keene-s/Samnee-a/Andrews-c 4.00

DEAD OF NIGHT FEATURING MAN-THING
Marvel Comics (MAX): Apr, 2008 - No. 4, July, 2008 ($3.99, limited series)
1-4: 1-Man-Thing origin re-told; Kano-a. 2-4-Jennifer Kale app. 4.00

DEAD OF NIGHT FEATURING WEREWOLF BY NIGHT
Marvel Comics (MAX): Mar, 2009 - No. 4, Jun, 2009 ($3.99, limited series)
1-4: 1-Werewolf By Night origin re-told; Swierczynski-s/Suayan-a 4.00

DEAD OR ALIVE - A CYBERPUNK WESTERN
Image Comics (Shok Studio): Apr, 1998 - No. 4, July, 1998 ($2.50, limited series)
1-4 3.00

DEADPOOL (See New Mutants #98 for 1st app.)
Marvel Comics: Aug, 1994 - No. 4, Nov, 1994 ($2.50, limited series)
1-4: Mark Waid's 1st Marvel work; Ian Churchill-c/a 4.00

DEADPOOL (... : Agent of Weapon X on cover #57-60) (title becomes Agent X)
Marvel Comics: Jan, 1997 - No. 69, Sept, 2002 ($2.95/$1.95/$1.99)
1-($2.95)-Wraparound-c 1 2 3 4 5 7
2-Begin-$1.95-c. 5.00
3-10,12-22,24: 4-Hulk-c/app. 12-Variant-c. 14-Begin McDaniel-a. 22-Cable app. 5.00
11-($3.99)-Deadpool replaces Spider-Man from Amazing Spider-Man #47; Kraven, Gwen Stacy app. 6.00
23,25-($2.99); 23-Dead Reckoning pt. 1; wraparound-c 4.00
26-40: 27-Wolverine-c/app. 37-Thor app. 3.00
41-53,56-60: 41-Begin $2.25-c. 44-Black Panther-c/app. 46-49-Chadwick-a 51-Cover swipe of Detective #38. 57-60-BWS-c 3.00
54,55-Punisher-c/app. 54-Dillon-c. 55-Bradstreet-c 3.00
61-69: 61-64-Funeral For a Freak on cover. 65-69-Udon Studios-a. 67-Dazzler-c/app. 3.00
#(-1) Flashback (7/97) Lopresti-a; Wade Wilson's early days 3.00
.../Death '98 Annual ($2.99) Kelly-s, ... Team-Up (12/98, $2.99) Widdle Wade-c/app., Baby's First Deadpool Book (12/98, $2.99), Encyclopædia Deadpoolica (12/98, $2.99) Synopses 4.00
.../GLI - Summer Fun Spectacular #1 (9/07, $3.99) short stories; Pelletier-c 4.00
... Classic Vol. 1 TPB (2008, $29.99) r/#1, New Mutants #98, Deadpool: The Circle Chase #1-4 and Deadpool (1994 series) #1-4 30.00
Mission Improbable TPB (9/98, $14.95) r/#1-5 15.00
Wizard #0 ('98, bagged with Wizard #87) 3.00

DEADPOOL
Marvel Comics: Nov, 2008 - Present ($3.99/$2.99)
1-($3.99) Medina-a; Secret Invasion x-over; 2 covers by Crain & Liefeld 4.00
2-24,26-33, 33.1,34,35-($2.99) Variant covers for most. 4-20-Pearson-c. 8,9-Thunderbolts x-over. 10-Dark Reign. 16-18-X-Men app. 19-21-Spider-Man & Hit-Monkey app. 26-Ghost Rider app. 27-29-Secret Avengers app. 30,31-Curse of the Mutants 3.00
25-($3.99) 3-D cover, fake 3-D glasses on back-c; back-up story w/Bond-a 4.00
900-(12/09, $4.99) Stories by various incl. Liefeld, Baker; wraparound-c by Johnson 5.00
1000-(10/10, $4.99) Stories by various; gallery of variant covers; Johnson-c 5.00
... & Cable #26 (4/11, $3.99) Swierczynski-s/Fernandez-a 4.00
... Family 1 (6/11, $3.99) short stories by various; Pearson-c 4.00
...: Games of Death 1 (5/09, $3.99) Benson-s/Crystal-a/Land-c 4.00
... MCG (7/10, $1.00) r/#1 with "Marvel's Greatest Comics" logo on cover 1.00

DEADPOOL CORPS (Continues from Prelude to Deadpool Corps series)
Marvel Comics: Jun, 2010 - No. 12, May, 2011 ($3.99/$2.99)
1-($3.99) Liefeld-a/c; Gischler-s; 2 covers by Liefeld 4.00
2-12-($2.99) 2-5,7,9-Liefeld-a. 6-Mychaels-a 3.00
...: Rank and Foul 1 (5/10, $3.99) Handbook-style profile pages of allies and enemies 4.00

DEADPOOL MAX
Marvel Comics: Dec, 2010 - Present ($3.99)
1-7-David Lapham-s/Kyle Baker-a/c. 6,7-Domino app. 4.00

Deadpool Team-Up #894 © MAR

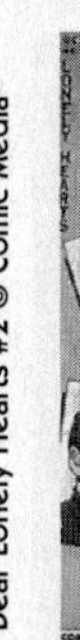
Dear Lonely Hearts #2 © Comic Media

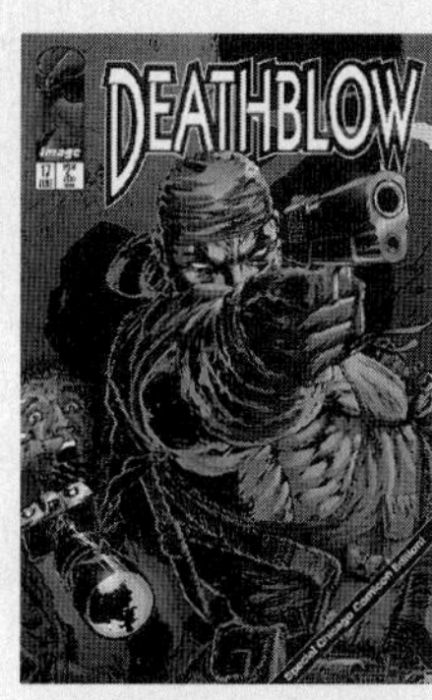

Deathblow #17 © WSP

	GD 2.0	VG 4.0	FN 6.0	VF 8.0	VF/NM 9.0	NM- 9.2

DEADPOOL: MERC WITH A MOUTH
Marvel Comics: Sept, 2009 - No. 13, Sept, 2010 ($3.99/$2.99)

1-($3.99) Suydam-c/Dazo-a; Zombie-head Deadpool & Ka-Zar app.; r/Deadpool #4 ('97) 4.00
2-6,8-12-($2.99) Suydam-c on all. 8-Deadpool goes to Zombie dimension 3.00
7-13-($3.99) 7-Covers by Suydam & Liefeld; art by Liefeld, Baker, Pastoras, Dazo 4.00

DEADPOOL PULP
Marvel Comics: Nov, 2010 - No. 4, Feb, 2011 ($3.99, limited series)

1-4-Alternate Deadpool in 1955; Glass & Benson-s/Laurence Campbell-a/Jae Lee-c 4.00

DEADPOOL: SUICIDE KINGS
Marvel Comics: Jun, 2009 - No. 5, Oct, 2009 ($3.99, limited series)

1-5-Barberi-a; Punisher, Daredevil, & Spider-Man app. 4.00

DEADPOOL TEAM-UP
Marvel Comics: No. 899, Jan, 2010 - No. 883, May, 2011 ($2.99, numbering runs in reverse)

899-883: 899-Hercules app.; Ramos-c. 897-Ghost Rider app. 894-Franken-Castle app. 887-Thor app. 883-Galactus & Silver Surfer app. 3.00

DEADPOOL: THE CIRCLE CHASE (See New Mutants #98)
Marvel Comics: Aug, 1993 - No. 4, Nov, 1993 ($2.00, limited series)

1-($2.50)-Embossed-c 6.00
2-4 4.00

DEADPOOL: WADE WILSON'S WAR
Marvel Comics: Aug, 2010 - No. 4, Nov, 2010 ($3.99, limited series)

1-4-Swierczynski-s/Pearson-a/c; Bullseye, Domino & Silver Sable app. 4.00

DEAD RIDER (See Deadlander)

DEAD ROMEO
DC Comics: June, 2009 - No. 6, Nov, 2009 ($2.99, limited series)

1-6-Ryan Benjamin-a/Jesse Snider-s 3.00
TPB (2010, $19.99) r/#1-6; cover gallery 20.00

DEAD, SHE SAID
IDW Publishing: May, 2008 - No. 3, Sept, 2008 ($3.99, limited series)

1-3-Bernie Wrightson-a/Steve Niles-s 4.00

DEADSHOT (See Batman #59, Detective Comics #474, & Showcase '93 #8)
DC Comics: Nov, 1988 - No. 4, Feb, 1989 ($1.00, limited series)

1-4 3.00

DEADSHOT
DC Comics: Feb, 2005 - No. 5, June 2005 ($2.95, limited series)

1-5-Zeck-c/Gage-s/Cummings-a. 3-Green Arrow app. 3.00

DEAD SPACE (Based on the Electronics Arts videogame)
Image Comics: Mar, 2008 - No. 6, Sept, 2008 ($2.99, limited series)

1-6-Templesmith-a/Johnston-s 3.00
... Extraction (9/09, $3.50) Templesmith-a/Johnston-s 3.50

DEAD WHO WALK, THE (See Strange Mysteries, Super Reprint #15, 16)
Realistic Comics: 1952 (one-shot)

	GD	VG	FN	VF	VF/NM	NM-
nn	54	108	162	343	574	825

DEADWORLD (Also see The Realm)
Arrow Comics/Caliber Comics: Dec, 1986 - No. 26 ($1.50/$1.95/#15-28: $2.50, B&W)

1-4 4.00
5-26-Graphic cover version 4.00
5-26-Tame cover version 3.00
...Archives 1-3 (1992, $2.50) 3.00

DEAN MARTIN & JERRY LEWIS (See Adventures of...)

DEAR BEATRICE FAIRFAX
Best/Standard Comics (King Features): No. 5, Nov, 1950 - No. 9, Sept, 1951 (Vern Greene art)

	GD	VG	FN	VF	VF/NM	NM-
5-All have Schomburg air brush-c	14	28	42	76	108	140
6-9	10	20	30	54	72	90

DEAR HEART (Formerly Lonely Heart)
Ajax: No. 15, July, 1956 - No. 16, Sept, 1956

	GD	VG	FN	VF	VF/NM	NM-
15,16	8	16	24	40	50	60

DEAR LONELY HEART (...Illustrated No. 1-6)
Artful Publications: Mar, 1951; No. 2, Oct, 1951 - No. 8, Oct, 1952

	GD	VG	FN	VF	VF/NM	NM-
1	17	34	51	98	154	210
2	10	20	30	54	72	90
3-Matt Baker Jungle Girl story	20	40	60	114	182	250
4-8	9	18	27	50	65	80

DEAR LONELY HEARTS (Lonely Heart #9 on)
Harwell Publ./Mystery Publ. Co. (Comic Media): Aug, 1953 -No. 8, Oct, 1954

	GD	VG	FN	VF	VF/NM	NM-
1	14	28	42	76	108	140
2-8	10	20	30	54	72	90

DEARLY BELOVED
Ziff-Davis Publishing Co.: Fall, 1952

	GD	VG	FN	VF	VF/NM	NM-
1-Photo-c	18	36	54	103	162	220

DEAR NANCY PARKER
Gold Key: June, 1963 - No. 2, Sept, 1963

	GD	VG	FN	VF	VF/NM	NM-
1-Painted-c on both	4	8	12	23	36	48
2	3	6	9	17	25	32

DEATH, THE ABSOLUTE... (From Neil Gaiman's Sandman titles)
DC Comics (Vertigo): 2009 ($99.99, oversized hardcover in slipcase)

nn-Reprints 1st app. in Sandman #8, Sandman #20, Death: The High Cost of Living #1-3, Death: the Time of Your Life #1-3, Death Talks About Life; short stories and pin-ups; merchandise pics; script and sketch art for Sandman #8; Gaiman afterword 100.00

DEATH: AT DEATH'S DOOR (See Sandman: The Season of Mists)
DC Comics (Vertigo): 2003 ($9.95, graphic novel one-shot, B&W, 7-1/2" x 5")

1-Jill Thompson-s/a/c; manga-style; Morpheus and the Endless app. 10.00

DEATHBLOW (Also see Batman/Deathblow and Darker Image)
Image Comics (WildStorm Productions): May (Apr. inside), 1993 - No. 29, Aug, 1996 ($1.75/$1.95/$2.50)

0-(8/96, $2.95, 32 pgs.)-r/Darker Image w/new story & art; Jim Lee & Trevor Scott-a; new Jim Lee-c 3.00
1-($2.50)-Red foil stamped logo on black varnish-c; Jim Lee-c/a; flip-book side has Cybernary -c/story (#2 also) 3.50
1-($1.95)-Newsstand version w/o foil-c & varnish 3.00
2-29: 2-(8/93)-Lee-a; with bound-in poster. 2-($1.75)-Newsstand version w/o poster. 4-Jim Lee-c/Tim Sale-a begin. 13-W/pinup poster by Tim Sale & Jim Lee. 16-($1.95 Newsstand & $2.50 Direct Market editions)-Wildstorm Rising Pt. 6. 17-Variant "Chicago Comicon" edition exists. 20,21-Gen 13 app. 23-Backlash-c/app. 24,25-Grifter-c/app; Gen 13 & Dane from Wetworks app. 28-Deathblow dies. 29-Memorial issue 3.00
5-Alternate Portacio-c (Forms larger picture when combined with alternate-c for Gen 13 #5, Kindred #3, Stormwatch #10, Team 7 #1, Union #0, Wetworks #2 & WildC.A.T.S #11) 6.00
...:Sinners and Saints TPB ('99, $19.95) r/#1-12; Sale-c 20.00

DEATHBLOW (Volume 2)
DC Comics (WildStorm): Dec, 2006 - No. 9, Apr, 2008 ($2.99)

1-9: 1-Azzarello-s/D'Anda-a; two covers by D'Anda & Platt 3.00
...: And Then You Live! TPB (2008, $19.99) r/#1-9 20.00

DEATHBLOW BY BLOWS
DC Comics (WildStorm): Nov, 1999 - No. 3, Jan, 2000 ($2.95, limited series)

1-3-Alan Moore-s/Jim Baikie-a 3.00

DEATHBLOW/WOLVERINE
Image Comics (WildStorm Productions)/ Marvel Comics: Sept, 1996 - No. 2, Feb, 1997 ($2.50, limited series)

1,2: Wiesenfeld-s/Bennett-a 3.00
TPB (1997, $8.95) r/#1,2 9.00

DEATHDEALER (Also see Frank Frazetta's...)
Verotik: July, 1995 - No. 4, July, 1997 ($5.95)

	GD	VG	FN	VF	VF/NM	NM-
1-Frazetta-c; Bisley-a	1	2	3	5	6	8
1-2nd print, 2-4-($6.95)-Frazetta-c; embossed logo	1	2	3	4	5	7

DEATH-DEFYING 'DEVIL, THE (Also see Project Superpowers)
Dynamite Entertainment: 2008 - No. 4, 2009 ($3.50, limited series)

1-4-Casey & Ross-s/Salazar-a; multiple covers; the Dragon app. 3.50

DEATH, JR.
Image Comics: Apr, 2005 - No. 3, Aug, 2005 ($4.99, squarebound, limited series)

1-3-Gary Whitta-s/Ted Naifeh-a 5.00
Vol. 1 TPB (2005, $14.99) r/series; concept and promotional art 15.00

DEATH, JR. (Volume 2)
Image Comics: Jul, 2006 - No. 3, May, 2007 ($4.99, squarebound, limited series)

1-3-Gary Whitta-s/Ted Naifeh-a. 1-Dan Brereton-c 5.00
Vol. 2 TPB (2007, $14.99) r/series; Halloween story w/Guy Davis-a; promotional art 15.00

DEATHLOK (Also see Astonishing Tales #25)

Deathlok (1999 series) #3 © MAR

Death of the New Gods #8 © DC

Death Valley #1 © Comic Media

	GD 2.0	VG 4.0	FN 6.0	VF 8.0	VF/NM 9.0	NM- 9.2

Marvel Comics: July, 1990 - No. 4, Oct, 1990 ($3.95, limited series, 52 pgs.)
1-4: 1,2-Guice-a(p). 3,4-Denys Cowan-a, c-4 4.00

DEATHLOK
Marvel Comics: July, 1991 - No. 34, Apr, 1994 ($1.75)
1-Silver ink cover; Denys Cowan-c/a(p) begins 3.50
2-18,20-24,26-34: 2-Forge (X-Men) app. 3-Vs. Dr. Doom. 5-X-Men & F.F. x-over. 6,7-Punisher x-over. 9,10-Ghost Rider-c/story. 16-Infinity War x-over. 17-Jae Lee-c. 22-Black Panther app. 27-Siege app. 3.00
19-($2.25)-Foil-c 3.50
25-($2.95, 52 pgs.)-Holo-grafx foil-c 4.00
Annual 1 (1992, $2.25, 68 pgs.)-Guice-p; Quesada-c(p) 4.00
Annual 2 (1993, $2.95, 68 pgs.)-Bagged w/card; intro Tracer 4.00
NOTE: *Denys Cowan a(p)-9-13, 15, Annual 1; c-9-12, 13p, 14.* ***Guice/Cowan*** *c-8.*

DEATHLOK
Marvel Comics: Sept, 1999 - No. 11, June, 2000 ($1.99)
1-11: 1-Casey-s/Manco-a. 2-Two covers. 4-Canete-a 3.00

DEATHLOK (... The Demolisher on cover)
Marvel Comics: Jan, 2010 - No. 7, Jul, 2010 ($3.99, limited series)
1-7-Huston-s/Medina-a/Peterson-c 4.00

DEATHLOK SPECIAL
Marvel Comics: May, 1991 - No. 4, June, 1991 ($2.00, bi-weekly lim. series)
1-4: r/1-4(1990) w/new Guice-c #1,2; Cowan c-3,4 3.00
1-2nd printing w/white-c 3.00

DEATHMASK
Future Comics: Mar, 2003 - No. 3, June, 2003 ($2.99)
1-3-Giordano-a(p)/Michelinie & Layton-s 3.00

DEATHMATE
Valiant (Prologue/Yellow/Blue)/Image Comics (Black/Red/Epilogue): Sept, 1993 - Epilogue (#6), Feb, 1994 ($2.95/$4.95, limited series)
Preview-(7/93, 8 pgs.) 3.00
Prologue (#1)–Silver foil; Jim Lee/Layton-c; B. Smith/Lee-a; Liefeld-a(p) 3.00
Prologue–Special gold foil ed. of silver ed. 4.00
Black (#2)-(9/93, $4.95, 52 pgs.)-Silvestri/Jim Lee-c; pencils by Peterson/Silvestri/Capullo/ Jim Lee/Portacio; 1st story app. Gen 13 telling their rebellion against the Troika (see WildC.A.T.S. Trilogy) 6.00
Black-Special gold foil edition 7.00
Yellow (#3)-(10/93, $4.95, 52 pgs)-Yellow foil-c; Indicia says Prologue Sept 1993 by mistake; 3rd app. Ninjak; Thibert-c(i) 5.00
Yellow-Special gold foil edition 6.00
Blue (#4)-(10/93, $4.95, 52 pgs.)-Thibert blue foil-c(i); Reese-a(i) 5.00
Blue-Special gold foil edition 6.00
Red (#5), Epilogue (#6)-(2/94, $2.95)-Silver foil Quesada/Silvestri-c; Silvestri-a(p) 3.00

DEATH METAL
Marvel Comics UK: Jan, 1994 - No. 4, Apr, 1994 ($1.95, limited series)
1-4: 1-Silver ink-c. Alpha Flight app. 3.00

DEATH METAL VS. GENETIX
Marvel Comics UK: Dec, 1993 - No. 2, Jan, 1994 (Limited series)
1-($2.95)-Polybagged w/2 trading cards 3.00
2-($2.50)-Polybagged w/2 trading cards 3.00

DEATH OF CAPTAIN MARVEL (See Marvel Graphic Novel #1)

DEATH OF DRACULA
Marvel Comics: Aug, 2010 ($3.99, one shot)
1-Gischler-s/Camuncoli-a/c 4.00

DEATH OF MR. MONSTER, THE (See Mr. Monster #8)

DEATH OF SUPERMAN (See Superman, 2nd Series)

DEATH OF THE NEW GODS (Tie-in to the Countdown series)
DC Comics: Early Dec, 2007 - No. 8, Jun, 2008 ($3.50, limited series)
1-8-Jim Starlin-s/a/c. 1-Barda killed. 6-Orion dies. 7-Scott Free and Metron die 3.50
TPB (2009, $19.99) r/#1-8; Starlin intro.; cover gallery 20.00

DEATH RACE 2020
Roger Corman's Cosmic Comics: Apr, 1995 - No. 8, Nov, 1995 ($2.50)
1-8: Sequel to the Movie 3.00

DEATH RATTLE (Formerly an Underground)
Kitchen Sink Press: V2#1, 10/85 - No. 18, 1988, 1994 ($1.95, Baxter paper, mature); V3#1, 11/95 - No. 5, 6/96 ($2.95, B&W)
V2#1-7,9-18: 1-Corben-c. 2-Unpubbed Spirit story by Eisner. 5-Robot Woman-r by Wolverton. 6-B&W issues begin. 10-Savage World-r by by Williamson/Torres/ Krenkel/Frazetta from Witzend #1. 16-Wolverton Spacehawk-r 5.00
8-(12/86)-1st app. Mark Schultz's Xenozoic Tales/Cadillacs & Dinosaurs 2 4 6 8 10 12
8-(1994)-r plus interview w/Mark Schultz 3.50
V3#1-5 ($2.95-c) 3.50

DEATH'S HEAD (See Daredevil #56, Dragon's Claws #5 & Incomplete...)(See Amazing Fantasy (2004) for Death's Head 3.0)
Marvel Comics: Dec, 1988 - No. 10, Sept, 1989 ($1.75)
1-Dragon's Claws spin-off 3.00
2-Fantastic Four app.; Dragon's Claws x-over 3.00
3-10: 8-Dr. Who app. 9-F. F. x-over; Simonson-c(p) 3.00

DEATH'S HEAD II (Also see Battletide)
Marvel Comics UK, Ltd.: Mar, 1992 - No. 4, June (May inside), 1992 ($1.75, color, lim. series)
1-4: 2-Fantastic Four app. 4-Punisher, Spider-Man, Daredevil, Dr. Strange, Capt. America & Wolverine in the year 2020 3.00
1,2-Silver ink 2nd printiings 3.00

DEATH'S HEAD II (Also see Battletide)
Marvel Comics UK, Ltd.: Dec, 1992 - No. 16, Mar, 1994 ($1.75/$1.95)
V2#1-13,15,16: 1-Gatefold-c. 1-4-X-Men app.15-Capt. America & Wolverine app. 3.00
14-($2.95)-Foil flip-c w/Death's Head II Gold #0 3.00
...Gold 1 (1/94, $3.95, 68 pgs.)-Gold foil-c 4.00

DEATH'S HEAD II & THE ORIGIN OF DIE CUT
Marvel Comics UK, Ltd.: Aug, 1993 - No. 2, Sept, 1993 (limited series)
1-($2.95)-Embossed-c 4.00
2 ($1.75) 3.00

DEATHSTROKE: THE TERMINATOR (Deathstroke: The Hunted #0-47; Deathstroke #48-60) (Also see Marvel & DC Present, New Teen Titans #2, New Titans, Showcase '93 #7,9 & Tales of the Teen Titans #42-44)
DC Comics: Aug, 1991 - No. 60, June, 1996 ($1.75-$2.25)
1-New Titans spin-off; Mike Zeck c-1-28 4.00
1-Gold ink 2nd printing ($1.75) 3.00
2 3.00
3-40,0(10/94),41(11/94)-49,51-60: 6,8-Batman cameo. 7,9-Batman-c/story. 9-1st brief app. new Vigilante (female). 10-1st full app. new Vigilante; Perez-i. 13-Vs. Justice League; Team Titans cameo on last pg. 14-Total Chaos, part 1; TeamTitans-c/story cont'd in New Titans #90. 40-(9/94). 0-(10/94)-Begin Deathstroke, The Hunted, ends #47. 3.00
50 ($3.50) 4.00
Annual 1-4 ('92-'95, 68 pgs.): 1-Nightwing & Vigilante app.; minor Eclipso app. 2-Bloodlines Deathstorm; 1st app. Gunfire. 3-Elseworlds story. 4-Year One story 4.00
NOTE: ***Golden*** *a-12.* ***Perez*** *a-11i.* ***Zeck*** *c-Annual 1, 2.*

DEATH: THE HIGH COST OF LIVING (See Sandman #8) (Also see the Books of Magic limited & ongoing series)
DC Comics (Vertigo): Mar, 1993 - No. 3, May, 1993 ($1.95, limited series)
1-Bachalo/Buckingham-a; Dave McKean-c; Neil Gaiman scripts in all 6.00
1-Platinum edition 40.00
2 3.50
3-Pgs. 19 & 20 had wrong placement 3.00
3-Corrected version w/pgs. 19 & 20 facing each other; has no-c & ads for Sebastion O & The Geek added 4.00
Death Talks About Life-giveaway about AIDS prevention 5.00
Hardcover (1994, $19.95)-r/#1-3 & Death Talks About Life; intro. by Tori Amos 20.00
Trade paperback (6/94, $12.95, Titan Books)-r/#1-3 & Death Talks About Life; prism-c 13.00

DEATH: THE TIME OF YOUR LIFE (See Sandman #8)
DC Comics (Vertigo): Apr, 1996 - No. 3, July, 1996 ($2.95, limited series)
1-3: Neil Gaiman story & Bachalo/Buckingham-a; Dave McKean-c. 2-(5/96) 3.00
Hardcover (1997, $19.95)-r/#1-3 w/3 new pages & gallery art by various 20.00
TPB (1997, $12.95)-r/#1-3 & Visions of Death gallery; Intro. by Claire Danes 13.00

DEATH 3
Marvel Comics UK: Sept, 1993 - No. 4, Dec, 1993 ($1.75, limited series)
1-($2.95)-Embossed-c 3.50
2-4 3.00

DEATH VALLEY (Cowboys and Indians)
Comic Media: Oct, 1953 - No. 6, Aug, 1954

	GD 2.0	VG 4.0	FN 6.0	VF 8.0	VF/NM 9.0	NM- 9.2
1-Billy the Kid; Morisi-a; Andru/Esposito-c/a	20	40	60	114	182	250
2-Don Heck-c	13	26	39	72	101	130
3-6: 3,5-Morisi-a. 5-Discount-a	12	24	36	67	94	120

Debbie Dean, Career Girl #1 © CSP

The Defenders #55 © MAR

Dellec #4 © Aspen MLT

GD VG FN VF VF/NM NM-
2.0 4.0 6.0 8.0 9.0 9.2

DEATH VALLEY (Becomes Frontier Scout, Daniel Boone No.10-13)
Charlton Comics: No. 7, 6/55 - No. 9, 10/55 (Cont'd from Comic Media series)
7-9: 8-Wolverton-a (half pg.) 10 20 30 54 72 90

DEATHWISH
DC Comics (Milestone Media): Dec, 1994 - No. 4, Mar, 1995 (2.50, lim. series)
1-4 3.00

DEATH WRECK
Marvel Comics UK: Jan, 1994 - No. 4, Apr, 1994 ($1.95, limited series)
1-4: 1-Metallic ink logo; Death's Head II app. 3.00

DEBBIE DEAN, CAREER GIRL
Civil Service Publ.: April, 1945 - No. 2, July, 1945
1,2-Newspaper reprints by Bert Whitman 14 28 42 76 108 140

DEBBI'S DATES (Also see Date With Debbi)
National Periodical Publications: Apr-May, 1969 - No. 11, Dec-Jan, 1970-71
1 6 12 18 41 66 90
2,3,5,7-11: 2-Last 12¢ issue 4 8 12 22 34 45
4-Neal Adams text illo 4 8 12 26 41 55
6-Superman cameo 6 12 18 39 62 85

DECADE OF DARK HORSE, A
Dark Horse Comics: Jul, 1996 - No. 4, Oct, 1996 ($2.95, B&W/color, lim. series)
1-4: 1-Sin City-c/story by Miller; Grendel by Wagner; Predator. 2-Star Wars wraparound-c. 3-Aliens-c/story; Nexus, Mask stories 3.00

DECAPITATOR (Randy Bowen's...)
Dark Horse Comics: Jun, 1998 - No. 4, ($2.95)
1-4-Bowen-s/art by various. 1-Mahnke-c. 3-Jones-c 4.00

DECEPTION, THE
Image Comics (Flypaper Press): 1999 - No. 3, 1999 ($2.95, B&W, mini-series)
1-3-Horley painted-c 3.00

DECIMATION: THE HOUSE OF M
Marvel Comics: Jan, 2006 ($3.99)
... - The Day After (one-shot) Claremont-s/Green-a 4.00

DEEP, THE (Movie)
Marvel Comics Group: Nov, 1977 (Giant)
1-Infantino-c/a 1 3 4 6 8 10

DEEP SLEEPER
Oni Press/Image Comics: Feb, 2004 - No. 4, Sept, 2004 ($3.50/$2.95, B&W, limited series)
1,2-(Oni Press, $3.50)-Hester-s/Huddleston-a 3.50
3,4-(Image Comics, $2.95) 3.00
... Omnibus (Image, 8/04, $5.95) r/#1,2 6.00
... Vol. 1 TPB (2005, $12.95) r/#1-4; cover gallery 13.00

DEFCON 4
Image Comics (WildStorm Productions): Feb, 1996 - No. 4, Sept, 1996 ($2.50, lim. series)
1/2 1 2 3 5 7 9
1/2 Gold-(1000 printed) 14.00
1-Main Cover by Mat Broome & Edwin Rosell 3.00
1-Hordes of Cymulants variant-c by Michael Golden 5.00
1-Backs to the Wall variant-c by Humberto Ramos & Alex Garner 5.00
1-Defcon 4-Way variant-c by Jim Lee 1 2 3 4 5 7
2-4 3.00

DEFENDERS, THE (TV)
Dell Publishing Co.: Sept-Nov, 1962 - No. 2, Feb-Apr, 1963
12-176-211(#1) 4 8 12 26 41 55
12-176-304(#2) 3 6 9 21 32 42

DEFENDERS, THE (Also see Giant-Size..., Marvel Feature, Marvel Treasury Edition, Secret Defenders & Sub-Mariner #34, 35; The New...#140-on)
Marvel Comics Group: Aug, 1972 - No. 152, Feb, 1986
1-The Hulk, Doctor Strange, Sub-Mariner begin 12 24 36 87 164 240
2-Silver Surfer x-over 7 14 21 49 80 110
3-5: 3-Silver Surfer x-over. 4-Valkyrie joins 5 10 15 32 51 70
6,7: 6-Silver Surfer x-over 4 8 12 22 34 45
8,9,11: 8-11-Defenders vs. the Avengers (Crossover with Avengers #115-118) 8,11-Silver Surfer x-over 4 8 12 28 44 60
10-Hulk vs. Thor battle 8 16 24 58 97 135
12-14: 12-Last 20¢ issue 3 6 9 14 19 24
15,16-Magneto & Brotherhood of Evil Mutants app. from X-Men 3 6 9 16 22 28
17-20: 17-Power Man x-over (11/74) 2 4 6 8 11 14
21-25: 24,25-Son of Satan app. 1 2 3 5 7 9
26-29-Guardians of the Galaxy app. (#26 is 8/75; pre-dates Marvel Presents #3): 28-1st full app. Starhawk (1st brief app. #27). 29-Starhawk joins Guardians 2 4 6 8 10 12
30-33,39-50: 31,32-Origin Nighthawk. 44-Hellcat joins. 45-Dr. Strange leaves. 47-49-Early Moon Knight app. (5/77). 48-50-(Reg. 30¢-c) 6.00
34-38-(Regular 25¢ editions): 35-Intro New Red Guardian 6.00
34-38-(30¢-c variants, limited distribution)(4-8/76) 3 6 9 20 30 40
48-52-(35¢-c variants, limited distribution)(6-10/77) 4 8 12 28 44 60
51-60: 51,52-(Reg. 30¢-c). 53-1st brief app. Lunatik (Lobo lookalike). 55-Origin Red Guardian; Lunatik cameo. 56-1st full Lunatik story 5.00
61-75: 61-Lunatik & Spider-Man app. 70-73-Lunatik (origin #71). 73-75-Foolkiller II app. (Greg Salinger). 74-Nighthawk resigns 4.00
76-93,95,97-99,102-119,123,124,126-149,151: 77-Origin Omega. 78-Original Defenders return thru #101. 104-The Beast joins. 105-Son of Satan joins. 106-Death of Nighthawk. 129-New Mutants cameo (3/84, early x-over) 3.00
94,101,120-122: 94-1st Gargoyle. 101-Silver Surfer-c & app. 120,121-Son of Satan-c/stories. 122-Final app. Son of Satan (2 pgs.) 4.00
96-Ghost Rider app. 4.00
100-(52 pgs.)-Hellcat (Patsy Walker) revealed as Satan's daughter 5.00
125,150: 125-(52 pgs.)-Intro new Defenders. 150-(52 pgs.)-Origin Cloud 4.00
152-(52 pgs.)-Ties in with X-Factor & Secret Wars II 4.00
Annual 1 (1976, 52 pgs.)-New book-length story 3 6 9 18 27 40
NOTE: ***Art Adams*** *c-142p.* ***Austin*** *a-53i; c-65i, 119i, 145i.* ***Frank Bolle*** *a-7i, 10i, 11i.* ***Buckler*** *c(p)-34, 38, 76, 77, 79-86, 90, 91.* ***J. Buscema*** *c-66.* ***Giffen*** *a-42-49p, 50, 51-54p.* ***Golden*** *a-53p, 54p; c-94, 96.* ***Guice*** *c-129.* ***G. Kane*** *c(p)-13, 16, 18, 19, 21-26, 31-33, 35-37, 40, 41, 52, 55.* ***Kirby*** *c-42-45.* ***Mooney*** *a-3i, 31-34i, 62i, 63i, 85i.* ***Nasser*** *c-88p.* ***Perez*** *c(p)-51, 53, 54.* ***Rogers*** *c-98.* ***Starlin*** *c-110.* ***Tuska*** *a-57p. Silver Surfer in No. 2, 3, 6, 8-11, 92, 98-101, 107, 112-115, 122-125.*

DEFENDERS, THE (Volume 2) (Continues in The Order)
Marvel Comics: Mar, 2001 - No. 12, Feb, 2002 ($2.99/$2.25)
1-Busiek & Larsen-s/Larsen & Janson-a/c 3.00
2-11: 2-Two covers by Larsen & Art Adams; Valkyrie app. 4-Frenz-a 3.00
12-($3.50) 'Nuff Said issue; back-up-s Reis-a 4.00

DEFENDERS, THE
Marvel Comics: Sept, 2005 - No. 5, Jan, 2006 ($2.99, limited series)
1-5-Giffen & DeMatteis-s/Maguire-a. 2-Dormammu app. 3.00
...: Indefensible HC (2006, $19.99, dust jacket) r/#1-5; Giffen & Maguire sketch page 20.00
...: Indefensible SC (2007, $13.99) r/#1-5; Giffen & Maguire sketch page 14.00

DEFENDERS OF DYNATRON CITY
Marvel Comics: Feb, 1992 - No. 6, July, 1992 ($1.25, limited series)
1-6-Lucasarts characters. 2-Origin 3.00

DEFENDERS OF THE EARTH (TV)
Marvel Comics (Star Comics): Jan, 1987 - No. 4, July, 1987
1-4: The Phantom, Mandrake The Magician, Flash Gordon begin. 3-Origin Phantom. 4-Origin Mandrake 4.00

DEFEX
Devil's Due Publ.: Oct, 2004 - No. 6, Apr, 2005 ($2.95)
1-6: 1-Wolfman-s/Caselli-a. 6-Pérez-c 3.00

DEFIANCE
Image Comics: Feb, 2002 - No. 8, Jun, 2003 ($2.95)
Preview Edition (12/01) 3.00
1-8-Barré-s/Kang & Suh-a 3.00

DEFINITIVE DIRECTORY OF THE DC UNIVERSE, THE (See Who's Who...)

DELECTA OF THE PLANETS (See Don Fortune & Fawcett Miniatures)

DELICATE CREATURES
Image Comics (Top Cow): 2001 ($16.95, hardcover with dust jacket)
nn-Fairy tale storybook; J. Michael Straczynski-s; Michael Zulli-a 17.00

DELLA VISION (...The Television Queen) (Patty Powers #4 on)
Atlas Comics: April, 1955 - No. 3, Aug, 1955
1-Al Hartley-c 15 30 45 92 144 195
2,3 11 22 33 62 86 110

DELLEC
Aspen MLT.: Aug, 2009 - Present ($2.50)
1-5-Gunnell-a/c 2.50

DELL GIANT COMICS
Dell Publishing began to release square bound comics in 1949 with a 132-page issue called

Dell Giant - Bugs Bunny's Christmas Funnies #2 © WB

Dell Giant - Pogo Parade #1 © Walt Kelly

Dell Giant - Raggedy Ann and Andy #1 © DELL

Christmas Parade #1. The covers were of a heavier stock to accommodate the increased number of pages. The books proved profitable at 25 cents, but the average number of pages was quickly reduced to 100. Ten years later they were converted to a numbering system similar to the Four Color Comics, for greater ease in distribution and the page counts cut back to mostly 84 pages. The label "Dell Giant" began to appear on the covers in 1954. Because of the size of the books and the heavier, less pliant cover stock, they are rarely found in high grade condition, and with the exception of a small quantity of copies released from Western Publishing's warehouse–are almost never found in near mint.

	GD 2.0	VG 4.0	FN 6.0	VF 8.0	VF/NM 9.0	NM- 9.2
Abraham Lincoln Life Story 1(3/58)	8	16	24	64	107	150
Bugs Bunny Christmas Funnies 1(11/50, 116pp)	19	38	57	152	261	370
...Christmas Funnies 2(11/51, 116pp)	11	22	33	88	157	225
...Christmas Funnies 3-5(11/52-11/54,)-Becomes Christmas Party #6	10	20	30	80	138	195
...Christmas Funnies 7-9(12/56-12/58)	9	18	27	72	124	175
...Christmas Party 6(11/55)-Formerly Bugs Bunny Christmas Funnies	9	18	27	72	124	175
...County Fair 1(9/57)	11	22	33	88	149	210
...Halloween Parade 1(10/53)	11	22	33	88	157	225
...Halloween Parade 2(10/54)-Trick 'N' Treat Halloween Fun #3 on	9	18	27	72	129	185
...Trick 'N' Treat Halloween Fun 3,4(10/55-10/56)-Formerly Halloween Parade #2	9	18	27	72	129	185
...Vacation Funnies 1(7/51, 112pp)	18	36	54	144	252	360
...Vacation Funnies 2('52)	13	26	39	104	180	255
...Vacation Funnies 3-5('53-'55)	10	20	30	80	138	195
...Vacation Funnies 6,7,9('56-'59)	9	18	27	72	124	175
...Vacation Funnies 8('58) 1st app. Beep Beep the Road Runner, Wile E. Coyote (1st meeting), Mathilda (Mrs. Beep Beep) and their 3 children who hatch from eggs; one month before Four Color #918	11	22	33	88	154	220
Cadet Gray of West Point 1(4/58)-Williamson-a, 10pgs.; Buscema-a; photo-c	8	16	24	64	107	150
Christmas In Disneyland 1(12/57)-Barks-a, 18 pgs.	25	50	75	200	350	500
Christmas Parade 1(11/49)(132 pgs.)(1st Dell Giant)-Donald Duck (25 pgs. by Barks, r-in G.K. Christmas Parade #5); Mickey Mouse & other film oriented stories; Cinderella (prior to movie), 7 Dwarfs, Bambi & Thumper, So Dear To My Heart, Flying Mouse, Dumbo, Cookieland & others	63	126	189	504	877	1250
Christmas Parade 2('50)-Donald Duck (132 pgs.)(25 pgs. by Barks, r-in Gold Key's Christmas Parade #6). Mickey, Pluto, Chip & Dale, etc. Contents shift to a holiday expansion of W.D. C&S type format	42	84	126	336	588	840
Christmas Parade 3-7('51-'55, #3-116pgs; #4-7, 100 pgs.)	14	28	42	112	196	280
Christmas Parade 8(12/56)-Barks-a, 8 pgs.	22	44	66	176	306	435
Christmas Parade 9(12/58)-Barks-a, 20 pgs.	25	50	75	200	350	500
Christmas Treasury, A 1(11/54)	9	18	27	72	126	180
Davy Crockett, King Of The Wild Frontier 1(9/55)-Fess Parker photo-c; Marsh-a	19	38	57	152	269	385
Disneyland Birthday Party 1(10/58)-Barks-a, 16 pgs. r-by Gladstone	25	50	75	200	350	500
Donald and Mickey In Disneyland 1(5/58)	11	22	33	88	157	225
Donald Duck Beach Party 1(7/54)-Has an Uncle Scrooge story (not by Barks) that prefigures the later rivalry with Flintheart Glomgold and tells of Scrooge's wild rivalry with another millionaire	16	32	48	128	224	320
...Beach Party 2(1955)-Lady & Tramp	11	22	33	88	157	225
...Beach Party 3-5(1956-58)	11	22	33	88	152	215
...Beach Party 6(8/59, 84pp)-Stapled	8	16	24	64	115	165
Donald Duck Fun Book 1,2 (1953 & 10/54)-Games, puzzles, comics & cut-outs (very rare in unused condition)(most copies commonly have defaced interior pgs.)	63	126	189	504	877	1250
Donald Duck In Disneyland 1(9/55)-1st Disneyland Dell Giant	15	30	45	120	210	300
Golden West Rodeo Treasury 1(10/57)	10	20	30	80	135	190
Huey, Dewey and Louie Back To School 1(9/58)	9	18	27	72	126	180
Lady and The Tramp 1(6/55)	17	34	51	136	233	330
Life Stories of American Presidents 1(11/57)-Buscema-a	8	16	24	64	107	150
Lone Ranger Golden West 3(8/55)-Formerly Lone Ranger Western Treasury	18	36	54	144	255	365
Lone Ranger Movie Story nn(3/56)-Origin Lone Ranger in text; Clayton Moore photo-c	36	72	108	288	507	725
...Western Treasury 1(9/53)-Origin Lone Ranger, Silver, & Tonto; painted cover	23	46	69	184	325	465
...Western Treasury 2(8/54)-Becomes Lone Ranger Golden West #3	18	36	54	144	255	365
Marge's Little Lulu & Alvin Story Telling Time 1(3/59)-r/#2,5,3,11,30,10,21,17,8, 14,16; Stanley-a	14	28	42	112	196	280
...& Her Friends 4(3/56)-Tripp-a	14	28	42	112	191	270
...& Her Special Friends 3(3/55)-Tripp-a	15	30	45	120	210	300
...& Tubby At Summer Camp 5,2: 5(10/57)-Tripp-a. 2(10/58)-Tripp-a	13	26	39	104	182	260
...& Tubby Halloween Fun 6,2: 6(10/57)-Tripp-a. 2(10/58)-Tripp-a	13	26	39	104	182	260
...& Tubby In Alaska 1(7/59)-Tripp-a	13	26	39	104	177	250
...On Vacation 1(7/54)-r/4C-110,14,4C-146,5,4C-97,4,4C-158,3,1;Stanley-a	25	50	75	200	350	500
...& Tubby Annual 1(3/53)-r/4C-165,4C-74,4C-146,4C-97,4C-158, 4C-139, 4C-131; Stanley-a (1st Lulu Dell Giant)	30	60	90	240	420	600
...& Tubby Annual 2('54)-r/4C-139,6,4C-115,4C-74,5,4C-97,3,4C-146,18; Stanley-a	25	50	75	200	350	500
Marge's Tubby & His Clubhouse Pals 1(10/56)-1st app. Gran'pa Feeb;1st app. Janie; written by Stanley; Tripp-a	15	30	45	120	210	300
Mickey Mouse Almanac 1(12/57)-Barks-a, 8pgs.	27	54	81	216	378	540
...Birthday Party 1(9/53)-r/entire 48pgs. of Gottfredson's "Mickey Mouse in Love Trouble" from WDC&S 36-39. Quality equal to original. Also reprints one story each from Four Color 27, 79, & 181 plus 6 panels of highlights in the career of Mickey Mouse	31	62	93	248	434	620
...Club Parade 1(12/55)-r/4-Color 16 with some death trap scenes redrawn by Paul Murry & recolored with night turned into day; quality less than original	22	44	66	176	308	440
...In Fantasy Land 1(5/57)	13	26	39	104	180	255
...In Frontier Land 1(5/56)-Mickey Mouse Club iss.	13	26	39	104	180	255
...Summer Fun 1(8/58)-Mobile cut-outs on back-c; becomes Summer Fun with #2; Canadian version exists with 30¢-c price	13	26	39	104	180	255
Moses & The Ten Commandments 1(8/57)-Not based on movie; Dell's adaptation; Sekowsky-a; variant version has "Gods of Egypt" comic back-c	8	16	24	64	107	150
Nancy & Sluggo Travel Time 1(9/58)	8	16	24	64	115	165
Peter Pan Treasure Chest 1(1/53, 212pp)-Disney; contains 54-page movie adaptation & other Peter Pan stories; plus Donald & Mickey stories w/P. Pan; a 32-page retelling of "D. Duck Finds Pirate Gold" with yellow beak, called "Capt. Hook & the Buried Treasure"	130	260	390	1040	1820	2600
Picnic Party 6,7(7/55-6/56)(Formerly Vacation Parade)-Uncle Scrooge, Mickey & Donald	12	24	36	96	166	235
Picnic Party 8(7/57)-Barks-a, 6pgs	21	42	63	168	289	410
Pogo Parade 1(9/53)-Kelly-a(r-/Pogo from Animal Comics in this order: #11,13,21,14,27,16,23,9,18,15,17)	25	50	75	200	350	500
Raggedy Ann & Andy 1(2/55)	16	32	48	128	224	320
Santa Claus Funnies 1(11/52)-Dan Noonan -A Christmas Carol adaptation	9	18	27	72	126	180
Silly Symphonies 1(9/52)-Redrawing of Gotfredson's Mickey Mouse strip of "The Brave Little Tailor;" 2 Good Housekeeping pages (from 1943); Lady and the Two Siamese Cats, three years before "Lady & the Tramp;" a retelling of Donald Duck's first app. in "The Wise Little Hen" & other stories based on 1930's Silly Symphony cartoons	30	60	90	240	420	600
Silly Symphonies 2(9/53)-M. Mouse in "The Sorcerer's Apprentice", 2 Good Housekeeping pages (from 1944); The Pelican & the Snipe, Elmer Elephant, Peculiar Penguins, Little Hiawatha, & others	24	48	72	192	336	480
Silly Symphonies 3(2/54)-r/Mickey & The Beanstalk (4-Color #157, 39pgs.), Little Minnehaha, Pablo, The Flying Gauchito, Pluto, & Bongo, & 2 Good Housekeeping pages (1944)	20	40	60	160	275	390
Silly Symphonies 4(8/54)-r/Dumbo (4-Color 234), Morris The Midget Moose, The Country Cousin, Bongo, & Clara Cluck	20	40	60	160	275	390
Silly Symphonies 5-8: 5(2/55)-r/Cinderella (4-Color 272), Bucky Bug, Pluto, Little Hiawatha, The 7 Dwarfs & Dumbo, Pinocchio. 6(8/55)-r/Pinocchio (WDC&S 63), The 7 Dwarfs & Thumper (WDC&S 45), M. Mouse "Adventures With Robin Hood" (40 pgs.), Johnny Appleseed, Pluto & Peter Pan, & Bucky Bug; Cut-out on back-c. 7(2/57)-r/Reluctant Dragon, Ugly Duckling, M. Mouse & Peter Pan, Jiminy Cricket, Peter & The Wolf, Brer Rabbit, Bucky Bug; Cut-out on back-c. 8(2/58)-r/Thumper Meets The 7 Dwarfs (4-Color #19), Jiminy Cricket, Niok, Brer Rabbit; Cut-out on back-c	16	32	48	128	224	320
Silly Symphonies 9(2/59)-r/Paul Bunyan, Humphrey Bear, Jiminy Cricket, The Social Lion, Goliath II; cut-out on back-c	15	30	45	120	210	300
Sleeping Beauty 1(4/59)	25	50	75	200	350	500
Summer Fun 2(8/59, 84pp, stapled binding)(Formerly Mickey Mouse...)-Barks-a(2), 24 pgs.	24	48	72	192	336	480
Tarzan's Jungle Annual 1(8/52)-Lex Barker photo on-c of #1,2	15	30	45	120	210	300
...Annual 2(8/53)	11	22	33	88	152	215
...Annual 3-7('54-9/58)(two No. 5s)-Manning-a-No. 3,5-7; Marsh-a in No. 1-7 plus painted-c 1-7	9	18	27	72	124	175

Dell Giant #45 © NYNS

Dell Junior Treasury #6 © DELL

The Demon (2nd series) #18 © DC

GD VG FN VF VF/NM NM-
2.0 4.0 6.0 8.0 9.0 9.2

Tom And Jerry Back To School 1(9/56) 2 different back-c, variant has "Apple for the Teacher" cut-out 12 24 36 96 168 240
...Picnic Time 1(7/58) 10 20 30 80 135 190
...Summer Fun 1(7/54)-Droopy written by Barks 15 30 45 120 205 290
...Summer Fun 2-4(7/55-7/57) 8 16 24 64 107 150
...Toy Fair 1(6/58) 9 18 27 72 126 180
...Winter Carnival 1(12/52)-Droopy written by Barks 20 40 60 160 280 400
...Winter Carnival 2(12/53)-Droopy written by Barks 16 32 48 128 224 320
...Winter Fun 3(12/54) 8 16 24 64 115 165
...Winter Fun 4-7(12/55-11/58) 7 14 21 56 101 145
Treasury of Dogs, A 1(10/56) 7 14 21 56 101 145
Treasury of Horses, A (9/55) 7 14 21 56 101 145
Uncle Scrooge Goes To Disneyland 1(8/57p)-Barks-a, 20 pgs. r-by Gladstone; 2 different back-c; variant shows 6 snapshots of Scrooge 26 52 78 208 359 510
Vacation In Disneyland 1(8/58) 11 22 33 88 157 225
Vacation Parade 1(7/50, 132pp)-Donald Duck & Mickey Mouse; Barks-a, 55 pgs. 95 190 285 760 1330 1900
Vacation Parade 2(7/51,116pp) 25 50 75 200 350 500
Vacation Parade 3-5(7/52-7/54)-Becomes Picnic Party No. 6 on. #4-Robin Hood Advs. 14 28 42 112 194 275
Western Roundup 1(6/52)-Photo-c; Gene Autry, Roy Rogers, Johnny Mack Brown, Rex Allen, & Bill Elliott begin; photo back-c begin, end No. 14,16,18 25 50 75 200 350 500
Western Roundup 2(2/53)-Photo-c 14 28 42 112 196 280
Western Roundup 3-5(7-9/53 - 1-3/54)-Photo-c 11 22 33 88 157 225
Western Roundup 6-10(4-6/54 - 4-6/55)-Photo-c 11 22 33 88 149 210
Western Roundup 11-17,25: 11-17-Photo-c; 11-13,16,17-Manning-a. 11-Flying A's Range Rider, Dale Evans begin 9 18 27 72 129 185
Western Roundup 18-Toth-a; last photo-c; Gene Autry ends 11 22 33 88 149 210
Western Roundup 19-24-Manning-a. 19-Buffalo Bill Jr. begins (7-9/57; early app.). 19,20,22-Toth-a. 21-Rex Allen, Johnny Mack Brown end. 22-Jace Pearson's Texas Rangers, Rin Tin Tin, Tales of Wells Fargo (2nd app., 4-6/58) & Wagon Train (2nd app.) begin 9 18 27 72 129 185
Woody Woodpecker Back To School 1(10/52) 10 20 30 80 140 200
...Back To School 2-4,6('53-10/57)-County Fair No. 5 8 16 24 64 112 160
...County Fair 5(9/56)-Formerly Back To School 8 16 24 64 112 160
...County Fair 2(11/58) 7 14 21 56 101 145

DELL GIANTS (Consecutive numbering)
Dell Publishing Co.: No. 21, Sept, 1959 - No. 55, Sept, 1961 (Most 84 pgs., 25¢)

21-(#1)-M.G.M.'s Tom & Jerry Picnic Time (84pp, stapled binding)-Painted-c 11 22 33 88 157 225
22-Huey, Dewey & Louie Back to School (Disney; 10/59, 84pp, square binding begins) 9 18 27 72 129 185
23-Marge's Little Lulu & Tubby Halloween Fun (10/59)-Tripp-a 12 24 36 96 168 240
24-Woody Woodpecker's Family Fun (11/59)(Walter Lantz) 8 16 24 64 112 160
25-Tarzan's Jungle World(11/59)-Marsh-a; painted-c 11 22 33 88 152 215
26-Christmas Parade(Disney; 12/59)-Barks-a, 16pgs.; Barks draws himself on wanted poster on pg. 13 21 42 63 168 289 410
27-Walt Disney's Man in Space (10/59) r-/4-Color 716,866, & 954 (100 pgs., 35¢)(TV) 9 18 27 72 129 185
28-Bugs Bunny's Winter Fun (2/60) 9 18 27 72 126 180
29-Marge's Little Lulu & Tubby in Hawaii (4/60)-Tripp-a 12 24 36 96 166 235
30-Disneyland USA(Disney; 6/60) 9 18 27 72 124 175
31-Huckleberry Hound Summer Fun (7/60)(TV)(HannaBarbera)-Yogi Bear & Pixie & Dixie app. 12 24 36 96 173 250
32-Bugs Bunny Beach Party 7 14 21 56 101 145
33-Daisy Duck & Uncle Scrooge Picnic Time (Disney; 9/60) 9 18 27 72 124 175
34-Nancy & Sluggo Summer Camp (8/60) 7 14 21 56 101 145
35-Huey, Dewey & Louie Back to School (Disney; 10/60)-1st app. Daisy Duck's Nieces, April, May & June 12 24 36 96 163 230
36-Marge's Little Lulu & Witch Hazel Halloween Fun (10/60)-Tripp-a 11 22 33 88 157 225
37-Tarzan, King of the Jungle (11/60)-Marsh-a; painted-c 9 18 27 72 129 185
38-Uncle Donald & His Nephews Family Fun (Disney; 11/60)-Cover painting based on a pencil sketch by Barks 12 24 36 96 173 250
39-Walt Disney's Merry Christmas (Disney; 12/60)-Cover painting based on a pencil sketch by Barks 12 24 36 96 173 250
40-Woody Woodpecker Christmas Parade (12/60)(Walter Lantz) 6 12 18 48 87 125
41-Yogi Bear's Winter Sports (12/60)(TV)(Hanna-Barbera)-Huckleberry Hound, Pixie & Dixie, Augie Doggie app. 12 24 36 96 173 250
42-Marge's Little Lulu & Tubby in Australia (4/61) 11 22 33 88 157 225
43-Mighty Mouse in Outer Space (5/61) 18 36 54 144 252 360
44-Around the World with Huckleberry and His Friends (7/61)(TV)(Hanna-Barbera)-Yogi Bear, Pixie & Dixie, Quick Draw McGraw, Augie Doggie app.; 1st app. Yakky Doodle 13 26 39 104 182 260
45-Nancy & Sluggo Summer Camp (8/61) 7 14 21 56 96 135
46-Bugs Bunny Beach Party (8/61) 7 14 21 56 96 135
47-Mickey & Donald in Vacationland (Disney; 8/61) 8 16 24 64 115 165
48-The Flintstones (No. 1)(Bedrock Bedlam)(7/61)(TV)(Hanna-Barbera) 1st app. in comics 19 38 57 152 269 385
49-Huey, Dewey & Louie Back to School (Disney; 9/61) 9 18 27 72 124 175
50-Marge's Little Lulu & Witch Hazel Trick 'N' Treat (10/61) 11 22 33 88 157 225
51-Tarzan, King of the Jungle by Jesse Marsh (11/61)-Painted-c 8 16 24 64 110 155
52-Uncle Donald & His Nephews Dude Ranch (Disney; 11/61) 8 16 24 64 115 165
53-Donald Duck Merry Christmas (Disney; 12/61) 8 16 24 64 112 160
54-Woody Woodpecker's Christmas Party (12/61)-Issued after No. 55 7 14 21 56 98 140
55-Daisy Duck & Uncle Scrooge Showboat (Disney; 9/61) 8 16 24 64 117 170

NOTE: All issues printed with & without ad on back cover.

DELL JUNIOR TREASURY
Dell Publishing Co.: June, 1955 - No. 10, Oct, 1957 (15¢) (All painted-c)

1-Alice in Wonderland; r/4-Color #331 (52 pgs.) 9 18 27 63 107 150
2-Aladdin & the Wonderful Lamp 7 14 21 49 80 110
3-Gulliver's Travels (1/56) 6 12 18 43 69 95
4-Adventures of Mr. Frog & Miss Mouse 7 14 21 45 73 100
5-The Wizard of Oz (7/56) 7 14 21 49 80 110
6-10: 6-Heidi (10/56). 7-Santa and the Angel. 8-Raggedy Ann and the Camel with the Wrinkled Knees. 9-Clementina the Flying Pig. 10-Adventures of Tom Sawyer 6 12 18 43 69 95

DEMOLITION MAN
DC Comics: Nov, 1993 - No. 4, Feb, 1994 ($1.75, color, limited series)

1-4-Movie adaptation 3.00

DEMON, THE (See Detective Comics No. 482-485)
National Periodical Publications: Aug-Sept, 1972 - V3#16, Jan, 1974

1-Origin; Kirby-c/a in all 7 14 21 49 80 110
2-5 4 8 12 26 41 55
6-16 3 6 9 19 29 38

DEMON, THE (1st limited series)(Also see Cosmic Odyssey #2)
DC Comics: Nov, 1986 - No. 4, Feb, 1987 (75¢, limited series)(#2 has #4 of 4 on-c)

1-4: Matt Wagner-a(p) & scripts in all. 4-Demon & Jason Blood become separate entities. 3.00

DEMON, THE (2nd Series)
DC Comics: July, 1990 - No. 58, May, 1995 ($1.50/$1.75/$1.95)

1-Grant scripts begin, ends #39: 1-4-Painted-c 5.00
2-18,20-27,29-39,41,42: 3,8-Batman app. (cameo #4). 12-Bisley painted-c. 12-15,21-Lobo app. (1 pg. cameo #11). 23-Robin app. 29-Superman app. 31,33-39-Lobo app. 3.00
19,28,40: 19-($2.50, 44 pgs.)-Lobo poster stapled inside. 28-Superman-c/story; begin $1.75-c. 40-Garth Ennis scripts begin 4.00
43-45-Hitman app. 1 2 3 5 7 9
46-48 Return of The Haunted Tank-c/s. 48-Begin $1.95-c. 5.00
49,51,0-(10/94),55-58: 51-(9/94) 3.00
50 ($2.95, 52 pgs.) 4.00
52-54-Hitman-s 5.00
Annual 1 (1992, $3.00, 68 pgs.)-Eclipso-c/story 4.00
Annual 2 (1993, $3.50, 68 pgs.)-1st app. of Hitman 2 4 6 9 13 16

NOTE: *Alan Grant scripts in #1-16, 20, 21, 23-25, 30-39, Annual 1.* ***Wagner*** *a/scripts-22.*

DEMON DREAMS
Pacific Comics: Feb, 1984 - No. 2, May, 1984

1,2-Mostly r-/Heavy Metal 3.00

DEMON: DRIVEN OUT
DC Comics: Nov, 2003 - No. 6, Apr, 2004 ($2.50, limited series)

1-6-Dysart-s/Mhan-a 3.00

Demon-Hunter #1 © Seaboard

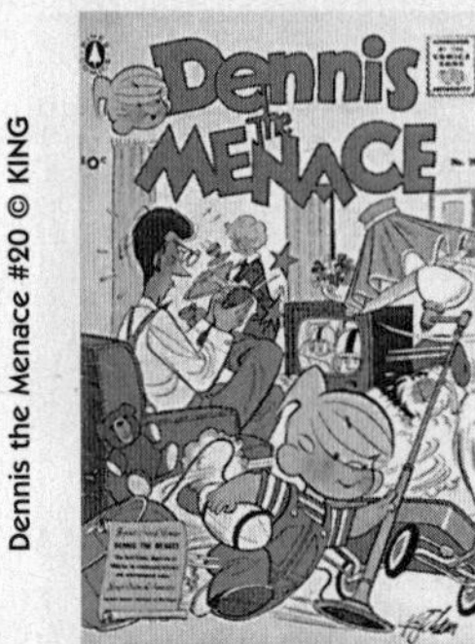

Dennis the Menace #20 © KING

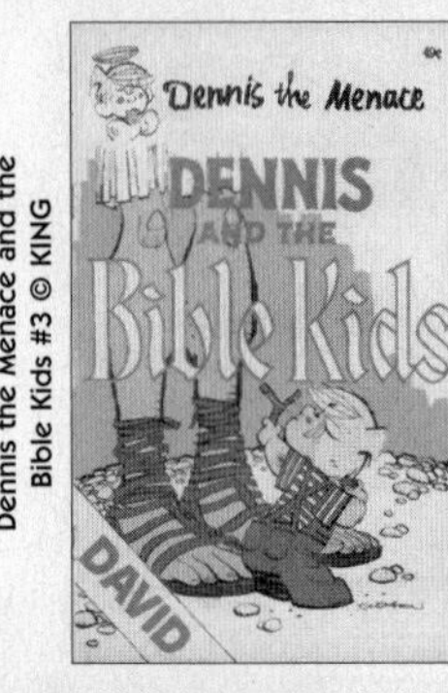

Dennis the Menace and the Bible Kids #3 © KING

	GD 2.0	VG 4.0	FN 6.0	VF 8.0	VF/NM 9.0	NM- 9.2

DEMON-HUNTER
Seaboard Periodicals (Atlas): Sept, 1975

	GD	VG	FN	VF	VF/NM	NM-
1-Origin/1st app. Demon-Hunter; Buckler-c/a	2	4	6	8	11	14

DEMON KNIGHT: A GRIMJACK GRAPHIC NOVEL
First Publishing: 1990 ($8.95, 52 pgs.)

	GD	VG	FN	VF	VF/NM	NM-
nn-Flint Henry-a						9.00

DEMONWARS (R.A. Salvatore's...) ("The Demon Awakens" on cover)
Devil's Due Publishing: Jan, 2007 - No. 3, May, 2007 ($4.99/$5.50, limited series)

	GD	VG	FN	VF	VF/NM	NM-
1-Daab-s/Seeley-a						5.50
2,3-($5.50)						5.50
Volume 2 (The Demon Spirit) (3/08 - Present, $5.50, B&W) 1-Balan-a						5.50

DEMONWARS: EYE FOR AN EYE (R.A. Salvatore's...)
CrossGeneration Comics (Code 6 Comics): Jun, 2003 - No. 5, Nov, 2003 ($2.95, lim. series)

	GD	VG	FN	VF	VF/NM	NM-
1-5-Ciencin-s/Tocchini-a						3.00

DEMONWARS: TRIAL BY FIRE (R.A. Salvatore's...)
CrossGeneration Comics (Code 6 Comics): Jan, 2003 - No. 5, May, 2003 ($2.95, lim. series)

	GD	VG	FN	VF	VF/NM	NM-
1-5-Ciencin-s/Wagner-a						3.00
TPB (2003, $9.95) r/#1-5; new short story by Salvatore						10.00

DENNIS THE MENACE (TV with 1959 issues) (Becomes ...Fun Fest Series; See The Best of... & The Very Best of...)(...Fun Fest on-c only to #156-166)
Standard Comics/Pines No.15-31/Hallden (Fawcett) No.32 on: 8/53 - #14, 1/56; #15, 3/56 - #31, 11/58; #32, 1/59 - #166, 11/79

	GD	VG	FN	VF	VF/NM	NM-
1-1st app. Dennis, Mr. & Mrs. Wilson, Ruff & Dennis' mom & dad; Wiseman-a, written by Fred Toole-most issues	97	194	291	621	1061	1500
2	37	74	111	222	361	500
3-10: 8-Last pre-code issue	20	40	60	118	192	265
11-20	14	28	42	82	121	160
21,23-30	11	22	33	60	83	105
22-1st app. Margaret w/blonde hair	14	28	42	78	112	145
31-1st app. Joey	14	28	42	78	112	145
32-38,40(1/60): 37-A-Bomb blast panel	8	16	24	42	54	65
39-1st app. Gina (11/59)	9	18	27	50	65	80
41-60(7/62)	4	8	12	21	30	40
61-80(9/65),100(1/69)	3	6	9	14	19	24
81-99	2	4	6	11	16	20
101-117: 102-Last 12¢ issue	2	4	6	9	12	15
118(1/72)-131 (All 52 pages)	2	4	6	10	14	18
132(1/74)-142,144-160	1	2	3	5	7	9
143(3/76) Olympic-c/s; low print	2	4	6	10	14	18
161-166	1	3	4	6	8	10

NOTE: *Wiseman c/a-1-46, 53, 68, 69.*

DENNIS THE MENACE (Giants) (No. 1 titled Giant Vacation Special; becomes Dennis the Menace Bonus Magazine No. 76 on)
(#1-8,18,23,25,30,38: 100 pgs.; rest to #41: 84 pgs.; #42-75: 68 pgs.)
Standard/Pines/Hallden(Fawcett): Summer, 1955 - No. 75, Dec, 1969

	GD	VG	FN	VF	VF/NM	NM-
nn-Giant Vacation Special(Summ/55-Standard)	18	36	54	103	162	220
nn-Christmas issue (Winter '55)	15	30	45	88	137	185
2-Giant Vacation Special (Summer '56-Pines)	14	28	42	78	112	145
3-Giant Christmas issue (Winter '56-Pines)	13	26	39	72	101	130
4-Giant Vacation Special (Summer '57-Pines)	12	24	36	67	94	120
5-Giant Christmas issue (Winter '57-Pines)	12	24	36	67	94	120
6-In Hawaii (Giant Vacation Special)(Summer '58-Pines)	11	22	33	62	86	110
6-In Hawaii (Summer '59-Hallden)-2nd printing; says 3rd large printing on-c 6-In Hawaii (Summer '60)-3rd printing; says 4th large printing on-c 6-In Hawaii (Summer '62)-4th printing; says 5th large printing on-c each....	8	16	24	42	54	65
6-Giant Christmas issue (Winter '58)	11	22	33	62	86	110
7-In Hollywood (Winter '59-Hallden)	5	10	15	32	51	70
7-In Hollywood (Summer '61)-2nd printing	3	6	9	21	32	42
8-In Mexico (Winter '60, 100 pgs.-Hallden/Fawcett)	5	10	15	32	51	70
8-In Mexico (Summer '62, 2nd printing)	3	6	9	21	32	42
9-Goes to Camp (Summer '61, 84 pgs.)-1st CCA approved issue	5	10	15	32	51	70
9-Goes to Camp (Summer '62)-2nd printing	3	6	9	21	32	42
10-12: 10-X-Mas issue (Winter '61), 11-Giant Christmas issue (Winter '62), 12-Triple Feature (Winter '62)	6	12	18	37	59	80
13-17: 13-Best of Dennis the Menace (Spring '63)-Reprints, 14-And His Dog Ruff (Summer '63), 15-In Washington, D.C. (Summer '63), 16-Goes to Camp (Summer '63)-Reprints No. 9, 17-& His Pal Joey (Winter '63)	4	8	12	24	37	50
18-In Hawaii (Reprints No. 6)	3	6	9	20	30	40
19-Giant Christmas issue (Winter '63)	4	8	12	24	37	50
20-Spring Special (Spring '64)	4	8	12	24	37	50
21-40 (Summer '66): 30-r/#6. #35-Xmas spec.Wint,'65	3	6	9	18	27	35
41-60 (Fall '68)	3	6	9	14	19	24
61-75 (12/69): 68-Partial-r/#6	2	4	6	11	16	20

NOTE: *Wiseman c/a-1-8, 12, 14, 15, 17, 20, 22, 27, 28, 31, 35, 36, 41, 49.*

DENNIS THE MENACE
Marvel Comics Group: Nov, 1981 - No. 13, Nov, 1982

	GD	VG	FN	VF	VF/NM	NM-
1-New-a	2	4	6	8	10	12
2-13: 2-New art. 3-Part-r. 4,5-r. 5-X-Mas-c & issue, 7-Spider Kid-c/sty	1	2	3	4	5	7

NOTE: *Hank Ketcham c-most; a-3, 12. Wiseman a-4, 5.*

DENNIS THE MENACE AND HIS DOG RUFF
Hallden/Fawcett: Summer, 1961

	GD	VG	FN	VF	VF/NM	NM-
1-Wiseman-c/a	5	10	15	32	51	70

DENNIS THE MENACE AND HIS FRIENDS
Fawcett Publ.: 1969; No. 5, Jan, 1970 - No. 46, April, 1980 (All reprints)

	GD	VG	FN	VF	VF/NM	NM-
Dennis the Menace & Joey No. 2 (7/69)	2	4	6	13	18	22
Dennis the Menace & Ruff No. 2 (9/69)	2	4	6	13	18	22
Dennis the Menace & Mr. Wilson No. 1 (10/69)	3	6	9	16	22	28
Dennis & Margaret No. 1 (Winter '69)	3	6	9	16	22	28
5-12: 5-Dennis the Menace & Margaret. 6-...& Joey. 7-...& Ruff. 8-...& Mr. Wilson	2	4	6	8	11	14
13-21-(52 pg Giants): 13-(1/72). 21-(1/74)	2	4	6	10	14	18
22-37	1	3	4	6	8	10
38-46 (Digest size, 148 pgs., 4/78, 95¢)	2	4	6	8	11	14

NOTE: *Titles rotate every four issues, beginning with No. 5. Joey issues: #2(7/69),6,10,14,18,22,26,30,34. Ruff issues: #2(9/69), 7,11,15,19,23,27,31,35. Mr. Wilson issues: #1(10/69),8,12,16,20,24,28,32,36. Margaret issues: #1(Wint./69),5,9,13,17,21,25,29,33,37.*

DENNIS THE MENACE AND HIS PAL JOEY
Fawcett Publ.: Summer, 1961 (10¢) (See Dennis the Menace Giants No. 45)

	GD	VG	FN	VF	VF/NM	NM-
1-Wiseman-c/a	5	10	15	34	55	75

DENNIS THE MENACE AND THE BIBLE KIDS
Word Books: 1977 (36 pgs.)

	GD	VG	FN	VF	VF/NM	NM-
1-6: 1-Jesus. 2-Joseph. 3-David. 4-The Bible Girls. 5-Moses. 6-More About Jesus	2	4	6	9	12	15
7-9-Low print run: 7-The Lord's Prayer. 8-Stories Jesus told. 9-Paul, God's Traveller	3	6	9	20	30	40
10-Low print run; In the Beginning	6	12	18	37	59	80

NOTE: *Ketcham c/a in all.*

DENNIS THE MENACE BIG BONUS SERIES
Fawcett Publications: No. 10, Feb, 1980 - No. 11, Apr, 1980

	GD	VG	FN	VF	VF/NM	NM-
10,11	1	2	3	5	6	8

DENNIS THE MENACE BONUS MAGAZINE (Formerly Dennis the Menace Giants Nos. 1-75) (...Big Bonus Series on-c for #174-194)
Fawcett Publications: No. 76, 1/70 - No. 95, 7/71; No. 95, 7/71; No. 97, '71; No. 194, 10/79; (No. 76-124: 68 pgs.; No. 125-163: 52 pgs.; No. 164 on: 36 pgs.)

	GD	VG	FN	VF	VF/NM	NM-
76-90(3/71)	2	4	6	10	14	18
91-95, 97-110(10/72): Two #95's with same date(7/71) A-Summer Games, and B-That's Our Boy. No #96	2	4	6	9	13	16
111-124	2	4	6	8	10	12
125-163-(52 pgs.)	2	4	6	8	10	12
164-194: 166-Indicia printed backwards	1	2	3	4	5	7

DENNIS THE MENACE COMICS DIGEST
Marvel Comics Group: April, 1982 - No. 3, Aug, 1982 ($1.25, digest-size)

	GD	VG	FN	VF	VF/NM	NM-
1-3-Reprints	1	3	4	6	8	10
1-Mistakenly printed with DC emblem on cover	2	4	6	10	12	15

NOTE: *Ketcham c-all. Wiseman a-all. A few thousand #1's were published with a DC emblem on cover.*

DENNIS THE MENACE FUN BOOK
Fawcett Publications/Standard Comics: 1960 (100 pgs.)

	GD	VG	FN	VF	VF/NM	NM-
1-Part Wiseman-a	6	12	18	41	66	90

DENNIS THE MENACE FUN FEST SERIES (Formerly Dennis the Menace #166)
Hallden (Fawcett): No. 16, Jan, 1980 - No. 17, Mar, 1980 (40¢)

	GD	VG	FN	VF	VF/NM	NM-
16,17-By Hank Ketcham	1	2	3	4	5	7

DENNIS THE MENACE POCKET FULL OF FUN!
Fawcett Publications (Hallden): Spring, 1969 - No. 50, March, 1980 (196 pgs.) (Digest size)

Desperado #4 © LEV

The Destructor #3 © Seaboard

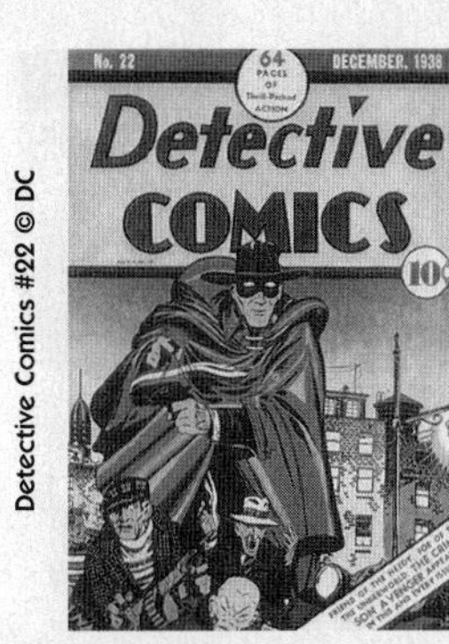

Detective Comics #22 © DC

	GD 2.0	VG 4.0	FN 6.0	VF 8.0	VF/NM 9.0	NM- 9.2
1-Reprints in all issues	6	12	18	37	59	80
2-10	4	8	12	24	37	50
11-20	3	6	9	16	22	28
21-28	2	4	6	11	16	20
29-50: 35,40,46-Sunday strip-r	2	4	6	8	11	14

NOTE: *No. 1-28 are 196 pgs.; No. 29-36: 164 pgs.; No. 37: 148 pgs.; No. 38 on: 132 pgs. No. 8, 11, 15, 21, 25, 29 all contain strip reprints.*

DENNIS THE MENACE TELEVISION SPECIAL
Fawcett Publ. (Hallden Div.): Summer, 1961 - No. 2, Spring, 1962 (Giant)

1	6	12	18	39	62	85
2	4	8	12	22	34	45

DENNIS THE MENACE TRIPLE FEATURE
Fawcett Publications: Winter, 1961 (Giant)

1-Wiseman-c/a 6 12 18 39 62 85

DEPUTY, THE (TV)
Dell Publishing Co.: No. 1077, Feb-Apr, 1960 - No. 1225, Oct-Dec, 1961 (all-Henry Fonda photo-c)

Four Color 1077 (#1)-Buscema-a	11	22	33	75	138	200
Four Color 1130 (9-11/60)-Buscema-a,1225	9	18	27	63	107	150

DEPUTY DAWG (TV) (Also see New Terrytoons)
Dell Publishing Co./Gold Key: Oct-Dec, 1961 - No. 1299, 1962; No. 1, Aug, 1965

Four Color 1238,1299	10	20	30	71	128	185
1(10164-508)(8/65)-Gold Key	10	20	30	71	128	185

DEPUTY DAWG PRESENTS DINKY DUCK AND HASHIMOTO-SAN (TV)
Gold Key: August, 1965

1(10159-508) 9 18 27 64 110 155

DESERT GOLD (See Zane Grey 4-Color 467)

DESIGN FOR SURVIVAL (Gen. Thomas S. Power's...)
American Security Council Press: 1968 (36 pgs. in color) (25¢)

nn-Propaganda against the Threat of Communism-Aircraft cover; H-Bomb panel	3	6	9	17	25	32
Twin Circle Edition-Cover shows panels from inside	2	4	6	11	16	20

DESOLATION JONES
DC Comics (WildStorm): July, 2005 - Present ($2.95/$2.99)

1-8: 1-6-Warren Ellis-s/J.H. Williams-a. 7,8-Zezelj-a 3.00
...: Made in England TPB (2006, $14.99) r/series; cover gallery 15.00

DESPERADO (Becomes Black Diamond Western No. 9 on)
Lev Gleason Publications: June, 1948 - No. 8, Feb, 1949 (All 52 pgs.)

1-Biro-c on all; contains inside photo-c of Charles Biro, Lev Gleason & Bob Wood	15	30	45	86	133	180
2	10	20	30	54	72	90
3-Story with over 20 killings	10	20	30	56	76	95
4-8	8	16	24	42	54	65

NOTE: ***Barry** a-2. **Fuje** a-4, 8. **Guardineer** a-5-7. **Kida** a-3-7. **Ed Moore** a-4, 6.*

DESPERADO PRIMER
Image Comics (Desperado): Apr, 2005 ($1.99, one-shot)

1-Previews of Roundeye, World Traveler, A Mirror To The Soul; Bolland-c 3.00

DESPERADOES
Image Comics (Homage): Sept, 1997 - No. 5, June, 1998 ($2.50/$2.95)

1-5-Mariotte-s/Cassaday-c/a: 1-($2.50-c). 2-5-($2.95) 3.00
...: A Moment's Sunlight TPB ('98, $16.95) r/#1-5 17.00
...: Epidemic! (11/99, $5.95) Mariotte-s 6.00

DESPERADOES: BANNERS OF GOLD
IDW Publishing: Dec, 2004 - No. 5, Apr, 2005 ($3.99, limited series)

1-5: Mariotte-s/Haun-a. 1-Cassaday-c 4.00

DESPERADOES: BUFFALO DREAMS
IDW Publishing: Jan, 2007 - No. 4, Apr, 2007 ($3.99, limited series)

1-4: Mariotte-s/Dose-a/c 4.00

DESPERADOES: QUIET OF THE GRAVE
DC Comics (Homage): Jul, 2001 - No. 5, Nov, 2001 ($2.95)

1-5-Jeff Mariotte-s/John Severin-c/a 3.00
TPB (2002, $14.95) r/#1-5; intro. by Brian Keene 15.00

DESPERATE TIMES (See Savage Dragon)
Image Comics: Jun, 1998 - No. 4, Dec, 1998; Nov, 2000 - No. 4, July, 2001 ($2.95, B&W)

1-4-Chris Eliopoulos-s/a 3.00

GD VG FN VF VF/NM NM-
2.0 4.0 6.0 8.0 9.0 9.2

(Vol. 2) 1-4 3.00
(Vol. 3) 0-(1/04, $3.50) Pages read sideways 3.50
(Vol. 3) 1-Pages read sideways 3.00

DESTINATION MOON (See Fawcett Movie Comics, Space Adventures #20, 23, & Strange Adventures #1)

DESTINY: A CHRONICLE OF DEATHS FORETOLD (See Sandman)
DC Comics (Vertigo): 1997 - No.3, 1998 ($5.95, limited series)

1-3-Alisa Kwitney-s in all: 1-Kent Williams & Michael Zulli-a, Williams painted-c. 2-Williams & Scott Hampton-painted-c/a. 3-Williams & Guay-a 6.00
TPB (2000, $14.95) r/series 15.00

DESTROY!!
Eclipse Comics: 1986 ($4.95, B&W, magazine-size, one-shot)

1 5.00
3-D Special 1-r-/#1 ($2.50) 5.00

DESTROYER
Marvel Comics: June, 2009 - No. 5, Oct, 2009 ($3.99, limited series)

1-5-Kirkman-s/Walker-a/Pearson-c 4.00

DESTROYER, THE
Marvel Comics (MAX): Nov, 1989 - No. 9, Jun, 1990 ($2.25, B&W, magazine, 52 pgs.)

1-Based on Remo Williams movie, paperbacks 6.00
2-9: 2-Williamson part inks. 4-Ditko-a 4.00

DESTROYER, THE
Marvel Comics: V2#1, March, 1991 ($1.95, 52 pgs.)
V3#1, Dec, 1991 - No. 4, Mar, 1992 ($1.95, mini-series)

V2#1,V3#1-4: Based on Remo Williams paperbacks. V3#1-4-Simonson-c. 3-Morrow-a 4.00

DESTROYER, THE (Also see Solar, Man of the Atom)
Valiant: Apr, 1995 ($2.95, color, one-shot)

0-Indicia indicates #1 3.00

DESTROYER DUCK
Eclipse Comics: Feb, 1982 - No. 7, May, 1984 (#2-7: Baxter paper) ($1.50)

1-Origin Destroyer Duck; 1st app. Groo; Kirby-c/a(p) 1 3 4 6 8 10
2-5: 2-Starling back-up begins; Kirby-c/a(p) thru #5 5.00
6,7 4.00

NOTE: ***Neal Adams** c-1i. **Kirby** c/a-1-5p. **Miller** c-7.*

DESTRUCTOR, THE
Atlas/Seaboard: February, 1975 - No. 4, Aug, 1975

1-Origin/1st app.; Ditko/Wood-a; Wood-c(i)	2	4	6	8	10	12
2-4: 2-Ditko/Wood-a. 3,4-Ditko-a(p)	2	3	4	6	8	10

DETECTIVE COMICS (Also see other Batman titles)
National Periodical Publications/DC Comics: Mar, 1937 - Present

1-(Scarce)-Slam Bradley & Spy by Siegel & Shuster, Speed Saunders by Stoner and Flessel, Cosmo, the Phantom of Disguise, Buck Marshall, Bruce Nelson begin; Chin Lung in 'Claws of the Red Dragon' serial begins; Vincent Sullivan-c	12,000	24,000	36,000	84,000	-	-
2 (Rare)-Creig Flessel-c begin; new logo	3400	6800	10,200	24,000	-	-
3 (Rare)	2600	5200	7800	18,000	-	-
4,5: 5-Larry Steele begins	1300	2600	3900	7150	10,075	13,000
6,7,9,10	920	1840	2760	5060	7130	9,200
8-Mister Chang-c; classic-c	1400	2800	4200	7700	10,850	14,000
11-17,19: 15,16-Have interior ad for Action Comics #1. 17-1st app. Fu Manchu in Detective	720	1440	2160	3960	5580	7200
18-Fu Manchu-c; last Flessel-c	1150	2300	3450	6325	8913	11,500
20-The Crimson Avenger begins (1st app.)	1050	2100	3150	5775	8138	10,500
21,23-25	580	1160	1740	3190	4495	5800
22-1st Crimson Avenger-c by Chambers (12/38)	770	1540	2310	4235	5968	7700
26	570	1140	1710	3135	4418	5700
27-The Bat-Man & Commissioner Gordon begin (1st app.), created by Bill Finger & Bob Kane (5/39); Batman-c (1st)(by Kane). Bat-Man's secret identity revealed as Bruce Wayne in six pg. story. Signed Rob't Kane (also see Det. PIcture Stories #5 & Funny Pages V3#1)	80,000	160,000	240,000	600,000	900,000	1,200,000

27-Reprint, Oversize 13-1/2x10". WARNING: This comic is an exact duplicate reprint of the original except for its size. DC published it in 1974 with a second cover titling it as Famous First Edition. There have been many reported cases of the outer cover being removed and the interior sold as the original edition. The reprint with the new outer cover removed is practically worthless; see Famous First Edition for value.

28-2nd app. The Batman (6 pg. story); non-Bat-Man-c; signed Rob't Kane	3000	6000	9000	22,500	39,250	56,000
29-1st app. Doctor Death-c/story, Batman's 1st name villain. 1st 2 part story (10 pgs.). 2nd Batman-c by Kane	4800	9600	14,400	36,000	62,000	88,000

30-Dr. Death app. Story concludes from issue #29. Classic Batman splash panel by Kane.

Detective Comics #46 © DC

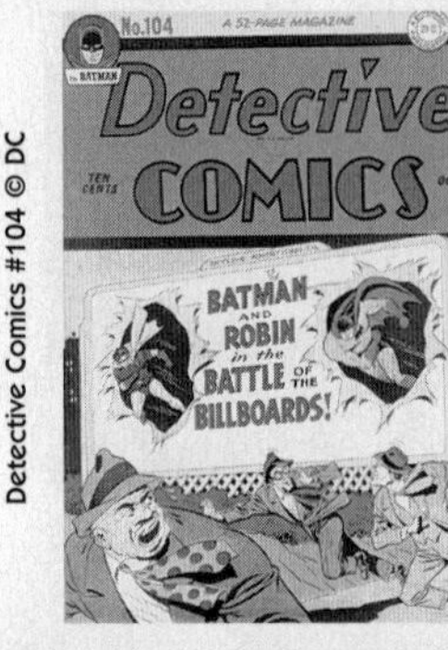

Detective Comics #104 © DC

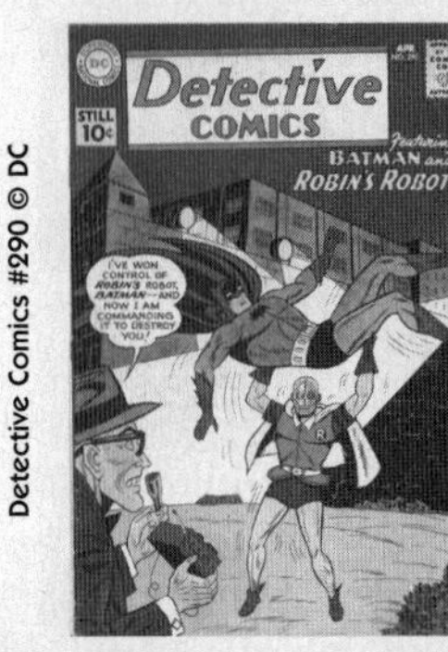

Detective Comics #290 © DC

	GD 2.0	VG 4.0	FN 6.0	VF 8.0	VF/NM 9.0	NM- 9.2
	1000	2000	3000	7600	13,800	20,000
31-Classic Batman over castle cover; 1st app. The Monk & 1st Julie Madison (Bruce Wayne's 1st love interest); 1st Batplane (Bat-Gyro) and Batarang; 2nd 2-part Batman adventure. Gardner Fox takes over script from Bill Finger. 1st mention of locale (New York City) where Batman lives	5500	11,000	16,500	42,000	71,000	100,000
32-Batman story concludes from issue #31. 1st app. Dala (Monk's assistant). Batman uses gun for 1st time to slay The Monk and Dala. This was the 1st time a costumed hero used a gun in comic books. 1st Batman head logo on cover	919	1838	2757	6709	11,855	17,000
33-Origin The Batman (2 pgs.)(1st told origin); Batman gun holster-c; Batman w/smoking gun panel at end of story. Batman story now 12 pgs. Classic Batman-c	5500	11,000	16,500	42,000	71,000	100,000
34-2nd Crimson Avenger-c by Creig Flessel and last non Batman-c. Story from issue #32 x-over as Bruce Wayne sees Julie Madison off to America from Paris. Classic Batman splash panel used later in Batman #1 for origin story. Steve Malone begins	676	1352	2028	4935	8718	12,500
35-Classic Batman hypodermic needle-c that reflects story in issue #34. Classic Batman with smoking .45 automatic splash panel. Batman-c begin	2500	5000	7500	18,750	32,375	46,000
36-Batman-c that reflects adventure in issue #35. Origin/1st app. of Dr. Hugo Strange (1st major villain, 2/40). 1st finned-gloves worn by Batman	1200	2400	3600	9000	15,500	22,000
37-Last solo Golden-Age Batman adventure in Detective Comics. Panel at end of story reflects solo Batman adventure in Batman #1 that was originally planned for Detective #38. Cliff Crosby begins	1000	2000	3000	7600	13,800	20,000
38-Origin/1st app. Robin the Boy Wonder (4/40); Batman and Robin-c begin; cover by Kane	4800	9600	14,400	36,000	62,000	88,000
39-Opium story; Clayface app. in 1 panel ad at the end of the Batman story	757	1514	2271	5526	9763	14,000
40-Origin & 1st app. Clayface (Basil Karlo); 1st Joker cover app. (6/40); Joker story intended for this issue was used in Batman #1 instead; cover is similar to splash page in 2nd Joker story in Batman #1	892	1784	2676	6512	11,506	16,500
41-Robin's 1st solo	417	834	1251	2918	5109	7300
42-44: 44-Crimson Avenger-new costume	309	618	927	2163	3782	5400
45-1st Joker story in Det. (3rd book app. & 4th story app. over all, 11/40)	423	846	1269	3067	5384	7700
46-50: 46-Death of Hugo Strange. 48-1st time car called Batmobile (2/41); Gotham City 1st mention in Detective (1st mentioned in Wow #1; also see Batman #4). 49-Last Clay Face	300	600	900	2040	3570	5100
51-57	219	438	657	1402	2401	3400
58-1st Penguin app. (12/41); last Speed Saunders; Fred Ray-c	514	1028	1542	3750	6625	9500
59,60: 59-Last Steve Malone; 2nd Penguin; Wing becomes Crimson Avenger's aide. 60-Intro. Air Wave; Joker app. (2nd in Det.)	226	452	678	1446	2473	3500
61,63: 63-Last Cliff Crosby; 1st app. Mr. Baffle	200	400	600	1280	2190	3100
62-Joker-c/story (2nd Joker-c, 4/42)	326	652	978	2282	3991	5700
64-Origin & 1st app. Boy Commandos by Simon & Kirby (6/42); Joker app.	400	800	1200	2800	4900	7000
65-1st Boy Commandos-c (S&K-a on Boy Commandos & Ray/Robinson-a on Batman & Robin on-c; 4 artists on one-c)	300	600	900	1980	3440	4900
66-Origin & 1st app. Two-Face	486	972	1458	3550	6275	9000
67-1st Penguin-c (9/42)	303	606	909	2121	3711	5300
68-Two-Face-c/story; 1st Two-Face-c	258	516	774	1651	2826	4000
69-Joker-c/story	284	568	852	1818	3109	4400
70	174	348	522	1114	1907	2700
71-Joker-c/story	277	554	831	1747	3024	4300
72,74,75: 74-1st Tweedledum & Tweedledee plus-c; S&K-a	148	296	444	947	1624	2300
73-Scarecrow-c/story (1st Scarecrow-c)	194	388	582	1242	2121	3000
76-Newsboy Legion & The Sandman x-over in Boy Commandos; S&K-a; Joker-c/story	232	464	696	1485	2543	3600
77-79: All S&K-a	139	278	417	883	1517	2150
80-Two-Face app.; S&K-a	158	316	474	1003	1727	2450
81,82,84,86-90: 81-1st Cavalier-c & app. 89-Last Crimson Avenger; 2nd Cavalier-c & app.	107	214	321	680	1165	1650
83-1st "skinny" Alfred (1/44)(see Batman #21; last S&K Boy Commandos (also #92,128); most issues #84 on signed S&K are not by them	113	226	339	718	1234	1750
85-Joker-c/story; last Spy; Kirby/Klech Boy Commandos	168	336	504	1075	1838	2600
91,102,109-Joker-c/stories	161	332	483	1030	1765	2500
92-98: 96-Alfred's last name 'Beagle' revealed, later changed to 'Pennyworth' in #214	87	174	261	553	952	1350
99-Penguin-c/story	145	290	435	921	1586	2250
100 (6/45)	126	252	378	806	1378	1950
101,103-108,110-113,115-117,119: 108-1st Bat-signal-c (2/46)	79	158	237	502	864	1225
114,118-Joker-c/stories. 114-1st small logo (8/46)	145	290	435	921	1586	2250
120-Penguin-c/story	148	296	444	947	1624	2300
121,123,125,127,129,130	76	152	228	486	831	1175
122-1st Catwoman-c (4/47)	200	400	600	1280	2190	3100
124,128-Joker-c/stories	129	258	387	826	1413	2000
126-Penguin-c	123	246	369	787	1344	1900
131-134,136,139	71	142	213	454	777	1100
135-Frankenstein-c/story	89	178	267	565	970	1375
137-Joker-c/story; last Air Wave	110	220	330	704	1202	1700
138-Origin Robotman (see Star Spangled #7 for 1st app.); series ends #202	113	226	339	718	1234	1750
140-The Riddler-c/story (1st app., 10/48)	541	1082	1623	3950	6975	10,000
141,143-148,150: 150-Last Boy Commandos	71	142	213	454	777	1100
142-2nd Riddler-c/story	152	304	456	965	1658	2350
149-Joker-c/story	110	220	330	704	1202	1700
151-Origin & 1st app. Pow Wow Smith, Indian lawman (9/49) & begins series	81	162	243	518	884	1250
152,154,155,157-160: 152-Last Slam Bradley	71	142	213	454	777	1100
153-1st app. Roy Raymond TV Detective (11/49); origin The Human Fly	74	148	222	470	810	1150
156(2/50)-The new classic Batmobile	100	200	300	635	1093	1550
161-167,169,170,172-176: Last 52 pg. issue	68	136	204	435	743	1050
168-Origin the Joker	423	846	1269	3000	5250	7500
171-Penguin-c	97	194	291	621	1061	1500
177-179,181-186,188,189,191,192,194-199,201,202,204,206-210,212,214-216: 184-1st app. Fire Fly. 185-Secret of Batman's utility belt. 187-Two-Face app. 202-Last Robotman & Pow Wow Smith. 215-1st app. of Batmen of all Nations. 216-Last precode (2/55)	65	130	195	416	708	1000
180,193-Joker-c/story	84	168	252	538	919	1300
187-Two-Face-c/story	74	148	222	470	810	1150
190-Origin Batman retold	87	174	261	553	952	1350
200(10/53), 205: 205-Origin Batcave	81	162	243	518	884	1250
203,211-Catwoman-c/stories	82	164	246	528	902	1275
213-Origin & 1st app. Mirror Man	76	152	228	486	831	1175
217-224: 218-Batman Jr. & Robin Sr. app.	55	110	165	352	601	850
225-(11/55)-1st app. Martian Manhunter (J'onn J'onzz); origin begins; also see Batman #78	410	820	1230	3700	7350	11,000
226-Origin Martian Manhunter cont'd (2nd app.)	152	304	456	965	1658	2350
227-229: Martian Manhunter stories in all	61	122	183	390	670	950
230-1st app. Mad Hatter; brief recap origin of Martian Manhunter	68	136	204	435	743	1050
231-Brief origin recap Martian Manhunter	50	100	150	315	533	750
232,234,237-240: 239-Early DC grey tone-c	47	94	141	296	498	700
233-Origin & 1st app. Batwoman (7/56)	194	388	582	1242	2121	3000
235-Origin Batman & his costume; tells how Bruce Wayne's father (Thomas Wayne) wore Bat costume & fought crime (reprinted in Batman #255)	76	152	228	486	831	1175
236-1st S.A. issue; J'onn J'onzz talks to parents and Mars-1st since being stranded on Earth; 1st app. Bat-Tank?	48	96	144	302	514	725
241-260: 246-Intro. Diane Meade, John Jones' girl. 249-Batwoman-c/app. 253-1st app. The Terrible Trio. 254-Bat-Hound-c/story. 257-Intro. & 1st app. Whirly Bats. 259-1st app. The Calendar Man	40	80	120	242	401	560
261-264,266,268-271: 261-J. Jones tie-in to sci/fi movie "Incredible Shrinking Man"; 1st app. Dr. Double X. 262-Origin Jackal. 268,271-Manhunter origin recap	33	66	99	194	317	440
265-Batman's origin retold with new facts	43	86	129	271	461	650
267-Origin & 1st app. Bat-Mite (5/59)	50	100	150	315	533	750
272,274,275,277-280	28	56	84	165	270	375
273-J'onn J'onzz i.d. revealed for 1st time	29	58	87	170	278	385
276-2nd app. Bat-Mite	34	68	102	199	325	450
281-292, 294-297: 286,292-Batwoman-c/app. 287-Origin J'onn J'onzz retold. 289-Bat-Mite-c/story. 292-Last Roy Raymond. 297-Last 10¢ issue (11/61)	22	44	66	132	216	300
293-(7/61)-Aquaman begins (pre #1); ends #300	23	46	69	136	223	310
298-(12/61)-1st modern Clayface (Matt Hagen)	26	52	78	186	373	560
299, 300-(2/62)-Aquaman ends	13	26	39	94	185	275
301-(3/62)-J'onn J'onzz returns to Mars (1st time since stranded on Earth six years before)	11	22	33	77	144	210
302-317,319-321,323,324,326,329,330: 302,307-Batwoman-c/app. 311-Intro. Zook in John Jones; 1st app. Cat-Man. 321-2nd Terrible Trio. 326-Last J'onn J'onzz, story cont'd in House of Mystery #143; intro. Idol-Head of Diabolu						

Detective Comics #486 © DC

Detective Comics #743 © DC

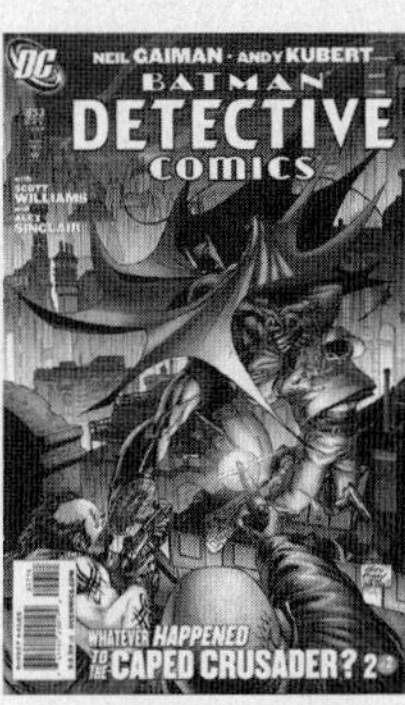

Detective Comics #853 © DC

	GD 2.0	VG 4.0	FN 6.0	VF 8.0	VF/NM 9.0	NM- 9.2
	10	20	30	69	122	175
318,322,325: 318,325-Cat-Man-c/story (2nd & 3rd app.); also 1st & 2nd app. Batwoman as the Cat-Woman. 322-Bat-Girl's 1st/only app. in Det. (6th in all); Batman cameo in J'onn J'onzz (only hero to app. in series)	10	20	30	70	125	180
327-(5/64)-Elongated Man begins, ends #383; 1st new look Batman with new costume; Infantino/Giella new look-a begins; Batman with gun	13	26	39	91	176	260
328-Death of Alfred; Bob Kane biog, 2 pgs.	12	24	36	87	164	240
331,333-340: 334-1st app. The Outsider	9	18	27	60	100	140
332,341,365-Joker-c/stories	10	20	30	70	125	180
342-358,360,361,366-368: 345-Intro Block Buster. 347-"What If" theme story (1/66). 350-Elongated Man new costume. 355-Zatanna x-over in Elongated Man. 356-Alfred brought back in Batman, early SA app.	8	16	24	53	86	120
359-Intro/origin Batgirl (Barbara Gordon)-c/story (1/67); 1st Silver Age app. Killer Moth	24	48	72	175	350	525
362,364-S.A. Riddler app. (early)	9	18	27	63	107	150
363-2nd app. new Batgirl	16	32	48	94	147	200
369(11/67)-N. Adams-a (Elongated Man); 3rd app. S.A. Catwoman (cameo; leads into Batman #197); 4th app. new Batgirl	11	22	33	80	150	220
370-1st Neal Adams-a on Batman (cover only, 12/67)	9	18	27	63	107	150
371-(1/68) 1st new Batmobile from TV show; classic Batgirl-c	11	22	33	75	138	200
372-376,378-386,389,390: 375-New Batmobile-c	6	12	18	43	69	95
377-S.A. Riddler-c/sty	8	16	24	52	86	120
387-r/1st Batman story from #27 (30th anniversary, 5/69); Joker-c; last 12¢ issue	9	18	27	65	113	160
388-Joker-c/story	9	18	27	61	103	145
391-394,396,398,399,401,403,405,406,409: 392-1st app. Jason Bard. 401-2nd Batgirl/Robin team-up. 405-Debut League of Assassins	6	12	18	37	59	80
395,397,402,404,407,408,410-Neal Adams-a. 404-Tribute to Enemy Ace	9	18	27	65	113	160
400-(6/70)-Origin & 1st app. Man-Bat; 1st Batgirl/Robin team-up (cont'd in #401); Neal Adams-a	18	36	54	131	266	400
411-(5/71) Intro. Talia, daughter of Ra's al Ghul (Ra's mentioned, but doesn't appear until Batman #232 (6/71); Bob Brown-a	6	12	18	41	66	90
412-413: 413-Last 15¢ issue	5	10	15	30	48	65
414-424: All-25¢, 52 pgs. 418-Creeper x-over. 424-Last Batgirl.	5	10	15	32	51	70
425-436: 426,430,436-Elongated Man app. 428,434-Hawkman begins, ends #467	5	10	15	30	48	65
437-New Manhunter begins (10-11/73, 1st app.) by Simonson, ends #443	6	12	18	37	59	80
438-445 (All 100 Page Super Spectaculars): 438-Kubert Hawkman-r. 439-Origin Manhunter. 440-G.A. Manhunter(Adv. #79) by S&K, Hawkman, Dollman, Green Lantern; Toth-a. 441-G.A. Plastic Man, Batman, Ibis-r. 442-G.A. Newsboy Legion, Black Canary, Elongated Man, Dr. Fate-r. 443-Origin The Creeper-r; death of Manhunter; G.A. Green Lantern, Spectre-r; Batman-r/Batman #18. 444-G.A. Kid Eternity-r. 445-G.A. Dr. Midnite-r	7	14	21	45	73	100
446-460: 457-Origin retold & updated	3	6	9	17	25	32
461-465,470,480: 480-(44 pgs.). 463-1st app. Black Spider. 464-2nd app. Black Spider 470-Intro. Silver St. Cloud.	3	6	9	16	22	28
466-468,471-474,478,479-Rogers-a in all: 466-1st app. Signalman since Batman #139. 470,471-1st modern app. Hugo Strange. 474-1st app. new Deadshot. 478-1st app. 3rd Clayface (Preston Payne). 479-(44 pgs.)	4	8	12	26	41	55
469-Intro/origin Dr. Phosphorous; Simonson-a	4	8	12	24	37	50
475,476-Joker-c/stories; Rogers-a	8	16	24	52	86	120
477-Neal Adams-a(r); Rogers-a (3 pgs.)	4	8	12	24	37	50
481-(Combined with Batman Family, 12-1/78-79, begin $1.00, 68 pg. issues, ends #495); 481-495-Batgirl, Robin solo stories	3	6	9	17	25	32
482-Starlin/Russell, Golden-a; The Demon begins (origin-r), ends #485 (by Ditko #483-485)	3	6	9	14	19	24
483-40th Anniversary issue; origin retold; Newton Batman begins	3	6	9	16	22	28
484-495 (68 pgs): 484-Origin Robin. 485-Death of Batwoman. 486-Killer Moth app. 487-The Odd Man by Ditko. 489-Robin/Batgirl team-up. 490-Black Lightning begins. 491-(#492 on inside). 493-Intro. The Swashbuckler	2	4	6	9	13	16
496-499: 496-Clayface app.	2	4	6	8	10	12
500-($1.50, 52 pgs.)-Batman/Deadman team-up with Infantino-a; new Hawkman story by Joe Kubert; incorrectly says 500th Anniv. of Det.	2	4	6	13	18	22
501-503,505-523: 509-Catman-c. 510-Mad Hatter-c. 512-2nd app. new Dr. Death. 519-Last Batgirl. 521-Green Arrow series begins. 523-Solomon Grundy app.	1	2	3	5	6	8
504-Joker-c/story	2	4	6	9	13	16
524-2nd app. Jason Todd (cameo)(3/83)	1	3	4	6	8	10
525-3rd app. Jason Todd (See Batman #357)	1	3	4	6	8	10
526-Batman's 500th app. in Detective Comics ($1.50, 68 pgs.); Death of Jason Todd's parents, Joker-c/story (55 pgs.); Bob Kane pin-up	3	6	9	14	19	24
527-531,533,534,536-568,571,573: 538-Cat-Man-c/story cont'd from Batman #371. 542-Jason Todd quits as Robin (becomes Robin again #547). 549,550-Alan Moore scripts (Green Arrow). 554-1st new Black Canary (9/85). 566-Batman villains profiled. 567-Harlan Ellison scripts.						6.00
532,569,570-Joker-c/stories	2	4	6	9	13	16
535-Intro new Robin (JasonTodd)-1st appeared in Batman	1	3	4	6	8	10
572-(3/87, $1.25, 60 pgs.)-50th Anniv. of Det. Comics	1	2	3	5	6	8
574-Origin Batman & Jason Todd retold	1	3	4	6	8	10
575-Year 2 begins, ends #578	3	6	9	16	22	28
576-578: McFarlane-c/a; The Reaper app.	3	6	9	16	22	28
579-597,599,601-610: 579-New bat wing logo. 583-1st app. villains Scarface & Ventriloquist. 589-595-(52 pgs.)-Each contain free 16 pg. Batman stories. 604-607-Mudpack storyline; 604,607-Contain Batman mini-posters. 610-Faked death of Penguin; artists names app. on tombstone on-c						4.00
598-($2.95, 84 pgs.)- "Blind Justice" storyline begins by Batman movie writer Sam Hamm, ends #600						5.00
600-(5/89, $2.95, 84 pgs.)-50th Anniv. of Batman in Det.; 1 pg. Neal Adams pin-up, among other artists						5.00
611-626,628-658: 612-1st new look Cat-Man; Catwoman app. 615- "The Penguin Affair" part 2 (See Batman #448,449). 617-Joker-c/story. 624-1st new Catwoman (w/death) & 1st new Batwoman. 626-Batman's 600th app. in Detective. 642-Return of Scarface, part 2. 644-Last $1.00-c. 652,653-Huntress-c/story w/new costume plus Charest-c on both						4.00
627-($2.95, 84 pgs.)-Batman's 601st app. in Det.; reprints 1st story/#27 plus 3 versions (2 new) of same story						5.00
659-664: 659-Knightfall part 2; Kelley Jones-c. 660-Knightfall part 4; Bane-c by Sam Kieth. 661-Knightfall part 6; brief Joker & Riddler app. 662-Knightfall part 8; Riddler app.; Sam Kieth-c. 663-Knightfall part 10; Kelley Jones-c. 664-Knightfall part 12; Bane-c/story; Joker app.; continued in Showcase 93 #7 & 8; Jones-c						4.00
665-675: 665,666-Knightfall parts 16 & 18; 666-Bane-c/story. 667-Knightquest: The Crusade & new Batman begins (1st app. in Batman #500). 669-Begin $1.50-c; Knightquest, cont'd in Robin #1. 671,673-Joker app.						3.00
675-($2.95)-Collectors edition w/foil-c						4.00
676-($2.50, 52 pgs.)-KnightsEnd pt. 3						4.00
677,678: 677-KnightsEnd pt. 9. 678-(9/94)-Zero Hour tie-in.						3.00
679-685: 679-(11/94). 682-Troika pt. 3						3.00
682-($2.50) Embossed-c Troika pt. 3						4.00
686-699,701-719: 686-Begin $1.95-c. 693,694-Poison Ivy-c/app. 695-Contagion pt. 2; Catwoman, Penguin app. 696-Contagion pt. 8. 698-Two-Face-c/app. 701-Legacy pt. 6; Batman vs. Bane-c/app. 702-Legacy Epilogue. 703-Final Night x-over. 705-707-Riddler-app. 714,715-Martian Manhunter-app.						3.00
700-($4.95, Collectors Edition)-Legacy pt. 1; Ra's Al Ghul-c/app; Talia & Bane app; book displayed at shops in envelope						6.00
700-($2.95, Regular Edition)-Different-c						4.00
720-740: 720,721-Cataclysm pts. 5,14. 723-Green Arrow app. 730-740-No Man's Land stories						3.00
741-($2.50) Endgame; Joker-c/app.						4.00
742-749,751-765: 742-New look Batman begins; 1st app. Crispus Allen (who later becomes the Spectre). 751,752-Poison Ivy app. 756-Superman-c/app. 759-762-Catwoman back-up						3.00
750-($4.95, 64 pgs.) Ra's al Ghul-c						6.00
766-772: 766,767-Bruce Wayne: Murderer pt. 1,8. 769-772-Bruce Wayne: Fugitive pts. 4,8,12,16						3.00
773,774,776-799: 773-Begin $2.75-c; Sienkiewicz-c. 777-784-Sale-c. 784-786-Alan Scott app. 787-Mad Hatter app. 793-Begin $2.95-c. 797-799-War Games						3.00
775-($3.50) Sienkiewicz-c						4.00
800-($3.50) Jock-c; aftermath of War Games; back-up by Lapham						4.00
801-816: 801-814-Lapham-s. 804-Mr. Freeze app. 809-War Crimes						3.00
817-849,851,852: 817-820: One Year Later 8-part x-over with Batman #651-654; Robinson-s/ Bianchi-c. 819-Begin $2.99-c. 820-Dini-s/Williams III-a. 825-Doctor Phosphorus app. 827-Debut of new Scarface. 831-Harley app.; Dini-s. 833,834-Zatanna & Joker app. 838,839-Resurrection of Ra's al Ghul x-over. 846-847-Batman R.I.P. x-over						3.00
817,818,838,839-2nd printings. 817-Combo-c of #817̳ cover images. 818-Combo-c of #818 and Batman #653 cover images. 838-Andy Kubert variant-c. 839-Red bkgd-c						3.00
850-($3.99) Batman vs. Hush; Dini-s/Nguyen-a						4.00
853-($3.99) Gaiman-s/Andy Kubert-a; continued from Batman #686; Kubert sketch pgs.						4.00
853-Variant-c with red background by Andy Kubert						12.00
854-872-($3.99) 854-Batwoman features begin; Rucka-a/J.H. Williams-a/c; The Question back-ups begin. 858-860-Batwoman origin						4.00
854,858,859,860-Variant-c: 854-JG Jones. 858-Hughes. 859-Jock. 860-Alex Ross						6.00
854-Special Edition (8/10, $1.00) reprints issue with "What's Next?" logo on cover						1.00
873,874-($2.99) 874-Francavilla-a						3.00

Detective Comics Annual #10 © DC

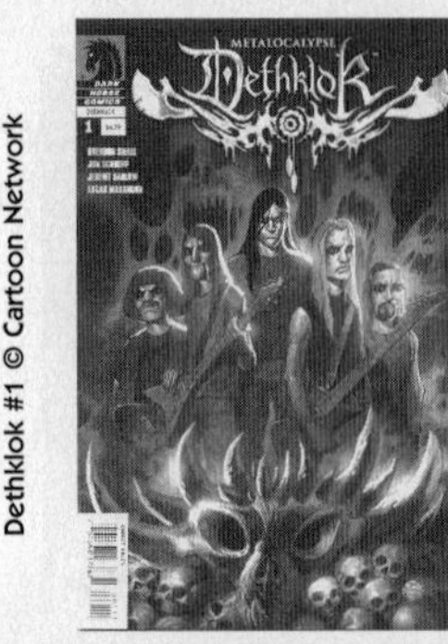

Dethklok #1 © Cartoon Network

Devil Kids Starring Hot Stuff #95 © HARV

	GD	VG	FN	VF	VF/NM	NM-
	2.0	4.0	6.0	8.0	9.0	9.2

GD VG FN VF VF/NM NM-
2.0 4.0 6.0 8.0 9.0 9.2

#0-(10/94) Zero Hour tie-in 3.00
#1,000,000 (11/98) 853rd Century x-over 3.00
Annual 1 (1988, $1.50) 5.00
Annual 2-7,9 ('89-'94, '96, 68 pgs.)-4-Painted-c. 5-Joker-c/story (54 pgs.) continued in Robin Annual #1; Sam Kieth-c; Eclipso app. 6-Azrael as Batman in new costume; intro Geist the Twilight Man; Bloodlines storyline. 7-Elseworlds story. 9-Legends of the Dead Earth story 4.00
Annual 8 (1995, $3.95, 68 pgs.)-Year One story 4.00
Annual 10 (1997, $3.95)-Pulp Heroes story 4.00
Annual 11 (12/09, $4.99)-Azrael & The Question app.; continued from Batman Ann. #27 5.00
Annual 12 (2/11, $4.99)-Nightrunner & The Question app.; continued in Batman Ann. #28 5.00

NOTE: ***Neal Adams** c-370, 372, 385, 389, 391, 392, 394-422, 439. **Aparo** a-437, 438, 444-446, 500, 625-632p, 638-643p; c-430, 437, 440-446, 448, 468-470, 480, 484(back), 492-502,508, 509, 515, 518-522, 641, 716, 719, 722, 724. **Austin** a(i)-450, 451, 463-468, 471-476; c(i)-474-476, 478. **Baily** a-443r. **Buckler** a-434, 446p, 479p; c(p)-467, 482, 505-507, 511, 513-516, 518. **Burnley** a(Batman)-65, 75, 78, 83, 100, 103, 125; c-62i, 63i, 64, 73i, 78, 83p, 96p, 103p, 105p, 106, 108, 121p, 123p, 125p. **Chaykin** a-441. **Colan** a(p)-510, 512, 517, 523, 528-538, 540-546, 555-567; c(p)-510, 512, 528, 530-535, 537, 538, 540, 541, 543-545, 556-558, 560-564. **J. Craig** a-488. **Ditko** a-443r, 483-485, 487. **Golden** a-482p; c-625, 626, 628-631, 633, 644-646. **Alan Grant** scripts-584-597, 601-621, 641, 642, Annual 5. **Grell** a-445, 455, 463p, 464p; c-455. **Guardineer** c-23, 24, 26, 28, 30, 32. **Gustavson** a-441r. **Infantino** a-354, 442(2)r, 500, 572. **Infantino/Anderson** c-333, 337-340, 343, 344, 347, 351, 352, 359, 361-368, 371. **Kelley Jones** c-651, 657i, 658i, 659, 661, 663-675. **Kaluta** c-423, 424, 426-428, 431, 434, 438, 484, 486, 572. **Bob Kane** a-Most early issues #27 on, 297r, 356r, 438-440r, 442r, 443r. **Kane/Robinson** c-33. **Gil Kane** a(p)-368, 370-374, 384, 385, 388-407, 438r, 439r, 520. **Kane/Anderson** c-369. **Sam Kieth** c-654-656 (657, 658 w/**Kelley Jones**), 660, 662, Annual #5. **Kubert** a-438r, 439r, 500; c-348, 350. **McFarlane** c/a(p)-576-578. **Meskin** a-420r. **Mignola** c-583. **Moldoff** c-233-354, 259, 266, 267, 275, 287, 289, 290, 297, 300. **Moldoff/Giella** a-328, 330, 332, 334, 336, 338, 340, 342, 344, 346, 348, 350, 352, 354, 356. **Mooney** a-444r. **Moreira** a-153-300, 419r, 444r, 445r. **Nasser/Netzer** a-654, 655, 657, 658. **Newton** a(p)-480, 481, 483-499, 501-509, 511, 513-516, 518-520, 524, 526, 539; c-526p. **Irv Novick** c-375-377, 383. **Robbins** a-426p, 429p. **Robinson** a-part: 66, 68, 71-73; all: 74-76, 79, 80; c-62, 64, 66, 68-74, 76, 79, 82, 86, 88, 442r, 443r. **Rogers** a-466-468, 471-479p, 481p; c-471p, 472p, 473, 474-479p. **Roussos** Airwave-76-105(most); c(i)-71, 72, 74-76, 79, 107. **Russell** a-481i, 482i. **Simon/Kirby** a-440r, 442r. **Simonson** a-437-443, 450, 469, 470, 500. **Dick Sprang** c-77, 82, 84, 85, 87, 89-93, 95-100, 102, 103i, 104i, 106, 108, 114, 117, 118, 122, 123, 128, 129, 131, 133, 135, 141, 148, 149, 168, 622-624. **Starlin** a-481p, 482p; c-503, 504, 567p. **Starr** a-444r. **Toth** a-442; r-414, 416, 418, 424, 440-441, 443, 444. **Tuska** a-486p, 490p. **Matt Wagner** c-647-649. **Wrightson** c-425.*

DETECTIVE DAN, SECRET OP. 48 (Also see Adventures of Detective Ace King and Bob Scully, The Two-Fisted Hick Detective)
Humor Publ. Co. (Norman Marsh): 1933 (10¢, 10x13", 36 pgs., B&W, one-shot) (3 color, cardboard-c)

	GD	VG	FN	VF	VF/NM	NM-
nn-By Norman Marsh, 1st comic w/ original-a; 1st newsstand-c; Dick Tracy look-alike; forerunner of Dan Dunn. (Title and Wu Fang character inspired Detective Comics #1 four years later.) (1st comic of a single theme)	1600	3200	4800	9600	-	-

DETECTIVE EYE (See Keen Detective Funnies)
Centaur Publications: Nov, 1940 - No. 2, Dec, 1940

	GD	VG	FN	VF	VF/NM	NM-
1-Air Man (see Keen Detective) & The Eye Sees begins; The Masked Marvel & Dean Denton app.	239	478	717	1530	2615	3700
2-Origin Don Rance and the Mysticape; Binder-a; Frank Thomas-c	126	252	378	806	1378	1950

DETECTIVE PICTURE STORIES (Keen Detective Funnies No. 8 on?)
Comics Magazine Company: Dec, 1936 - No. 5, Apr, 1937
(1st comic of a single theme)

	GD	VG	FN	VF	VF/NM	NM-
1 (all issues are very scarce)	580	1160	1740	3103	4502	5900
2-The Clock app. (1/37, early app.)	250	500	750	1338	1944	2550
3,4: 4-Eisner-a	170	340	510	901	1330	1750
5-The Clock-c/story (4/37); 1st detective/adventure art by Bob Kane; Bruce Wayne prototype app.(see Funny Pages V3/1)	195	390	585	1043	1522	2000

DETECTIVES, THE (TV)
Dell Publishing Co.: No. 1168, Mar-May, 1961 - No. 1240, Oct-Dec, 1961

	GD	VG	FN	VF	VF/NM	NM-
Four Color 1168 (#1)-Robert Taylor photo-c	9	18	27	65	113	160
Four Color 1219-Robert Taylor, Adam West photo-c	9	18	27	60	100	140
Four Color 1240-Tufts-a; Robert Taylor photo-c; 2 different back-c	8	16	24	56	93	130

DETECTIVES, INC. (See Eclipse Graphic Album Series)
Eclipse Comics: Apr, 1985 - No. 2, Apr, 1985 ($1.75, both w/April dates)

1,2: 2-Nudity 3.00

DETECTIVES, INC.: A TERROR OF DYING DREAMS
Eclipse Comics: Jun, 1987 - No. 3, Dec, 1987 ($1.75, B&W& sepia)

1-3: Colan-a 3.00
TPB ('99, $19.95) r/series 20.00

DETENTION COMICS
DC Comics: Oct, 1996 ($3.50, 56 pgs., one-shot)

1-Robin story by Dennis O'Neil & Norm Breyfogle; Superboy story by Ron Marz & Ron Lim; Warrior story by Ruben Diaz & Joe Phillips; Phillips-c 5.00

DETHKLOK (Based on the animated series Metalocalypse)
Dark Horse Comics: Oct, 2010 - No. 3 ($3.99, limited series)

1,2-Small & Schnepp-s; covers by Schnepp & Eric Powell 4.00
...: Versus the Goon 1-(7/09, $3.50) Powell-s/a/c; Dethklok visits the Goon universe 3.50
...: Versus the Goon 1-Variant cover by Jon Schnepp 5.00

DETONATOR (Mike Baron's...)
Image Comics: Nov, 2004 - No. 4 ($2.50/$2.95)

1-4-Mike Baron-s/Mel Rubi-a 3.00

DEUS EX (Based on the Square Enix videogame)
DC Comics: Apr, 2011 - No. 6 ($2.99)

1,2-Robbie Morrison-s/Trevor Hairsine-a 3.00

DEVASTATOR
Image Comics/Halloween: 1998 - No. 3 ($2.95, B&W, limited series)

1,2-Hudnall-s/Horn-c/a 3.00

DEVI (Shekhar Kapur's...)
Virgin Comics: July, 2006 - No. 20, Jun, 2008 ($2.99)

1-20: 1-Mukesh Singh-a/Siddharth Kotian-s. 2-Greg Horn-c 3.00
.../Witchblade (4/08, $2.99) Singh-a/Land-c; continued from Witchblade/Devi 3.00
... Vol. 1 TPB (5/07, $14.99) r/#1-5 and Story from Virgin Comics Preview #0 15.00
... Vol. 2 TPB (9/07, $14.99) r/#6-10; character and cover sketches 15.00

DEVIL CHEF
Dark Horse Comics: July, 1994 ($2.50, B&W, one-shot)

nn 3.00

DEVIL DINOSAUR
Marvel Comics Group: Apr, 1978 - No. 9, Dec, 1978

	GD	VG	FN	VF	VF/NM	NM-
1-Kirby/Royer-a in all; all have Kirby-c	3	6	9	16	23	30
2-9: 4-7-UFO/sci. fic. 8-Dinoriders-c/sty	2	4	6	9	13	16

... By Jack Kirby Omnibus HC (2007, $29.99, dustjacket) r/#1-9; intro. by Brevoort 30.00

DEVIL DINOSAUR SPRING FLING
Marvel Comics: June, 1997 ($2.99. one-shot)

1-(48pgs.) Moon-Boy-c/app. 4.00

DEVIL-DOG DUGAN (Tales of the Marines No. 4 on)
Atlas Comics (OPI): July, 1956 - No. 3, Nov, 1956

	GD	VG	FN	VF	VF/NM	NM-
1-Severin-c	14	28	42	80	115	150
2-Iron Mike McGraw x-over; Severin-c	9	18	27	50	65	80
3	8	16	24	44	57	70

DEVIL DOGS
Street & Smith Publishers: 1942

	GD	VG	FN	VF	VF/NM	NM-
1-Boy Rangers, U.S. Marines	29	58	87	170	278	385

DEVILINA (Magazine)
Atlas/Seaboard: Feb, 1975 - No. 2, May, 1975 (B&W)

	GD	VG	FN	VF	VF/NM	NM-
1-Art by Reese, Marcos; "The Tempest" adapt.	4	8	12	22	34	45
2 (Low printing)	4	8	12	24	37	50

DEVIL KIDS STARRING HOT STUFF
Harvey Publications (Illustrated Humor): July, 1962 - No. 107, Oct, 1981 (Giant-Size #41-55)

	GD	VG	FN	VF	VF/NM	NM-
1 (12¢ cover price #1-#41-9/69)	23	46	69	168	334	500
2	12	24	36	82	154	225
3-10 (1/64)	9	18	27	60	100	140
11-20	6	12	18	37	59	80
21-30	4	8	12	26	41	55
31-40: 40-(6/69)	3	6	9	20	30	40
41-50: All 68 pg. Giants	4	8	12	22	34	45
51-55: All 52 pg. Giants	3	6	9	20	30	40
56-70	2	4	6	11	16	20
71-90	2	4	6	8	11	14
91-107	1	2	3	5	6	8

DEVIL'S DUE FREE COMIC BOOK DAY
Devil's Due Publ.: May, 2005 (Free Comic Book Day giveaway)

nn-Short stories of G.I. Joe, Defex and Darkstalkers; Darkstalkers flip cover 2.50

DEVIL'S FOOTPRINTS, THE
Dark Horse Comics: March, 2003 - No. 4, June, 2003 ($2.99, limited series)

1-4-Paul Lee-c/a; Scott Allie-s 3.00

DEXTER COMICS
Dearfield Publ.: Summer, 1948 - No. 5, July, 1949

	GD	VG	FN	VF	VF/NM	NM-
1-Teen-age humor	12	24	36	67	94	120
2-Junie Prom app.	8	16	24	44	57	70

Diary Loves #5 © QUA

Dick Cole #2 © STAR

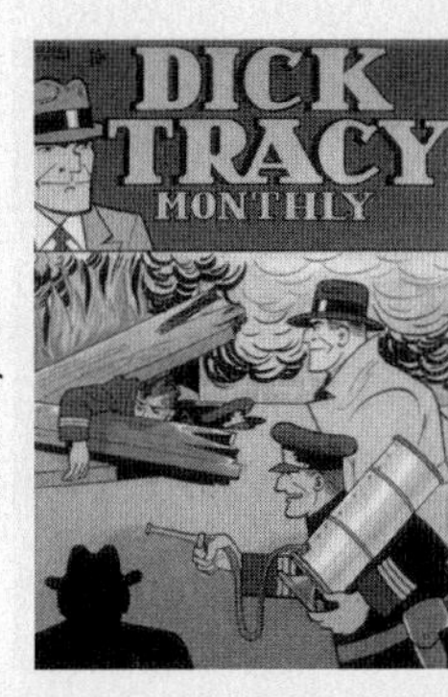

Dick Tracy #2 © NYNS

	GD 2.0	VG 4.0	FN 6.0	VF 8.0	VF/NM 9.0	NM- 9.2
3-5	7	14	21	37	46	55

DEXTER'S LABORATORY (Cartoon Network)
DC Comics: Sept, 1999 - No. 34, Apr, 2003 ($1.99/$2.25)

	GD	VG	FN	VF	VF/NM	NM-
1						4.00
2-10: 2-McCracken-s						3.00
11-24, 26-34: 31-Begin $2.25-c. 32-34-Wray-c						3.00
25-(50¢-c) Tartakovsky-s/a; Action Hank-c/app.						3.00

DEXTER THE DEMON (Formerly Melvin The Monster)(See Cartoon Kids & Peter the Little Pest)
Atlas Comics (HPC): No. 7, Sept, 1957

	GD	VG	FN	VF	VF/NM	NM-
7	8	16	24	44	57	70

DHAMPIRE: STILLBORN
DC Comics (Vertigo): 1996 ($5.95, one-shot, mature)

	GD	VG	FN	VF	VF/NM	NM-
1-Nancy Collins script; Paul Lee-c/a						6.00

DIARY CONFESSIONS (Formerly Ideal Romance)
Stanmor/Key Publ.(Medal Comics): No. 9, May, 1955 - No. 14, Apr, 1955

	GD	VG	FN	VF	VF/NM	NM-
9	9	18	27	50	65	80
10-14	8	16	24	40	50	60

DIARY LOVES (Formerly Love Diary #1; G. I. Sweethearts #32 on)
Quality Comics Group: No. 2, Nov, 1949 - No. 31, April, 1953

	GD	VG	FN	VF	VF/NM	NM-
2-Ward-c/a, 9 pgs.	19	38	57	109	172	235
3 (1/50)-Photo-c begin, end #27?	10	20	30	58	79	100
4-Crandall-a	11	22	33	64	90	115
5-7,10	9	18	27	52	69	85
8,9-Ward-a 6,8 pgs. 8-Gustavson-a; Esther Williams photo-c	14	28	42	80	115	150
11,13,14,17-20	9	18	27	50	65	80
12,15,16-Ward-a 9,7,8 pgs.	13	26	39	74	105	135
21-Ward-a, 7 pgs.	12	24	36	67	94	120
22-31: 31-Whitney-a	9	18	27	47	61	75

NOTE: *Photo c-3-10, 12-27.*

DIARY OF HORROR
Avon Periodicals: December, 1952

	GD	VG	FN	VF	VF/NM	NM-
1-Hollingsworth-c/a; bondage-c	45	90	135	284	480	675

DIARY SECRETS (Formerly Teen-Age Diary Secrets)(See Giant Comics Ed.)
St. John Publishing Co.: No. 10, Feb, 1952 - No. 30, Sept, 1955

	GD	VG	FN	VF	VF/NM	NM-
10-Baker-c/a most issues	29	58	87	170	278	385
11-16,18,19	21	42	63	126	206	285
17,20: Kubert-r/Hollywood Confessions #1. 17-r/Teen Age Romances #9	21	42	63	126	206	285
21-30: 22,27-Signed stories by Estrada. 28-Last precode (3/55)	16	32	48	94	147	200
nn-(25¢ giant, nd (1950?)-Baker-c & rebound St. John comics	77	154	231	493	847	1200

DICK COLE (Sport Thrills No. 11 on)(See Blue Bolt & Four Most #1)
Curtis Publ./Star Publications: Dec-Jan, 1948-49 - No. 10, June-July, 1950

	GD	VG	FN	VF	VF/NM	NM-
1-Sgt. Spook; L. B. Cole-c; McWilliams-a; Curt Swan's 1st work	34	68	102	199	325	450
2,5	15	30	45	92	144	195
3,4,6-10: All-L.B. Cole-c. 10-Joe Louis story	22	44	66	130	213	295
Accepted Reprint #7(V1#6 on-c)(1950's)-Reprints #7; L.B. Cole-c	9	18	27	47	61	75
Accepted Reprint #9(nd)-(Reprints #9 & #8-c)	9	18	27	47	61	75

NOTE: ***L. B. Cole** c-1, 3, 4, 6-10. **Al McWilliams** a-6. Dick Cole in 1-9. Baseball c-10. Basketball c-9. Football c-8.*

DICKIE DARE
Eastern Color Printing Co.: 1941 - No. 4, 1942 (#3 on sale 6/15/42)

	GD	VG	FN	VF	VF/NM	NM-
1-Caniff-a, bondage-c by Everett	61	122	183	390	670	950
2	29	58	87	170	278	385
3,4-Half Scorchy Smith by Noel Sickles who was very influential in Milton Caniff's development	31	62	93	182	296	410

DICK POWELL (Also see A-1 Comics)
Magazine Enterprises: No. 22, 1949 (one shot)

	GD	VG	FN	VF	VF/NM	NM-
A-1 22-Photo-c	22	44	66	132	216	300

DICK QUICK, ACE REPORTER (See Picture News #10)

DICKS
Caliber Comics: 1997 - No. 4, 1998 ($2.95, B&W)

	GD	VG	FN	VF	VF/NM	NM-
1-4-Ennis-s/McCrea-c/a; r/Fleetway						3.00
TPB ('98, $12.95) r/series						13.00

DICK'S ADVENTURES
Dell Publishing Co.: No. 245, Sept, 1949

	GD	VG	FN	VF	VF/NM	NM-
Four Color 245	6	12	18	41	66	90

DICK TRACY (See Famous Feature Stories, Harvey Comics Library, Limited Collectors' Ed., Mammoth Comics, Merry Christmas, The Original..., Popular Comics, Super Book No. 1, 7, 13, 25, Super Comics & Tastee-Freez)

DICK TRACY
David McKay Publications: May, 1937 - Jan, 1938

	GD	VG	FN	VF	VF/NM	NM-
Feature Books nn - 100 pgs., partially reprinted as 4-Color No. 1 (appeared before Large Feature Comics, 1st Dick Tracy comic book) (Very Rare-five known copies; two incomplete)	1025	2050	3075	7790	14,395	21,000
Feature Books 4 - Reprints nn issue w/new-c	135	270	405	864	1482	2100
Feature Books 6,9	97	194	291	621	1061	1500

DICK TRACY (...Monthly #1-24)
Dell Publishing Co.: 1939 - No. 24, Dec, 1949

	GD	VG	FN	VF	VF/NM	NM-
Large Feature Comic 1 (1939) -Dick Tracy Meets The Blank	187	374	561	1197	2049	2900
Large Feature Comic 4,8	97	194	291	621	1061	1500
Large Feature Comic 11,13,15	84	168	252	538	919	1300
Four Color 1(1939)('35-r)	1000	2000	3000	7400	13,200	19,000
Four Color 6(1940)('37-r)-(Scarce)	219	438	657	1402	2401	3400
Four Color 8(1940)('38-'39-r)	110	220	330	704	1202	1700
Large Feature Comic 3(1941, Series II)	84	168	252	538	919	1300
Four Color 21('41)('38-r)	81	162	243	518	884	1250
Four Color 34('43)('39-'40-r)	38	76	114	304	602	900
Four Color 56('44)('40-r)	35	70	105	273	537	800
Four Color 96('46)('40-r)	23	46	69	168	334	500
Four Color 133('47)('40-'41-r)	18	36	54	125	255	385
Four Color 163('47)('41-r)	16	32	48	111	226	340
Four Color 215('48)-Titled "Sparkle Plenty", Dick Tracy-r	11	22	33	77	144	210
1(1/48)('34-r)	35	70	105	273	537	800
2,3	18	36	54	131	266	400
4-10	16	32	48	111	226	340
11-18: 13-Bondage-c	13	26	39	89	170	250
19-1st app. Sparkle Plenty, B.O. Plenty & Gravel Gertie in a 3-pg. strip not by Gould	13	26	39	92	179	265
20-1st app. Sam Catchem; c/a not by Gould	12	24	36	87	164	240
21-24-Only 2 pg. Gould-a in each	12	24	36	84	157	230

NOTE: *No. 19-24 have a 2 pg. biography of a famous villain illustrated by **Gould**: 19-Little Face; 20-Flattop; 21-Breathless Mahoney; 22-Measles; 23-Itchy; 24-The Brow.*

DICK TRACY (Continued from Dell series)(...Comics Monthly #25-140)
Harvey Publications: No. 25, Mar, 1950 - No. 145, April, 1961

	GD	VG	FN	VF	VF/NM	NM-
25-Flat Top-c/story (also #26,27)	13	26	39	89	170	250
26-28,30: 28-Bondage-c. 28,29-The Brow-c/stories	10	20	30	71	128	185
29-1st app. Gravel Gertie in a Gould-r	12	24	36	82	154	225
31,32,34,35,37-40: 40-Intro/origin 2-way wrist radio (6/51)	9	18	27	61	103	145
33- "Measles the Teen-Age Dope Pusher"	10	20	30	71	128	185
36-1st app. B.O. Plenty in a Gould-r	10	20	30	71	128	185
41-50	8	16	24	54	90	125
51-56,58-80: 51-2pgs Powell-a	7	14	21	47	76	105
57-1st app. Sam Catchem in a Gould-r	8	16	24	54	90	125
81-99,101-140: 99-109-Painted-c	6	12	18	43	69	95
100, 141-145 (25¢)(titled "Dick Tracy")	7	14	21	47	76	105

NOTE: ***Powell** a(1-2pgs.)-43, 44, 104, 108, 109, 145. No. 110-120, 141-145 are all reprints from earlier issues.*

DICK TRACY ("Reuben Award" series)
Blackthorne Publishing: 12/84 - No. 24, 6/89 (1-12: $5.95; 13-24: $6.95, B&W, 76 pgs.)

	GD	VG	FN	VF	VF/NM	NM-
1-8-1st printings; hard-c ed. ($14.95)						20.00
1-3-2nd printings, 1986; hard-c ed.						20.00
1-12-1st & 2nd printings; squarebound. thick-c						12.00
13-24 ($6.95): 21,22-Regular-c & stapled						14.00

NOTE: ***Gould** daily & Sunday strip-r in all. 1-12 r-12/31/45-4/5/49; 13-24 r-7/13/41-2/20/44.*

DICK TRACY (Disney)
WD Publications: 1990 - No. 3, 1990 (color) (Book 3 adapts 1990 movie)

	GD	VG	FN	VF	VF/NM	NM-
Book One ($3.95, 52pgs.)-Kyle Baker-c/a						6.00
Book Two, Three ($5.95, 68pgs.)-Direct sale						6.00
Book Two, Three ($2.95, 68pgs.)-Newsstand						3.00

DICK TRACY ADVENTURES
Gladstone Publishing: May, 1991 ($4.95, 76 pgs.)

	GD	VG	FN	VF	VF/NM	NM-
1-Reprints strips 2/1/42-4/18/42						5.00

Die Hard: Year One #8 © 20th Century Fox

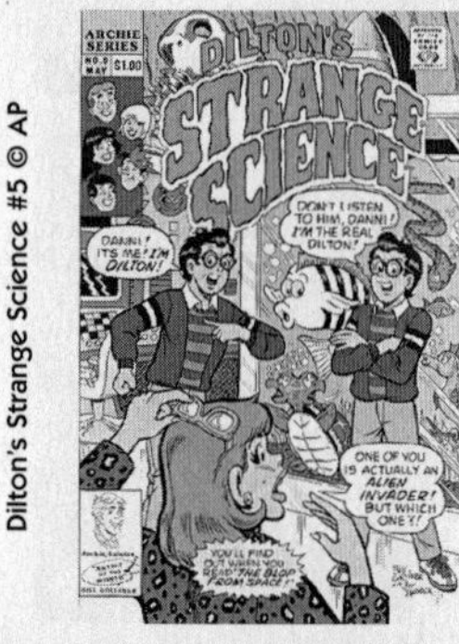

Dilton's Strange Science #5 © AP

Dino Island #1 © Jim Lawson

	GD 2.0	VG 4.0	FN 6.0	VF 8.0	VF/NM 9.0	NM- 9.2

DICK TRACY, EXPLOITS OF
Rosdon Books, Inc.: 1946 ($1.00, hard-c strip reprints)

1-Reprints the near complete case of "The Brow" from 6/12/44 to 9/24/44
(story starts a few weeks late) 25 50 75 147 241 335
with dust jacket... 39 78 117 240 395 550

DICK TRACY MONTHLY/WEEKLY
Blackthorne Publishing: May, 1986 - No. 99, 1989 ($2.00, B&W)
(Becomes Weekly #26 on)

1-60: Gould-r. 30,31-Mr. Crime app. 4.00
61-90 4.00
91-95 6.00
96-99-Low print 1 2 3 5 7 9
NOTE: *#1-10 reprint strips 3/10/40-7/13/41; #10(pg.8)-51 reprint strips 4/6/49-12/31/55; #52-99 reprint strips 12/26/56-4/26/64.*

DICK TRACY SPECIAL
Blackthorne Publ.: Jan, 1988 - No. 3, Aug. (no month), 1989 ($2.95, B&W)

1-3: 1-Origin D. Tracy; 4/strips 10/12/31-3/30/32 3.00

DICK TRACY: THE EARLY YEARS
Blackthorne Publishing: Aug, 1987 - No. 4, Aug (no month) 1989 ($6.95, B&W, 76 pgs.)

1-3: 1-4-r/strips 10/12/31(1st daily)-8/31/32 & Sunday strips 6/12/32-8/28/32;
Big Boy apps. in #1-3 1 2 3 4 5 7
4 ($2.95, 52pgs.) 4.00

DICK TRACY UNPRINTED STORIES
Blackthorne Publishing: Sept, 1987 - No. 4, June, 1988 ($2.95, B&W)

1-4: Reprints strips 1/1/56-12/25/56 3.00

DICK TURPIN (See Legend of Young...)

DIE-CUT
Marvel Comics UK, Ltd: Nov, 1993 - No. 4, Feb, 1994 ($1.75, limited series)

1-4: 1-Die-cut-c; The Beast app. 3.00

DIE-CUT VS. G-FORCE
Marvel Comics UK, Ltd: Nov, 1993 - No. 2, Dec, 1993 ($2.75, limited series)

1,2-($2.75)-Gold foil-c on both 3.00

DIE HARD: YEAR ONE (Based on the John McClane character)
BOOM! Studios: Aug, 2009 - No. 8, Mar, 2010 ($3.99, limited series)

1-8-Chaykin-s; Officier McClane in 1976 NYC; multiple covers on each 4.00

DIE, MONSTER, DIE (See Movie Classics)

DIGIMON DIGITAL MONSTERS (TV)
Dark Horse Comics: May, 2000 - No. 12, Nov, 2000 ($2.95/$2.99)

1-12 3.00

DIGITEK
Marvel UK, Ltd: Dec, 1992 - No. 4, Mar, 1993 ($1.95/$2.25, mini-series)

1-4: 3-Deathlock-c/story 3.00

DILLY (Dilly Duncan from Daredevil Comics; see Boy Comics #57)
Lev Gleason Publications: May, 1953 - No. 3, Sept, 1953

1-Teenage; Biro-c 7 14 21 37 46 55
2,3-Biro-c 5 10 15 24 30 35

DILTON'S STRANGE SCIENCE (See Pep Comics #78)
Archie Comics: May, 1989 - No. 5, May, 1990 (75¢/$1.00)

1-5 3.00

DIME COMICS
Newsbook Publ. Corp.: 1945; 1951

1-Silver Streak/Green Dragon-c/sty; Japanese WWII-c by L. B. Cole
129 258 387 826 1413 2000
1(1951) 14 28 42 80 115 150

DINGBATS (See 1st Issue Special)

DING DONG
Compix/Magazine Enterprises: Summer?, 1946 - No. 5, 1947 (52 pgs.)

1-Funny animal 28 56 84 165 270 375
2 (9/46) 15 30 45 83 124 165
3 (Wint '46-'47) - 5 12 24 36 69 97 125

DINKY DUCK (Paul Terry's...) (See Approved Comics, Blue Ribbon, Giant Comics Edition #5A & New Terrytoons)
St. John Publishing Co./Pines No. 16 on: Nov, 1951 - No. 16, Sept, 1955; No. 16, Fall, 1956; No. 17, May, 1957 - No. 19, Summer, 1958

1-Funny animal 13 26 39 72 101 130
2 8 16 24 42 54 65
3-10 6 12 18 29 36 42
11-16(9/55) 6 12 18 27 33 38
16 (Fall, '56) - 19 5 10 15 22 26 30

DINKY DUCK & HASHIMOTO-SAN (See Deputy Dawg Presents...)

DINO (TV)(The Flintstones)
Charlton Publications: Aug, 1973 - No. 20, Jan, 1977 (Hanna-Barbera)

1 3 6 9 18 27 35
2-10 2 4 6 10 14 18
11-20 2 4 6 8 10 12
Digest nn (w/Xerox Pub., 1974) (low print run) 2 4 6 11 16 20

DINO ISLAND
Mirage Studios: Feb, 1994 - No. 2, Mar, 1994 ($2.75, limited series)

1,2-By Jim Lawson 3.00

DINO RIDERS
Marvel Comics: Feb, 1989 - No. 3, 1989 ($1.00)

1-3: Based on toys 3.00

DINOSAUR REX
Upshot Graphics (Fantagraphics): 1986 - No. 3, 1986 ($2.00, limited series)

1-3 3.00

DINOSAURS, A CELEBRATION
Marvel Comics (Epic): Oct, 1992 - No. 4, Oct, 1992 ($4.95, lim. series, 52 pgs.)

1-4: 2-Bolton painted-c 5.00

DINOSAURS ATTACK! THE GRAPHIC NOVEL
Eclipse Comics: 1991 ($3.95, coated stock, stiff-c)

Book One- Based on Topps trading cards 4.00

DINOSAURS FOR HIRE
Malibu Comics: Feb, 1993 - No. 12, Feb, 1994 ($1.95/$2.50)

1-12: 1,10-Flip bk. 8-Bagged w/Skycap; Staton-c. 10-Flip book 3.00

DINOSAURS GRAPHIC NOVEL (TV)
Disney Comics: 1992 - No. 2, 1993 ($2.95, 52 pgs.)

1,2-Staton-a; based on Dinosaurs TV show 3.00

DINOSAURUS
Dell Publishing Co.: No. 1120, Aug, 1960

Four Color 1120-Movie, painted-c 8 16 24 56 93 130

DIPPY DUCK
Atlas Comics (OPI): October, 1957

1-Maneely-a; code approved 10 20 30 56 76 95

DIRECTORY TO A NONEXISTENT UNIVERSE
Eclipse Comics: Dec, 1987 ($2.00, B&W)

1 3.00

DIRTY DOZEN (See Movie Classics)

DIRTY PAIR (Manga)
Eclipse Comics: Dec, 1988 - No. 4, Apr, 1989 ($2.00, B&W, limited series)

1-4: Japanese manga with original stories 3.00
...: Start the Violence (Dark Horse, 9/99, $2.95) r/B&W stories in color from Dark Horse Presents #132-134; covers by Warren & Pearson 3.00

DIRTY PAIR: FATAL BUT NOT SERIOUS (Manga)
Dark Horse Comics: July, 1995 - No. 5, Nov, 1995 ($2.95, limited series)

1-5 3.00

DIRTY PAIR: RUN FROM THE FUTURE (Manga)
Dark Horse Comics: Jan, 2000 - No. 4, Mar, 2000 ($2.95, limited series)

1-4-Warren-s/c/a. Var.-c by Hughes(1), Stelfreeze(2), Timm(3), Ramos(4) 3.00

DIRTY PAIR: SIM HELL (Manga)
Dark Horse Comics: May, 1993 - No. 4, Aug, 1993 ($2.50, B&W, limited series)

1-4 3.00
...Remastered #1-4 (5/01 - 8/01) reprints in color, with pin-up gallery 3.00

DIRTY PAIR II (Manga)
Eclipse Comics: June, 1989 - No. 5, Mar, 1990 ($2.00, B&W, limited series)

1-5: 3-Cover is misnumbered as #1 3.00

DIRTY PAIR III, THE (A Plague of Angels) (Manga)
Eclipse Comics: Aug, 1990 - No. 5, Aug, 1991 ($2.00/$2.25, B&W, lim. series)

Disney's The Lion King #1 © DIS

A Distant Soil #21 © Colleen Doran

District X #1 © MAR

	GD 2.0	VG 4.0	FN 6.0	VF 8.0	VF/NM 9.0	NM- 9.2

1-5 3.00

DISHMAN
Eclipse Comics: Sept, 1988 ($2.50, B&W, 52 pgs.)

1 4.00

DISNEY AFTERNOON, THE (TV)
Marvel Comics: Nov, 1994 - No. 10?, Aug, 1995 ($1.50)

1-10: 3-w/bound-in Power Ranger Barcode Card 3.00

DISNEY COMIC ALBUM
Disney Comics: 1990(no month, year) - No. 8, 1991 ($6.95/$7.95)

1,2 ($6.95): 1-Donald Duck and Gyro Gearloose by Barks(r). 2-Uncle Scrooge by Barks(r); Jr. Woodchucks app. 9.00
3-8: 3-Donald Duck-r/F.C. 308 by Barks; begin $7.95-c. 4-Mickey Mouse Meets the Phantom Blot; r/M.M Club Parade (censored 1956 version of story). 5-Chip 'n' Dale Rescue Rangers; new-a. 6-Uncle Scrooge. 7-Donald Duck in Too Many Pets; Barks-r(4) including F.C. #29. 8-Super Goof; r/S.G. #1, D.D. #102 9.00

DISNEY COMIC HITS
Marvel Comics: Oct, 1995 - No. 16, Jan, 1997 ($1.50/$2.50)

1-16: 4-Toy Story. 6-Aladdin. 7-Pocahontas. 10-The Hunchback of Notre Dame (Same story in Disney's The Hunchback of Notre Dame). 13-Aladdin and the Forty Thieves 4.00

DISNEY COMICS
Disney Comics: June, 1990

Boxed set of #1 issues includes Donald Duck Advs., Ducktales, Chip 'n Dale Rescue Rangers, Roger Rabbit, Mickey Mouse Advs. & Goofy Advs.; limited to 10,000 sets 2 4 6 9 12 15

DISNEYLAND BIRTHDAY PARTY (Also see Dell Giants)
Gladstone Publishing Co.: Aug, 1985 ($2.50)

1-Reprints Dell Giant with new-photo-c 2 4 6 8 10 12
...Comics Digest #1-(Digest) 2 4 6 8 11 14

DISNEYLAND MAGAZINE
Fawcett Publications: Feb. 15, 1972 - ? (10-1/4"x12-5/8", 20 pgs, weekly)

1-One or two page painted art features on Dumbo, Snow White, Lady & the Tramp, the Aristocats, Brer Rabbit, Peter Pan, Cinderella, Jungle Book, Alice & Pinocchio. Most standard characters app. 3 6 9 16 23 30

DISNEYLAND, USA (See Dell Giant No. 30)

DISNEY MOVIE BOOK
Walt Disney Productions (Gladstone): 1990 ($7.95, 8-1/2"x11", 52 pgs.) (w/pull-out poster)

1-Roger Rabbit in Tummy Trouble; from the cartoon film strips adapted to the comic format. Ron Dias-c 2 4 6 8 10 12

DISNEY'S ACTION CLUB
Acclaim Books: 1997 - No. 4 ($4.50, digest size)

1-4: 1-Hercules. 4-Mighty Ducks 4.50

DISNEY'S ALADDIN (Movie)
Marvel Comics: Oct, 1994 - No. 11, 1995 ($1.50)

1-11 3.00

DISNEY'S BEAUTY AND THE BEAST (Movie)
Marvel Comics: Sept, 1994 - No. 13, 1995 ($1.50)

1-13 3.00

DISNEY'S BEAUTY AND THE BEAST HOLIDAY SPECIAL
Acclaim Books: 1997 ($4.50, digest size, one-shot)

1-Based on The Enchanted Christmas video 4.50

DISNEY'S COLOSSAL COMICS COLLECTION
Disney Comics: 1991 - No. 10, 1993 ($1.95, digest-size, 96/132 pgs.)

1-10: Ducktales, Talespin, Chip 'n Dale's Rescue Rangers. 4-r/Darkwing Duck #1-4. 6-Goofy begins. 8-Little Mermaid 5.00

DISNEY'S COMICS IN 3-D
Disney Comics: 1992 ($2.95, w/glasses, polybagged)

1-Infinity-c; Barks, Rosa, Gottfredson-r 5.00

DISNEY'S ENCHANTING STORIES
Acclaim Books: 1997 - No. 5 ($4.50, digest size)

1-5: 1-Hercules. 2-Pocahontas 4.50

DISNEY'S HERO SQUAD
BOOM! Studios: Jan, 2010 - No. 8, Aug, 2010 ($2.99)

1-8: 1-3-Phantom Blot app. 1-Back-up reprint of Super Goof #1 3.00

DISNEY'S NEW ADVENTURES OF BEAUTY AND THE BEAST (Also see Beauty and the Beast & Disney's Beauty and the Beast)
Disney Comics: 1992 - No. 2, 1992 ($1.50, limited series)

1,2-New stories based on movie 3.00

DISNEY'S POCAHONTAS (Movie)
Marvel Comics: 1995 ($4.95, one-shot)

1-Movie adaptation 1 2 3 4 5 7

DISNEY'S TALESPIN LIMITED SERIES: "TAKE OFF" (TV) (See Talespin)
W. D. Publications (Disney Comics): Jan, 1991 - No. 4, Apr, 1991 ($1.50, lim. series, 52 pgs.)

1-4: Based on animated series; 4 part origin 4.00

DISNEY'S TARZAN (Movie)
Dark Horse Comics: June, 1999 - No. 2, July, 1999 ($2.95, limited series)

1,2: Movie adaptation 3.00

DISNEY'S THE LION KING (Movie)
Marvel Comics: July, 1994 - No. 2, July, 1994 ($1.50, limited series)

1,2: 2-part movie adaptation 3.00
1-($2.50, 52 pgs.)-Complete story 5.00

DISNEY'S THE LITTLE MERMAID (Movie)
Marvel Comics: Sept, 1994 - No. 12, 1995 ($1.50)

1-12 4.00

DISNEY'S THE LITTLE MERMAID LIMITED SERIES (Movie)
Disney Comics: Feb, 1992 - No. 4, May, 1992 ($1.50, limited series)

1-4: Peter David scripts 3.00

DISNEY'S THE LITTLE MERMAID: UNDERWATER ENGAGEMENTS
Acclaim Books: 1997 ($4.50, digest size)

1-Flip book 4.50

DISNEY'S THE HUNCHBACK OF NOTRE DAME (Movie)(See Disney's Comic Hits #10)
Marvel Comics: July, 1996 ($4.95, squarebound, one-shot)

1-Movie adaptation. 1 2 3 4 5 7

NOTE: A different edition of this series was sold at Wal-Mart stores with new covers depicting scenes from the 1989 feature film. Inside contents and price were identical.

DISNEY'S THE THREE MUSKETEERS (Movie)
Marvel Comics: Jan, 1994 - No. 2, Feb, 1994 ($1.50, limited series)

1,2-Morrow-c; Spiegle-a; Movie adaptation 3.00

DISNEY'S TOY STORY (Movie)
Marvel Comics: Dec, 1995 ($4.95, one-shot)

nn-Adaptation of film 1 2 3 4 5 7

DISTANT SOIL, A (1st Series)
WaRP Graphics: Dec, 1983 - No. 9, Mar 1986 ($1.50, B&W)

1-Magazine size 4.00
2-9: 2-4 are magazine size 3.00

NOTE: Second printings exist of #1, 2, 3 & 6.

DISTANT SOIL, A
Donning (Star Blaze): Mar, 1989 ($12.95, trade paperback)

nn-new material 13.00

DISTANT SOIL, A (2nd Series)
Aria Press/Image Comics (Highbrow Entertainment) #15 on:
June, 1991 - Present ($1.75/$2.50/$2.95/$3.95, B&W)

1-27: 13-$2.95-c begins. 14-Sketchbook. 15-(8/96)-1st Image issue 4.00
29-33,35,37-($3.95) 4.00
34-($4.95, 64 pages) includes sketchbook pages 5.00
36,38-($4.50) 36-Back-up story by Darnall & Doran. 38-Includes sketch pages 4.50
The Aria ('01, $16.95,TPB) r/#26-31 17.00
The Ascendant ('98, $18.95,TPB) r/#13-25 19.00
The Gathering ('97, $18.95,TPB) r/#1-13; intro. Neil Gaiman 19.00
Vol. 4: Coda (2005, $17.99, TPB) r/#32-38 18.00

NOTE: Four separate printings exist for #1 and are clearly marked. Second printings exist of #2-4 and are also clearly marked.

DISTANT SOIL, A: IMMIGRANT SONG
Donning (Star Blaze): Aug, 1987 ($6.95, trade paperback)

nn-new material 7.00

DISTRICT X (Also see X-Men titles) (Also see Mutopia X)
Marvel Comics: July, 2004 - No. 14, Aug, 2005 ($2.99)

1-14: 1-3-Bishop app.; Yardin-a/Hine-s 3.00
...Vol. 1: Mr. M (2005, $14.99) r/#1-6; sketch page by Yardin 15.00

Divine Right #5 © WSP

DMZ #51 © Wood & Burchielli

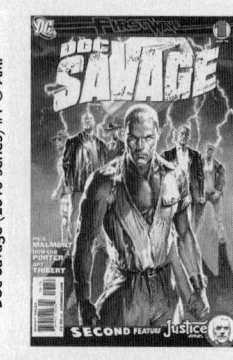

Doc Savage (2010 series) #1 © AMP

GD 2.0 | VG 4.0 | FN 6.0 | VF 8.0 | VF/NM 9.0 | NM- 9.2

...Vol. 2: Underground (2005, $19.99) r/#7-14; prologue from X-Men Unlimited #2 20.00

DIVER DAN (TV)
Dell Publishing Co.: Feb-Apr, 1962 - No. 2, June-Aug, 1962
Four Color 1254(#1), 2 5 10 15 34 55 75

DIVINE RIGHT
Image Comics (WildStorm Prod.): Sept, 1997 - No. 12, Nov, 1999 ($2.50)
Preview 5.00
1,2: 1-Jim Lee-s/a(p)/c, 1-Variant-c by Charest 4.00
1-($3.50)-Voyager Pack w/Stormwatch preview 3.50
1-American Entertainment Ed. 6.00
2-Variant-c of Exotica & Blaze 5.00
3-Chromium-c by Jim Lee 5.00
3-12: 3-5-Fairchild & Lynch app. 4-American Entertainment Ed. 8-Two covers. 9-1st DC issue. 11,12-Divine Intervention pt. 1,4 3.00
5-Pacific Comicon Ed. 6.00
6-Glow in the dark variant-c, European Tour Edition 20.00
...Book One TPB (2002, $17.95) r/#1-7 18.00
...Book Two TPB (2002, $17.95) r/#8-12 & Divine Intervention Gen13, ...Wildcats 18.00
...Collected Edition #1-3 ($5.95, TPB) 1-r/#1,2. 2-r/#3,4. 3-r/#5,6 6.00
Divine Intervention/Gen 13 (11/99, $2.50) Part 3; D'Anda-a 3.00
Divine Intervention/Wildcats (11/99, $2.50) Part 2; D'Anda-a 3.00

DIVISION 13 (See Comic's Greatest World)
Dark Horse Comics: Sept, 1994 - Jan, 1995 ($2.50, color)
1-4: Giffen story in all. 1-Art Adams-c 3.00

DIXIE DUGAN (See Big Shot, Columbia Comics & Feature Funnies)
McNaught Syndicate/Columbia/Publication Ent.: July, 1942 - No. 13, 1949
(Strip reprints in all)
1-Joe Palooka x-over by Ham Fisher 27 54 81 160 263 365
2 15 30 45 86 133 180
3 12 24 36 69 97 125
4,5(1945-46)-Bo strip-r 10 20 30 54 72 90
6-13(1/47-49): 6-Paperdoll cut-outs 9 18 27 47 61 75

DIXIE DUGAN
Prize Publications (Headline): V3#1, Nov, 1951 - V4#4, Feb, 1954
V3#1 10 20 30 54 72 90
2-4 7 14 21 35 43 50
V4#1-4(#5-8) 6 12 18 28 34 40

DIZZY DAMES
American Comics Group (B&M Distr. Co.): Sept-Oct, 1952 - No. 6, Jul-Aug, 1953
1-Whitney-c 18 36 54 103 162 220
2 11 22 33 62 86 110
3-6 9 18 27 52 69 85

DIZZY DON COMICS
F. E. Howard Publications/Dizzy Don Ent. Ltd (Canada): 1942 - No. 22, Oct, 1946; No. 3, Apr, 1947 - No. 4, Sept./Oct., 1947 (Most B&W)
1 (B&W) 22 44 66 132 216 300
2 (B&W) 14 28 42 80 115 150
4-21 (B&W) 12 24 36 67 94 120
22-Full color, 52 pgs. 22 44 66 132 216 300
3 (4/47), 4 (9-10/47)-Full color, 52 pgs. 22 44 66 132 216 300

DIZZY DUCK (Formerly Barnyard Comics)
Standard Comics: No. 32, Nov, 1950 - No. 39, Mar, 1952
32-Funny animal 10 20 30 54 72 90
33-39 6 12 18 31 38 45

DMZ
DC Comics (Vertigo): Jan, 2006 - Present ($2.99)
1-Brian Wood-s/Riccardo Burchielli-a 4.00
1-(2008, no cover price) Convention Exclusive promotional edition 3.00
2-49,51-63: 2-10-Brian Wood-s/Riccardo Burchielli-a. 11-Donaldson-a. 12-Wood-s/a 3.00
50-($3.99) Short stories by various incl. Risso, Moon, Gibbons, Bermejo, Jim Lee 4.00
...: Blood in the Game TPB (2009, $12.99) r/#29-34; intro. by Greg Palast 13.00
...: Body of a Journalist TPB (2007, $12.99) r/#6-12; intro. by D. Randall Blythe 13.00
...: Friendly Fire TPB (2008, $12.99) r/#18-22; intro. by Sgt. John G. Ford 13.00
...: Hearts and Minds TPB (2010, $16.99) r/#42-49; intro. by Morgan Spurlock 17.00
...: M.I.A. TPB (2011, $14.99) r/#50-54 15.00
...: On the Ground TPB (2006, $9.99) r/#1-5; intro. by Brian Azzarello 10.00
...: Public Works TPB (2007, $12.99) r/#13-17; intro. by Cory Doctorow 13.00
...: The Hidden War TPB (2008, $12.99) r/#23-28 13.00
...: War Powers TPB (2009, $14.99) r/#35-41 15.00

DNAGENTS (The New DNAgents V2/1 on)(Also see Surge)
Eclipse Comics: March, 1983 - No. 24, July, 1985 ($1.50, Baxter paper)
1,24: 1-Origin. 4-Amber app. 24-Dave Stevens-c 3.50
2-23: 8-Infinity-c 3.00
... Industrial Strength Edition TPB (Image, 2008, $24.99) B&W r/#1-14; Evanier intro. 25.00

DOBERMAN (See Sgt. Bilko's Private...)

DOBIE GILLIS (See The Many Loves of...)

DOC CHAOS: THE STRANGE ATTRACTOR
Vortex Comics: Apr, 1990 - No. 3, 1990 ($3.00, 32 pgs.)
1-3: The Lust For Order 3.00

DOC FRANKENSTEIN
Burlyman Entertainment: Nov, 2004 - No. 6 ($3.50)
1-6-Wachowski brothers-s/Skroce-a 3.50

DOCK WALLOPER (Ed Burns' ...)
Virgin Comics: Nov, 2007 - No. 5, Jun, 2008 ($2.99)
1-5-Burns & Palmiotti-s/Siju Thomas-a; Prohibition time 3.00

DOC MACABRE
IDW Publishing: Dec, 2010 - No. 3, Feb, 2011 ($3.99)
1-3-Steve Niles-s/Bernie Wrightson-a/c 4.00

DOC SAMSON (Also see Incredible Hulk)
Marvel Comics: Jan, 1996 - No. 4, Apr, 1996 ($1.95, limited series)
1-4: 1-Hulk c/app. 2-She-Hulk-c/app. 3-Punisher-c/app. 4-Polaris-c/app. 3.00

DOC SAMSON (Incredible Hulk)
Marvel Comics: Mar, 2006 - No. 5, July, 2006 ($2.99, limited series)
1-5: 1-DiFilippo-s/Fiorentino-a. 3-Conner-c 3.00

DOC SAVAGE
Gold Key: Nov, 1966
1-Adaptation of the Thousand-Headed Man; James Bama c-r/1964 Doc Savage paperback 11 22 33 75 138 200

DOC SAVAGE (Also see Giant-Size...)
Marvel Comics Group: Oct, 1972 - No. 8, Jan, 1974
1 3 6 9 20 30 40
2,3-Steranko-c 3 6 9 16 22 28
4-8 2 4 6 9 13 16
...: The Man of Bronze TPB (DC Comics, 2010, $17.99) r/#1-8 18.00
NOTE: *Gil Kane c-5, 6. Mooney a-1i. No. 1, 2 adapts pulp story "The Man of Bronze"; No. 3, 4 adapts "Death in Silver"; No. 5, 6 adapts "The Monsters"; No. 7, 8 adapts "The Brand of The Werewolf".*

DOC SAVAGE (Magazine)
Marvel Comics Group: Aug, 1975 - No. 8, Spring, 1977 ($1.00, B&W)
1-Cover from movie poster; Ron Ely photo-c 3 6 9 16 22 28
2-5: 3-Buscema-a. 5-Adams-a(1 pg.), Rogers-a(1 pg) 2 4 6 9 13 16
6-8 2 4 6 10 14 18

DOC SAVAGE
DC Comics: Nov, 1987 - No. 4, Feb, 1988 ($1.75, limited series)
1-4: Dennis O'Neil-s/Adam & Andy Kubert-a/c in all 3.00
...: The Silver Pyramid TPB (2009, $19.99) r/#1-4 20.00

DOC SAVAGE
DC Comics: Nov, 1988 - No. 24, Oct, 1990 ($1.75/$2.00: #13-24)
1-16,19-24 3.00
17,18-Shadow x-over 4.00
Annual 1 (1989, $3.50, 68 pgs.) 4.00

DOC SAVAGE (First Wave)
DC Comics: Jun, 2010 - Present ($3.99/$2.99)
1-9: 1-4-Malmont-s/Porter-a/J.G. Jones-c. Justice Inc. back-up; S. Hampton-a 4.00
1-6-Variant covers by Cassaday 5.00
10-12-($2.99) 10-Winslade-a 3.00

DOC SAVAGE COMICS (Also see Shadow Comics)
Street & Smith Publ.: May, 1940 - No. 20, Oct, 1943 (1st app. in Doc Savage pulp, 3/33)
1-Doc Savage, Cap Fury, Danny Garrett, Mark Mallory, The Whisperer, Captain Death, Billy the Kid, Sheriff Pete & Treasure Island begin; Norgil, the Magician app. 497 994 1491 3628 6414 9200
2-Origin & 1st app. Ajax, the Sun Man; Danny Garrett, The Whisperer end; classic sci-fi cover 203 406 609 1289 2220 3150
3 129 258 387 826 1413 2000

Doctor Fate (2nd series) #8 © DC

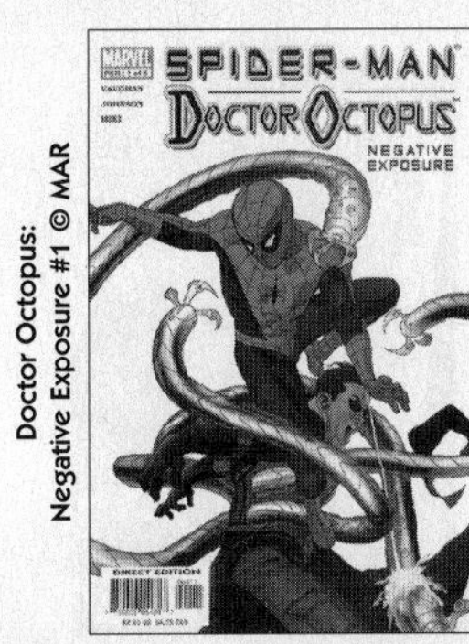

Doctor Octopus: Negative Exposure #1 © MAR

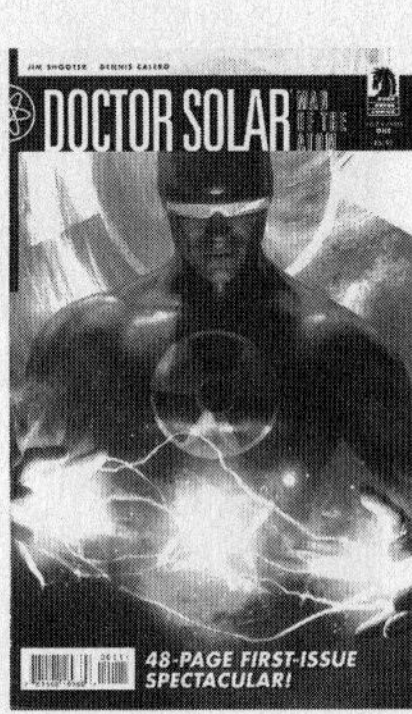

Doctor Solar, Man of the Atom (2010 series) #1 © RH

GD VG FN VF VF/NM NM-
2.0 4.0 6.0 8.0 9.0 9.2

4-Treasure Island ends; Tuska-a 103 206 309 659 1130 1600
5-Origin & 1st app. Astron, the Crocodile Queen, not in #9 & 11; Norgi the Magician app.; classic-c 94 188 282 597 1024 1450
6-10: 6-Cap Fury ends; origin & only app. Red Falcon in Astron story. 8-Mark Mallory ends; Charlie McCarthy app. on-c plus true life story. 9-Supersnipe app. 10-Origin & only app. The Thunderbolt 61 122 183 384 662 940
11,12 52 104 156 322 549 775
V2#1-6,8(#13-18,20): 15-Origin of Ajax the Sun Man; Jack Benny on-c; Hitler app. 16-The Pulp Hero, The Avenger app.; Fanny Brice story. 17-Sun Man ends; Nick Carter begins; Duffy's Tavern part photo-c & story. 18-Huckleberry Finn part-c/story. 19-Henny Youngman part photo-c & life story. 20-Only all funny-c w/Huckleberry Finn 47 94 141 296 498 700
V2#7-Classic Devil-c 52 104 156 322 549 775

DOC SAVAGE: CURSE OF THE FIRE GOD
Dark Horse Comics: Sept, 1995 - No, 4, Dec, 1995 ($2.95, limited series)
1-4 3.00

DOC SAVAGE: THE MAN OF BRONZE
Skylark Pub: Mar, 1979, 68pgs. (B&W comic digest, 5-1/4x7-5/8")(low print)
15406-0: Whitman-a, 60 pgs., new comics 4 8 12 24 37 50

DOC SAVAGE: THE MAN OF BRONZE
Millennium Publications: 1991 - No. 4, 1991 ($2.50, limited series)
1-4: 1-Bronze logo 3.00
...: The Manual of Bronze 1 ($2.50, B&W, color, one-shot)-Unpublished proposed Doc Savage strip in color, B&W strip-r 3.00

DOC SAVAGE: THE MAN OF BRONZE, DOOM DYNASTY
Millennium Publ.: 1992 (Says 1991) - No. 2, 1992 ($2.50, limited series)
1,2 3.00

DOC SAVAGE: THE MAN OF BRONZE - REPEL
Innovation Publishing: 1992 ($2.50)
1-Dave Dorman painted-c 3.00

DOC SAVAGE: THE MAN OF BRONZE THE DEVIL'S THOUGHTS
Millennium Publ.: 1992 (Says 1991) - No. 3, 1992 ($2.50, limited series)
1-3 3.00

DOC STEARN...MR. MONSTER (See Mr. Monster)

DR. ANTHONY KING, HOLLYWOOD LOVE DOCTOR
Minoan Publishing Corp./Harvey Publications No. 4: 1952(Jan) - No. 3, May, 1953; No. 4, May, 1954
1 15 30 45 84 127 170
2-4: 4-Powell-a 10 20 30 54 72 90

DR. ANTHONY'S LOVE CLINIC (See Mr. Anthony's...)

DR. BOBBS
Dell Publishing Co.: No. 212, Jan, 1949
Four Color 212 6 12 18 37 59 80

DOCTOR CYBORG
Attention! Publishing: 1996 - No. 5 ($2.95, B&W)
1-5 3.00
The Clone Conspiracy TPB (1998, $14.95) r/#1-5 15.00

DOCTOR DOOM AND THE MASTERS OF EVIL (All ages title)
Marvel Comics: Mar, 2009 - No. 4, Jun, 2009 ($2.99)
1-4: 1-Sinister Six app. 4-Magneto app. 3.00

DR. DOOM'S REVENGE
Marvel Comics: 1989 (Came w/computer game from Paragon Software)
V1#1-Spider-Man & Captain America fight Dr. Doom 3.00

DR. FATE (See 1st Issue Special, The Immortal..., Justice League, More Fun #55, & Showcase)

DOCTOR FATE
DC Comics: July, 1987 - No. 4, Oct, 1987 ($1.50, limited series, Baxter paper)
1-4: Giffen-c/a in all 3.00

DOCTOR FATE
DC Comics: Winter, 1988-'89 - No. 41, June, 1992 ($1.25/$1.50 #5 on)
1,15: 15-Justice League app. 3.50
2-14 3.00
16-41: 25-1st new Dr. Fate. 36-Original Dr. Fate returns 3.00
Annual 1(1989, $2.95, 68 pgs.)-Sutton-a 4.00

DOCTOR FATE
DC Comics: Oct, 2003 - No. 5, Feb, 2004 ($2.50, limited series)
1-5-Golden-s/Kramer-a 3.00

DR. FU MANCHU (See The Mask of...)
I.W. Enterprises: 1964
1-r/Avon's "Mask of Dr. Fu Manchu"; Wood-a 7 14 21 49 80 110

DR. GIGGLES (See Dark Horse Presents #64-66)
Dark Horse Comics: Oct, 1992 - No. 2, Oct, 1992 ($2.50, limited series)
1,2-Based on movie 3.00

DOCTOR GRAVES (Formerly The Many Ghosts of...)
Charlton Comics: No. 73, Sept, 1985 - No. 75, Jan, 1986
73-75-Low print run 1 2 3 5 6 8

DR. HORRIBLE (Based on Joss Whedon's internet feature)
Dark Horse Comics: Nov, 2009 ($3.50, one-shot)
1-Zack Whedon-s/Joëlle Jones-a; Captain Hammer pin-up by Gene Ha; 3 covers 3.50
... and other Horrible Stories TPB (9/10, $9.99) r/#1 and 3 stories from MySpace DHP 10.00

DR. JEKYLL AND MR. HYDE (See A Star Presentation & Supernatural Thrillers #4)

DR. KILDARE (TV)
Dell Publishing Co.: No. 1337, 4-6/62 - No. 9, 4-6/65 (All Richard Chamberlain photo-c)
Four Color 1337(#1, 1962) 8 16 24 58 97 135
2-9 6 12 18 43 69 95

DR. MASTERS (See The Adventures of Young...)

DOCTOR MID-NITE (Also see All-American #25)
DC Comics: 1999 - No. 3, 1999 ($5.95, square-bound, limited series)
1-3-Matt Wagner-s/John K. Snyder III-painted art 6.00
TPB (2000, $19.95) r/series 20.00

DOCTOR OCTOPUS: NEGATIVE EXPOSURE
Marvel Comics: Dec, 2003 - No. 5, Apr, 2004 ($2.99, limited series)
1-5-Vaughan-s/Staz Johnson-a; Spider-Man app. 3.00
Spider-Man/Doctor Octopus: Negative Exposure TPB (2004, $13.99) r/series 14.00

DR. ROBOT SPECIAL
Dark Horse Comics: Apr, 2000 ($2.95, one-shot)
1-Bernie Mireault-s/a; some reprints from Madman Comics #12-15 3.00

DOCTOR SOLAR, MAN OF THE ATOM (See The Occult Files of Dr. Spektor #14 & Solar)
Gold Key/Whitman No. 28 on: 10/62 - No. 27, 4/69; No. 28, 4/81 - No. 31, 3/82 (1-27 have painted-c)
1-(#10000-210)-Origin/1st app. Dr. Solar (1st original Gold Key character) 18 36 54 131 266 400
2-Prof. Harbinger begins 9 18 27 65 113 160
3,4 6 12 18 43 69 95
5-Intro. Man of the Atom in costume 7 14 21 45 73 100
6-10 5 10 15 35 55 75
11-14,16-20 4 8 12 26 41 55
15-Origin retold 4 8 12 28 44 60
21-23: 23-Last 12¢ issue 4 8 12 22 34 45
24-27 3 6 9 20 40 60
28-31: 29-Magnus Robot Fighter begins. 31-(3/82)The Sentinel app. 2 4 6 13 18 22
Hardcover Volume One (Dark Horse Books, 2004, $49.95) r/#1-7; creator bios 50.00
Hardcover Volume Two (Dark Horse Books, 6/05, $49.95) r/#8-14; Jim Shooter foreword 50.00
Hardcover Volume Three (Dark Horse Books, 9/05, $49.95) r/#15-22; Mike Baron foreword 50.00
Hardcover Volume Four (Dark Horse Books, 11/07, $49.95) r/#23-31 and The Occult Files of Dr. Spektor #14; Batton Lash foreword 50.00
NOTE: ***Frank Bolle*** *a-6-19, 29-31; c-29i, 30i.* ***Bob Fugitani*** *a-1-5.* ***Spiegle*** *a-29-31.* ***Al McWilliams*** *a-20-23.*

DOCTOR SOLAR, MAN OF THE ATOM
Valiant Comics: 1990 - No. 2, 1991 ($7.95, card stock-c, high quality, 96 pgs.)
1,2: Reprints Gold Key series 1 2 3 5 6 8

DOCTOR SOLAR, MAN OF THE ATOM
Dark Horse Comics: Jul, 2010 - Present ($3.50)
1-(48 pgs.) Shooter-s/Calero-a; back-up reprint of origin/1st app. in D.S. #1 (1962) 3.50
2-4-Roger Robinson-a 3.50
Free Comic Book Day Doctor Solar, Man of the Atom & Magnus, Robot Fighter (5/10, free) short story re-intros of Solar & Magnus; Shooter-s/Swanland-c; Calero & Reinhold-a 2.00

DOCTOR SPECTRUM (See Supreme Power)
Marvel Comics: Oct, 2004 - No. 6, Mar, 2005 ($2.99, limited series)
1-6-Origin; Sara Barnes-s/Travel Foreman-a 3.00

Doctor Strange #30 © MAR

Doctor Tomorrow #9 © Acclaim

Doctor Who (2011 series) #1 © BBC

GD VG FN VF VF/NM NM-
2.0 4.0 6.0 8.0 9.0 9.2

TPB (2005, $16.99) r/#1-6 17.00

DOCTOR SPEKTOR (See The Occult Files of..., & Spine-Tingling Tales)

DOCTOR STRANGE (Formerly Strange Tales #1-168) (Also see The Defenders, Giant-Size..., Marvel Fanfare, Marvel Graphic Novel, Marvel Premiere, Marvel Treasury Edition, Strange & Strange Tales, 2nd Series)
Marvel Comics Group: No. 169, 6/68 - No. 183, 11/69; 6/74 - No. 81, 2/87

169(#1)-Origin retold; panel swipe/M.D. #1-c 13 26 39 94 185 275
170-177: 177-New costume 5 10 15 32 51 70
178-183: 178-Black Knight app. 179-Spider-Man story-r. 180-Photo montage-c.
181-Brunner-c(part-i), last 12¢ issue 5 10 15 30 48 65
1(6/74, 2nd series)-Brunner-c/a 8 16 24 56 93 130
2 5 10 15 30 48 65
3-5 3 6 9 18 27 35
6-10 2 4 6 10 14 18
11-13,15-20: 13,15-17-(Regular 25¢ editions) 1 3 4 6 8 10
13,15-17-(30¢-c variants, limited distribution) 4 8 12 22 34 45
14-(5/76) Dracula app.; (regular 25¢ edition) 2 4 6 10 14 18
14-(30¢-c variant, limited distribution) 5 10 15 32 51 70
21-40: 21-Origin-r/Doctor Strange #169. 23-25-(Regular 30¢ editions). 31-Sub-Mariner-c/story 6.00
23-25-(35¢-c variants, limited distribution)(6,8,10/77) 2 4 6 8 10 12
41-57,63-77,79-81: 56-Origin retold 4.00
58-62: 58-Re-intro Hannibal King (cameo). 59-Hannibal King full app. 59-62-Dracula app. (Darkhold storyline). 61,62-Doctor Strange, Blade, Hannibal King & Frank Drake team-up to battle. Dracula. 62-Death of Dracula & Lilith 6.00
78-New costume 5.00
Annual 1(1976, 52 pgs.)-New Russell-a (35 pgs.) 3 6 9 14 20 25
...: From the Marvel Vault (4/11, $2.99) Stern-s/Vokes-a 3.00
.../Silver Dagger Special Edition 1 (3/83, $2.50)-r/#1,2,4,5; Wrightson-c 4.00
... Vs. Dracula TPB (2006, $19.99) r/#14,58-62 and Tomb of Dracula #44 20.00
...What Is It That Disturbs You, Stephen? #1 (10/97, $5.99, 48 pgs.) Russell-a/Andreyko & Russell-s, retelling of Annual #1 story 6.00

NOTE: ***Adkins*** *a-169, 170, 171i; c-169-171, 172i, 173.* ***Adams*** *a-4i.* ***Austin*** *a(i)-48-60, 66, 68, 70, 73; c(i)-38, 47-53, 55, 58-60, 70.* ***Brunner*** *a-1-5p; c-1-6, 22, 28-30, 33.* ***Colan*** *a(p)-172-178, 180-183, 6-18, 36-45, 47; c(p)-172, 174-183, 11-21, 23, 27, 35, 36, 47.* ***Ditko*** *a-179r, 3r.* ***Everett*** *c-183i.* ***Golden*** *a-46p, 55p; c-42-44, 46, 55p.* ***G. Kane*** *c(p)-8-10.* ***Miller*** *c-46p.* ***Nebres*** *a-20, 22, 23, 24i, 26i, 32i; c-32i, 34.* ***Rogers*** *a-48-53p; c-47p-53p.* ***Russell*** *a-34i, 46i, Annual 1.* ***B. Smith*** *c-179.* ***Paul Smith*** *a-54p, 56p, 65, 66p, 68p, 69, 71-73; c-56, 65, 66, 68, 71.* ***Starlin*** *a-23p, 26; c-25, 26.* ***Sutton*** *a-27-29p, 31i, 33, 34p. Painted c-62, 63.*

DOCTOR STRANGE (Volume 2)
Marvel Comics: Feb, 1999 - No. 4, May, 1999 ($2.99, limited series)

1-4: 1,2-Tony Harris-a/painted cover. 3,4-Chadwick-a 3.00

DOCTOR STRANGE CLASSICS
Marvel Comics Group: Mar, 1984 - No. 4, June, 1984 ($1.50, Baxter paper)

1-4: Ditko-r; Byrne-c. 4-New Golden pin-up 3.00
NOTE: ***Byrne*** *c-1i, 2-4.*

DOCTOR STRANGEFATE (See Marvel Versus DC #3 & DC Versus Marvel #4)
DC Comics (Amalgam): Apr, 1996 ($1.95)

1-Ron Marz script w/Jose Garcia-Lopez-(p) & Kevin Nowlan-(i). Access & Charles Xavier app. 3.00

DOCTOR STRANGE MASTER OF THE MYSTIC ARTS (See Fireside Book Series)

DOCTOR STRANGE, SORCERER SUPREME
Marvel Comics (Midnight Sons imprint #60 on): Nov, 1988 - No. 90, June, 1996 ($1.25/$1.50/$1.75/$1.95, direct sales only, Mando paper)

1 ($1.25) 5.00
2-9,12-14,16-25,27,29-40,42-49,51-64: 3-New Defenders app. 5-Guice-c/a begins. 14-18-Morbius story line. 31-36-Infinity Gauntlet x-overs. 31-Silver Surfer app. 33-Thanos-c & cameo. 36-Warlock app. 37-Silver Surfer app. 40-Daredevil x-over. 41-Wolverine-c/story. 42-47-Infinity War x-overs. 47-Gamora app. 52,53-Morbius-c/stories. 60,61-Siege of Darkness pt. 7 & 15. 60-Spot varnish-c. 61-New Doctor Strange begins (cameo, 1st app.). 62-Dr. Doom & Morbius app. 3.00
10,11,26,28,41: 10-Re-intro Morbius w/new costume (11/89). 11-Hobgoblin app. 26-Werewolf by Night app. 28-Ghost Rider-s cont'd from G.R. #12; published at same time as Doctor Strange/Ghost Rider Special #1(4/91) 4.00
15-Unauthorized Amy Grant photo-c 5.00
50-($2.95, 52 pgs.)-Holo-grafx foil-c; Hulk, Ghost Rider & Silver Surfer app.; leads into new Secret Defenders series 4.00
65-74, 76-90: 65-Begin $1.95-c; bound-in card sheet. 72-Silver ink-c. 80-82- Ellis-s. 84-DeMatteis story begins. 87-Death of Baron Mordo 3.00
75 ($2.50) 3.50
75 ($3.50)-Foil-c 4.00
Annual 2-4 ('92-'94, 68 pgs.)-2-Defenders app. 3-Polybagged w/card 4.00

GD VG FN VF VF/NM NM-
2.0 4.0 6.0 8.0 9.0 9.2

Ashcan (1995, 75¢) 3.00
.../Ghost Rider Special 1 (4/91, $1.50)-Same book as D.S.S.S. #28 3.00
...Vs. Dracula 1 (3/94, $1.75, 52 pgs.)-r/Tomb of Dracula #44 & Dr. Strange #14 4.00
NOTE: ***Colan*** *c/a-19.* ***Golden*** *c-28.* ***Guice*** *a-5-16, 18, 20-24; c-5-12, 20-24. See 1st series for Annual #1.*

DOCTOR STRANGE: THE OATH
Marvel Comics: Dec, 2006 - No. 5, Apr, 2007 ($2.99, limited series)

1-5-Vaughan-s/Martin-a; Night Nurse app. 3.00
TPB (2007, $13.99) r/#1-5; sketch pages and promotional art 14.00

DR. TOM BRENT, YOUNG INTERN
Charlton Publications: Feb, 1963 - No. 5, Oct, 1963

1 3 6 9 16 23 30
2-5 2 4 6 11 16 20

DR. TOMORROW
Acclaim Comics (Valiant): Sept, 1997 - No. 12 ($2.50)

1-12: 1-Mignola-c 3.00

DR. VOLTZ (See Mighty Midget Comics)

DOCTOR VOODOO: AVENGER OF THE SUPERNATURAL
Marvel Comics: Dec, 2009 - No. 5, Apr, 2010 ($2.99, limited series)

1-5-Dr. Doom, Son of Satan & Ghost Rider app.; Palo-a 3.00
Doctor Voodoo: The Origin of Jericho Drumm (1/10, $4.99) r/Strange Tales #169,170 5.00

DR. WEIRD
Big Bang Comics: Oct, 1994 - No. 2, May, 1995 ($2.95, B&W)

1,2: 1-Frank Brunner-c 4.00

DR. WEIRD SPECIAL
Big Bang Comics: Feb, 1994 ($3.95, B&W, 68 pgs.)

1-Origin-r by Starlin; Starlin-c. 4.00

DOCTOR WHO (Also see Marvel Premiere #57-60)
Marvel Comics Group: Oct, 1984 - No. 23, Aug, 1986 ($1.50, direct sales, Baxter paper)

1-15-British-r 4.00
16-23 5.00
Graphic Novel Voyager (1985, $8.95) color reprints of B&W comic pages from Doctor Who Magazine #88-99; Colin Baker afterword 12.00

DOCTOR WHO (Based on the 2005 TV series with David Tennant)
IDW Publishing: Jan, 2008 - No. 6, Jun, 2008 ($3.99)

1-6: 1-Nick Roche-a/Gary Russell-s; two covers 4.00

DOCTOR WHO (Based on the 2005 TV series with David Tennant)
IDW Publishing: Jul, 2009 - No. 16, Oct, 2010 ($3.99)

1-16-Grist-c on all. 3-5,13-16-Art by Matt Smith (not the actor) 4.00
... Annual 2010 (7/10, $7.99) short stories by various; Yates-c; cameo by 11th Doctor 8.00
...: Autopia (6/09, $3.99) Ostrander-s; Yates-a/c; variant photo-c 4.00
...: Black Death White Life (9/09, $3.99) Mandrake-a; Guy Davis- c; variant photo-c 4.00
...: Cold-Blooded War (8/09, $3.99) Salmon-a/c; variant photo-c 4.00
...: Room With a Déjà View (6/09, $3.99) Eric J-a; Mandrake-c; variant photo-c 4.00
...: The Whispering Gallery (2/09, $3.99) Moore & Reppion-s; Templesmith-a/2 covers 4.00
...: Time Machination (5/09, $3.99) Paul Grist-a/c; variant photo-c 4.00

DOCTOR WHO (Based on the 2010 TV series with Matt Smith)
IDW Publishing: Jan, 2011 - Present ($3.99)

1-Edwards & photo-c; Currie-a 4.00

DR. WHO & THE DALEKS (See Movie Classics)

DOCTOR WHO CLASSICS
IDW Publishing: Nov, 2005 - Present ($3.99)

1-10: Reprints from Doctor Who Weekly (1979); art by Gibbons, Neary and others 4.00
Series 2 (12/08 - No. 12, 11/09, $3.99) 1-12 4.00
Series 3 (3/10 - No. 6, 8/10, $3.99) 1-6 4.00
...: The Seventh Doctor (2/11, $3.99) 1-Furman-s/Ridgway-a; Sylvester McCoy-era 4.00

DOCTOR WHO: THE FORGOTTEN (Based on the 2005 TV series with David Tennant)
IDW Publishing: Aug, 2008 - No. 6, Jan, 2009 ($3.99)

1-6: 1,2-Pia Guerra-a/Tony Lee-s; two covers 4.00

DR. WONDER
Old Town Publishing: June, 1996 - No. 5 ($2.95, B&W)

1-5: 1-Intro & origin of Dr. Wonder; Dick Ayers-c/a; Irwin Hasen-a 3.00

DOCTOR ZERO
Marvel Comics (Epic Comics): Apr, 1988 - No. 8, Aug, 1989 ($1.25/$1.50)

1-8: 1-Sienkiewicz-c. 6,7-Spiegle-a 3.00
NOTE: ***Sienkiewicz*** *a-3i, 4i; c-1.* ***Spiegle*** *a-6, 7.*

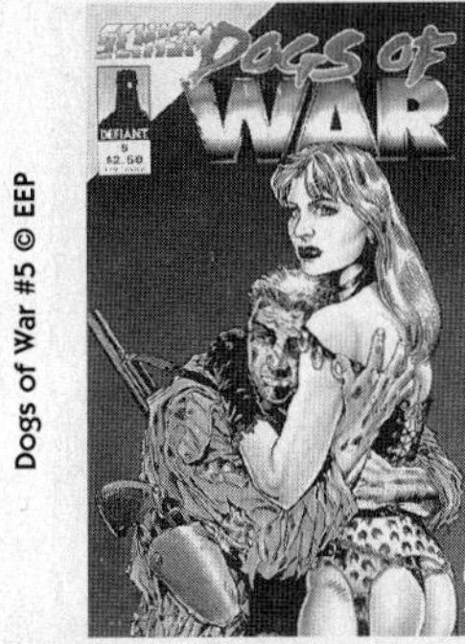

Dogs of War #5 © EEP

Doll Man Quarterly #1 © QUA

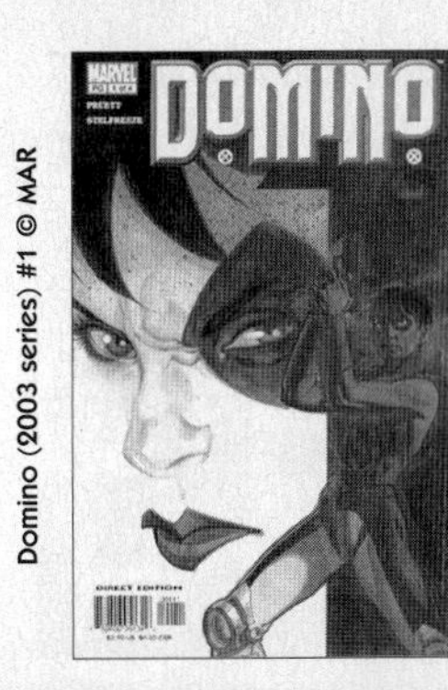

Domino (2003 series) #1 © MAR

GD 2.0 | VG 4.0 | FN 6.0 | VF 8.0 | VF/NM 9.0 | NM- 9.2

DO-DO (Funny Animal Circus Stories)
Nation-Wide Publishers: 1950 - No. 7, 1951 (5¢, 5x7-1/4" Miniature)

1 (52 pgs.) 26 52 78 154 252 350
2-7 15 30 45 85 130 175

DODO & THE FROG, THE (Formerly Funny Stuff; also see It's Game Time #2)
National Periodical Publications: No. 80, 9-10/54 - No. 88, 1-2/56; No. 89, 8-9/56; No. 90, 10-11/56; No. 91, 9/57; No. 92, 11/57 (See Comic Cavalcade and Captain Carrot)

80-1st app. Doodles Duck by Sheldon Mayer 20 40 60 114 182 250
81-91: Doodles Duck by Mayer in #81,83-90 14 28 42 76 108 140
92-(Scarce)-Doodles Duck by S. Mayer 18 36 54 105 165 225

DOGFACE DOOLEY
Magazine Enterprises: 1951 - No. 5, 1953

1(A-1 40) 8 16 24 40 50 60
2(A-1 43), 3(A-1 49), 4(A-1 53), 5(A-1 64) 6 12 18 28 34 40
I.W. Reprint #1('64), Super Reprint #17 2 4 6 9 13 16

DOG MOON
DC Comics (Vertigo): 1996 ($6.95, one-shot)

1-Robert Hunter-scripts; Tim Truman-c/a. 7.00

DOG OF FLANDERS, A
Dell Publishing Co.: No. 1088, Mar, 1960

Four Color 1088-Movie, photo-c 5 10 15 30 48 65

DOGPATCH (See Al Capp's... & Mammy Yokum)

DOGS OF WAR (Also see Warriors of Plasm)
Defiant: Apr, 1994 - No. 5, Aug, 1994 ($2.50)

1-5 3.00

DOGS-O-WAR
Crusade Comics: June, 1996 - No. 3, Jan, 1997 ($2.95, B&W, limited series)

1-3: 1,2-Photo-c 3.00

DOLLFACE & HER GANG (Betty Betz'...)
Dell Publishing Co.: No. 309, Jan, 1951

Four Color 309 5 10 15 35 55 75

DOLLMAN (Movie)
Eternity Comics: Sept, 1991 - No. 4, Dec, 1991 ($2.50, limited series)

1-4: Adaptation of film 3.00

DOLL MAN QUARTERLY, THE (Doll Man #17 on; also see Feature Comics #27 & Freedom Fighters)
Quality Comics: Fall, 1941 - No. 7, Fall, '43; No. 8, Spr, '46 - No. 47, Oct, 1953

1-Dollman (by Cassone), Justin Wright begin 331 662 993 2317 4059 5800
2-The Dragon begins; Crandall-a(5) 145 290 435 921 1586 2250
3,4 89 178 267 565 970 1375
5-Crandall-a 86 172 258 546 936 1325
6,7(1943) 54 108 162 343 574 825
8(1946)-1st app. Torchy by Bill Ward 165 330 495 1048 1799 2550
9 53 106 159 334 567 800
10-20 41 82 123 256 428 600
21-30: 28-Vs. The Flame 36 72 108 216 351 485
31-36,38,40: 31-(12/50)-Intro Elmo, the wonder dog (Dollman's faithful dog).
32-34-Jeb Rivers app.; 34 by Crandall(p) 33 66 99 194 317 440
37-Origin & 1st app. Dollgirl; Dollgirl bondage-c 47 94 141 296 498 700
39- "Narcotics...the Death Drug" c-/story 37 74 111 222 361 500
41-47 24 48 72 140 230 320
Super Reprint #11('64, r/#20),15(r/#23),17(r/#28): 15,17-Torchy app.; Andru/Esposito-c
3 6 9 20 30 40

NOTE: ***Ward*** *Torchy in 8, 9, 11, 12, 14-24, 27; by Fox-#26, 30, 35-47.* ***Crandall*** *a-2, 5, 10, 13 & Super #11, 17, 18.* ***Crandall/Cuidera*** *c-40-42.* ***Guardineer*** *a-3. Bondage c-27, 37, 38, 39.*

DOLLY
Ziff-Davis Publ. Co.: No. 10, July-Aug, 1951 (Funny animal)

10-Painted-c 9 18 27 47 61 75

DOLLY DILL
Marvel Comics/Newsstand Publ.: 1945

1 18 36 54 105 165 225

DOLLZ, THE
Image Comics: Apr, 2001 - No. 2, June, 2001 ($2.95)

1,2: 1-Four covers; Sniegoski & Green-s/Green-a 3.00

DOMINATION FACTOR
Marvel Comics: Nov, 1999 - 4.8, Feb, 2000 ($2.50, interconnected mini- series)

GD 2.0 | VG 4.0 | FN 6.0 | VF 8.0 | VF/NM 9.0 | NM- 9.2

1.1, 2.3, 3.5, 4.7-Fantastic Four; Jurgens-s/a 3.00
1.2, 2.4, 3.6, 4.8-Avengers; Ordway-s/a 3.00

DOMINIC FORTUNE
Marvel Comics (MAX): Oct, 2009 - No. 4, Jan, 2010 ($3.99, limited series)

1-4-Howard Chaykin-s/a/c 4.00

DOMINION
Image Comics: Jan, 2003 - No. 2 ($2.95)

1,2-Keith Giffen-s/a 3.00

DOMINION (Manga)
Eclipse Comics: Dec, 1990 - No. 6., July, 1990 ($2.00, B&W, limited series)

1-6 3.00

DOMINION: CONFLICT 1 (Manga)
Dark Horse Comics: Mar, 1996 - No. 6, Aug, 1996 ($2.95, B&W, limited series)

1-6: Shirow-c/a/scripts 3.00

DOMINIQUE: KILLZONE
Caliber Comics: May, 1995 ($2.95, B&W)

1 3.00

DOMINO (See X-Force)
Marvel Comics: Jan, 1997 - No. 3, Mar, 1997 ($1.95, limited series)

1-3: 2-Deathstrike-c/app. 3.00

DOMINO (See X-Force)
Marvel Comics: June, 2003 - No. 4, Aug, 2003 ($2.50, limited series)

1-4-Stelfreeze-c/a; Pruett-s. 3.00

DOMINO CHANCE
Chance Enterprises: May-June, 1982 - No. 9, May, 1985 (B&W)

1-9: 7-1st app. Gizmo, 2 pgs. 8-1st full Gizmo story. 1-Reprint, May, 1985 3.00

DONALD AND MICKEY IN DISNEYLAND (See Dell Giants)

DONALD AND SCROOGE
Disney Comics: 1992 ($8.95, squarebound, 100 pgs.)

nn-Don Rosa reprint special; r/U.S., D.D. Advs. 1 3 4 6 8 10
1-3 (1992, $1.50)-r/D.D. Advs. (Disney) #1,22,24 & U.S. #261-263,269 3.00

DONALD AND THE WHEEL (Disney)
Dell Publishing Co.: No. 1190, Nov, 1961

Four Color 1190-Movie, Barks-c 8 16 24 54 90 125

DONALD DUCK (See Adventures of Mickey Mouse, Cheerios, Donald & Mickey, Ducktales, Dynabrite Comics, Gladstone Comic Album, Mickey & Donald, Mickey Mouse Mag., Story Hour Series, Uncle Scrooge, Walt Disney's Comics & Stories, W. D.'s Donald Duck, Wheaties & Whitman Comic Books, Wise Little Hen, The)

DONALD DUCK
Whitman Publishing Co./Grosset & Dunlap/K.K.: 1935, 1936 (All pages on heavy linen-like finish cover stock in color;1st book ever devoted to Donald Duck; see Advs. of Mickey Mouse for 1st app.) (9-1/2x13")

978(1935)-16 pgs.; Illustrated text story book 206 412 618 1318 2259 3200
nn(1936)-36 pgs.plus hard cover & dust jacket. Story completely rewritten with B&W illos added. Mickey appears and his nephews are named Morty & Monty
Book only 194 388 582 1242 2121 3000
Dust jacket only.... 39 78 117 240 395 550

DONALD DUCK (Walt Disney's) (10¢)
Whitman/K.K. Publications: 1938 (8-1/2x11-1/2", B&W, cardboard-c)
(Has D. Duck with bubble pipe on-c)

nn-The first Donald Duck & Walt Disney comic book; 1936 & 1937 Sunday strip-r(in B&W); same format as the Feature Books; 1st strips with Huey, Dewey & Louie from 10/17/37
258 516 774 1651 2826 4000

DONALD DUCK (Walt Disney's...#262 on; see 4-Color listings for titles & Four Color No. 1109 for origin story)
Dell Publ. Co./Gold Key #85-216/Whitman #217-245/Gladstone #246 on: 1940 - No. 84, Sept-Nov, 1962; No. 85, Dec, 1962 - No. 245, July, 1984; No. 246, Oct, 1986 - No. 279, May, 1990; No. 280, Sept, 1993 - No. 307, Mar,1998

Four Color 4(1940)-Daily 1939 strip-r by Al Taliaferro
1600 3200 4800 12,000 18,500 25,000
Large Feature Comic 16(1/41?)-1940 Sunday strips-r in B&W
595 1190 1785 4350 7675 11,000
Large Feature Comic 20('41)-Comic Paint Book, r-single panels from Large Feature #16 at top of each pg. to color; daily strip-r across bottom of each pg. (Rare)
622 1244 1866 4541 8021 11,500
Four Color 9('42)- "Finds Pirate Gold"; 64 pgs. by Carl Barks & Jack Hannah (pgs. 1,2,5,12-40

Donald Duck #46 © DIS

Donald Duck #269 © DIS

Donald Duck and Friends #356 © DIS

GD 2.0 | VG 4.0 | FN 6.0 | VF 8.0 | VF/NM 9.0 | NM- 9.2

are by Barks, his 1st Donald Duck comic book art work; © 8/17/42) 1000 2000 3000 7600 13,800 20,000

Four Color 29(9/43)- "Mummy's Ring" by Barks; reprinted in Uncle Scrooge & Donald Duck #1('65), W. D. Comics Digest #44('73) & Donald Duck Advs. #14 757 1514 2271 5526 9763 14,000

Four Color 62(1/45)- "Frozen Gold"; 52 pgs. by Barks, reprinted in The Best of W.D. Comics & Donald Duck Advs. #4 212 424 636 1855 3778 5700

Four Color 108(1946)- "Terror of the River"; 52 pgs. by Carl Barks; reprinted in Gladstone Comic Album #2 148 296 444 1295 2648 4000

Four Color 147(5/47)-in "Volcano Valley" by Barks 104 208 312 884 1792 2700

Four Color 159(8/47)-in "The Ghost of the Grotto";52 pgs. by Carl Barks; reprinted in Best of Uncle Scrooge & Donald Duck #1 ('66) & The Best of W.D. Comics & D.D. Advs. #9; two Barks stories 89 178 267 757 1529 2300

Four Color 178(12/47)-1st app. Uncle Scrooge by Carl Barks; reprinted in Gold Key Christmas Parade #3 & The Best of Walt Disney Comics 119 238 357 1012 2056 3100

Four Color 189(6/48)-by Carl Barks; reprinted in Best of Donald Duck & Uncle Scrooge #1('64) & D.D. Advs. #19 73 146 219 621 1261 1900

Four Color 199(10/48)-by Carl Barks; mentioned in Love and Death; r/in Gladstone Comic Album #5 79 158 237 672 1361 2050

Four Color 203(12/48)-by Barks; reprinted as Gold Key Christmas Parade #4 56 112 168 476 963 1450

Four Color 223(4/49)-by Barks; reprinted as Best of Donald Duck #1 & Donald Duck Advs. #3 73 146 219 621 1261 1900

Four Color 238(8/49)-in "Voodoo Hoodoo" by Barks 56 112 168 476 963 1450

Four Color 256(12/49)-by Barks; reprinted in Best of Donald Duck & Uncle Scrooge #2('67), Gladstone Comic Album #16 & W.D. Comics Digest 44('73) 47 94 141 376 763 1150

Four Color 263(2/50)-Two Barks stories; r-in D.D. #278 46 92 138 368 747 1125

Four Color 275(5/50), 282(7/50), 291(9/50), 300(11/50)-All by Carl Barks; 275, 282 reprinted in W.D. Comics Digest #44('73). #275 r/in Gladstone Comic Album #10. #291 r/in D. Duck Advs. #16 45 90 135 360 730 1100

Four Color 308(1/51), 318(3/51)-by Barks; #318-reprinted in W.D. Comics Digest #34 & D.D. Advs. #2,19 42 86 126 336 681 1025

Four Color 328(5/51)-by Carl Barks 41 82 123 328 664 1000

Four Color 339(7-8/51), 379-2nd Uncle Scrooge-c; art not by Barks. 13 26 39 89 170 250

Four Color 348(9-10/51), 356,394-Barks-c only 20 40 60 144 290 435

Four Color 367(1-2/52)-by Barks; reprinted as Gold Key Christmas Parade #2 & #8 33 66 99 254 510 765

Four Color 408(7-8/52), 422(9-10/52)-All by Carl Barks. #408-r-in Best of Donald Duck & Uncle Scrooge #1('64) & Gladstone Comic Album #13 33 66 99 254 510 765

26(11-12/52)-In "Trick or Treat" (Barks-a, 36pgs.) 1st story r-in Walt Disney Digest #16 & Gladstone C.A. #23 33 66 99 254 510 765

27-30-Barks-c only 13 26 39 89 170 250

31-44,47-50 8 16 24 52 86 120

45-Barks-a (6 pgs.) 14 28 42 97 194 290

46- "Secret of Hondorica" by Barks, 24 pgs.; reprinted in Donald Duck #98 & 154 19 38 57 134 272 410

51-Barks-a,1/2 pg. 8 16 24 52 86 120

52- "Lost Peg-Leg Mine" by Barks, 10 pgs. 14 28 42 98 197 295

53,55-59 7 14 21 45 73 100

54- "Forbidden Valley" by Barks, 26 pgs. (10¢ & 15¢ versions exist) 15 30 45 110 223 335

60- "Donald Duck & the Titanic Ants" by Barks, 20 pgs. plus 6 more pgs. 15 30 45 110 223 335

61-67,69,70 6 12 18 39 62 85

68-Barks-a, 5 pgs. 10 20 30 72 131 190

71-Barks-r, 1/2 pg. 6 12 18 39 62 85

72-78,80,82-97,99,100: 96-Donald Duck Album 6 12 18 37 59 80

79,81-Barks-a, 1pg. 6 12 18 39 62 85

98-Reprints #46 (Barks) 6 12 18 39 62 85

101,103-111,113-135: 120-Last 12¢ issue. 134-Barks-r/#52 & WDC&S 194. 135-Barks-r/WDC&S 198, 19 pgs. 4 8 12 23 36 48

102-Super Goof. 112-1st Moby Duck 4 8 12 24 37 50

136-153,155,156,158: 149-20¢-c begin 3 6 9 14 20 26

154-Barks-r(#46) 3 6 9 17 25 32

157,159,160,164: 157-Barks-r(#45); 25¢-c begin. 159-Reprints/WDC&S #192 (10 pgs.). 160-Barks-r(#26). 164-Barks-r(#79) 3 6 9 14 20 26

161-163,165-173,175-187,189-191: 175-30¢-c begin. 187-Barks r/#68. 2 4 6 13 18 22

174,188: 174-r/4-Color #394. 3 6 9 14 19 24

192-Barks-r(40 pgs.) from Donald Duck #60 & WDC&S #226,234 (52 pgs.) 3 6 9 16 22 28

193-200,202-207,209-211,213-216 2 4 6 9 13 16

201,208,212: 201-Barks-r/Christmas Parade #26, 16pgs. 208-Barks-r/#60 (6 pgs.). 212-Barks-r/WDC&S #130 2 4 6 9 13 16

217-219: 217 has 216 on-c. 219-Barks-r/WDC&S #106,107, 10 pgs. ea. 2 4 6 10 14 18

220,225-228: 228-Barks-r/F.C. #275 2 4 6 13 18 22

221,223,224: Scarce; only sold in pre-packs. 221(8/80), 223(11/80), 224(12/80) 6 12 18 39 62 85

222-(9-10/80)-(Very low distribution) 16 32 48 111 226 340

229-240: 229-Barks-r/F.C. #282. 230-Barks-r/ #52 & WDC&S #194. 236(2/82), 237(2-3/82), 238(3/82), 239(4/82), 240(5/82) 2 4 6 9 13 16

241-245: 241(4/83), 242(5/83), 243(3/84), 244(4/84), 245(7/84)(low print) 3 6 9 14 19 24

246-(1st Gladstone issue)-Barks-r/FC #422 3 6 9 15 21 26

247-249,251: 248,249-Barks-r/DD #54 & 26. 251-Barks-r/1945 Firestone 2 4 6 9 13 16

250-($1.50, 68 pgs.)-Barks-r/4-Color #9 2 4 6 10 14 18

252-277,280: 254-Barks-r/FC #328. 256-Barks-r/FC #147. 257-($1.50, 52 pgs.)-Barks-r/ Vacation Parade #1. 261-Barks-r/FC #300. 275-Kelly-r/FC #92. 280 (#1, 2nd Series) 1 2 3 5 6 8

278,279,286: 278,279 ($1.95, 68 pgs.): 278-Rosa-a; Barks-r/FC #263. 279-Rosa-c; Barks-r/MOC #4. 286-Rosa-a 1 2 3 5 7 9

281,282,284 1 2 3 4 5 7

283-Don Rosa-a, part-c & scripts 1 2 3 5 6 8

285,287-307 5.00

286 ($2.95, 68 pgs.)-Happy Birthday, Donald 6.00

Mini-Comic #1(1976)-(3-1/4x6-1/2"); r/D.D. #150 2 4 6 8 11 14

NOTE: ***Carl Barks*** *wrote all issues he illustrated, but #117, 126, 138 contain his script only. Issues 4-Color #189, 199, 203, 223, 238, 256, 263, 275, 282, 308, 348, 356, 367, 394, 408, 422, 26-30, 35, 44, 46, 52, 55, 57, 60, 65, 70-73, 77-80, 83, 101, 103, 105, 106, 111, 126, 246r, 266r, 268r, 271r, 275r, 278r(F.C. 263) all have* ***Barks*** *covers.* ***Barks*** *r-263-267, 269-278-282, 284, 285. #96 titled "Comic Album", #99-"Christmas Album". New art issues (not reprints)-106-46, 148-63, 167, 169, 170, 172, 173, 175, 178, 179, 196, 209, 223, 225, 236.* ***Taliaferro*** *daily newspaper strips #258-260, 264, 284, 285; Sunday strips #247, 280-283.*

DONALD DUCK (Numbering continues from Donald Duck and Friends #362)
BOOM! Studios (Kaboom!): No. 363, Feb, 2011 - Present ($3.99)

363-365: 363-Barks reprints incl. "Mystery of the Loch". 364-Rosa-c 4.00

DONALD DUCK ADVENTURES (See Walt Disney's Donald Duck Adventures)

DONALD DUCK ALBUM (See Comic Album No. 1,3 & Duck Album)
Dell Publishing Co./Gold Key: 5-7/59 - F.C. No. 1239, 10-12/61; 1962; 8/63 - No. 2, Oct, 1963

Four Color 995 (#1) 6 12 18 43 69 95

Four Color 1099,1140,1239-Barks-c 7 14 21 45 73 100

Four Color 1182, 01204-207 (1962-Dell) 5 10 15 32 51 70

1(8/63-Gold Key)-Barks-c 6 12 18 39 62 85

2(10/63) 5 10 15 30 48 65

DONALD DUCK AND FRIENDS (Numbering continues from Walt Disney's ...)
BOOM! Studios: No. 347, Oct, 2009 - No. 362, Jan, 2011 ($2.99)

347-362: Two covers on most. Retitled "Donald Duck" with #363 3.00

DONALD DUCK AND THE BOYS (Also see Story Hour Series)
Whitman Publishing Co.: 1948 (5-1/4x5-1/2", 100pgs., hard-c; art & text)

845-(49) new illos by Barks based on his Donald Duck 10-pager in WDC&S #74, Expanded text not written by Barks; Cover not by Barks 50 100 150 350 600 850

(Prices vary widely on this book)

DONALD DUCK AND THE CHRISTMAS CAROL
Whitman Publishing Co.: 1960 (A Little Golden Book, 6-3/8"x7-5/8", 28 pgs.)

nn-Story book pencilled by Carl Barks with the intended title "Uncle Scrooge's Christmas Carol." Finished art adapted by Norman McGary. (Rare)-Reprinted in Uncle Scrooge in Color. 30 60 90 150 210 270

DONALD DUCK BEACH PARTY (Also see Dell Giants)
Gold Key: Sept, 1965 (12¢)

1(#10158-509)-Barks-r/WDC&S #45; painted-c 6 12 18 43 69 95

DONALD DUCK BOOK (See Story Hour Series)

DONALD DUCK COMICS DIGEST
Gladstone Publishing: Nov, 1986 - No. 5, July, 1987 ($1.25/$1.50, 96 pgs.)

1,3: 1-Barks-c/a-r 1 3 4 6 8 10

2,4,5: 4,5-$1.50-c 6.00

DONALD DUCK FUN BOOK (See Dell Giants)

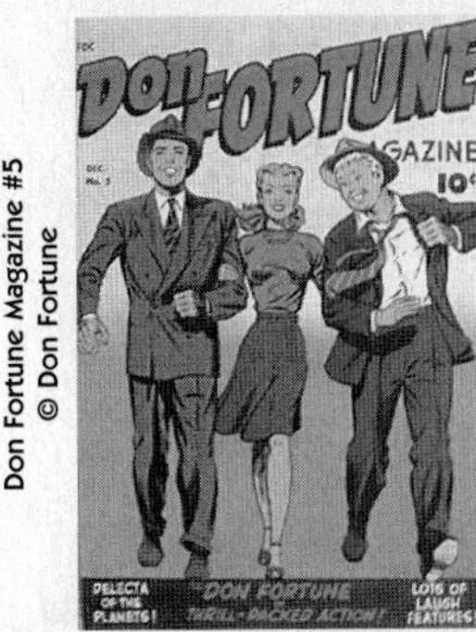

Don Fortune Magazine #5 © Don Fortune

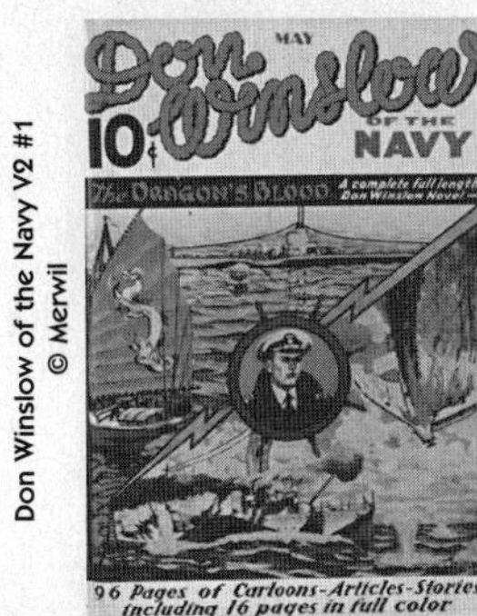

Don Winslow of the Navy V2 #1 © Merwil

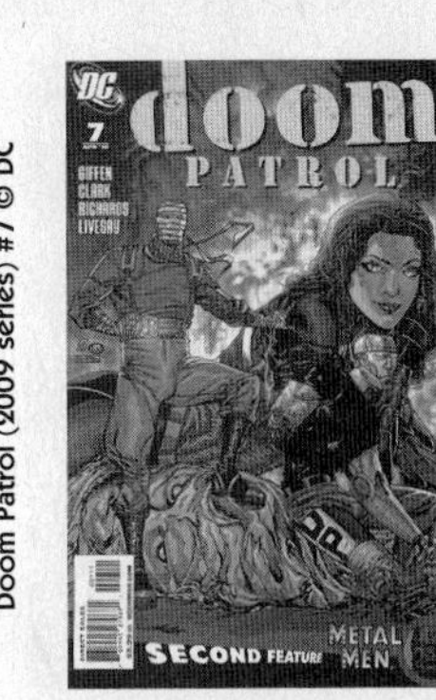

Doom Patrol (2009 series) #7 © DC

DONALD DUCK IN DISNEYLAND (See Dell Giants)

DONALD DUCK MARCH OF COMICS (See March of Comics #4,20,41,56,69,263)

DONALD DUCK MERRY CHRISTMAS (See Dell Giant No. 53)

DONALD DUCK PICNIC PARTY (See Picnic Party listed under Dell Giants)

DONALD DUCK TELLS ABOUT KITES (See Kite Fun Book)

DONALD DUCK, THIS IS YOUR LIFE (Disney, TV)
Dell Publishing Co.: No. 1109, Aug-Oct, 1960

	GD 2.0	VG 4.0	FN 6.0	VF 8.0	VF/NM 9.0	NM- 9.2
Four Color 1109-Gyro flashback to WDC&S #141; origin Donald Duck (1st told)	13	26	39	91	176	260

DONALD DUCK XMAS ALBUM (See regular Donald Duck No. 99)

DONALD IN MATHMAGIC LAND (Disney)
Dell Publishing Co.: No. 1051, Oct-Dec, 1959 - No. 1198, May-July, 1961

	GD 2.0	VG 4.0	FN 6.0	VF 8.0	VF/NM 9.0	NM- 9.2
Four Color 1051 (#1)-Movie	9	18	27	63	107	150
Four Color 1198-Reprint of above	6	12	18	43	69	95

DONATELLO, TEENAGE MUTANT NINJA TURTLE
Mirage Studios: Aug, 1986 ($1.50, B&W, one-shot, 44 pgs.)

	GD 2.0	VG 4.0	FN 6.0	VF 8.0	VF/NM 9.0	NM- 9.2
1	1	2	3	5	7	9

DONDI
Dell Publishing Co.: No. 1176, Mar-May, 1961 - No. 1276, Dec, 1961

	GD 2.0	VG 4.0	FN 6.0	VF 8.0	VF/NM 9.0	NM- 9.2
Four Color 1176 (#1)-Movie; origin, photo-c	5	10	15	35	55	75
Four Color 1276	4	8	12	22	34	45

DON FORTUNE MAGAZINE
Don Fortune Publishing Co.: Aug, 1946 - No. 6, Feb, 1947

	GD 2.0	VG 4.0	FN 6.0	VF 8.0	VF/NM 9.0	NM- 9.2
1-Delecta of the Planets by C.C. Beck in all	27	54	81	158	259	360
2	15	30	45	85	130	175
3-6: 3-Bondage-c	14	28	42	76	108	140

DONKEY KONG (See Blip #1)

DONNA MATRIX
Reactor, Inc.: Aug, 1993 ($2.95, 52 pgs.)

1-Computer generated-c/a by Mike Saenz; 3-D effects — 3.00

DON NEWCOMBE
Fawcett Publications: 1950 (Baseball)

	GD 2.0	VG 4.0	FN 6.0	VF 8.0	VF/NM 9.0	NM- 9.2
nn-Photo-c	45	90	135	284	480	675

DON ROSA'S COMICS AND STORIES
Fantagraphics Books (CX Comics): 1983 ($2.95)

	GD 2.0	VG 4.0	FN 6.0	VF 8.0	VF/NM 9.0	NM- 9.2
1,2: 1-(68 pgs.) Reprints Rosa's The Pertwillaby Papers episodes #128-133. 2-(60 pgs.) Reprints episodes #134-138	2	4	6	11	16	20

DON SIMPSON'S BIZARRE HEROES (Also see Megaton Man)
Fiasco Comics: May, 1990 - No. 17, Sept, 1996 ($2.50/$2.95, B&W)

1-10,0,11-17: 0-Begin $2.95-c; r/Bizarre Heroes #1. 17-(9/96)-Indicia also reads Megaton Man #0; intro Megaton Man and the Fiascoverse to new readers — 3.00

DON'T GIVE UP THE SHIP
Dell Publishing Co.: No. 1049, Aug, 1959

	GD 2.0	VG 4.0	FN 6.0	VF 8.0	VF/NM 9.0	NM- 9.2
Four Color 1049-Movie, Jerry Lewis photo-c	9	18	27	61	103	145

DON WINSLOW OF THE NAVY
Merwil Publishing Co.: Apr, 1937 - No. 2, May, 1937 (96 pgs.)(A pulp/comic book cross; stapled spine)

	GD 2.0	VG 4.0	FN 6.0	VF 8.0	VF/NM 9.0	NM- 9.2
V1#1-Has 16 pgs. comics in color. Captain Colorful & Jupiter Jones by Sheldon Mayer; complete Don Winslow novel	653	1306	1959	4900	-	-
2-Sheldon Mayer-a	177	354	531	1325	-	-

DON WINSLOW OF THE NAVY (See Crackajack Funnies, Famous Feature Stories, Popular Comics & Super Book #5,6)
Dell Publishing Co.: No. 2, Nov, 1939 - No. 22, 1941

	GD 2.0	VG 4.0	FN 6.0	VF 8.0	VF/NM 9.0	NM- 9.2
Four Color 2 (#1)-Rare	194	388	582	1242	2121	3000
Four Color 22	47	94	141	296	498	700

DON WINSLOW OF THE NAVY (See TV Teens; Movie, Radio, TV) (Fightin' Navy No. 74 on)
Fawcett Publications/Charlton No. 70 on: 2/43 - #64, 12/48; #65, 1/51 - #69, 9/51; #70, 3/55 - #73, 9/55

	GD 2.0	VG 4.0	FN 6.0	VF 8.0	VF/NM 9.0	NM- 9.2
1-(68 pgs.)-Captain Marvel on cover	112	224	336	706	1191	1675
2	42	84	126	265	445	625
3	34	68	102	199	325	450
4-6: 6-Flag-c	26	52	78	154	252	350
7-10: 8-Last 68 pg. issue?	20	40	60	114	182	250
11-20	15	30	45	90	140	190
21-40	14	28	42	76	108	140
41-43,45-64: 51,60-Singapore Sal (villain) app. 64-(12/48)	12	24	36	69	97	125
44-Classic spider-c	28	56	84	165	270	375
65(1/51)-Flying Saucer attack; photo-c	20	40	60	114	182	250
66 - 69(9/51): All photo-c. 66-sci-fi story	14	28	42	80	115	150
70(3/55)-73: 70-73 r-/#26,58 & 59	9	18	27	50	65	80

DOOM
Marvel Comics: Oct, 2000 - No. 3, Dec, 2000 ($2.99, limited series)

1-3-Dr. Doom; Dixon-s/Manco-a — 3.00

DOOM FORCE SPECIAL
DC Comics: July, 1992 ($2.95, 68 pgs., one-shot, mature) (X-Force parody)

1-Morrison scripts; Simonson, Steacy, & others-a; Giffen/Mignola-c — 4.00

DOOM PATROL, THE (Formerly My Greatest Adventure No. 1-85; see Brave and the Bold, DC Special Blue Ribbon Digest 19, Official... Index & Showcase No. 94-96)
National Periodical Publ.: No. 86, 3/64 - No. 121, 9-10/68; No. 122, 2/73 - No. 124, 6-7/73

	GD 2.0	VG 4.0	FN 6.0	VF 8.0	VF/NM 9.0	NM- 9.2
86-1 pg. origin (#86-121 are 12¢ issues)	11	22	33	75	138	200
87-98: 88-Origin The Chief. 91-Intro. Mento	8	16	24	58	97	135
99-Intro. Beast Boy (later becomes the Changeling in New Teen Titans)	10	20	30	68	119	170
100-Origin Beast Boy; Robot-Maniac series begins (12/65)	10	20	30	68	119	170
101-110: 102-Challengers of the Unknown app. 105-Robot-Maniac series ends. 106-Negative Man begins (origin)	6	12	18	43	69	95
111-120	5	10	15	35	55	75
121-Death of Doom Patrol; Orlando-c.	10	20	30	71	128	185
122-124: All reprints	2	4	6	8	11	14

DOOM PATROL
DC Comics (Vertigo imprint #64 on): Oct, 1987 - No, 87, Feb, 1995 (75¢-$1.95, new format)

	GD 2.0	VG 4.0	FN 6.0	VF 8.0	VF/NM 9.0	NM- 9.2
1-Wraparound-c; Lightle-a						6.00
2-18: 3-1st app. Lodestone. 4-1st app. Karma. 8,15,16-Art Adams-c(i). 18-Invasion tie-in						4.00
19-(2/89)-Grant Morrison scripts begin, ends #63; 1st app Crazy Jane; $1.50-c & new format begins.	1	2	3	5	6	8
20-30: 29-Superman app. 30-Night Breed fold-out						5.00
31-34,37-41,45-49,51-56,58-60: 39-World Without End preview						3.00
35-1st brief app. of Flex Mentallo						5.00
36-1st full app. of Flex Mentallo						6.00
42-44-Origin of Flex Mentallo						4.00
50,57 ($2.50, 52 pgs.)						4.00
61-87: 61,70-Photo-c. 73-Death cameo (2 panels)						3.00
...And Suicide Squad 1 (3/88, $1.50, 52 pgs.)-Wraparound-c						4.00
Annual 1 (1988, $1.50, 52 pgs.)						4.00
Annual 2 (1994, $3.95, 68 pgs.)-Children's Crusade tie-in.						4.00
...: Crawling From the Wreckage TPB (2004, $19.95) r/#19-25; Morrison-s						20.00
...: Down Paradise Way TPB (2005, $19.99) r/#35-41; Morrison-s						20.00
...: Magic Bus TPB (2007, $19.99) r/#51-57; Morrison-s; new Bolland-c						20.00
...: Musclebound TPB (2006, $19.99) r/#42-50; Morrison-s; new Bolland-c						20.00
...: Planet Love TPB (2008, $19.99) r/#58-63 & Doom Force Special #1; Morrison-s						20.00
...: The Painting That Ate Paris TPB (2004, $19.95) r/#26-34; Morrison-s						20.00

NOTE: ***Bisley** painted c-26-48, 55-58. **Bolland** c-64, 75. **Dringenberg** a-42(p). **Steacy** a-53.*

DOOM PATROL
DC Comics: Dec, 2001 - No. 22, Sept, 2003 ($2.50)

1-Intro. new team with Robotman; Tan Eng Huat-c/a; John Arcudi-s — 3.50
2-22: 4,5-Metamorpho & Elongated Man app. 13,14-Fisher-a. 20-Geary-a — 3.00

DOOM PATROL (see JLA #94-99)
DC Comics: Aug, 2004 - No. 18, Jan, 2006 ($2.50)

1-18-John Byrne-s/a. 1-Green Lantern, Batman app. — 3.00

DOOM PATROL
DC Comics: Oct, 2009 - Present ($3.99/$2.99)

1-7: 1-Giffen-s/Clark-a; back-up Metal Men feature w/Maguire-a. 1-Two covers. 4-5-Blackest Night. 6-Negative Man origin re-told — 4.00
8-20-($2.99) 11,12-Ambush Bug app. 16-Giffen-a — 3.00
...: Brotherhood TPB (2011, $17.99) r/#7-13 — 18.00
...: We Who Are About to Die TPB (2010, $14.99) r/#1-6; cover gallery; design art — 15.00

DOOM PATROL (See Tangent Comics/ Doom Patrol)

DOOMSDAY
DC Comics: 1995 ($3.95, one-shot)

1-Year One story by Jurgens, L. Simonson, Ordway, and Gil Kane; Superman app. — 4.00

Doom 2099 #20 © MAR

Dopey Duck #1 © MAR

Double Trouble #1 © STJ

GD VG FN VF VF/NM NM-
2.0 4.0 6.0 8.0 9.0 9.2

DOOMSDAY + 1 (Also see Charlton Bullseye)
Charlton Comics: July, 1975 - No. 6, June, 1976; No. 7, June, 1978 - No. 12, May, 1979
1: #1-5 are 25¢ issues 3 6 9 16 22 28
2-6: 4-Intro Lor. 5-Ditko-a(1 pg.) 6-Begin 30¢-c 2 4 6 10 14 18
V3#7-12 (reprints #1-6) 6.00
5 (Modern Comics reprint, 1977) 6.00
NOTE: *Byrne c/a-1-12; Painted covers-2-7.*

DOOMSDAY SQUAD, THE
Fantagraphics Books: Aug, 1986 - No. 7, 1987 ($2.00)
1,2,4-7: Byrne-a in all. 1,2-New Byrne-c. 4-Neal Adams-c. 5-7-Gil Kane-c 3.00
3-Usagi Yojimbo app. (1st in color); new Byrne-c 6.00

DOOM'S IV
Image Comics (Extreme): July, 1994 - No.4, Oct, 1994 ($2.50, limited series)
1-4-Liefeld story 3.00
1,2-Two alternate Liefeld-c each, 4 covers form 1 picture 5.00

DOOM: THE EMPEROR RETURNS
Marvel Comics: Jan, 2002 - No. 3, Mar, 2002 ($2.50, limited series)
1-3-Dixon-s/Manco-a; Franklin Richards app. 3.00

DOOM 2099 (See Marvel Comics Presents #118 & 2099: World of Tomorrow)
Marvel Comics: Jan, 1993 - No. 44, Aug, 1996 ($1.25/$1.50/$1.95)
1-24,26-44: 1-Metallic foil stamped-c. 4-Ron Lim-c(p). 17-bound-in trading card sheet. 40-Namor & Doctor Strange app. 41-Daredevil app., Namor-c/app. 44-Intro The Emissary; story contin'd in 2099: World of Tomorrow 3.00
1-2nd printing 3.00
18-Variant polybagged with Sega Sub-Terrania poster 4.00
25 ($2.25, 52 pgs.) 3.00
25 ($2.95, 52pgs.) Foil embossed cover 4.00
29 ($3.50)-acetate-c. 4.00

DOOMWAR
Marvel Comics: Apr, 2010 - No. 6, Sept, 2010 ($3.99, limited series)
1-6-Doctor Doom invades Wakanda; Black Panther & X-Men app.; Romita Jr.-c/Eaton-a 4.00

DOORWAY TO NIGHTMARE (See Cancelled Comic Cavalcade and Madame Xanadu)
DC Comics: Jan-Feb, 1978 - No. 5, Sept-Oct, 1978
1-Madame Xanadu in all 2 4 6 10 14 18
2-5: 4-Craig-a 2 4 6 8 10 12
NOTE: *Kaluta covers on all. Merged into The Unexpected with No. 190.*

DOPEY DUCK COMICS (Wacky Duck No. 3) (See Super Funnies)
Timely Comics (NPP): Fall, 1945 - No. 2, Apr, 1946
1,2-Casper Cat, Krazy Krow 25 50 75 150 245 340

DORK
Slave Labor: June, 1993 - Present ($2.50-$3.50, B&W, mature)
1-7,9-11: Evan Dorkin-c/a/scripts in all. 1(8/95),2(1/96)-(2nd printings). 1(3/97) (3rd printing). 1-Milk & Cheese app. 3-Eltingville Club starts. 6-Reprints 1st Eltingville Club app. from Instant Piano #1 3.00
8-($3.50) 3.50
Who's Laughing Now? TPB (2001, $11.95) reprints most of #1-5 12.00
The Collected Dork, Vol. 2: Circling the Drain (6/03, $13.95) r/most of #7-10 & other-s 14.00

DOROTHY LAMOUR (Formerly Jungle Lil)(Stage, screen, radio)
Fox Features Syndicate: No. 2, June, 1950 - No. 3, Aug, 1950
2,3-Wood-a(3) each, photo-c 27 54 81 158 259 360

DOT DOTLAND (Formerly Little Dot Dotland)
Harvey Publications: No. 62, Sept, 1974 - No. 63, Nov, 1974
62,63 2 4 6 9 12 15

DOTTY (...& Her Boy Friends)(Formerly Four Teeners; Glamorous Romances No. 41 on)
Ace Magazines (A. A. Wyn): No. 35, June, 1948 - No. 40, May, 1949
35-Teen-age 9 18 27 50 65 80
36-40: 37-Transvestism story 7 14 21 35 43 50

DOTTY DRIPPLE (Horace & Dotty Dripple No. 25 on)
Magazine Ent.(Life's Romances)/Harvey No. 3 on: 1946 - No. 24, June, 1952 (Also see A-1 No. 1, 3-8, 10)
1 (nd) (10¢) 12 24 36 67 94 120
2 8 16 24 40 50 60
3-10: 3,4-Powell-a 6 12 18 31 38 45
11-24 6 12 18 27 33 38

DOTTY DRIPPLE AND TAFFY
Dell Publishing Co.: No. 646, Sept, 1955 - No. 903, May, 1958
Four Color 646 (#1) 5 10 15 32 51 70
Four Color 691,718,746,801,903 4 8 12 22 34 45

DOUBLE ACTION COMICS
National Periodical Publications: No. 2, Jan, 1940 (68 pgs., B&W)
2-Contains original stories(?); pre-hero DC contents; same cover as Adventure No. 37. (seven known copies, five in high grade) (not an ashcan)
2050 4100 6150 12,500 16,500 20,500
NOTE: *The cover to this book was probably reprinted from Adventure #37. #1 exists as an ash can copy with B&W cover; contains a coverless comic on inside with 1st & last page missing. There is proof of at least limited newsstand distribution. #2 cover proof only sold in 2005 for $4,000.*

DOUBLE COMICS
Elliot Publications: 1940 - 1944 (132 pgs.)
1940 issues; Masked Marvel-c & The Mad Mong vs. The White Flash covers known
258 516 774 1651 2826 4000
1941 issues; Tornado Tim-c, Nordac-c, & Green Light covers known
171 342 513 1086 1868 2650
1942 issues 123 246 369 787 1344 1900
1943,1944 issues 100 200 300 635 1093 1550
NOTE: *Double Comics consisted of an almost endless combination of pairs of remaindered, unsold issues of comics representing most publishers and usually mixed publishers in the same book; e.g., a Captain America with a Silver Streak, or a Feature with a Detective, etc., could appear inside the same cover. The actual contents would have to determine its price. Prices listed are for average contents. Any containing rare origin or first issues are worth much more. Covers also vary in same year. Value would be approximately 50 percent of contents.*

DOUBLE-CROSS (See The Crusaders)

DOUBLE-DARE ADVENTURES
Harvey Publications: Dec, 1966 - No. 2, Mar, 1967 (35¢/25¢, 68 pgs.)
1-Origin Bee-Man, Glowing Gladiator, & Magic-Master; Simon/Kirby-a (last S&K art as a team?) 6 12 18 43 69 95
2-Torres-a; r/Alarming Adv. #3('63) 5 10 15 30 48 65
NOTE: *Powell a-1. Simon/Sparling c-1, 2.*

DOUBLE DRAGON
Marvel Comics: July, 1991 - No. 6, Dec, 1991 ($1.00, limited series)
1-6: Based on video game. 2-Art Adams-c 3.00

DOUBLE EDGE
Marvel Comics: Alpha, 1995; Omega, 1995 ($4.95, limited series)
Alpha ($4.95)- Punisher story, Nick Fury app. 5.00
Omega ($4.95)-Punisher, Daredevil, Ghost Rider app. Death of Nick Fury 5.00

DOUBLE IMAGE
Image Comics: Feb, 2001 - No. 5, July, 2001 ($2.95)
1-5: 1-Flip covers of Codeflesh (Casey-s/Adlard-a) and The Bod (Young-s). 2-Two covers. 5-"Trust in Me" begins; Chaudhary-a 3.00

DOUBLE LIFE OF PRIVATE STRONG, THE
Archie Publications/Radio Comics: June, 1959 - No. 2, Aug, 1959
1-Origin & re-intro The Shield; Simon & Kirby-c/a, their re-entry into the super-hero genre; intro./1st app. The Fly; 1st S.A. super-hero for Archie Publ.
41 82 123 326 656 985
2-S&K-c/a; Tuska-a; The Fly app. (2nd or 3rd?) 26 52 78 186 373 560

DOUBLE TROUBLE
St. John Publishing Co.: Nov, 1957 - No. 2, Jan-Feb, 1958
1,2: Tuffy & Snuffy by Frank Johnson; dubbed "World's Funniest Kids"
6 12 18 31 38 45

DOUBLE TROUBLE WITH GOOBER
Dell Publishing Co.: No. 417, Aug, 1952 - No. 556, May, 1954
Four Color 417 4 8 12 28 44 60
Four Color 471,516,556 4 8 12 22 34 45

DOUBLE UP
Elliott Publications: 1941 (Pocket size, 200 pgs.)
1-Contains rebound copies of digest sized issues of Pocket Comics, Speed Comics, & Spitfire Comics 84 168 252 538 919 1300

DOVER & CLOVER (See All Funny & More Fun Comics #93)

DOVER BOYS (See Adventures of the...)

DOVER THE BIRD
Famous Funnies Publishing Co.: Spring, 1955
1-Funny animal; code approved 7 14 21 35 43 50

DOWN
Image Comics (Top Cow): Dec, 2005 - No. 4, Mar, 2006 ($2.99)
1-4-Warren Ellis-s. 1-Tony Harris-a/c. 2-4-Cully Hamner-a 3.00

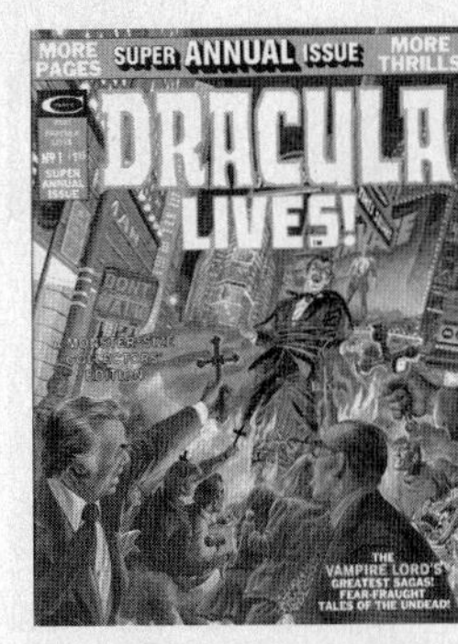

Dracula Lives! #1 © MAR

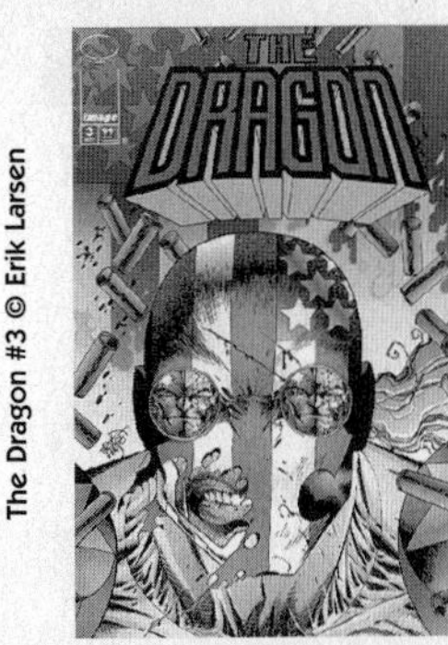

The Dragon #3 © Erik Larsen

Dragon Age #2 © EA

	GD 2.0	VG 4.0	FN 6.0	VF 8.0	VF/NM 9.0	NM- 9.2
Down & Top Cow's Best of Warren Ellis TPB (6/06, $15.99) r/#1-4 & Tales of the Witchblade #3,4; Ellis-s; script for Down #1 with Harris sketch pages						16.00

DOWN WITH CRIME
Fawcett Publications: Nov, 1952 - No. 7, Nov, 1953

	GD	VG	FN	VF	VF/NM	NM-
1	37	74	111	222	361	500
2,4,5: 2,4-Powell-a in each. 5-Bondage-c	19	38	57	111	176	240
3-Used in **POP**, pg. 106; "H is for Heroin" drug story	21	42	63	126	206	285
6,7: 6-Used in **POP**, pg. 80	16	32	48	94	147	200

DO YOU BELIEVE IN NIGHTMARES?
St. John Publishing Co.: Nov, 1957 - No. 2, Jan, 1958

	GD	VG	FN	VF	VF/NM	NM-
1-Mostly Ditko-c/a	51	102	153	322	549	775
2-Ayers-a	29	58	87	170	278	385

D.P. 7
Marvel Comics Group (New Universe): Nov, 1986 - No. 32, June, 1989

	GD	VG	FN	VF	VF/NM	NM-
1-20, Annual #1 (11/87)-Intro. The Witness						3.00
21-32-Low print						4.00
... Classic Vol. 1 TPB (2007, $24.99) r/#1-9; Mark Gruenwald-s/Paul Ryan-a in all						25.00

NOTE: ***Williamson** a-9i, 11i; c-9i.*

DRACULA (See Bram Stoker's Dracula, Giant-Size..., Little Dracula, Marvel Graphic Novel, Requiem for Dracula, Spider-Man Vs...., Stoker's..., Tomb of... & Wedding of...; also see Movie Classics under Universal Presents as well as Dracula)

DRACULA (See Movie Classics for #1)(Also see Frankenstein & Werewolf)
Dell Publ. Co.: No. 2, 11/66 - No. 4, 3/67; No. 6, 7/72 - No. 8, 7/73 (No #5)

	GD	VG	FN	VF	VF/NM	NM-
2-Origin & 1st app. Dracula (11/66) (super hero)	5	10	15	30	48	65
3,4: 4-Intro. Fleeta ('67)	3	6	9	20	30	40
6-('72)-r/#2 w/origin	3	6	9	15	21	26
7,8-r/#3, #4	2	4	6	11	16	20

DRACULA (Magazine)
Warren Publishing Co.: 1979 (120 pgs., full color)

	GD	VG	FN	VF	VF/NM	NM-
Book 1-Maroto art; Spanish material translated into English (mail order only)	6	12	18	41	66	90

DRACULA
Marvel Comics: Jul, 2010 - No. 4, Sept, 2010 ($3.99, limited series)

	GD	VG	FN	VF	VF/NM	NM-
1-4-Colored reprint of Bram Stoker's Classic Dracula adapt. from Dracula Lives!, Legion of Monsters and Stoker's Dracula; Thomas-s/Giordano-a; J. Djurdjevic-c						4.00

DRACULA CHRONICLES
Topps Comics: Apr, 1995 - No. 3, June, 1995 ($2.50, limited series)

	GD	VG	FN	VF	VF/NM	NM-
1-3-Linsner-c						3.00

DRACULA LIVES! (Magazine)(Also see Tomb of Dracula) (Reprinted in Stoker's Dracula)
Marvel Comics Group: 1973(no month) - No. 13, July, 1975 (75¢, B&W) (76 pgs.)

	GD	VG	FN	VF	VF/NM	NM-
1-Boris painted-c	8	16	24	52	86	120
2 (7/73)-1st time origin Dracula; Adams, Starlin-a	5	10	15	35	55	75
3-1st app. Robert E. Howard's Soloman Kane; Adams-c/a	5	10	15	35	55	75
4,5: 4-Ploog-a. 5(V2#1)-Bram Stoker's Classic Dracula adapt. begins	4	8	12	24	37	50
6-9: 6-8-Bram Stoker adapt. 9-Bondage-c	4	8	12	24	37	50
10 (1/75)-16 pg. Lilith solo (1st?)	4	8	12	28	44	60
11-13: 11-21 pg. Lilith solo sty. 12-31 pg. Dracula sty	4	8	12	24	37	50
Annual 1(Summer, 1975, $1.25, 92 pgs.)-Morrow painted-c; 6 Dracula stys. 25 pgs. Adams-a(r)	4	8	12	26	41	55

NOTE: ***N. Adams** a-2, 3i, 10i, Annual 1r(2, 3i). **Alcala** a-9. **Buscema** a-3p, 6p, Annual 1p. **Colan** a(p)-1, 2, 5, 6, 8. **Evans** a-7. **Gulacy** a-9. **Heath** a-1r, 13. **Pakula** a-6r. Sutton a-13.**Weiss** r-Annual 1p. 4 **Dracula** stories each in 1, 609; 3 **Dracula** stories each in 2, 4, 5,, 13.*

DRACULA: LORD OF THE UNDEAD
Marvel Comics: Dec, 1998 - No. 3, Dec, 1998 ($2.99, limited series)

	GD	VG	FN	VF	VF/NM	NM-
1-3-Olliffe & Palmer-a						3.00

DRACULA: RETURN OF THE IMPALER
Slave Labor Graphics: July, 1993 - No. 4, Oct, 1994 ($2.95, limited series)

	GD	VG	FN	VF	VF/NM	NM-
1-4						3.00

DRACULA'S REVENGE
IDW Publishing: Apr, 2004 - No. 3 ($3.99, limited series)

	GD	VG	FN	VF	VF/NM	NM-
1,2-Forbeck-s/Kudranski-a						4.00

DRACULA: THE COMPANY OF MONSTERS
BOOM! Studios: Aug, 2010 - Present ($3.99)

	GD	VG	FN	VF	VF/NM	NM-
1-6: 1-5-Busiek & Gregory-s/Godlewski-a. 1-Two covers by Brereton and Salas						4.00

DRACULA VERSUS ZORRO
Topps Comics: Oct, 1993 - No. 2, Nov, 1993 ($2.95, limited series)

	GD	VG	FN	VF	VF/NM	NM-
1,2: 1-Spot varnish & red foil-c. 2-Polybagged w/16 pg. Zorro #0						3.00

DRACULA VERSUS ZORRO
Dark Horse Comics: Sept, 1998 - No. 2, Oct, 1998 ($2.95, limited series)

	GD	VG	FN	VF	VF/NM	NM-
1,2						3.00

DRACULA: VLAD THE IMPALER (Also see Bram Stoker's Dracula)
Topps Comics: Feb, 1993 - No. 3, Apr, 1993 ($2.95, limited series)

	GD	VG	FN	VF	VF/NM	NM-
1-3-Polybagged with 3 trading cards each; Maroto-c/a						3.00

DRAFT, THE
Marvel Comics: 1988 ($3.50, one-shot, squarebound)

	GD	VG	FN	VF	VF/NM	NM-
1-Sequel to "The Pitt"						4.00

DRAFTED: ONE HUNDRED DAYS
Devil's Due Publishing: June, 2009 ($5.99, one-shot)

	GD	VG	FN	VF	VF/NM	NM-
1-Barack Obama on a post-galactic-war Earth; Powers-s						6.00

DRAG 'N' WHEELS (Formerly Top Eliminator)
Charlton Comics: No. 30, Sept, 1968 - No. 59, May, 1973

	GD	VG	FN	VF	VF/NM	NM-
30	4	8	12	28	44	60
31-40-Scot Jackson begins	3	6	9	19	29	38
41-50	3	6	9	17	25	32
51-59: Scot Jackson	2	4	6	13	18	22
Modern Comics Reprint 58('78)						5.00

DRAGON, THE (Also see The Savage Dragon)
Image Comics (Highbrow Ent.): Mar, 1996 - No. 5, July, 1996 (99¢, lim. series)

	GD	VG	FN	VF	VF/NM	NM-
1-5: Reprints Savage Dragon limited series w/new story & art. 5-Youngblood app; includes 5 pg. Savage Dragon story from 1984						3.00

DRAGON AGE (Based on the EA videogame)
IDW Publishing (EA Comics): Mar, 2010 - No. 6, Nov, 2010 ($3.99)

	GD	VG	FN	VF	VF/NM	NM-
1-6-Orson Scott Card & Aaron Johnston-s; Ramos-c						4.00

DRAGON ARCHIVES, THE (Also see The Savage Dragon)
Image Comics: Jun, 1998 - No. 4, Jan, 1999 ($2.95, B&W)

	GD	VG	FN	VF	VF/NM	NM-
1-4: Reprints early Savage Dragon app.						3.00

DRAGON BALL
Viz Comics: Mar, 1998 - Part 6: #2, Feb, 2003($2.95, B&W, Manga reprints read right to left)

	GD	VG	FN	VF	VF/NM	NM-
Part 1: 1-Akira Toriyama-s/a						6.00
2-12						5.00
1-12 (2nd & 3rd printings)						3.00
Part 2: 1-15: 15-($3.50-c)						4.00
Part 3: 1-14						3.00
Part 4: 1-10						3.00
Part 5: 1-7						3.00
Part 6: 1,2						3.50

DRAGON BALL Z
Viz Comics: Mar, 1998 - Part 5: #10, Oct, 2002 ($2.95, B&W, Manga reprints read right to left)

	GD	VG	FN	VF	VF/NM	NM-
Part 1: 1-Akira Toriyama-s/a	2	4	6	8	10	12
2-9						5.00
1-9 (2nd & 3rd printings)						3.00
Part 2: 1-14						4.00
Part 3: 1-10						3.00
Part 4: 1-15						3.00
Part 5: 1-10						3.00

DRAGON, THE: BLOOD & GUTS (Also see The Savage Dragon)
Image Comics (Highbrow Entertainment): Mar, 1995 - No. 3, May, 1995 ($2.50, lim. series)

	GD	VG	FN	VF	VF/NM	NM-
1-3: Jason Pearson-c/a/scripts						3.00

DRAGON CHIANG
Eclipse Books: 1991 ($3.95, B&W, squarebound, 52 pgs.)

	GD	VG	FN	VF	VF/NM	NM-
nn-Timothy Truman-c/a(p)						4.00

DRAGONFLIGHT
Eclipse Books: Feb, 1991 - No. 3, 1991 ($4.95, 52 pgs.)

	GD	VG	FN	VF	VF/NM	NM-
Book One - Three: Adapts 1968 novel						5.00

DRAGONFLY (See Americomics #4)
Americomics: Sum, 1985 - No. 8, 1986 ($1.75/$1.95)

	GD	VG	FN	VF	VF/NM	NM-
1						4.00
2-8						3.00

Dragon Lines #2 © MAR

Drakuun #19 © DH

Dreadstar #56 © FC

GD 2.0 | VG 4.0 | FN 6.0 | VF 8.0 | VF/NM 9.0 | NM- 9.2

DRAGONFORCE
Aircel Publishing: 1988 - No. 13, 1989 ($2.00)

1-Dale Keown-c/a/scripts in #1-12 3.50
2-13: 13-No Keown-a 3.00
...Chronicles Book 1-5 ($2.95, B&W, 60 pgs.): Dale Keown-r/Dragonring & Dragonforce 4.00

DRAGONHEART (Movie)
Topps Comics: May, 1996 - No. 2, June, 1996 ($2.95/$4.95, limited series)

1-($2.95, 24 pgs.)-Adaptation of the film; Hildebrandt Bros-c; Lim-a. 3.00
2-($4.95, 64 pgs.) 5.00

DRAGONLANCE (Also see TSR Worlds)
DC Comics: Dec, 1988 - No. 34, Sept, 1991 ($1.25/$1.50, Mando paper)

1-Based on TSR game 4.00
2-34: Based on TSR game. 30-32-Kaluta-c 3.00

DRAGONLANCE: CHRONICLES
Devil's Due Publ.: Aug, 2005 - No. 8, Mar, 2006 ($2.95)

1-8-Dabb-s/Kurth-a 3.00
...: Dragons of Autumn Twilight TPB (2006, $17.95) r/#1-8 18.00

DRAGONLANCE: CHRONICLES (Volume 2)
Devil's Due Publ.: July, 2006 - No. 4, Jan, 2007 ($4.95/$4.99, 48 pgs.)

1-4-Dragons of Winter Night; Dabb-s/Kurth-a 5.00
...: Dragons of Winter Night TPB (3/07, $18.99) r/#1-4; cover gallery 19.00

DRAGONLANCE: CHRONICLES (Volume 3)
Devil's Due Publ.: Mar, 2007 - No. 12, ($3.50)

1-11-Dragons of Spring Dawning; Dabb-s/Cope-a 3.50

DRAGONLANCE: THE LEGEND OF HUMA
Devil's Due Publ.: Jan, 2004 - No. 6, Oct, 2005 ($2.95)

1-6-Mike Miller & Rael-a 3.00

DRAGON LINES
Marvel Comics (Epic Comics/Heavy Hitters): May, 1993 - No. 4, Aug, 1993 ($1.95, limited series)

1-($2.50)-Embossed-c; Ron Lim-c/a in all 3.50
2-4 3.00

DRAGON LINES: WAY OF THE WARRIOR
Marvel Comics (Epic Comics/ Heavy Hitters): Nov, 1993 - No. 2, Jan, 1994 ($2.25, limited series)

1,2-Ron Lim-c/a(p) 3.00

DRAGON PRINCE
Image Comics (Top Cow): Sept, 2008 - No. 4, Jan, 2009 ($2.99)

1-4-Marz-s/Moder-a; two covers 3.00

DRAGONQUEST
Silverwolf Comics: Dec, 1986 - No. 2, 1987 ($1.50, B&W, 28 pgs.)

1,2-Tim Vigil-c/a in all 5.00

DRAGONRING
Aircel Publishing: 1986 - V2#15, 1988 ($1.70/$2.00, B&W/color)

1-6: 6-Last B&W issue, V2#1-15($2.00, color) 3.00

DRAGON'S CLAWS
Marvel UK, Ltd.: July, 1988 - No. 10, Apr, 1989 ($1.25/$1.50/$1.75, British)

1-10: 3-Death's Head 1 pg. strip on back-c (1st app.). 4-Silhouette of Death's Head on last pg. 5-1st full app. new Death's Head 3.00

DRAGON'S LAIR: SINGE'S REVENGE (Based on the Don Bluth video game)
CrossGen Comics: Sept, 2003 - No. 3 ($2.95, limited series)

1-3-Mangels-s/Laguna-a 3.00

DRAGONSLAYER (Movie)
Marvel Comics Group: October, 1981 - No. 2, Nov, 1981

1,2-Paramount Disney movie adaptation 3.00

DRAGOON WELLS MASSACRE
Dell Publishing Co.: No. 815, June, 1957

Four Color 815-Movie, photo-c 7 14 21 50 83 115

DRAGSTRIP HOTRODDERS (World of Wheels No. 17 on)
Charlton Comics: Sum, 1963; No. 2, Jan, 1965 - No. 16, Aug, 1967

1 7 14 21 49 80 110
2-5 4 8 12 26 41 55
6-16 4 8 12 22 34 45

GD 2.0 | VG 4.0 | FN 6.0 | VF 8.0 | VF/NM 9.0 | NM- 9.2

DRAIN
Image Comics: Nov, 2006 - No. 6, Mar, 2008 ($2.99)

1-6: 1-Cebulski-s/Takeda-a; two covers by Takeda and Finch 3.00
Vol. 1 TPB (2008, $16.99) r/#1-6; cover gallery and Takeda sketch art gallery 17.00

DRAKUUN
Dark Horse Comics: Feb, 1997 - No. 25, Mar, 1999 ($2.95, B&W, manga)

1-25; 1-6- Johji Manabe-s/a in all. Rise of the Dragon Princess series. 7-12-Revenge of Gustav. 13-18-Shadow of the Warlock. 19-25-The Hidden War 3.00

DRAMA
Sirius: June, 1994 ($2.95, mature)

1-1st full color Dawn app. in comics 2 4 6 11 16 20
1-Limited edition (1400 copies); signed & numbered; fingerprint authenticity 4 8 12 24 37 50

NOTE: *Dawn's 1st full color app. was a pin-up in Amazing Heroes' Swimsuit Special #5.*

DRAMA OF AMERICA, THE
Action Text: 1973 ($1.95, 224 pgs.)

1- "Students' Supplement to History" 1 3 4 6 8 10

DRAWING ON YOUR NIGHTMARES
Dark Horse Comics: Oct, 2003 ($2.99, one-shot)

1-Short stories; The Goon, Criminal Macabre, Tales of the Vampires; Templesmith-c 3.00

DRAX THE DESTROYER
Marvel Comics: Nov, 2005 - No. 4, Feb, 2006 ($2.99, limited series)

1-4-Giffen-s/Breitweiser-a 3.00
...: Earthfall TPB (2006, $10.99) r/#1-4; character design page 11.00

DREADLANDS (Also see Epic)
Marvel Comics (Epic Comics): 1992 - No. 4, 1992 ($3.95, lim. series, 52 pgs.)

1-4: Stiff-c 4.00

DREADSTAR (See Epic Illustrated #3 for 1st app. and Eclipse Graphic Album Series #5)
Marvel Comics (Epic Comics)/First Comics No. 27 on: Nov, 1982 - No. 64, Mar, 1991

1 4.00
2-5,8-49 3.00
6,7,51-64: 6,7-1st app. Interstellar Toybox; 8pgs. ea.; Wrightson-a. 51-64-Lower print run 4.00
50 5.00
Annual 1 (12/83)-r/The Price (Eclipse Graphic Album Series #5) 4.00

DREADSTAR
Malibu Comics (Bravura): Apr, 1994 - No. 6, Jan, 1995 ($2.50, limited series)

1-6-Peter David scripts: 1,2-Starlin-c 3.00

NOTE: *Issues 1-6 contain Bravura stamps.*

DREADSTAR AND COMPANY
Marvel Comics (Epic Comics): July, 1985 - No. 6, Dec, 1985

1-6: 1,3,6-New Starlin-a: 2-New Wrightson-c; reprints of Dreadstar series 3.00

DREAM BOOK OF LOVE (Also see A-1 Comics)
Magazine Enterprises: No. 106, June-July, 1954 - No. 123, Oct-Nov, 1954

A-1 106 (#1)-Powell, Bolle-a; Montgomery Clift, Donna Reed photo-c 14 28 42 80 115 150
A-1-114 (#2)-Guardineer, Bolle-a; Piper Laurie, Victor Mature photo-c 10 20 30 58 79 100
A-1 123 (#3)-Movie photo-c 10 20 30 54 72 90

DREAM BOOK OF ROMANCE (Also see A-1 Comics)
Magazine Enterprises: No. 92, 1954 - No. 124, Oct-Nov, 1954

A-1 92 (#5)-Guardineer-a; photo-c 14 28 42 76 108 140
A-1 101 (#6)(4-6/54)-Marlon Brando photo-c; Powell, Bolle, Guardineer-a 22 44 66 128 209 290
A-1 109,110,124: 109 (#7)(7-8/54)-Powell-a; movie photo-c. 110 (#8)(1/54)-Movie photo-c. 124 (#8)(10-11/54) 11 22 33 60 83 105

DREAMER, THE
Kitchen Sink Press: 1986 ($6.95, B&W, graphic novel)

nn-Will Eisner-s/a 12.00
DC Comics Reprint ($7.95, 6/00) 8.00

DREAMERY, THE
Eclipse Comics: Dec, 1986 - No. 14, Feb, 1989 ($2.00, B&W, Baxter paper)

1-14: 2-7-Alice In Wonderland adapt. 3.00

DREAMING, THE (See Sandman, 2nd Series)
DC Comics (Vertigo): June, 1996 - No. 60, May, 2001 ($2.50)

1-McKean-c on all.; LaBan scripts & Snejbjerg-a 4.00

The Dreaming #24 © DC

Droopy #1 © Turner Ent.

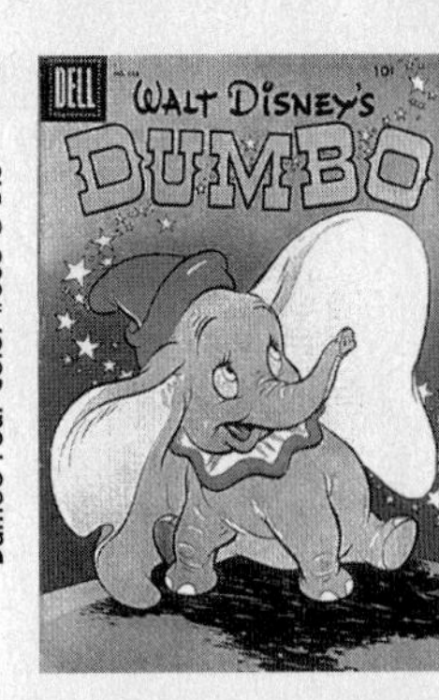

Dumbo Four Color #668 © DIS

GD 2.0 | VG 4.0 | FN 6.0 | VF 8.0 | VF/NM 9.0 | NM- 9.2

GD 2.0 | VG 4.0 | FN 6.0 | VF 8.0 | VF/NM 9.0 | NM- 9.2

2-30,32-60: 2,3-LaBan scripts & Snejbjerg-a. 4-7-Hogan scripts; Parkhouse-a. 8-Zulli-a. 9-11-Talbot-s/Taylor-a(p). 41-Previews Sandman: The Dream Hunters. 50-Hempel, Fegredo, McManus, Totleben-a 3.00
31-($3.95) Art by various 4.00
...Beyond The Shores of Night TPB ('97, $19.95) r/#1-8 20.00
...Special (7/98, $5.95, one-shot) Trial of Cain 6.00
...Through The Gates of Horn and Ivory TPB ('99, $19.95) r/#15-19,22-25 20.00

DREAM OF LOVE
I. W. Enterprises: 1958 (Reprints)

1,2,8: 1-r/Dream Book of Love #1; Bob Powell-a. 2-r/Great Lover's Romances #10. 8-Great Lover's Romances #1; also contains 2 Jon Juan stories by Siegel & Schomburg; Kinstler-c. 2 4 6 10 14 18
9-Kinstler-c; 1pg. John Wayne interview & Frazetta illo from John Wayne Adv. Comics #2 2 4 6 10 14 18

DREAM POLICE
Marvel Comics (Icon): Aug, 2005 ($3.99)

1-Straczynski-s/Deodato-a/c 4.00

DREAMS OF THE DARKCHYLDE
Darkchylde Entertainment: Oct, 2000 - No. 6, Sept, 2001 ($2.95)

1-6-Randy Queen-s in all. 1-Brandon Peterson-c/a 3.00

DREAM TEAM (See Battlezones: Dream Team 2)
Malibu Comics (Ultraverse): July, 1995 ($4.95, one-shot)

1-Pin-ups teaming up Marvel & Ultraverse characters by various artists including Allred, Romita, Darrow, Balent, Quesada & Palmiotti 5.00

DREAMWAVE PRODUCTIONS PREVIEW
Dreamwave Productions: May, 2002 ($1.00, one-shot)

nn-Previews Arkanium, Transformers: The War Within and other series 3.00

DRESDEN FILES (See Jim Butcher's...)

DRIFT FENCE (See Zane Grey 4-Color 270)

DRIFT MARLO
Dell Publishing Co.: May-July, 1962 - No. 2, Oct-Dec, 1962

01-232-207 (#1) 5 10 15 32 51 70
2 (12-232-212) 4 8 12 28 44 60

DRISCOLL'S BOOK OF PIRATES
David McKay Publ. (Not reprints): 1934 (B&W, hardcover; 124 pgs, 7x9")

nn-By Montford Amory 23 46 69 136 223 310

DROIDS (Based on Saturday morning cartoon) (Also see Dark Horse Comics)
Marvel Comics (Star Comics): April, 1986 - No. 8, June, 1987

1-R2D2 & C-3PO from Star Wars app. in all 2 4 6 11 16 20
2-8: 2,5,7,8-Williamson-a(i) 2 4 6 8 10 12
NOTE: ***Romita** a-3p. **Sinnott** a-3i.*

DROOPY (see Tom & Jerry #60)

DROOPY (Tex Avery's...)
Dark Horse Comics: Oct, 1995 - No. 3, Dec, 1995 ($2.50, limited series)

1-3: Characters created by Tex Avery; painted-c 3.00

DROPSIE AVENUE: THE NEIGHBORHOOD
Kitchen Sink Press: June, 1995 ($15.95/$24.95, B&W)

nn-Will Eisner (softcover) 16.00
nn-Will Eisner (hardcover) 25.00

DROWNED GIRL, THE
DC Comics (Piranha Press): 1990 ($5.95, 52 pgs, mature)

nn 6.00

DRUG WARS
Pioneer Comics: 1989 ($1.95)

1-Grell-c 3.00

DRUID
Marvel Comics: May, 1995 - No. 4, Aug, 1995 ($2.50, limited series)

1-4: Warren Ellis scripts. 3.00

DRUM BEAT
Dell Publishing Co.: No. 610, Jan, 1955

Four Color 610-Movie, Alan Ladd photo-c 8 16 24 56 93 130

DRUMS OF DOOM
United Features Syndicate: 1937 (25¢)(Indian)(Text w/color illos.)

nn-By Lt. F.A. Methot; Golden Thunder app.; Tip Top Comics ad in comic; nice-c 36 72 108 216 351 485

DRUNKEN FIST
Jademan Comics: Aug, 1988 - No. 54, Jan, 1993 ($1.50/$1.95, 68 pgs.)

1 5.00
2-50 4.00
51-54 4.00

DUCK ALBUM (See Donald Duck Album)
Dell Publishing Co.: No. 353, Oct, 1951 - No. 840, Sept, 1957

Four Color 353 (#1)-Barks-c; 1st Uncle Scrooge-c (also appears on back-c). 10 20 30 69 122 175
Four Color 450-Barks-c 7 14 21 49 80 110
Four Color 492,531,560,586,611,649,686, 6 12 18 41 66 90
Four Color 726,782,840 5 10 15 35 55 75

DUCKMAN
Dark Horse Comics: Sept, 1990 ($1.95, B&W, one-shot)

1-Story & art by Everett Peck 4.00

DUCKMAN
Topps Comics: Nov, 1994 - No. 5, May, 1995; No. 0, Feb, 1996 ($2.50)

0 (2/96, $2.95, B&W)-r/Duckman #1 from Dark Horse Comics 4.00
1-5: 1-w/ coupon #A for Duckman trading card. 2-w/Duckman 1st season episode guide 3.00

DUCKMAN: THE MOB FROG SAGA
Topps Comics: Nov, 1994 - No. 3, Feb, 1995 ($2.50, limited series)

1-3: 1-w/coupon #B for Duckman trading card, S. Shaw!-c 3.00

DUCKTALES
Gladstone Publ.: Oct, 1988 - No. 13, May, 1990 (1,2,9-11: $1.50; 3-8: 95¢)

1-Barks-r 6.00
2-11: 2-7,9-11-Barks-r 4.00
12,13 ($1.95, 68 pgs.)-Barks-r; 12-r/F.C. #495 5.00
Disney Presents Carl Barks' Greatest DuckTales Stories Vol. 1 (Gemstone Publ., 2006, $10.95) r/stories adapted for the animated TV series including "Back to the Klondike" 11.00
Disney Presents Carl Barks' Greatest DuckTales Stories Vol. 2 (Gemstone Publ., 2006, $10.95) r/stories adapted for the animated TV series; "Robot Robbers" app. 11.00

DUCKTALES (TV)
Disney Comics: June, 1990 - No. 18, Nov, 1991 ($1.50)

1-All new stories; Marv Wolfman-s 3.50
2-18 3.00
Disney's DuckTales by Marv Wolfman: Scrooge's Quest TPB (Gemstone, 9/07, $15.99) r/#1-7; intro. by Wolfman 16.00
Disney's DuckTales: The Gold Odyssey TPB (Gemstone, 10/08, $15.99) 16.00
The Movie nn (1990, $7.95, 68 pgs.)-Graphic novel adapting animated movie 8.00

DUDLEY (Teen-age)
Feature/Prize Publications: Nov-Dec, 1949 - No. 3, Mar-Apr, 1950

1-By Boody Rogers 15 30 45 84 127 170
2,3 10 20 30 56 76 95

DUDLEY DO-RIGHT (TV)
Charlton Comics: Aug, 1970 - No. 7, Aug, 1971 (Jay Ward)

1 9 18 27 61 103 145
2-7 6 12 18 43 69 95

DUEL MASTERS (Based on a trading card game) (Also see Free Comic Book Day Edition in the Promotional Comics section)
Dreamwave Productions: Nov, 2003 - Present ($2.95)

1-8: 1-Bagged with card; Augustyn-s 3.00

DUKE OF THE K-9 PATROL
Gold Key: Apr, 1963

1 (10052-304) 4 8 12 24 37 50

DUMBO (Disney; see Movie Comics, & Walt Disney Showcase #12)
Dell Publishing Co.: No. 17, 1941 - No. 668, Jan, 1958

Four Color 17 (#1)-Mickey Mouse, Donald Duck, Pluto app. 265 530 795 1694 2897 4100
Large Feature Comic 19 ('41)-Part-r 4-Color 17 297 594 891 1888 3244 4600
Four Color 234 ('49) 13 26 39 93 182 270
Four Color 668 (12/55)-1st of two printings. Dumbo on-c with starry sky. Same-c as #234 10 20 30 70 125 180
Four Color 668 (1/58)-2nd printing. Same cover altered with Timothy Mouse added. Same contents 7 14 21 45 73 100

Durango Kid #28 © ME

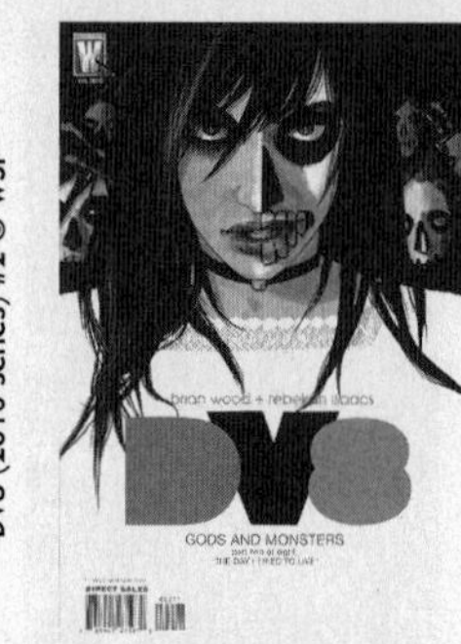

DV8 (2010 series) #2 © WSP

Dynamic Comics #9 © CHES

GD VG FN VF VF/NM NM-
2.0 4.0 6.0 8.0 9.0 9.2

DUMBO COMIC PAINT BOOK (See Dumbo, Large Feature Comic No. 19)

DUNC AND LOO (#1-3 titled "Around the Block with Dunc and Loo")
Dell Publishing Co.: Oct-Dec, 1961 - No. 8, Oct-Dec, 1963

1 8 16 24 52 86 120
2 6 12 18 37 59 80
3-8 4 8 12 28 44 60
NOTE: *Written by **John Stanley**; **Bill Williams** art.*

DUNE (Movie)
Marvel Comics: Apr, 1985 - No. 3, June, 1985

1-3-r/Marvel Super Special; movie adaptation 3.00

DUNGEONS & DRAGONS
IDW Publishing: No. 0, Aug, 2010 - Present ($1.00/$3.99)

0-(8/10, $1.00) Five covers; previews D&D series and Dark Sun mini-series 1.00
1-4: 1-(11/10, $3.99) Di Vito-a/Rogers-s; two covers. 2-Two covers 4.00

DURANGO KID, THE (Also see Best of the West, Great Western & White Indian)
(Charles Starrett starred in Columbia's Durango Kid movies)
Magazine Enterprises: Oct-Nov, 1949 - No. 41, Oct-Nov, 1955 (All 36 pgs.)

1-Charles Starrett photo-c; Durango Kid & his horse Raider begin; Dan Brand & Tipi (origin) begin by Frazetta & continue through #16 71 142 213 454 777 1100
2-Starrett photo-c. 34 68 102 199 325 450
3-5-All have Starrett photo-c. 29 58 87 172 281 390
6-10: 7-Atomic weapon-c/story 16 32 48 94 147 200
11-16-Last Frazetta issue 14 28 42 80 115 150
17-Origin Durango Kid 16 32 48 94 147 200
18-30: 18-Fred Meagher-a on Dan Brand begins.19-Guardineer-c/a(3) begins, end #41. 23-Intro. The Red Scorpion 10 20 30 54 72 90
31-Red Scorpion returns 9 18 27 52 69 85
32-41-Bolle/Frazetta*ish*-a (Dan Brand; true in later issues?) 9 18 27 50 65 80
NOTE: *#6, 8, 14, 15 contain **Frazetta** art not reprinted in White Indian. **Ayers** c-18. **Guardineer** a(3)-19-41; c-19-41. **Fred Meagher** a-18-29 at least.*

DURANGO KID, THE
AC Comics: 1990 - #2, 1990 ($2.50,$2.75, half-color)

1,2: 1-Starrett photo front/back-c; Guardineer-r. 2-B&W)-Starrett photo-c; White Indian-r by Frazetta; Guardineer-r (50th anniversary of films) 3.00

DUSTCOVERS: THE COLLECTED SANDMAN COVERS 1989-1997
DC Comics (Vertigo): 1997 ($39.95, Hardcover)

Reprints Dave McKean's Sandman covers with Gaiman text 40.00
Softcover (1998, $24.95) 25.00

DUSTY STAR
Image Comics (Desperado Studios): No. 0, Apr, 1997 - No. 1 ($2.95, B&W)

0,1-Pruett-s/Robinson-a 3.00

DUSTY STAR
Image Comics (Desperado Publishing): June, 2006 ($3.50)

1-Pruett-s/Robinson-s/a 3.50

DV8 (See Gen 13)
Image Comics (WildStorm Productions): Aug, 1996 - No. 25, Dec, 1998;
DC Comics (WildStorm Prod.): No. 0, Apr, 1999 - No. 32, Nov, 1999 ($2.50)

1/2 6.00
1-Warren Ellis scripts & Humberto Ramos-c/a(p) 4.00
1-(7-variant covers, w/1 by Jim Lee) ...each 4.00
2-4: 3-No Ramos-a 3.00
5-32: 14-Regular-c, 14-Variant-c by Charest. 26-(5/99)-McGuinness-c 3.00
14-($3.50) Voyager Pack w/Danger Girl preview 5.00
0-(4/99, $2.95) Two covers (Rio and McGuinness) 3.00
Annual 1 (1/98, $2.95) 4.00
Annual 1999 ($3.50) Slipstream x-over with Gen13 4.00
Rave-(7/96, $1.75)-Ramos-c; pinups & interviews 3.00
...: Neighborhood Threat TPB (2002, $14.95) r/#1-6 & #1/2; Ellis intro.; Ramos-c 15.00

DV8: GODS AND MONSTERS
DC Comics (WildStorm): June, 2010 - No. 8, Jan, 2011 ($2.99, limited series)

1-8-Wood-s/Issacs-a 3.00

DV8 VS. BLACK OPS
Image Comics (WildStorm): Oct, 1997 - No. 3, Dec, 1997 ($2.50, limited series)

1-3-Bury-s/Norton-a 3.00

DWIGHT D. EISENHOWER
Dell Publishing Co.: December, 1969

01-237-912 - Life story 5 10 15 30 48 65

DYNABRITE COMICS
Whitman Publishing Co.: 1978 - 1979 (69¢, 10x7-1/8", 48 pgs., cardboard-c)
(Blank inside covers)

11350 - Walt Disney's Mickey Mouse & the Beanstalk (4-C 157). 11350-1 - Mickey Mouse Album (4-C 1057, 1151,1246). 11351 - Mickey Mouse & His Sky Adventure (4-C 214, 343). 11354 - Goofy: A Gaggle of Giggles. 11354-1 - Super Goof Meets Super Thief. 11356 - (?). 11359 - Bugs Bunny-r. 11360 - Winnie the Pooh Fun and Fantasy (Disney-r).
each.... 2 4 6 9 12 15
11352 - Donald Duck (4-C 408, Donald Duck 45,52)-Barks-a. 11352-1 - Donald Duck (4-C 318, 10 pg. Barks/ WDC&S 125,128)-Barks-c(r). 11353 - Daisy Duck's Diary (4-C 1055,1150) Barks-a. 11355 - Uncle Scrooge (Barks-a/U.S. 12,33). 11355-1 - Uncle Scrooge (Barks-a/U.S. 13,16) - Barks-c(r). 11357 - Star Trek (r/-Star Trek 33,41). 11358 - Star Trek (r/-Star Trek 34,36). 11361 - Gyro Gearloose & the Disney Ducks (r/4-C 1047,1184)-Barks-c(r)
each.... 2 4 6 10 14 18

DYNAMIC ADVENTURES
I. W. Enterprises: No. 8, 1964 - No. 9, 1964

8-Kayo Kirby-r by Baker?/Fight Comics 53. 3 6 9 14 20 25
9-Reprints Avon's "Escape From Devil's Island"; Kinstler-c 3 6 9 16 23 30
nn (no date)-Reprints Risks Unlimited with Rip Carson, Senorita Rio; r/Fight #53 3 6 9 16 22 28

DYNAMIC CLASSICS (See Cancelled Comic Cavalcade)
DC Comics: Sept-Oct, 1978 (44 pgs.)

1-Neal Adams Batman, Simonson Manhunter-r 2 4 6 8 10 12

DYNAMIC COMICS (No #4-7)
Harry 'A' Chesler: Oct, 1941 - No. 3, Feb, 1942; No. 8, Mar, 1944 - No. 25, May, 1948

1-Origin Major Victory by Charles Sultan (reprinted in Major Victory #1), Dynamic Man & Hale the Magician; The Black Cobra only app.; Major Victory & Dynamic Man begin 213 426 639 1363 2332 3300
2-Origin Dynamic Boy & Lady Satan; intro. The Green Knight & sidekick Lance Cooper 97 194 291 621 1061 1500
3-1st small logo, resumes with #10 94 188 282 597 1024 1450
8-Classic-c; Dan Hastings, The Echo, The Master Key, Yankee Boy begin; Yankee Doodle Jones app.; hypo story 116 232 348 742 1271 1800
9-Mr. E begins; Mac Raboy-c 79 158 237 502 864 1225
10-Small logo begins 61 122 183 390 670 950
11-16: 15-The Sky Chief app. 16-Marijuana story 53 106 159 334 567 800
17(1/46)-Illustrated in **SOTI**, "The children told me what the man was going to do with the hot poker," but Wertham saw this in Crime Reporter #2 68 136 204 435 743 1050
18-Classic Airplanehead monster-c 57 114 171 362 619 875
19-Classic puppeteer-c by Gattuso 57 114 171 362 619 875
20-Bare-breasted woman-c 84 168 252 538 919 1300
21,22,25: 21-Dinosaur-c; new logo 42 84 126 265 445 625
23,24-(68 pgs.): 23-Yankee Girl app. 41 82 123 256 428 600
I.W. Reprint #1,8('64): 1-r/#23. 8-Exist? 3 7 10 18 27 35
NOTE: ***Kinstler** c-IW #1. **Tuska** art in many issues, #3, 9, 11, 12, 16, 19. Bondage c-16.*

DYNAMITE (Becomes Johnny Dynamite No. 10 on)
Comic Media/Allen Hardy Publ.: May, 1953 - No. 9, Sept, 1954

1-Pete Morisi-a; Don Heck-c; r-as Danger #6 37 74 111 222 361 500
2 20 40 60 114 182 250
3-Marijuana story; Johnny Dynamite (1st app.) begins by Pete Morisi(c/a); Heck text-a; man shot in face at close range 24 48 72 142 234 325
4-Injury-to-eye, prostitution; Morisi-c/a 22 44 66 132 216 300
5-9-Morisi-c/a in all. 7-Prostitute story & reprints 19 38 57 109 172 235

DYNAMO (Also see Tales of Thunder & T.H.U.N.D.E.R. Agents)
Tower Comics: Aug, 1966 - No. 4, June, 1967 (25¢)

1-Crandall/Wood, Ditko/Wood-a; Weed series begins; NoMan & Lightning cameos; Wood-c/a 9 18 27 63 107 150
2-4: Wood-c/a in all 6 12 18 39 62 85
NOTE: ***Adkins/Wood** a-2. **Ditko** a-4?. **Tuska** a-2, 3.*

DYNAMO 5 (See Noble Causes: Extended Family #2 for debut of Captain Dynamo)
Image Comics: Jan, 2007 - No. 25, Oct, 2009 ($3.50/$2.99)

1-Intro. the offspring of Captain Dynamo; Faerber-s/Asrar-a 8.00
2 5.00
3-7,11-24 : 5-Intro. Synergy. 13-Origin of Myriad. 21-Firebird app. 3.50
8-10-($2.99) 3.50
25-($4.99) Back-up short stories of team members 5.00
Annual #1 (4/08, $5.99) r/Captain Dynamo app. in Nobel Causes: Extended Family #2 and three new stories by Faerber & various; pin-up gallery 6.00

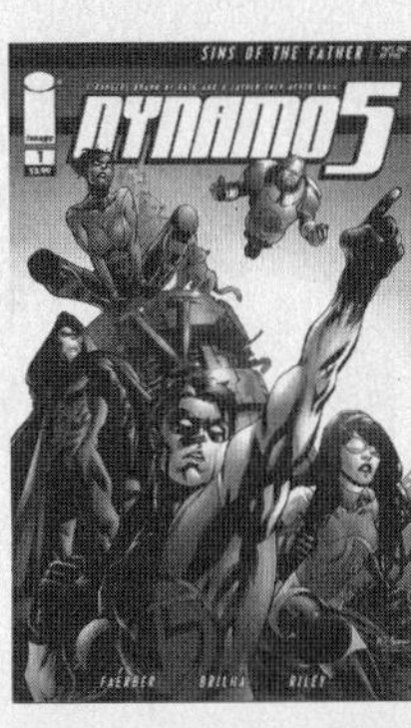

Dynamo 5: Sins of the Father #1 © Jay Faerber

The Eagle #2 © FOX

Echo #16 © Terry Moore

GD 2.0 | VG 4.0 | FN 6.0 | VF 8.0 | VF/NM 9.0 | NM- 9.2

#0 (2/09, 99¢) short story leading into #20; text synopsis of story so far 2.00
...: Holiday Special 2010 (12/10, $3.99) Faerber-s/Takara-a 4.00
... Vol. 1: Post-Nuclear Family TPB (2007, $9.99) r/#1-7; Kirkman intro. 10.00
... Vol. 2: Moments of Truth TPB (2008, $14.99) r/#8-13 15.00

DYNAMO 5: SINS OF THE FATHER
Image Comics: Jun, 2010 - No. 5, Oct, 2010 ($3.99, limited series)
1-5-Faerber-s/Brilha-a. 2-4-Invincible app. 4.00

DYNAMO JOE (Also see First Adventures & Mars)
First Comics: May, 1986 - No. 15, Jan, 1988 (#12-15: $1.75)
1-15: 4-Cargonauts begin, Special 1(1/87)-Mostly-r/Mars 3.00

DYNOMUTT (TV)(See Scooby-Doo (3rd series))
Marvel Comics Group: Nov, 1977 - No. 6, Sept, 1978 (Hanna-Barbera)
1-The Blue Falcon, Scooby Doo in all 4 8 12 26 41 55
2-6-All newsstand only 3 6 9 18 27 35

EAGLE, THE (1st Series) (See Science Comics & Weird Comics #8)
Fox Features Syndicate: July, 1941 - No. 4, Jan, 1942
1-The Eagle begins; Rex Dexter of Mars app. by Briefer; all issues feature German war covers 184 368 552 1168 2009 2850
2-The Spider Queen begins (origin) 87 174 261 553 952 1350
3,4: 3-Joe Spook begins (origin) 68 136 204 435 743 1050

EAGLE (2nd Series)
Rural Home Publ.: Feb-Mar, 1945 - No. 2, Apr-May, 1945
1-Aviation stories 50 100 150 315 533 750
2-Lucky Aces 27 54 81 158 259 360
NOTE: *L. B. Cole c/a in each.*

EAGLE
Crystal Comics/Apple Comics #17 on: Sept, 1986 - No. 23, 1989 ($1.50/1.75/1.95, B&W)
1-23: 12-Double size origin issue ($2.50) 3.00
1-Signed and limited 4.00

EARTH 4 (Also see Urth 4)
Continuity Comics: Dec, 1993 - No. 4, Jan, 1994 ($2.50)
1-4: 1-3 all listed as Dec, 1993 in indicia 3.00

EARTH 4 DEATHWATCH 2000
Continuity Comics: Apr, 1993 - No. 3, Aug, 1993 ($2.50)
1-3 3.00

EARTH MAN ON VENUS (An...) (Also see Strange Planets)
Avon Periodicals: 1951
nn-Wood-a (26 pgs.); Fawcette-c 142 284 426 909 1555 2200

EARTHWORM JIM (TV, cartoon)
Marvel Comics: Dec, 1995 - No. 3, Feb, 1996 ($2.25)
1-3: Based on video game and toys 3.00

EARTH X
Marvel Comics: No. 0, Mar, 1999 - No. 12, Apr, 2000 ($3.99/$2.99, lim. series)
nn- (Wizard supplement) Alex Ross sketchbook; painted-c 6.00
Sketchbook (2/99) New sketches and previews 6.00
0-(3/99)-Prelude; Leon-a(p)/Ross-c 1 2 3 4 5 7
1-(4/99)-Leon-a(p)/Ross-c 1 2 3 4 5 7
1-2nd printing 3.00
2-12 3.50
#1/2 (Wizard) Nick Fury on cover; Reinhold-a 6.00
#X (6/00, $3.99) 4.00
... Trilogy Companion TPB (2008, $29.99) r/#1/2; artwork and content from the Earth X, Paradise X and Universe X series; gallery of variant covers and promotional art 30.00
HC (2005, $49.99) r/#0,1-12, #1/2, X; foreword by Joss Whedon; Ross sketch pages 50.00
TPB (12/00, $24.95) r/#0,1-12, X; foreword by Joss Whedon 25.00

EASTER BONNET SHOP (See March of Comics No. 29)

EASTER WITH MOTHER GOOSE
Dell Publishing Co.: No. 103, 1946 - No. 220, Mar, 1949
Four Color 103 (#1)-Walt Kelly-a 16 32 48 111 226 340
Four Color 140 ('47)-Kelly-a 13 26 39 93 182 270
Four Color 185 ('48), 220-Kelly-a 12 24 36 87 164 240

EAST MEETS WEST
Innovation Publishing: Apr, 1990 - No. 2, 1990 ($2.50, limited series, mature)
1,2: 1-Stevens part-i; Redondo-c(i). 2-Stevens-c(i); 1st app. Cheech & Chong in comics 3.00

EC ARCHIVES (Also see EC Sampler in the Promotional Comics section)
Gemstone Publishing: 2006 - Present ($49.95, hardcover with dustjacket)
Crime SuspenStories Vol. 1 - Recolored reprints of #1-6; foreward by Max Allan Collins 50.00
Frontline Combat Vol. 1 - Recolored reprints of #1-6; foreward by Henry G. Franke III 50.00
Shock SuspenStories Vol. 1 - Recolored reprints of #1-6; foreward by Steven Spielberg 50.00
Shock SuspenStories Vol. 2 - Recolored reprints of #7-12; foreward by Dean Kamen 50.00
Tales From the Crypt Vol. 1 - Recolored reprints of Crypt of Terror #17-19 and Tales From the Crypt #20-22; foreward by John Carpenter; Al Feldstein behind-the-scenes info 50.00
Tales From the Crypt Vol. 2 - Recolored reprints of #23-28; foreward by Joe Dante 50.00
Tales From the Crypt Vol. 3 - Recolored reprints of #29-34; foreward by Bob Overstreet 50.00
Two-Fisted Tales Vol. 1 - Recolored reprints of #18-23; foreward by Stephen Geppi 50.00
Two-Fisted Tales Vol. 2 - Recolored reprints of #24-29; foreward by Rocco Versaci, Ph.D. 50.00
Vault of Horror Vol. 1 - Recolored reprints of #12-17; foreward by R.L. Stine 50.00
Weird Science Vol. 1 - Recolored reprints of #1-6; foreward by George Lucas 50.00
Weird Science Vol. 2 - Recolored reprints of #7-12; foreward by Paul Levitz 50.00
Weird Science Vol. 3 - Recolored reprints of #13-18; foreward by Jerry Weist 50.00

E. C. CLASSIC REPRINTS
East Coast Comix Co.: May, 1973 - No. 12, 1976 (E. C. Comics reprinted in color minus ads)
1-The Crypt of Terror #1 (Tales from the Crypt #46) 2 4 6 11 16 20
2-12: 2-Weird Science #15('52). 3-Shock SuspenStories #12. 4-Haunt of Fear #12. 5-Weird Fantasy #13('52). 6-Crime SuspenStories #25. 7-Vault of Horror #26. 8-Shock SuspenStories #6. 9-Two-Fisted Tales #34. 10-Haunt of Fear #23. 11-Weird Science 12(#1). 12-Shock SuspenStories #2 2 4 6 8 11 14

EC CLASSICS
Russ Cochran: Aug, 1985 - No. 12, 1986? (High quality paper; each-r 8 stories in color) (#2-12 were resolicited in 1990)($4.95, 56 pgs., 8x11")
1-12: 1-Tales From the Crypt. 2-Weird Science. 3-Two-Fisted Tales (r/31); Frontline Combat (r/9). 4-Shock SuspenStories. 5-Weird Fantasy. 6-Vault of Horror. 7-Weird Science-Fantasy (r/23,24). 8-Crime SuspenStories (r/17,18). 9-Haunt of Fear (r/14,15). 10-Panic (r/1,2). 11-Tales From the Crypt (r/23,24). 12-Weird Science (r/20,22) 1 2 3 4 5 7

ECHO
Image Comics (Dreamwave Prod.): Mar, 2000 - No. 5, Sept, 2000 ($2.50)
1-5: 1-3-Pat Lee-c 3.00
0-(7/00) 3.00

ECHO
Abstract Studio: Mar, 2008 - Present ($3.50)
1-Terry Moore-s/a/c 8.00
2-29 3.50
Terry Moore's Echo: Moon Lake TPB (2008, $15.95) r/#1-5; Moore sketch pages 16.00

ECHO OF FUTUREPAST
Pacific Comics/Continuity Com.: May, 1984 - No. 9, Jan, 1986 ($2.95, 52 pgs.)
1-9: Neal Adams-c/a in all? 6.00
NOTE: ***N. Adams** a-1-6,7i,9i; c-1-3, 5p,7i,8,9i. **Golden** a-1-6 (Bucky O'Hare); c-6. **Toth** a-6,7.*

ECLIPSE GRAPHIC ALBUM SERIES
Eclipse Comics: Oct, 1978 - 1989 (8-1/2x11") (B&W #1-5)
1-Sabre (10/78, B&W, 1st print.); Gulacy-a; 1st direct sale graphic novel 16.00
1-Sabre (2nd printing, 1/79) 8.00
1-Sabre (3rd printing, $5.95) 6.00
1-Sabre 30th Anniversary Edition (2008, $14.99, 9x6" HC) new McGregor & Gulacy intros. original script with sketch art 15.00
3,4: 3-Detectives, Inc. (5/80, B&W, $6.95)-Rogers-a. 4-Stewart The Rat (1980, B&W) -G. Colan-a 10.00
5-The Price (10/81, B&W)-Starlin-a 16.00
2,6,7,13: 2-Night Music (11/79, B&W)-Russell-a. 6-I Am Coyote (11/84, color)-Rogers-c/a. 7-The Rocketeer (2nd print, $7.95). 7-The Rocketeer (3rd print, 1991, $8.95). 13-The Sisterhood of Steel ('87, $8.95, color) 10.00
7-The Rocketeer (9/85, color)-Dave Stevens-a (r/chapters 1-5)(see Pacific Presents & Starslayer); has 7 pgs. new-a 14.00
7-The Rocketeer, signed & limited HC 60.00
7-The Rocketeer, hardcover (1986, $19.95) 20.00
7-The Rocketeer, unsigned HC (3rd, $32.95) 33.00
8-Zorro In Old California ('86, color) 14.00
8,12-Hardcover 18.00
9,10: 9-Sacred And The Profane ('86)-Steacy-a. 10-Somerset Holmes ('86, $15.95)-Adults, soft-c 16.00
9,10,12-Hardcover ($24.95). 12-signed & #'d 25.00
11-Floyd Farland, Citizen of the Future ('87, $2.95, B&W) Chris Ware-s/a 7.00
12,28,31,35: 12-Silverheels ('87, $7.95, color). 28-Miracleman Book I ($5.95). 31-Pigeons From Hell by R. E. Howard (11/88). 35-Rael: Into The Shadow of the Sun ('88, $7.95)10.00
14,16,18,20,23,24: 14-Samurai, Son of Death ('87, $4.95, B&W). 16,18,20,23-See Airfighters

Eclipso #11 © DC

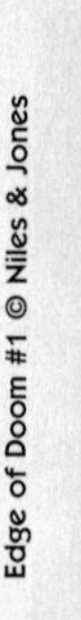
Edge of Doom #1 © Niles & Jones

Eerie #14 © AVON

	GD 2.0	VG 4.0	FN 6.0	VF 8.0	VF/NM 9.0	NM- 9.2

Classics #1-4. 24-Heartbreak ($4.95, B&W) 7.00
14 (2nd pr.),17,21: 14-Samurai, Son of Death ($3.95, 2nd printing). 17-Valkyrie, Prisoner of the Past SC ('88, $3.95, color). 21-XYR-Multiple ending comic ('88, $3.95, B&W) 6.00
15,22,27: 15-Twisted Tales (11/87, color)-Dave Stevens-c. 22-Alien Worlds #1 (5/88, $3.95, 52 pgs.)-Nudity. 27-Fast Fiction (She) ($5.95, B&W) 8.00
17-Valkyrie, Prisoner of the Past S&N Hardcover ('88, $19.95) 20.00
19-Scout: The Four Monsters ('88, $14.95, color)-r/Scout #1-7; soft-c 15.00
25,30,32-34: 25-Alex Toth's Zorro Vol. 1 ,2($10.95, B&W). 30-Brought To Light; Alan Moore scripts ('89). 32-Teenaged Dope Slaves and Reform School Girls. 33-Bogie. 34-Air Fighters Classics #5 12.00
29-Real Love: Best of Simon & Kirby Romance Comics(10/88, $12.95) 15.00
30,31: Limited hardcover ed. ($29.95). 31-signed 30.00
36-Dr. Watchstop: Adventures in Time and Space ('89, $8.95) 10.00

ECLIPSE MAGAZINE (Becomes Eclipse Monthly)
Eclipse Publishing: May, 1981 - No. 8, Jan, 1983 ($2.95, B&W, magazine)

1-8: 1-1st app. Cap'n Quick and a Foozle by Rogers, Ms. Tree by Beatty, and Dope by Trina Robbins. 2-1st app. I Am Coyote by Rogers. 7-1st app. Masked Man by Boyer 3.00

NOTE: ***Colan** a-3, 5, 8. **Golden** c/a-2. **Gulacy** a-6, c-1, 6. **Kaluta** c/a-5. **Mayerik** a-2, 3. **Rogers** a-1-8. **Starlin** a-1. **Sutton** a-6.*

ECLIPSE MONTHLY
Eclipse Comics: Aug, 1983 - No. 10, Jul, 1984 (Baxter paper, $2.00/$1.50/$1.75)

1-10: ($2.00, 52 pgs.)-Cap'n Quick and a Foozle by Rogers, Static by Ditko, Dope by Trina Robbins, Rio by Wildey, The Masked Man by Boyer begin. 3-Ragamuffins begins 4.00

NOTE: ***Boyer** c-6. **Ditko** a-1-3. **Rogers** a-1-4; c-2, 4, 7. **Wildey** a-1, 2, 5, 9, 10; c-5, 10.*

ECLIPSO (See Brave and the Bold #64, House of Secrets #61 & Phantom Stranger, 1987)
DC Comics: Nov, 1992 - No. 18, Apr, 1994 ($1.25)

1-18: 1-Giffen plots/breakdowns begin. 10-Darkseid app. Creeper in #3-6,9,11-13. 18-Spectre-c/s 3.00
Annual 1 (1993, $2.50, 68 pgs.)-Intro Prism 4.00
...: The Music of the Spheres TPB (2009, $19.99) r/stories from Countdown to Mystery #1-8 20.00

ECLIPSO: THE DARKNESS WITHIN
DC Comics: July, 1992 - No. 2, Oct, 1992 ($2.50, 68 pgs.)

1,2: 1-With purple gem attached to-c, 1-Without gem; Superman, Creeper app., 2-Concludes Eclipso storyline from annuals 4.00

EC SAMPLER - FREE COMIC BOOK DAY
Gemstone Publishing: May, 2008

Reprinted stories with restored color from Weird Science #6, Two-Fisted Tales #22, Crypt of Terror #17, Shock Suspenstories #6 2.50

E. C. 3-D CLASSICS (See Three Dimensional...)

ECTOKID (See Razorline)
Marvel Comics: Sept, 1993 - No. 9, May, 1994 ($1.75/$1.95)

1-($2.50)-Foil embossed-c; created by C. Barker 3.50
2-9: 2-Origin. 5-Saint Sinner x-over 3.00
...: Unleashed! 1 (10/94, $2.95, 52 pgs.) 4.00

ED "BIG DADDY" ROTH'S RATFINK COMIX (Also see Ratfink)
World of Fandom/ Ed Roth: 1991 - No. 3, 1991 ($2.50)

1-3: Regular Ed., 1-Limited double cover 1 3 4 6 8 10

EDDIE CAMPBELL'S BACCHUS
Eddie Campbell Comics: May, 1995 - No. 60, May, 2001 ($2.95, B&W)

1-Cerebus app. 1 2 3 5 6 8
1-2nd printing (5/97) 3.00
2-10: 9-Alex Ross back-c 5.00
11-60 3.00
Doing The Islands With Bacchus ('97, $17.95) 18.00
Earth, Water, Air & Fire ('98, $9.95) 10.00
King Bacchus ('99, $12.95) 13.00
The Eyeball Kid ('98, $8.50) 8.50

EDDIE STANKY (Baseball Hero)
Fawcett Publications: 1951 (New York Giants)

nn-Photo-c 34 68 102 204 332 460

EDEN'S TRAIL
Marvel Comics: Jan, 2003 - No. 6 ($2.99, limited series, Marvelscope-printed sideways)

1-5-Chuck Austen-s/Steve Uy-a 3.00

EDGAR ALLAN POE'S - THE FALL OF THE HOUSE OF USHER AND OTHER TALES OF HORROR
Catlan Communications Pub.: Sept. 1985 (hardcover graphic novel)

nn-Reprints of Poe story issues from Warren comic mags; all Richard Corben-a; numbered edition of 350 signed by Corben; 60 pgs. 130.00
nn-Softcover edition 60.00

EDGAR BERGEN PRESENTS CHARLIE McCARTHY
Whitman Publishing Co. (Charlie McCarthy Co.): No. 764, 1938 (36 pgs.; 15x10-1/2"; color)

764 76 152 228 486 831 1175

EDGAR RICE BURROUGHS' TARZAN: A TALE OF MUGAMBI
Dark Horse Comics: 1995 ($2.95, one-shot)

1 3.00

EDGAR RICE BURROUGHS' TARZAN: IN THE LAND THAT TIME FORGOT AND THE POOL OF TIME
Dark Horse Comics: 1996 ($12.95, trade paperback)

nn-r/Russ Manning-a 13.00

EDGAR RICE BURROUGHS' TARZAN OF THE APES
Dark Horse Comics: May, 1999 ($12.95, trade paperback)

nn-reprints 13.00

EDGAR RICE BURROUGHS' TARZAN: THE LOST ADVENTURE
Dark Horse Comics: Jan, 1995 - No. 4, Apr, 1995 ($2.95, B&W, limited series)

1-4: ERB's last Tarzan story, adapted by Joe Lansdale 3.00
Hardcover (12/95, $19.95) 20.00
Limited Edition Hardcover ($99.95)-signed & numbered 100.00

EDGAR RICE BURROUGHS' TARZAN: THE RETURN OF TARZAN
Dark Horse Comics: May, 1997 - No. 3, July, 1997 ($2.95, limited series)

1-3 3.00

EDGAR RICE BURROUGHS' TARZAN: THE RIVERS OF BLOOD
Dark Horse Comics: Nov, 1999 - No. 4, Feb, 2000 ($2.95, limited series)

1-4-Kordey-c/a 3.00

EDGE
Malibu Comics (Bravura): July, 1994 - No. 3, Apr, 1995 ($2.50/$2.95, unfinished lim.series)

1,2-S. Grant-story & Gil Kane-c/a; w/Bravura stamp 3.00
3-($2.95-c) 3.00

EDGE (Re-titled as Vector starting with #13)
CrossGeneration Comics: May, 2002 - No. 12, Apr, 2003 ($9.95/$11.95/$7.95, TPB)

1-3: Reprints from various CrossGen titles 10.00
4-8-($11.95) 12.00
9-12-($7.95, 8-1/4" x 5-1/2") digest-sized reprints 8.00

EDGE OF CHAOS
Pacific Comics: July, 1983 - No. 3, Jan, 1984 (Limited series)

1-3-Morrow c/a; all contain nudity 3.00

EDGE OF DOOM (Horror anthology)
IDW Publishing: Oct, 2010 - No. 4, Feb, 2011 ($3.99)

1-4-Steve Niles-s/Kelley Jones-a 4.00

ED WHEELAN'S JOKE BOOK STARRING FAT & SLAT (See Fat & Slat)

EERIE (Strange Worlds No. 18 on)
Avon Per.: No. 1, Jan, 1947; No. 1, May-June, 1951 - No. 17, Aug-Sept, 1954

1(1947)-1st supernatural comic; Kubert, Fugitani-a; bondage-c 459 918 1377 3350 5925 8500
1(1951)-Reprints story from 1947 #1 77 154 231 493 847 1200
2-Wood-c/a; bondage-c 79 158 237 502 864 1225
3-Wood-c; Kubert, Wood/Orlando-a 79 158 237 502 864 1225
4,5-Wood-c 61 122 183 390 670 950
6,8,13,14: 8-Kinstler-a; bondage-c; Phantom Witch Doctor story 36 72 108 216 351 485
7-Wood/Orlando-c; Kubert-a 47 94 141 296 498 700
9-Kubert-a; Check-c 39 78 117 236 388 540
10,11: 10-Kinstler-a. 11-Kinstlerish-a by McCann 36 72 108 216 351 485
12-Dracula story from novel, 25 pgs. 40 80 120 242 401 560
15-Reprints No. 1('51) minus-c(bondage) 24 48 72 142 234 325
16-Wood-a r-/No. 2 24 48 72 142 234 325
17-Wood/Orlando & Kubert-a; reprints #3 minus inside & outside Wood-c 24 48 72 142 234 325

NOTE: ***Hollingsworth** a-9-11; c-10, 11.*

EERIE
I. W. Enterprises: 1964

I.W. Reprint #1('64)-Wood-c(r); r-story/Spook #1 4 8 12 22 34 45

Eerie #60 © WP

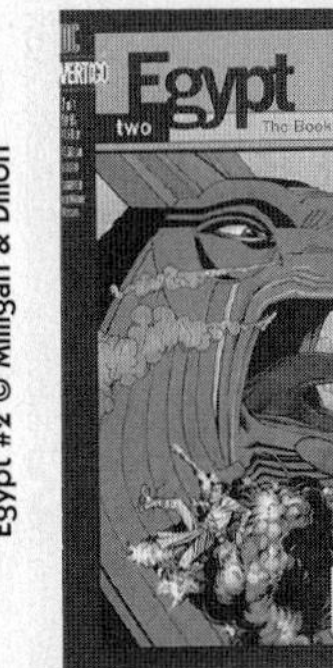

Egypt #2 © Milligan & Dillon

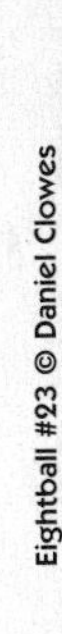
Eightball #23 © Daniel Clowes

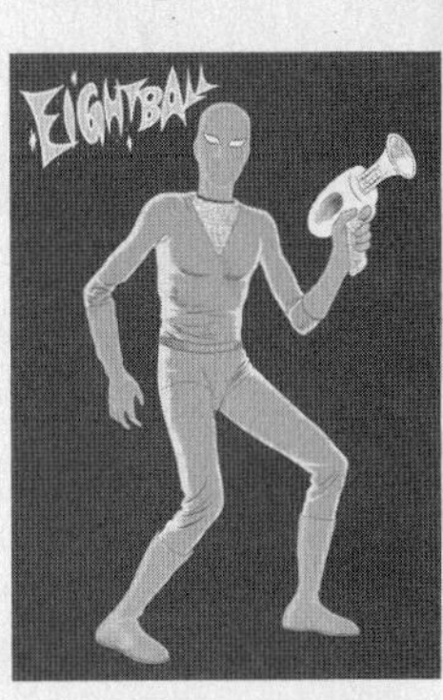

GD 2.0 | VG 4.0 | FN 6.0 | VF 8.0 | VF/NM 9.0 | NM- 9.2

I.W. Reprint #2,6,8: 8-Dr. Drew by Grandenetti from Ghost #9 3 6 9 20 30 40
I.W. Reprint #9-r/Tales of Terror #1(Toby); Wood-c 4 8 12 24 37 50

EERIE (Magazine)(See Warren Presents)
Warren Publ. Co.: No. 1, Sept, 1965; No. 2, Mar, 1966 - No. 139, Feb, 1983

1-24 pgs., black & white, small size (5-1/4x7-1/4"), low distribution; cover from inside back cover of Creepy No. 2; stories reprinted from Creepy No. 7, 8. At least three different versions exist.
First Printing - B&W, 5-1/4" wide x 7-1/4" high, evenly trimmed. On page 18, panel 5, in the upper left-hand corner, the large rear view of a bald headed man blends into solid black and is unrecognizable. Overall printing quality is poor. 43 86 129 344 697 1050
Second Printing - B&W, 5-1/4x7-1/4", with uneven, untrimmed edges (if one of these were trimmed evenly, the size would be less than as indicated). The figure of the bald headed man on page 18, panel 5 is clear and discernible. The staples have a 1/4" blue stripe. 15 30 45 106 216 325
Other unauthorized reproductions for comparison's sake would be practically worthless. One known version was probably shot off a first printing copy with some loss of detail; the finer lines tend to disappear in this version which can be determined by looking at the lower right-hand corner of page one, first story. The roof of the house is shaded with straight lines. These lines are sharp and distinct on original, but broken on this version.
NOTE: ***The Overstreet Comic Book Price Guide*** *recommends that, before buying a 1st issue, you consult an expert.*

2-Frazetta-c; Toth-a; 1st app. host Cousin Eerie 10 20 30 72 131 190
3-Frazetta-c & half pg. ad (rerun in #4); Toth, Williamson, Ditko-a 9 18 27 60 100 140
4-7: 4-Frazetta-a (1/2 pg. ad). 5,7-Frazetta-c. Ditko-a in all. 6 12 18 39 62 85
8-Frazetta-c; Ditko-a 6 12 18 43 69 95
9-11,25: 9,10-Neal Adams-a, Ditko-a. 11-Karloff Mummy adapt.-Wood-s/a. 25-Steranko-c 6 12 18 41 66 90
12-16,18-22,24,32-35,40,45: 12,13,20-Poe-s. 12-Bloch-s. 12,15-Jones-a. 13-Lovecraft-s. 14,16-Toth-a. 16,19,24-Stoker-s. 16,32,33,43-Corben-a. 34-Early Boris-c. 35-Early Brunner-a. 35,40-Early Ploog-a. 40-Frankenstein; Ploog-a (6/72, 6 months before Marvel's series) 4 8 12 28 44 60
17-(low distribution) 16 32 48 117 239 360
23-Frazetta-c; Adams-a(reprint) 7 14 21 47 76 105
26-31,36-38,43,44 4 8 12 24 37 50
39,41: 39-1st Dax the Warrior; Maroto-a. 41-(low distribution) 5 10 15 30 48 65
42,51: 42-('73 Annual, 84 pgs.) Spooktacular; Williamson-a. 51-('74 Annual, 76 pgs.) Color poster insert; Toth-a 4 8 12 28 44 60
46,48: 46-Dracula series by Sutton begins; 2pgs. Vampirella. 48-Begin "Mummy Walks" and "Curse of the Werewolf" series (both continue in #49,50,52,53) 4 8 12 24 37 50
47,49,50,52,53: 47-Lilith. 49-Marvin the Dead Thing. 50-Satanna, Daughter of Satan. 52-Hunter by Neary begins. 53-Adams-a 4 8 12 22 34 45
54,55-Color insert Spirit story by Eisner, reprints sections 12/21/47 & 6/16/46 54-Dr. Archaeus series begins 3 6 9 20 30 40
56,57,59,63,69,77,78: All have 8 pg. slick color insert. 56,57,77-Corben-a. 59-(100 pgs.) Summer Special, all Dax issue. 69-Summer Special, all Hunter issue, Neary-a. 78-All Mummy issue 3 6 9 20 30 40
58,60,62,68,72,: 8 pg. slick color insert & Wrightson-a in all. 58,60,62-Corben-a. 60-Summer Giant (9/74, $1.25) 1st Exterminator One; Wood-a. 62-Mummies Walk. 68-Summer Special (84 pgs.) 4 8 12 22 34 45
61,64-67,71: 61-Mummies Walk-s, Wood-a. 64-Corben-a. 64,65,67-Toth-a. 65,66-El Cid. 67-Hunter II. 71-Goblin-c/1st app. 3 6 9 18 27 35
70,73-75 3 6 9 14 20 26
76-1st app. Darklon the Mystic by Starlin-s/a 3 6 9 21 32 42
79,80-Origin Darklon the Mystic by Starlin 3 6 9 18 27 35
81,86,97: 81-Frazetta-c, King Kong; Corben-a. 86-(92 pgs.) All Corben issue. 97-Time Travel/ Dinosaur issue; Corben,Adams-a 3 6 9 16 23 30
82-Origin/1st app. The Rook 3 6 9 19 29 38
83,85,88,89,91-93,98,99: 98-Rook (31 pgs.). 99-1st Horizon Seekers. 2 4 6 10 14 18
84,87,90,96,100: 84,100-Starlin-a. 87-Hunter 3; Nino-a. 87,90-Corben-a. 96-Summer Special (92 pgs.). 100-(92 pgs.) Anniversary issue; Rook (30 pgs.) 2 4 6 13 18 22
94,95-The Rook & Vampirella team-up. 95-Vampirella-c; 1st MacTavish 3 6 9 17 25 32
101,106,112,115,118,120,121,128: 101-Return of Hunter II, Starlin-a. 106-Hard John Nuclear Hit Parade Special, Corben-a. 112-All Maroto issue, Luana-s. 115-All José Ortiz issues. 118-1st Haggarth. 120-1st Zud Kamish. 121-Hunter/Darklon. 128-Starlin-a, Hsu-a 2 4 6 10 14 18
102-105,107-111,113,114,116,117,119,122-124,126,127,129: 103-105,109-111-Gulacy-a. 104-Beast World. 2 4 6 9 13 16
125-(10/81, 84 pgs.) all Neal Adams issue 3 6 9 14 19 24
130-(76 pgs.) Vampirella-c/sty (54 pgs.); Pantha, Van Helsing, Huntress, Dax, Schreck, Hunter, Exterminator One, Rook app. 3 6 9 16 23 30
131-(Lower distr.); all Wood issue 3 6 9 14 20 26
132-134,136: 132-Rook returns. 133-All Ramon Torrents-a issue. 134,136-Color comic insert 2 4 6 10 14 18
135-(Lower distr., 10/82, 100 pgs.) All Ditko issue 3 6 9 14 20 26
137-139 (lower distr.):137-All Super-Hero issue. 138-Sherlock Holmes. 138,139-Color comic insert 2 4 6 13 18 22
Yearbook '70-Frazetta-c 6 12 18 37 59 80
Annual '71, '72-Reprints in both 4 8 12 26 41 55
... Archives - Volume One HC (Dark Horse, 3/09, $49.95, dustjacket) r/#1-5 50.00
... Archives - Volume Two HC (Dark Horse, 9/09, $49.95, dustjacket) r/#6-10; interview with Frank Frazetta from 1985 50.00
NOTE: *The above books contain art by many good artists:* ***N. Adams, Brunner, Corben, Craig (Taycee), Crandall, Ditko, Eisner, Evans, Jeff Jones, Krenkel, McWilliams, Morrow, Orlando, Ploog, Severin, Starlin, Torres, Toth, Williamson, Wood,*** *and* ***Wrightson****; covers by* ***Bode', Corben, Davis, Frazetta, Morrow,*** *and* ***Orlando. Frazetta*** *c-2, 3, 7, 8, 23. Annuals from 1973-on are included in regular numbering. 1970-74 Annuals are complete reprints. Annuals from 1975-on are in the format of the regular issues.*

EERIE ADVENTURES (Also see Weird Adventures)
Ziff-Davis Publ. Co.: Winter, 1951 (Painted-c)
1-Powell-a(2), McCann-a; used in **SOTI;** bondage-c; Krigstein back-c 53 106 159 334 567 800
NOTE: *Title dropped due to similarity to Avon's Eerie & legal action.*

EERIE TALES (Magazine)
Hastings Associates: 1959 (Black & White)
1-Williamson, Torres, Tuska-a, Powell(2), & Morrow(2)-a 15 30 45 90 140 190

EERIE TALES
Super Comics: 1963-1964
Super Reprint No. 10,11,12,18: 10('63)-r/Spook #27. Purple Claw in #11,12 ('63); #12-r/Avon's Eerie #1('51)-Kida-r 3 6 9 17 25 32
15-Wolverton-a, Spacehawk-r/Blue Bolt Weird Tales #113; Disbrow-a 5 10 15 30 48 65

EGBERT
Arnold Publications/Quality Comics Group: Spring, 1946 - No. 20, 1950
1-Funny animal; intro Egbert & The Count 19 38 57 112 179 245
2 11 22 33 62 86 110
3-10 9 18 27 47 61 75
11-20 7 14 21 37 46 55

EGON
Dark Horse Comics: Jan, 1998 - No.2, Feb, 1998 ($2.95, limited series)
1,2-Horley-painted-c 3.00

EGYPT
DC Comics (Vertigo): Aug, 1995 - No.7, Feb, 1996 ($2.50, lim. series, mature)
1-7: Milligan scripts in all. 3.00

EH! (...Dig This Crazy Comic) (From Here to Insanity No. 8 on)
Charlton Comics: Dec, 1953 - No. 7, Nov-Dec, 1954 (Satire)
1-Davis-*ish*-c/a by Ayers, Wood-*ish*-a by Giordano; Atomic Mouse app. 39 78 117 228 374 520
2-Ayers-c/a 21 42 63 126 206 285
3,5,7 20 40 60 114 182 250
4,6: Sexual innuendo-c. 6-Ayers-a 20 40 60 118 192 265

EIGHTBALL (Also see David Boring)
Fantagraphics Books: Oct, 1989 - Present ($2.75/$2.95/$3.95, semi-annually, mature)
1 (1st printing) Daniel Clowes-s/a in all 2 4 6 8 10 12
2,3 1 2 3 5 6 8
4-8 6.00
9-19: 17-(8/96) 4.00
20-($4.50) 4.50
21-($4.95) Concludes David Boring 3-parter 5.00
22-($5.95) 29 short stories 6.00
23-($7.00, 9" x 12") The Death Ray 7.00
Twentieth Century Eightball (2002, $19.00) r/Clowes strips 19.00

EIGHTH WONDER, THE
Dark Horse Comics: Nov, 1997 ($2.95, one-shot)
nn-Reprints stories from Dark Horse Presents #85-87 3.00

EIGHT IS ENOUGH KITE FUN BOOK (See Kite Fun Book 1979 in the Promotional Comics section)

EIGHT LEGGED FREAKS
DC Comics (WildStorm): 2002 ($6.95, one-shot, squarebound)

80 Page Giant #3 © DC

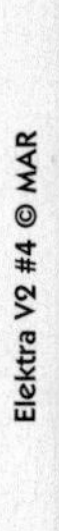
Elektra V2 #4 © MAR

Elementals #6 © Comico

	GD 2.0	VG 4.0	FN 6.0	VF 8.0	VF/NM 9.0	NM- 9.2

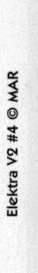

nn-Adaptation of 2002 mutant spider movie; Joe Phillips-a; intro by Dean Devlin 7.00

80 PAGE GIANT (...Magazine No. 2-15)
National Periodical Publications: 8/64 - No. 15, 10/65; No. 16, 11/65 - No. 89, 7/71 (25¢) (All reprints) (#1-56: 84 pgs.; #57-89: 68 pgs.)

	GD	VG	FN	VF	VF/NM	NM-
1-Superman Annual; originally planned as Superman Annual #9 (8/64)	37	74	111	284	562	840
2-Jimmy Olsen	20	40	60	140	283	425
3,4: 3-Lois Lane. 4-Flash-G.A.-r; Infantino-a	16	32	48	111	226	340
5-Batman; has Sunday newspaper strip; Catwoman-r; Batman's Life Story-r (25th anniversary special)	16	32	48	111	226	340
6-Superman	14	28	42	98	197	295
7-Sgt. Rock's Prize Battle Tales; Kubert-c/a	22	44	66	159	317	475
8-More Secret Origins-origins of JLA, Aquaman, Robin, Atom, & Superman; Infantino-a	28	56	84	204	415	625
9-15: 9-Flash (r/Flash #106,117,123 & Showcase #14); Infantino-a. 10-Superboy. 11-Superman; all Luthor issue. 12-Batman; has Sunday newspaper strip. 13-Jimmy Olsen. 14-Lois Lane. 15-Superman and Batman; Joker-c/story	13	26	39	94	185	275

Continued as part of regular series under each title in which that particular book came out, a Giant being published instead of the regular size. Issues No. 16 to No. 89 are listed for your information. See individual titles for prices. 16-JLA #39 (11/65), 17-Batman #176, 18-Superman #183, 19-Our Army at War #164, 20-Action #334, 21-Flash #160, 22-Superboy #129, 23-Superman #187, 24-Batman #182, 25-Jimmy Olsen #95, 26-Lois Lane #68, 27-Batman #185, 28-World's Finest #161, 29-JLA #48, 30-Batman #187, 31-Superman #193, 32-Our Army at War #177, 33-Action #347, 34-Flash #169, 35-Superboy #138, 36-Superman #197, 37-Batman #193, 38-Jimmy Olsen #104, 39-Lois Lane #77, 40-World's Finest #170, 41-JLA #58, 42-Superman #202, 43-Batman #198, 44-Our Army at War #190, 45-Action #360, 46-Flash #178, 47-Superboy #147, 48-Superman #207, 49-Batman #203, 50-Jimmy Olsen #113, 51-Lois Lane #86, 52-World's Finest #179, 53-JLA #67, 54-Superman #212, 55-Batman #208, 56-Our Army at War #203, 57-Action #373, 58-Flash #187, 59-Superboy #156, 60-Superman #217, 61-Batman #213, 62-Jimmy Olsen #122, 63-Lois Lane #95, 64-World's Finest #188, 65-JLA #76, 66-Superman #222, 67-Batman #218, 68-Our Army at War #216, 69-Adventure #390, 70-Flash #196, 71-Superboy #165, 72-Superman #227, 73-Batman #223, 74-Jimmy Olsen #131, 75-Lois Lane #104, 76-World's Finest #197, 77-JLA #85, 78-Superman #232, 79-Batman #228, 80-Our Army at War #229, 81-Adventure #403, 82-Flash #205, 83-Superboy #174, 84-Superman #239, 85-Batman #233, 86-Jimmy Olsen #140, 87-Lois Lane #113, 88-World's Finest #206, 89-JLA #93.

87TH PRECINCT (TV) (Based on the Ed McBain novels)
Dell Publishing Co.: Apr-June, 1962 - No. 2, July-Sept, 1962

	GD	VG	FN	VF	VF/NM	NM-
Four Color 1309(#1)-Krigstein-a	9	18	27	65	113	160
2	8	16	24	56	93	130

EL BOMBO COMICS
Standard Comics/Frances M. McQueeny: 1946

	GD	VG	FN	VF	VF/NM	NM-
nn(1946), 1(no date)	14	28	42	82	121	160

EL CAZADOR
CrossGen Comics: Oct, 2003 - No. 6, Jun, 2004 ($2.95)

1-Dixon-s/Epting-a 5.00
2-6: 5-Lady Death preview 3.00
Collected Edition (2003, $5.95) r/#1-3 6.00
...: The Bloody Ballad of Blackjack Tom 1 (4/04, $2.95, one-shot) Cariello-a 3.00

EL CID
Dell Publishing Co.: No. 1259, 1961

	GD	VG	FN	VF	VF/NM	NM-
Four Color 1259-Movie, photo-c	7	14	21	47	76	105

EL DIABLO (See All-Star Western #2 & Weird Western Tales #12)
DC Comics: Aug, 1989 - No. 16, Jan, 1991 ($1.50-$1.75, color)

1 ($2.50, 52pgs.)-Masked hero 4.00
2-16 3.00

EL DIABLO
DC Comics (Vertigo): Mar, 2001 - No. 4, Jun, 2001 ($2.50, limited series)

1-4-Azzarello-s/Zezelj-a/Sale-c 3.00
TPB (2008, $12.99) r/#1-4 13.00

EL DIABLO
DC Comics: Nov, 2008 - No. 6, Apr, 2009 ($2.99, limited series)

1-6-Nitz-s/Hester-a/c. 4,5-Freedom Fighters app. 3.00
...: The Haunted Horseman TPB (2009, $17.99) r/#1-6 18.00

EL DORADO (See Movie Classics)

ELECTRIC ANT
Marvel Comics: Jun, 2010 - No. 5, Oct, 201 ($3.99, Baxter paper)

1-5-Based on a Philip K. Dick story; David Mack-s/Pascal Alixe-a; Paul Pope-c 4.00

ELECTRIC UNDERTOW (See Strikeforce Moriturі: Electric Undertow)

ELECTRIC WARRIOR
DC Comics: May, 1986 - No. 18, Oct, 1987 ($1.50, Baxter paper)

1-18 3.00

ELECTROPOLIS
Image Comics: May, 2001 - No. 4, Jan, 2003 ($2.95/$5.95)

1-3-Dean Motter-s/a. 3-(12/01) 3.00
4-(1/03, $5.95, 72 pages) The Infernal Machine pts. 4-6 6.00

ELEKTRA (Also see Daredevil #319-325)
Marvel Comics: Mar, 1995 - No. 4, June, 1995 ($2.95, limited series)

1-4-Embossed-c; Scott McDaniel-a 3.00

ELEKTRA (Also see Daredevil)
Marvel Comics: Nov, 1996 - No. 19, Jun, 1998 ($1.95)

1-Peter Milligan scripts; Deodato-c/a 4.00
1-Variant-c 6.00
2-19: 4-Dr. Strange-c/app. 10-Logan-c/app. 3.00
#(-1) Flashback (7/97) Matt Murdock-c/app.; Deodato-c/a 3.00
.../Cyblade (Image, 3/97,$2.95) Devil's Reign pt. 7 3.00

ELEKTRA (Vol. 2) (Marvel Knights)
Marvel Comics: Sept, 2001 - No. 35, Jun, 2004 ($3.50/$2.99)

1-Bendis-s/Austen-a/Horn-c 4.00
2-6: 2-Two covers (Sienkiewicz and Horn) 3,4-Silver Samurai app. 3.00
3-Initial printing with panel of nudity; most copies pulped 18.00
7-35: 7-Rucka-s begin. 9,10,17-Bennett-a. 19-Meglia-a. 23-25-Chen-a; Sienkiewicz-c 3.00
...Vol. 1: Introspect TPB (2002, $16.99) r/#10-15; Marvel Knights: Double Shot #3 17.00
...Vol. 2: Everything Old is New Again TPB (2003, $16.99) r/#16-22 17.00
...Vol. 3: Relentless TPB (2004, $14.99) r/#23-28 15.00
...Vol. 4: Frenzy TPB (2004, $17.99) r/#29-35 18.00

ELEKTRA & WOLVERINE: THE REDEEMER
Marvel Comics: Jan, 2002 - No. 3, Mar, 2002 ($5.95, square-bound, lim. series)

1-3-Greg Rucka-s/Yoshitaka Amano-a/c 6.00
HC (5/02, $29.95, with dustjacket) r/#1-3, interview with Greg Rucka 30.00

ELEKTRA: ASSASSIN (Also see Daredevil)
Marvel Comics (Epic Comics): Aug, 1986 - No. 8, June, 1987 (Limited series, mature)

1,8-Miller scripts in all; Sienkiewicz-c/a. 6.00
2-7 5.00
Signed & numbered hardcover (Graphitti Designs, $39.95, 2000 print run)- reprints 1-8 50.00
TPB (2000, $24.95) 25.00

ELEKTRA: GLIMPSE & ECHO
Marvel Comics: Sept, 2002 - No. 4, Dec, 2002 ($2.99, limited series)

1-4-Scott Morse-s/painted-a 3.00

ELEKTRA LIVES AGAIN (Also see Daredevil)
Marvel Comics (Epic Comics): 1990 ($24.95, oversize, hardcover, 76 pgs.)(Produced by Graphitti Designs)

nn-Frank Miller-c/a/scripts; Lynn Varley painted-a; Matt Murdock & Bullseye app. 35.00
2nd printing (9/02, $24.99) 25.00

ELEKTRA MEGAZINE
Marvel Comics: Nov, 1996 - No. 2, Dec, 1996 ($3.95, 96 pgs., reprints, limited series)

1,2: Reprints Frank Miller's Elektra stories in Daredevil 4.00

ELEKTRA SAGA, THE
Marvel Comics Group: Feb, 1984 - No. 4, June, 1984 ($2.00, limited series, Baxter paper)

1-4-r/Daredevil 168-190; Miller-c/a 4.00

ELEKTRA: THE HAND
Marvel Comics: Nov, 2004 - No. 5, Feb, 2005 ($2.99, limited series)

1-5-Gossett-a/Sienkiewicz-c/Yoshida-s; origin of the Hand in the 16th century 3.00
TPB (2005, $13.99) r/#1-5 14.00

ELEKTRA: THE MOVIE
Marvel Comics: Feb, 2005 ($5.99)

1-Movie adaptation; McKeever-s/Perkins-a; photo-c 6.00
TPB (2005, $12.95) r/movie adaptation, Daredevil #168, 181 & Elektra #(-1) 13.00

ELEMENTALS, THE (See The Justice Machine & Morningstar Spec.)
Comico The Comic Co. : June, 1984 - No. 29, Sept, 1988; V2#1, Mar, 1989 - No. 28, 1994? ($1.50/$2.50, Baxter paper); V3#1, Dec, 1995 - No. 3 ($2.95)

1-Willingham-c/a, 1-8 5.00
2-29, V2#1-28: 9-Bissette-a(p). 10-Photo-c. V2#6-1st app. Strike Force America. 18-Prelude to Avalon mini-series. 27-Prequel to Strike Force America series 3.00
V3#1-3: 1-Daniel-a(p), bagged w/gaming card 3.00
Lingerie (5/96, $2.95) 3.00
Special 1,2 (3/86, 1/89)-1-Willingham-a(p) 3.00

ElfLord V1 #3 © Warp

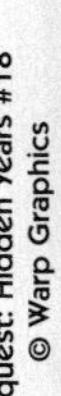
Elfquest 25th Anniversary Special © DC

Elfquest: Hidden Years #18 © Warp Graphics

	GD 2.0	VG 4.0	FN 6.0	VF 8.0	VF/NM 9.0	NM- 9.2

ELEMENTALS: (Title series), **Comico**
--GHOST OF A CHANCE, 12/95 ($5.95)-graphic novel, nn-Ross-c. 6.00
--HOW THE WAR WAS WON, 6/96 - No. 2, 8/96 ($2.95) 1,2-Tony Daniel-a, & 1-Variant-c; no logo 3.00
--SEX SPECIAL, 1991 - No. 4, Feb, 1993 ($2.95, color) 2 covers for each 3.00
--SEX SPECIAL, 5/97 - No. 2, 6/97 ($2.95, B&W) 1-Tony Daniel, Jeff Moy-a, 2-Robb Phipps, Adam McDaniel-a 3.00
--SWIMSUIT SPECTACULAR 1996, 6/96 ($2.95), 1-pin-ups, 1-Variant-c; no logo 3.00
--THE VAMPIRE'S REVENGE, 6/96 - No. 2 8/96 ($2.95) 1,2-Willingham-s, 1-Variant-c; no logo 3.00

ELEPHANTMEN
Image Comics: July, 2006 - Present ($2.99/$3.50) (Flip covers on most)
1-16: 1-Starkings-s/Moritat-a/Ladronn-c. 6-Campbell flip-c. 15-Sale flip-c 3.00
17-30-($3.50) 25-Flip book preview of Marineman 3.50
...: Man and Elephantman 1 (3/11, $3.99) Three covers 4.00
...: The Pilot (5/07, $2.99) short stories and pin-ups by various incl. Sale, Jim Lee, Jae Lee 3.00
...: War Toys (11/07 - No. 3, 4/08, $2.99) 1-3-Mappo war; Starkings-s/Moritat-a/Ladronn-c 3.00
... War Toys: Yvette (7/09, $3.50) Starkings-s/Moritat-a 3.50

1111 (ELEVEN ELEVEN)
Crusade Entertainment: Oct, 1996 ($2.95, B&W, one-shot)
1-Wrightson-c/a 4.00

ELEVEN OR ONE
Sirius: Apr, 1995 ($2.95)
1-Linsner-c/a 1 3 4 6 8 10
1-(6/96) 2nd printing 3.50

ELFLORD
Nightwind Productions: Jun, 1980 - Vol. 2 #1, 1982 (B&W, magazine-size)
1-1st Barry Blair-s/c/a in comics; B&W-c; limited print run for all 11 22 33 75 138 200
2-5-B&W-c 5 10 15 35 55 75
6-14: 9-14-Color-c 4 8 12 28 44 60
Vol. 2 #1 (1982) 4 8 12 24 37 50

ELFLORD
Aircel Publ.: 1986 - No. 6, Oct, 1989 ($1.70, B&W); V2#1- V2#31, 1995 ($2.00)
1 4.00
2-4,V2#1-20,22-30: 4-6: Last B&W issue. V2#1-Color-a begin. 22-New cast. 25-Begin B&W 3.00
1,2-2nd printings 3.00
21-Double size ($4.95) 5.00

ELFLORD
Warp Graphics: Jan, 1997-No.4, Apr, 1997 ($2.95, B&W, mini-series)
1-4 3.00

ELFLORD (CUTS LOOSE) (Vol. 2)
Warp Graphics: Sept, 1997 - No. 7, Apr, 1998 ($2.95, B&W, mini-series)
1-7 3.00

ELFLORD: DRAGON'S EYE
Night Wynd Enterprises: 1993 ($2.50, B&W)
1 3.00

ELFLORD: THE RETURN
Mad Monkey Press: 1996 ($6.95, magazine size)
1 7.00

ELFQUEST (Also see Fantasy Quarterly & Warp Graphics Annual)
Warp Graphics, Inc.: No. 2, Aug, 1978 - No. 21, Feb, 1985 (All magazine size)
No. 1, Apr, 1979
NOTE: ***Elfquest*** was originally published as one of the stories in **Fantasy Quarterly** #1. When the publisher went out of business, the creative team, Wendy and Richard Pini, formed WaRP Graphics and continued the series, beginning with **Elfquest** #2. **Elfquest** #1, which reprinted the story from **Fantasy Quarterly**, was published about the same time **Elfquest** #4 was released. Thereafter, most issues were reprinted as demand warranted, until Marvel announced it would reprint the entire series under its Epic imprint (Aug., 1985).
1(4/79)-Reprints Elfquest story from Fantasy Quarterly No. 1
1st printing ($1.00-c) 4 8 12 22 34 45
2nd printing ($1.25-c) 1 3 4 6 8 10
3rd printings ($1.50-c) 3.00
4th printing; different-c ($1.50-c) 3.00
2(8/78) 1st printing ($1.00-c) 3 6 9 18 27 35
2nd printings ($1.25-c) 4.00
3rd & 4th printings ($1.50-c)(all 4th prints 1989) 3.00
3-5: 1st printings ($1.00-c) 3 6 9 14 20 25
6-9: 1st printings ($1.25-c) 2 4 6 8 11 14
2nd printings ($1.50-c) 3.50
3rd printings ($1.50-c) 3.00
10-21: ($1.50-c); 16-8pg. preview of A Distant Soil 1 2 3 5 7 9
10-14: 2nd printings ($1.50) 3.00

ELFQUEST
Marvel Comics (Epic Comics): Aug, 1985 - No. 32, Mar, 1988
1-Reprints in color the Elfquest epic by Warp Graphics 4.00
2-32 3.00

ELFQUEST
DC Comics: 2003 - 2005
Archives Vol. 1 (2003, $49.95, HC) r/#1-5 50.00
Archives Vol. 2 (2005, $49.95, HC) r/#6-10 & Epic Illustrated #1 50.00
25th Anniversary Special (2003, $2.95) r/Elfquest #1 (Apr, 1979); interview w/Pinis 3.00

ELFQUEST (Title series), Warp Graphics
'89 - No. 4, '89 ($1.50, B&W) 1-4: R-original Elfquest series 3.00

ELFQUEST (Volume 2),**Warp Graphics:** V2#1, 5/96 - No. 33, 2/99 ($4.95/$2.95, B&W)
V2#1-31: 1,3,5,8,10,12,13,18,21,23,25-Wendy Pini-c 5.00
32,33-($2.95-c) 3.00
--BLOOD OF TEN CHIEFS, 7/93 - No. 20, 9/95 ($2.00/$2.50) 1-20-By Richard & Wendy Pini 3.00
--HIDDEN YEARS, 5/92 - No. 29, 3/96 ($2.00/$2.25)1-9,9 1/2, 10-29 3.00
--JINK, 11/94 - No. 12, 2/6 ($2.25/$2.50) 1-12-W. Pini/John Byrne-back-c 3.00
--KAHVI, 10/95 - No. 6,3/96 ($2.25, B&W) 1-6 3.00
--KINGS CROSS, 11/97 - No. 2, 12/97 ($2.95, B&W) 1,2 3.00
--KINGS OF THE BROKEN WHEEL, 6/90 - No. 9, 2/92 ($2.00, B&W) (3rd Elfquest saga) 1-9: By R. & W. Pini; 1-Color insert 3.00
1-2nd printing 3.00
--METAMORPHOSIS, 4/96 ($2.95, B&W) 1 3.00
--NEW BLOOD (...Summer Special on-c #1 only), 8/92 - No. 35, 1/96 ($2.00-$2.50, color/B&W) 1-($3.95, 68 pgs.,...Summer Special on-c)-Byrne-a/scripts (16 pgs.) 4.00
2-35: Barry Blair-a in all 3.00
1993 Summer Special ($3.95) Byrne-a/scripts 4.00
--SHARDS, 8/94 - No. 16, 3/96 ($2.25/$2.50) 1-16 3.00
--SIEGE AT BLUE MOUNTAIN, WaRP Graphics/Apple 3/87 - No. 8, 12/88 (1.75/ $1.95, B&W) 1-Staton-a(i) in all; 2nd Elfquest saga 4.00
1-3-2nd printing, 3-8 3.00
2 3.00
--THE REBELS, 11/94 - No. 12, 3/96 ($2.25/$2.50, B&W/color) 1-12 3.00
--TWO-SPEAR, 10/95 - No. 5, 2/96 ($2.25, B&W) 1-5 3.00
--WAVE DANCERS, 12/93 - No. 6, 3/96, 1-6: 1-Foil-c & poster 3.00
Special 1 ($2.95) 3.00
--WORLDPOOL, 7/97 ($2.95, B&W) 1-Richard Pini-s/Barry Blair-a 3.00

ELFQUEST: THE DISCOVERY
DC Comics: March,2006 - No. 4, Sept, 2006 ($3.99, limited series)
1-4-Wendy Pini-a/Wendy & Richard Pini-s 4.00
TPB (2006, $14.99) r/#1-4 15.00

ELFQUEST: THE GRAND QUEST
DC Comics: 2004 - Present ($9.95/$9.99, B&W, digest-size)
Vol. 1-6 ('04)1-r/Elfquest #1-5; new W. Pini-c. 2-r/#5-8. 3-r/#8-11. 4-r/#11-15. 5-r/#15-18 6-r/#18-20 10.00
Vol. 7-9 ('05) 1-r/Siege At Blue Mountain #1-3. 8-r/SABM #3-5. 9-r/SABM #6-8 10.00
Vol. 10-14 ('05) 10-r/Kings of the Broken Wheel #1-3. 11-KotBW #5-7 & Frazetta Fant. Ill. 12-r/Kings of the Broken Wheel #8&9. 13-r/Elfquest V2 #4-18. 14-r/Hidden Years #4-9 1/2 10.00

ELFQUEST: THE SEARCHER AND THE SWORD
DC Comics: 2004 ($24.95/$14.99, graphic novel)
HC (2004, $24.95, with dust jacket)-Wendy and Richard Pini-s/a/c 25.00
SC (2004, $14.99) 15.00

ELFQUEST: WOLFRIDER
DC Comics: 2003 - Present ($9.95, digest-size)
Volume 1 ('03, $9.95, digest-size) r/Elfquest V2#19,21,23,25,27,29,31; Blood of Ten Chiefs #2; Hidden Years #5; New Blood Special #1; New Blood 1993 Special #1; new W. Pini-c 10.00
Volume 2 ('03, $9.95, digest-size) r/Elfquest V2#33; Blood of Ten Chiefs #10,11,19; Warp

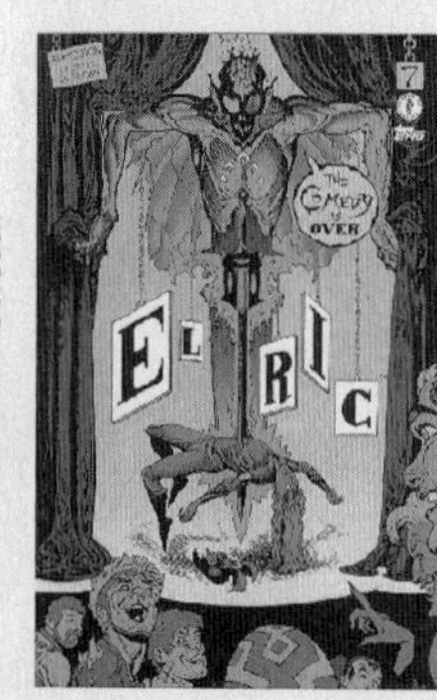

Elric, Stormbringer #7 © Michael Moorcock

Elseworld's Finest: Supergirl & Batgirl #1 © DC

Elvira's House of Mystery #7 © DC

	GD	VG	FN	VF	VF/NM	NM-
	2.0	4.0	6.0	8.0	9.0	9.2

Graphics Annual #1 10.00

ELF-THING
Eclipse Comics: March, 1987 ($1.50, B&W, one-shot)

1 3.00

ELIMINATOR (Also see The Solution #16 & The Night Man #16)
Malibu Comics (Ultraverse): Apr, 1995 - No. 3, Jul, 1995 ($2.95/$2.50, lim. series)

0-Mike Zeck-a in all 3.00
1-3-($2.50): 1-1st app. Siren 3.00
1-($3.95)-Black cover edition 4.00

ELIMINATOR FULL COLOR SPECIAL
Eternity Comics: Oct, 1991 ($2.95, one-shot)

1-Dave Dorman painted-c 3.00

ELLA CINDERS (See Comics On Parade, Comics Revue #1,4, Famous Comics Cartoon Book, Giant Comics Editions, Sparkler Comics, Tip Top & Treasury of Comics)

ELLA CINDERS
United Features Syndicate: 1938 - 1940

	GD	VG	FN	VF	VF/NM	NM-
Single Series 3(1938)	40	80	120	246	411	575
Single Series 21(#2 on-c, #21 on inside), 28('40)	35	70	105	208	339	470

ELLA CINDERS
United Features Syndicate: Mar, 1948 - No. 5, Mar, 1949

	GD	VG	FN	VF	VF/NM	NM-
1-(#2 on cover)	14	28	42	80	115	150
2	10	20	30	54	72	90
3-5	8	16	24	40	50	60

ELLERY QUEEN
Superior Comics Ltd.: May, 1949 - No. 4, Nov, 1949

	GD	VG	FN	VF	VF/NM	NM-
1-Kamen-c; L.B. Cole-a; r-in Haunted Thrills	52	104	156	328	557	785
2-4: 3-Drug use stories(2)	39	78	117	240	395	550

NOTE: *Iger shop art in all issues.*

ELLERY QUEEN (TV)
Ziff-Davis Publishing Co.: 1-3/52 (Spring on-c) - No. 2, Summer/52 (Saunders painted-c)

	GD	VG	FN	VF	VF/NM	NM-
1-Saunders-c	47	94	141	296	498	700
2-Saunders bondage, torture-c	39	78	117	231	378	525

ELLERY QUEEN (Also see Crackajack Funnies No. 23)
Dell Publishing Co.: No. 1165, Mar-May, 1961 - No.1289, Apr, 1962

	GD	VG	FN	VF	VF/NM	NM-
Four Color 1165 (#1)	10	20	30	69	122	175
Four Color 1243 (11-1/61-61), 1289	8	16	24	56	93	130

ELMER FUDD (Also see Camp Comics, Daffy, Looney Tunes #1 & Super Book #10, 22)
Dell Publishing Co.: No. 470, May, 1953 - No. 1293, Mar-May, 1962

	GD	VG	FN	VF	VF/NM	NM-
Four Color 470 (#1)	9	18	27	60	100	140
Four Color 558,628,689('56)	5	10	15	32	51	70
Four Color 725,783,841,888,938,977,1032,1081,1131,1171,1222,1293('62)	4	8	12	28	44	60

ELMO COMICS
St. John Publishing Co.: Jan, 1948 (Daily strip-r)

	GD	VG	FN	VF	VF/NM	NM-
1-By Cecil Jensen	10	20	30	58	79	100

ELONGATED MAN (See Flash #112 & Justice League of America #105)
DC Comics: Jan, 1992 - No. 4, Apr, 1992 ($1.00, limited series)

1-4: 3-The Flash app. 3.00

ELRIC (Of Melnibone)(See First Comics Graphic Novel #6 & Marvel Graphic Novel #2)
Pacific Comics: Apr, 1983 - No. 6, Apr, 1984 ($1.50, Baxter paper)

1-6: Russell-c/a(i) in all 3.00

ELRIC
Topps Comics: 1996 ($2.95, one-shot)

0--One Life: Russell-c/a; adapts Neil Gaiman's short story "One Life--Furnished in Early Moorcock." 3.00

ELRIC, SAILOR ON THE SEAS OF FATE
First Comics: June, 1985 - No. 7, June, 1986 ($1.75, limited series)

1-7: Adapts Michael Moorcock's novel 3.00

ELRIC, STORMBRINGER
Dark Horse Comics/Topps Comics: 1997 - No. 7, 1997($2.95, limited series)

1-7: Russell-c/s/a; adapts Michael Moorcock's novel 3.00

ELRIC: THE BANE OF THE BLACK SWORD
First Comics: Aug, 1988 - No. 6, June, 1989 ($1.75/$1.95, limited series)

1-6: Adapts Michael Moorcock's novel 3.00

	GD	VG	FN	VF	VF/NM	NM-
	2.0	4.0	6.0	8.0	9.0	9.2

ELRIC: THE VANISHING TOWER
First Comics: Aug, 1987 - No. 6, June, 1988 ($1.75, limited series)

1-6: Adapts Michael Moorcock's novel 3.00

ELRIC: WEIRD OF THE WHITE WOLF
First Comics: Oct, 1986 - No. 5, June, 1987 ($1.75, limited series)

1-5: Adapts Michael Moorcock's novel 3.00

EL SALVADOR - A HOUSE DIVIDED
Eclipse Comics: March, 1989 ($2.50, B&W, Baxter paper, stiff-c, 52 pgs.)

1-Gives history of El Salvador 3.00

ELSEWHERE PRINCE, THE (Moebius' Airtight Garage)
Marvel Comics (Epic): May, 1990 - No. 6, Oct, 1990 ($1.95, limited series)

1-6: Moebius scripts & back-up-a in all 3.00

ELSEWORLDS 80-PAGE GIANT
DC Comics: Aug, 1999 ($5.95, one-shot)

	GD	VG	FN	VF	VF/NM	NM-
1-Most copies destroyed by DC over content of the "Superman's Babysitter" story; some UK shipments sold before recall	11	22	33	75	138	200

ELSEWORLD'S FINEST
DC Comics: 1997 - No. 2, 1997 ($4.95, limited series)

1,2: Elseworld's story-Superman & Batman in the 1920's 5.00

ELSEWORLD'S FINEST: SUPERGIRL & BATGIRL
DC Comics: 1998 ($5.95, one-shot)

1-Haley-a 6.00

ELSIE THE COW
D. S. Publishing Co.: Oct-Nov, 1949 - No. 3, July-Aug, 1950

	GD	VG	FN	VF	VF/NM	NM-
1-(36 pgs.)	25	50	75	147	241	335
2,3	18	36	54	105	165	225

ELSINORE
Alias Entertainment: Apr, 2005 - No. 5, Apr, 2006 (75¢/$2.99/$3.25)

1-5: 1-(75¢-c) Brian Denham-a/Kenneth Lillie-Paetz-s. 2-($2.99-c). 4-($3.25-c) 5-Sparacio-a 3.25

ELSON'S PRESENTS
DC Comics: 1981 (100 pgs., no cover price)

	GD	VG	FN	VF	VF/NM	NM-
Series 1-6: Repackaged 1981 DC comics; 1-DC Comics Presents #29, Flash #303, Batman #331. 2-Superman #335, Ghosts #96, Justice League of America #186. 3-New Teen Titans #3, Secrets of Haunted House #32, Wonder Woman #275. 4-Secrets of the LSH #1, Brave & the Bold #170, New Adv. of Superboy #13. 5-LSH #271, Green Lantern #136, Super Friends #40. 6-Action #515, Mystery in Space #115, Detective #498	2	4	6	11	16	20

ELVEN (Also see Prime)
Malibu Comics (Ultraverse): Oct, 1994 - No. 4, Feb, 1995 ($2.50, lim. series)

0 ($2.95)-Prime app. 3.00
1-4: 2,4-Prime app. 3-Primevil app. 3.00
1-Limited Foil Edition- no price on cover 4.00

ELVIRA MISTRESS OF THE DARK
Marvel Comics: Oct, 1988 ($2.00, B&W, magazine size)

1-Movie adaptation 5.00

ELVIRA MISTRESS OF THE DARK
Claypool Comics (Eclipse): May, 1993 - No. 166, Feb, 2007 ($2.50, B&W)

1-Austin-a(i). Spiegle-a 6.00
2-6: Spiegle-a 4.00
7-99,101-166-Photo-c: 3.00
100-(8/01) Kurt Busiek back-up-s; art by DeCarlo and others 3.00
TPB ($12.95) 13.00

ELVIRA'S HOUSE OF MYSTERY
DC Comics: Jan, 1986 - No. 11, Jan, 1987

1,11: 11-Dave Stevens-c 6.00
2-10: 9-Photo-c, Special 1 (3/87, $1.25) 4.00

ELVIS MANDIBLE, THE
DC Comics (Piranha Press): 1990 ($3.50, 52 pgs., B&W, mature)

nn 4.00

ELVIS PRESLEY (See Career Girl Romances #32, Go-Go, Howard Chaykin's American Flagg #10, Humbug #8, I Love You #60 & Young Lovers #18)

EL ZOMBO FANTASMA
Dark Horse Comics (Rocket Comics): Apr, 2004 - No. 3, June, 2004 ($2.99)

E-Man #4 © CC

Emma #1 © MAR

Ender in Exile #2 © Orson Scott Card

	GD 2.0	VG 4.0	FN 6.0	VF 8.0	VF/NM 9.0	NM- 9.2

1-3-Wilkins-s&a/Munroe-s 3.00

E-MAN
Charlton Comics: Oct, 1973 - No. 10, Sept, 1975 (Painted-c No. 7-10)

	GD	VG	FN	VF	VF/NM	NM-
1-Origin & 1st app. E-Man; Staton c/a in all	3	6	9	16	23	30
2-5: 2,4,5-Ditko-a. 3-Howard-a. 5-Miss Liberty Belle app. by Ditko	2	4	6	9	12	15
6-10: 6,7,9,10-Early Byrne-a (#6 is 1/75). 6-Disney parody. 8-Full-length story; Nova begins as E-Man's partner	2	4	6	11	16	20
1-4,9,10 (Modern Comics reprints, '77)						4.00

NOTE: *Killjoy app.-No. 2, 4. Liberty Belle app.-No. 5. Rog 2000 app.-No. 6, 7, 9, 10. Travis app.-No. 3.* ***Sutton*** *a-1.*

E-MAN
Comico: Sept, 1989 ($2.75, one-shot, no ads, high quality paper)

1-Staton-c/a; Michael Mauser story 3.00

E-MAN
Comico: V4#1, Jan, 1990 - No. 3, Mar, 1990 ($2.50, limited series)

1-3: Staton-c/a 3.00

E-MAN
Alpha Productions: Oct, 1993 ($2.75)

V5#1-Staton-c/a; 20th anniversary issue 3.00

E-MAN COMICS (Also see Michael Mauser & The Original E-Man)
First Comics: Apr, 1983 - No. 25, Aug, 1985 ($1.00/$1.25, direct sales only)

1-25: 2-X-Men satire. 3-X-Men/Phoenix satire. 6-Origin retold. 8-Cutey Bunny app. 10-Origin Nova Kane. 24-Origin Michael Mauser 3.00

NOTE: ***Staton*** *a-1-5, 6-25p; c-1-25.*

E-MAN RETURNS
Alpha Productions: 1994 ($2.75, B&W)

1-Joe Staton-c/a(p) 3.00

EMERALD DAWN
DC Comics: 1991 ($4.95, trade paperback)

nn-Reprints Green Lantern: Emerald Dawn #1-6 5.00

EMERALD DAWN II (See Green Lantern...)

EMERGENCY (Magazine)
Charlton Comics: June, 1976 - No. 4, Jan, 1977 (B&W)

	GD	VG	FN	VF	VF/NM	NM-
1-Neal Adams-c/a; Heath, Austin-a	4	8	12	24	37	50
2,3: 2-N. Adams-c. 3-N. Adams-a.	3	6	9	19	29	38
4-Alcala-a	3	6	9	14	20	25

EMERGENCY (TV)
Charlton Comics: June, 1976 - No. 4, Dec, 1976

	GD	VG	FN	VF	VF/NM	NM-
1-Staton-c; early Byrne-a (22 pages)	3	6	9	20	30	40
2-4: 2-Staton-c. 2,3-Byrne text illos.	3	6	9	14	20	25

EMERGENCY DOCTOR
Charlton Comics: Summer, 1963 (one-shot)

	GD	VG	FN	VF	VF/NM	NM-
1	3	6	9	19	29	38

EMIL & THE DETECTIVES (See Movie Comics)

EMISSARY (Jim Valentino's...)
Image Comics (Shadowline): May, 2006 - Present ($3.50)

1-6: 1-Rand-s/Ferreyra-a. 4-6-Long-s 3.50

EMMA (Adaptation of the Jane Austen novel)
Marvel Comics: May, 2011 - No. 5 ($3.99)

1,2-Nancy Butler-s/Janet K. Lee-a 4.00

EMMA FROST
Marvel Comics: Aug, 2003 - No. 18, Feb, 2005 ($2.50/$2.99)

1-7-Emma in high school; Bollers-s/Green-a/Horn-c 3.00
8-18-($2.99) 3.00
... Vol. 1: Higher Learning TPB (2004, $7.99, digest size) r/#1-6 8.00
... Vol. 2: Mind Games TPB (2005, $7.99, digest size) r/#7-12 8.00
... Vol. 3: Bloom TPB (2005, $7.99, digest size) r/#13-18 8.00

EMMA PEEL & JOHN STEED (See The Avengers)

EMPEROR'S NEW CLOTHES, THE
Dell Publishing Co.: 1950 (10¢, 68 pgs., 1/2 size, oblong)

	GD	VG	FN	VF	VF/NM	NM-
nn - (Surprise Books series)	6	12	18	28	34	40

EMPIRE
Image Comics (Gorilla): May, 2000 - No. 2, Sept, 2000 ($2.50)
DC Comics: No. 0, Aug, 2003; Sept, 2003 - No. 6, Feb, 2004 ($4.95/$2.50, limited series)

1,2: 1 (5/00)-Waid-s/Kitson-a; w/Crimson Plague prologue 3.00
0-(8/03) reprints #1,2 5.00
1-6: 1-(9/03) new Waid-s/Kitson-a/c 3.00
TPB (DC, 2004, $14.95) r/series; Kitson sketch pages; Waid intro. 15.00

EMPIRE STRIKES BACK, THE (See Marvel Comics Super Special #16 & Marvel Special Edition)

EMPTY LOVE STORIES
Slave Labor #1 & 2/Funny Valentine Press: Nov, 1994 - Present ($2.95, B&W)

1,2: Steve Darnall scripts in all. 1-Alex Ross-c. 2-(8/96)-Mike Allred-c 4.00
1,2-2nd printing (Funny Valentine Press) 3.00
... 1999-Jeff Smith-c; Doran-a 3.00
..."Special" (2.95) Ty Templeton-c 3.00

ENCHANTED APPLES OF OZ, THE (See First Comics Graphic Novel #5)

ENCHANTER
Eclipse Comics: Apr, 1987 - No. 3, Aug. 1987 ($2.00, B&W, limited series)

1-3 3.00

ENCHANTING LOVE
Kirby Publishing Co.: Oct, 1949 - No. 6, July, 1950 (All 52 pgs.)

	GD	VG	FN	VF	VF/NM	NM-
1-Photo-c	16	32	48	94	147	200
2-Photo-c; Powell-a	10	20	30	58	79	100
3,4,6: 3-Jimmy Stewart photo-c	10	20	30	56	76	95
5-Ingels-a, 9 pgs.; photo-c	16	32	48	94	147	200

ENCHANTMENT VISUALETTES (Magazine)
World Editions: Dec, 1949 - No. 5, Apr, 1950 (Painted c-1)

	GD	VG	FN	VF	VF/NM	NM-
1-Contains two romance comic strips each	15	30	45	90	140	190
2	12	24	36	69	97	125
3-5	10	20	30	56	76	95

ENDER IN EXILE (ORSON SCOTT CARD'S...)
Marvel Comics: Aug, 2010 - No. 5, Dec, 2010 ($3.99, limited series)

1-5-Sequel to Ender's Game; Johnston-s/Mhan-a/Fiumara-c 4.00

ENDER'S GAME: BATTLE SCHOOL
Marvel Comics: Dec, 2008 - No. 5, Jun, 2009 ($3.99, limited series)

1-5-Adaptation of Orson Scott Card novel Ender's Game; Yost-s/Ferry-a. 1-Two covers 4.00
Ender's Game: Mazer in Prison Special (4/10, $3.99) Johnston-s/Mhan-a 4.00
Ender's Game: Recruiting Valentine (8/09, $3.99) Timothy Green-a 4.00
Ender's Game: The League War (6/10, $3.99) Aaron Johnston-s/Timothy Green-a 4.00
Ender's Game: War of Gifts Special (2/10, $4.99) Timothy Green-a 5.00

ENDER'S GAME: COMMAND SCHOOL
Marvel Comics: Nov, 2009 - No. 5, Apr, 2010 ($3.99, limited series)

1-5-Adaptation of Orson Scott Card novel Ender's Game; Yost-s/Ferry-a 4.00

ENDER'S SHADOW: BATTLE SCHOOL
Marvel Comics: Feb, 2009 - No. 5, Jun, 2009 ($3.99, limited series)

1-5-Adaptation of O.S. Card novel Ender's Shadow; Carey-s/Fiumara-a. 1-Two covers 4.00

ENDER'S SHADOW: COMMAND SCHOOL
Marvel Comics: Nov, 2009 - No. 5, Apr, 2010 ($3.99, limited series)

1-5-Adaptation of O.S. Card novel Ender's Shadow; Carey-s/Fiumara-a 4.00

END LEAGUE, THE
Dark Horse Comics: Dec, 2007 - No. 9, Nov, 2009 ($2.99/$3.99)

1-8: 1-Broome-c/a; Remender-s. 5,6-Canete-a 3.00
9-($3.99) MacDonald-a/Canete-c 4.00

ENEMY ACE SPECIAL (Also see Our Army at War #151, Showcase #57, 58 & Star Spangled War Stories #138)
DC Comics: 1990 ($1.00, one-shot)

1-Kubert-r/Our Army #151,153; c-r/Showcase 57 5.00

ENEMY ACE: WAR IDYLL
DC Comics: 1990 (Graphic novel)

Hardcover-George Pratt-s/painted-a/c 30.00
Softcover (1991, $14.95) 15.00

ENEMY ACE: WAR IN HEAVEN
DC Comics: 2001 - No. 2, 2001 ($5.95, squarebound, limited series)

1,2-Ennis-s; Von Hammer in WW2. 1-Weston & Alamy-a. 2-Heath-a 6.00
TPB (2003, $14.95) r/#1,2 & Star Spangled War Stories #139; Jim Dietz-painted-c 15.00

ENGINEHEAD
DC Comics: June, 2004 - No. 6, Nov, 2004 ($2.50, limited series)

1-6-Joe Kelly-s/Ted McKeever-a/c. 6-Metal Men app. 3.00

Enter the Heroic Age #1 © MAR

Epic Anthology #1 © MAR

Espers V3 #7 © James Hudnall

	GD 2.0	VG 4.0	FN 6.0	VF 8.0	VF/NM 9.0	NM- 9.2

ENIGMA
DC Comics (Vertigo): Mar, 1993 - No. 8, Oct, 1993 ($2.50, limited series)
1-8: Milligan scripts 3.00
Trade paperback ($19.95)-reprints 20.00

ENO AND PLUM (Also see Cud Comics)
Oni Press: Mar, 1998 ($2.95, B&W)
1-Terry LaBan-s/c/a 3.00

ENSIGN O'TOOLE (TV)
Dell Publishing Co.: Aug-Oct, 1963
1 3 6 9 20 30 40

ENSIGN PULVER (See Movie Classics)

ENTER THE HEROIC AGE
Marvel Comics: July, 2010 ($3.99, one-shot)
1-Short stories of Avengers Academy, Atlas, Black Widow, Thunderbolts; Hitch-c 4.00

EPIC
Marvel Comics (Epic Comics): 1992 - Book 4, 1992 ($4.95, lim. series, 52 pgs.)
Book One-Four: 2-Dorman painted-c 5.00
NOTE: *Alien Legion in #3. Cholly & Flytrap by* ***Burden****(scripts) &* ***Suydam****(art) in 3, 4. Dinosaurs in #4. Dreadlands in #1. Hellraiser in #1. Nightbreed in #2. Sleeze Brothers in #2. Stalkers in #1-4. Wild Cards in #1-4.*

EPIC ANTHOLOGY
Marvel Comics (Epic Comics): Apr, 2004 ($5.99)
1-Short stories by various 6.00

EPIC ILLUSTRATED (Magazine)
Marvel Comics Group: Spring, 1980 - No. 34, Feb, 1986 ($2.00/$2.50, B&W/color, mature)
1-Frazetta-c; Silver Surfer/Galactus-sty; Wendy Pini-s/a; Suydam-s/a; Metamorphosis Odyssey begins (thru #9) Starlin-a 2 4 6 8 10 12
2-10: 2-Bissette/Veitch-a; Goodwin-s. 3-1st app. Dreadstar. 4-Ellison 15 pg. story w/Steacy-a; Hempel-s/a; Veitch-s/a. 5-Hildebrandts-c/interview; Jusko-a; Vess-s/a. 6-Ellison-s (26 pgs). 7-Adams-s/a(16 pgs.); BWS interview. 8-Suydam-s/a; Vess-s/a. 9-Conrad-c. 10-Marada the She-Wolf-c/sty(21 pgs.) by Claremont/Bolton 1 2 3 4 5 7
11-20: 11-Wood-a; Jusko-a. 12-Wolverton Spacehawk-r edited & recolored w/article on him; Muth-a. 13-Blade Runner preview by Williamson. 14-Elric of Melnibone by Russell; Revenge of the Jedi preview. 15-Vallejo-c & interview; 1st Dreadstar solo story (cont'd in Dreadstar #1). 16-B. Smith-c/a(2); Sim-s/a. 17-Starslammers preview. 18-Go Nagai; Williams-a. 19-Jabberwocky w/Hampton-a; Cheech Wizard-s. 20-The Sacred & the Profane begins by Ken Steacy; Elric by Gould; Williams-a 1 2 3 5 6 8
21-30: 21-Vess-s/a. 22-Frankenstein w/Wrightson-a. 26-Galactus series begins (thru #34); Cerebus the Aardvark story by Dave Sim. 27-Groo. 28-Cerebus. 29-1st Sheeva. 30-Cerebus; History of Dreadstar, Starlin-s/a; Williams-a; Vess-a 1 3 4 6 8 10
31-33: 31-Bolton-c/a. 32-Cerebus portfolio. 2 4 6 8 10 12
34-R.E.Howard tribute by Thomas-s/Plunkett-a; Moore-s/Veitch-a; Cerebus; Cholly & Flytrap w/Suydam-a; BWS-a 2 4 6 10 14 18
Sampler (early 1980 8 pg. preview giveaway) same cover as #1 with "Sampler" text 6.00
NOTE: ***N. Adams*** *a-7; c-6.* ***Austin*** *a-15-20i.* ***Bode*** *a-19, 23, 27r.* ***Bolton*** *a-7, 10-12, 15, 18, 22-25; c-10, 18, 22, 23.* ***Boris*** *c/a-15.* ***Brunner*** *c-12.* ***Buscema*** *a-1p, 9p, 11-13p.* ***Byrne/Austin*** *a-26-34.* ***Chaykin*** *a-2; c-8.* ***Conrad*** *a-2-5, 7-9, 25-34; c-17.* ***Corben*** *a-15; c-2.* ***Frazetta*** *c-1.* ***Golden*** *a-3r.* ***Gulacy*** *c/a-3.* ***Jeff Jones*** *c-25.* ***Kaluta*** *a-17r, 21, 24r, 26; c-4, 28.* ***Nebres*** *a-1.* ***Reese*** *a-12.* ***Russell*** *a-2-4, 9, 14, 33; c-14.* ***Simonson*** *a-17.* ***B. Smith*** *c/a-7, 16.* ***Starlin*** *a-1-9, 14, 15, 34.* ***Steranko*** *c-19.* ***Williamson*** *a-13, 27, 34.* ***Wrightson*** *a-13p, 22, 25, 27, 34; c-30.*

EPIC LITE
Marvel Comics (Epic Comics): Sept, 1991 ($3.95, 52 pgs., one-shot)
1-Bob the Alien, Normalman by Valentino 4.00

EPICURUS THE SAGE
DC Comics (Piranha Press): Vol. 1, 1991 - Vol. 2, 1991 ($9.95, 8-1/8x10-7/8")
Volume 1,2-Sam Kieth-c/a; Messner-Loebs-s 10.00
TPB (2003, $19.95) r/ #1,2, Fast Forward Rising the Sun; new story 20.00

EPILOGUE
IDW Publishing: Sept, 2008 - No. 4, Dec, 2008 ($3.99)
1-4-Steve Niles-s/Kyle Hotz-a/c 4.00

ERADICATOR
DC Comics: Aug, 1996 - No. 3, Oct, 1996 ($1.75, limited series)
1-3: Superman app. 3.00

ERNIE COMICS (Formerly Andy Comics #21; All Love Romances #26 on)
Current Books/Ace Periodicals: No. 22, Sept, 1948 - No. 25, Mar, 1949
nn (9/48,11/48; #22,23)-Teenage humor 8 16 24 42 54 65
24,25 6 12 18 31 38 45

ESCAPADE IN FLORENCE (See Movie Comics)

	GD 2.0	VG 4.0	FN 6.0	VF 8.0	VF/NM 9.0	NM- 9.2

ESCAPE FROM DEVIL'S ISLAND
Avon Periodicals: 1952
1-Kinstler-c; r/as Dynamic Adventures #9 40 80 120 246 411 575

ESCAPE FROM THE PLANET OF THE APES (See Power Record Comics)

ESCAPE TO WITCH MOUNTAIN (See Walt Disney Showcase No. 29)

ESCAPISTS, THE (See Michael Chabon Presents The Amazing Adventures of the Escapist)
Dark Horse Comics: July, 2006 - No. 6, Dec, 2006 ($1.00/$2.99, limited series)
1-($1.00) Frank Miller-c; r/Vaughan story from Michael Chabon... #8 3.00
2-6($2.99) Vaughan-s/Rolston & Alexander-a. 2-James Jean-c. 3-Cassaday-c 3.00

ESPERS (Also see Interface)
Eclipse Comics: July, 1986 - No. 5, Apr, 1987 ($1.25/$1.75, Mando paper)
1-5-James Hudnall story & David Lloyd-a. 3.00

ESPERS
Halloween Comics: V2#1, 1996 - No. 6, 1997 ($2.95, B&W) (1st Halloween Comics series)
V2#1-6: James D. Hudnall scripts 3.00
Undertow TPB ('98, $14.95) r/#1-6 15.00

ESPERS
Image Comics: V3#1, 1997 - Present ($2.95, B&W, limited series)
V3#1-7: James D. Hudnall scripts 3.00
Black Magic TPB ('98, $14.95) r/#1-4 15.00

ESPIONAGE (TV)
Dell Publishing Co.: May-July, 1964
1 3 6 9 20 30 40

ESSENTIAL (Title series), **Marvel Comics**
--ANT-MAN, '02 (B&W- r) V1-Reprints app. from Tales To Astonish #27, #35-69; Kirby-c 15.00
--AVENGERS, '98 (B&W- r) V1-R-Avengers #1-24; new Immonen-c 15.00
V2(6/00)-Reprints Avengers #25-46, King-Size Special #1; Immonen-c 15.00
V3(3/01)-Reprints Avengers #47-68, Annual #2; Immonen-c 15.00
V4('04)-Reprints Avengers #69-97, Incredible Hulk #140; Neal Adams-c 17.00
V5('06)-Reprints Avengers #98-119, Daredevil #99, Defenders #8-11 17.00
V6('08)-Reprints Avengers #120-140, Giant Size #1-4, Capt. Marvel #33 & FF #150 17.00
--CAPTAIN AMERICA, '00 (B&W- r) V1-Reprints stories from Tales of Suspense #59-99, Captain America #100-102; new Romita & Milgrom-c 15.00
V2(1/02)-Reprints #103-126; Steranko-c 15.00
V3('06)-Reprints #127-153 17.00
V4('07)-Reprints #157-186 17.00
--CLASSIC X-MEN, '06 - Present (B&W- r) (See Essential Uncanny X-Men for V1)
V2-($16.99) R-X-Men #25-53 & Avengers #53; Gil Kane-c 17.00
--CONAN, '00 (B&W- r) V1-R-Conan the Barbarian#1-25; new Buscema-c 15.00
--DAREDEVIL, '02 - Present (B&W-r)
V1-R-Daredevil #1-25 15.00
V2-($16.99) R-Daredevil #26-48, Special #1, Fantastic Four #73 17.00
V3-($16.99) R-Daredevil #49-74, Iron Man #35-38 17.00
V4-($16.99) R-Daredevil #75-101, Avengers #111 17.00
--DAZZLER, '07 (B&W- r) V1-R/#1-21, X-Men #130-131, Amaz. Spider-Man #203 17.00
--DEFENDERS, '05 (B&W-r) V1-Reprints Doctor Strange #183, Sub-Mariner #22,34,35, Incredible Hulk #126, Marvel Feature #1-3, Defenders #1-14, Avengers #115-118 17.00
V2-($16.99) R- Defenders #15-30, Giant-Size Defenders #1-4, Marvel Two-In-One #6,7, Marvel Team-Up #33-35 and Marvel Treasury Edition #12 17.00
V3-($16.99) R- Defenders #31-60 and Annual #1 17.00
--DOCTOR STRANGE, '04 - Present (B&W-r)
V1-($15.95) Reprints Strange Tales #110,111,114-168 16.00
V1 (2nd printing)-(2006, $16.99) Reprints Strange Tales #110,111,114-168 17.00
V2-($16.99) R-Doctor Strange #169-178,180-183; Avengers #61, Sub-Mariner #22 Marvel Feature #1, Incredible Hulk #126 and Marvel Premiere #3-14 17.00
V3-($16.99) R-Doctor Strange #1-29 & Annual #1;Tomb of Dracula #44,45 17.00
--FANTASTIC FOUR, '98 - Present (B&W-r)
V1-Reprints FF #1-20, Annual #1; new Alan Davis-c; multiple printings exist 17.00
V2-Reprints FF #21-40, Annual #2; Davis and Farmer-c 15.00
V3-Reprints FF #41-63, Annual #3,4; Davis-c 15.00
V4-Reprints FF #64-83, Annual #5,6 17.00
V5-Reprints FF #84-110 17.00
V6-Reprints FF #111-137 17.00
--GHOST RIDER, '05 (B&W-r) V1-Reprints Marvel Spotlight #5-12, Ghost Rider #1-20 and Daredevil #138 17.00
V2-Reprints Ghost Rider #21-50 17.00

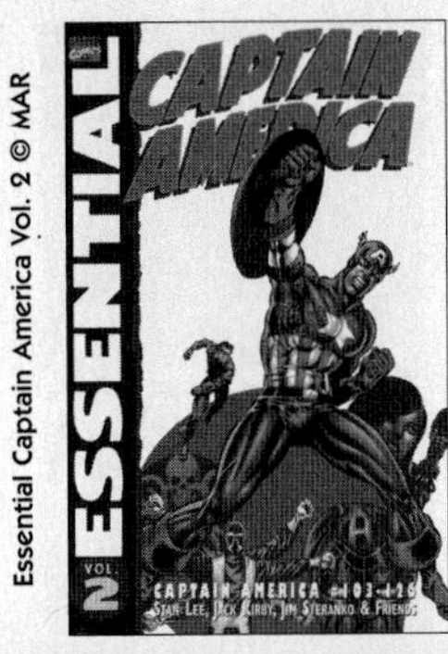

Essential Captain America Vol. 2 © MAR

Essential Tomb of Dracula Vol. 3 © MAR

The Eternal #2 © MAR

	GD 2.0	VG 4.0	FN 6.0	VF 8.0	VF/NM 9.0	NM- 9.2

--GODZILLA, '06 (B&W-r) V1-Godzilla #1-24 20.00

--HOWARD THE DUCK, '02 (B&W- r) V1-Reprints #1-27, Annual #1; plus stories from Marvel Treasury Ed. #12, Man-Thing #1, Giant-Size Man-Thing #4,5, Fear #19; Bolland-c 15.00

--HULK, '99 (B&W-r) V1-R-Incred. Hulk #1-6, Tales To Astonish stories; new Timm-c 15.00
V2-Reprints Tales To Astonish #102-117, Annual #1 15.00
V3-Reprints Incredible Hulk #118-142, Capt. Marvel #20&21, Avengers #88 17.00
V4-Reprints Incredible Hulk #143-170 17.00
V5-Reprints Incredible Hulk #171-200, Annual #5 17.00

--HUMAN TORCH, '03 (B&W-r) V1-Strange Tales #101-134 & Ann. 2; Kirby-c 15.00

--IRON MAN, '00 - Present (B&W-r)
V1-Reprints Tales Of Suspense #39-72; new Timm-c and back-c 15.00
V2-Reprints Tales Of Suspense #73-99, Tales To Astonish #82 & Iron Man #1-11 17.00
V3-Reprints Iron Man #12-38 & Daredevil #73 17.00

--KILLRAVEN, '05 (B&W-r) V1-Reprints Amazing Adventures V2 #18-39, Marvel Team-Up #45, Marvel Graphic Novel #7, Killraven #1 (2001) 17.00

--LUKE CAGE, POWER MAN, '05 (B&W-r) V1-Hero For Hire #1-16 & Power Man #17-27 17.00
V2-Reprints Power Man #28-49 & Annual #1 17.00

--MAN-THING, '06 (B&W-r) V1-Reprints Savage Tales #1, Astonishing Tales #12-13, Adventure Into Fear #10-19, Man-Thing #1-14, Giant-Size Man-Thing #1-2 & Monsters Unleashed #5,8,9 17.00
V2-R/Man-Thing #15-22 & #1-11 ('79 series), Giant-Size Man-Thing #3-5, Rampaging Hulk #7, Marvel Team-Up #68, Marvel Two-In-One #43 & Doctor Strange #41 17.00

--MARVEL HORROR, '06 (B&W-r) V1-R/#Ghost Rider #1-2, Marvel Spotlight #12-24, Son of Satan #1-8, Marvel Two-In-One #14, Marvel Team-Up #32,80,81, Vampire Tales #2-3, Haunt of Horror #2,4,5, Marvel Premiere #27, & Marvel Preview #7 17.00

--MARVEL SAGA, '08 (B&W-r) V1-R/#1-12 17.00

--MARVEL TEAM-UP, '02 - Present (B&W-r) V1('02, '06)-R/#1-24 17.00
V2-R/#25-51 and Marvel Two-In-One #17 17.00

--MARVEL TWO-IN-ONE, '05 - Present (B&W-r)
V1-Reprints Marvel Feature #11&12, Marvel Two-In-One #1-20,22-25 & Annual #1, Marvel Team-Up #47 and Fantastic Four Ann. #11 17.00
V2-R/#26-52 & Annual #2,3 17.00

--MONSTER OF FRANKENSTEIN, '04 (B&W-r) V1-Reprints Monster of Frankenstein #1-5, Frankenstein Monster #6-18, Giant-Size Werewolf #2, Monsters Unleashed #2,4-10 & Legion of Monsters #1 17.00

--MOON KNIGHT, '06 (B&W-r) V1-Reprints Moon Knight #1-10 and early apps. 17.00
V2-R/#11-30 17.00

--MS. MARVEL, '07 (B&W-r) V1-Reprints Ms. Marvel #1-23, Marvel Super-Heroes Magazine #10,11, and Avengers Annual #10 17.00

--NOVA, '06 (B&W-r) V1-Reprints Nova #1-25, AS-M #175, Marvel Two-In-One Ann. #3 17.00

--OFFICIAL HANDBOOK OF THE MARVEL UNIVERSE, '06 (B&W-r) V1-Reprints #1-15 profiling Abomination through Zzzax; dead and inactive characters; weapons & hardware; wraparound-c by Byrne 17.00

--OFFICIAL HANDBOOK OF THE MARVEL UNIVERSE - DELUXE EDITION, '06 (B&W-r)
V1-Reprints #1-7 profiling Abomination through Magneto; wraparound-c by Byrne 17.00
V2-Reprints #8-14 profiling Magus through Wolverine; wraparound-c by Byrne 17.00
V3-Reprints #15-20 profiling Wonder Man through Zzzax & Book of the Dead 17.00

--OFFICIAL HANDBOOK OF THE MARVEL UNIVERSE - MASTER EDITION, '08 (B&W-r)
V1-Reprints profiling Abomination through Gargoyle 17.00
V2-Reprints profiles 17.00

--OFFICIAL HANDBOOK OF THE MARVEL UNIVERSE - UPDATE '89, '06 (B&W-r)
V1-Reprints #1-8; wraparound-c by Frenz 17.00

--PETER PARKER, THE SPECTACULAR SPIDER-MAN, '05 (B&W-r) V1-Reprints #1-31 17.00
V2-Reprints #32-53 & Annual #1,2; Amazing Spider-Man Annual #13 17.00
V3-Reprints #54-74 & Annual #3; Frank Miller-c 17.00

--POWER MAN AND IRON FIST, '07 (B&W-r) V1-R/#50-72,74-75 17.00

--PUNISHER, '04, '06 - Present (B&W-r) V1-Reprints early app. in Amazing Spider-Man, Captain America, Daredevil, Marvel Preview and Punisher #1-5 (2 printings) 17.00
V2-Punisher #1-20, Annual #1 and Daredevil #257 17.00
V3-Punisher #21-40, Annual #2,3 17.00

--RAMPAGING HULK, '08 (B&W-r) V1-R/#1-9, The Hulk! #10-15 & Incredible Hulk #269 17.00

--SAVAGE SHE-HULK, '06 (B&W-r) V1-R/#1-25 17.00

--SILVER SURFER, '98 - Present (B&W-r)
V1-R-material from SS#1-18 and Fantastic Four Ann. #5 15.00
V2-R-SS#1(1982), SS#1-18 & Ann#1(1987), Epic Illustrated #1, Marvel Fanfare #51 17.00

--SPIDER-MAN, '96 - Present (B&W-r)
V1-R-AF #15, Amaz. S-M #1-20, Ann. #1 (2 printings) 15.00
V2-R-Amaz. Spider-Man #21-43, Annual #2,3 15.00
V3-R-Amaz. Spider-Man #44-68 15.00
V4-R-Amaz. Spider-Man #69-89; Annual #4,5; new Timm-f&b-c 15.00
V5-R-Amaz. Spider-Man #90-113; new Romita-c 15.00
V6-R-Amaz. Spider-Man #114-137, Giant-Size Super-Heroes #1 G-S S-M #1,2 17.00
V7-R-Amaz. Spider-Man #138-160, Annual #10; Giant-Size Spider-Man #3-5 17.00
V8-R-Amaz. Spider-Man #161-185, Annual #11; G-S Spider-Man #6; Nova #12 17.00

--SPIDER-WOMAN, '05 (B&W-r) V1-Reprints Marvel Spotlight #32, Marvel Two-In-One #29-33, Spider-Woman #1-25 17.00
V2-R-Spider-Woman #26-50, Marvel Team-Up #97 & Uncanny X-Men #148 17.00

--SUPER-VILLAIN TEAM-UP, '04 (B&W-r) V1-r/S-V T-U #1-14 & 16-17, Giant-Size S-V T-U #1,2; Avengers #154-156; Champions #16, & Astonishing Tales #1-8 17.00

--TALES OF THE ZOMBIE, '06 (B&W-r) V1-($16.99) r/#1-10 & Dracula Lives #1,2 17.00

--THOR, '01 (B&W-r) V1-R-Journey Into Mystery #83-112 15.00
V2-($16.99) R-Thor #113-136 & Annual #1,2 17.00
V3-($16.99) R-Thor #137-166 17.00

--TOMB OF DRACULA, '03 - Present (B&W-r) V1-R-Tomb of Dracula #1-25, Werewolf By Night #15, Giant-Size Chillers #1 15.00
V2-($16.99) R-Tomb of Dracula #26-49, Giant-Size Dracula #2-5, Dr. Strange #14 17.00
V3-($16.99) R-Tomb of Dracula #50-70, Tomb of Dracula Magazine #1-4 17.00
V4-($16.99) R/Stories from Tomb of Dracula Magazine #2-6, Dracula Lives! #1-13, and Frankenstein Monster #7-9 17.00

--UNCANNY X-MEN, '99 - Present (B&W reprints) (See Essential Classic X-Men for V2)
V1-Reprints X-Men (1st series) #1-24; Timm-c 15.00

ESSENTIAL VERTIGO: THE SANDMAN
DC Comics (Vertigo): Aug, 1996 - No. 32, Mar, 1999 ($1.95/$2.25, reprints)

1-13,15-31: Reprints Sandman, 2nd series 3.00
14-($2.95) 3.50
32-($4.50) Reprints Sandman Special #1 4.50

ESSENTIAL VERTIGO: SWAMP THING
DC Comics: Nov, 1996 - No. 24, Oct, 1998 ($1.95/$2.25,B&W, reprints)

1-11,13-24: 1-9-Reprints Alan Moore's Swamp Thing stories 3.00
12-($3.50) r/Annual #2 4.00

ESSENTIAL WEREWOLF BY NIGHT
Marvel Comics: 2005 - Present (B&W reprints)

V1-($16.99) r/Marvel Spotlight #2-4, Werewolf By Night 1-23, Marvel Team-Up #12, Tomb of Dracula #18, Giant-Size Creatures #1 17.00
V2-R/#22-43, Giant-Size Werewolf #2-5 and Marvel Premiere #28 17.00

ESSENTIAL WOLVERINE
Marvel Comics: 1999 - Present (B&W reprints)

V1-r/#1-23, V2-r/#24-47, V3-R/#48-69, V4-R/#70-90 17.00

ESSENTIAL X-FACTOR
Marvel Comics: 2005 - Present (B&W reprints)

V1-($16.99) r/X-Factor #1-16 & Annual #1, Avengers #262, Fantastic Four #286, Thor #373&374 and Power Pack #27 17.00
V2-Reprints X-Factor #17-35 & Annual #2, Thor #378 17.00

ESSENTIAL X-MEN
Marvel Comics: 1996 - Present (B&W reprints)

V1-V4: V1-R/Giant Size X-Men #1, X-Men #94-119. V2-R-X-Men #120-144. V3-R-Uncanny X-Men #145-161, Ann. #3-5. V4-Uncanny X-Men #162-179, Ann. #6 15.00
V5-($16.99) R/Uncanny X-Men #180-198, Ann. #7-8 17.00
V6-($16.99) R/Uncanny X-Men #199-213, Ann. #9, New Mutants Special Edition #1, X-Factor #9-11, New Mutants #46, Thor #373-374 and Power Pack #27 17.00
V7-($16.99) R/Uncanny X-Men #214-228, Ann. #10,11, and F.F. vs. The X-Men #1-4 17.00
V8-($16.99) R/Uncanny X-Men #229-243, Ann. #12 & X-Factor #36-39 17.00

ESTABLISHMENT, THE (Also see The Authority and The Monarchy)
DC Comics (WildStorm): Nov, 2001 - No. 13, Nov, 2002 ($2.50)

1-13-Edginton-s/Adlard-a 3.00

ETERNAL, THE
Marvel Comics (MAX): Aug, 2003 - No. 6, Jan, 2004 ($2.99, mature)

1-6-Austen-s/Walker-a 3.00

ETERNAL BIBLE, THE
Authentic Publications: 1946 (Large size) (16 pgs. in color)

	GD	VG	FN	VF	VF/NM	NM-
1	15	30	45	85	130	175

ETERNALS, THE

The Eternals #7 © MAR

Eternal Warrior #28 © VAL

Evil Ernie #1 © Chaos

Marvel Comics Group: July, 1976 - No. 19, Jan, 1978

	GD 2.0	VG 4.0	FN 6.0	VF 8.0	VF/NM 9.0	NM- 9.2
1-(Regular 25¢ edition)-Origin & 1st app. Eternals	3	6	9	16	23	30
1-(30¢-c variant, limited distribution)	4	8	12	22	34	45
2-(Reg. 25¢ edition)-1st app. Ajak & The Celestials	2	4	6	9	12	15
2-(30¢-c variant, limited distribution)	2	4	6	13	18	25
3-19: 14,15-Cosmic powered Hulk-c/story	2	4	6	8	10	12
12-16-(35¢-c variants, limited distribution)	2	4	6	10	14	18
Annual 1(10/77)	2	4	6	9	12	15
Eternals by Jack Kirby HC (2006, $75.00, dust jacket) r/#1-19 & Annual #1; intro by Royer; letter pages from #1,2,Annual #1; afterwords by Robert Greenberger						75.00

NOTE: *Kirby c/a(p) in all.*

ETERNALS, THE
Marvel Comics: Oct, 1985 - No. 12, Sept, 1986 (Maxi-series, mando paper)

	GD 2.0	VG 4.0	FN 6.0	VF 8.0	VF/NM 9.0	NM- 9.2
1,12 (52 pgs.): 12-Williamson-a(i)						4.00
2-11						3.00

ETERNALS
Marvel Comics: Aug, 2006 - No. 7, Mar, 2007 ($3.99, limited series)

	GD 2.0	VG 4.0	FN 6.0	VF 8.0	VF/NM 9.0	NM- 9.2
1-7-Neil Gaiman-s/John Romita Jr.-a/Rick Berry-c						4.00
1-7-Variant covers by Romita Jr.						4.00
1-Variant cover by Coipel						4.00
... Sketchbook (2006, $1.99, B&W) character sketches and sketch pages from #1						3.00
HC (2007, $29.99, dustjacket) r/#1-7; gallery of variant covers; sketches, Gaiman interview, Gaiman's original proposal; background essay on Kirby's Eternals						30.00

ETERNALS
Marvel Comics: Aug, 2008 - No. 9, May, 2009 ($2.99)

	GD 2.0	VG 4.0	FN 6.0	VF 8.0	VF/NM 9.0	NM- 9.2
1-9: 1-6-Acuña-a/c; Knauf-s. 2,4-Iron Man app. 7,8-Nguyen-a; X-Men app.						3.00
Annual 1 (1/09, $3.99) Alixe-a/McGuinness-c; & reprint from Eternals #7 ('77) Kirby-s/a						4.00

ETERNALS: THE HEROD FACTOR
Marvel Comics: Nov, 1991 ($2.50, 68 pgs.)

	GD 2.0	VG 4.0	FN 6.0	VF 8.0	VF/NM 9.0	NM- 9.2
1						4.00

ETERNAL WARRIOR (See Solar #10 & 11)
Valiant/Acclaim Comics (Valiant): Aug, 1992 - No. 50, Mar, 1996 ($2.25/$2.50)

	GD 2.0	VG 4.0	FN 6.0	VF 8.0	VF/NM 9.0	NM- 9.2
1-Unity x-over; Miller-c; origin Eternal Warrior & Aram (Armstrong)						4.00
1-($2.25-c) Gold logo						5.00
1-Gold foil logo on embossed cover; no cover price						6.00
2-8: 2-Unity x-over; Simonson-c. 3-Archer & Armstrong x-over. 4-1st brief app. Bloodshot (last pg.); see Rai #0 for 1st full app.; Cowan-c. 5-2nd full app. Bloodshot (12/92; see Rai #0). 6,7: 6-2nd app. Master Darque. 8-Flip book w/Archer & Armstrong #8						3.50
9-25,27-34: 9-1st Book of Geomancer. 14-16-Bloodshot app. 18-Doctor Mirage cameo. 19-Doctor Mirage app. 22-W/bound-in trading card. 25-Archer & Armstrong app.; cont'd from A&A #25						3.00
26-($2.75, 44 pgs.)-Flip book w/Archer & Armstrong						4.00
35-50: 35-Double-c; $2.50-c begins. 50-Geomancer app.						3.00
Special 1 (2/96, $2.50)-Wings of Justice; Art Holcomb script						3.00
Yearbook 1 (1993, $3.95), 2(1994, $3.95)						4.00

ETERNAL WARRIORS: BLACKWORKS
Acclaim Comics (Valiant Heroes): Mar, 1998 ($3.50, one-shot)

	GD 2.0	VG 4.0	FN 6.0	VF 8.0	VF/NM 9.0	NM- 9.2
1						3.50

ETERNAL WARRIORS: DIGITAL ALCHEMY
Acclaim Comics (Valiant Heroes): Vol. 2, Sep, 1997 ($3.95, one-shot, 64 pgs.)

	GD 2.0	VG 4.0	FN 6.0	VF 8.0	VF/NM 9.0	NM- 9.2
Vol. 2-Holcomb-s/Eaglesham-a(p)						4.00

ETERNAL WARRIORS: FIST AND STEEL
Acclaim Comics (Valiant): May, 1996 - No. 2, June, 1996 ($2.50, lim. series)

	GD 2.0	VG 4.0	FN 6.0	VF 8.0	VF/NM 9.0	NM- 9.2
1,2: Geomancer app. in both. 1-Indicia reads "June." 2-Bo Hampton-a						3.00

ETERNAL WARRIORS: TIME AND TREACHERY
Acclaim Comics (Valiant Heroes): Vol. 1, Jun, 1997 ($3.95, one-shot, 48 pgs.)

	GD 2.0	VG 4.0	FN 6.0	VF 8.0	VF/NM 9.0	NM- 9.2
Vol. 1-Reintro Aram, Archer, Ivar the Timewalker, & Gilad the Warmaster; 1st app. Shalla Redburn; Art Holcomb script						4.00

ETERNITY SMITH
Renegade Press: Sept, 1986 - No. 5, May, 1987 ($1.25/$1.50, 36 pgs.)

	GD 2.0	VG 4.0	FN 6.0	VF 8.0	VF/NM 9.0	NM- 9.2
1-5: 1st app. Eternity Smith. 5-Death of Jasmine						3.00

ETERNITY SMITH
Hero Comics: Sept, 1987 - No. 9, 1988 ($1.95)

	GD 2.0	VG 4.0	FN 6.0	VF 8.0	VF/NM 9.0	NM- 9.2
V2#1-9: 8-Indigo begins						3.00

ETTA KETT
King Features Syndicate/Standard: No. 11, Dec, 1948 - No. 14, Sept, 1949

	GD 2.0	VG 4.0	FN 6.0	VF 8.0	VF/NM 9.0	NM- 9.2
11-Teenage	12	24	36	67	94	120
12-14	9	18	27	50	65	80

EVA: DAUGHTER OF THE DRAGON
Dynamite Entertainment: 2007 ($4.99, one-shot)

	GD 2.0	VG 4.0	FN 6.0	VF 8.0	VF/NM 9.0	NM- 9.2
1-Two covers by Jo Chen and Edgar Salazar; Jerwa-s/Salazar-a						5.00

EVANGELINE (Also see Primer)
Comico/First Comics V2#1 on/Lodestone Publ.: 1984 - #2, 6/84; V2#1, 5/87 - V2#12, Mar, 1989 (Baxter paper)

	GD 2.0	VG 4.0	FN 6.0	VF 8.0	VF/NM 9.0	NM- 9.2
1,2, V2#1 (5/87) - 12, Special #1 (1986, $2.00)-Lodestone Publ.						3.00

EVA THE IMP
Red Top Comic/Decker: 1957 - No. 2, Nov, 1957

	GD 2.0	VG 4.0	FN 6.0	VF 8.0	VF/NM 9.0	NM- 9.2
1,2	5	10	14	20	24	28

EVEN MORE FUND COMICS (Benefit book for the Comic Book Legal Defense Fund) (Also see More Fund Comics)
Sky Dog Press: Sept, 2004 ($10.00, B&W, trade paperback)

	GD 2.0	VG 4.0	FN 6.0	VF 8.0	VF/NM 9.0	NM- 9.2
nn-Anthology of short stories and pin-ups by various; Spider-Man-c by Cho						10.00

E.V.E. PROTOMECHA
Image Comics (Top Cow): Mar, 2000 - No. 6, Sept, 2000 ($2.50)

	GD 2.0	VG 4.0	FN 6.0	VF 8.0	VF/NM 9.0	NM- 9.2
Preview ($5.95) Flip book w/Soul Saga preview	2	4	6	8	10	12
1-6: 1-Covers by Finch, Madureira, Garza. 2-Turner var-c						3.00
1-Another Universe variant-c						5.00
TPB (5/01, $17.95) r/#1-6 plus cover galley and sketch pages						18.00

EVERQUEST: ... (Based on online role-playing game)
DC Comics (WildStorm): 2002 ($5.95, one-shots)

	GD 2.0	VG 4.0	FN 6.0	VF 8.0	VF/NM 9.0	NM- 9.2
The Ruins of Kunark - Jim Lee & Dan Norton-a; McQuaid & Lee-s; Lee-c						6.00
Transformations - Philip Tan-a; Devin Grayson-s; Portacio-c						6.00

EVERYBODY'S COMICS (See Fox Giants)

EVERYMAN, THE
Marvel Comics (Epic Comics): Nov, 1991 ($4.50, one-shot, 52 pgs.)

	GD 2.0	VG 4.0	FN 6.0	VF 8.0	VF/NM 9.0	NM- 9.2
1-Mike Allred-a	1	2	3	4	5	7

EVERYTHING HAPPENS TO HARVEY
National Periodical Publications: Sept-Oct, 1953 - No. 7, Sept-Oct, 1954

	GD 2.0	VG 4.0	FN 6.0	VF 8.0	VF/NM 9.0	NM- 9.2
1	29	58	87	170	278	385
2	16	32	48	94	147	200
3-7	14	28	42	82	121	160

EVERYTHING'S ARCHIE
Archie Publications: May, 1969 - No. 157, Sept, 1991 (Giant issues No. 1-20)

	GD 2.0	VG 4.0	FN 6.0	VF 8.0	VF/NM 9.0	NM- 9.2
1-(68 pages)	8	16	24	56	93	130
2-(68 pages)	5	10	15	30	48	65
3-5-(68 pages)	4	8	12	26	41	55
6-13-(68 pages)	3	6	9	18	27	35
14-31-(52 pages)	2	4	6	13	18	22
32 (7/74)-50 (8/76)	2	4	6	8	10	12
51-80 (12/79),100 (4/82)	1	2	3	5	6	8
81-99						6.00
101-120						5.00
121-156: 142,148-Gene Colan-a						4.00
157-Last issue						5.00

EVERYTHING'S DUCKY (Movie)
Dell Publishing Co.: No. 1251, 1961

	GD 2.0	VG 4.0	FN 6.0	VF 8.0	VF/NM 9.0	NM- 9.2
Four Color 1251	5	10	15	30	48	65

EVIL DEAD, THE (Movie)
Dark Horse Comics: Jan, 2008 - No. 4, Apr, 2008 ($2.99, limited series)

	GD 2.0	VG 4.0	FN 6.0	VF 8.0	VF/NM 9.0	NM- 9.2
1-4-Adaptation of the Sam Raimi/Bruce Campbell movie; Bolton painted-a/c						3.00

EVIL ERNIE
Eternity Comics: Dec, 1991 - No. 5, 1992 ($2.50, B&W, limited series)

	GD 2.0	VG 4.0	FN 6.0	VF 8.0	VF/NM 9.0	NM- 9.2
1-1st app. Lady Death by Steven Hughes (12,000 print run); Lady Death app. in all issues	4	8	12	24	37	50
2,3: 2-1st Lady Death-c. 2,3-(7,000 print run)	3	6	9	14	20	25
4-(8,000 print run)	2	4	6	11	16	20
5	2	4	6	9	13	16
Special Edition 1	3	6	9	14	20	25
Youth Gone Wild! ($9.95, trade paperback)-r/#1-5	1	3	4	6	8	10
Youth Gone Wild! Director's Cut ($4.95)-Limited to 15,000, shows the making of the comic						5.00

EVIL ERNIE (Monthly series)
Chaos! Comics: July, 1998 - No. 10, Apr, 1999 ($2.95)

Evil Eye #3 © Richard Sala

Excalibur (2004 series) #2 © MAR

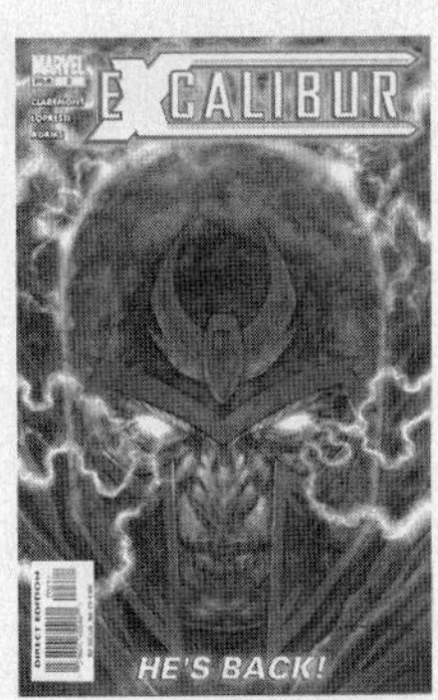

Exciting Comics #11 © STD

GD 2.0 | VG 4.0 | FN 6.0 | VF 8.0 | VF/NM 9.0 | NM- 9.2

1-10-Pulido & Nutman-s/Brewer-a 3.00
1-($10.00) Premium Ed. 10.00
... Baddest Battles (1/97, $1.50) Pin-ups; 2 covers 3.00
... Pieces of Me (11/00, $2.95, B&W) Flashback story; Pulido-s/Beck-a 3.00
... Relentless (5/02, $4.99, B&W) Pulido-s/Beck, Bonk, & Brewer-a 5.00
... Returns (10/01, $3.99, B&W) Pulido-s/Beck-a 4.00

EVIL ERNIE: DEPRAVED
Chaos! Comics: Jul, 1999 - No. 3, Sept, 1999 ($2.95, limited series)
1-3-Pulido-s/Brewer-a 3.00

EVIL ERNIE: DESTROYER
Chaos! Comics: Oct, 1997 - No. 9, Jun, 1998 ($2.95, limited series)
Preview ($2.50), 1-9-Flip cover 3.00

EVIL ERNIE: IN SANTA FE
Devil's Due Publ.: Sept, 2005 - Mar, 2006 ($2.95, limited series)
1-4-Alan Grant-s/Tommy Castillo-a/Alex Horley-c 3.00

EVIL ERNIE: REVENGE
Chaos! Comics: Oct, 1994 - No. 4, Feb, 1995 ($2.95, limited series)
1-Glow-in-the-dark-c; Lady Death app. 1-3-flip book w. Kilzone Preview (series of 3) 5.00
1-Commemorative-(4000 print run) 1 3 4 6 8 10
2-4 4.00
Trade paperback (10/95, $12.95) 13.00

EVIL ERNIE: STRAIGHT TO HELL
Chaos! Comics: Oct, 1995 - No. 5, May, 1996 ($2.95, limited series)
1-5: 1-fold-out-c 3.00
1,3:1-($19.95) Chromium Ed. 3-Chastity Chase-c-(4000 printed) 20.00
Special Edition (10,000) 20.00

EVIL ERNIE: THE RESURRECTION
Chaos! Comics: 1993 - No. 4, 1994 (Limited series)
0 5.00
1 2 4 6 8 10 12
1A-Gold 3 6 9 16 23 30
2-4 1 2 3 5 6 8

EVIL ERNIE VS. THE MOVIE MONSTERS
Chaos! Comics: Mar, 1997 ($2.95, one-shot)
1 3.00
1-Variant-"Chaos-Scope•Terror Vision" card stock-c 5.00

EVIL ERNIE VS. THE SUPER HEROES
Chaos! Comics: Aug, 1995; Sept, 1998 ($2.95)
1-Lady Death poster 3.00
1-Foil-c variant (limited to 10,000) 2 4 6 11 16 20
1-Limited Edition (1000) 2 4 6 11 16 20
2-(9/98) Ernie vs. JLA and Marvel parodies 3.00

EVIL ERNIE: WAR OF THE DEAD
Chaos! Comics: Nov, 1999 - No. 3, Jan, 2000 ($2.95, limited series)
1-3-Pulido & Kaminski-s/Brewer-a. 3-End of Evil Ernie 3.00

EVIL EYE
Fantagraphics Books: June, 1998 - Present ($2.95/$3.50/$3.95, B&W)
1-7-Richard Sala-s/a 4.00
8-10-($3.50) 4.00
11,12-($3.95) 4.00

EVO (Crossover from Tomb Raider #25 & Witchblade #60)
Image Comics (Top Cow): Feb, 2003 ($2.99, one-shot)
1-Silvestri-c/a(p); Endgame x-over pt. 3; Sara Pezzini & Lara Croft app. 3.00

EWOKS (Star Wars) (TV) (See Star Comics Magazine)
Marvel Comics (Star Comics): June, 1985 - No. 14, Jul, 1987 (75¢/$1.00)
1,10: 10-Williamson-a (From Star Wars) 2 4 6 9 12 15
2-9 2 4 6 8 10 12
11-14: 14-($1.00-c) 2 4 6 8 11 14

EXCALIBUR (Also see Marvel Comics Presents #31)
Marvel Comics: Apr, 1988; Oct, 1988 - No. 125, Oct, 1998 ($1.50/$1.75/$1.99)
Special Edition nn (The Sword is Drawn)(4/88, $3.25)-1st Excalibur comic 6.00
Special Edition nn (4/88)-no price on-c 1 3 4 6 8 10
Special Edition nn (2nd & print, 10/88, 12/89) 3.00
...The Sword is Drawn (Apr, 1992, $4.95) 5.00
1($1.50, 10/88)-X-Men spin-off; Nightcrawler, Shadowcat(Kitty Pryde), Capt. Britain, Phoenix & Meggan begin 6.00
2-4 5.00
5-10 4.00
11-49,51-70,72-74,76: 10,11-Rogers/Austin-a. 21-Intro Crusader X. 22-Iron Man x-over. 24-John Byrne app. in story. 26-Ron Lim-c/a. 27-B. Smith-a(p). 37-Dr. Doom & Iron Man app. 41-X-Men (Wolverine) app.; Cable cameo. 49-Neal Adams c-swipe. 52,57-X-Men (Cyclops, Wolverine) app. 53-Spider-Man-c/story. 58-X-Men (Wolverine, Gambit, Cyclops, etc.)-c/story. 61-Phoenix returns. 68-Starjammers-c/story 3.00
50-($2.75, 56 pgs.)-New logo 4.00
71-($3.95, 52 pgs.)-Hologram on-c; 30th anniversary 5.00
75-($3.50, 52 pgs.)-Holo-grafx foil-c 5.00
75-($2.25, 52 pgs.)-Regular edition 4.00
77-81,83-86: 77-Begin $1.95-c; bound-in trading card sheet. 83-86-Deluxe Editions and Standard Editions. 86-1st app. Pete Wisdom 3.00
82-($2.50)-Newsstand edition 3.00
82-($3.50)-Enhanced edition 4.00
87-89,91-99,101-110: 87-Return from Age of Apocalypse. 92-Colossus-c/app. 94-Days of Future Tense 95-X-Man-c/app. 96-Sebastian Shaw & the Hellfire Club app. 99-Onslaught app. 101-Onslaught tie-in. 102-w/card insert. 103-Last Warren Ellis scripts; Belasco app. 104,105-Hitch & Neary-c/a. 109-Spiral-c/app. 3.00
90,100-($2.95)-double-sized. 100-Onslaught tie-in; wraparound-c 4.00
111-124: 111-Begin $1.99-c, wraparound-c. 119-Califiore-a 3.00
125-($2.99) Wedding of Capt. Britain and Meggan 4.00
Annual 1,2 ('93, '94, 68 pgs.)-1st app. Khaos. 2-X-Men & Psylocke app. 4.00
#(-1) Flashback (7/97) 3.00
...Air Apparent nn (12/91, $4.95)-Simonson-c 5.00
...Mojo Mayhem nn (12/89, $4.50)-Art Adams/Austin-c/a 5.00
...: The Possession nn (7/91, $2.95, 52 pgs.) 4.00
...: XX Crossing (7/92, 5/92-inside, $2.50)-vs. The X-Men 3.00
...Classic Vol. 1: The Sword is Drawn TPB (2005, $19.99) r/#1-5 & Special Edition nn (The Sword is Drawn) 20.00
...Classic Vol. 2: Two-Edged Sword TPB (2006, $24.99) r/#6-11 25.00
...Classic Vol. 3: Cross-Time Caper Book 1 TPB (2007, $24.99) r/#12-20 25.00
...Classic Vol. 4: Cross-Time Caper Book 2 TPB (2007, $24.99) r/#21-28 25.00
...Classic Vol. 5 TPB (2008, $24.99) r/#29-34 & Marvel GN Excalibur: Weird War III 25.00

EXCALIBUR
Marvel Comics: Feb, 2001 - No. 4, May, 2001 ($2.99)
1-4-Return of Captain Britain; Raimondi-a 3.00

EXCALIBUR (X-Men Reloaded title) (Leads into House of M series, then New Excalibur)
Marvel Comics: July, 2004 - No. 14, July, 2005 ($2.99)
1-14: 1-Claremont-s/Lopresti-a/Park-c; Magneto returns. 6-11-Beast app. 13,14-Prelude to House of M; Dr. Strange app. 3.00
House of M Prelude: Excalibur TPB (2005, $11.99) r/#11-14 12.00
... Vol. 1: Forging the Sword (2004, $9.99) r/#1-4 10.00
... Vol. 2: Saturday Night Fever (2005, $14.99) r/#5-10 15.00

EXCITING COMICS
Nedor/Better Publications/Standard Comics: Apr, 1940 - No. 69, Sept, 1949
1-Origin & 1st app. The Mask, Jim Hatfield, Sgt. Bill King, Dan Williams begin; early Robot-c (see Smash #1) 420 840 1260 2959 5180 7400
2-The Sphinx begins; The Masked Rider app.; Son of the Gods begins, ends #8 174 348 522 1114 1907 2700
3-Robot-c 129 258 387 826 1413 2000
4-6 79 158 237 502 864 1225
7,8 63 126 189 403 689 975
9-Origin/1st app. of The Black Terror & sidekick Tim, begin series (5/41) (Black Terror c-9-21,23-52,54,55) 1000 2000 3000 7600 13,800 20,000
10-2nd app. Black Terror 300 600 900 2070 3635 5200
11 161 322 483 1030 1765 2500
12,13 116 232 348 742 1271 1800
14-Last Sphinx, Dan Williams 90 180 270 576 988 1400
15-The Liberator begins (origin) 129 258 387 826 1413 2000
16-20: 20-The Mask ends 68 136 204 435 743 1050
21,23-25: 25-Robot-c 53 106 159 334 567 800
22-Origin The Eaglet; The American Eagle begins 68 136 204 435 743 1050
26-Schomburg-c begin 103 206 309 659 1130 1600
27,29,30 90 180 270 576 988 1400
28-(Scarce) Crime Crusader begins, ends #58 181 362 543 1158 1979 2800
31-38: 35-Liberator ends, not in 31-33 71 142 213 454 777 1100
39-Nazis giving poison candy to kids on cover; origin Kara, Jungle Princess 168 336 504 1075 1838 2600
40-50: 42-The Scarab begins. 45-Schomburg Robot-c. 49-Last Kara, Jungle Princess. 50-Last American Eagle 64 128 192 406 696 985
51-Miss Masque begins (1st app.) 68 136 204 435 743 1050

Exiles (2009 series) #5 © MAR

Ex Machina #33 © Vaughan & Harris

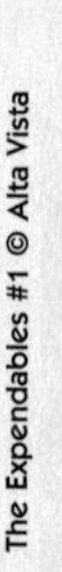

The Expendables #1 © Alta Vista

	GD 2.0	VG 4.0	FN 6.0	VF 8.0	VF/NM 9.0	NM- 9.2
52-54: Miss Masque ends. 53-Miss Masque-c	57	114	171	362	619	875
55-58: 55-Judy of the Jungle begins (origin), ends #69; 1 pg. Ingels-a; Judy of the Jungle c-56-66. 57,58-Airbrush-c	57	114	171	362	619	875
59-Frazetta art in Caniff style; signed Frank Frazeta (one t), 9 pgs.	57	114	171	364	625	885
60-66: 60-Rick Howard, the Mystery Rider begins. 66-Robinson/Meskin-a	52	102	156	328	557	785
67-69-All western covers	21	42	63	122	199	275

NOTE: ***Schomburg (Xela)** c-26-68; airbrush c-57-66. Black Terror by **R. Moreira**-#65. **Roussos** a-62. Bondage-c 9, 12, 13, 20, 23, 25, 30, 59.*

EXCITING ROMANCES
Fawcett Publications: 1949 (nd); No. 2, Spring, 1950 - No. 5, 10/50; No. 6 (1951, nd); No. 7, 9/51 -No. 12, 1/53

	GD 2.0	VG 4.0	FN 6.0	VF 8.0	VF/NM 9.0	NM- 9.2
1,3: 1(1949). 3-Wood-a	14	28	42	80	115	150
2,4,5-(1950)	10	20	30	54	72	90
6-12	9	18	27	47	61	75

NOTE: ***Powell** a-8-10. **Marcus Swayze** a-5, 6, 9. Photo c-1-7, 10-12.*

EXCITING ROMANCE STORIES (See Fox Giants)

EXCITING WAR (Korean War)
Standard Comics (Better Publ.): No. 5, Sept, 1952 - No. 8, May, 1953; No. 9, Nov, 1953

	GD 2.0	VG 4.0	FN 6.0	VF 8.0	VF/NM 9.0	NM- 9.2
5	11	22	33	62	86	110
6-Flamethrower/burning body-c	12	24	36	67	94	120
7,9	9	18	27	47	61	75
8-Toth-a	10	20	30	54	72	90

EXCITING X-PATROL
Marvel Comics (Amalgam): June, 1997 ($1.95, one-shot)

	GD 2.0	VG 4.0	FN 6.0	VF 8.0	VF/NM 9.0	NM- 9.2
1-Barbara Kesel-s/ Bryan Hitch-a						3.00

EXECUTIONER, THE (Don Pendleton's...)
IDW Publishing: Apr, 2008 - No. 5, Aug, 2008 ($3.99)

	GD 2.0	VG 4.0	FN 6.0	VF 8.0	VF/NM 9.0	NM- 9.2
1-5-Mack Bolan origin re-told; Gallant-a/Wojtowicz-s						4.00

EXECUTIVE ASSISTANT: IRIS
Aspen MLT: No. 0, Apr, 2009 - Present ($2.50/$2.99)

	GD 2.0	VG 4.0	FN 6.0	VF 8.0	VF/NM 9.0	NM- 9.2
0-($2.50) Wohl-s/Francisco-a; 3 covers						3.00
1-6-($2.99) Multiple covers on each						3.00

EXILES (Also see Break-Thru)
Malibu Comics (Ultraverse): Aug, 1993 - No. 4, Nov, 1993 ($1.95)

	GD 2.0	VG 4.0	FN 6.0	VF 8.0	VF/NM 9.0	NM- 9.2
1,2,4: 1,2-Bagged copies of each exist. 4-Team dies; story cont'd in Break-Thru #1						3.00
3-($2.50, 40 pgs.)-Rune flip-c/story by B. Smith (3 pgs.)						4.00
1-Holographic-c edition	1	2	3	5	6	8

EXILES (All New, The) (2nd Series) (Also see Black September)
Malibu Comics (Ultraverse): Sept, 1995 - V2#11, Aug, 1996 ($1.50)

	GD 2.0	VG 4.0	FN 6.0	VF 8.0	VF/NM 9.0	NM- 9.2
Infinity (9/95, $1.50)-Intro new team including Marvel's Juggernaut & Reaper						3.00
Infinity (2000 signed), V2#1 (2000 signed)	1	3	4	6	8	10
V2 #1-(10/95, 64 pgs.)-Reprint of Ultraforce V2#1 follows lead story						4.00
V2#2-4,6-11: 2-1st app. Hellblade. 8-Intro Maxis. 11-Vs. Maxis; Ripfire app.; cont'd in Ultraforce #12						3.00
V2#5-($2.50) Juggernaut returns to the Marvel Universe.						4.00

EXILES (Also see X-Men titles) (Leads into New Exiles series)
Marvel Comics: Aug, 2001 - No. 100, Feb, 2008 ($2.99/$2.25)

	GD 2.0	VG 4.0	FN 6.0	VF 8.0	VF/NM 9.0	NM- 9.2
1-($2.99) Blink and parallel world X-Men; Winick-s/McKone & McKenna-a	1	2	3	4	5	7
2-10-($2.25) 2-Two covers (McKone & JH Williams III). 5-Alpha Flight app.						3.50
11-24: 22-Blink leaves; Magik joins. 23,24-Walker-a; alternate Weapon-X app.						3.00
25-99: 25-Begin $2.99-c; Inhumans app.; Walker-a. 26-30-Austen-s. 33-Wolverine app. 35-37-Fantastic Four app. 37-Sunfire dies, Blink returns. 38-40-Hyperion app. 69-71-House of M. 77,78-Squadron Supreme app. 85,86-Multiple Wolverines. 90-Claremont-s begin; Psylocke app. 97-Shadowcat joins						3.00
100-($3.99) Last issue; Blink leaves; continues in Exiles (Days of Then and Now); r/#1						4.00
Annual 1 (2/07, $3.99) Bedard-s/Raney-a/c						4.00
Exiles #1 (Days of Then and Now) (3/08, $3.99) short stories by various						4.00
TPB (3/02, $12.95) r/#1-4						13.00
...: A World Apart TPB (7/02, $14.99) r/#5-11						15.00
...: Vol. 3: Out of Time TPB (2003, $17.99) r/#12-19						18.00
...: Vol. 4: Legacy TPB (2003, $12.99) r/#20-25						13.00
...: Vol. 5: Unnatural Instinct TPB (2003, $14.99) r/#26-30						15.00
...: Vol. 6: Fantastic Voyage TPB (2004, $17.99) r/#31-37						18.00
...: Vol. 7: A Blink in Time TPB (2004, $19.99) r/#38-45						20.00
...: Vol. 8: Earn Your Wings TPB (2004, $14.99) r/#46-51						15.00
...: Vol. 9: Bump in the Night TPB (2005, $17.99) r/#52-58						18.00
...: Vol. 10: Age of Apocalypse TPB ('05, $12.99) r/#59-61 & Official Handbook:AoA 2005						13.00
...: Vol. 11: Time Breakers TPB (2006, $17.99) r/#62-68						18.00
...: Vol. 12: World Tour Book 1 TPB (2006, $16.99) r/#69-74						17.00
...: Vol. 13: World Tour Book 2 TPB (2006, $23.99) r/#75-83						24.00
...: Vol. 14: The New Exiles TPB (2007, $14.99) r/#84-89 and Annual #1						15.00
...: Vol. 15: Enemy of the Stars TPB (2007, $13.99) r/#90-94						14.00
...: Vol. 16: Starting Over TPB (2008, $14.99) r/#95-100 & ...: Days of Then and Now						15.00

EXILES
Marvel Comics: Jun, 2009 - No. 6, Nov, 2009 ($2.99/$3.99)

	GD 2.0	VG 4.0	FN 6.0	VF 8.0	VF/NM 9.0	NM- 9.2
1,6-($3.99) Blink and parallel world Scarlet Witch, Beast and others; Bullock-c						4.00
2-5-($2.99)						3.00

EXILES VS. THE X-MEN
Malibu Comics (Ultraverse): Oct, 1995 (one-shot)

	GD 2.0	VG 4.0	FN 6.0	VF 8.0	VF/NM 9.0	NM- 9.2
0-Limited Super Premium Edition; signed w/certificate; gold foil logo, 0-Limited Premium Edition	1	3	4	6	8	10

EX MACHINA
DC Comics: Aug, 2004 - No. 50, Sept, 2010 ($2.95/$2.99)

	GD 2.0	VG 4.0	FN 6.0	VF 8.0	VF/NM 9.0	NM- 9.2
1-Intro. Mitchell Hundred; Vaughan-s/Harris-a/c						4.00
1-Special Edition (6/10, $1.00) Reprints #1 with "What's Next?" logo on cover						1.00
2-49: 12-Intro. Automaton. 33-Mitchell meets the Pope						3.00
50-($4.99) Wraparound-c						5.00
...: The Deluxe Edition Book One HC (2008, $29.99, dustjacket) r/#1-11; Vaughan's original proposal, Harris sketch pages; Brad Meltzer intro.						30.00
...: The Deluxe Edition Book Two HC (2009, $29.99, dustjacket) r/#12-20; Special #1,2; script and pencil art for #20; Wachowski Bros. intro.						30.00
...: The Deluxe Edition Book Three HC (2010, $29.99, dustjacket) r/#21-29; Special #3 and Ex Machina: Inside the Machine						30.00
...: The Deluxe Edition Book Four HC (2010, $29.99, dustjacket) r/#30-40; cover gallery						30.00
...: The Deluxe Edition Book Five HC (2011, $29.99, dustjacket) r/#41-50; Special #4						30.00
...: Inside the Machine (4/07, $2.99) script pages and Harris art and cover process						3.00
...: Masquerade Special (#3) (10/07, $3.50) John Paul Leon-a; Harris-c						3.50
... Special 1,2 (6/06 - No. 2, 8/06, $2.99) Sprouse-a; flashback to the Great Machine						3.00
... Special 4 (5/09, $3.99) Leon-a; Great Machine flashback; covers by Harris & Leon						4.00
...: Dirty Tricks TPB (2009, $12.99) r/#35-39 and Masquerade Special #3						13.00
...: Ex Cathedra TPB (2008, $12.99) r/#30-34						13.00
...: March To War TPB (2006, $12.99) r/#17-20 and Special #1,2						13.00
...: Power Down TPB (2008, $12.99) r/#26-29 & ...: Inside the Machine						13.00
...: Ring Out the Old TPB (2010, $14.99) r/#40-44 and Special #4						15.00
...: Smoke Smoke TPB (2007, $12.99) r/#21-25						13.00
...: The First Hundred Days TPB ('05, $9.95) r/#1-5; photo reference and sketch pages						10.00
...: Tag TPB (2005, $12.99) r/#6-10; Harris sketch pages						13.00
...: Term Limits TPB (2010, $14.99) r/#45-50						15.00

EX-MUTANTS
Malibu Comics: Nov, 1992 - No. 18, Apr, 1994 ($1.95/$2.25/$2.50)

	GD 2.0	VG 4.0	FN 6.0	VF 8.0	VF/NM 9.0	NM- 9.2
1-18: 1-Polybagged w/Skycap; prismatic cover						3.00

EXORCISTS (See The Crusaders)

EXOSQUAD (TV)
Topps Comics: No. 0, Jan, 1994 ($1.25)

	GD 2.0	VG 4.0	FN 6.0	VF 8.0	VF/NM 9.0	NM- 9.2
0-($1.00, 20 pgs.)-1st app.; Staton-a(p); wraparound-c						3.00

EXOTIC ROMANCES (Formerly True War Romances)
Quality Comics Group (Comic Magazines): No. 22, Oct, 1955-No. 31, Nov, 1956

	GD 2.0	VG 4.0	FN 6.0	VF 8.0	VF/NM 9.0	NM- 9.2
22	13	26	39	74	105	135
23-26,29	9	18	27	47	61	75
27,31-Baker-c/a	15	30	45	90	140	190
28,30-Baker-a	14	28	42	76	108	140

EXPENDABLES, THE (Movie)
Dynamite Entertainment: 2010 - No. 4, 2010 ($3.99, limited series)

	GD 2.0	VG 4.0	FN 6.0	VF 8.0	VF/NM 9.0	NM- 9.2
1-4-Chuck Dixon-s/Esteve Polls-a/Lucio Parrillo-c; prelude to the 2010 movie						4.00

EXPLOITS OF DANIEL BOONE
Quality Comics Group: Nov, 1955 - No. 6, Oct, 1956

	GD 2.0	VG 4.0	FN 6.0	VF 8.0	VF/NM 9.0	NM- 9.2
1-All have Cuidera-c(i)	20	40	60	114	182	250
2	14	28	42	82	121	160
3-6	13	26	39	74	105	135

EXPLOITS OF DICK TRACY (See Dick Tracy)

EXPLORER JOE
Ziff-Davis Comic Group (Approved Comics): Win, 1951 - No. 2, Oct-Nov, 1952

	GD 2.0	VG 4.0	FN 6.0	VF 8.0	VF/NM 9.0	NM- 9.2
1-2: Saunders painted covers; 2-Krigstein-a	14	28	42	76	108	140

Exposed #4 © DS

Extreme Justice #10 © DC

Fables #6 © Bill Willingham & DC

	GD 2.0	VG 4.0	FN 6.0	VF 8.0	VF/NM 9.0	NM- 9.2

EXPLORERS OF THE UNKNOWN (See Archie Giant Series #587, 599)
Archie Comics: June, 1990 - No. 6, Apr, 1991 ($1.00)

1-6: Featuring Archie and the gang 3.00

EXPOSED (...True Crime Cases; ...Cases in the Crusade Against Crime #5-9)
D. S. Publishing Co.: Mar-Apr, 1948 - No. 9, July-Aug, 1949

	GD 2.0	VG 4.0	FN 6.0	VF 8.0	VF/NM 9.0	NM- 9.2
1	25	50	75	150	245	340
2-Giggling killer story with excessive blood; two injury-to-eye panels; electrocution panel	32	64	96	188	307	425
3,8,9	15	30	45	83	124	165
4-Orlando-a	15	30	45	85	130	175
5-Breeze Lawson, Sky Sheriff by E. Good	15	30	45	85	130	175
6,7: 6-Ingels-a; used in **SOTI**, illo. "How to prepare an alibi" 7-Illo. in **SOTI**, "Diagram for housebreakers;" used by N.Y. Legis. Committee	34	68	102	206	336	465

EXTERMINATORS, THE
DC Comics (Vertigo): Mar, 2006 - No. 30, Aug, 2008 ($2.99)

1-30: Simon Oliver-s/Tony Moore-a in most. 11,12-Hawthorne-a 3.00
...: Bug Brothers TPB (2006, $9.99) r/#1-5; intro. by screenwriter Josh Olson 10.00
...: Bug Brothers Forever TPB (2008, $14.99) r/#24-30; intro. by Simon Oliver 15.00
...: Crossfire and Collateral TPB (2008, $14.99) r/#17-23 15.00
...: Insurgency TPB (2007, $12.99) r/#6-10 13.00
...: Lies of Our Fathers TPB (2007, $14.99) r/#11-16 15.00

EXTINCT!
New England Comics Press: Wint, 1991-92 - No. 2, Fall, 1992 ($3.50, B&W)

1,2-Reprints and background info of "perfectly awful" Golden Age stories 3.50

EXTINCTION EVENT
DC Comics (WildStorm): Sept, 2003 - No. 5, Jan, 2004 ($2.50, limited series)

1-5-Booth-a/Weinberg-s 3.00

EXTRA!
E. C. Comics: Mar-Apr, 1955 - No. 5, Nov-Dec, 1955

	GD 2.0	VG 4.0	FN 6.0	VF 8.0	VF/NM 9.0	NM- 9.2
1-Not code approved	20	40	60	160	255	350
2-5	13	26	39	104	165	225

NOTE: ***Craig, Crandall, Severin** art in all.*

EXTRA!
Gemstone Publishing: Jan, 2000 - No. 5, May, 2000 ($2.50)

1-5-Reprints E.C. series 3.00

EXTRA COMICS
Magazine Enterprises: 1948 (25¢, 3 comics in one)

	GD 2.0	VG 4.0	FN 6.0	VF 8.0	VF/NM 9.0	NM- 9.2
1-Giant; consisting of rebound ME comics. Two versions known; (1)-Funnyman by Siegel & Shuster, Space Ace, Undercover Girl, Red Fox by L.B. Cole, Trail Colt & (2)-All Funnyman	55	110	165	352	601	850

EXTREME
Image Comics (Extreme Studios): Aug, 1993 (Giveaway)

0 3.00

EXTREME DESTROYER
Image Comics (Extreme Studios): Jan, 1996 ($2.50)

Prologue 1-Polybagged w/card; Liefeld-c, Epilogue 1-Liefeld-c 3.00

EXTREME JUSTICE
DC Comics: No. 0, Jan, 1995 - No. 18, July, 1996 ($1.50/$1.75)

0-18 3.00

EXTREMELY YOUNGBLOOD
Image Comics (Extreme Studios): Sept, 1996 ($3.50, one-shot)

1 3.50

EXTREME SACRIFICE
Image Comics (Extreme Studios): Jan, 1995 ($2.50, limited series)

Prelude (#1)-Liefeld wraparound-c; polybagged w/ trading card 3.00
Epilogue (#2)-Liefeld wraparound-c; polybagged w/trading card 3.00
Trade paperback (6/95, $16.95)-Platt-a 17.00

EXTREME SUPER CHRISTMAS SPECIAL
Image Comics (Extreme Studios): Dec, 1994 ($2.95, one-shot)

1 3.00

EXTREMIST, THE
DC Comics (Vertigo): Sept, 1993 - No. 4, Dec, 1993 ($1.95, limited series)

1-4-Peter Milligan scripts; McKeever-c/a 3.00
1-Platinum Edition 5.00

EYE OF THE STORM
Rival Productions: Dec, 1994 - No. 7, June, 1995? ($2.95)

1-7: Computer generated comic 3.00

EYE OF THE STORM
DC Comics (WildStorm): Sept, 2003 ($4.95)

Annual 1-Short stories by various incl. Portacio, Johns, Coker, Pearson, Arcudi 5.00

FABLES
DC Comics (Vertigo): July, 2002 - Present ($2.50/$2.75/$2.99)

1-Willingham-s/Medina-a; two covers by Maleev & Jean 8.00
1: Special Edition (12/06, 25¢) r/#1 with preview of 1001 Nights of Snowfall 3.00
1: Special Edition (9/09, $1.00) r/#1 with preview of Peter & Max 3.00
1-Special Edition (8/10, $1.00) Reprints #1 with "What's Next?" logo on cover 1.00
2-Medina-a 5.00
3-5 4.00
6-37: 6-10-Buckingham-a. 11-Talbot-a. 18-Medley-a. 26-Preview of The Witching 3.00
6-RRP Edition wraparound variant-c; promotional giveaway for retailers (200 printed) 50.00
38-49,51-74,76-99,101-103: 38-Begin $2.75-c. 49-Begin $2.99-c. 57,58,76-Allred-a. 83-85-Crossover with Jack of Fables and The Literals. 101-Shanower-a 3.00
50-($3.99) Wedding of Snow White and Bigby Wolf; preview of Jack of Fables series 4.00
75-($4.99) Geppetto surrenders; pin-up gallery by Powell, Nowlan, Cooke & others 5.00
100-(1/11, $9.99, squarebound) Buckingham-a; short stories art by Hughes & others 10.00
Animal Farm (2003, $12.95, TPB) r/#6-10; sketch pages by Buckingham & Jean 13.00
...: Arabian Nights (And Days) (2006, $14.99, TPB) r/#42-47 15.00
...: Homelands (2005, $14.99, TPB) r/#34-41 15.00
Legends in Exile (2002, $9.95, TPB) r/#1-5; new short story Willingham-s/a 10.00
...: March of the Wooden Soldiers (2004, $17.95, TPB) r/#19-21 & ...: The Last Castle 18.00
...: 1001 Nights of Snowfall HC (2006, $19.99) short stories by Willingham with art by various incl. Bolton, Kaluta, Jean, McPherson, Thompson, Vess, Wheatley, Buckingham 20.00
...: 1001 Nights of Snowfall (2008, $14.99, TPB) short stories with art by various 15.00
...: Sons of Empire (2007, $17.99, TPB) r/#52-59 18.00
...: Storybook Love (2004, $14.95, TPB) r/#11-18 15.00
...: The Dark Ages (2009, $17.99, TPB) r/#76-82 18.00
...: The Deluxe Edition Book One HC (2009, $29.99, DJ) r/#1-10; character sketch-a 30.00
...: The Deluxe Edition Book Two HC (2010, $29.99, DJ) r/#11-18 & ...: The Last Castle 30.00
...: The Good Prince (2008, $17.99, TPB) r/#60-69 18.00
...: The Great Fables Crossover (2010, $17.99, TPB) r/#83-85, Jack of Fables #33-35 and The Literals #1-3; sneak preview of Peter & Max: A Fables Novel 18.00
...: The Last Castle (2003, $5.95) Hamilton-a/Willingham-s; prequel to title 6.00
...: The Mean Seasons (2005, $14.99, TPB) r/#22,28-33 15.00
...: War and Pieces (2008, $17.99, TPB) r/#70-75; sketch and pin-up pages 18.00
...: Witches (2010, $17.99, TPB) r/#86-93 18.00
...: Wolves (2006, $17.99, TPB) r/#48-51; script to #50 18.00

FACE, THE (Tony Trent, the Face No. 3 on) (See Big Shot Comics)
Columbia Comics Group: 1941 - No. 2, 1943

	GD 2.0	VG 4.0	FN 6.0	VF 8.0	VF/NM 9.0	NM- 9.2
1-The Face; Mart Bailey-c	90	180	270	576	988	1400
2-Bailey-c	51	102	153	321	543	765

FACES OF EVIL
DC Comics: Mar, 2009 ($2.99, series of one-shots)

...: Deathstroke 1 - Jeanty-a/Ladronn-c; Ravager app. 3.00
...: Kobra 1 - Jason Burr returns; Julian Lopez-a 3.00
...: Prometheus 1 - Gates-s/Dallacchio-a; origin re-told; Anima killed 3.00
...: Solomon Grundy 1 - Johns-s/Kolins-a; leads into Solomon Grundy mini-series 3.00

FACTOR X
Marvel Comics: Mar, 1995 - No. 4, July, 1995 ($1.95, limited series)

1-Age of Apocalypse 3.50
2-4 3.00

FACULTY FUNNIES
Archie Comics: June, 1989 - No. 5, May, 1990 (75¢/95¢ #2 on)

1-5: 1,2-The Awesome Four app. 3.00

FADE FROM GRACE
Beckett Comics: Aug, 2004 - No. 5, Mar, 2005 (99¢/$1.99)

1-(99¢) Jeff Amano-a/c; Gabriel Benson-s; origin of Fade 3.00
2-5-($1.99) 3.00
TPB (2005, $14.99) r/#1-5; cover gallery, afterword by David Mack 15.00

FAFHRD AND THE GREY MOUSER (Also see Sword of Sorcery & Wonder Woman #202)
Marvel Comics: Oct, 1990 - No. 4, 1991 ($4.50, 52 pgs., squarebound)

1-4: Mignola/Williamson-a; Chaykin scripts 4.50

FAGIN THE JAW

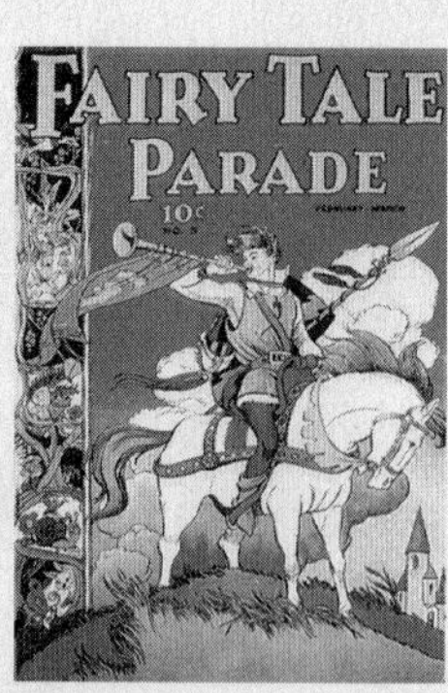

Fairy Tale Parade #5 © WEST

Fallen Son: The Death of Captain America #4 © MAR

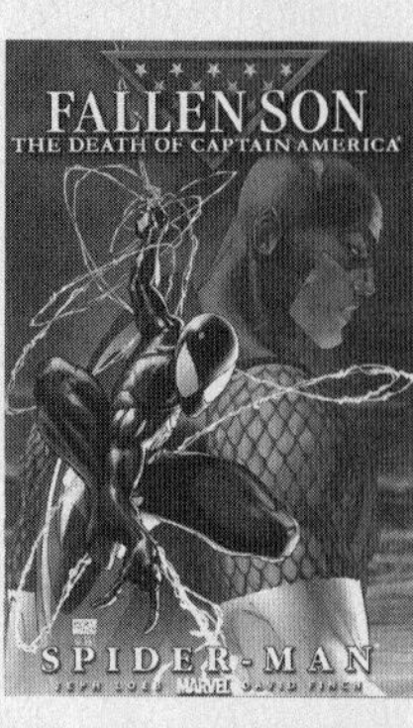

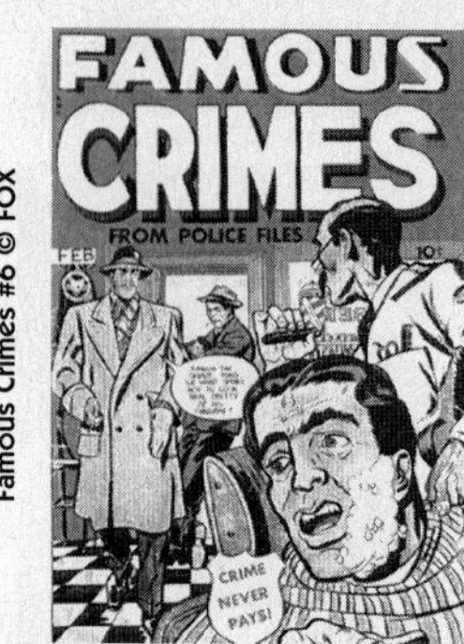

Famous Crimes #6 © FOX

	GD 2.0	VG 4.0	FN 6.0	VF 8.0	VF/NM 9.0	NM- 9.2

Doubleday: Oct, 2003 ($15.95, softcover graphic novel)

nn-Will Eisner-s/a; story of Fagin from Dickens' Oliver Twist						16.00

FAIRY TALE PARADE (See Famous Fairy Tales)
Dell Publishing Co.: June-July, 1942 - No. 121, Oct, 1946 (Most by Walt Kelly)

1-Kelly-a begins	92	184	276	782	1591	2400
2(8-9/42)	41	82	123	328	664	1000
3-5 (10-11/42 - 2-4/43)	30	60	90	231	458	685
6-9 (5-7/43 - 11-1/43-44)	24	48	72	175	350	525
Four Color 50('44),69('45), 87('45)	23	46	69	168	334	500
Four Color 104,114('46)-Last Kelly issue	18	36	54	125	255	385
Four Color 121('46)-Not by Kelly	12	24	36	82	154	225

NOTE: *#1-9, 4-Color #50, 69 have **Kelly** c/a; 4-Color #87, 104, 114-**Kelly** art only. #9 has a redrawn version of The Reluctant Dragon. This series contains all the classic fairy tales from Jack In The Beanstalk to Cinderella.*

FAIRY TALES
Ziff-Davis Publ. Co. (Approved Comics): No. 10, Apr-May, 1951 - No. 11, June-July, 1951

10,11-Painted-c	20	40	60	117	189	260

FAITH
DC Comics (Vertigo): Nov, 1999 - No. 5, Mar, 2000 ($2.50, limited series)

1-5-Ted McKeever-s/c/a						3.00

FAITHFUL
Marvel Comics/Lovers' Magazine: Nov, 1949 - No. 2, Feb, 1950 (52 pgs.)

1,2-Photo-c	12	24	36	69	97	125

FAKER
DC Comics (Vertigo): Sept, 2007 - No. 6, Feb, 2008 ($2.99, limited series)

1-6-Mike Carey-s/Jock-a/c						3.00
TPB (2008, $14.99) r/#1-6; Jock sketch pages						15.00

FALCON (See Marvel Premiere #49, Avengers #181 & Captain America #117 & 133)
Marvel Comics Group: Nov, 1983 - No. 4, Feb, 1984 (Mini-series)

1-4: 1-Paul Smith-c/a(p). 2-Paul Smith-c/Mark Bright-a. 3-Kupperberg-c						3.00

FALLEN ANGEL
DC Comics: Sept, 2003 - No. 20, July, 2005 ($2.50/$2.95)

1-9-Peter David-s/David Lopez-a/Stelfreeze-c; intro. Lee						3.00
10-20: 10-Begin $2.95-c. 13,17-Kaluta-c. 20-Last issue; Pérez-c						3.00
TPB (2004, $12.95) r/#1-6; intro. by Harlan Ellison						13.00
Down to Earth TPB (2007, $14.99) r/#7-12						15.00

FALLEN ANGEL
IDW Publ.: Dec, 2005 - No. 33, Dec, 2008 ($3.99)

1-33: 1-14-Peter David-s/J.K Woodward-a. Retailer variant-c for each. 15-Donaldson-a. 17-Flip cover with Shi story; Tucci-a. 25-Wraparound-c; character gallery						4.00
... Reborn 1-4 (7/09 - No. 4, 10/09, $3.99) David-s/Woodward-a; Illyria (from Angel) app.						4.00
... Return of the Son 1,2 (1/11 - Present, $3.99) David-s/Woodward-a;						4.00
...: To Serve in Heaven TPB (8/06, $19.99) r/#1-5; gallery of reg & variant covers						20.00

FALLEN ANGEL ON THE WORLD OF MAGIC: THE GATHERING
Acclaim (Armada): May, 1996 ($5.95, one-shot)

1-Nancy Collins story						6.00

FALLEN ANGELS
Marvel Comics Group: April, 1987 - No. 8, Nov, 1987 (Limited series)

1-8						3.00

FALLEN SON: THE DEATH OF CAPTAIN AMERICA
Marvel Comics: June, 2007 - No. 5, Aug, 2007 ($2.99, limited series)

1-5: Loeb-s in all. 1-Wolverine; Yu-a/c. 2-Avengers; McGuinness-a/c. 3-Captain America; Romita Jr.-a/c; Hawkeye app. 4-Spider-Man; Finch-c/a. 5-Cassaday-c/a						3.00
1-5-Variant covers by Turner						3.00
HC (2007, $19.99, dustjacket) r/#1-5						20.00
TPB (2008, $13.99) r/#1-5						14.00

FALLING IN LOVE
Arleigh Pub. Co./National Per. Pub.: Sept-Oct, 1955 - No. 143, Oct-Nov, 1973

1	40	80	120	242	401	560
2	21	42	63	124	202	280
3-10	14	28	42	82	121	160
11-20	12	24	36	69	97	125
21-40	10	20	30	56	76	95
41-47: 47-Last 10¢ issue	9	18	27	50	65	80
48-70	4	8	12	28	44	60
71-99,108: 108-Wood-a (4 pgs., 7/69)	3	6	9	19	29	38
100	4	8	12	24	37	50
101-107,109-124	3	6	9	14	20	26
134-143	2	4	6	13	18	22
125-133: 52 pgs.	3	6	9	21	32	42

NOTE: ***Colan** c/a-75, 81. 52 pgs.-#125-133.*

FALLING MAN, THE
Image Comics: Feb, 1998 ($2.95)

1-McCorkindale-s/Hester-a						3.00

FALL OF THE HOUSE OF USHER, THE (See A Corben Special & Spirit section 8/22/48)

FALL OF THE HULKS (Also see Hulk and Incredible Hulk)
Marvel Comics: Feb, 2010 - July, 2010 ($3.99, one-shots & limited series)

Alpha (2/10) Pelletier-a; The Leader, Dr. Doom, MODOK and The Thinker app.						4.00
Gamma (2/10) Romita Jr. -a; funeral for General Ross						4.00
Red Hulk (3/10 - No. 4, 6/10) 1-4: 1-A-Bomb app.						4.00
Savage She-Hulks (5/10 - No. 3, 7/10) 1-3: Cover tryptich by Campbell; Espin-a						4.00

FALL OF THE ROMAN EMPIRE (See Movie Comics)

FALL OUT TOY WORKS
Image Comics: Sept, 2009 - No. 5, Jun, 2010 ($3.99)

1-5-Co-created by Pete Wentz of the band Fall Out Boy; Basri-a. 5-Lau-c						4.00

FAMILY AFFAIR (TV)
Gold Key: Feb, 1970 - No. 4, Oct, 1970 (25¢)

1-With pull-out poster; photo-c	6	12	18	39	62	85
1-With poster missing	3	6	9	18	27	35
2-4-Photo-c	3	6	9	21	32	42

FAMILY DYNAMIC, THE
DC Comics: Oct, 2008 - No. 3, Dec, 2008 ($2.25)

1-3-J. Torres-s/Tim Levins-a						3.00

FAMILY FUNNIES
Parents' Magazine Institute: No. 9, Aug-Sept, 1946

9	6	12	18	28	34	40

FAMILY FUNNIES (Tiny Tot Funnies No. 9)
Harvey Publications: Sept, 1950 - No. 8, Apr, 1951

1-Mandrake (has over 30 King Feature strips)	10	20	30	58	79	100
2-Flash Gordon, 1 pg.	8	16	24	40	50	60
3-8: 4,5,7-Flash Gordon, 1 pg.	6	12	18	31	38	45

FAMILY GUY (TV)
Devil's Due Publ.: 2006 ($6.95)

nn-101 Ways to Kill Lois; 2-Peter Griffin's Guide to Parenting; 3-Books Don't Taste Very Good						7.00
... A Big Book o' Crap TPB (10/06, $16.95) r/nn,2,3						17.00

FAMILY MATTER
Kitchen Sink Press: 1998 ($24.95/$15.95, graphic novel)

Hardcover ($24.95) Will Eisner-s/a						25.00
Softcover ($15.95)						16.00

FAMOUS AUTHORS ILLUSTRATED (See Stories by...)

FAMOUS CRIMES
Fox Features Syndicate/M.S. Dist. No. 51,52: June, 1948 - No. 19, Sept, 1950; No. 20, Aug, 1951; No. 51, 52, 1953

1-Blue Beetle app. & crime story-r/Phantom Lady #16	53	106	159	334	567	800
2-Has woman dissolved in acid; lingerie-c/panels	42	84	126	265	445	625
3-Injury-to-eye story used in **SOTI**, pg. 112; has two electrocution stories	52	104	156	328	552	775
4-6	25	50	75	147	241	335
7- "Tarzan, the Wyoming Killer" (**SOTI**, pg. 44)	41	82	123	256	428	600
8-20: 17-Morisi-a. 20-Same cover as #15	20	40	60	114	182	250
51 (nd, 1953)	16	32	48	94	147	200
52 (Exist?)	16	32	48	94	147	200

FAMOUS FEATURE STORIES
Dell Publishing Co.: 1938 (7-1/2x11", 68 pgs.)

1-Tarzan, Terry & the Pirates, King of the Royal Mtd., Buck Jones, Dick Tracy, Smilin' Jack, Dan Dunn, Don Winslow, G-Man, Tailspin Tommy, Mutt & Jeff, Little Orphan Annie reprints - all illustrated text	75	140	210	455	710	965

FAMOUS FIRST EDITION (See Limited Collectors' Edition)
National Periodical Publications/DC Comics: ($1.00, 10x13-1/2", 72 pgs.) (No.6-8, 68 pgs.) 1974 - No. 8, Aug-Sept, 1975; C-61, 1979
(Hardbound editions with dust jackets are from Lyle Stuart, Inc.)

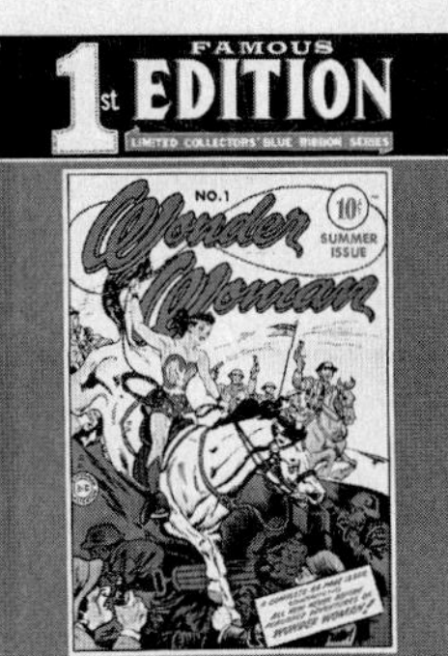

Famous First Edition F-6 © DC

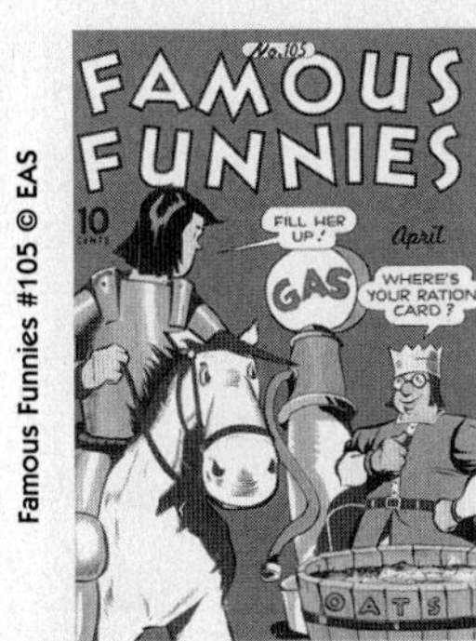

Famous Funnies #105 © EAS

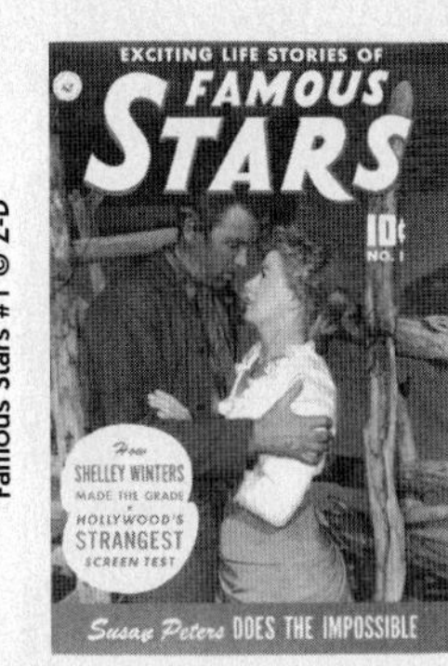

Famous Stars #1 © Z-D

	GD 2.0	VG 4.0	FN 6.0	VF 8.0	VF/NM 9.0	NM- 9.2

C-26-Action Comics #1; gold ink outer-c 6 12 18 41 66 90
C-26-Hardbound edition w/dust jacket 16 32 48 114 232 350
C-28-Detective #27; silver ink outer-c 6 12 18 41 66 90
C-28-Hardbound edition w/dust jacket 16 32 48 114 232 350
C-30-Sensation #1(1974); bronze ink outer-c 5 10 15 30 48 65
C-30-Hardbound edition w/dust jacket 14 28 42 97 194 290
F-4-Whiz Comics #2(#1)(10-11/74)-Cover not identical to original (dropped "Gangway for Captain Marvel" from cover); gold ink on outer-c 5 10 15 30 48 65
F-4-Hardbound edition w/dust jacket 14 28 42 97 194 290
F-5-Batman #1(F-6 inside); silver ink on outer-c 5 10 15 34 55 75
F-5-Hardbound edition w/dust jacket 14 28 42 97 194 290
V2#F-6-Wonder Woman #1 5 10 15 30 48 65
F-6-Wonder Woman #1 Hardbound w/dust jacket 14 28 42 97 194 290
F-7-All-Star Comics #3 5 10 15 30 48 65
F-8-Flash Comics #1(8-9/75) 5 10 15 30 48 65
V8#C-61-Superman #1(1979, $2.00) 4 8 12 26 41 55
V8#C-61 (Whitman variant) 4 8 12 28 44 60
V8#C-61 (SC in slipcase, edition of 250 copies) Each signed by Jerry Siegel and Joe Shuster 550.00

Warning: The above books are almost **exact** reprints of the originals that they represent except for the Giant-Size format. None of the originals are Giant-Size. The first five issues and C-61 were printed with two covers. Reprint information can be found on the outside cover, but not on the inside cover which was reprinted exactly like the original (inside and out).

FAMOUS FUNNIES
Eastern Color: 1934; July, 1934 - No. 218, July, 1955

A Carnival of Comics (See Promotional Comics section)

Series 1-(Very rare)(nd-early 1934)(68 pgs.) No publisher given (Eastern Color PrintingCo.); sold in chain stores for 10¢. 35,000 print run. Contains Sunday strip reprints of Mutt & Jeff, Reg'lar Fellers, Nipper, Hairbreadth Harry, Strange As It Seems, Joe Palooka, Dixie Dugan, The Nebbs, Keeping Up With the Jones, and others. Inside front and back covers and pages 1-16 of Famous Funnies Series 1, #s 49-64 reprinted from **Famous Funnies, A Carnival of Comics**, and most of pages 17-48 reprinted from **Funnies on Parade**.
4200 8400 12,600 31,000 - -

No. 1 (Rare)(7/34-on stands 5/34) - Eastern Color Printing Co. First monthly newsstand comic book. Contains Sunday strip reprints of Toonerville Folks, Mutt & Jeff, Hairbreadth Harry, S'Matter Pop, Nipper, Dixie Dugan, The Bungle Family, Connie, Ben Webster, Tailspin Tommy, The Nebbs, Joe Palooka, & others.
3100 6200 9300 23,000 - -
2 (Rare, 9/34) 680 1360 2040 5100 - -
3-Buck Rogers Sunday strip-r by Rick Yager begins, ends #218; not in #191-208; 1st comic book app. of Buck Rogers; the number of the 1st strip reprinted is pg. 190, Series No. 1
867 1754 2601 6500 - -
4 280 560 840 2100 - -
5-1st Christmas-c on a newsstand comic 293 586 879 2200 - -
6-10 187 374 561 1400 - -
11,12,18-Four pgs. of Buck Rogers in each issue, completes stories in Buck Rogers #1 which lacks these pages. 18-Two pgs. of Buck Rogers reprinted in Daisy Comics #1
102 204 306 612 1006 1400
13-17,19,20: 14-Has two Buck Rogers panels missing. 17-2nd Christmas-c on a newsstand comic (12/35) 79 158 237 474 787 1100
21,23-30: 27-(10/36)-War on Crime begins (4 pgs.); 1st true crime in comics (reprints); part photo-c. 29-X-Mas-c (12/36) 60 120 180 360 605 850
22-Four pgs. of Buck Rogers needed to complete stories in Buck Rogers #1
63 126 189 378 627 875
31,33,34,36,37,39,40: 33-Careers of Baby Face Nelson & John Dillinger traced
42 84 126 252 426 600
32-(3/37) 1st app. the Phantom Magician (costume hero) in Advs. of Patsy
46 92 138 276 463 650
35-Two pgs. Buck Rogers omitted in Buck Rogers #2
46 92 138 276 463 650
38-Full color portrait of Buck Rogers 44 88 132 264 445 625
41-60: 41,53-X-Mas-c. 55-Last bottom panel, pg. 4 in Buck Rogers redrawn in Buck Rogers #3 32 64 96 188 307 425
61,63,64,66,67,69,70 24 48 72 142 234 325
62,65,68,73-78-Two pgs. Kirby-a "Lightnin' & the Lone Rider". 65,77-X-Mas-c
26 52 78 154 252 350
71,79,80: 80-(3/41)-Buck Rogers story continues from Buck Rogers #5
20 40 60 114 182 250
72-Speed Spaulding begins by Marvin Bradley (artist), ends #88. This series was written by Edwin Balmer & Philip Wylie (later appeared as film & book "When Worlds Collide")
21 42 63 126 206 285
81-Origin & 1st app. Invisible Scarlet O'Neil (4/41); strip begins #82, ends #167; 1st non-funny-c (Scarlet O'Neil) 22 44 66 132 216 300
82-Buck Rogers-c 24 48 72 142 234 325
83-87,90: 86-Connie vs. Monsters on the Moon-c (sci/fi). 87 has last Buck Rogers full page-r. 90-Bondage-c 18 36 54 105 165 225
88,89: 88-Buck Rogers in "Moon's End" by Calkins, 2 pgs.(not reprints). Beginning with #88, all Buck Rogers pgs. have rearranged panels. 89-Origin & 1st app. Fearless Flint, the Flint Man 19 38 57 109 172 235
91-93,95,96,98-99,101,103-110: 105-Series 2 begins (Strip Page #1)
15 30 45 86 133 180
94-Buck Rogers in "Solar Holocaust" by Calkins, 3 pgs.(not reprints)
16 32 48 94 147 200
97-War Bond promotion, Buck Rogers by Calkins, 2 pgs.(not reprints)
16 32 48 94 147 200
100-1st comic to reach #100; 100th Anniversary cover features 11 major Famous Funnies characters, including Buck Rogers 20 40 60 117 189 260
102-Chief Wahoo vs. Hitler,Tojo & Mussolini-c (1/43) 68 136 204 435 743 1050
111-130 (5/45): 113-X-Mas-c 12 24 36 69 97 125
131-150 (1/47): 137-Strip page No. 110 omitted. 144-(7/46) 12th Anniversary cover
11 22 33 62 86 110
151-162,164-168 10 20 30 58 79 100
163-St. Valentine's Day-c 11 22 33 60 83 105
169,170-Two text illos. by Williamson, his 1st comic book work
13 26 39 74 105 135
171-190: 171-Strip pgs. 227,229,230, Series 2 omitted. 172-Strip Pg. 232 omitted. 190-Buck Rogers ends with start of strip pg. 302, Series 2; Oaky Doaks-c/story
10 20 30 54 72 90
191-197,199,201,203,206-208: No Buck Rogers. 191-Barney Carr, Space detective begins, ends #192. 9 18 27 52 69 85
198,200,202,205-One pg. Frazetta ads; no B. Rogers 10 20 30 54 72 90
204-Used in **POP**, pg. 79,99; war-c begin, end #208 10 20 30 56 76 95
209-216: Frazetta-c. 209-Buck Rogers begins (12/53) with strip pg. 480, Series 2; 211-Buck Rogers ads by Anderson begins, ends #217. #215-Contains B. Rogers strip pg. 515-518, series 2 followed by pgs.179-181, Series 3 119 238 357 762 1306 1850
217,218-B. Rogers ends with pg. 199, Series 3. 218-Wee Three-c/story
10 20 30 54 72 90

NOTE: ***Rick Yager** did the Buck Rogers Sunday strips reprinted in Famous Funnies. The Sundays were formerly done by Russ Keaton and Lt. Dick Calkins did the dailies, but would sometimes assist Yager on a panel or two from time to time. Strip No. 169 is Yager's first full Buck Rogers page. Yager did the strip until 1958 when **Murphy Anderson** took over. **Tuska** art from 4/26/59 - 1965. Virtually every panel was rewritten for Famous Funnies. Not identical to the original Sunday page. The Buck Rogers reprints run continuously through Famous Funnies issue No. 190 (Strip No. 302) with no break in story line. The story line has no continuity after No. 190. The Buck Rogers newspaper strips came out in four series: Series 1, 3/30/30 - 9/21/41 (No. 1 - 600); Series 2, 9/28/41 -10/21/51 (No. 1 -525)(Strip No. 110-1/2 (1/2 pg.) published in only a few newspapers); Series 3, 10/28/51 -2/9/58 (No. 100-428)(No No.1-99); Series 4, 2/16/58 - 6/13/65 (No numbers, dates only). **Everett** c-85, 86. **Moulton** a-100. Chief Wahoo c-93, 97, 102, 116, 136, 139, 151. Dickie Dare c-83, 88. Fearless Flint c-89. Invisible Scarlet O'Neil c-81, 87, 95, 121(part), 132. Scorchy Smith c-84, 90.*

FAMOUS FUNNIES
Super Comics: 1964

Super Reprint Nos. 15-18:17-r/Double Trouble #1. 18-Space Comics #?
2 4 6 9 12 15

FAMOUS GANGSTERS (Crime on the Waterfront No. 4)
Avon Periodicals/Realistic No. 3: Apr, 1951 - No. 3, Feb, 1952

1-3: 1-Capone, Dillinger; c-/Avon paperback #329. 2-Dillinger Machine Gun Killer; Wood-c/a (1 pg.); r/Saint #7 & retitled "Mike Strong". 3-Lucky Luciano & Murder, Inc; c-/Avon paperback #66 37 74 111 218 354 490

FAMOUS INDIAN TRIBES
Dell Publishing Co.: July-Sept, 1962; No. 2, July, 1972

12-264-209(#1) (The Sioux) 3 6 9 15 21 26
2(7/72)-Reprints above 1 3 4 6 8 10

FAMOUS STARS
Ziff-Davis Publ. Co.: Nov-Dec, 1950 - No. 6, Spring, 1952 (All have photo-c)

1-Shelley Winters, Susan Peters, Ava Gardner, Shirley Temple; Jimmy Stewart & Shelley Winters photo-c; Whitney-a 37 74 111 222 361 500
2-Betty Hutton, Bing Crosby, Colleen Townsend, Gloria Swanson; Betty Hutton photo-c; Everett-a(2) 24 48 72 140 230 320
3-Farley Granger, Judy Garland's ordeal (life story; she died 6/22/69 at the age of 47), Alan Ladd; Farley Granger photo-c; Whitney-a 30 60 90 177 289 400
4-Al Jolson, Bob Mitchum, Ella Raines, Richard Conte, Vic Damone; Jane Russell and Bob Mitchum photo-c; Crandall-a, 6pgs. 21 42 63 124 202 280
5-Liz Taylor, Betty Grable, Esther Williams, George Brent, Mario Lanza; Liz Taylor photo-c; Krigstein-a 45 90 135 284 480 675
6-Gene Kelly, Hedy Lamarr, June Allyson, William Boyd, Janet Leigh, Gary Cooper; Gene Kelly photo-c 20 40 60 114 182 250

FAMOUS STORIES (...Book No. 2)
Dell Publishing Co.: 1942 - No. 2, 1942

1,2: 1-Treasure Island. 2-Tom Sawyer 30 60 90 177 289 400

FAMOUS TV FUNDAY FUNNIES

Fanboy #1 © DC

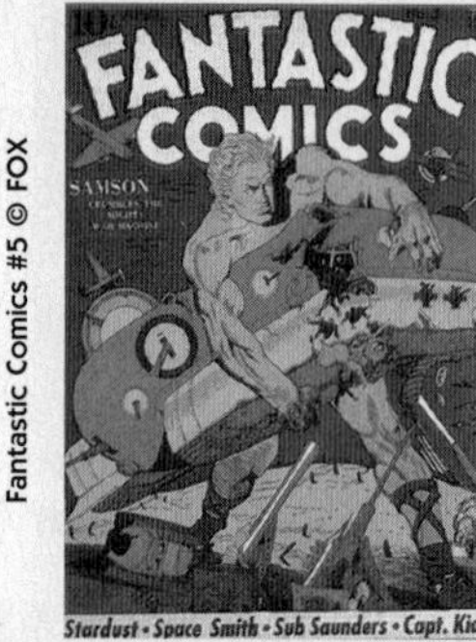

Fantastic Comics #5 © FOX

Fantastic Four #48 © MAR

GD VG FN VF VF/NM NM-
2.0 4.0 6.0 8.0 9.0 9.2

Harvey Publications: Sept, 1961 (25¢ Giant)

1-Casper the Ghost, Baby Huey, Little Audrey 6 12 18 39 62 85

FAMOUS WESTERN BADMEN (Formerly Redskin)
Youthful Magazines: No. 13, Dec, 1952 - No. 15, Apr, 1953

13-Redskin story 14 28 42 82 121 160
14,15: 15-The Dalton Boys story 11 22 33 60 83 105

FAN BOY
DC Comics: Mar, 1999 - No. 6, Aug, 1999 ($2.50, limited series)

1-6: 1-Art by Aragonés and various in all. 2-Green Lantern-c/a by Gil Kane. 3-JLA. 4-Sgt. Rock art by Heath, Marie Severin. 5-Batman art by Sprang, Adams, Miller, Timm. 6-Wonder Woman; art by Rude, Grell 3.00
TPB (2001, $12.95) r/#1-6 13.00

FANTASTIC (Formerly Captain Science; Beware No. 10 on)
Youthful Magazines: No. 8, Feb, 1952 - No. 9, Apr, 1952

8-Capt. Science by Harrison 43 86 129 271 461 650
9-Harrison-a; decapitation, shrunken head panels 36 72 108 211 343 475

FANTASTIC ADVENTURES
Super Comics: 1963 - 1964 (Reprints)

9,10,12,15,16,18: 9-r/? 10-r/He-Man #2(Toby). 11-Disbrow-a. 12-Unpublished Chesler material? 15-r/Spook #23. 16-r/Dark Shadows #2(Steinway); Briefer-a.18-r/Superior Stories #1 3 6 9 18 27 35
11-Wood-a; r/Blue Bolt #118 4 8 12 24 37 50
17-Baker-a(2) r/Seven Seas #6 4 8 12 24 37 50

FANTASTIC COMICS
Fox Features Syndicate: Dec, 1939 - No. 23, Nov, 1941

1-Intro/origin Samson; Stardust, The Super Wizard, Sub Saunders (by Kiefer), Space Smith, Capt. Kidd begin 497 994 1491 3628 6414 9200
2-Powell text illos 265 530 795 1694 2897 4100
3-Classic Lou Fine Robot-c; Powell text illos 1500 3000 4500 7500 11,250 15,000
4,5: Last Lou Fine-c 226 452 678 1446 2473 3500
6,7-Simon-c 155 310 465 992 1696 2400
8-10: 10-Intro/origin David, Samson's aide 97 194 291 621 1061 1500
11-17,19,20: 16-Stardust ends 79 178 237 502 864 1225
18,23: 18-1st app. Black Fury & sidekick Chuck; ends #23. 23-Origin The Gladiator 81 162 243 518 884 1250
21-The Banshee begins(origin); ends #23; Hitler-c 97 194 291 621 1061 1500
22-Hitler-c (likeness of Hitler as furnace on cover) 107 214 321 680 1165 1650
NOTE: *Lou Fine* c-1-5. *Tuska* a-3-5, 8. Bondage c-6, 8, 9. Issue #11 has indicia to Mystery Men Comics #15. All issues feature Samson covers.

FANTASTIC COMICS (Imagining of a 1941 issue by modern creators in Golden Age style)
Image Comics: No. 24, Jan, 2008 ($5.99, Golden Age sized, one-shot)

24-Samson, Yank Wilson, Stardust, Sub Saunders, Space Smith, Capt. Kidd app.; Larsen-c/a; art by Allred, Sienkiewicz, Yeates, Scioli, Hembeck, Ashley Wood & others 6.00

FANTASTIC COMICS (Fantastic Fears #1-9; Becomes Samson #12)
Ajax/Farrell Publ.: No. 10, Nov-Dec, 1954 - No. 11, Jan-Feb, 1955

10 (#1) 21 42 63 126 206 285
11-Robot-c 27 54 81 158 259 360

FANTASTIC FABLES
Silverwolf Comics: Feb, 1987 - No. 2, 1987 ($1.50, 28 pgs., B&W)

1,2: 1-Tim Vigil-a (6 pgs.). 2-Tim Vigil-a (7 pgs.) 4.00

FANTASTIC FEARS (Formerly Captain Jet) (Fantastic Comics #10 on)
Ajax/Farrell Publ.: No. 7, May, 1953 - No. 9, Sept-Oct, 1954

7(#1, 5/53)-Tales of Stalking Terror 52 104 156 322 549 775
8(#2, 7/53) 39 78 117 231 378 525
3,4 30 60 90 177 289 400
5-(1-2/54)-Ditko story (1st drawn) is written by Bruce Hamilton; r-in Weird V2#8 (1st pro work for Ditko but Daring Love #1 was published 1st) 103 206 309 659 1130 1600
6-Decapitation-girl's head w/paper cutter (classic) 60 120 180 381 658 935
7(5-6/54), 9(9-10/54) 30 60 90 177 289 400
8(7-8/54)-Contains story intended for Jo-Jo; name changed to Kaza; decapitation story 31 62 93 182 296 410

FANTASTIC FIVE
Marvel Comics: Oct, 1999 - No. 5, Feb, 2000 ($1.99)

1-5: 1-M2 Universe; recaps origin; Ryan-a. 2-Two covers 3.00
Spider-Girl Presents Fantastic Five: In Search of Doom (2006, $7.99, digest) r/#1-5 8.00

FANTASTIC FIVE
Marvel Comics: Sept, 2007 - No. 5, Nov, 2007 ($2.99, limited series)

1-5-DeFalco-s/Lim-a; Dr. Doom returns vs. the future Fantastic Five 3.00
...: The Final Doom TPB (2007, $13.99) r/#1-5; cover sketches with inks 14.00

FANTASTIC FORCE
Marvel Comics: Nov, 1994 - No. 18, Apr, 1996 ($1.75)

1-($2.50)-Foil wraparound-c; intro Fantastic Force w/Huntara, Delvor, Psi-Lord & Vibraxas 4.00
2-18: 13-She-Hulk app. 3.00

FANTASTIC FORCE (See Fantastic Four #558, Nu-World heroes from 500 years in the future)
Marvel Comics: Jun, 2009 - No. 4, Sept, 2009 ($3.99/$2.99, limited series)

1-($3.99)-Ahearne-s/Kurth-a/Hitch-c; Fantastic Four app. 4.00
2-4-($2.99) 3,4-Ego the Living Planet app. 3.00

FANTASTIC FOUR (See America's Best TV..., Fireside Book Series, Giant-Size..., Giant Size Super-Stars, Marvel Age..., Marvel Collectors Item Classics, Marvel Knights 4, Marvel Milestone Edition, Marvel's Greatest, Marvel Treasury Edition, Marvel Triple Action, Official Marvel Index to..., Power Record Comics & Ultimate...)

FANTASTIC FOUR
Marvel Comics Group: Nov, 1961 - No. 416, Sept, 1996 (Created by Stan Lee & Jack Kirby)

1-Origin & 1st app. The Fantastic Four (Reed Richards: Mr. Fantastic, Johnny Storm: The Human Torch, Sue Storm: The Invisible Girl, & Ben Grimm: The Thing–Marvel's 1st super-hero group since the G.A.; 1st app. S.A. Human Torch); origin/1st app. The Mole Man. 2500 5000 7500 24,000 52,000 80,000
1-Golden Record Comic Set Reprint (1966)-cover not identical to original 19 38 57 139 280 420
with Golden Record 28 56 84 207 419 630
2-Vs. The Skrulls (last 10¢ issue) 410 820 1230 3700 7350 11,000
3-Fantastic Four don costumes & establish Headquarters; brief 1pg. origin; intro. The Fantasti-Car; Human Torch drawn w/two left hands on-c 329 658 987 2961 6081 9200
4-1st S. A. Sub-Mariner app. (5/62) 357 714 1071 3213 6607 10,000
5-Origin & 1st app. Doctor Doom 520 1040 1560 4700 9350 14,000
6-Sub-Mariner, Dr. Doom team up; 1st Marvel villain team-up (2nd S.A. Sub-Mariner app. 196 392 588 1715 3508 5300
7-10: 7-1st app. Kurrgo. 8-1st app. Puppet-Master & Alicia Masters. 9-3rd Sub-Mariner app. 10-Stan Lee & Jack Kirby app. in story 139 278 417 1182 2391 3600
11-Origin/1st app. The Impossible Man (2/63) 135 270 405 1150 2325 3500
12-Fantastic Four vs. The Hulk (1st meeting); 1st Hulk x-over & ties w/Amazing Spider-Man #1 as 1st Marvel x-over; (3/63) 357 714 1071 3213 6607 10,000
13-Intro. The Watcher; 1st app. The Red Ghost 81 162 243 689 1395 2100
14,15,17,19: 14-Sub-Mariner x-over. 15-1st app. Mad Thinker. 19-Intro. Rama-Tut; Stan Lee & Jack Kirby cameo 50 100 150 425 863 1300
16-1st Ant-Man x-over (7/63); Wasp cameo 97 194 291 621 1111 1600
18-Origin/1st app. The Super Skrull 103 206 309 659 1180 1700
20-Origin/1st app. The Molecule Man 54 108 162 459 930 1400
21-Intro. The Hate Monger; 1st Sgt. Fury x-over (12/63) 47 94 141 376 763 1150
22-24: 22-Sue Storm gains more powers 33 66 99 254 502 750
25,26-The Hulk vs. The Thing (their 1st battle). 25-3rd Avengers x-over (1st time w/Captain America)(cameo, 4/64); 2nd S.A. app. Cap (takes place between Avengers #4 & 5.) 26-4th Avengers x-over 62 124 186 527 1064 1600
27-1st Doctor Strange x-over (6/64) 37 74 111 295 585 875
28-Early X-Men x-over (7/64); same date as X-Men #6 48 96 144 408 829 1250
29,30: 30-Intro. Diablo 27 54 81 197 399 600
31-40: 31-Early Avengers x-over (10/64). 33-1st app. Attuma; part photo-c. 35-Intro/1st app. Dragon Man. 36-Intro/1st app. Madam Medusa & the Frightful Four (Sandman, Wizard, Paste Pot Pete). 39-Wood inks on Daredevil (early x-over) 22 44 66 159 317 475
41-44,47: 41-43-Frightful Four app. 44-Intro. Gorgon 14 28 42 99 200 300
45-Intro/1st app. The Inhumans (c/story, 12/65); also see Incredible Hulk Special #1 & Thor #146, & 147 25 50 75 183 367 550
46-1st Black Bolt-c (Kirby) & 1st full app. 16 32 48 114 232 350
48-Partial origin/1st app. The Silver Surfer & Galactus (3/66) by Lee & Kirby; Galactus brief app. in last panel; 1st of 3 part story 58 116 174 493 997 1500
49-2nd app./1st cover Silver Surfer & Galactus 38 76 114 304 602 900
50-Silver Surfer battles Galactus; full S.S.-c 41 82 123 328 664 1000
51-Classic "This Man...This Monster" story 20 40 60 140 283 425
52-1st app. The Black Panther (7/66) 30 60 90 231 458 685
53-Origin & 2nd app. The Black Panther 17 34 51 122 249 375
54-Inhumans cameo 12 24 36 87 164 240
55-Thing battles Silver Surfer; 4th app. Silver Surfer 20 40 60 140 283 425
56-Silver Surfer cameo 12 24 36 86 161 235
57-60: Dr. Doom steals Silver Surfer's powers (also see Silver Surfer: Loftier Than Mortals). 59,60-Inhumans cameo 11 22 33 75 138 200

Fantastic Four #113 © MAR

Fantastic Four #249 © MAR

Fantastic Four #416 © MAR

	GD 2.0	VG 4.0	FN 6.0	VF 8.0	VF/NM 9.0	NM- 9.2
61-65,68-71: 61-Silver Surfer cameo; Sandman-c/s	9	18	27	63	107	150
66-Begin 2 part origin of Him (Warlock); does not app. (9/67)	12	24	36	87	164	240
66,67-2nd printings (1994)	2	4	6	8	10	12
67-Origin/1st brief app. Him (Warlock); 1 page; see Thor #165,166 for 1st full app.	12	24	36	87	164	240
72-Silver Surfer-c/story (pre-dates Silver Surfer #1)	12	24	36	87	164	240
73-Spider-Man, D.D., Thor x-over; cont'd from Daredevil #38	11	22	33	80	150	220
74-77: Silver Surfer app.(#77 is same date/S.S. #1)	10	20	30	71	128	185
78-80	7	14	21	47	76	105
81-88: 81-Crystal joins & dons costume. 82,83-Inhumans app. 84-87-Dr. Doom app. 88-Last 12¢ issue	6	12	18	43	69	95
89-99,101: 94-Intro. Agatha Harkness.	6	12	18	39	62	85
100 (7/70) F.F. vs Thinker and Puppet-Master	10	20	30	71	128	185
102-104: F.F. vs. Sub-Mariner. 104-Magneto-c/story	6	12	18	39	62	85
105-109,111: 108-Last Kirby issue (not in #103-107)	6	12	18	37	59	80
110-Initial version w/green Thing and blue faces and pink uniforms on-c	7	14	21	47	76	105
110-Corrected-c w/accurately colored faces and uniforms and orange Thing	6	12	18	39	62	85
112-Hulk Vs. Thing (7/71)	15	30	45	106	216	325
113-115: 115-Last 15¢ issue	5	10	15	30	48	65
116 (52 pgs.)	6	12	18	43	69	95
117-120	4	8	12	28	44	60
121-123-Silver Surfer-c/stories. 122,123-Galactus	5	10	15	32	51	70
124,125,127,129-140: 129-Intro. Thundra. 130-Sue leaves F.F. 131-Quicksilver app. 132-Medusa joins. 133-Thundra Vs. Thing	4	8	12	24	37	50
126-Origin F.F. retold; cover swipe of F.F. #1	4	8	12	26	41	55
128-Four pg. insert of F.F. Friends & Foes	4	8	12	26	41	55
141-149: 142-Kirbyish-a by Buckler begins. 143-Dr. Doom-c/story. 147-Sub-Mariner	4	8	12	22	34	45
150-Crystal & Quicksilver's wedding	4	8	12	26	41	55
151-154,158-160: 151-Origin Thundra. 159-Medusa leaves; Sue rejoins	3	6	9	16	22	28
155-157: Silver Surfer in all	3	6	9	20	30	40
161-165,168,174-180: 164-The Crusader (old Marvel Boy) revived (origin #165); 1st app. Frankie Raye. 168-170-Cage app. 176-Re-intro Impossible Man; Marvel artists app. 180-r/#101 by Kirby	2	4	6	10	14	18
166,167-vs. Hulk	3	6	9	17	25	32
169-173-(Regular 25¢ edition)(4-8/75)	2	4	6	10	14	18
169-173-(30¢-c, limited distribution)	3	6	9	18	27	36
181-199: 189-G.A. Human Torch app. & origin retold. 190,191-Fantastic Four break up	2	4	6	8	10	12
183-187-(35¢-c variants, limited dist.)(6-10/77)	4	8	12	24	37	50
200-(11/78, 52 pgs.)-F.F. re-united vs. Dr. Doom	2	4	6	10	14	18
201-208,219,222-231: 207-Human Torch vs. Spider-Man-c/story. 211-1st app. Terrax. 224-Contains unused alternate-c for FF #3 and pin-ups						6.00
209-216,218,220,221-Byrne-a. 209-1st Herbie the Robot. 220-Brief origin	1	2	3	5	6	8
217-Early app. Dazzler (4/80); by Byrne	1	2	3	5	6	8
232-Byrne-a begins	1	2	3	5	6	8
233-235,237-249,251-260: All Byrne-a. 238-Origin Frankie Raye. 244-Frankie Raye becomes Nova, Herald of Galactus. 252-Reads sideways; Annihilus app.; contains skin "Tattooz" decals						6.00
236-20th Anniversary issue(11/81, 68 pgs., $1.00)-Brief origin F.F.; Byrne-c/a(p); new Kirby-a(p)	1	2	3	5	6	8
250-(52 pgs)-Spider-Man x-over; Byrne-a; Skrulls impersonate New X-Men	1	2	3	5	6	8
261-285: 261-Silver Surfer. 262-Origin Galactus; Byrne writes & draws himself into story. 264-Swipes-c of F.F. #1. 274-Spider-Man's alien costume app. (4th app., 1/85, 2 pgs.)						4.00
286-2nd app. X-Factor continued from Avengers #263; story continues in X-Factor #1						5.00
287-295: 291-Action Comcis #1 cover swipe. 292-Nick Fury app. 293-Last Byrne-a						4.00
296-($1.50)-Barry Smith-c/a; Thing rejoins						5.00
297-318,321-330: 300-Johnny Storm & Alicia Masters wed. 306-New team begins (9/87). 311-Re-intro The Black Panther. 327-Mr. Fantastic & Invisible Girl return						3.00
319,320: 319-Double size. 320-Thing vs. Hulk						4.00
331-346,351-357,359,360: 334-Simonson-c/scripts begin. 337-Simonson-a begins. 342-Spider-Man cameo. 356-F.F. vs. The New Warriors; Paul Ryan-c/a begins. 360-Last $1.00-c						3.00
347-Ghost Rider, Wolverine, Spider-Man, Hulk-c/stories thru #349; Arthur Adams-c/a(p) in each						5.00
347,348-Gold 2nd printing						3.00
348-350: 350-($1.50, 52 pgs.)-Dr. Doom app.						4.00

	GD 2.0	VG 4.0	FN 6.0	VF 8.0	VF/NM 9.0	NM- 9.2
358-(11/91, $2.25, 88 pgs.)-30th anniversary issue; gives history of F.F.; die cut-c; Art Adams back-up story-a						4.00
361-368,370,372-374,376-380,382-386: 362-Spider-Man app. 367-Wolverine app. (brief). 370-Infinity War x-over; Thanos & Magus app. 374-Secret Defenders (Ghost Rider, Hulk, Wolverine) x-over						3.00
369-Infinity War x-over; Thanos app.						3.00
371-All white embossed-c ($2.00)						4.00
371-All red 2nd printing ($2.00)						3.00
375-($2.95, 52 pgs.)-Holo-grafx foil-c; ann. issue						4.00
376-($2.95)-Variant polybagged w/Dirt Magazine #4 and music tape						5.00
381-Death of Reed Richards (Mister Fantastic) & Dr. Doom						4.00
387-Newsstand ed. ($1.25)						3.00
387-($2.95)-Collector's Ed. w/Die-cut foil-c						4.00
388-393,395-397: 388-bound-in trading card sheet. 394-($1.50-c)						3.00
394,398,399: 394 ($2.95)-Collector's Edition-polybagged w/16 pg. Marvel Action Hour book and acetate print; pink logo. 398,399-Rainbow Foil-c						4.00
400-Rainbow-Foil-c						5.00
401-415: 401,402-Atlantis Rising. 407,408-Return of Reed Richards. 411-Inhumans app. 414-Galactus vs. Hyperstorm. 415-Onslaught tie-in; X-Men app.						3.00
416-($2.50)-Onslaught tie-in; Dr. Doom app.; wraparound-c						4.00
#500-up (See Fantastic Four Vol. 3; series resumed original numbering after Vol. 3 #70)						
Annual 1('63)-Origin F.F.; Ditko-i; early Spidey app.	71	142	213	604	1227	1850
Annual 2('64)-Dr. Doom origin & c/story	37	74	111	295	585	875
Annual 3('65)-Reed & Sue wed; r/#6,11	18	36	54	131	266	400
Special 4(11/66)-G.A. Torch x-over (1st S.A. app.) & origin retold; r/#25,26 (Hulk vs. Thing); Torch vs. Torch battle	13	26	39	89	170	250
Special 5(11/67)-New art; Intro. Psycho-Man; early Black Panther, Inhumans & Silver Surfer (1st solo story) app.	13	26	39	91	176	260
Special 6(11/68)-Intro. Annihilus; birth of Franklin Richards; new 48 pg. movie length epic; last non-reprint annual	9	18	27	63	107	150
Special 7(11/69)-r/F.F. #1,2; Marvel staff photos	5	10	15	32	51	70
Special 8-10: All reprints. 8(12/70)-F.F. vs. Sub-Mariner plus gallery of F.F. foes. 9(12/71). 10('73)	3	6	9	20	30	40
Annual 11-14: 11(1976)-New art begins again. 12(1978). 13(1978). 14(1979)	2	4	6	8	10	12
Annual 15-17: 15('80, 68 pgs.). 17(1983)-Byrne-c/a						6.00
Annual 18-27: 21(1988)-Evolutionary War x-over. 22-Atlantis Attacks x-over; Sub-Mariner & The Avengers app.; Buckler-a. 23-Byrne-c; Guice-p. 24-2 pg. origin recap of Fantastic Four; Guardians of the Galaxy x-over. 25-Moondragon story. 26-Bagged w/card						4.00
Best of the Fantastic Four Vol. 1 HC (2005, $29.99) oversized reprints of classic stories from FF#1,39,40,51,100,116,176,236,267, Ann.2, V3#56,60 and more; Brevoort intro.						30.00
Maximum Fantastic Four HC (2005, $49.99, dust jacket) r/Fantastic Four #1 with super-sized art; historical background from Walter Mosley and Mark Evanier; dust jacket unfolds to a poster: giant FF#1 cover on one side, gallery of interior pages on other						50.00
...: Monsters Unleashed nn (1992, $5.95)-r/F.F. #347-349 w/new Arthur Adams-c						6.00
...: Nobody Gets Out Alive (1994, $15.95) TPB r/ #387-392						16.00
... Omnibus Vol. 1 HC (2005, $99.99) r/#1-30 & Annual 1 plus letter pages; 3 intros. and a 1974 essay by Stan Lee; original plot synopsis for FF #1; essays and Kirby art						100.00
... Omnibus Vol. 2 HC (2007, $99.99) r/#31-60, Annual 2-4 and Not Brand Echh #1 plus letter pages and essays by Stan Lee, Reginald Hudlin, Roy Thomas and others						100.00
Special Edition 1(5/84)-r/Annual #1; Byrne-c/a						4.00
...: The Lost Adventure (4/08, $4.99) Lee & Kirby story partially used in flashback in FF #108 completed with additional art by Frenz & Sinnott; plus reprint of FF #108						5.00
... Visionaries: George Pérez Vol. 1 (2005, $19.99) r/#164-167,170,176-178,184-186						20.00
... Visionaries: George Pérez Vol. 2 (2006, $19.99) r/#187-188,191-192, Annual #14-15, Marvel Two-In-One #60 and back-up story from Adventures of the Thing #3						20.00
... Visionaries (11/01, $19.95) r/#232-240 by John Byrne						20.00
... Visionaries Vol. 2 (2004, $24.99) r/#241-250 by John Byrne						25.00
... Visionaries John Byrne Vol. 3 (2004, $24.99) r/#251-257; Annual #17; Avengers #233 and Thing #2						25.00
... Visionaries John Byrne Vol. 4 (2005, $24.99) r/#258-267; Alpha Flight #4 & Thing #10						25.00
... Visionaries John Byrne Vol. 5 (2005, $24.99) r/#268-275; Annual #18 & Thing #19						25.00
... Visionaries John Byrne Vol. 6 ('06, $24.99) r/#276-284; Secret Wars II #2 & Thing #23						25.00
... Visionaries John Byrne Vol. 7 ('07, $24.99) r/#285,286, Ann. #19, Avengers #263 & Ann. #14, and X-Factor #1						25.00
... Visionaries John Byrne Vol. 8 ('07, $24.99) r/#287-295						25.00
... Visionaries: Walter Simonson Vol. 1 (2007, $19.99) r/#334-341						20.00

NOTE: ***Arthur Adams*** *c/a-347-349p.* ***Austin*** *c(i)-232-236, 238, 240-242, 250i, 286i.* ***Buckler*** *c-151, 168.* ***John Buscema*** *a(p)-107, 108(w/**Kirby, Sinnott** & **Romita**),109-130, 132, 134-141, 160, 173-175, 202, 296-309p, Annual 11, 13; c(p)-107-122, 124-129, 133-139, 202, Annual 12p, Special 10.* ***Byrne*** *a-209-218p, 220p, 221p, 232-265, 266i, 267-273, 274-293p, Annual 17, 19; c-211-214p, 220p, 232-236p, 237, 238p, 239, 240-242p, 243-249, 250p, 251-267, 269-277, 278-281p, 283p, 284, 285, 286p, 288-293, Annual 17, 18.* ***Ditko*** *a-13i, 14i(w/**Kirby**-p), Annual 16.* ***G. Kane*** *c-145p, 146p, 150p, 160p.* ***Kirby*** *a-1-102p, 108p, 180r, 189r, 236p, Special 1-10; c-1-101, 164, 167, 171-177, 180, 181, 190, 200, Annual 11, Special 1-7, 9.* ***Marcos*** *a-Annual 14i.* ***Mooney*** *a-118i, 152i.* ***Perez*** *a(p)-164-167, 170-172, 176-178, 184-188, 191p, 192p. Annual 14p, 15p; c(p)-183-188, 191, 192, 194-197.* ***Simonson*** *a-337-341, 343, 344p, 345p, 346, 350p, 352-354; c-212, 334-341, 342p, 343-346, 350, 353, 354.* ***Steranko*** *c-130-*

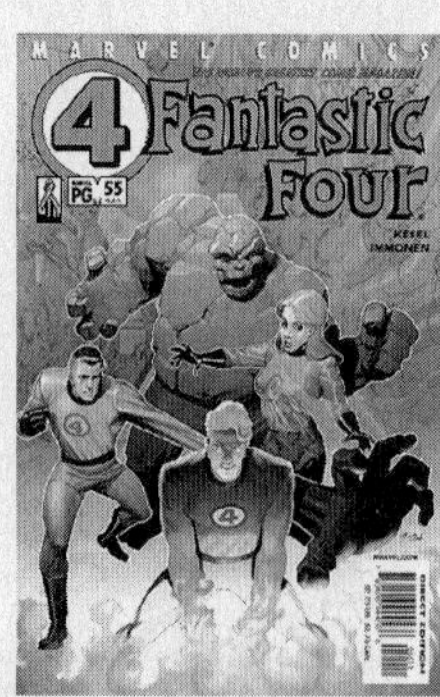
Fantastic Four V3 #55 © MAR

Fantastic Four #587 © MAR

Fantastic Four: Fireworks #1 © MAR

GD VG FN VF VF/NM NM-
2.0 4.0 6.0 8.0 9.0 9.2

*132p. **Williamson** c-357i.*

FANTASTIC FOUR (Volume Two)
Marvel Comics: V2#1, Nov, 1996 - No. 13, Nov, 1997 ($2.95/$1.95/$1.99) (Produced by WildStorm Productions)

1-($2.95)-Reintro Fantastic Four; Jim Lee-c/a; Brandon Choi scripts; Mole Man app. 5.00
1-($2.95)-Variant-c 1 2 3 4 5 7
2-9: 2-Namor-c/app. 3-Avengers-c/app. 4-Two covers; Dr. Doom cameo 3.00
10,11,13: All $1.99-c. 13-"World War 3"-pt. 1, x-over w/Image 3.00
12-($2.99) "Heroes Reunited"-pt. 1 4.00
...: Heroes Reborn (7/00, $17.95, TPB) r/#1-6 18.00
Heroes Reborn: Fantastic Four (2006, $29.99, TPB) r/#1-12; Jim Lee intro.; pin-ups 30.00

FANTASTIC FOUR (Volume Three)
Marvel Comics: V3#1, Jan, 1998 - No. 588, Apr, 2011 ($2.99/$1.99/$2.25)

1-($2.99)-Heroes Return; Lobdell-s/Davis & Farmer-a 1 2 3 5 6 8
1-Alternate Heroes Return-c 1 3 4 6 8 10
2-4,12: 2-2-covers. 4-Claremont-s/Larroca-a begin; Silver Surfer c/app. 12-($2.99) Wraparound-c by Larroca 5.00
5-11: 6-Heroes For Hire app. 9-Spider-Man-c/app. 4.00
13-24: 13,14-Ronan-c/app. 3.00
25-($2.99) Dr. Doom returns 4.00
26-49: 27-Dr. Doom marries Sue. 30-Begin $2.25-c. 32,42-Namor-c/app. 35-Regular cover; Pacheco-s/a begins. 37-Super-Skrull-c/app. 38-New Baxter Building 3.00
35-($3.25) Variant foil enhanced-c; Pacheco-s/a begins 4.00
50-($3.99, 64 pgs.) BWS-c; Grummett, Pacheco, Rude, Udon-a 4.00
51-53,55-59: 51-53-Bagley-a(p)/Wieringo-c; Inhumans app. 55,56-Immonen-a 57-59-Warren-s/Grant-a 3.00
54-($3.50, 100 pgs.) Birth of Valeria; r/Annual #6 birth of Franklin 4.00
60-(9¢-c) Waid-s/Wieringo-a begin 3.00
60-($2.25 newsstand edition)(also see Promotional Comics section) 3.00
61-70: 62-64-FF vs. Modulus. 65,66-Buckingham-a. 68-70-Dr. Doom app. 3.00
(After #70 [Aug, 2003] numbering reverted back to original Vol. 1 with #500, Sept, 2003)
500-($3.50) Regular edition; concludes Dr. Doom app.; Dr. Strange app.; Rivera painted-c 4.00
500-($4.99) Director's Cut Edition; chromium-c by Wieringo; sketch and script pages 8.00
501-516: 501,502-Casey Jones-a. 503-508-Porter-a. 509-Wieringo-c/a resumes. 512,513-Spider-Man app. 514-516-Ha-c/Medina-a 3.00
517-537: 517-Begin $2.99-c. 519-523-Galactus app. 527-Straczynski-s begins. 537-Dr. Doom. 3.00
527-Variant Edition with different McKone-c 3.00
527-Wizard World Philadelphia Edition with B&W McKone sketch-c 3.00
536-Variant cover by Bryan Hitch 5.00
537-B&W variant cover 5.00
538-542-Civil War. 538-Don Blake reclaims Thor's hammer 4.00
543-45th Anniversary; Black Panther and Storm replace Reed and Sue; Granov-c 4.00
544-553: 544-546-Silver Surfer app.; Turner-c 3.00
554-568-Millar-s/Hitch-a/c. 558-561-Dr. Doom-c/app. 562-Funeral & proposal 3.00
554-Variant-c by Bianchi 6.00
554-Variant Skrull-c by Suydam 30.00
569-($3.99) Wraparound-c; Immonen-a; Dr. Doom app. 4.00
570-586: 570-572,575-578-Eaglesham-a. 574-Spider-Man app. 584-586-Galactus app. 3.00
587-(3/11, $3.99) Death of Human Torch; Epting-a; issue is in black polybag; Davis-c 4.00
587-Variant-c by Cassaday 10.00
588-($3.99) Last issue; Dragotta-a; preview of FF #1; back-up w/Spider-Man; Davis-c 4.00
...'98 Annual ($3.50) Immonen-a 4.00
...'99 Annual ($3.50) Ladronn-a 4.00
...'00 Annual ($3.50) Larocca-a; Marvel Girl back-up story 4.00
...'01 Annual ($2.99) Maguire-a; Thing back-up w/Yu-a 4.00
... Annual 32 (8/10, $4.99) Hitch-a/c 5.00
... : A Death in the Family (7/06, $3.99, one-shot) Weeks-a/c; and r/F.F. #245 4.00
... By J. Michael Straczynski Vol. 1 (2005, $19.99, HC) r/#527-532 20.00
Civil War: Fantastic Four TPB (2007, $17.99) r/#538-543; 45th Anniversary Toasts 18.00
... Cosmic-Size Special 1 (2/09, $4.99) Cary Bates-s/Bing Cansino-a; r/F.F. #237 5.00
Fantastic 4th Voyage of Sinbad (9/01, $5.95) Claremont-s/Ferry-a 6.00
Flesh and Stone (8/01, $12.95, TPB) r/#35-39 13.00
... Giant-Size Adventures 1 (8/09, $3.99) Cifuentes & Coover-a; Egghead app. 4.00
... In...Ataque del M.O.D.O.K.! (11/10, $3.99) English & Spanish editions; Beland-s/Doe-a 4.00
... /Inhumans TPB (2007, $19.99) r/#51-54 and Inhumans ('00) #1-4 20.00
...: Isla De La Muerte! (2/08, $3.99) English & Spanish editions; Beland-s/Doe-a 4.00
... Presents: Franklin Richards 1 (11/05, $2.99) r/back-up stories from Power Pack #1-4 plus new 5 pg. story; Sumerak-s/Eliopoulos-a (Also see Franklin Richards) 3.00
...Special (2/06, $2.99) McDuffie-s/Casey Jones-a; dinner with Dr. Doom 3.00
...Tales Vol. 1 (2005, $7.99, digest) r/Marvel Age: FF Tales #1, Tales of the Thing #1-3, and Spider-Man Team-Up Special 8.00
...: The New Fantastic Four HC (2007, $19.99) r/#544-550; variant covers & sketch pgs. 20.00
...: The New Fantastic Four SC (2008, $15.99) r/#544-550; variant covers & sketch pgs. 16.00
... : The Wedding Special 1 (1/06, $5.00) 40th Anniversary new story & r/FF Annual #3 5.00
... Vol. 1 HC (2004, $29.99, dust jacket) oversized reprint /#60-70, 500-502; Mark Waid intro and series proposal; cover gallery 30.00
... Vol. 2 HC (2005, $29.99, d.j.) oversized r/#503-513; Waid intro.; deleted scenes 30.00
... Vol. 3 HC (2005, $29.99, d.j.) oversized r/#514-524; Waid commentaries; cover sketches 30.00
... Vol. 1: Imaginauts (2003, $17.99, TPB) r/#56,60-66; Mark Waid's series proposal 18.00
... Vol. 2: Unthinkable (2003, $17.99, TPB) r/#67-70,500-502; #500 Director's Cut extras 18.00
... Vol. 3: Authoritative Action (2004, $12.99, TPB) r/#503-508 13.00
... Vol. 4: Hereafter (2004, $11.99, TPB) r/#509-513 12.00
... Vol. 5: Disassembled (2004, $14.99, TPB) r/#514-519 15.00
... Vol. 6: Rising Storm (2005, $13.99, TPB) r/#520-524 14.00
...: The Beginning of the End TPB (2008, $14.99) r/#525,526,551-553 & Fantastic Four: Isla De La Muerte! one-shot 15.00
...: The Life Fantastic TPB (2006, $16.99) r/#533-535; The Wedding Special, Special (2/06) and A Death in the Family one-shots 17.00
Wizard #1/2 -Lim-a 10.00

FANTASTIC FOUR AND POWER PACK
Marvel Comics: Sept, 2007 - No. 4, Dec, 2007 ($2.99, limited series)

1-4-Gurihiru-a/Van Lente-s; the Wizard app. 3.00
...: Favorite Son TPB (2008, $7.99, digest size) r/#1-4 8.00

FANTASTIC FOUR: ATLANTIS RISING
Marvel Comics: June, 1995 - No. 2, July, 1995 ($3.95, limited series)

1,2: Acetate-c 5.00
Collector's Preview (5/95, $2.25, 52 pgs.) 4.00

FANTASTIC FOUR: BIG TOWN
Marvel Comics: Jan, 2001 - No. 4, Apr, 2001 ($2.99, limited series)

1-4:"What If?" story; McKone-a/Englehart-s 3.00

FANTASTIC FOUR: FIREWORKS
Marvel Comics: Jan, 1999 - No. 3, Mar, 1999 ($2.99, limited series)

1-3-Remix; Jeff Johnson-a 3.00

FANTASTIC FOUR: FIRST FAMILY
Marvel Comics: May, 2006 - No. 6, Oct, 2006 ($2.99, limited series)

1-6-Casey-s/Weston-a; flashback to the days after the accident 3.00
TPB (2006, $15.99) r/#1-6 16.00

FANTASTIC FOUR: FOES
Marvel Comics: Mar, 2005 - No. 6, Aug, 2005 ($2.99, limited series)

1-6-Kirkman-s/Rathburn-a. 1-Puppet Master app. 3-Super-Skrull app. 4-Mole Man app. 3.00
TPB (2005, $16.99) r/#1-6 17.00

FANTASTIC FOUR: HOUSE OF M (Reprinted in House of M: Fantastic Four/ Iron Man TPB)
Marvel Comics: Sept, 2005 - No. 3, Nov, 2005 ($2.99, limited series)

1-3: Fearsome Four, led by Doom; Scot Eaton-a 3.00

FANTASTIC FOUR INDEX (See Official...)

FANTASTIC FOUR/ IRON MAN: BIG IN JAPAN
Marvel Comics: Dec, 2005 - No. 4, Mar, 2006 ($3.50, limited series)

1-4-Seth Fisher-a/c; Zeb Wells-s; wraparound-c on each 3.50
TPB (2006, $12.99) r/#1-4 and Seth Fisher illustrated story from Spider-Man Unlimited #8 13.00

FANTASTIC FOUR: 1 2 3 4
Marvel Comics: Oct, 2001 - No. 4, Jan, 2002 ($2.99, limited series)

1-4-Morrison-s/Jae Lee-a. 2-4-Namor-c/app. 3.00
TPB (2002, $9.99) r/#1-4 10.00

FANTASTIC FOUR ROAST
Marvel Comics Group: May, 1982 (75¢, one-shot, direct sales)

1-Celebrates 20th anniversary of F.F.#1; X-Men, Ghost Rider & many others cameo; Golden, Miller, Buscema, Rogers, Byrne, Anderson art; Hembeck/Austin-c 4.00

FANTASTIC FOUR: THE END
Marvel Comics: Jan, 2007 - No. 6, May, 2007 ($2.99, limited series)

1-6-Alan Davis-s/a; last adventure of the future FF. 1-Dr. Doom-c/app. 3.00
Roughcut #1 ($3.99) B&W pencil art for full story and text script; B&W sketch cover 4.00
HC (2007, $19.99, dustjacket) r/#1-6 20.00
SC (2008, $14.99) r/#1-6 15.00

FANTASTIC FOUR: THE LEGEND
Marvel Comics: Oct, 1996 ($3.95, one-shot)

1-Tribute issue 4.00

FANTASTIC FOUR: THE MOVIE
Marvel Comics: Aug, 2005 ($4.99/$12.99, one-shot)

Fantastic Four: 1 2 3 4 #2 © MAR

Fantasy Masterpieces #9 © MAR

Farscape #9 © Jim Henson Co.

GD 2.0 | VG 4.0 | FN 6.0 | VF 8.0 | VF/NM 9.0 | NM- 9.2

1-($4.99) Movie adaptation; Jurgens-a; behind the scenes feature; Doom origin; photo-c 5.00
TPB-($12.99) Movie adaptation, r/Fantastic Four #5 & 190, and FF Vol. 3 #60, photo-c 13.00

FANTASTIC FOUR: TRUE STORY
Marvel Comics: Sept, 2008 - No. 4, Jan, 2009 ($2.99, limited series)

1-4-Cornell-s/Domingues-a/Henrichon-c 3.00

FANTASTIC FOUR 2099
Marvel Comics: Jan, 1996 - No. 8, Aug, 1996 ($3.95/$1.95)

1-($3.95)-Chromium-c; X-Nation preview 4.00
2-8: 4-Spider-Man 2099-c/app. 5-Doctor Strange app. 7-Thibert-c 3.00
NOTE: *Williamson a-1i; c-1i.*

FANTASTIC FOUR UNLIMITED
Marvel Comics: Mar, 1993 - No. 12, Dec, 1995 ($3.95, 68 pgs.)

1-12: 1-Black Panther app. 4-Thing vs. Hulk. 5-Vs. The Frightful Four. 6-Vs. Namor. 7, 9-12-Wraparound-c 4.00

FANTASTIC FOUR UNPLUGGED
Marvel Comics: Sept, 1995 - No. 6, Aug 1996 (99¢, bi-monthly)

1-6 3.00

FANTASTIC FOUR - UNSTABLE MOLECULES
(Indicia for #1 reads STARTLING STORIES: ... ; #2 reads UNSTABLE MOLECULES)
Marvel Comics: Mar, 2003 - No. 4, June, 2003 ($2.99, limited series)

1-4-Guy Davis-c/a 3.00
Fantastic Four Legends Vol. 1 TPB (2003, $13.99) r/#1-4, origin from FF #1 (1963) 14.00
TPB (2005, $13.99) r/#1-4 14.00

FANTASTIC FOUR VS. X-MEN
Marvel Comics: Feb, 1987 - No. 4, June, 1987 (Limited series)

1-4: 4-Austin-a(i) 4.00

FANTASTIC FOUR: WORLD'S GREATEST COMICS MAGAZINE
Marvel Comics: Feb, 2001 - No. 12 (Limited series)

1-12: Homage to Lee & Kirby era of F.F.; s/a by Larsen & various. 5-Hulk-c/app. 10-Thor app. 3.00

FANTASTIC GIANTS (Formerly Konga #1-23)
Charlton Comics: V2#24, Sept, 1966 (25¢, 68 pgs.)

V2#24-Special Ditko issue; origin Konga & Gorgo reprinted plus two new Ditko stories
7 14 21 45 73 100

FANTASTIC TALES
I. W. Enterprises: 1958 (no date) (Reprint, one-shot)

1-Reprints Avon's "City of the Living Dead" 3 6 9 20 30 40

FANTASTIC VOYAGE (See Movie Comics)
Gold Key: Aug, 1969 - No. 2, Dec, 1969

1 (TV) 4 8 12 28 44 60
2-Cover has the text "Civilian Miniaturized Defense Force" in yellow bar at top; back cover has painted art 3 6 9 20 30 40
2-Variant cover has text "In This Issue Sweepstakes..." along top; ad on back-c
4 8 12 24 37 50

FANTASTIC VOYAGES OF SINDBAD, THE
Gold Key: Oct, 1965 - No. 2, June, 1967

1-Painted-c on both 6 12 18 43 69 95
2 5 10 15 32 51 70

FANTASTIC WORLDS
Standard Comics: No. 5, Sept, 1952 - No. 7, Jan, 1953

5-Toth, Anderson-a 37 74 111 218 354 490
6-Toth-c/a 30 60 90 177 289 400
7 20 40 60 117 189 260

FANTASY FEATURES
Americomics: 1987 - No. 2, 1987 ($1.75)

1,2 3.00

FANTASY ILLUSTRATED
New Media Publ.: Spring 1982 ($2.95, B&W magazine)

1-P. Craig Russell-c/a; art by Ditko, Sekowsky, Sutton; Englehart-s
1 2 3 4 5 7

FANTASY MASTERPIECES (Marvel Super Heroes No. 12 on)
Marvel Comics Group: Feb, 1966 - No. 11, Oct, 1967; V2#1, Dec, 1979 - No. 14, Jan, 1981

1-Photo of Stan Lee (12¢-c #1,2) 8 16 24 56 93 130
2-r/1st Fin Fang Foom from Strange Tales #89 5 10 15 35 55 75
3-8: 3-G.A. Capt. America-r begin, end #11; 1st 25¢ Giant; Colan-r. 3-6-Kirby-c(p). 4-Kirby-c(p)(i). 7-Begin G.A. Sub-Mariner, Torch-r/M. Mystery. 8-Torch battles the Sub-Mariner-r/Marvel Mystery #9 6 12 18 37 59 80
9-Origin Human Torch-r/Marvel Comics #1 6 12 18 39 62 85
10,11: 10-r/origin & 1st app. All Winners Squad from All Winners #19. 11-r/origin of Toro (H.T. #1) & Black Knight #1 5 10 15 35 55 75
V2#1(12/79, 75¢, 52 pgs.)-r/origin Silver Surfer from Silver Surfer #1 with editing plus reprints cover; J. Buscema-a 1 3 4 6 8 10
2-14-Reprints Silver Surfer #2-14 w/covers 6.00
NOTE: *Buscema c-V2#7-9(in part).* ***Ditko*** *r-1-3, 7, 9.* ***Everett*** *r-1,7-9.* ***Matt Fox*** *r-9i.* ***Kirby*** *r-1-11; c(p)-3, 4i, 5, 6.* ***Starlin*** *r-8-13. Some direct sale V2#14's had a 50¢ cover price. #3-11 contain Capt. America-r/Capt. America #3-10. #7-11 contain G.A.Human Torch & Sub-Mariner-r.*

FANTASY QUARTERLY (Also see Elfquest)
Independent Publishers Syndicate: Spring, 1978 (B&W)

1-1st app. Elfquest; Dave Sim-a (6 pgs.) 8 16 24 52 86 120

FANTOMAN (Formerly Amazing Adventure Funnies)
Centaur Publications: No. 2, Aug, 1940 - No. 4, Dec, 1940

2-The Fantom of the Fair, The Arrow, Little Dynamite-r begin; origin The Ermine by Filchock; Fantoman app. in 2-4; Burgos, J. Cole, Ernst, Gustavson-a
110 220 330 704 1202 1700
3,4: Gustavson-r. 4-Red Blaze story 86 172 258 546 936 1325

FAREWELL MOONSHADOW (See Moonshadow)
DC Comics (Vertigo): Jan, 1997 ($7.95, one-shot)

nn-DeMatteis-s/Muth-c/a 8.00

FARGO KID (Formerly Justice Traps the Guilty)(See Feature Comics #47)
Prize Publications: V11#3(#1), June-July, 1958 - V11#5, Oct-Nov, 1958

V11#3(#1)-Origin Fargo Kid, Severin-c/a; Williamson-a(2); Heath-a
18 36 54 105 165 225
V11#4,5-Severin-c/a 13 26 39 74 105 135

FARMER'S DAUGHTER, THE
Stanhall Publ./Trojan Magazines: Feb-Mar, 1954 - No. 3, June-July, 1954; No. 4, Oct, 1954

1-Lingerie, nudity panel 43 86 129 271 461 650
2-4(Stanhall) 32 64 96 188 307 425

FARSCAPE (Based on TV series)
BOOM! Studios: Nov, 2008 - No. 4, Feb, 2009 ($3.99)

1-4-O'Bannon-s/Patterson-a; multiple covers 4.00

FARSCAPE (Based on TV series)
BOOM! Studios: Nov, 2009 - Present ($3.99)

1-18-O'Bannon-s/Sliney-a; multiple covers 4.00
...: D'Argo's Lament 1-4 (4/09 - No. 4, 7/09, $3.99) Edwards-a; three covers on each 4.00
...: D'Argo's Quest 1-4 (12/09 - No. 4, 3/10, $3.99) Cleveland-a; three covers on each 4.00
...: D'Argo's Trial 1-4 (8/09 - No. 4, 11/09, $3.99) Cleveland-a; multiple covers on each 4.00
...: Gone and Back 1-4 (7/09 - No. 4, 10/09, $3.99) Patterson-a; multiple covers on each 4.00
...: Scorpius 0-7 (4/10 - Present, $3.99) 0-3-Ruiz-a; multiple-c. 4-7-Purcell-a 4.00
...: Strange Detractors 1-4 (3/09 - No. 4, 6/09, $3.99) Sliney-a; three covers on each 4.00

FARSCAPE: WAR TORN (Based on TV series)
DC Comics (WildStorm): Apr, 2002 - No. 2, May, 2002 ($4.95, limited series)

1,2-Teranishi-a/Wolfman-s; photo-c 5.00

FASHION IN ACTION
Eclipse Comics: Aug, 1986 - Feb, 1987 (Baxter paper)

Summer Special 1 , Winter Special 1, each Snyder III-c/a 3.00

FASTBALL EXPRESS (Major League Baseball)
Ultimate Sports Force: 2000 ($3.95, one-shot)

1-Polybagged with poster; Johnson, Maddux, Park, Nomo, Clemens app. 4.00

FASTEST GUN ALIVE, THE (Movie)
Dell Publishing Co.: No. 741, Sept, 1956 (one-shot)

Four Color 741-Photo-c 7 14 21 47 76 105

FAST FICTION (...Action) (Stories by Famous Authors Illustrated #6 on)
Seaboard Publ./Famous Authors Ill.: Oct, 1949 - No. 5, Mar, 1950
(All have Kiefer-c)(48 pgs.)

1-Scarlet Pimpernel; Jim Lavery-c/a 28 56 84 135 270 375
2-Captain Blood; H. C. Kiefer-c/a 24 48 72 142 234 325
3-She, by Rider Haggard; Vincent Napoli-a 30 60 90 177 289 400
4-(1/50, 52 pgs.)-The 39 Steps; Lavery-c/a 19 38 57 112 176 240
5-Beau Geste; Kiefer-c/a 19 38 57 112 176 240
NOTE: ***Kiefer*** *a-2, 5; c-2, 3,5.* ***Lavery*** *c/a-1, 4.* ***Napoli*** *a-3.*

FAST FORWARD

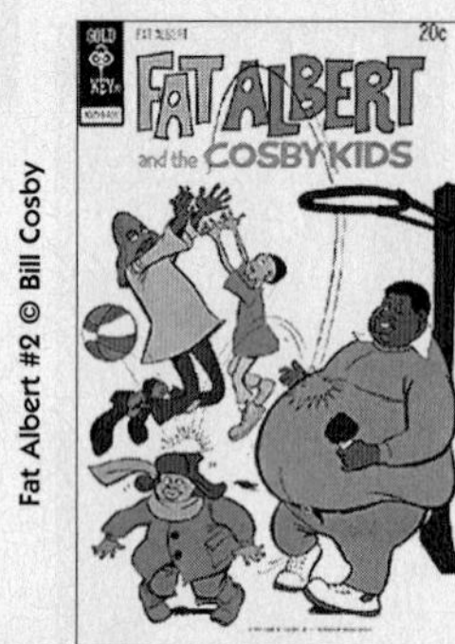

Fat Albert #2 © Bill Cosby

Fathom: Blue Descent #0 © Aspen MLT

Fawcett Movie Comics #9 © FAW

	GD 2.0	VG 4.0	FN 6.0	VF 8.0	VF/NM 9.0	NM- 9.2

DC Comics (Piranha Press): 1992 - No. 3, 1993 ($4.95, 68 pgs.)

1-3: 1-Morrison scripts; McKean-c/a. 3-Sam Kieth-a — 5.00

FAST WILLIE JACKSON
Fitzgerald Periodicals, Inc.: Oct, 1976 - No. 7, 1977

	GD	VG	FN	VF	VF/NM	NM-
1	3	6	9	16	23	30
2-7	2	4	6	10	16	20

FAT ALBERT (...& the Cosby Kids) (TV)
Gold Key: Mar, 1974 - No. 29, Feb, 1979

	GD	VG	FN	VF	VF/NM	NM-
1	4	8	12	24	37	50
2-10	3	6	9	14	20	26
11-29	2	4	6	10	14	18

FATALE (Also see Powers That Be #1 & Shadow State #1,2)
Broadway Comics: Jan, 1996 - No. 6, Aug, 1996 ($2.50)

1-6: J.G. Jones-c/a in all, Preview Edition 1 (11/95, B&W) — 3.00

FAT AND SLAT (Ed Wheelan) (Becomes Gunfighter No. 5 on)
E. C. Comics: Summer, 1947 - No. 4, Spring, 1948

	GD	VG	FN	VF	VF/NM	NM-
1-Intro/origin Voltage, Man of Lightning; "Comics" McCormick, the World's No. 1 Comic Book Fan begins, ends #4	39	78	117	231	378	525
2-4: 4-Comics McCormick-c feature	25	50	75	147	241	335

FAT AND SLAT JOKE BOOK
All-American Comics (William H. Wise): Summer, 1944 (52 pgs., one-shot)

	GD	VG	FN	VF	VF/NM	NM-
nn-by Ed Wheelan	29	58	87	170	278	385

FATE (See Hand of Fate & Thrill-O-Rama)

FATE
DC Comics: Oct, 1994 - No. 22, Sept, 1996 ($1.95/$2.25)

0,1-22: 8-Begin $2.25-c. 11-14-Alan Scott (Sentinel) app. 10,14-Zatanna app. 21-Phantom Stranger app. 22-Spectre app. — 3.00

FATHOM
Comico: May, 1987 - No. 3, July, 1987 ($1.50, limited series)

1-3 — 3.00

FATHOM
Image Comics (Top Cow Prod.): Aug, 1998 - No. 14, May, 2002 ($2.50)

	NM-
Preview	12.00
0-Wizard supplement	7.00
0-($6.95) DF Alternate	7.00
1/2 (Wizard) origin of Cannon; Turner-a	6.00
1/2 (3/03, $2.99) origin of Cannon	3.00
1-Turner-s/a; three covers; alternate story pages	6.00
1-Wizard World Ed.	9.00
2-14: 12-14-Witchblade app. 13,14-Tomb Raider app.	3.00
9-Green foil-c edition	15.00
9,12-Holofoil editions	18.00
12,13-DFE alternate-c	6.00
13,14-DFE Gold edition	8.00
14-DFE Blue	15.00
... Collected Edition 1 (3/99, $5.95) r/Preview & all three #1's	6.00
... Collected Edition 2-4 (3-12/99, $5.95) 2-r/#2,3. 3-r/#4,5. 4-r/#6,7	6.00
... Collected Edition 5 (4/00, $5.95) 5-r/#8,9	6.00
... Swimsuit Special (5/99, $2.95) Pin-ups by various	3.00
... Swimsuit Special 2000 (12/00, $2.95) Pin-ups by various; Turner-c	3.00
Michael Turner's Fathom HC ('01, $39.95) r/#1-9, black-c w/silver foil	40.00
Michael Turner's Fathom SC ('01, $24.95) r/#1-9, new Turner-c	25.00
Michael Turner's Fathom The Definitive Edition ('08, $49.95) r/Preview, #0,1/2,1-14, Swimsuit Special 1999 & 2000; cover gallery; foreword by Geoff Johns	50.00

FATHOM (MICHAEL TURNER'S...) (Volume 2)
Aspen MLT, Inc.: No. 0, Apr, 2005 - No. 11, Dec, 2006 ($2.50/$2.99)

	NM-
0-($2.50) Turnbull-a/Turner-c	3.00
1-11-($2.99) 1-Five covers. 2-Two covers. 4-Six covers	3.00
... Beginnings (2005, $1.99) Two covers; Turnbull-a	3.00
...: Killian's Vessel 1 (7/07, $2.99) 3 covers; Odagawa-a	3.00
... Prelude (6/05, $2.99) Seven covers; Garza-a	3.00

FATHOM (MICHAEL TURNER'S...) (Volume 3)
Aspen MLT, Inc.: No. 0, Jun, 2008 - No. 10, Feb, 2010 ($2.50/$2.99)

	NM-
0-($2.50) Garza-a/c	3.00
1-10-($2.99) Garza-a; multiple covers on each	3.00

FATHOM: BLUE DESCENT (MICHAEL TURNER'S...)
Aspen MLT, Inc.: Jun, 2010 - Present ($2.50/$2.99, limited series)

	NM-
0-($2.50) Scott Clark-a; covers by Clark & Benitez	3.00
1,2-($2.99) Alex Sanchez-a. 1-Covers by Clark & Finch	3.00

FATHOM: CANNON HAWKE (MICHAEL TURNER'S...)
Aspen MLT, Inc.: Nov, 2005 - No. 5, Feb, 2006 ($2.99)

	NM-
1-5-To-a/Turner-c	3.00
... Prelude (11/05, $2.50) Turner-c	3.00

FATHOM: DAWN OF WAR (MICHAEL TURNER'S...)
Aspen MLT, Inc.: Oct, 2004 - No. 3, Dec, 2004 ($2.99, limited series)

	NM-
0-Caldwell-a	3.00
1-3-Caldwell-a	3.00
...: Cannon Hawke #0 ('04, $2.50) Turner-c	3.00
... The Complete Saga Vol. 1 (2005, $9.99) r/series with cover gallery	10.00

FATHOM: KIANI (MICHAEL TURNER'S...)
Aspen MLT, Inc.: No. 0, Feb, 2007 - No. 4, Dec, 2007 ($2.99, limited series)

0-4-Marcus To-a. 1-Six covers — 3.00

FATHOM: KILLIAN'S TIDE
Image Comics (Top Cow Prod.): Apr, 2001 - No. 4, Nov, 2001 ($2.95)

	NM-
1-4-Caldwell-a(p); two covers by Caldwell and Turner. 2-Flip-book preview of Universe	3.00
1-DFE Blue, 1-Holographic logo	12.00
4-Foil-c	12.00

FATIMA...CHALLENGE TO THE WORLD
Catechetical Guild: 1951, 36 pgs. (15¢)

	GD	VG	FN	VF	VF/NM	NM-
nn (not same as 'Challenge to the World')	6	12	18	28	34	40

FATMAN, THE HUMAN FLYING SAUCER
Lightning Comics(Milson Publ. Co.): April, 1967 - No. 3, Aug-Sept, 1967 (68 pgs.)
(Written by Otto Binder)

	GD	VG	FN	VF	VF/NM	NM-
1-Origin/1st app. Fatman & Tinman by Beck	6	12	18	41	66	90
2-C. C. Beck-a	4	8	12	26	41	55
3-(Scarce)-Beck-a	6	12	18	43	69	95

FAULTLINES
DC Comics (Vertigo): May, 1997 - No. 6, Oct, 1997 ($2.50, limited series)

1-6-Lee Marrs-s/Bill Koeb-a in all — 3.00

FAUNTLEROY COMICS (Super Duck Presents...)
Close-Up/Archie Publications: 1950; No. 2, 1951; No. 3, 1952

	GD	VG	FN	VF	VF/NM	NM-
1-Super Duck-c/stories by Al Fagaly in all	9	18	27	52	69	85
2,3	6	12	18	31	38	45

FAUST
Northstar Publishing/Rebel Studios #7 on: 1989 - No 11, 1997 ($2.00/$2.25, B&W, mature themes)

	GD	VG	FN	VF	VF/NM	NM-
1-Decapitation-c; Tim Vigil-c/a in all	3	6	9	14	19	24
1-2nd - 4th printings						3.00
2	2	4	6	8	10	12
2-2nd & 3rd printings, 3,5-2nd printing						3.00
3	1	3	4	6	8	10
4-10: 7-Begin Rebel Studios series						5.00
11-($2.25)						3.00

FAWCETT MOTION PICTURE COMICS (See Motion Picture Comics)

FAWCETT MOVIE COMIC
Fawcett Publications: 1949 - No. 20, Dec, 1952 (All photo-c)

	GD	VG	FN	VF	VF/NM	NM-
nn- "Dakota Lil"; George Montgomery & Rod Cameron (1949)	20	40	60	114	182	250
nn- "Copper Canyon"; Ray Milland & Hedy Lamarr (1950)	15	30	45	86	133	180
nn- "Destination Moon" (1950)	61	122	183	390	670	950
nn- "Montana"; Errol Flynn & Alexis Smith (1950)	15	30	45	86	133	180
nn- "Pioneer Marshal"; Monte Hale (1950)	15	30	45	86	133	180
nn- "Powder River Rustlers"; Rocky Lane (1950)	20	40	60	114	182	250
nn- "Singing Guns"; Vaughn Monroe, Ella Raines & Walter Brennan (1950)	14	28	42	82	121	160
7- "Gunmen of Abilene"; Rocky Lane; Bob Powell-a (1950)	16	32	48	92	144	195
8- "King of the Bullwhip"; Lash LaRue; Bob Powell-a (1950)	21	42	63	126	206	285
9- "The Old Frontier"; Monte Hale; Bob Powell-a (2/51; mis-dated 2/50)	15	30	45	90	140	190
10- "The Missourians"; Monte Hale (4/51)	15	30	45	90	140	190
11- "The Thundering Trail"; Lash LaRue (6/51)	19	38	57	111	176	240

Fawcett's Funny Animals #5 © FAW

Fear Agent #30 © Remender & Moore

Fear Itself #1 © MAR

GD 2.0 | VG 4.0 | FN 6.0 | VF 8.0 | VF/NM 9.0 | NM- 9.2

12- "Rustlers on Horseback"; Rocky Lane (8/51) 15 30 45 90 140 190
13- "Warpath"; Edmond O'Brien & Forrest Tucker (10/51)
14 28 42 80 115 150
14- "Last Outpost"; Ronald Reagan (12/51) 32 64 96 188 307 425
15-(Scarce)- "The Man From Planet X"; Robert Clark; Schaffenberger-a (2/52)
245 490 735 1568 2684 3800
16- "10 Tall Men"; Burt Lancaster 13 26 39 74 105 135
17- "Rose of Cimarron"; Jack Buetel & Mala Powers 10 20 30 58 79 100
18- "The Brigand"; Anthony Dexter & Anthony Quinn; Schaffenberger-a
10 20 30 58 79 100
19- "Carbine Williams"; James Stewart; Costanza-a; James Stewart photo-c
11 22 33 62 86 110
20- "Ivanhoe"; Robert Taylor & Liz Taylor photo-c 18 36 54 105 165 225

FAWCETT'S FUNNY ANIMALS (No. 1-26, 80-on titled "Funny Animals"; becomes Li'l Tomboy No. 92 on?)
Fawcett Publications/Charlton Comics No. 84 on: 12/42 - #79, 4/53; #80, 6/53 - #83, 12?/53; #84, 4/54 - #91, 2/56

1-Capt. Marvel on cover; intro. Hoppy The Captain Marvel Bunny, cloned from Capt. Marvel; Billy the Kid & Willie the Worm begin 58 116 174 371 636 900
2-Xmas-c 36 72 108 211 343 475
3-5: 3(2/43)-Spirit of '43-c 25 50 75 150 245 340
6,7,9,10 15 30 45 88 137 185
8-Flag-c 16 32 48 92 144 195
11-20: 14-Cover is a 1944 calendar 12 24 36 69 97 125
21-40: 25-Xmas-c. 26-St. Valentine's Day-c 10 20 30 54 72 90
41-86,90,91 9 18 27 47 61 75
87-89(10-54-2/55)-Merry Mailman ish (TV/Radio)-part photo-c
10 20 30 54 72 90

NOTE: *Marvel Bunny in all issues to at least No. 68 (not in 49-54).*

FAZE ONE FAZERS
AC Comics: 1986 - No. 4, Sept, 1986 (Limited series)

1-4 3.00

F.B.I., THE
Dell Publishing Co.: Apr-June, 1965

1-Sinnott-a 3 6 9 18 27 35

F.B.I. STORY, THE (Movie)
Dell Publishing Co.: No. 1069, Jan-Mar, 1960

Four Color 1069-Toth-a; James Stewart photo-c 9 18 27 63 107 150

FEAR (Adventure into...)
Marvel Comics Group: Nov, 1970 - No. 31, Dec, 1975

1-Fantasy & Sci-Fi-r in early issues; 68 pg. Giant size; Kirby-a(r)
6 12 18 37 59 80
2-6: 2-4-(68 pgs.). 5,6-(52 pgs.) Kirby-a(r) 4 8 12 22 34 45
7-9-Kirby-a(r) 3 6 9 14 20 25
10-Man-Thing begins (10/72, 4th app.), ends #19; see Savage Tales #1 for 1st app.; 1st solo series; Chaykin/Morrow-c/a; 5 10 15 30 48 65
11,12: 11-N. Adams-c. 12-Starlin/Buckler-a 3 6 9 14 20 26
13,14,16-18: 17-Origin/1st app. Wundarr 2 4 6 13 18 22
15-1st full-length Man-Thing story (8/73) 3 6 9 16 22 28
19-Intro. Howard the Duck; Val Mayerik-a (12/73) 5 10 15 30 48 65
20-Morbius, the Living Vampire begins, ends #31; has history recap of Morbius with X-Men & Spider-Man 5 10 15 30 48 65
21-23,25 2 4 6 13 18 22
24-Blade-c/sty 3 6 9 20 30 40
26-31 2 4 6 10 14 18

NOTE: ***Bolle** a-13i. **Brunner** c-15-17. **Buckler** a-11p, 12i. **Chaykin** a-10i. **Colan** a-23r. **Craig** a-10p. **Ditko** a-6-8r. **Evans** a-30. **Everett** a-9, 10i, 21r. **Gulacy** a-20p. **Heath** a-12r. **Heck** a-8r, 13r. **Gil Kane** a-21p; c(p)-20, 21, 23-28, 31. **Kirby** a-1-9r. **Maneely** a-24r. **Mooney** a-11i, 26r. **Morrow** a-11i. **Paul Reinman** a-14r. **Robbins** a(p)-25-27, 31. **Russell** a-23p, 24p. **Severin** c-8. **Starlin** c-12p.*

FEAR AGENT
Image Comics (#1-11)/Dark Horse Comics.: Oct, 2005 - Present ($2.99/$3.50)

1-11: 1-Remender-s/Moore-a. 5-Opeña-a begins. 11-Francavilla-a 3.00
... The Last Goodbye 1-4 (Dark Horse, 6/07 - No. 4, 9/07) (#12-15) 3.00
Tales of the Fear Agent: Twelve Steps in One (#16), 17-27 3.00
28-30-($3.50) Hawthorne & Moore-a/Moore-c 3.50
... Vol 1.: Re-Ignition TPB (2006, $9.99) r/#1-4 10.00
... Vol 2.: My War TPB (Dark Horse Books, 2007, $14.95) r/#5-10; Opeña sketch pages 15.00

FEARBOOK
Eclipse Comics: April, 1986 ($1.75, one-shot, mature)

1-Scholastic Mag- r; Bissette-a 3.00

GD 2.0 | VG 4.0 | FN 6.0 | VF 8.0 | VF/NM 9.0 | NM- 9.2

FEAR EFFECT (Based on the video game)
Image Comics (Top Cow): May, 2000; March, 2001 ($2.95)

Retro Helix 1 (3/01), Special 1 (5/00) 3.00

FEAR IN THE NIGHT (See Complete Mystery No. 3)

FEAR ITSELF
Marvel Comics: Jun, 2011 - No. 7 ($3.99, limited series)

1-Fraction-s/Immonen-a/McNiven-c 4.00
1-Blank cover 4.00
...: Book of the Skull (5/11, $3.99) prequel to series; WWII flashback, Red Skull app. 4.00
... Spotlight 6/11, $3.99) Interviews with Fraction and Immonen; feature articles 4.00

FEAR ITSELF: THE HOME FRONT
Marvel Comics: Jun, 2011 - No. 7 ($3.99, limited series)

1-Short story anthology; Mayhew, Chaykin-a; Djurdjevic-c 4.00

FEARLESS FAGAN
Dell Publishing Co.: No. 441, Dec, 1952 (one-shot)

Four Color 441 4 8 12 24 37 50

FEATURE BOOK (Dell) (See Large Feature Comic)

FEATURE BOOKS (Newspaper-r, early issues)
David McKay Publications: May, 1937 - No. 57, 1948 (B&W)
(Full color, 68 pgs. begin #26 on)

Note: See individual alphabetical listings for prices

nn-Popeye & the Jeep (#1, 100 pgs.); reprinted as Feature Books #3(Very Rare; only 3 known copies, 1-VF, 2-in low grade)
nn-Dick Tracy (#1)-Reprinted as Feature Book #4 (100 pgs.) & in part as 4-Color #1 (Rare, less than 10 known copies)

NOTE: *Above books were advertised together with different covers from Feat. Books #3 & 4.*

1-King of the Royal Mtd. (#1)
2-Popeye (6/37) by Segar
3-Popeye (7/37) by Segar; same as nn issue but a new cover added
4-Dick Tracy (8/37)-Same as nn issue but a new cover added
5-Popeye (9/37) by Segar
6-Dick Tracy (10/37)
7-Little Orphan Annie (#1, 11/37) (Rare)-Reprints strips from 12/31/34 to 7/17/35
8-Secret Agent X-9 (12/37) -Not by Raymond
9-Dick Tracy (1/38)
10-Popeye (2/38)
11-Little Annie Rooney (#1, 3/38)
12-Blondie (#1) (4/38) (Rare)
13-Inspector Wade (5/38)
14-Popeye (6/38) by Segar
15-Barney Baxter (#1) (7/38)
16-Red Eagle (8/38)
17-Gangbusters (#1, 9/38) (1st app.)
18,19-Mandrake
20-Phantom (#1, 12/38)
21-Lone Ranger
22-Phantom
23-Mandrake
24-Lone Ranger (1941)
25-Flash Gordon (#1)-Reprints not by Raymond
26-Prince Valiant (1941)-Hal Foster -c/a; newspaper strips reprinted, pgs. 1-28,30-63; color & 68 pg. issues begin; Foster cover is only original comic book artwork by him
27-29,31,34-Blondie
30-Katzenjammer Kids (#1, 1942)
32,35,41,44-Katzenjammer Kids
33(nn)-Romance of Flying; World War II photos
36('43),38,40('44),42,43, 45,47-Blondie
37-Katzenjammer Kids; has photo & biog. of Harold H. Knerr (1883-1949) who took over strip from Rudolph Dirks in 1914
39-Phantom
46-Mandrake in the Fire World-(58 pgs.)
48-Maltese Falcon by Dashiell Hammett('46)
49,50-Perry Mason; based on Gardner novels
51,54-Rip Kirby; Raymond-c/s; origin-#51
52,55-Mandrake
53,56,57-Phantom

NOTE: *All Feature Books through #25 are over-sized 8-1/2x11-3/8" comics with color covers and black and white interiors. The covers are rough, heavy stock. The page counts, including covers, are as follows: nn, #3, 4-100 pgs.; #1, 2-52 pgs.; #5-25 are all 76 pgs. #33 was found in bound set from publisher. Reprints from 1980s exist.*

FEATURE COMICS (Formerly Feature Funnies)
Quality Comics Group: No. 21, June, 1939 - No. 144, May, 1950

21-The Clock, Jane Arden & Mickey Finn continue from Feature Funnies
66 132 198 363 582 800
22-26: 23-Charlie Chan begins (8/39, 1st app.) 46 92 138 253 402 550
26-(nn, nd)-Cover in one color, (10¢, 36 pgs.; issue No. blanked out. Two variations exist, each contain half of the regular #26) 46 92 138 253 402 550
27-(Rare)-Origin/1st app. Doll Man by Eisner (scripts) & Lou Fine (art); Doll Man begins, ends #139 514 1028 1542 3750 6625 9500
28-2nd app. Doll Man by Lou Fine 200 400 600 1280 2190 3100
29 107 214 321 680 1165 1650
30-1st Doll Man-c 174 348 522 1114 1907 2700

Feature Comics #70 © QUA

Felicia Hardy: The Black Cat #2 © MAR

Felix the Cat #14 © KING

	GD 2.0	VG 4.0	FN 6.0	VF 8.0	VF/NM 9.0	NM- 9.2
31-Last Clock & Charlie Chan issue (4/40); Charlie Chan moves to Big Shot #1 following month (5/40)	73	146	219	467	796	1125
32,34,36: Dollman covers. 32-Rusty Ryan & Samar begin. 34-Captain Fortune app.	69	138	207	442	759	1075
33,35,37: 37-Last Fine Doll Man	48	96	144	302	514	725

NOTE: *A 15¢ Canadian version of Feature Comics #37, made in the US, exists.*

	GD 2.0	VG 4.0	FN 6.0	VF 8.0	VF/NM 9.0	NM- 9.2
38,40-Dollman covers. 38-Origin the Ace of Space. 40-Bruce Blackburn in costume	54	108	162	343	574	825
39,41: 39-Origin The Destroying Demon, ends #40; X-Mas-c.	40	80	120	242	401	560
42,46,48,50-Dollman covers. 42-USA, the Spirit of Old Glory begins. 46-Intro. Boyville Brigadiers in Rusty Ryan. 48-USA ends	41	82	123	256	428	600
43,45,47,49: 47-Fargo Kid begins	30	60	90	177	289	400
44-Doll Man by Crandall begins, ends #63; Crandall-a(2)	53	106	159	334	567	800
51,53,55,57,59: 57-Spider Widow begins	22	44	66	128	209	290
52,54,56,58,60-Dollman covers. 56-Marijuana story in Swing Sisson strip. 60-Raven begins, ends #71	31	62	93	186	303	420
61,63,65,67	20	40	60	114	182	250
62,64,66,68-Dollman covers. 68-(5/43)	27	54	81	160	263	365
69,71-Phantom Lady x-over in Spider Widow	22	44	66	128	209	290
70-Dollman-c; Phantom Lady x-over	30	60	90	177	289	400
72,74,77-80,100-Dollman covers. 72-Spider Widow ends	22	44	66	128	209	290
73,75,76	16	32	48	94	147	200
81-99-All Dollman covers	16	32	48	94	147	200
101-144: 139-Last Doll Man & last Doll Man cover. 140-Intro. Stuntman Stetson (Stuntman Stetson c-140-144)	14	28	42	82	121	160

NOTE: ***Celardo** a-37-43. **Crandall** a-44-60, 62, 63-on(most). **Gustavson** a-(Rusty Ryan)- 32-134. **Powell** a-34, 64-73. The Clock c-25, 28, 29. Doll Man c-30, 32, 34, 36, 38, 40, 42, 44, 46, 48, 50, 52, 54, 56, 58, 60, 62, 64, 66, 68, 70, 72, 74, 77-139. Joe Palooka c-21, 24, 27.*

FEATURE FILMS
National Periodical Publ.: Mar-Apr, 1950 - No. 4, Sept-Oct, 1950 (All photo-c)

	GD 2.0	VG 4.0	FN 6.0	VF 8.0	VF/NM 9.0	NM- 9.2
1- "Captain China" with John Payne, Gail Russell, Lon Chaney & Edgar Bergen	66	132	198	416	701	985
2- "Riding High" with Bing Crosby	69	138	207	435	735	1035
3- "The Eagle & the Hawk" with John Payne, Rhonda Fleming & D. O'Keefe	66	132	198	416	701	985
4- "Fancy Pants"; Bob Hope & Lucille Ball	72	144	216	454	770	1085

FEATURE FUNNIES (Feature Comics No. 21 on)
Harry 'A' Chesler: Oct, 1937 - No. 20, May, 1939

	GD 2.0	VG 4.0	FN 6.0	VF 8.0	VF/NM 9.0	NM- 9.2
1(V9#1-indicia)-Joe Palooka, Mickey Finn (1st app.), The Bungles, Jane Arden, Dixie Dugan (1st app.), Big Top, Ned Brant, Strange As It Seems, & Off the Record strip reprints begin	322	644	966	1770	2635	3500
2-The Hawk app. (11/37); Goldberg-c	150	300	450	825	1213	1600
3-Hawks of Seas begins by Eisner, ends #12; The Clock begins; Christmas-c	117	234	351	644	947	1250
4,5	86	172	258	473	699	925
6-12: 11-Archie O'Toole by Bud Thomas begins, ends #22	67	134	201	369	542	715
13-Espionage, Starring Black X begins by Eisner, ends #20	71	142	213	391	578	765
14-20	50	100	150	275	408	540

NOTE: *Joe Palooka covers 1, 6, 9, 12, 15, 18.*

FEATURE PRESENTATION, A (Feature Presentations Magazine #6)
(Formerly Women in Love) (Also see Startling Terror Tales #11)
Fox Features Syndicate: No. 5, April, 1950

	GD 2.0	VG 4.0	FN 6.0	VF 8.0	VF/NM 9.0	NM- 9.2
5(#1)-Black Tarantula (scarce)	53	106	159	334	567	800

FEATURE PRESENTATIONS MAGAZINE (Formerly A Feature Presentation #5; becomes Feature Stories Magazine #3 on)
Fox Features Syndicate: No. 6, July, 1950

	GD 2.0	VG 4.0	FN 6.0	VF 8.0	VF/NM 9.0	NM- 9.2
6(#2)-Moby Dick; Wood-c	34	68	102	199	325	450

FEATURE STORIES MAGAZINE (Formerly Feature Presentations Mag. #6)
Fox Features Syndicate: No. 3, Aug, 1950

	GD 2.0	VG 4.0	FN 6.0	VF 8.0	VF/NM 9.0	NM- 9.2
3-Jungle Lil, Zegra stories; bondage-c	39	78	117	231	378	525

FEDERAL MEN COMICS
DC Comics: 1936

nn-Ashcan comic, not distributed to newsstands, only for in house use (no known sales)

FEDERAL MEN COMICS (See Adventure Comics #32, The Comics Magazine, New Adventure Comics, New Book of Comics, New Comics & Star Spangled Comics #91)
Gerard Publ. Co.: No. 2, 1945 (DC reprints from 1930's)

	GD 2.0	VG 4.0	FN 6.0	VF 8.0	VF/NM 9.0	NM- 9.2
2-Siegel/Shuster-a; cover redrawn from Det. #9	37	74	111	218	354	490

FELICIA HARDY: THE BLACK CAT
Marvel Comics: July, 1994 - No. 4, Oct, 1994 ($1.50, limited series)

	GD 2.0	VG 4.0	FN 6.0	VF 8.0	VF/NM 9.0	NM- 9.2
1-4: 1,4-Spider-Man app.						3.00

FELIX'S NEPHEWS INKY & DINKY
Harvey Publications: Sept, 1957 - No. 7, Oct, 1958

	GD 2.0	VG 4.0	FN 6.0	VF 8.0	VF/NM 9.0	NM- 9.2
1-Cover shows Inky's left eye with 2 pupils	10	20	30	58	79	100
2-7	7	14	21	37	46	55

NOTE: ***Messmer** art in 1-6. **Oriolo** a-1-7.*

FELIX THE CAT (See Cat Tales 3-D, The Funnies, March of Comics #24,36,51, New Funnies & Popular Comics)
Dell Publ. No. 1-19/Toby No. 20-61/Harvey No. 62-118/Dell No. 1-12:
1943 - No. 118, Nov, 1961; Sept-Nov, 1962 - No. 12, July-Sept, 1965

	GD 2.0	VG 4.0	FN 6.0	VF 8.0	VF/NM 9.0	NM- 9.2
Four Color 15	73	146	219	621	1261	1900
Four Color 46('44)	38	76	114	304	602	900
Four Color 77('45)	37	74	111	284	562	840
Four Color 119('46)-All new stories begin	31	62	93	242	476	710
Four Color 135('46)	22	44	66	159	317	475
Four Color 162(9/47)	16	32	48	114	232	350
1(2-3/48)(Dell)	25	50	75	180	360	540
2	13	26	39	89	170	250
3-5	10	20	30	71	128	185
6-19(2-3/51-Dell)	8	16	24	58	97	135
20-30,32,33,36,38-61(6/55)-All Messmer issues.(Toby): 28-(2/52)-Some copies have #29 on cover, #28 on inside (Rare in high grade)	15	30	45	103	209	315
31,34,35-No Messmer-a; Messmer-c only 31,34	8	16	24	58	97	135
37-(100 pgs., 25 ¢, 1/15/53, X-Mas-c, Toby; daily & Sunday-r (rare)	37	74	111	284	562	840
62(8/55)-80,100 (Harvey)	4	8	12	28	44	60
81-99	4	8	12	24	37	50
101-118(11/61): 101-117-Reprints. 118-All new-a	3	6	9	18	27	35
12-269-211(#1, 9-11/62)(Dell)-No Messmer	5	10	15	30	48	65
2-12(7-9/65)(Dell, TV)-No Messmer	4	8	12	24	37	50
3-D Comic Book 1(1953-One Shot, 25¢)-w/glasses	24	48	72	157	304	450
Summer Annual nn ('53, 25¢, 100 pgs., Toby)-Daily & Sunday-r	34	68	102	236	456	675
Winter Annual 2 ('54, 25¢, 100 pgs., Toby)-Daily & Sunday-r	32	64	96	218	422	625

(Special note: Despite the covers on Toby 37 and the Summer Annual above proclaiming "all new stories," they were actually reformatted newspaper strips)

NOTE: ***Otto Messmer** went to work for Universal Film as an animator in 1915 and then worked for the Pat Sullivan animation studio in 1916. He created a black cat in the cartoon short, Feline Follies in 1919 that became known as Felix in the early 1920s. The Felix Sunday strip began Aug. 14, 1923 and continued until Sept. 19, 1943 whjen **Messmer** took the character to Dell (Western Publishing) and began doing Felix comic books, first adapting strips to the comic format. The first all new Felix comic was Four Color #119 in 1946 (#4 in the Dell run). The daily Felix was begun on May 9, 1927 by another artist, but by the following year, **Messmer** did it too. King Features took the daily away from **Messmer** in 1954 and he began to do some of his most dynamic art for Toby Press. The daily was continued by **Joe Oriolo** who drew it until it was discontinued Jan. 9, 1967. **Oriolo** was **Messmer's** assistant for many years and inked some of **Messmer's** pencils through the Toby run, as well as doing some of the stories by himself. Though **Messmer** continued to work for Harvey, his contirubitons were limited, and no all **Messmer** stories appeared after the Toby run until some early Toby reprints were published in the 1990s Harvey revival of the title. 4-Color No. 15, 46, 77 and the Toby Annuals are all daily or Sunday newspaper reprints from the 1930's-1940's drawn by **Otto Messmer**. #101-r/#64; 102-r/#65; 103-r/#67; 104-117-r/#68-81. **Messmer**-a in all Dell/Toby/Harvey issues except #31, 34, 35, 97, 98, 100, 118. **Oriolo** a-20, 31-on.*

FELIX THE CAT (Also see The Nine Lives of...)
Harvey Comics/Gladstone: Sept, 1991 - No. 7, Jan, 1993 ($1.25/$1.50, bi-monthly)

	GD 2.0	VG 4.0	FN 6.0	VF 8.0	VF/NM 9.0	NM- 9.2
1: 1950s-r/Toby issues by Messmer begins. 1-Inky and Dinky back-up story (produced by Gladstone)						4.00
2-7, Big Book, V2#1 (9/92, $1.95, 52 pgs.)						3.00

FELIX THE CAT AND FRIENDS
Felix Comics: 1992 - No. 5, 1993 ($1.95)

	GD 2.0	VG 4.0	FN 6.0	VF 8.0	VF/NM 9.0	NM- 9.2
1-5: 1-Contains Felix trading cards						3.00

FELIX THE CAT & HIS FRIENDS (Pat Sullivan's...)
Toby Press: Dec, 1953 - No. 3, 1954 (Indicia title for #2&3 as listed)

	GD 2.0	VG 4.0	FN 6.0	VF 8.0	VF/NM 9.0	NM- 9.2
1 (Indicia title, "Felix and His Friends," #1 only)	29	58	87	170	278	385
2-3	18	36	54	105	165	225

FELIX THE CAT DIGEST MAGAZINE
Harvey Comics: July, 1992 ($1.75, digest-size, 98 pgs.)

	GD 2.0	VG 4.0	FN 6.0	VF 8.0	VF/NM 9.0	NM- 9.2
1-Felix, Richie Rich stories						6.00

FELIX THE CAT KEEPS ON WALKIN'
Hamilton Comics: 1991 ($15.95, 8-1/2"x11", 132 pgs.)

FF #1 © MAR

52 #20 © DC

Fight Against Crime #10 © Story

nn-Reprints 15 Toby Press Felix the Cat and Felix and His Friends stories in new color 16.00

FELL
Image Comics: Sept, 2005 - No. 9, Jan, 2008 ($1.99)
1-9-Warren Ellis-s/Ben Templesmith-a 3.00
..., Vol. 1: Feral City TPB (2007, $14.99) r/#1-8 15.00

FELON
Image Comics (Minotaur Press): Nov, 2001 - No. 4, Apr, 2002 ($2.95, B&W)
1-4-Rucka-s/Clark-a/c 3.00

FEM FANTASTIQUE
AC Comics: Aug, 1988 ($1.95, B&W)
V2#1-By Bill Black; Betty Page pin-up 4.00

FEMFORCE (Also see Untold Origin of the Femforce)
Americomics: Apr, 1985 - No. 109 (1.75-/2.95, B&W #16-56)
1-Black-a in most; Nightveil, Ms. Victory begin 1 3 4 6 8 10
2-10 4.00
11-43: 25-Origin/1st app. new Ms. Victory. 28-Colt leaves. 29,30-Camilla-r by Mayo from Jungle Comics. 36-(2.95, 52 pgs.) 4.00
44,64: 44-W/mini-comic, Catman & Kitten #0. 64-Re-intro Black Phantom 5.00
45-63,65-99: 50 (2.95, 52 pgs.)-Contains flexi-disc; origin retold; most AC characters app. 51-Photo-c from movie. 57-Begin color issues. 95-Photo-c 3.00
100-($3.95) 5.00
100-($6.90)-Polybagged 1 2 3 5 6 8
101-109-($4.95) 5.00
Special 1 (Fall, '84)(B&W, 52pgs.)-1st app. Ms. Victory, She-Cat, Blue Bulleteer, Rio Rita & Lady Luger 4.00
Bad Girl Backlash-(12/95, $5.00) 5.00
Frightbook 1 ('92, $2.95, B&W)-Halloween special, In the House of Horror 1 ('89, 2.50, B&W), Night of the Demon 1 ('90, 2.75, B&W), Out of the Asylum Special 1 ('87, B&W, $1.95), Pin-Up Portfolio 3.50
Pin-Up Portfolio (5 issues) 4.00

FEMFORCE UP CLOSE
AC Comics: Apr, 1992 - No. 11, 1995 ($2.75, quarterly)
1-11: 1-Stars Nightveil; inside f/c photo from Femforce movie. 2-Stars Stardust. 3-Stars Dragonfly. 4-Stars She-Cat 3.50

FERDINAND THE BULL (See Mickey Mouse Magazine V4#3)
Dell Publishing Co.: 1938 (10¢, large size, some color w/rest B&W)
nn 19 38 57 111 176 240

FERRET
Malibu Comics: Sept, 1992; May, 1993 - No. 10, Feb, 1994 ($1.95)
1-(1992, one-shot) 3.00
1-10: 1-Die-cut-c. 2-4-Collector's Ed. w/poster. 5-Polybagged w/Skycap 3.00
2-4-($1.95)-Newsstand Edition w/different-c 3.00

FERRYMAN
DC Comics (WildStorm): Early Dec, 2008 - No. 5, Mar, 2009 ($3.50)
1-5-Andreyko-s/Wayshak-a 3.50

FF (Fantastic Four after Human Torch's death)
Marvel Comics: May, 2011 - Present ($3.99)
1-Hickman-s/Epting-a; Spider-Man joins 4.00
1-Blank variant cover 4.00
1-Variant-c by Daniel Acuña 8.00
1-Variant-c by Stan Goldberg 6.00

F5
Image Comics/Dark Horse: Jan, 2000 - No. 4, Oct, 2000 ($2.50/$2.95)
Preview (1/00, $2.50) Character bios and b&w pages; Daniel-s/a 3.00
1-($2.95, 48 pages) Tony Daniel-s/a 4.00
1-($20.00) Variant bikini-c 20.00
2-4-($2.50) 3.00
F5 Origin (Dark Horse Comics, 11/01, $2.99) w/cove gallery & sketches 3.00

FIBBER McGEE & MOLLY (Radio)(Also see A-1 Comics)
Magazine Enterprises: No. 25, 1949 (one-shot)
A-1 25 12 24 36 67 94 120

FICTION ILLUSTRATED
Byron Preiss Visual Publ./Pyramid: No. 1, Jan, 1975 - No. 4, Jan, 1977 ($1.00, #1,2 are digest size, 132 pgs.; #3,4 are graphic novels for mail order and specialty bookstores only)
1,2: 1-Schlomo Raven; Sutton-a. 2-Starfawn; Stephen Fabian-a. 2 4 6 13 18 22
3-($1.00-c, 4 3/4 x 6 1/2" digest size) Chandler; new Steranko-a 3 6 9 14 20 26
3-($4.95-c, 8 1/2 x 11" graphic novel; low print) same contents and indicia, but "Chandler" is the cover feature title 5 10 15 34 55 75
4-($4.95-c, 8 1/2 x 11" graphic novel; low print) Son of Sherlock Holmes; Reese-a 4 8 12 28 44 60

FIERCE
Dark Horse Comics (Rocket Comics): July, 2004 - No. 4, Dec, 2004 ($2.99, limited series)
1-4-Jeremy Love-s/Robert Love-a 3.00

55 DAYS AT PEKING (See Movie Comics)

52 (Leads into Countdown series)
DC Comics: Week One, July, 2006 - Week Fifty-Two, Jul, 2007 ($2.50, weekly series)
1-Chronicles the year after Infinite Crisis; Johns, Morrison, Rucka & Waid-s; JG Jones-c 4.00
2-10: 2-History of the DC Universe back-up thru #11. 7-Intro. Kate Kane. 10-Supernova 3.00
11-Batwoman debut (single panel cameo in #9) 4.00
12-52: 12-Isis gains powers; back-up 2 pg. origins begin. 15-Booster Gold killed. 17-Lobo returns. 30-Batman-c/Robin & Nightwing app. 37-Booster Gold returns. 38-The Question dies. 42-Ralph Dibny dies. 44-Isis dies. 48-Renee becomes The Question. 50-World War III. 51-Mister Mind evolves. 52-The Multiverse is re-formed; wraparound-c 2.50
...: The Companion TPB (2007, $19.99) r/solo stories of series' prominent characters 20.00
...: Volume One TPB (2007, $19.99) r/#1-13; sample of page development; cover gallery 20.00
...: Volume Two TPB (2007, $19.99) r/#14-26; creator notes and sketches; cover gallery 20.00
...: Volume Three TPB (2007, $19.99) r/#27-39; notes and sketches; cover gallery 20.00
...: Volume Four TPB (2007, $19.99) r/#40-52; creator commentary; cover gallery 20.00

52 AFTERMATH: THE FOUR HORSEMEN (Takes place during 52 Week Fifty)
DC Comics: Oct, 2007 - No. 6, Mar, 2008 ($2.99, limited series)
1-6-Giffen-s/Olliffe-a; Superman, Batman & Wonder Woman app. 2-4,6-Van Sciver-c 3.00
TPB (2008, $19.99) r/#1-6 20.00

52/WWIII (Takes place during 52 Week Fifty)
DC Comics: Part One, Jun, 2007 - Part Four, Jun, 2007 ($2.50, 4 issues came out same day)
Part One - Part Four: Van Sciver-c; heroes vs. Black Adam. 3-Terra dies 3.00
DC: World War III TPB (2007, $17.99) r/Part One - Four and 52 Week 50 18.00

FIGHT AGAINST CRIME (Fight Against the Guilty #22, 23)
Story Comics: May, 1951 - No. 21, Sept, 1954
1-True crime stories #1-4 41 82 123 256 428 600
2 22 44 66 132 216 300
3,5: 5-Frazetta-a, 1 pg.; content change to horror & suspense 20 40 60 117 189 260
4-Drug story "Hopped Up Killers" 21 42 63 126 206 285
6,7: 6-Used in **POP**, pgs. 83,84 19 38 57 109 172 235
8-Last crime format issue 18 36 54 103 162 220
NOTE: *No. 9-21 contain violent, gruesome stories with blood, dismemberment, decapitation, E.C. style plot twists and several E.C. swipes. Bondage c-4, 6, 18, 19.*
9-11,13 41 82 123 256 428 600
12-Morphine drug story "The Big Dope" 43 86 129 271 461 650
14-Tothish art by Ross Andru; electrocution-c 42 84 126 268 452 635
15-B&W & color illos in **POP** 42 84 126 265 445 625
16-E.C. story swipe/Haunt of Fear #19; Tothish-a by Ross Andru; bondage-c 43 86 129 271 461 650
17-Wildey E.C. swipe/Shock SuspenStories #9; knife through neck-c (1/54) 46 92 138 290 488 685
18,19: 19-Bondage/torture-c 41 82 123 251 418 585
20-Decapitation cover; contains hanging, ax murder, blood & violence 90 180 270 576 988 1400
21-E.C. swipe 36 72 108 216 351 485
NOTE: ***Cameron** a-4, 5, 8. **Hollingsworth** a-3-7, 9, 10, 13. **Wildey** a-6, 15, 16.*

FIGHT AGAINST THE GUILTY (Formerly Fight Against Crime)
Story Comics: No. 22, Dec, 1954 - No. 23, Mar, 1955
22-Tothish-a by Ross Andru; Ditko-a; E.C. story swipe; electrocution-c (Last pre-code) 37 74 111 222 361 500
23-Hollingsworth-a 24 48 72 140 230 320

FIGHT COMICS
Fiction House Magazines: Jan, 1940 - No. 83, 11/52; No. 84, Wint, 1952-53; No. 85, Spring, 1953; No. 86, Summer, 1954
1-Origin Spy Fighter, Starring Saber; Jack Dempsey life story; Shark Brodie & Chip Collins begin; Fine-c; Eisner-a 343 686 1029 2400 4200 6000
2-Joe Louis life story; Fine/Eisner-c 124 248 372 787 1356 1925
3-Rip Regan, the Power Man begins (3/40) 113 226 339 718 1234 1750
4,5: 4-Fine-c 66 132 198 425 725 1025
6-10: 6,7-Powell-c 50 100 150 315 533 750

Fight For Love nn © UFS

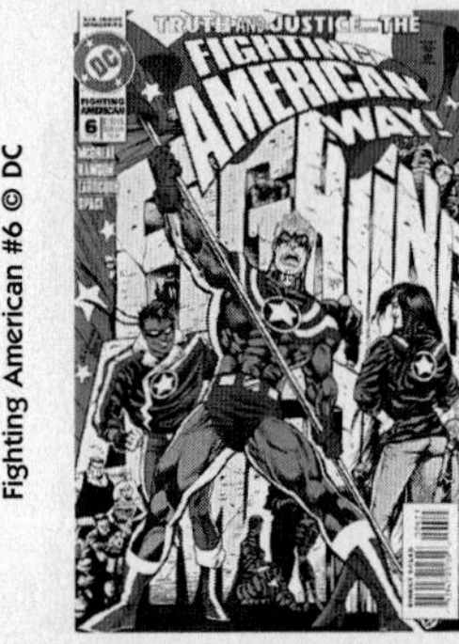

Fighting American #6 © DC

Fightin' Army #17 © CC

	GD 2.0	VG 4.0	FN 6.0	VF 8.0	VF/NM 9.0	NM- 9.2
11-14: Rip Regan ends	47	94	141	296	498	700
15-1st app. Super American plus-c (10/41)	60	120	180	382	659	935
16-Captain Fight begins (12/41); Spy Fighter ends	60	120	180	382	659	935
17,18: Super American ends	47	94	141	296	498	700
19-Captain Fight ends; Senorita Rio begins (6/42, origin & 1st app.); Rip Carson, Chute Trooper begins	49	98	147	309	525	740
20	42	84	126	265	445	625
21-30	39	78	117	240	395	550
31-Classic decapitation-c	116	232	348	742	1271	1800
32-Tiger Girl begins (6/44, 1st app.?)	40	80	120	246	411	575
33-50: 44-Capt. Fight returns. 48-Used in Love and Death by Legman. 49-Jungle-c begin, end #81	32	64	96	192	314	435
51-Origin Tiger Girl; Patsy Pin-Up app.	39	78	117	231	378	525
52-60,62-64-Last Baker issue	23	46	69	136	223	310
61-Origin Tiger Girl retold	24	48	72	142	234	325
65-78: 78-Used in **POP**, pg. 99	20	40	60	114	182	250
79-The Space Rangers app.	20	40	60	117	189	260
80-85: 81-Last jungle-c. 82-85-War-c/stories	17	34	51	98	154	210
86-Two Tigerman stories by Evans-r/Rangers Comics #40,41; Moreira-r/Rangers Comics #45	17	34	51	98	154	210

NOTE: *Bondage covers, Lingerie, headlights panels are common. Captain Fight by* ***Kamen****-51-66. Kayo Kirby by* ***Baker****-#43-64, 67(not by Baker). Senorita Rio by* ***Kamen****-#57-64; by* ***Grandenetti****-#65, 66. Tiger Girl by* ***Baker****-#36-60, 62-64;* ***Eisner*** *c-1-3, 5, 10, 11.* ***Kamen*** *a-54?, 57?* ***Tuska*** *a-1, 5, 8, 10, 21, 29, 34.* ***Whitman*** *c-73-84.* ***Zolnerwich*** *c-16, 17, 22. Power Man c-5, 6, 9. Super American c-15-17. Tiger Girl c-49-81.*

FIGHT FOR LOVE
United Features Syndicate: 1952 (no month)

	GD 2.0	VG 4.0	FN 6.0	VF 8.0	VF/NM 9.0	NM- 9.2
nn-Abbie & Slats newspaper-r	9	18	27	47	61	75

FIGHT FOR TOMORROW
DC Comics (Vertigo): Nov, 2002 - No. 6, Apr, 2003 ($2.50, limited series)

	GD 2.0	VG 4.0	FN 6.0	VF 8.0	VF/NM 9.0	NM- 9.2
1-6-Denys Cowan-a/Brian Wood-s. 1-Jim Lee-c. 5-Jo Chen-c						3.00
TPB (2008, $14.99) r/#1-6						15.00

FIGHTING AIR FORCE (See United States Fighting Air Force)

FIGHTIN' AIR FORCE (Formerly Sherlock Holmes?; Never Again? War and Attack #54 on)
Charlton Comics: No. 3, Feb, 1956 - No. 53, Feb-Mar, 1966

	GD 2.0	VG 4.0	FN 6.0	VF 8.0	VF/NM 9.0	NM- 9.2
V1#3	9	18	27	50	65	80
4-10	7	14	21	35	43	50
11(3/58, 68 pgs.)	8	16	24	44	57	70
12 (100 pgs.)-U.S. Nukes Russia	12	24	36	69	97	125
13-30: 13,24-Glanzman-a. 24-Glanzman-c	3	6	9	19	29	38
31-50: 50-American Eagle begins	3	6	9	14	20	26
51-53	2	4	6	13	18	22

FIGHTING AMERICAN
Headline Publ./Prize (Crestwood): Apr-May, 1954 - No. 7, Apr-May, 1955

	GD 2.0	VG 4.0	FN 6.0	VF 8.0	VF/NM 9.0	NM- 9.2
1-Origin & 1st app. Fighting American & Speedboy (Capt. America & Bucky clones); S&K-c/a(3); 1st super hero satire series	174	348	522	1114	1907	2700
2-S&K-a(3)	81	162	243	518	884	1250
3-5: 3,4-S&K-a(3). 5-S&K-a(2); Kirby/?-a	62	124	186	394	680	965
6-Origin-r (4 pgs.) plus 2 pgs. by S&K	59	118	177	375	643	910
7-Kirby-a	53	106	159	334	567	800

NOTE: ***Simon*** *&* ***Kirby*** *covers on all. 6 is last pre-code issue.*

FIGHTING AMERICAN
Harvey Publications: Oct, 1966 (25¢)

	GD 2.0	VG 4.0	FN 6.0	VF 8.0	VF/NM 9.0	NM- 9.2
1-Origin Fighting American & Speedboy by S&K-r; S&K-c/a(3); 1 pg. Neal Adams ad	6	12	18	37	59	80

FIGHTING AMERICAN
DC Comics: Feb, 1994 - No. 6, 1994 ($1.50, limited series)

	GD 2.0	VG 4.0	FN 6.0	VF 8.0	VF/NM 9.0	NM- 9.2
1-6						3.00

FIGHTING AMERICAN (Vol. 3)
Awesome Entertainment: Aug, 1997 - No. 2, Oct, 1997 ($2.50)

	GD 2.0	VG 4.0	FN 6.0	VF 8.0	VF/NM 9.0	NM- 9.2
Preview-Agent America (pre-lawsuit)	1	2	3	5	6	7
1-Four covers by Liefeld, Churchill, Platt, McGuinness						3.00
1-Platinum Edition, 1-Gold foil Edition						10.00
1-Comic Cavalcade Edition, 2-American Ent. Spice Ed.						4.00
2-Platt-c, 2-Liefeld variant-c						3.00

FIGHTING AMERICAN: DOGS OF WAR
Awesome-Hyperwerks: Sept, 1998 - No. 3, May, 1999 ($2.50)

	GD 2.0	VG 4.0	FN 6.0	VF 8.0	VF/NM 9.0	NM- 9.2
Limited Convention Special (7/98, B&W) Platt-a						2.50
1-3-Starlin-s/Platt-a/c						2.50

FIGHTING AMERICAN: RULES OF THE GAME
Awesome Entertainment: Nov, 1997 - No. 3, Mar, 1998 ($2.50, lim. series)

	GD 2.0	VG 4.0	FN 6.0	VF 8.0	VF/NM 9.0	NM- 9.2
1-3: 1-Loeb-s/McGuinness-a/c. 2-Flip book with Swat! preview						3.00
1-Liefeld SPICE variant-c, 1-Dynamic Forces Ed.; McGuinness-c						3.00
1-Liefeld Fighting American & cast variant-c						3.00

FIGHTIN' ARMY (Formerly Soldier and Marine Comics) (See Captain Willy Schultz)
Charlton Comics: No. 16, 1/56 - No. 127, 12/76; No. 128, 9/77 - No. 172, 11/84

	GD 2.0	VG 4.0	FN 6.0	VF 8.0	VF/NM 9.0	NM- 9.2
16	9	18	27	50	65	80
17-19,21-23,25-30	7	14	21	35	43	50
20-Ditko-a	9	18	27	50	65	80
24 (3/58, 68 pgs.)	8	16	24	42	54	65
31-45	3	6	9	19	28	38
46-60	3	6	9	16	23	30
61-74	3	6	9	14	19	24
75-1st The Lonely War of Willy Schultz	3	6	9	18	27	35
76-80: 76-92-The Lonely War of Willy Schultz. 79-Devil Brigade	3	6	9	14	19	24
81-88,91,93-99: 82,83-Devil Brigade	2	4	6	10	14	18
89,90,92-Ditko-a	3	6	9	14	20	26
100	2	4	6	13	18	22
101-127	2	4	6	8	11	14
128-140	1	2	3	5	7	9
141-165	1	2	3	4	5	7
166-172-Low print run	1	2	3	5	6	8
108(Modern Comics-1977)-Reprint						4.00

NOTE: ***Aparo*** *c-154.* ***Glanzman*** *a-77-88.* ***Montes/Bache*** *a-48, 49, 51, 69, 75, 76, 170r.*

FIGHTING CARAVANS (See Zane Grey 4-Color 632)

FIGHTING DANIEL BOONE
Avon Periodicals: 1953

	GD 2.0	VG 4.0	FN 6.0	VF 8.0	VF/NM 9.0	NM- 9.2
nn-Kinstler-c/a, 22 pgs.	18	36	54	105	165	225
I.W. Reprint #1-Reprints #1 above; Kinstler-c/a; Lawrence/Alascia-a	3	6	9	14	19	24

FIGHTING DAVY CROCKETT (Formerly Kit Carson)
Avon Periodicals: No. 9, Oct-Nov, 1955

	GD 2.0	VG 4.0	FN 6.0	VF 8.0	VF/NM 9.0	NM- 9.2
9-Kinstler-c	10	20	30	54	72	90

FIGHTIN' FIVE, THE (Formerly Space War) (Also see The Peacemaker)
Charlton Comics: July, 1964 - No. 41, Jan, 1967; No. 42, Oct, 1981 - No. 49, Dec, 1982

	GD 2.0	VG 4.0	FN 6.0	VF 8.0	VF/NM 9.0	NM- 9.2
V2#28-Origin/1st app. Fightin' Five; Montes/Bache-a	6	12	18	41	66	90
29-39,41-Montes/Bache-a in all	4	8	12	22	34	45
40-Peacemaker begins (1st app.)	6	12	18	43	69	95
41-Peacemaker (2nd app.)	5	10	15	30	48	65
42-49: Reprints						5.00

FIGHTING FRONTS!
Harvey Publications: Aug, 1952 - No. 5, Jan, 1953

	GD 2.0	VG 4.0	FN 6.0	VF 8.0	VF/NM 9.0	NM- 9.2
1	10	20	30	54	72	90
2-Extreme violence; Nostrand/Powell-a	11	22	33	60	83	105
3-5: 3-Powell-a	7	14	21	37	46	55

FIGHTING INDIAN STORIES (See Midget Comics)

FIGHTING INDIANS OF THE WILD WEST!
Avon Periodicals: Mar, 1952 - No. 2, Nov, 1952

	GD 2.0	VG 4.0	FN 6.0	VF 8.0	VF/NM 9.0	NM- 9.2
1-Geronimo, Chief Crazy Horse, Chief Victorio, Black Hawk begin; Larsen-a; McCann-a(2)	17	34	51	98	154	210
2-Kinstler-c & inside-c only; Larsen, McCann-a	12	24	36	69	97	125
100 Pg. Annual (1952, 25¢)-Contains three comics rebound; Geronimo, Chief Crazy Horse, Chief Victorio; Kinstler-c	36	72	108	211	343	475

FIGHTING LEATHERNECKS
Toby Press: Feb, 1952 - No. 6, Dec, 1952

	GD 2.0	VG 4.0	FN 6.0	VF 8.0	VF/NM 9.0	NM- 9.2
1- "Duke's Diary"; full pg. pin-ups by Sparling	14	28	42	80	115	150
2-5: 2- "Duke's Diary" full pg. pin-ups. 3-5- "Gil's Gals"; full pg. pin-ups	10	20	30	54	72	90
6-(Same as No. 3-5?)	10	20	30	54	72	90

FIGHTING MAN, THE (War)
Ajax/Farrell Publications(Excellent Publ.): May, 1952 - No. 8, July, 1953

	GD 2.0	VG 4.0	FN 6.0	VF 8.0	VF/NM 9.0	NM- 9.2
1	14	28	42	80	115	150
2	9	18	27	47	61	75
3-8	8	16	24	40	50	60
Annual 1 (1952, 25¢, 100 pgs.)	25	50	75	147	241	335

FIGHTIN' MARINES (Formerly The Texan; also see Approved Comics)
St. John(Approved Comics)/Charlton Comics No. 14 on:

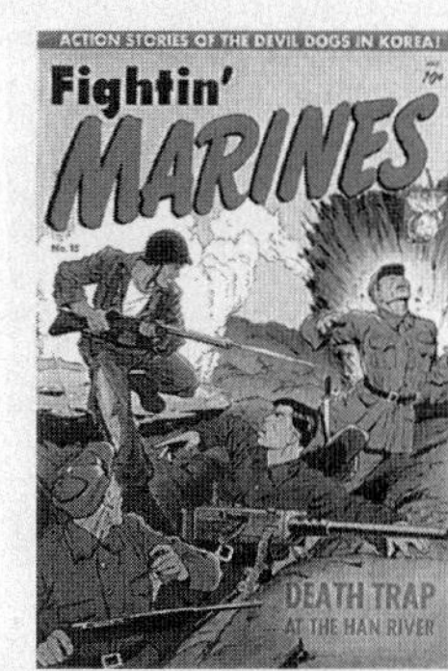

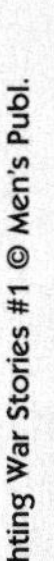
Fightin' Marines #1 © STJ

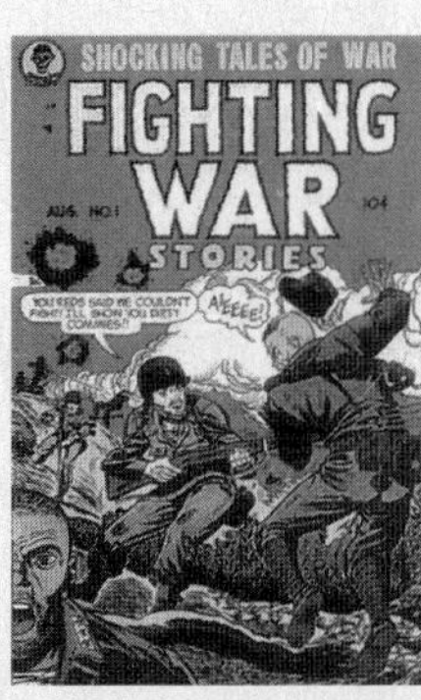

Fighting War Stories #1 © Men's Publ.

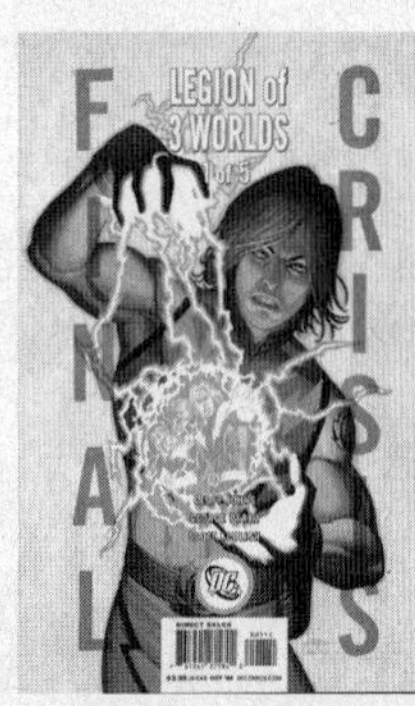

Final Crisis: Legion of 3 Worlds #1 © DC

GD VG FN VF VF/NM NM-
2.0 4.0 6.0 8.0 9.0 9.2

No. 15, 8/51 - No. 12, 3/53; No. 14, 5/55 - No. 132, 11/76; No. 133, 10/77 - No. 176, 9/84 (No #13?) (Korean War #1-3)

15(#1)-Matt Baker c/a "Leatherneck Jack"; slightly large size; Fightin' Texan No. 16 & 17? 44 88 132 277 469 660
2-1st Canteen Kate by Baker; slightly large size; partial Baker-c 53 106 159 334 567 800
3-9,11-Canteen Kate by Baker; Baker c-#2,3,5-11; 4-Partial Baker-c 31 62 93 186 303 420
10-Matt Baker-c 15 30 45 84 127 170
12-No Baker-a; Last St. John issue? 9 18 27 50 65 80
14 (5/55; 1st Charlton issue; formerly?)-Canteen Kate by Baker; all stories reprinted from #2 19 38 57 109 172 235
15-Baker-c 11 22 33 62 86 110
16,18-20-Not Baker-c 7 14 21 35 43 50
17-Canteen Kate by Baker 15 30 45 83 124 165
21-24 6 12 18 31 38 45
25-(68 pgs.)(3/58)-Check-a? 10 20 30 54 72 90
26-(100 pgs.)(8/58)-Check-a(5) 14 28 42 80 115 150
27-50 3 6 9 18 27 35
51-81: 78-Shotgun Harker & the Chicken series begin 3 6 9 16 22 28
82-85: 85-Last 12¢ issue 3 6 9 14 20 25
86-94: 94-Last 15¢ issue 2 4 6 10 14 18
95-100,122: 122-(1975) Pilot issue for "War" title (Fightin' Marines Presents War) 2 4 6 9 13 16
101-121 2 4 6 8 10 12
123-140 1 2 3 5 7 9
141-170 6.00
171-176-Low print run 1 2 3 5 6 8
120(Modern Comics reprint, 1977) 4.00

NOTE: *No. 14 & 16 (CC) reprint St. John issues; No. 16 reprints St. John insignia on cover.* ***Colan*** *a-3, 7.* ***Glanzman*** *c/a-92, 94.* ***Montes/Bache*** *a-48, 53, 55, 64, 65, 72-74, 77-83, 176r.*

FIGHTING MARSHAL OF THE WILD WEST (See The Hawk)

FIGHTIN' NAVY (Formerly Don Winslow)
Charlton Comics: No. 74, 1/56 - No. 125, 4-5/66; No. 126, 8/83 - No. 133, 10/84

74 6 12 18 37 59 80
75-81 4 8 12 22 34 45
82-Sam Glanzman-a (68 pg. Giant) 5 10 15 32 51 70
83-(100 pgs.) 7 14 21 47 76 105
84-99,101: 101-UFO-c/story 3 6 9 17 25 32
100 3 6 9 18 27 35
102-105,106-125('66) 3 6 9 14 19 24
126-133 (1984)-Low print run 1 2 3 5 6 8

NOTE: ***Montes/Bache*** *a-109.* ***Glanzman*** *a-82, 92, 96, 98, 100, 131r.*

FIGHTING PRINCE OF DONEGAL, THE (See Movie Comics)

FIGHTIN' TEXAN (Formerly The Texan & Fightin' Marines?)
St. John Publishing Co.: No. 16, Sept, 1952 - No. 17, Dec, 1952

16,17: Tuska-a each. 17-Cameron-c/a 8 16 24 44 57 70

FIGHTING UNDERSEA COMMANDOS (See Undersea Fighting...)
Avon Periodicals: May, 1952 - No. 5, April, 1953 (U.S. Navy frogmen)

1-Cover title is Undersea Fighting... #1 only 15 30 45 84 127 170
2 10 20 30 56 76 95
3-5: 1,3-Ravielli-c. 4-Kinstler-c 9 18 27 50 65 80

FIGHTING WAR STORIES
Men's Publications/Story Comics: Aug, 1952 - No. 5, 1953

1 12 24 36 67 94 120
2-5 8 16 24 40 50 60

FIGHTING YANK (See America's Best Comics & Startling Comics)
Nedor/Better Publ./Standard: Sept, 1942 - No. 29, Aug, 1949

1-The Fighting Yank begins; Mystico, the Wonder Man app; bondage-c 300 600 900 1950 3375 4800
2 123 246 369 787 1344 1900
3,4: 4-Schomburg-c begin 90 180 270 576 988 1400
5,6,8-10: 8,10-Bondage/torture-c 74 148 222 470 810 1150
7-Hitler special bomb-c; Grim Reaper app. 90 180 270 576 988 1400
11,13-20: 11-The Oracle app. 15-Bondage/torture-c. 18-The American Eagle app. 54 108 162 343 574 825
12-Hirohito bondage-c 90 180 270 576 988 1400
21,24: 21-Kara, Jungle Princess app.; lingerie-c. 24-Miss Masque app. 48 96 144 302 514 725
22-Miss Masque-c/story 54 108 162 343 574 825
23-Classic Schomburg hooded vigilante-c 81 162 243 518 884 1250
25-Robinson/Meskin-a; strangulation, lingerie panel; The Cavalier app. 53 106 159 334 567 800
26-29: All-Robinson/Meskin-a. 28-One pg. Williamson-a 43 86 129 271 461 650

NOTE: ***Schomburg (Xela)*** *c-4-29; airbrush-c 28, 29. Bondage c-1, 4, 8, 10, 11, 12, 15, 17.*

FIGHTMAN
Marvel Comics: June, 1993 ($2.00, one-shot, 52 pgs.)

1 4.00

FIGHT THE ENEMY
Tower Comics: Aug, 1966 - No. 3, Mar, 1967 (25¢, 68 pgs.)

1-Lucky 7 & Mike Manly begin 4 8 12 28 44 60
2-1st Boris Vallejo comic art; McWilliams-a 4 8 12 22 34 45
3-Wood-a (1/2 pg.); McWilliams, Bolle-a 4 8 12 22 34 45

FILM FUNNIES
Marvel Comics (CPC): Nov, 1949 - No. 2, Feb, 1950 (52 pgs.)

1-Krazy Krow, Wacky Duck 20 40 60 114 182 250
2-Wacky Duck 15 30 45 83 124 165

FILM STARS ROMANCES
Star Publications: Jan-Feb, 1950 - No. 3, May-June, 1950 (True life stories of movie stars)

1-Rudy Valentino & Gregory Peck stories; L. B. Cole-c; lingerie panels 43 86 129 271 461 650
2-Liz Taylor/Robert Taylor photo-c & true life story 57 114 171 362 619 875
3-Douglas Fairbanks story; photo-c 26 52 78 154 252 350

FILTH, THE
DC Comics (Vertigo): Aug, 2002 - No. 13, Oct, 2003 ($2.95, limited series)

1-13-Morrison-s/Weston & Erskine-a 3.00
TPB (2004, $19.95) r/#1-13 20.00

FINAL CRISIS
DC Comics: July, 2008 - No. 7, Mar, 2009 ($3.99, limited series)

1-Grant Morrison-s/J.G. Jones-a/c; Martian Manhunter killed; 2 covers 4.00
1-Director's Cut (10/08, $4.99) B&W printing of #1 with creator commentary 5.00
2-7: 2-Barry Allen-c/cameo; intro Big Science Action; two covers. 6-Batman zapped 4.00
SC (2010, $19.99) r/#1-7, FC: Superman Beyond #1,2, FC: Submit & FC Sketchbook 20.00
...: Rage of the Red Lanterns (12/08, $3.99) Atrocitus app.; intro. Blue Lantern; 3 covers 4.00
...: Requiem (9/08, $3.99) History, death and funeral of the Martian Manhunter; 2 covers 4.00
...: Resist (12/08, $3.99) Checkmate app; Rucka & Trautman-s/Sook-a; 2 covers 4.00
...: Secret Files (2/09, $3.99) origin of Libra; Wein-s/Shasteen-a; JG Jones sketch-a 4.00
... Sketchbook (7/08, $2.99) Jones development sketches with Morrison commentary 3.00
...: Submit (12/08, $3.99) Black Lightning & Tattooed Man team up; Morrison-s; 2 covers 4.00

FINAL CRISIS: DANCE (Final Crisis Aftermath)
DC Comics: Jul, 2009 - No. 6, Dec, 2009 ($2.99, limited series)

1-6-Super Young Team; Joe Casey-s/Chriscross-a/Stanley Lau-c 3.00
TPB (2009, $17.99) r/#1-6 18.00

FINAL CRISIS: ESCAPE (Final Crisis Aftermath)
DC Comics: Jul, 2009 - No. 6, Dec, 2009 ($2.99, limited series)

1-6-Nemesis & Cameron Chase app.; Ivan Brandon-s/Marco Rudy-a/Scott Hampton-c 3.00
TPB (2010, $17.99) r/#1-6 18.00

FINAL CRISIS: INK (Final Crisis Aftermath)
DC Comics: Jul, 2009 - No. 6, Dec, 2009 ($2.99, limited series)

1-6-The Tattooed Man; Eric Wallace-s/Fabrizio Florentino-a/Brian Stelfreeze-c 3.00
TPB (2010, $17.99) r/#1-6 18.00

FINAL CRISIS: LEGION OF THREE WORLDS
DC Comics: Oct, 2008 - No. 5, Sept, 2009 ($3.99, limited series)

1-Johns-s/Pérez-a; R.J. Brande killed; Time Trapper app.; two covers on each issue 5.00
2-5-Three Legions meet; two covers. 3-Bart Allen returns. 4-Superboy (Conner) returns 4.00
HC (2009, $19.99) r/#1-5; variant covers 20.00
SC (2010, $14.99) r/#1-5; variant covers 15.00

FINAL CRISIS: REVELATIONS
DC Comics: Oct, 2008 - No. 5, Feb, 2009 ($3.99, limited series)

1-5-Spectre and The Question; 2 covers on each. 1-Dr. Light killed; Rucka-s/Tan-a 4.00
HC (2009, $19.99, d.j.) r/#1-5; variant covers 20.00
SC (2010, $14.99) r/#1-5; variant covers 15.00

FINAL CRISIS: ROGUE'S REVENGE
DC Comics: Sept, 2008 - No. 3, Nov, 2008 ($3.99, limited series)

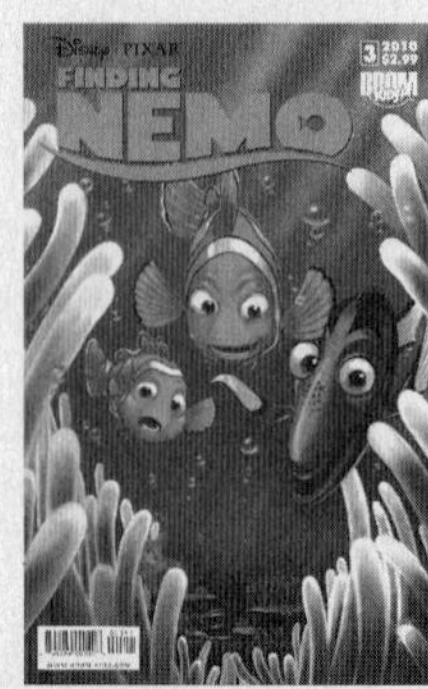
Finding Nemo #3 © DIS & Pixar

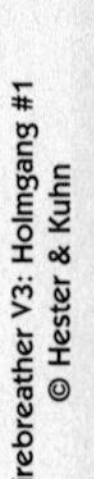
Firebreather V3: Holmgang #1 © Hester & Kuhn

Firestar (2010 series) #1 © MAR

	GD 2.0	VG 4.0	FN 6.0	VF 8.0	VF/NM 9.0	NM- 9.2

1-3-Johns-s/Kolins-a; Flash's Rogues, Zoom and Inertia app. 4.00
HC (2009, $19.99, d.j.) r/#1-3 & Flash #182,197; variant covers 20.00
SC (2010, $14.99) r/#1-3 & Flash #182,197; variant covers 15.00

FINAL CRISIS: RUN (Final Crisis Aftermath)
DC Comics: Jul, 2009 - No. 6, Dec, 2009 ($2.99, limited series)

1-6-The Human Flame on the run; Sturges-s/Williams-a/Kako-c 3.00
TPB (2010, $17.99) r/#1-6 18.00

FINAL CRISIS: SUPERMAN BEYOND
DC Comics: Oct, 2008 - No. 2, Mar, 2009 ($4.50, limited series)

1,2-Morrison-s/Mahnke-a; parallel-Earth Supermen app.; 3-D pages and glasses 4.50

FINAL NIGHT, THE (See DC related titles and Parallax: Emerald Night)
DC Comics: Nov, 1996 - No. 4, Nov, 1996 ($1.95, weekly limited series)

1-4: Kesel-s/Immonen-a(p) in all. 4-Parallax's final acts 3.50
Preview 3.00
TPB-(1998, $12.95) r/#1-4, Parallax: Emerald Night #1, and preview 13.00

FINALS (See Vertigo Resurrected:... for collected reprint)
DC Comics (Vertigo): Sept, 1999 - No. 4, Dec, 1999 ($2.95, limited series)

1-4-Will Pfeifer-s/Jill Thompson-a 3.00

FINDING NEMO (Based on the Pixar movie)
BOOM! Studios: Jul, 2010 - No. 4, Oct, 2010 ($2.99, limited series)

1-4-Michael Raicht & Brian Smith-s/Jake Myler-a.1-Three covers 3.00

FINDING NEMO: REEF RESCUE (Based on the Pixar movie)
BOOM! Studios: May, 2009 - No. 4, Aug, 2009 ($2.99, limited series)

1-4-Marie Croall-s/Erica Leigh Currey-a; 2 covers 3.00

FIN FANG FOUR RETURN!
Marvel Comics: Jul, 2009 ($3.99, one-shot)

1-Fin Fang Foom, Googam, Elektro, Gorgilla and Doc Samson app. 4.00

FIRE
Caliber Press: 1993 - No. 2, 1993 ($2.95, B&W, limited series, 52 pgs.)

1,2-Brian Michael Bendis-s/a 4.00
TPB (1999, 2001, $9.95) Restored reprints of series 10.00

FIREARM (Also see Codename: Firearm, Freex #15, Night Man #4 & Prime #10)
Malibu Comics (Ultraverse): Sept, 1993 - No. 18, Mar, 1995 ($1.95/$2.50)

0 ($14.95)-Came w/ video containing 1st half of story (comic contains 2nd half); 1st app. Duet 15.00
1,3-6: 1-James Robinson scripts begin; Cully Hamner-a; Chaykin-c; 1st app. Alec Swan. 3-Intro The Sportsmen; Chaykin-c. 4-Break-Thru x-over; Chaykin-c. 5-1st app. Ellen (Swan's girlfriend); 2 pg. origin of Prime. 6-Prime app. (story cont'd in Prime #10); Brereton-c 3.00
1-($2.50)-Newsstand edition polybagged w/card 3.50
1-Ultra Limited silver foil-c 5.00
2 ($2.50, 44 pgs.)-Hardcase app.;Chaykin-c; Rune flip-c/story by B. Smith (3 pgs.) 4.00
7-10,12-17: 12-The Rafferty Saga begins, ends #18; 1st app. Rafferty. 15-Night Man & Freex app. 17-Swan marries Ellen 3.00
11-($3.50, 68 pgs.)-Flip book w/Ultraverse Premiere #5 4.00
18-Death of Rafferty; Chaykin-c 4.00
NOTE: *Brereton* c-6. *Chaykin* c-1-4, 14, 16, 18. *Hamner* a-1-4. *Herrera* a-12. *James Robinson* scripts-0-18.

FIRE BALL XL5 (See Steve Zodiac & The ...)

FIREBIRDS (See Noble Causes)
Image Comics: Nov, 2004 ($5.95)

1-Faerber-s/Ponce-a/c; intro. Firebird 6.00

FIREBRAND (Also see Showcase '96 #4)
DC Comics: Feb, 1996 - No. 9, Oct, 1996 ($1.75)

1-9: Brian Augustyn scripts; Velluto-c/a in all. 9-Daredevil #319-c/swipe 3.00

FIREBREATHER
Image Comics: Jan, 2003 - No. 4, Apr, 2003 ($2.95)

1-4-Hester-s/Kuhn-a 3.00
...: The Iron Saint (12/04, $6.95, squarebound) Hester-s/Kuhn-a 7.00
TPB (7/04, $13.95) r/#1-4; foreword by Brad Meltzer; gallery and sketch pages 14.00

FIREBREATHER
Image Comics: Jun, 2008 - No. 4, Feb, 2009 ($2.99)

1-4-Hester-s/Kuhn-a 3.00

FIREBREATHER (Vol.3): HOLMGANG
Image Comics: Nov, 2010 - No. 4, ($3.99, limited series)

1,2-Hester-s/Kuhn-a 4.00

FIRE FROM HEAVEN
Image Comics (WildStorm Productions): Mar, 1996 ($2.50)

1,2-Moore-s 3.00

FIREHAIR COMICS (Formerly Pioneer West Romances #3-6; also see Rangers Comics)
Fiction House Magazines (Flying Stories): Winter/48-49; No. 2, Wint/49-50; No. 7, Spr/51 - No. 11, Spr/52

	GD	VG	FN	VF	VF/NM	NM-
1-Origin Firehair	34	68	102	199	325	450
2-Continues as Pioneer West Romances for #3-6	18	36	54	105	165	225
7-11	14	28	42	80	115	150
I.W. Reprint 8-(nd)-Kinstler-c; reprints Rangers #57; Dr. Drew story by Grandenetti	3	6	9	18	24	30

FIRESIDE BOOK SERIES (Hard and soft cover editions)
Simon and Schuster: 1974 - 1980 (130-260 pgs.), Square bound, color

		GD	VG	FN	VF	VF/NM	NM-
Amazing Spider-Man, The, 1979,	HC	8	16	24	56	93	130
130 pgs., $3.95, Bob Larkin-c	SC	6	12	18	37	59	80
America At War–The Best of DC War	HC	11	22	33	75	138	200
Comics, 1979, $6.95, 260 pgs, Kubert-c	SC	7	14	21	50	83	115
Best of Spidey Super Stories (Electric Company) 1978, $3.95,	SC	6	12	18	43	69	95
Bring On The Bad Guys (Origins of the	HC	8	16	24	54	90	125
Marvel Comics Villains) 1976, $6.95, 260 pgs.; Romita-c	SC	5	10	15	34	55	75
Captain America, Sentinel of Liberty,1979,	HC	8	16	24	56	93	130
130 pgs., $12.95, Cockrum-c	SC	6	12	18	37	59	80
Doctor Strange Master of the Mystic	HC	8	16	24	56	93	130
Arts, 1980, 130 pgs.	SC	6	12	18	37	59	80
Fantastic Four, The, 1979, 130 pgs.	HC	8	16	24	54	90	125
	SC	5	10	15	34	55	75
Heart Throbs–The Best of DC Romance	HC	14	28	42	97	194	290
Comics, 1979, 260 pgs., $6.95	SC	9	18	27	65	113	160
Incredible Hulk, The, 1978, 260 pgs.	HC	8	16	24	54	90	125
(8 1/4" x 11")	SC	5	10	15	34	55	75
Marvel's Greatest Superhero Battles,	HC	10	20	30	67	116	165
1978, 260 pgs., $6.95, Romita-c	SC	6	12	18	43	69	95
Mysteries in Space, 1980, $7,95,	HC	9	18	27	61	103	145
Anderson-c. r-DC sci/fi stories	SC	6	12	18	39	62	85
Origins of Marvel Comics, 1974, 260 pgs., $5.95. r-covers & origins of Fantastic Four, Hulk, Spider-Man, Thor,	HC	8	16	24	54	90	125
& Doctor Strange	SC	5	10	15	34	55	75
Silver Surfer, The, 1978, 130 pgs.,	HC	8	16	24	56	93	130
$4.95, Norem-c	SC	6	12	18	39	62	85
Son of Origins of Marvel Comics, 1975, 260 pgs., $6.95, Romita-c. Reprints covers & origins of X-Men, Iron Man,	HC	8	16	24	54	90	125
Avengers, Daredevil, Silver Surfer	SC	5	10	15	34	55	75
Superhero Women, The–Featuring the	HC	10	20	30	67	116	165
Fabulous Females of Marvel Comics, 1977, 260 pgs., $6.95, Romita-c	SC	6	12	18	43	69	95

Note: Prices listed are for 1st printings. Later printings have lesser value.

FIRESTAR
Marvel Comics Group: Mar, 1986 - No. 4, June, 1986 (75¢)(From Spider-Man TV series)

1,2: 1-X-Men & New Mutants app. 2-Wolverine-c (not real Wolverine?); Art Adams-a(p) 6.00
3,4: 3-Art Adams/Sienkiewicz-c. 4-B. Smith-c 4.00
X-Men: Firestar Digest (2006, $7.99, digest-size) r/#1-4; profile pages 8.00
1 (Jun, 2010, $3.99) Sean McKeever-s/Emma Rios-a 4.00

FIRESTONE (See Donald And Mickey Merry Christmas)

FIRESTORM (See Cancelled Comic Cavalcade, DC Comics Presents, Flash #289, The Fury of... & Justice League of America #179)
DC Comics: March, 1978 - No. 5, Oct-Nov, 1978

	GD	VG	FN	VF	VF/NM	NM-
1,5: 1-Origin & 1st app.	2	4	6	9	12	15
2-4: 2-Origin Multiplex. 3-Origin & 1st app. Killer Frost. 4-1st app. Hyena	1	2	3	5	7	9

FIRESTORM
DC Comics: July, 2004 - No. 35, June, 2007 ($2.50/$2.99)

1-24: 1-Intro. Jason Rusch; Jolley-s/ChrisCross-a. 6-Identity Crisis tie-in. 7-Bloodhound x-over. 8-Killer Frost returns. 9-Ronnie Raymond returns. 17-Villains United tie-in.

The First #10 © CRO

1st Issue Special #13 © DC

First Wave #1 © DC & AMP & WES

GD VG FN VF VF/NM NM-
2.0 4.0 6.0 8.0 9.0 9.2

21-Infinite Crisis. 24-One Year Later; Killer Frost app. 3.00
25-35: 25-Begin $2.99-c; Mr. Freeze app. 33-35-Mister Miracle & Orion app. 3.00
...: Reborn TPB (2007, $14.99) r/#23-27 15.00

FIRESTORM, THE NUCLEAR MAN (Formerly Fury of Firestorm)
DC Comics: No. 65, Nov, 1987 - No. 100, Aug, 1990

65-99: 66-1st app. Zuggernaut; Firestorm vs. Green Lantern. 67,68-Millennium tie-ins. 71-Death of Capt. X. 83-1st new look 3.00
100-($2.95, 68 pgs.) 4.00
Annual 5 (10/87)-1st app. new Firestorm 4.00

FIRST, THE
CrossGeneration Comics: Jan, 2001 - No. 37, Jan, 2004 ($2.95)

1-3: 1-Barbara Kesel-s/Bart Sears & Andy Smith-a 5.00
4-10 4.00
11-37 3.00
Preview (11/00, free) 8 pg. intro 3.00
Two Houses Divided Vol. 1 TPB (11/01, $19.95) r/#1-7; new Moeller-c 20.00
Magnificent Tension Vol. 2 TPB (2002, $19.95) r/#8-13 20.00
Sinister Motives Vol. 3 TPB (2003, $15.95) r/#14-19 16.00
Vol. 4 Futile Endeavors (2003, $15.95) r/#20-25 16.00
Vol. 5 Liquid Alliances (2003, $15.95) r/#26-31 16.00
Vol. 6 Ragnarok (2004, $15.95) r/#32-37 16.00

FIRST ADVENTURES
First Comics: Dec, 1985 - No. 5, Apr, 1986 ($1.25)

1-5: Blaze Barlow, Whisper & Dynamo Joe in all 3.00

FIRST AMERICANS, THE
Dell Publishing Co.: No. 843, Sept, 1957

Four Color 843-Marsh-a 8 16 24 56 93 130

FIRST BORN (See Witchblade and Darkness titles)
Image Comics (Top Cow): Aug, 2007 - No. 3 ($2.99, limited series)

... First Look (6/07, 99¢) Preview; The Darkness app.; Sejic-a; 2 covers (color & B&W) 3.00
1-3-($2.99) Two covers; Marz-s/Sejic-a. 3-Sara's baby is born 3.00
1-B&W variant Sejic cover 5.00
...: Aftermath (5/08, $3.99) short stories; Magdalena app.; two covers by Sook & Sejic 4.00

FIRST CHRISTMAS, THE (3-D)
Fiction House Magazines (Real Adv. Publ. Co.): 1953 (25¢, 8-1/4x10-1/4", oversize)(Came w/glasses)

nn-(Scarce)-Kelly Freas painted-c; Biblical theme, birth of Christ; Nativity-c
32 64 96 192 314 435

FIRST COMICS GRAPHIC NOVEL
First Comics: Jan, 1984 - No. 21? (52 pgs./176 pgs., high quality paper)

1,2: 1-Beowulf ($5.95)(both printings). 2-Time Beavers 9.00
3($11.95, 100 pgs.)-American Flagg! Hard Times (2nd printing exists) 15.00
4-Nexus ($6.95)-r/B&W 1-3 12.00
5,7: 5-The Enchanted Apples of Oz ($7.95, 52 pgs.)-Intro by Harlan Ellison (1986). 7-The Secret Island Of Oz ($7.95) 10.00
6-Elric of Melnibone ($14.95, 176 pgs.)-Reprints with new color 18.00
8,10,14,18: Teenage Mutant Ninja Turtles Book I -IV ($9.95, 132 pgs.)-8-r/TMNT #1-3 in color w/12 pgs. new-a; origin. 10-r/TMNT #4-6 in color. 14-r/TMNT #7,8 in color plus new 12 pg. story. 18-r/TMNT #10,11 plus 3 pg. fold-out 11.00
9-Time 2: The Epiphany by Chaykin (11/86, $7.95, 52pgs. - indicia says #8) 10.00
11-Sailor On The Sea of Fate ($14.95) 16.00
nn-Time 2: The Satisfaction of Black Mariah (9/87) 10.00
12-American Flagg! Southern Comfort (10/87, $11.95) 14.00
13,16,17,21: 13-The Ice King Of Oz. 16-The Forgotten Forest of Oz ($8.95). 17-Mazinger (68 pgs., $8.95). 21-Elric, The Weird of the White Wolf; r/#1-5 10.00
15,19: 15-Hex Breaker: Badger ($7.95). 19-The Original Nexus Graphic Novel ($7.95, 104 pgs.)-Reprints First Comics Graphic Novel #4 12.00
20-American Flagg!: State of the Union ($11.95, 96 pgs.); r/A.F. #7-9 15.00
NOTE: *Most or all issues have been reprinted.*

1ST FOLIO (The Joe Kubert School Presents...)
Pacific Comics: Mar, 1984 ($1.50, one-shot)

1-Joe Kubert-c/a(2 pgs.); Adam & Andy Kubert-a 3.00

1ST ISSUE SPECIAL
National Periodical Publications: Apr, 1975 - No. 13, Apr, 1976 (Tryout series)

1,6: 1-Intro. Atlas; Kirby-c/a/script. 6-Dingbats 2 4 6 11 16 20
2,12: 2-Green Team (see Cancelled Comic Cavalcade). 12-Origin/1st app. "Blue" Starman (2nd app. in Starman, 2nd Series #3); Kubert-c 2 4 6 8 11 14
3-Metamorpho by Ramona Fradon 2 4 6 8 11 14
4,10,11: 4-Lady Cop. 10-The Outsiders. 11-Code Name: Assassin; Grell-c
1 3 4 6 8 10
5-Manhunter; Kirby-c/a/script 3 6 9 14 20 26
7,9: 7-The Creeper by Ditko (c/a). 9-Dr. Fate; Kubert-c/Simonson-a.
2 4 6 11 16 20
8-Origin/1st app. The Warlord; Grell-c/a (11/75) 5 10 15 32 51 70
13-Return of the New Gods; Darkseid app.; 1st new costume Orion; predates New Gods #12 by more than a year 3 6 9 20 30 40

FIRST KISS
Charlton Comics: Dec, 1957 - No. 40, Jan, 1965

V1#1 4 8 12 28 44 60
V1#2-10 3 6 9 18 27 35
11-40 2 4 6 13 18 22

FIRST LOVE ILLUSTRATED
Harvey Publications(Home Comics)(True Love): 2/49 - No. 9, 6/50; No. 10, 1/51 - No. 86, 3/58; No. 87, 9/58 - No. 88, 11/58; No. 89, 11/62, No. 90, 2/63

1-Powell-a(2) 19 38 57 111 176 240
2-Powell-a 12 24 36 67 94 120
3-"Was I Too Fat To Be Loved" story 14 28 42 82 121 160
4-10 9 18 27 50 65 80
11-30: 13-"I Joined a Teen-age Sex Club" story. 30-Lingerie panel
8 16 24 40 50 60
31-34,37,39-49: 49-Last pre-code (2/55) 7 14 21 35 43 50
35-Used in **SOTI**, illo "The title of this comic book is First Love"
20 40 60 114 182 250
36-Communism story, "Love Slaves" 12 24 36 67 94 120
38-Nostrand-a 8 16 24 44 57 70
50-66,71-90 6 12 18 28 34 40
67-70-Kirby-c 8 16 24 40 50 60
NOTE: ***Disbrow** a-13. **Orlando** c-87. **Powell** a-1, 3-5, 7, 10, 11, 13-17, 19-24, 26-29, 33,35-41, 43, 45, 46, 50, 54, 55, 57, 58, 61-63, 65, 71-73, 76, 79r, 82, 84, 88.*

FIRST MEN IN THE MOON (See Movie Comics)

FIRST ROMANCE MAGAZINE
Home Comics(Harvey Publ.)/True Love: 8/49 - #6, 6/50; #7, 6/51 - #50, 2/58; #51, 9/58 - #52, 11/58

1 17 34 51 98 154 210
2 11 22 33 60 83 105
3-5 9 18 27 50 65 80
6-10,28: 28-Nostrand-a(Powell swipe) 8 16 24 40 50 60
11-20 7 14 21 35 43 50
21-27,29-32: 32-Last pre-code issue (2/55) 6 12 18 31 38 45
33-40,44-52 6 12 18 28 34 40
41-43-Kirby-c 8 16 24 40 50 60
NOTE: ***Powell** a-1-5, 8-10, 14, 18, 20-22, 24, 25, 28, 36, 46, 48, 51.*

FIRST TRIP TO THE MOON (See Space Adventures No. 20)

FIRST WAVE (Based on Sci-Fi Channel TV series)
Andromeda Entertainment: Dec, 2000 - No. 4, Jun, 2001 ($2.99)

1-4-Kuhoric-s/Parsons-a/Busch-c 3.00

FIRST WAVE
DC Comics: May, 2010 - No. 6, Mar, 2011 ($3.99, limited series)

1-6-Batman, Doc Savage and The Spirit app.; Azzarello-s/Morales-a/JG Jones-c 4.00

FISH POLICE (Inspector Gill of the...#2, 3)
Fishwrap Productions/Comico V2#5-17/Apple Comics #18 on:
Dec, 1985 - No. 11, Nov, 1987 ($1.50, B&W); V2#5, April, 1988 - V2#17, May, 1989 ($1.75, color) No. 18, Aug, 1989 - No. 26, Dec, 1990 ($2.25, B&W)

1-11, 1(5/86),2-2nd print, V2#5-17-(Color): V2#5-11. 12-17, new-a, 18-26 ($2.25-c, B&W). 18-Origin Inspector Gill 3.00
Special 1($2.50, 7/87, Comico) 3.00
Graphic Novel: Hairballs (1987, $9.95, TPB) r/#1-4 in color 10.00

FISH POLICE
Marvel Comics: V2#1, Oct, 1992 - No. 6, Mar, 1993 ($1.25)

V2#1-6: 1-Hairballs Saga begins; r/#1 (1985) 2.50

5 CENT COMICS (Also see Whiz Comics)
Fawcett Publ.: Feb, 1940 (8 pgs., reg. size, B&W)

nn - 1st app. Dan Dare. Ashcan comic, not distributed to newsstands, only for in-house use. A CGC certified 9.6 copy sold for $10,800 in 2003, and a CGC 9.4 sold for $11,500 in 2005.

5 RONIN (Marvel characters in Samurai setting)
Marvel Comics: May, 2011 - No. 5, May, 2011 ($2.99, weekly limited series)

The Flame #2 © FOX

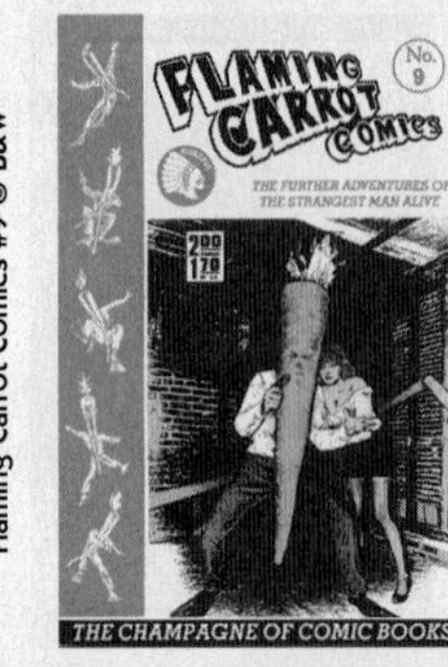

Flaming Carrot Comics #9 © B&W

The Flash #165 © DC

	GD	VG	FN	VF	VF/NM	NM-
	2.0	4.0	6.0	8.0	9.0	9.2

1-Wolverine. 2-Hulk. 3-Punisher. 4-Psylocke; Mack-c. 5-Deadpool 3.00

5-STAR SUPER-HERO SPECTACULAR (See DC Special Series No. 1)

FLAME, THE (See Big 3 & Wonderworld Comics)
Fox Features Synd.: Sum, 1940 - No. 8, Jan, 1942 (#1,2: 68 pgs; #3-8: 44 pgs.)

1-Flame stories reprinted from Wonderworld #5-9; origin The Flame; Lou Fine-a (36 pgs.), 300 600 900 2040 3570 5100
2-Fine-a(2); Wing Turner by Tuska; r/Wonderworld #3,10 121 242 363 768 1322 1875
3-8: 3-Powell-a 79 158 237 502 864 1225

FLAME, THE (Formerly Lone Eagle)
Ajax/Farrell Publications (Excellent Publ.): No. 5, Dec-Jan, 1954-55 - No. 3, April-May, 1955

5(#1)-1st app. new Flame 47 94 141 296 498 700
2,3 30 60 90 177 289 400

FLAMING CARROT COMICS (Also see Junior Carrot Patrol)
Killian Barracks Press: Summer-Fall, 1981 ($1.95, one shot) (Lg size, 8-1/2x11")

1-Bob Burden-c/a/scripts; serially #'ed to 6500 5 10 15 34 55 75

FLAMING CARROT COMICS (See Anything Goes, Cerebus, Teenage Mutant Ninja Turtles/Flaming Carrot Crossover & Visions)
Aardvark-Vanaheim/Renegade Press #6-17/Dark Horse #18-31:
May, 1984 - No. 5, Jan, 1985; No. 6, Mar, 1985 - No. 31, Oct, 1994 ($1.70/$2.00, B&W)

1-Bob Burden story/art 4 8 12 28 44 60
2 3 6 9 16 23 30
3 2 4 6 10 16 20
4-6 2 4 6 9 12 15
7-9 1 3 4 6 8 10
10-12 6.50
13-15 4.00
15-Variant without cover price 6.00
16-(6/87) 1st app. Mystery Men 1 2 3 5 6 8
17-20: 18-1st Dark Horse issue 4.00
21-23,25: 25-Contains trading cards; TMNT app. 3.00
24-(2.50, 52 pgs.)-10th anniversary issue 4.00
26-28: 26-Begin $2.25-c. 26,27-Teenage Mutant Ninja Turtles x-over. 27-McFarlane-c 3.00
29-31-(2.50-c) 3.00
Annual 1(1/97, $5.00) 5.00
... & Reid Fleming, World's Toughest Milkman (12/02, $3.99) listed as #32 in indicia 4.00
... :Fortune Favors the Bold (1998, $16.95, TPB) r/#19-24 17.00
... :Men of Mystery (7/97, $12.95, TPB) r/#1-3, + new material 13.00
... 's Greatest Hits (4/98, $17.95, TPB) r/#12-18, + new material 18.00
... :The Wild Shall Wild Remain (1997, $17.95, TPB) r/#4-11, + new s/a 18.00

FLAMING CARROT COMICS
Image Comics (Desperado): Dec, 2004 - Present ($2.95/$3.50, B&W)

1-3-Bob Burden story/art 3.00
4-($3.50-c) 3.50
... Special #1 (3/06, $3.50) All Photo comic 3.50
... Vol. 6 (2006, $14.99) r/1-4 & Special #1; intro. by Brian Bolland 15.00

FLAMING LOVE
Quality Comics Group (Comic Magazines): Dec, 1949 - No. 6, Oct, 1950 (Photo covers #2-6) (52 pgs.)

1-Ward-c/a (9 pgs.) 39 78 117 240 395 550
2 18 36 54 107 169 230
3-Ward-a (9 pgs.); Crandall-a 26 52 78 154 252 350
4-6: 4-Gustavson-a 15 30 45 90 140 190

FLAMING WESTERN ROMANCES (Formerly Target Western Romances)
Star Publications: No. 3, Mar-Apr, 1950

3-Robert Taylor, Arlene Dahl photo on-c with biographies inside; L. B. Cole-c 34 68 102 199 325 450

FLARE (Also see Champions for 1st app. & League of Champions)
Hero Comics/Hero Graphics Vol. 2 on: Nov, 1988 - No. 3, Jan, 1989 ($2.75, color, 52 pgs); V2#1, Nov, 1990 - No. 7, Nov, 1991 ($2.95/$3.50, color, mature, 52 pgs.);V2#8, Oct, 1992 - No. 16, Feb, 1994 ($3.50/$3.95, B&W, 36 pgs.)

V1#1-3, V2#1-16: 5-Eternity Smith returns. 6-Intro The Tigress 4.00
Annual 1(1992, $4.50, B&W, 52 pgs.)-Champions-r 4.50

FLARE ADVENTURES
Hero Graphics: Feb, 1992 - No. 12, 1993? ($3.50/$3.95)

1 (90¢, color, 20 pgs.) 3.00
2-12-Flip books w/Champions Classics 4.00

FLASH, THE (See Adventure Comics, The Brave and the Bold, Crisis On Infinite Earths, DC Comics Presents, DC Special, DC Special Series, DC Super-Stars, The Greatest Flash Stories Ever Told, Green Lantern, Impulse, JLA, Justice League of America, Showcase, Speed Force, Super Team Family, Titans & World's Finest)

FLASH, THE (1st Series)(Formerly Flash Comics)(See Showcase #4,8,13,14)
National Periodical Publ./DC: No. 105, Feb-Mar, 1959 - No. 350, Oct, 1985

105-(2-3/59)-Origin Flash(retold), & Mirror Master (1st app.) 575 1150 1725 5200 11,600 18,000
106-Origin Grodd & Pied Piper; Flash's 1st visit to Gorilla City; begin Grodd the Super Gorilla trilogy (Scarce) 193 386 579 1689 3445 5200
107-Grodd trilogy, part 2 110 220 330 935 1893 2850
108-Grodd trilogy ends 90 180 270 765 1558 2350
109-2nd app. Mirror Master 71 142 213 604 1227 1850
110-Intro/origin Kid Flash who later becomes Flash in Crisis On Infinite Earths #12; begin Kid Flash trilogy, ends #112 (also in #114,116,118); 1st app. & origin of The Weather Wizard 159 318 477 1391 2846 4300
111-2nd Kid Flash tryout; Cloud Creatures 50 100 150 425 863 1300
112-Origin & 1st app. Elongated Man (4-5/60); also apps. in #115,119,130 58 116 174 493 997 1500
113-Origin & 1st app. Trickster 48 96 144 400 813 1225
114-Captain Cold app. (see Showcase #8) 41 82 123 324 650 975
115,116,118-120: 119-Elongated Man marries Sue Dearborn. 120-Flash & Kid Flash team-up for 1st time 35 70 105 273 537 800
117-Origin & 1st app. Capt. Boomerang; 1st & only S.A. app. Winky Blinky & Noddy 37 74 111 295 585 875
121,122: 122-Origin & 1st app. The Top 27 54 81 197 399 600
123-(9/61)-Re-intro. Golden Age Flash; origins of both Flashes; 1st mention of an Earth II where DC G. A. heroes live 148 296 444 1295 2648 4000
124-Last 10¢ issue 22 44 66 162 324 485
125-128,130: 127-Return of Grodd-c/story. 128-Origin & 1st app. Abra Kadabra. 130-(7/62)-1st Gauntlet of Super-Villains (Mirror Master, Capt. Cold, The Top, Capt. Boomerang & Trickster) 21 42 63 150 300 450
129-2nd G.A. Flash x-over; J.S.A. cameo in flashback (1st S.A. app. G.A. Green Lantern, Hawkman, Atom, Black Canary & Dr. Mid-Nite. Wonder Woman (1st S.A. app.?) appears) 28 56 84 215 433 650
131-136,138,140: 131-Early Green Lantern x-over (9/62). 135-1st app. of Kid Flash's yellow costume (3/63). 136-1st Dexter Miles. 140-Origin & 1st app. Heat Wave 15 30 45 106 216 325
137-G.A. Flash x-over; J.S.A. cameo (1st S.A. app.)(1st real app. since 2-3/51); 1st S.A. app. Vandal Savage & Johnny Thunder; JSA team decides to re-form 37 74 111 295 585 875
139-Origin & 1st app. Prof. Zoom 16 32 48 114 232 350
141-150: 142-Trickster app. 147-2nd Prof. Zoom 13 26 39 89 170 250
151-Engagement of Barry Allen & Iris West; G.A. Flash vs. The Shade. 13 26 39 94 185 275
152-159: 159-Dr. Mid-Nite cameo 11 22 33 75 138 200
160-(80-Pg. Giant G-21); G.A. Flash & Johnny Quick-r 12 24 36 87 164 240
161-164,166,167: 167-New facts about Flash's origin 9 18 27 63 107 150
165-Barry Allen weds Iris West 9 18 27 65 113 160
168,170: 168-Green Lantern-c/app. 170-Dr. Mid-Nite, Dr. Fate, G.A. Flash x-over 9 18 27 63 107 150
169-(80-Pg. Giant G-34)-New facts about origin 10 20 30 67 116 165
171,172,174,176,177,179,180: 171-JLA, Green Lantern, Atom flashbacks. 174-Barry Allen reveals I.D. to wife. 179-(5/68)-Flash travels to Earth-Prime and meets DC editor Julie Schwartz; 1st unnamed app. Earth-Prime (See Justice League of America #123 for 1st named app. & 3rd app. overall) 8 16 24 54 90 125
173-G.A. Flash x-over 9 18 27 63 107 150
175-2nd Superman/Flash race (12/67) (See Superman #199 & World's Finest #198,199); JLA cameo; gold kryptonite used (on J'onn J'onzz impersonating Superman) 17 34 51 122 249 375
178-(80-Pg. Giant G-46) 9 18 27 61 103 145
181-186,188,189: 186-Re-intro. Sargon. 189-Last 12¢-c 6 12 18 39 62 85
187,196: (68-Pg. Giants G-58, G-70) 7 14 21 47 76 105
190-195,197-199 4 8 12 28 44 60
200 5 10 15 32 51 70
201-204,206,207: 201-New G.A. Flash story. 206-Elongated Man begins 207-Last 15¢ issue 4 8 12 22 34 45
205-(68-Pg. Giant G-82) 7 14 21 49 80 110
208-213-(52 pg.): 211-G.A. Flash origin-r/#104. 213-Reprints #137 4 8 12 26 41 55
214-DC 100 Page Super Spectacular DC-11; origin Metal Men-r/Showcase #37; never before published G.A. Flash story 9 18 27 63 107 150
215 (52 pgs.)-Flash-r/Showcase #4; G.A. Flash x-over, continued in #216 4 8 12 28 44 60

The Flash #305 © DC

The Flash (2nd series) #187 © DC

The Flash (2010 series) #1 © DC

	GD	VG	FN	VF	VF/NM	NM-
	2.0	4.0	6.0	8.0	9.0	9.2

216,220: 220-1st app. Turtle since Showcase #4 3 6 9 18 27 35
217-219: Neal Adams-a in all. 217-Green Lantern/Green Arrow series begins (9/72); 2nd G.L. & G.A. team-up series (see Green Lantern #76). 219-Last Green Arrow 5 10 15 30 48 65
221-225,227,228,230,231,233: 222-G. Lantern x-over. 228-(7-8/74)-Flash writer Cary Bates travels to Earth-One & meets Flash, Iris Allen & Trickster; 2nd unnamed app. Earth-Prime (See Justice League of America #123 for 1st named app. & 3rd app. overall) 3 6 9 14 19 24
226-Neal Adams-p 3 6 9 17 25 32
229,232-(100 pg. issues)-G.A. Flash-r & new-a 5 10 15 30 48 65
234-250: 235-Green Lantern x-over. 243-Death of The Top. 245-Origin The Floronic Man in Green Lantern back-up, ends #246. 246-Last Green Lantern. 247-Jay Garrick app. 250-Intro Golden Glider 2 4 6 10 14 18
251-274: 256-Death of The Top retold. 265-267-(44 pgs.). 267-Origin of Flash's uniform. 270-Intro The Clown 2 4 6 8 10 12
268,273-276,278,283,286-(Whitman variants; low print run; no issue #s shown on covers 2 4 6 8 11 14
275,276-Iris Allen dies 2 4 6 9 12 15
277-288,290: 286-Intro/origin Rainbow Raider 1 2 3 5 6 8
289-1st Pérez DC art (Firestorm); new Firestorm back-up series begins (9/80), ends #304 2 3 4 6 8 10
291-299,301-305: 291-1st app. Saber-Tooth (villain). 295-Gorilla Grodd-c/story. 298-Intro & origin new Shade. 301-Atomic bomb-c. 303-The Top returns. 304-Intro/origin Colonel Computron; 305-G.A. Flash x-over 6.00
300-(52 pgs.)-Origin Flash retold; 25th ann. issue 1 2 3 5 6 8
306-313-Dr. Fate by Giffen. 309-Origin Flash retold 6.00
314-340: 318-323-Creeper back-ups. 323,324-Two part Flash vs. Flash story. 324-Death of Reverse Flash (Professor Zoom). 328-Iris West Allen's death retold. 329-JLA app. 340-Trial of the Flash begins 5.00
341-349: 344-Origin Kid Flash 6.00
350-Double size ($1.25) Final issue 1 2 3 5 6 8
Annual 1 (10-12/63, 84 pgs.)-Origin Elongated Man & Kid Flash-r; origin Grodd; G.A. Flash-r 35 70 105 273 537 800
Annual 1 Replica Edition (2001, $6.95)-Reprints the entire 1963 Annual 7.00
...Chronicles SC Vol. 1 (2009, $14.99)-r/Showcase #4,8,13,14 and Flash #105,106 15.00
...Chronicles SC Vol. 2 (2010, $14.99)-r/Flash #107-112 15.00
The Flash Spectacular (See DC Special Series No. 11)
The Flash vs. The Rogues TPB (2009, $14.99) r/1st app. of classic rogues in Showcase #8 and Flash #105,106,110,113,117,122,140,155; new Van Sciver-c 15.00
The Life Story of the Flash (1997, $19.95, Hardcover) "Iris Allen's" chronicle of Barry Allen's life; comic panels w/additional text; Waid & Augustyn-s/ Kane & Staton-a/Orbik painted-c 20.00
The Life Story of the Flash (1998, $12.95, Softcover) New Orbik-c 13.00
NOTE: ***N. Adams*** *c-194, 195, 203, 204, 206-208, 211, 213, 215, 226p, 246.* ***M. Anderson*** *c-165, a(i)-195, 200-204, 206-208.* ***Austin*** *a-233i, 234i, 246i.* ***Buckler*** *a-271p, 272p; c(p)-247-250, 252, 253p, 255, 256p, 258, 262, 265-267, 269-271.* ***Giffen*** *a-306-313p; c-310p, 315.* ***Giordano*** *a-226i.* ***Sid Greene*** *a-167-174i, 229i(r).* ***Grell*** *a-237p, 238p, 240-243p; c-236.* ***Heck*** *a-198p.* ***Infantino/Anderson*** *a-135. c-135, 170-174, 192, 200, 201, 328-330.* ***Infantino/Giella*** *c-105-112, 163, 164, 166-168.* ***G. Kane*** *a-195p, 197-199p, 229r, 232r; c-197-199, 312p.* ***Kubert*** *a-108p, 215i(r); c-189-191.* ***Lopez*** *c-272.* ***Meskin*** *a-229r, 232r.* ***Perez*** *a-289-293p; c-293.* ***Starlin*** *a-294-296p.* ***Staton*** *c-263p, 264p. Green Lantern x-over-131, 143, 168, 171, 191.*

FLASH (2nd Series)(See Crisis on Infinite Earths #12 and All Flash #1)
DC Comics: June, 1987 - No. 230, Mar, 2006; No. 231, Oct, 2007 - No. 247, Feb, 2009

1-Guice-c/a begins; New Teen Titans app. 1 3 4 6 8 10
2-10: 3-Intro. Kilgore. 5-Intro. Speed McGee. 7-1st app. Blue Trinity. 8,9-Millennium tie-ins. 9-1st app. The Chunk 4.00
11-61: 12-Free extra 16 pg. Dr. Light story. 19-Free extra 16 pg. Flash story. 28-Capt. Cold app. 29-New Phantom Lady app. 40-Dr. Alchemy app. 50-($1.75, 52 pgs.) 4.00
62-78,80: 62-Flash: Year One begins, ends #65. 65-Last $1.00-c. 66-Aquaman app. 69,70-Green Lantern app. 70-Gorilla Grodd story ends. 73-Re-intro Barry Allen & begin saga ("Barry Allen's" true ID revealed in #78). 76-Re-intro of Max Mercury (Quality Comics' Quicksilver), not in uniform until #77. 80-($1.25-c) Regular Edition 4.00
79,80 ($2.50): 79-(68 pgs.) Barry Allen saga ends. 80-Foil-c 5.00
81-91,93,94,0,95-99,101: 81,82-Nightwing & Starfire app. 84-Razer app. 94-Zero Hour. 0-(10/94). 95-"Terminal Velocity" begins, ends #100. 96,98,99-Kobra app. 97-Origin Max Mercury; Chillblaine app. 4.00
92-1st Impulse 1 3 4 6 8 10
100 ($2.50)-Newstand edition; Kobra & JLA app. 4.00
100 ($3.50)-Foil-c edition; Kobra & JLA app. 5.00
102-131: 102-Mongul app.; begin-$1.75-c. 105-Mirror Master app. 107-Shazam app. 108-"Dead Heat" begins; 1st app. Savitar. 109-"Dead Heat" Pt. 2 (cont'd in Impulse #10). 110-"Dead Heat" Pt. 4 (cont'd in Impulse #11). 111-"Dead Heat" finale; Savitar disappears into the Speed Force; John Fox cameo (2nd app.). 112-"Race Against Time" begins, ends #118; re-intro John Fox. 113-Tornado Twins app. 119-Final Night x-over. 127-129-Rogue's Gallery & Neron. 128,129-JLA-app.130-Morrison & Millar-s begin 3.50
132-150: 135-GL & GA app. 142-Wally almost marries Linda; Waid-s return. 144-Cobalt Blue origin. 145-Chain Lightning begins.147-Professor Zoom app. 149-Barry Allen app. 150-($2.95) Final showdown with Cobalt Blue 3.00
151-162: 151-Casey-s. 152-New Flash-c. 154-New Flash ID revealed. 159-Wally marries Linda. 162-Last Waid-s. 3.00
163-187,189-196,198,199,201-206: 163-Begin $2.25-c. 164-186-Bolland-c. 183-New Trickster. 196-Winslade-a. 201-Dose-a begins. 205-Batman-c/app. 3.00
188-($2.95) Mirror Master, Weather Wizard, Trickster app. 4.00
197-Origin of Zoom (6/03) 6.00
200-($3.50) Flash vs. Zoom; Barry Allen & Hal Jordan app.; wraparound-c 4.00
207-230: 207-211-Turner-c/Porter-a. 209-JLA app. 210-Nightwing app. 212-Origin Mirror Master. 214-216-Identity Crisis x-over. 219-Wonder Woman app. 220-Rogue War 224-Zoom & Prof. Zoom app. 225-Twins born; Barry Allen app.; last Johns-s 3.00
231-247: 231-(10/07) Waid-s/Acuña-a. 240-Grodd app.; "Dark Side Club" 3.00
#1,000,000 (11/98) 853rd Century x-over 3.00
Annual 1-7,9: 2-('87-'94,'96, 68 pgs), 3-Gives history of G.A.,S.A., & Modern Age Flash in text. 4-Armaggedon 2001. 5-Eclipso-c/story. 7-Elseworlds story. 9-Legends of the Dead Earth story; J.H. Williams-a(p); Mick Gray-a(i) 4.00
Annual 8 (1995, $3.50)-Year One story 4.00
Annual 10 (1997, $3.95)-Pulp Heroes stories 4.00
Annual 11,12 ('98, '99)-11-Ghosts; Wrightson-c. 12-JLApe; Art Adams-c 4.00
Annual 13 ('00, $3.50) Planet DC; Alcatena-c/a 4.00
...: Blitz (2004, $19.95, TPB)-r/#192-200; Kolins-c 20.00
...: Blood Will Run (2002, 2008; $17.95, TPB)-r/#170-176, Secret Files #3, Iron Heights 18.00
...: Crossfire (2004, $17.95, TPB)-r/#183-191 & parts of Flash Secret Files #3 18.00
Dead Heat (2000, $14.95, TPB)-r/#108-111, Impulse #10,11 15.00
...80-Page Giant (8/98, $4.95) Flash family stories by Waid, Millar and others; Mhan-c 5.00
...80-Page Giant 2 (4/99, $4.95) Stories of Flash family, future Kid Flash, original Teen Titans and XS 5.00
...: Emergency Stop (2008, $12.99, TPB)-r/#130-135; Morrison & Millar-s 13.00
...: Ignition (2005, $14.95, TPB)-r/#201-206 15.00
...: Iron Heights (2001, $5.95)-Van Sciver-c/a; intro. Murmur 6.00
...: Mercury Falling (2009, $14.99, TPB)-r/Impulse #62-67 15.00
...: Our Worlds at War 1 (10/01, $2.95)-Jae Lee-c; Black Racer app. 3.00
...Plus 1 (1/1997, $2.95)-Nightwing-c/app. 3.00
Race Against Time (2001, $14.95, TPB)-r/#112-118 15.00
...: Rogues (2003, $14.95, TPB)-r/#177-182 15.00
...: Rogue War (2006, $17.99, TPB)-r/#1/2,212,218,220-225; cover gallery 18.00
...Secret Files 1 (11/97, $4.95) Origin-s & pin-ups 5.00
...Secret Files 2 (11/99, $4.95) Origin of Replicant 5.00
...Secret Files 3 (11/01; $4.95) Intro. Hunter Zolomon (who later becomes Zoom) 5.00
Special 1 (1990, $2.95, 84 pgs.)-50th anniversary issue; Kubert-c; 1st Flash story by Mark Waid; 1st app. John Fox (27th Century Flash) 4.00
Terminal Velocity (1996, $12.95, TPB)-r/#95-100. 13.00
...: The Greatest Stories Ever Told (2007, $19.99, TPB) reprints; Ross-c/Waid intro. 20.00
The Return of Barry Allen (1996, $12.95, TPB)-r/#74-79 13.00
The Secret of Barry Allen (2005, $19.99, TPB)-r/#207-211,213-217; Turner sketch page 20.00
...: The Wild Wests HC (2008, $24.99, dustjacket)-r/#231-237 25.00
...: Time Flies (2002, $5.95)-Seth Fisher-c/a; Rozum-s 6.00
TV Special 1 (1991, $3.95, 76 pgs.)-Photo-c plus behind the scenes photos of TV show; Saltares-a, Byrne scripts 4.00
Wizard #1/2 (2005) prelude to Rogue Wars; Justiano-a 10.00
...: Wonderland TPB (2007, $12.99, TPB)-r/#164-169 13.00
NOTE: ***Guice*** *a-1-9p, 11p, Annual 1p; c-1-9p, Annual 1p.* ***Perez*** *c-15-17, Annual 2i.* ***Charest*** *c/a-Annual 5p.*

FLASH, THE (Brightest Day)
DC Comics: Jun, 2010 - Present ($3.99/$2.99)

1-($3.99) Barry Allen vs. the 25th Century Rogues; Johns-s/Manapul-a/c 4.00
1-Variant-c by Tony Harris 10.00
2-9-($2.99) Capt. Boomerang app. 8-Reverse Flash origin retold 3.00
2-9-Variant covers. 2-Sook. 3-Horn. 4-Kolins. 5-Sook. 6-Garza. 7-Cooke 5.00
...: Secret Files and Origins 1 (5/10, $3.99) Johns-s/Kolins-a; profiles of the Rogues 4.00
...: The Dastardly Death of the Rogues HC (2011, $19.99, dj) r/#1-7 & Secret Files 20.00

FLASH: REBIRTH
DC Comics: Jun, 2009 - No. 6, Apr, 2010 ($3.99/$2.99, limited series)

1-($3.99) Barry Allen's return; Johns-s/Van Sciver-a; Flash-c by Van Sciver 4.00
1-Variant Barry Allen-c by Van Sciver 10.00
1-Second thru fourth printings 4.00
1-Special Edition (8/10, $1.00) reprints #1 with "What's Next?" logo on cover 1.00
2-6-($2.99) 3-Max Mercury returns 3.00
2-6-Variant covers by Van Sciver 8.00
HC (2010, $19.99, dustjacket) r/#1-6; Johns original proposal; sketch art; cover gallery 20.00

FLASH: THE FASTEST MAN ALIVE (3rd Series)(See Infinite Crisis)
DC Comics: Aug, 2006 - No. 13, Aug, 2007 ($2.99)

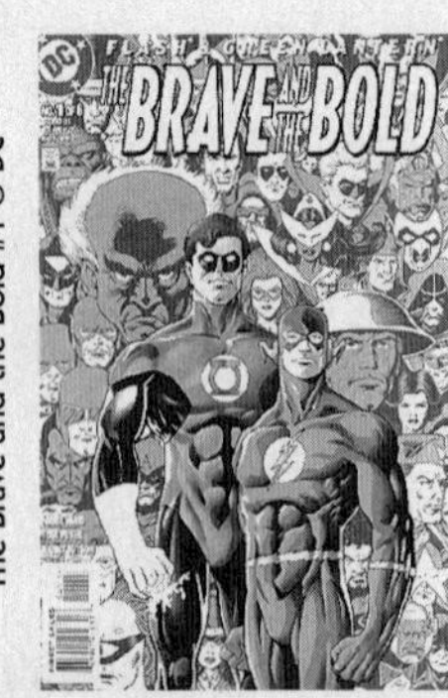

Flash and Green Lantern: The Brave and the Bold #1 © DC

Flash Comics #26 © DC

Flash Gordon (1950 series) #1 © KING

	GD 2.0	VG 4.0	FN 6.0	VF 8.0	VF/NM 9.0	NM- 9.2

1-Bart Allen becomes the Flash; Lashley-a/Bilson & Demeo-s 3.00
1-Variant-c by Joe and Andy Kubert 5.00
2-12: 5-Cyborg app. 7-Inertia returns. 10-Zoom app. 3.00
13-Bart Allen dies; 2 covers 3.00
13-DC Nation Edition from the 2007 San Diego Comic-Con 8.00
...: Full Throttle TPB (2007, $12.99) r/#7-13, All-Flash #1, DCU Infinite Holiday Spec. story 13.00
...: Lightning in a Bottle TPB (2007, $12.99) r/#1-6 13.00

FLASH, THE (See Tangent Comics/ The Flash)

FLASH AND GREEN LANTERN: THE BRAVE AND THE BOLD
DC Comics: Oct, 1999 - No. 6, Mar, 2000 ($2.50, limited series)

1-6-Waid & Peyer-s/Kitson-a. 4-Green Arrow app.; Grindberg-a(p) 3.00
TPB (2001, $12.95) r/#1-6 13.00

FLASH COMICS
DC Comics:. Dec. 1939

1-Ashcan comic, not distributed to newsstands, only for in-house use. Cover art is Adventure Comics #41 and interior from All-American Comics #8. A CGC certified 9.6 sold for $11,500 in 2004. A CGC certified 9.4 sold for $6,572.50 in 2008.

FLASH COMICS (Whiz Comics No. 2 on)
Fawcett Publications: Jan, 1940 (12 pgs., B&W, regular size)
(Not distributed to newsstands; printed for in-house use)

NOTE: ***Whiz Comics*** *#2 was preceded by two books,* ***Flash Comics*** *and* ***Thrill Comics****, both dated Jan, 1940, (12 pgs, B&W, regular size) and were not distributed. These two books are identical except for the title, and were sent out to major distributors as ad copies to promote sales. It is believed that the complete 68 page issue of Fawcett's* ***Flash*** *and* ***Thrill Comics*** *#1 was finished and ready for publication with the January date. Since DC Comics was also about to publish a book with the same date and title, Fawcett hurriedly printed up the black and white version of* ***Flash Comics*** *to secure copyright before DC. The inside covers are blank, with the covers and inside pages printed on a high quality uncoated paper stock.The eight page origin story of Captain Thunder is composed of pages 1-7 and 13 of the Captain Marvel story essentially as they appeared in the first issue of* ***Whiz Comics****. The balloon dialogue on page thirteen was relettered to tie the story into the end of page seven in* ***Flash*** *and* ***Thrill Comics*** *to produce a shorter version of the origin story for copyright purposes. Obviously, DC acquired the copyright and Fawcett dropped* ***Flash*** *as well as* ***Thrill*** *and came out with* ***Whiz Comics*** *a month later. Fawcett never used the cover to* ***Flash*** *and* ***Thrill*** *#1, designing a new cover for* ***Whiz Comics****. Fawcett also must have discovered that Captain Thunder had already been used by another publisher (Captain Terry Thunder by Fiction House). All references to Captain Thunder were relettered to Captain Marvel before appearing in* ***Whiz****.*

1 (nn on-c, #1 on inside)-Origin & 1st app. Captain Thunder. Cover by C.C. Beck. Eight copies of Flash and three copies of Thrill exist. All 3 copies of Thrill sold in 1986 for between $4,000-$10,000 each. A NM copy of Thrill sold in 1987 for $12,000. A VG copy of Thrill sold in 1987 for $9000 cash. A VF(8.0) copy of Thrill sold in 2003 for $11,400. A CGC certified 9.0 copy of the Flash Comics version sold for $10,117.50 in 2006. A CGC certified 9.4 copy of the Flash Comics version sold for $14,340 in 2008. A CGC certified 9.0 copy of the Thrill Comics version sold for $8,000 in 2006. A CGC certified 9.0 copy of the Thrill Comics version sold for $20,315 in 2008.

FLASH COMICS (The Flash No. 105 on) (Also see All-Flash)
National Periodical Publ./All-American: Jan, 1940 - No. 104, Feb, 1949

1-The Flash (origin/1st app.) by Harry Lampert, Hawkman (origin/1st app.) by Gardner Fox, The Whip, & Johnny Thunder (origin/1st app.) by Stan Asch; Cliff Cornwall by Moldoff, Flash Picture Novelets (later Minute Movies w/#12) begin; Moldoff (Shelly) cover; 1st app. Shiera Sanders who later becomes Hawkgirl, #24; reprinted in Famous First Edition (on sale 11/10/39); The Flash-c 8000 16,000 24,000 60,000 107,500 155,000
1-Reprint, Oversize 13-1/2x10". **WARNING:** This comic is an exact reprint of the original except for its size. DC published it in 1974 with a second cover titling it as a Famous First Edition. There have been many reported cases of the outer cover being removed and the interior sold as the original edition. The reprint with the new outer cover removed is practically worthless. See Famous First Edition for value.

2-Rod Rian begins, ends #11; Hawkman-c 838 1676 2514 6117 10,809 15,500
3-King Standish begins (1st app.), ends #41 (called The King #16-37,39-41); E.E. Hibbard-a begins on Flash 541 1082 1623 3950 6975 10,000
4-Moldoff (Shelly) Hawkman begins; The Whip-c 423 846 1269 3046 5323 7600
5-The King-c 354 708 1062 2478 4339 6200
6-2nd Flash-c (alternates w/Hawkman #6 on) 584 1168 1752 4263 7532 10,800
7-2nd Hawkman-c; 1st Moldoff Hawkman-c 568 1136 1704 4146 7323 10,500
8-New logo begins; classic Moldoff Flash-c 354 708 1062 2478 4339 6200
9,10: 9-Moldoff Hawkman-c; 10-Classic Moldoff Flash-c 366 732 1098 2562 4481 6400
11-13,15-20: 12-Les Watts begins; "Sparks" #16 on. 13-Has full page ad for All Star Comics #3. 17-Last Cliff Cornwall 239 478 717 1530 2615 3700
14-World War II cover 274 548 822 1740 2995 4250
21-Classic Hawkman-c 226 452 678 1446 2473 3500
22,23 200 400 600 1280 2190 3100
24-Shiera becomes Hawkgirl (12/41); see All-Star Comics #5 for 1st app. 242 484 726 1537 2644 3750
25-28,30: 28-Last Les Sparks. 135 270 405 864 1482 2100
29-Ghost Patrol begins (origin/1st app.), ends #104 139 278 417 883 1517 2150
31,33-Classic Hawkman-c. 33-Origin Shade 142 284 426 909 1555 2200
32,34-40: 36-1st app. Rag Doll 123 246 369 787 1344 1900
41-50 103 206 309 659 1130 1600
51-61: 52-1st computer in comics, c/s (4/44). 59-Last Minute Movies. 61-Last Moldoff Hawkman 90 180 270 576 988 1400
62-Hawkman by Kubert begins 116 232 348 742 1271 1800
63-85: 66-68-Hop Harrigan in all. 70-Mutt & Jeff app. 80-Atom begins, ends #104 81 162 243 518 884 1250
86-Intro. The Black Canary in Johnny Thunder (8/47); see All-Star #38. 300 600 900 1950 3375 4800
87,88,90: 87-Intro. The Foil. 88-Origin Ghost. 129 258 387 826 1413 2000
89-Intro villain The Thorn (scarce) 200 400 600 1280 2190 3100
91,93-99: 98-Atom & Hawkman don new costumes 135 270 405 864 1482 2100
92-1st solo Black Canary plus-c; rare in Mint due to black ink smearing on white-c 349 698 1047 2443 4272 6100
100 (10/48),103(Scarce)-52 pgs. each 297 594 891 1900 3250 4600
101,102(Scarce) 258 516 774 1651 2826 4000
104-Origin The Flash retold (Scarce) 676 1352 2028 4935 8718 12,500
NOTE: ***Irwin Hasen*** *a-Wheaties Giveaway. c-97, Wheaties Giveaway.* ***E.E. Hibbard*** *c-6, 12, 20, 24, 26, 28, 30, 44, 46, 48, 50, 62, 66, 68, 69, 72, 74, 76, 78, 80, 82.* ***Infantino*** *a-86p, 90, 93-95, 99-104; c-90, 92, 93, 97, 99, 101, 103.* ***Kinstler*** *a-87, 89(Hawkman); c-87.* ***Chet Kozlak*** *c-77, 79, 81.* ***Krigstein*** *a-94.* ***Kubert*** *a-62-76, 83, 85, 86, 88-104; c-63, 65, 67, 70, 71, 73, 75, 83, 85, 86, 88, 89, 91, 94, 96, 98, 100, 104.* ***Moldoff*** *a-3; c-3, 7-11, 13-17, plus odd #'s 19-61.* ***Martin Naydell*** *c-52, 54, 56, 58, 60, 64, 84.*

FLASH DIGEST, THE (See DC Special Series #24)

FLASH GORDON (See Defenders Of The Earth, Eat Right to Work..., Giant Comic Album, King Classics, King Comics, March of Comics #118, 133, 142, The Phantom #18, Street Comix & Wow Comics, 1st series)

FLASH GORDON
Dell Publishing Co.: No. 25, 1941; No. 10, 1943 - No. 512, Nov, 1953

Feature Books 25 (#1)(1941))-r-not by Raymond 129 258 387 826 1413 2000
Four Color 10(1942)-by Alex Raymond; reprints "The Ice Kingdom" 81 162 243 689 1395 2100
Four Color 84(1945)-by Alex Raymond; reprints "The Fiery Desert" 41 82 123 324 650 975
Four Color 173 18 36 54 131 266 400
Four Color 190-Bondage-c; "The Adventures of the Flying Saucers"; 5th Flying Saucer story (6/48)- see The Spirit 9/28/47(1st), Shadow Comics V7#10 (2nd, 1/48), Captain Midnight #60 (3rd, 2/48) & Boy Commandos #26 (4th, 3-4/48) 21 42 63 150 300 450
Four Color 204,247 14 28 42 99 200 300
Four Color 424-Painted-c 11 22 33 77 144 210
2(5-7/53-Dell)-Painted-c; Evans-a? 9 18 27 63 107 150
Four Color 512-Painted-c 9 18 27 63 107 150

FLASH GORDON (See Tiny Tot Funnies)
Harvey Publications: Oct, 1950 - No. 4, April, 1951

1-Alex Raymond-a; bondage-c; reprints strips from 7/14/40 to 12/8/40 39 78 117 231 378 525
2-Alex Raymond-a; r/strips 12/15/40-4/27/41 23 46 69 136 223 310
3,4-Alex Raymond-a; 3-bondage-c; r/strips 5/4/41-9/21/41. 4-r/strips 10/24/37-3/27/38 21 42 63 126 206 285
5-(Rare)-Small size-5-1/2x8-1/2"; B&W; 32 pgs.; Distributed to some mail subscribers only 77 154 231 493 847 1200
(Also see All-New No. 15, Boy Explorers No. 2, and Stuntman No. 3)

FLASH GORDON
Gold Key: June, 1965

1 (1947 reprint)-Painted-c 7 14 21 45 73 100

FLASH GORDON (Also see Comics Reading Libraries in the Promotional Comics section)
King #1-11/Charlton #12-18/Gold Key #19-23/Whitman #28 on:
9/66 - #11, 12/67; #12, 2/69 - #18, 1/70; #19, 9/78 - #37, 3/82 (Painted covers No. 19-30, 34)

1-1st S.A. app Flash Gordon; Williamson c/a(2); E.C. swipe/Incredible S.F. #32; Mandrake story 8 16 24 56 93 130
1-Army giveaway(1968)("Complimentary" on cover)(Same as regular #1 minus Mandrake story & back-c) 5 10 15 30 48 65
2-8: 2-Bolle, Gil Kane-c; Mandrake story. 3-Williamson-c. 4-Secret Agent X-9 begins, Williamson-c/a(3). 5-Williamson-c/a(2). 6,8-Crandall-a. 7-Raboy-a (last in comics?). 8-Secret Agent X-9-r 5 10 15 30 48 65
9-13: 9,10-Raymond-r. 10-Buckler's 1st pro work (11/67). 11-Crandall-a. 12-Crandall-c/a. 13-Jeff Jones-a (15 pgs.) 4 8 12 28 44 60
14,15: 15-Last 12¢ issue 3 6 9 20 30 40
16,17: 17-Brick Bradford story 3 6 9 17 25 32
18-Kaluta-a (3rd pro work?)(see Teen Confessions) 4 8 12 22 34 45
19(9/78, G.K.), 20-26 2 4 6 8 10 12
27-29,34-37: 34-37-Movie adaptation 2 4 6 8 11 14

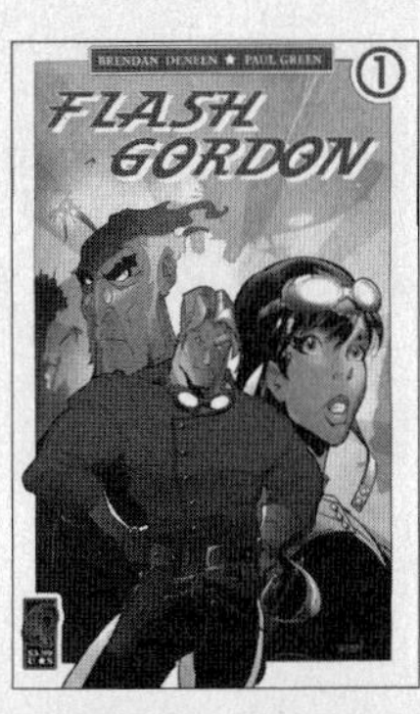

Flash Gordon (2008 series) #1 © KING

Flinch #12 © DC

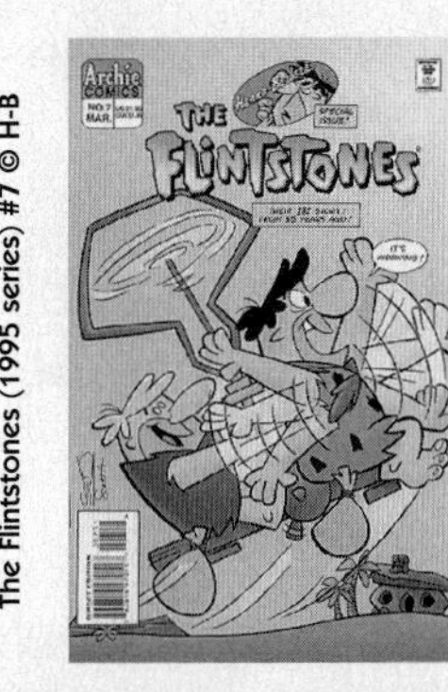

The Flintstones (1995 series) #7 © H-B

	GD 2.0	VG 4.0	FN 6.0	VF 8.0	VF/NM 9.0	NM- 9.2

30 (10/80) (scarce, from Whitman 3-pack only, 40¢-c) 3 6 9 20 30 40
30 (7/81; re-issue, 50¢-c), 31-33-single issues 2 4 6 8 11 14
31-33 (Bagged 3-pack): Movie adaptation; Williamson-a. 42.00
NOTE: *Aparo a-8. Bolle a-21, 22. Boyette a-14-18. Briggs c-10. Buckler a-10. Crandall c-6. Estrada a-3. Gene Fawcette a-29, 30, 34, 37. McWilliams a-31-33, 36.*

FLASH GORDON
DC Comics: June, 1988 - No. 9, Holiday, 1988-'89 ($1.25, mini-series)
1-9: 1,5-Painted-c 3.00

FLASH GORDON
Marvel Comics: June, 1995 - No. 2, July, 1995 ($2.95, limited series)
1,2: Schultz scripts; Williamson-a 3.00

FLASH GORDON
Ardden Entertainment: Aug, 2008 - No. 6, Jul, 2009 ($3.99)
1-6: 1-Deneen-s/Green-a; two covers 4.00

FLASH GORDON: INVASION OF THE RED SWORD
Ardden Entertainment: Jan, 2011 ($3.99)
1-Deneen-s/Garcia-a; two covers 4.00

FLASH GORDON THE MOVIE
Western Publishing Co.: 1980 (8-1/4 x 11", $1.95, 68 pgs.)
11294-Williamson-c/a; adapts movie 2 4 6 10 14 18
13743-Hardback edition 3 6 9 15 21 26

FLASH/ GREEN LANTERN: FASTER FRIENDS (See Green Lantern/Flash...)
DC Comics: No. 2, 1997 ($4.95, continuation of Green Lantern/Flash: Faster Friends #1)
2-Waid/Augustyn-s 5.00

FLASHPOINT (Elseworlds Flash)
DC Comics: Dec, 1999 - No. 3, Feb, 2000 ($2.95, limited series)
1-3-Paralyzed Barry Allen; Breyfogle-a/McGreal-s 3.00

FLAT-TOP
Mazie Comics/Harvey Publ.(Magazine Publ.) No. 4 on: 11/53 - No. 3, 5/54; No. 4, 3/55 - No. 7, 9/55
1-Teenage; Flat-Top, Mazie, Mortie & Stevie begin 9 18 27 50 65 80
2,3 6 12 18 28 34 40
4-7 5 10 15 24 30 35

FLESH & BLOOD
Brainstorm Comics: Dec, 1995 ($2.95, B&W, mature)
1-Balent-c; foil-c. 3.00

FLESH AND BONES
Upshot Graphics (Fantagraphics Books): June, 1986 - No. 4, Dec, 1986 (Limited series)
1-4: Alan Moore scripts (r) & Dalgoda by Fujitake 3.00

FLESH CRAWLERS
Kitchen Sink Press: Aug, 1993 - No. 3, 1995 ($2.50, B&W, limited series, mature)
1-3 3.00

FLEX MENTALLO (Man of Muscle Mystery) (See Doom Patrol, 2nd Series)
DC Comics (Vertigo): Jun, 1996 - No. 4, Sept, 1996 ($2.50, lim. series, mature)
1-4: Grant Morrison scripts & Frank Quitely-c/a in all; banned from reprints due to Charles Atlas legal action 2 4 6 9 13 16

FLINCH (Horror anthology)
DC Comics (Vertigo): Jun, 1999 - No. 16, Jan, 2001 ($2.50)
1-16: 1-Art by Jim Lee, Quitely, and Corben. 5-Sale-c. 11-Timm-a 3.00

FLINTSTONE KIDS, THE (TV) (See Star Comics Digest)
Star Comics/Marvel Comics #5 on: Aug, 1987 - No. 11, Apr, 1989
1-11 4.50

FLINTSTONES, THE (TV)(See Dell Giant #48 for No. 1)
Dell Publ. Co./Gold Key No. 7 (10/62) on: No. 2, Nov-Dec, 1961 - No. 60, Sept, 1970 (Hanna-Barbera)
2-2nd app. (TV show debuted on 9/30/60); 1st app. of Cave Kids; 15¢-c thru #5 10 20 30 69 122 175
3-6(7-8/62): 3-Perry Gunnite begins. 6-1st 12¢-c 7 14 21 45 73 100
7 (10/62; 1st GK) 7 14 21 45 73 100
8-10 6 12 18 37 59 80
11-1st app. Pebbles (6/63) 8 16 24 58 97 135
12-15,17-20 5 10 15 30 48 65
16-1st app. Bamm-Bamm (1/64) 8 16 24 54 90 125
21-23,25-30,33: 26,27-2nd & 3rd app. The Grusomes. 30-1st app. Martian Mopheads (10/65). 33-Meet Frankenstein & Dracula 4 8 12 28 44 60
24-1st app. The Grusomes 6 12 18 39 62 85
31,32,35-40: 31-Xmas-c. 36-Adaptation of "the Man Called Flintstone" movie. 39-Reprints 4 8 12 24 37 50
34-1st app. The Great Gazoo 6 12 18 39 62 85
41-60: 45-Last 12¢ issue 3 6 9 21 32 42
At N. Y. World's Fair ('64)-J.W. Books (25¢)-1st printing; no date on-c (29¢ version exists, 2nd print?) Most H-B characters app.; including Yogi Bear, Top Cat, Snagglepuss and the Jetsons 5 10 15 34 55 75
At N. Y. World's Fair (1965 on-c; re-issue; Warren Pub.)
NOTE: Warehouse find in 1984 2 4 6 10 14 18
Bigger & Boulder 1(#30013-211) (Gold Key Giant, 11/62, 25¢, 84 pgs.) 8 16 24 54 90 125
Bigger & Boulder 2-(1966, 25¢)-Reprints B&B No. 1 4 8 12 24 37 50
...On the Rocks (9/61, $1.00, 6-1/4x9", cardboard-c, high quality paper,116 pgs.) B&W new material 9 18 27 63 107 150
...With Pebbles & Bamm Bamm (100 pgs., G.K.)-30028-511 (paper-c, 25¢) (11/65) 7 14 21 45 73 100
NOTE: *(See Comic Album #16, Bamm-Bamm & Pebbles Flintstone, Dell Giant 48, Golden Comics Digest, March of Comics #229, 243, 271, 289, 299, 317, 327, 341, Pebbles Flintstone, Top Comics #2-4, and Whitman Comic Book.)*

FLINTSTONES, THE (TV)(...& Pebbles)
Charlton Comics: Nov, 1970 - No. 50, Feb, 1977 (Hanna-Barbera)
1 8 16 24 52 86 120
2 4 8 12 28 44 60
3-7,9,10 3 6 9 20 30 40
8- "Flintstones Summer Vacation" (Summer, 1971, 52 pgs.) 5 10 15 34 55 75
11-20,36: 36-Mike Zeck illos (early work) 3 6 9 16 23 30
21-35,38-41,43-45 3 6 9 14 19 24
37-Byrne text illos (early work; see Nightmare #20) 3 6 9 16 23 30
42-Byrne-a (2 pgs.) 3 6 9 16 23 30
46-50 2 4 6 13 18 22
Digest nn (1972, B&W, 100 pgs.) (low print run) 3 6 9 20 30 40
(Also see Barney & Betty Rubble, Dino, The Great Gazoo, & Pebbles & Bamm-Bamm)

FLINTSTONES, THE (TV)(See Yogi Bear, 3rd series) (Newsstand sales only)
Marvel Comics Group: October, 1977 - No. 9, Feb, 1979 (Hanna-Barbera)
1,7-9: 1-(30¢-c). 7-9-Yogi Bear app. 3 6 9 20 30 40
1-(35¢-c variant, limited distribution) 9 18 27 60 100 140
2,3,5,6: Yogi Bear app. 3 6 9 16 22 28
4-The Jetsons app. 3 6 9 17 25 32

FLINTSTONES, THE (TV)
Harvey Comics: Sept, 1992 - No. 13, Jun, 1994 ($1.25/$1.50) (Hanna-Barbera)
V2#1-13 4.00
...Big Book 1,2 (11/92, 3/93; both $1.95, 52 pgs.) 4.50
...Giant Size 1-3 (10/92, 4/93, 11/93; $2.25, 68 pgs.) 4.50

FLINTSTONES, THE (TV)
Archie Publications: Sept, 1995 - No. 22, June, 1997 ($1.50)
1-22 3.00

FLINTSTONES AND THE JETSONS, THE (TV)
DC Comics: Aug, 1997 - No. 21, May, 1999 ($1.75/$1.95/$1.99)
1 6.00
2-21: 19-Bizarro Elroy-c 3.00

FLINTSTONES CHRISTMAS PARTY, THE (See The Funtastic World of Hanna-Barbera No. 1)

FLIP
Harvey Publications: April, 1954 - No. 2, June, 1954 (Satire)
1,2-Nostrand-a each. 2-Powell-a 22 44 66 128 209 290

FLIPPER (TV)
Gold Key: Apr, 1966 - No. 3, Nov, 1967 (All have photo-c)
1 7 14 21 45 73 100
2,3 5 10 15 30 48 65

FLIPPITY & FLOP
National Per. Publ. (Signal Publ. Co.): 12-1/51-52 - No. 46, 8-10/59; No. 47, 9-11/60
1-Sam dog & his pets Flippity The Bird and Flop The Cat begin; Twiddle and Twaddle begin 27 54 81 162 266 370
2 15 30 45 86 133 180
3-5 14 28 42 78 112 145
6-10 11 22 33 64 90 115
11-20: 20-Last precode (3/55) 10 20 30 58 79 100
21-47 9 18 27 52 69 85

FLOATERS

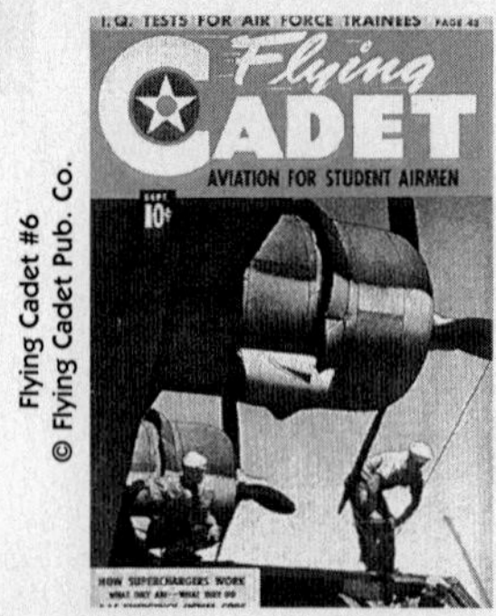

Flying Cadet #6 © Flying Cadet Pub. Co.

Foolkiller #2 © MAR

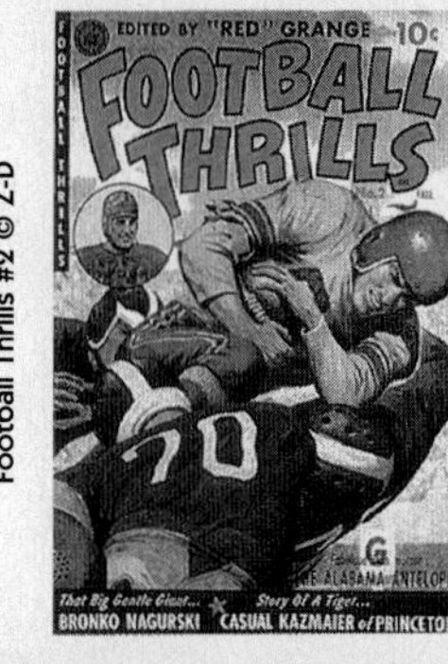

Football Thrills #2 © Z-D

GD 2.0 | VG 4.0 | FN 6.0 | VF 8.0 | VF/NM 9.0 | NM- 9.2

Dark Horse Comics: Sept, 1993 - No. 5, Jan, 1994 ($2.50, B&W, lim. series)
1-5 3.00

FLOYD FARLAND (See Eclipse Graphic Album Series #11)

FLY, THE (Also see Adventures of..., Blue Ribbon Comics & Flyman)
Archie Enterprises, Inc.: May, 1983 - No. 9, Oct, 1984
1,2: 1-Mr. Justice app; origin Shield; Kirby-a; Steranko-c. 2-Ditko-a; Flygirl app. 6.00
3-5: Ditko-a in all. 4,5-Ditko-c(p) 4.50
6-9: Ditko-a in all. 6-8-Ditko-c(p) 6.00
NOTE: ***Ayers** c-9. **Buckler** a-1, 2. **Kirby** a-1. **Nebres** c-3, 4, 5i, 6, 7i. **Steranko** c-1, 2.*

FLY, THE
Impact Comics (DC): Aug, 1991 - No. 17, Dec, 1992 ($1.00)
1 3.50
2-17: 4-Vs. The Black Hood. 9-Trading card inside 3.00
Annual 1 ('92, $2.50, 68 pgs.)-Impact trading card 4.00

FLYBOY (Flying Cadets)(Also see Approved Comics #5)
Ziff-Davis Publ. Co. (Approved): Spring, 1952 - No. 2, Oct-Nov, 1952
1-Saunders painted-c 20 40 60 114 182 250
2-(10-11/52)-Saunders painted-c 14 28 42 80 115 150

FLYING ACES (Aviation stories)
Key Publications: July, 1955 - No. 5, Mar, 1956
1 8 16 24 44 57 70
2-5: 2-Trapani-a 5 10 15 24 30 35

FLYING A'S RANGE RIDER, THE (TV)(See Western Roundup under Dell Giants)
Dell Publishing Co.: #404, 6-7/52; #2, June-Aug, 1953 - #24, Aug, 1959 (All photo-c)
Four Color 404(#1)-Titled "The Range Rider" 9 18 27 65 113 160
2 6 12 18 41 66 90
3-10 5 10 15 34 55 75
11-16,18-24 5 10 15 30 48 65
17-Toth-a 6 12 18 37 59 80

FLYING CADET (WW II Plane Photos)
Flying Cadet Publ. Co.; Jan, 1943 - V2#8, 1944 (Half photos, half comics)
V1#1-Painted-c 15 30 45 88 137 185
2-Photo-c 10 20 30 54 72 90
3-9 (Two #6's, Sept. & Oct.): 4,5,6a,6b-Photo-c 9 18 27 50 65 80
V2#1-7 (9/44)(#10-16): 1,2,4-7-Photo-c 8 16 24 44 57 70
7 (#17 on cover)-Bare-breasted woman-c 19 38 57 111 176 240

FLYING COLORS 10th ANNIVERSARY SPECIAL
Flying Colors Comics: Fall 1998 ($2.95, one-shot)
1-Dan Brereton-c; pin-ups by Jim Lee and Jeff Johnson 3.00

FLYIN' JENNY
Pentagon Publ. Co./Leader Enterprises #2: 1946 - No. 2, 1947 (1945 strip-r)
nn-Marcus Swayze strip-r (entire insides) 15 30 45 83 124 165
2-Baker-c; Swayze strip reprints 17 34 51 98 154 210

FLYING MODELS
H-K Publ. (Health-Knowledge Publs.): V61#3, May, 1954 (5¢, 16 pgs.)
V61#3 (Rare) 9 18 27 50 65 80

FLYING NUN (TV)
Dell Publishing Co.: Feb, 1968 - No. 4, Nov, 1968
1-Sally Field photo-c 7 14 21 45 73 100
2-4: 2-Sally Field photo-c 4 8 12 28 44 60

FLYING NURSES (See Sue & Sally Smith...)

FLYING SAUCERS (See The Spirit 9/28/47(1st app.), Shadow Comics V7#10 (2nd, 1/48), Captain Midnight #60 (3rd, 2/48), Boy Commandos #26 (4th, 3-4/48) & Flash Gordon Four Color 190 (5th, 6/48))

FLYING SAUCERS (See Out of This World Adventures #2)
Avon Periodicals/Realistic: 1950; 1952; 1953
1(1950)-Wood-a, 21 pgs.; Fawcette-c 84 168 252 538 919 1300
nn(1952)-Cover altered plus 2 pgs. of Wood-a not in original
46 92 138 290 488 685
nn(1953)-Reprints above (exist?) 35 70 105 208 339 470

FLYING SAUCERS (Comics)
Dell Publishing Co.: April, 1967 - No. 4, Nov, 1967; No. 5, Oct, 1969
1-(12¢-c) 4 8 12 28 44 60
2-5: 5-Has same cover as #1, but with 15¢ price 3 6 9 20 30 40

FLY MAN (Formerly Adventures of The Fly; Mighty Comics #40 on)
Mighty Comics Group (Radio Comics) (Archie): No. 32, July, 1965 - No. 39, Sept, 1966
(Also see Mighty Crusaders)
32,33-Comet, Shield, Black Hood, The Fly & Flygirl x-over. 33-Re-intro Wizard, Hangman (1st S.A. appearances) 6 12 18 39 62 85
34-39: 34-Shield begins. 35-Origin Black Hood. 36-Hangman x-over in Shield; re-intro. & origin of Web (1st S.A. app.). 37-Hangman, Wizard x-over in Flyman; last Shield issue. 38-Web story. 39-Steel Sterling (1st S.A. app.) 4 8 12 28 44 60

FOLLOW THE SUN (TV)
Dell Publishing Co.: May-July, 1962 - No. 2, Sept-Nov, 1962 (Photo-c)
01-280-207(No.1) 5 10 15 32 51 70
12-280-211(No.2) 4 8 12 28 44 60

FOODANG
Continum Comics: July, 1994 ($1.95, B&W, bi-monthly)
1 3.00

FOODINI (TV)(The Great...; see Jingle Dingle & Pinhead &...)
Continental Publ. (Holyoke): March, 1950 - No. 4, Aug, 1950 (All have 52 pgs.)
1-Based on TV puppet show (very early TV comic) 22 44 66 128 209 290
2-Jingle Dingle begins 14 28 42 78 112 145
3,4 10 20 30 56 76 95

FOOEY (Magazine) (Satire)
Scoff Publishing Co.: Feb, 1961 - No. 4, May, 1961
1 5 10 15 30 48 65
2-4 3 6 9 20 30 40

FOOFUR (TV)
Marvel Comics (Star Comics)/Marvel No. 5 on: Aug, 1987 - No. 6, Jun, 1988
1-6 3.00

FOOLKILLER (Also see The Amazing Spider-Man #225, The Defenders #73, Man-Thing #3 & Omega the Unknown #8)
Marvel Comics: Oct, 1990 - No. 10, Oct, 1991 ($1.75, limited series)
1-10: 1-Origin 3rd Foolkiller; Greg Salinger app; DeZuniga-a(i) in 1-4. 8-Spider-Man x-over 3.00

FOOLKILLER
Marvel Comics: Dec, 2007 - No. 5, Jul, 2008 ($3.99, limited series)
1-5-Hurwitz-s/Medina-a. 2-Origin 4.00

FOOLKILLER: WHITE ANGELS
Marvel Comics: Sept, 2008 - No. 5, Jan, 2009 ($3.99, limited series)
1-5-Hurwitz-s/Azaceta-a 4.00

FOOM (Friends Of Ol' Marvel)
Marvel Comics: 1973 - No. 22, 1979 (Marvel fan magazine)
1 8 16 24 56 93 130
2-Hulk-c by Steranko 6 12 18 37 59 80
3,4 5 10 15 35 55 75
5-11: 11-Kirby-a and interview 5 10 15 30 48 65
12-15: 12-Vision-c. 13-Daredevil-c. 14-Conan. 15-Howard the Duck
5 10 15 30 48 65
16-20: 16-Marvel bullpen. 17-Stan Lee issue. 19-Defenders
4 8 12 26 41 55
21-Star Wars 4 8 12 28 44 60
22-Spider-Man-c; low print run final issue 6 12 18 41 66 90

FOOTBALL THRILLS (See Tops In Adventure)
Ziff-Davis Publ. Co.: Fall-Winter, 1951-52 - No. 2, Fall, 1952 (Edited by "Red" Grange)
1-Powell a(2); Saunders painted-c; Red Grange, Jim Thorpe stories
27 54 81 158 259 360
2-Saunders painted-c 18 36 54 105 165 225

FOOT SOLDIERS, THE
Dark Horse Comics: Jan, 1996 - No. 4, Apr, 1996 ($2.95, limited series)
1-4: Krueger story & Avon Oeming-a. in all. 1-Alex Ross-c. 4-John K. Snyder, III-c 3.00

FOOT SOLDIERS, THE (Volume Two)
Image Comics: Sept, 1997 - No. 5, May, 1998 ($2.95, limited series)
1-5: 1-Yeowell-a. 2-McDaniel, Hester, Sienkiewicz, Giffen-a 3.00

FOR A NIGHT OF LOVE
Avon Periodicals: 1951
nn-Two stories adapted from the works of Emile Zola; Astarita, Ravielli-a; Kinstler-c
31 62 93 186 303 420

FORBIDDEN KNOWLEDGE: ADVENTURE BEYOND THE DOORWAY TO SOULS WITH RADICAL DREAMER (Also see Radical Dreamer)
Mark's Giant Economy Size Comics: 1996 ($3.50, B&W, one-shot, 48 pgs.)

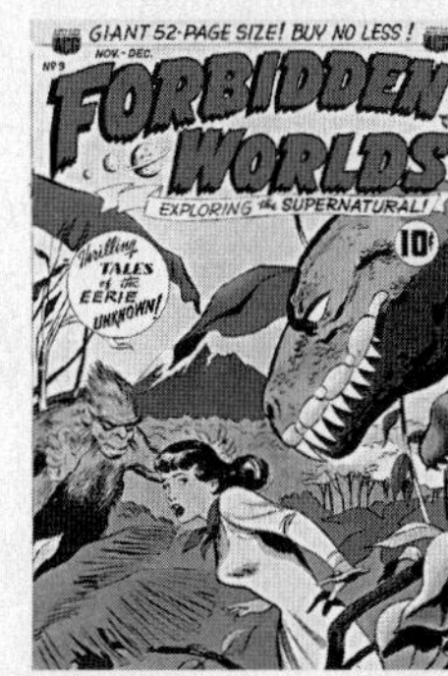

Forbidden Worlds #3 © ACG

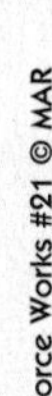
Force Works #21 © MAR

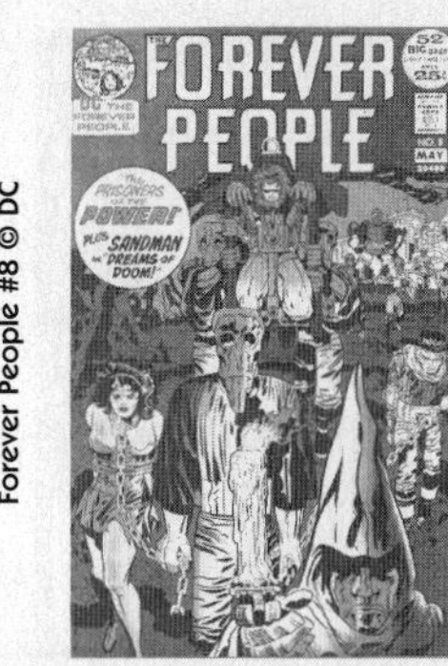

Forever People #8 © DC

	GD 2.0	VG 4.0	FN 6.0	VF 8.0	VF/NM 9.0	NM- 9.2
nn-Max Wrighter app.; Wheatley-c/a/script; painted infinity-c						4.00

FORBIDDEN LOVE
Quality Comics Group: Mar, 1950 - No. 4, Sept, 1950 (52 pgs.)

	GD 2.0	VG 4.0	FN 6.0	VF 8.0	VF/NM 9.0	NM- 9.2
1-(Scarce)-Classic photo-c; Crandall-a	77	154	231	493	847	1200
2-(Scarce)-Classic photo-c	65	130	195	416	708	1000
3-(Scarce)-Photo-c	41	82	123	251	418	585
4-(Scarce)-Ward/Cuidera-a; photo-c	41	82	123	256	428	600

FORBIDDEN LOVE (See Dark Mansion of...)

FORBIDDEN PLANET
Innovation Publishing: May, 1992 - No. 4, 1992 ($2.50, limited series)

	GD 2.0	VG 4.0	FN 6.0	VF 8.0	VF/NM 9.0	NM- 9.2
1-4: Adapts movie; painted-c						3.00

FORBIDDEN TALES OF DARK MANSION (Formerly Dark Mansion of Forbidden Love #1-4)
National Periodical Publ.: No. 5, May-June, 1972 - No. 15, Feb-Mar, 1974

	GD 2.0	VG 4.0	FN 6.0	VF 8.0	VF/NM 9.0	NM- 9.2
5-(52 pgs.)	6	12	18	39	62	85
6-15: 13-Kane/Howard-a	3	6	9	18	27	35

NOTE: ***N. Adams*** *c-9.* ***Alcala*** *a-9-11, 13.* ***Chaykin*** *a-7,15.* ***Evans*** *a-14.* ***Heck*** *a-5.* ***Kaluta*** *a-7i, 8-12; c-7, 8, 13.* ***G. Kane*** *a-13.* ***Kirby*** *a-6.* ***Nino*** *a-8, 12, 15.* ***Redondo*** *a-14.*

FORBIDDEN WORLDS
American Comics Group: 7-8/51 - No. 34, 10-11/54; No. 35, 8/55 - No. 145, 8/67 (No. 1-5: 52 pgs.; No. 6-8: 44 pgs.)

	GD 2.0	VG 4.0	FN 6.0	VF 8.0	VF/NM 9.0	NM- 9.2
1-Williamson/Frazetta-a (10 pgs.)	161	322	483	1030	1765	2500
2	66	132	198	419	722	1025
3-Williamson/Orlando-a (7 pgs.); Wood (2 panels); Frazetta (1 panel)	67	134	201	426	733	1040
4	43	86	129	271	461	650
5-Krenkel/Williamson-a (8 pgs.)	53	106	159	334	567	800
6-Harrison/Williamson-a (8 pgs.)	47	94	141	296	498	700
7,8,10: 7-1st monthly issue	32	64	96	192	314	435
9-A-Bomb explosion story	36	72	108	214	347	480
11-20	22	44	66	128	209	290
21-33: 24-E.C. swipe by Landau	18	36	54	105	165	225
34(10-11/54)(Scarce)(becomes Young Heroes #35 on)-Last pre-code issue; A-Bomb explosion story	20	40	60	115	185	255
35(8/55)-Scarce	19	38	57	112	179	245
36-62	13	26	39	74	105	135
63,69,76,78-Williamson-a in all; w/Krenkel #69	14	28	42	76	108	140
64,66-68,70-72,74,75,77,79-85,87-90	10	20	30	56	76	95
65- "There's a New Moon Tonight" listed in #114 as holding 1st record fan mail response	14	28	42	76	108	140
73-1st app. Herbie by Ogden Whitney	42	84	126	265	445	625
86-Flying saucer-c by Schaffenberger	11	22	33	62	86	110
91-93,95-100	5	10	15	34	55	75
94-Herbie (2nd app.)	11	22	33	75	138	200
101-109,111-113,115,117-120	4	8	12	28	44	60
110,116-Herbie app. 116-Herbie goes to Hell	8	16	24	52	86	120
114-1st Herbie-c; contains list of editor's top 20 ACG stories	9	18	27	65	113	160
121-123	4	8	12	22	34	45
124,127-130: 124-Magic Agent app.	4	8	12	24	37	50
125-Magic Agent app.; intro. & origin Magicman series, ends #141; Herbie app.	5	10	15	34	55	75
126-Herbie app.	4	8	12	28	44	60
131-139: 133-Origin/1st app. Dragonia in Magicman (1-2/66); returns in #138. 136-Nemesis x-over in Magicman	4	8	12	22	34	45
140-Mark Midnight app. by Ditko	4	8	12	24	37	50
141-145	3	6	9	20	30	40

NOTE: ***Buscema*** *a-75, 79, 81, 82, 140r.* ***Cameron*** *a-5.* ***Disbrow*** *a-10.* ***Ditko*** *a-137p, 138, 140.* ***Landau*** *a-24, 27-29, 31-34, 48, 86r, 96, 143-45.* ***Lazarus*** *a-18, 23, 24, 57.* ***Moldoff*** *a-27, 31, 139r.* ***Reinman*** *a-93.* ***Whitney*** *a-70, 115, 116, 137; c-40, 46, 57, 60, 68, 70, 78, 79, 90, 93, 94, 100, 102, 103, 106-108, 114, 129.*

FORCE, THE (See The Crusaders)

FORCE MAJEURE: PRAIRIE BAY (Also see Wild Stars)
Little Rocket Publications: May, 2002 ($2.95, B&W)

	GD 2.0	VG 4.0	FN 6.0	VF 8.0	VF/NM 9.0	NM- 9.2
1-Tierney-s/Gil-c/a						3.00

FORCE OF BUDDHA'S PALM THE
Jademan Comics: Aug, 1988 - No. 55, Feb, 1993 ($1.50/$1.95, 68 pgs.)

	GD 2.0	VG 4.0	FN 6.0	VF 8.0	VF/NM 9.0	NM- 9.2
1,55-Kung Fu stories in all						5.00
2-54						4.00

FORCE WORKS
Marvel Comics: July, 1994 - No. 22, Apr, 1996 ($1.50)

	GD 2.0	VG 4.0	FN 6.0	VF 8.0	VF/NM 9.0	NM- 9.2
1-($3.95)-Fold-out pop-up-c; Iron Man, Wonder Man, Spider-Woman, U.S. Agent & Scarlet Witch (new costume)						4.00
2-11, 13-22: 5-Blue logo & pink logo versions. 9-Intro Dreamguard. 13-Avengers app.						3.00
5-Pink logo ($2.95)-polybagged w/ 16pg. Marvel Action Hour Preview & acetate print						4.00
12 ($2.50)-Flip book w/War Machine.						4.00

FORD ROTUNDA CHRISTMAS BOOK (See Christmas at the Rotunda)

FOREIGN INTRIGUES (Formerly Johnny Dynamite; becomes Battlefield Action #16 on)
Charlton Comics: No. 14, 1956 - No. 15, Aug, 1956

	GD 2.0	VG 4.0	FN 6.0	VF 8.0	VF/NM 9.0	NM- 9.2
14,15-Johnny Dynamite continues	8	16	24	44	57	70

FOREMOST BOYS (See 4Most)

FOREVER AMBER
Image Comics: July, 1999 - Oct, 1999 ($2.95, B&W)

	GD 2.0	VG 4.0	FN 6.0	VF 8.0	VF/NM 9.0	NM- 9.2
1-4-Don Hudson-s/a						3.00

FOREVER DARLING (Movie)
Dell Publishing Co.: No. 681, Feb, 1956

	GD 2.0	VG 4.0	FN 6.0	VF 8.0	VF/NM 9.0	NM- 9.2
Four Color 681-w/Lucille Ball & Desi Arnaz; photo-c	11	22	33	77	144	210

FOREVER MAELSTROM
DC Comics: Jan, 2003 - No. 6, Jun, 2003 ($2.95, limited series)

	GD 2.0	VG 4.0	FN 6.0	VF 8.0	VF/NM 9.0	NM- 9.2
1-6-Chaykin & Tischman-s/Lucas & Barreto-a						3.00

FOREVER PEOPLE, THE
National Periodical Publications: Feb-Mar, 1971 - No. 11, Oct-Nov, 1972 (Fourth World) (#1-3, 10-11 are 36 pgs; #4-9 are 52 pgs.)

	GD 2.0	VG 4.0	FN 6.0	VF 8.0	VF/NM 9.0	NM- 9.2
1-1st app. Forever People; Superman x-over; Kirby-c/a begins; 1st full app. Darkseid (3rd anywhere, 3 weeks before New Gods #1); Darkseid storyline begins, ends #8 (app. in 1-4,6,8; cameos in 5,11)	7	14	21	49	80	110
2-9: 4-G.A. reprints thru #9. 9,10-Deadman app.	4	8	12	26	41	55
10,11	3	6	9	20	30	40
Jack Kirby's Forever People TPB ('99, $14.95, B&W&Grey) r/#1-11 plus cover gallery						15.00

NOTE: ***Kirby*** *c/a(p)-1-11; #4-9 contain Sandman reprints from Adventure #85, 84, 75, 80, 77, 74 in that order.*

FOREVER PEOPLE
DC Comics: Feb, 1988 - No. 6, July, 1988 ($1.25, limited series)

	GD 2.0	VG 4.0	FN 6.0	VF 8.0	VF/NM 9.0	NM- 9.2
1-6						3.00

FORGE
CrossGeneration Comics: Feb, 2002 - No. 13, May, 2003 ($9.95/$11.95/$7.95, TPB)

	GD 2.0	VG 4.0	FN 6.0	VF 8.0	VF/NM 9.0	NM- 9.2
1-3: Reprints from various CrossGen titles						10.00
4-8-($11.95)						12.00
9-13-($7.95, 8-1/4" x 5-1/2") digest-sized reprints						8.00

FOR GIRLS ONLY
Bernard Baily Enterprises: 11/53 - No. 2, 6/54 (100 pgs., digest size, 25¢)

	GD 2.0	VG 4.0	FN 6.0	VF 8.0	VF/NM 9.0	NM- 9.2
1-25% comic book, 75% articles, illos, games	16	32	48	94	147	200
2-Eddie Fisher photo & story.	12	24	36	69	97	125

FORGOTTEN FOREST OF OZ, THE (See First Comics Graphic Novel #16)

FORGOTTEN REALMS (Also see Avatar & TSR Worlds)
DC Comics: Sept, 1989 - No. 25, Sept, 1991 ($1.50/$1.75)

	GD 2.0	VG 4.0	FN 6.0	VF 8.0	VF/NM 9.0	NM- 9.2
1, Annual 1 (1990, $2.95, 68 pgs.)						4.00
2-25: Based on TSR role-playing game. 18-Avatar story						3.00

FORGOTTEN REALMS (Based on Wizards of the Coast game)
Devil's Due Publ.: June, 2005 - No. 3, Aug, 2005 ($4.95)

	GD 2.0	VG 4.0	FN 6.0	VF 8.0	VF/NM 9.0	NM- 9.2
1-3-Salvatore-s/Seeley-a						5.00
...Exile (11/05 - No. 3, 1/06, $4.95) 1-3-Daab-s/Seeley-a. 1-Flip cover						5.00
...: Legacy (2/08 - No. 3, 6/08, $5.50) 1-3-Daab-s/Atkins-a						5.50
The Legend of Drizzt Book II: Exile (2006, $14.95, TPB) r/#1-3						15.00
...Sojourn (3/06 - No. 3, 6/06, $4.95) 1-3-Daab-s/Seeley-a						5.00
...: Streams of Silver (12/06 - No. 3, $5.50) 1-3-Daab-s/Semeiks-a						5.50
...The Crystal Shard (8/06 - No. 3, 12/06, $4.95) 1-3-Daab-s/Semeiks-a						5.00
...The Halfling's Gem (8/07 - No. 3, 12/07, $5.50) 1-3-Daab-s/Seeley-a; two covers						5.50

FORLORN RIVER (See Zane Grey Four Color 395)

FOR LOVERS ONLY (Formerly Hollywood Romances)
Charlton Comics: No. 60, Aug, 1971 - No. 87, Nov, 1976

	GD 2.0	VG 4.0	FN 6.0	VF 8.0	VF/NM 9.0	NM- 9.2
60	3	6	9	20	30	40
61-80,82-87: 67-Morisi-a	2	4	6	11	16	20
81-Psychedelic cover	3	6	9	16	23	30

FORMERLY KNOWN AS THE JUSTICE LEAGUE
DC Comics: Sept, 2003 - No. 6, Feb, 2004 ($2.50, limited series)

1-Giffen & DeMatteis-s/Maguire-a; Booster Gold, Blue Beetle, Captain Atom, Mary Marvel,

Formic Wars: Burning Earth #1 © MAR

Four Color Comics Series 1 #2 © DELL

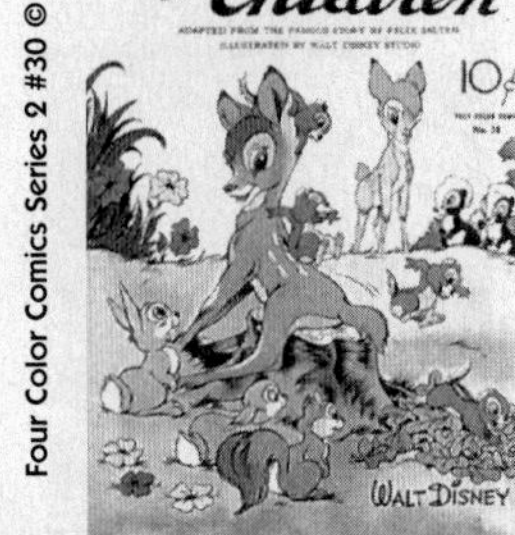

Four Color Comics Series 2 #30 © DIS

GD 2.0 | VG 4.0 | FN 6.0 | VF 8.0 | VF/NM 9.0 | NM- 9.2

Fire, and Elongated Man app. 3.50
2-6: 3,4-Roulette app. 6-JLA app. 3.00
TPB (2004, $12.95) r/#1-6 13.00

FORMIC WARS: BURNING EARTH
Marvel Comics: Apr, 2011 - No. 5 ($3.99, limited series)

1-4-Prequel to Orson Scott Card's novel Ender's Game. 1-Covers by Larroca & Hitch 4.00

FORT: PROPHET OF THE UNEXPLAINED
Dark Horse Comics: June, 2002 - No. 4, Sept, 2002 ($2.99, B&W, limited series)

1-4-Peter Lenkov-s/Frazer Irving-c/a 3.00
TPB (2003, $9.95) r/#1-4 10.00

FORTUNE AND GLORY
Oni Press: Dec, 1999 - No. 3, Apr, 2000 ($4.95, B&W, limited series)

1-3-Brian Michael Bendis in Hollywood 5.00
TPB ($14.95) 15.00

40 BIG PAGES OF MICKEY MOUSE
Whitman Publ. Co.: No. 945, Jan, 1936 (10-1/4x12-1/2", 44 pgs., cardboard-c)

945-Reprints Mickey Mouse Magazine #1, but with a different cover; ads were eliminated and some illustrated stories had expanded text. The book is 3/4" shorter than Mickey Mouse Mag. #1, but the reprints are same size (Rare) 164 328 492 1025 1663 2300

40 oz. COLLECTED
Image Comics: Nov, 2003 ($9.95, digest-size, B&W)

Vol. 1-Reprints Jim Mahfood's mini-comics plus 20 pgs. new material; Grrl Scouts app. 10.00

FOR YOUR EYES ONLY (See James Bond...)

FOUNTAIN, THE (Companion graphic novel to the Darren Aronofsky film)
DC Comics (Vertigo): 2005 ($39.99, hardcover with dust jacket)

1-Darren Aronofsky-s/Kent Williams-a 40.00

FOUR (Fantastic Four; See Marvel Knights 4 #28-30)

FOUR COLOR
Dell Publishing Co.: Sept?, 1939 - No. 1354, Apr-June, 1962
(Series I are all 68 pgs.)

NOTE: *Four Color only appears on issues #19-25, 1-99,101. Dell Publishing Co. filed these as Series I, #1-25, and Series II, #1-1354. Issues beginning with #710? were printed with and without ads on back cover. Issues without ads are worth more.*

SERIES I:
1(nn)-Dick Tracy 1000 2000 3000 7400 13,200 19,000
2(nn)-Don Winslow of the Navy (#1) (Rare) (11/39?)
194 388 582 1242 2121 3000
3(nn)-Myra North (1/40) 95 190 285 603 1039 1475
4-Donald Duck by Al Taliaferro (1940)(Disney)(3/40?)
1600 3200 4800 12,000 18,500 25,000
(Prices vary widely on this book)
5-Smilin' Jack (#1) (5/40?) 71 142 213 454 777 1100
6-Dick Tracy (Scarce) 219 438 657 1402 2401 3400
7-Gang Busters 50 100 150 315 533 750
8-Dick Tracy 110 220 330 704 1202 1700
9-Terry and the Pirates-r/Super #9-29 67 134 201 426 731 1035
10-Smilin' Jack 61 122 183 387 664 940
11-Smitty (#1) 45 90 135 284 480 675
12-Little Orphan Annie; reprints strips from 12/19/37 to 6/4/38
57 114 171 362 624 885
13-Walt Disney's Reluctant Dragon('41)-Contains 2 pgs. of photos from film; 2 pg. foreword to Fantasia by Leopold Stokowski; Donald Duck, Goofy, Baby Weems & Mickey Mouse (as the Sorcerer's Apprentice) app. (Disney) 219 438 657 1402 2401 3400
14-Moon Mullins (#1) 45 90 135 284 480 675
15-Tillie the Toiler (#1) 45 90 135 284 480 675
16-Mickey Mouse (#1) (Disney) by Gottfredson 1250 2500 3750 16,000 - -
17-Walt Disney's Dumbo, the Flying Elephant (#1)(1941)-Mickey Mouse, Donald Duck, & Pluto app. (Disney) 265 530 795 1694 2897 4100
18-Jiggs and Maggie (#1)(1936-38-r) 48 96 144 300 510 720
19-Barney Google and Snuffy Smith (#1)-(1st issue with Four Color on the cover)
47 94 141 296 498 700
20-Tiny Tim 37 74 111 218 354 490
21-Dick Tracy 81 162 243 518 884 1250
22-Don Winslow 47 94 141 296 498 700
23-Gang Busters 40 80 120 246 411 575
24-Captain Easy 50 100 150 315 533 750
25-Popeye (1942) 86 172 258 546 936 1325

SERIES II:

GD 2.0 | VG 4.0 | FN 6.0 | VF 8.0 | VF/NM 9.0 | NM- 9.2

1-Little Joe (1942) 50 100 150 425 863 1300
2-Harold Teen 28 56 84 204 415 625
3-Alley Oop (#1) 41 82 123 328 664 1000
4-Smilin' Jack 36 72 108 281 553 825
5-Raggedy Ann and Andy (#1) 44 88 132 352 714 1075
6-Smitty 20 40 60 142 286 430
7-Smokey Stover (#1) 26 52 78 186 373 560
8-Tillie the Toiler 22 44 66 155 310 465
9-Donald Duck Finds Pirate Gold, by Carl Barks & Jack Hannah (Disney) (© 8/17/42)
1000 2000 3000 7600 13,800 20,000
10-Flash Gordon by Alex Raymond; reprinted from "The Ice Kingdom"
81 162 243 689 1395 2100
11-Wash Tubbs 25 50 75 183 367 550
12-Walt Disney's Bambi (#1) 48 96 144 384 780 1175
13-Mr. District Attorney (#1)-See The Funnies #35 for 1st app.
26 52 78 186 373 560
14-Smilin' Jack 28 56 84 204 415 625
15-Felix the Cat (#1) 73 146 219 621 1261 1900
16-Porky Pig (#1)(1942)- "Secret of the Haunted House"
81 162 243 689 1395 2100
17-Popeye 41 82 123 324 650 975
18-Little Orphan Annie's Junior Commandos; Flag-c; reprints strips from 6/14/42 to 11/21/42 32 64 96 248 492 735
19-Walt Disney's Thumper Meets the Seven Dwarfs (Disney); reprinted in Silly Symphonies
43 86 129 344 697 1050
20-Barney Baxter 24 48 72 175 350 525
21-Oswald the Rabbit (#1)(1943) 40 80 120 320 643 965
22-Tillie the Toiler 16 32 48 111 226 340
23-Raggedy Ann and Andy 33 66 99 254 502 750
24-Gang Busters 26 52 78 186 373 560
25-Andy Panda (#1) (Walter Lantz) 48 96 144 392 796 1200
26-Popeye 41 82 123 324 650 975
27-Walt Disney's Mickey Mouse and the Seven Colored Terror
75 150 225 638 1294 1950
28-Wash Tubbs 17 34 51 118 242 365
29-Donald Duck and the Mummy's Ring, by Carl Barks (Disney) (9/43)
757 1514 2271 5526 9763 14,000
30-Bambi's Children (1943)-Disney 42 84 126 336 681 1025
31-Moon Mullins 16 32 48 111 226 340
32-Smitty 14 28 42 97 194 290
33-Bugs Bunny "Public Nuisance #1" 96 192 288 816 1658 2500
34-Dick Tracy 38 76 114 304 602 900
35-Smokey Stover 15 30 45 104 212 320
36-Smilin' Jack 21 42 63 148 297 445
37-Bringing Up Father 18 36 54 125 255 385
38-Roy Rogers (#1, © 4/44)-1st western comic with photo-c (see Movie Comics #3) 148 296 444 1295 2648 4000
39-Oswald the Rabbit (1944) 27 54 81 197 399 600
40-Barney Google and Snuffy Smith 20 40 60 140 283 425
41-Mother Goose and Nursery Rhyme Comics (#1)-All by Walt Kelly
21 42 63 150 300 450
42-Tiny Tim (1934-r) 15 30 45 103 209 315
43-Popeye (1938-'42-r) 28 56 84 204 415 625
44-Terry and the Pirates (1938-r) 32 64 96 250 495 740
45-Raggedy Ann 27 54 81 197 399 600
46-Felix the Cat and the Haunted Castle 38 76 114 304 602 900
47-Gene Autry (copyright 6/16/44) 33 66 99 254 477 700
48-Porky Pig of the Mounties by Carl Barks (7/44) 87 174 267 740 1495 2250
49-Snow White and the Seven Dwarfs (Disney) 47 94 141 376 763 1150
50-Fairy Tale Parade-Walt Kelly art (1944) 23 46 69 168 334 500
51-Bugs Bunny Finds the Lost Treasure 33 66 99 254 502 750
52-Little Orphan Annie; reprints strips from 6/18/38 to 11/19/38
24 48 72 175 355 535
53-Wash Tubbs 13 26 39 91 176 260
54-Andy Panda 27 54 81 197 399 600
55-Tillie the Toiler 12 24 36 88 167 245
56-Dick Tracy 35 70 105 273 537 800
57-Gene Autry 31 62 93 239 445 650
58-Smilin' Jack 21 42 63 148 297 445
59-Mother Goose and Nursery Rhyme Comics-Kelly-c/a
17 34 51 118 242 365
60-Tiny Folks Funnies 14 28 42 97 194 290
61-Santa Claus Funnies(11/44)-Kelly art 22 44 66 155 310 465
62-Donald Duck in Frozen Gold, by Carl Barks (Disney) (1/45)

Four Color Comics #126 © DELL

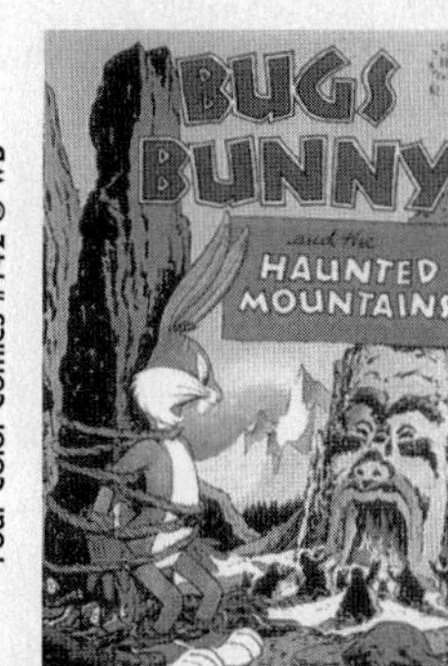

Four Color Comics #142 © WB

Four Color Comics #161 © ERB

	GD 2.0	VG 4.0	FN 6.0	VF 8.0	VF/NM 9.0	NM- 9.2
	212	424	636	1855	3778	5700
63-Roy Rogers; color photo-all 4 covers	37	74	111	286	568	850
64-Smokey Stover	12	24	36	87	164	240
65-Smitty	12	24	36	84	157	230
66-Gene Autry	31	62	93	239	445	650
67-Oswald the Rabbit	16	32	48	111	226	340
68-Mother Goose and Nursery Rhyme Comics, by Walt Kelly	17	34	51	118	242	365
69-Fairy Tale Parade, by Walt Kelly	23	46	69	168	334	500
70-Popeye and Wimpy	21	42	63	150	300	450
71-Walt Disney's Three Caballeros, by Walt Kelly (© 4/45)-(Disney)	60	120	180	510	1030	1550
72-Raggedy Ann	22	44	66	162	324	485
73-The Gumps (#1)	11	22	33	80	150	220
74-Marge's Little Lulu (#1)	127	254	381	1080	2190	3300
75-Gene Autry and the Wildcat	25	50	75	185	343	500
76-Little Orphan Annie; reprints strips from 2/28/40 to 6/24/40	20	40	60	142	286	430
77-Felix the Cat	37	74	111	284	562	840
78-Porky Pig and the Bandit Twins	25	50	75	183	367	550
79-Walt Disney's Mickey Mouse in The Riddle of the Red Hat by Carl Barks (8/45)	90	180	270	765	1558	2350
80-Smilin' Jack	13	26	39	94	185	275
81-Moon Mullins	10	20	30	71	128	185
82-Lone Ranger	37	74	111	286	568	850
83-Gene Autry in Outlaw Trail	25	50	75	185	343	500
84-Flash Gordon by Alex Raymond-Reprints from "The Fiery Desert"	41	82	123	324	650	975
85-Andy Panda and the Mad Dog Mystery	15	30	45	106	216	325
86-Roy Rogers; photo-c	27	54	81	197	391	585
87-Fairy Tale Parade by Walt Kelly; Dan Noonan-c	23	46	69	168	334	500
88-Bugs Bunny's Great Adventure (Sci/fi)	22	44	66	159	317	475
89-Tillie the Toiler	12	24	36	88	167	245
90-Christmas with Mother Goose by Walt Kelly (11/45)	16	32	48	111	226	340
91-Santa Claus Funnies by Walt Kelly (11/45)	16	32	48	111	226	340
92-Walt Disney's The Wonderful Adventures Of Pinocchio (1945); Donald Duck by Kelly, 16 pgs. (Disney)	47	94	141	376	763	1150
93-Gene Autry in The Bandit of Black Rock	22	44	66	157	291	425
94-Winnie Winkle (1945)	12	24	36	82	154	225
95-Roy Rogers Comics; photo-c	27	54	81	197	391	585
96-Dick Tracy	23	46	69	168	334	500
97-Marge's Little Lulu (1946)	52	104	156	442	896	1350
98-Lone Ranger, The	27	54	81	197	399	600
99-Smitty	10	20	30	71	128	185
100-Gene Autry Comics; 1st Gene Autry photo-c	24	48	72	181	336	490
101-Terry and the Pirates	20	40	60	144	290	435

NOTE: No. 101 is last issue to carry "Four Color" logo on cover; all issues beginning with No. 100 are marked "...O. S." (One Shot) which can be found in the bottom left-hand panel on the first page; the numbers following "O. S." relate to the year/month issued.

	GD 2.0	VG 4.0	FN 6.0	VF 8.0	VF/NM 9.0	NM- 9.2
102-Oswald the Rabbit-Walt Kelly art, 1 pg.	13	26	39	94	185	275
103-Easter with Mother Goose by Walt Kelly	16	32	48	111	226	340
104-Fairy Tale Parade by Walt Kelly	18	36	54	125	255	385
105-Albert the Alligator and Pogo Possum (#1) by Kelly (4/46)	48	96	144	408	829	1250
106-Tillie the Toiler (5/46)	10	20	30	68	119	170
107-Little Orphan Annie; reprints strips from 11/16/42 to 3/24/43	17	34	51	120	245	370
108-Donald Duck in The Terror of the River, by Carl Barks (Disney) (© 4/16/46)	148	296	444	1295	2648	4000
109-Roy Rogers Comics; photo-c	20	40	60	146	293	440
110-Marge's Little Lulu	37	74	111	286	568	850
111-Captain Easy	13	26	39	89	170	250
112-Porky Pig's Adventure in Gopher Gulch	15	30	45	106	216	325
113-Popeye; all new Popeye stories begin	13	26	39	92	179	265
114-Fairy Tale Parade by Walt Kelly	18	36	54	125	255	385
115-Marge's Little Lulu	36	72	108	281	553	825
116-Mickey Mouse and the House of Many Mysteries (Disney)	25	50	75	183	367	550
117-Roy Rogers Comics; photo-c	16	32	48	114	232	350
118-Lone Ranger, The	27	54	81	197	399	600
119-Felix the Cat; all new Felix stories begin	31	62	93	242	476	710
120-Marge's Little Lulu	30	60	90	228	457	685
121-Fairy Tale Parade-(not Kelly)	12	24	36	82	154	225

	GD 2.0	VG 4.0	FN 6.0	VF 8.0	VF/NM 9.0	NM- 9.2
122-Henry (#1) (10/46)	13	26	39	94	185	275
123-Bugs Bunny's Dangerous Venture	15	30	45	104	212	320
124-Roy Rogers Comics; photo-c	16	32	48	114	232	350
125-Lone Ranger, The	18	36	54	131	266	400
126-Christmas with Mother Goose by Walt Kelly (1946)	13	26	39	89	170	250
127-Popeye	13	26	39	92	179	265
128-Santa Claus Funnies- "Santa & the Angel" by Gollub; "A Mouse in the House" by Kelly	13	26	39	94	185	275
129-Walt Disney's Uncle Remus and His Tales of Brer Rabbit (#1) (1946)-Adapted from Disney movie "Song of the South"	24	48	72	175	350	525
130-Andy Panda (Walter Lantz)	11	22	33	77	144	210
131-Marge's Little Lulu	30	60	90	228	457	685
132-Tillie the Toiler (1947)	10	20	30	68	119	170
133-Dick Tracy	18	36	54	125	255	385
134-Tarzan and the Devil Ogre; Marsh-c/a	52	104	156	442	896	1350
135-Felix the Cat	22	44	66	159	317	475
136-Lone Ranger, The	18	36	54	131	266	400
137-Roy Rogers Comics; photo-c	16	32	48	114	232	350
138-Smitty	9	18	27	64	110	155
139-Marge's Little Lulu (1947)	29	58	87	218	439	660
140-Easter with Mother Goose by Walt Kelly	13	26	39	93	182	270
141-Mickey Mouse and the Submarine Pirates (Disney)	21	42	63	150	300	450
142-Bugs Bunny and the Haunted Mountain	15	30	45	104	212	320
143-Oswald the Rabbit & the Prehistoric Egg	9	18	27	63	107	150
144-Roy Rogers Comics (1947)-Photo-c	16	32	48	114	232	350
145-Popeye	13	26	39	92	179	265
146-Marge's Little Lulu	29	58	87	218	439	660
147-Donald Duck in Volcano Valley, by Carl Barks (Disney) (5/47)	104	208	312	884	1792	2700
148-Albert the Alligator and Pogo Possum by Walt Kelly (5/47)	40	80	120	320	635	950
149-Smilin' Jack	10	20	30	69	122	175
150-Tillie the Toiler (6/47)	9	18	27	63	107	150
151-Lone Ranger, The	16	32	48	111	226	340
152-Little Orphan Annie; reprints strips from 1/2/44 to 5/6/44	12	24	36	84	157	230
153-Roy Rogers Comics; photo-c	15	30	45	103	209	315
154-Walter Lantz Andy Panda	11	22	33	77	144	210
155-Henry (7/47)	10	20	30	68	119	170
156-Porky Pig and the Phantom	12	24	36	82	154	225
157-Mickey Mouse & the Beanstalk (Disney)	21	42	63	150	300	450
158-Marge's Little Lulu	29	58	87	218	439	660
159-Donald Duck in the Ghost of the Grotto, by Carl Barks (Disney) (8/47)	89	178	267	757	1529	2300
160-Roy Rogers Comics; photo-c	15	30	45	103	209	315
161-Tarzan and the Fires Of Tohr; Marsh-c/a	45	90	135	360	730	1100
162-Felix the Cat (9/47)	16	32	48	114	232	350
163-Dick Tracy	16	32	48	111	226	340
164-Bugs Bunny Finds the Frozen Kingdom	15	30	45	104	212	320
165-Marge's Little Lulu	29	58	87	218	439	660
166-Roy Rogers Comics (52 pgs.)-Photo-c	15	30	45	103	209	315
167-Lone Ranger, The	16	32	48	111	226	340
168-Popeye (10/47)	13	26	39	92	179	265
169-Woody Woodpecker (#1)- "Manhunter in the North"; drug use story	16	32	48	111	226	340
170-Mickey Mouse on Spook's Island (11/47)(Disney)-reprinted in Mickey Mouse #103	18	36	54	125	255	385
171-Charlie McCarthy (#1) and the Twenty Thieves	23	46	69	168	334	500
172-Christmas with Mother Goose by Walt Kelly (11/47)	13	26	39	89	170	250
173-Flash Gordon	18	36	54	131	266	400
174-Winnie Winkle	8	16	24	58	97	135
175-Santa Claus Funnies by Walt Kelly (1947)	13	26	39	94	185	275
176-Tillie the Toiler (12/47)	9	18	27	63	107	150
177-Roy Rogers Comics-(36 pgs.); Photo-c	14	28	42	99	200	300
178-Donald Duck "Christmas on Bear Mountain" by Carl Barks; 1st app. Uncle Scrooge (Disney)(12/47)	119	238	357	1012	2056	3100
179-Uncle Wiggily (#1)-Walt Kelly-c	14	28	42	97	194	290
180-Ozark Ike (#1)	10	20	30	67	116	165
181-Walt Disney's Mickey Mouse in Jungle Magic	18	36	54	125	255	385
182-Porky Pig in Never-Never Land (2/48)	12	24	36	82	154	225
183-Oswald the Rabbit (Lantz)	9	18	27	63	107	150

Four Color Comics #208 © DIS

Four Color Comics #275 © DIS

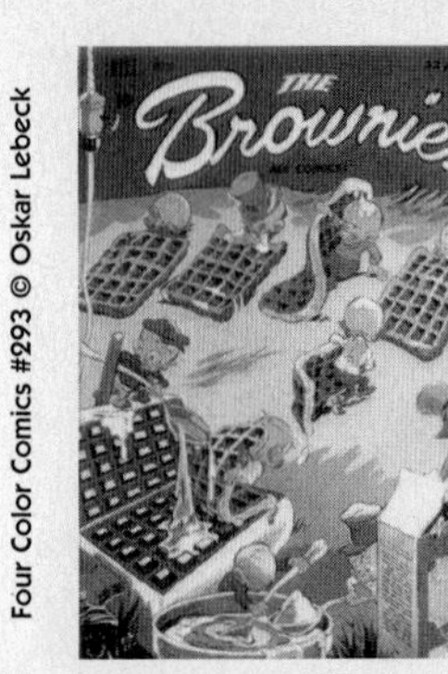

Four Color Comics #293 © Oskar Lebeck

	GD 2.0	VG 4.0	FN 6.0	VF 8.0	VF/NM 9.0	NM- 9.2
184-Tillie the Toiler	9	18	27	63	107	150
185-Easter with Mother Goose by Walt Kelly (1948)	12	24	36	87	164	240
186-Walt Disney's Bambi (4/48)-Reprinted as Movie Classic Bambi #3 (1956)	15	30	45	106	216	325
187-Bugs Bunny and the Dreadful Dragon	12	24	36	82	154	225
188-Woody Woodpecker (Lantz, 5/48)	11	22	33	75	138	200
189-Donald Duck in The Old Castle's Secret, by Carl Barks (Disney) (6/48)	73	146	219	621	1261	1900
190-Flash Gordon (6/48); bondage-c; "The Adventures of the Flying Saucers"; 5th Flying Saucer story- see The Spirit 9/28/47(1st), Shadow Comics V7#10 (2nd, 1/48),Captain Midnight #60 (3rd, 2/48) & Boy Commandos #26 (4th, 3-4/48)	21	42	63	150	300	450
191-Porky Pig to the Rescue	12	24	36	82	154	225
192-The Brownies (#1)-by Walt Kelly (7/48)	13	26	39	89	170	250
193-M.G.M. Presents Tom and Jerry (#1)(1948)	22	44	66	159	317	475
194-Mickey Mouse in The World Under the Sea (Disney)-Reprinted in Mickey Mouse #101	18	36	54	125	255	385
195-Tillie the Toiler	7	14	21	50	83	115
196-Charlie McCarthy in The Haunted Hide-Out; part photo-c	14	28	42	99	200	300
197-Spirit of the Border (#1) (Zane Grey) (1948)	11	22	33	75	138	200
198-Andy Panda	11	22	33	77	144	210
199-Donald Duck in Sheriff of Bullet Valley, by Carl Barks; Barks draws himself on wanted poster, last page; used in Love & Death (Disney) (10/48)	79	158	237	672	1361	2050
200-Bugs Bunny, Super Sleuth (10/48)	12	24	36	82	154	225
201-Christmas with Mother Goose by W. Kelly	11	22	33	75	138	200
202-Woody Woodpecker	8	16	24	58	97	135
203-Donald Duck in the Golden Christmas Tree, by Carl Barks (Disney) (12/48)	56	112	168	476	963	1450
204-Flash Gordon (12/48)	14	28	42	99	200	300
205-Santa Claus Funnies by Walt Kelly	12	24	36	87	164	240
206-Little Orphan Annie; reprints strips from 11/10/40 to 1/11/41	8	16	24	54	90	125
207-King of the Royal Mounted (#1) (12/48)	13	26	39	89	170	250
208-Brer Rabbit Does It Again (Disney) (1/49)	11	22	33	75	138	200
209-Harold Teen	6	12	18	39	62	85
210-Tippie and Cap Stubbs	5	10	15	32	51	70
211-Little Beaver (#1)	8	16	24	56	93	130
212-Dr. Bobbs	6	12	18	37	59	80
213-Tillie the Toiler	7	14	21	50	83	115
214-Mickey Mouse and His Sky Adventure (2/49)(Disney)-Reprinted in Mickey Mouse #105	14	28	42	96	191	285
215-Sparkle Plenty (Dick Tracy-r by Gould)	11	22	33	77	144	210
216-Andy Panda and the Police Pup (Lantz)	8	16	24	58	97	135
217-Bugs Bunny in Court Jester	12	24	36	82	154	225
218-Three Little Pigs and the Wonderful Magic Lamp (Disney) (3/49)(#1)	10	20	30	70	125	180
219-Swee'pea	8	16	24	56	93	130
220-Easter with Mother Goose by Walt Kelly	12	24	36	87	164	240
221-Uncle Wiggily-Walt Kelly cover in part	9	18	27	63	107	150
222-West of the Pecos (Zane Grey)	7	14	21	47	76	105
223-Donald Duck "Lost in the Andes" by Carl Barks (Disney-4/49) (square egg story)	73	146	219	621	1261	1900
224-Little Iodine (#1), by Hatlo (4/49)	11	22	33	77	144	210
225-Oswald the Rabbit (Lantz)	7	14	21	45	73	100
226-Porky Pig and Spoofy, the Spook	10	20	30	69	122	175
227-Seven Dwarfs (Disney)	9	18	27	65	113	160
228-Mark of Zorro, The (#1) (1949)	18	36	54	131	266	400
229-Smokey Stover	6	12	18	41	66	90
230-Sunset Pass (Zane Grey)	7	14	21	47	76	105
231-Mickey Mouse and the Rajah's Treasure (Disney)	14	28	42	96	191	285
232-Woody Woodpecker (Lantz, 6/49)	8	16	24	58	97	135
233-Bugs Bunny, Sleepwalking Sleuth	12	24	36	82	154	225
234-Dumbo in Sky Voyage (Disney)	13	26	39	93	182	270
235-Tiny Tim	6	12	18	37	59	80
236-Heritage of the Desert (Zane Grey) (1949)	7	14	21	47	76	105
237-Tillie the Toiler	7	14	21	50	83	115
238-Donald Duck in Voodoo Hoodoo, by Carl Barks (Disney) (8/49)	56	112	168	476	963	1450
239-Adventure Bound (8/49)	6	12	18	39	62	85
240-Andy Panda (Lantz)	8	16	24	58	97	135
241-Porky Pig, Mighty Hunter	10	20	30	69	122	175
242-Tippie and Cap Stubbs	4	8	12	26	41	55
243-Thumper Follows His Nose (Disney)	11	22	33	75	138	200
244-The Brownies by Walt Kelly	10	20	30	68	119	170
245-Dick's Adventures (9/49)	6	12	18	41	66	90
246-Thunder Mountain (Zane Grey)	5	10	15	32	51	70
247-Flash Gordon	14	28	42	99	200	300
248-Mickey Mouse and the Black Sorcerer (Disney)	14	28	42	96	191	285
249-Woody Woodpecker in the "Globetrotter" (10/49)	8	16	24	58	97	135
250-Bugs Bunny in Diamond Daze; used in **SOTI**, pg. 309	12	24	36	86	161	235
251-Hubert at Camp Moonbeam	7	14	21	49	80	110
252-Pinocchio (Disney)-not by Kelly; origin	10	20	30	71	128	185
253-Christmas with Mother Goose by W. Kelly	11	22	33	75	138	200
254-Santa Claus Funnies by Walt Kelly; Pogo & Albert story by Kelly (11/49)	12	24	36	87	164	240
255-The Ranger (Zane Grey) (1949)	5	10	15	32	51	70
256-Donald Duck in "Luck of the North" by Carl Barks (Disney) (12/49)-Shows #257 on inside	47	94	141	376	763	1150
257-Little Iodine	8	16	24	56	93	130
258-Andy Panda and the Balloon Race (Lantz)	8	16	24	58	97	135
259-Santa and the Angel (Gollub art-condensed from #128) & Santa at the Zoo (12/49) -two books in one	5	10	15	34	55	75
260-Porky Pig, Hero of the Wild West (12/49)	10	20	30	69	122	175
261-Mickey Mouse and the Missing Key (Disney)	14	28	42	96	191	285
262-Raggedy Ann and Andy	10	20	30	67	116	165
263-Donald Duck in "Land of the Totem Poles" by Carl Barks (Disney) (2/50)-Has two Barks stories	46	92	138	368	747	1125
264-Woody Woodpecker in the Magic Lantern (Lantz)	8	16	24	58	97	135
265-King of the Royal Mounted (Zane Grey)	8	16	24	58	97	135
266-Bugs Bunny on the "Isle of Hercules" (2/50)-Reprinted in Best of Bugs Bunny #1	10	20	30	68	119	170
267-Little Beaver; Harmon-c/a	5	10	15	34	55	75
268-Mickey Mouse's Surprise Visitor (1950)(Disney)	13	26	39	91	176	260
269-Johnny Mack Brown (#1)-Photo-c	20	40	60	140	283	425
270-Drift Fence (Zane Grey) (3/50)	5	10	15	32	51	70
271-Porky Pig in Phantom of the Plains	10	20	30	69	122	175
272-Cinderella (Disney) (4/50)	12	24	36	86	161	235
273-Oswald the Rabbit (Lantz)	7	14	21	45	73	100
274-Bugs Bunny, Hare-brained Reporter	10	20	30	68	119	170
275-Donald Duck in "Ancient Persia" by Carl Barks (Disney) (5/50)	45	90	135	360	730	1100
276-Uncle Wiggily	8	16	24	52	86	120
277-Porky Pig in Desert Adventure (5/50)	10	20	30	69	122	175
278-(Wild) Bill Elliott Comics (#1)-Photo-c	12	24	36	84	157	230
279-Mickey Mouse and Pluto Battle the Giant Ants (Disney); reprinted in Mickey Mouse #102 & 245	11	22	33	75	138	200
280-Andy Panda in The Isle Of Mechanical Men (Lantz)	8	16	24	58	97	135
281-Bugs Bunny in The Great Circus Mystery	10	20	30	68	119	170
282-Donald Duck and the Pixilated Parrot by Carl Barks (Disney) (© 5/23/50)	45	90	135	360	730	1100
283-King of the Royal Mounted (7/50)	8	16	24	58	97	135
284-Porky Pig in The Kingdom of Nowhere	10	20	30	69	122	175
285-Bozo the Clown & His Minikin Circus (#1) (TV)	17	34	51	122	249	375
286-Mickey Mouse in The Uninvited Guest (Disney	11	22	33	75	138	200
287-Gene Autry's Champion in The Ghost Of Black Mountain; photo-c	11	22	33	75	138	200
288-Woody Woodpecker in Klondike Gold (Lantz)	8	16	24	58	97	135
289-Bugs Bunny in "Indian Trouble"	10	20	30	68	119	170
290-The Chief (#1) (8/50)	8	16	24	52	86	120
291-Donald Duck in "The Magic Hourglass" by Carl Barks (Disney) (9/50)	45	90	135	360	730	1100
292-The Cisco Kid Comics (#1)	21	42	63	150	300	450
293-The Brownies-Kelly-c/a	10	20	30	68	119	170
294-Little Beaver	5	10	15	34	55	75
295-Porky Pig in President Porky (9/50)	10	20	30	69	122	175
296-Mickey Mouse in Private Eye for Hire (Disney)	11	22	33	75	138	200
297-Andy Panda in The Haunted Inn (Lantz, 10/50)	8	16	24	58	97	135
298-Bugs Bunny in Sheik for a Day	10	20	30	68	119	170
299-Buck Jones & the Iron Horse Trail (#1)	12	24	36	87	164	240
300-Donald Duck in "Big-Top Bedlam" by Carl Barks (Disney) (11/50)	45	90	135	360	730	1100
301-The Mysterious Rider (Zane Grey)	5	10	15	32	51	70

Four Color Comics #310 © KING

Four Color Comics #361 © WE

Four Color Comics #362 © DIS

	GD 2.0	VG 4.0	FN 6.0	VF 8.0	VF/NM 9.0	NM- 9.2
302-Santa Claus Funnies (11/50)	7	14	21	45	73	100
303-Porky Pig in The Land of the Monstrous Flies	8	16	24	54	90	125
304-Mickey Mouse in Tom-Tom Island (Disney) (12/50)						
	10	20	30	69	122	175
305-Woody Woodpecker (Lantz)	6	12	18	41	66	90
306-Raggedy Ann	7	14	21	50	83	115
307-Bugs Bunny in Lumber Jack Rabbit	9	18	27	60	100	140
308-Donald Duck in "Dangerous Disguise" by Carl Barks (Disney) (1/51)						
	42	86	126	336	681	1025
309-Betty Betz' Dollface and Her Gang (1951)	5	10	15	35	55	75
310-King of the Royal Mounted (1/51)	6	12	18	43	69	95
311-Porky Pig in Midget Horses of Hidden Valley	8	16	24	54	90	125
312-Tonto (#1)	10	20	30	72	131	190
313-Mickey Mouse in The Mystery of the Double-Cross Ranch (#1) (Disney) (2/51)						
	10	20	30	69	122	175

Note: Beginning with the above comic in 1951 Dell/Western began adding #1 in small print on the covers of several long running titles with the evident intention of switching these titles to their own monthly numbers, but when the conversions were made, there was no connection. It is thought that the post office may have stepped in and decreed the sequences should commence as though the first four colors printed had each begun with number one, or the first issues sold by subscription. Since the regular series' numbers don't correctly match to the numbers of earlier issues published, it's not known whether or not the numbering was in error.

	GD 2.0	VG 4.0	FN 6.0	VF 8.0	VF/NM 9.0	NM- 9.2
314-Ambush (Zane Grey)	5	10	15	32	51	70
315-Oswald the Rabbit (Lantz)	6	12	18	39	62	85
316-Rex Allen (#1)-Photo-c; Marsh-a	13	26	39	92	179	265
317-Bugs Bunny in Hair Today Gone Tomorrow (#1)	9	18	27	60	100	140
318-Donald Duck in "No Such Varmint" by Carl Barks (#1)-Indicia shows #317						
(Disney, © 1/23/51)	42	86	126	336	681	1025
319-Gene Autry's Champion; painted-c	6	12	18	41	66	90
320-Uncle Wiggily (#1)	8	16	24	52	86	120
321-Little Scouts (#1) (3/51)	5	10	15	30	48	65
322-Porky Pig in Roaring Rockets (#1 on-c)	8	16	24	54	90	125
323-Susie Q. Smith (#1) (3/51)	5	10	15	32	51	70
324-I Met a Handsome Cowboy (3/51)	8	16	24	56	93	130
325-Mickey Mouse in The Haunted Castle (#2) (Disney) (4/51)						
	10	20	30	69	122	175
326-Andy Panda (#1) (Lantz)	6	12	18	43	69	95
327-Bugs Bunny and the Rajah's Treasure (#2)	9	18	27	60	100	140
328-Donald Duck in Old California (#2) by Carl Barks-Peyote drug use issue						
(Disney) (5/51)	41	82	123	328	664	1000
329-Roy Roger's Trigger (#1)(5/51)-Painted-c	13	26	39	92	179	265
330-Porky Pig Meets the Bristled Bruiser (#2)	8	16	24	54	90	125
331-Alice in Wonderland (Disney) (1951)	14	28	42	97	194	290
332-Little Beaver	5	10	15	34	55	75
333-Wilderness Trek (Zane Grey) (5/51)	5	10	15	32	51	70
334-Mickey Mouse and Yukon Gold (Disney) (6/51)	10	20	30	69	122	175
335-Francis the Famous Talking Mule (#1, 6/51)-1st Dell non animated movie comic						
(all issues based on movie)	10	20	30	70	125	180
336-Woody Woodpecker (Lantz)	6	12	18	41	66	90
337-The Brownies-not by Walt Kelly	6	12	18	37	59	80
338-Bugs Bunny and the Rocking Horse Thieves	9	18	27	60	100	140
339-Donald Duck and the Magic Fountain-not by Carl Barks (Disney) (7-8/51)						
	13	26	39	89	170	250
340-King of the Royal Mounted (7/51)	6	12	18	43	69	95
341-Unbirthday Party with Alice in Wonderland (Disney) (7/51)						
	14	28	42	97	194	290
342-Porky Pig the Lucky Peppermint Mine; r/in Porky Pig #3						
	6	12	18	43	69	95
343-Mickey Mouse in The Ruby Eye of Homar-Guy-Am (Disney)-Reprinted in						
Mickey Mouse #104	9	18	27	60	100	140
344-Sergeant Preston from Challenge of The Yukon (#1) (TV)						
	11	22	33	77	144	210
345-Andy Panda in Scotland Yard (8-10/51) (Lantz)	6	12	18	43	69	95
346-Hideout (Zane Grey)	5	10	15	32	51	70
347-Bugs Bunny the Frigid Hare (8-9/51)	9	18	27	60	100	140
348-Donald Duck "The Crocodile Collector"; Barks-c only (Disney) (9-10/51)						
	20	40	60	144	290	435
349-Uncle Wiggily	6	12	18	43	69	95
350-Woody Woodpecker (Lantz)	6	12	18	41	66	90
351-Porky Pig & the Grand Canyon Giant (9-10/51)	6	12	18	43	69	95
352-Mickey Mouse in The Mystery of Painted Valley (Disney)						
	9	18	27	60	100	140
353-Duck Album (#1)-Barks-c (Disney)	10	20	30	69	122	175
354-Raggedy Ann & Andy	7	14	21	50	83	115

	GD 2.0	VG 4.0	FN 6.0	VF 8.0	VF/NM 9.0	NM- 9.2
355-Bugs Bunny Hot-Rod Hare	9	18	27	60	100	140
356-Donald Duck in "Rags to Riches"; Barks-c only	20	40	60	144	290	435
357-Comeback (Zane Grey)	4	8	12	28	44	60
358-Andy Panda (Lantz) (11-1/52)	6	12	18	43	69	95
359-Frosty the Snowman (#1)	9	18	27	63	107	150
360-Porky Pig in Tree of Fortune (11-12/51)	6	12	18	43	69	95
361-Santa Claus Funnies	7	14	21	45	73	100
362-Mickey Mouse and the Smuggled Diamonds (Disney)						
	9	18	27	60	100	140
363-King of the Royal Mounted	6	12	18	39	62	85
364-Woody Woodpecker (Lantz)	5	10	15	34	55	75
365-The Brownies-not by Kelly	6	12	18	37	59	80
366-Bugs Bunny Uncle Buckskin Comes to Town (12-1/52)						
	9	18	27	60	100	140
367-Donald Duck in "A Christmas for Shacktown" by Carl Barks (Disney) (1-2/52)						
	33	66	99	254	510	765
368-Bob Clampett's Beany and Cecil (#1)	22	44	66	159	317	475
369-The Lone Ranger's Famous Horse Hi-Yo Silver (#1); Silver's origin						
	10	20	30	70	125	180
370-Porky Pig in Trouble in the Big Trees	6	12	18	43	69	95
371-Mickey Mouse in The Inca Idol Case (1952) (Disney)						
	9	18	27	60	100	140
372-Riders of the Purple Sage (Zane Grey)	4	8	12	28	44	60
373-Sergeant Preston (TV)	8	16	24	52	86	120
374-Woody Woodpecker (Lantz)	5	10	15	34	55	75
375-John Carter of Mars (E. R. Burroughs)-Jesse Marsh-a; origin						
	25	50	75	183	367	550
376-Bugs Bunny, "The Magic Sneeze"	9	18	27	60	100	140
377-Susie Q. Smith	4	8	12	26	41	55
378-Tom Corbett, Space Cadet (#1) (TV)-McWilliams-a						
	15	30	45	106	216	325
379-Donald Duck in "Southern Hospitality"; Not by Barks (Disney)						
	13	26	39	89	170	250
380-Raggedy Ann & Andy	7	14	21	50	83	115
381-Marge's Tubby (#1)	18	36	54	131	266	400
382-Snow White and the Seven Dwarfs (Disney)-origin; partial reprint of Four Color #49						
(Movie)	9	18	27	65	113	160
383-Andy Panda (Lantz)	5	10	15	34	55	75
384-King of the Royal Mounted (3/52)(Zane Grey)	6	12	18	39	62	85
385-Porky Pig in The Isle of Missing Ships (3-4/52)	6	12	18	43	69	95
386-Uncle Scrooge (#1)-by Carl Barks (Disney) in "Only a Poor Old Man" (3/52)						
	185	370	555	1619	3310	5000
387-Mickey Mouse in High Tibet (Disney) (4-5/52)	9	18	27	60	100	140
388-Oswald the Rabbit (Lantz)	6	12	18	39	62	85
389-Andy Hardy Comics (#1)	5	10	15	34	55	75
390-Woody Woodpecker (Lantz)	5	10	15	34	55	75
391-Uncle Wiggily	6	12	18	43	69	95
392-Hi-Yo Silver	6	12	18	41	66	90
393-Bugs Bunny	9	18	27	60	100	140
394-Donald Duck in Malayalaya-Barks-c only (Disney)						
	20	40	60	144	290	435
395-Forlorn River(Zane Grey)-First Nevada (5/52)	4	8	12	28	44	60
396-Tales of the Texas Rangers(#1)(TV)-Photo-c	10	20	30	71	128	185
397-Sergeant Preston of the Yukon (TV) (5/52)	8	16	24	52	86	120
398-The Brownies-not by Kelly	6	12	18	37	59	80
399-Porky Pig in The Lost Gold Mine	6	12	18	43	69	95
400-Tom Corbett, Space Cadet (TV)-McWilliams-c/a	10	20	30	69	122	175
401-Mickey Mouse and Goofy's Mechanical Wizard (Disney) (6-7/52)						
	7	14	21	49	80	110
402-Mary Jane and Sniffles	7	14	21	50	83	115
403-Li'l Bad Wolf (Disney) (6/52)(#1)	7	14	21	47	76	105
404-The Range Rider (#1) (Flying A's...)(TV)-Photo-c	9	18	27	65	113	160
405-Woody Woodpecker (Lantz) (6-7/52)	5	10	15	34	55	75
406-Tweety and Sylvester (#1)	10	20	30	72	131	190
407-Bugs Bunny, Foreign-Legion Hare	7	14	21	50	83	115
408-Donald Duck and the Golden Helmet by Carl Barks (Disney) (7-8/52)						
	33	66	99	254	510	765
409-Andy Panda (7-9/52)	5	10	15	34	55	75
410-Porky Pig in The Water Wizard (7/52)	6	12	18	43	69	95
411-Mickey Mouse and the Old Sea Dog (Disney) (8-9/52)						
	7	14	21	49	80	110
412-Nevada (Zane Grey)	4	8	12	28	44	60
413-Robin Hood (Disney-Movie) (8/52)-Photo-c (1st Disney movie Four Color book)						
	9	18	27	65	113	160

Four Color Comics #470 © WB

Four Color Comics #517 © DIS

Four Color Comics #529 © DELL

	GD 2.0	VG 4.0	FN 6.0	VF 8.0	VF/NM 9.0	NM- 9.2
414-Bob Clampett's Beany and Cecil (TV)	13	26	39	94	185	275
415-Rootie Kazootie (#1) (TV)	9	18	27	65	113	160
416-Woody Woodpecker (Lantz)	5	10	15	34	55	75
417-Double Trouble with Goober (#1) (8/52)	4	8	12	28	44	60
418-Rusty Riley, a Boy, a Horse, and a Dog (#1)-Frank Godwin-a (strip reprints) (8/52)	5	10	15	32	51	70
419-Sergeant Preston (TV)	8	16	24	52	86	120
420-Bugs Bunny in The Mysterious Buckaroo (8-9/52)	7	14	21	50	83	115
421-Tom Corbett, Space Cadet(TV)-McWilliams-a	10	20	30	69	122	175
422-Donald Duck and the Gilded Man, by Carl Barks (Disney) (9-10/52) (#423 on inside)	33	66	99	254	510	765
423-Rhubarb, Owner of the Brooklyn Ball Club (The Millionaire Cat) (#1)-Painted cover	6	12	18	39	62	85
424-Flash Gordon-Test Flight in Space (9/52)	11	22	33	77	144	210
425-Zorro, the Return of	11	22	33	77	144	210
426-Porky Pig in The Scalawag Leprechaun	6	12	18	43	69	95
427-Mickey Mouse and the Wonderful Whizzix (Disney) (10-11/52)-Reprinted in Mickey Mouse #100	7	14	21	49	80	110
428-Uncle Wiggily	5	10	15	34	55	75
429-Pluto in "Why Dogs Leave Home" (Disney) (10/52)(#1)	9	18	27	65	113	160
430-Marge's Tubby, the Shadow of a Man-Eater	11	22	33	80	150	220
431-Woody Woodpecker (10/52) (Lantz)	5	10	15	34	55	75
432-Bugs Bunny and the Rabbit Olympics	7	14	21	50	83	115
433-Wildfire (Zane Grey) (11-1/52-53)	4	8	12	28	44	60
434-Rin Tin Tin "In Dark Danger" (#1) (TV) (11/52)-Photo-c	13	26	39	94	185	275
435-Frosty the Snowman (11/52)	6	12	18	37	59	80
436-The Brownies-not by Kelly (11/52)	5	10	15	34	55	75
437-John Carter of Mars (E.R. Burroughs)-Marsh-a	14	28	42	99	200	300
438-Annie Oakley (#1) (TV)	13	26	39	92	179	265
439-Little Hiawatha (Disney) (12/52)j(#1)	6	12	18	39	62	85
440-Black Beauty (12/52)	5	10	15	30	48	65
441-Fearless Fagan	4	8	12	24	37	50
442-Peter Pan (Disney) (Movie)	10	20	30	69	122	175
443-Ben Bowie and His Mountain Men (#1)	9	18	27	60	100	140
444-Marge's Tubby	11	22	33	80	150	220
445-Charlie McCarthy	6	12	18	39	62	85
446-Captain Hook and Peter Pan (Disney)(Movie)(1/53)	9	18	27	60	100	140
447-Andy Hardy Comics	4	8	12	26	41	55
448-Bob Clampett's Beany and Cecil (TV)	13	26	39	94	185	275
449-Tappan's Burro (Zane Grey) (2-4/53)	4	8	12	28	44	60
450-Duck Album; Barks-c (Disney)	7	14	21	49	80	110
451-Rusty Riley-Frank Godwin-a (strip-r) (2/53)	4	8	12	26	41	50
452-Raggedy Ann & Andy (1953)	7	14	21	50	83	115
453-Susie Q. Smith (2/53)	4	8	12	26	41	55
454-Krazy Kat Comics; not by Herriman	5	10	15	32	51	70
455-Johnny Mack Brown Comics(3/53)-Photo-c	7	14	21	47	76	105
456-Uncle Scrooge Back to the Klondike (#2) by Barks (3/53) (Disney)	92	184	276	782	1591	2400
457-Daffy (#1)	10	20	30	72	131	190
458-Oswald the Rabbit (Lantz)	5	10	15	32	51	70
459-Rootie Kazootie (TV)	7	14	21	47	76	105
460-Buck Jones (4/53)	6	12	18	41	66	90
461-Marge's Tubby	10	20	30	72	131	190
462-Little Scouts	4	8	12	24	37	50
463-Petunia (4/53)	4	8	12	28	44	60
464-Bozo (4/53)	10	20	30	67	116	165
465-Francis the Famous Talking Mule	6	12	18	41	66	90
466-Rhubarb, the Millionaire Cat; painted-c	5	10	15	34	55	75
467-Desert Gold (Zane Grey) (5-7/53)	4	8	12	28	44	60
468-Goofy (#1) (Disney)	11	22	33	77	144	210
469-Beetle Bailey (#1) (5/53	11	22	33	75	138	200
470-Elmer Fudd	9	18	27	60	100	140
471-Double Trouble with Goober	4	8	12	22	34	45
472-Wild Bill Elliott (6/53)-Photo-c	5	10	15	34	55	75
473-Li'l Bad Wolf (Disney) (6/53)(#2)	5	10	15	32	51	70
474-Mary Jane and Sniffles	7	14	21	47	76	105
475-M.G.M.'s The Two Mouseketeers (#1)	8	16	24	52	86	120
476-Rin Tin Tin (TV)-Photo-c	8	16	24	56	93	130
477-Bob Clampett's Beany and Cecil (TV)	13	26	39	94	185	275
478-Charlie McCarthy	6	12	18	39	62	85
479-Queen of the West Dale Evans (#1)-Photo-c	17	34	51	118	242	365
480-Andy Hardy Comics	4	8	12	26	41	55
481-Annie Oakley And Tagg (TV)	9	18	27	64	110	155
482-Brownies-not by Kelly	5	10	15	34	55	75
483-Little Beaver (7/53)	5	10	15	30	48	65
484-River Feud (Zane Grey) (8-10/53)	4	8	12	28	44	60
485-The Little People-Walt Scott (#1)	8	16	24	52	86	120
486-Rusty Riley-Frank Godwin strip-r	4	8	12	26	41	50
487-Mowgli, the Jungle Book (Rudyard Kipling's)	6	12	18	37	59	80
488-John Carter of Mars (Burroughs)-Marsh-a; painted-c	14	28	42	99	200	300
489-Tweety and Sylvester	6	12	18	43	69	95
490-Jungle Jim (#1)	7	14	21	49	80	110
491-Silvertip (#1) (Max Brand)-Kinstler-a (8/53)	8	16	24	52	86	120
492-Duck Album (Disney)	6	12	18	41	66	90
493-Johnny Mack Brown; photo-c	7	14	21	47	76	105
494-The Little King (#1)	9	18	27	60	100	140
495-Uncle Scrooge (#3) (Disney)-by Carl Barks (9/53)	62	124	186	527	1064	1600
496-The Green Hornet; painted-c	23	46	69	168	334	500
497-Zorro (Sword of...)-Kinstler-a	12	24	36	82	154	225
498-Bugs Bunny's Album (9/53)	6	12	18	41	66	90
499-M.G.M.'s Spike and Tyke (#1) (9/53)	7	14	21	45	73	100
500-Buck Jones	6	12	18	41	66	90
501-Francis the Famous Talking Mule	5	10	15	32	51	70
502-Rootie Kazootie (TV)	7	14	21	47	76	105
503-Uncle Wiggily (10/53)	5	10	15	34	55	75
504-Krazy Kat; not by Herriman	5	10	15	32	51	70
505-The Sword and the Rose (Disney) (10/53)(Movie)-Photo-c	8	16	24	56	93	130
506-The Little Scouts	4	8	12	24	37	50
507-Oswald the Rabbit (Lantz)	5	10	15	32	51	70
508-Bozo (10/53)	10	20	30	67	116	165
509-Pluto (Disney) (10/53)	6	12	18	41	66	90
510-Son of Black Beauty	4	8	12	26	41	55
511-Outlaw Trail (Zane Grey)-Kinstler-a	5	10	15	32	51	70
512-Flash Gordon (11/53)	9	18	27	63	107	150
513-Ben Bowie and His Mountain Men	5	10	15	32	51	70
514-Frosty the Snowman (11/53)	6	12	18	37	59	80
515-Andy Hardy	4	8	12	26	41	55
516-Double Trouble With Goober	4	8	12	22	34	45
517-Chip 'N' Dale (#1) (Disney)	11	22	33	75	138	200
518-Rivets (11/53)	4	8	12	24	37	50
519-Steve Canyon (#1)-Not by Milton Caniff	8	16	24	56	93	130
520-Wild Bill Elliott-Photo-c	5	10	15	34	55	75
521-Beetle Bailey (12/53)	7	14	21	45	73	100
522-The Brownies	5	10	15	34	55	75
523-Rin Tin Tin (TV)-Photo-c (12/53)	8	16	24	56	93	130
524-Tweety and Sylvester	6	12	18	43	69	95
525-Santa Claus Funnies	7	14	21	45	73	100
526-Napoleon	4	8	12	24	37	50
527-Charlie McCarthy	6	12	18	39	62	85
528-Queen of the West Dale Evans; photo-c	10	20	30	69	122	175
529-Little Beaver	5	10	15	30	48	65
530-Bob Clampett's Beany and Cecil (TV) (1/54)	13	26	39	94	185	275
531-Duck Album (Disney)	6	12	18	41	66	90
532-The Rustlers (Zane Grey) (2-4/54)	4	8	12	28	44	60
533-Raggedy Ann and Andy	7	14	21	50	83	115
534-Western Marshal(Ernest Haycox's)-Kinstler-a	6	12	18	39	62	85
535-I Love Lucy (#1) (TV) (2/54)-Photo-c	41	82	123	324	650	975
536-Daffy (3/54)	6	12	18	43	69	95
537-Stormy, the Thoroughbred... (Disney-Movie) on top 2/3 of each page; Pluto story on bottom 1/3 of each page (2/54)	5	10	15	30	48	65
538-The Mask of Zorro; Kinstler-a	12	24	36	82	154	225
539-Ben and Me (Disney) (3/54)	4	8	12	26	41	55
540-Knights of the Round Table (3/54) (Movie)-Photo-c	7	14	21	47	76	105
541-Johnny Mack Brown; photo-c	7	14	21	47	76	105
542-Super Circus Featuring Mary Hartline (TV) (3/54)	7	14	21	47	76	105
543-Uncle Wiggily (3/54)	5	10	15	34	55	75
544-Rob Roy (Disney-Movie)-Manning-a; photo-c	7	14	21	50	83	115
545-The Wonderful Adventures of Pinocchio-Partial reprint of Four Color #92 (Disney-Movie)	7	14	21	47	76	105
546-Buck Jones	6	12	18	41	66	90

Four Color Comics #559 © Desilu

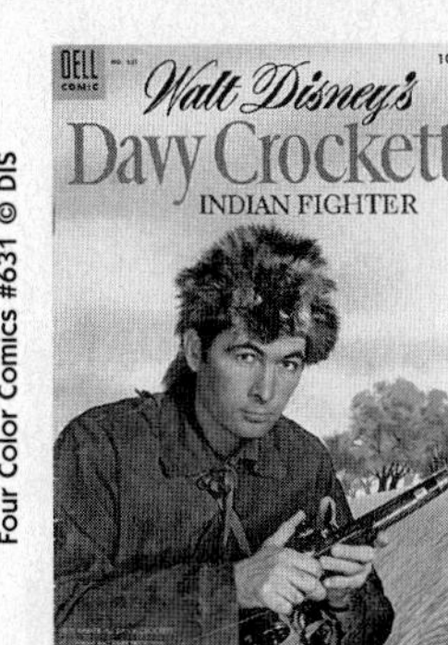

Four Color Comics #631 © DIS

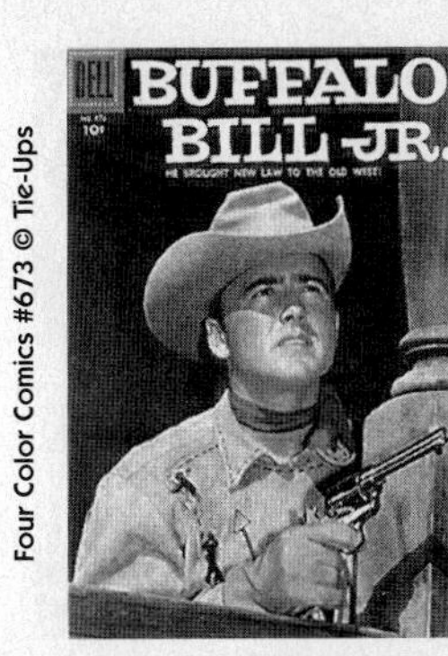

Four Color Comics #673 © Tie-Ups

	GD 2.0	VG 4.0	FN 6.0	VF 8.0	VF/NM 9.0	NM- 9.2
547-Francis the Famous Talking Mule	5	10	15	32	51	70
548-Krazy Kat; not by Herriman (4/54)	5	10	15	30	48	65
549-Oswald the Rabbit (Lantz)	5	10	15	32	51	70
550-The Little Scouts	4	8	12	24	37	50
551-Bozo (4/54)	10	20	30	67	116	165
552-Beetle Bailey	7	14	21	45	73	100
553-Susie Q. Smith	4	8	12	26	41	55
554-Rusty Riley (Frank Godwin strip-r)	4	8	12	26	41	50
555-Range War (Zane Grey)	4	8	12	28	44	60
556-Double Trouble With Goober (5/54)	4	8	12	22	34	45
557-Ben Bowie and His Mountain Men	5	10	15	32	51	70
558-Elmer Fudd (5/54)	5	10	15	32	51	70
559-I Love Lucy (#2) (TV)-Photo-c	26	52	78	190	383	575
560-Duck Album (Disney) (5/54)	6	12	18	41	66	90
561-Mr. Magoo (5/54)	10	20	30	68	119	170
562-Goofy (Disney)(#2)	7	14	21	47	76	105
563-Rhubarb, the Millionaire Cat (6/54)	5	10	15	34	55	75
564-Li'l Bad Wolf (Disney)(#3)	5	10	15	32	51	70
565-Jungle Jim	5	10	15	30	48	65
566-Son of Black Beauty	4	8	12	26	41	55
567-Prince Valiant (#1)-By Bob Fuje (Movie)-Photo-c	10	20	30	71	128	185
568-Gypsy Colt (Movie) (6/54)	5	10	15	32	51	70
569-Priscilla's Pop	4	8	12	26	41	55
570-Bob Clampett's Beany and Cecil (TV)	13	26	39	94	185	275
571-Charlie McCarthy	6	12	18	39	62	85
572-Silvertip (Max Brand) (7/54); Kinstler-a	5	10	15	30	48	65
573-The Little People by Walt Scott	5	10	15	32	51	70
574-The Hand of Zorro; Kinstler-a	12	24	36	82	154	225
575-Annie Oakley and Tagg (TV)-Photo-c	9	18	27	64	110	155
576-Angel (#1) (8/54)	4	8	12	26	41	55
577-M.G.M.'s Spike and Tyke	5	10	15	30	48	65
578-Steve Canyon (8/54)	5	10	15	34	55	75
579-Francis the Famous Talking Mule	5	10	15	32	51	70
580-Six Gun Ranch (Luke Short-8/54)	4	8	12	28	44	60
581-Chip 'N' Dale (#2) (Disney)	6	12	18	43	69	95
582-Mowgli Jungle Book (Kipling) (8/54)	5	10	15	30	48	65
583-The Lost Wagon Train (Zane Grey)	4	8	12	28	44	60
584-Johnny Mack Brown-Photo-c	7	14	21	47	76	105
585-Bugs Bunny's Album	6	12	18	41	66	90
586-Duck Album (Disney)	6	12	18	41	66	90
587-The Little Scouts	4	8	12	24	37	50
588-King Richard and the Crusaders (Movie) (10/54) Matt Baker-a; photo-c	9	18	27	63	107	150
589-Buck Jones	6	12	18	41	66	90
590-Hansel and Gretel; partial photo-c	6	12	18	43	69	95
591-Western Marshal(Ernest Haycox's)-Kinstler-a	5	10	15	34	55	75
592-Super Circus (TV)	6	12	18	43	69	95
593-Oswald the Rabbit (Lantz)	5	10	15	32	51	70
594-Bozo (10/54)	10	20	30	67	116	165
595-Pluto (Disney)	5	10	15	32	51	70
596-Turok, Son of Stone (#1)	52	104	156	442	896	1350
597-The Little King	5	10	15	34	55	75
598-Captain Davy Jones	5	10	15	30	48	65
599-Ben Bowie and His Mountain Men	5	10	15	32	51	70
600-Daisy Duck's Diary (#1) (Disney) (11/54)	7	14	21	47	76	105
601-Frosty the Snowman	6	12	18	37	59	80
602-Mr. Magoo and Gerald McBoing-Boing	10	20	30	68	119	170
603-M.G.M.'s The Two Mouseketeers	6	12	18	37	59	80
604-Shadow on the Trail (Zane Grey)	4	8	12	28	44	60
605-The Brownies-not by Kelly (12/54)	5	10	15	34	55	75
606-Sir Lancelot (not TV)	7	14	21	49	80	110
607-Santa Claus Funnies	7	14	21	45	73	100
608-Silvertip- "Valley of Vanishing Men" (Max Brand)-Kinstler-a	5	10	15	30	48	65
609-The Littlest Outlaw (Disney-Movie) (1/55)-Photo-c	6	12	18	43	69	95
610-Drum Beat (Movie); Alan Ladd photo-c	8	16	24	56	93	130
611-Duck Album (Disney)	6	12	18	41	66	90
612-Little Beaver (1/55)	5	10	15	30	48	65
613-Western Marshal (Ernest Haycox's) (2/55)-Kinstler-a	5	10	15	34	55	75
614-20,000 Leagues Under the Sea (Disney) (Movie) (2/55)-Painted-c	8	16	24	58	97	135

	GD 2.0	VG 4.0	FN 6.0	VF 8.0	VF/NM 9.0	NM- 9.2
615-Daffy	6	12	18	43	69	95
616-To the Last Man (Zane Grey)	4	8	12	28	44	60
617-The Quest of Zorro	11	22	33	77	144	210
618-Johnny Mack Brown; photo-c	7	14	21	47	76	105
619-Krazy Kat; not by Herriman	5	10	15	30	48	65
620-Mowgli Jungle Book (Kipling)	5	10	15	30	48	65
621-Francis the Famous Talking Mule (4/55)	4	8	12	28	44	60
622-Beetle Bailey	7	14	21	45	73	100
623-Oswald the Rabbit (Lantz)	4	8	12	28	44	60
624-Treasure Island(Disney-Movie)(4/55)-Photo-c	8	16	24	54	90	125
625-Beaver Valley (Disney-Movie)	6	12	18	41	66	90
626-Ben Bowie and His Mountain Men	5	10	15	32	51	70
627-Goofy (Disney) (5/55)	7	14	21	47	76	105
628-Elmer Fudd	5	10	15	32	51	70
629-Lady and the Tramp with Jock (Disney)	7	14	21	47	76	105
630-Priscilla's Pop	4	8	12	26	41	55
631-Davy Crockett, Indian Fighter (#1) (Disney) (5/55) (TV)-Fess Parker photo-c	15	30	45	106	216	325
632-Fighting Caravans (Zane Grey)	4	8	12	28	44	60
633-The Little People by Walt Scott (6/55)	5	10	15	32	51	70
634-Lady and the Tramp Album (Disney) (6/55)	5	10	15	32	51	70
635-Bob Clampett's Beany and Cecil (TV)	13	26	39	94	185	275
636-Chip 'N' Dale (Disney)	6	12	18	43	69	95
637-Silvertip (Max Brand)-Kinstler-a	5	10	15	30	48	65
638-M.G.M.'s Spike and Tyke (8/55)	5	10	15	30	48	65
639-Davy Crockett at the Alamo (Disney) (7/55) (TV)-Fess Parker photo-c	13	26	39	91	176	260
640-Western Marshal(Ernest Haycox's)-Kinstler-a	5	10	15	34	55	75
641-Steve Canyon (1955)-by Caniff	5	10	15	34	55	75
642-M.G.M.'s The Two Mouseketeers	6	12	18	37	59	80
643-Wild Bill Elliott; photo-c	5	10	15	30	48	65
644-Sir Walter Raleigh (5/55)-Based on movie "The Virgin Queen"; photo-c	7	14	21	45	73	100
645-Johnny Mack Brown; photo-c	7	14	21	47	76	105
646-Dotty Dripple and Taffy (#1)	5	10	15	32	51	70
647-Bugs Bunny's Album (9/55)	6	12	18	41	66	90
648-Jace Pearson of the Texas Rangers (TV)-Photo-c	6	12	18	41	66	90
649-Duck Album (Disney)	6	12	18	41	66	90
650-Prince Valiant; by Bob Fuje	7	14	21	50	83	115
651-King Colt (Luke Short) (9/55)-Kinstler-a	4	8	12	28	44	60
652-Buck Jones	5	10	15	32	51	70
653-Smokey the Bear (#1) (10/55)	10	20	30	70	125	180
654-Pluto (Disney)	5	10	15	32	51	70
655-Francis the Famous Talking Mule	4	8	12	28	44	60
656-Turok, Son of Stone (#2) (10/55)	29	58	87	223	449	675
657-Ben Bowie and His Mountain Men	5	10	15	32	51	70
658-Goofy (Disney)	7	14	21	47	76	105
659-Daisy Duck's Diary (Disney)(#2)	6	12	18	37	59	80
660-Little Beaver	5	10	15	30	48	65
661-Frosty the Snowman	6	12	18	37	59	80
662-Zoo Parade (TV)-Marlin Perkins (11/55)	5	10	15	32	51	70
663-Winky Dink (TV)	8	16	24	52	86	120
664-Davy Crockett in the Great Keelboat Race (TV) (Disney) (11/55)-Fess Parker photo-c	12	24	36	88	167	245
665-The African Lion (Disney-Movie) (11/55)	6	12	18	37	59	80
666-Santa Claus Funnies	7	14	21	45	73	100
667-Silvertip and the Stolen Stallion (Max Brand) (12/55)-Kinstler-a	5	10	15	30	48	65
668-Dumbo (Disney) (12/55)-First of two printings. Dumbo on cover with starry sky. Reprints 4-Color #234?; same-c as #234	10	20	30	70	125	180
668-Dumbo (Disney) (1/58)-Second printing. Same cover altered, with Timothy Mouse added. Same contents as above	7	14	21	45	73	100
669-Robin Hood (Disney-Movie) (12/55)-Reprints #413 plus-c; photo-c	6	12	18	37	59	80
670-M.G.M's Mouse Musketeers (#1) (1/56)-Formerly the Two Mouseketeers	5	10	15	34	55	75
671-Davy Crockett and the River Pirates (TV) (Disney) (12/55)-Jesse Marsh-a; Fess Parker photo-c	12	24	36	88	167	245
672-Quentin Durward (1/56) (Movie)-Photo-c	7	14	21	45	73	100
673-Buffalo Bill, Jr. (#1) (TV)-James Arness photo-c	9	18	27	60	100	140
674-The Little Rascals (#1) (TV)	9	18	27	60	100	140
675-Steve Donovan, Western Marshal (#1) (TV)-Kinstler-a; photo-c	8	16	24	52	86	120

Four Color Comics #684 © WB

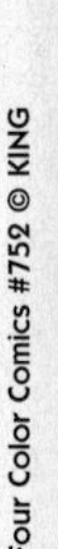
Four Color Comics #717 © WB

Four Color Comics #752 © KING

	GD 2.0	VG 4.0	FN 6.0	VF 8.0	VF/NM 9.0	NM- 9.2
676-Will-Yum!	4	8	12	26	41	55
677-Little King	5	10	15	34	55	75
678-The Last Hunt (Movie)-Photo-c	7	14	21	45	73	100
679-Gunsmoke (#1) (TV)-Photo-c	15	30	45	106	216	325
680-Out Our Way with the Worry Wart (2/56)	4	8	12	24	37	50
681-Forever Darling (Movie) with Lucille Ball & Desi Arnaz (2/56)-; photo-c	11	22	33	77	144	210
682-The Sword & the Rose (Disney-Movie)-Reprint of #505; Renamed When Knighthood Was in Flower for the novel; photo-c	7	14	21	47	76	105
683-Hi and Lois (3/56)	5	10	15	30	48	65
684-Helen of Troy (Movie)-Buscema-a; photo-c	9	18	27	65	113	160
685-Johnny Mack Brown; photo-c	7	14	21	47	76	105
686-Duck Album (Disney)	6	12	18	41	66	90
687-The Indian Fighter (Movie)-Kirk Douglas photo-c	7	14	21	50	83	115
688-Alexander the Great (Movie) (5/56)-Buscema-a; photo-c	7	14	21	49	80	110
689-Elmer Fudd (3/56)	5	10	15	32	51	70
690-The Conqueror (Movie) - John Wayne photo-c	14	28	42	99	200	300
691-Dotty Dripple and Taffy	4	8	12	22	34	45
692-The Little People-Walt Scott	5	10	15	32	51	70
693-Song of the South (Disney) (1956)-Partial reprint of #129	8	16	24	56	93	130
694-Super Circus (TV)-Photo-c	6	12	18	43	69	95
695-Little Beaver	5	10	15	30	48	65
696-Krazy Kat; not by Herriman (4/56)	5	10	15	30	48	65
697-Oswald the Rabbit (Lantz)	4	8	12	28	44	60
698-Francis the Famous Talking Mule (4/56)	4	8	12	28	44	60
699-Prince Valiant-by Bob Fuje	7	14	21	50	83	115
700-Water Birds and the Olympic Elk (Disney-Movie) (4/56)	5	10	15	34	55	75
701-Jiminy Cricket (#1) (Disney) (5/56)	8	16	24	56	93	130
702-The Goofy Success Story (Disney)	7	14	21	47	76	105
703-Scamp (#1) (Disney)	8	16	24	58	97	135
704-Priscilla's Pop (5/56)	4	8	12	26	41	55
705-Brave Eagle (#1) (TV)-Photo-c	6	12	18	43	69	95
706-Bongo and Lumpjaw (Disney) (6/56)	6	12	18	37	59	80
707-Corky and White Shadow (Disney) (5/56)-Mickey Mouse Club (TV); photo-c	7	14	21	47	76	105
708-Smokey the Bear	6	12	18	41	66	90
709-The Searchers (Movie) - John Wayne photo-c	21	42	63	150	300	450
710-Francis the Famous Talking Mule	4	8	12	28	44	60
711-M.G.M's Mouse Musketeers	4	8	12	26	41	55
712-The Great Locomotive Chase (Disney-Movie) (9/56)-Photo-c	7	14	21	47	76	105
713-The Animal World (Movie) (8/56)	4	8	12	26	41	55
714-Spin and Marty (#1) (TV) (Disney)-Mickey Mouse Club (6/56); photo-c	12	24	36	82	154	225
715-Timmy (8/56)	5	10	15	30	48	65
716-Man in Space (Disney)(A science feature from Tomorrowland)	8	16	24	56	93	130
717-Moby Dick (Movie)-Gregory Peck photo-c	8	16	24	56	93	130
718-Dotty Dripple and Taffy	4	8	12	22	34	45
719-Prince Valiant; by Bob Fuje (8/56)	7	14	21	50	83	115
720-Gunsmoke (TV)-James Arness photo-c	9	18	27	61	103	145
721-Captain Kangaroo (TV)-Photo-c	14	28	42	97	194	290
722-Johnny Mack Brown-Photo-c	7	14	21	47	76	105
723-Santiago (Movie)-Kinstler-a (9/56); Alan Ladd photo-c	9	18	27	63	107	150
724-Bugs Bunny's Album	5	10	15	34	55	75
725-Elmer Fudd (9/56)	4	8	12	28	44	60
726-Duck Album (Disney) (9/56)	5	10	15	35	55	75
727-The Nature of Things (TV) (Disney)-Jesse Marsh-a	5	10	15	34	55	75
728-M.G.M's Mouse Musketeers	4	8	12	26	41	55
729-Bob Son of Battle (11/56)	4	8	12	24	37	50
730-Smokey Stover	5	10	15	32	51	70
731-Silvertip and The Fighting Four (Max Brand)-Kinstler-a	5	10	15	30	48	65
732-Zorro, the Challenge of (10/56)	11	22	33	77	144	210
733-Buck Jones	5	10	15	32	51	70
734-Cheyenne (#1) (TV) (10/56)-Clint Walker photo-c	14	28	42	96	191	285
735-Crusader Rabbit (#1) (TV)	23	46	69	168	334	500
736-Pluto (Disney)	5	10	15	32	51	70

	GD 2.0	VG 4.0	FN 6.0	VF 8.0	VF/NM 9.0	NM- 9.2
737-Steve Canyon-Caniff-a	5	10	15	34	55	75
738-Westward Ho, the Wagons (Disney-Movie)-Fess Parker photo-c	9	18	27	63	107	150
739-Bounty Guns (Luke Short)-Drucker-a	4	8	12	26	41	55
740-Chilly Willy (#1) (Walter Lantz)	7	14	21	49	80	110
741-The Fastest Gun Alive (Movie)(9/56)-Photo-c	7	14	21	47	76	105
742-Buffalo Bill, Jr. (TV)-Photo-c	6	12	18	39	62	85
743-Daisy Duck's Diary (Disney) (11/56)	6	12	18	37	59	80
744-Little Beaver	5	10	15	30	48	65
745-Francis the Famous Talking Mule	4	8	12	28	44	60
746-Dotty Dripple and Taffy	4	8	12	22	34	45
747-Goofy (Disney)	7	14	21	47	76	105
748-Frosty the Snowman (11/56)	5	10	15	32	51	70
749-Secrets of Life (Disney-Movie)-Photo-c	5	10	15	32	51	70
750-The Great Cat Family (Disney-TV/Movie)-Pinocchio & Alice app.	6	12	18	43	69	95
751-Our Miss Brooks (TV)-Photo-c	7	14	21	50	83	115
752-Mandrake, the Magician	10	20	30	69	122	175
753-Walt Scott's Little People (11/56)	5	10	15	32	51	70
754-Smokey the Bear	6	12	18	41	66	90
755-The Littlest Snowman (12/56)	5	10	15	32	51	70
756-Santa Claus Funnies	7	14	21	45	73	100
757-The True Story of Jesse James (Movie)-Photo-c	8	16	24	58	97	135
758-Bear Country (Disney-Movie)	5	10	15	34	55	75
759-Circus Boy (TV)-The Monkees' Mickey Dolenz photo-c (12/56)	12	24	36	82	154	225
760-The Hardy Boys (#1) (TV) (Disney)-Mickey Mouse Club; photo-c	10	20	30	69	122	175
761-Howdy Doody (TV) (1/57)	10	20	30	72	131	185
762-The Sharkfighters (Movie) (1/57); Buscema-a; photo-c	7	14	21	50	83	115
763-Grandma Duck's Farm Friends (#1) (Disney)	8	16	24	52	86	120
764-M.G.M's Mouse Musketeers	4	8	12	26	41	55
765-Will-Yum!	4	8	12	26	41	55
766-Buffalo Bill, Jr. (TV)-Photo-c	6	12	18	39	62	85
767-Spin and Marty (TV) (Disney)-Mickey Mouse Club (2/57)	9	18	27	63	107	150
768-Steve Donovan, Western Marshal (TV)-Kinstler-a; photo-c	6	12	18	43	69	95
769-Gunsmoke (TV)-James Arness photo-c	9	18	27	61	103	145
770-Brave Eagle (TV)-Photo-c	4	8	12	26	41	55
771-Brand of Empire (Luke Short)(3/57)-Drucker-a	4	8	12	26	41	55
772-Cheyenne (TV)-Clint Walker photo-c	9	18	27	60	100	140
773-The Brave One (Movie)-Photo-c	5	10	15	34	55	75
774-Hi and Lois (3/57)	4	8	12	24	37	50
775-Sir Lancelot and Brian (TV)-Buscema-a; photo-c	9	18	27	65	113	160
776-Johnny Mack Brown; photo-c	7	14	21	47	76	105
777-Scamp (Disney) (3/57)	6	12	18	43	69	95
778-The Little Rascals (TV)	6	12	18	39	62	85
779-Lee Hunter, Indian Fighter (3/57)	5	10	15	34	55	75
780-Captain Kangaroo (TV)-Photo-c	12	24	36	86	161	235
781-Fury (#1) (TV) (3/57)-Photo-c	8	16	24	52	86	120
782-Duck Album (Disney)	5	10	15	35	55	75
783-Elmer Fudd	4	8	12	28	44	60
784-Around the World in 80 Days (Movie) (2/57)-Photo-c	7	14	21	50	83	115
785-Circus Boy (TV) (4/57)-The Monkees' Mickey Dolenz photo-c	10	20	30	69	122	175
786-Cinderella (Disney) (3/57)-Partial-r of #272	7	14	21	45	73	100
787-Little Hiawatha (Disney) (4/57)(#2)	5	10	15	30	48	65
788-Prince Valiant; by Bob Fuje	7	14	21	47	76	105
789-Silvertip-Valley Thieves (Max Brand) (4/57)-Kinstler-a	5	10	15	30	48	65
790-The Wings of Eagles (Movie) (John Wayne)-Toth-a; John Wayne photo-c; 10¢ & 15¢ editions exist	13	26	39	90	173	255
791-The 77th Bengal Lancers (TV)-Photo-c	7	14	21	47	76	105
792-Oswald the Rabbit (Lantz)	4	8	12	28	44	60
793-Morty Meekle	4	8	12	24	37	50
794-The Count of Monte Cristo (5/57) (Movie)-Buscema-a	8	16	24	56	93	130
795-Jiminy Cricket (Disney)(#2)	6	12	18	43	69	95
796-Ludwig Bemelman's Madeleine and Genevieve	4	8	12	24	37	50
797-Gunsmoke (TV)-Photo-c	9	18	27	61	103	145
798-Buffalo Bill, Jr. (TV)-Photo-c	6	12	18	39	62	85

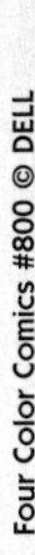
Four Color Comics #800 © DELL

Four Color Comics #815 © DELL

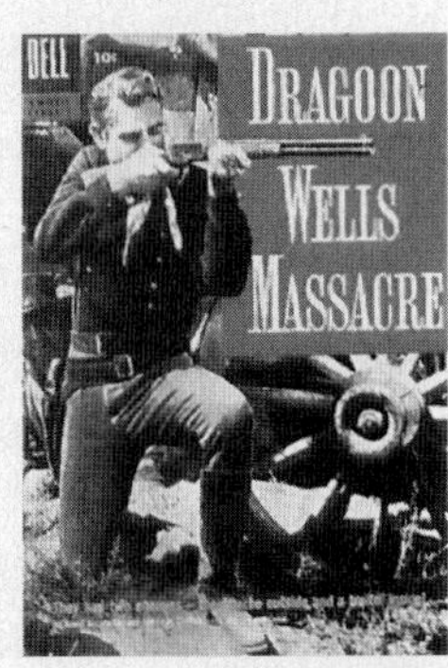

Four Color Comics #919 © Cal. Nat.

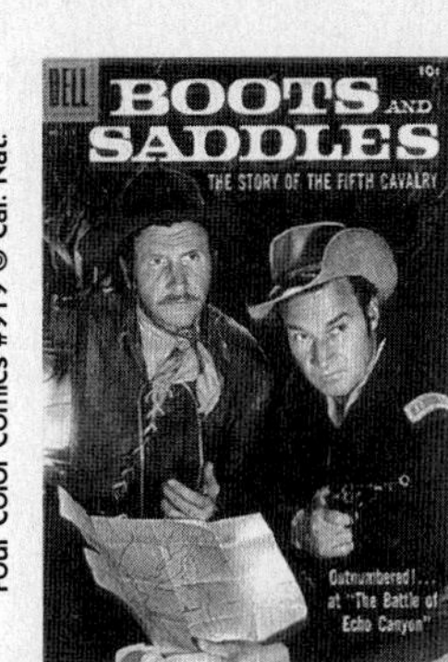

	GD 2.0	VG 4.0	FN 6.0	VF 8.0	VF/NM 9.0	NM- 9.2
799-Priscilla's Pop	4	8	12	26	41	55
800-The Buccaneers (TV)-Photo-c	7	14	21	47	76	105
801-Dotty Dripple and Taffy	4	8	12	22	34	45
802-Goofy (Disney) (5/57)	7	14	21	47	76	105
803-Cheyenne (TV)-Clint Walker photo-c	9	18	27	60	100	140
804-Steve Canyon-Caniff-a (1957)	5	10	15	34	55	75
805-Crusader Rabbit (TV)	17	34	51	124	252	380
806-Scamp (Disney) (6/57)	6	12	18	43	69	95
807-Savage Range (Luke Short)-Drucker-a	4	8	12	26	41	55
808-Spin and Marty (TV)(Disney)-Mickey Mouse Club; photo-c	9	18	27	63	107	150
809-The Little People (Walt Scott)	5	10	15	32	51	70
810-Francis the Famous Talking Mule	4	8	12	26	41	55
811-Howdy Doody (TV) (7/57)	10	20	30	72	131	185
812-The Big Land (Movie); Alan Ladd photo-c	9	18	27	60	100	140
813-Circus Boy (TV)-The Monkees' Mickey Dolenz photo-c	10	20	30	69	122	175
814-Covered Wagons, Ho! (Disney)-Donald Duck (TV) (6/57); Mickey Mouse app.	5	10	15	34	55	75
815-Dragoon Wells Massacre (Movie)-photo-c	7	14	21	50	83	115
816-Brave Eagle (TV)-photo-c	4	8	12	26	41	55
817-Little Beaver	5	10	15	30	48	65
818-Smokey the Bear (6/57)	6	12	18	41	66	90
819-Mickey Mouse in Magicland (Disney) (7/57)	6	12	18	39	62	85
820-The Oklahoman (Movie)-Photo-c	8	16	24	58	97	135
821-Wringle Wrangle (Disney)-Based on movie "Westward Ho, the Wagons"; Marsh-a; Fess Parker photo-c	8	16	24	52	86	120
822-Paul Revere's Ride with Johnny Tremain (TV) (Disney)-Toth-a	8	16	24	58	97	135
823-Timmy	4	8	12	26	41	55
824-The Pride and the Passion (Movie) (8/57)-Frank Sinatra & Cary Grant photo-c	9	18	27	63	107	150
825-The Little Rascals (TV)	6	12	18	39	62	85
826-Spin and Marty and Annette (TV) (Disney)-Mickey Mouse Club; Annette Funicello photo-c	20	40	60	140	283	425
827-Smokey Stover (8/57)	5	10	15	32	51	70
828-Buffalo Bill, Jr. (TV)-Photo-c	6	12	18	39	62	85
829-Tales of the Pony Express (TV) (8/57)-Painted-c	5	10	15	30	48	65
830-The Hardy Boys (TV) (Disney)-Mickey Mouse Club (8/57); photo-c	9	18	27	60	100	140
831-No Sleep 'Til Dawn (Movie)-Karl Malden photo-c	6	12	18	43	69	95
832-Lolly and Pepper (#1)	5	10	15	30	48	65
833-Scamp (Disney) (9/57)	6	12	18	43	69	95
834-Johnny Mack Brown; photo-c	7	14	21	47	76	105
835-Silvertip-The False Rider (Max Brand)	5	10	15	30	48	65
836-Man in Flight (Disney) (TV) (9/57)	7	14	21	47	76	105
837-Cotton Woods, (All-American Athlete...)	4	8	12	24	37	50
838-Bugs Bunny's Life Story Album (9/57)	5	10	15	34	55	75
839-The Vigilantes (Movie)	7	14	21	47	76	105
840-Duck Album (Disney) (9/57)	5	10	15	35	55	75
841-Elmer Fudd	4	8	12	28	44	60
842-The Nature of Things (Disney-Movie) ('57)-Jesse Marsh-a (TV series)	5	10	15	34	55	75
843-The First Americans (Disney) (TV)-Marsh-a	8	16	24	56	93	130
844-Gunsmoke (TV)-Photo-c	9	18	27	61	103	145
845-The Land Unknown (Movie)-Alex Toth-a	11	22	33	75	138	200
846-Gun Glory (Movie)-by Alex Toth; photo-c	8	16	24	58	97	135
847-Perri (squirrels) (Disney-Movie)-Two different covers published	5	10	15	35	55	75
848-Marauder's Moon (Luke Short)	4	8	12	26	41	55
849-Prince Valiant; by Bob Fuje	7	14	21	47	76	105
850-Buck Jones	5	10	15	32	51	70
851-The Story of Mankind (Movie) (1/58)-Hedy Lamarr & Vincent Price photo-c	7	14	21	47	76	105
852-Chilly Willy (2/58) (Lantz)	5	10	15	30	48	65
853-Pluto (Disney) (10/57)	5	10	15	32	51	70
854-The Hunchback of Notre Dame (Movie)-Photo-c	12	24	36	82	154	225
855-Broken Arrow (TV)-Photo-c	6	12	18	37	59	80
856-Buffalo Bill, Jr. (TV)-Photo-c	6	12	18	39	62	85
857-The Goofy Adventure Story (Disney) (11/57)	7	14	21	47	76	105
858-Daisy Duck's Diary (Disney) (11/57)	5	10	15	32	51	70
859-Topper and Neil (TV) (11/57)	5	10	15	30	48	65
860-Wyatt Earp (#1) (TV)-Manning-a; photo-c	9	18	27	65	113	160
861-Frosty the Snowman	5	10	15	32	51	70

	GD 2.0	VG 4.0	FN 6.0	VF 8.0	VF/NM 9.0	NM- 9.2
862-The Truth About Mother Goose (Disney-Movie) (11/57)	7	14	21	49	80	110
863-Francis the Famous Talking Mule	4	8	12	26	41	55
864-The Littlest Snowman	5	10	15	32	51	70
865-Andy Burnett (TV) (Disney) (12/57)-Photo-c	8	16	24	58	97	135
866-Mars and Beyond (Disney-TV)(A science feature from Tomorrowland)	8	16	24	56	93	130
867-Santa Claus Funnies	7	14	21	45	73	100
868-The Little People (12/57)	5	10	15	32	51	70
869-Old Yeller (Disney-Movie)-Photo-c	5	10	15	34	55	75
870-Little Beaver (1/58)	5	10	15	30	48	65
871-Curly Kayoe	4	8	12	24	37	50
872-Captain Kangaroo (TV)-Photo-c	12	24	36	86	161	235
873-Grandma Duck's Farm Friends (Disney)	6	12	18	37	59	80
874-Old Ironsides (Disney-Movie with Johnny Tremain) (1/58)	6	12	18	43	69	95
875-Trumpets West (Luke Short) (2/58)	4	8	12	26	41	55
876-Tales of Wells Fargo (#1)(TV)(2/58)-Photo-c	9	18	27	60	100	140
877-Frontier Doctor with Rex Allen (TV)-Alex Toth-a; Rex Allen photo-c	9	18	27	63	107	150
878-Peanuts (#1)-Schulz-c only (2/58)	22	44	66	159	317	475
879-Brave Eagle (TV) (2/58)-Photo-c	4	8	12	26	41	55
880-Steve Donovan, Western Marshal-Drucker-a (TV)-Photo-c	5	10	15	30	48	65
881-The Captain and the Kids (2/58)	4	8	12	28	44	60
882-Zorro (Disney)-1st Disney issue; by Alex Toth (TV) (2/58); photo-c	14	28	42	96	191	285
883-The Little Rascals (TV)	6	12	18	37	59	80
884-Hawkeye and the Last of the Mohicans (TV) (3/58); photo-c	7	14	21	47	76	105
885-Fury (TV) (3/58)-Photo-c	6	12	18	41	66	90
886-Bongo and Lumpjaw (Disney) (3/58)	5	10	15	30	48	65
887-The Hardy Boys (Disney) (TV)-Mickey Mouse Club (1/58)-Photo-c	9	18	27	60	100	140
888-Elmer Fudd (3/58)	4	8	12	28	44	60
889-Clint and Mac (Disney) (TV) (3/58)-Alex Toth-a; photo-c	11	22	33	75	138	200
890-Wyatt Earp (TV)-by Russ Manning; photo-c	7	14	21	49	80	110
891-Light in the Forest (Disney-Movie) (3/58)-Fess Parker photo-c	7	14	21	50	83	115
892-Maverick (#1) (TV) (4/58)-James Garner photo-c	20	40	60	140	283	425
893-Jim Bowie (TV)-Photo-c	6	12	18	39	62	85
894-Oswald the Rabbit (Lantz)	4	8	12	28	44	60
895-Wagon Train (#1) (TV) (3/58)-Photo-c	10	20	30	70	125	180
896-The Adventures of Tinker Bell (Disney)	8	16	24	56	93	130
897-Jiminy Cricket (Disney)	6	12	18	43	69	95
898-Silvertip (Max Brand)-Kinstler-a (5/58)	5	10	15	30	48	65
899-Goofy (Disney) (5/58)	5	10	15	32	51	70
900-Prince Valiant; by Bob Fuje	7	14	21	47	76	105
901-Little Hiawatha (Disney)	5	10	15	30	48	65
902-Will-Yum!	4	8	12	26	41	55
903-Dotty Dripple and Taffy	4	8	12	22	34	45
904-Lee Hunter, Indian Fighter	4	8	12	26	41	55
905-Annette (Disney) (TV) (5/58)-Mickey Mouse Club; Annette Funicello photo-c	23	46	69	168	334	500
906-Francis the Famous Talking Mule	4	8	12	26	41	55
907-Sugarfoot (#1) (TV)Toth-a; photo-c	11	22	33	79	147	215
908-The Little People and the Giant-Walt Scott (5/58)	5	10	15	32	51	70
909-Smitty	4	8	12	24	37	50
910-The Vikings (Movie)-Buscema-a; Kirk Douglas photo-c	8	16	24	54	90	125
911-The Gray Ghost (TV)-Photo-c	8	16	24	56	93	130
912-Leave It to Beaver (#1) (TV)-Photo-c	14	28	42	99	200	300
913-The Left-Handed Gun (Movie) (7/58); Paul Newman photo-c	9	18	27	63	107	150
914-No Time for Sergeants (Movie)-Andy Griffith photo-c; Toth-a	9	18	27	65	113	160
915-Casey Jones (TV)-Alan Hale photo-c	5	10	15	34	55	75
916-Red Ryder Ranch Comics (7/58)	5	10	15	30	48	65
917-The Life of Riley (TV)-Photo-c	10	20	30	69	122	175
918-Beep Beep, the Roadrunner (#1) (7/58)-Published with two different back covers	11	22	33	77	144	210
919-Boots and Saddles (#1) (TV)-Photo-c	7	14	21	50	83	115

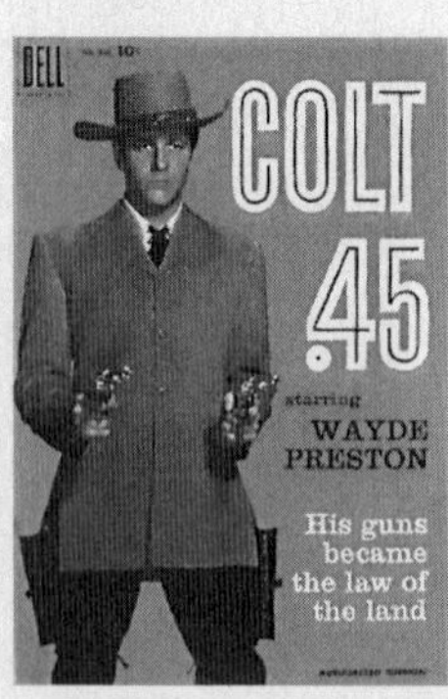

Four Color Comics #924 © WB

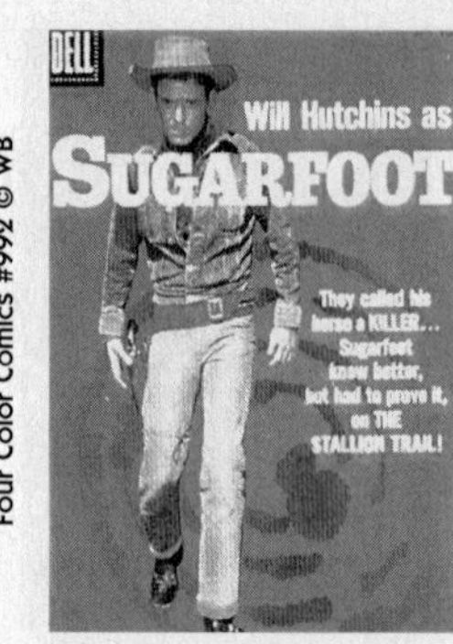

Four Color Comics #992 © WB

Four Color Comics #1040 © H-B

	GD 2.0	VG 4.0	FN 6.0	VF 8.0	VF/NM 9.0	NM- 9.2
920-Zorro (Disney) (TV) (6/58)Toth-a; photo-c	11	22	33	76	141	205
921-Wyatt Earp (TV)-Manning-a; photo-c	7	14	21	49	80	110
922-Johnny Mack Brown by Russ Manning; photo-c	7	14	21	49	80	110
923-Timmy	4	8	12	26	41	55
924-Colt .45 (#1) (TV) (8/58)-W. Preston photo-c	10	20	30	69	122	175
925-Last of the Fast Guns (Movie) (8/58)-Photo-c	6	12	18	43	69	95
926-Peter Pan (Disney)-Reprint of #442	4	8	12	28	44	60
927-Top Gun (Luke Short) Buscema-a	4	8	12	26	41	55
928-Sea Hunt (#1) (9/58) (TV)-Lloyd Bridges photo-c						
	11	22	33	75	138	200
929-Brave Eagle (TV)-Photo-c	4	8	12	26	41	55
930-Maverick (TV) (7/58)-James Garner photo-c	10	20	30	72	131	190
931-Have Gun, Will Travel (#1) (TV)-Photo-c	12	24	36	87	164	240
932-Smokey the Bear (His Life Story)	6	12	18	41	66	90
933-Zorro (Disney, 9/58) (TV)-Alex Toth-a; photo-c	11	22	33	76	141	205
934-Restless Gun (#1) (TV)-Photo-c	10	20	30	70	125	180
935-King of the Royal Mounted	4	8	12	28	44	60
936-The Little Rascals (TV)	6	12	18	37	59	80
937-Ruff and Reddy (#1) (9/58) (TV) (1st Hanna-Barbera comic book)						
	11	22	33	79	147	215
938-Elmer Fudd (9/58)	4	8	12	28	44	60
939-Steve Canyon - not by Caniff	5	10	15	34	55	75
940-Lolly and Pepper (10/58)	4	8	12	22	34	45
941-Pluto (Disney) (10/58)	4	8	12	28	44	60
942-Pony Express (Tales of the ...) (TV)	5	10	15	30	48	65
943-White Wilderness (Disney-Movie) (10/58)	6	12	18	43	69	95
944-The 7th Voyage of Sinbad (Movie) (9/58)-Buscema-a; photo-c						
	12	24	36	82	154	225
945-Maverick (TV)-James Garner/Jack Kelly photo-c	10	20	30	72	131	190
946-The Big Country (Movie)-Photo-c	7	14	21	47	76	105
947-Broken Arrow (TV)-Photo-c (11/58)	5	10	15	32	51	70
948-Daisy Duck's Diary (Disney) (11/58)	5	10	15	32	51	70
949-High Adventure(Lowell Thomas')(TV)-Photo-c	6	12	18	37	59	80
950-Frosty the Snowman	5	10	15	32	51	70
951-The Lennon Sisters Life Story (TV)-Toth-a, 32 pgs.; photo-c						
	12	24	36	87	164	240
952-Goofy (Disney) (11/58)	5	10	15	32	51	70
953-Francis the Famous Talking Mule	4	8	12	26	41	55
954-Man in Space-Satellites (TV)	7	14	21	47	76	105
955-Hi and Lois (11/58)	4	8	12	24	37	50
956-Ricky Nelson (#1) (TV)-Photo-c	16	32	48	111	226	340
957-Buffalo Bee (#1) (TV)	8	16	24	58	97	135
958-Santa Claus Funnies	6	12	18	41	66	90
959-Christmas Stories-(Walt Scott's Little People) (1951-56 strip reprints)						
	5	10	15	32	51	70
960-Zorro (Disney) (TV) (12/58)-Toth art; photo-c	11	22	33	76	141	205
961-Jace Pearson's Tales of the Texas Rangers (TV)-Spiegle-a; photo-c						
	6	12	18	37	59	80
962-Maverick (TV) (1/59)-James Garner/Jack Kelly photo-c						
	10	20	30	72	131	190
963-Johnny Mack Brown; photo-c	7	14	21	47	76	105
964-The Hardy Boys (TV) (Disney) (1/59)-Mickey Mouse Club; photo-c						
	9	18	27	60	100	140
965-Grandma Duck's Farm Friends (Disney)(1/59)	5	10	15	32	51	70
966-Tonka (starring Sal Mineo; Disney-Movie)-Photo-c						
	8	16	24	58	97	135
967-Chilly Willy (2/59) (Lantz)	5	10	15	30	48	65
968-Tales of Wells Fargo (TV)-Photo-c	8	16	24	56	93	130
969-Peanuts (2/59)	13	26	39	94	185	275
970-Lawman (#1) (TV)-Photo-c	12	24	36	82	154	225
971-Wagon Train (TV)-Photo-c	7	14	21	45	73	100
972-Tom Thumb (Movie)-George Pal (1/59)	8	16	24	58	97	135
973-Sleeping Beauty and the Prince(Disney)(5/59)	10	20	30	72	131	190
974-The Little Rascals (TV) (3/59)	6	12	18	37	59	80
975-Fury (TV)-Photo-c	6	12	18	41	66	90
976-Zorro (Disney) (TV)-Toth-a; photo-c	11	22	33	76	141	205
977-Elmer Fudd (3/59)	4	8	12	28	44	60
978-Lolly and Pepper	4	8	12	22	34	45
979-Oswald the Rabbit (Lantz)	4	8	12	28	44	60
980-Maverick (TV) (4-6/59)-James Garner/Jack Kelly photo-c						
	10	20	30	72	131	190
981-Ruff and Reddy (TV) (Hanna-Barbera)	8	16	24	52	86	120
982-The New Adventures of Tinker Bell (TV) (Disney)						
	8	16	24	52	86	120
983-Have Gun, Will Travel (TV) (4-6/59)-Photo-c	9	18	27	60	100	140
984-Sleeping Beauty's Fairy Godmothers (Disney)	9	18	27	61	103	145
985-Shaggy Dog (Disney-Movie)-Photo-all four covers; Annette on back-c(5/59)						
	7	14	21	50	83	115
986-Restless Gun (TV)-Photo-c	8	16	24	52	86	120
987-Goofy (Disney) (7/59)	5	10	15	32	51	70
988-Little Hiawatha (Disney)	5	10	15	30	48	65
989-Jiminy Cricket (Disney) (5-7/59)	6	12	18	43	69	95
990-Huckleberry Hound (#1)(TV)(Hanna-Barbera); 1st app. Huck, Yogi Bear,						
& Pixie & Dixie & Mr. Jinks	12	24	36	84	157	230
991-Francis the Famous Talking Mule	4	8	12	26	41	55
992-Sugarfoot (TV)-Toth-a; photo-c	10	20	30	73	134	195
993-Jim Bowie (TV)-Photo-c	5	10	15	35	55	75
994-Sea Hunt (TV)-Lloyd Bridges photo-c	8	16	24	54	90	125
995-Donald Duck Album (Disney) (5-7/59)(#1)	6	12	18	43	69	95
996-Nevada (Zane Grey)	4	8	12	28	44	60
997-Walt Disney Presents-Tales of Texas John Slaughter (#1) (TV) (Disney)-Photo-c;						
photo of W. Disney inside-c	7	14	21	49	80	110
998-Ricky Nelson (TV)-Photo-c	16	32	48	111	226	340
999-Leave It to Beaver (TV)-Photo-c	13	26	39	89	170	250
1000-The Gray Ghost (TV) (6-8/59)-Photo-c	8	16	24	56	93	130
1001-Lowell Thomas' High Adventure (TV) (8-10/59)-Photo-c						
	5	10	15	34	55	75
1002-Buffalo Bee (TV)	7	14	21	45	73	100
1003-Zorro (TV) (Disney)-Toth-a; photo-c	11	22	33	76	141	205
1004-Colt .45 (TV) (6-8/59)-Photo-c	8	16	24	56	93	130
1005-Maverick (TV)-James Garner/Jack Kelly photo-c						
	10	20	30	72	131	190
1006-Hercules (Movie)-Buscema-a; photo-c	9	18	27	60	100	140
1007-John Paul Jones (Movie)-Robert Stack photo-c	5	10	15	35	55	75
1008-Beep Beep, the Road Runner (7-9/59)	7	14	21	47	76	105
1009-The Rifleman (#1) (TV)-Photo-c	20	40	60	140	283	425
1010-Grandma Duck's Farm Friends (Disney)-by Carl Barks						
	12	24	36	82	154	225
1011-Buckskin (#1) (TV)-Photo-c	7	14	21	47	76	105
1012-Last Train from Gun Hill (Movie) (7/59)-Photo-c	8	16	24	56	93	130
1013-Bat Masterson (#1) (TV) (8/59)-Gene Barry photo-c						
	11	22	33	75	138	200
1014-The Lennon Sisters (TV)-Toth-a; photo-c	12	24	36	82	154	225
1015-Peanuts-Schulz-c	13	26	39	94	185	275
1016-Smokey the Bear Nature Stories	4	8	12	28	44	60
1017-Chilly Willy (Lantz)	5	10	15	30	48	65
1018-Rio Bravo (Movie)(6/59)-John Wayne; Toth-a; John Wayne, Dean Martin						
& Ricky Nelson photo-c	21	42	63	150	300	450
1019-Wagon Train (TV)-Photo-c	7	14	21	45	73	100
1020-Jungle Jim-McWilliams-a	4	8	12	26	41	55
1021-Jace Pearson's Tales of the Texas Rangers (TV)-Photo-c						
	6	12	18	37	59	80
1022-Timmy	4	8	12	26	41	55
1023-Tales of Wells Fargo (TV)-Photo-c	8	16	24	56	93	130
1024-Darby O'Gill and the Little People (Disney-Movie)-Toth-a; photo-c						
	9	18	27	65	113	160
1025-Vacation in Disneyland (8-10/59)-Carl Barks-a(24pgs.) (Disney)						
	15	30	45	103	209	315
1026-Spin and Marty (TV) (Disney) (9-11/59)-Mickey Mouse Club; photo-c						
	8	16	24	52	86	120
1027-The Texan (#1)(TV)-Photo-c	8	16	24	56	93	130
1028-Rawhide (#1) (TV) (9-11/59)-Clint Eastwood photo-c; Tufts-a						
	21	42	63	150	300	450
1029-Boots and Saddles (TV) (9/59)-Photo-c	5	10	15	34	55	75
1030-Spanky and Alfalfa, the Little Rascals (TV)	6	12	18	37	59	80
1031-Fury (TV)-Photo-c	6	12	18	41	66	90
1032-Elmer Fudd	4	8	12	28	44	60
1033-Steve Canyon-not by Caniff; photo-c	5	10	15	34	55	75
1034-Nancy and Sluggo Summer Camp (9-11/59)	5	10	15	32	51	70
1035-Lawman (TV)-Photo-c	8	16	24	54	90	125
1036-The Big Circus (Movie)-Photo-c	6	12	18	43	69	95
1037-Zorro (Disney) (TV)-Tufts-a; Annette Funicello photo-c						
	13	26	39	92	179	265
1038-Ruff and Reddy (TV)(Hanna-Barbera)(1959)	8	16	24	52	86	120
1039-Pluto (Disney) (11-1/60)	4	8	12	28	44	60
1040-Quick Draw McGraw (#1) (TV) (Hanna-Barbera) (12-2/60)						
	12	24	36	87	164	240
1041-Sea Hunt (TV) (10-12/59)-Toth-a; Lloyd Bridges photo-c						

Four Color Comics #1052 © Loew's

Four Color Comics #1085 © Loew's

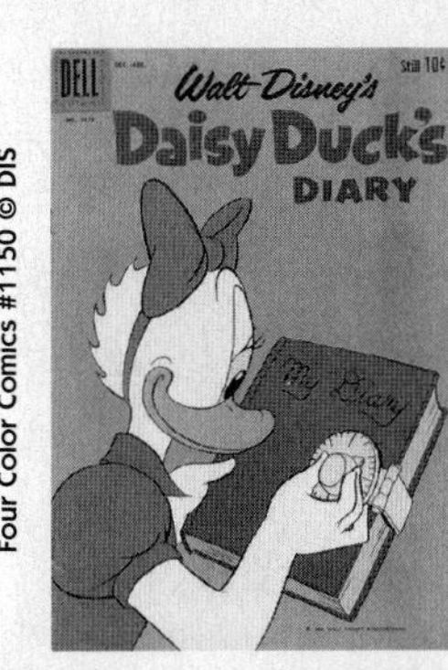

Four Color Comics #1150 © DIS

	GD 2.0	VG 4.0	FN 6.0	VF 8.0	VF/NM 9.0	NM- 9.2
	8	16	24	54	90	125
1042-The Three Chipmunks (Alvin, Simon & Theodore) (#1) (TV) (10-12/59)	8	16	24	56	93	130
1043-The Three Stooges (#1)-Photo-c	22	44	66	161	321	480
1044-Have Gun, Will Travel (TV)-Photo-c	9	18	27	60	100	140
1045-Restless Gun (TV)-Photo-c	8	16	24	52	86	120
1046-Beep Beep, the Road Runner (11-1/60)	7	14	21	47	76	105
1047-Gyro Gearloose (#1) (Disney)-All Barks-c/a	15	30	45	108	219	330
1048-The Horse Soldiers (Movie) (John Wayne)-Sekowsky-a; painted cover featuring John Wayne	12	24	36	87	164	240
1049-Don't Give Up the Ship (Movie) (8/59)-Jerry Lewis photo-c	9	18	27	61	103	145
1050-Huckleberry Hound (TV) (Hanna-Barbera) (10-12/59)	8	16	24	58	97	135
1051-Donald in Mathmagic Land (Disney-Movie)	9	18	27	63	107	150
1052-Ben-Hur (Movie) (11/59)-Manning-a	10	20	30	67	116	165
1053-Goofy (Disney) (11-1/60)	5	10	15	32	51	70
1054-Huckleberry Hound Winter Fun (TV) (Hanna-Barbera) (12/59)	8	16	24	58	97	135
1055-Daisy Duck's Diary (Disney)-by Carl Barks (11-1/60)	9	18	27	60	100	140
1056-Yellowstone Kelly (Movie)-Clint Walker photo-c	6	12	18	37	59	80
1057-Mickey Mouse Album (Disney)	5	10	15	35	55	75
1058-Colt .45 (TV)-Photo-c	8	16	24	56	93	130
1059-Sugarfoot (TV)-Photo-c	8	16	24	58	97	135
1060-Journey to the Center of the Earth (Movie)-Pat Boone & James Mason photo-c	10	20	30	71	128	185
1061-Buffalo Bee (TV)	7	14	21	45	73	100
1062-Christmas Stories (Walt Scott's Little People strip-r)	5	10	15	32	51	70
1063-Santa Claus Funnies	6	12	18	41	66	90
1064-Bugs Bunny's Merry Christmas (12/59)	5	10	15	34	55	75
1065-Frosty the Snowman	5	10	15	32	51	70
1066-77 Sunset Strip (#1) (TV)-Toth-a (1-3/60)-Efrem Zimbalist, Jr. & Edd "Kookie" Byrnes photo-c	10	20	30	70	125	180
1067-Yogi Bear (#1) (TV) (Hanna-Barbera)	11	22	33	75	138	200
1068-Francis the Famous Talking Mule	4	8	12	26	41	55
1069-The FBI Story (Movie)-Toth-a; James Stewart photo on-c	9	18	27	63	107	150
1070-Solomon and Sheba (Movie)-Sekowsky-a; photo-c	8	16	24	58	97	135
1071-The Real McCoys (#1) (TV) (1-3/60)-Toth-a; Walter Brennan photo-c	9	18	27	60	100	140
1072-Blythe (Marge's)	6	12	18	37	59	80
1073-Grandma Duck's Farm Friends-Barks-c/a (Disney)	12	24	36	82	154	225
1074-Chilly Willy (Lantz)	5	10	15	30	48	65
1075-Tales of Wells Fargo (TV)-Photo-c	8	16	24	56	93	130
1076-The Rebel (#1) (TV)-Sekowsky-a; photo-c	9	18	27	65	113	160
1077-The Deputy (#1) (TV)-Buscema-a; Henry Fonda photo-c	11	22	33	75	138	200
1078-The Three Stooges (2-4/60)-Photo-c	12	24	36	84	157	230
1079-The Little Rascals (TV) (Spanky & Alfalfa)	6	12	18	37	59	80
1080-Fury (TV) (2-4/60)-Photo-c	6	12	18	41	66	90
1081-Elmer Fudd	4	8	12	28	44	60
1082-Spin and Marty (Disney) (TV)-Photo-c	8	16	24	52	86	120
1083-Men into Space (TV)-Anderson-a; photo-c	5	10	15	34	55	75
1084-Speedy Gonzales	5	10	15	34	55	75
1085-The Time Machine (H.G. Wells) (Movie) (3/60)-Alex Toth-a; Rod Taylor photo-c	13	26	39	92	179	265
1086-Lolly and Pepper	4	8	12	22	34	45
1087-Peter Gunn (TV)-Photo-c	8	16	24	58	97	135
1088-A Dog of Flanders (Movie)-Photo-c	5	10	15	30	48	65
1089-Restless Gun (TV)-Photo-c	8	16	24	52	86	120
1090-Francis the Famous Talking Mule	4	8	12	26	41	55
1091-Jacky's Diary (4-6/60)	5	10	15	30	48	65
1092-Toby Tyler (Disney-Movie)-Photo-c	6	12	18	43	69	95
1093-MacKenzie's Raiders (Movie/TV)-Richard Carlson photo-c from TV show	6	12	18	43	69	95
1094-Goofy (Disney)	5	10	15	32	51	70
1095-Gyro Gearloose (Disney)-All Barks-c/a	10	20	30	67	116	165
1096-The Texan (TV)-Rory Calhoun photo-c	8	16	24	52	86	120
1097-Rawhide (TV)-Manning-a; Clint Eastwood photo-c	13	26	39	93	182	270
1098-Sugarfoot (TV)-Photo-c	8	16	24	58	97	135
1099-Donald Duck Album (Disney) (5-7/60)-Barks-c	7	14	21	45	73	100
1100-Annette's Life Story (Disney-Movie) (5/60)-Annette Funicello photo-c	18	36	54	131	266	400
1101-Robert Louis Stevenson's Kidnapped (Disney-Movie) (5/60); photo-c	6	12	18	43	69	95
1102-Wanted: Dead or Alive (#1) (TV) (5-7/60); Steve McQueen photo-c	12	24	36	82	154	225
1103-Leave It to Beaver (TV)-Photo-c	13	26	39	89	170	250
1104-Yogi Bear Goes to College (TV) (Hanna-Barbera) (6-8/60)	7	14	21	49	80	110
1105-Gale Storm (Oh! Susanna) (TV)-Toth-a; photo-c	11	22	33	76	136	195
1106-77 Sunset Strip(TV)(6-8/60)-Toth-a; photo-c	8	16	24	58	97	135
1107-Buckskin (TV)-Photo-c	6	12	18	43	69	95
1108-The Troubleshooters (TV)-Keenan Wynn photo-c	5	10	15	34	55	75
1109-This Is Your Life, Donald Duck (Disney) (TV) (8-10/60)-Gyro flashback to WDC&S #141; origin Donald Duck (1st told)	13	26	39	91	176	260
1110-Bonanza (#1) (TV) (6-8/60)-Photo-c	29	58	87	223	449	675
1111-Shotgun Slade (TV)-Photo-c	6	12	18	41	66	90
1112-Pixie and Dixie and Mr. Jinks (#1) (TV) (Hanna-Barbera) (7-9/60)	7	14	21	50	83	115
1113-Tales of Wells Fargo (TV)-Photo-c	8	16	24	56	93	130
1114-Huckleberry Finn (Movie) (7/60)-Photo-c	5	10	15	34	55	75
1115-Ricky Nelson (TV)-Manning-a; photo-c	13	26	39	92	179	265
1116-Boots and Saddles (TV) (8/60)-Photo-c	5	10	15	34	55	75
1117-Boy and the Pirates (Movie)-Photo-c	6	12	18	43	69	95
1118-The Sword and the Dragon (Movie) (6/60)-Photo-c	7	14	21	50	83	115
1119-Smokey the Bear Nature Stories	4	8	12	28	44	60
1120-Dinosaurus (Movie)-Painted-c	8	16	24	56	93	130
1121-Hercules Unchained (Movie) (8/60)-Crandall/Evans-a	9	18	27	60	100	140
1122-Chilly Willy (Lantz)	5	10	15	30	48	65
1123-Tombstone Territory (TV)-Photo-c	8	16	24	56	93	130
1124-Whirlybirds (#1) (TV)-Photo-c	8	16	24	56	93	130
1125-Laramie (#1) (TV)-Photo-c; G. Kane/Heath-a	8	16	24	58	97	135
1126-Hotel Deparee - Sundance (TV) (8-10/60)-Earl Holliman photo-c	6	12	18	43	69	95
1127-The Three Stooges-Photo-c (8-10/60)	12	24	36	84	157	230
1128-Rocky and His Friends (#1) (TV) (Jay Ward) (8-10/60)	27	54	81	197	399	600
1129-Pollyanna (Disney-Movie)-Hayley Mills photo-c	7	14	21	50	83	115
1130-The Deputy (TV)-Buscema-a; Henry Fonda photo-c	9	18	27	63	107	150
1131-Elmer Fudd (9-11/60)	4	8	12	28	44	60
1132-Space Mouse (Lantz) (8-10/60)	4	8	12	28	44	60
1133-Fury (TV)-Photo-c	6	12	18	41	66	90
1134-Real McCoys (TV)-Toth-a; photo-c	9	18	27	60	100	140
1135-M.G.M.'s Mouse Musketeers (9-11/60)	4	8	12	24	37	50
1136-Jungle Cat (Disney-Movie)-Photo-c	6	12	18	43	69	95
1137-The Little Rascals (TV)	6	12	18	37	59	80
1138-The Rebel (TV)-Photo-c	8	16	24	56	93	130
1139-Spartacus (Movie) (11/60)-Buscema-a; Kirk Douglas photo-c	12	24	36	82	154	225
1140-Donald Duck Album (Disney)-Barks-c	7	14	21	45	73	100
1141-Huckleberry Hound for President (TV) (Hanna-Barbera) (10/60)	8	16	24	52	86	120
1142-Johnny Ringo (TV)-Photo-c	7	14	21	47	76	105
1143-Pluto (Disney) (11-1/61)	4	8	12	28	44	60
1144-The Story of Ruth (Movie)-Photo-c	8	16	24	58	97	135
1145-The Lost World (Movie)-Gil Kane-a; photo-c; 1 pg. Conan Doyle biography by Torres	9	18	27	64	110	155
1146-Restless Gun (TV)-Photo-c; Wildey-a	8	16	24	52	86	120
1147-Sugarfoot (TV)-Photo-c	8	16	24	58	97	135
1148-I Aim at the Stars-the Wernher Von Braun Story (Movie) (11-1/61)-Photo-c	7	14	21	47	76	105
1149-Goofy (Disney) (11-1/61)	5	10	15	32	51	70
1150-Daisy Duck's Diary (Disney) (12-1/61) by Carl Barks	9	18	27	60	100	140
1151-Mickey Mouse Album (Disney) (11-1/61)	5	10	15	35	55	75
1152-Rocky and His Friends (TV) (Jay Ward) (12-2/61)	17	34	51	118	242	365

Four Color Comics #1179 © DIS

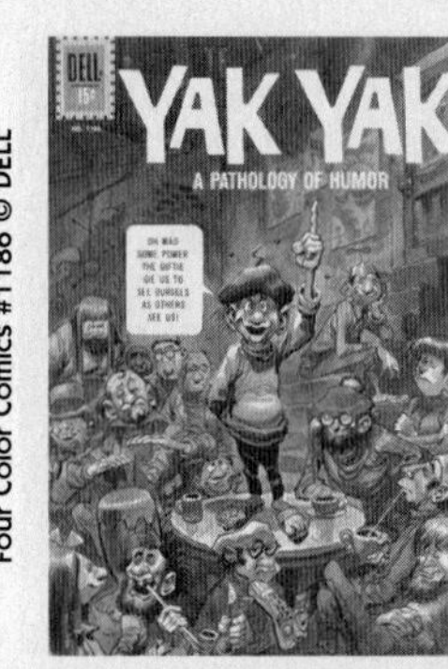

Four Color Comics #1186 © DELL

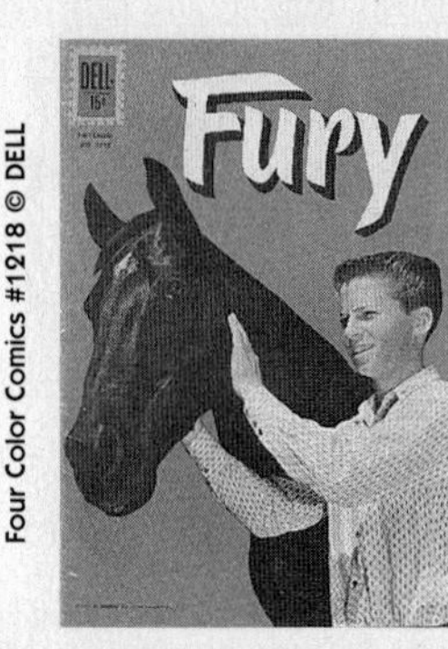

Four Color Comics #1218 © DELL

	GD 2.0	VG 4.0	FN 6.0	VF 8.0	VF/NM 9.0	NM- 9.2
1153-Frosty the Snowman	5	10	15	32	51	70
1154-Santa Claus Funnies	6	12	18	41	66	90
1155-North to Alaska (Movie)-John Wayne photo-c	15	30	45	103	209	315
1156-Walt Disney Swiss Family Robinson (Movie) (12/60)-Photo-c	7	14	21	49	80	110
1157-Master of the World (Movie) (7/61)	7	14	21	45	73	100
1158-Three Worlds of Gulliver (2 issues exist with different covers) (Movie)-Photo-c	7	14	21	45	73	100
1159-77 Sunset Strip (TV)-Toth-a; photo-c	8	16	24	58	97	135
1160-Rawhide (TV)-Clint Eastwood photo-c	13	26	39	93	182	270
1161-Grandma Duck's Farm Friends (Disney) by Carl Barks (2-4/61)	12	24	36	82	154	225
1162-Yogi Bear Joins the Marines (TV) (Hanna-Barbera) (5-7/61)	7	14	21	49	80	110
1163-Daniel Boone (3-5/61); Marsh-a	5	10	15	35	55	75
1164-Wanted: Dead or Alive (TV)-Steve McQueen photo-c	9	18	27	63	107	150
1165-Ellery Queen (#1) (3-5/61)	10	20	30	69	122	175
1166-Rocky and His Friends (TV) (Jay Ward)	17	34	51	118	242	365
1167-Tales of Wells Fargo (TV)-Photo-c	8	16	24	52	86	120
1168-The Detectives (TV)-Robert Taylor photo-c	9	18	27	65	113	160
1169-New Adventures of Sherlock Holmes	13	26	39	91	176	260
1170-The Three Stooges (3-5/61)-Photo-c	12	24	36	84	157	230
1171-Elmer Fudd	4	8	12	28	44	60
1172-Fury (TV)-Photo-c	6	12	18	41	66	90
1173-The Twilight Zone (#1) (TV) (5/61)-Crandall/Evans-c/a; Crandall tribute to Ingles	20	40	60	144	290	435
1174-The Little Rascals (TV)	5	10	15	30	48	65
1175-M.G.M.'s Mouse Musketeers (3-5/61)	4	8	12	24	37	50
1176-Dondi (Movie)-Origin; photo-c	5	10	15	35	55	75
1177-Chilly Willy (Lantz) (4-6/61)	5	10	15	30	48	65
1178-Ten Who Dared (Disney-Movie) (12/60)-Painted-c; cast member photo on back-c	7	14	21	49	80	110
1179-The Swamp Fox (TV) (Disney)-Leslie Nielsen photo-c	8	16	24	56	93	130
1180-The Danny Thomas Show (TV)-Toth-a; photo-c	14	28	42	96	191	285
1181-Texas John Slaughter (TV) (Walt Disney Presents...) (4-6/61)-Photo-c	6	12	18	39	62	85
1182-Donald Duck Album (Disney) (5-7/61)	5	10	15	32	51	70
1183-101 Dalmatians (Disney-Movie) (3/61)	10	20	30	67	116	165
1184-Gyro Gearloose; All Barks-c/a (Disney) (5-7/61) Two variations exist	10	20	30	67	116	165
1185-Sweetie Pie	5	10	15	30	48	65
1186-Yak Yak (#1) by Jack Davis (2 versions - one minus 3-pg. Davis-c/a)	8	16	24	58	97	135
1187-The Three Stooges (6-8/61)-Photo-c	12	24	36	84	157	230
1188-Atlantis, the Lost Continent (Movie) (5/61)-Photo-c	10	20	30	68	119	170
1189-Greyfriars Bobby (Disney-Movie) (11/61)-Photo-c (scarce)	7	14	21	47	76	105
1190-Donald and the Wheel (Disney-Movie) (11/61); Barks-c	8	16	24	54	90	125
1191-Leave It to Beaver (TV)-Photo-c	13	26	39	89	170	250
1192-Ricky Nelson (TV)-Manning-a; photo-c	13	26	39	92	179	265
1193-The Real McCoys (TV) (6-8/61)-Photo-c	8	16	24	56	93	130
1194-Pepe (Movie) (4/61)-Photo-c	4	8	12	24	37	50
1195-National Velvet (#1) (TV)-Photo-c	7	14	21	49	80	110
1196-Pixie and Dixie and Mr. Jinks (TV) (Hanna-Barbera) (7-9/61)	6	12	18	37	59	80
1197-The Aquanauts (TV) (5-7/61)-Photo-c	7	14	21	47	76	105
1198-Donald in Mathmagic Land (Disney-Movie)-Reprint of #1051	6	12	18	43	69	95
1199-The Absent-Minded Professor (Disney-Movie) (4/61)-Photo-c	8	16	24	56	93	130
1200-Hennessey (TV) (8-10/61)-Gil Kane-a; photo-c	7	14	21	47	76	105
1201-Goofy (Disney) (8-10/61)	5	10	15	32	51	70
1202-Rawhide (TV)-Clint Eastwood photo-c	13	26	39	93	182	270
1203-Pinocchio (Disney) (3/62)	5	10	15	34	55	75
1204-Scamp (Disney)	4	8	12	28	44	60
1205-David and Goliath (Movie) (7/61)-Photo-c	6	12	18	43	69	95
1206-Lolly and Pepper (9-11/61)	4	8	12	22	34	45
1207-The Rebel (TV)-Sekowsky-a; photo-c	8	16	24	56	93	130
1208-Rocky and His Friends (Jay Ward) (TV)	17	34	51	118	242	365

	GD 2.0	VG 4.0	FN 6.0	VF 8.0	VF/NM 9.0	NM- 9.2
1209-Sugarfoot (TV)-Photo-c (10-12/61)	8	16	24	58	97	135
1210-The Parent Trap (Disney-Movie) (8/61)-Hayley Mills photo-c	9	18	27	60	100	140
1211-77 Sunset Strip (TV)-Manning-a; photo-c	8	16	24	54	90	125
1212-Chilly Willy (Lantz) (7-9/61)	5	10	15	30	48	65
1213-Mysterious Island (Movie)-Photo-c	8	16	24	56	93	130
1214-Smokey the Bear	4	8	12	28	44	60
1215-Tales of Wells Fargo (TV) (10-12/61)-Photo-c	8	16	24	52	86	120
1216-Whirlybirds (TV)-Photo-c	8	16	24	52	86	120
1218-Fury (TV)-Photo-c	6	12	18	41	66	90
1219-The Detectives (TV)-Robert Taylor & Adam West photo-c	9	18	27	60	100	140
1220-Gunslinger (TV)-Photo-c	8	16	24	56	93	130
1221-Bonanza (TV) (9-11/61)-Photo-c	16	32	48	111	226	340
1222-Elmer Fudd (9-11/61)	4	8	12	28	44	60
1223-Laramie (TV)-Gil Kane-a; photo-c	6	12	18	43	69	95
1224-The Little Rascals (TV) (10-12/61)	5	10	15	30	48	65
1225-The Deputy (TV)-Henry Fonda photo-c	9	18	27	63	107	150
1226-Nikki, Wild Dog of the North (Disney-Movie) (9/61)-Photo-c	5	10	15	34	55	75
1227-Morgan the Pirate (Movie)-Photo-c	7	14	21	50	83	115
1229-Thief of Baghdad (Movie)-Crandall/Evans-a; photo-c	7	14	21	45	73	100
1230-Voyage to the Bottom of the Sea (#1) (Movie)-Photo insert on-c	10	20	30	70	125	180
1231-Danger Man (TV) (9-11/61)-Patrick McGoohan photo-c	10	20	30	70	125	180
1232-On the Double (Movie)	5	10	15	30	48	65
1233-Tammy Tell Me True (Movie) (1961)	6	12	18	43	69	95
1234-The Phantom Planet (Movie) (1961)	7	14	21	47	76	105
1235-Mister Magoo (#1) (12-2/62)	8	16	24	56	93	130
1235-Mister Magoo (3-5/65) 2nd printing; reprint of 12-2/62 issue	6	12	18	41	66	90
1236-King of Kings (Movie)-Photo-c	7	14	21	50	83	115
1237-The Untouchables (#1) (TV)-Not by Toth; photo-c	18	36	54	127	259	390
1238-Deputy Dawg (TV)	10	20	30	71	128	185
1239-Donald Duck Album (Disney) (10-12/61)-Barks-c	7	14	21	45	73	100
1240-The Detectives (TV)-Tufts-a; Robert Taylor photo-c	8	16	24	56	93	130
1241-Sweetie Pie	4	8	12	24	37	50
1242-King Leonardo and His Short Subjects (#1) (TV) (11-1/62)	11	22	33	79	147	215
1243-Ellery Queen	8	16	24	56	93	130
1244-Space Mouse (Lantz) (11-1/62)	4	8	12	28	44	60
1245-New Adventures of Sherlock Holmes	12	24	36	84	157	230
1246-Mickey Mouse Album (Disney)	5	10	15	35	55	75
1247-Daisy Duck's Diary (Disney) (12-2/62)	5	10	15	32	51	70
1248-Pluto (Disney)	4	8	12	28	44	60
1249-The Danny Thomas Show (TV)-Manning-a; photo-c	13	26	39	91	176	260
1250-The Four Horsemen of the Apocalypse (Movie)-Photo-c	6	12	18	43	69	95
1251-Everything's Ducky (Movie) (1961)	5	10	15	30	48	65
1252-The Andy Griffith Show (TV)-Photo-c; 1st show aired 10/3/60	34	68	102	262	519	775
1253-Space Man (#1) (1-3/62)	7	14	21	49	80	110
1254- "Diver Dan" (#1) (TV) (2-4/62)-Photo-c	5	10	15	34	55	75
1255-The Wonders of Aladdin (Movie) (1961)	6	12	18	43	69	95
1256-Kona, Monarch of Monster Isle (#1) (2-4/62)-Glanzman-a	9	18	27	65	113	160
1257-Car 54, Where Are You? (#1) (TV) (3-5/62)-Photo-c	8	16	24	56	93	130
1258-The Frogmen (#1)-Evans-a	8	16	24	52	86	120
1259-El Cid (Movie) (1961)-Photo-c	7	14	21	47	76	105
1260-The Horsemasters (TV, Movie) (Disney) (12-2/62)-Annette Funicello photo-c	12	24	36	82	154	225
1261-Rawhide (TV)-Clint Eastwood photo-c	13	26	39	93	182	270
1262-The Rebel (TV)-Photo-c	8	16	24	56	93	130
1263-77 Sunset Strip (TV) (12-2/62)-Manning-a; photo-c	8	16	24	54	90	125
1264-Pixie and Dixie and Mr. Jinks (TV) (Hanna-Barbera)	6	12	18	37	59	80

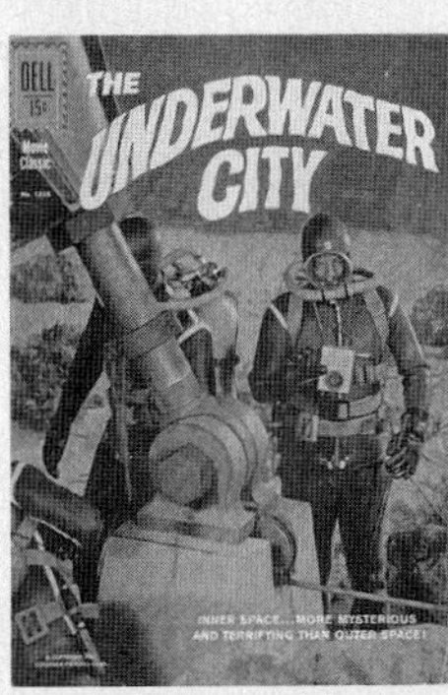

Four Color Comics #1328 © Columbia

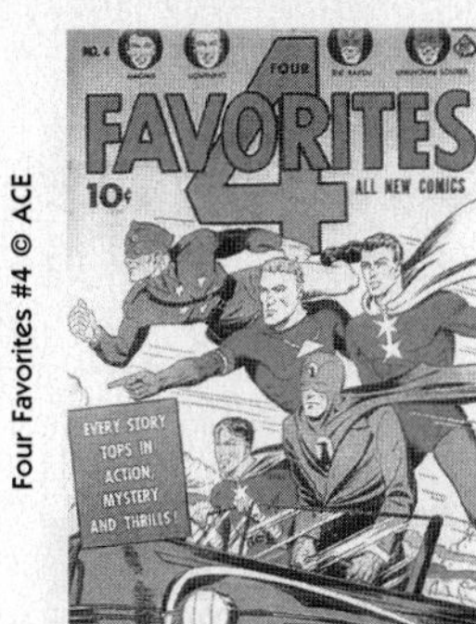

Four Favorites #4 © ACE

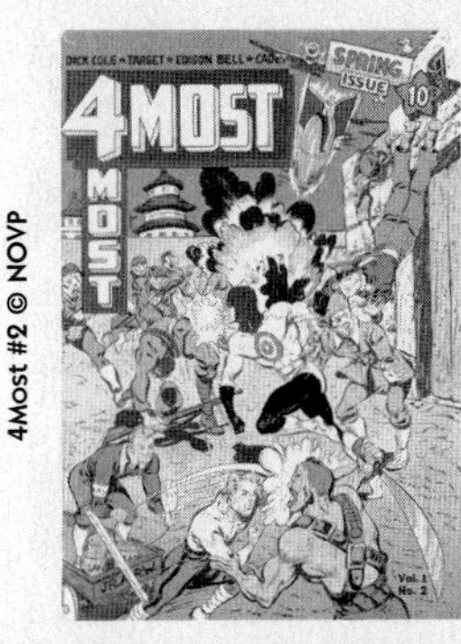

4Most #2 © NOVP

	GD 2.0	VG 4.0	FN 6.0	VF 8.0	VF/NM 9.0	NM- 9.2
1265-The Real McCoys (TV)-Photo-c	8	16	24	56	93	130
1266-M.G.M.'s Spike and Tyke (12-2/62)	4	8	12	24	37	50
1267-Gyro Gearloose; Barks-c/a, 4 pgs. (Disney) (12-2/62)	8	16	24	54	90	125
1268-Oswald the Rabbit (Lantz)	4	8	12	28	44	60
1269-Rawhide (TV)-Clint Eastwood photo-c	13	26	39	93	182	270
1270-Bullwinkle and Rocky (#1) (TV) (Jay Ward) (3-5/62)	17	34	51	122	249	375
1271-Yogi Bear Birthday Party (TV) (Hanna-Barbera) (11/61) (Given away for 1 box top from Kellogg's Corn Flakes)	6	12	18	37	59	80
1272-Frosty the Snowman	5	10	15	32	51	70
1273-Hans Brinker (Disney-Movie)-Photo-c (2/62)	6	12	18	43	69	95
1274-Santa Claus Funnies (12/61)	6	12	18	41	66	90
1275-Rocky and His Friends (TV) (Jay Ward)	17	34	51	118	242	365
1276-Dondi	4	8	12	22	34	45
1278-King Leonardo and His Short Subjects (TV)	11	22	33	79	147	215
1279-Grandma Duck's Farm Friends (Disney)	5	10	15	32	51	70
1280-Hennesey (TV)-Photo-c	6	12	18	43	69	95
1281-Chilly Willy (Lantz) (4-6/62)	5	10	15	30	48	65
1282-Babes in Toyland (Disney-Movie) (1/62); Annette Funicello photo-c	13	26	39	91	176	260
1283-Bonanza (TV) (2-4/62)-Photo-c	16	32	48	111	226	340
1284-Laramie (TV)-Heath-a; photo-c	6	12	18	43	69	95
1285-Leave It to Beaver (TV)-Photo-c	13	26	39	89	170	250
1286-The Untouchables (TV)-Photo-c	13	26	39	92	179	265
1287-Man from Wells Fargo (TV)-Photo-c	6	12	18	37	59	80
1288-Twilight Zone (TV) (4/62)-Crandall/Evans-c/a	12	24	36	82	154	225
1289-Ellery Queen	8	16	24	56	93	130
1290-M.G.M.'s Mouse Musketeers	4	8	12	24	37	50
1291-77 Sunset Strip (TV)-Manning-a; photo-c	8	16	24	54	90	125
1293-Elmer Fudd (3-5/62)	4	8	12	28	44	60
1294-Ripcord (TV)	7	14	21	47	76	105
1295-Mister Ed, the Talking Horse (#1) (TV) (3-5/62)-Photo-c	12	24	36	82	154	225
1296-Fury (TV) (3-5/62)-Photo-c	6	12	18	41	66	90
1297-Spanky, Alfalfa and the Little Rascals (TV)	5	10	15	30	48	65
1298-The Hathaways (TV)-Photo-c	5	10	15	30	48	65
1299-Deputy Dawg (TV)	10	20	30	71	128	185
1300-The Comancheros (Movie) (1961)-John Wayne photo-c	14	28	42	95	188	280
1301-Adventures in Paradise (TV) (2-4/62)	6	12	18	39	62	85
1302-Johnny Jason, Teen Reporter (2-4/62)	4	8	12	24	37	50
1303-Lad: A Dog (Movie)-Photo-c	4	8	12	28	44	60
1304-Nellie the Nurse (3-5/62)-Stanley-a	7	14	21	47	76	105
1305-Mister Magoo (3-5/62)	8	16	24	56	93	130
1306-Target: The Corruptors (#1) (TV) (3-5/62)-Photo-c	6	12	18	37	59	80
1307-Margie (TV) (3-5/62)	6	12	18	37	59	80
1308-Tales of the Wizard of Oz (TV) (3-5/62)	11	22	33	75	138	200
1309-87th Precinct (#1) (TV) (4-6/62)-Krigstein-a; photo-c	9	18	27	65	113	160
1310-Huck and Yogi Winter Sports (TV) (Hanna-Barbera) (3/62)	8	16	24	56	93	130
1311-Rocky and His Friends (TV) (Jay Ward)	17	34	51	118	242	365
1312-National Velvet (TV)-Photo-c	4	8	12	28	44	60
1313-Moon Pilot (Disney-Movie)-Photo-c	7	14	21	47	76	105
1328-The Underwater City (Movie) (1961)-Evans-a; photo-c	7	14	21	47	76	105
1329-See Gyro Gearloose #01329-207						
1330-Brain Boy (#1)-Gil Kane-a	11	22	33	75	138	200
1332-Bachelor Father (TV)	7	14	21	50	83	115
1333-Short Ribs (4-6/62)	5	10	15	34	55	75
1335-Aggie Mack (4-6/62)	5	10	15	30	48	65
1336-On Stage; not by Leonard Starr	5	10	15	30	48	65
1337-Dr. Kildare (#1) (TV) (4-6/62)-Photo-c	8	16	24	58	97	135
1341-The Andy Griffith Show (TV) (4-6/62)-Photo-c	32	64	96	246	486	725
1348-Yak Yak (#2)-Jack Davis-c/a	8	16	24	52	86	120
1349-Yogi Bear Visits the U.N. (TV) (Hanna-Barbera) (1/62)-Photo-c	8	16	24	58	97	135
1350-Comanche (Disney-Movie)(1962)-Reprints 4-Color #966 (title change from "Tonka" to "Comanche") (4-6/62)-Sal Mineo photo-c	5	10	15	35	55	75
1354-Calvin & the Colonel (#1) (TV) (4-6/62)	8	16	24	56	93	130

NOTE: *Missing numbers probably do not exist.*

4-D MONKEY, THE (Adventures of... #? on)
Leung's Publications: 1988 - No. 11, 1990 ($1.80/$2.00, 52 pgs.)

	GD 2.0	VG 4.0	FN 6.0	VF 8.0	VF/NM 9.0	NM- 9.2
1-11: 1-Karate Pig, Ninja Flounder & 4-D Monkey (48 pgs., centerfold is a Christmas card). 2-4 (52 pgs.)						4.00

FOUR FAVORITES (Crime Must Pay the Penalty No. 33 on)
Ace Magazines: Sept, 1941 - No. 32, Dec, 1947

	GD 2.0	VG 4.0	FN 6.0	VF 8.0	VF/NM 9.0	NM- 9.2
1-Vulcan, Lash Lightning (formerly Flash Lightning in Sure-Fire), Magno the Magnetic Man & The Raven begin; flag/Hitler-c	187	374	561	1197	2049	2900
2-The Black Ace only app.	65	130	195	416	708	1000
3-Last Vulcan	53	106	159	334	567	800
4,5: 4-The Raven & Vulcan end; Unknown Soldier begins (see Our Flag), ends #28. 5-Captain Courageous begins (5/42), ends #28 (moves over from Captain Courageous #6); not in #6	47	94	141	296	498	700
6-8: 6-The Flag app.; Mr. Risk begins (7/42)	43	86	129	271	461	650
9-Kurtzman-a (Lash Lightning); robot-c	48	96	144	302	514	725
10-Classic Kurtzman-c/a (Magno & Davey)	60	120	180	381	653	925
11-Kurtzman-a; Hitler, Mussolini, Hirohito-c; L.B. Cole-a; Unknown Soldier by Kurtzman	97	194	291	621	1061	1500
12-L.B. Cole-a	40	80	120	246	411	575
13-L.B. Cole-c (his first cover?)	65	130	195	416	708	1000
14-20: 18,20-Palais-c/a	37	74	111	222	361	500
21-No Unknown Soldier; The Unknown app.	26	52	78	154	252	350
22-26: 22-Captain Courageous drops costume. 23-Unknown Soldier drops costume. 25-29-Hap Hazard app. 26-Last Magno	26	52	78	154	252	350
27-29: Hap Hazard app. in all	21	42	63	122	199	275
30-32: 30-Funny-c begin (teen humor), end #32	15	30	45	83	124	165

NOTE: ***Dave Berg** c-5. **Jim Mooney** a-6; c-1-3. **Palais** a-18-20; c-18-25. Torture chamber c-5.*

FOUR HORSEMEN, THE (See The Crusaders)

FOUR HORSEMEN
DC Comics (Vertigo): Feb, 2000 - No. 4, May, 2000 ($2.50, limited series)

	GD 2.0	VG 4.0	FN 6.0	VF 8.0	VF/NM 9.0	NM- 9.2
1-4-Essad Ribic-c/a; Robert Rodi-s						3.00

FOUR HORSEMEN OF THE APOCALYPSE, THE (Movie)
Dell Publishing Co.: No. 1250, Jan-Mar, 1962 (one-shot)

	GD 2.0	VG 4.0	FN 6.0	VF 8.0	VF/NM 9.0	NM- 9.2
Four Color 1250-Photo-c	6	12	18	43	69	95

4MOST (Foremost Boys No. 32-40; becomes Thrilling Crime Cases #41 on)
Novelty Publications/Star Publications No. 37-on:
Winter, 1941-42 - V8#5(#36), 9-10/49; #37, 11-12/49 - #40, 4-5/50

	GD 2.0	VG 4.0	FN 6.0	VF 8.0	VF/NM 9.0	NM- 9.2
V1#1-The Target by Sid Greene, The Cadet & Dick Cole begin with origins retold; produced by Funnies Inc.; quarterly issues begin, end V6#3	152	304	456	965	1658	2350
2-Last Target (Spr/42); WWII cover	63	126	189	403	689	975
3-Dan'l Flannel begins; flag-c	47	94	141	296	498	700
4-1pg. Dr. Seuss (signed) (Aut/42); fish in the face-c	49	98	147	309	522	735
V2#1-3	20	40	60	114	182	250
4-Hitler, Tojo & Mussolini app. as pumpkins on-c	43	86	129	271	461	650
V3#1-4	15	30	45	88	137	185
V4#1-4: 2-Walter Johnson-c	13	26	39	74	105	135
V5#1-4: 1-The Target & Targeteers app.	11	22	33	64	90	115
V6#1-4	10	20	30	56	76	95
5-L. B. Cole-c	20	40	60	114	182	250
V7#1,3,5, V8#1, 37	10	20	30	56	76	95
2,4,6-L. B. Cole-c. 6-Last Dick Cole	20	40	60	114	182	250
V8#2,3,5-L. B. Cole-c/a	22	44	66	132	216	300
4-L. B. Cole-a	15	30	45	83	124	165
38-40: 38-Johnny Weismuller (Tarzan) life story & Jim Braddock (boxer) life story. 38-40-L.B. Cole-c. 40-Last White Rider	17	34	51	98	154	210
Accepted Reprint 38-40 (nd): 40-r/Johnny Weismuller life story; all have L.B. Cole-c	10	20	30	56	76	95

411
Marvel Comics: June, 2003 - No. 3 ($3.50, limited series)

	GD 2.0	VG 4.0	FN 6.0	VF 8.0	VF/NM 9.0	NM- 9.2
1,2-Tributes to peacemakers; s/a by various. 1-Millar, Quitely, Mack, Winslade & others-s/a. 2-Harris, Phillips, Manco, Bruce Jones.						3.50

FOUR-STAR BATTLE TALES
National Periodical Publications: Feb-Mar, 1973 - No. 5, Nov-Dec, 1973

	GD 2.0	VG 4.0	FN 6.0	VF 8.0	VF/NM 9.0	NM- 9.2
1-Reprints begin	3	6	9	17	25	32
2-5	2	4	6	11	16	20

NOTE: ***Drucker** r-1, 3-5. **Heath** r-2, 5; c-1. **Krigstein** r-5. **Kubert** r-4; c-2.*

FOUR STAR SPECTACULAR
National Periodical Publications: Mar-Apr, 1976 - No. 6, Jan-Feb, 1977

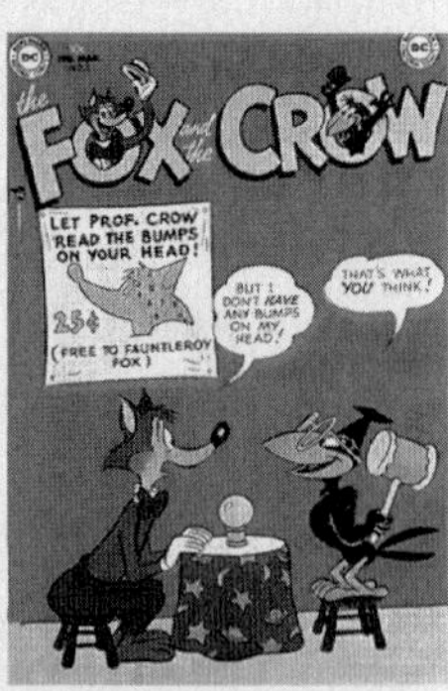

Fox and the Crow #2 © DC

Fox Giants - Love Problems © FOX

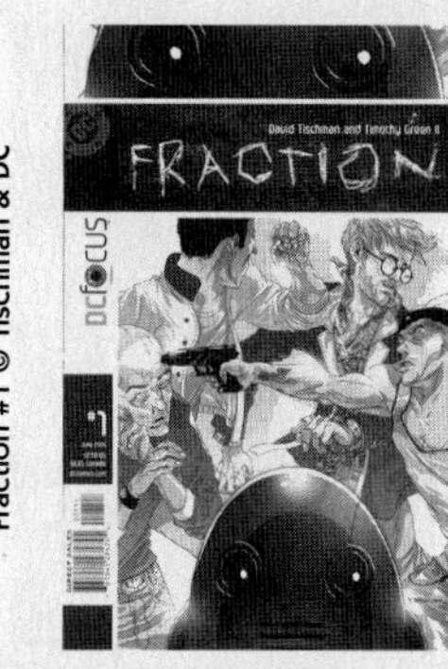

Fraction #1 © Tischman & DC

	GD 2.0	VG 4.0	FN 6.0	VF 8.0	VF/NM 9.0	NM- 9.2
1-Includes G.A. Flash story with new art	2	4	6	11	16	20
2-6: Reprints in all. 2-Infinity cover	2	4	6	8	10	12

NOTE: *All contain DC Superhero reprints. #1 has 68 pgs.; #2-6, 52 pgs.. #1, 4-Hawkman app.; #2-Kid Flash app.; #3-Green Lantern app; #2, 4, 5-Wonder Woman, Superboy app; #5-Green Arrow, Vigilante app; #6-Blackhawk G.A.-r.*

FOUR TEENERS (Formerly Crime Must Pay The Penalty; Dotty No. 35 on)
A. A. Wyn: No. 34, April, 1948 (52 pgs.)

	GD	VG	FN	VF	VF/NM	NM-
34-Teen-age comic; Dotty app.; Curly & Jerry continue from Four Favorites	10	20	30	54	72	90

FOURTH WORLD GALLERY, THE (Jack Kirby's...)
DC Comics: 1996 (9/96) ($3.50, one-shot)

	GD	VG	FN	VF	VF/NM	NM-
nn-Pin-ups of Jack Kirby's Fourth World characters (New Gods, Forever People & Mister Miracle) by John Byrne, Rick Burchett, Dan Jurgens, Walt Simonson & others						3.50

FOUR WOMEN
DC Comics (Homage): Dec, 2001 - No. 5, Apr, 2002 ($2.95, limited series)

	GD	VG	FN	VF	VF/NM	NM-
1-5-Sam Kieth-s/a						3.00
TPB (2002, $17.95) r/series; foreward by Kieth						18.00

FOX AND THE CROW (Stanley & His Monster No. 109 on) (See Comic Cavalcade & Real Screen Comics)
National Periodical Publications: Dec-Jan, 1951-52 - No. 108, Feb-Mar, 1968

	GD	VG	FN	VF	VF/NM	NM-
1	123	246	369	787	1344	1900
2(Scarce)	55	110	165	352	601	850
3-5	37	74	111	222	361	500
6-10	26	52	78	154	252	350
11-20	20	40	60	114	182	250
21-30: 22-Last precode issue (2/55)	15	30	45	83	124	165
31-40	12	24	36	69	97	125
41-60	6	12	18	43	69	95
61-80	5	10	15	34	55	75
81-94: 94-(11/65)-The Brat Finks begin	4	8	12	26	41	55
95-Stanley & His Monster begins (origin & 1st app)	6	12	18	37	59	80
96-99,101-108	3	6	9	20	30	40
100 (10-11/66)	4	8	12	22	34	45

NOTE: *Many later covers by* ***Mort Drucker.***

FOX AND THE HOUND, THE (Disney)(Movie)
Whitman Publishing Co.: Aug, 1981 - No. 3, Oct, 1981

	GD	VG	FN	VF	VF/NM	NM-
11292- Golden Press Graphic Novel	2	4	6	8	10	12
1-3-Based on animated movie	1	2	3	5	7	9

FOXFIRE (See The Phoenix Resurrection)
Malibu Comics (Ultraverse): Feb, 1996 - No. 4, May, 1996 ($1.50)

	GD	VG	FN	VF	VF/NM	NM-
1-4: Sludge, Ultraforce app. 4-Punisher app.						3.00

FOX GIANTS (Also see Giant Comics Edition)
Fox Features Syndicate: 1944 - 1950 (25¢, 132 - 196 pgs.)

	GD	VG	FN	VF	VF/NM	NM-
Album of Crime nn(1949, 132p)	53	106	159	334	567	800
Album of Love nn(1949, 132p)	50	100	150	315	533	750
All Famous Crime Stories nn('49, 132p)	53	106	159	334	567	800
All Good Comics 1(1944, 132p)(R.W. Voigt)-The Bouncer, Purple Tigress,Rick Evans, Puppeteer, Green Mask; Infinity-c	53	106	159	334	567	800
All Great nn(1944, 132p)-Capt. Jack Terry, Rick Evans, Jaguar Man	42	84	126	265	445	625
All Great nn(Chicago Nite Life News)(1945, 132p)-Green Mask, Bouncer, Puppeteer, Rick Evans, Rocket Kelly	42	84	126	265	445	625
All-Great Confessions nn(1949, 132p)	48	96	144	302	514	725
All Great Crime Stories nn('49, 132p)	53	106	159	334	567	800
All Great Jungle Adventures nn('49, 132p)	57	114	171	362	619	875
All Real Confession Magazine 3 (3/49, 132p)	48	96	144	302	514	725
All Real Confession Magazine 4 (4/49, 132p)	48	96	144	302	514	725
All Your Comics 1(1944, 132p)-The Puppeteer, Red Robbins, & Merciless the Sorcerer	42	84	126	265	445	625
Almanac Of Crime nn(1948, 148p)-Phantom Lady	60	120	180	381	653	925
Almanac Of Crime 1(1950, 132p)	52	104	156	328	557	785
Book Of Love nn(1950, 132p)	47	94	141	296	498	700
Burning Romances 1(1949, 132p)	54	108	162	343	574	825
Crimes Incorporated nn(1950, 132p)	48	96	144	302	514	725
Daring Love Stories nn(1950, 132p)	47	94	141	296	498	700
Everybody's Comics 1(1944, 50¢, 196p)-The Green Mask, The Puppeteer, The Bouncer, Rocket Kelly, Rick Evans	50	100	150	315	533	750
Everybody's Comics 1(1946, 196p)-Green Lama, The Puppeteer	41	82	123	251	418	585
Everybody's Comics 1(1946, 196p)-Same as 1945 Ribtickler	32	64	96	188	307	425
Everybody's Comics nn(1947, 132p)-Jo-Jo, Purple Tigress, Cosmo Cat, Bronze Man	42	84	126	265	445	625
Exciting Romance Stories nn(1949, 132p)	50	100	150	315	533	750
Famous Love nn(1950, 132p)	47	94	141	296	498	700
Intimate Confessions nn(1950, 132p)	47	94	141	296	498	700
Journal Of Crime nn(1949, 132p)	53	106	159	334	567	800
Love Problems nn(1949, 132p)	48	96	144	302	514	725
Love Thrills nn(1950, 132p)	47	94	141	296	498	700
March of Crime nn('48, 132p)-Female w/rifle-c	53	106	159	334	567	800
March of Crime nn('49, 132p)-Cop w/pistol-c	50	100	150	315	533	750
March of Crime nn(1949, 132p)-Coffin & man w/machine-gun-c	50	100	150	315	533	750
Revealing Love Stories nn(1950, 132p)	47	94	141	296	498	700
Ribtickler nn(1945, 50¢, 196p)-Chicago Nite Life News; Marvel Mutt, Cosmo Cat, Flash Rabbit, The Nebbs app.	40	80	120	246	411	575
Romantic Thrills nn(1950, 132p)	47	94	141	296	498	700
Secret Love Stories nn(1949, 132p)	50	100	150	315	533	750
Strange Love nn(1950, 132p)-Photo-c	55	110	165	352	601	850
Sweetheart Scandals nn(1950, 132p)	47	94	141	296	498	700
Teen-Age Love nn(1950, 132p)	47	94	141	296	498	700
Throbbing Love nn(1950, 132p)-Photo-c; used in **POP**, pg. 107	57	114	171	362	619	875
Truth About Crime nn(1949, 132p)	53	106	159	334	567	800
Variety Comics 1(1946, 132p)-Blue Beetle, Jungle Jo	43	86	129	271	461	650
Variety Comics nn(1950, 132p)-Jungle Jo, My Secret Affair (w/Harrison/Wood-a), Crimes by Women & My Story	42	84	126	265	445	625
Western Roundup nn('50, 132p)-Hoot Gibson; Cody of the Pony Express app.	40	80	120	246	411	575

NOTE: *Each of the above usually contain four remaindered Fox books minus covers. Since these missing covers often had the first page of the first story, most Giants therefore are incomplete. Approximate values are listed. Books with appearances of Phantom Lady, Rulah, Jo-Jo, etc. could bring more.*

FOXHOLE (Becomes Never Again #8?)
Mainline/Charlton No. 5 on: 9-10/54 - No. 4, 3-4/55; No. 5, 7/55 - No. 7, 3/56

	GD	VG	FN	VF	VF/NM	NM-
1-Classic Kirby-c	52	104	156	328	557	785
2-Kirby-c/a(2); Kirby scripts based on his war time experiences	37	74	111	222	361	500
3-5-Kirby-c only	23	46	69	136	223	310
6-Kirby-c/a(2)	32	64	96	192	314	435
7	13	26	39	74	105	135
Super Reprints #10,15-17: 10-r/? 15,16-r/United States Marines #5,8. 17-r/Monty Hall #?	2	4	6	11	16	20
11,12,18-r/Foxhole #1,2,3; Kirby-c	3	6	9	17	25	32

NOTE: ***Kirby*** *a(r)-Super #11, 12.* ***Powell*** *a(r)-Super #15, 16. Stories by actual veterans.*

FOXY FAGAN COMICS (Funny Animal)
Dearfield Publishing Co.: Dec, 1946 - No. 7, Summer, 1948

	GD	VG	FN	VF	VF/NM	NM-
1-Foxy Fagan & Little Buck begin	13	26	39	72	101	130
2	8	16	24	42	54	65
3-7: 6-Rocket ship-c	7	14	21	37	46	55

FRACTION
DC Comics (Focus): June, 2004 - No. 6, Nov, 2004 ($2.50, limited series)

	GD	VG	FN	VF	VF/NM	NM-
1-6-David Tischman-s/Timothy Green II-a						3.00
SC (2011, $17.99) r/#1-6; cover gallery						18.00

FRACTURED FAIRY TALES (TV)
Gold Key: Oct, 1962 (Jay Ward)

	GD	VG	FN	VF	VF/NM	NM-
1 (10022-210)-From Bullwinkle TV show	10	20	30	70	125	180

FRAGGLE ROCK (TV)
Marvel Comics (Star Comics)/Marvel V2#1 on: Apr, 1985 - No. 8, Sept, 1986; V2#1, Apr, 1988 - No. 5, Aug, 1988

	GD	VG	FN	VF	VF/NM	NM-
1-6 (75¢-c)						5.00
7,8						6.00
V2#1-5-($1.00): Reprints 1st series						3.00

FRANCIS, BROTHER OF THE UNIVERSE
Marvel Comics Group: 1980 (75¢, 52 pgs., one-shot)

	GD	VG	FN	VF	VF/NM	NM-
nn-John Buscema/Marie Severin-a; story of Francis Bernadone celebrating his 800th birthday in 1982						6.00

FRANCIS THE FAMOUS TALKING MULE (All based on movie)
Dell Publishing Co.: No. 335 (#1), June, 1951 - No. 1090, March, 1960

	GD	VG	FN	VF	VF/NM	NM-
Four Color 335 (#1)	10	20	30	70	125	180

Frankenstein Comics #10 © PRIZE

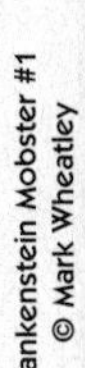
Frankenstein Mobster #1 © Mark Wheatley

Fray #7 © Joss Whedon

	GD 2.0	VG 4.0	FN 6.0	VF 8.0	VF/NM 9.0	NM- 9.2
Four Color 465	6	12	18	41	66	90
Four Color 501,547,579	5	10	15	32	51	70
Four Color 621,655,698,710,745	4	8	12	28	44	60
Four Color 810,863,906,953,991,1068,1090	4	8	12	26	41	55

FRANK
Nemesis Comics (Harvey): Apr (Mar inside), 1994 - No. 4, 1994 ($1.75/$2.50, limited series)

	GD 2.0	VG 4.0	FN 6.0	VF 8.0	VF/NM 9.0	NM- 9.2
1-4-($2.50, direct sale): 1-Foil-c Edition						3.50
1-4-($1.75)-Newsstand Editions; Cowan-a in all						3.00

FRANK
Fantagraphics Books: Sept, 1996 ($2.95, B&W)

	GD 2.0	VG 4.0	FN 6.0	VF 8.0	VF/NM 9.0	NM- 9.2
1-Woodring-c/a/scripts						3.00

FRANK BUCK (Formerly My True Love)
Fox Features Syndicate: No. 70, May, 1950 - No. 3, Sept, 1950

	GD 2.0	VG 4.0	FN 6.0	VF 8.0	VF/NM 9.0	NM- 9.2
70-Wood a(p)(3 stories)-Photo-c	32	64	96	188	307	425
71-Wood-a (9 pgs.); photo/painted-c	18	36	54	105	165	225
3: 3-Photo/painted-c	14	28	42	80	115	150

NOTE: *Based on "Bring 'Em Back Alive" TV show.*

FRANKEN-CASTLE (See The Punisher, 2009 series)

FRANKENSTEIN (See Dracula, Movie Classics & Werewolf)
Dell Publishing Co.: Aug-Oct, 1964; No. 2, Sept, 1966 - No. 4, Mar, 1967

	GD 2.0	VG 4.0	FN 6.0	VF 8.0	VF/NM 9.0	NM- 9.2
1(12-283-410)(1964)(2nd printing; see Movie Classics for 1st printing)	5	10	15	34	55	75
2-Intro. & origin super-hero character (9/66)	4	8	12	28	44	60
3,4	3	6	9	20	30	40

FRANKENSTEIN (The Monster of...; also see Monsters Unleashed #2, Power Record Comics, Psycho & Silver Surfer #7)
Marvel Comics Group: Jan, 1973 - No. 18, Sept, 1975

	GD 2.0	VG 4.0	FN 6.0	VF 8.0	VF/NM 9.0	NM- 9.2
1-Ploog-c/a begins, ends #6	8	16	24	52	86	120
2	4	8	12	28	44	60
3-5	4	8	12	22	34	45
6,7,10: 7-Dracula cameo	3	6	9	18	27	35
8,9-Dracula c/sty. 9-Death of Dracula	5	10	15	30	48	65
11-17	3	6	9	16	22	28
18-Wrightson-c(i)	3	6	9	17	25	32

NOTE: ***Adkins** c-17i. **Buscema** a-7-10p. **Ditko** a-12r. **G. Kane** c-15p. **Orlando** a-8r. **Ploog** a-1-3, 4p, 5p, 6; c-1-6. **Wrightson** c-18i.*

FRANKENSTEIN (Mary Wollstonecraft Shelley's...; A Marvel Illustrated Novel)
Marvel Pub.: 1983 ($8.95, B&W, 196 pgs., 8x11" TPB)

	GD 2.0	VG 4.0	FN 6.0	VF 8.0	VF/NM 9.0	NM- 9.2
nn-Wrightson-a; 4 pg. intro. by Stephen King	5	10	15	30	48	65
Limited HC Edition						175.00

FRANKENSTEIN COMICS (Also See Prize Comics)
Prize Publ. (Crestwood/Feature): Sum, 1945 - V5#5(#33), Oct-Nov, 1954

	GD 2.0	VG 4.0	FN 6.0	VF 8.0	VF/NM 9.0	NM- 9.2
1-Frankenstein begins by Dick Briefer (origin); Frank Sinatra parody	129	258	387	826	1413	2000
2	58	116	174	371	636	900
3-5	43	86	129	271	461	650
6-10: 7-S&K a(r)/Headline Comics. 8(7-8/47)-Superman satire	39	78	117	236	388	540
11-17(1-2/49)-11-Boris Karloff parody-c/story. 17-Last humor issue	34	68	102	206	439	465
18(3/52)-New origin, horror series begins	46	92	138	290	488	685
19,20(V3#4, 8-9/52)	30	60	90	177	289	400
21(V3#5), 22(V3#6), 23(V4#1) - #28(V4#6)	28	56	84	165	270	375
29(V5#1) - #33(V5#5)	27	54	81	160	263	365

NOTE: ***Briefer** c/a-all. **Meskin** a-21, 29.*

FRANKENSTEIN/DRACULA WAR, THE
Topps Comics: Feb, 1995 - No. 3, May, 1995 ($2.50, limited series)

	GD 2.0	VG 4.0	FN 6.0	VF 8.0	VF/NM 9.0	NM- 9.2
1-3						3.00

FRANKENSTEIN, JR. (...& the Impossibles) (TV)
Gold Key: Jan, 1966 (Hanna-Barbera)

	GD 2.0	VG 4.0	FN 6.0	VF 8.0	VF/NM 9.0	NM- 9.2
1-Super hero (scarce)	10	20	30	73	134	195

FRANKENSTEIN MOBSTER
Image Comics: No. 0, Oct, 2003 - No. 7, Dec, 2004 ($2.95)

	GD 2.0	VG 4.0	FN 6.0	VF 8.0	VF/NM 9.0	NM- 9.2
0-7: 0-Two covers by Wheatley and Hughes; Wheatley-s/a. 1-Variant-c by Wieringo						3.00

FRANKENSTEIN: OR THE MODERN PROMETHEUS
Caliber Press: 1994 ($2.95, one-shot)

	GD 2.0	VG 4.0	FN 6.0	VF 8.0	VF/NM 9.0	NM- 9.2
1						3.00

FRANK FRAZETTA FANTASY ILLUSTRATED (Magazine)
Quantum Cat Entertainment: Spring 1998 - No. 8 ($5.95, quarterly)

	GD 2.0	VG 4.0	FN 6.0	VF 8.0	VF/NM 9.0	NM- 9.2
1-Anthology; art by Corben, Horley, Jusko	1	2	3	4	5	7
1-Linsner variant-c						10.00
2-Battle Chasers by Madureira; Harris-a						8.00
2-Madureira Battle Chasers variant-c						12.00
3-8-Frazetta-c						6.00
3-Tony Daniel variant-c						15.00
5,6-Portacio variant-c, 7,8-Alex Nino variant-c						10.00
8-Alex Ross Chicago Comicon variant-c						10.00

FRANK FRAZETTA'S DEATH DEALER
Image Comics: Mar, 2007 - No. 6, Jan, 2008 ($3.99)

	GD 2.0	VG 4.0	FN 6.0	VF 8.0	VF/NM 9.0	NM- 9.2
1-6-Nat Jones-a; 3 covers (Frazetta, Jones, Jones sketch)						4.00

FRANK FRAZETTA'S...
Fantagraphics Books/Image Comics: one-shots

	GD 2.0	VG 4.0	FN 6.0	VF 8.0	VF/NM 9.0	NM- 9.2
... Creatures 1 (Image Comics, 7/08, $3.99) Bergting-a; covers by Frazetta & Bergting						4.00
... Dark Kingdom 1-4 (Image, 4/08 - No. 4, 1/10, $3.99) Vigil-a; covers by Frazetta & Vigil						4.00
... Dracula Meets the Wolfman 1 (Image, 8/08, $3.99) Francavilla-a; 2 covers						4.00
... Moon Maid 1 (Image, 1/09, $3.99) Tim Vigil-a; covers by Frazetta & Vigil						4.00
... Neanderthal 1 (Image, 4/09, $3.99) Fotos & Vigil-a; covers by Frazetta & Fotos						4.00
... Sorcerer 1 (Image, 8/09, $3.99) Medors-a; covers by Frazetta & Medors						4.00
... Swamp Demon 1 (Image, 7/08, $3.99) Medors-a; covers by Frazetta & Medors						4.00
... Thun'da Tales 1 (Fantagraphics Books, 1987, $2.00) Frazetta-r						6.00
... Untamed Love 1 (Fantagraphics Books, 11/87, $2.00) r/1950's romance comics						6.00

FRANKIE COMICS (...& Lana No. 13-15) (Formerly Movie Tunes; becomes Frankie Fuddle No. 16 on)
Marvel Comics (MgPC): No. 4, Wint, 1946-47 - No. 15, June, 1949

	GD 2.0	VG 4.0	FN 6.0	VF 8.0	VF/NM 9.0	NM- 9.2
4-Mitzi, Margie, Daisy app.	16	32	48	94	147	200
5-9	11	22	33	62	86	110
10-15: 13-Anti-Wertham editorial	10	20	30	58	79	100

FRANKIE DOODLE (See Sparkler, both series)
United Features Syndicate: No. 7, 1939

	GD 2.0	VG 4.0	FN 6.0	VF 8.0	VF/NM 9.0	NM- 9.2
Single Series 7	33	66	99	194	317	440

FRANKIE FUDDLE (Formerly Frankie & Lana)
Marvel Comics: No. 16, Aug, 1949 - No. 17, Nov, 1949

	GD 2.0	VG 4.0	FN 6.0	VF 8.0	VF/NM 9.0	NM- 9.2
16,17	10	20	30	58	79	100

FRANKLIN RICHARDS (Fantastic Four)
Marvel Comics: April, 2006 - Present ($2.99/$3.99, one-shots)

	GD 2.0	VG 4.0	FN 6.0	VF 8.0	VF/NM 9.0	NM- 9.2
...: April Fools (6/09, $3.99) Eliopoulos-s/a						4.00
...: Collected Chaos (2008, $8.99, digest) reprints various one-shots						9.00
...: Fall Football Fiasco (1/08, $2.99) Eliopoulos-a/Sumerak-s						3.00
...: Happy Franksgiving (1/07, $2.99) Thanksgiving stories by Eliopoulos-a/Sumerak-s						3.00
...: It's Dark Reigning Cats & Dogs (4/09, $3.99) Eliopoulos-s/a						4.00
...: Lab Brat (2007, $7.99, digest) reprints one-shots and Masked Marvel back-ups						8.00
...: March Madness (5/07, $2.99) More science gone wrong by Eliopoulos-a/Sumerak-s						3.00
...: Monster Mash (11/07, $2.99) Science mishaps by Eliopoulos-a/Sumerak-s						3.00
...: Not-So-Secret Invasion (7/08, $2.99) Skrull cover; The Wizard app.						3.00
... One Shot (4/06, $2.99) short stories by Eliopoulos-a/Sumerak-s						3.00
...: School's Out (4/09, $3.99) Eliopoulos-s/a; Katie Power app.						4.00
...: Sons of Geniuses (1/09, $3.99) parallel dimension alternate version hijinks						4.00
...: Spring Break (5/08, $2.99) short stories by Eliopoulos-a/Sumerak-s						3.00
...: Summer Smackdown (10/08, $2.99) short stories by Eliopoulos-a/Sumerak-s						3.00
...: Super Summer Spectacular (9/06, $2.99) short stories by Eliopoulos-a/Sumerak-s						3.00
...: World Be Warned (8/07, $2.99) short stories by Eliopoulos-a/Sumerak-s; Hulk app.						3.00

FRANK LUTHER'S SILLY PILLY COMICS (See Jingle Dingle...)
Children's Comics (Maltex Cereal): 1950 (10¢)

	GD 2.0	VG 4.0	FN 6.0	VF 8.0	VF/NM 9.0	NM- 9.2
1-Characters from radio, records, & TV	9	18	27	47	61	75

FRANK MERRIWELL AT YALE (Speed Demons No. 5 on?)
Charlton Comics: June, 1955 - No. 4, Jan, 1956 (Also see Shadow Comics)

	GD 2.0	VG 4.0	FN 6.0	VF 8.0	VF/NM 9.0	NM- 9.2
1	7	14	21	37	46	55
2-4	5	10	15	24	30	35

FRANTIC (Magazine) (See Ratfink & Zany)
Pierce Publishing Co.: Oct, 1958 - V2#2, Apr, 1959 (Satire)

	GD 2.0	VG 4.0	FN 6.0	VF 8.0	VF/NM 9.0	NM- 9.2
V1#1	12	24	36	69	97	125
2	9	18	27	52	69	85
V2#1,2: 1-Burgos-a, Severin-c/a; Powell-a?	8	16	24	42	54	65

FRAY (Also see Buffy the Vampire Slayer "season eight" #16-19)
Dark Horse Comics: June, 2001 - No. 8, July, 2003 ($2.99, limited series)

Freaks of the Heartland #1 © Niles & Ruth

Freedom Fighters #2 © DC

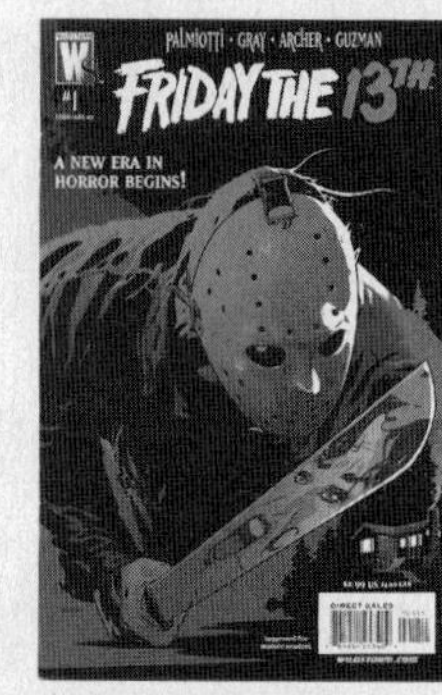

Friday the 13th #1 © New Line

GD VG FN VF VF/NM NM-
2.0 4.0 6.0 8.0 9.0 9.2

GD VG FN VF VF/NM NM-
2.0 4.0 6.0 8.0 9.0 9.2

1-Joss Whedon-s/Moline & Owens-a 1 2 3 5 6 8
1-DF Gold edition 2 4 6 9 12 15
2-8: 6-(3/02). 7-(4/03) 4.00
TPB (11/03, $19.95) r/#1-8; intros by Whedon & Loeb; Moline sketch pages 20.00

FREAK FORCE (Also see Savage Dragon)
Image Comics (Highbrow Ent.): Dec, 1993 - No. 18, July, 1995 ($1.95/$2.50)

1-18-Superpatriot & Mighty Man in all; Erik Larsen scripts in all. 4-Vanguard app. 8-Begin $2.50-c. 9-Cyberforce-c & app. 13-Variant-c 3.00

FREAK FORCE (Also see Savage Dragon)
Image Comics: Apr, 1997 - No. 3, July, 1997 ($2.95)

1-3-Larsen-s 3.00

FREAK OUT, USA (See On the Scene Presents...)

FREAK SHOW
Image Comics (Desperado): 2006 ($5.99, B&W, one-shot)

nn-Bruce Jones-s/Bernie Wrightson-c/a 6.00

FREAKS OF THE HEARTLAND
Dark Horse Comics: Jan, 2004 - No. 6, Nov, 2004 ($2.99)

1-6-Steve Niles-s/Greg Ruth-a 3.00

FRECKLES AND HIS FRIENDS (See Crackajack Funnies, Famous Comics Cartoon Book, Honeybee Birdwhistle... & Red Ryder)

FRECKLES AND HIS FRIENDS
Standard Comics/Argo: No. 5, 11/47 - No. 12, 8/49; 11/55 - No. 4, 6/56

5-Reprints 9 18 27 50 65 80
6-12-Reprints. 7-9-Airbrush-c (by Schomburg?). 11-Lingerie panels 7 14 21 35 43 50

NOTE: *Some copies of No. 8 & 9 contain a printing oddity. The negatives were elongated in the engraving process, probably to conform to page dimensions on the filler pages. Those pages only look normal when viewed at a 45 degree angle.*

1(Argo,'55)-Reprints (NEA Service) 6 12 18 28 34 40
2-4 4 8 12 18 22 25

FREDDY (Formerly My Little Margie's Boy Friends) (Also see Blue Bird)
Charlton Comics: V2#12, June, 1958 - No. 47, Feb, 1965

V2#12 4 8 12 22 34 45
13-15 3 6 9 16 22 28
16-47 2 4 6 11 16 20

FREDDY
Dell Publishing Co.: May-July, 1963 - No. 3, Oct-Dec, 1964

1 3 6 9 19 29 38
2,3 3 6 9 14 20 26

FREDDY KRUEGER'S A NIGHTMARE ON ELM STREET
Marvel Comics: Oct, 1989 - No. 2, Dec, 1989 ($2.25, B&W, movie adaptation, magazine)

1,2: Origin Freddy Krueger; Buckler/Alcala-a 1 2 3 4 5 7

FREDDY'S DEAD: THE FINAL NIGHTMARE
Innovation Publishing: Oct, 1991 - No. 3, Dec 1991 ($2.50, color mini-series, adapts movie)

1-3: Dismukes (film poster artist) painted-c 3.00

FREDDY VS. JASON VS. ASH (Freddy Krueger, Friday the 13th, Army of Darkness)
DC Comics (WildStorm): Early Jan, 2008 - No. 6, May, 2008 ($2.99, limited series)

1-Three covers by J. Scott Campbell; Kuhoric-s/Craig-a 5.00
1-Second printing with 3 covers combined sideways 4.00
2-6: 2-4-Eric Powell-c. 5,6-Richard Friend-c 3.00
2-4-Second printings with B&W covers 3.00
TPB (2008, $17.99) r/#1-6; creators' interview afterword 18.00

FREDDY VS. JASON VS. ASH: THE NIGHTMARE WARRIORS
DC Comics (WildStorm): Aug, 2009 - No. 6, Jan, 2010 ($3.99, limited series)

1-6-Katz & Kuhoric-s/Craig-a. 1-Suydam-c 4.00
TPB (2010, $17.99) r/#1-6; cover gallery 18.00

FRED HEMBECK DESTROYS THE MARVEL UNIVERSE
Marvel Comics: July, 1989 ($1.50, one-shot)

1-Punisher app.; Staton-i (5 pgs.) 3.00

FRED HEMBECK SELLS THE MARVEL UNIVERSE
Marvel Comics: Oct, 1990 ($1.25, one-shot)

1-Punisher, Wolverine parodies; Hembeck/Austin-c 3.00

FREEDOM AGENT (Also see John Steele)
Gold Key: Apr, 1963 (12¢)

1 (10054-304)-Painted-c 4 8 12 26 41 55

FREEDOM FIGHTERS (See Justice League of America #107,108)
National Periodical Publ./DC Comics: Mar-Apr, 1976 - No. 15, July-Aug, 1978

1-Uncle Sam, The Ray, Black Condor, Doll Man, Human Bomb, & Phantom Lady begin (all former Quality characters) 3 6 9 14 19 24
2-9: 4,5-Wonder Woman x-over. 7-1st app. Crusaders 2 4 6 9 12 15
10-15: 10-Origin Doll Man; Cat-Man-c/story (4th app; 1st revival since Detective #325). 11-Origin The Ray. 12-Origin Firebrand. 13-Origin Black Condor. 14-Batgirl & Batwoman app. 15-Batgirl & Batwoman app.; origin Phantom Lady 2 4 6 9 13 16

NOTE: ***Buckler** c-5-11p, 13p, 14p.*

FREEDOM FIGHTERS (Also see "Uncle Sam and the Freedom Fighters")
DC Comics: Nov, 2010 - Present ($2.99)

1-7-Dave Johnson-c/Travis Moore-a 3.00

FREEDOM FORCE
Image Comics: Jan, 2005 - No. 6, June, 2005 ($2.95)

1-6-Eric Dieter-s/Tom Scioli-a 3.00

FREEMIND
Future Comics: No. 0, Aug, 2002; Nov, 2002 - No. 7, June, 2003 ($3.50)

0-($2.25) Giordano-c 3.00
0-($2.25) Variant-c by Layton 3.00
1-7 ($3.50) 1-Two covers by Giordano & Layton; Giordano-a thru #3. 4,5-Leeke-a 3.50

FREEREALMS
DC Comics (WildStorm): Sept, 2009 - No. 12, Oct, 2010 ($3.99, limited series)

1-12-Based on the online game; Jon Buran-a 4.00
... Book One TPB (2010, $19.99) r/#1-6 20.00
... Book Two TPB (2010, $19.99) r/#7-12 20.00

FREEX
Malibu Comics (Ultraverse): July, 1993 - No. 18, Mar, 1995 ($1.95)

1-3,5-14,16-18: 1-Polybagged w/trading card. 2-Some were polybagged w/card. 6-Nightman-c/story. 7-2 pg. origin Hardcase by Zeck. 17-Rune app. 3.00
1-Holographic-c edition 6.00
1-Ultra 5,000 limited silver ink-c 4.00
4-($2.50, 48 pgs.)-Rune flip-c/story by B. Smith (3 pgs.); 3 pg. Night Man preview 4.00
15 ($3.50)-w/Ultraverse Premiere #9 flip book; Alec Swan & Rafferty app. 4.00
Giant Size 1 (1994, $2.50)-Prime app. 4.00

NOTE: ***Simonson** c-1.*

FRENEMY
Oni Press: May, 2010 - Present ($3.99)

1-3-Rashida Jones, Christina Weir & Nunzio DeFilippis-s 4.00

FRENZY (Magazine) (Satire)
Picture Magazine: Apr, 1958 - No. 6, Mar, 1959

1 13 26 39 72 101 130
2-6 8 16 24 44 57 70

FRESHMEN
Image Comics: Jul, 2005 - No. 6, Mar, 2006 ($2.99)

1-Sterbakov-s/Kirk-a; co-created by Seth Green; covers by Pérez, Migliari, Linsner 3.00
2-6-Migliari-c 3.00
... Yearbook (1/06, $2.99) profile pages of characters; art by various incl. Chaykin, Kirk 3.00
... Vol. 1 (3/06, $16.99, TPB) r/#1-6 & Yearbook; cover gallery with concept art 17.00

FRESHMEN (Volume 2)
Image Comics: Nov, 2006 - No. 6, Aug, 2007 ($2.99)

1-6: 1-Sterbakov-s/Conrad-a; 4 covers 3.00
...: Summer Vacation Special (7/08, $4.99) Sterbakov-s; bonus pin-ups by various 5.00
... Vol. 2 Fundamentals of Fear (6/07, $16.99, TPB) r/#1-6; cover gallery, journals 17.00

FRIDAY FOSTER
Dell Publishing Co.: October, 1972

1 4 8 12 24 37 50

FRIDAY THE 13TH (Based on the horror movie franchise)
DC Comics (WildStorm): Feb, 2007 - No. 6, July, 2007 ($2.99, mature)

1-6: 1-Two covers by Sook and Bradstreet; Gray & Palmiotti-s 3.00
...: Abuser and The Abused (6/08, $3.50) Fialkov-s/Andy B. -a 3.50
...: Bad Land 1,2 (3/08 - No. 2, 4/08, $2.99) Marz-s/Huddleston-a/McKone-c 3.00
...: How I Spent My Summer Vacation 1,2 (11/07 - No. 2, 12/07, $2.99) Aaron-s/Archer-a 3.00
...: Pamela's Tale 1,2 (9/07 - No. 2, 10/07, $2.99) Andreyko-s/Moll-a/Nguyen-c 3.00

FRIENDLY GHOST, CASPER, THE (Becomes Casper... #254 on)
Harvey Publications: Aug, 1958 - No. 224, Oct, 1982; No. 225, Oct, 1986 - No. 253, June, 1990

Friendly Neighborhood Spider-Man #1 © MAR

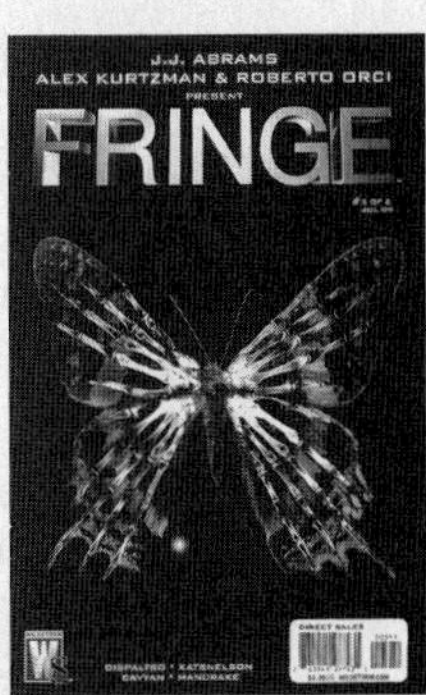

Fringe #5 © WB

Frisky Fables V2 #4 © STAR

	GD 2.0	VG 4.0	FN 6.0	VF 8.0	VF/NM 9.0	NM- 9.2
1-Infinity-c	37	74	111	286	568	850
2	16	32	48	114	232	350
3-10: 6-X-Mas-c	10	20	30	69	122	175
11-20: 18-X-Mas-c	8	16	24	52	86	120
21-30	5	10	15	34	55	75
31-50	4	8	12	24	37	50
51-70,100: 54-X-Mas-c	3	6	9	20	30	40
71-99	3	6	9	16	23	30
101-131: 131-Last 12¢ issue	3	6	9	14	20	26
132-159	2	4	6	11	16	20
160-163: All 52 pg. Giants	3	6	9	14	20	26
164-199: 173,179,185-Cub Scout Specials	2	4	6	8	10	12
200	2	4	6	8	11	14
201-224	1	2	3	5	7	9
225-237: 230-X-mas-c. 232-Valentine's-c						5.00
238-253: 238-Begin $1.00-c. 238,244-Halloween-c. 243-Last new material						4.00

FRIENDLY NEIGHBORHOOD SPIDER-MAN
Marvel Comics: Dec, 2005 - No. 24, Nov, 2007 ($2.99)

	GD 2.0	VG 4.0	FN 6.0	VF 8.0	VF/NM 9.0	NM- 9.2
1-Evolve or Die pt. 1; Peter David-s/Mike Wieringo-a; Morlun app.						4.00
1-Variant Wieringo-c with regular costume						3.00
2-4: 2-New Avengers app. 3-Spider-Man dies						3.00
2-4-var-c: 2-Bag-Head Fantastic Four costume. 3-Captain Universe. 4-Wrestler						5.00
5-10: 6-Red & gold costume. 8-10-Uncle Ben app.						3.00
11-23: 17-Black costume; Sandman app.						3.00
24-($3.99) "One More Day" part 2; Quesada-a; covers by Quesada & Djurdjevic						4.00
Annual 1 (7/07, $3.99) Origin of The Sandman; back-up w/Doran-a						4.00
... Vol. 1: Derailed (2006, $14.99) r/#5-10; Wieringo sketch pages						15.00
... Vol. 2: Mystery Date (2007, $13.99) r/#11-16						14.00

FRIENDS OF MAXX (Also see Maxx)
Image Comics (I Before E): Apr, 1996 - No. 3, Mar, 1997 ($2.95)

	GD 2.0	VG 4.0	FN 6.0	VF 8.0	VF/NM 9.0	NM- 9.2
1-3: Sam Kieth-c/a/scripts. 1-Featuring Dude Japan						3.00

FRIGHT
Atlas/Seaboard Periodicals: June, 1975 (Aug. on inside)

	GD 2.0	VG 4.0	FN 6.0	VF 8.0	VF/NM 9.0	NM- 9.2
1-Origin/1st app. The Son of Dracula; Frank Thorne-c/a	2	4	6	10	14	18

FRIGHT NIGHT
Now Comics: Oct, 1988 - No. 22, 1990 ($1.75)

	GD 2.0	VG 4.0	FN 6.0	VF 8.0	VF/NM 9.0	NM- 9.2
1-22: 1,2 Adapts movie. 8, 9-Evil Ed horror photo-c from movie						3.00

FRIGHT NIGHT II
Now Comics: 1989 ($3.95, 52 pgs.)

	GD 2.0	VG 4.0	FN 6.0	VF 8.0	VF/NM 9.0	NM- 9.2
1-Adapts movie sequel						4.00

FRINGE (Based on the 2008 FOX television series)
DC Comics (WildStorm): Oct, 2008 - No. 6, Aug, 2009 ($2.99, limited series)

	GD 2.0	VG 4.0	FN 6.0	VF 8.0	VF/NM 9.0	NM- 9.2
1-6-Anthology by various. 1-Mandrake & Coleby-a						3.00
TPB (2009, $19.99) r/#1-6; intro. by TV series co-creators Kurtzman & Orci						20.00

FRINGE: TALES FROM THE FRINGE (Based on the 2008 FOX television series)
DC Comics (WildStorm): Aug, 2010 - No. 6, Jan, 2011 ($3.99, limited series)

	GD 2.0	VG 4.0	FN 6.0	VF 8.0	VF/NM 9.0	NM- 9.2
1-6-Anthology by various; LaTorre-c. 1-Reg & photo-c						4.00
2-6-Variant covers from parallel world. 2-Death of Batman. 3-Superman/Dark Knight Returns. 4-Crisis #7 Supergirl holding dead Superman. 5-Justice League #1 w/Jonah Hex. 6-Red Lantern/Red Arrow #76						10.00
TPB (2011, $14.99) r/#1-6 with variant cover gallery and sketch art						15.00

FRISKY ANIMALS (Formerly Frisky Fables; Super Cat #56 on)
Star Publications: No. 44, Jan, 1951 - No. 55, Sept, 1953

	GD 2.0	VG 4.0	FN 6.0	VF 8.0	VF/NM 9.0	NM- 9.2
44-Super Cat; L.B. Cole	20	40	60	114	182	250
45-Classic L. B. Cole-c	28	56	84	165	270	375
46-51,53-55: Super Cat. 54-Super Cat-c begin	19	38	57	109	172	235
52-L. B. Cole-c/a, 3 1/2 pgs.; X-Mas-c	20	40	60	114	182	250

NOTE: *All have* ***L. B. Cole****-c. No. 47-No Super Cat.* ***Disbrow*** *a-49, 52.* ***Fago*** *a-51.*

FRISKY ANIMALS ON PARADE (Formerly Parade Comics; becomes Superspook)
Ajax-Farrell Publ. (Four Star Comic Corp.): Sept, 1957 - No. 3, Dec-Jan, 1957-1958

	GD 2.0	VG 4.0	FN 6.0	VF 8.0	VF/NM 9.0	NM- 9.2
1-L. B. Cole-c	17	34	51	98	154	210
2-No L. B. Cole-c	10	20	30	56	76	95
3-L. B. Cole-c	15	30	45	85	130	175

FRISKY FABLES (Frisky Animals No. 44 on)
Premium Group/Novelty Publ./Star Publ. V5#4 on: Spring, 1945 - No. 43, Oct, 1950

	GD 2.0	VG 4.0	FN 6.0	VF 8.0	VF/NM 9.0	NM- 9.2
V1#1-Funny animal; Al Fago-c/a #1-38	22	44	66	132	216	300
2,3(Fall & Winter, 1945)	14	28	42	76	108	140
V2#1(#4, 4/46) - 9,11,12(#15, 3/47): 4-Flag-c	10	20	30	58	79	100
10-Christmas-c. 12-Valentine's-c	11	22	33	60	83	105
V3#1(#16, 4/47) - 12(#27, 3/48): 4-Flag-c. 7,9-Infinity-c. 10-X-Mas-c. 12-Washington crossing the Delaware parody-c	9	18	27	50	65	80
V4#1(#28, 4/48) - 7(#34, 2-3/49)	9	18	27	47	61	75
V5#1(#35, 4-5/49) - 4(#38, 10-11/49)	9	18	27	47	61	75
39-43-L. B. Cole-c; 40-Xmas-c	20	40	60	114	182	250
Accepted Reprint No. 43 (nd); L.B. Cole-c	10	20	30	54	72	90

FRITZI RITZ (See Comics On Parade, Single Series #5, 1(reprint), Tip Top & United Comics)

FRITZI RITZ (United Comics No. 8-26) (Also see Tip Topper for early Peanuts by Schulz)
United Features Synd./St. John No. 37-55/Dell No. 56 on:
1939; Fall, 1948; No. 3, 1949 - No. 7, 1949; No. 27, 3-4/53 - No. 36, 9-10/54; No. 37 - No. 55, 9-11/57; No. 56, 12-2/57-58 - No. 59, 9-11/58

	GD 2.0	VG 4.0	FN 6.0	VF 8.0	VF/NM 9.0	NM- 9.2
Single Series #5 (1939)	32	64	96	192	314	435
nn(1948)-Special Fall issue; by Ernie Bushmiller	18	36	54	105	165	225
3(#1)	13	26	39	74	105	135
4-7(1949): 6-Abbie & Slats app.	10	20	30	54	72	90
27(1953)-33,37-50,57-59-Early Peanuts (1-4 pgs.) by Schulz. 29-Five pg. Abbie & Slats; 1 pg. Mamie by Russell Patterson. 38(9/55)-41(4/56)-Low print run	12	24	36	69	97	125
34-36,51-56: 36-1 pg. Mamie by Patterson	8	16	24	44	57	70

NOTE: *Abbie & Slats in #6,7, 27-31. Li'l Abner in #32-36.*

FROGMAN COMICS
Hillman Periodicals: Jan-Feb, 1952 - No. 11, May, 1953

	GD 2.0	VG 4.0	FN 6.0	VF 8.0	VF/NM 9.0	NM- 9.2
1	15	30	45	86	133	180
2	10	20	30	54	72	90
3,4,6-11: 4-Meskin-a	8	16	24	42	54	65
5-Krigstein-a	9	18	27	47	61	75

FROGMEN, THE
Dell Publishing Co.: No. 1258, Feb-Apr, 1962 - No. 11, Nov-Jan, 1964-65 (Painted-c)

	GD 2.0	VG 4.0	FN 6.0	VF 8.0	VF/NM 9.0	NM- 9.2
Four Color 1258(#1)-Evans-a	8	16	24	52	86	120
2,3-Evans-a; part Frazetta inks in #2,3	6	12	18	37	59	80
4,6-11	4	8	12	24	37	50
5-Toth-a	4	8	12	28	44	60

FROM BEYOND THE UNKNOWN
National Periodical Publications: 10-11/69 - No. 25, 11-12/73

	GD 2.0	VG 4.0	FN 6.0	VF 8.0	VF/NM 9.0	NM- 9.2
1	6	12	18	37	59	80
2-6	3	6	9	20	30	40
7-11: (64 pgs.) 7-Intro Col. Glenn Merrit	4	8	12	22	34	45
12-17: (52 pgs.) 13-Wood-a(i)(r). 17-Pres. Nixon-c	3	6	9	18	27	35
18-25: Star Rovers-r begin #18,19. Space Museum in #23-25	2	4	6	13	18	22

NOTE: ***N. Adams*** *c-3, 6, 8, 9.* ***Anderson*** *c-2, 4, 5, 10, 11i, 15-17, 22; reprints-3, 4, 6-8, 10, 11, 13-16, 24, 25.* ***Infantino*** *r-1-5, 7-19, 23-25; c-11p.* ***Kaluta*** *c-18, 19.* ***Gil Kane*** *a-9r.* ***Kubert*** *c-1, 7, 12-14.* ***Toth*** *a-2r.* ***Wood*** *a-13i. Photo c-22.*

FROM DUSK TILL DAWN (Movie)
Big Entertainment: 1996 ($4.95, one-shot)

	GD 2.0	VG 4.0	FN 6.0	VF 8.0	VF/NM 9.0	NM- 9.2
nn-Adaptation of the film; Brereton-c						5.00
nn-($9.95)Deluxe Ed. w/ new material						10.00

FROM HELL
Mad Love/Tundra Publishing/Kitchen Sink: 1991 - No. 11, Sept, 1998 (B&W)

	GD 2.0	VG 4.0	FN 6.0	VF 8.0	VF/NM 9.0	NM- 9.2
1-Alan Moore and Eddie Campbell's Jack The Ripper story collected from the Taboo anthology series	2	4	6	11	16	20
1-(2nd printing)	2	4	6	8	10	12
1-(3rd printing)	1	2	3	4	5	7
2	1	2	3	5	6	8
2-(2nd printing)						6.00
2-(3rd printing)						4.00
3-1st Kitchen Sink Press issue	1	2	3	5	6	8
3-(2nd printing)						5.00
4-10: 10-(8/96)	1	2	3	4	5	7
11-Dance of the Gull Catchers (9/98, $4.95) Epilogue	2	4	6	9	12	15
Tundra Publishing reprintings 1-5 ('92)	1	2	3	4	5	7
HC						125.00
HC Ltd. Edition of 1,000 (signed and numbered)						225.00
TPB-1st printing (11/99)						60.00
TPB-2nd printing (3/00)						50.00
TPB-3rd printing (11/00)						40.00
TPB-4th printing (7/01) Regular and movie covers						35.00
TPB-5th printing - Regular and movie covers						35.00

Frontier Fighters #3 © DC

Frontline Combat #4 © WMG

Fun Comics #10 © STAR

FROM HERE TO INSANITY (Satire) (Formerly Eh! #1-7) (See Frantic & Frenzy)
Charlton Comics: No. 8, Feb, 1955 - V3#1, 1956

	GD 2.0	VG 4.0	FN 6.0	VF 8.0	VF/NM 9.0	NM- 9.2
8	19	38	57	109	172	235
9	17	34	51	98	154	210
10-Ditko-c/a (3 pgs.)	26	52	78	154	252	350
11,12-All Kirby except 4 pgs.	36	72	108	211	343	475
V3#1(1956)-Ward-c/a(2) (signed McCartney); 5 pgs. Wolverton-a; 3 pgs. Ditko-a; magazine format (cover says "Crazy, Man, Crazy" and becomes Crazy, Man, Crazy with V2#2)	41	82	123	256	428	600

FROM THE PIT
Fantagor Press: 1994 ($4.95, one-shot, mature)

	GD 2.0	VG 4.0	FN 6.0	VF 8.0	VF/NM 9.0	NM- 9.2
1-R. Corben-a; HP Lovecraft back-up story	1	2	3	5	6	8

FRONTIER DOCTOR (TV)
Dell Publishing Co.: No. 877, Feb, 1958 (one-shot)

	GD 2.0	VG 4.0	FN 6.0	VF 8.0	VF/NM 9.0	NM- 9.2
Four Color 877-Toth-a, Rex Allen photo-c	9	18	27	63	107	150

FRONTIER FIGHTERS
National Periodical Publications: Sept-Oct, 1955 - No. 8, Nov-Dec, 1956

	GD 2.0	VG 4.0	FN 6.0	VF 8.0	VF/NM 9.0	NM- 9.2
1-Davy Crockett, Buffalo Bill (by Kubert), Kit Carson begin (Scarce)	55	110	165	352	601	850
2	37	74	111	222	361	500
3-8	34	68	102	199	325	450

NOTE: *Buffalo Bill by* ***Kubert*** *in all.*

FRONTIER ROMANCES
Avon Periodicals/I. W.: Nov-Dec, 1949 - No. 2, Feb-Mar, 1950 (Painted-c)

	GD 2.0	VG 4.0	FN 6.0	VF 8.0	VF/NM 9.0	NM- 9.2
1-Used in **SOTI**, pg. 180 (General reference) & illo. "Erotic spanking in a western comic book"	50	100	150	315	533	750
2 (Scarce)-Woodish-a by Stallman	37	74	111	222	361	500
I.W. Reprint #1-Reprints Avon's #1	4	8	12	22	34	45
I.W. Reprint #9-Reprints ?	3	6	9	16	22	28

FRONTIER SCOUT: DAN'L BOONE (Formerly Death Valley; The Masked Raider No. 14 on)
Charlton Comics: No. 10, Jan, 1956 - No. 13, Aug, 1956; V2#14, Mar, 1965

	GD 2.0	VG 4.0	FN 6.0	VF 8.0	VF/NM 9.0	NM- 9.2
10	10	20	30	54	72	90
11-13(1956)	6	12	18	31	38	45
V2#14(3/65)	5	10	14	20	24	28

FRONTIER TRAIL (The Rider No. 1-5)
Ajax/Farrell Publ.: No. 6, May, 1958

	GD 2.0	VG 4.0	FN 6.0	VF 8.0	VF/NM 9.0	NM- 9.2
6	6	12	18	28	34	40

FRONTIER WESTERN
Atlas Comics (PrPI): Feb, 1956 - No. 10, Aug, 1957

	GD 2.0	VG 4.0	FN 6.0	VF 8.0	VF/NM 9.0	NM- 9.2
1	19	38	57	111	176	240
2,3,6-Williamson-a, 4 pgs. each	14	28	42	80	115	150
4,7,9,10: 10-Check-a	10	20	30	56	76	95
5-Crandall, Baker, Davis-a; Williamson text illos	14	28	42	76	108	140
8-Crandall, Morrow, & Wildey-a	10	20	30	58	79	100

NOTE: ***Baker*** *a-9.* ***Colan*** *a-2, 6.* ***Drucker*** *a-3, 4.* ***Heath*** *c-5.* ***Maneely*** *c/a-2, 7, 9.* ***Maurera*** *a-2.* ***Romita*** *a-7.* ***Severin*** *c-6, 8, 10.* ***Tuska*** *a-2.* ***Wildey*** *a-5, 8. Ringo Kid in No. 4.*

FRONTLINE COMBAT
E. C. Comics: July-Aug, 1951 - No. 15, Jan, 1954

	GD 2.0	VG 4.0	FN 6.0	VF 8.0	VF/NM 9.0	NM- 9.2
1-Severin/Kurtzman-a	71	142	213	568	909	1250
2	37	74	111	296	473	650
3	29	58	87	232	366	500
4-Used in **SOTI**, pg. 257; contains "Airburst" by Kurtzman which is his personal all-time favorite story	27	54	81	216	346	475
5-John Severin and Bill Elder bios.	23	46	69	184	292	400
6-10: 6-Kurtzman bio. 9-Civil War issue	20	40	60	160	255	350
11-15: 11-Civil War issue	15	30	45	120	193	265

NOTE: ***Davis*** *a-in all; c-11, 12.* ***Evans*** *a-10-15.* ***Heath*** *a-1.* ***Kubert*** *a-14.* ***Kurtzman*** *a-1-5; c-1-9.* ***Severin*** *a-5-7, 9, 13, 15.* ***Severin/Elder*** *a-2-11; c-10.* ***Toth*** *a-8, 12.* ***Wood*** *a-1-4, 6-10, 12-15; c-13-15. Special issues: No. 7 (Iwo Jima), No. 9 (Civil War), No. 12 (Air Force).*
(Canadian reprints known; see Table of Contents.)

FRONTLINE COMBAT
Russ Cochran/Gemstone Publishing: Aug, 1995 - No. 14 ($2.00/$2.50)

	GD 2.0	VG 4.0	FN 6.0	VF 8.0	VF/NM 9.0	NM- 9.2
1-14-E.C. reprints in all						3.00

FRONT PAGE COMIC BOOK
Front Page Comics (Harvey): 1945

	GD 2.0	VG 4.0	FN 6.0	VF 8.0	VF/NM 9.0	NM- 9.2
1-Kubert-a; intro. & 1st app. Man in Black by Powell; Fuje-c	40	80	120	246	411	575

FROST AND FIRE (See DC Science Fiction Graphic Novel)

FROSTY THE SNOWMAN
Dell Publishing Co.: No. 359, Nov, 1951 - No. 1272, Dec-Feb?/1961-62

	GD 2.0	VG 4.0	FN 6.0	VF 8.0	VF/NM 9.0	NM- 9.2
Four Color 359 (#1)	9	18	27	63	107	150
Four Color 435,514,601,661	6	12	18	37	59	80
Four Color 748,861,950,1065,1153,1272	5	10	15	32	51	70

FRUITMAN SPECIAL (See Bunny #2 for 1st app.)
Harvey Publications: Dec, 1969 (68 pgs.)

	GD 2.0	VG 4.0	FN 6.0	VF 8.0	VF/NM 9.0	NM- 9.2
1-Funny super hero	4	8	12	24	37	50

F-TROOP (TV)
Dell Publishing Co.: Aug, 1966 - No. 7, Aug, 1967 (All have photo-c)

	GD 2.0	VG 4.0	FN 6.0	VF 8.0	VF/NM 9.0	NM- 9.2
1	9	18	27	64	110	155
2-7	6	12	18	39	62	85

FUGITIVES FROM JUSTICE
St. John Publishing Co.: Feb, 1952 - No. 5, Oct, 1952

	GD 2.0	VG 4.0	FN 6.0	VF 8.0	VF/NM 9.0	NM- 9.2
1	22	44	66	132	216	300
2-Matt Baker-r/Northwest Mounties #2; Vic Flint strip reprints begin	22	44	66	128	209	290
3-Reprints panel from Authentic Police Cases that was used in **SOTI** with changes; Tuska-a	21	42	63	124	202	280
4	13	26	39	74	105	135
5-Last Vic Flint-r; bondage-c	14	28	42	81	118	155

FUGITOID
Mirage Studios: 1985 (B&W, magazine size, one-shot)

	GD 2.0	VG 4.0	FN 6.0	VF 8.0	VF/NM 9.0	NM- 9.2
1-Ties into Teenage Mutant Ninja Turtles #5	2	3	4	6	8	10

FULL OF FUN
Red Top (Decker Publ.)(Farrell)/I. W. Enterprises: Aug, 1957 - No. 2, Nov, 1957; 1964

	GD 2.0	VG 4.0	FN 6.0	VF 8.0	VF/NM 9.0	NM- 9.2
1(1957)-Funny animal; Dave Berg-a	7	14	21	37	46	55
2-Reprints Bingo, the Monkey Doodle Boy	5	10	15	22	26	30
8-I.W. Reprint('64)	2	4	6	9	12	15

FUN AT CHRISTMAS (See March of Comics No. 138)

FUN CLUB COMICS (See Interstate Theatres...)

FUN COMICS (Formerly Holiday Comics #1-8; Mighty Bear #13 on)
Star Publications: No. 9, Jan, 1953 - No. 12, Oct, 1953

	GD 2.0	VG 4.0	FN 6.0	VF 8.0	VF/NM 9.0	NM- 9.2
9-(25¢ Giant)-L. B. Cole X-Mas-c; X-Mas issue	22	44	66	132	216	300
10-12-L. B. Cole-c. 12-Mighty Bear-c/story	18	36	54	105	165	225

FUNDAY FUNNIES (See Famous TV..., and Harvey Hits No. 35,40)

FUN-IN (TV)(Hanna-Barbera)
Gold Key: Feb, 1970 - No. 10, Jan, 1972; No. 11, 4/74 - No. 15, 12/74

	GD 2.0	VG 4.0	FN 6.0	VF 8.0	VF/NM 9.0	NM- 9.2
1-Dastardly & Muttley in Their Flying Machines; Perils of Penelope Pitstop in #1-4; It's the Wolf in all	7	14	21	49	80	110
2-4,6-Cattanooga Cats in 2-4	4	8	12	22	34	45
5,7-Motormouse & Autocat, Dastardly & Muttley in both; It's the Wolf in #7	4	8	12	24	37	50
8,10-The Harlem Globetrotters, Dastardly & Muttley in #10	4	8	12	24	37	50
9-Where's Huddles?, Dastardly & Muttley, Motormouse & Autocat app.	4	8	12	24	37	50
11-Butch Cassidy	3	6	9	20	30	40
12-15: 12,15-Speed Buggy. 13-Hair Bear Bunch. 14-Inch High Private Eye	3	6	9	20	30	40

FUNKY PHANTOM, THE (TV)
Gold Key: Mar, 1972 - No. 13, Mar, 1975 (Hanna-Barbera)

	GD 2.0	VG 4.0	FN 6.0	VF 8.0	VF/NM 9.0	NM- 9.2
1	5	10	15	32	51	75
2-5	3	6	9	18	27	38
6-13	3	6	9	15	21	28

FUNLAND
Ziff-Davis (Approved Comics): No date (1940s) (25¢)

	GD 2.0	VG 4.0	FN 6.0	VF 8.0	VF/NM 9.0	NM- 9.2
nn-Contains games, puzzles, cut-outs, etc.	19	38	57	111	176	240

FUNLAND COMICS
Croyden Publishers: 1945

	GD 2.0	VG 4.0	FN 6.0	VF 8.0	VF/NM 9.0	NM- 9.2
1-Funny animal	15	30	45	88	137	185

FUNNIES, THE (New Funnies No. 65 on)
Dell Publishing Co.: Oct, 1936 - No. 64, May, 1942

	GD 2.0	VG 4.0	FN 6.0	VF 8.0	VF/NM 9.0	NM- 9.2
1-Tailspin Tommy, Mutt & Jeff, Alley Oop (1st app?), Capt. Easy (1st app.), Don Dixon begin	400	800	1200	2300	3650	5000
2 (11/36)-Scribbly by Mayer begins (see Popular Comics #6 for 1st app.)						

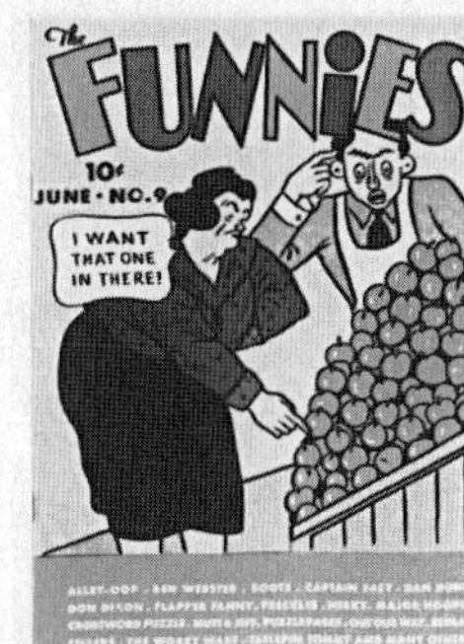

The Funnies #9 © DELL

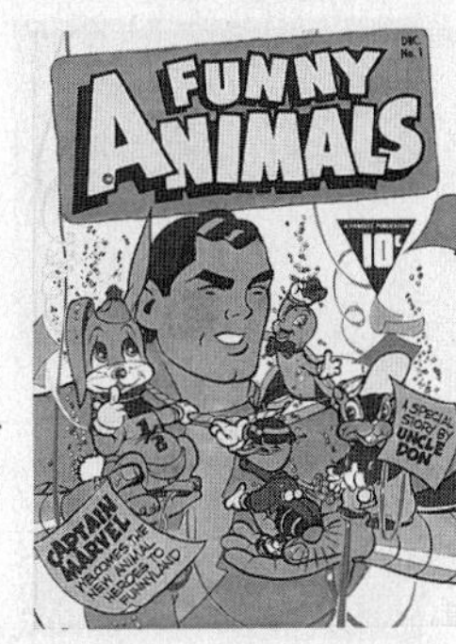

Funny Animals #1 © FAW

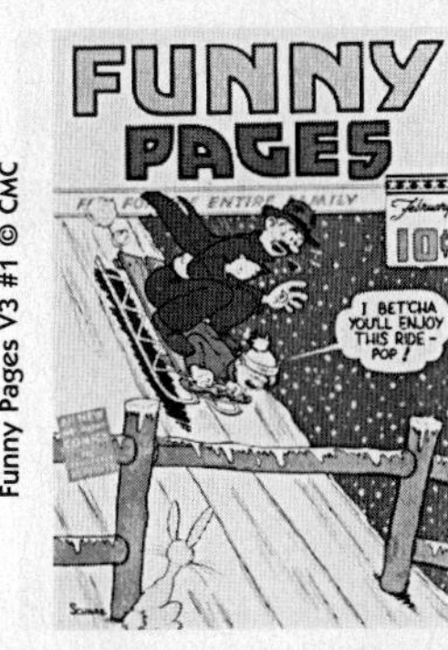

Funny Pages V3 #1 © CMC

	GD 2.0	VG 4.0	FN 6.0	VF 8.0	VF/NM 9.0	NM- 9.2
	180	360	540	1035	1643	2250
3	124	248	372	713	1132	1550
4,5: 4(1/37)-Christmas-c	92	184	276	529	840	1150
6-10	70	140	210	403	639	875
11-20: 16-Christmas-c	65	130	195	374	597	820
21-29: 25-Crime Busters by McWilliams(4pgs.)	52	104	156	299	475	650
30-John Carter of Mars (origin/1st app.) begins by Edgar Rice Burroughs; Jim Gary-a Warner Bros.' Bosko-c (4/39)	152	304	456	965	1658	2350
31-34,36-44: 31,32-Gary-a. 33-John Coleman Burroughs art begins on John Carter. 34-Last funny-c	81	162	243	518	884	1250
35-(9/39)-Mr. District Attorney begins; based on radio show; 1st cover app. John Carter of Mars	90	180	270	576	988	1400
45-Origin/1st app. Phantasmo, the Master of the World (Dell's 1st super-hero, 7/40) & his sidekick Whizzer McGee	94	188	282	597	1024	1450
46-50: 46-The Black Knight begins, ends #62	58	116	174	371	636	900
51-56-Last ERB John Carter of Mars	47	94	141	296	498	700
57-Intro. & origin Captain Midnight (7/41)	349	698	1047	2443	4272	6100
58-60: 58-Captain Midnight-c begin, end #63	87	174	261	553	952	1350
61-Andy Panda begins by Walter Lantz; WWII-c	103	206	309	659	1130	1600
62,63: 63-Last Captain Midnight-c; bondage-c	68	136	204	435	743	1050
64-Format change; Oswald the Rabbit, Felix the Cat, Li'l Eight Ball app.; origin & 1st app. Woody Woodpecker in Oswald; last Capt. Midnight; Oswald, Andy Panda, Li'l Eight Ball-c	148	296	444	947	1624	2300

NOTE: ***Mayer*** *c-26, 48.* ***McWilliams*** *art in many issues on "Rex King of the Deep". Alley Oop c-17, 20. Captain Midnight c-57(i/2), 58-63. John Carter c-35-37, 40. Phantasmo c-45-56, 57(1/2), 58-61(part). Rex King c-38, 39, 42. Tailspin Tommy c-41.*

FUNNIES ANNUAL, THE
Avon Periodicals: 1959 ($1.00, approx. 7x10", B&W; tabloid-size)

	GD 2.0	VG 4.0	FN 6.0	VF 8.0	VF/NM 9.0	NM- 9.2
1-(Rare)-Features the best newspaper comic strips of the year: Archie, Snuffy Smith, Beetle Bailey, Henry, Blondie, Steve Canyon, Buz Sawyer, The Little King, Hi & Lois, Popeye, & others. Also has a chronological history of the comics from 2000 B.C. to 1959.	43	86	129	271	461	650

FUNNIES ON PARADE (See Promotional Comics section)

FUNNY ANIMALS (See Fawcett's Funny Animals)
Charlton Comics: Sept, 1984 - No. 2, Nov, 1984

	GD 2.0	VG 4.0	FN 6.0	VF 8.0	VF/NM 9.0	NM- 9.2
1,2-Atomic Mouse-r; low print						6.00

FUNNYBONE (... The Laugh-Book of Comical Comics)
La Salle Publishing Co.: 1944 (25¢, 132 pgs.)

	GD 2.0	VG 4.0	FN 6.0	VF 8.0	VF/NM 9.0	NM- 9.2
nn	30	60	90	177	289	400

FUNNY BOOK (...Magazine for Young Folks) (Hocus Pocus No. 9)
Parents' Magazine Press (Funny Book Publishing Corp.):
Dec, 1942 - No. 9, Aug-Sept, 1946 (Comics, stories, puzzles, games)

	GD 2.0	VG 4.0	FN 6.0	VF 8.0	VF/NM 9.0	NM- 9.2
1-Funny animal; Alice In Wonderland app.	15	30	45	86	133	180
2-Gulliver in Giant-Land	10	20	30	56	76	95
3-9: 4-Advs. of Robin Hood. 9-Hocus-Pocus strip	9	18	27	47	61	75

FUNNY COMICS
Modern Store Publ.: 1955 (7¢, 5x7", 36 pgs.)

	GD 2.0	VG 4.0	FN 6.0	VF 8.0	VF/NM 9.0	NM- 9.2
1-Funny animal	4	8	12	22	34	45

FUNNY COMIC TUNES (See Funny Tunes)

FUNNY FABLES
Decker Publications (Red Top Comics): Aug, 1957 - V2#2, Nov, 1957

	GD 2.0	VG 4.0	FN 6.0	VF 8.0	VF/NM 9.0	NM- 9.2
V1#1	6	12	18	31	38	45
V1#2,V2#1,2: V1#2 (11/57)-Reissue of V1#1	5	10	14	20	24	28

FUNNY FILMS (Features funny animal characters from films)
American Comics Group(Michel Publ./Titan Publ.): Sept-Oct, 1949 - No. 29, May-June, 1954 (No. 1-4: 52 pgs.)

	GD 2.0	VG 4.0	FN 6.0	VF 8.0	VF/NM 9.0	NM- 9.2
1-Puss An' Boots, Blunderbunny begin	18	36	54	105	165	225
2	11	22	33	62	86	110
3-10: 3-X-Mas-c	9	18	27	47	61	75
11-20	7	14	21	35	43	50
21-29	6	12	18	28	34	40

FUNNY FOLKS
DC Comics: Feb, 1946

nn-Ashcan comic, not distributed to newsstands, only for in house use (no known sales)

FUNNY FOLKS (Hollywood... on cover only No. 16-26; becomes Hollywood Funny Folks No. 27 on)
National Periodical Publ.: April-May, 1946 - No. 26, June-July, 1950 (52 pgs., #15 on)

	GD 2.0	VG 4.0	FN 6.0	VF 8.0	VF/NM 9.0	NM- 9.2
1-Nutsy Squirrel begins (1st app.) by Rube Grossman; Grossman-a in most issues	39	78	117	240	395	550
2	20	40	60	114	182	250
3-5: 4-1st Nutsy Squirrel-c	15	30	45	84	127	170
6-10: 6,9-Nutsy Squirrel-c begin	11	22	33	62	86	110
11-26: 15-Begin 52 pg. issues (8-9/48)	10	20	30	54	72	90

NOTE: ***Sheldon Mayer*** *a-in some issues.* ***Post*** *a-18. Christmas c-12.*

FUNNY FROLICS
Timely/Marvel Comics (SPI): Summer, 1945 - No. 5, Dec, 1946

	GD 2.0	VG 4.0	FN 6.0	VF 8.0	VF/NM 9.0	NM- 9.2
1-Sharpy Fox, Puffy Pig, Krazy Krow	26	52	78	154	252	350
2	15	30	45	85	130	175
3,4	13	26	39	72	101	130
5-Kurtzman-a	14	28	42	78	112	145

FUNNY FUNNIES
Nedor Publishing Co.: April, 1943 (68 pgs.)

	GD 2.0	VG 4.0	FN 6.0	VF 8.0	VF/NM 9.0	NM- 9.2
1-Funny animals; Peter Porker app.	19	38	57	111	176	240

FUNNYMAN (Also see Cisco Kid Comics & Extra Comics)
Magazine Enterprises: Dec, 1947; No. 1, Jan, 1948 - No. 6, Aug, 1948

nn(12/47)-Prepublication B&W undistributed copy by Siegel & Shuster-(5-3/4x8"), 16 pgs.; Sold at auction in 1997 for $575.00

	GD 2.0	VG 4.0	FN 6.0	VF 8.0	VF/NM 9.0	NM- 9.2
1-Siegel & Shuster-a in all; Dick Ayers 1st pro work (as assistant) on 1st few issues	47	94	141	296	498	700
2	28	56	84	165	270	375
3-6	24	48	72	142	234	325

FUNNY MOVIES (See 3-D Funny Movies)

FUNNY PAGES (Formerly The Comics Magazine)
Comics Magazine Co./Ultem Publ.(Chesler)/Centaur Publications:
No. 6, Nov, 1936 - No. 42, Oct, 1940

	GD 2.0	VG 4.0	FN 6.0	VF 8.0	VF/NM 9.0	NM- 9.2
V1#6 (nn, nd)-The Clock begins (2 pgs., 1st app.), ends #11; The Clock is the 1st masked comic book hero	271	542	813	1734	2967	4200
7-11	103	206	309	659	1130	1600
V2#1-V2#3: V2#1 (9/37)(V2#2 on-c; V2#1 in indicia). V2#2 (10/37)(V2#3 on-c; V2#2 in indicia). V2#3(11/37)-5	73	146	219	467	796	1125
6(1st Centaur, 3/38)	95	190	285	603	1039	1475
7-9	73	146	219	467	796	1125
10(Scarce, 9/38)-1st app. of The Arrow by Gustavson (Blue costume)	366	732	1098	2562	4481	6400
11,12	129	258	387	826	1413	2000
V3#1-Bruce Wayne prototype in "Case of the Missing Heir," by Bob Kane, 3 months before app. Batman (See Det. Pic. Stories #5)	139	278	417	883	1517	2150
2-6,8: 6,8-Last funny covers	113	226	339	718	1234	1750
7-1st Arrow-c (9/39)	300	600	900	2070	3635	5200
9-Tarpe Mills jungle-c	129	258	387	826	1413	2000
10-2nd Arrow-c	284	568	852	1818	3109	4400
V4#1(1/40, Arrow-c)-(Rare)-The Owl & The Phantom Rider app.; origin Mantoka, Maker of Magic by Jack Cole. Mad Ming begins, ends #42; Tarpe Mills-a	300	600	900	2010	3505	5000
35-Classic Arrow-c	300	600	900	2010	3505	5000
36-38-Mad Ming-c	129	258	387	826	1413	2000
39-41-Arrow-c	232	464	696	1485	2543	3600
42 (Scarce,10/40)-Last Arrow; Arrow-c	239	478	717	1530	2615	3700

NOTE: ***Biro*** *c-V2#9.* ***Burgos*** *c-V3#10.* ***Jack Cole*** *a-V2#3, 7, 8, 10, 11, V3#2, 6, 9, 10, V4#1, 37; c-V3#2, 4.* ***Eisner*** *a-V1#7, 8?, 10.* ***Ken Ernst*** *a-V1#7, 8.* ***Everett*** *a-V2#11 (illos).* ***Filchock*** *c-V2#10, V3#6.* ***Gill Fox*** *a-V2#11.* ***Sid Greene*** *a-39.* ***Guardineer*** *a-V2#2, 3, 5.* ***Gustavson*** *a-V2#5, 11, 12, V3#1-10, 35, 38-42; c-V3#7, 35, 39-42.* ***Bob Kane*** *a-V3#1.* ***McWilliams*** *a-V2#12, V3#1, 3-6.* ***Tarpe Mills*** *a-V3#8-10, V4#1; c-V3#9.* ***Ed Moore Jr.*** *a-V2#12.* ***Schwab*** *c-V3#1.* ***Bob Wood*** *a-V2#2, 3, 8, 11, V3#6, 9, 10; c-V2#6, 7. Arrow c-V3#7, 10, V4#1, 35, 40-42.*

FUNNY PICTURE STORIES (Comic Pages V3#4 on)
Comics Magazine Co./Centaur Publications: Nov, 1936 - V3#3, May, 1939

	GD 2.0	VG 4.0	FN 6.0	VF 8.0	VF/NM 9.0	NM- 9.2
V1#1-The Clock begins (c-feature)(see Funny Pages for 1st app.)	366	732	1098	2562	4481	6400
2	135	270	405	864	1482	2100
3-6(4/37): 4-Eisner-a; X-Mas-c.	90	180	270	576	988	1400
7-(6/37) (Rare) Racial humor-c	181	362	543	1158	1979	2800
V2#1 (9/37; V1#10 on-c; V2#1 in indicia)-Jack Strand begins	58	116	174	371	636	900
2 (10/37; V1#11 on-c; V2#2 in indicia)	58	116	174	371	636	900
3-5,7-11(11/38): 4-Xmas-c	53	106	159	334	567	800
6-(1st Centaur, 3/38)	81	162	243	518	884	1250
V3#1(1/39)-3	52	104	156	328	552	775

NOTE: ***Biro*** *c-V2#1, 8, 9, 11.* ***Guardineer*** *a-V1#11; c-V2#6, V3#5.* ***Bob Wood*** *c/a-V1#11, V2#2; c-V2#3, 5.*

FUNNY STUFF (Becomes The Dodo & the Frog No. 80)
All-American/National Periodical Publications No. 7 on: Summer, 1944 - No. 79, July-Aug,

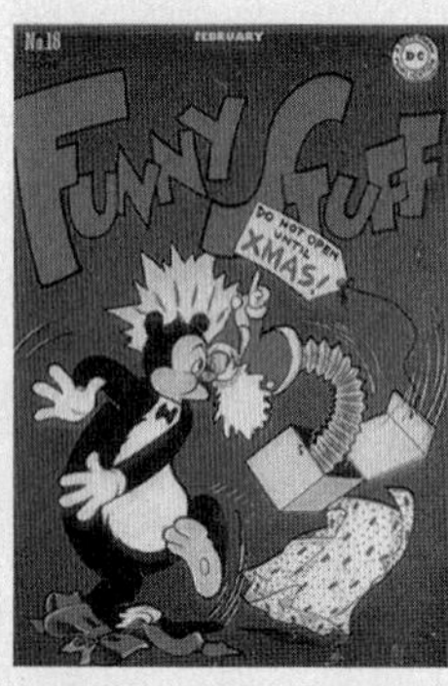

Funny Stuff #18 © DC

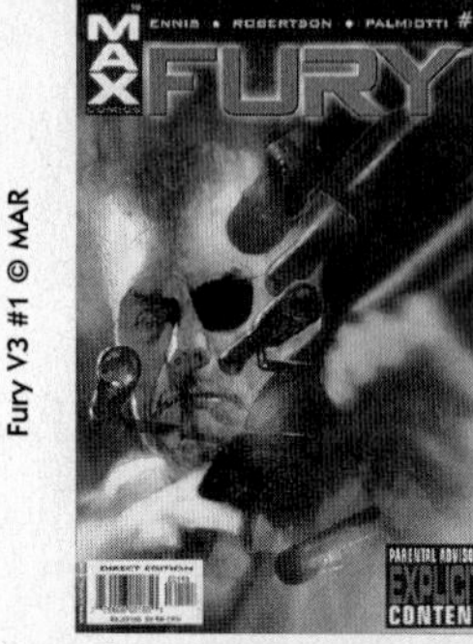

Fury V3 #1 © MAR

Futurama Comics #40 © Bongo

	GD 2.0	VG 4.0	FN 6.0	VF 8.0	VF/NM 9.0	NM- 9.2
1954 (#1-7 are quarterly)						
1-The Three Mouseketeers (ends #28) & The "Terrific Whatzit" begin; Sheldon Mayer-a; Grossman-a in most issues	89	178	267	565	970	1375
2-Sheldon Mayer-a	42	84	126	265	445	625
3-5: 3-Flash parody. 5-All Mayer-a/scripts issue	30	60	90	177	289	400
6-10 10-(6/46)	20	40	60	114	182	250
11-17,19	15	30	45	90	140	190
18-The Dodo & the Frog (2/47, 1st app?) begin?; X-Mas-c	27	54	81	160	263	365
19-1st Dodo & the Frog-c (3/47)	18	36	54	105	165	225
20-2nd Dodo & the Frog-c (4/47)	14	28	42	80	115	150
21,23-30: 24-Infinity-c. 30-Christmas-c	11	22	33	62	86	110
22-Superman cameo	37	74	111	222	361	500
31-79: 70-1st Bo Bunny by Mayer & begins	10	20	30	56	76	95

NOTE: *Mayer a-1-8, 55, ,57, 58, 61, 62, 64, 65, 68, 70, 72, 74-79; c-2, 5, 6, 8.*

FUNNY STUFF STOCKING STUFFER
DC Comics: Mar, 1985 ($1.25, 52 pgs.)

1-Almost every DC funny animal featured — 4.00

FUNNY 3-D
Harvey Publications: December, 1953 (25¢, came with 2 pair of glasses)

	GD	VG	FN	VF	VF/NM	NM-
1-Shows cover in 3-D on inside	11	22	33	62	86	110

FUNNY TUNES (Animated Funny Comic Tunes No. 16-22; Funny Comic Tunes No. 23, on covers only; Oscar No. 24 on)
U.S.A. Comics Magazine Corp. (Timely): No. 16, Summer, 1944 - No. 23, Fall, 1946

	GD	VG	FN	VF	VF/NM	NM-
16-Silly Seal, Ziggy Pig, Krazy Krow begin	18	36	54	105	165	225
17 (Fall/44)-Becomes Gay Comics #18 on?	14	28	42	82	121	160
18-22: 21-Super Rabbit app.	13	26	39	74	105	135
23-Kurtzman-a	14	28	42	80	115	150

FUNNY TUNES (Becomes Space Comics #4 on)
Avon Periodicals: July, 1953 - No. 3, Dec-Jan, 1953-54

	GD	VG	FN	VF	VF/NM	NM-
1-Space Mouse, Peter Rabbit, Merry Mouse, Spotty the Pup, Cicero the Cat begin; all continue in Space Comics	11	22	33	60	83	105
2,3	8	16	24	44	57	70

FUNNY WORLD
Marbak Press: 1947 - No. 3, 1948

	GD	VG	FN	VF	VF/NM	NM-
1-The Berrys, The Toodles & other strip-r begin	9	18	27	47	61	75
2,3	6	12	18	31	38	45

FUNTASTIC WORLD OF HANNA-BARBERA, THE (TV)
Marvel Comics Group: Dec, 1977 - No. 3, June, 1978 ($1.25, oversized)

	GD	VG	FN	VF	VF/NM	NM-
1-3: 1-The Flintstones Christmas Party(12/77). 2-Yogi Bear's Easter Parade(3/78). 3-Laff-a-lympics(6/78)	4	8	12	26	41	55

FUN TIME
Ace Periodicals: Spring, 1953; No. 2, Sum, 1953; No. 3(nn), Fall, 1953; No. 4, Wint, 1953-54

	GD	VG	FN	VF	VF/NM	NM-
1-(25¢, 100 pgs.)-Funny animal	19	38	57	111	176	240
2-4 (All 25¢, 100 pgs.)	15	30	45	88	137	185

FUN WITH SANTA CLAUS (See March of Comics No. 11, 108, 325)

FURTHER ADVENTURES OF CYCLOPS AND PHOENIX (Also see Adventures of Cyclops and Phoenix, Uncanny X-Men & X-Men)
Marvel Comics: June, 1996 - No. 4, Sept, 1996 ($1.95, limited series)

1-4: Origin of Mr. Sinister; Milligan scripts; John Paul Leon-c/a(p). 2-4-Apocalypse app. — 3.00
Trade Paperback (1997, $14.99) r/1-4 — 15.00

FURTHER ADVENTURES OF INDIANA JONES, THE (Movie) (Also see Indiana Jones and the Last Crusade & Indiana Jones and the Temple of Doom)
Marvel Comics Group: Jan, 1983 - No. 34, Mar, 1986

1-Byrne/Austin-a; Austin-c — 6.00
2-34: 2-Byrne/Austin-c/a — 4.00

NOTE: ***Austin** a-1i, 2i, 6i, 9i; c-1, 2i, 6i, 9i. **Byrne** a-1p, 2p; c-2p. **Chaykin** a-6p; c-6p, 8p-10p. **Ditko** a-21p, 25-28, 34. **Golden** c-24, 25. **Simonson** c-9. Painted c-14.*

FURTHER ADVENTURES OF NYOKA, THE JUNGLE GIRL, THE (See Nyoka)
AC Comics: 1988 - No. 5, 1989 ($1.95, color; $2.25/$2.50, B&W)

1-5 : 1,2-Bill Black-a plus reprints. 3-Photo-c. 5-(B&W)-Reprints plus movie photos — 3.00

FURY (Straight Arrow's Horse...) (See A-1 No. 119)

FURY (TV) (See March Of Comics #200)
Dell Publishing Co./Gold Key: No. 781, Mar, 1957 - Nov, 1962 (All photo-c)

	GD	VG	FN	VF	VF/NM	NM-
Four Color 781	8	16	24	52	86	120
Four Color 885,975,1031,1080,1133,1172,1218,1296	6	12	18	41	66	90
01292-208(#1-'62), 10020-211(11/62-G.K.)	6	12	18	37	59	80

FURY
Marvel Comics: May, 1994 ($2.95, one-shot)

1-Iron Man, Red Skull, FF, Hatemonger, Logan app.; Origin Nick Fury — 3.00

FURY (Volume 3)
Marvel Comics (MAX): Nov, 2001 - No. 6, Apr, 2002 ($2.99, mature content)

1-6-Ennis-s/Robertson-a — 3.00

FURY/ AGENT 13
Marvel Comics: June, 1998 - No. 2, July, 1998 ($2.99, limited series)

1,2-Nick Fury returns — 3.00

FURY OF FIRESTORM, THE (Becomes Firestorm The Nuclear Man on cover with #50, in indicia with #65) (Also see Firestorm)
DC Comics: June, 1982 - No. 64, Oct, 1987 (75¢ on)

1-Intro The Black Bison; brief origin — 6.00
2-40,43-64: 4-JLA x-over. 17-1st app. Firehawk. 21-Death of Killer Frost. 22-Origin. 23-Intro. Byte. 24-(6/84)-1st app. Blue Devil & Bug (origin); origin Byte. 34-1st app./origin Killer Frost II. 39-Weasel's ID revealed. 48-Intro. Moonbow. 53-Origin/1st app. Silver Shade. 55,56-Legends x-over. 58-1st app./origin new Parasite — 3.00
41,42-Crisis x-over — 3.50

	GD	VG	FN	VF	VF/NM	NM-
61-Test cover variant; Superman logo	4	8	12	22	34	45

Annual 1-4: 1(1983), 2(1984), 3(1985), 4(1986) — 4.00

NOTE: ***Colan** a-19p, Annual 4p. **Giffen** a-Annual 4p. **Gil Kane** c-30. **Nino** a-37. **Tuska** a-(p)-17, 18, 32, 45.*

FURY OF SHIELD
Marvel Comics: Apr, 1995 - No. 4, July, 1995 ($2.50/$1.95, limited series)

1 ($2.50)-Foil-c — 3.50
2-4: 4-Bagged w/ decoder — 3.00

FURY: PEACEMAKER
Marvel Comics: Apr, 2006 - No. 6, Sept, 2006 ($3.50, limited series)

1-6-Flashback to WW2; Ennis-s/Robertson-a. 1-Deodato-c. 2-Texeira-c. 5-Dillon-c — 3.50
TPB (2006, $17.99) r/#1-6 — 18.00

FUSED
Image Comics: Mar, 2002 - No. 4, Jan, 2003 ($2.95)

1-4-Steve Niles-s. 1,2-Paul Lee-a. 3-Brad Rader-a. 4-Templesmith-a — 3.00
Canned Heat TPB (Dark Horse, 6/04, $12.95) r/series; Dan Wickline intro. — 13.00

FUSED
Dark Horse Comics: Dec, 2003 - No. 4, Mar, 2004 ($2.95)

1-4-Steve Niles-s/Josh Medors-a. 1-Powell-c — 3.00

FUSION
Eclipse Comics: Jan, 1987 - No. 17, Oct, 1989 ($2.00, B&W, Baxter paper)

1-17: 11-The Weasel Patrol begins (1st app.?) — 3.00

FUSION
Image Comics (Top Cow): May, 2009 - No. 3, Jul, 2009 ($2.99, limited series)

1-3-Avengers, Thunderbolts, Cyberforce and Hunter-Killer meet; Kirkham-a — 3.00

FUTURAMA (TV)
Bongo Comics: 2000 - Present ($2.50/$2.99, bi-monthly)

1-Based on the FOX-TV animated series; Groening/Morrison-c — 4.00
1-San Diego Comic-Con Premiere Edition — 5.00
2-54: 8-CGC cover spoof; X-Men parody. 40-Santa app. 50-52-Poster included — 3.00
Futurama Adventures TPB (2004, $14.95) r/#5-9 — 15.00
Futurama Conquers the Universe TPB (2007, $14.95) r/#10-13 — 15.00
Futurama-O-Rama TPB (2002, $12.95) r/#1-4; sketch pages of Fry's development — 13.00
...: The Time Bender Trilogy TPB (2006, $14.95) r/#16-19; cover gallery — 15.00

FUTURAMA/SIMPSONS INFINITELY SECRET CROSSOVER CRISIS (TV) (See Simpsons/ Futurama Crossover Crisis II for sequel)
Bongo Comics: 2002 - No. 2, 2002 ($2.50, limited series)

1,2-Evil Brain Spawns put Futurama crew into the Simpsons' Springfield — 3.00

FUTURE COMICS
David McKay Publications: June, 1940 - No. 4, Sept, 1940

	GD	VG	FN	VF	VF/NM	NM-
1-(6/40, 64 pgs.)-Origin The Phantom (1st in comics) (4 pgs.); The Lone Ranger (8 pgs.) & Saturn Against the Earth (4 pgs.) begin	300	600	900	1920	3310	4700
2	123	246	369	787	1344	1900
3,4	87	174	261	553	952	1350

FUTURE COP L.A.P.D. (Electronic Arts video game) (Also see Promotional Comics section)
DC Comics (WildStorm): Jan, 1999 ($4.95, magazine sized)

FX #1 © Monkeyboard Inc.

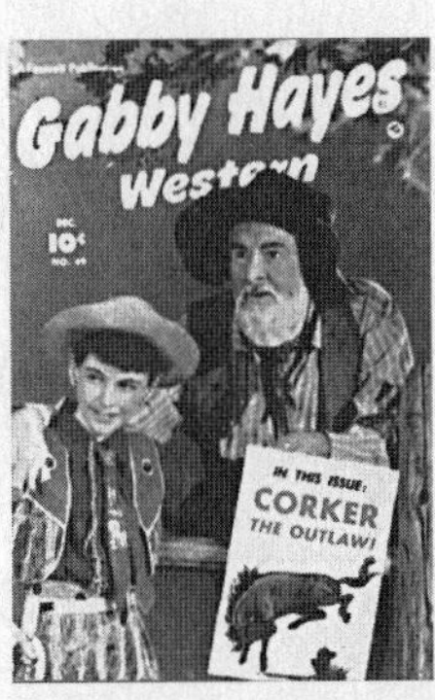

Gabby Hayes Western #49 © FAW

Gambit (2004 series) #1 © MAR

GD 2.0 | VG 4.0 | FN 6.0 | VF 8.0 | VF/NM 9.0 | NM- 9.2

1-Stories & art by various 5.00

FUTURE SHOCK
Image Comics: 2006 (Free Comic Book Day giveaway)
...: FCBD 2006 Edition; Spawn, Invincible, Savage Dragon & others short stories 2.50

FUTURE WORLD COMICS
George W. Dougherty: Summer, 1946 - No. 2, Fall, 1946
1,2: H. C. Kiefer-c; preview of the World of Tomorrow 29 58 87 170 278 385

FUTURE WORLD COMIX (Warren Presents...)
Warren Publications: Sept, 1978 (B&W magazine, 84 pgs.)
1-Corben, Maroto, Morrow, Nino, Sutton-a; Todd-c/a; contains nudity panels
2 4 6 8 11 14

FUTURIANS, THE (See Marvel Graphic Novel #9)
Lodestone Publishing/Eternity Comics: Sept, 1985 - No. 3, 1985 ($1.50)
1-3: Indicia title "Dave Cockrum's..." 3.00
Graphic Novel 1 ($9.95, Eternity)-r/#1-3, plus never published #4 issue 10.00

FX
IDW Publishing: Mar, 2008 - No. 6, Aug, 2008 ($3.99)
1-6-John Byrne-a/c; Wayne Osborne-s 4.00

G-8 (Listed at G-Eight)

GABBY (Formerly Ken Shannon) (Teen humor)
Quality Comics Group: No. 11, Jul, 1953; No. 2, Sep, 1953 - No. 9, Sep, 1954
11(#1)(7/53) 9 18 27 47 61 75
2 6 12 18 31 38 45
3-9 5 10 15 24 30 35

GABBY GOB (See Harvey Hits No. 85, 90, 94, 97, 100, 103, 106, 109)

GABBY HAYES ADVENTURE COMICS
Toby Press: Dec, 1953
1-Photo-c 15 30 45 88 137 185

GABBY HAYES WESTERN (Movie star)(See Monte Hale, Real Western Hero & Western Hero)
Fawcett Publications/Charlton Comics No. 51 on: Nov, 1948 - No. 50, Jan, 1953; No. 51, Dec, 1954 - No. 59, Jan, 1957
1-Gabby & his horse Corker begin; photo front/back-c begin
40 80 120 246 411 575
2 20 40 60 118 192 265
3-5 15 30 45 88 137 185
6-10: 9-Young Falcon begins 14 28 42 78 112 145
11-20: 19-Last photo back-c 11 22 33 64 90 115
21-49: 20,22,24,26,28,29-(52 pgs.) 9 18 27 52 69 85
50-(1/53)-Last Fawcett issue; last photo-c? 10 20 30 58 79 100
51-(12/54)-1st Charlton issue; photo-c 11 22 33 60 83 105
52-59(1955-57): 53,55-Photo-c. 58-Swayze-a 8 16 24 42 54 65

GAGS
United Features Synd./Triangle Publ. No. 9 on: Jul, 1937 - V3#10, Oct, 1944 (13-3/4x10-3/4")
1(7/37)-52 pgs.; 20 pgs. Grin & Bear It, Fellow Citizen
11 22 33 62 86 110
V1#9 (36 pgs.) (7/42) 7 14 21 35 43 50
V3#10 6 12 18 31 38 45

GALACTA: DAUGHTER OF GALACTUS
Marvel Comics: July, 2010 ($3.99, one-shot)
1-Adam Warren-s/Hector Sevilla-a; Warren & Sevilla-c : Wolverine and the FF app. 4.00

GALACTICA 1980 (Based on the Battlestar Galactica TV series)
Dynamite Entertainment: 2009 - No. 4, 2009 ($3.50)
1-4-Guggenheim-s/Razek-a 3.50

GALACTICA: THE NEW MILLENNIUM
Realm Press: Sept, 1999 ($2.99)
1-Stories by Shooter, Braden, Kuhoric 3.00

GALACTIC GUARDIANS
Marvel Comics: July, 1994 - No. 4, Oct, 1994 ($1.50, limited series)
1-4 3.00

GALACTIC WARS COMIX (Warren Presents... on cover)
Warren Publications: Dec, 1978 (B&W magazine, 84 pgs.)
nn-Wood, Williamson-r; Battlestar Galactica/Flash Gordon photo/text stories
2 4 6 8 11 14

GALACTUS THE DEVOURER
Marvel Comics: Sept, 1999 - No. 6, Mar, 2000 ($3.50/$2.50, limited series)
1-($3.50) L. Simonson-s/Muth & Sienkiewicz-a 4.00
2-5-($2.50) Buscema & Sienkiewicz-a 3.00
6-($3.50) Death of Galactus; Buscema & Sienkiewicz-a 4.00

GALAXIA (Magazine)
Astral Publ.: 1981 ($2.50, B&W, 52 pgs.)
1-Buckler/Giordano-c; Texeira/Guice-a; 1st app. Astron, Sojourner, Bloodwing, Warlords; Buckler-s/a 2 4 6 9 13 16

GALAXY QUEST: GLOBAL WARNING! (Based on the 1999 movie)
IDW Publishing: Aug, 2008 - No. 5, Dec, 2008 ($3.99)
1-5-Lobdell-s/Kyriazis-a 4.00

GALLANT MEN, THE (TV)
Gold Key: Oct, 1963 (Photo-c)
1(1008-310)-Manning-a 4 8 12 22 34 45

GALLEGHER, BOY REPORTER (Disney, TV)
Gold Key: May, 1965
1(10149-505)-Photo-c 3 6 9 18 27 35

GAMBIT (See X-Men #266 & X-Men Annual #14)
Marvel Comics: Dec, 1993 - No. 4, Mar, 1994 ($2.00, limited series)
1-($2.50)-Lee Weeks-c/a in all; gold foil stamped-c. 6.00
1 (Gold) 2 4 6 9 12 15
2-4 4.00

GAMBIT
Marvel Comics: Sept, 1997 - No. 4, Dec, 1997 ($2.50, limited series)
1-4-Janson-a/Mackie & Kavanagh-s 3.00

GAMBIT
Marvel Comics: Feb, 1999 - No. 25, Feb, 2001 ($2.99/$1.99)
1-($2.99) Five covers; Nicieza-a/Skroce-a 5.00
2-11,13-16-($1.99): 2-Two covers (Skroce & Adam Kubert) 3.00
12-($2.99) 4.00
17-24: 17-Begin $2.25-c. 21-Mystique-c/app. 3.00
25-($2.99) Leads into "Gambit & Bishop" 4.00
...1999 Annual ($3.50) Nicieza-s/McDaniel-a 4.00
...2000 Annual ($3.50) Nicieza-s/Derenick & Smith-a 4.00

GAMBIT
Marvel Comics: Nov, 2004 - No. 12, Aug, 2005 ($2.99)
1-12: 1-Jeanty-a/Land-c/Layman-s. 5-Wolverine-c/app. 9-Brother Voodoo-c/app. 3.00
...: Hath No Fury TPB (2005, $14.99) r/#7-12 15.00
...: House of Cards TPB (2005, $14.99) r/#1-6; Land cover sketches; unused covers 15.00

GAMBIT & BISHOP (... : Sons of the Atom on cover)
Marvel Comics: Feb, 2001 - No. 6, May, 2001 ($2.25, bi-weekly limited series)
Alpha (2/01) Prelude to series; Nord-a 3.00
1-6-Jeanty-a/Williams-c 3.00
Genesis (3/01, $3.50) reprints their first apps. and first meeting 4.00

GAMBIT AND THE X-TERNALS
Marvel Comics: Mar, 1995 - No. 4, July, 1995 ($1.95, limited series)
1-4-Age of Apocalypse 3.00

GAMEBOY (Super Mario covers on all)
Valiant: 1990 - No. 5 ($1.95, coated-c)
1-5: 3,4-Layton-c. 4-Morrow-a. 5-Layton-c(i) 8.00

GAMEKEEPER (Guy Ritchie's...)
Virgin Comics: Mar, 2007 - No. 5, Sept, 2007; Mar, 2008 - Present ($2.99)
1-5-Andy Diggle-s/Mukesh Singh-a; 2 covers on each 3.00
1-Extended Edition (6/07, $2.99) r/#1 with script excerpt and sketch art 3.00
Series 2 (3/08 - Present) 1-5-Parker-s/Randle-a 3.00
Vol. 1 TPB (10/07, $14.99) r/#1-5; script and sketch pages; Guy Ritchie intro. 15.00

GAMERA
Dark Horse Comics: Aug, 1996 - No. 4, Nov, 1996 ($2.95, limited series)
1-4 3.00

GAMMARAUDERS
DC Comics: Jan, 1989 - No. 10, Dec, 1989 ($1.25/$1.50/$2.00)
1-10-Based on TSR game 3.00

GAMORRA SWIMSUIT SPECIAL
Image Comics (WildStorm Productions): June, 1996 ($2.50, one-shot)

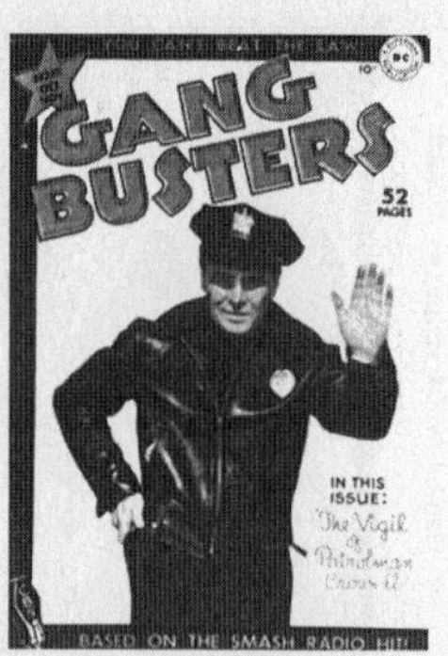

Gang Busters #12 © DC

Gay Comics #32 © MAR

Gears of War #9 © Epic Comics

	GD 2.0	VG 4.0	FN 6.0	VF 8.0	VF/NM 9.0	NM- 9.2
1-Campbell wraparound-c; pinups						3.00

GANDY GOOSE (Movies/TV)(See All Surprise, Giant Comics Edition #5A &10, Paul Terry's Comics & Terry-Toons)
St. John Publ. Co./Pines No. 5,6: Mar, 1953 - No. 5, Nov, 1953; No. 5, Fall, 1956 - No. 6, Sum/58

	GD	VG	FN	VF	VF/NM	NM-
1-All St. John issues are pre-code	10	20	30	58	79	100
2	7	14	21	35	43	50
3-5(1953)(St. John)	6	12	18	31	38	45
5,6(1956-58)(Pines)-CBS Television Presents...	5	10	15	24	30	35

GANG BUSTERS (See Popular Comics #38)
David McKay/Dell Publishing Co.: 1938 - 1943

	GD	VG	FN	VF	VF/NM	NM-
Feature Books 17(McKay)('38)-1st app.	68	136	204	435	743	1050
Large Feature Comic 10('39)-(Scarce)	68	136	204	435	743	1050
Large Feature Comic 17('41)	47	94	141	296	498	700
Four Color 7(1940)	50	100	150	315	533	750
Four Color 23('42)	40	80	120	246	411	575
Four Color 24('43)	26	52	78	186	373	560

GANG BUSTERS (Radio/TV)(Gangbusters #14 on)
National Periodical Publ.: Dec-Jan, 1947-48 - No. 67, Dec-Jan, 1958-59 (No. 1-23: 52 pgs.)

	GD	VG	FN	VF	VF/NM	NM-
1	84	168	252	538	919	1300
2	39	78	117	240	395	550
3-5	28	56	84	165	270	375
6-10: 9-Dan Barry-a. 9,10-Photo-c	21	42	63	122	199	275
11-13-Photo-c	17	34	51	100	158	215
14,17-Frazetta-a, 8 pgs. each. 14-Photo-c	36	72	108	211	343	475
15,16,18-20,26: 26-Kirby-a	15	30	45	85	130	175
21-25,27-30	14	28	42	76	108	140
31-44: 44-Last Pre-code (2-3/55)	12	24	36	67	94	120
45-67	10	20	30	54	72	90

NOTE: ***Barry** a-6, 8, 10. **Drucker** a-51. **Moreira** a-48, 50, 59. **Roussos** a-8.*

GANGLAND
DC Comics (Vertigo): Jun, 1998 - No. 4, Sept, 1998 ($2.95, limited series)

	GD	VG	FN	VF	VF/NM	NM-
1-4:Crime anthology by various. 2-Corben-a						3.00
TPB-(2000, $12.95) r/#1-4; Bradstreet-c						13.00

GANGSTERS AND GUN MOLLS
Avon Per./Realistic Comics: Sept, 1951 - No. 4, June, 1952 (Painted c-1-3)

	GD	VG	FN	VF	VF/NM	NM-
1-Wood-a, 1 pg; c-/Avon paperback #292	50	100	150	315	533	750
2-Check-a, 8 pgs.; Kamen-a; Bonnie Parker story	40	80	120	242	401	560
3-Marijuana mentioned; used in **POP**, pg. 84,85	39	78	117	231	378	525
4-Syd Shores-c	30	60	90	177	289	400

GANGSTERS CAN'T WIN
D. S. Publishing Co.: Feb-Mar, 1948 - No. 9, June-July, 1949 (All 52 pgs?)

	GD	VG	FN	VF	VF/NM	NM-
1-True crime stories	37	74	111	222	361	500
2	20	40	60	114	182	250
3,5,6	18	36	54	103	162	220
4-Acid in face story	22	44	66	132	216	300
7-9	15	30	45	84	127	170

NOTE: ***Ingles** a-5, 6. **McWilliams** a-5, 7, 8. **Reinman** c-6.*

GANG WORLD
Standard Comics: No. 5, Nov, 1952 - No. 6, Jan, 1953

	GD	VG	FN	VF	VF/NM	NM-
5-Bondage-c	19	38	57	109	172	235
6	15	30	45	83	124	165

GARGOYLE (See The Defenders #94)
Marvel Comics Group: June, 1985 - No. 4, Sept, 1985 (75¢, limited series)

	GD	VG	FN	VF	VF/NM	NM-
1-Wrightson-c; character from Defenders						4.00
2-4						3.00

GARGOYLES (TV cartoon)
Marvel Comics: Feb, 1995 - No. 11, Dec, 1995 ($2.50)

	GD	VG	FN	VF	VF/NM	NM-
1-11: Based on animated series						3.00

GARRISON
DC Comics (WildStorm): Jun, 2010 - No. 6, Nov, 2010 ($2.99)

	GD	VG	FN	VF	VF/NM	NM-
1-6-Mariotte-s/Francavilla-a/c						3.00

GARRISON'S GORILLAS (TV)
Dell Publishing Co.: Jan, 1968 - No. 4, Oct, 1968; No. 5, Oct, 1969 (Photo-c)

	GD	VG	FN	VF	VF/NM	NM-
1	5	10	15	30	48	65
2-5: 5-Reprints #1	3	6	9	20	30	40

GARY GIANNI'S THE MONSTERMEN
Dark Horse Comics: Aug, 1999 ($2.95, one-shot)

	GD	VG	FN	VF	VF/NM	NM-
1-Gianni-s/c/a; back-up Hellboy story by Mignola						3.00

GASM (Sci-Fi, Horror, Fantasy comics magazine)(Mature content)
Stories, Layouts & Press, Inc.: Nov, 1977 - nn (No. 5), Jun, 1978 (B&W/color)

	GD	VG	FN	VF	VF/NM	NM-
1-Mark Wheatley-s/a; Gene Day-s/a; Workman-a	3	6	9	14	19	24
2 (12/77) Wheatley-a; Winnick-s/a; Workman-a	2	4	6	11	16	20
nn(#3, 2/78) Day-s/a; Wheatley-a; Workman-a	2	4	6	10	14	18
nn(#4, 4/78) Day-s/a; Wheatley-a; Corben-a	3	6	9	14	20	26
nn(#5, 6/78) Hempel-a; Howarth-a; Corben-a	3	6	9	16	22	28

GASOLINE ALLEY (Top Love Stories No. 3 on?)
Star Publications: Sept-Oct, 1950 - No. 2, Dec, 1950 (Newspaper-r)

	GD	VG	FN	VF	VF/NM	NM-
1-Contains 1 pg. intro. history of the strip (The Life of Skeezix); reprints 15 scenes of highlights from 1921-1935, plus an adventure from 1935 and 1936 strips; a 2-pg. filler is included on the life of the creator Frank King, with photo of the cartoonist.	20	40	60	115	185	255
2-(1936-37 reprints)-L. B. Cole-c	22	44	66	128	209	290

(See Super Book No. 21)

GASP!
American Comics Group: Mar, 1967 - No. 4, Aug, 1967 (12¢)

	GD	VG	FN	VF	VF/NM	NM-
1	5	10	15	32	51	70
2-4	4	8	12	22	34	45

GATECRASHER
Black Bull Entertainment: Mar, 2000 - No. 4, Jun, 2000 ($2.50, limited series)

	GD	VG	FN	VF	VF/NM	NM-
1,2-Waid-s/Conner & Palmiotti-c/a; 1,2-variant-c by J.G. Jones						3.00
3,4: 3-Jusko var-c. 4-Linsner-c						3.00
... Ring of Fire TPB (11/00, $12.95) r/#1-4; Hughes-c; Ennis intro.						13.00

GATECRASHER (Regular series)
Black Bull Entertainment: Aug, 2000 - No. 6, Jan, 2001 ($2.50, limited series)

	GD	VG	FN	VF	VF/NM	NM-
1-6-Waid-s/Conner & Palmiotti-c/a; 1-3-Variant-c by Fabry. 4-Hildebrandts variant-c. 5-Art Adams var-c. 6-Texeira var-c						3.00

GAY COMICS (Honeymoon No. 41)
Timely Comics/USA Comic Mag. Co. No. 18-24: Mar, 1944 (no month); No. 18, Fall, 1944 - No. 40, Oct, 1949

	GD	VG	FN	VF	VF/NM	NM-
1-Wolverton's Powerhouse Pepper; Tessie the Typist begins; 1st app. Willie (one shot)	57	114	171	362	619	875
18-(Formerly Funny Tunes #17?)-Wolverton-a	39	78	117	231	378	525
19-29: Wolverton-a in all. 21,24-6 pg., 7 pg. Powerhouse Pepper; additional 2 pg. story in 24). 23-7 pg Wolverton story & 2 two pg stories(total of 11pgs.). 24,29-Kurtzman-a (24-"Hey Look"(2))	36	72	108	211	343	475
30,33,36,37-Kurtzman's "Hey Look"	15	30	45	85	130	175
31-Kurtzman's "Hey Look" (1), Giggles 'N' Grins (1-1/2)	15	30	45	85	130	175
32,35,38-40: 35-Nellie The Nurse begins?	14	28	42	82	121	160
34-Three Kurtzman's "Hey Look"	15	30	45	88	137	185

GAY COMICS (Also see Smile, Tickle, & Whee Comics)
Modern Store Publ.: 1955 (7¢, 5x7-1/4", 52 pgs.)

	GD	VG	FN	VF	VF/NM	NM-
1	4	8	12	22	34	45

GAY PURR-EE (See Movie Comics)

GEARS OF WAR (Based on the video game)
DC Comics (WildStorm): Dec, 2008 - Present ($3.99/$2.99)

	GD	VG	FN	VF	VF/NM	NM-
1-15: 1-Liam Sharp-a/Joshua Ortega-s. 1-Two covers						4.00
16-($2.99) Traviss-s/Gopez-a						3.00
... Reader (4/09, $3.99) r/#1 & 2 in flipbook						4.00
... Sourcebook (8/09, $3.99) character pin-ups by various; Platt-c						4.00
Book One HC (2009, $19.99, dustjacket) r/#1-6 & Sourcebook						20.00
Book One SC (2010, $14.99) r/#1-6 & Sourcebook						15.00
Book Two HC (2011, $24.99, dustjacket) r/#7-13						25.00

GEAR STATION, THE
Image Comics: Mar, 2000 - No. 5, Nov, 2000 ($2.50)

	GD	VG	FN	VF	VF/NM	NM-
1-Four covers by Ross, Turner, Pat Lee, Fraga						3.00
1-($6.95) DF Cover						7.00
2-5: 2-Two covers by Fraga and Art Adams						3.00

GEEK, THE (See Brother Power... & Vertigo Visions)

GEEKSVILLE (Also see 3 Geeks, The)
3 Finger Prints/ Image: Aug, 1999 - No. 6, Mar, 2001 ($2.75/$2.95, B&W)

	GD	VG	FN	VF	VF/NM	NM-
1,2,4-6-The 3 Geeks by Koslowski; Innocent Bystander by Sassaman						3.00
3-Includes "Babes & Blades" mini-comic						5.00

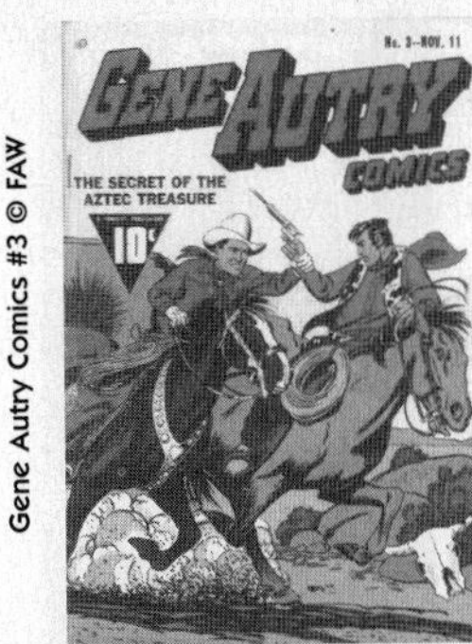

Gene Autry Comics #3 © FAW

Generation Hope #1 © MAR

Generation X #6 © MAR

GD 2.0 | VG 4.0 | FN 6.0 | VF 8.0 | VF/NM 9.0 | NM- 9.2

0-(3/00) First Image issue 3.00
(Vol. 2) 1-4-($2.95) 3-Mini-comic insert by the Geeks. 4-Steve Borock app. 3.00

G-8 AND HIS BATTLE ACES (Based on pulps)
Gold Key: Oct, 1966
1 (10184-610)-Painted-c 4 8 12 26 41 55

G-8 AND HIS BATTLE ACES
Blazing Comics: 1991 ($1.50, one-shot)
1-Glanzman-a; Truman-c 3.00
NOTE: *Flip book format with "The Spider's Web" #1 on other side w/**Glanzman**-a, **Truman**-c.*

GEISHA (Also see Oni Press Summer Vacation Supercolor Fun Special)
Oni Press: Sept, 1998 - No. 4, Dec, 1998 ($2.95, limited series)
1-4-Andi Watson-s/a. 2-Adam Warren-c 3.00
...One Shot (5/00, $4.50) 4.50
The Complete Geisha TPB (5/03, $15.95, digest size) r/#1-4, One Shot & story from Oni Press Summer Vacation Supercolor Fun Special 16.00

GEM COMICS
Spotlight Publishers: Apr, 1945 (52 pgs)
1-Little Mohee, Steve Strong app.; Jungle bondage-c
52 104 156 328 557 785

GEMINAR
Image Comics: July, 2000 ($4.95, B&W)
1-(72-Page Special) Terry Collins-s/Al Bigley-a 5.00

GEMINI BLOOD
DC Comics (Helix): Sept, 1996 - No. 9, May, 1997 ($2.25, limited series)
1-9: 5-Simonson-c 3.00

GEN ACTIVE
DC Comics (WildStorm): May, 2000 - No. 6, Aug, 2001 ($3.95)
1-6: 1-Covers by Campbell and Madureira; Gen 13 & DV8 app. 5-Mahfood-a; Quitely and Stelfreeze-c. 6-Portacio-a/c 4.00

GENE AUTRY (See March of Comics No. 25, 28, 39, 54, 78, 90, 104, 120, 135, 150 in the Promotional Comics section & Western Roundup under Dell Giants)

GENE AUTRY COMICS (Movie, Radio star; singing cowboy)
Fawcett Publications: Jan, 1942 (On sale 12/17/41) - No. 10, 1943 (68 pgs.) (Dell takes over with No. 11)
1 (Scarce)-Gene Autry & his horse Champion begin; photo back-c
556 1112 1668 4003 7002 10,000
2-(1942) 127 254 381 800 1350 1900
3-5: 3-(11/1/42) 67 134 201 422 711 1000
6-10 53 106 159 334 567 800

GENE AUTRY COMICS (...& Champion No. 102 on)
Dell Publishing Co.: No. 11, 1943 - No. 121, Jan-Mar, 1959 (TV - later issues)
11 (1943, 60 pgs.)-Continuation of Fawcett series; photo back-c; first Dell issue
38 76 114 293 547 800
12 (2/44, 60 pgs.) 33 66 99 254 477 700
Four Color 47 (1944, 60 pgs.) 33 66 99 254 477 700
Four Color 57 (11/44),66('45)(52 pgs. each) 31 62 93 239 445 650
Four Color 75,83 ('45, 36 pgs. each) 25 50 75 185 343 500
Four Color 93 ('45, 36 pgs.) 22 44 66 157 291 425
Four Color 100 ('46, 36 pgs.) First Gene Autry photo-c
24 48 72 181 336 490
1 (5-6/46, 52 pgs.) 33 66 99 254 477 700
2 (7-8/46)-Photo-c begin, end #111 17 34 51 120 223 325
3-5: 4-Intro Flapjack Hobbs 14 28 42 99 175 250
6-10 11 22 33 79 140 200
11-20: 20-Panhandle Pete begins 10 20 30 71 126 180
21-29 (36 pgs.) 9 18 27 61 103 145
30-40 (52 pgs.) 8 16 24 52 86 120
41-56 (52 pgs.) 7 14 21 45 73 100
57-66 (36 pgs.): 58-X-mas-c 6 12 18 39 62 85
67-80 (52 pgs.): 70-X-mas-c 6 12 18 39 62 85
81-90 (52 pgs.): 82-X-mas-c. 87-Blank inside-c 5 10 15 34 55 75
91-99 (36 pgs. No. 91-on). 94-X-mas-c 5 10 15 30 48 65
100 5 10 15 32 51 70
101-111-Last Gene Autry photo-c 4 8 12 28 44 60
112-121-All Champion painted-c, most by Savitt 4 8 12 26 41 55
NOTE: *Photo back covers 4-18, 20-45, 48-65.* ***Manning** a-118.* ***Jesse Marsh** art: 4-Color No. 66, 75, 93, 100, No. 1-25, 27-37, 39, 40.*

GENE AUTRY'S CHAMPION (TV)

GD 2.0 | VG 4.0 | FN 6.0 | VF 8.0 | VF/NM 9.0 | NM- 9.2

Dell Publ. Co.: No. 287, 8/50; No. 319, 2/51; No. 3, 8-10/51 - No. 19, 8-10/55
Four Color 287(#1)('50, 52 pgs.)-Photo-c 11 22 33 75 138 200
Four Color 319(#2, '51), 3: 2-Painted-c begin, most by Sam Savitt
6 12 18 41 66 90
4-19: 19-Last painted-c 5 10 15 30 48 65

GENE COLAN TRIBUTE BOOK (Produced for The Hero Initiative)
Marvel Comics: 2008 ($9.99, one-shot)
1-Spotlighted stories from Tales of Suspense #89,90, Doctor Strange #174 and others 10.00

GENE DOGS
Marvel Comics UK: Oct, 1993 - No. 4, Jan, 1994 ($1.75, limited series)
1-($2.75)-Polybagged w/4 trading cards 3.50
2-4: 2-Vs. Genetix 3.00

GENE POOL
IDW Publishing: Oct, 2003 ($6.99, squarebound)
nn-Wein & Wolfman-s/Cummings-a 7.00

GENERAL DOUGLAS MACARTHUR
Fox Features Syndicate: 1951
nn-True life story 20 40 60 114 182 250

GENERIC COMIC, THE
Marvel Comics Group: Apr, 1984 (one-shot)
1 3.00

GENERATION HEX
DC Comics (Amalgam): June, 1997 ($1.95, one-shot)
1-Milligan-s/ Pollina & Morales-a 3.00

GENERATION HOPE (See X-Men titles and Cable)
Marvel Comics: Jan, 2011 - Present ($3.99/$2.99)
1-($3.99) Gillen-s/Espin-a; Coipel-c; back-up bio of Hope Summers 4.00
1-Variant-c by Greg Land 8.00
2-6-($2.99) 5-McKelvie-a 3.00

GENERATION M (Follows House of M x-over)
Marvel Comics: Jan, 2006 - No. 5, May, 2006 ($2.99, limited series)
1-5-Jenkins-s/Bachs-a. 1-Chamber app. 2-Jubilee app. 3-Blob-c. 4-Angel-c 3.00
Decimation: Generation M TPB (2006, $13.99) r/#1-5 14.00

GENERATION NEXT
Marvel Comics: Mar, 1995 - No. 4, June, 1995 ($1.95, limited series)
1-4-Age of Apocalypse; Scott Lobdell scripts & Chris Bachalo-c/a 3.00

GENERATION X (See Gen [13]/ Generation X)
Marvel Comics: Oct, 1994 - No. 75, June, 2001 ($1.50/$1.95/$1.99/$2.25)
Collectors Preview ($1.75), "Ashcan" Edition 3.00
-1(7/97) Flashback story 3.00
1/2 (San Diego giveaway) 2 4 6 8 10 12
1-($3.95)-Wraparound chromium-c; Scott Lobdell scripts & Chris Bachalo-a begins 6.00
2-($1.95)-Deluxe edition, Bachalo-a 4.00
3,4-($1.95)-Deluxe Edition; Bachalo-a 4.00
2-10: 2-4-Standard Edition. 5-Returns from "Age of Apocalypse," begin $1.95-c. 6-Bachalo-a(p) ends, returns #17. 7-Roger Cruz-a(p). 10-Omega Red-c/app. 3.00
11-24, 26-28: 13,14-Bishop-app. 17-Stan Lee app. (Stan Lee scripts own dialogue); Bachalo/Buckingham-a; Onslaught update. 18-Toad cameo. 20-Franklin Richards app; Howard the Duck cameo. 21-Howard the Duck app. 22-Nightmare app. 3.00
25-($2.99)-Wraparound-c. Black Tom, Howard the Duck app. 4.00
29-37: 29-Begin $1.99-c, "Operation Zero Tolerance". 33-Hama-s 3.00
38-49: 38-Dodson-a begins. 40-Penance ID revealed. 49-Maggott app. 3.00
50,57-($2.99): 50-Crossover w/X-Man #50 4.00
51-56, 58-62: 59-Avengers & Spider-Man app. 3.00
63-74: 63-Ellis-s begin. 64-Begin $2.25-c. 69-71-Art Adams-c 3.00
75-($2.99) Final issue; Chamber joins the X-Men; Lim-a 4.00
'95 Special-($3.95) 4.00
'96 Special-($2.95)-Wraparound-c; Jeff Johnson-c/a 4.00
'97 Special-($2.99)-Wraparound-c; 4.00
'98 Annual-($3.50)-vs. Dracula 4.00
'99 Annual-($3.50)-Monet leaves 4.00
75¢ Ashcan Edition 3.00
...Holiday Special 1 (2/99, $3.50) Pollina-a 4.00
...Underground Special 1 (5/98, $2.50, B&W) Mahfood-a 3.00

GENERATION X/ GEN [13] (Also see Gen [13]/ Generation X)
Marvel Comics: 1997 ($3.99, one-shot)
1-Robinson-s/Larroca-a(p) 4.00

Genext: United #1 © MAR

Gen 13 #9 © WSP

Gen 13 V4 #13 © WSP

	GD	VG	FN	VF	VF/NM	NM-
	2.0	4.0	6.0	8.0	9.0	9.2

GENE RODDENBERRY'S LOST UNIVERSE
Tekno Comix: Apr, 1995 - No. 7, Oct, 1995 ($1.95)
1-7: 1-3-w/ bound-in game piece & trading card. 4-w/bound-in trading card 3.00

GENE RODDENBERRY'S XANDER IN LOST UNIVERSE
Tekno Comix: No. 0, Nov, 1995; No. 1, Dec, 1995 - No. 8, July, 1996 ($2.25)
0,1-8: 1-5-Jae Lee-c. 4-Polybagged. 8-Pt. 5 of The Big Bang x-over 3.00

GENESIS (See DC related titles)
DC Comics: Oct, 1997 - No. 4, Oct, 1997 ($1.95, weekly limited series)
1-4: Byrne-s/Wagner-a(p) in all. 3.00

GENESIS: THE #1 COLLECTION (WildStorm Archives)
WildStorm Productions: 1998 ($9.99, TPB, B&W)
nn-Reprints #1 issues of WildStorm titles and pin-ups 10.00

GENETIX
Marvel Comics UK: Oct, 1993 - No. 6, Mar, 1994 ($1.75, limited series)
1-($2.75)-Polybagged w/4 cards; Dark Guard app. 3.50
2-6: 2-Intro Tektos. 4-Vs. Gene Dogs 3.00

GENEXT (Next generation of X-Men)
Marvel Comics: July, 2008 - No. 5, Nov, 2008 ($3.99, limited series)
1-5: 1-Claremont-s/Scherberger-a; character profile pages 4.00

GENEXT: UNITED
Marvel Comics: July, 2009 - No. 5, Dec, 2009 ($3.99, limited series)
1-5: 1-Claremont-s/Meyers-a; Beast app. 4.00

GEN 12 (Also see Gen 13 and Team 7)
Image Comics (WildStorm Productions): Feb, 1998 - No. 5, June, 1998 ($2.50, lim. series)
1-5: 1-Team 7 & Gen 13 app.; wraparound-c 3.00

GEN 13 (Also see Wild C.A.T.S. #1 & Deathmate Black #2)
Image Comics (WildStorm Productions): Feb, 1994 - No. 5, July 1994 ($1.95, limited series)
0 (8/95, $2.50)-Ch. 1 w/Jim Lee-p; Ch. 4 w/Charest-p 3.00
1/2 1 2 3 4 5 7
1-($2.50)-Created by Jim Lee 1 3 4 6 8 10
1-2nd printing 3.00
1-"3-D" Edition (9/97, $4.95)-w/glasses 5.00
2-($2.50) 1 2 3 4 5 7
3-Pitt-c & story 4.00
4-Pitt-c & story; wraparound-c 4.00
5 4.00
5-Alternate Portacio-c; see Deathblow #5 6.00
...Collected Edition ('94, $12.95)-r/#1-5 13.00
...Rave ($1.50, 3/95)-wraparound-c 3.00
...: Who They Are And How They Came To Be... (2006, $14.99) r/#1-5; sketch gallery 15.00
NOTE: *Issues 1-4 contain coupons redeemable for the ashcan edition of Gen 13 #0. Price listed is for a complete book.*

GEN 13
Image Comics (WildStorm Productions): Mar, 1995 - No. 36, Dec, 1998;
DC Comics (WildStorm): No. 37, Mar, 1999 - No. 77, Jul, 2002 ($2.95/$2.50)
1-A (Charge)-Campbell/Garner-c 5.00
1-B (Thumbs Up)-Campbell/Garner-c 5.00
1-C-1-F,1-I-1-M: 1-C (Lil' GEN 13)-Art Adams-c. 1-D (Barbari-GEN)-Simon Bisley-c. 1-E (Your Friendly Neighborhood Grunge)-Cleary-c. 1-F (GEN 13 Goes Madison Ave.)-Golden-c. 1-I (That's the way we became GEN 13)-Campbell/Gibson-c. 1-J (All Dolled Up)-Campbell/McWeeney-c. 1-K (Verti-GEN)-Dunn-c. 1-L (Picto-Fiction). 1-M (Do it Yourself Cover) 1 2 3 4 5 7
1-G (Lin-GEN-re)-Michael Lopez-c 2 4 6 8 10 12
1-H (GEN-et Jackson)-Jason Pearson-c 2 4 6 8 10 12
1-Chromium-c by Campbell 4 8 12 28 44 60
1-Chromium-c by Jim Lee 6 12 18 37 59 80
1-"3-D" Edition (2/98, $4.95)-w/glasses 5.00
2 ($1.95, Newsstand)-WildStorm Rising Pt. 4; bound-in card 3.00
2-12: 2-($2.50, Direct Market)-WildStorm Rising Pt. 4, bound-in card. 6,7-Jim Lee-c/a(p). 9-Ramos-a. 10,11-Fire From Heaven Pt. 3. & Pt.9 4.00
11-($4.95)-Special European Tour Edition; chromium-c 2 4 6 10 14 18
13A,13B,13C-($1.30, 13 pgs.): 13A-Archie & Friends app. 13B-Bone-c/app.; Teenage Mutant Ninja Turtles, Madman, Spawn & Jim Lee app. 4.00
14-24: 20-Last Campbell-a 3.00
25-($3.50)-Two covers by Campbell and Charest 4.00
25-($3.50)-Voyager Pack w/Danger Girl preview 5.00
25-Foil-c 10.00
26-32,34: 26-Arcudi-s/Frank-a begins. 34-Back-up story by Art Adams 3.00
33-Flip book w/Planetary preview 4.00
35-49: 36,38,40-Two covers. 37-First DC issue. 41-Last Frank-a 3.00
50-($3.95) Two covers by Lee and Benes; art by various 4.00
51-76: 51-Moy-a; Fairchild loses her powers. 60-Warren-s/a. 66-Art by various incl. Campbell (3 pgs.). 70,75,76-Mays-a. 76-Original team dies 3.00
77-($3.50) Mays, Andrews, Warren-a 4.00
Annual 1 (1997, $2.95) Ellis-s/ Dillon-c/a. 4.00
Annual 1999 ($3.50, DC) Slipstream x-over w/ DV8 4.00
Annual 2000 ($3.50) Devil's Night x-over w/WildStorm titles; Bermejo-c 4.00
...: A Christmas Caper (1/00, $5.95, one-shot) McWeeney-s/a 6.00
... Archives (4/98, $12.99) B&W reprints of mini-series, #0,1/2,1-13ABC; includes cover gallery and sourcebook 13.00
...: Carny Folk (2/00, $3.50) Collect back-up stories 3.50
... European Vacation TPB ($6.95) r/#6,7 7.00
.../ Fantastic Four (2001, $5.95) Maguire-s/c/a(p) 6.00
...: Going West (6/99, $2.50, one-shot) Pruett-s 3.00
...: Grunge Saves the World (5/99, $5.95, one-shot) Altieri-c/a 6.00
... I Love New York TPB ($9.95) r/part #25, 26-29; Frank-c 10.00
... London, New York, Hell TPB ($6.95) r/Annual #1 & Bootleg Ann. #1 7.00
... Lost in Paradise TPB ($6.95) r/#3-5 7.00
.../ Maxx (12/95, $3.50, one-shot) Messner-Loebs-s, 1st Coker-c/a. 4.00
...: Meanwhile (2003, $17.95) r/#43,44,66-70; all Warren-s; art by various 18.00
...: Medicine Song (2001, $5.95) Brent Anderson-c/a(p)/Raab-s 6.00
... Science Friction (2001, $5.95) Haley & Lopresti-a 6.00
... Starting Over TPB ($14.95) r/#1-7 15.00
... Superhuman Like You TPB ($12.95) r/#60-65; Warren-c 13.00
... #13 A,B&C Collected Edition ($6.95, TPB) r/#13A,B&C 7.00
... 3-D Special (1997, $4.95, one-shot) Art Adams-s/a(p) 5.00
...: The Unreal World (7/96, $2.95, one-shot) Humberto Ramos-c/a 3.00
... We'll Take Manhattan TPB ($14.95) r/#45-50; new Benes-c 15.00
...: Wired (4/99, $2.50, one-shot) Richard Bennett-c/a 3.00
... Yearbook 1997 (6/97, $2.50) College-themed stories and pin-ups by various 3.00
....: 'Zine (12/96, $1.95, B&W, digest size) Campbell/Garner-c 3.00
Variant Collection-Four editions (all 13 variants w/Chromium variant-limited, signed) 100.00

GEN 13
DC Comics (WildStorm): No. 0, Sept, 2002 - No. 16, Feb, 2004 ($2.95)
0-(13¢-c) Intro. new team; includes previews of 21 Down & The Resistance 3.00
1-Claremont-s/Garza-c/a; Fairchild app. 3.00
2-16: 8-13-Bachs-a. 16-Original team returns 3.00
...: September Song TPB (2003, $19.95) r/#0-6; Garza sketch pages 20.00

GEN 13 (Volume 4)
DC Comics (WildStorm): Dec, 2006 - No. 39, Feb, 2011 ($2.99)
1-39: 1-Simone-s/Caldwell-a; re-intro the original team; Caldwell-c. 8-The Authority app. 3.00
1-Variant-c by J. Scott Campbell 5.00
...: Armageddon (1/08, $2.99) Gage-s/Meyers-a; future Gen13 app. 3.00
...: Best of a Bad Lot TPB (2007, $14.99) r/#1-6 15.00
...: 15 Minutes TPB (2008, $14.99) r/#14-20 15.00
...: Road Trip TPB (2008, $14.99) r/#7-13 15.00
...: World's End TPB (2009, $17.99) r/#21-26 18.00

GEN 13 BOOTLEG
Image Comics (WildStorm): Nov, 1996 - No. 20, Jul, 1998 ($2.50)
1-Alan Davis-a; alternate costumes-c 3.00
1-Team falling variant-c 3.50
2-7: 2-Alan Davis-a. 5,6-Terry Moore-s. 7-Robinson-s/Scott Hampton-a 3.00
8-10-Adam Warren-s/a 4.00
11-20: 11,12-Lopresti-s/a & Simonson-s. 13-Wieringo-s/a. 14-Mariotte-s/Phillips-a. 15,16-Strnad-s/Shaw-a. 18-Altieri-s/a(p)/c, 18-Variant-c by Bruce Timm 3.00
Annual 1 (2/98, $2.95) Ellis-s/Dillon-c/a 4.00
... Grunge: The Movie (12/97, $9.95) r/#8-10, Warren-c 10.00
...Vol. 1 TPB (10/98, $11.95) r/#1-4 12.00

GEN 13/ GENERATION X (Also see Generation X / Gen 13)
Image Comics (WildStorm Publications): July, 1997 ($2.95, one-shot)
1-Choi-s/ Art Adams-p/Garner-i. Variant covers by Adams/Garner and Campbell/McWeeney 3.00
1-($4.95) 3-D Edition w/glasses; Campbell-c 5.00

GEN 13 INTERACTIVE
Image Comics (WildStorm): Oct, 1997 - No. 3, Dec, 1997 ($2.50, lim. series)
1-3-Internet voting used to determine storyline 3.00
... Plus! (7/98, $11.95) r/series & 3-D Special (in 2-D) 12.00

GEN 13 : MAGICAL DRAMA QUEEN ROXY

Gen 13/Monkeyman & O'Brien #2 © Aegis

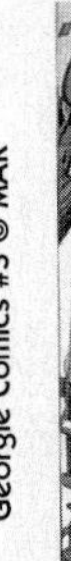
Georgie Comics #3 © MAR

Ghost #4 © FH

	GD 2.0	VG 4.0	FN 6.0	VF 8.0	VF/NM 9.0	NM- 9.2

Image Comics (WildStorm): Oct, 1998 - No. 3, Dec, 1998 ($3.50, lim. series)

1-3-Adam Warren-s/c/a; manga style, 2-Variant-c by Hiroyuki Utatane 3.50
1-($6.95) Dynamic Forces Ed. w/Variant Warren-c 7.00

GEN [13] /MONKEYMAN & O'BRIEN
Image Comics (WildStorm): Jun, 1998 - No. 2, July, 1998 ($2.50, lim. series)

1,2-Art Adams-s/a(p); 1-Two covers 3.00
1-($4.95) Chromium-c 5.00
1-($6.95) Dynamic Forces Ed. 7.00

GEN [13]: ORDINARY HEROES
Image Comics (WildStorm Publications): Feb, 1996 - No. 2, July, 1996 ($2.50, lim. series)

1,2-Adam Hughes-c/a/scripts 3.00
TPB (2004, $14.95) r/series, Gen13 Bootleg #1&2 and Wildstorm Thunderbook; new Hughes-c and art pages 15.00

GENTLE BEN (TV)
Dell Publishing Co.: Feb, 1968 - No. 5, Oct, 1969 (All photo-c)

1 4 8 12 26 41 55
2-5: 5-Reprints #1 3 6 9 16 23 30

GEOMANCER (Also see Eternal Warrior: Fist & Steel)
Valiant: Nov, 1994 - No. 8, June, 1995 ($3.75/$2.25)

1 ($3.75)-Chromium wraparound-c; Eternal Warrior app. 4.00
2-8 3.00

GEORGE OF THE JUNGLE (TV)(See America's Best TV Comics)
Gold Key: Feb, 1969 - No. 2, Oct, 1969 (Jay Ward)

1 9 18 27 65 113 160
2 6 12 18 41 66 90

GEORGE PAL'S PUPPETOONS (Funny animal puppets)
Fawcett Publications: Dec, 1945 - No. 18, Dec, 1947; No. 19, 1950

1-Captain Marvel-c 42 84 126 265 445 625
2 23 46 69 136 223 310
3-10 15 30 45 86 133 180
11-19 13 26 39 74 105 135

GEORGIE COMICS (...& Judy Comics #20-35?; see All Teen & Teen Comics)
Timely Comics/GPI No. 1-34: Spr, 1945 - No. 39, Oct, 1952 (#1-3 are quarterly)

1-Dave Berg-a 31 62 93 186 303 420
2 17 34 51 98 154 210
3-5,7,8 15 30 45 86 133 180
6-Georgie visits Timely Comics 17 34 51 98 154 210
9,10-Kurtzman's "Hey Look" (1 & ?); Millie the Model & Margie app.
15 30 45 88 137 185
11,12: 11-Margie, Millie app. 13 26 39 72 101 130
13-Kurtzman's "Hey Look", 3 pgs. 14 28 42 76 108 140
14-Wolverton-a(1 pg.); Kurtzman's "Hey Look" 14 28 42 80 115 150
15,16,18-20 12 24 36 67 94 120
17,29-Kurtzman's "Hey Look", 1 pg. 13 26 39 72 101 130
21-24,27,28,30-39: 21-Anti-Wertham editorial. 33-38-Hy Rosen-c
11 22 33 62 86 110
25-Painted-c by classic pin-up artist Peter Driben 14 28 42 80 115 150
26-Logo design swipe from Archie Comics 11 22 33 64 90 115

GERALD McBOING-BOING AND THE NEARSIGHTED MR. MAGOO (TV)
(Mr. Magoo No. 6 on)
Dell Publishing Co.: Aug-Oct, 1952 - No. 5, Aug-Oct, 1953

1 10 20 30 72 131 190
2-5 9 18 27 63 107 150

GERONIMO (See Fighting Indians of the Wild West!)
Avon Periodicals: 1950 - No. 4, Feb, 1952

1-Indian Fighter; Maneely-a; Texas Rangers-r/Cowpuncher #1; Fawcette-c
19 38 57 109 172 235
2-On the Warpath; Kit West app.; Kinstler-c/a 13 26 39 74 105 135
3-And His Apache Murderers; Kinstler-c/a(2); Kit West-r/Cowpuncher #6
13 26 39 74 105 135
4-Savage Raids of; Kinstler-c & inside front-c; Kinstlerish-a by McCann(3)
12 24 36 69 97 125

GERONIMO JONES
Charlton Comics: Sept, 1971 - No. 9, Jan, 1973

1 2 4 6 13 18 22
2-9 2 4 6 8 10 12
Modern Comics Reprint #7('78) 4.00

GETALONG GANG, THE (TV)
Marvel Comics (Star Comics): May, 1985 - No. 6, Mar, 1986

1-6: Saturday morning TV stars 3.00

GET LOST
Mikeross Publications/New Comics: Feb-Mar, 1954 - No. 3, June-July, 1954 (Satire)

1-Andru/Esposito-a in all? 32 64 96 188 307 425
2-Andru/Esposito-c; has 4 pg. E.C. parody featuring "The Sewer Keeper"
21 42 63 126 206 285
3-John Wayne 'Hondo' parody 18 36 54 105 165 225
1,2 (10,12/87-New Comics)-B&W r-original 4.00

GET SMART (TV)
Dell Publ. Co.: June, 1966 - No. 8, Sept, 1967 (All have Don Adams photo-c)

1 10 20 30 69 122 175
2,3-Ditko-a 7 14 21 47 76 105
4-8: 8-Reprints #1 (cover and insides) 6 12 18 37 59 80

GHOST (...Comics #9)
Fiction House Magazines: 1951(Winter) - No. 11, Summer, 1954

1-Most covers by Whitman 81 162 243 518 884 1250
2-Ghost Gallery & Werewolf Hunter stories 41 82 123 256 428 600
3-9: 3,6,7,9-Bondage-c. 9-Abel, Discount-a 36 72 108 216 351 485
10,11-Dr. Drew by Grandenetti in each, reprinted from Rangers; 11-Evans-r/Rangers #39; Grandenetti-r/Rangers #49 29 58 87 170 278 385

GHOST (See Comic's Greatest World)
Dark Horse Comics: Apr, 1995 - No. 36, Apr, 1998 ($2.50/$2.95)

1-Adam Hughes-a 1 2 3 5 6 8
2,3-Hughes-a 4.00
4-24: 4-Barb Wire app. 5,6-Hughes-c. 12-Ghost/Hellboy preview. 15,21-X app. 18,19-Barb Wire app. 3.00
25-($3.50)-48 pgs. special 4.00
26-36: 26-Begin $2.95-c. 29-Flip book w/Timecop. 33-36-Jade Cathedral; Harris painted-c 3.00
Special 1 (7/94, $3.95, 48 pgs.) 1 2 3 4 5 7
Special 2 (6/98, $3.95) Barb Wire app. 4.00
... Black October (1/99, $14.95, trade paperback)-r/#6-9,26,27 15.00
... Nocturnes (1996, $9.95, trade paperback)-r/#1-3 & 5 10.00
... Omnibus Vol. 1 (10/08, $24.95, 9x6") r/#1-12; Special 1 and Decade of Dark Horse #2 25.00
...Stories (1995, $9.95, trade paperback)-r/Early Ghost app. 10.00

GHOST (Volume 2)
Dark Horse Comics: Sept, 1998 - No. 22, Aug, 2000 ($2.95)

1-22: 1-4-Ryan Benjamin-c/Zanier-a 3.00
Handbook (8/99, $2.95) guide to issues and characters 3.00
Special 3 (12/98, $3.95) 4.00

GHOST AND THE SHADOW
Dark Horse Comics: Dec, 1995 ($2.95, one-shot)

1-Moench scripts 3.00

GHOST/BATGIRL
Dark Horse Comics: Aug, 2000 - No. 4, Dec, 2000 ($2.95, limited series)

1-4-New Batgirl; Oracle & Bruce Wayne app.; Benjamin-c/a 3.00

GHOST/HELLBOY
Dark Horse Comics: May, 1996 - No. 2, June, 1996 ($2.50, limited series)

1,2: Mike Mignola-c/scripts & breakdowns; Scott Benefiel finished-a 3.00

GHOST BREAKERS (Also see Racket Squad in Action, Red Dragon & (CC) Sherlock Holmes Comics)
Street & Smith Publications: Sept, 1948 - No. 2, Dec, 1948 (52 pgs.)

1-Powell-c/a(3); Dr. Neff (magician) app. 42 84 126 265 445 625
2-Powell-c/a(2); Maneely-a 34 68 102 206 336 465

GHOSTBUSTERS (TV) (Also, see Real...and Slimer)
First Comics: Feb, 1987 - No. 6, Aug, 1987 ($1.25)

1-6: Based on new animated TV series 3.00

GHOSTBUSTERS
IDW Publishing: (one-shots)

...: Con-Volution (6/10, $3.99) Josh Howard-a 4.00
...: Tainted Love (2/10, $3.99) Salgood Sam-a 4.00
...: What in Samhain Just Happened? (10/10, $3.99) Peter David-s/Dan Schoening-a 4.00

GHOSTBUSTERS: DISPLACED AGGRESSION
IDW Publishing: Sept, 2009 - No. 4, Dec, 2009 ($3.99)

1-3-Lobdell-s/Kyriazis-a 4.00

Ghostbusters: Infestation #1 © Columbia Picts.

Ghost in the Shell #2 © DH

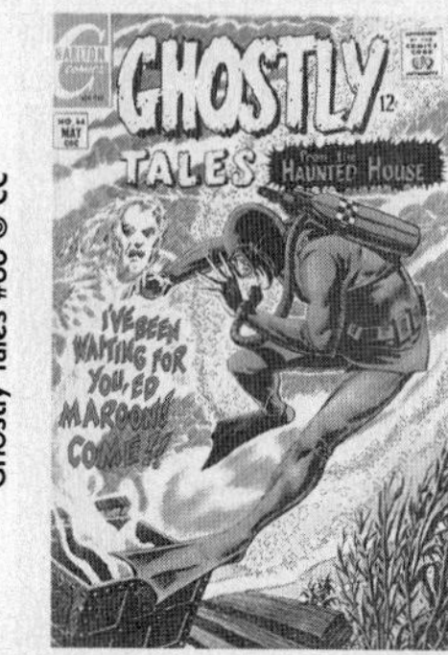

Ghostly Tales #66 © CC

GHOSTBUSTERS: INFESTATION (Zombie x-over with Star Trek, G.I. Joe & Transformers)
IDW Publishing: Mar, 2011 - No. 2 ($3.99, limited series)

	GD 2.0	VG 4.0	FN 6.0	VF 8.0	VF/NM 9.0	NM- 9.2
1-Kyle Hotz-a; covers by Hotz and Snyder III						4.00

GHOSTBUSTERS: LEGION (Movie)
88 MPH Studios: Feb, 2004 - No. 4, May, 2004 ($2.95/$3.50)

	GD 2.0	VG 4.0	FN 6.0	VF 8.0	VF/NM 9.0	NM- 9.2
1-4-Steve Kurth-a/Andrew Dabb-s						3.00
1-3-($3.50) Brereton variant-c						3.50

GHOSTBUSTERS: THE OTHER SIDE
IDW Publishing: Oct, 2008 - No. 4, Jan, 2009 ($3.99)

	GD 2.0	VG 4.0	FN 6.0	VF 8.0	VF/NM 9.0	NM- 9.2
1-4-Champagne-s/Nguyen-a						4.00

GHOSTBUSTERS II
Now Comics: Oct, 1989 - No. 3, Dec, 1989 ($1.95, mini-series)

	GD 2.0	VG 4.0	FN 6.0	VF 8.0	VF/NM 9.0	NM- 9.2
1-3: Movie Adaptation						3.00

GHOST CASTLE (See Tales of...)

GHOST IN THE SHELL (Manga)
Dark Horse: Mar, 1995 - No. 8, Oct, 1995 ($3.95, B&W/color, lim. series)

	GD 2.0	VG 4.0	FN 6.0	VF 8.0	VF/NM 9.0	NM- 9.2
1,2	3	6	9	14	20	25
3	2	4	6	9	12	15
4-8	1	3	4	6	8	10

GHOST IN THE SHELL 2: MAN-MADE INTERFACE (Manga)
Dark Horse Comics: Jan, 2003 - No. 11, Dec, 2003 ($3.50, color/B&W, lim. series)

	GD 2.0	VG 4.0	FN 6.0	VF 8.0	VF/NM 9.0	NM- 9.2
1-11-Masamune Shirow-s/a. 5-B&W						5.00

GHOSTLY HAUNTS (Formerly Ghost Manor)
Charlton Comics: #20, 9/71 - #53, 12/76; #54, 9/77 - #55, 10/77; #56, 1/78 - #58, 4/78

	GD 2.0	VG 4.0	FN 6.0	VF 8.0	VF/NM 9.0	NM- 9.2
20	3	6	9	19	29	38
21	2	4	6	13	18	22
22-25,27,31-34,36,37-Ditko-c/a. 27-Dr. Graves x-over. 32-New logo. 33-Back to old logo	3	6	9	16	22	28
26,29,30,35-Ditko-c	2	4	6	13	18	22
28,38-40-Ditko-a. 39-Origin & 1st app. Destiny Fox	2	4	6	11	16	20
41,42: 41-Sutton-c; Ditko-a. 42-Newton-c/a	2	4	6	13	18	22
43-46,48,50,52-Ditko-a	2	4	6	10	14	18
47,54,56-Ditko-c/a. 56-Ditko-a(r).	3	6	9	14	19	24
49,51,53,55,57	2	4	6	8	10	12
58 (4/78) Last issue	3	6	9	14	19	24
40,41(Modern Comics-r, 1977, 1978)						6.00

NOTE: ***Ditko** a-22-25, 27, 28, 31-34, 36-41, 43-48, 50, 52, 54, 56r; c-22-27, 29, 30, 33-37, 47, 54, 56. **Glanzman** a-20. **Howard** a-27, 30, 35, 40-43, 48, 54, 57. **Kim** a-38, 41, 57. **Larson** a-48, 50. **Newton** c/a-42. **Staton** a-32, 35; c-28, 46. **Sutton** c-33, 37, 39, 41.*

GHOSTLY TALES (Formerly Blue Beetle No. 50-54)
Charlton Comics: No. 55, 4-5/66 - No. 124, 12/76; No. 125, 9/77 - No. 169, 10/84

	GD 2.0	VG 4.0	FN 6.0	VF 8.0	VF/NM 9.0	NM- 9.2
55-Intro. & origin Dr. Graves; Ditko-a	8	16	24	52	86	120
56-58,60,61,70,71-Ditko-a. 70-Dr. Graves ends. 71-Last 12¢ issue	4	8	12	26	41	55
59,62-66,68	3	6	9	18	27	35
67,69-Ditko-c/a	4	8	12	28	44	60
72,75,76,79-82,85-Ditko-a	3	6	9	16	22	28
73,77,78,83,84,86-90,92-95,97,99-Ditko-c/a	3	6	9	19	29	38
74,91,98,119,123,124,127-130: 127,130-Sutton-a	2	4	6	10	14	18
96-Ditko-c	3	6	9	16	22	28
100-Ditko-c; Sutton-a	3	6	9	16	23	30
101,103-105-Ditko-a	2	4	6	13	18	22
102,109-Ditko-c/a	3	6	9	16	22	28
110,113-Sutton-c; Ditko-a	2	4	6	13	18	22
106-Ditko & Sutton-a; Sutton-c	2	4	6	13	18	22
107-Ditko, Wood, Sutton-a	3	6	9	14	19	24
108,116,117,126-Ditko-a	2	4	6	13	18	22
111,118,120-122,125-Ditko-c/a	3	6	9	16	22	28
112,114,115: 112,114-Ditko, Sutton-a. 114-Newton-a. 115-Newton, Ditko-a.	2	4	6	13	18	22
131-134,151,157,163-Ditko-c/a	2	4	6	11	16	20
135,142,145-150,153,154,156,158-160	1	2	3	5	7	9
136-141,143,144,152,155-Ditko-a	2	4	6	8	10	12
161,162,164-168-Lower print run. 162-Nudity panel	2	4	6	9	12	15
169 (10/84) Last issue; lower print run	2	4	6	11	16	20

NOTE: ***Aparo** a-65, 66, 68, 72, 137, 141r, 142r; c-71, 72, 74-76, 81, 146r, 149. **Ditko** a-55-58, 60, 61, 67, 69-73, 75-90, 92-95, 97, 99-118, 120-122, 125r, 126r, 131-141r, 143r, 144r, 146, 147, 149-152, 154-157, 159-161, 163; c-67, 69, 73, 77, 78, 83, 84, 86-90, 92-97, 99, 102, 109, 111, 118, 120-122, 125, 131-133, 147, 148, 151, 157-160, 163. **Glanzman** a-167. **Howard** a-95, 98, 99, 108, 117, 129, 131; c-98, 107, 120, 121, 161. **Larson** a-117, 119, 136, 159; c-136. **Morisi** a-83, 84, 86. **Newton** a-114; c-115(painted). **Palais** a-61. **Staton** a-161; c-117. **Sutton** a-106, 107, 111-114, 127, 130, 162; c-100, 106, 110, 113(painted). **Wood** a-107.*

GHOSTLY WEIRD STORIES (Formerly Blue Bolt Weird)
Star Publications: No. 120, Sept, 1953 - No. 124, Sept, 1954

	GD 2.0	VG 4.0	FN 6.0	VF 8.0	VF/NM 9.0	NM- 9.2
120-Jo-Jo-r	40	80	120	246	411	575
121-124: 121-Jo-Jo-r. 122-The Mask-r/Capt. Flight #5; Rulah-r; has 1pg. story 'Death and the Devil Pills'-r/Western Outlaws #17. 123-Jo-Jo; Disbrow-a(2). 124-Torpedo Man	37	74	111	222	361	500

NOTE: ***Disbrow** a-120-124. **L. B. Cole** covers-all issues (#122 is a sci-fi cover).*

GHOST MANOR (Ghostly Haunts No. 20 on)
Charlton Comics: July, 1968 - No. 19, July, 1971

	GD 2.0	VG 4.0	FN 6.0	VF 8.0	VF/NM 9.0	NM- 9.2
1	6	12	18	41	66	90
2-6: 6-Last 12¢ issue	4	8	12	22	34	45
7-12,17: 17-Morisi-a	3	6	9	18	27	35
13,14,16-Ditko-a	3	6	9	21	32	42
15,18,19-Ditko-c/a	4	8	12	26	41	55

GHOST MANOR (2nd Series)
Charlton Comics: Oct, 1971-No. 32, Dec, 1976; No. 33, Sept, 1977-No. 77, 11/84

	GD 2.0	VG 4.0	FN 6.0	VF 8.0	VF/NM 9.0	NM- 9.2
1	5	10	15	32	51	70
2,3,5-7,9-Ditko-c	3	6	9	18	27	35
4,10-Ditko-c/a	4	8	12	22	34	45
8-Wood, Ditko-a; Sutton-c	3	6	9	20	40	60
11,14-Ditko-c/a	3	6	9	17	25	32
12,17,27,30	2	4	6	9	13	16
13,15,16,23-26,29: 13-Ditko-a. 15,16-Ditko-c. 23-Sutton-a. 24-26,29-Ditko-a. 26-Early Zeck-a; Boyette-c	2	4	6	13	18	22
18-(3/74) Newton 1st pro art; Ditko-a; Sutton-c	3	6	9	16	22	28
19-21: 19-Newton, Sutton-a; nudity panels. 20-Ditko-a. 21-E-Man, Blue Beetle, Capt. Atom cameos; Ditko-a.	2	4	6	13	18	22
22-Newton-c/a; Ditko-a	3	6	9	14	19	24
25,28,31,37,38-Ditko-c/a: 28-Nudity panels	3	6	9	14	19	24
32-36,39,41,45,48-50,53: 34-Black Cat by Kim	2	4	6	8	10	12
40-Ditko-a; torture & drug use	2	4	6	13	18	22
42,43,46,47,51,52,60,62,69-Ditko-c/a	2	4	6	11	16	20
44,54,71-Ditko-a	2	4	6	8	11	14
55,56,58,59,61,63,65-68,70	1	2	3	5	7	9
57-Wood, Ditko, Howard-a	2	4	6	9	12	15
64-Ditko & Newton-a	2	4	6	8	11	14
71-76 (low print)	2	3	4	6	8	10
77-(11/84) Last issue Aparo-r/Space Adventures V3#60 (Paul Mann)	2	4	6	9	13	16
19 (Modern Comics reprint, 1977)						6.00

NOTE: ***Ditko** a-4, 8, 10, 11(2), 13, 14, 18, 20-22, 24-26, 28, 29, 31, 37r, 38r, 40r, 42-44r, 46r, 47, 51r, 52r, 54r, 57, 60, 62(4), 64r, 69, 71; c-2-7, 9-11, 14-16, 28, 31, 37, 38, 42, 43, 46, 47, 51, 52, 60, 62, 64. **Howard** a-4, 8, 12, 17, 19-21, 31, 41, 45, 57. **Newton** a-18-20, 22, 64; c-22. **Staton** a-13, 38, 44, 45. **Sutton** a-19, 23, 25, 45;c-8, 18.*

GHOST RIDER (See A-1 Comics, Best of the West, Black Phantom, Bobby Benson, Great Western, Red Mask & Tim Holt)
Magazine Enterprises: 1950 - No. 14, 1954

NOTE: *The character was inspired by Vaughn Monroe's "Ghost Riders in the Sky", and Disney's movie "The Headless Horseman".*

	GD 2.0	VG 4.0	FN 6.0	VF 8.0	VF/NM 9.0	NM- 9.2
1(A-1 #27)-Origin Ghost Rider	116	232	348	742	1271	1800
2-5: 2(A-1 #29), 3(A-1 #31), 4(A-1 #34), 5(A-1 #37)-All Frazetta-c only	74	148	222	470	810	1150
6,7: 6(A-1 #44)-Loco weed story, 7(A-1 #51)	34	68	102	199	325	450
8,9: 8(A-1 #57)-Drug use story, 9(A-1 #69)	29	58	87	170	278	385
10(A-1 #71)-Vs. Frankenstein	32	64	96	188	307	425
11-14: 11(A-1 #75). 12(A-1 #80)-Bondage-c; one-eyed Devil-c. 13(A-1 #84). 14(A-1 #112)	25	50	75	150	245	340

NOTE: ***Dick Ayers** art in all; c-1, 6-14.*

GHOST RIDER, THE (See Night Rider & Western Gunfighters)
Marvel Comics Group: Feb, 1967 - No. 7, Nov, 1967 (Western hero)(12¢)

	GD 2.0	VG 4.0	FN 6.0	VF 8.0	VF/NM 9.0	NM- 9.2
1-Origin & 1st app. Ghost Rider; Kid Colt-reprints begin	9	18	27	63	107	150
2	5	10	15	34	55	75
3-7: 6-Last Kid Colt-r; All Ayers-c/a(p)	5	10	15	30	48	65

GHOST RIDER (See The Champions, Marvel Spotlight #5, Marvel Team-Up #15, 58, Marvel Treasury Edition #18, Marvel Two-In-One #8, The Original Ghost Rider & The Original Ghost Rider Rides Again)
Marvel Comics Group: Sept, 1973 - No. 81, June, 1983 (Super-hero)

	GD 2.0	VG 4.0	FN 6.0	VF 8.0	VF/NM 9.0	NM- 9.2
1-Johnny Blaze, the Ghost Rider begins; 1st brief app. Daimon Hellstrom (Son of Satan)	15	30	45	106	216	325

2-1st full app. Daimon Hellstrom; gives glimpse of costume (1 panel); story continues in

Ghost Rider #31 © MAR

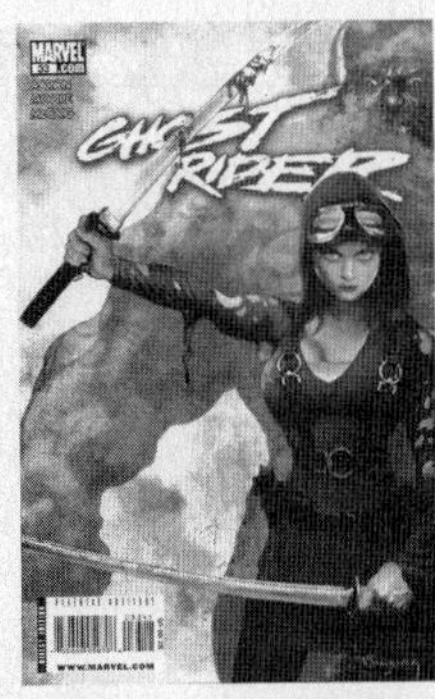

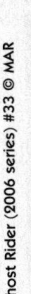

Ghost Rider (2006 series) #33 © MAR

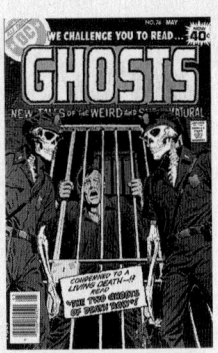

Ghosts #76 © DC

	GD 2.0	VG 4.0	FN 6.0	VF 8.0	VF/NM 9.0	NM- 9.2
Marvel Spotlight #12	7	14	21	49	80	110
3-5: 3-Ghost Rider gains power to make cycle of fire; Son of Satan app.	5	10	15	32	51	70
6-10: 10-Hulk on cover; reprints origin/1st app. from Marvel Spotlight #5; Ploog-a	4	8	12	22	34	45
11-16: 11-Hulk app.	3	6	9	14	20	25
17,19-(Reg. 25¢ editions)(4,8/76)	3	6	9	14	20	25
17,19-(30¢-c variants, limited distribution)	4	8	12	28	44	60
18-(Reg. 25¢ edition)(6/76). Spider-Man-c & app.	3	6	9	16	22	28
18-(30¢-c variant, limited distribution)	5	10	15	32	51	70
20-Daredevil x-over; ties into D.D. #138; Byrne-a	3	6	9	18	27	35
21-30: 22-1st app. Enforcer. 29,30-Vs. Dr. Strange	2	4	6	9	12	15
24-26-(35¢-c variants, limited distribution)	4	8	12	26	41	55
31-34,36-49	2	3	4	6	8	10
35-Death Race classic; Starlin-c/a/sty	2	4	6	9	13	16
50-Double size	2	4	6	8	10	12
51-76: 68-Origin retold						6.00
77-80: 77-Origin retold. 80-Brief origin recap	1	2	3	5	6	8
81-Death of Ghost Rider (Demon leaves Blaze)	3	6	9	16	23	30
... Team Up TPB (2007, $15.99) r/#27, 50, Marvel Team-Up #91, Marvel Two-In-One #80, Avengers #214 and Marvel Premiere #28; Night Rider app.; cover gallery						16.00

NOTE: ***Anderson** c-64p. **Infantino** a(p)-43, 44, 51. **G. Kane** a-21p; c(p)-1, 2, 4, 5, 8, 9, 11-13, 19, 20, 24, 25. **Kirby** c-21-23. **Mooney** a-2-9p, 30i. **Nebres** c-26i. **Newton** a-23i. **Perez** c-26p. **Shores** a-2i. J. **Sparling** a-62p, 64p, 65p. **Starlin** a(p)-35. **Sutton** a-1p, 44i, 64i, 65i, 66, 67i. **Tuska** a-13p, 14p, 16p.*

GHOST RIDER (Volume 2) (Also see Doctor Strange/Ghost Rider Special, Marvel Comics Presents & Midnight Sons Unlimited)
Marvel Comics (Midnight Sons imprint #44 on): V2#1, May, 1990 - No. 93, Feb, 1998 ($1.50/$1.75/$1.95)

	GD	VG	FN	VF	VF/NM	NM-
1-($1.95, 52 pgs.)-Origin/1st app. new Ghost Rider; Kingpin app.						6.00
1-2nd printing (not gold)						3.00
2-5: 3-Kingpin app. 5-Punisher app.; Jim Lee-c						4.00
5-Gold background 2nd printing						3.00
6-14,16-24,29,30,32-39: 6-Punisher app. 6,17-Spider-Man/Hobgoblin-c/story. 9-X-Factor app. 10-Reintro Johnny Blaze on the last pg. 11-Stroman-c/a(p). 12,13-Dr. Strange x-over cont'd in D.S. #28. 13-Painted-c. 14-Johnny Blaze vs. Ghost Rider; origin recap 1st Ghost Rider (Blaze). 18-Painted-c by Nelson. 29-Wolverine-c/story. 32-Dr. Strange x-over; Johnny Blaze app. 34-Williamson-a(i). 36-Daredevil app. 37-Archangel app.						3.00
15-Glow in the dark-c						4.00
25-27: 25-($2.75)-Contains pop-up scene insert. 26,27-X-Men x-over; Lee/Williams-c on both						4.00
28,31-($2.50, 52 pgs.)-Polybagged w/poster; part 1 & part 6 of Rise of the Midnight Sons storyline (see Ghost Rider/Blaze #1)						4.00
40-Outer-c is Darkhold envelope made of black parchment w/gold ink; Midnight Massacre; Demogoblin app.						3.00
41-48: 41-Lilith & Centurious app.; begin $1.75-c. 41-43-Neon ink-c. 43-Has free extra 16 pg. insert on Siege of Darkness. 44,45-Siege of Darkness parts 2 & 10. 44-Spot varnish-c. 46-Intro new Ghost Rider. 48-Spider-Man app.						3.00
49,51-60,62-74: 49-Begin $1.95-c; bound-in trading card sheet; Hulk app. 55-Werewolf by Night app. 65-Punisher app. 67,68-Gambit app. 68-Wolverine app. 73,74-Blaze, Vengeance app.						3.00
50,61: 50-($2.50, 52 pgs.)-Regular edition						4.00
50-($2.95, 52 pgs.)-Collectors Ed. die cut foil-c						4.00
75-89: 76-Vs. Vengeance. 77,78-Dr. Strange-app. 78-New costume						3.00
90-92						6.00
93-($2.99)-Last issue; Saltares & Texeira-a	2	4	6	8	10	12
(#94, see Ghost Rider Finale for unpublished story)						
#(-1) Flashback (7/97) Saltares-a						3.00
Annual 1,2 ('93, '94, $2.95, 68 pgs.) 1-Bagged w/card						4.00
...And Cable 1 (9/92, $3.95, stiff-c, 68 pgs.)-Reprints Marvel Comics Presents #90-98 w/new Kieth-c						4.00
...:Crossroads (11/95, $3.95) Die cut cover; Nord-a						5.00
... Finale (2007, $3.99) r/#93 and the story meant for the unpublished #94; Saltares-a						4.00
Highway to Hell (2001, $3.50) Reprints origin from Marvel Spotlight #5						3.50
...: Resurrected TPB (2001, $12.95) r/#1-7						13.00

NOTE: ***Andy & Joe Kubert** c/a-28-31. **Quesada** c-21. **Williamson** a(i)-33-35; c-33i.*

GHOST RIDER (Volume 3)
Marvel Comics: Aug, 2001 - No. 6, Jan, 2002 ($2.99, limited series)

1-6-Grayson-s/Kaniuga-a/c	3.00
...: The Hammer Lane TPB (6/02, $15.95) r/#1-6	16.00

GHOST RIDER
Marvel Comics: Nov, 2005 - No. 6, Apr, 2006 ($2.99, limited series)

1-6-Garth Ennis-s/Clayton Crain-a/c. 1-Origin retold	3.00
1 (Director's Cut) (2005, $3.99) r/#1 with Ennis pitch and script and Crain art process	4.00
...: Road to Damnation HC (2006, $19.99, dust jacket) r/#1-6; variant covers & concept-a	20.00
...: Road to Damnation SC (2007, $14.99) r/#1-6; variant covers & concept-a	15.00

GHOST RIDER
Marvel Comics: Sept, 2006 - No. 35, Jul, 2009 ($2.99)

1-11: 1-Daniel Way-s/Saltares & Texeira-a. 2-4-Dr. Strange app. 6,7-Corben-a	3.00
12-27,29-35: 12,13-World War Hulk; Saltares-a/Dell'Otto-c. 23-Danny Ketch returns	3.00
28-($3.99) Silvestri-c/Huat-a; back-up history of Danny Ketch	4.00
Annual 1 (1/08, $3.99) Ben Oliver-a/c/Stuart Moore-s	4.00
Annual 2 (10/08, $3.99) Spurrier-s/Robinson-a; r/Ghost Rider #35 (1979)	4.00
... Vol. 1: Vicious Cycle TPB (2007, $13.99) r/#1-5	14.00
... Vol. 2: The Life and Death of Johnny Blaze TPB (2007, $13.99) r/#6-11	14.00
... Vol. 3: Apocalypse Soon TPB (2008, $10.99) r/#12,13 & Annual #1	11.00
... Vol. 4: Revelations TPB (2008, $14.99) r/#14-19	15.00

GHOST RIDER/BALLISTIC
Marvel Comics: Feb, 1997 ($2.95, one-shot)

1-Devil's Reign pt. 3	3.00

GHOST RIDER/BLAZE: SPIRITS OF VENGEANCE (Also see Blaze)
Marvel Comics (Midnight Sons imprint #17 on): Aug, 1992 - No. 23, June, 1994 ($1.75)

1-($2.75, 52 pgs.)-Polybagged w/poster; part 2 of Rise of the Midnight Sons storyline; Adam Kubert-c/a begins	4.00
2-11,14-21: 4-Art Adams & Joe Kubert-p. 5,6-Spirits of Venom parts 2 & 4 cont'd from Web of Spider-Man #95,96 w/Demogoblin. 14-17-Neon ink-c. 15-Intro Blaze's new costume & power. 17,18-Siege of Darkness parts 8 & 13. 17-Spot varnish-c	3.00
12-($2.95)-Glow-in-the-dark-c	4.00
13-($2.25)-Outer-c is Darkhold envelope made of black parchment w/gold ink; Midnight Massacre x-over	3.00
22,23: 22-Begin $1.95-c; bound-in trading card sheet	3.00

NOTE: ***Adam & Joe Kubert** c-7, 8. **Adam Kubert/Steacy** c-6. **J. Kubert** a-13p(6 pgs.)*

GHOST RIDER/CAPTAIN AMERICA: FEAR
Marvel Comics: Oct, 1992 ($5.95, 52 pgs.)

nn-Wraparound gatefold-c; Williamson inks	6.00

GHOST RIDER: DANNY KETCH
Marvel Comics: Dec, 2008 - No. 5, Apr, 2009 ($3.99, limited series)

1-5-Saltares-a	4.00

GHOST RIDER: HEAVEN'S ON FIRE
Marvel Comics: Oct, 2009 - No. 6, Mar, 2010 ($3.99, limited series)

1-6: 1-Jae Lee-c/Boschi-a/Aaron-s; Hellstorm app.; r/pages from Ghost Rider #1 ('73)	4.00

GHOST RIDER: TRAIL OF TEARS
Marvel Comics: Apr, 2007 - No. 6, Sept, 2007 ($2.99, limited series)

1-6-Garth Ennis-s/Clayton Crain-a/c; Civil War era tale	3.00
HC (2007, $19.99) r/series	20.00
SC (2008, $14.99) r/series	15.00

GHOST RIDER 2099
Marvel Comics: May, 1994 - No. 25, May, 1996 ($1.50/$1.95)

1 ($2.25)-Collector's Edition w/prismatic foil-c	4.00
1 ($1.50)-Regular Edition; bound-in trading card sheet	3.00
2-24: 7-Spider-Man 2099 app.	3.00
2-(Variant; polybagged with Sega Sub-Terrania poster)	5.00
25 ($2.95)	4.00

GHOST RIDER, WOLVERINE, PUNISHER: THE DARK DESIGN
Marvel Comics: Dec, 1994 ($5.95, one-shot)

nn-Gatefold-c	6.00

GHOST RIDER; WOLVERINE; PUNISHER: HEARTS OF DARKNESS
Marvel Comics: Dec, 1991 ($4.95, one-shot, 52 pgs.)

1-Double gatefold-c; John Romita, Jr.-c/a(p)	5.00

GHOSTS (Ghost No. 1)
National Periodical Publications/DC Comics: Sept-Oct, 1971 - No. 112, May, 1982 (No. 1-5: 52 pgs.)

	GD 2.0	VG 4.0	FN 6.0	VF 8.0	VF/NM 9.0	NM- 9.2
1-Aparo-a	13	26	39	89	170	250
2-Wood-a(i)	8	16	24	52	86	120
3-5-(52 pgs.)	7	14	21	45	73	100
6-10	3	6	9	20	40	60
11-20	3	6	9	14	20	25
21-39	2	4	6	9	13	16
40-(68 pgs.)	3	6	9	16	23	30
41-60	2	4	6	8	10	12
61-96	1	2	3	5	6	8

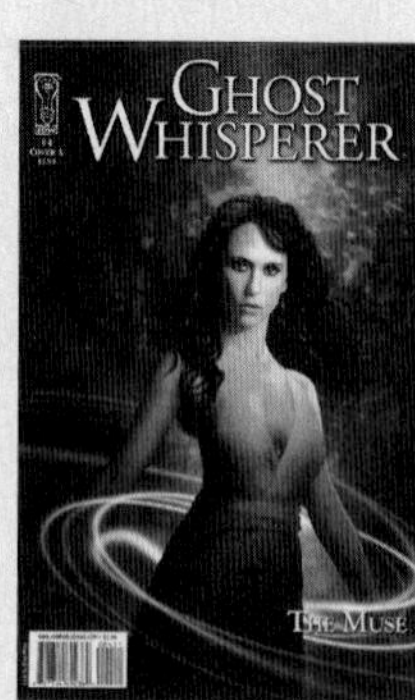

Ghost Whisperer: The Muse #4 © CBS

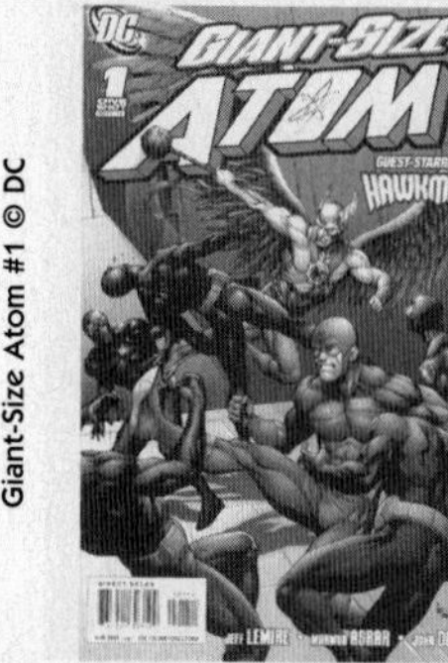

Giant-Size Atom #1 © DC

Giant-Size Daredevil #1 © MAR

GD VG FN VF VF/NM NM-
2.0 4.0 6.0 8.0 9.0 9.2

97-99-The Spectre vs. Dr. 13 by Aparo. 97,98-Spectre-c by Aparo. 2 4 6 10 14 18
100-Infinity-c 2 3 4 6 8 10
101-112 1 2 3 5 6 8
NOTE: *B. Baily a-77. Buckler c-99, 100. J. Craig a-108. Ditko a-77, 111. Giffen a-104p, 106p, 111p. Glanzman a-2. Golden a-88. Infantino a-8. Kaluta c-7, 93, 101. Kubert a-8; c-89, 105-108, 111. Mayer a-111. McWilliams a-99. Win Mortimer a-89, 91, 94. Nasser/Netzer a-97. Newton a-92p, 94p. Nino a-35, 37, 57. Orlando a-74i; c-80. Redondo a-8, 13, 45. Sparling a(p)-90, 93, 94. Spiegle a-103, 105. Tuska a-2i. Dr. 13, the Ghostbreaker back-ups in 95-99, 101.*

GHOSTS SPECIAL (See DC Special Series No. 7)

GHOST STORIES (See Amazing Ghost Stories)

GHOST STORIES
Dell Publ. Co.: Sept-Nov, 1962; No. 2, Apr-June, 1963 - No. 37, Oct, 1973

12-295-211(#1)-Written by John Stanley 7 14 21 45 73 100
2 4 8 12 24 37 50
3-10: Two No. 6's exist with different c/a(12-295-406 & 12-295-503) #12-295-503 is actually #9 with indicia to #6 3 6 9 20 30 40
11-21: 21-Last 12¢ issue 3 6 9 16 23 30
22-37 2 4 6 13 18 22
NOTE: *#21-34, 36, 37 all reprint earlier issues.*

GHOST WHISPERER (Based on the CBS television series)
IDW Publishing: Mar, 2008 - No. 5, July, 2008 ($3.99)

1-5: 1-Two covers by Casagrande & Ho; Casagrande-a 4.00

GHOST WHISPERER: THE MUSE
IDW Publishing: Dec, 2008 - No. 4, Mar, 2009 ($3.99)

1-4-Two covers (photo & art) for each; Barbara Kesel-s/ Adriano Loyola-a 4.00

GHOUL, THE
IDW Publishing: Nov, 2009 - No. 3, Mar, 2010 ($3.99, limited series)

1-3-Niles-s/Wrightson-a 4.00

GHOUL TALES (Magazine)
Stanley Publications: Nov, 1970 - No. 5, July, 1971 (52 pgs.) (B&W)

1-Aragon pre-code reprints; Mr. Mystery as host; bondage-c 8 16 24 52 86 120
2,3: 2-(1/71)Reprint/Climax #1. 3-(3/71) 4 8 12 28 44 60
4-(5/71)Reprints story "The Way to a Man's Heart" used in **SOTI** 5 10 15 32 51 70
5-ACG reprints 4 8 12 22 34 45
NOTE: *No. 1-4 contain pre-code Aragon reprints.*

GIANT BOY BOOK OF COMICS (Also see Boy Comics)
Newsbook Publications (Gleason): 1945 (240 pgs., hard-c)

1-Crimebuster & Young Robin Hood; Biro-c 94 188 282 597 1024 1450

GIANT COMIC ALBUM
King Features Syndicate: 1972 (59¢, 11x14", 52 pgs., B&W, cardboard-c)

Newspaper reprints: Barney Google, Little Iodine, Katzenjammer Kids, Henry, Beetle Bailey, Blondie, & Snuffy Smith each... 3 6 9 20 30 40
Flash Gordon ('68-69 Dan Barry) 4 8 12 26 41 55
Mandrake the Magician ('59 Falk), Popeye 4 8 12 24 37 50

GIANT COMICS
Charlton Comics: Summer, 1957 - No. 3, Winter, 1957 (25¢, 100 pgs.)

1-Atomic Mouse, Hoppy app. 21 42 63 126 206 285
2,3: 2-Romance. 3-Christmas Book; Atomic Mouse, Atomic Rabbit, Li'l Genius, Li'l Tomboy & Atom the Cat stories 15 30 45 90 140 190
NOTE: *The above may be rebound comics; contents could vary.*

GIANT COMICS (See Wham-O Giant Comics)

GIANT COMICS EDITION (See Terry-Toons) (Also see Fox Giants)
St. John Publishing Co.: 1947 - No. 17, 1950 (25¢, 100-164 pgs.)

1-Mighty Mouse 52 104 156 328 552 775
2-Abbie & Slats 28 56 84 165 270 375
3-Terry-Toons Album; 100 pgs. 40 80 120 246 411 575
4-Crime comics; contains Red Seal No. 16, used & illo. in **SOTI** 57 114 171 362 619 875
5-Police Case Book (4/49, 132 pgs.)-Contents varies; contains remaindered St. John books - some volumes contain 5 copies rather than 4, with 160 pages; Matt Baker-c 58 116 174 371 636 900
5A-Terry-Toons Album (132 pgs.)-Mighty Mouse, Heckle & Jeckle, Gandy Goose & Dinky stories 37 74 111 222 361 500
6-Western Picture Stories; Baker-c/a(3); Tuska-a; The Sky Chief, Blue Monk, Ventrilo app., 132 pgs. 52 104 156 328 557 785

GD VG FN VF VF/NM NM-
2.0 4.0 6.0 8.0 9.0 9.2

7-Contains a teen-age romance plus 3 Mopsy comics 36 72 108 211 343 475
8-The Adventures of Mighty Mouse (10/49) 37 74 111 222 361 500
9-Romance and Confession Stories; Kubert-a(4); Baker-a; photo-c (132 pgs.) 90 180 270 576 988 1400
10-Terry-Toons Album (132 pgs.)-Mighty Mouse, Heckle & Jeckle, Gandy Goose stories 37 74 111 222 361 500
11-Western Picture Stories-Baker-c/a(4); The Sky Chief, Desperado, & Blue Monk app.; another version with Son of Sinbad by Kubert (132 pgs.) 52 104 156 328 557 785
12-Diary Secrets; Baker prostitute-c; 4 St. John romance comics; Baker-a 300 600 900 1950 3375 4800
13-Romances; Baker, Kubert-a 74 148 222 470 810 1150
14-Mighty Mouse Album (132 pgs.) 36 72 108 216 351 485
15-Romances (4 love comics)-Baker-c 81 162 243 518 884 1250
16-Little Audrey; Abbott & Costello, Casper 40 80 120 242 401 560
17(nn)-Mighty Mouse Album (nn, no date, but did follow No. 16); 100 pgs. on cover but has 148 pgs. 36 72 108 216 351 485
NOTE: *The above books contain remaindered comics and contents could vary with each issue. No. 11, 12 have part photo magazine insides.*

GIANT COMICS EDITIONS
United Features Syndicate: 1940's (132 pgs.)

1-Abbie & Slats, Abbott & Costello, Jim Hardy, Ella Cinders, Iron Vic, Gordo, & Bill Bumlin 39 78 117 240 395 550
2-Jim Hardy, Ella Cinders, Elmo & Gordo 27 54 81 158 259 360
NOTE: *Above books contain rebound copies; contents can vary.*

GIANT GRAB BAG OF COMICS (See Archie All-Star Specials under Archie Comics)

GIANTKILLER
DC Comics: Aug, 1999 - No. 6, Jan, 2000 ($2.50, limited series)

1-6-Story and painted art by Dan Brereton 3.00
...A to Z: A Field Guide to Big Monsters (8/99) 3.00
...Vol. 1 TPB (Image Comics, 2006, $14.99) r/#1-6 & A-Z; gallery of concept art 15.00

GIANTS (See Thrilling True Story of the Baseball...)

GIANT-SIZE ATOM
DC Comics: May, 2011 ($4.99, one-shot)

1-Gary Frank-c; Hawkman app.; Lemire-s/Asrar-a 5.00

GIANT-SIZE...
Marvel Comics Group: May, 1974 - Dec, 1975 (35/50¢, 52/68 pgs.)
(Some titles quarterly) (Scarce in strict NM or better due to defective cutting, gluing and binding; warping, splitting and off-center pages are common)

Avengers 1(8/74)-New-a plus G.A. H. Torch-r; 1st modern app. The Whizzer; 1st & only modern app. Miss America; 2nd app. Invaders; Kang, Rama-Tut, Mantis app. 6 12 18 43 69 95
Avengers 2,3,5: 2(11/74)-Death of the Swordsman; origin of Rama-Tut. 3(2/75). 5(12/75)-Reprints Avengers Special #1 4 8 12 26 41 55
Avengers 4 (6/75)-Vision marries Scarlet Witch. 5 10 15 32 51 70
Captain America 1(12/75)-r/stories T.O.S. 59-63 by Kirby (#63 reprints origin) 4 8 12 28 44 60
Captain Marvel 1(12/75)-r/Capt. Marvel #17, 20, 21 by Gil Kane (p) 4 8 12 23 36 48
Chillers 1(6/74, 52 pgs)-Curse of Dracula; origin/1st app. Lilith, Dracula's daughter; Heath-r, Colan-c/a(p); becomes Giant-Size Dracula #2 on 6 12 18 41 66 90
Chillers 1(2/75, 50¢, 68 pgs.)-Alcala-a 4 8 12 24 37 50
Chillers 2(5/75)-All-r; Everett-r from Advs. into Weird Worlds 3 6 9 19 29 38
Chillers 3(8/75)-Wrightson-c(new)/a(r); Colan, Kirby, Smith-r 4 8 12 24 37 50
Conan 1(9/74)-B. Smith-r/#3; start adaptation of Howard's "Hour of the Dragon" (ends #4); 1st app. Belit; new-a begins 4 8 12 23 36 48
Conan 2(12/74)-B. Smith-r/#5; Sutton-a(i)(#1 also); Buscema-c 3 6 9 19 29 38
Conan 3-5: 3(4/75)-B. Smith-r/#6; Sutton-a(i). 4(6/75)-B. Smith-r/#7. 5(1975)-B. Smith-r/#14,15; Kirby-c 3 6 9 17 25 32
Creatures 1(5/74, 52 pgs.)-Werewolf app; 1st app. Tigra (formerly Cat); Crandall-r; becomes Giant-Size Werewolf w/#2 5 10 15 30 48 65
Daredevil 1(1975)-Reprints Daredevil Annual #1 3 6 9 21 32 42
Defenders 1(7/74)-Silver Surfer app.; Starlin-a; Ditko, Everett & Kirby reprints 5 10 15 32 51 70
Defenders 2(10/74, 68 pgs.)-New G. Kane-c/a(p); Son of Satan app.; Sub-Mariner-r by Everett; Ditko-r/Strange Tales #119 (Dr. Strange); Maneely-r 4 8 12 23 36 48

Giant-Size X-Men #2 © MAR

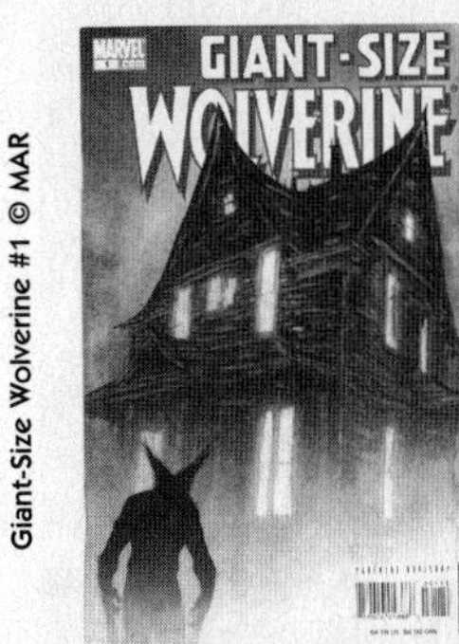

Giant-Size Wolverine #1 © MAR

G.I. Combat #12 © QUA

GD 2.0 VG 4.0 FN 6.0 VF 8.0 VF/NM 9.0 NM- 9.2

Defenders 3-5: 3(1/75)-1st app. Korvac.; Newton, Starlin-a; Ditko, Everett-r. 4(4/75)-Ditko, Everett-r; G. Kane-c. 5-(7/75)-Guardians app. 3 6 9 21 32 42
Doc Savage 1(1975, 68 pgs.)-r/#1,2; Mooney-r 3 6 9 17 25 32
Doctor Strange 1(11/75)-Reprints stories from Strange Tales #164-168; Lawrence, Tuska-r 3 6 9 19 29 38
Dracula 2(9/74, 50¢)-Formerly Giant-Size Chillers 4 8 12 23 36 48
Dracula 3(12/74)-Fox-r/Uncanny Tales #6 3 6 9 21 32 42
Dracula 4(3/75)-Ditko-r(2) 3 6 9 21 32 42
Dracula 5(6/75)-1st Byrne art at Marvel 6 12 18 37 59 80
Fantastic Four 2-4: 2(8/74)-Formerly Giant-Size Super-Stars; Ditko-r. 2,4-Buscema-a. 3(11/74)-Buckler-a. 4(2/75)-1st Madrox. 4 8 12 26 41 55
Fantastic Four 5,6: 5(5/75)-All-r; Kirby, G. Kane-r. 6(10/75)-All-r; Kirby-r 3 6 9 21 32 42
Hulk 1(1975) r/Hulk Special #1 4 8 12 23 36 48
Invaders 1(6/75, 50¢, 68 pgs.)-Origin; G.A. Sub-Mariner-r/Sub-Mariner #1; intro Master Man 4 8 12 28 44 60
Iron Man 1(1975)-Ditko reprint 4 8 12 23 36 48
Kid Colt 1-3: 1(1/75). 2(4/75). 3(7/75)-new Ayers-a 8 16 24 56 93 130
Man-Thing 1(8/74)-New Ploog-c/a (25 pgs.); Ditko-r/Amazing Adv. #11; Kirby-r/ Strange Tales Ann. #2 & T.O.S. #15; (#1-5 all have new Man-Thing stories, pre-hero-r & are 68 pgs.) 4 8 12 28 44 60
Man-Thing 2,3: 2(11/74)-Buscema-c/a(p); Kirby, Powell-r. 3(2/75)-Alcala-a; Ditko, Kirby, Sutton-r; Gil Kane-c 3 6 9 21 32 42
Man-Thing 4,5: 4(5/75)-Howard the Duck by Brunner-c/a; Ditko-r. 5(8/75)-Howard the Duck by Brunner (p); Dracula cameo in Howard the Duck; Buscema-a(p); Sutton-a(i); G. Kane-c 4 8 12 28 44 60
Marvel Triple Action 1,2: 1(5/75). 2(7/75) 3 6 9 17 25 32
Master of Kung Fu 1(9/74)-Russell-a; Yellow Claw-r in #1-4; Gulacy-a in #1,2 4 8 12 26 41 55
Master of Kung Fu 2-4: 2-(12/74)-r/Yellow Claw #1. 3(3/75)-Gulacy-a; Kirby-a. 4(6/75)-Kirby-a 3 6 9 21 32 42
Power Man 1(1975) 3 6 9 19 29 38
Spider-Man 1(7/74)-Spider-Man /Human Torch-r by Kirby/Ditko; Byrne-r plus new-a (Dracula-c/story) 7 14 21 47 76 105
Spider-Man 2,3: 2(10/74)-Shang-Chi-c/app. 3(1/75)-Doc Savage-c/app.; Daredevil/ Spider-Man-r w/Ditko-a 4 8 12 28 44 60
Spider-Man 4(4/75)-3rd Punisher app.; Byrne, Ditko-r 11 22 33 77 144 210
Spider-Man 5,6: 5(7/75)-Man-Thing/Lizard-c. 6(9/75) 4 8 12 24 37 50
Super-Heroes Featuring Spider-Man 1(6/74, 35¢, 52 pgs.)-Spider-Man vs. Man-Wolf; Morbius, the Living Vampire app.; Ditko-r; G. Kane-a(p); Spidey villains app. 6 12 18 43 69 95
Super-Stars 1(5/74, 35¢, 52 pgs.)-Fantastic Four; Thing vs. Hulk; Kirbyish-c/a by Buckler/Sinnott; F.F. villains profiled; becomes Giant-Size Fantastic Four #2 on 6 12 18 41 66 90
Super-Villain Team-Up 1(3/75, 68 pgs.)-Craig-r(i) (Also see Fantastic Four #6 for 1st super-villain team-up) 3 6 9 21 32 42
Super-Villain Team-Up 2(6/75, 68 pgs.)-Dr. Doom, Sub-Mariner app.; Spider-Man-r from Amazing Spider-Man #8 by Ditko; Sekowsky-a(p) 3 6 9 18 27 35
Thor 1(7/75) 4 8 12 26 41 55
Werewolf 2(10/74, 68 pgs.)-Formerly Giant-Size Creatures; Ditko-r; Frankenstein app. 3 6 9 20 30 40
Werewolf 3,5: 3(1/75, 68 pgs.). 5(7/75, 68 pgs.) 3 6 9 20 30 40
Werewolf 4(4/75, 68 pgs.)-Morbius the Living Vampire app. 4 8 12 22 34 45
X-Men 1(Summer, 1975, 50¢, 68 pgs.)-1st app. new X-Men; intro. Nightcrawler, Storm, Colossus & Thunderbird; 2nd full app. Wolverine after Incredible Hulk #181 50 100 150 425 863 1300
X-Men 2 (11/75)-N. Adams-r (51 pgs) 9 18 27 63 107 150
Giant Size Marvel TPB (2005, $24.99) reprints stories from Giant-Size Avengers #1, G-S Fantastic Four #4, G-S Defenders #4, G-S Super-Heroes #1, G-S Invaders #1, G-S X-Men #1 and Giant-Size Creatures #1 25.00

GIANT-SIZE...
Marvel Comics: 2005 - Present ($4.99/$3.99)

Astonishing X-Men 1 (7/08, $4.99) Concludes story from Astonishing X-Men #24; Whedon-s/ Cassaday-a/wraparound-c; Spider-Man, FF, Dr. Strange app.; variant cover gallery 5.00
Astonishing X-Men 1 (7/08, $4.99) Variant B&W cover 5.00
Avengers 1 (2/08, $4.99) new short stories and r/Avengers #58, 201; Hitch-c 5.00
Avengers/Invaders 1 ('08, $3.99) r/Avengers #71; Invaders #10, Ann. 1 & G-S #2 4.00
Hulk 1 (8/06, $4.99)-2 new stories; Planet Hulk (David-s/Santacruz-a) & Hulk vs. The Champions (Pak-s/Lopresti-a; r/Incredible Hulk: The End) 5.00
Incredible Hulk 1 (7/08, $3.99)-1 new story; r/Incredible Hulk Annual #7; Frank-c 4.00
Invaders 2 ('05, $4.99)-new Thomas-s/Weeks-a; r/Invaders #1&2 & All-Winners #1&2 5.00
Marvel Adventures The Avengers (9/07, $3.99) Agents of Atlas and Kang app.; Kirk-a: reprint of 1st Namora app. from Marvel Mystery Comics #82; reprint from Venus #1 4.00
Spider-Woman ('05, $4.99)-new Bendis-s/Mays-a; r/Marvel Spotlight #32 & S-W #1,37,38 5.00
Wolverine (12/06, $4.99)-new Lapham-s/Aja-a; r/X-Men #6,7 5.00
X-Men 3 ('05, $4.99)-new Whedon-s/N. Adams-a; r/team-ups; Cockrum & Cassaday-c 5.00

GIANT SPECTACULAR COMICS (See Archie All-Star Special under Archie Comics)

GIANT SUMMER FUN BOOK (See Terry-Toons...)

G. I. COMBAT
Quality Comics Group: Oct, 1952 - No. 43, Dec, 1956

1-Crandall-c; Cuidera a-1-43i 90 180 270 576 988 1400
2 41 82 123 256 428 600
3-5,10-Crandall-c/a 39 78 117 231 378 525
6-Crandall-a 35 70 105 208 339 470
7-9 31 62 93 186 303 420
11-20 23 46 69 136 223 310
21-31,33,35-43: 41-1st S.A. issue 21 42 63 126 206 285
32-Nuclear attack-c/story "Atomic Rocket Assault" 24 48 72 142 234 325
34-Crandall-a 22 44 66 132 216 300

G. I. COMBAT (See DC Special Series #22)
National Periodical Publ./DC Comics: No. 44, Jan, 1957 - No. 288, Mar, 1987

44-Grey tone-c 69 138 207 587 1194 1800
45 34 68 102 262 519 775
46-50 28 56 84 215 433 650
51-Grey tone-c 38 76 114 304 602 900
52-54,59,60 26 52 78 190 383 575
55-Minor Sgt. Rock prototype by Finger 27 54 81 197 399 600
56-Sgt. Rock prototype by Kanigher/Kubert 32 64 96 246 486 725
57,58-Pre-Sgt. Rock Easy Co. stories 31 62 93 239 470 700
61-65,70-73 20 40 60 140 283 425
66-Pre-Sgt. Rock Easy Co. story 28 56 84 215 433 650
67-1st Tank Killer 36 72 108 281 553 825
68-(1/59) Introduces "The Rock", Sgt. Rock prototype by Kanigher/Kubert; once considered his actual 1st app. (see Our Army at War #82,83) 96 192 288 816 1658 2500
69-Grey tone-c 34 68 102 262 519 775
74-American flag-c 22 44 66 159 317 475
75-80: 75-Grey tone-c begin, end #109 29 58 87 223 449 675
81,82,84-86 26 52 78 190 383 575
83-1st Big Al, Little Al, & Charlie Cigar; grey tone-c 33 66 99 254 502 750
87-(4-5/61) 1st Haunted Tank; series begins; classic Heath washtone-c 115 230 345 978 1989 3000
88-(6-7/61) 2nd Haunted Tank 40 80 120 320 635 950
89,90: 90-Last 10¢ issue 27 54 81 197 399 600
91-(12/61-1/62)1st Haunted Tank-c 48 96 144 392 796 1200
92-95,99-Grey tone-c 24 48 72 175 350 525
96-98 18 36 54 125 255 385
100,108: 100-(6-7/63). 108-1st Sgt. Rock x-over 21 42 63 150 300 450
101-103,105-107 15 30 45 106 216 325
104,109-Grey tone-c 20 40 60 140 283 425
110-112,115-118,120 13 26 39 89 170 250
113-Grey tone-c 16 32 48 114 232 350
114-Origin Haunted Tank 31 62 93 239 470 700
119-Grey tone-c 15 30 45 106 216 325
121-136: 121-1st app. Sgt. Rock's father. 125-Sgt. Rock app. 136-Last 12¢ issue 9 18 27 63 107 150
137,139,140 6 12 18 39 62 85
138-Intro. The Losers (Capt. Storm, Gunner/Sarge, Johnny Cloud) in Haunted Tank (10-11/69) 13 26 39 89 170 250
141-143 4 8 12 24 37 50
144-148 (68 pgs.) 5 10 15 30 48 65
149,151-154 (52 pgs.): 151-Capt. Storm story. 151,153-Medal of Honor series by Maurer 4 8 12 24 37 50
150- (52 pgs.) Ice Cream Soldier story (tells how he got his name); Death of Haunted Tank-c/s 5 10 15 30 48 65
155-167,169,170 3 6 9 14 20 25
168-Neal Adams-c 3 6 9 18 27 35
171-192,194-199: 195-Haunted Tank & War That Time Forgot 2 4 6 11 16 20
193-(10/76) Haunted Tank meets War That Time Forgot; Dinosaur-c/s; Kubert-a 3 6 9 14 20 25
200-(3/77) Haunted Tank-c/s; Sgt. Rock and the Losers app.; Kubert-c 3 6 9 16 23 30
201,202 ($1.00 size) Neal Adams-c 3 6 9 16 23 30
203-210 ($1.00 size) 3 6 9 14 20 25

Gift Comics #1 © FAW

G.I. Jane #5 © Stanhall

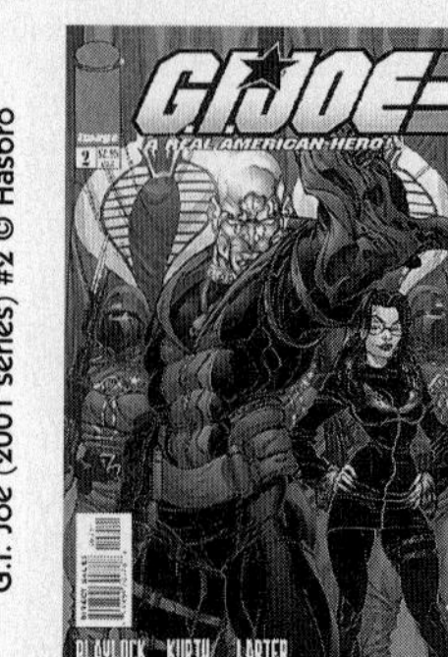

G.I. Joe (2001 series) #2 © Hasbro

	GD 2.0	VG 4.0	FN 6.0	VF 8.0	VF/NM 9.0	NM- 9.2
211-230 ($1.00 size)	2	4	6	11	16	20
231-259 ($1.00 size).232-Origin Kana the Ninja. 244-Death of Slim Stryker; 1st app. The Mercenaries. 246-(76 pgs., $1.50)-30th Anniversary issue. 257-Intro. Stuart's Raiders	2	4	6	9	13	16
260-281: 260-Begin $1.25, 52 pg. issues, end #281. 264-Intro Sgt. Bullet; origin Kana. 269-Intro. The Bravos of Vietnam. 274-Cameo of Monitor from Crisis on Infinite Earths	2	4	6	8	10	12
282-288 (75¢): 282-New advs. begin	1	2	3	5	7	9

NOTE: ***N. Adams*** *c-168, 201, 202.* ***Check*** *a-168, 173.* ***Drucker*** *a-48, 61, 63, 66, 71, 72, 76, 134, 140, 141, 144, 147, 148, 153.* ***Evans*** *a-135, 138, 158, 164, 166, 201, 202, 204, 205, 215, 256. Giffen a-267.* ***Glanzman*** *a-most issues.* ***Kubert/Heath*** *a-most issues;* ***Kubert*** *covers most issues.* ***Morrow*** *a-159-161(2 pgs.).* ***Redondo*** *a-189, 240i, 243i.* ***Sekowsky*** *a-162p.* ***Severin*** *a-147, 152, 154.* ***Simonson*** *c-169.* ***Thorne*** *a-152, 156.* ***Wildey*** *a-153. Johnny Cloud app.-112, 115, 120. Mlle. Marie app.-123, 132, 200. Sgt. Rock app.-111-113, 115, 120, 125, 141, 146, 147, 149, 200. USS Stevens by* ***Glanzman****-145, 150-153, 157.* ***Grandenetti*** *c-44-48.*

G. I. COMBAT
DC Comics: Nov, 2010 ($3.99, one-shot)

	GD 2.0	VG 4.0	FN 6.0	VF 8.0	VF/NM 9.0	NM- 9.2
1-Haunted Tank and General J.E.B. Stuart app.; Sturges-s/Winslade-a/Darrow-c						4.00

GIDGET (TV)
Dell Publishing Co.: Apr, 1966 - No. 2, Dec, 1966

	GD 2.0	VG 4.0	FN 6.0	VF 8.0	VF/NM 9.0	NM- 9.2
1-Sally Field photo-c	9	18	27	60	100	140
2	6	12	18	43	69	95

GIFT COMICS
Fawcett Publications: 1942 - No. 4, 1949 (50¢/25¢, 324 pgs./152 pgs.)

	GD 2.0	VG 4.0	FN 6.0	VF 8.0	VF/NM 9.0	NM- 9.2
1-Captain Marvel, Bulletman, Golden Arrow, Ibis the Invincible, Mr. Scarlet, & Spy Smasher begin; not rebound, remaindered comics, printed at same time as originals; 50¢-c & 324 pgs. begin, end #3.	290	580	870	1856	3178	4500
2-Commando Yank, Phantom Eagle, others app.	171	342	513	1086	1868	2650
3-(50¢, 324 pgs.)	116	232	348	742	1271	1800
4-(25¢, 152 pgs.)-The Marvel Family, Captain Marvel, etc.; each issue can vary in contents	71	142	213	454	777	1100

GIFTS FROM SANTA (See March of Comics No. 137)

GIFTS OF THE NIGHT
DC Comics (Vertigo): Feb, 1999 - No. 4, May, 1999 ($2.95, limited series)

	GD 2.0	VG 4.0	FN 6.0	VF 8.0	VF/NM 9.0	NM- 9.2
1-4-Bolton-c/a; Chadwick-s						3.00

GIGANTIC
Dark Horse Comics: Nov, 2008 - No. 5, Jan, 2010 ($3.50, limited series)

	GD 2.0	VG 4.0	FN 6.0	VF 8.0	VF/NM 9.0	NM- 9.2
1-5-Remender-s/Nguyen-a; Earth as a reality show						3.50

GIGGLE COMICS (Spencer Spook No. 100) (Also see Ha Ha Comics)
Creston No.1-63/American Comics Group No. 64 on; Oct, 1943 - No. 99, Jan-Feb, 1955

	GD 2.0	VG 4.0	FN 6.0	VF 8.0	VF/NM 9.0	NM- 9.2
1-Funny animal	34	68	102	204	332	460
2	18	36	54	103	162	220
3-5: Ken Hultgren-a begins?	14	28	42	80	115	150
6-10: 9-1st Superkatt (6/44)	11	22	33	64	90	115
11-20	10	20	30	56	76	95
21-40: 32-Patriotic-c. 37,61-X-Mas-c	9	18	27	50	65	80
41-54,56-59,61-99: Spencer Spook app. in many	8	16	24	44	57	70
55,60-Milt Gross-a	10	20	30	56	76	95

G-I IN BATTLE (G-I No. 1 only)
Ajax-Farrell Publ./Four Star: Aug, 1952 - No. 9, July, 1953; Mar, 1957 - No. 6, May, 1958

	GD 2.0	VG 4.0	FN 6.0	VF 8.0	VF/NM 9.0	NM- 9.2
1	14	28	42	76	108	140
2	8	16	24	44	57	70
3-9	8	16	24	40	50	60
Annual 1(1952, 25¢, 100 pgs.)	26	52	78	154	252	350
1(1957-Ajax)	8	16	24	42	54	65
2-6	6	12	18	28	34	40

G. I. JANE
Stanhall/Merit No. 11: May, 1953 - No. 11, Mar, 1955 (Misdated 3/54)

	GD 2.0	VG 4.0	FN 6.0	VF 8.0	VF/NM 9.0	NM- 9.2
1-PX Pete begins; Bill Williams-c/a	15	30	45	84	127	170
2-7(5/54)	9	18	27	52	69	85
8-10(12/54, Stanhall)	9	18	27	47	61	75
11 (3/55, Merit)	8	16	24	44	57	70

G. I. JOE (Also see Advs. of..., Showcase #53, 54 & The Yardbirds)
Ziff-Davis Publ. Co. (Korean War): No. 10, 1950; No. 11, 4-5/51 - No. 51, 6/57(52pgs.: 10-14,6-17?)

	GD 2.0	VG 4.0	FN 6.0	VF 8.0	VF/NM 9.0	NM- 9.2
10(#1, 1950)-Saunders painted-c begin	17	34	51	98	154	210
11-14(#2-5, 10/51): 11-New logo. 12-New logo	12	24	36	67	94	120
V2#6(12/51)-17-(11/52; Last 52 pgs.?)	10	20	30	58	79	100
18-(25¢, 100 pg. Giant, 12-1/52-53)	25	50	75	147	241	335
19-30: 20-22,24,28-31-The Yardbirds app.	9	18	27	52	69	85
31-47,49-51	9	18	27	50	65	80
48-Atom bomb story	9	18	27	52	69	85

NOTE: ***Powell*** *a-V2#7, 8, 11.* ***Norman Saunders*** *painted c-10-14, V2#6-14, 26, 30, 31, 35, 38, 39.* ***Tuska*** *a-7. Bondage c-29, 35, 38.*

G. I. JOE (America's Movable Fighting Man)
Custom Comics: 1967 (5-1/8x8-3/8", 36 pgs.)

	GD 2.0	VG 4.0	FN 6.0	VF 8.0	VF/NM 9.0	NM- 9.2
nn-Schaffenberger-a; based on Hasbro toy	4	8	12	22	34	45

G.I. JOE
Dark Horse Comics: Dec, 1995 - No. 4, Apr, 1996 ($1.95, limited series)

	GD 2.0	VG 4.0	FN 6.0	VF 8.0	VF/NM 9.0	NM- 9.2
1-4: Mike W. Barr scripts. 1-Three Frank Miller covers with title logos in red, white and blue. 2-Breyfogle-c. 3-Simonson-c						3.00

G.I. JOE
Dark Horse Comics: V2#1, June, 1996 - V2#4, Sept, 1996 ($2.50)

	GD 2.0	VG 4.0	FN 6.0	VF 8.0	VF/NM 9.0	NM- 9.2
V2#1-4: Mike W. Barr scripts. 4-Painted-c						3.00

G.I. JOE
Image Comics/Devil's Due Publishing: 2001 - No. 43, May, 2005 ($2.95)

	GD 2.0	VG 4.0	FN 6.0	VF 8.0	VF/NM 9.0	NM- 9.2
1-Campbell-c; back-c painted by Beck; Blaylock-s	2	4	6	8	10	12
1-2nd printing with front & back covers switched						6.00
2,3						5.00
4-($3.50)						4.00
5-20,22-41: 6-SuperPatriot preview. 18-Brereton-c. 31-33-Wraith back-up; Caldwell-a						3.00
21-Silent issue; Zeck-a; two covers by Campbell and Zeck						3.00
42,43-($4.50)-Dawn of the Red Shadows; leads into G.I. Joe Vol. 2						4.50
...:Cobra Reborn (1/04, $4.95) Bradstreet-c/Jenkins-s						5.00
...:G.I. Joe Reborn (2/04, $4.95) Bradstreet-c/Bennett & Saltares-a						5.00
...: Malfunction (2003, $15.95) r/#11-15						16.00
... M. I. A. (2002, $4.95) r/#1&2; Beck back-c from #1 on cover						5.00
...: Players & Pawns (11/04, $12.95) r/#28-33; cover gallery						13.00
...: Reborn (2004, $9.95) r/Cobra Reborn & G.I. Joe Reborn						10.00
...: Reckonings (2002, $12.95) r/#6-9; Zeck-c						13.00
...: Reinstated (2002, $14.95) r/#1-4						15.00
...: The Return of Serpentor (9/04, $12.95) r/#16,22-25; cover gallery						13.00
...Vol. 8: The Rise of the Red Shadows (1/06, $14.95) r/#42,43 & prologue pgs. from #37-41						15.00

G.I. JOE (Volume 2) (Also see Snake Eyes: Declassified)
Devil's Due Publishing: No. 0, June, 2005 - No. 36, June, 2008 (25¢/$2.95/$3.50/$4.50)

	GD 2.0	VG 4.0	FN 6.0	VF 8.0	VF/NM 9.0	NM- 9.2
0-(25¢-c) Casey-s/Caselli-a						3.00
1-4,7-19 ($2.95): 1-Four covers; Casey-s/Caselli-a. 4-R. Black-c						3.00
5,6-($4.50) 6-Wraparound-c						4.50
20-29,31-35-($3.50) 25-Wraparound-c World War III part 1						3.50
30,36-($5.50) 30-Double-sized World War III part 6. 36-Double-sized WW III part 12						5.50
...America's Elite Vol. 1: The Newest War TPB ('06, $14.95) r/#0-5; cover gallery						15.00
...America's Elite Vol. 2: The Ties That Bind TPB (8/06, $15.95) r/#6-12; cover gallery						16.00
...America's Elite Vol. 3: In Sheep's Clothing TPB (2007, $18.99) r/#13-18; cover gallery						19.00
...America's Elite Vol. 4: Truth and Consequences TPB (9/07, $18.99) r/#19-24; covers						19.00
... Data Desk Handbook (10/05, $2.95) character profile pages						3.00
... Data Desk Handbook A-M (10/07, $5.50) character profile pages						5.50
... Data Desk Handbook N-Z (11/07, $3.50) character profile pages						3.50
... :Scarlett: Declassified (7/06, $4.95) Scarlett's childhood and training; Noto-c/a						5.00
... Special Missions (2/06, $4.95) short stories and profile pages by various						5.00
... Special Missions Antarctica (12/06, $4.95) short stories and profile pages by various						5.00
... Special Missions Brazil (4/07, $5.50) short stories and profile pages by various						5.50
... Special Missions: The Enemy (9/07, $5.50) two stories and profile pages by various						5.50
... Special Missions Tokyo (9/06, $4.95) short stories and profile pages by various						5.00
...: The Hunt For Cobra Commander (5/06, 25¢) short story and character profiles						3.00

G.I. JOE
IDW Publishing: No. 0, Oct, 2008; No. 1, Jan, 2009 - Present ($1.00/$3.99)

	GD 2.0	VG 4.0	FN 6.0	VF 8.0	VF/NM 9.0	NM- 9.2
0-($1.00) Short stories by Dixon & Hama; creator interviews and character sketches						3.00
1-27-($3.99) 1-Dixon-s/Atkins-a; covers by Johnson, Atkins and Dell'Otto						4.00
...: Special - Helix (8/09, $3.99) Reed-s/Suitor-a						4.00

G. I. JOE AND THE TRANSFORMERS
Marvel Comics Group: Jan, 1987 - No. 4, Apr, 1987 (Limited series)

	GD 2.0	VG 4.0	FN 6.0	VF 8.0	VF/NM 9.0	NM- 9.2
1-4						6.00

G. I. JOE, A REAL AMERICAN HERO (...Starring Snake-Eyes on-c #135 on)
Marvel Comics Group: June, 1982 - No. 155, Dec, 1994

	GD 2.0	VG 4.0	FN 6.0	VF 8.0	VF/NM 9.0	NM- 9.2
1-Printed on Baxter paper; based on Hasbro toy	3	6	9	20	30	40
2-Printed on regular paper; 1st app. Kwinn	3	6	9	18	27	35
3-10: 6-1st app. Oktober Guard	3	6	9	14	20	25
11-20: 11-Intro Airborne. 13-1st Destro (cameo). 14-1st full app. Destro. 15-1st app. Major Blood. 16-1st app. Cover Girl and Trip-Wire	2	4	6	10	14	18

G.I. Joe, A Real American Hero #158 © Hasbro

G.I. Joe: Origins #14 © Hasbro

G.I. Joe vs. The Transformers #2 © Hasbro

	GD 2.0	VG 4.0	FN 6.0	VF 8.0	VF/NM 9.0	NM- 9.2
21-1st app. Storm Shadow; silent issue	4	8	12	26	41	55
22-1st app. Duke and Roadblock	2	4	6	10	14	18
23-25,28-30,60: 25-1st full app. Zartan, 1st app of Cutter, Deep Six, Mutt and Junkyard, and The Dreadnoks. 60-Todd McFarlane-a	2	3	4	6	8	10
26,27-Origin Snake-Eyes parts 1 & 2	3	6	9	14	19	24
31-50: 31-1st Spirit Iron-Knife. 32-1st Blowtorch, Lady J, Recondo, Ripcord. 33-New headquarters. 40-1st app. of Shipwreck, Barbecue. 48-1st app. Sgt. Slaughter. 49-1st app. of Lift-Ticket, Slipstream, Leatherneck, Serpentor						6.00
51-59,61-90						5.00
91,92,94-99: 94-96-Snake Eyes Trilogy						6.00
93-Snake-Eyes' face first revealed	2	4	6	11	16	20
100,135-138: 135-138-($1.75)-Bagged w/trading card. 138-Transformers app.	2	4	6	9	13	16
101-134: 101-New Oktober Guard app. 110-1st Garney-a. 117- Debut G.I. Joe Ninja Force	2	3	4	6	8	10
139-142-New Transformers app.	2	4	6	13	18	22
143,145-149: 145-Intro. G.I. Joe Star Brigade	2	4	6	9	13	16
144-Origin Snake-Eyes	3	6	9	14	19	24
150-Low print thru #155	3	6	9	20	30	40
151-154: 152-30th Anniversary (of doll) issue, original G.I. Joe General Joseph Colton app. (also app. in #151)	3	6	9	19	29	38
155-Last issue	5	10	15	35	55	75
All 2nd printings						3.00
Special #1 (2/95, $1.50) r/#60 w/McFarlane-a. Cover swipe from Spider-Man #1	4	8	12	26	41	55
Special Treasury Edition (1982)-r/#1	3	6	9	20	30	40
Volume 1 TPB (4/02, $24.95) r/#1-10; new cover by Michael Golden						25.00
Volume 2 TPB (6/02, $24.95) r/#11-20; new cover by J. Scott Campbell						25.00
Volume 3 TPB (2002, $24.99) r/#21-30; new cover by J. Scott Campbell						25.00
Volume 4 TPB (2002, $25.99) r/#31-40; new cover by J. Scott Campbell						26.00
Volume 5 TPB (2002, $24.99) r/#42-50; new cover by J. Scott Campbell						25.00
Yearbook 1-4: (3/85-3/88)-r/#1; Golden-c. 2-Golden-c/a						5.00

NOTE: ***Garney** a(p)-110. **Golden** c-23, 29, 34, 36. **Heath** a-24. **Rogers** a(p)-75, 77-82, 84, 86; c-77.*

G. I. JOE, A REAL AMERICAN HERO
IDW Publishing: No. 156, Jul, 2010 - Present ($3.99)

156-163-Continuation of story from Marvel series #155 (1994); Hama-s — 4.00

G.I. JOE: BATTLE FILES
Image Comics: 2002 - No. 3, 2002 ($5.95)

1-3-Profile pages of characters and history; Beck-c — 6.00

G.I. JOE: COBRA (#5-on is continuation of G.I. Joe: Cobra II #4, not G.I. Joe: Cobra #4)
IDW Publishing: Mar, 2009 - No. 13, Feb, 2011 ($3.99)

1-13: 1-4-Gage & Costa-s/Fuso-a/covers by Chaykin & Fuso. 5-8-Carrera-a — 4.00
... Special (9/09, $3.99) Costa-s/Fuso-a — 4.00
... Special 2 - Chameleon (9/10, $3.99) Costa-s/Fuso-a — 4.00
... II (1/10 - No. 4, 4/10, $3.99) 1-4-Gage & Costa-s/Fuso-a/covers by Chaykin & Fuso — 4.00

G. I. JOE COMICS MAGAZINE
Marvel Comics Group: Dec, 1986 - No. 13, 1988 ($1.50, digest-size)

	GD	VG	FN	VF	VF/NM	NM-
1-13: G.I. Joe-r	2	4	6	8	10	12

G.I. JOE DECLASSIFIED
Devil's Due Publishing: June, 2006 - No. 3 ($4.95, bi-monthly)

1-3-New "early" adventures of the team; Hama-s; Quinn & DeLandro-a; var-c for each — 5.00
TPB (1/07, $18.99) r/#1-3; cover gallery — 19.00

G.I. JOE DREADNOKS: DECLASSIFIED
Devil's Due Publishing: Nov, 2006 - No. 3, Mar, 2007 ($4.95/$4.99/$5.50, bi-monthly)

1,2-Secret history of the team; Blaylock-s; var-c for each — 5.00
3-($5.50) — 5.50

G.I. JOE EUROPEAN MISSIONS (Action Force in indicia) (Series reprints Action Force)
Marvel Comics Ltd. (British): Jun, 1988 - No. 15, Dec, 1989 ($1.50/$1.75)

	GD	VG	FN	VF	VF/NM	NM-
1,3-Snake Eyes & Storm Shadow-c/s	1	2	3	5	7	9
2,4-15						6.00

G.I. JOE: FRONT LINE
Image Comics: 2002 - No. 18, Dec, 2003 ($2.95)

1-18: 1-Jurgens-a/Hama-s. 1-Two covers by Dorman & Sharpe. 7,8-Harris-c — 3.00
...Vol. 1 - The Mission That Never Was TPB (2003, $14.95) r/ #1-4; script pages — 15.00
...Vol. 2 - Icebound TPB (3/04, $12.95) r/ #5-8 — 13.00
...Vol. 3 - History Repeating TPB (4/04, $9.95) r/#11-14 — 10.00
...Vol. 4 - One-Shots TPB (5/04, $15.95) r/#9,10,15-18 — 16.00

G.I. JOE: FUTURE NOIR SPECIAL
IDW Publishing: Nov, 2010 - No. 2, Dec, 2010 ($3.99, limited series, greytone art)

1,2-Schmidt-s/Bevilacqua-a — 4.00

G. I. JOE: HEARTS & MINDS
IDW Publishing: May, 2010 - No. 5, Sept, 2010 ($3.99)

1-5: Short origin stories; Brooks-s; Chaykin & Fuso-a — 4.00

G. I. JOE: INFESTATION (Zombie x-over with Star Trek, Ghostbusters & Transformers)
IDW Publishing: Mar, 2011 - No. 2 ($3.99, limited series)

1-Timpano-a; covers by Timpano and Snyder III — 4.00

G.I. JOE: MASTER & APPRENTICE
Image Comics: May, 2004 - No. 4, Aug, 2004 ($2.95)

1-4-Caselli-a/Jerwa-s — 3.00

G.I. JOE: MASTER & APPRENTICE 2
Image Comics: Feb, 2005 - No. 4, May, 2005 ($2.95, limited series)

1-4: Stevens & Vedder-a/Jerwa-s — 3.00

G.I. JOE MOVIE PREQUEL...
IDW Publishing: Mar, 2009 - No. 4, June, 2009 ($3.99, limited series)

1-4-Two covers on each: 1-Duke. 2-Destro. 3-The Baroness. 4-SnakeEyes — 4.00

G.I. JOE: OPERATION HISS
IDW Publishing: Feb, 2010 - No. 5, Jun, 2010 ($3.99, limited series)

1-5: 1-4-Reed-s/Padilla-a; covers by Corroney & Padilla. 5-Guglotta-a — 4.00

G. I. JOE ORDER OF BATTLE, THE
Marvel Comics Group: Dec, 1986 - No. 4, Mar, 1987 (limited series)

1-4 — 6.00

G.I. JOE: ORIGINS
IDW Publishing: Feb, 2009 - No. 23, Jan, 2011 ($3.99)

1-23: 1-Origin of Snake Eyes; Hama-s. 12-Templesmith-a. 19-Benitez-a — 4.00

G.I. JOE: RELOADED
Image Comics: Mar, 2004 -No. 14, Apr, 2005 ($2.95)

1-14: 1-3-Granov-c/Ney Rieber-s. 5,6-Rieber-s/Saltares-a. 8-Origin of the Baroness — 3.00
Vol. 1 In the Name of Patriotism (11/04, $12.95) r/#1-6; cover gallery — 13.00

G.I. JOE: RISE OF COBRA MOVIE ADAPTATION
IDW Publishing: July, 2009 - No. 4, July, 2009 ($3.99, weekly limited series)

1-4-Tipton-s/Maloney-a; two covers — 4.00

G.I. JOE SIGMA 6 (Based on the cartoon TV series)
Devil's Due Publishing: Dec, 2005 - No. 6, May, 2006 ($2.95, limited series)

1-6-Andrew Daab-s — 3.00
TPB Vol. 1 (10/06, $10.95, 8-1/4" x 5-3/4") r/#1-6; cover gallery — 11.00

G.I. JOE: SNAKE EYES
IDW Publishing: Oct, 2009 - No. 4, Jan, 2010 ($3.99, limited series)

1-4-Ray Park & Kevin VanHook-s/Lee Ferguson-a; two covers — 4.00

G. I. JOE SPECIAL MISSIONS (Indicia title: Special Missions)
Marvel Comics Group: Oct, 1986 - No. 28, Dec, 1989 ($1.00)

1-20 — 4.00
21-28 — 5.00

G.I. JOE VS. THE TRANSFORMERS
Image Comics: Jun, 2003 - No. 6, Nov, 2003 ($2.95, limited series)

1-Blaylock-s/Mike Miller-a; three covers by Miller, Campbell & Andrews — 3.00
1-2nd printing; black cover with logo; back-c by Campbell — 3.00
2-6: 2-Two covers by Miller & Brooks — 3.00
TPB (3/04, $15.95) r/series; sketch pages — 16.00

G.I. JOE VS. THE TRANSFORMERS (Volume 2)
Devil's Due Publ.: Sept, 2004 - No. 4, Dec, 2004 ($4.95/$2.95, limited series)

1-($4.95) Three covers; Jolley-s/Su & Seeley-a — 5.00
2-4-($2.95) Two covers by Su & Pollina — 3.00
Vol. 2 TPB (4/05, $14.95) r/series; interview with creators; sketch pages and covers — 15.00

G.I. JOE VS. THE TRANSFORMERS (Volume 3) THE ART OF WAR
Devil's Due Publ.: Mar, 2006 - No. 5, July, 2006 ($2.95, limited series)

1-5: 1-Three covers; Seeley-s/Ng-a — 3.00
TPB (8/06, $14.95) r/series; cover gallery — 15.00

G.I. JOE VS. THE TRANSFORMERS (Volume 4) BLACK HORIZON
Devil's Due Publ.: Jan, 2007 - No. 2, Feb, 2007 ($5.50, limited series)

1,2: 1-Three covers; Seeley-s/Wildman-a. 2-Two covers — 5.50

G. I. JUNIORS (See Harvey Hits No. 86,91,95,98,101,104,107,110,112,114,116,118,120,122)

Ginger #5 © AP

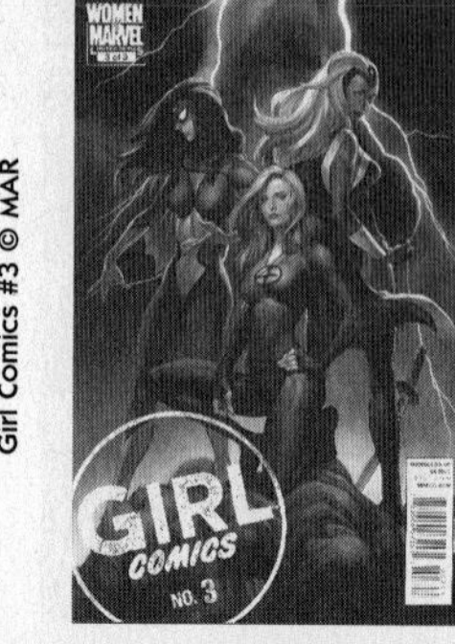

Girl Comics #3 © MAR

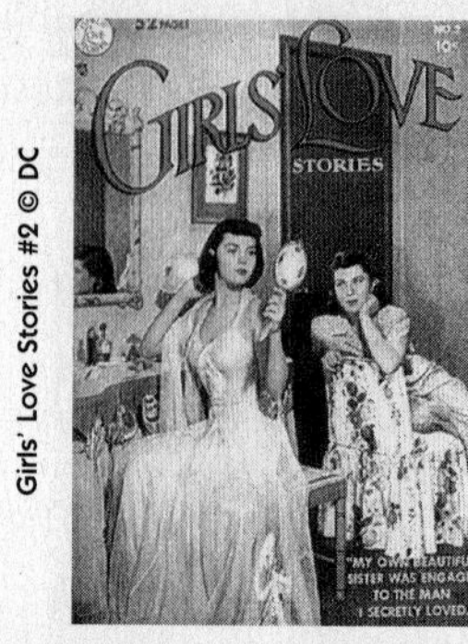

Girls' Love Stories #2 © DC

	GD 2.0	VG 4.0	FN 6.0	VF 8.0	VF/NM 9.0	NM- 9.2

GD VG FN VF VF/NM NM- 2.0 4.0 6.0 8.0 9.0 9.2

GILGAMESH II
DC Comics: 1989 - No. 4, 1989 ($3.95, limited series, prestige format, mature)

1-4: Starlin-c/a/scripts						4.00

GIL THORP
Dell Publishing Co.: May-July, 1963

1-Caniff-*ish* art	4	8	12	24	37	50

GINGER
Archie Publications: 1951 - No. 10, Summer, 1954

1-Teenage humor	15	30	45	84	127	170
2-(1952)	9	18	27	52	69	85
3-6: 6-(Sum/53)	8	16	24	44	57	70
7-10-Katy Keene app.	10	20	30	56	76	95

GINGER FOX (Also see The World of Ginger Fox)
Comico: Sept, 1988 - No. 4, Dec, 1988 ($1.75, limited series)

1-4: Part photo-c on all						3.00

G.I. R.A.M.B.O.T.
Wonder Color Comics/Pied Piper #2: Apr, 1987 - No. 2? ($1.95)

1,2: 2-Exist?						3.00

GIRL
DC Comics (Vertigo Verite): Jul, 1996 - No. 3, 1996 ($2.50, lim. series, mature)

1-3: Peter Milligan scripts; Fegredo-c/a						3.00

GIRL COMICS (Becomes Girl Confessions No. 13 on)
Marvel/Atlas Comics(CnPC): Oct, 1949 - No. 12, Jan, 1952 (#1-4: 52 pgs.)

1-Photo-c	23	46	69	136	223	310
2-Kubert-a; photo-c	14	28	42	81	118	155
3-Everett-a; Liz Taylor photo-c	32	64	96	192	314	435
4-11: 4-Photo-c. 10-12-Sol Brodsky-c	12	24	36	67	94	120
12-Krigstein-a; Al Hartley-c	13	26	39	72	101	130

GIRL COMICS
Marvel Comics: May, 2010 - No. 3, Sept, 2010 ($4.99, limited series)

1-3-Anthology of short stories by women creators. 1-Conner-c. 2-Thompson-c. 3-Chen-c						5.00

GIRL CONFESSIONS (Formerly Girl Comics)
Atlas Comics (CnPC/ZPC): No. 13, Mar, 1952 - No. 35, Aug, 1954

13-Everett-a	14	28	42	78	112	145
14,15,19,20	10	20	30	58	79	100
16-18-Everett-a	12	24	36	67	94	120
21-35: Robinson-a	9	18	27	50	65	80

GIRL CRAZY
Dark Horse Comics: May, 1996 - No. 3, July, 1996 ($2.95, B&W, limited series)

1-3: Gilbert Hernandez-a/scripts.						3.00

GIRL FROM U.N.C.L.E., THE (TV) (Also see The Man From...)
Gold Key: Jan, 1967 - No. 5, Oct, 1967

1-McWilliams-a; Stephanie Powers photo front/back-c & pin-ups (no ads, 12¢)	8	16	24	52	86	120
2-5-Leonard Swift-Courier No. 5. 4-Back-c pin-up	6	12	18	37	59	80

GIRLS
Image Comics: May, 2005 - No. 24, Apr, 2007 ($2.95/$2.99)

1-Luna Brothers-s/a/c						4.00
2-24						3.00
Image Firsts: Girls #1 (4/10, $1.00) r/#1 with "Image Firsts" cover logo						1.00
... Vol. 1: Conception TPB (2005, $14.99) r/#1-6						15.00
... Vol. 2: Emergence TPB (2006, $14.99) r/#7-12						15.00
... Vol. 3: Survival TPB (2006, $14.99) r/#13-18						15.00
... Vol. 4: Extinction TPB (2007, $14.99) r/#19-24						15.00

GIRLS' FUN & FASHION MAGAZINE (Formerly Polly Pigtails)
Parents' Magazine Institute: V5#44, Jan, 1950 - V5#48, Sept., 1950

V5#44	7	14	21	37	46	55
45-48	6	12	18	27	33	38

GIRLS IN LOVE
Fawcett Publications: May, 1950 - No. 2, July, 1950

1-Photo-c	12	24	36	69	97	125
2-Photo-c	10	20	30	54	72	90

GIRLS IN LOVE (Formerly G. I. Sweethearts No. 45)
Quality Comics Group: No. 46, Sept, 1955 - No. 57, Dec, 1956

46	10	20	30	54	72	90
47-53,55,56	8	16	24	40	50	60
54- 'Commie' story	9	18	27	52	69	85
57-Matt Baker-c/a	14	28	42	76	108	140

GIRLS IN WHITE (See Harvey Comics Hits No. 58)

GIRLS' LIFE (Patsy Walker's Own Magazine For Girls!)
Atlas Comics (BFP): Jan, 1954 - No. 6, Nov, 1954

1	14	28	42	82	121	160
2-Al Hartley-c	9	18	27	50	65	80
3-6	8	16	24	44	57	70

GIRLS' LOVE STORIES
National Comics(Signal Publ. No. 9-65/Arleigh No. 83-117): Aug-Sept, 1949 - No. 180, Nov-Dec, 1973 (No. 1-13: 52 pgs.)

1-Toth, Kinstler-a, 8 pgs. each; photo-c	56	112	168	350	595	840
2-Kinstler-a?	31	62	93	182	296	410
3-10: 1-9-Photo-c	21	42	63	122	199	275
11-20	16	32	48	94	147	200
21-33: 21-Kinstler-a. 33-Last pre-code (1-2/55)	13	26	39	72	101	130
34-50	11	22	33	60	83	105
51-70	10	20	30	54	72	90
71-99: 83-Last 10¢ issue	5	10	15	32	51	70
100	5	10	15	34	55	75
101-146: 113-117-April O'Day app.	3	6	9	20	30	40
147-151- "Confessions" serial. 150-Wood-a	3	6	9	21	32	42
152-160,171-179	3	6	9	16	22	28
161-170 (52 pgs.)	4	8	12	22	34	45
180 Last issue	3	6	9	20	30	40
Ashcan (8-9/49) not distributed to newsstands, only for in house use						(no known sales)

GIRLS' ROMANCES
National Periodical Publ.(Signal Publ. No. 7-79/Arleigh No. 84): Feb-Mar, 1950 - No. 160, Oct, 1971 (No. 1-11: 52 pgs.)

1-Photo-c	53	106	159	334	567	800
2-Photo-c; Toth-a	30	60	90	177	289	400
3-10: 3-6-Photo-c	21	42	63	122	199	275
11,12,14-20	15	30	45	86	133	180
13-Toth-c	15	30	45	90	140	190
21-31: 31-Last pre-code (2-3/55)	13	26	39	72	101	130
32-50	7	14	21	45	73	100
51-99: 80-Last 10¢ issue	5	10	15	32	51	70
100	5	10	15	34	55	75
101-108,110-120	3	6	9	20	30	40
109-Beatles-c/story	12	24	36	87	164	240
121-133,135-140	3	6	9	18	27	35
134-Neal Adams-c (splash pg. is same as-c)	5	10	15	34	55	75
141-158	3	6	9	16	22	28
159,160-52 pgs.	4	8	12	22	34	45

GIRL WHO WOULD BE DEATH, THE
DC Comics (Vertigo): Dec, 1998 - No. 4, March, 1999 ($2.50, lim. series)

1-4-Kiernan-s/Ormston-a						3.00

G. I. SWEETHEARTS (Formerly Diary Loves; Girls In Love #46 on)
Quality Comics Group: No. 32, June, 1953 - No. 45, May, 1955

32	10	20	30	58	79	100
33-45: 44-Last pre-code (3/55)	8	16	24	42	54	65

G.I. TALES (Formerly Sgt. Barney Barker No. 1-3)
Atlas Comics (MCI): No. 4, Feb, 1957 - No. 6, July, 1957

4-Severin-a(4)	10	20	30	54	72	90
5	8	16	24	40	50	60
6-Orlando, Powell, & Woodbridge-a	8	16	24	42	54	65

GIVE ME LIBERTY (Also see Dark Horse Presents Fifth Anniversary Special, Dark Horse Presents #100-4, Happy Birthday Martha Washington, Martha Washington Goes to War, Martha Washington Stranded In Space & San Diego Comicon Comics #2)
Dark Horse Comics: June, 1990 - No. 4, 1991 ($4.95, limited series, 52 pgs.)

1-4: 1st app. Martha Washington; Frank Miller scripts, Dave Gibbons-c/a in all						5.00

G. I. WAR BRIDES
Superior Publishers Ltd.: Apr, 1954 - No. 8, June, 1955

1	10	20	30	58	79	100
2	8	16	24	40	50	60
3-8: 4-Kamen*esque*-a; lingerie panels	7	14	21	35	43	50

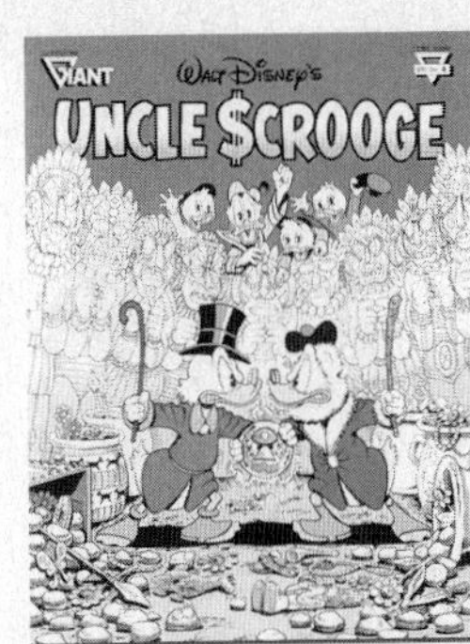

Gladstone Comic Album #4 © DIS

Glamourpuss #15 © Dave Sim

Global Frequency #12 © Warren Ellis & DC

G. I. WAR TALES
National Periodical Publications: Mar-Apr, 1973 - No. 4, Oct-Nov, 1973

1-Reprints in all; dinosaur-c/s 3 6 9 18 27 35
2-N. Adams-a(r) 2 4 6 13 18 22
3,4: 4-Krigstein-a(r) 2 4 6 11 16 20
NOTE: ***Drucker** a-3r, 4r. **Heath** a-4r. **Kubert** a-2, 3; c-4r.*

GIZMO (Also see Domino Chance)
Chance Ent.: May-June, 1985 (B&W, one-shot)

1 6.00

GIZMO
Mirage Studios: 1986 - No. 6, July, 1987 ($1.50, B&W)

1-6 3.00

G.L.A. (Great Lakes Avengers)(Also see GLX-Mas Special)
Marvel Comics: June, 2005 - No. 4, Sept, 2005 ($2.99, limited series)

1-4-Slott-s/Pelletier-a 3.00
...: Misassembled TPB (2005, $14.99) r/#1-4, West Coast Avengers #46 (1st app.) and Marvel Super-Heroes #8 (1st app. Squirrel Girl; Ditko-a) 15.00

GLADSTONE COMIC ALBUM
Gladstone: 1987 - No. 28, 1990 ($5.95/$9.95, 8-1/2x11")(All Mickey Mouse albums are by Gottfredson)

1-10: 1-Uncle Scrooge; Barks-r; Beck-c. 2-Donald Duck; r/F.C. #108 by Barks. 3-Mickey Mouse-r by Gottfredson. 4-Uncle Scrooge; r/F.C. #456 by Barks w/unedited story. 5-Donald Duck Advs.; r/F.C. #199. 6-Uncle Scrooge-r by Barks. 7-Donald Duck-r by Barks. 8-Mickey Mouse-r. 9-Bambi; r/F.C. #186? 10-Donald Duck Advs.; r/F.C. #275 1 3 4 6 8 10
11-20: 11-Uncle Scrooge; r/U.S. #4. 12-Donald And Daisy; r/F.C. #1055, WDC&S. 13-Donald Duck Advs.; r/F.C. #408. 14-Uncle Scrooge; Barks-r/U.S #21. 15-Donald And Gladstone; Barks-r. 16-Donald Duck Advs.; r/F.C. #238. 17-Mickey Mouse strip-r (The World of Tomorrow, The Pirate Ghost Ship). 18-Donald Duck and the Junior Woodchucks; Barks-r. 19-Uncle Scrooge; r/U.S. #12; Rosa-c. 20-Uncle Scrooge; r/F.C. #386; Barks-c/a(r) 1 3 4 6 8 10
21-25: 21-Donald Duck Family; Barks-c/a(r). 22-Mickey Mouse strip-r. 23-Donald Duck; Barks-r/D.D. #26 w/unedited story. 24-Uncle Scrooge; Barks-r; Rosa-c. 25-D. Duck; Barks-c/a-r/F.C. #367 1 3 4 6 8 10
26-28: All have $9.95-c. 26-Mickey & Donald; Gottfredson-c/a(r). 27-Donald Duck; r/WDC&S by Barks; Barks painted-c. 28-Uncle Scrooge & Donald Duck; Rosa-c/a (4 stories) 1 3 4 6 8 10
Special 1-7: 1 ('89-'90, $9.95/13.95)-1-Donald Duck Finds Pirate Gold; r/F.C. #9. 2 ('89, $8.95)-Uncle Scrooge and Donald Duck; Barks-r/Uncle Scrooge #5; Rosa-c. 3 ('89, $8.95)-Mickey Mouse strip-r. 4 ('89, $11.95)-Uncle Scrooge; Rosa-c/a-r/Son of the Sun from U.S. #219 plus Barks-r/U.S. 5 ('90, $11.95)-Donald Duck Advs.; Barks-r/F.C. #282 & 422 plus Barks painted-c. 6 ('90, $12.95)-Uncle Scrooge; Barks-c/a-r/Uncle Scrooge. 7 ('90, $13.95)-Mickey Mouse; Gottfredson strip-r 2 4 6 9 11 14

GLADSTONE COMIC ALBUM (2nd Series)(Also see The Original Dick Tracy)
Gladstone Publishing: 1990 ($5.95, 8-1/2 x 11," stiff-c, 52 pgs.)

1,2-The Original Dick Tracy. 2-Origin of the 2-way wrist radio 6.00
3-D Tracy Meets the Mole-r by Gould ($6.95). 1 2 3 5 6 8

GLAMOROUS ROMANCES (Formerly Dotty)
Ace Magazines (A. A. Wyn): No. 41, July, 1949 - No. 90, Oct, 1956 (Photo-c 68-90)

41-Dotty app. 12 24 36 67 94 120
42-72,74-80: 44-Begin 52 pg. issues. 45,50-61-Painted-c. 80-Last pre-code (2/55) 9 18 27 50 65 80
73-L.B. Cole-r/All Love #27 9 18 27 52 69 85
81-90 9 18 27 47 61 75

GLAMOURPUSS
Aardvark-Vanaheim Inc.: Apr, 2008 - Present ($3.00, B&W)

1-18: 1-Two covers; Dave Sim-s/a/c. 9,10-Gene Colan-c. 1-Heath-c 3.00
1-Comics Industry Preview Edition (Diamond Dateline supplement) 4.00

GLOBAL FREQUENCY
DC Comics (WildStorm): Dec, 2002 - No. 12, Aug, 2004 ($2.95, limited series)

1-12-Warren Ellis-s. 1-Leach-a. 2-Fabry-a. 3-Dillon-a. 5-Muth-a. 7-Bisley-a. 12-Ha-a 3.00
1-RRP Edition variant-c; promotional giveaway for retailers (200 printed) 10.00
...: Detonation Radio TPB (2005, $14.95) r/#7-12 15.00
...: Planet Ablaze TPB (2003, $14.95) r/#1-6 15.00

GLORY
Image Comics (Extreme Studios)/Maximum Press: Mar, 1995 - No. 22, Apr, 1997 ($2.50)

0-Deodato-c/a, 1-(3/95)-Deodato-a 3.00
1A-Variant-c 4.00
2-11,13-22: 4-Variant-c by Quesada & Palmiotti. 5-Bagged w/Youngblood gaming card. 7,8-Deodato-c/a(p). 8-Babewatch x-over. 9-Cruz-c; Extreme Destroyer Pt. 5; polybagged w/card. 10-Angela-c/app. 11-Deodato-c. 3.00
12-($3.50)-Photo-c 3.50
... & Friends Christmas Special (12/95, $2.50) Deodato-c 3.00
... & Friends Lingerie Special (9/95, $2.95) Pin-ups w/photos; photo-c; varant-c exists 3.00
... /Angela: Angels in Hell (4/96, $2.50) Flip book w/Darkchylde #1 3.00
... /Avengelyne (10/95, $3.95) 1-Chromium-c, 1-Regular-c 4.00
Trade Paperback (1995, $9.95)-r/#1-4 10.00

GLORY
Awesome Comics: Mar, 1999 ($2.50)

0-Liefeld-c; story and sketch pages 3.00

GLORY (ALAN MOORE'S...)
Avatar Press: Dec, 2001 - No. 2 ($3.50)

Preview-(9/01, $1.99) B&W pages and cover art; Alan Moore-s 3.00
0-Four regular covers 3.50
1,2: 1-Alan Moore-s/Mychaels & Gebbie-a; nine covers by various. 2-Five covers 3.50

GLORY & FRIENDS BIKINI FEST
Image Comics (Extreme): Sept, 1995 - No. 2, Oct, 1995 ($2.50, limited series)

1,2: 1-Photo-c; centerfold photo; pin-ups 3.00

GLORY/CELESTINE: DARK ANGEL
Image Comics/Maximum Press (Extreme Studios): Sept, 1996 - No. 3, Nov, 1996 ($2.50, limited series)

1-3 3.00

GLX-MAS SPECIAL (Great Lakes Avengers)
Marvel Comics: Feb, 2006 ($3.99, one-shot)

1-Christmas themed stories by various incl. Haley, Templeton, Grist, Wieringo 4.00

G-MAN: CAPE CRISIS
Image Comics: Aug, 2009 - No. 5, Jan, 2010 ($2.99, limited series)

1-5-Chris Giarrusso-s/a; back-up short strips by various 3.00

GNOME MOBILE, THE (See Movie Comics)

GOBBLEDYGOOK
Mirage Studios: 1984 - No. 2, 1984 (B&W)(1st Mirage comics, published at same time)

1-(24 pgs.)-(distribution of approx. 50) Teenage Mutant Ninja Turtles app. on full page back-c ad; Teenage Mutant Ninja Turtles do not appear inside. 1st app of Fugitoid 185 370 555 1619 3310 5000
2-(24 pgs.)-Teenage Mutant Ninja Turtles on full page back-c ad 77 154 231 655 1328 2000
NOTE: Counterfeit copies exist. Originals feature both black & white covers and interiors. Signed and numbered copies do not exist.

GOBBLEDYGOOK
Mirage Studios: Dec, 1986 ($3.50, B&W, one-shot, 100 pgs.)

1-New 8 pg. TMNT story plus a Donatello/Michaelangelo 7 pg. story & a Gizmo story; Corben-i(r)/TMNT #7 1 2 3 5 6 8

GOBLIN, THE
Warren Publishing Co.: June, 1982 - No. 3, Dec, 1982 ($2.25, B&W magazine with 8 pg. color insert comic in all)

1-The Gremlin app. Philo Photon & the Troll Patrol, Micro-Buccaneers & Wizard Wormglow begin & app. in all. Tin Man app. Golden-a(p). Nebres-c/a in all 2 4 6 13 18 22
2,3: 2-1st Hobgoblin. 3-Tin Man app. 2 4 6 9 12 15
NOTE: ***Bermejo** a-1-3. **Elias** a-1-3. **Laxamana** a-1-3. **Nino** a-3.*

GOD COMPLEX
Image Comics: Dec, 2009 - No. 7, Jun, 2010 ($2.99)

1-7-Oeming & Berman-s/Broglia-a/Oeming-c 3.00

GODDESS
DC Comics (Vertigo): June, 1995 - No. 8, Jan, 1996 ($2.95, limited series)

1-Garth Ennis scripts; Phil Winslade-c/a in all 5.00
2-8 4.00
TPB (2002, $19.95) r/#1-8; foreword and sketch pages by Winslade 20.00

GODFATHERS, THE (See The Crusaders)

GOD IS
Spire Christian Comics (Fleming H. Revell Co.): 1973, 1975 (35-49¢)

nn-(1973) By Al Hartley 2 4 6 10 14 18
nn-(1975) 2 4 6 8 10 12

GODLAND

Godland #28 © Casey & Scioli

Go-Go #7 © CC

The Golden Age #2 © DC

	GD 2.0	VG 4.0	FN 6.0	VF 8.0	VF/NM 9.0	NM- 9.2

Image Comics: July, 2005 - Present ($2.99)

1-15,17-34-Joe Casey-s; Kirby-esque art by Tom Scioli. 13-Var-c by Giffen & Larsen. 33-"Dogland" on cover 3.00
16-(60¢-c) Re-cap/origin issue 3.00
Image Firsts: Godland #1 (9/10, $1.00) r/#1 with "Image Firsts" cover logo 1.00
...: Celestial Edition One HC (2007, $34.99) r/#1-12 and story from Image Holiday Special; intro. by Grant Morrison; cover gallery, developmental art and original story pitches 35.00
... Vol. 1: Hello Cosmic! TPB (1/06, $14.99) r/#1-6; sketch development pages 15.00
... Vol. 2: Another Sunny Delight TPB (8/06, $14.99) r/#7-12; early Christmas story 15.00
... Vol. 3: Proto-Plastic Party TPB (2007, $14.99) r/#13-18 15.00
... Vol. 4: Amplified Now TPB (2008, $14.99) r/#19-24 15.00

GOD OF WAR (Based on the Sony videogame)
DC Comics (WildStorm): May, 2010 - No. 6, Mar, 2011 ($3.99/$2.99, limited series)

1-6-Wolfman-s/Sorrentino-a/Park-c. 6-($2.99) 4.00
TPB (2011, $14.99) r/#1-6; cover gallery 15.00

GOD SAVE THE QUEEN
DC Comics (Vertigo): 2007 ($19.99, hardcover with dustjacket, graphic novel)

HC-Mike Carey-s/John Bolton-painted art 20.00
SC-(2008, $12.99) Different Bolton painted-c 13.00

GOD'S COUNTRY (Also see Marvel Comics Presents)
Marvel Comics: 1994 ($6.95)

nn-P. Craig Russell-a; Colossus story; r/Marvel Comics Presents #10-17 7.00

GOD'S HEROES IN AMERICA
Catechetical Guild Educational Society: 1956 (nn) (25¢/35¢, 68 pgs.)

307 3 6 9 16 23 30

GOD'S SMUGGLER (Religious)
Spire Christian Comics/Fleming H. Revell Co.: 1972 (35¢/39¢/40¢)

1-Three variations exist 2 4 6 10 14 18

GODWHEEL
Malibu Comics (Ultraverse): No. 0, Jan, 1995 - No. 3, Feb, 1995 ($2.50, limited series)

0-3: 0-Flip-c. 1-1st app. of Primevil; Thor cameo (1 panel). 3-Perez-a in Chapter 3, Thor app. 3.00

GODZILLA (Movie)
Marvel Comics : August, 1977 - No. 24, July, 1979 (Based on movie series)

1-(Regular 30¢ edition)-Mooney-i 3 6 9 20 30 40
1-(35¢-c variant, limited distribution) 6 12 18 37 59 80
2-(Regular 30¢ edition)-Tuska-i. 2 4 6 9 13 16
2,3-(35¢-c variant, limited distribution) 3 6 9 20 30 40
3-(30¢-c) Champions app.(w/o Ghost Rider) 2 4 6 10 14 18
4-10: 4,5-Sutton-a 2 4 6 8 11 14
11-23: 14-Shield app. 20-F.F. app. 21,22-Devil Dinosaur app. 2 4 6 8 10 12
24-Last issue 2 4 6 9 13 16

GODZILLA (Movie)
Dark Horse Comics: May, 1988 - No. 6, 1988 ($1.95, B&W, limited series) (Based on movie series)

1 6.00
2-6 4.00
...Collection (1990, $10.95)-r/1-6 with new-c 11.00
...Color Special 1 (Sum, 1992, $3.50, color, 44 pgs.)-Arthur Adams wraparound-c/a & part scripts 5.00
...King Of The Monsters Special (8/87, $1.50)-Origin; Bissette-c/a 4.00
...Vs. Barkley nn (12/93, $2.95, color)-Dorman painted-c 4.00

GODZILLA (King of the Monsters) (Movie)
Dark Horse Comics: May, 1995 - No. 16, Sept, 1996 ($2.50) (Based on movies)

0-16: 0-r/Dark Horse Comics #10,11. 1-3-Kevin Maguire scripts. 3-8-Art Adams-c 4.00
...Vs. Hero Zero ($2.50) 3.00

GOG (VILLAINS) (See Kingdom Come)
DC Comics: Feb, 1998 ($1.95, one-shot)

1-Waid-s/Ordway-a(p)/Pearson-c 3.00

GO GIRL!
Image Comics: Aug, 2000 - No. 5 ($3.50, B&W, quarterly)

1-5-Trina Robbins-s/Anne Timmons-a; pin-up gallery 3.50

GO-GO
Charlton Comics: June, 1966 - No. 9, Oct, 1967

1-Miss Bikini Luv begins w/Jim Aparo's 1st published work; Rolling Stones, Beatles, Elvis, Sonny & Cher, Bob Dylan, Sinatra, parody; Herman's Hermits pin-ups; D'Agostino-c/a in #1-8 8 16 24 58 97 135
2-Ringo Starr, David McCallum & Beatles photos on cover; Beatles story and photos 8 16 24 58 97 135
3,4: 3-Blooperman begins, ends #6; 1 pg. Batman & Robin satire; full pg. photo pin-ups Lovin' Spoonful & The Byrds 5 10 15 35 55 75
5,7,9: 5 (2/67)-Super Hero & TV satire by Jim Aparo & Grass Green begins. 6-8-Aparo-a. 7-Photo of Brian Wilson of Beach Boys on-c & Beach Boys photo inside f/b-c. 9-Aparo-c/a 5 10 15 35 55 75
6-Parody of JLA & DC heroes vs. Marvel heroes; Aparo-a; Elvis parody; Petula Clark photo-c 6 12 18 39 62 85
8-Monkees photo on-c & photo inside f/b-c 6 12 18 43 69 95

GO-GO AND ANIMAL (See Tippy's Friends...)

GOING STEADY (Formerly Teen-Age Temptations)
St. John Publ. Co.: No. 10, Dec, 1954 - No. 13, June, 1955; No. 14, Oct, 1955

10(1954)-Matt Baker-c/a 30 60 90 177 289 400
11(2/55, last precode), 12(4/55)-Baker-c 19 38 57 109 172 235
13(6/55)-Baker-c/a 24 48 72 142 234 325
14(10/55)-Matt Baker-c/a, 25 pgs. 28 56 84 165 270 375

GOING STEADY (Formerly Personal Love)
Prize Publications/Headline: V3#3, Feb, 1960 - V3#6, Aug, 1960; V4#1, Sept-Oct, 1960

V3#3-6, V4#1 3 6 9 19 29 38

GOING STEADY WITH BETTY (Becomes Betty & Her Steady No. 2)
Avon Periodicals: Nov-Dec, 1949 (Teen-age)

1-Partial photo-c 16 32 48 94 147 200

GOLDEN AGE, THE (TPB also reprinted in 2005 as JSA: The Golden Age)
DC Comics (Elseworlds): 1993 - No. 4, 1994 ($4.95, limited series)

1-4: James Robinson scripts; Paul Smith-c/a; gold foil embossed-c 6.00
Trade Paperback (1995, $19.95) intro by Howard Chaykin 20.00

GOLDEN AGE SECRET FILES
DC Comics: Feb, 2001 ($4.95, one-shot)

1-Origins and profiles of JSA members and other G.A. heroes; Lark-c 5.00

GOLDEN ARROW (See Fawcett Miniatures, Mighty Midget & Whiz Comics)

GOLDEN ARROW (...Western No. 6)
Fawcett Publications: Spring, 1942 - No. 6, Spring, 1947 (68 pgs.)

1-Golden Arrow begins 47 94 141 296 498 700
2-(1943) 22 44 66 132 216 300
3-5: 3-(Win/45-46). 4-(Spr/46). 5-(Fall/46) 15 30 45 90 140 190
6-Krigstein-a 16 32 48 94 147 200
Ashcan (1942) not distributed to newsstands, only for in house use. A CGC certified 9.0 sold for $3,734.38 in 2008.

GOLDEN COMICS DIGEST
Gold Key: May, 1969 - No. 48, Jan, 1976

NOTE: *Whitman editions exist of many titles and are generally valued the same.*

1-Tom & Jerry, Woody Woodpecker, Bugs Bunny 6 12 18 37 59 80
2-Hanna-Barbera TV Fun Favorites; Space Ghost, Flintstones, Atom Ant, Jetsons, Yogi Bear, Banana Splits, others app. 7 14 21 49 80 110
3-Tom & Jerry, Woody Woodpecker 3 6 9 17 25 32
4-Tarzan; Manning & Marsh-a 5 10 15 30 48 65
5,8-Tom & Jerry, W. Woodpecker, Bugs Bunny 3 6 9 16 23 30
6-Bugs Bunny 3 6 9 16 23 30
7-Hanna-Barbera TV Fun Favorites 6 12 18 37 59 80
9-Tarzan 5 10 15 30 48 65
10,12-17: 10-Bugs Bunny. 12-Tom & Jerry, Bugs Bunny, W. Woodpecker Journey to the Sun. 13-Tom & Jerry. 14-Bugs Bunny Fun Packed Funnies. 15-Tom & Jerry, Woody Woodpecker, Bugs Bunny. 16-Woody Woodpecker Cartoon Special. 17-Bugs Bunny 3 6 9 16 23 30
11-Hanna-Barbera TV Fun Favorites 6 12 18 39 62 85
18-Tom & Jerry; Barney Bear-r by Barks 3 6 9 17 25 32
19-Little Lulu 4 8 12 26 41 55
20-22: 20-Woody Woodpecker Falltime Funtime. 21-Bugs Bunny Showtime. 22-Tom & Jerry Winter Wingding 3 6 9 16 23 30
23-Little Lulu & Tubby Fun Fling 4 8 12 26 41 55
24-26,28: 24-Woody Woodpecker Fun Festival. 25-Tom & Jerry. 26-Bugs Bunny Halloween Hulla-Boo-Loo; Dr. Spektor article, also #25. 28-Tom & Jerry 3 6 9 14 20 26
27-Little Lulu & Tubby in Hawaii 4 8 12 25 39 52
29-Little Lulu & Tubby 4 8 12 25 39 52
30-Bugs Bunny Vacation Funnies 3 6 9 14 20 26

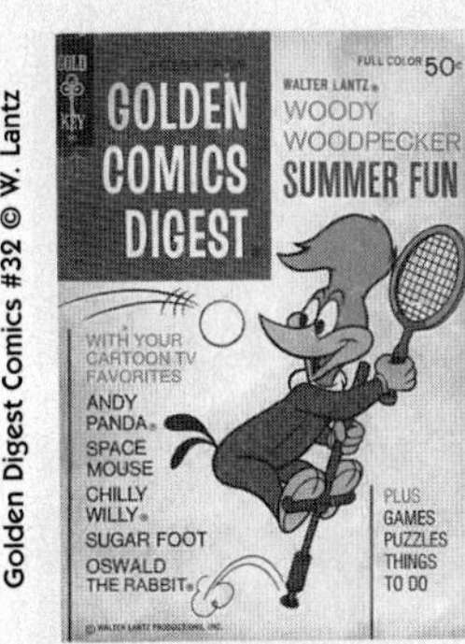

Golden Digest Comics #32 © W. Lantz

Golden Picture Story Book ST-3 © DIS

Gon Again © Kodansha Ltd.

GD 2.0 | VG 4.0 | FN 6.0 | VF 8.0 | VF/NM 9.0 | NM- 9.2

31-Turok, Son of Stone; r/4-Color #596,656; c-r/#9 4 8 12 28 44 60
32-Woody Woodpecker Summer Fun 3 6 9 14 20 26
33,36: 33-Little Lulu & Tubby Halloween Fun; Dr. Spektor app. 36-Little Lulu & Her Friends
4 8 12 25 39 52
34,35,37-39: 34-Bugs Bunny Winter Funnies. 35-Tom & Jerry Snowtime Funtime. 37-Woody Woodpecker County Fair. 39-Bugs Bunny Summer Fun
3 6 9 14 20 26
38-The Pink Panther 3 6 9 17 25 32
40,43: 40-Little Lulu & Tubby Trick or Treat; all by Stanley. 43-Little Lulu in Paris
4 8 12 25 39 52
41,42,44,47: 41-Tom & Jerry Winter Carnival. 42-Bugs Bunny. 44-Woody Woodpecker Family Fun Festival. 47-Bugs Bunny 3 6 9 14 20 25
45-The Pink Panther 3 6 9 17 25 32
46-Little Lulu & Tubby 4 8 12 22 34 45
48-The Lone Ranger 3 6 9 18 27 35

NOTE: *#1-30, 164 pgs.; #31 on, 132 pgs..*

GOLDEN LAD
Spark/Fact & Fiction Publ.: July, 1945 - No. 5, June, 1946 (#4, 5: 52 pgs.)

1-Origin & 1st app. Golden Lad & Swift Arrow; Sandusky and the Senator begins
60 120 180 381 653 925
2-Mort Meskin-c/a 30 60 90 177 289 400
3,4-Mort Meskin-c/a 27 54 81 158 259 360
5-Origin & 1st app. Golden Girl; Shaman & Flame app.
30 60 90 177 289 400

NOTE: *All have* **Robinson,** *and* **Roussos** *art plus* **Meskin** *covers and art.*

GOLDEN LEGACY
Fitzgerald Publishing Co.: 1966 - 1972 (Black History) (25¢)

1-12,14-16: 1-Toussaint L'Ouverture (1966), 2-Harriet Tubman (1967), 3-Crispus Attucks & the Minutemen (1967), 4-Benjamin Banneker (1968), 5-Matthew Henson (1969), 6-Alexander Dumas & Family (1969), 7-Frederick Douglass, Part 1 (1969), 8-Frederick Douglass, Part 2 (1970), 9-Robert Smalls (1970), 10-J. Cinque & the Amistad Mutiny (1970), 11-Men in Action: White, Marshall J. Wilkins (1970), 12-Black Cowboys (1972), 14-The Life of Alexander Pushkin (1971), 15-Ancient African Kingdoms (1972), 16-Black Inventors (1972) each.... 3 6 9 20 30 40
13-The Life of Martin Luther King, Jr. (1972) 4 8 12 24 37 50
1-10,12,13,15,16(1976)-Reprints 2 4 6 8 10 12

GOLDEN LOVE STORIES (Formerly Golden West Love)
Kirby Publishing Co.: No. 4, April, 1950

4-Powell-a; Glenn Ford/Janet Leigh photo-c 17 34 51 98 154 210

GOLDEN PICTURE CLASSIC, A
Western Printing Co. (Simon & Shuster): 1956-1957 (Text stories w/illustrations in color; 100 pgs. each)

CL-401: Treasure Island 11 22 33 64 90 115
CL-402,403: 402: Tom Sawyer. 403: Black Beauty 10 20 30 54 72 90
CL-404, 405: CL-404: Little Women. CL-405: Heidi 10 20 30 54 72 90
CL-406: Ben Hur 8 16 24 44 57 70
CL-407: Around the World in 80 Days 8 16 24 44 57 70
CL-408: Sherlock Holmes 9 18 27 50 65 80
CL-409: The Three Musketeers 8 16 24 44 57 70
CL-410: The Merry Advs. of Robin Hood 8 16 24 44 57 70
CL-411,412: 411: Hans Brinker. 412: The Count of Monte Cristo
9 18 27 50 65 80
(Both soft & hardcover editions are valued the same)

NOTE: *Recent research has uncovered new information. Apparently #s 1-6 were issued in 1956 and #7-12 in 1957. But they can be found in five different series listings: CL-1 to CL-12 (softbound); CL-401 to CL-412 (also softbound); CL-101 to CL-112 (hardbound); plus two new series discoveries: A Golden Reading Adventure, publ. by Golden Press; edited down to 60 pages and reduced in size to 6x9"; only #s discovered so far are #381 (CL-4), #382 (CL-6) & #387 (CL-3). They have no reorder list and some have covers different from GPC. There have also been found British hardbound editions of GPC with dust jackets. Copies of all five listed series vary from scarce to very rare. Some editions of some series have not yet been found at all.*

GOLDEN PICTURE STORY BOOK
Racine Press (Western): Dec, 1961 (50¢, Treasury size, 52 pgs.) (All are scarce)

ST-1-Huckleberry Hound (TV); Hokey Wolf, Pixie & Dixie, Quick Draw McGraw, Snooper and Blabber, Augie Doggie app. 16 32 48 114 232 350
ST-2-Yogi Bear (TV); Snagglepuss, Yakky Doodle, Quick Draw McGraw, Snooper and Blabber, Augie Doggie app. 16 32 48 114 232 350
ST-3-Babes in Toyland (Walt Disney's...)-Annette Funicello photo-c
21 42 63 150 300 450
ST-4-(...of Disney Ducks)-Walt Disney's Wonderful World of Ducks (Donald Duck, Uncle Scrooge, Donald's Nephews, Grandma Duck, Ludwig Von Drake, & Gyro Gearloose stories) 21 42 63 150 300 450

GOLDEN RECORD COMIC (See Amazing Spider-Man #1, Avengers #4, Fantastic Four #1, Journey Into Mystery #83)

GOLDEN STORY BOOKS
Western Printing Co. (Simon & Shuster): 1949-1950 (Heavy covers, digest size, 128 pgs.) (Illustrated text in color)

7-Walt Disney's Mystery in Disneyville, a book-length adventure starring Donald and Nephews, Mickey and Nephews, and with Minnie, Daisy and Goofy. Art by Dick Moores & Manuel Gonzales (scarce) 30 60 90 177 289 400
10-Bugs Bunny's Treasure Hunt, a book-length adventure starring Bugs & Porky Pig, with Petunia Pig & Nephew, Cicero. Art by Tom McKimson (scarce)
21 42 63 122 199 275
11,12 ('50): 11-M-G-M's Tom & Jerry. 12-Walt Disney's "So Dear My Heart"
20 40 60 114 182 250

GOLDEN WEST LOVE (Golden Love Stories No. 4)
Kirby Publishing Co.: Sept-Oct, 1949 - No. 3, Feb, 1950 (All 52 pgs.)

1-Powell-a in all; Roussos-a; painted-c 22 44 66 128 209 290
2,3: Photo-c 17 34 51 98 154 210

GOLDEN WEST RODEO TREASURY (See Dell Giants)

GOLDFISH (See A.K.A. Goldfish)

GOLDILOCKS (See March of Comics No. 1)

GOLD KEY CHAMPION
Gold Key: Mar, 1978 - No. 2, May, 1978 (50¢, 52pgs.)

1,2: 1-Space Family Robinson; half-r. 2-Mighty Samson; half-r
1 3 4 6 8 10

GOLD KEY SPOTLIGHT
Gold Key: May, 1976 - No. 11, Feb, 1978

1-Tom, Dick & Harriet 2 4 6 8 11 14
2-11: 2-Wacky Advs. of Cracky. 3-Wacky Witch. 4-Tom, Dick & Harriet. 5-Wacky Advs. of Cracky. 6-Dagar the Invincible; Santos-a; origin Demonomicon. 7-Wacky Witch & Greta Ghost. 8-The Occult Files of Dr. Spektor, Simbar, Lu-sai; Santos-a. 9-Tragg. 10-O. G. Whiz. 11-Tom, Dick & Harriet 2 4 6 8 10 12

GOLD MEDAL COMICS
Cambridge House: 1945 (25¢, one-shot, 132 pgs.)

nn-Captain Truth by Fugitani as well as Stallman and Howie Post, Crime Detector, The Witch of Salem, Luckyman, others app. 32 64 96 188 307 425

GOMER PYLE (TV)
Gold Key: July, 1966 - No. 3, Oct, 1967

1-Photo front/back-c 8 16 24 54 90 125
2,3 6 12 18 39 62 85

GON
DC Comics (Paradox Press): July, 1996 - No. 4, Oct, 1996; No. 5, 1997 ($5.95, B&W, digest-size, limited series)

1-5: Misadventures of baby dinosaur; 1-Gon. 2-Gon Again. 3-Gon: Here Today, Gone Tomorrow. 4-Gon: Going, Going...Gon. 5-Gon Swimmin'. Tanaka-c/a/scripts in all
1 2 3 5 6 8

GON COLOR SPECTACULAR
DC Comics (Paradox Press): 1998 ($5.95, square-bound)

nn-Tanaka-c/a/scripts 1 2 3 5 6 8

GON ON SAFARI
DC Comics (Paradox Press): 2000 ($7.95, B&W, digest-size)

nn-Tanaka-c/a/scripts 1 2 3 5 6 8

GON UNDERGROUND
DC Comics (Paradox Press): 1999 ($7.95, B&W, digest-size)

nn-Tanaka-c/a/scripts 1 2 3 5 6 8

GON WILD
DC Comics (Paradox Press): 1997 ($9.95, B&W, digest-size)

nn-Tanaka-c/a/scripts in all. (Rep. Gon #3,4) 1 3 4 6 8 10

GOODBYE, MR. CHIPS (See Movie Comics)

GOOD GIRL ART QUARTERLY
AC Comics: Summer, 1990 - No. 15, Spring, 1994 (B&W/color, 52 pgs.)

1,3-15 ($3.50)-All have one new story (often FemForce) & rest reprints by Baker, Ward & other "good girl" artists 4.00
2 ($3.95) 4.00

GOOD GIRL COMICS (Formerly Good Girl Art Quarterly)
AC Comics: No. 16, Summer, 1994 - No. 18, 1995 (B&W)

16-18 4.00

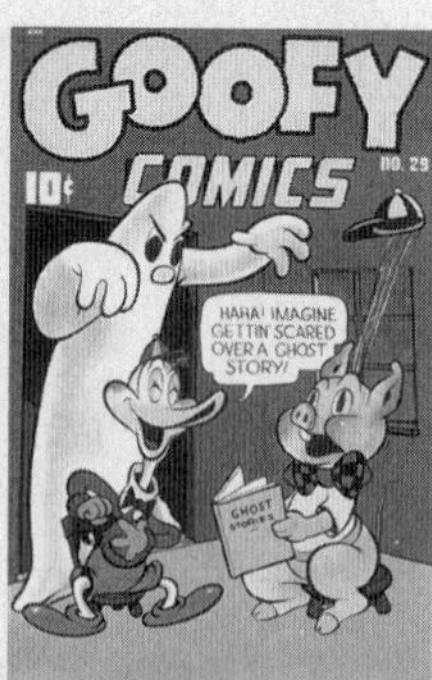

Goofy Comics #25 © STD

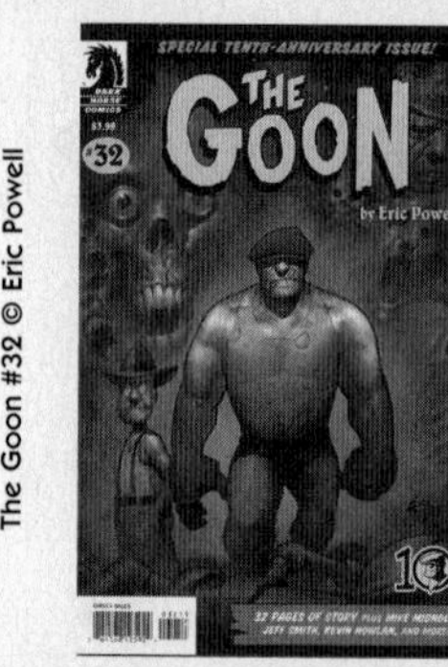

The Goon #32 © Eric Powell

Gotham City Sirens #12 © DC

GD VG FN VF VF/NM NM-
2.0 4.0 6.0 8.0 9.0 9.2

GOOD GUYS, THE
Defiant: Nov, 1993 - No. 9, July, 1994 ($2.50/$3.25/$3.50)
1-($3.50, 52 pgs.)-Glory x-over from Plasm 4.00
2,3,5-9: 9-Pre-Schism issue 3.00
4-($3.25, 52 pgs.) 4.00

GOOD, THE BAD AND THE UGLY, THE (Also see Man With No Name)
Dynamite Entertainment: 2009 - No. 8 ($3.50)
1-8: 1-Character from the 1966 Clint Eastwood movie; Dixon-s/Polls-a; three covers 3.50

GOOD TRIUMPHS OVER EVIL! (Also see Narrative Illustration)
M.C. Gaines: 1943 (12 pgs., 7-1/4"x10", B&W) (not a comic book) (Rare)
nn-A pamphlet, sequel to Narrative Illustration 110 220 330 704 1202 1700
NOTE: ***Print, A Quarterly Journal of the Graphic Arts*** *Vol. 3 No. 3 (64 pg. square bound) features 1st printing of Good Triumphs Over Evil! A VG copy sold for $350 in 2005.*

GOOFY (Disney)(See Dynabrite Comics, Mickey Mouse Magazine V4#7, Walt Disney Showcase #35 & Wheaties)
Dell Publishing Co.: No. 468, May, 1953 - Sept-Nov, 1962
Four Color 468 (#1) 11 22 33 77 144 210
Four Color 562,627,658,702,747,802,857 7 14 21 47 76 105
Four Color 899,952,987,1053,1094,1149,1201 5 10 15 32 51 70
12-308-211(Dell, 9-11/62) 5 10 15 32 51 70

GOOFY ADVENTURES
Disney Comics: June, 1990 - No. 17, 1991 ($1.50)
1-17: Most new stories. 2-Joshua Quagmire-a w/free poster. 7-WDC&S-r plus new-a. 9-Gottfredson-r. 14-Super Goof story. 15-All Super Goof issue. 17-Gene Colan-a(p) 3.00

GOOFY ADVENTURE STORY (See Goofy No. 857)

GOOFY COMICS (Companion to Happy Comics)(Not Disney)
Nedor Publ. Co. No. 1-14/Standard No. 14-48: June, 1943 - No. 48, 1953
(Animated Cartoons)
1-Funny animal; Oriolo-c 30 60 90 177 289 400
2 16 32 48 94 147 200
3-10 14 28 42 80 115 150
11-19 11 22 33 60 83 105
20-35-Frazetta text illos in all 12 24 36 67 94 120
36-48 9 18 27 52 69 85

GOOFY SUCCESS STORY (See Goofy No. 702)

GOON, THE
Avatar Press: Mar, 1999 - No. 3, July, 1999 ($3.00, B&W)
1-Eric Powell-s/a 20.00
2 12.00
3 8.00
...: Rough Stuff (Albatross, 1/03, $15.95) r/Avatar Press series #1-3 16.00
...: Rough Stuff (Dark Horse, 2/04, $12.95) r/Avatar Press series #1-3 newly colored 13.00

GOON, THE (2nd series)
Albatross Exploding Funny Books: Oct, 2002 - No. 4, Feb, 2003 ($2.95)
1-Eric Powell-s/a 10.00
2-4 6.00
...Color Special 1 (8/02) 10.00
...: Nothin' But Misery Vol. 1 (Dark Horse, 7/03, $15.95, TPB) - Reprints The Goon #1-4 (Albatross series), Color Special, and story from DHP #157 16.00

GOON, THE (3rd series) (Also see Dethklok Versus the Goon)
Dark Horse Comics: June, 2003 - Present ($2.99)
1-Eric Powell-s/a in all 6.00
2-4 4.00
5-31: 7-Hellboy-c/app; framing seq. by Mignola 14-Two covers 3.00
32-($3.99, 3/09) Tenth Anniversary issue; with sketch pages and pin-ups 4.00
33-($3.50) Silent issue 3.50
... 25¢ Edition (9/05, 25¢) 3.00
...: Chinatown and the Mystery of Mr. Wicker HC (11/07, $19.95) original GN; Powell-s/a 20.00
...: Fancy Pants Edition HC (10/05, $24.95, dust jacket) r/#1,2 of 2nd series & #1,3,5,9 of 3rd series; Powell intro.; sketch pages and cover gallery 25.00
...: Heaps of Ruination (5/05, $12.95, TPB) r/#5-8; intro. by Frank Darabont 13.00
...: My Murderous Childhood (And Other Grievous Yarns) (5/04, $13.95, TPB) r/#1-4 and short story from Drawing on Your Nightmares one-shot; intro. by Frank Cho 14.00
...: One For One (8/10, $1.00) r/#1 with red cover frame 1.00
...: Virtue and the Grim Consequences Thereof (2/06, $16.95) r/#9-13 17.00
...: Wicked Inclinations (12/06, $14.95) r/#14-18; intro. by Mike Allred 15.00

GOON NOIR, THE (Dwight T. Albatross's...)
Dark Horse Comics: Sept, 2006 - No. 3, Jan, 2007 ($2.99, B&W, limited series)

GD VG FN VF VF/NM NM-
2.0 4.0 6.0 8.0 9.0 9.2

1-3-Anthology 1-Oswalt-s/Ploog-a; Sniegoski-s/Powell-a; Morrison-s/a; Niles-s/Sook-a. 2-Nowlan, Barta-a. 3-Ramos, Guy Davis-a; Nelson, Posehn, Thomas Lennon-s 3.00
TPB (7/07, $12.95) r/#1-3; sketch pages; intros by "Dwight" 13.00

GOOSE (Humor magazine)
Cousins Publ. (Fawcett): Sept, 1976 - No. 3, 1976 (75¢, 52 pgs., B&W)
1-Nudity in all 3 6 9 16 23 30
2,3: 2-(10/76) Fonz-c/s; Lone Ranger story. 3-Wonder Woman, King Kong, Six Million Dollar Man stories 2 4 6 11 16 20

GORDO (See Comics Revue No. 5 & Giant Comics Edition)

GORGO (Based on M.G.M. movie) (See Return of...)
Charlton Comics: May, 1961 - No. 23, Sept, 1965
1-Ditko-a, 22 pgs. 22 44 66 159 317 475
2,3-Ditko-c/a 13 26 39 89 170 250
4-Ditko-c 9 18 27 65 113 160
5-11,13-16: 11,13-16-Ditko-a 8 16 24 56 93 130
12,17-23: 12-Reptisaurus x-over; Montes/Bache-a-No. 17-23. 20-Giordano-c 6 12 18 37 59 80
Gorgo's Revenge('62)-Becomes Return of... 7 14 21 47 76 105

GORILLA MAN (From Agents of Atlas)
Marvel Comics: Sept, 2010 - No. 3, Nov, 2010 ($3.99, limited series)
1-3-Parker-s/Caracuzzo-a. 1-Johnson-c. 3-Dell'Otto-c 4.00

GOSPEL BLIMP, THE
Spire Christian Comics (Fleming H. Revell Co.): 1973,1975 (35¢/39¢, 36 pgs.)
nn-(1973) 2 4 6 11 16 20
nn-(1975) 2 4 6 8 10 12

GOTHAM BY GASLIGHT (A Tale of the Batman)(See Batman: Master of...)
DC Comics: 1989 ($3.95, one-shot, squarebound, 52 pgs.)
nn-Mignola/Russell-a; intro by Robert Bloch 4.00

GOTHAM CENTRAL
DC Comics: Early Feb, 2003 - No. 40, Apr, 2006 ($2.50)
1-40-Stories of Gotham City Police. 1-Brubaker & Rucka-s/Lark-c/a. 10-Two-Face app. 13,15-Joker-c. 18-Huntress app. 27-Catwoman-c. 32-Poison Ivy app. 34-Teen Titans-c/app. 38-Crispus Allen killed (becomes The Spectre in Infinite Crisis #5) 3.00
... Book One: In the Line of Duty HC (2008, $29.99, dustjacket) r/#1-10; sketch pages 70.00
... Book One: In the Line of Duty SC (2008, $19.99) r/#1-10; sketch pages 20.00
... Book Two: Jokers and Madmen HC (2009, $29.99, dustjacket) r/#11-22 30.00
... Book Three: On the Freak Beat HC (2010, $29.99, dustjacket) r/#23-31 30.00
... Book Four: Corrigan HC (2011, $29.99, dustjacket) r/#32-40 30.00
...: Dead Robin (2007, $17.99, TPB) r/#33-40; cover gallery 18.00
...: Half a Life (2005, $14.99, TPB) r/#6-10, Batman Chronicles #16 and Detective #747 15.00
...: In The Line of Duty (2004, $9.95, TPB) r/#1-5, cover gallery & sketch pages 10.00
...: The Quick and the Dead TPB (2006, $14.99) r/#23-25,28-31 15.00
...: Unresolved Targets (2006, $14.99, TPB) r/#12-15,19-22, cover gallery 15.00

GOTHAM CITY SIRENS (Batman:Reborn)
DC Comics: Aug, 2009 - Present ($2.99)
1-20: 1-Catwoman, Harley Quinn and Poison Ivy; Dini-s/March-a/c 3.00
1-Variant-c by JG Jones 5.00
...: Song of the Sirens HC (2010, $19.99, dustjacket) r/#8-13 & Catwoman #83 20.00
...: Union HC (2010, $19.99, dustjacket) r/#1-7 20.00

GOTHAM GAZETTE (Battle For The Cowl crossover in Batman titles)
DC Comics: May, 2009; Jul, 2009 ($2.99, one-shots)
1-Short stories of Gotham without Batman; Nguyen, March, ChrisCross & others-a 3.00
...: Batman Alive? (7/09) Vicki Vale app.; Nguyen, March, ChrisCross & others-a 3.00

GOTHAM GIRLS
DC Comics: Oct, 2002 - No. 5, Feb, 2003 ($2.25, limited series)
1-5-Catwoman, Batgirl, Poison Ivy, Harley Quinn from animated series 3.00

GOTHAM NIGHTS (See Batman: Gotham Nights II)
DC Comics: Mar, 1992 - No. 4, June, 1992 ($1.25, limited series)
1-4: Featuring Batman 3.00

GOTHAM UNDERGROUND
DC Comics: Dec, 2007 - No. 9, Aug, 2008 ($2.99, limited series)
1-9-Nine covers interlock for single image; Tieri-s/Calafiore-a/c. 7,8-Vigilante app. 3.00
Batman: Gotham Underground TPB (2008, $19.99) r/#1-9; interlocked image cover 20.00

GOTHIC ROMANCES (Also see My Secrets)
Atlas/Seaboard Publ.: Dec, 1974 (75¢, B&W, magazine, 76 pgs.)
1-Text w/ illos by N. Adams, Chaykin, Heath (2 pgs. ea.); painted cover from Ravenwood

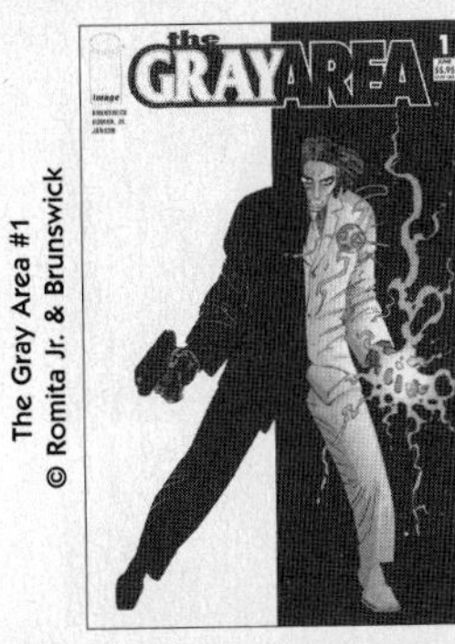

The Gray Area #1 © Romita Jr. & Brunswick

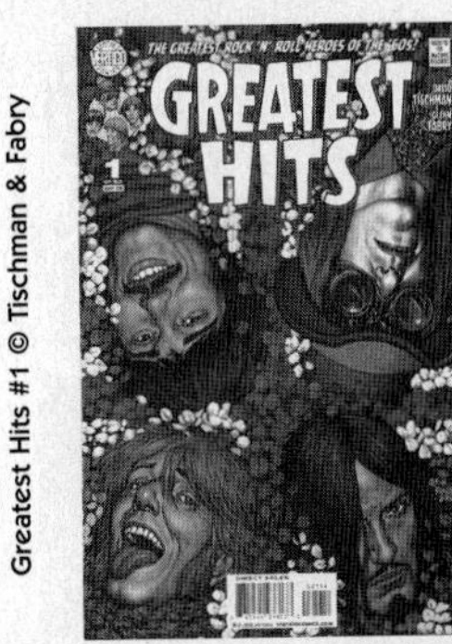

Greatest Hits #1 © Tischman & Fabry

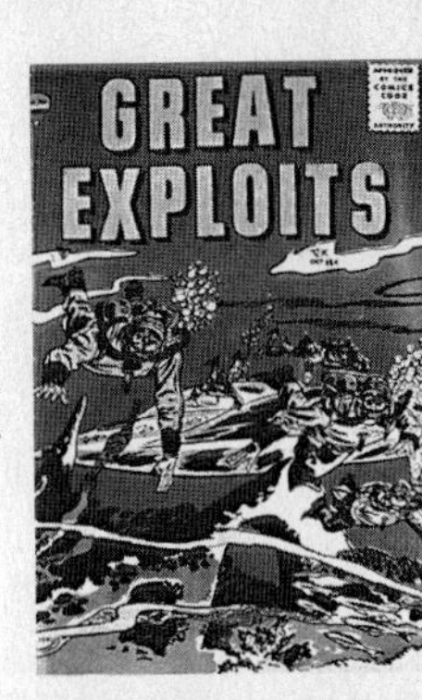

Great Exploits #1 © Decker

	GD 2.0	VG 4.0	FN 6.0	VF 8.0	VF/NM 9.0	NM- 9.2
Gothic paperback "The Conservatory"(scarce)	21	42	63	150	300	450

GOTHIC TALES OF LOVE (Magazine)
Marvel Comics: Apr, 1975 - No. 3, 1975 (B&W, 76 pgs.)

	GD	VG	FN	VF	VF/NM	NM-
1-3-Painted-c/a (scarce)	24	48	72	175	350	525

GOVERNOR & J. J., THE (TV)
Gold Key: Feb, 1970 - No. 3, Aug, 1970 (Photo-c)

	GD	VG	FN	VF	VF/NM	NM-
1	4	8	12	26	41	55
2,3	3	6	9	19	29	38

GRACKLE, THE
Acclaim Comics: Jan, 1997 - No. 4, Apr, 1997 ($2.95, B&W)

	GD	VG	FN	VF	VF/NM	NM-
1-4: Mike Baron scripts & Paul Gulacy-c/a. 1-4-Doublecross						3.00

GRAFIK MUSIK
Caliber Press: Nov, 1990 - No. 4, Aug, 1991 ($3.50/$2.50)

	GD	VG	FN	VF	VF/NM	NM-
1-($3.50, 48 pgs., color) Mike Allred-c/a/scripts-1st app. in color of Frank Einstein (Madman)	3	6	9	14	20	25
2-($2.50, 24 pgs., color)	2	4	6	9	12	15
3,4-($2.50, 24 pgs., B&W)	2	4	6	8	10	12

GRANDMA DUCK'S FARM FRIENDS(See Walt Disney's C&S 293 & Wheaties)
Dell Publishing Co.: No. 763, Jan, 1957 - No. 1279, Feb, 1962 (Disney)

	GD	VG	FN	VF	VF/NM	NM-
Four Color 763 (#1)	8	16	24	52	86	120
Four Color 873	6	12	18	37	59	80
Four Color 965,1279	5	10	15	32	51	70
Four Color 1010,1073,1161-Barks-a; 1073,1161-Barks c/a	12	24	36	82	154	225

GRAND PRIX (Formerly Hot Rod Racers)
Charlton Comics: No. 16, Sept, 1967 - No. 31, May, 1970

	GD	VG	FN	VF	VF/NM	NM-
16-Features Rick Roberts	4	8	12	22	34	45
17-20	3	6	9	18	27	35
21-31	3	6	9	16	23	30

GRAPHIQUE MUSIQUE
Slave Labor Graphics: Dec, 1989 - No. 3, May, 1990 ($2.95, 52 pgs.)

	GD	VG	FN	VF	VF/NM	NM-
1-Mike Allred-c/a/scripts	3	6	9	20	30	40
2,3	3	6	9	16	23	30

GRAVESLINGER
Image Comics (Shadowline): Oct, 2007 - No. 4, Mar, 2008 ($3.50, limited series)

	GD	VG	FN	VF	VF/NM	NM-
1-4-Denton & Mariotte-s/Cboins-a						3.50

GRAVE TALES
Hamilton Comics: Oct, 1991 - No. 3, Feb, 1992 ($3.95, B&W, mag., 52 pgs.)

	GD	VG	FN	VF	VF/NM	NM-
1-Staton-c/a	2	3	4	6	8	10
2,3: 2-Staton-a; Morrow-c	1	2	3	5	6	8

GRAVITY (Also see Beyond! limited series)
Marvel Comics: Aug, 2005 - No. 5, Dec, 2005 ($2.99, limited series)

	GD	VG	FN	VF	VF/NM	NM-
1-5: 1-Intro. Gravity; McKeever-s/Norton-a. 2-Rhino-c/app. 5-Spider-Man app.						3.00
...: Big-City Super Hero (2005, $7.99, digest) r/#1-5						8.00

GRAY AREA, THE
Image Comics: Jun, 2004 - No. 3, Oct, 2004 ($5.95/$3.95, limited series)

	GD	VG	FN	VF	VF/NM	NM-
1,3-($5.95) Romita, Jr.-a/Brunswick-s; sketch pages and script pages. 3-Pin-up pages						6.00
2-($3.95)						4.00
...Vol. 1: All Of This Can Be Yours (2005, $14.95) r/series & sketch,script & pin-up pages						15.00

GRAY GHOST, THE
Dell Publishing Co.: No. 911, July, 1958; No. 1000, June-Aug, 1959

	GD	VG	FN	VF	VF/NM	NM-
Four Color 911 (#1), 1000-Photo-c each	8	16	24	56	93	130

GREAT ACTION COMICS
I. W. Enterprises: 1958 (Reprints with new covers)

	GD	VG	FN	VF	VF/NM	NM-
1-Captain Truth reprinted from Gold Medal #1	3	6	9	16	23	30
8,9-Reprints Phantom Lady #15 & 23	7	14	21	49	80	110

GREAT AMERICAN COMICS PRESENTS - THE SECRET VOICE
Peter George 4-Star Publ./American Features Syndicate: 1945 (10¢)

	GD	VG	FN	VF	VF/NM	NM-
1-Anti-Nazi; "What Really Happened to Hitler"	41	82	123	256	428	600

GREAT AMERICAN WESTERN, THE
AC Comics: 1987 - No. 4, 1990? ($1.75/$2.95/$3.50, B&W with some color)

	GD	VG	FN	VF	VF/NM	NM-
1-4: 1-Western-r plus Bill Black-a. 2-Tribute to ME comics; Durango Kid photo-c 3-Tribute to Tom Mix plus Roy Rogers, Durango Kid; Billy the Kid-r by Severin; photo-c. 4- ($3.50, 52 pgs., 16 pgs. color)-Tribute to Lash LaRue; photo-c & interior photos; Fawcett-r						4.00
...Presents 1 (1991, $5.00) New Sunset Carson; film history						5.00

GREAT CAT FAMILY, THE (Disney-TV/Movie)
Dell Publishing Co.: No. 750, Nov, 1956 (one-shot)

	GD	VG	FN	VF	VF/NM	NM-
Four Color 750-Pinocchio & Alice app.	6	12	18	43	69	95

GREAT COMICS
Great Comics Publications: Nov, 1941 - No. 3, Jan, 1942

	GD	VG	FN	VF	VF/NM	NM-
1-Origin/1st app. The Great Zarro; Madame Strange & Guy Gorham, Wizard of Science & The Great Zarro begin	135	270	405	864	1482	2100
2-Buck Johnson, Jungle Explorer app.; X-Mas-c	68	136	204	435	743	1050
3-Futuro Takes Hitler to Hell-c/s; "The Lost City" movie story (starring William Boyd); continues in Choice Comics #3 (scarce)	459	918	1377	3350	5925	8500

GREAT COMICS
Novack Publishing Co./Jubilee Comics/Knockout/Barrel O' Fun: 1945

	GD	VG	FN	VF	VF/NM	NM-
1-(Four publ. variations: Barrel O-Fun, Jubilee, Knockout & Novack)-The Defenders, Capt. Power app.; L. B. Cole-c	32	64	96	188	307	425
1-(Jubilee)-Same cover; Boogey Man, Satanas, & The Sorcerer & His Apprentice	26	52	78	152	249	345
1-(Barrel O' Fun)-L. B. Cole-c; Barrel O' Fun overprinted in indicia; Li'l Cactus, Cuckoo Sheriff (humorous)	18	36	54	105	165	225

GREAT DOGPATCH MYSTERY (See Mammy Yokum & the...)

GREATEST AMERICAN HERO (Based on the 1981-1986 TV series)
Catastrophic Comics: Dec, 2008 - No. 3, May, 2009 ($3.50/$3.95)

	GD	VG	FN	VF	VF/NM	NM-
1-3-Origin re-told; William Katt and others-s. 3-Obama-c/app.						4.00

GREATEST BATMAN STORIES EVER TOLD, THE
DC Comics

	GD	VG	FN	VF	VF/NM	NM-
Hardcover ($24.95)						50.00
Softcover ($15.95) "Greatest DC Stories Vol. 2" on spine						20.00
Vol. 2 softcover (1992, $16.95) "Greatest DC Stories Vol. 7" on spine						20.00

GREATEST FLASH STORIES EVER TOLD, THE
DC Comics: 1991

	GD	VG	FN	VF	VF/NM	NM-
nn-Hardcover ($29.95); Infantino-c						45.00
nn-Softcover ($14.95)						20.00

GREATEST GOLDEN AGE STORIES EVER TOLD, THE
DC Comics: 1990 ($24.95, hardcover)

	GD	VG	FN	VF	VF/NM	NM-
nn-Ordway-c						60.00

GREATEST HITS
DC Comics (Vertigo): Dec, 2008 - No. 6, Apr, 2009 ($2.99, limited series)

	GD	VG	FN	VF	VF/NM	NM-
1-6-Intro. The Mates superhero team in 1967 England; Tischman-s/Fabry-a/c						3.00

GREATEST JOKER STORIES EVER TOLD, THE (See Batman)
DC Comics: 1983

	GD	VG	FN	VF	VF/NM	NM-
Hardcover ($19.95)-Kyle Baker painted-c						45.00
Softcover ($14.95)						20.00
Stacked Deck...Expanded Edition (1992, $29.95)-Longmeadow Press Publ.						32.00

GREATEST 1950s STORIES EVER TOLD, THE
DC Comics: 1990

	GD	VG	FN	VF	VF/NM	NM-
Hardcover ($29.95)-Kubert-c						55.00
Softcover ($14.95) "Greatest DC Stories Vol. 5" on spine						22.00

GREATEST TEAM-UP STORIES EVER TOLD, THE
DC Comics: 1989

	GD	VG	FN	VF	VF/NM	NM-
Hardcover ($24.95)-DeVries and Infantino painted-c						55.00
Softcover ($14.95) "Greatest DC Stories Vol. 4" on spine; Adams-c						22.00

GREATEST SUPERMAN STORIES EVER TOLD, THE
DC Comics: 1987

	GD	VG	FN	VF	VF/NM	NM-
Hardcover ($24.95)						50.00
Softcover ($15.95)						22.00

GREAT EXPLOITS
Decker Publ./Red Top: Oct, 1957

	GD	VG	FN	VF	VF/NM	NM-
1-Krigstein-a(2) (re-issue on cover); reprints Daring Advs. #6 by Approved Comics	6	12	18	31	38	45

GREAT FOODINI, THE (See Foodini)

GREAT GAZOO, THE (The Flintstones)(TV)
Charlton Comics: Aug, 1973 - No. 20, Jan, 1977 (Hanna-Barbera)

	GD	VG	FN	VF	VF/NM	NM-
1	4	8	12	24	37	50
2-10	3	6	9	14	19	24

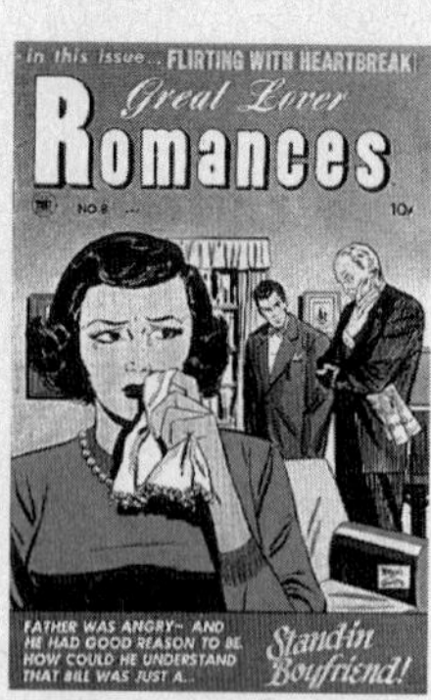

Great Lover Romances #8 © TOBY

Great Western #11 © ME

Green Arrow (2010 series) #1 © DC

GD VG FN VF VF/NM NM-
2.0 4.0 6.0 8.0 9.0 9.2

11-20 2 4 6 10 14 18

GREAT GRAPE APE, THE (TV)(See TV Stars #1)
Charlton Comics: Sept, 1976 - No. 2, Nov, 1976 (Hanna-Barbera)
1 4 8 12 22 34 45
2 3 6 9 14 20 25

GREAT LOCOMOTIVE CHASE, THE (Disney)
Dell Publishing Co.: No. 712, Sept, 1956 (one-shot)
Four Color 712-Movie, photo-c 7 14 21 47 76 105

GREAT LOVER ROMANCES (Young Lover Romances #4,5)
Toby Press: 3/51; #2, 1951(nd); #3, 1952 (nd); #6, Oct?, 1952 - No. 22, May, 1955 (Photo-c #1-5, 10 ,13, 15, 17) (no #4, 5)
1-Jon Juan story-r/Jon Juan #1 by Schomburg; Dr. Anthony King app.
19 38 57 111 176 240
2-Jon Juan, Dr. Anthony King app. 12 24 36 67 94 120
3,7,9-14,16-22: 10-Rita Hayworth photo-c. 17-Rita Hayworth & Aldo Ray photo-c
9 18 27 52 69 85
6-Kurtzman-a (10/52) 11 22 33 64 90 115
8-Five pgs. of "Pin-Up Pete" by Sparling 11 22 33 64 90 115
15-Liz Taylor photo-c (scarce) 41 82 123 256 428 600

GREAT RACE, THE (See Movie Classics)

GREAT SCOTT SHOE STORE (See Bulls-Eye)

GREAT SOCIETY COMIC BOOK, THE (Political parody)
Pocket Books Inc./Parallax Pub.: 1966 ($1.00, 36 pgs., 7"x10", one-shot)
nn-Super-LBJ-c/story; 60s politicians app. as super-heroes; Tallarico-a
3 6 9 18 27 35

GREAT TEN, THE (Characters from Final Crisis)
DC Comics: Jan, 2010 - No. 9, Sept, 2010 ($2.99, limited series)
1-9-Super team of China; Bedard-s/McDaniel-a/Stanley Lau-c 3.00

GREAT WEST (Magazine)
M. F. Enterprises: 1969 (B&W, 52 pgs.)
V1#1 2 4 6 10 14 18

GREAT WESTERN
Magazine Enterprises: No. 8, Jan-Mar, 1954 - No. 11, Oct-Dec, 1954
8(A-1 93)-Trail Colt by Guardineer; Powell Red Hawk-r/Straight Arrow begins, ends #11; Durango Kid story 18 36 54 103 162 220
9(A-1 105), 11(A-1 127)-Ghost Rider, Durango Kid app. in each. 9-Red Mask-c, but no app.
15 30 45 83 124 165
10(A-1 113)-The Calico Kid by Guardineer-r/Tim Holt #8; Straight Arrow, Durango Kid app.
12 24 36 69 97 125
I.W. Reprint #1,2 9: 1,2-r/Straight Arrow #36,42. 9-r/Straight Arrow #?
3 6 9 16 22 28
I.W. Reprint #8-Origin Ghost Rider(r/Tim Holt #11); Tim Holt app.; Bolle-a
3 6 9 17 25 32
NOTE: ***Guardineer** c-8. **Powell** a(r)-8-11 (from Straight Arrow).*

GREEK STREET
DC Comics (Vertigo): Sept, 2009 - No. 16, Dec, 2010 ($1.00/$2.99)
1-16: 1-($1.00) Milligan-s/Gianfelice-a. 2: Begin $2.99-c 3.00
...: Blood Calls For Blood SC (2010, $9.99) r/#1-5; Mike Carey intro.; sketch art 10.00
...: Cassandra Complex SC (2010, $14.99) r/#6-11 15.00

GREEN ARROW (See Action #440, Adventure, Brave & the Bold, DC Super Stars #17, Detective #521, Flash #217, Green Lantern #76, Justice League of America #4, Leading Comics, More Fun #73 (1st app.), Showcase '95 #9 & World's Finest Comics)

GREEN ARROW
DC Comics: May, 1983 - No. 4, Aug, 1983 (limited series)
1-Origin; Speedy cameo; Mike W. Barr scripts, Trevor Von Eeden-c/a 5.00
2-4 4.00

GREEN ARROW
DC Comics: Feb, 1988 - No. 137, Oct, 1998 ($1.00-$2.50) (Painted-c #1-3)
1-Mike Grell scripts begin, ends #80 6.00
2-49,51-74,76-86: 27,28-Warlord app. 35-38-Co-stars Black Canary; Bill Wray-i. 40-Grell-a. 47-Begin $1.50-c. 63-No longer has mature readers on-c. 63-66-Shado app. 81-Aparo-a begins, ends #100; Nuklon app. 82-Intro & death of Rival. 83-Huntress-c/story. 84, 85-Deathstroke app. 86-Catwoman-c/story w/Jim Balent layouts 3.00
50,75-($2.50, 52 pgs.): Anniversary issues. 75-Arsenal (Roy Harper) & Shado app. 4.00
0,87-96: 87-$1.95-c begins. 88-Guy Gardner, Martian Manhunter, & Wonder Woman-c/app.; Flash-c. 89-Anarky app. 90-(9/94)-Zero Hour tie-in. 0-(10/94)-1st app. Connor Hawke; Aparo-a(p). 91-(11/94). 93-1st app. Camorouge. 95-Hal Jordan cameo. 96-Intro new Force of July; Hal Jordan (Parallax) app; Oliver Queen learns that Connor Hawke is his son 3.00
97-99,102-109: 97-Begin $2.25-c; no Aparo-a. 97-99-Arsenal app. 102,103-Underworld Unleashed x-over. 104-GL(Kyle Rayner)-c/app. 105-Robin-c/app. 107-109-Thorn app. 109-Lois Lane cameo; Weeks-c. 3.00
100-($3.95)-Foil-c; Superman app. 1 3 4 6 8 10
101-Death of Oliver Queen; Superman app. 3 6 9 16 23 30
110,111-124: 110,111-GL x-over. 110-Intro Hatchet. 114-Final Night. 115-117-Black Canary & Oracle app. 3.00
125-($3.50, 48 pgs)-GL x-over cont. in GL #92 4.00
126-136: 126-Begin $2.50-c. 130-GL & Flash x-over. 132,133-JLA app. 134,135-Brotherhood of the Fist pts. 1,5. 136-Hal Jordan-c/app. 3.00
137-Last issue; Superman app.; last panel cameo of Oliver Queen
2 4 6 9 12 15
#1,000,000 (11/98) 853rd Century x-over 3.00
Annual 1-6 ('88-'94, 68 pgs.)-1-No Grell scripts. 2-No Grell scripts; recaps origin Green Arrow, Speedy, Black Canary & others. 3-Bill Wray-a. 4-50th anniversary issue. 5-Batman, Eclipso app. 6-Bloodlines; Hook app. 4.00
Annual 7-('95, $3.95)-Year One story 4.00
NOTE: ***Aparo** a-0, 81-85, 86 (partial),87p, 88p, 91-95, 96i, 98-100p, 109p; c-81,98-100p. **Austin** c-96i. **Balent** layouts-86. **Burchett** c-91-95. **Campanella** a-100-108i, 110-113i; c-99i, 101-108i,110-113i. **Denys Cowan** a-39p, 41-43p, 47p, 48p, 60p; c-41-43. **Damaggio** a(p)-97p, 100-108p, 110-112p; c-97-99p, 101-108p, 110-113p. **Mike Grell** c-1-4, 10p, 11, 39, 40, 44, 45, 47-80, Annual 4, 5. **Nasser/Netzer** a-89, 96. **Sienkiewicz** a-109i. **Springer** a-67, 68. **Weeks** c-109.*

GREEN ARROW
DC Comics: Apr, 2001 - No. 75, Aug, 2007 ($2.50/$2.99)
1-Oliver Queen returns; Kevin Smith-s/Hester-a/Wagner-painted-c
2 4 6 9 13 16
1-2nd-4th printings 3.00
2-Batman cameo 1 2 3 4 5 7
2-2nd printing 3.00
3-5: 4-JLA app. 5.00
6-15: 7-Barry Allen & Hal Jordan app. 9,10-Stanley & his Monster app. 10-Oliver regains his soul. 12-Hawkman-c/app. 3.00
16-25: 16-Brad Meltzer-s begin; The Shade app. 18-Solomon Grundy-c/app. 19-JLA app. 22-Beatty-s; Count Vertigo app. 23-25-Green Lantern app.; Raab-s/Adlard-a 3.00
26-49: 26-Winick-s begin. 35-37-Riddler app. 43-Mia learns she's HIV+. 45-Mia becomes the new Speedy. 46-Teen Titans app. 49-The Outsiders app. 3.00
50-($3.50) Green Arrow's team and the Outsiders vs. The Riddler and Drakon 4.00
51-59: 51-Anarky app. 52-Zatanna-c/app. 55-59-Dr. Light app. 3.00
60-74: 60-One Year Later starts. 62-Begin $2.99-c; Deathstroke app. 69-Batman app. 3.00
75-($3.50) Ollie proposes to Dinah (see Black Canary mini-series); JLA app. 4.00
...: City Walls SC (2005, $17.95) r/#32, 34-39 18.00
...: Crawling Through the Wreckage SC (2007, $12.99) r/#60-65 13.00
...: Heading Into the Light SC (2006, $12.99) r/#52,54-59 13.00
...: Moving Targets SC (2006, $17.99) r/#40-50 18.00
...: Quiver HC (2002, $24.95) r/#1-10; Smith intro. 25.00
...: Quiver SC (2003, $17.95) r/#1-10; Smith intro. 18.00
...: Road to Jericho SC (2007, $17.99) r/#66-75 18.00
...Secret Files & Origins 1-(12/02, $4.95) Origin stories & profiles; Wagner-c 5.00
...: Sounds of Violence HC (2003, $19.95) r/#11-15; Hester intro. & sketch pages 20.00
...: Sounds of Violence SC (2003, $12.95) r/#11-15; Hester intro. & sketch pages 13.00
...: Straight Shooter SC (2004, $12.95) r/#26-31 13.00
...: The Archer's Quest HC (2003, $19.95) r/#16-21; pitch, script and sketch pages 20.00
...: The Archer's Quest SC (2004, $14.95) r/#16-21; pitch, script and sketch pages 15.00

GREEN ARROW (Brightest Day)
DC Comics: Aug, 2010 - Present ($3.99/$2.99)
1-Oliver Queen in the Star City forest; Green Lantern app.; Neves-a/Cascioli-c 4.00
1-Variant-c by Van Sciver 8.00
2-9-($2.99) 2-Green Lantern app. 7-Mayhew-a. 8,9-The Demon app. 3.00

GREEN ARROW/BLACK CANARY (Titled Green Arrow for #30-32)
DC Comics: Dec, 2007 - No. 32, Jun, 2010 ($3.50/$2.99)
1-($3.50) Connor Hawke & Black Canary; follows Wedding Special; Winick-s/Chang-a 4.00
2-21-($2.99) 3-Two covers; Connor shot. 5-Dinah & Ollie's real wedding 3.00
22-30-($3.99) Back-up stories begin. 28-Origin of Cupid. 30-Blackest Night 4.00
30-Variant cover by Mike Grell 8.00
31-32-($2.99) Rise and Fall; Dallocchio-a 3.00
...: A League of Their Own TPB (2009, $17.99) r/#11-14 & G.A. Secret Files & Origins 18.00
...: Big Game TPB (2010, $19.99) r/#21-26 20.00
...: Enemies List TPB (2009, $17.99) r/#15-20 18.00
...: Family Business TPB (2008, $17.99) r/#5-10 18.00
...: Five Stages TPB (2010, $17.99) r/#27-30 18.00
...: Road To The Altar TPB (2008, $17.99) r/proposal pages from Green Arrow #75, Birds of Prey #109, Black Canary #1-4 and Black Canary Wedding Planner #1 18.00

Green Hornet (2010 series) #3 © Green Hornet Inc.

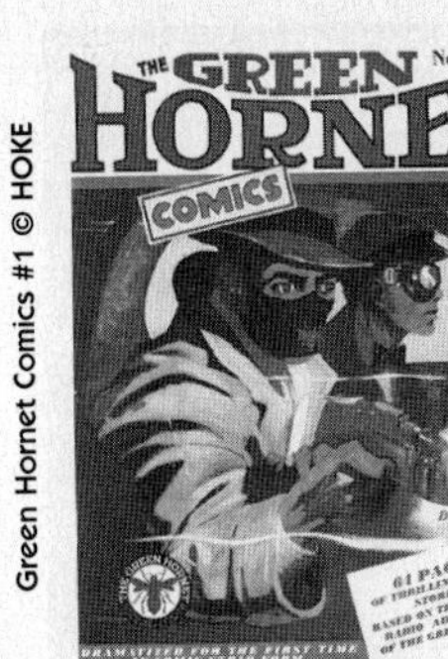
Green Hornet Comics #1 © HOKE

Green Lama #6 © Spark

GD VG FN VF VF/NM NM-
2.0 4.0 6.0 8.0 9.0 9.2

GD VG FN VF VF/NM NM-
2.0 4.0 6.0 8.0 9.0 9.2

...: The Wedding Album HC (2008, $19.99, dustjacket) r/#1-5 & Wedding Special #1 20.00
...: The Wedding Album SC (2009, $17.99) r/#1-5 & Wedding Special #1 18.00
... Wedding Special 1 (11/07, $3.99) Winick-s/Conner-a/c; Dinah & Ollie's "wedding" 4.00
... Wedding Special 1 (11/07, $3.99) 2nd printing with Ryan Sook variant-c 4.00

GREEN ARROW: THE LONG BOW HUNTERS
DC Comics: Aug, 1987 - No. 3, Oct, 1987 ($2.95, limited series, mature)

1-Grell-c/a in all 6.00
1,2-2nd printings 3.00
2,3 4.00
Trade paperback (1989, $12.95)-r/#1-3 13.00

GREEN ARROW: THE WONDER YEAR
DC Comics: Feb, 1993 - No. 4, May, 1993 ($1.75, limited series)

1-4: Mike Grell-a(p)/scripts & Gray Morrow-a(i) 3.00

GREEN ARROW: YEAR ONE
DC Comics: Early Sept, 2007 - No. 6, Late Nov, 2007 ($2.99, bi-weekly limited series)

1-6-Origin re-told; Diggle-s/Jock-a 3.00
HC (2008, $24.99) r/#1-6; intro. by Brian K. Vaughan; script and sketch pages 25.00
SC (2009, $14.99) r/#1-6; intro. by Brian K. Vaughan; script and sketch pages 15.00

GREEN BERET, THE (See Tales of...)

GREEN GIANT COMICS (Also see Colossus Comics)
Pelican Publ. (Funnies, Inc.): 1940 (No price on cover; distributed in New York City only)

1-Dr. Nerod, Green Giant, Black Arrow, Mundoo & Master Mystic app.; origin Colossus (Rare)
1150 2300 3450 8600 15,800 23,000

NOTE: *The idea for this book came from George Kapitan. Printed by Moreau Publ. of Orange, N.J. as an experiment to see if they could profitably use the idle time of their 40-page Hoe color press. The experiment failed due to the difficulty of obtaining good quality color registration and Mr. Moreau believes the book never reached the stands. The book has no price or date which lends credence to this. Contains five pages reprinted from Motion Picture Funnies Weekly.*

GREEN GOBLIN
Marvel Comics: Oct, 1995 - No. 13, Oct, 1996 ($2.95/$1.95)

1-($2.95)-Scott McDaniel-c/a begins, ends #7; foil-c 4.00
2-13: 2-Begin $1.95-c. 4-Hobgoblin-c/app; Thing app. 6-Daredevil-c/app. 8-Robertson-a; McDaniel-c. 12,13-Onslaught x-over. 13-Green Goblin quits; Spider-Man app. 3.00

GREENHAVEN
Aircel Publishing: 1988 - No. 3, 1988 ($2.00, limited series, 28 pgs.)

1-3 3.00

GREEN HORNET, THE (TV)
Dell Publishing Co./Gold Key: Sept, 1953; Feb, 1967 - No. 3, Aug, 1967

Four Color 496-Painted-c. 23 46 69 168 334 500
1-Bruce Lee photo-c and back-c pin-up 17 34 51 122 249 375
2,3-Bruce Lee photo-c 12 24 36 82 154 225

GREEN HORNET, THE (Also see Kato of the... & Tales of the...)
Now Comics: Nov, 1989 - No. 14, Feb, 1991 ($1.75)
V2#1, Sept, 1991 - V2#40, Jan, 1995 ($1.95)

1 ($2.95, double-size)-Steranko painted-c; G.A. Green Hornet 6.00
1,2: 1-2nd printing ('90, $3.95)-New Butler-c 4.00
3-14: 5-Death of original ('30s) Green Hornet. 6-Dave Dorman painted-c. 11-Snyder-c 4.00
V2#1-11,13-21,24-26,28-30,32-37: 1-Butler painted-c. 9-Mayerik-c 3.00
12-($2.50)-Color Green Hornet button polybagged inside 4.00
22,23-($2.95)-Bagged w/color hologravure card 4.00
27-($2.95)-Newsstand ed. polybagged w/multi-dimensional card (1993 Anniversary Special on cover), 27-($2.95)-Direct Sale ed. polybagged w/multi-dimensional card; cover variations 4.00
31,38: 31-($2.50)-Polybagged w/trading card 4.00
39,40-Low print run 6.00
1-($2.50)-Polybagged w/button (same as #12) 4.00
2,3-($1.95)-Same as #13 & 14 3.00
Annual 1 (12/92, $2.50), Annual 1994 (10/94, $2.95) 4.00

GREEN HORNET
Dynamite Entertainment: 2010 - Present ($3.99)

1-Kevin Smith-s/Jonathan Lau-a; multiple covers by Alex Ross, Cassaday, Campbell and Segovia 4.00
2-15-Multiple covers by Ross and others on each. 11-Hester-s begins 4.00
Annual 1 (2010, $5.99) Hester-s/Netzer & Rafael-a 6.00
... FCBD Edition; 5 previews of various new Green Hornet series; Cassaday-c 2.50

GREEN HORNET: AFTERMATH
Dynamite Entertainment: 2011 - Present ($1.99)

1-Nitz-s/Raynor-a; Green Hornet & Kato after the 2011 movie 2.00

GREEN HORNET: BLOOD TIES
Dynamite Entertainment: 2010 - No. 4, 2011 ($3.99)

1-4-Ande Parks-s/Johnny Desjardins-a; original Green Hornet & Kato 4.00

GREEN HORNET COMICS (...Racket Buster #44) (Radio, movies)
Helnit Publ. Co.(Holyoke) No. 1-6/Family Comics(Harvey) No. 7-on:
Dec, 1940 - No. 47, Sept, 1949 (See All New #13,14)(Early issues: 68 pgs.)

1-1st app. Green Hornet & Kato; origin of Green Hornet on inside front-c; intro the Black Beauty (Green Hornet's car); painted-c 568 1136 1704 4146 7323 10,500
2-Early issues based on radio adventures 232 464 696 1485 2543 3600
3 161 322 483 1030 1765 2500
4-6: 6-(8/41) 129 258 387 826 1413 2000
7 (6/42)-Origin The Zebra & begins; Robin Hood, Spirit of '76, Blonde Bomber & Mighty Midgets begin; new logo 107 214 321 680 1165 1650
8,10 92 184 276 584 1005 1425
9-Kirby-c 116 232 348 742 1271 1800
11,12-Mr. Q in both 87 174 261 553 952 1350
13-1st Nazi-c; shows Hitler poster on-c 103 206 309 659 1130 1600
14-19 71 142 213 454 777 1100
20-Classic-c 82 164 246 528 902 1275
21-23 53 106 159 334 567 800
24-Sci-Fi-c 55 110 165 352 601 850
25-30 47 94 141 296 498 700
31-The Man in Black Called Fate begins (11-12/45, early app.)
50 100 150 315 533 750
32-36 36 72 108 216 351 485
37,38: Shock Gibson app. by Powell. 37-S&K Kid Adonis reprinted from Stuntman #3. 38-Kid Adonis app. 36 72 108 211 343 475
39-Stuntman story by S&K 39 78 117 236 388 540
40-47: 42-47-Kerry Drake in all. 45-Boy Explorers on-c only. 46- "Case of the Marijuana Racket" cover/story; Kerry Drake app. 27 51 81 158 259 360

NOTE: ***Fuje** a-23, 24, 26. **Henkle** c-7-9. **Kubert** a-20, 30. **Powell** a-7-10, 12, 14, 16-21, 30, 31(2), 32(3), 33, 34(3), 35, 36, 37(2), 38. **Robinson** a-27. **Schomburg** c-15, 17-23. Kirbyish c-7, 15. Bondage c-8, 14, 18, 26, 36.*

GREEN HORNET: DARK TOMORROW
Now Comics: Jun, 1993 - No. 3, Aug, 1993 ($2.50, limited series)

1-3: Future Green Hornet 3.00

GREEN HORNET: GOLDEN AGE RE-MASTERED
Dynamite Entertainment: 2010 - No. 8, 2011 ($3.99)

1-8-Re-colored reprints of 1940's Green Hornet Comics; new Rubenstein-c 4.00

GREEN HORNET: PARALLEL LIVES
Dynamite Entertainment: 2010 - No. 5, 2010 ($3.99, limited series)

1-5-Jai Nitz-s/Nigel Raynor-a; semi-prequel to the 2011 movie; Kato's origin 4.00

GREEN HORNET: SOLITARY SENTINEL, THE
Now Comics: Dec, 1992 - No. 3, 1993 ($2.50, limited series)

1-3 3.00

GREEN HORNET STRIKES!
Dynamite Entertainment: 2010 - No. 10 ($3.99, limited series)

1-7-Matthews-s/Padilla-a/Cassaday-c; future Green Hornet 4.00

GREEN HORNET: YEAR ONE
Dynamite Entertainment: 2010 - Present ($3.99, limited series)

1-9-Matt Wagner-s/Aaron Campbell-a; Cassaday-c; 1940s' Green Hornet & Kato 4.00

GREEN JET COMICS, THE (See Comic Books, Series 1 in the Promotional Comics section)

GREEN LAMA (Also see Comic Books, Series 1, Daring Adventures #17 & Prize Comics #7)
Spark Publications/Prize No. 7 on: Dec, 1944 - No. 8, Mar, 1946

1-Intro. Lt. Hercules & The Boy Champions; Mac Raboy-c/a #1-8
116 232 348 742 1271 1800
2-Lt. Hercules borrows the Human Torch's powers for one panel
62 124 186 394 680 965
3-5,8: 4-Dick Tracy take-off in Lt. Hercules story by H. L. Gold (science fiction writer). 5-Lt. Hercules story; Little Orphan Annie, Smilin' Jack & Snuffy Smith take-off (5/45) 50 100 150 315 533 750
6-Classic Raboy swastika-c 53 106 159 334 567 800
7-X-mas-c; Raboy craft tint-c/a (note: a small quantity of NM copies surfaced)
34 68 102 199 325 450
... Archives Featuring the Art of Mac Raboy Vol. 1 HC (Dark Horse Books, 4/08, $49.95) r/#1-4 including back-up features; foreward by Chuck Rozanski 50.00
... Archives Featuring the Art of Mac Raboy Vol. 2 HC (Dark Horse Books, 1/09, $49.95) r/#5-8; foreward by Chuck Rozanski 50.00

NOTE: ***Robinson** a-3-5, 8. Roussos a-8. Formerly a pulp hero who began in 1940.*

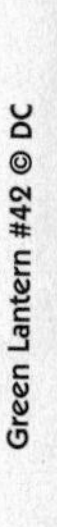
Green Lantern #1 © DC

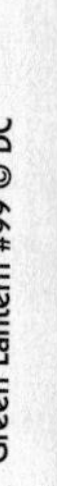
Green Lantern #42 © DC

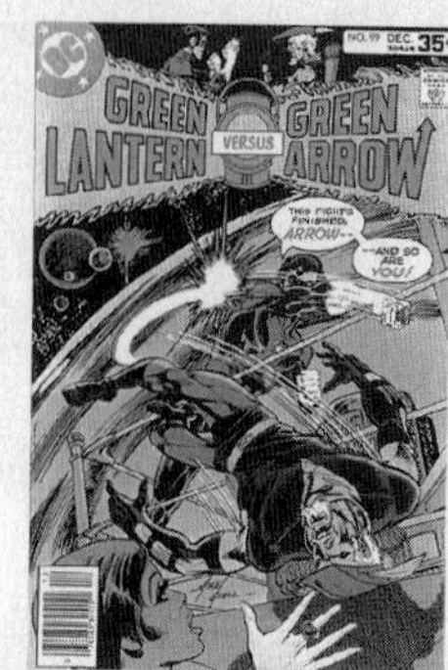

Green Lantern #99 © DC

	GD 2.0	VG 4.0	FN 6.0	VF 8.0	VF/NM 9.0	NM- 9.2

GREEN LANTERN (1st Series) (See All-American, All Flash Quarterly, All Star Comics, The Big All-American & Comic Cavalcade)
National Periodical Publications/All-American: Fall, 1941 - No. 38, May-June, 1949 (#1-18 are quarterly)

	GD 2.0	VG 4.0	FN 6.0	VF 8.0	VF/NM 9.0	NM- 9.2
1-Origin retold; classic Purcell-c	3000	6000	9000	22,000	38,000	64,000
2-1st book-length story	676	1352	2028	4935	8718	12,500
3-Classic German war-c by Mart Nodell	568	1136	1704	4146	7323	10,500
4-Green Lantern & Doiby Dickles join the Army	400	800	1200	2800	4900	7000
5	300	600	900	2070	3635	5200
6,8: 8-Hop Harrigan begins; classic-c	258	516	774	1651	2826	4000
7-Classic robot-c.	290	580	870	1856	3178	4500
9,10: 10-Origin/1st app. Vandal Savage	226	452	678	1446	2473	3500
11-15: 12-Origin/1st app. Gambler	161	322	483	1030	1765	2500
16-Classic jungle-c (scarce in high grade)	168	336	504	1075	1838	2600
17,19,20	135	270	405	864	1482	2100
18-Christmas-c	184	368	552	1168	2009	2850
21-26,28	126	252	378	806	1378	1950
27-Origin/1st app. Sky Pirate	142	284	426	909	1555	2200
29-All Harlequin issue; classic Harlequin-c	161	322	483	1030	1765	2500
30-Origin/1st app. Streak the Wonder Dog by Toth (2-3/48) (Rare)	300	600	900	2010	3505	5000
31-35: 35-Kubert-c. 35-38-New logo	113	226	339	718	1234	1750
36-38: 37-Sargon the Sorcerer app.	129	258	387	826	1413	2000

NOTE: *Book-length stories #2-7.* ***Mayer/Moldoff*** *c-9.* ***Mayer/Purcell*** *c-8.* ***Purcell*** *c-1.* ***Mart Nodell*** *c-2, 3, 7.* ***Paul Reinman*** *c-11, 12, 15-22.* ***Toth*** *a-28, 30, 31, 34-38; c-28, 30, 34p, 36-38p. Cover to #8 says Fall while the indicia says Summer Issue. Streak the Wonder Dog c-30 (w/Green Lantern), 34, 36, 38.*

GREEN LANTERN (See Action Comics Weekly, Adventure Comics, Brave & the Bold, Day of Judgment, DC Special, DC Special Series, Flash, Guy Gardner, Guy Gardner Reborn, JLA, JSA, Justice League of America, Parallax: Emerald Night, Showcase, Showcase '93 #12 & Tales of The...Corps)

GREEN LANTERN (2nd Series)(Green Lantern Corps #206 on) (See Showcase #22-24)
National Periodical Publ./DC Comics: Jul/Aug. 1960 - No. 89, Apr/May 1972; No. 90, Aug/Sept. 1976 - No. 205, Oct, 1986

	GD 2.0	VG 4.0	FN 6.0	VF 8.0	VF/NM 9.0	NM- 9.2
1-(7-8/60)-Origin retold; Gil Kane-c/a continues; 1st app. Guardians of the Universe	450	900	1350	4000	8250	12,500
2-1st Pieface	85	170	255	723	1462	2200
3-Contains readers poll	48	96	144	392	796	1200
4,5: 5-Origin/1st app. Hector Hammond	40	80	120	320	635	950
6-Intro Tomar-Re the alien G.L.	37	74	111	286	568	850
7-Origin/1st app. Sinestro (7-8/61)	48	96	144	392	796	1200
8-1st 5700 A.D. story; grey tone-c	34	68	102	262	519	775
9,10: 9-1st Jordan Brothers; last 10¢ issue	28	56	84	215	433	650
11,12	21	42	63	150	300	450
13-Flash x-over	33	66	99	254	502	750
14,15,17-20: 14-Origin/1st app. Sonar. 20-Flash x-over	17	34	51	122	249	375
16-Origin & 1st app. (Silver Age) Star Sapphire	23	46	69	168	334	500
21,22,24-28,30: 21-Origin & 1st app. Dr. Polaris. 24-Origin & 1st app. Shark	13	26	39	92	179	265
23-1st Tattooed Man	14	28	42	96	191	285
29-JLA cameo; 1st Blackhand	14	28	42	99	200	300
31-39: 37-1st app. Evil Star (villain)	12	24	36	82	154	225
40-Origin of Infinite Earths (10/65); 2nd solo G.A. Green Lantern in Silver Age (see Showcase #55); origin The Guardians; Doiby Dickles app.	47	94	141	376	763	1150
41-44,46-50: 42-Zatanna x-over. 43-Flash x-over	10	20	30	70	125	180
45-2nd S.A. app. G.A. Green Lantern in title (6/66)	14	28	42	99	200	300
51,53-58	9	18	27	60	100	140
52-G.A. Green Lantern x-over; Sinestro app.	10	20	30	71	128	185
59-1st app. Guy Gardner (3/68)	16	32	48	114	232	350
60,62-69: 69-Wood inks; last 12¢ issue	7	14	21	45	73	100
61-G.A. Green Lantern x-over	8	16	24	52	86	120
70-75	6	12	18	39	62	85
76-(4/70)-Begin Green Lantern/Green Arrow series (by Neal Adams #76-89) ends #122 (see Flash #217 for 2nd series)	96	192	288	816	1658	2500
77	12	24	36	86	161	235
78-80	11	22	33	76	141	200
81-84: 82-Wrightson-i(1 pg.). 83-G.L. reveals i.d. to Carol Ferris. 84-N. Adams/Wrightson-a (22 pgs.); last 15¢-c; partial photo-c	10	20	30	67	116	165
85,86-(52 pgs.)-Anti-drug issues. 86-G.A. Green Lantern-r; Toth-a	12	24	36	82	154	225
87-(52 pgs.): 2nd app. Guy Gardner (cameo); 1st app. John Stewart (12-1/71-72) (becomes 3rd Green Lantern in #182)	10	20	30	69	122	175
88-(2-3/72, 52 pgs.)-Unpubbed G.A. Green Lantern story; Green Lantern-r/Showcase #23. N. Adams-c/a (1 pg.)	7	14	21	49	80	110
89-(4-5/72, 52 pgs.)-G.A. Green Lantern-r; Green Lantern & Green Arrow move to Flash #217 (2nd team-up series)	9	18	27	63	107	150
90 (8-9/76)-Begin 3rd Green Lantern/Green Arrow team-up series; Mike Grell-c/a begins, ends #111	3	6	9	16	23	30
91-99	2	4	6	10	14	18
100-(1/78, Giant)-1st app. Air Wave II	3	6	9	16	22	28
101-107,111,113-115,117-119: 107-1st Tales of the G.L. Corps story	2	4	6	8	10	12
108-110-(44 pgs)-G.A. Green Lantern back-ups in each. 111-Origin retold; G.A. Green Lantern app.	2	4	6	9	12	15
112-G.A. Green Lantern origin retold	2	4	6	11	16	20
116-1st app. Guy Gardner as a G.L. (5/79)	4	8	12	28	44	60
116-Whitman variant; issue # on cover	5	10	15	35	55	75
117-119,121-(Whitman variants; low print run; none have issue # on cover)	2	4	6	10	14	18
120-122,124-150: 122-Last Green Lantern/Green Arrow team-up. 130-132-Tales of the G.L. Corps. 132-Adam Strange series begins, ends147. 136,137-1st app. Citadel; Space Ranger app. 141-1st app. Omega Men (6/81). 142,143-Omega Men app.;Perez-c. 144-Omega Men cameo. 148-Tales of the G.L. Corps begins, ends #173. 150-Anniversary issue, 52 pgs.; no G.L. Corps	1	2	3	5	7	9
123-Green Lantern back to solo action; 2nd app. Guy Gardner as Green Lantern	2	4	6	9	12	15
151-180,183,184,186,187: 159-Origin Evil Star. 160,161-Omega Men app.						6.00
181,182,185,188,191: 181-Hal Jordan resigns as G.L. 182-John Stewart becomes new G.L.; origin recap of Hal Jordan as G.L. 185-Origin new G.L. (John Stewart).188-I.D. revealed; Alan Moore back-up scripts. 191-Re-intro Star Sapphire (cameo)	1	2	3	5	6	8
189,190,193,196-199,201-205: 194,198-Crisis x-over. 199-Hal Jordan returns as a member of G.L. Corps (3 G.L.s now). 201-Green Lantern Corps begins (is cover title, says premiere issue); intro. Kilowog						5.00
192-Re-intro & origin of Star Sapphire (1st full app.)	2	4	6	9	13	16
194-Hal Jordan/Guy Gardner battle; Guardians choose Guy Gardner to become new Green Lantern	1	2	3	5	6	8
195-Guy Gardner becomes Green Lantern; Crisis on Infinite Earths x-over	2	4	6	9	13	16
200-Double-size						6.00
Annual 1 (Listed as Tales Of The Green Lantern Corps Annual 1)						
Annual 2,3 (See Green Lantern Corps Annual #2,3)						5.00
Special 1 (1988), 2 (1989)-(Both $1.50, 52 pgs.)						4.00
... Chronicles TPB (2009, $14.99) r/Showcase #22-24 & Green Lantern #1-3						15.00
... Chronicles Vol. 2 TPB (2009, $14.99) r/Green Lantern #4-9						15.00
... Chronicles Vol. 3 TPB (2010, $14.99) r/Green Lantern #10-14 and Flash #131						15.00

NOTE: ***N. Adams*** *a-76, 77-87p, 89; c-63, 76-89.* ***M. Anderson*** *a-137i.* ***Austin*** *a-93i, 94i, 171i.* ***Chaykin*** *c-196.* ***Greene*** *a-39-49i, 58-63i; c-54-58i.* ***Grell*** *a-90-100, 106, 108-111; c-90-106, 108-112.* ***Heck*** *a-120-122p.* ***Infantino*** *a-137p, 145-147p, 151, 152p.* ***Gil Kane*** *a-1-49p, 50-57, 58-61p, 68-75p, 85p(r), 87p(r), 88p(r), 156, 177, 184p; c-1-52, 54-61p, 67-75, 123, 154, 156, 165-171, 177, 184.* ***Newton*** *a-148p, 149p, 181.* ***Perez*** *c-132p, 141-144.* ***Sekowsky*** *a-65p, 170p.* ***Simonson*** *c-200.* ***Sparling*** *a-63p.* ***Starlin*** *c-129, 133.* ***Staton*** *a-117p, 123-127p, 128, 129-131p, 132-139, 140p, 141-146, 147p, 148-150, 151-155p; c-107p, 117p, 135(i), 136p, 145p, 146, 147, 148-152p, 155p.* ***Toth*** *a-86r, 171p.* ***Tuska*** *a-166-168p, 170p.*

GREEN LANTERN (3rd Series)
DC Comics: June, 1990 - No. 181, Nov, 2004 ($1.00/$1.25/$1.50/$1.75/$1.95/$1.99/$2.25)

	NM- 9.2
1-Hal Jordan, John Stewart & Guy Gardner return; Batman & JLA app.	6.00
2-18,20-26: 9-12-Guy Gardner solo story. 13-(52 pgs.). 18-Guy Gardner solo story. 25-($1.75, 52 pgs.)-Hal Jordan/Guy Gardner battle	4.00
19-($1.75, 52 pgs.)-50th anniversary issue; Mart Nodell (original G.A. artist) part-p on G.A. Green Lantern; G. Kane-c	5.00
27-45,47: 30,31-Gorilla Grodd-c/story(see Flash #69). 38,39-Adam Strange-c/story. 42-Deathstroke-c/s. 47-Green Arrow x-over	4.00
46,48,49,50: 46-Superman app. cont'd in Superman #82. 48-Emerald Twilight part 1. 50-($2.95, 52 pgs.)-Glow-in-the-dark-c	6.00
0, 51-62: 51-1st app. New Green Lantern (Kyle Rayner) with new costume. 53-Superman-c/story. 55-(9/94)-Zero Hour. 0-(10/94). 56-(11/94)	4.00
63,64-Kyle Rayner vs. Hal Jordan.	4.00
65-80,82-92: 63-Begin $1.75-c. 65-New Titans app. 66,67-Flash app. 71-Batman & Robin app. 72-Shazam!-c/app. 73-Wonder Woman-c/app. 73-75-Adam Strange app. 76,77-Green Arrow x-over. 80-Final Night. 87-JLA app. 91-Genesis x-over. 92-Green Arrow x-over	3.00
81-(Regular Ed.)-Memorial for Hal Jordan (Parallax); most DC heroes app.	5.00
81-($3.95, Deluxe Edition)-Embossed prism-c	6.00
93-99: 93-Begin $1.95-c; Deadman app. 94-Superboy app. 95-Starlin-a(p). 98,99-Legion of Super-Heroes-c/app.	3.00
100-($2.95) Two covers (Jordan & Rayner); vs. Sinestro	6.00
101-106: 101-106-Hal Jordan-c/app. 103-JLA-c/app. 104-Green Arrow app. 105,106-Parallax app.	3.00
107-126: 107-Jade becomes a Green Lantern. 119-Hal Jordan/Spectre app. 125-JLA app.	3.00
127-149: 127-Begin $2.25-c. 129-Winick-s begin. 134-136-JLA-c/app. 143-Joker: Last Laugh; Lee-c. 145-Kyle becomes The Ion. 149-Superman-c/app.	3.00

Green Lantern (3rd series) #156 © DC

Green Lantern (4th series) #29 Special Edition © DC

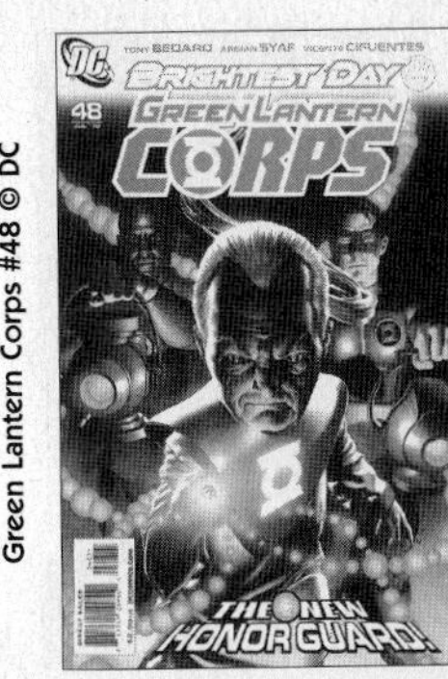

Green Lantern Corps #48 © DC

	GD	VG	FN	VF	VF/NM	NM-
	2.0	4.0	6.0	8.0	9.0	9.2

150-($3.50) Jim Lee-c; Kyle becomes Green Lantern again; new costume 4.00
151-181: 151-155-Jim Lee-c: 154-Terry attacked. 155-Spectre-c/app. 162-164-Crossover with Green Arrow #23-25. 165-Raab-s begin. 169-Kilowog returns 3.00
#1,000,000 (11/98) 853rd Century x-over; Hitch & Neary-a/c 3.00
Annual 1-3: ('92-'94, 68 pgs.)-1-Eclipso app. 2 -Intro Nightblade. 3-Elseworlds story 4.00
Annual 4 (1995, $3.50)-Year One story 4.00
Annual 5,7,8 ('96, '98, '99, $2.95): 5-Legends of the Dead Earth. 7-Ghosts; Wrightson-c. 8-JLApe; Art Adams-c 4.00
Annual 6 (1997, $3.95)-Pulp Heroes story 5.00
Annual 9 (2000, $3.50) Planet DC 4.00
...80 Page Giant (12/98, $4.95) Stories by various 5.00
...80 Page Giant 2 (6/99, $4.95) Team-ups 5.00
...80 Page Giant 3 (8/00, $5.95) Darkseid vs. the GL Corps 6.00
...: 1001 Emerald Nights (2001, $6.95) Elseworlds; Guay-a/c; LaBan-s 7.00
...3-D #1 (12/98, $3.95) Jeanty-a 4.00
...: A New Dawn TPB (1998, $9.95)-r/#50-55 10.00
...: Baptism of Fire TPB (1999, $12.95)-r/#59,66,67,70-75 13.00
...: Brother's Keeper (2003, $12.95)-r/#151-155; Green Lantern Secret Files #3 13.00
...: Emerald Allies TPB (2000, $14.95)-r/GL/GA team-ups 15.00
...: Emerald Knights TPB (1998, $12.95)-r/Hal Jordan's return 13.00
...: Emerald Twilight nn (1994, $5.95)-r/#48-50 6.00
...: Emerald Twilight/New Dawn TPB (2003, $19.95)-r/#48-55 20.00
...: Ganthet's Tale nn (1992, $5.95, 68 pgs.)-Silver foil logo; Niven scripts; Byrne-c/a 6.00
.../Green Arrow Vol. 1 (2004, $12.95) -r/GL #76-82; intro. by O'Neil 13.00
.../Green Arrow Vol. 2 (2004, $12.95) -r/GL #83-87,89 & Flash #217-219, 226; cover gallery with 1983-84 GL/GA covers #1-7; intro. by Giordano 13.00
.../Green Arrow Collection, Vol. 2-r/GL #84-87,89 & Flash #217-219 & GL/GA #5-7 by O'Neil/Adams/Wrightson 13.00
...: New Journey, Old Path TPB (2001, $12.95)-r/#129-136 13.00
... : Our Worlds at War (8/01, $2.95) Jae Lee-c; prelude to x-over 3.00
...: Passing The Torch (2004, $12.95, TPB) r/#156,158-161 & GL Secret Files #2 13.00
...Plus 1 (12/1996, $2.95)-The Ray & Polaris-c/app. 3.00
...Secret Files 1-3 (7/98-7/02, $4.95)1-Origin stories & profiles. 2-Grell-c 5.00
.../Superman: Legend of the Green Flame (2000, $5.95) 1988 unpub. Neil Gaiman story of Hal Jordan with new art by various; Frank Miller-c 6.00
...: The Power of Ion (2003, $14.95, TPB) r/#142-150 50.00
...The Road Back nn (1992, $8.95)-r/1-8 w/covers 9.00
...: Traitor TPB (2001, $12.95) r/Legends of the DCU #20,21,28,29,37,38 13.00
...: Willworld (2001, $24.95, HC) Seth Fisher-a/J.M. DeMatteis-s; Hal Jordan 25.00
...: Willworld (2003, $17.95, SC) Seth Fisher-a/J.M. DeMatteis-s; Hal Jordan 18.00
NOTE: *Staton a(p)-9-12; c-9-12.*

GREEN LANTERN (See Tangent Comics/ Green Lantern)

GREEN LANTERN (4th Series) (Follows Hal Jordan's return in Green Lantern: Rebirth)
DC Comics: July, 2005 - Present ($3.50/$2.99)

1-($3.50) Two covers by Pacheco and Ross; Johns-s/Van Sciver and Pacheco-a 5.00
2-20-($2.99) 2-4-Manhunters app. 6-Bianchi-a. 7,8-Green Arrow app. 8-Bianchi-c. 9-Batman app.; two covers by Bianchi and Van Sciver. 10,11-Reis-a. 17-19-Star Sapphire returns. 18-Acuna-a; Sinestro Corps back-ups begin 3.00
8-Variant-c by Neal Adams 8.00
21-Sinestro Corps War pt. 2 5.00
21-2nd printing with variant green hued background-c 3.00
22-24: 22-Sinestro Corps War pt. 4; green hued-c. 23-Part 6. 24-Part 8 4.00
22,23-2nd printings. 22-Yellow hued-c. 23-B&W Hal Jordan with colored rings 3.00
25-($4.99) Sinestro Corps War conclusion; Ivan Reis-c 6.00
25-($4.99) Variant cover by Gary Frank; Sinestro Corps War conclusion 8.00
26-43: 26-Alpha Lanterns. 29-35-Childhood & origin re-told; Sinestro app. 41-Origin Larfleeze. 43-Prologue to Blackest Night, origin of Black Hand; Mahnke-a 3.00
29-Special Edition (6/10, $1.00) reprints #29 with "What's Next?" logo on cover 1.00
29-Special Edition (2010 San Diego Comic-Con giveaway) reprints #29 with new Van Sciver cover and Geoff Johns intro on inside front cover 3.00
39-43-Variant covers: 39,40-Migliari. 41-42-Barrows 12.00
44-49,51,52-Blackest Night. 44-Flash app. 46-Sinestro vs. Mongul. 47-Black Lantern Abin Sur. 49-Art by Benes & Ordway; Atom and Mera app. 51-Nekron app. 3.00
44-49,51-Variant covers: 44-Tan. 45-Manapul. 46. Andy Kubert. 47-Benes. 48-Morales. 49-Migliari. 51-Horn. 52-Shane Davis 8.00
50-($3.99)-Black Lantern Spectre & Parallax app.; Mahnke-a/c 4.00
50-Variant-c by Jim Lee 12.00
53-64: 53-62-Brightest Day. 54,55-Lobo app. 58-60-Flash app. 60-Krona returns 3.00
FCBD 2011 Green Lantern Flashpoint Special Edition (6/11, giveaway) r/#30 and previews Flashpoint x-over; Andy Kubert-a 2.00
...: Larfleeze Christmas Special 1 (2/11, $3.99) Johns-s/Booth-a/Ha-c 4.00
.../Plastic Man: Weapons of Mass Deception (2/11, $4.99) Brent Anderson-a 5.00
...Secret Files and Origins 2005 (6/05, $4.99) Johns-s/Cooke & Van Sciver-a; profiles with art by various incl. Chaykin, Gibbons, Gleason, Igle; Pacheco-c 5.00
.../Sinestro Corps: Secret Files 1 (2/08, $4.99) Profiles of Green Lanterns and Corps info 5.00
...: Agent Orange HC (2009, $19.99) r/#38-42 & Blackest Night #0; sketch art 20.00
...: Agent Orange SC (2010, $14.99) r/#38-42 & Blackest Night #0; sketch art 15.00
Blackest Night: Green Lantern HC (2010, $24.99) r/#43-52; variant covers; sketch art 25.00
...: In Brightest Day SC (2008, $19.99) r/stories selected by Geoff Johns w/commentary 20.00
...: No Fear HC (2006, $24.99) r/#1-6 & Secret Files and Origins 25.00
...: No Fear SC (2008, $12.99) r/#1-6 & Secret Files and Origins 13.00
...: Rage of the Red Lanterns HC (2009, $24.99) r/#26-28,36-38 & Final Crisis: Rage... 25.00
...: Rage of the Red Lanterns SC (2010, $14.99) r/#26-28,36-38 & Final Crisis: Rage... 15.00
...: Revenge of the Green Lanterns HC (2006, $19.99) r/#7-13; variant cover gallery 20.00
...: Revenge of the Green Lanterns SC (2008, $12.99) r/#7-13; variant cover gallery 13.00
...: Secret Origin HC (2008, $19.99) r/#29-35 20.00
...: Secret Origin (New Edition) HC (2010, $19.99) r/#29-35; intro. by Ryan Reynolds 20.00
...: Secret Origin SC (2008, $14.99) r/#29-35 15.00
...: Secret Origin (New Edition) SC (2011, $14.99) r/#29-35; intro. by Ryan Reynolds; photo-c of Reynolds from movie; movie preview photo gallery 15.00
...: Tales of the Sinestro Corps HC (2008, $29.99, d.j.) r/back-up stories from #18-20, Tales of the Sinestro Corps series, Green Lantern: Sinestro Corps Special and Sinestro Corps: Secret Files 30.00
...: Tales of the Sinestro Corps SC (2009, $14.99) same contents as HC 15.00
...: The Sinestro Corps War Vol. 1 HC (2008, $24.99, d.j.) r/#21-23, Green Lantern Corps #14-15 and Green Lantern: Sinestro Corps Special 25.00
...: The Sinestro Corps War Vol. 1 SC (2009, $14.99) same contents as HC 15.00
...: The Sinestro Corps War Vol. 2 HC (2008, $24.99, d.j.) r/#24,25, Green Lantern Corps #16-19; interview with the creators and sketch art 25.00
... - Wanted: Hal Jordan HC (2007, $19.99) r/#14-20 without Sinestro Corps back-ups 20.00
... - Wanted: Hal Jordan SC (2008, $14.99) r/#14-20 without Sinestro Corps back-ups 15.00

GREEN LANTERN ANNUAL NO. 1, 1963
DC Comics: 1998 ($4.95, one-shot)

1-Reprints Golden Age & Silver Age stories in 1963-style 80 pg. Giant format; new Gil Kane sketch art 5.00

GREEN LANTERN: BRIGHTEST DAY; BLACKEST NIGHT
DC Comics: 2002 ($5.95, squarebound, one-shot)

nn-Alan Scott vs. Solomon Grundy in 1944; Snyder III-c/a; Seagle-s 1 2 3 5 6 8

GREEN LANTERN: CIRCLE OF FIRE
DC Comics: Early Oct, 2000 - No. 2, Late Oct, 2000 (limited series)

1-($4.95) Intro. other Green Lanterns 5.00
2-($3.75) 4.00
Green Lantern (x-overs)- .../Adam Strange; .../Atom; .../Firestorm; ... /Green Lantern, Winick-s; .../Power Girl (all $2.50-c) 3.00
TPB (2002, $17.95) r/#1,2 & x-overs 18.00

GREEN LANTERN CORPS, THE (Formerly Green Lantern; see Tales of...)
DC Comics: No. 206, Nov, 1986 - No. 224, May, 1988

206-223: 212-John Stewart marries Katma Tui. 220,221-Millennium tie-ins 4.00
224-Double-size last issue 5.00
...Corps Annual 2,3- (12/86,8/87) 1-Formerly Tales of ...Annual #1; Alan Moore scripts. 3-Indicia says Green Lantern Annual #3; Moore scripts; Byrne-a 4.00
NOTE: ***Austin** a-Annual 3i. **Gil Kane** a-223, 224p; c-223, 224, Annual 2. **Russell** a-Annual 3i. **Staton** a-207-213p, 217p, 221p, 222p, Annual 3; c-207-213p, 217p, 221p, 222p. **Willingham** a-213p, 219p, 220p, 218p, 219p, Annual 2, 3p; c-218p, 219p.*

GREEN LANTERN CORPS
DC Comics: Aug, 2006 - Present ($2.99)

1,14-19: 1-Gibbons-s. 14-19-Sinestro Corps War pts. 3,5,7,9,10, Epilogue 4.00
2-13: 2-6,10,11-Gibbons-s. 9-Darkseid app. 3.00
20-38: 20-Mongul app. 3.00
20-Second printing with sketch-c 3.00
34-38: 34-37-Variant covers by Migliari. 38-Fabry var-c 10.00
39-45-Blackest Night. 43-45-Red Lantern Guy Gardner 3.00
39-45-Variant covers: 39-Jusko. 40-Tucci. 41,42,44-Horn. 43-Ladronn. 45 Bolland 8.00
46,47-($3.99) 46-Blackest Night. 47-Brightest Day 4.00
48-58-($2.99) 48-Migliari-c; Ganthet joins the Corps. 49-52-Cyborg Superman app. 3.00
Blackest Night: Green Lantern Corps HC (2010, $24.99, d.j.) r/#39-47, cover gallery 25.00
...: Emerald Eclipse HC (2009, $24.99) r/#33-39; gallery of variant covers 25.00
...: Emerald Eclipse SC (2010, $14.99) r/#33-39; gallery of variant covers 15.00
...: Ring Quest TPB (2008, $14.99) r/#19,20,23-26 15.00
...: The Dark Side of Green TPB (2007, $12.99) r/#7-13 13.00
...: To Be a Lantern TPB (2007, $12.99) r/#1-6 13.00

GREEN LANTERN CORPS QUARTERLY
DC Comics: Summer, 1992 - No. 8, Spring, 1994 ($2.50/$2.95, 68 pgs.)

Green Lantern: Rebirth #1 © DC

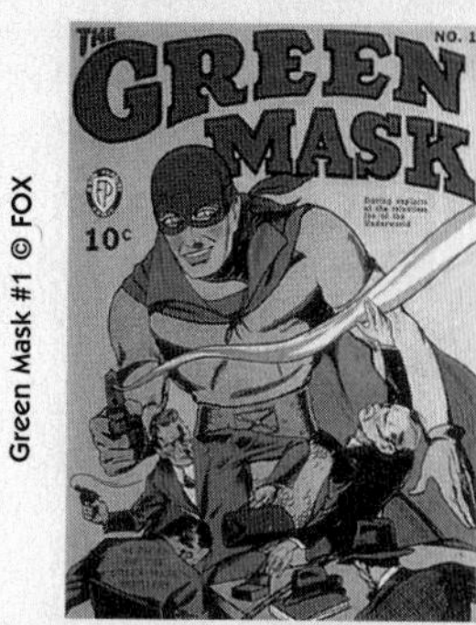

Green Mask #1 © FOX

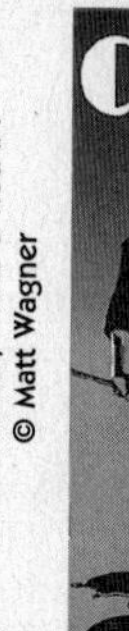
Grendel: Black, White & Red #4 © Matt Wagner

GD VG FN VF VF/NM NM-
2.0 4.0 6.0 8.0 9.0 9.2

1-G.A. Green Lantern story; Staton-a(p) 5.00
2-8: 2-G.A. G.L.-c/story; Austin-c(i); Gulacy-a(p). 3-G.A. G.L. story. 4-Austin-i. 7-Painted-c; Tim Vigil-a. 8-Lobo-c/s 4.00

GREEN LANTERN CORPS: RECHARGE
DC Comics: Nov, 2005 - No. 5, Mar, 2006 ($3.50/$2.99, limited series)
1-($3.50) Kyle Rayner, Guy Gardner & Kilowog app.; Gleason-a 4.00
2-5-($2.99) 3.00
TPB (2006, $12.99) r/series 13.00

GREEN LANTERN: DRAGON LORD
DC Comics: 2001 - No. 3, 2001 ($4.95, squarebound, limited series)
1-3: A G.L. in ancient China; Moench-s/Gulacy-c/a 5.00

GREEN LANTERN: EMERALD DAWN (Also see Emerald Dawn)
DC Comics: Dec, 1989 - No. 6, May, 1990 ($1.00, limited series)
1-Origin retold; Giffen plots in all 6.00
2-6: 4-Re-intro. Tomar-Re 4.00

GREEN LANTERN: EMERALD DAWN II (Emerald Dawn II #1 & 2)
DC Comics: Apr, 1991 - No. 6, Sept, 1991 ($1.00, limited series)
1-6 3.00
TPB (2003, $12.95) r/#1-6; Alan Davis-c 13.00

GREEN LANTERN: EMERALD WARRIORS
DC Comics: Oct, 2010 - Present ($3.99/$2.99)
1-5-($3.99) Guy Gardner's exploits; Migliari-c. 1-Bermejo variant-c. 2-5-Massaferra var-c 4.00
6-7-($2.99) Covers by Migliari & Massaferra 3.00

GREEN LANTERN: EVIL'S MIGHT (Elseworlds)
DC Comics: 2002 - No. 3 ($5.95, squarebound, limited series)
1-3-Kyle Rayner in 19th century NYC; Rogers-a; Chaykin & Tischman-s 6.00

GREEN LANTERN: FEAR ITSELF
DC Comics: 1999 (Graphic novel)
Hardcover ($24.95) Ron Marz-s/Brad Parker painted-a 25.00
Softcover ($14.95) 15.00

GREEN LANTERN/FLASH: FASTER FRIENDS (See Flash/Green Lantern...)
DC Comics: 1997 ($4.95, limited series)
1-Marz-s 5.00

GREEN LANTERN GALLERY
DC Comics: Dec, 1996 ($3.50, one-shot)
1-Wraparound-c; pin-ups by various 3.50

GREEN LANTERN/GREEN ARROW (Also see The Flash #217)
DC Comics: Oct, 1983 - No. 7, April, 1984 (52-60 pgs.)
1-7- r-Green Lantern #76-89 4.00
NOTE: ***Neal Adams** r-1-7; c-1-4. **Wrightson** r-4, 5.*

GREEN LANTERN • LEGACY: THE LAST WILL & TESTAMENT OF HAL JORDAN
DC Comics: 2002 ($24.95, hardcover graphic novel)
Hardcover-Anderson & Sienkiewicz-a/c; Kelly-s; Return of Oa 25.00
Softcover (2004, $17.95) 18.00

GREEN LANTERN: MOSAIC (Also see Cosmic Odyssey #2)
DC Comics: June, 1992 - No. 18, Nov, 1993 ($1.25)
1-18: Featuring John Stewart. 1-Painted-c by Cully Hamner 3.00

GREEN LANTERN: REBIRTH
DC Comics: Dec, 2004 - No. 6, May, 2005 ($2.95, limited series)
1-Johns-s/Van Sciver-a; Hal Jordan as The Spectre on-c 8.00
1-2nd printing; Hal Jordan as Green Lantern on-c 4.00
1-3rd printing; B&W-c version of 1st printing 3.00
1 Special Edition (9/09, $1.00) r/#1 with "After Watchmen" cover frame 3.00
2-Guy Gardner becomes a Green Lantern again; JLA app. 5.00
2-2nd & 3rd printings 3.00
3-6: 3-Sinestro returns. 4-6-JLA & JSA app. 3.00
HC (2005, $24.99, dust jacket) r/series & Wizard preview; intro. by Brad Meltzer 25.00
SC (2007, 2010, $14.99) r/series & Wizard preview; intro. by Brad Meltzer 15.00

GREEN LANTERN/SENTINEL: HEART OF DARKNESS
DC Comics: Mar, 1998 - No. 3, May, 1998 ($1.95, limited series)
1-3-Marz-s/Pelletier-a 3.00

GREEN LANTERN/SILVER SURFER: UNHOLY ALLIANCES
DC Comics: 1995 ($4.95, one-shot)(Prelude to DC Versus Marvel)
nn-Hal Jordan app. 5.00

GD VG FN VF VF/NM NM-
2.0 4.0 6.0 8.0 9.0 9.2

GREEN LANTERN SINESTRO CORPS SPECIAL (Continues in Green Lantern #21)
DC Comics: Aug, 2007 ($4.99, one-shot)
1-Kyle Rayner becomes Parallax; Cyborg Superman & Earth-Prime Superboy app.; Johns-s; Van Sciver-a/c; back-up story origin of Sinestro; Gibbons-a; Sinestro on cover 8.00
1-(2nd printing) Kyle Rayner as Parallax on cover 6.00
1-(3rd printing) Sinestro cover with muted colors 5.00

GREEN LANTERN: THE GREATEST STORIES EVER TOLD
DC Comics: 2006 ($19.99, TPB)
SC-Reprints Showcase #22; G.L. #1,31,74,87,172; ('90 series) #3, and others; Ross-c 20.00

GREEN LANTERN: THE NEW CORPS
DC Comics:1999 - No. 2, 1999 ($4.95, limited series)
1,2-Kyle recruits new GLs; Eaton-a 5.00

GREEN LANTERN VS. ALIENS
Dark Horse Comics: Sept, 2000 - No. 4, Dec, 2000 ($2.95, limited series)
1-4: 1-Hal Jordan and GL Corps vs. Aliens; Leonardi-p. 2-4-Kyle Rayner 3.00

GREEN MASK, THE (See Mystery Men)
Summer, 1940 - No. 9, 2/42; No. 10, 8/44 - No. 11, 11/44;
Fox Features Syndicate: V2#1, Spring, 1945 - No. 6, 10-11/46

	GD	VG	FN	VF	VF/NM	NM-
V1#1-Origin The Green Mask & Domino; reprints/Mystery Men #1-3,5-7; Lou Fine-c	337	674	1011	2359	4130	5900
2-Zanzibar The Magician by Tuska	132	264	396	838	1444	2050
3-Powell-a; Marijuana story	84	168	252	538	919	1300
4-Navy Jones begins, ends #6	65	130	195	416	708	1000
5	53	106	159	334	567	800
6-The Nightbird begins, ends #9; bondage/torture-c	45	90	135	284	480	675
7-9: 9(2/42)-Becomes The Bouncer #10(nn) on? & Green Mask #10 on	39	78	117	231	378	525
10,11: 10-Origin One Round Hogan & Rocket Kelly	30	60	90	177	289	400
V2#1	23	46	69	136	223	310
2-6	19	38	57	112	179	245

GREEN PLANET, THE
Charlton Comics: 1962 (one-shot) (12¢)

	GD	VG	FN	VF	VF/NM	NM-
nn-Giordano-c; sci-fi	7	14	21	45	73	100

GREEN TEAM (See Cancelled Comic Cavalcade & 1st Issue Special)

GREEN WOMAN, THE
DC Comics (Vertigo): 2010 ($24.99, HC graphic novel)
HC-John Bolton-a/Peter Straub & Michael Easton-s 25.00

GREETINGS FROM SANTA (See March of Comics No. 48)

GRENDEL (Also see Primer #2, Mage and Comico Collection)
Comico: Mar, 1983 - No. 3, Feb, 1984 ($1.50, B&W)(#1 has indicia to Skrog #1)

	GD	VG	FN	VF	VF/NM	NM-
1-Origin Hunter Rose	10	20	30	72	131	190
2,3: 2-Origin Argent	8	16	24	54	90	125

GRENDEL
Comico: Oct, 1986 - No. 40, Feb, 1990 ($1.50/$1.95/$2.50, mature)

	GD	VG	FN	VF	VF/NM	NM-
1	1	2	3	5	7	9
1,2: 2nd printings						3.00
2,3,5-15: 13-15-Ken Steacy-c.						4.00
4,16: 4-Dave Stevens-c(i). 16-Re-intro Mage (series begins, ends #19)						6.00
17-40: 24-25,27-28,30-31-Snyder-c/a						3.00
Devil by the Deed (Graphic Novel, 10/86, $5.95, 52 pgs.)-r/Grendel back-ups/ Mage 6-14; Alan Moore intro.	1	2	3	4	5	7
Devil's Legacy ($14.95, 1988, Graphic Novel)	2	4	6	9	12	15
Devil's Vagary (10/87, B&W & red)-No price; included in Comico Collection	2	4	6	8	10	12

GRENDEL (Title series): **Dark Horse Comics**
--ARCHIVES, 5/07 ($14.95, HC) r/1st apps. in Primer #2 and Grendel #1-3; Wagner intro. 15.00
--BEHOLD THE DEVIL, No. 0, 7/07 - No. 8, 6/08 ($3.50/50¢, B&W&Red)
0-(50¢-c) Prelude to series; Matt Wagner-s/a; interview with Wagner 3.00
1-8-Matt Wagner-s/a/c in all 3.50
--BLACK, WHITE, AND RED, 11/98 - No. 4, 2/99 ($3.95, anthology)
1-Wagner-s in all. Art by Sale, Leon and others 5.00
2-4: 2-Mack, Chadwick-a. 3-Allred, Kristensen-a. 4-Pearson, Sprouse-a 4.00
--CLASSICS, 7/95 - 8/95 ($3.95, mature) 1,2-reprints; new Wagner-c 4.00
--CYCLE, 10/95 ($5.95) 1-nn-history of Grendel by M. Wagner & others 6.00

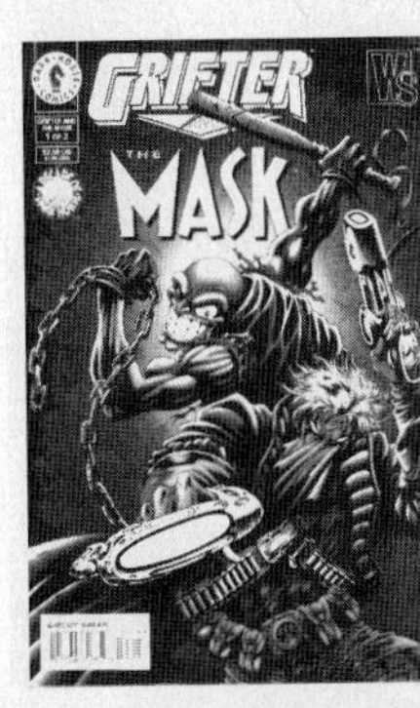

Grifter & The Mask #1 © DH/WSP

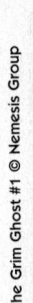

The Grim Ghost #1 © Nemesis Group

Grimjack #2 © FC

GD 2.0 | VG 4.0 | FN 6.0 | VF 8.0 | VF/NM 9.0 | NM- 9.2

--DEVIL BY THE DEED, 7/93 ($3.95, varnish-c) 1-nn-M. Wagner-c/a/scripts; r/Grendel back-ups from Mage #6-14 4.00
Reprint (12/97, $3.95) w/pin-ups by various 4.00
Hardcover (2007, $12.95) reprint recolored to B&W&red; includes covers and intros from previously reprinted editions 13.00

--DEVIL CHILD, 6/99 - No. 2, 7/99 ($2.95, mature) 1,2-Sale & Kristiansen-a/Schutz-s 3.00

--DEVIL QUEST, 11/95 ($4.95) 1-nn-Prequel to Batman/Grendel II; M. Wagner story & art; r/back-up story from Grendel Tales series. 5.00

--DEVILS AND DEATHS, 10/94 - 11/94 ($2.95, mature) 1,2 3.00

: DEVIL'S LEGACY, 3/00 - No. 12, 2/01 ($2.95, reprints 1986 series, recolored)
1-12-Wagner-s/c; Pander Bros.-a 3.00

: DEVIL'S REIGN, 5/04 - No. 7, 12/04 ($3.50, repr. 1989 series #34-40, recolored)
1-7-Sale-c/a. 3.50

: GOD AND THE DEVIL, No. 0, 1/03 - No. 10, 12/03 ($3.50/$4.99, repr. 1986 series, recolored)
0-9: 0-Sale-c/a; r/#23. 1-9-Snyder-c 3.50
10-($4.99) Double-sized; Snyder-c 5.00

--RED, WHITE & BLACK, 9/02 - No. 4, 12/02 ($4.99, anthology)
1-4-Wagner-s in all. 1-Art by Thompson, Sakai, Mahfood and others. 2-Kelley Jones, Watson, Brereton, Hester & Parks-a. 3-Oeming, Noto, Cannon, Ashley Wood, Huddleston-a 4-Chiang, Dalrymple, Robertson, Snyder III and Zulli-a 5.00
TPB (2005, $19.95) r/#1-4; cover gallery, artist bios 20.00

--TALES: DEVIL'S CHOICES, 3/95 - 6/95 ($2.95, mature) 1-4 3.00

--TALES: FOUR DEVILS, ONE HELL, 8/93 - 1/94 ($2.95, mature)
1-6-Wagner painted-c 3.00
TPB (12/94, $17.95) r/#1-6 18.00

--TALES: HOMECOMING, 12/94 - 2/95 ($2.95, mature) 1-3 3.00

--TALES: THE DEVIL IN OUR MIDST, 5/94 - 9/95 ($2.95, mature) 1-5-Wagner painted-c 3.00

--TALES: THE DEVIL MAY CARE, 12/95 - No. 6, 5/96 ($2.95, mature)
1-6-Terry LaBan scripts. 5-Batman/Grendel II preview 3.00

--TALES: THE DEVIL'S APPRENTICE, 9/97 - No. 3, 11/97 ($2.95, mature)
1-3 3.00

: THE DEVIL INSIDE, 9/01 - No. 3, 11/01 ($2.99)
1-3-r/#13-15 with new Wagner-c 3.00

: WAR CHILD, 8/92 - No. 10, 6/93 ($2.50, lim. series, mature)
1-9: 1-4-Bisley painted-c; Wagner-i & scripts in all 3.00
10-($3.50, 52 pgs.) Wagner-c 4.00
Limited Edition Hardcover ($99.95) 100.00

GREYFRIARS BOBBY (Disney)(Movie)
Dell Publishing Co.: No. 1189, Nov, 1961 (one-shot)
Four Color 1189-Photo-c (scarce) 7 14 21 47 76 105

GREYLORE
Sirius: 12/85 - No. 5, Sept, 1986 ($1.50/$1.75, high quality paper)
1-5: Bo Hampton-a in all 3.00

GREYSHIRT: INDIGO SUNSET (Also see Tomorrow Stories)
America's Best Comics: Dec, 2001 - No. 6, Aug, 2002 ($3.50, limited series)
1-6-Veitch-s/a. 4-Back-up w/John Severin-a. 6-Cho-a 3.50
TPB (2002, $19.95) r/#1-6; preface by Alan Moore 20.00

GRIDIRON GIANTS
Ultimate Sports Ent.: 2000 - No. 2 ($3.95, cardstock covers)
1,2-NFL players Sanders, Marino, Plummer, T. Davis battle evil 4.00

GRIFFIN, THE
DC Comics: 1991 - No. 6, 1991 ($4.95, limited series, 52 pgs.)
Book 1-6: Matt Wagner painted-c 5.00

GRIFTER (Also see Team 7 & WildC.A.T.S)
Image Comics (WildStorm Prod.): May, 1995 - No. 10, Mar, 1996 ($1.95)
1 ($1.95, Newsstand)-WildStorm Rising Pt. 5 3.00
1-10:1 ($2.50, Direct)-WildStorm Rising Pt. 5, bound-in trading card 3.00
...: One Shot (1/95, $4.95) Flip-c 5.00

GRIFTER
Image Comics (WildStorm Prod.): V2#1, July, 1996 - No. 14, Aug, 1997 ($2.50)
V2#1-14: Steven Grant scripts 3.00

GRIFTER & MIDNIGHTER
DC Comics (WildStorm Prod.): May, 2007 - No. 6, Oct, 2007 ($2.99, limited series)
1-6-Dixon-s/Benjamin-a/c. 1,3-The Authority app. 3.00

TPB (2008, $17.99) r/#1-6 18.00

GRIFTER AND THE MASK
Dark Horse Comics: Sept, 1996 - No. 2, Oct, 1996 ($2.50, limited series)
(1st Dark Horse Comics/Image x-over)
1,2: Steve Seagle scripts 3.00

GRIFTER/BADROCK (Also see WildC.A.T.S & Youngblood)
Image Comics (Extreme Studios): Oct, 1995 - No.2, Nov, 1995 ($2.50, unfinished lim. series)
1,2: 2-Flip book w/Badrock #2 3.00

GRIFTER/SHI
Image Comics (WildStorm Productions): Apr, 1996 - No. 2, May, 1996 ($2.95, limited series)
1,2: 1-Jim Lee-c/a(p); Travis Charest-a(p). 2-Billy Tucci-c/a(p); Travis Charest-a(p) 3.00

GRIM GHOST, THE
Atlas/Seaboard Publ.: Jan, 1975 - No. 3, July, 1975
1-3: Fleisher-s in all. 1-Origin. 2-Son of Satan; Colan-a. 3-Heath-c
2 4 6 8 11 14

GRIM GHOST
Ardden Entertainment (Atlas Comics): Mar, 2011 - Present ($2.99)
1-Isabella & Susco-s/Kelley Jones-a; re-intro. Matthew Dunsinane 3.00
... Issue Zero - NY Comicon Edtion (10/10, $2.99) Qing Ping Mui-a; prequel to #1 3.00

GRIMJACK (Also see Demon Knight & Starslayer)
First Comics: Aug, 1984 - No. 81, Apr, 1991 ($1.00/$1.95/$2.25)
1-John Ostrander scripts & Tim Truman-c/a begins. 4.00
2-25: 20-Sutton-c/a begins. 22-Bolland-a. 3.00
26-2nd color Teenage Mutant Ninja Turtles 6.00
27-74,76-81 (Later issues $1.95, $2.25): 30-Dynamo Joe x-over; 31-Mandrake-c/a begins. 73,74-Kelley Jones-a 3.00
75-($5.95, 52 pgs.)-Fold-out map; coated stock 6.00
The Legend of Grimjack Vol. 1 (IDW Publishing, 2004, $19.99) r/Starslayer #10-18; 8 new pages & art 20.00
The Legend of Grimjack Vol. 2 (IDW, 2005, $19.99) r/#1-7; unpublished art 20.00
The Legend of Grimjack Vol. 3 (IDW, 2005, $19.99) r/#8-14; cover gallery 20.00
The Legend of Grimjack Vol. 4 (IDW, 2005, $24.99) r/#15-21; cover gallery 25.00
The Legend of Grimjack Vol. 5 (IDW, 5/06, $24.99) r/#22-30; cover gallery 25.00
The Legend of Grimjack Vol. 6 (IDW, 1/07, $24.99) r/#31-37; cover gallery 25.00
The Legend of Grimjack Vol. 7 (IDW, 4/07, $24.99) r/#38-46; covers; "Rough Trade" 25.00
NOTE: *Truman c/a-1-17.*

GRIMJACK CASEFILES
First Comics: Nov, 1990 - No. 5, Mar, 1991 ($1.95, limited series)
1-5 Reprints 1st stories from Starslayer #10 on 3.00

GRIMJACK: KILLER INSTINCT
IDW Publ.: Jan, 2005 - No. 6, June, 2005 ($3.99, limited series)
1-6-Ostrander-s/Truman-a 4.00

GRIMJACK: THE MANX CAT
IDW Publ.: Aug, 2009 - No. 6, Jan, 2010 ($3.99, limited series)
1-6-Ostrander-s/Truman-a 4.00

GRIMM'S GHOST STORIES (See Dan Curtis)
Gold Key/Whitman No. 55 on: Jan, 1972 - No. 60, June, 1982 (Painted-c #1-42,44,46-56)

	GD	VG	FN	VF	VF/NM	NM-
1	4	8	12	22	34	45
2-5,8: 5,8-Williamson-a	2	4	6	13	18	22
6,7,9,10	2	4	6	11	16	20
11-20	2	4	6	8	11	14
21-42,45-54: 32,34-Reprints. 45-Photo-c	1	3	4	6	8	10
43,44,55-60: 43,44-(52 pgs.). 43-Photo-c. 58(2/82). 59(4/82)-Williamson-a(r/#8). 60(6/82)	2	4	6	8	11	14
Mini-Comic No. 1 (3-1/4x6-1/2", 1976)	1	3	4	6	8	10

NOTE: *Reprints-#32?, 34?, 39, 43, 44, 47?, 53; 56-60(1/3).* **Bolle** *a-8, 17, 22-25, 27, 29(2), 33, 35, 41, 43r, 45(2), 48(2), 50, 52, 57.* **Celardo** *a-17, 26, 28p, 30, 31, 43(2), 45.* **Lopez** *a-24, 25.* **McWilliams** *a-33, 44r, 48, 54(2), 57, 58.* **Win Mortimer** *a-31, 33, 49, 51, 55, 56, 58(2), 59, 60.* **Roussos** *a-25, 30.* **Sparling** *a-23, 24, 28, 30, 31, 33, 43r, 44, 45, 51(2), 52, 56-58, 59(2), 60.* **Spiegle** *a-44.*

GRIN (The American Funny Book) (Satire)
APAG House Pubs: Nov, 1972 - No. 3, April, 1973 (Magazine, 52 pgs.)

	GD	VG	FN	VF	VF/NM	NM-
1-Parodies-Godfather, All in the Family	3	6	9	17	25	32
2,3	2	4	6	11	16	20

GRIN & BEAR IT (See Gags)
Dell Publishing Co.: No. 28, 1941
Large Feature Comic 28 16 32 48 94 147 200

GRIPS (Extreme violence)

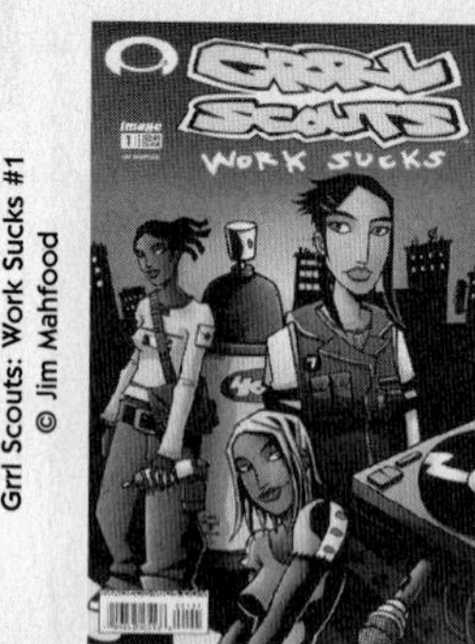

Grrl Scouts: Work Sucks #1 © Jim Mahfood

Guardians of the Galaxy #55 © MAR

The Guild #1 © The Guild

GD 2.0 VG 4.0 FN 6.0 VF 8.0 VF/NM 9.0 NM- 9.2

GD 2.0 VG 4.0 FN 6.0 VF 8.0 VF/NM 9.0 NM- 9.2

Silverwolf Comics: Sept, 1986 - No. 4, Dec, 1986 ($1.50, B&W, mature)
1-Tim Vigil-c/a in all 6.00
2-4 4.00

GRIP: THE STRANGE WORLD OF MEN
DC Comics (Vertigo): Jan, 2002 - No. 5, May, 2002 ($2.50, limited series)
1-4-Gilbert Hernandez-s/a 3.00

GRIT GRADY (See Holyoke One-Shot No. 1)

GROO (Also see Sergio Aragonés' Groo...)

GROO (Sergio Aragonés'...)
Image Comics: Dec, 1994 - No. 12, Dec, 1995 ($1.95)
1-12: 2-Indicia reads #1, Jan, 1995; Aragonés-c/a in all 3.50

GROO (Sergio Aragonés'...)
Dark Horse Comics: Jan, 1998 - No. 4, Apr, 1998 ($2.95)
1-4: Aragonés-c/a in all 4.00
...: One For One (9/10, $1.00) reprints #1 with red cover frame 1.00

GROO CHRONICLES, THE (Sergio Aragonés)
Marvel Comics (Epic Comics): June, 1989 - No. 6, Feb, 1990 ($3.50)
Book 1-6: Reprints early Pacific issues 3.50

GROO SPECIAL
Eclipse Comics: Oct, 1984 ($2.00, 52 pgs., Baxter paper)
1-Aragonés-c/a 3 6 9 16 22 28

GROO THE WANDERER (See Destroyer Duck #1 & Starslayer #5)
Pacific Comics: Dec, 1982 - No. 8, Apr, 1984
1-Aragonés-c/a(p) in all; Aragonés bio., photo 2 4 6 13 18 22
2-5: 5-Deluxe paper (1.00-c) 2 4 6 9 12 15
6-8 2 4 6 10 14 18

GROO THE WANDERER (Sergio Aragonés'...) (See Marvel Graphic Novel #32)
Marvel Comics (Epic Comics): March, 1985 - No. 120, Jan, 1995
1-Aragonés-c/a in all 2 4 6 9 13 16
2-10 1 2 3 5 6 8
11-20,50-($1.50, double size) 5.00
21-49,51-99: 87-direct sale only, high quality paper 3.00
100-($2.95, 52 pgs.) 5.00
101-120 4.00
Groo Carnival, The (12/91, $8.95)-r/#9-12 11.00
Groo Garden, The (4/94, $10.95)-r/#25-28 11.00

GROOVY (Cartoon Comics - not CCA approved)
Marvel Comics Group: March, 1968 - No. 3, July, 1968
1-Monkees, Ringo Starr, Sonny & Cher, Mamas & Papas photos
9 18 27 60 100 140
2,3 6 12 18 41 66 90

GROSS POINT
DC Comics: Aug, 1997 - No. 14, Aug, 1998 ($2.50)
1-14: 1-Waid/Augustyn-s 3.00

GROUNDED
Image Comics: July, 2005 - No. 6, May, 2006 ($2.95/$2.99, limited series)
1-6-Mark Sable-s/Paul Azaceta-a. 1-Mike Oeming-c 3.00
Vol. 1: Powerless TPB (2006, $14.99) r/#1-6; sketch pages and creator bios 15.00

GRRL SCOUTS (Jim Mahfood's...) (Also see 40 oz. Collected)
Oni Press: Mar,1999 - No. 4, Dec, 1999 ($2.95, B&W, limited series)
1-4-Mahfood-s/c/a 3.00
TPB (2003, $12.95) r/#1-4; pin-ups by Warren, Winick, Allred, Fegredo and others 13.00

GRRL SCOUTS: WORK SUCKS
Image Comics: Feb, 2003 - No. 4, May, 2003 ($2.95, B&W, limited series)
1-4-Mahfood-s/c/a 3.00
TPB (2004, $12.95) r/#1-4; pin-ups by Oeming, Dwyer, Tennapel and others 13.00

GUADALCANAL DIARY (See American Library)

GUARDIAN ANGEL
Image Comics: May, 2002 - No. 2, July, 2002 ($2.95)
1,2-Peterson-s/Wiesenfeld-a 3.00

GUARDIANS
Marvel Comics: Sept, 2004 - No. 5, Dec, 2004 ($2.99, limited series)
1-5-Sumerak-s/Casey Jones-a 3.00

GUARDIANS OF METROPOLIS
DC Comics: Nov, 1995 - Feb, 1995 ($1.50, limited series)
1-4: 1-Superman & Granny Goodness app. 3.00

GUARDIANS OF THE GALAXY (Also see The Defenders #26, Marvel Presents #3, Marvel Super-Heroes #18, Marvel Two-In-One #5)
Marvel Comics: June, 1990 - No. 62, July, 1995 ($1.00/$1.25)
1-Valentino-c/a(p) begin. 4.00
2-15: 2-Zeck-c(i). 5-McFarlane-c(i). 7-Intro Malevolence (Mephisto's daughter); Perez-c(i). 8-Intro Rancor (descendant of Wolverine) in cameo. 9-1st full app. Rancor; Rob Liefeld-c(i). 10-Jim Lee-c(i). 13,14-1st app. Spirit of Vengeance (futuristic Ghost Rider). 14-Spirit of Vengeance vs. The Guardians. 15-Starlin-c(i) 3.00
16-($1.50, 52 pgs.)-Starlin-c(i) 4.00
17-24,26-38,40-47: 17-20-31st century Punishers storyline. 20-Last $1.00-c. 21-Rancor app. 22-Reintro Starhawk. 24-Silver Surfer-c/story; Ron Lim-c. 26-Origin retold. 27-28-Infinity War x-over; 27-Inhumans app. 43-Intro Wooden (son of Thor) 3.00
25-($2.50)-Prism foil-c; Silver Surfer/Galactus-c/s 4.00
25-($2.50)-Without foil-c; newsstand edition 3.00
39-($2.95, 52 pgs.)-Embossed & holo-grafx foil-c; Dr. Doom vs. Rancor 4.00
48,49,51-62: 48-bound-in trading card sheet 3.00
50-($2.00, 52 pgs.)-Newsstand edition 4.00
50-($2.95, 52 pgs.)-Collectors ed. w/foil embossed-c 5.00
Annual 1-4: ('91-'94, 68 pgs.)-1-Origin. 2-Spirit of Vengeance-c/story. 3,4-Bagged w/card 4.00

GUARDIANS OF THE GALAXY (See Annihilation series)
Marvel Comics: July, 2008 - No. 25, Jun, 2010 ($2.99)
1-25: 1-Pelletier-a/Abnett & Lanning-s; 2nd printing exists. 24-Thanos returns 3.00

GUARDING THE GLOBE (See Invincible)
Image Comics: Aug, 2010 - Present ($3.50)
1-4-Kirkman & Cereno-s/Getty-a; back-c swipe of Avengers #4 w/Obama 3.50

GUERRILLA WAR (Formerly Jungle War Stories)
Dell Publishing Co.: No. 12, July-Sept, 1965 - No. 14, Mar, 1966
12-14 3 6 9 16 22 28

GUILD, THE (Based on the web-series)
Dark Horse Comics: Mar, 2010 - No. 3, May, 2010 ($3.50, limited series)
1-3-Felicia Day-s/Jim Rugg-a; two covers on each 3.50
... Vork 1 (12/10, $3.50) Robertson-a/c; variant-c by Hernandez 3.50

GUILTY (See Justice Traps the Guilty)

GULLIVER'S TRAVELS (See Dell Jr. Treasury No. 3)
Dell Publishing Co.: Sept-Nov, 1965
1 5 10 15 34 55 75

GUMBY
Wildcard Ink: July, 2006 - No. 3 ($3.99)
1-3-Bob Burden & Rick Geary-s&a 4.00

GUMBY'S SUMMER FUN SPECIAL
Comico: July, 1987 ($2.50)
1-Art Adams-c/a; B. Burden scripts 5.00

GUMBY'S WINTER FUN SPECIAL
Comico: Dec, 1988 ($2.50, 44 pgs.)
1-Art Adams-c/a 5.00

GUMPS, THE (See Merry Christmas..., Popular & Super Comics)
Dell Publ. Co./Bridgeport Herald Corp.: No. 73, 1945; Mar-Apr, 1947 - No. 5, Nov-Dec, 1947
Four Color 73 (Dell)(1945) 11 22 33 80 150 220
1 (3-4/47) 15 30 45 88 137 185
2-5 11 22 33 60 83 105

GUN CANDY (Also see The Ride)
Image Comics: July, 2005 - Present ($5.99)
1,2-Stelfreeze-c/a; flip book with The Ride (1-Pearson-c. 2-Noto-c) 6.00

GUNFIGHTER (Fat & Slat #1-4) (Becomes Haunt of Fear #15 on)
E. C. Comics (Fables Publ. Co.): No. 5, Sum, 1948 - No. 14, Mar-Apr, 1950
5,6-Moon Girl in each 54 108 162 343 574 825
7-14: 14-Bondage-c 40 80 120 246 411 575
NOTE: *Craig & H. C. Kiefer art in most issues. Craig c-5, 6, 13, 14. Feldstein/Craig a-10. Feldstein a-7-11. Harrison/Wood a-13, 14. Ingels a-5-14; c-7-12.*

GUNFIGHTERS, THE
Super Comics (Reprints): 1963 - 1964

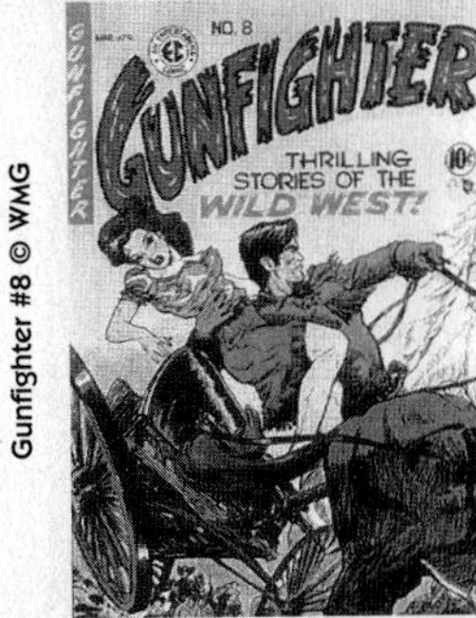

Gunfighter #8 © WMG

Gunsmoke #25 © CBS

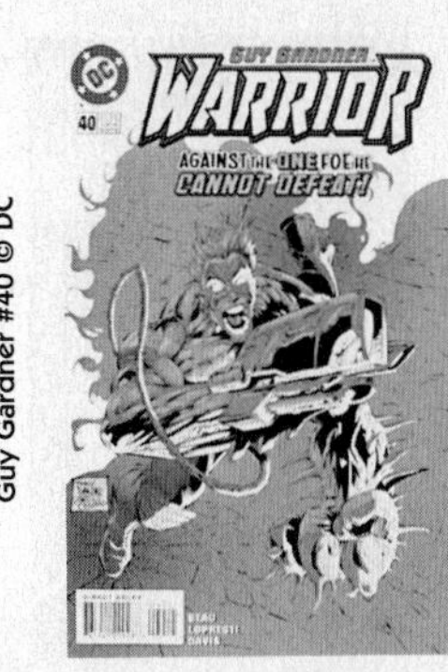

Guy Gardner #40 © DC

GD 2.0 | VG 4.0 | FN 6.0 | VF 8.0 | VF/NM 9.0 | NM- 9.2

10-12,15,16,18: 10,11-r/Billy the Kid #s? 12-r/The Rider #5(Swift Arrow). 15-r/Straight Arrow #42; Powell-r. 16-r/Billy the Kid #?(Toby). 18-r/The Rider #3; Severin-c
2 4 6 10 14 18

GUNFIGHTERS, THE (Formerly Kid Montana)
Charlton Comics: No. 51, 10/66 - No. 52, 10/67; No. 53, 6/79 - No. 85, 7/84

51,52 2 4 6 11 16 20
53,54,56:53,54-Williamson/Torres-r/Six Gun Heroes #47,49. 56-Williamson/Severin-c; Severin-r/Sheriff of Tombstone #1 1 3 4 6 8 10
55,57-80 6.00
81-84-Lower print run 1 2 3 5 6 8
85-S&K-r/1955 Bullseye 1 3 4 6 8 10

GUNFIRE (See Deathstroke Annual #2 & Showcase 94 #1,2)
DC Comics: May, 1994 - No. 13, June, 1995 ($1.75/$2.25)

1-5,0,6-13: 2-Ricochet-c/story. 5-(9/94). 0-(10/94). 6-(11/94) 3.00

GUN GLORY (Movie)
Dell Publishing Co.: No. 846, Oct, 1957 (one-shot)

Four Color 846-Toth-a, photo-c. 8 16 24 58 97 135

GUNHAWK, THE (Formerly Whip Wilson)(See Wild Western)
Marvel Comics/Atlas (MCI): No. 12, Nov, 1950 - No. 18, Dec, 1951
(Also see Two-Gun Western #5)

12 18 36 54 105 165 225
13-18: 13-Tuska-a. 16-Colan-a. 18-Maneely-c 14 28 42 76 108 140

GUNHAWKS (Gunhawk No. 7)
Marvel Comics Group: Oct, 1972 - No. 7, October, 1973

1,6: 1-Reno Jones, Kid Cassidy; Shores-c/a(p). 6-Kid Cassidy dies
3 6 9 16 23 30
2-5,7: 7-Reno Jones solo 2 4 6 11 16 20

GUNMASTER (Becomes Judo Master #89 on)
Charlton Comics: 9/64 - No. 4, 1965; No. 84, 7/65 - No. 88, 3-4/66; No. 89, 10/67

V1#1 4 8 12 22 34 45
2,4, V5#84-86: 84-Formerly Six-Gun Heroes 3 6 9 16 22 28
V5#87-89 2 4 6 11 16 20
NOTE: *Vol. 5 was originally cancelled with #88 (3-4/66). #89 on, became Judo Master, then later in 1967, Charlton issued #89 as a Gunmaster one-shot.*

GUN RUNNER
Marvel Comics UK: Oct, 1993 - No. 6, Mar, 1994 ($1.75, limited series)

1-($2.75)-Polybagged w/4 trading cards; Spirits of Vengeance app. 3.50
2-6: 2-Ghost Rider & Blaze app. 3.00

GUNS AGAINST GANGSTERS (True-To-Life Romances #8 on)
Curtis Publications/Novelty Press: Sept-Oct, 1948 - No. 6, July-Aug, 1949; V2#1, Sept-Oct, 1949

1-Toni & Greg Gayle begins by Schomburg; L.B. Cole-c
39 78 117 240 395 550
2-L.B. Cole-c 28 56 84 165 270 375
3-6, V2#1: 6-Toni Gayle-c by Cole 25 50 75 147 241 335
NOTE: ***L. B. Cole** c-1-6, V2#1, 2; a-1, 2, 3(2), 4-6.*

GUNSLINGER
Dell Publishing Co.: No. 1220, Oct-Dec, 1961 (one-shot)

Four Color 1220-Photo-c 8 16 24 56 93 130

GUNSLINGER (Formerly Tex Dawson...)
Marvel Comics Group: No. 2, Apr, 1973 - No. 3, June, 1973

2,3 2 4 6 13 18 22

GUNSLINGERS
Marvel Comics: Feb, 2000 ($2.99)

1-Reprints stories of Two-Gun Kid, Rawhide Kid and Caleb Hammer 3.00

GUNSMITH CATS: (Title series), **Dark Horse Comics**

--BAD TRIP (Manga), 6/98 - No. 6, 11/98 ($2.95, B&W) 1-6 3.00
--BEAN BANDIT (Manga), 1/99 - No. 9 ($2.95, B&W, limited series) 1-9 3.00
--GOLDIE VS. MISTY (Manga), 11/97 - No. 7, 5/98 ($2.95, B&W) 1-7 3.00
--KIDNAPPED (Manga), 11/99 - No. 10, 8/00 ($2.95, B&W) 1-10 3.00
--MISTER V (Manga), 10/00 - No. 11, 8/01 ($3.50/$2.99), B&W) 1-7,9-11 3.50
8-($2.99) 3.00
--THE RETURN OF GRAY (Manga), 8/96 - No. 7, 2/97 ($2.95, B&W) 1-7 3.00
--SHADES OF GRAY (Manga), 5/97 - No. 5, 9/97 ($2.95, B&W) 1-5 3.00

GD 2.0 | VG 4.0 | FN 6.0 | VF 8.0 | VF/NM 9.0 | NM- 9.2

--SPECIAL (Manga) Nov, 2001 ($2.99, B&W, one-shot) 3.00

GUNSMOKE (Blazing Stories of the West)
Western Comics (Youthful Magazines): Apr-May, 1949 - No. 16, Jan, 1952

1-Gunsmoke & Masked Marvel begin by Ingels; Ingels bondage-c
47 94 141 296 498 700
2-Ingels-c/a(2) 31 62 93 182 296 410
3-Ingels bondage-c/a 26 52 78 154 252 350
4-6: Ingels-c 20 40 60 120 195 270
7-10 14 28 42 80 115 150
11-16: 15,16-Western/horror stories 14 28 42 76 108 140
NOTE: ***Stallman** a-11, 14. **Wildey** a-15, 16.*

GUNSMOKE (TV)
Dell Publishing Co./Gold Key (All have James Arness photo-c): No. 679, Feb, 1956 - No. 27, Feb, 1969 - No. 6, Feb, 1970

Four Color 679(#1) 15 30 45 106 216 325
Four Color 720,769,797,844 (#2-5),6(11-1/57-58) 9 18 27 61 103 145
7,8,9,11,12-Williamson-a in all, 4 pgs. each 9 18 27 63 107 150
10-Williamson/Crandall-a, 4 pgs. 9 18 27 63 107 150
13-27 8 16 24 52 86 120
1 (Gold Key) 6 12 18 41 66 90
2-6('69-70) 4 8 12 22 34 45

GUNSMOKE TRAIL
Ajax-Farrell Publ./Four Star Comic Corp.: June, 1957 - No. 4, Dec, 1957

1 11 22 33 60 83 105
2-4 7 14 21 35 43 50

GUNSMOKE WESTERN (Formerly Western Tales of Black Rider)
Atlas Comics No. 32-35(CPS/NPI); Marvel No. 36 on: No. 32, Dec, 1955 - No. 77, July, 1963

32-Baker & Drucker-a 18 36 54 105 165 225
33,35,36-Williamson-a in each: 5,6 & 4 pgs. plus Drucker-a #33. 33-Kinstler-a?
14 28 42 82 121 160
34-Baker-a, 4 pgs.; Severin-c 14 28 42 82 121 160
37-Davis-a(2); Williamson text illo 12 24 36 67 94 120
38,39: 39-Williamson text illo (unsigned) 10 20 30 54 72 90
40-Williamson/Mayo-a (4 pgs.) 10 20 30 58 79 100
41,42,45,46,48,49,52-54,57,58,60: 49,52-Kid from Texas story. 57-1st Two Gun Kid by Severin. 60-Sam Hawk app. in Kid Colt 8 16 24 44 57 70
43,44-Torres-a 8 16 24 44 57 70
47,51,59,61: 47,51,59-Kirby-a. 61-Crandall-a 9 18 27 52 69 85
50-Kirby, Crandall-a 10 20 30 58 79 100
55,56-Matt Baker-a 10 20 30 58 79 100
62-67,69,71-73,77-Kirby-a. 72-Origin Kid Colt 5 10 15 35 55 75
68,70,74-76: 68-(10¢-c) 4 8 12 28 44 60
68-(10¢ cover price blacked out, 12¢ printed on) 9 18 27 60 100 140
NOTE: ***Colan** a-35-37, 39, 72, 76. **Davis** a-37, 52, 54, 55; c-50, 54. **Ditko** a-66; c-56p. **Drucker** a-.32-34. **Heath** c-33. **Jack Keller** a-34, 35, 40, 55, 56, 60, 61, 65, 68, 71, 72, 74, 75, 77; c-72. **Kirby** a-47, 50, 51, 59, 62(3), 63-67, 69, 71, 73, 77; c-56(w/**Ditko**), 57, 58, 60, 61(w/**Ayers**), 62, 63, 65, 66, 68, 69, 71-77. **Maleely** c-455. **Robinson** a-35. **Severin** a-35, 59-61; c-34, 35, 39, 42, 43. **Tuska** a-34. **Wildey** a-10, 37, 42, 56, 57. Kid Colt in all. Two-Gun Kid in No. 57, 59, 60-63. Wyatt Earp in No. 45, 48, 49, 52, 54, 55, 56, 58.*

GUNS OF FACT & FICTION (Also see A-1 Comics)
Magazine Enterprises: No. 13, 1948 (one-shot)

A-1 13-Used in **SOTI**, pg. 19; Ingels & J. Craig-a 27 54 81 158 259 360

GUNS OF THE DRAGON
DC Comics: Oct, 1998 - No. 4, Jan, 1999 ($2.50, limited series)

1-4-DCU in the 1920's; Enemy Ace & Bat Lash app. 3.00

GUN THEORY
Marvel Comics (Epic): Oct, 2003 - No. 4 ($2.50, limited series)

1,2-Daniel Way-s/Jon Proctor-a 3.00

GUNWITCH, THE : OUTSKIRTS OF DOOM (See The Nocturnals)
Oni Press: June, 2001 - No. 3, Oct, 2001 ($2.95, B&W, limited series)

1-3-Brereton-s/painted-c/Naifeh-s 3.00

GUY GARDNER (Guy Gardner: Warrior #17 on)(Also see Green Lantern #59)
DC Comics: Oct, 1992 - No. 44, July, 1996 ($1.25/$1.50/$1.75)

1-Staton-c/a(p) begins 4.00
2-24,0,26-30: 6-Guy vs. Hal Jordan. 8-Vs. Lobo-c/story. 15-JLA x-over, begin $1.50-c. 18-Begin 4-part Emerald Fallout story; splash page x-over GL #50. 18-21-Vs. Hal Jordan. 24-(9/94)-Zero Hour. 0-(10/94) 3.00
25 (11/94, $2.50, 52 pgs.) 4.00
29 ($2.95)-Gatefold-c 4.00
29-Variant-c (Edward Hopper's Nighthawks) 3.00

Hack/Slash (2011 series) #1 © Hack/Slash Inc.

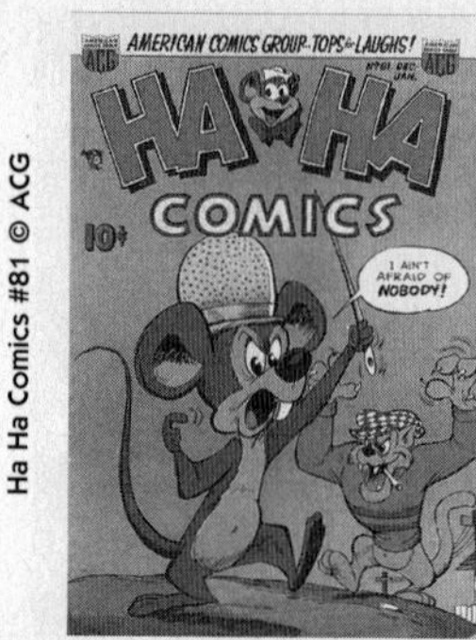

Ha Ha Comics #81 © ACG

Halo: Blood Line #5 © Microsoft

	GD 2.0	VG 4.0	FN 6.0	VF 8.0	VF/NM 9.0	NM- 9.2

31-44: 31-$1.75-c begins. 40-Gorilla Grodd-c/app. 44-Parallax-app. (1 pg.) 3.00
Annual 1 (1995, $3.50)-Year One story 4.00
Annual 2 (1996, $2.95)-Legends of the Dead Earth story 4.00

GUY GARDNER: COLLATERAL DAMAGE
DC Comics: 2006 - No. 2 ($5.99, square-bound, limited series)
1,2-Howard Chaykin-s/a 6.00

GUY GARDNER REBORN
DC Comics: 1992 - Book 3, 1992 ($4.95, limited series)
1-3: Staton-c/a(p). 1-Lobo-c/cameo. 2,3-Lobo-c/s 5.00

GYPSY COLT
Dell Publishing Co.: No. 568, June, 1954 (one-shot)

	GD	VG	FN	VF	VF/NM	NM-
Four Color 568--Movie	5	10	15	32	51	70

GYRO GEARLOOSE (See Dynabrite Comics, Walt Disney's C&S #140 &Walt Disney Showcase #18)
Dell Publishing Co.: No. 1047, Nov-Jan/1959-60 - May-July, 1962 (Disney)

	GD	VG	FN	VF	VF/NM	NM-
Four Color 1047 (No. 1)-All Barks-c/a	15	30	45	108	219	330
Four Color 1095,1184-All by Carl Barks	10	20	30	67	116	165
Four Color 1267-Barks c/a, 4 pgs.	8	16	24	54	90	125
01329-207 (#1, 5-7/62)-Barks-c only (intended as 4-Color 1329?)	6	12	18	41	66	90

HACKER FILES, THE
DC Comics: Aug, 1992 - No. 12, July, 1993 ($1.95)
1-12: 1-Sutton-a(p) begins; computer generated-c 3.00

HACK/SLASH
Devil's Due Publishing: Apr. 2004 - No. 32, Mar, 2010 ($3.25/$4.95)
1-Seeley-s/Caselli-a/c 5.00
...: (The Series) 1-24,26-32 (5/07-No. 32, 3/10, $3.50) Flashack to Cassie's childhood and origin. 12-Milk & Cheese cameo. 15-Re-Animator app. 3.50
25-($5.50) Double sized issue; Baugh-a; two covers 5.50
...: Comic Book Carnage (3/05) Manfredi-a/Seeley-s; Robert Kirkman & Steve Niles app. 5.00
...: First Cut TPB (10/05, $14.95) r/one-shots with sketch pages , designs, interviews 15.00
...: Girls Gone Dead (10/04, $4.95) Manfredi-a/Seeley-s 5.00
...: Land of Lost Toys 1-3 (11/05 - No. 3, 1/06, $3.25) Crossland-a/Seeley-s 3.25
...: New Reader Halloween Treat #1 (10/08, $3.50) origin retold; Cassie's diary pages 3.50
...: The Final Revenge of Evil Ernie (6/05, $4.95) Salman-a/Seeley-s; two covers 5.00
...: Trailers (2/05, $3.25) short stories by Seeley; art by various; three covers 3.25
...: Slice Hard (12/05, $4.95) Seeley-s 5.00
...: Slice Hard Pre-Sliced 25¢ Special (2/06, 25¢) origin story by Seeley; sketch pages 3.00
...: Vs Chucky (3/07, $5.50) Seeley-s/Merhoff-a; 3 covers 5.50
...: Vol. 2 Death By Sequel TPB (1/07, $18.99) r/Land of Lost Toys #1-3, Trailers, Slice Hard 19.00
...: Vol. 3 Friday the 31st TPB (10/07, $18.99) r/The Series #1-4 & ... Vs Chucky 19.00

HACK/SLASH
Image Comics: Jun, 2010 - Present ($3.50)
1-3: 1-(2/11, $3.50) Seeley-s/Leister-a 3.50
...: Me Without You (1/11, $3.50) Leister-a/Seeley-s; 2 covers 3.50
...: My First Maniac 1-4 (6/10- No. 4, 9/10) Leister-a/Seeley-s 3.50
...: Trailers #2 (11/10, $6.99) short stories; story & art by various; Seeley-c 7.00
... Annual 2010: Murder Messiah (10/10, $5.99) Seeley-s/Morales-a 6.00
Image Firsts: Hack/Slash #1 (10/10, $1.00) r/#1 (2004) with "Image Firsts" cover frame 1.00

HAGAR THE HORRIBLE (See Comics Reading Libraries in the Promotional Comics section)

HA HA COMICS (Teepee Tim No. 100 on; also see Giggle Comics)
Scope Mag.(Creston Publ.) No. 1-80/American Comics Group: Oct, 1943 - No. 99, Jan, 1955

	GD	VG	FN	VF	VF/NM	NM-
1-Funny animal	34	68	102	204	332	460
2	18	36	54	103	162	220
3-5: Ken Hultgren-a begins?	14	28	42	80	115	150
6-10	11	22	33	64	90	115
11-20: 14-Infinity-c	10	20	30	56	76	95
21-40	9	18	27	50	65	80
41-94,96-99: 49,61-X-Mas-c	8	16	24	44	57	70
95-3-D effect-c	15	30	45	90	140	190

HAIR BEAR BUNCH, THE (TV) (See Fun-In No. 13)
Gold Key: Feb, 1972 - No. 9, Feb, 1974 (Hanna-Barbera)

	GD	VG	FN	VF	VF/NM	NM-
1	4	8	12	24	37	50
2-9	3	6	9	17	25	32

HALCYON
Image Comics: Nov, 2010 - No. 3, Jan, 2011 ($2.99)

	GD 2.0	VG 4.0	FN 6.0	VF 8.0	VF/NM 9.0	NM- 9.2

1-3-Guggenheim & Butters-s/Bodenheim-a 3.00

HALF DEAD
Marvel Comics (Dabel Brothers Prods.): March, 2007 ($10.99, softcover, graphic novel)
SC-Barb Lien-Cooper & Park Cooper-s/Jimmy Bott-a 11.00

HALLELUJAH TRAIL, THE (See Movie Classics)

HALL OF FAME FEATURING THE T.H.U.N.D.E.R. AGENTS
JC Productions(Archie Comics Group): May, 1983 - No. 3, Dec, 1983
1-3: Thunder Agents-r(Crandall, Kane, Tuska, Wood-a). 2-New Ditko-c 3.00

HALLOWEEN (Movie)
Chaos! Comics: Nov, 2000; Apr, 2001 ($2.95/$2.99, one-shots)
1-Brewer-a; Michael Myers childhood at the Sanitarium 3.00
...II: The Blackest Eyes (4/01, $2.99) Beck-a 3.00
...III: The Devil's Eyes (11/01, $2.99) Justiniano-a 3.00

HALLOWEEN (Halloween Nightdance on cover)(Movie)
Devils Due Publishing: Mar, 2008 - No. 4, May, 2008 ($3.50, limited series)
1-4-Seeley-a/Hutchinson-s; multiple covers on each 3.50
...: 30 Years of Terror (8/08, $5.50) short stories by various incl. Seeley 5.50

HALLOWEEN HORROR
Eclipse Comics: Oct, 1987 (Seduction of the Innocent #7)($1.75)
1-Pre-code horror-r 4.00

HALLOWEEN MEGAZINE
Marvel Comics: Dec, 1996 ($3.95, one-shot, 96 pgs.)
1-Reprints Tomb of Dracula 4.00

HALO GRAPHIC NOVEL (Based on video game)
Marvel Publishing Inc.: 2006 ($24.99, hardcover with dust jacket)
HC-Anthology set in the Halo universe; art by Bisley, Moebius and others; pin-up gallery by various incl. Darrow, Pratt, Williams and Van Fleet; Phil Hale painted-c 25.00

HALO: BLOOD LINE (Based on video game)
Marvel Comics: Feb, 2010 - No. 5, Jul, 2010 ($3.99, limited series)
1-5-Van Lente-s/Portela-a 4.00

HALO: FALL OF REACH - BOOT CAMP (Based on video game)
Marvel Comics: Nov, 2010 - No. 4, Apr, 2011 ($3.99, limited series)
1-4-Reed-s/Ruiz-a 4.00

HALO: HELLJUMPER (Based on video game)
Marvel Comics: Sept, 2009 - No. 5, Jan, 2010 ($3.99, limited series)
1-5-Peter David-s/Eric Nguyen-a 4.00

HALO: UPRISING (Based on video game) (Also see Marvel Spotlight: Halo)
Marvel Comics: Oct, 2007 - No. 4, Jun, 2009 ($3.99, limited series)
1-4-Bendis-s/Maleev-a; takes pllace between the *Halo 2* and *Halo 3* video games 4.00

HALO JONES (See The Ballad of...)

HAMMER, THE
Dark Horse Comics: Oct, 1997 - No. 4, Jan, 1998 ($2.95, limited series)
1-4-Kelley Jones-s/c/a, ...: Uncle Alex (8/98, $2.95) 3.00

HAMMER, THE: THE OUTSIDER
Dark Horse Comics: Feb, 1999 - No. 3, Apr, 1999 ($2.95, limited series)
1-3-Kelley Jones-s/c/a 3.00

HAMMERLOCKE
DC Comics: Sept, 1992 - No. 9, May, 1993 ($1.75, limited series)
1-($2.50, 52 pgs.)-Chris Sprouse-c/a in all 4.00
2-9 3.00

HAMMER OF GOD (Also see Nexus)
First Comics: Feb, 1990 - No. 4, May, 1990 ($1.95, limited series)
1-4 3.00

HAMMER OF GOD: BUTCH
Dark Horse Comics: May, 1994 - No. 4, Aug, 1994 ($2.50, limited series)
1-3 3.00

HAMMER OF GOD: PENTATHLON
Dark Horse Comics: Jan, 1994 ($2.50, one shot)
1-Character from Nexus 3.00

HAMMER OF GOD: SWORD OF JUSTICE
First Comics: Feb 1991 - Mar 1991 ($4.95, lim. series, squarebound, 52 pgs.)

Hammer of the Gods #3 © Oeming & Wheatley

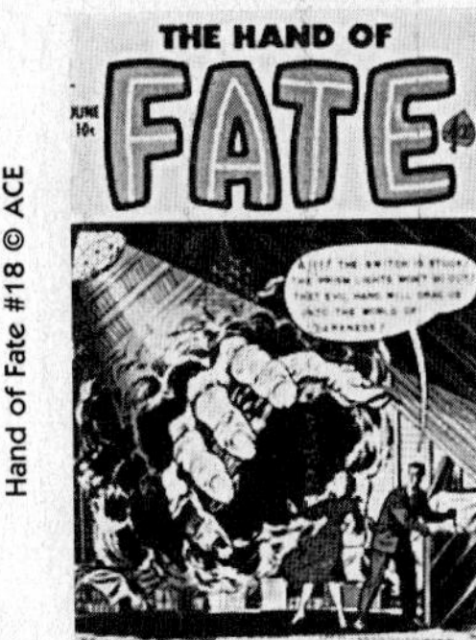

Hand of Fate #18 © ACE

Hap Hazard Comics #1 © ACE

V2#1,2 5.00

HAMMER OF THE GODS
Insight Studio Groups: 2001 - No. 5, 2001 ($2.95, limited series)
1-Michael Oeming & Mark Wheatley-s/a; Frank Cho-c 6.00
2-5: 3-Hughes-c. 5-Dave Johnson-c 3.00
The ColorSaga (2002, $4.95) r/"Enemy of the Gods" internet strip 5.00
Mortal Enemy TPB (2002, $18.95) r/#1-5; intro. by Peter David; afterword by Raven 19.00

HAMMER OF THE GODS: HAMMER HITS CHINA
Image Comics: Feb, 2003 - No. 3, Sept, 2003 ($2.95, limited series)
1-3-Oeming & Wheatley-s/a; Oeming-c. 2-Frankenstein Mobster by Wheatley 3.00

HANDBOOK OF THE CONAN UNIVERSE, THE
Marvel Comics: June, 1985; Jan, 1986 ($1.25, one-shot)
1-(6/85) Kaluta-c (2 printings) 4.00
1-(1/86) Kaluta-c 6.00
nn-(no date, circa '87-88, B&W, 36 pgs.) reprints '86 with changes; new painted cover 1 2 3 5 6 8

HAND OF FATE (Formerly Men Against Crime)
Ace Magazines: No. 8, Dec, 1951 - No. 25, Dec, 1954 (Weird/horror stories) (Two #25's)
8-Surrealistic text story 43 86 129 271 461 650
9,10,21-Necronomicon sty; drug belladonna used 27 54 81 158 259 360
11-18,20,22,23 22 44 66 132 216 300
19-Bondage, hypo needle scenes 24 48 72 140 230 320
24-Electric chair-c 34 68 102 199 325 450
25a(11/54), 25b(12/54)-Both have Cameron-a 19 38 57 109 172 235
NOTE: ***Cameron** a-9, 10, 19-25a, 25b; c-13. **Sekowsky** a-8, 9, 13, 14.*

HAND OF FATE
Eclipse Comics: Feb, 1988 - No. 3, Apr, 1988 ($1.75/$2.00, Baxter paper)
1-3; 3-B&W 3.00

HANDS OF THE DRAGON
Seaboard Periodicals (Atlas): June, 1975
1-Origin/1st app.; Craig-a(p)/Mooney inks 2 4 6 9 12 15

HANGMAN COMICS (Special Comics No. 1; Black Hood No. 9 on)
(Also see Flyman, Mighty Comics, Mighty Crusaders & Pep Comics)
MLJ Magazines: No. 2, Spring, 1942 - No. 8, Fall, 1943
2-The Hangman, Boy Buddies begin 213 426 639 1363 2332 3300
3-Beheading splash pg.; 1st Nazi war-c 181 362 543 1158 1979 2800
4-Classic Nazi WWII hunchback torture-c 161 322 483 1030 1765 2500
5-8: 5-1st Japan war-c. 8-2nd app. Super Duck (ties w/Jolly Jingles #11) 129 258 387 826 1413 2000
NOTE: ***Fuje** a-7(3), 8(3); c-3. **Reinman** c/a-3. Bondage c-3. **Sahle** c-6.*

HANK
Pentagon Publishing Co.: 1946
nn-Coulton Waugh's newspaper reprint 8 16 24 44 57 70

HANNA-BARBERA (See Golden Comics Digest No. 2, 7, 11)

HANNA-BARBERA ALL-STARS
Archie Publications: Oct, 1995 - No. 4, Apr, 1996 ($1.50, bi-monthly)
1-4 4.00

HANNA-BARBERA BANDWAGON (TV)
Gold Key: Oct, 1962 - No. 3, Apr, 1963
1-Giant, 84 pgs. 1-Augie Doggie app.; 1st app. Lippy the Lion, Touché Turtle & Dum Dum, Wally Gator, Loopy de Loop, 12 24 36 82 154 225
2-Giant, 84 pgs.; Mr. & Mrs. J. Evil Scientist (1st app.) in Snagglepuss story; Yakky Doodle, Ruff and Reddy and others app. 9 18 27 60 100 140
3-Regular size; Mr. & Mrs. J. Evil Scientist app. (pre-#1), Snagglepuss, Wally Gator and others app. 7 14 21 47 76 105

HANNA-BARBERA GIANT SIZE
Harvey Comics: Oct, 1992 - No. 3 ($2.25, 68 pgs.)
V2#1-3:Flintstones, Yogi Bear, Magilla Gorilla, Huckleberry Hound, Quick Draw McGraw, Yakky Doodle & Chopper, Jetsons & others 6.00

HANNA-BARBERA HI-ADVENTURE HEROES (See Hi-Adventure...)

HANNA-BARBERA PARADE (TV)
Charlton Comics: Sept, 1971 - No. 10, Dec, 1972
1 7 14 21 49 80 110
2,4-10 4 8 12 26 41 55
3-(52 pgs.)- "Summer Picnic" 6 12 18 37 59 80
NOTE: *No. 4 (1/72) went on sale late in 1972 with the January 1973 issues.*

HANNA-BARBERA PRESENTS
Archie Publications: Nov, 1995 - No. 8 ($1.50, bi-monthly)
1-8: 1-Atom Ant & Secret Squirrel. 2-Wacky Races. 3-Yogi Bear. 4-Quick Draw McGraw & Magilla Gorilla. 5-A Pup Named Scooby-Doo. 6-Superstar Olympics. 7-Wacky Races. 8-Frankenstein Jr. & the Impossibles 3.00

HANNA-BARBERA SPOTLIGHT (See Spotlight)

HANNA-BARBERA SUPER TV HEROES (TV)
Gold Key: Apr, 1968 - No. 7, Oct, 1969 (Hanna-Barbera)
1-The Birdman, The Herculoids(ends #6; not in #3), Moby Dick, Young Samson & Goliath (ends #2,4), and The Mighty Mightor begin; Spiegle-a in all 13 26 39 89 170 250
2-The Galaxy Trio app.; Shazzan begins; 12¢ & 15¢ versions exist 9 18 27 65 113 160
3,6,7-The Space Ghost app. 9 18 27 60 100 140
4,5 8 16 24 52 86 120
NOTE: *Birdman in #1,2,4,5. Herculoids in #2,4-7. Mighty Mightor in #1,2,4-7. Moby Dick in all. Shazzan in #2-5. Young Samson & Goliath in #1,3.*

HANNA-BARBERA TV FUN FAVORITES (See Golden Comics Digest #2,7,11)

HANNA-BARBERA (TV STARS) (See TV Stars)

HANS BRINKER (Disney)
Dell Publishing Co.: No. 1273, Feb, 1962 (one-shot)
Four Color 1273-Movie, photo-c 6 12 18 43 69 95

HANS CHRISTIAN ANDERSEN
Ziff-Davis Publ. Co.: 1953 (100 pgs., Special Issue)
nn-Danny Kaye (movie)-Photo-c; fairy tales 16 32 48 94 147 200

HANSEL & GRETEL
Dell Publishing Co.: No. 590, Oct, 1954 (one-shot)
Four Color 590-Partial photo-c 6 12 18 43 69 95

HANSI, THE GIRL WHO LOVED THE SWASTIKA
Spire Christian Comics (Fleming H. Revell Co.): 1973, 1976 (39¢/49¢)
1973 edition with 39¢-c 6 12 18 41 66 90
1976 edition with 49¢-c 4 8 12 24 37 50

HAP HAZARD COMICS (Real Love No. 25 on)
Ace Magazines (Readers' Research): Summer, 1944 - No. 24, Feb, 1949
(#1-6 are quarterly issues)
1 15 30 45 84 127 170
2 9 18 27 52 69 85
3-10 8 16 24 44 57 70
11-13,15-24 8 16 24 40 50 60
14-Feldstein-c (4/47) 10 20 30 56 76 95

HAP HOPPER (See Comics Revue No. 2)

HAPPIEST MILLIONAIRE, THE (See Movie Comics)

HAPPI TIM (See March of Comics No. 182)

HAPPY BIRTHDAY MARTHA WASHINGTON (Also see Give Me Liberty, Martha Washington Goes To War, & Martha Washington Stranded In Space)
Dark Horse Comics: Mar, 1995 ($2.95, one-shot)
1-Miller script; Gibbons-c/a 3.00

HAPPY COMICS (Happy Rabbit No. 41 on)
Nedor Publ./Standard Comics (Animated Cartoons): Aug, 1943 - No. 40, Dec, 1950
(Companion to Goofy Comics)
1-Funny animal 27 54 81 158 259 360
2 15 30 45 86 133 180
3-10 12 24 36 67 94 120
11-19 10 20 30 54 72 90
20-31,34-37-Frazetta text illos in all (2 in #34&35, 3 in #27,28,30). 27-Al Fago-a 11 22 33 64 90 115
32-Frazetta-a, 7 pgs. plus 2 text illos; Roussos-a 20 40 60 120 195 270
33-Frazetta-a(2), 6 pgs. each (Scarce) 28 56 84 165 270 375
38-40 9 18 27 47 61 75

HAPPYDALE: DEVILS IN THE DESERT
DC Comics (Vertigo): 1999 - No. 2, 1999 ($6.95, limited series)
1,2-Andrew Dabb-s/Seth Fisher-a 7.00

HAPPY DAYS (TV)(See Kite Fun Book)
Gold Key: Mar, 1979 - No. 6, Feb, 1980
1-Photo-c of TV cast; 35¢-c 3 6 9 16 23 30

Harbinger #14 © Voyager Comm.

The H.A.R.D. Corps #8 © Voyager Comm.

Harley Quinn #25 © DC

GD 2.0 | VG 4.0 | FN 6.0 | VF 8.0 | VF/NM 9.0 | NM- 9.2

2-6-(40¢-c) 2 4 6 9 12 15

HAPPY HOLIDAY (See March of Comics No. 181)

HAPPY HOULIHANS (Saddle Justice No. 3 on; see Blackstone, The Magician Detective)
E. C. Comics: Fall, 1947 - No. 2, Winter, 1947-48

1-Origin Moon Girl (same date as Moon Girl #1) 55 110 165 352 601 850
2 32 64 96 188 307 425

HAPPY JACK
Red Top (Decker): Aug, 1957 - No. 2, Nov, 1957

V1#1,2 5 10 15 22 26 30

HAPPY JACK HOWARD
Red Top (Farrell)/Decker: 1957

nn-Reprints Handy Andy story from E. C. Dandy Comics #5, renamed "Happy Jack" 5 10 15 22 26 30

HAPPY RABBIT (Formerly Happy Comics)
Standard Comics (Animated Cartoons): No. 41, Feb, 1951 - No. 48, Apr, 1952

41-Funny animal 8 16 24 44 57 70
42-48 7 14 21 35 43 50

HARBINGER (Also see Unity)
Valiant: Jan, 1992 - No. 41, June, 1995 ($1.95/$2.50)

0-Prequel to the series; available by redeeming coupons in #1-6; cover image has pink sky; title logo is blue 4 8 12 24 37 50
0-(2nd printing) cover has blue sky & red logo 5.00
1-1st app. 2 4 6 8 10 12
2-4: 4-Low print run 1 2 3 5 7 9
5,6: 5-Solar app. 6-Torque dies 1 2 3 4 5 7
7-10: 8,9-Unity x-overs. 8-Miller-c. 9-Simonson-c. 10-1st app. H.A.R.D Corps (10/92) 5.00
11-24,26-41: 14-1st app. Stronghold. 18-Intro Screen. 19-1st app. Stunner. 22-Archer & Armstrong app. 24-Cover similar to #1. 26-Intro New Harbingers. 29-Bound-in trading card. 30-H.A.R.D. Corps app. 32-Eternal Warrior app. 33-Dr. Eclipse app. 3.00
25-($3.50, 52 pgs.)-Harada vs. Sting 4.00
...Files 1,2 (8/94,2/95 $2.50) 3.00
...: The Beginning HC (2007, $24.95) recolored reprints #0-7 and Story of Harada from coupons from #1-6; new "Origin of Harada" story by Shooter and Bob Hall 25.00
Trade paperback nn (11/92, $9.95)-Reprints #1-4 & comes polybagged with a copy of Harbinger #0 w/new-c. Price for TPB only 10.00
NOTE: *Issues 1-6 have coupons with origin of Harada and are redeemable for Harbinger #0 .*

HARD BOILED
Dark Horse Comics: Sept, 1990 - No. 3, Mar, 1992 ($4.95/$5.95, 8 1/2x11", lim. series)

1-3-Miller-s; Darrow-c/a; sexually explicit & violent 1 2 3 4 5 7
TPB (5/93, $15.95) 16.00
Big Damn Hard Boiled (12/97, $29.95, B&W) r/#1-3 30.00

HARDCASE (See Break Thru, Flood Relief & Ultraforce, 1st Series)
Malibu Comics (Ultraverse): June, 1993 - No. 26, Aug, 1995 ($1.95/$2.50)

1-Intro Hardcase; Dave Gibbons-c; has coupon for Ultraverse Premiere #0; Jim Callahan-a(p) begin, ends #3 3.00
1-With coupon missing 2.00
1-Platinum Edition 4.00
1-Holographic Cover Edition; 1st full-c holograph tied w/Prime 1 & Strangers 1 7.00
1-Ultra Limited silver foil-c 4.00
2,3-Callahan-a, 2-($2.50)-Newsstand edition bagged w/trading card 3.00
4,6-15, 17-19: 4-Strangers app. 7-Break-Thru x-over. 8-Solution app. 9-Vs. Turf. 12-Silver foil logo, wraparound-c. 17-Prime app. 3.00
5-($2.50, 48 pgs.)-Rune flip-c/story by B. Smith (3 pgs.) 4.00
16 ($3.50, 68 pgs.)-Rune pin-up 4.00
20-26: 23-Loki app. 3.00
NOTE: *Perez a-8(2); c-20i.*

HARDCORE STATION
DC Comics: July, 1998 - No. 6, Dec, 1998 ($2.50, limited series)

1-6-Starlin-s/a(p). 3-Green Lantern-c/app. 5,6-JLA-c/app. 3.00

H.A.R.D. CORPS, THE (See Harbinger #10)
Valiant: Dec, 1992 - No. 30, Feb, 1995 ($2.25) (Harbinger spin-off)

1-($2.50)-Gatefold-c by Jim Lee & Bob Layton 3.00
1-Gold variant 5.00
2-30: 5-Bloodshot-c/story cont'd from Bloodshot #3. 5-Variant edition; came w/Comic Defense System. 10-Turok app. 17-vs. Armorines. 18-Bound-in trading card. 20-Harbinger app. 3.00

HARD TIME
DC Comics (Focus): Apr, 2004 - No. 12, Mar, 2005 ($2.50)

1-12-Gerber-s/Hurtt-a; 1-Includes previews of other DC Focus series 3.00
...: 50 to Life (2004, $9.95, TPB) r/#1-6; cover gallery with sketches 10.00

HARD TIME: SEASON TWO
DC Comics: Feb, 2006 - No. 7, Aug, 2006 ($2.50/$2.99)

1-5-Gerber-s/Hurtt-a 3.00
6,7-($2.99) 7-Ethan paroled in 2053 3.00

HARDWARE
DC Comics (Milestone): Apr, 1993 - No. 50, Apr, 1997 ($1.50/$1.75/$2.50)

1-($2.95)-Collector's Edition polybagged w/poster & trading card (direct sale only) 4.00
1-Platinum Edition 6.00
1-15,17-19: 11-Shadow War x-over. 11,14-Simonson-c. 12-Buckler-a(p). 17-Worlds Collide Pt. 2. 18-Simonson-c; Worlds Collide Pt. 9. 15-1st Humberto Ramos DC work 3.00
16,50-($3.95, 52 pgs.)-16-Collector's Edition w/gatefold 2nd cover by Byrne; new armor; Icon app. 4.00
16,20-24,26-49: 16-($2.50, 52 pgs.)-Newsstand Ed. 49-Moebius-c 3.00
25-($2.95, 52 pgs.) 4.00
...: The Man in the Machine TPB (2010, $19.99) r/#1-8 20.00

HARDY BOYS, THE (Disney
Dell Publ. Co.: No. 760, Dec, 1956 - No. 964, Jan, 1959 (Mickey Mouse Club)

Four Color 760 (#1)-Photo-c 10 20 30 69 122 175
Four Color 830(8/57), 887(1/58), 964-Photo-c 9 18 27 60 100 140

HARDY BOYS, THE (TV)
Gold Key: Apr, 1970 - No. 4, Jan, 1971

1 4 8 12 28 44 60
2-4 3 6 9 18 27 35

HARLAN ELLISON'S DREAM CORRIDOR
Dark Horse Comics: Mar, 1995 - No. 5, July, 1995 ($2.95, anthology)

1-5: Adaptation of Ellison stories. 1-4-Byrne-a. 3.00
Special (1/95, $4.95) 5.00
Trade paperback-(1996, $18.95, 192 pgs)-r/#1-5 & Special #1 19.00

HARLAN ELLISON'S DREAM CORRIDOR QUARTERLY
Dark Horse Comics: V2#1, Aug, 1996 ($5.95, anthology, squarebound)

V2#1-Adaptations of Ellison's stories w/new material; Neal Adams-a 6.00
Volume 2 TPB (3/07, $19.95) r/V2#1 and unpublished material incl. last Swan-a 20.00

HARLEM GLOBETROTTERS (TV) (See Fun-In No. 8, 10)
Gold Key: Apr, 1972 - No. 12, Jan, 1975 (Hanna-Barbera)

1 4 8 12 26 41 55
2-5 3 6 9 16 22 28
6-12 2 4 6 13 18 22
NOTE: *#4, 8, and 12 contain 16 extra pages of advertising.*

HARLEQUIN ROMANCE
Dark Horse Comics: Nov, 2001 ($10.95, hardcover, one-shot)

nn-Neil Gaiman-s; painted-a/c by John Bolton 11.00

HARLEY QUINN (Also see Gotham City Sirens)
DC Comics: Dec, 2000 - No. 38, Jan, 2004 ($2.95/$2.25/$2.50)

1-Joker and Poison Ivy app.; Terry & Rachel Dodson-a/c 6.00
2-11-($2.25). 2-Two-Face-c/app. 3-Slumber party. 6,7-Riddler app. 3.00
12-($2.95) Batman app. 4.00
13-38: 13-Joker: Last Laugh. 17,18-Bizarro-c/app. 23-Begin $2.50-c. 23,24-Martian Manhunter app. 25,32-Joker-c/app. 3.00
Harley & Ivy: Love on the Lam (2001, $5.95) Winick-s/Chiodo-c/a 6.00
...: Our Worlds at War (10/01, $2.95) Jae Lee-c; art by various 3.00

HAROLD TEEN (See Popular Comics, & Super Comics)
Dell Publishing Co.: No. 2, 1942 - No. 209, Jan, 1949

Four Color 2 28 56 84 204 415 625
Four Color 209 6 12 18 39 62 85

HARROWERS, THE (See Clive Barker's...)

HARSH REALM (Inspired 1999 TV series)
Harris Comics: 1993- No. 6, 1994 ($2.95, limited series)

1-6: Painted-c. Hudnall-s/Paquette & Ridgway-a 3.50
TPB (2000, $14.95) r/series 15.00

HARVEY
Marvel Comics: Oct, 1970; No. 2, 12/70; No. 3, 6/72 - No. 6, 12/72

1 10 20 30 69 122 175
2-6 7 14 21 47 76 105

HARVEY COLLECTORS COMICS (Titled Richie Rich Collectors Comics on cover of #6-on)

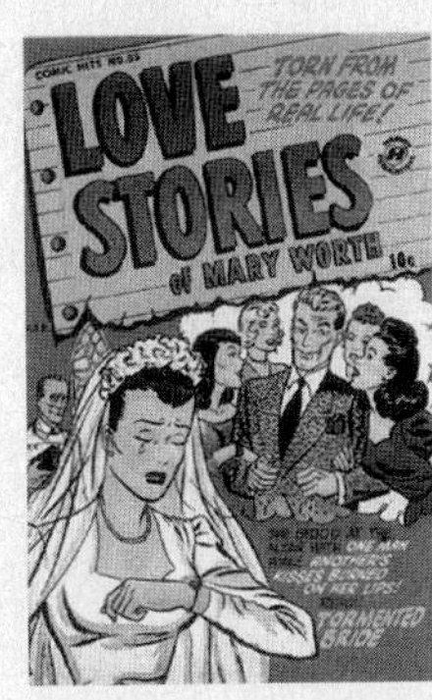

Harvey Comics Hits #55 © HARV

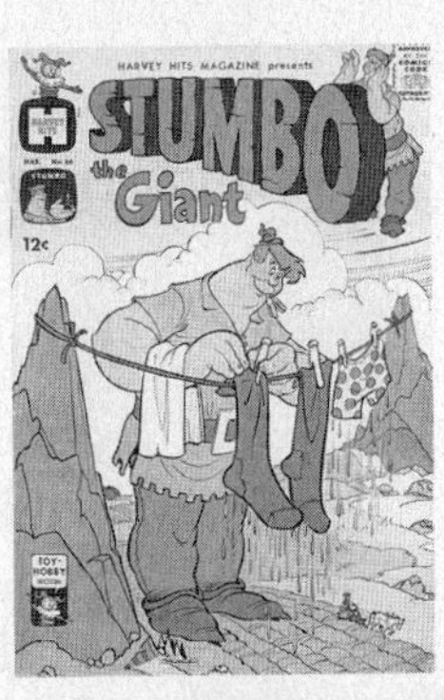

Harvey Hits #66 © HARV

Harvey Pop Comics #1 © HARV

GD 2.0 | VG 4.0 | FN 6.0 | VF 8.0 | VF/NM 9.0 | NM- 9.2

Harvey Publ.: Sept, 1975 - No. 15, Jan, 1978; No. 16, Oct, 1979 (52 pgs.)

1-Reprints Richie Rich #1,2 2 4 6 13 18 22
2-10: 7-Splash pg. shows cover to Friendly Ghost Casper #1 2 4 6 8 11 14
11-16: 16-Sad Sack-r 1 2 3 5 7 9

NOTE: *All reprints: Casper-#2, 7, Richie Rich-#1, 3, 5, 6, 8-15, Sad Sack-#16. Wendy-#4.*

HARVEY COMICS HITS (Formerly Joe Palooka #50)
Harvey Publications: No. 51, Oct, 1951 - No. 62, Apr, 1953

51-The Phantom 31 62 93 184 300 415
52-Steve Canyon's Air Power(Air Force sponsored) 13 26 39 72 101 130
53-Mandrake the Magician 20 40 60 114 182 250
54-Tim Tyler's Tales of Jungle Terror 13 26 39 74 105 135
55-Love Stories of Mary Worth 11 22 33 62 86 110
56-The Phantom; bondage-c 26 52 78 154 252 350
57-Rip Kirby Exposes the Kidnap Racket; entire book by Alex Raymond 15 30 45 85 130 175
58-Girls in White (nurses stories) 11 22 33 62 86 110
59-Tales of the Invisible featuring Scarlet O'Neil 12 24 36 67 94 120
60-Paramount Animated Comics #1 (9/52) (3rd app. Baby Huey); 2nd Harvey app. Baby Huey & Casper the Friendly Ghost (1st in Little Audrey #25 (8/52)); 1st app. Herman & Catnip (c/story) & Buzzy the Crow 45 90 135 284 480 675
61-Casper the Friendly Ghost #6 (3rd Harvey Casper, 10/52)-Casper-c 47 94 141 296 498 700
62-Paramount Animated Comics #2; Herman & Catnip, Baby Huey & Buzzy the Crow 17 34 51 98 154 210

HARVEY COMICS LIBRARY
Harvey Publications: Apr, 1952 - No. 2, 1952

1-Teen-Age Dope Slaves as exposed by Rex Morgan, M.D.; drug propaganda story; used in **SOTI**, pg. 27 174 348 522 1114 1907 2700
2-Dick Tracy Presents Sparkle Plenty in "Blackmail Terror" 20 40 60 114 182 250

HARVEY COMICS SPOTLIGHT
Harvey Comics: Sept, 1987 - No. 4, Mar, 1988 (75¢/$1.00)

1-New material; begin 75ç, ends #3; Sand Sack 5.00
2-4: 2,4-All new material. 2-Baby Huey. 3-Little Dot; contains reprints w/5 pg. new story. 4-$1.00-c; Little Audrey 4.00

NOTE: No. 5 was advertised but not published.

HARVEY HITS (Also see Tastee-Freez Comics in the Promotional Comics section)
Harvey Publications: Sept, 1957 - No. 122, Nov, 1967

1-The Phantom 24 48 72 175 350 525
2-Rags Rabbit (10/57) 5 10 15 34 55 75
3-Richie Rich (11/57)-r/Little Dot; 1st book devoted to Richie Rich; see Little Dot for 1st app. 131 262 393 1114 2257 3400
4-Little Dot's Uncles (12/57) 15 30 45 106 216 325
5-Stevie Mazie's Boy Friend (1/58) 4 8 12 28 44 60
6-The Phantom (2/58); Kirby-c; 2pg. Powell-a 16 32 48 111 226 340
7-Wendy the Good Little Witch (3/58, pre-dates Wendy #1; 1st book devoted to Wendy) 27 54 81 197 399 600
8-Sad Sack's Army Life; George Baker-c 7 14 21 50 83 115
9-Richie Rich's Golden Deeds; (2nd book devoted to Richie Rich) reprints Richie Rich story from Tastee-Freez #1 50 100 150 425 863 1300
10-Little Lotta's Lunch Box 11 22 33 75 138 200
11-Little Audrey Summer Fun (7/58) 9 18 27 60 100 140
12-The Phantom; Kirby-c; 2pg. Powell-a (8/58) 13 26 39 94 185 275
13-Little Dot's Uncles (9/58); Richie Rich 1pg. 11 22 33 75 138 200
14-Herman & Katnip (10/58, TV/movies) 4 8 12 28 44 60
15-The Phantom (12/58)-1 pg. origin 13 26 39 94 185 275
16-Wendy the Good Little Witch (1/59); Casper app. 11 22 33 77 144 210
17-Sad Sack's Army Life (2/59) 6 12 18 39 62 85
18-Buzzy & the Crow 4 8 12 26 41 55
19-Little Audrey (4/59) 6 12 18 37 59 80
20-Casper & Spooky 8 16 24 52 86 120
21-Wendy the Witch 8 16 24 52 86 120
22-Sad Sack's Army Life 5 10 15 30 48 65
23-Wendy the Witch (8/59) 8 16 24 52 86 120
24-Little Dot's Uncles (9/59); Richie Rich 1pg. 9 18 27 60 100 140
25-Herman & Katnip (10/59) 4 8 12 22 34 45
26-The Phantom (11/59) 10 20 30 71 128 185
27-Wendy the Good Little Witch (12/59) 7 14 21 50 83 115
28-Sad Sack's Army Life (1/60) 4 8 12 26 41 55
29-Harvey-Toon (No.1)('60); Casper, Buzzy 5 10 15 34 55 75
30-Wendy the Witch (3/60) 7 14 21 50 83 115
31-Herman & Katnip (4/60) 3 6 9 20 30 40
32-Sad Sack's Army Life (5/60) 4 8 12 22 34 45
33-Wendy the Witch (6/60) 7 14 21 47 76 105
34-Harvey-Toon (7/60) 4 8 12 24 37 50
35-Funday Funnies (8/60) 3 6 9 20 30 40
36-The Phantom (1960) 10 20 30 68 119 170
37-Casper & Nightmare 6 12 18 37 59 80
38-Harvey-Toon 4 8 12 24 37 50
39-Sad Sack's Army Life (12/60) 3 6 9 21 32 42
40-Funday Funnies (1/61) 3 6 9 17 25 32
41-Herman & Katnip 3 6 9 17 25 32
42-Harvey-Toon (3/61) 3 6 9 19 29 38
43-Sad Sack's Army Life (4/61) 3 6 9 19 29 38
44-The Phantom (5/61) 9 18 27 65 113 160
45-Casper & Nightmare 5 10 15 30 48 65
46-Harvey-Toon (7/61) 3 6 9 17 25 32
47-Sad Sack's Army Life (8/61) 3 6 9 17 25 32
48-The Phantom (9/61) 9 18 27 65 113 160
49-Stumbo the Giant (1st app. in Hot Stuff) 9 18 27 65 113 160
50-Harvey-Toon (11/61) 3 6 9 16 23 30
51-Sad Sack's Army Life (12/61) 3 6 9 16 23 30
52-Casper & Nightmare 4 8 12 28 44 60
53-Harvey-Toons (2/62) 3 6 9 16 23 30
54-Stumbo the Giant 5 10 15 34 55 75
55-Sad Sack's Army Life (4/62) 3 6 9 16 23 30
56-Casper & Nightmare 4 8 12 26 41 55
57-Stumbo the Giant 5 10 15 34 55 75
58-Sad Sack's Army Life 3 6 9 16 23 30
59-Casper & Nightmare (7/62) 4 8 12 26 41 55
60-Stumbo the Giant (9/62) 5 10 15 34 55 75
61-Sad Sack's Army Life 3 6 9 16 22 28
62-Casper & Nightmare 4 8 12 23 36 48
63-Stumbo the Giant 4 8 12 28 44 60
64-Sad Sack's Army Life (1/63) 3 6 9 16 22 28
65-Casper & Nightmare 4 8 12 23 36 48
66-Stumbo The Giant (3/63) 4 8 12 28 44 60
67-Sad Sack's Army Life (4/63) 3 6 9 16 22 28
68-Casper & Nightmare 4 8 12 23 36 48
69-Stumbo the Giant (6/63) 4 8 12 28 44 60
70-Sad Sack's Army Life (7/63) 3 6 9 16 22 28
71-Casper & Nightmare (8/63) 3 6 9 21 32 42
72-Stumbo the Giant 4 8 12 28 44 60
73-Little Sad Sack (10/63) 3 6 9 16 22 28
74-Sad Sack's Muttsy... (11/63) 3 6 9 16 22 28
75-Casper & Nightmare 3 6 9 19 29 38
76-Little Sad Sack 3 6 9 16 22 28
77-Sad Sack's Muttsy... 3 6 9 16 22 28
78-Stumbo the Giant (3/64); JFK caricature 4 8 12 28 44 60
79-87: 79-Little Sad Sack (4/64). 80-Sad Sack's Muttsy... (5/64). 81-Little Sad Sack. 82-Sad Sack's Muttsy... 83-Little Sad Sack(8/64). 84-Sad Sack's Muttsy... 85-Gabby Gob (#1) (10/64). 86-G. I. Juniors (#1)(11/64). 87-Sad Sack's Muttsy... (12/64) 3 6 9 16 22 28
88-Stumbo the Giant (1/65) 4 8 12 28 44 60
89-122: 89-Sad Sack's Muttsy... 90-Gabby Gob. 91-G. I. Juniors. 92-Sad Sack's Muttsy... (5/65). 93-Sadie Sack (6/65). 94-Gabby Gob. 95-G. I. Juniors (8/65). 96-Sad Sack's Muttsy... (9/65). 97-Gabby Gob (10/65). 98-G. I. Juniors (11/65). 99-Sad Sack's Muttsy... (12/65). 100-Gabby Gob(1/66). 101-G. I. Juniors (2/66). 102-Sad Sack's Muttsy... (3/66). 103-Gabby Gob. 104- G. I. Juniors. 105-Sad Sack's Muttsy... 106-Gabby Gob (7/66). 107-G. I. Juniors (8/66). 108-Sad Sack's Muttsy...109-Gabby Gob. 110-G. I. Juniors (11/66). 111-Sad Sack's Muttsy... (12/66). 112-G. I. Juniors. 113-Sad Sack's Muttsy... 114-G. I. Juniors. 115-Sad Sack's Muttsy... 116-G. I. Juniors (5/67). 117-Sad Sack's Muttsy... 118-G. I. Juniors. 119-Sad Sack's Muttsy... (8/67). 120-G. I. Juniors (9/67). 121-Sad Sack's Muttsy... (10/67). 122-G. I. Juniors (11/67) 2 4 6 10 14 18

HARVEY HITS COMICS
Harvey Publications: Nov, 1986 - No. 6, Oct, 1987

1-Little Lotta, Little Dot, Wendy & Baby Huey 1 2 3 4 5 7
2-6: 3-Xmas-c 4.50

HARVEY POP COMICS (Rock Happening) (Teen Humor)
Harvey Publications: Oct, 1968 - No. 2, Nov, 1969 (Both are 68 pg. Giants)

1-The Cowsills 6 12 18 39 62 85
2-Bunny 5 10 15 34 55 75

HARVEY 3-D HITS (See Sad Sack)

Haunt #9 © TMP

Haunted Tank (2009 series) #1 © DC

The Haunt of Fear #8 © WMG

GD VG FN VF VF/NM NM-
2.0 4.0 6.0 8.0 9.0 9.2

HARVEY-TOON (...S) (See Harvey Hits No. 29, 34, 38, 42, 46, 50, 53)

HARVEY WISEGUYS (...Digest #? on)
Harvey Comics: Nov, 1987; #2, Nov, 1988; #3, Apr, 1989 - No. 4, Nov, 1989 (98 pgs., digest-size, $1.25/$1.75)

1-Hot Stuff, Spooky, etc. 2 3 4 6 8 10
2-4: 2 (68 pgs.) 1 2 3 4 5 7

HATARI (See Movie Classics)

HATE
Fantagraphics Books: Spr, 1990 - No. 30, 1998 ($2.50/$2.95, B&W/color)

1 2 4 6 10 12 15
2-3 1 2 3 5 6 8
4-10 5.00
11-20: 16- color begins 4.00
21-29 3.00
30-($3.95) Last issue 4.00
Annual 1 (2/01, $3.95) Peter Bagge-s/a 4.00
Annual 2-7 (12/01-Present; $4.95) Peter Bagge-s/a 5.00
Buddy Bites the Bullet! (2001, $16.95) r/Buddy stories in color 17.00
Buddy Go Home! (1997, $16.95) r/Buddy stories in color 17.00
Hate-Ball Special Edition ($3.95, giveaway)-reprints 4.00
Hate Jamboree (10/98, $4.50) old & new cartoons 4.50

HATHAWAYS, THE (TV)
Dell Publishing Co.: No. 1298, Feb-Apr, 1962 (one-shot)

Four Color 1298-Photo-c 5 10 15 30 48 65

HAUNTED (See This Magazine Is Haunted)

HAUNT
Image Comics: Oct, 2009 - Present ($2.99)

1-McFarlane & Kirkman-s/Capullo & Ottley-a/McFarlane-a(i)/c; two variant-c 3.00
2-14: 2-Two covers. 13-($1.99) 3.00
Image Firsts: Haunt #1 (10/10, $1.00) r/#1 with "Image First" cover logo 1.00

HAUNTED (Baron Weirwulf's Haunted Library on-c #21 on)
Charlton Comics: 9/71 - No. 30, 11/76; No. 31, 9/77 - No. 75, 9/84

1-All Ditko issue 5 10 15 35 55 75
2-7-Ditko-c/a 3 6 9 19 29 38
8,12,28-Ditko-a 2 4 6 11 16 20
9,19 2 4 6 8 11 14
10,20,15,18: 10,20-Sutton-a. 15-Sutton-c 2 4 6 8 11 14
11,13,14,16-Ditko-c/a 3 6 9 14 20 25
17-Sutton-c/a; Newton-a 2 4 6 9 12 15
21-Newton-c/a; Sutton-a; 1st Baron Weirwulf 3 6 9 16 23 30
22-Newton-c/a; Sutton-a 2 4 6 9 13 16
23,24-Sutton-c; Ditko-a 2 4 6 9 13 16
25-27,29,32,33 1 3 4 6 8 10
30,41,47,49-52,60,74-Ditko-c/a: 51-Reprints #1 2 4 6 11 16 20
31,35,37,38-Sutton-a 1 3 4 6 8 10
34,36,39,40,42,57-Ditko-a 2 4 6 8 10 12
43-46,48,53-56,58,59,61-73: 59-Newton-a. 64-Sutton-c. 71-73-Low print
1 2 3 5 6 8
75-(9/84) Last issue; low print 2 4 6 9 13 16

NOTE: ***Aparo*** *c-45.* ***Ditko*** *a-1-8, 11-16, 18, 23, 24, 28, 30, 34r, 36r, 39-42r, 47r, 49-52r, 57, 60, 74. c-1-7, 11, 13, 14, 16, 30, 41, 47, 49-52, 74.* ***Howard*** *a-6, 9, 18, 22, 25, 32.* ***Kim*** *a-9, 19.* ***Morisi*** *a-13.* ***Newton*** *a-17, 21, 59r; c-21, 22(painted).* ***Staton*** *a-11, 12, 18, 21, 22, 30, 33, 35, 38; c-18, 33, 38.* ***Sutton*** *a-10, 17, 20-22, 31, 35, 37, 38; c-15, 17, 18, 23(painted), 24(painted), 27, 64r. #49 reprints Tales of the Mysterious Traveler #4.*

HAUNTED, THE
Chaos! Comics: Jan, 2002 - No. 4, Apr, 2002 ($2.99, limited series)

1-4-Peter David-s/Nat Jones-a 3.00
...: Gray Matters (7/02, $2.99) David-s/Jones-a 3.00

HAUNTED LOVE
Charlton Comics: Apr, 1973 - No. 11, Sept, 1975

1-Tom Sutton-a (16 pgs.) 6 12 18 37 59 80
2,3,6,7,10,11 3 6 9 18 27 35
4,5-Ditko-a 4 8 12 22 34 45
8,9-Newton-c 3 6 9 19 29 38
Modern Comics #1(1978) 2 3 4 6 8 10

NOTE: ***Howard*** *a-8i.* ***Kim*** *a-7-9.* ***Newton*** *c-8, 9.* ***Staton*** *a-1-6.* ***Sutton*** *a-1, 3-5, 10, 11.*

HAUNTED TANK, THE
DC Comics (Vertigo): Feb, 2009 - No. 5, June, 2009 ($2.99, limited series)

1-5-Marraffino-s/Flint-a. 1-Two covers by Flint and Joe Kubert 3.00
TPB (2010, $14.99) r/#1-5 15.00

GD VG FN VF VF/NM NM-
2.0 4.0 6.0 8.0 9.0 9.2

HAUNTED THRILLS (Tales of Horror and Terror)
Ajax/Farrell Publications: June, 1952 - No. 18, Nov-Dec, 1954

1-r/Ellery Queen #1 60 120 180 381 653 925
2-L. B. Cole-a r-/Ellery Queen #1 40 80 120 242 401 560
3,4: 3-Drug use story 36 72 108 216 351 485
5-Classic skull-c 37 74 111 222 361 500
6-10,12: 7-Hitler story. 32 64 96 188 307 425
11-Nazi death camp story 34 68 102 199 325 450
13-18: 18-Lingerie panels. 14-Jesus Christ apps. in story by Webb. 15-Jo-Jo-r
27 54 81 158 259 360

NOTE: ***Kamenish*** *art in most issues.* ***Webb*** *a-12.*

HAUNT OF FEAR (Formerly Gunfighter)
E. C. Comics: No. 15, May-June, 1950 - No. 28, Nov-Dec, 1954

15(#1, 1950)(Scarce) 291 582 873 2328 3714 5100
16-1st app. "The Witches Cauldron" & the Old Witch (by Kamen); begin series as hostess of Haunt of Fear 120 240 360 960 1530 2100
17-Origin of Crypt of Terror, Vault of Horror, & Haunt of Fear; used in **SOTI**, pg. 43; last pg. Ingels-a used by N.Y. Legis. Comm.; story "Monster Maker" based on Frankenstein. Old Witch by Feldstein 120 240 360 960 1530 2100
4-Ingels becomes regular artist for Old Witch. 1st Vault Keeper & Crypt Keeper app. in HOF; begin series 77 154 231 616 983 1350
5-Injury-to-eye panel, pg. 4 of Wood story 61 122 183 488 782 1075
6,7,9,10: 6-Crypt Keeper by Feldstein begins. 9-Crypt Keeper by Davis begins. 10-Ingels biog. 47 94 141 376 601 825
8-Classic Feldstein Shrunken Head-c 51 102 153 408 654 900
11,12: Classic Ingels-c; 11-Kamen biog. 12-Feldstein biog.
40 80 120 320 510 700
13,15,16,20: 16-Ray Bradbury adaptation. 20-Feldstein-r/Vault of Horror #12
37 74 111 296 473 650
14-Origin Old Witch by Ingels; classic-Ingels-c 50 100 150 400 638 875
17-Classic Ingels-c 40 80 120 320 510 700
18-Old Witch-c; Ray Bradbury adaptation & biography
39 78 117 312 499 685
19-Used in **SOTI**, ill. "A comic book baseball game" & Senate investigation on juvenile delinq. bondage/decapitation-c 47 94 141 376 601 825
21-27: 23-EC version of the Hansel and Gretel story; **SOTI**, pg. 241 discusses the original Grimm tale in relation to comics. 24-Used in Senate Investigative Report, pg.8. 26-Contains anti-censorship editorial, 'Are you a Red Dupe?' 27-Cannibalism story; Vault Keeper shown reading **SOTI** 27 54 81 216 346 475
28-Low distribution 35 70 105 280 445 610

NOTE: *(Canadian reprints known; see Table of Contents).* ***Craig*** *a-15-17, 5, 7, 10, 12, 13; c-15-17, 5-7.* ***Crandall*** *a-20, 21, 26, 27.* ***Davis*** *a-4-26, 28.* ***Evans*** *a-15-19, 22-25, 27.* ***Feldstein*** *a-15-17, 20; c-4, 8-10.* ***Ingels*** *a-16, 17, 4-28; c-11-28.* ***Kamen*** *a-16, 4, 6, 7, 9-11, 13-19, 21-28.* ***Krigstein*** *a-28.* ***Kurtzman*** *a-15(#1), 17(#3).* ***Orlando*** *a-9, 12.* ***Wood*** *a-15, 16, 4-6.*

HAUNT OF FEAR, THE
Gladstone Publishing: May, 1991 - No. 2, July, 1991 ($2.00, 68 pgs.)

1,2: 1-Ghastly Ingels-c(r); 2-Craig-c(r) 4.00

HAUNT OF FEAR
Russ Cochran/Gemstone Publ.: Sept, 1991 - No. 5, 1992 ($2.00, 68 pgs.); Nov, 1992 - No. 28, Aug, 1998 ($1.50/$2.00/$2.50)

1-28: 1-Ingels-c(r). 1-3-r/HOF #15-17 with original-c. 4,5-r/HOF #4,5 with original-c 4.00
Annual 1-5: 1- r/#1-5. 2- r/#6-10. 3- r/#11-15. 4- r/#16-20. 5- r/#21-25 14.00
Annual 6-r/#26-28 9.00

HAUNT OF HORROR, THE (Digest)
Marvel Comics: Jun, 1973 - No. 2, Aug, 1973 (164 pgs.; text and art)

1-Morrow painted skull-c; stories by Ellison, Howard, and Leiber; Brunner-a
4 8 12 24 37 50
2-Kelly Freas painted bondage-c; stories by McCaffrey, Goulart, Leiber, Ellison; art by Simonson, Brunner, and Buscema 3 6 9 17 25 32

HAUNT OF HORROR, THE (Magazine)
Cadence Comics Publ. (Marvel): May, 1974 - No. 5, Jan, 1975 (75¢) (B&W)

1,2: 2-Origin & 1st app. Gabriel the Devil Hunter; Satana begins
3 6 9 14 20 26
3-5: 4-Neal Adams-a. 5-Evans-a(2) 3 6 9 18 27 35

NOTE: ***Alcala*** *a-2.* ***Colan*** *a-2p.* ***Heath*** *r-1.* ***Krigstein*** *r-3.* ***Reese*** *a-1.* ***Simonson*** *a-1.*

HAUNT OF HORROR: EDGAR ALLAN POE
Marvel Comics (MAX): July, 2006 - No. 3, Sept, 2006 ($3.99, B&W, limited series)

1-3- Poe-inspired/adapted stories with Richard Corben-a 4.00
HC (2006, $19.99) r/series; cover sketches 20.00

HAUNT OF HORROR: LOVECRAFT

The Hawk #3 © Z-D

Hawkeye: Blindspot #1 © MAR

Hawkman V4 #8 © DC

GD 2.0 | VG 4.0 | FN 6.0 | VF 8.0 | VF/NM 9.0 | NM- 9.2

Marvel Comics (MAX): Aug, 2008 - No. 3, Oct, 2008 ($3.99, B&W, limited series)

1-3-Lovecraft-inspired/adapted stories with Richard Corben-a 4.00

HAVE GUN, WILL TRAVEL (TV)
Dell Publishing Co.: No. 931, 8/58 - No. 14, 7-9/62 (All Richard Boone photo-c)

	GD	VG	FN	VF	VF/NM	NM-
Four Color 931 (#1)	12	24	36	87	164	240
Four Color 983,1044 (#2,3)	9	18	27	60	100	140
4 (1-3/60) - 10	8	16	24	54	90	125
11-14	8	16	24	52	86	120

HAVEN: THE BROKEN CITY (See JLA/Haven: Arrival and JLA/Haven: Anathema)
DC Comics: Feb, 2002 - No. 9, Oct, 2002 ($2.50, limited series)

1-9-Olivetti-c/a: 1- JLA app. Series concludes in JLA/Haven: Anathema 3.00

HAVOK & WOLVERINE - MELTDOWN (See Marvel Comics Presents #24)
Marvel Comics (Epic Comics): Mar, 1989 - No. 4, Oct, 1989 ($3.50, mini-series, squarebound, mature)

1-4: Art by Kent Williams & Jon J. Muth; story by Walt & Louise Simonson 4.00

HAWAIIAN DICK
Image Comics: Dec, 2002 - No. 3, Feb, 2003 ($2.95, limited series)

1-3-B. Clay Moore-s/Steven Griffin-a 3.00
...: Byrd of Paradise TPB (8/03, $14.95) r/#1-3, script & sketch pages 15.00

HAWAIIAN DICK: SCREAMING BLACK THUNDER
Image Comics: Nov, 2007 - No. 5, Oct, 2008 ($2.99, limited series)

1-5-B. Clay Moore-s/Scott Chantler-a 3.00

HAWAIIAN DICK: THE LAST RESORT
Image Comics: Aug, 2004 - No. 4, June, 2006 ($2.95/$2.99, limited series)

1-4-B. Clay Moore-s/Steven Griffin-a 3.00
Vol. 2 TPB (10/06, $14.99) r/#1-4 & the original series pitch 15.00

HAWAIIAN EYE (TV)
Gold Key: July, 1963 (Troy Donahue, Connie Stevens photo-c)

	GD	VG	FN	VF	VF/NM	NM-
1 (10073-307)	5	10	15	34	55	75

HAWAIIAN ILLUSTRATED LEGENDS SERIES
Hogarth Press: 1975 (B&W)(Cover printed w/blue, yellow, and green)

1-Kalelealuaka, the Mysterious Warrior 5.00

HAWK, THE (Also see Approved Comics #1, 7 & Tops In Adventure)
Ziff-Davis/St. John Publ. Co. No. 4 on: Wint/51 - No. 3, 11-12/52; No. 4, 1-2/53; No. 8, 9/54 - No. 12, 5/55 (Painted c-1-4)(#5-7 don't exist)

	GD	VG	FN	VF	VF/NM	NM-
1-Anderson-a	20	40	60	114	182	250
2 (Sum, '52)-Kubert, Infantino-a	12	24	36	69	97	125
3-4	10	20	30	56	76	95
8-12: 8(9/54)-Reprints #3 w/different-c by Baker. 9-Baker-c/a; Kubert-a(r)/#2. 10-Baker-c/a; r/one story from #2. 11-Baker-c; Buckskin Belle & The Texan app. 12-Baker-c/a; Buckskin Belle app.	15	30	45	85	130	175
3-D 1(11/53, 25¢)-Came w/glasses; Baker-c	32	64	96	188	307	425

NOTE: *Baker c-8-12. Larsen a-10. Tuska a-1, 9, 12. Painted c-1, 4, 7.*

HAWK AND THE DOVE, THE (See Showcase #75 & Teen Titans) (1st series)
National Periodical Publications: Aug-Sept, 1968 - No. 6, June-July, 1969

	GD	VG	FN	VF	VF/NM	NM-
1-Ditko-c/a	8	16	24	54	90	125
2-6: 5-Teen Titans cameo	5	10	15	32	51	70

NOTE: *Ditko c/a-1, 2. Gil Kane a-3p, 4p, 5, 6p; c-3-6.*

HAWK AND DOVE (2nd Series)
DC Comics: Oct, 1988 - No. 5, Feb, 1989 ($1.00, limited series)

1-Rob Liefeld-c/a(p) in all 4.00
2-5 3.00
Trade paperback ('93, $9.95)-Reprints #1-5 10.00

HAWK AND DOVE
DC Comics: June, 1989 - No. 28, Oct, 1991 ($1.00)

1-28 3.00
Annual 1,2 ('90, '91; $2.00) 1-Liefeld pin-up. 2-Armageddon 2001 x-over 4.00

HAWK AND DOVE
DC Comics: Nov, 1997 - No. 5, Mar, 1998 ($2.50, limited series)

1-5-Baron-s/Zachary & Giordano-a 3.00

HAWK AND WINDBLADE (See Elfford)
Warp Graphics: Aug, 1997 - No.2, Sept, 1997 ($2.95, limited series)

1,2-Blair-s/Chan-c/a 3.00

HAWKEYE (See The Avengers #16 & Tales Of Suspense #57)
Marvel Comics Group: Sept, 1983 - No. 4, Dec, 1983 (limited series)

GD 2.0 | VG 4.0 | FN 6.0 | VF 8.0 | VF/NM 9.0 | NM- 9.2

1-4: Mark Gruenwald-a/scripts. 1-Origin Hawkeye. 3-Origin Mockingbird. 4-Hawkeye & Mockingbird elope 3.00

HAWKEYE
Marvel Comics: Jan, 1994 - No. 4, Apr, 1994 ($1.75, limited series)

1-4 3.00

HAWKEYE (Volume 2)
Marvel Comics: Dec, 2003 - No. 8, Aug, 2004 ($2.99)

1-8: 1-6-Nicieza-s/Raffaele-a. 7,8-Bennett-a; Black Widow app. 3.00

HAWKEYE AND MOCKINGBIRD (Avengers) (Leads into Widowmaker mini-series)
Marvel Comics: Aug, 2010 - No. 6, Jan, 2011 ($3.99/$2.99)

1-($3.99) Heroic Age; Jim McCann-s/David Lopez-a; history of the characters 4.00
2-6-($2.99) Phantom Rider, Dominic Fortune & Crossfire app. 3.00

HAWKEYE & THE LAST OF THE MOHICANS (TV)
Dell Publishing Co.: No. 884, Mar, 1958 (one-shot)

	GD	VG	FN	VF	VF/NM	NM-
Four Color 884-Lon Chaney Jr. photo-c	7	14	21	47	76	105

HAWKEYE: BLINDSPOT (Avengers)
Marvel Comics: Apr, 2011 - No. 4 ($2.99, limited series)

1-3: 1-McCann-s/Diaz-a; Zemo app. 2-Diaz & Dragotta-a 3.00

HAWKEYE: EARTH'S MIGHTIEST MARKSMAN
Marvel Comics: Oct, 1998 ($2.99, one-shot)

1-Justice and Firestar app.; DeFalco-s 3.00

HAWKGIRL (Title continued from Hawkman #49, Apr, 2006)
DC Comics: No. 50, May, 2006 - No. 66, Sept, 2007 ($2.50/$2.99)

50-66: 50-Chaykin-a/Simonson-s begin; One Year Later. 52-Begin $2.99-c. 57,58-Bennett-a. 59-Blackfire app. 63-Batman app. 64-Superman app. 3.00
...: Hath-Set TPB (2008, $17.99) r/#61-66 18.00
...: Hawkman Returns TPB (2007, $17.99) r/#57-60 & JSA Classified #21,22 18.00
...: The Maw TPB (2007, $17.99) r/#50-56 18.00

HAWKMAN (See Atom & Hawkman, The Brave & the Bold, DC Comics Presents, Detective Comics, Flash Comics, Hawkworld, JSA, Justice League of America #31, Legend of the Hawkman, Mystery in Space, Shadow War Of..., Showcase, & World's Finest #256)

HAWKMAN (1st Series) (Also see The Atom #7 & Brave & the Bold #34-36, 42-44, 51)
National Periodical Publications: Apr-May, 1964 - No. 27, Aug-Sept, 1968

	GD	VG	FN	VF	VF/NM	NM-
1-(4-5/64)-Anderson-c/a begins, ends #21	54	108	162	459	930	1400
2	22	44	66	159	317	475
3,5: 5-2nd app. Shadow Thief	14	28	42	99	200	300
4-Origin & 1st app. Zatanna (10-11/64)	17	34	51	122	249	375
6	11	22	33	77	144	210
7	10	20	30	70	125	180
8-10: 9-Atom cameo; Hawkman & Atom learn each other's I.D.; 3rd app. Shadow Thief	9	18	27	63	107	150
11-15	7	14	21	47	76	105
16-27: 18-Adam Strange x-over (cameo #19). 25-G.A. Hawkman-r by Moldoff. 26-Kirby-a(r). 27-Kubert-c	6	12	18	37	59	80

HAWKMAN (2nd Series)
DC Comics: Aug, 1986 - No. 17, Dec, 1987

1-17: 10-Byrne-c, Special #1 (1986, $1.25) 3.00
Trade paperback (1989, $19.95)-r/Brave and the Bold #34-36,42-44 by Kubert; Kubert-c 20.00

HAWKMAN (4th Series)(See both Hawkworld limited & ongoing series)
DC Comics: Sept, 1993 - No. 33, July, 1996 ($1.75/$1.95/$2.25)

1-($2.50)-Gold foil embossed-c; storyline cont'd from Hawkworld ongoing series; new costume & powers. 4.00
2-13,0,14-33: 2-Green Lantern x-over. 3-Airstryke app. 4,6-Wonder Woman app. 13-(9/94)-Zero Hour. 0-(10/94). 14-(11/94). 15-Aquaman-c & app. 23-Wonder Woman app. 25-Kent Williams-c. 29,30-Chaykin-c. 32-Breyfogle-c 3.00
Annual 1 (1993, $2.50, 68 pgs.)-Bloodlines Earthplague 4.00
Annual 2 (1995, $3.95)-Year One story 4.00

HAWKMAN (Title continues as Hawkgirl #50-on) (See JSA #23 for return)
DC Comics: May, 2002 - No. 49, Apr, 2006 ($2.50)

1-Johns & Robinson-s/Morales-a 5.00
1-2nd printing 3.00
2-40: 2-4-Shadow Thief app. 5,6-Green Arrow-c/app. 8-Atom-c/app. 13-Van Sciver-a. 14-Gentleman Ghost app. 15-Hawkwoman app. 16-Byth returns. 23-25-Black Reign x-over with JSA #56-58. 26-Byrne-c/a. 29,30-Land-c. 37-Golden Eagle returns 3.00
41-49: 41-Hawkman killed. 43-Golden Eagle origin. 46-49-Adam Kubert-c 3.00
...: Allies & Enemies TPB (2004, $14.95) r/#7-14 & pages from Secret Files and Origins 15.00
...: Endless Flight TPB (2003, $12.95) r/#1-6 & Secret Files and Origins 13.00

Headline Comics #8 © PRIZE

Heart of Empire #6 © Bryan Talbot

Heart Throbs #100 © DC

	GD 2.0	VG 4.0	FN 6.0	VF 8.0	VF/NM 9.0	NM- 9.2
...: Rise of the Golden Eagle TPB (2006, $17.99) r/#37-45						18.00
... Secret Files and Origins (10/02, $4.95) profiles and pin-ups by various						5.00
... Special 1 (10/08, $3.50) Tie-in to Rann-Thanagar Holy War series; Starlin-s/a(p)						3.50
...: Wings of Fury TPB (2005, $17.99) r/#15-22						18.00

HAWKMOON: THE JEWEL IN THE SKULL
First Comics: May, 1986 - No. 4, Nov, 1986 ($1.75, limited series, Baxter paper)

1-4: Adapts novel by Michael Moorcock 3.00

HAWKMOON: THE MAD GOD'S AMULET
First Comics: Jan, 1987 - No. 4, July, 1987 ($1.75, limited series, Baxter paper)

1-4: Adapts novel by Michael Moorcock 3.00

HAWKMOON: THE RUNESTAFF
First Comics: Jun, 1988 -No. 4, Dec, 1988 ($1.75-$1.95, lim. series, Baxter paper)

1-4: ($1.75) Adapts novel by Michael Moorcock. 3,4 ($1.95) 3.00

HAWKMOON: THE SWORD OF DAWN
First Comics: Sept, 1987 - No. 4, Mar, 1988 ($1.75, lim. series, Baxter paper)

1-4: Dorman painted-c; adapts Moorcock novel 3.00

HAWKS OF THE SEAS (WILL EISNER'S...)
Dark Horse Comics: July, 2003 ($19.95, B&W, hardcover)

nn-Reprints 1937-1939 weekly Pirate serial by Will Eisner; Williamson intro. 20.00

HAWKWORLD
DC Comics: 1989 - No. 3, 1989 ($3.95, prestige format, limited series)

Book 1-3: 1-Tim Truman story & art in all; Hawkman dons new costume; reintro Byth 4.00
TPB (1991, $16.95) r/#1-3 17.00

HAWKWORLD (3rd Series)
DC Comics: June, 1990 - No. 32, Mar, 1993 ($1.50/$1.75)

1-Hawkman spin-off; story cont'd from limited series. 4.00
2-32: 15,16-War of the Gods x-over. 22-J'onn J'onzz app. 3.00
Annual 1-3 ('90-'92, $2.95, 68 pgs.), 2-2nd printing with silver ink-c 4.00
NOTE: *Truman a-30-32; c-27-32, Annual 1.*

HAYWIRE
DC Comics: Oct, 1988 - No. 13, Sept, 1989 ($1.25, mature)

1-13 3.00

HAZARD
Image Comics (WildStorm Prod.): June, 1996 - No. 7, Nov, 1996 ($1.75)

1-7: 1-Intro Hazard; Jeff Mariotte scripts begin; Jim Lee-c(p) 3.00

HEADHUNTERS
Image Comics: Apr, 1997 - No. 3, June, 1997 ($2.95, B&W)

1-3: Chris Marrinan-s/a 3.00

HEADLINE COMICS
DC Comics: Jan. 1942

nn - Ashcan comic, not distributed to newsstands, only for in-house use. Cover art is More Fun Comics #73 with interior being Star Spangled Comics #2 (no known sales)

HEADLINE COMICS (...For the American Boy) (...Crime No. 32-39)
Prize Publ./American Boys' Comics: Feb, 1943 - No. 22, Nov-Dec, 1946; No. 23, 1947 - No. 77, Oct, 1956

	GD 2.0	VG 4.0	FN 6.0	VF 8.0	VF/NM 9.0	NM- 9.2
1-Junior Rangers-c/stories begin; Yank & Doodle x-over in Junior Rangers (Junior Rangers are Uncle Sam's nephews)	61	128	183	390	670	950
2	36	72	108	211	343	475
3-Used in **POP**, pg. 84	24	48	72	142	234	325
4-7,9,10: 4,9,10-Hitler stories in each	20	40	60	120	195	270
8-Classic Hitler-c	129	258	387	826	1413	2000
11,12	19	38	57	111	176	240
13-15-Blue Streak in all	20	40	60	114	182	250
16-Origin & 1st app. Atomic Man (11-12/45)	30	60	90	177	289	400
17,18,20,21: 21-Atomic Man ends (9-10/46)	17	34	51	98	154	210
19-S&K-a	32	64	96	188	307	425
22-Last Junior Rangers; Kiefer-c	15	30	45	83	124	165
23,24: (All S&K-a). 23-Valentine's Day Massacre story; content changes to true crime. 24-Dope-crazy killer story	32	64	96	188	307	425
25-35-S&K-c/a. 25-Powell-a	29	58	87	170	278	385
36-S&K-a; photo-c begin	21	42	63	124	202	280
37-1 pg. S&K, Severin-a; rare Kirby photo-c app.	22	44	66	128	209	290
38,40-Meskin-a	11	22	33	60	83	105
39,41-43,46-50,52-55: 41-J. Edgar Hoover 26th Anniversary Issue with photo on-c. 43,49-Meskin-a. 48-Meskin-c	9	18	27	52	69	85
44-S&K-c; Severin/Elder, Meskin-a	15	30	45	84	127	170
45-Kirby-a	13	26	39	72	101	130
51-Kirby-c	13	26	39	72	101	130
56-S&K-a	14	28	42	81	118	155
57-77: 72-Meskin-c/a(i)	8	16	24	44	57	70

NOTE: ***Hollingsworth*** *a-30. Photo c-36-43.* ***H. C. Kiefer*** *c-12-16, 22. Atomic Man c-17-19.*

HEADMAN
Innovation Publishing: 1990 ($2.50, mature)

1-Sci/fi 3.00

HEAP, THE
Skywald Publications: Sept, 1971 (52 pgs.)

	GD 2.0	VG 4.0	FN 6.0	VF 8.0	VF/NM 9.0	NM- 9.2
1-Kinstler-r/Strange Worlds #8; new-s w/Sutton-a	4	8	12	24	37	50

HEART AND SOUL
Mikeross Publications: April-May, 1954 - No. 2, June-July, 1954

	GD 2.0	VG 4.0	FN 6.0	VF 8.0	VF/NM 9.0	NM- 9.2
1,2	9	18	27	50	65	80

HEARTBREAKERS (Also see Dark Horse Presents)
Dark Horse Comics: Apr, 1996 - No. 4, July, 1996 ($2.95, limited series)

1-4: 1-W/paper doll & pin-up. 2-Alex Ross pin-up. 3-Evan Dorkin pin-ups. 4-Brereton-c; Matt Wagner pin-up 3.00
...Superdigest (7/98, $9.95, digest-size) new stories 10.00

HEARTLAND (See Hellblazer)
DC Comics (Vertigo): Mar, 1997 ($4.95, one-shot, mature)

1-Garth Ennis-s/Steve Dillon-c/a 5.00

HEART OF DARKNESS
Hardline Studios: 1994 ($2.95)

1-Brereton-c 3.00

HEART OF EMPIRE
Dark Horse Comics: Apr, 1999 - No. 9, Dec, 1999 ($2.95, limited series)

1-9-Bryan Talbot-s/a 3.00

HEART OF THE BEAST, THE
DC Comics (Vertigo): 1994 ($19.95, hardcover, mature)

1-Dean Motter scripts 20.00

HEARTS OF DARKNESS (See Ghost Rider; Wolverine; Punisher: Hearts of...)

HEART THROBS (Love Stories No. 147 on)
Quality Comics/National Periodical #47(4-5/57) on (Arleigh #48-101): 8/49 - No. 8, 10/50; No. 9, 3/52 - No. 146, Oct, 1972

	GD 2.0	VG 4.0	FN 6.0	VF 8.0	VF/NM 9.0	NM- 9.2
1-Classic Ward-c, Gustavson-a, 9 pgs.	43	86	129	271	461	650
2-Ward-c/a (9 pgs); Gustavson-a	27	54	81	158	259	360
3-Gustavson-a	14	28	42	80	115	150
4,6,8-Ward-a, 8-9 pgs.	17	34	51	98	154	210
5,7	12	24	36	67	94	120
9-Robert Mitchum, Jane Russell photo-c	14	28	42	82	121	160
10,15-Ward-a	14	28	42	82	121	160
11-14,16-20: 12 (7/52)	10	20	30	56	76	95
21-Ward-c	14	28	42	80	115	150
22,23-Ward-a(p)	11	22	33	60	83	105
24-33: 33-Last pre-code (3/55)	10	20	30	54	72	90
34-39,41-44,46 (12/56; last Quality issue)	9	18	27	52	69	85
40-Ward-a; r-7 pgs./#21	10	20	30	56	76	95
45-Baker-a	7	14	21	45	73	100
47-(4-5/57; 1st DC issue)	20	40	60	144	290	435
48-60, 100	9	18	27	65	113	160
61-70	7	14	21	47	76	105
71-99: 74-Last 10 cent issue	6	12	18	41	66	90
101-The Beatles app. on-c	13	26	39	93	182	270
102-120: 102-123-(Serial)-Three Girls, Their Lives, Their Loves	4	8	12	26	41	55
121-132,143-146	4	8	12	22	34	45
133-142-(52 pgs.)	4	8	12	28	44	60

NOTE: ***Gustavson*** *a-8.* ***Tuska*** *a-128. Photo c-4, 5, 8-10, 15, 17.*

HEART THROBS - THE BEST OF DC ROMANCE COMICS (See Fireside Book Series)

HEART THROBS
DC Comics (Vertigo): Jan, 1999 - No. 4, Apr, 1999 ($2.95, lim. series)

1-4-Romance anthology. 1-Timm-c. 3-Corben-a 3.00

HEATHCLIFF (See Star Comics Magazine)
Marvel Comics (Star Comics)/Marvel Comics No. 23 on: Apr, 1985 - No. 56, Feb, 1991 (#16-on, $1.00)

	GD 2.0	VG 4.0	FN 6.0	VF 8.0	VF/NM 9.0	NM- 9.2
1-Post-a most issues	1	2	3	4	5	7

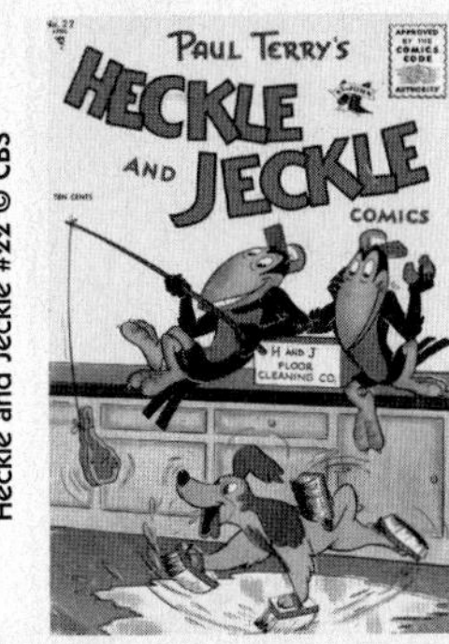

Heckle and Jeckle #22 © CBS

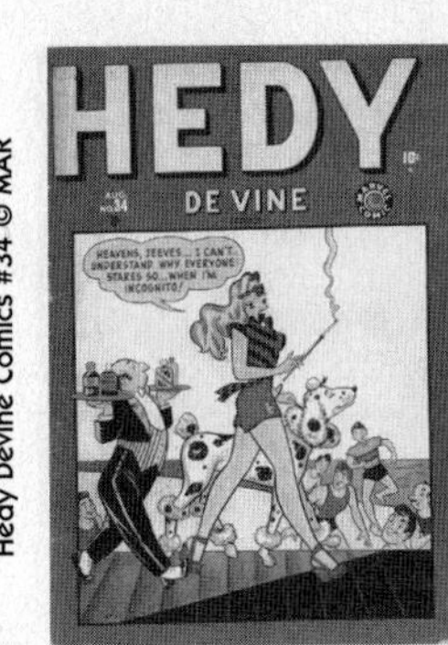

Hedy Devine Comics #34 © MAR

Hellblazer #232 © DC

2-10,47: 47-Batman parody (Catman vs. the Soaker) 5.00
11-46,48-56: 43-X-Mas issue 4.00
Annual 1 ('87) 4.00

HEATHCLIFF'S FUNHOUSE
Marvel Comics (Star Comics)/Marvel No. 6 on: May, 1987 - No. 10, 1988
1 5.00
2-10 4.00

HEAVEN'S DEVILS
Image Comics: Sept, 2003 - No. 4, July, 2004 ($2.95/$3.50, B&W, limited series)
1-3-($2.95) Jai Nitz-s/Zach Howard-a 3.00
4-($3.50) Kevin Sharpe-a 3.50

HEAVY HITTERS
Marvel Comics (Epic Comics): 1993 ($3.75, 68 pgs.)
1-Bound w/trading card; Lawdog, Feud, Alien Legion, Trouble With Girls, & Spyke 4.00

HEAVY LIQUID
DC Comics (Vertigo): Oct, 1999 - No. 5, Feb, 2000 ($5.95, limited series)
1-5-Paul Pope-s/a; flip covers 6.00
TPB (2001, $29.95) r/#1-5 30.00
TPB (2009, $24.95) r/#1-5; development sketches and cover gallery; new cover 25.00
HC (2008, $39.99, dustjacket) r/#1-5; development sketches and cover gallery 40.00

HECKLE AND JECKLE (Paul Terry's...)(See Blue Ribbon, Giant Comics Edition #5A & 10, Paul Terry's, Terry-Toons Comics)
St. John Publ. Co. No. 1-24/Pines No. 25 on: No. 3, 2/52 - No. 24, 10/55; No. 25, Fall/56 - No. 34, 6/59

	GD	VG	FN	VF	VF/NM	NM-
3(#1)-Funny animal	24	48	72	140	230	320
4(6/52), 5	13	26	39	74	105	135
6-10(4/53)	9	18	27	50	65	80
11-20	8	16	24	40	50	60
21-34: 25-Begin CBS Television Presents on-c	7	14	21	35	43	50

HECKLE AND JECKLE (TV) (See New Terrytoons)
Gold Key/Dell Publ. Co.: 11/62 - No. 4, 8/63; 5/66; No. 2, 10/66; No. 3, 8/67

	GD	VG	FN	VF	VF/NM	NM-
1 (11/62; Gold Key)	6	12	18	43	69	95
2-4	4	8	12	22	34	45
1 (5/66; Dell)	4	8	12	26	41	55
2,3	3	6	9	19	29	38

(See March of Comics No. 379, 472, 484)

HECKLE AND JECKLE 3-D
Spotlight Comics: 1987 - No. 2?, 1987 ($2.50)
1,2 5.00

HECKLER, THE
DC Comics: Sept, 1992 - No. 6, Feb, 1993 ($1.25)
1-6-T&M Bierbaum-s/Keith Giffen-c/a 3.00

HECTIC PLANET
Slave Labor Graphics 1998 ($12.95/$14.95)
Book 1,2-r-Dorkin-s/a from Pirate Corp$ Vol. 1 & 2 15.00

HECTOR COMICS (The Keenest Teen in Town)
Key Publications: Nov, 1953 - No. 3, 1954

	GD	VG	FN	VF	VF/NM	NM-
1-Teen humor	7	14	21	37	46	55
2,3	5	10	15	22	26	30

HECTOR HEATHCOTE (TV)
Gold Key: Mar, 1964

	GD	VG	FN	VF	VF/NM	NM-
1 (10111-403)	7	14	21	47	76	105

HECTOR THE INSPECTOR (See Top Flight Comics)

HEDGE KNIGHT, THE
Image Comics: Aug, 2003 - No. 6, Apr, 2004 ($2.95, limited series)
1-6-George R.R. Martin-s/Mike S. Miller-a. 1-Two covers by Kaluta and Miller 3.00
George R.R. Martin's The Hedge Knight HC (Marvel, 2006, $19.99) r/series; 2 covers 20.00
George R.R. Martin's The Hedge Knight SC (Marvel, 2007, $14.99) r/series 15.00
TPB (2004, $14.95) r/series plus new short story 15.00

HEDGE KNIGHT II: SWORN SWORD
Marvel Comics (Dabel Brothers): Jun, 2007 - No. 6, Jun, 2008 ($2.99, limited series)
1-6-George R.R. Martin-s/Mike Miller-a. 1-Two covers by Yu & Miller, plus Miller B&W-c 3.00
... HC (2008, $19.99) r/series; 2 covers 20.00

HEDY DEVINE COMICS (Formerly All Winners #21? or Teen #22?(6/47); Hedy of Hollywood #36 on; also see Annie Oakley, Comedy & Venus)
Marvel Comics (RCM)/Atlas #50: No. 22, Aug, 1947 - No. 50, Sept, 1952

	GD	VG	FN	VF	VF/NM	NM-
22-1st app. Hedy Devine (also see Joker #32)	34	68	102	199	325	450
23,24,27-30: 23-Wolverton-a, 1 pg; Kurtzman's "Hey Look", 2 pgs. 24,27-30- "Hey Look" by Kurtzman, 1-3 pgs.	20	40	60	117	189	260
25-Classic "Hey Look" by Kurtzman, "Optical Illusion"	21	42	63	126	206	285
26- "Giggles 'n' Grins" by Kurtzman	18	36	54	103	162	220
31-34,36-50: 32-Anti-Wertham editorial	14	28	42	76	108	140
35-Four pgs. "Rusty" by Kurtzman	17	34	51	98	154	210

HEDY-MILLIE-TESSIE COMEDY (See Comedy Comics)

HEDY WOLFE (Also see Patsy & Hedy & Miss America Magazine V1#2)
Atlas Publishing Co. (Emgee): Aug, 1957

	GD	VG	FN	VF	VF/NM	NM-
1-Patsy Walker's rival; Al Hartley-c	13	26	39	72	101	130

HEE HAW (TV)
Charlton Press: July, 1970 - No. 7, Aug, 1971

	GD	VG	FN	VF	VF/NM	NM-
1	4	8	12	28	44	60
2-7	3	6	9	19	29	38

HEIDI (See Dell Jr. Treasury No. 6)

HELEN OF TROY (Movie)
Dell Publishing Co.: No. 684, Mar, 1956 (one-shot)

	GD	VG	FN	VF	VF/NM	NM-
Four Color 684-Buscema-a, photo-c	9	18	27	65	113	160

HELL
Dark Horse Comics: July, 2003 - No. 4, Mar, 2004 ($2.99, limited series)
1-4-Augustyn-s/Demong-a/Meglia-c 3.00

HELLBLAZER (John Constantine) (See Saga of Swamp Thing #37)
(Also see Books of Magic limited series)
DC Comics (Vertigo #63 on): Jan, 1988 - Present ($1.25-$2.99)

	GD	VG	FN	VF	VF/NM	NM-
1-(44 pgs.)-John Constantine; McKean-c thru #21	2	4	6	9	12	15
1-Special Edition (7/10, $1.00) r/#1 with "What's Next?" cover logo						1.00
2-5	1	2	3	5	7	9
6-8,10: 10-Swamp Thing cameo						6.00
9,19: 9-X-over w/Swamp Thing #76. 19-Sandman app.	1	2	3	5	6	8
11-18,20						6.00
21-26,28-30: 22-Williams-c. 24-Contains bound-in Shocker movie poster. 25,26-Grant Morrison scripts.						5.00
27-Gaiman scripts; Dave McKean-a; low print run	2	4	6	10	12	15
31-39: 36-Preview of World Without End.						4.00
40-($2.25, 52 pgs.)-Dave McKean-a & colors; preview of Kid Eternity						5.00
41-Ennis scripts begin; ends #83						5.00
42-49,51-74,76-99,101-119: 44,45-Sutton-a(i). 52-Glenn Fabry painted-c begin. 62-Special Death insert by McKean. 63-Silver metallic ink on-c. 77-Totleben-c. 84-Sean Phillips-c/a begins; Delano story. 85-88-Eddie Campbell story. 89-Paul Jenkins scripts begin						3.50
50,75,100,120: 50-($3.00, 52 pgs.). 75-($2.95, 52 pgs.). 100,120 ($3.50,48 pgs.)						4.00
121-199, 201-249, 251-274,276,277: 129-Ennis-s. 141-Bradstreet-a. 146-150-Corben-a. 151-Azzarello-s begin. 175-Carey-s begin; Dillon-a. 176-Begin $2.75-c. 182,183-Bermejo-a. 216-Mina-s begins. 220-Begin $2.99-c. 229-Carey-s/Leon-a. 234-Initial printing (white title logo) has missing text; corrected printing has lt. blue title logo. 265,266,271-274-Bisley-a. 268-271-Shade the Changing Man app.						3.00
200-($4.50) Carey-s/Dillon, Frusin, Manco-a						4.50
250-($3.99) Short stories by various; art by Lloyd, Phillips, Milligan; Bermejo-c						4.00
275-($4.99) Constatine's wedding; Bisley-c						5.00
Annual 1 (1989, $2.95, 68 pgs.)-Bryan Talbot's 1st work in American comics						5.00
Special 1 (1993, $3.95, 68 pgs.)-Ennis story; w/pin-ups.						4.00
...Black Flowers (2005, $14.99, TPB) r/#181-186						15.00
...Bloodlines (2007, $19.99, TPB) r/#47-50,52-55,59-61						20.00
...Damnation's Flame (1999, $16.95, TPB) r/#72-77						17.00
...Dangerous Habits (1997, $14.95, TPB) r/#41-46						15.00
...Fear and Loathing (1997, $14.95, TPB) r/#62-67						18.00
...Fear and Loathing (2nd printing, $17.95)						18.00
...: Freezes Over (2003, $14.95, TPB) r/#157-163						15.00
...Good Intentions (2002, $12.95, TPB) r/#151-156						13.00
...Hard Time (2001, $9.95, TPB) r/#146-150						10.00
...Haunting (2003, $12.95, TPB) r/#134-139						13.00
...Highwater (2004, $19.95, TPB) r/#164-174						20.00
John Constantine Hellblazer: All His Engines HC (2005, $24.95, with dustjacket) new graphic novel; Mike Carey-s/Leonardo Manco-a						25.00
John Constantine Hellblazer: All His Engines SC (2006, $14.99) new graphic novel						15.00
John Constantine Hellblazer: Empathy is the Enemy SC (2006, $14.99) r/#216-222						15.00

Hellblazer Special: Lady Constantine #4 © DC

Hellboy: FCBD 2008 © Mike Mignola

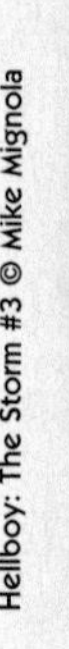
Hellboy: The Storm #3 © Mike Mignola

	GD	VG	FN	VF	VF/NM	NM-
	2.0	4.0	6.0	8.0	9.0	9.2

John Constantine Hellblazer: Hooked SC (2010, $14.99) r/#256-260 15.00
John Constantine Hellblazer: India SC (2010, $14.99) r/#261-266 15.00
John Constantine Hellblazer: Joyride SC (2008, $14.99) r/#230-237 15.00
John Constantine Hellblazer: Pandemonium HC (2010, $24.99,with dustjacket) new graphic novel; Jamie Delano-s/Jock-a 25.00
John Constantine Hellblazer: Pandemonium SC (2011, $7.99) new graphic novel 18.00
John Constantine Hellblazer: Scab SC (2009, $14.99) r/#250-255 15.00
John Constantine Hellblazer: The Devil You Know SC (2007, $19.99) r/#10-13, Annual #1 and The Horrorist miniseries #1,2 20.00
John Constantine Hellblazer: The Family Man SC (2008, $19.99, TPB) r/#23,24,28-33 20.00
John Constantine Hellblazer: The Fear Machine SC (2008, $19.99, TPB) r/#14-22 20.00
John Constantine Hellblazer: The Red Right Hand SC (2007, $14.99) r/#223-228 15.00
John Const. Hellblazer: The Roots of Coincidence SC ('09, $14.99) r/#243,244,247-249 15.00
...Original Sins (1993, $19.95, TPB) r/#1-9 20.00
...Original Sins (2011, $19.99, TPB) r/#1-9 20.00
...Rake at the Gates of Hell (2003, $19.95, TPB) r/#78-83; Heartland #1 20.00
...: Rare Cuts (2005, $14.95, TPB) r/#11,25,26,35,56,84 & Vertigo Secret Files: Hellblazer 15.00
...: Reasons To Be Cheerful (2007, $14.99, TPB) r/#201-206 15.00
...: Red Sepulchre (2005, $12.99, TPB) r/#175-180 13.00
...: Setting Sun (2004, $12.95, TPB) r/#140-143 13.00
...: Son of Man (2004, $12.95, TPB) r/#129-133 13.00
...: Stations of the Cross (2006, $14.99, TPB) r/#194-200 15.00
...: Staring At The Wall (2005, $14.99, TPB) r/#187-193 15.00
...Tainted Love (1998, $16.95, TPB) r/#68-71, Vertigo Jam #1 and Hellblazer Special #1 17.00
NOTE: ***Alcala*** *a-8i, 9i, 18-22i.* ***Gaiman*** *scripts-27.* ***McKean*** *a-27,40; c-1-21.* ***Sutton*** *a-44i, 45i.* ***Talbot*** *a-Annual 1.*

HELLBLAZER: CITY OF DEMONS
DC Comics (Vertigo): Early Dec, 2010 - No. 5, Feb, 2011 ($2.99, limited series)
1-5-Si Spencer-s/Sean Murphy-a/c 3.00

HELLBLAZER SPECIAL: BAD BLOOD
DC Comics (Vertigo): Sept, 2000 - No. 4, Dec, 2000 ($2.95, limited series)
1-4-Delano-s/Bond-a; Constantine in 2025 London 3.00

HELLBLAZER SPECIAL: CHAS
DC Comics (Vertigo): Sept, 2008 - No. 5, Jan, 2009 ($2.99, limited series)
1-5-Story of Constantine's cab driver; Oliver-s/Sudzuka-a/Fabry-c 3.00
... - The Knowledge TPB (2009, $14.99) r/#1-5 15.00

HELLBLAZER SPECIAL: LADY CONSTANTINE
DC Comics (Vertigo): Feb, 2003 - No. 4, May, 2003 ($2.95, limited series)
1-4-Story of Johanna Constantine in 1785; Diggle-s/Sudzuka-a/Noto-c 3.00

HELLBLAZER/THE BOOKS OF MAGIC
DC Comics (Vertigo): Dec, 1997 - No. 2, Jan, 1998 ($2.50, limited series)
1,2-John Constantine and Tim Hunter 3.00

HELLBOY (Also see Batman/Hellboy/Starman, Danger Unlimited #4, Dark Horse Presents, Gen[13] #13B, Ghost/Hellboy, John Byrne's Next Men, San Diego Comic Con #2, & Savage Dragon)

HELLBOY
Dark Horse Comics: Apr, 2008
... : Free Comic Book Day; Three short stories; Mignola-c; art by Fegredo, Davis, Azaceta 2.50

HELLBOY: ALMOST COLOSSUS
Dark Horse Comics (Legend): Jun, 1997 - No. 2, Jul, 1997 ($2.95, lim. series)
1,2-Mignola-s/a 4.00

HELLBOY/BEASTS OF BURDEN
Dark Horse Comics: Oct, 2010 ($3.50, one-shot)
... Sacrifice - Evan Dorkin & Mignola-s/Jill Thompson-a 3.50

HELLBOY: BOX FULL OF EVIL
Dark Horse Comics: Aug, 1999 - No. 2, Sept, 1999 ($2.95, lim. series)
1,2-Mignola-s/a; back-up story w/ Matt Smith-a 4.00

HELLBOY CHRISTMAS SPECIAL
Dark Horse Comics: Dec, 1997 ($3.95, one-shot)
nn-Christmas stories by Mignola, Gianni, Darrow, Purcell 5.00

HELLBOY: CONQUEROR WORM
Dark Horse Comics: May, 2001 - No. 4, Aug, 2001 ($2.99, lim. series)
1-4-Mignola-s/a/c 3.00

HELLBOY: DARKNESS CALLS
Dark Horse Comics: Apr, 2007 - No. 6, Nov, 2007 ($2.99, lim. series)
1-6-Mignola-s/Fegredo-a 3.00

HELLBOY: DOUBLE FEATURE OF EVIL
Dark Horse Comics: Nov, 2010 ($3.50, one-shot)
1-Mignola-s; Corben-a/c 3.50

HELLBOY IN MEXICO
Dark Horse Comics: May, 2010 ($3.50, one-shot)
1-Mignola-s; Corben-a/c; Mexican wrestlers vs. monsters 3.50

HELLBOY: IN THE CHAPEL OF MOLOCH
Dark Horse Comics: Oct, 2008 ($2.99, one-shot)
nn-Mignola-s/a/c 3.00

HELLBOY, JR.
Dark Horse Comics: Oct, 1999 - No. 2, Nov, 1999 ($2.95, limited series)
1,2-Stories and art by various 4.00
TPB (1/04, $14.95) r/#1&2, Halloween; sketch pages; intro. by Steve Niles; Bill Wray-c 15.00

HELLBOY, JR., HALLOWEEN SPECIAL
Dark Horse Comics: Oct, 1997 ($3.95, one-shot)
nn-"Harvey" style renditions of Hellboy characters; Bill Wray, Mike Mignola & various-s/a; wraparound-c by Wray 5.00

HELLBOY: MAKOMA, OR A TALE TOLD...
Dark Horse Comics: Feb, 2006 - No. 2, Mar, 2006 ($2.99, lim. series)
1,2-Mignola-s/c; Mignola & Corben-a 3.00

HELLBOY PREMIERE EDITION
Dark Horse Comics (Wizard): 2004 (no price, one-shot)
nn- Two covers by Mignola & Davis; Mignola-s/a; BPRD story w/Arcudi-s/Davis-a 5.00
Wizard World Los Angeles-Movie photo-c; Mignola-s/a; BPRD story w/Arcudi-s/Davis-a 10.00

HELLBOY: SEED OF DESTRUCTION (First Hellboy series)
Dark Horse Comics (Legend): Mar, 1994 - No. 4, Jun, 1994 ($2.50, lim. series)
1-4-Mignola-c/a w/Byrne scripts; Monkeyman & O'Brien back-up story (origin) by Art Adams. 6.00
Hellboy: One for One (8/10, $1.00) r/#1 Hellboy story with red cover frame 1.00
Trade paperback (1994, $17.95)-collects all four issues plus r/Hellboy's 1st app. in San Diego Comic Con #2 & pin-ups 18.00
Limited edition hardcover (1995, $99.95)-includes everything in trade paperback plus additional material. 100.00

HELLBOY STRANGE PLACES
Dark Horse Books: Apr, 2006 ($17.95, TPB)
SC - Reprints Hellboy: The Third Wish #1,2 and Hellboy: The Island #1,2; sketch pages 18.00

HELLBOY: THE BRIDE OF HELL
Dark Horse Comics: Dec, 2009 ($3.50, one-shot)
1-Mignola-s/c; Corben-a; preview of The Marquis: Inferno 3.50

HELLBOY: THE CHAINED COFFIN AND OTHERS
Dark Horse Comics (Legend): Aug, 1998 ($17.95, TPB)
nn-Mignola-c/a/s; reprints out-of-print one shots; pin-up gallery 18.00

HELLBOY: THE COMPANION
Dark Horse Books: May, 2008 ($14.95, 9"x6", TPB)
nn-Overview of Hellboy history, characters, stories, mythology; text with Mignola panels 15.00

HELLBOY: THE CORPSE
Dark Horse Comics: Mar, 2004 (25¢, one-shot)
nn-Mignola-c/a/scripts; reprints "The Corpse" serial from Capitol City's Advance Comics catalog; development sketches and photos of the Corpse from the Hellboy movie 3.00

HELLBOY: THE CORPSE AND THE IRON SHOES
Dark Horse Comics (Legend): Jan, 1996 ($2.95, one-shot)
nn-Mignola-c/a/scripts; reprints "The Corpse" serial w/new story 4.00

HELLBOY: THE CROOKED MAN
Dark Horse Comics: Jul, 2008 - No. 3, Sept, 2008 ($2.99, lim. series)
1-3-Mignola-s/Corben-a/c 3.00

HELLBOY: THE GOLDEN ARMY
Dark Horse Comics: Jan, 2008 (no cover price)
nn-Prelude to the 2008 movie; Del Toro & Mignola-s/Velasco-a; 3 photo covers 3.00

HELLBOY: THE ISLAND
Dark Horse Comics: June, 2005 - No. 2, July, 2005 ($2.99, lim. series)
1,2: Mignola-c/a & scripts 3.00

HELLBOY: THE RIGHT HAND OF DOOM
Dark Horse Comics (Legend): Apr, 2000 ($17.95, TPB)
nn-Mignola-c/a/s; reprints 18.00

HELLBOY: THE SLEEPING AND THE DEAD

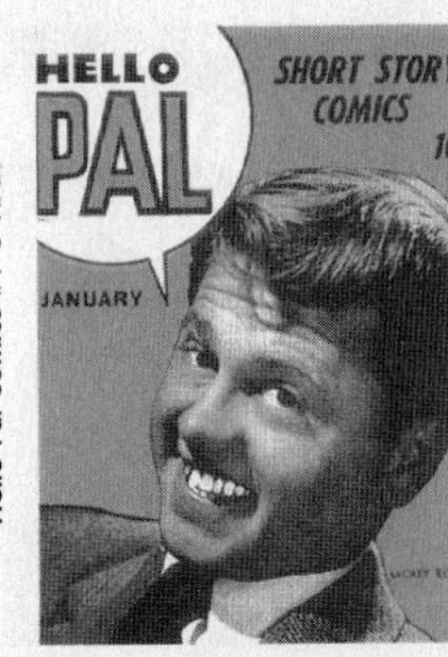

Hello Pal Comics #1 © HARV

Hellstorm #18 © MAR

Henry #27 © DELL

	GD 2.0	VG 4.0	FN 6.0	VF 8.0	VF/NM 9.0	NM- 9.2

Dark Horse Comics: Dec, 2010 - No. 2, Feb, 2011 ($3.50, lim. series)
1,2-Mignola-s/Scott Hampton-a 3.50

HELLBOY: THE STORM
Dark Horse Comics: Jul, 2010 - No. 3, Sept, 2010 ($2.99, lim. series)
1-3-Mignola-s/Fegredo-a 3.00

HELLBOY: THE THIRD WISH
Dark Horse Comics (Maverick): July, 2002 - No. 2, Aug, 2002 ($2.99, limited series)
1,2-Mignola-c/a/s 3.00

HELLBOY THE TROLL WITCH AND OTHERS
Dark Horse Books: Nov, 2007 ($17.95, TPB)
SC - Reprints Hellboy: Makoma, Hellboy Premiere Edition and stories from Dark Horse Book of Hauntings, DHB of Witchcraft, DHB of the Dead, DHB of Monsters 18.00

HELLBOY: THE WILD HUNT
Dark Horse Comics: Dec, 2008 - No. 8, Nov, 2009 ($2.99, lim. series)
1-8: Mignola-c/s; Fegredo-a 3.00

HELLBOY: THE WOLVES OF ST. AUGUST
Dark Horse Comics (Legend): 1995 ($4.95, squarebound, one-shot)
nn-Mignola--c/a/scripts; r/Dark Horse Presents #88-91 with additional story 5.00

HELLBOY: WAKE THE DEVIL (Sequel to Seed of Destruction)
Dark Horse Comics (Legend): Jun, 1996 - No. 5, Oct, 1996 ($2.95, lim. series)
1-5: Mignola-c/a & scripts; The Monstermen back-up story by Gary Gianni 5.00
TPB (1997, $17.95) r/#1-5 18.00

HELLBOY: WEIRD TALES
Dark Horse Comics: Feb, 2003 - No. 8, Apr, 2004 ($2.99, limited series, anthology)
1-8-Hellboy stories from other creators. 1-Cassaday-c/s/a; Watson-s/a. 6-Cho-c 3.00
... Vol. 1 (2004, 17.95) r/#1-4 18.00
... Vol. 2 (2004, 17.95) r/#5-8 and Lobster Johnson serial from #1-8 18.00

HELLCAT
Marvel Comics: Sept, 2000 - No. 3, Nov, 2000 ($2.99)
1-3-Englehart-s/Breyfogle-a; Hedy Wolfe app. 3.00

HELLCOP
Image Comics (Avalon Studios): Aug, 1998 - No. 4, Mar, 1999 ($2.50)
1-4: 1-(Oct. on-c) Casey-s 3.00

HELL ETERNAL
DC Comics (Vertigo Verité): 1998 ($6.95, squarebound, one-shot)
1-Delano-s/Phillips-a 7.00

HELLGATE: LONDON (Based on the video game)
Dark Horse Comics: No. 0, May 2006 - No. 3, Mar, 2007 ($2.99)
0-3-Edginton-s/Pugh-a/Briclot-c 3.00

HELLHOUNDS (...: Panzer Cops #3-6)
Dark Horse Comics: 1994 - No. 6, July, 1994 ($2.50, B&W, limited series)
1-6: 1-Hamner-c. 3-(4/94). 2-Joe Phillips-c 3.00

HELLHOUND, THE REDEMPTION QUEST
Marvel Comics (Epic Comics): Dec, 1993 - No. 4, Mar, 1994 ($2.25, lim. series, coated stock)
1-4 3.00

HELLO BUDDIES
Harvey Publications: 1953 (25¢, small size)

1	2	4	6	11	16	20

HELLO, I'M JOHNNY CASH
Spire Christian Comics (Fleming H. Revell Co.): 1976 (39¢/49¢)

nn-(39¢-c)	3	6	9	16	22	28
nn-(49¢-c)	2	4	6	10	14	18

HELL ON EARTH (See DC Science Fiction Graphic Novel)

HELLO PAL COMICS (Short Story Comics)
Harvey Publications: Jan, 1943 - No. 3, May, 1943 (Photo-c)

1-Rocketman & Rocketgirl begin; Yankee Doodle Jones app.; Mickey Rooney photo-c	63	126	189	403	689	975
2-Charlie McCarthy photo-c (scarce)	56	112	168	349	595	840
3-Bob Hope photo-c (scarce)	60	120	180	384	660	935

HELLRAISER/NIGHTBREED – JIHAD (Also see Clive Barker's...)
Epic Comics (Marvel Comics): 1991 - Book 2, 1991 ($4.50, 52 pgs.)
Book 1,2 4.50

HELL-RIDER (Motorcycle themed magazine)
Skywald Publications: Aug, 1971 - No. 2, Oct, 1971 (B&W, 68 pgs.)

1-Origin & 1st app.; Butterfly & the Wild Bunch begin; 1st Hell-Rider by Andru, Esposito and Friedrich	6	12	18	41	66	90
2-Andru, Ayers, Buckler, Shores-a	4	8	12	28	44	60

NOTE: *#3 advertised in Psycho #5 but did not come out.* ***Buckler*** *a-1, 2.* ***Rosenbaum*** *c-1,2.*

HELL'S ANGEL (Becomes Dark Angel #6 on)
Marvel Comics UK: July, 1992 - No. 5, Nov, 1993 ($1.75)
1-5: X-Men (Wolverine, Cyclops)-c/stories. 1-Origin. 3-Jim Lee cover swipe 3.00

HELLSHOCK
Image Comics: July, 1994 - No. 4, Nov, 1994 ($1.95, limited series)
1-4-Jae Lee-c/a & scripts. 4-Variant-c. 3.00

HELLSHOCK
Image Comics: Jan, 1997 - No. 3, Jan, 1998 ($2.95/$2.50, limited series)
1-($2.95)-Jae Lee-c/s/a, Villarrubia-painted-a 4.00
2-($2.50) 3.00
Book 3: The Science of Faith (1/98, $2.50) Jae Lee-c/s/a, Villarrubia-painted-a 3.00
Vol. 1 HC (2006, $49.99) r/#1-3 re-colored, with unpublished 22 pg. conclusion; cover gallery and sketches; alternate opening art; intro. by Jim Lee 50.00

HELLSPAWN
Image Comics: Aug, 2000 - No. 16, Apr, 2003 ($2.50)
1-Bendis-s/Ashley Wood-c/a; Spawn and Clown app. 3.00
2-9: 6-Last Bendis-s; Mike Moran (Miracleman app.). 7-Niles-s 3.00
10-16-Templesmith-a 3.00
...: The Ashley Wood Collection Vol. 1 (4/06, $24.95, TPB) r/#1-10; sketch & cover gallery 25.00

HELLSTORM: PRINCE OF LIES (See Ghost Rider #1 & Marvel Spotlight #12)
Marvel Comics: Apr, 1993 - No. 21, Dec, 1994 ($2.00)
1-($2.95)-Parchment-c w/red thermographic ink 4.00
2-21: 14-Bound-in trading card sheet. 18-P. Craig Russell-c 3.00

HELLSTORM: SON OF SATAN
Marvel Comics (MAX): Dec, 2006 - No. 5, Apr, 2007 ($3.99, limited series)
1-5-Suydam-c/Irvine-s/Braun & Janson-a 4.00
... - Equinox TPB (2007, $17.99) r/#1-5; interviews with the creators 18.00

HELMET OF FATE, THE (Series of one-shots following Doctor Fate's helmet)
DC Comics: Mar, 2007 - May 2007 ($2.99, one-shots)
...: Black Alice (5/07) Simone-s/Rouleau-a/c 3.00
...: Detective Chimp (3/07) Willingham-s/McManus-a/Bolland-c 3.00
...: Ibis the Invincible (3/07) Williams-s/Winslade-a; the Ibistick returns 3.00
...: Sargon the Sorcerer (4/07) Niles-s/Scott Hampton-s; debut new Sargon 3.00
...: Zauriel (4/07) Gerber-s/Snejbjerg-a/Kaluta-c; leads into new Doctor Fate series 3.00
TPB (2007, $14.99) r/one-shots 15.00

HE-MAN (See Masters Of The Universe)

HE-MAN (Also see Tops In Adventure)
Ziff-Davis Publ. Co. (Approved Comics): Fall, 1952

1-Kinstler painted-c; Powell-a	16	32	48	94	147	200

HE-MAN
Toby Press: May, 1954 - No. 2, July, 1954 (Painted-c by B. Safran)

1	15	30	45	88	137	185
2-Shark-c	15	30	45	85	130	175

HENNESSEY (TV)
Dell Publishing Co.: No. 1200, Aug-Oct, 1961 - No. 1280, Mar-May, 1962

Four Color 1200-Gil Kane-a, photo-c	7	14	21	47	76	105
Four Color 1280-Photo-c	6	12	18	43	69	95

HENRY (Also see Little Annie Rooney)
David McKay Publications: 1935 (52 pgs.) (Daily B&W strip reprints)(10"x10" cardboard-c)

1-By Carl Anderson	39	78	117	240	395	550

HENRY (See King Comics & Magic Comics)
Dell Publishing Co.: No. 122, Oct, 1946 - No. 65, Apr-June, 1961

Four Color 122-All new stories begin	13	26	39	94	185	275
Four Color 155 (7/47), 1 (1-3/48)-All new stories	10	20	30	68	119	170
2	6	12	18	41	66	90
3-10	5	10	15	34	55	75
11-20: 20-Infinity-c	4	8	12	28	44	60
21-30	4	8	12	22	34	45

Henry Aldrich Comics #3 © DELL

Herc #1 © MAR

Here's Howie Comics #5 © DC

GD 2.0 | VG 4.0 | FN 6.0 | VF 8.0 | VF/NM 9.0 | NM- 9.2

31-40 3 6 9 19 29 38
41-65 3 6 9 16 23 30

HENRY (See Giant Comic Album and March of Comics No. 43, 58, 84, 101, 112, 129, 147, 162, 178, 189)

HENRY ALDRICH COMICS (TV)
Dell Publishing Co.: Aug-Sept, 1950 - No. 22, Sept-Nov, 1954
1-Part series written by John Stanley; Bill Williams-a
9 18 27 65 113 160
2 6 12 18 37 59 80
3-5 5 10 15 30 48 65
6-10 4 8 12 26 41 55
11-22 4 8 12 22 34 45

HENRY BREWSTER
Country Wide (M.F. Ent.): Feb, 1966 - V2#7, Sept, 1967 (All 25¢ Giants)
1 3 6 9 19 29 38
2-6(12/66), V2#7-Powell-a in most 2 4 6 13 18 22

HEPCATS
Antarctic Press: Nov, 1996 - No. 12 ($2.95, B&W)
0-12-Martin Wagner-c/s/a: 0-color 3.00
0-($9.95) CD Edition 10.00

HERALDS
Marvel Comics: Aug, 2010 - No. 5, Aug, 2010 ($2.99, weelky limited series)
1-5-Kathryn Immonen-s/Zonjic & Harren-a; She-Hulk, Hellcat, Emma Frost, Photon app. 3.00

HERBIE (See Forbidden Worlds #73,94,110,114,116 & Unknown Worlds #20)
American Comics Group: April-May, 1964 - No. 23, Feb, 1967 (All 12¢)
1-Whitney-c/a in most issues 15 30 45 106 216 325
2-4 9 18 27 65 113 160
5-Beatles parody (10 pgs.), Dean Martin, Frank Sinatra app. (10-11/64)
10 20 30 71 128 185
6,7,9,10 8 16 24 56 93 130
8-Origin & 1st app. The Fat Fury 9 18 27 64 110 155
11-23: 14-Nemesis & Magicman app. 17-r/2nd Herbie from Forbidden Worlds #94. 23-r/1st Herbie from F.W. #73 6 12 18 43 69 95
... Archives Volume One HC (Dark Horse, 8/08, $49.95, dust jacket) r/earliest apps. in Forbidden Worlds, Unknown Worlds, and Herbie #1-5; Scott Shaw intro. 50.00

HERBIE
Dark Horse Comics: Oct, 1992 - No. 12, 1993 ($2.50, limited series)
1-Whitney-r plus new-c/a in all; Byrne-c/a & scripts 4.00
2-6: 3-Bob Burden-c/a. 4-Art Adams-c 3.00

HERBIE GOES TO MONTE CARLO, HERBIE RIDES AGAIN (See Walt Disney Showcase No. 24, 41)

HERC (Hercules from the Avengers)
Marvel Comics: Jun, 2011 - Present ($2.99)
1-Pak & Van Lente-s; Hobgoblin app. 3.00

HERCULES (See Hit Comics #1-21, Journey Into Mystery Annual, Marvel Graphic Novel #37, Marvel Premiere #26 & The Mighty...)

HERCULES (See Charlton Classics)
Charlton Comics: Oct, 1967 - No. 13, Sept, 1969; Dec, 1968
1-Thane of Bagarth begins; Glanzman-a in all 4 8 12 26 41 55
2-13: 1-5,7-10-Aparo-a. 8-(12¢-c) 3 6 9 16 23 50
8-(Low distribution)(12/68, 35¢, B&W); magazine format; new Hercules story plus-r story/#1; Thane-r/#1-3 6 12 18 37 59 80
Modern Comics reprint 10('77), 11('78) 6.00

HERCULES (Prince of Power) (Also see The Champions)
Marvel Comics Group: V1#1, Sept, 1982 - V1#4, Dec, 1982; V2#1, Mar, 1984 - V2#4, Jun, 1984 (color, both limited series)
1-4, V2#1-4: Layton-c/a. 4-Death of Zeus. 3.00
NOTE: ***Layton*** *a-1, 2, 3p, 4p, V2#1-4; c-1-4, V2#1-4.*

HERCULES
Marvel Comics: Jun, 2005 - No. 5, Sept, 2005 ($2.99, limited series)
1-5-Texeira-a/c; Tieri-s. 4-Capt. America, Wolverine and New Avengers app. 3.00
...: New Labors of Hercules TPB (2005, $13.99) r/#1-5 14.00

HERCULES: HEART OF CHAOS
Marvel Comics: Aug, 1997 - No. 3, Oct, 1997 ($2.50, limited series)
1-3-DeFalco-s, Frenz-a 3.00

HERCULES: OFFICIAL COMICS MOVIE ADAPTION
Acclaim Books: 1997 ($4.50, digest size)
nn-Adaption of the Disney animated movie 4.50

GD 2.0 | VG 4.0 | FN 6.0 | VF 8.0 | VF/NM 9.0 | NM- 9.2

HERCULES: THE LEGENDARY JOURNEYS (TV)
Topps Comics: June, 1996 - No. 5, Oct, 1996 ($2.95)
1-2: 1-Golden-c. 3.00
3-Xena-c/app. 1 2 3 4 5 7
3-Variant-c 2 4 6 9 12 15
4,5: Xena-c/app. 5.00

HERCULES UNBOUND
National Periodical Publications: Oct-Nov, 1975 - No. 12, Aug-Sept, 1977
1-Wood-i begins 2 4 6 9 13 16
2-12: 7-Adams ad. 10-Atomic Knights x-over 2 3 4 6 8 10
NOTE: ***Buckler*** *c-7p.* ***Layton*** *inks-No. 9, 10.* ***Simonson*** *a-7-10p, 11, 12; c- 8p, 9-12.* ***Wood*** *a-1-8i; c-7i, 8i.*

HERCULES (...Unchained #1121) (Movie)
Dell Publishing Co.: No. 1006, June-Aug, 1959 - No.1121, Aug, 1960
Four Color 1006-Buscema-a, photo-c 9 18 27 60 100 140
Four Color 1121-Crandall/Evans-a 9 18 27 60 100 140

HERCULES: FALL OF AN AVENGER (Continues in Heroic Age: Prince of Power)
Marvel Comics: May, 2010 - No. 2, June, 2010 ($3.99, limited series)
1,2-Follows Hercules' demise in Incredible Hercules #141; Olivetti-c/a 4.00

HERCULES: TWILIGHT OF A GOD
Marvel Comics: Aug, 2010 - No. 4, Nov, 2010 ($3.99, limited series)
1-4-Layton-s/a(i); Lim-a; Galactus app. 4.00

HERCULIAN
Image Comics: Mar, 2011 ($4.99, oversized, one-shot)
1-Golden Age style superhero stories and humor pages; Erik Larsen-s/a/c 5.00

HERE COMES SANTA (See March of Comics No. 30, 213, 340)

HERE'S HOWIE COMICS
National Periodical Publications: Jan-Feb, 1952 - No. 18, Nov-Dec, 1954
1 28 56 84 165 270 375
2 15 30 45 88 137 185
3-5: 5-Howie in the Army issues begin (9-10/52) 14 28 42 76 108 140
6-10 11 22 33 64 90 115
11-18 11 22 33 50 83 105
Ashcan (1,2/51) not distributed to newsstands, only for in house use (no known sales)

HERETIC, THE
Dark Horse (Blanc Noir): Nov, 1996 - No. 4, Mar, 1997 ($2.95, lim. series)
1-4:-w/back-up story 3.00

HERITAGE OF THE DESERT (See Zane Grey, 4-Color 236)

HERMAN & KATNIP (See Harvey Comics Hits #60 & 62, Harvey Hits #14,25,31,41 & Paramount Animated Comics #1)

HERMES VS. THE EYEBALL KID
Dark Horse Comics: Dec, 1994 - No. 3,Feb, 1995 ($2.95, B&W, limited series)
1-3: Eddie Campbell-c/a/scripts 3.00

H-E-R-O (Dial H For HERO)
DC Comics: Apr, 2003 - No. 22, Jan, 2005 ($2.50)
1-Will Pfeiffer-s/Kano-a/Van Fleet-c 3.50
2-22: 2-6-Kano-a. 7,8-Gleason-a. 12-14-Kirk-a. 15-22-Robby Reed app. 3.00
...: Double Feature (6/03, $4.95) r/#1&2 5.00
...: Powers and Abilities (2003, $9.95) r/#1-6; intro. by Geoff Johns 10.00

HERO (Warrior of the Mystic Realms)
Marvel Comics: May, 1990 - No. 6, Oct, 1990 ($1.50, limited series)
1-6: 1-Portacio-i 3.00

HERO ALLIANCE, THE
Sirius Comics: Dec, 1985 - No. 2, Sept, 1986 (B&W)
1,2: 2-($1.50), Special Edition 1 (7/86, color) 3.00

HERO ALLIANCE
Wonder Color Comics: May, 1987 ($1.95)
1-Ron Lim-a 3.00

HERO ALLIANCE
Innovation Publishing: V2#1, Sept, 1989 - V2#17, Nov, 1991 ($1.95, 28 pgs.)
V2#1-17: 1,2-Ron Lim-a 3.00
Annual 1 (1990, $2.75, 36 pgs.)-Paul Smith-c/a 3.00
Special 1 (1992, $2.50, 32 pgs.)-Stuart Immonen-a (10 pgs.) 3.00

HERO ALLIANCE: END OF THE GOLDEN AGE
Innovation Publ.: July, 1989 - No. 3, Aug, 1989 ($1.75, bi-weekly lim. series)

Her-oes #4 © MAR

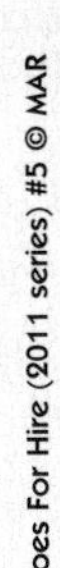

Heroes For Hire (2011 series) #5 © MAR

Heroic Comics #3 © EAS

	GD 2.0	VG 4.0	FN 6.0	VF 8.0	VF/NM 9.0	NM- 9.2

1-3: Bart Sears & Ron Lim-c/a; reprints & new-a 3.00

HERO COMICS (Hero Initiative benefit book)
IDW Publishing: 2009 ($3.99)

1-Short story anthology by various incl. Colan, Chaykin; covers by Wagner & Campbell 4.00

HEROES
Marvel Comics: Dec, 2001 ($3.50, magazine-size, one-shot)

1-Pin-up tributes to the rescue workers of the Sept. 11 tragedy; art and text by various; cover by Alex Ross 5.00
1-2nd and 3rd printings 3.50

HEROES (Also see Shadow Cabinet & Static)
DC Comics (Milestone): May, 1996 - No. 6, Nov, 1996 ($2.50, limited series)

1-6: 1-Intro Heroes (Iota, Donner, Blitzen, Starlight, Payback & Static) 3.00

HEROES (Based on the NBC TV series)
DC Comics (WildStorm): 2007; 2009 ($29.99, hardcover with dustjacket)

Vol. 1 - Collects 34 installments of the online graphic novel; art by various; two covers by Jim Lee and Alex Ross; intro. by Masi Oka; Jeph Loeb interview 30.00
Vol. 2 - (2009) Collects 46 installments of the online graphic novel; art by various incl. Gaydos, Grummett, Gunnell, Odagawa; two covers by Tim Sale and Gene Ha 30.00

HER-OES
Marvel Comics: Jun, 2010 - No. 4, Sept, 2010 ($2.99, limited series)

1-4-Randolph-s/Rousseau-a; Wasp, She-Hulk, Namora as teenagers 3.00

HEROES AGAINST HUNGER
DC Comics: 1986 ($1.50; one-shot for famine relief)

1-Superman, Batman app.; Neal Adams-c(p); includes many artists work; Jeff Jones assist (2 pg.) on B. Smith-a; Kirby-a 5.00

HEROES ALL CATHOLIC ACTION ILLUSTRATED
Heroes All Co.: 1943 - V6#5, Mar 10, 1948 (paper covers)

	GD	VG	FN	VF	VF/NM	NM-
V1#1-(16 pgs., 8x11")	24	48	72	142	234	325
V1#2-(16 pgs., 8x11")	19	38	57	111	176	240
V2#1(1/44)-3(3/44)-(16 pgs., 8x11")	15	30	45	94	147	200
V3#1(1/45)-10(12/45)-(16 pgs., 8x11")	15	30	45	85	130	175
V4#1-35 (12/20/46)-(16 pgs.)	14	28	42	80	115	150
V5#1(1/10/47)-8(2/28/47)-(16 pgs.), V5#9(3/7/47)-20(11/25/47)-(32 pgs.), V6#1(1/10/48)-5(3/10/48)-(32 pgs.)	12	24	36	69	97	125

HEROES ANONYMOUS
Bongo Comics: 2003 - No. 6, 2004 ($2.99, limited series)

1-6-($2.99)-Bill Morrison-c. 2-Guerra-a. 3-Pepoy-a 3.00

HEROES FOR HIRE
Marvel Comics: July, 1997 - No. 19, Jan, 1999 ($2.99/$1.99)

1-($2.99)-Wraparound cover 5.00
2-19: 2-Variant cover. 7-Thunderbolts app. 9-Punisher-c/app. 10,11-Deadpool-c/app. 18,19-Wolverine-c/app. 3.00
.../Quicksilver '98 Annual ($2.99) Siege of Wundagore pt.5 4.00

HEROES FOR HIRE
Marvel Comics: Oct, 2006 - No. 15, Dec, 2007 ($2.99)

1-5-Tucci-a/c; Black Cat, Shang-Chi, Tarantula, Humbug & Daughters of the Dragon app. 3.00
6-15: 6-8-Sparacio-c. 9,10-Golden-c. 11-13-World War Hulk x-over. 13-Takeda-c 3.00
... Vol. 1: Civil War (2007, $13.99) r/#1-5 14.00
... Vol. 2: Ahead of the Curve (2007, $13.99) r/#6-10 14.00
... Vol. 3: World War Hulk (2008, $13.99) r/#11-15 14.00

HEROES FOR HIRE
Marvel Comics: Feb, 2011 - Present ($3.99/$2.99)

1-($3.99) Abnett & Lanning-s/Walker-a; back-up history of the various teams 4.00
2-5-($2.99) 2-Silver Sable & Ghost Rider app. 5-Punisher app. 3.00

HEROES FOR HOPE STARRING THE X-MEN
Marvel Comics Group: Dec, 1985 ($1.50, one-shot, 52 pgs., proceeds donated to famine relief)

1-Stephen King scripts; Byrne, Miller, Corben-a; Wrightson/J. Jones-a (3 pgs.); Art Adams-c; Starlin back-c 5.00

HEROES, INC. PRESENTS CANNON
Wally Wood/CPL/Gang Publ.:1969 - No. 2, 1976 (Sold at Army PX's)

	GD	VG	FN	VF	VF/NM	NM-
nn-Ditko, Wood-a; Wood-c; Reese-a(p)	2	4	6	9	12	15
2-Wood-c; Ditko, Byrne, Wood-a; 8-1/2x10-1/2"; B&W; $2.00	3	6	9	16	23	30

NOTE: *First issue not distributed by publisher; 1,800 copies were stored and 900 copies were stolen from warehouse. Many copies have surfaced in recent years.*

HEROES OF THE WILD FRONTIER (Formerly Baffling Mysteries)
Ace Periodicals: No. 27, Jan, 1956 - No. 2, Apr, 1956

	GD	VG	FN	VF	VF/NM	NM-
27(#1),2-Davy Crockett, Daniel Boone, Buffalo Bill	6	12	18	29	36	42

HEROES REBORN (one-shots)
Marvel Comics: Jan, 2000 ($1.99)

...:Ashema; ...:Doom; ...:Doomsday; ...:Masters of Evil; ...:Rebel; ...:Remnants; ...:Young Allies 3.00

HEROES REBORN: THE RETURN (Also see Avengers, Fantastic Four, Iron Man & Captain America titles for issues and TPBs)
Marvel Comics: Dec, 1997 - No. 4 ($2.50, weekly mini-series)

1-4-Avengers, Fantastic Four, Iron Man & Captain America rejoin regular Marvel Universe; Peter David-s/Larocca-c/a 4.00
1-4-Variant-c for each 6.00

	GD	VG	FN	VF	VF/NM	NM-
Wizard 1/2	1	2	3	5	7	9

Return of the Heroes TPB ('98, $14.95) r/#1-4 15.00

HERO FOR HIRE (Power Man No. 17 on; also see Cage)
Marvel Comics Group: June, 1972 - No. 16, Dec, 1973

	GD	VG	FN	VF	VF/NM	NM-
1-Origin & 1st app. Luke Cage; Tuska-a(p)	12	24	36	87	164	240
2-Tuska-a(p)	6	12	18	41	66	90
3-5: 3-1st app. Mace. 4-1st app. Phil Fox of the Bugle	4	8	12	28	44	60
6-10: 8,9-Dr. Doom app. 9-F.F. app.	3	6	9	18	27	35
11-16: 14-Origin retold. 15-Everett Sub-Mariner-r('53). 16-Origin Stilletto; death of Rackham	3	6	9	14	20	25

HERO HOTLINE (1st app. in Action Comics Weekly #637)
DC Comics: April, 1989 - No. 6, Sept, 1989 ($1.75, limited series)

1-6: Super-hero humor; Schaffenberger-i 3.00

HEROIC ADVENTURES (See Adventures)

HEROIC AGE
Marvel Comics: Nov, 2010 ($3.99, limited series)

... Heroes 1 (11/10, $3.99) profile of heroes, bios, pros, cons, "power grid"; Raney-c 4.00
... Villains 1 (1/11, $3.99) profile of villains, bios, pros, cons, "power grid"; Jae Lee-c 4.00
... X-Men 1 (2/11, $3.99) profile of members in Steve Rogers journal entries,; Jae Lee-c 4.00

HEROIC AGE: PRINCE OF POWER (Continued from Hercules: Fall of an Avenger)
Marvel Comics: Jul, 2010 - No. 4, Oct, 2010 ($3.99, limited series)

1-4-Van Lente & Pak-s; Thor app.; leads into Chaos War #1 4.00

HEROIC COMICS (Reg'lar Fellers...#1-15; New Heroic #41 on)
Eastern Color Printing Co./Famous Funnies(Funnies, Inc. No. 1):
Aug, 1940 - No. 97, June, 1955

	GD	VG	FN	VF	VF/NM	NM-
1-Hydroman (origin) by Bill Everett, The Purple Zombie (origin) & Mann of India by Tarpe Mills begins (all 1st apps.)	200	400	600	1280	2190	3100
2	82	164	246	528	902	1275
3,4	52	104	156	328	557	785
5,6	44	88	132	277	469	660
7-Origin & 1st app. Man O'Metal (1 pg.)	47	94	141	296	498	700
8-10: 10-Lingerie panels	36	72	108	214	347	480
11,13	33	66	99	194	317	440
12-Music Master (origin/1st app.) begins by Everett, ends No. 31; last Purple Zombie & Mann of India	37	74	111	222	361	500
14,15-Hydroman x-over in Rainbow Boy. 14-Origin & 1st app. Rainbow Boy (super hero). 15-1st app. Downbeat	36	72	108	214	347	480
16-20: 16-New logo. 17-Rainbow Boy x-over in Hydroman. 19-Rainbow Boy x-over in Hydroman & vice versa	25	50	75	147	241	335
21-30:25-Rainbow Boy x-over in Hydroman. 28-Last Man O'Metal. 29-Last Hydroman	19	38	57	111	176	240
31,34,38	9	18	27	47	61	75
32,36,37-Toth-a (3-4 pgs. each)	10	20	30	54	72	90
33,35-Toth-a (8 & 9 pgs.)	10	20	30	56	76	95
39-42-Toth, Ingels-a	10	20	30	56	76	95
43,46,47,49-Toth-a (2-4 pgs.). 47-Ingels-a	9	18	27	52	69	85
44,45,50-Toth-a (6-9 pgs.)	10	20	30	54	72	90
48,53,54	8	16	24	44	57	70
51-Williamson-a	10	20	30	54	72	90
52-Williamson-a (3 pg. story)	9	18	27	47	61	75
55-Toth-a	9	18	27	52	69	85
56-60: 60-Everett-a	9	18	27	47	61	75
61-Everett-a	8	16	24	44	57	70
62,64-Everett-c/a	9	18	27	52	69	85
63-Everett-c	9	18	27	50	65	80

Hickory #1 © QUA

High Roads #3 © Leinil Yu

Hi-Jinx #5 © ACG

GD VG FN VF VF/NM NM-
2.0 4.0 6.0 8.0 9.0 9.2

GD VG FN VF VF/NM NM-
2.0 4.0 6.0 8.0 9.0 9.2

65-Williamson/Frazetta-a; Evans-a (2 pgs.) 12 24 36 69 97 125
66,75,94-Frazetta-a (2 pgs. each) 9 18 27 50 65 80
67,73-Frazetta-a (4 pgs. each) 10 20 30 58 79 100
68,74,76-80,84,85,88-93,95-97: 95-Last pre-code 8 16 24 44 57 70
69,72-Frazetta-a (6 & 8 pgs. each); 1st (?) app. Frazetta Red Cross ad 12 24 36 69 97 125
70,71,86,87-Frazetta, 3-4 pgs. each; 1 pg. ad by Frazetta in #70 10 20 30 54 72 90
81,82-Frazetta art (1 pg. each): 81-1st (?) app. Frazetta Boy Scout ad (tied w/ Buster Crabbe #9 9 18 27 47 61 75
83-Frazetta-a (1/2 pg.) 9 18 27 47 61 75

NOTE: ***Evans** a-64, 65. **Everett** a-(Hydroman-c/a-No. 1-9), 44, 60-64; c-1-9, 62-64. **Harvey Fuller** c-28-35. **Sid Greene** a-38-43, 46. **Guardineer** a-42(3), 43, 44, 45(2), 49(3), 50, 60, 61(2), 65, 67(2) 70-72. **Ingels** c-41. **Kiefer** a-46, 48; c-19-22, 24, 44, 46, 48, 51-53, 65, 67-69, 71-74, 76, 77, 79, 80, 82, 85, 86, 88, 89, 94, 95. **Mort Lawrence** a-45. **Tarpe Mills** a-2(2), 3(2), 10. **Ed Moore** a-49, 52-54, 56-63, 65-69, 72-74, 76, 77. **H.G. Peter** a-58-74, 76, 77, 87. **Paul Reinman** a-49. **Rico** a-31. Captain Tootsie by **Beck**-31, 32. Painted-c #16 on. Hydroman c-1-11. Music Master c-12, 13, 15. Rainbow Boy c-14.*

HERO INITIATIVE: MIKE WIERINGO BOOK (Also see Hero Comics)
Marvel Comics: Aug, 2008 ($4.99)
1-The "What If" Fantastic Four story with Wieringo-a (7 pgs.) finished by other artists after his passing; art by Davis, Immonen, Ramos, Kitson and others; written tributes 5.00

HERO ZERO (Also see Comics' Greatest World & Godzilla Versus Hero Zero)
Dark Horse Comics: Sept, 1994 ($2.50)
0 3.00

HEX (Replaces Jonah Hex)
DC Comics: Sept, 1985 - No. 18, Feb, 1987 (Story cont'd from Jonah Hex # 92)
1-Hex in post-atomic war world; origin 2 4 6 8 10 12
2-10,14-18: 6-Origin Stiletta 1 2 3 4 5 7
11-13: All contain future Batman storyline. 13-Intro The Dogs of War (origin #15) 1 3 4 6 8 10
NOTE: ***Giffen** a(p)-15-18; c(p)-15,17,18. **Texeira** a-1, 2p, 3p, 5-7p, 9p, 11-14p; c(p)-1, 2, 4-7, 12.*

HEXBREAKER (See First Comics Graphic Novel #15)

HEY THERE, IT'S YOGI BEAR (See Movie Comics)

HI-ADVENTURE HEROES (TV)
Gold Key: May, 1969 - No. 2, Aug, 1969 (Hanna-Barbera)
1-Three Musketeers, Gulliver, Arabian Knights 5 10 15 32 51 70
2-Three Musketeers, Micro-Venture, Arabian Knights 4 8 12 28 44 60

HI AND LOIS
Dell Publishing Co.: No. 683, Mar, 1956 - No. 955, Nov, 1958
Four Color 683 (#1) 5 10 15 30 48 65
Four Color 774(3/57),955 4 8 12 24 37 50

HI AND LOIS
Charlton Comics: Nov, 1969 - No. 11, July, 1971
1 3 6 9 14 20 25
2-11 2 4 6 9 12 15

HICKORY (See All Humor Comics)
Quality Comics Group: Oct, 1949 - No. 6, Aug, 1950
1-Sahl-c/a in all; Feldstein?-a 19 38 57 112 176 240
2 12 24 36 67 94 120
3-6 10 20 30 56 76 95

HIDDEN CREW, THE (See The United States Air Force Presents:...)

HIDE-OUT (See Zane Grey, Four Color No. 346)

HIDING PLACE, THE
Spire Christian Comics (Fleming H. Revell Co.): 1973 (39¢/49¢)
nn 2 4 6 9 13 16

HIGH ADVENTURE
Red Top(Decker) Comics (Farrell): Oct, 1957
1-Krigstein-r from Explorer Joe (re-issue on-c) 5 10 15 23 28 32

HIGH ADVENTURE (TV)
Dell Publishing Co.: No. 949, Nov, 1958 - No. 1001, Aug-Oct, 1959 (Lowell Thomas)
Four Color 949 (#1)-Photo-c 6 12 18 37 59 80
Four Color 1001-Lowell Thomas'...(#2) 5 10 15 34 55 75

HIGH CHAPPARAL (TV)
Gold Key: Aug, 1968 (Photo-c)
1 (10226-808)-Tufts-a 5 10 15 35 55 75

HIGHLANDER
Dynamite Entertainment: No. 0, 2006 - No. 12, 2007 (25¢/$2.99)
0-(25¢-c) Takes place after the first movie; photo-c and Dell'Otto painted-c 3.00
1-12: 1-($2.99) Three covers; Moder-a/Jerwa & Oeming-s. 2-Three covers 3.00
... Origins: The Kurgan 1,2 (2009 - No. 2, 2009, $4.99) Three covers; Rafael-a 5.00
...: Way of the Sword (2007 - No. 4, 2008, $3.50) Two interlocking covers for each 3.50

HIGH ROADS
DC Comics (Cliffhanger): June, 2002 - No. 6, Nov, 2002 ($2.95, limited series)
1-6-Leinil Yu-c/a; Lobdell-s 3.00
TPB (2003, $14.95) r/#1-6; sketch pages 15.00

HIGH SCHOOL CONFIDENTIAL DIARY (Confidential Diary #12 on)
Charlton Comics: June, 1960 - No. 11, Mar, 1962
1 4 8 12 28 44 60
2-11 3 6 9 18 27 35

HIGHWAYMEN
DC Comics (WildStorm): Aug, 2007 - No. 5, Dec, 2007 ($2.99)
1-5-Bernardin & Freeman-s/Garbett-a 3.00
TPB (2008, $17.99) r/#1-5 18.00

HI HI PUFFY AMIYUMI (Based on Cartoon Network animated series)
DC Comics: Apr, 2006 - No. 3, June, 2006 ($2.25, limited series)
1-3-Phil Moy-a 3.00

HI-HO COMICS
Four Star Publications: nd (2/46?) - No. 3, 1946
1-Funny Animal; L. B. Cole-c 37 74 111 222 361 500
2,3: 2-L. B. Cole-c 21 42 63 122 199 275

HI-JINX (Teen-age Animal Funnies)
La Salle Publ. Co./B&I Publ. Co. (American Comics Group)/Creston: 1945; July-Aug, 1947 - No. 7, July-Aug, 1948
nn-(© 1945, 25 cents, 132 Pgs.)(La Salle) 25 50 75 147 241 335
1-Teen-age, funny animal 18 36 54 105 165 225
2,3 12 24 36 69 97 125
4-7-Milt Gross. 4-X-Mas-c 17 34 51 98 154 210

HI-LITE COMICS
E. R. Ross Publishing Co.: Fall, 1945
1-Miss Shady 20 40 60 117 189 260

HILLBILLY COMICS
Charlton Comics: Aug, 1955 - No. 4, July, 1956 (Satire)
1-By Art Gates 9 18 27 52 69 85
2-4 7 14 21 35 43 50

HILLY ROSE'S SPACE ADVENTURES
Astro Comics: May, 1995 - No. 9 ($2.95, B&W)
1 1 2 3 5 7 9
2-9 5.00
Trade Paperback (1996, $12.95)-r/#1-5 13.00

HIP FLASK UNNATURAL SELECTION
Active Images: Sept, 2002 ($2.99)
1-Casey & Starkings-s/Ladronn-a; var.-c by Madureira, Campbell, Churchill 3.00

HIP-IT-TY HOP (See March of Comics No. 15)

HIRE, THE (BMWfilms.com's...)
Dark Horse Comics: July, 2004 - No. 6 ($2.99)
1-4: 1-Matt Wagner-s/Wagner & Velasco-a. 2-Bruce Campbell-s/Plunkett-a. 3-Waid-s 3.00
TPB (4/06, $17.95) r/#1-4 18.00

HI-SCHOOL ROMANCE (...Romances No. 41 on)
Harvey Publ./True Love(Home Comics): Oct, 1949 - No. 5, June, 1950; No. 6, Dec, 1950 - No. 73, Mar, 1958; No. 74, Sept, 1958 - No. 75, Nov, 1958
1-Photo-c 15 30 45 90 140 190
2-Photo-c 10 20 30 56 76 95
3-9: 3-5-Photo-c 9 18 27 47 61 75
10-Rape story 10 20 30 56 76 95
11-20 8 16 24 40 50 60
21-31 6 12 18 31 38 45
32- "Unholy passion" story 9 18 27 50 65 80
33-36: 36-Last pre-code (2/55) 6 12 18 29 36 42
37-53,59-72,74,75 5 10 15 24 30 35
54-58,73-Kirby-c 6 12 18 31 38 45
NOTE: ***Powell** a-1-3, 5, 8, 12-16, 18, 21-23, 25-27, 30-34, 36, 37, 39, 45-48, 50-52, 57, 58, 60, 64, 65, 67, 69.*

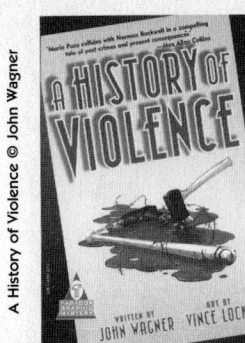

A History of Violence © John Wagner

Hit Comics #6 © QUA

Hit Monkey (mini-series) #1 © MAR

GD 2.0 | VG 4.0 | FN 6.0 | VF 8.0 | VF/NM 9.0 | NM- 9.2

GD 2.0 | VG 4.0 | FN 6.0 | VF 8.0 | VF/NM 9.0 | NM- 9.2

HI-SCHOOL ROMANCE DATE BOOK
Harvey Publications: Nov, 1962 - No. 3, Mar, 1963 (25¢ Giants)

1-Powell, Baker-a 6 12 18 41 66 90
2,3 4 8 12 22 34 45

HIS NAME IS SAVAGE (Magazine format)
Adventure House Press: June, 1968 (35¢, 52 pgs.)

1-Gil Kane-a 5 10 15 34 55 75

HI-SPOT COMICS (Red Ryder No. 1 & No. 3 on)
Hawley Publications: No. 2, Nov, 1940

2-David Innes of Pellucidar; art by J. C. Burroughs; written by Edgar Rice Burroughs
129 258 387 826 1413 2000

HISTORY OF THE DC UNIVERSE (Also see Crisis on Infinite Earths)
DC Comics: Sept, 1986 - No. 2, Nov, 1986 ($2.95, limited series)

1,2: 1-Perez-c/a 4.00
Limited Edition hardcover 4 8 12 26 41 55
Softcover (2002, $9.95) new Alex Ross wraparound-c 10.00
Softcover (2009, $12.99) Alex Ross wraparound-c 13.00

HISTORY OF VIOLENCE, A (Inspired the 2005 movie)
DC Comics (Paradox Press) 1997 ($9.95, B&W graphic novel)

nn-Paperback ($9.95) John Wagner-s/Vince Locke-a 15.00

HITCHHIKERS GUIDE TO THE GALAXY (See Life, the Universe and Everything & Restaurant at the End of the Universe)
DC Comics: 1993 - No. 3, 1993 ($4.95, limited series)

1-3: Adaptation of Douglas Adams book 5.00
TPB (1997, $14.95) r/#1-3 15.00

HIT COMICS
Quality Comics Group: July, 1940 - No. 65, July, 1950

1-Origin/1st app. Neon, the Unknown & Hercules; intro. The Red Bee; Bob & Swab, Blaze Barton, the Strange Twins, X-5 Super Agent, Casey Jones & Jack & Jill (ends #7) begin
811 1622 2433 5920 10,460 15,000
2-The Old Witch begins, ends #14 290 580 870 1856 3178 4500
3-Casey Jones ends; transvestism story "Jack & Jill"
277 554 831 1759 3030 4300
4-Super Agent (ends #17), & Betty Bates (ends #65) begin; X-5 ends
239 478 717 1530 2615 3700
5-Classic Lou Fine cover 703 1406 2109 5132 9066 13,000
6-10: 10-Old Witch by Crandall (4 pgs.); 1st work in comics (4/41)
200 400 600 1280 2190 3100
11-Classic cover 226 452 678 1446 2473 3500
12-17: 13-Blaze Barton ends. 17-Last Neon; Crandall Hercules in all; Last Lou Fine-c
126 252 378 806 1378 1950
18-Origin & 1st app. Stormy Foster, the Great Defender (12/41); The Ghost of Flanders begins; Crandall-c 132 264 396 838 1444 2050
19,20 103 206 309 659 1130 1600
21-24: 21-Last Hercules. 24-Last Red Bee & Strange Twins
100 200 300 635 1093 1550
25-Origin & 1st app. Kid Eternity and begins by Moldoff (12/42); 1st app. The Keeper (Kid Eternity's aide) 187 374 561 1197 2049 2900
26-Blackhawk x-over in Kid Eternity 97 194 291 621 1061 1500
27-29 49 98 147 309 522 735
30,31- "Bill the Magnificent" by Kurtzman, 11 pgs. in each
45 90 135 284 480 675
32-40: 32-Plastic Man x-over. 34-Last Stormy Foster
30 60 90 177 289 400
41-50 21 42 63 126 206 285
51-60-Last Kid Eternity 20 40 60 120 195 270
61-63-Crandall-c/a; 61-Jeb Rivers begins 21 42 63 124 202 280
64,65-Crandall-a 20 40 60 120 195 270

NOTE: ***Crandall*** *a-11-17(Hercules), 23, 24(Stormy Foster); c-18-20, 23, 24.* ***Fine*** *c-1-14, 16, 17(most).* ***Ward*** *c-33. Bondage c-7, 64. Hercules c-3, 10-17. Jeb Rivers c-61-65. Kid Eternity c-25-60 (w/Keeper-28-34, 36, 39-43, 45-55). Neon the Unknown c-2, 4, 8, 9. Red Bee c-1, 5-7. Stormy Foster c-18-24.*

HITLER'S ASTROLOGER (See Marvel Graphic Novel #35)

HITMAN (Also see Bloodbath #2, Batman Chronicles #4, Demon #43-45 & Demon Annual #2)
DC Comics: May, 1996 - No. 60, Apr, 2001 ($2.25/$2.50)

1-Garth Ennis-s & John McCrea-c/a begin; Batman app.
2 4 6 8 10 12
2-Joker-c;Two Face, Mad Hatter, Batman app. 1 2 3 5 6 8
3-5: 3-Batman-c/app.; Joker app. 4-1st app. Nightfist 5.00
6-20: 8-Final Night x-over. 10-GL cameo. 11-20: 11,12-GL-c/app. 15-20-"Ace of Killers".
16-18-Catwoman app. 17-19-Demon-app. 4.00
21-59: 34-Superman-c/app. 2.50
60-($3.95) Final issue; includes pin-ups by various 4.00
#1,000,000 (11/98) Hitman goes to the 853rd Century 3.00
Annual 1 (1997, $3.95) Pulp Heroes 5.00
.../Lobo: That Stupid Bastich (7/00, $3.95) Ennis-s/Mahnke-a 4.00
TPB-(1997, $9.95) r/#1-3, Demon Ann. #2, Batman Chronicles #4 10.00
Ace of Killers TPB ('00, $17.95) r/#15-22 18.00
Local Heroes TPB ('99, $17.95) r/#9-14 & Annual #1 18.00
10,000 Bullets TPB ('98, $9.95) r/#4-8 10.00
Ten Thousand Bullets TPB ('10, $17.99) r/#4-8 & Annual #1; intro, by Kevin Smith 18.00
Who Dares Wins TPB ('01, $12.95) r/#23-28 13.00

HIT-MONKEY (See Deadpool)
Marvel Comics: Apr, 2010; Sept, 2010 - No. 3, Nov, 2010 ($3.99/$2.99)

1-(4/10, $3.99) Printing of story from Marvel Digital Comics; Frank Cho-c; origin revealed 4.00
1-3-Daniel Way-s/Talajic-a/Johnson-c; Bullseye app. 3.00

HI-YO SILVER (See Lone Ranger's Famous Horse... and The Lone Ranger; and March of Comics No. 215 in the Promotional Comics section)

HOBBIT, THE
Eclipse Comics: 1989 - No. 3, 1990 ($4.95, squarebound, 52 pgs.)

Book 1-3: Adapts novel; Wenzel-a 8.00
Book 1-Second printing 5.00
Graphic Novel (1990, Ballantine)-r/#1-3 25.00

HOCUS POCUS (See Funny Book #9)

HOGAN'S HEROES (TV) (Also see Wild!)
Dell Publishing Co.: June, 1966 - No. 8, Sept, 1967; No. 9, Oct, 1969

1: #1-7 photo-c 8 16 24 56 93 130
2,3-Ditko-a(p) 6 12 18 37 59 80
4-9: 9-Reprints #1 5 10 15 30 48 65

HOKUM & HEX (See Razorline)
Marvel Comics (Razorline): Sept, 1993 - No. 9, May, 1994 ($1.75/$1.95)

1-($2.50)-Foil embossed-c; by Clive Barker 3.50
2-9: 5-Hyperkind x-over 3.00

HOLIDAY COMICS
Fawcett Publications: 1942 (25¢, 196 pgs.)

1-Contains three Fawcett comics plus two page portrait of Captain Marvel; Capt. Marvel, Jungle Girl #1, & Whiz. Not rebound, remaindered comics; printed at the same time as originals 258 516 774 1651 2826 4000

HOLIDAY COMICS (Becomes Fun Comics #9-12)
Star Publications: Jan, 1951 - No. 8, Oct, 1952

1-Funny animal contents (Frisky Fables) in all; L. B. Cole X-Mas-c
29 58 87 170 278 385
2-Classic L. B. Cole-c 31 62 93 186 303 420
3-8: 5,8-X-Mas-c; all L.B. Cole-c 19 38 57 109 172 235
Accepted Reprint 4 (nd)-L.B. Cole-c 10 20 30 58 79 100

HOLIDAY DIGEST
Harvey Comics: 1988 ($1.25, digest-size)

1 1 2 3 5 7 9

HOLIDAY PARADE (Walt Disney's...)
W. D. Publications (Disney): Winter, 1990-91(no year given) - No. 2, Winter, 1990-91 ($2.95, 68 pgs.)

1-Reprints 1947 Firestone by Barks plus new-a 5.00
2-Barks-r plus other stories 4.00

HOLI-DAY SURPRISE (Formerly Summer Fun)
Charlton Comics: V2#55, Mar, 1967 (25¢ Giant)

V2#55 4 8 12 24 37 50

HOLLYWOOD COMICS
New Age Publishers: Winter, 1944 (52 pgs.)

1-Funny animal 18 36 54 105 165 225

HOLLYWOOD CONFESSIONS
St. John Publishing Co.: Oct, 1949 - No. 2, Dec, 1949

1-Kubert-c/a (entire book) 34 68 102 199 325 450
2-Kubert-c/a (entire book) (Scarce) 36 72 108 211 343 475

HOLLYWOOD DIARY
Quality Comics Group: Dec, 1949 - No. 5, July-Aug, 1950

1-No photo-c 21 42 63 126 206 285

Hollywood Secrets #1 © QUA

Holyoke One-Shot #1 © HOKE

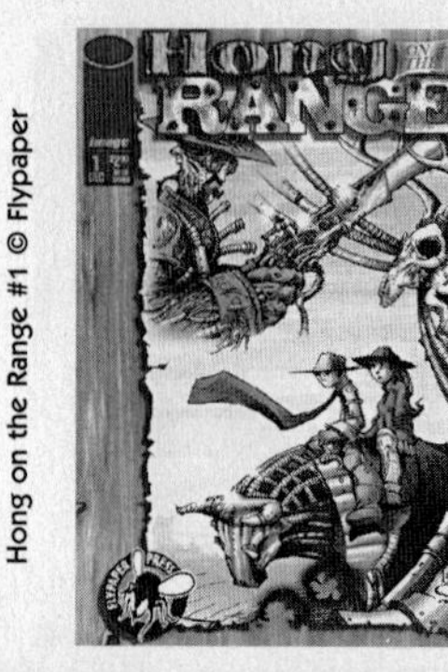

Hong on the Range #1 © Flypaper

	GD 2.0	VG 4.0	FN 6.0	VF 8.0	VF/NM 9.0	NM- 9.2
2-Photo-c	15	30	45	83	124	165
3-5-Photo-c. 5-June Allyson/Peter Lawford photo-c	14	28	42	76	108	140

HOLLYWOOD FILM STORIES
Feature Publications/Prize: April, 1950 - No. 4, Oct, 1950 (All photo-c; "Fumetti" type movie comic)

	GD	VG	FN	VF	VF/NM	NM-
1-June Allyson photo-c	20	40	60	117	189	260
2-4: 2-Lizabeth Scott photo-c. 3-Barbara Stanwick photo-c. 4-Betty Hutton photo-c	15	30	45	85	130	175

HOLLYWOOD FUNNY FOLKS (Formerly Funny Folks; Becomes Nutsy Squirrel #61 on)
National Periodical Publ.: No. 27, Aug-Sept, 1950 - No. 60, July-Aug, 1954

	GD	VG	FN	VF	VF/NM	NM-
27	14	28	42	76	108	140
28-40	10	20	30	54	72	90
41-60	9	18	27	47	61	75

NOTE: ***Rube Grossman** a-most issues. **Sheldon Mayer** a-27-35, 37-40, 43-46, 48-51, 53, 56, 57, 60.*

HOLLYWOOD LOVE DOCTOR (See Doctor Anthony King...)

HOLLYWOOD PICTORIAL (...Romances on cover)
St. John Publishing Co.: No. 3, Jan, 1950

	GD	VG	FN	VF	VF/NM	NM-
3-Matt Baker-a; photo-c	28	56	84	165	270	375

(Becomes a movie magazine - Hollywood Pictorial Western with No. 4.)

HOLLYWOOD ROMANCES (Formerly Brides In Love; becomes For Lovers Only #60 on)
Charlton Comics: V2#46, 11/66; #47, 10/67; #48, 11/68;V3#49,11/69-V3#59, 6/71

	GD	VG	FN	VF	VF/NM	NM-
V2#46-Rolling Stones-c/story	9	18	27	65	113	160
V2#47-V3#59: 56- "Born to Heart Break" begins	3	6	9	14	19	24

HOLLYWOOD SECRETS
Quality Comics Group: Nov, 1949 - No. 6, Sept, 1950

	GD	VG	FN	VF	VF/NM	NM-
1-Ward-c/a (9 pgs.)	36	72	108	211	343	475
2-Crandall-a, Ward-c/a (9 pgs.)	24	48	72	142	234	325
3-6: All photo-c. 5-Lex Barker (Tarzan)-c	14	28	42	80	115	150
...of Romance, I.W. Reprint #9; r/#2 above w/Kinstler-c	2	4	6	11	16	20

HOLLYWOOD SUPERSTARS
Marvel Comics (Epic Comics): Nov, 1990 - No. 5, Apr, 1991 ($2.25)

	GD	VG	FN	VF	VF/NM	NM-
1-($2.95, 52 pgs.)-Spiegle-c/a in all; Aragones-a, inside front-c plus 2-4 pgs.						4.00
2-5 ($2.25)						3.00

HOLO-MAN (See Power Record Comics)

HOLYOKE ONE-SHOT
Holyoke Publishing Co. (Tem Publ.): 1944 - No. 10, 1945 (All reprints)

	GD	VG	FN	VF	VF/NM	NM-
1,2: 1-Grit Grady (on cover only), Miss Victory, Alias X (origin)-All reprints from Captain Fearless. 2-Rusty Dugan (Corporal); Capt. Fearless (origin), Mr. Miracle (origin) app.	24	48	72	142	234	325
3-Miss Victory; r/Crash #4; Cat Man (origin), Solar Legion by Kirby app.; Miss Victory on cover only (1945)	37	74	111	222	361	500
4,6,8: 4-Mr. Miracle; The Blue Streak app. 6-Capt. Fearless, Alias X, Capt. Stone (splash used as-c to #10); Diamond Jim & Rusty Dugan (splash from cover of #2). 8-Blue Streak, Strong Man (story matches cover to #7)-Crash reprints	21	42	63	122	199	275
5,7: 5-U.S. Border Patrol Comics (Sgt. Dick Carter of the...), Miss Victory (story matches cover to #3), Citizen Smith, & Mr. Miracle app. 7-Secret Agent Z-2, Strong Man, Blue Streak (story matches cover to #8); Reprints from Crash #2	22	44	66	132	216	300
9-Citizen Smith, The Blue Streak, Solar Legion by Kirby & Strongman, the Perfect Human app.; reprints from Crash #4 & 5; Citizen Smith on cover only-from story in #5 (1944-before #3)	25	50	75	147	241	335
10-Captain Stone; r/Crash; Solar Legion by S&K	25	50	75	147	241	335

HOMER COBB (See Adventures of...)

HOMER HOOPER
Atlas Comics: July, 1953 - No. 4, Dec, 1953

	GD	VG	FN	VF	VF/NM	NM-
1-Teenage humor	10	20	30	58	79	100
2-4	8	16	24	40	50	60

HOMER, THE HAPPY GHOST (See Adventures of...)
Atlas(ACI/PPI/WPI)/Marvel: 3/55 - No. 22, 11/58; V2#1, 11/69 - V2#4, 5/70

	GD	VG	FN	VF	VF/NM	NM-
V1#1-Dan DeCarlo-c/a begins, ends #22	22	44	66	132	216	300
2-1st code approved issue	14	28	42	80	115	150
3-10	13	26	39	72	101	130
11-22	11	22	33	62	86	110
V2#1 (11/69)	11	22	33	75	138	200
2-4	7	14	21	45	73	100

HOME RUN (Also see A-1 Comics)
Magazine Enterprises: No. 89, 1953 (one-shot)

	GD	VG	FN	VF	VF/NM	NM-
A-1 89 (#3)-Powell-a; Stan Musial photo-c	15	30	45	85	130	175

HOMICIDE (Also see Dark Horse Presents)
Dark Horse Comics: Apr, 1990 ($1.95, B&W, one-shot)

	GD	VG	FN	VF	VF/NM	NM-
1-Detective story						3.00

HONEYMOON (Formerly Gay Comics)
A Lover's Magazine(USA) (Marvel): No. 41, Jan, 1950

	GD	VG	FN	VF	VF/NM	NM-
41-Photo-c; article by Betty Grable	12	24	36	69	97	125

HONEYMOONERS, THE (TV)
Lodestone: Oct, 1986 ($1.50)

	GD	VG	FN	VF	VF/NM	NM-
1-Photo-c						5.00

HONEYMOONERS, THE (TV)
Triad Publications: Sept, 1987 - No. 13? ($2.00)

	GD	VG	FN	VF	VF/NM	NM-
1-13						5.00

HONEYMOON ROMANCE
Artful Publications (Canadian): Apr, 1950 - No. 2, July, 1950 (25¢, digest size)

	GD	VG	FN	VF	VF/NM	NM-
1,2-(Rare)	50	100	150	315	533	750

HONEY WEST (TV)
Gold Key: Sept, 1966 (Photo-c)

	GD	VG	FN	VF	VF/NM	NM-
1 (10186-609)	9	18	27	60	100	140

HONEY WEST (TV)
Moonstone: 2010 ($5.99)

	GD	VG	FN	VF	VF/NM	NM-
1-Trina Robbins-s/Cynthia Martin-a; two art covers & two photo covers						6.00

HONG KONG PHOOEY (TV)
Charlton Comics: June, 1975 - No. 9, Nov, 1976 (Hanna-Barbera)

	GD	VG	FN	VF	VF/NM	NM-
1	5	10	15	34	55	75
2	3	6	9	19	29	38
3-9	3	6	9	16	22	28

HONG ON THE RANGE
Image/Flypaper Press: Dec, 1997 - No. 3, Feb, 1998 ($2.50, lim. series)

	GD	VG	FN	VF	VF/NM	NM-
1-3: Wu-s/Lafferty-a						3.00

HOOD, THE
Marvel Comics (MAX): Jul, 2002 - No. 6, Dec, 2002 ($2.99, limited series)

	GD	VG	FN	VF	VF/NM	NM-
1-6-Vaughan-s/Hotz-c/a						3.00
Vol. 1 Blood From Stones HC (2007, $19.99, dustjacket) r/#1-6; production sketch art						20.00
Vol. 1 Blood From Stones TPB (2003, $14.99) r/#1-6						15.00

HOODED HORSEMAN, THE (Formerly Blazing West)
American Comics Group (Michel Publ.): No. 21, 1-2/52 - No. 27, 1-2/54; No. 18, 12-1/54-55 - No. 22, 8-9/55

	GD	VG	FN	VF	VF/NM	NM-
21(1-2/52)-Hooded Horseman, Injun Jones cont.	15	30	45	83	124	165
22	10	20	30	56	76	95
23,24,27(1-2/54)	9	18	27	50	65	80
25 (9-10/53)-Cowboy Sahib on cover only; Hooded Horseman i.d. revealed	9	18	27	52	69	85
26-Origin/1st app. Cowboy Sahib by L. Starr	11	22	33	62	86	110
18(12-1/54-55)(Formerly Out of the Night)	10	20	30	54	72	90
19,21,22: 19-Last precode (1-2/55)	8	16	24	44	57	70
20-Origin Johnny Injun	9	18	27	50	65	80

NOTE: ***Whitney** c/a-21('52), 20-22.*

HOODED MENACE, THE (Also see Daring Adventures)
Realistic/Avon Periodicals: 1951 (one-shot)

	GD	VG	FN	VF	VF/NM	NM-
nn-Based on a band of hooded outlaws in the Pacific Northwest, 1900-1906; reprinted in Daring Advs. #15	50	100	150	315	533	750

HOODS UP (See the Promotional Comics section)

HOOK (Movie)
Marvel Comics: Early Feb, 1992 - No. 4, Late Mar, 1992 ($1.00, limited series)

	GD	VG	FN	VF	VF/NM	NM-
1-4: Adapts movie; Vess-c; 1-Morrow-a(p)						3.00
nn (1991, $5.95, 84 pgs.)-Contains #1-4; Vess-c						6.00
1 (1991, $2.95, magazine, 84 pgs.)-Contains #1-4; Vess-c (same cover as nn issue)						4.00

HOOT GIBSON'S WESTERN ROUNDUP (See Western Roundup under Fox Giants)

HOOT GIBSON WESTERN (Formerly My Love Story)
Fox Features Syndicate: No. 5, May, 1950 - No. 3, Sept, 1950

Hopalong Cassidy #9 © FAW

Horrific #12 © Comic Media

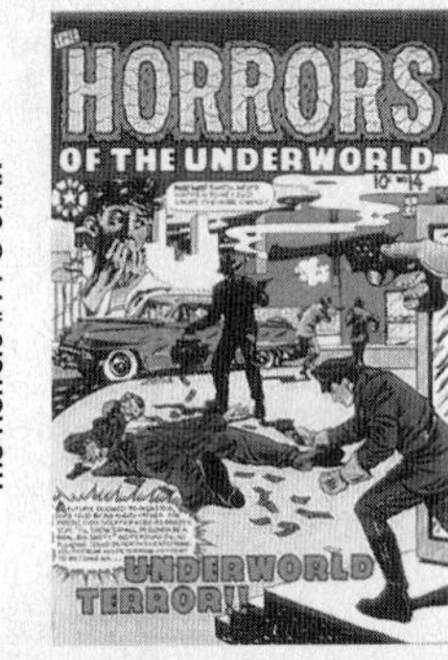

The Horrors #14 © STAR

GD 2.0 | VG 4.0 | FN 6.0 | VF 8.0 | VF/NM 9.0 | NM- 9.2

5,6(#1,2): 5-Photo-c. 6-Photo/painted-c 21 42 63 123 197 270
3-Wood-a; painted-c 22 44 66 131 211 290

HOPALONG CASSIDY (Also see Bill Boyd Western, Master Comics, Real Western Hero, Six Gun Heroes & Western Hero; Bill Boyd starred as Hopalong Cassidy in movies, radio & TV)
Fawcett Publications: Feb, 1943; No. 2, Summer, 1946 - No. 85, Nov, 1953

1 (1943, 68 pgs.)-H. Cassidy & his horse Topper begin (on sale 1/8/43)-Captain Marvel app. on-c 343 686 1029 2400 4200 6000
2-(Sum, '46) 53 106 159 334 567 800
3,4: 3-(Fall, '46, 52 pgs. begin) 26 52 78 154 252 350
5- "Mad Barber" story mentioned in **SOTI**, pgs. 308,309; photo-c 24 48 72 142 234 325
6-10: 8-Photo-c 18 36 54 105 165 225
11-19: 11,13-19-Photo-c 15 30 45 85 130 175
20-29 (52 pgs.)-Painted/photo-c 14 28 42 76 108 140
30,31,33,34,37-39,41 (52 pgs.)-Painted-c 11 22 33 64 90 115
32,40 (36pgs.)-Painted-c 10 20 30 58 79 100
35,42,43,45-47,49-51,53,54,56 (52 pgs.)-Photo-c 11 22 33 60 83 105
36,44,48 (36 pgs.)-Photo-c 10 20 30 56 76 95
52,55,57-70 (36 pgs.)-Photo-c 9 18 27 52 69 85
71-84-Photo-c 8 16 24 44 57 70
85-Last Fawcett issue; photo-c 10 20 30 54 72 90
NOTE: *Line-drawn c-1-4, 6, 7, 9, 10, 12.*
... & The 5 Men of Evil (AC Comics, 1991, $12.95) r/newspaper strips and Fawcett story "Signature of Death" 13.00

HOPALONG CASSIDY
National Periodical Publications: No. 86, Feb, 1954 - No. 135, May-June, 1959 (All-36 pgs.)

86-Gene Colan-a begins, ends #117; photo covers continue 36 72 108 216 351 485
87 20 40 60 118 189 260
88-91: 91-1 pg. Superboy-sty (7/54) 15 30 45 83 124 165
92-99 (98 has #93 on-c; last precode issue, 2/55). 95-Reversed photo-c to #52. 98-Reversed photo-c to #61. 99-Reversed photo-c to #60 14 28 42 76 108 140
100-Same cover as #50 15 30 45 83 124 165
101-108: 105-Same photo-c as #54. 107-Same photo-c as #51. 108-Last photo-c 7 14 21 45 73 100
109-130: 118-Gil Kane-a begins. 123-Kubert-a (2 pgs.). 124-Painted-c 6 12 18 41 66 90
131-135 6 12 18 43 69 95

HOPELESS SAVAGES (Also see Too Much Hopeless Savages)
Oni Press: Aug, 2001 - No. 4, Nov, 2001 ($2.95, B&W, limited series)

1-4-Van Meter-s/Norrie-a/Clugston-Major-a/Watson-c 3.00
Free Comic Book Day giveaway (5/02) r/#1 with "Free Comic Book Day" banner on-c 2.50
TPB (2002, $13.95, 8" x 5.75") r/#1-4; plus color stories; Watson-c 14.00

HOPELESS SAVAGES: GROUND ZERO
Oni Press: June, 2002 - No. 4, Oct, 2002 ($2.95, B&W, limited series)

1-4-Van Meter-s/O'Malley-a/Dodson-c. 1-Watson-a 3.00
TPB (2003, $11.95, 8" x 5.75") r/#1-4; Dodson-c 12.00

HOPE SHIP
Dell Publishing Co.: June-Aug, 1963

1 3 6 9 16 22 28

HOPPY THE MARVEL BUNNY (See Fawcett's Funny Animals)
Fawcett Publications: Dec, 1945 - No. 15, Sept, 1947

1 28 56 84 165 270 375
2 14 28 42 82 121 160
3-15: 7-Xmas-c 12 24 36 67 94 120

HORACE & DOTTY DRIPPLE (Dotty Dripple No. 1-24)
Harvey Publications: No. 25, Aug, 1952 - No. 43, Oct, 1955

25-43 4 9 13 18 22 26

HORIZONTAL LIEUTENANT, THE (See Movie Classics)

HOROBI
Viz Premiere Comics: 1990 - No. 8, 1990 ($3.75, B&W, mature readers, 84 pgs.) V2#1, 1990 - No. 7, 1991 ($4.25, B&W, 68 pgs.)

1-8: Japanese manga, Part Two, #1-7 4.50

HORRIFIC (Terrific No. 14 on)
Artful/Comic Media/Harwell/Mystery: Sept, 1952 - No. 13, Sept, 1954

1 65 130 195 416 708 1000
2 41 82 123 256 428 600
3-Bullet in head-c 81 162 243 518 884 1250
4,5,7,9,10: 4-Shrunken head-c. 7-Guillotine-c 39 78 117 231 378 525
6-Jack The Ripper story 39 78 117 236 388 540
8-Origin & 1st app. The Teller (E.C. parody) 41 82 123 256 428 600
11-13: 11-Swipe/Witches Tales #6,27; Devil-c 32 64 96 188 307 425
NOTE: ***Don Heck** a-8; c-3-13. **Hollingsworth** a-4. **Morisi** a-8. **Palais** a-5, 7-12.*

HORRORCIDE
IDW Publishing: Sept, 2004 ($6.99)

1-Steve Niles short stories; art by Templesmith, Medors and Chee 7.00

HORROR FROM THE TOMB (Mysterious Stories No. 2 on)
Premier Magazine Co.: Sept, 1954

1-Woodbridge/Torres, Check-a; The Keeper of the Graveyard is host 43 86 129 271 461 650

HORRORIST, THE (Also see Hellblazer)
DC Comics (Vertigo): Dec, 1995 - No. 2, Jan, 1996 ($5.95, lim. series, mature)

1,2: Jamie Delano scripts, David Lloyd-c/a; John Constantine (Hellblazer) app. 6.00

HORROR OF COLLIER COUNTY
Dark Horse Comics: Oct, 1999 - No. 5, Feb, 2000 ($2.95, B&W, limited series)

1-5-Rich Tommaso-s/a 3.00

HORRORS, THE (Formerly Startling Terror Tales #10)
Star Publications: No. 11, Jan, 1953 - No. 15, Apr, 1954

11-Horrors of War; Disbrow-a(2) 30 60 90 177 289 400
12-Horrors of War; color illo in **POP** 28 56 84 165 270 375
13-Horrors of Mystery; crime stories 26 52 78 154 252 350
14,15-Horrors of the Underworld; crime stories 28 56 84 165 270 375
NOTE: *All have **L. B. Cole** covers; a-12. **Hollingsworth** a-13. **Palais** a-13r.*

HORROR TALES (Magazine)
Eerie Publications: V1#7, 6/69 - V6#6, 12/74; V7#1, 2/75; V7#2, 5/76 - V8#5, 1977; V9#1-3, 8/78; V10#1(2/79) (V1-V6: 52 pgs.; V7, V8#2: 112 pgs.; V8#4 on: 68 pgs.) (No V5#3, V8#1,3)

V1#7 7 14 21 45 73 100
V1#8,9 5 10 15 30 48 65
V2#1-6('70), V3#1-6('71), V4#1-3,5-7('72) 4 8 12 26 41 55
V4#4-LSD story reprint/Weird V3#5 5 10 15 35 55 75
V5#1,2,4,5(6/73),5(10/73),6(12/73),V6#1-6('74),V7#1,2,4('76),V7#3('76)-Giant issue, V8#2,4,5('77) 4 8 12 26 41 55
V9#1-3(11/78, $1.50), V10#1(2/79) 4 8 12 28 44 60
NOTE: *Bondage-c-V6#1, 3, V7#2.*

HORSE FEATHERS COMICS
Lev Gleason Publ.: Nov, 1945 - No. 4, July(Summer on-c), 1948 (52 pgs.) (#2,3 are oversized)

1-Wolverton's Scoop Scuttle, 2 pgs. 19 38 57 109 172 235
2 11 22 33 60 83 105
3,4: 3-(5/48) 9 18 27 47 61 75

HORSEMAN
Crusade Comics/Kevlar Studios: Mar, 1996 - No. 3, Nov, 1997 ($2.95)

0-1st Kevlar Studios issue, 1-(3/96)-Crusade issue; Shi-c/app., 1-(11/96)-3-(11/97)-Kevlar Studios 3.00

HORSEMASTERS, THE (Disney)(TV, Movie)
Dell Publishing Co.: No. 1260, Dec-Feb, 1961/62

Four Color 1260-Annette Funicello photo-c 12 24 36 82 154 225

HORSE SOLDIERS, THE
Dell Publishing Co.: No. 1048, Nov-Jan, 1959/60 (John Wayne movie)

Four Color 1048-Painted-c, Sekowsky-a 12 24 36 87 164 240

HORSE WITHOUT A HEAD, THE (See Movie Comics)

HOT DOG
Magazine Enterprises: June-July, 1954 - No. 4, Dec-Jan, 1954-55

1(A-1 #107) 9 18 27 47 61 75
2,3(A-1 #115),4(A-1 #136) 6 12 18 31 38 45

HOT DOG (See Jughead's Pal, Hotdog)

HOTEL DEPAREE - SUNDANCE (TV)
Dell Publishing Co.: No. 1126, Aug-Oct, 1960 (one-shot)

Four Color 1126-Earl Holliman photo-c 6 12 18 43 69 95

HOT ROD AND SPEEDWAY COMICS
Hillman Periodicals: Feb-Mar, 1952 - No. 5, Apr-May, 1953

1 27 54 81 158 259 360
2-Krigstein-a 18 36 54 105 165 225
3-5 13 26 39 72 101 130

Hot Rods and Racing Cars #8 © CC

Hot Stuff, The Little Devil #3 © HARV

House of M: Avengers #4 © MAR

HOT ROD COMICS (...Featuring Clint Curtis) (See XMas Comics)
Fawcett Publications: Nov, 1951 (no month given) - V2#7, Feb, 1953

	GD 2.0	VG 4.0	FN 6.0	VF 8.0	VF/NM 9.0	NM- 9.2
nn (V1#1)-Powell-c/a in all	29	58	87	170	278	385
2 (4/52)	15	30	45	90	140	190
3-6, V2#7	13	26	39	72	101	130

HOT ROD KING (Also see Speed Smith the Hot Rod King)
Ziff-Davis Publ. Co.: Fall, 1952

	GD 2.0	VG 4.0	FN 6.0	VF 8.0	VF/NM 9.0	NM- 9.2
1-Giacoia-a; Saunders painted-c	25	50	75	150	245	340

HOT ROD RACERS (Grand Prix No. 16 on)
Charlton Comics: Dec, 1964 - No. 15, July, 1967

	GD 2.0	VG 4.0	FN 6.0	VF 8.0	VF/NM 9.0	NM- 9.2
1	8	16	24	54	90	125
2-5	5	10	15	32	51	70
6-15	4	8	12	24	37	50

HOT RODS AND RACING CARS
Charlton Comics (Motor Mag. No. 1): Nov, 1951 - No. 120, June, 1973

	GD 2.0	VG 4.0	FN 6.0	VF 8.0	VF/NM 9.0	NM- 9.2
1-Speed Davis begins; Indianapolis 500 story	28	56	84	165	270	375
2	15	30	45	86	133	180
3-10	12	24	36	67	94	120
11-20	10	20	30	54	72	90
21-33,36-40	8	16	24	44	57	70
34, 35 (? & 6/58, 68 pgs.)	11	22	33	60	83	105
41-60	7	14	21	37	46	55
61-80	3	6	9	20	30	40
81-100	3	6	9	16	23	30
101-120	3	6	9	14	19	24

HOT SHOT CHARLIE
Hillman Periodicals: 1947 (Lee Elias)

	GD 2.0	VG 4.0	FN 6.0	VF 8.0	VF/NM 9.0	NM- 9.2
1	12	24	36	67	94	120

HOT SHOTS: AVENGERS
Marvel Comics: Oct, 1995 ($2.95, one-shot)

	GD 2.0	VG 4.0	FN 6.0	VF 8.0	VF/NM 9.0	NM- 9.2
nn-pin-ups						3.00

HOTSPUR
Eclipse Comics: Jun, 1987 - No. 3, Sep, 1987 ($1.75, lim. series, Baxter paper)

	GD 2.0	VG 4.0	FN 6.0	VF 8.0	VF/NM 9.0	NM- 9.2
1-3						3.00

HOT STUFF (See Stumbo Tinytown)
Harvey Comics: V2#1, Sept, 1991 - No. 12, June, 1994 ($1.00)

	GD 2.0	VG 4.0	FN 6.0	VF 8.0	VF/NM 9.0	NM- 9.2
V2#1-Stumbo back-up story						5.00
2-12 ($1.50)						4.00
...Big Book 1 (11/92), 2 (6/93) (Both $1.95, 52 pgs.)						5.00

HOT STUFF CREEPY CAVES
Harvey Publications: Nov, 1974 - No. 7, Nov, 1975

	GD 2.0	VG 4.0	FN 6.0	VF 8.0	VF/NM 9.0	NM- 9.2
1	4	8	12	22	34	45
2-7	3	6	9	15	21	26

HOT STUFF DIGEST
Harvey Comics: July, 1992 - No. 5, Nov, 1993 ($1.75, digest-size)

	GD 2.0	VG 4.0	FN 6.0	VF 8.0	VF/NM 9.0	NM- 9.2
V2#1-Hot Stuff, Stumbo, Richie Rich stories						6.00
2-5						4.00

HOT STUFF GIANT SIZE
Harvey Comics: Oct, 1992 - No. 3, Oct, 1993 ($2.25, 68 pgs.)

	GD 2.0	VG 4.0	FN 6.0	VF 8.0	VF/NM 9.0	NM- 9.2
V2#1-Hot Stuff & Stumbo stories						5.00
2,3						4.00

HOT STUFF SIZZLERS
Harvey Publications: July, 1960 - No. 59, Mar, 1974; V2#1, Aug, 1992

	GD 2.0	VG 4.0	FN 6.0	VF 8.0	VF/NM 9.0	NM- 9.2
1- 84 pgs. begin, ends #5; Hot Stuff, Stumbo begin	14	28	42	99	200	300
2-5	8	16	24	58	97	135
6-10: 6-68 pgs. begin, ends #45	6	12	18	41	66	90
11-20	4	8	12	28	44	60
21-45	3	6	9	20	30	40
46-52: 52 pgs. begin	3	6	9	16	23	30
53-59	2	4	6	10	14	18
V2#1-(8/92, $1.25)-Stumbo back-up						5.00

HOT STUFF, THE LITTLE DEVIL (Also see Devil Kids & Harvey Hits)
Harvey Publications (Illustrated Humor): 10/57 - No. 141, 7/77; No. 142, 2/78 - No. 164, 8/82; No. 165, 10/86 - No. 171, 11/87; No. 172, 11/88; No. 173, Sept, 1990 - No. 177, 1/91

	GD 2.0	VG 4.0	FN 6.0	VF 8.0	VF/NM 9.0	NM- 9.2
1	54	108	162	459	930	1400
2-Stumbo-like giant 1st app. (12/57)	24	48	72	175	350	525
3-Stumbo the Giant debut (2/58)	20	40	60	140	283	425
4,5	18	36	54	125	255	385
6-10	11	22	33	77	144	210
11-20	9	18	27	60	100	140
21-40	6	12	18	39	62	85
41-60	4	8	12	26	41	55
61-80	3	6	9	20	30	40
81-105	3	6	9	16	22	28
106-112: All 52 pg. Giants	3	6	9	18	27	35
113-125	2	4	6	9	12	15
126-141	1	2	3	5	7	9
142-177: 172-177-($1.00)						6.00
Harvey Comics Classics Vol. 3 TPB (Dark Horse Books, 3/08, $19.95) Reprints Hot Stuff's earliest appearances in this title and Devil Kids, mostly B&W with some color stories; history, early concept drawings; foreword by Mark Arnold						20.00

HOT WHEELS (TV)
National Periodical Publications: Mar-Apr, 1970 - No. 6, Jan-Feb, 1971

	GD 2.0	VG 4.0	FN 6.0	VF 8.0	VF/NM 9.0	NM- 9.2
1	10	20	30	68	119	170
2,4,5	6	12	18	39	62	85
3-Neal Adams-c	7	14	21	49	80	110
6-Neal Adams-c/a	8	16	24	58	97	135

NOTE: *Toth a-1p, 2-5; c-1p, 5.*

HOURMAN (Justice Society member, see Adventure Comics #48)

HOURMAN (See JLA and DC One Million)
DC Comics: Apr, 1999 - No. 25, Apr, 2001 ($2.50)

	GD 2.0	VG 4.0	FN 6.0	VF 8.0	VF/NM 9.0	NM- 9.2
1-25: 1-JLA app.; McDaniel-c. 2-Tomorrow Woman-c/app. 6,7-Amazo app. 11-13-Justice Legion A app. 16-Silver Age flashback. 18,19-JSA-c/app. 22-Harris-c/a. 24-Hourman Vs. Rex Tyler						3.00

HOUSE OF M (Also see miniseries with Fantastic Four, Iron Man and Spider-Man)
Marvel Comics: Aug, 2005 - No. 8, Dec, 2005 ($2.99, limited series)

	GD 2.0	VG 4.0	FN 6.0	VF 8.0	VF/NM 9.0	NM- 9.2
1-Bendis-s/Coipel-a/Ribic-c; Scarlet Witch changes reality; Quesada variant-c						3.00
2-8-Variant covers for each. 3-Hawkeye returns						3.00
... MGC #1 (6/11, $1.00) r/#1 with "Marvel's Greatest Comics" logo on cover						1.00
Secrets Of The House Of M (2005, $3.99, one-shot) profile pages and background info						4.00
... Sketchbook (6/05) B&W preview sketches by Coipel, Davis, Hairsine, Quesada						3.00
TPB (2006, $24.99) r/#1-8 and The Pulse: House of M Special Edition newspaper						25.00
...: Fantastic Four/ Iron Man TPB (2006, $13.99) r/ both House of M mini-series						14.00
...: World of M Featuring Wolverine TPB (2006, $13.99) r/2005 x-over issues Wolverine #33-35, Black Panther #7, Captain America #10 and The Pulse #10						14.00
HC (2008, $29.99, oversized with d.j.) r/#1-8, The Pulse: House of M Special Edition newspaper and Secrets Of The House Of M one-shot; script pages; cover gallery						30.00

HOUSE OF M: AVENGERS
Marvel Comics: Jan, 2008 - No. 5, Apr, 2008 ($2.99, limited series)

	GD 2.0	VG 4.0	FN 6.0	VF 8.0	VF/NM 9.0	NM- 9.2
1-5-Gage-s/Perkins-a; Luke Cage, Iron Fist, Hawkeye, Tigra, Misty Knight, Shang-Chi						3.00

HOUSE OF M: MASTERS OF EVIL
Marvel Comics: Oct, 2009 - No. 4, Jan, 2010 ($3.99, limited series)

	GD 2.0	VG 4.0	FN 6.0	VF 8.0	VF/NM 9.0	NM- 9.2
1-4-Gage-s/Garcia-a/Perkins-c; The Hood app.						4.00

HOUSE OF MYSTERY
DC Comics: Dec/Jan. 1951

nn - Ashcan comic, not distributed to newsstands, only for in-house use. Cover art is Danger Trail #3 with interior being Star Spangled Comics #109. A VG+ copy sold for $2,357.50 in 2002.

HOUSE OF MYSTERY (See Brave and the Bold #93, Elvira's House of Mystery, Limited Collectors' Edition & Super DC Giant)

HOUSE OF MYSTERY, THE
National Periodical Publications/DC Comics: Dec-Jan, 1951-52 - No. 321, Oct, 1983 (No. 194-203: 52 pgs.)

	GD 2.0	VG 4.0	FN 6.0	VF 8.0	VF/NM 9.0	NM- 9.2
1-DC's first horror comic	252	504	756	1613	2757	3900
2	95	190	285	603	1039	1475
3	65	130	195	416	708	1000
4,5	53	106	159	334	567	800
6-10	47	94	141	296	498	700
11-15	40	80	120	246	411	575
16(7/53)-25	34	68	102	199	325	450
26-35(2/55)-Last pre-code issue; 30-Woodish-a	26	52	78	154	252	350
36-50: 50-Text story of Orson Welles' War of the Worlds broadcast	14	28	42	95	188	280
51-60: 55-1st S.A. issue	12	24	36	84	157	230
61,63,65,66,69,70,72,76,85-Kirby-a	13	26	39	91	176	260
62,64,67,68,71,73-75,77-83,86-99	11	22	33	75	138	200
84-Prototype of Negative Man (Doom Patrol)	13	26	39	91	176	260

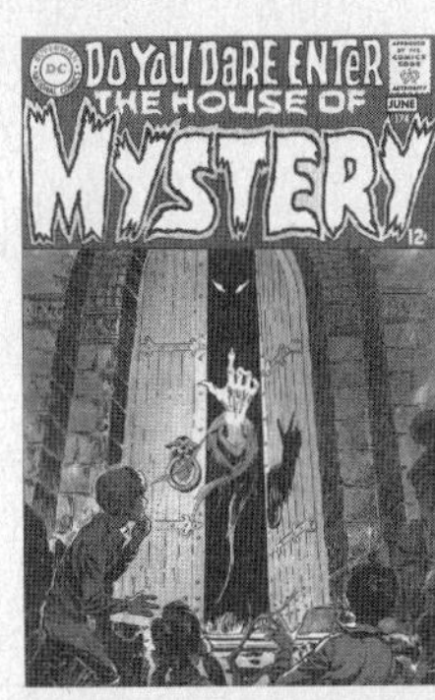

House of Mystery #174 © DC

House of Mystery (2008 series) #1 © DC

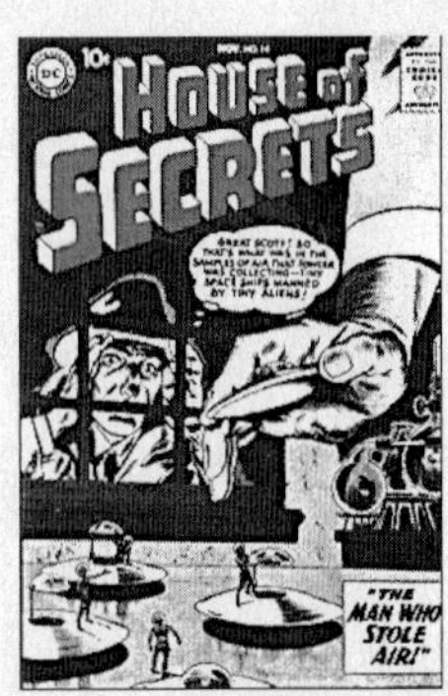

House of Secrets #14 © DC

	GD 2.0	VG 4.0	FN 6.0	VF 8.0	VF/NM 9.0	NM- 9.2
100 (7/60)	11	22	33	80	150	220
101-116: 109-Toth, Kubert-a. 116-Last 10¢ issue	10	20	30	69	122	175
117-130: 117-Swipes-c to HOS #20. 120-Toth-a	9	18	27	64	110	155
131-142	8	16	24	58	97	135
143-J'onn J'onzz, Manhunter begins (6/64), ends #173; story continues from Detective #326; intro. Idol-Head of Diabolu	18	36	54	131	266	400
144	9	18	27	60	100	140
145-155,157-159: 149-Toth-a. 155-The Human Hurricane app. (12/65), Red Tornado prototype. 158-Origin Diabolu Idol-Head	6	12	18	41	66	90
156-Robby Reed begins (origin/1st app.), ends #173	8	16	24	52	86	120
160-(7/66)-Robby Reed becomes Plastic Man in this issue only; 1st S.A. app. Plastic Man; intro Marco Xavier (Martian Manhunter) & Vulture Crime Organization; ends #173	9	18	27	65	113	160
161-173: 169-Origin/1st app. Gem Girl	5	10	15	30	48	65
174-Mystery format begins.	11	22	33	80	150	220
175-1st app. Cain (House of Mystery host); Adams-c	9	18	27	65	113	160
176,177-Neal Adams-c	9	18	27	60	100	140
178-Neal Adams-c/a (2/69)	9	18	27	65	113	160
179-Neal Adams/Orlando, Wrightson-a (1st pro work, 3 pgs.); Adams-c	11	22	33	75	138	200
180,181,183: Wrightson-a (3,10, & 3 pgs.); Adams-c. 180-Last 12¢ issue; Kane/Wood-a(2). 183-Wood-a	9	18	27	60	100	140
182,184-Adams-c. 182-Toth-a. 184-Kane/Wood, Toth-a	6	12	18	43	69	95
185-Williamson/Kaluta-a; Howard-a (3 pgs.); Adams-c	7	14	21	47	76	105
186-N. Adams-c/a; Wrightson-a (10 pgs.)	9	18	27	65	113	160
187,190: Adams-c. 187-Toth-a. 190-Toth-a(r)	6	12	18	41	66	90
188-Wrightson-a (8 & 3pgs.); Adams-c	8	16	24	52	86	120
189,192,197: Adams-c on all. 189-Wood-a(i). 192-Last 15¢-c	6	12	18	41	66	90
191-Wrightson-a (8 & 3pgs.); Adams-c	8	16	24	52	86	120
193-Wrightson-c	6	12	18	41	66	90
194-Wrightson-c; 52 pgs begin, end #203; Toth,Kirby-a	8	16	24	54	90	125
195: Wrightson-c. Swamp creature story by Wrightson similar to Swamp Thing (10 pgs.)(10/71)	10	20	30	67	116	165
196,198	5	10	15	35	55	75
199-Adams-c; Wood-a(8pgs.); Kirby-a	7	14	21	45	73	100
200-(25¢, 52 pgs.)-One third-r (3/72)	6	12	18	43	69	95
201-203-(25¢, 52 pgs.)-One third-r	5	10	15	30	48	65
204-Wrightson-c/a, 9 pgs.	5	10	15	35	55	75
205,206,208,210,212,215,216,218	3	6	9	20	30	40
207-Wrightson-c/a; Starlin, Redondo-a	5	10	15	35	55	75
209,211,213,214,217,219-Wrightson-c	4	8	12	28	44	60
220,222,223	3	6	9	18	27	35
221-Wrightson/Kaluta-a(8 pgs.); Wrightson-c	5	10	15	32	51	70
224-229: 224-Wrightson-r from Spectre #9; Dillin/Adams-r from House of Secrets #82; begin 100 pg. issues; Phantom Stranger-r. 225,227-(100 pgs.): 225-Spectre app. 226-Wrightson/Redondo-a Phantom Stranger-r. 228-N. Adams inks; Wrightson-r. 229-Wrightson-a(r); Toth-r; last 100 pg. issue	6	12	18	39	62	85
230,232-235,237-250	2	4	6	13	18	22
231-Classic Wrightson-c	5	10	15	32	51	70
236-Wrightson-c; Ditko-a(p); N. Adams-i	4	8	12	24	37	50
251-254-(84 pgs.)-Adams-c. 251-Wood-a	4	8	12	26	41	55
255,256-(84 pgs.)-Wrightson-c	4	8	12	26	41	55
257-259-(84 pgs.)	3	6	9	18	27	35
260-289: 282-(68 pgs.)-Has extra story "The Computers That Saved Metropolis" Radio Shack giveaway by Jim Starlin	2	4	6	8	10	12
290-1st "I, Vampire"	3	6	9	16	23	30
291-299: 291,293,295-299- "I, Vampire"	2	4	6	10	14	18
300,319-"I, Vampire"	2	4	6	11	16	20
301-318,320: 301-318-"I, Vampire"	2	4	6	10	14	18
321-Death of "I, Vampire"	3	6	9	14	20	25
Welcome to the House of Mystery (7/98, $5.95) reprints stories with new framing story by Gaiman and Aragonés						6.00

NOTE: ***Neal Adams*** *a-236i; c-175-192, 197, 199, 251-254.* ***Alcala*** *a-209, 217, 219, 224, 227.* ***M. Anderson*** *a-212; c/a-37.* ***Aparo*** *a-209.* ***Aragones*** *a-185, 186, 194, 196, 200, 202, 229, 251.* ***Baily*** *a-279p.* ***Cameron*** *a-76, 79.* ***Colan*** *a-202r.* ***Craig*** *a-263, 275, 295, 300.* ***Dillin/Adams*** *r-224.* ***Ditko*** *a-236p, 247, 254, 258, 276; c-277.* ***Drucker*** *a-37.* ***Evans*** *c-218.* ***Fradon*** *a-251.* ***Giffen*** *a-284.* ***Giunta*** *a-199, 227r.* ***Golden*** *a-257, 259.* ***Heath*** *a-194r; c-203.* ***Howard*** *a-182, 185, 187, 196, 229r, 247i, 254, 279i.* ***Kaluta*** *a-195, 200, 250r; c-200-202, 210, 212, 233, 260, 261, 263, 265, 267, 268, 273, 276, 284, 287, 288, 293-295, 300, 302, 304, 305, 309-319, 321.* ***Bob Kane*** *a-84.* ***Gil Kane*** *a-196p, 253p, 300p.* ***Kirby*** *a-194r, 199r; c-65, 76, 78, 79, 85.* ***Kubert*** *c-282, 283, 285, 286, 289-292, 297-299, 301, 303, 306-308.* ***Maneely*** *a-68, 227r.* ***Mayer*** *a-317p.* ***Meskin*** *a-52-144 (most), 195r, 224r, 229r; c-63, 66, 124, 127.* ***Mooney*** *a-24, 159, 160.* ***Moreira*** *a-3, 4, 20-50, 58, 59, 62, 68, 77, 79, 90, 108, 113, 123, 201r, 228; c-4-28, 44, 47, 50, 54, 59, 62, 64, 68, 70, 73.* ***Morrow*** *a-192, 196, 255, 320i.* ***Mortimer*** *a-204(3 pgs.).* ***Nasser*** *a-276.* ***Newton*** *a-259, 272.* ***Nino*** *a-204, 212, 213, 220, 224, 225, 245, 250, 252-256, 283.* ***Orlando*** *a-175(2 pgs.), 178, 240i; c-240, 258p, 262, 264p, 270p, 271, 272, 274, 275, 278, 296i.* ***Redondo*** *a-194, 195, 197, 202, 203, 207, 211, 214, 217, 219, 226, 227, 229, 235, 241, 287(layout), 302p, 303i, 308; c-229.* ***Reese*** *a-195, 200, 205i.* ***Rogers*** *a-254, 274, 277.* ***Roussos*** *a-65, 84, 224i.* ***Sekowsky*** *a-282p.* ***Sparling*** *a-203.* ***Starlin*** *a-207(2 pgs.), 282p; c-281.* ***Leonard Starr*** *a-9.* ***Staton*** *a-300p.* ***Sutton*** *a-189, 271, 290, 291, 293, 295, 297-299, 302, 303, 306-309, 310-313i, 314.* ***Tuska*** *a-293p, 294p, 316p.* ***Wrightson*** *c-193-195, 204, 207, 209, 211, 213, 214, 217, 219, 221, 231, 236, 255, 256; r-224.*

HOUSE OF MYSTERY
DC Comics (Vertigo): Jul, 2008 - Present ($2.99)

	GD 2.0	VG 4.0	FN 6.0	VF 8.0	VF/NM 9.0	NM- 9.2
1-12,14-35: 1-Cain & Abel app.; Rossi-a/Weber-c. 9-Wrightson-a (6 pgs.). 16-Corben-a						3.00
1-Variant-c by Bernie Wrightson						5.00
13-Art by Neal Adams, Ralph Reese, Eric Powell, Sergio Aragonés						3.00
13-Variant-c by Neal Adams						5.00
... Halloween Annual #1 (12/09, $4.99) short stories by various incl. Hadley, Allred, Nowlan						5.00
... Halloween Annual #2 (12/10, $4.99) short stories by various incl. Carey, Allred, Gross						5.00
...: Love Stories for Dead People TPB (2009, $14.99) r/#6-10						15.00
...: Room and Boredom TPB (2008, $9.99) r/#1-5						10.00
...: The Beauty of Decay TPB (2010, $17.99) r/#16-20 & Halloween Annual #1						18.00
...: The Space Between TPB (2010, $14.99) r/#11-15; sketch pages						15.00
...: Under New Management TPB (2011, $14.99) r/#20-25						15.00

HOUSE OF SECRETS (Combined with The Unexpected after #154)
National Periodical Publications/DC Comics: 11-12/56 - No. 80, 9-10/66; No. 81, 8-9/69 - No. 140, 2-3/76; No. 141, 8-9/76 - No. 154, 10-11/78

	GD 2.0	VG 4.0	FN 6.0	VF 8.0	VF/NM 9.0	NM- 9.2
1-Drucker-a; Moreira-c	112	224	336	952	1926	2900
2-Moreira-a	40	80	120	320	635	950
3-Kirby-c/a	34	68	102	267	526	785
4-Kirby-a	25	50	75	183	367	550
5-7	18	36	54	125	255	385
8-Kirby-a	20	40	60	140	283	425
9-11: 11-Lou Cameron-a (unsigned)	16	32	48	111	226	340
12-Kirby-c/a; Lou Cameron-a	17	34	51	118	242	365
13-15: 14-Flying saucer-c	13	26	39	89	170	250
16-20	12	24	36	82	154	225
21,22,24-30	11	22	33	75	138	200
23-1st app. Mark Merlin & begin series (8/59)	11	22	33	77	144	210
31-50: 48-Toth-a. 50-Last 10¢ issue	10	20	30	69	122	175
51-60: 58-Origin Mark Merlin	9	18	27	60	100	140
61-First Eclipso (7-8/63) and begin series	14	28	42	99	200	300
62	8	16	24	54	90	125
63-65-Toth-a on Eclipso (see Brave and the Bold #64)	6	12	18	43	69	95
66-1st Eclipso-c (also #67,70,78,79); Toth-a	8	16	24	54	90	125
67,73: 67-Toth-a on Eclipso. 73-Mark Merlin becomes Prince Ra-Man (1st app.)	6	12	18	43	69	95
68-72,74-80: 76-Prince Ra-Man vs. Eclipso. 80-Eclipso, Prince Ra-Man end	6	12	18	39	62	85
81-Mystery format begins; 1st app. Abel (House Of Secrets host); (cameo in DC Special #4)	12	24	36	82	154	225
82-84: 82-Neal Adams-c(i)	7	14	21	49	80	110
85,90: 85-N. Adams-a(i). 90-Buckler (early work)/N. Adams-a(i)	7	14	21	50	83	115
86,88,89,91	6	12	18	43	69	95
87-Wrightson & Kaluta-a	8	16	24	52	86	120
92-1st app. Swamp Thing-c/story (8 pgs.)(6-7/71) by Berni Wrightson(p) w/JeffJones/Kaluta/Weiss ink assists; classic-c.	47	94	141	376	763	1150
93,94,96-(52 pgs.)-Wrightson-c. 94-Wrightson-a(i); 96-Wood-a	7	14	21	49	80	110
95,97,98-(52 pgs.)	5	10	15	35	55	75
99-Wrightson splash pg.	5	10	15	32	51	70
100-Classic Wrightson-c	8	16	24	52	86	120
101,102,104,105,108-111,113-120	3	6	9	18	27	35
103,106,107-Wrightson-c	5	10	15	30	48	65
112-Grey tone-c	3	6	9	20	30	40
121-133	2	4	6	11	16	20
134-Wrightson-a	3	6	9	18	27	35
135,136,139-Wrightson-a/c	3	6	9	20	30	40
137,138,141-153	2	4	6	8	10	12
140-1st solo origin of the Patchworkman (see Swamp Thing #3)	3	6	9	16	23	30
154 (10-11/78, 44 pgs.) Last issue	2	4	6	9	13	16

NOTE: ***Neal Adams*** *c-81, 82, 84-88, 90, 91.* ***Alcala*** *a-104-107.* ***Anderson*** *a-91. Aparo a-93, 97, 105.* ***B. Bailey*** *a-107.* ***Cameron*** *a-13, 15.* ***Colan*** *a-63.* ***Ditko*** *a-139p, 148.* ***Elias*** *a-58.* ***Evans*** *a-118.* ***Finlay*** *a-7r(Real Fact?).* ***Glanzman*** *a-91.* ***Golden*** *a-151.* ***Heath*** *a-31.* ***Heck*** *a-85.* ***Kaluta*** *a-87, 98, 99; c-98, 99, 101, 102, 105, 149, 151, 154.* ***Bob Kane*** *a-18, 21.* ***G. Kane*** *a-85p.* ***Kirby*** *c-3, 11, 12.* ***Kubert*** *a-39.* ***Meskin*** *a-2-68 (most), 94r; c-55-60.* ***Moreira*** *a-7, 8, 51, 54, 102-104, 106, 108, 113, 116, 118, 121, 123, 127; c-1, 2, 4-10, 13-20.* ***Morrow*** *a-86, 89, 90; c-89, 146-148.* ***Nino*** *a-101, 103, 106, 109, 115, 117, 126, 128, 131, 147, 153.* ***Redondo*** *a-95, 99, 102, 104p, 113, 116, 134, 136, 139, 140.* ***Reese*** *a-85.* ***Severin*** *a-91.* ***Starlin*** *c-150.* ***Sutton*** *a-154.* ***Toth*** *a-63-67, 83, 93r, 94r,*

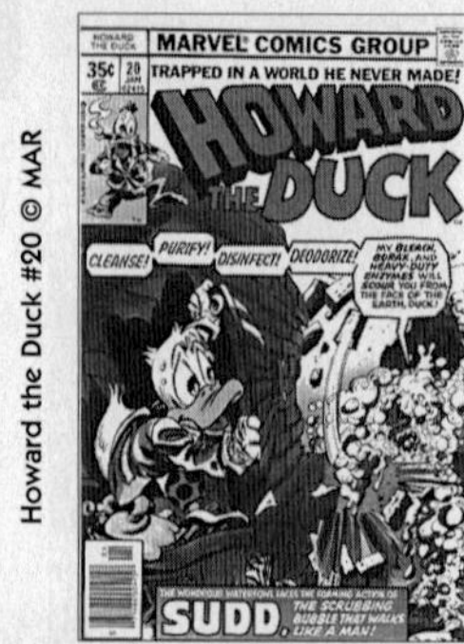

Howard the Duck #20 © MAR

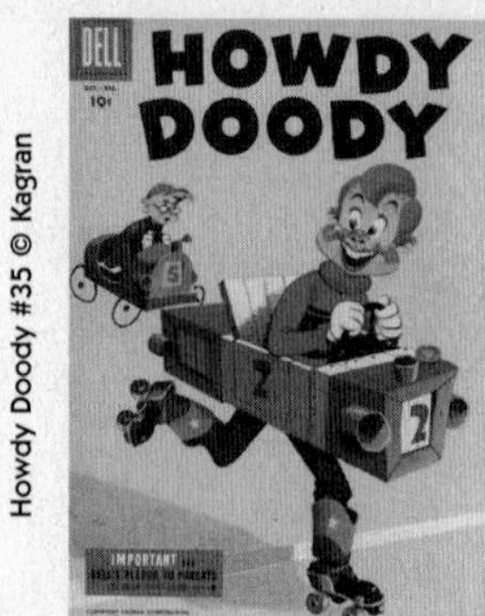

Howdy Doody #35 © Kagran

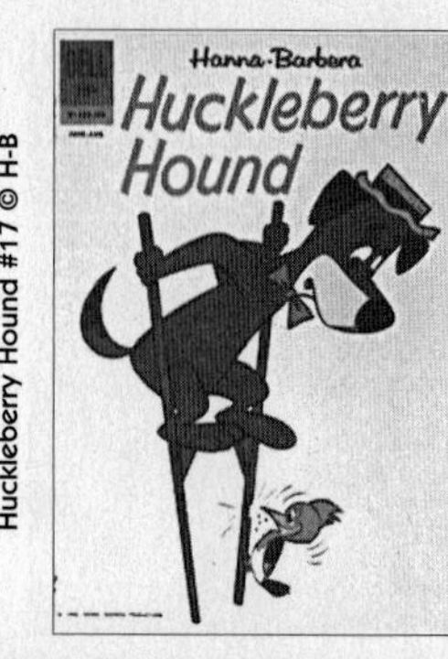

Huckleberry Hound #17 © H-B

GD 2.0 | VG 4.0 | FN 6.0 | VF 8.0 | VF/NM 9.0 | NM- 9.2

GD 2.0 | VG 4.0 | FN 6.0 | VF 8.0 | VF/NM 9.0 | NM- 9.2

96r-98r, 123. ***Tuska*** *a-90, 104.* ***Wrightson*** *a-134; c-92-94, 96, 100, 103, 106, 107, 135, 136, 139.*

HOUSE OF SECRETS
DC Comics (Vertigo): Oct, 1996 - No. 25, Dec, 1998 ($2.50) (Creator-owned series)

1-Steven Seagle-s/Kristiansen-c/a. 3.50
2-25: 5,7-Kristiansen-c/a. 6-Fegrado-a 3.00
TPB-(1997, $14.95) r/1-5 15.00

HOUSE OF SECRETS: FACADE
DC Comics (Vertigo): 2001 - No. 2, 2001 ($5.95, limited series)

1,2-Steven Seagle-s/Teddy Kristiansen-c/a. 6.00

HOUSE OF TERROR (3-D)
St. John Publishing Co.: Oct, 1953 (25¢, came w/glasses)

1-Kubert, Baker-a 27 54 81 158 259 360

HOUSE OF YANG, THE (See Yang)
Charlton Comics: July, 1975 - No. 6, June, 1976; 1978

1-Sanho Kim-a in all 2 4 6 13 18 22
2-6 2 4 6 8 10 12
Modern Comics #1,2(1978) 6.00

HOUSE ON THE BORDERLAND
DC Comics (Vertigo): 2000 ($29.95, hardcover, one-shot)

HC-Adaptation of William Hope Hodgson book; Corben-a 30.00
SC (2003, $19.95) 20.00

HOUSE II: THE SECOND STORY
Marvel Comics: Oct, 1987 (One-shot)

1-Adapts movie 3.00

HOWARD CHAYKIN'S AMERICAN FLAGG (See American Flagg!)
First Comics: V2#1, May, 1988 - V2#12, Apr, 1989 ($1.75/$1.95, Baxter paper)

V2#1-9,11,12-Chaykin-c(p) in all 3.00
10-Elvis Presley photo-c 4.00

HOWARD THE DUCK (See Bizarre Adventures #34, Crazy Magazine, Fear, Man-Thing, Marvel Treasury Edition & Sensational She-Hulk #14-17)
Marvel Comics Group: Jan, 1976 - No. 31, May, 1979; No. 32, Jan, 1986; No. 33, Sept, 1986

1-Brunner-c/a; Spider-Man x-over (low distr.) 4 8 12 24 37 50
2-Brunner-c/a 2 4 6 11 16 20
3,4-(Regular 25¢ edition). 3-Buscema-a(p), (7/76) 2 4 6 8 11 14
3,4-(30¢-c, limited distribution) 3 6 9 16 22 28
5 2 4 6 8 11 14
6-11: 8-Howard The Duck for president. 9-1st Sgt. Preston Dudley of RCMP. 10-Spider-Man-c/sty 1 2 3 5 7 9
12-1st brief app. Kiss (3/77) 4 8 12 24 37 50
13-(30¢-c) 1st full app. Kiss (6/77); Daimon Hellstrom app. plus cameo of Howard as Son of Satan 4 8 12 28 44 60
13-(35¢-c, limited distribution) 9 18 27 65 113 160
14-32: 14-17-(Regular 30¢-c). 14-Howard as Son of Satan-c/story; Son of Satan app. 16-Album issue; 3 pgs. comics. 22,23-Man-Thing-c/stories; Star Wars parody. 30,32-P. Smith-a 6.00
14-17-(35¢-c, limited distribution) 3 6 9 14 20 25
33-Last issue; low print run 1 2 3 5 6 8
Annual 1(1977, 52 pgs.)-Mayerik-a 2 3 4 6 8 10
... Omnibus HC (2008, $99.99, dustjacket) r/#1-33 & Annual #1, Adventure Into Fear #19, Man-Thing #1, Giant-Size Man-Thing #4&5, Marvel Treasury Ed. #12, Marvel Team-Up #96 and FOOM #15; Gerber foreword; creator interviews; bonus art; 2 covers 100.00

NOTE: ***Austin*** *c-29i.* ***Bolland*** *c-33.* ***Brunner*** *a-1p, 2p; c-1, 2.* ***Buckler*** *c-3p.* ***Buscema*** *a-3p.* ***Colan*** *a(p)-4-15, 17-20, 24-27, 30, 31; c(p)-4-31, Annual 1p.* ***Leialoha*** *a-1-13i; c(i)-3-5, 8-11.* ***Mayerik*** *a-22, 23, 33.* ***Paul Smith*** *a-30p, 32. Man-Thing app. in #22, 23.*

HOWARD THE DUCK (Magazine)
Marvel Comics Group: Oct, 1979 - No. 9, Mar, 1981 (B&W, 68 pgs.)

1-Art by Colan, Janson, Golden. Kidney Lady app. 2 4 6 8 10 12
2,3,5-9 (nudity in most): 2-Mayerick-c. 3-Xmas issue; Jack Davis-c; Duck World flashback. 5-Dracula app. 6-1st Street People back-up story. 7-Has pin-up by Byrne; Man-Thing-c/s (46 pgs.). 8-Batman parody w/Marshall Rogers-a; Dave Sim-a (1 pg.). 9-Marie Severin-a; John Pound painted-c 6.00
4-Beatles, John Lennon, Elvis, Kiss & Devo cameos; Hitler app. 2 4 6 9 12 15

NOTE: ***Buscema*** *a-4p.* ***Colan*** *a-1-5p, 7-9p.* ***Jack Davis*** *c-3.* ***Golden*** *a(p)-1, 5, 6(51pgs.).* ***Rogers*** *a-7, 8.* ***Simonson*** *a-7.*

HOWARD THE DUCK (Volume 2)
Marvel Comics: Mar, 2002 - No. 6, Aug, 2002 ($2.99)

1-Gerber-s/Winslade-a/Fabry-c 4.00
2-6: 2,4-6-Gerber-s/Winslade-a/Fabry-c. 3-Fabry-a/c 3.00
TPB (9/02, $14.99) r/#1-6 15.00

HOWARD THE DUCK (Volume 3)
Marvel Comics: Dec, 2007 - No. 4, Feb, 2008 ($2.99, limited series)

1-4-Templeton-s/Bobillo-a/c; She-Hulk app. 3.00
...: Media Duckling TPB (2008, $11.99) r/#1-4; Howard the Duck #1 (1/76) and pages from Civil War: Choosing Sides 12.00

HOWARD THE DUCK HOLIDAY SPECIAL
Marvel Comics: Feb, 1997 ($2.50, one-shot)

1-Wraparound-c; Hama-s 4.00

HOWARD THE DUCK: THE MOVIE
Marvel Comics Group: Dec, 1986 - No. 3, Feb, 1987 (Limited series)

1-3: Movie adaptation; r/Marvel Super Special 3.00

HOW BOYS AND GIRLS CAN HELP WIN THE WAR
The Parents' Magazine Institute: 1942 (10¢, one-shot)

1-All proceeds used to buy war bonds 27 54 81 158 259 360

HOWDY DOODY (TV)(See Jackpot of Fun-- & Poll Parrot)(Some have stories by John Stanley)
Dell Publishing Co.: 1/50 - No. 38, 7-9/56; No. 761, 1/57; No. 811, 7/57

1-(Scarce)-Photo-c; 1st TV comic 77 154 231 655 1328 2000
2-Photo-c 37 74 111 284 562 840
3-5: All photo-c 21 42 63 153 307 460
6-Used in **SOTI**, pg. 309; classic-c; painted covers begin 23 46 69 168 334 500
7-10 14 28 42 96 191 285
11-20: 13-X-Mas-c 12 24 36 84 157 230
21-38, Four Color 761,811 10 20 30 72 131 185

HOW IT BEGAN
United Features Syndicate: No. 15, 1939 (one-shot)

Single Series 15 34 68 102 199 325 450

HOW SANTA GOT HIS RED SUIT (See March of Comics No. 2)

HOW THE WEST WAS WON (See Movie Comics)

HOW TO DRAW FOR THE COMICS
Street and Smith: No date (1942?) (10¢, 64 pgs., B&W & color, no ads)

nn-Art by Robert Winsor McCay (recreating his father's art), George Marcoux (Supersnipe artist), Vernon Greene (The Shadow artist), Jack Binder (with biog.), Thorton Fisher, Jon Small, & Jack Farr; has biographies of each artist 30 60 90 177 289 400

H. P. LOVECRAFT'S CTHULHU
Millennium Publications: Dec, 1991 - No. 3, May, 1992 ($2.50, limited series)

1-3: 1-Contains trading cards on thin stock 3.00

H. R. PUFNSTUF (TV) (See March of Comics #360)
Gold Key: Oct, 1970 - No. 8, July, 1972

1-Photo-c 11 22 33 75 138 200
2-8-Photo-c on all. 6-8-Both Gold Key and Whitman editions exist 8 16 24 54 90 125

HUBERT AT CAMP MOONBEAM
Dell Publishing Co.: No. 251, Oct, 1949 (one shot)

Four Color 251 7 14 21 49 80 110

HUCK & YOGI JAMBOREE (TV)
Dell Publishing Co.: Mar, 1961 ($1.00, 6-1/4x9", 116 pgs., cardboard-c, high quality paper) (B&W original material)

nn (scarce) 9 18 27 63 107 150

HUCK & YOGI WINTER SPORTS (TV)
Dell Publishing Co.: No. 1310, Mar, 1962 (Hanna-Barbara) (one-shot)

Four Color 1310 8 16 24 56 93 130

HUCK FINN (See The New Adventures of... & Power Record Comics)

HUCKLEBERRY FINN (Movie)
Dell Publishing Co.: No. 1114, July, 1960

Four Color 1114-Photo-c 5 10 15 34 55 75

HUCKLEBERRY HOUND (See Dell Giant #31,44, Golden Picture Story Book, Kite Fun Book, March of Comics #199, 214, 235, Spotlight #1 & Whitman Comic Books)

HUCKLEBERRY HOUND (TV)
Dell/Gold Key No. 18 (10/62) on: No. 990, 5-7/59 - No. 43, 10/70 (Hanna-Barbera)

Four Color 990(#1)-1st app. Huckleberry Hound, Yogi Bear, & Pixie & Dixie & Mr. Jinks 12 24 36 84 157 230

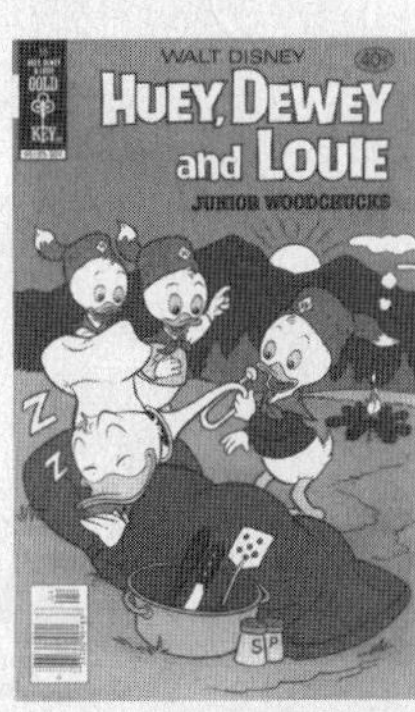

Huey, Dewey, and Louie Junior Woodchucks #55 © DIS

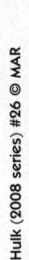

Hulk (2008 series) #26 © MAR

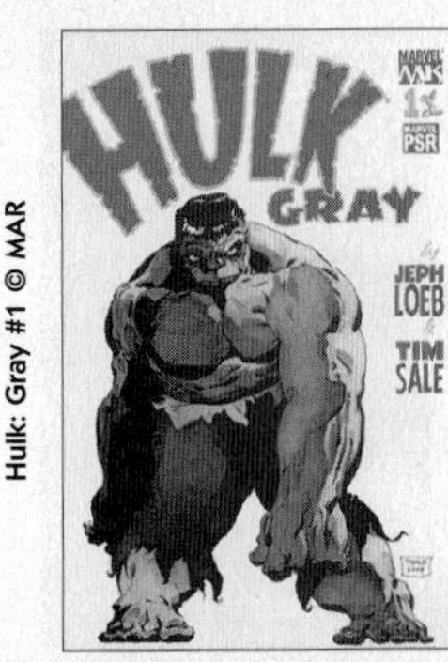

Hulk: Gray #1 © MAR

	GD 2.0	VG 4.0	FN 6.0	VF 8.0	VF/NM 9.0	NM- 9.2
Four Color 1050,1054 (12/59)	8	16	24	58	97	135
3(1-2/60) - 7 (9-10/60), Four Color 1141 (10/60)	8	16	24	52	86	120
8-10	6	12	18	43	69	95
11,13-17 (6-8/62)	5	10	15	32	51	70
12-1st Hokey Wolf & Ding-a-Ling	6	12	18	37	59	80
18,19 (84pgs.; 18-20 titled ...Chuckleberry Tales)	8	16	24	52	86	120
20-Titled Chuckleberry Tales	5	10	15	30	48	65
21-30: 28-30-Reprints	4	8	12	24	37	50
31-43: 31,32,35,37-43-Reprints	3	6	9	20	30	40

HUCKLEBERRY HOUND (TV)
Charlton Comics: Nov, 1970 - No. 8, Jan, 1972 (Hanna-Barbera)

	GD 2.0	VG 4.0	FN 6.0	VF 8.0	VF/NM 9.0	NM- 9.2
1	5	10	15	32	51	70
2-8	3	6	9	18	27	35

HUEY, DEWEY, & LOUIE (See Donald Duck, 1938 for 1st app. Also see Mickey Mouse Magazine V4#2, V5#7 & Walt Disney's Junior Woodchucks Limited Series)

HUEY, DEWEY, & LOUIE BACK TO SCHOOL (See Dell Giant #22, 35, 49 & Dell Giants)

HUEY, DEWEY, AND LOUIE JUNIOR WOODCHUCKS (Disney)
Gold Key No. 1-61/Whitman No. 62 on: Aug, 1966 - No. 81, July, 1984
(See Walt Disney's Comics & Stories #125)

	GD 2.0	VG 4.0	FN 6.0	VF 8.0	VF/NM 9.0	NM- 9.2
1	6	12	18	41	66	90
2,3(12/68)	4	8	12	22	34	45
4,5(4/70)-r/two WDC&S D.Duck stories by Barks	3	6	9	20	30	40
6-17	3	6	9	18	27	35
18,27-30	3	6	9	15	21	26
19-23,25-New storyboarded scripts by Barks, 13-25 pgs. per issue	3	6	9	19	29	38
24,26: 26-r/Barks Donald Duck WDC&S stories	3	6	9	16	23	30
31-57,60,61: 35,41-r/Barks J.W. scripts	2	4	6	8	11	14
58,59: 58-r/Barks Donald Duck WDC&S stories	2	4	6	9	13	16
62-64 (Whitman)	2	4	6	9	13	16
65-(9/80), 66 (Pre-pack? scarce)	4	8	12	22	34	45
67 (1/81),68	2	4	6	9	13	16
67-40¢ cover variant	4	8	12	17	21	24
69-74: 72(2/82), 73(2-3/82), 74(3/82)	2	4	6	8	11	14
75-81 (all #90183; pre-pack; nd, nd code; scarce): 75(4/83), 76(5/83), 77(7/83), 78(8/83), 79(4/84), 80(5/84), 81(7/84)	3	6	9	14	20	25

HUGGA BUNCH (TV)
Marvel Comics (Star Comics): Oct, 1986 - No. 6, Aug, 1987

1-6 ... 4.00

HULK (Magazine)(Formerly The Rampaging Hulk)(Also see The Incredible Hulk)
Marvel Comics: No. 10, Aug., 1978 - No. 27, June, 1981 ($1.50)

	GD 2.0	VG 4.0	FN 6.0	VF 8.0	VF/NM 9.0	NM- 9.2
10-18: 10-Bill Bixby interview. 11-Moon Knight begins. 12-15,17,18-Moon Knight stories. 12-Lou Ferrigno interview.	2	4	6	10	14	18
19-27: 20-Moon Knight story. 23-Last full color issue; Banner is attacked. 24-Part color, Lou Ferrigno interview. 25-Part color. 26,27-are B&W	2	4	6	9	12	15

NOTE: #10-20 have fragile spines which split easily. ***Alcala*** *a(i)-15, 17-20, 22, 24-27.* ***Buscema*** *a-23; c-26.* ***Chaykin*** *a-21-25.* ***Colan*** *a(p)-11, 19, 24-27.* ***Jusko*** *painted c-12.* ***Nebres*** *a-16.* ***Severin*** *a-19i. Moon Knight by* ***Sienkiewicz*** *in 13-15, 17, 18, 20.* ***Simonson*** *a-27; c-23. Dominic Fortune appears in #21-24.*

HULK (Becomes Incredible Hulk Vol. 2 with issue #12) (Also see Marvel Age Hulk)
Marvel Comics: Apr, 1999 - No. 11, Feb, 2000 ($2.99/$1.99)

	NM- 9.2
1-($2.99) Byrne-s/Garney-a	5.00
1-Variant-c	9.00
1-DFE Remarked-c	50.00
1-Gold foil variant	10.00
2-7-($1.99): 2-Two covers. 5-Art by Jurgens, Buscema & Texeira. 7-Avengers app.	4.00
8-Hulk battles Wolverine	7.00
9-11: 11-She-Hulk app.	3.00
1999 Annual ($3.50) Chapter One story; Byrne-s/Weeks-a	4.00
Hulk Vs. The Thing (12/99, $3.99, TPB) reprints their notable battles	4.00

HULK (Also see Fall of the Hulks and King-Size Hulk)
Marvel Comics: Mar, 2008 - Present ($2.99/$3.99)

	NM- 9.2
1-Red Hulk app.; Abomination killed; Loeb-s/McGuinness-a/c	5.00
1-Variant-c by Acuña	10.00
1-Variant-c with Incredible Hulk #1 cover swipe by McGuinness	20.00
1,2-2nd printings with wraparound McGuinness variant-c	3.00
2-22: 2-Iron Man app.; Rick Jones becomes the new Abomination. 4,6-Red Hulk vs. green Hulk; two covers (each Hulk); Thor app. 7-9-Art Adams & Cho-a (2 covers) 10-Defenders re-form. 14,15-X-Force, Elektra & Deadpool app. 15-Red She-Hulk app. 19-21-Fall of the Hulks x-over. 19-FF app. 22-World War Hulks	4.00
2-9: 2-Variant-c by Djurdjevic. 3-Var-c by Finch. 5-Var-c by Coipel. 6,7-Var-c by Turner 8-Var-c by Sal Buscema. 9-Two covers w/Hulks as Santa	6.00
23-($4.99) Origin of the Red Hulk; art by Sale, Romita, Deodato, Trimpe, Yu, others	5.00
24-31-($3.99): 24-World war Hulks. 25,26-Iron Man app. 26-Thor app.	4.00
30.1, 32-($2.99) Parker-s/Hardman-a	3.00
... Family: Green Genes 1 (2/09, $4.99) new She-Hulk, Scorpion, Skaar & Mr. Fixit stories	5.00
... Let the Battle Begin 1 (5/10, $3.99) Snider-s/Kurth-a; Del Mundo-c; McGuinness-a	4.00
... MGC #1 (6/10, $1.00) r/#1 with "Marvel's Greatest Comics" logo on cover	1.00
... Monster-Size Special (12/08, $3.99) monster-themed stories by Niles, David & others	4.00
...: Raging Thunder 1 (8/08, $3.99) Hulk vs. Thundra; Breitweiser-a; r/FF #133; Land-c	4.00
... Vs. Fin Fang Foom (2/08, $3.99) new re-telling of first meeting; r/Strange Tales #89	4.00
... Vs. Hercules (6/08, $3.99) Djurdjevic-c; new story w/art by various; r/Tales To Ast. #79	4.00
...: Winter Guard (2/10, $3.99) Darkstar, Crimson Dynamo app. Steve Ellis-a/c	4.00
Hulk 100 Project (2008, $10.00, SC, charity book for the HERO Initiative) collection of 100 variant covers by Adams, Romita Sr. & Jr., Cho, McGuinness and more	10.00

HULK AND POWER PACK (All ages series)
Marvel Comics: May, 2007 - No. 4, Aug, 2007 ($2.99, limited series)

	NM- 9.2
1-4-Sumerak-s. 1,2,4-Williams-a. 1-Absorbing Man app. 3-Kuhn-a; Abomination app.	3.00
...: Pack Smash! (2007, $6.99, digest) r/#1-4	7.00

HULK & THING: HARD KNOCKS
Marvel Comics: Nov, 2004 - No. 4, Feb, 2005 ($3.50, limited series)

	NM- 9.2
1-4-Bruce Jones-s/Jae Lee-a/c	3.50
TPB (2005, $13.99) r/#1-4 and Giant-Size Super-Stars #1	14.00

HULK: BROKEN WORLDS
Marvel Comics: May, 2009 -No. 2, July, 2009 ($3.99, limited series)

1,2-Short stories of alternate world Hulks by various, incl. Trimpe, David, Warren ... 4.00

HULK CHRONICLES: WWH
Marvel Comics: Oct, 2008 - No. 6, Mar, 2009 ($4.99, limited series)

1-6-Reprints stories from World War Hulk x-over. 1-R/Inc. Hulk #106 & WWH Prologue ... 5.00

HULK: DESTRUCTION
Marvel Comics: Sept, 2005 - No. 4, Dec, 2005 ($2.99, limited series)

1-4-Origin of the Abomination; Peter David-s/Jim Muniz-a ... 3.00

HULKED-OUT HEROES
Marvel Comics: Jun, 2010 - No. 2, Jun, 2010 ($3.99, limited series)

1,2-World War Hulks tie-in; Deadpool app.; Ramos-a ... 4.00

HULK: FUTURE IMPERFECT
Marvel Comics: Jan, 1993 - No. 2, Dec, 1992 (In error) ($5.95, 52 pgs., squarebound, limited series)

	GD 2.0	VG 4.0	FN 6.0	VF 8.0	VF/NM 9.0	NM- 9.2
1,2: Embossed-c; Peter David story & George Perez-c/a. 1-1st app. Maestro.	1	2	3	5	6	8

HULK: GRAY
Marvel Comics: Dec, 2003 - No. 6, Apr, 2004 ($3.50, limited series)

	NM- 9.2
1-6-Hulk's origin & early days; Loeb-s/Sale-a/c	3.50
HC (2004, $21.99, with dust jacket) oversized r/#1-6	22.00
SC (2005, $19.99) r/#1-6	20.00

HULK: NIGHTMERICA
Marvel Comics: Aug, 2003 - No. 6, May, 2004 ($2.99, limited series)

1-6-Brian Ashmore painted-a/c ... 3.00

HULK/ PITT
Marvel Comics: 1997 ($5.99, one-shot)

1-David-s/Keown-c/a ... 6.00

HULK SMASH
Marvel Comics: Mar, 2001 - No. 2, Apr, 2001 ($2.99, limited series)

1,2-Ennis-s/McCrea & Janson-a/Nowlan painted-c ... 3.00

HULK: THE MOVIE
Marvel Comics

	NM- 9.2
...Adaptation (8/03, $3.50) Bruce Jones-s/Bagley-a/Keown-c	3.50
TPB (2003, $12.99) r/Adaptation, Ultimates #5, Inc. Hulk #34, Ult. Marvel Team-Up #2&3	13.00

HULK 2099
Marvel Comics: Dec, 1994 - No. 10, Sept, 1995 ($1.50/$1.95)

	NM- 9.2
1-($2.50)-Green foil-c	3.50
2-10: 2-A. Kubert-c	3.00

HULK/WOLVERINE: 6 HOURS
Marvel Comics: Mar, 2003 - No. 4, May, 2003 ($2.99, limited series)

1-4-Bruce Jones-s/Scott Kolins-a; Bisley-c ... 3.00

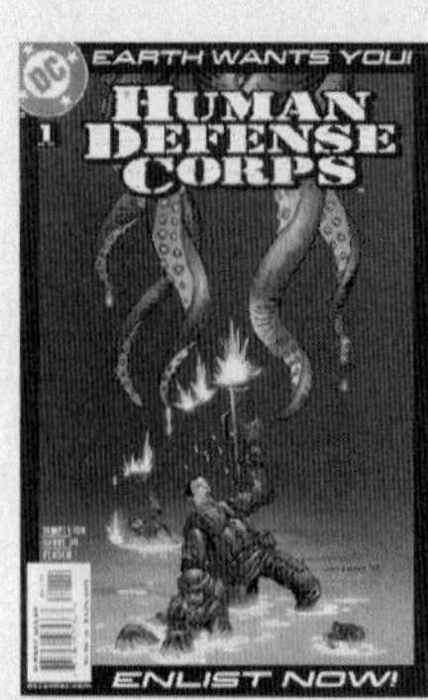

Human Defense Corps #1 © DC

The Human Torch #32 © MAR

Humphrey Comics #16 © HARV

GD VG FN VF VF/NM NM-
2.0 4.0 6.0 8.0 9.0 9.2

GD VG FN VF VF/NM NM-
2.0 4.0 6.0 8.0 9.0 9.2

Hulk Legends Vol. 1: Hulk/Wolverine: 6 Hours (2003, $13.99, TPB) r/#1-4 & 1st Wolverine app. from Incredible Hulk #181 14.00

HUMAN DEFENSE CORPS
DC Comics: Jul, 2003 - No. 6, Dec, 2003 ($2.50, limited series)

1-6-Ty Templeton-s/Sauve, Jr & Vlasco-a. 1-Lois Lane app. 3.00

HUMAN FLY
I.W. Enterprises/Super: 1963 - 1964 (Reprints)

I.W. Reprint #1-Reprints Blue Beetle #44('46) 2 4 6 13 18 22
Super Reprint #10-R/Blue Beetle #46('47) 2 4 6 13 18 22

HUMAN FLY, THE
Marvel Comics Group: Sept, 1977 - No. 19, Mar, 1979

1,2,9,19: 1,2-(Regular 30¢-c). 1-Origin; Spider-Man x-over. 2-Ghost Rider app. 9-Daredevil x-over; Byrne-c(p). 19-Last issue 2 3 4 6 8 10
1,2-(35¢-c, limited distribution) 3 6 9 20 30 40
3-8,10-18 5.00

NOTE: ***Austin** c-4i, 9i. **Elias** a-1, 3p, 4p, 7p, 10-12p, 15p, 18p, 19p. **Layton** c-19.*

HUMANKIND
Image Comics (Top Cow): Sept, 2004 - No. 5, Mar, 2005 ($2.99, limited series)

1-5-Tony Daniel-a. 1-Three covers by Daniel, Silvestri, and Land 3.00

HUMAN RACE, THE
DC Comics: May, 2005 - No. 7, Nov, 2005 ($2.99, limited series)

1-7-Raab-s/Justiniano-a/c 3.00

HUMAN TARGET
DC Comics (Vertigo): Apr, 1999 - No. 4, July, 1999 ($2.95, limited series)

1-4-Milligan-s/Bradstreet-c/Biukovic-a 3.00
1-Special Edition (6/10, $1.00) r/#1 with "What's Next?" logo on cover 1.00
TPB (2000, $12.95) new Bradstreet-c 13.00
...: Chance Meetings TPB (2010, $14.99) r/#1-4 and Human Target: Final Cut GN 15.00

HUMAN TARGET
DC Comics (Vertigo): Oct, 2003 - No. 21, June, 2005 ($2.95)

1-21: 1-5-Milligan-s/Pulido-a/c. 6-Chiang-a 3.00
...: Living in Amerika TPB (2004, $14.95) r/#6-10; Chiang sketch pages 15.00
...: Second Chances TPB (2011, $19.99) r/#1-10; Chiang sketch pages 20.00
...: Strike Zones TPB (2004, $9.95) r/#1-5 10.00

HUMAN TARGET (Based on the Fox TV series)
DC Comics: Apr, 2010 - No. 6, Sept, 2010 ($2.99, limited series)

1-6-Wein-s/Redondo-a; back-up stories by various. 1-Bermejo-c. 5-Sook-c 3.00
TPB (2010, $17.99) r/#1-6 18.00

HUMAN TARGET: FINAL CUT
DC Comics (Vertigo): 2002 ($29.95/$19.95, graphic novel)

Hardcover (2002, $29.95) Milligan-s/Pulido-a/c 30.00
Softcover (2003, $19.95) 20.00

HUMAN TARGET SPECIAL (TV)
DC Comics: Nov, 1991 ($2.00, 52 pgs., one-shot)

1 3.00

HUMAN TORCH, THE (Red Raven #1)(See All-Select, All Winners, Marvel Mystery, Men's Adventures, Mystic Comics (2nd series), Sub-Mariner, USA & Young Men)
Timely/Marvel Comics (TP 2,3/TCI 4-9/SePI 10/SnPC 11-25/CnPC 26-35/Atlas Comics (CPC 36-38)): No. 2, Fall, 1940 - No. 15, Spring, 1944; No. 16, Fall, 1944 - No. 35, Mar, 1949 (Becomes Love Tales #36 on); No. 36, April, 1954 - No. 38, Aug, 1954

2(#1)-Intro & Origin Toro; The Falcon, The Fiery Mask, Mantor the Magician, & Microman only app.; Human Torch by Burgos, Sub-Mariner by Everett begin (origin of each in text) 3250 6500 9750 24,400 44,700 65,000
3(#2)-40 pg. H.T. story; H.T. & S.M. battle over who is best artist in text-Everett or Burgos 584 1168 1752 4263 7532 10,800
4(#3)-Origin The Patriot in text; last Everett Sub-Mariner; Sid Greene-a 449 898 1347 3278 5789 8300
5(#4)-The Patriot app; Angel x-over in Sub-Mariner (Summer, 1941); 1st Nazi war-c this title; back-c ad for Young Allies #1 with diff. cover-a 389 778 1167 2723 4762 6800
5-Human Torch battles Sub-Mariner (Fall, '41); 60 pg. story 622 1244 1866 4541 8021 11,500
6,9 300 600 900 2010 3505 5100
7-1st Japanese war-c 300 600 900 2070 3635 5200
8-Human Torch battles Sub-Mariner; 52 pg. story; Wolverton-a, 1 pg. 420 840 1260 2959 5181 7400
10-Human Torch battles Sub-Mariner, 45 pg. story; Wolverton-a, 1 pg. 331 662 993 2317 4059 5800
11,13-15: 14-1st Atlas Globe logo (Winter, 1943-44; see All Winners #11 also) 258 516 774 1651 2826 4000
12-Classic-c 400 800 1200 2800 4900 7000
16-20: 20-Last War issue 174 348 522 1114 1907 2700
21,22,24-30: 27-2nd app. (1st-c) Asbestos Lady (see Capt. America Comics #63 for 1st app.) 145 290 435 921 1586 2250
23 (Sum/46)-Becomes Junior Miss 24? Classic Schomburg Robot-c 174 348 522 1114 1907 2700
31,32: 31-Namora x-over in Sub-Mariner (also #30); last Toro. 32-Sungirl, Namora app.; Sungirl-c 126 252 378 806 1378 1950
33-Capt. America x-over 132 264 396 838 1444 2050
34-Sungirl solo 121 242 363 768 1322 1875
35-Captain America & Sungirl app. (1949) 126 252 378 806 1378 1950
36-38(1954)-Sub-Mariner in all 107 214 321 680 1165 1650

NOTE: ***Ayers** Human Torch in 36(3). **Brodsky** c-25, 31-33?, 37, 38, **Burgos** c-36. **Everett** a-1-3, 27, 28, 30, 37, 38. **Powell** a-36(Sub-Mariner). **Schomburg** c-1-3, 5-8, 10-23. **Sekowsky** c-28, 34?, 35? **Shores** c-24, 26, 27, 29, 30. **Mickey Spillane** text 4-6. Bondage c-2, 12, 19.*

HUMAN TORCH, THE (Also see Avengers West Coast, Fantastic Four, The Invaders, Saga of the Original... & Strange Tales #101)
Marvel Comics Group: Sept, 1974 - No. 8, Nov, 1975

1: 1-8-r/stories from Strange Tales #101-108 3 6 9 16 22 28
2-8: 1st H.T. title since G.A. 7-vs. Sub-Mariner 2 4 6 10 14 18

NOTE: *Golden Age & Silver Age Human Torch-r #1-8. **Ayers** r-6, 7. **Kirby/Ayers** r-1-5, 8.*

HUMAN TORCH (From the Fantastic Four)
Marvel Comics: June, 2003 - No. 12, Jun, 2004 ($2.50/$2.99)

1-7-Skottie Young-c/a; Karl Kesel-s 3.00
8-12-($2.99) 8,10-Dodd-a. 9-Young-a. 11-Porter-a. 12-Medina-a 3.00
... Vol. 1: Burn TPB (2005, $7.99, digest size) r/#1-6 8.00

HUMAN TORCH COMICS 70TH ANNIVERSARY SPECIAL
Marvel Comics: July, 2009 ($3.99, one-shot)

1-Covers by Granov and Martin; new story and r/1st app Toro from Human Torch #2 4.00

HUMBUG (Satire by Harvey Kurtzman)
Humbug Publications: Aug, 1957 - No. 9, May, 1958; No. 10, June, 1958; No. 11, Oct, 1958

1-Wood-a (intro pgs. only) 27 54 81 158 259 360
2 15 30 45 85 130 175
3-9: 8-Elvis in Jailbreak Rock 14 28 42 76 108 140
10,11-Magazine format. 10-Photo-c 15 30 45 90 140 190
Bound Volume(#1-9)(extremely rare) 65 130 195 416 708 1000

NOTE: ***Davis** a-1-11. **Elder** a-2-4, 6-9, 11. **Heath** a-2, 4-8, 10. **Jaffee** a-2, 4-9. **Kurtzman** a-11.*

HUMDINGER (Becomes White Rider and Super Horse #3 on?)
Novelty Press/Premium Group: May-June, 1946 - V2#2, July-Aug, 1947

1-Jerkwater Line, Mickey Starlight by Don Rico, Dink begin 36 72 108 211 343 475
2 16 32 48 94 147 200
3-6, V2#1,2 12 24 36 69 97 125

HUMONGOUS MAN
Alternative Press (Ikon Press): Sept, 1997 -No. 3 ($2.25, B&W)

1-3-Stepp & Harrison-c/s/a. 3.00

HUMOR (See All Humor Comics)

HUMPHREY COMICS (Joe Palooka Presents...; also see Joe Palooka)
Harvey Publications: Oct, 1948 - No. 22, Apr, 1952

1-Joe Palooka's pal (r); (52 pgs.)-Powell-a 14 28 42 80 115 150
2,3: Powell-a 9 18 27 47 61 75
4-Boy Heroes app.; Powell-a 9 18 27 50 65 80
5-8,10: 5,6-Powell-a. 7-Little Dot app. 8 16 24 40 50 60
9-Origin Humphrey 9 18 27 47 61 75
11-22 7 14 21 37 46 55

HUNCHBACK OF NOTRE DAME, THE
Dell Publishing Co.: No. 854, Oct, 1957 (one shot)

Four Color 854-Movie, photo-c 12 24 36 82 154 225

HUNGER, THE
Speakeasy Comics: May, 2005 ($2.99)

1-Andy Bradshaw-s/a; Eric Powell-c 3.00

HUNGER DOGS, THE (See DC Graphic Novel #4)

HUNK
Charlton Comics: Aug, 1961 - No. 11, 1963

1 4 8 12 24 37 50
2-11 3 6 9 14 20 25

The Huntress #17 © DC

I Am An Avenger #1 © MAR

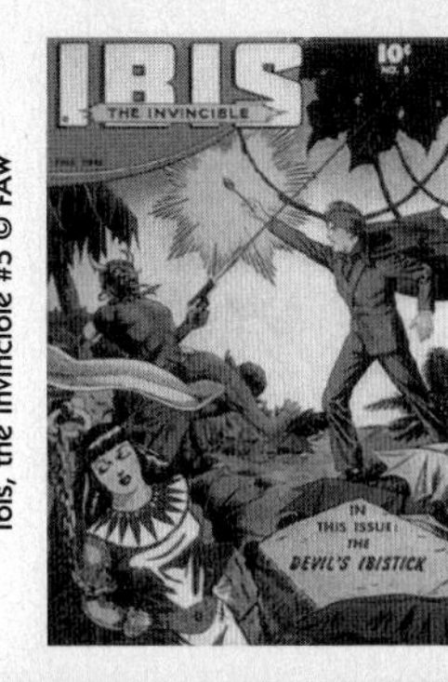

Ibis, the Invincible #5 © FAW

HUNTED (Formerly My Love Memoirs)
Fox Features Syndicate: No. 13, July, 1950; No. 2, Sept, 1950

13(#1)-Used in **SOTI**, pg. 42 & illo. "Treating police contemptuously" (lower left);
Hollingsworth bondage-c 37 74 111 218 354 490
2 18 36 54 103 162 220

HUNTER-KILLER
Image Comics (Top Cow): Nov, 2004 - No. 12, Mar, 2007 ($2.99)

0-(11/04, 25¢) Prelude with Silvestri sketch page and Waid afterword 3.00
1-12: 1-(3/05, $2.99) Waid-s/Silvestri-a; four covers. 2-Linsner variant-c 3.00
... Collected Edition Vol. 1 (9/05, $4.99) r/#0-3 5.00
...Dossier 1 (9/05, $2.99) character profiles with art by various; Migliari-c 3.00
... Volume 1 TPB (1/08, $24.99) r/#0-12; Dossier and Script Book; variant covers 25.00

HUNTER: THE AGE OF MAGIC (See Books of Magic)
DC Comics (Vertigo): Sept, 2001 - No. 25, Sept, 2003 ($2.50/$2.75)

1-25: Horrocks-s/Case-a. 1-8-Bolton-c. 14-Begin $2.75-c. 19-Bachalo-c 3.00

HUNTRESS, THE (See All-Star Comics #69, Batman Family, DC Super Stars #17, Detective #652, Infinity, Inc. #1 & Wonder Woman #271)
DC Comics: Apr, 1989 - No. 19, Oct, 1990 ($1.00, mature)

1-16: Staton-c/a(p) in all 3.00
17-19-Batman-c/stories 3.00
..: Darknight Daughter TPB (2006, $19.99) r/origin & early apps. in DC Super Stars #17,
Batman Family #18-20 & Wonder Woman #271-287,289,290,294,295; Bolland-c 20.00

HUNTRESS, THE
DC Comics: June, 1994 - No. 4, Sept, 1994 ($1.50, limited series)

1-4-Netzer-c/a: 2-Batman app. 3.00

HUNTRESS: YEAR ONE
DC Comics: Early July, 2008 - No. 6, Late Sept, 2008 ($2.99, limited series)

1-6-Origin re-told; Cliff Richards-a/Ivory Madison-s 3.00
TPB (2009, $17.99) r/#1-6; intro. by Paul Levitz 18.00

HURRICANE COMICS
Cambridge House: 1945 (52 pgs.)

1-(Humor, funny animal) 23 46 69 136 223 310

HUSK
Marvel Comics (Soleil): May, 2010 - No. 2, Jun, 2010 ($5.99, limited series)

1,2-English version of French comic; L'Homme-s/Boudoiron-a 6.00

HYBRIDS
Continunity Comics: Jan, 1994 ($2.50, one-shot)

1-Neal Adams-c(p) & part-a(i); embossed-c. 3.50

HYBRIDS DEATHWATCH 2000
Continuity Comics: Apr, 1993 - No. 3, Aug, 1993 ($2.50)

0-(Giveaway)-Foil-c; Neal Adams-c(i) & plots (also #1,2) 3.50
1-3: 1-Polybagged w/card; die-cut-c. 2-Thermal-c. 3-Polybagged w/card;
indestructible-c; Adams plot 3.00

HYBRIDS ORIGIN
Continunity Comics: 1993 - No. 5, Jan, 1994 ($2.50)

1-5: 2,3-Neal Adams-c. 4,5-Valeria the She-Bat app. Adams-c(i) 3.00

HYDE
IDW Publ.: Oct, 2004 ($7.49, one-shot)

1-Steve Niles-s/Nick Stakal 7.50

HYDE-25
Harris Publications: Apr, 1995 ($2.95, one-shot)

0-coupon for poster; r/Vampirella's 1st app. 3.00

HYDROMAN (See Heroic Comics)

HYPERKIND (See Razorline)
Marvel Comics: Sept, 1993 - No. 9, May, 1994 ($1.75/$1.95)

1-($2.50)-Foil embossed-c; by Clive Barker 3.50
2-9 3.00

HYPERKIND UNLEASED
Marvel Comics: Aug, 1994 ($2.95, 52 pgs., one-shot)

1 4.00

HYPER MYSTERY COMICS
Hyper Publications: May, 1940 - No. 2, June, 1940 (68 pgs.)

1-Hyper, the Phenomenal begins; Calkins-a 206 412 618 1318 2259 3200
2 103 206 309 659 1130 1600

HYPERSONIC
Dark Horse Comics: Nov, 1997 - No. 4, Feb, 1998 ($2.95, limited series)

1-4: Abnett & White/Erskine-a 3.00

I AIM AT THE STARS (Movie)
Dell Publishing Co.: No. 1148, Nov-Jan/1960-61 (one-shot)

Four Color 1148-The Werner Von Braun Sty-photo-c 7 14 21 47 76 105

I AM AN AVENGER (See Avengers, Young Avengers and Pet Avengers)
Marvel Comics: Nov, 2010 - No. 5, Mar, 2011 ($3.99, limited series)

1-5-Short stories by various. 1-Yu-c. 2-Land-c. 2-4-Mayhew-a. 3-Noto-c. 4-Acuña-c 4.00

I AM COYOTE (See Eclipse Graphic Album Series & Eclipse Magazine #2)

I AM LEGEND
Eclipse Books: 1991 - No. 4, 1991 ($5.95, B&W, squarebound, 68 pgs.)

1-4: Based on 1954 novel by Richard Matheson 1 2 3 5 6 8

I AM LEGION (English version of French graphic novel Je Suis Légion)
Devils Due Publishing: Jan, 2009 - No. 6, July, 2009 ($3.50)

1-6-John Cassaday-a/Fabien Nury-s; two covers 3.50

IBIS, THE INVINCIBLE (See Fawcett Miniatures, Mighty Midget & Whiz)
Fawcett Publications: 1942 (Fall?); #2, Mar.,1943; #3, Wint, 1945 - #5, Fall, 1946; #6, Spring, 1948

1-Origin Ibis; Raboy-c; on sale 1/2/43 239 478 717 1530 2615 3700
2-Bondage-c (on sale 2/5/43) 103 206 309 659 1130 1600
3-Wolverton-a #3-6 (4 pgs. each) 74 148 222 470 810 1150
4-6: 5-Bondage-c 50 100 150 315 533 750

NOTE: *Mac Raboy c(p)-3-5.* ***Schaffenberger** c-6.*

I-BOTS (See Isaac Asimov's I-BOTS)

ICE AGE ON THE WORLD OF MAGIC: THE GATHERING (See Magic The Gathering)

ICE KING OF OZ, THE (See First Comics Graphic Novel #13)

ICEMAN (Also see The Champions & X-Men #94)
Marvel Comics Group: Dec, 1984 - No. 4, June, 1985 (Limited series)

1,2,4: Zeck covers on all 4.00
3-The Defenders, Champions (Ghost Rider) & the original X-Men x-over 5.00

ICEMAN (X-Men)
Marvel Comics: Dec, 2001 - No. 4, Mar, 2002 ($2.50, limited series)

1-4-Abnett & Lanning-s/Kerschl-a 3.00

ICEMAN AND ANGEL (X-Men)
Marvel Comics: May, 2011 ($2.99, one-shot)

1-Brian Clevinger-s/Juan Doe-a; Goom & Googam app. 3.00

ICON
DC Comics (Milestone): May, 1993 - No. 42, Feb, 1997($1.50/$1.75/$2.50)

1-($2.95)-Collector's Edition polybagged w/poster & trading card (direct sale only) 4.00
1-24,30-42: 9-Simonson-c. 15,16-Worlds Collide Pt. 4 & 11. 15-Superboy app.
16-Superman-c/story. 40-Vs. Blood Syndicate 3.00
25-($2.95, 52 pgs.) 4.00
... A Hero's Welcome SC (2009, $19.99) r/#1-8; intro. by Reginald Hudlin 20.00
...: Mothership Connection SC (2010, $24.99) r/#13,19-22,24-27,30 25.00

IDAHO
Dell Publishing Co.: June-Aug, 1963 - No. 8, July-Sept, 1965

1 3 6 9 17 25 32
2-8: 5-7-Painted-c 2 4 6 9 13 16

IDEAL (... a Classical Comic) (2nd Series) (Love Romances No. 6 on)
Timely Comics: July, 1948 - No. 5, March, 1949 (Feature length stories)

1-Antony & Cleopatra 37 74 111 222 361 500
2-The Corpses of Dr. Sacotti 31 62 93 186 303 420
3-Joan of Arc; used in **SOTI**, pg. 310 'Boer War' 29 58 87 172 281 390
4-Richard the Lion-hearted; titled "...the World's Greatest Comics";
The Witness story 40 80 120 246 411 575
5-Ideal Love & Romance; change to love; photo-c 20 40 60 117 189 260

IDEAL COMICS (1st Series) (Willie Comics No. 5 on)
Timely Comics (MgPC): Fall, 1944 - No. 4, Spring, 1946

1-Funny animal; Super Rabbit in all 28 56 84 165 270 375
2 15 30 45 88 137 185
3,4 15 30 45 85 130 175

IDEAL LOVE & ROMANCE (See Ideal, A Classical Comic)

IDEAL ROMANCE (Formerly Tender Romance)

Identity Crisis #5 © DC

I Feel Sick #1 © Jhonen Vasquez

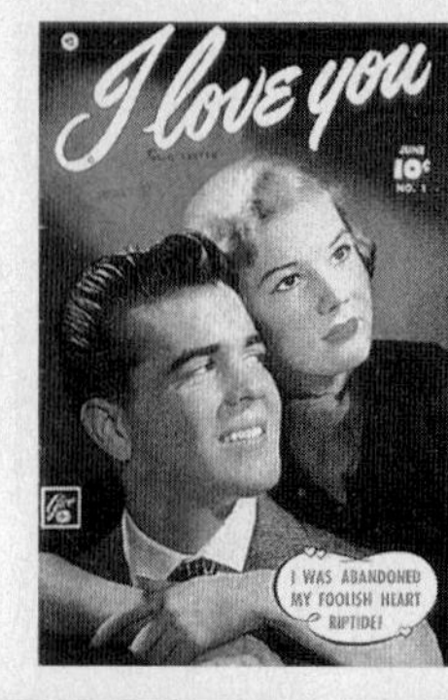

I Love You #1 © FAW

Key Publ.: No. 3, April, 1954 - No. 8, Feb, 1955 (Diary Confessions No. 9 on)

	GD 2.0	VG 4.0	FN 6.0	VF 8.0	VF/NM 9.0	NM- 9.2
3-Bernard Baily-c	10	20	30	54	72	90
4-8: 4-6-B. Baily-c	8	16	24	40	50	60

IDEALS (Secret Stories)
Ideals Publ., USA: 1981 (68 pgs, graphic novels, 7x10", stiff-c)

	GD 2.0	VG 4.0	FN 6.0	VF 8.0	VF/NM 9.0	NM- 9.2
Captain America - Star Spangled Super Hero	3	6	9	18	27	35
Fantastic Four - Cosmic Quartet	3	6	9	18	27	35
Incredible Hulk - Gamma Powered Goliath	3	6	9	18	27	35
Spider-Man - World Famous Wall Crawler	4	8	12	22	34	45

IDENTITY CRISIS
DC Comics: Aug, 2004 - No. 7, Feb, 2005 ($3.95, limited series)

	NM- 9.2
1-Meltzer-s/Morales-a/Turner-c in all; Sue Dibny murdered	5.00
1-(Second printing) black-c with white sketch lines	5.00
1-(3rd & 4th) 3rd-Bloody broken photo glass image-c by Morales. 4th-Turner red-c	4.00
1-Diamond Retailer Summit Edition with sketch-c	30.00
1-Special Edition (6/09, $1.00) r/#1 with "After Watchmen" cover frame	1.00
2-7: 2-4-Deathstroke app. 5-Firestorm, Jack Drake, Capt. Boomerang killed	4.00
2-(Second printing) new Morales sketch-c	4.00
Final printings for all issues with red background variant covers	4.00
HC (2005, $24.99, dust jacket) r/series; Director's Cut extras; cover gallery; Whedon intro.; 2 covers: Direct Market-c by Turner, Bookstore-c with Morales-a	25.00
SC (2006, $14.99) r/series; Director's Cut extras; cover gallery; Whedon intro	15.00

IDENTITY DISC
Marvel Comics: Aug, 2004 - No. 5, Dec, 2004 ($2.99, limited series)

	NM- 9.2
1-5-Sabretooth, Bullseye, Sandman, Vulture, Deadpool, Juggernaut app.; Higgins-a	4.00
TPB (2004, $13.99) r/#1-5	14.00

IDES OF BLOOD
DC Comics (WildStorm): Oct, 2010 - No. 6, Mar, 2011 ($3.99/$2.99, limited series)

	NM- 9.2
1-6-Stuart Paul-s/Christian Duce-a/Michael Geiger-c; Roman Empire vampires	4.00

I DIE AT MIDNIGHT (Vertigo V2K)
DC Comics (Vertigo): 2000 ($6.95, prestige format, one-shot)

	NM- 9.2
1-Kyle Baker-s/a	7.00

IDOL
Marvel Comics (Epic Comics): 1992 - No. 3, 1992 ($2.95, mini-series, 52 pgs.)

	NM- 9.2
Book 1-3	4.00

I DREAM OF JEANNIE (TV)
Dell Publishing Co.: Apr, 1965 - No. 2, Dec, 1966 (Photo-c)

	GD 2.0	VG 4.0	FN 6.0	VF 8.0	VF/NM 9.0	NM- 9.2
1-Barbara Eden photo-c, each	13	26	39	91	176	260
2	10	20	30	73	134	195

I FEEL SICK
Slave Labor Graphics: Aug, 1999 - No. 2, May, 2000 ($3.95, limited series)

	NM- 9.2
1,2-Jhonen Vasquez-s/a	4.00

I HATE GALLANT GIRL
Image Comics (Shadowline): Nov, 2008 - No. 3, Jan, 2009 ($3.50, limited series)

	NM- 9.2
1-3-Kat Cahill-s/Seth Damoose-a	3.50

I (heart) MARVEL
Marvel Comics: Apr, 2006; May, 2006 ($2.99, one-shots)

	NM- 9.2
...: Marvel AI 1 (4/06) Cebulski-s; manga art by various; Vision, Daredevil, Elektra app.	3.00
...: Masked Intentions 1 (5/06) Squirrel Girl, Speedball, Firestar, Justice app.; Nicieza-s	3.00
...: My Mutant Heart 1 (4/06) Wolverine, Cannonball, Doop app.	3.00
...: Outlaw Love 1 (4/06) Bullseye, The Answer, Ruby Thursday app.; Nicieza-s	3.00
...: Web of Romance 1 (4/06) Spider-Man, Mary Jane, The Avengers app.	3.00

ILLUMINATOR
Marvel Comics/Nelson Publ.: 1993 - No. 4, 1993 ($4.99/$2.95, 52 pgs.)

	NM- 9.2
1,2-($4.99) Religious themed	5.00
3,4	4.00

ILLUSTRATED GAGS
United Features Syndicate: No. 16, 1940

	GD 2.0	VG 4.0	FN 6.0	VF 8.0	VF/NM 9.0	NM- 9.2
Single Series 16	16	32	48	94	147	200

ILLUSTRATED LIBRARY OF..., AN (See Classics Illustrated Giants)

ILLUSTRATED STORIES OF THE OPERAS
Baily (Bernard) Publ. Co.: 1943 (16 pgs.; B&W) (25 cents) (cover-B&W & red)

	GD 2.0	VG 4.0	FN 6.0	VF 8.0	VF/NM 9.0	NM- 9.2
nn-(Rare)(4 diff. issues)-Faust (part-r in Cisco Kid #1), nn-Aida, nn-Carmen; Baily-a, nn-Rigoleito	57	114	171	362	619	875

ILLUSTRATED STORY OF ROBIN HOOD & HIS MERRY MEN, THE (See Classics Giveaways, 12/44)

ILLUSTRATED TARZAN BOOK, THE (See Tarzan Book)

I LOVED (Formerly Rulah; Colossal Features Magazine No. 33 on)
Fox Features Syndicate: No. 28, July, 1949 - No. 32, Mar, 1950

	GD 2.0	VG 4.0	FN 6.0	VF 8.0	VF/NM 9.0	NM- 9.2
28	14	28	42	80	115	150
29-32	10	20	30	58	79	100

I LOVE LUCY
Eternity Comics : 6/90 - No. 6, 1990;V2#1, 11/90 - No. 6, 1991 ($2.95, B&W, mini-series)

	GD 2.0	VG 4.0	FN 6.0	VF 8.0	VF/NM 9.0	NM- 9.2
1-6: Reprints 1950s comic strip; photo-c						4.00
Book II #1-6: Reprints comic strip; photo-c						4.00
...In Full Color 1 (1991, $5.95, 52 pgs.)-Reprints I Love Lucy Comics #4,5,8,16; photo-c with embossed logo (2 versions exist, one with pgs. 18 & 19 reversed, the other corrected)	1	2	3	5	6	8
...In 3-D 1 (1991, $3.95, w/glasses)-Reprints I Love Lucy Comics; photo-c; bagged						6.00

I LOVE LUCY COMICS (TV) (Also see The Lucy Show)
Dell Publishing Co.: No. 535, Feb, 1954 - No. 35, Apr-June, 1962 (Lucille Ball photo-c on all)

	GD 2.0	VG 4.0	FN 6.0	VF 8.0	VF/NM 9.0	NM- 9.2
Four Color 535(#1)	41	82	123	324	650	975
Four Color 559(#2, 5/54)	26	52	78	190	383	575
3 (8-10/54) - 5	15	30	45	106	216	325
6-10	13	26	39	91	176	260
11-20	10	20	30	71	128	185
21-35	9	18	27	63	107	150

I LOVE NEW YORK
Linsner.com: 2002 ($2.95, B&W, one-shot)

	NM- 9.2
1-Linsner-s/a; benefit book for the Sept. 11 charities	3.00

I LOVE YOU
Fawcett Publications: June, 1950 (one-shot)

	GD 2.0	VG 4.0	FN 6.0	VF 8.0	VF/NM 9.0	NM- 9.2
1-Photo-c	15	30	45	83	124	165

I LOVE YOU (Formerly In Love)
Charlton Comics: No. 7, 9/55 - No. 121, 12/76; No. 122, 3/79 - No. 130, 5/80

	GD 2.0	VG 4.0	FN 6.0	VF 8.0	VF/NM 9.0	NM- 9.2
7-Kirby-c; Powell-a	9	18	27	63	107	150
8-10	5	10	15	32	51	70
11-16,18-20	4	8	12	28	44	60
17-(68 pg. Giant)	7	14	21	49	80	110
21-50: 26-No Torres-a	3	6	9	21	32	42
51-59	3	6	9	16	23	30
60-(1/66)-Elvis Presley line drawn c/story	15	30	45	104	212	320
61-85	2	4	6	11	16	20
86-90,92-98,100-110	2	4	6	8	10	12
91-(5/71) Ditko-a (5 pgs.)	2	4	6	13	18	22
99-David Cassidy pin-up	2	4	6	10	14	18
111-113,115-130	1	3	4	6	8	10
114-Psychedelic cover	3	6	9	16	23	30

I, LUSIPHUR (Becomes Poison Elves, 1st series #8 on)
Mulehide Graphics: 1991 - No. 7, 1992 (B&W, magazine size)

	GD 2.0	VG 4.0	FN 6.0	VF 8.0	VF/NM 9.0	NM- 9.2
1-Drew Hayes-c/a/scripts	4	8	12	26	41	55
2,4,5	3	6	9	14	20	25
3-Low print run	4	8	12	28	44	60
6,7	2	4	6	8	11	14
Poison Elves: Requiem For An Elf (Sirius Ent., 6/96, $14.95, trade paperback) -Reprints I, Lusiphur #1,2 as text, and 3-6						15.00

I'M A COP
Magazine Enterprises: 1954 - No. 3, 1954

	GD 2.0	VG 4.0	FN 6.0	VF 8.0	VF/NM 9.0	NM- 9.2
1(A-1 #111)-Powell-c/a in all	15	30	45	88	137	185
2(A-1 #126), 3(A-1 #128)	10	20	30	56	76	95

IMAGE COMICS HARDCOVER
Image Comics: 2005 ($24.99, hardcover with dust jacket)

	NM- 9.2
Vol. 1-New Spawn by McFarlane-s/a; Savage Dragon origin by Larsen; CyberForce by Silvestri; ShadowHawk by Valentino; intro by Marder; Image timeline	25.00

IMAGE COMICS SUMMER SPECIAL
Image Comics: July, 2004 (Free Comic Book Day giveaway)

	NM- 9.2
1-New short stories of Spawn, Invincible, Savage Dragon and Witchblade	2.50

IMAGE FIRST
Image Comics: 2005 ($6.99, TPB)

	NM- 9.2
Vol. 1 (2005) r/Strange Girl #1, Sea of Red #1, The Walking Dead #1 and Girls #1	7.00

IMAGE GRAPHIC NOVEL
Image Int.: 1984 ($6.95)(Advertised as Pacific Comics Graphic Novel #1)

Image United #3 © Image

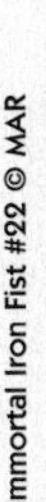
Immortal Iron Fist #22 © MAR

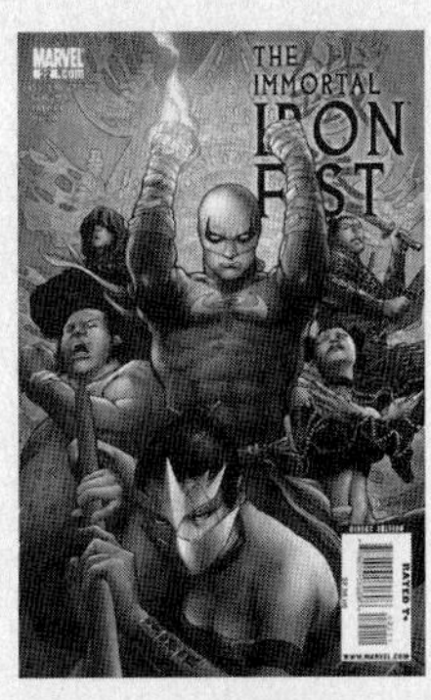

Incognito #1 © Brubaker & Phillips

	GD 2.0	VG 4.0	FN 6.0	VF 8.0	VF/NM 9.0	NM- 9.2

1-The Seven Samuroid; Brunner-c/a 7.00

IMAGE HOLIDAY SPECIAL 2005
Image Comics: 2005 ($9.99, TPB)
nn-Holiday-themed short stories by various incl. Larsen, Kurtz, Kirkman, Valentino 10.00

IMAGE INTRODUCES...
Image Comics: Oct, 2001 - June, 2002 ($2.95, anthology)
Believer #1-Schamberger-s/Thurman & Molder-a; Legend of Isis preview 3.00
Cryptopia #1-Raab-s/Quinn-a 3.00
Dog Soldiers #1-Hunter-s/Pachoumis-a 3.00
Legend of Isis #1-Valdez-a 3.00
Primate #1-Two covers; Beau Smith & Bernhardt-s/Byrd-a 3.00

IMAGES OF A DISTANT SOIL
Image Comics: Feb, 1997 ($2.95, B&W, one-shot)
1-Sketches by various 3.00

IMAGES OF SHADOWHAWK (Also see Shadowhawk)
Image Comics: Sept, 1993 - No. 3, 1994 ($1.95, limited series)
1-3: Keith Giffen-c/a; Trencher app. 3.00

IMAGE TWO-IN-ONE
Image Comics: Mar, 2001 ($2.95, 48 pgs., B&W, one-shot)
1-Two stories; 24 pages produced in 24 hrs. by Larsen and Eliopoulos 4.00

IMAGE UNITED
Image Comics: No. 0, Mar, 2010; Nov, 2009 - No. 6 ($3.99, limited series)
0-(3/10, $2.99) Fortress and Savage Dragon app. 3.00
1-3-($3.99) Image character crossover; Kirkman-s; art by Larsen, Liefeld, McFarlane, Portacio, Silvestri and Valentino; Spawn, Witchblade, Savage Dragon, Youngblood, Cyberforce and Shadowhawk app. Multiple covers on each 4.00
1-Jim Lee variant-c 8.00

IMAGE ZERO
Image Comics: 1993 (Received through mail w/coupons from Image books)
0-Savage Dragon, StormWatch, Shadowhawk, Strykeforce; 1st app. Troll; 1st app. McFarlane's Freak, Blotch, Sweat and Bludd 5.00

IMAGINARIES, THE
Image Comics: Mar, 2005 - No. 4, June, 2005 ($2.95, limited series)
1-4-Mike S. Miller & Ben Avery-s; Miller & Titus-a 3.00

I'M DICKENS - HE'S FENSTER (TV)
Dell Publishing Co.: May-July, 1963 - No. 2, Aug-Oct, 1963 (Photo-c)

	GD	VG	FN	VF	VF/NM	NM-
1	6	12	18	37	59	80
2	5	10	15	32	51	70

I MET A HANDSOME COWBOY
Dell Publishing Co.: No. 324, Mar, 1951

	GD	VG	FN	VF	VF/NM	NM-
Four Color 324	8	16	24	56	93	130

IMMORTAL DOCTOR FATE, THE
DC Comics: Jan, 1985 - No. 3, Mar, 1985 ($1.25, limited series)
1-3: 1-Simonson-c/a. 2-Giffen-c/a(p) 4.00

IMMORTAL IRON FIST, THE (Also see Iron Fist)
Marvel Comics: Jan, 2007 - No. 27, Aug, 2009 ($2.99/$3.99)
1-Brubaker & Fraction-s/Aja-c/a; origin retold; intro. Orson Randall 5.00
1-Variant-c by Dell'Otto 8.00
1-Director's Cut ($3.99) r/#1 and 8-page story from Civil War: Choosing Sides; script excerpt; character designs; sketch and inks art; cover variant and concepts 4.00
2-13,15-26: 6,17-20-Flashback-a by Heath. 21-Green-a 3.00
14,27: 14-($3.99) Heroes For Hire app. 27-Last issue; 2 covers; Foreman & Lapham-a 4.00
Annual 1 (11/07, $3.99) Brubaker & Fraction-s/Chaykin, Brereton & J. Djurdjevic-a 4.00
... Orson Randall and the Death Queen of California (11/08, $3.99) art by Camuncoli 4.00
... Orson Randall and the Green Mist of Death (4/08, $3.99) art by Heath and various 4.00
...: The Origin of Danny Rand (2008, $3.99) r/Marvel Premiere #15-16 recolored 4.00
... Vol. 1: The Last Iron Fist Story HC (2007, $19.99, dustjacket) r/#1-6, story from Civil War: Choosing Sides; sketch pages 20.00
... Vol. 1: The Last Iron Fist Story SC (2007, $14.99) same content as HC 15.00
... Vol. 2: The Seven Capital Cities HC (2008, $24.99, dustjacket) r/#8-14 & Annual #1 25.00

IMMORTALIS (See Mortigan Goth: Immortalis)

IMMORTAL II
Image Comics: Apr, 1997 - No. 5, Feb, 1998 ($2.50, B&W&Grey, limited series)
1-5: 1-B&W w/ color pull-out poster 3.00

IMMORTAL WEAPONS (Also see Immortal Iron Fist)
Marvel Comics: Sept, 2009 - No. 5, Jan, 2010 ($3.99, limited series)
1-5: Back-up Iron Fist stories in all. 1-Origin of Fat Cobra. 2-Brereton-a 4.00

IMPACT
E. C. Comics: Mar-Apr, 1955 - No. 5, Nov-Dec, 1955

	GD	VG	FN	VF	VF/NM	NM-
1-Not code approved	18	36	54	144	232	320
2	11	22	33	88	139	190
3-5: 4-Crandall-a	10	20	30	80	125	170

NOTE: ***Crandall*** *a-1-4.* ***Davis*** *a-2-4; c-1-5.* ***Evans*** *a-1, 4, 5.* ***Ingels*** *a-in all.* ***Kamen*** *a-3.* ***Krigstein*** *a-1, 5.* ***Orlando*** *a-2, 5.*

IMPACT
Gemstone Publishing: Apr, 1999 - No. 5, Aug, 1999 ($2.50)
1-5-Reprints E.C. series 3.00

IMPACT CHRISTMAS SPECIAL
DC Comics (Impact Comics): 1991 ($2.50, 68 pgs.)
1-Gift of the Magi by Infantino/Rogers; The Black Hood, The Fly, The Jaguar, & The Shield stories 4.00

IMPERIAL GUARD
Marvel Comics: Jan, 1997 - No. 3, Mar, 1997 ($1.95, limited series)
1-3: Augustyn-s in all; 1-Wraparound-c 3.00

IMPOSSIBLE MAN SUMMER VACATION SPECTACULAR, THE
Marvel Comics: Aug, 1990; No. 2, Sept, 1991 ($2.00, 68 pgs.) (See Fantastic Four#11)
1-Spider Man, Quasar, Dr. Strange, She-Hulk, Punisher & Dr. Doom stories; Barry Crain, Guice-a; Art Adams-c(i) 4.00
2-Ka Zar & Thor app.; Cable Wolverine-c app. 4.00

IMPULSE (See Flash #92, 2nd Series for 1st app.) (Also see Young Justice)
DC Comics: Apr, 1995 - No. 89, Oct, 2002 ($1.50/$1.75/$1.95/$2.25/$2.50)
1-Mark Waid scripts & Humberto Ramos-c/a(p) begin; brief retelling of origin 6.00
2-12: 9-XS from Legion (Impulse's cousin) comes to the 20th Century, returns to the 30th Century in #12. 10-Dead Heat Pt. 3 (cont'd in Flash #110). 11-Dead Heat Pt. 4 (cont'd in Flash #111); Johnny Quick dies. 4.00
13-25: 14-Trickster app. 17-Zatanna-c/app. 21-Legion-c/app. 22-Jesse Quick-c/app. 24-Origin; Flash app. 25-Last Ramos-a. 3.00
26-55: 26-Rousseau-a begins. 28-1st new Arrowette (see World's Finest #113). 30-Genesis x-over. 47-Superman-c/app. 50-Batman & Joker-c/app. Van Sciver-a begins 3.00
56-62: 56-Young Justice app. 3.00
63-89: 63-Begin $2.50-c. 66-JLA,JSA-c/app. 68,69-Adam Strange, GL app. 77-Our Worlds at War x-over; Young Justice-c/app. 85-World Without Young Justice x-over pt. 2. 3.00
#1,000,000 (11/98) John Fox app. 3.00
Annual 1 (1996, $2.95)-Legends of the Dead Earth; Parobeck-a 4.00
Annual 2 (1997, $3.95)-Pulp Heroes stories; Orbik painted-c 4.00
.../Atom Double-Shot 1(2/98, $1.95) Jurgens-s/Mhan-a 3.00
...: Bart Saves the Universe (4/99, $5.95) JSA app. 6.00
...Plus(9/97, $2.95) w/Gross Out (Scare Tactics)-c/app. 3.00
...Reckless Youth (1997, $14.95, TPB) r/Flash #92-94, Impulse #1-6 15.00

INCAL, THE
Marvel Comics (Epic): Nov, 1988 - No. 3, Jan, 1989 ($10.95/$12.95, mature)
1-3: Moebius-c/a in all; sexual content 16.00

INCOGNEGRO
DC Comics (Vertigo): 2008 ($19.99, B&W, hardcover graphic novel with dustjacket)
HC-Mat Johnson-s/Warren Pleece-a 20.00

INCOGNITO
Marvel Comics (Icon): Dec, 2008 - No. 6, Aug, 2009 ($3.50/$3.99, limited series)
1-5-Brubaker-s/Phillips-a/c; pulp noir-style 3.50
6-($3.99) Bonus history of the Zeppelin pulps 4.00
...: Bad Influences (10/10 - No. 5, 4/11, $3.50) 1-5 Brubaker-s/Phillips-a/c 3.50

INCOMPLETE DEATH'S HEAD (Also see Death's Head)
Marvel Comics UK: Jan, 1993 - No. 12, Dec, 1993 ($1.75, limited series)
1-($2.95, 56 pgs.)-Die-cut cover 4.00
2-11: 2-Re-intro original Death's Head. 3-Original Death's Head vs. Dragon's Claws 3.00
12-($2.50, 52 pgs.)-She Hulk app. 4.00

INCORRUPTIBLE (Also see Irredeemable)
BOOM! Studios: Dec, 2000 - Present ($3.99)
1-16: 1-Waid-s/Diaz-a; 3 covers 4.00

INCREDIBLE HERCULES (Continued from Incredible Hulk #112, Jan, 2008)
Marvel Comics: No. 113, Feb, 2008 - No. 141, Apr, 2010 ($2.99/$3.99)
113-125: 113-Ares and Wonder Man app.; Art Adams-c. 116-Romita Jr-c; Eternals app. 3.00

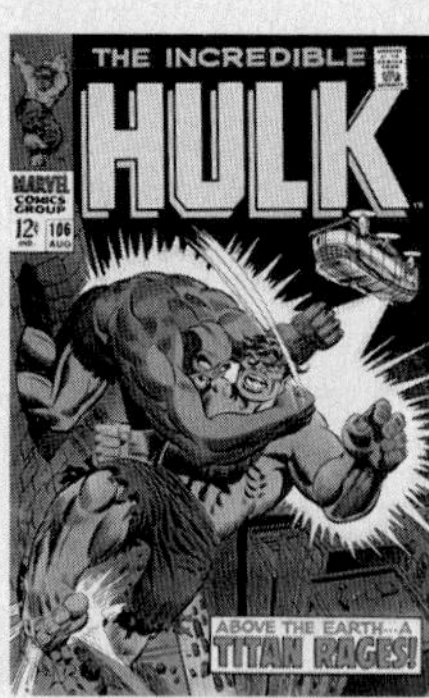

Incredible Hulk #106 © MAR

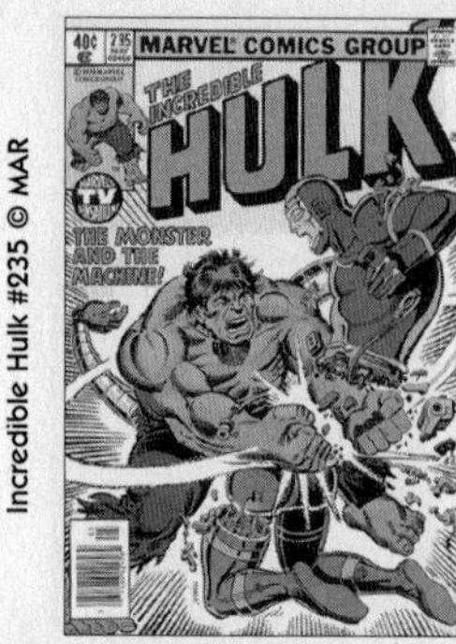

Incredible Hulk #235 © MAR

Incredible Hulk #421 © MAR

GD VG FN VF VF/NM NM-
2.0 4.0 6.0 8.0 9.0 9.2

113-Variant-c by Pham 5.00
126-($3.99) Hercules origin retold; back-up story w/Miyazawa-a 4.00
127-137: 128-Dark Avengers app. 132-Replacement Thor. 136-Thor app. 3.00
138-141-($3.99) Assault on New Olympus; Avengers app. 4.00

INCREDIBLE HULK, THE (See Aurora, The Avengers #1, The Defenders #1, Giant-Size..., Hulk, Marvel Collectors Item Classics, Marvel Comics Presents #26, Marvel Fanfare, Marvel Treasury Edition, Power Record Comics, Rampaging Hulk, She-Hulk, 2099 Unlimited & World War Hulk)

INCREDIBLE HULK, THE
Marvel Comics: May, 1962 - No. 6, Mar, 1963; No. 102, Apr, 1968 - No. 474, Mar, 1999

1-Origin & 1st app. (skin is grey colored); Kirby pencils begin, end #5
1700 3400 5100 20,000 47,500 75,000
2-1st green skinned Hulk; Kirby/Ditko-a 296 592 888 2590 5295 8000
3-Origin retold; 1st app. Ringmaster (9/62) 185 370 555 1619 3310 5000
4,5: 4-Brief origin retold 163 326 489 1426 2913 4400
6-(3/63) Intro. Teen Brigade; all Ditko-a 174 348 522 1523 3112 4700
102-(4/68) (Formerly Tales to Astonish)-Origin retold; story continued from
Tales to Astonish #101 22 44 66 159 317 475
103 10 20 30 71 128 185
104-Rhino app. 10 20 30 71 128 185
105-108: 105-1st Missing Link. 107-Mandarin app.(9/68). 108-Mandarin & Nick Fury app.
(10/68) 8 16 24 52 86 120
109,110: 109-Ka-Zar app. 7 14 21 45 73 100
111-117: 117-Last 12¢ issue 6 12 18 37 59 80
118-Hulk vs. Sub-Mariner 7 14 21 47 76 105
119-121,123-125 4 8 12 28 44 60
122-Hulk battles Thing (12/69) 9 18 27 60 100 140
126-1st Barbara Norriss (Valkyrie) 5 10 15 30 48 65
127-139: 131-Hulk vs. Iron Man; 1st Jim Wilson, Hulk's new sidekick. 136-1st Xeron,
The Star-Slayer 3 6 9 20 30 40
140-Written by Harlan Ellison; 1st Jarella, Hulk's love 4 8 12 22 34 45
140-2nd printing (1994) 2 4 6 8 10 12
141-1st app. Doc Samson (7/71) 10 20 30 67 116 165
142-144: 144-Last 15¢ issue 3 6 9 19 29 38
145-(52 pgs.)-Origin retold 5 10 15 30 48 65
146-160: 149-1st app. The Inheritor. 155-1st app. Shaper. 158-Warlock cameo(12/72)
3 6 9 17 25 32
161-The Mimic dies; Beast app. 5 10 15 30 48 65
162-1st app. The Wendigo (4/73); Beast app. 7 14 21 50 83 115
163-171,173-176: 163-1st app. The Gremlin. 164-1st Capt. Omen & Colonel John D. Armbruster. 166-1st Zzzax. 168-1st The Harpy; nudity panels of Betty Ross. 169-1st app. Bi-Beast.176-Warlock cameo (2 panels only); same date as Strange Tales #178 (6/74)
3 6 9 14 20 26
172-X-Men cameo; origin Juggernaut retold 4 8 12 28 44 60
177-1st actual death of Warlock (last panel only) 3 6 9 16 22 28
178-Rebirth of Warlock 3 6 9 16 22 28
179 3 6 9 14 19 24
180-(10/74)-1st brief app. Wolverine (last pg.) 16 32 48 114 232 350
181-(11/74)-1st full Wolverine story; Trimpe-a 80 160 240 680 1190 1700
182-Wolverine cameo; see Giant-Size X-Men #1 for next app.; 1st Crackajack Jackson
11 22 33 77 144 210
183-199: 185-Death of Col. Armbruster. 195,196-Abomination app. 197,198-Man-Thing-c/s
2 4 6 10 14 18
198,199, 201,202-(30¢-c variants, lim. distribution) 3 6 9 18 27 35
200-(25¢-c) Silver Surfer app.; anniversary issue 3 6 9 20 30 40
200-(30¢-c variant, limited distribution)(6/76) 6 12 18 39 62 85
201-220: 201-Conan swipe-c/sty. 212-1st app. The Constrictor
1 2 3 5 7 9
212-216-(35¢-c variant, limited distribution) 4 8 12 24 37 50
221-249: 227-Original Avengers app. 232-Capt. America x-over from C.A. #230. 233-Marvel Man app. 234-(4/79)-1st app. Quasar (formerly called Marvel Man. 243-Cage app.
1 2 3 4 5 7
250-Giant size; Silver Surfer app. 2 4 6 9 12 15
251-277,280-299: 271-Rocket Raccoon app. 272-Sasquatch & Wendigo app.; Wolverine & Alpha Flight cameo in flashback. 282-284-She-Hulk app. 293-F.F. app. 5.00
278,279-Most Marvel characters app. (Wolverine in both). 279-X-Men & Alpha Flight cameos 6.00
300-(11/84, 52 pgs.)-Spider-Man app in new black costume on-c & 2 pg. cameo
1 2 3 5 6 8
301-313: 312-Origin Hulk retold 4.00
314-Byrne-c/a begins, ends #319 6.00
315-319: 319-Bruce Banner & Betty Talbot wed 5.00
320-323,325,327-329 4.00
324-1st app. Grey Hulk since #1 (c-swipe of #1) 2 4 6 8 10 12
326-Grey vs. Green Hulk 6.00

GD VG FN VF VF/NM NM-
2.0 4.0 6.0 8.0 9.0 9.2

330,331: 330-1st McFarlane ish (4/87); Thunderbolt Ross dies. 331-Grey Hulk series begins
3 6 9 17 25 32
332-334,336-339: 336,337-X-Factor app. 2 4 6 9 12 15
335-No McFarlane-a 6.00
340-Hulk battles Wolverine by McFarlane 4 8 12 26 41 55
341-346: 345-($1.50, 52 pgs.). 346-Last McFarlane issue
1 3 4 6 8 10
347-349,351-358,360-366: 347-1st app. Marlo 3.00
350-Hulk/Thing battle 6.00
359-Wolverine app. (illusion only) 3.00
367,372,377: 367-1st Dale Keown-a on Hulk (3/90). 372-Green Hulk app.;Keown-c/a.
377-1st all new Hulk; fluorescent-c; Keown-c/a 1 2 3 5 6 8
368-371,373-376: 368-Sam Kieth-c/a, 1st app. Pantheon. 369,370-Dale Keown-c/a.
370,371-Original Defenders app. 371,373-376: Keown-c/a. 376-Green vs. Grey Hulk 5.00
377-Fluorescent green logo 2nd printing 3.00
378,380,389: No Keown-a. 380-Doc Samson app. 3.00
379,381-388,390-392-Keown-a. 385-Infinity Gauntlet x-over. 389-Last $1.00-c.
392-X-Factor app. 4.00
393-($2.50, 72 pgs.)-30th anniversary issue; green foil stamped-c; swipes-c to #1;
has pin-ups of classic battles; Keown-c/a 6.00
393,400-2nd printings: 400-2nd print-Diff. color foil-c. 4.00
394-399: 394-No Keown-c/a; intro Trauma. 395,396-Punisher-c/stories; Keown-c/a.
397-Begin "Ghost of the Past" 4-part sty; Keown c/a. 398-Last Keown-c/a 3.00
400-($2.50, 68 pgs.)-Holo-grafx foil-c & r/TTA #63 3.00
400-416: 402-Return of Doc Samson 3.00
417-424: 417-Begin $1.50-c; Rick Jones' bachelor party; Hulk returns from "Future Imperfect"; bound-in trading card sheet. 418-(Regular edition)-Rick Jones marries Marlo; includes cameo apps of various Marvel characters as well as DC's Death & Peter David. 420-Death of Jim Wilson 3.00
418-($2.50)-Collector's Edition w/gatefold die-cut-c 4.00
425 ($2.25, 52 pgs.) 4.00
425 ($3.50, 52 pgs.)-Holographic-c 5.00
426-434, 436-442: 426-Begin $1.95-c. 427, 428-Man-Thing app. 431,432-Abomination app. 434-Funeral for Nick Fury. 436-Ghosts of the Future begins, ends #440. 439-Hulk becomes Maestro, Avengers app. 440-Thor-c/app. 441,442-She-Hulk-c/app. 3.00
435 ($2.50)-Rhino-app; excerpt from "What Savage Beast" 4.00
443,446-448: 443-Begin $1.50-c; re-app. of Hulk. 446-w/card insert. 447-Begin Deodato-c/a(p) 3.00
444,445: 444-Cable-c/app.; "Onslaught". 445-"Onslaught" 4.00
447-Variant cover 4.00
449-1st app. Thunderbolts 6.00
450-($2.95)-Thunderbolts app.; 2 stories; Heroes Reborn-c/app. 5.00
451-470: 455-X-Men-c/app. 460-Bruce Banner returns. 464-Silver Surfer-c/app. 466,467: Betty dies. 467-Last Peter David-s/Kubert-a. 468-Casey-s/Pulido-a begin 3.00
471-473 4.00
474-($2.99) Last issue; Abomination app. 5.00
#(-1) Flashback (7/97) Kubert-a 3.00
Special 1 (10/68, 25¢, 68 pg.)-New 51 pg. story, Hulk battles The Inhumans (early app.);
Steranko-c. 11 22 33 75 138 200
Special 2 (10/69, 25¢, 68 pg.)-Origin retold 6 12 18 41 66 90
Special 3,4: 3-(1/71, 25¢, 68 pg.). 4-(1/72, 52pgs.) 3 6 9 21 32 42
Annual 5 (1976) 2 4 6 10 14 18
Annual 6-8 ('77-79): 7-Byrne/Layton-c/a; Iceman & Angel app. in book-length story.
8-Book-length Sasquatch-c/sty 2 4 6 8 10 12
Annual 9,10: 9('80). 10 ('81) 6.00
Annual 11('82)-Doc Samson back-up by Miller(p)(5 pgs.); Spider-Man & Avengers app.
Buckler-a(p) 6.00
Annual 12-17: 12 ('83). 13('84). 14('85). 15('86). 16('90, $2.00, 68 pgs.)-She-Hulk app.
17(1991, $2.00)-Origin retold 4.00
Annual 18-20 ('92-'94 68 pgs.)-18-Return of the Defenders, Pt. I; no Keown-c/a
19-Bagged w/card 4.00
...'97 ($2.99) Pollina-c 4.00
...And Wolverine 1 (10/86, $2.50)-r/1st app. (#180-181) 1 3 4 6 8 10
...: Beauty and the Behemoth ('98, $19.95, TPB) r/Bruce & Betty stories 20.00
...Ground Zero ('95, $12.95) r/#340-346 13.00
...Hercules Unleashed (10/96, $2.50) David-s/Deodato-c/a 4.00
... Omnibus Vol. 1 HC (2008, $99.99, dustjacket) r/#1-6 & 102, Tales To Astonish #59-101 bonus art, cover reprints; afterword by Peter David; 2 covers (Kirby & Ross swipe) 100.00
.../Sub-Mariner '98 Annual ($2.99) 3.00
...Versus Quasimodo 1 (3/83, one-shot)-Based on Saturday morning cartoon 4.00
...Vs. Superman 1 (7/99, $5.95, one-shot)-painted-c by Rude 6.00
...Versus Venom 1 (4/94, $2.50, one-shot)-Embossed-c; red foil logo 4.00
... Visionaries: Peter David Vol. 1 (2005, $19.99) r/#331-339 written by Peter David 20.00
... Visionaries: Peter David Vol. 2 (2005, $19.99) r/#340-348 20.00

Incredible Hulk V2 #49 © MAR

Incredible Hulk #626 © MAR

The Incredibles #12 © DIS & Pixar

	GD 2.0	VG 4.0	FN 6.0	VF 8.0	VF/NM 9.0	NM- 9.2

... Visionaries: Peter David Vol. 3 (2006, $19.99) r/#349-354, Web of Spider-Man #44, and Fantastic Four #320 — 20.00
... Visionaries: Peter David Vol. 4 (2007, $19.99) r/#355-363 and Marvel Comics Presents #26,45 — 20.00
... Visionaries: Peter David Vol. 5 (2008, $19.99) r/#364-372 and Annual #16 — 20.00
Wizard #1 Ace Edition - Reprints #1 with new Andy Kubert-c — 14.00
Wizard #181 Ace Edition - Reprints #181 with new Chen-c — 14.00
(Also see titles listed under **Hulk**)

NOTE: ***Adkins*** *a-111-116i.* ***Austin*** *a(i)-350, 351, 353, 354; c-302i, 350i.* ***Ayers*** *a-3-5i.* ***Buckler*** *a-Annual 5; c-252.* ***John Buscema*** *c-202p.* ***Byrne*** *a-314-319p; c-314-316, 318, 319, 359, Annual 14i.* ***Colan*** *c-363.* ***Ditko*** *a-2i, 6, 249, Annual 2r(5), 3r, 9p; c-2i, 6, 235, 249.* ***Everett*** *c-133i.* ***Golden*** *c-248, 251.* ***Kane*** *c(p)-193, 194, 196, 198.* ***Dale Keown*** *a(p)-367, 369-377, 379, 381-388, 390-393, 395-398; c-369-377p, 381, 382p, 384, 385, 386, 387p, 388, 390p, 391-393, 395p, 396, 397p, 398.* ***Kirby*** *a-1-5p, Special 2, 3p, Annual 5p; c-1-5, Annual 5.* ***McFarlane*** *a-330-334p, 336-339p, 340-343, 344-346p; c-330p, 340p, 341-343, 344p, 345, 346p.* ***Mignola*** *c-302, 305, 313.* ***Miller*** *c-258p, 261, 264, 268.* ***Mooney*** *a-230p, 287i, 288i.* ***Powell*** *a-Special 3r(2).* ***Romita*** *a-Annual 17p.* ***Severin*** *a(i)-108-110, 131-133, 141-151, 153-155; c(i)-109, 110, 132, 142, 144-155.* ***Simonson*** *c-283, 364-367.* ***Starlin*** *a-222p; c-217.* ***Staton*** *a(i)-187-189, 191-209.* ***Tuska*** *a-102i, 105i, 106i, 218p.* ***Williamson*** *a-310i; c-310i, 311i.* ***Wrightson*** *c-197.*

INCREDIBLE HULK (Vol. 2) (Formerly Hulk #1-11; becomes Incredible Hercules with #113) (Re-titled Incredible Hulks #612-on)(Also see World War Hulk)
Marvel Comics: No. 12, Mar, 2000 - No. 112, Jan, 2008 ($1.99-$3.50)
No. 600, Sept, 2009 - Present ($3.99/$4.99)

12-Jenkins-s/Garney & McKone-a — 4.00
13,14-($1.99) Garney & Buscema-a — 3.00
15-24,26-32: 15-Begin $2.25-c. 21-Maximum Security x-over. 24-($1.99-c) — 3.00
25-($2.99) Hulk vs. The Abomination; Romita Jr.-a — 4.00
33-($3.50, 100 pgs.) new Bogdanove-a/Priest-s; reprints — 4.00
34-Bruce Jones-s begin; Romita Jr.-a — 5.00
35-49,51-54: 35-39-Jones-s/Romita Jr.-a. 40-43-Weeks-a. 44-49-Immonen-a — 3.00
50-($3.50) Deodato-a begins; Abomination app. thru #54 — 4.00
55-74,77-91: 55(25¢-c) Absorbing Man returns; Fernandez-a. 60-65,70-72-Deodato-a. 66-69-Braithwaite-a. 71-74-Iron Man app. 77-($2.99-c) Peter David-s begin/Weeks-a. 80-Wolverine-c. 82-Jae Lee-c/a. 83-86-House of M x-over. 87-Scorpion app. — 3.00
75,76-($3.50) The Leader app. 75-Robertson-a/Frank-c. 76-Braithwaite-a — 4.00
92-Planet Hulk begins; Ladronn-c — 5.00
92-2nd printing with variant-c by Bryan Hitch — 4.00
93-99,101-105 Planet Hulk; Ladronn-c — 3.00
100-($3.99) Planet Hulk continues; back-up w/Frank-a; r/#152,153; Ladronn-c — 5.00
100-($3.99) Green Hulk variant-c by Michael Turner — 10.00
100-($3.99) Gray Hulk variant-c by Michael Turner — 30.00
106-World War Hulk begins; Gary Frank-a/c — 6.00
106-2nd printing with new cover of Hercules and Angel — 3.00
107-112: 107-Hercules vs. Hulk. 108-Rick Jones app. 112-Art Adams-c — 3.00
600-(9/09, $4.99) Covers by Ross, Sale and wraparound-c by McGuinness; back-up with Stan Lee-s; r/Hulk: Gray #1; cover gallery — 5.00
601-611-($3.99): 601-605-Olivetti-a. 603-Wolverine app. 606-608-Fall of the Hulks — 4.00
(Title becomes Incredible Hulks with #612, Nov, 2010)
612-621: 612-617-Dark Son. 618-620-Chaos War. 621-Hercules app. — 4.00
622-626-($2.99) 623-625-Ka-Zar app.; Eaglesham-a. 626-Grummett-a — 3.00
Annual 2000 ($3.50) Texeira-a/Jenkins-s; Avengers app. — 4.00
Annual 2001 ($2.99) Thor-c/app.; Larsen-s/Williams III-c — 4.00
... : Boiling Point (Volume 2, 2002, $8.99, TPB) r/#40-43; Andrews-c — 9.00
Dogs of War (6/01, $19.95, TPB) r/#12-20 — 20.00
House of M (2006, $13.99) r/House of M tie-in issues Incredible Hulk #83-87 — 14.00
Hulk: Planet Hulk HC (2007, $39.99, dustjacket) oversized r/#92-105, Planet Hulk: Gladiator Guidebook, stories from Amazing Fantasy (2004) #15 and Giant-Size Hulk #1 — 40.00
Hulk: Planet Hulk SC (2008, $34.99) same content as HC — 35.00
Planet Hulk: Gladiator Guidebook (2006, $3.99) bios of combatants and planet history — 4.00
...: Prelude to Planet Hulk (2006, $13.99, TPB) r/#88-91 & Official Handbook: Hulk 2004 — 14.00
...: Return of the Monster (7/02, $12.99, TPB) r/#34-39 — 13.00
...: The End (8/02, $5.95) David-s/Keown-a; Hulk in the far future — 6.00
...: The End HC (2008, $19.99, dustjacket) r/The End and Hulk: Future Imperfect #1-2 — 20.00
...Volume 1 HC (2002, $29.99, oversized) r/#34-43 & Startling Stories: Banner #1-4 — 30.00
...Volume 2 HC (2003, $29.99, oversized) r/#44-54; sketch pages and cover gallery — 30.00
Volume 3: Transfer of Power (2003, $12.99, TPB) r/#44-49 — 13.00
Volume 4: Abominable (2003, $11.99, TPB) r/#50-54; Abomination app.; Deodato-a — 12.00
Volume 5: Hide in Plain Sight (2003, $11.99, TPB) r/#55-59; Fernandez-a — 12.00
Volume 6: Split Decisions (2004, $12.99, TPB) r/#60-65; Deodato-a — 13.00
Volume 7: Dead Like Me (2004, $12.99, TPB) r/#66-69 & Hulk Smash #1&2 — 13.00
Volume 8: Big Things (2004, $17.99, TPB) r/#70-76; Iron Man app. — 18.00
Volume 9: Tempest Fugit (2005, $14.99, TPB) r/#77-82 — 15.00

INCREDIBLE HULKS: ENIGMA FORCE
Marvel Comics: Nov, 2010 - No. 3, Jan, 2011 ($3.99, limited series)

1-3-Reed-s/Munera-a/Pagulayan-c; Bug app. — 4.00

INCREDIBLE MR. LIMPET, THE (See Movie Classics)

INCREDIBLES, THE
Image Comics: Nov, 2004 - No. 4, Feb, 2005 ($2.99, limited series)

1-4-Adaptation of 2004 Pixar movie; Ricardo Curtis-a — 3.00
TPB (2005, $12.95) r/#1-4; cover gallery — 13.00

INCREDIBLES, THE (Pixar characters)
BOOM! Studios: No. 0, Jul, 2009 - Present ($2.99)

0-15: 0-3-City of Incredibles; Waid & Walker-s. 0,1-Wagner-c. 8-15-Walker-s — 3.00
...: Family Matters 1-4 (3/09 - No. 4, 6/09) Waid-s/Takara-a. 1-Five covers — 3.00

INCREDIBLE SCIENCE FICTION (Formerly Weird Science-Fantasy)
E. C. Comics: No. 30, July-Aug, 1955 - No. 33, Jan-Feb, 1956

	GD 2.0	VG 4.0	FN 6.0	VF 8.0	VF/NM 9.0	NM- 9.2
30-Davis-c begin, end #32	39	78	117	312	499	685
31-Williamson/Krenkel-a, Wood-a(2)	40	80	120	320	510	700
32-Williamson/Krenkel-a	40	80	120	320	510	700
33-Classic Wood-c; "Judgment Day" story-r/Weird Fantasy #18; final issue & last E.C. comic book	41	82	123	328	524	720

NOTE: ***Davis*** *a-30, 32, 33; c-30-32.* ***Krigstein*** *a-in all.* ***Orlando*** *a-30, 32, 33.* ***Wood*** *a-30, 31, 33; c-33.*

INCREDIBLE SCIENCE FICTION (Formerly Weird Science-Fantasy)
Russ Cochran/Gemstone Publ.: No. 8, Aug, 1994 - No. 11, May, 1995 ($2.00)

8-11: Reprints #30-33 of E.C. series — 3.00

INDEPENDENCE DAY (Movie)
Marvel Comics: No. 0, June, 1996 - No. 2, Aug, 1996 ($1.95, limited series)

0-Special Edition; photo-c — 5.00
0-2 — 3.00

INDIANA JONES (Title series), **Dark Horse Comics**
--ADVENTURES, 6/08 ($6.95, digest-sized) Vol. 1 - new all-ages adventures; Beavers-a — 7.00
--AND THE ARMS OF GOLD, 2/94 - 5/94 ($2.50) 1-4 — 3.00
--AND THE FATE OF ATLANTIS, 3/91 - 9/91 ($2.50) 1-4-Dorman painted-c on all; contain trading cards (#1 has a 2nd printing, 10/91) — 3.00
--AND THE GOLDEN FLEECE, 6/94 - 7/94 ($2.50) 1,2 — 3.00
--AND THE IRON PHOENIX, 12/94 - 3/95 ($2.50) 1-4 — 3.00

INDIANA JONES AND THE KINGDOM OF THE CRYSTAL SKULL
Dark Horse Comics: May, 2008 - No. 2, May, 2008 ($5.99, limited series, movie adaptation)

1,2-Luke Ross-a/John Jackson Miller-adapted-s; two covers by Struzan & Fleming — 6.00
TPB (5/08, $12.95) r/#1,2; Struzan-c — 13.00

INDIANA JONES AND THE LAST CRUSADE
Marvel Comics: 1989 - No. 4, 1989 ($1.00, limited series, movie adaptation)

1-4: Williamson-i assist — 3.00
1-(1989, $2.95, B&W mag., 80 pgs.) — 4.00

--AND THE SHRINE OF THE SEA DEVIL: Dark Horse, 9/94 ($2.50, one shot)
1-Gary Gianni-a — 3.00
--AND THE SARGASSO PIRATES: Dark Horse, 12/95 - 3/96 ($2.50) 1-4: 1,2-Ross-c — 3.00
--AND THE SPEAR OF DESTINY: Dark Horse, 4/95 - 8/95 ($2.50) 1-4 — 3.00
--AND THE TOMB OF THE GODS, 6/08 - No. 4, 3/09 ($2.99) 1-4: 1-Tony Harris-c — 3.00
--THUNDER IN THE ORIENT: Dark Horse, 9/93 - '94 ($2.50)
1-6: Dan Barry story & art in all; 1-Dorman painted-c — 3.00

INDIANA JONES AND THE TEMPLE OF DOOM
Marvel Comics Group: Sept, 1984 - No. 3, Nov, 1984 (Movie adaptation)

1-3-r/Marvel Super Special; Guice-a — 3.00

INDIANA JONES OMNIBUS
Dark Horse Books: Feb, 2008; June 2008; Feb, 2009 ($24.95, digest-size)

Volume One - Reprints Indiana Jones and the Fate of Atlantis, Indiana Jones: Thunder in the Orient; and Indiana Jones and the Arms of Gold mini-series — 25.00
Volume Two - Reprints I.J. and the Golden Fleece, I.J. and the Shrine of the Sea Devil, I.J. and the Iron Phoenix, I.J. and the Spear of Destiny, I.J. and the Sargasso Pirates — 25.00
The Further Adventures Volume One - (2/09) r/Raiders of the Lost Ark #1-3 & The Further Adventures of Indiana Jones #1-12 — 25.00

INDIAN BRAVES (Baffling Mysteries No. 5 on)
Ace Magazines: March, 1951 - No. 4, Sept, 1951

	GD 2.0	VG 4.0	FN 6.0	VF 8.0	VF/NM 9.0	NM- 9.2
1-Green Arrowhead begins, apps. in all	15	30	45	84	127	170
2	9	18	27	52	69	85
3,4	8	16	24	44	57	70
I.W. Reprint #1 (nd)-r/Indian Braves #4	2	4	6	9	13	16

INDIAN CHIEF (White Eagle...) (Formerly The Chief, Four Color 290)

Indians #8 © FH

Infestation #1 © IDW

Infinite Vacation #1 © Spencer & Ward

GD VG FN VF VF/NM NM-
2.0 4.0 6.0 8.0 9.0 9.2

GD VG FN VF VF/NM NM-
2.0 4.0 6.0 8.0 9.0 9.2

Dell Publ. Co.: No. 3, July-Sept, 1951 - No. 33, Jan-Mar, 1959 (All painted-c)

3 5 10 15 34 55 75
4-11: 6-White Eagle app. 4 8 12 28 44 60
12-1st White Eagle(10-12/53)-Not same as earlier character
5 10 15 34 55 75
13-29 4 8 12 23 36 48
30-33-Buscema-a 4 8 12 24 37 50

INDIAN CHIEF (See March of Comics No. 94, 110, 127, 140, 159, 170, 187)

INDIAN FIGHTER, THE (Movie)
Dell Publishing Co.: No. 687, May, 1956 (one-shot)

Four Color 687-Kirk Douglas photo-c 7 14 21 50 83 115

INDIAN FIGHTER
Youthful Magazines: May, 1950 - No. 11, Jan, 1952

1 15 30 45 84 127 170
2-Wildey-a/c(bondage) 11 22 33 60 83 105
3-11: 3,4-Wildey-a 9 18 27 47 61 75
NOTE: ***Hollingsworth** a-5. **Walter Johnson** c-1, 3, 4, 6. **Palais** a-10. **Stallman** a-5-8. **Wildey** a-2-4; c-2, 5.*

INDIAN LEGENDS OF THE NIAGARA (See American Graphics)

INDIANS
Fiction House Magazines (Wings Publ. Co.): Spring, 1950 - No. 17, Spr, 1953 (1-8: 52 pgs.)

1-Manzar The White Indian, Long Bow & Orphan of the Storm begin
30 60 90 177 289 400
2-Starlight begins 15 30 45 90 140 190
3-5: 5-17-Most-c by Whitman 14 28 42 81 118 155
6-10 13 26 39 72 101 130
11-17 11 22 33 64 90 115

INDIANS OF THE WILD WEST
I. W. Enterprises: Circa 1958? (no date) (Reprints)

9-Kinstler-c; Whitman-a; r/Indians #? 2 4 6 10 14 18

INDIANS ON THE WARPATH
St. John Publishing Co.: No date (Late 40s, early 50s) (132 pgs.)

nn-Matt Baker-c; contains St. John comics rebound. Many combinations possible
39 78 117 231 378 525

INDIAN TRIBES (See Famous Indian Tribes)

INDIAN WARRIORS (Formerly White Rider and Super Horse; becomes Western Crime Cases #9)
Star Publications: No. 7, June, 1951 - No. 8, Sept, 1951

7-White Rider & Superhorse continue; "Last of the Mohicans" serial begins;
L.B. Cole-c 18 36 54 105 165 225
8-L. B. Cole-c 17 34 51 98 154 210
3-D 1(12/53, 25¢)-Came w/glasses; L. B. Cole-c 34 68 102 199 325 450
Accepted Reprint(nn)(inside cover shows White Rider & Superhorse #11)-r/cover to #7;
origin White Rider &...; L. B. Cole-c 8 16 24 40 50 60
Accepted Reprint #8 (nd); L.B. Cole-c (r-cover to #8) 8 16 24 40 50 60

INDOORS-OUTDOORS (See Wisco)

INDOOR SPORTS
National Specials Co.: nd (6x9", 64 pgs., B&W-r, hard-c)

nn-By Tad 5 10 15 24 30 35

INDUSTRIAL GOTHIC
DC Comics (Vertigo): Dec, 1995 - No. 5, Apr, 1996 ($2.50, limited series)

1-5: Ted McKeever-c/a/scripts 3.00

INFAMOUS (Based on the Sony videogame)
DC Comics: Early May, 2011 - No. 6 ($2.99, limited series)

1,2-William Harms-s/Eric Nguyen-a/Doug Mahnke-c 3.00

INFERIOR FIVE, THE (Inferior 5 #11, 12) (See Showcase #62, 63, 65)
National Periodical Publications (#1-10: 12¢): 3-4/67 - No. 10, 9-10/68; No. 11, 8-9/72 - No. 12, 10-11/72

1-(3-4/67)-Sekowsky-a(p); 4th app. 6 12 18 37 59 80
2-5: 2-Plastic Man, F.F. app. 4-Thor app. 3 6 9 20 30 40
6-9: 6-Stars DC staff 3 6 9 16 23 30
10-Superman x-over; F.F., Spider-Man & Sub-Mariner app.
3 6 9 19 29 38
11,12: Orlando-c/a; both r/Showcase #62,63 2 4 6 11 16 20

INFERNO
Caliber Comics: 1995 - No. 5 ($2.95, B&W)

1-5 3.00

INFERNO (See Legion of Super-Heroes)
DC Comics: Oct, 1997 - No. 4, Feb, 1998 ($2.50, limited series)

1-Immonen-s/c/a in all 4.00
2-4 3.00

INFERNO: HELLBOUND
Image Comics (Top Cow): Jan, 2002 - No. 3 ($2.50/$2.99)

1,2: 1-Seven covers; Silvestri-a/Silvestri and Wohl-s 3.00
3-($2.99) Tan-a 3.00
#0 (7/02, $3.00) Tan-a 3.00
Wizard #0- Previews series; bagged with Wizard Top Cow Special mag 3.00

INFESTATION (Zombie crossover with G.I. Joe, Star Trek, Transformers and Ghostbusters)
IDW Publishing: Jan, 2011 - No. 2, Apr, 2011 ($3.99, limited series)

1,2-Abnett & Lanning-s/Messina-a; two covers by Messina & Snyder III 4.00

INFINITE CRISIS
DC Comics: Dec, 2005 - No. 7, Jun, 2006 ($3.99, limited series)

1-Johns-s/Jimenez-a; two covers by Jim Lee and George Pérez 5.00
1-RRP Edition with Jim Lee sketch-c 275.00
2-7: 4-New Spectre; Earth-2 returns. 5-Earth-2 Lois dies; new Blue Beetle debut. 6-Superboy killed, new Earth formed. 7-Earth-2 Superman dies 4.00
HC (2006, $24.99, dustjacket) r/#1-7; DiDio intro.; sketch cover gallery; interview/commentary with Johns, Jimenez and editors; sketch art 25.00
... Companion TPB (2006, $14.99) r/Day of Vengeance: Infinite Crisis Special #1, Rann-Thanagar War: ICS #1, The Omac Project: ICS #1, Villains United: ICS #1 15.00
... Secret Files 2006 (4/06, $5.99) tie-in story with Earth-2 Lois and Superman, Earth-Prime Superboy and Alexander Luthor; art by various; profile pages 6.00

INFINITE CRISIS AFTERMATH (See Crisis Aftermath:...)

INFINITE VACATION
Image Comics (Shadowline): Jan, 2011 - Present ($3.50)

1,2-Nick Spencer-s/Christian Ward-a/c 3.50

INFINITY ABYSS (Also see Marvel Universe: The End)
Marvel Comics: Aug, 2002 - No. 6, Oct, 2002 ($2.99, limited series)

1-5-Starlin-s/a; Thanos, Captain Marvel, Spider-Man, Dr. Strange app. 3.00
6-($3.50) 3.50
Thanos Vol. 2: Infinity Abyss TPB (2003, $17.99) r/ #1-6 25.00

INFINITY CRUSADE
Marvel Comics: June, 1993 - No. 6, Nov, 1993 ($2.50, limited series, 52 pgs.)

1-6: By Jim Starlin & Ron Lim 4.00

INFINITY GAUNTLET (The... #2 on; see Infinity Crusade, The Infinity War & Warlock & the Infinity Watch)
Marvel Comics: July, 1991 - No. 6, Dec, 1991 ($2.50, limited series)

1-6:Thanos-c/stories in all; Starlin scripts in all; 5,6-Ron Lim-c/a 4.00
TPB (4/99, $24.95) r/#1-6 25.00
NOTE: ***Lim** a-3p(part), 5p, 6p; c-5i, 6i. **Perez** a-1-3p, 4p(part); c-1(painted), 2-4, 5i, 6i.*

INFINITY, INC. (See All-Star Squadron #25)
DC Comics: Mar, 1984 - No. 53, Aug, 1988 ($1.25, Baxter paper, 36 pgs.)

1-Brainwave, Jr., Fury, The Huntress, Jade, Northwind, Nuklon, Obsidian, Power Girl, Silver Scarab & Star Spangled Kid begin 4.00
2-13,38-49,51-53: 2-Dr. Midnite, G.A. Flash, W. Woman, Dr. Fate, Hourman, Green Lantern, Wildcat app. 5-Nudity panels. 46,47-Millennium tie-ins 3.00
14-Todd McFarlane-a (5/85, 2nd full story) 1 2 3 6 8 9
15-37-McFarlane-a (20,23,24: 5 pgs. only; 33: 2 pgs.); 18-24-Crisis x-over. 21-Intro new Hourman & Dr. Midnight. 26-New Wildcat app. 31-Star Spangled Kid becomes Skyman. 32-Green Fury becomes Green Flame. 33-Origin Obsidian. 35-1st modern app. G.A. Fury 4.00
50 ($2.50, 52 pgs.) 4.00
Annual 1,2: 1(12/85)-Crisis x-over. 2('88, $2.00), Special 1 ('87, $1.50) 4.00
NOTE: ***Kubert** r-4. **McFarlane** a-14-37p, Annual 1p; c(p)-14-19, 22, 25, 26, 31-33, 37, Annual 1. **Newton** a-12p, 13p(last work 4/85). **Tuska** a-11p. JSA app. 3-10.*

INFINITY, INC. (See 52)
DC Comics: Nov, 2007 - No. 12, Oct, 2008 ($2.99)

1-12: 1-Milligan-s; Steel app. 3.00
...: Luthor's Monsters TPB (2008, $14.99) r/#1-5 15.00
...: The Bogeyman TPB (2008, $14.99) r/#6-10 15.00

INFINITY WAR, THE (Also see Infinity Gauntlet & Warlock and the Infinity...)
Marvel Comics: June, 1992 - No. 6, Nov, 1992 ($2.50, mini-series)

1-Starlin scripts, Lim-c/a(p), Thanos app. in all 4.00
2-6: All have wraparound gatefold covers 4.00

The Inhumans #5 © MAR

Instant Piano #3 © DH

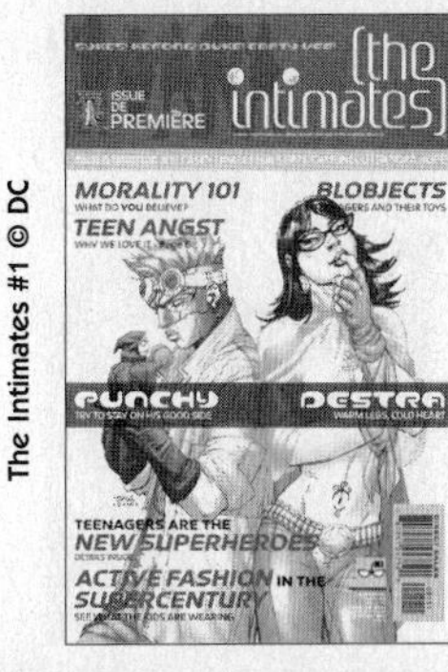

The Intimates #1 © DC

	GD 2.0	VG 4.0	FN 6.0	VF 8.0	VF/NM 9.0	NM- 9.2
TPB (2006, $29.99) r/#1-6, Marvel Comics Presents #108-111, Warlock and the Infinity Watch #7-10; cover gallery and synopses of Infinity War crossovers						30.00

INFORMER, THE
Feature Television Productions: April, 1954 - No. 5, Dec, 1954

	GD	VG	FN	VF	VF/NM	NM-
1-Sekowsky-a begins	12	24	36	69	97	125
2	9	18	27	47	61	75
3-5	8	16	24	42	54	65

IN HIS STEPS
Spire Christian Comics (Fleming H. Revell Co.): 1973, 1977 (39/49¢)

	GD	VG	FN	VF	VF/NM	NM-
nn	2	4	6	9	13	16

INHUMANOIDS, THE (TV)
Marvel Comics (Star Comics): Jan, 1987 - No. 4, July 1987

	GD	VG	FN	VF	VF/NM	NM-
1-4: Based on Hasbro toys						3.00

INHUMANS, THE (See Amazing Adventures, Fantastic Four #54 & Special #5, Incredible Hulk Special #1, Marvel Graphic Novel & Thor #146)
Marvel Comics Group: Oct, 1975 - No. 12, Aug, 1977

	GD	VG	FN	VF	VF/NM	NM-
1: #1-4,6 are 25¢ issues	3	6	9	16	22	28
2-4-Peréz-a	2	4	6	8	11	14
5-12: 9-Reprints Amazing Adventures #1,2('70). 12-Hulk app.	2	4	6	8	10	12
4-(30¢-c variant, limited distribution)(4/76) Peréz-a	3	6	9	17	25	32
6-(30¢-c variant, limited distribution)(8/76)	3	6	9	17	25	32
11,12-(35¢-c variants, limited distribution)	4	8	12	24	37	50
Special 1(4/90, $1.50, 52 pgs.)-F.F. cameo						4.00
...: The Great Refuge (5/95, $2.95)						4.00

NOTE: ***Buckler** c-2-4p, 5. **Gil Kane** a-5-7p; c-1p, 7p, 8p. **Kirby** a-9r. **Mooney** a-11i. **Perez** a-1-4p, 8p.*

INHUMANS (Marvel Knights)
Marvel Comics: Nov, 1998 - No. 12, Oct, 1999 ($2.99, limited series)

	GD	VG	FN	VF	VF/NM	NM-
1-Jae Lee-c/a; Paul Jenkins-s						10.00
1-($6.95) DF Edition; Jae Lee variant-c						7.00
2-Two covers by Lee and Darrow						4.00
3-12						3.00
TPB (10/00, $24.95) r/#1-12						25.00

INHUMANS (Volume 3)
Marvel Comics: Jun, 2000 - No. 4, Oct, 2000 ($2.99, limited series)

	GD	VG	FN	VF	VF/NM	NM-
1-4-Ladronn-c/Pacheco & Marin-s. 1-3-Ladronn-a. 4-Lucas-a						3.00

INHUMANS (Volume 6)
Marvel Comics: Jun, 2003 - No. 12, Jun, 2004 ($2.50/$2.99)

	GD	VG	FN	VF	VF/NM	NM-
1-12: 1-6-McKeever-s/Clark-a/JH Williams III-c. 7-Begin $2.99-c. 7,8-Teranishi-a						3.00
Vol. 1: Culture Shock (2005, $7.99, digest) r/#1-6; story pitch and sketch pages						8.00

INHUMANS 2099
Marvel Comics: Nov, 2004 ($2.99, one-shot)

	GD	VG	FN	VF	VF/NM	NM-
1-Kirkman-s/Rathburn-a/Pat Lee-c						3.00

INKY & DINKY (See Felix's Nephews...)

IN LOVE (...Magazine on-c; I Love You No. 7 on)
Mainline/Charlton No. 5 (5/55)-on: Aug-Sept, 1954 - No. 6, July, 1955 ('Adult Reading' on-c)

	GD	VG	FN	VF	VF/NM	NM-
1-Simon & Kirby-a; book-length novel in all issues	40	80	120	246	411	575
2,3-S&K-a. 3-Last pre-code (12-1/54-55)	24	48	72	142	234	325
4-S&K-a.(Rare)	27	54	81	158	259	360
5-S&K-c only	14	28	42	82	121	160
6-No S&K-a	10	20	30	56	76	95

INNOVATION SPECTACULAR
Innovation Publishing: 1991 - No. 2, 1991 ($2.95, squarebound, 100 pgs.)

	GD	VG	FN	VF	VF/NM	NM-
1,2: Contains rebound comics w/o covers						4.00

INNOVATION SUMMER FUN SPECIAL
Innovation Publishing: 1991 ($3.50, B&W/color, squarebound)

	GD	VG	FN	VF	VF/NM	NM-
1-Contains rebound comics (Power Factory)						4.00

IN SEARCH OF THE CASTAWAYS (See Movie Comics)

INSIDE CRIME (Formerly My Intimate Affair)
Fox Features Syndicate (Hero Books): No. 3, July, 1950 - No. 2, Sept, 1950

	GD	VG	FN	VF	VF/NM	NM-
3-Wood-a (10 pgs.); L. B. Cole-c	30	60	90	177	289	400
2-Used in **SOTI**, pg. 182,183; r/Spook #24	23	46	69	136	223	310
nn(no publ. listed, nd)	11	22	33	62	86	110

INSPECTOR, THE (TV) (Also see The Pink Panther)
Gold Key: July, 1974 - No. 19, Feb, 1978

	GD	VG	FN	VF	VF/NM	NM-
1	3	6	9	19	29	38
2-5	2	4	6	13	18	22
6-9	2	4	6	10	14	18
10-19: 11-Reprints	2	4	6	8	10	12

INSPECTOR GILL OF THE FISH POLICE (See Fish Police)

INSPECTOR WADE
David McKay Publications: No. 13, May, 1938

	GD	VG	FN	VF	VF/NM	NM-
Feature Books 13	29	58	87	170	278	385

INSTANT PIANO
Dark Horse Comics: Aug, 1994 - No. 4, Feb, 1995 ($3.95, B&W, bimonthly, mature)

	GD	VG	FN	VF	VF/NM	NM-
1-4						4.00

INTERFACE
Marvel Comics (Epic Comics): Dec, 1989 - No. 8, Dec, 1990 ($1.95, mature, coated paper)

	GD	VG	FN	VF	VF/NM	NM-
1-8: Cont. from 1st ESPers series; painted-c/a						3.00
Espers: Interface TPB ('98, $16.95) r/#1-6						17.00

INTERNATIONAL COMICS (...Crime Patrol No. 6)
E. C. Comics: Spring, 1947 - No. 5, Nov-Dec, 1947

	GD	VG	FN	VF	VF/NM	NM-
1-Schaffenberger-a begins, ends #4	63	126	189	403	689	975
2	43	86	129	271	461	650
3-5	40	80	120	243	402	560

INTERNATIONAL CRIME PATROL (Formerly International Comics #1-5; becomes Crime Patrol No. 7 on)
E. C. Comics: No. 6, Spring, 1948

	GD	VG	FN	VF	VF/NM	NM-
6-Moon Girl app.	63	126	189	403	689	975

IN THE DAYS OF THE MOB (Magazine)
Hampshire Dist. Ltd. (National): Fall, 1971 (B&W)

	GD	VG	FN	VF	VF/NM	NM-
1-Kirby-a; John Dillinger wanted poster inside (1/2 value if poster is missing)	8	16	24	52	86	120

IN THE PRESENCE OF MINE ENEMIES
Spire Christian Comics/Fleming H. Revell Co.: 1973 (35/49¢)

	GD	VG	FN	VF	VF/NM	NM-
nn	2	4	6	8	11	14

IN THE SHADOW OF EDGAR ALLAN POE
DC Comics (Vertigo): 2002 (Graphic novel)

	GD	VG	FN	VF	VF/NM	NM-
Hardcover (2002, $24.95) Fuqua-s/Phillips and Parke photo-a						25.00
Softcover (2003, $17.95)						18.00

INTIMATE
Charlton Comics: Dec, 1957 - No. 3, May, 1958

	GD	VG	FN	VF	VF/NM	NM-
1	6	12	18	28	34	40
2,3	4	8	12	18	22	25

INTIMATE CONFESSIONS (See Fox Giants)

INTIMATE CONFESSIONS
Country Press Inc.: 1942

nn-Ashcan comic, not distributed to newsstands, only for in house use. A VF copy sold for $1,000 in 2007, and a VF+ copy sold for $1,525 in 2007.

INTIMATE CONFESSIONS
Realistic Comics: July-Aug, 1951 - No. 7, Aug, 1952; No. 8, Mar, 1953 (All painted-c)

	GD	VG	FN	VF	VF/NM	NM-
1-Kinstler-a; c/Avon paperback #222	103	206	309	659	1130	1600
2	26	52	78	154	252	350
3-c/Avon paperback #250; Kinstler-c/a	30	60	90	177	289	400
4-8: 4-c/Avon paperback #304; Kinstler-c. 6-c/Avon paperback #120. 8-c/Avon paperback #375; Kinstler-a	25	50	75	150	245	340

INTIMATE CONFESSIONS
I. W. Enterprises/Super Comics: 1964

	GD	VG	FN	VF	VF/NM	NM-
I.W. Reprint #9,10, Super Reprint #10,12,18	2	4	6	11	16	20

INTIMATE LOVE
Standard Comics: No. 5, 1950 - No. 28, Aug, 1954

	GD	VG	FN	VF	VF/NM	NM-
5-8: 6-8-Severin/Elder-a	10	20	30	58	79	100
9	8	16	24	42	54	65
10-Jane Russell, Robert Mitchum photo-c	14	28	42	80	115	150
11-18,20,23,25,27,28	8	16	24	40	50	60
19,21,22,24,26-Toth-a	9	18	27	47	61	75

NOTE: ***Celardo** a-8, 10. **Colletta** a-23. **Moreira** a-13(2). Photo-c-6, 7, 10, 12, 14, 15, 18-20, 24, 26, 27.*

INTIMATES, THE
DC Comics (WildStorm): Jan, 2005 - No. 12, Dec, 2005 ($2.95/$2.99)

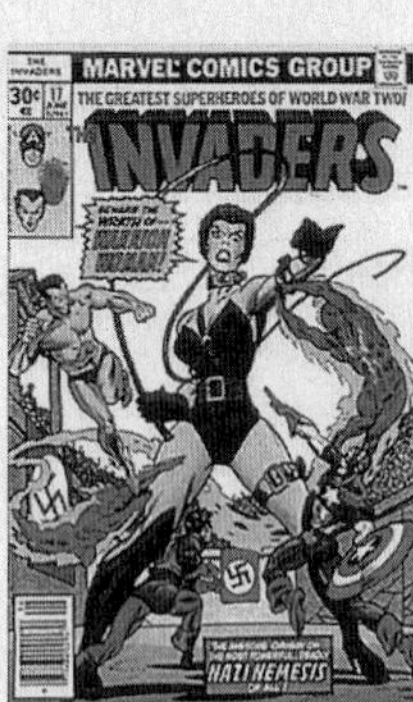

The Invaders #17 © MAR

Invincible #72 © Kirkman & Walker

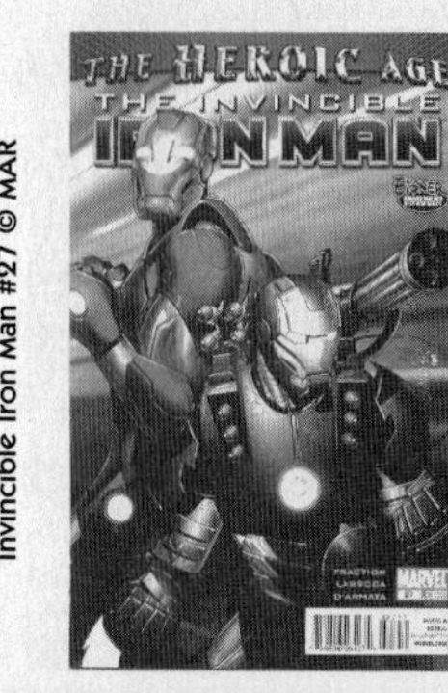

Invincible Iron Man #27 © MAR

GD VG FN VF VF/NM NM-
2.0 4.0 6.0 8.0 9.0 9.2

1-12: 1-Joe Casey-s/Jim Lee-c/Lee and Giuseppe Camuncoli-a 3.00

INTIMATE SECRETS OF ROMANCE
Star Publications: Sept, 1953 - No. 2, Apr, 1954
1,2-L. B. Cole-c 19 38 57 109 172 235

INTRIGUE
Quality Comics Group: Jan, 1955
1-Horror; Jack Cole reprint/Web of Evil 34 68 102 199 325 450

INTRIGUE
Image Comics: Aug, 1999 - No. 3, Feb, 2000 ($2.50/$2.95)
1,2: 1-Two covers (Andrews, Wieringo); Shum-s/Andrews-a 3.00
3-($2.95) 3.00

INTRUDER
TSR, Inc.: 1990 - No. 10, 1991 ($2.95, 44 pgs.)
1-10 4.00

INVADERS, THE (TV)
Gold Key: Oct, 1967 - No. 4, Oct, 1968 (All have photo-c)
1-Spiegle-a in all 9 18 27 60 100 140
2-4: 2-Pin-up on back-c 6 12 18 41 66 90

INVADERS, THE (Also see The Avengers #71 & Giant-Size Invaders)
Marvel Comics Group: August, 1975 - No. 40, May, 1979; No. 41, Sept, 1979
1-Captain America & Bucky, Human Torch & Toro, & Sub-Mariner begin; cont'd. from Giant Size Invaders #1; #1-7 are 25¢ issues 6 12 18 43 69 95
2-5: 2-1st app. Brain-Drain. 3-Battle issue; Cap vs. Namor vs. Torch; intro U-Man 3 6 9 18 27 35
6-10: 6,7-(Regular 25¢ edition). 6-(7/76) Liberty Legion app. 7-Intro Baron Blood & intro/1st app. Union Jack; Human Torch origin retold. 8-Union Jack-c/story. 9-Origin Baron Blood. 10-G.A. Capt. America-r/C.A #22 2 4 6 11 16 20
6,7-(30¢-c variants, limited distribution) 4 8 12 24 37 50
11-19: 11-Origin Spitfire; intro The Blue Bullet. 14-1st app. The Crusaders. 16-Re-intro The Destroyer. 17-Intro Warrior Woman. 18-Re-intro The Destroyer w/new origin. 19-Hitler-c/story 2 4 6 8 11 14
17-19,21-(35¢-c variants, limited distribution) 4 8 12 28 44 60
20-(Regular 30¢-c) Reprints origin/1st app. Sub-Mariner from Motion Picture Funnies Weekly with color added & brief write-up about MPFW; 1st app. new Union Jack II 2 4 6 10 14 18
20-(35¢-c variant, limited distribution) 5 10 15 32 51 70
21-(Regular 30¢ edition)-r/Marvel Mystery #10 (battle issue) 2 4 6 9 13 16
22-30,34-40: 22-New origin Toro. 24-r/Marvel Mystery #17 (team-up issue; all-r). 25-All new-a begins. 28-Intro new Human Top & Golden Girl. 29-Intro Teutonic Knight. 34-Mighty Destroyer joins. 35-The Whizzer app. 1 2 3 5 7 9
31-33: 31-Frankenstein-c/sty. 32,33-Thor app. 2 4 6 8 11 14
41-Double size last issue 3 6 9 14 19 24
Annual 1 (9/77)-Schomburg, Rico stories (new); Schomburg-c/a (1st for Marvel in 30 years); Avengers app.; re-intro The Shark & The Hyena 5 10 15 35 55 75
... Classic Vol. 1 TPB (2007, $24.99) r/#1-9, Giant-Size Invaders #1 and Marvel Premiere #29,30; cover pencils and cover inks 25.00
NOTE: ***Buckler** a-5. **Everett** r-20('39), 21(1940), 24, Annual 1. **Gil Kane** c(p)-13, 17, 18, 20-27. **Kirby** c(p)-3-12, 14-16, 32, 33. **Mooney** a-5i, 16, 22. **Robbins** a-1-4, 6-9, 10(3 pg.), 11-15, 17-21, 23, 25-28; c-28.*

INVADERS (See Namor, the Sub-Mariner #12)
Marvel Comics Group: May, 1993 - No. 4, Aug, 1993 ($1.75, limited series)
1-4 3.00

INVADERS (2004 title - see New Invaders)

INVADERS FROM HOME
DC Comics (Piranha Press): 1990 - No. 6, 1990 ($2.50, mature)
1-6 3.00

INVADERS NOW! (See Avengers/Invaders and The Torch series)
Marvel Comics: Nov, 2010 - No. 5, Mar, 2011 ($3.99, limited series)
1-5-Alex Ross-c; Steve Rogers, Bucky, Human Torch & Toro, Sub-Mariner app. 4.00

INVASION
DC Comics: Holiday, 1988-'89 - No. 3, Jan, 1989 ($2.95, lim. series, 84 pgs.)
1-3:1-McFarlane/Russell-a. 2-McFarlane/Russell & Giffen/Gordon-a 4.00
Invasion! TPB (2008, $24.99) r/#1-3 25.00

INVINCIBLE (Also see The Pact #4)
Image Comics: Jan, 2003 - Present ($2.95/$2.99)
1-Kirkman-s/Walker-a 40.00
2-8-Kirkman-s/Walker-a. 4-Preview of The Moth 12.00
9-14: 11-Origin of Omni-Man. 14-Cho-c 6.00
15-24,26-41,43-49: 33-Tie-in w/Marvel Team-Up #14 4.00
25-($4.95) Science Dog app.; back-up stories w/origins of Science Dog and teammates 6.00
42-($1.99) Includes re-cap of the entire series 3.00
50-(6/08, $4.99) Two covers; back-up origin of Cecil Stedman; Science Dog app. 6.00
51-59,61-74,76-79: 51-Jim Lee-c; new costumes. 57-Continues in Astounding Wolf-Man #11. 71-74-Viltrumite War 3.00
60-($3.99) Invincible War; Witchblade, Savage Dragon, Spawn, Youngblood app. 4.00
75-($5.99) Viltrumite War; Science Dog back-up; 2 covers 6.00
#0-(4/05, 50¢) Origin of Invincible; Ottley-a 3.00
Image Firsts: Invincible #1 (4/10, $1.00) r/#1 with "Image Firsts" cover logo 1.00
Official Handbook of the Invincible Universe 1,2 (11/06, 1/07, $4.99) profile pages 5.00
Official Handbook of the Invincible Universe Vol. 1 (2007, $12.99) r/#1-2; sketch pages 13.00
... Presents Atom Eve 1,2 (12/07, 3/08, $2.99) origin of Atom Eve; Bellegarde-a 3.00
... Presents Atom Eve & Rex Splode 1-3 (10/09 - 2/10, $2.99) origin of Rex 3.00
... Returns (4/10, $3.99) Leads into Viltrumite War in #71; 4 covers 4.00
... Universe Primer 1 (5/08, $5.99) r/Invincible #1, Brit #1, Astounding Wolf-Man #1 6.00
The Complete Invincible Library Vol. 1 Slipcase HC (2006, $125.00) oversized r/#1-24, #0 and story from Image Comics Summer Special (FCBD 2004); sketch pages; script for #1 125.00
..., Ultimate Collection Vol. 1 HC (2005, $34.95) oversized r/#1-13; sketch pages 35.00
..., Ultimate Collection Vol. 2 HC (2006, $34.99) oversized r/#14-24, #0 and story from Image Comics Summer Special (FCBD 2004); sketch pages and script for #23; intro by Damon Lindelof; afterword by Robert Kirkman 35.00
..., Ultimate Collection Vol. 3 HC (2007, $34.95) oversized r/#25-35 & The Pact #4; sketch pages and script for #28; afterword by Robert Kirkman 35.00
..., Ultimate Collection Vol. 4 HC (2008, $34.99) oversized r/#36-47; sketch & script pgs. 35.00
Vol. 1: Family Matters TPB (8/03, $12.95) r/#1-4; intro. by Busiek; sketch pages 13.00
Vol. 2: Eight in Enough TPB (3/04, $12.95) r/#5-8; intro. by Larsen; sketch pages 13.00
Vol. 3: Perfect Strangers TPB (2004, $12.95) r/#9-12; intro. by Brevoort; sketch pages 13.00
Vol. 4: Head of the Class TPB (1/05, $14.95) r/#14-19; intro. by Waid; sketch pages 15.00
Vol. 5: The Facts of Life TPB (2005, $14.99) r/#0,20-24; intro. by Wieringo; sketch pages 15.00
Vol. 6: A Different World TPB (2006, $14.99) r/#25-30; intro. by Brubaker; sketch pages 15.00
Vol. 7: Three's Company TPB (2006, $14.99) r/#31-35 & The Pact #4; sketch pages 15.00
Vol. 8: My Favorite Martian TPB (2007, $14.99) r/#36-41; sketch pages 15.00
Vol. 9: Out of This World TPB (2008, $14.99) r/#42-47; sketch pages 15.00

INVINCIBLE FOUR OF KUNG FU & NINJA
Leung Publications: April, 1988 - No. 6, 1989 ($2.00)
1-($2.75) 4.00
2-6: 2-Begin $2.00-c 3.00

INVINCIBLE IRON MAN
Marvel Comics: July, 2008 - No. 33, Feb, 2011; No. 500, Mar, 2011 - Present ($2.99/$3.99)
1-Fraction-s/Larroca-a; covers by Larroca & Quesada 4.00
1-Downey movie photo wraparound 5.00
1-Secret Movie Variant white-c with movie cast 30.00
2-18: 2-War Machine and Thor app. 7-Spider-Man app. 8-10-Dark Reign. 11-War Machine app.; Pepper gets her armor suit. 12-Namor app. 3.00
19,20-($3.99) 20-Stark Disassembled starts; back-up synopsis of recent storylines 4.00
21-24-Covers by Larocca and Zircher: 21-Thor & Capt. America app. 22-Dr. Strange app. 3.00
25-($3.99) Fraction-s/Larroca-a; new armor 4.00
26-31-($2.99) 29-New Rescue armor 3.00
32,33-($3.99)-War Machine app.; back-up w/McKelvie-a 4.00
(After #33, numbering reverts to original Vol. 1 as #500)
500-(3/11, $4.99) Two covers by Larroca; Mandarin & Spider-Man app.; cover gallery 5.00
500-Variant-c by Romita Jr. 10.00
500.1 (4/11, $2.99) Histroy re-told; Fraction-s/Larroca-a/c 3.00
501-503-($3.99) 501-503-Doctor Octopus app. 503-Back-up w/Chaykin-a 4.00
Annual 1 (8/10, $4.99) Larroca-c; history of the Mandarin; Di Giandomenico-a 5.00
...MGC #1 (4/10, free) r/#1 with "Marvel's Greatest Comics" cover logo 1.00

INVISIBLE BOY (See Approved Comics)

INVISIBLE MAN, THE (See Superior Stories #1 & Supernatural Thrillers #2)

INVISIBLE PEOPLE
Kitchen Sink Press: 1992 (B&W, lim. series)
Book One: Sanctum; Book Two: "The Power": Will Eisner-s/a in all 3.00
Book Three: "Mortal Combat" 4.00
Hardcover ($34.95) 35.00
TPB (DC Comics, 9/00, $12.95) reprints series 13.00

INVISIBLES, THE (1st Series)
DC Comics (Vertigo): Sept, 1994 - No. 25, Oct, 1996 ($1.95/$2.50, mature)
1-($2.95, 52 pgs.)-Intro King Mob, Ragged Robin, Boy, Lord Fanny & Dane (Jack Frost); Grant Morrison scripts in all 6.00
2-8: 4-Includes bound-in trading cards. 5-1st app. Orlando; brown paper-c 4.00

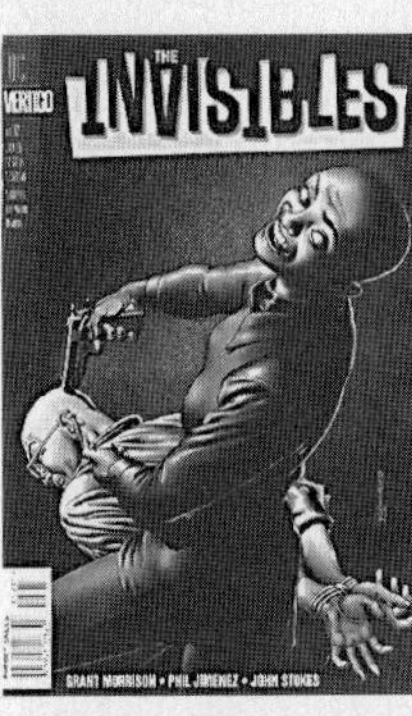

The Invisibles (2nd series) #12 © Grant Morrison

Iron Fist #2 © MAR

Iron Man #125 © MAR

GD 2.0 | VG 4.0 | FN 6.0 | VF 8.0 | VF/NM 9.0 | NM- 9.2

9-25: 10-Intro Jim Crow. 13-15-Origin Lord Fanny. 19-Origin King Mob; polybagged. 20-Origin Boy. 21-Mister Six revealed. 25-Intro Division X 3.00
Apocalipstick (2001, $19.95, TPB)-r/#9-16; Bolland-c 20.00
Entropy in the U.K. (2001, $19.95, TPB)-r/#17-25; Bolland-c 20.00
Say You Want A Revolution (1996, $17.50, TPB)-r/#1-8 18.00
NOTE: *Buckingham a-25p. Rian Hughes c-1, 5. Phil Jimenez a-17p-19p. Paul Johnson a-16, 21. Sean Phillips c-2-4, 6-25. Weston a-10p. Yeowell a-1p-4p, 22p-24p.*

INVISIBLES, THE (2nd Series)
DC Comics (Vertigo): V2#1, Feb, 1997 - No. 22, Feb, 1999 ($2.50, mature)

1-Intro Jolly Roger; Grant Morrison scripts, Phil Jimenez-a, & Brian Bolland-c begins 4.00
2-22: 9,14-Weston-a 3.00
Bloody Hell in America TPB ('98, $12.95) r/#1-4 13.00
Counting to None TPB ('99, $19.95) r/#5-13 20.00
Kissing Mr. Quimper TPB ('00, $19.95) r/#14-22 20.00

INVISIBLES, THE (3rd Series) (Issue #'s go in reverse from #12 to #1)
DC Comics (Vertigo): V3#12, Apr, 1999 - No. 1, June, 2000 ($2.95, mature)

1-12-Bolland-c; Morrison-s on all. 1-Quitely-a. 2-4-Art by various. 5-8-Phillips-a. 9-12-Phillip Bond-a. 3.00
The Invisible Kingdom TPB ('02, $19.95) r/#12-1; new Bolland-c 20.00

INVISIBLE SCARLET O'NEIL (Also see Famous Funnies #81 & Harvey Comics Hits #59)
Famous Funnies (Harvey): Dec, 1950 - No. 3, Apr, 1951 (2-3 pgs. of Powell-a in each issue.)

1 15 30 45 86 133 180
2,3 12 24 36 67 94 120

ION (Green Lantern Kyle Rayner) (See Countdown)
DC Comics: Jun, 2006 - No. 12, May, 2007 ($2.99)

1-12: 1-Marz-s/Tocchini-a. 3-Mogo app. 9,10-Tangent Green Lantern app. 12-Monitor app. 3.00
...: The Torchbearer TPB (2007, $14.99) r/#1-6 15.00

I, PAPARAZZI
DC Comics (Vertigo): 2001 ($29.95, HC, digitally manipulated photographic art)

nn-Pat McGreal-s/Steven Parke-digital-a/Stephen John Phillips-photos 30.00

IRON AND THE MAIDEN
Aspen MLT: Sept, 2007 - No. 4, Dec, 2007 ($3.99)

1-4: 1-Two covers by Manapul and Madureira/Matsuda; Jason Rubin-s 4.00
...: Brutes, Bims and the City (2/08, $2.99) character backgrounds/development art 3.00

IRON CORPORAL, THE (See Army War Heroes #22)
Charlton Comics: No. 23, Oct, 1985 - No. 25, Feb, 1986

23-25: Glanzman-a(r); low print 6.00

IRON FIST (See Immortal Iron Fist, Deadly Hands of Kung Fu, Marvel Premiere & Power Man)
Marvel Comics: Nov, 1975 - No. 15, Sept, 1977

1-Iron Fist battles Iron Man (#1-6: 25¢) 7 14 21 47 76 105
2 4 8 12 24 37 50
3-10: 4-6-(Regular 25¢ edition)(4-6/76). 8-Origin retold 3 6 9 19 29 38
4-6-(30¢-c variant, limited distribution) 6 12 18 37 59 80
11,13: 13-(30¢-c) 3 6 9 16 23 30
12-Capt. America app. 3 6 9 19 29 38
13-(35¢-c variant, limited distribution) 7 14 21 49 80 110
14-1st app. Sabretooth (8/77)(see Power Man) 14 28 42 99 200 300
14-(35¢-c variant, limited distribution) 64 128 192 544 1097 1650
15-(Regular 30¢ ed.) X-Men app., Byrne-a 7 14 21 49 80 110
15-(35¢-c variant, limited distribution) 17 34 51 122 249 375
NOTE: *Adkins a-8p, 10i, 13i; c-8i. Byrne a-1-15p; c-8p, 15p. G. Kane c-4-6p. McWilliams a-1i.*

IRON FIST
Marvel Comics: Sept, 1996 - No. 2, Oct, 1996 ($1.50, limited series)

1,2 3.00

IRON FIST
Marvel Comics: Jul, 1998 - No. 3, Sept, 1998 ($2.50, limited series)

1-3: Jurgens-s/Guice-a 3.00

IRON FIST (Also see Immortal Iron Fist)
Marvel Comics: May, 2004 - No. 6, Oct, 2004 ($2.99)

1-6: 1-4,6-Kevin Lau-c/a. 5-Mays-c/a 3.00

IRON FIST: WOLVERINE
Marvel Comics: Nov, 2000 - No. 4, Feb, 2001 ($2.99, limited series)

1-4-Igle-c/a; Kingpin app. 2-Iron Man app. 3,4-Capt. America app. 3.00

IRON GHOST
Image Comics: Apr, 2005 - No. 6, Mar, 2006 ($2.95/$2.99, limited series)

1-6-Chuck Dixon-s/Sergio Cariello-a; flip cover on each 3.00

IRONHAND OF ALMURIC (Robert E. Howard's...)
Dark Horse Comics: Aug, 1991 - No. 4, 1991 ($2.00, B&W, mini-series)

1-4: 1-Conrad painted-c 3.00

IRON HORSE (TV)
Dell Publishing Co.: March, 1967 - No. 2, June, 1967

1-Dale Robertson photo covers on both 3 6 9 18 27 35
2 3 6 9 15 21 26

IRONJAW (Also see The Barbarians)
Atlas/Seaboard Publ.: Jan, 1975 - No. 4, July, 1975

1,2-Neal Adams-c. 1-1st app. Iron Jaw; Sekowsky-a(p); Fleisher-s 2 4 6 10 14 18
3,4-Marcos. 4-Origin 2 4 6 8 10 12

IRON LANTERN
Marvel Comics (Amalgam): June, 1997 ($1.95, one-shot)

1-Kurt Busiek-s/Paul Smith & Al Williamson-a 2.50

IRON MAN (Also see The Avengers #1, Giant-Size..., Marvel Collectors Item Classics, Marvel Double Feature, Marvel Fanfare, Tales of Suspense #39 & Uncanny Tales #52)
Marvel Comics: May, 1968 - No. 332, Sept, 1996

1-Origin; Colan-c/a(p); story continued from Iron Man & Sub-Mariner #1 38 76 114 304 602 900
2 14 28 42 99 200 300
3 10 20 30 71 128 185
4,5 9 18 27 63 107 150
6-10: 9-Iron Man battles green Hulk-like android 7 14 21 49 80 110
11-15: 15-Last 12¢ issue 6 12 18 41 66 90
16-20 5 10 15 32 51 70
21-24,26-30: 22-Death of Janice Cord. 27-Intro Firebrand 4 8 12 24 37 50
25-Iron Man battles Sub-Mariner 4 8 12 28 44 60
31-42: 33-1st app. Spymaster. 35-Nick Fury & Daredevil x-over. 42-Last 15¢ issue 3 6 9 18 27 35
43-Intro The Guardsman; 25¢ giant (52 pgs.) 4 8 12 28 44 60
44-46,48-50: 43-Giant-Man back-up by Ayers. 44-Ant-Man by Tuska. 46-The Guardsman dies. 50-Princess Python app. 3 6 9 16 23 30
47-Origin retold; Barry Smith-a(p) 3 6 9 20 30 40
51-53: 53-Starlin part pencils 3 6 9 14 20 25
54-Iron Man battles Sub-Mariner; 1st app. Moondragon (1/73) as Madame MacEvil; Everett part-c 5 10 15 32 51 70
55-1st app. Thanos, Drax the Destroyer, Mentor, Starfox & Kronos (2/73); Starlin-c/a 15 30 45 106 216 325
56-Starlin-a 5 10 15 32 51 70
57-65,67-70: 59-Firebrand returns. 65-Origin Dr. Spectrum. 67-Last 20¢ issue. 68-Sunfire & Unicorn app.; origin retold; Starlin-c 2 4 6 11 16 20
66-Iron Man vs. Thor. 3 6 9 19 29 38
71-84: 72-Cameo portraits of N. Adams. 73-Rename Stark Industries to Stark International; Brunner. 76-r/#9. 2 4 6 9 13 16
85-89-(Regular 25¢ editions): 86-1st app. Blizzard. 87-Origin Blizzard. 88-Thanos app. 89-Daredevil app.; last 25¢-c 2 4 6 9 13 16
85-89-(30¢-c variants, limited distribution)(4-8/76) 4 8 12 22 34 45
90-99: 96-1st app. new Guardsman 2 4 6 8 11 14
99,101-103-(35¢-c variants, limited dist.) 4 8 12 28 44 60
100-(7/77)-Starlin-c 3 6 9 20 30 40
100-(35¢-c variant, limited dist.) 9 18 27 60 100 140
101-117: 101-Intro DreadKnight. 109-1st app. new Crimson Dynamo; 1st app. Vanguard. 110-Origin Jack of Hearts retold; death of Count Nefaria. 114-Avengers app. 2 4 6 8 10 12
118-Byrne-a(p); 1st app. Jim Rhodes 3 6 9 16 22 28
119-127: 120,121-Sub-Mariner x-over. 122-Origin. 123-128-Tony Stark treated for alcohol problem. 125-Ant-Man app. 3 6 9 14 19 24
128-(11/79) Classic Tony Stark alcoholism cover 3 6 9 20 30 40
129,130,134-149 1 2 3 5 6 8
131-133: 131,132-Hulk x-over. 133-Hulk/Ant Man-c 1 3 4 6 8 10
150-Double size 2 4 6 8 10 12
151-168: 152-New armor. 161-Moon Knight app. 167-Tony Stark alcohol problem resurfaces 6.00
169-New Iron Man (Jim Rhodes replaces Tony Stark) 1 3 4 6 8 10
170,171 6.00
172-199: 172-Captain America x-over. 186-Intro Vibro. 190-Scarlet Witch app. 191-198-Tony Stark returns as original Iron Man. 192-Both Iron Men battle 5.00
200-(11/85, $1.25, 52 pgs.)-Tony Stark returns as new Iron Man (red & white armor)

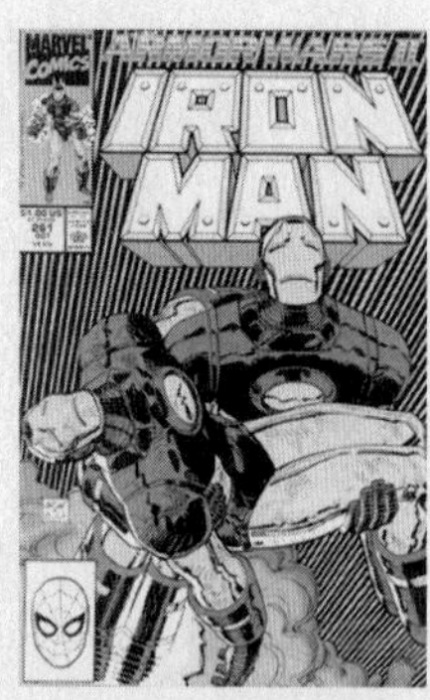
Iron Man #261 © MAR

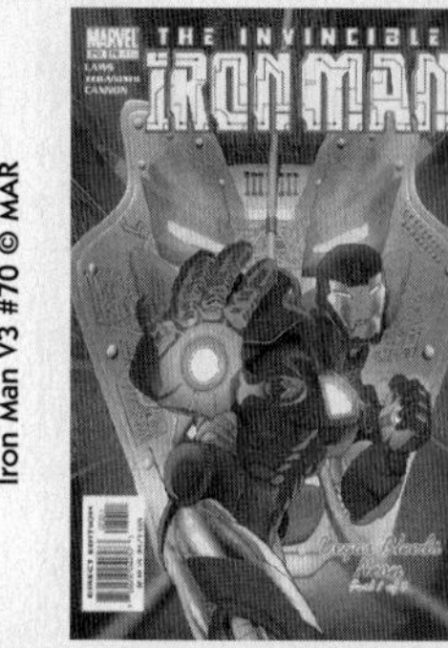

Iron Man V3 #70 © MAR

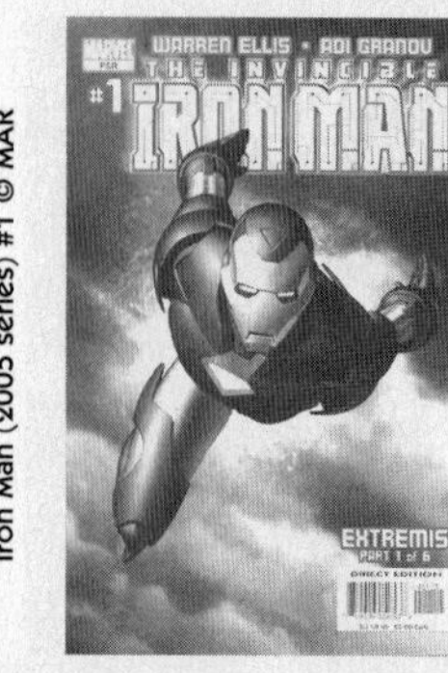

Iron Man (2005 series) #1 © MAR

	GD 2.0	VG 4.0	FN 6.0	VF 8.0	VF/NM 9.0	NM- 9.2

thru #230 1 2 3 5 6 8
201-213,215-224: 213-Intro new Dominic Fortune 4.00
214,225,228,231,234,247: 214-Spider-Woman app. in new black costume (1/87). 225-Double size ($1.25). 228-vs. Capt. America. 231-Intro new Iron Man. 234-Spider-Man x-over. 247-Hulk x-over 5.00
226,227,229,230,232,233,235-243,245,246,248,249: 233-Ant-Man app. 243-Tony Stark loses use of legs 3.00
244-($1.50, 52 pgs.)-New Armor makes him walk 4.00
250-($1.50, 52 pgs.)-Dr. Doom-c/story 4.00
251-274,276-281,283,285-287,289,291-299: 258-277-Byrne scripts. 271-Fin Fang Foom app. 276-Black Widow-c/story; last $1.00-c. 281-1st brief app. War Machine. 283-2nd full app. War Machine 3.00
275-($1.50, 52 pgs.) 4.00
282-1st full app. War Machine (7/92) 5.00
284-Death of Iron Man (Tony Stark) 5.00
288-($2.50, 52pg.)-Silver foil stamped-c; Iron Man's 350th app. in comics 4.00
290-($2.95, 52pg.)-Gold foil stamped-c; 30th ann. 4.00
300-($3.95, 68 pgs.)-Collector's Edition w/embossed foil-c; anniversary issue; War Machine-c/story 5.00
300-($2.50, 68 pgs.)-Newsstand Edition 4.00
301-303: 302-Venom-c/story (cameo #301) 3.00
304-316,318-324,326-331: 304-Begin $1.50-c; bound-in trading card sheet; Thunderstrike-c/story. 310-Orange logo. 312-w/bound-in Power Ranger Card. 319-Prologue to "The Crossing." 326-New Tony Stark; Pratt-c. 330-War Machine & Stockpile app; return of Morgan Stark 3.00
310,325: 310 ($2.95)-Polybagged w/ 16 pg. Marvel Action Hour preview & acetate print; white logo. 325-($2.95)-Wraparound-c 4.00
317-($2.50)-Flip book 4.00
332-Onslaught x-over 5.00
Special 1 (8/70)-Sub-Mariner x-over; Everett-c 5 10 15 32 51 70
Special 2 (11/71, 52 pgs.)-r/TOS #81,82,91 (all-r) 3 6 9 19 29 38
Annual 3 (1976)-Man-Thing app. 3 6 9 14 20 25
King Size 4 (8/77)-The Champions (w/Ghost Rider) app.; Newton-a(i) 2 4 6 11 16 20
Annual 5 ('82) New-a 1 2 3 5 6 8
Annual 6-8: ('83-'85) 6-New Iron Man (J. Rhodes) app. 8-X-Factor app. 5.00
Annual 9-15: ('86-'94) 10-Atlantis Attacks x-over; P. Smith-a; Layton/Guice-a; Sub-Mariner app. 11-(1990)-Origin of Mrs. Arbogast by Ditko (p&i). 12-1 pg. origin recap; Ant-Man back-up-s. 13-Darkhawk & Avengers West Coast app.; Colan/Williamson-a. 14-Bagged w/card 4.00
...: Armor Wars TPB (2007, $24.99) r/#225-232; Michelinie intro. 25.00
Manual 1 (1993, $1.75)-Operations handbook 3.00
Graphic Novel: Crash (1988, $12.95, Adults, 72 pgs.)-Computer generated art & color; violence & nudity 13.00
...Collector's Preview 1(11/94, $1.95)-wraparound-c; text & illos-no comics 3.00
...: Demon in a Bottle HC (2008, $24.99) r/#120-128; two covers 25.00
...: Demon in a Bottle TPB (2006, $24.99) r/#120-128 25.00
...: Many Armors of Iron Man (2008, $24.99) r/#47, 142-144, 152-153, 200, 218 25.00
...Vs. Dr. Doom (12/94, $12.95)-r/#149-150, 249,250. Julie Bell-c 13.00
...Vs. Dr. Doom: Doomquest HC (2008, $19.99, dustjacket)-r/#149-150, 249,250; new Michelinie intro.; bonus art 20.00
...: War Machine TPB (2008, $29.99) r/#280-291 30.00
The Invincible Iron Man Omnibus Vol. 1 HC (2008, $99.99, dustjacket) r/Iron Man stories from Tales of Suspense #39-83 & Tales To Astonish #82; 1992 intro. by Stan Lee; 1975 essay by Lee; 2008 essay by Layton; gallery of original art and covers; creator bios 100.00

NOTE: **Austin** *c-105i, 109-111i, 151i.* **Byrne** *a-118p; c-109p, 197, 253.* **Colan** *a-1p, 253, Special 1p(3); c-1p.* **Craig** *a-1i, 2-4, 5-13i, 14, 15-19i, 24p, 25p, 26-28i; c-2-4.* **Ditko** *a-160p.* **Everett** *c-29.* **Guice** *a-233-241p.* **G. Kane** *c(p)-52-54, 63, 67, 72-75, 77-79, 88, 98.* **Kirby** *a-Special 1p; c-13, 80p, 90, 92-95.* **Mooney** *a-40i, 43i, 47i.* **Perez** *c-103p.* **Simonson** *c-Annual 8.* **B. Smith** *a-232p, 243i; c-232.* **P. Smith** *a-159p, 245p, Annual 10p; c-159.* **Starlin** *a-53p(part), 55p, 56p; c-55p, 160, 163.* **Tuska** *a-5-13p, 15-23p, 24i, 32p, 38-46p, 48-54p, 57-61p, 63-69p, 70-72p, 78p, 86-92p, 95-106p, Annual 4p.* **Wood** *a-Special 1i.*

IRON MAN (The Invincible...) (Volume Two)
Marvel Comics: Nov, 1996 - No. 13, Nov, 1997 ($2.95/$1.95/$1.99)
(Produced by WildStorm Productions)

V2#1-3-Heroes Reborn begins; Scott Lobdell scripts & Whilce Portacio-c/a begin; new origin Iron Man & Hulk. 2-Hulk app. 3-Fantastic Four app. 4.00
1-Variant-c 5.00
4-11: 4-Two covers. 6-Fantastic Four app.; Industrial Revolution; Hulk app. 7-Return of Rebel. 11-($1.99) Dr. Doom-c/app. 3.00
12-($2.99) "Heroes Reunited"-pt. 3; Hulk-c/app. 4.00
13-($1.99) "World War 3"-pt. 3, x-over w/Image 3.00
Heroes Reborn: Iron Man (2006, $29.99, TPB) r/#1-12; Heroes Reborn #1/2; pin-ups 30.00

IRON MAN (The Invincible...) (Volume Three)
Marvel Comics: Feb, 1998 - No. 89, Dec, 2004 ($2.99/$1.99/$2.25)

V3#1-($2.99)-Follows Heroes Return; Busiek scripts & Chen-c/a begin; Deathsquad app. 6.00

	GD 2.0	VG 4.0	FN 6.0	VF 8.0	VF/NM 9.0	NM- 9.2

1-Alternate Ed. 1 2 3 5 7 9
2-12: 2-Two covers. 6-Black Widow-c/app. 7-Warbird-c/app. 8-Black Widow app. 9-Mandarin returns 4.00
13-($2.99) battles the Controller 5.00
14-24: 14-Fantastic Four-c/app. 3.00
25-($2.99) Iron Man and Warbird battle Ultimo; Avengers app. 4.00
26-30-Quesada-s. 28-Whiplash killed. 29-Begin $2.25-c. 3.00
31-45,47-49,51-54: 35-Maximum Security x-over; FF-c/app. 41-Grant-a begins. 44-New armor debut. 48-Ultron-c/app. 3.00
46-($3.50, 100 pgs.) Sentient armor returns; r/V1#78,140,141 4.00
50-($3.50) Grell-s begin; Black Widow app. 4.00
55-($3.50) 400th issue; Asamiya-c; back-up story Stark reveals ID; Grell-a 4.00
56-66: 56-Reis-a. 57,58-Ryan-a. 59-61-Grell-c/a. 62,63-Ryan-a. 64-Davis-a; Thor-c/app. 3.00
67-89: 67-Begin $2.99-c; Gene Ha-c. 75-83-Granov-c. 84-Avengers Disassembled prologue 85-89-Avengers Disassembled. 85-88-Harris-a. 86-89-Pat Lee-c. 87-Rumiko killed 3.00
.../Captain America '98 Annual ($3.50) vs. Modok 4.00
1999, 2000 Annual ($3.50) 4.00
2001 Annual ($2.99) Claremont-s/Ryan-a 4.00
Avengers Disassembled: Iron Man TPB (2004, $14.99) r/#84-89 15.00
Mask in the Iron Man (5/01, $14.95, TPB) r/#26-30, #1/2 15.00

IRON MAN (The Invincible...)
Marvel Comics: Jan, 2005 - No. 35, Jan, 2009 ($3.50/$2.99)

1-($3.50-c) Warren Ellis-s/Adi Granov-c/a 4.00
2-14-($2.99) 5-Flashback to origin; Stark gets new abilities. 7-Knauf-s/Zircher-a 13,14-Civil War 3.00
15-24,26,27,29-35: 15-Stark becomes Director of S.H.I.E.L.D. 19,20-World War Hulk. 33-Secret Invasion; War Machine app. 34,35-War Machine title logo 3.00
25,28-($3.99) 25-Includes movie preview & armor showcase. 28-Red & white armor 4.00
All-New Iron Manual (2/08, $4.99) Handbook-style guide to characters & armor suits 5.00
... By Design 1 (11/10, $3.99) Gallery of 2010 variant covers with artist commentary 4.00
.../Captain America: Casualities of War (2/07, $3.99) two covers; flashbacks 4.00
...: Director of S.H.I.E.L.D. Annual 1 (1/08, $3.99) Madame Hydra app.; Cheung-c 4.00
Free Comic Book Day 2010 (Iron Man: Supernova) #1 (5/10, 9-1/2" x 6-1/4") Nova app. 2.00
Free Comic Book Day 2010 (Iron Man/Thor) #1 (5/10, 9-1/2" x 6-1/4") Romita Jr.-a/c 2.00
...Golden Avenger 1 (11/08, $2.99) Santacruz-a; movie photo-c 3.00
.../Hulk/Fury 1 (2/09, $3.99) crossover of movie-version characters 4.00
Indomitable Iron Man (4/10, $3.99) B&W stories; Chaykin-s/a; Rosado-a; Parrillo-c 4.00
Iron Manual Mark 3 (6/10, $3.99) Handbook-format profiles of characters 4.00
...: Iron Protocols (12/09, $3.99) Olivetti-c/Nelson-a 4.00
...: Kiss and Kill (8/10, $3.99) Black Widow and Wolverine app. 4.00
...: Requiem (2009, $4.99) r/TOS #39, Iron Man #144 (1981); armor profiles 5.00
...: The End (1/09, $4.99) future Tony Stark retires; Michelinie-s/Chang & Layton-a 5.00
...: Titanium! 1 (12/10, $4.99) short stories by various; Yardin-c 5.00
Civil War: Iron Man TPB (2007, $11.99) r/#13,14, .../Captain America: Casualities of War, and Civil War: The Confession 12.00
HC (2006, $19.99, dust jacket) r/#1-6 and Granov covers from Iron Man V3 #75-83 20.00
...: Director of S.H.I.E.L.D. TPB (2007, $14.99) r/#15-18; Strange Tales #135 (1965) and Iron Man #129; profile pages for Iron Man and S.H.I.E.L.D.; creator interviews 15.00
...: Extremis SC (2007, $14.99) r/#1-6 and Granov covers from Iron Man V3 #75-83 15.00
...: Execute Program SC (2007, $14.99) r/#7-12; cover layouts and sketches 15.00

IRON MAN AND POWER PACK
Marvel Comics: Jan, 2008 - No. 4, Apr, 2008 ($2.99, limited series)

1-4-Gurihiru-c/Sumerak-s; Puppet Master app.; Mini Marvels back-ups in each 3.00
...: Armored and Dangerous TPB (2008, $7.99, digest size) r/series 8.00

IRON MAN & SUB-MARINER
Marvel Comics Group: Apr, 1968 (12¢, one-shot) (Pre-dates Iron Man #1 & Sub-Mariner #1)

1-Iron Man story by Colan/Craig continued from Tales of Suspense #99 & continued in Iron Man #1; Sub-Mariner story by Colan continued from Tales to Astonish #101 & continued in Sub-Mariner #1; Colan/Everett-c 15 30 45 104 212 320

IRON MAN AND THE ARMOR WARS
Marvel Comics: Oct, 2009 - No. 4, Jan, 2010 ($2.99, limited series)

1-4-Rousseau-a; Crimson Dynamo & Omega Red app. 3.00

IRON MAN: ARMORED ADVENTURES
Marvel Comics: Sept, 2009 ($3.99, one-shot)

1-Based on the 2009 cartoon; Brizuela-a; Nick Fury & Living Laser app. 4.00

IRON MAN: BAD BLOOD
Marvel Comics: Sept, 2000 - No. 4, Dec, 2000 ($2.99, limited series)

1-4-Micheline-s/Layton-a 3.00

IRON MAN: ENTER THE MANDARIN
Marvel Comics: Nov, 2007 - No. 6, Apr, 2008 ($2.99, limited series)

Iron Man 2.0 #1 © MAR

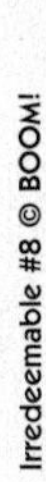
Irredeemable #8 © BOOM!

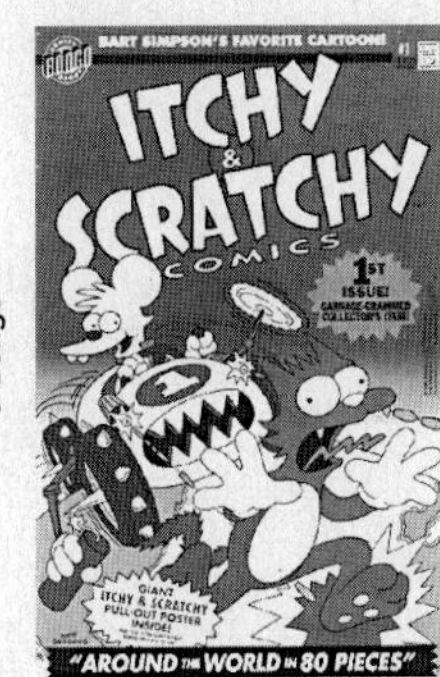

Itchy and Scratchy Comics #1 © Bongo

	GD 2.0	VG 4.0	FN 6.0	VF 8.0	VF/NM 9.0	NM- 9.2

1-6-Casey-s/Canete-a; retells first meeting 3.00
TPB (2008, $14.99) r/#1-6 15.00

IRON MAN: EXTREMIS DIRECTOR'S CUT
Marvel Comics: Jun, 2010 - No. 6, Sept, 2010 ($3.99, limited series)
1-6-Reprints Iron Man #1-6 (2005 series) with script pages and design art 4.00

IRON MAN: HOUSE OF M (Also see House of M and related x-overs)
(Reprinted in House of M: Fantastic Four/ Iron Man TPB)
Marvel Comics: Sept, 2005 - No. 3, Nov, 2005 ($2.99, limited series)
1-3-Pat Lee-a/c; Greg Pak-s 3.00

IRON MAN: HYPERVELOCITY
Marvel Comics: Mar, 2007 - No. 6, Aug, 2007 ($2.99, limited series)
1-6-Adam Warren-s/Brian Denham-a/c 3.00
TPB (2007, $14.99) r/#1-6; layout pages and armor design sketches 15.00

IRON MAN: I AM IRON MAN
Marvel Comics: Mar, 2010 - No. 2, Apr, 2010 ($3.99, limited series)
1,2-Adaptation of the first movie; Peter David-s/Sean Chen-a/Adi Granov-c 4.00

IRON MAN: INEVITABLE
Marvel Comics: Feb, 2006 - No. 6, July, 2006 ($2.99, limited series)
1-6-Joe Casey-s/Frazer Irving; Spymaster and the Living Laser app. 3.00
TPB (2006, $14.99) r/#1-6; cover sketches 15.00

IRON MAN: LEGACY
Marvel Comics: Jun, 2010 - No. 11, Apr, 2011 ($3.99/$2.99)
1-Van Lente-s/Kurth-a; Dr. Doom app.; back-up r/debut in Tales of Suspense #39 4.00
2-11-($2.99) 4-Titanium Man & Crimson Dynamo app. 6-The Pride app. 3.00

IRON MAN: LEGACY OF DOOM
Marvel Comics: Jun, 2008 - No. 4, Sept, 2008 ($2.99, limited series)
1-4-Michelinie-s/Lim & Layton-a; Dr. Doom app. 3.00

IRON MAN NOIR
Marvel Comics: Jun, 2010 - No. 4, Sept, 2010 ($3.99, limited series)
1-4-Pulp-style set in 1939; Snyder-s/Garcia-a 4.00

IRON MAN: RAPTURE
Marvel Comics: Jan, 2011 - No. 4, Feb, 2011 ($3.99, limited series)
1-4-Irvine-s/Medina-a/Bradstreet-c. 3,4-War Machine app. 4.00

IRON MAN: THE IRON AGE
Marvel Comics: Aug, 1998 - No. 2, Sept, 1998 ($5.99, limited series)
1,2-Busiek-s; flashback story from gold armor days 6.00

IRON MAN: THE LEGEND
Marvel Comics: Sept, 1996 ($3.95, one-shot)
1-Tribute issue 4.50

IRON MAN/ THOR
Marvel Comics: Jan, 2011 - No. 4, Apr, 2011 ($3.99, limited series)
1-4-Eaton-a; Crimson Dynamo & Diablo app. 4.00

IRON MAN 2: ... (Follows the first movie)
Marvel Comics: Jun, 2010 - Nov, 2010 ($3.99, limited series)
Agents of S.H.I.E.L.D. 1 (11/10, $3.99) Nick Fury, Agent Coulson & Black Widow app. 4.00
Public Identity (6/10 - No. 3, 7/10, $3.99) 1-3-Kitson & Lim-a/Granov-c 4.00
Spotlight (4/10, $3.99) Interviews with Granov, Guggenheim, Fraction, Ellis, Michelinie 4.00

IRON MAN 2.0
Marvel Comics: Apr, 2011 - Present ($3.99/$2.99)
1-($3.99) Spencer-s/Kitson-c; back-up history of War Machine 4.00
1-Variant-c by Djurdjevic 6.00
2-4-($2.99) 2,3-Kitson, Kano & Di Giandomenico-a. 4-Olivetta-a 3.00

IRON MAN 2020 (Also see Machine Man limited series)
Marvel Comics: June, 1994 ($5.95, one-shot)
nn 6.00

IRON MAN: VIVA LAS VEGAS
Marvel Comics: Jul, 2008 - No. 4 ($3.99, limited series)
1,2-Jon Favreau-s/Adi Granov-a/c 4.00

IRON MAN VS WHIPLASH
Marvel Comics: Jan, 2010 - No. 4, Apr, 2010 ($3.99, limited series)
1-4-Briones-a/Peterson-c; origin of new Whiplash 4.00

IRON MAN/X-O MANOWAR: HEAVY METAL (See X-O Manowar/Iron Man: In Heavy Metal)
Marvel Comics: Sept, 1996 ($2.50, one-shot) (1st Marvel/Valiant x-over)
1-Pt. II of Iron Man/X-O Manowar x-over; Fabian Nicieza scripts; 1st app. Rand Banion 3.00

IRON MARSHALL
Jademan Comics: July, 1990 - No. 32, Feb, 1993 ($1.75, plastic coated-c)
1,32: Kung Fu stories. 1-Poster centerfold 4.00
2-31-Kung Fu stories in all 3.00

IRON VIC (See Comics Revue No. 3 & Giant Comics Editions)
United Features Syndicate/St. John Publ. Co.: 1940

	GD 2.0	VG 4.0	FN 6.0	VF 8.0	VF/NM 9.0	NM- 9.2
Single Series 22	34	68	102	199	325	450

IRONWOLF
DC Comics: 1986 ($2.00, one shot)
1-r/Weird Worlds 8-10; Chaykin story & art 3.00

IRONWOLF: FIRES OF THE REVOLUTION (See Weird Worlds #8-10)
DC Comics: 1992 ($29.95, hardcover)
nn-Chaykin/Moore story, Mignola-a w/Russell inks. 30.00

IRREDEEMABLE (Also see Incorruptible)
BOOM! Studios: Apr, 2009 - Present ($3.99)
1-24: 1-Waid-s/Krause-a; 3 covers; Grant Morrison afterword. 2-24-Three covers 4.00
... Special 1 (4/10, $3.99) Art by Azaceta, Rios & Chaykin; three covers 4.00

IRREDEEMABLE ANT-MAN, THE
Marvel Comics: Dec, 2006 - No. 12, Nov, 2007 ($2.99)
1-12-Kirkman-s/Hester-a/c; intro. Eric O'Grady as the new Ant-Man. 7-Ms. Marvel app. 10-World War Hulk x-over 3.00
... Vol. 1: Lowlife (2007, $9.99, digest) r/#1-6 10.00
... Vol. 2: Small-Minded (2007, $9.99, digest) r/#7-12 10.00

ISAAC ASIMOV'S I-BOTS
Tekno Comix: Dec, 1995 - No. 7, May, 1996 ($1.95)
1-7: 1-6-Perez-c/a. 2-Chaykin variant-c exists. 3-Polybagged. 7-Lady Justice-c/app. 3.00

ISAAC ASIMOV'S I-BOTS
BIG Entertainment: V2#1, June, 1996 - No. 9, Feb, 1997 ($2.25)
V2#1-9: 1-Lady Justice-c/app. 6-Gil Kane-c 3.00

ISIS (TV) (Also see Shazam)
National Per.l Publ./DC Comics: Oct-Nov, 1976 - No. 8, Dec-Jan, 1977-78

	GD 2.0	VG 4.0	FN 6.0	VF 8.0	VF/NM 9.0	NM- 9.2
1-Wood inks	2	4	6	10	14	18
2-8: 5-Isis new look. 7-Origin	2	3	4	6	8	10

ISLAND AT THE TOP OF THE WORLD (See Walt Disney Showcase #27)

ISLAND OF DR. MOREAU, THE (Movie)
Marvel Comics Group: Oct, 1977 (52 pgs.)

	GD 2.0	VG 4.0	FN 6.0	VF 8.0	VF/NM 9.0	NM- 9.2
1-Gil Kane-c	1	2	3	5	6	8

I SPY (TV)
Gold Key: Aug, 1966 - No. 6, Sept, 1968 (All have photo-c)

	GD 2.0	VG 4.0	FN 6.0	VF 8.0	VF/NM 9.0	NM- 9.2
1-Bill Cosby, Robert Culp photo covers	11	22	33	77	144	210
2-6: 3,4-McWilliams-a. 5-Last 12¢-c	7	14	21	45	73	100

IT! (See Astonishing Tales No. 21-24 & Supernatural Thrillers No. 1)

ITCHY & SCRATCHY COMICS (The Simpsons TV show)
Bongo Comics: 1993 - No. 3, 1993 ($1.95)
1-3: 1-Bound-in jumbo poster. 3-w/decoder screen trading card 4.00
Holiday Special ('94, $1.95) 4.00

IT GIRL (Also see Atomics, and Madman Comics)
Oni Press: May, 2002 ($2.95, one-shot)
1-Allred-s/Clugston-Major-c/a; Atomics and Madman app. 3.00

IT REALLY HAPPENED
William H. Wise No. 1,2/Standard (Visual Editions): 1944 - No. 11, Oct, 1947

	GD 2.0	VG 4.0	FN 6.0	VF 8.0	VF/NM 9.0	NM- 9.2
1-Kit Carson & Ben Franklin stories	23	46	69	136	223	310
2	14	28	42	81	118	155
3,4,6,9,11: 4-D-Day story. 6-Joan of Arc story. 9-Captain Kidd & Frank Buck stories	12	24	36	69	97	125
5-Lou Gehrig & Lewis Carroll stories	17	34	51	100	158	215
7-Teddy Roosevelt story	14	28	42	80	115	150
8-Story of Roy Rogers	17	34	51	98	154	210
10-Honus Wagner & Mark Twain stories	15	30	45	85	130	175

NOTE: ***Guardineer** a-7(2), 8(2), 10, 11. **Schomburg** c-1-7, 9-11.*

IT RHYMES WITH LUST (Also see Bold Stories & Candid Tales)
St. John Publishing Co.: 1950 (Digest size, 128 pgs., 25¢)

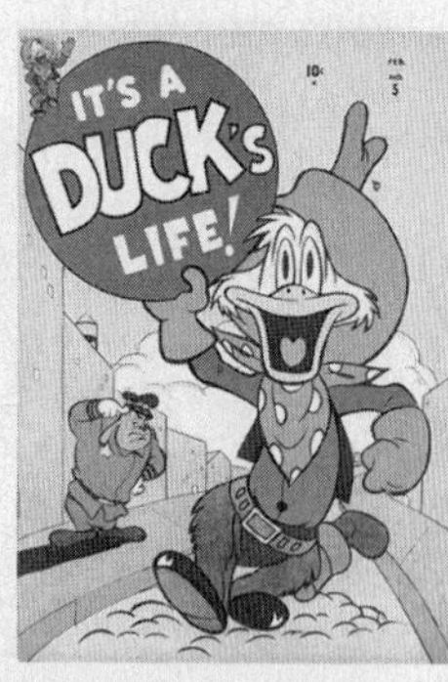

It's a Duck's Life #5 © MAR

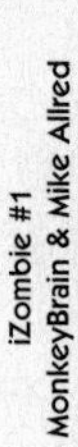
iZombie #1
© MonkeyBrain & Mike Allred

Jack of Fables #10
© Bill Willingham & DC

GD VG FN VF VF/NM NM-
2.0 4.0 6.0 8.0 9.0 9.2

nn (Rare)-Matt Baker & Ray Osrin-a 129 258 387 826 1413 2000

IT'S A BIRD...
DC Comics: 2004 ($24.95, hardcover with dust jacket)
HC-Semi-autobiographical story of Steven Seagle writing Superman; Kristiansen-a 25.00
SC-($17.95) 18.00

IT'S ABOUT TIME (TV)
Gold Key: Jan, 1967
1 (10195-701)-Photo-c 4 8 12 28 44 60

IT'S A DUCK'S LIFE
Marvel Comics/Atlas(MMC): Feb, 1950 - No. 11, Feb, 1952
1-Buck Duck, Super Rabbit begin 15 30 45 90 140 190
2 10 20 30 56 76 95
3-11 9 18 27 52 69 85

IT'S GAMETIME
National Periodical Publications: Sept-Oct, 1955 - No. 4, Mar-Apr, 1956
1-(Scarce)-Infinity-c; Davy Crockett app. in puzzle 84 168 252 538 919 1300
2,3 (Scarce): 2-Dodo & The Frog 61 122 183 390 670 950
4 (Rare) 65 130 195 416 708 1000

IT'S LOVE, LOVE, LOVE
St. John Publishing Co.: Nov, 1957 - No. 2, Jan, 1958 (10¢)
1,2 7 14 21 35 43 50

IT! THE TERROR FROM BEYOND SPACE
IDW Publishing: Jul, 2010 - No. 3, Sept, 2010 ($3.99, limited series)
1-3-Naraghi-s/Dos Santos-a/Mannion-c 4.00

IVANHOE (See Fawcett Movie Comics No. 20)

IVANHOE
Dell Publishing Co.: July-Sept, 1963
1 (12-372-309) 3 6 9 21 32 42

IWO JIMA (See Spectacular Features Magazine)

I, ZOMBIE (Also see House of Mystery Halloween Annual #1)
DC Comics (Vertigo): July, 2010 - Present ($1.00/$2.99)
1-($1.00) Allred-a/Roberson-s; 2 covers by Allred & Cooke 3.00
2-11-($2.99) Allred-c/a 3.00
...: Dead to the World TPB (2011, $14.99) r/#1-5 & House of Mystery Hall. Ann. #1 15.00

JACE PEARSON OF THE TEXAS RANGERS (Radio/TV)(4-Color #396 is titled Tales of the Texas Rangers; ...'s Tales of ... #11-on)(See Western Roundup under Dell Giants)
Dell Publishing Co.: No. 396, 5/52 - No. 1021, 8-10/59 (No #10) (All-Photo-c)
Four Color 396 (#1) 10 20 30 71 128 185
2(5-7/53) - 9(2-4/55) 7 14 21 47 76 105
Four Color 648(#10, 9/55) 6 12 18 41 66 90
11(11-2/55-56) - 14,17-20(6-8/58) 6 12 18 37 59 80
15,16-Toth-a 6 12 18 39 62 85
Four Color 961,1021: 961-Spiegle-a 6 12 18 37 59 80
NOTE: *Joel McCrea photo c-1-9, F.C. 648 (starred on radio show only); Willard Parker photo c-11-on (starred on TV series).*

JACK ARMSTRONG (Radio)(See True Comics)
Parents' Institute: Nov, 1947 - No. 9, Sept, 1948; No. 10, Mar, 1949 - No. 13, Sept, 1949
1-(Scarce) (odd size) Cast intro. inside front-c; Vic Hardy's Crime Lab begins
43 86 129 271 461 650
2 20 40 60 114 182 250
3-5 15 30 45 83 124 165
6-13 13 26 39 72 101 130

JACK CROSS
DC Comics: Oct, 2005 - No. 4, Jan, 2006 ($2.50)
1-4-Warren Ellis-s/Gary Erskine-a 3.00
DC Comics Presents: Jack Cross #1 (12/10, $7.99, squarebound) r/#1-4 8.00

JACK HUNTER
Blackthorne Publishing: July, 1987 - No. 3 ($1.25)
1-3 3.00

JACKIE CHAN'S SPARTAN X
Topps Comics: May, 1997 - No. 3 ($2.95, limited series)
1-3-Michael Golden-s/a; variant photo-c 3.00

JACKIE CHAN'S SPARTAN X: HELL BENT HERO FOR HIRE
Image Comics (Little Eva Ink): Mar, 1998 - No. 3 ($2.95, B&W)
1-3-Michael Golden-s/a: 1-variant photo-c 3.00

JACKIE GLEASON (TV) (Also see The Honeymooners)
St. John Publishing Co.: Sept, 1955 - No. 4, Dec, 1955?
1(1955)(TV)-Photo-c 62 124 186 394 680 965
2-4 42 84 126 265 445 625

JACKIE GLEASON AND THE HONEYMOONERS (TV)
National Periodical Publications: June-July, 1956 - No. 12, Apr-May, 1958
1-1st app. Ralph Kramden 90 180 270 576 988 1400
2 53 106 159 334 567 800
3-11: 8-Statue of Liberty-c 42 84 126 265 445 625
12 (Scarce) 60 120 180 380 653 925

JACKIE JOKERS (Became Richie Rich &...)
Harvey Publications: March, 1973 - No. 4, Sept, 1973 (#5 was advertised, but not published)
1-1st app. 3 6 9 16 22 28
2-4: 2-President Nixon app. 2 4 6 8 11 14

JACKIE ROBINSON (Famous Plays of...) (Also see Negro Heroes #2 & Picture News #4)
Fawcett Publications: May, 1950 - No. 6, 1952 (Baseball hero) (All photo-c)
nn 97 194 291 621 1061 1500
2 55 110 165 352 601 850
3-6 47 94 141 296 498 700

JACK IN THE BOX (Formerly Yellowjacket Comics #1-10; becomes Cowboy Western Comics #17 on)
Frank Comunale/Charlton Comics No. 11 on: Feb, 1946; No. 11, Oct, 1946 - No. 16, Nov-Dec, 1947
1-Stitches, Marty Mouse & Nutsy McKrow 19 38 57 111 176 240
11-Yellowjacket (early Charlton comic) 21 42 63 126 206 285
12,14,15 13 26 39 74 105 135
13-Wolverton-a 21 42 63 122 199 275
16-12 pg. adapt. of Silas Marner; Kiefer-a 14 28 42 80 115 150

JACK KIRBY'S FOURTH WORLD (See Mister Miracle & New Gods, 3rd Series)
DC Comics: Mar, 1997 - No. 20, Oct, 1998 ($1.95/$2.25)
1-20: 1-Byrne-a/scripts & Simonson-c begin; story cont'd from New Gods, 3rd Series #15; retells "The Pact" (New Gods, 1st Series #7); 1st brief DC app. Thor. 2-Thor vs. Big Barda; "Apokolips Then" back-up begins; Kirby-c/swipe (Thor #126) 8-Genesis x-over. 10-Simonson-s/a 13-Simonson back-up story. 20-Superman-c/app. 3.00

JACK KIRBY'S FOURTH WORLD OMNIBUS
DC Comics: 2007 - Vol. 4, 2008 ($49.99, hardcovers with dustjackets)
Vol. 1 ('07) Recolored reprints in chronological order of Superman's Pal, Jimmy Olsen #133-139, Forever People #1-3, New Gods #1-3, and Mister Miracle #1-3; Morrison intro, bonus art 50.00
Vol. 2 ('07) r/Jimmy Olsen #141-145, F.P. #4-6, N.G. #4-6 & M.M. #4-6; bonus art 50.00
Vol. 3 ('07) r/Jimmy Olsen #146-148, F.P. #7-10, N.G. #7-10 & M.M. #7-9; bonus art 50.00
Vol. 4 ('08) r/F.P. #11, M.M. #10-18, N.G. #11 & reprint series #6, & DC Graphic Novel #6 (The Hunger Dogs); Levitz intro.; Evanier afterword; character profile pages 50.00

JACK KIRBY'S GALACTIC BOUNTY HUNTERS
Marvel Comics (Icon): July, 2006 - No. 6, Nov, 2007 ($3.99)
1-6-Based on a Kirby concept; Mike Thibodeaux-a; Lisa Kirby, Thibodeaux and others-s 4.00
HC (2007, $24.99) r/series; pin-ups and supplemental art and interviews 25.00

JACK KIRBY'S SECRET CITY SAGA
Topps Comics (Kirbyverse): No. 0, Apr, 1993; No. 1, May, 1993 - No. 4, Aug, 1993 ($2.95, limited series)
0-(No cover price, 20 pgs.)-Simonson-c/a 3.00
0-Red embossed-c (limited ed.) 5.00
1-4-Bagged w/3 trading cards; Ditko-c/a: 1-Ditko/Art Adams-c. 2-Ditko/Byrne-c; has coupon for Pres. Clinton holo-foil trading card. 3-Dorman poster; has coupon for Gore holo-foil trading card. 4-Ditko/Perez-c 3.00
NOTE: *Issues #1-4 contain coupons redeemable for Kirbychrome version of #1*

JACK KIRBY'S SILVER STAR (Also see Silver Star)
Topps Comics (Kirbyverse): Oct, 1993 ($2.95)(Intended as a 4-issue limited series)
1-Silver ink-c; Austin-c/a(i); polybagged w/3 cards 3.00

JACK KIRBY'S TEENAGENTS (See Satan's Six)
Topps Comics (Kirbyverse): Aug, 1993 - No. 4, Nov, 1993 ($2.95, limited series)
1-4: Bagged with/3 trading cards; Busiek-s/Austin-c(i): 3-Liberty Project app. 3.00

JACK OF FABLES (See Fables)
DC Comics (Vertigo): Sept, 2006 - Present ($2.99)
1-49: 1-Willingham & Sturges-s/Akins-a. 33-35-Crossover with Fables and The Literals 3.00
1-Special Edition (8/10, $1.00) r/#1 with "What's Next?" logo on cover 1.00
...: Americana TPB (2008, $14.99) r/#17-21 15.00
...: Jack of Hearts TPB (2007, $14.99) r/#6-11 15.00

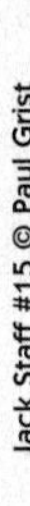

Jack Staff #15 © Paul Grist

Jane Arden #1 © UFS

Jason and the Argobots #1 © Torres & Norton

	GD 2.0	VG 4.0	FN 6.0	VF 8.0	VF/NM 9.0	NM- 9.2

...: The Bad Prince TPB (2008, $14.99) r/#12-16 15.00
...: The Big Book of War TPB (2009, $14.99) r/#28-32 15.00
...: The Fulminate Blade TPB (2011, $14.99) r/#41-45 15.00
...: The (Nearly) Great Escape TPB (2007, $14.99) r/#1-5; Akins sketch pages 15.00
...: The New Adventures of Jack and Jack TPB (2010, $14.99) r/#36-40 15.00
...: Turning Pages TPB (2009, $14.99) r/#22-27 15.00

JACK OF HEARTS (Also see The Deadly Hands of Kung Fu #22 & Marvel Premiere #44)
Marvel Comics Group: Jan, 1984 - No. 4, Apr, 1984 (60¢, limited series)
1-4 3.00

JACKPOT COMICS (Jolly Jingles #10 on)
MLJ Magazines: Spring, 1941 - No. 9, Spring, 1943
1-The Black Hood, Mr. Justice, Steel Sterling & Sgt. Boyle begin; Biro-c 326 652 978 2282 3991 5700
2-S. Cooper-c 148 296 444 947 1624 2300
3-Hubbell-c 110 220 330 704 1202 1700
4-Archie begins (Win/41; on sale 12/41)-(also see Pep Comics #22); 1st app. Mrs. Grundy, the principal; Novick-c 486 972 1458 3550 6275 9000
5-Hitler, Tojo, Mussolini-c by Montana; 1st definitive Mr. Weatherbee; 1st brief app. Reggie in 1 panel 206 412 618 1318 2259 3200
6-9: 6,7-Bondage-c by Novick. 8,9-Sahle-c 116 232 348 742 1271 1800

JACK Q FROST (See Unearthly Spectaculars)

JACK STAFF (Vol. 2; previously published in Britain)
Image Comics: Feb, 2003 - No. 20, May, 2009 ($2.95/$3.50)
1-5-Paul Grist-s/a 3.50
6-20-($3.50) 6-Flashback to the WW2 Freedom Fighters 3.50
... Special 1 (1/08, $3.50) Molachi the Immortal app. 3.50
The Weird World of Jack Staff King Size Special 1 (7/07, $5.99, B&W) r/story serialized in Comics International magazine; afterword by Grist 6.00
Vol. 1: Everything Used to Be Black and White TPB (12/03, $19.95) r/British issues 20.00
Vol. 2: Soldiers TPB (2005, $15.95) r/#1-5; cover gallery 16.00
Vol. 3: Echoes of Tomorrow TPB (2006, $16.99) r/#6-12; cover gallery 17.00

JACK THE GIANT KILLER (See Movie Classics)

JACK THE GIANT KILLER (New Adventures of...)
Bimfort & Co.: Aug-Sept, 1953
V1#1-H. C. Kiefer-c/a 24 48 72 144 237 330

JACKY'S DIARY
Dell Publishing Co.: No. 1091, Apr-June, 1960 (one-shot)
Four Color 1091 5 10 15 30 48 65

JADEMAN COLLECTION
Jademan Comics: Dec, 1989 - No. 3, 1990 ($2.50, plastic coated-c, 68 pgs.)
1-3: 1-Wraparound-c w/fold-out poster 4.00

JADEMAN KUNG FU SPECIAL
Jademan Comics: 1988 ($1.50, 64 pgs.)
1 4.00

JADE WARRIORS (Mike Deodato's...)
Image Comics (Glass House Graphics): Nov, 1999 - No. 3, 2000 ($2.50)
1-3-Deodato-a 3.00
1-Variant-c 3.00

JAGUAR, THE (Also see The Adventures of...)
Impact Comics (DC): Aug, 1991 - No. 14, Oct, 1992 ($1.00)
1-14: 4-The Black Hood x-over. 7-Sienkiewicz-c. 9-Contains Crusaders trading card 3.00
Annual 1 (1992, $2.50, 68 pgs.)-With trading card 4.00

JAGUAR GOD
Verotik: Mar, 1995 - No. 7, June, 1997 ($2.95, mature)
0 (2/96, $3.50)-Embossed Frazetta-c; Bisley-a; w/pin-ups. 5.00
1-Frazetta-c. 5.00
2-7: 2-Frazetta-c. 3-Bisley-c. 4-Emond-c. 7-($2.95)-Frazetta-c 4.00

JAKE THRASH
Aircel Publishing: 1988 - No. 3, 1988 ($2.00)
1-3 3.00

JAM, THE (...Urban Adventure)
Slave Labor Nos. 1-5/Dark Horse Comics Nos. 6-8/Caliber Comics No. 9 on: Nov, 1989 - No. 14, 1997 ($1.95/$2.50/$2.95, B&W)
1-14: Bernie Mireault-c/a/scripts. 6-1st Dark Horse issue. 9-1st Caliber issue 3.00

JAMBOREE
Round Publishing Co.: Feb, 1946(no month given) - No. 3, Apr, 1946
1-Funny animal 21 42 63 122 199 275
2,3 15 30 45 85 130 175

JAMES BOND 007: A SILENT ARMAGEDDON
Dark Horse Comics/Acme Press: Mar, 1993 - Apr 1993 (limited series)
1,2 3.50

JAMES BOND 007: GOLDENEYE (Movie)
Topps Comics: Jan, 1996 ($2.95, unfinished limited series of 3)
1-Movie adaptation; Stelfreeze-c 3.00

JAMES BOND 007: SERPENT'S TOOTH
Dark Horse Comics/Acme Press: July 1992 - Aug 1992 ($4.95, limited series)
1-3-Paul Gulacy-c/a 5.00

JAMES BOND 007: SHATTERED HELIX
Dark Horse Comics: Jun 1994 - July 1994 ($2.50, limited series)
1,2 3.00

JAMES BOND 007: THE QUASIMODO GAMBIT
Dark Horse Comics: Jan 1995 - May 1995 ($3.95, limited series)
1-3 4.50

JAMES BOND FOR YOUR EYES ONLY
Marvel Comics Group: Oct, 1981 - No. 2, Nov, 1981
1,2-Movie adapt.; r/Marvel Super Special #19 4.00

JAMES BOND JR. (TV)
Marvel Comics: Jan, 1992 - No. 12, Dec, 1992 (#1: $1.00, #2-on: $1.25)
1-12: Based on animated TV show 3.00

JAMES BOND: LICENCE TO KILL (See Licence To Kill)

JAMES BOND: PERMISSION TO DIE
Eclipse Comics/ACME Press: 1989 - No. 3, 1991 ($3.95, lim. series, squarebound, 52 pgs.)
1-3: Mike Grell-c/a/scripts in all. 3-($4.95) 5.00

JAM, THE: SUPER COOL COLOR INJECTED TURBO ADVENTURE #1 FROM HELL!
Comico: May, 1988 ($2.50, 44 pgs., one-shot)
1 4.00

JANE ARDEN (See Feature Funnies & Pageant of Comics)
St. John (United Features Syndicate): Mar, 1948 - No. 2, June, 1948
1-Newspaper reprints 15 30 45 88 137 185
2 12 24 36 67 94 120

JANE WIEDLIN'S LADY ROBOTIKA
Image Comics: Jul, 2010 - No. 2, Aug, 2010 ($3.50, unfinished limited series)
1,2-Wiedlin & Bill Morrison-s. 1-Morrison & Rodriguez-a. 2-Moy-a 3.50

JANN OF THE JUNGLE (Jungle Tales No. 1-7)
Atlas Comics (CSI): No. 8, Nov, 1955 - No. 17, June, 1957
8(#1) 36 72 108 216 351 485
9,11-15 20 40 60 118 192 265
10-Williamson/Colletta-c 20 40 60 120 195 270
16,17-Williamson/Mayo-a(3), 5 pgs. each 21 42 63 124 202 280
NOTE: ***Everett** c-15-17. **Heck** a-8, 15, 17. **Maneely** c-11. **Shores** a-8.*

JASON & THE ARGOBOTS
Oni Press: Aug, 2002 - No. 4, Dec, 2002 ($2.95, B&W, limited series)
1-4-Torres-s/Norton-c/a 3.00
Vol. 1 Birthquake TPB (6/03, $11.95, digest size) r/#1-4, Sunday comic strips 12.00
Vol. 2 Machina Ex Deus TPB (9/03, $11.95, digest size) new story 12.00

JASON & THE ARGONAUTS (See Movie Classics)

JASON GOES TO HELL: THE FINAL FRIDAY (Movie)
Topps Comics: July, 1993 - No. 3, Sept, 1993 ($2.95, limited series)
1-3: Adaptation of film. 1-Glow-in-the-dark-c 3.00

JASON'S QUEST (See Showcase #88-90)

JASON VS. LEATHERFACE
Topps Comics: Oct, 1995 - No. 3, Jan, 1996 ($2.95, limited series)
1-3: Collins scripts; Bisley-c 5.00

JAWS 2 (See Marvel Comics Super Special, A)

JAY & SILENT BOB (See Clerks, Oni Double Feature, and Tales From the Clerks)
Oni Press: July, 1998 - No. 4, Oct, 1999 ($2.95, B&W, limited series)

Jeanie Comics #15 © MAR

Jennifer Blood #1 © Spitfire & DE

Jet Fighters #5 © STD

	GD 2.0	VG 4.0	FN 6.0	VF 8.0	VF/NM 9.0	NM- 9.2
1-Kevin Smith-s/Fegredo-a; photo-c & Quesada/Palmiotti-c						8.00
1-San Diego Comic Con variant covers (2 different covers, came packaged with action figures)						10.00
1-2nd & 3rd printings, 2-4: 2-Allred-c. 3-Flip-c by Jaime Hernandez						3.00
Chasing Dogma TPB (1999, $11.95) r/#1-4; Alanis Morissette intro.						12.00
Chasing Dogma TPB (2001, $12.95) r/#1-4 in color; Morissette intro.						13.00
Chasing Dogma HC (1999, $69.95, S&N) r/#1-4 in color; Morissette intro.						70.00

JCP FEATURES
J.C. Productions (Archie): Feb, 1982-c; Dec, 1981-indicia ($2.00, one-shot, B&W magazine)

	GD 2.0	VG 4.0	FN 6.0	VF 8.0	VF/NM 9.0	NM- 9.2
1-T.H.U.N.D.E.R. Agents; Black Hood by Morrow & Neal Adams; Texeira-a; 2 pgs. S&K-a from Fly #1	2	4	6	8	10	12

JEANIE COMICS (Formerly All Surprise; Cowgirl Romances #28)
Marvel Comics/Atlas(CPC): No. 13, April, 1947 - No. 27, Oct, 1949

	GD 2.0	VG 4.0	FN 6.0	VF 8.0	VF/NM 9.0	NM- 9.2
13-Mitzi, Willie begin	22	44	66	128	209	290
14,15	15	30	45	88	137	185
16-Used in Love and Death by Legman; Kurtzman's "Hey Look"	18	36	54	105	165	225
17-19,21,22-Kurtzman's "Hey Look" (1-3 pgs. each)	14	28	42	81	118	155
20,23-27	14	28	42	75	108	140

JEEP COMICS (Also see G.I. Comics and Overseas Comics)
R. B. Leffingwell & Co.: Winter, 1944, No. 2, Spring, 1945 - No. 3, Mar-Apr, 1948

	GD 2.0	VG 4.0	FN 6.0	VF 8.0	VF/NM 9.0	NM- 9.2
1-Capt. Power, Criss Cross & Jeep & Peep (costumed) begin	63	126	189	403	689	975
2- Jeep & Peep-c	40	80	120	246	411	575
3-L. B. Cole dinosaur-c	50	100	150	315	533	750

JEFF JORDAN, U.S. AGENT
D. S. Publishing Co.: Dec, 1947 - Jan, 1948

	GD 2.0	VG 4.0	FN 6.0	VF 8.0	VF/NM 9.0	NM- 9.2
1	15	30	45	86	133	180

JEMM, SON OF SATURN
DC Comics: Sept, 1984 - No. 12, Aug, 1985 (Maxi-series, mando paper)

	GD 2.0	VG 4.0	FN 6.0	VF 8.0	VF/NM 9.0	NM- 9.2
1-12: 3-Origin						3.00

NOTE: ***Colan*** *a-1-12p; c-1-5, 7-12p.*

JENNIFER BLOOD
Dynamite Entertainment: 2011 - Present ($3.99)

	GD 2.0	VG 4.0	FN 6.0	VF 8.0	VF/NM 9.0	NM- 9.2
1,2-Garth Ennis-s/Adriano Batista-a; four covers on each						4.00

JENNY FINN
Oni Press: June, 1999 - No. 2, Sept, 1999 ($2.95, B&W, unfinished lim. series)

	GD 2.0	VG 4.0	FN 6.0	VF 8.0	VF/NM 9.0	NM- 9.2
1,2-Mignola & Nixey-s/Nixey-a/Mignola-c						3.00
...: Doom (Atomeka, 2005, $6.99, TPB) r/#1 & 2 with new supplemental material						7.00

JENNY SPARKS: THE SECRET HISTORY OF THE AUTHORITY
DC Comics (WildStorm): Aug, 2000 - No. 5, Mar, 2001 ($2.50, limited series)

	GD 2.0	VG 4.0	FN 6.0	VF 8.0	VF/NM 9.0	NM- 9.2
1-Millar-s/McCrea & Hodgkins-a/Hitch & Neary-c						3.50
1-Variant-c by McCrea	1	3	4	6	8	10
2-5: 2-Apollo & Midnighter. 3-Jack Hawksmoor. 4-Shen. 5-Engineer						3.00
TPB (2001, $14.95) r/#1-5; Ellis intro.						15.00

JERICHO (Based on the TV series)
Devil's Due Publishing/IDW Publishing: Oct, 2009 - Present ($3.99)

	GD 2.0	VG 4.0	FN 6.0	VF 8.0	VF/NM 9.0	NM- 9.2
... Redux (IDW, 2/11, $7.99) r/Season 3: Civil War #1-3						8.00
... Season 3: Civil War 1-4: 1-Story by the show's writing staff						4.00

JERRY DRUMMER (Formerly Soldier & Marine V2#9)
Charlton Comics: V2#10, Apr, 1957 - V3#12, Oct, 1957

	GD 2.0	VG 4.0	FN 6.0	VF 8.0	VF/NM 9.0	NM- 9.2
V2#10, V3#11,12: 11-Whitman-c/a	6	12	18	29	36	42

JERRY IGER'S... (All titles, Blackthorne/First)(Value: cover or less)

JERRY LEWIS (See The Adventures of...)

JERSEY GODS
Image Comics: Feb, 2009 - No. 12, May, 2010 ($3.50)

	GD 2.0	VG 4.0	FN 6.0	VF 8.0	VF/NM 9.0	NM- 9.2
1-11: 1-Brunswick-s/McDaid-a; two covers by McDaid and Allred						3.50
12-($4.99) Wraparound cover swipe of Superman #252 by Allred						5.00

JESSE JAMES (The True Story Of..., also seeThe Legend of...)
Dell Publishing Co.: No. 757, Dec, 1956 (one shot)

	GD 2.0	VG 4.0	FN 6.0	VF 8.0	VF/NM 9.0	NM- 9.2
Four Color 757-Movie, photo-c	8	16	24	58	97	135

JESSE JAMES (See Badmen of the West & Blazing Sixguns)
Avon Periodicals: 8/50 - No. 9, 11/52; No. 15, 10/53 - No. 29, 8-9/56

	GD 2.0	VG 4.0	FN 6.0	VF 8.0	VF/NM 9.0	NM- 9.2
1-Kubert Alabam-r/Cowpuncher #1	17	34	51	98	154	210
2-Kubert-a(3)	14	28	42	80	115	150
3-Kubert Alabam-r/Cowpuncher #2	14	28	42	76	108	140
4,9-No Kubert	8	16	24	44	57	70
5,6-Kubert Jesse James-a(3); 5-Wood-a(1pg.)	14	28	42	76	108	140
7-Kubert Jesse James-a(2)	12	24	36	67	94	120
8-Kinstler-a(3)	9	18	27	50	65	80
15-Kinstler-r/#3	8	16	24	40	50	60
16-Kinstler-r/#3 & story-r/Butch Cassidy #1	8	16	24	42	54	65
17-19,21: 17-Jesse James-r/#4; Kinstler-c idea from Kubert splash in #6. 18-Kubert Jesse James-r/#5. 19-Kubert Jesse James-r/#6. 21-Two Jesse James-r/#4, Kinstler-r/#4	7	14	21	37	46	55
20-Williamson/Frazetta-a; r/Chief Vic. Apache Massacre; Kubert Jesse James-r/#6; Kit West story by Larsen	14	28	42	80	115	150
22-29: 22,23-No Kubert. 24-New McCarty strip by Kinstler; Kinstler-r. 25-New McCarty Jesse James strip by Kinstler; Jesse James-r/#7,9. 26,27-New McCarty Jesse James strip plus a Kinstler/McCann Jesse James-r. 28-Reprints most of Red Mountain, Featuring Quantrells Raiders	7	14	21	37	46	55
Annual nn (1952; 25¢, 100 pgs.)- "...Brings Six-Gun Justice to the West"- 3 earlier issues rebound; Kubert, Kinstler-a(3)	29	58	87	170	278	385

NOTE: *Mostly reprints #10 on.* ***Fawcette*** *c-1, 2.* ***Kida*** *a-5.* ***Kinstler*** *a-3, 4, 7-9, 15r, 16r(2), 21-27; c-3, 4, 9, 17-27. Painted c-5-8. 22 has 2 stories r/Sheriff Bob Dixon's Chuck Wagon #1 with name changed to Sheriff Bob Trent.*

JESSE JAMES
Realistic Publications: July, 1953

	GD 2.0	VG 4.0	FN 6.0	VF 8.0	VF/NM 9.0	NM- 9.2
nn-Reprints Avon's #1; same-c, colors different	9	18	27	52	69	85

JEST (Formerly Snap; becomes Kayo #12)
Harry 'A' Chesler: No. 10, 1944; No. 11, 1944

	GD 2.0	VG 4.0	FN 6.0	VF 8.0	VF/NM 9.0	NM- 9.2
10-Johnny Rebel & Yankee Boy app. in text	17	34	51	100	158	215
11-Little Nemo in Adventure Land	17	34	51	100	158	215

JESTER
Harry 'A' Chesler: No. 10, 1945

	GD 2.0	VG 4.0	FN 6.0	VF 8.0	VF/NM 9.0	NM- 9.2
10	15	30	45	88	137	185

JESUS
Spire Christian Comics (Fleming H. Revell Co.): 1979 (49¢)

	GD 2.0	VG 4.0	FN 6.0	VF 8.0	VF/NM 9.0	NM- 9.2
nn	2	4	6	10	14	18

JET (See Jet Powers)

JET (Crimson from Wildcore & Backlash)
DC Comics (WildStorm): Nov, 2000 - No. 4, Feb, 2001 ($2.50, limited series)

	GD 2.0	VG 4.0	FN 6.0	VF 8.0	VF/NM 9.0	NM- 9.2
1-4-Nguyen-a/Abnett & Lanning-s						3.00

JET ACES
Fiction House Magazines: 1952 - No. 4, 1953

	GD 2.0	VG 4.0	FN 6.0	VF 8.0	VF/NM 9.0	NM- 9.2
1- Sky Advs. of American War Aces (on sale 6/20/52)	16	32	48	94	147	200
2-4	11	22	33	60	83	105

JETCAT CLUBHOUSE (Also see Land of Nod, The)
Oni Press: Apr, 2001 - No. 3, Aug, 2001 ($3.25)

	GD 2.0	VG 4.0	FN 6.0	VF 8.0	VF/NM 9.0	NM- 9.2
1-3-Jay Stephens-s/a. 1-Wraparound-c						3.25
TPB (8/02, $10.95, 8 3/4" x 5 3/4") r/#1-3 & stories from Nickelodeon mag. & other						11.00

JET DREAM (...and Her Stunt-Girl Counterspies)(See The Man from Uncle #7)
Gold Key: June, 1968 (12¢)

	GD 2.0	VG 4.0	FN 6.0	VF 8.0	VF/NM 9.0	NM- 9.2
1-Painted-c	4	8	12	22	34	45

JET FIGHTERS (Korean War)
Standard Magazines: No. 5, Nov, 1952 - No. 7, Mar, 1953

	GD 2.0	VG 4.0	FN 6.0	VF 8.0	VF/NM 9.0	NM- 9.2
5,7-Toth-a. 5-Toth-c	12	24	36	69	97	125
6-Celardo-a	8	16	24	44	57	70

JET POWER
I.W. Enterprises: 1963

	GD 2.0	VG 4.0	FN 6.0	VF 8.0	VF/NM 9.0	NM- 9.2
I.W. Reprint 1,2-r/Jet Powers #1,2	3	6	9	17	25	32

JET POWERS (American Air Forces No. 5 on)
Magazine Enterprises: 1950 - No. 4, 1951

	GD 2.0	VG 4.0	FN 6.0	VF 8.0	VF/NM 9.0	NM- 9.2
1(A-1 #30)-Powell-c/a begins	38	76	114	226	368	510
2(A-1 #32) Classic Powell dinosaur-c/a	38	76	114	226	368	510
3(A-1 #35)-Williamson/Evans-a	40	80	120	244	407	570
4(A-1 #38)-Williamson/Wood-a; "The Rain of Sleep" drug story	40	80	120	244	407	570

JET PUP (See 3-D Features)

JETSONS, THE (TV) (See March of Comics #276, 330, 348 & Spotlight #3)
Gold Key: Jan, 1963 - No. 36, Oct, 1970 (Hanna-Barbera)

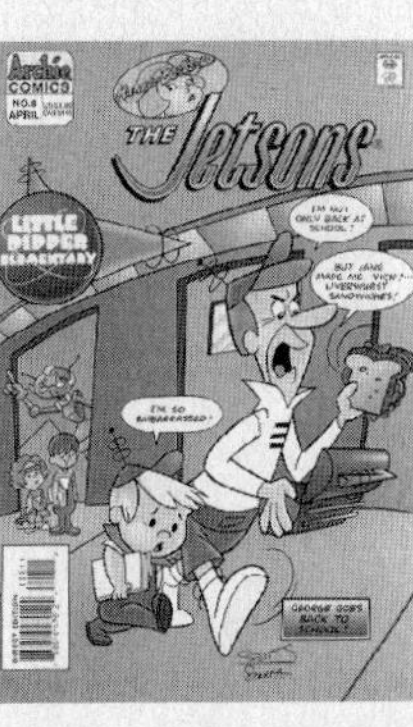

The Jetsons (1995 series) #8 © H-B

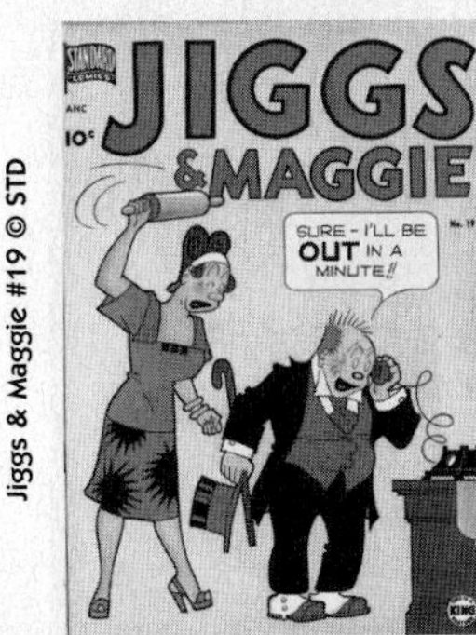

Jiggs & Maggie #19 © STD

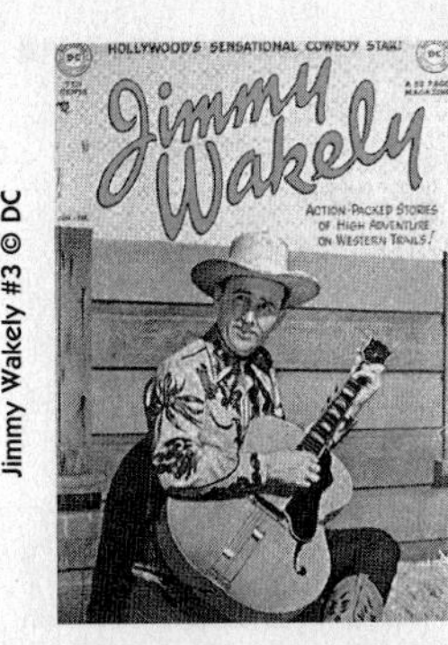

Jimmy Wakely #3 © DC

	GD 2.0	VG 4.0	FN 6.0	VF 8.0	VF/NM 9.0	NM- 9.2
1-1st comic book app.	21	42	63	150	300	450
2	11	22	33	77	144	210
3-10	9	18	27	60	100	140
11-22	7	14	21	47	76	105
23-36-Reprints	4	8	12	28	44	60

JETSONS, THE (TV) (Also see Golden Comics Digest)
Charlton Comics: Nov, 1970 - No. 20, Dec, 1973 (Hanna-Barbera)

	GD	VG	FN	VF	VF/NM	NM-
1	8	16	24	56	93	130
2	5	10	15	30	48	65
3-10	3	6	9	21	32	42
11-20	3	6	9	17	25	32
nn (1973, digest, 60¢, 100 pgs.) B&W one page gags	4	8	12	24	37	50

JETSONS, THE (TV)
Harvey Comics: V2#1, Sept, 1992 - No. 5, Nov, 1993 ($1.25/$1.50) (Hanna-Barbera)

	NM-
V2#1-5	5.00
...Big Book V2#1,2,3 ($1.95, 52 pgs.): 1-(11/92). 2-(4/93). 3-(7/93)	5.00
...Giant Size 1,2,3 ($2.25, 68 pgs): 1-(10/92). 2-(4/93). 3-(10/93)	5.00

JETSONS, THE (TV)
Archie Comics: Sept, 1995 - No. 8, Apr, 1996 ($1.50)

	NM-
1-8	3.00

JETTA OF THE 21ST CENTURY
Standard Comics: No. 5, Dec, 1952 - No. 7, Apr, 1953 (Teen-age Archie type)

	GD	VG	FN	VF	VF/NM	NM-
5-Dan DeCarlo-a	23	46	69	136	223	310
6,7: 6-Robot-c	15	30	45	84	127	170
TPB (Airwave Publ., 2006, $9.99) B&W reprint of series; Bill Morrison intro./back-c						10.00

JEZEBEL JADE (Hanna-Barbara)
Comico: Oct, 1988 - No. 3, Dec, 1988 ($2.00, mini-series)

	NM-
1-3: Johnny Quest spin-off	3.00

JEZEBELLE (See Wildstorm 2000 Annuals)
DC Comics (WildStorm): Mar, 2001 - No. 6, Aug, 2001 ($2.50, limited series)

	NM-
1-6-Ben Raab-s/Steve Ellis-a	3.00

JIGGS & MAGGIE
Dell Publishing Co.: No. 18, 1941 (one shot)

	GD	VG	FN	VF	VF/NM	NM-
Four Color 18 (#1)-(1936-38-r)	48	96	144	300	510	720

JIGGS & MAGGIE
Standard Comics/Harvey Publications No. 22 on: No. 11, 1949 (June) - No. 21, 2/53; No. 22, 4/53 - No. 27, 2-3/54

	GD	VG	FN	VF	VF/NM	NM-
11	15	30	45	86	133	180
12-15,17-21	10	20	30	58	79	100
16-Wood text illos.	11	22	33	60	83	105
22-24-Little Dot app.	10	20	30	58	79	100
25,27	10	20	30	54	72	90
26-Four pgs. partially in 3-D	14	28	42	80	115	150

NOTE: *Sunday page reprints by McManus loosely blended into story continuity. Based on Bringing Up Father strip. Advertised on covers as "All New."*

JIGSAW (Big Hero Adventures)
Harvey Publ. (Funday Funnies): Sept, 1966 - No. 2, Dec, 1966 (36 pgs.)

	GD	VG	FN	VF	VF/NM	NM-
1-Origin & 1st app.; Crandall-a (5 pgs.)	4	8	12	22	34	45
2-Man From S.R.A.M.	3	6	9	16	22	28

JIGSAW OF DOOM (See Complete Mystery No. 2)

JIM BOWIE (Formerly Danger?; Black Jack No. 20 on)
Charlton Comics: No. 16, Mar, 1956 - No. 19, Apr, 1957

	GD	VG	FN	VF	VF/NM	NM-
16	8	16	24	42	54	65
17-19: 18-Giordano-c	6	12	18	29	36	42

JIM BOWIE (TV, see Western Tales)
Dell Publishing Co.: No. 893, Mar, 1958 - No. 993, May-July, 1959

	GD	VG	FN	VF	VF/NM	NM-
Four Color 893 (#1)	6	12	18	39	62	85
Four Color 993-Photo-c	5	10	15	35	55	75

JIM BUTCHER'S THE DRESDEN FILES: FOOL MOON (Based on the Dresden Files novels)
Dynamite Entertainment: 2011 - Present ($3.99, limited series)

	NM-
1-Jim Butcher & Mark Powers-s/Chase Conley-a/Brett Booth-c	4.00

JIM BUTCHER'S THE DRESDEN FILES: STORM FRONT (Based on the Dresden Files novels)
Dabel Bros. Productions: Oct, 2008 (Nov. on-c) - No. 4, Apr, 2009 ($3.99, limited series)

	NM-
1-4-Jim Butcher & Mark Powers-s/Ardian Syaf-a; covers by Syaf & Tsai	4.00
Vol. 2: 1,2 (7/09 - No. 4)	4.00

JIM BUTCHER'S THE DRESDEN FILES: WELCOME TO THE JUNGLE
Dabel Bros. Productions: Mar, 2008 (Apr. on-c) - No. 4, Jul, 2008 ($3.99, limited series)

	NM-
1-Jim Butcher-s/Ardian Syaf-a; Ardian Syaf-c	5.00
1-Variant-c by Chris McGrath	8.00
1-New York Comic-Con 2008 variant-c	15.00
1-Second printing	4.00
2-4-Two covers on each	4.00
HC (2008, $19.95, dustjacket) r/#1-4; Butcher intro.; concept art pages	20.00

JIM DANDY
Dandy Magazine (Lev Gleason): May, 1956 - No. 3, Sept, 1956 (Charles Biro)

	GD	VG	FN	VF	VF/NM	NM-
1-Jim Dandy adventures w/Cup, an alien & his flying saucer (both invisible) from the planet Zikalug begins; ends #3. Biro-c. 1,2-Bammy Boozle app.	9	18	27	50	65	80
2,3: 2-Two pg. actual flying saucer reports	6	12	18	31	38	45

JIM HARDY (See Giant Comics Eds., Sparkler & Treasury of Comics #2 & 5)
United Features Syndicate/Spotlight Publ.: 1939; 1942; 1947 - No. 2, 1947

	GD	VG	FN	VF	VF/NM	NM-
Single Series 6 ('39)	41	82	123	256	428	600
Single Series 27('42)	36	72	108	211	343	475
1('47)-Spotlight Publ.	15	30	45	85	130	175
2	10	20	30	54	72	90

JIM HARDY
Spotlight/United Features Synd.: 1944 (25¢, 132 pgs.) (Tip Top, Sparkler-r)

	GD	VG	FN	VF	VF/NM	NM-
nn-Origin Mirror Man; Triple Terror app.	40	80	120	231	378	525

JIMINY CRICKET (Disney,, see Mickey Mouse Mag. V5#3 & Walt Disney Showcase #37)
Dell Publishing Co.: No. 701, May, 1956 - No. 989, May-July, 1959

	GD	VG	FN	VF	VF/NM	NM-
Four Color 701	8	16	24	56	93	130
Four Color 795, 897, 989	6	12	18	43	69	95

JIM LEE SKETCHBOOK
DC Comics (WildStorm): 2002 (no price, 16 pgs.)

	NM-
nn-Various DC and WildStorm character sketches by Lee	3.00

JIMMY CORRIGAN (See Acme Novelty Library)

JIMMY DURANTE (Also see A-1 Comics)
Magazine Enterprises: No. 18, 1949 - No. 20, 1949

	GD	VG	FN	VF	VF/NM	NM-
A-1 18,20-Photo-c (scarce)	47	94	141	296	498	700

JIMMY OLSEN (See Superman's Pal...)

JIMMY OLSEN: ADVENTURES BY JACK KIRBY
DC Comics: 2003, 2004 ($19.95, TPB)

	NM-
nn-(2003) Reprints Jack Kirby's early issues of Superman's Pal Jimmy Olsen #133-139,141; Mark Evanier intro.; cover by Kirby and Steve Rude	20.00
Vol. 2 (2004) Reprints #142-148; Evanier intro.; cover gallery and sketch pages	20.00

JIMMY WAKELY (Cowboy movie star)
National Per. Publ.: Sept-Oct, 1949 - No. 18, July-Aug, 1952 (1-13: 52pgs.)

	GD	VG	FN	VF	VF/NM	NM-
1-Photo-c, 52 pgs. begin; Alex Toth-a; Kit Colby Girl Sheriff begins	58	116	174	371	636	900
2-Toth-a	24	48	72	142	234	325
3,4,6,7-Frazettà-a in all, 3 pgs. each; Toth-a in all. 7-Last photo-c. 4-Kurtzman "Pot-Shot Pete", 1 pg; Toth-a	30	60	90	177	289	400
5,8-15-Toth-a; 12,14-Kubert-a (3 & 2 pgs.)	20	40	60	114	182	250
16-18	17	34	51	98	154	210

NOTE: *Gil Kane c-10-18p.*

JIM RAY'S AVIATION SKETCH BOOK
Vital Publishers: Mar-Apr, 1946 - No. 2, May-June, 1946 (15¢)

	GD	VG	FN	VF	VF/NM	NM-
1-Picture stories of planes and pilots	39	78	117	231	378	525
2-Story of General "Nap" Arnold	25	50	75	147	241	335

JIM SOLAR (See Wisco/Klarer in the Promotional Comics section)

JINGLE BELLE (Paul Dini's...)
Oni Press/Top Cow: Nov, 1999 - No. 2, Dec, 1999 ($2.95, B&W, limited series)

	NM-
1,2-Paul Dini-s. 2-Alex Ross flip-c	3.00
Jingle Belle: Dash Away All (12/03, $11.95, digest-size) Dini-s/Garibaldi-a	12.00
Jingle Belle: Santa Claus vs. Frankenstein (Top Cow, 12/08, $2.99) Dini-s/Gladden-a	3.00
Jingle Belle's Cool Yule (11/02, $13.95,TPB) r/All-Star Holiday Hullabaloo, The Mighty Elves, and Jubilee; internet strips and a color section w/DeStefano-a	14.00
Paul Dini's Jingle Belle Jubilee (11/01, $2.95) Dini-s; art by Rolston, DeCarlo, Morrison and Bone; pin-ups by Thompson and Aragonés	3.00
Paul Dini's Jingle Belle's All-Star Holiday Hullabaloo (11/00, $4.95) stories by various including Dini, Aragonés, Jeff Smith, Bill Morrison; Frank Cho-c	5.00

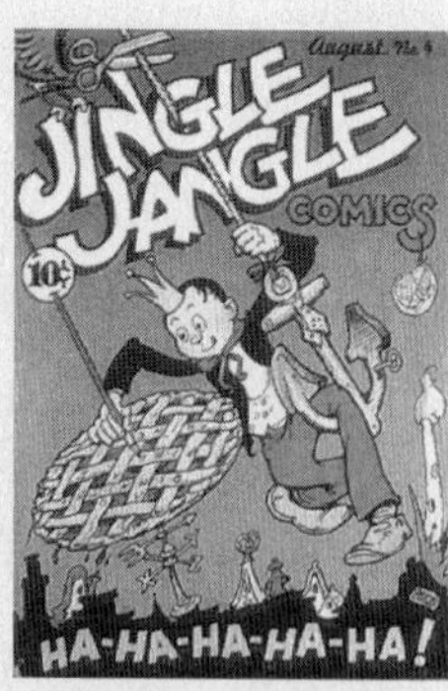

Jingle Jangle Comics #4 © EAS

Jinx #5 © Brian M. Bendis

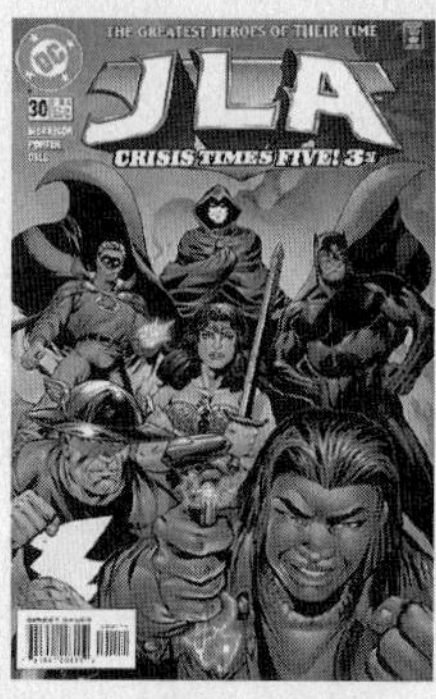

JLA #30 © DC

GD VG FN VF VF/NM NM-
2.0 4.0 6.0 8.0 9.0 9.2

Paul Dini's Jingle Belle: The Fight Before Christmas (12/05, $2.99) Dini-s/Bone & others-a 3.00
Paul Dini's Jingle Belle: The Mighty Elves (7/01, $2.95) Dini-s/Bone-a 3.00
Paul Dini's Jingle Belle Winter Wingding (11/02, $2.95) Dini-s/Clugston-Major-c 3.00
The Bakers Meet Jingle Belle (12/06, $2.99) Dini-s/Kyle Baker-a 3.00
TPB (10/00, $8.95) r/#1&2, and app. from Oni Double Feature #13 9.00

JINGLE BELLE (Paul Dini's...)
Dark Horse Comics: Nov, 2004 - No. 4, Apr, 2005 ($2.99, limited series)
1-4-Paul Dini-s/Jose Garibaldi-a 3.00
TPB (9/05, $12.95) r/#1-4 13.00

JINGLE BELLS (See March of Comics No. 65)

JINGLE DINGLE CHRISTMAS STOCKING COMICS (See Foodini #2)
Stanhall Publications: V2#1, 1951 (no date listed) (25¢, 100 pgs.; giant-size) (Publ. annually)
V2#1-Foodini & Pinhead, Silly Pilly plus games & puzzles 20 40 60 114 182 250

JINGLE JANGLE COMICS (Also see Puzzle Fun Comics)
Eastern Color Printing Co.: Feb, 1942 - No. 42, Dec, 1949
1-Pie-Face Prince of Old Pretzleburg, Jingle Jangle Tales by George Carlson, Hortense, & Benny Bear begin 44 88 132 277 469 660
2-4: 2,3-No Pie-Face Prince. 4-Pie-Face Prince-c 20 40 60 120 195 270
5 (10/42) 19 38 57 111 176 240
6-10: 8-No Pie-Face Prince 15 30 45 85 130 175
11-15 12 24 36 69 97 125
16-30: 17,18-No Pie-Face Prince. 24,30-XMas-c 10 20 30 56 76 95
31-42: 36,42-Xmas-c 9 18 27 52 69 85
NOTE: ***George Carlson** a-(2) in all except No. 2, 3, 8; c-1-6. **Carlson** 1 pg. puzzles in 9, 10, 12-15, 18, 20. **Carlson** illustrated a series of Uncle Wiggily books in 1930's.*

JING PALS
Victory Publishing Corp.: Feb, 1946 - No. 4, Aug?, 1946 (Funny animal)
1-Wishing Willie, Puggy Panda & Johnny Rabbit begin 15 30 45 86 133 180
2-4 10 20 30 54 72 90

JINKS, PIXIE, AND DIXIE (See Kite Fun Book & Whitman Comic Books)

JINX
Caliber Press: 1996 - No. 7, 1996 ($2.95, B&W, 32 pgs.)
1-7: Brian Michael Bendis-c/a/scripts. 2-Photo-c 3.00

JINX (Volume 2)
Image Comics: 1997 - No. 5, 1998 ($2.95, B&W, bi-monthly)
1-4: Brian Michael Bendis-c/a/scripts. 3.00
5-($3.95) Brereton-c 4.00
...Buried Treasures ('98, $3.95) short stories, ...Confessions ('98, $3.95) short stories, ...Pop Culture Hoo-Hah ('98, $3.95) humor shorts 4.00
TPB (1997, $10.95) r/Vol 1,#1-4 11.00
...: The Definitive Collection ('01, $24.95) remastered #1-5, sketch pages, art gallery, script excerpts, Mack intro. 25.00

JINX: TORSO
Image Comics: 1998 - No. 6, 1999 ($3.95/$4.95, B&W)
1-6-Based on Eliot Ness' pursuit of America's first serial killer; Brian Michael Bendis & Marc Andreyko-s/Bendis-a. 3-6-($4.95) 5.00
Softcover (2000, $24.95) r/#1-6; intro. by Greg Rucka; photo essay of the actual murders and police documents 25.00
Hardcover (2000, $49.95) signed & numbered 50.00

JLA (See Justice League of America and Justice Leagues)
DC Comics: Jan, 1997 - No. 125, Apr, 2006 ($1.95/$1.99/$2.25/$2.50)
1-Morrison-s/Porter & Dell-a. The Hyperclan app. 2 4 6 9 12 15
2 1 3 4 6 8 10
3,4 1 2 3 5 7 9
5-Membership drive; Tomorrow Woman app. 6.00
6-9: 8-Green Arrow joins. 6.00
10-21: 10-Rock of Ages begins. 11-Joker and Luthor-c/app. 15-($2.95) Rock of Ages concludes. 16-New members join; Prometheus app. 17,20-Jorgensen-a. 18-21-Waid-s. 20,21-Adam Strange c/app. 5.00
22-40: 22-Begin $1.99-c; Sandman (Daniel) app. 27-Amazo app. 28-31-JSA app. 35-Hal Jordan/Spectre app. 36-40-World War 3 3.00
41-($2.99) Conclusion of World War 3; last Morrison-s 4.00
42-46: 43-Waid-s; Ra's al Ghul app. 44-Begin $2.25-c. 46-Batman leaves 3.00
47-49: 47-Hitch & Neary-a begins; JLA battles Queen of Fables 3.00
50-($3.75) JLA vs. Dr. Destiny; art by Hitch & various 4.00
51-74: 52-55-Hitch-a. 59-Joker: Last Laugh. 61-68-Kelly-s/Mahnke-a. 69-73-Hunt for Aquaman; bi-monthly with alternating art by Mahnke and Guichet 3.00
75-(1/03, $3.95) leads into Aquaman (4th series) #1 4.00
76-93: 76-Firestorm app. 77-Banks-a. 79-Kanjar Ro app. 91-93-O'Neil-s/Huat-a 3.00
94-99-Byrne & Ordway-a/Claremont-s; Doom Patrol app. 3.00
100-($3.50) Intro. Vera Black; leads into Justice League Elite #1 4.00
101-114: 101-106-Austen-s/Garney-a/c. 107-114-Crime Syndicate app.; Busiek-s 3.00
115-125: 115-Begin $2.50-c; Johns & Heinberg-s;Secret Society of Super-Villains app. 3.00
#1,000,000 (11/98) 853rd Century x-over 3.00
Annual 1 (1997, $3.95) Pulp Heroes; Augustyn-s/Olivetti & Ha-a 4.00
Annual 2 (1998, $2.95) Ghosts; Wrightson-c 4.00
Annual 3 (1999, $2.95) JLApe; Art Adams-c 4.00
Annual 4 (2000, $3.50) Planet DC x-over; Steve Scott-c/a 4.00
... American Dreams (1998, $7.95, TPB) r/#5-9 8.00
...: Crisis of Conscience TPB (2006, $12.99) r/#115-119 13.00
.../ Cyberforce (DC/Top Cow, 2005, $5.99) Kelly-s/Mahnke-a/Silvestri-c 6.00
Divided We Fall (2001, $17.95, TPB) r/#47-54 18.00
...80-Page Giant 1 (7/98, $4.95) stories & art by various 6.00
...80-Page Giant 2 (11/99, $4.95) Green Arrow & Hawkman app. Hitch-c 6.00
...80-Page Giant 3 (10/00, $5.95) Pariah & Harbinger; intro. Moon Maiden 6.00
...Foreign Bodies (1999, $5.95, one-shot) Kobra app.; Semeiks-a 6.00
...Gallery (1997, $2.95) pin-ups by various; Quitely-c 3.00
...God & Monsters (2001, $6.95, one-shot) Benefiel-a/c 7.00
Golden Perfect (2003, $12.95, TPB) r/#61-65 13.00
.../ Haven: Anathema (2002, $6.95) Concludes the Haven: The Broken City series 7.00
.../ Haven: Arrival (2001, $6.95) Leads into the Haven: The Broken City series 7.00
...In Crisis Secret Files 1 (11/98, $4.95) recap of JLA in DC x-overs 5.00
...: Island of Dr. Moreau, The (2002, $6.95, one-shot) Elseworlds; Pugh-c/a; Thomas-s 7.00
.../ JSA Secret Files & Origins (1/03, $4.95) prelude to JLA/JSA: Virtue & Vice; short stories and pin-ups by various; Pacheco-c 5.00
.../ JSA: Virtue and Vice HC (2002, $24.95) Teams battle Despero & Johnny Sorrow; Goyer & Johns-s/Pacheco-a/c 25.00
.../ JSA: Virtue and Vice SC (2003, $17.95) 18.00
Justice For All (1999, $14.95, TPB) r/#24-33 15.00
New World Order (1997, $5.95, TPB) r/#1-4 6.00
...: Obsidian Age Book One, The (2003, $12.95) r/#66-71 13.00
...: Obsidian Age Book Two, The (2003, $12.95) r/#72-76 13.00
One Million (2004, $19.95, TPB) r/#DC One Million #1-4 and other #1,000,000 x-overs 20.00
...: Our Worlds at War (9/01, $2.95) Jae Lee-c; Aquaman presumed dead 3.00
...: Pain of the Gods (2005, $12.99) r/#101-106 13.00
...Primeval (1999, $5.95, one-shot) Abnett & Lanning-s/Olivetti-a 6.00
...: Riddle of the Beast HC (2001, $24.95) Grant-s/painted-a by various; Sweet-c 25.00
...: Riddle of the Beast SC (2003, $14.95) Grant-s/painted-a by various; Kaluta-c 15.00
Rock of Ages (1998, $9.95, TPB) r/#10-15 10.00
Rules of Engagement (2004, $12.95, TPB) r/#77-82 13.00
...: Seven Caskets (2000, $5.95, one-shot) Brereton-s/painted-c/a 6.00
...: Shogun of Steel (2002, $6.95, one-shot) Elseworlds; Justiniano-c/a 7.00
...Showcase 80-Page Giant (2/00, $4.95) Hitch-c 5.00
Strength in Numbers (1998, $12.95, TPB) r/#16-23, Secret Files #2 and Prometheus #1 13.00
...Superpower (1999, $5.95, one-shot) Arcudi-s/Eaton-a; Mark Antaeus joins 6.00
Syndicate Rules (2005, $17.99, TPB) r/#107-114, Secret Files #4 18.00
Terror Incognita (2002, $12.95, TPB) r/#55-60 13.00
...: The Deluxe Edition Vol. 1 HC (2008, $29.99, dustjacket) oversized r/#1-9 and JLA Secret Files #1 30.00
...: The Deluxe Edition Vol. 2 HC (2009, $29.99, dustjacket) oversized r/#10-17, JLA/Wildcats, and Prometheus #1 30.00
...: The Deluxe Edition Vol. 3 HC (2010, $29.99, dustjacket) oversized r/#22-26, 28-31 & #1,000,000 30.00
...: The Deluxe Edition Vol. 4 HC (2010, $34.99, dustjacket) oversized r/#34, 36-41, JLA Classified #1-3 and JLA: Earth 2 GN 35.00
The Tenth Circle (2004, $12.95, TPB) r/#94-99 13.00
...: The Greatest Stories Ever Told TPB (2006, $19.99) r/Justice League of America #19,71,122, 166-168,200, Justice League #1, JLA Secret Files #1 and JLA #61; Alex Ross-c 20.00
Tower of Babel (2001, $12.95, TPB) r/#42-46, Secret Files #3, 80-Page Giant #1 13.00
Trial By Fire (2004, $12.95, TPB) r/#84-89 13.00
...Vs. Predator (DC/Dark Horse, 2000, $5.95, one-shot) Nolan-c/a 6.00
...: Welcome to the Working Week (2003, $6.95, one-shot) Patton Oswalt-s 7.00
...: World War III (2000, $12.95, TPB) r/#34-41 13.00
...: World Without a Justice League (2006, $12.99, TPB) r/#120-125 13.00
...: Zatanna's Search (2003, $12.95, TPB) rep. Zatanna's early app. & origin; Bolland-c 13.00

JLA: ACT OF GOD
DC Comics: 2000 - No. 3, 2001 ($4.95, limited series)
1-3-Elseworlds; metahumans lose their powers; Moench-s/Dave Ross-a 5.00

JLA: AGE OF WONDER

JLA/Avengers #3 © DC/MAR

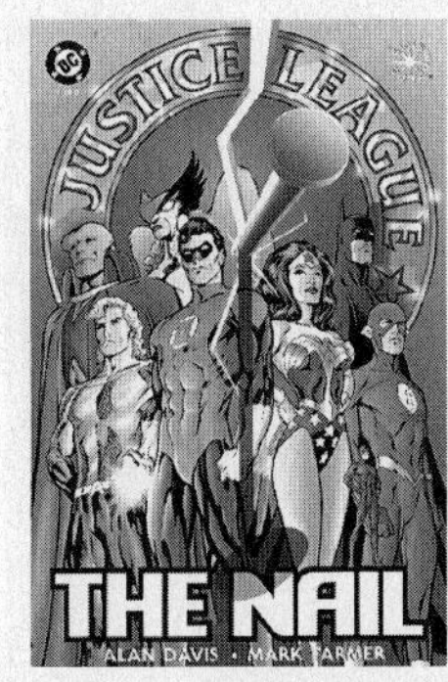

JLA: The Nail #1 © DC

Joe College #1 © HILL

GD VG FN VF VF/NM NM-
2.0 4.0 6.0 8.0 9.0 9.2

DC Comics: 2003 - No. 2, 2003 ($5.95, limited series)
1,2-Elseworlds; Superman and the League of Science during the Industrial Revolution 6.00

JLA: A LEAGUE OF ONE
DC Comics: 2000 (Graphic novel)
Hardcover ($24.95) Christopher Moeller-s/painted-a 25.00
Softcover (2002, $14.95) 15.00

JLA/AVENGERS (See Avengers/JLA for #2 & #4)
Marvel Comics: Sept, 2003; No. 3, Dec, 2003 ($5.95, limited series)
1-Busiek-s/Pérez-a; wraparound-c; Krona, Starro, Grandmaster, Terminus app. 6.00
3-Busiek-s/Pérez-a; wraparound-c; Phantom Stranger app. 6.00
SC (2008, $19.99) r/4-issue series; cover gallery; intros by Stan Lee & Julius Schwartz 20.00

JLA: BLACK BAPTISM
DC Comics: May, 2001 - No. 4, Aug, 2001 ($2.50, limited series)
1-4-Saiz-a(p)/Bradstreet-c; Zatanna app. 3.00

JLA: CLASSIFIED
DC Comics: Jan, 2005 - No. 54, May, 2008 ($2.95/$2.99)
1-3-Morrison-s/McGuinness-a/c; Ultramarines app. 3.00
4-9-"I Can't Believe It's Not The Justice League," Giffen & DeMatteis-s/Maguire-a 3.00
10-31,33-54: 10-15-New Maps of Hell; Ellis-s/Guice-a. 16-21-Garcia-Lopez-a. 22-25-Detroit League & Royal Flush Gang app.; Englehart-s. 26-28-Chaykin-s. 37-41-Kid Amazo. 50-54-Byrne-a/Middleston-c 3.00
32-($3.99) Dr. Destiny app.; Jurgens-a 4.00
I Can't Believe It's Not The Justice League TPB (2005, $12.99) r/#4-9 13.00
...: Kid Amazo TPB (2007, $12.99) r/#37-41 13.00
...: New Maps of Hell TPB (2006, $12.99) r/#10-15 13.00
...: That Was Now, This Is Then TPB (2008, $14.99) r/#50-54 15.00
...: The Hypothetical Woman TPB (2008, $12.99) r/#16-21 13.00
...: Ultramarine Corps TPB (2007, $14.99) r/#1-3, JLA/WildC.A.T.s #1 and JLA Secret Files 2004 #1 15.00

JLA CLASSIFIED: COLD STEEL
DC Comics: 2005 - No. 2, 2006 ($5.99, limited series, prestige format)
1,2-Chris Moeller-s/a; giant robot Justice League 6.00

JLA: CREATED EQUAL
DC Comics: 2000 - No. 2, 2000 ($5.95, limited series, prestige format)
1,2-Nicieza-s/Maguire-a; Elseworlds-Superman as the last man on Earth 6.00

JLA: DESTINY
DC Comics: 2002 - No. 4, 2002 ($5.95, prestige format, limited series)
1-4-Elseworlds; Arcudi-s/Mandrake-a 6.00

JLA: EARTH 2
DC Comics: 2000 (Graphic novel)
Hardcover ($24.95) Morrison-s/Quitely-a; Crime Syndicate app. 25.00
Softcover ($14.95) 15.00

JLA: GATEKEEPER
DC Comics: 2001 - No. 3, 2001 ($4.95, prestige format, limited series)
1-3-Truman-s/a 5.00

JLA: HEAVEN'S LADDER
DC Comics: 2000 ($9.95, Treasury-size one-shot)
nn-Bryan Hitch & Paul Neary-c/a; Mark Waid-s 10.00

JLA/HITMAN (Justice League/Hitman in indicia)
DC Comics: Nov, 2007 - No. 2, Dec, 2007 ($3.99, limited series)
1,2-Ennis-s/McCrea-a; Bloodlines creatures return 4.00

JLA: INCARNATIONS
DC Comics: Jul, 2001 - No. 7, Feb, 2002 ($3.50, limited series)
1-7-Ostrander-s/Semeiks-a; different eras of the Justice League 3.50

JLA: LIBERTY AND JUSTICE
DC Comics: Nov, 2003 ($9.95, Treasury-size one-shot)
nn-Alex Ross-c/a; Paul Dini-s; story of the classic Justice League 10.00

JLA PARADISE LOST
DC Comics: Jan, 1998 - No. 3, Mar, 1998 ($1.95, limited series)
1-3-Millar-s/Olivetti-a 3.00

JLA: SCARY MONSTERS
DC Comics: May, 2003 - No. 6, Oct, 2003 ($2.50, limited series)
1-6-Claremont-s/Art Adams-c 3.00

JLA SECRET FILES

GD VG FN VF VF/NM NM-
2.0 4.0 6.0 8.0 9.0 9.2

DC Comics: Sept, 1997 - 2004 ($4.95)
1-Standard Ed. w/origin-s & pin-ups 5.00
1-Collector's Ed. w/origin-s & pin-ups; cardstock-c 6.00
2,3: 2-(8/98) origin-s of JLA #16's newer members. 3-(12/00) 5.00
... 2004 (11/04) Justice League Elite app.; Mahnke & Byrne-a; Crime Syndicate app. 5.00

JLA: SECRET ORIGINS
DC Comics: Nov, 2002 ($7.95, Treasury-size one-shot)
nn-Alex Ross 2-page origins of Justice League members; text by Paul Dini 8.00

JLA: SECRET SOCIETY OF SUPER-HEROES
DC Comics: 2000 - No. 2, 2000 ($5.95, limited series, prestige format)
1,2-Elseworlds JLA; Chaykin and Tischman-s/McKone-a 6.00

JLA /SPECTRE: SOUL WAR
DC Comics: 2003 - No. 2, 2003 ($5.95, limited series, prestige format)
1,2-DeMatteis-s/Banks & Neary-a 6.00

JLA: THE NAIL (Elseworlds) (Also see Justice League of America: Another Nail)
DC Comics: Aug, 1998 - No. 3, Oct, 1998 ($4.95, prestige format)
1-3-JLA in a world without Superman; Alan Davis-s/a(p) 5.00
TPB ('98, $12.95) r/series w/new Davis-c 13.00

JLA / TITANS
DC Comics: Dec, 1998 - No. 3, Feb, 1999 ($2.95, limited series)
1-3-Grayson-s; P. Jimenez-c/a 3.00
...:The Technis Imperative ('99, $12.95, TPB) r/#1-3; Titans Secret Files 13.00

JLA: TOMORROW WOMAN (Girlfrenzy)
DC Comics: June, 1998 ($1.95, one-shot)
1-Peyer-s; story takes place during JLA #5 3.00

JLA / WILDC.A.T.S
DC Comics: 1997 ($5.95, one-shot, prestige format)
1-Morrison-s/Semeiks & Conrad-a 6.00

JLA /WITCHBLADE
DC Comics/Top Cow: 2000 ($5.95, prestige format, one-shot)
1-Pararillo-c/a 6.00

JLA / WORLD WITHOUT GROWN-UPS (See Young Justice)
DC Comics: Aug, 1998 - No. 2, Sept, 1998 ($4.95, prestige format)
1,2-JLA, Robin, Impulse & Superboy app.; Ramos & McKone-a 6.00
TPB ('98, $9.95) r/series & Young Justice: The Secret #1 10.00

JLA: YEAR ONE
DC Comics: Jan, 1998 - No. 12, Dec, 1998 ($2.95/$1.95, limited series)
1-($2.95)-Waid & Augustyn-s/Kitson-a 5.00
1-Platinum Edition 10.00
2-8-($1.95): 5-Doom Patrol-c/app. 7-Superman app. 4.00
9-12 3.00
TPB ('99,'09; $19.95/$19.99) r/#1-12; Busiek intro. 20.00

JLA-Z
DC Comics: Nov, 2003 - No. 3, Jan, 2004 ($2.50, limited series)
1-3-Pin-ups and info on current and former JLA members and villains; art by various 3.00

JLX
DC Comics (Amalgam): Apr, 1996 ($1.95, one-shot)
1-Mark Waid scripts 3.00

JLX UNLEASHED
DC Comics (Amalgam): June, 1997 ($1.95, one-shot)
1-Priest-s/ Oscar Jimenez & Rodriquez/a 3.00

JOAN OF ARC (Also see A-1 Comics & Ideal a Classical Comic)
Magazine Enterprises: No. 21, 1949 (one shot)
A-1 21-Movie adaptation; Ingrid Bergman photo-covers & interior photos; Whitney-a 29 58 87 170 278 385

JOE COLLEGE
Hillman Periodicals: Fall, 1949 - No. 2, Wint, 1950 (Teen-age humor, 52 pgs.)
1-Powell-a; Briefer-a 12 24 36 69 97 125
2-Powell-a 10 20 30 54 72 90

JOE JINKS
United Features Syndicate: No. 12, 1939
Single Series 12 31 62 93 182 296 410

JOE LOUIS (See Fight Comics #2, Picture News #6 & True Comics #5)

Joe Palooka #43 © HARV

Joe the Barbarian #4 © Grant Morrison & DC

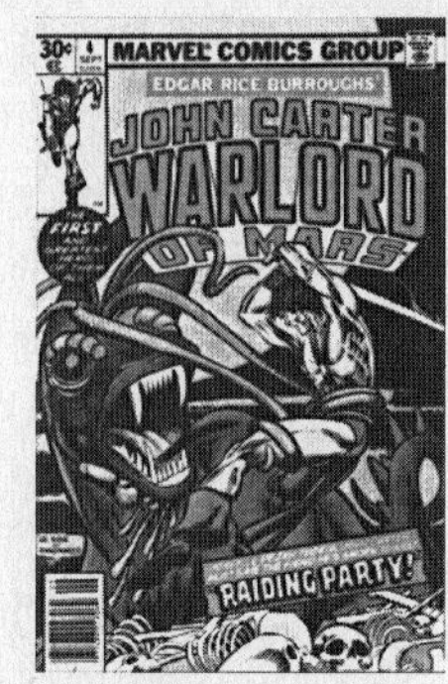

John Carter, Warlord of Mars #4 © ERB

GD 2.0 | VG 4.0 | FN 6.0 | VF 8.0 | VF/NM 9.0 | NM- 9.2

Fawcett Publications: Sept, 1950 - No. 2, Nov, 1950 (Photo-c) (Boxing champ) (See Dick Cole #10)

1-Photo-c; life story 55 110 165 352 601 850
2-Photo-c 39 78 117 240 395 550

JOE PALOOKA (1st Series)(Also see Big Shot Comics, Columbia Comics & Feature Funnies)
Columbia Comic Corp. (Publication Enterprises): 1942 - No. 4, 1944

1-1st to portray American president; gov't permission required
100 200 300 635 1093 1550
2 (1943)-Hitler-c 65 130 195 416 708 1000
3-Nazi Sub-c 40 80 120 246 411 575
4 34 68 102 199 325 450

JOE PALOOKA (2nd Series) (Battle Adv. #68-74; ...Advs. #75, 77-81, 83-85, 87; Champ of the Comics #76, 82, 86, 89-93) (See All-New)
Harvey Publications: Nov, 1945 - No. 118, Mar, 1961

1-By Ham Fisher 48 96 144 302 514 725
2 24 48 72 142 234 325
3,4,6,7-1st Flyin' Fool, ends #25 16 32 48 94 147 200
5-Boy Explorers by S&K (7-8/46) 21 42 63 122 199 275
8-10 14 28 42 80 115 150
11-14,16,18-20: 14-Black Cat text-s(2). 18-Powell-a.; Little Max app. 19-Freedom Train-c
11 22 33 64 90 115
15-Origin & 1st app. Humphrey (12/47); Super-heroine Atoma app. by Powell
15 30 45 90 140 190
17-Humphrey vs. Palooka-c/s; 1st app. Little Max 15 30 45 90 140 190
21-26,29,30: 22-Powell-a. 30-Nude female painting 10 20 30 56 76 95
27-Little Max app.; Howie Morenz-s 10 20 30 58 79 100
28-Babe Ruth 4 pg. sty. 10 20 30 58 79 100
31,39,51: 31-Dizzy Dean 4 pg. sty. 39-(12/49) Humphrey & Little Max begin; Sonny Baugh football-s; Sherlock Max-s. 51-Babe Ruth 2 pg. sty; Jake Lamotta 1/2 pg. sty
9 18 27 50 65 80
32-38,40-50,52-61: 35-Little Max-c/story(4 pgs.); Joe Louis 1 pg. sty. 36-Humphrey story. 41-Bing Crosby photo on-c. 44-Palooka marries Ann Howe. 50-(11/51)-Becomes Harvey Comics Hits #51 8 16 24 44 57 70
62-S&K Boy Explorers-r 9 18 27 50 65 80
63-65,73-80,100: 79-Story of 1st meeting with Ann 8 16 24 40 50 60
66,67-'Commie' torture story "Drug-Diet Horror" 11 22 33 60 83 105
68,70-72: 68,70-Joe vs. "Gooks"-c. 71-Bloody bayonets-c. 72-Tank-c
10 20 30 58 79 100
69-1st "Battle Adventures" issue; torture & bondage 11 22 33 60 83 105
81-99,101-115: 104,107-Humphrey & Little Max-s 7 14 21 37 46 55
116-S&K Boy Explorers-r (Giant, '60) 9 18 27 47 61 75
117-(84 pg. Giant) r/Commie issues #66,67; Powell-a 9 18 27 50 65 80
118-(84 pg. Giant) Jack Dempsey 2 pg. sty, Powell-a 9 18 27 47 61 75
...Visits the Lost City nn (1945)(One Shot)(50¢)-164 page continuous story strip reprint. Has biography & photo of Ham Fisher; possibly the single longest comic book story published in that era (159 pgs.?) (scarce) 194 388 582 1242 2121 3000

NOTE: *Nostrand/Powell a-73.* ***Powell*** *a-7, 8, 10, 12, 14, 17, 19, 26-45, 47-53, 70, 73 at least. Black Cat text stories #8, 12, 13, 19.*

JOE PSYCHO & MOO FROG
Goblin Studios: 1996 - No. 5, 1997 ($2.50, B&W)

1-5: 4-Two covers 3.00
...Full Color Extravagarbonzo ($2.95, color) 3.00

JOE THE BARBARIAN
DC Comics (Vertigo): Mar, 2010 - No. 8, May, 2011 ($1.00/$2.99/$3.99)

1-($1.00) Grant Morrison-s/Sean Murphy-a 3.00
2-7-($2.99) 3.00
8-($3.99) 4.00

JOE YANK (Korean War)
Standard Comics (Visual Editions): No. 5, Mar, 1952 - No. 16, 1954

5-Toth, Celardo, Tuska-a 10 20 30 54 72 90
6-Toth, Severin/Elder-a 9 18 27 52 69 85
7-Pinhead Perkins by Dan DeCarlo (in all?) 8 16 24 40 50 60
8-Toth-c 8 16 24 44 57 70
9-16: 9-Andru-c. 12-Andru-a 7 14 21 37 46 55

JOHN BOLTON'S HALLS OF HORROR
Eclipse Comics: June, 1985 - No. 2, June, 1985 ($1.75, limited series)

1,2-British-r; Bolton-c/a 3.00

JOHN BOLTON'S STRANGE WINK
Dark Horse Comics: Mar, 1998 - No. 3, May, 1998 ($2.95, B&W, limited series)

1-3-Anthology; Bolton-s/c/a 3.00

JOHN BYRNE'S NEXT MEN (See Dark Horse Presents #54)
Dark Horse Comics (Legend imprint #19 on): Jan, 1992 - No. 30, Dec, 1994 ($2.50, mature)

1-Silver foil embossed-c; Byrne-c/a/scripts in all 4.00
1-4: 1-2nd printing with gold ink logo 3.00
0-(2/92)-r/chapters 1-4 from DHP w/new Byrne-c 3.00
5-20,22-30: 7-10-MA #1-4 mini-series on flip side. 16-Origin of Mark IV. 17-Miller-c. 19-22-Faith storyline. 23-26-Power storyline. 27-30-Lies storyline Pt. 1-4 3.00
21-(12/93) 1st Hellboy; cover and Hellboy pages by Mike Mignola; Byrne other pages
4 8 12 22 34 45
...Parallel, Book 2 ($16.95)-TPB; r/#7-12 17.00
...Fame, Book 3($16.95)-TPB r/#13-18 17.00
...Faith, Book 4($14.95)-TPB r/#19-22 15.00

NOTE: *Issues 1 through 6 contain certificates redeemable for an exclusive Next Men trading card set by Byrne. Prices are for complete books.* ***Cody*** *painted c-23-26.* ***Mignola*** *a-21(part); c-21.*

JOHN BYRNE'S NEXT MEN
IDW Publishing: Dec, 2010 - No. 4, Mar, 2011 ($3.99, limited series)

1-4-John Byrne-s/a/c in all. 1-Origin retold 4.00

JOHN BYRNE'S 2112
Dark Horse Comics (Legend): Oct, 1994 ($9.95, TPB)

1-Byrne-c/a/s 10.00

JOHN CARTER OF MARS (See The Funnies & Tarzan #207)
Dell Publishing Co.: No. 375, Mar-May, 1952 - No. 488, Aug-Oct, 1953 (Edgar Rice Burroughs)

Four Color 375 (#1)-Origin; Jesse Marsh-a 25 50 75 183 367 550
Four Color 437, 488-Painted-c 14 28 42 99 200 300

JOHN CARTER OF MARS
Gold Key: Apr, 1964 - No. 3, Oct, 1964

1(10104-404)-r/4-Color #375; Jesse Marsh-a 6 12 18 41 66 90
2(407), 3(410)-r/4-Color #437 & 488; Marsh-a 4 8 12 28 44 60

JOHN CARTER OF MARS
House of Greystroke: 1970 (10-1/2x16-1/2", 72 pgs., B&W, paper-c)

1941-42 Sunday strip-r; John Coleman Burroughs-a 4 8 12 22 34 45

JOHN CARTER, WARLORD OF MARS (Also see Tarzan #207-209 and Weird Worlds)
Marvel Comics: June, 1977 - No. 28, Oct, 1979

1,18: 1-Origin. 18-Frank Miller-a(p)(1st publ. Marvel work)
2 4 6 8 10 12
1-(35¢-c variant, limited dist.) 4 8 12 22 34 45
2-5-(35¢-c variants, limited dist.) 3 6 9 18 27 35
2-17,19-28: 11-Origin Dejah Thoris 6.00
Annuals 1-3: 1(1977). 2(1978). 3(1979)-All 52 pgs. with new book-length stories 6.00
Edgar Rice Burroughs' John Carter of Mars: Weird Worlds TPB (Dark Horse Books, Jan. 2011, $14.99) r/stories from Tarzan #207-209 and Weird Worlds #1-7; Marv Wolfman intro. 15.00

NOTE: ***Austin*** *c-24i.* ***Gil Kane*** *a-1-10p; c-1p, 2p, 3, 4-9p, 10, 15p, Annual 1p.* ***Layton*** *a-17i.* ***Miller*** *c-25, 26p.* ***Nebres*** *a-2-4i, 8-16i; c(i)-6-9, 11-22, 25, Annual 1.* ***Perez*** *c-24p.* ***Simonson*** *a-15p.* ***Sutton*** *a-7i.*

JOHN CONSTANTINE - HELLBLAZER SPECIAL: PAPA MIDNITE
DC Comics (Vertigo): April, 2005 - No. 5, Aug, 2005 ($2.95/$2.99, limited series)

1-5-Origin of Papa Midnite; Akins-a/Johnson-s 3.00

JOHN F. KENNEDY, CHAMPION OF FREEDOM
Worden & Childs: 1964 (no month) (25¢)

nn-Photo-c 8 16 24 52 86 120

JOHN F. KENNEDY LIFE STORY
Dell Publishing Co.: Aug-Oct, 1964; Nov, 1965; June, 1966 (12¢)

12-378-410-Photo-c 7 14 21 47 76 105
12-378-511 (reprint, 11/65) 4 8 12 22 34 45
12-378-606 (reprint, 6/66) 3 6 9 20 30 40

JOHN FORCE (See Magic Agent)

JOHN HIX SCRAP BOOK, THE
Eastern Color Printing Co. (McNaught Synd.): Late 1930's (no date) (10¢, 68 pgs., regular size)

1-Strange As It Seems (resembles Single Series books)
39 78 117 231 378 525
2-Strange As It Seems 25 50 75 147 241 335

JOHN JAKES' MULLKON EMPIRE
Tekno Comix: Sept, 1995 - No. 6, Feb, 1996 ($1.95)

1-6 3.00

JOHN LAW DETECTIVE (See Smash Comics #3)
Eclipse Comics: April, 1983 ($1.50, Baxter paper)

Johnny Hazard #6 © STD

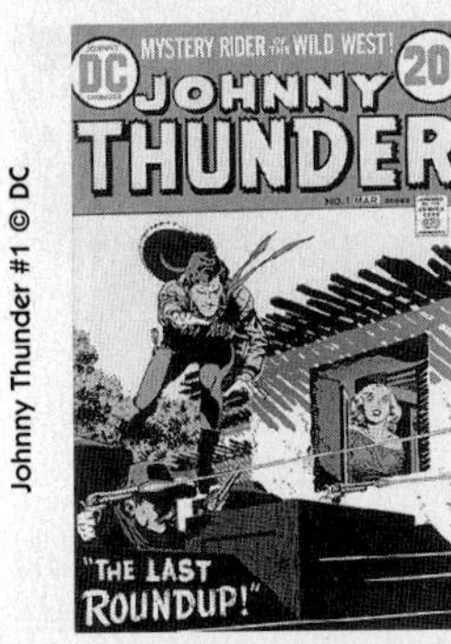

Johnny Thunder #1 © DC

The Joker #6 © DC

	GD 2.0	VG 4.0	FN 6.0	VF 8.0	VF/NM 9.0	NM- 9.2

1-Three Eisner stories originally drawn in 1948 for the never published John Law #1; original cover pencilled in 1948 & inked in 1982 by Eisner 3.00

JOHN McCAIN (See Presidential Material: John McCain)

JOHNNY APPLESEED (See Story Hour Series)

JOHNNY CASH (See Hello, I'm...)

JOHNNY DANGER (See Movie Comics, 1946)
Toby Press: 1950 (Based on movie serial)

1-Photo-c; Sparling-a 19 38 57 111 176 240

JOHNNY DANGER PRIVATE DETECTIVE
Toby Press: Aug, 1954 (Reprinted in Danger #11 by Super)

1-Photo-c; Opium den story 16 32 48 94 147 200

JOHNNY DYNAMITE (Formerly Dynamite #1-9; Foreign Intrigues #14 on)
Charlton Comics: No. 10, June, 1955 - No. 12, Oct, 1955

10-12 12 24 36 67 94 120

JOHNNY DYNAMITE
Dark Horse Comics: Sept, 1994 - Dec, 1994 ($2.95, B&W & red, limited series)

1-4: Max Allan Collins scripts in all; Terry Beatty-a 3.00
...: Underworld GN (AiT/Planet Lar, 3/03, $12.95, B&W) r/#1-4 in B&W without red 13.00

JOHNNY HAZARD
Best Books (Standard Comics) (King Features): No. 5, Aug, 1948 - No. 8, May, 1949; No. 35, date?

5-Strip reprints by Frank Robbins (c/a) 18 36 54 105 165 225
6,8-Strip reprints by Frank Robbins 15 30 45 88 137 185
7,35: 7-New art, not Robbins 12 24 36 67 94 120

JOHNNY JASON (...Teen Reporter)
Dell Publishing Co.: Feb-Apr, 1962 - No. 2, June-Aug, 1962

Four Color 1302, 2(01380-208) 4 8 12 24 37 50

JOHNNY LAW, SKY RANGER
Good Comics (Lev Gleason): Apr, 1955 - No. 3, Aug, 1955; No. 4, Nov, 1955

1-Edmond Good-c/a 10 20 30 56 76 95
2-4 7 14 21 35 43 50

JOHNNY MACK BROWN (Western star; see Western Roundup under Dell Giants)
Dell Publishing Co.: No. 269, Mar, 1950 - No. 963, Feb, 1959 (All Photo-c)

Four Color 269(#1)(3/50, 52pgs.)-Johnny Mack Brown & his horse Rebel begin; photo front/back-c begin; Marsh-a in #1-9 20 40 60 140 283 425
2(10-12/50, 52pgs.) 11 22 33 75 138 200
3(1-3/51, 52pgs.) 9 18 27 63 107 150
4-10 (9-11/52)(36pgs.), Four Color 455,493,541,584,618,645,685,722,776,834,963 7 14 21 47 76 105
Four Color 922-Manning-a 7 14 21 49 80 110

JOHNNY NEMO
Eclipse Comics: Sept, 1985 - No. 3, Feb, 1986 (Mini-series)

1-3 3.00

JOHNNY PERIL (See Comic Cavalcade #15, Danger Trail #5, Sensation Comics #107 & Sensation Mystery)

JOHNNY RINGO (TV)
Dell Publishing Co.: No. 1142, Nov-Jan, 1960/61 (one shot)

Four Color 1142-Photo-c 7 14 21 47 76 105

JOHNNY STARBOARD (See Wisco)

JOHNNY THE HOMICIDAL MANIAC (Also see Squee)
Slave Labor Graphics: Aug, 1995 - No. 7, Jan, 1997 ($2.95, B&W, lim. series)

1-Jhonen Vasquez-c/s/a 1 3 4 6 8 10
1-Signed & numbered edition 2 4 6 9 12 15
2,3: 2-(11/95). 3-(2/96) 6.00
4-7: 4-(5-96). 5-(8/96) 4.00
Hardcover-($29.95) r/#1-7 30.00
TPB-($19.95) 20.00

JOHNNY THUNDER
National Periodical Publications: Feb-Mar, 1973 - No. 3, July-Aug, 1973

1-Johnny Thunder & Nighthawk-r. in all 2 4 6 13 18 22
2,3: 2-Trigger Twins app. 2 4 6 8 11 14

NOTE: *All contain 1950s DC reprints from All-American Western.* ***Drucker*** *r-2, 3.* ***G. Kane*** *r-2, 3.* ***Moreira*** *r-1.* ***Toth*** *r-1, 3; c-1r, 3r. Also see All-American, All-Star Western, Flash Comics, Western Comics, World's Best & World's Finest.*

JOHN PAUL JONES
Dell Publishing Co.: No. 1007, July-Sept, 1959 (one-shot)

Four Color 1007-Movie, Robert Stack photo-c 5 10 15 35 55 75

JOHN ROMITA JR. 30TH ANNIVERSARY SPECIAL
Marvel Comics: 2006 ($3.99, one-shot)

nn-r/1st story in Amazing Spider-Man Annual #11; timeline, sketch pages, interviews 4.00

JOHN STEED & EMMA PEEL (See The Avengers, Gold Key series)

JOHN STEELE SECRET AGENT (Also see Freedom Agent)
Gold Key: Dec, 1964

1-Freedom Agent 6 12 18 37 59 80

JOHN WAYNE ADVENTURE COMICS (Movie star; See Big Tex, Oxydol-Dreft, Tim McCoy, & With The Marines...#1)
Toby Press: Winter, 1949-50 - No. 31, May, 1955 (Photo-c: 1-12,17,25-on)

1 (36pgs.)-Photo-c begin (1st time in comics on-c) 161 322 483 1030 1765 2500
2-4: 2-(4/50, 36pgs.)-Williamson/Frazetta-a(2) 6 & 2 pgs. (one story-r/Billy the Kid #1); photo back-c. 3-(36pgs.)-Williamson/Frazetta-a(2), 16 pgs. total; photo back-c. 4-(52pgs.)-Williamson/Frazetta-a(2), 16 pgs. total 69 138 207 442 759 1075
5 (52pgs.)-Kurtzman-a-(Alfred "L" Newman in Potshot Pete) 51 102 153 321 541 760
6 (52pgs.)-Williamson/Frazetta-a (10 pgs.); Kurtzman-a "Pot-Shot Pete", (5 pgs.); & "Genius Jones", (1 pg.) 60 120 180 381 653 925
7 (52pgs.)-Williamson/Frazetta-a (10 pgs.) 52 104 156 328 557 785
8 (36pgs.)-Williamson/Frazetta-a(2) (12 & 9 pgs.) 64 128 192 406 696 985
9-11: Photo western-c 39 78 117 230 375 520
12,14-Photo war-c. 12-Kurtzman-a(2 pg.) "Genius" 39 78 117 230 375 520
13,15: 13,15-Line-drawn-c begin, end #24 32 64 96 192 314 435
16-Williamson/Frazetta-r/Billy the Kid #1 36 72 108 211 343 475
17-Photo-c 36 72 108 211 343 475
18-Williamson/Frazetta-a (r/#4 & 8, 19 pgs.) 39 78 117 234 385 535
19-24: 23-Evans-a? 28 56 84 168 274 380
25-Photo-c resume; end #31; Williamson/Frazetta-r/Billy the Kid #3 39 78 117 234 385 535
26-28,30-Photo-c 32 64 96 192 314 435
29,31-Williamson/Frazetta-a in each (r/#4, 2) 37 74 111 222 361 500

NOTE: *Williamsonish art in later issues by* ***Gerald McCann.***

JO-JO COMICS (...Congo King #7-29; My Desire #30 on)(Also see Fantastic Fears and Jungle Jo)
Fox Feature Syndicate: 1945 - No. 29, July, 1949 (Two No.7's; no #13)

nn(1945)-Funny animal, humor 20 40 60 114 182 250
2(Sum,'46)-6(4-5/47): Funny animal. 2-Ten pg. Electro story (Fall/46) 14 28 42 80 115 150
7(7/47)-Jo-Jo, Congo King begins (1st app.); Bronze Man & Purple Tigress app. 94 188 282 597 1024 1450
7(#8) (9/47) 68 136 204 435 743 1050
8(#9) Classic Kamen mountain of skulls-c; Tanee begins 52 104 156 328 552 775
9,10(#10,11) 57 114 171 362 619 875
11,12(#12,13),14,16: 11,16-Kamen bondage-c 50 100 150 315 533 750
15,17: 15-Cited by Dr. Wertham in 5/47 Saturday Review of Literature. 17-Kamen bondage-c 52 104 156 322 549 775
18-20 50 100 150 315 533 750
21-29: 21-Hollingsworth-a(4 pgs.; 23-1 pg.) 41 82 123 249 417 585

NOTE: *Many bondage-c/a by* ***Baker/Kamen/Feldstein/Good.*** *No. 7's have Princesses Gwenna, Geesa, Yolda, & Safra before settling down on Tanee.*

JOKEBOOK COMICS DIGEST ANNUAL (...Magazine No. 5 on)
Archie Publications: Oct, 1977 - No. 13, Oct, 1983 (Digest Size)

1(10/77)-Reprints; Neal Adams-a 2 4 6 13 18 22
2(4/78)-5 2 4 6 9 12 15
6-13 1 3 4 6 8 10

JOKER
DC Comics: 2008 ($19.99, hardcover graphic novel with dustjacket)

HC-Joker is released from Arkham; Azzarello-s/Bermejo-a 20.00

JOKER, THE (See Batman #1, Batman: The Killing Joke, Brave & the Bold, Detective, Greatest Joker Stories & Justice League Annual #2)
National Periodical Publications: May, 1975 - No. 9, Sept-Oct, 1976

1-Two-Face app. 6 12 18 41 66 90
2,3: 3-The Creeper app. 4 8 12 22 34 45
4-9: 4-Green Arrow-c/sty. 6-Sherlock Holmes-c/sty. 7-Lex Luthor-c/story. 8-Scarecrow-c/story. 9-Catwoman-c/story 3 6 9 18 27 35
...: The Greatest Stories Ever Told TPB (2008, $19.99) r/Batman #1 and other apps. 20.00

JOKER, THE (See Tangent Comics/ The Joker)

Joker's Asylum: Poison Ivy #1 © DC

Jolly Jingles #12 © MLJ

Jonah Hex (2006 series) #29 © DC

GD VG FN VF VF/NM NM-
2.0 4.0 6.0 8.0 9.0 9.2

JOKER COMICS (Adventures Into Terror No. 43 on)
Timely/Marvel Comics No. 36 on (TCI/CDS): Apr, 1942 - No. 42, Aug, 1950
1-(Rare)-Powerhouse Pepper (1st app.) begins by Wolverton; Stuporman app. from Daring Comics 300 600 900 1950 3375 4800
2-Wolverton-a; 1st app. Tessie the Typist & begin series 100 200 300 635 1093 1550
3-5-Wolverton-a 55 110 165 352 601 850
6-10-Wolverton-a. 6-Tessie-c begin 43 86 129 271 456 640
11-20-Wolverton-a 40 80 120 242 401 560
21,22,24-27,29,30-Wolverton cont'd. & Kurtzman's "Hey Look" in #23-27 35 70 105 206 339 470
23-1st "Hey Look" by Kurtzman; Wolverton-a 37 74 111 222 361 500
28,32,34,37-41: 28-Millie the Model begins. 32-Hedy begins. 41-Nellie the Nurse app. 15 30 45 90 140 190
31-Last Powerhouse Pepper; not in #28 29 58 87 170 278 385
33,35,36-Kurtzman's "Hey Look" 16 32 48 94 147 200
42-Only app. 'Patty Pinup,' clone of Millie the Model 16 32 48 94 147 200

JOKER: DEVIL'S ADVOCATE
DC Comics: 1996 ($24.95/$12.95, one-shot)
nn-(Hardcover)-Dixon scripts/Nolan & Hanna-a 25.00
nn-(Softcover) 13.00

JOKER: LAST LAUGH (See Batman: The Joker's Last Laugh for TPB)
DC Comics: Dec, 2001 - No. 6, Jan, 2002 ($2.95, weekly limited series)
1-6: 1,6-Bolland-c 3.00
...Secret Files (12/01, $5.95) Short stories by various; Simonson-c 6.00

JOKER / MASK
Dark Horse Comics: May, 2000 - No. 4, Aug, 2000 ($2.95, limited series)
1-4-Batman, Harley Quinn, Poison Ivy app. 3.00

JOKER'S ASYLUM
DC Comics: Sept, 2008 ($2.99, weekly limited series of one-shots)
...: Joker - Andy Kubert-c, Sanchez-a; ...: Penguin - Pearson-c/a; ...: Poison Ivy - Guillem March-c/a; ...: Scarecrow - Juan Doe-c/a; ...: Two-Face - Andy Clarke-c/a 3.00
Batman: The Joker's Asylum TPB (2008, $14.99) r/one-shots 15.00

JOKER'S ASYLUM II
DC Comics: Aug, 2010 ($2.99, weekly limited series of one-shots)
...: Clayface - Kelley Jones-c/a; ...: Harley Quinn - Quinones-a; ...: Killer Croc - Mattina-c; Mad Hatter - Giffen & Sienkiewicz-a, Sienkiewicz-c; ...: Riddler - Van Sciver-c 3.00
Batman: The Joker's Asylum Volume 2 TPB (2011, $14.99) r/one-shots 15.00

JOLLY CHRISTMAS, A (See March of Comics No. 269)

JOLLY COMICS: **Four Star Publishing Co.:** 1947 (Advertised, not published)

JOLLY JINGLES (Formerly Jackpot Comics)
MLJ Magazines: No. 10, Sum, 1943 - No. 16, Wint, 1944/45
10-Super Duck begins (origin & 1st app.); Woody The Woodpecker begins (not same as Lantz character) 40 80 120 246 411 575
11 (Fall, '43)-2nd Super Duck(see Hangman #8) 21 42 63 122 199 275
12-Hitler-c 39 78 117 240 395 550
13-16: 13-Sahle-c. 15,16-Vigoda-c 15 30 45 83 124 165

JONAH HEX (See All-Star Western, Hex and Weird Western Tales)
National Periodical Pub./DC Comics: Mar-Apr, 1977 - No. 92, Aug, 1985
1 12 24 36 82 154 225
2 7 14 21 45 73 100
3,4,9: 9-Wrightson-c. 6 12 18 37 59 80
5,6,10: 5-Rep 1st app. from All-Star Western #10 5 10 15 32 51 70
7,8-Explains Hex's face disfigurement (origin) 6 12 18 41 66 90
11-20: 12-Starlin-c 3 6 9 20 30 40
21-32: 31,32-Origin retold 2 4 6 13 18 22
33-50 2 4 6 8 11 14
51-80 1 2 3 5 7 9
81-91: 89-Mark Texeira-a. 91-Cover swipe from Superman #243 (hugging a mystery woman) 2 4 6 8 10 12
92-Story cont'd in Hex #1 3 6 9 20 30 40
*NOTE: **Ayers** a(p)-35-37, 40, 41, 44-53, 56, 58-82. **Buckler** a-11; c-11, 13-16. **Kubert** c-43-46. **Morrow** a-90-92; c-10. **Spiegle(Tothish)** a-34, 38, 40, 49, 52. **Texeira** a-89p. Batlash back-ups in 49, 52. El Diablo back-ups in 48, 56-60, 73-75. Scalphunter back-ups in 40, 41, 45-47.*

JONAH HEX
DC Comics: Jan, 2006 - Present ($2.99)
1-Justin Gray & Jimmy Palmiotti-s/Luke Ross-a/Quitely-c 5.00
1-Special Edition (7/10, $1.00) r/#1 with "What's Next?" logo on cover 1.00

GD VG FN VF VF/NM NM-
2.0 4.0 6.0 8.0 9.0 9.2

2-49,51-65: 3-Bat Lash app. 10,16,17,19,20,22-Noto-a. 11-El Diablo app.; Beck-a. 13-15-Origin retold. 21,23,27,30,32,37,38,42,52,54,57,59,61,63-Bernet-a. 33-Darwyn Cooke-a/c. 34-Sparacio-a. 51-Giordano-c. 53-Tucci-c/a. 62-Risso-a 3.00
50-($3.99) Darwyn Cooke-a/c 4.00
...: Bullets Don't Lie TPB (2009, $14.99) r/#31-36 15.00
...: Counting Corpses TPB (2010, $14.99) r/#43,50-54 15.00
...: Face Full of Violence TPB (2006, $12.99) r/#1-6 13.00
...: Guns of Vengeance TPB (2007, $12.99) r/#7-12 13.00
...: Lead Poisoning TPB (2009, $14.99) r/#37-42 15.00
...: Luck Runs Out TPB (2008, $12.99) r/#25-30 13.00
...: No Way Back HC (2010, $19.99) new GN; Gray & Palmiotti-s/DeZuniga-a 20.00
...: Only the Good Die Young TPB (2008, $12.99) r/#19-24 13.00
...: Origins TPB (2007, $12.99) r/#13-18 13.00
...: The Six Gun War TPB (2010, $14.99) r/#44-49 15.00
...: Welcome to Paradise TPB (2010, $17.99) r/debut in All-Star Western #10 plus early apps. in Weird Western Tales and Jonah Hex #2,4 (1977 series) 18.00

JONAH HEX AND OTHER WESTERN TALES (Blue Ribbon Digest)
DC Comics: Sept-Oct, 1979 - No. 3, Jan-Feb, 1980 (100 pgs.)
1-3: 1-Origin Scalphunter-r, Ayers/Evans, Neal Adams-a.; painted-c. 2-Weird Western Tales-r; Neal Adams, Toth, Aragones-a. 3-Outlaw-r, Scalphunter-r; Gil Kane, Wildey-a 2 4 6 11 16 20

JONAH HEX: RIDERS OF THE WORM AND SUCH
DC Comics (Vertigo): Mar, 1995 - No. 5, July, 1995 ($2.95, limited series)
1-5-Lansdale story, Truman -a 4.00

JONAH HEX: SHADOWS WEST
DC Comics (Vertigo): Feb, 1999 - No. 3, Apr, 1999 ($2.95, limited series)
1-3-Lansdale-s/Truman -a 4.00

JONAH HEX SPECTACULAR (See DC Special Series No. 16)

JONAH HEX: TWO-GUN MOJO
DC Comics (Vertigo): Aug, 1993 - No. 5, Dec, 1993 ($2.95, limited series)
1-Lansdale scripts in all; Truman/Glanzman-a in all w/Truman-c 6.00
1-Platinum edition with no price on cover 20.00
2-5 4.00
TPB-(1994, $12.95) r/#1-5 13.00

JONESY (Formerly Crack Western)
Comic Favorite/Quality Comics Group: No. 85, Aug, 1953; No. 2, Oct, 1953 - No. 8, Oct, 1954
85(#1)-Teen-age humor 8 16 24 44 57 70
2 6 12 18 27 33 38
3-8 5 10 15 23 28 32

JON JUAN (Also see Great Lover Romances)
Toby Press: Spring, 1950
1-All Schomburg-a (signed Al Reid on-c); written by Siegel; used in **SOTI**, pg. 38 (Scarce) 64 128 192 406 696 985

JONNI THUNDER (...A.K.A. Thunderbolt)
DC Comics: Feb, 1985 - No. 4, Aug, 1985 (75¢, limited series)
1-4: 1-Origin & 1st app. 3.00

JONNY DOUBLE
DC Comics (Vertigo): Sept, 1998 - No. 4, Dec, 1998 ($2.95, limited series)
1-4-Azzarello-s 3.00
TPB (2002, $12.95) r/#1-4; Chiarello-c 13.00

JONNY QUEST (TV)
Gold Key: Dec, 1964 (Hanna-Barbera)
1 (10139-412) 29 58 87 223 449 675

JONNY QUEST (TV)
Comico: June 1986 - No. 31, Dec, 1988 ($1.50/$1.75)(Hanna-Barbera)
1 5.00
2,3,5: 3,5-Dave Stevens-c 4.00
4,6-31: 30-Adapts TV episode 3.00
Special 1(9/88, $1.75), 2(10/88, $1.75) 4.00
*NOTE: **M. Anderson** a-9. **Mooney** a-Special 1. **Pini** a-2. **Quagmire** a-31p. **Rude** a-1; c-2i. **Sienkiewicz** c-11. **Spiegle** a-7, 12, 21; c-21 **Staton** a-2i, 11p. **Steacy** c-8. **Stevens** a-4i; c-3,5. **Wildey** a-1, c-1, 7, 12. **Williamson** a-4i; c-4i.*

JONNY QUEST CLASSICS (TV)
Comico: May, 1987 - No. 3, July, 1987 ($2.00) (Hanna-Barbera)
1-3: Wildey-c/a; 3-Based on TV episode 3.00

JON SABLE, FREELANCE (Also see Mike Grell's Sable & Sable)

Journey Into Fear #20 © SUPR

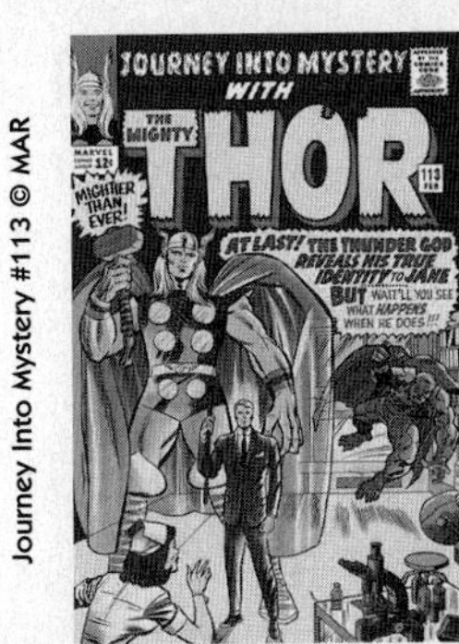

Journey Into Mystery #113 © MAR

Journey Into Mystery #622 © MAR

GD VG FN VF VF/NM NM-
2.0 4.0 6.0 8.0 9.0 9.2

First Comics: 6/83 - No. 56, 2/88 (#1-17, $1; #18-33, $1.25, #34-on, $1.75)
1-Mike Grell-c/a/scripts 4.00
2-56: 3-5-Origin, parts 1-3. 6-Origin, part 4. 11-1st app. of Maggie the Cat. 14-Mando paper begins. 16-Maggie the Cat. app. 25-30-Shatter app. 34-Deluxe format begins ($1.75) 3.00
The Complete Jon Sable, Freelance: Vol. 1 (IDW, 2005, $19.99) r/#1-6 20.00
The Complete Jon Sable, Freelance: Vol. 2 (IDW, 2005, $19.99) r/#7-11 20.00
The Complete Jon Sable, Freelance: Vol. 3 (IDW, 2005, $19.99) r/#12-16 20.00
The Complete Jon Sable, Freelance: Vol. 4 (IDW, 2005, $19.99) r/#17-21 20.00
NOTE: *Aragones a-33; c-33(part).* ***Grell*** *a-1-43;c-1-52, 53p, 54-56.*

JON SABLE, FREELANCE
IDW Publ.: (Limited series)
...: Ashes of Eden 1-5 (2009 - No. 5, 2/10, $3.99) Mike Grell-c/a/scripts 4.00
...: Bloodtrail 1-6 (4/05 - No. 6, 11/05, $3.99) Mike Grell-c/a/scripts 4.00
...: Bloodtrail TPB (4/06, $19.99) r/#1-6; cover gallery 20.00

JOSEPH & HIS BRETHREN (See The Living Bible)

JOSIE (She's... #1-16) (...& the Pussycats #45 on) (See Archie's Pals 'n' Gals #23 for 1st app.) (Also see Archie Giant Series Magazine #528, 540, 551, 562, 571, 584, 597, 610, 622)
Archie Publ./Radio Comics: Feb, 1963; No. 2, Aug, 1963 - No. 106, Oct, 1982
1 14 28 42 99 200 300
2 9 18 27 63 107 150
3-5 7 14 21 47 76 105
6-10: 6-(5/64) Book length Haunted Mansion-c/s. 7-(8/64) 1st app. Alexandra Cabot? 5 10 15 32 51 70
11-20 4 8 12 24 37 50
21, 23-30 3 6 9 19 29 38
22 (9/66)-Mighty Man & Mighty (Josie Girl) app. 4 8 12 26 41 55
31-44 3 6 9 16 23 30
45 (12/69)-Josie and the Pussycats begins (Hanna Barbera TV cartoon); 1st app. of the Pussycats 11 22 33 75 138 200
46-2nd app./1st cover Pussycats 8 16 24 54 90 125
47-3rd app. of the Pussycats 6 12 18 37 59 80
48,49-Pussycats band-c/s 6 12 18 41 66 90
50-J&P-c; go to Hollywood, meet Hanna & Barbera 7 14 21 47 76 105
51-54 3 6 9 19 29 38
55-74 (2/74)(52 pg. issues) 3 6 9 19 29 38
75-90(8/76) 2 4 6 13 18 22
91-99 2 4 6 10 14 18
100 (10/79) 2 4 6 13 18 22
101-106 2 4 6 11 16 20

JOSIE & THE PUSSYCATS (TV)
Archie Comics: 1993 - No. 2, 1994 ($2.00, 52 pgs.)(Published annually)
1,2-Bound-in pull-out poster in each. 2-(Spr/94) 5.00

JOURNAL OF CRIME (See Fox Giants)

JOURNEY
Aardvark-Vanaheim #1-14/Fantagraphics Books #15-on: 1983 - No. 14, Sept, 1984; No. 15, Apr, 1985 - No. 27, July, 1986 (B&W)
1 3.50
2-27: 20-Sam Kieth-a 3.00

JOURNEY INTO FEAR
Superior-Dynamic Publications: May, 1951 - No. 21, Sept, 1954
1-Baker-r(2) 68 136 204 435 743 1050
2 47 94 141 296 498 700
3,4 40 80 120 242 401 560
5-10,15: 15-Used in **SOTI**, pg. 389 32 64 96 188 307 425
11-14,16-21 29 58 87 170 278 385
NOTE: *Kamenish 'headlight'-a most issues.* ***Robinson*** *a-10.*

JOURNEY INTO MYSTERY (1st Series) (Thor Nos. 126-502)
Atlas(CPS No. 1-48/AMI No. 49-68/Marvel No. 69 (6/61) on): 6/52 - No. 48, 8/57; No. 49, 11/58 - No. 125, 2/66; 503, 11/96 - No. 521, June, 1998
1-Weird/horror stories begin 331 662 993 2317 4059 5800
2 113 226 339 718 1234 1750
3,4 84 168 252 538 919 1300
5-11 58 116 174 371 636 900
12-20,22: 15-Atomic explosion panel. 22-Davis*esque*-a; last pre-code issue (2/55) 47 94 141 296 498 700
21-Kubert-a; Tothish-a by Andru 47 94 141 298 504 710
23-32,35-38,40: 24-Torres?-a. 38-Ditko-a 37 74 111 218 354 490
33-Williamson-a; Ditko-a (his 1st for Atlas?) 39 78 117 231 378 525
34,39: 34-Krigstein-a. 39-1st S.A. issue; Wood-a 37 74 111 222 361 500
41-Crandall-a; Frazetta*esque*-a by Morrow 19 38 57 139 280 420
42,46,48: 42,48-Torres-a. 46-Torres & Krigstein-a 19 38 57 134 272 410
43,44-Williamson/Mayo-a in both. 43-Invisible Woman prototype 19 38 57 139 280 420
45,47 18 36 54 131 266 400
49-Matt Fox, Check-a 19 38 57 134 272 410
50,52-54: Ditko/Kirby-a. 50-Davis-a. 54-Williamson-a 22 44 66 159 317 475
51-Kirby/Wood-a 22 44 66 162 324 485
55-61,63-65,67-69,71,72,74,75: 74-Contents change to Fantasy. 75-Last 10¢ issue 22 44 66 159 317 475
62-Prototype ish. (The Hulk); 1st app. Xemnu (Titan) called "The Hulk" 30 60 90 228 457 685
66-Prototype ish. (The Hulk)-Return of Xemnu "The Hulk" 27 54 81 194 399 600
70-Prototype ish. (The Sandman)(7/61); similar to Spidey villain 26 52 78 186 376 560
73-Story titled "The Spider" where a spider is exposed to radiation & gets powers of a human and shoots webbing; a reverse prototype of Spider-Man's origin 37 74 111 295 585 875
76,77,80-82: 80-Anti-communist propaganda story 18 36 54 131 266 400
76-(10¢ cover price blacked out, 12¢ printed on) 38 76 114 304 602 900
78-The Sorceror (Dr. Strange prototype) app. (3/62) 26 52 78 190 383 575
79-Prototype issue. (Mr. Hyde) 23 46 69 168 334 500
83-Origin & 1st app. The Mighty Thor by Kirby (8/62) and begin series; Thor-c also begin 1035 2070 3105 10,350 20,175 30,000
83-Reprint from the Golden Record Comic Set 16 32 48 114 232 350
With the record (1966) 24 48 72 175 350 525
84-2nd app. Thor 204 408 612 1785 3643 5500
85-1st app. Loki & Heimdall; 1st brief app. Odin (1 panel); 1st app. Asgard 135 270 405 1150 2325 3500
86-1st full app. Odin 81 162 243 689 1395 2100
87-89: 89-Origin Thor retold 65 130 195 553 1127 1700
90-No Kirby-a 52 104 156 442 896 1350
91,92,94,96-Sinnott-a 41 82 123 324 650 975
93,97-Kirby-a; Tales of Asgard series begins #97 (origin which concludes in #99); origin/1st app. Lava Man 45 90 135 360 730 1100
95-Sinnott-a; Thor vs. Thor 45 90 135 360 730 1100
98,99-Kirby/Heck-a. 98-Origin/1st app. The Human Cobra. 99-1st app. Surtur & Mr. Hyde 35 70 105 273 537 800
100-Kirby/Heck-a; Thor battles Mr. Hyde 35 70 105 273 537 800
101,108: 101-(2/64)-2nd Avengers x-over (w/o Capt. America); see Tales Of Suspense #49 for 1st x-over. 108-(9/64)-Early Dr. Strange & Avengers x-over; ten extra pgs. Kirby-a 24 48 72 175 350 525
102,104-107,110: 102-Intro Sif. 105-109-Ten extra pgs. Kirby-a in each. 107-1st app. Grey Gargoyle. 110,111-Two part battle vs. The Human Cobra & Mr. Hyde 23 46 69 168 334 500
103-1st app. Enchantress 27 54 81 197 399 600
109-Magneto-c & app. (1st x-over, 10/64) 45 90 135 360 730 1100
111,113: 113-Origin Loki 18 36 54 131 266 400
112-Thor Vs. Hulk (1/65); Origin Loki 54 108 162 459 930 1400
114-Origin/1st app. Absorbing Man 24 48 72 175 350 525
115-Detailed origin of Loki 22 44 66 159 317 475
116,117,120-123,125 15 30 45 106 216 325
118-1st app. Destroyer 21 42 63 150 300 450
119-Intro Hogun, Fandral, Volstagg; 2nd Destroyer 16 32 48 117 239 360
124-Hercules-c/story 16 32 48 111 226 340
503-521: 503-(11/96, $1.50)-The Lost Gods begin; Tom DeFalco scripts & Deodato Studios-c/a. 505-Spider-Man-c/app. 509-Loki-c/app. 514-516-Shang-Chi 3.00
#(-1) Flashback (7/97) Tales of Asgard Donald Blake app. 3.00
Annual 1(1965, 25¢, 72 pgs.)-New Thor vs. Hercules(1st app.)-c/story (see Incredible Hulk #3); Kirby-c/a; r/#85,93,95,97 23 46 69 168 334 500
NOTE: ***Ayers*** *a-14, 39, 64i, 71i, 74i, 80i.* ***Bailey*** *a-43.* ***Briefer*** *a-5, 12.* ***Cameron*** *a-35.* ***Check*** *a-17.* ***Colan*** *a-23, 81; c-14.* ***Ditko*** *a-33, 38, 50-96; c-58, 67, 71, 88i.* ***Kirby/Ditko*** *a-50-83.* ***Everett*** *a-20, 48; c-4-7, 9, 36, 37, 39-42, 44, 45, 47.* ***Forte*** *a-19, 35, 40, 53.* ***Heath*** *a-4-6, 11, 14; c-1, 8, 11, 15, 51.* ***Heck*** *a-53, 73.* ***Kirby*** *a(p)-51, 52, 56, 57-60, 62-64, 66, 67, 69-89, 93, 97, 98, 100(w/**Heck**), 101-125; c-50-57, 59-66, 68-70, 72-82, 88(w/**Ditko**), 83 & 84(w/**Sinnott**), 85-96(w/**Ayers**), 97-125p.* ***Leiber/Fox*** *a-93, 98-102.* ***Maneely*** *c-20-22.* ***Morisi*** *a-42.* ***Morrow*** *a-41, 42.* ***Orlando*** *a-30, 45, 57.* ***Mac Pakula*** *(Tothish) a-9, 35, 41.* ***Powell*** *a-20, 27, 34.* ***Reinman*** *a-39, 87, 92, 96i.* ***Robinson*** *a-9.* ***Roussos*** *a-39.* ***Robert Sale*** *a-14.* ***Severin*** *a-27; c-30.* ***Sinnott*** *a-41; c-50.* ***Tuska*** *a-11.* ***Wildey*** *a-16.*

JOURNEY INTO MYSTERY (Series and numbering continue from Thor #621)
Marvel Comics: No. 622, Jun, 2011 - Present ($3.99)
622-Reincarnated young Loki; Thor app.; Braithwaite-a; Hans-c 4.00
622-Variant covers by Art Adams and Lee Weeks 6.00

JOURNEY INTO MYSTERY (2nd Series)
Marvel Comics: Oct, 1972 - No. 19, Oct, 1975

JSA #23 © DC

JSA: All Stars #1 © DC

Jubilee #1 © MAR

GD 2.0 VG 4.0 FN 6.0 VF 8.0 VF/NM 9.0 NM- 9.2

1-Robert Howard adaptation; Starlin/Ploog-a 4 8 12 22 34 45

2-5: 2,3,5-Bloch adapt. 4-H. P. Lovecraft adapt. 3 6 9 16 22 28

6-19: Reprints 2 4 6 13 18 22

NOTE: ***N. Adams*** *a-2i.* ***Ditko*** *r-7, 10, 12, 14, 15, 19; c-10.* ***Everett*** *r-9, 14.* ***G. Kane*** *a-1p, 2p; c-1-3p.* ***Kirby*** *r-7, 13, 15, 18, 19; c-7.* ***Mort Lawrence*** *r-2.* ***Maneely*** *r-3.* ***Orlando*** *r-16.* ***Reese*** *a-1, 2i.* ***Starlin*** *a-1p, 3p.* ***Torres*** *r-16.* ***Wildey*** *r-9, 14.*

JOURNEY INTO UNKNOWN WORLDS (Formerly Teen)
Atlas Comics (WFP): No. 36, Sept, 1950 - No. 38, Feb, 1951;
No. 4, Apr, 1951 - No. 59, Aug, 1957

36(#1)-Science fiction/weird; "End Of The Earth" c/story
265 530 795 1694 2897 4100

37(#2)-Science fiction; "When Worlds Collide" c/story; Everett-c/a; Hitler story
107 214 321 727 1189 1650

38(#3)-Science fiction 90 180 270 576 988 1400

4-6,8,10-Science fiction/weird 55 110 165 352 601 850

7-Wolverton-a "Planet of Terror", 6 pgs; electric chair c-inset/story
92 184 276 584 1005 1425

9-Giant eyeball story 71 142 213 454 777 1100

11,12-Krigstein-a 41 82 123 256 428 600

13,16,17,20 37 74 111 222 361 500

14-Wolverton-a "One of Our Graveyards Is Missing", 4 pgs; Tuska-a
68 136 204 435 743 1050

15-Wolverton-a "They Crawl by Night", 5 pgs.; 2 pg. Maneely s/f story
68 136 204 435 743 1050

18,19-Matt Fox-a 41 82 123 256 428 600

21-33: 21-Decapitation-c. 24-Sci/fic story. 26-Atom bomb panel. 27-Sid Check-a. 33-Last pre-code (2/55) 27 54 81 162 266 370

34-Kubert, Torres-a 22 44 66 128 209 290

35-Torres-a 20 40 60 117 189 260

36-45,48,50,53,55,59: 43-Krigstein-a. 44-Davis-a. 45,55,59-Williamson-a in all; with Mayo #55,59. 55-Crandall-a. 48,53-Crandall-a (4 pgs. #48). 48-Check-a. 50-Davis, Crandall-a
20 40 60 114 182 250

46,47,49,52,54,56-58: 54-Torres-a 18 36 54 105 165 225

51-Ditko, Wood-a 21 42 63 122 199 275

NOTE: ***Ayers*** *a-24, 43,* ***Berg*** *a-38(#3), 43.* ***Lou Cameron*** *a-33.* ***Colan*** *a-37(#2), 6, 17, 19, 20, 23, 39.* ***Ditko*** *a-45, 51.* ***Drucker*** *a-35, 58.* ***Everett*** *a-37(#2), 11, 14, 41, 55, 56; c-37(#2), 11, 13, 14, 17, 22, 47, 48, 50, 53-55, 59.* ***Forte*** *a-49.* ***Fox*** *a-21i.* ***Heath*** *a-36(#1), 4, 6-8, 17, 20, 22, 36i; c-18.* ***Keller*** *a-15.* ***Mort Lawrence*** *a-38, 39.* ***Maneely*** *a-7, 8, 15, 16, 22, 49, 58; c-19, 25, 52.* ***Morrow*** *a-48.* ***Orlando*** *a-44, 57.* ***Pakula*** *a-36.* ***Powell*** *a-42, 53, 54.* ***Reinman*** *a-8.* ***Rico*** *a-21.* ***Robert Sale*** *a-24, 49.* ***Sekowsky*** *a-4, 5, 9.* ***Severin*** *a-38, 51; c-38, 48i, 56.* ***Sinnott*** *a-9, 21, 24.* ***Tuska*** *a-38(#3), 14.* ***Wildey*** *a-25, 43, 44.*

JOURNEYMAN
Image Comics: Aug, 1999 - No. 3, Oct, 1999 ($2.95, B&W, limited series)

1-3-Brandon McKinney-s/a 3.00

JOURNEY TO THE CENTER OF THE EARTH (Movie)
Dell Publishing Co.: No. 1060, Nov-Jan, 1959/60 (one-shot)

Four Color 1060-Pat Boone & James Mason photo-c 10 20 30 71 128 185

JSA (Justice Society of America) (Also see All Star Comics)
DC Comics: Aug, 1999 - No. 87, Sept, 2006 ($2.50/$2.99)

1-Robinson and Goyer-s; funeral of Wesley Dodds 2 4 6 8 10 12

2-5: 4-Return of Dr. Fate 6.00

6-24: 6-Black Adam-c/app. 11,12-Kobra. 16-20-JSA vs. Johnny Sorrow. 19,20-Spectre app. 22-Hawkgirl origin. 23-Hawkman returns 4.00

25-($3.75) Hawkman rejoins the JSA 1 2 3 5 7 9

26-36, 38-49: 27-Capt. Marvel app. 29-Joker: Last Laugh. 31,32-Snejbjerg-a. 33-Ultra-Humanite. 34-Intro. new Crimson Avenger and Hourman. 42-G.A. Mr. Terrific and the Freedom Fighters app. 46-Eclipso returns 3.00

37-($3.50) Johnny Thunder merges with the Thunderbolt; origin new Crimson Avenger 4.00

50-($3.95) Wraparound-c by Pacheco; Sentinel becomes Green Lantern again 4.00

51-74,76-82: 51-Kobra killed. 54-JLA app. 55-Ma Hunkle (Red Tornado) app. 56-58-Black Reign x-over with Hawkman #23-25. 64-Sand returns. 67-Identity Crisis tie-in; Gibbons-a. 68,69,72-81-Ross-c. 73,74-Day of Vengeance tie-in. 76-OMAC tie-in. 82-Infinite Crisis x-over; Levitz-s/Perez-a 3.00

75-($2.99) Day of Vengeance tie-in; Alex Ross Spectre-c 4.00

83-87: One Year Later; Pérez-c. 83-85,87-Morales-a; Gentleman Ghost app. 85-Begin $2.99-c; Earth-2 Batman, Atom, Sandman, Mr. Terrific app. 86,87-Ordway-a. 3.00

Annual 1 (10/00, $3.50) Planet DC; intro. Nemesis 4.00

...: Black Reign TPB (2005, $12.99) r/#56-58, Hawkman #23-25; Watson cover gallery 13.00

...: Black Vengeance TPB (2006, $19.99) r/#66-75 20.00

...: Darkness Falls TPB (2002, $19.95) r/#6-15 20.00

...: Fair Play TPB (2003, $14.95) r/#26-31 & Secret Files #2 15.00

...: Ghost Stories TPB (2006, $14.99) r/#82-87 15.00

...: Justice Be Done TPB (2000, $14.95) r/Secret Files & #1-5 15.00

...: Lost TPB (2005, $19.99) r/#59-67 20.00

...: Mixed Signals TPB (2006, $14.99) r/#76-81 15.00

...: Our Worlds at War 1 (9/01, $2.95) Jae Lee-c; Saltares-a 3.00

... Presents Green Lantern TPB (2008, $14.99) r/JSA Classified #25,32,33 and Green Lantern: Brightest Day, Blackest Night 15.00

...: Princes of Darkness TPB (2005, $19.95) r/#46-55 20.00

...: Savage Times TPB (2004, $14.95) r/#39-45 15.00

... Secret Files 1 (8/99, $4.95) Origin stories and pin-ups; death of Wesley Dodds (G.A. Sandman); intro new Hawkgirl 5.00

... Secret Files 2 (9/01, $4.95) Short stories and profile pages 5.00

...: Stealing Thunder TPB (2003, $14.95) r/#32-38; JSA vs. The Ultra-Humanite 15.00

...: The Golden Age TPB (2005, $19.99) r/"The Golden Age" Elseworlds mini-series 20.00

...: The Return of Hawkman TPB (2002, $19.95) r/#16-26 & Secret Files #1 20.00

JSA: ALL STARS
DC Comics: July, 2003 - No. 8, Feb, 2004 ($2.50/$3.50, limited series, back-up stories in Golden Age style)

1-6,8-Goyer & Johns-s/Cassaday-c. 1-Velluto-a; intro. Legacy. 2-Hawkman by Loeb/Sale 3-Dr. Fate by Cooke. 4-Starman by Robinson/Harris. 5-Hourman by Chaykin. 6-Dr. Mid-nite by Azzarello/Risso 3.00

7-($3.50) Mr. Terrific back-up story by Chabon; Lark-a 4.00

TPB (2004, $14.95) r/#1-8 15.00

JSA: ALL STARS
DC Comics: Feb, 2010 - Present ($3.99/$2.99)

1-13-Younger JSA members form team. 1-Covers by Williams and Sook 4.00

14-16-($2.99) 3.00

...: Constellations TPB (2010, $14.99) r/#1-6 and sketch art 15.00

JSA: CLASSIFIED (Issues #1-4 reprinted in Power Girl TPB)
DC Comics: Sept, 2005 - No. 39, Aug, 2008 ($2.50/$2.99)

1-(1st printing) Conner-c/a; origin of Power Girl 3.00

1-(1st printing) Adam Hughes variant-c 5.00

1-(2nd & 3rd printings) 2nd-Hughes B&W sketch-c. 3rd-Close-up of Conner-c 3.00

2-11: 2-LSH app. 4-Leads into Infinite Crisis #2. 5-7-Injustice Society app. 10-13-Vandal Savage origin retold; Gulacy-a/c 3.00

12-39: 12-Begin $2.99-c. 17,18-Bane app. 19,20-Morales-a. 21,22-Simonson-s/a 3.00

...: Honor Among Thieves TPB (2007, $14.99) r/#5-9 15.00

JSA STRANGE ADVENTURES
DC Comics: Oct, 2004 - No. 6, Mar, 2005 ($3.50, limited series)

1-6-Johnny Thunder as pulp writer; Kitson-a/Watson-c/ Kevin Anderson-s 3.50

TPB (2010, $14.99) r/#1-6 15.00

JSA: THE LIBERTY FILE (Elseworlds)
DC Comics: Feb, 2000 - No. 2, Mar, 2000 ($6.95, limited series)

1,2-Batman, Dr. Mid-Nite and Hourman vs. WW2 Joker; Tony Harris-c/a 7.00

JSA: The Liberty Files TPB (2004, $19.95) r/The Liberty File and The Unholy Three series 20.00

JSA: THE UNHOLY THREE (Elseworlds)(Sequel to JSA: The Liberty File)
DC Comics: 2003 - No. 2, 2003 ($6.95, limited series)

1,2-Batman, Superman and Hourman; Tony Harris-c/a 7.00

JSA VS. KOBRA
DC Comics: Aug, 2009 - No. 6, Jan, 2010 ($2.99, limited series)

1-6-Kramer-a/Ha-c; Jason Burr app. 3.00

TPB (2010, $14.99) r/#1-6; cover gallery 15.00

J2 (Also see A-Next and Juggernaut)
Marvel Comics: Oct, 1998 - No. 12, Sept, 1999 ($1.99)

1-12:1-Juggernaut's son; Lim-a. 2-Two covers; X-People app. 3-J2 battles the Hulk 3.00

Spider-Girl Presents Juggernaut Jr. Vol.1: Secrets & Lies (2006, $7.99, digest) r/#1-6 8.00

JUBILEE (X-Men)
Marvel Comics: Nov, 2004 - No. 6, Apr, 2005 ($2.99)

1-6: 1-Jubilee in a Los Angeles high school; Kirkman-s; Casey Jones-c 3.00

JUDENHASS
Aardvark-Vanaheim Press: 2008 ($4.00, B&W, squarebound)

nn-Dave Sim-writer/artist; The Shoah and Jewish persecution through history 4.00

JUDE, THE FORGOTTEN SAINT
Catechetical Guild Education Soc.: 1954 (16 pgs.; 8x11"; full color; paper-c)

nn 6 12 18 28 34 40

J.U.D.G.E.: THE SECRET RAGE
Image Comics: Mar, 2000 - No. 3, May, 2000 ($2.95)

1-3-Greg Horn-s/c/a 3.00

JUDGE COLT

Judo Joe #1 © Jay-Jay Corp.

Jughead #241 © AP

Jughead Comics. Night at GEM © AP

	GD 2.0	VG 4.0	FN 6.0	VF 8.0	VF/NM 9.0	NM- 9.2

Gold Key: Oct, 1969 - No. 4, Sept, 1970

1	3	6	9	16	23	30
2-4	2	4	6	9	13	16

JUDGE DREDD (...Classics #62 on; also see Batman - Judge Dredd, The Law of Dredd & 2000 A.D. Monthly)
Eagle Comics/IPC Magazines Ltd./Quality Comics #34-35, V2#1-37/ Fleetway #38 on: Nov, 1983 - No. 35, 1986; V2#1, Oct, 1986 - No. 77, 1993

1-Bolland-c/a 6.00
2-35 3.00
V2#1-77: 1-('86)-New look begins. 20-Begin $1.50-c. 21/22, 23/24-Two issue numbers in one. 28-1st app. Megaman (super-hero). 39-Begin $1.75-c. 51-Begin $1.95-c. 53-Bolland-a. 57-Reprints 1st published Judge Dredd story 3.00
Special 1 3.00
NOTE: *Bolland a-1-6, 8, 10; c-1-10, 15.* ***Guice*** *c-V2#23/24, 26, 27.*

JUDGE DREDD (3rd Series)
DC Comics: Aug, 1994 - No. 18, Jan, 1996 ($1.95)

1-18: 12-Begin $2.25-c 3.00
nn ($5.95)-Movie adaptation, Sienkiewicz-c 6.00

JUDGE DREDD'S CRIME FILE
Eagle Comics: Aug, 1989 - No. 6, Feb, 1986 ($1.25, limited series)

1-6: 1-Byrne-a 3.00

JUDGE DREDD: LEGENDS OF THE LAW
DC Comics: Dec, 1994 - No. 13, Dec, 1995 ($1.95)

1-13: 1-5-Dorman-c 3.00

JUDGE DREDD: THE EARLY CASES
Eagle Comics: Feb, 1986 - No. 6, Jul, 1986 ($1.25, Mega-series, Mando paper)

1-6: 2000 A.D.-r 3.00

JUDGE DREDD: THE JUDGE CHILD QUEST (Judge Child in indicia)
Eagle Comics: Aug, 1984 - No. 5, Oct, 1984 ($1.25, Lim. series, Baxter paper)

1-5: 2000A.D.-r; Bolland-c/a 3.00

JUDGE DREDD: THE MEGAZINE
Fleetway/Quality: 1991 - Present ($4.95, stiff-c, squarebound, 52 pgs.)

1-3 5.00

JUDGE DREDD VS. ALIENS: INCUBUS
Dark Horse Comics: March, 2003 - No. 4, June, 2003 ($2.99, limited series)

1-4-Flint-a/Wagner & Diggle-s 3.00

JUDGE PARKER
Argo: Feb, 1956 - No. 2, 1956

1-Newspaper strip reprints	7	14	21	35	43	50
2	5	10	15	24	30	35

JUDGMENT DAY
Awesome Entertainment: June, 1997 - No. 3, Oct, 1997 ($2.50, limited series)

1-3: 1 Alpha-Moore-s/Liefeld-c/a(p) flashback art by various in all. 2 Omega. 3 Final Judgment. All have a variant cover by Dave Gibbons 3.00
...Aftermath-($3.50) Moore-s/Kane-a; Youngblood, Glory, New Men, Maximage, Allies and Spacehunter short stories. Also has a variant cover by Dave Gibbons 3.50
TPB (Checker Books, 2003, $16.95) r/series 17.00

JUDO JOE
Jay-Jay Corp.: Aug, 1953 - No. 3, Dec, 1953 (Judo lessons in each issue)

1-Drug ring story	11	22	33	62	86	110
2,3: 3-Hypo needle story	8	16	24	42	54	65

JUDOMASTER (Gun Master #84-89) (Also see Crisis on Infinite Earths, Sarge Steel #6 & Special War Series)
Charlton Comics: No. 89, May-June, 1966 - No. 98, Dec, 1967 (Two No. 89's)

89-3rd app. Judomaster	4	8	12	26	41	55
90-Origin of Thunderbolt	4	8	12	24	37	50
91-Sarge Steel begins	4	8	12	22	34	45
92-98: 93-Intro. Tiger	3	6	9	21	32	42
93,94,96,98 (Modern Comics reprint, 1977)						6.00

NOTE: *Morisi Thunderbolt #90. #91 has 1 pg. biography on writer/artist Frank McLaughlin.*

JUDY CANOVA (Formerly My Experience) (Stage, screen, radio)
Fox Features Syndicate: No. 23, May, 1950 - No. 3, Sept, 1950

23(#1)-Wood-c,a(p)?	24	48	72	140	230	320
24-Wood-a(p)	23	46	69	136	223	310
3-Wood-c; Wood/Orlando-a	25	50	75	150	245	340

JUDY GARLAND (See Famous Stars)

JUDY JOINS THE WAVES
Toby Press: 1951 (For U.S. Navy)

nn	7	14	21	35	43	50

JUGGERNAUT (See X-Men)
Marvel Comics: Apr, 1997, Nov, 1999 ($2.99, one-shots)

1-(4/97) Kelly-s/ Rouleau-a 3.00
1-(11/99) Casey-s; Eighth Day x-over; Thor, Iron Man, Spidey app. 3.00

JUGHEAD (Formerly Archie's Pal...)
Archie Publications: No. 127, Dec, 1965 - No. 352, June, 1987

127-130: 129-LBJ on cover	3	6	9	18	27	35
131,133,135-160(9/68)	3	6	9	16	22	28
132,134: 132-Shield-c; The Fly & Black Hood app.; Shield cameo. 134-Shield-c	4	8	12	26	41	55
161-180	2	4	6	13	18	22
181-199	2	4	6	9	13	16
200(1/'72)	2	4	6	11	16	20
201-240(5/75)	2	4	6	8	10	12
241-270(11/77)	1	2	3	5	7	9
271-299	1	2	3	4	5	7
300(5/80)-Anniversary issue; infinity-c	1	2	3	5	6	8
301-320(1/82)						5.00
321-324,326-352						4.00
325-(10/82) Cheryl Blossom app. (not on cover); same month as intro. (cover & story) in Archie's Girls, Betty & Veronica #320; Jason Blossom app.; DeCarlo-a	3	6	9	20	30	40

JUGHEAD (2nd Series)(Becomes Archie's Pal Jughead Comics #46 on)
Archie Enterprises: Aug, 1987 - No. 45, May, 1993 (.75/$1.00/$1.25)

1	1	2	3	4	5	7
2-10						4.00
11-45: 4-X-Mas issue. 17-Colan-c/a						3.00

JUGHEAD & FRIENDS DIGEST MAGAZINE
Archie Publ.: June, 2005 - No. 38, Aug, 2010 ($2.39/$2.49/$2.69, digest-size)

1-38: 1-That Wilkin Boy app. 3.00

JUGHEAD AS CAPTAIN HERO (See Archie as Pureheart the Powerful, Archie Giant Series Magazine #142 & Life With Archie)
Archie Publications: Oct, 1966 - No. 7, Nov, 1967

1-Super hero parody	8	16	24	52	86	110
2	5	10	15	30	48	65
3-7	4	8	12	26	41	55

JUGHEAD COMICS. NIGHT AT GEPPI'S ENTERTAINMENT MUSEUM
Archie Comic Publ. Inc: 2008

Free Comic Book Day giveaway - New story; Archie gang visits GEM; Steve Geppi app. 2.50

JUGHEAD JONES COMICS DIGEST, THE (...Magazine No. 10-64; Jughead Jones Digest Magazine #65)
Archie Publ.: June, 1977 - No. 100, May, 1996 ($1.35/$1.50/$1.75, digest-size, 128 pgs.)

1-Neal Adams-a; Capt. Hero-r	3	6	9	21	32	42
2(9/77)-Neal Adams-a	3	6	9	16	22	28
3-6,8-10	2	4	6	11	16	20
7-Origin Jaguar-r; N. Adams-a.	2	4	6	13	18	22
11-20: 13-r/1957 Jughead's Folly	2	4	6	8	10	12
21-50	1	2	3	4	5	7
51-70						5.00
71-100						3.00

JUGHEAD'S BABY TALES
Archie Comics: Spring, 1994 - No. 2, Wint. 1994 ($2.00, 52 pgs.)

1,2: 1-Bound-in pull-out poster 4.00

JUGHEAD'S DINER
Archie Comics: Apr, 1990 - No. 7, Apr, 1991 ($1.00)

1 4.00
2-7 3.00

JUGHEAD'S DOUBLE DIGEST (...Magazine #5)
Archie Comics: Oct, 1989 - Present ($2.25 - $3.69)

1	2	4	6	8	10	12
2-10: 2,5-Capt. Hero stories	1	2	3	5	6	8
11-25						5.00

26-170: 58-Begin $2.99-c. 66-Begin $3.19-c. 91-Begin $3.59-c. 138-Reprints entire

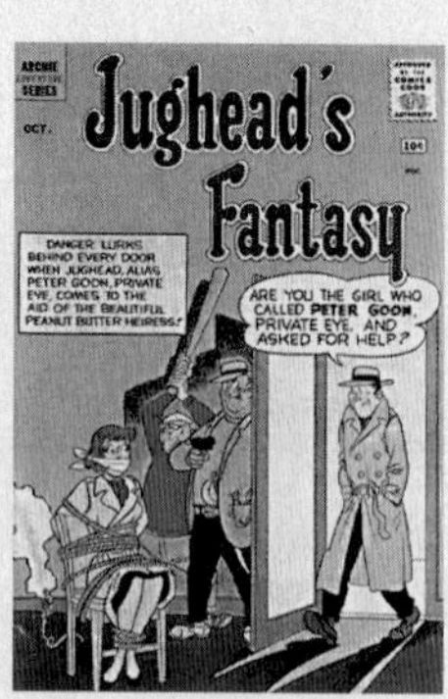

Jughead's Fantasy #2 © AP

Jumbo Comics #9 © FH

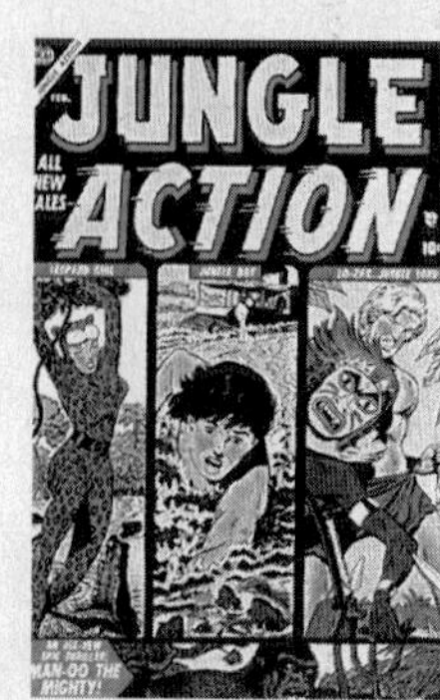

Jungle Action #3 © FH

	GD 2.0	VG 4.0	FN 6.0	VF 8.0	VF/NM 9.0	NM- 9.2
Jughead #1 (1949). 139-142-"New Look" Jughead; Staton-a. 148-Begin $3.99-c						4.00
Archie New Look Series Book 2, Jughead "The Matchmakers" TPB (2009, $10.95) r/new look series in #139-142; new cover by Staton & Milgrom						11.00

JUGHEAD'S EAT-OUT COMIC BOOK MAGAZINE (See Archie Giant Series Magazine No. 170)

JUGHEAD'S FANTASY
Archie Publications: Aug, 1960 - No. 3, Dec, 1960

	GD 2.0	VG 4.0	FN 6.0	VF 8.0	VF/NM 9.0	NM- 9.2
1	15	30	45	106	216	325
2	10	20	30	72	131	190
3	9	18	27	63	107	150

JUGHEAD'S FOLLY
Archie Publications (Close-Up): 1957 (36 pgs.)(one-shot)

	GD 2.0	VG 4.0	FN 6.0	VF 8.0	VF/NM 9.0	NM- 9.2
1-Jughead a la Elvis (Rare) (1st reference to Elvis in comics?)	53	106	154	334	567	800

JUGHEAD'S JOKES
Archie Publications: Aug, 1967 - No. 78, Sept, 1982
(No. 1-8, 38 on: reg. size; No. 9-23: 68 pgs.; No. 24-37: 52 pgs.)

	GD 2.0	VG 4.0	FN 6.0	VF 8.0	VF/NM 9.0	NM- 9.2
1	6	12	18	43	69	95
2	4	8	12	24	37	50
3-8	3	6	9	17	25	32
9,10 (68 pgs.)	3	6	9	19	29	38
11-23(4/71) (68 pgs.)	3	6	9	16	23	30
24-37(1/74) (52 pgs.)	2	4	6	11	16	20
38-50(9/76)	1	3	4	6	8	10
51-78						6.00

JUGHEAD'S PAL HOT DOG (See Laugh #14 for 1st app.)
Archie Comics: Jan, 1990 - No. 5, Oct, 1990 ($1.00)

	GD 2.0	VG 4.0	FN 6.0	VF 8.0	VF/NM 9.0	NM- 9.2
1						4.00
2-5						3.00

JUGHEAD'S SOUL FOOD
Spire Christian Comics (Fleming H. Revell Co.): 1979 (49¢/59¢)

	GD 2.0	VG 4.0	FN 6.0	VF 8.0	VF/NM 9.0	NM- 9.2
nn-Low print run	2	4	6	13	18	22

JUGHEAD'S TIME POLICE
Archie Comics: July, 1990 - No. 6, May, 1991 ($1.00, bi-monthly)

	GD 2.0	VG 4.0	FN 6.0	VF 8.0	VF/NM 9.0	NM- 9.2
1						4.00
2-6: Colan a-3-6p; c-3-6						3.00

JUGHEAD WITH ARCHIE DIGEST (...Plus Betty & Veronica & Reggie Too No. 1,2; ...Magazine #33-?, 101-on; ...Comics Digest Mag.)
Archie Pub.: Mar, 1974 - No. 200, May, 2005 ($1.00-$2.39)

	GD 2.0	VG 4.0	FN 6.0	VF 8.0	VF/NM 9.0	NM- 9.2
1	5	10	15	34	55	75
2	4	8	12	22	34	45
3-10	3	6	9	18	27	35
11-13,15-17,19,20: Capt. Hero-r in #14-16; Capt. Pureheart #17,19	2	4	6	10	14	18
14,18,21,22-Pureheart the Powerful in #18,21,22	2	4	6	11	16	20
23-30: 29-The Shield-r. 30-The Fly-r	1	3	4	6	8	10
31-50,100	1	2	3	5	6	8
51-99	1	2	3	4	5	7
101-121						4.00
122-200: 156-Begin $2.19-c. 180-Begin $2.39-c						3.00

JUKE BOX COMICS
Famous Funnies: Mar, 1948 - No. 6, Jan, 1949

	GD 2.0	VG 4.0	FN 6.0	VF 8.0	VF/NM 9.0	NM- 9.2
1-Toth-c/a; Hollingsworth-a	37	74	111	222	361	500
2-Transvestism story	22	44	66	132	216	300
3-6: 3-Peggy Lee story. 4-Jimmy Durante line drawn-c. 6-Features Desi Arnaz plus Arnaz line drawn-c	18	36	54	105	165	225

JUMBO COMICS (Created by S.M. Iger)
Fiction House Magazines (Real Adv. Publ. Co.): Sept, 1938 - No. 167, Mar, 1953 (No. 1-3: 68 pgs.; No. 4-8: 52 pgs.)(No. 1-8 oversized-10-1/2x14-1/2"; black & white)

	GD 2.0	VG 4.0	FN 6.0	VF 8.0	VF/NM 9.0	NM- 9.2
1-(Rare)-Sheena Queen of the Jungle(1st app.) by Meskin, Hawks of the Seas (The Hawk #10 on; see Feature Funnies #3) by Eisner, The Hunchback by Dick Briefer (ends #8), Wilton of the West (ends #24), Inspector Dayton (ends #67) & ZX-5 (ends #140) begin; 1st comic art by Jack Kirby (Count of Monte Cristo & Wilton of the West); Mickey Mouse appears (1 panel) with brief biography of Walt Disney; 1st app. Peter Pupp by Bob Kane. Note: Sheena was created by Iger for publication in England as a newspaper strip. The early issues of Jumbo contain Sheena strip-r; multiple panel-c 1,2,7	2150	4300	6450	21,500	-	-
2-(Rare)-Origin Sheena. Diary of Dr. Hayward by Kirby (also #3) plus 2 other stories; contains strip from Universal Film featuring Edgar Bergen & Charlie McCarthy plus-c (preview of film)	700	1400	2100	7000	-	-
3-Last Kirby issue	500	1000	1500	5000	-	-
4-(Scarce)-Origin The Hawk by Eisner; Wilton of the West by Fine (ends #14)(1st comic work); Count of Monte Cristo by Fine (ends #15); The Diary of Dr. Hayward by Fine (cont'd #8,9)	460	920	1380	4600	-	-
5-Christmas-c	400	800	1200	4000	-	-
6-8-Last B&W issue. #8 was a 1939 N. Y. World's Fair Special Edition; Frank Buck's Jungleland story	360	720	1080	3600	-	-
9-Stuart Taylor begins by Fine (ends #140); Fine-c; 1st color issue (8-9/39)-1st Sheena (jungle) cover; 8-1/4x10-1/4" (oversized in width only)	350	700	1050	3500	-	-
10-Regular size 68 pg. issues begin; Sheena dons new costume w/origin costume; Stuart Taylor sci/fi-c; classic Lou Fine-c.	219	438	657	1402	2401	3400
11-13: 12-The Hawk-c by Eisner. 13-Eisner-c	135	270	405	864	1482	2100
14-Intro. Lightning (super-hero) on-c only	139	278	417	883	1517	2150
15,17-20: 15-1st Lightning story and begins, ends #41. 17-Lightning part-c	86	172	258	546	936	1325
16-Lightning-c	100	200	300	635	1093	1550
21-30: 22-1st Tom, Dick & Harry; origin The Hawk retold. 25-Midnight the Black Stallion begins, ends #65	64	128	192	406	696	985
31-40: 31-(9/41)-1st app. Mars God of War in Stuart Taylor story (see Planet Comics #15. 35-Shows V2#11 (correct number does not appear)	53	106	159	334	567	800
41-50: 42-Ghost Gallery begins, ends #167	41	82	123	256	428	600
51-60: 52-Last Tom, Dick & Harry	37	74	111	222	361	500
61-70: 68-Sky Girl begins, ends #130; not in #79	30	60	90	177	289	400
71-93,95-99: 89-ZX5 becomes a private eye.	24	48	72	142	234	325
94-Used in Love and Death by Legman	26	52	78	154	252	350
100	26	52	78	154	252	350
101-121	21	42	63	126	206	285
121-140,150-158: 155-Used in **POP**, pg. 98	20	40	60	114	182	250
141-149-Two Sheena stories. 141-Long Bow, Indian Boy begins, ends #160	20	40	60	117	189	260
159-163: Space Scouts serial in all. 160-Last jungle-c (6/52). 161-Ghost Gallery covers begin, end #167. 163-Suicide Smith app.	18	36	54	105	165	225
164-The Star Pirate begins, ends #165	18	36	54	105	165	225
165-167: 165,167-Space Rangers app.	18	36	54	105	165	225

NOTE: *Bondage covers, negligee panels, torture, etc. are common in this series. Hawks of the Seas, Inspector Dayton, Spies in Action, Sports Shorts, & Uncle Otto by Eisner, #1-7. Hawk by* ***Eisner****-#10-15.* ***Eisner*** *c-1-8, 12-14. 1pg. Patsy pin-ups in 92-97, 99-101. Sheena by* ***Meskin****-#1, 4; by* ***Powell****-#2, 3, 5-28;* ***Powell*** *c-14, 16, 17, 19.* ***Powell/Eisner*** *c-15. Sky Girl by* ***Matt Baker****-#69-78, 80-130. ZX-5 & Ghost Gallery by* ***Kamen****-#90-130.* ***Bailey*** *a-3-8.* ***Briefer*** *a-1-8, 10.* ***Fine*** *a-14; c-9-11.* ***Kamen*** *a-101, 105, 123, 132; c-105, 121-145.* ***Bob Kane*** *a-1-8.* ***Whitman*** *c-146-167(most). Jungle c-9, 13, 15, 17 on.*

JUMPER: JUMPSCARS
Oni Press: Jan, 2008 ($14.95, graphic novel)

	GD 2.0	VG 4.0	FN 6.0	VF 8.0	VF/NM 9.0	NM- 9.2
SC-Prelude to 2008 movie Jumper; Brian Hurtt-a/c						15.00

JUNGLE ACTION
Atlas Comics (IPC): Oct, 1954 - No. 6, Aug, 1955

	GD 2.0	VG 4.0	FN 6.0	VF 8.0	VF/NM 9.0	NM- 9.2
1-Leopard Girl begins by Al Hartley (#1,3); Jungle Boy by Forte; Maneely-a in all	37	74	111	222	361	500
2-(3-D effect cover)	37	74	111	222	361	500
3-6: 3-Last precode (2/55)	24	48	72	140	230	320

NOTE: ***Maneely*** *c-1, 2, 5, 6.* ***Romita*** *a-3, 6.* ***Shores*** *a-3, 6; c-3, 4?.*

JUNGLE ACTION (...& Black Panther #18-21?)
Marvel Comics Group: Oct, 1972 - No. 24, Nov, 1976

	GD 2.0	VG 4.0	FN 6.0	VF 8.0	VF/NM 9.0	NM- 9.2
1-Lorna, Jann-r (All reprints in 1-4)	3	6	9	14	20	25
2-4	2	4	6	9	12	15
5-Black Panther begins (r/Avengers #62)	3	6	9	20	30	40
6-New solo Black Panther stories begin	3	6	9	18	27	35
7,9,10: 9-Contains pull-out centerfold ad by Mark Jewelers	2	4	6	11	16	20
8-Origin Black Panther	3	6	9	14	20	26
11-20,23,24: 19-23-KKK x-over. 23-r/#22. 24-1st Wind Eagle; story contd in Marvel Premiere #51-#53	2	4	6	8	11	14
21,22-(Regular 25¢ edition)(5,7/76)	2	4	6	8	11	14
21,22-(30¢-c variant, limited distribution)	3	6	9	18	27	35

NOTE: ***Buckler*** *a-6-9p, 22; c-8p, 12p.* ***Buscema*** *a-5p; c-22.* ***Byrne*** *c-23.* ***Gil Kane*** *a-8p; c-2, 4, 10p, 11p, 13-17, 19, 24.* ***Kirby*** *c-18.* ***Maneely*** *r-1.* ***Russell*** *a-13i.* ***Starlin*** *c-3p.*

JUNGLE ADVENTURES
Super Comics: 1963 - 1964 (Reprints)

10,12,15,17,18: 10-r/Terrors of the Jungle #4 & #10(Rulah). 12-r/Zoot #14(Rulah).15-r/Kaanga from Jungle #152 & Tiger Girl. 17-All Jo-Jo-r. 18-Reprints/White Princess of the Jungle #1; no Kinstler-a; origin of both White Princess & Cap'n Courage

Jungle Comics #30 © FH

Jungle Girl Season 2 #1 © Jungle Girl LLC

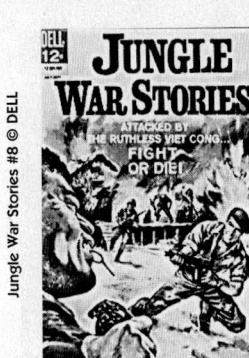

Jungle War Stories #8 © DELL

GD VG FN VF VF/NM NM-
2.0 4.0 6.0 8.0 9.0 9.2

3 6 9 19 29 38

JUNGLE ADVENTURES
Skywald Comics: Mar, 1971 - No. 3, June, 1971 (25¢, 52 pgs.) (Pre-code reprints & new-s)
1-Zangar origin; reprints of Jo-Jo, Blue Gorilla(origin)/White Princess #3, Kinstler-r/White Princess #2 3 6 9 18 27 35
2,3: 2-Zangar, Sheena-r/Sheena #17 & Jumbo #162, Jo-Jo, origin Slave Girl-r. 3-Zangar, Jo-Jo, White Princess, Rulah-r 3 6 9 14 20 25

JUNGLE BOOK (See King Louie and Mowgli, Movie Comics, Mowgli..., Walt Disney Showcase #45 & Walt Disney's The Jungle Book)

JUNGLE CAT (Disney)
Dell Publishing Co.: No. 1136, Sept-Nov, 1960 (one shot)
Four Color 1136-Movie, photo-c 6 12 18 43 69 95

JUNGLE COMICS
Fiction House Magazines: 1/40 - No. 157, 3/53; No. 158, Spr, 1953 - No. 163, Summer, 1954
1-Origin The White Panther, Kaanga, Lord of the Jungle, Tabu, Wizard of the Jungle; Wambi, the Jungle Boy, Camilla & Capt. Terry Thunder begin (all 1st app.). Lou Fine-c 476 952 1428 3475 6138 8800
2-Fantomah, Mystery Woman of the Jungle begins, ends #51; The Red Panther begins, ends #26 174 348 522 1114 1907 2700
3,4 139 278 417 883 1517 2150
5-Classic Eisner-c 155 310 465 992 1696 2400
6-10: 7,8-Powell-c 81 162 243 518 884 1250
11-20: 13-Tuska-c 55 110 165 352 601 850
21-30: 25-Shows V2#1 (correct number does not appear). #27-New origin Fantomah, Daughter of the Pharoahs; Camilla dons new costume 47 94 141 296 498 700
31-40 39 78 117 231 378 525
41,43-50 34 68 102 199 325 450
42-Kaanga by Crandall, 12 pgs. 36 72 108 211 343 475
51-60 30 60 90 177 289 400
61-70: 67-Cover swipes Crandall splash pg. in #42 26 52 78 154 252 350
71-80: 79-New origin Tabu 23 46 69 136 223 310
81-97,99 22 44 66 128 209 290
98-Used in **SOTI**, pg. 185 & illo "In ordinary comic books, there are pictures within pictures for children who know how to look;" used by N.Y. Legis. Comm. 34 68 102 199 325 450
100 26 52 78 154 252 350
101-110: 104-In Camilla story, villain is Dr. Wertham 21 42 63 124 202 280
111-120: 118-Clyde Beatty app. 20 40 60 118 192 265
121-130 20 40 60 114 182 250
131-163: 135-Desert Panther begins in Terry Thunder (origin), not in #137; ends (dies) #138. 139-Last 52 pg. issue. 141-Last Tabu. 143,145-Used in **POP**, pg. 99. 151-Last Camilla & Terry Thunder. 152-Tiger Girl begins. 158-Last Wambi; Sheena app. 18 36 54 105 165 225
I.W. Reprint #1,9: 1-r/? 9-r/#151 3 6 9 17 25 32
NOTE: *Bondage covers, negligee panels, torture, etc. are common to this series. Camilla by* ***Fran Hopper****-#70-92; by* ***Baker****-#69, 100-113, 115, 116; by* ***Lubbers****-#97-99 by* ***Tuska****-#63, 65. Kaanga by* ***John Celardo****-#80-113; by* ***Larsen****-#71, 75-79; by* ***Moreira****-#58, 60, 61, 63-70, 72-74; by* ***Tuska****-#37, 62; by* ***Whitman****-#114-163. Tabu by* ***Larsen****-#59-75, 82-92; by* ***Whitman****-#93-115. Terry Thunder by* ***Hopper****-#71, 72; by* ***Celardo****-#78, 79; by* ***Lubbers****-#80-85. Tiger Girl-r by* ***Baker****-#152, 153, 155-157, 159. Wambi by* ***Baker****-#62-67, 74.* ***Astarita*** *c-45, 46.* ***Celardo*** *a-78; c-98-113.* ***Crandall*** *c-67 from splash pg.* ***Eisner*** *c-2, 5, 6.* ***Fine*** *c-1.* ***Larsen*** *a-65, 66, 71, 72, 74, 75, 79, 83, 84, 87-90.* ***Moreira*** *c-43, 44.* ***Morisi*** *a-51.* ***Powell*** *c-7, 8.* ***Sultan*** *c-3, 4.* ***Tuska*** *c-13.* ***Whitman*** *c-132-163(most).* ***Zolnerowich*** *c-11, 12, 18-41.*

JUNGLE COMICS
Blackthorne Publishing: May, 1988 - No. 4 ($2.00, B&W/color)
1-Dave Stevens-c; B. Jones scripts in all. 5.00
2-4: 2-B&W-a begins 3.00

JUNGLE GIRL (See Lorna, the...)

JUNGLE GIRL (Nyoka, Jungle Girl No. 2 on)
Fawcett Publications: Fall, 1942 (one-shot)(No month listed)
1-Bondage-c; photo of Kay Aldridge who played Nyoka in movie serial app. on-c. Adaptation of the classic Republic movie serial Perils of Nyoka. 1st comic to devote entire contents to a movie serial adaptation 126 252 378 806 1378 1950

JUNGLE GIRL
Dynamite Entertainment: No. 0, 2007 - 2009 (25¢/$2.99/$3.50)
0-(25¢-c) Eight page preview; preview of Superpowers w/Alex Ross-a 3.00
1-5-Frank Cho-plot/cover; Batista-a/variant-c 3.00
... Season 2 ($3.50) 1-5-Two covers by Cho & Batista 3.50

JUNGLE GIRLS
AC Comics: 1989 - No. 16, 1993 (B&W)
1-16: 1-4,10,13-16-New story & "good girl" reprints. 5-9,11,12-All g.g. reprints (Baker, Powell, Lubbers, others) 3.00

JUNGLE JIM (Also see Ace Comics)
Standard Comics (Best Books): No. 11, Jan, 1949 - No. 20, Apr, 1951
11 11 22 33 62 86 110
12-20 8 16 24 42 54 65

JUNGLE JIM
Dell Publishing Co.: No. 490, 8/53 - No. 1020, 8-10/59 (Painted-c)
Four Color 490(#1) 7 14 21 49 80 110
Four Color 565(#2, 6/54) 5 10 15 30 48 65
3(10-12/54)-5 4 8 12 28 44 60
6-19(1-3/59), Four Color 1020(#20) 4 8 12 26 41 55

JUNGLE JIM
King Features Syndicate: No. 5, Dec, 1967
5-Reprints Dell #5; Wood-c 2 4 6 10 14 18

JUNGLE JIM (Continued from Dell series)
Charlton Comics: No. 22, Feb, 1969 - No. 28, Feb, 1970 (#21 was an overseas edition only)
22-Dan Flagg begins; Ditko/Wood-a 3 6 9 21 32 42
23-26: 23-Last Dan Flagg; Howard-c. 24-Jungle People begin 3 6 9 15 21 26
27,28: 27-Ditko/Howard-a. 28-Ditko-a 3 6 9 17 25 32
NOTE: *Ditko cover of #22 reprints story panels*

JUNGLE JO
Fox Feature Syndicate (Hero Books): Mar, 1950 - No. 3, Sept, 1950
nn-Jo-Jo blanked out in titles of interior stories, leaving Congo King; came out after Jo-Jo #29 (intended as Jo-Jo #30?) 53 106 159 334 567 800
1-Tangi begins; part Wood-a 54 108 162 343 574 825
2,3 41 82 123 256 428 600

JUNGLE LIL (Dorothy Lamour #2 on; also see Feature Stories Magazine)
Fox Feature Syndicate (Hero Books): April, 1950
1 43 86 129 271 461 650

JUNGLE TALES (Jann of the Jungle No. 8 on)
Atlas Comics (CSI): Sept, 1954 - No. 7, Sept, 1955
1-Jann of the Jungle 39 78 117 236 388 540
2-7: 3-Last precode (1/55) 27 54 81 158 259 360
NOTE: ***Heath*** *c-5.* ***Heck*** *a-6, 7.* ***Maneely*** *a-2; c-1, 3.* ***Shores*** *a-5-7; c-4, 6.* ***Tuska*** *a-2.*

JUNGLE TALES OF TARZAN
Charlton Comics: Dec, 1964 - No. 4, July, 1965
1 6 12 18 37 59 80
2-4 4 8 12 24 37 50
NOTE: ***Giordano*** *c-3p.* ***Glanzman*** *a-1-3.* ***Montes/Bache*** *a-4.*

JUNGLE TERROR (See Harvey Comics Hits No. 54)

JUNGLE THRILLS (Formerly Sports Thrills; Terrors of the Jungle #17 on)
Star Publications: No. 16, Feb, 1952; Dec, 1953; No. 7, 1954
16-Phantom Lady & Rulah story-reprint/All Top No. 15; used in **POP**, pg. 98,99; L. B. Cole-c 50 100 150 315 533 750
3-D 1(12/53, 25¢)-Came w/glasses; Jungle Lil & Jungle Jo appear; L. B. Cole-c 50 100 150 315 533 750
7-Titled 'Picture Scope Jungle Adventures;' (1954, 36 pgs, 15¢)-3-D effect c/stories; story & coloring book; Disbrow-a/script; L.B. Cole-c 50 100 150 315 533 750

JUNGLE TWINS, THE (Tono & Kono)
Gold Key/Whitman No. 18: Apr, 1972 - No. 17, Nov, 1975; No. 18, May, 1982
1 3 6 9 16 22 28
2-5 2 4 6 8 11 14
6-18: 18(Whitman, 5/82)-Reprints 1 2 3 5 7 9
NOTE: *UFO c/story No. 13. Painted-c No. 1-17.* ***Spiegle*** *c-18.*

JUNGLE WAR STORIES (Guerrilla War No. 12 on)
Dell Publishing Co.: July-Sept, 1962 - No. 11, Apr-June, 1965 (Painted-c)
01-384-209 (#1) 4 8 12 22 34 45
2-11 3 6 9 16 23 30

JUNIE PROM (Also see Dexter Comics)
Dearfield Publishing Co.: Winter, 1947-48 - No. 7, Aug, 1949
1-Teen-age 14 28 42 82 121 160
2 9 18 27 50 65 80
3-7 8 16 24 42 54 65

JUNIOR

Junior Miss #34 © MAR

Jurassic Park (2010 series) #4 © Universal

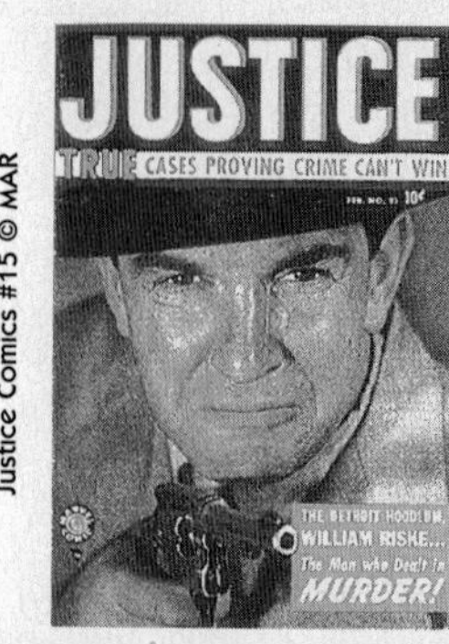

Justice Comics #15 © MAR

	GD 2.0	VG 4.0	FN 6.0	VF 8.0	VF/NM 9.0	NM- 9.2

Fantagraphics Books: June, 2000 - No. 5, Jan, 2001 ($2.95, B&W)

1-5-Peter Bagge-s/a						3.00

JUNIOR CARROT PATROL (Jr. Carrot Patrol #2)
Dark Horse Comics: May, 1989; No. 2, Nov, 1990 ($2.00, B&W)

1,2-Flaming Carrot spin-off. 1-Bob Burden-c(i)						3.00

JUNIOR COMICS (Formerly Li'l Pan; becomes Western Outlaws with #17)
Fox Feature Syndicate: No. 9, Sept, 1947 - No. 16, July, 1948

9-Feldstein-c/a; headlights-c	135	270	405	864	1482	2100
10-16-Feldstein-c/a; headlights-c on all	123	246	369	787	1344	1900

JUNIOR FUNNIES (Formerly Tiny Tot Funnies No. 9)
Harvey Publ. (King Features Synd.): No. 10, Aug, 1951 - No. 13, Feb, 1952

10-Partial reprints in all; Blondie, Dagwood, Daisy, Henry, Popeye, Felix, Katzenjammer Kids	6	12	18	28	34	40
11-13	5	10	15	24	30	35

JUNIOR HOPP COMICS
Stanmor Publ.: Feb, 1952 - No. 3, July, 1952

1-Teenage humor	10	20	30	58	79	100
2,3: 3-Dave Berg-a	7	14	21	35	43	50

JUNIOR MEDICS OF AMERICA, THE
E. R. Squire & Sons: No. 1359, 1957 (15¢)

1359	4	8	12	17	21	24

JUNIOR MISS
Timely/Marvel (CnPC): Wint, 1944; No. 24, Apr, 1947 - No. 39, Aug, 1950

1-Frank Sinatra & June Allyson life story	31	62	93	186	303	420
24-Formerly The Human Torch #23?	15	30	45	90	140	190
25-38: 29,31,34-Cindy-c/stories (others?)	10	20	30	58	79	100
39-Kurtzman-a	12	24	36	67	94	120

NOTE: *Painted-c 35-37. 35, 37-all romance. 36, 38-mostly teen humor.* ***Louise Alston*** *c-36.*

JUNIOR PARTNERS (Formerly Oral Roberts' True Stories)
Oral Roberts Evangelistic Assn.: No. 120, Aug, 1959 - V3#12, Dec, 1961

120(#1)	4	8	12	24	37	50
2(9/59)	3	6	9	17	25	32
3-12(7/60)	2	4	6	13	18	22
V2#1(8/60)-5(12/60)	2	4	6	9	13	16
V3#1(1/61)-12	2	4	6	8	10	12

JUNIOR TREASURY (See Dell Junior...)

JUNIOR WOODCHUCKS GUIDE (Walt Disney's...)
Danbury Press: 1973 (8-3/4"x5-3/4", 214 pgs., hardcover)

nn-Illustrated text based on the long-standing J.W. Guide used by Donald Duck's nephews Huey, Dewey & Louie by Carl Barks. The guidebook was a popular plot device to enable the nephews to solve problems facing their uncle or Scrooge McDuck (scarce)	5	10	15	35	55	75

JUNIOR WOODCHUCKS LIMITED SERIES (Walt Disney's...)
W. D. Publications (Disney): July, 1991 - No. 4, Oct, 1991 ($1.50, limited series; new & reprint-a)

1-4: 1-The Beagle Boys app.; Barks-r						3.00

JUNIOR WOODCHUCKS (See Huey, Dewey & Louie...)

JURASSIC PARK
Topps Comics: June, 1993 - No. 4, Aug, 1993; No. 5, Oct, 1994 - No. 10, Feb, 1995

1-($2.50)-Newsstand Edition; Kane/Perez-a in all; 1-4: movie adaptation						3.00
1-($2.95)-Collector's Ed.; polybagged w/3 cards						4.00
1-Amberchrome Edition w/no price or ads	1	2	3	4	5	7
2-4-($2.50)-Newsstand Edition						3.00
2,3-($2.95)-Collector's Ed.; polybagged w/3 cards						4.00
4-10: 4-($2.95)-Collector's Ed.; polybagged w/1 of 4 different action hologram trading card; Gil Kane/Perez-a. 5-becomes Advs. of						3.00
Annual 1 ($3.95, 5/95)						4.00
Trade paperback (1993, $9.95)-r/#1-4; bagged w/#0						10.00

JURASSIC PARK
IDW Publishing: Jun, 2010 - No. 5, Oct, 2010 ($3.99, limited series)

1-5: Takes place 13 years after the first movie; Schreck-s. 1-Covers by Yeates & Miller						4.00

JURASSIC PARK: RAPTOR
Topps Comics: Nov, 1993 - No. 2, Dec, 1993 ($2.95, limited series)

1,2: 1-Bagged w/3 trading cards & Zorro #0; Golden c-1,2						3.00

JURASSIC PARK: RAPTORS ATTACK
Topps Comics: Mar, 1994 - No. 4, June, 1994 ($2.50, limited series)

1-4-Michael Golden-c/frontispiece						3.00

JURASSIC PARK: RAPTORS HIJACK
Topps Comics: July, 1994 - No. 4, Oct, 1994 ($2.50, limited series)

1-4: Michael Golden-c/front piece						3.00

JURASSIC PARK: THE DEVILS IN THE DESERT
IDW Publishing: Jan, 2011 - No. 4, Apr, 2011 ($3.99, limited series)

1-4-John Byrne-s/a/c						4.00

JUST A PILGRIM
Black Bull Entertainment: May, 2001 - No. 5, Sept, 2001 ($2.99)

Limited Preview Edition (12/00, $7.00) Ennis & Ezquerra interviews						7.00
1-Ennis-s/Ezquerra-a; two covers by Texeira & JG Jones						3.00
2-5: 2-Fabry-c. 3-Nowlan-c. 4-Sienkiewicz-c						3.00
TPB (11/01, $12.99) r/#1-5; Waid intro.						13.00

JUST A PILGRIM: GARDEN OF EDEN
Black Bull Entertainment: May, 2002 - No. 4, Aug, 2002 ($2.99, limited series)

Limited Preview Ed. (1/02, $7.00) Ennis & Ezquerra interviews; Jones-c						7.00
1-4-Ennis-s/Ezquerra-a						3.00
TPB (11/02, $12.99) r/#1-4; Gareb Shamus intro.						13.00

JUSTICE
Marvel Comics Group (New Universe): Nov, 1986 - No. 32, June, 1989

1-32: 26-32-$1.50-c (low print run)						3.00

JUSTICE
DC Comics: Oct, 2005 - No. 12, Aug, 2007 ($2.99/$3.50/$3.99, bi-monthly maxi-series)

1-Classic Justice League vs. The Legion of Doom; Alex Ross & Doug Braithwaite-a; Jim Krueger-s; two covers by Ross; Ross sketch pages						5.00
1-2nd & 3rd printings						4.00
2-($3.50)						4.00
2 (2nd printing), 3-11-($3.50)						3.50
12-($3.99) Two covers (Heroes & Villains)						4.00
Absolute Justice HC (2009, $99.99, slipcased book with dustjacket) oversized r/#1-12; afterwords by creators; Ross sketch and design art; photo gallery of action figures						100.00
... Volume One HC (2006, $19.99, dustjacket) r/#1-4; Krueger intro.; sketch pages						20.00
... Volume One SC (2008, $14.99) r/#1-4; Krueger intro.; sketch pages						15.00
... Volume Two HC (2007, $19.99, dustjacket) r/#5-8; Krueger intro.; sketch pages						20.00
... Volume Two SC (2008, $14.99) r/#5-8; Krueger intro.; sketch pages						15.00
... Volume Three HC (2007, $19.99, dustjacket) r/#9-12; Ross intro.; sketch pages						20.00
... Volume Three SC (2007, $14.99) r/#9-12; Ross intro.; sketch pages						15.00

JUSTICE COMICS (Formerly Wacky Duck; Tales of Justice #53 on)
Marvel/Atlas Comics (NPP 7-9,4-19/CnPC 20-23/MjMC 24-38/Male 39-52:
No. 7, Fall/47 - No. 9, 6/48; No. 4, 8/48 - No. 52, 3/55

7(#1, 1947)	30	60	90	177	289	400
8(#2)-Kurtzman-a "Giggles 'n' Grins" (3)	20	40	60	117	189	260
9(#3, 6/48)	18	36	54	105	165	225
4	16	32	48	94	147	200
5(9/48)-9: 8-Anti-Wertham editorial	15	30	45	83	124	165
10-15-Photo-c	13	26	39	72	101	130
16-30	11	22	33	62	86	110
31-40,42-52: 35-Gene Colan-a. 48-Last precode; Pakula & Tuska-a.	10	20	30	58	79	100
41-Electrocution-c	17	34	51	98	154	210

NOTE: ***Hartley*** *a-48.* ***Heath*** *a-24.* ***Maneely*** *c-44, 52.* ***Pakula*** *a-43, 45, 47, 48.* ***Louis Ravielli*** *a-39, 47.* ***Robinson*** *a-22, 25, 41.* ***Sale*** *c-45.* ***Shores*** *c-7(#1), 8(#2)?* ***Tuska*** *a-41, 48.* ***Wildey*** *a-52.*

JUSTICE: FOUR BALANCE
Marvel Comics: Sept, 1994 - No. 4, Dec, 1994 ($1.75, limited series)

1-4: 1-Thing & Firestar app.						3.00

JUSTICE, INC. (The Avenger) (Pulp)
National Periodical Publications: May-June, 1975 - No. 4, Nov-Dec, 1975

1-McWilliams-a, Kubert-c; origin	2	4	6	11	16	20
2-4: 2-4-Kirby-a(p), c-2,3p. 4-Kubert-c	2	4	6	11	16	20

NOTE: *Adapted from Kenneth Robeson novel, creator of Doc Savage.*

JUSTICE, INC. (Pulp)
DC Comics: 1989 - No. 2, 1989 ($3.95, 52 pgs., squarebound, mature)

1,2: Re-intro The Avenger; Andrew Helfer scripts & Kyle Baker-c/a						4.00

JUSTICE LEAGUE (...International #7-25; ...America #26 on)
DC Comics: May, 1987 - No. 113, Aug, 1996 (Also see Legends #6)

1-Batman, Green Lantern (Guy Gardner), Blue Beetle, Mr. Miracle, Capt. Marvel & Martian

Justice League Adventures #1 © DC

Justice League Elite #1 © DC

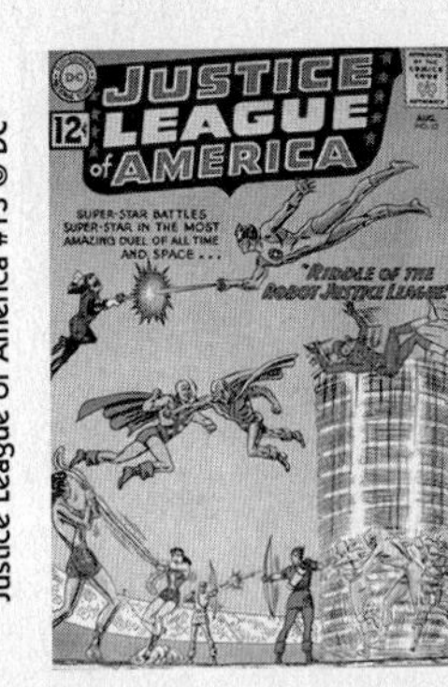

Justice League of America #13 © DC

	GD 2.0	VG 4.0	FN 6.0	VF 8.0	VF/NM 9.0	NM- 9.2

Manhunter begin 1 2 3 5 6 8
2,3: 3-Regular-c (white background) 5.00
3-Limited-c (yellow background, Superman logo) 4 8 12 24 37 50
4-6,8-10: 4-Booster Gold joins. 5-Origin Gray Man; Batman vs. Guy Gardner; Creeper app. 9,10-Millennium x-over 4.00
7-($1.25, 52 pgs.)-Capt. Marvel & Dr. Fate resign; Capt. Atom & Rocket Red join 5.00
11-17,22,23,25-49,51-68,71-82: 16-Bruce Wayne-c/story. 31,32-J. L. Europe x-over. 58-Lobo app. 61-New team begins; swipes-c to J.L. of A. #1('60). 70-Newsstand version w/o outer-c. 71-Direct sales version w/black outer-c. 71-Newsstand version w/o outer-c. 80-Intro new Booster Gold. 82,83-Guy Gardner-c/stories 3.00
18-21,24,50: 18-21-Lobo app. 24-($1.50)-1st app. Justice League Europe. 50-($1.75, 52 pgs.) 4.00
69-Doomsday tie-in; takes place between Superman: The Man of Steel #18 & Superman #74 5.00
69,70-2nd printings 3.00
70-Funeral for a Friend part 1; red 3/4 outer-c 4.00
83-99,101-113: 92-(9/94)-Zero Hour x-over; Triumph app. 113-Green Lantern, Flash & Hawkman app. 3.00
100 ($3.95)-Foil-c; 52 pgs. 5.00
100 ($2.95)-Newstand 4.00
#0-(10/94) Zero Hour (publ between #92 & #93); new team begins (Hawkman, Flash, Wonder Woman, Metamorpho, Nuklon, Crimson Fox, Obsidian & Fire) 3.00
Annual 1-8,10 ('87-'94, '96, 68 pgs.): 2-Joker-c/story; Batman cameo. 5-Armageddon 2001 x-over; Silver ink 2nd print. 7-Bloodlines x-over. 8-Elseworlds story. 10-Legends of the Dead Earth 4.00
Annual 9 (1995, $3.50)-Year One story 4.00
Special 1,2 ('90,'91, 52 pgs.): 1-Giffen plots. 2-Staton-a(p) 4.00
Spectacular 1 (1992, $1.50, 52 pgs.)-Intro new JLI & JLE teams; ties into JLI #61 & JLE #37; two interlocking covers by Jurgens 4.00
A New Beginning Trade Paperback (1989, $12.95)-r/#1-7 13.00
... International Vol. 1 HC (2008, $24.99) r/#1-7; new intro. by Giffen 25.00
... International Vol. 1 SC (2009, $17.99) r/#1-7; new intro. by Giffen 18.00
... International Vol. 2 HC (2008, $24.99) r/#8-13, Annual #1 and Suicide Squad #13 25.00
... International Vol. 2 SC (2009, $17.99) r/#8-13, Annual #1 and Suicide Squad #13 18.00
... International Vol. 3 SC (2009, $19.99) r/#14-22 20.00
... International Vol. 4 SC (2010, $17.99) r/#23-30 18.00
... International Vol. 5 SC (2011, $19.99) r/#Annual #2,3 & Justice League Europe #1-6 20.00
NOTE: *Anderson c-61i. Austin a-1i, 60i; c-1i. Giffen a-13; c-21p. Guice a-62i. Maguire a-1-12, 16-19, 22, 23. Russell a-Annual 1i; c-54i. Willingham a-30p, Annual 2.*

JUSTICE LEAGUE ADVENTURES (Based on Cartoon Network series)
DC Comics: Jan, 2002 - No. 34, Oct, 2004 ($1.99/$2.25)

1-Timm & Ross-c 4.00
2-32: 3-Nicieza-s. 5-Starro app. 10-Begin $2.25-c. 14-Includes 16 pg. insert for VERB with Haberlin CG-art. 15,29-Amancio-a. 16-McCloud-s. 20-Psycho Pirate app. 25,26-Adam Strange-c/app. 28-Legion of Super-Heroes app. 30-Kamandi app. 3.00
Free Comic Book Day giveaway - (5/02) r/#1 with "Free Comic Book Day" banner on-c 4.00
TPB (2003, $9.95) r/#1,3,6,10-13; Timm/Ross-c from #1 10.00
...Vol. 1: The Magnificent Seven (2004, $6.95) digest-size reprints #3,6,10-12 7.00
...Vol. 2: Friends and Foes (2004, $6.95) digest-size reprints #13,14,16,19,20 7.00

JUSTICE LEAGUE: A MIDSUMMER'S NIGHTMARE
DC Comics: Sept, 1996 - No. 3, Nov, 1996 ($2.95, limited series, 38 pgs.)

1-3: Re-establishes Superman, Batman, Green Lantern, The Martian Manhunter, Flash, Aquaman & Wonder Woman as the Justice League; Mark Waid & Fabian Nicieza co-scripts; Jeff Johnson & Darick Robertson-a(p); Kevin Maguire-c 5.00
TPB-(1997, $8.95) r/1-3 9.00

JUSTICE LEAGUE: CRY FOR JUSTICE
DC Comics: Sept, 2009 - No. 7, Apr, 2010 ($3.99, limited series)

1-7-James Robinson-s/Mauro Cascioli-a/c. 1-Two covers; Congorilla origin 4.00
HC (2010, $24.99, d.j.) r/#1-7, Face of Evil: Prometheus 25.00

JUSTICE LEAGUE ELITE (See JLA #100 and JLA Secret Files 2004)
DC Comics: Sept, 2004 - No. 12, Aug, 2005 ($2.50)

1-12-Flash, Green Arrow, Vera Black and others; Kelly-s/Mahnke-a. 5,6-JSA app. 2.50
JL Elite TPB (2005, $19.99) r/#1-4, Action #775, JLA #100, JLA Secret Files 2004 20.00
... Vol. 2 TPB (2007, $19.99) r/#5-12 20.00

JUSTICE LEAGUE EUROPE (Justice League International #51 on)
DC Comics: Apr, 1989 - No. 68, Sept., 1994 (75¢/ $1.00/$1.25/$1.50)

1-Giffen plots in all, breakdowns in #1-8,13-30; Justice League #1-c/swipe 4.00
2-10: 7-9-Batman app. 7,8-JLA x-over. 8,9-Superman app. 3.00
11-49: 12-Metal Men app. 20-22-Rogers-c/a(p). 33,34-Lobo vs. Despero. 37-New team begins; swipes-c to JLA #9; see JLA Spectacular 3.00
50-($2.50, 68 pgs.)-Battles Sonar 4.00
51-68: 68-Zero Hour x-over; Triumph joins Justice League Task Force (See JLTF #17) 3.00
Annual 1-5 ('90-'94, 68 pgs.)-1-Return of the Global Guardians; Giffen plots/breakdowns. 2-Armageddon 2001; Giffen-a(p); Rogers-a(p); Golden-a(i). 5-Elseworlds story 4.00
NOTE: *Phil Jimenez a-68p. Rogers c/a-20-22. Sears a-1-12, 14-19, 23-29; c-1-10, 12, 14-19, 23-29.*

JUSTICE LEAGUE: GENERATION LOST (Brightest Day)
DC Comics: Early July, 2010 - Present ($2.99, bi-weekly limited series)

1-22: 1-Maxwell Lord's return; Winick & Giffen-s. 1-5,7-Harris-c. 13-Magog killed 3.00

JUSTICE LEAGUE INTERNATIONAL (See Justice League Europe)

JUSTICE LEAGUE OF AMERICA (See Brave & the Bold #28-30, Mystery In Space #75 & Official... Index) (See Crisis on Multiple Earths TPBs for reprints of JLA/JSA crossovers)
National Periodical Publ./DC Comics: Oct-Nov, 1960 - No. 261, Apr, 1987 (#91-99,139-157: 52 pgs.)

1-(10-11/60)-Origin & 1st app. Despero; Aquaman, Batman, Flash, Green Lantern, J'onn J'onzz, Superman & Wonder Woman continue from Brave and the Bold 533 1066 1600 4800 9900 15,000
2 112 224 336 952 1926 2900
3-Origin/1st app. Kanjar Ro (see Mystery in Space #75)(scarce in high grade due to black-c) 96 192 288 816 1658 2500
4-Green Arrow joins JLA 64 128 192 544 1097 1650
5-Origin & 1st app. Dr. Destiny 52 104 156 442 896 1350
6-8,10: 6-Origin & 1st app. Prof. Amos Fortune. 7-(10-11/61)-Last 10¢ issue. 10-(3/62)-Origin & 1st app. Felix Faust; 1st app. Lord of Time 41 82 123 328 664 1000
9-(2/62)-Origin JLA (1st origin) 48 96 144 408 829 1250
11-15: 12-(6/62)-Origin & 1st app. Dr. Light. 13-(8/62)-Speedy app. 14-(9/62)-Atom joins JLA. 28 56 84 204 415 625
16-20: 17-Adam Strange flashback 24 48 72 175 350 525
21-(8/63)-"Crisis on Earth-One"; re-intro. of JSA in this title (see Flash #129) (1st S.A. app. Hourman & Dr. Fate) 38 76 114 304 602 900
22- "Crisis on Earth-Two"; JSA x-over (story continued from #21) 33 66 99 254 502 750
23-28: 24-Adam Strange app. 27-Robin app. 17 34 51 122 249 375
29-JSA x-over; 1st S.A. app. Starman; "Crisis on Earth-Three" 21 42 63 150 300 450
30-JSA x-over 20 40 60 140 283 425
31-Hawkman joins JLA, Hawkgirl cameo (11/64) 14 28 42 99 200 300
32,34: 32-Intro & Origin Brain Storm. 34-Joker-c/sty 12 24 36 82 154 225
33,35,36,40,41: 40-3rd S.A. Penguin app. 41-Intro & origin The Key 11 22 33 77 144 210
37-39: 37,38-JSA x-over. 37-1st S.A. app. Mr. Terrific; Batman cameo. 38-"Crisis on Earth-A". 39-Giant G-16; r/B&B #28,30 & JLA #5 13 26 39 92 179 265
42-45: 42-Metamorpho app. 43-Intro. Royal Flush Gang 9 18 27 65 113 160
46-JSA x-over; 1st S.A. app. Sandman; 3rd S.A. app. of G.A. Spectre (8/66) 13 26 39 89 170 250
47-JSA x-over; 4th S.A. app of G.A. Spectre. 10 20 30 70 125 180
48-Giant G-29; r/JLA #2,3 & B&B #29 10 20 30 68 119 170
49-54,57,59,60 8 16 24 54 90 125
55-Intro. Earth 2 Robin (1st G.A. Robin in S.A.) 10 20 30 67 116 165
56-JLA vs. JSA (1st G.A. Wonder Woman in S.A.) 9 18 27 61 103 145
58-Giant G-41; r/JLA #6,8,1 9 18 27 61 103 145
61-63,66,68-72: 69-Wonder Woman quits. 71-Manhunter leaves. 72-Last 12¢ issue 6 12 18 41 66 90
64,65-JSA story. 64-(8/68)-Origin/1st app. S.A. Red Tornado 6 12 18 43 69 95
67-Giant G-53; r/JLA #4,14,31 8 16 24 54 90 125
73-1st S.A. app. of G.A. Superman 7 14 21 47 76 105
74-Black Canary joins; Larry Lance dies; 1st meeting of G.A. & S.A. Superman; Neal Adams-c 7 14 21 50 83 115
75-2nd app. Green Arrow in new costume (see Brave & the Bold #85) 7 14 21 47 76 105
76-Giant G-65 7 14 21 45 73 100
77-80: 78-Re-intro Vigilante (1st S.A. app?) 4 8 12 28 44 60
81-84,86-90: 82-1st S.A. app. of G.A. Batman (cameo). 83-Apparent death of The Spectre. 90-Last 15¢ issue 4 8 12 26 41 55
85,93-(Giant G-77,G-89; 68 pgs.) 5 10 15 35 55 75
91,92: 91-1st meeting of the G.A. & S.A. Robin; begin 25¢, 52 pgs. issues, ends #99. 92-S.A. Robin tries on costume that is similar to that of G.A. Robin in All Star Comics #58 5 10 15 30 48 65
94-Reprints 1st Sandman story (Adv. #40) & origin/1st app. Starman (Adventure #61); Deadman x-over; N. Adams-a (4 pgs.) 9 18 27 61 103 145
95,96: 95-Origin Dr. Fate & Dr. Midnight -r/ More Fun #67, All-American #25). 96-Origin Hourman (Adv. #48); Wildcat-r 5 10 15 32 51 70
97-99: 97-Origin JLA retold; Sargon, Starman-r. 98-G.A. Sargon, Starman-r.

Justice League of America #138 © DC

Justice League of America (2006 series) #41 © DC

Justice League: Another Nail #1 © DC

GD 2.0 | VG 4.0 | FN 6.0 | VF 8.0 | VF/NM 9.0 | NM- 9.2

99-G.A. Sandman, Atom-r; last 52 pg. issue 4 8 12 28 44 60
100-(8/72)-1st meeting of G.A. & S.A. W. Woman 5 10 15 32 51 70
101,102: JSA x-overs. 102-Red Tornado destroyed 4 8 12 26 41 55
103-106,109: 103-Rutland Vermont Halloween x-over; Phantom Stranger joins. 105-Elongated Man joins. 106-New Red Tornado joins. 109-Hawkman resigns 3 6 9 18 27 35
107,108-JSA x-over; 1st revival app. of G.A. Uncle Sam, Black Condor, The Ray, Dollman, Phantom Lady & The Human Bomb 3 6 9 20 30 40
110,112-116: All 100 pgs. 112-Amazo app; Crimson Avenger, Vigilante-r; origin Starman-r/ Adv. #81. 115-Martian Manhunter app. 5 10 15 32 51 70
111-JLA vs. Injustice Gang; intro. Libra (re-appears in 2008's Final Crisis); Shining Knight, Green Arrow-r 5 10 15 35 55 75
117-122,125-134: 117-Hawkman rejoins. 120,121-Adam Strange app. 125,126-Two-Face-app. 128-Wonder Woman rejoins. 129-Destruction of Red Tornado 3 6 9 16 22 28
123-(10/75),124: JLA/JSA x-over. DC editor Julie Schwartz & JLA writers Cary Bates & Elliot S! Maggin appear in story as themselves. 1st named app. Earth-Prime (3rd app. after Flash; 1st Series #179 & 228) 3 6 9 17 25 32
135-136: 135-137-G.A. Bulletman, Bulletgirl, Spy Smasher, Mr. Scarlet, Pinky & Ibis x-over, 1st appearances since G.A. 3 6 9 17 25 32
137-Superman battles G.A. Capt. Marvel 3 6 9 19 29 38
138-Adam Strange app. w/c by Neal Adams; 1st app. Green Lantern of the 73rd Century 3 6 9 16 23 30
139-157: 139-157-(52 pgs.): 139-Adam Strange app. 144-Origin retold; origin J'onn J'onzz. 145-Red Tornado resurrected. 147,148-Legion of Super-Heroes x-over 2 4 6 10 14 18
158-160-(44 pgs.) 2 4 6 8 11 14
158,160-162,169,171,172,173,176-179,181-(Whitman variants; low print run, none show issue # on cover) 2 4 6 10 14 18
161-165,169-182: 161-Zatanna joins & new costume. 171,172-JSA x-over. 171-Mr. Terrific murdered. 178-Cover similar to #1; J'onn J'onzz app. 179-Firestorm joins. 181-Green Arrow leaves JLA 1 2 3 5 6 8
166-168- "Identity Crisis (2004)" precursor; JSA app. vs. Secret Society of Super-Villains 3 6 9 14 20 25
166-168-Whitman variants (no issue # on covers) 4 8 12 24 37 50
183-185-JSA/New Gods/Darkseid/Mr. Miracle x-over 2 4 6 8 10 12
186-194,198,199: 192,193-Real origin Red Tornado. 193-1st app. All-Star Squadron as free 16 pg. insert 6.00
195-197-JSA app. vs. Secret Society of Super-Villains 1 2 3 5 6 8
200 ($1.50, Anniversary issue, 76 pgs.)-JLA origin retold; Green Arrow rejoins; Bolland, Aparo, Giordano, Gil Kane, Infantino, Kubert-a; Pérez-c/a 1 3 4 6 8 10
201-206,209-243,246-259: 203-Intro/origin new Royal Flush Gang. 219,220-True origin Black Canary. 228-Re-intro Martian Manhunter. 228-230-War of the Worlds storyline; JLA Satellite destroyed by Martians. 233-Story cont'd from Annual #2. 243-Aquaman leaves. 250-Batman rejoins. 253-Origin Despero. 258-Death of Vibe. 258-261-Legends x-over 5.00
207,208-JSA, JLA, & All-Star Squadron team-up 1 2 3 4 5 7
244,245-Crisis x-over 6.00
260-Death of Steel 1 2 3 4 5 7
261-Last issue 1 3 4 6 8 10
Annual 1-3 ('83-'85), 2-Intro new J.L.A. (Aquaman, Martian Manhunter, Steel, Gypsy, Vixen, Vibe, Elongated Man & Zatanna). 3-Crisis x-over 4.00
... Hereby Elects (2006, $14.99, TPB) reprints issues where new members joined; JLofA #4,75,105,106,146,161,173&174; roster of various incarnations; Ordway-c 15.00

NOTE: ***Neal Adams** c-63, 66, 67, 70, 74, 79, 81, 82, 86-89, 91, 92, 94, 96-98, 138, 139. **M. Anderson** c-1-4, 6, 7, 10, 12-14. **Aparo** a-200. **Austin** a-200i. **Baily** a-96r. **Bolland** a-200. **Buckler** c-158, 163, 164. **Burnley** r-94, 98, 99. **Greene** a-46-61i, 64-73i, 110i(r). **Grell** c-117, 122. **Kaluta** c-154p. **Gil Kane** a-200. **Krigstein** a-96(r/Sensation #84). **Kubert** a-200; c-72, 73. **Nino** a-228i, 230i. **Orlando** c-151i. **Perez** a-184-186p, 192-197p, 200p; c-184p, 186, 192-195, 196p, 197p, 199, 200, 201p, 202, 203-205p, 207-209, 212-215, 217, 219, 220. **Reinman** r-97. **Roussos** a-62i. **Sekowsky** a-37, 38, 44-63p, 110-112p(r); c-46-48p, 51p. **Sekowsky/Anderson** c-5, 8, 9, 11, 15. **B. Smith** c-185i. **Starlin** c-178-180, 183, 185p. **Staton** a-244p; c-157p, 244p. **Toth** r-110. **Tuska** a-153, 228p, 241-243p. JSA x-overs-21, 22, 29, 30, 37, 38, 46, 47, 55, 56, 64, 65, 73, 74, 82, 83, 91, 92, 100, 101, 102, 107, 108, 110, 113, 115, 123, 124, 135-137, 147, 148, 159, 160, 171, 172, 183-185, 195-197, 207-209, 219, 220, 231, 232, 244.*

JUSTICE LEAGUE OF AMERICA
DC Comics: No. 0, Sept, 2006 - Present ($2.99/$3.99)

0-Meltzer-s; history of the JLA; art by various incl. Lee, Giordano, Benes; Turner-c 5.00
0-Variant-c by Campbell 12.00
1-($3.99) Two interlocking covers by Benes; Benes-a 5.00
1-Variant-c by Turner 8.00
1-RRP Edition; sideways composite of both Benes covers 80.00
1-Second printing; Benes cover image between black bars 4.00
2-5-($2.99) Turner-c 4.00
2-5: Variant-c: 2-Jimenez. 3-Sprouse. 4-JG Jones. 5-Art Adams 5.00
6,7-($3.50) 6-JLA vs. Amazo; covers by Turner and Hughes. 7-Roster picked, new HQs; two Benes covers and Turner cover. 4.00
8-11,13-24,26-38-($2.99) 8-11-JLA/JSA team-up; covers by Turner & Jimenez. 10-Wally West returns. 13-Two covers. 13-15-Injustice Gang. 16-Tangent Flash. 20-Queen Bee app. 21-Libra app.; leads into Final Crisis #1. 35,36-Royal Flush Gang app. 38-Bagley-a begins 3.00
12-($3.50) Two Ross covers; origin retold with Wight-a; Benes-a 4.00
25-($3.99) McDuffie-s/art by various; Benes-c 4.00
39-49,51,52-($3.99) 39,40-Blackest Night. 41-New team; 2 covers. 44-48-Justice Society app. 44-Jade returns. 4.00
50-($4.99) Crime Syndicate app.; Bagley-a; wraparound-c by Van Sciver 5.00
50-Variant-c by Bagley, swipe of Quitely's JLA: Earth 2 cover 8.00
50-Variant-c by Jim Lee; swipe of Brave and the Bold #28 Starro cover 12.00
53-55-($2.99) 54-Booth-a; Eclipso returns. 55-Doomsday app. 3.00
... 80 Page Giant (11/09, $5.99) Anacleto-c; short stories by various; Ra's al Ghul app. 6.00
Free Comic Book Day giveaway - (2007) r/#0 with "Free Comic Book Day" banner on-c 2.50
Justice League Wedding Special 1 (11/07, $3.99) McKone-a; Injustice League forms 4.00
...: Dark Things HC (2011, $24.99, dustjacket) r/#44-48 & J.S.A. #41,42 25.00
...: The Injustice Gang HC (2008, $19.99, dustjacket) r/#13-16; Wedding Special 20.00
...: The Lightning Saga HC (2008, $24.99, dustjacket) r/#0,8-12 & Justice Society of America #5,6; intro. by Patton Oswalt 25.00
...: The Lightning Saga SC (2008, $17.99) r/#0,8-12 & J.S.A. #5,6; intro. by Oswalt 18.00
...: Sanctuary SC (2009, $14.99) r/#17-21 15.00
...: Second Coming HC (2009, $19.99, dustjacket) r/#22-26 20.00
...: Second Coming SC (2010, $17.99) r/#22-26 18.00
...: Team History HC (2010, $19.99, dustjacket) r/#38-43 20.00
...: The Tornado's Path HC (2007, $24.99, dustjacket) r/#1-7; variant cover gallery; Lindelof intro.; commentary by Meltzer & Benes 25.00
...: The Tornado's Path SC (2008, $17.99) r/#1-7; variant cover gallery; Lindelof intro.; commentary by Meltzer & Benes 18.00
...: When Worlds Collide HC (2009, $24.99, dustjacket) r/#27,28,30-34 25.00
...: When Worlds Collide SC (2010, $14.99) r/#27,28,30-34 15.00

JUSTICE LEAGUE OF AMERICA : ANOTHER NAIL (Elseworlds) (Also see JLA: The Nail)
DC Comics: 2004 - No. 3, 2004 ($5.95, prestige format)

1-3-Sequel to JLA: The Nail; Alan Davis-s/a(p) 6.00
TPB (2004, $12.95) r/series 13.00

JUSTICE LEAGUE OF AMERICA SUPER SPECTACULAR
DC Comics: 1999 ($5.95, mimics format of DC 100 Page Super Spectaculars)

1-Reprints Silver Age JLA and Golden Age JSA 6.00

JUSTICE LEAGUE OF AMERICA/ THE 99
DC Comics: Dec, 2010 - No. 6 ($3.99/$2/99, limited series)

1-3-($3.99) Derenick-a/Massaferra-c; JLA meets Teshkeel Comics characters 4.00
4,5-($2.99) Starro app. 3.00

JUSTICE LEAGUE QUARTERLY (...International Quarterly #6 on)
DC Comics: Winter, 1990-91 - No. 17, Winter, 1994 ($2.95/$3.50, 84 pgs.)

1-12,14-17: 1-Intro The Conglomerate (Booster Gold, Praxis, Gypsy, Vapor, Echo, Maxi-Man, & Reverb); Justice League #1-c/swipe. 1,2-Keith Giffen plots/breakdowns. 3-Giffen plot; 72 pg. story. 4-Rogers/Russell-a in back-up. 5,6-Mark Waid scripts. 8,17-Global Guardians app. 4.00
13-Linsner-c 6.00
NOTE: ***Phil Jimenez** a-17p. **Sprouse** a-1p.*

JUSTICE LEAGUE: RISE AND FALL
DC Comics: 2010, 2011

Justice League: The Rise and Fall Special #1 (5/10, $3.99) Hunt for Green Arrow 4.00
HC-(2011, $24.99) Reprints Justice League of America #43, Justice League: The Rise and Fall Special #1, Green Arrow #31,32 and Justice League: The Rise of Arsenal #1-4 25.00

JUSTICE LEAGUES...
DC Comics: Mar, 2001 ($2.50, limited series)

JL?, Justice League of Amazons, Justice League of Atlantis, Justice League of Arkham, Justice League of Aliens, JLA: JLA split by the Advance Man; Perez-c in all; s&a by various 3.00

JUSTICE LEAGUE TASK FORCE
DC Comics: June, 1993 - No. 37, Aug, 1996 ($1.25/$1.50/$1.75)

1-16,0,17-37: Aquaman, Nightwing, Flash, J'onn J'onzz, & Gypsy form team. 5,6-Knight-quest tie-ins (new Batman cameo #5, 1 pg.). 15-Triumph cameo. 16-(9/94)-Zero Hour x-over; Triumph app. 0-(10/94). 17-(11/94)-Triumph becomes part of Justice League Task Force (See JLE #68). 26-Impulse app. 35-Warlord app. 37-Triumph quits team 3.00

JUSTICE LEAGUE: THE NEW FRONTIER SPECIAL (Also see DC: The New Frontier)
DC Comics: May, 2008 ($4.99, one-shot)

1-Short stories by Darwyn Cooke, J.Bone and Dave Bullock; bonus storyboards from the

Justice League Unlimited #41 © DC

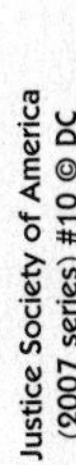

Justice Society of America (2007 series) #10 © DC

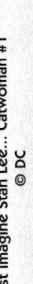

Just Imagine Stan Lee... Catwoman #1 © DC

GD VG FN VF VF/NM NM-
2.0 4.0 6.0 8.0 9.0 9.2

GD VG FN VF VF/NM NM-
2.0 4.0 6.0 8.0 9.0 9.2

movie 5.00

JUSTICE LEAGUE: THE RISE OF ARSENAL (Follows Justice League: Cry For Justice)
DC Comics: May, 2010 - No. 4, Aug, 2010 ($3.99, limited series)

1-4-Horn-c/Borges-a/Krul-s. 2,3-Cheshire app. 4.00

JUSTICE LEAGUE UNLIMITED (Based on Cartoon Network animated series)
DC Comics: Nov, 2004 - No. 46, Aug, 2008 ($2.25)

1-46: 1-Zatanna app. 2,23,42-Royal Flush Gang app. 4-Adam Strange app. 10-Creeper app. 17-Freedom Fighters app. 18-Space Cabby app. 27-Black Lightning app. 34-Zod app. 3.00
Free Comic Book Day giveaway (5/06) r/#1 with "Free Comic Book Day" banner on-c 3.00
Jam Packed Action (2005, $7.99, digest) adaptations of two TV episodes 8.00
... Vol. 1: United They Stand (2005, $6.99, digest) r/#1-5 7.00
... Vol. 2: World's Greatest Heroes (2006, $6.99, digest) r/#6-10 7.00
... Vol. 3: Champions of Justice (2006, $6.99, digest) r/#11-15 7.00
...: Heroes (2009, $12.99, full-size) r/#23-29 13.00
...: The Ties That Bind (2008, $12.99, full-size) r/#16-22 13.00

JUSTICE MACHINE, THE
Noble Comics: June, 1981 - No. 5, Nov, 1983 ($2.00, nos. 1-3 are mag. size)

	GD	VG	FN	VF	VF/NM	NM-
1-Byrne-c(p)	3	6	9	15	21	26
2-Austin-c(i)	2	4	6	9	12	15
3	1	3	4	6	8	10

4,5, Annual 1: Ann. 1-(1/84, 68 pgs.)(published by Texas Comics); 1st app. The Elementals; Golden-c(p); new Thunder Agents story (43 pgs.) 6.00

JUSTICE MACHINE (Also see The New Justice Machine)
Comico/Innovation Publishing: Jan, 1987 - No. 29, May 1989 ($1.50/$1.75)

1-29 3.00
Annual 1(6/89, $2.50, 36 pgs.)-Last Comico ish. 3.00
Summer Spectacular 1 ('89, $2.75)-Innovation Publ.; Byrne/Gustovich-c 3.00

JUSTICE MACHINE, THE
Innovation Publishing: 1990 - No. 4, 1990 ($1.95/$2.25, deluxe format, mature)

1-4: Gustovich-c/a in all 3.00

JUSTICE MACHINE FEATURING THE ELEMENTALS
Comico: May, 1986 - No. 4, Aug, 1986 ($1.50, limited series)

1-4 3.00

JUSTICE RIDERS
DC Comics: 1997 ($5.95, one-shot, prestige format)

1-Elseworlds; Dixon-s/Williams & Gray-a 6.00

JUSTICE SOCIETY
DC Comics: 2006; 2007 ($14.99, TPB)

Vol. 1 - Rep. from 1976 revival in All Star Comics #58-67 & DC Special #29; Bolland-c 15.00
Vol. 2 - R/All Star Comics #68-74 & Adventure Comics #461-466; new Bolland-c 15.00

JUSTICE SOCIETY OF AMERICA (See Adventure #461 & All-Star #3)
DC Comics: April, 1991 - No. 8, Nov, 1991 ($1.00, limited series)

1-8: 1-Flash. 2-Black Canary. 3-Green Lantern. 4-Hawkman. 5-Flash/Hawkman. 6-Green Lantern/Black Canary. 7-JSA 3.00

JUSTICE SOCIETY OF AMERICA (Also see Last Days of the... Special)
DC Comics: Aug, 1992 - No. 10, May, 1993 ($1.25)

1-10 3.00

JUSTICE SOCIETY OF AMERICA (Follows JSA series)
DC Comics: Feb, 2007 - Present ($3.99/$2.99)

1-($3.99) New team selected; intro. Maxine Hunkle; Alex Ross-c 4.00
1-Variant-c by Eaglesham 6.00
2-48: 1-Covers by Ross and Eaglesham. 3,4-Vandal Savage app. 5,6-JLA/JSA team-up. 9-22-Kingdom Come Superman app.18-Magog app. 22-Superman returns to Kingdom Come Earth; Ross partial art. 23-25-Ordway-a. 26-Triptych cover by Ross. 33-Team splits. 34,35-Mordru app. 41,42-Justice League x-over 3.00
JSA Annual 1 (9/08, $3.99) Power Girl on Earth-2; Ross-c/Ordway-a 4.00
JSA Annual 2 (4/10, $4.99) All Star team app.; Magog quits; Williams-a 5.00
... 80 Page Giant (1/10, $5.99) short stories by various incl. Ordway, S. Hampton 6.00
... 80 Page Giant 2010 (12/10, $5.99) short stories by various 6.00
... Special (11/10, $4.99) Scott Kolins-s/a; spotlight on Magog 5.00
...: Axis of Evil SC (2010, $14.99) r/#34-40 15.00
...: Black Adam and Isis HC (2009, $19.99, d.j.) r/#23-28 20.00
...: Black Adam and Isis SC (2010, $14.99) r/#23-28 15.00
... Kingdom Come Special: Magog (1/09, $3.99) Pasarin-a; origin re-told; 2 covers 4.00
... Kingdom Come Special: Superman (1/09, $3.99) Lois' death re-told; Alex Ross-s/a/c; thumbnails, photo references, sketch art 4.00
... Kingdom Come Special: Superman (1/09, $3.99) Eaglesham variant cover 8.00
... Kingdom Come Special: The Kingdom (1/09, $3.99) Pasarin-a; 2 covers 4.00
...: The Bad Seed SC (2010, $14.99) r/#29-33 15.00
...: The Next Age SC (2008, $14.99) r/#1-4; Ross and Eaglesham sketch pages 15.00
...: Thy Kingdom Come Part One HC (2008, $19.99, d.j.) r/#7-12; Ross sketch pages 20.00
...: Thy Kingdom Come Part One SC (2009, $14.99) r/#7-12; Ross sketch pages 15.00
...: Thy Kingdom Come Part Two HC (2008, $24.99, d.j.) r/#13-18 & Annual #1; Ross sketch pages 25.00
...: Thy Kingdom Come Part Two SC (2009, $19.99) r/#13-18 & Ann. #1; Ross sketch-a 20.00
...: Thy Kingdom Come Part Three HC (2009, $24.99, d.j.) r/#19-22 & K.C. Specials - Superman, Magog and The Kingdom; Ross sketch pages 25.00
...: Thy Kingdom Come Part Three SC (2010, $19.99) same contents as HC 20.00

JUSTICE SOCIETY OF AMERICA 100-PAGE SUPER SPECTACULAR
DC Comics: 2000 ($6.95, mimics format of DC 100 Page Super Spectaculars)

1-"1975 Issue" reprints Flash team-up and Golden Age JSA 7.00

JUSTICE SOCIETY RETURNS, THE (See All Star Comics (1999) for related titles)
DC Comics: 2003 ($19.95, TPB)

TPB-Reprints 1999 JSA x-over from All-Star Comics #1,2 and related one-shots 20.00

JUSTICE TRAPS THE GUILTY (Fargo Kid V11#3 on)
Prize/Headline Publications: Oct-Nov, 1947 - V11#2(#92), Apr-May, 1958 (True FBI Cases)

	GD	VG	FN	VF	VF/NM	NM-
V2#1-S&K-c/a; electrocution-c	61	122	183	390	670	950
2-S&K-c/a	36	72	108	216	351	485
3-5-S&K-c/a	34	68	102	199	325	450
6-S&K-c/a; Feldstein-a	36	72	108	211	343	475
7,9-S&K-c/a. 7-9-V2#1-3 in indicia; #7-9 on-c	30	60	90	177	289	400
8-Krigstein-a; S&K-c; electric chair-c	27	54	81	160	263	365
10-Krigstein-a; S&K-c/a	30	60	90	177	289	400
11,18,19-S&K-c	17	34	51	98	154	210
12,14-17,20-No S&K. 14-Severin/Elder-a (8pg.)	11	22	33	62	86	110
13-Used in **SOTI**, pg. 110-111	13	26	39	74	105	135
21,30-S&K-c/a	18	36	54	103	162	220
22,23-S&K-c	14	28	42	78	112	145
24-26,27,29,31-50: 32-Meskin story	11	22	33	60	83	105
28-Kirby-c	13	26	39	74	105	135
51-55,57,59-70	10	20	30	54	72	90
56-Ben Oda, Joe Simon, Joe Genola, Mort Meskin & Jack Kirby app. in police line-up on classic-c	14	28	42	82	121	160
58-Illo. in **SOTI**, "Treating police contemptuously" (top left); text on heroin	26	52	78	154	252	350
71-92: 76-Orlando-a	8	16	24	44	57	70

NOTE: ***Bailey** a-12, 13. **Elder** a-8. **Kirby** a-19p. **Meskin** a-22, 27, 63, 64; c-45, 46. **Robinson/Meskin** a-5, 19. **Severin** a-8, 11p. Photo c-12, 15-17.*

JUST IMAGINE STAN LEE WITH... (Stan Lee re-invents DC icons)
DC Comics: 2001 - 2002 ($5.95, prestige format, one-shots)
(Adam Hughes back-c on all)(Michael Uslan back-up stories in all, diff. artists)

Scott McDaniel Creating **Aquaman**- Back-up w/Fradon-a 6.00
Joe Kubert Creating **Batman**- Back-up w/Kaluta-a 6.00
Chris Bachalo Creating **Catwoman**- Back-up w/Cooke & Allred-a 6.00
John Cassaday Creating **Crisis**- no back-up story 6.00
Kevin Maguire Creating **The Flash**- Back-up w/Aragonés-a 6.00
Dave Gibbons Creating **Green Lantern**- Back-up w/Giordano-a 6.00
Jerry Ordway Creating **JLA** 6.00
John Byrne Creating **Robin**- Back-up w/John Severin-a 6.00
Walter Simonson Creating **Sandman**- Back-up w/Corben-a 6.00
Gary Frank Creating **Shazam!**- Back-up w/Kano-a 6.00
John Buscema Creating **Superman**- Back-up w/Kyle Baker-a 6.00
Jim Lee Creating **Wonder Woman**- Back-up w/Gene Colan-a 6.00
Secret Files and Origins #1 (3/02, $4.95) Crisis prologue; Jurgens-a 5.00
TPB -Just Imagine Stan Lee Creating the DC Universe: Book One (2002, $19.95) r/Batman, Wonder Woman, Superman, Green Lantern 20.00
TPB -Just Imagine Stan Lee Creating the DC Universe: Book Two (2003, $19.95) r/Flash, JLA, Secret Files and Origins, Robin, Shazam; sketch pages 20.00
TPB -Just Imagine Stan Lee Creating the DC Universe: Book Three (2004, $19.95) r/Aquaman, Catwoman, Sandman, Crisis; profile pages 20.00

JUST MARRIED
Charlton Comics: January, 1958 - No. 114, Dec, 1976

	GD	VG	FN	VF	VF/NM	NM-
1	6	12	18	41	66	90
2	4	8	12	22	34	45
3-10	3	6	9	18	27	35
11-30	3	6	9	14	20	26
31-50	2	4	6	11	16	20

Ka'a'nga Comics #9 © FH

Kamandi, The Last Boy on Earth #28 © DC

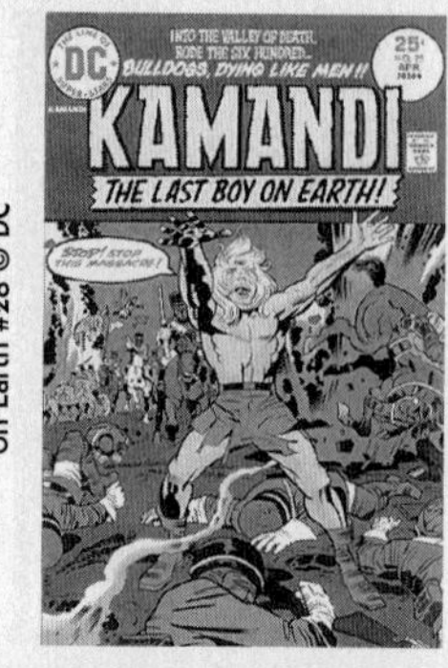

Kane & Lynch #1 © SquareEnix

	GD 2.0	VG 4.0	FN 6.0	VF 8.0	VF/NM 9.0	NM- 9.2
51-70	2	4	6	9	13	16
71-78,80-89	2	4	6	8	11	14
79-Ditko-a (7 pages)	2	4	6	10	14	18
90-Susan Dey and David Cassidy full page poster	2	4	6	11	16	20
91-114	2	4	6	8	10	12

KA'A'NGA COMICS (...Jungle King)(See Jungle Comics)
Fiction House Magazines (Glen-Kel Publ. Co.): Spring, 1949 - No. 20, Summer, 1954

	GD 2.0	VG 4.0	FN 6.0	VF 8.0	VF/NM 9.0	NM- 9.2
1-Ka'a'nga, Lord of the Jungle begins	52	104	156	323	549	775
2 (Winter, '49-'50)	30	60	90	177	289	400
3,4	22	44	66	132	216	300
5-Camilla app.	21	42	63	122	199	275
6-10: 7-Tuska-a. 9-Tabu, Wizard of the Jungle app. 10-Used in **POP**, pg. 99	15	30	45	88	137	185
11-15: 15-Camilla-r by Baker/Jungle #106	14	28	42	78	112	145
16-Sheena app.	14	28	42	81	118	155
17-20	13	26	39	72	101	130
I.W. Reprint #1,8: 1-r/#18; Kinstler-c. 8-r/#10	3	6	9	14	20	25

NOTE: ***Celardo** c-1. **Whitman** c-8-20(most).*

KABOOM
Awesome Entertainment: Sept, 1997 - No. 3, Nov, 1997 ($2.50)

	GD 2.0	VG 4.0	FN 6.0	VF 8.0	VF/NM 9.0	NM- 9.2
1-3: 1-Matsuda-a/Loeb-s; 4 covers exist (Matsuda, Sale, Pollina and McGuinness), 1-Dynamic Forces Edition, 2-Regular, 2-Alicia Watcher variant-c, 2-Gold logo variant-c, 3-Two covers by Liefeld & Matsuda, 3-Dynamic Forces Ed., Prelude Ed.						3.00
Prelude Gold Edition						4.00

KABOOM (2nd series)
Awesome Entertainment: July, 1999 - No. 3, Dec, 1999 ($2.50)

	GD 2.0	VG 4.0	FN 6.0	VF 8.0	VF/NM 9.0	NM- 9.2
1-3: 1-Grant-a(p); at least 4 variant covers						3.00

KABUKI
Caliber: Nov, 1994 ($3.50, B&W, one-shot)

	GD 2.0	VG 4.0	FN 6.0	VF 8.0	VF/NM 9.0	NM- 9.2
nn-(Fear The Reaper) 1st app.; David Mack-c/a/s	1	2	3	5	6	8
Color Special (1/96, $2.95)-Mack-c/a/scripts; pin-ups by Tucci, Harris & Quesada						4.00
Gallery (8/95, $2.95)- pinups from Mack, Bradstreet, Paul Pope & others						3.00

KABUKI
Image Comics: Oct, 1997 - No. 9, Mar, 2000 ($2.95, color)

	GD 2.0	VG 4.0	FN 6.0	VF 8.0	VF/NM 9.0	NM- 9.2
1-David Mack-c/s/a						5.00
1-($10.00)-Dynamic Forces Edition	1	3	4	6	8	10
2-5						4.00
6-9						3.00
#1/2 (9/01, $2.95) r/Wizard 1/2; Eklipse Mag. article; bio						3.00
...Classics (2/99, $3.95) Reprints Fear the Reaper						4.00
...Classics 2 (3/99, $3.95) Reprints Dance of Dance						4.00
...Classics 3-5 (3-6/99, $4.95) Reprints Circle of Blood-Acts 1-3						5.00
...Classics 6-12 (7/99-3/00, $3.25) Various reprints						3.25
...Images (6/98, $4.95) r/#1 with new pin-ups						5.00
...Images 2 (1/99, $4.95) r/#1 with new pin-ups						5.00
...Metamorphosis TPB (10/00, $24.95) r/#1-9; Sienkiewicz intro.; 2nd printing exists						25.00
...Reflections 1-4 (7/98-5/02; $4.95) new story plus art techniques						5.00
... The Ghost Play (11/02, $2.95) new story plus interview						3.00

KABUKI
Marvel Comics (Icon): July, 2004 - Present ($2.99, color)

	GD 2.0	VG 4.0	FN 6.0	VF 8.0	VF/NM 9.0	NM- 9.2
1-9: 1-David Mack-c/s/a in all; variant-c by Alex Maleev. 4-Variant-c by Adam Hughes. 6-Variant-c by Mignola. 8-Variant-c by Kent Williams. 9-Allred var-c						3.00
...: The Alchemy HC (2008, $29.99, dust jacket) oversized r/#1-9; bonus art & content						30.00
... Reflections 5-15 (7/05-10/09, $5.99) paintings & sketches of recent work; photos						6.00

KABUKI AGENTS (SCARAB)
Image Comics: Aug, 1999 - No. 8, Aug, 2001 ($2.95, B&W)

	GD 2.0	VG 4.0	FN 6.0	VF 8.0	VF/NM 9.0	NM- 9.2
1-8-David Mack-s/Rick Mays-a						3.00
Lost in Translation HC (3/02, $29.95) r/#1-8; intro. by Paul Pope						30.00
Lost in Translation SC (3/02, $19.95) r/#1-8; intro. by Paul Pope						20.00

KABUKI: CIRCLE OF BLOOD
Caliber Press: Jan, 1995 - No. 6, Nov, 1995 ($2.95, B&W)

	GD 2.0	VG 4.0	FN 6.0	VF 8.0	VF/NM 9.0	NM- 9.2
1-David Mack story/a in all						5.00
2-6: 3-#1 on inside indicia.						3.00
6-Variant-c						3.00
TPB ($16.95) r/#1-6, intro. by Steranko						17.00
TPB (1997, $17.95) Image Edition-r/#1-6, intro. by Steranko						18.00
TPB ($24.95) Deluxe Edition						25.00

KABUKI: DANCE OF DEATH
London Night Studios: Jan, 1995 ($3.00, B&W, one-shot)

	GD 2.0	VG 4.0	FN 6.0	VF 8.0	VF/NM 9.0	NM- 9.2
1-David Mack-c/a/scripts	1	2	3	5	6	8

KABUKI: DREAMS
Image Comics: Jan, 1998 ($4.95, TPB)

	GD 2.0	VG 4.0	FN 6.0	VF 8.0	VF/NM 9.0	NM- 9.2
nn-Reprints Color Special & Dreams of the Dead						5.00

KABUKI: DREAMS OF THE DEAD
Caliber: July, 1996 ($2.95, one-shot)

	GD 2.0	VG 4.0	FN 6.0	VF 8.0	VF/NM 9.0	NM- 9.2
nn-David Mack-c/a/scripts						3.00

KABUKI FAN EDITION
Gemstone Publ./Caliber: Feb, 1997 (mail-in offer, one-shot)

	GD 2.0	VG 4.0	FN 6.0	VF 8.0	VF/NM 9.0	NM- 9.2
nn-David Mack-c/a/scripts						4.00

KABUKI: MASKS OF THE NOH
Caliber: May, 1996 - No. 4, Feb, 1997 ($2.95, limited series)

	GD 2.0	VG 4.0	FN 6.0	VF 8.0	VF/NM 9.0	NM- 9.2
1-4: 1-Three-c (1A-Quesada, 1B-Buzz, &1C-Mack). 3-Terry Moore pin-up						3.00
TPB-(4/98, $10.95) r/#1-4; intro by Terry Moore						11.00

KABUKI: SKIN DEEP
Caliber Comics: Oct, 1996 - No. 3, May, 1997 ($2.95)

	GD 2.0	VG 4.0	FN 6.0	VF 8.0	VF/NM 9.0	NM- 9.2
1-3:David Mack-c/a/scripts. 2-Two-c (1-Mack, 1-Ross)						3.00
TPB-(5/98, $9.95) r/#1-3; intro by Alex Ross						10.00

KAMANDI: AT EARTH'S END
DC Comics: June, 1993 - No. 6, Nov, 1993 ($1.75, limited series)

	GD 2.0	VG 4.0	FN 6.0	VF 8.0	VF/NM 9.0	NM- 9.2
1-6: Elseworlds storyline						3.00

KAMANDI, THE LAST BOY ON EARTH (Also see Alarming Tales #1, Brave and the Bold #120 & 157, Cancelled Comic Cavalcade & Wednesday Comics)
National Periodical Publ./DC Comics: Oct-Nov, 1972 - No. 59, Sept-Oct, 1978

	GD 2.0	VG 4.0	FN 6.0	VF 8.0	VF/NM 9.0	NM- 9.2
1-Origin & 1st app. Kamandi	8	16	24	52	86	120
2,3	5	10	15	30	48	65
4,5: 4-Intro. Prince Tuftan of the Tigers	4	8	12	26	41	55
6-10	3	6	9	19	29	38
11-20	3	6	9	16	22	28
21-28,30,31,33-40: 24-Last 20¢ issue. 31-Intro Pyra.	2	4	6	13	18	22
29,32: 29-Superman x-over. 32-(68 pgs.)-r/origin from #1 plus one new story; 4 pg. biog. of Jack Kirby with B&W photos	3	6	9	14	20	26
41-57	2	4	6	10	14	18
58-(44 pgs.)-Karate Kid x-over from LSH	3	6	9	14	19	24
59-(44 pgs.)-Cont'd in B&B #157; The Return of Omac back-up by Starlin-c/a(p)	3	6	9	14	19	24

NOTE: ***Ayers** a(p)-48-59 (most). **Giffen** a-44p, 45p. **Kirby** a-1-40p; c-1-33. **Kubert** c-34-41. **Nasser** a-45p, 46p. **Starlin** a-59p; c-57, 59p.*

KAMUI (Legend Of...#2 on)
Eclipse Comics/Viz Comics: May 12, 1987 - No. 37, Nov. 15, 1988 ($1.50, B&W, bi-weekly)

	GD 2.0	VG 4.0	FN 6.0	VF 8.0	VF/NM 9.0	NM- 9.2
1-37: 1-3 have 2nd printings						3.00

KANE & LYNCH (Based on the video games)
DC Comics (WildStorm): Oct, 2010 - No. 6, Apr, 2011 ($3.99/$2.99, limited series)

	GD 2.0	VG 4.0	FN 6.0	VF 8.0	VF/NM 9.0	NM- 9.2
1-4-($3.99) Templesmith-c/Edginton-s/Mitten-a						4.00
5,6-($2.99)						3.00

KAOS MOON (Also see Negative Burn #34)
Caliber Comics: 1996 - No. 4, 1997 ($2.95, B&W)

	GD 2.0	VG 4.0	FN 6.0	VF 8.0	VF/NM 9.0	NM- 9.2
1-4-David Boller-s/a						3.00
3,4-Limited Alternate-c						4.00
3,4-Gold Alternate-c, Full Circle TPB ($5.95) r/#1,2						6.00

KARATE KID (See Action, Adventure, Legion of Super-Heroes, & Superboy)
National Periodical Publications/DC Comics: Mar-Apr, 1976 - No. 15, July-Aug, 1978 (Legion of Super-Heroes spin-off)

	GD 2.0	VG 4.0	FN 6.0	VF 8.0	VF/NM 9.0	NM- 9.2
1,15: 1-Meets Iris Jacobs; Estrada/Staton-a. 15-Continued into Kamandi #58	2	4	6	11	16	20
2-14: 2-Major Disaster app. 14-Robin x-over	2	3	4	6	8	10

NOTE: ***Grell** c-1-4, 5p, 6p, 7, 8. **Staton** a-1-9i. Legion x-over-No. 1, 2, 4, 6, 10, 12, 13. Princess Projectra x-over-#8, 9.*

KATHY
Standard Comics: Sept, 1949 - No. 17, Sept, 1955

	GD 2.0	VG 4.0	FN 6.0	VF 8.0	VF/NM 9.0	NM- 9.2
1-Teen-age	15	30	45	84	127	170
2-Schomburg-c	11	22	33	64	90	115
3-5	9	18	27	47	61	75
6-17: 17-Code approved	8	16	24	42	54	65

KATHY (The Teenage Tornado)
Atlas Comics/Marvel (ZPC): Oct, 1959 - No. 27, Feb, 1964 (most issues contain paper dolls and pin-up pages)

Kato #1 © Green Hornet Inc.

Katy Keene #38 © AP

Ka-Zar V2 #6 © MAR

	GD 2.0	VG 4.0	FN 6.0	VF 8.0	VF/NM 9.0	NM- 9.2
1-The Teen-age Tornado; Goldberg-c/a in all	9	18	27	60	100	140
2	5	10	15	35	55	75
3-15	4	8	12	28	44	60
16-23,25,27	3	6	9	21	32	42
24-(8/63) Frank Sinatra, Cary Grant, Ed Sullivan & Liz Taylor-c	4	8	12	26	41	55
26-(12/63) Kathy becomes a model; Millie app.	4	8	12	22	34	45

KAT KARSON
I. W. Enterprises: No date (Reprint)

	GD	VG	FN	VF	VF/NM	NM-
1-Funny animals	2	4	6	10	12	15

KATO (Also see The Green Hornet)
Dynamite Entertainment: 2010 - Present ($3.99)

	GD	VG	FN	VF	VF/NM	NM-
1-9: 1-Kato and daughter origin; Garza-a/Parks-s. 2-9 Bernard-a						4.00
Annual 1 (2011, $4.99) Parks-s/Salazar-a						5.00

KATO OF THE GREEN HORNET (Also see The Green Hornet)
Now Comics: Nov, 1991 - No. 4, Feb, 1992 ($2.50, mini-series)

	GD	VG	FN	VF	VF/NM	NM-
1-4: Brent Anderson-c/a						3.00

KATO OF THE GREEN HORNET II (Also see The Green Hornet)
Now Comics: Nov, 1992 - No. 2, Dec, 1993 ($2.50, mini-series)

	GD	VG	FN	VF	VF/NM	NM-
1,2-Baron-s/Mayerik & Sherman-a						3.00

KATO ORIGINS (Also see The Green Hornet: Year One)
Dynamite Entertainment: 2010 - Present ($3.99, mini-series)

	GD	VG	FN	VF	VF/NM	NM-
1-7-Kato in 1942; Jai Nitz-s/Colton Worley-a; covers by Worley & Francavilla						4.00

KATY KEENE (Also see Kasco Komics, Laugh, Pep, Suzie, & Wilbur)
Archie Publ./Close-Up/Radio Comics: 1949 - No. 4, 1951; No. 5, 3/52 - No. 62, Oct, 1961 (50-53-Adventures of...on-c) (Cut and missing pages are common)

	GD	VG	FN	VF	VF/NM	NM-
1-Bill Woggon-c/a begins; swipes-c to Mopsy #1	168	336	504	1075	1838	2600
2-(1950)	61	122	183	390	670	950
3-5: 3-(1951). 4-(1951)	50	100	150	315	533	750
6-10	37	74	111	222	361	500
11,13-21: 21-Last pre-code issue (3/55)	31	62	93	182	296	410
12-(Scarce)	37	74	111	222	361	500
22-40	21	42	63	126	206	285
41-60: 54-Wedding Album plus wedding pin-up	18	36	54	103	162	220
61,62: 62-Robot-c	20	40	60	114	182	250
Annual 1('54, 25¢)-All new stories; last pre-code	55	110	165	352	601	850
Annual 2-6('55-59, 25¢)-All new stories	32	64	96	188	307	425
3-D 1(1953, 25¢, large size)-Came w/glasses	39	78	117	231	378	525
Charm 1(9/58)-Woggon-c/a; new stories, and cut-outs	29	58	87	170	278	385
Glamour 1(1957)-Puzzles, games, cut-outs	29	58	87	170	278	385
Spectacular 1('56)	30	60	90	177	289	400

NOTE: *Debby's Diary in #45, 47-49, 52, 57.*

KATY KEENE COMICS DIGEST MAGAZINE
Close-Up, Inc. (Archie Ent.): 1987 - No. 10, July, 1990 ($1.25/$1.35/$1.50, digest size)

	GD	VG	FN	VF	VF/NM	NM-
1	2	4	6	10	14	18
2-10	1	3	4	6	8	10

NOTE: *Many used copies are cut-up inside.*

KATY KEENE FASHION BOOK MAGAZINE
Radio Comics/Archie Publications: 1955 - No. 13, Sum, '56 - N. 23, Wint, '58-59 (nn 3-10)

	GD	VG	FN	VF	VF/NM	NM-
1-Bill Woggon-c/a	54	108	162	343	574	825
2	31	62	93	182	296	410
11-18: 18-Photo Bill Woggon	22	44	66	132	216	300
19-23	19	38	57	111	176	240

KATY KEENE HOLIDAY FUN (See Archie Giant Series Magazine No. 7, 12)

KATY KEENE MODEL BEHAVIOR
Archie Comic Publications: 2008 ($10.95, TPB)

	GD	VG	FN	VF	VF/NM	NM-
Vol. 1 - New story and reprinted apps./pin-ups from Archie & Friends #101-112						11.00

KATY KEENE PINUP PARADE
Radio Comics/Archie Publications: 1955 - No. 15, Summer, 1961 (25¢)
(Cut-out & missing pages are common)

	GD	VG	FN	VF	VF/NM	NM-
1-Cut-outs in all?; last pre-code issue	54	108	162	343	574	825
2-(1956)	31	62	93	182	296	410
3-5: 3-(1957)	26	52	78	154	252	350
6-10,12-14: 8-Mad parody. 10-Bill Woggon photo	22	44	66	128	209	290
11-Story of how comics get CCA approved, narrated by Katy	27	54	81	158	259	360
15(Rare)-Photo artist & family	41	82	123	251	418	585

KATY KEENE SPECIAL (Katy Keene #7 on; see Laugh Comics Digest)
Archie Ent.: Sept, 1983 - No. 33, 1990 (Later issues published quarterly)

	GD	VG	FN	VF	VF/NM	NM-
1-10: 1-Woggon-r; new Woggon-c. 3-Woggon-r						5.00
11-25: 12-Spider-Man parody						6.00
26-32-(Low print run)	1	2	3	5	7	9
33	2	4	6	8	10	12

KATZENJAMMER KIDS, THE (See Captain & the Kids & Giant Comic Album)
David McKay Publ./Standard No. 12-21(Spring/'50 - 53)/Harvey No. 22, 4/53 on: 1945-1946; Summer, 1947 - No. 27, Feb-Mar, 1954

	GD	VG	FN	VF	VF/NM	NM-
Feature Books 30	20	40	60	114	182	250
Feature Books 32,35('45),41,44('46)	18	36	54	103	162	220
Feature Book 37-Has photos & biography of Harold Knerr	19	38	57	109	172	235
1(1947)-All new stories begin	19	38	57	109	172	235
2	11	22	33	64	90	115
3-11	9	18	27	52	69	85
12-14(Standard)	8	16	24	42	54	65
15-21(Standard)	8	16	24	40	50	60
22-25,27(Harvey): 22-24-Henry app.	7	14	21	35	43	50
26-Half in 3-D	16	32	48	94	147	200

KAYO (Formerly Bullseye & Jest; becomes Carnival Comics)
Harry 'A' Chesler: No. 12, Mar, 1945

	GD	VG	FN	VF	VF/NM	NM-
12-Green Knight, Capt. Glory, Little Nemo (not by McCay)	19	38	57	111	176	240

KA-ZAR (Also see Marvel Comics #1, Savage Tales #6 & X-Men #10)
Marvel Comics Group: Aug, 1970 - No. 3, Mar, 1971 (Giant-Size, 68 pgs.)

	GD	VG	FN	VF	VF/NM	NM-
1-Reprints earlier Ka-Zar stories; Avengers x-over in Hercules; Daredevil, X-Men app.; hidden profanity-c	4	8	12	28	44	60
2,3-Daredevil-r. 2-r/Daredevil #13 w/Kirby layouts; Ka-Zar origin, Angel-r from X-Men by Tuska. 3-Romita & Heck-a (no Kirby)	3	6	9	18	27	35

NOTE: ***Buscema** r-2. **Colan** a-1p(r). **Kirby** c/a-1, 2. #1-Reprints X-Men #10 & Daredevil #24*

KA-ZAR
Marvel Comics Group: Jan, 1974 - No. 20, Feb, 1977 (Regular Size)

	GD	VG	FN	VF	VF/NM	NM-
1	3	6	9	14	19	24
2-10	2	4	6	8	10	12
11-14,16,18-20: 16-Only a 30 ¢ edition exists	1	2	3	5	6	8
15,17-(Regular 25¢ edition)(8/76)	1	2	3	5	6	8
15,17-(30¢-c variants, limited distribution)	3	6	9	14	20	25

NOTE: ***Alcala** a-6i, 8i. **Brunner** c-4. **J. Buscema** a-6-10p; c-1, 5, 7. **Heath** a-12. **G. Kane** c(p)-3, 5, 8-11, 15, 20. **Kirby** c-12p. **Reinman** a-1p.*

KA-ZAR (Volume 2)
Marvel Comics: May, 1997 - No. 20, Dec, 1998 ($1.95/$1.99)

	GD	VG	FN	VF	VF/NM	NM-
1-Waid-s/Andy Kubert-c/a. thru #4						4.00
1-2nd printing; new cover						3.00
2,4: 2-Two-c						3.00
3-Alpha Flight #1 preview						4.00
5-13,15-20: 8-Includes Spider-Man Cybercomic CD-ROM. 9-11-Thanos app. 15-Priest-s/Martinez & Rodriguez-a begin; Punisher app.						3.00
14-($2.99) Last Waid/Kubert issue; flip book with 2nd story previewing new creative team of Priest-s/Martinez & Rodriguez-a						4.00
'97 Annual ($2.99)-Wraparound-c						4.00

KA-ZAR OF THE SAVAGE LAND
Marvel Comics: Feb, 1997 ($2.50, one-shot)

	GD	VG	FN	VF	VF/NM	NM-
1-Wraparound-c						4.00

KA-ZAR: SIBLING RIVALRY
Marvel Comics: July, 1997 ($1.95, one-shot)

	GD	VG	FN	VF	VF/NM	NM-
(# -1) Flashback story w/Alpha Flight #1 preview						3.00

KA-ZAR THE SAVAGE (See Marvel Fanfare)
Marvel Comics Group: Apr, 1981 - No. 34, Oct, 1984 (Regular size)(Mando paper #10 on)

	GD	VG	FN	VF	VF/NM	NM-
1						5.00
2-20,24,27,28,30-34: 11-Origin Zabu. 12-One of two versions with panel missing on pg. 10. 20-Kraven the Hunter-c/story (also apps. in #21)						3.00
12-Version with panel on pg. 10 (1600 printed)	1	2	3	5	6	8
21-23, 25,26-Spider-Man app. 26-Photo-c.						4.00
29-Double size; Ka-Zar & Shanna wed						4.00

NOTE: ***B. Anderson** a-1-15p, 18, 19; c-1-17, 18p, 20(back). **G. Kane** a(back-up)-11, 12, 14.*

KEEN DETECTIVE FUNNIES (Formerly Detective Picture Stories?)
Centaur Publications: No. 8, July, 1938 - No. 24, Sept, 1940

V1#8-The Clock continues-r/Funny Picture Stories #1; Roy Crane-a (1st?)

Keen Detective Funnies #9 © CEN

The Kents #1 © DC

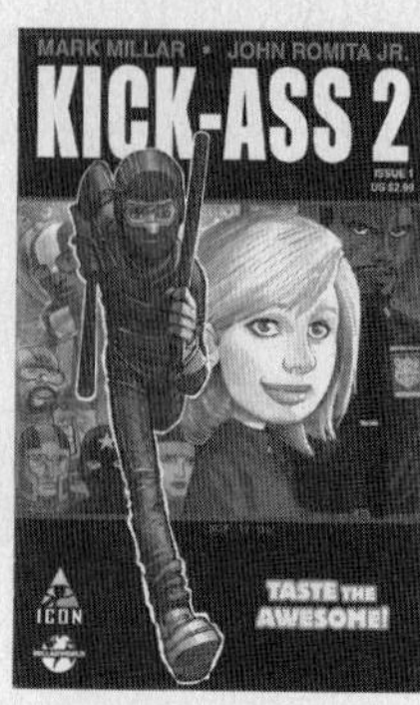

Kick-Ass 2 #1 © Millarworld & John Romita Jr.

	GD 2.0	VG 4.0	FN 6.0	VF 8.0	VF/NM 9.0	NM- 9.2
	252	504	756	1613	2757	3900
9-Tex Martin by Eisner; The Gang Buster app.	92	184	276	584	1005	1425
10,11: 11-Dean Denton story (begins?)	84	168	252	538	919	1300
V2#1,2-The Eye Sees by Frank Thomas begins; ends #23(Not in V2#3&5). 2-Jack Cole-a	77	154	231	493	847	1200
3-6: 3-TNT Todd begins. 4-Gabby Flynn begins. 5,6-Dean Denton story	73	146	219	467	796	1125
7-The Masked Marvel by Ben Thompson begins (7/39, 1st app.)(scarce)	258	516	774	1651	2826	4000
8-Nudist ranch panel w/four girls	92	184	276	584	1005	1425
9-11	82	164	246	528	902	1275
12(12/39)-Origin The Eye Sees by Frank Thomas; death of Masked Marvel's sidekick ZL	100	200	300	635	1093	1550
V3#1,2	73	146	219	467	796	1125
18-Bondage/torture-c	77	154	231	493	847	1200
19,21,22	73	146	219	467	796	1125
20-Classic Eye Sees-c by Thomas	110	220	330	704	1202	1700
23-Air Man begins (intro); Air Man-c	97	194	291	621	1061	1500
24-(scarce) Air Man-c	103	206	309	659	1130	1600

NOTE: ***Burgos*** *a-V2#2.* ***Jack Cole*** *a-V2#2.* ***Eisner*** *a-10, V2#6r.* ***Ken Ernst*** *a-V2#4-7, 9, 10, 19, 21; c-V2#4.* ***Everett*** *a-V2#6, 7, 9, 11, 12, 20.* ***Guardineer*** *a-V2#5, 66.* ***Gustavson*** *a-V2#4-6.* ***Simon*** *c-V3#1.* ***Thompson*** *c-V2#7, 9, 10, 22.*

KEEN KOMICS
Centaur Publications: V2#1, May, 1939 - V2#3, Nov, 1939

	GD	VG	FN	VF	VF/NM	NM-
V2#1(Large size)-Dan Hastings (s/f), The Big Top, Bob Phantom the Magician, The Mad Goddess app.	103	206	309	659	1130	1600
V2#2(Reg. size)-The Forbidden Idol of Machu Picchu; Cut Carson by Burgos begins	64	128	192	406	696	985
V2#3-Saddle Sniffl by Jack Cole, Circus Pays, Kings Revenge app.	64	128	192	406	696	985

NOTE: ***Binder*** *a-V2#2.* ***Burgos*** *a-V2#2, 3.* ***Ken Ernst*** *a-V2#3.* ***Gustavson*** *a-V2#2.* ***Jack Cole*** *a-V2#3.*

KEEN TEENS (Girls magazine)
Life's Romances Publ./Leader/Magazine Ent.: 1945 - No. 6, Aug-Sept, 1947

	GD	VG	FN	VF	VF/NM	NM-
nn (#1)-14 pgs. Claire Voyant (cont'd. in other nn issue) movie photos, Dotty Dripple, Gertie O'Grady & Sissy; Van Johnson, Sinatra photo-c	40	80	120	242	401	560
nn (#2, 1946)-16 pgs. Claire Voyant & 16 pgs. movie photos	29	58	87	170	278	385
3-6: 4-Glenn Ford photo-c. 5-Perry Como-c	15	30	45	85	130	175

KELLYS, THE (Formerly Rusty Comics; Spy Cases No. 26 on)
Marvel Comics (HPC): No. 23, Jan, 1950 - No. 25, June, 1950 (52 pgs.)

	GD	VG	FN	VF	VF/NM	NM-
23-Teenage	14	28	42	80	115	150
24,25: 24-Margie app.	10	20	30	54	72	90

KEN MAYNARD WESTERN (Movie star)(See Wow Comics, 1936)
Fawcett Publ.: Sept, 1950 - No. 8, Feb, 1952 (All 36 pgs; photo front/back-c)

	GD	VG	FN	VF	VF/NM	NM-
1-Ken Maynard & his horse Tarzan begin	37	74	111	222	361	500
2	20	40	60	120	195	270
3-8: 6-Atomic bomb explosion panel	15	30	45	88	137	185

KEN SHANNON (Becomes Gabby #11 on) (Also see Police Comics #103)
Quality Comics Group: Oct, 1951 - No. 10, Apr, 1953 (A private eye)

	GD	VG	FN	VF	VF/NM	NM-
1-Crandall-a	40	80	120	242	401	560
2-Crandall c/a(2)	30	60	90	177	289	400
3-Horror-c; Crandall-a	32	64	96	188	307	425
4,5-Crandall-a	22	44	66	128	209	290
6-Crandall-c/a; "The Weird Vampire Mob"-c/s	30	60	90	177	289	400
7-"The Ugliest Man Alive"-c; Crandall-a	21	42	63	126	206	285
8,9: 8-Opium den drug use story	18	36	54	105	165	225
10-Crandall-c	19	38	57	109	172	235

NOTE: ***Crandall/Cuidera*** *c-1-10.* ***Jack Cole*** *a-1-9. #1-15 published after title change to Gabby.*

KEN STUART
Publication Enterprises: Jan, 1949 (Sea Adventures)

	GD	VG	FN	VF	VF/NM	NM-
1-Frank Borth-c/a	10	20	30	54	72	90

KENT BLAKE OF THE SECRET SERVICE (Spy)
Marvel/Atlas Comics (20CC): May, 1951 - No. 14, July, 1953

	GD	VG	FN	VF	VF/NM	NM-
1-Injury to eye, bondage, torture; Brodsky-c	21	42	63	126	206	285
2-Drug use w/hypo scenes; Brodsky-c	15	30	45	88	137	185
3-14: 8-R.Q. Sale-a (2 pgs.)	10	20	30	58	79	100

NOTE: ***Heath*** *c-5, 7, 8.* ***Infantino*** *c-12.* ***Maneely*** *c-3.* ***Sinnott*** *a-2(3).* ***Tuska*** *a-8(3pg.).*

KENTS, THE
DC Comics: Aug, 1997 - No. 12, July, 1998 ($2.50, limited series)

	GD	VG	FN	VF	VF/NM	NM-
1-12-Ostrander-s/art by Truman and Bair (#1-8), Mandrake (#9-12)						3.00
TPB ($19.95) r/#1-12						20.00

KERRY DRAKE (Also see A-1 Comics)
Argo: Jan, 1956 - No. 2, March, 1956

	GD	VG	FN	VF	VF/NM	NM-
1,2-Newspaper-r	8	16	24	44	57	70

KERRY DRAKE DETECTIVE CASES (...Racket Buster No. 32,33)
(Also see Chamber of Clues & Green Hornet Comics #42-47)
Life's Romances/Com/Magazine Ent. No.1-5/Harvey No.6 on: 1944 - No. 5, 1944; No. 6, Jan, 1948 - No. 33, Aug, 1952

	GD	VG	FN	VF	VF/NM	NM-
nn(1944)(A-1 Comics)(slightly over-size)	30	60	90	177	289	400
2	18	36	54	107	169	230
3-5(1944)	15	30	45	90	140	190
6,8(1948): Lady Crime by Powell. 8-Bondage-c	12	24	36	67	94	120
7-Kubert-a; biog of Andriola (artist)	13	26	39	74	105	135
9,10-Two-part marijuana story; Kerry smokes marijuana in #10	15	30	45	88	137	185
11-15	10	20	30	58	79	100
16-33	9	18	27	50	65	80

NOTE: ***Andiola*** *c-6-9.* ***Berg*** *a-5.* ***Powell*** *a-10-23, 28, 29.*

KEWPIES
Will Eisner Publications: Spring, 1949

	GD	VG	FN	VF	VF/NM	NM-
1-Feiffer-a; Kewpie Doll ad on back cover; used in **SOTI**, pg. 35	48	96	144	302	514	725

KEY COMICS
Consolidated Magazines: Jan, 1944 - No. 5, Aug, 1946

	GD	VG	FN	VF	VF/NM	NM-
1-The Key, Will-O-The-Wisp begin	43	86	129	271	456	640
2 (3/44)	24	48	72	140	230	320
3,4: 4-(5/46)-Origin John Quincy The Atom (begins); Walter Johnson c-3-5	21	42	63	122	199	275
5-4pg. Faust Opera adaptation; Kiefer-a; back-c advertises "Masterpieces Illustrated" by Lloyd Jacquet after he left Classic Comics (no copies of Masterpieces Illustrated known)	26	52	78	154	252	350

KEY RING COMICS
Dell Publishing Co.: 1941 (16 pgs.; two colors) (sold 5 for 10¢)

	GD	VG	FN	VF	VF/NM	NM-
1-Sky Hawk, 1-Viking Carter, 1-Features Sleepy Samson, 1-Origin Greg Gilday; r/War Comics #2	9	18	27	50	65	80
1-Radior (Super hero)	10	20	30	58	79	100

NOTE: *Each book has two holes in spine to put in binder.*

KICK-ASS
Marvel Comics (Icon): April, 2008 - No. 8, Mar, 2010 ($2.99)

	GD	VG	FN	VF	VF/NM	NM-
1-Mark Millar-s/John Romita Jr.-a/c						15.00
1-Red variant cover by McNiven						20.00
1-2nd printing						4.00
1-Director's Cut (8/08, $3.99) r/#1 with script and sketch pages; Millar afterword						4.00
2						8.00
3-8: 5-Intro. Red Mist						4.00

NOTE: *Multiple printings exist for most issues.*

KICK-ASS 2
Marvel Comics (Icon): Dec, 2010 - Present ($2.99)

	GD	VG	FN	VF	VF/NM	NM-
1,2-Mark Millar-s/John Romita Jr.-a/c						3.00
1,2-Variant covers. 1-Edwards. 2-Yu						5.00

KID CARROTS
St. John Publishing Co.: September, 1953

	GD	VG	FN	VF	VF/NM	NM-
1-Funny animal	8	16	24	44	57	70

KID COLT ONE-SHOT
Marvel Comics: Sept, 2009 ($3.99)

	GD	VG	FN	VF	VF/NM	NM-
1-DeFalco-s/Burchett-a/Luke Ross-c						4.00

KID COLT OUTLAW (Kid Colt #1-4; ...Outlaw #5-on)(Also see All Western Winners, Best Western, Black Rider, Giant-Size..., Two-Gun Kid, Two-Gun Western, Western Winners, Wild Western, Wisco)
Marvel Comics(LCC) 1-16; Atlas(LMC) 17-102; Marvel 103-on: 8/48 - No. 139, 3/68; No. 140, 11/69 - No. 229, 4/79

	GD	VG	FN	VF	VF/NM	NM-
1-Kid Colt & his horse Steel begin.	123	246	369	787	1344	1900
2	55	110	165	352	601	850
3-5: 4-Anti-Wertham editorial; Tex Taylor app. 5-Blaze Carson app.	45	90	135	284	480	675
6-8: 6-Tex Taylor app; 7-Nimo the Lion begins, ends #10	32	64	96	188	307	425

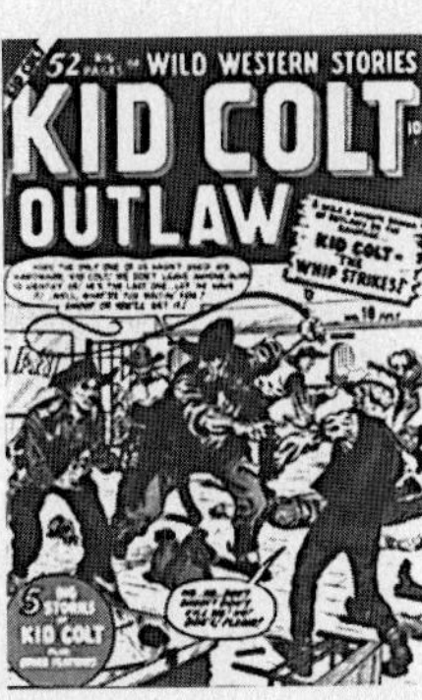

Kid Colt Outlaw #10 © MAR

Kid Eternity #11 © QUA

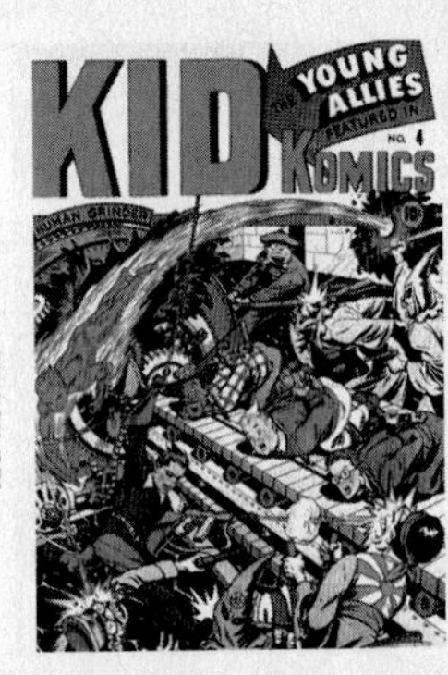

Kid Komics #4 © MAR

	GD 2.0	VG 4.0	FN 6.0	VF 8.0	VF/NM 9.0	NM- 9.2
9,10 (52 pgs.)	32	64	96	188	307	425
11-Origin	37	74	111	222	361	500
12-20	21	42	63	126	206	285
21-32	18	36	54	105	165	225
33-45: Black Rider in all	15	30	45	84	127	170
46,47,49,50	14	28	42	76	108	140
48-Kubert-a	14	28	42	78	112	145
51-53,55,56	11	22	33	62	86	110
54-Williamson/Maneely-c	12	24	36	67	94	120
57-60,66: 4-pg. Williamson-a in all	8	16	24	54	90	125
61-63,67-78,80-86: 70-Severin-c. 69,73-Maneely-c. 86-Kirby-a(r).	6	12	18	43	69	95
64,65-Crandall-a	7	14	21	45	73	100
79,87: 79-Origin retold. 87-Davis-a(r)	7	14	21	45	73	100
88,89-Williamson-a in both (4 pgs.). 89-Redrawn Matt Slade #2	7	14	21	47	76	105
90-99,101-106,108,109: 91-Kirby/Ayers-c. 95-Kirby/Ayers-c/story. 102-Last 10¢ issue	6	12	18	39	62	85
100	6	12	18	43	69	95
107-Only Kirby sci-fi cover of title; Kirby-a.	8	16	24	52	86	120
110-(5/63)-1st app. Iron Mask (Iron Man type villain)	7	14	21	47	76	105
111-120: 114-(1/64)-2nd app. Iron Mask	5	10	15	35	55	75
121-129,133-139: 121-Rawhide Kid x-over. 125-Two-Gun Kid x-over. 139-Last 12¢ issue	4	8	12	28	44	60
130-132 (68 pgs.)-one new story each. 130-Origin	6	12	18	37	59	80
140-155: 140-Reprints begin (later issues mostly-r). 155-Last 15¢ issue	3	6	9	16	22	28
156-Giant; reprints (52 pgs.)	3	6	9	20	30	40
157-180,200: 170-Origin retold.	3	6	9	14	19	24
181-199	2	4	6	11	16	20
201-229: 201-New material w/Rawhide Kid app; Kane-c. 229-Rawhide Kid-r	2	4	6	10	14	18
205-209-(30¢-c variants, limited dist.)	6	12	18	37	59	80
218-220-(35¢-c variants, limited dist.)	9	18	27	60	100	140
...Album (no date; 1950's; Atlas Comics)-132 pgs.; random binding, cardboard cover, B&W stories; contents can vary (Rare)	97	194	291	621	1061	1500

NOTE: ***Ayers** a-many. **Colan** a-52, 53, 84, 112, 114; c(p)-223, 228, 229. **Crandall** a-140r, 167r. **Everett** a-90, 137i, 225i(r). **Heath** a-8(2); c-34, 35, 39, 44, 46, 48, 49, 57, 64. **Heck** a-135, 139. **Jack Keller** a-25(2), 26-68(3-4), 73, 78, 84, 85, 88, 92, 94p, 98, 99, 101, 106-108, 110-112, 114, 115, 117-127, 129, 130, 132, 140-150r. **Kirby** a-86r, 93, 96, 107, 119, 176(part); c-87, 92-95, 97, 99-112, 114-117, 121-123, 197r; w/**Ditko** c-89. **Maneely** a-12, 68, 81; c-17, 19, 40-43, 47, 52, 53, 62, 65, 68, 73, 78, 81, 142r, 150r. **Morrow** a-173r, 216r. **Rico** a-13, 18. **Severin** c-55, 58, 59, 84, 143, 148, 149i. **Shores** a-39, 41-43, 143r; c-1-10(most), 24. **Sutton** a-136, 137p, 225p(r). **Wildey** a-47, 54, 82, 144r. **Williamson** r-147, 170, 172, 216. **Woodbridge** a-64, 81. Black Rider in #33-45, 74, 86. Iron Mask in #110, 114, 121, 127. Sam Hawk in #80, 84, 101, 111, 121, 146, 174, 181, 188.*

KID COWBOY (Also see Approved Comics #4 & Boy Cowboy)
Ziff-Davis Publ./St. John (Approved Comics) #11,14: 1950 - No. 11, Wint, '52-'53; No. 13, April 1953; No. 14, June, 1954 (No #12) (Painted covers #1-10,13,14)

	GD 2.0	VG 4.0	FN 6.0	VF 8.0	VF/NM 9.0	NM- 9.2
1-Lucy Belle & Red Feather begin	16	32	48	94	147	200
2-Maneely-c	11	22	33	62	86	110
3-11,13,14: (#3, spr. '51). 5-Berg-a. 14-Code approved	10	20	30	56	76	95

KID DEATH & FLUFFY HALLOWEEN SPECIAL
Event Comics: Oct, 1997 ($2.95, B&W, one-shot)

	GD 2.0	VG 4.0	FN 6.0	VF 8.0	VF/NM 9.0	NM- 9.2
1-Variant-c by Cebollero & Quesada/Palmiotti						3.00

KID DEATH & FLUFFY SPRING BREAK SPECIAL
Event Comics: July, 1996 ($2.50, B&W, one-shot)

	GD 2.0	VG 4.0	FN 6.0	VF 8.0	VF/NM 9.0	NM- 9.2
1-Quesada & Palmiotti-c/scripts						3.00

KIDDIE KAPERS
Kiddie Kapers Co., 1945/Decker Publ. (Red Top-Farrell): 1945?(nd); Oct, 1957; 1963 - 1964

	GD 2.0	VG 4.0	FN 6.0	VF 8.0	VF/NM 9.0	NM- 9.2
1(nd, 1945-46?, 36 pgs.)-Infinity-c; funny animal	10	20	30	54	72	90
1(10/57)(Decker)-Little Bit-r from Kiddie Karnival	5	10	15	22	26	30
Super Reprint #7, 10('63), 12, 14('63), 15,17('64), 18('64): 10, 14-r/Animal Adventures #1. 15-Animal Advs. #? 17-Cowboys 'N' Injuns #?	2	4	6	8	11	14

KIDDIE KARNIVAL
Ziff-Davis Publ. Co. (Approved Comics): 1952 (25¢, 100 pgs.) (One Shot)

	GD 2.0	VG 4.0	FN 6.0	VF 8.0	VF/NM 9.0	NM- 9.2
nn-Rebound Little Bit #1,2; painted-c	36	72	108	211	343	475

KID ETERNITY (Becomes Buccaneers) (See Hit Comics)
Quality Comics Group: Spring, 1946 - No. 18, Nov, 1949

	GD 2.0	VG 4.0	FN 6.0	VF 8.0	VF/NM 9.0	NM- 9.2
1	90	180	270	576	988	1400
2	39	78	117	240	395	550
3-Mac Raboy-a	40	80	120	246	411	575
4-10	25	50	75	147	241	335
11-18	19	38	57	112	179	245

KID ETERNITY
DC Comics: 1991 - No. 3, Nov, 1991 ($4.95, limited series)

	GD 2.0	VG 4.0	FN 6.0	VF 8.0	VF/NM 9.0	NM- 9.2
1-3: Grant Morrison scripts/Duncan Fegredo-a/c						6.00
TPB (2006, $14.99) r/#1-3						15.00

KID ETERNITY
DC Comics (Vertigo): May, 1993 - No. 16, Sept, 1994 ($1.95, mature)

	GD 2.0	VG 4.0	FN 6.0	VF 8.0	VF/NM 9.0	NM- 9.2
1-16: 1-Gold ink-c. 6-Photo-c. All Sean Phillips-c/a except #15 (Phillips-c/i only)						3.00

KID FROM DODGE CITY, THE
Atlas Comics (MMC): July, 1957 - No. 2, Sept, 1957

	GD 2.0	VG 4.0	FN 6.0	VF 8.0	VF/NM 9.0	NM- 9.2
1-Don Heck-c	10	20	30	56	76	95
2-Everett-c	7	14	21	37	46	55

KID FROM TEXAS, THE (A Texas Ranger)
Atlas Comics (CSI): June, 1957 - No. 2, Aug, 1957

	GD 2.0	VG 4.0	FN 6.0	VF 8.0	VF/NM 9.0	NM- 9.2
1-Powell-a; Severin-c	10	20	30	56	76	95
2	7	14	21	37	46	55

KID KOKO
I. W. Enterprises: 1958

	GD 2.0	VG 4.0	FN 6.0	VF 8.0	VF/NM 9.0	NM- 9.2
Reprint #1,2-(r/M.E.'s Koko & Kola #4, 1947)	2	4	6	8	11	14

KID KOMICS (Kid Movie Komics No. 11)
Timely Comics (USA 1,2/FCI 3-10): Feb, 1943 - No. 10, Spring, 1946

	GD 2.0	VG 4.0	FN 6.0	VF 8.0	VF/NM 9.0	NM- 9.2
1-Origin Captain Wonder & sidekick Tim Mullrooney, & Subbie; intro the Sea-Going Lad, Pinto Pete, & Trixie Trouble; Knuckles & Whitewash Jones (from Young Allies) app.; Wolverton-a (7 pgs.)	423	846	1269	3088	5444	7800
2-The Young Allies, Red Hawk, & Tommy Tyme begin; last Captain Wonder & Subbie; Schomburg Japanese WWII bondage-c	219	438	657	1402	2401	3400
3-The Vision, Daredevils & Red Hawk app.	155	310	465	992	1696	2400
4-The Destroyer begins; Sub-Mariner app.; Red Hawk & Tommy Tyme end; classic Schomburg WWII human meat grinder-c	161	322	483	1030	1765	2500
5,6: 5-Tommy Tyme begins, ends #10	103	206	309	659	1130	1600
7-10: 7,10-The Whizzer app. Destroyer not in #7,8. 10-Last Destroyer, Young Allies & Whizzer	87	174	261	553	952	1350

NOTE: ***Brodsky** c-5. **Schomburg** c-2-4, 6-10. **Shores** c-1. Captain Wonder c-1, 2. The Young Allies c-3-10.*

KID MONTANA (Formerly Davy Crockett Frontier Fighter; The Gunfighters No. 51 on)
Charlton Comics: V2#9, Nov, 1957 - No. 50, Mar, 1965

	GD 2.0	VG 4.0	FN 6.0	VF 8.0	VF/NM 9.0	NM- 9.2
V2#9 (#1)	4	8	12	28	44	60
10	3	6	9	20	30	40
11,12,14-20	3	6	9	16	22	28
13-Williamson-a	3	6	9	20	30	40
21-35: 25,31-Giordano-c. 32-Origin Kid Montana. 34-Geronimo-c/s. 35-Snow Monster-c/s	2	4	6	11	16	20
36-50: 36-Dinosaur-c/s. 37,48-Giordano-c	2	4	6	9	12	15

NOTE: *Title change to Montana Kid on cover only #44 & 45; remained Kid Montana on inside. **Chasal** a-29,30. **Giordano** c-25,31,37,48. **Giordano/Alascia** c-12. **Mastroserio** a-9,11,13,14,22; c-11,14. **Masulli/Mastroserio** c-13. **Montes/Bache** c-42. **Morisi** c-16,32-34,36?,40,41,44,46; a-13,15;16,31-50. **Nicholas/Alascia** a-44,48.*

KID MOVIE KOMICS (Formerly Kid Komics; Rusty Comics #12 on)
Timely Comics: No. 11, Summer, 1946

	GD 2.0	VG 4.0	FN 6.0	VF 8.0	VF/NM 9.0	NM- 9.2
11-Silly Seal & Ziggy Pig; 2 pgs. Kurtzman "Hey Look" plus 6 pg. "Pigtales" story	27	54	81	158	259	360

KIDNAPPED (See Marvel Illustrated: Kidnapped)

KIDNAPPED (Robert Louis Stevenson's...also see Movie Comics)(Disney)
Dell Publishing Co.: No. 1101, May, 1960

	GD 2.0	VG 4.0	FN 6.0	VF 8.0	VF/NM 9.0	NM- 9.2
Four Color 1101-Movie, photo-c	6	12	18	43	69	95

KIDNAP RACKET (See Harvey Comics Hits No. 57)

KID SLADE GUNFIGHTER (Formerly Matt Slade...)
Atlas Comics (SPI): No. 5, Jan, 1957 - No. 8, July, 1957

	GD 2.0	VG 4.0	FN 6.0	VF 8.0	VF/NM 9.0	NM- 9.2
5-Maneely, Roth, Severin-a in all; Maneely-c	13	26	39	72	101	130
6,8-Severin-c	8	16	24	44	57	70
7-Williamson/Mayo-a, 4 pgs.	10	20	30	56	76	95

KID SUPREME (See Supreme)
Image Comics (Extreme Studios): Mar, 1996 - No. 3, July, 1996 ($2.50)

	GD 2.0	VG 4.0	FN 6.0	VF 8.0	VF/NM 9.0	NM- 9.2
1-3: Fraga-a/scripts. 3-Glory-c/app.						3.00

KID TERRIFIC
Image Comics: Nov, 1998 ($2.95, B&W)

	GD 2.0	VG 4.0	FN 6.0	VF 8.0	VF/NM 9.0	NM- 9.2
1-Snyder & Diliberto-s/a						3.00

Killapalooza #4 © Beechen & Hairsine

Killraven (2002 series) #1 © MAR

King Comics #35 © KING

	GD 2.0	VG 4.0	FN 6.0	VF 8.0	VF/NM 9.0	NM- 9.2

KID ZOO COMICS
Street & Smith Publications: July, 1948 (52 pgs.)

1-Funny Animal	32	64	96	188	307	425

KILL ALL PARENTS
Image Comics: June, 2008 ($3.99, one-shot)

1-Marcelo Di Chiara-a/Mark Andrew Smith-s 4.00

KILLAPALOOZA
DC Comics (WildStorm): July, 2009 - No. 6, Dec, 2009 ($2.99, limited series)

1-6: 1-Beechen-s/Hairsine-a/c 3.00
TPB (2010, $19.99) r/#1-6

KILLER (...Tales By Timothy Truman)
Eclipse Comics: March, 1985 ($1.75, one-shot, Baxter paper)

1-Timothy Truman-c/a 3.00

KILLER INSTINCT (Video game)
Acclaim Comics: June, 1996 - No. 6 ($2.50, limited series)

1-6: 1-Bart Sears-a(p). 4-Special #1. 5-Special #2. 6-Special #3 3.00

KILLERS, THE
Magazine Enterprises: 1947 - No. 2, 1948 (No month)

1-Mr. Zin, the Hatchet Killer; mentioned in **SOTI**, pgs. 179,180; used by N.Y. Legis. Comm.; L. B. Cole-c	129	258	387	826	1413	2000
2-(Scarce)-Hashish smoking story; "Dying, Dying, Dead" drug story; Whitney, Ingels-a; Whitney hanging-c	103	206	309	659	1130	1600

KILLING GIRL
Image Comics: Aug, 2007 - No. 5, Dec, 2007 ($2.99, limited series)

1-5: 1-Frank Espinosa-a/Glen Brunswick-s; covers by Espinosa and Frank Cho 3.00

KILLING JOKE, THE (See Batman: The Killing Joke under Batman one-shots)

KILLPOWER: THE EARLY YEARS
Marvel Comics UK: Sept, 1993 - No. 4, Dec, 1993 ($1.75, mini-series)

1-($2.95)-Foil embossed-c 3.50
2-4: 2-Genetix app. 3-Punisher app. 3.00

KILLRAVEN (See Amazing Adventures #18 (5/73))
Marvel Comics: Feb, 2001 ($2.99, one-shot)

1-Linsner-s/a/c 3.00

KILLRAVEN
Marvel Comics: Dec, 2002 - No. 6, May, 2003 ($2.99, limited series)

1-6-Alan Davis-s/a(p)/Mark Farmer-i 3.00
HC (2007, $19.99) r/#1-6; cover gallery, pencil art; foreward by Alan Davis 20.00

KILLRAZOR
Image Comics (Top Cow Productions): Aug, 1995 ($2.50, one-shot)

1 3.00

KILL YOUR BOYFRIEND
DC Comics (Vertigo): June, 1995 ($4.95, one-shot)

1-Grant Morrison story 6.00
1 ($5.95, 1998) 2nd printing 6.00

KILROY (Volume 2)
Caliber Press: 1998 ($2.95, B&W)

1-Pruett-s 3.00

KILROY IS HERE
Caliber Press: 1995 ($2.95, B&W)

1-10 3.00

KILROYS, THE
B&I Publ. Co. No. 1-19/American Comics Group: June-July, 1947 - No. 54, June-July, 1955

1	22	44	66	132	216	300
2	14	28	42	80	115	150
3-5: 5-Gross-a	13	26	39	72	101	130
6-10: 8-Milt Gross's Moronica	10	20	30	56	76	95
11-20: 14-Gross-a	9	18	27	50	65	80
21-30	8	16	24	44	57	70
31-47,50-54	8	16	24	42	54	65
48,49-(3-D effect-c/stories)	18	36	54	103	162	220

KILROY: THE SHORT STORIES
Caliber Press: 1995 ($2.95, B&W)

1 3.00

KIN
Image Comics (Top Cow): Mar, 2000 - No. 6, Sept, 2000 ($2.95)

1-5-Gary Frank-s/c/a 3.00
1-($6.95) DF Alternate footprint cover 7.00
6-($3.95) 4.00
... Descent of Man TPB (2002, $19.95) r/ #1-6 20.00

KINDRED, THE
Image Comics (WildStorm Productions): Mar, 1994 - No. 4, July, 1995 ($1.95, lim. series)

1-($2.50)-Grifter & Backlash app. in all; bound-in trading card 3.00
2-4 3.00
2,3: 2-Variant-c. 3-Alternate-c by Portacio, see Deathblow #5 4.00
Trade paperback (2/95, $9.95) 10.00
NOTE: ***Booth** c/a-1-4. The first four issues contain coupons redeemable for a Jim Lee Grifter/Backlash print.*

KINDRED II, THE
DC Comics (WildStorm): Mar, 2002 - No. 4, June, 2002 ($2.50, limited series)

1-4-Booth-s/Booth & Regla-a 3.00

KINETIC
DC Comics (Focus): May, 2004 - No. 8, Dec, 2004 ($2.50)

1-8-Puckett-s/Pleece-a/c 3.00
TPB (2005, $9.99) r/#1-8; cover gallery and sketch pages 10.00

KING (Magazine)
Skywald Publ.: Mar, 1971 - No. 2, July, 1971

1-Violence; semi-nudity; Boris Vallejo-a (2 pgs.)	5	10	15	35	55	75
2-Photo-c	4	8	12	22	34	45

KING ARTHUR AND THE KNIGHTS OF JUSTICE
Marvel Comics UK: Dec, 1993 - No. 3, Feb, 1994 ($1.25, limited series)

1-3: TV adaptation 3.00

KING CLASSICS
King Features : 1977 (36 pgs., cardboard-c) (Printed in Spain for U.S. distr.)

1-Connecticut Yankee, 2-Last of the Mohicans, 3-Moby Dick, 4-Robin Hood, 5-Swiss Family Robinson, 6-Robinson Crusoe, 7-Treasure Island, 8-20,000 Leagues, 9-Christmas Carol, 10-Huck Finn, 11-Around the World in 80 Days, 12-Davy Crockett, 13-Don Quixote, 14-Gold Bug, 15-Ivanhoe, 16-Three Musketeers, 17-Baron Munchausen, 18-Alice in Wonderland, 19-Black Arrow, 20-Five Weeks in a Balloon, 21-Great Expectations, 22-Gulliver's Travels, 23-Prince & Pauper, 24-Lawrence of Arabia (Originals, 1977-78) each....	2	4	6	10	14	18
Reprints (1979; HRN-24)	2	4	6	8	10	12

NOTE: *The first eight issues were not numbered. Issues No. 25-32 were advertised but not published. The 1977 originals have HRN 32a; the 1978 originals have HRN 32b.*

KING COLT (See Luke Short's Western Stories)

KING COMICS (Strip reprints)
David McKay Publications/Standard #156-on: 4/36 - No. 155, 11-12/49; No. 156, Spr/50 - No. 159, 2/52 (Winter on-c)

1-1st app. Flash Gordon by Alex Raymond; Brick Bradford (1st app.), Popeye, Henry (1st app.) & Mandrake the Magician (1st app.) begin; Popeye-c begin	1250	2500	3750	10,000	-	-
2	360	720	1080	1980	2790	3600
3	245	490	735	1348	1899	2450
4	190	380	570	1045	1473	1900
5	140	280	420	770	1085	1400
6-10: 9-X-Mas-c	95	190	285	523	737	950
11-20	75	150	225	413	582	750
21-30: 21-X-Mas-c	55	110	165	303	427	550
31-40: 33-Last Segar Popeye	45	90	135	248	349	450
41-50: 46-Text illos by Marge Buell contain characters similar to Lulu, Alvin & Tubby. 50-The Lone Ranger begins	31	62	93	182	296	410
51-60: 52-Barney Baxter begins?	22	44	66	130	213	295
61-The Phantom begins	23	46	69	136	223	310
62-80: 76-Flag-c. 79-Blondie begins	17	34	51	98	154	210
81-99	14	28	42	81	118	155
100	16	32	48	92	144	195
101-114: 114-Last Raymond issue (1 pg.); Flash Gordon by Austin Briggs begins, ends #155	14	28	42	76	108	140
115-145: 117-Phantom origin retold	10	20	30	56	76	95
146,147-Prince Valiant in both	9	18	27	50	65	80
148-155: 155-Flash Gordon ends (11-12/49)	9	18	27	50	65	80
156-159: 156-New logo begins (Standard)	9	18	27	47	61	75

NOTE: *Marge Buell text illos in No. 24-46 at least.*

KING CONAN (Conan The King No. 20 on)
Marvel Comics Group: Mar, 1980 - No. 19, Nov, 1983 (52 pgs.)

1	1	2	3	5	6	8

The Kingdom #2 © DC

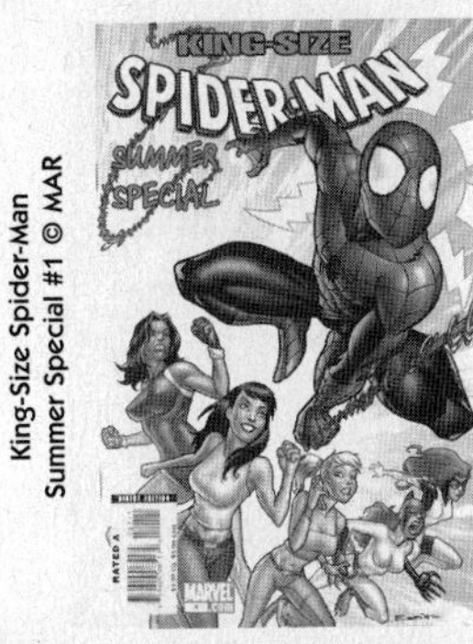

King-Size Spider-Man Summer Special #1 © MAR

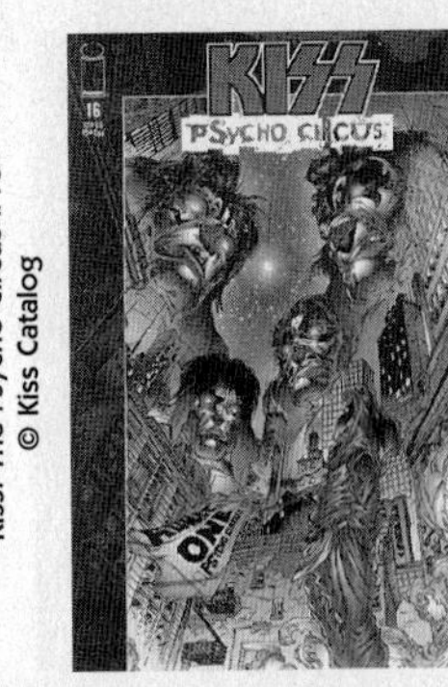

Kiss: The Psycho Circus #16 © Kiss Catalog

GD VG FN VF VF/NM NM-
2.0 4.0 6.0 8.0 9.0 9.2

2-19: 4-Death of Thoth Amon. 7-1st Paul Smith-a, 1 pg. pin-up (9/81) 5.00
NOTE: ***J. Buscema** a-1-9p, 17p; c(p)-1-5, 7-9, 14, 17. **Kaluta** c-19. **Nebres** a-17i, 18, 19i. **Severin** c-18. **Simonson** c-6.*

KING DAVID
DC Comics (Vertigo): 2002 ($19.95, 8 1/2" x 11")
nn-Story of King David; Kyle Baker-s/a 20.00

KINGDOM, THE
DC Comics: Feb, 1999 - No. 2, Feb, 1999 ($2.95/$1.99, limited series)
1,2-Waid-s; sequel to Kingdom Come; introduces Hypertime 4.00
...: Kid Flash 1 (2/99, $1.99) Waid-s/Pararillo-a, ...: Nightstar 1 (2/99, $1.99) Waid-s/Haley-a, ...: Offspring 1 (2/99, $1.99) Waid-s/Quitely-a, ...: Planet Krypton 1 (2/99, $1.99) Waid-s/ Kitson-a, ...: Son of the Bat 1 (2/99, $1.99) Waid-s/Apthorp-a 3.00

KINGDOM COME (Also see Justice Society of America #9-22)
DC Comics: 1996 - No. 4, 1996 ($4.95, painted limited series)
1-Mark Waid scripts & Alex Ross-painted c/a in all; tells the last days of the DC Universe; 1st app. Magog 1 2 3 5 6 8
2-Superman forms new Justice League 1 2 3 4 5 7
3-Return of Captain Marvel 6.00
4-Final battle of Superman and Captain Marvel 1 2 3 4 5 7
Deluxe Slipcase Edition-($89.95) w/Revelations companion book, 12 new story pages, foil stamped covers, signed and numbered 120.00
Hardcover Edition-($29.95)-Includes 12 new story pages and artwork from Revelations, new cover artwork with gold foil inlay 35.00
Hardcover 2nd printing 30.00
Softcover Ed.-($14.95)-Includes 12 new story pgs. & artwork from Revelations, new c-artwork 15.00
Softcover Ed.-(2008, $17.99)-New wraparound gatefold cover by Ross 18.00

KING KONG (See Movie Comics)

KING KONG: THE 8TH WONDER OF THE WORLD (Adaptation of 2005 movie)
Dark Horse Comics: Dec, 2005 ($3.99, planned limited series completed in TPB)
1-Photo-c; Dustin Weaver-a/Christian Gossett-s 4.00
TPB (11/06, $12.95) r/#1 and unpublished parts 2&3; photo-c; Dorman paintings 13.00

KING LEONARDO & HIS SHORT SUBJECTS (TV)
Dell Publishing Co./Gold Key: Nov-Jan, 1961-62 - No. 4, Sept, 1963
Four Color 1242,1278 11 22 33 79 147 215
01390-207(5-7/62)(Dell) 9 18 27 61 103 145
1 (10/62) 10 20 30 70 125 180
2-4 8 16 24 56 93 130

KING LOUIE & MOWGLI (See Jungle Book under Movie Comics)
Gold Key: May, 1968 (Disney)
1 (#10223-805)-Characters from Jungle Book 3 6 9 20 30 40

KING OF DIAMONDS (TV)
Dell Publishing Co.: July-Sept, 1962
01-391-209-Photo-c 4 8 12 26 41 55

KING OF KINGS (Movie)
Dell Publishing Co.: No. 1236, Oct-Nov, 1961
Four Color 1236-Photo-c 7 14 21 50 83 115

KING OF THE BAD MEN OF DEADWOOD
Avon Periodicals: 1950 (See Wild Bill Hickok #16)
nn-Kinstler-c; Kamen/Feldstein-r/Cowpuncher #2 15 30 45 94 147 200

KING OF THE ROYAL MOUNTED (See Famous Feature Stories, King Comics, Red Ryder #3 & Super Book #2, 6)

KING OF THE ROYAL MOUNTED (Zane Grey's...)
David McKay/Dell Publishing Co.: No. 1, May, 1937; No. 9, 1940; No. 207, Dec, 1948 - No. 935, Sept-Nov, 1958
Feature Books 1 (5/37)(McKay) 90 180 270 576 988 1400
Large Feature Comic 9 (1940) 47 94 141 296 498 700
Four Color 207(#1, 12/48) 13 26 39 89 170 250
Four Color 265,283 8 16 24 58 97 135
Four Color 310,340 6 12 18 43 69 95
Four Color 363,384, 8(6-8/52)-10 6 12 18 39 62 85
11-20 5 10 15 34 55 75
21-28(3-5/58), Four Color 935(9-11/58) 4 8 12 28 44 60
NOTE: *4-Color No. 207, 265, 283, 310, 340, 363, 384 are all newspaper reprints with **Jim Gary** art. No. 8 on are all Dell originals. Painted c-No. 9-on.*

KINGPIN
Marvel Comics: Nov, 1997 ($5.99, squarebound, one-shot)
nn-Spider-Man & Daredevil vs. Kingpin; Stan Lee-s/ John Romita Sr.-a 6.00

KINGPIN
Marvel Comics: Aug, 2003 - No. 7, Jan, 2004 ($2.50/$2.99, limited series)
1-6-Bruce Jones-s/Sean Phillips & Klaus Janson-a 3.00
7-($2.99) 3.00

KING RICHARD & THE CRUSADERS
Dell Publishing Co.: No. 588, Oct, 1954
Four Color 588-Movie, Matt Baker-a, photo-c 9 18 27 63 107 150

KING-SIZE CABLE SPECTACULAR (Takes place between Cable (2008 series) #6 & #7)
Marvel Comics: Nov, 2008 ($4.99, one-shot)
1-Lashley-a; Deadpool #1 preview; cover gallery of variants from 2008 series 5.00

KING-SIZE HULK (Takes place between Hulk (2008 series) #3 & #4)
Marvel Comics: July, 2008 ($4.99, one-shot)
1-Art Adams, Frank Cho, & Herb Trimpe-a; double-c by Cho & Adams; Red Hulk, She-Hulk & Wendigo app.; origin Abomination; r/Incr. Hulk #180,181 & Avengers #83 5.00

KING-SIZE SPIDER-MAN SUMMER SPECIAL
Marvel Comics: Oct, 2008 ($4.99, one-shot)
1-Short stories by various; Falcon app.; Burchett, Giarrusso & Coover-a 5.00

KINGS OF THE NIGHT
Dark Horse Comics: 1990 - No. 2, 1990 ($2.25, limited series)
1,2-Robert E. Howard adaptation; Bolton-c 3.00

KING SOLOMON'S MINES (Movie)
Avon Periodicals: 1951
nn (#1 on 1st page) 40 80 120 242 401 560

KIPLING, RUDYARD (See Mowgli, The Jungle Book)

KISS (See Crazy Magazine, Howard the Duck #12, 13, Marvel Comics Super Special #1, 5, Rock Fantasy Comics #10 & Rock N' Roll Comics #9)

KISS
Dark Horse Comics: June, 2002 - No. 13, Sept, 2003 ($2.99, limited series)
1-Photo-c and J. Scott Campbell-c; Casey-s 5.00
2-13: 2-Photo-c and J. Scott Campbell-c. 3-Photo-c and Leinil Yu-c 4.00
...: Men and Monsters TPB (9/03, $12.95) r/#7-10 13.00
...: Rediscovery TPB (2003, $9.95) r/#1-3 10.00
...: Return of the Phantom TPB (2003, $9.95) r/#4-6 10.00
...: Unholy War TPB (2004, $9.95) r/#11-13 10.00

KISS 4K
Platinum Studios Comics: May, 2007 - No. 6, Apr, 2008 ($3.99/$2.99)
1-Sprague-s/Crossley & Campos-a/Migliari-c 4.00
1-B&W sketch-c 6.00
1-Destroyer Edition ($50.00, 30"x18", edition of 5000) 50.00
2-6-($2.99) 3.00
KISSMAS (12/07, $4.99) Christmas-themed issue; re-cap of issues #1-4 5.00

KISS: THE PSYCHO CIRCUS
Image Comics: Aug, 1997 - No. 31, June, 2000 ($1.95/$2.25/$2.50)
1-Holguin-s/Medina-a(p) 1 3 4 6 8 10
1-2nd & 3rd printings 3.00
2 6.00
3,4: 4-Photo-c 5.00
5-8: 5-Begin $2.25-c 4.00
9-29 4.00
30,31: 30-Begin $2.50-c 4.00
Book 1 TPB ('98, $12.95) r/#1-6 13.00
Book 2 Destroyer TPB (8/99, $9.95) r/#10-13 10.00
Book 3 Whispered Scream TPB ('00, $9.95) r/#7-9,18 10.00
...Magazine 1 ($6.95) r/#1-3 plus interviews 7.00
...Magazine 2-5 ($4.95) 2-r/#4,5 plus interviews. 3-r/#6,7. 4-r/#8,9 5.00
Wizard Edition ('98, supplement) Bios, tour preview and interviews 3.00

KISSING CHAOS
Oni Press: Sept, 2001 - No. 8, Mar, 2002 ($2.25, B&W, 6" x 9", limited series)
1-8-Arthur Dela Cruz-s/a 3.00
...: Nine Lives (12/03, $2.99, regular comic-sized) 3.00
...: 1000 Words (7/03, $2.99, regular comic-sized) 3.00
TPB (9/02, $17.95) r/#1-8 18.00

KISSING CHAOS: NONSTOP BEAUTY
Oni Press: Oct, 2002 - No. 4, March, 2003 ($2.95, B&W, 6" x 9", limited series)
1-4-Arthur Dela Cruz-s/a 3.00

Klaws of the Panther #1 © MAR

Knight and Squire #1 © DC

Kobalt #6 © Milestone

	GD 2.0	VG 4.0	FN 6.0	VF 8.0	VF/NM 9.0	NM- 9.2

TPB (9/03, $11.95) r/#1-4 12.00

KISS KISS BANG BANG
CrossGen Comics: Feb, 2004 - No. 5, Jun, 2004 ($2.95)

1-5-Bedard-s/Perkins-a 3.00

KISSYFUR (TV)
DC Comics: 1989 (Sept.) ($2.00, 52 pgs., one-shot)

1-Based on Saturday morning cartoon 4.00

KIT CARSON (Formerly All True Detective Cases No. 4; Fighting Davy Crockett No. 9; see Blazing Sixguns & Frontier Fighters)
Avon Periodicals: 1950; No. 2, 8/51 - No. 3, 12/51; No. 5, 11-12/54 - No. 8, 9/55 (No #4)

nn(#1) (1950)- "...Indian Scout" ; r-Cowboys 'N' Injuns #? 14 28 42 76 108 140
2(8/51) 10 20 30 56 76 95
3(12/51)- "...Fights the Comanche Raiders" 9 18 27 50 65 80
5-6,8(11-12/54-9/55): 5-Formerly All True Detective Cases (last pre-code); titled "...and the Trail of Doom" 9 18 27 47 61 75
7-McCann-a? 9 18 27 47 61 75
I.W. Reprint #10('63)-r/Kit Carson #1; Severin-c 2 4 6 11 16 20
NOTE: *Kinstler c-1-3, 5-8.*

KIT CARSON & THE BLACKFEET WARRIORS
Realistic: 1953

nn-Reprint; Kinstler-c 9 18 27 52 69 85

KIT KARTER
Dell Publishing Co.: May-July, 1962

1 3 6 9 19 29 38

KITTY
St. John Publishing Co.: Oct, 1948

1-Teenage; Lily Renee-c/a 9 18 27 47 61 75

KITTY PRYDE, AGENT OF S.H.I.E.L.D. (Also see Excalibur and Mekanix)
Marvel Comics: Dec, 1997 - No. 3, Feb, 1998 ($2.50, limited series)

1-3-Hama-s 3.00

KITTY PRYDE AND WOLVERINE (Also see Uncanny X-Men & X-Men)
Marvel Comics Group: Nov, 1984 - No. 6, Apr, 1985 (Limited series)

1-6: Characters from X-Men 4.50
X-Men: Kitty Pryde and Wolverine HC (2008, $19.99) r/series 20.00

KLARER GIVEAWAYS (See Wisco in the Promotional Comics section)

KLAWS OF THE PANTHER (Also see Black Panther)
Marvel Comics: Dec, 2010 - No. 4, Feb, 2011 ($3.99, limited series)

1-4-Maberry-s/Gugliotta-a/Del Mundo-c. 1-Ka-Zar & Shanna app. 3-Spider-Man app. 4.00

KNIGHT AND SQUIRE (Also see Batman #667-669)
DC Comics: Dec, 2010 - No. 6, May, 2011 ($2.99, limited series)

1-6-Cornell-s/Broxton-a. 1-Two covers by Paquette & Tucci. 5,6-Joker app. 3.00

KNIGHTHAWK
Acclaim Comics (Windjammer): Sept, 1995 - No. 6, Nov, 1995 ($2.50, lim. series)

1-6: 6-origin 3.00

KNIGHTMARE
Antarctic Press: July, 1994 - May, 1995 ($2.75, B&W, mature readers)

1-6 3.00

KNIGHTMARE
Image Comics (Extreme Studios): Feb, 1995 - No. 5, June, 1995 ($2.50)

0 ($3.50) 4.00
1-5: 4-Quesada & Palmiotti variant-c, 5-Flip book w/Warcry 3.00

KNIGHTS 4 (See Marvel Knights 4)

KNIGHTS OF PENDRAGON, THE (Also see Pendragon)
Marvel Comics Ltd.: July, 1990 - No. 18, Dec, 1991 ($1.95)

1-18: 1-Capt. Britain app. 2,8-Free poster inside. 9,10-Bolton-c. 11,18-Iron Man app. 2.50

KNIGHTS OF THE ROUND TABLE
Dell Publishing Co.: No. 540, Mar, 1954

Four Color 540-Movie, photo-c 7 14 21 47 76 105

KNIGHTS OF THE ROUND TABLE
Pines Comics: No. 10, April, 1957

10 5 10 15 24 30 35

KNIGHTS OF THE ROUND TABLE
Dell Publishing Co.: Nov-Jan, 1963-64

1 (12-397-401)-Painted-c 3 6 9 21 32 42

KNIGHTSTRIKE (Also see Operation: Knightstrike)
Image Comics (Extreme Studios): Jan, 1996 ($2.50)

1-Rob Liefeld & Eric Stephenson story; Extreme Destroyer Part 6. 3.00

KNIGHT WATCHMAN (See Big Bang Comics & Dr. Weird)
Image Comics: June, 1998 - No. 4, Oct, 1998 ($2.95/$3.50, B&W, lim. series)

1-3-Ben Torres-c/a in all 3.00
4-($3.50) 3.50

KNIGHT WATCHMAN: GRAVEYARD SHIFT
Caliber Press: 1994 ($2.95, B&W)

1,2-Ben Torres-a 3.00

KNOCK KNOCK (...Who's There?)
Dell Publ./Gerona Publications: No. 801, 1936 (52 pgs.) (8x9", B&W)

801-Joke book; Bob Dunn-a 10 20 30 58 79 100

KNOCKOUT ADVENTURES
Fiction House Magazines: Winter, 1953-54

1-Reprints Fight Comics #53 w/Rip Carson-c/s 14 28 42 76 108 140

KNUCKLES (Spin-off of Sonic the Hedgehog)
Archie Publications: Apr, 1997 - No. 32, Feb, 2000 ($1.50/$1.75/$1.79)

1-32 4.00

KNUCKLES' CHAOTIX
Archie Publications: Jan, 1996 ($2.00, annual)

1 5.00

KOBALT
DC Comics (Milestone): June, 1994 - No. 16, Sept, 1995 ($1.75/$2.50)

1-16: 1-Byrne-c. 4-Intro Page. 16-Kent Williams-c 3.00

KOBRA (Unpublished #8 appears in DC Special Series No. 1)
National Periodical Publications: Feb-Mar, 1976 - No. 7, Mar-Apr, 1977

1-1st app.; Kirby-a redrawn by Marcos; only 25¢-c 2 4 6 8 11 14
2-7: (All 30¢ issues) 3-Giffen-a 1 2 3 5 6 8
...: Resurrection TPB (2010, $19.99) r/#1, DC Special Series No. 1 and later apps. in Checkmate #23-25, Faces of Evil: Kobra #1 and various Who's Who issues 20.00
NOTE: *Austin a-3i. Buckler a-5p; c-5p. Kubert c-4. Nasser a-6p, 7; c-7.*

KOKEY KOALA (...and the Magic Button)
Toby Press: May, 1952

1-Funny animal 12 24 36 67 94 120

KOKO AND KOLA (Also see A-1 Comics #16 & Tick Tock Tales)
Com/Magazine Enterprises: Fall, 1946 - No. 5, May, 1947; No. 6, 1950

1-Funny animal 13 26 39 72 101 130
2-X-Mas-c 9 18 27 50 65 80
3-6: 6(A-1 28) 8 16 24 44 57 70

KO KOMICS
Gerona Publications: Oct, 1945 (scarce)

1-The Duke of Darkness & The Menace (hero) 74 148 222 470 810 1150

KOLCHAK: THE NIGHT STALKER (TV)
Moonstone: 2002 - Present ($6.50/$6.95)

1-($6.50) Jeff Rice-s/Gordon Purcell-a 6.50
... Black & White & Read All Over (2005, $4.95) short stories by various; 2 covers 5.00
... Devil in the Details (2003, $6.95) Trevor Von Eeden-a 7.00
... Eve of Terror (2005, $5.95) Gentile-s/Figueroa-a/Beck-c 6.00
... Fever Pitch (2002, $6.95) Christopher Jones-a 7.00
... Get of Belial (2002, $6.95) Art Nichols-a 7.00
... Lambs to the Slaughter (2003, $6.95) Trevor Von Eeden-a 7.00
... Pain Most Human (2004, $6.95) Greg Scott-a 7.00
... Tales: The Frankenstein Agenda 1 (2007 - No. 3, $3.50) Michelinie-s 3.50
... Tales of the Night Stalker 1-7 (2003-Present, $3.50) two covers by Moore & Ulanski 3.50
TPB (2004, $17.95) r/#1, Get of Belial & Fever Pitch 18.00
Vol. 2: Terror Within TPB (2006, $16.95) r/Pain Most Human, Pain Without Tears & Devil in the Details 17.00

KOMIC KARTOONS
Timely Comics (EPC): Fall, 1945 - No. 2, Winter, 1945

1,2-Andy Wolf, Bertie Mouse 22 44 66 132 216 300

KOMIK PAGES (Formerly Snap; becomes Bullseye #11)

Konga #2 © CC

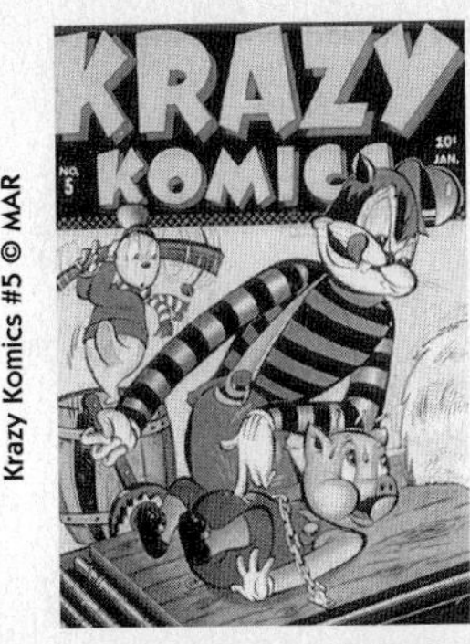

Krazy Komics #5 © MAR

Kull #6 © Kull Prods.

Harry 'A' Chesler, Jr. (Our Army, Inc.): Apr, 1945 (All reprints)

Issue	GD 2.0	VG 4.0	FN 6.0	VF 8.0	VF/NM 9.0	NM- 9.2
10(#1 on inside)-Land O' Nod by Rick Yager (2 pgs.), Animal Crackers, Foxy GrandPa, Tom, Dick & Mary, Cheerio Minstrels, Red Starr plus other 1-2 pg. strips; Cole-a	23	46	69	136	223	310

KONA (...Monarch of Monster Isle)
Dell Publishing Co.: Feb-Apr, 1962 - No. 21, Jan-Mar, 1967 (Painted-c)

Issue	GD 2.0	VG 4.0	FN 6.0	VF 8.0	VF/NM 9.0	NM- 9.2
Four Color 1256 (#1)	9	18	27	65	113	160
2-10: 4-Anak begins. 6-Gil Kane-c	6	12	18	37	59	80
11-21	5	10	15	30	48	65

NOTE: *Glanzman a-all issues.*

KONGA (Fantastic Giants No. 24) (See Return of...)
Charlton Comics: 1960; No. 2, Aug, 1961 - No. 23, Nov, 1965

Issue	GD 2.0	VG 4.0	FN 6.0	VF 8.0	VF/NM 9.0	NM- 9.2
1(1960)-Based on movie; Giordano-c	23	46	69	168	334	500
2-5: 2-Giordano-c; no Ditko-a	11	22	33	77	144	210
6-9-Ditko-c/a	10	20	30	68	119	170
10-15	9	18	27	63	107	150
16-23	6	12	18	41	66	90

NOTE: *Ditko a-1, 3-15; c-4, 6-9. Glanzman a-12. Montes & Bache a-16-23.*

KONGA'S REVENGE (Formerly Return of...)
Charlton Comics: No. 2, Summer, 1963 - No. 3, Fall, 1964; Dec, 1968

Issue	GD 2.0	VG 4.0	FN 6.0	VF 8.0	VF/NM 9.0	NM- 9.2
2,3: 2-Ditko-c/a	8	16	24	52	86	120
1(12/68)-Reprints Konga's Revenge #3	3	6	9	17	25	32

KONG THE UNTAMED
National Periodical Publications: June-July, 1975 - V2#5, Feb-Mar, 1976

Issue	GD 2.0	VG 4.0	FN 6.0	VF 8.0	VF/NM 9.0	NM- 9.2
1-1st app. Kong; Wrightson-c; Alcala-a	2	4	6	11	16	20
2-Wrightson-c; Alcala-a	2	4	6	9	13	16
3-5: 3-Alcala-a	1	2	3	5	6	8

KOOKABURRA K
Marvel Comics (Soleil): 2009 - No. 3, 2010 ($5.99, limited series)

Issue	GD 2.0	VG 4.0	FN 6.0	VF 8.0	VF/NM 9.0	NM- 9.2
1-3-Humbertos Ramos-a/c						6.00

KOOKIE
Dell Publishing Co.: Feb-Apr, 1962 - No. 2, May-July, 1962 (15 cents)

Issue	GD 2.0	VG 4.0	FN 6.0	VF 8.0	VF/NM 9.0	NM- 9.2
1-Written by John Stanley; Bill Williams-a	8	16	24	54	90	125
2	7	14	21	49	80	110

KOOSH KINS
Archie Comics: Oct, 1991 - No. 3, Feb, 1992 ($1.00, bi-monthly, limited series)

Issue	GD 2.0	VG 4.0	FN 6.0	VF 8.0	VF/NM 9.0	NM- 9.2
1-3						3.00

NOTE: *No. 4 was planned, but cancelled.*

KORAK, SON OF TARZAN (Edgar Rice Burroughs)(See Tarzan #139)
Gold Key: Jan, 1964 - No. 45, Jan, 1972 (Painted-c No. 1-?)

Issue	GD 2.0	VG 4.0	FN 6.0	VF 8.0	VF/NM 9.0	NM- 9.2
1-Russ Manning-a	9	18	27	65	113	160
2-5-Russ Manning-a	6	12	18	37	59	80
6-11-Russ Manning-a	5	10	15	32	51	70
12-23: 12,13-Warren Tufts-a. 14-Jon of the Kalahari ends. 15-Mabu, Jungle Boy begins. 21-Manning-a. 23-Last 12¢ issue	4	8	12	28	44	60
24-30	4	8	12	22	34	45
31-45	3	6	9	18	27	35

KORAK, SON OF TARZAN (Tarzan Family #60 on; see Tarzan #230)
National Periodical Publications: V9#46, May-June, 1972 - V12#56, Feb-Mar, 1974; No. 57, May-June, 1975 - No. 59, Sept-Oct, 1975 (Edgar Rice Burroughs)

Issue	GD 2.0	VG 4.0	FN 6.0	VF 8.0	VF/NM 9.0	NM- 9.2
46-(52 pgs.)-Carson of Venus begins (origin), ends #56; Pellucidar feature; Weiss-a	3	6	9	16	22	28
47-59: 49-Origin Korak retold	2	4	6	8	11	14

NOTE: *All have covers by* ***Joe Kubert. Manning*** *strip reprints-No. 57-59.* ***Murphy Anderson*** *a-52.* ***Michael Kaluta*** *a-46-56.* ***Frank Thorne*** *a-46-51.*

KORE
Image Comics: Apr, 2003 - No. 5, Sept, 2003 ($2.95)

Issue	GD 2.0	VG 4.0	FN 6.0	VF 8.0	VF/NM 9.0	NM- 9.2
1-5: 1-Two covers by Capullo and Seeley; Seeley-a (p)						3.00

KORG: 70,000 B. C. (TV)
Charlton Publications: May, 1975 - No. 9, Nov, 1976 (Hanna-Barbera)

Issue	GD 2.0	VG 4.0	FN 6.0	VF 8.0	VF/NM 9.0	NM- 9.2
1,2: 1-Boyette-c/a. 2-Painted-c; Byrne text illos	2	4	6	11	16	20
3-9	2	4	6	8	11	14

KORNER KID COMICS: Four Star Publications: 1947 (Advertised, not pub.)

KOSMIC KAT ACTIVITY BOOK (See Deity)
Image Comics: Aug, 1999 ($2.95, one-shot)

Issue	GD 2.0	VG 4.0	FN 6.0	VF 8.0	VF/NM 9.0	NM- 9.2
1-Stories and games by various						3.00

KRAZY KAT
Holt: 1946 (Hardcover)

Issue	GD 2.0	VG 4.0	FN 6.0	VF 8.0	VF/NM 9.0	NM- 9.2
Reprints daily & Sunday strips by Herriman	56	112	168	353	597	840
dust jacket only	42	84	126	265	445	625

KRAZY KAT (See Ace Comics & March of Comics No. 72, 87)

KRAZY KAT COMICS (...& Ignatz the Mouse early issues)
Dell Publ. Co./Gold Key: May-June, 1951 - F.C. #696, Apr, 1956; Jan, 1964 (None by Herriman)

Issue	GD 2.0	VG 4.0	FN 6.0	VF 8.0	VF/NM 9.0	NM- 9.2
1(1951)	9	18	27	61	103	145
2-5 (#5, 8-10/52)	5	10	15	35	55	75
Four Color 454,504	5	10	15	32	51	70
Four Color 548,619,696 (4/56)	5	10	15	30	48	65
1(10098-401)(1/64-Gold Key)(TV)	4	8	12	26	41	55

KRAZY KOMICS (1st Series) (Cindy Comics No. 27 on) (Also see Ziggy Pig)
Timely Comics (USA No. 1-21/JPC No. 22-26): July, 1942 - No. 26, Spr, 1947

Issue	GD 2.0	VG 4.0	FN 6.0	VF 8.0	VF/NM 9.0	NM- 9.2
1-Toughy Tomcat, Ziggy Pig (by Jaffee) & Silly Seal begin	77	154	231	493	847	1200
2	36	72	108	211	343	475
3-8,10	24	48	72	142	234	325
9-Hitler parody-c	26	52	78	154	252	350
11,13,14	18	36	54	105	165	225
12-Timely's entire art staff drew themselves into a Creeper story	29	58	87	170	278	385
15-(8-9/44)-Has "Super Soldier" by Pfc. Stan Lee	19	38	57	109	172	235
16-24,26: 16-(10-11/44). 26-Super Rabbit-c/story	15	30	45	86	133	180
25-Wacky Duck-c/story & begin; Kurtzman-a (6pgs.)	18	36	54	105	165	225

KRAZY KOMICS (2nd Series)
Timely/Marvel Comics: Aug, 1948 - No. 2, Nov, 1948

Issue	GD 2.0	VG 4.0	FN 6.0	VF 8.0	VF/NM 9.0	NM- 9.2
1-Wolverton (10 pgs.) & Kurtzman (8 pgs.)-a; Eustice Hayseed begins (Li'l Abner swipe)	44	88	132	277	469	660
2-Wolverton-a (10 pgs.); Powerhouse Pepper cameo	32	64	96	188	307	425

KRAZY KROW (Also see Dopey Duck, Film Funnies, Funny Frolics & Movie Tunes)
Marvel Comics (ZPC): Summer, 1945 - No. 3, Wint, 1945/46

Issue	GD 2.0	VG 4.0	FN 6.0	VF 8.0	VF/NM 9.0	NM- 9.2
1	22	44	66	132	216	300
2,3	15	30	45	85	130	175
I.W. Reprint #1('57), 2('58), 7	2	4	6	11	16	20

KRAZYLIFE (Becomes Nutty Life #2)
Fox Feature Syndicate: 1945 (no month)

Issue	GD 2.0	VG 4.0	FN 6.0	VF 8.0	VF/NM 9.0	NM- 9.2
1-Funny animal	21	42	63	126	206	285

KREE/SKRULL WAR STARRING THE AVENGERS, THE
Marvel Comics: Sept, 1983 - No. 2, Oct, 1983 ($2.50, 68 pgs., Baxter paper)

Issue	GD 2.0	VG 4.0	FN 6.0	VF 8.0	VF/NM 9.0	NM- 9.2
1,2						4.00

NOTE: ***Neal Adams*** *p-1r, 2.* ***Buscema*** *a-1r, 2r.* ***Simonson*** *a-1p; c-1p.*

KROFFT SUPERSHOW (TV)
Gold Key: Apr, 1978 - No. 6, Jan, 1979

Issue	GD 2.0	VG 4.0	FN 6.0	VF 8.0	VF/NM 9.0	NM- 9.2
1-Photo-c	3	6	9	18	27	35
2-6: 6-Photo-c	3	6	9	14	19	24

KRULL
Marvel Comics Group: Nov, 1983 - No. 2, Dec, 1983

Issue	GD 2.0	VG 4.0	FN 6.0	VF 8.0	VF/NM 9.0	NM- 9.2
1,2-Adaptation of film; r/Marvel Super Special. 1-Photo-c from movie						3.00

KRUSTY COMICS (TV)(See Simpsons Comics)
Bongo Comics: 1995 - No. 3, 1995 ($2.25, limited series)

Issue	GD 2.0	VG 4.0	FN 6.0	VF 8.0	VF/NM 9.0	NM- 9.2
1-3						3.00

KRYPTON CHRONICLES
DC Comics: Sept, 1981 - No. 3, Nov, 1981

Issue	GD 2.0	VG 4.0	FN 6.0	VF 8.0	VF/NM 9.0	NM- 9.2
1-3: 1-Buckler-c(p)						4.00

KRYPTO THE SUPERDOG (TV)
DC Comics: Nov, 2006 - No. 6, Apr, 2007 ($2.25)

Issue	GD 2.0	VG 4.0	FN 6.0	VF 8.0	VF/NM 9.0	NM- 9.2
1-6-Based on Cartoon Network series. 1-Origin retold						3.00

KULL
Dark Horse Comics: Nov, 2008 - No. 6, May, 2009 ($2.99)

Issue	GD 2.0	VG 4.0	FN 6.0	VF 8.0	VF/NM 9.0	NM- 9.2
1-6: 1-Nelson-s/Conrad-a; two covers by Andy Brase and Joe Kubert						3.00

KULL AND THE BARBARIANS
Marvel Comics: May, 1975 - No. 3, Sept, 1975 ($1.00, B&W, magazine)

Kull The Conqueror #1 © Kull Prods.

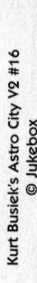

Kurt Busiek's Astro City V2 #16 © Jukebox

Lady Deadpool #1 © MAR

	GD 2.0	VG 4.0	FN 6.0	VF 8.0	VF/NM 9.0	NM- 9.2

1-(84 pgs.) Andru/Wood-r/Kull #1; 2 pgs. Neal Adams; Gil Kane(p), Marie & John Severin-a(r); Krenkel text illo. 3 6 9 17 25 32
2,3: 2-(84 pgs.) Red Sonja by Chaykin begins; Solomon Kane by Weiss/Adams; Gil Kane-a; Solomon Kane pin-up by Wrightson. 3-(76 pgs.) Origin Red Sonja by Chaykin; Adams-a; Solomon Kane app. 3 6 9 14 19 24

KULL THE CONQUEROR (...the Destroyer #11 on; see Conan #1, Creatures on the Loose #10, Marvel Preview, Monsters on the Prowl)
Marvel Comics Group: June, 1971 - No. 2, Sept, 1971; No. 3, July, 1972 - No. 15, Aug, 1974; No. 16, Aug, 1976 - No. 29, Oct, 1978

1-Andru/Wood-a; 2nd app. & origin Kull; 15¢ issue 6 12 18 41 66 90
2-5: 2-3rd Kull app. Last 15¢ iss. 3-13: 20¢ issues. 3-Thulsa Doom-c/app. 3 6 9 18 27 35
6-10: 7-Thulsa Doom-c/app 2 4 6 10 14 18
11-15: 11-15-Ploog-a. 14,15: 25¢ issues 2 4 6 8 11 14
16-(Regular 25¢ edition)(8/76) 2 3 4 6 8 10
16-(30¢-c variant, limited distribution) 3 6 9 14 20 25
17-29: 21-23-(Reg. 30¢ editions) 2 3 4 6 8 10
21-23-(35¢-c variants, limited distribution) 3 6 9 20 40 60
NOTE: *No. 1, 2, 7-9, 11 are based on Robert E. Howard stories.* ***Alcala*** *a-17p, 18-20i; c-24.* ***Ditko*** *a-12r, 15r.* ***Gil Kane*** *c-15p, 21.* ***Nebres*** *a-22i-27i; c-25i, 27i.* ***Ploog*** *c-11, 12p, 13.* ***Severin*** *a-2-9i; c-2-10i, 19.* ***Starlin*** *c-14.*

KULL THE CONQUEROR
Marvel Comics Group: Dec, 1982 - No. 2, Mar, 1983 (52 pgs., Baxter paper)
1,2: 1-Buscema-a(p) 4.00

KULL THE CONQUEROR (No. 9,10 titled "Kull")
Marvel Comics Group: 5/83 - No. 10, 6/85 (52 pgs., Baxter paper)
V3#1-10: Buscema-a in #1-3,5-10 4.00
NOTE: Bolton a-4. Golden painted c-3-8. Guice a-4p. Sienkiewicz a-4; c-2.

KULL: THE HATE WITCH
Dark Horse Comics: Nov, 2010 - Present ($3.50)
1,2-Lapham-s/Guzman-a/Fleming-c 3.50

KUNG FU (See Deadly Hands of..., & Master of...)

KUNG FU FIGHTER (See Richard Dragon...)

KURT BUSIEK'S ASTRO CITY (Limited series) (Also see Astro City: Local Heroes)
Image Comics (Juke Box Productions): Aug, 1995 - No. 6, Jan, 1996 ($2.25)
1-Kurt Busiek scripts, Brent Anderson-a & Alex Ross front & back-c begins; 1st app. Samaritan & Honor Guard (Cleopatra, MHP, Beautie, The Black Rapier, Quarrel & N-Forcer) 2 4 6 8 10 12
2-6: 2-1st app. The Silver Agent, The Old Soldier, & the "original" Honor Guard (Max O'Millions, Starwoman, the "original" Cleopatra, the "original" N-Forcer, the Bouncing Beatnik, Leopardman & Kitkat). 3-1st app. Jack-in-the-Box & The Deacon. 4-1st app. Winged Victory (cameo), The Hanged Man & The First Family. 5-1st app. Crackerjack, The Astro City Irregulars, Nightingale & Sunbird. 6-Origin Samaritan; 1st full app. Winged Victory 1 3 4 6 8 10
Life In The Big City-(8/96, $19.95, trade paperback)-r/Image Comics limited series w/sketchbook & cover gallery; Ross-c 20.00
Life In The Big City-(8/96, $49.95, hardcover, 1000 print run)-r/Image Comics limited series w/sketchbook & cover gallery; Ross-c 50.00

KURT BUSIEK'S ASTRO CITY (1st Homage Comics series)
Image Comics (Homage Comics): V2#1, Sept, 1996 - No. 15, Dec, 1998;
DC Comics (Homage Comics): No. 16, Mar, 1999 - No. 22, Aug, 2000 ($2.50)
1/2-(10/96)-The Hanged Man story; 1st app. The All-American & Slugger, The Lamplighter, The Time-Keeper & Eterneon 1 3 4 6 8 10
1/2-(1/98) 2nd printing w/new cover 3.00
1- Kurt Busiek scripts, Alex Ross-c, Brent Anderson-p & Will Blyberg-i begin; intro The Gentleman, Thunderhead & Helia. 1 2 3 5 6 8
1-(12/97, $4.95) "3-D Edition" w/glasses 5.00
2-Origin The First Family; Astra story 1 2 3 4 5 7
3-5: 4-1st app. The Crossbreed, Ironhorse, Glue Gun & The Confessor (cameo) 6.00
6-10 5.00
11-22: 14-20-Steeljack story arc. 16-(3/99) First DC issue 3.00
TPB-($19.95) Ross-c, r/#4-9, #1/2 w/sketchbook 20.00
Family Album TPB ($19.95) r/#1-3,10-13 20.00
The Tarnished Angel HC ($29.95) r/#14-20; new Ross dust jacket; sketch pages by Anderson & Ross; cover gallery with reference photos 30.00
The Tarnished Angel SC ($19.95) r/#14-20; new Ross-c 20.00

LABMAN
Image Comics: Nov, 1996 ($3.50, one-shot)
1-Allred-c 4.00

LAB RATS
DC Comics: June, 2002 - No. 8, Jan, 2003 ($2.50)
1-8-John Byrne-s/a. 5,6-Superman app. 3.00

LABYRINTH
Marvel Comics Group: Nov, 1986 - No. 3, Jan, 1987 (Limited series)
1-3: David Bowie movie adaptation; r/Marvel Super Special #40 5.00

LA COSA NOSTROID (See Scud: The Disposible Assassin)
Fireman Press: Mar, 1996 - No. 9, 1998 ($2.95, B&W)
1-9-Dan Harmon-s/Rob Schrab-c/a 3.00

LAD: A DOG (Movie)
Dell Publishing Co.: 1961 - No. 2, July-Sept, 1962
Four Color 1303 4 8 12 28 44 60
2 4 8 12 24 37 50

LADY AND THE TRAMP (Disney, See Dell Giants & Movie Comics)
Dell Publishing Co.: No. 629, May, 1955 - No. 634, June, 1955
Four Color 629 (#1)-..with Jock 7 14 21 47 76 105
Four Color 634-...Album 5 10 15 32 51 70

LADY COP (See 1st Issue Special)

LADY DEADPOOL
Marvel Comics: Sept, 2010 ($3.99, one-shot)
1-Land-c/Lashley-a 4.00

LADY DEATH (See Evil Ernie)
Chaos! Comics: Jan, 1994 - No. 3, Mar, 1994 ($2.75, limited series)
1/2-S. Hughes-c/a in all, 1/2 Velvet 1 2 3 4 5 7
1/2 Gold 1 3 4 6 8 10
1/2 Signed Limited Edition 2 4 6 8 10 12
1-($3.50)-Chromium-c 2 4 6 10 14 18
1-Commemorative 2 4 6 9 13 16
1-(9/96, $2.95) "Encore Presentation"; r/#1 3.00
2 1 2 3 5 6 8
3 5.00
... And Jade (4/02, $2.99) Augustyn-s/Reis-a 3.00
...And The Women of Chaos! Gallery #1 (11/96, $2.25) pin-ups by various 3.00
.../Bad Kitty (9/01, $2.99) Mota-c/a 3.00
.../Bedlam (6/02, $2.99) Augustyn-s/Reis-c 3.00
...By Steven Hughes (6/00, $2.95) Tribute issue to Steven Hughes 3.00
...By Steven Hughes Deluxe Edition(6/00, $15.95) 16.00
.../Chastity (1/02, $2.99) Mota-c/a; Augustyn-s 3.00
...Death Becomes Her #0 (11/97, $2.95) Hughes-c/a 3.00
...FAN Edition: All Hallow's Eve #1 (1/97, mail-in) 5.00
...In Lingerie #1 (8/95, $2.95) pin-ups, wraparound-c 3.00
...In Lingerie #1-Leather Edition (10,000) 12.00
...In Lingerie #1-Micro Premium Edition; Lady Demon-c (2,000) 35.00
...: Love Bites (3/01, $2.99) Kaminski-s/Luke Ross-a 3.00
.../Medieval Witchblade (8/01, $3.50) covers by Molenaar and Silvestri 3.50
.../Medieval Witchblade Preview Ed. (8/01, $1.99) Molenaar-c 3.00
...: Mischief Night (11/01, $2.99) Ostrander-s/Reis-a 3.00
...: Re-Imagined (7/02, $2.99) Gossett-c 3.00
...: River of Fear (4/01, $2.99) Bennett-a(p)/Cleavenger-c 3.00
...Swimsuit Special #1-($2.50)-Wraparound-c 3.00
...Swimsuit Special #1-Red velvet-c 14.00
...Swimsuit 2001 #1-(2/01, $2.99)-Reis-c; art by various 3.00
...: The Reckoning (7/94, $6.95)-r/#1-3 7.00
...: The Reckoning (8/95, $12.95)- new printing including Lady Death 1/2 & Swimsuit Special #1 13.00
.../Vampirella (3/99, $3.50) Hughes-c/a 3.50
.../Vampirella 2 (3/00, $3.50) Deodato-c/a 3.50
... Vs. Purgatori (12/99, $3.50) Deodato-a 3.50
... Vs. Vampirella Preview (2/00, $1.00) Deodato-a/c 3.00

LADY DEATH (Ongoing series)
Chaos! Comics: Feb, 1998 - No. 16, May, 1999 ($2.95)
1-16: 1-4: Pulido-s/Hughes-c/a. 5-8,13-16-Deodato-a. 9-11-Hughes-a 3.00
...Retribution (8/98, $2.95) Jadsen-a 3.00
...Retribution Premium Ed. 6.00

LADY DEATH
Boundless Comics: No. 0, Nov, 2010 - Present ($3.99)
0-4-Pulido & Wolfer-s/Mueller-a; multiple covers on all 4.00
... Premiere (7/10, free) previews series; five covers 1.00

LADY DEATH: ALIVE

Lady Death (2011) #1 © Avatar

Lady Mechanika #0 © Aspen MLT

Lana #7 © MAR

GD VG FN VF VF/NM NM-
2.0 4.0 6.0 8.0 9.0 9.2

Chaos! Comics: May, 2001 - No. 4, Aug, 2001 ($2.99, limited series)
1-4-Ivan Reis-a; Lady Death becomes mortal 3.00

LADY DEATH: A MEDIEVAL TALE (Brian Pulido's...)
CG Entertainment: Mar, 2003 - No. 12, Apr, 2004 ($2.95)
1-12: 1-Brian Pulido-s/Ivan Reis-a; Lady Death in the CrossGen Universe 3.00
Vol.1 TPB (2003, $9.95) digest-sized reprint of #1-6 10.00

LADY DEATH: DARK ALLIANCE
Chaos! Comics: July, 2002 - No. 5, ($2.99, limited series)
1-3-Reis-a/Ostrander-s 3.00

LADY DEATH: DARK MILLENNIUM
Chaos! Comics: Feb, 2000 - No. 3, Apr, 2000 ($2.95, limited series)
Preview (6/00, $5.00) 5.00
1-3-Ivan Reis-a 3.00

LADY DEATH: GODDESS RETURNS
Chaos! Comics: Jun, 2002 - No. 2, Aug, 2002 ($2.99, limited series)
1,2-Mota-a/Ostrander-s 3.00

LADY DEATH: HEARTBREAKER
Chaos! Comics: Mar, 2002 - No. 4, ($2.99, limited series)
1-Molenaar-a/Ostrander-s 3.00

LADY DEATH: JUDGEMENT WAR
Chaos! Comics: Nov, 1999 - No. 3, Jan, 2000 ($2.95, limited series)
Prelude (10/99) two covers 3.00
1-3-Ivan Reis-a 3.00

LADY DEATH: LAST RITES
Chaos! Comics: Oct, 2001 - No. 4, Feb, 2001 ($2.99, limited series)
1-4-Ivan Reis-a/Ostrander-s 3.00

LADY DEATH: THE CRUCIBLE
Chaos! Comics: Nov, 1996 - No. 6, Oct, 1997 ($3.50/$2.95, limited series)
1/2 4.00
1/2 Cloth Edition 8.00
1-Wraparound silver foil embossed-c 4.00
2-6-($2.95) 3.00

LADY DEATH: THE GAUNTLET
Chaos! Comics: Apr, 2002 - No. 2, May, 2002 ($2.99, limited series)
1,2: 1-J. Scott Campbell-c/redesign of Lady Death's outfit; Mota-a 3.00

LADY DEATH: THE ODYSSEY
Chaos! Comics: Apr, 1996 - No. 4, Aug, 1996 ($3.50/$2.95)
1-($1.50)-Sneak Peek Preview 3.00
1-($1.50)-Sneak Peek Preview Micro Premium Edition (2500 print run)
2 4 6 8 10 12
1-($3.50)-Embossed, wraparound goil foil-c 5.00
1-Black Onyx Edition (200 print run) 6 12 18 37 59 80
1-($19.95)-Premium Edition (10,000 print run) 20.00
2-4-($2.95) 3.00

LADY DEATH: THE RAPTURE
Chaos! Comics: Jun, 1999 - No. 4, Sept, 1999 ($2.95, limited series)
1-4-Ivan Reis-c/a; Pulido-s 3.00

LADY DEATH: THE WILD HUNT (Brian Pulido's...)
CG Entertainment: Apr, 2004 - No. 2, May, 2005 ($2.95)
1-2: 1-Brian Pulido-s/Jim Cheung-a 3.00

LADY DEATH: TRIBULATION
Chaos! Comics: Dec, 2000 - No. 4, Mar, 2001 ($2.95, limited series)
1-4-Ivan Reis-a; Kaminski-s 3.00

LADY DEATH II: BETWEEN HEAVEN & HELL
Chaos! Comics: Mar, 1995 - No. 4, July, 1995 ($3.50, limited series)
1-Chromium wraparound-c; Evil Ernie cameo 5.00
1-Commemorative (4,000), 1-Black Velvet-c 2 4 6 10 14 18
1-Gold 1 3 4 6 8 10
1-"Refractor" edition (5,000) 2 4 6 11 16 20
2-4 3.50
4-Lady Demon variant-c 1 2 3 5 7 9
Trade paperback-($12.95)-r/#1-4 13.00

LADY DEMON
Chaos! Comics: Mar, 2000 - No. 3, May, 2000 ($2.95, limited series)
1-3-Kaminski-s/Brewer-a 3.00
1-Premium Edition 10.00

LADY FOR A NIGHT (See Cinema Comics Herald)

LADY JUSTICE (See Neil Gaiman's...)

LADY LUCK (Formerly Smash #1-85) (Also see Spirit Sections #1)
Quality Comics Group: No. 86, Dec, 1949 - No. 90, Aug, 1950
86(#1) 94 188 282 597 1024 1450
87-90 65 130 195 416 708 1000

LADY MECHANIKA
Aspen MLT: No. 0, Oct, 2010 - Present ($2.50/$2.99)
0-Joe Benitez-s/a; two covers; Benitez interview and sketch pages 2.50
1-(1/11, $2.99) Multiple covers 3.00

LADY PENDRAGON
Maximum Press: Mar, 1996 ($2.50)
1-Matt Hawkins script 2.50

LADY PENDRAGON
Image Comics: Nov, 1998 - No. 3, Jan, 1999 ($2.50, mini-series)
Preview (6/98) Flip book w/ Deity preview 3.00
1-3: 1-Matt Hawkins-s/Stinsman-a 3.00
1-($6.95) DF Ed. with variant-c by Jusko 7.00
2-($4.95)Variant edition 5.00
0-(3/99) Origin; flip book 3.00

LADY PENDRAGON (Volume 3)
Image Comics: Apr, 1999 - No. 9, Mar, 2000 ($2.50, mini-series)
1,2,4-6,8-10: 1-Matt Hawkins-s/Stinsman-a. 2-Peterson-c 3.00
3-Flip book w/Alley Cat preview (1st app.) 4.00
7-($3.95) Flip book; Stinsman-a/Cleavenger painted-a 4.00
Gallery Edition (10/99, $2.95) pin-ups 3.00
...Merlin (1/00, $2.95) Stinsman-a 3.00
.../ More Than Mortal (5/99, $2.50) Scott-s/Norton-a; 2 covers by Norton & Finch 3.00
.../ More Than Mortal Preview (2/99) Diamond Dateline supplement 3.00
Pilot Season: Lady Pendragon (5/08, $3.99) Hawkins-s/Eru-a; wraparound-c by Struzan 4.00

LADY RAWHIDE
Topps Comics: July, 1995 - No. 5, Mar, 1996 ($2.95, bi-monthly, limited series)
1-5: Don McGregor scripts & Mayhew-a. in all. 2-Stelfreeze-c. 3-Hughes-c. 4-Golden-c. 5-Julie Bell-c. 3.00
It Can't Happen Here TPB (8/99, $16.95) r/#1-5 17.00
Mini Comic 1 (7/95) Maroto-a; Zorro app. 3.00
Special Edition 1 (6/95, $3.95)-Reprints 4.00

LADY RAWHIDE (Volume 2)
Topps Comics: Oct, 1996 -No. 5, June, 1997 ($2.95, limited series)
1-5: 1-Julie Bell-c. 3.00

LADY RAWHIDE OTHER PEOPLE'S BLOOD (ZORRO'S ...)
Image Comics: Mar, 1999 - No. 5, July, 1999 ($2.95, B&W)
1-5-Reprints Lady Rawhide series in B&W 3.00

LADY SUPREME (See Asylum)(Also see Supreme & Kid Supreme)
Image Comics (Extreme): May, 1996 - No. 2, June, 1996 ($2.50, limited series)
1,2-Terry Moore -s: 1-Terry Moore-c. 2-Flip book w/Newmen preview 3.00

LAFF-A-LYMPICS (TV)(See The Funtastic World of Hanna-Barbera)
Marvel Comics: Mar, 1978 - No. 13, Mar, 1979 (Newsstand sales only)
1-Yogi Bear, Scooby Doo, Pixie & Dixie, etc. 3 6 9 18 27 35
2-8 3 6 9 14 19 24
9-13: 11-Jetsons x-over; 1 pg. illustrated bio of Mighty Mightor, Herculoids, Shazzan, Galaxy Trio & Space Ghost 3 6 9 16 23 30

LAFFY-DAFFY COMICS
Rural Home Publ. Co.: Feb, 1945 - No. 2, Mar, 1945
1-Funny animal 11 22 33 60 83 105
2-Funny animal 10 20 30 56 76 95

LANA (Little Lana No. 8 on)
Marvel Comics (MjMC): Aug, 1948 - No. 7, Aug, 1949 (Also see Annie Oakley)
1-Rusty, Millie begin 28 56 84 165 270 375
2-Kurtzman's "Hey Look" (1); last Rusty 15 30 45 88 137 185
3-7: 3-Nellie begins 12 24 36 69 97 125

LANCELOT & GUINEVERE (See Movie Classics)

LANCELOT LINK, SECRET CHIMP (TV)

Land of the Giants #1 © DELL

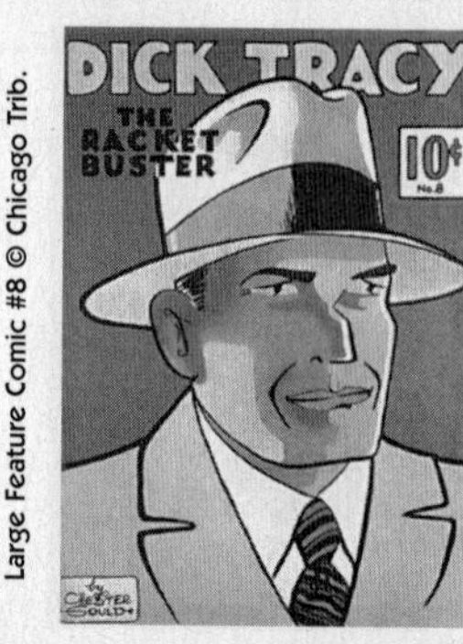

Large Feature Comic #8 © Chicago Trib.

Lash Larue Western #46 © FAW

	GD 2.0	VG 4.0	FN 6.0	VF 8.0	VF/NM 9.0	NM- 9.2

Gold Key: Apr, 1971 - No. 8, Feb, 1973

1-Photo-c	6	12	18	41	66	90
2-8: 2-Photo-c	4	8	12	24	37	50

LANCELOT STRONG (See The Shield)

LANCE O'CASEY (See Mighty Midget & Whiz Comics)
Fawcett Publications: Spring, 1946 - No. 3, Fall, 1946; No. 4, Summer, 1948

1-Captain Marvel app. on-c	26	52	78	154	252	350
2	16	32	48	94	147	200
3,4	14	28	42	80	115	150

NOTE: *The cover for the 1st issue was done in 1942 but was not published until 1946. The cover shows 68 pages but actually has only 36 pages.*

LANCER (TV)(Western)
Gold Key: Feb, 1969 - No. 3, Sept, 1969 (All photo-c)

1	4	8	12	24	37	50
2,3	3	6	9	18	27	35

LAND OF NOD, THE
Dark Horse Comics: July, 1997 - No. 3, Feb, 1998 ($2.95, B&W)

1-3-Jetcat; Jay Stephens-s/a — 3.00

LAND OF OZ
Arrow Comics: 1998 - No. 9 ($2.95, B&W)

1-9-Bishop-s/Bryan-s/a — 3.00

LAND OF THE DEAD (George A. Romaro's...)
IDW Publishing: Aug, 2005 - No. 5 ($3.99, limited series)

1-4-Adaptation of 2005 movie; Ryall-s/Rodriguez-a — 4.00
TPB (3/06, $19.99) r/#1-5; cover gallery — 20.00

LAND OF THE GIANTS (TV)
Gold Key: Nov, 1968 - No. 5, Sept, 1969 (All have photo-c)

1	6	12	18	43	69	95
2-5	4	8	12	26	41	55

LAND OF THE LOST COMICS (Radio)
E. C. Comics: July-Aug, 1946 - No. 9, Spring, 1948

1	39	78	117	236	388	540
2	24	48	72	142	234	325
3-9	21	42	63	122	199	275

LAND UNKNOWN, THE (Movie)
Dell Publishing Co.: No. 845, Sept, 1957

Four Color 845-Alex Toth-a	11	22	33	75	138	200

LA PACIFICA
DC Comics (Paradox Press): 1994/1995 ($4.95, B&W, limited series, digest size, mature)

1-3 — 5.00

LARAMIE (TV)
Dell Publishing Co.: Aug, 1960 - July, 1962 (All photo-c)

Four Color 1125-Gil Kane/Heath-a	8	16	24	58	97	135
Four Color 1223,1284, 01-418-207 (7/62)	6	12	18	43	69	95

LAREDO (TV)
Gold Key: June, 1966

1 (10179-606)-Photo-c	4	8	12	22	34	45

LARGE FEATURE COMIC (Formerly called Black & White in previous guides)
Dell Publishing Co.: 1939 - No. 13, 1943

Note: See individual alphabetical listings for prices

1 (Series I)-Dick Tracy Meets the Blank
2-Terry and the Pirates (#1)
3-Heigh-Yo Silver! The Lone Ranger (text & ill.)(76 pgs.); also exists as a Whitman #710; based on radio
4-Dick Tracy Gets His Man
5-Tarzan of the Apes (#1) by Harold Foster (origin); reprints 1st Tarzan dailies from 1929
6-Terry & the Pirates & The Dragon Lady; reprints dailies from 1936
7-(Scarce, 52 pgs.)-Hi-Yo Silver the Lone Ranger to the Rescue; also exists as a Whitman #715, based on radio program
8-Dick Tracy the Racket Buster
9-King of the Royal Mounted (Zane Grey's...)
10-(Scarce)-Gang Busters (No. appears on inside front cover); first slick cover (based on radio program)
11-Dick Tracy Foils the Mad Doc Hump
12-Smilin' Jack; no number on-c
13-Dick Tracy and Scottie of Scotland Yard
14-Smilin' Jack Helps G-Men Solve a Case!
15-Dick Tracy and the Kidnapped Princes
16-Donald Duck; 1st app. Daisy Duck on back cover (6/41-Disney)
17-Gang Busters (1941)
18-Phantasmo (see The Funnies #45)
19-Dumbo Comic Paint Book
20-Donald Duck Comic Paint Book (rarer than #16) (Disney)
21,22: 21-Private Buck. 22-Nuts & Jolts
24-Popeye in "Thimble Theatre" by Segar
26-Smitty
28-Grin and Bear It
30-Tillie the Toiler
2-Winnie Winkle (#1)
3-Dick Tracy
4-Tiny Tim (#1)
6-Terry and the Pirates; Caniff-a
8-Bugs Bunny (#1)('42)
9-Bringing Up Father
10-Popeye (Thimble Theatre)
11-Barney Google and Snuffy Smith
13-(nn)-1001 Hours Of Fun; puzzles & games; by A. W. Nugent. This book was bound as #13 with Large Feature Comics in publisher's files
(Disney); partial-r from 4-Color #17
23-The Nebbs
25-Smilin' Jack-1st issue to show title on-c
27-Terry and the Pirates; Caniff-c/a
29-Moon Mullins
1 (Series II)-Peter Rabbit by Harrison Cady; arrival date-3/27/42
5-Toots and Casper
7-Pluto Saves the Ship (#1) (Disney)-Written by Carl Barks, Jack Hannah, & Nick George (Barks' 1st comic book work)
12-Private Buck

NOTE: *The Black & White Feature Books are oversized 8-1/2x11-3/8" comics with color covers and black and white interiors. The first nine issues all have rough, heavy stock covers and, except for #7, all have 76 pages, including covers. #7 and #10-on all have 52 pages. Beginning with #10 the covers are slick and thin and, because of their size, are difficult to handle without damaging. For this reason, they are seldom found in fine to mint condition. The paper stock, unlike Wow #1 and Capt. Marvel #1, is itself not unstable ...just thin. Issues #2,6, and 27 were reprinted in the early 1980s, identical except for the copyright notice on the first page.*

LARRY DOBY, BASEBALL HERO
Fawcett Publications: 1950 (Cleveland Indians)

nn-Bill Ward-a; photo-c	77	154	231	493	847	1200

LARRY HARMON'S LAUREL AND HARDY (...Comics)
National Periodical Publ.: July-Aug, 1972 (Digest advertised, not published)

1-Low print run	9	18	27	63	107	150

LARS OF MARS
Ziff-Davis Publishing Co.: No. 10, Apr-May, 1951 - No. 11, July-Aug, 1951 (Painted-c) (Created by Jerry Siegel, editor)

10-Origin; Anderson-a(3) in each; classic robot-c	90	180	270	576	988	1400
11-Gene Colan-a; classic-c	68	136	204	435	743	1050

LARS OF MARS 3-D
Eclipse Comics: Apr, 1987 ($2.50)

1-r/Lars of Mars #10,11 in 3-D plus new story — 4.00
2-D limited edition (B&W, 100 copies) — 10.00

LASER ERASER & PRESSBUTTON (See Axel Pressbutton & Miracle Man 9)
Eclipse Comics: Nov, 1985 - No. 6, 1987 (95¢/$2.50, limited series)

1-6: 5,6-(95¢) — 3.00
...In 3-D 1 (8/86, $2.50) — 4.00
2-D 1 (B&W, limited to 100 copies signed & numbered) — 10.00

LASH LARUE WESTERN (Movie star; King of the bullwhip)(See Fawcett Movie Comic, Motion Picture Comics & Six-Gun Heroes)
Fawcett Publications: Sum, 1949 - No. 46, Jan, 1954 (36 pgs., 1-6,9,13,16-on)

1-Lash & his horse Black Diamond begin; photo front/back-c begin	58	116	174	371	636	900
2(11/49)	28	56	84	165	270	375
3-5	21	42	63	126	206	285
6,9: 6-Last photo back-c; intro. Frontier Phantom (Lash's twin brother)	19	38	57	109	172	235
7,8,10 (52pgs.)	20	40	60	114	182	250
11,12,14,15 (52pgs.)	15	30	45	84	127	170
13,16-20 (36pgs.)	14	28	42	80	115	150
21-30: 21-The Frontier Phantom app.	12	24	36	69	97	125
31-45	11	22	33	60	83	105
46-Last Fawcett issue & photo-c	11	22	33	64	90	115

LASH LARUE WESTERN (Continues from Fawcett series)
Charlton Comics: No. 47, Mar-Apr, 1954 - No. 84, June, 1961

47-Photo-c	14	28	42	80	115	150
48	11	22	33	60	83	105
49-60, 67,68-(68 pgs.). 68-Check-a	9	18	27	52	69	85
61-66,69,70: 52-r/#8; 53-r/#22	9	18	27	47	61	75
71-83	8	16	24	40	50	60
84-Last issue	9	18	27	47	61	75

LASH LARUE WESTERN

Lassie #27 © MGM

The Last Defenders #3 © MAR

The Last Phantom #1 © KING

GD VG FN VF VF/NM NM-
2.0 4.0 6.0 8.0 9.0 9.2

GD VG FN VF VF/NM NM-
2.0 4.0 6.0 8.0 9.0 9.2

AC Comics: 1990 ($3.50, 44 pgs) (24 pgs. of color, 16 pgs. of B&W)
1-Photo covers; r/Lash #6; r/old movie posters 4.00
Annual 1 (1990, $2.95, B&W, 44 pgs.)-Photo covers 4.00

LASSIE (TV)(M-G-M's... #1-36; see Kite Fun Book)
Dell Publ. Co./Gold Key No. 59 (10/62) on: June, 1950 - No. 70, July, 1969
1 (52 pgs.)-Photo-c; inside lists One Shot #282 in error
16 32 48 114 232 350
2-Painted-c begin 8 16 24 58 97 135
3-10 6 12 18 39 62 85
11-19: 12-Rocky Langford (Lassie's master) marries Gerry Lawrence. 15-1st app. Timbu
5 10 15 30 48 65
20-22-Matt Baker-a 5 10 15 34 55 75
23-38: 33-Robinson-a. 4 8 12 28 44 60
39-1st app. Timmy as Lassie picks up her TV family; photo-c
6 12 18 39 62 85
40-50-Photo-c on all 4 8 12 28 44 60
51-58-Photo-c on all 4 8 12 26 41 55
59 (10/62)-1st Gold Key 4 8 12 28 44 60
60-70: 63-Last Timmy (10/63). 64-r/#19. 65-Forest Ranger Corey Stuart begins, ends #69. 70-Forest Rangers Bob Ericson & Scott Turner app. (Lassie's new masters)
4 8 12 24 37 50
11193(1978, $1.95, 224 pgs., Golden Press)-Baker-r (92 pgs.)
4 8 12 26 41 55
NOTE: *Also see March of Comics #210, 217, 230, 254, 266, 278, 296, 308, 324,334, 346, 358, 370, 381, 394, 411, 432.*

LAST AMERICAN, THE
Marvel Comics (Epic): Dec, 1990 - No. 4, March, 1991 ($2.25, mini-series)
1-4: Alan Grant scripts 3.00

LAST AVENGERS STORY, THE (Last Avengers #1)
Marvel Comics: Nov, 1995 - No. 2, Dec, 1995 ($5.95, painted, limited series) (Alterniverse)
1,2: Peter David story; acetate-c in all. 1-New team (Hank Pym, Wasp, Human Torch, Cannonball, She-Hulk, Hotshot, Bombshell, Tommy Maximoff, Hawkeye & Mockingbird) forms to battle Ultron 59, Kang the Conqueror, The Grim Reaper & Oddball 6.00

LAST CHRISTMAS, THE
Image Comics: May, 2006 - No. 5, Oct, 2006 ($2.99, limited series)
1-5-Gerry Duggan & Brian Posehn-s/Rick Remender & Hilary Barta-a 3.00
TPB (2006, $14.99) r/#1-5; Patton Oswalt intro.; sketch pages and art 15.00

LAST DAY IN VIETNAM
Dark Horse Books: July, 2000 ($10.95, graphic novel)
nn-Will Eisner-s/a/c 11.00

LAST DAYS OF ANIMAL MAN, THE
DC Comics: July, 2009 - No. 6, Dec, 2009 ($2.99, limited series)
1-6: 1-Conway-s/Batista-a/Bolland-c. 3,4-Starfire app. 5,6-Future Justice League app. 3.00
TPB (2010, $17.99) r/#1-6 18.00

LAST DAYS OF THE JUSTICE SOCIETY SPECIAL
DC Comics: 1986 ($2.50, one-shot, 68 pgs.)
1-62 pg. JSA story plus unpubbed G.A. pg. 2 4 6 8 10 12

LAST DEFENDERS, THE
Marvel Comics: May, 2008 - No. 6, Oct, 2008 ($2.99, limited series)
1-6-Nighthawk, She-Hulk, Colossus, and Blazing Skull; Muniz-a. 2-Deodato-c 3.00

LAST FANTASTIC FOUR STORY, THE
Marvel Comics: Oct, 2007 ($4.99, one-shot)
1-Stan Lee-s/John Romita, Jr.-a/c; Galactus app. 5.00

LAST GENERATION, THE
Black Tie Studios: 1986 - No. 5, 1989 ($1.95, B&W, high quality paper)
1-5 3.00
Book 1 (1989, $6.95)-By Caliber Press 7.00

LAST HERO STANDING (Characters from Spider-Girl's M2 universe)
Marvel Comics: Aug, 2005 - No. 5, Aug, 2005 ($2.99, weekly limited series)
1-5: 1-DeFalco-s/Olliffe-a. 4-Thor app. 5-Capt. America dies 3.00
TPB (2005, $13.99) r/#1-5 14.00

LAST HUNT, THE
Dell Publishing Co.: No. 678, Feb, 1956
Four Color 678-Movie, photo-c 7 14 21 45 73 100

LAST KISS
ACME Press (Eclipse): 1988 ($3.95, B&W, squarebound, 52 pgs.)
1-One story adapts E.A. Poe's The Black Cat 4.00

LAST OF THE COMANCHES (Movie) (See Wild Bill Hickok #28)
Avon Periodicals: 1953
nn-Kinstler-c/a, 21pgs.; Ravielli-a 15 30 45 88 137 185

LAST OF THE ERIES, THE (See American Graphics)

LAST OF THE FAST GUNS, THE
Dell Publishing Co.: No. 925, Aug, 1958
Four Color 925-Movie, photo-c 6 12 18 43 69 95

LAST OF THE MOHICANS (See King Classics & White Rider and...)

LAST OF THE VIKING HEROES, THE (Also see Silver Star #1)
Genesis West Comics: Mar, 1987 - No. 12 ($1.50/$1.95)
1-4,5A,5B,6-12: 4-Intro The Phantom Force, 1-Signed edition ($1.50), 5A-Kirby/Stevens-c. 5B,6 ($1.95). 7-Art Adams-c. 8-Kirby back-c. 4.00
Summer Special 1-3: 1-(1988)-Frazetta-c & illos. 2 (1990, $2.50)-A TMNT app. 3 (1991, $2.50)-Teenage Mutant Ninja Turtles 4.00
Summer Special 1-Signed edition (sold for $1.95) 4.00
NOTE: ***Art Adams** c-7. **Byrne** c-3. **Kirby** c-1p, 5p. **Perez** c-2i. **Stevens** c-5Ai.*

LAST ONE, THE
DC Comics (Vertigo): July, 1993 - No. 6, Dec, 1993 ($2.50, lim. series, mature)
1-6 3.00

LAST PHANTOM, THE (Lee Falk's Phantom)
Dynamite Entertainment: 2010 - Present ($3.99)
1-6-Beatty-s/Ferigato-a; 1-Two covers by Alex Ross; Neves & Prado var. covers 4.00

LAST PLANET STANDING
Marvel Comics: July, 2006 - No. 5, Sept, 2006 ($2.99, limited series)
1-5-Galactus threatens Spider-Girl & Fantastic Five's M2 Earth; Avengers app.; Olliffe-a 3.00
TPB (2006, $13.99) r/series 14.00

LAST SHOT
Image Comics: Aug, 2001 - No. 4, Mar, 2002 ($2.95, limited series)
1-4: 1-Wraparound-c; by Studio XD 3.00
...: First Draw (5/01, $2.95) Introductory one-shot 3.00

LAST STARFIGHTER, THE
Marvel Comics Group: Oct, 1984 - No. 3, Dec, 1984 (75¢, movie adaptation)
1-3: r/Marvel Super Special; Guice-c 3.00

LAST TEMPTATION, THE
Marvel Comics: 1994 - No. 3, 1994 ($4.95, limited series)
1-3-Alice Cooper story; Neil Gaiman scripts; McKean-c; Zulli-a: 1-Two covers 5.00
HC (Dark Horse Comics, 2005, $14.95) r/#1-3; Gaiman intro. 15.00

LAST TRAIN FROM GUN HILL
Dell Publishing Co.: No. 1012, July, 1959
Four Color 1012-Movie, photo-c 8 16 24 56 93 130

LAST TRAIN TO DEADSVILLE: A CAL McDONALD MYSTERY (See Criminal Macabre)
Dark Horse Comics: May, 2004 - No. 4, Sept, 2004 ($2.99, limited series)
1-4-Steve Niles-s/Kelley Jones-a/c 3.00
TPB (2005, $14.95) r/series 15.00

LATEST ADVENTURES OF FOXY GRANDPA (See Foxy Grandpa)

LATEST COMICS (Super Duper No. 3?)
Spotlight Publ./Palace Promotions (Jubilee): Mar, 1945 - No. 2, 1945?
1-Super Duper 16 32 48 94 147 200
2-Bee-29 (nd); Jubilee in indicia blacked out 14 28 42 76 108 140

LAUGH
Archie Enterprises: June, 1987 - No. 29, Aug, 1991 (75¢/$1.00)
V2#1 5.00
2-10,14,24: 5-X-Mas issue. 14-1st app. Hot Dog. 24-Re-intro Super Duck 4.00
11-13,15-23,25-29: 19-X-Mas issue 3.00

LAUGH COMICS (Teenage) (Formerly Black Hood #9-19) (Laugh #226 on)
Archie Publications (Close-Up): No. 20, Fall, 1946 - No. 400, Apr, 1987
20-Archie begins; Katy Keene & Taffy begin by Woggon; Suzie & Wilbur also begin; Archie covers begin 84 168 252 538 919 1300
21-23,25 41 82 123 250 418 585
24- "Pipsy" by Kirby (6 pgs.) 41 82 123 256 428 600
26-30 27 54 81 158 259 360
31-40 20 40 60 114 182 250
41-60: 41,54-Debbi by Woggon 15 30 45 83 124 165

Laugh Comics #35 © AP

Laurel and Hardy #3 © DELL

Law Against Crime #1 © Essenkay

	GD 2.0	VG 4.0	FN 6.0	VF 8.0	VF/NM 9.0	NM- 9.2
61-80: 67-Debbi by Woggon	11	22	33	62	86	110
81-99	6	12	18	41	66	90
100	7	14	21	45	73	100
101-105,110,112,114-126: 125-Debbi app.	5	10	15	30	48	65
106-109,111,113-Neal Adams-a (1 pg.) in each	5	10	15	32	51	70
127-144: Super-hero app. in all (see note)	6	12	18	39	62	85
145-(4/63) Josie by DeCarlo begins	6	12	18	39	62	85
146-149-early Josie app. by DeCarlo	4	8	12	28	44	60
150,162,163,165,167,169,170-No Josie	3	6	9	19	29	38
151-161,164,168-Josie app. by DeCarlo	4	8	12	24	37	50
166-Beatles-c (1/65)	6	12	18	41	66	90
171-180, 200 (12/67)	3	6	9	17	25	32
181-199	3	6	9	14	20	26
201-240(3/71)	2	4	6	11	16	20
241-280(7/74)	2	4	6	9	13	16
281-299	2	4	6	8	10	12
300(3/76)	2	4	6	8	11	14
301-340 (7/79)	1	2	3	5	7	9
341-370 (1/82)	1	2	3	4	5	7
371-379,385-399						5.00
380-Cheryl Blossom app.	1	2	3	5	6	8
381-384,400: 381-384-Katy Keene app.; by Woggon-381,382						6.00

NOTE: *The Fly app. in 128, 129, 132, 134, 138, 139. Flygirl app. in 136, 137, 143. Flyman app. in 137. The Jaguar app. in 127, 130, 131, 133, 135, 140-142, 144. Josie app. in 145-149, 151-161, 164, 168. Katy Keene app. in 20-125, 129, 130, 133. Horror/Sci-Fi covers on 128-135, 137, 139. Many issues contain paper dolls.* ***Al Fagaly*** *c-20-29.* ***Montana*** *c-33, 36, 37, 42.* ***Bill Vigoda*** *c-30, 50.*

LAUGH COMICS DIGEST (...Magazine #23-89; Laugh Digest Mag. #90 on)
Archie Publ. (Close-Up No. 1, 3 on): 8/74; No. 2, 9/75; No. 3, 3/76 - No. 200, Apr, 2005 (Digest-size) (Josie and Sabrina app. in most issues)

	GD	VG	FN	VF	VF/NM	NM-
1-Neal Adams-a	5	10	15	34	55	75
2,7,8,19-Neal Adams-a	3	6	9	20	30	40
3-6,9,10	3	6	9	16	22	28
11-18,20	2	4	6	11	16	20
21-40	2	4	6	9	13	16
41-60	1	3	4	6	8	10
61-80	1	2	3	5	6	8
81-99						5.00
100						6.00
101-138						4.00
139-200: 139-Begin $1.95-c. 148-Begin $1.99-c. 156-Begin $2.19-c. 180-Begin $2.39-c						3.00

NOTE: *Katy Keene in 23, 25, 27, 32-38, 40, 45-48, 50. The Fly-r in 19, 20. The Jaguar-r in 25, 27. Mr. Justice-r in 21. The Web-r in 23.*

LAUGH COMIX (Laugh Comics inside)(Formerly Top Notch Laugh; Suzie Comics No. 49 on)
MLJ Magazines: No. 46, Summer, 1944 - No. 48, Winter, 1944-45

	GD	VG	FN	VF	VF/NM	NM-
46-Wilbur & Suzie in all; Harry Sahle-c	24	48	72	142	234	325
47,48: 47-Sahle-c. 48-Bill Vigoda-c	17	34	51	98	154	210

LAUGH-IN MAGAZINE (TV)(Magazine)
Laufer Publ. Co.: Oct, 1968 - No. 12, Oct, 1969 (50¢) (Satire)

	GD	VG	FN	VF	VF/NM	NM-
V1#1	5	10	15	32	51	70
2-12	4	8	12	22	34	45

LAUREL & HARDY (See Larry Harmon's... & March of Comics No. 302, 314)

LAUREL AND HARDY (...Comics)
St. John Publ. Co.: 3/49 - No. 3, 9/49; No. 26, 11/55 - No. 28, 3/56 (No #4-25)

	GD	VG	FN	VF	VF/NM	NM-
1	74	148	222	470	810	1150
2	40	80	120	242	401	560
3	31	62	93	182	296	410
26-28 (Reprints)	15	30	45	92	144	195

LAUREL AND HARDY (TV)
Dell Publishing Co.: Oct, 1962 - No. 4, Sept-Nov, 1963

	GD	VG	FN	VF	VF/NM	NM-
12-423-210 (8-10/62)	6	12	18	43	69	95
2-4 (Dell)	4	8	12	28	44	60

LAUREL AND HARDY (Larry Harmon's...)
Gold Key: Jan, 1967 - No. 2, Oct, 1967

	GD	VG	FN	VF	VF/NM	NM-
1-Photo back-c	4	8	12	28	44	60
2	4	8	12	22	34	45

LAUREL AND HARDY DIGEST: DC Comics. 1972 (Advertised, not published)

L.A.W., THE (LIVING ASSAULT WEAPONS)
DC Comics: Sept, 1999 - No. 6, Feb, 2000 ($2.50, limited series)

1-6-Blue Beetle, Question, Judomaster, Capt. Atom app.; Giordano-a. 5-JLA app. 3.00

LAW AGAINST CRIME (Law-Crime on cover)
Essenkay Publishing Co.: April, 1948 - No. 3, Aug, 1948 (Real Stories from Police Files)

	GD	VG	FN	VF	VF/NM	NM-
1-(#1-3 are half funny animal, half crime stories)-L. B. Cole-c/a in all; electrocution-c	76	152	228	486	831	1175
2-L. B. Cole-c/a	55	110	165	352	601	850
3-Used in **SOTI**, pg. 180,181 & illo "The wish to hurt or kill couples in lovers' lanes;" reprinted in All-Famous Crime #9	69	138	207	442	759	1075

LAW AND ORDER
Maximum Press: Sept, 1995 - No. 2, 1995 ($2.50, unfinished limited series)

1,2 3.00

LAWBREAKERS (...Suspense Stories No. 10 on)
Law and Order Magazines (Charlton): Mar, 1951 - No. 9, Oct-Nov, 1952

	GD	VG	FN	VF	VF/NM	NM-
1	41	82	123	256	428	600
2	24	48	72	142	234	325
3,5,6,8,9	20	40	60	118	192	265
4- "White Death" junkie story	27	54	81	158	259	360
7- "The Deadly Dopesters" drug story	27	54	81	158	259	360

LAWBREAKERS ALWAYS LOSE!
Marvel Comics (CBS): Spring, 1948 - No. 10, Oct, 1949

	GD	VG	FN	VF	VF/NM	NM-
1-2pg. Kurtzman-a, "Giggles 'n' Grins"	37	74	111	222	361	500
2	20	40	60	114	182	250
3-5: 4-Vampire story	15	30	45	90	140	190
6(2/49)-Has editorial defense against charges of Dr. Wertham	17	34	51	100	158	215
7-Used in **SOTI**, illo "Comic-book philosophy"	32	64	96	188	307	425
8-10: 9,10-Photo-c	15	30	45	83	124	165

NOTE: ***Brodsky*** *c-4, 5.* ***Shores*** *c-1-3, 6-8.*

LAWBREAKERS SUSPENSE STORIES (Formerly Lawbreakers; Strange Suspense Stories No. 16 on)
Capitol Stories/Charlton Comics: No. 10, Jan, 1953 - No. 15, Nov, 1953

	GD	VG	FN	VF	VF/NM	NM-
10	42	84	126	265	445	625
11 (3/53)-Severed tongues-c/story & woman negligee scene	168	336	504	1075	1838	2600
12-14: 13-Giordano-c begin, end #15	29	58	87	170	278	385
15-Acid-in-face-c/story; hands dissolved in acid story	61	122	183	390	670	950

LAW-CRIME (See Law Against Crime)

LAWDOG
Marvel Comics (Epic Comics): May, 1993 - No. 10, Feb, 1993

1-10 3.00

LAWDOG/GRIMROD: TERROR AT THE CROSSROADS
Marvel Comics (Epic Comics): Sept, 1993 ($3.50)

1 3.50

LAWMAN (TV)
Dell Publishing Co.: No. 970, Feb, 1959 - No. 11, Apr-June, 1962 (All photo-c)

	GD	VG	FN	VF	VF/NM	NM-
Four Color 970(#1)	12	24	36	82	154	225
Four Color 1035('60), 3(2-4/60)-Toth-a	8	16	24	54	90	125
4-11	6	12	18	43	69	95

LAW OF DREDD, THE (Also see Judge Dredd)
Quality Comics/Fleetway #8 on: 1989 - No. 33, 1992 ($1.50/$1.75)

1-33: Bolland a-1-6,8,10-12,14(2 pg),15,19 3.00

LAWRENCE (See Movie Classics)

LAZARUS CHURCHYARD
Tundra Publishing: June, 1992 - No. 3, 1992 ($3.95, 44 pgs., coated stock)

1-3 4.00
The Final Cut (Image, 1/01, $14.95, TPB) Reprints Ellis/D'Israeli strips 15.00

LAZARUS FIVE
DC Comics: July, 2000 - No. 5, Nov, 2000 ($2.50, limited series)

1-5-Harris-c/Abell-a(p) 3.00

LEADING COMICS
DC Comics: Jan. 1942

nn - Ashcan comic, not distributed to newsstands, only for in-house use. Cover art is Detective Comics #57 with interior being Star Spangled Comics #2 (no known sales)

LEADING COMICS (...Screen Comics No. 42 on)
National Periodical Publications: Winter, 1941-42 - No. 41, Feb-Mar, 1950

1-Origin The Seven Soldiers of Victory; Crimson Avenger, Green Arrow & Speedy, Shining

Leading Comics #5 © DC

Leave It To Binky #9 © DC

Legacy #1 © Roaring Studios

	GD 2.0	VG 4.0	FN 6.0	VF 8.0	VF/NM 9.0	NM- 9.2

Knight, The Vigilante, Star Spangled Kid & Stripesy begin; The Dummy (Vigilante villain)
1st app. 343 686 1029 2400 4200 6000
2-Meskin-a; Fred Ray-c 116 232 348 742 1271 1800
3 90 180 270 576 988 1400
4,5 65 130 195 416 708 1000
6-10 50 100 150 315 533 750
11,12,14(Spring, 1945) 39 78 117 240 395 550
13-Classic robot-c 87 174 261 553 952 1350
15-(Sum,'45)-Contents change to funny animal 26 52 78 154 252 350
16-22,24-30: 16-Nero Fox-c begin, end #22 14 28 42 80 115 150
23-1st app. Peter Porkchops by Otto Feuer & begins 26 52 78 154 252 350
31,32,34-41: 34-41-Leading Screen... on-c only 12 24 36 67 94 120
33-(Scarce) 20 40 60 114 182 250
NOTE: ***Otto Feuer**-a most #15-on; **Rube Grossman**-a most #15-on;c-15-41. **Post** a-23-37, 39, 41.*

LEADING MAN
Image Comics: June, 2006 - No. 5, Feb, 2007 ($3.50, limited series)
1-5-B. Clay Moore-s/Jeremy Haun-a 3.50
TPB (2/07, $14.95) r/#1-5; sketch gallery 15.00

LEADING SCREEN COMICS (Formerly Leading Comics)
National Periodical Publ.: No. 42, Apr-May, 1950 - No. 77, Aug-Sept, 1955
42-Peter Porkchops-c/stories continue 12 24 36 67 94 120
43-77 11 22 33 60 83 105
NOTE: ***Grossman** a-most. **Mayer** a-45-48, 50, 54-57, 60, 62-74, 75(3), 76, 77.*

LEAGUE OF CHAMPIONS, THE (Also see The Champions)
Hero Graphics: Dec, 1990 - No. 12, 1992 ($2.95, 52 pgs.)
1-12: 1-Flare app. 2-Origin Malice 4.00

LEAGUE OF EXTRAORDINARY GENTLEMEN, THE
America's Best Comics: Mar, 1999 - No. 6, Sept, 2000 ($2.95, limited series)
1-Alan Moore-s/Kevin O'Neill-a 2 4 6 8 10 12
1-DF Edition ($10.00) O'Neill-c 2 4 6 9 12 15
2,3 6.00
4-6: 5-Revised printing with "Amaze 'Whirling Spray' Syringe" parody ad 4.00
5-Initial printing recalled because of "Marvel Co. Syringe" parody ad
13 26 39 93 182 270
... Compendium 1,2: 1-r/#1,2. 2-r/#3,4 6.00
Hardcover (2000, $24.95) r/#1-6 plus cover gallery 25.00

LEAGUE OF EXTRAORDINARY GENTLEMEN, THE (Volume 2)
America's Best Comics: Sept, 2002 - No. 6, Nov, 2003 ($3.50, limited series)
1-6-Alan Moore-s/Kevin O'Neill-a 4.00
... Bumper Compendium 1,2: 1-r/#1,2. 2-r/#3,4 6.00
... Black Dossier (HC, 2007, $29.99) new graphic novel; 3-D section with glasses; extras 30.00

LEAGUE OF EXTRAORDINARY GENTLEMEN CENTURY: 1910
Top Shelf Productions/Knockabout Comics: 2009 ($7.95, squarebound one-shot)
1-Alan Moore-s/Kevin O'Neill-a 8.00

LEAGUE OF JUSTICE
DC Comics (Elseworlds): 1996 - No. 2, 1996 ($5.95, 48 pgs., squarebound)
1,2: Magic-based alternate DC Universe story; Giordano-i 6.00

LEATHERFACE
Arpad Publishing: May (April on-c), 1991 - No. 4, May, 1992 ($2.75, painted-c)
1-4-Based on Texas Chainsaw movie; Dorman-c 1 2 3 5 7 9

LEATHERNECK THE MARINE (See Mighty Midget Comics)

LEAVE IT TO BEAVER (TV)
Dell Publishing Co.: No. 912, June, 1958; May-July, 1962 (All photo-c)
Four Color 912 14 28 42 99 200 300
Four Color 999,1103,1191,1285, 01-428-207 13 26 39 89 170 250

LEAVE IT TO BINKY (Binky No. 72 on) (Super DC Giant) (No. 1-22: 52 pgs.)
National Periodical Publications: 2-3/48 - #60, 10/58; #61, 6-7/68 - #71, 2-3/70 (Teen-age humor)
1-Lucy wears Superman costume 36 72 108 216 351 485
2 20 40 60 114 182 250
3,4 14 28 42 80 115 150
5-Superman cameo 18 36 54 105 165 225
6-10 12 24 36 69 97 125
11-14,16-22: Last 52 pg. issue 11 22 33 60 83 105
15-Scribbly story by Mayer 12 24 36 69 97 125
23-28,30-45: 45-Last pre-code (2/55) 9 18 27 52 69 85
29-Used in **POP**, pg. 78 10 20 30 54 72 90
46-60: 60-(10/58) 6 12 18 37 59 80
61 (6-7/68) 1950's reprints with art changes 6 12 18 39 62 85
62-69: 67-Last 12¢ issue 4 8 12 28 44 60
70-7pg. app. Bus Driver who looks like Ralph from Honeymooners
5 10 15 32 51 70
71-Last issue 5 10 15 30 48 65
NOTE: ***Aragones**-a-61, 62, 67. **Drucker** a-28. **Mayer** a-1, 2, 15. Created by **Mayer**.*

LEAVE IT TO CHANCE
Image Comics (Homage Comics): Sept, 1996 - No. 11, Sept, 1998; No. 13, July, 2002
DC Comics (Homage Comics): No. 12, Jun, 1999 ($2.50/$2.95/$4.95)
1-3: 1-Intro Chance Falconer & St. George; James Robinson scripts & Paul Smith-c/a 5.00
4-12: 12-(6/99) 3.00
13-(7/02, $4.95) includes sketch pages and pin-ups 5.00
Free Comic Book Day Edition (2003) - James Robinson-s/Paul Smith-a 2.50
Shaman's Rain TPB (1997, $9.95) r/#1-4 10.00
Shaman's Rain HC (2002, $14.95, over-sized 8 1/4" x 12") r/#1-4 15.00
Trick or Threat TPB (1997, $12.95) r/#5-8 13.00
Trick or Threat HC (2002, $14.95, over-sized 8 1/4" x 12") r/#5-8 15.00
Vol. 3: Monster Madness and Other Stories HC (2003, $14.95, 8 1/4" x 12") r/#9-11 15.00

LEE HUNTER, INDIAN FIGHTER
Dell Publishing Co.: No. 779, Mar, 1957; No. 904, May, 1958
Four Color 779 (#1) 5 10 15 34 55 75
Four Color 904 4 8 12 26 41 55

LEFT-HANDED GUN, THE (Movie)
Dell Publishing Co.: No. 913, July, 1958
Four Color 913-Paul Newman photo-c 9 18 27 63 107 150

LEGACY
Majestic Entertainment: Oct, 1993 - No. 2, Nov, 1993; No. 0, 1994 ($2.25)
1-2,0: 1-Glow-in-the-dark-c. 0-Platinum 3.00

LEGACY
Image Comics: May, 2003 - No. 4, Feb, 2004 ($2.95)
1-4: 1-Francisco-a/Treffiletti-s 3.00

LEGACY OF KAIN (Based on the Eidos video game)
Top Cow Productions: Oct, 1999; Jan, 2004 ($2.99)
...Defiance 1 (1/04, $2.99) Cha-c; Kirkham-a 3.00
...Soul Reaver 1 (10/99, Diamond Dateline supplement) Benitez-c 3.00

LEGEND
DC Comics (WildStorm): Apr, 2005 - No. 4, July, 2005 ($5.95/$5.99, limited series)
1-4-Howard Chaykin-s/Russ Heath-a; inspired by Philip Wylie's novel "Gladiator" 6.00

LEGENDARY TALESPINNERS
Dynamite Entertainment: 2010 - No. 3, 2010 ($3.99)
1-3-Kuhoric-s/Bond-a; two covers 4.00

LEGEND OF CUSTER, THE (TV)
Dell Publishing Co.: Jan, 1968
1-Wayne Maunder photo-c 3 6 9 18 27 35

LEGEND OF ISIS
Alias Entertainment: May, 2005 - No. 5 ($2.99)
1-5: 1-Three covers; Ottney-s/Fontana-a 3.00
...: Beginnings TPB (5/05, $9.99) Ottney-s 10.00

LEGEND OF JESSE JAMES, THE (TV)
Gold Key: Feb, 1966
10172-602-Photo-c 3 6 9 18 27 35

LEGEND OF KAMUI, THE (See Kamui)

LEGEND OF LOBO, THE (See Movie Comics)

LEGEND OF MOTHER SARAH (Manga)
Dark Horse Comics: Apr, 1995 - No. 8, Nov, 1995 ($2.50, limited series)
1-8: Katsuhiro Otomo scripts 4.00

LEGEND OF MOTHER SARAH: CITY OF THE ANGELS (Manga)
Dark Horse Comics: Oct, 1996 - No. 9 ($3.95, B&W, limited series)
1(10/96), 2(12/97),3-9: Otomo scripts 4.00

LEGEND OF MOTHER SARAH: CITY OF THE CHILDREN (Manga)
Dark Horse Comics: Jan, 1996 - No. 7, July, 1996 ($3.95, B&W, limited series)
1-7: Otomo scripts 4.00

LEGEND OF SUPREME
Image Comics (Extreme): Dec, 1994 - No. 3, Feb, 1995 ($2.50, limited series)

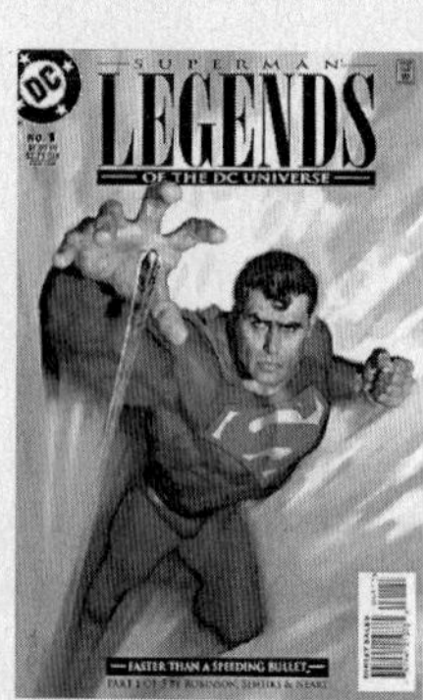

Legends of the DC Universe #1 © DC

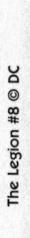

The Legion #8 © DC

Legionnaires #55 © DC

	GD 2.0	VG 4.0	FN 6.0	VF 8.0	VF/NM 9.0	NM- 9.2

1-3 3.00

LEGEND OF THE ELFLORD
DavDez Arts: July, 1998 - No. 2, Sept, 1998 ($2.95)
1,2-Barry Blair & Colin Chin-s/a 3.00

LEGEND OF THE HAWKMAN
DC Comics: 2000 - No. 3, 2000 ($4.95, limited series)
1-3-Raab-s/Lark-c/a 5.00

LEGEND OF THE SHIELD, THE
DC Comics (Impact Comics): July, 1991 - No. 16, Oct, 1992 ($1.00)
1-16: 6,7-The Fly x-over. 12-Contains trading card 4.00
Annual 1 (1992, $2.50, 68 pgs.)-Snyder-a; w/trading card 4.00

LEGEND OF WONDER WOMAN, THE
DC Comics: May, 1986 - No. 4, Aug, 1986 (75¢, limited series)
1-4 4.00

LEGEND OF YOUNG DICK TURPIN, THE (Disney)(TV)
Gold Key: May, 1966
1 (10176-605)-Photo/painted-c 3 6 9 18 27 35

LEGEND OF ZELDA, THE (Link: The Legend... in indicia)
Valiant Comics: 1990 - No. 4, 1990 ($1.95, coated stiff-c) V2#1, 1990 - No. 5, 1990 ($1.50)
1-4: 4-Layton-c(i) 6.00
V2#1-5 4.00

LEGENDS
DC Comics: Nov, 1986 - No. 6, Apr, 1987 (75¢, limited series)
1-5: 1-Byrne-c/a(p) in all; 1st app. new Capt. Marvel. 3-1st app. new Suicide Squad; death of Blockbuster 5.00
6-1st app. new Justice League 1 2 3 4 5 7

LEGENDS OF DANIEL BOONE, THE (...Frontier Scout)
National Periodical Publications: Oct-Nov, 1955 - No. 8, Dec-Jan, 1956-57
1 (Scarce)-Nick Cardy c-1-8 54 108 162 346 591 835
2 (Scarce) 40 80 120 246 411 575
3-8 (Scarce) 34 68 102 199 325 450

LEGENDS OF NASCAR, THE
Vortex Comics: Nov, 1990 - No. 14, 1992? (#1 3rd printing (1/91) says 2nd printing inside)
1-Bill Elliott biog.; Trimpe-a ($1.50) 5.00
1-2nd printing (11/90, $2.00) 3.00
1-3rd print; contains Maxx racecards ($3.00) 3.00
2-14: 2-Richard Petty. 3-Ken Schrader (7/91). 4-Bobby Allison; Spiegle-a(p); Adkins part-i. 5-Sterling Marlin. 6-Bill Elliott. 7-Junior Johnson; Spiegle-c/a. 8-Benny Parsons; Heck-a3.00
1-13-Hologram cover versions. 2-Hologram shows Bill Elliott's car by mistake (all are numbered & limited) 5.00
2-Hologram corrected version 5.00
Christmas Special ($5.95) 6.00

LEGENDS OF THE DARK CLAW
DC Comics (Amalgam): Apr, 1996 ($1.95)
1-Jim Balent-c/a 3.00

LEGENDS OF THE DARK KNIGHT (See Batman: ...)

LEGENDS OF THE DC UNIVERSE
DC Comics: Feb, 1998 - No. 41, June, 2001 ($1.95/$1.99/$2.50)
1-13,15-21: 1-3-Superman; Robinson-s/Semeiks-a/Orbik-painted-c. 4,5-Wonder Woman; Deodato-a/Rude painted-c. 8-GL/GA, O'Neil-s. 10,11-Batgirl; Dodson-a. 12,13-Justice League. 15-17-Flash. 18-Kid Flash; Guice-a. 19-Impulse; prelude to JLApe Annuals. 20,21-Abin Sur 4.00
14-($3.95) Jimmy Olsen; Kirby-esque-c by Rude 5.00
22-27,30: 22,23-Superman; Rude-c/Ladronn-a. 26,27-Aquaman/Joker 3.00
28,29: Green Lantern & the Atom; Gil Kane-a; covers by Kane and Ross 3.00
31,32: 32-Begin $2.50-c; Wonder Woman; Texeira-c 3.00
33-36-Hal Jordan as The Spectre; DeMatteis-s/Zulli-a; Hale painted-c 3.00
37-41: 37,38-Kyle Rayner. 39-Superman. 40,41-Atom; Harris-c 3.00
... Crisis on Infinite Earths 1 (2/99, $4.95) Untold story during and after Crisis on Infinite Earths #4; Wolfman-s/Ryan-a/Orbik-c 5.00
... 80 Page Giant 1 (9/98, $4.95) Stories and art by various incl. Ditko, Perez, Gibbons, Mumy; Joe Kubert-c 5.00
... 80 Page Giant 2 (1/00, $4.95) Stories and art by various incl. Challengers by Art Adams; Sean Phillips-c 5.00
... 3-D Gallery (12/98, $2.95) Pin-ups w/glasses 3.00

LEGENDS OF THE LEGION (See Legion of Super-Heroes)
DC Comics: Feb, 1998 - No. 4, May, 1998 ($2.25, limited series)
1-4:1-Origin-s of Ultra Boy. 2-Spark. 3-Umbra. 4-Star Boy 3.00

LEGENDS OF THE STARGRAZERS (See Vanguard Illustrated #2)
Innovation Publishing: Aug, 1989 - No. 6, 1990 ($1.95, limited series, mature)
1-6: 1-Redondo part inks 3.00

LEGENDS OF THE WORLD'S FINEST (See World's Finest)
DC Comics: 1994 - No. 3, 1994 ($4.95, squarebound, limited series)
1-3: Simonson scripts; Brereton-c/a; embossed foil logos 6.00
TPB-(1995, $14.95) r/#1-3 15.00

L.E.G.I.O.N. (The # to right of title represents year of print)(Also see Lobo & R.E.B.E.L.S.)
DC Comics: Feb, 1989 - No. 70, Sept, 1994 ($1.50/$1.75)
1-Giffen plots/breakdowns in #1-12,28 5.00
2-22,24-47: 3-Lobo app. #3 on. 4-1st Lobo-c this title. 5-Lobo joins L.E.G.I.O.N. 13-Lar Gand app. 16-Lar Gand joins L.E.G.I.O.N., leaves #19. 31-Capt. Marvel app. 35-L.E.G.I.O.N. '92 begins 3.00
23,70-($2.50, 52 pgs.)-L.E.G.I.O.N. '91 begins. 70-Zero Hour 4.00
48,49,51-69: 48-Begin $1.75-c. 63-L.E.G.I.O.N. '94 begins; Superman x-over 3.00
50-($3.50, 68 pgs.) 4.00
Annual 1-5 ('90-94, 68 pgs.): 1-Lobo, Superman app. 2-Alan Grant scripts. 5-Elseworlds story; Lobo app. 4.00
NOTE: *Alan Grant scripts in #1-39, 51, Annual 1, 2.*

LEGION, THE (Continued from Legion Lost & Legion Worlds)
DC Comics: Dec, 2001 - No. 38, Oct, 2004 ($2.50)
1-Abnett & Lanning-s; Coipel & Lanning-c/a 4.00
2-24: 3-8-Ra's al Ghul app. 5-Snejbjerg-a. 9-DeStefano-a. 12-Legion vs. JLA. 16-Fatal Five app.; Walker-a 17,18-Ra's al Ghul app. 20-23-Universo app. 3.00
25-($3.95) Art by Harris, Cockrum, Rivoche; teenage Clark Kent app.; Harris-c 4.00
26-38-Superboy in classic costume. 26-30-Darkseid app. 31-Giffen-a. 35-38-Jurgens-a 3.00
...Secret Files 3003 (1/04, $4.95) Kirk-a, Harris-c/a; Superboy app. 5.00
...Foundations TPB (2004, $19.95) r/#25-30 & Secret Files 3003; Harris-c 20.00

LEGION LOST (Continued from Legion of Super-Heroes [4th series] #125)
DC Comics: May, 2000 - No. 12, Apr, 2001 ($2.50, limited series)
1-Abnett & Lanning-s. Coipel & Lanning-c/a 1 2 3 4 5 7
2-12-Abnett & Lanning-s. Coipel & Lanning-c/a in most. 4,9-Alixe-a 3.00

LEGIONNAIRES (See Legion of Super-Heroes #40, 41 & Showcase 95 #6)
DC Comics: Apr, 1992 - No. 81, Mar, 2000 ($1.25/$1.50/$2.25)
0-(10/94)-Zero Hour restart of Legion; released between #18 & #19 3.00
1-49,51-77: 1-(4/92)-Chris Sprouse-c/a; polybagged w/SkyBox trading card. 11-Kid Quantum joins. 18-(9/94)-Zero Hour. 19(11/94). 37-Valor (Lar Gand) becomes M'onel (5/96). 43-Legion tryouts; reintro Princess Projectra, Shadow Lass & others. 47-Forms one cover image with LSH #91. 60-Karate Kid & Kid Quantum join. 61-Silver Age & 70's Legion app. 76-Return of Wildfire. 79,80-Coipel-c/a; Legion vs. the Blight 3.00
50-($3.95) Pullout poster by Davis/Farmer 4.00
#1,000,000 (11/98) Sean Phillips-a 3.00
Annual 1,3 ('94,'96 $2.95)-1-Elseworlds-s. 3-Legends of the Dead Earth-s 4.00
Annual 2 (1995, $3.95)-Year One-s 4.50

LEGIONNAIRES THREE
DC Comics: Jan, 1986 - No. 4, May, 1986 (75¢, limited series)
1-4 3.00

LEGION OF MONSTERS (Also see Marvel Premiere #28 & Marvel Preview #8)
Marvel Comics Group: Sept, 1975 ($1.00, B&W, magazine, 76 pgs.)
1-Origin & 1st app. Legion of Monsters; Neal Adams-c; Morrow-a; origin & only app. The Manphibian; Frankenstein by Mayerik; Bram Stoker's Dracula adaptation; Reese-a; painted-c (#2 was advertised with Morbius & Satana, but was never published) 6 12 18 39 62 85

LEGION OF MONSTERS (One-shots)
Marvel Comics: Apr, 2007 - Sept, 2007 ($2.99)
... Man-Thing (5/07) Huston-s/Janson-a/Land-c; Simon Garth: Zombie by Ted McKeever 3.00
... Morbius (9/07) Cahill-s/Gaydos-a/Land-c; Dracula w/Finch-a/Cebulski-s 3.00
... Satana (8/07) Furth-s/Andrasofszky-a/Land-c; Living Mummy by Hickman 3.00
... Werewolf By Night (4/07) Carey-s/Land-a/c; Monster of Frankenstein by Skottie Young 3.00
HC (2007, $24.99, dustjacket) oversized r/series and classic stories; sketch pages 25.00

LEGION OF NIGHT, THE
Marvel Comics: Oct, 1991 - No. 2, Oct, 1991 ($4.95, 52 pgs.)
1,2-Whilce Portacio-c/a(p) 5.00

LEGION OF SUBSTITUTE HEROES SPECIAL (See Adventure Comics #306)
DC Comics: July, 1985 ($1.25, one-shot, 52 pgs.)

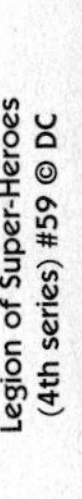
Legion of Super-Heroes (4th series) #59 © DC

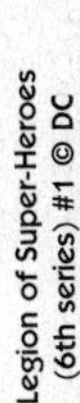
Legion of Super-Heroes (6th series) #1 © DC

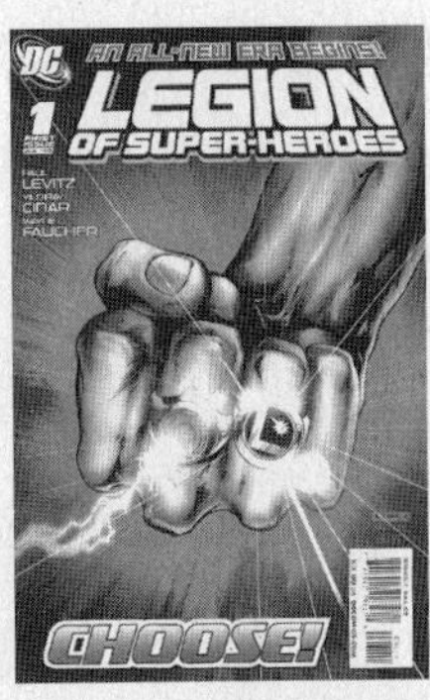

Lenore #8 © Roman Dirge

GD 2.0 VG 4.0 FN 6.0 VF 8.0 VF/NM 9.0 NM- 9.2

1-Giffen-c/a(p) 4.00

LEGION OF SUPER-HEROES (See Action Comics, Adventure, All New Collectors Edition, Legionnaires, Legends of the Legion, Limited Collectors Edition, Secrets of the..., Superboy & Superman)
National Periodical Publications: Feb, 1973 - No. 4, July-Aug, 1973

1-Legion & Tommy Tomorrow reprints begin 3 6 9 18 27 35
2-4: 2-Forte-r. 3-r/Adv. #340. Action #240. 4-r/Adv. #341, Action #233; Mooney-r 2 4 6 11 16 20

LEGION OF SUPER-HEROES, THE (Formerly Superboy and...; Tales of The Legion No. 314 on)
DC Comics: No. 259, Jan, 1980 - No. 313, July, 1984

259(#1)-Superboy leaves Legion 2 4 6 8 11 14
260-270,285-289: 265-Contains 28 pg. insert "Superman & the TRS-80 computer"; origin Tyroc; Tyroc leaves Legion 6.00
261,263,264,266-(Whitman variants; low print run; no cover #'s) 2 4 6 8 11 14
271-284: 272-Blok joins; origin; 20 pg. insert-Dial 'H' For Hero. 277-Intro. Reflecto. 280-Superboy re-joins Legion. 282-Origin Reflecto. 283-Origin Wildfire 6.00
290-294-Great Darkness saga. 294-Double size (52 pgs.) 1 2 3 5 7 9
295-299,301-313: 297-Origin retold. 298-Free 16 pg. Amethyst preview. 306-Brief origin Star Boy (Swan art). 311-Colan-a 4.00
300-(68 pgs., Mando paper)-Anniversary issue; has c/a by almost everyone at DC 5.00
Annual 1-3(82-84, 52 pgs.)-1-Giffen-c/a; 1st app./origin new Invisible Kid who joins Legion. 2-Karate Kid & Princess Projectra wed & resign 4.00
...The Great Darkness Saga (1989, $17.95, 196 pgs.)-r/LSH #287,290-294 & Annual #3; Giffen-c/a 2 4 6 10 14 18
...The Great Darkness Saga The Deluxe Edition HC (2010, $39.99, dj)-r/LSH #284-296 & Annual #1; new intro. by Levitz, script for #290, Giffen design sketches 40.00

NOTE: ***Aparo** c-282, 283, 300(part). **Austin** c-268i. **Buckler** c-273p, 274p, 276p. **Colan** a-311p. **Ditko** a(p)-267, 268, 272, 274, 276, 281. **Giffen** a-285-313p, Annual 1p; c-287p, 288p, 289, 290p, 291p, 292, 293, 294-299p, 300, 301-313p, Annual 1p, 2p. **Perez** c-268p, 277-280, 281p. **Starlin** a-265. **Staton** a-259p, 260p, 280. **Tuska** a-308p.*

LEGION OF SUPER-HEROES (3rd Series) (Reprinted in Tales of the Legion)
DC Comics: Aug, 1984 - No. 63, Aug, 1989 ($1.25/$1.75, deluxe format)

1-Silver ink logo 5.00
2-36,39-44,46-49,51-62: 4-Death of Karate Kid. 5-Death of Nemesis Kid. 12-Cosmic Boy, Lightning Lad, & Saturn Girl resign. 14-Intro new members: Tellus, Sensor Girl, Quislet. 15-17-Crisis tie-ins. 18-Crisis x-over. 25-Sensor Girl i.d. revealed as Princess Projectra. 35-Saturn Girl rejoins. 42,43-Millennium tie-ins. 44-Origin Quislet 3.00
37,38-Death of Superboy 2 4 6 8 11 14
45,50: 45 ($2.95, 68 pgs.)-Anniversary ish. 50-Double size ($2.50-c) 4.00
63-Final issue 4.00
Annual 1-4 (10/85-'88, 52 pgs.)-1-Crisis tie-in 4.00
...: An Eye For An Eye TPB (2007, $17.99)-r/#1-6; intro by Paul Levitz; cover gallery 18.00
...: The More Things Change TPB (2008, $17.99)-r/#7-13; cover gallery 18.00

NOTE: ***Byrne** c-36p. **Giffen** a(p)-1, 2, 50-55, 57-63, Annual 1p, 2; c-1-5p, 54p, Annual 1. **Orlando** a-6p. **Steacy** c-45-50, Annual 3.*

LEGION OF SUPER-HEROES (4th Series)
DC Comics: Nov, 1989 - No. 125, Mar, 2000 ($1.75/$1.95/$2.25)

0-(10/94)-Zero Hour restart of Legion; released between #61 & #62 3.00
1-Giffen-c/a(p)/scripts begin (4 pg.-a only #18) 6.00
2-20,26-49,51-53,55-58: 4-Mon-El (Lar Gand) destroys Time Trapper, changes reality. 5-Alt. reality story where Mordru rules all; Ferro Lad app. 6-1st app. of Laurel Gand (Lar Gand's cousin). 8-Origin. 13-Free poster by Giffen showing new costumes. 15-(2/91)-1st reference of Lar Gand as Valor. 26-New map of headquarters. 34-Six pg. preview of Timber Wolf mini-series. 40-Minor Legionnaires app. 41-(3/93)-SW6 Legion renamed Legionnaires w/new costumes and some new code-names 4.00
21-25: 21-24-Lobo & Darkseid storyline. 24-Cameo SW6 younger Legion duplicates. 25-SW6 Legion full intro. 4.50
50-($3.50, 68 pgs.) 5.00
54-($2.95)-Die-cut & foil stamped-c 5.00
59-99: 61-(9/94)-Zero Hour. 62-(11/94). 75-XS travels back to the 20th Century (cont'd in Impulse #9). 77-Origin of Brainiac 5. 81-Reintro Sun Boy. 85-Half of the Legion sent to the 20th century, Superman-c/app. 86-Final Night. 87-Deadman-c/app. 88-Impulse-c/app. Adventure Comics #247 cover swipe. 91-Forms one cover image with Legionnaires #47. 96-Wedding of Ultra Boy and Apparition. 99-Robin, Impulse, Superboy app. 3.00
100-($5.95, 96 pgs.)-Legionnaires return to the 30th Century; gatefold-c; 5 stories-art by Simonson, Davis and others 1 2 3 4 5 7
101-121: 101-Armstrong-a(p) begins. 105-Legion past & present vs. Time Trapper. 109-Moder-a. 110-Thunder joins. 114,115-Bizarro Legion. 120,121-Fatal Five. 3.00
122-124: 122,123-Coipel-c/a. 124-Coipel-c 3.50
125-Leads into "Legion Lost" maxi-series; Coipel-c 5.00
#1,000,000 (11/98) Giffen-a 3.00
Annual 1-5 (1990-1994, $3.50, 68 pgs.): 4-Bloodlines. 5-Elseworlds story 4.00
Annual 6 (1995,$3.95)-Year One story 4.00
Annual 7 (1996, $3.50, 48 pgs.)-Legends of the Dead Earth story; intro 75th Century Legion of Super-Heroes; Wildfire app. 4.00
Legion: Secret Files 1 (1/98, $4.95) Retold origin & pin-ups 5.00
Legion: Secret Files 2 (6/99, $4.95) Story and profile pages 5.00
The Beginning of Tomorrow TPB ('99, $17.95) r/post-Zero Hour reboot 18.00

NOTE: ***Giffen** a-1-24; breakdowns-26-32, 34-36; c-1-7, 8(part), 9-24. **Brandon Peterson** a(p)-15(1st for DC), 16, 18, Annual 2(54 pgs.); c-Annual 2p. **Swan/Anderson** c-8(part).*

LEGION OF SUPER-HEROES (5th Series) (Title becomes Supergirl and the Legion of Super-Heroes #16-36) (Intro. in Teen Titans/Legion Special)
DC Comics: Feb, 2005 - No. 15, Apr, 2006; No. 37, Feb, 2008 - No. 50, Mar, 2009 ($2.95/$2.99)

1-15: 1-Waid-s/Kitson-a/c. 4-Kirk & Gibbons-a. 9-Jeanty-a. 15-Dawnstar, Tyroc, Blok-c 3.00
37-50: 37-Shooter-s/Manapul-a begin; two interlocking covers. 50-Wraparound cover 3.00
44-Variant-c by Neal Adams 5.00
... Death of a Dream TPB ('06, $14.99) r/#7-13 15.00
... Enemy Manifest HC ('09, $24.99, dustjacket) r/#45-50 25.00
... Enemy Manifest SC ('10, $14.99) r/#45-50 15.00
... Enemy Rising HC ('08, $19.99, dustjacket) r/#37-44 20.00
... Enemy Rising SC ('09, $14.99) r/#37-44 15.00
...: 1050 Years of the Future TPB ('08, $19.99) r/greatest tales of their 50 year history 20.00
... Teenage Revolution TPB ('05, $14.99) r/#1-6 & Teen Titans/Legion Spec.; sketch pages 15.00

LEGION OF SUPER-HEROES (6th Series)
DC Comics: Jul, 2010 - Present ($3.99/$2.99)

1-9: 1-Earth-Man app.; Titan destroyed; Levitz-s/Cinar-a/c. 6-Jimenez back-up-a 4.00
1-6-Variant covers by Jim Lee 8.00
10,11-($2.99) 3.00
Annual 1 (2/11, $4.99) New Emerald Empress; Levitz-s/Giffen-a 5.00

LEGION OF SUPER-HEROES IN THE 31ST CENTURY (Based on the animated series)
DC Comics: June, 2007 - No. 20, Jan, 2009 ($2.25)

1-20: 1-Chynna Clugston-a; Fatal Five app. 6-Green Lantern Corps app. 15-Impulse app. 3.00
1-(6/07) Free Comic Book Day giveaway 2.50
...: Tomorrow's Heroes (2008, $14.99) r/#1-7; cover gallery 15.00

LEGION OF SUPER-VILLAINS
DC Comics: May, 2011 ($4.99, one-shot)

1-Levitz-s/Portela-a; Saturn Queen, Lightning Lord, Sun-Killer, Micro Lad app. 5.00

LEGION: PROPHETS (Prelude to 2010 movie)
IDW Publishing: Nov, 2009 - No. 4, Dec, 2009 ($3.99, limited series)

1-4: Stewart & Waltz-s. 1-Muriel-a. 2-Holder-a. 3-Paronzini-a. 4-Gaydos-a 4.00

LEGION: SCIENCE POLICE (See Legion of Super-Heroes)
DC Comics: Aug, 1998 - No. 4, Nov, 1998 ($2.25, limited series)

1-4-Ryan-a 3.00

LEGION WORLDS (Follows Legion Lost series)
DC Comics: Jun, 2001 - No. 6, Nov, 2001 ($3.95, limited series)

1-6-Abnett & Lanning-s; art by various. 5-Dillon-a. 6-Timber Wolf app. 4.00

LEMONADE KID, THE (See Bobby Benson's B-Bar-B Riders)
AC Comics: 1990 ($2.50, 28 pgs.)

1-Powell-c(r); Red Hawk-r by Powell; Lemonade Kid-r/Bobby Benson by Powell (2 stories) 3.00

LENNON SISTERS LIFE STORY, THE
Dell Publishing Co.: No. 951, Nov, 1958 - No. 1014, Aug, 1959

Four Color 951 (#1)-Toth-a, 32pgs, photo-c 12 24 36 87 164 240
Four Color 1014-Toth-a, photo-c 12 24 36 82 154 225

LENORE
Slave Labor Graphics: Feb, 1998 - Present ($2.95/$3.95, B&W, color #13-on)

1-12: 1-Roman Dirge-s/a, 1,2-2nd printing 3.00
13-($3.95, color) 4.00
Vol. 2 (8/09 - Present) 1,2: 1-1st and 2nd printings; Lenore's origin 4.00
...: Noogies TPB ($11.95) r/#1-4 12.00
...: Wedgies TPB (2000, $13.95) r/#5-8 14.00
...: Cooties TPB (3/06, $13.95) r/#9-12; pin-ups by various 14.00

LEONARD NIMOY'S PRIMORTALS
Tekno Comix: Mar, 1995 - No. 15, May, 1996 ($1.95)

1-15: Concept by Leonard Nimoy & Isaac Asimov 1-3-w/bound-in game piece & trading card. 4-w/Teknophage Steel Edition coupon. 13,14-Art Adams-c. 15-Simonson-c 3.00

Leonard Nimoy's Primortals #3 © Tekno

Let Me In: Crossroads #1 © Hammer LMI

Liberty Meadows #25 © Creators Synd.

	GD 2.0	VG 4.0	FN 6.0	VF 8.0	VF/NM 9.0	NM- 9.2

LEONARD NIMOY'S PRIMORTALS
BIG Entertainment: V2#0, June, 1996 - No. 8, Feb, 1997 ($2.25)

V2#0-8: 0-Includes Pt. 9 of "The Big Bang" x-over. 0,1-Simonson-c. 3-Kelley Jones-c 3.00

LEONARD NIMOY'S PRIMORTALS ORIGINS
Tekno Comix: Nov, 1995 - No. 2, Dec, 1995 ($2.95, limited series)

1,2: Nimoy scripts; Art Adams-c; polybagged 3.00

LEONARDO (Also see Teenage Mutant Ninja Turtles)
Mirage Studios: Dec, 1986 ($1.50, B&W, one-shot)

1 6.00

LEO THE LION
I. W. Enterprises: No date(1960s) (10¢)

	GD 2.0	VG 4.0	FN 6.0	VF 8.0	VF/NM 9.0	NM- 9.2
1-Reprint	2	4	6	9	13	16

LEROY (Teen-age)
Standard Comics: Nov, 1949 - No. 6, Nov, 1950

	GD 2.0	VG 4.0	FN 6.0	VF 8.0	VF/NM 9.0	NM- 9.2
1	14	28	42	82	121	160
2-Frazetta text illo.	10	20	30	58	79	100
3-6: 3-Lubbers-a	9	18	27	52	69	85

LETHAL (Also see Brigade)
Image Comics (Extreme Studios): Feb, 1996 ($2.50, unfinished limited series)

1-Marat Mychaels-c/a. 3.00

LETHAL FOES OF SPIDER-MAN (Sequel to Deadly Foes of Spider-Man)
Marvel Comics: Sept, 1993 - No. 4, Dec, 1993 ($1.75, limited series)

1-4 3.00

LETHARGIC LAD
Crusade Ent.: June, 1996 - No. 3, Sept, 1996 ($2.95, B&W, limited series)

1,2 3.00
3-Alex Ross-c/swipe (Kingdom Come) 4.00
...Jumbo Sized Annual #1 (Summer 2002, $3.99) prints comic stories from internet 4.00

LETHARGIC LAD ADVENTURES
Crusade Ent./Destination Ent.#3 on: Oct, 1997 - No. 12, Sept./Oct. 1999 ($2.95, B&W)

1-12-Hyland-s/a. 9-Alex Ross sketch page & back-c 3.00

LET ME IN: CROSSROADS (Based on the 2010 movie Let Me In)
Dark Horse Comics: Dec, 2010 - No. 4 ($3.99, limited series)

1,2-Prelude to the film; Andreyko-s/Reynolds-a/Phillips-c 4.00

LET'S PRETEND (CBS radio)
D. S. Publishing Co.: May-June, 1950 - No. 3, Sept-Oct, 1950

	GD 2.0	VG 4.0	FN 6.0	VF 8.0	VF/NM 9.0	NM- 9.2
1	18	36	54	105	165	225
2,3	14	28	42	82	121	160

LET'S READ THE NEWSPAPER
Charlton Press: 1974

	GD 2.0	VG 4.0	FN 6.0	VF 8.0	VF/NM 9.0	NM- 9.2
nn-Features Quincy by Ted Sheares	1	3	4	6	8	10

LET'S TAKE A TRIP (TV) (CBS Television Presents)
Pines Comics: Spring, 1958

	GD 2.0	VG 4.0	FN 6.0	VF 8.0	VF/NM 9.0	NM- 9.2
1-Marv Levy-c/a	5	10	15	23	28	32

LETTERS TO SANTA (See March of Comics No. 228)

LEX LUTHOR: MAN OF STEEL
DC Comics: May, 2005 - No. 5, Sept, 2005 ($2.99, limited series)

1-5: 1-Azzarello-s/Bermejo-a/c in all. 3-Batman-c/app. 3.00
TPB (2005, $12.99) r/series 13.00
Luthor HC (2010, $19.99, d.j.) r/#1-5 with 10 new story pages; cover gallery & sketch-a 20.00

LEX LUTHOR: THE UNAUTHORIZED BIOGRAPHY
DC Comics: 1989 ($3.95, 52 pgs., one-shot, squarebound)

1-Painted-c; Clark Kent app. 4.00

LIBERTY COMICS (Miss Liberty No. 1)
Green Publishing Co.: No. 5, May, '46 - No. 15, July, 1946 (MLJ & other-r)

	GD 2.0	VG 4.0	FN 6.0	VF 8.0	VF/NM 9.0	NM- 9.2
5 (5/46)-The Prankster app; Starr-a	21	42	63	126	206	285
10-Hangman & Boy Buddies app.; reprints 3 Hangman stories, incl. Hangman #8	22	44	66	132	216	300
11 (V2#2, 1/46)-Wilbur in women's clothes	18	36	54	105	165	225
12 (V2#4)-Black Hood & Suzie app.; classic Skull-c	60	120	180	381	653	925
14,15-Patty of Airliner; Starr-a in both	18	36	54	105	165	225

LIBERTY COMICS (The CBLDF Presents...)
Image Comics: July, 2008; Oct, 2009 ($3.99/$4.99, Comic Book Legal Defense Fund benefit)

1-Two covers by Campbell & Mignola; art by Cooke, Aragones, A. Adams & others 4.00
1-(12/08) Second printing with Thor-c by Simonson 4.00
2-(10/09, $4.99) two covers by Romita Jr. & Sale; art by Allred, Templesmith, Jim Lee 5.00

LIBERTY COMICS
Heroic Publishing: Sept, 2007 ($4.50)

1-Mark Sparacio-c 4.50

LIBERTY GIRL
Heroic Publishing: Aug, 2006 - No. 3, May, 2007 ($3.25/$2.99)

1-3-Mark Sparacio-c/a 3.25

LIBERTY GUARDS
Chicago Mail Order: No date (1946?)

	GD 2.0	VG 4.0	FN 6.0	VF 8.0	VF/NM 9.0	NM- 9.2
nn-Reprints Man of War #1 with cover of Liberty Scouts #1; Gustavson-c	34	68	102	206	336	465

LIBERTY MEADOWS
Insight Studios Group/Image Comics #27 on: 1999 - Present ($2.95, B&W)

	GD 2.0	VG 4.0	FN 6.0	VF 8.0	VF/NM 9.0	NM- 9.2
1-Frank Cho-s/a; reprints newspaper strips	3	6	9	14	20	25
1-2nd & 3rd printings	1	2	3	4	5	7
2,3	2	4	6	8	11	14
4-10	1	2	3	4	5	7

11-25,27-37: 20-Adam Hughes-c. 22-Evil Brandy vs. Brandy. 27-1st Image issue, printed sideways 3.00
..., Cover Girl HC (Image, 2006, $24.99, with dustjacket) r/color covers of #1-19,21-37 along with B&W inked versions, sketches and pin-up art 25.00
...: Eden Book 1 SC (Image, 2002, $14.95) r/#1-9; sketch gallery 15.00
...: Eden Book 1 SC 2nd printing (Image, 2004, $19.95) r/#1-9; sketch gallery 20.00
...: Eden Book 1 HC (Image, 2003, $24.95, with dustjacket) r/#1-9; sketch gallery 25.00
...: Creature Comforts Book 2 HC (Image, 2004, $24.95, with d.j.) r/#10-18; sketch gallery 25.00
...: Creature Comforts Book 2 SC (Image, 12/04, $14.95) r/#10-18; sketch gallery 15.00
...Book 3: Summer of Love HC (Image, 12/04, $24.95) r/#19-27; sketch gallery 25.00
...Book 3: Summer of Love SC (Image, 7/05, $14.95) r/#19-27; sketch gallery 15.00
...Book 4: Cold, Cold Heart HC (Image, 9/05, $24.95) r/#28-36; sketch gallery 25.00
...Book 4: Cold, Cold Heart SC (Image, 2006, $14.99) r/#28-36; sketch gallery 15.00
Image Firsts: Liberty Meadows #1 (9/10, $1.00) r/#1 1.00
... Sourcebook (5/04, $4.95) character info and unpublished strips 5.00
... Wedding Album (#26) (2002, $2.95) 3.00

LIBERTY PROJECT, THE
Eclipse Comics: June, 1987 - No. 8, May, 1988 ($1.75, color, Baxter paper)

1-8: 6-Valkyrie app. 3.00

LIBERTY SCOUTS (See Liberty Guards & Man of War)
Centaur Publications: No. 2, June, 1941 - No. 3, Aug, 1941

	GD 2.0	VG 4.0	FN 6.0	VF 8.0	VF/NM 9.0	NM- 9.2
2(#1)-Origin The Fire-Man, Man of War; Vapo-Man & Liberty Scouts begin; intro Liberty Scouts; Gustavson-c/a in both	129	258	387	826	1413	2000
3(#2)-Origin & 1st app. The Sentinel	90	180	270	576	988	1400

LICENCE TO KILL (James Bond 007) (Movie)
Eclipse Comics: 1989 ($7.95, slick paper, 52 pgs.)

	GD 2.0	VG 4.0	FN 6.0	VF 8.0	VF/NM 9.0	NM- 9.2
nn-Movie adaptation; Timothy Dalton photo-c	1	2	3	5	6	8
Limited Hardcover ($24.95)						25.00

LIDSVILLE (TV)
Gold Key: Oct, 1972 - No. 5, Oct, 1973

	GD 2.0	VG 4.0	FN 6.0	VF 8.0	VF/NM 9.0	NM- 9.2
1-Photo-c	5	10	15	35	55	75
2-5	4	8	12	22	34	45

LIEUTENANT, THE (TV)
Dell Publishing Co.: April-June, 1964

	GD 2.0	VG 4.0	FN 6.0	VF 8.0	VF/NM 9.0	NM- 9.2
1-Photo-c	3	6	9	18	27	35

LIEUTENANT BLUEBERRY (Also see Blueberry)
Marvel Comics (Epic Comics): 1991 - No. 3, 1991 (Graphic novel)

	GD 2.0	VG 4.0	FN 6.0	VF 8.0	VF/NM 9.0	NM- 9.2
1,2 ($8.95)-Moebius-a in all	2	4	6	11	16	20
3 ($14.95)	3	6	9	16	22	28

LT. ROBIN CRUSOE, U.S.N. (See Movie Comics & Walt Disney Showcase #26)

LIFE EATERS, THE
DC Comics (WildStorm): 2003 ($29.95, hardcover with dust jacket)

HC-David Brin-s; Scott Hampton-painted-a/c; Norse Gods team with the Nazis 30.00
SC-(2004, $19.95) 20.00

LIFE OF CAPTAIN MARVEL, THE
Marvel Comics Group: Aug, 1985 - No. 5, Dec, 1985 ($2.00, Baxter paper)

1-5: 1-All reprint Starlin issues of Iron Man #55, Capt. Marvel #25-34 plus Marvel Feature #12

Life Story #2 © FAW

Life With Archie #2 © AP

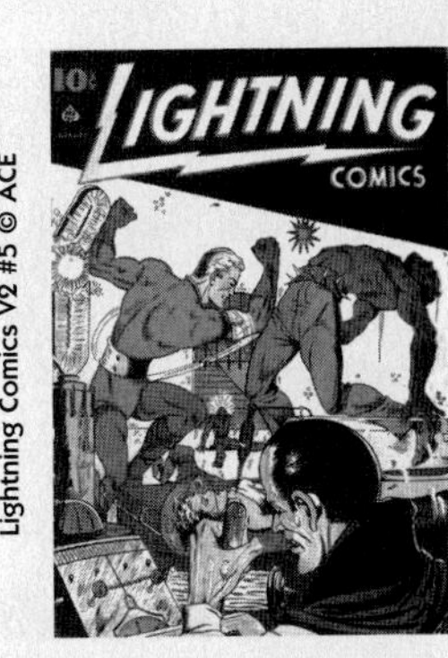

Lightning Comics V2 #5 © ACE

(all with Thanos). 4-New Thanos back-c by Starlin 3.00

LIFE OF CHRIST, THE
Catechetical Guild Educational Society: No. 301, 1949 (35¢, 100 pgs.)
301-Reprints from Topix(1949)-V5#11,12 9 18 27 50 65 80

LIFE OF CHRIST: THE CHRISTMAS STORY, THE
Marvel Comics/Nelson: Feb, 1993 ($2.99, slick stock)
nn 5.00

LIFE OF CHRIST: THE EASTER STORY, THE
Marvel Comics/Nelson: 1993 ($2.99, slick stock)
nn 5.00

LIFE OF CHRIST VISUALIZED
Standard Publishers: 1942 - No. 3, 1943
1-3: All came in cardboard case, each... 9 18 27 50 65 80
Case only..... 10 20 30 54 72 90

LIFE OF CHRIST VISUALIZED
The Standard Publ. Co.: 1946? (48 pgs. in color)
nn 7 14 21 37 46 55

LIFE OF ESTHER VISUALIZED
The Standard Publ. Co.: No. 2062, 1947 (48 pgs. in color)
2062 7 14 21 37 46 55

LIFE OF JOSEPH VISUALIZED
The Standard Publ. Co.: No. 1054, 1946 (48 pgs. in color)
1054 7 14 21 37 46 55

LIFE OF PAUL (See The Living Bible)

LIFE OF POPE JOHN PAUL II, THE
Marvel Comics Group: Jan, 1983 ($1.50/$1.75)
1 1 3 4 6 8 10

LIFE OF RILEY, THE (TV)
Dell Publishing Co.: No. 917, July, 1958
Four Color 917-Photo-c 10 20 30 69 122 175

LIFE ON ANOTHER PLANET
Kitchen Sink Press: 1978 (B&W, graphic novel, magazine size)
nn-Will Eisner-s/a 13.00
Reprint (DC Comics, 5/00, $12.95) 13.00

LIFE'S LIKE THAT
Croyden Publ. Co.: 1945 (25¢, B&W, 68 pgs.)
nn-Newspaper Sunday strip-r by Neher 7 14 21 35 43 50

LIFE STORIES OF AMERICAN PRESIDENTS (See Dell Giants)

LIFE STORY
Fawcett Publications: Apr, 1949 - V8#46, Jan, 1953; V8#47, Apr, 1953 (All have photo-c?)
V1#1 15 30 45 84 127 170
2 9 18 27 52 69 85
3-6, V2#7-12 8 16 24 44 57 70
V3#13-Wood-a 15 30 45 84 127 170
V3#14-18, V4#19-24, V5#25-30, V6#31-35 8 16 24 40 50 60
V6#36- "I sold drugs" on-c 11 22 33 64 90 115
V7#37,40-42, V8#44,45 7 14 21 37 46 55
V7#38, V8#43-Evans-a 8 16 24 40 50 60
V7#39-Drug Smuggling & Junkie story 10 20 30 56 76 95
V8#46,47 (Scarce) 9 18 27 50 65 80
NOTE: ***Powell*** *a-13, 23, 24, 26, 28, 30, 32, 39.* ***Marcus Swayze*** *a-1-3, 10-12, 15, 16, 20, 21, 23-25, 31, 35, 37, 40, 44, 46.*

LIFE, THE UNIVERSE AND EVERYTHING (See Hitchhikers Guide to the Galaxy & Restaurant at the End of the Universe)
DC Comics: 1996 - No. 3, 1996 ($6.95, squarebound, limited series)
1-3: Adaptation of novel by Douglas Adams. 1 2 3 4 5 7

LIFE WITH ARCHIE
Archie Publications: Sept, 1958 - No. 286, Sept, 1991
1 25 50 75 183 367 550
2-(9/59) 13 26 39 91 176 260
3-5: 3-(7/60) 10 20 30 67 116 165
6-8,10 8 16 24 54 90 125
9,11-Horror/SciFi-c 9 18 27 63 107 150
12-20 6 12 18 43 69 95
21(7/63)-30 5 10 15 35 55 75
31-34,36-38,40,41 4 8 12 28 44 60
35,39-Horror/Sci-Fi-c 6 12 18 37 59 80
42-Pureheart begins (1st app.-c/s, 10/65) 8 16 24 54 90 125
43,44 6 12 18 37 59 80
45(1/66) 1st Man From R.I.V.E.R.D.A.L.E. 7 14 21 45 73 100
46-Origin Pureheart 6 12 18 37 59 80
47-49 4 8 12 28 44 60
50-United Three begin: Pureheart (Archie), Superteen (Betty), Captain Hero (Jughead) 6 12 18 39 62 85
51-59: 59-Pureheart ends 4 8 12 28 44 60
60-Archie band begins, ends #66 6 12 18 37 59 80
61-66: 61-Man From R.I.V.E.R.D.A.L.E.-c/s 4 8 12 24 37 50
67-80 3 6 9 17 25 32
81-99 3 6 9 16 22 28
100 (8/70), 113-Sabrina & Salem app. 3 6 9 19 29 38
101-112, 114-130(2/73), 139(11/73)-Archie Band c/s 2 4 6 11 16 20
131,134-138,140-146,148-161,164-170(6/76) 2 4 6 9 12 15
132,133,147,163-all horror-c/s 3 6 9 14 20 26
162-UFO c/s 3 6 9 14 19 24
171,173-175,177-184,186,189,191-194,196 2 3 4 6 8 10
172,185,197 : 172-(9/77)-Bi-Cent. spec. ish, 185-2nd 24th cent.-c/s, 197-Time machine/SF-c/s 2 4 6 8 10 12
176(12/76)-1st app. Capt. Archie of Starship Rivda, in 24th century c/s; 1st app. Stella the Robot 3 6 9 14 19 24
187,188,195,198,199-all horror-c/s 2 4 6 9 13 16
190-1st Dr. Doom-c/s 2 4 6 9 13 16
200 (12/78) Maltese Pigeon-s 2 4 6 8 11 14
201-203,205-237,239,240(1/84): 208-Reintro Veronica 1 2 3 5 6 8
204-Flying saucer-c/s 2 3 4 6 8 10
238-(9/83)-25th anniversary issue; Ol' Betsy (jalopy) replaced 1 2 3 5 7 9
241-278,280-285: 250-Comic book convention-s 5.00
279,286: 279-Intro Mustang Sally ($1.00, 7/90) 6.00
NOTE: ***Gene Colan*** *a-272-279, 285, 286. Horror/Sci-Fi-c 9, 11, 35, 39, 162.*

LIFE WITH ARCHIE (The Married Life) (Magazine)
Archie Publications: Sept, 2010 - Present ($3.99, magazine-size)
1-10: Continuation of Married Life stories from Archie #600-605; articles/interviews 4.00

LIFE WITH MILLIE (Formerly A Date With Millie) (Modeling With Millie #21 on)
Atlas/Marvel Comics Group: No. 8, Dec, 1960 - No. 20, Dec, 1962
8-Teenage 9 18 27 60 100 140
9-11 6 12 18 43 69 95
12-20 6 12 18 39 62 85

LIFE WITH SNARKY PARKER (TV)
Fox Feature Syndicate: Aug, 1950
1-Early TV comic; photo-c from TV puppet show 27 54 81 158 259 360

LIGHT AND DARKNESS WAR, THE
Marvel Comics (Epic Comics): Oct, 1988 - No. 6, Dec, 1989 ($1.95, lim. series)
1-6 3.00

LIGHT BRIGADE, THE
DC Comics: 2004 - No. 4, 2004 ($5.95, limited series)
1-4-Archangels in World War II; Tomasi-s/Snejbjerg-a 6.00
TPB (2005, 2009, $19.99) r/series; cover galery 20.00

LIGHT FANTASTIC, THE (Terry Pratchett's)
Innovation Publishing: June, 1992 - No. 4, Sept, 1992 ($2.50, mini-series)
1-4: Adapts 2nd novel in Discworld series 3.00

LIGHT IN THE FOREST (Disney)
Dell Publishing Co.: No. 891, Mar, 1958
Four Color 891-Movie, Fess Parker photo-c 7 14 21 50 83 115

LIGHTNING COMICS (Formerly Sure-Fire No. 1-3)
Ace Magazines: No. 4, Dec, 1940 - No. 13(V3#1), June, 1942
4-Characters continue from Sure-Fire 102 204 306 648 1112 1575
5,6: 6-Dr. Nemesis begins 69 138 207 442 759 1075
V2#1-6: 2- "Flash Lightning" becomes "Lash..." 55 110 165 352 601 850
V3#1-Intro. Lightning Girl & The Sword 55 110 165 352 601 850
NOTE: ***Anderson*** *a-V2#6.* ***Mooney*** *c-V1#5, 6, V2#1-6, V3#1. Bondage c-V2#6. Lightning-c on all.*

LIGHTNING COMICS PRESENTS
Lightning Comics: May, 1994 ($3.50)
1-Red foil-c distr. by Diamond Distr., 1-Black/yellow/blue-c distrib. by Capital Distr.,

Limited Collectors' Edition C-32 © DC

The Literals #2 © Bill Willingham & DC

Li'l Abner #62 © TOBY

	GD 2.0	VG 4.0	FN 6.0	VF 8.0	VF/NM 9.0	NM- 9.2

1-Red/yellow-c distributed by H. World, 1-Platinum 3.50

LI'L ... (Listed under Little ...)

LILI
Image Comics: No. 0, 1999 ($4.95, B&W)
0-Bendis & Yanover-s 5.00

LILLITH (See Warrior Nun...)
Antarctic Press: Sept, 1996 - No. 3, Feb, 1997 ($2.95, limited series)
1-3: 1-Variant-c 3.00

LIMITED COLLECTORS' EDITION (See Famous First Edition, Marvel Treasury #28, Rudolph The Red-Nosed Reindeer, & Superman Vs. The Amazing Spider-Man; becomes All-New Collectors' Edition)
National Periodical Publications/DC Comics:
(#21-34,51-59: 84 pgs.; #35-41: 68 pgs.; #42-50: 60 pgs.)
C-21, Summer, 1973 - No. C-59, 1978 ($1.00) (10x13-1/2")
(Rudolph...C-20 (implied), 12/72)-See Rudolph The Red-Nosed Reindeer
C-21: Shazam (TV); r/Captain Marvel Jr. #11 by Raboy; C.C. Beck-c, biog. & photo 3 6 9 20 30 40
C-22: Tarzan; complete origin reprinted from #207-210; all Kubert-c/a; Joe Kubert biography & photo inside 3 6 9 17 25 32
C-23: House of Mystery; Wrightson, N. Adams/Orlando, G. Kane/Wood, Toth, Aragones, Sparling reprints 4 8 12 24 37 50
C-24: Rudolph The Red-Nosed Reindeer 7 14 21 45 73 100
C-25: Batman; Neal Adams-c/a(r); G.A. Joker-r; Batman/Enemy Ace-r; Novick-a(r); has photos from TV show 4 8 12 26 41 55
C-26: See Famous First Edition C-26 (same contents)
C-27,C-29,C-31: C-27: Shazam (TV); G.A. Capt. Marvel & Mary Marvel-r; Beck-r. C-29: Tarzan; reprints "Return of Tarzan" from #219-223 by Kubert; Kubert-c. C-31: Superman; origin-r; Giordano-a; photos of George Reeves from 1950s TV show on inside b/c; Burnley, Boring-r 3 6 9 16 23 30
C-32: Ghosts (new-a) 4 8 12 22 34 45
C-33: Rudolph The Red-Nosed Reindeer(new-a) 6 12 18 41 66 90
C-34: Christmas with the Super-Heroes; unpublished Angel & Ape story by Oksner & Wood; Batman & Teen Titans-r 3 6 9 16 23 30
C-35: Shazam (TV); photo cover features TV's Captain Marvel, Jackson Bostwick; Beck-r; TV photos inside b/c 3 6 9 16 22 28
C-36: The Bible; all new adaptation beginning with Genesis by Kubert, Redondo & Mayer; Kubert-c 3 6 9 16 22 28
C-37: Batman; r-1946 Sundays; inside b/c photos of Batman TV show villains (all villain issue; r/G.A. Joker, Catwoman, Penguin, Two-Face, & Scarecrow stories plus 1946 Sundays-r) 3 6 9 18 27 35
C-38: Superman; 1 pg. N. Adams; part photo-c; photos from TV show on inside back-c 3 6 9 16 22 28
C-39: Secret Origins of Super-Villains; N. Adams-i(r); collection reprints 1950's Joker origin, Luthor origin from Adv. Comics #271, Captain Cold origin from Showcase #8 among others; G.A. Batman-r; Beck-r 3 6 9 16 22 28
C-40: Dick Tracy by Gould featuring Flattop; newspaper-r from 12/21/43 - 5/17/44; biog. of Chester Gould 3 6 9 16 22 28
C-41: Super Friends (TV); JLA-r(1965); Toth-c/a 3 6 9 16 23 30
C-42: Rudolph 4 8 12 28 44 60
C-43-C-47: C-43: Christmas with the Super-Heroes; Wrightson, S&K, Neal Adams-a. C-44: Batman; N. Adams-p(r) & G.A.-r; painted-c. C-45: More Secret Origins of Super-Villains; Flash-r/#105; G.A. Wonder Woman & Batman/Catwoman-r. C-46: Justice League of America(1963-r); 3 pgs. Toth-a C-47: Superman Salutes the Bicentennial (Tomahawk interior); 2 pgs. new-a 3 6 9 14 20 26
C-48,C-49: C-48: Superman Vs. The Flash (Superman/Flash race); swipes-c to Superman #199; r/Superman #199 & Flash #175; 6 pgs. Neal Adams-a. C-49: Superboy & the Legion of Super-Heroes 3 6 9 16 23 30
C-50: Rudolph The Red-Nosed Reindeer; contains poster (1/2 price if poster is missing) 4 8 12 28 44 60
C-51: Batman; Neal Adams-c/a 3 6 9 17 25 32
C-52,C-57: C-52: The Best of DC; Neal Adams-c/a; Toth, Kubert-a. C-57: Welcome Back, Kotter-r(TV)(5/78) includes unpublished #11 3 6 9 16 22 28
C-53 thru C-56, C-58, C-60 thru C-62 (See All-New Collectors' Edition)
C-59: Batman's Strangest Cases; N. Adams-r; Wrightson-r/Swamp Thing #7; N. Adams/Wrightson-c 3 6 9 16 22 28
NOTE: *All-r with exception of some special features and covers.* **Aparo** *a-52r; c-37.* **Grell** *c-49.* **Infantino** *a-25, 39, 44, 45, 52.* **Bob Kane** *r-25.* **Robinson** *r-25, 44.* **Sprang** *r-44. Issues #21-31, 35-39, 45, 48 have back cover cut-outs.*

LINDA (Everybody Loves...) (Phantom Lady No. 5 on)
Ajax-Farrell Publ. Co.: Apr-May, 1954 - No. 4, Oct-Nov, 1954
1-Kamenish-a 15 30 45 85 130 175
2-Lingerie panel 13 26 39 72 101 130
3,4 10 20 30 56 76 95

LINDA CARTER, STUDENT NURSE
Atlas Comics (AMI): Sept, 1961 - No. 9, Jan, 1963
1-Al Hartley-c 6 12 18 41 66 90
2-9 4 8 12 28 44 60

LINDA LARK
Dell Publishing Co.: Oct-Dec, 1961 - No. 8, Aug-Oct, 1963
1 3 6 9 19 29 38
2-8 3 6 9 14 19 24

LINUS, THE LIONHEARTED (TV)
Gold Key: Sept, 1965
1 (10155-509) 7 14 21 45 73 100

LION, THE (See Movie Comics)

LIONHEART
Awesome Comics: Sept, 1999 - No. 2, Dec, 1999 ($2.99/$2.50)
1-Ian Churchill-story/a, Jeph Loeb-s; Coven app. 3.50
2-Flip book w/Coven #4 3.00

LION OF SPARTA (See Movie Classics)

LIPPY THE LION AND HARDY HAR HAR (TV)
Gold Key: Mar, 1963 (12¢) (See Hanna-Barbera Band Wagon #1)
1 (10049-303) 8 16 24 54 90 125

LISA COMICS (TV)(See Simpsons Comics)
Bongo Comics: 1995 ($2.25)
1-Lisa in Wonderland 3.00

LITERALS, THE (See Fables and Jack of Fables)
DC Comics (Vertigo): June, 2009 - No. 3, Aug, 2009 ($2.99)
1-3-Crossover with Fables #83-85 and Jack of Fables #33-35; Buckingham-c/a 3.00

LI'L ABNER (See Comics on Parade, Sparkle, Sparkler Comics, Tip Top Comics & Tip Topper)
United Features Syndicate: 1939 - 1940
Single Series 4 ('39) 77 154 231 493 847 1200
Single Series 18 ('40) (#18 on inside, #2 on-c) 60 120 180 381 653 925

LI'L ABNER (Al Capp's; continued from Comics on Parade #58)
Harvey Publ. No. 61-69 (2/49)/Toby Press No. 70 on: No. 61, Dec, 1947 - No. 97, Jan, 1955
(See Oxydol-Dreft in Promotional Comics section)
61(#1)-Wolverton & Powell-a 23 46 69 136 223 310
62-65: 63-The Wolf Girl app. 65-Powell-a 15 30 45 85 130 175
66,67,69,70 14 28 42 82 121 160
68-Full length Fearless Fosdick-c/story 15 30 45 88 137 185
71-74,76,80 13 26 39 74 105 135
75,77-79,86,91-All with Kurtzman art; 86-Sadie Hawkins Day. 91-r/#77 15 30 45 83 124 165
81-85,87-90,92-94,96,97: 83-Evil-Eye Fleegle & Double Whammy app. 88-Cousin Weakeyes goes hunting. 94-Six lessons from Adam Lazonga. 96-Football issue 12 24 36 69 97 125
95-Full length Fearless Fosdick story 14 28 42 76 108 140

LI'L ABNER
Toby Press: 1951
1 18 36 54 103 162 220

LI'L ABNER'S DOGPATCH (See Al Capp's...)

LITTLE AL OF THE F.B.I.
Ziff-Davis Publications: No. 10, 1950 (no month) - No. 11, Apr-May, 1951 (Saunders painted-c)
10(1950) 16 32 48 94 147 200
11(1951) 14 28 42 78 112 145

LITTLE AL OF THE SECRET SERVICE
Ziff-Davis Publications: No. 10, 7-8/51; No, 2, 9-10/51; No. 3, Winter, 1951 (Saunders painted-c)
10(#1) 16 32 48 92 144 195
2,3 14 28 42 76 108 140

LITTLE AMBROSE
Archie Publications: September, 1958
1-Bob Bolling-c 15 30 45 84 127 170

LITTLE ANGEL
Standard (Visual Editions)/Pines: No. 5, Sept, 1954; No. 6, Sept, 1955 - No. 16, Sept, 1959
5-Last pre-code issue 8 16 24 40 50 60

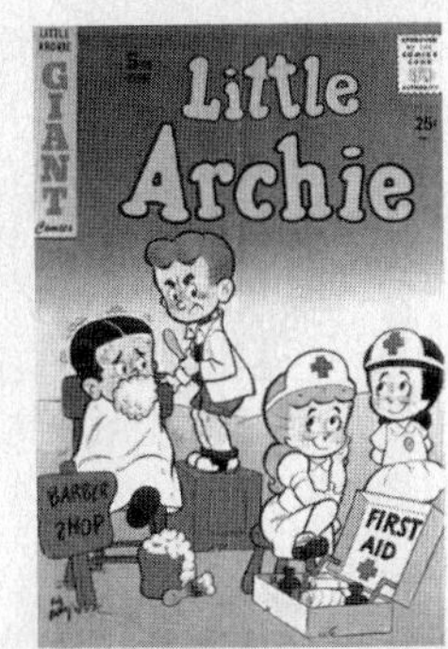

Little Archie #5 © AP

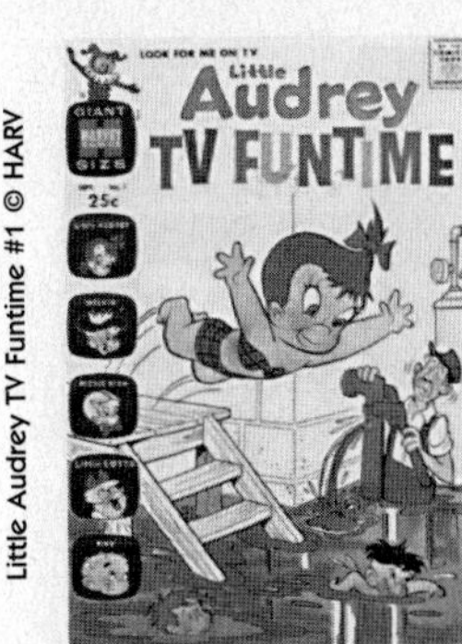

Little Audrey TV Funtime #1 © HARV

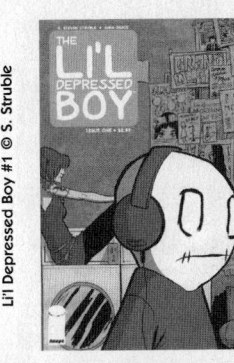

Li'l Depressed Boy #1 © S. Struble

	GD 2.0	VG 4.0	FN 6.0	VF 8.0	VF/NM 9.0	NM- 9.2
6-16	5	10	15	24	30	35

LITTLE ANNIE ROONEY (Also see Henry)
David McKay Publ.: 1935 (25¢, B&W dailies, 48 pgs.)(10"x10", cardboard-c)

	GD	VG	FN	VF	VF/NM	NM-
Book 1-Daily strip-r by Darrell McClure	38	76	114	226	368	510

LITTLE ANNIE ROONEY (See King Comics & Treasury of Comics)
David McKay/St. John/Standard: 1938; Aug, 1948 - No. 3, Oct, 1948

	GD	VG	FN	VF	VF/NM	NM-
Feature Books 11 (McKay, 1938)	39	78	117	231	378	525
1 (St. John)	15	30	45	88	137	185
2,3	10	20	30	54	72	90

LITTLE ARCHIE (The Adventures of... #13-on) (See Archie Giant Series Mag. #527, 534, 538, 545, 549, 556, 560, 566, 570, 583, 594, 596, 607, 609, 619)
Archie Publications: 1956 - No. 180, Feb, 1983 (Giants No. 3-84)

	GD	VG	FN	VF	VF/NM	NM-
1-(Scarce)	58	116	174	493	997	1500
2 (1957)	24	48	72	175	350	525
3-5: 3-(1958)-Bob Bolling-c & giant issues begin	14	28	42	99	200	300
6-10	11	22	33	77	144	210
11-17,19,21 (84 pgs.)	9	18	27	50	100	140
18,20,22 (84 pgs.)-Horror/Sci-Fi-c	10	20	30	69	122	175
23-39 (68 pgs.)	7	14	21	45	73	100
40 (Fall/66)-Intro. Little Pureheart-c/s (68 pgs.)	7	14	21	49	80	110
41,44-Little Pureheart (68 pgs.)	6	12	18	43	69	95
42-Intro The Little Archies Band, ends #66 (68 pgs.)	7	14	21	47	76	105
43-1st Boy From R.I.V.E.R.D.A.L.E. (68 pgs.)	7	14	21	45	73	100
45-58 (68 pgs.)	5	10	15	35	55	75
59 (68 pgs.)-Little Sabrina begins	8	16	24	56	93	130
60-66 (68 pgs.)	4	8	12	28	44	60
67(9/71)-84: 84-Last 52pg. Giant-Size (2/74)	3	6	9	18	27	35
85-99	2	4	6	10	14	18
100	2	4	6	13	18	22
101-112,114-116,118-129	2	4	6	8	10	12
113,117,130: 113-Halloween Special issue(12/76). 117-Donny Osmond-c cameo 130-UFO cover (5/78)	2	4	6	9	13	16
131-150(1/80), 180(Last issue, 2/83)	1	2	3	5	7	9
151-179						5.00
...In Animal Land 1 (1957)	13	26	39	91	176	260
...In Animal Land 17 (Winter, 1957-58)-19 (Summer,1958)-Formerly Li'l Jinx	8	16	24	56	93	130
Archie Classics - The Adventures of Little Archie Vol. 1 TPB (2004, $10.95) reprints						11.00
Vol. 2 TPB (2008, $9.95) reprints plus new 22 pg. story with Bolling-s/a						10.00

NOTE: *Little Archie Band app. 42-66. Little Sabrina in 59-78,80-180*

LITTLE ARCHIE CHRISTMAS SPECIAL (See Archie Giant Series #581)

LITTLE ARCHIE COMICS DIGEST ANNUAL (...Magazine #5 on)
Archie Publications: 10/77 - No. 48, 5/91 (Digest-size, 128 pgs., later issues $1.35-$1.50)

	GD	VG	FN	VF	VF/NM	NM-
1(10/77)-Reprints	3	6	9	20	30	40
2(4/78,3(11/78)-Neal Adams-a. 3-The Fly-r by S&K	3	6	9	14	20	26
4(4/79) - 10	2	4	6	10	14	18
11-20	2	4	6	8	10	12
21-30: 28-Christmas-c	1	2	3	5	6	8
31-48: 40,46-Christmas-c						5.00

NOTE: *Little Archie, Little Jinx, Little Jughead & Little Sabrina in most issues.*

LITTLE ARCHIE DIGEST MAGAZINE
Archie Comics: July, 1991 - No. 21, Mar, 1998 ($1.50/$1.79/$1.89, digest size, bi-annual)

	GD	VG	FN	VF	VF/NM	NM-
V2#1						6.00
2-10						4.00
11-21						3.00

LITTLE ARCHIE MYSTERY
Archie Publications: Aug, 1963 - No. 2, Oct, 1963 (12¢ issues)

	GD	VG	FN	VF	VF/NM	NM-
1	10	20	30	72	131	190
2	6	12	18	43	69	95

LITTLE ASPIRIN (See Little Lenny & Wisco)
Marvel Comics (CnPC): July, 1949 - No. 3, Dec, 1949 (52 pgs.)

	GD	VG	FN	VF	VF/NM	NM-
1-Oscar app.; Kurtzman-a (4 pgs.)	17	34	51	98	154	210
2-Kurtzman-a (4 pgs.)	11	22	33	60	83	105
3-No Kurtzman-a	9	18	27	47	61	75

LITTLE AUDREY (Also see Playful...)
St. John Publ.: Apr, 1948 - No. 24, May, 1952

	GD	VG	FN	VF	VF/NM	NM-
1-1st app. Little Audrey	55	110	165	352	601	850
2	27	54	81	158	259	360
3-5	18	36	54	107	169	230
6-10	14	28	42	81	118	155
11-20: 16-X-Mas-c	11	22	33	60	83	105
21-24	10	20	30	54	72	90

LITTLE AUDREY (See Harvey Hits #11, 19)
Harvey Publications: No. 25, Aug, 1952 - No. 53, April, 1957

	GD	VG	FN	VF	VF/NM	NM-
25-(Paramount Pictures Famous Star... on-c); 1st Harvey Casper and Baby Huey (1 month earlier than Harvey Comic Hits #60(9/52))	13	26	39	94	185	275
26-30: 26-28-Casper app.	8	16	24	54	90	125
31-40: 32-35-Casper app.	7	14	21	45	73	100
41-53	5	10	15	34	55	75
...Clubhouse 1 (9/61, 68 pg. Giant)-New stories & reprints	9	18	27	60	100	140

LITTLE AUDREY
Harvey Comics: Aug, 1992 - No. 8, July, 1994 ($1.25/$1.50)

	GD	VG	FN	VF	VF/NM	NM-
V2#1						3.50
2-8						3.00

LITTLE AUDREY (...Yearbook)
St. John Publishing Co.: 1950 (50¢, 260 pgs.)

	GD	VG	FN	VF	VF/NM	NM-
Contains 8 complete 1949 comics rebound; Casper, Alice in Wonderland, Little Audrey, Abbott & Costello, Pinocchio, Moon Mullins, Three Stooges (from Jubilee), Little Annie Rooney app. (Rare)	103	206	309	659	1130	1600

(Also see All Good & Treasury of Comics)

NOTE: *This book contains remaindered St. John comics; many variations possible.*

LITTLE AUDREY & MELVIN (Audrey & Melvin No. 62)
Harvey Publications: May, 1962 - No. 61, Dec, 1973

	GD	VG	FN	VF	VF/NM	NM-
1	10	20	30	68	119	170
2-5	6	12	18	39	62	85
6-10	5	10	15	30	48	65
11-20	3	6	9	19	29	38
21-40: 22-Richie Rich app.	3	6	9	14	20	26
41-50,55-61	2	4	6	11	16	20
51-54: All 52 pg. Giants	3	6	9	14	20	26

LITTLE AUDREY TV FUNTIME
Harvey Publ.: Sept, 1962 - No. 33, Oct, 1971 (#1-31: 68 pgs.; #32,33: 52 pgs.)

	GD	VG	FN	VF	VF/NM	NM-
1-Richie Rich app.	10	20	30	68	119	170
2,3: Richie Rich app.	6	12	18	39	62	85
4,5: 5-25¢ & 35¢ issues exist	5	10	15	32	51	70
6-10	3	6	9	21	32	42
11-20	3	6	9	16	23	28
21-33	3	6	9	14	19	24

LITTLE BAD WOLF (Disney; see Walt Disney's C&S #52, Walt Disney Showcase #21 & Wheaties)
Dell Publishing Co.: No. 403, June, 1952 - No. 564, June, 1954

	GD	VG	FN	VF	VF/NM	NM-
Four Color 403 (#1)	7	14	21	47	76	105
Four Color 473 (6/53), 564	5	10	15	32	51	70

LITTLE BEAVER
Dell Publishing Co.: No. 211, Jan, 1949 - No. 870, Jan, 1958 (All painted-c)

	GD	VG	FN	VF	VF/NM	NM-
Four Color 211('49)-All Harman-a	8	16	24	56	93	130
Four Color 267,294,332(5/51)	5	10	15	34	55	75
3(10-12/51)-8(1-3/53)	5	10	15	32	51	70
Four Color 483(8-10/53),529	5	10	15	30	48	65
Four Color 612,660,695,744,817,870	5	10	15	30	48	65

LITTLE BIT
Jubilee/St. John Publishing Co.: Mar, 1949 - No. 2, June, 1949

	GD	VG	FN	VF	VF/NM	NM-
1-Kid humor	10	20	30	54	72	90
2	8	16	24	40	50	60

LI'L DEPRESSED BOY
Image Comics: Feb, 2011 - Present ($2.99)

	GD	VG	FN	VF	VF/NM	NM-
1-3-S. Steven Struble-s/Sina Grace-a						3.00

LITTLE DOT (See Humphrey, Li'l Max, Sad Sack, and Tastee-Freez Comics)
Harvey Publications: Sept, 1953 - No. 164, Apr, 1976

	GD	VG	FN	VF	VF/NM	NM-
1-Intro./1st app. Richie Rich & Little Lotta	314	628	942	2198	3849	5500
2-1st app. Freckles & Pee Wee (Richie Rich's poor friends)	103	206	309	659	1130	1600
3	63	126	189	403	689	975
4	57	114	171	362	619	875
5-Origin dots on Little Dot's dress	63	126	189	403	689	975
6-Richie Rich, Little Lotta, & Little Dot all on cover; 1st Richie Rich cover featured						

Little Dot #13 © HARV

Little Eva #2 © STJ

Li'l Ghost #1 © STJ

	GD 2.0	VG 4.0	FN 6.0	VF 8.0	VF/NM 9.0	NM- 9.2
	63	126	189	403	689	975
7-10: 9-Last pre-code issue (1/55)	39	78	117	240	395	550
11-20	28	56	84	165	270	375
21-30	18	36	54	105	165	225
31-40	14	28	42	80	115	150
41-50	11	22	33	62	86	110
51-60	9	18	27	52	69	85
61-80	4	8	12	28	44	60
81-100	3	6	9	20	30	40
101-141	3	6	9	16	23	30
142-145: All 52 pg. Giants	3	6	9	18	27	35
146-164	2	4	6	11	16	20

NOTE: *Richie Rich & Little Lotta in all.*

LITTLE DOT
Harvey Comics: Sept, 1992 - No. 7, June, 1994 ($1.25/$1.50)

	GD 2.0	VG 4.0	FN 6.0	VF 8.0	VF/NM 9.0	NM- 9.2
V2#1-Little Dot, Little Lotta, Richie Rich in all						3.50
2-7 ($1.50)						3.00

LITTLE DOT DOTLAND (Dot Dotland No. 62, 63)
Harvey Publications: July, 1962 - No. 61, Dec, 1973

	GD 2.0	VG 4.0	FN 6.0	VF 8.0	VF/NM 9.0	NM- 9.2
1-Richie Rich begins	12	24	36	87	164	240
2,3	8	16	24	52	86	120
4,5	6	12	18	41	66	90
6-10	5	10	15	32	51	70
11-20	4	8	12	24	37	50
21-30	3	6	9	18	27	35
31-50	3	6	9	16	23	30
51-54: All 52 pg. Giants	3	6	9	18	27	35
55-61	2	4	6	11	16	20

LITTLE DOT'S UNCLES & AUNTS (See Harvey Hits No. 4, 13, 24)
Harvey Enterprises: Oct, 1961; No. 2, Aug, 1962 - No. 52, Apr, 1974

	GD 2.0	VG 4.0	FN 6.0	VF 8.0	VF/NM 9.0	NM- 9.2
1-Richie Rich begins; 68 pgs. begin	14	28	42	95	188	280
2,3	9	18	27	60	100	140
4,5	6	12	18	41	66	90
6-10	5	10	15	34	55	75
11-20	4	8	12	24	37	50
21-37: Last 68 pg. issue	3	6	9	19	29	38
38-52: All 52 pg. Giants	3	6	9	16	23	30

LITTLE DRACULA
Harvey Comics: Jan, 1992 - No. 3, May, 1992 ($1.25, quarterly, mini-series)

	GD 2.0	VG 4.0	FN 6.0	VF 8.0	VF/NM 9.0	NM- 9.2
1-3						3.00

LITTLE ENDLESS STORYBOOK, THE (See The Sandman titles)
DC Comics: 2001 ($5.95, Prestige format, one-shot)

	GD 2.0	VG 4.0	FN 6.0	VF 8.0	VF/NM 9.0	NM- 9.2
nn-Jill Thompson-s/painted-a/c; puppy Barnabas searches for Delirium						20.00

LITTLE EVA
St. John Publishing Co.: May, 1952 - No. 31, Nov, 1956

	GD 2.0	VG 4.0	FN 6.0	VF 8.0	VF/NM 9.0	NM- 9.2
1	16	32	48	94	147	200
2	10	20	30	58	79	100
3-5	9	18	27	47	61	75
6-10	8	16	24	42	54	65
11-31	7	14	21	37	46	55
3-D 1,2(10/53, 11/53, 25¢)-Both came w/glasses. 1-Infinity-c	18	36	54	107	169	230
I.W. Reprint #1-3,6-8: 1-r/Little Eva #28. 2-r/Little Eva #29. 3-r/Little Eva #24	2	4	6	8	11	14
Super Reprint #10,12('63),14,16,18('64): 18-r/Little Eva #25.	2	4	6	8	11	14

LI'L GENIUS (Formerly Super Brat; Summer Fun No. 54) (See Blue Bird & Giant Comics #3)
Charlton Comics: 1954 - No. 52, 1/65; No. 53, 10/65; No. 54, 10/85 - No. 55, 1/86

	GD 2.0	VG 4.0	FN 6.0	VF 8.0	VF/NM 9.0	NM- 9.2
5(#1?)	11	22	33	62	86	110
6-10	7	14	21	37	46	55
11-15,19,20	6	12	18	29	36	42
16,17-(68 pgs.)	8	16	24	40	50	60
18-(100 pgs., 10/58)	11	22	33	60	83	105
21-35	3	6	9	16	22	28
36-53	2	4	6	10	14	18
54,55 (Low print)						5.00

LI'L GHOST
St. John Publ. Co./Fago No. 1 on: 2/58; No. 2,1/59 - No. 3, Mar, 1959

	GD 2.0	VG 4.0	FN 6.0	VF 8.0	VF/NM 9.0	NM- 9.2
1(St. John)	9	18	27	50	65	80
2,3	6	12	18	28	34	40

LITTLE GIANT COMICS
Centaur Publications: 7/38 - No. 3, 10/38; No. 4, 2/39 (132 pgs.) (6-3/4x4-1/2")

	GD 2.0	VG 4.0	FN 6.0	VF 8.0	VF/NM 9.0	NM- 9.2
1-B&W with color-c; stories, puzzles, magic	116	232	348	742	1271	1800
2,3-B&W with color-c	77	154	231	493	847	1200
4 (6-5/8x9-3/8")(68 pgs., B&W inside)	77	154	231	493	847	1200

NOTE: ***Filchock** c-2, 4. **Gustavson** a-1. **Pinajian** a-4. **Bob Wood** a-1.*

LITTLE GIANT DETECTIVE FUNNIES
Centaur Publ.: Oct, 1938; No. 4, Jan, 1939 (6-3/4x4-1/2", 132 pgs., B&W)

	GD 2.0	VG 4.0	FN 6.0	VF 8.0	VF/NM 9.0	NM- 9.2
1-B&W with color-c	116	232	348	742	1271	1800
4(1/39, B&W; color-c; 68 pgs., 6-1/2x9-1/2")-Eisner-r	77	154	231	493	847	1200

LITTLE GIANT MOVIE FUNNIES
Centaur Publ.: Aug, 1938 - No. 2, Oct, 1938 (6-3/4x4-1/2", 132 pgs., B&W)

	GD 2.0	VG 4.0	FN 6.0	VF 8.0	VF/NM 9.0	NM- 9.2
1-Ed Wheelan's "Minute Movies" reprints	116	232	348	742	1271	1800
2-Ed Wheelan's "Minute Movies" reprints	77	154	231	493	847	1200

LITTLE GROUCHO (...the Red-Headed Tornado; ...Grouchy No. 2)
Reston Publ. Co.: No. 16; Feb-Mar, 1955 - No. 2, June-July, 1955 (See Tippy Terry)

	GD 2.0	VG 4.0	FN 6.0	VF 8.0	VF/NM 9.0	NM- 9.2
16, 1 (2-3/55)	8	16	24	42	54	65
2(6-7/55)	6	12	18	27	33	38

LITTLE HIAWATHA (Disney; see Walt Disney's C&S #143)
Dell Publishing Co.: No. 439, Dec, 1952 - No. 988, May-July, 1959

	GD 2.0	VG 4.0	FN 6.0	VF 8.0	VF/NM 9.0	NM- 9.2
Four Color 439 (#1)	6	12	18	39	62	85
Four Color 787 (4/57), 901 (5/58), 988	5	10	15	30	48	65

LITTLE IKE
St. John Publishing Co.: April, 1953 - No. 4, Oct, 1953

	GD 2.0	VG 4.0	FN 6.0	VF 8.0	VF/NM 9.0	NM- 9.2
1-Kid humor	10	20	30	54	72	90
2	6	12	18	31	38	45
3,4	5	10	15	24	30	35

LITTLE IODINE (See Giant Comic Album)
Dell Publ. Co.: No. 224, 4/49 - No. 257, 1949: 3-5/50 - No. 56, 4-6/62 (1-4-52pgs.)

	GD 2.0	VG 4.0	FN 6.0	VF 8.0	VF/NM 9.0	NM- 9.2
Four Color 224-By Jimmy Hatlo	11	22	33	77	144	210
Four Color 257	8	16	24	56	93	130
1(3-5/50)	9	18	27	65	113	160
2-5	6	12	18	37	59	80
6-10	4	8	12	28	44	60
11-20	4	8	12	22	34	45
21-30: 27-Xmas-c	3	6	9	20	30	40
31-40	3	6	9	18	27	35
41-56	3	6	9	16	23	30

LITTLE JACK FROST
Avon Periodicals: 1951

	GD 2.0	VG 4.0	FN 6.0	VF 8.0	VF/NM 9.0	NM- 9.2
1	11	22	33	64	90	115

LI'L JINX (Little Archie in Animal Land #17) (Also see Pep Comics #62)
Archie Publications: No. 1(#11), Nov, 1956 - No. 16, Sept, 1957

	GD 2.0	VG 4.0	FN 6.0	VF 8.0	VF/NM 9.0	NM- 9.2
1(#11)-By Joe Edwards; "First Issue" on cover	14	28	42	80	115	150
12(1/57)-16	10	20	30	54	72	90

LI'L JINX (See Archie Giant Series Magazine No. 223)

LI'L JINX CHRISTMAS BAG (See Archie Giant Series Mag. No. 195, 206, 219)

LI'L JINX GIANT LAUGH-OUT (See Archie Giant Series Mag. No. 176, 185)
Archie Publications: No. 33, Sept, 1971 - No. 43, Nov, 1973 (52 pgs.)

	GD 2.0	VG 4.0	FN 6.0	VF 8.0	VF/NM 9.0	NM- 9.2
33-43 (52 pgs.)	2	4	6	13	18	22

LITTLE JOE (See Popular Comics & Super Comics)
Dell Publishing Co.: No. 1, 1942

	GD 2.0	VG 4.0	FN 6.0	VF 8.0	VF/NM 9.0	NM- 9.2
Four Color 1	50	100	150	425	863	1300

LITTLE JOE
St. John Publishing Co.: Apr, 1953

	GD 2.0	VG 4.0	FN 6.0	VF 8.0	VF/NM 9.0	NM- 9.2
1	6	12	18	28	34	40

LI'L KIDS (Also see Li'l Pals)
Marvel Comics Group: 8/70 - No. 2, 10/70; No. 3, 11/71 - No. 12, 6/73

	GD 2.0	VG 4.0	FN 6.0	VF 8.0	VF/NM 9.0	NM- 9.2
1	8	16	24	52	86	120
2-9	4	8	12	28	44	60
10-12-Calvin app.	5	10	15	30	48	65

LITTLE KING
Dell Publishing Co.: No. 494, Aug, 1953 - No. 677, Feb, 1956

Little Lotta #1 © HARV

Little Lulu #221 © M. Buell

Little Max Comics #68 © HARV

	GD 2.0	VG 4.0	FN 6.0	VF 8.0	VF/NM 9.0	NM- 9.2
Four Color 494 (#1)	9	18	27	60	100	140
Four Color 597, 677	5	10	15	34	55	75

LITTLE LANA (Formerly Lana)
Marvel Comics (MjMC): No. 8, Nov, 1949; No. 9, Mar, 1950

	GD	VG	FN	VF	VF/NM	NM-
8,9	12	24	36	69	97	125

LITTLE LENNY
Marvel Comics (CDS): June, 1949 - No. 3, Nov, 1949

	GD	VG	FN	VF	VF/NM	NM-
1-Little Aspirin app.	13	26	39	74	105	135
2,3	9	18	27	47	61	75

LITTLE LIZZIE
Marvel Comics (PrPI)/Atlas (OMC): 6/49 - No. 5, 4/50; 9/53 - No. 3, Jan, 1954

	GD	VG	FN	VF	VF/NM	NM-
1-Kid humor	14	28	42	82	121	160
2-5	9	18	27	50	65	80
1 (9/53, 2nd series by Atlas)-Howie Post-c	10	20	30	56	76	95
2,3	8	16	24	42	54	65

LITTLE LOTTA (See Harvey Hits No. 10)
Harvey Publications: 11/55 - No. 110, 11/73; No. 111, 9/74 - No. 120, 5/76
V2#1, Oct, 1992 - No. 4, July, 1993 ($1.25)

	GD	VG	FN	VF	VF/NM	NM-
1-Richie Rich (r) & Little Dot begin	37	74	111	286	568	850
2,3	16	32	48	114	232	350
4,5	11	22	33	77	144	210
6-10	8	16	24	54	90	125
11-20	6	12	18	41	66	90
21-40	4	8	12	24	37	50
41-60	3	6	9	19	29	38
61-80: 62-1st app. Nurse Jenny	3	6	9	16	22	28
81-99	2	4	6	11	16	20
100-103: All 52 pg. Giants	3	6	9	14	19	24
104-120	2	4	6	8	10	12
V2#1-4 (1992-93)						4.00

NOTE: *No. 121 was advertised, but never released.*

LITTLE LOTTA FOODLAND
Harvey Publications: 9/63 - No. 14, 10/67; No. 15, 10/68 - No. 29, Oct, 1972

	GD	VG	FN	VF	VF/NM	NM-
1-Little Lotta, Little Dot, Richie Rich, 68 pgs. begin	12	24	36	87	164	240
2,3	9	18	27	60	100	140
4,5	7	14	21	45	73	100
6-10	5	10	15	32	51	70
11-20	3	6	9	20	30	40
21-26: 26-Last 68 pg. issue	3	6	9	16	23	30
27,28: Both 52 pgs.	3	6	9	14	19	24
29-(36 pgs.)	2	4	6	9	13	16

LITTLE LULU (Formerly Marge's Little Lulu)
Gold Key 207-257/Whitman 258 on: No. 207, Sept, 1972 - No. 268, Mar, 1984

	GD	VG	FN	VF	VF/NM	NM-
207,209,220-Stanley-r. 207-1st app. Henrietta	2	4	6	11	16	20
208,210-219: 208-1st app. Snobbly, Wilbur's butler	2	4	6	9	12	15
221-240,242-249, 250(r/#166), 251-254(r/#206)	1	3	4	6	8	10
241,263-Stanley-r	2	4	6	8	10	12
255-257(Gold Key): 256-r/#212	1	2	3	5	7	9
258,259,262(50¢-c),264(2/82),265(3/82) (Whitman)	2	4	6	9	13	16
260-(9/80)(Whitman pre-pack only - low distribution)	13	26	39	92	179	265
261-(11/80)(Whitman pre-pack only)	4	8	12	28	44	60
262-(1/81) Variant 40¢-c price error (reg. ed. 50¢-c)	3	6	9	14	19	24
266-268 (All #90028 on-c; no date, no date code; 3-pack): 266(7/83). 267(8/83). 268(3/84)-Stanley-r	3	6	9	16	23	30

LITTLE LULU
Dark Horse Books: Nov, 2004 - Present ($9.95/$10.95, B&W, digest-size TPB)

	GD	VG	FN	VF	VF/NM	NM-
Vol. 1 -B&W reprints of Marge's Little Lulu #6-12; John Stanley-s/a & Irving Tripp-a						10.00
...: (Vol. 2) Lulu Takes a Trip (2/05) -B&W r/Marge's Little Lulu #13-16						10.00
...: (Vol. 3) My Dinner With Lulu (4/05) -B&W r/Four Color #74,97,110,115,120						10.00
...: (Vol. 4) Sunday Afternoon (6/05) -B&W r/Four Color #131,139,146,158						10.00
...: (Vol. 5) Lulu in the Doghouse (8/05) -B&W r/Four Color #165 & Marge's Little Lulu #1-5						10.00
...: (Vol. 6) Letters to Santa (10/05) -B&W r/Marge's Little Lulu #18-22						10.00
...: (Vol. 7) Lulu's Umbrella Service (12/05) -B&W r/Marge's Little Lulu #23-27						10.00
...: (Vol. 8) Late For School (2/06) -B&W r/Marge's Little Lulu #28-32						10.00
...: (Vol. 9) Lucky Lulu (4/06) -B&W r/Marge's Little Lulu #33-37						10.00
...: (Vol. 10) All Dressed Up (6/06) -B&W r/Marge's Little Lulu #38-42						10.00
...: (Vol. 11) April Fools (8/06) -B&W r/Marge's Little Lulu #43-48						10.00
...: (Vol. 12) Leave It to Lulu (10/06) -B&W r/Marge's Little Lulu #49-53						10.00
...: (Vol. 13) Too Much Fun (12/06) -B&W r/Marge's Little Lulu #54-58						10.00
...: (Vol. 14) Queen Lulu (2/07) -B&W r/Marge's Little Lulu #59-63						10.00
...: (Vol. 15) The Explorers (4/07) -B&W r/Marge's Little Lulu #64-68						10.00
...: (Vol. 16) A Handy Kid (7/07, $10.95) -B&W r/Marge's Little Lulu #69-74						11.00
...: (Vol. 17) The Valentine (10/07, $10.95) -B&W r/Marge's Little Lulu #75-81						11.00
...: (Vol. 18) The Expert (1/08, $10.95) -B&W r/Marge's Little Lulu #82-87						11.00
Color Special (9/06, $13.95, standard size) r/various stories from Marge's Little Lulu						14.00

LITTLE MARY MIXUP (See Comics On Parade)
United Features Syndicate: No. 10, 1939, - No. 26, 1940

	GD	VG	FN	VF	VF/NM	NM-
Single Series 10, 26	34	68	102	199	325	450

LITTLE MAX COMICS (Joe Palooka's Pal; see Joe Palooka)
Harvey Publications: Oct, 1949 - No. 73, Nov, 1961

	GD	VG	FN	VF	VF/NM	NM-
1-Infinity-c; Little Dot begins; Joe Palooka on-c	22	44	66	128	209	290
2-Little Dot app.; Joe Palooka on-c	14	28	42	78	112	145
3-Little Dot app.; Joe Palooka on-c	10	20	30	58	79	100
4-10: 5-Little Dot app., 1pg.	9	18	27	47	61	75
11-20	8	16	24	40	50	60
21-40: 23-Little Dot app. 38-r/#20	6	12	18	31	38	45
41-62,66	3	6	9	18	27	35
63-65,67-73-Include new five pg. Richie Rich stories. 70-73-Little Lotta app.	3	6	9	19	29	38

LI'L MENACE
Fago Magazine Co.: Dec, 1958 - No. 3, May, 1959

	GD	VG	FN	VF	VF/NM	NM-
1-Peter Rabbit app.	8	16	24	44	57	70
2-Peter Rabbit (Vincent Fago's)	7	14	21	35	43	50
3	6	12	18	28	34	40

LITTLE MERMAID, THE (Walt Disney's...; also see Disney's...)
W. D. Publications (Disney): 1990 (no date given)($5.95, no ads, 52 pgs.)

	GD	VG	FN	VF	VF/NM	NM-
nn-Adapts animated movie	1	2	3	4	5	7
nn-Comic version ($2.50)						3.00

LITTLE MERMAID, THE
Disney Comics: 1992 - No. 4, 1992 ($1.50, mini-series)

	GD	VG	FN	VF	VF/NM	NM-
1-4: Based on movie						3.50
1-4: 2nd printings sold at Wal-Mart w/different-c						3.00

LITTLE MISS MUFFET
Best Books (Standard Comics)/King Features Synd.: No. 11, Dec, 1948 - No. 13, March, 1949

	GD	VG	FN	VF	VF/NM	NM-
11-Strip reprints; Fanny Cory-c/a	9	18	27	50	65	80
12,13-Strip reprints; Fanny Cory-c/a	7	14	21	35	43	50

LITTLE MISS SUNBEAM COMICS
Magazine Enterprises/Quality Bakers of America: June-July, 1950 - No. 4, Dec-Jan, 1950-51

	GD	VG	FN	VF	VF/NM	NM-
1	15	30	45	94	147	200
2-4	10	20	30	56	76	95
...Advs. In Space ('55)	7	14	21	35	43	50

LITTLE MONSTERS, THE (See March of Comics #423, Three Stooges #17)
Gold Key: Nov, 1964 - No. 44, Feb, 1978

	GD	VG	FN	VF	VF/NM	NM-
1	6	12	18	37	59	80
2	3	6	9	20	30	40
3-10	3	6	9	17	25	32
11-20	3	6	9	15	21	26
21-30: 19-21-Reprints	2	4	6	11	16	20
31-44: 34-39,43-Reprints	2	4	6	8	11	14

LITTLE MONSTERS (Movie)
Now Comics: 1989 - No. 6, June, 1990 ($1.75)

	GD	VG	FN	VF	VF/NM	NM-
1-6: Photo-c from movie						3.00

LITTLE NEMO (See Cocomalt, Future Comics, Help, Jest, Kayo, Punch, Red Seal, & Superworld; most by Winsor McCay Jr., son of famous artist) (Other McCay books: see Little Sammy Sneeze & Dreams of the Rarebit Fiend)

LITTLE NEMO (...in Slumberland)
McCay Features/Nostalgia Press('69): 1945 (11x7-1/4", 28 pgs., B&W)

	GD	VG	FN	VF	VF/NM	NM-
1905 & 1911 reprints by Winsor McCay	10	20	30	56	76	95
1969-70 (Exact reprint)	2	4	6	9	12	15

LITTLE ORPHAN ANNIE (See Annie, Famous Feature Stories, Marvel Super Special, Merry Christmas..., Popular Comics, Super Book #7, 11, 23 & Super Comics)

LITTLE ORPHAN ANNIE
David McKay Publ./Dell Publishing Co.: No. 7, 1937 - No. 3, Sept-Nov, 1948; No. 206, Dec, 1948

	GD	VG	FN	VF	VF/NM	NM-
Feature Books(McKay) 7-(1937) (Rare)	97	194	291	621	1061	1500
Four Color 12(1941)	57	114	171	362	624	885

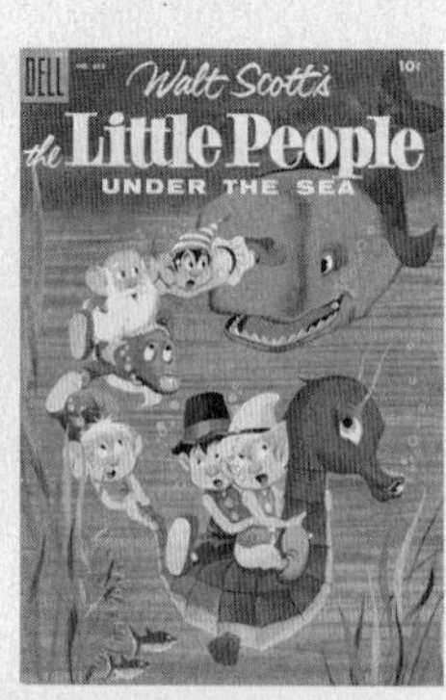

Little People FC #633 © DELL

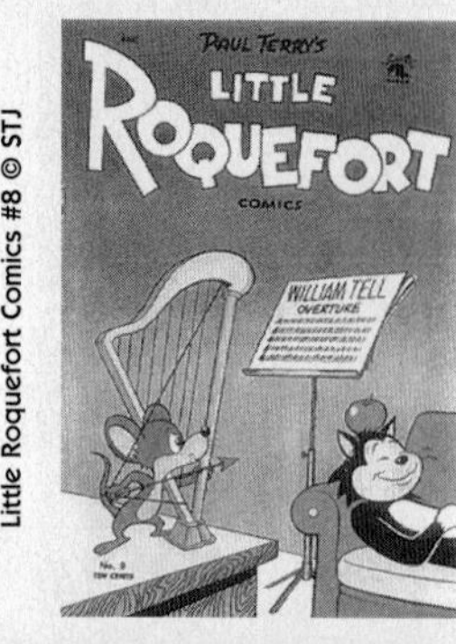

Little Roquefort Comics #8 © STJ

Lobo #26 © DC

	GD 2.0	VG 4.0	FN 6.0	VF 8.0	VF/NM 9.0	NM- 9.2
Four Color 18(1943)-Flag-c	32	64	96	248	492	735
Four Color 52(1944)	24	48	72	175	355	535
Four Color 76(1945)	20	40	60	142	286	430
Four Color 107(1946)	17	34	51	120	245	370
Four Color 152(1947)	12	24	36	84	157	230
1(3-5/48)-r/strips from 5/7/44 to 7/30/44	12	24	36	82	154	225
2-r/strips from 7/21/40 to 9/9/40	9	18	27	60	100	140
3-r/strips from 9/10/40 to 11/9/40	9	18	27	60	100	140
Four Color 206(12/48)	8	16	24	54	90	125

LI'L PALS (Also see Li'l Kids)
Marvel Comics Group: Sept, 1972 - No. 5, May, 1973

	GD 2.0	VG 4.0	FN 6.0	VF 8.0	VF/NM 9.0	NM- 9.2
1	7	14	21	45	73	100
2-5	4	8	12	28	44	60

LI'L PAN (Formerly Rocket Kelly; becomes Junior Comics with #9)
Fox Features Syndicate: No. 6, Dec-Jan, 1946-47 - No. 8, Apr-May, 1947
(Also see Wotalife Comics)

	GD 2.0	VG 4.0	FN 6.0	VF 8.0	VF/NM 9.0	NM- 9.2
6	11	22	33	60	83	105
7,8: 7-Atomic bomb story; robot-c	9	18	27	47	61	75

LITTLE PEOPLE (Also see Darby O'Gill & the...)
Dell Publishing Co.: No. 485, Aug-Oct, 1953 - No. 1062, Dec, 1959 (Walt Scott's)

	GD 2.0	VG 4.0	FN 6.0	VF 8.0	VF/NM 9.0	NM- 9.2
Four Color 485 (#1)	8	16	24	52	86	120
Four Color 573(7/54), 633(6/55)	5	10	15	32	51	70
Four Color 692(3/56),753(11/56),809(7/57),868(12/57),908(5/58), 959(12/58), 1062	5	10	15	32	51	70

LITTLE RASCALS
Dell Publishing Co.: No. 674, Jan, 1956 - No. 1297, Mar-May, 1962

	GD 2.0	VG 4.0	FN 6.0	VF 8.0	VF/NM 9.0	NM- 9.2
Four Color 674 (#1)	9	18	27	60	100	140
Four Color 778(3/57),825(8/57)	6	12	18	39	62	85
Four Color 883(3/58),936(9/58),974(3/59),1030(9/59),1079(2-4/60),1137(9-11/60)	6	12	18	37	59	80
Four Color 1174(3-5/61),1224(10-12/61),1297	5	10	15	30	48	65

LI'L RASCAL TWINS (Formerly Nature Boy)
Charlton Comics: No. 6, 1957 - No. 18, Jan, 1960

	GD 2.0	VG 4.0	FN 6.0	VF 8.0	VF/NM 9.0	NM- 9.2
6-Li'l Genius & Tomboy in all	6	12	18	29	36	42
7-18: 7-Timmy the Timid Ghost app.	4	8	12	18	22	25

LITTLE RED HOT: (CHANE OF FOOLS)
Image Comics: Feb, 1999 - No. 3, Apr, 1999 ($2.95/$3.50, B&W, limited series)

	GD 2.0	VG 4.0	FN 6.0	VF 8.0	VF/NM 9.0	NM- 9.2
1-3-Dawn Brown-s/a. 2,3-($3.50-c)						3.50
The Foolish Collection TPB ($12.95) r/#1-3						13.00

LITTLE RED HOT: BOUND
Image Comics: July, 2001 - No. 3, Nov, 2001 ($2.95, color, limited series)

	GD 2.0	VG 4.0	FN 6.0	VF 8.0	VF/NM 9.0	NM- 9.2
1-3-Dawn Brown-s/a.						3.00

LITTLE ROQUEFORT COMICS (See Paul Terry's Comics #105)
St. John Publishing Co.(all pre-code)/Pines No. 10: June, 1952 - No. 9, Oct, 1953; No. 10, Summer, 1958

	GD 2.0	VG 4.0	FN 6.0	VF 8.0	VF/NM 9.0	NM- 9.2
1-By Paul Terry; Funny Animal	10	20	30	54	72	90
2	6	12	18	31	38	45
3-10: 10-CBS Television Presents on-c	5	10	15	24	30	35

LITTLE SAD SACK (See Harvey Hits No. 73, 76, 79, 81, 83)
Harvey Publications: Oct, 1964 - No. 19, Nov, 1967

	GD 2.0	VG 4.0	FN 6.0	VF 8.0	VF/NM 9.0	NM- 9.2
1-Richie Rich app. on cover only	5	10	15	32	51	70
2-10	3	6	9	18	27	35
11-19	3	6	9	16	22	28

LITTLE SCOUTS
Dell Publishing Co.: No. 321, Mar, 1951 - No. 587, Oct, 1954

	GD 2.0	VG 4.0	FN 6.0	VF 8.0	VF/NM 9.0	NM- 9.2
Four Color 321 (#1, 3/51)	5	10	15	30	48	65
2(10-12/51) - 6(10-12/52)	4	8	12	24	37	50
Four Color 462,506,550,587	4	8	12	24	37	50

LITTLE SHOP OF HORRORS SPECIAL (Movie)
DC Comics: Feb, 1987 ($2.00, 68 pgs.)

	GD 2.0	VG 4.0	FN 6.0	VF 8.0	VF/NM 9.0	NM- 9.2
1-Colan-c/a						4.00

LITTLE SPUNKY
I. W. Enterprises: No date (1963?) (10¢)

	GD 2.0	VG 4.0	FN 6.0	VF 8.0	VF/NM 9.0	NM- 9.2
1-r/Frisky Fables #1	2	4	6	8	11	14

LITTLE STAR
Oni Press: Feb, 2005 - No. 6, Dec, 2005 ($2.99, B&W, limited series)

	GD 2.0	VG 4.0	FN 6.0	VF 8.0	VF/NM 9.0	NM- 9.2
1-6-Andi Watson-s/a						3.00
TPB (4/06, $19.95) r/#1-6						20.00

LITTLE STOOGES, THE (The Three Stooges' Sons)
Gold Key: Sept, 1972 - No. 7, Mar, 1974

	GD 2.0	VG 4.0	FN 6.0	VF 8.0	VF/NM 9.0	NM- 9.2
1-Norman Maurer cover/stories in all	3	6	9	19	29	38
2-7	2	4	6	13	18	22

LITTLEST OUTLAW (Disney)
Dell Publishing Co.: No. 609, Jan, 1955

	GD 2.0	VG 4.0	FN 6.0	VF 8.0	VF/NM 9.0	NM- 9.2
Four Color 609-Movie, photo-c	6	12	18	43	69	95

LITTLEST SNOWMAN, THE
Dell Publishing Co.: No. 755, 12/56; No. 864, 12/57; 12-2/1963-64

	GD 2.0	VG 4.0	FN 6.0	VF 8.0	VF/NM 9.0	NM- 9.2
Four Color 755,864, 1(1964)	5	10	15	32	51	70

LI'L TOMBOY (Formerly Fawcett's Funny Animals; see Giant Comics #3)
Charlton Comics: V14#92, Oct, 1956; No. 93, Mar, 1957 - No. 107, Feb, 1960

	GD 2.0	VG 4.0	FN 6.0	VF 8.0	VF/NM 9.0	NM- 9.2
V14#92	6	12	18	27	33	38
93-107: 97-Atomic Bunny app.	5	10	14	20	24	28

LI'L WILLIE COMICS (Formerly & becomes Willie Comics #22 on)
Marvel Comics (MgPC): No. 20, July, 1949 - No. 21, Sept, 1949

	GD 2.0	VG 4.0	FN 6.0	VF 8.0	VF/NM 9.0	NM- 9.2
20,21: 20-Little Aspirin app.	14	28	42	76	108	140

LITTLE WOMEN (See Power Record Comics)

LIVE IT UP
Spire Christian Comics (Fleming H. Revell Co.): 1973, 1974 (39-49 cents)

	GD 2.0	VG 4.0	FN 6.0	VF 8.0	VF/NM 9.0	NM- 9.2
nn-1973 Edition	2	4	6	10	14	18
nn-1974 Edition	2	4	6	8	10	12

LIVEWIRES
Marvel Comics: Apr, 2005 - No. 6, Sept, 2005 ($2.99, limited series)

	GD 2.0	VG 4.0	FN 6.0	VF 8.0	VF/NM 9.0	NM- 9.2
1-6-Adam Warren-s/c; Rick Mays-a						3.00
...: Clockwork Thugs, Yo (2005, $7.99, digest) r/#1-6						8.00

LIVING BIBLE, THE
Living Bible Corp.: Fall, 1945 - No. 3, Spring, 1946

	GD 2.0	VG 4.0	FN 6.0	VF 8.0	VF/NM 9.0	NM- 9.2
1-The Life of Paul; all have L. B. Cole-c	39	78	117	231	378	525
2-Joseph & His Brethren; Jonah & the Whale	27	54	81	158	259	360
3-Chaplains At War (classic-c)	40	80	120	246	411	575

LIVING WITH THE DEAD
Dark Horse Comics: Oct, 2007 - No. 3, Nov, 2007 ($2.99, limited series)

	GD 2.0	VG 4.0	FN 6.0	VF 8.0	VF/NM 9.0	NM- 9.2
1-3-Zombies; Mike Richardson-s/Ben Stenbeck-a/Richard Corben-c						3.00

LOADED BIBLE
Image Comics: Apr, 2006; May, 2007; Feb, 2008 ($4.99)

	GD 2.0	VG 4.0	FN 6.0	VF 8.0	VF/NM 9.0	NM- 9.2
...: Jesus vs. Vampires (4/06) Tim Seeley-s/Nate Bellegarde-a						5.00
...2: Blood of Christ (5/07) Seeley-s/Mike Norton-a. ...3: Communion (2/08)						5.00

LOBO
Dell Publishing Co.: Dec, 1965; No. 2, Oct, 1966

	GD 2.0	VG 4.0	FN 6.0	VF 8.0	VF/NM 9.0	NM- 9.2
1-1st black character to have his own title	4	8	12	28	44	60
2	3	6	9	20	30	40

LOBO (Also see Action #650, Adventures of Superman, Demon (2nd series), Justice League, L.E.G.I.O.N., Mister Miracle, Omega Men #3 & Superman #41)
DC Comics: Nov, 1990 - No. 4, Feb, 1991 ($1.50, color, limited series)

	GD 2.0	VG 4.0	FN 6.0	VF 8.0	VF/NM 9.0	NM- 9.2
1-(99¢)-Giffen plots/Breakdowns in all						5.00
1-2nd printing						3.00
2-4: 2-Legion '89 spin-off. 1-4 have Bisley painted covers & art						3.00
...: Blazing Chain of Love 1 (9/92, $1.50)-Denys Cowan-c/a; Alan Grant scripts, ...Convention Special 1 (1993, $1.75), ...: Portrait of a Victim 1 (1993, $1.75)						3.00
... Paramilitary Christmas Special 1 (1991, $2.39, 52 pgs.) Bisley-c/a						4.00
...: Portrait of a Bastich TPB (2008, $19.99) r/#1-4 & Lobo's Back #1-4						20.00

LOBO (Also see Showcase '95 #9)
DC Comics: Dec, 1993 - No. 64, Jul, 1999 ($1.75/$1.95/$2.25/$2.50, mature)

	GD 2.0	VG 4.0	FN 6.0	VF 8.0	VF/NM 9.0	NM- 9.2
1 ($2.95)-Foil enhanced-c; Alan Grant scripts begin						4.00
2-9,0,10-64: 2-7-Alan Grant scripts. 9-(9/94). 0-(10/94)-Origin retold. 50-Lobo vs. the DCU. 58-Giffen-a						3.00
#1,000,000 (11/98) 853rd Century x-over						3.00
Annual 1 (1993, $3.50, 68 pgs.)-Bloodlines x-over						4.00
Annual 2 (1994, $3.50)-21 artists (20 listed on-c); Alan Grant script; Elseworlds story						4.00
Annual 3 (1995, $3.95)-Year One story						4.00
.../Authority: Holiday Hell TPB (2006, $17.99) r/Lobo Paramilitary Christmas Special; Authority/Lobo: Jingle Hell and Spring Break Massacre; WildStorm Winter Special						18.00

Logan: Shadow Society #1 © MAR

Loki (2010 series) #1 © MAR

Lone Ranger Large Feature Comic #7 © L.R. Inc.

	GD 2.0	VG 4.0	FN 6.0	VF 8.0	VF/NM 9.0	NM- 9.2

...Big Babe Spring Break Special (Spr, '95, $1.95)-Balent-a 3.00
...Bounty Hunting for Fun and Profit ('95)-Bisley-c 5.00
... Chained (5/97, $2.50)-Alan Grant story 3.00
.../Deadman: The Brave And The Bald (2/95, $3.50) 4.00
.../Demon: Helloween (12/96, $2.25)-Giarrano-a 3.00
...Fragtastic Voyage 1 ('97, $5.95)-Mejia painted-c/a 6.00
...Gallery (9/95, $3.50)-pin-ups. 3.50
...In the Chair 1 (8/94, $1.95, 36 pgs.), ...I Quit-(12/95, $2.25) 3.00
.../Judge Dredd ('95, $4.95). 5.00
...Lobocop 1 (2/94, $1.95)-Alan Grant scripts; painted-c 3.00

LOBO: (Title Series), DC Comics

--A CONTRACT ON GAWD, 4/94 - 7/94 (mature) 1-4: Alan Grant scripts. 3-Groo cameo 3.00

--DEATH AND TAXES, 10/96 - No. 4, 1/97, 1-4-Giffen/Grant scripts 3.00

--GOES TO HOLLYWOOD, 8/96 ($2.25), 1-Grant scripts 3.00

--HIGHWAY TO HELL, 1/10 - No. 2, 2/10 ($6.99), 1,2-Scott Ian-s/Sam Keith-a/c 7.00
TPB (2010, $19.99) r/#1,2; intro. by Scott Ian; Kieth B&W art pages 20.00

--INFANTICIDE, 10/92 - 1/93 ($1.50, mature), 1-4-Giffen-c/a; Grant scripts 3.00

--/ MASK, 2/97 - No. 2, 3/97 ($5.95), 1,2 6.00

--'S BACK, 5/92 - No. 4, 11/92 ($1.50, mature), 1-4: 1-Has 3 outer covers. Bisley painted-c 1,2; a-1-3. 3-Sam Kieth-c; all have Giffen plots/breakdown & Grant scripts 3.00
Trade paperback (1993, $9.95)-r/1-4 10.00

--THE DUCK, 6/97 ($1.95), 1-A. Grant-s/V. Semeiks & R. Kryssing-a 3.00

--UNAMERICAN GLADIATORS, 6/93 - No. 4, 9/93 ($1.75, mature), 1-4-Mignola-c; Grant/Wagner scripts 3.00

--UNBOUND, 8/03 - No. 6, 5/04 ($2.95), 1-6-Giffen-s/Horley-c/a. 4-6-Ambush Bug app. 3.00

LOBSTER JOHNSON: THE IRON PROMETHEUS (See B.P.R.D. and Hellboy titles)
Dark Horse Comics: Sept, 2007 - No. 5, Jan, 2008 ($2.99, limited series)

1-5-Mignola-s/c; Armstrong-a 3.00

LOCKE & KEY
IDW Publ.: Feb, 2008 - No. 6, July, 2008 ($3.99, limited series)

1-Joe Hill-s/Gabriel Rodriguez-a 10.00
1-Second printing 4.00
2-6 4.00
...: Free Comic Book day Edition (5/11) r/story from Crown of Shadows 2.00
...: Welcome to Lovecraft Legacy Edition #1 (8/10, $1.00) r/#1; synopsis of later issues 2.00
...: Welcome to Lovecraft Special Edition #1 SC (9/09, $5.99) Hill-s/Rodriguez-a; script; back-up story with final art from Seth Fisher 6.00

LOCKE & KEY: CROWN OF SHADOWS
IDW Publ.: Nov, 2009 - No. 6, Apr, 2010 ($3.99, limited series)

1-6-Joe Hill-s/Gabriel Rodriguez-a 4.00

LOCKE & KEY: HEAD GAMES
IDW Publ.: Jan, 2009 - No. 6, Jun, 2009 ($3.99, limited series)

1-6-Joe Hill-s/Gabriel Rodriguez-a. 3-EC style-c 4.00

LOCKE & KEY: KEYS TO THE KINGDOM
IDW Publ.: Sept, 2010 - Present ($3.99, limited series)

1-5-Joe Hill-s/Gabriel Rodriguez-a 4.00

LOCKJAW AND THE PET AVENGERS (Also see Tails of the Pet Avengers)
Marvel Comics: July, 2009 - No. 4, Oct, 2009 ($2.99, limited series)

1-4-Lockheed, Frog Thor, Zabu, Lockjaw and Redwing team up; 2 covers on each 3.00

LOCKJAW AND THE PET AVENGERS UNLEASHED
Marvel Comics: May, 2010 - No. 4, Aug, 2010 ($2.99, limited series)

1-4-Eliopoulos-s/Guara-a; 2 covers on each 3.00

LOCO (Magazine) (Satire)
Satire Publications: Aug, 1958 - V1#3, Jan, 1959

	GD	VG	FN	VF	VF/NM	NM-
V1#1-Chic Stone-a	9	18	27	47	61	75
V1#2,3-Severin-a, 2 pgs. Davis; 3-Heath-a	7	14	21	35	43	50

LOGAN (Wolverine)
Marvel Comics: May, 2008 - No. 3, Jul, 2008 ($3.99, limited series)

1-3-Vaughan-s/Risso-a/c; regular & B&W editions for each 4.00

LOGAN: PATH OF THE WARLORD
Marvel Comics: Feb, 1996 ($5.95, one-shot)

1-John Paul Leon-a 6.00

LOGAN: SHADOW SOCIETY
Marvel Comics: 1996 ($5.95, one-shot)

1 6.00

LOGAN'S RUN
Marvel Comics Group: Jan, 1977 - No. 7, July, 1977

	GD	VG	FN	VF	VF/NM	NM-
1: 1-5-Based on novel & movie	2	4	6	8	10	12
2-5,7: 6,7-New stories adapted from novel	1	2	3	5	6	8
6-1st Thanos (also see Iron Man #55) solo story (back-up) by Zeck (6/77)	4	8	12	24	37	50
6-(35¢-c variant, limited distribution)	8	16	24	54	90	125
7-(35¢-c variant, limited distribution)	3	6	9	20	30	40

NOTE: **Austin** a-6i. **Gulacy** c-6. **Kane** c-7p. **Perez** a-1-5p; c-1-5p. **Sutton** a-6p, 7p.

LOIS & CLARK, THE NEW ADVENTURES OF SUPERMAN
DC Comics: 1994 ($9.95, one-shot)

	GD	VG	FN	VF	VF/NM	NM-
1-r/Man of Steel #2, Superman Ann. 1, Superman #9 & 11, Action #600 & 655, Adventures of Superman #445, 462 & 466	1	3	4	6	8	10

LOIS LANE (Also see Daring New Adventures of Supergirl, Showcase #9,10 & Superman's Girlfriend...)
DC Comics: Aug, 1986 - No. 2, Sept, 1986 ($1.50, 52 pgs.)

1,2-Morrow-c/a in each 4.00

LOKI (Thor)
Marvel Comics: Sept, 2004 - No. 4, Nov, 2004 ($3.50)

1-4-Rodi-s/Ribic-a/c 3.50
HC (2005, $17.99, with dustjacket) oversized r/#1-4; original proposal and sketch pages 18.00
SC (2007, $12.99) r/#1-4; original proposal and sketch pages 13.00

LOKI (Thor)
Marvel Comics: Dec, 2010 - No. 4, May, 2011 ($3.99, limited series)

1-4-Aguirre-Sacasa-s/Fiumara-a. 2-Balder dies 4.00

LOLLY AND PEPPER
Dell Publishing Co.: No. 832, Sept, 1957 - July, 1962

	GD	VG	FN	VF	VF/NM	NM-
Four Color 832(#1)	5	10	15	30	48	65
Four Color 940,978,1086,1206	4	8	12	22	34	45
01-459-207 (7/62)	3	6	9	18	27	35

LOMAX (See Police Action)

LONDON'S DARK
Escape/Titan: 1989 ($8.95, B&W, graphic novel)

	GD	VG	FN	VF	VF/NM	NM-
nn-James Robinson script; Paul Johnson-c/a	1	2	3	5	7	9

LONE
Dark Horse Comics: Sept, 2003 - No. 6, Mar, 2004 ($2.99)

1-6-Stuart Moore-s/Jerome Opeña-a/Templesmith-c 3.00

LONE EAGLE (The Flame No. 5 on)
Ajax/Farrell Publications: Apr-May, 1954 - No. 4, Oct-Nov, 1954

	GD	VG	FN	VF	VF/NM	NM-
1	13	26	39	74	105	135
2-4: 3-Bondage-c	9	18	27	50	65	80

LONE GUNMEN, THE (From the X-Files)
Dark Horse Comics: June, 2001 ($2.99, one-shot)

1-Paul Lee-a; photo-c 3.00

LONELY HEART (Formerly Dear Lonely Hearts; Dear Heart #15 on)
Ajax/Farrell Publ. (Excellent Publ.): No. 9, Mar, 1955 - No. 14, Feb, 1956

	GD	VG	FN	VF	VF/NM	NM-
9-Kamen*esque*-a; (Last precode)	10	20	30	58	79	100
10-14	8	16	24	40	50	60

LONE RANGER, THE (See Ace Comics, Aurora, Dell Giants,Future Comics, Golden Comics Digest #48, King Comics, Magic Comics & March of Comics #165, 174, 193, 208, 225, 238, 310, 322, 338, 350)

LONE RANGER, THE
Dell Publishing Co.: No. 3, 1939 - No. 167, Feb, 1947

	GD	VG	FN	VF	VF/NM	NM-
Large Feature Comic 3(1939)-Heigh-Yo Silver; text with illus. by Robert Weisman; also exists as a Whitman #710	187	374	561	1197	2049	2900
Large Feature Comic 7(1939)-Illustr. by Henry Vallely; Hi-Yo Silver the Lone Ranger to the Rescue; also exists as a Whitman #715	174	348	522	1114	1907	2700
Feature Book 21(1940), 24(1941)	90	180	270	576	988	1400
Four Color 82(1945)	37	74	111	286	568	850
Four Color 98(1945),118(1946)	27	54	81	197	399	600
Four Color 125(1946),136(1947)	18	36	54	131	266	400
Four Color 151,167(1947)	16	32	48	111	226	340

LONE RANGER, THE (Movie, radio & TV; Clayton Moore starred as Lone Ranger in the movies; No. 1-37: strip reprints)(See Dell Giants)
Dell Publishing Co.: Jan-Feb, 1948 - No. 145, May-July, 1962

Lone Ranger (2006 series) #24 © Classic Media

Lone Rider #8 © SUPR

Lone Wolf and Cub #15 © FC

	GD 2.0	VG 4.0	FN 6.0	VF 8.0	VF/NM 9.0	NM- 9.2
1 (36 pgs.)-The Lone Ranger, his horse Silver, companion Tonto & his horse Scout begin	54	108	162	459	930	1400
2 (52 pgs. begin, end #41)	27	54	81	192	389	585
3-5	21	42	63	150	300	450
6,7,9,10	16	32	48	117	239	360
8-Origin retold; Indian back-c begin, end #35	19	38	57	139	280	420
11-20: 11- "Young Hawk" Indian boy serial begins, ends #145	13	26	39	89	170	250
21,22,24-31: 51-Reprint. 31-1st Mask logo	10	20	30	72	131	190
23-Origin retold	13	26	39	89	170	250
32-37: 32-Painted-c begin. 36-Animal photo back-c begin, end #49. 37-Last newspaper-r issue; new outfit; red shirt becomes blue; most known copies show the blue shirt on-c & inside	9	18	27	65	113	160
37-Variant issue; Long Ranger wears a red shirt on-c and inside. A few copies of the red shirt outfit were printed before catching the mistake and changing the color to blue (rare)	16	32	48	114	232	350
38-41 (All 52 pgs.) 38-Paul S. Newman-s (wrote most of the stories #38-on)	9	18	27	63	107	150
42-50 (36 pgs.)	8	16	24	54	90	125
51-74 (52 pgs.): 56-One pg. origin story of Lone Ranger & Tonto. 71-Blank inside-c	7	14	21	50	83	115
75,77-99: 79-X-mas-c	7	14	21	47	76	105
76-Classic flag-c	7	14	21	50	83	115
100	8	16	24	54	90	125
101-111: Last painted-c	6	12	18	43	69	95
112-Clayton Moore photo-c begin, end #145	16	32	48	114	232	350
113-117: 117-10¢ &15¢-c exist	10	20	30	70	125	180
118-Origin Lone Ranger, Tonto, & Silver retold; Special anniversary issue	21	42	63	150	300	450
119-140: 139-Fran Striker-s	9	18	27	65	113	160
141-145	10	20	30	68	119	170

NOTE: ***Hank Hartman*** *painted c(signed)-65, 66, 70, 75, 82; unsigned-64?, 67-69?, 71, 72, 73?, 74?, 76-78, 80, 81, 83-91, 92?, 93-111.* ***Ernest Nordli*** *painted c(signed)-42, 50, 52, 53, 56, 59, 60; unsigned-39-41, 44-49, 51, 54, 55, 57, 58, 61-63?*

LONE RANGER, THE
Gold Key (Reprints in #13-20): 9/64 - No. 16, 12/69; No. 17, 11/72; No. 18, 9/74 - No. 28, 3/77

	GD 2.0	VG 4.0	FN 6.0	VF 8.0	VF/NM 9.0	NM- 9.2
1-Retells origin	6	12	18	41	66	90
2	4	8	12	22	34	45
3-10: Small Bear-r in #6-12. 10-Last 12¢ issue	3	6	9	20	30	40
11-17	3	6	9	16	22	28
18-28	2	4	6	11	16	20
Golden West 1(30029-610, 10/66)-Giant; r/most Golden West #3 including Clayton Moore photo front/back-c	7	14	21	45	73	100

LONE RANGER
Dynamite Entertainment: 2006 - Present ($2.99/$3.50/$3.99)

	GD 2.0	VG 4.0	FN 6.0	VF 8.0	VF/NM 9.0	NM- 9.2
1-Retells origin; Carriello-a/Matthews-s; badge cover by Cassaday						4.00
1-Variant mask cover by Cassaday						5.00
1-Baltimore Comic-Con 2006 variant cover with masked face and horse silhouette						12.00
1-Directors' Cut ($4.99) r/#1 with comments at page bottoms, script and sketches						5.00
2-23: 2-Origin continues; Tonto app.						3.50
24-($3.99)						4.00
... and Tonto 1-4 (200-2010, $4.99) Cassaday-c						5.00
... Volume 1: Now and Forever TPB (2007, $19.99) r/#1-6; sketch pages						20.00

LONE RANGER AND TONTO, THE
Topps Comics: Aug, 1994 - No. 4, Nov, 1994 ($2.50, limited series)

	GD 2.0	VG 4.0	FN 6.0	VF 8.0	VF/NM 9.0	NM- 9.2
1-4: 3-Origin of Lone Ranger; Tonto leaves; Lansdale story, Truman-c/a in all.						3.00
1-4: Silver logo. 1-Signed by Lansdale and Truman						6.00
Trade paperback (1/95, $9.95)						10.00

LONE RANGER AND ZORRO: THE DEATH OF ZORRO, THE
Dynamite Entertainment: 2011 - No. 5 ($3.99, limited series)

	GD 2.0	VG 4.0	FN 6.0	VF 8.0	VF/NM 9.0	NM- 9.2
1,2: 1-Four covers by Alex Ross and others; Parks-s/Polls-a						4.00

LONE RANGER'S COMPANION TONTO, THE (TV)
Dell Publishing Co.: No. 312, Jan, 1951 - No. 33, Nov-Jan/58-59 (All painted-c)

	GD 2.0	VG 4.0	FN 6.0	VF 8.0	VF/NM 9.0	NM- 9.2
Four Color 312(#1, 1/51)	10	20	30	72	131	190
2(8-10/51),3: (#2 titled "Tonto")	6	12	18	43	69	95
4-10	6	12	18	37	59	80
11-20	5	10	15	32	51	70
21-33	4	8	12	28	44	60

NOTE: ***Ernest Nordli*** *painted c(signed)-2, 7; unsigned-3-6, 8-11, 12?, 13, 14, 18?, 22-24?*
See Aurora Comic Booklets.

LONE RANGER'S FAMOUS HORSE HI-YO SILVER, THE (TV)
Dell Publishing Co.: No. 369, Jan, 1952 - No. 36, Oct-Dec, 1960 (All painted-c, most by Sam Savitt) (Lone Ranger appears in most issues)

	GD 2.0	VG 4.0	FN 6.0	VF 8.0	VF/NM 9.0	NM- 9.2
Four Color 369(#1)-Silver's origin as told by The Lone Ranger	10	20	30	70	125	180
Four Color 392(#2, 4/52)	6	12	18	41	66	90
3(7-9/52)-10(4-6/52)	5	10	15	35	55	75
11-36	4	8	12	28	44	60

LONE RIDER (Also see The Rider)
Superior Comics(Farrell Publ.): Apr, 1951 - No. 26, Jul, 1955 (#3-on: 36 pgs.)

	GD 2.0	VG 4.0	FN 6.0	VF 8.0	VF/NM 9.0	NM- 9.2
1 (52 pgs.)-The Lone Rider & his horse Lightnin' begin; Kamenish-a begins	32	64	96	188	307	425
2 (52 pgs.)-The Golden Arrow begins (origin)	20	40	60	120	195	220
3-6: 6-Last Golden Arrow	17	34	51	98	154	210
7-Golden Arrow becomes Swift Arrow; origin of his shield	20	40	60	120	195	220
8-Origin Swift Arrow	18	36	54	107	169	230
9,10	12	24	36	69	97	125
11-14	10	20	30	54	72	90
15-Golden Arrow origin-r from #2, changing name to Swift Arrow	10	20	30	58	79	100
16-20,22-26: 23-Apache Kid app.	9	18	27	50	65	80
21-3-D effect-c	16	32	48	94	147	200

LONERS, THE
Marvel Comics: June, 2007 - No. 6, Jan, 2008 ($2.99, limited series)

	GD 2.0	VG 4.0	FN 6.0	VF 8.0	VF/NM 9.0	NM- 9.2
1-6-Cebulski-s/Moline-a/Pearson-c; Lightspeed, Spider-Woman, Ricochet app.						3.00
...: The Secret Lives of Super Heroes TPB (2008, $14.99) r/#1-6; sketch pages						15.00

LONE WOLF AND CUB
First Comics: May, 1987 - No. 45, Apr, 1991 ($1.95-$3.25, B&W, deluxe size)

	GD 2.0	VG 4.0	FN 6.0	VF 8.0	VF/NM 9.0	NM- 9.2
1-Frank Miller-c & intro.; reprints manga series by Koike & Kojima	1	2	3	6	8	10
1-2nd print, 3rd print, 2-2nd print						3.25
2-12: 6-72 pgs. origin issue						5.50
13-38,40: 40-Ploog-c						4.00
39-($5.95, 120 pgs.)-Ploog-c						6.50
41-44: 41-($3.95, 84 pgs.)-Ploog-c. 42-Ploog-c						6.00
45-Last issue; low print	2	4	6	8	10	12
Deluxe Edition ($19.95, B&W)						20.00

NOTE: ***Sienkiewicz*** *c-13-24.* ***Matt Wagner*** *c-25-30.*

LONE WOLF AND CUB (Trade paperbacks)
Dark Horse Comics: Aug, 2000 - No. 28 ($9.95, B&W, 4" x 6", approx. 300 pgs.)

	GD 2.0	VG 4.0	FN 6.0	VF 8.0	VF/NM 9.0	NM- 9.2
1-Collects First Comics reprint series; Frank Miller-c						18.00
1-(2nd printing)						12.00
1-(3rd-5th printings)						10.00
2,3-(1st printings)						12.00
2,3-(2nd printings)						10.00
4-28						10.00

LONE WOLF 2100 (Also see Reveal)
Dark Horse Comics: May, 2002 - No. 11, Dec, 2003 ($2.99, color)

	GD 2.0	VG 4.0	FN 6.0	VF 8.0	VF/NM 9.0	NM- 9.2
1-New homage to Lone Wolf and Cub; Kennedy-s/Velasco-a						4.00
2-11						3.00
...: The Red File (1/03, $2.99) character and story background files						3.00
... Vol. 1 - Shadows on Saplings TPB (2003, $12.95, 6" x 9") r/#1-4						13.00
... Vol. 2 - The Language of Chaos TPB (2003, $12.95, 6" x 9") r/#5-8, Dirty Tricks short story from Reveal						13.00

LONG BOW (...Indian Boy)(See Indians & Jumbo Comics #141)
Fiction House Mag. (Real Adventures Publ.): 1951 - No. 9, Wint, 1952/53

	GD 2.0	VG 4.0	FN 6.0	VF 8.0	VF/NM 9.0	NM- 9.2
1-Most covers by Maurice Whitman	17	34	51	98	154	210
2	11	22	33	60	83	105
3-9	10	20	30	54	72	90

LONG HOT SUMMER, THE
DC Comics (Milestone): Jul, 1995 - No. 3, Sept, 1995 ($2.95/$2.50, lim. series)

	GD 2.0	VG 4.0	FN 6.0	VF 8.0	VF/NM 9.0	NM- 9.2
1-3: 1-($2.95-c). 2,3-($2.50-c)						3.00

LONG JOHN SILVER & THE PIRATES (Formerly Terry & the Pirates)
Charlton Comics: No. 30, Aug, 1956 - No. 32, March, 1957 (TV)

	GD 2.0	VG 4.0	FN 6.0	VF 8.0	VF/NM 9.0	NM- 9.2
30-32: Whitman-c	10	20	30	54	72	90

LONGSHOT (Also see X-Men, 2nd Series #10)
Marvel Comics: Sept, 1985 - No. 6, Feb, 1986 (60¢, limited series)

1-6: 1-Art Adams/Whilce Portacio-c/a in all. 4-Spider-Man app. 6-Double size

Looney Tunes #70 © WB

Lorna, The Jungle Girl #7 © MAR

Lost in Space #1 © CBS

	GD 2.0	VG 4.0	FN 6.0	VF 8.0	VF/NM 9.0	NM- 9.2
	1	2	3	4	5	7
Trade Paperback (1989, $16.95)-r/#1-6						17.00

LONGSHOT
Marvel Comics: Feb, 1998 ($3.99, one-shot)

	GD 2.0	VG 4.0	FN 6.0	VF 8.0	VF/NM 9.0	NM- 9.2
1-DeMatteis-s/Zulli-a						4.00

LOOKING GLASS WARS: HATTER M
Image Comics (Desperado): Dec, 2005 - No. 4, Nov, 2006 ($3.99)

	GD 2.0	VG 4.0	FN 6.0	VF 8.0	VF/NM 9.0	NM- 9.2
1-4-Templesmith-a/c						4.00

LOONEY TUNES (2nd Series) (TV)
Gold Key/Whitman: April, 1975 - No. 47, June, 1984

	GD 2.0	VG 4.0	FN 6.0	VF 8.0	VF/NM 9.0	NM- 9.2
1-Reprints	4	8	12	22	34	45
2-10: 2,4-reprints	2	4	6	13	18	22
11-20: 16-reprints	2	4	6	9	12	15
21-30	2	3	4	6	8	10
31,32,36-42(2/82)	1	2	3	5	6	8
33-(8/80)-35 (Whitman pre-pack only, scarce)	3	6	9	17	25	32
43(4/82),44(6/83) (low distribution)	2	4	6	9	13	16
45-47 (All #90296 on-c; nd, nd code, pre-pack) 45(8/83), 46(3/84), 47(6/84)	3	6	9	14	20	26

LOONEY TUNES (3rd Series) (TV)
DC Comics: Apr, 1994 - Present ($1.50/$1.75/$1.95/$1.99/$2.25/$2.50/$2.99)

	GD 2.0	VG 4.0	FN 6.0	VF 8.0	VF/NM 9.0	NM- 9.2
1-10,120: 1-Marvin Martian-c/sty; Bugs Bunny, Roadrunner, Daffy begin. 120-($2.95-C)						4.00
11-119,121-187: 23-34-($1.75-c). 35-43-($1.95-c). 44-Begin $1.99-c. 93-Begin $2.25-c. 100-Art by various incl. Kyle Baker, Marie Severin, Darwyn Cooke, Jill Thompson						3.00
188-196: 188-Begin $2.99-c; Scooby-Doo spoof. 193-Christmas-c						3.00
...Back In Action Movie Adaptation (12/03, $3.95) photo-c						4.00

LOONEY TUNES AND MERRIE MELODIES COMICS ("Looney Tunes" #166(8/55) on)
(Also see Porky's Duck Hunt)
Dell Publishing Co.: 1941 - No. 246, July-Sept, 1962

	GD 2.0	VG 4.0	FN 6.0	VF 8.0	VF/NM 9.0	NM- 9.2
1-Porky Pig, Bugs Bunny, Daffy Duck, Elmer Fudd, Mary Jane & Sniffles, Pat Patsy and Pete begin (1st comic book app. of each). Bugs Bunny story by Win Smith (early Mickey Mouse artist)	1125	2250	3375	8500	15,500	22,500
2 (11/41)	152	304	456	1330	2715	4100
3-Kandi the Cave Kid begins by Walt Kelly; also in #4-6,8,11,15	110	220	330	935	1893	2850
4-Kelly-a	110	220	330	935	1893	2850
5-Bugs Bunny The Super-Duper Rabbit story (1st funny animal super hero, 3/42; also see Coo Coo); Kelly-a	83	166	249	706	1428	2150
6,8-Kelly-a	65	130	195	553	1127	1700
7,9,10: 9-Painted-c. 10-Flag-c	48	96	144	408	829	1250
11,15-Kelly-a; 15-X-Mas-c	49	98	147	417	846	1275
12-14,16-19	38	76	114	304	602	900
20-25: Pat, Patsy & Pete by Walt Kelly in all. 20-War Bonds-c	33	66	99	254	502	750
26-30	25	50	75	180	360	540
31-40: 33-War Bonds-c. 39-X-Mas-c	20	40	60	144	290	435
41-50: 45-War Bonds-c	15	30	45	106	216	325
51-60	13	26	39	89	170	250
61-80	9	18	27	65	113	160
81-99: 87-X-Mas-c	8	16	24	58	97	135
100	9	18	27	61	103	145
101-120	7	14	21	47	76	105
121-150	6	12	18	41	67	90
151-200: 159-X-Mas-c	6	12	18	37	59	80
201-240	5	10	15	34	55	75
241-246	6	12	18	37	59	80

LOONY SPORTS (Magazine)
3-Strikes Publishing Co.: Spring, 1975 (68 pgs.)

	GD 2.0	VG 4.0	FN 6.0	VF 8.0	VF/NM 9.0	NM- 9.2
1-Sports satire	2	4	6	8	11	14

LOOSE CANNON (Also see Action Comics Annual #5 & Showcase '94 #5)
DC Comics: June, 1995 - No. 4, Sept, 1995 ($1.75, limited series)

	GD 2.0	VG 4.0	FN 6.0	VF 8.0	VF/NM 9.0	NM- 9.2
1-4: Adam Pollina-a. 1-Superman app.						3.00

LOOY DOT DOPE
United Features Syndicate: No. 13, 1939

	GD 2.0	VG 4.0	FN 6.0	VF 8.0	VF/NM 9.0	NM- 9.2
Single Series 13	30	60	90	177	289	400

LORD JIM (See Movie Comics)

LORD PUMPKIN
Malibu Comics (Ultraverse): Oct, 1994 ($2.50, one-shot)

	GD 2.0	VG 4.0	FN 6.0	VF 8.0	VF/NM 9.0	NM- 9.2
0-Two covers						3.00

LORD PUMPKIN/NECROMANTRA
Malibu Comics (Ultraverse): Apr, 1995 - No. 4, July, 1995 ($2.95, limited series, flip book)

	GD 2.0	VG 4.0	FN 6.0	VF 8.0	VF/NM 9.0	NM- 9.2
1-4						3.00

LORDS OF AVALON: KNIGHT OF DARKNESS
Marvel Comics: Jan, 2008 - No. 6, July, 2009 ($3.99, limited series)

	GD 2.0	VG 4.0	FN 6.0	VF 8.0	VF/NM 9.0	NM- 9.2
1-6-($3.99)-Kenyon & Furth-s; Ohtsuka-a/c						4.00

LORDS OF AVALON: SWORD OF DARKNESS
Marvel Comics: Apr, 2008 - No. 6, Sept, 2006 ($3.99/$2.99, limited series)

	GD 2.0	VG 4.0	FN 6.0	VF 8.0	VF/NM 9.0	NM- 9.2
1-($3.99)-Adaptation of Sherrilyn Kenyon's Arthurian fantasy; Ohtsuka-a/c						4.00
2-6-($2.99)						3.00
HC (2008, $19.99) r/#1-6; two covers						20.00

LORNA, RELIC WRANGLER
Image Comics: Mar, 2011 ($3.99, one-shot)

	GD 2.0	VG 4.0	FN 6.0	VF 8.0	VF/NM 9.0	NM- 9.2
1-Micah Harris-s; J. Bone-c						4.00

LORNA THE JUNGLE GIRL (...Jungle Queen #1-5)
Atlas Comics (NPI 1/OMC 2-11/NPI 12-26): July, 1953 - No. 26, Aug, 1957

	GD 2.0	VG 4.0	FN 6.0	VF 8.0	VF/NM 9.0	NM- 9.2
1-Origin & 1st app.	40	80	120	242	401	560
2-Intro. & 1st app. Greg Knight	20	40	60	118	192	265
3-5	18	36	54	105	165	225
6-11: 11-Last pre-code (1/55)	15	30	45	86	133	180
12-17,19-26: 14-Colletta & Maneely-c	14	28	42	80	115	150
18-Williamson/Colletta-c	14	28	42	82	121	160

NOTE: ***Brodsky*** *c-1-3, 5, 9.* ***Everett*** *c-21, 23-26.* ***Heath*** *c-6, 7.* ***Maneely*** *c-12, 15.* ***Romita*** *a-18, 20, 22, 24, 26.* ***Shores*** *a-14-16, 18, 24, 26; c-11, 13, 16.* ***Tuska*** *a-6.*

LOSERS (Inspired the 2010 movie)
DC Comics (Vertigo): Aug, 2003 - No. 32, Mar, 2006 ($2.95/$2.99)

	GD 2.0	VG 4.0	FN 6.0	VF 8.0	VF/NM 9.0	NM- 9.2
1-Andy Diggle-s/Jock-a						4.00
1-Special Edition (6/10, $1.00) r/#1 with "What's Next?" logo on cover						1.00
2-32: 15-Bagged with Sky Captain CD. 20-Oliver-a. 27-Wilson-a						3.00
...: Ante Up TPB (2004, $9.95) r/#1-6						10.00
...: Book Two TPB (2010, $24.99) r/#13-32; Ian Rankin intro.; preliminary art pages						25.00
...: Close Quarters TPB (2005, $14.99) r/#20-25						15.00
...: Double Down TPB (2004, $12.95) r/#7-12						13.00
...: Endgame TPB (2006, $14.99) r/#26-32						15.00
...: Trifecta TPB (2005, $14.99) r/#13-19						15.00
...: Volumes One and Two TPB (2010, $19.99) r/#1-12; new intro. by Diggle						20.00

LOSERS SPECIAL (See Our Fighting Forces #123)(Also see G.I. Combat & Our Fighting Forces)
DC Comics: Sept, 1985 ($1.25, one-shot)

	GD 2.0	VG 4.0	FN 6.0	VF 8.0	VF/NM 9.0	NM- 9.2
1-Capt. Storm, Gunner & Sarge; Crisis on Infinite Earths x-over						6.00

LOST, THE
Chaos! Comics: Dec, 1997 - No. 3 ($2.95, B&W, unfinished limited series)

	GD 2.0	VG 4.0	FN 6.0	VF 8.0	VF/NM 9.0	NM- 9.2
1-3-Andreyko-script: 1-Russell back-c						3.00

LOST BOYS: REIGN OF FROGS (Based on the 1987 vampire movie)
DC Comics (WildStorm): Jul, 2008 - No. 4, Oct, 2008 ($3.50, limited series)

	GD 2.0	VG 4.0	FN 6.0	VF 8.0	VF/NM 9.0	NM- 9.2
1-4-Rodionoff-s/Gomez-a; Edgar Frog app.						3.50
TPB (2009, $12.99) r/#1-4						13.00

LOST CONTINENT
Eclipse Int'l: Sept, 1990 - No. 6, 1991 ($3.50, B&W, squarebound, 60 pgs.)

	GD 2.0	VG 4.0	FN 6.0	VF 8.0	VF/NM 9.0	NM- 9.2
1-6: Japanese story translated to English						3.50

LOST IN SPACE (Movie)
Dark Horse Comics: Apr, 1998 - No. 3, July, 1998 ($2.95, limited series)

	GD 2.0	VG 4.0	FN 6.0	VF 8.0	VF/NM 9.0	NM- 9.2
1-3-Continuation of 1998 movie; Erskine-c						3.00

LOST IN SPACE (TV)(Also see Space Family Robinson)
Innovation Publishing: Aug, 1991 - No. 12, Jan, 1993 ($2.50, limited series)

	GD 2.0	VG 4.0	FN 6.0	VF 8.0	VF/NM 9.0	NM- 9.2
1-12: Bill Mumy (Will Robinson) scripts in #1-9. 9-Perez-c						3.00
1,2-Special Ed.; r/#1,2 plus new art & new-c						3.00
Annual 1,2 (1991, 1992, $2.95, 52 pgs.)						4.00
...: Project Robinson (11/93, $2.50) 1st & only part of intended series						3.00

LOST IN SPACE: VOYAGE TO THE BOTTOM OF THE SOUL
Innovation Publishing: No. 13, Aug, 1993 - No. 18, 1994 ($2.50, limited series)

	GD 2.0	VG 4.0	FN 6.0	VF 8.0	VF/NM 9.0	NM- 9.2
13(V1#1, $2.95)-Embossed silver logo edition; Bill Mumy scripts begin; painted-c						3.00
13(V1#1, $4.95)-Embossed gold logo edition bagged w/poster						5.00
14-18: Painted-c						3.00

NOTE: *Originally intended to be a 12 issue limited series.*

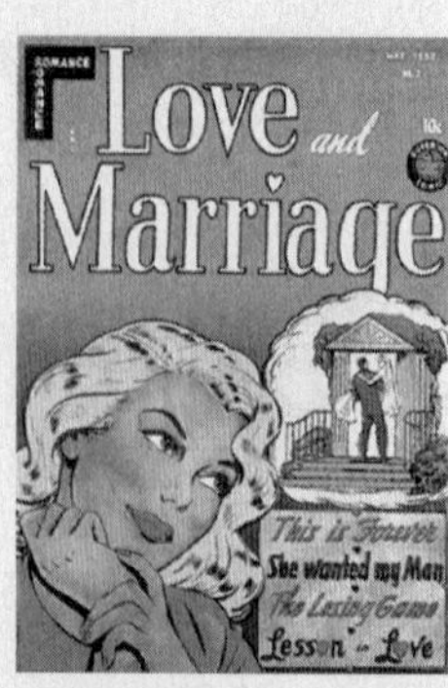

Love and Marriage #2 © SUPR

Love Confessions #4 © QUA

Love Diary #34 © OPC

LOST ONES, THE
Image Comics: Mar, 2000 ($2.95)

	GD 2.0	VG 4.0	FN 6.0	VF 8.0	VF/NM 9.0	NM- 9.2
1-Ken Penders-s/a						3.00

LOST PLANET
Eclipse Comics: 5/87 - No. 5, 2/88; No. 6, 3/89 (Mini-series, Baxter paper)

	GD 2.0	VG 4.0	FN 6.0	VF 8.0	VF/NM 9.0	NM- 9.2
1-6-Bo Hampton-c/a in all						3.00

LOST WAGON TRAIN, THE (See Zane Grey Four Color 583)

LOST WORLD, THE
Dell Publishing Co.: No. 1145, Nov-Jan, 1960-61

	GD 2.0	VG 4.0	FN 6.0	VF 8.0	VF/NM 9.0	NM- 9.2
Four Color 1145-Movie, Gil Kane-a, photo-c; 1pg. Conan Doyle biography by Torres	9	18	27	64	110	155

LOST WORLD, THE (See Jurassic Park)
Topps Comics: May, 1997 - No. 4, Aug, 1997 ($2.95, limited series)

	GD 2.0	VG 4.0	FN 6.0	VF 8.0	VF/NM 9.0	NM- 9.2
1-4-Movie adaption						3.00

LOST WORLDS (Weird Tales of the Past and Future)
Standard Comics: No. 5, Oct, 1952 - No. 6, Dec, 1952

	GD 2.0	VG 4.0	FN 6.0	VF 8.0	VF/NM 9.0	NM- 9.2
5- "Alice in Terrorland" by Alex Toth; J. Katz-a	44	88	132	277	469	660
6-Toth-a	36	72	108	216	351	485

LOTS 'O' FUN COMICS
Robert Allen Co.: 1940's? (5¢, heavy stock, blue covers)

nn-Contents can vary; Felix, Planet Comics known; contents would determine value. Similar to Up-To-Date Comics. Remainders - re-packaged.

LOU GEHRIG (See The Pride of the Yankees)

LOVE ADVENTURES (Actual Confessions #13)
Marvel (IPS)/Atlas Comics (MPI): Oct, 1949; No. 2, Jan, 1950; No. 3, Feb, 1951 - No. 12, Aug, 1952

	GD 2.0	VG 4.0	FN 6.0	VF 8.0	VF/NM 9.0	NM- 9.2
1-Photo-c	18	36	54	105	165	225
2-Powell-a; Tyrone Power, Gene Tierney photo-c	15	30	45	86	133	180
3-8,10-12: 8-Robinson-a	10	20	30	58	79	100
9-Everett-a	11	22	33	60	83	105

LOVE AND MARRIAGE
Superior Comics Ltd. (Canada): Mar, 1952 - No. 16, Sept, 1954

	GD 2.0	VG 4.0	FN 6.0	VF 8.0	VF/NM 9.0	NM- 9.2
1	15	30	45	85	130	175
2	9	18	27	52	69	85
3-10	9	18	27	47	61	75
11-16	8	16	24	42	54	65
I.W. Reprint #1,2,8,11,14: 8-r/Love and Marriage #3. 11-r/Love and Marriage #11	2	4	6	9	13	16
Super Reprint #10('63),15,17('64):15-Love and Marriage #?	2	4	6	9	13	16

NOTE: *All issues have* **Kamenish** *art.*

LOVE AND ROCKETS
Fantagraphics Books: July, 1982 - No. 50, May, 1996 ($2.95/$2.50/$4.95, B&W, mature)

	GD 2.0	VG 4.0	FN 6.0	VF 8.0	VF/NM 9.0	NM- 9.2
1-B&W-c (6/82, $2.95; small size, publ. by Hernandez Bros.)(800 printed)	6	12	18	41	66	90
1 (Fall, '82; color-c)	4	8	12	22	34	45
1-2nd & 3rd printing, 2-11,29-31: 2nd printings						3.00
2	2	4	6	11	16	20
3-10	1	3	4	6	8	10
11-49: 30 ($2.95, 52 pgs.)						5.00
50-($4.95)						6.00

LOVE AND ROCKETS (Volume 2)
Fantagraphics Books: Spring, 2001 - Present ($3.95-$7.99, B&W, mature)

	GD 2.0	VG 4.0	FN 6.0	VF 8.0	VF/NM 9.0	NM- 9.2
1-9-Gilbert, Jaime and Mario Hernandez-s/a						5.00
10-($5.95)						6.00
11-19-($4.50)						4.50
20-($7.99)						8.00

LOVE AND ROMANCE
Charlton Comics: Sept, 1971 - No. 24, Sept, 1975

	GD 2.0	VG 4.0	FN 6.0	VF 8.0	VF/NM 9.0	NM- 9.2
1	3	6	9	18	27	35
2-5,7-10	2	4	6	10	14	18
6-David Cassidy pin-up; grey-tone cover	3	6	9	14	19	24
11,13-24	2	4	6	8	10	12
12-Susan Dey poster	2	4	6	10	14	18

LOVE AT FIRST SIGHT
Ace Magazines (RAR Publ. Co./Periodical House): Oct, 1949 - No. 43, Nov, 1956 (Photo-c: 18-42)

	GD 2.0	VG 4.0	FN 6.0	VF 8.0	VF/NM 9.0	NM- 9.2
1-Painted-c	17	34	51	98	154	210
2-Painted-c	11	22	33	60	83	105
3-10: 4,7-Painted-c	10	20	30	54	72	90
11-20	9	18	27	50	65	80
21-33: 33-Last pre-code	9	18	27	47	61	75
34-43	8	16	24	44	57	70

LOVE BUG, THE (See Movie Comics)

LOVEBUNNY AND MR. HELL
Devil's Due Publ./Image Comics: 2002 - 2004 ($2.95, B&W, one-shots)

	GD 2.0	VG 4.0	FN 6.0	VF 8.0	VF/NM 9.0	NM- 9.2
1-Tim Seeley-s						3.00
...: A Day in the Lovelife (Image, 2003) Blaylock-a						3.00
...: Savage Love (Image, 2003) Seeley-s/a; Savage Dragon app.; Seeley & Larsen-c						3.00
TPB (4/04, $9.95, digest-sized) reprints						10.00

LOVE CLASSICS
A Lover's Magazine/Marvel: Nov, 1949 - No. 2, Feb, 1950 (Photo-c, 52 pgs.)

	GD 2.0	VG 4.0	FN 6.0	VF 8.0	VF/NM 9.0	NM- 9.2
1,2: 2-Virginia Mayo photo-c; 30 pg. story "I Turned Into a Small-Town Flirt"	16	32	48	94	147	200

LOVE CONFESSIONS
Quality Comics: Oct, 1949 - No. 54, Dec, 1956 (Photo-c: 3,4,6,7,9,11-18,21,24,25)

	GD 2.0	VG 4.0	FN 6.0	VF 8.0	VF/NM 9.0	NM- 9.2
1-Ward-c/a, 9 pgs; Gustavson-a	32	64	96	188	307	425
2-Gustavson-a; Ward-c	16	32	48	94	147	200
3	11	22	33	64	90	115
4-Crandall-a	13	26	39	72	101	130
5-Ward-a, 7 pgs.	14	28	42	80	115	150
6,7,9,11-13,15,16,18: 7-Van Johnson photo-c. 8-Robert Mitchum & Jane Russell photo-c	10	20	30	54	72	90
8,10-Ward-a (2 stories in #10)	14	28	42	80	115	150
14,17,19,22-Ward-a; 17-Faith Domerque photo-c	14	28	42	76	108	140
20-Ward-a(2)	14	28	42	80	115	150
21,23-28,30-38,40-42: Last precode, 4/55	9	18	27	47	61	75
29-Ward-a	13	26	39	72	101	130
39,53-Matt Baker-a	11	22	33	62	86	110
43,44,46,47,50-52,54: 47-Ward-c?	8	16	24	44	57	70
45,48-Ward-a	10	20	30	54	72	90
49-Baker-c/a	13	26	39	74	105	135

LOVECRAFT
DC Comics: 2003 (graphic novel)

	GD 2.0	VG 4.0	FN 6.0	VF 8.0	VF/NM 9.0	NM- 9.2
Hardcover ($24.95) Rodionoff & Giffen-s/Breccia-a; intro. by John Carpenter						25.00
Softcover ($17.95)						18.00

LOVE DIARY
Our Publishing Co./Toytown/Patches: July, 1949 - No. 48, Oct, 1955 (Photo-c: 1-24,27-29) (52 pgs. #1-11?)

	GD 2.0	VG 4.0	FN 6.0	VF 8.0	VF/NM 9.0	NM- 9.2
1-Krigstein-a	21	42	63	124	202	280
2,3-Krigstein & Mort Leav-a in each	15	30	45	83	124	165
4-8	11	22	33	60	83	105
9,10-Everett-a	11	22	33	64	90	115
11-15,17-20	10	20	30	54	72	90
16- Mort Leav-a, 3 pg. Baker-sty. Leav-a	10	20	30	58	79	100
21-30,32-48: 45-Leav-a. 47-Last precode(12/54)	9	18	27	50	65	80
31-John Buscema headlights-c	11	22	33	62	86	110

LOVE DIARY (Diary Loves #2 on; title change due to previously published title)
Quality Comics Group: Sept, 1949

	GD 2.0	VG 4.0	FN 6.0	VF 8.0	VF/NM 9.0	NM- 9.2
1-Ward-c/a, 9 pgs.	33	64	96	188	307	425

LOVE DIARY
Charlton Comics: July, 1958 - No. 102, Dec, 1976

	GD 2.0	VG 4.0	FN 6.0	VF 8.0	VF/NM 9.0	NM- 9.2
1	11	22	33	62	86	110
2	8	16	24	40	50	60
3-5,7-10: 10-Photo-c	7	14	21	35	43	50
6-Torres-a	7	14	21	37	46	55
11-20: 20-Photo-c	3	6	9	18	27	35
21-40	3	6	9	16	22	28
41-60	2	4	6	13	18	22
61-78,80,100-102	2	4	6	9	13	16
79-David Cassidy pin-up	2	4	6	13	18	22
81,83,84,86-99	2	4	6	8	10	12
82,85: 82-Partridge Family poster. 85-Danny poster	2	4	6	10	14	18

LOVE DOCTOR (See Dr. Anthony King...)

LOVE DRAMAS (True Secrets No. 3 on?)
Marvel Comics (IPS): Oct, 1949 - No. 2, Jan, 1950

Love Experiences #6 © ACE

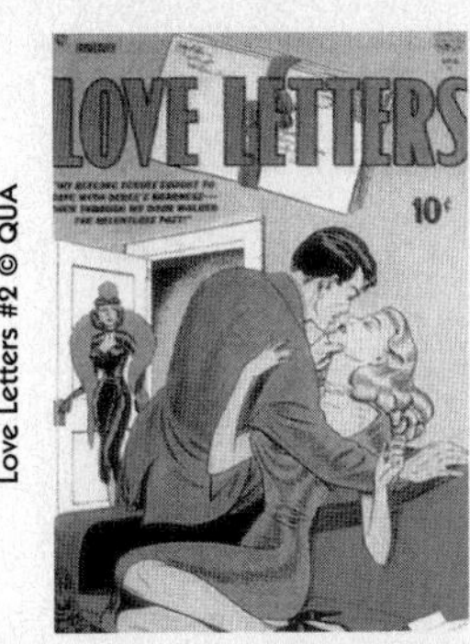

Love Letters #2 © QUA

Lovers' Lane #4 © LEV

	GD 2.0	VG 4.0	FN 6.0	VF 8.0	VF/NM 9.0	NM- 9.2
1-Jack Kamen-a; photo-c	19	38	57	111	176	240
2-Photo-c	14	28	42	80	115	150

LOVE EXPERIENCES (Challenge of the Unknown No. 6)
Ace Periodicals (A.A. Wyn/Periodical House): Oct, 1949 - No. 5, June, 1950; No. 6, Apr, 1951 - No. 38, June, 1956

	GD 2.0	VG 4.0	FN 6.0	VF 8.0	VF/NM 9.0	NM- 9.2
1-Painted-c	16	32	48	94	147	200
2	10	20	30	58	79	100
3-5: 5-Painted-c	10	20	30	54	72	90
6-10	9	18	27	50	65	80
11-30: 30-Last pre-code (2/55)	8	16	24	44	57	70
31-38: 38-Indicia date-6/56; c-date-8/56	8	16	24	42	54	65

NOTE: ***Anne Brewster** a-15. Photo c-4, 15-35, 38.*

LOVE FIGHTS (Also see Free Comic Book Day Edition in the Promotional Comics section)
Oni Press: June, 2003 - No. 12, Aug, 2004 ($2.99, B&W)

	GD 2.0	VG 4.0	FN 6.0	VF 8.0	VF/NM 9.0	NM- 9.2
1-12-Andi Watson-s/a						3.00
Vol. 1 TPB (4/04, $14.95, digest-size) r/#1-6						15.00

LOVE JOURNAL
Our Publishing Co.: No. 10, Oct, 1951 - No. 25, July, 1954

	GD 2.0	VG 4.0	FN 6.0	VF 8.0	VF/NM 9.0	NM- 9.2
10	15	30	45	83	124	165
11-15,17-25: 19-Mort Leav-a	10	20	30	58	76	95
16-Buscema headlight-c	12	24	36	67	94	120

LOVELAND
Mutual Mag./Eye Publ. (Marvel): Nov, 1949 - No. 2, Feb, 1950 (52 pgs.)

	GD 2.0	VG 4.0	FN 6.0	VF 8.0	VF/NM 9.0	NM- 9.2
1,2-Photo-c	14	28	42	78	112	145

LOVELESS
DC Comics: Dec, 2005 - No. 24, Jun, 2008 ($2.99)

	GD 2.0	VG 4.0	FN 6.0	VF 8.0	VF/NM 9.0	NM- 9.2
1-24: 1-Azzarello-s/Frusin-a. 6-8,15,22,23,24-Zezelj-a. 11,12,16-21-Dell'Edera-a						3.00
...: A Kin of Homecoming TPB (2006, $9.99) r/#1-5						10.00
...: Blackwater Falls TPB (2008, $19.99) r/#13-24						20.00
...: Thicker Than Blackwater TPB (2007, $14.99) r/#6-12						15.00

LOVE LESSONS
Harvey Comics/Key Publ. No. 5: Oct, 1949 - No. 5, June, 1950

	GD 2.0	VG 4.0	FN 6.0	VF 8.0	VF/NM 9.0	NM- 9.2
1-Metallic silver-c printed over the cancelled covers of Love Letters #1; indicia title is "Love Letters"	15	30	45	85	130	175
2-Powell-a; photo-c	9	18	27	52	69	85
3-5: 3,4-Photo-c	8	16	24	42	54	65

LOVE LETTERS (10/49, Harvey; advertised but never published; covers were printed before cancellation and were used as the cover to Love Lessons #1)

LOVE LETTERS (Love Secrets No. 32 on)
Quality Comics: 11/49 - #6, 9/50; #7, 3/51 - #31, 6/53; #32, 2/54 - #51, 12/56

	GD 2.0	VG 4.0	FN 6.0	VF 8.0	VF/NM 9.0	NM- 9.2
1-Ward-c, Gustavson-a	25	50	75	150	245	340
2-Ward-c, Gustavson-a	20	40	60	120	195	270
3-Gustavson-a	15	30	45	85	130	175
4-Ward-a, 9 pgs.; photo-c	19	38	57	112	179	245
5-8,10	11	22	33	60	83	105
9-One pg. Ward "Be Popular with the Opposite Sex"; Robert Mitchum photo-c	12	24	36	67	94	120
11-Ward-r/Broadway Romances #2 & retitled	12	24	36	67	94	120
12-15,18-20	10	20	30	54	72	90
16,17-Ward-a; 16-Anthony Quinn photo-c. 17-Jane Russell photo-c	15	30	45	83	124	165
21-29	9	18	27	52	69	85
30,31(6/53)-Ward-a	11	22	33	60	83	105
32(2/54)-39: 37-Ward-a. 38-Crandall-a. 39-Last precode (4/55)	9	18	27	47	61	75
40-48	8	16	24	44	57	70
49-51: 49,50-Baker-a. 51-Baker-c	12	24	36	69	97	125

NOTE: *Photo-c on most 3-28.*

LOVE LIFE
P. L. Publishing Co.: Nov, 1951

	GD 2.0	VG 4.0	FN 6.0	VF 8.0	VF/NM 9.0	NM- 9.2
1	11	22	33	60	83	105

LOVELORN (Confessions of the Lovelorn #52 on)
American Comics Group (Michel Publ./Regis Publ.): Aug-Sept, 1949 - No. 51, July, 1954 (No. 1-26: 52 pgs.)

	GD 2.0	VG 4.0	FN 6.0	VF 8.0	VF/NM 9.0	NM- 9.2
1	17	34	51	98	154	210
2	11	22	33	60	83	105
3-10	9	18	27	52	69	85
11-20,22-48: 18-Drucker-a(2 pgs.). 46-Lazarus-a	8	16	24	44	57	70
21-Prostitution story	10	20	30	58	79	100
49-51-Has 3-D effect-c/stories	17	34	51	98	154	210

LOVE MEMORIES
Fawcett Publications: 1949 (no month) - No. 4, July, 1950 (All photo-c)

	GD 2.0	VG 4.0	FN 6.0	VF 8.0	VF/NM 9.0	NM- 9.2
1	15	30	45	88	137	185
2-4: 2-(Win/49-50)	10	20	30	56	76	95

LOVE ME TENDERLOIN: A CAL McDONALD MYSTERY
Dark Horse Comics: Jan, 2004 ($2.99, one-shot)

	GD 2.0	VG 4.0	FN 6.0	VF 8.0	VF/NM 9.0	NM- 9.2
1-Niles-s/Templesmith-a/c						3.00

LOVE MYSTERY
Fawcett Publications: June, 1950 - No. 3, Oct, 1950 (All photo-c)

	GD 2.0	VG 4.0	FN 6.0	VF 8.0	VF/NM 9.0	NM- 9.2
1-George Evans-a	21	42	63	124	202	280
2,3-Evans-a. 3-Powell-a	16	32	48	92	144	195

LOVE PROBLEMS (See Fox Giants)

LOVE PROBLEMS AND ADVICE ILLUSTRATED (see True Love...)

LOVE ROMANCES (Formerly Ideal #5)
Timely/Marvel/Atlas(TCI No. 7-71/Male No. 72-106): No. 6, May, 1949 - No. 106, July, 1963

	GD 2.0	VG 4.0	FN 6.0	VF 8.0	VF/NM 9.0	NM- 9.2
6-Photo-c	19	38	57	111	176	240
7-Photo-c; Kamen-a	13	26	39	72	101	130
8-Kubert-a; photo-c	13	26	39	72	101	130
9-20: 9-12-Photo-c	11	22	33	64	90	115
21,24-Krigstein-a	12	24	36	67	94	120
22,23,25-35,37,39,40	11	22	33	60	83	105
36,38-Krigstein-a	11	22	33	62	86	110
41-44,46,47: Last precode (2/55)	10	20	30	58	79	100
45,57-Matt Baker-a	12	24	36	69	97	125
48,50-52,54-56,58-74	6	12	18	39	62	85
49,53-Toth-a, 6 & ? pgs.	6	12	18	43	69	95
75,77,82-Matt Baker-a	7	14	21	50	83	115
76,78-81,86,88-90,92-95: 80-Heath-c. 95-Last 10¢-c?	6	12	18	37	59	80
83,84,87,91-Kirby-c. 83-Severin-a	7	14	21	47	76	105
85,96,97,99-106-Kirby-c/a. 97-10¢ cover price blacked out, 12¢ printed on cover	8	16	24	54	90	125
98-Kirby-c/a	8	16	24	54	90	125

NOTE: ***Anne Brewster** a-67, 72. **Colletta** a-37, 40, 42, 44, 67(2); c-42, 44, 49, 54, 80. **Everett** c-70. **Hartley** c-20, 21, 30, 31. **Heath** a-87. **Kirby** c-80, 85, 88. **Robinson** a-29.*

LOVERS (Formerly Blonde Phantom)
Marvel Comics No. 23,24/Atlas No. 25 on (ANC): No. 23, May, 1949 - No. 86, Aug?, 1957

	GD 2.0	VG 4.0	FN 6.0	VF 8.0	VF/NM 9.0	NM- 9.2
23-Photo-c begin, end #29	19	38	57	111	176	240
24-Toth-*ish* plus Robinson-a	12	24	36	67	94	120
25,30-Kubert-a; 7, 10 pgs.	12	24	36	69	97	125
26-29,31-36,39,40: 35-Maneely-c	11	22	33	60	83	105
37,38-Krigstein-a	12	24	36	67	94	120
41-Everett-a(2)	12	24	36	67	94	120
42,44-65: 65-Last pre-code (1/55)	9	18	27	52	69	85
43-Frazetta 1 pg. ad	10	20	30	54	72	90
66,68-80,82-86	9	18	27	50	65	80
67-Toth-a	10	20	30	54	72	90
81-Baker-a	10	20	30	56	76	95

NOTE: ***Anne Brewster** a-86. **Colletta** a-54, 59, 62, 64, 65, 69, 85; c-61, 64, 65, 75. **Hartley** c-37, 53, 54. **Heath** a-61. **Maneely** a-57. **Powell** a-27, 30. **Robinson** a-42, 54, 56.*

LOVERS' LANE
Lev Gleason Publications: Oct, 1949 - No. 41, June, 1954 (No. 1-18: 52 pgs.)

	GD 2.0	VG 4.0	FN 6.0	VF 8.0	VF/NM 9.0	NM- 9.2
1-Biro-c	15	30	45	86	133	180
2-Biro-c	10	20	30	56	76	95
3-20: 3,4-Painted-c. 20-Frazetta 1 pg. ad	9	18	27	52	69	85
21-38,40,41	8	16	24	44	57	70
39-Story narrated by Frank Sinatra	10	20	30	56	76	95

NOTE: ***Briefer** a-6, 13, 21. **Esposito** a-5. **Fuje** a-4, 16; c-many. **Guardineer** a-1, 3. **Kinstler** c-41. **Sparling** a-3. **Tuska** a-6. Painted c-3-18. Photo c-19-22, 26-28.*

LOVE SCANDALS
Quality Comics: Feb, 1950 - No. 5, Oct, 1950 (Photo-c #2-5) (All 52 pgs.)

	GD 2.0	VG 4.0	FN 6.0	VF 8.0	VF/NM 9.0	NM- 9.2
1-Ward-c/a, 9 pgs.	27	54	81	158	259	360
2,3: 2-Gustavson-a	14	28	42	78	112	145
4-Ward-a, 18 pgs; Gil Fox-a	21	42	63	122	199	275
5-C. Cuidera-a; tomboy story "I Hated Being a Woman"	15	30	45	85	130	175

LOVE SECRETS
Marvel Comics(IPC): Oct, 1949 - No. 2, Jan, 1950 (52 pgs., photo-c)

Lucifer #9 © DC

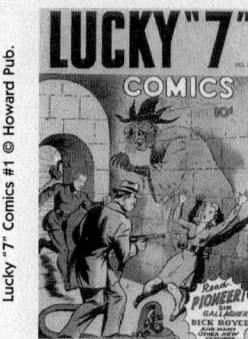

Lucky "7" Comics #1 © Howard Pub.

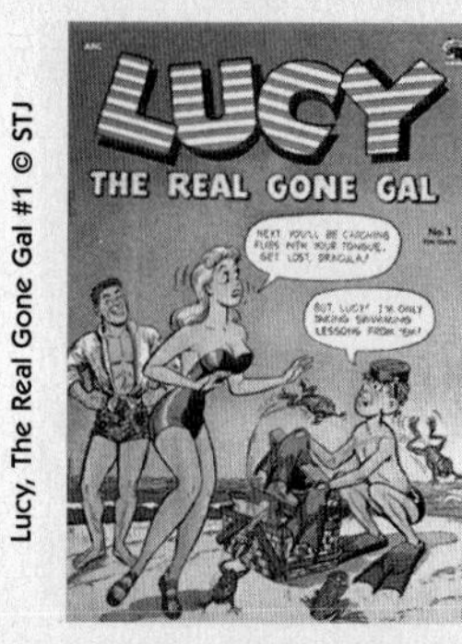

Lucy, The Real Gone Gal #1 © STJ

	GD 2.0	VG 4.0	FN 6.0	VF 8.0	VF/NM 9.0	NM- 9.2
1	17	34	51	98	154	210
2	12	24	36	67	94	120

LOVE SECRETS (Formerly Love Letters #31)
Quality Comics Group: No. 32, Aug, 1953 - No. 56, Dec, 1956

	GD 2.0	VG 4.0	FN 6.0	VF 8.0	VF/NM 9.0	NM- 9.2
32	13	26	39	74	105	135
33,35-39	9	18	27	52	69	85
34-Ward-a	13	26	39	74	105	135
40-Matt Baker-c	13	26	39	72	101	130
41-43: 43-Last precode (3/55)	9	18	27	52	69	85
44,47-50,53,54	8	16	24	44	57	70
45-Ward-a	11	22	33	60	83	105
46-Ward-a; Baker-a	12	24	36	67	94	120
51,52-Ward(r). 52-r/Love Confessions #17	9	18	27	52	69	85
55,56: 55-Baker-a. 56-Baker-c	11	22	33	62	86	110

LOVE STORIES (See Top Love Stories)

LOVE STORIES (Formerly Heart Throbs)
National Periodical Publ.: No. 147, Nov, 1972 - No. 152, Oct-Nov, 1973

	GD 2.0	VG 4.0	FN 6.0	VF 8.0	VF/NM 9.0	NM- 9.2
147-152	3	6	9	14	20	26

LOVE STORIES OF MARY WORTH (See Harvey Comics Hits #55 & Mary Worth)
Harvey Publications: Sept, 1949 - No. 5, May, 1950

	GD 2.0	VG 4.0	FN 6.0	VF 8.0	VF/NM 9.0	NM- 9.2
1-1940's newspaper reprints-#1-4	9	18	27	47	61	75
2-5: 3-Kamen/Baker-a?	6	12	18	31	38	45

LOVE TALES (Formerly The Human Torch #35)
Marvel/Atlas Comics (ZPC No. 36-50/MMC No. 67-75): No. 36, 5/49 - No. 58, 8/52; No. 59, date? - No. 75, Sept, 1957

	GD 2.0	VG 4.0	FN 6.0	VF 8.0	VF/NM 9.0	NM- 9.2
36-Photo-c	18	36	54	103	162	220
37	11	22	33	62	86	110
38-44,46-50: 39-41-Photo-c	10	20	30	58	79	100
45,51,52,69: 45-Powell-a. 51,69-Everett-a. 52-Krigstein-a	11	22	33	60	83	105
53-60: 60-Last pre-code (2/55)	9	18	27	50	65	80
61-68,70-75: 75-Brewster, Cameron, Colletta-a	9	18	27	47	61	75

LOVE THRILLS (See Fox Giants)

LOVE TRAILS (Western romance)
A Lover's Magazine (CDS)(Marvel): Dec, 1949 - No. 2, Mar, 1950 (52 pgs.)

	GD 2.0	VG 4.0	FN 6.0	VF 8.0	VF/NM 9.0	NM- 9.2
1,2: 1-Photo-c	15	30	45	85	130	175

LOWELL THOMAS' HIGH ADVENTURE (See High Adventure)

LT. (See Lieutenant)

LUCIFER (See The Sandman #4)
DC Comics (Vertigo): Jun, 2000 - No. 75, Aug, 2006 ($2.50/$2.75)

	GD 2.0	VG 4.0	FN 6.0	VF 8.0	VF/NM 9.0	NM- 9.2
1-Carey-s/Weston-a/Fegredo-c						8.00
2,3-Carey-s/Weston-a/Fegredo-c						5.00
4-10: 4-Pleece-a. 5-Gross-a						4.00
11-49,51-73: 16-Moeller-c begin. 25,26-Death app. 45-Naifeh-a. 53-Kaluta-c begin. 62-Doran-a. 63-Begin $2.75-c						3.00
50-($3.50) P. Craig Russell-a; Mazikeen app.						4.00
74-($2.99) Kaluta-c						3.00
75-($3.99) Last issue; Lucifer's origins retold; Morpheus app.; Gross-a/Moeller-c						4.00
Preview-16 pg. flip book w/Swamp Thing Preview						3.00
...: A Dalliance With the Damned TPB ('02, $14.95) r/#14-20						15.00
...: Children and Monsters TPB ('01, $17.95) r/#5-13						18.00
...: Crux TPB (2006, $14.99) r/#55-61						15.00
...: Devil in the Gateway TPB ('01, $14.95) r/#1-4 & Sandman Presents:..#1-3						15.00
...: Evensong TPB (2007, $14.99) r/#70-75 & Lucifer: Nirvana one-shot						15.00
...: Exodus TPB (2005, $14.95) r/#42-44,46-49						15.00
...: Inferno TPB (2003, $14.95) r/#29-35						15.00
...: Mansions of the Silence TPB (2004, $14.95) r/#36-41						15.00
...: Morningstar TPB (2006, $14.99) r/#62-69						15.00
...: Nirvana (2002, $5.95) Carey-s/Muth-painted-c/a; Daniel app.						6.00
...: The Divine Comedy TPB (2003, $17.95) r/#21-28						18.00
...: The Wolf Beneath the Tree TPB (2005, $14.99) r/#45,50-54						15.00

LUCIFER'S HAMMER (Larry Niven & Jerry Pournelle's...)
Innovation Publishing: Nov, 1993 - No. 6, 1994 ($2.50, painted, limited series)

	GD 2.0	VG 4.0	FN 6.0	VF 8.0	VF/NM 9.0	NM- 9.2
1-6: Adaptatin of novel, painted-c & art						3.00

LUCKY COMICS
Consolidated Magazines: Jan, 1944; No. 2, Sum, 1945 - No. 5, Sum, 1946

	GD 2.0	VG 4.0	FN 6.0	VF 8.0	VF/NM 9.0	NM- 9.2
1-Lucky Starr & Bobbie begin	22	44	66	132	216	300
2-5: 5-Devil-c by Walter Johnson	14	28	42	80	115	150

LUCKY DUCK
Standard Comics (Literary Ent.): No. 5, Jan, 1953 - No. 8, Sept, 1953

	GD 2.0	VG 4.0	FN 6.0	VF 8.0	VF/NM 9.0	NM- 9.2
5-Funny animal; Irving Spector-a	11	22	33	60	83	105
6-8-Irving Spector-a	10	20	30	54	72	90

NOTE: *Harvey Kurtzman tried to hire Spector for Mad #1.*

LUCKY "7" COMICS
Howard Publishers Ltd.: 1944 (No date listed)

	GD 2.0	VG 4.0	FN 6.0	VF 8.0	VF/NM 9.0	NM- 9.2
1-Pioneer, Sir Gallagher, Dick Royce, Congo Raider, Punch Powers; bondage-c	40	80	120	242	401	560

LUCKY STAR (Western)
Nation Wide Publ. Co.: 1950 - No. 7, 1951; No. 8, 1953 - No. 14, 1955 (5x7-1/4"; full color, 5¢)

	GD 2.0	VG 4.0	FN 6.0	VF 8.0	VF/NM 9.0	NM- 9.2
nn (#1)-(5¢, 52 pgs.)-Davis-a	19	38	57	111	176	240
2,3-(5¢, 52 pgs.)-Davis-a	13	26	39	74	105	135
4-7-(5¢, 52 pgs.)-Davis-a	12	24	36	69	97	125
8-14-(36 pgs.)(Exist?)	12	24	36	69	97	125
Given away with Lucky Star Western Wear by the Juvenile Mfg. Co.	7	14	21	35	43	50

LUCY SHOW, THE (TV) (Also see I Love Lucy)
Gold Key: June, 1963 - No. 5, June, 1964 (Photo-c: 1,2)

	GD 2.0	VG 4.0	FN 6.0	VF 8.0	VF/NM 9.0	NM- 9.2
1	12	24	36	82	154	225
2	7	14	21	49	80	110
3-5: Photo back c-1,2,4,5	6	12	18	43	69	95

LUCY, THE REAL GONE GAL (Meet Miss Pepper #5 on)
St. John Publishing Co.: June, 1953 - No. 4, Dec, 1953

	GD 2.0	VG 4.0	FN 6.0	VF 8.0	VF/NM 9.0	NM- 9.2
1-Negligee panels	15	30	45	86	133	180
2	10	20	30	54	72	90
3,4: 3-Drucker-a	9	18	27	50	65	80

LUDWIG BEMELMAN'S MADELEINE & GENEVIEVE
Dell Publishing Co.: No. 796, May, 1957

	GD 2.0	VG 4.0	FN 6.0	VF 8.0	VF/NM 9.0	NM- 9.2
Four Color 796	4	8	12	24	37	50

LUDWIG VON DRAKE (TV)(Disney)(See Walt Disney's C&S #256)
Dell Publishing Co.: Nov-Dec, 1961 - No. 4, June-Aug, 1962

	GD 2.0	VG 4.0	FN 6.0	VF 8.0	VF/NM 9.0	NM- 9.2
1	7	14	21	45	73	100
2-4	5	10	15	32	51	70

LUFTWAFFE: 1946 (Volume 1)
Antarctic Press: July, 1996 - No. 4, Jan, 1997 ($2.95, B&W, limited series)

	GD 2.0	VG 4.0	FN 6.0	VF 8.0	VF/NM 9.0	NM- 9.2
1-4-Ben Dunn & Ted Nomura-s/a, ...Special Ed.						3.00

LUFTWAFFE: 1946 (Volume 2)
Antarctic Press: Mar, 1997 - No. 18 ($2.95/$2.99, B&W, limited series)

	GD 2.0	VG 4.0	FN 6.0	VF 8.0	VF/NM 9.0	NM- 9.2
1-18: 8-Reviews Tigers of Terra series						3.00
Annual 1 (4/98, $2.95)-Reprints early Nomura pages						3.00
...Color Special (4/98)						3.00
...Technical Manual 1,2 (2/98, 4/99)						4.00

LUGER
Eclipse Comics: Oct, 1986 - No. 3, Feb, 1987 ($1.75, miniseries, Baxter paper)

	GD 2.0	VG 4.0	FN 6.0	VF 8.0	VF/NM 9.0	NM- 9.2
1-3: Bruce Jones scripts; Yeates-c/a						3.00

LUKE CAGE (See Cage & Hero for Hire)

LUKE CAGE NOIR
Marvel Comics: Oct, 2009 - No. 4, Jan, 2010 ($3.99, limited series)

	GD 2.0	VG 4.0	FN 6.0	VF 8.0	VF/NM 9.0	NM- 9.2
1-4-Glass & Benson-a/Martinbrough-a; covers by Bradstreet and Calero						4.00

LUKE SHORT'S WESTERN STORIES
Dell Publishing Co.: No. 580, Aug, 1954 - No. 927, Aug, 1958

	GD 2.0	VG 4.0	FN 6.0	VF 8.0	VF/NM 9.0	NM- 9.2
Four Color 580(8/54), 651(9/55)-Kinstler-a	4	8	12	28	44	60
Four Color 739,771,807,848,875,927	4	8	12	26	41	55

LUNATIC FRINGE, THE
Innovation Publishing: July, 1989 - No. 2, 1989 ($1.75, deluxe format)

	GD 2.0	VG 4.0	FN 6.0	VF 8.0	VF/NM 9.0	NM- 9.2
1,2						3.00

LUNATICKLE (Magazine) (Satire)
Whitstone Publ.: Feb, 1956 - No. 2, Apr, 1956

	GD 2.0	VG 4.0	FN 6.0	VF 8.0	VF/NM 9.0	NM- 9.2
1,2-Kubert-a (scarce)	9	18	27	47	61	75

LUNATIK
Marvel Comics: Dec, 1995 - No. 3, Feb, 1996 ($1.95, limited series)

	GD 2.0	VG 4.0	FN 6.0	VF 8.0	VF/NM 9.0	NM- 9.2
1-3						3.00

LURKERS, THE

Lynch Mob #2 © Chaos!

Machete #1 © Fifth Brain

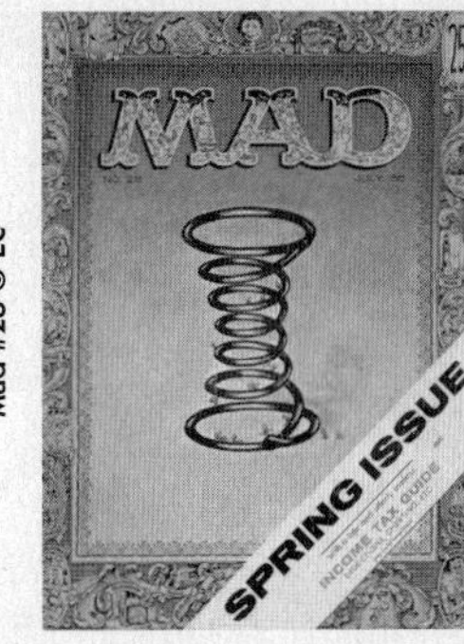

Mad #28 © EC

GD VG FN VF VF/NM NM-
2.0 4.0 6.0 8.0 9.0 9.2

IDW Publ.: Oct, 2004 - No. 4, Jan, 2005 ($3.99)
1-4-Niles-s/Casanova-a 4.00

LUST FOR LIFE
Slave Labor Graphics: Feb, 1997 - No. 4, Jan, 1998 ($2.95, B&W)
1-4: 1-Jeff Levin-s/a 3.00

LUTHOR (See Lex Luthor: Man of Steel)

LYCANTHROPE LEO
Viz Communications: 1994 - No. 7($2.95, B&W, limited series, 44 pgs.)
1-7 4.00

LYNCH (See Gen 13)
Image Comics (WildStorm Productions): May, 1997 ($2.50, one-shot)
1-Helmut-c/app. 3.00

LYNCH MOB
Chaos! Comics: June, 1994 - No. 4, Sept, 1994 ($2.50, limited series)
1-4 5.00
1-Special edition full foil-c 1 2 3 5 6 8

LYNDON B. JOHNSON
Dell Publishing Co.: Mar, 1965
12-445-503-Photo-c 3 6 9 20 30 40

M
Eclipse Books: 1990 - No. 4, 1991 ($4.95, painted, 52 pgs.)
1-Adapts movie; contains flexi-disc ($5.95) 6.00
2-4 5.00

MACE GRIFFIN BOUNTY HUNTER (Based on video game)
Image Comics (Top Cow): May, 2003 ($2.99, one-shot)
1-Nocon-a 3.00

MACHETE (Based on the Robert Rodriguez movie)
IDW Publishing: No. 0, Sept, 2010 ($3.99)
0-Origin story; Rodriguez & Kaufman-s/Sayger-a; 3 covers 4.00

MACHINE, THE
Dark Horse Comics: Nov, 1994 - No. 4, Feb, 1995 ($2.50, limited series)
1-4 3.00

MACHINE MAN (Also see 2001, A Space Odyssey)
Marvel Comics Group: Apr, 1978 - No. 9, Dec, 1978; No. 10, Aug, 1979 - No. 19, Feb, 1981
1-Jack Kirby-c/a/scripts begin; end #9 3 6 9 16 23 30
2-9-Kirby-c/a/s. 9-(12/78) 2 4 6 9 12 15
10-17: 10-(8/79) Marv Wolfman scripts & Ditko-a begins
1 3 4 6 8 10
18-Wendigo, Alpha Flight-ties into X-Men #140 3 6 9 16 23 30
19-Intro/1st app. Jack O'Lantern (Macendale), later becomes 2nd Hobgoblin
3 6 9 14 20 25

NOTE: ***Austin** c-7i, 19i. **Buckler** c-17p, 18p. **Byrne** c-14p. **Ditko** a-10-19; c-10-13, 14i, 15, 16. **Kirby** a-1-9p; c-1-5, 7-9p. **Layton** c-7i. **Miller** c-19p. **Simonson** c-6.*

MACHINE MAN (Also see X-51)
Marvel Comics Group: Oct, 1984 - No. 4, Jan, 1985 (limited series)
1-4-Barry Smith-c/a(i) & colors in all 5.00
TPB (1988, $6.95) r/ #1-4; Barry Smith-c 7.00
.../Bastion '98 Annual ($2.99) wraparound-c 4.00

MACHINE MAN 2020
Marvel Comics: Aug, 1994 - Nov, 1994 ($2.00, 52 pgs., limited series)
1-4: Reprints Machine Man limited series; Barry Windsor-Smith-c/i(r) 4.00

MACHINE TEEN
Marvel Comics: July, 2005 - No. 5, Nov, 2005 ($2.99, limited series)
1-5-Sumerak-s/Hawthorne-a. 1-James Jean-c 3.00
...: History (2005, $7.99, digest) r/#1-5 8.00

MACK BOLAN: THE EXECUTIONER (Don Pendleton's...)
Innovation Publishing: July, 1993 ($2.50)
1-3-($2.50) 3.00
1-($3.95)-Indestructible Cover Edition 4.00
1-($2.95)-Collector's Gold Edition; foil stamped 3.00
1-($3.50)-Double Cover Edition; red foil outer-c 3.50

MACKENZIE'S RAIDERS (Movie, TV)
Dell Publishing Co.: No. 1093, Apr-June, 1960
Four Color 1093-Richard Carlson photo-c from TV show

GD VG FN VF VF/NM NM-
2.0 4.0 6.0 8.0 9.0 9.2

6 12 18 43 69 95

MACROSS (Becomes Robotech: The Macross Saga #2 on)
Comico: Dec, 1984 ($1.50)(Low print run)
1-Early manga app. 3 6 9 14 20 25

MACROSS II
Viz Select Comics: 1992 - No. 10, 1993 ($2.75, B&W, limited series)
1-10: Based on video series 3.00

MAD (Tales Calculated to Drive You...)
E. C. Comics (Educational Comics): Oct-Nov, 1952 - Present (No. 24-on are magazine format) (Kurtzman editor No. 1-28, Feldstein No. 29 - No. ?)
1-Wood, Davis, Elder start as regulars 417 834 1251 3336 5318 7300
2-Dick Tracy cameo 110 220 330 880 1403 1925
3,4: 3-Stan Lee mentioned. 4-Reefer mention story "Flob Was a Slob" by Davis; Superman parody 77 154 231 616 983 1350
5-Low distr.; W.M. Gaines biog. 157 314 471 1256 2003 2750
6-11: 6-Popeye cameo. 7,8- "Hey Look" reprints by Kurtzman. 11-Wolverton-a; Davis story was-r/Crime Suspenstories #12 w/new Kurtzman dialogue
60 120 180 480 765 1050
12-15: 15,18-Pot Shot Pete-r by Kurtzman 48 96 144 384 612 840
16-23(5/55): 18-Alice in Wonderland by Jack Davis. 21-1st app. Alfred E. Neuman on-c in fake ad. 22-All by Elder plus photo-montages by Kurtzman.
23-Special cancel announcement 40 80 120 320 510 700
24(7/55)-1st magazine issue (25¢); Kurtzman logo & border on-c; 1st "What? Me Worry?" on-c; 2nd printing exists 94 188 282 752 1201 1650
25-Jaffee starts as regular writer 44 88 132 352 564 775
26,27: 27-Jaffee starts as story artist; new logo 39 78 117 312 499 685
28-Last issue edited by Kurtzman; (three cover variations exist with different wording on contents banner on lower right of cover; value of each the same)
37 74 111 231 358 485
29-Kamen-a; Don Martin starts as regular; Feldstein editing begins
37 74 111 231 358 485
30-1st A. E. Neuman cover by Mingo; last Elder-a; Bob Clarke starts as regular; Disneyland & Elvis Presley spoof 58 116 174 363 557 750
31-Freas starts as regular; last Davis-a until #99 34 68 102 213 324 435
32,33: 32-Orlando, Drucker, Woodbridge start as regulars; Wood back-c. 33-Orlando back-c
29 58 87 181 276 370
34-Berg starts as regular 23 46 69 144 222 300
35-Mingo wraparound-c; Crandall-a 23 46 69 144 222 300
36-40 (7/58): 39-Beall-c 17 34 51 106 166 225
41-50: 42-Danny Kaye-s. 44-Xmas-c. 47-49-Sid Caesar-s. 48-Uncle Sam-c.
50 (10/59)-Peter Gunn-s 15 30 45 94 142 190
51-59: 52-Xmas-c; 77 Sunset Strip. 53-Rifleman-s. 54-Jaffee-a begins. 55-Sid Caesar-s. 59-Strips of Superman, Flash Gordon, Donald Duck & others. 59-Halloween/Headless Horseman-c 12 24 36 75 113 150
60 (1/61)-JFK/Nixon flip-c; 1st Spy vs. Spy by Prohias, who starts as regular
14 28 42 88 134 180
61-70: 64-Rickard starts as regular. 65-JFK-s. 66-JFK-c. 68-Xmas-c by Martin. 70-Route 66-s
9 18 27 56 83 110
71-75,77-80 (7/63): 72-10th Anniv. special; 1/3 pg. strips of Superman, Tarzan & others.
73-Bonanza-s. 74-Dr. Kildare-s 5 10 15 34 55 75
76-Aragonés starts as regular 6 12 18 39 62 85
81-85: 81-Superman strip. 82-Castro-c. 85-Lincoln-c 5 10 15 30 48 65
86-1st Fold-in; commonly creased back covers makes these and later issues scarcer in NM
6 12 18 37 59 80
87,88 5 10 15 34 55 75
89,90: 89-One strip by Walt Kelly; Frankenstein-c; Fugitive-s. 90-Ringo back-c by Frazetta; Beatles app. 6 12 18 37 59 80
91,94,96,100: 94-King Kong-c. 96-Man From U.N.C.L.E. 100-(1/66)-Anniversary issue
5 10 15 30 48 65
92,93,95,97-99: 99-Davis-a resumes 4 8 12 28 44 60
101,104,106,108,114,115,119,121: 101-Infinity-c; Voyage to the Bottom of the Sea-s. 104-Lost in Space-s. 106-Tarzan back-c by Frazetta; 2 pg. Batman by Aragonés. 108-Hogan's Heroes by Davis. 114-Rat Patrol-s. 115-Star Trek. 119-Invaders (TV). 121-Beatles-c; Ringo pin-up; flip-c of Sik-Teen; Flying Nun-s 3 6 9 21 32 42
102,103,107,109-113,116-118,120(7/68): 118-Beatles cameo
3 6 9 19 29 38
105-Batman-c/s, TV show parody (9/66) 4 8 12 24 37 50
122,124,126,128,129,131-134,136,137,139,140: 122-Ronald Reagan photo inside; Drucker & Mingo-c. 126-Family Affair-s. 128-Last Orlando. 131-Reagan photo back-c. 132-Xmas-c.
133-John Wayne/True Grit. 136-Room 222 3 6 9 16 22 28
123-Four different covers 3 6 9 16 23 30
125,127,130,135,138: 125-2001 Space Odyssey; Hitler back-c. 127-Mod Squad-c/s. 130-Land

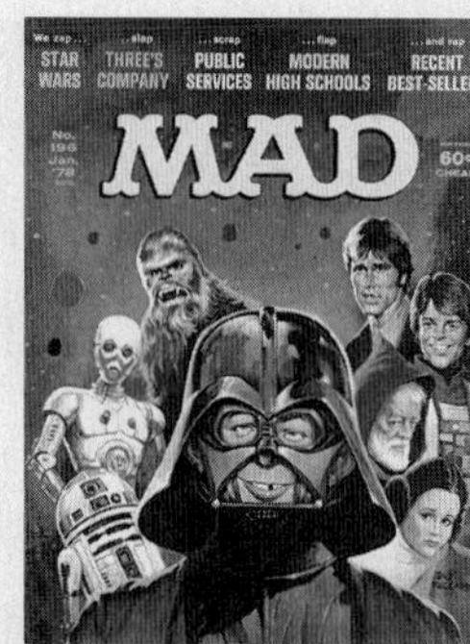

Mad #196 © EC

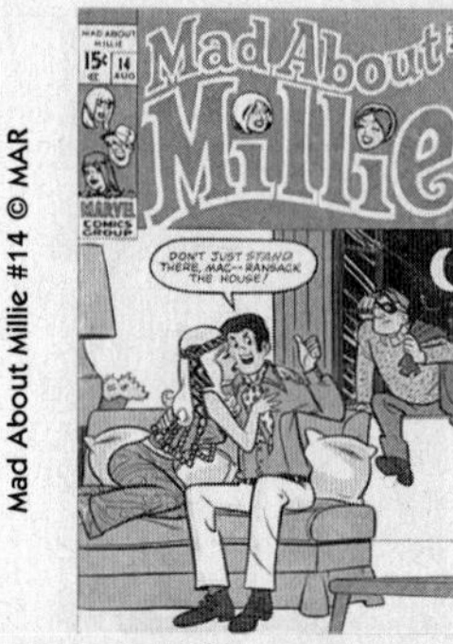

Mad About Millie #14 © MAR

Madame Xanadu #22 © DC

GD VG FN VF VF/NM NM-
2.0 4.0 6.0 8.0 9.0 9.2

of the Giants-s; Torres begins as reg. 135-Easy Rider-c by Davis. 138-Snoopy-c; MASH-s 3 6 9 17 25 32
141-149,151-156,158-165,167-170: 141-Hawaii Five-0. 147-All in the Family-s. 153-Dirty Harry-s. 155-Godfather-c/s. 156-Columbo-s. 159-Clockwork Orange-c/s. 161-Tarzan-s. 164-Kung Fu (TV)-s. 165-James Bond-s; Dean Martin-c. 169-Drucker-c; McCloud-s. 170-Exorcist-s 3 6 9 14 19 24
150-(4/72) Partridge Family-s 3 6 9 15 21 26
157-(3/73) Planet of the Apes-c/s 3 6 9 16 23 30
166-(4/74) Classic finger-c 3 6 9 16 23 30
171-185,187,189-192,194,195,198,199: 172-Six Million Dollar Man-s; Hitler back-c. 178-Godfather II-c/s. 180-Jaws-c/s (1/76). 182-Bob Jones starts as regular.185-Starsky & Hutch-s. 187-Fonz/Happy Days-c/s; Harry North starts as regular. 189-Travolta/Kotter-c/s. 190-John Wayne-c/s. 192-King Kong-c/s. 194-Rocky-c/s; Laverne & Shirley-s. 199-James Bond-s 2 4 6 10 14 18
186,188,197,200: 186-Star Trek-c/s. 188-Six Million Dollar Man/ Bionic Woman. 197-Spock-s; Star Wars-s. 200-Close Encounters 2 4 6 13 18 22
193,196: 193-Farrah/Charlie's Angels-c/s. 196-Star Wars-c/s 3 6 9 14 19 24
201,203,205,220: 201-Sat. Night Fever-c/s. 203-Star Wars. 205-Travolta/Grease. 220-Yoda-c, Empire Strikes Back-s 2 4 6 9 13 16
202,204,206,207,209,211-219,221-227,229,230: 204-Hulk TV show. 206-Tarzan. 208-Superman movie. 209-Mork & Mindy. 212-Spider-Man-s; Alien (movie)-s. 213-James Bond, Dracula, Rocky II-s 216-Star Trek. 219-Martin-c. 221-Shining-s. 223-Dallas-c/s. 225-Popeye. 226-Superman II. 229-James Bond. 230-Star Wars 1 3 4 6 8 10
208,228: 208-Superman movie-c/s; Battlestar Galactica-s. 228-Raiders of the Lost Ark-c/s 2 4 6 9 12 15
210-Lord of the Rings 2 4 6 9 13 16
231-235,237-241,243-249,251-260: 233-Pac-Man-c. 234-MASH-c/s. 235-Flip-c with Rocky III & Conan; Boris-a. 239-Mickey Mouse-c. 241-Knight Rider-s. 243-Superman III. 245- Last Rickard-a. 247-Seven Dwarfs-c. 253-Supergirl movie-s; Prince/Purple Rain-s. 254-Rock stars-s. 255-Reagan-c; Cosby-s. 256-Last issue edited by Feldstein; Dynasty, Bev. Hills Cop. 259-Rambo. 260-Back to the Future-c/s; Honeymooners-s 1 2 3 5 6 8
236,242,250: 236-E.T.-c/s;Star Trek II-s. 242-Star Wars/A-Team-c/s. 250-Temple of Doom-c/s; Tarzan-s 1 2 3 5 7 9
261-267,269-276,278-288,290-297: 261-Miami Vice. 262-Rocky IV-c/s, Leave It To Beaver-s. 263-Young Sherlock Holmes-s. 264-Hulk Hogan-c; Rambo-s. 267-Top Gun. 271-Star Trek IV-c/s. 272-ALF-c; Get Smart-s. 273-Pee Wee Herman-c/s. 274-Last Martin-a. 281-California Raisins-c. 282-Star Trek:TNG-s; ALF-s. 283-Rambo III-c/s. 284-Roger Rabbit-c/s. 285-Hulk Hogan-c. 287-3 pgs. Eisner-a. 291-TMNT-c; Indiana Jones-s. 292-Super Mario Bros.-c; Married with Children-s. 295-Back to the Future II. 297-Mike Tyson-c 1 2 3 4 5 7
268,277,289,298-300: 268-Aliens-c/s. 277-Michael Jackson-c/s; Robocop-s. 289-Batman movie parody. 298-Gremlins II-c/s; Robocop II. Batman-s. 299-Simpsons-c/story; Total Recall-s. 300(1/91) Casablanca-s, Dick Tracy-s, Wizard of Oz-s, Gone With The Wind-s 1 2 3 5 6 8
300-303 (1/91-6/91)-Special Hussein Asylum Editions; only distributed to the troops in the Middle East (see Mad Super Spec.) 2 4 6 13 18 22
301-310,312,313,315-320,322,324,326-334,337-349: 303-Home Alone-c/s. 305-Simpsons-s. 306-TMNT II movie. 308-Terminator II. 315-Tribute to William Gaines. 316-Photo-c. 319-Dracula-c/s. 320-Disney's Aladdin-s. 322-Batman Animated series. 327-Seinfeld-s; X-Men-s. 331-Flintstones-c/s. 332-O.J. Simpson-c/s; Simpsons app. in Lion King. 334-Frankenstein-c/s. 338-Judge Dredd-c by Frazetta. 341-Pocahontas-s. 345-Beatles app. (1 pg.) 347-Broken Arrow & Mission Impossible 5.00
311,314,321,323,325,335,336,350,354,358: 311-Addams Family-c/story, Home Improvement-s. 314-Batman Returns-c/story. 321-Star Trek DS9-c/s. 323-Jurassic Park-c/s. 325,336-Beavis & Butthead-c/s. 335-X-Files-s; Pulp Fiction-s; Interview with the Vampire-s. 336-Lois & Clark-s. 350-Polybagged w/CD Rom. 354-Star Wars; Beavis & Butthead-s. 358-X-Files 6.00
351-353,355-357,359-500 5.00
501-503-($5.99) 6.00
Mad About Super Heroes (2002, $9.95) r/super hero app.; Alex Ross-c 10.00
NOTE: ***Aragones*** *c-210, 293.* ***Beall*** *c-39.* ***Davis*** *c-2, 27, 135, 139, 173, 178, 212, 213, 219, 246, 260, 296, 308.* ***Drucker*** *a-35-62; c-122, 169, 176, 225, 234, 264, 266, 274, 280, 285, 297, 299, 303, 314, 315, 321.* ***Elder*** *c-5, 259, 261, 268.* ***Elder/Kurtzman*** *a-258-274.* ***Jules Feiffer*** *a(r)-42.* ***Freas*** *c-40-59, 62-67, 69-70, 72, 74.* ***Heath*** *a-14, 27.* ***Jaffee*** *c-199, 217, 224, 258.* ***Kamen*** *a-29.* ***Krigstein*** *a-12, 17, 24, 26.* ***Kurtzman*** *c-1, 3, 4, 6-10, 13, 16, 18.* ***Martin*** *a-29-62; c-68, 165, 229.* ***Mingo*** *c-30-37, 61, 71, 75-80, 82-114, 117-124, 126, 129, 131, 133, 134, 136, 140, 143-148, 150-162, 164, 166-168, 171, 172, 174, 175, 177, 179, 181, 183, 185, 198, 206, 209, 211, 214, 218, 221, 222, 300.* ***John Severin*** *a-1-6, 9, 10.* ***Wolverton*** *c-11; a-11, 17, 29, 31, 36, 40, 82, 137.* ***Wood*** *a-1-21, 23-62; c-26, 28, 29.* ***Woodbridge*** *a-35-62. Issues 1-23 are 36 pgs.; 24-28 are 58 pgs.; 29 on are 52 pgs.*

MAD (See Mad Follies, ...Special, More Trash from..., and The Worst from...)

MAD ABOUT MILLIE (Also see Millie the Model)
Marvel Comics Group: April, 1969 - No. 16, Nov, 1970

1-Giant issue 9 18 27 65 113 160
2,3 (Giants) 6 12 18 43 69 95

GD VG FN VF VF/NM NM-
2.0 4.0 6.0 8.0 9.0 9.2

4-10 5 10 15 30 48 65
11-16: 16-r 4 8 12 28 44 60
Annual 1(11/71, 52 pgs.) 5 10 15 30 48 65

MADAME MIRAGE
Image Comics (Top Cow): June, 2007 - No. 6, May, 2008 ($2.99)

1-6: 1-Paul Dini-s/Kenneth Rocafort-a; two covers by Horn and Rocafort 3.00
... First Look (5/07, 99¢) preview of series; Dini interview; cover gallery 2.25
Volume 1 TPB (7/08, $14.99) r/#1-6; cover gallery; cover and design sketches 15.00

MADAME XANADU
DC Comics: July, 1981 ($1.00, no ads, 36 pgs.)

1-Marshall Rogers-a (25 pgs.); Kaluta-c/a (2pgs.); pin-up 1 2 3 5 6 8

MADAME XANADU (Also see Doorway to Nightmare)
DC Comics (Vertigo): Aug, 2008 - No. 29, Jan, 2011 ($2.99)

1-Matt Wagner-s/Amy Reeder Hadley-a/c; Phantom Stranger app. 4.00
1,2-Variant covers. 1-Wagner. 2-Kaluta 5.00
2-29: 2-10-Amy Reeder Hadley-a/c; Phantom Stranger app. 6-Death (from The Sandman) app.; covers by Hadley & Quitely. 9-Zatara app. 10-Jim Corrigan becomes The Spectre. 11-15-Kaluta-a. 14,15-Sandman (Wesley Dodds) app. 16-18-Hadley-a; Det. Jones app. 3.00
...: Broken House of Cards TPB (2011, $17.99) r/#16-23 and story from House of Mystery Halloween Annual #1 18.00
...: Disenchanted TPB (2009, $12.99) r/#1-10; James Robinson intro.; Hadley sketch-a 13.00
...: Exodus TPB (2010, $12.99) r/#11-15; Chris Roberson intro. 13.00

MADBALLS
Star Comics/Marvel Comics #9 on: Sept, 1986 - No. 3, Nov, 1986; No. 4, June, 1987 - No. 10, June, 1988

1-10: Based on toys. 9-Post-a 4.00

MAD DISCO
E.C. Comics: 1980 (one-shot, 36 pgs.)

1-Includes 30 minute flexi-disc of Mad disco music 2 4 6 11 16 20

MAD-DOG
Marvel Comics: May, 1993 - No. 6, Oct, 1993 ($1.25)

1-6-Flip book w/2nd story "created" by Bob Newhart's character from his TV show "Bob" set at a comic book company; actual s/a-Ty Templeton 3.00

MAD DOGS
Eclipse Comics: Feb, 1992 - No. 3, July, 1992 ($2.50, B&W, limited series)

1-3 3.00

MAD 84 (Mad Extra)
E.C. Comics: 1984 (84 pgs.)

1 1 3 4 6 8 10

MAD FOLLIES (Special)
E. C. Comics: 1963 - No. 7, 1969

nn(1963)-Paperback book covers 21 42 63 148 297 445
2(1964)-Calendar 16 32 48 111 226 340
3(1965)-Mischief Stickers 13 26 39 89 170 250
4(1966)-Mobile; Frazetta-r/back-c Mad #90 10 20 30 67 116 165
5,6: 5(1967)-Stencils. 6(1968)-Mischief Stickers 8 16 24 52 86 120
7(1969)-Nasty Cards 8 16 24 52 86 120
(If bonus is missing, issue is half price)
NOTE: ***Clarke*** *c-4.* ***Frazetta*** *r-4, 6 (1 pg. ea.).* ***Mingo*** *c-1-3.* ***Orlando*** *a-5.*

MAD HATTER, THE (Costumed Hero)
O. W. Comics Corp.: Jan-Feb, 1946; No. 2, Sept-Oct, 1946

1-Freddy the Firefly begins; Giunta-c/a 77 154 231 493 847 1200
2-Has ad for E.C.'s Animal Fables #1 40 80 120 246 411 575

MADHOUSE
Ajax/Farrell Publ. (Excellent Publ./4-Star): 3-4/54 - No. 4, 9-10/54; 6/57 - No. 4, Dec?, 1957

1(1954) 32 64 96 188 307 425
2,3 18 36 54 105 165 225
4-Surrealistic-c 24 48 72 140 230 320
1(1957, 2nd series) 14 28 42 82 121 160
2-4 (#4 exist?) 10 20 30 56 76 95

MAD HOUSE (Formerly Madhouse Glads; ...Comics #104? on)
Red Circle Productions/Archie Publications: No. 95, 9/74 - No. 97, 1/75; No. 98, 8/75 - No. 130, 10/82

95,96-Horror stories through #97; Morrow-c 2 4 6 11 16 20
97-Intro. Henry Hobson; Morrow-a/c, Thorne-a 2 4 6 10 14 18

Madman Atomic Comics #6 © Mike Allred

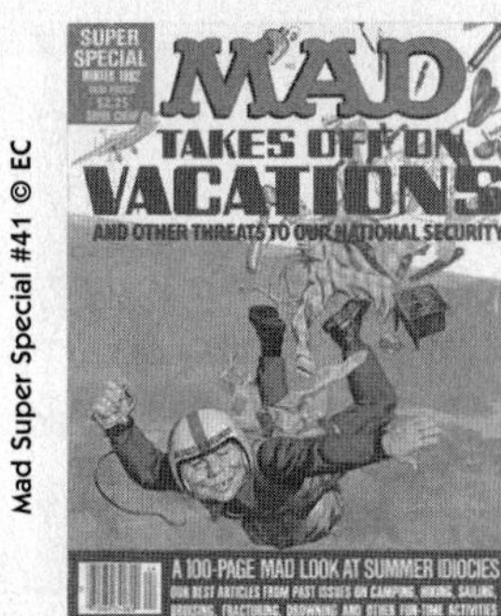

Mad Super Special #41 © EC

The Magdalena V3 #1 © TCOW

GD 2.0 VG 4.0 FN 6.0 VF 8.0 VF/NM 9.0 NM- 9.2

98,99,101-120-Satire/humor stories. 110-Sabrina app.,1pg. 1 3 4 6 8 10
100 2 4 6 8 10 12
121-129 2 4 6 8 10 12
130 2 4 6 9 13 16
Annual 8(1970-71)-Formerly Madhouse Ma-ad Annual; Sabrina app. (6 pgs.) 4 8 12 26 41 55
Annual 9-12(1974-75): 11-Wood-a(r) 3 6 9 14 20 25
...Comics Digest 1('75-76) 2 4 6 10 14 18
2-8(8/82)(...Mag. #5 on)-Sabrina in many 2 4 6 8 11 14
NOTE: ***B. Jones** a-96. **McWilliams** a-97. **Wildey** a-95, 96. See Archie Comics Digest #1, 13.*

MADHOUSE GLADS (Formerly ...Ma-ad; Madhouse #95 on)
Archie Publ.: No. 73, May, 1970 - No. 94, Aug, 1974 (No. 78-92: 52 pgs.)
73-77,93,94: 74-1 pg. Sabrina 2 4 6 9 13 16
78-92 (52 pgs.) 2 4 6 11 16 20

MADHOUSE MA-AD (...Jokes #67-70; ...Freak-Out #71-74) (Formerly Archie's Madhouse) (Becomes Madhouse Glads #73 on)
Archie Publications: No. 67, April, 1969 - No. 72, Jan, 1970
67-71: 70-1 pg. Sabrina 3 6 9 16 22 28
72-6 pgs. Sabrina 4 8 12 26 41 55
...Annual 7(1969-70)-Formerly Archie's Madhouse Annual; becomes Madhouse Annual; 6 pgs. Sabrina 4 8 12 28 44 60

MADMAN (See Creatures of the Id #1)
Tundra Publishing: Mar, 1992 - No. 3, 1992 ($3.95, duotone, high quality, lim. series, 52 pgs.)
1-Mike Allred-c/a in all 2 4 6 8 10 12
1-2nd printing 4.00
2,3 6.00

MADMAN ADVENTURES
Tundra Publishing: 1992 - No. 3, 1993 ($2.95, limited series)
1-Mike Allred-c/a in all 1 2 3 5 7 9
2,3 5.00
TPB (Oni Press, 2002, $14.95) r/#1-3 & first app. of Frank Einstein from Creatures of the Id in color; gallery pages 15.00

MADMAN ATOMIC COMICS (Also see The Atomics)
Image Comics: Apr, 2007 - Present ($2.99/$3.50)
1-12-Mike Allred-s/c/a. 1-Origin re-told; pin-ups by Rivoche and Powell. 3-Sale back-c 3.50
13-17-($3.50) Wraparound-c. 14-Back up w/Darwyn Cooke-a 3.50
All-New Giant-Size Super Ginchy Special (4/11, $5.99) Allred-s/a; back-ups/pin-ups 6.00
... Vol. 1 (2008, $19.99) r/#1-7; bonus art; Jamie Rich intro. 20.00

MADMAN COMICS (Also see The Atomics)
Dark Horse Comics (Legend No. 2 on): Apr, 1994 - No. 20, Dec, 2000 ($2.95/$2.99)
1-Allred-c/a; F. Miller back-c. 1 2 3 5 6 8
2-3: 3-Alex Toth back-c. 5.00
4-11: 4-Dave Stevens back-c. 6,7-Miller/Darrow's Big Guy app. 6-Bruce Timm back-c. 7-Darrow back-c. 8-Origin?; Bagge back-c. 10-Allred/Ross-c; Ross back-c. 11-Frazetta back-c 4.00
12-16: 12-(4/99) 3.50
17-20: 17-The G-Men From Hell #1 on cover; Brereton back-c. 18-(#2). 19,20-($2.99-c). 20-Clowes back-c 3.50
... Boogaloo TPB (6/99, $8.95) r/Nexus Meets Madman & Madman/The Jam 9.00
... Gargantua! (2007, $125.00, HC with dustjacket) r/Madman#1-3, Madman Adventures #1-3, Madman Comics #1-20 and Madman King-Size Super Groovy Special; pin-ups 125.00
Image Firsts: Madman #1 (10/10, $1.00) r/#1 1.00
Ltd. Ed. Slipcover (1997, $99.95, signed and numbered) w/Vol.1 & Vol. 2. Vol.1- reprints #1-5; Vol. 2- reprints #6-10 100.00
The Complete Madman Comics: Vol. 2 (11/96, $17.95, TPB) r/#6-10 plus new material 18.00
Madman King-Size Super Groovy Special (Oni Press, 7/03, $6.95) new short stories by Allred, Derington, Krall and Weissman 7.00
Madman Picture Exhibition No. 1-4 (4-7/02, $3.95) pin-ups by various 4.00
Madman Picture Exhibition Limited Edition (10/02, $29.95) Hardcover collects MPE #1-4 30.00
... Volume 2 SC (2007, $17.99) r/#1-11; Erik Larsen intro. 18.00
... Volume 3 SC (2007, $17.99) r/#12-20 and story from King-Size Groovy; Allred intro. 18.00
Yearbook '95 (1996, $17.95, TPB)-r/#1-5, intro by Teller 18.00

MADMAN / THE JAM
Dark Horse Comics: Jul, 1998 - No. 2, Aug, 1998 ($2.95, mini-series)
1,2-Allred & Mireault-s/a 4.00

MAD MONSTER PARTY (See Movie Classics)

MADNESS IN MURDERWORLD
Marvel Comics: 1989 (Came with computer game from Paragon Software)
V1#1-Starring The X-Men 3.00

MADRAVEN HALLOWEEN SPECIAL
Hamilton Comics: Oct, 1995 ($2.95, one-shot)
nn-Morrow-a 3.00

MADROX (from X-Factor)
Marvel Comics (Marvel Knights): Nov, 2004 - No. 5, Mar, 2005 ($2.99)
1-5-Peter David-s/Pablo Raimondi-a; Strong Guy app. 3.00
...: Multiple Choice TPB (2005, $13.99) r/#1-5 14.00
X-Factor: Madrox - Multiple Choice HC (2008, $19.99) r/#1-5 20.00

MAD SPECIAL (...Super Special)
E. C. Publications, Inc.: Fall, 1970 - No. 141, Nov, 1999 (84 - 116 pgs.)
(If bonus is missing, issue is one half price)
Fall 1970(#1)-Bonus-Voodoo Doll; contains 17 pgs. new material 10 20 30 68 119 170
Spring 1971(#2)-Wall Nuts; 17 pgs. new material 6 12 18 37 59 80
3-Protest Stickers 6 12 18 37 59 80
4-8: 4-Mini Posters. 5-Mad Flag. 6-Mad Mischief Stickers. 7-Presidential candidate posters, Wild Shocking Message posters. 8-TV Guise 5 10 15 32 51 70
9(1972)-Contains Nostalgic Mad #1 (28 pgs.) 4 8 12 26 41 55
10-13: 10-Nonsense Stickers (Don Martin). 13-Sickie Stickers; 3 pgs. Wolverton-r/Mad #137. 11-Contains 33-1/3 RPM record. 12-Contains Nostalgic Mad #2 (36 pgs.); Davis, Wolverton-a 3 6 9 20 30 40
14,16-21,24: 4-Vital Message posters & Art Depreciation paintings. 16-Mad-hesive Stickers. 17-Don Martin posters. 20-Martin Stickers. 18-Contains Nostalgic Mad #4 (36 pgs.). 21,24-Contains Nostalgic Mad #5 (28 pgs.) & #6 (28 pgs.) 3 6 9 16 23 30
15-Contains Nostalgic Mad #3 (28 pgs.) 3 6 9 17 25 32
22,23,25,27-29,30: 22-Diplomas. 23-Martin Stickers. 25-Martin Posters. 27-Mad Shock-Sticks. 28-Contains Nostalgic Mad #7 (36 pgs.). 29-Mad Collectable-Connectables Posters. 30-The Movies 2 4 6 9 13 16
26-Has 33-1/3 RPM record 2 4 6 13 18 22
31,33-35,37-50 2 4 6 8 11 14
32-Contains Nostalgic Mad #8. 36-Has 96 pgs. of comic book & comic strip spoofs: titles "The Comics" on-c 2 4 6 9 13 16
51-70 1 3 4 6 8 10
71-88,90-100: 71-Batman parodies-r by Wood, Drucker. 72-Wolverton-c r-from 1st panel in Mad #11; Wolverton-s r/new dialogue. 83-All Star Trek spoof issue 1 2 3 5 6 8
76-(Fall, 1991)-Special Hussein Asylum Edition; distributed only to the troops in the Middle East (see Mad #300-303) 2 4 6 13 18 22
89-($3.95)-Polybaged w/1st of 3 Spy vs. Spy hologram trading cards (direct sale only issue) (other cards came w/card set) 1 3 4 6 8 10
101-141: 117-Sci-Fi parodies-r. 4.00
NOTE: *#28-30 have no number on cover. **Freas** c-76. **Mingo** c-9, 11, 15, 19, 23.*

MAGDALENA, THE (See The Darkness #15-18)
Image Comics (Top Cow): Apr, 2000 - No. 3, Jan, 2001 ($2.50)
Preview Special ('00, $4.95) Flip book w/Blood Legacy preview 5.00
1-Benitez-c/a; variant covers by Silvestri & Turner 3.00
2,3: 2-Two covers 3.00
.../Angelus #1/2 (11/01, $2.95) Benitez-c/Ching-a 3.00
...Blood Divine (2002, $9.95) r/#1-3 & #1/2; cover gallery 10.00
.../Vampirella (7/03, $2.99) Wohl-s/Benitez-a; two covers 3.00

MAGDALENA, THE (Volume 2)
Image Comics (Top Cow): Aug, 2003 - No. 4, Dec, 2003 ($2.99)
Preview (6/03) B&W preview; Wizard World East logo on cover 3.00
1-4-Holguin-s/Basaldua-a 3.00
1-Variant-c by Jim Silke benefitting ACTOR charity 5.00
TPB Volume 1 (12/06, $19.99) r/both series, Darkness #15-18 & Magdalena/Angelus 20.00
.../Daredevil (5/08, $3.99) Phil Hester-s/a; Hester & Sejic-c 4.00
.../Vampirella (12/04, $2.99) Kirkman-s/Manapul-a; two covers by Manapul and Bachalo 3.00
... Vs. Dracula Monster War 2005 (6/05, $2.99) four covers; Joyce Chin-a 3.00

MAGDALENA, THE (Volume 3)
Image Comics (Top Cow): Apr, 2010 - Present ($3.99)
1-5: 1-Marz-s/Blake-a/Sook-c 4.00

MAGE (The Hero Discovered...; also see Grendel #16)
Comico: Feb, 1984 (no month) - No. 15, Dec, 1986 ($1.50, Mando paper)
1-Comico's 1st color comic 2 4 6 8 11 14
2-5: 3-Intro Edsel. 6.00
6-Grendel begins (1st in color) 3 6 9 14 20 25
7-1st new Grendel story 2 4 6 8 10 12

Mage (The Hero Defined) #6 © Matt Wagner

Magic Comics #19 © KING

Magneto (2011) #1 © MAR

	GD 2.0	VG 4.0	FN 6.0	VF 8.0	VF/NM 9.0	NM- 9.2
8-14: 13-Grendel dies. 14-Grendel story ends						6.00
15-($2.95) Double size w/pullout poster	1	2	3	5	6	8
Image Firsts: Mage - The Hero Discovered #1 (10/10, $1.00) r/#1 w/"Image Firsts" logo						1.00
TPB Volume 1-4 (Image, $5.95) 1- r/#1,2. 2- r/#3,4. 3- r/#5,6. 4- r/#7,8						7.00
TPB Volume 5-7 (Image, $6.95) 5- r/#9,10. 6- r/#11,12. 7- r/#13,14						7.00
TPB Volume 8 (Image, 9/99, $7.50) r/#15						7.50
..., Vol. 1 TPB (Image, 2004, $29.99) r/#1-15; cover gallery, promo artwork, bonus art						30.00

MAGE (The Hero Defined) (Volume 2)
Image Comics: July, 1997 - No. 15, Oct, 1999 ($2.50)

0-(7/97, $5.00) American Ent. Ed. 5.00
1-14:Matt Wagner-c/s/a in all. 13-Three covers 3.00
1-"3-D Edition" (2/98, $4.95) w/glasses 5.00
15-($5.95) Acetate cover 6.00
Volume 1,2 TPB ('98,'99, $9.95) 1- r/#1-4. 2-r/#5-8 10.00
Volume 3 TPB ('00, $12.95) r/#9-12 13.00
Volume 4 TPB ('01, $14.95) r/#13-15 15.00
Hardcover Vol. 2 (2005, $49.95) r/#1-15; cover gallery, character design & sketch pages 50.00

MAGE KNIGHT: STOLEN DESTINY (Based on the fantasy game Mage Knight)
Idea + Design Works: Oct, 2002 - No. 5, Feb, 2003 ($3.50, limited series)

1-5: 1-J. Scott Campbell-c; Cabrera-a/Dezago-s, 2-Dave Johnson-c 3.50

MAGGIE AND HOPEY COLOR SPECIAL (See Love and Rockets)
Fantagraphics Books: May, 1997 ($3.50, one-shot)

1 3.50

MAGGIE THE CAT (Also see Jon Sable, Freelance #11 & Shaman's Tears #12)
Image Comics (Creative Fire Studio): Jan, 1996 - No. 2, Feb, 1996 ($2.50, unfinished limited series)

1,2: Mike Grell-c/a/scripts 3.00

MAGICA DE SPELL (See Walt Disney Showcase #30)

MAGIC AGENT (See Forbidden Worlds & Unknown Worlds)
American Comics Group: Jan-Feb, 1962 - No. 3, May-June, 1962

	GD	VG	FN	VF	VF/NM	NM-
1-Origin & 1st app. John Force	4	8	12	26	41	55
2,3	3	6	9	19	29	38

MAGICAL POKÉMON JOURNEY
Viz Comics: 2000 - Present ($4.95, B&W, magazine-size)

1-4 5.00
Part 2: 1-3; Part 3: 1-4: 1-Includes color poster; Part 4: 1-4; Part 5: 1-4; Part 6: 1-4 5.00

MAGIC COMICS
David McKay Publications: Aug, 1939 - No. 123, Nov-Dec, 1949

	GD	VG	FN	VF	VF/NM	NM-
1-Mandrake the Magician, Henry, Popeye , Blondie, Barney Baxter, Secret Agent X-9 (not by Raymond), Bunky by Billy DeBeck & Thornton Burgess text stories illustrated by Harrison Cady begin; Henry covers begin	350	700	1050	2013	3107	4200
2	124	248	372	713	1099	1485
3	92	184	276	528	814	1100
4	73	146	219	420	648	875
5	60	120	180	345	535	725
6-10: 8-11,21-Mandrake/Henry-c	48	96	144	276	426	575
11-16,18,20: 12-Mandrake-c begin.	40	80	120	230	353	475
17-The Lone Ranger begins	46	92	138	265	400	535
19-Classic robot-c (scarce)	100	200	300	575	888	1200
21-30: 25-Only Blondie-c. 26-Dagwood-c begin	27	54	81	158	259	360
31-40: 36-Flag-c	19	38	57	109	172	235
41-50	15	30	45	85	130	175
51-60	14	28	42	76	108	140
61-70	11	22	33	62	86	110
71-99, 107,108-Flash Gordon app; not by Raymond	9	18	27	52	69	85
100	10	20	30	56	76	95
101-106,109-123: 123-Last Dagwood-c	9	18	27	47	61	75

MAGIC FLUTE, THE (See Night Music #9-11)

MAGICIAN: APPRENTICE
Dabel Brothers/Marvel Comics (Dabel Brothers) #3 on: Mar, 2007 - No. 12, Dec, 2007 ($2.95/$2.99)

1-12-Adaptation of the Raymond E. Feist Riftwar Saga series 3.00
1,2-($5.95) 1-Wraparound variant-c by Maitz. 2-Wraparound variant-c by Booth 6.00
Collected Edition (10/06, $3.99) r/#1&2 4.00
Vol. 1 HC (2007, $19.99, dustjacket) r/#1-6; foreword by Feist 20.00
Vol. 1 SC (2007, $15.99) r/#1-6; foreword by Feist 16.00
Vol. 2 HC (2008, $19.99, dustjacket) r/#7-12 20.00

MAGIC PICKLE
Oni Press: Sept, 2001 - No. 4, Dec, 2001 ($2.95, limited series)

1-4-Scott Morse-s/a; Mahfood-a (2 pgs.) 3.00

MAGIC SWORD, THE (See Movie Classics)

MAGIC THE GATHERING (Title Series), **Acclaim Comics (Armada)**

...ANTIQUITIES WAR,11/95 - 2/96 ($2.50), 1-4-Paul Smith-a(p) 3.00
...ARABIAN NIGHTS, 12/95 - 1/96 ($2.50), 1,2 3.00
...COLLECTION ,'95 ($4.95), 1,2-polybagged 5.00
...CONVOCATIONS, '95 ($2.50), 1-nn-pin-ups 3.00
...ELDER DRAGONS ,'95 ($2.50), 1,2-Doug Wheatley-a 3.00
...FALLEN ANGEL ,'95 ($5.95), nn 6.00
...FALLEN EMPIRES ,9/95 - 10/95 ($2.75), 1,2 3.00
...Collection ($4.95)-polybagged 5.00
...HOMELANDS ,'95 ($5.95), nn-polybagged w/card; Hildebrandts-c 6.00
... ICE AGE (On The World of...) ,7/5 -11/95 ($2.50), 1-4: 1,2-bound-in Magic Card. 3,4-bound-in insert 3.00
...LEGEND OF JEDIT OJANEN, '96 ($2.50), 1,2 3.00
...NIGHTMARE, '95 ($2.50, one shot), 1 3.00
...THE SHADOW MAGE, 7/95 - 10/95 ($2.50), 1-4-bagged w/Magic The Gathering card 3.00
...Collection 1,2 (1995, $4.95)-Trade paperback; polybagged 5.00
...SHANDALAR ,'96 ($2.50), 1,2 3.00
...WAYFARER ,11/95 - 2/96 ($2.50), 1-5 3.00

MAGIC: THE GATHERING: GERRARD'S QUEST
Dark Horse Comics: Mar, 1998 - No. 4, June, 1998 ($2.95, limited series)

1-4: Grell-s/Mhan-a 3.00

MAGIK (Illyana and Storm Limited Series)
Marvel Comics Group: Dec, 1983 - No. 4, Mar, 1984 (60¢, limited series)

1-4: 1-Characters from X-Men; Inferno begins; X-Men cameo (Buscema pencils in #1,2; c-1p. 2-4: 2-Nightcrawler app. & X-Men cameo 4.00

MAGIK (See Black Sun mini-series)
Marvel Comics: Dec, 2000 - No. 4, Mar, 2001 ($2.99, limited series)

1-4-Liam Sharp-a/Abnett & Lanning-s; Nightcrawler app. 3.00

MAGILLA GORILLA (TV) (See Kite Fun Book)
Gold Key: May, 1964 - No. 10, Dec, 1968 (Hanna-Barbera)

	GD	VG	FN	VF	VF/NM	NM-
1-1st comic app.	9	18	27	65	113	160
2-4: 3-Vs. Yogi Bear for President. 4-1st Punkin Puss & Mushmouse, Ricochet Rabbit & Droop-a-Long	6	12	18	37	59	80
5-10: 10-Reprints	5	10	15	30	48	65

MAGILLA GORILLA (TV)(See Spotlight #4)
Charlton Comics: Nov, 1970 - No. 5, July, 1971 (Hanna-Barbera)

	GD	VG	FN	VF	VF/NM	NM-
1	5	10	15	34	55	75
2-5	4	8	12	22	34	45

MAGNETIC MEN FEATURING MAGNETO
Marvel Comics (Amalgam): June, 1997 ($1.95, one-shot)

1-Tom Peyer-s/Barry Kitson & Dan Panosian-a 3.00

MAGNETO (See X-Men #1)
Marvel Comics: nd (Sept, 1993) (Giveaway) (one-shot)

0-Embossed foil-c by Sienkiewicz; r/Classic X-Men #19 & 12 by Bolton 5.00

MAGNETO
Marvel Comics: Nov, 1996 - No. 4, Feb, 1997 ($1.95, limited series)

1-4: Peter Milligan scripts & Kelley Jones-a(p) 3.00

MAGNETO
Marvel Comics: Mar, 2011 ($2.99, one-shot)

1-Howard Chaykin-s/a; Roger Cruz-c 3.00

MAGNETO AND THE MAGNETIC MEN
Marvel Comics (Amalgam): Apr, 1996 ($1.95, one-shot)

1-Jeff Matsuda-a(p) 3.00

MAGNETO ASCENDANT
Marvel Comics: May, 1999 ($3.99, squarebound one-shot)

1-Reprints early Magneto appearances 4.00

MAGNETO: DARK SEDUCTION
Marvel Comics: Jun, 2000 - No. 4, Sept, 2000 ($2.99, limited series)

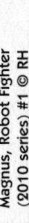

Magnus, Robot Fighter (2010 series) #1 © RH

Major Bummer #4 © Arcudi & Mahnke

Man Comics #15 © MAR

GD 2.0 | VG 4.0 | FN 6.0 | VF 8.0 | VF/NM 9.0 | NM- 9.2

1-4: Nicieza-s/Cruz-a. 3,4-Avengers-c/app. 3.00

MAGNETO REX
Marvel Comics: Apr, 1999 - No. 3, July, 1999 ($2.50, limited series)
1-3-Rogue, Quicksilver app.; Peterson-a(p) 3.00

MAGNUS, ROBOT FIGHTER (...4000 A.D.)(See Doctor Solar)
Gold Key: Feb, 1963 - No. 46, Jan, 1977 (All painted covers except #5,30,31)
1-Origin & 1st app. Magnus; Aliens (1st app.) series begins
22 44 66 159 317 475
2,3 10 20 30 73 134 195
4-10: 10-Simonson fan club illo (5/65, 1st-a?) 7 14 21 49 80 110
11-20 5 10 15 35 55 75
21,24-28: 28-Aliens ends 4 8 12 23 36 48
22,23: 22-Origin-r/#1; last 12¢ issue 4 8 12 24 37 50
29-46-Mostly reprints 2 4 6 13 18 22
...: One For One (Dark Horse Comics, 9/10, $1.00) r/#1 1.00
Russ Manning's Magnus Robot Fighter - Vol. 1 HC (Dark Horse, 2004, $49.95) r/#1-7 70.00
Russ Manning's Magnus Robot Fighter - Vol. 2 HC (DH, 6/05, $49.95) r/#8-14; forward by Steve Rude 50.00
Russ Manning's Magnus Robot Fighter - Vol. 3 HC (Dark Horse, 10/06, $49.95) r/#15-21 50.00
NOTE: *Manning a-1-22, 28-43(r). **Spiegle** a-23, 44r.*

MAGNUS ROBOT FIGHTER (Also see Vintage Magnus)
Valiant/Acclaim Comics: May, 1991 - No. 64, Feb, 1996 ($1.75/$1.95/$2.25/$2.50)
1-Nichols/Layton-c/a; 1-8 have trading cards 1 2 3 5 7 9
2-8: 4-Rai cameo. 5-Origin & 1st full app. Rai (10/91); 5-8 are in flip book format and back-c & half of book are Rai #1-4 mini-series. 6-1st Solar x-over. 7-Magnus vs. Rai-c/story; 1st X-O Armor 6.00
0-Origin issue; Layton-a; ordered through mail w/coupons from 1st 8 issues plus 50¢; B. Smith trading card 2 4 6 11 16 20
0-Sold thru comic shops without trading card 2 4 6 8 10 12
9-11 4.00
12-(3.25, 44 pgs.)-Turok-c/story (1st app. in Valiant universe, 5/92); has 8 pg. Magnus story insert 2 4 6 9 12 15
13-24,26-48: 14-1st app. Isak. 15,16-Unity x-overs. 15-Miller-c. 16-Birth of Magnus. 21-New direction & new logo. 21-Gold ink variant. 24-Story cont'd in Rai & the Future Force #9. 33-Timewalker app.36-Bound-in trading cards. 37-Rai & Starwatchers app. 44-Bound-in sneak peek card. 3.00
25-($2.95)-Embossed silver foil-c; new costume 4.00
49-63 3.00
64-($2.50): 64-Magnus dies? 4.00
...Invasion (1994, $9.95)-r/Rai #1-4 & Magnus #5-8 10.00
Magnus Steel Nation (1994, $9.95) r/#1-4 10.00
Yearbook (1994, $3.95, 52 pgs.) 4.00
NOTE: ***Ditko/Reese** a-18. **Layton** a(i)-5; c-6-9i, 25; back(i)-5-8. **Reese** a(i)-22, 25, 28; c(i)-22, 24, 28. **Simonson** c-16. Prices for issues 1-8 are for trading cards and coupons intact.*

MAGNUS ROBOT FIGHTER
Acclaim Comics (Valiant Heroes): V2#1, May, 1997 - No. 18, Jun, 1998 ($2.50)
1-18: 1-Reintro Magnus; Donavon Wylie (X-O Manowar) cameo; Tom Peyer scripts & Mike McKone-c/a begin; painted variant-c exists 3.00

MAGNUS ROBOT FIGHTER
Dark Horse Comics: Aug, 2010 - Present ($3.50)
1,2: 1-Shooter-s/Reinhold-a; covers by Swanland & Reinhold; back-up r/#1 (1963) 3.50

MAGNUS ROBOT FIGHTER/NEXUS
Valiant/Dark Horse Comics: Dec, 1993 - No. 2, Apr, 1994 ($2.95, lim. series)
1,2: Steve Rude painted-c & pencils in all 3.00

MAGOG (See Justice Society of America 2007 series)(Continues in Justice Society Special #1)
DC Comics: Nov, 2009 - No.12, Ot. 2010 ($2.99)
1-12: 1-Giffen-s/Porter-a/Fabry-c; variant-c by Porter. 7-Zatanna app. 3.00
...: Lethal Force TPB (2010, $14.99) r/#1-5 15.00

MAID OF THE MIST (See American Graphics)

MAI, THE PSYCHIC GIRL
Eclipse Comics: May, 1987 - No. 28, July, 1989 ($1.50, B&W, bi-weekly, 44pgs.)
1-28, 1,2-2nd print 4.00

MAJESTIC (Mr. Majestic from WildCATS)
DC Comics: Oct, 2004 - No. 4, Jan, 2005 ($2.95, limited series)
1-4-Kerschl-a/Abnett & Lanning-s. 1-Superman app.; Superman #1 cover swipe 3.00
...: Strange New Visitor TPB (2005, $14.99) r/#1-4 & Action #811, Advs. of Superman #624 & Superman #201 15.00

MAJESTIC (Mr. Majestic from WildCATS)

GD 2.0 | VG 4.0 | FN 6.0 | VF 8.0 | VF/NM 9.0 | NM- 9.2

DC Comics (WildStorm): Mar, 2005 - No. 17, July, 2006 ($2.95/$2.99)
1-17: 1-Googe-a/Abnett & Lanning-s; Superman app. 9-Jeanty-a; Zealot app. 3.00
...: Meanwhile, Back on Earth... TPB (2006, $14.99) r/#8-12 15.00
...: The Final Cut TPB (2007, $14.99) r/#13-17 & story fro WildStorm Winter Special 15.00
...: While You Were Out TPB (2006, $12.99) r/#1-7 13.00

MAJOR BUMMER
DC Comics: Aug, 1997 - No. 15, Oct, 1998 ($2.50)
1-15: 1-Origin and 1st app. Major Bummer 3.00

MAJOR HOOPLE COMICS (See Crackajack Funnies)
Nedor Publications: nd (Jan, 1943)
1-Mary Worth, Phantom Soldier app. by Moldoff 38 76 114 219 352 485

MAJOR VICTORY COMICS (Also see Dynamic Comics)
H. Clay Glover/Service Publ./Harry 'A' Chesler: 1944 - No. 3, Summer, 1945
1-Origin Major Victory (patriotic hero) by C. Sultan (reprint from Dynamic #1); 1st app. Spider Woman 65 130 195 416 708 1000
2-Dynamic Boy app. 40 80 120 242 401 560
3-Rocket Boy app. 37 74 111 222 361 500

MALIBU ASHCAN: RAFFERTY (See Firearm #12)
Malibu Comics (Ultraverse): Nov, 1994 (99¢, B&W w/color-c; one-shot)
1-Previews "The Rafferty Saga" storyline in Firearm; Chaykin-c 3.00

MALTESE FALCON
David McKay Publications: No. 48, 1946
Feature Books 48-by Dashiell Hammett 86 172 258 546 936 1325

MALU IN THE LAND OF ADVENTURE
I. W. Enterprises: 1964 (See White Princess of Jungle #2)
1-r/Avon's Slave Girl Comics #1; Severin-c 5 10 15 30 48 65

MAMMOTH COMICS
Whitman Publishing Co.(K. K. Publ.): 1938 (84 pgs.) (B&W, 8-1/2x11-1/2")
1-Alley Oop, Terry & the Pirates, Dick Tracy, Little Orphan Annie, Wash Tubbs, Moon Mullins, Smilin' Jack, Tailspin Tommy, Don Winslow, Dan Dunn, Smokey Stover & other reprints (scarce) 200 400 600 1280 2190 3100

MAN AGAINST TIME
Image Comics (Motown Machineworks): May, 1996 - No. 4, Aug, 1996 ($2.25, lim. series)
1-4: 1-Simonson-c. 2,3-Leon-c. 4-Barreto & Leon-c 3.00

MAN-BAT (See Batman Family, Brave & the Bold, & Detective #400)
National Periodical Publ./DC Comics: Dec-Jan, 1975-76 - No. 2, Feb-Mar, 1976; Dec, 1984
1-Ditko-a(p); Aparo-c; Batman app.; 1st app. She-Bat?
3 6 9 16 23 30
2-Aparo-c 2 4 6 10 14 18
1 (12/84)-N. Adams-r(3)/Det.(Vs. Batman on-c) 5.00

MAN-BAT
DC Comics: Feb, 1996 - No. 3, Apr, 1996 ($2.25, limited series)
1-3: Dixon scripts in all. 2-Killer Croc-c/app. 3.00

MAN-BAT
DC Comics: Jun, 2006 - No. 5, Oct, 2006 ($2.99, limited series)
1-5: Bruce Jones-s/Mike Huddleston-a/c. 1-Hush app. 3.00

MAN CALLED A-X, THE
Malibu Comics (Bravura): Nov, 1994 - No. 4, Jun, 1995 ($2.95, limited series)
0-4: Marv Wolfman scripts & Shawn McManus-c/a. 0-(2/95). 1-"1A" on cover 3.00

MAN CALLED A-X, THE
DC Comics: Oct, 1997 - No. 8, May, 1998 ($2.50)
1-8: Marv Wolfman scripts & Shawn McManus-c/a. 3.00

MAN CALLED KEV, A (See The Authority)
DC Comics (WildStorm): Sept, 2006 - No. 5, Feb, 2007 ($2.99, limited series)
1-5-Ennis-s/Ezquerra-a/Fabry-c 3.00
TPB (2007, $14.99) r/#1-5; cover gallery 15.00

MAN COMICS
Marvel/Atlas Comics (NPI): Dec, 1949 - No. 28, Sept, 1953 (#1-6: 52 pgs.)
1-Tuska-a 24 48 72 140 230 320
2-Tuska-a 15 30 45 83 124 165
3-6 12 24 36 69 97 125
7,8 11 22 33 64 90 115
9-13,15: 9-Format changes to war 10 20 30 54 72 90
14-Henkel (3 pgs.); Pakula-a 10 20 30 56 76 95

The Man From UNCLE #18 © GK

Manhunt! #3 © ME

Manhunter (2004 series) #21 © DC

	GD	VG	FN	VF	VF/NM	NM-
	2.0	4.0	6.0	8.0	9.0	9.2

16-21,23-28: 28-Crime issue (Bob Brant) 9 18 27 50 65 80
22-Krigstein-a, 5 pgs. 10 20 30 58 79 100

NOTE: *Berg a-14, 15, 19. Colan a-9, 21, 23. Everett a-8, 22; c-22, 25. Heath a-11, 13, 16, 17, 21. Kubertish a-by Bob Brown-3. Maneely a-11-13; c-10, 11, 16. Reinman a-11. Robinson a-7, 10, 14. Robert Sale a-9, 11. Sinnott a-22, 23. Tuska a-14, 23.*

MANDRAKE THE MAGICIAN (See Defenders Of The Earth, 123, 46, 52, 55, Giant Comic Album, King Comics, Magic Comics, The Phantom #21, Tiny Tot Funnies & Wow Comics, '36)

MANDRAKE THE MAGICIAN (See Harvey Comics Hits #53)
David McKay Publ./Dell/King Comics (All 12¢): 1938 - 1948; Sept, 1966 - No. 10, Nov, 1967

Feature Books 18,19,23 (1938) 73 146 219 467 796 1125
Feature Books 46 47 94 141 296 498 700
Feature Books 52,55 39 78 117 240 395 550
Four Color 752 (11/56) 10 20 30 69 122 175
1-Begin S.O.S. Phantom, ends #3 6 12 18 37 59 80
2-7,9: 4-Girl Phantom app. 5-Flying Saucer-c/story. 5,6-Brick Bradford app. 7-Origin Lothar. 9-Brick Bradford app. 4 8 12 22 34 45
8-Jeff Jones-a (4 pgs.) 4 8 12 24 37 50
10-Rip Kirby app.; Raymond-a (14 pgs.) 4 8 12 28 44 60

MANDRAKE THE MAGICIAN
Marvel Comics: Apr, 1995 - No. 2, May, 1995 ($2.95, unfinished limited series)

1,2: Mike Barr scripts 3.00

MAN-EATING COW (See Tick #7,8)
New England Comics: July, 1992 - No. 10, 1994? ($2.75, B&W, limited series)

1-10 3.00
Man-Eating Cow Bonanza (6/96, $4.95, 128 pgs.)-r/#1-4. 5.00

MAN FROM ATLANTIS (TV)
Marvel Comics: Feb, 1978 - No. 7, Aug, 1978

1-(84 pgs.)-Sutton-a(p), Buscema-c; origin & cast photos 2 4 6 8 12 12
2-7 6.00

MAN FROM PLANET X, THE
Planet X Productions: 1987 (no price; probably unlicensed)

1-Reprints Fawcett Movie Comic 3.00

MAN FROM U.N.C.L.E., THE (TV) (Also see The Girl From Uncle)
Gold Key: Feb, 1965 - No. 22, Apr, 1969 (All photo-c)

1 12 24 36 87 164 240
2-Photo back c-2-8 7 14 21 50 83 115
3-10: 7-Jet Dream begins (1st app., also see Jet Dream) (all new stories) 6 12 18 37 59 80
11-22: 19-Last 12¢ issue. 21,22-Reprint #10 & 7 5 10 15 32 51 70

MAN FROM U.N.C.L.E., THE (TV)
Entertainment Publishing: 1987 - No. 11 ($1.50/$1.75, B&W)

1-7 ($1.50), 8-11 ($1.75) 4.00

MAN FROM WELLS FARGO (TV)
Dell Publishing Co.: No. 1287, Feb-Apr, 1962 - May-July, 1962 (Photo-c)

Four Color 1287, #01-495-207 6 12 18 37 59 80

MANGA DARKCHYLDE (Also see Darkchylde titles)
Dark Horse Comics: Feb, 2005 - No. 5 ($2.99, limited series)

1,2-Randy Queen-s/a; manga-style pre-teen Ariel Chylde 3.00

MANGA SHI (See Tomoe)
Crusade Entertainment: Aug, 1996 ($2.95)

1-Printed backwards (manga-style) 3.00

MANGA SHI 2000
Crusade Entertainment: Feb, 1997 - No. 3, June, 1997 ($2.95, mini-series)

1-3: 1-Two covers 3.00

MANGA ZEN (Also see Zen Intergalactic Ninja)
Zen Comics (Fusion Studios): 1996 - No. 3, 1996 ($2.50, B&W)

1-3 3.00

MANGAZINE
Antarctic Press: Aug, 1985 - No. 4, Sept, 1986 (B&W)

1-Soft paper-c 2 4 6 11 16 20
2-4 2 4 6 8 11 14

MANGLE TANGLE TALES
Innovation Publishing: 1990 ($2.95, deluxe format)

1-Intro by Harlan Ellison 3.00

MANHUNT! (Becomes Red Fox #15 on)
Magazine Enterprises: 10/47 - No. 11, 8/48; #13,14, 1953 (no #12)

1-Red Fox by L. B. Cole, Undercover Girl by Whitney, Space Ace begin (1st app.); negligee panels 53 106 159 334 567 800
2-Electrocution-c 41 82 123 256 428 600
3-6: 6-Bondage-c 34 68 102 199 325 450
7-10: 7-Space Ace ends. 8-Trail Colt begins (intro/1st app., 5/48) by Guardineer; Trail Colt-c. 10-G. Ingels-a 29 58 87 170 278 385
11(8/48)-Frazetta-a, 7 pgs.; The Duke, Scotland Yard begin 41 82 123 250 418 585
13(A-1 #63)-Frazetta, r-/Trail Colt #1, 7 pgs. 39 78 117 231 378 525
14(A-1 #77)-Bondage/hypo-c; last L. B. Cole Red Fox; Ingels-a 40 80 120 242 401 560

NOTE: *Guardineer a-1-5; c-8. Whitney a-2-14; c-1-6, 10. Red Fox by L. B. Cole-#1-14. #15 was advertised but came out as Red Fox #15.*

MANHUNTER (See Adventure #58, 73, Brave & the Bold, Detective Comics, 1st Issue Special, House of Mystery #143 and Justice League of America)
DC Comics: 1984 ($2.50, 76 pgs; high quality paper)

1-Simonson-c/a(r)/Detective; Batman app. 4.00

MANHUNTER
DC Comics: July, 1988 - No. 24, Apr, 1990 ($1.00)

1-24: 8,9-Flash app. 9-Invasion. 17-Batman-c/sty 3.00

MANHUNTER
DC Comics: No. 0, Nov, 1994 - No. 12, Nov, 1995 ($1.95/$2.25)

0-12 3.00

MANHUNTER (Also see Batman: Streets of Gotham)
DC Comics: Oct, 2004 - No. 38, Mar, 2009 ($2.50/$2.99)

1-21: 1-Intro. Kate Spencer; Saiz-a/Jae Lee-c/Andreyko-s. 2,3 Shadow Thief app. 13,14-Omac x-over. 20-One Year Later 3.00
22-30: 22-Begin $2.99-c. 23-Sandra Knight app. 27-Chaykin-c. 28-Batman app. 3.00
31-38: 31-(8/08) Gaydos-a. 33,34-Suicide Squad app. 3.00
...: Forgotten (2009, $17.99) r/#31-38 18.00
...: Origins (2007, $17.99) r/#15-23 18.00
...: Street Justice (2005, $12.99) r/#1-5; Andreyko intro. 13.00
...: Trial By Fire (2007, $17.99) r/#6-14 18.00
...: Unleashed (2008, $17.99) r/#24-30 18.00

MANHUNTER: ...
DC Comics: 1979, 1999

The Complete Saga TPB (1979) Reprints stories from Detective Comics #437-443 by Goodwin and Simonson 40.00
The Special Edition TPB (1999, $9.95) r/stories from Detective Comics #437-443 10.00

MANIFEST ETERNITY
DC Comics: Aug, 2006 - No. 6, Jan, 2007 ($2.99)

1-6-Lobdell-s/Nguyen-a/c 3.00

MAN IN BLACK (See Thrill-O-Rama) (Also see All New Comics, Front Page, Green Hornet #31, Strange Story & Tally-Ho Comics)
Harvey Publications: Sept, 1957 - No. 4, Mar, 1958

1-Bob Powell-c/a 18 36 54 105 165 225
2-4: Powell-c/a 14 28 42 80 115 150

MAN IN BLACK
Lorne-Harvey Publications (Recollections): 1990 - No. 2, July, 1991 (B&W)

1,2 4.00

MAN IN FLIGHT (Disney, TV)
Dell Publishing Co.: No. 836, Sept, 1957

Four Color 836 7 14 21 47 76 105

MAN IN SPACE (Disney, TV, see Dell Giant #27)
Dell Publishing Co.: No. 716, Aug, 1956 - No. 954, Nov, 1958

Four Color 716-A science feat. from Tomorrowland 8 16 24 56 93 130
Four Color 954-Satellites 7 14 21 47 76 105

MANKIND (WWF Wrestling)
Chaos Comics: Sept, 1999 ($2.95, one-shot)

1-Regular and photo-c 3.00
1-Premium Edition ($10.00) Dwayne Turner & Danny Miki-c 10.00

MANN AND SUPERMAN
DC Comics: 2000 ($5.95, prestige format, one-shot)

nn-Michael T. Gilbert-s/a 6.00

MAN OF STEEL, THE (Also see Superman: The Man of Steel)

Man-Thing #14 © MAR

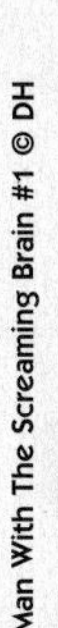

Man With The Screaming Brain #1 © DH

The Many Ghosts of Doctor Graves #41 © CC

GD 2.0 VG 4.0 FN 6.0 VF 8.0 VF/NM 9.0 NM- 9.2

DC Comics: 1986 (June release) - No. 6, 1986 (75¢, limited series)

1-6: 1-Silver logo; Byrne-c/a/scripts in all; origin, 1-Alternate-c for newsstand sales,1-Distr. to toy stores by So Much Fun, 2-6: 2-Intro. Lois Lane, Jimmy Olsen. 3-Intro/origin Magpie; Batman-c/story. 4-Intro. new Lex Luthor 4.00
1-6-Silver Editions (1993, $1.95)-r/1-6 3.00
...The Complete Saga nn-Contains #1-6, given away in contest 60.00
Limited Edition, softcover 4 8 12 28 44 60
NOTE: *Issues 1-6 were released between Action #583 (9/86) & Action #584 (1/87) plus Superman #423 (9/86) & Advs. of Superman #424 (1/87).*

MAN OF THE ATOM (See Solar, Man of the Atom Vol. 2)

MAN OF WAR (See Liberty Guards & Liberty Scouts)
Centaur Publications: Nov, 1941 - No. 2, Jan, 1942

1-The Fire-Man, Man of War, The Sentinel, Liberty Guards, & Vapo-Man begin; Gustavson-c/a; Flag-c 174 348 522 1114 1907 2700
2-Intro The Ferret; Gustavson-c/a 126 252 378 806 1378 1950

MAN OF WAR
Eclipse Comics: Aug, 1987 - No. 3, Feb, 1988 ($1.75, Baxter paper)

1-3: Bruce Jones scripts 3.00

MAN OF WAR (See The Protectors)
Malibu Comics: 1993 - No, 8, Feb, 1994 ($1.95/$2.50/$2.25)

1-5 ($1.95)-Newsstand Editions w/different-c 3.00
1-8: 1-5-Collector's Edi. w/poster. 6-8 ($2.25): 6-Polybagged w/Skycap. 8-Vs. Rocket Rangers 4.00

MAN O' MARS
Fiction House Magazines: 1953; 1964

1-Space Rangers; Whitman-c 46 90 138 290 488 685
I.W. Reprint #1-r/Man O'Mars #1 & Star Pirate; Murphy Anderson-a 6 12 18 37 59 80

MANTECH ROBOT WARRIORS
Archie Enterprises, Inc.: Sept, 1984 - No. 4, Apr, 1985 (75¢)

1-4: Ayers-c/a(p). 1-Buckler-c(i) 3.00

MAN-THING (See Fear, Giant-Size..., Marvel Comics Presents, Marvel Fanfare, Monsters Unleashed, Power Record Comics & Savage Tales)
Marvel Comics Group: Jan, 1974 - No. 22, Oct, 1975; V2#1, Nov, 1979 - V2#11, July, 1981

1-Howard the Duck(2nd app.) cont'd/Fear #19 6 12 18 41 66 90
2 3 6 9 18 27 35
3-1st app. original Foolkiller 3 6 9 16 22 28
4-Origin Foolkiller; last app. 1st Foolkiller 3 6 9 14 20 26
5-11-Ploog-a. 11-Foolkiller cameo (flashback) 3 6 9 14 20 26
12-22: 19-1st app. Scavenger. 20-Spidey cameo. 21-Origin Scavenger, Man-Thing. 22-Howard the Duck cameo 2 4 6 9 13 16
V2#1(1979) 2 4 6 8 10 12
V2#2-11: 4-Dr. Strange-c/app. 11-Mayerik-a 6.00
NOTE: ***Alcala** a-14. **Brunner** c-1. J. **Buscema** a-12p, 13p, 16p. **Gil Kane** c-4p, 10p, 12-20p, 21. **Mooney** a-17, 18, 19p, 20-22, V2#1-3p. **Ploog** Man-Thing-5p, 6p, 7, 8, 9-11p; c-5, 6, 8, 9, 11. **Sutton** a-13i. No. 19 says #10 in indicia.*

MAN-THING (Volume Three, continues in Strange Tales #1 (9/98))
Marvel Comics: Dec, 1997 - No. 8, July, 1998 ($2.99)

1-8-DeMatteis-s/Sharp-a. 2-Two covers. 6-Howard the Duck-c/app. 3.00

MAN-THING (Prequel to 2005 movie)
Marvel Comics: Sept, 2004 - No. 3, Nov, 2004 ($2.99, limited series)

1-3-Hans Rodionoff-s/Kyle Hotz-a 3.00
...: Whatever Knows Fear... (2005, $12.99, TPB) r/#1-3, Savage Tales #1, Adv. Into Fear #16 13.00

MANTRA
Malibu Comics (Ultraverse): July, 1993 - No. 24, Aug, 1995 ($1.95/$2.50)

1-Polybagged w/trading card & coupon 4.00
1-Newsstand edition w/o trading card or coupon 3.00
1-Full cover holographic edition 1 3 4 6 8 10
1-Ultra-limited silver foil-c 5.00
2-9,11-24: 3-Intro Warstrike & Kismet. 6-Break-Thru x-over. 2-($2.50-Newsstand edition bagged w/card. 4-($2.50, 48 pgs.)-Rune flip-c/story by B. Smith (3 pgs.). 7-Prime app.; origin Prototype by Jurgens/Austin (2 pgs.). 11-New costume. 17-Intro NecroMantra & Pinnacle; prelude to Godwheel 3.00
10-($3.50, 68 pgs.)-Flip-c w/Ultraverse Premiere #2 4.00
Giant Size 1 (7/94, $2.50, 44 pgs.) 4.00
...Spear of Destiny 1,2 (4/95, $2.50, 36pgs.) 3.00

MANTRA (2nd Series) (Also See Black September)
Malibu Comics (Ultraverse): Infinity, Sept, 1995 - No. 7, Apr, 1996 ($1.50)

Infinity (9/95, $1.50)-Black September x-over, Intro new Mantra 3.00
1-7: 1-(10/95). 5-Return of Eden (original Mantra). 6,7-Rush app. 3.00

MAN WITH NO NAME, THE (Based on the Clint Eastwood gunslinger character)
Dynamite Entertainment: 2008 - No. 11, 2009 ($3.50)

1-11: 1-Gage-s/Dias-a/Isanove-c. 7-Bernard-a 3.50

MAN WITH THE SCREAMING BRAIN (Based on screenplay by Bruce Campbell & David Goodman)
Dark Horse Comics: Apr, 2005 - No. 4, July, 2005 ($2.99, limited series)

1-4-Campbell & Goodman-s; Remender-a/c. 1-Variant-c by Noto. 3-Powell var-c. 4-Mignola var-c 3.00
TPB (11/05, $13.95) r/#1-4; David Goodman intro.; cover gallery 14.00

MAN WITH THE X-RAY EYES, THE (See X,... under Movie Comics)

MANY GHOSTS OF DR. GRAVES, THE (Doctor Graves #73 on)
Charlton Comics: 5/67 - No. 60, 12/76; No. 61, 9/77 - No. 62, 10/77; No. 63, 2/78 - No. 65, 4/78; No. 66, 6/81 - No. 72, 5/82

1-Ditko-a; Palais-a; early issues 12¢-c 7 14 21 45 73 100
2-6,8,10 3 6 9 20 30 40
7,9-Ditko-a 4 8 12 24 37 50
11-13,16-18-Ditko-c/a 3 6 9 20 30 40
14,19,23,25 2 4 6 10 14 18
15,20,21-Ditko-a 3 6 9 14 20 25
22,24,26,27,29-35,38,40-Ditko-c/a 3 6 9 16 22 28
28-Ditko-c 3 6 9 14 20 25
36,46,56,57,59,61,66,67,69,71 2 4 6 8 10 12
37,41,43,51,60-Ditko-a 2 4 6 9 13 16
39,58-Ditko-c. 39-Sutton-a. 58-Ditko-a 2 4 6 9 13 16
42,44,53-Sutton-c; Ditko-a. 42-Sutton-a 2 4 6 9 13 16
45-(5/74) 2nd Newton comic work (8 pgs.); new logo; Sutton-c 2 4 6 11 16 20
47-Newton, Sutton, Ditko-a 2 4 6 10 14 18
48-Ditko, Sutton-a 2 4 6 9 13 16
49-Newton-c/a; Sutton-a. 2 4 6 8 11 14
50-Sutton-a 2 4 6 8 10 12
52-Newton-c; Ditko-a 2 4 6 9 13 16
54-Early Byrne-c; Ditko-a 2 4 6 10 14 18
55-Ditko-c; Sutton-a 2 4 6 9 13 16
62-65,68-Ditko-c/a. 65-Sutton-a 2 4 6 11 16 20
70,72-Ditko-a 2 4 6 10 14 18
Modern Comics Reprint 12,25 (1978) 6.00
NOTE: ***Aparo** a-4, 5, 7, 8, 66r, 69r; c-8, 14, 19, 66r, 67r. **Byrne** c-54. **Ditko** a-1, 7, 9, 11-13, 15-18, 20-22, 24, 26, 27, 29, 30-35, 37, 38, 40-44, 47, 48, 51-54, 58, 60r-65r, 70, 72; c-11-13, 16-18, 22, 24, 26-35, 38, 40, 55, 58, 62-65. **Howard** a-38, 39, 45i, 65; c-48. **Kim** a-36, 46, 52. **Larson** a-58. **Morisi** a-13, 14, 23, 26. **Newton** a-45, 47p, 49p; c-49, 52. **Staton** a-36, 37, 41, 43. **Sutton** a-39, 42, 47-50, 55, 65; c-42, 44, 45; painted c-53. **Zeck** a-56, 59.*

MANY LOVES OF DOBIE GILLIS (TV)
National Periodical Publications: May-June, 1960 - No. 26, Oct, 1964

1-Most covers by Bob Oskner 21 42 63 150 300 450
2-5 12 24 36 82 154 225
6-10: 10-Last 10¢-c 9 18 27 60 100 140
11-26: 20-Drucker-a. 24-(3-4/64). 25-(9/64) 8 16 24 54 90 125

MANY WORLDS OF TESLA STRONG, THE (Also see Tom Strong)
America's Best Comics: July, 2003 ($5.95, one-shot)

1-Two covers by Timm & Art Adams; art by various incl. Campbell, Cho, Noto, Hughes 6.00

MARAUDER'S MOON (See Luke Short, Four Color #848)

MARCH OF COMICS (See Promotional Comics section)

MARCH OF CRIME (Formerly My Love Affair #1-6) (See Fox Giants)
Fox Features Synd.: No. 7, July, 1950 - No. 2, Sept, 1950; No. 3, Sept, 1951

7(#1)(7/50)-True crime stories; Wood-a 41 82 123 250 418 585
2(9/50)-Wood-a (exceptional) 40 80 120 242 401 560
3(9/51) 20 40 60 117 189 260

MARCO POLO
Charlton Comics Group: 1962 (Movie classic)

nn (Scarce)-Glanzman-c/a (25 pgs.) 10 20 30 68 119 170

MARC SILVESTRI SKETCHBOOK
Image Comics (Top Cow): Jan, 2004 ($2.99, one-shot)

1-Character sketches, concept artwork, storyboards of Witchblade, Darkness & others 3.00

MARC SPECTOR: MOON KNIGHT (Also see Moon Knight)
Marvel Comics: June, 1989 - No. 60, Mar, 1994 ($1.50/$1.75, direct sales)

1-24,26-49,51-54,58,59: 4-Intro new Midnight. 8,9-Punisher app. 15-Silver Sable app.

Marge's Little Lulu #25 © M. Buell

Marge's Tubby #22 © M. Buell

Marineman #1 © Ian Churchill

GD VG FN VF VF/NM NM-
2.0 4.0 6.0 8.0 9.0 9.2

19-21-Spider-Man & Punisher app. 32,33-Hobgoblin II (Macendale) & Spider-Man (in black costume) app. 35-38-Punisher story. 42-44-Infinity War x-over. 46-Demogoblin app.
51,53-Gambit app. 55-New look. 57-Spider-Man-c/story. 60-Moon Knight dies 3.00
25,50: 25-(52 pgs.)-Ghost Rider app. 50-(56 pgs.)-Special die-cut-c 4.00
55-57,60-Platt a 4.00
...: Divided We Fall ($4.95, 52 pgs.) 5.00
Special 1 (1992, $2.50) 4.00

NOTE: *Cowan c(p) 20-23. Guice c-20. Heath c/a-4. Platt -a 55-57,60; c-55-60.*

MARGARET O'BRIEN (See The Adventures of...)

MARGE'S LITTLE LULU (Continues as Little Lulu from #207 on)
Dell Publishing Co./Gold Key #165-206: No. 74, 6/45 - No. 164, 7-9/62; No. 165, 10/62 - No. 206, 8/72

Marjorie Henderson Buell, born in Philadelphia, Pa., in 1904, created Little Lulu, a cartoon character that appeared weekly in the Saturday Evening Post from Feb. 23, 1935 through Dec. 30, 1944. She was not responsible for any of the comic books. **John Stanley** did pencils only on all Little Lulu comics through at least #135 (1959). He did pencils and inks on Four Color #74 & 97. **Irving Tripp** began inking stories from #1 on, and remained the comic's illustrator throughout its entire run. **Stanley** did storyboards (layouts), pencils, and scripts in all cases and inking only on covers. His word balloons were written in cursive. **Tripp** and occasionally other artists at Western Publ. in Poughkeepsie, N.Y. blew up the pencilled pages, inked the blowups, and lettered them. **Arnold Drake** did storyboards, pencils and scripts starting with #197 (1970) on, amidst reprinted issues. **Buell** sold her rights exclusively to Western Publ. in Dec., 1971. The earlier issues had to be approved by **Buell** prior to publication.

Four Color 74('45)-Intro Lulu, Tubby & Alvin 127 254 381 1080 2190 3300
Four Color 97(2/46) 52 104 156 442 896 1350
(Above two books are all John Stanley - cover, pencils, and inks.)
Four Color 110('46)-1st Alvin Story Telling Time; 1st app. Willy; variant cover exists
37 74 111 286 568 850
Four Color 115-1st app. Boys' Clubhouse 36 72 108 281 553 825
Four Color 120, 131: 120-1st app. Eddie 30 60 90 228 457 685
Four Color 139('47),146,158 29 58 87 218 439 660
Four Color 165 (10/47)-Smokes doll hair & has wild hallucinations. 1st Tubby detective story
29 58 87 218 439 660
1(1-2/48)-Lulu's Diary feature begins 65 130 195 553 1127 1700
2-1st app. Gloria; 1st app. Miss Feeny 29 58 87 223 449 675
3-5 27 54 81 197 399 600
6-10: 7-1st app. Annie; Xmas-c 22 44 66 162 324 485
11-20: 18-X-Mas-c. 19-1st app. Wilbur. 20-1st app. Mr. McNabbem
17 34 51 122 249 375
21-30: 26-r/F.C. 110. 30-Xmas-c 15 30 45 106 216 325
31-38,40: 35-1st Mumday story 13 26 39 90 173 255
39-Intro. Witch Hazel in "That Awful Witch Hazel" 13 26 39 91 176 260
41-60: 42-Xmas-c. 45-2nd Witch Hazel app. 49-Gives Stanley & others credit
11 22 33 77 144 210
61-80: 63-1st app. Chubby (Tubby's cousin). 68-1st app. Prof. Cleff.
78-Xmas-c. 80-Intro. Little Itch (2/55) 9 18 27 65 113 160
81-99: 90-Xmas-c 8 16 24 54 90 125
100 8 16 24 58 97 135
101-130: 123-1st app. Fifi 6 12 18 43 69 95
131-164: 135-Last Stanley-p 6 12 18 37 59 80
165-Giant; ...in Paris ('62) 10 20 30 71 128 185
166-Giant; ...Christmas Diary (1962 - '63) 10 20 30 71 128 185
167-169 5 10 15 30 48 65
170,172,175,176,178-196,198-200-Stanley-r. 182-1st app. Little Scarecrow Boy
3 6 9 18 27 35
171,173,174,177,197 3 6 9 16 23 30
201,203,206-Last issue to carry Marge's name 3 6 9 14 20 26
202,204,205-Stanley-r 3 6 9 16 23 30
...& Tubby in Japan (12¢)(5-7/62) 01476-207 8 16 24 52 86 120
...Summer Camp 1(8/67-G.K.-Giant) '57-58-r 6 12 18 41 66 90
...Trick 'N' Treat 1(12¢)(12/62-Gold Key) 7 14 21 47 76 105

NOTE: *See Dell Giant Comics #23, 29, 36, 42, 50, & Dell Giants for annuals. All Giants not by Stanley from L.L. on Vacation (7/54) on. Irving Tripp a-#1-on. Christmas c-7, 18, 30, 42, 78, 90, 126, 166, 250. Summer Camp issues #173, 177, 181, 189, 197, 201, 206.*

MARGE'S LITTLE LULU (See Golden Comics Digest #19, 23, 27, 29, 33, 36, 40, 43, 46, & March of Comics #251, 267, 275, 293, 307, 323, 335, 349, 355, 369, 385, 406, 417, 427, 439, 456, 468, 475, 488)

MARGE'S TUBBY (Little Lulu)(See Dell Giants)
Dell Publishing Co./Gold Key: No. 381, Aug, 1952 - No. 49, Dec-Feb, 1961-62

Four Color 381(#1)-Stanley script; Irving Tripp-a 18 36 54 131 266 400
Four Color 430,444-Stanley-a 11 22 33 80 150 220
Four Color 461 (4/53)-1st Tubby & Men From Mars story; Stanley-a
10 20 30 72 131 190
5 (7-9/53)-Stanley-a 9 18 27 61 103 145
6-10 8 16 24 52 86 120
11-20 6 12 18 39 62 85
21-30 5 10 15 32 51 70
31-49 4 8 12 28 44 60
...& the Little Men From Mars No. 30020-410(10/64-G.K.)-25¢, 68 pgs.
8 16 24 52 86 120

NOTE: ***John Stanley** did all storyboards & scripts through at least #35 (1959). **Lloyd White** did all art except F.C. 381, 430, 444, 461 & #5.*

MARGIE (See My Little...)

MARGIE (TV)
Dell Publ. Co.: No. 1307, Mar-May, 1962 - No. 2, July-Sept, 1962 (Photo-c)

Four Color 1307(#1) 6 12 18 37 59 80
2 5 10 15 30 48 65

MARGIE COMICS (Formerly Comedy Comics; Reno Browne #50 on)
(Also see Cindy Comics & Teen Comics)
Marvel Comics (ACI): No. 35, Winter, 1946-47 - No. 49, Dec, 1949

35 19 38 57 111 176 240
36-38,42,45,47-49 12 24 36 67 94 120
39,41,43(2),44,46-Kurtzman's "Hey Look" 13 26 39 74 105 135
40-Three "Hey Looks", three "Giggles 'n' Grins" by Kurtzman
14 28 42 81 118 155

MARINEMAN (Ian Churchill's...)
Image Comics: Dec, 2010 - Present ($3.99)

1-4-Ian Churchill-s/a/c 4.00

MARINES (See Tell It to the...)

MARINES ATTACK
Charlton Comics: Aug, 1964 - No. 9, Feb-Mar, 1966

1-Glanzman-a begins 4 8 12 22 34 45
2-9 3 6 9 14 19 24

MARINES AT WAR (Formerly Tales of the Marines #4)
Atlas Comics (OPI): No. 5, Apr, 1957 - No. 7, Aug, 1957

5-7 10 20 30 54 72 90

NOTE: ***Colan** a-5. **Drucker** a-5. **Everett** a-5. **Maneely** a-5. **Orlando** a-7. **Severin** c-5.*

MARINES IN ACTION
Atlas News Co.: June, 1955 - No. 14, Sept, 1957

1-Rock Murdock, Boot Camp Brady begin 13 26 39 74 105 135
2-14 10 20 30 54 72 90

NOTE: ***Berg** a-2, 8, 9, 11, 14. **Heath** c-2, 9. **Maneely** c-1, 3. **Severin** a-4; c-7-11, 14.*

MARINES IN BATTLE
Atlas Comics (ACI No. 1-12/WPI No. 13-25): Aug, 1954 - No. 25, Sept, 1958

1-Heath-c; Iron Mike McGraw by Heath; history of U.S. Marine Corps. begins
22 44 66 128 209 290
2-Heath-c 14 28 42 80 115 150
3-6,8-10: 4-Last precode (2/55); Romita-a 11 22 33 60 83 105
7-Kubert/Moskowitz-a (6 pgs.) 11 22 33 62 86 110
11-16,18-21,24 10 20 30 56 76 95
17-Williamson-a (3 pgs.) 11 22 33 64 90 115
22,25-Torres-a 10 20 30 56 76 95
23-Crandall-a; Mark Murdock app. 10 20 30 58 79 100

NOTE: ***Berg** a-22. **G. Colan** a-22, 23. **Drucker** a-6. **Everett** a-4, 15; c-21. **Heath** c-1, 2, 4. **Maneely** c-23, 24. **Orlando** a-14. **Pakula** a-6, 23. **Powell** a-16. **Severin** a-22; c-12. **Sinnott** a-23. **Tuska** a-15.*

MARINE WAR HEROES (Charlton Premiere #19 on)
Charlton Comics: Jan, 1964 - No. 18, Mar, 1967

1-Montes/Bache-c/a 4 8 12 23 36 48
2-18: 14,18-Montes/Bache-a 3 6 9 14 20 26

MARK, THE (Also see Mayhem)
Dark Horse Comics: Dec, 1993 - No. 4, Mar, 1994 ($2.50, limited series)

1-4 3.00

MARK HAZZARD: MERC
Marvel Comics Group: Nov, 1986 - No. 12, Oct, 1987 (75¢)

1-12: Morrow-a 3.00
Annual 1 (11/87, $1.25) 4.00

MARK OF CHARON (See Negation)
CG Entertainment: Apr, 2003 - No. 5, Aug, 2003 ($2.95, limited series)

1-5-Bedard-s/Bennett-a 3.00

MARK OF ZORRO (See Zorro, Four Color #228)

MARK 1 COMICS (Also see Shaloman)
Mark 1 Comics: Apr, 1988 - No. 3, Mar, 1989 ($1.50)

1-3: Early Shaloman app. 2-Origin 3.00

MARKSMAN, THE (Also see Champions)

Marmaduke Mouse #41 © QUA

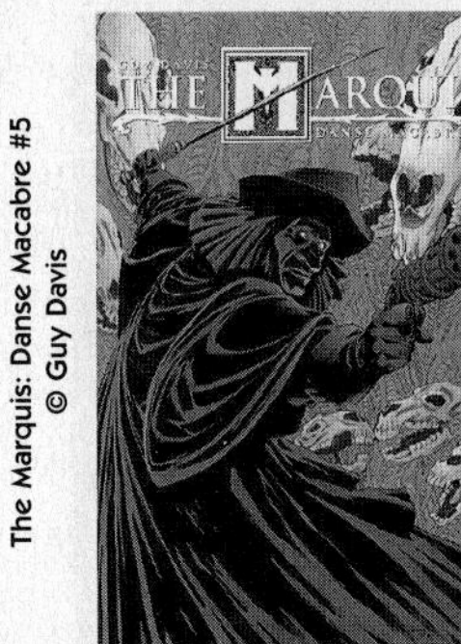

The Marquis: Danse Macabre #5 © Guy Davis

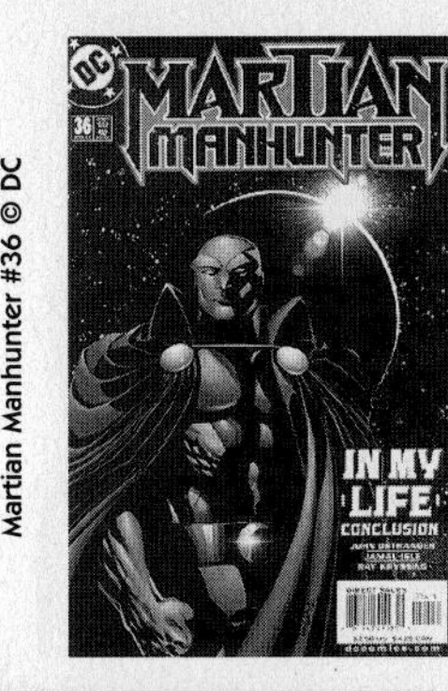

Martian Manhunter #36 © DC

	GD 2.0	VG 4.0	FN 6.0	VF 8.0	VF/NM 9.0	NM- 9.2

Hero Comics: Jan, 1988 - No. 5, 1988 ($1.95)
1-5: 1-Rose begins. 1-3-Origin The Marksman 3.00
Annual 1 ('88, $2.75, 52pgs)-Champions app. 4.00

MARK TRAIL
Standard Magazines (Hall Syndicate)/Fawcett Publ. No. 5: Oct, 1955; No. 5, Summer, 1959
1(1955)-Sunday strip-r 7 14 21 37 46 55
5(1959) 5 10 15 22 26 30
...Adventure Book of Nature 1 (Summer, 1958, 25¢, Pines)-100 pg. Giant; Special Camp Issue; contains 78 Sunday strip-r 9 18 27 52 69 85

MARMADUKE MONK
I. W. Enterprises/Super Comics: No date; 1963 (10¢)
I.W. Reprint 1 (nd) 2 4 6 8 11 14
Super Reprint 14 (1963)-r/Monkeyshines Comics #? 2 4 6 8 10 12

MARMADUKE MOUSE
Quality Comics Group (Arnold Publ.): Spring, 1946 - No. 65, Dec, 1956 (Early issues: 52 pgs.)
1-Funny animal 17 34 51 98 154 210
2 11 22 33 60 83 105
3-10 9 18 27 47 61 75
11-30 7 14 21 35 43 50
31-65: Later issues are 36 pgs. 6 12 18 28 34 40
Super Reprint #14(1963) 2 4 6 9 12 15

MARQUIS, THE
Oni Press
...: A Sin of One ($2.99, 5/03) Guy Davis-s/a; Michael Gaydos-c 3.00
...: Intermezzo TPB ($11.95, 12/03) r/A Sin of One and Hell's Courtesan #1,2 12.00

MARQUIS, THE: DANSE MACABRE
Oni Press: May, 2000 - No. 5, Feb, 2001 ($2.95, B&W, limited series)
1-5-Guy Davis-s/a. 1-Wagner-c. 2-Mignola-c. 3-Vess-c. 5-K. Jones-c 3.00
TPB (8/2001, $18.95) r/1-5 & Les Preludes; Seagle intro. 19.00

MARQUIS, THE: DEVIL'S REIGN: HELL'S COURTESAN
Oni Press: Feb, 2002 - No. 2, Apr, 2002 ($2.95, B&W, limited series)
1,2-Guy Davis-s/a 3.00

MARRIAGE OF HERCULES AND XENA, THE
Topps Comics: July, 1998 ($2.95, one-shot)
1-Photo-c; Lopresti-a; Alex Ross pin-up, 1-Alex Ross painted-c 3.00
1-Gold foil logo-c 5.00

MARRIED ... WITH CHILDREN (TV)(Based on Fox TV show)
Now Comics: June, 1990 - No. 7, Feb, 1991(12/90 inside) ($1.75)
V2#1, Sept, 1991 - No. 12, 1992 ($1.95)
1-7: 2-Photo-c, 1,2-2nd printing, V2#1-12: 1,4,5,9-Photo-c 3.00
...Buck's Tale (6/94, $1.95) 3.00
...1994 Annual nn (2/94, $2.50, 52 pgs.)-Flip book format 4.00
Special 1 (7/92, $1.95)-Kelly Bundy photo-c/poster 3.00

MARRIED ... WITH CHILDREN: KELLY BUNDY
Now Comics: Aug, 1992 - No. 3, Oct, 1992 ($1.95, limited series)
1-3: Kelly Bundy photo-c & poster in each 3.00

MARRIED ... WITH CHILDREN: QUANTUM QUARTET
Now Comics: Oct, 1993 - No. 4, 1994, ($1.95, limited series)
1-4: Fantastic Four parody 3.00

MARRIED ... WITH CHILDREN: 2099
Now Comics: June, 1993 - No. 3, Aug, 1993 ($1.95, limited series)
1-3 3.00

MARS
First Comics: Jan, 1984 - No. 12, Jan, 1985 ($1.00, Mando paper)
1-12: Marc Hempel & Mark Wheatley story & art. 2-The Black Flame begins. 10-Dynamo Joe begins 3.00
TPB (IDW Publ., 8/05, $39.99) r/#1-12, creator commentary; bonus art; new Hempel-c 40.00

MARS & BEYOND (Disney, TV)
Dell Publishing Co.: No. 866, Dec, 1957
Four Color 866-A Science feat. from Tomorrowland 8 16 24 56 93 130

MARS ATTACKS
Topps Comics: May, 1994 - No. 5, Sept, 1994 ($2.95, limited series)
1-5-Giffen story; flip books 5.00
Special Edition 2 4 6 8 10 12
Trade paperback (12/94, $12.95)-r/limited series plus new 8 pg. story 13.00

MARS ATTACKS
Topps Comics: V2#1, 8/95 - V2#3, 10/95; V2#4, 1/96 - No. 7, 5/96($2.95, bi-monthly #6 on)
V2#1-7: 1-Counterstrike storyline begins. 4-(1/96). 5-(1/96). 5,7-Brereton-c. 6-(3/96)-Simonson-c. 7-Story leads into Baseball Special #1 3.00
Baseball Special 1 (6/96, $2.95)-Bisley-c. 3.00

MARS ATTACKS HIGH SCHOOL
Topps Comics: May, 1997 - No. 2, Sept, 1997 ($2.95, B&W, limited series)
1,2-Stelfreeze-c 3.00

MARS ATTACKS IMAGE
Topps Comics: Dec, 1996 - No. 4, Mar, 1997 ($2.50, limited series)
1-4-Giffen-s/Smith/Sienkiewicz-a 3.00

MARS ATTACKS THE SAVAGE DRAGON
Topps Comics: Dec, 1996 - No. 4, Mar, 1997 ($2.95, limited series)
1-4: 1-w/bound-in card 3.00

MARSHAL BLUEBERRY (See Blueberry)
Marvel Comics (Epic Comics): 1991 ($14.95, graphic novel)
1-Moebius-a 3 6 9 14 19 24

MARSHAL LAW (Also see Crime And Punishment: Marshall Law...)
Marvel Comics (Epic Comics): Oct, 1987 - No. 6, May, 1989 ($1.95, mature)
1-6 3.00

M.A.R.S. PATROL TOTAL WAR (Formerly Total War #1,2)
Gold Key: No. 3, Sept, 1966 - No. 10, Aug, 1969 (All-Painted-c except #7)
3-Wood-a; aliens invade USA 6 12 18 41 66 90
4-10 4 8 12 24 37 50
Wally Wood's M.A.R.S. Patrol Total War TPB (Dark Horse, 9/04, $12.95) r/#3 & Total War #1&2; foreward by Batton Lash; afterword by Dan Adkins 13.00

MARTHA WASHINGTON (Also see Dark Horse Presents Fifth Anniversary Special, Dark Horse Presents #100-4, Give Me Liberty, Happy Birthday Martha Washington & San Diego Comicon Comics #2)

MARTHA WASHINGTON... (one-shots)
Dark Horse Comics (Legend): ($2.95/$3.50, one-shots)
... Dies (7/07, $3.50) Miller-s/Gibbons-a; r/Miller's original outline for Give Me Liberty 3.50
... Stranded in Space (11/95, $2.95) Miller-s/Gibbons-a; Big Guy app. 3.00

MARTHA WASHINGTON GOES TO WAR
Dark Horse Comics (Legend): May, 1994 - No. 5, Sep, 1994 ($2.95, lim. series)
1-5-Miller scripts; Gibbons-c/a 3.00
TPB ($17.95) r/#1-5 18.00

MARTHA WASHINGTON SAVES THE WORLD
Dark Horse Comics: Dec, 1997 - No. 3, Feb, 1998 ($2.95/$3.95, lim. series)
1,2-Miller scripts; Gibbons-c/a in all 3.00
3-($3.95) 4.00

MARTHA WAYNE (See The Story of...)

MARTIAN MANHUNTER (See Detective Comics & Showcase '95 #9)
DC Comics: May, 1988 - No. 4, Aug,. 1988 ($1.25, limited series)
1-4: 1,4-Batman app. 2-Batman cameo 3.00
Special 1-(1996, $3.50) 4.00

MARTIAN MANHUNTER (See JLA)
DC Comics: No. 0, Oct, 1998 - No. 36, Nov, 2001 ($1.99)
0-(10/98) Origin retold; Ostrander-s/Mandrake-c/a 3.00
1-36: 1-(12/98). 6-9-JLA app. 18,19-JSA app. 24-Mahnke-a 3.00
#1,000,000 (11/98) 853rd Century x-over 3.00
Annual 1,2 (1998,1999; $2.95) 1-Ghosts; Wrightson-c. 2-JLApe 4.00

MARTIAN MANHUNTER (See DCU Brave New World)
DC Comics: Oct, 2006 - No. 8, May, 2007 ($2.99, limited series)
1-8-Lieberman-s/Barrionuevo-a/c 3.00
...: The Others Among Us TPB (2007, $19.99) r/#1-8 & story from DCU Brave New World 20.00

MARTIAN MANHUNTER: AMERICAN SECRETS
DC Comics: 1992 - Book Three, 1992 ($4.95, limited series, prestige format)
1-3: Barreto-a 5.00

MARTIN KANE (William Gargan as... Private Eye)(Stage/Screen/Radio/TV)
Fox Features Syndicate (Hero Books): No. 4, June, 1950 - No. 2, Aug, 1950 (Formerly My Secret Affair)
4(#1)-True crime stories; Wood-c/a(2); used in **SOTI**, pg. 160; photo back-c 32 64 96 188 307 425

Marvel Adventures Spider-Man (2010 series) #1 © MAR

Marvel Adventures Super Heroes #2 © MAR

Marvel Age Fantastic Four #1 © MAR

	GD	VG	FN	VF	VF/NM	NM-
	2.0	4.0	6.0	8.0	9.0	9.2

2-Wood/Orlando story, 5 pgs; Wood-a(2) 23 46 69 136 223 310

MARTIN MYSTERY
Dark Horse (Bonelli Comics): Mar, 1999 - No. 6, Aug, 1999 ($4.95, B&W, digest size)

1-6-Reprints Italian series in English; Gibbons-c on #1-3 5.00

MARTY MOUSE
I. W. Enterprises: No date (1958?) (10¢)

1-Reprint 2 4 6 9 12 15

MARVEL ACTION HOUR FEATURING IRON MAN (TV cartoon)
Marvel Comics: Nov, 1994 - No. 8, June, 1995 ($1.50/$2.95)

1-8: Based on cartoon series 3.00
1 ($2.95)-Polybagged w/16 pg Marvel Action Hour Preview & acetate print 4.00

MARVEL ACTION HOUR FEATURING THE FANTASTIC FOUR (TV cartoon)
Marvel Comics: Nov, 1994 - No. 8, June, 1995 ($1.50/$2.95)

1-8: Based on cartoon series 3.00
1-($2.95)-Polybagged w/ 16 pg. Marvel Action Hour Preview & acetate print 4.00

MARVEL ACTION UNIVERSE (TV cartoon)
Marvel Comics: Jan, 1989 ($1.00, one-shot)

1-r/Spider-Man And His Amazing Friends 4.00

MARVEL ADVENTURES
Marvel Comics: Apr, 1997 - No. 18, Sept, 1998 ($1.50)

1-18-"Animated style": 1,4,7-Hulk-c/app. 2,11-Spider-Man. 3,8,15-X-Men. 5-Spider-Man & X-Men. 6-Spider-Man & Human Torch. 9,12-Fantastic Four. 10,16-Silver Surfer. 13-Spider-Man & Silver Surfer. 14-Hulk & Dr. Strange. 18-Capt. America 3.00

MARVEL ADVENTURES...
Marvel Comics: 2007, 2008 (Free Comic Book Day giveaways)

... Free Comic Book Day 2007 (6/07) 1-Iron Man, Hulk and Franklin Richards app. 2.50
... Free Comic Book Day 2008 - Iron Man, Hulk, Ant-Man and Spider-Man app. 2.50

MARVEL ADVENTURES FANTASTIC FOUR (All ages title)
Marvel Comics: No. 0, July, 2005 - No. 48, July, 2009 ($1.99/$2.50/$2.99)

0-($1.99) Movie version characters; Dr. Doom app.; Eaton-a 3.00
1-10-($2.50) 1-Skrulls app.; Pagulayan-a. 7-Namor app. 3.00
11-48-($2.99) 12,42-Dr. Doom app. 24-Namor app. 26,28-Silver Surfer app. 3.00
... Vol. 1: Family of Heroes (2005, $6.99, digest) r/#1-4 7.00
... Vol. 2: Fantastic Voyages (2006, $6.99, digest) r/#5-8 7.00
... Vol. 3: World's Greatest (2006, $6.99, digest) r/#9-12 7.00
... Vol. 4: Cosmic Threats (2006, $6.99, digest) r/#13-16 7.00
... Vol. 5: All 4 One, 4 For All (2007, $6.99, digest) r/#17-20 7.00
... Vol. 6: Monsters & Mysteries (2007, $6.99, digest) r/#21-24 7.00
... Vol. 7: The Silver Surfer (2007, $6.99, digest) r/#25-28 7.00
... Vol. 8: Monsters, Moles, Cowboys & Coupons (2008, $7.99, digest) r/#29-32 8.00

MARVEL ADVENTURES FLIP MAGAZINE (All ages title)
Marvel Comics: Aug, 2005 - Present ($3.99/$4.99)

1-11: 1-10-Rep. Marvel Advs. Fantastic Four and Marvel Advs. Spider-Man in flip format 4.00
12-14-($4.99) Reprints Marvel Advs. Spider-Man & X-Men/Power Pack in flip format 5.00
15-26-Rep. Marvel Advs. Fantastic Four and Marvel Advs. Spider-Man in flip format 5.00

MARVEL ADVENTURES HULK (All ages title)
Marvel Comics: Sept, 2007 - No. 16, Dec, 2008 ($2.99)

1-16: 1-New version of Hulk's origin; Pagulayan-c. 2-Jamie Madrox app. 13-Mummies 3.00
... Vol. 1: Misunderstood Monster (2007, $6.99, digest) r/#1-4 7.00

MARVEL ADVENTURES IRON MAN (All ages title)
Marvel Comics: July, 2007 - No. 13, Jul, 2008 ($2.99)

1-13: 1-4-Michael Golden-c. 1-New version of Iron Man's origin. 2-Intro. the Mandarin 3.00
... Vol. 1: Heart of Steel (2007, $6.99, digest) r/#1-4 7.00
... Vol. 2: Iron Armory (2008, $7.99, digest) r/#5-8 8.00

MARVEL ADVENTURES SPIDER-MAN (All ages title)
Marvel Comics: May, 2005 - No. 61, May, 2010 ($2.50/$2.99)

1-13-Lee & Ditko stories retold with new art. 13-Conner-c 3.00
14-48: 14-Begin $2.99-c. 14-16-Conner-c. 22,23-Black costume. 35-Venom app. 3.00
50-($3.99) Sinister Six app.; back-up w/Sonny Liew-a 4.00
51-61: 53-Emma Frost becomes a regular; intro. Chat; Skottie Young-c begin 3.00
... Vol. 1 HC (2006, $19.99, with dustjacket) r/#1-8; plot for #7; sketch pages from #6,8 20.00
... Vol. 1: The Sinister Six (2005, $6.99, digest) r/#1-4 7.00
... Vol. 2: Power Struggle (2005, $6.99, digest) r/#5-8 7.00
... Vol. 3: Doom With a View (2006, $6.99, digest) r/#9-12 7.00
... Vol. 4: Concrete Jungle (2006, $6.99, digest) r/#13-16 7.00
... Vol. 5: Monsters on the Prowl (2007, $6.99, digest) r/#17-20 7.00

	GD	VG	FN	VF	VF/NM	NM-
	2.0	4.0	6.0	8.0	9.0	9.2

... Vol. 6: The Black Costume (2007, $6.99, digest) r/#21-24 7.00
... Vol. 7: Secret Identity (2007, $6.99, digest) r/#25-28 7.00
... Vol. 8: Forces of Nature (2008, $7.99, digest) r/#29-32 8.00
... Vol. 9: Fiercest Foes (2008, $7.99, digest) r/#33-36 8.00

MARVEL ADVENTURES SPIDER-MAN (All ages title)
Marvel Comics: June, 2010 - Present ($3.99/$2.99)

1-($3.99) Tobin-s; Franklin Richards back-up 4.00
2-12-($2.99): 3,7-Wolverine app. 3,4-Bullseye app. 6-Doctor Octopus app. 3.00

MARVEL ADVENTURES STARRING DAREDEVIL (...Adventure #3 on)
Marvel Comics Group: Dec, 1975 - No. 6, Oct, 1976

1 2 4 6 8 10 12
2-6-r/Daredevil #22-27 by Colan. 3-5-(25¢-c) 1 2 3 5 6 8
3-5-(30¢-c variants, limited distribution)(4,6,8/76) 2 4 6 11 16 20

MARVEL ADVENTURES SUPER HEROES (All ages title)
Marvel Comics: Sept, 2008 - No. 21, May, 2010 ($2.99)

1-21: 1-4: Spider-Man, Hulk and Iron Man team-ups. 1-Hercules app. 5-Dr. Strange app. 6-Ant-Man origin re-told. 7-Thor. 8,12-Capt. America. 17-Avengers begin 3.00

MARVEL ADVENTURES SUPER HEROES (All ages title)
Marvel Comics: June, 2010 - Present ($3.99/$2.99)

1-($3.99) Iron Man and Avengers vs. Magneto 4.00
2-13-($2.99) 4-Deadpool app. 5-Rhino app. 11,12-Hulk app. 13-Thor 3.00

MARVEL ADVENTURES THE AVENGERS (All ages title)
Marvel Comics: July, 2006 - No. 39, Oct, 2009 ($2.99)

1-39-Spider-Man, Wolverine, Hulk, Iron Man, Capt. America, Storm, Giant-Girl app. 3.00
... Vol. 1: Heroes Assembled (2006, $6.99, digest) r/#1-4 7.00
... Vol. 2: Mischief (2007, $6.99, digest) r/#5-8 7.00
... Vol. 3: Bizarre Adventures (2007, $6.99, digest) r/#9-12 7.00
... Vol. 4: The Dream Team (2007, $6.99, digest) r/#13-15 & Giant-Size #1 7.00
... Vol. 5: Some Assembling Required (2008, $7.99, digest) r/#16-19 8.00

MARVEL ADVENTURES TWO-IN-ONE
Marvel Comics: Oct, 2007 - Present ($4.99, bi-weekly)

1-18: 1-9-Reprints Marvel Adventures Spider-Man and Fantastic Four stories. 10-Hulk 5.00

MARVEL AGE FANTASTIC FOUR (All ages title)
Marvel Comics: Jun, 2004 - No. 12, Mar, 2005 ($2.25)

1-12-Lee & Kirby stories retold with new art by various. 11-Impossible Man app. 3.00
...Tales (4/05, $2.25) retells first meeting with the Black Panther; O'Hare & Lim-a 3.00
Vol. 1: All For One TPB (2004, $5.99, digest size) r/#1-4 6.00
Vol. 2: Doom TPB (2004, $5.99, digest size) r/#5-8 6.00
Vol. 3: The Return of Doctor Doom TPB (2005, $5.99, digest size) r/#9-12 6.00

MARVEL AGE HULK (All ages title)
Marvel Comics: Nov, 2004 - No. 4, Feb, 2005 ($1.75)

1-3-Lee & Kirby stories retold with new art by various 3.00
Vol. 1: Incredible TPB (2005, $5.99, digest size) r/#1-4 6.00
Vol. 2: Defenders (2008, $7.99, digest) r/#5-8 8.00

MARVEL AGE SPIDER-MAN (All ages title)
Marvel Comics: May, 2004 - No. 20, Mar, 2005 ($2.25)

1-20-Lee & Ditko stories retold with new art. 4-Doctor Doom app. 5-Lizard app. 3.00
1-(Free Comic Book Day giveaway, 8/04) Spider-Man vs. The Vulture; Brooks-a 2.50
Vol. 1 TPB (2004, $5.99, digest) 1-r/#1-4 6.00
Vol. 2: Everyday Hero TPB (2004, $5.99, digest) r/#5-8 6.00
Vol. 3: Swingtime TPB (2004, $5.99, digest) r/#9-12 6.00
Spidey Strikes Back TPB (2005, 5.99, digest) r/#17-20 6.00

MARVEL AGE SPIDER-MAN TEAM-UP (Marvel Adventures on cover)
Marvel Comics: June, 2005 (Free Comic Book Day giveaway)

1-Spider-Man meets the Fantastic Four 2.50

MARVEL AGE TEAM-UP (All ages Spider-Man team-ups) (Also see Free Comic Book Day edition in the Promotional Comics section)
Marvel Comics: Nov, 2004 - No. 5, Apr, 2005 ($1.75)

1-5-Stories retold with new art by various. 1-Fantastic Four app. 3-Kitty Pryde app. 3.00
... Vol. 1: A Little Help From My Friends (2005, $7.99, digest) r/#1-5 8.00

MARVEL AND DC PRESENT FEATURING THE UNCANNY X-MEN AND THE NEW TEEN TITANS
Marvel Comics/DC Comics: 1982 ($2.00, 68 pgs., one-shot, Baxter paper)

1-3rd app. Deathstroke the Terminator; Darkseid app.; Simonson/Austin-c/a 2 4 6 11 16 20

MARVEL APES

Marvel Boy #2 © MAR

Marvel Classics Comics #28 © MAR

Marvel Comics Presents #43 © MAR

Marvel Comics: Nov, 2008 - No. 4, Dec, 2008 ($3.99, limited series)

	GD 2.0	VG 4.0	FN 6.0	VF 8.0	VF/NM 9.0	NM- 9.2
1-4: 1-Kesel-s/Bachs-a; back-up history story with Peyer-s/Kitson-a; two covers						4.00
1-($10.00) Hero Initiative edition with Daredevil gorilla cover by Mike Wieringo						10.00
#0-(2008, $3.99) r/Amazing Spider-Man #110,111; gallery of Marvel Apes variant covers						4.00
...: Amazing Spider-Monkey Special1 (6/09, $3.99) Sandmonk and the Apevengers app.						4.00
...: Grunt Line 1 (7/09, $3.99) Kesel-s; Charles Darwin app.						4.00
...: Speedball Special 1 (5/09, $3.99) Bachs & Hardin-a						4.00

MARVEL ASSISTANT-SIZED SPECTACULAR
Marvel Comics: Jun, 2009 - No. 2, Jun, 2009 ($3.99, limited series)

	GD 2.0	VG 4.0	FN 6.0	VF 8.0	VF/NM 9.0	NM- 9.2
1,2-Short stories by various incl. Isanove, Giarrusso, Nauck, Wyatt Cenak, Warren						4.00

MARVEL ATLAS (Styled after the Official Marvel Handbooks)
Marvel Comics: 2007 - No. 2, 2008 ($3.99, limited series)

	GD 2.0	VG 4.0	FN 6.0	VF 8.0	VF/NM 9.0	NM- 9.2
1,2-Profiles and maps of countries in the Marvel Universe						4.00

MARVEL BOY (Astonishing #3 on; see Marvel Super Action #4)
Marvel Comics (MPC): Dec, 1950 - No. 2, Feb, 1951

	GD 2.0	VG 4.0	FN 6.0	VF 8.0	VF/NM 9.0	NM- 9.2
1-Origin Marvel Boy by Russ Heath	116	232	348	742	1271	1800
2-Everett-a	81	162	243	518	884	1250

MARVEL BOY (Marvel Knights)
Marvel Comics: Aug, 2000 - No. 6, Mar, 2001 ($2.99, limited series)

	GD 2.0	VG 4.0	FN 6.0	VF 8.0	VF/NM 9.0	NM- 9.2
1-Intro. Marvel Boy; Morrison-s/J.G. Jones-c/a						3.50
1-DF Variant-c						5.00
2-6						3.00
TPB (6/01, $15.95)						16.00

MARVEL BOY: THE URANIAN (Agents of Atlas)
Marvel Comics: Mar, 2010 - No. 3, May, 2010 ($2.99, limited series)

	GD 2.0	VG 4.0	FN 6.0	VF 8.0	VF/NM 9.0	NM- 9.2
1-3-Origin re-told; back-up reprints from 1950s; Heath & Everett-a						3.00

MARVEL CHILLERS (Also see Giant-Size Chillers)
Marvel Comics Group: Oct, 1975 - No. 7, Oct, 1976 (All 25¢ issues)

	GD 2.0	VG 4.0	FN 6.0	VF 8.0	VF/NM 9.0	NM- 9.2
1-Intro. Modred the Mystic, ends #2; Kane-c(p)	3	6	9	14	19	24
2,4,5,7: 4-Kraven app. 5,6-Red Wolf app. 7-Kirby-c; Tuska-p	2	4	6	8	11	14
3-Tigra, the Were-Woman begins (origin), ends #7 (see Giant-Size Creatures #1). Chaykin/Wrightson-c.	3	6	9	18	27	35
4-6-(30¢-c variants, limited distribution)(4-8/76)	3	6	9	18	27	35
6-Byrne-a(p); Buckler-c(p)	2	4	6	11	16	20

NOTE: ***Bolle*** *a-1.* ***Buckler*** *c-2.* ***Kirby*** *c-7.*

MARVEL CLASSICS COMICS SERIES FEATURING...
(Also see Pendulum Illustrated Classics)
Marvel Comics Group: 1976 - No. 36, Dec, 1978 (52 pgs., no ads)

	GD 2.0	VG 4.0	FN 6.0	VF 8.0	VF/NM 9.0	NM- 9.2
1-Dr. Jekyll and Mr. Hyde	2	4	6	10	14	18
2-10,28: 28-1st Golden-c/a; Pit and the Pendulum	2	4	6	8	10	12
11-27,29-36	1	2	3	5	7	9

NOTE: ***Adkins*** *c-1i, 4i, 12i.* ***Alcala*** *a-34i; c-34.* ***Bolle*** *a-35.* ***Buscema*** *c-17p, 19p, 26p.* ***Golden*** *c/a-28.* ***Gil Kane*** *c-1-16p, 21p, 22p, 24p, 32p.* ***Nebres*** *a-5; c-24i.* ***Nino*** *a-2, 8, 12.* ***Redondo*** *a-1, 9. No. 1-12 were reprinted from Pendulum Illustrated Classics.*

MARVEL COLLECTIBLE CLASSICS: AVENGERS
Marvel Comics: 1998 ($10.00, reprints with chromium wraparound-c)

	GD 2.0	VG 4.0	FN 6.0	VF 8.0	VF/NM 9.0	NM- 9.2
1-Reprints Avengers Vol.3, #1; Perez-c						10.00

MARVEL COLLECTIBLE CLASSICS: SPIDER-MAN
Marvel Comics: 1998 ($10.00, reprints with chromium wraparound-c)

	GD 2.0	VG 4.0	FN 6.0	VF 8.0	VF/NM 9.0	NM- 9.2
1-Reprints Amazing Spider-Man #300; McFarlane-c						10.00
2-Reprints Spider-Man #1; McFarlane-c						10.00

MARVEL COLLECTIBLE CLASSICS: X-MEN
Marvel Comics: 1998 ($10.00, reprints with chromium wraparound-c)

	GD 2.0	VG 4.0	FN 6.0	VF 8.0	VF/NM 9.0	NM- 9.2
1-6: 1-Reprints (Uncanny) X-Men #1 & 2; Adam Kubert-c. 2-Reprints Uncanny X-Men #141 & 142; Byrne-c. 3-Reprints (Uncanny) X-Men #137; Larroca-c. 4-Reprints X-Men #25; Andy Kubert-c. 5-Reprints Giant Size X-Men #1; Gary Frank-c. 6-Reprints X-Men V2#1; Ramos-c						10.00

MARVEL COLLECTOR'S EDITION
Marvel Comics: 1992 (Ordered thru mail with Charleston Chew candy wrapper)

	GD 2.0	VG 4.0	FN 6.0	VF 8.0	VF/NM 9.0	NM- 9.2
1-Flip-book format; Spider-Man, Silver Surfer, Wolverine (by Sam Kieth), & Ghost Rider stories; Wolverine back-c by Kieth						5.00

MARVEL COLLECTORS' ITEM CLASSICS (Marvel's Greatest #23 on)
Marvel Comics Group(ATF): Feb, 1965 - No. 22, Aug, 1969 (25¢, 68 pgs.)

	GD 2.0	VG 4.0	FN 6.0	VF 8.0	VF/NM 9.0	NM- 9.2
1-Fantastic Four, Spider-Man, Thor, Hulk, Iron Man-r begin	11	22	33	75	138	200
2 (4/66)	7	14	21	45	73	100
3,4	6	12	18	37	59	80
5-10	5	10	15	32	51	70
11-22: 22-r/The Man in the Ant Hill/TTA #27	4	8	12	26	41	55

NOTE: *All reprints;* ***Ditko, Kirby*** *art in all.*

MARVEL COMICS (Marvel Mystery Comics #2 on)
Timely Comics (Funnies, Inc.): Oct, Nov, 1939

NOTE: The first issue was originally dated October 1939. Most copies have a black circle stamped over the date (on cover and inside) with "November" printed over it. However, some copies do not have the November overprint and could have a higher value. Most No. 1's have printing defects, i.e., tilted pages which caused trimming into the panels usually on right side and bottom. Covers exist with and without gloss finish.

	GD 2.0	VG 4.0	FN 6.0	VF 8.0	VF/NM 9.0	NM- 9.2
1-Origin Sub-Mariner by Bill Everett(1st newsstand app.); 1st 8 pgs. were produced for Motion Picture Funnies Weekly #1 which was probably not distributed outside of advance copies; intro Human Torch by Carl Burgos, Kazar the Great (1st Tarzan clone), & Jungle Terror(only app.); intro. The Angel by Gustavson, The Masked Raider & his horse Lightning (ends #12); cover by sci/fi pulp illustrator Frank R. Paul	21,000	42,000	63,000	135,000	235,000	460,000

MARVEL COMICS
Marvel Comics: 1990 ($17.95, hardcover)

	GD 2.0	VG 4.0	FN 6.0	VF 8.0	VF/NM 9.0	NM- 9.2
1-Reprint of entire Marvel Comics #1	3	6	9	16	23	30

MARVEL COMICS 70th ANNIVERARY SPECIAL
Marvel Comics: Oct, 2009 ($3.99, one-shot)

	GD 2.0	VG 4.0	FN 6.0	VF 8.0	VF/NM 9.0	NM- 9.2
1-Re-colored reprint of entire Marvel Comics #1; cover swipe by Jelena Djurdjevic						4.00

MARVEL COMICS PRESENTS
Marvel Comics (Midnight Sons imprint #143 on): Early Sept, 1988 - No. 175, Feb, 1995 ($1.25/$1.50/$1.75, bi-weekly)

	GD 2.0	VG 4.0	FN 6.0	VF 8.0	VF/NM 9.0	NM- 9.2
1-Wolverine by Buscema in #1-10	1	2	3	5	6	8
2-5						5.00
6-10: 6-Sub-Mariner app. 10-Colossus begins						4.00
11-47,51-71: 17-Cyclops begins. 19-1st app. Damage Control. 24-Havok begins. 25-Origin/1st app. Nth Man. 26-Hulk begins by Rogers. 29-Quasar app. 31-Excalibur begins by Austin (i). 32-McFarlane-a(p). 33-Capt. America; Jim Lee-a. 37-Devil-Slayer app. 38-Wolverine begins by Buscema; Hulk app. 39-Spider-Man app. 46-Liefeld Wolverine-c. 51-53-Wolverine by Rob Liefeld. 54-61-Wolverine/Hulk story: 54-Werewolf by Night begins; The Shroud by Ditko. 58-Iron Man by Ditko. 59-Punisher. 62-Deathlok & Wolverine stories 63-Wolverine. 64-71-Wolverine/Ghost Rider 8-part story. 70-Liefeld Ghost Rider/ Wolverine-c						3.00
48-50-Wolverine & Spider-Man team-up by Erik Larsen-c/a. 48-Wasp app. 49,50-Savage Dragon prototype app. by Larsen. 50-Silver Surfer. 50-53-Comet Man; Mumy scripts						5.00
72-Begin 13-part Weapon-X story (Wolverine origin) by B. Windsor-Smith (prologue)						5.00
73-Weapon-X part 1; Black Knight, Sub-Mariner						4.00
74-84: 74-Weapon-X part 2; Black Knight, Sub-Mariner. 76-Death's Head story. 77-Mr. Fantastic story. 78-Iron Man by Steacy. 80,81-Capt. America by Ditko/Austin. 81-Daredevil by Rogers/Williamson. 82-Power Man. 83-Human Torch by Ditko(a&scripts); $1.00-c direct, $1.25 newsstand. 84-Last Weapon-X (24 pg. conclusion)						3.00
85-Begin 8-part Wolverine story by Sam Kieth (c/a); 1st Kieth-a on Wolverine; begin 8-part Beast story by Jae Lee(p) with Liefeld part pencils #85,86; 1st Jae Lee-a (assisted w/Liefeld, 1991)						4.00
86-90: 86-89-Wolverine, Beast stories continue. 90-Begin 8-part Ghost Rider & Cable story, ends #97; begin flip book format w/two-c						3.00
91-175: 93-Begin 6-part Wolverine story, ends #98. 98-Begin 2-part Ghost Rider story. 99-Spider-Man story. 100-Full-length Ghost Rider/Wolverine story by Sam Kieth w/Tim Vigil assists; anniversary issue, non flip-book. 101-Begin 6-part Ghost Rider/Dr. Strange story & begin 8-part Wolverine/Nightcrawler story by Colan/Williamson; Punisher story. 107-Begin 6-part Ghost Rider/Werewolf by Night story. 109-Begin 8 part Wolverine/Typhoid Mary story. 111-Iron Fist. 113-Begin 6-part Giant-Man & begin 6-part Ghost Rider/Iron Fist stories. 117-Preview of Ravage 2099 (1st app.); begin 6 part Wolverine/Venom story w/Kieth-a. 118-Preview of Doom 2099 (1st app.). 119-Begin Ghost Rider/Cloak & Dagger by Colan. 120,136,138-Spider-Man. 123-Begin 8-part Ghost Rider/Typhoid Mary story; begin 4-part She Hulk story; begin 8-part Wolverine/Lynx story. 125-Begin 6-part Iron Fist story. 130-Begin 6-part Ghost Rider/ Cage story. 136-Daredevil. 137-Begin 6-part Wolverine story & 6-part Ghost Rider story. 147-Begin 2-part Vengeance-c/story w/new Ghost Rider. 149-Vengeance-c/story w/new Ghost Rider. 150-Silver ink-c; begin 2-part Bloody Mary story w/Typhoid Mary,Wolverine, Daredevil, new Ghost Rider; intro Steel Raven. 152-Begin 4-part Wolverine, 4-part War Machine, 4-part Vengeance, 3-part Moon Knight stories; same date as War Machine #1. 143-146: Siege of Darkness parts 3,6,11,14; all have spot-varnished-c. 143-Ghost Rider/Scarlet Witch; intro new Werewolf. 144-Begin 2-part Morbius story. 145-Begin 2-part Nightstalkers story. 153-155-Bound-in Spider-Man trading card sheet						3.00
...Colossus: God's Country (1994, $6.95) r/#10-17	1	2	3	4	5	7
...: Wolverine Vol. 1 TPB (2005, $12.99) r/Wolverine stories from #1-10						13.00
...: Wolverine Vol. 2 TPB (2006, $12.99) r/from #39-50 and Marvel Age Annual #4						13.00
...: Wolverine Vol. 3 TPB (2006, $12.99) r/from #51-61						13.00

Marvel Divas #1 © MAR

Marvel Family #13 © FAW

Marvel Fanfare #52 © MAR

GD 2.0 | VG 4.0 | FN 6.0 | VF 8.0 | VF/NM 9.0 | NM- 9.2

...: Wolverine Vol. 4 TPB (2006, $12.99) r/from #62-71 13.00

NOTE: ***Austin*** *a-31-37i; c(i)-48, 50, 99, 122.* ***Buscema*** *a-1-10, 38-47; c-6.* ***Byrne*** *a-79; c-71.* ***Colan*** *a(p)-36, 37.* ***Colan/Williamson*** *a-101-108.* ***Ditko*** *a-7p, 10, 56p, 58, 80, 81, 83.* ***Guice*** *a-62.* ***Sam Kieth*** *a-85-92, 117-122; c-85-98, 99p, 100-108, 117, 118, 120-122; back c-109-113, 117.* ***Jae Lee*** *c-129(back).* ***Liefeld*** *a-51, 52, 53p(2), 85p; c-46, 70.* ***McFarlane*** *c-32.* ***Mooney*** *a-73.* ***Rogers*** *a-26, 38, 46i, 81p.* ***Russell*** *a-10-14,16,17i; c-4,19, 30,31i.* ***Saltares*** *a-8p(early), 38-45p.* ***Simonson*** *c-1.* ***B. Smith*** *a-72-84; c-72-84.* ***P. Smith*** *c-34.* ***Sparling*** *a-33.* ***Starlin*** *a-89i.* ***Staton*** *a-74.* ***Steacy*** *a-78.* ***Sutton*** *a-101-105.* ***Williamson*** *c-62i. Two Gun Kid by* ***Gil Kane*** *in #116, 122.*

MARVEL COMICS PRESENTS
Marvel Comics: Nov, 2007 - No. 12, Oct, 2008 ($3.99)

1-12-Short stories by various. 1-Wraparound-c by Campbell 4.00

MARVEL COMICS SUPER SPECIAL, A (Marvel Super Special #5 on)
Marvel Comics: Sept, 1977 - No. 41(?), Nov, 1986 (nn 7) ($1.50, magazine)

1-Kiss, 40 pgs. comics plus photos & features; John Buscema-a(p); also see Howard the Duck #12; ink contains real KISS blood; Dr. Doom, Spider-Man, Avengers, Fantastic Four, Mephisto app. 12 24 36 82 154 225
2-Conan (1978) 3 6 9 14 19 24
3-Close Encounters of the Third Kind (1978); Simonson-a 2 4 6 9 13 16
4-The Beatles Story (1978)-Perez/Janson-a; has photos & articles 5 10 15 32 51 70
5-Kiss (1978)-Includes poster 12 24 36 82 154 225
6-Jaws II (1978) 2 4 6 9 13 16
7-Sgt. Pepper; Beatles movie adaptation; withdrawn from U.S. distribution (French ed. exists)
8-Battlestar Galactica; tabloid size ($1.50, 1978); adapts TV show 2 4 6 13 18 20
8-Modern-r of tabloid size 2 4 6 10 14 18
8-Battlestar Galactica; publ. in regular magazine format; low distribution ($1.50, 8-1/2x11") 3 6 9 14 19 24
9-Conan 2 4 6 11 16 20
10-Star-Lord 2 4 6 9 13 16
11-13-Weirdworld begins #11; 25 copy special press run of each with gold seal and signed by artists (Proof quality), Spring-June, 1979 8 16 24 54 90 125
11-15: 11-13-Weirdworld (regular issues): 11-Fold-out centerfold. 14-Miller-c(p); adapts movie "Meteor." 15-Star Trek with photos & pin-ups ($1.50-c) 1 3 4 6 8 10
15-With $2.00 price; the price was changed at tail end of a 200,000 press run 2 4 6 8 10 12
16-Empire Strikes Back adaption; Williamson-a 2 4 6 9 12 15
17-20 (Movie adaptations): 17-Xanadu. 18-Raiders of the Lost Ark. 19-For Your Eyes Only (James Bond). 20-Dragonslayer 6.00
21-26,28-30 (Movie adaptations): 21-Conan. 22-Blade Runner; Williamson-a; Steranko-c. 23-Annie. 24-The Dark Crystal. 25-Rock and Rule-w/photos; artwork is from movie. 26-Octopussy (James Bond). 28-Krull; photo-c. 29-Tarzan of the Apes (Greystoke movie). 30-Indiana Jones and the Temple of Doom 1 2 3 4 5 7
27,31-41: 27-Return of the Jedi. 31-The Last Star Fighter. 32-The Muppets Take Manhattan. 33-Buckaroo Banzai. 34-Sheena. 35-Conan The Destroyer. 36-Dune. 37-2010. 38-Red Sonja. 39-Santa Claus:The Movie. 40-Labyrinth. 41-Howard The Duck 1 2 3 5 7 9

NOTE: ***J. Buscema*** *a-1, 2, 9, 11-13, 18p, 21, 35, 40; c-11(part), 12.* ***Chaykin*** *a-9, 19p; c-18, 19.* ***Colan*** *a(p)-6, 10, 14.* ***Morrow*** *a-34; c-1i, 34.* ***Nebres*** *a-11.* ***Spiegle*** *a-29.* ***Stevens*** *a-27.* ***Williamson*** *a-27. #22-28 contain photos from movies.*

MARVEL COMICS: 2001
Marvel Comics: 2001 (no cover price, one-shot)

1-Previews new titles for Fall 2001; Wolverine-c 3.00

MARVEL DABEL BROTHERS SAMPLER
Marvel Comics: Dec, 2006 (no cover price, one-shot)

1-Profiles and sample pages of Anita Blake, Magician: Apprentice, Red Prophet, Ptolus 3.00

MARVEL DIVAS
Marvel Comics: Sept, 2009 - No. 4, Dec, 2009 ($3.99, limited series)

1-4-Black Cat, Firestar, Hellcat and Photon app. 1-Campbell-c 4.00

MARVEL DOUBLE FEATURE
Marvel Comics Group: Dec, 1973 - No. 21, Mar, 1977

1-Capt. America, Iron Man-r/T.O.S. begin 2 4 6 11 16 20
2-10: 3-Last 20¢ issue 2 4 6 8 10 12
11-17,20,21:17-Story-r/Iron Man & Sub-Mariner #1; last 25¢ issue 1 2 3 5 6 8
15-17-(30¢-c variants, limited distribution)(4,6,8/76) 2 4 6 9 13 16
18,19-Colan/Craig-r from Iron Man #1 in both 2 3 4 6 8 10

NOTE: ***Colan*** *r-1-19p.* ***Craig*** *r-17-19i.* ***G. Kane*** *r-15p; c-15p.* ***Kirby*** *r-1-16p, 20, 21; c-17-20.*

MARVEL DOUBLE SHOT
Marvel Comics: Jan, 2003 - No. 4, April, 2003 ($2.99, limited series)

GD 2.0 | VG 4.0 | FN 6.0 | VF 8.0 | VF/NM 9.0 | NM- 9.2

1-4: 1-Hulk by Haynes; Thor w/Asamiya-a; Jusko-c. 2-Dr. Doom by Rivera; Simpsons-style Avengers by Bill Morrison 3.00

MARVEL FAMILY (Also see Captain Marvel Adventures No. 18)
Fawcett Publications: Dec, 1945 - No. 89, Jan, 1954

1-Origin Captain Marvel, Captain Marvel Jr., Mary Marvel, & Uncle Marvel retold; origin/1st app. Black Adam 181 362 543 1158 1979 2800
2-The 3 Lt. Marvels & Uncle Marvel app. 77 154 231 493 847 1200
3 54 108 162 343 574 825
4,5 44 88 132 277 469 660
6-10: 7-Shazam app. 39 78 117 230 375 520
11-20 29 58 87 170 278 385
21-30 25 50 75 150 245 340
31-40 21 42 63 124 202 280
41-46,48-50 18 36 54 107 169 230
47-Flying Saucer-c/story (5/50) 24 48 72 140 230 320
51-76 17 34 51 98 154 210
77-Communist Threat-c 27 54 81 158 259 360
78,81-Used in **POP**, pg. 92,93. 20 40 60 114 182 250
79,80,82-88: 79-Horror satire-c 19 38 57 111 176 240
89-Last issue; last Fawcett Captain Marvel app. (low distribution) 22 44 66 132 216 300

MARVEL FANFARE (1st Series)
Marvel Comics Group: Mar, 1982 - No. 60, Jan, 1992 ($1.25/$2.25, slick paper, direct sales)

1-Spider-Man/Angel team-up; 1st Paul Smith-a (1st full story; see King Conan #7); Daredevil app. (many copies were printed missing the centerfold) 1 3 4 6 8 10
2-Spider-Man, Ka-Zar, The Angel. F.F. origin retold 1 2 3 5 6 8
3,4-X-Men & Ka-Zar. 4-Deathlok, Spidey app. 6.00
5-14: 5-Dr. Strange, Capt. America. 6-Spider-Man, Scarlet Witch. 7-Incredible Hulk; D.D. back-up(also 15). 8-Dr. Strange; Wolf Boy begins. 9-Man-Thing. 10-13-Black Widow. 14-The Vision 4.00
15,24,33: 15-The Thing by Barry Smith, c/a. 24-Weirdworld; Wolverine back-up. 33-X-Men, Wolverine app.; Punisher pin-up 5.00
16-23,25-32,34-44,46-50: 16,17-Skywolf. 16-Sub-Mariner back-up. 17-Hulk back-up. 18-Capt. America by Miller. 19-Cloak and Dagger. 20-Thing/Dr. Strange. 21-Thing/Dr. Strange /Hulk. 22,23-Iron Man vs. Dr. Octopus. 25,26-Weirdworld. 27-Daredevil/Spider-Man. 28-Alpha Flight. 29-Hulk. 30-Moon Knight. 31,32-Captain America. 34-37-Warriors Three. 38-Moon Knight/Dazzler. 39-Moon Knight/Hawkeye. 40-Angel/Rogue & Storm. 41-Dr. Strange. 42-Spider-Man. 43-Sub-Mariner/Human Torch. 44-Iron Man vs. Dr. Doom by Ken Steacy. 46-Fantastic Four. 47-Hulk. 48-She-Hulk/Vision. 49-Dr. Strange/Nick Fury. 50-X-Factor 3.00
45-All pin-up issue by Steacy, Art Adams & others 5.00
51-($2.95, 52 pgs.)-Silver Surfer; Fantastic Four & Capt. Marvel app.; 51,52-Colan/Williamson back-up (Dr. Strange) 4.00
52,53,56-60: 52,53-Black Knight; 53-Iron Man back up. 56-59-Shanna the She-Devil. 58-Vision & Scarlet Witch back-up. 60-Black Panther/Rogue/Daredevil stories 3.00
54,55-Wolverine back-ups. 54-Black Knight. 55-Power Pack 4.00
... Vol. 1 TPB (2008, $24.99) r/#1-7 25.00

NOTE: ***Art Adams*** *c-13.* ***Austin*** *a-1i, 4i, 33i, 38i; c-8i, 33i.* ***Buscema*** *a-51p.* ***Byrne*** *a-1p, 29, 48; c-29.* ***Chiodo*** *painted c-56-59.* ***Colan*** *a-51p.* ***Cowan/Simonson*** *c/a-60.* ***Golden*** *a-1, 2, 4p, 47; c-1, 2, 47.* ***Infantino*** *c/a(p)-8.* ***Gil Kane*** *a-8-11p.* ***Miller*** *a-18; c-1(Back-c), 18.* ***Perez*** *a-10, 11p, 12, 13p; c-10-13p.* ***Rogers*** *a-5p; c-5p.* ***Russell*** *a-5i, 6i, 8-11i, 43i; c-5i, 6.* ***Paul Smith*** *a-1p, 4p, 32, 60; c-4p. Staton c/a-50(p).* ***Williamson*** *a-30i, 51i.*

MARVEL FANFARE (2nd Series)
Marvel Comics: Sept, 1996 - No. 6, Feb, 1997 (99¢)

1-6: 1-Capt. America & The Falcon-c/story; Deathlok app. 2-Wolverine & Hulk-c/app. 3-Ghost Rider & Spider-Man-c/app. 5-Longshot-c/app. 6-Sabretooth, Power Man, & Iron Fist-c/app 3.00

MARVEL FEATURE (See Marvel Two-In-One)
Marvel Comics Group: Dec, 1971 - No. 12, Nov, 1973 (1,2: 25¢, 52 pg. giants) (#1-3: quarterly)

1-Origin/1st app. The Defenders (Sub-Mariner, Hulk & Dr. Strange); see Sub-Mariner #34,35 for prequel; Dr. Strange solo story (predates Dr.Strange #1) plus 1950s Sub-Mariner-r; Neal Adams-c 16 32 48 114 232 350
2-2nd app. Defenders; 1950s Sub-Mariner-r. Rutland, Vermont Halloween x-over 9 18 27 65 113 160
3-Defenders ends 7 14 21 47 76 105
4-Re-intro Antman (1st app. since 1960s), begin series; brief origin; Spider-Man app. 5 10 15 32 51 70
5-7,9,10: 6-Wasp app. & begins team-ups. 9-Iron Man app. 10-Last Antman 3 6 9 20 30 40
8-Origin Antman & Wasp-r/TTA #44; Kirby-a 4 8 12 22 34 45
11-Thing vs. Hulk; 1st Thing solo book (9/73); origin Fantastic Four retold 8 16 24 56 93 130

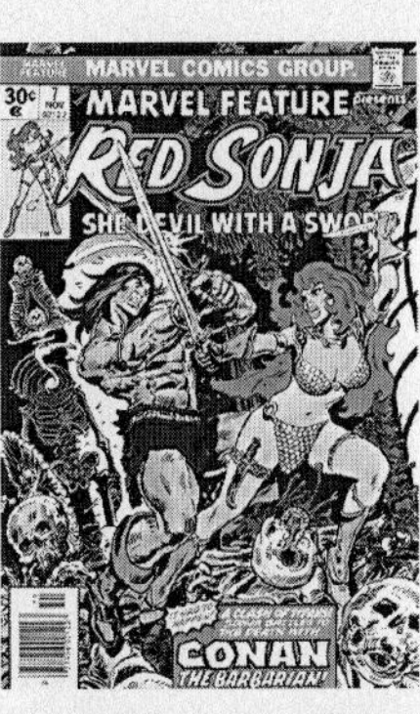

Marvel Feature (2nd series) #7 © MAR

Marvel Graphic Novel #19 © Conan Prop.

Marvel Holiday Special 1994 © MAR

GD 2.0 | VG 4.0 | FN 6.0 | VF 8.0 | VF/NM 9.0 | NM- 9.2

12-Thing/Iron Man; early Thanos app.; occurs after Capt. Marvel #33; Starlin-a(p) 5 10 15 35 55 75

NOTE: *Bolle a-9i. Everett a-1i, 3i. Hartley r-10. Kane c-3p, 7p. Russell a-7-10p. Starlin a-8, 11, 12; c-8.*

MARVEL FEATURE (Also see Red Sonja)
Marvel Comics: Nov, 1975 - No. 7, Nov, 1976 (Story cont'd in Conan #68)

1,7: 1-Red Sonja begins (pre-dates Red Sonja #1); adapts Howard short story; Adams-r/Savage Sword of Conan #1. 7-Battles Conan 2 4 6 8 11 14
2-6: Thorne-c/a in #2-7. 4,5-(Regular 25¢ edition)(5,7/76) 1 2 3 5 6 8
4,5-(30¢-c variants, limited distribution) 3 6 9 14 20 25

MARVEL FRONTIER COMICS UNLIMITED
Marvel Frontier Comics: Jan, 1994 ($2.95, 68 pgs.)

1-Dances with Demons, Immortalis, Children of the Voyager, Evil Eye, The Fallen stories 4.00

MARVEL FUMETTI BOOK
Marvel Comics Group: Apr, 1984 ($1.00, one-shot)

1-All photos; Stan Lee photo-c; Art Adams touch-ups 5.00

MARVEL FUN & GAMES
Marvel Comics Group: 1979/80 (color comic for kids)

1,11: 1-Games, puzzles, etc. 11-X-Men-c 2 3 4 6 8 10
2-10,12,13: (beware marked pages) 1 2 3 4 5 7

MARVEL GIRL
Marvel Comics: Apr, 2011 ($2.99, one-shot)

1-Early X-Men days of Jean Grey; Fialkov-s/Plati-a/Cruz-c 3.00

MARVEL GRAPHIC NOVEL
Marvel Comics Group (Epic Comics): 1982 - No. 38, 1990? ($5.95/$6.95)

1-Death of Captain Marvel (2nd Marvel graphic novel); Capt. Marvel battles Thanos by Jim Starlin (c/a/scripts) 3 6 9 14 19 24
1 (2nd & 3rd printings) 1 2 3 5 6 8
2-Elric: The Dreaming City 2 4 6 8 10 12
3-Dreadstar; Starlin-c/a, 52 pgs. 2 4 6 8 11 14
4-Origin/1st app. The New Mutants (1982) 2 4 6 8 11 14
4,5-2nd printings 1 2 3 4 5 7
5-X-Men; book-length story (1982) 3 6 9 14 20 25
6-15,20,23,25,30,31: 6-The Star Slammers. 7-Killraven. 8-Super Boxers; Byrne scripts. 9-The Futurians. 10-Heartburst. 11-Void Indigo. 12-Dazzler. 13-Starstruck. 14-The Swords Of The Swashbucklers. 15-The Raven Banner (a Tale of Asgard). 20-Greenberg the Vampire. 23-Dr. Strange. 25-Alien Legion. 30-A Sailor's Story. 31-Wolfpack 1 2 3 5 7 9
16,17,21,29: 16-The Aladdin Effect (Storm, Tigra, Wasp, She-Hulk). 17-Revenge Of The Living Monolith (Spider-Man, Avengers, FF app.). 21-Marada the She-Wolf. 29-The Big Chance (Thing vs. Hulk) 1 2 3 5 7 9
18,19,26-28: 18-She Hulk. 19-Witch Queen of Acheron (Conan). 26-Dracula. 27-Avengers (Emperor Doom). 28-Conan the Reaver 2 4 6 9 11 13
22-Amaz. Spider-Man in Hooky by Wrightson 2 4 6 9 12 15
24-Love and War (Daredevil); Miller scripts 2 4 6 8 11 14
32-Death of Groo 2 4 6 9 12 15
32-2nd printing ($5.95) 1 2 3 5 6 8
33,34,36,37: 33-Thor. 34-Predator & Prey (Cloak & Dagger). 36-Willow (movie adapt.). 37-Hercules 1 3 4 6 8 10
35-Hitler's Astrologer (The Shadow, $12.95, HC) 2 4 6 9 13 16
35-Soft-c reprint (1990, $10.95) 2 4 6 8 10 12
38-Silver Surfer (Judgement Day)($14.95, HC) 2 4 6 10 14 18
38-Soft-c reprint (1990, $10.95) 2 4 6 8 11 14
nn-Abslom Daak: Dalak Killer (1990, $8.95) Dr. Who 1 3 4 6 8 10
nn-Arena by Bruce Jones (1989, $5.95) Dinosaurs 1 2 3 5 6 8
nn- A-Team Storybook Comics Illustrated (1983) r/ A-Team mini-series #1-3 1 3 4 6 8 10
nn-Ax (1988, $5.95) Ernie Colan-s/a 1 3 4 6 8 10
nn-Black Widow Coldest War (4/90, $9.95) 2 4 6 8 10 12
nn-Chronicles of Genghis Grimtoad (1990, $8.95)-Alan Grant-s 1 3 4 6 8 10
nn-Conan the Barbarian in the Horn of Azoth (1990, $8.95) 2 4 6 8 11 16
nn-Conan of Isles ($8.95) 2 4 6 8 11 16
nn-Conan Ravagers of Time (1992, $9.95) Kull & Red Sonja app. 2 4 6 8 11 16
nn-Conan -The Skull of Set 2 4 6 8 11 16
nn-Doctor Strange and Doctor Doom Triumph and Torment (1989, $17.95, HC) 2 4 6 13 18 22
nn-Dreamwalker (1989, $6.95)-Morrow-a 1 2 3 5 7 9
nn-Excalibur Weird War III (1990, $9.95) 2 4 6 8 10 12
nn-G.I. Joe - The Trojan Gambit (1983, 68 pgs.) 2 4 6 8 10 12
nn-Harvey Kurtzman Strange Adventures (Epic, $19.95, HC) Aragonés, Crumb 3 6 9 14 20 25
nn-Hearts and Minds (1990, $8.95) Heath-a 1 3 4 6 8 10
nn-Inhumans (1988, $7.95)-Williamson-i 1 2 3 5 7 9
nn-Jhereg (Epic, 1990, $8.95) 1 3 4 6 8 10
nn-Kazar-Guns of the Savage Land (7/90, $8.95) 1 3 4 6 8 10
nn-Kull-The Vale of Shadow ('89, $6.95) 2 4 6 8 10 12
nn-Last of the Dragons (1988, $6.95) Austin-a(i) 1 2 3 4 5 7
nn-Nightraven: House of Cards (1991, $14.95) 2 4 6 9 12 15
nn-Nightraven: The Collected Stories (1990, $9.95) Bolton-r/British Hulk mag.; David Lloyd-c/a 2 4 6 8 10 12
nn-Original Adventures of Cholly and Flytrap (Epic, 1991, $9.95) Suydam-s/c/a 2 4 6 9 12 15
nn-Rick Mason Agent (1989, $9.95) 1 3 4 6 8 10
nn-Roger Rabbit In The Resurrection Of Doom (1989, $8.95) 1 3 4 6 8 10
nn-A Sailor's Story Book II: Winds, Dreams and Dragons ('86, $6.95, softcover) Glansman-s/c/a 1 3 4 6 8 10
nn-Squadron Supreme: Death of a Universe (1989, $9.95) Gruenwald-s; Ryan & Williamson-a 3 6 9 14 20 25
nn-Who Framed Roger Rabbit (1989, $6.95) 1 3 4 6 8 10

NOTE: *Aragones a-27, 32. Buscema a-38. Byrne c/a-18. Heath a-35i. Kaluta a-13, 35p; c-13. Miller a-24p. Simonson a-6; c-6. Starlin c/a-1,3. Williamson a-34. Wrightson c-29i.*

MARVEL HEARTBREAKERS
Marvel Comics: Apr, 2010 ($3.99, one-shot)

1-Romance short stories; Spider-Man, MJ & Gwen app.; Casagrande-a; Beast app. 4.00

MARVEL-HEROES & LEGENDS
Marvel Comics: Oct, 1996; 1997 ($2.95)

nn-Wraparound-c, ...1997 ($2.99) -Original Avengers story 3.00

MARVEL HEROES FLIP MAGAZINE
Marvel Comics: Aug, 2005 - No. 26, Sept, 2007 ($3.99/$4.99)

1-11-Reprints New Avengers and Captain America (2005 series) in flip format thru #13 4.00
12-26: 14-19-Reprints New Avengers and Young Avengers in flip format. 20-Ghost Rider 5.00

MARVEL HOLIDAY SPECIAL
Marvel Comics: No. 1, 1991 ($2.25, 84 pgs.) - Present

1-X-Men, Fantastic Four, Punisher, Thor, Capt. America, Ghost Rider, Capt. Ultra, Spidey stories; Art Adams-c/a 4.00
nn (1/93)-Wolverine, Thanos (by Starlin/Lim/Austin) 4.00
nn (1994)-Capt. America, X-Men, Silver Surfer 4.00
...1996-Spider-Man by Waid & Olliffe; X-Men, Silver Surfer 4.00
...2004-Spider-Man by DeFalco & Miyazawa; X-Men, Fantastic Four 4.00
...2004 TPB ($15.99) r/M.H.S. 2004 & past Christmas-themed stories 16.00
1 (1/06, $3.99) new Christmas-themed stories by various; Immonen-c 4.00
....2006 (2/07, $3.99) Fin Fang Foom, Hydra, AIM app.; gallery of past covers; Irving-c 4.00
....2007 (2/08, $3.99) Spider-Man & Wolverine stories; Hembeck-a 4.00
Marvel Holiday (2006, $7.99, digest) reprints from M.H.S. 2004, 2006 & TPB 8.00
Marvel Holiday Spectacular Magazine (2009, $9.99, magazine) reprints from M.H.S. '93, '94, & Amazing Spider-Man #166; and new material w/Doe, Semeiks & Nauck-a 10.00

NOTE: *Art Adams c-'93. Golden a-'93. Perez c-'94.*

MARVEL ILLUSTRATED...
Marvel Comics: 2007 ($2.99)

...Jungle Book - reprints from Marvel Fanfare #8-11; Gil Kane-s/a(p); P. Craig Russell-i 3.00

MARVEL ILLUSTRATED: KIDNAPPED (Title changes to Kidnapped with #5)
Marvel Comics: Jan, 2009 - No. 5, May, 2009 ($3.99, limited series)

1-5-Adaptation of the Stevenson novel; Roy Thomas-s/Mario Gully-a/Parel-c 4.00

MARVEL ILLUSTRATED: LAST OF THE MOHICANS
Marvel Comics: July, 2007 - No. 6, Dec, 2007 ($2.99, limited series)

1-6-Adaptation of the Cooper novel; Roy Thomas-s/Steve Kurth-a. 1-Jo Chen-c 3.00
HC (2008, $19.99) r/#1-6 20.00

MARVEL ILLUSTRATED: MOBY DICK
Marvel Comics: Apr, 2008 - No. 6, Sept, 2008 ($2.99, limited series)

1-6-Adaptation of the Melville novel; Roy Thomas-s/Alixe-a/Watson-c 3.00

MARVEL ILLUSTRATED: PICTURE OF DORIAN GRAY
Marvel Comics: Jan, 2008 - No. 6, July, 2008 ($2.99, limited series)

1-6-Adaptation of the Wilde novel; Roy Thomas-s/Fiumara-a. 1-Parel-c 3.00

Marvel Knights 4 #1 © MAR

Marvel Mangaverse: Spider-Man #1 © MAR

Marvel Masterpieces 2 #2 © MAR

	GD	VG	FN	VF	VF/NM	NM-
	2.0	4.0	6.0	8.0	9.0	9.2

MARVEL ILLUSTRATED: SWIMSUIT ISSUE (Also see Marvel Swimsuit Special)
Marvel Comics: 1991 ($3.95, magazine, 52 pgs.)

V1#1-Parody of Sports Illustrated swimsuit issue; Mary Jane Parker centerfold pin-up by Jusko; 2nd print exists 1 3 4 6 8 10

MARVEL ILLUSTRATED: THE ILIAD
Marvel Comics: Feb, 2008 - No. 8, Sept, 2008 ($2.99, limited series)

1-8-Adaptation of Homer's Epic Poem; Roy Thomas-s/Sepulveda-a/Rivera-c 3.00

MARVEL ILLUSTRATED: THE MAN IN THE IRON MASK
Marvel Comics: Sept, 2007 - No. 6, Feb, 2008 ($2.99, limited series)

1-6-Adaptation of the Dumas novel; Roy Thomas-s/Hugo Petrus-a. 1-Djurdjevic-c 3.00
HC (2008, $19.99) r/#1-6 20.00

MARVEL ILLUSTRATED: THE ODYSSEY (Title changes to The Odyssey with #7)
Marvel Comics: Nov, 2008 - No. 8, June, 2009 ($3.99, limited series)

1-8-Adaptation of Homer's Epic Poem; Roy Thomas-s/Greg Tocchini-a/c 4.00

MARVEL ILLUSTRATED: THE THREE MUSKETEERS
Marvel Comics: Aug, 2008 - No. 6, Jan, 2009 ($3.99, limited series)

1-6-Adaptation of the Dumas novel; Roy Thomas-s/Hugo Petrus-a/Parel-c 4.00

MARVEL ILLUSTRATED: TREASURE ISLAND
Marvel Comics: Aug, 2007 - No. 6, Jan, 2008 ($2.99, limited series)

1-6-Adaptation of the Stevenson novel; Roy Thomas-s/Mario Gully-a/Greg Hildebrandt-c 3.00
HC (2008, $19.99) r/#1-6 20.00

MARVEL KNIGHTS (See Black Panther, Daredevil, Inhumans, & Punisher)
Marvel Comics: 1998 (Previews for upcoming series)

Sketchbook-Wizard suppl.; Quesada & Palmiotti-c 3.00
Tourbook-($2.99) Interviews and art previews 3.00

MARVEL KNIGHTS
Marvel Comics: July, 2000 - No. 15, Sept, 2001 ($2.99)

1-Daredevil, Punisher, Black Widow, Shang-Chi, Dagger app. 4.00
2-15: 2-Two covers by Barreto & Quesada 3.00
.../Marvel Boy Genesis Edition (6/00) Sketchbook preview 3.00
...: Millennial Visions (2/02, $3.99) Pin-ups by various; Harris-c 4.00

MARVEL KNIGHTS (Volume 2)
Marvel Comics: May, 2002 - No. 6, Oct, 2002 ($2.99)

1-6-Daredevil, Punisher, Black Widow app.; Ponticelli-a 3.00

MARVEL KNIGHTS: DOUBLE SHOT
Marvel Comics: June, 2002 - No. 4, Sept, 2002 ($2.99, limited series)

1-4: 1-Punisher by Ennis & Quesada; Daredevil by Haynes; Fabry-c 3.00

MARVEL KNIGHTS 4 (Fantastic Four) (Issues #1&2 are titled **Knights 4**) (#28-30 titled **Four**)
Marvel Comics: Apr, 2004 - No. 30, July, 2006 ($2.99)

1-30: 1-7-McNiven-c/a; Aguirre-Sacasa-a. 8,9-Namor app. 13-Cho-c. 14-Land-c. 21-Flashback meeting with Black Panther. 30-Namor app. 3.00
...Vol. 1: The Wolf at the Door (2004, $16.99, TPB) r/#1-7 17.00
...Vol. 2: The Stuff of Nightmares (2005, $13.99, TPB) r/#8-12 14.00
...Vol. 3: Divine Time (2005, $14.99, TPB) r/#13-18 15.00
...Vol. 4: Impossible Things Happen Every Day (2006, $14.99, TPB) r/#19-24 15.00
Fantastic Four: The Resurrection of Nicholas Scratch TPB (2006, $14.99) r/#25-30 15.00

MARVEL KNIGHTS MAGAZINE
Marvel Comics: May, 2001 - No. 6, Oct, 2001 ($3.99, magazine size)

1-6-Reprints of recent Daredevil, Punisher, Black Widow, Inhumans 4.00

MARVEL KNIGHTS SPIDER-MAN (Title continues in Sensational Spider-Man #23)
Marvel Comics: Jun, 2004 - No. 22, Mar, 2006 ($2.99)

1-Wraparound-c by Dodson; Millar-s/Dodson-a; Green Goblin app. 4.00
2-12: 2-Avengers app. 2,3-Vulture & Electro app. 5,8-Cho-c/a. 6-8-Venom app. 3.00
13-18-Reginald Hudlin-s/Billy Tan-a. 13,14,18-New Avengers app. 15-Punisher app. 3.00
19-22-The Other x-over pts. 2,5,8,11; Pat Lee-a 3.00
19-22-var-c: 19-Black costume. 20-Scarlet Spider. 21-Spider-Armor. 22-Peter Parker 5.00
... Vol. 1 HC (2005, $29.99, over-sized with d.j.) r/#1-12; Stan Lee intro.; Dodson & Cho sketch pages 30.00
... Vol. 1: Down Among the Dead Men (2004, $9.99, TPB) r/#1-4 10.00
... Vol. 2: Venomous (2005, $9.99, TPB) r/#5-8 10.00
... Vol. 3: The Last Stand (2005, $9.99, TPB) r/#9-12 10.00
... Vol. 4: Wild Blue Yonder (2005, $14.99, TPB) r/#13-18 15.00

MARVEL KNIGHTS 2099
Marvel Comics: 2005 ($13.99, TPB)

nn-Reprints one shots: Daredevil 2099, Punisher 2099, Black Panther 2099, Inhumans 2099 and Mutant 2099; Pat Lee-c 14.00

MARVEL LEGACY: ...
Marvel Comics: 2006, 2007 ($4.99, one-shots)

... The 1960s Handbook - Profiles of 1960s iconic and minor characters; info thru 1969 5.00
... The 1970s Handbook - Profiles of 1970s iconic and minor characters; info thru 1979 5.00
... The 1980s Handbook - Profiles of 1980s iconic and minor characters; info thru 1989 5.00
... The 1990s Handbook - Profiles of 1990s iconic and minor characters; Lim-c 5.00
...: The 1960s-1990s Handbook TPB (207, $19.99) r/one-shots 20.00

MARVELMAN CLASSIC
Marvel Comics: 2010 ($34.99, B&W)

HC-(2010, $34.99) Reprints of 1950s British Marvelman stories; character history 35.00
... Primer (8/10, $3.99) Character history; Mick Anglo interview; Quesada-c 4.00

MARVELMAN FAMILY'S FINEST
Marvel Comics: 2010 - No. 6 ($3.99, B&W, limited series)

1-6-Reprints of 1950s Marvelman, Young Marvelman and Marvelman Family stories 4.00

MARVEL MANGAVERSE:... (one-shots)
Marvel Comics: March, 2002 ($2.25, manga-inspired one-shots)

Avengers Assemble! - Udon Studio-s/a 3.00
Eternity Twilight ($3.50) - Ben Dunn-s/a/wrap-around-c 3.50
Fantastic Four - Adam Warren-s/Keron Grant-a 3.00
Ghost Riders - Chuck Austen-s/a 3.00
Punisher - Peter David-s/Lea Hernandez-a 3.00
Spider-Man - Kaare Andrews-s/a 3.00
X-Men - C.B. Cebulski-s/Jeff Matsuda-a 3.00

MARVEL MANGAVERSE (Manga series)
Marvel Comics: June, 2002 - No. 6, Nov., 2002 ($2.25)

1-6: 1-Ben Dunn-s/a; intro. manga Captain Marvel 3.00
Vol. 1 TPB (2002, $24.95) r/one-shots 25.00
Vol. 2 TPB (2002, $12.99) r/#1-6 13.00
Vol. 3: Spider-Man-Legend of the Spider-Clan (2003, $11.99, TPB) r/series 12.00

MARVEL MASTERPIECES COLLECTION, THE
Marvel Comics: May, 1993 - No. 4, Aug, 1993 ($2.95, coated paper, lim. series)

1-4-Reprints Marvel Masterpieces trading cards w/ new Jusko paintings in each; Jusko painted-c/a 3.00

MARVEL MASTERPIECES 2 COLLECTION, THE
Marvel Comics: July, 1994 - No. 3, Sept, 1994 ($2.95, limited series)

1-3: 1-Kaluta-c; r/trading cards; new Steranko centerfold 3.00

MARVEL MILESTONE EDITION
Marvel Comics: 1991 - 1999 ($2.95, coated stock)(r/originals with original ads w/silver ink-c)

...: X-Men #1-Reprints X-Men #1 (1991) 3.00
...: Giant Size X-Men #1-(1991, $3.95, 68 pgs.) 4.00
...: Fantastic Four #1 (11/91), ...: Incredible Hulk #1 (3/92, says 3/91 by error), ...: Amazing Fantasy #15 (3/92), ...: Fantastic Four #5 (11/92), ...: Amazing Spider-Man #129 (11/92), ...: Iron Man #55 (11/92), ...: Iron Fist #14 (11/92), ...: Amazing Spider-Man #1 (1/93), ...: Amazing Spider-Man #1 (1/93) variation- no price on-c, ...: Tales of Suspense #39 (3/93), ...: Avengers #1 (9/93), ...: X-Men #9 (10/93), ...: Avengers #16 (10/93), ...:Amazing Spider-Man #149 (11/94, $2.95), ...:X-Men #28 (11/94, $2.95) 3.00
...:Captain America #1 (3/95, $3.95) 4.00
...:Amazing Spider-Man #3 (3/95, $2.95), ...:Avengers #4 (3/95, $2.95), ...:Strange Tales-r/Dr. Strange stories from #110, 111, 114, & 115 3.00
....:Hulk #181 (8/99, $2.99) 3.00

MARVEL MILESTONES
Marvel Comics: 2005 - Present ($3.99, coated stock)(r/originals w/silver ink-c)

...: Beast & Kitty Pryde-r/from Amazing Adventures #11 & Uncanny X-Men #153 4.00
...: Black Panther, Storm & Ka-Zar-r/from Black Panther #26, Marvel Team-Up #100 and Marvel Mystery Comics #7 4.00
...: Blade, Man-Thing & Satana-r/from Tomb of Dracula #10, Adv. Into Fear #16 and Vampire Tales #2 4.00
...: Captain Britain, Psylocke & Sub-Mariner-r/from Spect. Spidey #114, Uncanny X-Men #213 and Human Torch #2 4.00
...: Doom, Sub-Mariner & Red Skull -r/from FF Ann. #2, Sub-Mariner Comics #1, Captain America Comics #1 4.00
...: Dragon Lord, Speedball and The Man in the Sky -r/from Marvel Spotlight #5, Speedball #1 and Amazing Adult Fantasy #14; Ditko-a on all 4.00
...: Dr. Strange, Silver Surfer, Sub-Mariner, & Hulk -r/from Marvel Premiere #3, FF Ann. #5, Marvel Comics #1, Incredible Hulk #3 4.00
...: Ghost Rider, Black Widow & Iceman -r/from Marvel Spotlight #5, Daredevil #81, X-Men #47 4.00
...: Iron Man, Ant-Man & Captain America -r/from TOS #39,40, TTA #27, Capt. America #1 4.00

Marvel Must Haves: NYX #4-5 © MAR

Marvel Mystery Comics #3 © MAR

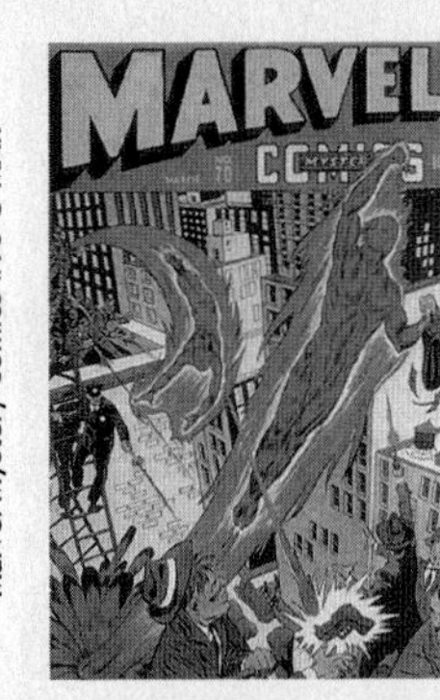

Marvel Mystery Comics #70 © MAR

GD 2.0 | VG 4.0 | FN 6.0 | VF 8.0 | VF/NM 9.0 | NM- 9.2

...: Legion of Monsters, Spider-Man and Brother Voodoo -r/Marvel Premiere #28 & others 4.00
...: Millie the Model & Patsy Walker-r/from Millie the Model #100, Defenders #65 4.00
...: Onslaught -r/Onslaught: Marvel; wraparound-c 4.00
...: Rawhide Kid & Two-Gun Kid-r/Two-Gun Kid #60 and Rawhide Kid #17 4.00
...: Special: Bloodstone, X-51 & Captain Marvel II ($4.99) -r/from Marvel Presents #1, Machine Man #1, Amazing Spider-Man Ann. #19, and Bloodstone #1 5.00
...: Star Brand & Quasar -r/from Star Brand #1 & Quasar #1 4.00
...: Ultimate Spider-Man, Ult. X-Men, Microman & Mantor -r/from Ultimate Spider-Man #1/2, Ultimate X-Men #1/2 and Human Torch #2 4.00
...: Venom & Hercules -r/Marvel S-H Secret Wars #8, Journey Into Mystery Ann. #1 4.00
...: Wolverine, X-Men & Tuk: Caveboy -r/from Marvel Comics Presents #1, Uncanny X-Men #201, Capt. America Comics #1,2 4.00
...: (Jim Lee and Chris Claremont) X-Men and the Starjammers Pt. 1 -r/Unc. X-Men #275 4.00
...: X-Men and the Starjammers Pt. 2 -r/Unc. X-Men #276,277 4.00

MARVEL MINI-BOOKS (See Promotional Comics section)

MARVEL MONSTERS:... (one-shots)
Marvel Comics: Dec, 2005 ($3.99)

...Devil Dinosaur 1 - Hulk app.; Eric Powell-c/a; Sniegoski-s; r/Journey Into Mystery #62 5.00
...Fin Fang Four 1 - FF app.; Powell-c; Langridge-s/Gray-a; r/Strange Tales #89 5.00
...From the Files of Ulysses Bloodstone 1 - Guide to classic Marvel monsters; Powell-c 5.00
...Monsters on the Prowl 1 - Niles-s/Fegredo-a/Powell-c; Thing, Hulk, Giant-Man & Beast app. 5.00
...Where Monsters Dwell 1 - Giffen-s/a; David-s/Pander-a; Parker-s/Braun-s; Powell-c 5.00
HC (2006, $20.99, dust jacket) r/one-shots 21.00

MARVEL MOVIE PREMIERE (Magazine)
Marvel Comics Group: Sept, 1975 (B&W, one-shot)

1-Burroughs' "The Land That Time Forgot" adapt. 2 4 6 9 13 16

MARVEL MOVIE SHOWCASE FEATURING STAR WARS
Marvel Comics Group: Nov, 1982 - No. 2, Dec, 1982 ($1.25, 68 pgs.)

1,2-Star Wars movie adaptation; reprints Star Wars #1-6 by Chaykin; 1-Reprints-c to Star Wars #1. 2-Stevens-r 4.00

MARVEL MOVIE SPOTLIGHT FEATURING RAIDERS OF THE LOST ARK
Marvel Comics Group: Nov, 1982 ($1.25, 68 pgs.)

1-Edited-r/Raiders of the Lost Ark #1-3; Buscema-c/a(p); movie adapt. 4.00

MARVEL MUST HAVES (Reprints of recent sold-out issues)
Marvel Comics: Dec, 2001 - Present ($2.99/$3.99/$4.99)

1,2,4-6: 1-r/Wolverine: Origin #1, Startling Stories: Banner #1, Tangled Web #4 and Cable #97. 2-Amazing Spider-Man #36 and others. 4-Truth #1, Capt. America V4 #1, and The Ultimates #1. 5-r/Ultimate War #1, Ult. X-Men #26, Ult Spider-Man #33. 6-Ult. Spider-Man #33-36 4.00
3-r/Call of Duty: The Brotherhood #1 & Daredevil #32,33 3.00
Amazing Spider-Man #30-32; Incredible Hulk #34-36; The Ultimates #1-3; Ultimate Spider-Man #1-3; Ultimate X-Men #1-3; (New) X-Men #114-116 each.... 4.00
NYX #1-3; NYX #4-5 with sketch & cover gallery; Ultimates 2 #1-3 each... 5.00
Spider-Man and the Black Cat #1-3; preview of #4 5.00

MARVEL MYSTERY COMICS (Formerly Marvel Comics) (Becomes Marvel Tales No. 93 on)
Timely /Marvel Comics (TP #2-17/TCI #18-54/MCI #55-92): No. 2, Dec, 1939 - No. 92, June, 1949 (Some material from #8-10 reprinted in 2004's Marvel 65th Anniversary Special #1)

2-(Rare)-American Ace begins, ends #3; Human Torch (blue costume) by Burgos, Sub-Mariner by Everett continue; 2 pg. origin recap of Human Torch
3200 6400 9600 24,000 46,000 68,000
3-New logo from Marvel pulp begins; 1st app. of television in comics? in Human Torch story (1/40) 1900 3800 5700 14,000 26,000 38,000
4-Intro. Electro, the Marvel of the Age (ends #19), The Ferret, Mystery Detective (ends #9); 1st Sub-Mariner-c by Schomburg; 2nd German swastika on-c of a comic (2/40); one month after Top-Notch Comics #2 1650 3300 4950 12,500 22,750 33,000
5 Classic Schomburg-c (Scarce) 2700 5400 8100 20,000 38,500 57,000
6,7: 6-Gustavson Angel story 970 1940 2910 7180 12,590 18,000
8-1st Human Torch & Sub-Mariner battle(6/40) 1350 2700 4050 10,000 18,500 27,000
9-(Scarce)-Human Torch & Sub-Mariner battle (cover/story); classic-c
4200 8400 12,600 32,000 56,000 80,000
10-Human Torch & Sub-Mariner battle, conclusion; Terry Vance, the Schoolboy Sleuth begins, ends #57 1250 2500 3750 9500 17,250 25,000
11 423 846 1269 3000 5250 7500
12-Classic Kirby-c 459 918 1377 3350 5925 8500
13-Intro. of The Vision by S&K (11/40); Sub-Mariner dons new costume, ends #15
622 1244 1866 4541 8021 11,500
14-16: 14-Shows-c to Human Torch #1 on-c (12/40). 15-S&K Vision, Gustavson Angel story
326 652 978 2282 3991 5700
17-Human Torch/Sub-Mariner team-up by Burgos/Everett; Human Torch pin-up on back-c; shows-c to Human Torch #2 on-c 354 708 1062 2478 4339 6200

GD 2.0 | VG 4.0 | FN 6.0 | VF 8.0 | VF/NM 9.0 | NM- 9.2

18 303 606 909 2121 3711 5300
19,20: 19-Origin Toro in text; shows-c to Sub-Mariner #1 on-c. 20-Origin The Angel in text
309 618 927 2163 3782 5400
21-The Patriot begins, (intro. in Human Torch #4 (#3)); not in #46-48; Sub-Mariner pin-up on back-c (7/41) 303 606 909 2121 3711 5300
22-25: 23-Last Gustavson Angel; origin The Vision in text. 24-Injury-to-eye story
300 600 900 2040 3570 5100
26-30: 27-Ka-Zar ends; last S&K Vision who battles Satan. 28-Jimmy Jupiter in the Land of Nowhere begins, ends #48; Sub-Mariner vs. The Flying Dutchman. 30-1st Japanese war-c
300 600 900 1950 3375 4800
31-33,35,36,38,39: 31-Sub-Mariner by Everett ends, resumes #84. 32-1st app. The Boboes
284 568 852 1818 3109 4400
34-Everett, Burgos, Martin Goodman, Funnies, Inc. office appear in story & battles Hitler; last Burgos Human Torch 300 600 900 1950 3375 4800
37-Classic Hitler-c 300 600 900 2040 3570 5100
40-Classic Zeppelin-c 300 600 900 2010 3505 5000
41-43,45,47 252 504 756 1613 2757 3900
44-Classic Super Plane-c 300 600 900 1920 3310 4700
46-Classic Hitler-c 300 600 900 2010 3505 5000
48-Last Vision; flag-c 258 516 774 1651 2826 4000
49-Origin Miss America 265 530 795 1694 2897 4100
50-Mary becomes Miss Patriot (origin) 252 504 756 1613 2757 3900
51-60: 54-Bondage-c 213 426 639 1363 2332 3300
61,62,64-Last German war-c 194 388 582 1242 2121 3000
63-Classic Hitler War-c; The Villainess Cat-Woman only app.
245 490 735 1568 2684 3800
65,66-Last Japanese War-c 194 388 582 1242 2121 3000
67-78: 74-Last Patriot. 75-Young Allies begin. 76-Ten Chapter Miss America serial begins, ends #85 129 258 387 826 1413 2000
79-New cover format; Super Villains begin on cover; last Angel
142 284 426 909 1555 2200
80-1st app. Capt. America in Marvel Comics 158 316 474 1003 1727 2450
81-Captain America app. 129 258 387 826 1413 2000
82-Origin & 1st app. Namora (5/47); 1st Sub-Mariner/Namora team-up; Captain America app.
300 600 900 1920 3310 4700
83,85: 83-Last Young Allies. 85-Last Miss America; Blonde Phantom app.
119 238 357 762 1306 1850
84-Blonde Phantom begins (on-c of #84,88,89); Sub-Mariner by Everett begins; Captain America app.; Everett-c 158 316 474 1003 1727 2450
86-Blonde Phantom i.d. revealed; Captain America app.; last Bucky app.
126 252 378 806 1378 1950
87-1st Capt. America/Golden Girl team-up; last Toro app. (8/48)
135 270 405 864 1482 2100
88-Golden Girl, Namora, & Sun Girl (1st in Marvel Comics) x-over; Captain America, Blonde Phantom app. 127 254 381 807 1391 1975
89-1st Human Torch/Sun Girl team-up; 1st Captain America solo; Blonde Phantom app.
126 252 378 806 1378 1950
90,91: 90-Blonde Phantom un-masked; Captain America app. 91-Capt. America app.; Blonde Phantom & Sub-Mariner end; early Venus app. (4/49) (scarce)
181 362 543 1158 1979 2800
92-Feature story on the birth of the Human Torch and the death of Professor Horton (his creator); 1st app. The Witness in Marvel Comics; Captain America app. (scarce)
343 686 1029 2400 4200 6000
132 Pg. issue, B&W, 25¢ (1943-44)-printed in N. Y.; square binding, blank inside covers); has Marvel No. 33-c in color; contains Capt. America #18 & Marvel Mystery Comics #33; same contents as Captain America Annual (Less than 5 copies known to exist)
6333 12,667 19,000 38,000 - -
132 Pg. issue (with variant contents), B&W, 25¢ (1942-'43)- square binding, blank inside covers; has same Marvel No. 33-c in color but contains Capt. America #22 & Marvel Mystery Comics #41 instead (possibly scarcer than other version)
(a VG+ copy sold in 2007 for $28,680 and a VG copy sold in 2009 for $19,120)

NOTE: *Brodsky c-49, 72, 86, 88-92.* ***Crandall*** *a-26i.* ***Everett*** *c-7, 27, 84.* ***Gabrielle*** *c-30-32.* ***Schomburg*** *c-3-11, 13-29, 33-36, 39-48, 50-59, 63-69, 74, 76, 132 pg. issue.* ***Shores*** *c-37, 38, 75p, 77, 78p, 79p, 80, 81p, 82-84, 85p, 87p.* ***Sekowsky*** *c-73. Bondage covers-3, 4, 7, 12, 28, 29, 49, 50, 52, 56, 57, 58, 59, 65. Angel c-2, 3, 8, 12. Remember Pearl Harbor issues-#30-32.*

MARVEL MYSTERY COMICS
Marvel Comics: Dec, 1999 ($3.95, reprints)

1-Reprints original 1940s stories; Schomburg-c from #74 4.00

MARVEL MYSTERY COMICS 70th ANNIVERARY SPECIAL
Marvel Comics: Jul, 2009 ($3.99, one-shot)

1-Rivera-c; new Sub-Mariner/Human Torch team-up set in 1941; reps. from #4 & 5 4.00

MARVEL MYSTERY HANDBOOK: 70th ANNIVERARY SPECIAL
Marvel Comics: 2009 ($4.99, one-shot)

Marvel 1985 #6 © MAR

Marvelous Land of Oz #1 © MAR

Marvel Premiere #50 © MAR

GD VG FN VF VF/NM NM-
2.0 4.0 6.0 8.0 9.0 9.2

GD VG FN VF VF/NM NM-
2.0 4.0 6.0 8.0 9.0 9.2

1-Official Handbook-style profile pages of characters from Marvel's first year 5.00

MARVEL NEMESIS: THE IMPERFECTS (EA Games characters)
Marvel Comics: July, 2005 - No. 6, Dec, 2005 ($2.99, limited series)

1-6-Jae Lee-c/Greg Pak-s/Renato Arlem-a; Spider-Man, Thing, Wolverine, Elektra app 3.00
Digest (2005, $7.99) r/#1-6 8.00

MARVEL 1985
Marvel Comics: July, 2008 - No. 6, Dec, 2008 ($3.99, limited series)

1-6: 1-Marvel villains come to the real world; Millar-s/Edwards-a; three covers 4.00
HC (2009, $24.99) r/#1-6; intro. by Lindelof; Edwards production art 25.00

MARVEL NO-PRIZE BOOK, THE (The Official... on-c)
Marvel Comics Group: Jan, 1983 (one-shot, direct sales only)

1-Golden-c; Kirby-a 4.00

MARVELOUS ADVENTURES OF GUS BEEZER
Marvel Comics: May, 2003; Feb, 2004 ($2.99, one-shots)

...: Gus Beezer & Spider-Man 1 - (5/03) Gurihiru-a 3.00
...: Hulk 1 - (5/03) Simone-s/Lethcoe-a; She-Hulk app. 3.00
...: Spider-Man 1 - (5/03) Simone-s/Lethcoe-a; The Lizard & Dr. Doom app. 3.00
...: X-Men 1 - (5/03) Simone-s/Lethcoe-a 3.00

MARVELOUS LAND OF OZ (Sequel to Wonderful Wizard of Oz)
Marvel Comics: Jan, 2010 - No. 8, Sept, 2010 ($3.99, limited series)

1-8-Eric Shanower-a/Skottie Young-a/c. 1-Two covers by Young 4.00
1-Variant Pumpkinhead/Saw-Horse cover by McGuinness 6.00

MARVEL PETS HANDBOOK (Also see "Lockjaw and the Pet Avengers")
Marvel Comics: 2009 ($3.99, one-shot)

1-Official Handbook-style profile pages of animal characters 4.00

MARVEL PREMIERE
Marvel Comics Group: April, 1972 - No. 61, Aug, 1981 (A tryout book for new characters)

1-Origin Warlock (pre-#1) by Gil Kane/Adkins; origin Counter-Earth; Hulk & Thor cameo
(#1-14 are 20¢-c) 8 16 24 52 86 120
2-Warlock ends; Kirby Yellow Claw-r 4 8 12 26 41 55
3-Dr. Strange series begins (pre #1, 7/72), B. Smith-c/a(p)
8 16 24 52 86 120
4-Smith/Brunner-a 4 8 12 23 36 48
5-9: 8-Starlin-c/a(p) 3 6 9 17 25 32
10-Death of the Ancient One 3 6 9 19 29 38
11-14: 11-Dr. Strange origin-r by Ditko. 14-Last Dr. Strange (3/74), gets own title
3 months later 2 4 6 13 18 22
15-Origin/1st app. Iron Fist (5/74), ends #25 9 18 27 65 113 160
16,25: 16-2nd app. Iron Fist; origin cont'd from #15; Hama's 1st Marvel-a. 25-1st Byrne
Iron Fist (moves to own title next) 5 10 15 30 48 65
17-24: Iron Fist in all 3 6 9 21 32 42
26-Hercules. 2 4 6 8 10 12
27-Satana 2 4 6 9 12 15
28-Legion of Monsters (Ghost Rider, Man-Thing, Morbius, Werewolf)
3 6 9 19 29 38
29-46,49: 29,30-The Liberty Legion. 29-1st modern app. Patriot. 31-1st app. Woodgod; last 25¢ issue. 32-1st app. Monark Starstalker. 33,34-1st color app. Solomon Kane (Robert E. Howard adaptation "Red Shadows".) 35-Origin/1st app. 3-D Man. 36,37-3-D Man. 38-1st Weirdworld. 39,40-Torpedo. 41-1st Seeker 3000! 42-Tigra. 43-Paladin. 44-Jack of Hearts (1st solo book, 10/78). 45,46-Man-Wolf. 49-The Falcon (1st solo book, 8/79) 6.00
29-31-(30¢-c variants, limited distribution)(4,6,8/76) 2 4 6 11 16 20
36-38-(35¢-c variants, limited distribution)(6,8,10/77) 3 6 9 18 27 35
47,48-Byrne-a: 47-Origin/1st app. new Ant-Man. 48-Ant-Man
2 4 6 11 16 20
50-1st app. Alice Cooper; co-plotted by Alice 2 4 6 9 13 16
51-56,58-61: 51-53-Black Panther. 54-1st Caleb Hammer. 55-Wonder Man. 56-1st color app. Dominic Fortune. 58-60-Dr. Who. 61-Star Lord 5.00
57-Dr. Who (2nd U.S. app.-see Movie Classics) 1 3 4 6 8 10

NOTE: ***N. Adams*** *(Crusty Bunkers) part inks-10, 12, 13.* ***Austin*** *a-50i, 56i; c-46i, 50i, 56i, 58.* ***Brunner*** *a-4i, 6p, 9-14p; c-9-14.* ***Byrne*** *a-47p, 48p.* ***Chaykin*** *a-32-34; c-32, 33, 56.* ***Giffen*** *a-31p, 44p; c-44.* ***Gil Kane*** *a(p)-1, 2, 15; c(p)-1, 2, 15, 16, 22-24, 27, 36, 37.* ***Kirby*** *c-26, 29-31, 35.* ***Layton*** *a-47i, 48i; c-47.* ***McWilliams*** *a-25i.* ***Miller*** *c-49p, 53p, 58p.* ***Nebres*** *a-44i; c-38i.* ***Nino*** *a-38i.* ***Perez*** *c/a-38p, 45p, 46p.* ***Ploog*** *a-38; c-5-7.* ***Russell*** *a-7p.* ***Simonson*** *a-60(2pgs.); c-57.* ***Starlin*** *a-8p; c-8.* ***Sutton*** *a-41, 43, 50p, 61; c-50p, 61. #57-60 publ'd w/two different prices on-c.*

MARVEL PRESENTS
Marvel Comics: October, 1975 - No. 12, Aug, 1977 (#1-6 are 25¢ issues)

1-Origin & 1st app. Bloodstone 2 4 6 9 13 16
2-Origin Bloodstone continued; Kirby-c 2 3 4 6 8 10
3-Guardians of the Galaxy (1st solo book, 2/76) begins, ends #12
2 4 6 11 16 20
4-7,9-12: 9,10-Origin Starhawk 2 3 4 6 8 10
4-6-(30¢-c variants, limited distribution)(4-8/76) 3 6 9 16 23 30
8-r/story from Silver Surfer #2 plus 4 pgs. new-a 2 3 4 6 8 10
11,12-(35¢-c variants, limited distribution)(6,8/77) 4 8 12 24 37 50

NOTE: ***Austin*** *a-6i.* ***Buscema*** *r-8p.* ***Chaykin*** *a-5p.* ***Kane*** *c-1p.* ***Starlin*** *layouts-10.*

MARVEL PREVIEW (Magazine) (Bizarre Adventures #25 on)
Marvel Comics: Feb (no month), 1975 - No. 24, Winter, 1980 (B&W) ($1.00)

1-Man-Gods From Beyond the Stars; Crusty Bunkers (Neal Adams)-a(i) & cover; Nino-a
3 6 9 16 23 30
2-1st origin The Punisher (see Amaz. Spider-Man #129 & Classic Punisher);
1st app. Dominic Fortune; Morrow-c 11 22 33 75 138 200
3,8,10: 3-Blade the Vampire Slayer. 8-Legion of Monsters; Morbius app. 10-Thor the Mighty;
Starlin frontispiece 3 6 9 18 27 35
4,5: 4-Star-Lord & Sword in the Star (origins & 1st app.). 5,6-Sherlock Holmes.
3 6 9 14 19 24
6,9: 6-Sherlock Holmes; N. Adams frontispiece. 9-Man-God; origin Star Hawk, ends #20
2 4 6 11 16 20
7-Satana, Sword in the Star app. 2 4 6 13 18 22
11,12,16,19,21,23: 11-Star-Lord; Byrne-a; Starlin frontispiece. 12-Haunt of Horror. 16-Masters of Terror. 19-Kull. 21-Moon Knight (Spr/80)-Predates Moon Knight #1; The Shroud by Ditko. 23-Bizarre Advs.; Miller-a. 2 4 6 8 10 12
13-15,17,18,20,22,24: 14,15-Star-Lord. 14-Starlin painted-c. 17-Blackmark by G. Kane (see SSOC #1-3). 18-Star-Lord; Sienkiewicz-a; Veitch & Bissette-a. 20-Bizarre Advs. 22-King Arthur. 24-Debut Paradox 1 2 3 5 6 8

NOTE: ***N. Adams*** *(C. Bunkers) r-20i.* ***Buscema*** *a-22, 23.* ***Byrne*** *a-11.* ***Chaykin*** *a-20r; c-20 (new).* ***Colan*** *a-8, 16p(3), 18p, 23p; c-16p.* ***Elias*** *a-18.* ***Giffen*** *a-7.* ***Infantino*** *a-14p.* ***Kaluta*** *a-12; c-15.* ***Miller*** *a-23.* ***Morrow*** *a-8i; c-2-4.* ***Perez*** *a-20p.* ***Ploog*** *a-8.* ***Starlin*** *c-13, 14. Nudity in some issues.*

MARVEL RIOT
Marvel Comics: Dec, 1995 ($1.95, one-shot)

1-"Age of Apocalypse" spoof; Lobdell script 3.00

MARVEL ROMANCE
Marvel Comics: 2006 ($19.99, TPB)

nn-Reprints romance stories from 1960-1972; art by Kirby, Buscema, Colan, Romita 20.00

MARVEL ROMANCE REDUX (Humor stories using art reprinted from Marvel romance comics)
Marvel Comics: Apr, 2006 - Aug, 2006 ($2.99, one-shots)

...: But I Thought He Loved Me Too (4/06) art by Kirby, Colan, Buscema & Romita; Giffen-c 3.00
...: Guys & Dolls (5/06) art by Starlin, Heck, Colan & Buscema; Conner-c 3.00
...: I Should Have Been a Blonde (7/06) art by Brodsky Colletta & Colan; Cho-c 3.00
...: Love is a Four Letter Word (8/06) art by Kirby, Buscema, Colan & Heck; Land-c 3.00
...: Restraining Orders are For Other Girls (6/06) art by Giordano, Kirby; Baker-c 3.00
...: Another Kind of Love TPB (2007, $13.99) r/one-shots 14.00

MARVELS (Also see Marvels: Eye of the Camera)
Marvel Comics: Jan, 1994 - No. 4, Apr, 1994 ($5.95, painted lim. series)
No. 1 (2nd Printing), Apr, 1996 - No. 4 (2nd Printing), July, 1996 ($2.95)

1-4: Kurt Busiek scripts & Alex Ross painted-c/a in all; double-c w/acetate overlay
1 2 3 5 6 8
Marvel Classic Collectors Pack ($11.90)-Issues #1 & 2 boxed (1st printings).
2 4 6 9 13 16
0-(8/94, $2.95)-no acetate overlay. 4.00
1-4-(2nd printing): r/original limited series w/o acetate overlay 3.00
Hardcover (1994, $59.95)-r/#0-4; w/intros by Stan Lee, John Romita, Sr., Kurt Busiek & Scott McCloud. 60.00
...: 10th Anniversary Edition (2004, $49.99, hardcover w/dustjacket) r/#0-4; scripts and commentaries; Ross sketch pages, cover gallery, behind the scenes art 50.00
Trade paperback ($19.95) 20.00

MARVEL SAGA, THE
Marvel Comics Group: Dec, 1985 - No. 25, Dec, 1987

1,21-25 3.00
2-20 3.00

NOTE: ***Williamson*** *a(i)-9, 10; c(i)-7, 10-12, 14, 16.*

MARVELS COMICS: ... (Marvel-type comics read in the Marvel Universe)
Marvel Comics: Jul, 2000 ($2.25, one-shots)

...Captain America #1 -Frenz & Sinnott-a; ...Daredevil #1 -Isabella-s/Newell-a; ...Fantastic Four #1 -Kesel-s/Paul Smith-a; Spider-Man #1 -Oliff-a; ...Thor #1 -Templeton-s/Aucoin-a 3.00
...X-Men #1 -Millar-s/ Sean Phillips & Duncan Fegredo-a 3.00
The History of Marvels Comics (no cover price)-Faux history; previews titles 3.00

MARVEL SELECT FLIP MAGAZINE
Marvel Comics: Aug, 2005 - No. 24 ($3.99/$4.99)

1-11-Reprints Astonishing X-Men and New X-Men: Academy X in flip format 4.00
12-24-($4.99) Reprints recent X-Men mini-series in flip format 5.00

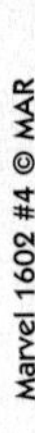

Marvel 1602 #4 © MAR

Marvel Spotlight #32 © MAR

Marvel Spotlight: Dark Reign © MAR

GD VG FN VF VF/NM NM-
2.0 4.0 6.0 8.0 9.0 9.2

MARVEL SELECTS:
Marvel Comics: Jan, 2000 - No. 6, June, 2000 ($2.75/$2.99, reprints)

...Fantastic Four 1-6: Reprints F.F. #107-112; new Davis-c 3.00
...Spider-Man 1,2,4-6: Reprints AS-M #100,101,103,104,93; Wieringo-c 3.00
...Spider-Man 3 ($2.99): Reprints AS-M #102; new Wieringo-c 3.00

MARVELS: EYE OF THE CAMERA (Sequel to Marvels)
Marvel Comics: Feb, 2009 - No. 6, Apr, 2010 ($3.99, limited series)

1-6-Kurt Busiek-s/Jay Anacleto-a; continuing story of photographer Phil Sheldon 4.00
1-6-B&W edition 4.00

MARVEL'S GREATEST COMICS (Marvel Collectors' Item Classics #1-22)
Marvel Comics Group: No. 23, Oct, 1969 - No. 96, Jan, 1981

23-34 (Giants). Begin Fantastic Four-r/#30s?-116 3 6 9 17 25 32
35-37-Silver Surfer-r/Fantastic Four #48-50 2 4 6 8 11 14
38-50: 42-Silver Surfer-r/F.F.(others?) 1 2 3 5 7 9
51-70: 63,64-(25¢ editions) 6.00
63,64-(30¢-c variants, limited distribution)(5,7/76) 2 4 6 11 16 20
71-96: 71-73-(30¢ editions) 5.00
71-73-(35¢-c variants, limited distribution)(7,9-10/77) 3 6 9 18 27 35
...: Fantastic Four #52 (2006, $2.99) reprints entire comic with ads and letter column 3.00

NOTE: *Dr. Strange, Fantastic Four, Iron Man, Watcher-#23, 24. Capt. America, Dr. Strange, Iron Man, Fantastic Four-#25-28. Fantastic Four-#38-96.* ***Buscema*** *r-85-92; c-87-92r.* ***Ditko*** *r-23-28.* ***Kirby*** *r-23-82; c-75, 77p, 80p. #81 reprints Fantastic Four #100.*

MARVEL'S GREATEST SUPERHERO BATTLES (See Fireside Book Series)

MARVEL: SHADOWS AND LIGHT
Marvel Comics: Feb, 1997 ($2.95, B&W, one-shot)

1-Tony Daniel-c 3.00

MARVEL 1602
Marvel Comics: Nov, 2003 - No. 8, June, 2004 ($3.50, limited series)

1-8-Neil Gaiman-s; Andy Kubert & Richard Isanove-a 3.50
... MGC #1 (7/10, $1.00) r/#1 with "Marvel's Greatest Comics" logo on cover 1.00
HC (2004, $24.99) r/series; script pages for #1, sketch pages and Gaiman afterword 25.00
SC (2005, $19.99) 20.00

MARVEL 1602: FANTASTICK FOUR
Marvel Comics: Nov, 2006 - No. 5, Mar, 2007s ($3.50, limited series)

1-5-Peter David-s/Pascal Alixe-a/Leinil Yu-c 3.50
TPB (2007, $14.99) r/#1-5; sketch page 15.00

MARVEL 1602: NEW WORLD
Marvel Comics: Oct, 2005 - No. 5, Jan, 2006 ($3.50, limited series)

1-5-Greg Pak-s/Greg Tocchini-a; "Hulk" and "Iron Man" app. 3.50
TPB (2006, $14.99) r/#1-5 15.00

MARVEL 65TH ANNIVERSARY SPECIAL
Marvel Comics: 2004 ($4.99, one-shot)

1-Reprints Sub-Mariner & Human Torch battle from Marvel Mystery Comics #8-10 5.00

MARVELS OF SCIENCE
Charlton Comics: March, 1946 - No. 4, June, 1946

1-A-Bomb story 23 46 69 136 223 310
2-4 14 28 42 80 115 150

MARVEL SPECIAL EDITION FEATURING... (Also see Special Collectors' Ed.)
Marvel Comics Group: 1975 - 1978 (84 pgs.) (Oversized)

1-The Spectacular Spider-Man ($1.50); r/Amazing Spider-Man #6,35,
Annual 1; Ditko-a(r) 3 6 9 20 30 40
1,2-Star Wars ('77,'78; r/Star Wars #1-3 & #4-6; regular edition and Whitman variant exist
2 4 6 11 16 20
3-Star Wars ('78, $2.50, 116 pgs.); r/S. Wars #1-6; regular edition and Whitman variant exist
3 6 9 14 20 26
3-Close Encounters of the Third Kind (1978, $1.50, 56 pgs.)-Movie adaptation;
Simonson-a(p) 2 4 6 10 14 18
V2#2(Spring, 1980, $2.00, oversized)- "Star Wars: The Empire Strikes Back";
r/Marvel Comics Super Special #16 3 6 9 16 23 30

NOTE: ***Chaykin*** *c/a(r)-1(1977), 2, 3.* ***Stevens*** *a(r)-2i, 3i.* ***Williamson*** *a(r)-V2#2.*

MARVEL SPECTACULAR
Marvel Comics Group: Aug, 1973 - No. 19, Nov, 1975

1-Thor-r from mid-sixties begin by Kirby 2 4 6 8 11 14
2-19 1 2 3 5 6 8

MARVELS: PORTRAITS
Marvel Comics: Mar, 1995 - No. 4, June, 1995 ($2.95, limited series)

1-4:Different artists renditions of Marvel characters 3.00

GD VG FN VF VF/NM NM-
2.0 4.0 6.0 8.0 9.0 9.2

MARVEL SPOTLIGHT (...& Son of Satan #19, 20, 23, 24)
Marvel Comics Group: Nov, 1971 - No. 33, Apr, 1977; V2#1, July, 1979 - V2#11, Mar, 1981
(A try-out book for new characters)

1-Origin Red Wolf (western hero)(1st solo book, pre-#1); Wood inks, Neal Adams-c;
only 15¢ issue 6 12 18 39 62 85
2-(25¢, 52 pgs.)-Venus-r by Everett; origin/1st app. Werewolf By Night (begins) by Ploog;
N. Adams-c 20 40 60 140 283 425
3,4: 4-Werewolf By Night ends (6/72); gets own title 9/72
7 14 21 47 76 105
5-Origin/1st app. Ghost Rider (8/72) & begins 25 50 75 183 367 550
6-8: 6-Origin G.R. retold. 8-Last Ploog issue 8 16 24 58 97 135
9-11-Last Ghost Rider (gets own title next mo.) 6 12 18 43 69 95
12-Origin & 2nd full app. The Son of Satan (10/73); story cont'd from Ghost Rider #2 & into
#3; series begins, ends #24 4 8 12 28 44 60
13-24: 13-Partial origin Son of Satan. 14-Last 20¢ issue. 22-Ghost Rider-c & cameo
(5 panels). 24-Last Son of Satan (10/75); gets own title 12/75
2 4 6 9 12 15
25,27,30,31: 27-(Regular 25¢-c), Sub-Mariner app. 30-The Warriors Three. 31-Nick Fury 6.00
26-Scarecrow 1 3 4 6 8 10
27-(30¢-c variant, limited distribution) 2 4 6 13 18 22
28-(Regular 25¢-c) 1st solo Moon Knight app. 4 8 12 24 37 50
28-(30¢-c variant, limited distribution) 8 16 24 54 90 125
29-(Regular 25¢-c) (8/76) Moon Knight app.; last 25¢ issue
3 6 9 16 23 30
29-(30¢-c variant, limited distribution) 6 12 18 41 66 90
32-1st app./partial origin Spider-Woman (2/77); Nick Fury app.
3 6 9 16 22 28
33-Deathlok; 1st app. Devil-Slayer 2 3 4 6 8 10
V2#1-7,9-11: 1-4-Capt. Marvel. 5-Dragon Lord. 6,7-StarLord; origin #6. 9-11-Capt. Universe
(see Micronauts #8) 4.00
1-Variant copy missing issue #1 on cover 2 4 6 9 12 15
8-Capt. Marvel; Miller-c/a(p) 1 2 3 5 6 8

NOTE: ***Austin*** *c-V2#2i, 8.* ***J. Buscema*** *c/a-30p.* ***Chaykin*** *a-31; c-26, 31.* ***Colan*** *a-18p, 19p.* ***Ditko*** *a-V2#4, 5, 9-11; c-V2#4, 9-11.* ***Kane*** *c-21p, 32p.* ***Kirby*** *c-29p.* ***McWilliams*** *a-20i.* ***Miller*** *a-V2#8p; c(p)-V2#2, 5, 7, 8.* ***Mooney*** *a-8i, 10i, 14p, 15, 16p, 17p, 24p, 27, 32i.* ***Nasser*** *a-33p.* ***Ploog*** *a-2-5, 6-8p; c-3-9.* ***Romita*** *c-13.* ***Sutton*** *a-9-11p, V2#6, 7. #29-25¢ & 30¢ issues exist.*

MARVEL SPOTLIGHT (Most issues spotlight one Marvel artist and one Marvel writer)
Marvel Comics: 2005 - Present ($2.99/$3.99)

...Brian Bendis/Mark Bagley; Daniel Way/Olivier Coipel; David Finch/Roberto Aguirre-Sacasa; Ed Brubaker/Billy Tan; John Cassaday/Sean McKeever; Joss Whedon/Michael Lark; Laurell K. Hamilton/George R.R. Martin; Neil Gaiman/Salvador Larroca; Robert Kirkman/Greg Land; Stan Lee/Jack Kirby; Warren Ellis/Jim Cheung each... 3.00
...Steve McNiven/Mark Millar - Civil War 10.00
...: Captain America (2009) interviews with Brubaker & Hitch; Reborn preview 3.00
...: Captain America Remembered (2007) character features; creator interviews 3.00
...: Civil War Aftermath (2007) Top 10 Moments, casualty list, previews of upcoming series 3.00
...: Dark Reign (2009) features on the Avengers, Fury and others; creator interview 4.00
...: Dark Tower (2007) previews the Stephen King adaptation; creator interviews 5.00
...: Deadpool (2009) character features; interviews with Kelly, Way, Medina & Benson 3.00
...: Fantastic Four and Silver Surfer (2007) character features; creator interviews 3.00
...: Ghost Rider (2007) character and movie features; creator interviews 3.00
...: Halo (2007) a World of Halo feature; Bendis & Maleev interviews 3.00
...: Heroes Reborn/Onslaught Reborn (2006) 3.00
...: Hulk Movie (2008) character and movie features; comic & movie creator interviews 3.00
...: Iron Man Movie (2008) character and movie features; Terrence Howard interview 3.00
...: Iron Man 2 (4/10) movie preview; Granov, Fraction interviews; Whiplash profile 4.00
...: Marvel Knights 10th Anniversary (2008) Quesada interview; series synopsies 3.00
...: Marvel Zombies/Mystic Arcana (2008) character features; creator interviews 3.00
...: Marvel Zombies Return (2009) character features; creator interviews 3.00
...: New Mutants (2009) character features; Claremont & McLeod interviews 3.00
...: Punisher Movie (2008) character and movie features; creator interviews 3.00
...: Secret Invasion (2008) features on the Skrulls; Bendis, Reed & Yu interviews 3.00
...: Secret Invasion Aftermath (2008) Skrull profiles; Bendis, Reed & Diggle interviews 4.00
...: Spider-Man (2007) character features; creator interviews; Ditko art showcase 3.00
...: Spider-Man - Brand New Day (2008) storyline features; Romitas interviews 3.00
...: Spider-Man-One More Day/Brand New Day (2008) storyline features; interviews 3.00
...: Summer Events (2009, $3.99) 2009 title previews; creator interviews 4.00
...: Thor (2007) character features; Straczynski interview; Romita Jr. art showcase 3.00
...: Ultimates 3 (2008) character features; Loeb & Madureira interviews 3.00
...: Ultimatum (2008) previews the limited series; Loeb & Bendis interviews 3.00
...: Uncanny X-Men 500 Issues Celebration (2008) creator interviews; timeline 3.00
...: War of Kings (2009) character features; Abnett, Lanning, Pelletier interviews 3.00
...: Wolverine (2009, $3.99) preview of 2009 Wolverine stories; creator interviews 4.00
...: World War Hulk (2007) character features; creator interviews; early art showcase 3.00

Marvel Super-Heroes #77 © MAR

Marvel Super Hero Squad #4 © MAR

Marvel Tales #120 © MAR

GD 2.0 | VG 4.0 | FN 6.0 | VF 8.0 | VF/NM 9.0 | NM- 9.2

...: X-Men: Messiah Complex (2008) X-Men crossover features; creator interviews 3.00

MARVELS PROJECT, THE
Marvel Comics: Oct, 2009 - No. 8, July, 2010 ($3.99, limited series)

1-8-Emergence of Marvel heroes in 1939-40; Brubaker-s/Epting-a; Epting & McNiven-c 4.00
1-8-Variant covers by Parel 5.00

MARVEL SUPER ACTION (Magazine)
Marvel Comics Group: Jan, 1976 (B&W, 76 pgs.)

1-2nd app. Dominic Fortune (see Marvel Preview); early Punisher app.; Weird World & The Huntress; Evans, Ploog-a 8 16 24 58 97 135

MARVEL SUPER ACTION
Marvel Comics Group: May, 1977 - No. 37, Nov, 1981

1-Reprints Capt. America #100 by Kirby 2 4 6 9 13 16
2-13: 2,3,5-13 reprint Capt. America #101,102,103-111. 4-Marvel Boy-r(origin)/M. Boy #1. 11-Origin-r. 12,13-Classic Steranko-c/a(r). 1 2 3 5 7 9
2,3-(35¢-c variants, limited distribution)(6,8/77) 4 8 12 22 34 45
14-20: r/Avengers #55,56, Annual 2, others 6.00
21-37: 30-r/Hulk #6 from U.K. 5.00

NOTE: ***Buscema** a(r)-14p, 15p; c-18-20, 22, 35r-37. **Everett** a-4. **Heath** a-4r. **Kirby** r-1-3, 5-11. **B. Smith** a-27r, 28r. **Steranko** a(r)-12p, 13p; c-12r, 13r.*

MARVEL SUPER HERO CONTEST OF CHAMPIONS
Marvel Comics Group: June, 1982 - No. 3, Aug, 1982 (Limited series)

1-3: Features nearly all Marvel characters currently appearing in their comics; 1st Marvel limited series 1 2 3 5 6 8

MARVEL SUPER HEROES
Marvel Comics Group: October, 1966 (25¢, 68 pgs.) (1st Marvel one-shot)

1-r/origin Daredevil from D.D. #1; r/Avengers #2; G.A. Sub-Mariner-r/Marvel Mystery #8 (Human Torch app.). Kirby-a 11 22 33 77 144 210

MARVEL SUPER-HEROES (Formerly Fantasy Masterpieces #1-11)
(Also see Giant-Size Super Heroes) (#12-20: 25¢, 68 pgs.)
Marvel Comics: No. 12, 12/67 - No. 31, 11/71; No. 32, 9/72 - No. 105, 1/82

12-Origin & 1st app. Capt. Marvel of the Kree; G.A. Human Torch, Destroyer, Capt. America, Black Knight, Sub-Mariner-r (#12-20 all contain new stories and reprints) 13 26 39 91 176 260
13-2nd app. Capt. Marvel; G.A. Black Knight, Torch, Vision, Capt. America, Sub-Mariner-r 8 16 24 56 93 130
14-Amazing Spider-Man (5/68, new-a by Andru/Everett); G.A. Sub-Mariner, Torch, Mercury (1st Kirby-a at Marvel), Black Knight, Capt. America reprints 10 20 30 71 128 185
15-17: 15-Black Bolt cameo in Medusa (new-a); Black Knight, Sub-Mariner, Black Marvel, Capt. America-r. 16-Origin & 1st app. S. A. Phantom Eagle; G.A. Torch, Capt. America, Black Knight, Patriot, Sub-Mariner-r. 17-Origin Black Knight (new-a); G.A. Torch, Sub-Mariner-r; reprint from All-Winners Squad #21 (cover & story) 5 10 15 32 51 70
18-Origin/1st app. Guardians of the Galaxy (1/69); G.A. Sub-Mariner, All-Winners Squad-r 7 14 21 50 83 115
19-Ka-Zar (new-a); G.A. Torch, Marvel Boy, Black Knight, Sub-Mariner reprints; Smith-c(p); Tuska-a(r) 4 8 12 26 41 55
20-Doctor Doom (5/69); r/Young Men #24 w/-c 5 10 15 30 48 65
21-31: All-r issues. 21-X-Men, Daredevil, Iron Man-r begin, end #31. 31-Last Giant issue 3 6 9 16 23 30
32-50: 32-Hulk/Sub-Mariner-r begin from TTA. 1 2 3 5 7 9
51-70,100: 56-r/origin Hulk/Inc. Hulk #102; Hulk-r begin 6.00
57,58-(30¢-c variants, limited distribution)(5,7/76) 2 4 6 11 16 20
65,66-(35¢-c variants, limited distribution)(7,9/77) 3 6 9 17 25 32
71-99,101-105 5.00

NOTE: ***Austin** a-104. **Colan** a(p)-12, 13, 15, 18; c-12, 13, 15, 18. **Everett** a-14i(new); r-14, 15i, 18, 19, 33; c-85(r). New **Kirby** c-22, 27, 54. **Maneely** r-14, 15, 19. **Severin** r-83-85i, 100-102; c-100-102r. **Starlin** c-47. **Tuska** a-19p. Black Knight-r by **Maneely** in 12-16, 19. Sub-Mariner-r by **Everett** in 12-20.*

MARVEL SUPER-HEROES
Marvel Comics: May, 1990 - V2#15, Oct, 1993 ($2.95/$2.50, quart., 68-84 pgs.)

1-Moon Knight, Hercules, Black Panther, Magik, Brother Voodoo, Speedball (by Ditko) & Hellcat; Hembeck-a 4.00
2,4,5,V2#3,6-15: 2-Summer Special(7/90); Rogue, Speedball (by Ditko), Iron Man, Falcon, Tigra & Daredevil. 4-Spider-Man/Nick Fury, Daredevil,Speedball, Wonder Man, Spitfire & Black Knight; Byrne-c. 5-Thor, Dr. Strange, Thing & She-Hulk; Speedball by Ditko(p). V2#3-Retells origin Capt. America w/new facts; Blue Shield, Capt. Marvel,Speedball, Wasp; Hulk by Ditko/Rogers V2#6-9: 6-8-$2.25-c. 6,7-X-Men, Cloak & Dagger, The Shroud (by Ditko) & Marvel Boy in each. 8-X-Men, Namor & Iron Man (by Ditko); Larsen-c. 9-West Coast Avengers, Iron Man app.; Kieth-c(p). V2#10-Ms. Marvel/Sabretooth-c/story (intended for Ms. Marvel #24; shows-c to #24); Namor, Vision, Scarlet Witch stories. V2#11,12 :11-Original Ghost Rider-c/story; Giant-Man, Ms. Marvel stories. 12-Dr. Strange, Falcon, Iron Man. V2#13-15 ($2.75, 84 pgs.): 13-All Iron Man 30th anniversary. 15-Iron Man/Thor/Volstagg/Dr. Druid 4.00

MARVEL SUPER-HEROES MEGAZINE
Marvel Comics: Oct, 1994 - No. 6, Mar, 1995 ($2.95, 100 pgs.)

1-6: 1-r/FF #232, DD #159, Iron Man #115, Incred. Hulk #314 4.00

MARVEL SUPER-HEROES SECRET WARS (See Secret Wars II)
Marvel Comics Group: May, 1984 - No. 12, Apr, 1985 (limited series)

1 1 2 3 5 6 8
1-3-(2nd printings, sold in multi-packs) 3.00
2-6,9-11: 6-The Wasp dies 6.00
7,12: 7-Intro. new Spider-Woman. 12-($1.00, 52 pgs.) 1 2 3 4 5 7
8-Spider-Man's new black costume explained as alien costume (1st app. Venom as alien costume) 3 6 9 20 30 40
Secret Wars Omnibus HC (2008, $99.99, dustjacket) r/#1-12, Thor #383, She-Hulk (2004) #10 and What If? (1989) #4 & #114; photo gallery of related toys; pencil-a from #1 100.00

NOTE: ***Zeck** a-1-12; c-1,3,8-12. Additional artists (John Romita Sr., Art Adams and others) had uncredditted art in #12.*

MARVEL SUPER HERO SQUAD (All ages)
Marvel Comics: Mar, 2009; Nov, 2009 - No. 4, Feb, 2010 ($3.99/$2.99)

1-4-Based on the animated series; back-up humor strips and pin-ups 3.00
...Hero Up! (3/09, $3.99) Collects humor strips from MarvelKids.com; 2 covers 4.00

MARVEL SUPER HERO SQUAD (All ages)
Marvel Comics: Mar, 2010 - No. 12, Feb, 2011 ($2.99)

1-12-Based on the animated series. 1-Wraparound-c 3.00
Super Hero Squad Spectacular 1 (4/11, $3.99) The Beyonder app. 4.00

MARVEL SUPER SPECIAL, A (See Marvel Comics Super...)

MARVEL SWIMSUIT SPECIAL (Also see Marvel Illustrated...)
Marvel Comics: 1992 - No. 4, 1995 ($3.95/$4.50, magazine, 52 pgs.)

1-4-Silvestri-c; pin-ups by diff. artists. 2-Jusko-c. 3-Hughes-c 1 3 4 6 8 10

MARVEL TAILS STARRING PETER PORKER THE SPECTACULAR SPIDER-HAM
(Also see Peter Porker...)
Marvel Comics Group: Nov, 1983 (one-shot)

1-Peter Porker, the Spectacular Spider-Ham, Captain Americat, Goose Rider, Hulk Bunny app. 4.00

MARVEL TALES (Formerly Marvel Mystery Comics #1-92)
Marvel/Atlas Comics (MCI): No. 93, Aug, 1949 - No. 159, Aug, 1957

93-Horror/weird stories begin 155 310 465 992 1696 2400
94-Everett-a 97 194 291 621 1061 1500
95-New logo 71 142 213 454 777 1100
96,99,101,103,105 60 120 180 381 653 925
97-Sun Girl, 2 pgs; Kirbyish-a; one story used in N.Y. State Legislative document 81 162 243 518 884 1250
98,100: 98-Krigstein-a 61 122 183 387 664 940
102-Wolverton-a "The End of the World", (6 pgs.) 86 172 258 546 936 1325
104-Wolverton-a "Gateway to Horror", (6 pgs.) 86 172 258 546 936 1325
106,107-Krigstein-a. 106-Decapitation story 49 98 147 309 522 735
108-120: 116-(7/53) Werewolf By Night story. 118-Hypo-c/panels in End of World story. 120-Jack Katz-a 37 74 111 222 361 500
121,123-131: 128-Flying Saucer-c. 131-Last precode (2/55) 29 58 87 172 281 390
122-Kubert-a 30 60 90 177 289 400
132,133,135-141,143,145 22 44 66 128 209 290
134-Krigstein, Kubert-a; flying saucer-c 24 48 72 140 230 320
142-Krigstein-a 22 44 66 132 216 300
144-Williamson/Krenkel-a, 3 pgs. 22 44 66 132 216 300
146,148-151,154-156,158: 150-1st S.A. issue. 156-Torres-a 18 36 54 105 165 225
147,152: 147-Ditko-a. 152-Wood, Morrow-a 20 40 60 117 189 260
153-Everett End of World c/story 22 44 66 128 209 290
157,159-Krigstein-a 19 38 57 111 176 240

NOTE: ***Andru** a-103. **Briefer** a-118. **Check** a-147. **Colan** a-102, 105, 107, 118, 120, 121, 127, 131. **Drucker** a-127, 135, 141, 146, 150. **Everett** a-98, 104, 106(2), 108(2), 131, 148, 151, 153, 155; c-107, 109, 111, 112, 114, 117, 127, 143, 147-151, 153, 155, 156. **Forte** a-119, 125, 130, 158. **Heath** a-110, 113, 118, 119; c-104-106, 110, 130. **Gil Kane** a-117. **Lawrence** a-130. **Maneely** a-111, 126, 129; c-108, 116, 120, 129, 152. **Mooney** a-114. **Morisi** a-153. **Morrow** a-150, 152, 156. **Orlando** a-149, 151, 157. **Pakula** a-119, 121, 133, 135, 144, 150, 152, 156. **Powell** a-136, 137, 150, 154. **Ravielli** a-117, 123. **Rico** a-97, 99. **Romita** a-108. **Sekowsky** a-96-98. **Shores** a-110; c-96. **Sinnott** a-105, 116, 144. **Tuska** a-114. **Whitney** a-107. **Wildey** a-126, 138.*

MARVEL TALES (...Annual #1,2; ...Starring Spider-Man #123 on)

Marvel Tales (2nd series) #91 © MAR

Marvel Tales (2nd series) #289 © MAR

Marvel Team-Up #68 © MAR

GD VG FN VF VF/NM NM-
2.0 4.0 6.0 8.0 9.0 9.2

Marvel Comics Group (NPP earlier issues): 1964 - No. 291, Nov, 1994 (No. 1-32: 72 pgs.)
(#1-3 have Canadian variants; back & inside-c are blank, same value)

1-Reprints origins of Spider-Man/Amazing Fantasy #15, Hulk/Inc. Hulk#1, Ant-Man/T.T.A. #35, Giant Man/T.T.A. #49, Iron Man/T.O.S. #39,48, Thor/J.I.M. #83 & r/Sgt. Fury #1 — 28 56 84 215 433 650
2 ('65)-r/X-Men #1(origin), Avengers #1(origin), origin Dr. Strange-r/Strange Tales #115 & origin Hulk(Hulk #3) — 11 22 33 75 138 200
3 (7/66)-Spider-Man, Strange Tales (H. Torch), Journey into Mystery (Thor), Tales to Astonish (Ant-Man)-r begin (r/Strange Tales #101) — 7 14 21 45 73 100
4,5 — 5 10 15 32 51 70
6-8,10: 10-Reprints 1st Kraven/Amaz. S-M #15 — 4 8 12 22 34 45
9-r/Amazing Spider-Man #14 w/cover — 4 8 12 24 37 50
11-33: 11-Spider-Man battles Daredevil-r/Amaz. Spider-Man #16. 13-Origin Marvel Boy-r from M. Boy #1. 22-Green Goblin-c/story-r/Amaz. Spider-Man #27. 30-New Angel story (x-over w/Ka-Zar #2,3). 32-Last 72 pg. iss. 33-(52 pgs.) Kraven-r — 3 6 9 16 23 30
34-50: 34-Begin regular size issues — 2 3 4 6 8 10
51-65 — 6.00
66-70-(Regular 25¢ editions)(4-8/76) — 5.00
66-70-(30¢-c variants, limited distribution) — 2 4 6 11 16 20
71-105: 75-Origin Spider-Man-r. 77-79-Drug issues-r/Amaz. Spider-Man #96-98. 98-Death of Gwen Stacy-r/Amaz. Spider-Man #121 (Green Goblin). 99-Death Green Goblin-r/Amaz. Spider-Man #122. 100-(52 pgs.)-New Hawkeye/Two Gun Kid story. 101-105-All Spider-Man-r — 5.00
80-84-(35¢-c variants, limited distribution)(6-10/77) — 3 6 9 16 23 30
106-r/1st Punisher-Amazing Spider-Man #129 — 1 2 3 5 7 9
107-136: 107-133-All Spider-Man-r. 111,112-r/Spider-Man #134,135 (Punisher). 113,114-r/Spider-Man #136,137(Green Goblin). 126-128-r/clone story from Amazing Spider-Man #149-151. 134-136-Dr. Strange-r begin; SpM stories continue. 134-Dr. Strange-r/Strange Tales #110 — 4.00
137-Origin-r Dr. Strange; shows original unprinted-c & origin Spider-Man/Amazing Fantasy #15 — 1 2 3 5 6 8
137-Nabisco giveaway — 1 2 3 5 6 8
138-Reprints all Amazing Spider-Man #1; begin reprints of Spider-Man with covers similar to originals — 6.00
139-144: r/Amazing Spider-Man #2-7 — 5.00
145-149,151-190,193-199: Spider-Man-r continue w/#8 on. 149-Contains skin "Tattooz" decals. 153-r/1st Kraven/Spider-Man #15. 155-r/2nd Green Goblin/Spider-Man #17. 161,164,165-Gr. Goblin-c/stories-r/Spider-Man #23,26,27. 178,179-Green Goblin-c/story-r/ Spider-Man #39,40. 187,189-Kraven-r. 193-Byrne-r/Marvel Team-Up begin w/scripts — 4.00
150,191,192,200: 150-($1.00, 52pgs.)-r/Spider-Man Annual #1(Kraven app.). 191-($1.50, 68 pgs.)-r/Spider-Man #96-98. 192-($1.25, 52 pgs.)-r/Spider-Man #121,122. 200-Double size ($1.25)-Miller-c & r/Annual #14 — 5.00
201-249,251,252,254-257: 208-Last Byrne-r. 210,211-r/Spidey #134,135. 212,213-r/Giant-Size Spidey #4. 213-r/1st solo Silver Surfer story/F.F. Annual #5. 214,215-r/Spidey #161,162. 222-Reprints origin Punisher/Spect. Spider-Man #83; last Punisher reprint. 209-Reprints 1st app. The Punisher/Amazing Spider-Man #129; Punisher reprints begin, end #222. 223-McFarlane-c begins, end #239. 233-Spider-Man/X-Men team-ups begin; r/X-Men #35. 234-r/Marvel Team-Up #4. 235,236-r/M. Team-Up Annual #1. 237,238-r/M. Team-Up #150. 239,240-r/M. Team-Up #38,90(Beast). 242-r/M.Team-Up #89. 243-r/M. Team-Up #117 (Wolverine). 251-r/Spider-Man #100 (Green Goblin-c/story). 252-r/1st app. Morbius/Amaz. Spider-Man #101. 254-r/M. Team-Up #15(Ghost Rider); new painted-c. 255,256-Spider-Man & Ghost Rider-r/Marvel Team-Up #58,91. 257-Hobgoblin-r begin (r/ASM #238) — 3.00
250.253: 250-($1.50, 52 pgs.)-r/1st Karma/M. Team-Up #100. 253-($1.50, 52 pgs.) -r/Amaz. S-M #102 — 4.00
258-291: 258-261-r/A. Spider-Man #239,249-251(Hobgoblin). 262,263-r/Marv. Team-Up #53,54. 262-New X-Men vs. Sunstroke story. 263-New Woodgod origin story. 264,265-r/Amazing Spider-Man Annual 5. 266-273-Reprints alien costume stories/A. S-M 252-259. 277-r/1st Silver Sable/A. S-M 265. 283-r/A. S-M 275 (Hobgoblin). 284-r/A. S-M 276 (Hobgoblin) — 3.00
285-variant w/Wonder-Con logo on c-no price-giveaway — 3.00
286-($2.95)-p/bagged w/16 page insert & animation print — 4.00

NOTE: *All contain reprints; some have new art. #89-97-r/Amazing Spider-Man #110-118; #98-136-r/#121-159; #137-150-r/Amazing Fantasy #15, #1-12 & Annual 1; #151-167-r/#13-28 & Annual 2; #168-186-r/#29-46.* ***Austin*** *a-100i; c-272i, 273i.* ***Byrne*** *a(r)-193-198p, 201-208p.* ***Ditko*** *a-1-30, 83, 100, 137-155.* ***G. Kane*** *a-71, 81, 98-101p, 249r; c-125-127p, 130p, 137-155.* ***Sam Kieth*** *c-255, 262, 263.* ***Ron Lim*** *c-266p-281p, 283p-285p.* ***McFarlane*** *c-223-239.* ***Mooney*** *a-63, 95-97i, 103(i).* ***Nasser*** *a-100p.* ***Nebres*** *a-242i.* ***Perez*** *c-259-261.* ***Rogers*** *c-240, 241, 243-252.*

MARVEL TALES FLIP MAGAZINE
Marvel Comics: Sept, 2005 - No. 25, Sept, 2007 ($3.99/$4.99)

1-6-Reprints Amazing Spider-Man #30-up and Amazing Fantasy (2004) in flip format — 4.00
7-10-Reprints Amazing Spider-Man #36-up and Runaways Vol. 2 in flip format — 4.00
11-25-($4.99) Reprints Amazing Spider-Man #36-up and Runaways Vol. 2 in flip format — 5.00

MARVEL TAROT, THE
Marvel Comics: 2007 ($3.99, one-shot)

1-Marvel characters featured in Tarot deck images; Djurdjevic-c — 4.00

MARVEL TEAM-UP (See Marvel Treasury Edition #18 & Official Marvel Index To...)
(Replaced by Web of Spider-Man)
Marvel Comics Group: March, 1972 - No. 150, Feb, 1985
NOTE: *Spider-Man team-ups in all but Nos. 18, 23, 26, 29, 32, 35, 97, 104, 105, 137.*

1-Human Torch — 13 26 39 91 176 260
2-Human Torch — 6 12 18 41 66 90
3-Spider-Man/Human Torch vs. Morbius (part 1); 3rd app. of Morbius (7/72) — 7 14 21 49 80 110
4-Spider-Man/X-Men vs. Morbius (part 2 of story); 4th app. of Morbius — 7 14 21 49 80 110
5-10: 5-Vision. 6-Thing. 7-Thor. 8-The Cat (4/73, came out between The Cat #3 & 4). 9-Iron Man. 10-H-T — 3 6 9 21 32 42
11,13,14,16-20: 11-Inhumans. 13-Capt. America. 14-Sub-Mariner. 16-Capt. Marvel. 17-Mr. Fantastic. 18-H-T/Hulk. 19-Ka-Zar. 20-Black Panther; last 20¢ issue — 2 4 6 13 18 22
12-Werewolf (By Night) (8/73) — 3 6 9 20 30 40
15-1st Spider-Man/Ghost Rider team-up (11/73) — 3 6 9 21 32 42
21-30: 21-Dr. Strange. 22-Hawkeye. 23-H-T/Iceman (X-Men cameo). 24-Brother Voodoo. 25-Daredevil. 26-H-T/Thor. 27-Hulk. 28-Hercules. 29-H-T/Iron Man. 30-Falcon — 2 4 6 8 10 12
31-45,47-50: 31-Iron Fist. 32-H-T/Son of Satan. 33-Nighthawk. 34-Valkyrie. 35-H-T/Dr. Strange. 36-Frankenstein. 37-Man-Wolf. 38-Beast. 39-H-T. 40-Sons of the Tiger/H-T. 41-Scarlet Witch. 42-The Vision. 43-Dr. Doom; retells origin. 44-Moondragon. 45-Killraven. 47-Thing. 48-Iron Man; last 25¢ issue. 49-Dr. Strange; Iron Man app. 50-Iron Man; Dr. Strange app. — 1 2 3 5 6 8
44-48-(30¢-c variants, limited distribution)(4-8/76) — 3 6 9 20 30 40
46-Spider-Man/Deathlok team-up — 1 2 3 5 7 9
51,52,56,57: 51-Iron Man; Dr. Strange app. 52-Capt. America. 56-Daredevil. 57-Black Widow — 1 2 3 4 5 7
53-Hulk; Woodgod & X-Men app., 1st Byrne-a on X-Men (1/77) — 3 6 9 20 30 40
54,55,58-60: 54,59,60: 54-Hulk; Woodgod app. 59-Yellowjacket/The Wasp. 60-The Wasp (Byrne-a in all). 55-Warlock-c/story; Byrne-a. 58-Ghost Rider — 2 3 4 6 8 10
58-62-(35¢-c variants, limited distribution)(6-10/77) — 5 10 15 30 48 65
61-70: All Byrne-a; 61-H-T. 62-Ms. Marvel; last 30¢ issue. 63-Iron Fist. 64-Daughters of the Dragon. 65-Capt. Britain (1st U.S. app.). 66-Capt. Britain; 1st app. Arcade. 67-Tigra; Kraven the Hunter app. 68-Man-Thing. 69-Havok (from X-Men). 70-Thor — 1 2 3 5 7 9
71-74,76-78,80: 71-Falcon. 72-Iron Man. 73-Daredevil. 74-Not Ready for Prime Time Players (Belushi). 76-Dr. Strange. 77-Ms. Marvel. 78-Wonder Man. 80-Dr. Strange/Clea; last 35¢ issue — 6.00
75,79,81: Byrne-a(p). 75-Power Man; Cage app. 79-Mary Jane Watson as Red Sonja; Clark Kent cameo (1 panel, 3/79). 81-Death of Satana — 1 2 3 5 6 8
82-99: 82-Black Widow. 83-Nick Fury. 84-Shang-Chi. 86-Guardians of the Galaxy. 89-Nightcrawler (from X-Men). 91-Ghost Rider. 92-Hawkeye. 93-Werewolf by Night. 94-Spider-Man vs. The Shroud. 95-Mockingbird (intro.); Nick Fury app. 96-Howard the Duck; last 40¢ issue. 97-Spider-Woman/ Hulk. 98-Black Widow. 99-Machine Man. 85-Shang-Chi/ Black Widow/Nick Fury. 87-Black Panther. 88-Invisible Girl. 90-Beast — 5.00
100-(Double-size)-Fantastic Four/Storm/Black Panther; origin/1st app. Karma, one of the New Mutants; origin Storm; X-Men x-over; Miller-c/a(p); Byrne-a (on X-Men app. only) — 1 3 4 6 8 10
101-116: 101-Nighthawk(Ditko-a). 102-Doc Samson. 103-Ant-Man. 104-Hulk/Ka-Zar. 105-Hulk/Powerman/Iron Fist. 106-Capt. America. 107-She-Hulk. 108-Paladin; Dazzler cameo. 109-Dazzler; Paladin app. 110-Iron Man. 111-Devil-Slayer. 112-King Kull; last 50¢ issue. 113-Quasar. 114-Falcon. 115-Thor. 116-Valkyrie — 4.00
117-Wolverine-c/story — 2 4 6 8 10 12
118-140,142-149: 118-Professor X; Wolverine app. (4 pgs.); X-Men cameo. 119-Gargoyle. 120-Dominic Fortune. 121-Human Torch. 122-Man-Thing. 123-Daredevil. 124-The Beast. 125-Tigra. 126-Hulk & Powerman/Son of Satan. 127-The Watcher. 128-Capt. America; Spider-Man/Capt. America photo-c. 129-The Vision. 130-Scarlet Witch. 131-Frogman. 132-Mr. Fantastic. 133-Fantastic Four. 134-Jack of Hearts. 135-Kitty Pryde; X-Men cameo. 136-Wonder Man. 137-Aunt May/Franklin Richards. 138-Sandman. 139-Nick Fury. 140-Black Widow. 142-Capt. Marvel. 143-Starfox. 144-Moon Knight. 145-Iron Man. 146-Nomad. 147-Human Torch; Spider-Man back to old costume. 148-Thor. 149-Cannonball — 4.00
141-Daredevil; SpM/Black Widow app. (Spidey in new black costume; ties w/ Amazing Spider-Man #252 for 1st black costume) — 2 4 6 10 14 18
150-X-Men ($1.00, double-size); B. Smith-c — 6.00
Annual 1 (1976)-Spider-Man/X-Men (early app.) — 4 8 12 22 34 45
Annual 2 (1979)-Spider-Man/Hulk — 1 3 4 6 8 10
Annuals 3,4: 3 (1980)-Hulk/Power Man/Machine Man/Iron Fist; Miller-c(p). 4 (1981)-Spider-

Marvel Treasury Edition #21 © MAR

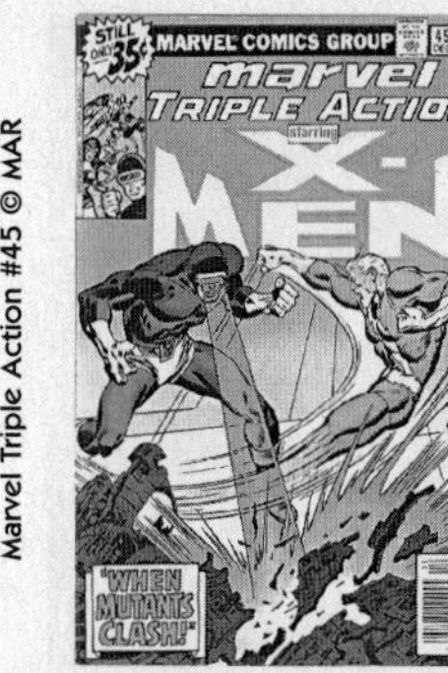

Marvel Triple Action #45 © MAR

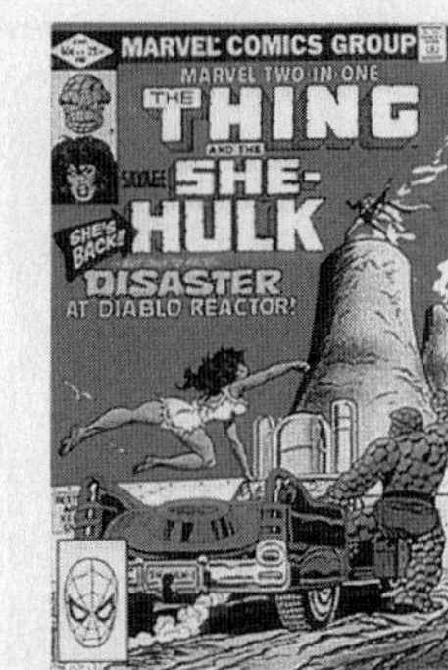

Marvel Two-In-One #88 © MAR

GD 2.0 VG 4.0 FN 6.0 VF 8.0 VF/NM 9.0 NM- 9.2

Man /Daredevil/Moon Knight/Power Man/Iron Fist; brief origins of each; Miller-c; Miller scripts on Daredevil 1 2 3 4 5 7
Annuals 5-7: 5 (1982)-SpM/The Thing/Scarlet Witch/Dr. Strange/Quasar. 6 (1983)-Spider-Man/ New Mutants (early app.), Cloak & Dagger. 7(1984)-Alpha Flight; Byrne-c(i) 6.00
NOTE: ***Art Adams*** *c-141p.* ***Austin*** *a-79i; c-76i, 79i, 96i, 101i, 112i, 130i.* ***Bolle*** *a-9i.* ***Byrne*** *a(p)-53-55, 59-70, 75, 79, 100; c-68p, 70p, 72p, 75, 76p, 79p, 129i, 133i.* ***Colan*** *a-87p.* ***Ditko*** *a-101.* ***Kane*** *a(p)-4-6, 13, 14, 16-19, 23; c(p)-4, 13, 14, 17-19, 23, 25, 26, 32-35, 37, 41, 44, 45, 47, 53, 54.* ***Miller*** *a-100p; c-95p, 99p, 100p, 102p, 106.* ***Mooney*** *a-2i, 7i, 8, 10p, 11p, 16i, 24-31p, 72, 93i, Annual 5i.* ***Nasser*** *a-89p; c-101p.* ***Simonson*** *c-99i, 148.* ***Paul Smith*** *c-131, 132.* ***Starlin*** *c-27.* ***Sutton*** *a-93p. "H-T" means Human Torch; "SpM" means Spider-Man; "S-M" means Sub-Mariner.*

MARVEL TEAM-UP (2nd Series)
Marvel Comics: Sept, 1997 - No. 11, July, 1998 ($1.99)

1-11: 1-Spider-Man team-ups begin, Generation x-app. 2-Hercules-c/app.; two covers. 3-Sandman. 4-Man-Thing. 7-Blade. 8-Namor team-ups begin, Dr. Strange app. 9-Capt. America. 10-Thing. 11-Iron Man 3.00

MARVEL TEAM-UP
Marvel Comics: Jan, 2005 - No. 25, Dec, 2006 ($2.25/$2.99)

1-7,9: 1,2-Spider-Man & Wolverine; Kirkman-s/Kolins-a. 5,6-X-23 app. 3.00
8,10-25 ($2.99-c) 10-Spider-Man & Daredevil. 12-Origin of Titannus. 14-Invincible app. 3.00
... Vol. 1: The Golden Child TPB (2005, $12.99) r/#1-6 13.00
... Vol. 2: Master of the Ring TPB (2005, $17.99) r/#7-13 18.00
... Vol. 3: League of Losers TPB (2006, $13.99) r/#14-18 14.00
... Vol. 4: Freedom Ring TPB (2007, $17.99) r/#19-25 18.00

MARVEL: THE LOST GENERATION
Marvel Comics: No. 12, Mar, 2000 - No. 1, Feb, 2001 ($2.99, issue #s go in reverse)

1-12-Stern-s/Byrne-s/a; untold story of The First Line. 5-Thor app. 3.00

MARVEL/ TOP COW CROSSOVERS
Image Comics (Top Cow): Nov, 2005 ($24.99, TPB)

Vol. 1-Reprints crossovers with Wolverine, Witchblade, Hulk, Darkness; Devil's Reign 25.00

MARVEL TREASURY EDITION
Marvel Comics Group/Whitman #17,18: 1974; #2, Dec, 1974 - #28, 1981 ($1.50/$2.50, 100 pgs., oversized, new-a &-r)(Also see Amazing Spider-Man, The, Marvel Spec. Ed. Feat.--, Savage Fists of Kung Fu, Superman Vs. , & 2001, A Space Odyssey)

1-Spectacular Spider-Man; story-r/Marvel Super-Heroes #14; Romita-c/a(r); G. Kane, Ditko-r; Green Goblin/Hulk-r 6 12 18 37 59 80
1-1,000 numbered copies signed by Stan Lee & John Romita on front-c & sold thru mail for $5.00; these were the1st 1,000 copies off the press 11 22 33 75 138 200
2-10: 2-Fantastic Four-r/F.F. 6,11,48-50(Silver Surfer). 3-The Mighty Thor-r/Thor #125-130. 4-Conan the Barbarian; Barry Smith-c/a(r)/Conan #11. 5-The Hulk (origin-r/Hulk #3). 6-Dr. Strange. 7-Mighty Avengers. 8-Giant Superhero Holiday Grab-Bag; Spider-Man, Hulk, Nick Fury. 9-Giant; Super-hero Team-up. 10-Thor; r/Thor #154-157 3 6 9 18 27 35
11-20: 11-Fantastic Four. 12-Howard the Duck (r/#H. the Duck #1 & G.S. Man-Thing #4,5) plus new Defenders story. 13-Giant Super-Hero Holiday Grab-Bag. 14-The Sensational Spider-Man; r/1st Morbius from Amazing S-M #101,102 plus #100 & r/Not Brand Echh #6. 15-Conan; B. Smith, Neal Adams-i; r/Conan #24. 16-The Defenders (origin) & Valkyrie; r/Defenders #1,4,13,14. 17-Incredible Hulk; Blob, Havok, Rhino and The Leader app. 18-The Astonishing Spider-Man; r/Spider-Man's 1st team-ups with Iron Fist, The X-Men, Ghost Rider & Werewolf by Night; inside back-c has photos from 1978 Spider-Man TV show. 19-Conan the Barbarian. 20-Hulk 3 6 9 14 20 25
21-24,27: 21-Fantastic Four. 22-Spider-Man. 23-Conan. 24-Rampaging Hulk. 27-Spider-Man 3 6 9 14 20 25
25-Spider-Man vs. The Hulk new story 3 6 9 16 23 30
26-The Hulk; 6 pg. new Wolverine/Hercules-s 3 6 9 16 22 28
28-Spider-Man/Superman; (origin of each) 5 10 15 32 51 70
NOTE: *Reprints-2, 3, 5, 7-9, 13, 14, 16, 17.* ***Neal Adams*** *a(i)-6, 15.* ***Brunner*** *a-6, 12; c-6.* ***Buscema*** *a-15, 19, 28; c-28.* ***Colan*** *a-6r; c-12p.* ***Ditko*** *a-1, 6.* ***Gil Kane*** *c-16p.* ***Kirby*** *a-1-3, 5, 7, 9-11; c-7.* ***Perez*** *a-26.* ***Romita*** *c-1, 5.* ***B. Smith*** *a-4, 15, 19; c-4, 19.*

MARVEL TREASURY OF OZ FEATURING THE MARVELOUS LAND OF OZ
Marvel Comics Group: 1975 ($1.50, oversized) (See MGM's Marvelous...)

1-Roy Thomas-s/Alfredo Alcala-a; Romita-c & bk-c 3 6 9 16 23 30

MARVEL TREASURY SPECIAL (Also see 2001: A Space Odyssey)
Marvel Comics Group: 1974; 1976 ($1.50, oversized, 84 pgs.)

Vol. 1-Spider-Man, Torch, Sub-Mariner, Avengers "Giant Superhero Holiday Grab-Bag"; Wood, Colan/Everett, plus 2 Kirby-r; reprints Hulk vs. Thing from Fantastic Four #25,26 3 6 9 17 25 32
Vol. 1-... Featuring Captain America's Bicentennial Battles (6/76)-Kirby-a; B. Smith inks, 11 pgs. 3 6 9 18 27 35

MARVEL TRIPLE ACTION (See Giant-Size...)
Marvel Comics Group: Feb, 1972 - No. 24, Mar, 1975; No. 25, Aug, 1975 - No. 47, Apr, 1979

GD 2.0 VG 4.0 FN 6.0 VF 8.0 VF/NM 9.0 NM- 9.2

1-(25¢ giant, 52 pgs.)-Dr. Doom, Silver Surfer, The Thing begin, end #4 ('66 reprints from Fantastic Four) 4 8 12 24 37 50
2-5 2 4 6 10 14 18
6-10 1 2 3 5 6 8
11-47: 45-r/X-Men #45. 46-r/Avengers #53(X-Men) 6.00
29,30-(30¢-c variants, limited distribution)(5,7/76) 3 6 9 14 20 25
36,37-(35¢-c variants, limited distribution)(7,9/77) 3 6 9 20 30 40
NOTE: *#5-44, 46, 47 reprint Avengers #11 thru ?. #40-r/Avengers #48(1st Black Knight).* ***Buscema*** *a(r)-35p, 36p, 38p, 39p, 41, 42, 43p, 44p, 46p, 47p.* ***Ditko*** *a-2r; c-47.* ***Kirby*** *a(r)-1-4p; c-1-4, 9-19, 22, 24, 29.* ***Starlin*** *c-7.* ***Tuska*** *a(r)-40p, 43i, 46i, 47i. #2 through #17 are 20¢-c.*

MARVEL TRIPLE ACTION
Marvel Comics: May, 2009 - No. 2, Jun, 2009 ($5.99, limited series)

1,2-Reprints stories from Wolverine First Class, Marvel Adventures Avengers & Marvel Super Heroes 6.00

MARVEL TV: GALACTUS - THE REAL STORY
Marvel Comics: Apr, 2009 ($3.99, one-shot)

1-The "hoax" of Galactus, Tieri-s/Santacruz-a; r/Fantastic Four #50 4.00

MARVEL TWO-IN-ONE (...Featuring ... #82 on; also see The Thing)
Marvel Comics Group: January, 1974 - No. 100, June, 1983

1-Thing team-ups begin; Man-Thing 7 14 21 49 80 110
2,3: 2-Sub-Mariner; last 20¢ issue. 3-Daredevil 3 6 9 21 32 42
4-6: 4-Capt. America. 5-Guardians of the Galaxy (9/74, 2nd app.?). 6-Dr. Strange (11/74) 3 6 9 16 22 28
7,9,10 2 4 6 10 14 18
8-Early Ghost Rider app. (3/75) 3 6 9 16 22 28
11-14,19,20: 13-Power Man. 14-Son of Satan (early app.) 1 3 4 6 8 10
15-18-(Regular 25¢ editions)(5-7/76) 17-Spider-Man. 1 3 4 6 8 10
15-18-(30¢-c variants, limited distribution) 3 6 9 18 27 35
21-29: 27-Deathlok. 29-Master of Kung Fu; Spider-Woman cameo 1 2 3 4 5 7
28,29,31-(35¢-c variants, limited distribution) 4 8 12 24 37 50
30-2nd full app. Spider-Woman (see Marvel Spotlight #32 for 1st app.) 2 4 6 8 10 12
30-(35¢-c variant, limited distribution)(8/77) 5 10 15 32 51 70
31-33-Spider-Woman app. 1 3 4 6 8 10
34-40: 39-Vision 1 2 3 4 5 7
41,42,44,45,47-49: 42-Capt. America. 45-Capt. Marvel 5.00
43,50,53,55-Byrne-a(p). 53-Quasar(7/79, 2nd app.) 1 2 3 5 7 9
46-Thing battles Hulk-c/story 2 4 6 8 10 12
51-The Beast, Nick Fury, Ms. Marvel; Miller-p 1 2 3 5 7 9
52-Moon Knight app. 5.00
54-Death of Deathlok; Byrne-a 2 4 6 8 10 12
56-60,64-74,76-79,81,82: 60-Intro. Impossible Woman. 68-Angel. 69-Guardians of the Galaxy. 71-1st app. Maelstrom. 76-Iceman 4.00
61-63: 61-Starhawk (from Guardians); "The Coming of Her" storyline begins, ends #63; cover similar to F.F. #67 (Him-c). 62-Moondragon; Thanos & Warlock cameo in flashback; Starhawk app. 63-Warlock revived shortly; Starhawk & Moondragon app. 5.00
75-Avengers (52 pgs.) 5.00
80,90,100: 80-Ghost Rider. 90-Spider-Man. 100-Double size, Byrne-s 5.00
83-89,91-99: 83-Sasquatch. 84-Alpha Flight app. 93-Jocasta dies. 96-X-Men-c & cameo 4.00
Annual 1 (1976, 52 pgs.)-Thing/Liberty Legion; Kirby-c 2 4 6 9 13 16
Annual 2 (1977, 52 pgs.)-Thing/Spider-Man; 2nd death of Thanos; end of Thanos saga; Warlock app.; Starlin-c/a 5 10 15 35 55 75
Annual 3,4 (1978-79, 52 pgs.): 3-Nova. 4-Black Bolt 1 2 3 4 5 7
Annual 5-7 (1980-82, 52 pgs.): 5-Hulk. 6-1st app. American Eagle. 7-The Thing/Champion; Sasquatch, Colossus app.; X-Men cameo (1 pg.) 5.00
NOTE: ***Austin*** *c(i)-42, 54, 56, 58, 61, 63, 66.* ***John Buscema*** *a-30p, 45; c-30p.* ***Byrne*** *(p)-43, 50, 53-55; c-43, 53p, 56p, 98i, 99i.* ***Gil Kane*** *a-1p, 2p; c(p)-1-3, 9, 11, 14, 28.* ***Kirby*** *c-10, 12, 19p, 20, 25, 27.* ***Mooney*** *a-18i, 38i, 90i.* ***Nasser*** *a-70p.* ***Perez*** *a(p)-56-58, 60, 64, 65; c(p)-32, 33, 42, 50-52, 54, 55, 57, 58, 61-66, 70.* ***Roussos*** *a-Annual 1i.* ***Simonson*** *c-43i, 97p, Annual 6i.* ***Starlin*** *c-6, Annual 1.* ***Tuska*** *a-6p.*

MARVEL TWO-IN-ONE
Marvel Comics: Sept, 2007 - Present ($4.99, 64 pgs.)

1-8,13-16-Reprints Marvel Adventures Avengers and X-Men: First Class stories 5.00
9-12,17-Reprints Marvel Adventures Iron Man and Avengers stories 5.00

MARVEL UNIVERSE (See Official Handbook Of The...)

MARVEL UNIVERSE (Title on variant covers for newsstand editions of some 2001 Marvel titles. See indicia for actual titles and issue numbers)

MARVEL UNIVERSE
Marvel Comics: June, 1998 - No. 7, Dec, 1998 ($2.99/$1.99)

1-($2.99)-Invaders stories from WW2; Stern-s 4.00
2-7-($1.99): 2-Two covers. 4-7-Monster Hunters; Manley-a/Stern-s 3.00

Marvel Universe vs. The Punisher #1 © MAR

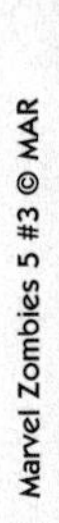
Marvel Zombies 5 #3 © MAR

Mary Jane #1 © MAR

	GD	VG	FN	VF	VF/NM	NM-
	2.0	4.0	6.0	8.0	9.0	9.2

MARVEL UNIVERSE: MILLENNIAL VISIONS
Marvel Comics: Feb, 2002 ($3.99, one-shot)

1-Pin-ups by various; wraparound-c by JH Williams & Gray 4.00

MARVEL UNIVERSE: THE END (Also see Infinity Abyss)
Marvel Comics: May, 2003 - No. 6, Aug, 2003 ($3.50/$2.99, limited series)

1-($3.50)-Thanos, X-Men, FF, Avengers, Spider-Man, Daredevil app.; Starlin-s/a(p) 3.50
2-6-($2.99) Akhenaten, Eternity, Living Tribunal app. 3.00
Thanos Vol. 3: Marvel Universe - The End (2003, $16.99) r/#1-6 17.00

MARVEL UNIVERSE VS. THE PUNISHER
Marvel Comics: Oct, 2010 - No. 4, Nov, 2010 ($3.99, limited series)

1-4-Punisher vs. Marvel Zombies; Maberry-s/Parlov-a/c 4.00

MARVEL UNLIMITED (Title on variant covers for newsstand editions of some 2001 Daredevil issues. See indicia for actual titles and issue numbers)

MARVEL VALENTINE SPECIAL
Marvel Comics: Mar, 1997 ($2.99, one-shot)

1-Valentine stories w/Spider-Man, Daredevil, Cyclops, Phoenix 3.00

MARVEL VERSUS DC (See DC Versus Marvel) (Also see Amazon, Assassins, Bruce Wayne: Agent of S.H.I.E.L.D., Bullets & Bracelets, Doctor Strangefate, JLX, Legend of the Dark Claw, Magneto & The Magnetic Men, Speed Demon, Spider-Boy, Super Soldier, & X-Patrol)
Marvel Comics: No. 2, 1996 - No. 3, 1996 ($3.95, limited series)

2,3: 2-Peter David script. 3-Ron Marz script; Dan Jurgens-a(p). 1st app. of Super Soldier, Spider-Boy, Dr. Doomsday, Doctor Strangefate, The Dark Claw, Nightcreeper, Amazon, Wraith & others. Storyline continues in Amalgam books. 4.00

MARVEL VISIONARIES
Marvel Comics: 2002 - Present (various prices, HC and TPB)

...: Chris Claremont (2005, $29.99) r/X-Men #137, Uncanny X-Men #153,205,268 & Ann. #12, Iron Fist #14, Wolverine #3, New Mutants #21 and other highlights 30.00
...: Gil Kane (8/02, $24.95) r/Amazing Spider-Man #99, Marvel Premiere #1,#15, TOA #76 & others; plus sketch pages and a cover gallery 25.00
...: Jack Kirby HC (2004, $29.99) r/career highlights- Red Raven Comics #1 (1st work), Captain America Comics #1, Avengers #4, Fantastic Four #48-50 and more 30.00
...: Jack Kirby Vol. 2 HC (2006, $34.99) r/career highlights- Captain America, Two-Gun Kid, Fantastic Four, Thor, Fin Fang Foom, Devil Dinosaur, romance and more 35.00
...: Jim Steranko (9/02, $14.95) r/Captain America #110,111,113; X-Men #50,51 and stories from Tower of Shadows #1 and Our Love Story #5; plus a cover gallery 15.00
...: John Buscema (2007, $34.99) r/career highlights-Avengers, Silver Surfer, Thor, FF, Hulk, Wolverine and others; Roy Thomas intro.; sketch pages and pin-up art 35.00
...: John Romita Jr. (2005, $29.99) r/various stories 1977-2002; debut in AS-M Ann. #11; Iron Man #128, AS-M V2 #36, issues of Hulk, Daredevil: The Man Without Fear, Punisher; sketch pages; intro. by John Romita Sr. 30.00
...: John Romita Sr. (2005, $29.99) r/various stories 1951-1997 including Young Men #24&26, Daredevil #16, ASM #39,42,50; sketch pages; intro. by John Romita Jr. 30.00
...: Roy Thomas (2006, $34.99) r/career highlights; intro. by Stan Lee 35.00
...: Steve Ditko (2005, $29.99) r/various stories 1961-1992; intro. by Blake Bell 30.00
...: Stan Lee HC (2005, $29.99) r/career highlights- Captain America Comics #3 (1st work), and various Spider-Man, FF, Thor, Daredevil stories; 1940-1995; Roy Thomas intro. 30.00

MARVEL WEDDINGS
Marvel Comics: 2005 ($19.99, TPB)

TPB-Reprints weddings of Peter & Mary Jane, Reed & Sue, Scott & Jean, and others 20.00

MARVEL WESTERNS: ...
Marvel Comics: 2006 ($3.99, one-shots)

... Kid Colt and the Arizona Girl 1 (9/06) 2 short stories & 3 Kirby/Ayers reps.; Powell-c 4.00
... Outlaw Files-Profiles and essays about Marvel western characters 4.00
... Strange Westerns Starring The Black Rider 1 (10/06) Englehart-s/Rogers-a & 2 Kirby Rawhide Kid reprints; Rogers-c 4.00
... The Two-Gun Kid 1 (8/06) 2 short stories & a Kirby/Ayers reprint; Powell-c 4.00
... Western Legends 1 (9/06) 2 short stories & r/Rawhide Kid origin by Kirby; Powell-c 4.00
HC (2006, $20.99, dustjacket) r/one-shots 21.00

MARVEL X-MEN COLLECTION, THE
Marvel Comics: Jan, 1994 - No. 3, Mar, 1994 ($2.95, limited series)

1-3-r/X-Men trading cards by Jim Lee 3.00

MARVEL - YEAR IN REVIEW (Magazine)
Marvel Comics: 1989 - No. 3, 1991 (52 pgs.)

1-3: 1-Spider-Man-c by McFarlane. 2-Capt. America-c. 3-X-Men/Wolverine-c 5.00

MARVEL: YOUR UNIVERSE
Marvel Comics: 2008; May, 2009 - No. 3, July, 2009 ($5.99)

1-3-Reprints of 5 recent comics (Ms. Marvel, Nova, Immortal Iron Fist & others) 6.00

...Saga (2008, no cover price) - Re-caps of crossovers (Secret War thru Secret Invasion) 3.00

MARVEL ZOMBIES (See Ultimate Fantastic Four #21-23, 30-32)
Marvel Comics: Feb, 2006 - No. 5, June, 2006 ($2.99, limited series)

1-Zombies vs. Magneto; Kirkman-s/Phillips-a/Suydam-c swipe of A.F. #15 20.00
1-(2nd-4th printings) Variant Suydam-c swipes of Spider-Man #1, Amazing Spider-Man #50 and Incredible Hulk #1 5.00
2-Avengers #4 cover swipe by Suydam 10.00
3-5: 3-Inc. Hulk #340 c-swipe. 4-X-Men #1 c-swipe. 5-AS-M Ann. #21 c-swipe 6.00
3-5-(2nd printings) 3-Daredevil #179 c-swipe. 4-AS-M #39 c-swipe. 5-Silver Surfer #1 3.00
...: Dead Days (7/07, $3.99) Early days of the plaque; Kirkman-s/Phillips-a/Suydam-c 5.00
...: Dead Days HC (2008, $29.99, oversized) r/Dead Days one-shot, Ultimate Fantastic Four #21-23, 30-32, and Black Panther #28-30 30.00
...: Evil Evolution (1/10, $4.99) Apes vs. Zombies; Marcos Martin-c 5.00
... MGC #1 (7/10, $1.00) r/#1 with "Marvel's Greatest Comics" logo on cover 1.00
...: The Book of Angels, Demons and Various Monstrosities (2007, $3.99) profile pages 5.00
...: The Covers HC (2007, $19.99, d.j.) Suydam's covers with originals and commentary 20.00
HC (2006, $19.99) r/#1-5; Kirkman foreword; cover gallery with variants 20.00

MARVEL ZOMBIES 2
Marvel Comics: Dec, 2007 - No. 5, Apr, 2008 ($2.99, limited series)

1-5-Kirkman-s/Phillips-a/Suydam zombie-fied cover swipes 5.00
HC (2008, $19.99) r/#1-5; cover swipe gallery 20.00

MARVEL ZOMBIES 3
Marvel Comics: Dec, 2008 - No. 4, Mar, 2009 ($3.99, limited series)

1-4-Van Lente-s/Walker-a/Land-c; Machine Man, Jocasta and Morbius app. 5.00

MARVEL ZOMBIES 4
Marvel Comics: Jun, 2009 - No. 4, Sept, 2009 ($3.99, limited series)

1-4-Van Lente-s/Walker-a/Land-c; Zombie Deadpool head app. 4.00

MARVEL ZOMBIES 5
Marvel Comics: Jun, 2010 - No. 5, Sept, 2010 ($3.99, limited series)

1-5-Van Lente-s; Machine Man and Howard the Duck app. 3-Kaluta-a 4.00

MARVEL ZOMBIES / ARMY OF DARKNESS
Marvel Comics/Dynamite Entertainment: May, 2007 - No. 5, Aug, 2007($2.99, limited series)

1-Zombies vs. Ash during the start of the plaque; Layman-s/Neves-a/Suydam-c 7.00
1-Second printing with Suydam zombie-fied Captain America Comics #1 cover swipe 3.00
2-5-Suydam zombie-fied cover swipes on all 5.00
HC (2007, $19.99) r/#1-5; cover gallery with variants and non-zombied original covers 20.00

MARVEL ZOMBIES RETURN
Marvel Comics: Nov, 2009 - No. 5, Nov, 2009 ($3.99, weekly limited series)

1-5-Suydam-c. 1-Zombie Spider-Man eats the Earth-Z Sinister Six; Dragotta-a. 4.00

MARVEL ZOMBIES SUPREME
Marvel Comics: May, 2011 - No. 5 ($3.99, limited series)

1-3-Zombie plague in Squadrom Supreme dimension; Blanco-a/Komarck-c 4.00

MARVILLE
Marvel Comics: Nov, 2002 - No. 7, Jul, 2003 ($2.25, limited series)

1-6-Satire on DC/AOL-Time-Warner; Jemas-a/Bright-a/Horn-c 3.00
1-($3.95) Variant foil cover by Udon Studios; bonus sketch pages and Jemas afterword 4.00
7-($2.99) Intro. to Epic Comics line with submission guidelines 3.00

MARVIN MOUSE
Atlas Comics (BPC): September, 1957

1-Everett-c/a; Maneely-a 14 28 42 80 115 150

MARY JANE (Spider-Man) (Also see Spider-Man Loves Mary Jane)
Marvel Comics: Aug, 2004 - No. 4, Nov, 2004 ($2.25, limited series)

1-4-Marvel Age series with teen-age MJ Watson; Miyazawa-c/a; McKeever-s 3.00
... Vol. 1: Circle of Friends (2004, $5.99, digest-size) r/#1-4 6.00

MARY JANE & SNIFFLES (See Looney Tunes)
Dell Publishing Co.: No. 402, June, 1952 - No. 474, June, 1953

Four Color 402 (#1) 7 14 21 50 83 115
Four Color 474 7 14 21 47 76 105

MARY JANE: HOMECOMING (Spider-Man)
Marvel Comics: May, 2005 - No. 4, Aug, 2005 ($2.99, limited series)

1-4-Teen-age MJ Watson in high school; Miyazawa-c/a; McKeever-s 3.00
... Vol. 2 (2005, $6.99, digest-size) r/#1-4 7.00

MARY MARVEL COMICS (Monte Hale #29 on) (Also see Captain Marvel #18, Marvel Family, Shazam, & Wow Comics)
Fawcett Publications: Dec, 1945 - No. 28, Sept, 1948

Mary Marvel Comics #16 © FAW

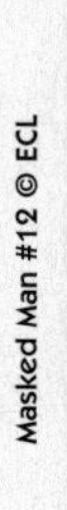

Masked Man #12 © ECL

Master Comics #1 © FAW

	GD	VG	FN	VF	VF/NM	NM-
	2.0	4.0	6.0	8.0	9.0	9.2

1-Captain Marvel introduces Mary on-c; intro/origin Georgia Sivana 219 438 657 1402 2401 3400
2 80 160 240 508 874 1240
3,4: 3-New logo 53 106 159 334 567 800
5-8: 8-Bulletgirl x-over in Mary Marvel; X-Mas-c 40 80 120 244 402 560
9,10 37 74 111 218 354 490
11-20 25 50 75 147 241 335
21-28: 28-Western-c 21 42 63 124 202 280

MARY POPPINS (See Movie Comics & Walt Disney Showcase No. 17)

MARY SHELLEY'S FRANKENSTEIN
Topps Comics: Oct, 1994 - Jan, 1995 ($2.95, limited series)
1-4-polybagged w/3 trading cards 4.00
1-4 ($2.50)-Newstand ed. 3.00

MARY WORTH (See Harvey Comics Hits #55 & Love Stories of...)
Argo: March, 1956 (Also see Romantic Picture Novelettes)
1 8 16 24 42 54 65

MASK (TV)
DC Comics: Dec, 1985 - No. 4, Mar, 1986; Feb, 1987 - No. 9, Oct, 1987
1-4; 1-9 (2nd series)-Sat. morning TV show. 3.00

MASK, THE (Also see Mayhem)
Dark Horse Comics: Aug, 1991 - No. 4, Oct, 1991; No. 0, Dec, 1991 ($2.50, 36 pgs., limited series)
1-4: 1-1st app. Lt. Kellaway as The Mask (see Dark Horse Presents #10 for 1st app.) 5.00
0-(12/91, B&W, 56 pgs.)-r/Mayhem #1-4 4.00
...Omnibus Vol. 1 (8/08, $24.95) r/#1-4, Mask Returns and Mask Strikes Back series 25.00
...Omnibus Vol. 2 (4/09, $24.95) r/#1-4, The Hunt For Green October, World Tour, Southern Discomfort, Toys in the Attic series and short stories from DHP 25.00

...: HUNT FOR GREEN OCTOBER July, 1995 - Oct, 1995 ($2.50, lim. series)
1-4-Evan Dorkin scripts 3.00

../ MARSHALL LAW Feb, 1998 - No. 2, Mar, 1998 ($2.95, lim. series)
1,2-Mills-s/O'Neill-a 3.00

...: OFFICIAL MOVIE ADAPTATION July, 1994 - Aug, 1994 ($2.50, lim. series)
1,2 3.00

... RETURNS Oct, 1992 - No. 4, Mar, 1993 ($2.50, limited series)
1-4 4.00

... SOUTHERN DISCOMFORT Mar, 1996 - No. 4, July, 1996 ($2.50, lim. series)
1-4 3.00

... STRIKES BACK Feb, 1995 - No. 5, Jun, 1995 ($2.50, limited series)
1-5 3.00

... SUMMER VACATION July, 1995 ($10.95, one shot, hard-c)
1-nn-Rick Geary-c/a 11.00

... TOYS IN THE ATTIC Aug, 1998 - No. 4, Nov, 1998 ($2.95, limited series)
1-4-Fingerman-s 3.00

... VIRTUAL SURREALITY July, 1997 ($2.95, one shot)
nn-Mignola, Aragonés, and others-s/a 3.00

... WORLD TOUR Dec, 1995 - No. 4, Mar, 1996 ($2.50, limited series)
1-4: 3-X & Ghost-c/app. 3.00

MASK COMICS
Rural Home Publ.: Feb-Mar, 1945 - No. 2, Apr-May, 1945; No. 2, Fall, 1945
1-Classic L. B. Cole Satan-c/a; Palais-a 300 600 900 2010 3505 5000
2-(Scarce)-Classic L. B. Cole Satan-c; Black Rider, The Boy Magician, & The Collector app. 206 412 618 1318 2259 3200
2-(Fall, 1945)-No publ.-same as regular #2; L. B. Cole-c 161 322 483 1030 1765 2500

MASKED BANDIT, THE
Avon Periodicals: 1952
nn-Kinstler-a 16 32 48 94 147 200

MASKED MAN, THE
Eclipse Comics: 12/84 - #10, 4/86; #11, 10/87; #12, 4/88 ($1.75/$2.00, color/B&W #9 on, Baxter paper)
1-12: 1-Origin retold. 3-Origin Aphid-Man; begin $2.00-c 3.00

MASKED MARVEL (See Keen Detective Funnies)
Centaur Publications: Sept, 1940 - No. 3, Dec, 1940
1-The Masked Marvel begins 168 336 504 1075 1838 2600
2,3: 2-Gustavson, Tarpe Mills-a 110 220 330 704 1202 1700

MASKED RAIDER, THE (Billy The Kid #9 on; Frontier Scout, Daniel Boone #10-13) (Also see Blue Bird)
Charlton Comics: June, 1955 - No. 8, July, 1957; No. 14, Aug, 1958 - No. 30, June, 1961
1-Masked Raider & Talon the Golden Eagle begin; painted-c 13 26 39 72 101 130
2 8 16 24 42 54 65
3-8,15: 8-Billy The Kid app. 15-Williamson-a, 7 pgs. 6 12 18 31 38 45
14,16-30: 22-Rocky Lane app. 5 10 15 24 30 35

MASKED RANGER
Premier Magazines: Apr, 1954 - No. 9, Aug, 1955
1-The Masked Ranger, his horse Streak, & The Crimson Avenger (origin) begin, end #9; Woodbridge/Frazetta-a 40 80 120 242 401 560
2,3 15 30 45 86 133 180
4-8-All Woodbridge-a. 5-Jesse James by Woodbridge. 6-Billy The Kid by Woodbridge. 7-Wild Bill Hickok by Woodbridge. 8-Jim Bowie's Life Story 15 30 45 88 137 185
9-Torres-a; Wyatt Earp by Woodbridge; Says Death of Masked Ranger on-c 16 32 48 94 147 200
NOTE: *Check a-1. Woodbridge c/a-1, 4-9.*

MASK OF DR. FU MANCHU, THE (See Dr. Fu Manchu)
Avon Periodicals: 1951
1-Sax Rohmer adapt.; Wood-c/a (26 pgs.); Hollingsworth-a 97 194 291 621 1061 1500

MASK OF ZORRO, THE
Image Comics: Aug, 1998 - No. 4, Dec, 1998 ($2.95, limited series)
1-4-Movie adapt. Photo variant-c 3.00

MASKS: TOO HOT FOR TV!
DC Comics (WildStorm): Feb, 2004 ($4.95)
1-Short stories by various incl. Thompson, Brubaker, Mahnke, Conner; Fabry-c 5.00

MASQUE OF THE RED DEATH (See Movie Classics)

MASQUERADE (See Project Superpowers)
Dynamite Entertainment: 2009 - No. 4, 2009 ($3.50, limited series)
1-4-Alex Ross & Phil Hester-s/Carlos Paul-a; covers by Ross & others 3.50

MASS EFFECT: REDEMPTION (Based on the EA video game)
Dark Horse Comics: Jan, 2010 - No. 4, Apr, 2010 ($3.50, limited series)
1-4-Walters & Jackson Miller-s/Francia-a 3.50

MASTER COMICS (Combined with Slam Bang Comics #7 on)
Fawcett Publications: Mar, 1940 - No. 133, Apr, 1953 (No. 1-6: oversized issues) (#1-3: 15¢, 52 pgs.; #4-6: 10¢, 36 pgs.; #7-Begin 68 pg. issues)
1-Origin & 1st app. Master Man; The Devil's Dagger, El Carim, Master of Magic, Rick O'Say, Morton Murch, White Rajah, Shipwreck Roberts, Frontier Marshal, Streak Sloan, Mr. Clue begin (all features end #6) 800 1600 2400 5840 10,320 14,800
2 248 496 744 1575 2713 3850
3-6: 6-Last Master Man 177 354 531 1124 1937 2750
NOTE: *#1-6 rarely found in near mint or very fine condition due to large-size format.*
7-(10/40)-Bulletman, Zoro, the Mystery Man (ends #22), Lee Granger, Jungle King, & Buck Jones begin; only app. The War Bird & Mark Swift & the Time Retarder; Zoro, Lee Granger, Jungle King & Mark Swift all continue from Slam Bang; Bulletman moves from Nickel 300 600 900 1920 3310 4700
8-The Red Gaucho (ends #13), Captain Venture (ends #22) & The Planet Princess begin 158 316 474 1003 1727 2450
9,10: 10-Lee Granger ends 126 252 378 806 1378 1950
11-Origin & 1st app. Minute-Man (2/41) 271 542 813 1734 2967 4200
12 129 258 387 826 1413 2000
13-Origin & 1st app. Bulletgirl; Hitler-c 213 426 639 1363 2332 3300
14-16: 14-Companions Three begins, ends #31 113 226 339 718 1234 1750
17-20: 17-Raboy-a on Bulletman begins. 20-Captain Marvel cameo app. in Bulletman 103 206 309 659 1130 1600
21-(12/41; Scarce)-Captain Marvel & Bulletman team up against Capt. Nazi; origin & 1st app. Capt. Marvel Jr's most famous nemesis Captain Nazi who will cause creation of Capt. Marvel Jr. in Whiz #25. Part I of trilogy origin of Capt. Marvel Jr.; 1st Mac Raboy-c for Fawcett; Capt. Nazi-c 595 1190 1785 4350 7675 11,000
22-(1/42)-Captain Marvel Jr. moves over from Whiz #25 & teams up with Bulletman against Captain Nazi; part III of trilogy origin of Capt. Marvel Jr. & his 1st cover and adventure 541 1082 1623 3950 6975 10,000
23-Capt. Marvel Jr. c/stories begin (1st solo story); fights Capt. Nazi by himself. 300 600 900 1950 3375 4800
24,25 108 216 324 686 1181 1675
26-28,30-Captain Marvel Jr. vs. Capt. Nazi. 28-Liberty Bell-c. 30-Flag-c

Master Comics #96 © FAW

Master of Kung-Fu #18 © MAR

Masters of the Universe V3 #3 © Mattel

GD VG FN VF VF/NM NM-
2.0 4.0 6.0 8.0 9.0 9.2

100 200 300 635 1093 1550
29-Hitler & Hirohito-c 148 296 444 947 1624 2300
31-33,35: 32-Last El Carim & Buck Jones; intro Balbo, the Boy Magician in El Carim story; classic Eagle-c by Raboy. 33-Balbo, the Boy Magician (ends #47), Hopalong Cassidy (ends #49) begins 81 162 243 518 884 1250
34-Capt. Marvel Jr. vs. Capt. Nazi-c/story; 1st mention of Capt. Nippon
87 174 261 553 952 1350
36-39 65 130 195 416 708 1000
40-Classic flag-c 77 154 231 493 847 1200
41-(8/43)-Bulletman, Capt. Marvel Jr. & Bulletgirl x-over in Minute-Man; only app. Crime Crusaders Club (Capt. Marvel Jr., Minute-Man, Bulletman & Bulletgirl)
68 136 204 435 743 1050
42-47,49: 47-Hitler becomes Corpl. Hitler Jr. 49-Last Minute-Man
42 84 126 265 445 625
48-Intro. Bulletboy; Capt. Marvel cameo in Minute-Man
48 96 144 302 514 725
50-Intro Radar & Nyoka the Jungle Girl & begin series (5/44); Radar also intro in Captain Marvel #35 (same date); Capt. Marvel x-over in Radar; origin Radar; Capt. Marvel & Capt. Marvel, Jr. introduce Radar on-c 42 84 126 265 450 635
51-58 26 52 78 154 252 350
59-62: Nyoka serial "Terrible Tiara" in all; 61-Capt. Marvel Jr. 1st meets Uncle Marvel
28 56 84 165 270 375
63-80 20 40 60 118 192 265
81,83-87,89-91,95-99: 88-Hopalong Cassidy begins (ends #94). 95-Tom Mix begins (cover only in #123, ends #133) 18 36 54 107 169 230
82,88,92-94-Krigstein-a 19 38 57 111 176 240
100 19 38 57 111 176 240
101-106-Last Bulletman (not in #104) 18 36 54 103 162 220
107-120: 118-Mary Marvel 17 34 51 98 154 210
121-131-(lower print run): 123-Tom Mix-c only 18 36 54 107 169 230
132-B&W and color illos in **POP**; last Nyoka 19 38 57 109 172 235
133-Bill Battle app. 23 46 69 136 223 310
NOTE: ***Mac Raboy*** *a-15-39, 40(part), 42, 58. c-21-49, 51, 52, 54, 56, 58, 68(part), 69(part). Bulletman c-7-11, 13(half), 15, 18(part), 19, 20, 21(w/Capt. Marvel & Capt. Nazi), 22(w/Capt. Marvel, Jr.). Capt. Marvel, Jr. c-23-133. Master Man c-1-6. Minute Man c-12, 13(half), 14, 16, 17, 18(part).*

MASTER DARQUE
Acclaim Comics (Valiant): Feb, 1998 ($3.95)
1-Manco-a/Christina Z.-s 4.00

MASTER DETECTIVE
Super Comics: 1964 (Reprints)
17-r/Criminals on the Loose V4 #2; r/Young King Cole #?; McWilliams-r
2 4 6 8 11 14

MASTER OF KUNG FU (Formerly Special Marvel Edition; see Deadly Hands of Kung Fu & Giant-Size...)
Marvel Comics Group: No. 17, April, 1974 - No. 125, June, 1983
17-Starlin-a; intro Black Jack Tarr; 3rd Shang-Chi (ties w/Deadly Hands #1)
4 8 12 26 41 55
18,20 3 6 9 16 22 28
19-Man-Thing-c/story 3 6 9 18 27 35
21-23,25-30 2 4 6 10 14 18
24-Starlin, Simonson-a 2 4 6 11 16 20
31-50: 33-1st Leiko Wu. 43-Last 25¢ issue 1 3 4 6 8 10
39-43-(30¢-c variants, limited distribution)(5-7/76) 3 6 9 16 22 28
51-75 6.00
53-57-(35¢-c variants, limited distribution)(6-10/77) 3 6 9 18 27 35
76-99 5.00
100,118,125-Double size 6.00
101-117,119-124 4.00
Annual 1(4/76)-Iron Fist app. 3 6 9 18 27 35
NOTE: ***Austin*** *c-63i, 74i.* ***Buscema*** *c-44p.* ***Gulacy*** *a(p)-18-20, 22, 25, 29-31, 33-35, 38, 39, 40(p&i), 42-50, 53r(#20); c-51, 55, 64, 67.* ***Gil Kane*** *c(p)-20, 38, 39, 42, 45, 59, 63.* ***Nebres*** *c-73i.* ***Starlin*** *a-17p, 24; c-54.* ***Sutton*** *a-42i. #53 reprints #20.*

MASTER OF KUNG-FU, SHANG-CHI:... (2002 series, see Shang Chi:...)

MASTER OF KUNG-FU: BLEEDING BLACK
Marvel Comics: Feb, 1991 ($2.95, 84 pgs., one-shot)
1-The Return of Shang-Chi 4.00

MASTER OF THE WORLD
Dell Publishing Co.: No. 1157, July, 1961
Four Color 1157-Movie based on Jules Verne's "Master of the World" and "Robur the Conqueror" novels; with Vincent Price & Charles Bronson 7 14 21 45 73 100

MASTERS OF TERROR (Magazine)
Marvel Comics Group: July, 1975 - No. 2, Sept, 1975 (B&W) (All reprints)
1-Brunner, Barry Smith-a; Morrow/Steranko-c; Starlin-a(p); Gil Kane-a
3 6 9 18 27 35
2-Reese, Kane, Mayerik-a; Adkins/Steranko-c 2 4 6 13 18 22

MASTERS OF THE UNIVERSE (See DC Comics Presents #47 for 1st app.)
DC Comics: Dec, 1982 - No. 3, Feb, 1983 (Mini-series)
1 6.00
2,3: 2-Origin He-Man & Ceril 4.00
NOTE: ***Alcala*** *a-1i,, 2i.* ***Tuska*** *a-1-3p; c-1-3p. #2 has 75 & 95 cent cover price.*

MASTERS OF THE UNIVERSE (Comic Album)
Western Publishing Co.: 1984 (8-1/2x11", $2.95, 64 pgs.)
11362-Based on Mattel toy & cartoon 2 4 6 11 16 20

MASTERS OF THE UNIVERSE
Star Comics/Marvel #7 on: May 1986 - No. 13, May, 1988 (75¢/$1.00)
1 1 2 3 5 6 8
2-11: 8-Begin $1.00-c 6.00
12-Death of He-Man (1st Marvel app.) 2 4 6 8 11 14
13-Return of He-Man & death of Skeletor 2 4 6 8 11 14
The Motion Picture (11/87, $2.00)-Tuska-p 1 2 3 4 5 7

MASTERS OF THE UNIVERSE
Image Comics: Nov, 2002 - No. 4, March, 2003 ($2.95, limited series)
1-($2.95) Two covers by Santalucia and Campbell; Santalucia-a 3.00
1-($5.95) Variant-c by Norem w/gold foil logo 6.00
2-4($2.95) 2-Two covers by Santalucia and Manapul. 3,4-Two covers 3.00
TPB (CrossGen, 2003, $9.95, 8-1/4" x 5-1/2") digest-sized reprints #1-4 10.00

MASTERS OF THE UNIVERSE (Volume 2)
Image Comics: March, 2003 - No. 6, Aug, 2003 ($2.95)
1-6-($2.95) 1-Santalucia-c. 2-Two covers by Santalucia & JJ Kirby 3.00
1-($5.95) Wraparound variant-c by Struzan w/silver foil logo 6.00
3,4-($5.95) Wraparound variant holofoil-c. 3-By Edwards 4-By Boris Vallejo & Julie Bell 6.00
Volume 2 Dark Reflections TPB (2004, $18.95) r/#1-6 19.00

MASTERS OF THE UNIVERSE (Volume 3)
MVCreations: Apr, 2004 - No. 8, Dec, 2004 ($2.95)
1-8: 1-Santalucia-c 3.00

MASTERS OF THE UNIVERSE...
CrossGen Comics
...Rise of the Snake-Men (Nov, 2003 - No. 3, $2.95) Meyers-a 3.00
...The Power of Fear (12/03, $2.95, one-shot) Santalucia-a 3.00

MASTERS OF THE UNIVERSE, ICONS OF EVIL
Image Comics/CrossGen Comics: 2003 ($4.95, one-shots)
...Beastman -(Image) Origin of Beast Man; Tony Moore-a 5.00
...Mer-Man -(CrossGen) 5.00
...Trapjaw -(CrossGen) 5.00
...Tri-Klops -(CrossGen) Walker-c 5.00
TPB (3/04, $18.95, MVCreations) r/one-shots; sketch pages 19.00

MASTERWORKS SERIES OF GREAT COMIC BOOK ARTISTS, THE
Sea Gate Dist./DC Comics: May, 1983 - No. 3, Dec, 1983 (Baxter paper)
1-3: 1,2-Shining Knight by Frazetta r-/Adventure. 2-Tomahawk by Frazetta-r. 3-Wrightson-c/a(r) 6.00

MATADOR
DC Comics (WildStorm): July, 2005 - No. 6, May, 2006 ($2.99, limited series)
1-6-Devin Grayson-s/Brian Stelfreeze-a/c 3.00

MATRIX COMICS, THE (Movie)
Burlyman Entertainment: 2003; 2004 ($21.95, trade paperback)
nn-Short stories by various incl. Wachowskis, Darrow, Gaiman, Sienkiewicz, Bagge 22.00
...Volume One Preview (7/03, no cover price) bios of creators; Chadwick-s/a 3.00
Volume 2-(2004) Short stories by various incl. Wachowskis, Sale, McKeever, Dorman 22.00

MATT SLADE GUNFIGHTER (Kid Slade Gunfighter #5 on; See Western Gunfighters)
Atlas Comics (SPI): May, 1956 - No. 4, Nov, 1956
1-Intro Matt & horse Eagle; Williamson/Torres-a 18 36 54 107 169 230
2-Williamson-a 13 26 39 74 105 135
3,4 10 20 30 56 76 95
NOTE: ***Maneely*** *a-1, 3, 4; c-1, 2, 4.* ***Roth*** *a-2-4.* ***Severin*** *a-1, 3, 4.* ***Maneely*** *c/a-1. Issue #s stamped on cover after printing.*

MAUS: A SURVIVOR'S TALE (First graphic novel to win a Pulitzer Prize)
Pantheon Books: 1986, 1991 (B&W)

Maximage #6 © Rob Liefeld

Mazie #8 © Mag. Pub.

MD #3 © WMG

GD VG FN VF VF/NM NM-
2.0 4.0 6.0 8.0 9.0 9.2

GD VG FN VF VF/NM NM-
2.0 4.0 6.0 8.0 9.0 9.2

Vol. 1-(...: My Father Bleeds History)(1986) Art Spiegelman-s/a; recounts stories of Spiegelman's father in 1930s-40s Nazi-occupied Poland; collects first six stories serialized in Raw Magazine from 1980-1985 20.00
Vol. 2-(...: And Here My Troubles Began)(1991) 20.00
Complete Maus Survivor's Tale -HC Vols. 1& 2 w/slipcase 35.00
Hardcover Vol. 1 (1991) 24.00
Hardcover Vol. 2 (1991) 24.00
TPB (1992, $14.00) Vols. 1& 2 14.00

MAVERICK (TV)
Dell Publishing Co.: No. 892, 4/58 - No. 19, 4-6/62 (All have photo-c)

Four Color 892 (#1)-James Garner photo-c begin 20 40 60 140 283 425
Four Color 930,945,962,980,1005 (6-8/59): 945-James Garner/Jack Kelly photo-c begin 10 20 30 72 131 190
7 (10-12/59) - 14: 11-Variant edition has "Time For Change" comic strip on back-c. 14-Last Garner/Kelly-c 9 18 27 63 107 150
15-18: Jack Kelly/Roger Moore photo-c 8 16 24 52 86 120
19-Jack Kelly photo-c (last issue) 8 16 24 54 90 125

MAVERICK (See X-Men)
Marvel Comics: Jan, 1997 ($2.95, one-shot)

1-Hama-s 3.00

MAVERICK (See X-Men)
Marvel Comics: Sept, 1997 - No. 12, Aug, 1998 ($2.99/$1.99)

1,12: 1-($2.99)-Wraparound-c. 12-($2.99) Battles Omega Red 4.00
2-11: 2-Two covers. 4-Wolverine app. 6,7-Sabretooth app. 3.00

MAVERICK MARSHAL
Charlton Comics: Nov, 1958 - No. 7, May, 1960

1 6 12 18 33 41 48
2-7 5 10 15 23 28 32

MAVERICKS
Daggar Comics Group: Jan, 1994 - No. 5, 1994 (#1-$2.75, #2-5-$2.50)

1-5: 1-Bronze. 1-Gold. 1-Silver 3.00

MAX BRAND (See Silvertip)

MAX HAMM FAIRY TALE DETECTIVE
Nite Owl Comix: 2002 - 2004 ($4.95, B&W, 6 1/2" x 8")

1-(2002) Frank Cammuso-s/a 5.00
Vol. 2 #1-3 (2003-2004) Frank Cammuso-s/a 5.00

MAXIMAGE
Image Comics (Extreme Studios): Dec, 1995 - No. 7, June 1996 ($2.50)

1-7: 1-Liefeld-c. 2-Extreme Destroyer Pt. 2; polybagged w/card. 4-Angela & Glory-c/app. 3.00

MAXIMO
Dreamwave Prods.: Jan, 2004 ($3.95, one-shot)

1-Based on the Capcom video game 4.00

MAXIMUM SECURITY (Crossover)
Marvel Comics: Oct, 2000 - No. 3, Jan, 2001 ($2.99)

1-3-Busiek-s/Ordway-a; Ronan the Accuser, Avengers app. 3.00
...Dangerous Planet 1: Busiek-s/Ordway-a; Ego, the Living Planet 3.00
Thor vs. Ego (11/00, $2.99) Reprints Thor #133,160,161; Kirby-a 3.00

MAXX (Also see Darker Image, Primer #5, & Friends of Maxx)
Image Comics (I Before E): Mar, 1993 - No. 35, Feb, 1998 ($1.95)

1/2 1 3 4 6 8 10
1/2 (Gold) 20.00
1-Sam Kieth-c/a/scripts 4.00
1-Glow-in-the-dark variant 2 4 6 8 10 12
1-"3-D Edition" (1/98, $4.95) plus new back-up story 5.00
2-12: 6-Savage Dragon cameo(1 pg.). 7,8-Pitt-c & story 3.00
13-16 3.00
17-35: 21-Alan Moore-s 3.00
Volume 1 TPB (DC/WildStorm, 2003, $17.95) r/#1-6 18.00
Volume 2 TPB (DC/WildStorm, 2004, $17.95) r/#7-13 18.00
Volume 3 TPB (DC/WildStorm, 2004, $17.95) r/#14-20 18.00
Volume 4 TPB (DC/WildStorm, 2005, $17.95) r/#21-27 18.00
Volume 5 TPB (DC/WildStorm, 2005, $19.99) r/#28-35 20.00
Volume 6 TPB (DC/WildStorm, 2006, $19.99) r/Friends of Maxx #1-3 & The Maxx 3-D 20.00

MAYA (See Movie Classics)
Gold Key: Mar, 1968

1 (10218-803)(TV) 3 6 9 17 25 32

MAYHEM
Dark Horse Comics: May, 1989 - No. 4, Sept, 1989 ($2.50, B&W, 52 pgs.)

1- Four part Stanley Ipkiss/Mask story begins; Mask-c 1 3 4 6 8 10
2-4: 2-Mask 1/2 back-c. 4-Mask-c 1 2 3 5 7 9

MAYHEM (Tyrese Gibson's...)
Image Comics: Aug, 2009 - No. 3, Oct, 2009 ($2.99, limited series)

1-3-Tyrese Gibson co-writer; Tone Rodriguez-a/c 3.00

MAZE AGENCY, THE
Comico/Innovation Publ. #8 on: Dec, 1988 - No. 20, 1991 ($1.95-$2.50, color)

1-20: 9-Ellery Queen app. 7 ($2.50)-Last Comico issue 3.00
Annual 1 (1990, $2.75)-Ploog-c; Spirit tribute ish 4.00
Special 1 (1989, $2.75)-Staton-p (Innovation) 4.00
TPB (IDW Publ., 11/05, $24.99) r/#1-5 25.00

MAZE AGENCY, THE (Vol. 2)
Caliber Comics: July, 1997 - No. 3, 1998 ($2.95, B&W)

1-3: 1-Barr-s/Gonzales-a(p). 3-Hughes-c 3.00

MAZE AGENCY, THE
Caliber Comics: Nov, 2005 - No. 3, Jan, 2006 ($3.99, limited series)

1-3-Barr-s/Padilla-a(p)/c 4.00

MAZIE (...& Her Friends) (See Flat-Top, Mortie, Stevie & Tastee-Freez)
Mazie Comics(Magazine Publ.)/Harvey Publ. No. 13-on: 1953 - #12, 1954; #13, 12/54 - #22, 9/56; #23, 9/57 - #28, 8/58

1-(Teen-age)-Stevie's girlfriend 10 20 30 58 79 100
2 7 14 21 35 43 50
3-10 6 12 18 31 38 45
11-28 5 10 15 24 30 35

MAZIE
Nation Wide Publishers: 1950 - No. 7, 1951 (5¢) (5x7-1/4"-miniature)(52 pgs.)

1-Teen-age 17 34 51 98 154 210
2-7 11 22 33 62 86 110

MAZINGER (See First Comics Graphic Novel #17)

'MAZING MAN
DC Comics: Jan, 1986 - No. 12, Dec, 1986

1-11: 7,8-Hembeck-a 3.00
12-Dark Knight part-c by Miller 3.50
Special 1 ('87), 2 (4/88), 3 ('90)-All $2.00, 52pgs. 3.00

McCANDLESS & COMPANY
Mandalay Books: 2001 ($7.95)

...: Dead Razor - J.C. Vaughn-s/Busch & Sheehan-a; 3 covers 8.00
Crime Scenes: A McCandless & Company Reader TPB (Spring 2006, $17.95) Vaughn-s 18.00

McHALE'S NAVY (TV) (See Movie Classics)
Dell Publ. Co.: May-July, 1963 - No. 3, Nov-Jan, 1963-64 (All have photo-c)

1 7 14 21 45 73 100
2,3 5 10 15 32 51 70

McKEEVER & THE COLONEL (TV)
Dell Publishing Co.: Feb-Apr, 1963 - No. 3, Aug-Oct, 1963

1-Photo-c 6 12 18 39 62 85
2,3 5 10 15 30 48 65

McLINTOCK (See Movie Comics)

MD
E. C. Comics: Apr-May, 1955 - No. 5, Dec-Jan, 1955-56

1-Not approved by code; Craig-c 15 30 45 120 195 270
2-5 10 20 30 80 128 175

NOTE: ***Crandall, Evans, Ingels, Orlando*** art in all issues; ***Craig*** c-1-5.

MD
Russ Cochran/Gemstone Publishing: Sept, 1999 - No. 5, Jan, 2000 ($2.50)

1-5-Reprints original EC series 3.00
Annual 1 (1999, $13.50) r/#1-5 14.00

MEASLES
Fantagraphics Books: Christmas 1998 - No. 8 ($2.95, B&W, quarterly)

1-8-Anthology: 1-Venus-s by Hernandez 3.00

MECHA (Also see Mayhem)
Dark Horse Comics: June, 1987 - No. 6, 1988 ($1.50/$1.95, color/B&W)

Medal of Honor #2 © DH

Megamind: Bad. Blue. Brilliant #1 © DreamWorks

Megaton #5 © Gary Carlson

GD VG FN VF VF/NM NM-
2.0 4.0 6.0 8.0 9.0 9.2

1-6: 1,2 ($1.95, color), 3,4-($1.75, B&W), 5,6-($1.50, B&W) 3.00

MECHANIC, THE
Image Comics: 1998 ($5.95, one-shot, squarebound)
1-Chiodo-painted art; Peterson-s 6.00
1-($10.00) DF Alternate Cover Ed. 10.00

MECHA SPECIAL
Dark Horse Comics: May, 1995 ($2.95, one-shot)
1 3.00

MECH DESTROYER
Image Comics: Apr, 2001 - No. 4, Sept, 2001 ($2.95, limited series)
1-4-Jae Kim-c/a; Robert Chong-s 3.00

MEDAL FOR BOWZER, A (See Promotional Comics section)

MEDAL OF HONOR COMICS
A. S. Curtis: Spring, 1946
1-War stories 14 28 42 76 108 140

MEDAL OF HONOR SPECIAL
Dark Horse Comics: 1994 ($2.50, one-shot)
1-Kubert-c/a (first story) 3.00

MEDIA STARR
Innovation Publ.: July, 1989 - No. 3, Sept, 1989 ($1.95, mini-series, 28 pgs.)
1-3: Deluxe format 3.00

MEDIEVAL SPAWN/WITCHBLADE
Image Comics (Top Cow Productions): May, 1996 - No. 3, June, 1996 ($2.95, limited series)
1-3-Garth Ennis scripts in all 6.00
1-Platinum foil-c (500 copies from Pittsburgh Con) 35.00
1-Gold 10.00
1-ETM Exclusive Edition; gold foil logo 7.00
TPB ($9.95) r/#1-3 10.00

MEET ANGEL (Formerly Angel & the Ape)
National Periodical Publications: No. 7, Nov-Dec, 1969
7-Wood-a(i) 3 6 9 20 30 40

MEET CORLISS ARCHER (Radio/Movie)(My Life #4 on)
Fox Features Syndicate: Mar, 1948 - No. 3, July, 1948
1-(Teen-age)-Feldstein-c/a; headlight-c 113 226 339 718 1234 1750
2 57 114 171 362 619 875
3-Part Feldstein-c only 53 106 159 334 567 800
NOTE: *No. 1-3 used in Seduction of the Innocent, pg. 39.*

MEET HERCULES (See Three Stooges)

MEET MERTON
Toby Press: Dec, 1953 - No. 4, June, 1954
1-(Teen-age)-Dave Berg-c/a 10 20 30 54 72 90
2-Dave Berg-c/a 6 12 18 31 38 45
3,4-Dave Berg-c/a 6 12 18 28 34 40
I.W. Reprint #9, Super Reprint #11('63), 18 2 4 6 8 11 14

MEET MISS BLISS (Becomes Stories Of Romance #5 on)
Atlas Comics (LMC): May, 1955 - No. 4, Nov, 1955
1-Al Hartley-c/a 14 28 42 80 115 150
2-4 10 20 30 54 72 90

MEET MISS PEPPER (Formerly Lucy, The Real Gone Gal)
St. John Publishing Co.: No. 5, April, 1954 - No. 6, June, 1954
5-Kubert/Maurer-a 21 42 63 122 199 275
6-Kubert/Maurer-a; Kubert-c 18 36 54 105 165 225

MEGACITY909
Devil's Due Publ.: Sept, 2004 - No. 8, Aug, 2005 ($2.95)
1-8-Kano Kang & Zack Suh-a 3.00

MEGA DRAGON & TIGER
Image Comics: Mar, 1999 - No. 5 ($2.95)
1-5-Tony Wong-s/a 3.00

MEGAHURTZ
Image Comics: Aug, 1997 - No. 3, Oct, 1997 ($2.95, B&W)
1-3-St. Pierre-s 3.00

MEGALITH (Megalith Deathwatch 2000 #1,2 of second series)
Continuity: 1989 - No. 9, Mar, 1992; No, 0, Apr, 1993 - No. 7, Jan, 1994
1-9-($2.00-c) 1-Neal Adams & Mark Texiera-c/Texiera & Nebres-a 3.00
2nd series: 0-(4/93)-Foil-c; no c-price, giveaway; Adams plot 3.00
1-7: 1-3-Bagged w/card: 1-Gatefold-c by Nebres; Adams plot. 2-Fold-out-c; Adams plot. 3-Indestructible-c. 4-7-Embossed-c: 4-Adams/Nebres-c; Adams part-i. 5-Sienkiewicz-i. 6-Adams part-i. 7-Adams-c(p); Adams plot 3.00

MEGAMAN
Dreamwave Productions: Sept, 2003 - No. 4, Dec, 2003 ($2.95)
1-4-Brian Augustyn-s/Mic Fong-a 3.00
1-($5.95) Chromium wraparound variant-c 6.00

MEGA MAN (Based on the Capcom video game character)
Archie Comics Publications: Jul, 2011 - Present ($2.99)
1-Spaziante-a 3.00

MEGAMIND: BAD. BLUE. BRILLIANT (DreamWorks'...) (Based on the 2010 movie)
Ape Entertainment: 2010 - No. 4 ($3.95)
1-High school flashback 4.00
nn-($6.95, 9x6") Prequel to the movie; Joe Kelly-s 7.00

MEGA MORPHS
Marvel Comics: Oct, 2005 - No. 4, Dec, 2005 ($2.99, limited series)
1-4-Giant robots based on action figures; McKeever-s; Kang-a 3.00
Digest (2006, $7.99) r/#1-4 plus mini-comics 8.00

MEGATON (A super hero)
Megaton Publ.: Nov, 1983; No. 2, Oct, 1985 - No. 8, Aug, 1987 (B&W)
1-($2.00, 68 pgs.)-Erik Larsen's 1st pro work; Vanguard by Larsen begins (1st app.), ends #4; 1st app. Megaton, Berzerker, & Ethrian; Guice-c/a(p); Gustovich-a(p) in #1,2 2 4 6 10 14 18
2-($2.00, 68 pgs.)-1st brief app. The Dragon (1 pg.) by Larsen (later The Savage Dragon in Image Comics); Guice-c/a(p) 2 4 6 9 12 15
3-(44 pgs.)-1st full app. Savage Dragon-c/story by Larsen; 1st comic book work by Angel Medina (pin-up) 2 4 6 13 18 22
4-(52 pgs.)-2nd full app. Savage Dragon by Larsen; 4,5-Wildman by Grass Green 2 4 6 8 10 12
5-1st Liefeld published-a (inside f/c, 6/86) 1 2 3 5 7 9
6,7: 6-Larsen-c 1 2 3 4 5 7
8-1st Liefeld story-a (7 pg. super hero story) plus 1 pg. Youngblood ad 1 3 4 6 8 10
...Explosion (6/87, 16 pg. color giveaway)-1st app. Youngblood by Rob Liefeld (2 pg. spread); shows Megaton heroes 3 6 9 14 20 25
...Holiday Special 1 (1994, $2.95, color, 40 pgs., publ. by Entity Comics)-Gold foil logo; bagged w/Kelley Jones card; Vanguard, Megaton plus shows unpublished-c to 1987 Youngblood #1 by Liefeld/Ordway 5.00
NOTE: *Copies of Megaton Explosion were also released in early 1992 all signed by Rob Liefeld and were made available to retailers.*

MEGATON MAN (See Don Simpson's Bizarre Heroes)
Kitchen Sink Enterprises: Nov, 1984 - No. 10, 1986
1-10, 1-2nd printing (1989) 3.00
...Meets The Uncategorizable X-Thems 1 (4/89, $2.00) 3.00

MEGATON MAN: BOMB SHELL
Image Comics: Jul, 1999 - No. 2 ($2.95, B&W, mini-series)
1-Reprints stories from Megaton Man internet site 3.00

MEGATON MAN: HARD COPY
Image Comics: Feb, 1999 - No. 2, Apr, 1999 ($2.95, B&W, mini-series)
1,2-Reprints stories from Megaton Man internet site 3.00

MEGATON MAN VS. FORBIDDEN FRANKENSTEIN
Fiasco Comics: Apr, 1996 ($2.95, B&W, one-shot)
1-Intro The Tomb Team (Forbidden Frankenstein, Drekula, Bride of the Monster, & Moon Wolf). 3.00

MEK (See Reload/Mek flipbook for TPB reprint)
DC Comics (Homage): Jan, 2003 - No. 3, Mar, 2003 ($2.95, limited series)
1-3-Warren Ellis-s/Steve Rolston-a 3.00

MEKANIX (See X-Men titles) (See X-Treme X-Men Vol. 4 for TPB)
Marvel Comics: Dec, 2002 - No. 6, May, 2003 ($2.99, limited series)
1-6-Kitty Pryde in college; Claremont-s/Bobillo & Sosa-a 3.00

MEL ALLEN SPORTS COMICS (The Voice of the Yankees)
Standard Comics: No. 5, Nov, 1949; No. 6, June, 1950
5(#1 on inside)-Tuska-a 23 46 69 136 223 310
6(#2)-Lou Gehrig story 16 32 48 94 147 200

Menace #11 © MAR

Men's Adventures #21 © MAR

Meridian #23 © CRO

	GD	VG	FN	VF	VF/NM	NM-
	2.0	4.0	6.0	8.0	9.0	9.2

GD VG FN VF VF/NM NM-
2.0 4.0 6.0 8.0 9.0 9.2

MELTDOWN
Image Comics: Dec, 2006 - No. 2, Jan, 2007 ($5.95, squarebound, limited series)
1,2-Schwartz-s/Wang-a. 1-Bachalo-c. 2-Horn-c 6.00

MELVIN MONSTER
Dell Publishing Co.: Apr-June, 1965 - No. 10, Oct, 1969
1-By John Stanley 7 14 21 47 76 105
2-10-All by Stanley. #10-r/#1 5 10 15 32 51 70

MELVIN THE MONSTER (See Peter, the Little Pest & Dexter The Demon #7)
Atlas Comics (HPC): July, 1956 - No. 6, July, 1957
1-Maneely-c/a 14 28 42 80 115 150
2-6: 4-Maneely-c/a 10 20 30 54 72 90

MENACE
Atlas Comics (HPC): Mar, 1953 - No. 11, May, 1954
1-Horror & sci/fi stories begin; Everett-c/a 77 154 231 493 847 1200
2-Post-atom bomb disaster by Everett; anti-Communist propaganda/torture scenes; Sinnott sci/fi story "Rocket to the Moon" 52 104 156 322 549 775
3,4,6-Everett-a. 4-Sci/fi story "Escape to the Moon". 6-Romita sci/fi story "Science Fiction" 42 84 126 265 445 625
5-Origin & 1st app. The Zombie by Everett (reprinted in Tales of the Zombie #1)(7/53); 5-Sci/fi story "Rocket Ship" 60 120 180 381 653 925
7,8,10,11: 7-Frankenstein story. 8-End of world story; Heath 3-D art(3 pgs.). 10-H-Bomb panels 36 72 108 211 343 475
9-Everett-a r-in Vampire Tales #1 39 78 117 231 378 525
NOTE: ***Brodsky** c-7, 8, 11. **Colan** a-6; c-9. **Everett** a-1-6, 9; c-1-6. **Heath** a-1-8; c-10. **Katz** a-11. **Maneely** a-3, 5, 7-9. **Powell** a-11. **Romita** a-3, 6, 8, 11. **Shelly** a-10. **Shores** a-7. **Sinnott** a-2, 7. **Tuska** a-1, 2, 5.*

MENACE
Awesome-Hyperwerks: Nov, 1998 ($2.50)
1-Jada Pinkett Smith-s/Fraga-a 3.00

MEN AGAINST CRIME (Formerly Mr. Risk; Hand of Fate #8 on)
Ace Magazines: No. 3, Feb, 1951 - No. 7, Oct, 1951
3-Mr. Risk app. 11 22 33 60 83 105
4-7: 4-Colan-a; entire book-r as Trapped! #4. 5-Meskin-a 8 16 24 44 57 70

MEN, GUNS, & CATTLE (See Classics Illustrated Special Issue)

MEN IN ACTION (Battle Brady #10 on)
Atlas Comics (IPS): April, 1952 - No. 9, Dec, 1952 (War stories)
1-Berg, Reinman-a 18 36 54 103 162 220
2,3: 3-Heath-c/a 11 22 33 62 86 110
4-6,8,9 10 20 30 56 76 95
7-Krigstein-a; Heath-c 11 22 33 62 86 110
NOTE: ***Brodsky** a-3; c-1, 4-6. **Maneely** c-5. **Pakula** a-1, 6. **Robinson** c-8. **Shores** c-9. **Sinnott** a-6.*

MEN IN ACTION
Ajax/Farrell Publications: April, 1957 - No. 6, 1958
1 10 20 30 56 76 95
2 7 14 21 35 43 50
3-6 6 12 18 31 38 45

MEN IN BLACK, THE (1st series)
Aircel Comics (Malibu): Jan, 1990 - No. 3 Mar, 1990 ($2.25, B&W, lim. series)
1-Cunningham-s/a in all 4 8 12 28 44 60
2,3 3 6 9 17 25 32
Graphic Novel (Jan, 1991) r/#1-3 3 6 9 16 22 28

MEN IN BLACK (2nd series)
Aircel Comics (Malibu): May, 1991 - No. 3, Jul, 1991 ($2.50, B&W, lim. series)
1-Cunningham-s/a in all 3 6 9 17 25 32
2,3 2 4 6 9 13 16

MEN IN BLACK: FAR CRY
Marvel Comics: Aug, 1997 ($3.99, color, one-shot)
1-Cunningham-s 4.00

MEN IN BLACK: RETRIBUTION
Marvel Comics: Dec, 1997 ($3.99, color, one-shot)
1-Cunningham-s; continuation of the movie 4.00

MEN IN BLACK: THE MOVIE
Marvel Comics: Oct, 1997 ($3.99, one-shot, movie adaptation)
1-Cunningham-s 4.00

MEN INTO SPACE
Dell Publishing Co.: No. 1083, Feb-Apr, 1960
Four Color 1083-Anderson-a, photo-c 5 10 15 34 55 75

MEN OF BATTLE (Also see New Men of Battle)
Catechetical Guild: V1#5, March, 1943 (Hardcover)
V1#5-Topix reprints 6 12 18 28 34 40

MEN OF WAR
DC Comics, Inc.: August, 1977 - No. 26, March, 1980 (#9,10: 44 pgs.)
1-Enemy Ace, Gravedigger (origin #1,2) begin 3 6 9 16 23 30
2-4,8-10,12-14,19,20: All Enemy Ace stories. 4-1st Dateline Frontline. 9-Unknown Soldier app. 2 4 6 10 14 18
5-7,11,15-18,21-25: 17-1st app. Rosa 2 4 6 8 11 14
26-Sgt. Rock & Easy Co.-c/s 3 6 9 14 19 24
NOTE: ***Chaykin** a-9, 10, 12-14, 19, 20. **Evans** c-25. **Kubert** c-2-23, 24p, 26.*

MEN'S ADVENTURES (Formerly True Adventures)
Marvel/Atlas Comics (CCC): No. 4, Aug, 1950 - No. 28, July, 1954
4(#1)(52 pgs.) 34 68 102 199 325 450
5-Flying Saucer story 22 44 66 128 209 290
6-8: 7-Buried alive story. 8-Sci/fic story 20 40 60 117 189 260
9-20: All war format 14 28 42 81 118 155
21,22,24,26: All horror format 23 46 69 136 223 310
23-Crandall-a; Fox-a(i); horror format 24 48 72 140 230 320
25-Shrunken head-c 37 74 111 222 361 500
27,28-Human Torch & Toro-c/stories; Captain America & Sub-Mariner stories in each (also see Young Men #24-28) 123 246 369 787 1344 1900
NOTE: ***Ayers** a-20, 27(H. Torch). **Berg** a-15, 16. **Brodsky** c-4-9, 11, 12, 16-18, 24. **Burgos** c-27, 28 (Human Torch). **Colan** a-13, 14, 19. **Everett** a-10, 14, 22, 25, 28; c-14, 21-23. **Hartley** a-12. **Heath** a-8, 11, 24; c-13, 20, 26. **Lawrence** a-23; 27(Captain America). **Maneely** a-24; c-10, 15. **Mac Pakula** a-15, 25. **Post** a-23. **Powell** a-27(Sub-Mariner). **Reinman** a-11, 12. **Robinson** c-19. **Romita** a-22. **Sale** a-12. **Shores** c-25. **Sinnott** a-13, 21. **Tuska** a-24. Adventure-#4-8; War-#9-20; Weird/Horror-#21-26.*

MENZ INSANA
DC Comics (Vertigo): 1997 ($7.95, one-shot)
nn-Fowler-s/Bolton painted art 1 2 3 5 6 8

MEPHISTO VS... (See Silver Surfer #3)
Marvel Comics Group: Apr, 1987 - No. 4, July, 1987 ($1.50, mini-series)
1-4: 1-Fantastic Four; Austin-i. 2-X-Factor. 3-X-Men. 4-Avengers 3.00

MERC (See Mark Hazzard: Merc)

MERCENARIES (Based on the Pandemic video game)
Dynamite Entertainment: 2007 - No. 3, 2008 ($3.99, limited series)
1-3-Michael Turner-c; Brian Reed-s/Edgar Salazar-a 4.00

MERCHANTS OF DEATH
Acme Press (Eclipse): Jul, 1988 - No. 4, Nov, 1988 ($3.50, B&W/16 pgs. color, 44 pg. mag.)
1-4: 4-Toth-c 3.50

MERCY THOMPSON: HOMECOMING (Patricia Briggs'...)
Dabel Brothers Prods.: Oct, 2008 (Nov. on-c) - No. 4 ($3.99, limited series)
1-Characters from the Patricia Briggs werewolf novels; Francis Tsai-a 4.00

MERIDIAN
CrossGeneration Comics: Jul, 2000 - No. 44, Apr, 2004 ($2.95)
1-44: Barbara Kesel-s 3.00
Flying Solo Vol. 1 TPB (2001, $19.95) r/#1-7; cover by Steve Rude 20.00
Going to Ground Vol. 2 TPB (2002, $19.95) r/#8-14 20.00
Taking the Skies Vol. 3 TPB (2002, $15.95) r/#15-20 16.00
Vol. 4: Coming Home (12/02, $15.95) r/#21-26 16.00
Vol. 5: Minister of Cadador (7/03, $15.95) r/#27-32 16.00
Vol. 6: Changing Course (1/04, $15.95) r/#33-38 16.00
Traveler Vol. 1-4 ($9.95): Digest-size reprints of TPBs 10.00

MERLIN JONES AS THE MONKEY'S UNCLE (See Movie Comics and The Misadventures of... under Movie Comics)

MERRILL'S MARAUDERS (See Movie Classics)

MERRY CHRISTMAS (See A Christmas Adventure, Donald Duck..., Dell Giant #39, & March of Comics #153 in the Promotional Comics section)

MERRY COMICS
Carlton Publishing Co.: Dec, 1945 (10¢)
nn-Boogeyman app. 20 40 60 114 182 250

MERRY COMICS: Four Star Publications: 1947 (Advertised, not published)

MERRY-GO-ROUND COMICS
LaSalle Publ. Co./Croyden Publ./Rotary Litho.: 1944 (25¢, 132 pgs.); 1946; 9-10/47 - No. 2, 1948
nn(1944)(LaSalle)-Funny animal; 29 new features 18 36 54 105 165 225

Metal Men #41 © DC

Metamorpho #2 © DC

Mice Templar V3 #1 © Glass & Oeming

	GD 2.0	VG 4.0	FN 6.0	VF 8.0	VF/NM 9.0	NM- 9.2
21 (Publisher?)	9	18	27	47	61	75
1(1946)(Croyden)-Al Fago-c; funny animal	11	22	33	60	83	105
V1#1,2(1947-48; 52 pgs.)(Rotary Litho. Co. Ltd., Canada); Ken Hultgren-a	9	18	27	47	61	75

MERRY MAILMAN (See Fawcett's Funny Animals #87-89)

MERRY MOUSE (Also see Funny Tunes & Space Comics)
Avon Periodicals: June, 1953 - No. 4, Jan-Feb, 1954

1-1st app.; funny animal; Frank Carin-c/a	10	20	30	54	72	90
2-4	7	14	21	35	43	50

MERV PUMPKINHEAD, AGENT OF D.R.E.A.M. (See The Sandman)
DC Comics (Vertigo): 2000 ($5.95, one-shot)

1-Buckingham-a(p); Nowlan painted-c 6.00

META-4
First Comics: Feb, 1991 - No. 4, 1991 ($2.25)

1-($3.95, 52pgs.) 4.00
2-4 3.00

METAL GEAR SOLID (Based on the video game)
IDW Publ.: Sept, 2004 - No. 12, Aug, 2005 ($3.99)

1-12: 1-Two covers; Ashley Wood-a/Kris Oprisko-s 4.00
1-Retailer edition with foil cover 20.00

METAL GEAR SOLID: SONS OF LIBERTY
IDW Publ.: Sept, 2005 - No. 12, Sept, 2007 ($3.99)

#0 (9/05) profile pages on characters; Ashley Wood-a 4.00
1-12: 1-Two covers; Ashley Wood-a/Alex Garner-s 4.00

METALLIX
Future Comics: Dec, 2002 - No. 6, June, 2003 ($3.50)

0-6-Ron Lim-a. 0-(6/03) Origin. 1-Layton-c 3.50
1-Collector's Edition with variant cover by Lim 3.50
1-Free Comic Book Day Edition (4/03) Layton-c 2.50

METAL MEN (See Brave & the Bold, DC Comics Presents, and Showcase #37-40)
National Periodical Publications/DC Comics: 4-5/63 - No. 41, 12-1/69-70; No. 42, 2-3/73 - No. 44, 7-8/73; No. 45, 4-5/76 - No. 56, 2-3/78

1-(4-5/63)-5th app. Metal Men	54	108	162	459	930	1400
2	22	44	66	155	310	465
3-5	14	28	42	99	200	300
6-10	10	20	30	69	122	175
11-20: 12-Beatles cameo (2-3/65)	8	16	24	54	90	125
21-Batman, Robin & Flash x-over	6	12	18	43	69	95
22-26,28-30	6	12	18	39	62	85
27-Origin Metal Men retold	7	14	21	50	83	115
31-41(1968-70): 38-Last 12¢ issue. 41-Last 15¢	5	10	15	34	55	75
42-44(1973)-Reprints	2	4	6	10	14	18
45('76)-49-Simonson-a in all: 48,49-Re-intro Eclipso	2	4	6	10	14	18
50-56: 50-Part-r. 54,55-Green Lantern x-over	2	4	6	9	12	15

NOTE: ***Andru/Esposito** c-1-30. **Aparo** c-53-56. **Giordano** c-45, 46. **Kane/Esposito** a-30, 31; c-31. **Simonson** a-45-49; c-47-52. **Staton** a-50-56.*

METAL MEN (Also see Tangent Comics/ Metal Men)
DC Comics: Oct, 1993 - No. 4, Jan, 1994 ($1.25, mini-series)

1-($2.50)-Multi-colored foil-c 4.00
2-4: 2-Origin 3.00

METAL MEN (Also see 52)
DC Comics: Oct, 2007 - No. 8, Jul, 2008 ($2.99, limited series)

1-8-Duncan Rouleau-s/a; origin re-told. 3-Chemo returns 3.00
HC (2008, $24.99, dustjacket) r/#1-8; cover gallery and sketch pages 25.00
SC (2009, $14.99) r/#1-8; cover gallery and sketch pages 15.00

METAMORPHO (See Action Comics #413, Brave & the Bold #57,58, 1st Issue Special, & World's Finest #217)
National Periodical Publications: July-Aug, 1965 - No. 17, Mar-Apr, 1968 (All 12¢ issues)

1-(7-8/65)-3rd app. Metamorpho	13	26	39	91	176	260
2,3	8	16	24	52	86	120
4-6,10:10-Origin & 1st app. Element Girl (1-2/67)	6	12	18	43	69	95
7-9	6	12	18	37	59	80
11-17: 17-Sparling-c/a	5	10	15	32	51	70

NOTE: ***Ramona Fradon** a-B&B 57, 58, 1-4. **Orlando** a-5, 6; c-5-9, 11. **Trapani** a(p)-7-16; i-16.*

METAMORPHO
DC Comics: Aug, 1993 - No. 4, Nov, 1993 ($1.50, mini-series)

1-4 3.00

METAMORPHO: YEAR ONE
DC Comics: Early Dec, 2007 - No. 6, Late Feb, 2008 ($2.99, limited series)

1-6-Origin re-told; Jurgens-s/Jurgens & Delperdang-a/Nowlan-c. 6-Justice League app. 3.00
TPB ('08, $14.99) r/#1-6 15.00

METAPHYSIQUE
Malibu Comics (Bravura): Apr, 1995 - No. 6, Oct, 1995 ($2.95, limited series)

1-6: Norm Breyfogle-c/a/scripts 3.00

METEOR COMICS
L. L. Baird (Croyden): Nov, 1945

1-Captain Wizard, Impossible Man, Race Wilkins app.; origin Baldy Bean, Capt. Wizard's sidekick; bare-breasted mermaids story	40	80	120	242	401	560

METEOR MAN
Marvel Comics: Aug, 1993 - No. 6, Jan, 1994 ($1.25, limited series)

1-6: 1-Regular unbagged. 4-Night Thrasher-c/story. 6-Terry Austin-c(i) 3.00
1-Polybagged w/button & rap newspaper 4.00
...: The Movie (4/93 [7/93 on cover], $2.25) movie adaptation 3.00

METROPOL (See Ted McKeever's...)

METROPOL A.D. (See Ted McKeever's...)

METROPOLIS S.C.U. (Also see Showcase '96 #1)
DC Comics: Nov, 1995 - No. 4, Feb, 1996 ($1.50, limited series)

1-4:1-Superman-c & app. 3.00

MEZZ: GALACTIC TOUR 2494 (Also See Nexus)
Dark Horse Comics: May, 1994 ($2.50, one-shot)

1 3.00

MGM'S MARVELOUS WIZARD OF OZ (See Marvel Treasury of Oz)
Marvel Comics Group/National Periodical Publications: 1975 ($1.50, 84 pgs.; oversize)

1-Adaptation of MGM's movie; J. Buscema-a	3	6	9	16	23	30

M.G.M'S MOUSE MUSKETEERS (Formerly M.G.M.'s The Two Mouseketeers)
Dell Publishing Co.: No. 670, Jan, 1956 - No. 1290, Mar-May, 1962

Four Color 670 (#4)	5	10	15	34	55	75
Four Color 711,728,764	4	8	12	26	41	55
8 (4-6/57) - 21 (3-5/60)	4	8	12	24	37	50
Four Color 1135,1175,1290	4	8	12	24	37	50

M.G.M.'S SPIKE AND TYKE (also see Tom & Jerry #79)
Dell Publishing Co.: No. 499, Sept, 1953 - No. 1266, Dec-Feb, 1961-62

Four Color 499 (#1)	7	14	21	45	73	100
Four Color 577,638	5	10	15	30	48	65
4(12-2/55-56)-10	4	8	12	26	41	55
11-24(12-2/60-61)	4	8	12	22	34	45
Four Color 1266	4	8	12	24	37	50

M.G.M.'S THE TWO MOUSKETEERS
Dell Publishing Co.: No. 475, June, 1953 - No. 642, July, 1955

Four Color 475 (#1)	8	16	24	52	86	120
Four Color 603 (11/54), 642	6	12	18	37	59	80

MICE TEMPLAR, THE
Image Comics: Sept, 2007 - No. 6, Oct, 2008 ($3.99/$2.99)

1-($3.99)-Bryan Glass-s/Michael Avon Oeming-a/c 4.00
2-6-($2.99) 3.00

MICE TEMPLAR, THE , VOLUME 2: DESTINY
Image Comics: July, 2009 - No. 9, May, 2010 ($3.99/$2.99/$4.99)

1,2-($3.99) 1-Bryan Glass-s/Oeming & Santos-a; 2 covers. 2-Santos-a 4.00
3-8-($2.99)-Santos-a; 2 covers by Oeming & Santos 3.00
9-($4.99) 5.00

MICE TEMPLAR, THE , VOLUME 3: A MIDWINTER NIGHT'S DREAM
Image Comics: Dec, 2010 - Present ($3.99/$2.99)

1-($3.99) 1-Bryan Glass-s/Oeming & Santos-a; 2 covers 4.00
2,3-($2.99)-Santos-a; 2 covers by Oeming & Santos 3.00

MICHAELANGELO CHRISTMAS SPECIAL (See Teenage Mutant Ninja Turtles Christmas Special)

MICHAELANGELO, TEENAGE MUTANT NINJA TURTLE
Mirage Studios: 1986 (One shot) ($1.50, B&W)

1	1	2	3	5	6	8
1-2nd printing ('89, $1.75)-Reprint plus new-a						3.00

MICHAEL CHABON PRESENTS THE AMAZING ADVENTURES OF THE ESCAPIST
Dark Horse Comics: Feb, 2004 - Present ($8.95, squarebound)

Michael Turner, A Tribute To... © Aspen MLT

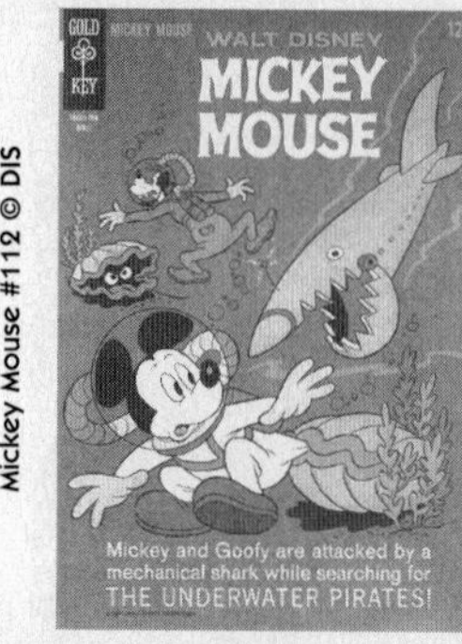

Mickey Mouse #112 © DIS

Mickey Mouse and Friends #300 © DIS

GD VG FN VF VF/NM NM-
2.0 4.0 6.0 8.0 9.0 9.2

1-5,7,8-Short stories by Chabon and various incl. Chaykin, Starlin, Brereton, Baker 9.00
6-Includes 6 pg. Spirit & Escapist story (Will Eisner's last work); Spirit on cover 9.00
... Vol. 1 (5/04, $17.95, digest-size) r/#1&2; wraparound-c by Chris Ware 18.00
... Vol. 2 (11/04, $17.95, digest-size) r/#3&4; wraparound-c by Matt Kindt 18.00
... Vol. 3 (4/06, $14.95, digest-size) r/#5&6; Tim Sale-c 15.00

MICHAEL MOORCOCK'S ELRIC: THE MAKING OF A SORCEROR
DC Comics: 2004 - No. 4, 2006 ($5.95, prestige format, limited series)
1-4-Moorcock-s/Simonson-a 6.00
TPB (2007, $19.99) r/#1-4 20.00

MICHAEL MOORCOCK'S MULTIVERSE
DC Comics (Helix): Nov, 1997 - No. 12, Oct, 1998 ($2.50, limited series)
1-12: Simonson, Reeve & Ridgway-a 3.00
TPB (1999, $19.95) r/#1-12 20.00

MICHAEL TURNER, A TRIBUTE TO...
Aspen MLT: 2008 ($8.99, squarebound)
nn-Pin-ups and tributes from Turner's colleagues and friends; Turner & Ross-c 9.00

MICHAEL TURNER PRESENTS: ASPEN (See Aspen)

MICKEY AND DONALD (See Walt Disney's...)

MICKEY AND DONALD IN VACATIONLAND (See Dell Giant No. 47)

MICKEY & THE BEANSTALK (See Story Hour Series)

MICKEY & THE SLEUTH (See Walt Disney Showcase #38, 39, 42)

MICKEY FINN (Also see Big Shot Comics #74 & Feature Funnies)
Eastern Color 1-4/McNaught Synd. #5 on (Columbia)/Headline V3#2:
Nov?, 1942 - V3#2, May, 1952
1 30 60 90 177 289 400
2 15 30 45 90 140 190
3-Charlie Chan story 12 24 36 69 97 125
4 10 20 30 56 76 95
5-10 9 18 27 47 61 75
11-15(1949): 12-Sparky Watts app. 8 16 24 40 50 60
V3#1,2(1952) 6 12 18 31 38 45

MICKEY MALONE
Hale Nass Corp.: 1936 (Color, punchout-c) (B&W-a on back)
nn-1pg. of comics 200 400 800 - - -

MICKEY MANTLE (See Baseball's Greatest Heroes #1)

MICKEY MOUSE (See Adventures of Mickey Mouse, The Best of Walt Disney Comics, Cheerios giveaways, Donald and ..., Dynabrite Comics, 40 Big Pages..., Gladstone Comic Album, Merry Christmas From..., Walt Disney's Mickey and Donald, Walt Disney's Comics & Stories, Walt Disney's..., & Wheaties)

MICKEY MOUSE (...Secret Agent #107-109; Walt Disney's... #148-205?)
(See Dell Giants for annuals) (#204 exists from both G.K. & Whitman)
Dell Publ. Co./Gold Key #85-204/Whitman #204-218/Gladstone #219 on:
#16, 1941 - #84, 7-9/62; #85, 11/62 - #218, 6/84; #219, 10/86 - #256, 4/90
Four Color 16(1941)-1st Mickey Mouse comic book; "...vs. the Phantom Blot" by Gottfredson 1250 2500 3750 16,000 - -
Four Color 27(1943)- "7 Colored Terror" 75 150 225 638 1294 1950
Four Color 79(1945)-By Carl Barks (1 story) 90 180 270 765 1558 2350
Four Color 116(1946) 25 50 75 183 367 550
Four Color 141,157(1947) 21 42 63 150 300 450
Four Color 170,181,194('48) 18 36 54 125 255 385
Four Color 214('49),231,248,261 14 28 42 96 191 285
Four Color 268-Reprints/WDC&S #22-24 by Gottfredson ("Surprise Visitor") 13 26 39 91 176 260
Four Color 279,286,296 11 22 33 75 138 200
Four Color 304,313(#1),325(#2),334 10 20 30 69 122 175
Four Color 343,352,362,371,387 9 18 27 60 100 140
Four Color 401,411,427(10-11/52) 7 14 21 49 80 110
Four Color 819-Mickey Mouse in Magicland 6 12 18 39 62 85
Four Color 1057,1151,1246(1959-61)-Album; #1057 has 10¢ & 12¢ editions; back covers are different 5 10 15 35 55 75
28(12-1/52-53)-32,34 6 12 18 43 69 95
33-(Exists with 2 dates, 10-11/53 & 12-1/54) 6 12 18 43 69 95
35-50 6 12 18 39 62 85
51-73,75-80 5 10 15 32 51 70
74-Story swipe "The Rare Stamp Search" from 4-Color #422- "The Gilded Man" 5 10 15 35 55 75
81-105: 93,95-titled "Mickey Mouse Club Album". 100-105: Reprint 4-Color #427,194,279, 170,343,214 in that order 4 8 12 26 41 55
106-120 3 6 9 20 30 40
121-130 3 6 9 16 23 30
131-146 3 6 9 14 20 25
147,148: 147-Reprints "The Phantom Fires" from WDC&S #200-202.148-Reprints "The Mystery of Lonely Valley" from WDC&S #208-210 3 6 9 14 20 25
149-158 2 4 6 10 14 18
159-Reprints "The Sunken City" from WDC&S #205-207 2 4 6 10 14 18
160-178: 162-165,167-170-r 2 4 6 10 14 18
179-(52 pgs.) 2 4 6 11 16 20
180-203: 200-r/Four Color #371 2 4 6 8 10 12
204-(Whitman or G.K.), 205,206 2 4 6 9 13 16
207(8/80), 209(pre-pack?) 4 8 12 26 41 55
208-(8-12/80)-Only distr. in Whitman 3-pack 9 18 27 65 113 160
210(2/81),211-214 2 4 6 9 13 16
215-218: 215(2/82), 216(4/82), 217(3/84), 218(misdated 8/82; actual date 7/84) 2 4 6 10 14 18
219-1st Gladstone issue; The Seven Ghosts serial-r begins by Gottfredson 2 4 6 11 16 20
220,221 2 3 4 6 8 10
222-225: 222-Editor-in Grief strip-r 5.00
226-230 5.00
231-243,246-254: 240-r/March of Comics #27. 245-r/F.C. #279. 250-r/F.C. #248 4.00
244 (1/89, $2.95, 100 pgs.)-Squarebound 60th anniversary issue; gives history of Mickey 5.00
245, 256: 245-r/F.C. #279. 256-$1.95, 68 pgs. 5.00
255 ($1.95, 68 pgs.) 5.00
NOTE: *Reprints #195-197, 198(2/3), 199(1/3), 200-208, 211(1/2), 212, 213, 215(1/3), 216-on.* ***Gottfredson*** *Mickey Mouse serials in #219-239, 241-244, 246-249, 251-253, 255.*
Album 01-518-210(Dell), 1(10082-309)(9/63-Gold Key) 4 8 12 22 34 45
...Club 1(1/64-Gold Key)(TV) 4 8 12 23 36 48
Mini Comic 1(1976)(3-1/4x6-1/2")-Reprints 158 1 2 3 5 6 8
Surprise Party 1(30037-901, G.K.)(1/69)-40th Anniversary (see Walt Disney Showcase #47) 3 6 9 21 32 42
Surprise Party 1(1979)-r/1969 issue 1 2 3 5 6 8

MICKEY MOUSE (Continued from Mickey Mouse and Friends)
BOOM! Studios: No. 304, Jan, 2011 - Present ($3.99)
304-307: 304-Peg-Leg Pete app. 4.00

MICKEY MOUSE ADVENTURES
Disney Comics: June, 1990 - No. 18, Nov, 1991 ($1.50)
1,8,9: 1-Bradbury, Murry-r/M.M. #45,73 plus new-a. 8-Byrne-c. 9-Fantasia 50th ann. issue w/new adapt. of movie 4.00
2-7,10-18: 2-Begin all new stories. 10-r/F.C. #214 3.00

MICKEY MOUSE AND FRIENDS (Continued from Walt Disney's Mickey Mouse and Friends)
(Title continues as Mickey Mouse #304-on)
BOOM! Studios: No. 296, Sept, 2009 - No. 303, Dec, 2010 ($2.99/$3.99)
296-299,301-303: 296-299-Wizards of Mickey stories. 301-Conclusion to story in #300 3.00
300-($3.99, 9/10) Petrucha-s/Pelaez-a; back-up Tanglefoot story w/Gottfredson-a 4.00
300 Deluxe Edition ($6.99) Variant cover by Daan Jippes 7.00

MICKEY MOUSE CLUB FUN BOOK
Golden Press: 1977 (1.95, 228 pgs.)(square bound)
11190-1950s-r; 20,000 Leagues, M. Mouse Silly Symphonys, The Reluctant Dragon, etc. 4 8 12 28 44 60

MICKEY MOUSE CLUB MAGAZINE (See Walt Disney...)

MICKEY MOUSE COMICS DIGEST
Gladstone: 1986 - No. 5, 1987 (96 pgs.)
1 ($1.25-c) 1 2 3 5 6 8
2-5: 3-5 ($1.50-c) 5.00

MICKEY MOUSE IN COLOR
Another Rainbow/Pantheon: 1988 (Deluxe, 13"x17", hard-c, $250.00)
(Trade, 9-7/8"x11-1/2", hard-c, $39.95)
Deluxe limited edition of 3,000 copies signed by Floyd Gottfredson and Carl Barks, designated as the "Official Mickey Mouse 60th Anniversary" book. Mickey Sunday and daily reprints, plus Barks "Riddle of the Red Hat" from Four Color #79. Comes with 45 r.p.m. record interview with Gottfredson and Barks. 240 pgs. 14 28 42 100 188 275
Deluxe, limited to 100 copies, as above, but with a unique colored pencil original drawing of Mickey Mouse by Carl Barks. 800.00
Pantheon trade edition, edited down & without Barks, 192 pgs. 3 6 9 20 30 40

MICKEY MOUSE MAGAZINE (Becomes Walt Disney's Comics & Stories)(Also see 40 Big Pages of Mickey Mouse)

Mickey Mouse Magazine V4 #7 © DIS

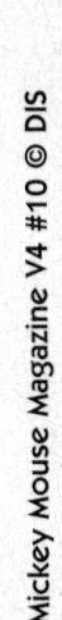
Mickey Mouse Magazine V4 #10 © DIS

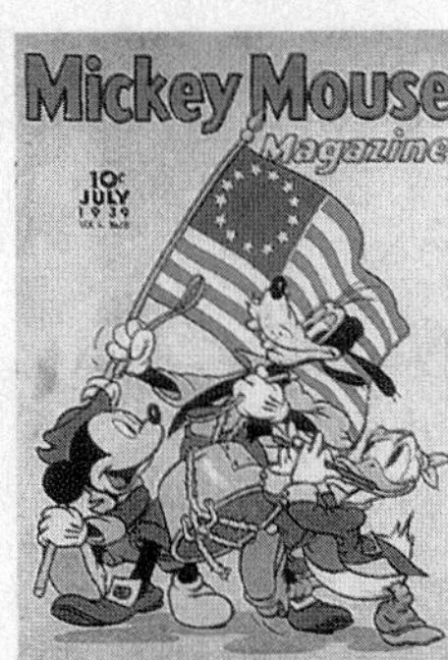

Micronauts #32 © MAR

GD 2.0 | VG 4.0 | FN 6.0 | VF 8.0 | VF/NM 9.0 | NM- 9.2

GD 2.0 | VG 4.0 | FN 6.0 | VF 8.0 | VF/NM 9.0 | NM- 9.2

K. K. Publ./Western Publishing Co.: Summer, 1935 (June-Aug, indicia) - V5#12, Sept, 1940; V1#1-5, V3#11,12, V4#1-3 are 44 pgs; V2#3-100 pgs; V5#12-68 pgs; rest are 36 pgs.(No V3#1, V4#6)

V1#1 (Large size, 13-1/4x10-1/4"; 25¢)-Contains puzzles, games, cels, stories & comics of Disney characters. Promotional magazine for Disney cartoon movies and paraphernalia 1425 2850 4275 9200 19,000 -

Note: *Some copies were autographed by the editors & given away with all early one year subscriptions.*

2 (Size change, 11-1/2x8-1/2"; 10/35; 10¢)-High quality paper begins; Messmer-a 282 564 846 2400 - -

3,4: 3-Messmer-a 153 306 459 1300 - -

5-1st Donald Duck solo-c; 2nd cover app. ever; last 44 pg. & high quality paper issue 271 542 813 2300 - -

6-9: 6-36 pg. issues begin; Donald becomes editor. 8-2nd Donald solo-c. 9-1st Mickey/Minnie-c 141 282 423 1200 - -

10-12, V2#1,2: 11-1st Pluto/Mickey-c; Donald fires himself and appoints Mickey as editor 135 270 405 1150 - -

V2#3-Special 100 pg. Christmas issue (25¢); Messmer-a; Donald becomes editor of Wise Quacks 447 894 1341 3800 - -

4-Mickey Mouse Comics & Roy Ranger (adventure strip) begin; both end V2#9; Messmer-a 115 230 345 975 - -

5-9: 5-Ted True (adventure strip, ends V2#9) & Silly Symphony Comics (ends V3#3) begin. 6-1st solo Minnie-c. 6-9-Mickey Mouse Movies cut-out in each 54 108 162 343 584 825

10-1st full color issue; Mickey Mouse (by Gottfredson; ends V3#12) & Silly Symphony (ends V3#3) full color Sunday-r, Peter The Farm Detective (ends V5#8) & Ole Of The North (ends V3#3) begins 81 162 243 518 884 1250

11-13: 12-Hiawatha-c & feature story 53 106 159 334 567 800

V3#2-Big Bad Wolf Halloween-c 60 120 180 381 653 925

3 (12/37)-1st app. Snow White & The Seven Dwarfs (before release of movie) (possibly 1st in print); Mickey X-Mas-c 107 214 321 680 1165 1650

4 (1/38)-Snow White & The Seven Dwarfs serial begins (on stands before release of movie); Ducky Symphony (ends V3#11) begins 89 178 267 565 970 1375

5-1st Snow White & Seven Dwarfs-c (St. Valentine's Day) 107 214 321 680 1165 1650

6-Snow White serial ends; Lonesome Ghosts app. (2 pp.) 60 120 180 381 658 935

7-Seven Dwarfs Easter-c 56 112 168 355 615 875

8-10: 9-Dopey-c. 10-1st solo Goofy-c 48 96 144 302 514 725

11,12 (44 pgs; 8 more pgs. color added). 11-Mickey the Sheriff serial (ends V4#3) & Donald Duck strip-r (ends V3#12) begin. Color feature on Snow White's Forest Friends 52 104 156 328 552 775

V4#1 (10/38; 44 pgs.)-Brave Little Tailor-c/feature story, nominated for Academy Award; Bobby & Chip by Otto Messmer (ends V4#2) & The Practical Pig (ends V4#2) begin 52 104 156 328 552 775

2 (44 pgs.)-1st Huey, Dewey & Louie-c 53 106 159 334 567 800

3 (12/38, 44 pgs.)-Ferdinand The Bull-c/feature story, Academy Award winner; Mickey Mouse & The Whalers serial begins, ends V4#12 52 104 156 328 552 775

4-Spotty, Mother Pluto strip-r begin, end V4#8 48 96 144 302 514 725

5-St. Valentine's day-c. 1st Pluto solo-c 54 108 162 343 584 825

7 (3/39)-The Ugly Duckling-c/feature story, Academy Award winner 52 104 156 328 552 775

7 (4/39)-Goofy & Wilbur The Grasshopper classic-c/feature story from 1st Goofy solo cartoon movie; Timid Elmer begins, ends V5#5 52 104 156 328 552 775

8-Big Bad Wolf-c from Practical Pig movie poster; Practical Pig feature story 52 104 156 328 552 775

9-Donald Duck & Mickey Mouse Sunday-r begin; The Pointer feature story, nominated for Academy Award 52 104 156 328 552 775

10-Classic July 4th drum & fife-c; last Donald Sunday-r 62 124 186 394 680 965

11-1st slick-c; last over-sized issue 48 96 144 302 514 725

12 (9/39; format change, 10-1/4x8-1/4")-1st full color, cover to cover issue; Donald's Penguin-c/feature story 55 110 165 352 601 850

V5#1-Black Pete-c; Officer Duck-c/feature story; Autograph Hound feature story; Robinson Crusoe serial begins 54 108 162 346 591 835

2-Goofy-c; 1st brief app. Pinocchio 71 142 213 454 777 1100

3 (12/39)-Pinocchio Christmas-c (Before movie release). 1st app. Jiminy Cricket; Pinocchio serial begins 84 168 252 538 919 1300

4,5: 5-Jiminy Cricket-c; Pinocchio serial ends; Donald's Dog Laundry feature story 56 112 168 348 594 840

6,7: 6-Tugboat Mickey feature story; Rip Van Winkle feature begins, ends V5#8. 7-2nd Huey, Dewey & Louie-c 54 108 162 336 573 810

8-Last magazine size issue; 2nd solo Pluto-c; Figaro & Cleo feature story 56 112 168 348 594 840

9-11: 9 (6/40; change to comic book size)-Jiminy Cricket feature story; Donald-c & Sunday-r begin. 10-Special Independence Day issue. 11-Hawaiian Holiday & Mickey's Trailer feature stories; last 36 pg. issue 60 120 180 381 653 925

12 (Format change)-The transition issue (68 pgs.) becoming a comic book. With only a title change to follow, becomes Walt Disney's Comics & Stories #1 with the next issue 465 930 1395 3395 5998 8600

NOTE: ***Otto Messmer**-a is in many issues of the first two-three years. The following story titles and issues have gags created by **Carl Barks:** V4#3(12/38)-'Donald's Better Self' & 'Donald's Golf Game;' V4#4(1/39)-'Donald's Lucky Day;' V4#7(3/39)-'Hockey Champ;' V4#7(4/39)-'Donald's Cousin Gus;' V4#9(6/39)-'Sea Scouts;' V4#12(9/39)-'Donald's Penguin;' V5#9 (6/40)-'Donald's Vacation;' V5#10(7/40)-'Bone Trouble;' V5#12(9/40)-'Window Cleaners.'*

MICKEY MOUSE MAGAZINE (Russian Version)
May 16, 1991 (1st Russian printing of a modern comic book)

1-Bagged w/gold label commemoration in English 10.00

MICKEY MOUSE MARCH OF COMICS (See March of Comics #8,27,45,60,74)

MICKEY MOUSE'S SUMMER VACATION (See Story Hour Series)

MICKEY MOUSE SUMMER FUN (See Dell Giants)

MICKEY SPILLANE'S MIKE DANGER
Tekno Comix: Sept, 1995 - No. 11, May, 1996 ($1.95)

1-11: 1-Frank Miller-c. 7-polybagged; Simonson-c. 8,9-Simonson-c 3.00

MICKEY SPILLANE'S MIKE DANGER
Big Entertainment: V2#1, June, 1996 - No. 10, Apr, 1997 ($2.25)

V2#1-10: Max Allan Collins scripts 3.00

MICKEY'S TWICE UPON A CHRISTMAS (Disney)
Gemstone Publishing: 2004 ($3.95, square-bound, one-shot)

nn-Christmas short stories with Mickey, Minnie, Donald, Uncle Scrooge, Goofy and others 4.00

MICROBOTS, THE
Gold Key: Dec, 1971 (one-shot)

1 (10271-112) 3 6 9 16 22 28

MICRONAUTS (Toys)
Marvel Comics Group: Jan, 1979 - No. 59, Aug, 1984 (Mando paper #53 on)

1-Intro/1st app. Baron Karza 1 2 3 4 5 7

2-10,35,37,57: 7-Man-Thing app. 8-1st app. Capt. Universe (8/79). 9-1st app. Cilicia. 35-Double size; origin Microverse; intro Death Squad; Dr. Strange app. 37-Nightcrawler app.; X-Men cameo (2 pgs.). 57-(52 pgs.) 4.00

11-34,36,38-56,58,59: 13-1st app. Jasmine. 15-Death of Microtron. 15-17-Fantastic Four app. 17-Death of Jasmine. 20-Ant-Man app. 21-Microverse series begins. 25-Origin Baron Karza. 25-29-Nick Fury app. 27-Death of Biotron. 34-Dr. Strange app. 38-First direct sale. 40-Fantastic Four app. 48-Early Guice-a begins. 59-Golden painted-c 3.00

nn-Blank UPC; diamond on top 3.00

Annual 1,2 (12/79,10/80)-Ditko-c/a 4.00

NOTE: *#38-on distributed only through comic shops. **N. Adams** c-7i. **Chaykin** a-13-18p. **Ditko** a-39p. **Giffen** a-36p, 37p(part). **Golden** a-1-12p; c-2-7p, 8-23, 24p, 38, 39, 59. **Guice** a-48-58p; c-49-58. **Gil Kane** a-38, 40-45p; c-40-45. **Layton** c-33-37. **Miller** c-31.*

MICRONAUTS (Micronauts: The New Voyages on cover)
Marvel Comics Group: Oct, 1984 - No. 20, May, 1986

V2#1-20 3.00

NOTE: ***Kelley Jones** a-1; c-1, 6. **Guice** a-4p; c-2p.*

MICRONAUTS
Image Comics: 2002 - No. 11, Sept, 2003 ($2.95)

2002 Convention Special (no cover price, B&W) previews series 3.00

1-11: 1-3-Hanson-a; Dave Johnson-c. 4-Su-a; 2 covers by Linsner & Hanson 3.00

...Vol. 1: Revolution (2003, $12.95, digest size) r/#1-5 13.00

MICRONAUTS (Volume 2)
Devil's Due Publishing: Mar, 2004 - No. 3, May, 2004 ($2.95)

1-3-Jolley-s/Broderick-a 3.00

MICRONAUTS: KARZA
Image Comics: Feb, 2003 - No. 4, May, 2003 ($2.95)

1-4-Krueger-s/Kurth-a 3.00

MICRONAUTS SPECIAL EDITION
Marvel Comics Group: Dec, 1983 - No. 5, Apr, 1984 ($2.00, limited series, Baxter paper)

1-5: r-/original series 1-12; Guice-c(p)-all 4.00

MIDGET COMICS (Fighting Indian Stories)
St. John Publishng Co.: Feb, 1950 - No. 2, Apr, 1950 (5-3/8x7-3/8", 68 pgs.)

Midnight Nation #5 © JM Straczynski & TCOW

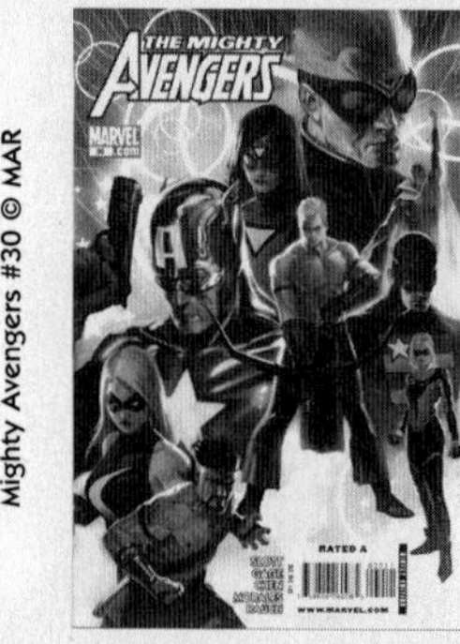
Mighty Avengers #30 © MAR

The Mighty Crusaders (2010 series) #1 © AP

GD VG FN VF VF/NM NM-
2.0 4.0 6.0 8.0 9.0 9.2

1-Fighting Indian Stories; Matt Baker-c 20 40 60 117 189 260
2-Tex West, Cowboy Marshal (also in #1) 11 22 33 62 86 110

MIDNIGHT (See Smash Comics #18)

MIDNIGHT
Ajax/Farrell Publ. (Four Star Comic Corp.): Apr, 1957 - No. 6, June, 1958
1-Reprints from Voodoo & Strange Fantasy with some changes
15 30 45 88 137 185
2-6 10 20 30 58 79 100

MIDNIGHTER (See The Authority)
DC Comics (WildStorm): Jan, 2007 - No. 20, Aug, 2008 ($2.99)
1-20: 1-Ennis-s/Sprouse-a/c. 6-Fabry-a. 7-Vaughan-s. 8-Gage-s. 9-Stelfreeze-a 3.00
1-4-Variant covers. 1-Michael Golden. 2-Art Adams 3-Jason Pearson. 4-Glenn Fabry 4.00
...: Anthem TPB (2008, $14.99) r/#7,10-15 15.00
...: Armageddon (12/07, $2.99) Gage-s/Coleby-a/McKone-c 3.00
...: Assassin8 TPB (2009, $14.99) r/#16-20 15.00
...: Killing Machine TPB (2008, $14.99) r/#1-6 15.00

MIDNIGHT MASS
DC Comics (Vertigo): Jun, 2002 - No. 8, Jan, 2003 ($2.50)
1-8-Rozum-s/Saiz & Palmiotti-a 3.00

MIDNIGHT MASS: HERE THERE BE MONSTERS
DC Comics (Vertigo): March, 2004 - No. 6, Aug, 2004 ($2.95, limited series)
1-6-Rozum-s/Paul Lee-a 3.00

MIDNIGHT MEN
Marvel Comics (Epic Comics/Heavy Hitters): June, 1993 - No. 4, Sept, 1993 ($2.50/$1.95, limited series)
1-($2.50)-Embossed-c; Chaykin-c/a & scripts in all 4.00
2-4 3.00

MIDNIGHT MYSTERY
American Comics Group: Jan-Feb, 1961 - No. 7, Oct, 1961
1-Sci/Fi story 8 16 24 58 97 135
2-7: 7-Gustavson-a 5 10 15 30 48 65
NOTE: ***Reinman*** *a-1, 3.* ***Whitney*** *a-1, 4-6; c-1-3, 5, 7.*

MIDNIGHT NATION
Image Comics (Top Cow): Oct, 2000 - No. 12, July, 2002 ($2.50/$2.95)
1-Straczynski-s/Frank-a; 2 covers 3.50
2-11: 9-Twin Towers cover 3.00
12-($2.95)Last issue 3.00
Wizard #1/2 (2001) Michael Zulli-a; two covers by Frank 3.00
Vol. 1 ('03, $29.99, TPB) r/#1-12 & Wizard #1/2; cover gallery; afterword by Straczynski 30.00

MIDNIGHT SONS UNLIMITED
Marvel Comics (Midnight Sons imprint #4 on): Apr, 1993 - No. 9, May, 1995 ($3.95, 68 pgs.)
1-9: Blaze, Darkhold (by Quesada #1), Ghost Rider, Morbius & Nightstalkers in all. 1-Painted-c. 3-Spider-Man app. 4-Siege of Darkness part 17; new Dr. Strange & new Ghost Rider app.; spot varnish-c 4.00
NOTE: ***Sears*** *a-2.*

MIDNIGHT TALES
Charlton Press: Dec, 1972 - No. 18, May, 1976
V1#1 3 6 9 16 23 30
2-10 2 4 6 10 14 18
11-18: 11-14-Newton-a(p) 2 4 6 8 11 14
12,17(Modern Comics reprint, 1977) 6.00
NOTE: ***Adkins*** *a-12i, 13i.* ***Ditko*** *a-12.* ***Howard*** *(Wood imitator) a-1-15, 17, 18; c-1-18.* ***Don Newton*** *a-11-14p.* ***Staton*** *a-1, 3-11, 13.* ***Sutton*** *a-3-10.*

MIGHTY, THE
DC Comics: Apr, 2009 - No. 12, Mar, 2010 ($2.99)
1-12: Tomasi & Champagne-s/Dave Johnson-c. 1-4-Snejbjerg-a. 5-12-Samnee-a 3.00
...: Volume 1 TPB (2009, $17.99) r/#1-6 18.00
...: Volume 2 TPB (2010, $17.99) r/#7-12 18.00

MIGHTY ATOM, THE (...& the Pixies #6) (Formerly The Pixies #1-5)
Magazine Enterprises: No. 6, 1949; Nov, 1957 - No. 6, Aug-Sept, 1958
6(1949-M.E.)-no month (1st Series) 7 14 21 35 43 50
1-6(2nd Series)-Pixies-r 4 8 12 18 22 25
I.W. Reprint #1(nd) 2 4 6 8 11 14

MIGHTY AVENGERS
Marvel Comics: May, 2007 - No. 36, Jun, 2010 ($3.99/$2.99)
1-($3.99) Iron Man, Ms. Marvel select new team; Bendis-s/Cho-a/c; Mole Man app. 5.00

GD VG FN VF VF/NM NM-
2.0 4.0 6.0 8.0 9.0 9.2

2-6-($2.99) Ultron returns 3.00
7-15: 7-Bagley-a begins; Venom on-c. 9-11-Dr. Doom app. 3.00
12-20-Secret Invasion: 12,13-Maleev-a. 15-Romita Jr.-a. 16-Elektra. 20-Wasp funeral 3.00
21-($3.99) Dark Reign; Scarlet Witch returns; new team assembled; Pham-a 4.00
22-36: 25,26-Fantastic Four app. 35,36-Siege; Ultron returns 3.00
...: Most Wanted Files (2007, $3.99) profiles of members, accomplices & adversaries 4.00
... Vol. 1: The Ultron Initiative HC (2008, $19.99) r/#1-6; variant covers and sketch art 20.00
... Vol. 2: Venom Bomb HC (2008, $19.99) r/#7-11; B&W cover art 20.00

MIGHTY BEAR (Formerly Fun Comics; becomes Unsane #15)
Star Publ. No. 13,14/Ajax-Farrell (Four Star): No. 13, Jan, 1954 - No. 14, Mar, 1954; 9/57 - No. 3, 2/58
13,14-L. B. Cole-c 18 36 54 103 162 220
1-3('57-58)Four Star; becomes Mighty Ghost #4 7 14 21 35 43 50

MIGHTY COMICS (...Presents) (Formerly Flyman)
Radio Comics (Archie): No. 40, Nov, 1966 - No. 50, Oct, 1967 (All 12¢ issues)
40-Web 5 10 15 30 48 65
41-50: 41-Shield, Black Hood. 42-Black Hood. 43-Shield, Web & Black Hood. 44-Black Hood, Steel Sterling & The Shield. 45-Shield & Hangman; origin Web retold. 46-Steel Sterling, Web & Black Hood. 47-Black Hood & Mr. Justice. 48-Shield & Hangman; Wizard x-over in Shield. 49-Steel Sterling & Fox; Black Hood x-over in Steel Sterling. 50-Black Hood & Web; Inferno x-over in Web 4 8 12 28 44 60
NOTE: ***Paul Reinman*** *a-40-50.*

MIGHTY CRUSADERS, THE (Also see Adventures of the Fly, The Crusaders & Fly Man)
Mighty Comics Group (Radio Comics): Nov, 1965 - No. 7, Oct, 1966 (All 12¢)
1-Origin The Shield 7 14 21 49 80 110
2-Origin Comet 4 8 12 28 44 60
3,5-7: 3-Origin Fly-Man. 5-Intro. Ultra-Men (Fox, Web, Capt. Flag) & Terrific Three (Jaguar, Mr. Justice, Steel Sterling). 7-Steel Sterling feature; origin Fly-Girl
4 8 12 26 41 55
4-1st S.A. app. Fireball, Inferno & Fox; Firefly, Web, Bob Phantom, Blackjack, Hangman, Zambini, Kardak, Steel Sterling, Mr. Justice, Wizard, Capt. Flag, Jaguar x-over
4 8 12 28 44 60
Volume 1: Origin of a Super Team TPB (2003, $12.95) r/#1 & Fly Man #31-33 13.00
NOTE: ***Reinman*** *a-6.*

MIGHTY CRUSADERS, THE (All New Advs. of...#2)
Red Circle Prod./Archie Ent. No. 6 on: Mar, 1983 - No. 13, Sept, 1985 ($1.00, 36 pgs, Mando paper)
1-Origin Black Hood, The Fly, Fly Girl, The Shield, The Wizard, The Jaguar, Pvt. Strong & The Web. 1 2 3 4 5 7
2-10: 2-Mister Midnight begins. 4-Darkling replaces Shield. 5-Origin Jaguar, Shield begins. 7-Untold origin Jaguar. 10-Veitch-a 5.00
11-13-Lower print run 6.00
NOTE: ***Buckler*** *a-1-3, 4i, 5p, 7p, 8i, 9i; c-1-10p.*

MIGHTY CRUSADERS, THE (Also see The Shield, The Web and The Red Circle)
DC Comics: Sept, 2010 - No. 6, Feb, 2011 ($3.99, limited series)
1-6-The Shield, The Web, Fly-Girl, Inferno, War Eagle & The Comet team-up 4.00
... Special 1 (7/10, $4.99) Prequel to series; Pina-a/Lau-c 5.00

MIGHTY GHOST (Formerly Mighty Bear #1-3)
Ajax/Farrell Publ.: No. 4, June, 1958
4 7 14 21 35 43 50

MIGHTY HERCULES, THE (TV)
Gold Key: July, 1963 - No. 2, Nov, 1963
1 (10072-307) 13 26 39 89 170 255
2 (10072-311) 12 24 36 87 164 240

MIGHTY HEROES, THE (TV) (Funny)
Dell Publishing Co.: Mar, 1967 - No. 4, July, 1967
1-Also has a 1957 Heckle & Jeckle-r 11 22 33 75 138 200
2-4: 4-Has two 1958 Mighty Mouse-r 8 16 24 52 86 120

MIGHTY HEROES
Spotlight Comics: 1987 (B&W, one-shot)
1-Heckle & Jeckle backup 5.00

MIGHTY HEROES
Marvel Comics: Jan, 1998 ($2.99, one-shot)
1-Origin of the Mighty Heroes 3.00

MIGHTY LOVE
DC Comics: 2003 ($24.99/$17.95, graphic novel)
HC-($24.95) Howard Chaykin-s/a; intro. Skylark and the Iron Angel 25.00

Mighty Marvel Western #1 © MAR

Mighty Mouse #72 © Viacom

Mighty Samson #1 © RH

GD VG FN VF VF/NM NM-
2.0 4.0 6.0 8.0 9.0 9.2

SC-($17.95) 18.00

MIGHTY MAN (From Savage Dragon titles)
Image Comics: Dec, 2004 ($7.95, one-shot)

1-Reprints seriaizedl back-up from Savage Dragon #109-118 8.00

MIGHTY MARVEL TEAM-UP THRILLERS
Marvel Comics: 1983 ($5.95, trade paperback)

1-Reprints team-up stories 3 6 9 19 29 38

MIGHTY MARVEL WESTERN, THE
Marvel Comics Group (LMC earlier issues): Oct, 1968 - No. 46, Sept, 1976 (#1-14: 68 pgs.; #15,16: 52 pgs.)

1-Begin Kid Colt, Rawhide Kid, Two-Gun Kid-r 6 12 18 37 59 80
2-5: (2-14 are 68 pgs.) 4 8 12 26 41 55
6-16: (15,16 are 52 pgs.) 4 8 12 22 34 45
17-20 2 4 6 13 18 22
21-30,32,37: 24-Kid Colt-r end. 25-Matt Slade-r begin. 32-Origin-r/Rawhide Kid #23; Williamson-r/Kid Slade #7. 37-Williamson, Kirby-r/Two-Gun Kid 51
2 4 6 9 13 16
31,33-36,38-46: 31-Baker-r. 2 4 6 8 11 14
45-(30¢-c variant, limited distribution)(6/76) 4 8 12 26 41 55

NOTE: ***Jack Davis** a(r)-21-24. **Keller** r-1-13, 22. **Kirby** a(r)-1-3, 6, 9, 12-14, 16, 25-29, 32-38, 40, 41, 43-46; c-29. **Maneely** a(r)-22. **Severin** c-3i, 9. No Matt Slade-#43.*

MIGHTY MIDGET COMICS, THE (Miniature)
Samuel E. Lowe & Co.: No date; circa 1942-1943 (Sold 2 for 5¢, B&W and red, 36 pgs, approx. 5x4")

Bulletman #11(1943)-r/cover/Bulletman #3 16 32 48 94 147 200
Captain Marvel Adventures #11 16 32 48 94 147 200
Captain Marvel #11 (Same as above except for full color ad on back cover; this issue was glued to cover of Captain Marvel #20 and is not found in fine-mint condition)
340 680 1020 - - -
Captain Marvel Jr. #11 (Same-c as Master #27 16 32 48 94 147 200
Captain Marvel Jr. #11 (Same as above except for full color ad on back-c; this issue was glued to cover of Captain Marvel #21 and is not found in fine-mint condition)
340 680 1020 - - -
Golden Arrow #11 15 30 45 86 133 180
Golden Arrow #11 (Same as above except for full color ad on back-c; this issue was glued to cover of Captain Marvel #21 and is not found in fine-mint condition)
280 560 840 - - -
Ibis the Invincible #11(1942)-Origin; reprints cover to Ibis #1 (Predates Fawcett's Ibis the Invincible #1). 16 32 48 94 147 200
Spy Smasher #11(1942) 16 32 48 94 147 200

NOTE: *The above books came in a box called "box full of books" and was distributed with other Samuel Lowe puzzles, paper dolls, coloring books, etc. They are not titled Mighty Midget Comics. All have a war bond seal on back cover which is otherwise blank. These books came in a "Mighty Midget" flat cardboard counter display rack.*

Balbo, the Boy Magician #12 (1943)-1st book devoted entirely to character.
10 20 30 54 72 90
Bulletman #12 12 24 36 69 97 125
Commando Yank #12 (1943)-Only comic devoted entirely to character.
10 20 30 56 76 95
Dr. Voltz the Human Generator (1943)-Only comic devoted entirely to character.
10 20 30 54 72 90
Lance O'Casey #12 (1943)-1st comic devoted entirely to character (Predates Fawcett's Lance O'Casey #1). 10 20 30 54 72 90
Leatherneck the Marine (1943)-Only comic devoted entirely to character.
10 20 30 54 72 90
Minute Man #12 12 24 36 67 94 120
Mister "Q" (1943)-Only comic devoted entirely to character.
10 20 30 54 72 90
Mr. Scarlet and Pinky #12 (1943)-Only comic devoted entirely to character.
10 20 30 58 79 100
Pat Wilton and His Flying Fortress (1943)-1st comic devoted entirely to character. 10 20 30 54 72 90
The Phantom Eagle #12 (1943)-Only comic devoted entirely to character.
10 20 30 54 72 90
State Trooper Stops Crime (1943)-Only comic devoted entirely to character.
10 20 30 54 72 90
Tornado Tom (1943)-Origin, r/from Cyclone #1-3; only comic devoted entirely to character.
10 20 30 54 72 90

MIGHTY MORPHIN' POWER RANGERS: THE MOVIE (Also see Saban's Mighty Morphin' Power Rangers)
Marvel Comics: Sept, 1995 ($3.95, one-shot)

nn-Adaptation of movie 4.00

MIGHTY MOUSE (See Adventures of..., Dell Giant #43, Giant Comics Edition, March of Comics #205, 237, 247, 257, 447, 459, 471, 483, Oxydol-Dreft, Paul Terry's, & Terry-Toons Comics)

MIGHTY MOUSE (1st Series)
Timely/Marvel Comics (20th Century Fox): Fall, 1946 - No. 4, Summer, 1947

1 181 362 543 1158 1979 2800
2 69 138 207 442 759 1075
3,4 43 86 129 271 461 650

MIGHTY MOUSE (2nd Series) (Paul Terry's... #62-71)
St. John Publishing Co./Pines No. 68 (3/56) on (TV issues #72 on): Aug, 1947 - No. 67, 11/55; No. 68, 3/56 - No. 83, 6/59

5(#1) 39 78 117 240 395 550
6-10: 10-Over-sized issue 20 40 60 117 189 260
11-19 14 28 42 80 115 150
20 (11/50) - 25-(52 pg. editions) 11 22 33 62 86 110
20-25-(36 pg. editions) 10 20 30 54 72 90
26-37: 35-Flying saucer-c 9 18 27 50 65 80
38-45-(100 pgs.) 18 36 54 107 169 230
46-83: 62-64,67-Painted-c. 82-Infinity-c 9 18 27 47 61 75
Album nn (nd, 1952/53?, St. John)(100 pgs.)(Rebound issues w/new cover)
22 44 66 128 209 290
Album 1(10/52, 25¢, 100 pgs., St. John)-Gandy Goose app.
28 56 84 165 270 375
Album 2,3(11/52 & 12/52, St. John) (100 pgs.) 22 44 66 128 209 290
Fun Club Magazine 1(Fall, 1957-Pines, 25¢, 100 pgs.) (CBS TV)-Tom Terrific, Heckle & Jeckle, Dinky Duck, Gandy Goose 15 30 45 90 140 190
Fun Club Magazine 2-6(Winter, 1958-Pines) 11 22 33 62 86 110
3-D 1-(1st printing-9/53, 25¢)(St. John)-Came w/glasses; stiff covers; says World's First! on-c; 1st 3-D comic 28 56 84 165 270 375
3-D 1-(2nd printing-10/53, 25¢)-Came w/glasses; slick, glossy covers, slightly smaller
20 40 60 114 182 250
3-D 2,3(11/53, 12/53, 25¢)-(St. John)-With glasses 20 40 60 114 182 250

MIGHTY MOUSE (TV)(3rd Series)(Formerly Adventures of Mighty Mouse)
Gold Key/Dell Publ. Co. No. 166-on: No. 161, Oct, 1964 - No. 172, Oct, 1968

161(10/64)-165(9/65)-(Becomes Adventures of... No. 166 on)
5 10 15 30 48 65
166(3/66), 167(6/66)-172 3 6 9 21 32 42

MIGHTY MOUSE (TV)
Spotlight Comics: 1987 - No. 2, 1987 ($1.50, color)

1,2-New stories 4.00
...And Friends Holiday Special (11/87, $1.75) 4.00

MIGHTY MOUSE (TV)
Marvel Comics: Oct, 1990 - No. 10, July, 1991 ($1.00)(Based on Sat. cartoon)

1-10: 1-Dark Knight-c parody. 2-10: 3-Intro Bat-Bat; Byrne-c. 4,5-Crisis-c/story parodies w/Perez-c. 6-Spider-Man-c parody. 7-Origin Bat-Bat 3.00

MIGHTY MOUSE ADVENTURE MAGAZINE
Spotlight Comics: 1987 ($2.00, B&W, 52 pgs., magazine size, one-shot)

1-Deputy Dawg, Heckle & Jeckle backup stories 5.00

MIGHTY MOUSE ADVENTURES (Adventures of... #2 on)
St. John Publishing Co.: November, 1951

1 36 72 108 211 343 475

MIGHTY MOUSE ADVENTURE STORIES (Paul Terry's... on-c only)
St. John Publishing Co.: 1953 (50¢, 384 pgs.)

nn-Rebound issues 47 94 141 296 498 700

MIGHTY MUTANIMALS (See Teenage Mutant Ninja Turtles Adventures #19)
May, 1991 - No. 3, July, 1991 ($1.00, limited series)
Archie Comics: Apr, 1992 - No. 8, June, 1993 ($1.25)

1-3: 1-Story cont'd from TMNT Advs. #19. 6.00
1-4 (1992) 6.00
5-8: 7-1st app. Merdude 1 2 3 5 7 9

MIGHTY SAMSON (Also see Gold Key Champion)
Gold Key/Whitman #32: July, 1964 - No. 20, Nov, 1969; No. 21, Aug, 1972; No. 22, Dec, 1973 - No. 31, Mar, 1976; No. 32, Aug, 1982 (Painted-c #1-31)

1-Origin/1st app.; Thorne-a begins 8 16 24 54 90 125
2-5 5 10 15 30 48 65
6-10: 7-Tom Morrow begins, ends #20 3 6 9 20 30 40
11-20 3 6 9 16 23 30
21-31: 21,22-r 2 4 6 11 16 20
32(Whitman, 8/82)-r 2 4 6 8 10 12

The Mighty Thor #1 © MAR

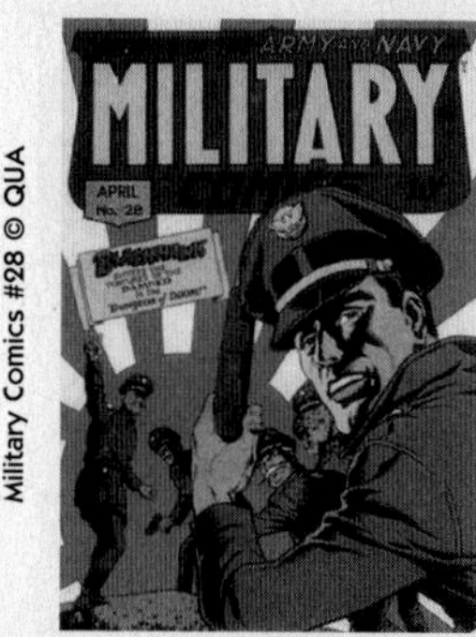

Military Comics #28 © QUA

Millie the Model #135 © MAR

MIGHTY SAMSON
Dark Horse Comics: Dec, 2010 - Present ($3.50)

	GD 2.0	VG 4.0	FN 6.0	VF 8.0	VF/NM 9.0	NM- 9.2
1-Origin retold; Shooter & Vaughn-s/Olliffe-a/Swanland-c; reprints 1st app. from 1964						3.50
1-Variant-c by Olliffe						6.00

MIGHTY THOR, THE
Marvel Comics: Jun, 2011 - Present ($3.99)

	GD 2.0	VG 4.0	FN 6.0	VF 8.0	VF/NM 9.0	NM- 9.2
1-Fraction-s/Coipel-a; Silver Surfer app.' bonus concept art from the movie						4.00
1-Variant-c by Charest						6.00
1-Variant-c by Simonson						10.00

MIKE BARNETT, MAN AGAINST CRIME (TV)
Fawcett Publications: Dec, 1951 - No. 6, Oct, 1952

	GD 2.0	VG 4.0	FN 6.0	VF 8.0	VF/NM 9.0	NM- 9.2
1	19	38	57	111	176	240
2	13	26	39	74	105	135
3,4,6	11	22	33	60	83	105
5- "Market for Morphine" cover/story	14	28	42	82	121	160

MIKE DANGER (See Mickey Spillane's...)

MIKE DEODATO'S...
Caliber Comics: 1996, ($2.95, B&W)

	GD 2.0	VG 4.0	FN 6.0	VF 8.0	VF/NM 9.0	NM- 9.2
...FALLOUT 3000 #1, **...JONAS** (mag. size) #1,**...PRIME CUTS** (mag. size) #1, **...PROTHEUS** #1,2, **...RAMTHAR** #1,**...RAZOR NIGHTS** #1						3.00

MIKE GRELL'S SABLE (Also see Jon Sable & Sable)
First Comics: Mar, 1990 - No. 10, Dec, 1990 ($1.75)

	GD 2.0	VG 4.0	FN 6.0	VF 8.0	VF/NM 9.0	NM- 9.2
1-10: r/Jon Sable Freelance #1-10 by Grell						3.00

MIKE MIST MINUTE MIST-ERIES (See Ms. Tree/Mike Mist in 3-D)
Eclipse Comics: April, 1981 ($1.25, B&W, one-shot)

	GD 2.0	VG 4.0	FN 6.0	VF 8.0	VF/NM 9.0	NM- 9.2
1						3.00

MIKE SHAYNE PRIVATE EYE
Dell Publishing Co.: Nov-Jan, 1962 - No. 3, Sept-Nov, 1962

	GD 2.0	VG 4.0	FN 6.0	VF 8.0	VF/NM 9.0	NM- 9.2
1	4	8	12	24	37	50
2,3	3	6	9	17	25	32

MILESTONE FOREVER
DC Comics: Apr, 2010 - No. 2, May, 2010 ($5.99, squarebound, limited series)

	GD 2.0	VG 4.0	FN 6.0	VF 8.0	VF/NM 9.0	NM- 9.2
1,2-McDuffie-s/Leon & Bright-a; Icon, Blood Syndicate, Hardware and Static app.						6.00

MILITARY COMICS (Becomes Modern Comics #44 on)
Quality Comics Group: Aug, 1941 - No. 43, Oct, 1945

	GD 2.0	VG 4.0	FN 6.0	VF 8.0	VF/NM 9.0	NM- 9.2
1-Origin/1st app. Blackhawk by C. Cuidera (Eisner scripts); Miss America, The Death Patrol by Jack Cole (also #2-7,27-30), & The Blue Tracer by Guardineer; X of the Underground, The Yankee Eagle, Q-Boat & Shot & Shell, Archie Atkins, Loops & Banks by Bud Ernest (Bob Powell)(ends #13) begin	568	1136	1704	4146	7323	10,500
2-Secret War News begins (by McWilliams #2-16); Cole-a; new uniform with yellow circle & hawk's head for Blackhawk	174	348	522	1114	1907	2700
3-Origin/1st app. Chop Chop (9/41)	155	310	465	992	1696	2400
4	123	246	369	787	1344	1900
5-The Sniper begins; Miss America in costume #4-7	103	206	309	659	1130	1600
6-9: 8-X of the Underground begins (ends #13). 9-The Phantom Clipper begins (ends #16)	71	142	213	454	777	1100
10-Classic Eisner-c	90	180	270	576	988	1400
11-Flag-c	68	136	204	435	743	1050
12-Blackhawk by Crandall begins, ends #22	71	142	213	454	777	1100
13-15: 14-Private Dogtag begins (ends #83)	58	116	174	371	636	900
16-20: 16-Blue Tracer ends. 17-P.T. Boat begins	53	106	159	334	567	800
21-31: 22-Last Crandall Blackhawk. 23-Shrunken head-c. 27-Death Patrol revived	47	94	141	296	498	700
32-43	41	82	123	256	428	600

NOTE: *Berg a-6.* ***Al Bryant*** *c-31-34, 38, 40-43.* ***J. Cole*** *a-1-3, 27-32.* ***Crandall*** *a-12-22; c-13-20.* ***Cuidera*** *c-2-9.* ***Eisner*** *c-1, 2(part), 9, 10.* ***Kotsky*** *c-21-29, 35, 37, 39.* ***McWilliams*** *a-2-16.* ***Powell*** *a-1-13.* ***Ward*** *Blackhawk-30, 31(15 pgs. each); c-30.*

MILK AND CHEESE (Also see Cerebus Bi-Weekly #20)
Slave Labor: 1991 - Present ($2.50, B&W)

	GD 2.0	VG 4.0	FN 6.0	VF 8.0	VF/NM 9.0	NM- 9.2
1-Evan Dorkin story & art in all	4	8	12	24	37	50
1-2nd-6th printings						4.00
2-"Other #1"	3	6	9	16	23	30
2-reprint						3.00
3-"Third #1"	2	4	6	11	16	20
4-"Fourth #1", 5-"First Second Issue"	1	3	4	6	8	10
6,7: 6-"#666"						5.00

NOTE: *Multiple printings of all issues exist and are worth cover price unless listed here.*

MILKMAN MURDERS, THE
Dark Horse Comics: Jun, 2004 - No. 4, Aug, 2004 ($2.99, limited series)

	GD 2.0	VG 4.0	FN 6.0	VF 8.0	VF/NM 9.0	NM- 9.2
1-4-Casey-s/Parkhouse-a						3.00

MILLENNIUM
DC Comics: Jan, 1988 - No. 8, Feb, 1988 (Weekly limited series)

	GD 2.0	VG 4.0	FN 6.0	VF 8.0	VF/NM 9.0	NM- 9.2
1-Englehart-s/Staton c/a(p)						4.00
2-8						3.00
TPB (2008, $19.99) r/#1-8						20.00

MILLENNIUM EDITION:... (Reprints of classic DC issues)
DC Comics: Feb, 2000 - Feb, 2001 (gold foil cover stamps)

	GD 2.0	VG 4.0	FN 6.0	VF 8.0	VF/NM 9.0	NM- 9.2
Action Comics #1, Adventure Comics #61, All Star Comics #3, All Star Comics #8, Batman #1, Detective Comics #1, Detective Comics #27, Detective Comics #38, Flash Comics #1, Military Comics #1, More Fun Comics #73, Police Comics #1, Sensation Comics #1, Superman #1, Whiz Comics #2, Wonder Woman #1 -($3.95-c)						4.00
Action Comics #252, Adventure Comics #247, Brave and the Bold #28, Brave and the Bold #85, Crisis on Infinte Earths #1, Detective #225, Detective #327, Detective #359, Detective #395, Flash #123, Gen13 #1, Green Lantern #76, House of Mystery #1, House of Secrets #92, JLA #1, Justice League #1, Mad #1, Man of Steel #1, Mysterious Suspense #1, New Gods, #1, New Teen Titans #1, Our Army at War #81, Plop! #1, Saga of the Swamp Thing #21, Shadow #1, Showcase #4, Showcase #9, Showcase #22, Superman #233, Superman (2nd) #75, Superman's Pal Jimmy Olsen #1, Watchmen #1, WildC.A.T.s #1, Wonder Woman (2nd) #1, World's Finest #71 -($2.50-c)						3.00
All-Star Western #10, Hellblazer #1, More Fun Comics #101, Preacher #1, Sandman #1, Spirit #1, Superboy #1, Superman #76, Young Romance #1-($2.95-c)						3.00
Batman: The Dark Knight Returns #1, Kingdom Come #1 -($5.95-c)						6.00
All Star Comics #3, Batman #1, Justice League #1: Chromium cover						10.00
Crisis on Infinite Earths #1 Chromium cover						20.00

MILLENNIUM FEVER
DC Comics (Vertigo): Oct, 1995 - No.4, Jan, 1996 ($2.50, limited series)

	GD 2.0	VG 4.0	FN 6.0	VF 8.0	VF/NM 9.0	NM- 9.2
1-4: Duncan Fegredo-c/a						3.00

MILLENNIUM INDEX
Independent Comics Group: Mar, 1988 - No. 2, Mar, 1988 ($2.00)

	GD 2.0	VG 4.0	FN 6.0	VF 8.0	VF/NM 9.0	NM- 9.2
1,2						3.00

MILLENNIUM 2.5 A.D.
ACG Comics: No. 1, 2000 ($2.95)

	GD 2.0	VG 4.0	FN 6.0	VF 8.0	VF/NM 9.0	NM- 9.2
1-Reprints 1934 Buck Rogers daily strips #1-48						3.00

MILLIE, THE LOVABLE MONSTER
Dell Publishing Co.: Sept-Nov, 1962 - No. 6, Jan, 1973

	GD 2.0	VG 4.0	FN 6.0	VF 8.0	VF/NM 9.0	NM- 9.2
12-523-211-Bill Woggon c/a in all	5	10	15	34	55	75
2(8-10/63)	5	10	15	30	48	65
3(8-10/64)	4	8	12	26	41	55
4(7/72), 5(10/72), 6(1/73)	3	6	9	14	19	24

NOTE: ***Woggon*** *a-3-6; c-3-6. 4 reprints 1; 5 reprints 2; 6 reprints 3.*

MILLIE THE MODEL (See Comedy Comics, A Date With..., Joker Comics #28, Life With..., Mad About..., Marvel Mini-Books, Misty & Modeling With...)
Marvel/Atlas/Marvel Comics(CnPC #1)(SPI/Male/VPI):1945 - No. 207, Dec, 1973

	GD 2.0	VG 4.0	FN 6.0	VF 8.0	VF/NM 9.0	NM- 9.2
1-Origin	100	200	300	635	1093	1550
2 (10/46)-Millie becomes The Blonde Phantom to sell Blonde Phantom perfume; a pre-Blonde Phantom app. (see All-Select #11, Fall, 1946)	45	90	135	284	480	675
3-8,10: 4-7-Willie app. 7-Willie smokes extra strong tobacco. 8,10-Kurtzman's "Hey Look". 8-Willie & Rusty app.	36	72	108	211	343	475
9-Powerhouse Pepper by Wolverton, 4 pgs.	37	74	111	222	361	500
11-Kurtzman-a, "Giggles 'n' Grins"	21	42	63	126	206	285
12,15,17,19,20: 12-Rusty & Hedy Devine app.	18	36	54	107	169	230
13,14,16,18: 13,14,16-Kurtzman's "Hey Look". 13-Hedy Devine app. 18-Dan DeCarlo-a begins	19	38	57	111	176	240
21-30	14	28	42	82	121	160
31-40	8	16	24	58	97	135
41-60	7	14	21	47	76	105
61-99	6	12	18	39	62	85
100	6	12	18	43	69	95
101-106,108-130	5	10	15	35	55	75
107-Jack Kirby app. in story	6	12	18	39	62	85
131-134,136,138-153: 141-Groovy Gears-c/s	4	8	12	28	44	60
135-(2/66) 1st app. Groovy Gears	5	10	15	35	55	75
137-2nd app. Groovy Gears	5	10	15	30	48	65
154-New Millie begins (10/67)	6	12	18	43	69	95
155-190	4	8	12	28	44	60

Mindfield #0 © Aspen MLT

Miracleman #1 © ECL

Miss America Comics #1 © MAR

	GD 2.0	VG 4.0	FN 6.0	VF 8.0	VF/NM 9.0	NM- 9.2
191,193-199,201-206	4	8	12	24	37	50
192-(52 pgs.)	4	8	12	28	44	60
200,207(Last issue)	4	8	12	28	44	60
(Beware: cut-up pages are common in all Annuals)						
Annual 1(1962)-Early Marvel annual (2nd?)	18	36	54	131	266	400
Annual 2(1963)	13	26	39	89	170	250
Annual 3-5 (1964-1966)	9	18	27	63	107	150
Annual 6-10(1967-11/71)	7	14	21	49	80	110
Queen-Size 11(9/74), 12(1975)	6	12	18	43	69	95

NOTE: ***Dan DeCarlo*** *a-18-93.*

MILLION DOLLAR DIGEST (Richie Rich... #23 on; also see Richie Rich...)
Harvey Publications: 11/86 - No. 7, 11/87; No. 8, 4/88 - No. 34, Nov, 1994 ($1.25/$1.75, digest size)

1	1	2	3	5	6	8
2-8: 8-(68 pgs.)						6.00
9-20: 9-Begin $1.75-c. 14-May not exist	1	2	3	4	5	7
21-34	1	3	4	6	8	10

MILT GROSS FUNNIES (Also see Picture News #1)
Milt Gross, Inc. (ACG?): Aug, 1947 - No. 2, Sept, 1947

1	22	44	66	128	209	290
2	15	30	45	88	137	185

MILTON THE MONSTER & FEARLESS FLY (TV)
Gold Key: May, 1966

1 (10175-605)	9	18	27	63	107	150

MINDFIELD
Aspen MLT: No. 0, May, 2010 - No. 6 ($2.50/$2.99)

0-($2.50) Krul-s/Konat-a; 3 covers						2.50
1-5-($2.99) Multiples covers on each						3.00

MINIMUM WAGE
Fantagraphics Books: V1#1, July, 1995 ($9.95, B&W, graphic novel, mature)
V2#1, 1995 - Present ($2.95, B&W, mature)

V1#1-Bob Fingerman story & art	1	3	4	6	8	10
V2#1-9($2.95): Bob Fingerman story & art. 2-Kevin Nowlan back-c. 4-w/pin-ups. 5-Mignola back-c						3.00
Book Two TPB ('97, $12.95) r/V2#1-5						13.00

MINISTRY OF SPACE
Image Comics: Apr, 2001 - No. 3, Apr, 2004 ($2.95, limited series)

1-3-Warren Ellis-s/Chris Weston-a						3.00
...Vol. 1 Omnibus (3/04, $4.95) r/1&2						5.00
TPB (12/04, $12.95) r/series; sketch & design pages; intro by Mark Millar						13.00

MINOR MIRACLES
DC Comics: 2000 ($12.95, B&W, squarebound)

nn-Will Eisner-s/a						13.00

MINUTE MAN (See Master Comics & Mighty Midget Comics)
Fawcett Publications: Summer, 1941 - No. 3, Spring, 1942 (68 pgs.)

1	213	426	639	1363	2332	3300
2,3: 2-Japanese WWII-c	123	246	369	787	1344	1900

MINX, THE
DC Comics (Vertigo): Oct, 1998 - No. 8, May, 1999 ($2.50, limited series)

1-8-Milligan-s/Phillips-c/a						3.00

MIRACLE COMICS
Hillman Periodicals: Feb, 1940 - No. 4, Mar, 1941

1-Sky Wizard Master of Space, Dash Dixon, Man of Might, Pinkie Parker, Dusty Doyle, The Kid Cop, K-7, Secret Agent, The Scorpion, & Blandu, Jungle Queen begin; Masked Angel only app. (all 1st app.)	194	388	582	1242	2121	3000
2	97	194	291	621	1061	1500
3,4: 3-Bill Colt, the Ghost Rider begins. 4-The Veiled Prophet & Bullet Bob (by Burnley) app.	82	164	246	528	902	1275

MIRACLEMAN
Eclipse Comics: Aug, 1985 - No. 15, Nov, 1988; No. 16, Dec, 1989 - No. 24, Aug, 1993

1-r/British Marvelman series; Alan Moore scripts in #1-16	2	3	4	6	8	10
1-Gold variant (edition of 400, signed by Alan Moore, came with signed & #'d certificate of authenticity)	58	116	174	493	997	1500
1-Blue variant (edition of 600, came with signed certificate of authenticity)	35	70	105	273	537	800
2-10: 8-Airboy preview. 6,9,10-Origin Miracleman. 9-Shows graphic scenes of childbirth. 10-Snyder-c	1	2	3	5	6	8
11-14(5/87-4/88) Totleben-a	2	4	6	11	16	20
15-($1.75-c, scarce) end of Kid Miracleman	6	12	18	41	66	90
16-Last Alan Moore-s; 1st $1.95-c (low print)	3	6	9	16	23	30
17-22: 17-"The Golden Age" begins, ends #22. Dave McKean-c begins, end #22; Neil Gaiman scripts in #17-24	2	4	6	10	14	18
23-"The Silver Age" begins; Barry W. Smith-c	2	4	6	11	16	20
24-Last issue; Smith-c	3	6	9	14	20	25
3-D #1 (12/85)	1	2	3	5	7	9
3-D #1 Blue variant (edition of 99)	3	6	9	16	23	30
3-D #1 Gold variant (edition of 199)	2	4	6	11	16	20

NOTE: *Miracleman 3-D #1 (12/85) (2D edition) Interior is the same as the 3-D version except in non 3-D format. Indicia are the same for both versions of the book with only the non 3-D art distinguishing this book from the standard 3-D version. Standard 3-D edition has house ad mentioning the non 3-D edition. Two known copies exist, one in the Michigan State University Special Collection Department. (No known sales)*

Book One: A Dream of Flying (1988, $9.95, TPB) r/#1-5; Leach-c	22.00
Book One: A Dream of Flying-Hardcover (1988, $29.95) r/#1-5	70.00
Book Two: The Red King Syndrome (1990, $12.95, TPB) r/#6-10; Bolton-c	30.00
Book Two: The Red King Syndrome-Hardcover (1990, $30.95) r/#6-10	85.00
Book Three: Olympus (1990, $12.95, TPB) r/#11-16	130.00
Book Three: Olympus-Hardcover (1990, $30.95) r/#11-16	250.00
Book Four: The Golden Age (1992, $15.95, TPB) r/#17-22	30.00
Book Four: The Golden Age Hardcover (1992, $33.95) r/#17-22	50.00
Book Four: The Golden Age (1993, $12.99, TPB) new McKean-c	15.00

NOTE: *Eclipse archive copies exist for #4,5,8,17,23. Each has a small Miracleman image foil-stamped on the cover.* ***Chaykin*** *c-3.* ***Gulacy*** *c-7.* ***McKean*** *c-17-22.* ***B. Smith*** *c-23, 24.* ***Starlin*** *c-4.* ***Totleben*** *a-11-13; c-9, 11-13.* ***Truman*** *c-6.*

MIRACLEMAN: APOCRYPHA
Eclipse Comics: Nov, 1991 - No. 3, Feb, 1992 ($2.50, limited series)

1-3: 1-Stories by Neil Gaiman, Mark Buckingham, Alex Ross & others. 3-Stories by James Robinson, Kelley Jones, Matt Wagner, Neil Gaiman, Mark Buckingham & others	1	2	3	4	5	7
TPB (12/92, $15.95) r/#1-3; Buckingham-c						20.00

MIRACLEMAN FAMILY
Eclipse Comics: May, 1988 - No. 2, Sept, 1988 ($1.95, lim. series, Baxter paper)

1,2: 2-Gulacy-c						5.00

MIRACLE OF THE WHITE STALLIONS, THE (See Movie Comics)

MIRROR'S EDGE (Based on the EA video game)
DC Comics (WildStorm): Dec, 2008 - No. 6, Jun, 2009 ($3.99, limited series)

1-6: 1-Origin of Faith; Rhianna Pratchett-s/Matthew Dow Smith-a						4.00
TPB (2009, $19.99) r/#1-6						20.00

MISADVENTURES OF MERLIN JONES, THE (See Movie Comics & Merlin Jones as the Monkey's Uncle under Movie Comics)

MISPLACED
Image Comics: May, 2003 - No. 4, Dec, 2004 ($2.95)

1-4: 1-Three covers by Blaylock, Green and Clugston-Major; Blaylock-s/a						3.00
... @17 (12/04, $4.95) Nara from "Dead @17 " app.; Blaylock-s/a						5.00

MISS AMERICA COMICS (Miss America Magazine #2 on; also see Blonde Phantom & Marvel Mystery Comics)
Marvel Comics (20CC): 1944 (one-shot)

1-2 pgs. pin-ups	194	388	582	1242	2121	3000

MISS AMERICA COMICS 70th ANNIVERARY SPECIAL
Marvel Comics: Aug, 2009 ($3.99, one-shot)

1-Eaglesham-c; new Miss America & Whizzer story; reps. from All Winners #9-11						4.00

MISS AMERICA MAGAZINE (Formerly Miss America; Miss America #51 on)
Miss America Publ. Corp./Marvel/Atlas (MAP): V1#2, Nov, 1944 - No. 93, Nov, 1958

V1#2-Photo-c of teenage girl in Miss America costume; Miss America, Patsy Walker (intro.) comic stories plus movie reviews & stories; intro. Buzz Baxter & Hedy Wolfe; 1 pg. origin Miss America	148	296	444	947	1624	2300
3-5-Miss America & Patsy Walker stories	63	126	189	403	689	975
6-Patsy Walker only	36	72	108	211	343	475
V2#1(4/45)-6(9/45)-Patsy Walker continues	15	30	45	85	130	175
V3#1(10/45)-6(4/46)	14	28	42	76	108	140
V4#1(5/46),2,5(9/46)	12	24	36	69	97	125
V4#3(7/46)-Liz Taylor photo-c	32	64	96	188	307	425
V4#4 (8/46; 68 pgs.), V4#6 (10/46; 92 pgs.)	11	22	33	64	90	115
V5#1(11/46)-6(4/47), V6#1(5/47)-3(7/47)	11	22	33	62	86	110
V7#1(8/47)-23(#56, 6/49)	11	22	33	60	83	105
V7#24(#57, 7/49)-Kamen-a (becomes Best Western #58 on?)	11	22	33	62	86	110

Miss Fury #6 © MAR

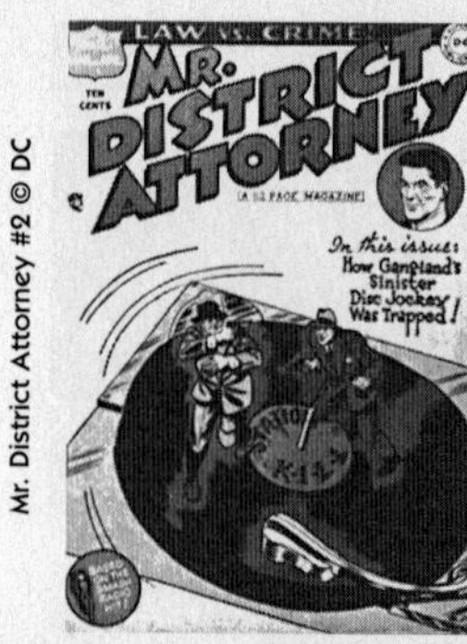

Mr. District Attorney #2 © DC

Mister Miracle #19 © DC

	GD 2.0	VG 4.0	FN 6.0	VF 8.0	VF/NM 9.0	NM- 9.2
V7#25(8/49), 27-44(3/52), VII,nn(5/52)	10	20	30	58	79	100
V7#26(9/49)-All comics	11	22	33	64	90	115
V1,nn(7/52)-V1,nn(1/53)(#46-49), V7#50(Spring '53), V1#51-V7?#54(7/53), 55-93	10	20	30	56	76	95

NOTE: *Photo-c #1, 4, V2#1, 4, 5, V3#5, V4#3, 4, 6, V7#15, 16, 24, 26, 34, 37, 38. Painted c-3.* ***Powell*** *a-V7#31.*

MISS BEVERLY HILLS OF HOLLYWOOD (See Adventures of Bob Hope)
National Periodical Publ.: Mar-Apr, 1949 - No. 9, July-Aug, 1950 (52 pgs.)

	GD 2.0	VG 4.0	FN 6.0	VF 8.0	VF/NM 9.0	NM- 9.2
1 (Meets Alan Ladd)	58	116	174	371	636	900
2-William Holden photo on-c	42	84	126	265	450	635
3-5: 2-9-Part photo-c. 5-Bob Hope photo on-c	39	78	117	232	381	530
6,7,9: 6-Lucille Ball photo on-c	35	70	105	208	339	470
8-Reagan photo on-c	39	78	117	240	395	550

NOTE: *Beverly meets Alan Ladd in #1, Eve Arden #2, Betty Hutton #4, Bob Hope #5.*

MISS CAIRO JONES
Croyden Publishers: 1945

	GD 2.0	VG 4.0	FN 6.0	VF 8.0	VF/NM 9.0	NM- 9.2
1-Bob Oksner daily newspaper-r (1st strip story); lingerie panels	20	40	60	114	182	250

MISS FURY COMICS (Newspaper strip reprints)
Timely Comics (NPI 1/CmPI 2/MPC 3-8): Winter, 1942-43 - No. 8, Winter, 1946 (Published twice a year)

	GD 2.0	VG 4.0	FN 6.0	VF 8.0	VF/NM 9.0	NM- 9.2
1-Origin Miss Fury by Tarpe' Mills (68 pgs.) in costume w/paper dolls with cut-out costumes	411	822	1233	2877	5039	7200
2-(60 pgs.)-In costume w/paper dolls; hooded Nazi-c	213	426	639	1363	2332	3300
3-(60 pgs.)-In costume w/paper dolls; Hitler-c	168	336	504	1075	1838	2600
4-(52 pgs.)-Classic Nazi WWII-c with giant swastika, Tojo & Hitler photo on wall; in costume, 2 pgs. w/paper dolls	145	290	435	921	1586	2250
5-(52 pgs.)-In costume w/paper dolls; Japanese WWII-c	110	220	330	704	1202	1700
6-(52 pgs.)-Not in costume in inside stories, w/paper dolls	100	200	300	635	1093	1550
7,8-(36 pgs.)-In costume 1 pg. each; no paper dolls	82	164	246	528	902	1275

NOTE: ***Schomburg*** *c-1, 5, 6.*

MISS FURY
Adventure Comics: 1991 - No. 4, 1991 ($2.50, limited series)

	GD 2.0	VG 4.0	FN 6.0	VF 8.0	VF/NM 9.0	NM- 9.2
1-4: 1-Origin; granddaughter of original Miss Fury						3.00
1-Limited ed. ($4.95)						5.00

MISSION IMPOSSIBLE (TV) (Also see Wild!)
Dell Publ. Co.: May, 1967 - No. 4, Oct, 1968; No. 5, Oct, 1969 (All have photo-c)

	GD 2.0	VG 4.0	FN 6.0	VF 8.0	VF/NM 9.0	NM- 9.2
1	8	16	24	58	97	135
2-5: 5-Reprints #1	6	12	18	41	66	90

MISSION IMPOSSIBLE (Movie) (1st Paramount Comics book)
Marvel Comics (Paramount Comics): May, 1996 ($2.95, one-shot)

	GD 2.0	VG 4.0	FN 6.0	VF 8.0	VF/NM 9.0	NM- 9.2
1-Liefeld-c & back-up story						3.00

MISS LIBERTY (Becomes Liberty Comics)
Burten Publishing Co.: 1945 (MLJ reprints)

	GD 2.0	VG 4.0	FN 6.0	VF 8.0	VF/NM 9.0	NM- 9.2
1-The Shield & Dusty, The Wizard, & Roy, the Super Boy app.; r/Shield-Wizard #13	29	58	87	170	278	385

MISS MELODY LANE OF BROADWAY (See The Adventures of Bob Hope)
National Periodical Publ.: Feb-Mar, 1950 - No. 3, June-July, 1950 (52 pgs.)

	GD 2.0	VG 4.0	FN 6.0	VF 8.0	VF/NM 9.0	NM- 9.2
1-Movie stars photos app. on all-c.	58	116	174	371	636	900
2,3: 3-Ed Sullivan photo on-c.	39	78	117	231	378	525

MISS PEACH
Dell Publishing Co.: Oct-Dec, 1963; 1969

	GD 2.0	VG 4.0	FN 6.0	VF 8.0	VF/NM 9.0	NM- 9.2
1-Jack Mendelsohn-a/script	8	16	24	52	86	120
...Tells You How to Grow (1969; 25¢)-Mel Lazarus-a; also given away (36 pgs.)	5	10	15	32	51	70

MISS PEPPER (See Meet Miss Pepper)

MISS SUNBEAM (See Little Miss...)

MISS VICTORY (See Captain Fearless #1,2, Holyoke One-Shot #3, Veri Best Sure Fire & Veri Best Sure Shot Comics)

MISTER AMERICA
Endeavor Comics: Apr, 1994 - No. 2, May, 1994 ($2.95, limited series)

	GD 2.0	VG 4.0	FN 6.0	VF 8.0	VF/NM 9.0	NM- 9.2
1,2						3.00

MR. & MRS. BEANS
United Features Syndicate: No. 11, 1939

	GD 2.0	VG 4.0	FN 6.0	VF 8.0	VF/NM 9.0	NM- 9.2
Single Series 11	34	68	102	199	325	450

MR. & MRS. J. EVIL SCIENTIST (TV)(See The Flintstones & Hanna-Barbera Band Wagon #3)
Gold Key: Nov, 1963 - No. 4, Sept, 1966 (Hanna-Barbera, all 12¢)

	GD 2.0	VG 4.0	FN 6.0	VF 8.0	VF/NM 9.0	NM- 9.2
1	6	12	18	41	66	90
2-4	4	8	12	24	37	50

MR. ANTHONY'S LOVE CLINIC (Based on radio show)
Hillman Periodicals: Nov, 1949 - No. 5, Apr-May, 1950 (52 pgs.)

	GD 2.0	VG 4.0	FN 6.0	VF 8.0	VF/NM 9.0	NM- 9.2
1-Photo-c on all	16	32	48	94	147	200
2	11	22	33	62	86	110
3-5	10	20	30	58	79	100

MISTER BLANK
Amaze Ink: No. 0, Jan, 1996 - No. 14, May, 2000 ($1.75/$2.95, B&W)

	GD 2.0	VG 4.0	FN 6.0	VF 8.0	VF/NM 9.0	NM- 9.2
0-($1.75, 16 pgs.) Origin of Mr. Blank						3.00
1-14-($2.95) Chris Hicks-s/a						3.00

MR. DISTRICT ATTORNEY (Radio/TV)
National Per. Publ.: Jan-Feb, 1948 - No. 67, Jan-Feb, 1959 (1-23: 52 pgs.)

	GD 2.0	VG 4.0	FN 6.0	VF 8.0	VF/NM 9.0	NM- 9.2
1-Howard Purcell c-5-23 (most)	87	174	261	553	952	1350
2	41	82	123	256	428	600
3-5	29	58	87	170	278	385
6-10	22	44	66	132	216	300
11-20	17	34	51	98	154	210
21-43: 43-Last pre-code (1-2/55)	14	28	42	76	108	140
44-67	11	22	33	62	86	110

MR. DISTRICT ATTORNEY (SeeThe Funnies #35)
Dell Publishing Co.: No. 13, 1942

	GD 2.0	VG 4.0	FN 6.0	VF 8.0	VF/NM 9.0	NM- 9.2
Four Color 13-See The Funnies #35 for 1st app.	26	52	78	186	373	560

MISTER E (Also see Books of Magic limited series)
DC Comics: Jun, 1991- No. 4, Sept, 1991($1.75, limited series)

	GD 2.0	VG 4.0	FN 6.0	VF 8.0	VF/NM 9.0	NM- 9.2
1-4-Snyder III-c/a; follow-up to Books of Magic limited series						3.00

MISTER ED, THE TALKING HORSE (TV)
Dell Publishing Co./Gold Key: Mar-May, 1962 - No. 6, Feb, 1964 (All photo-c; photo back-c: 1-6)

	GD 2.0	VG 4.0	FN 6.0	VF 8.0	VF/NM 9.0	NM- 9.2
Four Color 1295	12	24	36	82	154	225
1(11/62) (Gold Key)-Photo-c	9	18	27	60	100	140
2-6: Photo-c	6	12	18	37	59	80

(See March of Comics #244, 260, 282, 290)

MR. GUM (From The Atomics)
Oni Press: April, 2003 ($2.99, one-shot)

	GD 2.0	VG 4.0	FN 6.0	VF 8.0	VF/NM 9.0	NM- 9.2
1-Mike Allred-s/J. Bone-a; Madman & The Atomics app.						3.00

MR. HERO, THE NEWMATIC MAN (See Neil Gaiman's...)

MR. MAGOO (TV) (The Nearsighted..., ...& Gerald McBoing Boing 1954 issues; formerly Gerald McBoing-Boing And ...)
Dell Publishing Co.: No. 6, Nov-Jan, 1953-54; 5/54 - 3-5/62; 9-11/63 - 3-5/65

	GD 2.0	VG 4.0	FN 6.0	VF 8.0	VF/NM 9.0	NM- 9.2
6	10	20	30	68	119	170
Four Color 561(5/54),602(11/54)	10	20	30	68	119	170
Four Color 1235(#1, 12-2/62),1305(#2, 3-5/62)	8	16	24	56	93	130
3(9-11/63) - 5	7	14	21	50	83	115
Four Color 1235(12-536-505)(3-5/65)-2nd Printing	6	12	18	41	66	90

MR. MAJESTIC (See WildC.A.T.S.)
DC Comics (WildStorm): Sept, 1999 - No. 9, May, 2000 ($2.50)

	GD 2.0	VG 4.0	FN 6.0	VF 8.0	VF/NM 9.0	NM- 9.2
1-9: 1-McGuinness-a/Casey & Holguin-s. 2-Two covers						3.00
TPB (2002, $14.95) r/#1-6 & Wildstorm Spotlight #1						15.00

MISTER MIRACLE (1st series) (See Cancelled Comic Cavalcade)
National Periodical Publications/DC Comics: 3-4/71 - V4#18, 2-3/74; V5#19, 9/77 - V6#25, 8-9/78; 1987 (Fourth World)

	GD 2.0	VG 4.0	FN 6.0	VF 8.0	VF/NM 9.0	NM- 9.2
1-1st app. Mr. Miracle (#1-3 are 15¢)	8	16	24	56	93	130
2,3: 2-Intro. Granny Goodness. 3-Last 15¢ issue	5	10	15	30	48	65
4-8: 4-Intro. Barda; Boy Commandos-r begin; all 52 pgs.	5	10	15	30	48	65
9-18: 9-Origin Mr. Miracle; Darkseid cameo. 15-Intro/1st app. Shilo Norman. 18-Barda & Scott Free wed; New Gods app. & Darkseid cameo; Last Kirby issue.	3	6	9	16	23	30
19-25 (1977-78)	2	4	6	8	10	12
Special 1(1987, $1.25, 52 pgs.)						4.00
Jack Kirby's Fourth World TPB ('01, $12.95) B&W&Grey-toned reprint of #11-18; Mark Evanier intro.						13.00
Jack Kirby's Mister Miracle TPB ('98, $12.95) B&W&Grey-toned reprint of #1-10; David Copperfield intro.						13.00

Mister Mystery #15 © Media Pub.

Mr. T and the T-Force #1 © NOW

Mitzi's Romances #8 © MAR

GD VG FN VF VF/NM NM-
2.0 4.0 6.0 8.0 9.0 9.2

GD VG FN VF VF/NM NM-
2.0 4.0 6.0 8.0 9.0 9.2

NOTE: ***Austin*** *a-19i.* ***Ditko*** *a-6r.* ***Golden*** *a-23-25p; c-25p.* ***Heath*** *a-24i, 25i; c-25i.* ***Kirby*** *a(p)/c-1-18.* ***Nasser*** *a-19i.* ***Rogers*** *a-19-22p; c-19, 20p, 21p, 22-24. 4-8 contain* ***Simon & Kirby*** *Boy Commandos reprints from Detective 82,76, Boy Commandos 1, 3 & Detective 64 in that order.*

MISTER MIRACLE (2nd Series) (See Justice League)
DC Comics: Jan, 1989 - No. 28, June, 1991 ($1.00/$1.25)
1-28: 13,14-Lobo app. 22-1st new Mr. Miracle w/new costume 3.00

MISTER MIRACLE (3rd Series)
DC Comics: Apr, 1996 - No. 7, Oct, 1996 ($1.95)
1-7: 2-Vs. JLA. 6-Simonson-c 3.00

MR. MIRACLE (See Capt. Fearless #1 & Holyoke One-Shot #4)

MR. MONSTER (1st Series)(Doc Stearn... #7 on; See Airboy-Mr. Monster Special, Dark Horse Presents, Super Duper Comics & Vanguard Illustrated #7)
Eclipse Comics: Jan, 1985 - No. 10, June, 1987 ($1.75, Baxter paper)
1-3: 1-1st story-r from Vanguard Ill. #7(1st app.). 2-Dave Stevens-c. 3-Alan Moore scripts; Wolverton-r/Weird Mysteries #5. 5.00
4-10: 6-Ditko-r/Fantastic Fears #5 plus new Giffen-a. 10- "6-D" issue 4.00

MR. MONSTER
Dark Horse Comics: Feb, 1988 - No. 8, July, 1991 ($1.75, B&W)
1-7 3.00
8-($4.95, 60 pgs.)-Origins conclusion 5.00

MR. MONSTER ATTACKS! (Doc Stearn...)
Tundra Publ.: Aug, 1992 - No. 3, Oct, 1992 ($3.95, limited series, 32 pgs.)
1-3: Michael T. Gilbert-a/scripts; Gilbert/Dorman painted-c 4.00

MR. MONSTER PRESENTS (CRACK-A-BOOM!)
Caliber Comics: 1997 - No. 3, 1997 ($2.95, B&W&Red, limited series)
1-3: Michael T. Gilbert-a/scripts: 1-Wraparound-c 3.00

MR. MONSTER'S GAL FRIDAY...KELLY!
Image Comics: Jan, 2000 - No. 3, May, 2004 ($3.50, B&W)
1-3-Michael T. Gilbert-c; story & art by various. 3-Alan Moore-s 3.50

MR. MONSTER'S SUPER-DUPER SPECIAL
Eclipse Comics: May, 1986 - No. 8, July, 1987
1-(5/86)...3-D High Octane Horror #1 5.00
1-(5/86)...2-D version, 100 copies 2 4 6 9 13 16
2-(8/86)...High Octane Horror #1, 3-(9/86)...True Crime #1, 4-(11/86)...True Crime #2, 5-(1/87)...Hi-Voltage Super Science #1, 6-(3/87)...High Shock Schlock #1, 7-(5/87)...High Shock Schlock #2, 8-(7/87)...Weird Tales Of The Future #1 4.00
NOTE: ***Jack Cole*** *r-3, 4.* ***Evans*** *a-2r.* ***Kubert*** *a-1r.* ***Powell*** *a-5r.* ***Wolverton*** *a-2r, 7r, 8r.*

MR. MONSTER VS. GORZILLA
Image Comics: July, 1998 ($2.95, one-shot)
1-Michael T. Gilbert-a 3.00

MR. MONSTER: WORLDS WAR TWO
Atomeka Press: 2004 ($6.99, one-shot)
nn-Michael T. Gilbert-s/George Freeman-a; two covers by Horley & Dorman 7.00

MR. MUSCLES (Formerly Blue Beetle #18-21)
Charlton Comics: No. 22, Mar, 1956; No. 23, Aug, 1956
22,23 9 18 27 50 65 80

MR. MXYZPTLK (VILLAINS)
DC Comics: Feb, 1998 ($1.95, one-shot)
1-Grant-s/Morgan-a/Pearson-c 3.00

MISTER MYSTERY (Tales of Horror and Suspense)
Mr. Publ. (Media Publ.) No. 1-3/SPM Publ./Stanmore (Aragon): Sept, 1951 - No. 19, Oct, 1954
1-Kurtzman*esque* horror story 97 194 291 621 1061 1500
2,3-Kurtzman*esque* story. 3-Anti-Wertham edit. 65 130 195 416 708 1000
4-Bondage-c 65 130 195 416 708 1000
5,8,10 57 114 171 362 624 885
6-Classic torture-c 82 164 246 528 902 1275
7- "The Brain Bats of Venus" by Wolverton; partially re-used in Weird Tales of the Future #7
129 258 387 826 1413 2000
9-Nostrand-a 57 114 171 362 624 885
11-Wolverton "Robot Woman" story/Weird Mysteries #2, cut up, rewritten & partially redrawn
87 174 261 553 952 1350
12-Classic injury to eye-c 161 322 483 1030 1765 2500
13-17,19: 15- "Living Dead" junkie story. 16-Bondage-c. 17-Severed heads-c. 19-Reprints
46 92 138 290 488 685
18- "Robot Woman" by Wolverton reprinted from Weird Mysteries #2; decapitation, bondage-c
68 136 204 435 743 1050
NOTE: ***Andru*** *a-1, 2p, 3p.* ***Andru/Esposito*** *c-1-3.* ***Baily*** *c-10-18(most).* ***Mortellaro*** *c-5-7. Bondage c-7, 16. Some issues have graphic dismemberment scenes.*

MR. PUNCH
DC Comics (Vertigo): 1994 ($24.95, one-shot)
nn (Hard-c)-Gaiman scripts; McKean-c/a 40.00
nn (Soft-c) 15.00

MISTER Q (See Mighty Midget Comics & Our Flag Comics #5)

MR. RISK (Formerly All Romances; Men Against Crime #3 on)(Also see Our Flag Comics & Super-Mystery Comics)
Ace Magazines: No. 7, Oct, 1950; No. 2, Dec, 1950
7,2 11 22 33 64 90 115

MR. SCARLET & PINKY (See Mighty Midget Comics)

MR. T
APComics: May, 2005 ($3.50)
1-Chris Bunting-s/Neil Edwards-a 3.50

MR. T AND THE T-FORCE
Now Comics: June, 1993 - No. 10, May, 1994 ($1.95, color)
1-10-Newsstand editions: 1-7-polybagged with photo trading card in each. 1,2-Neal Adams-c/a(p). 3-Dave Dorman painted-c 3.00
1-10-Direct Sale editions polybagged w/line drawn trading cards. 1-Contains gold foil trading card by Neal Adams 3.00

MISTER UNIVERSE (Professional wrestler)
Mr. Publications Media Publ. (Stanmor, Aragon): July, 1951; No. 2, Oct, 1951 - No. 5, April, 1952
1 22 44 66 132 216 300
2- "Jungle That Time Forgot", (24 pg. story); Andru/Esposito-c
14 28 42 82 121 160
3-Marijuana story 14 28 42 82 121 160
4,5- "Goes to War" cover/stories 11 22 33 64 90 115

MISTER X (See Vortex)
Mr. Publications/Vortex Comics/Caliber V3#1 on: 6/84 - No. 14, 8/88 ($1.50/$2.25, direct sales, coated paper);V2#1, Apr, 1989 - V2#12, Mar, 1990 ($2.00/$2.50, B&W, newsprint) V3#1, 1996 - Present ($2.95, B&W)
1-14: 11-Dave McKean story & art (6 pgs.) 4.00
V2 #1-12: 1-11 (Second Coming, B&W): 1-Four diff.-c. 10-Photo-c 3.00
V3 #1-4 3.00
Return of... ($11.95, graphic novel)-r/V1#1-4 12.00
Return of... ($34.95, hardcover limited edition)-r/1-4 35.00
Special (no date, 1990?) 3.00

MISTER X: CONDEMNED
Dark Horse Comics: Dec, 2008 - No. 4, Mar, 2009 ($3.50, limited series)
1-4-Dean Motter-s/a 3.50

MISTY
Marvel Comics (Star Comics): Dec, 1985 - No. 6, May, 1986 (Limited series)
1-6: Millie The Model's niece 4.00

MITZI COMICS (Becomes Mitzi's Boy Friend #2-7)(See All Teen)
Timely Comics: Spring, 1948 (one-shot)
1-Kurtzman's "Hey Look" plus 3 pgs. "Giggles 'n' Grins"
28 56 84 165 270 375

MITZI'S BOY FRIEND (Formerly Mitzi Comics; becomes Mitzi's Romances)
Marvel Comics (TCI): No. 2, June, 1948 - No. 7, April, 1949
2 15 30 45 86 133 180
3-7 14 28 42 76 108 140

MITZI'S ROMANCES (Formerly Mitzi's Boy Friend)
Timely/Marvel Comics (TCI): No. 8, June, 1949 - No. 10, Dec, 1949
8-Becomes True Life Tales #8 (10/49) on? 14 28 42 80 115 150
9,10: 10-Painted-c 12 24 36 67 94 120

MNEMOVORE
DC Comics (Vertigo): Jun, 2005 - No. 6, Nov, 2005 ($2.99, limited series)
1-6-Rodionoff & Fawkes-s/Huddleston-a/c 3.00

MOBY DICK (See Feature Presentations #6, and King Classics)
Dell Publishing Co.: No. 717, Aug, 1956
Four Color 717-Movie, Gregory Peck photo-c 8 16 24 56 93 130

MOBY DUCK (See Donald Duck #112 & Walt Disney Showcase #2,11)
Gold Key (Disney): Oct, 1967 - No. 11, Oct, 1970; No. 12, Jan, 1974 - No. 30, Feb, 1978

Modern Comics #69 © QUA

Mod Wheels #17 © GK

The Monkees #8 © DELL

	GD 2.0	VG 4.0	FN 6.0	VF 8.0	VF/NM 9.0	NM- 9.2
1	3	6	9	21	32	42
2-5	2	4	6	11	16	20
6-11	2	4	6	9	13	16
12-30: 21,30-r	1	3	4	6	8	10

MODEL FUN (With Bobby Benson)
Harle Publications: No. 2, Fall, 1954 - No. 5, July, 1955

	GD 2.0	VG 4.0	FN 6.0	VF 8.0	VF/NM 9.0	NM- 9.2
2-Bobby Benson	7	14	21	35	43	50
3-5-Bobby Benson	5	10	15	23	28	32

MODELING WITH MILLIE (Formerly Life With Millie)
Atlas/Marvel Comics (Male Publ.): No. 21, Feb, 1963 - No. 54, June, 1967

	GD 2.0	VG 4.0	FN 6.0	VF 8.0	VF/NM 9.0	NM- 9.2
21	9	18	27	63	107	150
22-30	6	12	18	37	59	80
31-53	5	10	15	30	48	65
54-Last issue; Gears-c & 6 pg. story; Beatles swipe imitators; FF #63 comic appears in story; "Millie the Marvel" 6 pg. story as super-hero	5	10	15	35	55	75

MODELS, INC.
Marvel Comics: Oct, 2009 - No. 4, Jan, 2010 ($3.99, limited series)

	GD 2.0	VG 4.0	FN 6.0	VF 8.0	VF/NM 9.0	NM- 9.2
1-4-Millie the Model, Patsy Walker, Mary Jane Watson app.; Land-c. 1-Tim Gunn app.						4.00

MODERN COMICS (Formerly Military Comics #1-43)
Quality Comics Group: No. 44, Nov, 1945 - No. 102, Oct, 1950

	GD 2.0	VG 4.0	FN 6.0	VF 8.0	VF/NM 9.0	NM- 9.2
44-Blackhawk continues	52	104	156	328	557	785
45-52: 49-1st app. Fear, Lady Adventuress	38	76	114	228	369	510
53-Torchy by Ward begins (9/46)	42	84	126	265	445	625
54-60: 55-J. Cole-a	32	64	96	192	314	435
61-Classic-c	39	78	117	231	378	525
62-64,66-77,79,80: 73-J. Cole-a	31	62	93	182	296	410
65-Classic Grim Reaper Skull-c	47	94	141	296	498	700
78-1st app. Madame Butterfly	34	68	102	199	325	450
81-99,101: 82,83-One pg. J. Cole-a. 83-Last 52 pg. issue 99-Blackhawks on the moon-c/story	29	58	87	170	278	385
100	31	62	93	186	303	420
102-(Scarce)-J. Cole-a; Spirit by Eisner app.	38	76	114	229	375	520

NOTE: ***Al Bryant** c-44-51, 54, 55, 66, 69. **Jack Cole** a-55, 73. **Crandall** Blackhawk-#46, 47, 50, 51, 54, 56, 58-60, 64, 67-70, 73, 74, 76-78, 80-83; c-60-65, 67, 68, 70-95. **Crandall/Cuidera** c-56-59, 96-102. **Gustavson** a-47, 49. **Ward** Blackhawk-#52, 53, 55 (15 pgs. each). Torchy in #53-102; by **Ward** only in #53-89(9/49); by **Gil Fox** #92, 93, 102.*

MODERN LOVE
E. C. Comics: June-July, 1949 - No. 8, Aug-Sept, 1950

	GD 2.0	VG 4.0	FN 6.0	VF 8.0	VF/NM 9.0	NM- 9.2
1-Feldstein, Ingels-a	84	168	252	538	919	1300
2-Craig/Feldstein-c/s	53	106	159	334	567	800
3	47	94	141	296	498	700
4-6 (Scarce): 4-Bra/panties panels	58	116	174	371	636	900
7,8	47	94	141	296	498	700

NOTE: ***Craig** a-3. **Feldstein** a-in most issues; c-1, 2i, 3-8. **Harrison** a-4. **Iger** a-6-8. **Ingels** a-1, 2, 4-7. **Palais** a-5. **Wood** a-7. **Wood/Harrison** a-5-7. (Canadian reprints known; see Table of Contents.)*

MODERN WARFARE 2: GHOST (Based on the videogame)
DC Comics (WildStorm): Jan, 2010 - No. 6, Sept, 2010 ($3.99, limited series)

	GD 2.0	VG 4.0	FN 6.0	VF 8.0	VF/NM 9.0	NM- 9.2
1-6: 1-Two covers; Lapham-s/West-a						4.00
TPB (2010, $17.99) r/#1-6; cover sketches and sketch art						18.00

MOD LOVE
Western Publishing Co.: 1967 (50¢, 36 pgs.)

	GD 2.0	VG 4.0	FN 6.0	VF 8.0	VF/NM 9.0	NM- 9.2
1-(Low print)	6	12	18	39	62	85

MODNIKS, THE
Gold Key: Aug, 1967 - No. 2, Aug, 1970

	GD 2.0	VG 4.0	FN 6.0	VF 8.0	VF/NM 9.0	NM- 9.2
10206-708(#1)	4	8	12	22	34	45
2	3	6	9	16	22	28

M.O.D.O.K.: REIGN DELAY
Marvel Comics: Nov, 2009 ($3.99, one-shot)

	GD 2.0	VG 4.0	FN 6.0	VF 8.0	VF/NM 9.0	NM- 9.2
1-M.O.D.O.K. cartoony humor stories from Marvel Digital Comics; Ryan Dunlavey-s/a						4.00

MOD SQUAD (TV)
Dell Publishing Co.: Jan, 1969 - No. 3, Oct, 1969 - No. 8, April, 1971

	GD 2.0	VG 4.0	FN 6.0	VF 8.0	VF/NM 9.0	NM- 9.2
1-Photo-c	7	14	21	45	73	100
2-4: 2-4-Photo-c	4	8	12	28	44	60
5-8: 8-Photo-c; Reprints #2	4	8	12	24	37	50

MOD WHEELS
Gold Key: Mar, 1971 - No. 19, Jan, 1976

	GD 2.0	VG 4.0	FN 6.0	VF 8.0	VF/NM 9.0	NM- 9.2
1	4	8	12	26	41	55
2-9	3	6	9	16	23	30
10-19: 11,15-Extra 16 pgs. ads	3	6	9	14	19	24

MOE & SHMOE COMICS
O. S. Publ. Co.: Spring, 1948 - No. 2, Summer, 1948

	GD 2.0	VG 4.0	FN 6.0	VF 8.0	VF/NM 9.0	NM- 9.2
1	9	18	27	47	61	75
2	6	12	18	31	38	45

MOEBIUS (Graphic novel)
Marvel Comics (Epic Comics): Oct, 1987 - No. 6, 1988; No. 7, 1990; No. 8, 1991 ($9.95, 8x11", mature)

	GD 2.0	VG 4.0	FN 6.0	VF 8.0	VF/NM 9.0	NM- 9.2
1,2,4-6,8: (#2, 2nd printing, $9.95)	3	6	9	16	22	28
3,7,0: 3-(1st & 2nd printings, $12.95). 0 (1990, $12.95)	3	6	9	17	25	32
Moebius I-Signed & #'d hard-c ($45.95, Graphitti Designs, 1,500 copies printed)-r/#1-3	5	10	15	32	51	70

MOEBIUS COMICS
Caliber: May, 1996 - No. 6 ($2.95, B&W)

	GD 2.0	VG 4.0	FN 6.0	VF 8.0	VF/NM 9.0	NM- 9.2
1-6: Moebius-c/a. 1-William Stout-a						4.00

MOEBIUS: THE MAN FROM CIGURI
Dark Horse Comics: 1996 ($7.95, digest-size)

	GD 2.0	VG 4.0	FN 6.0	VF 8.0	VF/NM 9.0	NM- 9.2
nn-Moebius-c/a	1	2	3	5	7	9

MOLLY MANTON'S ROMANCES (Romantic Affairs #3)
Marvel Comics (SePI): Sept, 1949 - No. 2, Dec, 1949 (52 pgs.)

	GD 2.0	VG 4.0	FN 6.0	VF 8.0	VF/NM 9.0	NM- 9.2
1-Photo-c (becomes Blaze the Wonder Collie #2 (10/49) on? & Molly Manton's Romances #2	18	36	54	105	165	225
2-Titled "Romances of..."; photo-c	14	28	42	76	108	140

MOLLY O'DAY (Super Sleuth)
Avon Periodicals: February, 1945 (1st Avon comic)

	GD 2.0	VG 4.0	FN 6.0	VF 8.0	VF/NM 9.0	NM- 9.2
1-Molly O'Day, The Enchanted Dagger by Tuska (r/Yankee #1), Capt'n Courage, Corporal Grant app.	58	116	174	371	636	900

MOMENT OF SILENCE
Marvel Comics: Feb, 2002 ($3.50, one-shot)

	GD 2.0	VG 4.0	FN 6.0	VF 8.0	VF/NM 9.0	NM- 9.2
1-Tributes to the heroes and victims of Sept. 11; s/a by various						3.50

MONARCHY, THE (Also see The Authority and StormWatch)
DC Comics (WildStorm): Apr, 2001 - No. 12, May, 2002 ($2.50)

	GD 2.0	VG 4.0	FN 6.0	VF 8.0	VF/NM 9.0	NM- 9.2
1-12: 1-McCrea & Leach-a/Young-s						3.00
Bullets Over Babylon TPB (2001, $12.95) r/#1-4, Authority #21						13.00

MONKEES, THE (TV)(Also see Circus Boy, Groovy, Not Brand Echh #3, Teen-Age Talk, Teen Beam & Teen Beat)
Dell Publishing Co.: March, 1967 - No. 17, Oct, 1969

	GD 2.0	VG 4.0	FN 6.0	VF 8.0	VF/NM 9.0	NM- 9.2
1-Photo-c	10	20	30	69	122	175
2-17: All photo-c. 17-Reprints #1	6	12	18	43	69	95

MONKEY AND THE BEAR, THE
Atlas Comics (ZPC): Sept, 1953 - No. 3, Jan, 1954

	GD 2.0	VG 4.0	FN 6.0	VF 8.0	VF/NM 9.0	NM- 9.2
1-Howie Post-c/a in all; funny animal	10	20	30	54	72	90
2,3	8	16	24	40	50	60

MONKEYMAN AND O'BRIEN (Also see Dark Horse Presents #80, 100-5, Gen^{13}/..., Hellboy: Seed of Destruction, & San Diego Comic Con #2)
Dark Horse Comics (Legend): Jul, 1996 - No. 3, Sept, 1996 ($2.95, lim. series)

	GD 2.0	VG 4.0	FN 6.0	VF 8.0	VF/NM 9.0	NM- 9.2
1-3: New stories; Art Adams-c/a/scripts						4.00
nn-(2/96, $2.95)-r/back-up stories from Hellboy: Seed of Destruction; Adams-c/a/scripts						4.00

MONKEYSHINES COMICS
Ace Periodicals/Publishers Specialists/Current Books/Unity Publ.: Summer, 1944 - No. 27, July, 1949

	GD 2.0	VG 4.0	FN 6.0	VF 8.0	VF/NM 9.0	NM- 9.2
1-Funny animal	15	30	45	83	124	165
2-(Aut/44)	9	18	27	52	69	85
3-10: 3-(Win/44)	9	18	27	47	61	75
11-18,20-27: 23,24-Fago-c/a	8	16	24	40	50	60
19-Frazetta-a	9	18	27	50	65	80

MONKEY'S UNCLE, THE (See Merlin Jones As... under Movie Comics)

MONOLITH, THE
DC Comics: Apr, 2004 - No. 12, Mar, 2005 ($3.50/$2.95)

	GD 2.0	VG 4.0	FN 6.0	VF 8.0	VF/NM 9.0	NM- 9.2
1-($3.50) Palmiotti & Gray-s/Winslade-a						3.50
2-12-($2.95): 6-8-Batman app.; Coker-a						3.00

MONROES, THE (TV)
Dell Publishing Co.: Apr, 1967

Monster Hunters #16 © CC

Monsters on the Prowl #16 © MAR

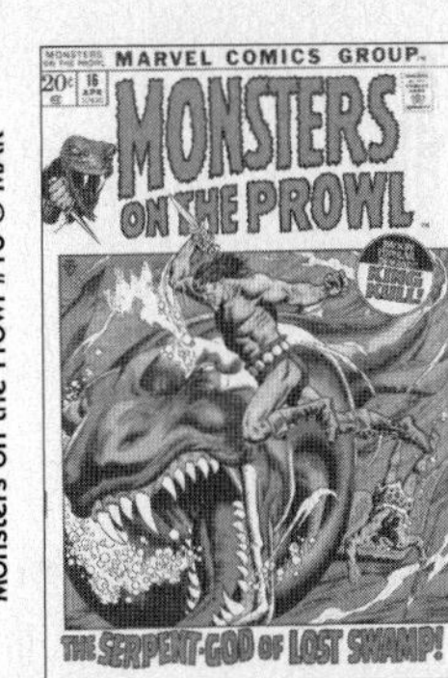

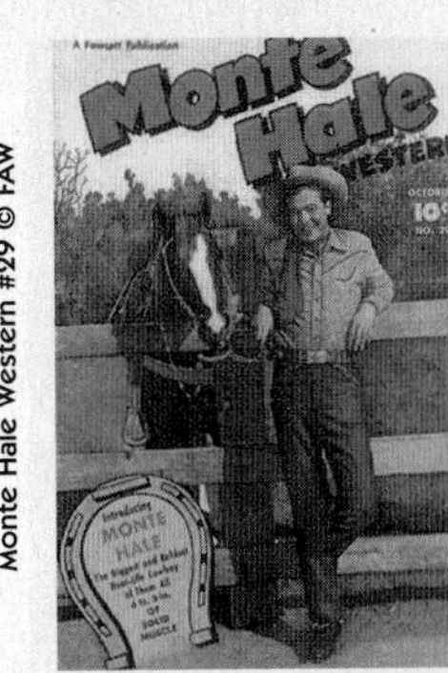

Monte Hale Western #29 © FAW

GD VG FN VF VF/NM NM-
2.0 4.0 6.0 8.0 9.0 9.2

1-Photo-c 3 6 9 18 27 35

MONSTER
Fiction House Magazines: 1953 - No. 2, 1953

1-Dr. Drew by Grandenetti; reprint from Rangers Comics #48; Whitman-c
52 104 156 325 550 775
2-Whitman-c 39 78 117 240 395 550

MONSTER CRIME COMICS (Also see Crime Must Stop)
Hillman Periodicals: Oct, 1952 (15¢, 52 pgs.)

1 (Scarce) 174 348 522 1114 1907 2700

MONSTER HOUSE (Companion to the 2006 movie)
IDW Publishing: June, 2006 ($7.99, one-shot)

nn-Two stories about Bones and Skull by Joshua Dysart and Simeon Wilkins 8.00

MONSTER HOWLS (Magazine)
Humor-Vision: December, 1966 (Satire) (35¢, 68 pgs.)

1 6 12 18 39 62 85

MONSTER HUNTERS
Charlton Comics: Aug, 1975 - No. 9, Jan, 1977; No. 10, Oct, 1977 - No. 18, Feb, 1979

1-Howard-a; Newton-c; 1st Countess Von Bludd and Colonel Whiteshroud
3 6 9 18 27 35
2-Sutton-c/a; Ditko-a 3 6 9 14 19 24
3,4,5,7: 4-Sutton-c/a 2 4 6 9 12 15
6,8,10: 6,8,10-Ditko-a 2 4 6 10 14 18
9,11,12 1 3 4 6 8 10
13,15,18-Ditko-c/a. 18-Sutton-a 2 4 6 10 14 18
14-Special all-Ditko issue 3 6 9 17 25 32
16,17-Sutton-a 2 3 4 6 8 10
1,2 (Modern Comics reprints, 1977) 6.00

NOTE: ***Ditko*** *a-2, 6, 8, 10, 13-15r, 18r; c-13-15, 18.* ***Howard*** *a-1, 3, 17; r-13.* ***Morisi*** *a-1.* ***Staton*** *a-1, 13.* ***Sutton*** *a-2, 4; c-2, 4; r-16-18.* ***Zeck*** *a-4-9. Reprints in #12-18.*

MONSTER MADNESS (Magazine)
Marvel Comics: 1972 - No. 3, 1973 (60¢, B&W)

1-3: Stories by "Sinister" Stan Lee 4 8 12 26 41 55

MONSTER MAN
Image Comics (Action Planet): Sept, 1997 ($2.95, B&W)

1-Mike Manley-c/s/a 3.00

MONSTER MASTERWORKS
Marvel Comics: 1989 ($12.95, TPB)

nn-Reprints 1960's monster stories; art by Kirby, Ditko, Ayers, Everett 20.00

MONSTER MATINEE
Chaos! Comics: Oct, 1997 - No. 3, Oct, 1997 ($2.50, limited series)

1-3: pin-ups 3.00

MONSTER MENACE
Marvel Comics: Dec, 1993 - No. 4, Mar, 1994 ($1.25, limited series)

1-4: Pre-code Atlas horror reprints. 6.00

NOTE: ***Ditko****-r &* ***Kirby****-r in all.*

MONSTER OF FRANKENSTEIN (See Frankenstein and Essential Monster of Frankenstein)

MONSTER PILE-UP
Image Comics: Aug, 2008 ($1.99)

1-New short stories of Astounding Wolf-Man, Firebreather, Perhapanauts, Proof 3.00

MONSTERS ATTACK (Magazine)
Globe Communications Corpse: Sept, 1989 - No. 5, Dec, 1990 (B&W)

1-5-Ditko, Morrow, J. Severin-a. 5-Toth, Morrow-a 1 2 3 4 5 7

MONSTERS, INC. (Based on the Disney/Pixar movie)
BOOM! Studios: Jun, 2009 - No. 4, Nov, 2009 ($2.99, limited series)

...: Laugh Factory 1-4: 1,3-Three covers. 2,4-Two covers 3.00

MONSTERS ON THE PROWL (Chamber of Darkness #1-8)
Marvel Comics Group (No. 13,14: 52 pgs.): No. 9, 2/71 - No. 27, 11/73; No. 28, 6/74 - No. 30, 10/74

9-Barry Smith inks 4 8 12 26 41 55
10-12,15: 12-Last 15¢ issue 3 6 9 16 23 30
13,14-(52 pgs.) 3 6 9 19 29 38
16-(4/72)-King Kull 4th app.; Severin-c 3 6 9 19 29 38
17-30 3 6 9 14 19 24

NOTE: ***Ditko*** *r-9, 14, 16.* ***Kirby*** *r-10-17, 21, 23, 25, 27, 28, 30; c-9, 25.* ***Kirby/Ditko*** *r-14, 17-20, 22, 24, 26, 29.* ***Marie/John Severin*** *a-16(Kull). 9-13, 15 contain one new story. Woodish art by* ***Reese****-11. King Kull created by Robert E. Howard.*

GD VG FN VF VF/NM NM-
2.0 4.0 6.0 8.0 9.0 9.2

MONSTERS TO LAUGH WITH (Magazine) (Becomes Monsters Unlimited #4)
Marvel Comics Group: 1964 - No. 3, 1965 (B&W)

1-Humor by Stan Lee 8 16 24 52 86 120
2,3 5 10 15 32 51 70

MONSTERS UNLEASHED (Magazine)
Marvel Comics Group: July, 1973 - No. 11, Apr, 1975; Summer, 1975 (B&W)

1-Soloman Kane sty; Werewolf app. 5 10 15 30 48 65
2-4: 2-The Frankenstein Monster begins, ends #10. 3-Neal Adams-c/a; The Man-Thing begins (origin-r); Son of Satan preview. 4-Werewolf app. 4 8 12 24 37 50
5-7: Werewolf in all. 5-Man-Thing. 7-Williamson-a(r) 3 6 9 18 27 35
8-11: 8-Man-Thing; N. Adams-r. 9-Man-Thing; Wendigo app. 10-Origin Tigra
3 6 9 19 29 38
Annual 1 (Summer,1975, 92 pgs.)-Kane-a 3 6 9 18 27 35

NOTE: ***Boris*** *c-2, 6.* ***Brunner*** *a-2; c-11.* ***J. Buscema*** *a-2p, 4p, 5p.* ***Colan*** *a-1, 4r.* ***Davis*** *a-3r.* ***Everett*** *a-2r.* ***G. Kane*** *a-3.* ***Krigstein*** *r-4.* ***Morrow*** *a-3; c-1.* ***Perez*** *a-8.* ***Ploog*** *a-6.* ***Reese*** *a-1, 2.* ***Tuska*** *a-3p.* ***Wildey*** *a-1r.*

MONSTERS UNLIMITED (Magazine) (Formerly Monsters To Laugh With)
Marvel Comics Group: No. 4, 1965 - No. 7, 1966 (B&W)

4-7 5 10 15 32 51 70

MONSTER WORLD
DC Comics (WildStorm): Jul, 2001 - No. 4, Oct, 2001 ($2.50, limited series)

1-4-Lobdell-s/Meglia-c/a 3.00

MONTANA KID, THE (See Kid Montana)

MONTE HALE WESTERN (Movie star; Formerly Mary Marvel #1-28; also see Fawcett Movie Comic, Motion Picture Comics, Picture News #8, Real Western Hero, Six-Gun Heroes, Western Hero & XMas Comics)
Fawcett Publ./Charlton No. 83 on: No. 29, Oct, 1948 - No. 88, Jan, 1956

29-(#1, 52 pgs.)-Photo-c begin, end #82; Monte Hale & his horse Pardner begin
26 52 78 154 252 350
30-(52 pgs.)-Big Bow and Little Arrow begin, end #34; Captain Tootsie by Beck
14 28 42 80 115 150
31-36,38-40-(52 pgs.): 34-Gabby Hayes begins, ends #80. 39-Captain Tootsie by Beck
12 24 36 67 94 120
37,41,45,49-(36 pgs.) 10 20 30 54 72 90
42-44,46-48,50-(52 pgs.): 47-Big Bow & Little Arrow app.
10 20 30 58 79 100
51,52,54-56,58,59-(52 pgs.) 9 18 27 52 69 85
53,57-(36 pgs.): 53-Slim Pickens app. 8 16 24 44 57 70
60-81: 36 pgs. #60-on. 80-Gabby Hayes ends 8 16 24 42 54 65
82-Last Fawcett issue (6/53) 9 18 27 52 69 85
83-1st Charlton issue (2/55); B&W photo back-c begin. Gabby Hayes returns, ends #86
10 20 30 58 79 100
84 (4/55) 8 16 24 44 57 70
85-86 8 16 24 42 54 65
87,88: 87-Wolverton-r, 1/2 pg. 88-Last issue 8 16 24 44 57 70

NOTE: ***Gil Kane*** *a-33?, 34? Rocky Lane -1 pg. (Carnation ad)-38, 40, 41, 43, 44, 46, 55.*

MONTY HALL OF THE U.S. MARINES (See With the Marines...)
Toby Press: Aug, 1951 - No. 11, Apr, 1953

1 12 24 36 69 97 125
2 8 16 24 42 54 65
3-5 8 16 24 40 50 60
6-11 7 14 21 37 46 55

NOTE: *Full page pin-ups (Pin-Up Pete) by* ***Jack Sparling*** *in #1-9.*

MOON, A GIRL...ROMANCE, A (Becomes Weird Fantasy #13 on; formerly Moon Girl #1-8)
E. C. Comics: No. 9, Sept-Oct, 1949 - No. 12, Mar-Apr, 1950

9-Moon Girl cameo 82 164 246 528 902 1275
10,11 68 136 204 435 743 1050
12-(Scarce) 82 164 246 528 902 1275

NOTE: ***Feldstein, Ingels*** *art in all.* ***Feldstein*** *c-9-12.* ***Wood/Harrison*** *a-10-12. Canadian reprints known; see Table of Contents.*

MOON GIRL AND THE PRINCE (#1) (Moon Girl #2-6; Moon Girl Fights Crime #7, 8; becomes A Moon, A Girl, Romance #9 on)(Also see Animal Fables #7, Int. Crime Patrol #6, Happy Houlihans & Tales From The Crypt #22)
E. C. Comics: Fall, 1947 - No. 8, Summer, 1949

1-Origin Moon Girl (see Happy Houlihans #1). Intro Santana, Queen of the Underworld
110 220 330 704 1202 1700
2-Moon Girl battles Futureman 63 126 189 403 689 975
3,4: 3-Santana, Queen of the Underworld returns. 4-Moon Girl vs. a vampire
54 108 162 346 591 835
5-E.C.'s 1st horror story, "Zombie Terror" 119 238 357 762 1306 1850
6-8 (Scarce): 7-Origin Star (Moongirl's sidekick) 63 126 189 403 689 975

Moon Knight (4th series) #27 © MAR

Moon Mullins #8 © ACG

More Fun Comics #48 © DC

GD 2.0 | VG 4.0 | FN 6.0 | VF 8.0 | VF/NM 9.0 | NM- 9.2

NOTE: ***Craig** a-2, 5; c-1, 2. **Moldoff** a-1-8; c-3-8 (Shelly). **Wheelan's** Fat and Slat app. in #3, 4, 6. #2 & #3 are 52 pgs., #4 on, 36 pgs. Canadian reprints known; (see Table of Contents).*

MOON KNIGHT (Also see The Hulk, Marc Spector..., Marvel Preview #21, Marvel Spotlight & Werewolf by Night #32)
Marvel Comics Group: Nov, 1980 - No. 38, Jul, 1984 (Mando paper #33 on)

1-Origin resumed in #4 6.00
2-15,25,35: 4-Intro Midnight Man. 25-Double size. 35-($1.00, 52 pgs.)-X-Men app.; F.F. cameo 4.00
16-24,26-28,30-34,36-38: 16-The Thing app. 3.00
29,30-Werewolf By Night app. 4.00

NOTE: ***Austin** c-27i, 31i. **Cowan** a-16; c-16, 17. **Kaluta** c-36-38; back c-35. **Miller** c-9, 12p, 13p, 15p, 27p. **Ploog** back c-35. **Sienkiewicz** a-1-15, 17-20, 22-26, 28-30, 33i, 36(4), 37; c-1-5, 7, 8, 10, 11, 14-16, 18-26, 28-30, 31p, 33, 34.*

MOON KNIGHT
Marvel Comics Group: June, 1985 - V2#6, Dec, 1985

V2#1-6: 1-Double size; new costume. 6-Sienkiewicz painted-c 3.00

MOON KNIGHT
Marvel Comics: Jan, 1998 - No. 4, Apr, 1998 ($2.50, limited series)

1-4-Moench-s/Edwards-c/a 3.00

MOON KNIGHT (Volume 3)
Marvel Comics: Jan, 1999 - No. 4, Feb, 1999 ($2.99, limited series)

1-4-Moench-s/Texeira-a(p) 3.00

MOON KNIGHT (Fourth series) (Leads into Vengeance of the Moon Knight)
Marvel Comics: June, 2006 - No. 30, Jul, 2009 ($2.99, limited series)

1-Finch-a/c; Huston-s 4.00
1-B&W sketch variant-c 6.00
2-19,21-26: 7-Spider-Man app. 9,10-Punisher app. 13-Suydam-c begin. 23-25-Bullseye 3.00
20-($3.99) Deodato-a; back-up r/1st app. in Werewolf By Night #32,33 4.00
Annual 1 (1/08, $3.99) Swierczynski-s/Palo-a 4.00
... Saga (2009, free) synopsis of origin and major storylines 3.00
...: Silent Knight 1 (1/09, $3.99) Milligan-s/Laurence Campbell-a/Crain-c 4.00
... Vol. 1: The Bottom HC (2006, $19.99) r/#1-6; Huston afterword; 2 covers 20.00
... Vol. 1: The Bottom SC (2007, $14.99) r/#1-6; Huston afterword 15.00
... Vol. 2: Midnight Sun HC (2008, $19.99) r/#7-13 & Annual #1 20.00
... Vol. 2: Midnight Sun SC (2008, $14.99) r/#7-13 & Annual #1 15.00

MOON KNIGHT: DIVIDED WE FALL
Marvel Comics: 1992 ($4.95, 52 pgs.)

nn-Denys Cowan-c/a(p) 5.00

MOON KNIGHT SPECIAL
Marvel Comics: Oct, 1992 ($2.50, 52 pgs.)

1-Shang Chi, Master of Kung Fu-c/story 4.00

MOON KNIGHT SPECIAL EDITION
Marvel Comics Group: Nov, 1983 - No. 3, Jan, 1984 ($2.00, limited series, Baxter paper)

1-3: Reprints from Hulk mag. by Sienkiewicz 4.00

MOON MULLINS (See Popular Comics, Super Book #3 & Super Comics)
Dell Publishing Co.: 1941 - 1945

	GD 2.0	VG 4.0	FN 6.0	VF 8.0	VF/NM 9.0	NM- 9.2
Four Color 14(1941)	45	90	135	284	480	675
Large Feature Comic 29(1941)	36	72	108	211	343	475
Four Color 31(1943)	16	32	48	111	226	340
Four Color 81(1945)	10	20	30	71	128	185

MOON MULLINS
Michel Publ. (American Comics Group)#1-6/St. John #7,8: Dec-Jan, 1947-48 - No. 8, 1949 (52 pgs)

	GD 2.0	VG 4.0	FN 6.0	VF 8.0	VF/NM 9.0	NM- 9.2
1-Alternating Sunday & daily strip-r	22	44	66	128	209	290
2	14	28	42	78	112	145
3-8: 7,8-St. John Publ. 8-...Featuring Kayo on-c	13	26	39	74	105	135

NOTE: ***Milt Gross** a-2-6, 8. **Frank Willard** r-all.*

MOON PILOT
Dell Publishing Co.: No. 1313, Mar-May, 1962

	GD 2.0	VG 4.0	FN 6.0	VF 8.0	VF/NM 9.0	NM- 9.2
Four Color 1313-Movie, photo-c	7	14	21	47	76	105

MOONSHADOW (Also see Farewell, Moonshadow)
Marvel Comics (Epic Comics): 5/85 - #12, 2/87 ($1.50/$1.75, mature) (1st fully painted comic book)

1-Origin; J. M. DeMatteis scripts & Jon J. Muth painted-c/a. 6.00
2-12: 11-Origin 4.00
Trade paperback (1987?)-r/#1-12 14.00

	GD 2.0	VG 4.0	FN 6.0	VF 8.0	VF/NM 9.0	NM- 9.2
Signed & #ed HC ($39.95, 1,200 copies)-r/#1-12	4	8	12	28	44	60

MOONSHADOW

GD 2.0 | VG 4.0 | FN 6.0 | VF 8.0 | VF/NM 9.0 | NM- 9.2

DC Comics (Vertigo): Oct, 1994 - No. 12, Aug, 1995 ($2.25/$2.95)

1-11: Reprints Epic series. 3.00
12 ($2.95)-w/expanded ending 4.00
The Complete Moonshadow TPB ('98, $39.95) r/#1-12 and Farewell Moonshadow; new Muth painted-c 40.00

MOON-SPINNERS, THE (See Movie Comics)

MOONSTONE MONSTERS
Moonstone: 2003 - 2005 ($2.95, B&W)

...: Demons ($2.95) - Short stories by various; Frenz-c 3.00
...: Ghosts ($2.95) - Short stories by various; Frenz-c 3.00
...: Sea Creatures ($2.95) - Short stories by various; Frenz-c 3.00
...: Witches ($2.95) - Short stories by various; Frenz-c 3.00
...: Zombies ($2.95) - Short stories by various; Frenz-c 3.00
Volume 1 (2004, $16.95, TPB) r/short stories from series; Wolak-c 17.00

MOONSTONE NOIR
Moonstone: 2003 - Present ($2.95/$4.95/$5.50, B&W)

...: Bulldog Drummond (2004, $4.95) - Messner-Loebs-s/Barkley-a 5.00
...: Johnny Dollar ($4.95) - Gallaher-s/Theriault-a 5.00
...: Mr. Keen, Tracer of Lost Persons 1,2 ($2.95, limited series) - Ferguson-a 3.00
...: Mysterious Traveler (2003, $5.50) - Trevor Von Eeden-a/Joe Gentile-s 5.50
...: Mysterious Traveler Returns (2004, $4.95) - Trevor Von Eeden-a/Joe Gentile-s 5.00
...: The Lone Wolf ($4.95) - Jolley-s/Croall-a 5.00

MOPSY (See Pageant of Comics & TV Teens)
St. John Publ. Co.: Feb, 1948 - No. 19, Sept, 1953

	GD 2.0	VG 4.0	FN 6.0	VF 8.0	VF/NM 9.0	NM- 9.2
1-Part-r; reprints "Some Punkins" by Neher	18	36	54	103	162	220
2	11	22	33	62	86	110
3-10(1953): 8-Lingerie panels	10	20	30	56	76	95
11-19: 19-Lingerie-c	9	18	27	52	69	85

NOTE: *#1-7, 13, 18, 19 have paper dolls.*

MORBIUS REVISITED
Marvel Comic: Aug, 1993 - No. 5, Dec, 1993 ($1.95, mini-series)

1-5-Reprints Fear #27-31 3.00

MORBIUS: THE LIVING VAMPIRE (Also see Amazing Spider-Man #101,102, Fear #20, Marvel Team-Up #3, 4, Midnight Sons Unl. & Vampire Tales)
Marvel Comics (Midnight Sons imprint #16 on): Sep, 1992 - No. 32, Apr, 1995 ($1.75/$1.95)

1-($2.75, 52 pgs.)-Polybagged w/poster; Ghost Rider & Johnny Blaze x-over (part 3 of Rise of the Midnight Sons) 4.00
2-11,13-24,26-32: 3,4-Vs. Spider-Man-c/s.15-Ghost Rider app. 16-Spot varnish-c. 16,17-Siege of Darkness, parts 5 &13. 18-Deathlok app. 21-Bound-in Spider-Man trading card sheet; Spider-Man app. 3.00
12-($2.25)-Outer-c is a Darkhold envelope made of black parchment w/gold ink; Midnight Massacre x-over 3.00
25-($2.50, 52 pgs.)-Gold foil logo 4.00

MORE FUN COMICS (Formerly New Fun Comics #1-6)
National Periodical Publs: No. 7, Jan, 1936 - No. 127, Nov-Dec, 1947 (No. 7,9-11: paper-c)

	GD 2.0	VG 4.0	FN 6.0	VF 8.0	VF/NM 9.0	NM- 9.2
7(1/36)-Oversized, paper-c; 1 pg. Kelly-a	825	1650	2475	6600	-	-
8(2/36)-Oversized (10x12"), paper-c; 1 pg. Kelly-a; Sullivan-c	825	1650	2475	6600	-	-
9(3-4/36)(Very rare, 1st standard-sized comic book with original material)-Last multiple panel-c	1000	2000	3000	8000	-	-
10,11(7/36): 10-Last Henri Duval by Siegel & Shuster. 11-1st "Calling All Cars" by Siegel & Shuster; new classic logo begins	588	1176	1764	4700	-	-
12(8/36)-Slick-c begin	463	926	1389	3700	-	-
V2#1(9/36, #13) 1 pg. Fred Astaire photo/bio	425	850	1275	3400	-	-
2(10/36, #14)-Dr. Occult in costume (1st in color)(Superman proto-type; 1st DC appearance) continues from The Comics Magazine, ends #17	1938	3876	5814	15,500	-	-
V2#3(11/36, #15), 17(V2#5)	788	1576	2364	6300	-	-
16(V2#4)-Cover numbering begins; ties with New Comics #11 as 1st DC Christmas-c; last Superman tryout issue	813	1626	2439	6500	-	-
18-20(V2#8, 5/37)	338	676	1014	2700	-	-
21(V2#9)-24(V2#12, 9/37)	276	552	828	1518	2309	3100
25(V3#1, 10/37)-27(V3#3, 12/37): 27-Xmas-c	276	552	828	1518	2309	3100
28-30: 30-1st non-funny cover	250	500	750	1375	2088	2800
31-Has ad for Action Comics #1	265	530	795	1458	2204	2950
32-35: 32-Last Dr. Occult	250	500	750	1375	2088	2800
36-40: 36-(10/38)-The Masked Ranger & sidekick Pedro begins; Ginger Snap by Bob Kane (2 pgs.; 1st-a?). 39-Xmas-c	250	500	750	1375	2088	2800
41-50: 41-Last Masked Ranger	212	424	636	1166	1833	2500

More Fun Comics #117 © DC

Morlocks #4 © MAR

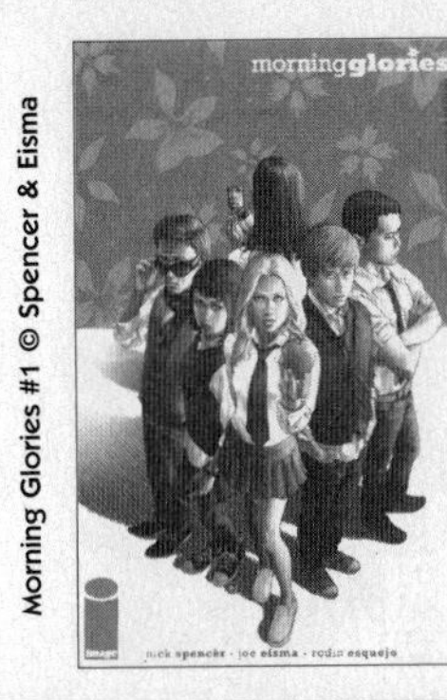

Morning Glories #1 © Spencer & Eisma

	GD 2.0	VG 4.0	FN 6.0	VF 8.0	VF/NM 9.0	NM- 9.2

51-The Spectre app. (in costume) in one panel ad at end of Buccaneer story
741 1482 2223 4076 6038 8000
52-(2/40)-Origin/1st app. The Spectre (in costume splash panel only), part 1 by Bernard Baily (parts 1 & 2 written by Jerry Siegel; Spectre's costume changes color from purple & blue to green & grey; last Wing Brady; Spectre-c 7500 15,000 22,500 56,250 100,625 145,000
53-Origin The Spectre (in costume at end of story), part 2; Capt. Desmo begins; Spectre-c 3250 6500 9750 22,750 48,875 75,000
54-The Spectre in costume; last King Carter; classic-Spectre-c
1750 3500 5250 13,125 23,563 34,000
55-(Scarce, 5/40)-Dr. Fate begins (1st app.); last Bulldog Martin; Spectre-c
1700 3400 5100 12,750 22,875 33,000
56-1st Dr. Fate-c (classic), origin continues. Congo Bill begins (6/40), 1st app.;
838 1676 2514 6117 10,809 15,500
57-60-All Spectre-c 432 864 1296 3154 5577 8000
61,65: 61-Classic Dr. Fate-c. 65-Classic Spectre-c 411 822 1233 2877 5039 7200
62-64,66: 63-Last Lt. Bob Neal. 64-Lance Larkin begins; all Spectre-c
331 662 993 2317 4059 5800
67-(5/41)-Origin (1st) Dr. Fate; last Congo Bill & Biff Bronson (Congo Bill continues in Action Comics #37, 6/41)-Spectre-c 811 1622 2433 5920 10,460 15,000
68-70: 68-Clip Carson begins. 70-Last Lance Larkin; all Dr. Fate-c
290 580 870 1856 3178 4500
71-Origin & 1st app. Johnny Quick by Mort Weisinger (9/41); classic sci/fi Dr. Fate-c
524 1048 1572 3825 6763 9700
72-Dr. Fate's new helmet; last Sgt. Carey, Sgt. O'Malley & Captain Desmo; German submarine-c (Nazi war-c) 284 568 852 1818 3109 4400
73-Origin & 1st app. Aquaman (11/41) by Paul Norris; intro. Green Arrow & Speedy; Dr. Fate-c 1600 3200 4800 12,000 21,500 31,000
74-2nd Aquaman; 1st Percival Popp, Supercop; Dr. Fate-c
300 600 900 2010 3505 5000
75,76: 75-New origin Spectre; Nazi spy ring cover w/Hitler's photo. 76-Last Dr. Fate-c; Johnny Quick (by Meskin #76-97) begins, ends #107; last Clip Carson
258 516 774 1651 2826 4000
77-80: 77-Green Arrow-c begin 194 388 582 1242 2121 3000
81-83,85,88,90: 81-Last large logo. 82-1st small logo.
132 264 396 838 1444 2050
84-Green Arrow Japanese war-c 135 270 405 864 1482 2100
86,87-Johnny Quick-c. 87-Last Radio Squad 132 264 396 838 1444 2050
89-Origin Green Arrow & Speedy Team-up 139 278 417 883 1517 2150
91-97,99: 91-1st bi-monthly issue. 93-Dover & Clover begin (1st app., 9-10/43). 97-Kubert-a 87 174 261 553 952 1350
98-Last Dr. Fate (scarce) 107 214 321 680 1165 1650
100 (11-12/44)-Johnny Quick-c 118 236 354 749 1287 1825
101-Origin & 1st app. Superboy (1-2/45)(not by Siegel & Shuster); last Spectre issue; Green Arrow-c 919 1838 2757 6709 11,855 17,000
102-2nd Superboy app; 1st Dover & Clover-c 145 290 435 921 1586 2250
103-3rd Superboy app; last Green Arrow-c 103 206 309 659 1130 1600
104-1st Superboy-c w/Dover & Clover 90 180 270 576 988 1400
105,106-Superboy-c 82 164 246 528 902 1275
107-Last Johnny Quick & Superboy 82 164 246 528 902 1275
108-120: 108-Genius Jones begins; 1st c-app. (3-4/46; cont'd from Adventure Comics #102)
26 52 78 154 252 350
121-124,126: 121-123,126-Post funny animal (Jimminy & the Magic Book)-c
24 48 72 142 234 325
125-Superman c-app.w/Jimminy 82 164 246 528 902 1275
127-(Scarce)-Post-c/a 39 78 117 231 378 525
NOTE: *All issues are scarce to rare. Cover features: The Spectre-#52-55, 57-60, 62-67. Dr. Fate-#56, 61, 68-76. The Green Arrow & Speedy-#77-85, 88-97, 99, 101 (w/Dover & Clover-#98, 103). Johnny Quick-#86, 87, 100. Dover & Clover-#102, (104, 106 w/Superboy), 107, 108(w/Genius Jones), 110, 112, 114, 117, 119. Genius Jones-#109, 111, 113, 115, 116, 118, 120.* ***Baily*** *a-45, 52-on; c-52-55, 57-60, 62-67.* ***Al Capp*** *a-45(signed Koppy).* ***Ellsworth*** *c-7.* ***Creig Flessel*** *c-30, 31, 35-48(most).* ***Guardineer*** *c-47, 49, 50.* ***Kiefer*** *a-20.* ***Meskin*** *c-86, 87, 100?* ***Moldoff*** *c-51.* ***George Papp*** *c-77-85.* ***Post*** *c-121-127.* ***Vincent Sullivan*** *c-8-28, 32-34.*

MORE FUND COMICS (Benefit book for the Comic Book Legal Defense Fund)
(Also see Even More Fund Comics)
Sky Dog Press: Sept, 2003 ($10.00, B&W, trade paperback)
nn-Anthology of short stories and pin-ups by various; Hulk-c by Pérez 10.00

MORE SEYMOUR (See Seymour My Son)
Archie Publications: Oct, 1963
1-DeCarlo-a? 3 6 9 20 30 40

MORE THAN MORTAL (Also see Lady Pendragon/...)
Liar Comics: June, 1997 - No. 4, Apr, 1998 ($2.95, limited series)
Image Comics: No. 5, Dec, 1999 - Present ($2.95)
1-Blue forest background-c, 1-Variant-c 4.00
1-White-c 6.00
1-2nd printing; purple sky cover 3.00
2-4: 3-Silvestri-c, 4-Two-c, one by Randy Queen 3.00
5,6: 5-1st Image Comics issue 3.00

MORE THAN MORTAL: OTHERWORLDS
Image Comics: July, 1999 - No. 4, Dec, 1999 ($2.95, limited series)
1-4-Firchow-a. 1-Two covers 3.00

MORE THAN MORTAL SAGAS
Liar Comics: Jun, 1998 - No. 3, Dec, 1998 ($2.95, limited series)
1,2-Painted art by Romano. 2-Two-c, one by Firchow 3.00
1-Variant-c by Linsner 5.00

MORE THAN MORTAL TRUTHS AND LEGENDS
Liar Comics: Aug, 1998 - No. 6, Apr, 1999 ($2.95)
1-6-Firchow-a(p) 3.00
1-Variant-c by Dan Norton 4.50

MORE TRASH FROM MAD (Annual)
E. C. Comics: 1958 - No. 12, 1969
(Note: Bonus missing = half price)
nn(1958)-8 pgs. color Mad reprint from #20 18 36 54 125 255 385
2(1959)-Market Product Labels 13 26 39 89 170 250
3(1960)-Text book covers 12 24 36 82 154 225
4(1961)-Sing Along with Mad booklet 12 24 36 82 154 225
5(1962)-Window Stickers; r/from Mad #39 9 18 27 63 107 150
6(1963)-TV Guise booklet 9 18 27 63 107 150
7(1964)-Alfred E. Neuman commemorative stamps 8 16 24 52 86 120
8(1965)-Life size poster-Alfred E. Neuman 6 12 18 41 66 90
9-12: 9,10(1966-67)-Mischief Sticker. 11(1968)-Campaign poster & bumper sticker. 12(1969)-Pocket medals 6 12 18 41 66 90
NOTE: ***Kelly Freas*** *c-1, 2, 4.* ***Mingo*** *c-3, 5-9, 12.*

MORGAN THE PIRATE (Movie)
Dell Publishing Co.: No. 1227, Sept-Nov, 1961
Four Color 1227-Photo-c 7 14 21 50 83 115

MORLOCKS
Marvel Comics: June, 2002 - No. 4, Sept, 2002 ($2.50, limited series)
1-4-Johns-s/Martinbrough-c/a 3.00

MORLOCK 2001
Atlas/Seaboard Publ.: Feb, 1975 - No. 3, July, 1975
1,2: 1-(Super-hero)-Origin & 1st app.; Milgrom-c 2 4 6 8 11 14
3-Ditko/Wrightson-a; origin The Midnight Man & The Mystery Men
2 4 6 13 18 22

MORNING GLORIES
Image Comics: Aug, 2010 - Present ($3.99/$3.50/$2.99)
1-($3.99) Nick Spencer-s/Joe Eisma-a/Rodin Esquejo-c; group cover 8.00
1-Second-Fourth printings 4.00
2-($3.50) Regular cover and white background 2nd printing 5.00
3-6-Regular covers and white background 2nd printings 4.00
7,8-($2.99) 3.00
...Vol. 1 TPB (2/11, $9.99) r/#1-6 10.00

MORNINGSTAR SPECIAL
Comico: Apr, 1990 ($2.50)
1-From the Elementals; Willingham-c/a/scripts 3.00

MORTAL KOMBAT
Malibu Comics: July, 1994 - No. 6, Dec, 1994 ($2.95)
1-6: 1-Two diff. covers exist 3.00
1-Limited edition gold foil embossed-c 4.00
0 (12/94), Special Edition 1 (11/94) 3.00
Tournament Edition I12/94, $3.95), II('95)($3.95) 4.00
...: **BARAKA** ,June, 1995 ($2.95, one-shot) #1; ...**BATTLEWAVE** ,2/95 - No. 6, 7/95 , #1-6; ...**GORO, PRINCE OF PAIN** ,9/94 - No. 3, 11/94, #1-3; ...**KITANA AND MILEENA** ,8/95 , ...**KUNG LAO** ,7/95 , #1; ... **RAYDON & KANO** ,3/95 - No. 3, 5/95, #1-3: ...(all $2.95-c) 3.00
...: **U.S. SPECIAL FORCES** ,1/95 - No. 2, ($3.50), #1,2 3.50

MORTIE (Mazie's Friend; also see Flat-Top)
Magazine Publishers: Dec, 1952 - No. 4, June, 1953?
1 9 18 27 50 65 80
2-4 6 12 18 28 34 40

MORTIGAN GOTH: IMMORTALIS (See Marvel Frontier Comics Unlimited)
Marvel Comics: Sept, 1993 - No. 4, Mar, 1994 ($1.95, mini-series)

Motel Hell #1 © MGM

Motion Picture Comics #114 © FAW

Movie Classics - Mad Monster Party © DELL

GD VG FN VF VF/NM NM-
2.0 4.0 6.0 8.0 9.0 9.2

1-($2.95)-Foil-c 3.50
2-4 3.00

MORT THE DEAD TEENAGER
Marvel Comics: Nov, 1993 - No. 4, Mar, 1994 ($1.75, mini-series)
1-4 3.00

MORTY MEEKLE
Dell Publishing Co.: No. 793, May, 1957
Four Color 793 4 8 12 24 37 50

MOSES & THE TEN COMMANDMENTS (See Dell Giants)

MOSTLY WANTED
DC Comics (WildStorm): Jul, 2000 - No. 4, Nov, 2000 ($2.50, limited series)
1-4-Lobdell-s/Flores-a 3.00

MOTEL HELL (Based on the 1980 movie)
IDW Publishing: Oct, 2010 - No. 3, Dec, 2010 ($3.99, limited series)
1-3-Matt Nixon-s/Chris Moreno-a. 1,2-Bradstreet-c. 3-Moreno-c 4.00

MOTH, THE
Dark Horse Comics: Apr, 2004 - No. 4, Aug, 2004 ($2.99)
1-4-Steve Rude-c/a; Gary Martin-s 3.00
... Special (3/04, $4.95) 5.00
TPB (5/05, $12.95) r/#1-4 and Special; gallery of extras 13.00

MOTH, THE
Rude Dude Productions: May 2008 (Free Comic Book Day giveaway)
... Special Edition - Steve Rude-s/a; sketch pages 2.50

MOTHER GOOSE AND NURSERY RHYME COMICS (See Christmas With Mother Goose)
Dell Publishing Co.: No. 41, 1944 - No. 862, Nov, 1957
Four Color 41-Walt Kelly-c/a 21 42 63 150 300 450
Four Color 59, 68-Kelly c/a 17 34 51 118 242 365
Four Color 862-The Truth About..., Movie (Disney) 7 14 21 49 80 110

MOTHER TERESA OF CALCUTTA
Marvel Comics Group: 1984
1-(52 pgs.) No ads 1 2 3 5 6 8

MOTION PICTURE COMICS (See Fawcett Movie Comics)
Fawcett Publications: No. 101, 1950 - No. 114, Jan, 1953 (All-photo-c)
101- "Vanishing Westerner"; Monte Hale (1950) 15 30 45 90 140 190
102- "Code of the Silver Sage"; Rocky Lane (1/51) 15 30 45 83 124 165
103- "Covered Wagon Raid"; Rocky Lane (3/51) 15 30 45 83 124 165
104- "Vigilante Hideout"; Rocky Lane (5/51)-Book length Powell-a
15 30 45 83 124 165
105- "Red Badge of Courage"; Audie Murphy; Bob Powell-a (7/51)
18 36 54 105 165 225
106- "The Texas Rangers"; George Montgomery (9/51)
15 30 45 83 124 165
107- "Frisco Tornado"; Rocky Lane (11/51) 14 28 42 80 115 150
108- "Mask of the Avenger"; John Derek 12 24 36 69 97 125
109- "Rough Rider of Durango"; Rocky Lane 14 28 42 80 115 150
110- "When Worlds Collide"; George Evans-a (5/52); Williamson & Evans drew themselves in story; (also see Famous Funnies No. 72-88) 77 154 231 493 847 1200
111- "The Vanishing Outpost"; Lash LaRue 15 30 45 90 140 190
112- "Brave Warrior"; Jon Hall & Jay Silverheels 12 24 36 67 94 120
113- "Walk East on Beacon"; George Murphy; Schaffenberger-a
10 20 30 54 72 90
114- "Cripple Creek"; George Montgomery (1/53) 10 20 30 58 79 100

MOTION PICTURE FUNNIES WEEKLY (See Promotional Comics section)

MOTORHEAD (See Comic's Greatest World)
Dark Horse Comics: Aug, 1995 - No. 6, Jan, 1996 ($2.50)
1-6: Bisley-c on all. 1-Predator app. 3.00
Special 1 (3/94, $3.95, 52pgs.)-Jae Lee-c; Barb Wire, The Machine & Wolf Gang app. 4.00

MOTORMOUTH (... & Killpower #7? on)
Marvel Comics UK: June, 1992 - No. 12, May, 1993 ($1.75)
1-13: 1,2-Nick Fury app. 3-Punisher-c/story. 5,6-Nick Fury & Punisher app. 6-Cable cameo. 7-9-Cable app. 3.00

MOUNTAIN MEN (See Ben Bowie)

MOUSE MUSKETEERS (See M.G.M.'s...)

MOUSE ON THE MOON, THE (See Movie Classics)

MOVIE CARTOONS
DC Comics: Dec, 1944 (cover only ashcan)
nn-Ashcan comic, not distributed to newsstands, only for in house use. Covers were produced, but not the rest of the book. A copy sold in 2006 for $500.

MOVIE CLASSICS
Dell Publishing Co.: Apr, 1956; May-Jul, 1962 - Dec, 1969
(Before 1963, most movie adaptations were part of the 4-Color series)
(Disney movie adaptations after 1970 are in Walt Disney Showcase)
Around the World Under the Sea 12-030-612 (12/66) 3 6 9 20 30 40
Bambi 3(4/56)-Disney; r/4-Color #186 4 8 12 24 37 50
Battle of the Bulge 12-056-606 (6/66) 3 6 9 21 32 42
Beach Blanket Bingo 12-058-509 7 14 21 47 76 105
Bon Voyage 01-068-212 (12/62)-Disney; photo-c 4 8 12 22 34 45
Castilian, The 12-110-401 3 6 9 20 30 40
Cat, The 12-109-612 (12/66) 3 6 9 19 29 38
Cheyenne Autumn 12-112-506 (4-6/65) 5 10 15 34 55 75
Circus World, Samuel Bronston's 12-115-411; John Wayne app.; John Wayne photo-c
9 18 27 65 113 160
Countdown 12-150-710 (10/67)-James Caan photo-c 3 6 9 21 32 42
Creature, The 1 (12-142-302) (12-2/62-63) 9 18 27 60 100 140
Creature, The 12-142-410 (10/64) 5 10 15 32 51 70
David Ladd's Life Story 12-173-212 (10-12/62)-Photo-c
7 14 21 47 76 105
Die, Monster, Die 12-175-603 (3/66)-Photo-c 5 10 15 34 55 75
Dirty Dozen 12-180-710 (10/67) 4 8 12 28 44 60
Dr. Who & the Daleks 12-190-612 (12/66)-Peter Cushing photo-c; 1st U.S. app. of Dr. Who
10 20 30 72 131 190
Dracula 12-231-212 (10-12/62) 8 16 24 54 90 125
El Dorado 12-240-710 (10/67)-John Wayne; photo-c 11 22 33 78 139 200
Ensign Pulver 12-257-410 (8-10/64) 3 6 9 19 29 38
Frankenstein 12-283-305 (3-5/63)(see Frankenstein 8-10/64 for 2nd printing)
8 16 24 56 93 130
Great Race, The 12-299-603 (3/66)-Natallie Wood, Tony Curtis photo-c
4 8 12 28 44 60
Hallelujah Trail, The 12-307-602 (2/66) (Shows 1/66 inside); Burt Lancaster, Lee Remick photo-c
5 10 15 32 51 70
Hatari 12-340-301 (1/63)-John Wayne 8 16 24 52 86 120
Horizontal Lieutenant, The 01-348-210 (10/62) 3 6 9 19 29 38
Incredible Mr. Limpet, The 12-370-408; Don Knotts photo-c
5 10 15 30 48 65
Jack the Giant Killer 12-374-301 (1/63) 8 16 24 52 86 120
Jason & the Argonauts 12-376-310 (8-10/63)-Photo-c
9 18 27 61 103 145
Lancelot & Guinevere 12-416-310 (10/63) 5 10 15 32 51 70
Lawrence 12-426-308 (8/63)-Story of Lawrence of Arabia; movie ad on back-c; not exactly like movie
5 10 15 32 51 70
Lion of Sparta 12-439-301 (1/63) 4 8 12 22 34 45
Mad Monster Party 12-460-801 (9/67)-Based on Kurtzman's screenplay
9 18 27 60 100 140
Magic Sword, The 01-496-209 (9/62) 5 10 15 35 55 75
Masque of the Red Death 12-490-410 (8-10/64)-Vincent Price photo-c
6 12 18 41 66 90
Maya 12-495-612 (12/66)-Clint Walker & Jay North part photo-c
4 8 12 24 37 50
McHale's Navy 12-500-412 (10-12/64) 4 8 12 28 44 60
Merrill's Marauders 12-510-301 (1/63)-Photo-c 3 6 9 19 29 38
Mouse on the Moon, The 12-530-312 (10/12/63)-Photo-c
4 8 12 22 34 45
Mummy, The 12-537-211 (9-11/62) 2 versions with different back-c
8 16 24 58 97 135
Music Man, The 12-538-301 (1/63) 3 6 9 20 30 40
Naked Prey, The 12-545-612 (12/66)-Photo-c 5 10 15 34 55 75
Night of the Grizzly, The 12-558-612 (12/66)-Photo-c 4 8 12 22 34 45
None But the Brave 12-565-506 (4-6/65) 5 10 15 34 55 75
Operation Bikini 12-597-310 (10/63)-Photo-c 3 6 9 20 30 40
Operation Crossbow 12-590-512 (10-12/65) 3 6 9 20 30 40
Prince & the Pauper, The 01-654-207 (5-7/62)-Disney
4 8 12 22 34 45
Raven, The 12-680-309 (9/63)-Vincent Price photo-c 6 12 18 39 62 85
Ring of Bright Water 01-701-910 (10/69) (inside shows #12-701-909)
4 8 12 22 34 45
Runaway, The 12-707-412 (10-12/64) 3 6 9 19 29 38
Santa Claus Conquers the Martians #? (1964)-Photo-c
10 20 30 67 116 165

Movie Comics #1 © DC

Movie Comics #3 © FH

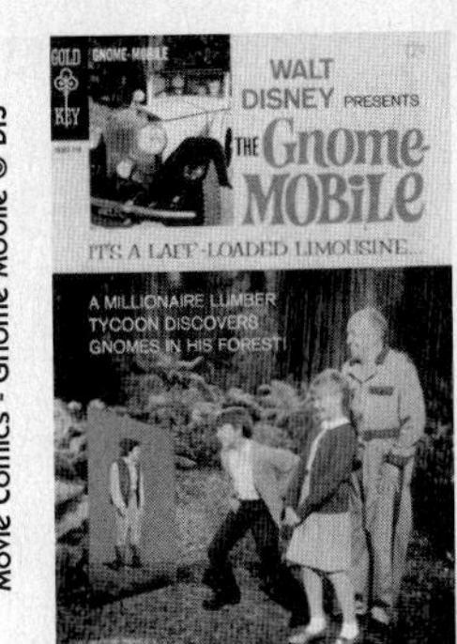

Movie Comics - Gnome Mobile © DIS

GD VG FN VF VF/NM NM-
2.0 4.0 6.0 8.0 9.0 9.2

Santa Claus Conquers the Martians 12-725-603 (3/66, 12¢)-Reprints 1964 issue; photo-c 7 14 21 47 76 105
Another version given away with a Golden Record, SLP 170, nn, no price (3/66)-Complete with record 12 24 36 82 154 225
Six Black Horses 12-750-301 (1/63)-Photo-c 3 6 9 20 30 40
Ski Party 12-743-511 (9-11/65)-Frankie Avalon photo-c; photo inside-c; Adkins-a 5 10 15 30 48 65
Smoky 12-746-702 (2/67) 3 6 9 19 29 38
Sons of Katie Elder 12-748-511 (9-11/65); John Wayne app.; photo-c 11 22 33 75 138 200
Tales of Terror 12-793-302 (2/63)-Evans-a 5 10 15 34 55 75
Three Stooges Meet Hercules 01-828-208 (8/62)-Photo-c 9 18 27 60 100 140
Tomb of Ligeia 12-830-506 (4-6/65) 5 10 15 34 55 75
Treasure Island 01-845-211 (7-9/62)-Disney; r/4-Color #624 3 6 9 20 30 40
Twice Told Tales (Nathaniel Hawthorne) 12-840-401 (11-1/63-64); Vincent Price photo-c 6 12 18 37 59 80
Two on a Guillotine 12-850-506 (4-6/65) 4 8 12 22 34 45
Valley of Gwangi 01-880-912 (12/69) 9 18 27 60 100 140
War Gods of the Deep 12-900-509 (7-9/65) 3 6 9 20 30 40
War Wagon, The 12-533-709 (9/67); John Wayne app. 8 16 24 54 90 125
Who's Minding the Mint? 12-924-708 (8/67) 3 6 9 19 29 38
Wolfman, The 12-922-308 (6-8/63) 8 16 24 56 93 130
Wolfman, The 1(12-922-410)(8-10/64)-2nd printing; r/#12-922-308 4 8 12 23 36 48
Zulu 12-950-410 (8-10/64)-Photo-c 7 14 21 49 80 110

MOVIE COMICS (See Cinema Comics Herald & Fawcett Movie Comics)

MOVIE COMICS
National Periodical Publications/Picture Comics: April, 1939 - No. 6, Sept-Oct, 1939 (Most all photo-c)

1- "Gunga Din", "Son of Frankenstein", "The Great Man Votes", "Fisherman's Wharf", & "Scouts to the Rescue" part 1; Wheelan "Minute Movies" begin 366 732 1098 2562 4481 6400
2- "Stagecoach", "The Saint Strikes Back", "King of the Turf","Scouts to the Rescue" part 2, "Arizona Legion", Andy Devine photo-c 252 504 756 1613 2757 3900
3- "East Side of Heaven", "Mystery in the White Room", "Four Feathers", "Mexican Rose" with Gene Autry, "Spirit of Culver", "Many Secrets", "The Mikado" (1st Gene Autry photo cover) 177 354 531 1124 1937 2750
4- "Captain Fury", Gene Autry in "Blue Montana Skies", "Streets of N.Y." with Jackie Cooper, "Oregon Trail" part 1 with Johnny Mack Brown, "Big Town Czar" with Barton MacLane, & "Star Reporter" with Warren Hull 148 296 444 947 1624 2300
5- "The Man in the Iron Mask", "Five Came Back", "Wolf Call", "The Girl & the Gambler", "The House of Fear", "The Family Next Door", "Oregon Trail" part 2 161 322 483 1030 1765 2500
6- "The Phantom Creeps", "Chumps at Oxford", & "The Oregon Trail" part 3; 2nd Robot-c 206 412 618 1318 2259 3200

NOTE: *Above books contain many original movie stills with dialogue from movie scripts. All issues are scarce.*

MOVIE COMICS
Fiction House Magazines: Dec, 1946 - No. 4, 1947

1-Big Town (by Lubbers), Johnny Danger begin; Celardo-a; Mitzi of the Movies by Fran Hopper 41 82 123 256 428 600
2-(2/47)- "White Tie & Tails" with William Bendix; Mitzi of the Movies begins 31 62 93 186 303 420
3-(6/47)-Andy Hardy starring Mickey Rooney 31 62 93 186 303 420
4-Mitzi In Hollywood by Matt Baker; Merton of the Movies with Red Skelton; Yvonne DeCarlo & George Brent in "Slave Girl" 39 78 117 231 378 525

MOVIE COMICS
Gold Key/Whitman: Oct, 1962 - 1984

Alice in Wonderland 10144-503 (3/65)-Disney; partial reprint of 4-Color #331 4 8 12 22 34 45
Alice In Wonderland #1 (Whitman pre-pack, 3/84) 2 4 6 10 14 18
Aristocats, The 1 (30045-103)(3/71)-Disney; with pull-out poster (25¢) (No poster = half price) 7 14 21 47 76 105
Bambi 1 (10087-309)(9/63)-Disney; r/4-C #186 4 8 12 24 37 50
Bambi 2 (10087-607)(7/66)-Disney; r/4-C #186 3 6 9 20 30 40
Beneath the Planet of the Apes 30044-012 (12/70)-with pull-out poster; photo-c (No poster = half price) 9 18 27 61 103 145
Big Red 10026-211 (11/62)-Disney; photo-c 3 6 9 20 30 40
Big Red 10026-503 (3/65)-Disney; reprints 10026-211; photo-c 3 6 9 16 23 30

Blackbeard's Ghost 10222-806 (6/68)-Disney 3 6 9 19 29 38
Bullwhip Griffin 10181-706 (6/67)-Disney; Spiegle-a; photo-c 4 8 12 22 34 45
Captain Sindbad 10077-309 (9/63)-Manning-a; photo-c 6 12 18 41 66 90
Chitty Chitty Bang Bang 1 (30038-902)(2/69)-with pull-out poster; Disney; photo-c (No poster = half price) 6 12 18 43 69 95
Cinderella 10152-508 (8/65)-Disney; r/4-C #786 4 8 12 26 41 55
Darby O'Gill & the Little People 10251-001(1/70)-Disney; reprints 4-Color #1024 (Toth-a); photo-c 5 10 15 30 48 65
Dumbo 1 (10090-310)(10/63)-Disney; r/4-C #668 3 6 9 21 32 42
Emil & the Detectives 10120-502 (11/64)-Disney; photo-c & back-c photo pin-up 3 6 9 20 30 40
Escapade in Florence 1 (10043-301)(1/63)-Disney; starring Annette Funicello 8 16 24 52 86 120
Fall of the Roman Empire 10118-407 (7/64); Sophia Loren photo-c 4 8 12 24 37 50
Fantastic Voyage 10178-702 (2/67)-Wood/Adkins-a; photo-c 6 12 18 37 59 80
55 Days at Peking 10081-309 (9/63)-Photo-c 3 6 9 20 30 40
Fighting Prince of Donegal, The 10193-701 (1/67)-Disney 3 6 9 19 29 38
First Men in the Moon 10132-503 (3/65)-Fred Fredericks-a; photo-c 4 8 12 24 37 50
Gay Purr-ee 30017-301(1/63, 84 pgs.) 5 10 15 32 51 70
Gnome Mobile, The 10207-710 (10/67)-Disney; Walter Brennan photo-c & back-c photo pin-up 4 8 12 22 34 45
Goodbye, Mr. Chips 10246-006 (6/70)-Peter O'Toole photo-c 3 6 9 20 30 40
Happiest Millionaire, The 10221-804 (4/68)-Disney 4 8 12 22 34 45
Hey There, It's Yogi Bear 10122-409 (9/64)-Hanna-Barbera 6 12 18 43 69 95
Horse Without a Head, The 10109-401 (1/64)-Disney 3 6 9 19 29 38
How the West Was Won 10074-307 (7/63)-Based on the L'Amour novel; Tufts-a 4 8 12 28 44 60
In Search of the Castaways 10048-303 (3/63)-Disney; Hayley Mills photo-c 6 12 18 43 69 95
Jungle Book, The 1 (6022-801)(1/68-Whitman)-Disney; large size (10x13-1/2"); 59¢ 6 12 18 43 69 95
Jungle Book, The 1 (30033-803)(3/68, 68 pgs.)-Disney; same contents as Whitman #1 4 8 12 24 37 50
Jungle Book, The 1 (6/78, $1.00 tabloid) 3 6 9 16 23 30
Jungle Book (7/84)-r/Giant; Whitman pre-pack 2 4 6 10 14 18
Kidnapped 10080-306 (6/63)-Disney; reprints 4-Color #1101; photo-c 3 6 9 20 30 40
King Kong 30036-809(9/68-68 pgs.)-painted-c 4 8 12 26 41 55
King Kong nn-Whitman Treasury($1.00, 68 pgs.,1968), same cover as Gold Key issue 5 10 15 34 55 75
King Kong 11299(#1-786, 10x13-1/4", 68 pgs., $1.00, 1978) 3 6 9 18 27 35
Lady and the Tramp 10042-301 (1/63)-Disney; r/4-Color #629 3 6 9 21 32 42
Lady and the Tramp 1 (1967-Giant; 25¢)-Disney; reprints part of Dell #1 5 10 15 34 55 75
Lady and the Tramp 2 (10042-203)(3/72)-Disney; r/4-Color #629 3 6 9 16 23 30
Legend of Lobo, The 1 (10059-303)(3/63)-Disney; photo-c 3 6 9 16 23 30
Lt. Robin Crusoe, U.S.N. 10191-610 (10/66)-Disney; Dick Van Dyke photo-c & back-c photo pin-up 3 6 9 18 27 35
Lion, The 10035-301 (1/63)-Photo-c 3 6 9 17 25 32
Lord Jim 10156-509 (9/65)-Photo-c 3 6 9 17 25 32
Love Bug, The 10237-906 (6/69)-Disney; Buddy Hackett photo-c 4 8 12 22 34 45
Mary Poppins 10136-501 (1/65)-Disney; photo-c 5 10 15 30 48 65
Mary Poppins 30023-501 (1/65-68 pgs.)-Disney; photo-c 7 14 21 47 76 105
McLintock 10110-403 (3/64); John Wayne app.; John Wayne & Maureen O'Hara photo-c 11 22 33 77 144 210
Merlin Jones as the Monkey's Uncle 10115-510 (10/65)-Disney; Annette Funicello front/back photo-c 6 12 18 39 62 85
Miracle of the White Stallions, The 10065-306 (6/63)-Disney 3 6 9 19 29 38
Misadventures of Merlin Jones, The 10115-405 (5/64)-Disney; Annette Funicello

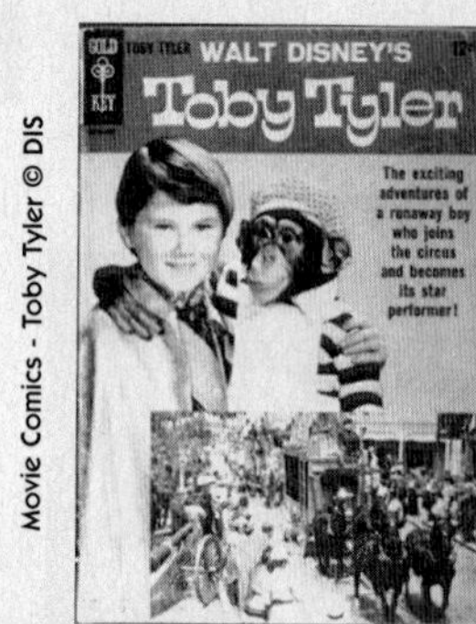

Movie Comics - Toby Tyler © DIS

Movie Love #11 © FF

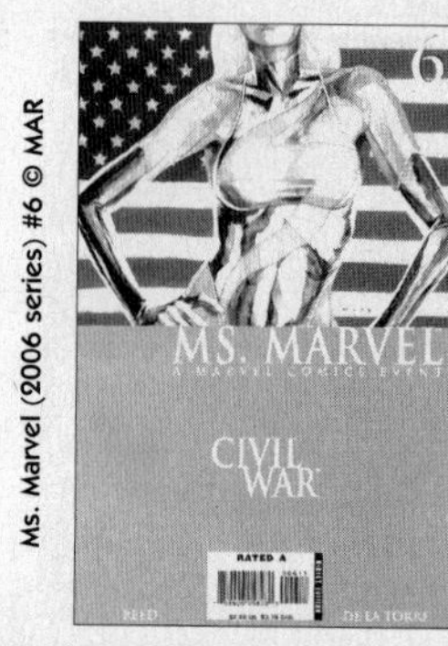

Ms. Marvel (2006 series) #6 © MAR

GD 2.0 | VG 4.0 | FN 6.0 | VF 8.0 | VF/NM 9.0 | NM- 9.2

photo front/back-c 6 12 18 39 62 85
Moon-Spinners, The 10124-410 (10/64)-Disney; Hayley Mills photo-c
6 12 18 43 69 95
Mutiny on the Bounty 1 (10040-302)(2/63)-Marlon Brando photo-c
4 8 12 22 34 45
Nikki, Wild Dog of the North 10141-412 (12/64)-Disney; reprints 4-Color #1226
3 6 9 16 23 30
Old Yeller 10168-601 (1/66)-Disney; reprints 4-Color #869; photo-c
3 6 9 16 23 30
One Hundred & One Dalmations 1 (10247-002) (2/70)-Disney; reprints Four Color #1183
3 6 9 18 27 35
Peter Pan 1 (10086-309)(9/63)-Disney; reprints Four Color #442
3 6 9 21 32 42
Peter Pan 2 (10086-909)(9/69)-Disney; reprints Four Color #442
3 6 9 16 23 30
Peter Pan 1 (3/84)-r/4-Color #442; Whitman pre-pack 2 4 6 11 16 20
P.T. 109 10123-409 (9/64)-John F. Kennedy 5 10 15 30 48 65
Rio Conchos 10143-503(3/65) 4 8 12 22 34 45
Robin Hood 10163-506 (6/65)-Disney; reprints Four Color #413
3 6 9 17 25 32
Shaggy Dog & the Absent-Minded Professor 30032-708 (8/67-Giant, 68 pgs.) Disney;
reprints 4-Color #985,1199 5 10 15 32 51 70
Sleeping Beauty 1 (30042-009)(9/70)-Disney; reprints Four Color #973; with pull-out poster
(No poster = half price) 6 12 18 43 69 95
Snow White & the Seven Dwarfs 1 (10091-310)(10/63)-Disney; reprints Four Color #382
3 6 9 20 30 40
Snow White & the Seven Dwarfs 10091-709 (9/67)-Disney; reprints Four Color #382
3 6 9 16 23 30
Snow White & the Seven Dwarfs 90091-204 (2/84)-Reprints Four Color #382;
Whitman pre-pack 2 4 6 11 16 20
Son of Flubber 1 (10057-304)(4/63)-Disney; sequel to "The Absent-Minded Professor"
4 8 12 22 34 45
Summer Magic 10076-309 (9/63)-Disney; Hayley Mills photo-c; Manning-a
6 12 18 43 69 95
Swiss Family Robinson 10236-904 (4/69)-Disney; reprints Four Color #1156; photo-c
3 6 9 18 27 35
Sword in the Stone, The 30019-402 (2/64-Giant, 68 pgs.)-Disney (see March of Comics #258
& Wart and the Wizard 6 12 18 43 69 95
That Darn Cat 10171-602 (2/66)-Disney; Hayley Mills photo-c
6 12 18 43 69 95
Those Magnificent Men in Their Flying Machines 10162-510 (10/65); photo-c
3 6 9 20 30 40
Three Stooges in Orbit 30016-211 (11/62-Giant, 32 pgs.)-All photos from movie; stiff-photo-c
9 18 27 65 113 160
Tiger Walks, A 10117-406 (6/64)-Disney; Torres?, Tufts-a; photo-c
4 8 12 24 37 50
Toby Tyler 10142-502 (2/65)-Disney; reprints Four Color #1092; photo-c
3 6 9 18 27 35
Treasure Island 1 (10200-703)(3/67)-Disney; reprints Four Color #624; photo-c
3 6 9 16 23 30
20,000 Leagues Under the Sea 1 (10095-312)(12/63)-Disney; reprints Four Color #614
3 6 9 18 27 35
Wonderful Adventures of Pinocchio, The 1 (10089-310)(10/63)-Disney; reprints Four Color #545
(see Wonderful Advs. of...) 3 6 9 21 32 42
Wonderful Adventures of Pinocchio, The 10089-109 (9/71)-Disney; reprints Four Color #545
3 6 9 16 23 30
Wonderful World of the Brothers Grimm 1 (10008-210)(10/62)
4 8 12 28 44 60
X, the Man with the X-Ray Eyes 10083-309 (9/63)-Ray Milland photo on-c
7 14 21 49 80 110
Yellow Submarine 35000-902 (2/69-Giant, 68 pgs.)-With pull-out poster;
The Beatles cartoon movie; Paul S. Newman-s 20 40 60 144 290 435
Without poster 9 18 27 64 110 155

MOVIE FABLES
DC Comics: Dec, 1944 (cover only ashcan)
nn-Ashcan comic, not distributed to newsstands, only for in house use. Covers were produced, but not the rest of the book. A copy sold in 2006 for $500.

MOVIE GEMS
DC Comics: Dec, 1944 (cover only ashcan)
nn-Ashcan comic, not distributed to newsstands, only for in house use. Covers were produced, but not the rest of the book. A copy sold in 2006 for $500.

MOVIE LOVE (Also see Personal Love)
Famous Funnies: Feb, 1950 - No. 22, Aug, 1953 (All photo-c)

GD 2.0 | VG 4.0 | FN 6.0 | VF 8.0 | VF/NM 9.0 | NM- 9.2

1-Dick Powell, Evelyn Keyes, & Mickey Rooney photo-c
18 36 54 107 169 230
2-Myrna Loy photo-c 11 22 33 64 90 115
3-7,9: 6-Ricardo Montalban photo-c. 9-Gene Tierney, John Lund, Glenn Ford,
& Rhonda Fleming photo-c. 11 22 33 60 83 105
8-Williamson/Frazetta-a, 6 pgs. 46 92 138 290 488 685
10-Frazetta-a, 6 pgs. 47 94 141 296 498 700
11,14-16: 14-Janet Leigh photo-c 10 20 30 58 79 100
12-Dean Martin & Jerry Lewis photo-c (12/51, pre-dates Advs. of Dean Martin &
Jerry Lewis comic) 20 40 60 117 189 260
13-Ronald Reagan photo-c with 1 pg. biog. 26 52 78 154 252 350
17-Leslie Caron & Ralph Meeker photo-c; 1 pg. Frazetta ad
11 22 33 60 83 105
18-22: 19-John Derek photo-c. 20-Donald O'Connor & Debbie Reynolds photo-c.
21-Paul Henreid & Patricia Medina photo-c. 22-John Payne & Coleen Gray photo-c
10 20 30 56 76 95
NOTE: *Each issue has a full-length movie adaptation with photo covers.*

MOVIE MONSTERS (Magazine)
Atlas/Seaboard: Dec, 1974 - No. 4, Aug, 1975 (B&W; Film, photo & article magazine)
1-(84 pages) Planet of the Apes, King Kong, Sindbad & Harryhausen, Christopher Lee Dracula, Star Trek, Werewolf, Creature from the Black Lagoon, Hammer's Mummy, Gorgo, & Exorcist 3 6 9 18 27 35
2-(2/1975) 2001: Planet of the Apes-c; 2001: A Space Odyssey; Doc Savage; Frankenstein; Rodan; One Million Years BC; (lower print run) 4 8 12 22 34 45
3-(4/1975) Phantom of the Opera-c; Wolfman, Godzilla, Boris Karloff, Batman, Forbidden Planet, Jack the Giant Killer 4 8 12 22 34 45
4-(8/1975) Thing, Flash Gordon, Lon Chaney Jr., Lost Worlds, Loch Ness Monster, Day the Earth Stood Still, Star Trek 4 8 12 22 34 45

MOVIE THRILLERS (Movie)
Magazine Enterprises: 1949
1-Adaptation of "Rope of Sand" w/Burt Lancaster; Burt Lancaster photo-c
28 56 84 165 270 375

MOVIE TOWN ANIMAL ANTICS (Formerly Animal Antics; becomes Raccoon Kids #52 on)
National Periodical Publ.: No. 24, Jan-Feb, 1950 - No. 51, July-Aug, 1954
24-Raccoon Kids continue 12 24 36 67 94 120
25-51 10 20 30 54 72 90
NOTE: ***Sheldon Mayer** a-28-33, 35, 37-41, 43, 44, 47, 49-51.*

MOVIE TUNES COMICS (Formerly Animated...; Frankie No. 4 on)
Marvel Comics (MgPC): No. 3, Fall, 1946
3-Super Rabbit, Krazy Krow, Silly Seal & Ziggy Pig 15 30 45 86 133 180

MOWGLI JUNGLE BOOK (Rudyard Kipling's...)
Dell Publ. Co.: No. 487, Aug-Oct, 1953 - No. 620, Apr, 1955
Four Color 487 (#1) 6 12 18 37 59 80
Four Color 582 (8/54), 620 5 10 15 30 48 65

MR. (See Mister)

M. REX
Image Comics: July, 1999 - No. 2, Dec, 1999 ($2.95)
Preview ($5.00) B&W pages and sketchbook; Rouleau-a 5.00
1,2-($2.95) 1-Joe Kelly-s/Rouleau-a/Anacleto-c. 2-Rouleau-c 3.00

MS. MARVEL (Also see The Avengers #183)
Marvel Comics Group: Jan, 1977 - No. 23, Apr, 1979
1-1st app. Ms. Marvel; Scorpion app. in #1,2 2 4 6 10 14 18
2-10: 2-Origin. 5-Vision app. 6-10-(Reg. 30¢-c). 10-Last 30¢ issue
1 2 3 5 7 9
6-10-(35¢-c variants, limited dist.)(6/77) 4 8 12 22 34 45
11-15,19-23: 19-Capt. Marvel app. 20-New costume. 23-Vance Astro (leader of the Guardians) app. 6.00
16,17-1st brief app. Mystique 3 6 9 16 22 28
18-1st full app. Mystique; Avengers x-over 5 10 15 30 48 65
NOTE: ***Austin** c-14i, 16i, 17i, 22i. **Buscema** a-1-3p; c(p)-2, 4, 6, 7, 15. **Infantino** a-14p, 19p. **Gil Kane** c-8. **Mooney** a-4-8p, 13p, 15-18p. **Starlin** c-12.*

MS. MARVEL (Also see New Avengers)
Marvel Comics: May, 2006 - Present ($2.99)
1-24: 1-Cho-c/Reed-s/De La Torre-a; Stilt-Man app. 4,5-Dr. Strange app. 6,7-Araña app. 3.00
1-Variant cover by Michael Turner 5.00
25-($3.99) Two covers by Horn and Dodson; Secret Invasion 4.00
26-49: 26-31-Secret Invasion. 34-Spider-Man app. 35-Dark Reign. 37-Carol explodes. 39,40,46,48,49-Takeda-a. 41-Carol returns. 47-Spider-Man app. 3.00
50-($3.99) Mystique and Captain Marvel app.; Takeda & Oliver-a 4.00

Ms. Tree #33 © Collins & Beatty

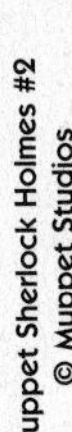
Muppet Sherlock Holmes #2 © Muppet Studios

Murderland #2 © Stephen Scott

GD VG FN VF VF/NM NM-
2.0 4.0 6.0 8.0 9.0 9.2

... Annual 1 (11/08, $3.99) Spider-Man app.; Horn-c 4.00
... Special (3/07, $2.99) Reed-s/Camuncoli-a/c 3.00
... Storyteller (1/09, $2.99) Reed-s/Camuncoli-a/c 3.00
... Vol. 1: Best of the Best HC (2006, $19.99) r/#1-5 & Giant-Size Ms. Marvel #1 20.00
... Vol. 1: Best of the Best SC (2007, $14.99) r/#1-5 & Giant-Size Ms. Marvel #1 15.00
... Vol. 2: Civil War HC (2007, $19.99) r/#6-10 & Ms. Marvel Special #1 20.00
... Vol. 2: Civil War SC (2007, $14.99) r/#6-10 & Ms. Marvel Special #1 15.00
... Vol. 3: Operation Lightning Storm HC (2007, $19.99) r/#11-17 20.00
... Vol. 4: Monster Smash HC (2008, $19.99) r/#18-24 20.00

MS. MYSTIC
Pacific Comics: Oct, 1982 - No. 2, Feb, 1984 ($1.00/$1.50)
1,2: Neal Adams-c/a/script. 1-Origin; intro Erth, Ayre, Fyre & Watr 4.00

MS. MYSTIC
Continuity Comics: 1988 - No. 9, May, 1992 ($2.00)
1-9: 1,2-Reprint Pacific Comics issues 3.00

MS. MYSTIC
Continunity Comics: V2#1, Oct, 1993 - V2#4, Jan, 1994 ($2.50)
V2#1-4: 1-Adams-c(i)/part-i. 2-4-Embossed-c. 2-Nebres part-i. 3-Adams-c(i)/plot. 4-Adams-c(p)/plot 3.00

MS. MYSTIC DEATHWATCH 2000 (Ms. Mystic #3)
Continuity: May, 1993 - No. 3, Aug, 1993 ($2.50)
1-3-Bagged w/card; Adams plots 3.00

MS. TREE QUARTERLY / SPECIAL
DC Comics: Summer, 1990 -No. 10, 1992 ($3.95/$3.50, 84 pgs, mature)
1-10: 1-Midnight story; Batman text story, Grell-a. 2,3-Midnight stories; The Butcher text stories 4.00
NOTE: ***Cowan** c-2. **Grell** c-1, 6. **Infantino** a-8.*

MS. TREE'S THRILLING DETECTIVE ADVS (Ms. Tree #4 on; also see The Best of Ms. Tree) (Baxter paper #4-9)
Eclipse Comics/Aardvark-Vanaheim 10-18/Renegade Press 19 on:
2/83 - #9, 7/84; #10, 8/84 - #18, 5/85; #19, 6/85 - #50, 6/89
1 4.00
2-49: 2-Schythe begins. 9-Last Eclipse & last color issue. 10,11-two-tone 3.00
50-Contains flexi-disc ($3.95, 52 pgs.) 4.00
Summer Special 1 (8/86) 3.00
1950s 3-D Crime (7/87, no glasses)-Johnny Dynamite in 3-D 3.00
Mike Mist in 3-D (8/85)-With glasses 3.00
NOTE: ***Miller** pin-up 1-4. Johnny Dynamite-r begin #36 by **Morisi**.*

MS. VICTORY SPECIAL(Also see Capt. Paragon & Femforce)
Americomics: Jan, 1985 (nd)
1 3.00

MUCHA LUCHA (Based on Kids WB animated TV show)
DC Comics: Jun, 2003 - No. 3, Aug, 2003 ($2.25, limited series)
1-3-Rikochet, Buena Girl and The Flea app. 3.00

MUGGSY MOUSE (Also see Tick Tock Tales)
Magazine Enterprises: 1951 - No. 3, 1951; No. 4, 1954 - No. 5, 1954; 1963

	GD 2.0	VG 4.0	FN 6.0	VF 8.0	VF/NM 9.0	NM- 9.2
1(A-1 #33)	9	18	27	52	69	85
2(A-1 #36)-Racist-c	14	28	42	76	108	140
3(A-1 #39), 4(A-1 #95), 5(A-1 #99)	7	14	21	37	46	55
Super Reprint #14(1963), I.W. Reprint #1,2 (nd)	2	4	6	8	11	14

MUGGY-DOO, BOY CAT
Stanhall Publ.: July, 1953 - No. 4, Jan, 1954

	GD 2.0	VG 4.0	FN 6.0	VF 8.0	VF/NM 9.0	NM- 9.2
1-Funny animal; Irving Spector-a	9	18	27	47	61	75
2-4	6	12	18	27	33	38
Super Reprint #12('63), 16('64)	2	4	6	8	11	14

MULLKON EMPIRE (See John Jake's...)

MUMMY, THE (See Universal Presents... under Dell Giants & Movie Classics)

MUMMY, THE: THE RISE AND FALL OF XANGO'S AX (Based on the Brendan Fraser movies)
IDW Publishing: Apr, 2008 - No. 4, July, 2008 ($3.99, limited series)
1-4-Prequel to '08 movie The Mummy: Tomb of the Dragon Emperor; Stephen Mooney-a 4.00

MUNDEN'S BAR ANNUAL
First Comics: Apr, 1988; 1989 ($2.95/$5.95)
1-($2.95)-r/from Grimjack; Fish Police story; Ordway-c 3.00
2-($5.95)-Teenage Mutant Ninja Turtles app. 6.00

MUNSTERS, THE (TV)
Gold Key: Jan, 1965 - No. 16, Jan, 1968 (All photo-c)

	GD 2.0	VG 4.0	FN 6.0	VF 8.0	VF/NM 9.0	NM- 9.2
1 (10134-501)	16	32	48	111	226	340
2	9	18	27	65	113	160
3-5	8	16	24	54	90	125
6-16	7	14	21	47	76	105

MUNSTERS, THE (TV)
TV Comics!: Aug, 1997 - No. 4 ($2.95, B&W)
1-4-All have photo-c 3.00
1,4-($7.95)-Variant-c 8.00
2-Variant-c w/Beverly Owens as Marilyn 3.00
Special Comic Con Ed. (7/97, $9.95) 10.00

MUPPET... (TV)
BOOM! Studios
... King Arthur 1-4 (12/09 - No. 4, 3/10, $2.99) Benjamin & Storck-s/Alvarez-a; 2 covers 3.00
... Peter Pan 1-4 (8/09 - No. 4, 11/09, $2.99) Randolph-s/Mebberson-a; multiple covers 3.00
... Robin Hood 1-4 (4/09 - No. 4, 7/09, $2.99) Beedle-s/Villavert Jr.-a; multiple covers 3.00
... Sherlock Holmes 1-4 (8/10 - No. 4, 11/10, $2.99) Storck-s/Mebberson-a/c 3.00
... Snow White 1-4 (4/10 - No. 4, 7/10, $2.99) Snider & Storck-s/Paroline-a; 2 covers 3.00

MUPPET BABIES, THE (TV)(See Star Comics Magazine)
Marvel Comics (Star Comics)/Marvel #18 on: Aug, 1985 - No. 26, July, 1989 (Children's book)
1-26 4.00

MUPPET SHOW, THE (TV)
BOOM! Studios: Mar, 2009 - No. 4, Jun, 2009 ($2.99, limited series)
1-4-Roger Landridge-s/a; multiple covers 3.00
...: The Treasure of Peg Leg Wilson (7/09 - No. 4, 10/09) 1-4-Landridge-s/a; multiple-c 3.00

MUPPET SHOW COMIC BOOK, THE (TV)
BOOM! Studios: No. 0, Nov, 2009 - Present ($2.99)
0-11: 0-3-Roger Landridge-s/a; multiple covers. 0-Paroline-a; Pigs in Space 3.00

MUPPETS TAKE MANHATTAN, THE
Marvel Comics (Star Comics): Nov, 1984 - No. 3, Jan, 1985
1-3-Movie adapt. r-/Marvel Super Special 4.00

MURCIELAGA, SHE-BAT
Heroic Publishing: Jan, 1993 - No. 2, 1993 (B&W)
1-($1.50, 28 pgs.) 3.00
2-($2.95, 36 pgs.)-Coated-c 3.00

MURDER CAN BE FUN
Slave Labor Graphics: Feb, 1996 - No. 12 ($2.95, B&W)
1-12: 1-Dorkin-c. 2-Vasquez-c. 3.00

MURDER INCORPORATED (My Private Life #16 on)
Fox Feature Syndicate: 1/48 - No. 15, 12/49; (2 No.9's); 6/50 - No. 3, 8/51

	GD 2.0	VG 4.0	FN 6.0	VF 8.0	VF/NM 9.0	NM- 9.2
1 (1st Series); 1,2 have 'For Adults Only' on-c	52	104	156	328	552	775
2-Electrocution story	40	80	120	242	401	560
3-7,9(4/49),10(5/49),11-15	24	48	72	140	230	320
8-Used in **SOTI**, pg. 160	27	54	81	158	259	360
9(3/49)-Possible use in **SOTI**, pg. 145; r/Blue Beetle #56('48)	24	48	72	140	230	320
5(#1, 6/50)(2nd Series)-Formerly My Desire #4; bondage-c.	20	40	60	117	189	260
2(8/50)-Morisi-a	18	36	54	107	169	230
3(8/51)-Used in **POP**, pg. 81; Rico-a; lingerie-c/panels	20	40	60	120	195	270

MURDERLAND
Image Comics: Aug, 2010 - No. 3, Nov, 2010 ($2.99)
1-3-Stephen Scott-s/David Haun-a 3.00

MURDER ME DEAD
El Capitán Books: July, 2000 - No. 9, Oct, 2001 ($2.95/$4.95, B&W)
1-8-David Lapham-s/a 3.00
9-($4.95) 5.00

MURDEROUS GANGSTERS
Avon Per./Realistic No. 3 on: Jul, 1951; No. 2, Dec, 1951 - No. 4, Jun, 1952

	GD 2.0	VG 4.0	FN 6.0	VF 8.0	VF/NM 9.0	NM- 9.2
1-Pretty Boy Floyd, Leggs Diamond; 1 pg. Wood-a	45	90	135	284	480	675
2-Baby-Face Nelson; 1 pg. Wood-a; painted-c	29	58	87	170	278	385
3-Painted-c	24	48	72	140	230	320
4- "Murder by Needle" drug story; Mort Lawrence-a; Kinstler-c	30	60	90	177	289	400

Music Box #1 © Lovespell & IDW

Muties #1 © MAR

Mutt and Jeff #6 © DC

GD VG FN VF VF/NM NM-
2.0 4.0 6.0 8.0 9.0 9.2

GD VG FN VF VF/NM NM-
2.0 4.0 6.0 8.0 9.0 9.2

MURDER MYSTERIES (Neil Gaiman's...)
Dark Horse Comics: 2002 ($13.95, HC, one-shot)
HC-Adapts Gaiman story; P. Craig Russell-script/art 14.00

MURDER TALES (Magazine)
World Famous Publications: V1#10, Nov, 1970 - V1#11, Jan, 1971 (52 pgs.)
V1#10-One pg. Frazetta ad 4 8 12 28 44 60
11-Guardineer-r; bondage-c 4 8 12 24 37 50

MUSHMOUSE AND PUNKIN PUSS (TV)
Gold Key: September, 1965 (Hanna-Barbera)
1 (10153-509) 8 16 24 58 97 135

MUSIC BOX (Jennifer Love Hewitt's...)
IDW Publishing: Nov, 2009 - No. 5, Apr, 2010 ($3.99, lim. series)
1-5-Anthology; Scott Lobdell-s/art by various. 1-Gaydos-a. 3-Archer-a 4.00

MUSIC MAN, THE (See Movie Classics)

MUTANT CHRONICLES (Video game)
Acclaim Comics (Armada): May, 1996 - No. 4, Aug, 1996 ($2.95, lim. series)
1-4: Simon Bisley-c on all, Sourcebook (#5) 3.00

MUTANT EARTH (Stan Winston's...)
Image Comics: April, 2002 - No. 4, Jan, 2003 ($2.95)
1-4-Flip book w/Realm of the Claw 3.00
Trakk...His Adventures in Mutant Earth TPB (2003, $16.95) r/#1-4; Winston interview 17.00

MUTANT MISADVENTURES OF CLOAK AND DAGGER, THE
(Becomes Cloak and Dagger #14 on)
Marvel Comics: Oct, 1988 - No. 19, Aug, 1991 ($1.25/$1.50)
1-8,10-15: 1-X-Factor app. 10-Painted-c. 12-Dr. Doom app. 14-Begin new direction 3.00
9,16-19: 9-(52 pgs.) The Avengers x-over; painted-c. 16-18-Spider-Man x-over. 18-Infinity Gauntlet x-over; Thanos cameo; Ghost Rider app. 19-(52 pgs.) Origin Cloak & Dagger 4.00
NOTE: ***Austin** a-12i; c(i)-4, 12, 13; scripts-all. **Russell** a-2i. **Williamson** a-14i-16i; c-15i.*

MUTANTS & MISFITS
Silverline Comics (Solson): 1987 - No. 3, 1987 ($1.95)
1-3 3.00

MUTANTS VS. ULTRAS
Malibu Comics (Ultraverse): Nov, 1995 ($6.95, one-shot)
1-r/Exiles vs. X-Men, Night Man vs. Wolverine, Prime vs. Hulk 7.00

MUTANT, TEXAS: TALES OF SHERIFF IDA RED (Also see Jingle Belle)
Oni Press: May, 2002 - No. 4, Nov, 2002 ($2.95, B&W, limited series)
1-4-Paul Dini-s/J. Bone-c/a 3.00
TPB (2003, $11.95) r/#1-4; intro. by Joe Lansdale 12.00

MUTANT 2099
Marvel Comics (Marvel Knights): Nov, 2004 ($2.99, one-shot)
1-Kirkman-s/Pat Lee-c 3.00

MUTANT X (See X-Factor)
Marvel Comics: Nov, 1998 - No. 32, June, 2001 ($2.99/$1.99/$2.25)
1-($2.99) Alex Summers with alternate world's X-Men 4.00
2-11,13-19-($1.99): 2-Two covers. 5-Man-Spider-c/app. 3.00
12,25-($2.99): 12-Pin-up gallery by Kaluta, Romita, Byrne 4.00
20-24,26-32: 20-Begin $2.25-c. 28-31-Logan-c/app. 32-Last issue 3.00
Annual '99, '00 (5/99,'00, $3.50) '00-Doran-a(p) 4.00
Annual 2001 ($2.99) Story occurs between #31 & #32; Dracula app. 4.00

MUTANT X (Based on TV show)
Marvel Comics: May, 2002; June, 2002 ($3.50)
...: Dangerous Decisions (6/02) -Kuder-s/Immonen-a 3.50
...: Origin (5/02) -Tischman & Chaykin-s/Ferguson-a 3.50

MUTATIS
Marvel Comics (Epic Comics): 1992 - No. 3, 1992 ($2.25, mini-series)
1-3: Painted-c 3.00

MUTIES
Marvel Comics: Apr, 2002 - No. 6, Sept, 2002 ($2.50)
1-6: 1-Bollars-s/Ferguson-a. 2-Spaziante-a. 3-Haspiel-a. 4-Kanuiga-a 3.00

MUTINY (Stormy Tales of the Seven Seas)
Aragon Magazines: Oct, 1954 - No. 3, Feb, 1955
1 16 32 48 94 147 200
2,3: 2-Capt. Mutiny. 3-Bondage-c 14 28 42 76 108 140

MUTINY ON THE BOUNTY (See Classics Illustrated #100 & Movie Comics)

MUTOPIA X (Also see House of M and related titles)
Marvel Comics: Sept, 2005 - No. 5, Jan, 2006 ($2.99, limited series)
1-5-Medina-a/Hine-s 3.00
House of M: Mutopia X (2006, $13.99, TPB) r/series 14.00

MUTT AND JEFF (See All-American, All-Flash #18, Cicero's Cat, Comic Cavalcade, Famous Feature Stories, The Funnies, Popular & Xmas Comics)
All American/National 1-103(6/58)/Dell 104(10/58)-115 (10-12/59)/ Harvey 116(2/60)-148: Summer, 1939 (nd) - No. 148, Nov, 1965
1(nn)-Lost Wheels 145 290 435 921 1586 2250
2(nn)-Charging Bull (Summer, 1940, nd; on sale 6/20/40) 69 138 207 442 759 1075
3(nn)-Bucking Broncos (Summer, 1941, nd) 50 100 150 315 533 750
4(Winter, '41), 5(Summer, '42) 46 92 138 289 487 685
6-10: 6-Includes Minute Man Answers the Call 27 54 81 159 259 360
11-20: 20-X-Mas-c 20 40 60 114 182 250
21-30 15 30 45 86 133 180
31-50: 32-X-Mas-c 14 28 42 76 108 140
51-75-Last Fisher issue. 53-Last 52 pgs. 11 22 33 60 83 105
76-99,101-103: 76-Last pre-code issue(1/55) 6 12 18 37 59 80
100 6 12 18 39 62 85
104-115,132-148 5 10 15 30 48 65
116-131-Richie Rich app. 5 10 15 32 51 70
...Jokes 1-3(8/60-61, Harvey)-84 pgs.; Richie Rich in all; Little Dot in #2,3; Lotta in #2 5 10 15 30 48 65
...New Jokes 1-4(10/63-11/65, Harvey)-68 pgs.; Richie Rich in #1-3; Stumbo in #1 4 8 12 24 37 50
NOTE: *Most all issues by **Al Smith**. Issues from 1963 on have **Fisher** reprints. Clarification: early issues signed by Fisher are mostly drawn by Smith.*

MY BROTHERS' KEEPER
Spire Christian Comics (Fleming H. Revell Co.): 1973 (35/49¢, 36 pgs.)
nn 2 4 6 9 13 16

MY CONFESSIONS (My Confession #7&8; formerly Western True Crime; A Spectacular Feature Magazine #11)
Fox Feature Syndicate: No. 7, Aug, 1949 - No. 10, Jan-Feb, 1950
7-Wood-a (10 pgs.) 24 48 72 144 237 330
8,9: 8-Harrison/Wood-a (19 pgs.). 9-Wood-a 22 44 66 132 216 300
10 14 28 42 76 108 140

MY DATE COMICS (Teen-age)
Hillman Periodicals: July, 1947 - V1#4, Jan, 1948 (2nd Romance comic; see Young Romance)
1-S&K-c/a 39 78 117 236 388 540
2-4-S&K-c/a; Dan Barry-a 27 54 81 158 259 360

MY DESIRE (Formerly Jo-Jo Comics; becomes Murder, Inc. #5 on)
Fox Feature Syndicate: No. 30, Aug, 1949 - No. 4, April, 1950
30(#1) 18 36 54 105 165 225
31 (#2, 10/49),3(2/50),4 14 28 42 80 115 150
31 (Canadian edition) 9 18 27 47 61 75
32(12/49)-Wood-a 22 44 66 128 209 290

MY DIARY (Becomes My Friend Irma #3 on?)
Marvel Comics (A Lovers Mag.): Dec, 1949 - No. 2, Mar, 1950
1,2-Photo-c 15 30 45 88 137 185

MY EXPERIENCE (Formerly All Top; becomes Judy Canova #23 on)
Fox Feature Syndicate: No. 19, Sept, 1949 - No. 22, Mar, 1950
19,21: 19-Wood-a. 21-Wood-a(2) 26 52 78 152 249 345
20 14 28 42 80 115 150
22-Wood-a (9 pgs.) 22 44 66 128 209 290

MY FAITH IN FRANKIE
DC Comics (Vertigo): March, 2004 - No. 4, June, 2004 ($2.95, limited series)
1-4-Mike Carey-s/Sonny Liew & Marc Hempel-a 3.00
TPB (2004, $6.95, digest-size) r/series in B&W; Dead Boy Detectives preview 7.00

MY FAVORITE MARTIAN (TV)
Gold Key: 1/64; No.2, 7/64 - No. 9, 10/66 (No. 1,3-9 have photo-c)
1-Russ Manning-a 12 24 36 82 154 225
2 7 14 21 49 80 110
3-9 6 12 18 41 66 90

MY FRIEND IRMA (Radio/TV) (Formerly My Diary? and/or Western Life Romances?)
Marvel/Atlas Comics (BFP): No. 3, June, 1950 - No. 47, Dec, 1954; No. 48, Feb, 1955

My Intimate Affair #1 © FOX

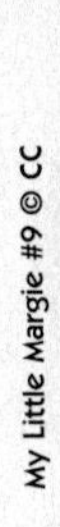

My Little Margie #9 © CC

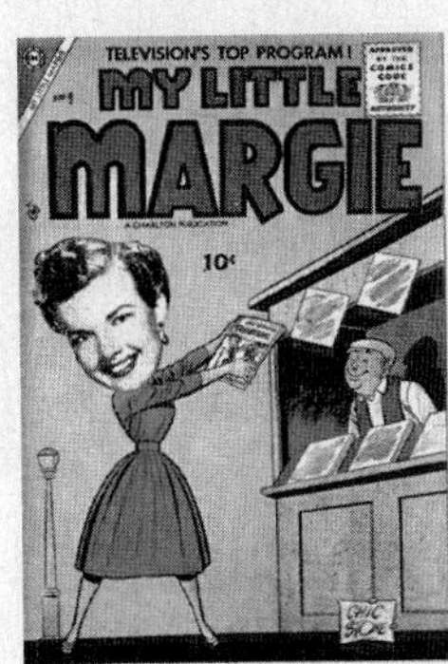

My Love Story #2 © FOX

	GD 2.0	VG 4.0	FN 6.0	VF 8.0	VF/NM 9.0	NM- 9.2
3-Dan DeCarlo-a in all; 52 pgs. begin, end ?	20	40	60	115	185	255
4-Kurtzman-a (10 pgs.)	19	38	57	111	176	240
5- "Egghead Doodle" by Kurtzman (4 pgs.)	15	30	45	86	133	180
6,8-10: 9-Paper dolls, 1 pg; Millie app. (5 pgs.)	13	26	39	74	105	135
7-One pg. Kurtzman-a	14	28	42	76	108	140
11-23: 23-One pg. Frazetta-a	10	20	30	57	76	95
24-48: 41,48-Stan Lee & Dan DeCarlo app.	9	18	27	50	65	80

MY GIRL PEARL
Atlas Comics: 4/55 - #4, 10/55; #5, 7/57 - #6, 9/57; #7, 8/60 - #11, ?/61

	GD	VG	FN	VF	VF/NM	NM-
1-Dan DeCarlo-c/a in #1-6	15	30	45	90	140	190
2	10	20	30	56	76	95
3-6	9	18	27	47	61	75
7-11	5	10	15	30	48	65

MY GREATEST ADVENTURE (Doom Patrol #86 on)
National Periodical Publications: Jan-Feb, 1955 - No. 85, Feb, 1964

	GD	VG	FN	VF	VF/NM	NM-
1-Before CCA	123	246	369	1046	2123	3200
2	45	90	135	360	730	1100
3-5	33	66	99	260	513	765
6-10: 6-Science fiction format begins	27	54	81	197	399	600
11-14: 12-1st S.A. issue	20	40	60	146	293	440
15-17: Kirby-a in all	22	44	66	159	317	475
18-Kirby-c/a	25	50	75	180	360	540
19,23-25	17	34	51	118	242	365
20,21,28-Kirby-a	20	40	60	144	290	435
22-Space Ranger prototype (7-8/58)(see Showcase #15 for Space Ranger debut)	18	36	54	125	255	385
26,27,29,30	13	26	39	94	185	275
31-40	11	22	33	80	150	220
41,42,44-57,59	10	20	30	69	122	175
43-Kirby-a	10	20	30	72	131	190
58,60,61-Toth-a; Last 10¢ issue	10	20	30	70	125	180
62-76,78,79: 79-Promotes "Legion of the Strange" for next issue; renamed Doom Patrol for #80	8	16	24	56	93	130
77-Toth-a; Robotman prototype	8	16	24	58	97	135
80-(6/63)-Intro/origin Doom Patrol and begin series; origin & 1st app. Negative Man, Elasti-Girl & S.A. Robotman	48	96	144	392	796	1200
81,85-Toth-a	18	36	54	125	255	385
82-84	16	32	48	117	239	360

NOTE: ***Anderson** a-42. **Cameron** a-24. **Colan** a-77. **Meskin** a-25, 26, 32, 39, 45, 50, 56, 57, 61, 64, 70, 73, 74, 76, 79; c-76. **Moreira** a-11, 12, 15, 17, 20, 23, 25, 27, 37, 40-43, 46, 48, 55-57, 59, 60, 62-65, 67, 69, 70; c-1-4, 7-10. **Roussos** c/a-71-73. **Wildey** a-32.*

MY GREAT LOVE (Becomes Will Rogers Western #5)
Fox Feature Syndicate: Oct, 1949 - No. 4, Apr, 1950

	GD	VG	FN	VF	VF/NM	NM-
1	16	32	48	94	147	200
2-4	10	20	30	58	79	100

MY INTIMATE AFFAIR (Inside Crime #3)
Fox Feature Syndicate: Mar, 1950 - No. 2, May, 1950

	GD	VG	FN	VF	VF/NM	NM-
1	16	32	48	94	147	200
2	10	20	30	58	79	100

MY LIFE (Formerly Meet Corliss Archer)
Fox Feature Syndicate: No. 4, Sept, 1948 - No. 15, July, 1950

	GD	VG	FN	VF	VF/NM	NM-
4-Used in **SOTI**, pg. 39; Kamen/Feldstein-a	41	82	123	256	428	600
5-Kamen-a	25	50	75	150	245	340
6-Kamen/Feldstein-a	28	56	84	165	270	375
7-Wood-a; wash cover	22	44	66	128	209	290
8,9,11-15	14	28	42	76	108	140
10-Wood-a	20	40	60	115	185	255

MY LITTLE MARGIE (TV)
Charlton Comics: July, 1954 - No. 54, Nov, 1964

	GD	VG	FN	VF	VF/NM	NM-
1-Photo front/back-c	37	74	111	218	354	490
2-Photo front/back-c	18	36	54	107	169	230
3-7,10	12	24	36	69	97	125
8,9-Infinity-c	13	26	39	72	101	130
11-14: Part-photo-c (#13, 8/56). 14-UFO cover	10	20	30	58	79	100
15-19	10	20	30	54	72	90
20-(25¢, 100 pg. issue)	15	30	45	86	133	180
21-40: 40-Last 10¢ issue	5	10	15	32	51	70
41-53	4	8	12	28	44	60
54-(11/64) Beatles on cover; lead story spoofs the Beatle haircut craze of the 1960's; Beatles app. (scarce)	15	30	45	106	216	325

NOTE: *Doll cut-outs in 32, 33, 40, 45, 50.*

MY LITTLE MARGIE'S BOY FRIENDS (TV) (Freddy V2#12 on)
Charlton Comics: Aug, 1955 - No. 11, Apr?, 1958

	GD	VG	FN	VF	VF/NM	NM-
1-Has several Archie swipes	15	30	45	84	127	170
2	9	18	27	52	69	85
3-11	8	16	24	44	57	70

MY LITTLE MARGIE'S FASHIONS (TV)
Charlton Comics: Feb, 1959 - No. 5, Nov, 1959

	GD	VG	FN	VF	VF/NM	NM-
1	14	28	42	76	108	140
2-5	8	16	24	44	57	70

MY LOVE (Becomes Two Gun Western #5 (11/50) on?)
Marvel Comics (CLDS): July, 1949 - No. 4, Apr, 1950 (All photo-c)

	GD	VG	FN	VF	VF/NM	NM-
1	17	34	51	98	154	210
2,3	12	24	36	67	94	120
4-Bettie Page photo-c (see Cupid #2)	41	82	123	256	428	600

MY LOVE
Marvel Comics Group: Sept, 1969 - No. 39, Mar, 1976

	GD	VG	FN	VF	VF/NM	NM-
1	8	16	24	52	86	120
2-9: 4-6-Colan-a	4	8	12	28	44	60
10-Williamson-r/My Own Romance #71; Kirby-a	5	10	15	30	48	65
11-13,15-19	4	8	12	24	37	50
14(52 pgs.)-Woodstock-c/sty; Morrow-c/a; Kirby/Colletta-r	6	12	18	39	62	85
20-Starlin-a	4	8	12	26	41	55
21,22,24-27,29-38: 38-Reprints	3	6	9	21	32	42
23-Steranko-r/Our Love Story #5	4	8	12	24	37	50
28-Kirby-a	4	8	12	22	34	45
39-Last issue; reprints	4	8	12	22	34	45
Special 1 (12/71)(52 pgs.)	5	10	15	35	55	75

NOTE: ***John Buscema** a-1-7, 10, 18-21, 22r(2), 24r, 25r, 29r, 34r, 36r, 37r, Spec. (r)(4); c-13, 15, 25, 27, Spec. **Colan** a-4, 5, 6, 8, 9, 16, 17, 20, 21, 22, 24r, 27r, 30r, 35r, 39r. **Colan/Everett** a-13, 15, 16, 27(r/#13). **Kirby** a-(r)-10, 14, 26, 28. **Romita** a-1-3, 19, 20, 25, 34, 38; c-1-3, 15.*

MY LOVE AFFAIR (March of Crime #7 on)
Fox Feature Syndicate: July, 1949 - No. 6, May, 1950

	GD	VG	FN	VF	VF/NM	NM-
1	16	32	48	94	147	200
2	10	20	30	58	79	100
3-6-Wood-a. 5-(3/50)-Becomes Love Stories #6	19	38	57	112	179	245

MY LOVE LIFE (Formerly Zegra)
Fox Feature Synd.: No. 6, June, 1949 - No. 13, Aug, 1950; No. 13, Sept, 1951

	GD	VG	FN	VF	VF/NM	NM-
6-Kamenish-a	16	32	48	94	147	200
7-13	10	20	30	58	79	100
13 (9/51)(Formerly My Story #12)	10	20	30	54	72	90

MY LOVE MEMOIRS (Formerly Women Outlaws; Hunted #13 on)
Fox Feature Syndicate: No. 9, Nov, 1949 - No. 12, May, 1950

	GD	VG	FN	VF	VF/NM	NM-
9,11,12-Wood-a	19	38	57	112	179	245
10	10	20	30	58	79	100

MY LOVE SECRET (Formerly Phantom Lady; Animal Crackers #31)
Fox Feature Syndicate/M. S. Distr.: No. 24, June, 1949 - No. 30, June, 1950; No. 53, 1954

	GD	VG	FN	VF	VF/NM	NM-
24-Kamen/Feldstein-a	20	40	60	115	185	255
25-Possible caricature of Wood on-c?	14	28	42	76	108	140
26,28-Wood-a	19	38	57	112	179	245
27,29,30: 30-Photo-c	12	24	36	67	94	120
53-(Reprint, M.S. Distr.) 1954? nd given; formerly Western Thrillers; becomes Crimes by Women #54; photo-c	8	16	24	40	50	60

MY LOVE STORY (Hoot Gibson Western #5 on)
Fox Feature Syndicate: Sept, 1949 - No. 4, Mar, 1950

	GD	VG	FN	VF	VF/NM	NM-
1	16	32	48	94	147	200
2	10	20	30	58	79	100
3,4-Wood-a	19	38	57	112	179	245

MY LOVE STORY
Atlas Comics (GPS): April, 1956 - No. 9, Aug, 1957

	GD	VG	FN	VF	VF/NM	NM-
1	14	28	42	76	108	140
2	8	16	24	44	57	70
3,7: Matt Baker-a. 7-Toth-a	11	22	33	60	83	105
4-6,8,9	8	16	24	42	54	65

NOTE: ***Brewster** a-3. **Colletta** a-1(2), 3, 4(2), 5; c-3.*

MY NAME IS BRUCE
Dark Horse Comics: Sept, 2008 ($3.50, one-shot)

	NM-
nn-Adaptation of the Bruce Campbell movie; Cliff Richards-a/Bart Sears-c	3.50

My Only Love #9 © CC

My Secret Confession #1 © Sterling

Mysteries #3 © SUPR

MY NAME IS HOLOCAUST
DC Comics: May, 1995 - No. 5, Sept, 1995 ($2.50, limited series)

	GD 2.0	VG 4.0	FN 6.0	VF 8.0	VF/NM 9.0	NM- 9.2
1-5						3.00

MY ONLY LOVE
Charlton Comics: July, 1975 - No. 9, Nov, 1976

	GD 2.0	VG 4.0	FN 6.0	VF 8.0	VF/NM 9.0	NM- 9.2
1	3	6	9	14	19	24
2,4-9	2	4	6	9	13	16
3-Toth-a	2	4	6	11	16	20

MY OWN ROMANCE (Formerly My Romance; Teen-Age Romance #77 on)
Marvel/Atlas (MjPC/RCM No. 4-59/ZPC No. 60-76): No. 4, Mar, 1949 - No. 76, July, 1960

	GD 2.0	VG 4.0	FN 6.0	VF 8.0	VF/NM 9.0	NM- 9.2
4-Photo-c	16	32	48	94	147	200
5-10: 5,6,8-10-Photo-c	11	22	33	62	86	110
11-20: 14-Powell-a	10	20	30	56	76	95
21-42,55: 42-Last precode (2/55). 55-Toth-a	9	18	27	52	69	85
43-54,56-60	5	10	15	32	51	70
61-70,72,73,75,76	4	8	12	28	44	60
71-Williamson-a	5	10	15	34	55	75
74-Kirby-a	5	10	15	34	55	75

NOTE: ***Brewster** a-59. **Colletta** a-45(2), 48, 50, 55, 57(2), 59; c-58i, 59, 61. **Everett** a-25; c-58p. **Kirby** c-71, 75, 76. **Morisi** a-18. **Orlando** a-61. **Romita** a-36. **Tuska** a-10.*

MY PAL DIZZY (See Comic Books, Series I)

MY PAST (...Confessions) (Formerly Western Thrillers)
Fox Feature Syndicate: No. 7, Aug, 1949 - No. 11, Apr, 1950 (Crimes Inc. #12)

	GD 2.0	VG 4.0	FN 6.0	VF 8.0	VF/NM 9.0	NM- 9.2
7	16	32	48	94	147	200
8-10	10	20	30	58	79	100
11-Wood-a	19	38	57	112	179	245

MY PERSONAL PROBLEM
Ajax/Farrell/Steinway Comic: 11/55; No. 2, 2/56; No. 3, 9/56 - No. 4, 11/56; 10/57 - No. 3, 5/58

	GD 2.0	VG 4.0	FN 6.0	VF 8.0	VF/NM 9.0	NM- 9.2
1	9	18	27	52	69	85
2-4	7	14	21	35	43	50
1-3('57-'58)-Steinway	6	12	18	28	34	40

MY PRIVATE LIFE (Formerly Murder, Inc.; becomes Pedro #18)
Fox Feature Syndicate: No. 16, Feb, 1950 - No. 17, April, 1950

	GD 2.0	VG 4.0	FN 6.0	VF 8.0	VF/NM 9.0	NM- 9.2
16,17	14	28	42	80	115	150

MYRA NORTH (See The Comics, Crackajack Funnies & Red Ryder)
Dell Publishing Co.: No. 3, Jan, 1940

	GD 2.0	VG 4.0	FN 6.0	VF 8.0	VF/NM 9.0	NM- 9.2
Four Color 3	95	190	285	603	1039	1475

MY REAL LOVE
Standard Comics: No. 5, June, 1952 (Photo-c)

	GD 2.0	VG 4.0	FN 6.0	VF 8.0	VF/NM 9.0	NM- 9.2
5-Toth-a, 3 pgs.; Tuska, Cardy, Vern Greene-a	14	28	42	76	108	140

MY ROMANCE (Becomes My Own Romance #4 on)
Marvel Comics (RCM): Sept, 1948 - No. 3, Jan, 1949

	GD 2.0	VG 4.0	FN 6.0	VF 8.0	VF/NM 9.0	NM- 9.2
1	20	40	60	114	182	250
2,3: 2-Anti-Wertham editorial (11/48)	14	28	42	76	108	140

MY ROMANTIC ADVENTURES (Formerly Romantic Adventures)
American Comics Group: No. 68, 8/56 - No. 115, 12/60; No. 116, 7/61 - No. 138, 3/64

	GD 2.0	VG 4.0	FN 6.0	VF 8.0	VF/NM 9.0	NM- 9.2
68	8	16	24	42	54	65
69-85	7	14	21	35	43	50
86-Three pg. Williamson-a (2/58)	8	16	24	44	57	70
87-100	3	6	9	20	30	40
101-138	3	6	9	16	23	30

NOTE: ***Whitney** art in most issues.*

MY SECRET (Becomes Our Secret #4 on)
Superior Comics, Ltd.: Aug, 1949 - No. 3, Oct, 1949

	GD 2.0	VG 4.0	FN 6.0	VF 8.0	VF/NM 9.0	NM- 9.2
1	17	34	51	98	154	210
2,3	14	28	42	76	108	140

MY SECRET AFFAIR (Becomes Martin Kane #4)
Hero Book (Fox Feature Syndicate): Dec, 1949 - No. 3, April, 1950

	GD 2.0	VG 4.0	FN 6.0	VF 8.0	VF/NM 9.0	NM- 9.2
1-Harrison/Wood-a (10 pgs.)	24	48	72	140	230	320
2,3-Wood-a	19	38	57	112	179	245

MY SECRET CONFESSION
Sterling Comics: September, 1955

	GD 2.0	VG 4.0	FN 6.0	VF 8.0	VF/NM 9.0	NM- 9.2
1-Sekowsky-a	9	18	27	52	69	85

MY SECRET LIFE (Formerly Western Outlaws; Romeo Tubbs #26 on)
Fox Feature Syndicate: No. 22, July, 1949 - No. 27, July, 1950; No. 27, 9/51

	GD 2.0	VG 4.0	FN 6.0	VF 8.0	VF/NM 9.0	NM- 9.2
22	14	28	42	76	108	140
23,26-Wood-a, 6 pgs.	19	38	57	112	179	245
24,25,27	12	24	36	67	94	120
27 (9/51)	10	20	30	56	76	95

NOTE: *The title was changed to Romeo Tubbs after #25 even though #26 & 27 did come out.*

MY SECRET LIFE (Formerly Young Lovers; Sue & Sally Smith #48)
Charlton Comics: No. 19, Aug, 1957 - No. 47, Sept, 1962

	GD 2.0	VG 4.0	FN 6.0	VF 8.0	VF/NM 9.0	NM- 9.2
19	4	8	12	26	41	55
20-35	3	6	9	16	23	30
36-47: 44-Last 10¢ issue	3	6	9	14	20	26

MY SECRET MARRIAGE
Superior Comics, Ltd.: May, 1953 - No. 24, July, 1956 (Canadian)

	GD 2.0	VG 4.0	FN 6.0	VF 8.0	VF/NM 9.0	NM- 9.2
1	14	28	42	82	121	160
2	9	18	27	50	65	80
3-24	8	16	24	42	54	65
I.W. Reprint #9	2	4	6	8	11	14

NOTE: *Many issues contain **Kamen-ish** art.*

MY SECRET ROMANCE (Becomes A Star Presentation #3)
Hero Book (Fox Feature Syndicate): Jan, 1950 - No. 2, March, 1950

	GD 2.0	VG 4.0	FN 6.0	VF 8.0	VF/NM 9.0	NM- 9.2
1	15	30	45	90	140	190
2-Wood-a	19	38	57	112	179	245

MY SECRETS (Magazine) (Also see Gothic Romances)
Atlas/Seaboard: Feb, 1975 (B&W, 68 pgs.)

	GD 2.0	VG 4.0	FN 6.0	VF 8.0	VF/NM 9.0	NM- 9.2
Vol. 1 #1	7	14	21	47	76	105

MY SECRET STORY (Formerly Captain Kidd #25; Sabu #30 on)
Fox Feature Syndicate: No. 26, Oct, 1949 - No. 29, April, 1950

	GD 2.0	VG 4.0	FN 6.0	VF 8.0	VF/NM 9.0	NM- 9.2
26	15	30	45	86	133	180
27-29	10	20	30	58	79	100

MYSPACE DARK HORSE PRESENTS
Dark Horse Books: Sept, 2008 - Feb, 2011 ($19.95/$19.99, TPB)

	GD 2.0	VG 4.0	FN 6.0	VF 8.0	VF/NM 9.0	NM- 9.2
Vol. 1 - Short stories previously appearing on Dark Horse's MySpace.com webpage; s/a by various incl. Whedon, Bá, Bagge, Mignola, Moon, Nord, Trimpe, Warren, Way						20.00
Vol. 2 - Collects stories from online #7-12; s/a by Way, Niles, Dorkin, Hotz & others						20.00
Vol. 3 - Collects stories from online #13-19; s/a by Mignola, Cloonan & others						20.00
Vol. 4 - Collects stories from online #20-24; s/a by Whedon, Chen & others						20.00
Vol. 5 - Collects stories from online #25-30; s/a by Thompson, Aragonés & others						20.00
Vol. 6 - Collects stories from online #31-36; s/a by Sakai, Dorkin & others						20.00

MYSTERIES (...Weird & Strange)
Superior/Dynamic Publ. (Randall Publ. Ltd.): May, 1953 - No. 11, Jan, 1955

	GD 2.0	VG 4.0	FN 6.0	VF 8.0	VF/NM 9.0	NM- 9.2
1-All horror stories	42	84	126	265	445	625
2-A-Bomb blast story	27	54	81	158	259	360
3-11: 10-Kamenish-c/a reprinted from Strange Mysteries #2; cover is from a panel in Strange Mysteries #2	24	48	72	140	230	320

MYSTERIES IN SPACE (See Fireside Book Series)

MYSTERIES OF SCOTLAND YARD (Also see A-1 Comics)
Magazine Enterprises: No. 121, 1954 (one shot)

	GD 2.0	VG 4.0	FN 6.0	VF 8.0	VF/NM 9.0	NM- 9.2
A-1 121-Reprinted from Manhunt (5 stories)	15	30	45	85	130	175

MYSTERIES OF UNEXPLORED WORLDS (See Blue Bird)(Becomes Son of Vulcan V2#49 on)
Charlton Comics: Aug, 1956; No. 2, Jan, 1957 - No. 48, Sept, 1965

	GD 2.0	VG 4.0	FN 6.0	VF 8.0	VF/NM 9.0	NM- 9.2
1	37	74	111	222	361	500
2-No Ditko	16	32	48	94	147	200
3,4,8,9 Ditko-a. 3-Diko c/a (4). 4-Ditko c/a (2).	30	60	90	177	289	400
5,6,10,11: 5,6-Ditko-c/a (all). 10-Ditko-c/a(4). 11-Ditko-c/a(3); signed J. Kotdi	31	62	93	186	303	420
7-(2/58, 68 pgs.) 4 stories w/Ditko-a	34	68	102	204	332	460
12-Ditko sty (3); Baker story "The Charm Bracelet"	30	60	90	177	289	400
13-18,20	10	20	30	56	76	95
19,21-24,26-Ditko-a	23	46	69	136	223	310
25,27-30	5	10	15	34	55	75
31-45	4	8	12	26	41	55
46(5/65)-Son of Vulcan begins (origin/1st app.)	4	8	12	28	44	60
47,48	4	8	12	23	34	45

NOTE: ***Ditko** c-3-6, 10, 11, 19, 21-24. Covers to #19, 21-24 reprint story panels.*

MYSTERIOUS ADVENTURES
Story Comics: Mar, 1951 - No. 24, Mar, 1955; No. 25, Aug, 1955

	GD 2.0	VG 4.0	FN 6.0	VF 8.0	VF/NM 9.0	NM- 9.2
1-All horror stories	76	152	228	486	831	1175
2-(6/51)	41	82	123	256	428	600
3,4,6,10	40	80	120	242	404	565

Mysterious Adventures #9 © Story

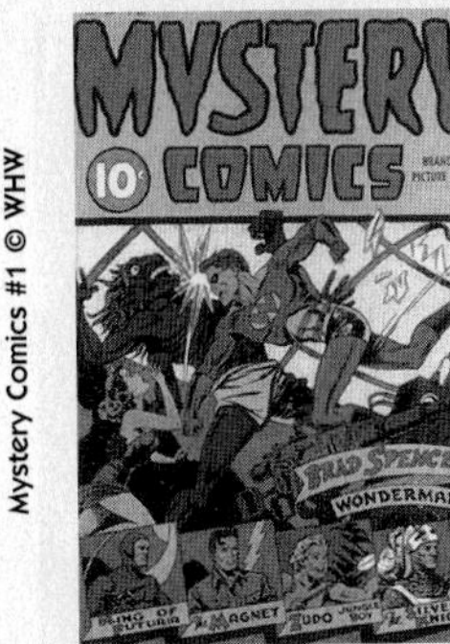

Mystery Comics #1 © WHW

Mystery In Space #117 © DC

GD 2.0 | VG 4.0 | FN 6.0 | VF 8.0 | VF/NM 9.0 | NM- 9.2

5-Bondage-c 41 82 123 256 428 600
7-Dagger in eye panel; dismemberment stories 46 92 138 290 488 685
8-Eyeball story 52 104 156 328 557 785
9-Extreme violence (8/52) 42 84 126 265 445 625
11-(12/52)-Used in **SOTI**, pg. 84 42 84 126 265 445 625
12,14: 14-E.C. Old Witch swipe 40 80 120 242 404 565
13-Classic skull-c 50 100 150 315 533 750
15-21: 18-Used in Senate Investigative report, pgs. 5,6; E.C. swipe/TFTC #35; The Coffin-Keeper & Corpse (hosts). 20-Electric chair-c; used by Wertham in the Senate hearings. 21-Bondage/beheading-c 44 88 132 277 469 660
22- "Cinderella" parody 40 80 120 246 411 575
23-Disbrow-a (6 pgs.); E.C. swipe "The Mystery Keeper's Tale" (host) and "Mother Ghoul's Nursery Tale" 40 80 120 246 411 575
24,25 30 60 90 177 289 400

NOTE: ***Tothish** art by **Ross Andru**-#22, 23. **Bache** a-8. **Cameron** a-5-7. **Harrison** a-12. **Hollingsworth** a-3-8, 12. **Schaffenberger** a-24, 25. **Wildey** a-15, 17.*

MYSTERIOUS ISLAND
Dell Publishing Co.: No. 1213, July-Sept, 1961

Four Color 1213-Movie, photo-c 8 16 24 56 93 130

MYSTERIOUS ISLE
Dell Publishing Co.: Nov-Jan, 1963/64 (Jules Verne)

1 4 8 12 22 34 45

MYSTERIOUS RIDER, THE (See Zane Grey, 4-Color 301)

MYSTERIOUS STORIES (Formerly Horror From the Tomb #1)
Premier Magazines: No. 2, Dec-Jan, 1954-1955 - No. 7, Dec, 1955

2-Woodbridge-c; last pre-code issue 49 98 147 309 522 735
3-Woodbridge-c/a 34 68 102 206 336 465
4-7: 5-Cinderella parody. 6-Woodbridge-c 32 64 96 188 307 425

NOTE: ***Hollingsworth** a-2, 4.*

MYSTERIOUS STRANGER
DC Comics: Aug/Sept. 1952

nn-Ashcan comic, not distributed to newsstands, only for in-house use. Cover art is All Star Western #60 with interior being Sensation Comics #100. A FN/VF copy sold for $2,357.50 in 2002.

MYSTERIOUS SUSPENSE (Also see Blue Beetle #1 (1967))
Charlton Comics: Oct, 1968 (12¢)

1-Return of the Question by Ditko (c/a) 7 14 21 47 76 105

MYSTERIOUS TRAVELER (See Tales of the...)

MYSTERIOUS TRAVELER COMICS (Radio)
Trans-World Publications: Nov, 1948

1-Powell-c/a(2); Poe adaptation, "Tell Tale Heart" 61 122 183 390 670 950

MYSTERIUS
DC Comics (WildStorm): Mar, 2009 - No. 6, Aug, 2009 ($2.99, limited series)

1-6-Jeff Parker-a/Tom Fowler-a 3.00
TPB (2010, $17.99) r/#1-6 18.00

MYSTERY COMICS
William H. Wise & Co.: 1944 - No. 4, 1944 (No months given)

1-The Magnet, The Silver Knight, Brad Spencer, Wonderman, Dick Devins, King of Futuria, & Zudo the Jungle Boy begin (all 1st app.); Schomburg-c on all 126 252 378 806 1378 1950
2-Bondage-c 71 142 213 454 777 1100
3,4: 3-Lance Lewis, Space Detective begins (1st app.); Robot-c. 4(V2#1 inside) 65 130 195 416 708 1000

MYSTERY COMICS DIGEST
Gold Key/Whitman?: Mar, 1972 - No. 26, Oct, 1975

1-Ripley's Believe It or Not; reprint of Ripley's #1 origin Ra-Ka-Tep the Mummy; Wood-a 4 8 12 26 41 55
2-9: 2-Boris Karloff Tales of Mystery; Wood-a; 1st app. Werewolf Count Wulfstein. 3-Twilight Zone (TV); Crandall, Toth & George Evans-a; 1st app. Tragg & Simbar the Lion Lord; (2) Crandall/Frazetta-r/Twilight Zone #1 4-Ripley's Believe It or Not; 1st app. Baron Tibor, the Vampire. 5-Boris Karloff Tales of Mystery; 1st app. Dr. Spektor. 6-Twilight Zone (TV); 1st app. U.S. Marshal Reid & Sir Duane; Evans-r. 7-Ripley's Believe It or Not; origin The Lurker in the Swamp; 1st app. Duroc. 8-Boris Karloff Tales of Mystery; McWilliams-r; Orlando-r. 9-Twilight Zone (TV); Williamson, Crandall, McWilliams-a; 2nd Tragg app.;Torres, Evans, Heck/Tuska-r 3 6 9 20 30 40
10-26: 10,13-Ripley's Believe It or Not: 13-Orlando-r. 11,14-Boris Karloff Tales of Mystery. 14-1st app. Xorkon. 12,15-Twilight Zone (TV). 16,19,22,25-Ripley's Believe It or Not. 17-Boris Karloff Tales of Mystery; Williamson-r; Orlando-r. 18,21,24-Twilight Zone (TV). 20,23,26-Boris Karloff Tales of Mystery 3 6 9 16 23 30

NOTE: *Dr. Spektor app.-#5, 10-12, 21. Durak app.-#15. Duroc app.-#14 (later called Durak). King George 1st app.-#8.*

MYSTERY IN SPACE (Also see Fireside Book Series and Pulp Fiction Library: ...)
National Periodical Pub.: 4-5/51 - No. 110, 9/66; No. 111, 9/80 - No. 117, 3/81 (#1-3: 52 pgs.)

1-Frazetta-a, 8 pgs.; Knights of the Galaxy begins, ends #8 237 474 711 2074 4237 6400
2 85 170 255 723 1462 2200
3 65 130 195 553 1127 1700
4,5 54 108 162 459 930 1400
6-10: 7-Toth-a 41 82 123 328 664 1000
11-15 34 68 102 262 519 775
16-18,20-25: Interplanetary Insurance feature by Infantino in all. 21-1st app. Space Cabbie. 24-Last pre-code issue 29 58 87 223 449 675
19-Virgil Finlay-a 32 64 96 246 486 725
26-40: 26-Space Cabbie feature begins. 34-1st S.A. issue 24 48 72 175 350 525
41-52: 47-Space Cabbie feature ends 18 36 54 125 255 385
53-Adam Strange begins (8/59, 10pg. sty); robot-c 156 312 468 1365 2783 4200
54 44 88 132 352 714 1075
55-Grey tone-c 41 82 123 324 650 975
56-60: 59-Kane/Anderson-a 23 46 69 168 334 500
61-71: 61-1st app. Adam Strange foe Ulthoon. 62-1st app. A.S. foe Mortan. 63-Origin Vandor. 66-Star Rovers begin (1st app.). 68-1st app. Dust Devils (6/61). 69-1st Mailbag. 70-2nd app. Dust Devils. 71-Last 10¢ issue 18 36 54 131 266 400
72-74,76-80 13 26 39 94 185 275
75-JLA x-over in Adam Strange (5/62)(sequel to J.L.A. #3, 2nd app. of Kanjar Ro) 23 46 69 168 334 500
81-86 11 22 33 75 138 200
87-(11/63)-Adam Strange/Hawkman double feat begins; 3rd Hawkman tryout series 16 32 48 111 226 340
88-Adam Strange & Hawkman stories 14 28 42 99 200 300
89-Adam Strange & Hawkman stories 14 28 42 97 194 290
90-Book-length Adam Strange & Hawkman story; 1st team-up (3/64); Hawkman moves to own title next month; classic-c 16 32 48 111 226 340
91-102: 91-End Infantino art on Adam Strange; double-length Adam Strange story. 92-Space Ranger begins (6/64), ends #103. 92-94,96,98-Space Ranger-c. 94,98-Adam Strange/ Space Ranger team-up. 102-Adam Strange ends (no Space Ranger) 7 14 21 49 80 110
103-Origin Ultra, the Multi-Alien; last Space Ranger 6 12 18 41 66 90
104-110: 110-(9/66)-Last 12¢ issue 5 10 15 32 51 70
V17#111(9/80)-117: 117-Newton-a(3 pgs.) 2 4 6 8 11 14

NOTE: ***Anderson** a-2, 4, 8-10, 12-17, 19, 45-48, 51, 57, 59i, 61-64, 70, 76, 87-91; c-9, 10, 15-25, 87, 89, 105-108, 110. **Aparo** a-111. **Austin** a-112i. **Bolland** a-115. **Craig** a-114, 116. **Ditko** a-111, 114-116. **Drucker** a-13, 14. **Elias** a-98, 102, 103. **Golden** a-113p. **Sid Greene** a-78, 91. **Infantino** a-1-8, 11, 14-25, 27-46, 48, 49, 51, 53-91, 103, 117; c-60-86, 88, 90, 91, 105, 107. **Gil Kane** a-14p, 15p, 18p, 19p, 26p, 29-59p(most), 100-102; c-52, 101. **Kubert** a-113; c-111-115. **Moreira** c-27, 28. **Rogers** a-111. **Sekowsky** a-52. **Simon & Kirby** a-4(2 pgs.). **Spiegle** a-111, 114. **Starlin** c-116. **Sutton** a-112. **Tuska** a-115p, 117p.*

MYSTERY IN SPACE
DC Comics: Nov, 2006 - No. 8, Jul, 2007 ($3.99, limited series)

1-8: 1-Captain Comet's rebirth; Starlin-s/Shane Davis-a; The Weird by Starlin 4.00
1-Variant cover by Neal Adams 10.00
Volume One TPB (2007, $17.99) r/#1-5 18.00
Volume Two TPB (2007, $17.99) r/#6-8 and The Weird from #1-4 18.00

MYSTERY MEN COMICS
Fox Features Syndicate: Aug, 1939 - No. 31, Feb, 1942

1-Intro. & 1st app. The Blue Beetle, The Green Mask, Rex Dexter of Mars by Briefer, Zanzibar by Tuska, Lt. Drake, D-13-Secret Agent by Powell, Chen Chang, Wing Turner, & Captain Denny Scott 1000 2000 3000 7400 13,200 19,000
2-Robot & sci/fi-c (2nd Robot-c w/Movie #6) 343 686 1029 2400 4200 6000
3 (10/39)-Classic Lou Fine-c 443 886 1329 3234 5717 8200
4,5: 4-Capt. Savage begins (11/39) 284 568 852 1818 3109 4400
6-Tuska-c 232 464 696 1485 2543 3600
7-1st Blue Beetle-c app. 297 594 891 1901 3251 4600
8-Lou Fine bondage-c 271 542 813 1734 2967 4200
9-The Moth begins; Lou Fine-c 135 270 405 864 1482 2100
10-12: All Joe Simon-c. 10-Wing Turner by Kirby; Simon bondage-c. 11-Intro. Domino 113 226 339 718 1234 1750
13-Intro. Lynx & sidekick Blackie (8/40) 68 136 204 435 743 1050
14-18 64 128 192 406 696 985
19-Intro. & 1st app. Miss X (ends #21) 68 136 204 435 743 1050
20-31: 26-The Wraith begins 61 122 183 390 670 950

NOTE: ***Briefer** a-1-15, 20, 24; c-9. **Cuidera** a-22. **Lou Fine** c-1-5,8,9. **Powell** a-1-15, 24. **Simon** c-10-12. **Tuska** a-1-16, 22, 24, 27; c-6. Bondage-c 1, 3, 7, 8, 10, 25, 27-29, 31. Blue Beetle c-7, 8, 10-31. D-13 Secret Agent c-6. Green Mask c-1, 3-5. Rex Dexter of Mars c-2, 9.*

Mystery Society #1 © Steve Niles

Mystical Tales #6 © MAR

Mystic #23 © CRO

MYSTERY MEN MOVIE ADAPTION
Dark Horse Comics: July, 1999 - No. 2, Aug, 1999 ($2.95, mini-series)

	GD 2.0	VG 4.0	FN 6.0	VF 8.0	VF/NM 9.0	NM- 9.2
1,2-Fingerman-s; photo-c						3.00

MYSTERY PLAY, THE
DC Comics (Vertigo): 1994 ($19.95, one-shot)

	GD 2.0	VG 4.0	FN 6.0	VF 8.0	VF/NM 9.0	NM- 9.2
nn-Hardcover-Morrison-s/Muth-painted art						25.00
Softcover ($9.95)-New Muth cover						10.00

MYSTERY SOCIETY
IDW Publishing: May, 2010 - No. 5, Oct, 2010 ($3.99, limited series)

	GD 2.0	VG 4.0	FN 6.0	VF 8.0	VF/NM 9.0	NM- 9.2
1-5-Niles-s/Staples-a						4.00

MYSTERY TALES
Atlas Comics (20CC): Mar, 1952 - No. 54, Aug, 1957

	GD 2.0	VG 4.0	FN 6.0	VF 8.0	VF/NM 9.0	NM- 9.2
1-Horror/weird stories in all	92	184	276	584	1005	1425
2-Krigstein-a	48	96	144	302	514	725
3-10: 6-A-Bomb panel. 10-Story similar to "The Assassin" from Shock SuspenStories	43	86	129	271	461	650
11,13-21: 14-Maneely s/f story. 20-Electric chair issue. 21-Matt Fox-a; decapitation story	31	62	93	182	296	410
12,22: 12-Matt Fox-a. 22-Forte/Matt Fox-c; a(i)	34	68	102	204	332	460
23-26 (2/55)-Last precode issue	24	48	72	144	237	330
27,29-35,37,38,41-43,48,49: 43-Morisi story contains Frazetta art swipes from Untamed Love	20	40	60	117	189	260
28,36,39,40,45: 28-Jack Katz-a. 36,39-Krigstein-a. 40,45-Ditko-a (#45 is 3 pgs. only)	20	40	60	120	195	270
44,51-Williamson/Krenkel-a	21	42	63	126	206	285
46-Williamson/Krenkel-a; Crandall text illos	21	42	63	126	206	285
47-Crandall, Ditko, Powell-a	21	42	63	126	206	285
50,52,53: 50-Torres, Morrow-a	20	40	60	117	189	260
54-Crandall, Check-a	20	40	60	120	195	270

NOTE: ***Ayers*** *a-18, 49, 52.* ***Berg*** *a-17, 51.* ***Colan*** *a-1, 3, 18, 35, 43.* ***Colletta*** *a-18.* ***Drucker*** *a-41.* ***Everett*** *a-2, 29, 33, 35, 41; c-8-11, 14, 38, 39, 41, 43, 44, 46, 48-51, 53.* ***Fass*** *a-16.* ***Forte*** *a-21, 22, 45, 46.* ***Matt Fox*** *a-12?, 21, 22; c-22.* ***Heath*** *a-3; c-3, 15, 17, 26.* ***Heck*** *a-25.* ***Kinstler*** *a-15.* ***Mort Lawrence*** *a-26, 32, 34.* ***Maneely*** *a-1, 9, 14, 22; c-12, 23, 24, 27.* ***Mooney*** *a-3, 40.* ***Morisi*** *a-43, 49, 52.* ***Morrow*** *a-50.* ***Orlando*** *a-51.* ***Pakula*** *a-16.* ***Powell*** *a-21, 29, 37, 38, 47.* ***Reinman*** *a-1, 14, 17.* ***Robinson*** *a-7p, 42.* ***Romita*** *a-37.* ***Roussos*** *a-4, 44.* ***R.Q. Sale*** *a-45, 46, 49.* ***Severin*** *c-52.* ***Shores*** *a-17, 45.* ***Tuska*** *a-10, 12, 14.* ***Whitney*** *a-2.* ***Wildey*** *a-37.*

MYSTERY TALES
Super Comics: 1964

	GD 2.0	VG 4.0	FN 6.0	VF 8.0	VF/NM 9.0	NM- 9.2
Super Reprint #16,17('64): 16-r/Tales of Horror #2. 17-r/Eerie #14(Avon), 18-Kubert-r/Strange Terrors #4	3	6	9	14	20	25

MYSTERY TRAIL
DC Comics: Feb/Mar 1950

nn - Ashcan comic, not distributed to newsstands, only for in-house use. Cover art is Danger Trail #3 with interior being Star Spangled Comics #109. A FN/VF copy sold for $2,357.50 in 2002.

MYSTIC (3rd Series)
Marvel/Atlas Comics (CLDS 1/CSI 2-21/OMC 22-35/CSI 35-61): March, 1951 - No. 61, Aug, 1957

	GD 2.0	VG 4.0	FN 6.0	VF 8.0	VF/NM 9.0	NM- 9.2
1-Atom bomb panels; horror/weird stories in all	97	194	291	621	1061	1500
2	52	104	156	328	552	775
3-Eyes torn out	47	94	141	296	498	700
4- "The Devil Birds" by Wolverton (6 pgs.)	82	164	246	528	902	1275
5,7-10	39	78	117	231	378	525
6- "The Eye of Doom" by Wolverton (7 pgs.)	82	164	246	528	902	1275
11-20: 16-Bondage/torture c/story	31	62	93	182	296	410
21-25,27-36-Last precode (3/55). 25-E.C. swipe	24	48	72	144	237	330
26-Atomic War story; severed head story/cover	30	60	90	177	289	400
37-51,53-56,61	20	40	60	120	195	270
52-Wood-a; Crandall-a?	22	44	66	128	209	290
57-Story "Trapped in the Ant-Hill" (1957) is very similar to "The Man in the Ant Hill" in TTA #27	24	48	72	144	237	330
58,59-Krigstein-a	21	42	63	122	199	275
60-Williamson/Mayo-a (4 pgs.)	21	42	63	124	202	280

NOTE: ***Andru*** *a-23, 25.* ***Ayers*** *a-35, 53; c-8.* ***Berg*** *a-49.* ***Cameron*** *a-49, 51.* ***Check*** *a-31, 60.* ***Colan*** *a-3, 7, 12, 21, 37, 60.* ***Colletta*** *a-29.* ***Drucker*** *a-46, 52, 56.* ***Everett*** *a-8, 9, 17, 40, 44, 57; c-13, 18, 21, 42, 47, 49, 51-55, 57-59, 61.* ***Forte*** *a-35, 52, 58.* ***Fox*** *a-24i.* ***Al Hartley*** *a-35.* ***Heath*** *a-10; c-10, 20, 22, 23, 25, 30.* ***Infantino*** *a-12.* ***Kane*** *a-8, 24p.* ***Jack Katz*** *a-31, 33.* ***Mort Law.rence*** *a-19, 37.* ***Maneely*** *a-22, 24, 58; c-7, 15, 28, 29, 31.* ***Moldoff*** *a-29.* ***Morisi*** *a-48, 49, 52.* ***Morrow*** *a-51.* ***Orlando*** *a-57, 61.* ***Pakula*** *a-52, 57, 59.* ***Powell*** *a-52, 54-56.* ***Robinson*** *a-5.* ***Romita*** *a-11, 15.* ***R.Q. Sale*** *a-35, 53, 58.* ***Sekowsky*** *a-1, 2, 4, 5.* ***Severin*** *c-56, 60.* ***Tuska*** *a-15.* ***Whitney*** *a-33.* ***Wildey*** *a-28, 30.* ***Ed Win*** *a-17, 20. Canadian reprints known-title 'Startling.'*

MYSTIC (Also see CrossGen Chronicles)
CrossGeneration Comics: Jul, 2000 - No. 43, Jan, 2004 ($2.95)

	GD 2.0	VG 4.0	FN 6.0	VF 8.0	VF/NM 9.0	NM- 9.2
1-43: 1-Marz-s/Peterson & Dell-a. 15-Cameos by DC & Marvel characters						3.00
...: Rite of Passage Vol. 1 TPB (5/01, $19.95) r/#1-7; Linsner-c						20.00
...: The Demon Queen Vol. 2 TPB (2002, $19.95) r/#8-14						20.00
...: Siege of Scales Vol. 3 TPB (2002, $15.95) r/#15-20						16.00
...: Out All Night Vol.4 TPB (2003, $15.95) r/#21-26						16.00
Vol. 5: Master Class (2003, $15.95) r/#27-32						16.00

MYSTICAL TALES
Atlas Comics (CCC 1/EPI 2-8): June, 1956 - No. 8, Aug, 1957

	GD 2.0	VG 4.0	FN 6.0	VF 8.0	VF/NM 9.0	NM- 9.2
1-Everett-c/a	48	96	144	302	514	725
2-4: 2-Berg-a. 3,4-Crandall-a.	26	52	78	154	252	350
5-Williamson-a (4 pgs.)	28	56	84	165	270	375
6-Torres, Krigstein-a	25	50	75	147	241	335
7-Bolle, Forte, Torres, Orlando-a	24	48	72	142	234	325
8-Krigstein, Check-a	25	50	75	147	241	335

NOTE: ***Everett*** *a-1; c-1-4, 6, 7.* ***Orlando*** *a-1, 2, 7.* ***Pakula*** *a-3.* ***Powell*** *a-1, 4.*

MYSTIC ARCANA
Marvel Comics: Aug, 2007 - Jan, 2008 ($2.99)

	GD 2.0	VG 4.0	FN 6.0	VF 8.0	VF/NM 9.0	NM- 9.2
1-Magik on-c; art by Scott and Nguyen; Ian McNee and Dani Moonstar app.						3.00
(#2)...: Black Knight 1 (9/07, $2.99) Djurdjevic-c/Grummett & Hanna-a; origin retold						3.00
3-("Scarlet Witch" on cover)(10/07, $2.99) Djurdjevic-c/Santacruz-a; childhood						3.00
(#4)...: Sister Grimm 1 (1/08, $2.99) Nico Minoru from Runaways; Djurdjevic-c/Noto-a						3.00
...: The Book of Marvel Magic ('07, $3.99) Official Handbook profiles of the magic-related						4.00
HC (2007, $24.99, d.j.) r/series and ...: The Book of Marvel Magic						25.00

MYSTIC COMICS (1st Series)
Timely Comics (TPI 1-5/TCI 8-10): March, 1940 - No. 10, Aug, 1942

	GD 2.0	VG 4.0	FN 6.0	VF 8.0	VF/NM 9.0	NM- 9.2
1-Origin The Blue Blaze, The Dynamic Man, & Flexo the Rubber Robot; Zephyr Jones, 3X's & Deep Sea Demon app.; The Magician begins (all 1st app.); c-from Spider pulp V18#1, 6/39	1400	2800	4200	10,700	19,350	28,000
2-The Invisible Man & Master Mind Excello begin; Space Rangers, Zara of the Jungle, Taxi Taylor app. (scarce)	514	1028	1542	3750	6625	9500
3-Origin Hercules, who last appears in #4	360	720	1080	2520	4410	6300
4-Origin The Thin Man & The Black Widow; Merzak the Mystic app.; last Flexo, Dynamic Man, Invisible Man & Blue Blaze (some issues have date sticker on cover; others have July w/August overprint in silver color); Roosevelt assassination-c	400	800	1200	2800	4900	7000
5-(3/41)-Origin The Black Marvel, The Blazing Skull, The Sub-Earth Man, Super Slave & The Terror; The Moon Man & Black Widow app.; 5-German war-c begin, end #10	371	742	1113	2600	4550	6500
6-(10/41)-Origin The Challenger & The Destroyer (1st app.?; also see All-Winners #2, Fall, 1941)	423	846	1269	3088	5444	7800
7-The Witness begins (12/41, origin & 1st app.); origin Davey & the Demon; last Black Widow; Hitler opens his trunk of terror-c by Simon & Kirby (classic-c)	476	952	1428	3475	6138	8800
8,10: 10-Father Time, World of Wonder, & Red Skeleton app.; last Challenger & Terror	300	600	900	1920	3310	4700
9-Gary Gaunt app.; last Black Marvel, Mystic & Blazing Skull; Hitler-c	309	618	927	2163	3782	5400

NOTE: ***Gabrielle*** *c-8-10.* ***Kirby/Schomburg*** *c-6.* ***Rico*** *a-9(2).* ***Schomburg*** *a-1-4; c-1-5.* ***Sekowsky*** *a-9.* ***Sekowsky/Klein*** *a-8(Challenger). Bondage c-1, 2, 9.*

MYSTIC COMICS (2nd Series)
Timely Comics (ANC): Oct, 1944 - No. 3, Win, 1944-45; No. 4, Mar, 1945

	GD 2.0	VG 4.0	FN 6.0	VF 8.0	VF/NM 9.0	NM- 9.2
1-The Angel, The Destroyer, The Human Torch, Terry Vance the Schoolboy Sleuth, & Tommy Tyme begin	277	554	831	1759	3030	4300
2-(Fall/44)-Last Human Torch & Terry Vance; bondage/hypo-c	142	284	426	909	1555	2200
3-Last Angel (two stories) & Tommy Tyme	127	254	381	807	1391	1975
4-The Young Allies-c & app.; Schomburg-c	116	232	348	742	1271	1800

MYSTIC COMICS 70th ANNIVERARY SPECIAL
Marvel Comics: Oct, 2009 ($3.99, one-shot)

	GD 2.0	VG 4.0	FN 6.0	VF 8.0	VF/NM 9.0	NM- 9.2
1-New story of The Vision; r/G.A. Vision app. from Marvel Myst. Comics #13 & 16						4.00

MYSTIC EDGE (Manga)
Antarctic Press: Oct, 1998 ($2.95, one-shot)

	GD 2.0	VG 4.0	FN 6.0	VF 8.0	VF/NM 9.0	NM- 9.2
1-Ryan Kinnaird-s/a/c						3.00

MYSTIC HANDS OF DR. STRANGE
Marvel Comics: May, 2010 ($3.99, B&W, one-shot)

	GD 2.0	VG 4.0	FN 6.0	VF 8.0	VF/NM 9.0	NM- 9.2
1-Short stories; art by Irving, Brunner, McKeever & Marcos Martin; Parrillo-c						4.00

MYSTIQUE (See X-Men titles)
Marvel Comics: June, 2003 - No. 24, Apr, 2005 ($2.99)

1-24: 1-6-Linsner-c/Vaughan-s/Lucas-a. 7-Ryan-a begins. 8-Horn-c. 9-24-Mayhew-c

Mythos: Fantastic Four #1 © MAR

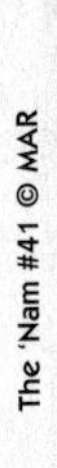

The 'Nam #41 © MAR

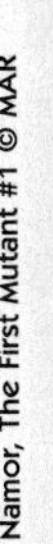

Namor, The First Mutant #1 © MAR

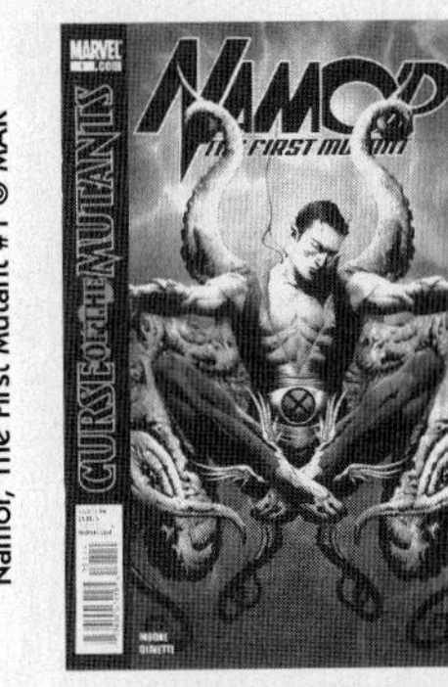

GD 2.0 | VG 4.0 | FN 6.0 | VF 8.0 | VF/NM 9.0 | NM- 9.2

23-Wolverine & Rogue app. 3.00
... Vol. 1: Drop Dead Gorgeous TPB (2004, $14.99) r/#1-6 15.00
... Vol. 2: Tinker, Tailor, Mutant, Spy TPB (2004, $17.99) r/#7-13 18.00
... Vol. 3: Unnatural TPB (2004, $13.99) r/#14-18 14.00

MYSTIQUE & SABRETOOTH (Sabretooth and Mystique on-c)
Marvel Comics: Dec, 1996 - No. 4, Mar, 1997 ($1.95, limited series)
1-4: Characters from X-Men 3.00

MY STORY (...True Romances in Pictures #5,6; becomes My Love Life #13) (Formerly Zago)
Hero Books (Fox Features Syndicate): No. 5, May, 1949 - No. 12, Aug, 1950
5-Kamen/Feldstein-a 21 42 63 126 206 285
6-8,11,12: 12-Photo-c 12 24 36 69 97 125
9,10-Wood-a 19 38 57 112 179 245

MYTHOS
Marvel Comics: Mar, 2006 - Dec, 2007 ($3.99)
1-Retelling of X-Men #1 with painted-a by Paolo Rivera; Paul Jenkins-s 4.00
...: Captain America 1 (8/08) Retelling of origin; painted-a by Rivera; Jenkins-s 4.00
...: Fantastic Four 1 (12/07) Retelling of Fantastic Four #1; painted-a by Rivera; Jenkins-s 4.00
...: Ghost Rider 1 (3/07) Retelling of Marvel Spotlight #5; painted-a by Rivera; Jenkins-s 4.00
...: Hulk 1 (10/06) Retelling of Incredible Hulk #1; painted-a by Rivera; Jenkins-s 4.00
...: Spider-Man 1 (8/07) Retelling of Amazing Fantasy #15; painted-a by Rivera; Jenkins-s 4.00

MYTHOS: THE FINAL TOUR
DC Comics/Vertigo: Dec, 1996 - No. 3, Feb, 1997 ($5.95, limited series)
1-3: 1-Ney Rieber-s/Amaro-a. 2-Snejbjerg-a; Constantine-app. 3-Kristiansen-a; Black Orchid-app. 6.00

MYTHSTALKERS
Image Comics: Mar, 2003 - No. 8, Mar, 2004 ($2.95)
1-8-Jiro-a 3.00

MY TRUE LOVE (Formerly Western Killers #64; Frank Buck #70 on)
Fox Features Syndicate: No. 65, July, 1949 - No. 69, March, 1950
65 16 32 48 94 147 200
66,68,69: 69-Morisi-a 12 24 36 67 94 120
67-Wood-a 19 38 57 112 179 245

NAIL, THE
Dark Horse Comics: June, 2004 - No. 4, Oct, 2004 ($2.99, limited series)
1-4-Rob Zombie & Steve Niles-s/Nat Jones-a/Simon Bisley-c 3.00
TPB (2005, $12.95) r/series 13.00

NAKED BRAIN (Marc Hempel's...)
Insight Studios Group: 2002 - No. 3, 2002 ($2.95, B&W, limited series)
1-3-Marc Hempel cartoons and sketches; Tug & Buster app. 3.00

NAKED PREY, THE (See Movie Classics)

'NAM, THE (See Savage Tales #1, 2nd series & Punisher Invades...)
Marvel Comics Group: Dec, 1986 - No. 84, Sept, 1993
1-Golden a(p)/c begins, ends #13 6.00
1 (2nd printing) 3.00
2-7,9-19,21-66,70-74: 7-Golden-a (2 pgs.). 32-Death R. Kennedy. 52,53-Frank Castle (The Punisher) app. 52,53-Gold 2nd printings. 58-Silver logo. 65-Heath-c/a. 70-Lomax scripts begin 3.00
8-1st app. Fudd Verzyl, Tunnel Rat 5.00
20-2nd app. Fudd Verzyl, Tunnel Rat 4.00
67-69-Punisher 3 part story 4.00
75-($2.25, 52 pgs.) 6.00
76-84 3.00
Trade Paperback 1,2: 1-r/#1-4. 2-r/#5-8 5.00
TPB ('99, $14.95) r/#1-4; recolored 15.00

'NAM MAGAZINE, THE
Marvel Comics: Aug, 1988 - No. 10, May, 1989 ($2.00, B&W, 52pgs.)
1-10: Each issue reprints 2 issues of the comic 4.00

NAMELESS, THE
Image Comics: May, 1997 - No. 5, Sept, 1997 ($2.95, B&W)
1-5: Pruett/Hester-s/a 3.00
...: The Director's Cut TPB (2006, $15.99) r/#1-5; original proposal by Pruett 16.00

NAMES OF MAGIC, THE (Also see Books of Magic)
DC Comics (Vertigo): Feb, 2001 - No. 5, June, 2001 ($2.50, limited series)
1-5: Bolton painted-c on all; Case-a; leads into Hunter: The Age of Magic 3.00
TPB (2002, $14.95) r/#1-5 15.00

NAME OF THE GAME, THE
DC Comics: 2001 ($29.95, graphic novel)
Hardcover ($29.95) Will Eisner-s/a 30.00

NAMOR (Volume 2)
Marvel Comics: June, 2003 - No. 12, May, 2004 (25¢/$2.25/$2.99)
1-(25¢-c)Young Namor in the 1920s; Larroca-c/a 3.00
2-6-($2.25) Larroca-a 3.00
7-12-($2.99): 7-Olliffe-a begins 3.00

NAMORA (See Marvel Mystery Comics #82 & Sub-Mariner Comics)
Marvel Comics (PrPl): Fall, 1948 - No. 3, Dec, 1948
1-Sub-Mariner x-over in Namora; Namora by Everett(2), Sub-Mariner by Rico (10 pgs.) 277 554 831 1759 3030 4300
2-The Blonde Phantom & Sub-Mariner story; Everett-a 155 310 465 992 1696 2400
3-(Scarce)-Sub-Mariner app.; Everett-a 161 322 483 1030 1765 2500

NAMORA (See Agents of Atlas)
Marvel Comics: Aug, 2010 ($3.99, one-shot)
1-Parker-s/Pichelli-a 4.00

NAMOR: THE FIRST MUTANT (Curse of the Mutants x-over with X-Men titles)
Marvel Comics: Oct, 2010 - Present ($3.99/$2.99)
1-($3.99) Olivetti-a/Stuart Moore-s/Jae Lee-c; back-up retelling of origin and history 4.00
2-8-($2.99) 2-Emma Frost app. 5-Mayhew-c. 6-8-Noto-c 3.00

NAMOR, THE SUB-MARINER (See Prince Namor & Sub-Mariner)
Marvel Comics: Apr, 1990 - No. 62, May, 1995 ($1.00/$1.25/$1.50)
1-Byrne-c/a/scripts in 1-25 (scripts only #26-32) 5.00
2-5: 5-Iron Man app. 4.00
6-11,13-23,25,27-49,51-62: 16-Re-intro Iron Fist (8-cameo only). 18-Punisher cameo (1 panel); 21-23,25-Wolverine cameos. 22,23-Iron Fist app. 28-Iron Fist-c/story. 31-Dr. Doom-c/story. 33,34-Iron Fist cameo. 35-New Tiger Shark-c/story. 37-Aqua holografx foil-c. 48-The Thing app. 3.00
12,24: 12-(52pgs.)-Re-intro. The Invaders. 24-Namor vs. Wolverine 4.00
26-Namor w/new costume; 1st Jae Lee-c/a this title (5/92) & begins 4.00
50-($1.75, 52 pgs.)-Newsstand ed.; w/bound-in S-M trading card sheet (both versions) 4.00
50-($2.95, 52 pgs.)-Collector edition w/foil-c 4.00
Annual 1-4 ('91-94, 68 pgs.): 1-3 pg. origin recap. 2-Return/Defenders. 3-Bagged w/card. 4-Painted-c 4.00
NOTE: *Jae Lee a-26-30p, 31-37, 38p, 39, 40; c-26-40.*

NANCY AND SLUGGO (See Comics On Parade & Sparkle Comics)
United Features Syndicate: No. 16, 1949 - No. 23, 1954
16(#1) 10 20 30 58 79 100
17-23 8 16 24 40 50 60

NANCY & SLUGGO (Nancy #146-173; formerly Sparkler Comics)
St. John/Dell #146-187/Gold Key #188 on: No. 121, Apr, 1955-No. 192, Oct, 1963
121(4/55)(St. John) 10 20 30 54 72 90
122-145(7/57)(St. John) 8 16 24 44 57 70
146(9/57)-Peanuts begins, ends #192 (Dell) 9 18 27 65 113 160
147-161 (Dell) Peanuts in all 8 16 24 52 86 120
162-165,177-180-John Stanley-a 8 16 24 52 86 120
166-176-Oona & Her Haunted House series; Stanley-a 8 16 24 58 97 135
181-187(3-5/62)(Dell) 6 12 18 41 66 90
188(10/62)-192 (Gold Key) 6 12 18 41 66 90
Four Color 1034(9-11/59)-Summer Camp 5 10 15 32 51 70
(See Dell Giant #34, 45 & Dell Giants)

NANNY AND THE PROFESSOR (TV)
Dell Publishing Co.: Aug, 1970 - No. 2, Oct, 1970 (Photo-c)
1-(01-546-008) 5 10 15 32 51 70
2 4 8 12 26 41 55

NAPOLEON
Dell Publishing Co.: No. 526, Dec, 1953
Four Color 526 4 8 12 24 37 50

NAPOLEON & SAMANTHA (See Walt Disney Showcase No. 10)

NAPOLEON & UNCLE ELBY (See Clifford McBride's...)
Eastern Color Printing Co.: July, 1942 (68 pgs.) (One Shot)
1 43 86 129 268 454 640
1945-American Book-Strafford Press (128 pgs.) (8x10-1/2"; B&W reprints; hardcover) 15 30 45 83 124 165

NARRATIVE ILLUSTRATION, THE STORY OF THE COMICS (Also see Good Triumphs

Nathaniel Dusk II #3 © DC

National Comics #23 © QUA

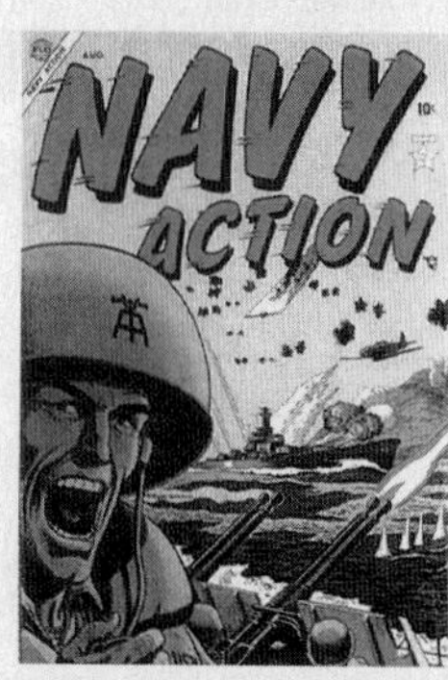

Navy Action #1 © MAR

GD VG FN VF VF/NM NM-
2.0 4.0 6.0 8.0 9.0 9.2

Over Evil!)
M.C. Gaines: Summer, 1942 (32 pgs., 7-1/4"x10", B&W w/color inserts)

nn-16 pgs. text with illustrations of ancient art, strips and comic covers; 4 pg. WWII War Bond promo, "The Minute Man Answers the Call" color comic drawn by Shelly and a special 8-page color comic insert of "The Story of Saul" (from Picture Stories from the Bible #10 or soon to appear in PS #10) or "Noah and His Ark" or "The Story of Ruth". Insert has special title page indicating it was part of a Sunday newspaper supplement insert series that had already run in a New England "Sunday Herald." Another version exists with insert from Picture Stories from the Bible #7.
(very rare) Estimated value... 1500.00

NOTE: ***Print, A Quarterly Journal of the Graphic Arts*** *Vol. 3 No. 2 (88 pg., square bound) features the 1st printing of Narrative Illustration, The Story of The Comics. A VG+ copy sold for $750 in 2005.*

NASCAR HEROES
Starbridge Media: 2007 - No. 3 ($3.95)

1-3: 1-Origin of fictional racer Jimmy Dash. 3-Origin of the Daytona 500; DeStefano-s 4.00
nn-(2008, Free Comic Book Day giveaway) The Mystery of Driver Z 2.50

NASH (WCW Wrestling)
Image Comics: July, 1999 - No. 2, July, 1999 ($2.95)

1,2-Regular and photo-c 3.00
1-($6.95) Photo-split-cover Edition 7.00

NATHANIEL DUSK
DC Comics: Feb, 1984 - No. 4, May, 1984 ($1.25, mini-series, direct sales, Baxter paper)

1-4: 1-Intro/origin; Gene Colan-c/a in all 3.00

NATHANIEL DUSK II
DC Comics: Oct, 1985 - No. 4, Jan, 1986 ($2.00, mini-series, Baxter paper)

1-4: Gene Colan-c/a in all 3.00

NATIONAL COMICS
Quality Comics Group: July, 1940 - No. 75, Nov, 1949

1-Uncle Sam begins (1st app.); origin sidekick Buddy by Eisner; origin Wonder Boy & Kid Dixon; Merlin the Magician (ends #45); Cyclone, Kid Patrol, Sally O'Neil Policewoman, Pen Miller (by Klaus Nordling; ends #22), Prop Powers (ends #26), & Paul Bunyan (ends #22) begin 541 1082 1623 3950 6975 10,000
2 245 490 735 1568 2684 3800
3-Last Eisner Uncle Sam 171 342 513 1086 1868 2650
4-Last Cyclone 135 270 405 864 1482 2100
5-(11/40)-Quicksilver begins (1st app.; 3rd w/lightning speed?; re-intro'd by DC in 1993 as Max Mercury in Flash #76, 2nd series); origin Uncle Sam; bondage-c 155 310 465 992 1696 2400
6,8-11: 8-Jack & Jill begins (ends #22). 9-Flag-c 129 258 387 826 1413 2000
7-Classic Lou Fine-c 258 516 774 1651 2826 4000
12 87 174 261 553 952 1350
13-16-Lou Fine-a 89 178 267 565 970 1375
17,19-22: 21-Classic Nazi swastika cover. 22-Last Pen Miller (moves to Crack #23) 68 136 204 435 743 1050
18-(12/41)-Shows Asians attacking Pearl Harbor; on stands one month before actual event 135 270 405 864 1482 2100
23-The Unknown & Destroyer 171 begin 69 138 207 442 759 1075
24-Japanese War-c 69 138 207 442 759 1075
25-30: 25-Nazi drug usage/hypodermic needle in story. 26-Wonder Boy ends. 27- G-2 the Unknown begins (ends #46). 29-Origin The Unknown 50 100 150 315 533 750
31-33: 33-Chic Carter begins (ends #47) 45 90 135 284 480 675
34-37,40: 35-Last Kid Patrol 40 80 120 242 401 560
38-Hitler, Tojo, Mussolini-c 63 126 189 403 689 975
39-Hitler-c 65 130 195 416 708 1000
41,43-50: 48-Origin The Whistler 27 54 81 158 259 360
42-The Barker begins (1st app?, 5/44); The Barker covers begin 40 80 120 246 411 575
51-Sally O'Neil by Ward, 8 pgs. (12/45) 30 60 90 117 289 400
52-60 20 40 60 118 192 265
61-67: 67-Format change; Quicksilver app. 15 30 45 90 140 190
68-75: The Barker ends 14 28 42 82 121 160

NOTE: ***Cole*** *Quicksilver-13; Barker-43; c-43, 46, 47, 49-51.* ***Crandall*** *Uncle Sam-11-13 (with* ***Fine****), 25, 26; c-24-26, 30-33, 43.* ***Crandall*** *Paul Bunyan-10-13.* ***Fine*** *Uncle Sam-13 (w/****Crandall****), 17, 18; c-1-14, 16, 18, 21.* ***Gill Fox*** *c-69-74.* ***Guardineer*** *Quicksilver-27, 35.* ***Gustavson*** *Quicksilver-14-26.* ***McWilliams*** *a-23-28, 55, 57. Uncle Sam c-1-41. Barker c-42-75.*

NATIONAL COMICS (Also see All Star Comics 1999 crossover titles)
DC Comics: May, 1999 ($1.99, one-shot)

1-Golden Age Flash and Mr. Terrific; Waid-s/Lopresti-a 3.00

NATIONAL CRUMB, THE (Magazine-Size)
Mayfair Publications: August, 1975 (52 pgs., B&W) (Satire)

GD VG FN VF VF/NM NM-
2.0 4.0 6.0 8.0 9.0 9.2

1-Grandenetti-c/a, Ayers-a 2 4 6 11 16 20

NATIONAL VELVET (TV)
Dell Publishing Co./Gold Key: May-July, 1961 - No. 2, Mar, 1963 (All photo-c)

Four Color 1195 (#1) 7 14 21 49 80 110
Four Color 1312, 01-556-207, 12-556-210 (Dell) 4 8 12 28 44 60
1,2: 1(12/62) (Gold Key). 2(3/63) 4 8 12 28 44 60

NATION OF SNITCHES
Piranha Press (DC): 1990 ($4.95, color, 52 pgs.)

nn 5.00

NATION X (X-Men on the Utopia island)
Marvel Comics: Feb, 2010 - No. 4, May, 2010 ($3.99, limited series)

1-4-Short stories by various. 1,4-Allred-a. 2-Choi, Cloonan-a. 4-Doop app. 4.00
...: X-Factor (3/10, $3.99) David-s/DeLandro-a 4.00

NATURE BOY (Formerly Danny Blaze; Li'l Rascal Twins #6 on)
Charlton Comics: No. 3, March, 1956 - No. 5, Feb, 1957

3-Origin; Blue Beetle story; Buscema-c/a 22 44 66 130 213 295
4,5 15 30 45 92 144 195

NOTE: ***John Buscema*** *a-3, 4p, 5; c-3.* ***Powell*** *a-4.*

NATURE OF THINGS (Disney, TV/Movie)
Dell Publishing Co.: No. 727, Sept, 1956 - No. 842, Sept, 1957

Four Color 727 (#1), 842-Jesse Marsh-a 5 10 15 34 55 75

NAUSICAA OF THE VALLEY OF WIND
Viz Comics: 1988 - No. 7, 1989; 1989 - No. 4, 1990 ($2.50, B&W, 68pgs.)

Book 1-7: 1-Contains Moebius poster 4.00
Part II, Book 1-4 ($2.95) 4.00

NAVY ACTION (Sailor Sweeney #12-14)
Atlas Comics (CDS): Aug, 1954 - No. 11, Apr, 1956; No. 15, 1/57 - No. 18, 8/57

1-Powell-a 20 40 60 114 182 250
2-Lawrence-a; RQ Sale-a 12 24 36 69 97 125
3-11: 4-Last precode (2/55) 10 20 30 56 76 95
15-18 10 20 30 54 72 90

NOTE: ***Berg*** *a-7, 9.* ***Colan*** *a-8.* ***Drucker*** *a-7, 17.* ***Everett*** *a-3, 7, 16; c-16, 17.* ***Heath*** *c-1, 2, 5, 6.* ***Maneely*** *a-5, 7, 8, 18; c-9, 11.* ***Pakula*** *a-2, 3, 9.* ***Reinman*** *a-17.*

NAVY COMBAT
Atlas Comics (MPI): June, 1955 - No. 20, Oct, 1958

1-Torpedo Taylor begins by Don Heck 20 40 60 114 182 250
2 12 24 36 69 97 125
3-10 10 20 30 56 76 95
11,13-16,18-20: 14-Torres-a 10 20 30 54 72 90
12-Crandall-a 11 22 33 60 83 105
17-Williamson-a, 4 pgs.; Torres-a 10 20 30 58 79 100

NOTE: ***Ayers*** *a-15.* ***Berg*** *a-10, 11.* ***Colan*** *a-11.* ***Drucker*** *a-7.* ***Everett*** *a-3, 20; c-8 & 9 w/****Tuska****, 10, 13-16.* ***Forte*** *a-15, 18.* ***Heck*** *a-11(2), 15, 19.* ***Maneely*** *c-1, 6, 11, 17.* ***Morisi*** *a-8.* ***Pakula*** *a-7, 18.* ***Powell*** *a-20.* ***Reinman*** *a-18.*

NAVY HEROES
Almanac Publishing Co.: 1945

1-Heavy in propaganda 14 28 42 80 115 150

NAVY PATROL
Key Publications: May, 1955 - No. 4, Nov, 1955

1 8 16 24 44 57 70
2-4 6 12 18 28 34 40

NAVY TALES
Atlas Comics (CDS): Jan, 1957 - No. 4, July, 1957

1-Everett-c; Berg, Powell-a 17 34 51 98 154 210
2-Williamson/Mayo-a(5 pgs); Crandall-a 14 28 42 80 115 150
3,4-Reinman-a; Severin-c. 4-Crandall-a 12 24 36 69 97 125

NOTE: ***Colan*** *a-4.* ***Maneely*** *c-2.* ***Reinman*** *a-2-4.* ***Sinnott*** *a-4.*

NAVY TASK FORCE
Stanmor Publications/Aragon Mag. No. 4-8: Feb, 1954 - No. 8, April, 1956

1 9 18 27 50 65 80
2 6 12 18 31 38 45
3-8: #8-r/Navy Patrol #1 6 12 18 28 34 40

NAVY WAR HEROES
Charlton Comics: Jan, 1964 - No. 7, Mar-Apr, 1965

1 3 6 9 20 30 40
2-7 3 6 9 14 19 24

NAZA (Stone Age Warrior)

Necromancer Pilot Season #1 © TCOW

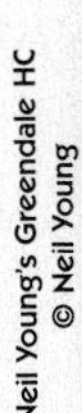

Neil Young's Greendale HC © Neil Young

Nemesis #1 © Millar & McNiven

GD 2.0 | VG 4.0 | FN 6.0 | VF 8.0 | VF/NM 9.0 | NM- 9.2

Dell Publishing Co.: Nov-Jan, 1963-64 - No. 9, March, 1966

12-555-401 (#1)-Painted-c 5 10 15 34 55 75
2-9: 2-4-Painted-c 4 8 12 24 37 50

NEBBS, THE (Also see Crackajack Funnies)
Dell Publishing Co./Croydon Publishing Co.: 1941; 1945

Large Feature Comic 23(1941) 21 42 63 122 199 275
1(1945, 36 pgs.)-Reprints 13 26 39 74 105 135

NECESSARY EVIL
Desperado Publishing: Oct, 2007 - No. 9, Nov, 2008 ($3.99)

1-9: 1-Joshua Williamson-s/Marcus Harris-a/Dustin Nguyen-c 4.00

NECROMANCER
Image Comics (Top Cow): Sept, 2005 - No. 6, July 2006 ($2.99)

1-6: 1-Manapul-a/Ortega-s; three covers by Manapul, Horn & Bachalo 3.00
... Pilot Season Vol. 1 #1 (11/07, $2.99) Ortega-s/Meyers-a/Manapul-c 3.00

NECROMANCER: THE GRAPHIC NOVEL
Marvel Comics (Epic Comics): 1989 ($8.95)

nn 9.00

NECROWAR
Dreamwave Productions: July, 2003 - No. 3, Sept, 2003 ($2.95)

1-3-Furman-s/Granov-digital art 3.00

NEGATION
CrossGeneration Comics: Dec, 2001 - No. 27, Mar, 2004 ($2.95)

Prequel (12/01) 3.00
1-27: 1-(1/02) Pelletier-a/Bedard & Waid-s 3.00
... Lawbringer (11/02, $2.95) Nebres-a 3.00
Vol. 1: Bohica! (10/02, $19.95, TPB) r/ Prequel & #1-6 20.00
Vol. 2: Baptism of Fire (5/03, $15.95, TPB) r/#7-12 16.00
Vol. 3: Hounded (12/03, $15.95, TPB) r/#13-18 16.00

NEGATION WAR
CrossGeneration Comics: Apr, 2004 - No. 6 ($2.95)

1-4-Bedard-s/Pelletier-a 3.00

NEGATIVE BURN
Caliber: 1993 - No. 50, 1997 ($2.95, B&W, anthology)

1,2,4-12,14-47: Anthology by various including Bolland, Burden, Doran, Gaiman, Moebius, Moore, & Pope 4.00
3,13: 3-Bone story. 13-Strangers in Paradise story 2 4 6 8 10 12
48,49-($4.95) 5.00
50-($6.95, 96 pgs.)-Gaiman, Robinson, Bolland 7.00
...Summer Special 2005 (Image, 2005, $9.99) new short stories by various 10.00
...: The Best From 1993-1998 (Image, 1/05, $19.95) r/short stories by various 20.00
...Winter Special 2005 (Image, 2005, $9.95) new short stories by various 10.00

NEGATIVE BURN
Image Comics (Desperado): May, 2006 - Present ($5.99, B&W, anthology)

1-21: 1-Art by Bolland, Powell, Luna, Smith, Hester. 2-Milk & Cheese by Dorkin 6.00

NEGRO (See All-Negro)

NEGRO HEROES (Calling All Girls, Real Heroes, & True Comics reprints)
Parents' Magazine Institute: Spring, 1947 - No. 2, Summer, 1948

1 116 232 348 742 1271 1800
2-Jackie Robinson-c/story 129 258 387 826 1413 2000

NEGRO ROMANCE (Negro Romances #4)
Fawcett Publications: June, 1950 - No. 3, Oct, 1950 (All photo-c)

1-Evans-a (scarce) 142 284 426 909 1555 2200
2,3 (scarce) 110 220 330 704 1202 1700

NEGRO ROMANCES (Formerly Negro Romance; Romantic Secrets #5 on)
Charlton Comics: No. 4, May, 1955

4-Reprints Fawcett #2 (scarce) 71 142 213 454 777 1100

NEIL GAIMAN AND CHARLES VESS' STARDUST
DC Comics (Vertigo): 1997 - No. 4, 1998 ($5.95/$6.95, square-bound, lim. series)

1-4: Gaiman text with Vess paintings in all 7.00
Hardcover (1998, $29.95) r/series with new sketches 35.00
Softcover (1999, $19.95) oversized; new Vess-c 20.00

NEIL GAIMAN'S LADY JUSTICE
Tekno Comix: Sept, 1995 - No. 11, May, 1996 ($1.95/$2.25)

1-11: 1-Sienkiewicz-c; pin-ups. 1-5-Brereton-c. 7-Polybagged. 11-The Big Bang Pt. 7 3.00

NEIL GAIMAN'S LADY JUSTICE
BIG Entertainment: V2#1, June, 1996 - No. 9, Feb, 1997 ($2.25)

V2#1-9: Dan Brereton-c on all. 6-8-Dan Brereton script 3.00

NEIL GAIMAN'S MIDNIGHT DAYS
DC Comics (Vertigo): 1999 ($17.95, trade paperback)

nn-Reprints Gaiman's short stories; new Swamp Thing w/ Bissette-a 18.00

NEIL GAIMAN'S MR. HERO-THE NEWMATIC MAN
Tekno Comix: Mar, 1995 - No. 17, May, 1996 ($1.95/$2.25)

1-17: 1-Intro Mr. Hero & Teknophage; bound-in game piece and trading card. 4-w/Steel edition Neil Gaiman's Teknophage #1 coupon. 13-Polybagged 3.00

NEIL GAIMAN'S MR. HERO-THE NEWMATIC MAN
BIG Entertainment: V2#1, June, 1996 ($2.25)

V2#1-Teknophage destroys Mr. Hero; includes The Big Bang Pt. 10 3.00

NEIL GAIMAN'S NEVERWHERE
DC Comics (Vertigo): Aug, 2005 - No. 9, Sept, 2006 ($2.99, limited series)

1-9-Adaptation of Gaiman novel; Carey-s/Fabry-a/c 3.00
TPB (2007, $19.99) r/series; intro. by Carey 20.00

NEIL GAIMAN'S PHAGE-SHADOWDEATH
BIG Entertainment: June, 1996 - No. 6, Nov, 1996 ($2.25, limited series)

1-6: Bryan Talbot-c & scripts in all. 1-1st app. Orlando Holmes 3.00

NEIL GAIMAN'S TEKNOPHAGE
Tekno Comix: Aug, 1995 - No. 10, Mar, 1996 ($1.95/$2.25)

1-6-Rick Veitch scripts & Bryan Talbot-c/a. 3.00
1-Steel Edition 4.00
7-10: Paul Jenkins scripts in all. 8-polybagged 3.00

NEIL GAIMAN'S WHEEL OF WORLDS
Tekno Comix: Apr, 1995 - No. 1, May, 1996 ($2.95/$3.25)

0-1st app. Lady Justice; 48 pgs.; bound-in poster 4.00
0-Regular edition 3.00
1 ($3.25, 5/96)-Bruce Jones scripts; Lady Justice & Teknophage app.; CGI photo-c 4.00

NEIL THE HORSE (See Charlton Bullseye #2)
Aardvark-Vanaheim #1-10/Renegade Press #11 on: 2/83 - No. 10, 12/84; No. 11, 4/85 - #15, 1985 (B&W)

1($1.40) 4.00
1-2nd print 3.00
2-12: 11-w/paperdolls 3.00
13-15: Double size ($3.00). 13-w/paperdolls. 15 is a flip book(2-c) 4.00

NEIL YOUNG'S GREENDALE
DC Comics (Vertigo): 2010 ($19.99, hardcover graphic novel)

HC-Story based on the Neil Young album; Dysart-s/Chiang-a; intro. by Neil Young 20.00

NELLIE THE NURSE (Also see Gay Comics & Joker Comics)
Marvel/Atlas Comics (SPI/LMC): 1945 - No. 36, Oct, 1952; 1957

1-(1945) 45 90 135 284 480 675
2-(Spring/46) 23 46 69 136 223 310
3,4: 3-New logo (9/46) 19 38 57 109 172 235
5-Kurtzman's "Hey Look" (3); Georgie app. 20 40 60 114 182 250
6-8,10: 7,8-Georgie app. 10-Millie app. 18 36 54 103 162 220
9-Wolverton-a (1 pg.); Mille the Model app. 18 36 54 105 165 225
11,14-16,18-Kurtzman's "Hey Look" 18 36 54 107 169 230
12- "Giggles 'n' Grins" by Kurtzman 18 36 54 103 162 220
13,17,19,20: 17-Annie Oakley app. 14 28 42 82 121 160
21-30: 28-Mr. Nexdoor-r (3 pgs.) by Kurtzman/Rusty #22 13 26 39 72 101 130
31-36: 36-Post-c 11 22 33 62 86 110
1('57)-Leading Mag. (Atlas)-Everett-a, 20 pgs 12 24 36 67 94 120

NELLIE THE NURSE
Dell Publishing Co.: No. 1304, Mar-May, 1962

Four Color 1304-Stanley-a 7 14 21 47 76 105

NEMESIS (Millar & McNiven's...)
Marvel Comics (Icon): May, 2010 - No. 4, Feb, 2011 ($2.99)

1-4-Millar-s/McNiven-a 3.00
1,2-Variant covers: 1-Yu. 2-Cassaday 8.00

NEMESIS ARCHIVES (Listed with Adventures Into the Unknown)

NEMESIS: THE IMPOSTERS
DC Comics: May, 2010 - No. 4, Aug, 2010 ($2.99, limited series)

New Adventure Comics #17 © DC

New Adventures of Superboy #5 © DC

New Avengers #11 © MAR

	GD 2.0	VG 4.0	FN 6.0	VF 8.0	VF/NM 9.0	NM- 9.2

1-4-Richards-a/Luvisi-c. 1-Joker app. 2-4-Batman app. 3.00

NEMESIS THE WARLOCK (Also see Spellbinders)
Eagle Comics: Sept, 1984 - No. 7, Mar, 1985 (limited series, Baxter paper)

1-7: 2000 A.D. reprints 3.00

NEMESIS THE WARLOCK
Quality Comics/Fleetway Quality #2 on: 1989 - No. 19, 1991 ($1.95, B&W)

1-19 3.00

NEUTRO
Dell Publishing Co.: Jan, 1967

1-Jack Sparling-c/a (super hero); UFO-s 4 8 12 26 41 55

NEVADA (See Zane Grey's Four Color 412, 996 & Zane Grey's Stories of the West #1)

NEVADA (Also see Vertigo Winter's Edge #1)
DC Comics (Vertigo): May, 1998 - No. 6, Oct, 1998 ($2.50, limited series)

1-6-Gerber-s/Winslade-c/a 3.00
TPB-(1999, $14.95) r/#1-6 & Vertigo Winter's Edge preview 15.00

NEVER AGAIN (War stories; becomes Soldier & Marine V2#9)
Charlton Comics: Aug, 1955; No. 8, July, 1956 (No #2-7)

1	10	20	30	54	72	90
8-(Formerly Foxhole?)	6	12	18	31	38	45

NEVERMEN, THE (See Dark Horse Presents #148-150)
Dark Horse Comics: May, 2000 - No. 4, Aug, 2000 ($2.95, limited series)

1-4-Phil Amara-s/Guy Davis-a 3.00

NEVERMEN, THE: STREETS OF BLOOD
Dark Horse Comics: Jan, 2003 - No. 3, Apr, 2003 ($2.99, limited series)

1-3-Phil Amara-s/Guy Davis-a 3.00
TPB (7/03, $9.95) r/#1-3; Paul Jenkins intro.; Davis sketch pages 10.00

NEVERMORE (DEAN KOONTZ'S:...)
Dabel Brothers Prods.: Mar, 2009 - No. 5 ($3.99, limited series)

1-Keith Champagne-s/Andy Smith-a 4.00

NEW ADVENTURE COMICS (Formerly New Comics; becomes Adventure Comics #32 on; V1#12 indicia says NEW COMICS #12)
National Periodical Publications: V1#12, Jan, 1937 - No. 31, Oct, 1938

V1#12-Federal Men by Siegel & Shuster continues; Jor-L mentioned; Whitney Ellsworth-c begin, end #14	533	1066	1600	4300	-	-
V2#1(2/37, #13)-(Rare)	507	1014	1521	4100	-	-
V2#2 (#14)	450	900	1350	3700	-	-
15(V2#3)-20(V2#8): 15-1st Adventure logo; Craig Flessel-c begin, end #31. 16-1st non-funny cover. 17-Nadir, Master of Magic begins, ends #30	360	720	1080	1980	3140	4300
21(V2#9),22(V2#10, 2/37): 22-X-Mas-c	320	640	960	1760	2830	3900
23-25,28-31	270	540	810	1485	2443	3400

26(5/38) (scarce) has house ad for Action Comics #1 showing B&W image of cover (early published image of Superman)(prices vary widely on this book) (A CGC 5.0 sold in 2006 for $5377.50)

27(6/38) has house ad for Action Comics #1 showing B&W image of cover (scarce) (early published image of Superman)	450	900	1350	2700	3600	4500

NEW ADVENTURES OF ABRAHAM LINCOLN, THE
Image Comics (Homage): 1998 ($19.95, one-shot)

1-Scott McCloud-s/computer art 20.00

NEW ADVENTURES OF CHARLIE CHAN, THE (TV)
National Periodical Publications: May-June, 1958 - No. 6, Mar-Apr, 1959

1 (Scarce)-John Broome-s/Sid Greene-a in all	74	148	222	470	810	1150
2 (Scarce)	47	94	141	296	498	700
3-6 (Scarce)-Greene/Giella-a	40	80	120	246	411	575

NEW ADVENTURES OF HUCK FINN, THE (TV)
Gold Key: December, 1968 (Hanna-Barbera)

1- "The Curse of Thut"; part photo-c 4 8 12 22 34 45

NEW ADVENTURES OF PINOCCHIO (TV)
Dell Publishing Co.: Oct-Dec, 1962 - No. 3, Sept-Nov, 1963

12-562-212(#1)	8	16	24	56	93	130
2,3	7	14	21	45	73	100

NEW ADVENTURES OF ROBIN HOOD (See Robin Hood)

NEW ADVENTURES OF SHERLOCK HOLMES (Also see Sherlock Holmes)
Dell Publishing Co.: No. 1169, Mar-May, 1961 - No. 1245, Nov-Jan, 1961/62

Four Color 1169(#1)	13	26	39	91	176	260
Four Color 1245	12	24	36	84	157	230

NEW ADVENTURES OF SPEED RACER
Now Comics: Dec, 1993 - No. 7, 1994? ($1.95)

1-7 3.00
0-(Premiere)-3-D cover 3.00

NEW ADVENTURES OF SUPERBOY, THE (Also see Superboy)
DC Comics: Jan, 1980 - No. 54, June, 1984

1 5.00
2-6,8-10 4.00
11-49,51-54: 11-Superboy gets new power. 14-Lex Luthor app. 15-Superboy gets new parents. 28-Dial "H" For Hero begins, ends #49. 45-47-1st app. Sunburst. 48-Begin 75¢-c. 3.00
1,2,5,6,8 (Whitman variants; low print run; no issue # shown on cover) 2 4 6 8 10 12
7,50: 7-Has extra story "The Computers That Saved Metropolis" by Starlin (Radio Shack giveaway w/indicia). 50-Legion app. 5.00

NOTE: *Buckler a-9p; c-36p. Giffen a-50; c-50. 40i. Gil Kane c-32p, 33p, 35, 39, 41-49. Miller c-51. Starlin a-7. Krypto back-ups in 17, 22. Superbaby in 11, 14, 19, 24.*

NEW ADVENTURES OF THE PHANTOM BLOT, THE (See The Phantom Blot)

NEW AMERICA
Eclipse Comics: Nov, 1987 - No. 4, Feb, 1988 ($1.75, Baxter paper)

1-4: Scout limited series 3.00

NEW ARCHIES, THE (TV)
Archie Comic Publications: Oct, 1987 - No. 22, May, 1990 (75¢)

1 5.00
2-10: 3-Xmas issue 4.00
11-22: 17-22 (95¢-$1.00): 21-Xmas issue 3.00

NEW ARCHIES DIGEST (TV)(...Comics Digest Magazine #4?-10; ...Digest Magazine #11 on)
Archie Comics: May, 1988 - No. 14, July, 1991 ($1.35/$1.50, quarterly)

1 6.00
2-14: 6-Begin $1.50-c 3.50

NEW AVENGERS, THE (Also see Promotional section for military giveaway)
Marvel Comics: Jan, 2005 - No. 64, Jun, 2010 ($2.25/$2.50/$2.99/$3.99)

1-Bendis-s/Finch-a; Spider-Man app.; re-intro The Sentry; 4 covers by McNiven, Quesada & Finch; variants from #1-6 combine for one team image 5.00
1-Director's Cut ($3.99) includes alternate covers, script, villain gallery 4.00
1-MGC (6/10 $1.00) r/#1 with "Marvel's Greatest Comics" cover logo 1.00
2-20: 2-6-Finch-a. 5-Wolverine app. 7-10-Origin of the Sentry; McNiven-a. 11-Debut of Ronin. 14,15-Cho-c/a. 17-20-Deodato-a 3.00
21-48: 21-26-Civil War. 21-Chaykin-a/c. 26-Maleev-a. 27-31-Yu-a; Echo & "Elektra" app. 33-37-The Hood app. 38-Gaydos-a. 39-Mack-a. 40-47-Secret Invasion 3.00
49-($3.99) Dark Reign 4.00
50-($4.99) Dark Reign; Tan, Hitch, McNiven, Yu, Horn & others-a; Tan wraparound-c 5.00
50-($4.99) Adam Kubert variant-c 6.00
51-64-($3.99) Dark Reign. 51,52-Tan & Bachalo-a. 54-Brother Voodoo becomes Sorceror Supreme. 56-Wrecking Crew app. 61-64-Siege; Steve Rogers app. 4.00
51-54-Variant covers by Bachalo 7.00
56,57-Variant covers. 56-70th Anniversary frame. 57-Super Hero Squad 6.00
Annual 1 (6/06, $3.99) Wedding of Luke Cage and Jessica Jones; Bendis-s/Coipel-a 4.00
Annual 2 (2/08, $3.99) Avengers vs. The Hood's gang; Bendis-s/Pagulayan-a 4.00
Annual 3 (2/10, $4.99) Mayhew-c/a; Dark Avengers app.; Siege preview 5.00
... Finale (6/10, $4.99) Follows Siege #4; Bendis-s/Hitch-a/c; Count Nefaria app. 5.00
...: Illuminati (5/06, $3.99) Bendis-s/Maleev-a; leads into Planet Hulk; Civil War preview 4.00
... Most Wanted Files (2006, $3.99) profile pages of Avenger villains 4.00
... Vol. 1: Breakout HC (2005, $19.99) r/#1-6; gallery of variant covers 20.00
... Vol. 1: Breakout SC (2006, $14.99) r/#1-6; gallery of variant covers 15.00
... Vol. 2: Sentry HC (2006, $19.99) r/#7-10 & ... Most Wanted Files 20.00
... Vol. 2: Sentry SC (2006, $14.99) r/#7-10 & ... Most Wanted Files 15.00
... Vol. 3: Secrets and Lies HC (2006, $19.99) r/#11-15 & Giant-Size Spider-Woman #1 20.00
... Vol. 3: Secrets and Lies SC (2006, $14.99) r/#11-15 & Giant-Size Spider-Woman #1 15.00
... Vol. 4: The Collective HC (2006, $19.99) r/#16-20 20.00
... Vol. 4: The Collective SC (2007, $14.99) r/#16-20 15.00
... Vol. 5: Civil War HC (2007, $19.99) r/#21-25 20.00
... Vol. 5: Civil War SC (2007, $14.99) r/#21-25 15.00
... Vol. 6: Revolution HC (2007, $19.99) r/#26-31 20.00
... Vol. 6: Revolution SC (2007, $14.99) r/#26-31 15.00
... Volume 1 HC (2007, $29.99) oversized r/#1-10, ... Most Wanted Files, and ... Guest Starring the Fantastic Four (militiary giveaway); new intro. by Bendis; script & sketch pages 30.00
... Volume 2 HC (2008, $29.99) oversized r/#11-20, ... Annual #1, and story from Giant-Size

New Avengers (2010 series) #4 © MAR

New Comics #1 © DC

New Gods #5 © DC

GD 2.0 | VG 4.0 | FN 6.0 | VF 8.0 | VF/NM 9.0 | NM- 9.2

Spider-Woman; variant covers & sketch pages 30.00

NEW AVENGERS (The Heroic Age)
Marvel Comics: Aug, 2010 - Present ($3.99)

1-Bendis-s/Immonen-a/c; Luke Cage forms new team; back-up text Avengers history 4.00
1-Variant-c by Djurdjevic 6.00
2-11: Hellstrom & Doctor Voodoo app.; back-up text Avengers history. 6-Doctor Voodoo killed. 9-11-Nick Fury flashback w/Chaykin-a 4.00

NEW AVENGERS: ILLUMINATI (Also see Civil War and Secret Invasion)
Marvel Comics: Feb, 2007 - No. 5, Jan, 2008 ($2.99, limited series)

1-5-Bendis & Reed-s/Cheung-a. 3-Origin of The Beyonder. 5-Secret Invasion 3.00
HC (2008, $19.99, dustjacket) r/#1-5; cover sketch art 20.00
SC (2008, $14.99) r/#1-5; cover sketch art 15.00

NEW AVENGERS: LUKE CAGE
Marvel Comics: Jun, 2010 - No. 3, Aug, 2010 ($3.99, limited series)

1-3-Arcudi-s/Canete-a; Spider-Man & Ronin app. 4.00

NEW AVENGERS: THE REUNION
Marvel Comics: May, 2009 - No. 4, Aug, 2009 ($3.99, limited series)

1-4-Mockingbird and Ronin (Hawkeye); McCann-s/López-a/Jo Chen-c 4.00

NEW AVENGERS/TRANSFORMERS
Marvel Comics: Sept, 2007 - No. 4, Dec, 2007 ($2.99, limited series)

1-4-Kirkham-a; Capt. America app. 1-Cheung-c. 2-Pearson-c 3.00
TPB (2008, $10.99) r/#1-4 11.00

NEW BOOK OF COMICS (Also see Big Book Of Fun)
National Periodical Publ.: 1937; No. 2, Spring, 1938 (100 pgs. each) (Reprints)

1(Rare)-1st regular size comic annual; 2nd DC annual; contains r/New Comics #1-4 & More Fun #9; r/Federal Men (8 pgs.), Henri Duval (1 pg.), & Dr. Occult in costume (1 pg.) by Siegel & Shuster; Moldoff, Sheldon Mayer (15 pgs.)-a
1850 3700 5550 12,000 21,000 30,000
2-Contains-r/More Fun #15 & 16; r/Dr. Occult in costume (a Superman prototype), & Calling All Cars (4 pgs.) by Siegel & Shuster 950 1900 2850 6175 11,088 16,000

NEW COMICS (New Adventure #12 on)
National Periodical Publ.: 12/35 - No. 11, 12/36 (No. 1-6: paper cover) (No. 1-5: 84 pgs.)

V1#1-Billy the Kid, Sagebrush 'n' Cactus, Jibby Jones, Needles, The Vikings, Sir Loin of Beef, Now-When I Was a Boy, & other 1-2 pg. strips; 2 pgs. Kelly art(1st)-(Gulliver's Travels); Sheldon Mayer-a(1st)(2 2pg. strips); Vincent Sullivan-c(1st)
2857 5714 8571 20,000 - -
2-1st app. Federal Men by Siegel & Shuster & begins (also see The Comics Magazine #2); Mayer, Kelly-a (Rare)(1/36) 1229 2458 3687 8600 - -
3-6: 3,4-Sheldon Mayer-a which continues in The Comics Magazine #1. 3-Vincent Sullivan-c. 4-Dickens' "A Tale of Two Cities" adaptation begins. 5-Junior Federal Men Club; Kiefer-a. 6- "She" adaptation begins 886 1772 2658 6200 - -
7-10 629 1258 1887 4400 - -
11-Ties with More Fun #16 as DC's 1st Christmas-c 671 1342 2013 4700 - -
NOTE: *#1-6 rarely occur in mint condition.* ***Whitney Ellsworth*** *c-4-11.*

NEW DEFENDERS (See Defenders)

NEW DNAGENTS, THE (Formerly DNAgents)
Eclipse Comics: V2#1, Oct, 1985 - V2#17, Mar, 1987 (Whole #s 25-40; Mando paper)

V2#1-17: 1-Origin recap. 7-Begin 95 cent-c. 9,10-Airboy preview 3.00
3-D 1 (1/86, $2.25) 3.00
2-D 1 (1/86)-Limited ed. (100 copies) 10.00

NEW DYNAMIX
DC Comics (WildStorm): May, 2008 - No. 5, Sept, 2008 ($2.99, limited series)

1-5-Warner-s/J.J. Kirby-a/c. 1-Variant-c by Jim Lee. 1-Convention Ed. with Lee-c 3.00

NEW ETERNALS: APOCALYPSE NOW (Also see Eternals, The)
Marvel Comics: Feb, 2000 ($3.99, one-shot)

1-Bennett & Hanna-a; Ladronn-c 4.00

NEW EXCALIBUR
Marvel Comics: Jan, 2006 - No. 24, Dec, 2007 ($2.99)

1-24: 1-Claremont-s/Ryan-a; Dazzler app. 3-Juggernaut app. 4-Lionheart app. 3.00
... Vol. 1: Defenders of the Realm TPB (2006, $17.99) r/#1-7 18.00
... Vol. 2: Last Days of Camelot TPB (2007, $19.99) r/#8-15 20.00
... Vol. 3: Battle for Eternity TPB (2007, $24.99) r/#16-24; sketch pages 25.00

NEW EXILES (Continued from Exiles #100 and Exiles - Days of Then and Now)
Marvel Comics: Mar, 2008 - No. 18, Apr, 2009 ($2.99)

1-18: 1-Claremont-s/Grummett-a; 2 covers by Land & Golden; new team 3.00
1-2nd printing with Grummett-c 3.00

GD 2.0 | VG 4.0 | FN 6.0 | VF 8.0 | VF/NM 9.0 | NM- 9.2

Annual 1 (2/09, $3.99) Claremont-s/Grummett-a 4.00

NEWFORCE (Also see Newmen)
Image Comics (Extreme Studios): Jan, 1996-No. 4, Apr, 1996 ($2.50, lim. series)

1-4: 1-"Extreme Destroyer" Pt. 8; polybagged w/gaming card. 4-Newforce disbands 3.00

NEW FUN COMICS (More Fun #7 on; see Big Book of Fun Comics)
National Periodical Publications: Feb, 1935 - No. 6, Oct, 1935 (10x15", No. 1-4,: slick-c) (No. 1-5: 36 pgs; 40 pgs. No. 6)

V1#1 (1st DC comic); 1st app. Oswald The Rabbit; Jack Woods (cowboy) begins
7429 14,858 22,287 52,000 - -
2(3/35)-(Very Rare) 3214 6428 9642 22,500 - -
3-5(8/35): 3-Don Drake on the Planet Soro-c/story (sci/fi, 4/35); early (maybe 1st) DC letter column. 5-Soft-c 1857 3714 5571 13,000 - -
6(10/35)-1st Dr. Occult by Siegel & Shuster (Leger & Reuths); last "New Fun" title. "New Comics" #1 begins in Dec. which is reason for title change to More Fun; Henri Duval (ends #10) by Siegel & Shuster begins; paper-c
3500 7000 10,500 24,500 - -

NEW FUNNIES (The Funnies #1-64; Walter Lantz...#109 on; New TV... #259, 260, 272, 273; TV Funnies #261-271)
Dell Publishing Co.: No. 65, July, 1942 - No. 288, Mar-Apr, 1962

65(#1)-Andy Panda in a world of real people, Raggedy Ann & Andy, Oswald the Rabbit (with Woody Woodpecker x-overs), Li'l Eight Ball & Peter Rabbit begin; Bugs Bunny and Elmer app. 69 138 207 587 1194 1800
66-70: 66-Felix the Cat begins. 67-Billy & Bonny Bee by Frank Thomas begins. 69-Kelly-a (2 pgs.); The Brownies begin (not by Kelly) 32 64 96 246 486 725
71-75: 72-Kelly illos. 75-Brownies by Kelly? 22 44 66 159 317 475
76-Andy Panda (Carl Barks & Pabian-a); Woody Woodpecker x-over in Oswald ends
71 142 213 604 1227 1850
77,78: 77-Kelly-c. 78-Andy Panda in a world with real people ends
21 42 63 150 300 450
79-81 14 28 42 97 194 290
82-Brownies by Kelly begins 15 30 45 110 210 310
83-85-Brownies by Kelly in ea. 83-X-mas-c; Homer Pigeon begins. 85-Woody Woodpecker, 1 pg. strip begins 14 28 42 100 203 305
86-90: 87-Woody Woodpecker stories begin 11 22 33 80 150 220
91-99 10 20 30 67 116 165
100 (6/45) 10 20 30 69 122 175
101-120: 119-X-Mas-c 8 16 24 54 90 125
121-150: 131,143-X-Mas-c 7 14 21 47 76 105
151-200: 155-X-Mas-c. 167-X-Mas-c. 182-Origin & 1st app. Knothead & Splinter. 191-X-Mas-c 6 12 18 41 66 90
201-240 6 12 18 37 59 80
241-288: 270,271-Walter Lantz c-app. 281-1st story swipes/WDC&S #100
5 10 15 32 51 70
NOTE: *Early issues written by* ***John Stanley.***

NEW GODS, THE (1st Series)(New Gods #12 on)(See Adventure #459, DC Graphic Novel #4, 1st Issue Special #13 & Super-Team Family)
National Periodical Publications/DC Comics: 2-3/71 - V2#11, 10-11/72; V3#12, 7/77 - V3#19, 7-8/78 (Fourth World)

1-Intro/1st app. Orion; 4th app. Darkseid (cameo; 3 weeks after Forever People #1) (#1-3 are 15¢ issues) 9 18 27 65 113 160
2-Darkseid-c/story (2nd full app., 4-5/71) 5 10 15 35 55 75
3-1st app. Black Racer; last 15¢ issue 4 8 12 24 37 50
4-9: (25¢, 52 pg. giants): 4-Darkseid cameo; origin Manhunter-r. 5,7,8-Young Gods feature. 7-Darkseid app. (2-3/72); origin Orion; 1st origin of all New Gods as a group. 9-1st app. Forager 4 8 12 24 37 50
10,11: 11-Last Kirby issue. 3 6 9 20 30 40
12-19: Darkseid storyline w/minor apps. 12-New costume Orion (see 1st Issue Special #13 for 1st new costume). 19-Story continued in Adventure Comics #459,460
2 4 6 8 10 12
Jack Kirby's New Gods TPB ('98, $11.95, B&W&Grey) r/#1-11 plus cover gallery of original series and "84 reprints 12.00
NOTE: *#4-9(25¢, 52 pgs.) contain Manhunter-r by* ***Simon*** *&* ***Kirby*** *from Adventure #73, 74, 75, 76, 77, 78 with covers in that order.* ***Adkins*** *i-12-14, 17-19.* ***Buckler*** *a(p)-15.* ***Kirby*** *c/a-1-11p.* ***Newton*** *a(p)-12-14, 16-19.* ***Starlin*** *c-17.* ***Staton*** *c-19p.*

NEW GODS (Also see DC Graphic Novel #4)
DC Comics: June, 1984 - No. 6, Nov, 1984 ($2.00, Baxter paper)

1-5: New Kirby-c; r/New Gods #1-10. 4.00
6-Reprints New Gods #11 w/48 pgs of new Kirby story & art; leads into DC Graphic Novel #4
2 4 6 8 10 12

NEW GODS (2nd Series)
DC Comics: Feb, 1989 - No. 28, Aug, 1991 ($1.50)

New Gods (2nd series) #10 © DC

The New Mutants #10 © MAR

New Mutants Forever #2 © MAR

	GD 2.0	VG 4.0	FN 6.0	VF 8.0	VF/NM 9.0	NM- 9.2

1-28 3.00

NEW GODS (3rd Series) (Becomes Jack Kirby's Fourth World) (Also see Showcase '94 #1 & Showcase '95 #7)
DC Comics: Oct, 1995 - No. 15, Feb, 1997 ($1.95)

1-11,13-15: 9-Giffen-a(p). 10,11-Superman app. 13-Takion, Mr. Miracle & Big Barda app. 13-15-Byrne-a(p)/scripts & Simonson-c. 15-Apokolips merged w/ New Genesis; story cont'd in Jack Kirby's Fourth World 3.00
12-(11/96, 99¢)-Byrne-a(p)/scripts & Simonson-c begin; Takion cameo; indicia reads October 1996 3.00
...Secret Files 1 (9/98, $4.95) Origin-s 5.00

NEW GUARDIANS, THE
DC Comics: Sept, 1988 - No. 12, Sept, 1989 ($1.25)

1-($2.00, 52 pgs)-Staton-c/a in #1-9 4.00
2-12 3.00

NEW HEROIC (See Heroic)

NEW INVADERS (Titled Invaders for #0 & #1) (See Avengers V3#83,84)
Marvel Comics: No. 0, Aug, 2004 - No. 9, June, 2005 ($2.99)

0-9-Roster of U.S. Agent, Sub-Mariner, Blazing Skull and others. 0-Avengers app. 3.00

NEW JUSTICE MACHINE, THE (Also see The Justice Machine)
Innovation Publishing: 1989 - No. 3, 1989 ($1.95, limited series)

1-3 3.00

NEW KIDS ON THE BLOCK, THE (Also see Richie Rich and...)
Harvey Comics: Dec, 1990 - No. 8, Dec, 1991 ($1.25)

1-8 4.00
...**Back Stage Pass** 1(12/90) - 7(11/91) **Chillin'** 1(12/90) - 7(12/91): 1-Photo-c ...**Comic Tour** '90/91 1 (12/90) - 7(12/91) **Digest** 1(1/91) - 5(1/92) **Hanging Tough** 1 (2/91) **Magic Summer Tour** 1 (Fall/90) **Magic Summer Tour** nn (Fall/90, sold at concerts) **Step By Step** 1 (Fall/90, one-shot) **Valentine Girl** 1 (Fall/90, one-shot)-Photo-c 4.00

NEW LINE CINEMA'S TALES OF HORROR (Anthology)
DC Comics (WildStorm): Nov, 2007 ($2.99, one-shot)

1-Freddy Krueger and Leatherface app.; Darick Robertson-c 3.00

NEW LOVE (See Love & Rockets)
Fantagraphics Books: Aug, 1996 - No. 6, Dec, 1997 ($2.95, B&W, lim. series)

1-6: Gilbert Hernandez-s/a 3.00

NEWMAN
Image Comics (Extreme Studios): Jan, 1996 - No. 4, Apr, 1996 ($2.50, lim. series)

1-4: 1-Extreme Destroyer Pt. 3; polybagged w/card. 4-Shadowhunt tie-in; Eddie Collins becomes new Shadowhawk 3.00

NEW MANGVERSE (Also see Marvel Mangaverse)
Marvel Comics: Mar, 2006 - No. 5, July, 2006 ($2.99, lim. series)

1-5: Cebulski-s/Ohtsuka-a; The Hand and Elektra app. 3.00
...: The Rings of Fate (2006, $7.99, digest) r/#1-5 8.00

NEWMEN (becomes The Adventures Of The...#22)
Image Comics (Extreme Studios): Apr, 1994 - No. 20, Nov, 1995; No. 21, Nov, 1996 ($1.95/$2.50)

1-21: 1-5: Matsuda-c/a. 10-Polybagged w/trading card. 11-Polybagged. 20-Has a variant-c; Babewatch! x-over. 21-(11/96)-Series relaunch; Chris Sprouse-a begins; pin-up. 16-Has a variant-c by Quesada & Palmiotti 3.00
TPB-(1996, $12.95) r/#1-4 w/pin-ups 13.00

NEW MEN OF BATTLE, THE
Catechetical Guild: 1949 (nn) (Carboard-c)

nn(V8#1-3,5,6)-192 pgs.; contains 5 issues of Topix rebound 9 18 27 50 65 80
nn(V8#7-V8#11)-160 pgs.; contains 5 iss. of Topix 9 18 27 50 65 80

NEW MUTANTS, THE (See Marvel Graphic Novel #4 for 1st app.)(Also see X-Force & Uncanny X-Men #167)
Marvel Comics Group: Mar, 1983 - No. 100, Apr, 1991

1 6.00
2-10: 3,4-Ties into X-Men #167. 10-1st app. Magma 4.00
11-17,19,20: 13-Kitty Pryde app. 16-1st app. Warpath (w/out costume); see X-Men #193 3.00
18,21: 18-Intro. new Warlock. 21-Double size; origin new Warlock; newsstand version has cover price written in by Sienkiewicz 4.00
22-24,27-30: 23-25-Cloak & Dagger app. 3.00
25,26: 25-1st brief app. Legion. 26-1st full Legion app. 5.00
31-49,51-58: 35-Magneto intro'd as new headmaster. 43-Portacio-i. 58-Contains pull-out mutant registration form 3.00
50,73: 50-Double size. 73-(52 pgs.). 4.00
59-61: Fall of The Mutants series. 60-(52 pgs.) 4.00
62-72,74-85: 68-Intro Spyder. 63-X-Men & Wolverine clones app. 76-X-Factor & X-Terminator app. 85-Liefeld-c begin 3.00
86-Rob Liefeld-a begins; McFarlane-c(i) swiped from Ditko splash pg.; 1st brief app. Cable (last page teaser) 1 2 3 5 6 8
87-1st full app. Cable (3/90) 3 6 9 14 20 25
87-2nd printing; gold metallic ink-c ($1.00) 3.00
88-2nd app. Cable 1 3 4 6 8 10
92-No Liefeld-a; Liefeld-c 4.00
89,90,91,93-97,99,100: 89-3rd app. Cable. 90-New costumes. 90,91-Sabretooth app. 93,94-Cable vs. Wolverine. 95-97-X-Tinction Agenda x-over. 95-Death of new Warlock. 97-Wolverine & Cable-c, but no app. 99-1st app. of Feral (of X-Force); Byrne-c/swipe (X-Men, 1st Series #138). 100-(52 pgs.)-1st brief app. X-Force 5.00
95,100-Gold 2nd printing. 100-Silver ink 3rd printing 3.00
98-1st app. Deadpool, Gideon & Domino (2/91); 2nd Shatterstar (cameo); Liefeld-c/a 3 6 9 16 23 30
Annual 1 (1984) 5.00
Annual 2 (1986, $1.25)-1st Psylocke 1 3 4 6 8 10
Annual 3,4,6,7 ('87, '88,'90,'91, 68 pgs.): 4-Evolutionary War x-over. 6-1st new costumes by Liefeld (3 pgs.); 1st brief app. Shatterstar (of X-Force). 7-Liefeld pin-up only; X-Terminators back-up story; 2nd app. X-Force (cont'd in New Warriors Annual #1) 4.00
Annual 5 (1989, $2.00, 68 pgs.)-Atlantis Attacks; 1st Liefeld-a on New Mutants 5.00
... Classic Vol. 1 TPB (2006, $24.99) r/#1-7, Marvel Graphic Novel #4, Uncanny X-Men #167 25.00
... Classic Vol. 2 TPB (2007, $24.99) r/#8-17 25.00
... Classic Vol. 3 TPB (2008, $24.99) r/#18-25 & Annual #1 25.00
Special 1-Special Edition ('85, 68 pgs.)-Ties in w/X-Men Alpha Flight limited series; cont'd in X-Men Annual #9; Art Adams/Austin-a 5.00
Summer Special 1(Sum/90, $2.95, 84 pgs.) 4.00
NOTE: ***Art Adams** c-38, 39. **Austin** c-57i. **Byrne** c/a-75p. **Liefeld** a-86-91p, 93-96p, 98-100, Annual 5p, 6(3 pgs.); c-85-91p, 92, 93p, 94, 95, 96p, 97-100, Annual 5, 6p. **McFarlane** c-85-89i, 93i. **Portacio** a(i)-43. **Russell** a-48i. **Sienkiewicz** a-18-31, 35-38i; c-17-31, 35i, 37i, Annual 1. **Simonson** c-11p. **B. Smith** c-36, 40-48. **Williamson** a(i)-69, 71-73, 78-80, 82, 83; c(i)-69, 72, 73, 78i.*

NEW MUTANTS (Continues as New X-Men (Academy X))
Marvel Comics: July, 2003 - No. 13, June, 2004 ($2.50/$2.99)

1-7: 1-6-Josh Middleton-c. 7-Bachalo-c 3.00
8-13 ($2.99) 8-11-Bachalo-c 3.00
... Vol. 1: Back To School TPB (2005, $16.99) r/#1-6; new Middleton-c 17.00

NEW MUTANTS
Marvel Comics: July, 2009 - Present ($3.99/$2.99)

1-($3.99) Neves-a; Legion app.; covers by Ross, Adam Kubert, McLeod, Benjamin 4.00
2-23-($2.99) 2-10-Adam Kubert-c. 11-Siege; Dodson-c. 12-14-Second Coming 3.00
... Saga (2009, giveaway) New Mutants character profiles and story synopsies; Neves-c 3.00

NEW MUTANTS FOREVER
Marvel Comics: Oct, 2010 - No. 5, Feb, 2011 ($3.99, limited series)

1-5-Claremont-s/Rio & McLeod-a; Red Skull app. 1-Back-up history of New Mutants 4.00

NEW MUTANTS, THE: TRUTH OR DEATH
Marvel Comics: Nov, 1997 - No. 3, Jan, 1998 ($2.50, limited series)

1-3-Raab-s/Chang-a(p) 3.00

NEW ORDER, THE
CFD Publishing: Nov, 1994 ($2.95)

1 3.00

NEW PEOPLE, THE (TV)
Dell Publishing Co.: Jan, 1970 - No. 2, May, 1970

1 3 6 9 17 25 32
2-Photo-c 3 6 9 15 21 26

NEW ROMANCES
Standard Comics: No. 5, May, 1951 - No. 21, May, 1954

5-Photo-c 15 30 45 88 137 185
6-9: 6-Barbara Bel Geddes, Richard Basehart "Fourteen Hours" photo-c. 7-Ray Milland & Joan Fontaine photo-c. 9-Photo-c from '50s movie 11 22 33 60 83 105
10,14,16,17-Toth-a 11 22 33 64 90 115
11-Toth-a; Liz Taylor, Montgomery Clift photo-c 30 60 90 177 289 400
12,13,15,18-21 10 20 30 56 76 95
NOTE: ***Celardo** a-9. **Moreira** a-6. **Tuska** a-7, 20. Photo c-5-16.*

NEWSBOY LEGION BY JOE SIMON AND JACK KIRBY, THE
DC Comics: 2010 ($49.99, hardcover with dustjacket)

Vol. 1 - Reprints apps. in Star Spangled Comics #7-32; new intro. by Joe Simon 50.00

New Teen Titans #27 © DC

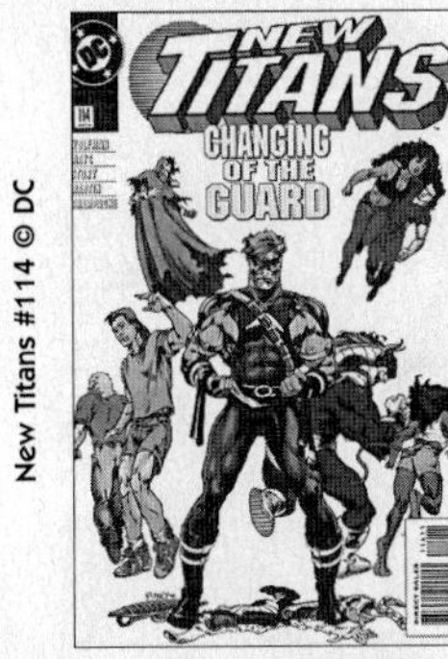

New Titans #114 © DC

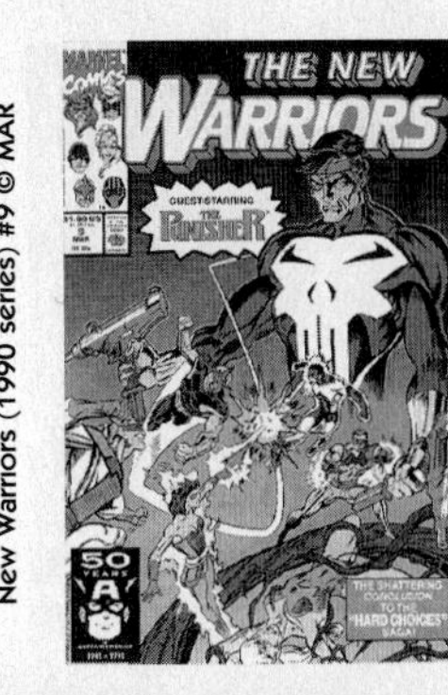

New Warriors (1990 series) #9 © MAR

GD VG FN VF VF/NM NM-
2.0 4.0 6.0 8.0 9.0 9.2

NEW SHADOWHAWK, THE (Also see Shadowhawk & Shadowhunt)
Image Comics (Shadowline Ink): June, 1995 - No. 7, Mar, 1996 ($2.50)

1-7: Kurt Busiek scripts in all 3.00

NEW STATESMEN, THE
Fleetway Publications (Quality Comics): 1989 - No. 5, 1990 ($3.95, limited series, mature readers, 52pgs.)

1-5: Futuristic; squarebound; 3-Photo-c 4.00

NEWSTRALIA
Innovation Publ.: July, 1989 - No. 5, 1989 ($1.75, color)(#2 on, $2.25, B&W)

1-5: 1,2: Timothy Truman-c/a; Gustovich-i 3.00

NEW TALENT SHOWCASE (Talent Showcase #16 on)
DC Comics: Jan, 1984 - No. 19, Oct, 1985 (Direct sales only)

1-19: Features new strips & artists. 18-Williamson-c(i) 3.00

NEW TEEN TITANS, THE (See DC Comics Presents #26, Marvel and DC Present & Teen Titans; Tales of the Teen Titans #41 on)
DC Comics: Nov, 1980 - No. 40, Mar, 1984

1-Robin, Kid Flash, Wonder Girl, The Changeling (1st app.), Starfire, The Raven, Cyborg begin; partial origin 3 6 9 16 22 28
2-1st app. Deathstroke the Terminator 3 6 9 21 32 42
3-10: 3-Origin Starfire; Intro The Fearsome Five. 4-Origin continues; J.L.A. app. 6-Origin Raven. 7-Cyborg origin. 8-Origin Kid Flash retold. 9-Minor app. Deathstroke on last pg. 10-2nd app. Deathstroke the Terminator (see Marvel & DC Present for 3rd app.); origin Changeling retold 1 3 4 6 8 10
11-20: 13-Return of Madame Rouge & Capt. Zahl; Robotman revived. 14-Return of Mento; origin Doom Patrol. 15-Death of Madame Rouge & Capt. Zahl; intro. new Brotherhood of Evil. 16-1st app. Captain Carrot (free 16 pg. preview). 18-Return of Starfire. 19-Hawkman teams-up 1 2 3 4 5 7
21-40: 21-Intro Night Force in free 16 pg. insert; intro Brother Blood. 23-1st app. Vigilante (not in costume), & Blackfire. 24-Omega Men app. 25-Omega Men cameo; free 16 pg. preview Masters of the Universe. 26-1st app. Terra. 27-Free 16 pg. preview Atari Force. 29-The New Brotherhood of Evil & Speedy app. 30-Terra joins the Titans. 34-4th app. Deathstroke the Terminator.37-Batman & The Outsiders x-over. 38-Origin Wonder Girl. 39-Last Dick Grayson as Robin; Kid Flash quits 5.00
Annual 1(11/82)-Omega Men app. 6.00
Annual V2#2(9/83)-1st app. Vigilante in costume; 1st app. Lyla 6.00
Annual 3 (See Tales of the Teen Titans Annual #3)
...: Terra Incognito TPB (2006, $19.99) r/#26,28-34 & Annual #2 20.00
...: The Judas Contract TPB (2003, $19.95) r/#39,40 plus Tales of the Teen Titans #41-44 & Annual #3 20.00
...: Who is Donna Troy? TPB (2005, $19.99) r/#38,Tales of the Teen Titans #50, New Titans #50-55 and Teen Titans/Outsiders Secret Files 2003 20.00

NOTE: ***Pérez** a-1-4p, 6-34p, 37-40p, Annual 1p, 2p; c-1-12, 13-17p, 18-21, 22p, 23p, 24-37, 38, 39(painted), 40, Annual 1, 2.*

NEW TEEN TITANS, THE (Becomes The New Titans #50 on)
DC Comics: Aug, 1984 - No. 49, Nov, 1988 ($1.25/$1.75; deluxe format)

1-New storyline; Pérez-c/a begins 1 3 4 6 8 10
2,3: 2-Re-intro Lilith 6.00
4-10: 5-Death of Trigon. 7-9-Origin Lilith. 8-Intro Kole. 10-Kole joins 5.00
11-49: 13,14-Crisis x-over. 20-Robin (Jason Todd) joins; original Teen Titans return. 38-Infinity, Inc. x-over. 47-Origin of all Titans; Titans (East & West) pin-up by Pérez 4.00
Annual 1-4 (9/85-'88): 1-Intro. Vanguard. 2-Byrne c/a(p); origin Brother Blood; intro new Dr. Light. 3-Intro. Danny Chase. 4-Pérez-c 4.00
...: The Terror of Trigon TPB (2003, $17.95) r/#1-5; new cover by Phil Jimenez 18.00

NOTE: ***Buckler** c-10. **Kelley Jones** a-47, Annual 4. **Erik Larsen** a-33. **Orlando** c-33p. **Perez** a-1-5; c-1-7, 19-23, 43. **Steacy** c-47.*

NEW TERRYTOONS (TV)
Dell Publishing Co./Gold Key: 6-8/60 - No. 8, 3-5/62; 10/62 - No. 54, 1/79

1(1960-Dell)-Deputy Dawg, Dinky Duck & Hashimoto-San begin (1st app. of each) 10 20 30 68 119 170
2-8(1962) 6 12 18 43 69 95
1(30010-210)(10/62-Gold Key, 84 pgs.)-Heckle & Jeckle begins 9 18 27 65 113 160
2(30010-301)-84 pgs. 8 16 24 58 97 135
3-5 4 8 12 28 44 60
6-10 4 8 12 22 34 45
11-20 3 6 9 16 22 28
21-30 2 4 6 9 13 16
31-43 1 3 4 6 8 10
44-54: Mighty Mouse-c/s in all 2 4 6 8 11 14

NOTE: *Reprints: #4-12, 38, 40, 47. (See March of Comics #379, 393, 412, 435)*

NEW TESTAMENT STORIES VISUALIZED
Standard Publishing Co.: 1946 - 1947

"New Testament Heroes–Acts of Apostles Visualized, Book I"
"New Testament Heroes–Acts of Apostles Visualized, Book II"
"Parables Jesus Told" Set.... 17 34 51 98 154 210

NOTE: *All three are contained in a cardboard case, illustrated on front and info about the set.*

NEW THUNDERBOLTS (Continues in Thunderbolts #100)
Marvel Comics: Jan, 2005 - No. 18, Apr, 2006 ($2.99)

1-18: 1-Grummett-a/Nicieza-s. 1-Captain Marvel app. 2-Namor app. 4-Wolverine app. 3.00
... Vol. 1: One Step Forward (2005, $14.99) r/#1-6 15.00
... Vol. 2: Modern Marvels (2005, $14.99) r/#7-12 15.00
... Vol. 3: Right of Power (2006, $17.99) r/#13-18 & Thunderbolts #100 18.00

NEW TITANS, THE (Formerly The New Teen Titans)
DC Comics: No. 50, Dec, 1988 - No. 130, Feb, 1996 ($1.75/$2.25)

50-Perez-c/a begins; new origin Wonder Girl 6.00
51-59: 50-55-Painted-c. 55-Nightwing (Dick Grayson) forces Danny Chase to resign; Batman app. in flashback, Wonder Girl becomes Troia 4.00
60,61: 60-A Lonely Place of Dying Part 2 continues from Batman #440; new Robin tie-in; Timothy Drake app. 61-A Lonely Place of Dying Part 4 4.00
62-70,72-99,101-124,126-130: 62-65: Deathstroke the Terminator app. 65-Tim Drake (Robin) app. 70-1st Deathstroke solo cover/sty. 72-79-Deathstroke in all: 74-Intro. Pantha. 79-Terra brought back to life; 1 panel cameo Team Titans (1st app.). Deathstroke in #80-84,86. 80-2nd full app. Team Titans. 83,84-Deathstroke kills his son, Jericho. 85-Team Titans app. 86-Deathstroke vs. Nightwing-c/story; last Deathstroke app. 87-New costume Nightwing. 90-92-Parts 2,5,8 Total Chaos (Team Titans). 115-(11/94) 3.00
71-(44 pgs.)-10th anniversary issue; Deathstroke cameo 4.00
100-($3.50, 52 pgs.)-Holo-grafx foil-c 4.00
125 (3.50)-wraparound-c 4.00
#0-(10/94) Zero Hour, released between #114 & 115 3.00
Annual 5-10 ('89-'94, 68 pgs.. 7-Armaggedon 2001 x-over; 1st full app. Teen (Team) Titans (new group). 8-Deathstroke app.; Eclipso app. (minor). 10-Elseworlds story 4.00
Annual 11 (1995, $3.95)-Year One story 4.00

NOTE: ***Perez** a-50-55p, 57,60p, 58,59,61(layouts); c-50-61, 62-67i, Annual 5i; co-plots-66.*

NEW TV FUNNIES (See New Funnies)

NEW TWO-FISTED TALES, THE
Dark Horse Comics/Byron Preiss:1993 ($4.95, limited series, 52 pgs.)

1-Kurtzman-r & new-a 5.00

NOTE: ***Eisner** c-1i. **Kurtzman** c-1p, 2.*

NEWUNIVERSAL
Marvel Comics: Feb, 2007 - No. 6, July, 2007 ($2.99)

1-6-Warren Ellis-s/Salvador Larroca-a. 1,2-Variant covers by Ribic 3.00
...: 1959 (9/08, $3.99) Aftermath of the White Event of 1953; Tony Stark app. 4.00
...: Conqueror (10/08, $3.99) The White Event of 2689 B.C.; Eric Nguyen-a 4.00
... : Everything Went White HC (2007, $19.99) r/#1-6; sketch pages 20.00
... : Everything Went White SC (2008, $14.99) r/#1-6; sketch pages 15.00

NEWUNIVERSAL: SHOCKFRONT
Marvel Comics: Jul, 2008 - Present ($2.99)

1,2-Warren Ellis-s/Steve Kurth-a 3.00

NEW WARRIORS, THE (See Thor #411,412)
Marvel Comics: July, 1990 - No. 75, 1996 ($1.00/$1.25/$1.50)

1-Williamson-i; Bagley-c/a(p) in 1-13, Annual 1 6.00
1-Gold 2nd printing (7/91) 3.00
2-5: 1,3-Guice-c(i). 2-Williamson-c/a(i). 4.00
6-24,26-49,51-75: 7-Punisher cameo (last pg.). 8,9-Punisher app. 14-Darkhawk & Namor x-over. 17-Fantastic Four & Silver Surfer x-over. 19-Gideon (of X-Force) app. 28-Intro Turbo & Cardinal. 31-Cannonball & Warpath app. 42-Nova vs. Firelord. 46-Photo-c. 47-Bound-in S-M trading card sheet. 52-12 pg. ad insert. 62-Scarlet Spider-c/app. 70-Spider-Man-c/app. 72-Avengers-c/app. 3.00
25-($2.50, 52 pgs.)-Die-cut cover 4.00
40,60: 40-($2.25)-Gold foil collector's edition 4.00
50-($2.95, 52 pgs.)-Glow in the dark-c 4.00
Annual 1-4('91-'94,68 pgs.)-1-Origins all members; 3rd app. X-Force (cont'd from New Mutants Ann. #7 & cont'd in X-Men Ann. #15); x-over before X-Force #1. 3-Bagged w/card 4.00

NEW WARRIORS, THE
Marvel Comics: Oct, 1999 - No. 10, July, 2000 ($2.99/$2.50)

0-Wizard supplement; short story and preview sketchbook 3.00
1-($2.99) 4.00
2-10: 2-Two covers. 5-Generation X app. 9-Iron Man-c 3.00

NEW WARRIORS (See Civil War #1)

New X-Men (Academy X) #2 © MAR

New York Five #1 © Wood & Kelly

Nexus #24 © FC

GD VG FN VF VF/NM NM-
2.0 4.0 6.0 8.0 9.0 9.2

Marvel Comics: Aug, 2005 - No. 6, Feb, 2006 ($2.99, limited series)

1-6-Scottie Young-a 3.00
...: Reality Check TPB (2006, $14.99) r/#1-6 15.00

NEW WARRIORS (The Initiative)
Marvel Comics: Aug, 2007 - No. 20, Mar, 2009 ($2.99)

1-19: 1-Medina-a; new team is formed. 2-Jubilee app. 14-16-Secret Invasion 3.00
20-($3.99) 4.00
...: Defiant TPB (2008, $14.99) r/#1-6 15.00

NEW WAVE, THE
Eclipse Comics: 6/10/86 - No. 13, 3/87 (#1-8: bi-weekly, 20pgs; #9-13: monthly)

1-13:1-Origin, concludes #5. 6-Origin Megabyte. 8,9-The Heap returns. 13-Snyder-c 3.00
...Versus the Volunteers 3-D #1,2(4/87): 1-Snyder-c 3.00

NEW WEST, THE
Black Bull Comics: Mar, 2005 - No. 2, Jun, 2005 ($4.99, limited series)

1,2-Phil Noto-a/c; Jimmy Palmiotti-s 5.00

NEW WORLD (See Comic Books, series I)

NEW WORLDS
Caliber: 1996 - No. 6 ($2.95/$3.95, 80 pgs., B&W, anthology)

1-6: 1-Mister X & other stories 4.00

NEW X-MEN (See X-Men *2nd series* #114-156)

NEW X-MEN (Academy X) (Continued from New Mutants)
Marvel Comics: July, 2004 - Present ($2.99)

1-46: 1,2-Green-c/a. 16-19-House of M. 20,21-Decimation. 40-Endangered Species back-ups begin. 44-46-Messiah Complex x-over; Ramos-a 3.00
Yearbook 1 (12/05, $3.99) new story and profile pages 4.00
...: Childhood's End Vol. 1 TPB (2006, $10.99) r/#20-23 11.00
...: Childhood's End Vol. 2 TPB (2006, $10.99) r/#24-27 11.00
...: Childhood's End Vol. 3 TPB (2006, $10.99) r/#28-32 11.00
...: Childhood's End Vol. 4 TPB (2007, $10.99) r/#33-36 11.00
...: Childhood's End Vol. 5 TPB (2007, $17.99) r/#37-43 18.00
House of M: New X-Men TPB (2006, $13.99) r/#16-19 and selections from Secrets Of The House of M one-shot 14.00
... Vol. 1: Choosing Sides TPB (2004, $14.99) r/#1-6 15.00
... Vol. 2: Haunted TPB (2005, $14.99) r/#7-12 15.00
... Vol. 3: X-Posed TPB (2006, $14.99) r/#12-15 & Yearbook Special 15.00

NEW X-MEN: HELLIONS
Marvel Comics: July, 2005 - No. 4, Oct, 2005 ($2.99, limited series)

1-4-Henry-a/Weir & DeFilippis-s 3.00
TPB (2006, $9.99) r/#1-4 10.00

NEW YORK FIVE, THE
DC Comics (Vertigo): Mar, 2011 - No. 4 ($2.99, B&W, limited series)

1-3-Brian Wood-s/Ryan Kelly-a 3.00

NEW YORK GIANTS (See Thrilling True Story of the Baseball Giants)

NEW YORK STATE JOINT LEGISLATIVE COMMITTEE TO STUDY THE PUBLICATION OF COMICS, THE
N.Y. State Legislative Document: 1951, 1955

This document was referenced by Wertham for **Seduction of the Innocent.** Contains numerous repros from comics showing violence, sadism, torture, and sex. 1955 version (196p, No. 37, 2/23/55) - Sold for $180 in 1986.

NEW YORK, THE BIG CITY
Kitchen Sink Press: 1986 ($10.95, B&W); **DC Comics:** July, 2000 ($12.95, B&W)

nn-Will Eisner-s/a 13.00

NEW YORK WORLD'S FAIR (Also see Big Book of Fun & New Book of Fun)
National Periodical Publ.: 1939, 1940 (100 pgs.; cardboard covers)
(DC's 4th & 5th annuals)

1939-Scoop Scanlon, Superman (blond haired Superman on-c), Sandman, Zatara, Slam Bradley, Ginger Snap by Bob Kane begin; 1st published app. The Sandman (see Adventure #40 for his 1st drawn story); Vincent Sullivan-c; cover background by Guardineer
1700 3400 5100 12,750 29,000 –
1940-Batman, Hourman, Johnny Thunderbolt, Red, White & Blue & Hanko (by Creig Flessel) app.; Superman, Batman & Robin-c (1st time they all appear together); early Robin app.; 1st Burnley-c/a (per Burnley) 922 1844 2766 6915 15,500 –

NOTE: *The 1939 edition was published 4/29/39 and released 4/30/39, the day the fair opened, at 25¢, and was first sold only at the fair. Since all other comics were 10¢, it didn't sell. Remaining copies were advertised beginning in the August issues of most DC comics for 25¢, but soon the price was dropped to 15¢. Everyone that sent a quarter through the mail for it received a free Superman #1 or a #2 to make up the dime difference. 15¢ stickers were placed over the 25¢ price. Four variations on the 15¢ stickers are known. The 1940 edition was published 5/11/40 and was priced at 15¢. It was a precursor to World's Best #1.*

GD VG FN VF VF/NM NM-
2.0 4.0 6.0 8.0 9.0 9.2

NEW YORK: YEAR ZERO
Eclipse Comics: July, 1988 - No. 4, Oct, 1988 ($2.00, B&W, limited series)

1-4 3.00

NEXT, THE
DC Comics: Sept, 2006 - No. 6, Feb, 2007 ($2.99, limited series)

1-6-Tad Williams-s/Dietrich Smith-a; Superman app. 3.00

NEXT MEN (See John Byrne's...)

NEXT NEXUS, THE
First Comics: Jan, 1989 - No. 4, April, 1989 ($1.95, limited series, Baxter paper)

1-4: Mike Baron scripts & Steve Rude-c/a. 3.00
TPB (10/89, $9.95) r/series 10.00

NEXTWAVE: AGENTS OF H.A.T.E
Marvel Comics: Mar, 2006 - No. 12, Mar, 2007 ($2.99)

1-12-Warren Ellis-s/Stuart Immonen-a. 2-Fin Fang Foom app. 12-Devil Dinosaur app. 3.00
Vol. 1 - This Is What They Want HC (2006, $19.99) r/#1-6; Ellis original pitch 20.00
Vol. 1 - This Is What They Want SC (2007, $14.99) r/#1-6; Ellis original pitch 15.00
Vol. 2 - I Kick Your Face HC (2007, $19.99) r/#7-12 20.00
Vol. 2 - I Kick Your Face SC (2008, $14.99) r/#7-12 15.00

NEXUS (See First Comics Graphic Novel #4, 19 & The Next Nexus)
Capital Comics/First Comics No. 7 on: June, 1981 - No. 6, Mar, 1984; No. 7, Apr, 1985 - No. 80?, May, 1991 (Direct sales only, 36 pgs.; V2#1('83)-printed on Baxter paper)

1-B&W version; mag. size; w/double size poster 3 6 9 14 20 26
1-B&W 1981 limited edition; 500 copies printed and signed; same as above except this version has a 2-pg. poster & a pencil sketch on paperboard by Steve Rude
4 8 12 24 37 50
2-B&W, magazine size 2 4 6 11 16 20
3-B&W, magazine size; Brunner back-c; contains 33-1/3 rpm record ($2.95 price)
2 4 6 9 13 16
V2#1-Color version 4.00
2-49,51-80: 2-Nexus' origin begins. 67-Snyder-c/a 3.00
50-($3.50, 52 pgs.) 4.00
Hardcover Volume One (Dark Horse Books, 11/05, $49.95) r/#1-3 & V2 #1-4; creator bios 50.00
HC Volume Two (Dark Horse Books, 3/06, $49.95) r/V2 #5-11; creator bios 50.00
HC Volume Three (Dark Horse Books, 5/06, $49.95) r/V2 #12-18; Marz forward 50.00
HC Volume Four (Dark Horse Books, 8/06, $49.95) r/V2 #19-25; Powell forward 50.00
HC Volume Five (Dark Horse Books, 2/07, $49.95) r/V2 #26-32; Brubaker forward 50.00
HC Volume Six (Dark Horse Books, 2/07, $49.95) r/V2 #33-39; Evanier forward 50.00
HC Volume Seven (Dark Horse Books, 2/08, $49.95) r/V2 #40-46; Brunning forward 50.00
HC Volume Eight (Dark Horse Books, 1/09, $49.95) r/V2 #47-52 and The Next Nexus #1; interview with original publishers John Davis and Milton Griepp 50.00
HC Volume Nine (Dark Horse Books, 8/09, $49.95) r/V2 #53-57 & The Next Nexus #2-4 50.00

NOTE: ***Bissette** c-V2#29. **Giffen** c/a-V2#23. **Gulacy** c-1 (B&W), 2(B&W). **Mignola** c/a-V2#28. **Rude** c-3(B&W), V2#1-22, 24-27, 33-36, 39-42, 45-48, 50, 58-60, 75; a-1-3, V2#1-7, 8-16p, 18-22p, 24-27p, 33-36p, 39-42p, 45-48p, 50, 58, 59p, 60. **Paul Smith** a-V2#37, 38, 43, 44, 51-55p; c-V2#37, 38, 43, 44, 51-55.*

NEXUS
Rude Dude Productions: No. 99, July, 2007 - No. 102, Jun, 2009 ($2.99)

99-Mike Baron scripts & Steve Rude-c/a 3.00
100-($4.99) Part 2 of Space Opera; back-up feature: History of Nexus 5.00
101/102-(6/09, $4.95) Combined issue 5.00
..., Free Comic Book Day 2007 - Excerpts from previous issues and preview of #99 3.00
... Greatest Hits (8/07, $1.99) same content as Free Comic Book Day 2007 3.00
...: The Origin (11/07, $3.99) reprints the 7/96 one-shot 4.00

NEXUS: ALIEN JUSTICE
Dark Horse Comics: Dec, 1992 - No. 3, Feb, 1993 ($3.95, limited series)

1-3: Mike Baron scripts & Steve Rude-c/a 4.00

NEXUS: EXECUTIONER'S SONG
Dark Horse Comics: June, 1996 - No. 4, Sept, 1996 ($2.95, limited series)

1-4: Mike Baron scripts & Steve Rude-c/a 3.00

NEXUS FILES
First Comics: 1989 ($4.50, color/16pgs. B&W, one-shot, squarebound, 52 pgs.)

1-New Rude-a; info on Nexus 4.50

NEXUS: GOD CON
Dark Horse Comics: Apr, 1997 - No. 2, May, 1997 ($2.95, limited series)

1,2-Baron-s/Rude-c/a 3.00

NEXUS LEGENDS
First Comics: May, 1989 - No. 23, Mar, 1991 ($1.50, Baxter paper)\

1-23: R/1-3(Capital) & early First Comics issues w/new Rude covers #1-6,9,10 3.00

Nickel Comics #2 © FAW

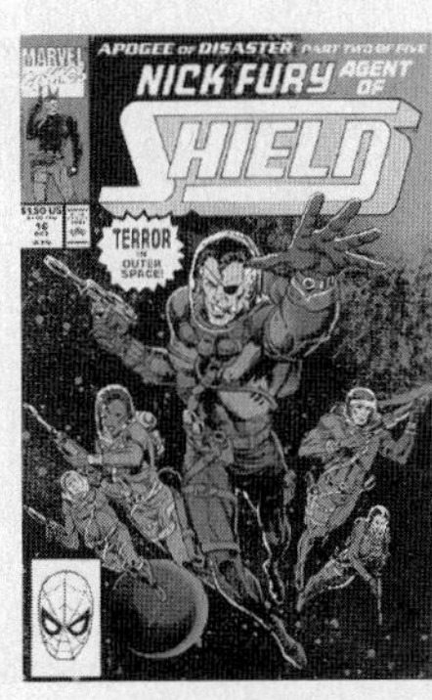

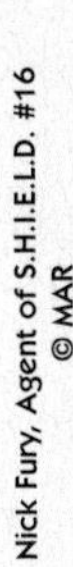
Nick Fury, Agent of S.H.I.E.L.D. #16 © MAR

Nightcrawler (2004 series) #1 © MAR

GD VG FN VF VF/NM NM-
2.0 4.0 6.0 8.0 9.0 9.2

NEXUS MEETS MADMAN (...Special)
Dark Horse Comics: May, 1996 ($2.95, one-shot)
nn-Mike Baron & Mike Allred scripts, Steve Rude-c/a. 3.00

NEXUS: NIGHTMARE IN BLUE
Dark Horse Comics: July, 1997 - No. 4, Oct, 1997 ($2.95, limited series)
1-4: 1,2,4-Adam Hughes-c 3.00

NEXUS: THE LIBERATOR
Dark Horse Comics: Aug, 1992 - No. 4, Nov, 1992 ($2.95, limited series)
1-4 3.00

NEXUS: THE ORIGIN
Dark Horse Comics: July, 1996 ($3.95, one-shot)
nn-Mike Baron- scripts, Steve Rude-c/a. 4.00

NEXUS: THE WAGES OF SIN
Dark Horse Comics: Mar, 1995 - No. 4, June, 1995 ($2.95, limited series)
1-4 3.00

NFL SUPERPRO
Marvel Comics: Oct, 1991 - No. 12, Sept, 1992 ($1.00)
1-12: 1-Spider-Man-c/app. 3.00
Special Edition (9/91, $2.00) Jusko painted-c 4.00
Super Bowl Edition (3/91, squarebound) Jusko painted-c 4.00

NICKEL COMICS
Dell Publishing Co.: 1938 (Pocket size - 7-1/2x5-1/2")(68 pgs.)
1- "Bobby & Chip" by Otto Messmer, Felix the Cat artist. Contains some English reprints
81 162 243 518 884 1250

NICKEL COMICS
Fawcett Publications: Feb 1940
nn - Ashcan comic, not distributed to newsstands, only for in-house use. A CGC certified 9.6 copy sold for $7,200 in 2003. In 2008, a CGC certified 8.5 sold for $2,390 and an uncertified Near Mint copy sold for $3,100.

NICKEL COMICS
Fawcett Publications: May, 1940 - No. 8, Aug, 1940 (36 pgs.; Bi-Weekly; 5¢)
1-Origin/1st app. Bulletman 371 742 1113 2600 4550 6500
2 118 236 354 749 1287 1825
3 86 172 258 546 936 1325
4-The Red Gaucho begins 68 136 204 435 743 1050
5-7 67 134 201 426 731 1035
8-World's Fair-c; Bulletman moved to Master Comics #7 in October (scarce)
89 178 267 565 970 1375
NOTE: ***Beck*** *c-5-8.* ***Jack Binder*** *c-1-4. Bondage c-5. Bulletman c-1-8.*

NICK FURY, AGENT OF SHIELD (See Fury, Marvel Spotlight #31 & Shield)
Marvel Comics Group: 6/68 - No. 15, 11/69; No. 16, 11/70 - No. 18, 3/71
1 13 26 39 94 185 275
2-4: 4-Origin retold 8 16 24 56 93 130
5-Classic-c 9 18 27 50 100 140
6,7: 7-Salvador Dali painting swipe 8 16 24 52 86 120
8-11,13: 9-Hate Monger begins, ends #11. 10-Smith layouts/pencil. 11-Smith-c.
13-1st app. Super-Patriot; last 12¢ issue 5 10 15 30 48 65
12-Smith-c/a 5 10 15 32 51 70
14-Begin 15¢ issues 4 8 12 26 41 55
15-1st app. & death of Bullseye-c/story(11/69); Nick Fury shot & killed; last 15¢ issue
8 16 24 56 93 130
16-18-(25¢, 52 pgs.)-r/Str. Tales #135-143 3 6 9 21 32 42
TPB (May 2000, $19.95) r/ Strange Tales #150-168 20.00
...: Who is Scorpio? TPB (11/00, $12.95) r/#1-3,5; Steranko-c 13.00
NOTE: ***Adkins*** *a-3i.* ***Craig*** *a-10i.* ***Sid Greene*** *a-12i.* ***Kirby*** *a-16-18r.* ***Springer*** *a-4, 6, 7, 8p, 9, 10p, 11; c-8, 9.* ***Steranko*** *a(p)-1-3, 5; c-1-7.*

NICK FURY AGENT OF SHIELD (Also see Strange Tales #135)
Marvel Comics: Dec, 1983 - No. 2, Jan, 1984 (2.00, 52 pgs., Baxter paper)
1,2-r/Nick Fury #1-4; new Steranko-c 4.00

NICK FURY, AGENT OF S.H.I.E.L.D.
Marvel Comics: Sept, 1989 - No. 47, May, 1993 ($1.50/$1.75)
V2#1-26,30-47: 10-Capt. America app. 13-Return of The Yellow Claw. 15-Fantastic Four app. 30,31-Deathlok app. 36-Cage app. 37-Woodgod c/story. 38-41-Flashes back to pre-Shield days after WWII. 44-Capt. America-c/s. 45-Viper-c/s. 46-Gideon x-over 3.00
27-29-Wolverine-c/stories 4.00
NOTE: ***Alan Grant*** *scripts-11.* ***Guice*** *a(p)-20-23, 25, 26; c-20-28.*

NICK FURY'S HOWLING COMMANDOS
Marvel Comics: Dec, 2005 - No. 6, May, 2006 ($2.99)
1-6: 1-Giffen-s/Francisco-a 3.00
1-Director's Cut ($3.99) r/#1 with original script and sketch design pages 4.00

NICK FURY VS. S.H.I.E.L.D.
Marvel Comics: June, 1988 - No. 6, Nov, 1988 ($3.50, 52 pgs, deluxe format)
1,2: 1-Steranko-c. 2-(Low print run) Sienkiewicz-c 5.00
3-6 4.00

NICK HALIDAY (Thrill of the Sea)
Argo: May, 1956
1-Daily & Sunday strip-r by Petree 8 16 24 44 57 70

NIGHT AND THE ENEMY (Graphic Novel)
Comico: 1988 (8-1/2x11") ($11.95, color, 80 pgs.)
1-Harlan Ellison scripts/Ken Steacy-c/a; r/Epic Illustrated & new-a (1st & 2nd printings) 12.00
1-Limited edition ($39.95) 40.00

NIGHT BEFORE CHRISTMAS, THE (See March of Comics No. 152 in the Promotional Comics section)

NIGHT BEFORE CHRISTMASK, THE
Dark Horse Comics: Nov, 1994 ($9.95, one-shot)
nn-Hardcover book; The Mask; Rick Geary-c/a 10.00

NIGHTBREED (See Clive Barker's Nightbreed)

NIGHT CLUB
Image Comics: Apr, 2005 - No. 4, Dec, 2006 ($2.95/$2.99, limited series)
1-4: 1-Mike Baron-s/Mike Norton-a 3.00

NIGHTCRAWLER (X-Men)
Marvel Comics Group: Nov, 1985 - No. 4, Feb, 1986 (Mini-series from X-Men)
1-4: 1-Cockrum-c/a 4.00

NIGHTCRAWLER (Volume 2)
Marvel Comics: Feb, 2002 - No. 4, May, 2002 ($2.50, limited series)
1-4-Matt Smith-a 3.00

NIGHTCRAWLER
Marvel Comics: Nov, 2004 - No. 12, Jan, 2006 ($2.99)
1-12: 1-6-Robertson-a/Land-c. 2-Magik app. 8-Wolverine app. 10-Man-Thing app. 3.00
...: The Devil Inside TPB (2005, $14.99) r/#1-6 15.00
...: The Winding Way TPB (2006, $14.99) r/#7-12 15.00

NIGHTFALL: THE BLACK CHRONICLES
DC Comics (Homage): Dec, 1999 - No. 3, Feb, 2000 ($2.95, limited series)
1-3-Coker-a/Gilmore-s 3.00

NIGHT FORCE, THE (See New Teen Titans #21)
DC Comics: Aug, 1982 - No. 14, Sept, 1983 (60¢)
1 4.00
2-14: 13-Origin Baron Winter. 14-Nudity panels 3.00
NOTE: ***Colan*** *c/a-1-14p.* ***Giordano*** *c-1i, 2i, 4i, 5i, 7i, 12i.*

NIGHT FORCE
DC Comics: Dec, 1996 - No. 12, Nov, 1997 ($2.25)
1-12: 1-3-Wolfman-s/Anderson-a(p). 8-"Convergence" part 2 3.00

NIGHT GLIDER
Topps Comics (Kirbyverse): April, 1993 ($2.95, one-shot)
1-Kirby c-1, Heck-a; polybagged w/Kirbychrome trading card 3.00

NIGHTHAWK
Marvel Comics: Sept, 1998 - No. 3, Nov, 1998 ($2.99, mini-series)
1-3-Krueger-s; Daredevil app. 3.00

NIGHTINGALE, THE
Henry H. Stansbury Once-Upon-A-Time Press, Inc.: 1948 (10¢, 7-1/4x10-1/4", 14 pgs., 1/2 B&W)
(Very Rare)-Low distribution; distributed to Westchester County & Bronx, N.Y. only; used in **Seduction of the Innocent**, pg. 312,313 as the 1st and only "good" comic book ever published. Ill. by Dong Kingman; 1,500 words of text, printed on high quality paper & no word balloons. Copyright registered 10/22/48, distributed week of 12/5/48. (By Hans Christian Andersen)
Estimated value........ 250.00

NIGHT MAN, THE (See Sludge #1)
Malibu Comics (Ultraverse): Oct, 1993 - No. 23, Aug, 1995 ($1.95/$2.50)
1-($2.50, 48 pgs.)-Rune flip-c/story by B. Smith (3 pgs.) 3.00
1-Ultra-Limited silver foil-c 6.00
2-15, 17: 3-Break-Thru x-over; Freex app. 4-Origin Firearm (2 pgs.) by Chaykin. 6-TNTNT app. 8-1st app. Teknight 3.00

Nightmare #7 © Skywald

Nightmask #4 © MAR

Nightstalkers #11 © MAR

GD 2.0 | VG 4.0 | FN 6.0 | VF 8.0 | VF/NM 9.0 | NM- 9.2

16 ($3.50)-flip book (Ultraverse Premiere #11) 4.00
...:The Pilgrim Conundrum Saga (1/95, $3.95, 68 pgs.)-Strangers app. 4.00
18-23: 22-Loki-c/app. 3.00
Infinity ($1.50) 3.00
...Vs. Wolverine #0-Kelley Jones-c; mail in offer 1 3 4 6 8 10
NOTE: Zeck a-16.

NIGHT MAN, THE
Malibu Comics (Ultraverse): Sept, 1995 - No.4, Dec, 1995 ($1.50, lim. series)
1-4: Post Black September storyline 3.00

NIGHT MAN, THE /GAMBIT
Malibu Comics (Ultraverse): Mar, 1996 - No. 3, May, 1996 ($1.95, lim. series)
0-Limited Premium Edition 4.00
1-3: David Quinn scripts in all. 3-Rhiannon discovered to be The Night Man's mother 3.00

NIGHTMARE
Ziff-Davis (Approved Comics)/St. John No. 3: Summer, 1952 - No. 3, Winter, 1952, 53 (Painted-c)
1-1 pg. Kinstler-a; Tuska-a(2) 57 114 171 362 619 875
2-Kinstler-a-Poe's "Pit & the Pendulum" 40 80 120 246 411 575
3-Kinstler-a 37 74 111 222 361 500

NIGHTMARE (Weird Horrors #1-9) (Amazing Ghost Stories #14 on)
St. John Publishing Co.: No. 10, Dec, 1953 - No. 13, Aug, 1954
10-Reprints Ziff-Davis Weird Thrillers #2 w/new Kubert-c plus 2 pgs. Kinstler-a; Anderson, Colan & Toth-a 54 108 162 343 574 825
11-Krigstein-a; painted-c; Poe adapt., "Hop Frog" 40 80 120 246 411 575
12-Kubert bondage-c; adaptation of Poe's "The Black Cat"; Cannibalism story 39 78 117 240 395 550
13-Reprints Z-D Weird Thrillers #3 with new cover; Powell-a(2), Tuska-a; Baker-c 30 60 90 177 289 400

NIGHTMARE (Magazine) (Also see Psycho)
Skywald Publishing Corp.: Dec, 1970 - No. 23, Feb, 1975 (B&W, 68 pgs.)
1-Everett-a; Heck-a; Shores-a 10 20 30 68 119 170
2-5,8,9: 2,4-Decapitation story. 5-Nazi-s; Boris Karloff 4 pg. photo/text-s. 8-Features E.C. movie "Tales From the Crypt"; reprints some E.C. comics panels. 9-Wrightson-a; bondage-c; 1st Lovecraft Saggoth Chronicles/Cthulhu 6 12 18 39 62 85
6-Kaluta-a; Jeff Jones-c, photo & interview; 1st Living Gargoyle; Love Witch-s w/nudity; Boris Karloff-s 6 12 18 41 66 90
7 5 10 15 32 51 70
10-Wrightson-a (1 pg.); Princess of Earth-c/s; Edward & Mina Sartyros, the Human Gargoyles series continues from Psycho #8 6 12 18 41 66 90
11-19: 12-Excessive gore, severed heads. 13-Lovecraft-s. 15-Dracula-c/s. 17-Vampires issue; Autobiography of a Vampire series begins 4 8 12 26 41 55
20-John Byrne's 1st artwork (2 pgs.)(8/74); severed head-c; Hitler app. 8 16 24 56 93 130
21-23: 21-(1974 Summer Special)-Kaluta-a. 22-Tomb of Horror issue. 23-(1975 Winter Special) 5 10 15 30 48 65
Annual 1(1972)-Squarebound; B. Jones-a 5 10 15 30 48 65
Winter Special 1(1973)-All new material 4 8 12 26 41 55
Yearbook nn(1974)-B. Jones, Reese, Wildey-a 4 8 12 26 41 55
NOTE: ***Adkins** a-5. **Boris** c-2, 3, 5 (#4 is not by Boris). **Buckler** a-3, 15. **Byrne** a-20p. **Everett** a-1, 2, 4, 5, 12. **Jeff Jones** a-6, 21r(Psycho #6); c-6. **Katz** a-3, 5, 21. **Reese** a-4, 5. **Wildey** a-4, 5, 6, 21, '74 Yearbook. **Wrightson** a-9, 10.*

NIGHTMARE (Alex Nino's)
Innovation Publishing: 1989 ($1.95)
1-Alex Nino-a 3.00

NIGHTMARE
Marvel Comics: Dec, 1994 - No. 4, Mar, 1995 ($1.95, limited series)
1-4 3.00

NIGHTMARE & CASPER (See Harvey Hits #71) (Casper & Nightmare #6 on) (See Casper The Friendly Ghost #19)
Harvey Publications: Aug, 1963 - No. 5, Aug, 1964 (25¢)
1-All reprints? 8 16 24 54 90 125
2-5: All reprints? 5 10 15 32 51 70

NIGHTMARE ON ELM STREET, A (Also see Freddy Krueger's...)
DC Comics (WildStorm): Dec, 2006 - Present ($2.99)
1-8: 1-Two covers by Harris & Bradstreet; Dixon-s/West-a 3.00

NIGHTMARES (See Do You Believe in Nightmares)

NIGHTMARES
Eclipse Comics: May, 1985 - No. 2, May, 1985 ($1.75, Baxter paper)
1,2 3.00

NIGHTMARE THEATER
Chaos! Comics: Nov, 1997 - No. 4, Nov, 1997 ($2.50, mini-series)
1-4-Horror stories by various; Wrightson-a 3.00

NIGHTMARK: BLOOD & HONOR
Alpha Productions: 1994 - No. 3, 1994 ($2.50, B&W, mini-series)
1,2 3.00

NIGHTMARK MYSTERY SPECIAL
Alpha Productions: Jan, 1994 ($2.50, B&W)
1 3.00

NIGHTMASK
Marvel Comics Group: Nov, 1986 - No. 12, Oct, 1987
1-12 3.00

NIGHT MASTER
Silverwolf: Feb, 1987 ($1.50, B&W)
1-Tim Vigil-c/a 3.00

NIGHTMASTER (See Shadowpact)
DC Comics: Jan, 2011 ($2.99, one-shot)
1-Wrightson-c/Beechen-s/Dwyer-a; Shadowpact app. 3.00

NIGHT MUSIC (See Eclipse Graphic Album Series, The Magic Flute)
Eclipse Comics: Dec, 1984 - No. 11, 1990 ($1.75/$3.95/$4.95, Baxter paper)
1-7: 3-Russell's Jungle Book adapt. 4,5-Pelleas And Melisande (double titled) 6-Salomé (double titled). 7-Red Dog #1 3.00
8-($3.95) Ariane and Bluebeard 4.00
9-11-($4.95) The Magic Flute; Russell adapt. 5.00

NIGHT NURSE
Marvel Comics Group: Nov, 1972 - No. 4, May, 1973
1 12 24 36 82 154 225
2-4 9 18 27 63 107 150

NIGHT OF MYSTERY
Avon Periodicals: 1953 (no month) (one-shot)
nn-1 pg. Kinstler-a, Hollingsworth-c 47 94 141 296 498 700

NIGHT OF THE GRIZZLY, THE (See Movie Classics)

NIGHTRAVEN (See Marvel Graphic Novel)

NIGHT RIDER (Western)
Marvel Comics Group: Oct, 1974 - No. 6, Aug, 1975
1: 1-6 reprint Ghost Rider #1-6 (#1-origin) 2 4 6 10 14 18
2-6 2 4 6 8 10 12

NIGHT'S CHILDREN: THE VAMPIRE
Millenium: July, 1995 - No. 2, Aug, 1995 ($2.95, B&W)
1,2: Wendy Snow-Lang story & art 3.00

NIGHTSIDE
Marvel Comics: Dec, 2001 - No. 4, Mar, 2002 ($2.99)
1-4: 1-Weinberg-s/Derenick-a; intro Sydney Taine 3.00

NIGHTS INTO DREAMS (Based on video game)
Archie Comics: Feb, 1998 -No. 6, Oct, 1998 ($1.75, limited series)
1-6 3.00

NIGHTSTALKERS (Also see Midnight Sons Unlimited)
Marvel Comics (Midnight Sons #14 on): Nov, 1992 - No. 18, Apr, 1994 ($1.75)
1-($2.75, 52 pgs.)-Polybagged w/poster; part 5 of Rise of the Midnight Sons storyline; Garney/Palmer-c/a begins; Hannibal King, Blade & Frank Drake begin (see Tomb of Dracula for & Dr. Strange) 4.00
2-9,11-18: 5-Punisher app. 7-Ghost Rider app. 8,9-Morbius app. 14-Spot varnish-c. 14,15-Siege of Darkness Pts 1 & 9 3.00
10-($2.25)-Outer-c is a Darkhold envelope made of black parchment w/gold ink; Midnight Massacre part 1 3.00

NIGHT TERRORS,THE
Chanting Monks Studios: 2000 ($2.75, B&W)
1-Bernie Wrightson-c; short stories, one by Wrightson-s/a 3.00

NIGHT THRASHER (Also see The New Warriors)
Marvel Comics: Aug, 1993 - No. 21, Apr, 1995 ($1.75/$1.95)
1-($2.95, 52 pgs.)-Red holo-grafx foil-c; origin 4.00
2-21: 2-Intro Tantrum. 3-Gideon (of X-Force) app. 10-Bound-in trading card sheet; Iron Man

Nightwing #148 © DC

9-11: Emergency Relief © Alternative

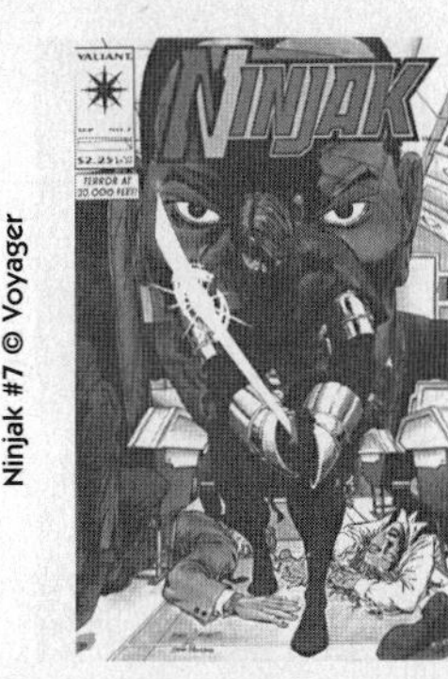

Ninjak #7 © Voyager

GD 2.0 | VG 4.0 | FN 6.0 | VF 8.0 | VF/NM 9.0 | NM- 9.2

app. 15-Hulk app. 3.00

NIGHT THRASHER: FOUR CONTROL
Marvel Comics: Oct, 1992 - No. 4, Jan, 1993 ($2.00, limited series)

1-4: 2-Intro Tantrum. 3-Gideon (of X-Force) app. 3.00

NIGHT TRIBES
DC Comics (WildStorm): July, 1999 ($4.95, one-shot)

1-Golden & Sniegoski-s/Chin-a 5.00

NIGHTVEIL (Also see Femforce)
Americomics/AC Comics: Nov, 1984 - No. 7, 1987 ($1.75)

1-7 3.00
...'s Cauldron Of Horror 1 (1989, B&W)-Kubert, Powell, Wood-r plus new Nightveil story 3.00
...'s Cauldron Of Horror 2 (1990, $2.95, B&W)-Pre-code horror-r by Kubert & Powell 3.00
...'s Cauldron Of Horror 3 (1991) 3.00
Special 1 ('88, $1.95)-Kaluta-c 3.00
One Shot ('96, $5.95)-Flip book w/ Colt 6.00

NIGHTWATCH
Marvel Comics: Apr, 1994 - No. 12, Mar, 1995 ($1.50)

1-($2.95)-Collectors edition; foil-c; Ron Lim-c/a begins; Spider-Man app. 4.00
1-12-Regular edition. 2-Bound-in S-M trading card sheet; 5,6-Venom-c & app. 7,11-Cardiac app. 3.00

NIGHTWING (Also see New Teen Titans, New Titans, Showcase '93 #11,12, Tales of the New Teen Titans & Teen Titans Spotlight)
DC Comics: Sept, 1995 - No. 4, Dec, 1995 ($2.25, limited series)

1-Dennis O'Neil story/Greg Land-a in all 5.00
2-4 4.00
...: Alfred's Return (7/95, $3.50) Giordano-a 4.00
...Ties That Bind (1997, $12.95, TPB) r/mini-series & Alfred's Return 13.00

NIGHTWING
DC Comics: Oct, 1996 - No. 153, Apr, 2009 ($1.95/$1.99/$2.25/$2.50/$2.99)

1-Chuck Dixon scripts & Scott McDaniel-c/a 2 4 6 9 11 12
2,3 6.00
4-10: 6-Robin-c/app. 5.00
11-20: 13-15-Batman app. 19,20-Cataclysm pts. 2,11 4.00
21-49,51-64: 23-Green Arrow app. 26-29-Huntress-c/app. 30-Superman-c/app. 35-39-No Man's Land. 41-Land/Geraci-a begins. 46-Begin $2.25-c. 47-Texiera-c. 52-Catwoman-c/app. 54-Shrike app. 3.00
50-($3.50) Nightwing battles Torque 4.00
65-74,76-99: 65,66-Bruce Wayne: Murderer x-over pt. 3,9. 68,69: B.W.: Fugitive pt. 6,9. 70-Last Dixon-s. 71-Devin Grayson-s begin. 81-Batgirl vs. Deathstroke. 93-Blockbuster killed. 94-Copperhead app. 96-Bagged w/CD. 96-98-War Games 3.00
75-(1/03, $2.95) Intro. Tarantula 4.00
100-(2/05, $2.95) Tarantula app. 4.00
101-117: 101-Year One begins. 103-Jason Todd & Deadman app. 107-110-Hester-a. 109-Begin $2.50-c. 109,110-Villains United tie-ins. 112-Deathstroke app. 3.00
118-149,151-153: 118-One Year Later; Jason Todd as 2nd Nightwing. 120-Begin $2.99-c. 138,139-Resurrection of Ra's al Ghul x-over. 138-2nd printing. 147-Two-Face app. 3.00
150-($3.99) Batman R.I.P. x-over; Nightwing vs. Two-Face; Tan-c 4.00
#1,000,000 (11/98) teams with future Batman 3.00
Annual 1(1997, $3.95) Pulp Heroes 4.00
Annual 2 (6/07, $3.99) Dick Grayson and Barbara Gordon's shared history 4.00
...Eighty Page Giant 1 (12/00, $5.95) Intro. of Hella; Dixon-s/Haley-c 6.00
...: Big Guns (2004, $14.95, TPB) r/#47-50; Secret Files 1, Eighty Page Giant 1 15.00
...: Brothers in Blood (2007, $14.99, TPB) r/#118-124 15.00
...: A Darker Shade of Justice (2001, $19.95, TPB) r/#30-39, Secret Files #1 20.00
...: Freefall (2008, $17.99, TPB) r/#140-146 18.00
...: A Knight in Blüdhaven (1998, $14.95, TPB) r/#1-8 15.00
...: Love and Bullets (2000, $17.95, TPB) r/#1/2, 19,21,22,24-29 18.00
...: Love and War (2007, $14.99, TPB) r/#125-132 15.00
...: On the Razor's Edge (2005, $14.99, TPB) r/#52,54-60 15.00
...: Our Worlds at War (9/01, $2.95) Jae Lee-c 3.00
...: Renegade TPB (2006, $17.95) r/#112-117 18.00
...: Rough Justice (1999, $17.95, TPB) r/#9-18 18.00
Secret Files 1 (10/99, $4.95) Origin-s and pin-ups 5.00
...: The Great Leap (2009, $19.99) r/#147-153 20.00
...: The Hunt for Oracle (2003, $14.95, TPB) r/#41-46 & Birds of Prey #20,21 15.00
...: The Lost Year (2008, $14.99) r/#133-137 & Annual #2 15.00
...: The Target (2001, $5.95) McDaniel-c/a 6.00
Wizard 1/2 (Mail offer) 5.00
...: Year One (2005, $14.99) r/#101-106 15.00

NIGHTWING (See Tangent Comics/ Nightwing)

NIGHTWING AND HUNTRESS
DC Comics: May, 1998 - No. 4, Aug, 1998 ($1.95, limited series)

1-4-Grayson-s/Land & Sienkiewicz-a 3.00
TPB (2003, $9.95) r/#1/4; cover gallery 10.00

NIGHTWINGS (See DC Science Fiction Graphic Novel)

NIKKI, WILD DOG OF THE NORTH (Disney, see Movie Comics)
Dell Publishing Co.: No. 1226, Sept, 1961

Four Color 1226-Movie, photo-c 5 10 15 34 55 75

9-11 - ARTISTS RESPOND
Dark Horse Comics: 2002 ($9.95, TPB, proceeds donated to charities)

Volume 1-Short stories about the September 11 tragedies by various Dark Horse, Chaos! and Image writers and artists; Eric Drooker-c 10.00

9-11: EMERGENCY RELIEF
Alternative Comics: 2002 ($14.95, TPB, proceeds donated to the Red Cross)

nn-Short stories by various inc. Pekar, Eisner, Hester, Oeming, Noto; Cho-c 15.00

9-11 - THE WORLD'S FINEST COMIC BOOK WRITERS AND ARTISTS TELL STORIES TO REMEMBER
DC Comics: 2002 ($9.95, TPB, proceeds donated to charities)

Volume 2-Short stories about the September 11 tragedies by various DC, MAD, and WildStorm writers and artists ; Alex Ross-c 10.00

NINE RINGS OF WU-TANG
Image Comics: July, 1999 - No. 5, July, 2000 ($2.95)

Preview (7/99, $5.00, B&W) 5.00
1-5: 1-(11/99, $2.95) Clayton Henry-a 3.00
Tower Records Variant-c 5.00
Wizard #0 Prelude 3.00
TPB (1/01, $19.95) r/#1-5, Preview & Prelude; sketchbook & cover gallery 20.00

1963
Image Comics (Shadowline Ink): Apr, 1993 - No. 6, Oct, 1993 ($1.95, lim. series)

1-6: Alan Moore scripts; Veitch, Bissette & Gibbons-a(p) 3.00
1-Gold 4.00

NOTE: ***Bissette** a-2-4; **Gibbons** a-1i, 2i, 6i; c-2.*

1984 (Magazine) (1994 #11 on)
Warren Publishing Co.: June, 1978 - No. 10, Jan, 1980 ($1.50, B&W with color inserts, mature content with nudity; 84 pgs. except #4 has 92 pgs.)

1-Nino-a in all; Mutant World begins by Corben 3 6 9 14 19 24
2-10: 4-Rex Havoc begins. 7-1st Ghita of Alizarr by Thorne. 9-1st Starfire 2 4 6 9 13 16

NOTE: ***Alcala** a-1-3,5,7i. **Corben** a-1-8; c-1,2. **Nebres** a-1-8,10. **Thorne** a-7,8,10. **Wood** a-1,2,5i.*

1994 (Formerly 1984) (Magazine)
Warren Publishing Co.: No. 11, Feb, 1980 - No. 29, Feb, 1983 (B&W with color; mature; #11-(84 pgs.); #12-16,18-21,24-(76 pgs.); #17,22,23,25-29-(68 pgs.)

11,17,18,20,22,23,29: 11,17-8 pgs. color insert. 18-Giger-c. 20-1st Diana Jacklighter Manhuntress by Maroto. 22-1st Sigmund Pavlov by Nino; 1st Ariel Hart by Hsu. 23-All Nino issue 2 4 6 8 11 14
12-16,19,21,24-28: 21-1st app. Angel by Nebres. 27-The Warhawks return 1 3 4 6 8 10

NOTE: ***Corben** c-26. **Maroto** a-20, 21, 24-28. **Nebres** a-11-13, 15, 16, 18, 21, 22, 25, 28. **Nino** a-11-19, 20(2), 21, 25, 26, 28; c-21. **Redondo** c-20. **Thorne** a-11-14, 17-21, 24-26, 28, 29.*

NINJA BOY
DC Comics (WildStorm): Oct, 2001 - No. 6, Mar, 2002 ($3.50/$2.95)

1-($3.50) Ale Garza-a/c 3.50
2-6-($2.95) 3.00
...: Faded Dreams TPB (2003, $14.95) r/#1-6; sketch pages 15.00

NINJA HIGH SCHOOL (1st series)
Antarctic Press: 1986 - No. 3, Aug, 1987 (B&W)

1-Ben Dunn-s/c/a; early Manga series 2 4 6 9 12 15
2,3 1 3 4 6 8 10

NINJAK (See Bloodshot #6, 7 & Deathmate)
Valiant/Acclaim Comics (Valiant) No. 16 on: Feb, 1994 - No. 26, Nov. 1995 ($2.25/$2.50)

1 ($3.50)-Chromium-c; Quesada-c/a(p) in #1-3 3.50
1-Gold 5.00
2-13: 3-Batman, Spawn & Random (from X-Factor) app. as costumes at party (cameo). 4-w/bound-in trading card. 5,6-X-O app. 3.00
0,00,14-26: 14-(4/95)-Begin $2.50-c. 0-(6/95, $2.50). 00-(6/95, $2.50) 3.00
Yearbook 1 (1994, $3.95) 4.00

NINJAK

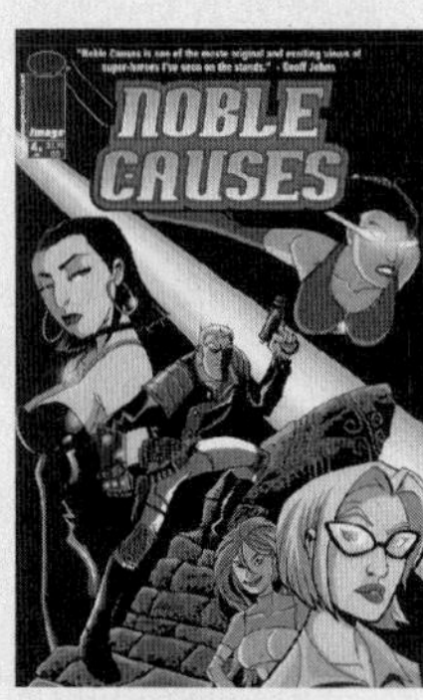

Noble Causes #4 © Jay Faerber

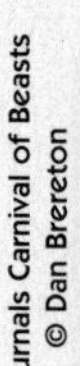
Nocturnals Carnival of Beasts © Dan Brereton

Nomad: Girl Without a World #1 © MAR

Acclaim Comics (Valiant Heroes): V2#1, Mar, 1997 -No. 12, Feb, 1998 ($2.50)

V2#1-12: 1-Intro new Ninjak; 1st app. Brutakon; Kurt Busiek scripts begin; painted variant-c exists. 2-1st app. Karnivor & Zeer. 3-1st app. Gigantik, Shurikai, & Nixie. 4-Origin; 1st app. Yasuiti Motomiya; intro The Dark Dozen; Colin King cameo. 9-Copycat-c 3.00

NINJA SCROLL
DC Comics (WildStorm): Nov, 2006 - No. 12, Oct, 2007 ($2.99)

1-12: 1-J. Torres-s/Michael Chang Ting Yu-a/c. 11-Puckett-s/Meyers-a 3.00
1-3-Variant covers by Jim Lee 5.00
TPB (2007, $19.99) r/#1-3,5-7 20.00

NINTENDO COMICS SYSTEM (Also see Adv. of Super Mario Brothers)
Valiant Comics: Feb, 1990 - No. 9, Oct, 1991 ($4.95, card stock-c, 68pgs.)

1-9: 1-Featuring Game Boy, Super Mario, Clappwall. 3-Layton-c. 5-8-Super Mario Bros. 9-Dr. Mario 1st app. 5.00

NOAH'S ARK
Spire Christian Comics/Fleming H. Revell Co.: 1973 (35/49¢)

nn-By Al Hartley 2 4 6 9 13 16

NOBLE CAUSES
Image Comics: July, 2001; Jan, 2002 - No. 4, May, 2002 ($2.95)

...First Impressions (7/01) Intro. the Noble family; Faerber-s 3.00
1-4: 1-(1/02) Back-up-s with Conner-a. 2-Igle back-up-a. 2-4-Two covers 3.00
...: Extended Family (5/03, $6.95) short stories by various 7.00
...: Extended Family 2 (6/04, $7.95) short stories by various 8.00
Vol. 1: In Sickness and in Health (2003, $12.95) r/#1-4 & ...First Impresssions 13.00

NOBLE CAUSES (Volume 3)
Image Comics: July, 2004 - No. 40, Mar, 2009 ($3.50)

1-24,26-40-Faerber-s. 1-Two covers. 2-Venture app. 5-Invincible app. 3.50
25-($4.99) Art by various; Randolph-c 5.00
Vol. 4: Blood and Water (2005, $14.95) r/#1-6 15.00
Vol. 5: Betrayals (2006, $14.99) r/#7-12 & The Pact V2 #2 15.00
Vol. 6: Hidden Agendas (2006, $15.99) r/#13-18 and Image Holiday Spec. 2005 story 16.00
Vol. 7: Powerless (2007, $15.99) r/#19-25; Wieringo sketch page 16.00

NOBLE CAUSES: DISTANT RELATIVES
Image Comics: Jul, 2003 - No. 4, Oct, 2003 ($2.95, B&W, limited series)

1-4-Faerber-s/Richardson & Ponce-a 3.00
Vol. 3: Distant Relatives (1/05, $12.95) r/#1-4; intro. by Joe Casey 13.00

NOBLE CAUSES: FAMILY SECRETS
Image Comics: Oct, 2002 - No. 4, Jan, 2003 ($2.95, limited series)

1-4-Faerber-s/Oeming-c. 1-Variant cover by Walker. 2,3-Valentino var-c. 4-Hester var-c 3.00
Vol. 2: Family Secrets (2004, $12.95) r/#1-4; sketch pages 13.00

NOBODY (Amado, Cho & Adlard's...)
Oni Press: Nov, 1998 - No. 4, Feb, 1999 ($2.95, B&W, mini-series)

1-4 3.00

NOCTURNALS, THE
Malibu Comics (Bravura): Jan, 1995 - No. 6, Aug, 1995 ($2.95, limited series)

1-6: Dan Brereton painted-c/a & scripts 3.00
1-Glow-in-the-Dark premium edition 5.00

NOCTURNALS, THE
Dark Horse Comics/Image Comics/Oni Press: one-shots and trade paperbacks

Black Planet TPB (Oni Press, 1998, $19.95) r/#1-6 (Malibu Comics series) 20.00
Black Planet and Other Stories HC (Olympian Publ.; 7/07, $39.95) r/Black Planet & Witching Hour contents; cover & sketch gallery with Brereton interviews 40.00
Carnival of Beasts (Image, 7/08, $6.99) short stories; Brereton-s/Brereton & others-a 7.00
Troll Bridge (Oni Press, 2000, $4.95, B&W & orange) Brereton-s/painted-c; art by Brereton, Chin, Art Adams, Sakai, Timm, Warren, Thompson, Purcell, Stephens and others 5.00
Unhallowed Eve TPB (Oni Press, 10/02, $9.95) r/Witching Hour & Troll Bridge one-shots 10.00
Witching Hour (Dark Horse, 5/98, $4.95) Brereton-s/a; reprints DHP stories + 8 new pgs. 5.00

NOCTURNALS: THE DARK FOREVER
Oni Press: Jul, 2001 -No. 3, Feb, 2002 ($2.95, limited series)

1-3-Brereton-s/painted-a/c 3.00
TPB (5/02, $9.95) r/#1-3; afterword & pin-ups by Alex Ross 10.00

NOCTURNE
Marvel Comics: June, 1995 - No. 4, Sept. 1995 ($1.50, limited series)

1-4 3.00

NO ESCAPE (Movie)
Marvel Comics: June, 1994 - No. 3, Aug, 1994 ($1.50)

1-3: Based on movie 3.00

NO HONOR
Image Comics (Top Cow): Feb, 2001 - No. 4, July, 2001 ($2.50)

Preview (12/00, B&W) Silvestri-c 3.00
1-4-Avery-s/Crain-a 3.00
TPB (8/03, $12.99) r/#1-4; intro. by Straczynski 13.00

NOMAD (See Captain America #180)
Marvel Comics: Nov, 1990 - No. 4, Feb, 1991 ($1.50, limited series)

1-4: 1,4-Captain America app. 3.00

NOMAD
Marvel Comics: V2#1, May, 1992 - No. 25, May, 1994 ($1.75)

V2#1-25: 1-Has gatefold-c w/map/wanted poster. 4-Deadpool x-over. 5-Punisher vs. Nomad-c/story. 6-Punisher & Daredevil-c/story cont'd in Punisher War Journal #48. 7-Gambit-c/story. 10-Red Wolf app. 21-Man-Thing-c/story. 25-Bound-in trading card sheet 3.00

NOMAD: GIRL WITHOUT A WORLD (Rikki Barnes from Captain America V2 Heroes Reborn)
Marvel Comics: Nov, 2009 - No. 4, Feb, 2010 ($3.99, limited series)

1-4-McKeever-s. 2-Falcon app. 4-Young Avengers app. 4.00

NOMAN (See Thunder Agents)
Tower Comics: Nov, 1966 - No. 2, March, 1967 (25¢, 68 pgs.)

1-Wood/Williamson-c; Lightning begins; Dynamo cameo; Kane-a(p) & Whitney-a
9 18 27 63 107 150
2-Wood-c only; Dynamo x-over; Whitney-a 6 12 18 39 62 85

NONE BUT THE BRAVE (See Movie Classics)

NOODNIK COMICS (See Pinky the Egghead)
Comic Media/Mystery/Biltmore: Dec, 1953; No. 2, Feb, 1954 - No. 5, Aug, 1954

3-D(1953, 25¢; Comic Media)(#1)-Came w/glasses 29 58 87 170 278 385
2-5 9 18 27 52 69 85

NORMALMAN (See Cerebus the Aardvark #55, 56)
Aardvark-Vanaheim/Renegade Press #6 on: Jan, 1984 - No. 12, Dec, 1985 ($1.70/$2.00)

1-12: 1-Jim Valentino-c/a in all. 6-12 ($2.00, B&W): 10-Cerebus cameo; Sim-a (2 pgs.) 3.00
...- Megaton Man Special 1 (Image Comics, 8/94, $2.50) 3.00
...3-D 1 (Annual, 1986, $2.25) 3.00
...Twentieth Anniversary Special (7/04, $2.95) 3.00

NORTH AVENUE IRREGULARS (See Walt Disney Showcase #49)

NORTH 40
DC Comics (WildStorm): Sept, 2009 - No. 6, Feb, 2010 ($2.99)

1-6-Aaron Williams-s/Fiona Staples-a 3.00
TPB (2010, $17.99) r/#1-6 18.00

NORTHLANDERS
DC Comics (Vertigo): Feb, 2008 - Present ($2.99)

1-38: 1-Vikings in 980 A.D.; Wood-s/Gianfelice-a; covers by Carnivale. 35-Cloonan-a 3.00
1-3-Variant covers. 1-Adam Kubert. 2-Andy Kubert. 3-Dave Gibbons 5.00
...: Blood in the Snow TPB (2010, $14.99) r/#9,10,17-20 15.00
...: Sven the Returned TPB (2008, $9.99) r/#1-8; cover gallery 10.00
...: The Cross + The Hammer TPB (2009, $14.99) r/#11-16 15.00
...: The Plague Widow TPB (2010, $16.99) r/#21-28 17.00

NORTHSTAR
Marvel Comics: Apr, 1994 - No. 4, July, 1994 ($1.75, mini-series)

1-4: Character from Alpha Flight 3.00

NORTH TO ALASKA
Dell Publishing Co.: No. 1155, Dec, 1960

Four Color 1155-Movie, John Wayne photo-c 15 30 45 103 209 315

NORTHWEST MOUNTIES (Also see Approved Comics #12)
Jubilee Publications/St. John: Oct, 1948 - No. 4, July, 1949

1-Rose of the Yukon by Matt Baker; Walter Johnson-a; Lubbers-c
47 94 141 296 498 700
2-Baker-a; Lubbers-c. Ventrilo app. 39 78 117 231 378 525
3-Bondage-c, Baker-a; Sky Chief, K-9 app. 39 78 117 240 395 550
4-Baker-c/a(2 pgs.); Blue Monk & The Desperado app.
41 82 123 256 428 600

NO SLEEP 'TIL DAWN
Dell Publishing Co.: No. 831, Aug, 1957

Four Color 831-Movie, Karl Malden photo-c 6 12 18 43 69 95

NOSTALGIA ILLUSTRATED
Marvel Comics: Nov, 1974 - V2#8, Aug, 1975 (B&W, 76 pgs.)

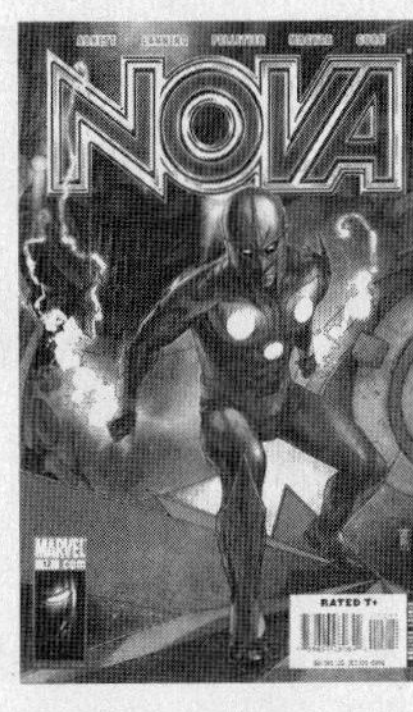

Nova (2007 series) #12 © MAR

Number of the Beast #2 © WSP

Nyoka, The Jungle Girl #76 © FAW

	GD 2.0	VG 4.0	FN 6.0	VF 8.0	VF/NM 9.0	NM- 9.2
V1#1	4	8	12	22	34	45
V1#2, V2#1-8	3	6	9	16	22	28

NOT BRAND ECHH (Brand Echh #1-4; See Crazy, 1973)
Marvel Comics Group (LMC): Aug, 1967 - No. 13, May, 1969
(1st Marvel parody book)

	GD	VG	FN	VF	VF/NM	NM-
1: 1-8 are 12¢ issues	7	14	21	49	80	110
2-8: 3-Origin Thor, Hulk & Capt. America; Monkees, Alfred E. Neuman cameo. 4-X-Men app. 5-Origin/intro. Forbush Man. 7-Origin Fantastical-4 & Stuporman. 8-Beatles cameo; X-Men satire; last 12¢-c	4	8	12	26	41	55
9-13 (25¢, 68 pgs., all Giants) 9-Beatles cameo. 10-All-r; The Old Witch, Crypt Keeper & Vault Keeper cameos. 12,13-Beatles cameo	5	10	15	32	51	70

NOTE: *Colan a(p)-4, 5, 8, 9, 13.* ***Everett*** *a-1i.* ***Kirby*** *a(p)-1, 3, 5-7, 10r; c-1p.* ***J. Severin*** *a-1; c-3, 6-8, 11.* ***M. Severin*** *a-1-13; c-2, 9, 10, 12, 13.* ***Sutton*** *a-3, 4, 5i, 6i, 8, 9, 10r, 11-13; c-5. Archie satire in #9. Avengers satire in #8, 12.*

NOTHING CAN STOP THE JUGGERNAUT
Marvel Comics: 1989 ($3.95)

1-r/Amazing Spider-Man #229 & 230 — 4.00

NO TIME FOR SERGEANTS (TV)
Dell Publ. Co.: No. 914, July, 1958; Feb-Apr, 1965 - No. 3, Aug-Oct, 1965

	GD	VG	FN	VF	VF/NM	NM-
Four Color 914 (Movie)-Toth-a; Andy Griffith photo-c	9	18	27	65	113	160
1(2-4/65) (TV): Photo-c	6	12	18	39	62	85
2,3 (TV): Photo-c	5	10	15	30	48	65

NOVA (The Man Called... No. 22-25)(See New Warriors)
Marvel Comics Group: Sept, 1976 - No. 25, May, 1979

	GD	VG	FN	VF	VF/NM	NM-
1-Origin/1st app. Nova	3	6	9	14	20	25
2-4,12: 4-Thor x-over. 12-Spider-Man x-over	2	4	6	8	10	12
5-11	1	2	3	5	7	9
10,11-(35¢-c variants, limited distribution)(6,7/77)	4	8	12	26	41	55
12-(35¢-c variant, limited distribution)(8/77)	5	10	15	32	51	70
13,14-(Regular 30¢ editions)(9/77) 13-Intro Crime-Buster	1	2	3	5	6	8
13,14-(35¢-c variants, limited distribution)	4	8	12	24	37	50
15-24: 18-Yellow Claw app. 19-Wally West (Kid Flash) cameo	1	2	3	5	6	8
25-Last issue	2	3	4	6	8	10

NOTE: ***Austin*** *c-21i, 23i.* ***John Buscema*** *a(p)-1-3, 8, 21; c-1p, 2, 15.* ***Infantino*** *a(p)-15-20, 22-25; c-17-20, 21p, 23p, 24p.* ***Kirby*** *c-4p, 5, 7.* ***Nebres*** *c-25i.* ***Simonson*** *a-23i.*

NOVA
Marvel Comics: Jan, 1994 - June, 1995 ($1.75/$1.95) (Started as 4-part mini-series)

1-($2.95, 52 pgs.)-Collector's Edition w/gold foil-c; new Nova costume — 5.00
1-($2.25, 52 pgs.)-Newsstand Edition w/o foil-c — 4.00
2-18: 3-Spider-Man-c/story. 5-Stan Lee app. 5-Bound-in card sheet. 13-Firestar & Night Thrasher app.14-Darkhawk — 3.00

NOVA
Marvel Comics: May, 1999 - No. 7, Nov, 1999 ($2.99/$1.99)

1-($2.99) Larsen-s/Bennett-a; wraparound-c by Larsen — 4.00
2-7-($1.99): 2-Two covers; Capt. America app. 5-Spider-Man. 7-Venom — 3.00

NOVA (See Secret Avengers and The Thanos Imperative)
Marvel Comics: June, 2007 - No. 36, Jun, 2010 ($2.99)

1-36: 1-Sean Chen-a/Granov-c. 2,3-Iron Man app. 3-Thunderbolts app. 14,15-Silver Surfer & Galactus app. 16-18-Secret Invasion. 21-Fantastic Four app. 23-28-War of Kings — 3.00
... Annual 1 (4/08, $3.99) Origin retold; Annihilation: Conquest tie-in — 4.00
...: Origin of Richard Rider (2009, $4.99) origin retold from Nova #1 & 4 ('76) — 5.00
... Vol. 1: Annihilation - Conquest TPB (2007, $17.99) r/#1-7; cover sketches — 18.00

NOW AGE ILLUSTRATED (See Pendulum Illustrated Classics)

NOW AGE BOOKS ILLUSTRATED (See Pendulum Illustrated Classics)

NTH MAN THE ULTIMATE NINJA (See Marvel Comics Presents #25)
Marvel Comics: Aug, 1989 - No. 16, Sept, 1990 ($1.00)

1-16-Ninja mercenary. 8-Dale Keown's 1st Marvel work (1/90, pencils) — 3.00

NUCLEUS (Also see Cerebus)
Heiro-Graphic Publications: May, 1979 ($1.50, B&W, adult fanzine)

	GD	VG	FN	VF	VF/NM	NM-
1-Contains "Demonhorn" by Dave Sim; early app. of Cerebus The Aardvark (4 pg. story)	6	12	18	37	59	80

NUKLA
Dell Publishing Co.: Oct-Dec, 1965 - No. 4, Sept, 1966

	GD	VG	FN	VF	VF/NM	NM-
1-Origin & 1st app. Nukla (super hero)	5	10	15	30	48	65
2,3	3	6	9	20	30	40
4-Ditko-a, c(p)	4	8	12	24	37	50

NUMBER OF THE BEAST
DC Comics (WildStorm): June, 2008 - No. 8, Sept, 2008 ($2.99, limited series)

1-8-Beatty-s/Sprouse-a/c. 1-Variant-c by Mahnke. 6-The Authority app. — 3.00
TPB (2008, $19.99) r/#1-8; character dossiers — 20.00

NURSE BETSY CRANE (Formerly Teen Secret Diary) (Also see Registered Nurse for reprints)
Charlton Comics: V2#12, Aug, 1961 - V2#27, Mar, 1964 (See Soap Opera Romances)

	GD	VG	FN	VF	VF/NM	NM-
V2#12-27	3	6	9	16	23	30

NURSE HELEN GRANT (See The Romances of...)

NURSE LINDA LARK (See Linda Lark)

NURSERY RHYMES
Ziff-Davis Publ. Co. (Approved Comics): No. 10, July-Aug, 1951 - No. 2, Winter, 1951 (Painted-c)

	GD	VG	FN	VF	VF/NM	NM-
10 (#1), 2: 10-Howie Post-a	16	32	48	94	147	200

NURSES, THE (TV)
Gold Key: April, 1963 - No. 3, Oct, 1963 (Photo-c: #1,2)

	GD	VG	FN	VF	VF/NM	NM-
1	4	8	12	24	37	50
2,3	3	6	9	18	27	35

NUTS! (Satire)
Premiere Comics Group: March, 1954 - No. 5, Nov, 1954

	GD	VG	FN	VF	VF/NM	NM-
1-Hollingsworth-a	31	62	93	182	296	410
2,4,5: 5-Capt. Marvel parody	20	40	60	118	192	265
3-Drug "reefers" mentioned	20	40	60	120	195	270

NUTS (Magazine) (Satire)
Health Knowledge: Feb, 1958 - No. 2, April, 1958

	GD	VG	FN	VF	VF/NM	NM-
1	10	20	30	54	72	90
2	7	14	21	37	46	55

NUTS & JOLTS
Dell Publishing Co.: No. 22, 1941

	GD	VG	FN	VF	VF/NM	NM-
Large Feature Comic 22	18	36	54	103	162	220

NUTSY SQUIRREL (Formerly Hollywood Funny Folks)(See Comic Cavalcade)
National Periodical Publications: #61, 9-10/54 - #69, 1-2/56; #70, 8-9/56 - #71, 10-11/56; #72, 11/57

	GD	VG	FN	VF	VF/NM	NM-
61-Mayer-a; Grossman-a in all	14	28	42	76	108	140
62-72: Mayer a-62,65,67-72	10	20	30	54	72	90

NUTTY COMICS
Fawcett Publications: Winter, 1946

	GD	VG	FN	VF	VF/NM	NM-
1-Capt. Kidd story; 1 pg. Wolverton-a	14	28	42	80	115	150

NUTTY COMICS
Home Comics (Harvey Publications): 1945; No. 4, May-June, 1946 - No. 8, June-July, 1947 (No #2,3)

	GD	VG	FN	VF	VF/NM	NM-
nn-Helpful Hank, Bozo Bear & others (funny animal)	9	18	27	50	65	80
4	7	14	21	37	46	55
5-Rags Rabbit begins(1st app.); infinity-c	8	16	24	40	50	60
6-8	6	12	18	31	38	45

NUTTY LIFE (Formerly Krazy Life #1; becomes Wotalife Comics #3 on)
Fox Features Syndicate: No. 2, Summer, 1946

	GD	VG	FN	VF	VF/NM	NM-
2	16	32	48	94	147	200

NYOKA, THE JUNGLE GIRL (Formerly Jungle Girl; see The Further Adventures of..., Master Comics #50 & XMas Comics)
Fawcett Publications: No. 2, Winter, 1945 - No. 77, June, 1953 (Movie serial)

	GD	VG	FN	VF	VF/NM	NM-
2	60	120	180	381	653	925
3	34	68	102	199	325	450
4,5	28	56	84	165	270	375
6-11,13,14,16-18-Krigstein-a: 17-Sam Spade ad by Lou Fine	20	40	60	114	182	250
12,15,19,20	18	36	54	105	165	225
21-30: 25-Clayton Moore photo-c?	14	28	42	76	108	140
31-40	11	22	33	62	86	110
41-50	10	20	30	56	76	95
51-60	9	18	27	50	65	80
61-77	8	16	24	44	57	70

NOTE: *Photo-c from movies 25, 30-70, 72, 75-77. Bondage c-4, 5, 7, 8, 14, 24.*

NYOKA, THE JUNGLE GIRL (Formerly Zoo Funnies; Space Adventures #23 on)
Charlton Comics: No. 14, Nov, 1955 - No. 22, Nov, 1957

	GD	VG	FN	VF	VF/NM	NM-
14	11	22	33	62	86	110

NYX: No Way Home #1 © MAR

The Occultist #1 © DH

Official Handbook of the Marvel Universe : X-Men 2004 © MAR

GD 2.0 | VG 4.0 | FN 6.0 | VF 8.0 | VF/NM 9.0 | NM- 9.2

15-22 9 18 27 52 69 85

NYX (Also see X-23 title)
Marvel Comics: Nov, 2003 - No. 7, Oct, 2005 ($2.99)
1,2: 1-Quesada-s/Middleton-a/c; intro. Kiden Nixon 3.00
3-1st app. X-23 1 3 4 6 8 10
4-6: 5,6-Teranishi-a 3.00
7-($3.99) Teranishi-a 4.00
NYX X-23 (2005, $34.99, oversized with d.j.) r/X-23 #1-6 & NYX #1-7; intro by Craig Kyle; sketch pages, development art and unused covers 35.00
...: Wannabe TPB (2006, $19.99) r/#1-7; development art and unused covers 20.00

NYX: NO WAY HOME
Marvel Comics: Oct, 2008 - No. 6, Apr, 2009 ($3.99)
1-6: 1-Andrasofszky-a/Liu-s/Urusov-c; sketch pages, character and cover design art 4.00

OAKLAND PRESS FUNNYBOOK, THE
The Oakland Press: 9/17/78 - 4/13/80 (16 pgs.) (Weekly)
Full color in comic book form; changes to tabloid size 4/20/80-on
Contains Tarzan by Manning, Marmaduke, Bugs Bunny, etc. (low distribution); 9/23/79 - 4/13/80 contain Buck Rogers by Gray Morrow & Jim Lawrence 3.00

OAKY DOAKS (See Famous Funnies #190)
Eastern Color Printing Co.: July, 1942 (One Shot)
1 34 68 102 199 325 450

OBERGEIST: RAGNAROK HIGHWAY
Image Comics (Top Cow/Minotaur): May, 2001 - No. 6, Nov, 2001 ($2.95, limited series)
Preview ('01, B&W, 16 pgs.) Harris painted-c 3.00
1-6-Harris-c/a/Jolley-s. 1-Three covers 3.00
... :The Directors' Cut (2002, $19.95, TPB) r/#1-6; Bruce Campbell intro. 20.00
... :The Empty Locket (3/02, $2.95, B&W) Harris & Snyder-a 3.00

OBIE
Store Comics: 1953 (6¢)
1 6 12 18 28 34 40

OBJECTIVE FIVE
Image Comics: July, 2000 - No. 6, Jan, 2001($2.95)
1-6-Lizalde-a 3.00

OBLIVION
Comico: Aug, 1995 - No. 3, May, 1996 ($2.50)
1-3: 1-Art Adams-c. 2-(1/96)-Bagged w/gaming card. 3-(5/96)-Darrow-c 3.00

OBNOXIO THE CLOWN (Character from Crazy Magazine)
Marvel Comics Group: April, 1983 (one-shot)
1-Vs. the X-Men 4.00

OCCULT CRIMES TASKFORCE
Image Comics: July, 2006 - No. 4, May, 2007 ($2.99, limited series)
1-4-Rosario Dawson & David Atchison-s/Tony Shasteen-a 3.00
... Vol. 1 TPB (2007, $14.99) r/#1-4; sketch and cover development art 15.00

OCCULTIST, THE
Dark Horse Comics: Dec, 2010 ($3.50, one-shot)
1-Richardson & Seeley-sDrujiniu-a/Morris-c 3.50

OCCULT FILES OF DR. SPEKTOR, THE
Gold Key/Whitman No. 25: Apr, 1973 - No. 24, Feb, 1977; No. 25, May, 1982 (Painted-c #1-24)
1-1st app. Lakota; Baron Tibor begins 5 10 15 32 51 70
2-5: 3-Mummy-c/s. 5-Jekyll & Hyde-c/s 3 6 9 18 27 35
6-10: 6,9-Frankenstein. 8,9-Dracula c/s. 9.-Jekyll & Hyde c/s. 9,10-Mummy-c/s 3 6 9 14 20 25
11-13,15-17,19-22,24: 11-1st app. Spektor as Werewolf. 11-13-Werewolf-c/s. 12,16-Frankenstein c/s. 17-Zombie/Voodoo-c. 19-Sea monster-c/s. 20-Mummy-s. 21-Swamp monster-c/s. 24-Dragon-c/s 2 4 6 10 14 18
14-Dr. Solar app. 3 6 9 16 23 30
18,23-Dr. Solar cameo 2 4 6 11 16 20
22-Return of the Owl c/s 2 4 6 11 16 20
25(Whitman, 5/82)-r/#1 with line drawn-c 2 4 6 8 11 14
NOTE: *Also see Dan Curtis, Golden Comics Digest 33, Gold Key Spotlight, Mystery Comics Digest 5, & Spine Tingling Tales.*

OCEAN
DC Comics (WildStorm): Dec, 2005 - No. 6, Sept, 2005 ($2.95/$2.99/$3.99, limited series)
1-5-Warren Ellis-s/Chris Sprouse-a 3.00
6-($3.99) Conclusion 4.00

ODELL'S ADVENTURES IN 3-D (See Adventures in 3-D)

GD 2.0 | VG 4.0 | FN 6.0 | VF 8.0 | VF/NM 9.0 | NM- 9.2

ODYSSEY, THE (See Marvel Illustrated: The Odyssey)

OFFCASTES
Marvel Comics (Epic Comics/Heavy Hitters): July, 1993 - No. 3, Sept, 1993 ($1.95, limited series)
1-3: Mike Vosburg-c/a/scripts in all 3.00

OFFICIAL CRISIS ON INFINITE EARTHS INDEX, THE
Independent Comics Group (Eclipse): Mar, 1986 ($1.75)
1 5.00

OFFICIAL CRISIS ON INFINITE EARTHS CROSSOVER INDEX, THE
Independent Comics Group (Eclipse): July, 1986 ($1.75)
1-Perez-c. 5.00

OFFICIAL DOOM PATROL INDEX, THE
Independent Comics Group (Eclipse): Feb, 1986 - No. 2, Mar, 1986 ($1.50, limited series)
1,2: Byrne-c. 4.00

OFFICIAL HANDBOOK OF THE CONAN UNIVERSE (See Handbook of...)

OFFICIAL HANDBOOK OF THE MARVEL UNIVERSE, THE
Marvel Comics Group: Jan, 1983 - No. 15, May, 1984 (Limited series)
1-Lists Marvel heroes & villains (letter A) 5.00
2-15: 2 (B-C, 3-(C-D). 4-(D-G). 5-(H-J), 6-(K-L). 7-(M). 8-(N-P); Punisher-c. 9-(Q-S), 10-(S). 11-(S-U). 12-(V-Z); Wolverine-c. 13,14-Book of the Dead. 15-Weaponry catalogue 4.00
NOTE: ***Bolland** a-8. **Byrne** c/a(p)-1-14; c-15p. **Grell** a-6, 9. **Kirby** a-1, 3. **Layton** a-2, 5, 7. **Mignola** a-3, 4, 5, 6, 8, 12. **Miller** a-4-6, 8, 10. **Nebres** a-3, 4, 8. **Redondo** a-3, 4, 8, 13, 14. **Simonson** a-1, 4, 6-13. **Paul Smith** a-1-12. **Starlin** a-5, 7, 8, 10, 13, 14. **Steranko** a-8p. **Zeck**-2-14.*

OFFICIAL HANDBOOK OF THE MARVEL UNIVERSE, THE
Marvel Comics Group: Dec, 1985 - No. 20, Feb, 1988 ($1.50, maxi-series)
V2#1-Byrne-c 5.00
2-20: 2,3-Byrne-c 4.00
Trade paperback Vol. 1-10 ($6.95) 1 3 4 6 8 10
NOTE: ***Art Adams** a-7, 8, 11, 12, 14. **Bolland** a-8, 10, 13. **Buckler** a-1, 3, 5, 10. **Buscema** a-1, 5, 8, 9, 10, 13, 14. **Byrne** a-1-14; c-1-11. **Ditko** a-1, 2, 4, 6, 7, 11, 13. a-7, 11. **Mignola** a-2, 4, 9, 11, 13. **Miller** a-2, 4, 12. **Simonson** a-1, 2, 4-13, 15. **Paul Smith** a-1-5, 7-12, 14. **Starlin** a-6, 8, 9, 12, 16. **Zeck** a-1-4, 6, 7, 9-14, 16.*

OFFICIAL HANDBOOK OF THE MARVEL UNIVERSE, THE
Marvel Comics: July, 1989 - No. 8, Mid-Dec, 1990 ($1.50, lim. series, 52 pgs.)
V3#1-8: 1-McFarlane-a (2 pgs.) 4.00

OFFICIAL HANDBOOK OF THE MARVEL UNIVERSE, THE (Also see Spider-Man)
Marvel Comics: 2004 - Present ($3.99, one-shots)
...: Alternate Universes 2005 - Profile pages of 1602, MC2, 2099, Earth X, Mangaverse, Days of Future Past, Squadron Supreme, Spider-Ham's Larval Earth and others 4.00
...: Avengers 2004 - Profile pages; art by various; lists of character origins and 1st apps. 4.00
...: Avengers 2005 - Profile pages and info for New Avengers, Young Avengers & others 4.00
...: Book of the Dead 2004 - Profile pages of deceased Marvel characters; art by various; 4.00
...: Daredevil 2004 - Profile pages; art by various; lists of character origins and 1st apps. 4.00
...: Fantastic Four 2005 - Profile pages of members, friends & enemies 4.00
...: Golden Age 2005 - Profile pages; art by various; lists of character origins and 1st apps. 4.00
...: Horror 2005 - Profile pages; art by various; lists of character origins and 1st apps. 4.00
...: Hulk 2004 - Profile pages; art by various; lists of character origins and 1st apps. 4.00
...: Marvel Knights 2005 - Profile pages of characters from Marvel Knights line 4.00
...: Spider-Man 2004 - Profile pages; art by various; lists of character origins and 1st apps. 4.00
...: Spider-Man 2005 - Profile pages of Spidey's friends and foes, emphasizing the recent 4.00
...: Wolverine 2004 - Profile pages; art by various; lists of character origins and 1st apps. 4.00
...: Teams 2005 - Profile pages of Avengers, X-Men and other teams 4.00
...: Women of Marvel 2005 - Profile pages; art by various; Greg Land-c 4.00
...: X-Men 2004 - Profile pages; art by various; lists of character origins and 1st apps. 4.00
...: X-Men 2005 - Profile pages; art by various; lists of character origins and 1st apps. 4.00
...: X-Men - The Age of Apocalypse 2005 - Profile pages of characters plus Exiles 4.00

OFFICIAL HANDBOOK OF THE MARVEL UNIVERSE A-Z UPDATE
Marvel Comics: Apr, 2010 - No. 5, 2010 ($3.99, limited series)
1-5-Profile pages; Andrasofszky-c 4.00

OFFICIAL HANDBOOK OF THE ULTIMATE MARVEL UNIVERSE, THE
Marvel Comics: 2005 ($3.99, one-shots)
... 2005: The Fantastic Four and Spider-Man - Profile pages; art by various 4.00
... The Ultimates and X-Men 2005 - Profile pages; art by various; Bagley-c 4.00

OFFICIAL HAWKMAN INDEX, THE
Independent Comics Group: Nov, 1986 - No. 2, Dec, 1986 ($2.00)
1,2 4.00

OFFICIAL INDEX TO THE MARVEL UNIVERSE (Also see "Avengers, Thor...")
Marvel Comics: 2009 - No. 14, April, 2010 ($3.99)

Official Legion of Super-Heroes Index #1 © DC

Oh My Goddess! Part 6 #3 © Fujishima

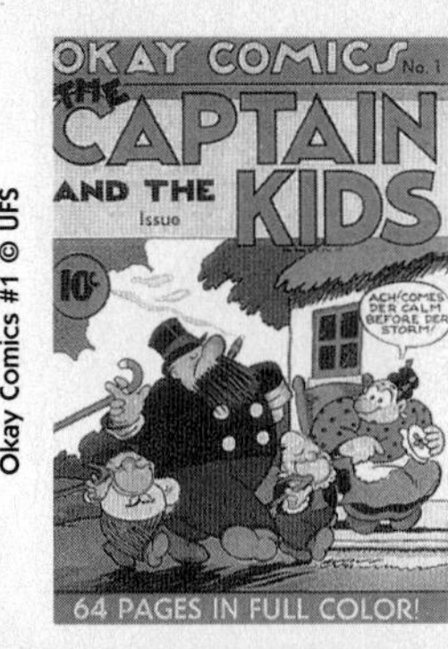

Okay Comics #1 © UFS

GD VG FN VF VF/NM NM-
2.0 4.0 6.0 8.0 9.0 9.2

1-14-Each issue has chronological synopsies, creator credits, character lists for 40-50 issues of apps. for Iron Man, Spider-Man and the X-Men starting with 1st apps. in issue #1 4.00

OFFICIAL JUSTICE LEAGUE OF AMERICA INDEX, THE
Independent Comics Group (Eclipse): April, 1986 - No. 8, Mar, 1987 ($2.00, Baxter paper)
1-8: 1,2-Perez-c. 6.00

OFFICIAL LEGION OF SUPER-HEROES INDEX, THE
Independent Comics Group (Eclipse): Dec, 1986 - No. 5, 1987 ($2.00, limited series)
(No Official in Title #2 on)
1-5: 4-Mooney-c 6.00

OFFICIAL MARVEL INDEX TO MARVEL TEAM-UP
Marvel Comics Group: Jan, 1986 - No. 6, 1987 ($1.25, limited series)
1-6 4.00

OFFICIAL MARVEL INDEX TO THE AMAZING SPIDER-MAN
Marvel Comics Group: Apr, 1985 - No. 9, Dec, 1985 ($1.25, limited series)
1 ($1.00)-Byrne-c. 4.00
2-9: 5,6,8,9-Punisher-c. 3.00

OFFICIAL MARVEL INDEX TO THE AVENGERS, THE
Marvel Comics: Jun, 1987 - No. 7, Aug, 1988 ($2.95, limited series)
1-7 5.00

OFFICIAL MARVEL INDEX TO THE AVENGERS, THE
Marvel Comics: V2#1, Oct, 1994 - V2#6, 1995 ($1.95, limited series)
V2#1-#6 3.00

OFFICIAL MARVEL INDEX TO THE FANTASTIC FOUR
Marvel Comics Group: Dec, 1985 - No. 12, Jan, 1987 ($1.25, limited series)
1-12: 1-Byrne-c. 1,2-Kirby back-c (unpub. art) 3.00

OFFICIAL MARVEL INDEX TO THE X-MEN, THE
Marvel Comics: May, 1987 - No. 7, July, 1988 ($2.95, limited series)
1-7 5.00

OFFICIAL MARVEL INDEX TO THE X-MEN, THE
Marvel Comics: V2#1, Apr, 1994 - V2#5, 1994 ($1.95, limited series)
V2#1-5: 1-Covers X-Men #1-51. 2-Covers #52-122,Special #1,2,Giant-Size #1,2. 3-Byrne-c; covers #123-177, Annuals 3-7, Spec. Ed. #1. 4-Covers Uncanny X-Men #178-234, Annuals 8-12. 5-Covers #235-287, Annuals 13-15 3.00

OFFICIAL SOUPY SALES COMIC (See Soupy Sales)

OFFICIAL TEEN TITANS INDEX, THE
Indep. Comics Group (Eclipse): Aug, 1985 - No. 5, 1986 ($1.50, lim. series)
1-5 4.00

OFFICIAL TRUE CRIME CASES (Formerly Sub-Mariner #23; All-True Crime Cases #26 on)
Marvel Comics (OCI): No. 24, Fall, 1947 - No. 25, Winter, 1947-48
24(#1)-Burgos-a; Syd Shores-c 23 46 69 136 223 310
25-Syd Shores-c; Kurtzman's "Hey Look" 18 36 54 107 169 230

OF SUCH IS THE KINGDOM
George A. Pflaum: 1955 (15¢, 36 pgs.)
nn-Reprints from 1951 Treasure Chest 4 7 10 14 17 20

O.G. WHIZ (See Gold Key Spotlight #10)
Gold Key: 2/71 - No. 6, 5/72; No. 7, 5/78 - No. 11, 1/79 (No. 7: 52 pgs.)
1-John Stanley script 5 10 15 34 55 75
2-John Stanley script 4 8 12 24 37 50
3-6(1972) 3 6 9 18 27 35
7-11(1978-79)-Part-r: 9-Tubby issue 2 4 6 9 12 15

OH, BROTHER! (Teen Comedy)
Stanhall Publ.: Jan, 1953 - No. 5, Oct, 1953
1-By Bill Williams 9 18 27 50 65 80
2-5 6 12 18 33 41 48

OH MY GODDESS! (Manga)
Dark Horse Comics: Aug, 1994 - Present ($2.50-$3.99, B&W)
1-6-Kosuke Fujishima-s/a in all 3.00
... PART II 2/95 - No. 9, 9/95 ($2.50, B&W, lim.series) #1-9 3.00
... PART III 11/95 - No. 11, 9/96 ($2.95, B&W, lim. series) #1-11 3.00
... PART IV 12/96 - No. 8, 7/97 ($2.95, B&W, lim. series) #1-8 3.00
... PART V 9/97 - Np. 12, 8/98 ($2.95, B&W, lim. series)
1,2,5,8: 5-Ninja Master pt. 1 3.00
3,4,6,7,10-12-($3.95, 48 pgs.) 10-Fallen Angel. 11-Play The Game 4.00
9-($3.50) "It's Lonely At The Top" 3.50
... PART VI 10/98 - No. 5, 3/99 ($3.50/$2.95, B&W, lim. series)
1-($3.50) 3.50
2-6-($2.95)-6-Super Urd one-shot 3.00
... PART VII 5/99 - No. 8, 12/99 ($2.95, B&W, lim. series) #1-3 3.00
4-8-($3.50) 3.50
... PART VIII 1/00 - No. 6, 6/00 ($3.50, B&W, lim. series) #1-3,5,7 3.50
4-($2.95) "Hail To The Chief" begins 3.00
... PART IX 7/00 - No. 7, 1/01 ($3.50/$2.99) #1-4: 3-Queen Sayoko 3.50
5-7-($2.99) 3.00
... PART X 2/01 - No. 5, 6/01 ($3.50) #1-5 3.50
... PART XI 10/01 - No. 10, 3/02 ($3.50) #1,2,7,8 3.50
3-6,9-($2.99) Mystery Child 3.00
10-($3.99) 4.00
(Series adapts new numbering) 88-90-($3.50) Learning to Love 3.50
91-94,96-103,105,107-110: 91-94 ($2.99) Traveler. 96-98-The Phantom Racer 3.00
95,104,106-($3.50) 95-Traveler pt. 5 3.50
111,112-($3.99) 4.00

OH SUSANNA (TV)
Dell Publishing Co.: No. 1105, June-Aug, 1960 (Gale Storm)
Four Color 1105-Toth-a, photo-c 11 22 33 76 136 195

OKAY COMICS
United Features Syndicate: July, 1940
1-Captain & the Kids & Hawkshaw the Detective reprints 45 90 135 279 465 650

O.K. COMICS
Hit Publications: May, 1940 (ashcan)
nn-Ashcan comic, not distributed to newsstands, only for in house use. A CGC certified 8.0 copy sold in 2003 for $1,000.

O.K. COMICS
United Features Syndicate/Hit Publications: July, 1940 - No. 2, Oct, 1940
1-Little Giant (w/super powers), Phantom Knight, Sunset Smith, & The Teller Twins begin 76 152 228 486 831 1175
2 (Rare)-Origin Mister Mist by Chas. Quinlan 77 154 231 493 847 1200

OKLAHOMA KID
Ajax/Farrell Publ.: June, 1957 - No. 4, 1958
1 11 22 33 60 83 105
2-4 7 14 21 37 46 55

OKLAHOMAN, THE
Dell Publishing Co.: No. 820, July, 1957
Four Color 820-Movie, photo-c 8 16 24 58 97 135

OKTANE
Dark Horse Comics: Aug, 1995 - Nov, 1995 ($2.50, color, limited series)
1-4-Gene Ha-a 3.00

OKTOBERFEST COMICS
Now & Then Publ.: Fall 1976 (75¢, Canadian, B&W, one-shot)
1-Dave Sim-s/a; Gene Day-a; 1st app. Uncle Hans & Natter P. Bombast; The Beavers sty; 1st Cap'n Riverrat, Sim-s/Day-a 3 6 9 16 23 30

OLD GLORY COMICS
DC Comics: 1941
nn - Ashcan comic, not distributed to newsstands, only for in-house use. Cover art is Flash Comics #12 with interior being Action Comics #37 (no known sales)

OLD IRONSIDES (Disney)
Dell Publishing Co.: No. 874, Jan, 1958
Four Color 874-Movie w/Johnny Tremain 6 12 18 43 69 95

OLD YELLER (Disney, see Movie Comics, and Walt Disney Showcase #25)
Dell Publishing Co.: No. 869, Jan, 1958
Four Color 869-Movie, photo-c 5 10 15 34 55 75

OMAC (One Man Army; ...Corps. #4 on; also see Kamandi #59 & Warlord)
(See Cancelled Comic Cavalcade)
National Periodical Publications: Sept-Oct, 1974 - No. 8, Nov-Dec, 1975
1-Origin 6 12 18 37 59 80
2-8: 8-2 pg. Neal Adams ad 3 6 9 18 27 35
Jack Kirby's Omac: One Man Army Corps HC (2008, $24.99, d.j.) r/#1-8; Evanier intro. 25.00
NOTE: *Kirby a-1-8p; c-1-7p.* *Kubert c-8.*

OMAC (See DCU Brave New World)
DC Comics: Sept, 2006 - No. 8, Apr, 2007 ($2.99, limited series)

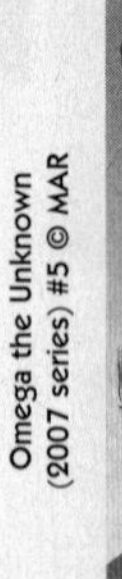

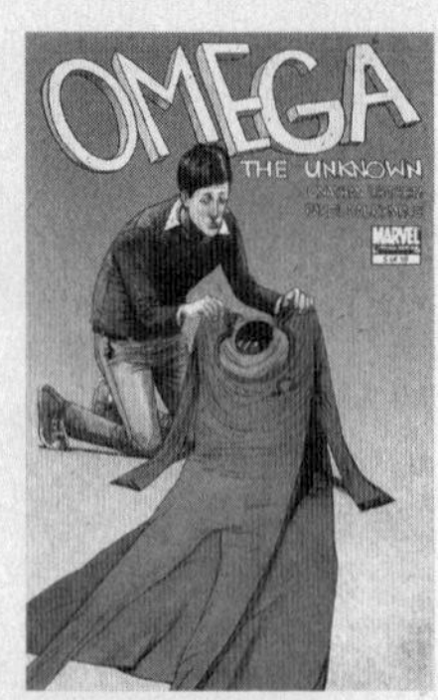

100 Bullets #86 © Azzarello & Risso

One Month to Live #3 © MAR

	GD 2.0	VG 4.0	FN 6.0	VF 8.0	VF/NM 9.0	NM- 9.2

1-8: 1-Bruce Jones-s/Renato Guedes-a. 1-3-Firestorm & Cyborg app. 8-Superman app. 3.00

OMAC: ONE MAN ARMY CORPS
DC Comics: 1991 - No. 4, 1991 ($3.95, B&W, mini-series, mature, 52 pgs.)

Book One - Four: John Byrne-c/a & scripts 4.00

OMAC PROJECT, THE
DC Comics: June, 2005 - No. 6, Nov, 2005 ($2.50, limited series)

1-6-Prelude to Infinite Crisis x-over; Rucka-s/Saiz-a 3.00
...: Infinite Crisis Special 1 (5/06, $4.99) Rucka-s/Saiz-a; follows destruction of satellite 5.00
TPB (2005, $14.99) r/#1-6, Countdown to Infinite Crisis, Wonder Woman #219 15.00

O'MALLEY AND THE ALLEY CATS
Gold Key: April, 1971 - No. 9, Jan, 1974 (Disney)

1 3 6 9 16 23 30
2-9 2 4 6 9 13 16

OMEGA ELITE
Blackthorne Publishing: 1987 ($1.25)

1-Starlin-c 3.00

OMEGA FLIGHT
Marvel Comics: Jun, 2007 - No. 5, Oct, 2007 ($2.99, limited series)

1-Oeming-s/Kolins-a; Wrecking Crew app. 4.00
1-Second printing with Sasquatch variant-c 3.00
2-5: 5-Beta Ray Bill app. 3.00
...: Alpha to Omega TPB ('07, $13.99) r/#1-5, USAgent story/Civil War: Choosing Sides 14.00

OMEGA MEN, THE (See Green Lantern #141)
DC Comics: Dec, 1982 - No. 38, May, 1986 ($1.00/$1.25/$1.50; Baxter paper)

1,20: 20-2nd full Lobo story 4.00
2,4-9,11-19,21-25,28-30,32,33,36,38: 2-Origin Broot. 5,9-2nd & 3rd app. Lobo (cameo, 2 pgs. each). 7-Origin The Citadel. 19-Lobo cameo. 30-Intro new Primus 3.00
3-1st app. Lobo (5 pgs.)(6/83); Lobo-c 1 2 3 4 5 7
10-1st full Lobo story 5.00
26,27,31,34,35: 26,27-Alan Moore scripts. 31-Crisis x-over. 34,35-Teen Titans x-over 4.00
37-1st solo Lobo story (8 pg. back-up by Giffen) 4.00
Annual 1(11/84, 52 pgs.), 2(11/85) 4.00
NOTE: *Giffen* c/a-1-6p. *Morrow* a-24r. *Nino* c/a-16, 21; a-Annual 1i.

OMEGA MEN, THE
DC Comics: Dec, 2006 - No. 6, May, 2007 ($2.99, limited series)

1-6: 1-Superman, Wonder Girl, Green Lantern app.; Flint-a/Gabrych-s 3.00

OMEGA THE UNKNOWN
Marvel Comics Group: March, 1976 - No. 10, Oct, 1977

1-1st app. Omega 2 4 6 11 16 20
2,3-(Regular 25¢ editions). 2-Hulk-c/story. 3-Electro-c/story.
2 3 4 6 8 10
2,3-(30¢-c variants, limited distribution) 3 6 9 18 27 35
4-10: 8-1st brief app. 2nd Foolkiller (Greg Salinger), 1 panel only. 9,10-(Reg. 30¢ editions). 9-1st full app. 2nd Foolkiller 1 2 3 5 6 8
9,10-(35¢-c variants, limited distribution) 4 8 12 22 34 45
... Classic TPB (2005, $29.99) r/#1-10 30.00
NOTE: *Kane* c(p)-3, 5, 8, 9. *Mooney* a-1-3, 4p, 5, 6p, 7, 8i, 9, 10.

OMEGA: THE UNKNOWN
Marvel Comics: Dec, 2007 - No. 10, Sept, 2008 ($2.99, limited series)

1-10-Jonathan Lethem-s/Farel Dalrymple-a 3.00

OMEN
Northstar Publishing: 1989 - No. 3, 1989 ($2.00, B&W, mature)

1-Tim Vigil-c/a in all 1 2 3 5 7 9
1, (2nd printing) 3.00
2,3 6.00

OMEN, THE
Chaos! Comics: May, 1998 - No. 5, Sept, 1998 ($2.95, limited series)

1-5: 1-Six covers, ...: Vexed (10/98, $2.95) Chaos! characters appear 3.00

OMNI MEN
Blackthorne Publishing: 1987 - No. 3, 1987 ($1.25)

1-3 3.00
Graphic Novel (1989, $3.50) 4.00

ONE, THE
Marvel Comics (Epic Comics): July, 1985 - No. 6, Feb, 1986 (Limited series, mature)

1-6: Post nuclear holocaust super-hero. 2-Intro The Other 3.00

ONE-ARM SWORDSMAN, THE
Victory Prod./Lueng's Publ. #4 on: 1987 - No. 12, 1990 ($2.75/$1.80, 52 pgs.)

1-3 ($2.75) 4.00
4-12: 4-6-$1.80-c. 7-12-$2.00-c 4.00

ONE HUNDRED AND ONE DALMATIANS (Disney, see Cartoon Tales, Movie Comics, and Walt Disney Showcase #9, 51)
Dell Publishing Co.: No. 1183, Mar, 1961

Four Color 1183-Movie 10 20 30 67 116 165

101 DALMATIONS (Movie)
Disney Comics: 1991 (52 pgs., graphic novel)

nn-($4.95, direct sales)-r/movie adaptation & more 5.00
1-($2.95, newsstand edition) 3.00

101 WAYS TO END THE CLONE SAGA (See Spider-Man)
Marvel Comics: Jan, 1997 ($2.50, one-shot)

1 3.00

100 BULLETS
DC Comics (Vertigo): Aug, 1999 - No. 100, Jun, 2009 ($2.50/$2.75/$2.99)

1-Azzarello-s/Risso-a/Dave Johnson-c 4.00
2-5 3.00
6-49,51-61: 26-Series summary; art by various. 45-Preview of Losers 3.00
50-($3.50) History of the Trust 4.00
62-71: 62-Begin $2.75-c. 64-Preview of Loveless 3.00
72-99: 72-Begin $2.99-c 3.00
100-($4.99) Final issue 5.00
...#1/Crime Line Sampler Flip-Book (9/09, $1.00) r/#1 with previews of upcoming GNs 3.00
...: A Foregone Tomorrow TPB (2002, $17.95) r/#20-30 18.00
...: Decayed TPB (2006, $14.99) r/#68-75; Darwyn Cooke intro. 15.00
...: First Shot, Last Call TPB (2000, $9.95) r/#1-5, Vertigo Winter's Edge #3 10.00
...: Hang Up on the Hang Low TPB (2001, $9.95) r/#15-19; Jim Lee intro. 10.00
...: Once Upon a Crime TPB (2007, $12.99) r/#76-83 13.00
...: Samurai TPB (2003, $12.95) r/#43-49 13.00
...: Six Feet Under the Gun TPB (2003, $12.95) r/#37-42 13.00
...: Split Second Chance TPB (2001, $14.95) r/#6-14 15.00
...: Strychnine Lives TPB (2006, $14.99) r/#59-67; Manuel Ramos intro. 15.00
...: The Counterfifth Detective TPB (2003, $12.95) r/#31-36 13.00
...: The Hard Way TPB (2005, $14.99) r/#50-58 15.00
...: Wilt TPB (2009, $19.99) r/#89-100; Azzarello intro. 20.00

100 GREATEST MARVELS OF ALL TIME
Marvel Comics: Dec, 2001 ($7.50/$3.50, limited series)

1-5-Reprints top #6-#25 stories voted by poll for Marvel's 40th ann. 7.50
6-($3.50) (#5 on-c) Reprints X-Men (2nd series) #1 3.50
7-($3.50) (#4 on-c) Reprints Giant-Size X-Men #1 3.50
8-($3.50) (#3 on-c) Reprints (Uncanny) X-Men #137 (Death of Jean Grey) 3.50
9-($3.50) (#2 on-c) Reprints Fantastic Four #1 3.50
10-($3.50) (#1 on-c) Reprints Amazing Fantasy #15 (1st app. Spider-Man) 3.50

100 PAGES OF COMICS
Dell Publishing Co.: 1937 (Stiff covers, square binding)

101(Found on back cover)-Alley Oop, Wash Tubbs, Capt. Easy, Og Son of Fire, Apple Mary, Tom Mix, Dan Dunn, Tailspin Tommy, Doctor Doom
147 294 441 934 1605 2275

100 PAGE SUPER SPECTACULAR (See DC 100 Page Super Spectacular)

100%
DC Comics (Vertigo): Aug, 2002 - No. 5, July, 2003 ($5.95, B&W, limited series)

1-5-Paul Pope-s/a 6.00
HC (2009, $39.99, dustjacket) r/#1-5; sketch pages and background info 40.00
TPB (2005, $24.99) r/#1-5; sketch pages and background info 25.00
TPB (2009, $29.99) r/#1-5; sketch pages and background info 30.00

100% TRUE?
DC Comics (Paradox Press): Summer 1996 - No. 2 ($4.95, B&W)

1,2-Reprints stories from various Paradox Press books. 5.00

$1,000,000 DUCK (See Walt Disney Showcase #5)

ONE MILLION YEARS AGO (Tor #2 on)
St. John Publishing Co.: Sept, 1953

1-Origin & 1st app. Tor; Kubert-c/a; Kubert photo inside front cover
18 36 54 105 165 225

ONE MONTH TO LIVE ("Heroic Age: ..." in indicia)
Marvel Comics: Nov, 2010 - No. 5, Nov, 2010 ($2.99, weekly limited series)

1-5-Remender-s; Spider-Man and the Fantastic Four app. 3.00

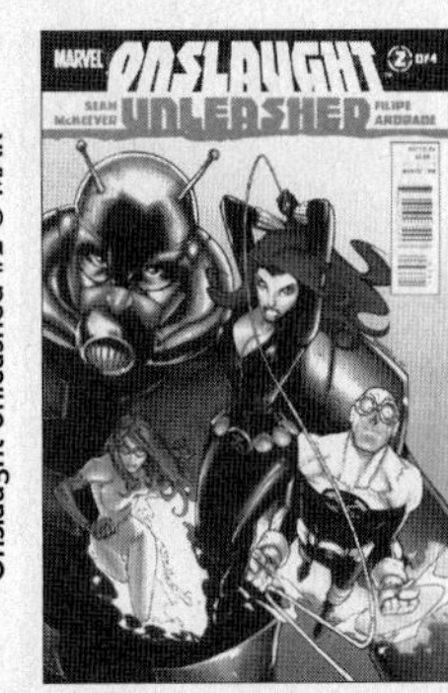

Onslaught Unleashed #2 © MAR

Operation Peril #2 © ACG

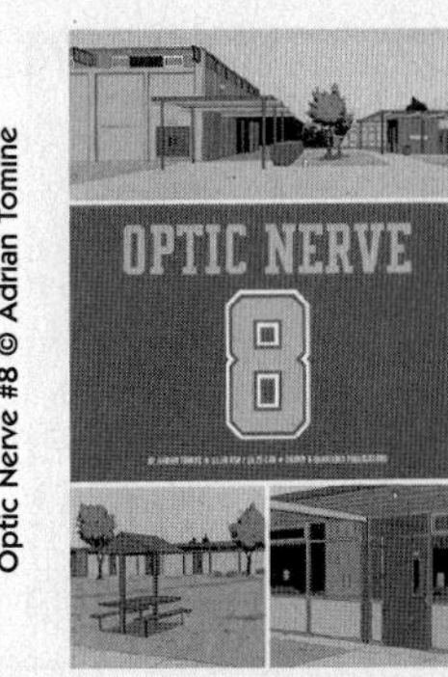

Optic Nerve #8 © Adrian Tomine

GD 2.0 | VG 4.0 | FN 6.0 | VF 8.0 | VF/NM 9.0 | NM- 9.2

ONE PLUS ONE
Oni Press: Sept, 2002 - No. 5, March, 2003 ($2.95, B&W, limited series)
1-5-Shaffer-s/Krall-a 3.00
TPB (9/03, $14.95, digest-size) r/#1-5 & story from Oni Press Color Special 2002 15.00

ONE SHOT (See Four Color...)

1001 HOURS OF FUN
Dell Publishing Co.: No. 13, 1943
Large Feature Comic 13 (nn)-Puzzles & games; by A.W. Nugent. This book was bound as #13 w/Large Feature Comics in publisher's files 28 56 84 165 270 375

ONE TRICK RIP OFF, THE (See Dark Horse Presents)

ONI (Adaption of video game)
Dark Horse Comics: Feb, 2001 - No. 3, Apr, 2001 ($2.99, limited series)
1-3-Sunny Lee-a(p) 3.00

ONI DOUBLE FEATURE (See Clerks: The Comic Book and Jay & Silent Bob)
Oni Press: Jan, 1998 - No. 13, Sept, 1999 ($2.95, B&W)
1-Jay & Silent Bob; Kevin Smith-s/Matt Wagner-a 1 3 4 6 8 10
1-2nd printing 3.00
2-11,13: 2,3-Paul Pope-s/a. 3,4-Nixey-s/a. 4,5-Sienkewicz-s/a. 6,7-Gaiman-s. 9-Bagge-c. 13-All Paul Dini-s; Jingle Belle 3.00
12-Jay & Silent Bob as Bluntman & Chronic; Smith-s/Allred-a 5.00

ONI PRESS COLOR SPECIAL
Oni Press: Jun, 2001; Jul, 2002 ($5.95, annual)
...2001-Oeming "Who Killed Madman?" cover; stories & art by various 6.00
...2002-Allred wraparound-c; stories & art by various 6.00

ONSLAUGHT: EPILOGUE
Marvel Comics: Feb, 1997 ($2.95, one-shot)
1-Hama-s/Green-a; Xavier-c; Bastion-app. 3.00

ONSLAUGHT: MARVEL
Marvel Comics: Oct, 1996 ($3.95, one-shot)
1-Conclusion to Onslaught x-over; wraparound-c 1 2 3 4 5 7

ONSLAUGHT REBORN
Marvel Comics: Jan, 2007 - No. 5, Feb, 2008 ($2.99, limited series)
1-5-Loeb-s/Liefeld-a; female Bucky app. 2-Variant-c by Joe Madureira. 3-McGuiness var-c. 4-Campbell var-c. 5-Bianchi var-c; female Bucky goes to regular Marvel Universe 3.00
1-Variant-c by Michael Turner 4.00
HC (2008, $19.99) r/#1-5; sketch pages; foreword by Liefeld 20.00

ONSLAUGHT UNLEASHED
Marvel Comics: Apr, 2011 - No. 4 ($3.99, limited series)
1-3-McKeever-s/Andrade-a/Ramos-c; Secret Avengers & Young Allies app. 4.00

ONSLAUGHT: X-MEN
Marvel Comics: Aug, 1996 ($3.95, one-shot)
1-Waid & Lobdell script; Fantastic Four & Avengers app.; Xavier as Onslaught 5.00
1-Variant-c 2 4 6 8 10 12

ON STAGE
Dell Publishing Co.: No. 1336, Apr-June, 1962
Four Color 1336-Not by Leonard Starr 5 10 15 30 48 65

ON THE DOUBLE (Movie)
Dell Publishing Co.: No. 1232, Sept-Nov, 1961
Four Color 1232 5 10 15 30 48 65

ON THE ROAD TO PERDITION (Movie)
DC Comics (Paradox Press): 2003 - Book 3, 2004 ($7.95, 8"x5 1/2", B&W, limited series)
...: Oasis, Book 1-Max Allan Collins-s/José Luis García-López-a/David Beck-c 8.00
...: Sanctuary, Book 2-Max Allan Collins-s/Steve Lieber-a/José Luis García-López-c 8.00
...: Detour, Book 3-Max Allan Collins-s/José Luis García-López-a/Steve Lieber-c/a(i) 8.00
Road to Perdition 2: On the Road (2004, $14.95) r/series; Collins intro. 15.00

ON THE ROAD WITH ANDRAE CROUCH
Spire Christian Comics (Fleming H. Revell): 1973, 1974 (39¢)
nn-1973 Edition 2 4 6 10 14 18
nn-1974 Edition 2 4 6 8 10 12

ON THE SCENE PRESENTS:...
Warren Publishing Co.: Oct, 1966 - No. 2, 1967 (B&W magazine, two #1 issues)
#1 "Super Heroes" (68 pgs.) Batman 1966 movie photo-c/s; has articles/photos/comic art from serials on Superman, Flash Gordon, Capt. America, Capt. Marvel and The Phantom 5 10 15 30 48 65
#1 "Freak Out, USA" (Fall/1966, 60 pgs.) (lower print run) articles on musicians like Zappa, Jefferson Airplane, Supremes 5 10 15 32 51 70
#2 "Freak Out, USA" (2/67, 52 pgs.) Beatles, Country Joe, Doors/Jim Morrison, Bee Gees 5 10 15 32 51 70

ON THE SPOT (Pretty Boy Floyd...)
Fawcett Publications: Fall, 1948
nn-Pretty Boy Floyd photo on-c; bondage-c 34 68 102 199 325 450

ONYX OVERLORD
Marvel Comics (Epic): Oct, 1992 - No. 4, Jan, 1993 ($2.75, mini-series)
1-4: Moebius scripts 3.00

OPEN SPACE
Marvel Comics: Mid-Dec, 1989 - No. 4, Aug, 1990 ($4.95, bi-monthly, 68 pgs.)
1-4: 1-Bill Wray-a; Freas-c 5.00
0-(1999) Wizard supplement; unpubl. early Alex Ross-a; new Ross-c 3.00

OPERATION BIKINI (See Movie Classics)

OPERATION BUCHAREST (See The Crusaders)

OPERATION CROSSBOW (See Movie Classics)

OPERATION: KNIGHTSTRIKE (See Knightstrike)
Image Comics (Extreme Studios): May, 1995 - No.3, July, 1995 ($2.50)
1-3 3.00

OPERATION PERIL
American Comics Group (Michel Publ.): Oct-Nov, 1950 - No. 16, Apr-May, 1953 (#1-5: 52 pgs.)
1-Time Travelers, Danny Danger (by Leonard Starr) & Typhoon Tyler (by Ogden Whitney) begin 40 80 120 242 401 560
2-War-c 23 46 69 136 223 310
3-War-c; horror story 21 42 63 126 206 285
4,5-Sci/fi-c/story 23 46 69 136 223 310
6-10: 6,8,9,10-Sci/fi-c. 6-Dinosaur-c. 7-Sabretooth-c 21 42 63 122 199 275
11,12-War-c; last Time Travelers 14 28 42 80 115 150
13-16: All war format 10 20 30 56 76 95
NOTE: *Starr a-2, 5. Whitney a-1, 2, 5-10, 12; c-1, 3, 5, 8, 9.*

OPERATION: STORMBREAKER
Acclaim Comics (Valiant Heroes): Aug, 1997 ($3.95, one-shot)
1-Waid/Augustyn-s, Braithwaite-a 4.00

OPTIC NERVE
Drawn and Quarterly: Apr, 1995 - Present ($2.95-$3.95, bi-annual)
1-7: Adrian Tomine-c/a/scripts in all 3.00
8-11: 8-($3.50). 9-11-($3.95) 4.00
32 Stories-($9.95, trade paperback)-r/Optic Nerve mini-comics 10.00
32 Stories-($29.95, hardcover)-r/Optic Nerve mini-comics; signed & numbered 30.00

ORACLE: THE CURE
DC Comics: May, 2009 - No. 3, Jul, 2009 ($2.99, limited series)
1-3-Guillem March-c; Calculator app. 3.00
TPB (2010, $17.99) r/#1-3 and Birds of Prey #126,127 18.00

ORAL ROBERTS' TRUE STORIES (Junior Partners #120 on)
TelePix Publ. (Oral Roberts' Evangelistic Assoc./Healing Waters): 1956 (no month) - No. 119, 7/59 (15¢)(No. 102: 25¢)
V1#1(1956)-(Not code approved)- "The Miracle Touch" 19 38 57 109 172 235
102-(Only issue approved by code, 10/56) "Now I See" 13 26 39 74 105 135
103-119: 115-(114 on inside) 10 20 30 54 72 90
NOTE: *Also see Happiness & Healing For You.*

ORANGE BIRD, THE
Walt Disney Educational Media Co.: No date (1980) (36 pgs.; in color; slick cover)
nn-Included with educational kit on foods, ...in Nutrition Adventures nn (1980) ...and the Nutrition Know-How Revue nn (1983) 3.00

ORB (Magazine)
Orb Publishing: 1974 - No. 6, Mar/Apr 1976 (B&W/color)
1-1st app. Northern Light & Kadaver, both series begin 5 10 15 32 51 70
2,3 (72 pgs.) 3 6 9 16 23 30
4-6 (60 pgs.): 4,5-origin Northern Light 2 4 6 10 14 18
NOTE: ***Allison** a-1-3. **Gene Day** a-1-6. **P. Hsu** a-4-6. **Steacy** s/a-3,4.*

ORBIT
Eclipse Books: 1990 - No. 3, 1990 ($4.95, 52 pgs., squarebound)

The Order #1 © MAR

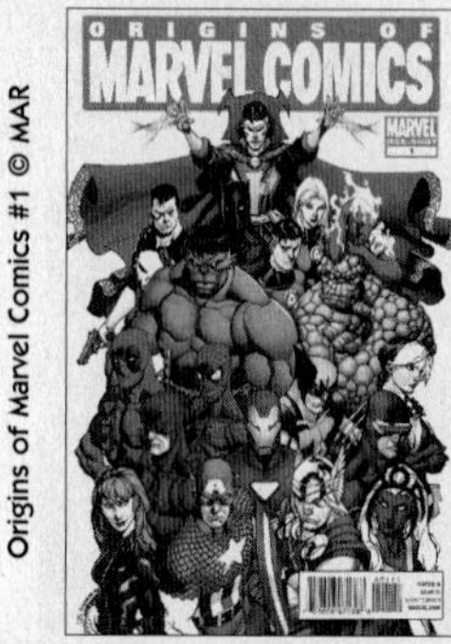

Origins of Marvel Comics #1 © MAR

Osborn #1 © MAR

	GD 2.0	VG 4.0	FN 6.0	VF 8.0	VF/NM 9.0	NM- 9.2

1-3: Reprints from Isaac Asimov's Science Fiction Magazine; 1-Dave Stevens-c, Bolton-a. 3-Bolton-c/a, Yeates-a 5.00

ORBITER
DC Comics (Vertigo): 2003 ($24.95, hardcover with dust jacket)

HC-Warren Ellis-s/Colleen Doran-a 25.00
SC-(2004, $17.95) Warren Ellis-s/Colleen Doran-a 18.00

ORDER, THE (cont'd from Defenders V2#12)
Marvel Comics: Apr, 2002 - No. 6, Sept, 2002 ($2.25, limited series)

1-6: 1-Haley-a/Duffy & Busiek-s. 3-Avengers-c/app. 4-Jurgens-a 3.00

ORDER, THE (The Initiative following Civil War)
Marvel Comics: Sept, 2007 - No. 10, Jun, 2008 ($2.99)

1-10-California's Initiative team; Fraction-s/Kitson-a/c 3.00
... Vol. 1: The Next Right Thing TPB (2008, $14.99) r/#1-7 15.00

ORIENTAL HEROES
Jademan Comics: Aug, 1988 - No. 55, Feb, 1993 ($1.50/$1.95, 68 pgs.)

1,55 5.00
2-54 4.00

ORIGINAL ADVENTURES OF CHOLLY & FLYTRAP, THE
Image Comics: Feb, 2006 - No. 2, June, 2006 ($5.99, limited series)

1,2-Arthur Suydam-s/a; interview with Suydam and art pages 6.00

ORIGINAL ASTRO BOY, THE
Now Comics: Sept, 1987 - No. 20, Jun, 1989 ($1.50/$1.75)

1-20-All have Ken Steacy painted-c/a 3.00

ORIGINAL BLACK CAT, THE
Recollections: Oct. 6, 1988 - No. 9, 1992 ($2.00, limited series)

1-9: Elias-r; 1-Bondage-c. 2-Murphy Anderson-c 4.00

ORIGINAL DICK TRACY, THE
Gladstone Publishing: Sept, 1990 - No. 5, 1991 ($1.95, bi-monthly, 68pgs.)

1-5: 1-Vs. Pruneface. 2-& the Evil influence; begin $2.00-c 4.00
NOTE: *#1 reprints strips 7/16/43 - 9/30/43. #2 reprints strips 12/1/46 - 2/2/47. #3 reprints 8/31/46 - 11/14/46. #4 reprints 9/17/45 - 12/23/45. #5 reprints 6/10/46 - 8/28/46.*

ORIGINAL DOCTOR SOLAR, MAN OF THE ATOM, THE
Valiant: Apr, 1995 ($2.95, one-shot)

1-Reprints Doctor Solar, Man of the Atom #1,5; Bob Fugitani-r; Paul Smith-c; afterword by Seaborn Adamson 4.00

ORIGINAL E-MAN AND MICHAEL MAUSER, THE
First Comics: Oct, 1985 - No. 7, April, 1986 ($1.75/$2.00, Baxter paper)

1-6: 1-Has r-/Charlton's E-Man, Vengeance Squad. 2-Shows #4 in indicia by mistake 3.00
7-($2.00, 44 pgs.)-Staton-a 4.00

ORIGINAL GHOST RIDER, THE
Marvel Comics: July, 1992 - No. 20, Feb, 1994 ($1.75)

1-20: 1-7-r/Marvel Spotlight #5-11 by Ploog w/new-c. 3-New Phantom Rider (former Night Rider) back-ups begin by Ayers. 4-Quesada-c(p). 8-Ploog-c. 8,9-r/Ghost Rider #1,2. 10-r/Marvel Spotlight #12. 11-18,20-r/Ghost Rider #3-12. 19-r/Marvel Two-in-One #8 3.00

ORIGINAL GHOST RIDER RIDES AGAIN, THE
Marvel Comics: July, 1991 - No. 7, Jan, 1992, ($1.50, limited series, 52 pgs.)

1-7: 1-r/Ghost Rider #68(origin),69 w/covers. 2-7: R/ G.R. #70-81 w/covers 4.00

ORIGINAL MAGNUS ROBOT FIGHTER, THE
Valiant: Apr, 1995 ($2.95, one-shot)

1-Reprints Magnus, Robot Fighter 4000 #2; Russ Manning-r; Rick Leonardi-c; afterword by Seaborn Adamson 4.00

ORIGINAL NEXUS GRAPHIC NOVEL (See First Comics Graphic Novel #19)

ORIGINALS, THE
DC Comics (Vertigo): 2004 ($24.95/$17.99, B&W graphic novel)

HC (2004, $24.95) Dave Gibbons-s/a 25.00
SC (2005, $17.99) 18.00

ORIGINAL SHIELD, THE
Archie Enterprises, Inc.: Apr, 1984 - No. 4, Oct, 1984

1-4: 1,2-Origin Shield; Ayers p-1-4, Nebres c-1,2 4.00

ORIGINAL SWAMP THING SAGA, THE (See DC Special Series #2, 14, 17, 20)

ORIGINAL TUROK, SON OF STONE, THE
Valiant: Apr, 1995 - No. 2, May, 1995 ($2.95, limited series)

1,2: 1-Reprints Turok, Son of Stone #24,25,42; Alberto Gioletti-r; Rags Morales-c; afterword by Seaborn Adamson. 2-Reprints Turok, Son of Stone #24,33; Gioletti-r; McKone-c 4.00

ORIGIN OF GALACTUS (See Fantastic Four #48-50)
Marvel Comics: Feb, 1996 ($2.50, one-shot)

1-Lee & Kirby reprints w/pin-ups 4.00

ORIGIN OF THE DEFIANT UNIVERSE, THE
Defiant Comics: Feb, 1994 ($1.50, 20 pgs., one-shot)

1-David Lapham, Adam Pollina & Alan Weiss-a; Weiss-c 5.00
NOTE: *The comic was originally published as Defiant Genesis and was distributed at the 1994 Philadelphia ComicCon.*

ORIGINS OF MARVEL COMICS (Also see Fireside Book Series)
Marvel Comics: July, 2010 ($3.99, one-shot)

1-Single page origins of prominent Marvel characters; text and art by various 4.00
...: X-Men (11/10, $3.99) single page origins of X-Men and other mutants; s/a-various 4.00

ORION (Manga)
Dark Horse Comics: Sept, 1992 - No. 6, July, 1993 ($2.95/$3.95, B&W, bimonthly, lim. series)

1-6:1,2,6-Squarebound): 1-Masamune Shirow-c/a/s in all 4.00

ORION (See New Gods)
DC Comics: June, 2000 - No. 25, June, 2002 ($2.50)

1-14-Simonson-s/a. 3-Back-up story w/Miller-a. 4-Gibbons-a back-up. 7-Chaykin back-up. 8-Loeb/Liefeld back-up. 10-A. Adams back-up-a 12-Jim Lee back-up-a. 13-JLA-c/app.; Byrne-a 3.00
15-($3.95) Black Racer app.; back-up story w/J.P. Leon-a 4.00
16-24-Simonson-s/a: 19-Joker: Last Laugh x-over 3.00
25-($3.95) Last issue; Mister Miracle-c/app. 4.00
The Gates of Apocalypse (2001, $12.95, TPB) r/#1-5 & various short-s 13.00

ORORO: BEFORE THE STORM (Storm from X-Men)
Marvel Comics: Aug, 2005 - No. 4, Nov, 2005 ($2.99, limited series)

1-4-Barberi-a/Sumerak-s; young Storm in Egypt 3.00
... Digest (2006, $6.99) r/#1-4 7.00

OSBORN (Green Goblin)
Marvel Comics: Jan, 2011 - No. 5 ($3.99, limited series)

1-4-Deconnick-s/Rios-a/Oliver-c 4.00

OSBORN JOURNALS (See Spider-Man titles)
Marvel Comics: Feb, 1997 ($2.95, one-shot)

1-Hotz-c/a 3.00

OSCAR COMICS (Formerly Funny Tunes; Awful...#11 & 12) (Also see Cindy Comics)
Marvel Comics: No. 24, Spring, 1947 - No. 10, Apr, 1949; No. 13, Oct, 1949

	GD 2.0	VG 4.0	FN 6.0	VF 8.0	VF/NM 9.0	NM- 9.2
24(#1, Spring, 1947)	18	36	54	107	169	230
25(#2, Sum, 1947)-Wolverton-a plus Kurtzman's "Hey Look"	20	40	60	114	182	250
26(#3)-Same as regular #3 except #26 was printed over in black ink with #3 appearing on-c below the over print	14	28	42	76	108	140
3-9,13: 8-Margie app.	14	28	42	76	108	140
10-Kurtzman's "Hey Look"	14	28	42	82	121	160

OSWALD THE RABBIT (Also see New Fun Comics #1)
Dell Publishing Co.: No. 21, 1943 - No. 1268, 12-2/61-62 (Walter Lantz)

	GD 2.0	VG 4.0	FN 6.0	VF 8.0	VF/NM 9.0	NM- 9.2
Four Color 21(1943)	40	80	120	320	643	965
Four Color 39(1943)	27	54	81	197	399	600
Four Color 67(1944)	16	32	48	111	226	340
Four Color 102(1946)-Kelly-a, 1 pg.	13	26	39	94	185	275
Four Color 143,183	9	18	27	63	107	150
Four Color 225,273	7	14	21	45	73	100
Four Color 315,388	6	12	18	39	62	85
Four Color 458,507,549,593	5	10	15	32	51	70
Four Color 623,697,792,894,979,1268	4	8	12	28	44	60

OSWALD THE RABBIT (See The Funnies, March of Comics #7, 38, 53, 67, 81, 95, 111, 126, 141, 156, 171, 186, New Funnies & Super Book #8, 20)

OTHER SIDE, THE
DC Comics (Vertigo): Dec, 2006 - No. 5, Apr, 2007 ($2.99, limited series)

1-5-Soldiers from both sides of the Vietnam War; Aaron-s/Stewart-a/c 3.00
TPB (2007, $12.99) r/#1-5; sketch pages, Stewart's travelogue to Saigon 13.00

OTHERWORLD
DC Comics (Vertigo): May, 2005 - No. 7, Nov, 2005 ($2.99)

1-7-Phil Jimenez-s/a(p) 3.00
...: Book One TPB (2006, $19.99) r/#1-7; cover gallery 20.00

OUR ARMY AT WAR (Becomes Sgt. Rock #302 on; also see Army At War)

Our Army at War #15 © DC

Our Army at War #158 © DC

Our Fighting Forces #3 © DC

National Periodical Publications: Aug, 1952 - No. 301, Feb, 1977

	GD 2.0	VG 4.0	FN 6.0	VF 8.0	VF/NM 9.0	NM- 9.2
1	185	370	555	1619	3310	5000
2	81	162	243	689	1395	2100
3,4: 4-Krigstein-a	60	120	180	510	1030	1550
5-7	48	96	144	400	813	1225
8-11,14-Krigstein-a	47	94	141	376	763	1150
12,15-20	41	82	123	324	650	975
13-Krigstein-c/a; flag-c	48	96	144	392	796	1200
21-31: Last precode (2/55)	28	56	84	215	433	650
32-40	25	50	75	180	360	540
41-60: 51-1st S.A. issue	22	44	66	159	317	475
61-70: 61-(8/57) Pre-Sgt. Rock Easy Co.-c/s. 67-Minor Sgt. Rock prototype	20	40	60	140	283	425
71-80	17	34	51	122	249	375
81-(4/59)-Sgt. Rocky of Easy Co. app. by Andru & Esposito-a/ Haney-s; (the last Sgt. Rock prototype)	267	534	801	2336	4768	7200
82-1st Sgt. Rock app., in name only, in Easy Co. story (6 panels) by Kanigher & Drucker	71	142	213	604	1227	1850
83-(6/59)-1st true Sgt. Rock app. in "The Rock and the Wall" by Kubert & Kanigher; (most similar to prototype in G.I. Combat #68)	230	460	690	2013	4107	6200
84-Kubert-c	45	90	135	360	730	1100
85-Origin & 1st app. Ice Cream Soldier	52	104	156	442	896	1350
86,87-Early Sgt. Rock; Kubert-a	42	84	126	336	681	1025
88-1st Sgt. Rock-c; Kubert-c/a	56	112	168	476	963	1450
89	38	76	114	304	602	900
90-Kubert-c/a; How Rock got his stripes	48	96	144	408	829	1250
91-All-Sgt. Rock issue; Grandenetti-c/Kubert-a	96	192	288	816	1658	2500
92,94,96-99: 97-Regular Kubert-c begin	27	54	81	197	399	600
93-1st Zack Nolan	28	56	84	204	415	625
95,100: 95-1st app. Bulldozer	28	56	84	209	422	635
101,105,108,113,114: 101-1st app. Buster. 105-1st app. Junior. 113-1st app. Wildman & Jackie Johnson	22	44	66	159	317	475
102-104,106,107,109,110,114,116-120: 104-Nurse Jane-c/s. 109-Pre Easy Co. Sgt. Rock-s. 118-Sunny injured	20	40	60	140	283	425
111-1st app. Wee Willie & Sunny	27	54	81	193	389	585
112-Classic Easy Co. roster-c	29	58	87	223	449	675
115-Rock revealed as orphan; 1st x-over Mlle. Marie. 1st Sgt. Rock's battle family	26	52	78	190	383	575
121-125,129-139,141-150: 138-1st Sparrow. 141-1st Shaker. 147,148-Rock becomes a General	14	28	42	99	200	300
126-1st app. Canary; grey tone-c	18	36	54	131	266	400
127-2nd all-Sgt. Rock issue; 1st app. Little Sure Shot	21	42	63	150	300	450
128-Training & origin Sgt. Rock; 1st Sgt. Krupp	37	74	111	286	568	850
140-3rd all-Sgt. Rock issue	16	32	48	114	232	350
151-Intro. Enemy Ace by Kubert (2/65), black-c	43	86	129	344	697	1050
152-4th all-Sgt. Rock issue	15	30	45	105	216	325
153-2nd app. Enemy Ace (4/65)	22	44	66	159	317	475
154,156,157,159-161,165-167: 157-2 pg. centerfold spread pin-up as part of story. 159-1st Nurse Wendy Winston-c/s. 165-2nd Iron Major	11	22	33	75	138	200
155-3rd app. Enemy Ace (6/65)(see Showcase)	15	30	45	106	216	325
158-Origin & 1st app. Iron Major(9/65), formerly Iron Captain	12	24	36	86	161	235
162,163-Viking Prince x-over in Sgt. Rock	12	24	36	82	154	225
164-Giant G-19	16	32	48	114	232	350
168-1st Unknown Soldier app.; referenced in Star-Spangled War Stories #157; (Sgt. Rock x-over) (6/66)	16	32	48	111	226	340
169,170	9	18	27	65	113	160
171-176,178-181: 171-1st Mad Emperor	9	18	27	60	100	140
177-(80 pg. Giant G-32)	11	22	33	75	138	200
182,183,186-Neal Adams-a. 186-Origin retold	10	20	30	67	116	165
184-Wee Willie dies	10	20	30	71	128	185
185,187,188,193-195,197-199	7	14	21	49	80	110
189,191,192,196: 189-Intro. The Teen-age Underground Fighters of Unit 3. 196-Hitler cameo	7	14	21	50	83	115
190-(80 pg. Giant G-44)	9	18	27	63	107	150
200-12 pg. Rock story told in verse; Evans-a	8	16	24	52	86	120
201,202,204-207: 201-Krigstein-r/#14. 204,205-All reprints; no Sgt. Rock. 207-Last 12¢ cover	6	12	18	39	62	85
203-(80 pg. Giant G-56)-All-r, Sgt. Rock story	8	16	24	56	93	130
208-215	4	8	12	28	44	60
216,229-(80 pg. Giants G-68, G-80): 216-Has G-58 on-c by mistake	7	14	21	47	76	105
217-219: 218-1st U.S.S. Stevens	4	8	12	26	41	55
220-Classic dinosaur/Sgt. Rock-c/s	5	10	15	30	48	65
221-228,230-234: 231-Intro/death Rock's brother. 234-Last 15¢ issue	4	8	12	22	34	45
235-239,241: 52 pg. Giants	4	8	12	28	44	60
240-Neal Adams-a; 52 pg. Giant	5	10	15	35	55	75
242-Also listed as DC 100 Page Super Spectacular #9	10	20	30	68	119	170
243-246: (All 52 pgs.) 244-No Adams-a	4	8	12	26	41	55
247-250,254-268,270: 247-Joan of Arc	3	6	9	16	22	28
251-253-Return of Iron Major	3	6	9	17	25	32
269,275-(100 pgs.)	5	10	15	35	55	75
271,272,274,276-279	3	6	9	14	19	24
273-Crucifixion-c	3	6	9	17	25	32
280-(68 pgs.)-200th app. Sgt. Rock; reprints Our Army at War #81,83	4	8	12	25	36	48
281-299,301: 295-Bicentennial cover	2	4	6	13	18	22
300-Sgt. Rock-s by Kubert (2/77)	3	6	9	16	22	28
... (War One-Shot) 1 (11/10, $3.99) Joe Kubert-c; Marts-s/Ibáñez-a						4.00

NOTE ***Alcala** a-251. **Drucker** a-27, 67, 68, 79, 82, 83, 96, 164, 177, 203, 212, 243r, 244, 269r, 275r, 280r. **Evans** a-165-175, 200, 266, 269, 270, 274, 276, 278, 280. **Glanzman** a-218, 220, 222, 223, 225, 227, 230-232, 238-241, 244, 247, 248, 256-259, 261, 265-267, 271, 282, 283, 298. **Grandenetti** c-91,120. **Grell** a-287. **Heath** a-50, 164, & most 176-281. **Kubert** a-38, 59, 67, 68 & most issues from 83-165, 171, 233, 236, 267, 275, 300; c-84, 280. **Maurer** a-233, 237, 239, 240, 45, 280, 284, 288, 290, 291, 295. **Severin** a-236, 252, 265, 267, 269r, 272. **Toth** a-235, 241, 254. **Wildey** a-283-285, 287p. **Wood** a-249.*

OUR FIGHTING FORCES
National Per. Publ./DC Comics: Oct-Nov, 1954 - No. 181, Sept-Oct, 1978

	GD 2.0	VG 4.0	FN 6.0	VF 8.0	VF/NM 9.0	NM- 9.2
1-Grandenetti-c/a	127	254	381	1080	2190	3300
2	48	96	144	392	796	1200
3-Kubert-c; last precode issue (3/55)	41	82	123	324	650	975
4,5	35	70	105	273	537	800
6-9: 7-1st S.A. issue	28	56	84	215	433	650
10-Wood-a	29	58	87	218	439	660
11-19	25	50	75	183	367	550
20-Grey tone-c (4/57)	33	66	99	254	502	750
21-30	20	40	60	144	290	435
31-40	18	36	54	125	255	385
41-Unknown Soldier tryout	21	42	63	153	307	460
42-44	16	32	48	117	239	360
45-1st app. of Gunner & Sarge, app. thru #94	50	100	150	425	863	1300
46	23	46	69	168	334	500
47	18	36	54	131	266	400
48,50	15	30	45	110	223	335
49-1st Pooch	22	44	66	159	317	475
51-Grey tone-c	21	42	63	150	300	450
52-64: 64-Last 10¢ issue	13	26	39	91	176	260
65-70	10	20	30	71	128	185
71-Classic grey tone-c; Pooch fires machine gun	14	28	42	99	200	300
72-80	9	18	27	61	103	145
81-90	7	14	21	49	80	110
91-98: 95-Devil-Dog begins, ends #98.	6	12	18	41	66	90
99-Capt. Hunter begins, ends #106	6	12	18	43	69	95
100	6	12	18	43	69	95
101-105,107-120: 116-Mlle. Marie app. 120-Last 12¢ issue	5	10	15	30	48	65
106-Hunters Hellcats begin	5	10	15	32	51	70
121,122: 121-Intro. Heller	4	8	12	26	41	55
123-The Losers (Capt. Storm, Gunner & Sarge, Johnny Cloud) begin	9	18	27	60	100	140
124-132: 132-Last 15¢ issue	4	8	12	22	34	45
133-137 (Giants). 134-Toth-a	4	8	12	26	41	55
138-145,147-150	3	6	9	16	22	28
146-Classic "Burma Sky" story; Toth-a/Goodwin-s	3	6	9	17	25	32
151-162-Kirby a(p)	3	6	9	18	27	35
163-180	2	4	6	13	18	22
181-Last issue	3	6	9	16	22	28
... (War One-Shot) 1 (11/10, $3.99) The Losers app.; B. Clay Moore-s/Chad Hardin-a						4.00

NOTE: ***N. Adams** c-147. **Drucker** a-28, 37, 39, 42-44, 49, 53, 133r. **Evans** a-149, 164-174, 177-181. **Glanzman** a-125-128, 132, 134, 138-141, 143, 144. **Heath** a-2, 16, 18, 28, 41, 44, 49, 114, 135-138r; c-51. **Kirby** a-151-162p; c-152-159. **Kubert** c/a in many issues. **Maurer** a-135. **Redondo** a-166. **Severin** a-123-130, 131i, 132-150.*

OUR FIGHTING MEN IN ACTION (See Men In Action)

OUR FLAG COMICS
Ace Magazines: Aug, 1941 - No. 5, April, 1942

	GD 2.0	VG 4.0	FN 6.0	VF 8.0	VF/NM 9.0	NM- 9.2
1-Captain Victory, The Unknown Soldier (intro.) & The Three Cheers begin	258	516	774	1651	2826	4000
2-Origin The Flag (patriotic hero); 1st app?	110	220	330	704	1202	1700

Our Gang Comics #2 © Loew's

Our Love Story #1 © MAR

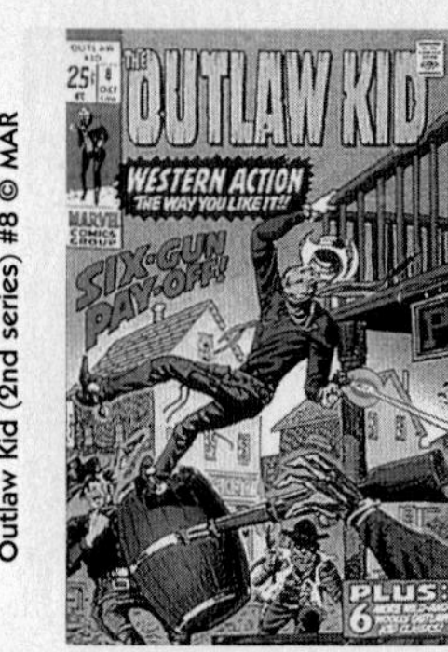

Outlaw Kid (2nd series) #8 © MAR

	GD 2.0	VG 4.0	FN 6.0	VF 8.0	VF/NM 9.0	NM- 9.2
3-5: 5-Intro & 1st app. Mr. Risk	84	168	252	538	919	1300

NOTE: ***Anderson** a-1, 4. **Mooney** a-1, 2; c-2.*

OUR GANG COMICS (With Tom & Jerry #39-59; becomes Tom & Jerry #60 on; based on film characters)
Dell Publishing Co.: Sept-Oct, 1942 - No. 59, June, 1949

	GD 2.0	VG 4.0	FN 6.0	VF 8.0	VF/NM 9.0	NM- 9.2
1-Our Gang & Barney Bear by Kelly, Tom & Jerry, Pete Smith, Flip & Dip, The Milky Way begin (all 1st app.)	65	130	195	553	1127	1700
2-Benny Burro begins (#2 by Kelly)	34	68	102	262	519	775
3-5	23	46	69	171	341	510
6-Bumbazine & Albert only app. by Kelly	31	62	93	242	476	710
7-No Kelly story	17	34	51	122	249	375
8-Benny Burro begins by Barks	40	80	120	320	635	950
9-Barks-a(2): Benny Burro & Happy Hound; no Kelly story	37	74	111	284	562	840
10-Benny Burro by Barks	27	54	81	197	399	600
11-1st Barney Bear & Benny Burro by Barks (5-6/44); Happy Hound by Barks	37	74	111	284	562	840
12-20	17	34	51	118	242	365
21-30: 30-X-Mas-c	13	26	39	90	173	255
31-36-Last Barks issue	10	20	30	73	134	195
37-40	8	16	24	52	86	120
41-50	7	14	21	45	73	100
51-57	6	12	18	41	66	90
58,59-No Kelly art or Our Gang stories	6	12	18	37	59	80
Our Gang Volume 1 (Fantagraphics Books, 2006, $12.95, TPB) r/Our Gang stories written and by Walt Kelly from #1-8; Leonard Maltin intro.; Jeff Smith-c						13.00
Our Gang Volume 2 (Fantagraphics Books, 2007, $12.95, TPB) r/Our Gang stories written and by Walt Kelly from #9-15; Steve Thompson intro.; Jeff Smith-c						13.00
Our Gang Volume 3 (Fantagraphics Books, 2008, $14.99, TPB) r/Our Gang stories written and by Walt Kelly from #16-23; Steve Thompson intro.; Jeff Smith-c						15.00

NOTE: ***Barks** art in part only. **Barks** did not write Barney Bear stories #30-34. (See March of Comics #3, 26). Early issues have photo back-c.*

OUR LADY OF FATIMA
Catechetical Guild Educational Society: 3/11/55 (15¢) (36 pgs.)

	GD 2.0	VG 4.0	FN 6.0	VF 8.0	VF/NM 9.0	NM- 9.2
395	6	12	18	28	34	40

OUR LOVE (True Secrets #3 on? or Romantic Affairs #3 on?)
Marvel Comics (SPC): Sept, 1949 - No. 2, Jan, 1950

	GD 2.0	VG 4.0	FN 6.0	VF 8.0	VF/NM 9.0	NM- 9.2
1-Photo-c	17	34	51	98	154	210
2-Photo-c	12	24	36	67	94	120

OUR LOVE STORY
Marvel Comics Group: Oct, 1969 - No. 38, Feb, 1976

	GD 2.0	VG 4.0	FN 6.0	VF 8.0	VF/NM 9.0	NM- 9.2
1	8	16	24	56	93	130
2-4,6-8,10,11	4	8	12	28	44	60
5-Steranko-a	11	22	33	75	138	200
9,12-Kirby-a	5	10	15	30	48	65
13-(10/71, 52 pgs.)	5	10	15	35	55	75
14-New story by Gary Fredrich & Tarpe' Mills	5	10	15	30	48	65
15-20,27:27-Colan/Everett-a(r?); Kirby/Colletta-r	3	6	9	21	32	42
21-26,28-37	3	6	9	19	29	38
38-Last issue	4	8	12	23	36	48

NOTE: ***J. Buscema** a-1-3, 5-7, 9, 13r, 16r, 19r(2), 21r, 22r(2), 23r, 34r, 35r; c-11, 13, 16, 22, 23, 24, 27, 35. **Colan** a-3-6, 21r(#6), 22r, 23r(#3), 24r(#4), 27; c-19. **Katz** a-17. **Maneely** a-13r. **Romita** a-13r; c-1, 2, 4-6. **Weiss** a-16, 17, 29r(#17).*

OUR MEN AT WAR
DC Comics: Aug/Sept 1952

nn - Ashcan comic, not distributed to newsstands, only for in-house use. Cover art is All Star Western #60 with interior being Detective Comics #181 (no known sales)

OUR MISS BROOKS
Dell Publishing Co.: No. 751, Nov, 1956

	GD 2.0	VG 4.0	FN 6.0	VF 8.0	VF/NM 9.0	NM- 9.2
Four Color 751-Photo-c	7	14	21	50	83	115

OUR SECRET (Exciting Love Stories)(Formerly My Secret)
Superior Comics Ltd.: No. 4, Nov, 1949 - No. 8, Jun, 1950

	GD 2.0	VG 4.0	FN 6.0	VF 8.0	VF/NM 9.0	NM- 9.2
4-Kamen-a; spanking scene	19	38	57	111	176	240
5,6,8	12	24	36	69	97	125
7-Contains 9 pg. story intended for unpublished Ellery Queen #5; lingerie panels	13	26	39	74	105	135

OUTBREED 999
Blackout Comics: May, 1994 - No. 6, 1994 ($2.95)

	GD 2.0	VG 4.0	FN 6.0	VF 8.0	VF/NM 9.0	NM- 9.2
1-6: 4-1st app. of Extreme Violet in 7 pg. backup story						3.00

OUTCAST, THE
Valiant: Dec, 1995 ($2.50, one-shot)

	GD 2.0	VG 4.0	FN 6.0	VF 8.0	VF/NM 9.0	NM- 9.2
1-Breyfogle-a.						3.00

OUTCASTS
DC Comics: Oct, 1987 - No. 12, Sept, 1988 ($1.75, limited series)

	GD 2.0	VG 4.0	FN 6.0	VF 8.0	VF/NM 9.0	NM- 9.2
1-12: John Wagner & Alan Grant scripts in all						3.00

OUTER LIMITS, THE (TV)
Dell Publishing Co.: Jan-Mar, 1964 - No. 18, Oct, 1969 (Most painted-c)

	GD 2.0	VG 4.0	FN 6.0	VF 8.0	VF/NM 9.0	NM- 9.2
1	12	24	36	82	154	225
2-5	7	14	21	49	80	110
6-10	6	12	18	41	66	90
11-18: 17-Reprints #1. 18-r/#2	5	10	15	34	55	75

OUTER SPACE (Formerly This Magazine Is Haunted, 2nd Series)
Charlton Comics: No. 17, May, 1958 - No. 25, Dec, 1959; Nov, 1968

	GD 2.0	VG 4.0	FN 6.0	VF 8.0	VF/NM 9.0	NM- 9.2
17-Williamson/Wood style art; not by them (Sid Check?)	14	28	42	80	115	150
18-20-Ditko-a	23	46	69	136	223	310
21-Ditko-c	20	40	60	114	182	250
22-25	14	28	42	80	115	150
V2#1(11/68)-Ditko-a, Boyette-c	5	10	15	32	51	70

OUT FOR BLOOD
Dark Horse: Sept, 1999 - No. 4, Dec, 1999 ($2.95, B&W, limited series)

	GD 2.0	VG 4.0	FN 6.0	VF 8.0	VF/NM 9.0	NM- 9.2
1-4-Kelley Jones-c; Erskine-a						3.00

OUTLANDERS (Manga)
Dark Horse Comics: Dec, 1988 - No. 33, Sept,1991 ($2.00-$2.50, B&W, 44 pgs.)

	GD 2.0	VG 4.0	FN 6.0	VF 8.0	VF/NM 9.0	NM- 9.2
1-33: Japanese Sci-fi manga						4.00

OUTLAW (See Return of the...)

OUTLAW FIGHTERS
Atlas Comics (IPC): Aug, 1954 - No. 5, Apr, 1955

	GD 2.0	VG 4.0	FN 6.0	VF 8.0	VF/NM 9.0	NM- 9.2
1-Tuska-a	14	28	42	76	108	140
2-5: 5-Heath-c/a, 7 pgs.	9	18	27	50	65	80

NOTE: ***Hartley** a-3. **Heath** c/a-5. **Maneely** c-2. **Pakula** a-2. **Reinman** a-2. **Tuska** a-1-3.*

OUTLAW KID, THE (1st Series; see Wild Western)
Atlas Comics (CCC No. 1-11/EPI No. 12-29): Sept, 1954 - No. 19, Sept, 1957

	GD 2.0	VG 4.0	FN 6.0	VF 8.0	VF/NM 9.0	NM- 9.2
1-Origin; The Outlaw Kid & his horse Thunder begin; Black Rider app.	27	54	81	158	259	360
2-Black Rider app.	14	28	42	80	115	150
3-7,9: 3-Wildey-a(3)	12	24	36	69	97	125
8-Williamson/Woodbridge-a, 4 pgs.	13	26	39	74	105	135
10-Williamson-a	13	26	39	74	105	135
11-17,19: 13-Baker text illo. 15-Williamson text illo (unsigned)	9	18	27	52	69	85
18-Williamson/Mayo-a	10	20	30	56	76	95

NOTE: ***Berg** a-4, 7, 13. **Maneely** c-1-3, 5-8, 11-13, 15, 16, 18. **Pakula** a-3. **Severin** c-10, 17, 19. **Shores** a-1. **Wildey** a-1(3), 2-8, 10, 11, 12(4), 13(4), 15-19(4 each); c-4.*

OUTLAW KID, THE (2nd Series)
Marvel Comics Group: Aug, 1970 - No. 30, Oct, 1975

	GD 2.0	VG 4.0	FN 6.0	VF 8.0	VF/NM 9.0	NM- 9.2
1-Reprints; 1-Orlando-r, Wildey-r(3)	3	6	9	20	30	40
2,3,9: 2-Reprints. 3,9-Williamson-a(r)	2	4	6	13	18	22
4-7: 7-Last 15¢ issue	2	4	6	11	16	20
8-Double size (52 pgs.); Crandall-r	3	6	9	17	25	32
10-Origin	3	6	9	20	30	40
11-20: new-a in #10-16	2	4	6	13	18	22
21-30: 27-Origin-r/#10	2	4	6	9	13	16

NOTE: ***Ayers** a-10, 27r. **Berg** a-7, 25r. **Everett** a-2(2 pgs.). **Gil Kane** c-10, 11, 15, 27r, 28. **Roussos** a-10i, 27i(r). **Severin** c-1, 9, 20, 25. **Wildey** r-1-4, 6-9, 19-22, 25, 26. **Williamson** a-28r. **Woodbridge/Williamson** a-9r.*

OUTLAW NATION
DC Comics (Vertigo): Nov, 2000 - No. 19, May, 2002 ($2.50)

	GD 2.0	VG 4.0	FN 6.0	VF 8.0	VF/NM 9.0	NM- 9.2
1-19-Fabry painted-c/Delano-s/Sudzuka-a						3.00
TPB (Image Comics, 11/06, $15.99) B&W reprint of #1-19; Delano intro.						16.00

OUTLAWS
D. S. Publishing Co.: Feb-Mar, 1948 - No. 9, June-July, 1949

	GD 2.0	VG 4.0	FN 6.0	VF 8.0	VF/NM 9.0	NM- 9.2
1-Violent & suggestive stories	34	68	102	204	332	460
2-Ingels-a; Baker-a	34	68	102	204	332	460
3,5,6: 3-Not Frazetta. 5-Sky Sheriff by Good app. 6-McWilliams-a	17	34	51	98	154	210
4-Orlando-a	18	36	54	103	162	220
7,8-Ingels-a in each	24	48	72	142	234	325
9-(Scarce)-Frazetta-a (7 pgs.)	48	96	144	302	514	725

Out of the Shadows #5 © STD

Out of This World #2 © CC

Outsiders (2009 series) #29 © DC

	GD 2.0	VG 4.0	FN 6.0	VF 8.0	VF/NM 9.0	NM- 9.2

NOTE: *Another #3 was printed in Canada with* ***Frazetta*** *art "Prairie Jinx," 7 pgs.*

OUTLAWS, THE (Formerly Western Crime Cases)
Star Publishing Co.: No. 10, May, 1952 - No. 13, Sep, 1953; No. 14, Apr, 1954

10-L. B. Cole-c	21	42	63	122	199	275
11-14-L. B. Cole-c. 14-Reprints Western Thrillers #4 (Fox) w/new L.B. Cole-c; Kamen, Feldstein-r	16	32	48	92	144	195

OUTLAWS
DC Comics: Sept, 1991 - No. 8, Apr, 1992 ($1.95, limited series)

1-8: Post-apocalyptic Robin Hood. 3.00

OUTLAWS OF THE WEST (Formerly Cody of the Pony Express #10)
Charlton Comics: No. 11, 7/57 - No. 81, 5/70; No. 82, 7/79 - No. 88, 4/80

11	8	16	24	44	57	70
12,13,15-17,19,20	6	12	18	27	33	38
14-(68 pgs., 2/58)	9	18	27	50	65	80
18-Ditko-a	10	20	30	56	76	95
21-30	3	6	9	16	23	30
31-50: 34-Gunmaster app.	2	4	6	13	18	22
51-63,65,67-70: 54-Kid Montana app.	2	4	6	10	14	18
64,66: 64-Captain Doom begins (1st app.). 68-Kid Montana series begins	2	4	6	13	18	22
71-79: 73-Origin & 1st app. The Sharp Shooter, last app. #74. 75-Last Capt. Doom	2	4	6	9	12	15
80,81-Ditko-a	2	4	6	13	18	22
82-88						6.00
64,79(Modern Comics-r, 1977, '78)						4.00

OUTLAWS OF THE WILD WEST
Avon Periodicals: 1952 (25¢, 132 pgs.) (4 rebound comics)

1-Wood back-c; Kubert-a (3 Jesse James-r)	34	68	102	204	332	460

OUTLAW TRAIL (See Zane Grey 4-Color 511)

OUT OF SANTA'S BAG (See March of Comics #10 in the Promotional Comics section)

OUT OF THE NIGHT (The Hooded Horseman #18 on)
Amer. Comics Group (Creston/Scope): Feb-Mar, 1952 - No. 17, Oct-Nov, 1954

1-Williamson/LeDoux-a (9 pgs.)	66	132	198	419	722	1025
2-Williamson-a (5 pgs.)	47	94	141	296	498	700
3,5-10: 9-Sci/Fic story	29	58	87	172	281	390
4-Williamson-a (7 pgs.)	40	80	120	243	402	560
11-17: 13-Nostrand-a? 17-E.C. Wood swipe	22	44	66	128	209	290

NOTE: ***Landau*** *a-14, 16, 17.* ***Shelly*** *a-12.*

OUT OF THE SHADOWS
Standard Comics/Visual Editions: No. 5, July, 1952 - No. 14, Aug, 1954

5-Toth-p; Moreira, Tuska-a; Roussos-c	56	112	168	356	611	865
6-Toth/Celardo-a; Katz-a(2)	40	80	120	246	411	575
7,9: 7-Jack Katz-c/a(2). 9-Crandall-a(2)	34	68	102	204	332	460
8-Katz shrunken head-c	54	108	162	348	594	840
10-Spider-c; Sekowsky-a	36	72	108	211	343	475
11-Toth-a, 2 pgs.; Katz-a; Andru-c	34	68	102	204	332	460
12-Toth/Peppe-a(2); Katz-a	40	80	120	246	411	575
13-Cannabalism story; Sekowsky-a; Roussos-c	39	78	117	233	384	535
14-Toth-a	34	68	102	204	332	460

OUT OF THE VORTEX (Comics' Greatest World:... #1-4)
Dark Horse Comics: Oct., 1993 - No. 12, Oct, 1994 ($2.00, limited series)

1-11: 1-Foil logo. 4-Dorman-c(p). 6-Hero Zero x-over 3.00
12 ($2.50) 3.00

NOTE: ***Art Adams*** *c-7.* ***Golden*** *c-8.* ***Mignola*** *c-2.* ***Simonson*** *c-3.* ***Zeck*** *c-10.*

OUT OF THIS WORLD
Charlton Comics: Aug, 1956 - No. 16, Dec, 1959

1	27	54	81	158	259	360
2	15	30	45	85	130	175
3-6-Ditko-c/a (3) each	32	64	96	188	307	425
7-(2/58, 15¢, 68 pgs.)-Ditko-c/a(4)	34	68	102	199	325	450
8-(5/58, 15¢, 68 pgs.)-Ditko-a(2)	30	60	90	177	289	400
9,10,12,16-Ditko-a	23	46	69	136	223	310
11-Ditko c/a (3)	27	54	81	158	259	360
13-15	13	26	39	72	101	130

NOTE: ***Ditko*** *c-3-12, 16.* ***Reinman*** *a-10.*

OUT OF THIS WORLD
Avon Periodicals: June, 1950; Aug, 1950

1-Kubert-a(2) (one reprinted/Eerie #1, 1947) plus Crom the Barbarian by Gardner Fox & John Giunta (origin); Fawcette-c	77	154	231	493	847	1200
1-(8/50) Reprint; no month on cover	47	94	141	296	498	700

OUT OF THIS WORLD ADVENTURES
Avon Periodicals: July, 1950 - No. 2, Apr, 1951 (25¢ sci-fi pulp magazine with 32-page color comic insert)

1-Kubert-a(2); Crom the Barbarian by Fox & Giunta; text stories by Cummings, Van Vogt, del Rey, Chandler	71	142	213	454	777	1100
2-Kubert-a plus The Spider God of Akka by Gardner Fox & John Giunta pulp magazine w/comic insert; Wood-a (21 pgs.); mentioned in **SOTI**, page 120	50	100	150	315	533	750

OUT OUR WAY WITH WORRY WART
Dell Publishing Co.: No. 680, Feb, 1956

Four Color 680	4	8	12	24	37	50

OUTPOSTS
Blackthorne Publishing: June, 1987 - No. 4, 1987 ($1.25)

1-4: 1-Kaluta-c(p) 3.00

OUTSIDERS, THE
DC Comics: Nov, 1985 - No. 28, Feb, 1988

1 4.00
2-17 3.00
18-28: 18-26-Batman returns. 21-Intro. Strike Force Kobra; 1st app. Clayface IV 22-E.C. parody; Orlando-a. 21- 25-Atomic Knight app. 27,28-Millennium tie-ins 3.00
Annual 1 (12/86, $2.50), Special 1 (7/87, $1.50) 4.00

NOTE: ***Aparo*** *a-1-7, 9-14, 17-22, 25, 26; c-1-7, 9-14, 17, 19-26.* ***Byrne*** *a-11.* ***Bolland*** *a-6, 18; c-16.* ***Ditko*** *a-13p.* ***Erik Larsen*** *a-24, 27 28; c-27, 28.* ***Morrow*** *a-12.*

OUTSIDERS
DC Comics: Nov, 1993 - No. 24, Nov, 1995 ($1.75/$1.95/$2.25)

1-11,0,12-24: 1-Alpha; Travis Charest-c. 1-Omega; Travis Charest-c. 5-Atomic Knight app. 8-New Batman-c/story. 11-(9/94)-Zero Hour. 0-(10/94).12-(11/94). 21-Darkseid cameo. 22-New Gods app. 3.00

OUTSIDERS (See Titans/Young Justice: Graduation Day)(Leads into Batman and the Outsiders)
DC Comics: Aug, 2003 - No. 50, Nov, 2007 ($2.50/$2.99)

1-Nightwing, Arsenal, Metamorpho app.; Winick-s/Raney-a 5.00
2-Joker and Grodd app. 3.50
3-33: 3-Joker-c. 5,6-ChrisCross-a. 8-Huntress app. 9,10-Capt. Marvel Jr. app. 24,25-X-over with Teen Titans. 26,27-Batman & old Outsiders 3.00
34-50: 34-One Year Later. 36-Begin $2.99-c. 37-Superman app. 44-Red Hood app. 3.00
Annual 1 (6/07, $3.99) McDaniel-a; Black LIghtning app. 4.00
.../Checkmate: Checkout TPB (2008, $14.99) r/#47-49 & Checkmate #13-15 15.00
... Double Feature (10/03, $4.95) r/#1,2 5.00
...: Crisis Intervention TPB (2006, $12.99) r/#29-33 13.00
...: Looking For Trouble TPB (2004, $12.95) r/#1-7 & Teen Titans/Outsiders Secret Files & Origins 2003; intro. by Winick 13.00
...: Pay As You Go TPB (2007, $14.99) r/#42-46 & Annual #1 15.00
...: Sum of All Evil TPB (2004, $14.95) r/#8-15 15.00
...: The Good Fight TPB (2006, $14.99) r/#34-41 15.00
...: Wanted TPB (2005, $14.99) r/#16-23 15.00

OUTSIDERS, THE (Continued from Batman and the Outsiders #14)
DC Comics: No. 15, Apr, 2009 - Present ($2.99)

15-23,26-37: 15-Alfred assembles a new team; Garbett-a. 17-19-Deathstroke app. 3.00
24,25-($3.99) Blackest Night; Terra rises as a Black Lantern 4.00
...: The Deep TPB (2009, $14.99) r/#15-20 & Batman and the Outsiders Special #1 15.00
...: The Hunt TPB (2010, $14.99) r/#21-25 15.00
...: The Road to Hell TPB (2010, $14.99) r/#26-31 15.00

OUTSIDERS: FIVE OF A KIND (Bridges Outsiders #49 & 50)
DC Comics: Oct, 2007 ($2.99, weekly limited series)

...Katana/Shazam! (part 2 of 5) - Barr-s/Sharpe-a 3.00
...Metamorpho/Aquaman (part 4 of 5) - Wilson-s/Middleton-a 3.00
...Nightwing/Captain Boomerang (part 1 of 5) - DeFilippis & Weir-s/Willams-a 3.00
...Thunder/Martian Manhunter (part 3 of 5) - Bedard-s/Turnbull-a; Grayven app. 3.00
...Wonder Woman/Grace (part 5 of 5) - Andreyko-s/Richards-a 3.00
TPB (2008, $14.99) r/series & Outsiders #50 15.00

OUT THERE
DC Comics(Cliffhanger): July, 2001 - No. 18, Aug, 2003 ($2.50/$2.95)

1-Humberto Ramos-c/a; Brian Augustyn-s 3.00
1-Variant-c by Carlos Meglia 4.00
2-8: 3-Variant-c by Bruce Timm 3.00
9-18: 9-Begin $2.95-c 3.00
...: The Evil Within TPB (2002, $12.95) r/#1-6; Ramos sketch pages 13.00

Over the Edge #7 © MAR

Ozma of Oz #1 © MAR

Painkiller Jane #2 © Quesada & Palmiotti

	GD 2.0	VG 4.0	FN 6.0	VF 8.0	VF/NM 9.0	NM- 9.2

OVERKILL: WITCHBLADE/ ALIENS/ DARKNESS/ PREDATOR
Image Comics/Dark Horse Comics: Dec, 2000 - No. 2, 2001 ($5.95)

1,2-Jenkins-s/Lansing, Ching & Benitez-a 6.00

OVER THE EDGE
Marvel Comics: Nov, 1995 - No. 10, Aug, 1996 (99¢)

1-10: 1,6,10-Daredevil-c/story. 2,7-Dr. Strange-c/story. 3-Hulk-c/story. 4,9-Ghost Rider-c/story. 5-Punisher-c/story. 8-Elektra-c/story 3.00

OWL, THE (See Crackajack Funnies #25, Popular Comics #72 and Occult Files of Dr. Spektor #22)
Gold Key: April, 1967; No. 2, April, 1968

1-Written by Jerry Siegel; '40s super hero	6	12	18	39	62	85
2	5	10	15	30	48	65

OZ (See First Comics Graphic Novel, Marvel Treaury Of Oz & MGM's Marvelous...)

OZ
Caliber Press: 1994 - 1997 ($2.95, B&W)

0-20: 0-Released between #10 & #11 3.00
1 ($5.95)-Limited Edition; double-c 6.00
...Specials: Freedom Fighters. Lion. Scarecrow. Tin Man 3.00

OZARK IKE
Dell Publishing Co./Standard Comics B11 on: Feb, 1948; Nov, 1948 - No. 24, Dec, 1951; No. 25, Sept, 1952

Four Color 180(1948-Dell)	10	20	30	67	116	165
B11, B12, 13-15	10	20	30	54	72	90
16-25	9	18	27	47	61	75

OZ: DAEMONSTORM
Caliber Press: 1997 ($3.95, B&W, one-shot)

1 4.00

OZMA OF OZ (Dorothy Gale from Wonderful Wizard of Oz)
Marvel Comics: Jan, 2011 - No. 8 ($3.99, limited series)

1-5-Eric Shanower-s/Skottie Young-a/c 4.00
Oz Primer (5/11, $3.99) creator interviews and character profiles 4.00

OZ: ROMANCE IN RAGS
Caliber Press: 1996 ($2.95, B&W, limited series)

1-3, ..Special 3.00

OZ SQUAD
Brave New Worlds/Patchwork Press: 1992 - No. 4, 1994 ($2.50/$2.75, B&W)

1-4-Patchwork Press 3.00

OZ SQUAD
Patchwork Press: Dec, 1995 - No. 10, 1996 ($3.95/$2.95, B&W)

1-($3.95) 4.00
2-10 3.00

OZ: STRAW AND SORCERY
Caliber Press: 1997 ($2.95, B&W, limited series)

1-3 3.00

OZ-WONDERLAND WARS, THE
DC Comics: Jan, 1986 - No. 3, March, 1986 (Mini-series)(Giants)

1-3-Capt. Carrot app.; funny animals 4.00

OZZIE & BABS (TV Teens #14 on)
Fawcett Publications: Dec, 1947 - No. 13, Fall, 1949

1-Teen-age	10	20	30	54	72	90
2	6	12	18	31	38	45
3-13	6	12	18	27	33	38

OZZIE AND HARRIET (The Adventures of... on cover) (Radio)
National Periodical Publications: Oct-Nov, 1949 - No. 5, June-July, 1950

1-Photo-c	94	188	282	597	1024	1450
2	47	94	141	296	498	700
3-5	39	78	117	240	395	550

OZZY OSBOURNE (Todd McFarlane Presents)
Image Comics (Todd McFarlane Prod.): June, 1999 ($4.95, magazine-sized)

1-Bio, interview and comic story; Ormston painted-a; Ashley Wood-c 5.00

PACIFIC COMICS GRAPHIC NOVEL (See Image Graphic Novel)

PACIFIC PRESENTS (Also see Starslayer #2, 3)
Pacific Comics: Oct, 1982 - No. 2, Apr, 1983; No. 3, Mar, 1984 - No. 4, Jun, 1984

1-Chapter 3 of The Rocketeer; Stevens-c/a; Bettie Page model	2	3	4	6	8	10
2-Chapter 4 of The Rocketeer (4th app.); nudity; Stevens-c/a	2	3	4	6	8	10

3,4: 3-1st app. Vanity 3.00
NOTE: *Conrad a-3, 4; c-3. **Ditko** a-1-3; c-1(1/2). **Dave Stevens** a-1, 2; c-1(1/2), 2.*

PACT, THE
Image Comics: Feb, 1994 - No. 3, June, 1994 ($1.95, limited series)

1-3: Valentino co-scripts & layouts 3.00

PACT, THE
Image Comics: Apr, 2005 - No. 4, Jan, 2006 ($2.99/$2.95)

1-4: Invincible, Shadowhawk, Firebreather & Zephyr team-up. 1-Valentino-s/a 3.00

PAGEANT OF COMICS (See Jane Arden & Mopsy)
Archer St. John: Sept, 1947 - No. 2, Oct, 1947

1,2: 1-Mopsy strip-r. 2-Jane Arden strip-r	10	20	30	56	76	95

PAINKILLER JANE
Event Comics: June, 1997 - No. 5, Nov, 1997 ($3.95/$2.95)

1-Augustyn/Waid-s/Leonardi/Palmiotti-a, variant-c 4.00
2-5: Two covers (Quesada, Leonardi) 3.00
0-(1/99, $3.95) Retells origin; two covers 4.00
Essential Painkiller Jane TPB (2007, $19.99) r/#0-5; cover gallery and pin-ups 20.00

PAINKILLER JANE
Dynamite Entertainment: 2006 - No. 3, 2006 ($2.99)

1-3-Quesada & Palmiotti-s/Moder-a. 1-Four covers by Q&P, Moder, Tan and Conner 3.00
Volume #1 TPB (2007, $9.99) r/#1-3; cover gallery and Palmiotti interview 10.00

PAINKILLER JANE
Dynamite Entertainment: No. 0, 2007 - Present ($3.50)

0-(25¢) Quesada & Palmiotti-s/Moder-a 3.00
1-5-($3.50) 1-Continued from #0; 5 covers. 4,5-Crossover with Terminator 2 #6,7 3.50
Volume #2 TPB (2007, $11.99) r/#0-3; cover gallery 12.00

PAINKILLER JANE / DARKCHYLDE
Event Comics: Oct, 1998 ($2.95, one-shot)

Preview-($6.95) DF Edition, 1-($6.95) DF Edition 7.00
1-Three covers; J.G. Jones-a 3.00

PAINKILLER JANE / HELLBOY
Event Comics: Aug, 1998 ($2.95, one-shot)

1-Leonardi & Palmiotti-a 3.00

PAINKILLER JANE VS. THE DARKNESS
Event Comics: Apr, 1997 ($2.95, one-shot)

1-Ennis-s; four variant-c (Conner, Hildebrandts, Quesada, Silvestri) 3.50

PAKKINS' LAND
Caliber Comics (Tapestry): Oct, 1996 - No. 6, July, 1997 ($2.95, B&W)

1-Gary and Rhoda Shipman-s/a 6.00
2,3 4.00
1-3-2nd printing 3.00
4-6 3.00
0-(6/97, $1.95) 3.00

PAKKINS' LAND
Alias Enterprises: Apr, 2005 - No. 2 ($2.99)

1,2-Gary Shipman-s/a 3.00

PAKKINS' LAND: FORGOTTEN DREAMS
Caliber Comics/Image Comics #4: Apr, 1998 - No. 4, Mar, 2000 ($2.95, B&W)

1-4-Gary and Rhoda Shipman-s/a 3.00

PAKKINS' LAND: QUEST FOR KINGS
Caliber Comics: Aug, 1997 - No. 6, Mar, 1998 ($2.95, B&W)

1-6: 1-Gary and Rhoda Shipman-s/a; Jeff Smith var-c 3.00

PANCHO VILLA
Avon Periodicals: 1950

nn-Kinstler-c	23	46	69	136	223	310

PANHANDLE PETE AND JENNIFER (TV) (See Gene Autry #20)
J. Charles Laue Publishing Co.: July, 1951 - No. 3, Nov, 1951

1	10	20	30	54	72	90
2,3: 2-Interior photo-cvrs	7	14	21	37	46	55

PANIC (Companion to Mad)

Panic #2 © WMG

Pantheon #1 © IDW

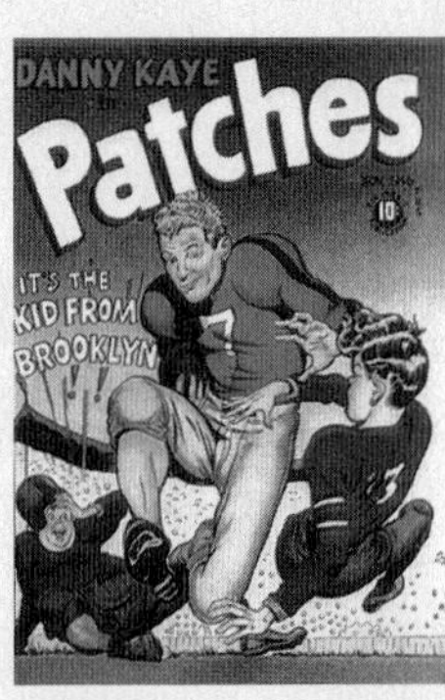

Patches #5 © Rural Home

	GD 2.0	VG 4.0	FN 6.0	VF 8.0	VF/NM 9.0	NM- 9.2

E. C. Comics (Tiny Tot Comics): Feb-Mar, 1954 - No. 12, Dec-Jan, 1955-56

1-Used in Senate Investigation hearings; Elder draws entire E. C. staff; Santa Claus & Mickey Spillane parody	34	68	102	272	436	600
2	16	32	48	128	207	285
3,4: 3-Senate Subcommittee parody; Davis draws Gaines, Feldstein & Kelly, 1 pg.; Old King Cole smokes marijuana. 4-Infinity-c; John Wayne parody	13	26	39	104	167	230
5-11: 8-Last pre-code issue (5/55). 9-Superman, Smilin' Jack & Dick Tracy app. on-c; has photo of Walter Winchell on-c. 11-Wheedies cereal box-c	12	24	36	96	153	210
12 (Low distribution; thousands were destroyed)	15	30	45	120	195	270

NOTE: ***Davis** a-1-12; c-12. **Elder** a-1-12. **Feldstein** c-1-3, 5. **Kamen** a-1. **Orlando** a-1-9. **Wolverton** c-4, panel-3. **Wood** a-2-9, 11, 12.*

PANIC (Magazine) (Satire)
Panic Publ.: July, 1958 - No. 6, July, 1959; V2#10, Dec, 1965 - V2#12, 1966

1	14	28	42	76	108	140
2-6	9	18	27	50	65	80
V2#10-12: Reprints earlier issues	3	6	9	18	27	35

NOTE: ***Davis** a-3(2 pgs.), 4, 5, 10; c-10. **Elder** a-5. **Powell** a-V2#10, 11. **Torres** a-1-5. **Tuska** a-V2#11.*

PANIC
Gemstone Publishing: March, 1997 - No. 12, Dec, 1999 ($2.50, quarterly)

1-12: E.C. reprints 3.00

PANTHA (See Vampirella-The New Monthly #16,17)

PANTHA: HAUNTED PASSION (Also see Vampirella Monthly #0)
Harris Comics: May, 1997 ($2.95, B&W, one-shot)

1-r/Vampirella #30,31 3.00

PANTHEON
IDW Publishing: Apr, 2010 - No. 5, Aug, 2010 ($3.99)

1-5-Andreyko-s/Molnar-a; co-created by Michael Chiklis 4.00

PAPA MIDNITE (See John Constantine - Hellblazer Special:...)

PARADE (See Hanna-Barbera...)

PARADE COMICS (See Frisky Animals on Parade)

PARADE OF PLEASURE
Derric Verschoyle Ltd., London, England: 1954 (192 pgs.) (Hardback book)

By Geoffrey Wagner. Contains section devoted to the censorship of American comic books with illustrations in color and black and white. (Also see **Seduction of the Innocent**). Distributed in USA by Library Publishers, N. Y.	113	226	339	486	581	675
with dust jacket....	208	416	624	894	1072	1250

PARADISE TOO!
Abstract Studios: 2000 - No. 14, 2003 ($2.95, B&W)

1-14-Terry Moore's unpublished newspaper strips and sketches 3.00
...: Checking For Weirdos TPB (4/03, $14.95) r/#8-12 15.00
...: Drunk Ducks! TPB (7/02, $15.95) r/#1-7 16.00

PARADISE X (Also see Earth X and Universe X)
Marvel Comics: Apr, 2002 - No. 12, Aug, 2003 ($4.50/$2.99)

0-Ross-c; Braithwaite-a 4.50
1-12-($2.99) Ross-c; Braithwaite-a. 7-Punisher on-c. 10-Kingpin on-c 3.00
...:A (10/03, $2.99) Braithwaite-a; Ross-c 3.00
...:Devils (11/02, $4.50) Sadowski-a; Ross-c 4.50
...:Ragnarok 1,2 (3/02, 4/03; $2.99) Yeates-a; Ross-c 3.00
...:X (11/03, $2.99) Braithwaite-a; Ross-c; conclusion of story 3.00
...:Xen (7/02, $4.50) Yeowell & Sienkiewicz-a; Ross-c 4.50
Earth X Vol. 4: Paradise X Book 1 (2003, $29.99, TPB) r/#0,1-5, ...: Xen; Heralds #1-3 30.00
Vol. 5: Paradise X Book 2 (2004, $29.99, TPB) r/#6-12, Ragnarok #1&2; Devils, A & X 30.00

PARADISE X: HERALDS (Also see Earth X and Universe X)
Marvel Comics: Dec, 2001 - No. 3, Feb, 2002 ($3.50)

1-3-Prelude to Paradise X series; Ross-c; Pugh-a 3.50
Special Edition (Wizard preview) Ross-c 3.00

PARADOX
Dark Visions Publ: June, 1994 - No. 2, Aug, 1994 ($2.95, B&W, mature)

1,2: 1-Linsner-c. 2-Boris-c. 3.00

PARALLAX: EMERALD NIGHT (See Final Night)
DC Comics: Nov, 1996 ($2.95, one-shot, 48 pgs.)

1-Final Night tie-in; Green Lantern (Kyle Rayner) app. 4.00

PARAMOUNT ANIMATED COMICS (See Harvey Comics Hits #60, 62)
Harvey Publications: No. 3, Feb, 1953 - No. 22, July, 1956

3-Baby Huey, Herman & Katnip, Buzzy the Crow begin	24	48	72	140	230	320
4-6	14	28	42	76	108	140
7-Baby Huey becomes permanent cover feature; cover title becomes Baby Huey with #9	22	44	66	132	216	300
8-10: 9-Infinity-c	12	24	36	69	97	125
11-22	10	20	30	54	72	90

PARENT TRAP, THE (Disney)
Dell Publishing Co.: No. 1210, Oct-Dec, 1961

Four Color 1210-Movie, Hayley Mills photo-c	9	18	27	60	100	140

PARLIAMENT OF JUSTICE
Image Comics: Mar, 2003 ($5.95, B&W, one-shot, square-bound)

1-Michael Avon Oeming-c/s; Neil Vokes-a 6.00

PARODY
Armour Publishing: Mar, 1977 - No. 3, Aug, 1977 (B&W humor magazine)

1	3	6	9	14	19	24
2,3: 2-King Kong, Happy Days. 3-Charlie's Angels, Rocky	2	4	6	10	14	18

PAROLE BREAKERS
Avon Periodicals/Realistic #2 on: Dec, 1951 - No. 3, July, 1952

1(#2 on inside)-r-c/Avon paperback #283 (painted-c)	43	86	129	271	461	650
2-Kubert-a; r-c/Avon paperback #114 (photo-c)	30	60	90	177	289	400
3-Kinstler-c	27	54	81	158	259	360

PARTRIDGE FAMILY, THE (TV)(Also see David Cassidy)
Charlton Comics: Mar, 1971 - No. 21, Dec, 1973

1-(2 versions: B&W photo-c & tinted color photo-c)	7	14	21	49	80	110
2-4,6-10	4	8	12	26	41	55
5-Partridge Family Summer Special (52 pgs.); The Shadow, Lone Ranger, Charlie McCarthy, Flash Gordon, Hopalong Cassidy, Gene Autry & others app.	8	16	24	54	90	125
11-21	4	8	12	22	34	45

PARTS OF A HOLE
Caliber Press: 1991 ($2.50, B&W)

1-Short stories & cartoons by Brian Michael Bendis 3.00

PARTS UNKNOWN
Eclipse Comics/FX: July, 1992 - No. 4, Oct, 1992 ($2.50, B&W, mature)

1-4: All contain FX gaming cards 3.00

PARTS UNKNOWN
Image Comics: May, 2000 - Present ($2.95, B&W)

...: Killing Attractions 1 (5/00) Beau Smith-s/Brad Gorby-a 3.00
...: Hostile Takeover 1-4 (6-9/00) 3.00

PASSION, THE
Catechetical Guild: No. 394, 1955

394	6	12	18	31	38	45

PASSOVER (See Avengelyne)
Maximum Press: Dec, 1996 ($2.99, one-shot)

1 3.00

PAT BOONE (TV)(Also see Superman's Girlfriend Lois Lane #9)
National Per. Publ.: Sept-Oct, 1959 - No. 5, May-Jun, 1960 (All have photo-c)

1	42	84	126	265	445	625
2-5: 3-Fabian, Connie Francis & Paul Anka photos on-c. 4-Previews "Journey To The Center Of The Earth". 4-Johnny Mathis & Bobby Darin photos on-c. 5-Dick Clark & Frankie Avalon photos on-c	34	68	102	199	325	450

PATCHES
Rural Home/Patches Publ. (Orbit): Mar-Apr, 1945 - No. 11, Nov, 1947

1-L. B. Cole-c	39	78	117	240	395	550
2	15	30	45	88	137	185
3,4,6,8-11: 6-Henry Aldrich story. 8-Smiley Burnette-c/s (6/47); pre-dates Smiley Burnette #1. 9-Mr. District Attorney story (radio). Leav/Keigstein-a (16 pgs.). 9-11-Leav-c. 10-Jack Carson (radio) c/story; Leav-c. 11-Red Skelton story	15	30	45	85	130	175
5-Danny Kaye-c/story; L.B. Cole-c.	20	40	60	115	185	255
7-Hopalong Cassidy-c/story	18	36	54	103	162	220

PATH, THE (Also see Negation War)
CrossGeneration Comics: Apr, 2002 - No. 23, Apr, 2004 ($2.95)

1-23: 1-Ron Marz-s/Bart Sears-a. 13-Matthew Smith-a begins 3.00

Patsy and Hedy #4 © MAR

Paul the Samurai #4 © NEC

Peanuts #1 © UFS

	GD 2.0	VG 4.0	FN 6.0	VF 8.0	VF/NM 9.0	NM- 9.2
Vol. 1: Crisis of Faith (2002, $15.95, TPB) r/#1-6						16.00
Vol. 2: Blood on Snow (5/03, $15.95, TPB) r/#7-12						16.00
Vol. 3: Death and Dishonor ('03, $15.95, TPB) r/#13-18						16.00

PATHWAYS TO FANTASY
Pacific Comics: July, 1984

	GD 2.0	VG 4.0	FN 6.0	VF 8.0	VF/NM 9.0	NM- 9.2
1-Barry Smith-c/a; Jeff Jones-a (4 pgs.)						4.00

PATIENT ZERO
Image Comics: Mar, 2004 - No. 4, Jun, 2004 ($2.95, limited series)

	GD 2.0	VG 4.0	FN 6.0	VF 8.0	VF/NM 9.0	NM- 9.2
1-4-Brent White-a/John McLean-Foreman-s						3.00

PATORUZU (See Adventures of...)

PATRIOTS, THE
DC Comics (WildStorm): Jan, 2000 - No. 10, Oct, 2000 ($2.50)

	GD 2.0	VG 4.0	FN 6.0	VF 8.0	VF/NM 9.0	NM- 9.2
1-10-Choi and Peterson-s/Ryan-a						3.00

PATSY & HEDY (Teenage)(Also see Hedy Wolfe)
Atlas Comics/Marvel (GPI/Male): Feb, 1952 - No. 110, Feb, 1967

	GD 2.0	VG 4.0	FN 6.0	VF 8.0	VF/NM 9.0	NM- 9.2
1-Patsy Walker & Hedy Wolfe; Al Jaffee-c	26	52	78	154	252	350
2	15	30	45	84	127	170
3-10: 3,7,8,9-Al Jaffee-c	13	26	39	74	105	135
11-20: 17,19,20-Al Jaffee-c	11	22	33	62	86	110
21-40	10	20	30	54	72	90
41-50	6	12	18	37	59	80
51-60	5	10	15	35	55	75
61-80,100: 88-Lingerie panel	5	10	15	30	48	65
81-87,89-99,101-110	4	8	12	28	44	60
Annual 1(1963)-Early Marvel annual	9	18	27	65	113	160

PATSY & HER PALS (Teenage)
Atlas Comics (PPI): May, 1953 - No. 29, Aug, 1957

	GD 2.0	VG 4.0	FN 6.0	VF 8.0	VF/NM 9.0	NM- 9.2
1-Patsy Walker	20	40	60	114	182	250
2	12	24	36	69	97	125
3-10	11	22	33	62	86	110
11-29: 24-Everett-c	10	20	30	54	72	90

PATSY WALKER (See All Teen, A Date With Patsy, Girls' Life, Miss America Magazine, Patsy & Hedy, Patsy & Her Pals & Teen Comics)
Marvel/Atlas Comics (BPC): 1945 (no month) - No. 124, Dec, 1965

	GD 2.0	VG 4.0	FN 6.0	VF 8.0	VF/NM 9.0	NM- 9.2
1-Teenage	58	116	174	371	636	900
2	32	64	96	192	314	435
3,4,6-10	26	52	78	154	252	350
5-Injury-to-eye-c	30	60	90	177	289	400
11,12,15,16,18	16	32	48	94	147	200
13,14,17,19-22-Kurtzman's "Hey Look"	17	34	51	98	154	210
23,24	14	28	42	82	121	160
25-Rusty by Kurtzman; painted-c	17	34	51	98	154	210
26-29,31: 26-31: 52 pgs.	13	26	39	72	101	130
30(52 pgs.)-Egghead Doodle by Kurtzman (1 pg.)	14	28	42	76	108	140
32-57: Last precode (3/55)	10	20	30	58	79	100
58-80,100	6	12	18	37	59	80
81-99: 92,98-Millie x-over. 99-Linda Carter x-over	5	10	15	32	51	70
101-124	5	10	15	30	48	65
Fashion Parade 1(1966, 68 pgs.) (Beware cut-out & marked pages)	8	16	24	58	97	135

NOTE: *Painted c-25-28. Anti-Wertham editorial in #21. Georgie app. in #8, 11. Millie app. in #10, 92, 98. Mitzi app. in #11. Rusty app. in #12, 25. Willie app. in #12.* ***Al Jaffee*** *c-44, 47, 49, 57, 58.*

PATSY WALKER: HELLCAT
Marvel Comics: Sept, 2008 - No. 5, Feb, 2009 ($2.99, limited series)

	GD 2.0	VG 4.0	FN 6.0	VF 8.0	VF/NM 9.0	NM- 9.2
1-5-Lafuente-a/Kathryn Immonen-s/Stuart Immonen-c; Hellcat joins The Initiative						3.00

PAT THE BRAT (Adventures of Pipsqueak #34 on)
Archie Publications (Radio): June, 1953; Summer, 1955 - No. 4, 5/56; No. 15, 7/56 - No. 33, 7/59

	GD 2.0	VG 4.0	FN 6.0	VF 8.0	VF/NM 9.0	NM- 9.2
nn(6/53)	14	28	42	76	108	140
1(Summer, 1955)	10	20	30	54	72	90
2-4-(5/56) (#5-14 not published). 3-Early Bolling-a	7	14	21	37	46	55
15-(7/56)-33: 18-Early Bolling-a	4	8	12	22	34	45

PAT THE BRAT COMICS DIGEST MAGAZINE
Archie Publications: October, 1980

	GD 2.0	VG 4.0	FN 6.0	VF 8.0	VF/NM 9.0	NM- 9.2
1-Li'l Jinx & Super Duck app.	2	4	6	9	13	16

PATTY CAKE
Permanent Press: Mar, 1995 - No. 9, Jul, 1996 ($2.95, B&W)

	GD 2.0	VG 4.0	FN 6.0	VF 8.0	VF/NM 9.0	NM- 9.2
1-9: Scott Roberts-s/a						3.00

PATTY CAKE
Caliber Press (Tapestry): Oct, 1996 - No. 3, Apr, 1997 ($2.95, B&W)

	GD 2.0	VG 4.0	FN 6.0	VF 8.0	VF/NM 9.0	NM- 9.2
1-3: Scott Roberts-s/a, ...Christmas (12/96)						3.00

PATTY CAKE & FRIENDS
Slave Labor Graphics: Nov, 1997 - Present ($2.95, B&W)

	GD 2.0	VG 4.0	FN 6.0	VF 8.0	VF/NM 9.0	NM- 9.2
Here There Be Monsters (10/97), 1-14: Scott Roberts-s/a						3.00
Volume 2 #1 (11/00, $4.95)						5.00

PATTY POWERS (Formerly Della Vision #3)
Atlas Comics: No. 4, Oct, 1955 - No. 7, Oct, 1956

	GD 2.0	VG 4.0	FN 6.0	VF 8.0	VF/NM 9.0	NM- 9.2
4	11	22	33	62	86	110
5-7	8	16	24	40	50	60

PAT WILTON (See Mighty Midget Comics)

PAUL
Spire Christian Comics (Fleming H. Revell Co.): 1978 (49¢)

	GD 2.0	VG 4.0	FN 6.0	VF 8.0	VF/NM 9.0	NM- 9.2
nn	2	4	6	9	13	16

PAULINE PERIL (See The Close Shaves of...)

PAUL REVERE'S RIDE (TV, Disney, see Walt Disney Showcase #34)
Dell Publishing Co.: No. 822, July, 1957

	GD 2.0	VG 4.0	FN 6.0	VF 8.0	VF/NM 9.0	NM- 9.2
Four Color 822-w/Johnny Tremain, Toth-a	8	16	24	58	97	135

PAUL TERRY (See Heckle and Jeckle)

PAUL TERRY'S ADVENTURES OF MIGHTY MOUSE (See Adventures of...)

PAUL TERRY'S COMICS (Formerly Terry-Toons Comics; becomes Adventures of Mighty Mouse No. 126 on)
St. John Publishing Co.: No. 85, Mar, 1951 - No. 125, May, 1955

	GD 2.0	VG 4.0	FN 6.0	VF 8.0	VF/NM 9.0	NM- 9.2
85,86-Same as Terry-Toons #85, & 86 with only a title change; published at same time?; Mighty Mouse, Heckle & Jeckle & Gandy Goose continue from Terry-Toons	12	24	36	67	94	120
87-99	9	18	27	50	65	80
100	10	20	30	54	72	90
101-104,107-125: 121,122,125-Painted-c	9	18	27	47	61	75
105,106-Giant Comics Edition (25¢, 100 pgs.) (9/53 & ?). 105-Little Roquefort-c/story	18	36	54	105	165	225

PAUL TERRY'S MIGHTY MOUSE (See Mighty Mouse)

PAUL TERRY'S MIGHTY MOUSE ADVENTURE STORIES (See Mighty Mouse Adventure Stories)

PAUL THE SAMURAI (See The Tick #4)
New England Comics: July, 1992 - No. 6, July, 1993 ($2.75, B&W)

	GD 2.0	VG 4.0	FN 6.0	VF 8.0	VF/NM 9.0	NM- 9.2
1-6						3.00

PAWNEE BILL
Story Comics (Youthful Magazines?): Feb, 1951 - No. 3, July, 1951

	GD 2.0	VG 4.0	FN 6.0	VF 8.0	VF/NM 9.0	NM- 9.2
1-Bat Masterson, Wyatt Earp app.	13	26	39	72	101	130
2,3: 3-Origin Golden Warrior; Cameron-a	8	16	24	42	54	65

PAY-OFF (This Is the..., ...Crime, ...Detective Stories)
D. S. Publishing Co.: July-Aug, 1948 - No. 5, Mar-Apr, 1949 (52 pgs.)

	GD 2.0	VG 4.0	FN 6.0	VF 8.0	VF/NM 9.0	NM- 9.2
1-True Crime Cases #1,2	26	52	78	154	252	350
2	15	30	45	94	147	200
3-5-Thrilling Detective Stories	14	28	42	82	121	160

PEACEMAKER, THE (Also see Fightin' Five)
Charlton Comics: V3#1, Mar, 1967 - No. 5, Nov, 1967 (All 12¢ cover price)

	GD 2.0	VG 4.0	FN 6.0	VF 8.0	VF/NM 9.0	NM- 9.2
1-Fightin' Five begins	5	10	15	34	55	75
2,3,5	3	6	9	21	32	42
4-Origin The Peacemaker	4	8	12	26	41	55
1,2(Modern Comics reprint, 1978)						6.00

PEACEMAKER (Also see Crisis On Infinite Earths & Showcase '93 #7,9,10)
DC Comics: Jan, 1988 - No. 4, Apr, 1988 ($1.25, limited series)

	GD 2.0	VG 4.0	FN 6.0	VF 8.0	VF/NM 9.0	NM- 9.2
1-4						3.00

PEANUTS (Charlie Brown) (See Fritzi Ritz, Nancy & Sluggo, Sparkle & Sparkler, Tip Top, Tip Topper & United Comics)
United Features Syndicate/Dell Publishing Co./Gold Key: 1953-54; No. 878, 2/58 - No. 13, 5-7/62; 5/63 - No. 4, 2/64

	GD 2.0	VG 4.0	FN 6.0	VF 8.0	VF/NM 9.0	NM- 9.2
1(U.F.S.)(1953-54)-Reprints United Features' Strange As It Seems, Willie, Ferdnand	23	46	69	168	334	500
Four Color 878(#1) (Dell) Schulz-s/a, with assistance from Dale Hale and Jim Sasseville thru #4	22	44	66	159	317	475
Four Color 969,1015('59)	13	26	39	94	185	275
4(2-4/60) Schulz-s/a; one story by Anthony Pocrnich, Schulz's assistant cartoonist						

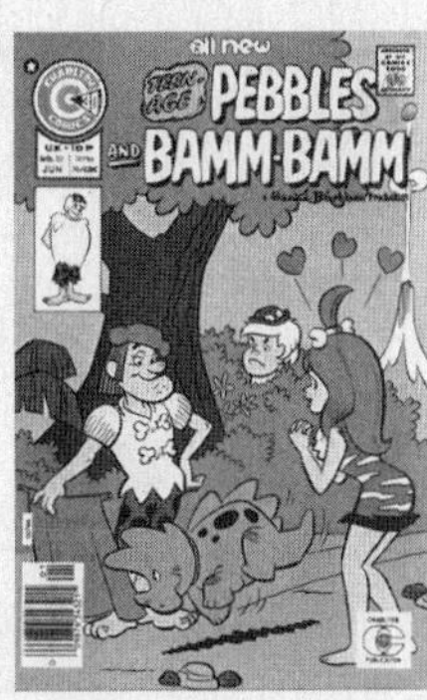

Pebbles and Bamm-Bamm #33 © H-B

Penny #1 © AVON

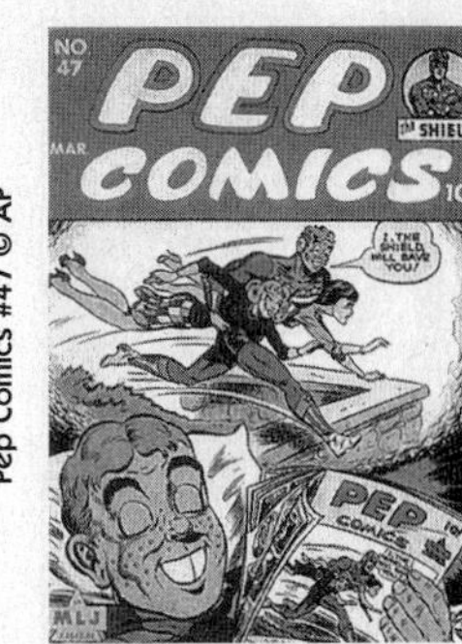

Pep Comics #47 © AP

	GD 2.0	VG 4.0	FN 6.0	VF 8.0	VF/NM 9.0	NM- 9.2
	12	24	36	86	161	235
5-13-Schulz-c only; s/a by Pocrnich	10	20	30	72	131	190
1(Gold Key, 5/63)	11	22	33	77	144	210
2-4	8	16	24	56	93	130

PEBBLES & BAMM BAMM (TV) (See Cave Kids #7, 12)
Charlton Comics: Jan, 1972 - No. 36, Dec, 1976 (Hanna-Barbera)

	GD	VG	FN	VF	VF/NM	NM-
1-From the Flintstones; "Teen Age..." on cover	5	10	15	30	48	65
2-10	3	6	9	17	25	32
11-20	2	4	6	13	18	22
21-36	2	4	6	9	13	16
nn (1973, digest, 100 pgs.) B&W one page gags	3	6	9	18	27	35

PEBBLES & BAMM BAMM (TV)
Harvey Comics: Nov, 1993 - No. 3, Mar, 1994 ($1.50) (Hanna-Barbera)

V2#1-3 3.00
...Giant Size 1 (10/93, $2.25, 68 pgs.)("Summer Special" on-c) 4.00

PEBBLES FLINTSTONE (TV) (See The Flintstones #11)
Gold Key: Sept, 1963 (Hanna-Barbera)

	GD	VG	FN	VF	VF/NM	NM-
1 (10088-309)-Early Pebbles app.	9	18	27	60	100	140

PEDRO (Formerly My Private Life #17; also see Romeo Tubbs)
Fox Features Syndicate: No. 18, June, 1950 - No. 2, Aug, 1950?

	GD	VG	FN	VF	VF/NM	NM-
18(#1)-Wood-c/a(p)	22	44	66	132	216	300
2-Wood-a?	15	30	45	88	137	185

PEE-WEE PIXIES (See The Pixies)

PELLEAS AND MELISANDE (See Night Music #4, 5)

PENALTY (See Crime Must Pay the...)

PENANCE: RELENTLESS (See Civil War, Thunderbolts and related titles)
Marvel Comics: Nov, 2007 - No. 5 ($2.99)

1-5-Speedball/Penance; Jenkins-s/Gulacy-a. 3-Wolverine app. 3.00
TPB (2008, $13.99) r/#1-5 14.00

PENDRAGON (Knights of... #5 on; also see Knights of...)
Marvel Comics UK, Ltd.: July, 1992 - No. 15, Sept, 1993 ($1.75)

1-15: 1-4-Iron Man app. 6-8-Spider-Man app. 3.00

PENDULUM ILLUSTRATED BIOGRAPHIES
Pendulum Press: 1979 (B&W)

19-355x-George Washington/Thomas Jefferson, 19-3495-Charles Lindbergh/Amelia Earhart, 19-3509-Harry Houdini/Walt Disney, 19-3517-Davy Crockett/Daniel Boone-Redondo-a, 19-3525-Elvis Presley/Beatles, 19-3533-Benjamin Franklin/Martin Luther King Jr, 19-3541-Abraham Lincoln/Franklin D. Roosevelt, 19-3568-Marie Curie/Albert Einstein-Redondo-a, 19-3576-Thomas Edison/Alexander Graham Bell-Redondo-a, 19-3584-Vince Lombardi/Pele, 19-3592-Babe Ruth/Jackie Robinson, 19-3606-Jim Thorpe/Althea Gibson

	GD	VG	FN	VF	VF/NM	NM-
Softback						5.00
Hardback	1	2	3	4	5	7

PENDULUM ILLUSTRATED CLASSICS (Now Age Illustrated)
Pendulum Press: 1973 - 1978 (75¢, 62pp, B&W, 5-3/8x8")
(Also see Marvel Classics)

64-100x(1973)-Dracula-Redondo art, 64-131x-The Invisible Man-Nino art, 64-0968-Dr. Jekyll and Mr. Hyde-Redondo art, 64-1005-Black Beauty, 64-1010-Call of the Wild, 64-1020-Frankenstein, 64-1025-Hucklebury Finn, 64-1030-Moby Dick-Nino-a, 64-1040-Red Badge of Courage, 64-1045-The Time Machine-Nino-a, 64-1050-Tom Sawyer, 64-1055-Twenty Thousand Leagues Under the Sea, 64-1069-Treasure Island, 64-1328(1974)-Kidnapped, 64-1336-Three Musketeers-Nino art, 64-1344-A Tale of Two Cities, 64-1352-Journey to the Center of the Earth, 64-1360-The War of the Worlds-Nino-a, 64-1379-The Greatest Advs. of Sherlock Holmes-Redondo art, 64-1387-Mysterious Island, 64-1395-Hunchback of Notre Dame, 64-1409-Helen Keller-story of my life, 64-1417-Scarlet Letter, 64-1425-Gulliver's Travels, 64-2618(1977)-Around the World in Eighty Days, 64-2626-Captains Courageous, 64-2634-Connecticut Yankee, 64-2642-The Hound of the Baskervilles, 64-2650-The House of Seven Gables, 64-2669-Jane Eyre, 64-2677-The Last of the Mohicans, 64-2685-The Best of O'Henry, 64-2693-The Best of Poe-Redondo-a, 64-2707-Two Years Before the Mast, 64-2715-White Fang, 64-2723-Wuthering Heights, 64-3126(1978)-Ben Hur-Redondo art, 64-3134-A Christmas Carol, 64-3142-The Food of the Gods, 64-3150-Ivanhoe, 64-3169-The Man in the Iron Mask, 64-3177-The Prince and the Pauper, 64-3185-The Prisoner of Zenda, 64-3193-The Return of the Native, 64-3207-Robinson Crusoe, 64-3215-The Scarlet Pimpernel, 64-3223-The Sea Wolf, 64-3231-The Swiss Family Robinson, 64-3851-Billy Budd, 64-386x-Crime and Punishment, 64-3878-Don Quixote, 64-3886-Great Expectations, 64-3894-Heidi, 64-3908-The Iliad, 64-3916-Lord Jim, 64-3924-The Mutiny on Board H.M.S. Bounty, 64-3932-The Odyssey, 64-3940-Oliver Twist, 64-3959-Pride and Prejudice, 64-3967-The Turn of the Screw

	GD	VG	FN	VF	VF/NM	NM-
Softback						6.00
Hardback	1	2	3	5	6	8

NOTE: *All of the above books can be ordered from the publisher; some were reprinted as Marvel Classic Comics #1-12. In 1972 there was another brief series of 12 titles which contained Classics Ill. artwork. They were entitled* ***Now Age Books*** *Illustrated, but can be easily distinguished from later series by the small Classics Illustrated logo at the top of the front cover. The format is the same as the later series. The 48 pg. C.I. art was stretched out to make 62 pgs. After Twin Circle Publ. terminated the Classics Ill. series in 1971, they made a one year contract with Pendulum Press to print these twelve titles of C.I. art. Pendulum was unhappy with the contract, and at the end of 1972 began their own art series, utilizing the talents of the Filipino artist group. One detail which makes this rather confusing is that when they redid the art in 1973, they gave it the same identifying no. as the 1972 series. All 12 of the 1972 C.I. editions have new covers, taken from internal art panels. In spite of their recent age, all of the 1972 C.I. series are very rare. Mint copies would fetch at least $50. Here is a list of the 1972 series, with C.I. title no. counterpart:*

64-1005 (CI#60-A2) 64-1010 (CI#91) 64-1015 (CI-Jr #503) 64-1020 (CI#26)
64-1025 (CI#19-A2) 64-1030 (CI#5-A2) 64-1035 (CI#169) 64-1040 (CI#98)
64-1045 (CI#133) 64-1050 (CI#50-A2) 64-1055 (CI#47) 64-1060 (CI-Jr#535)

PENDULUM ILLUSTRATED ORIGINALS
Pendulum Press: 1979 (In color)

94-4254-Solarman: The Beginning (See Solarman) 6.00

PENDULUM'S ILLUSTRATED STORIES
Pendulum Press: 1990 - No. 72, 1990? (No cover price ($4.95), squarebound, 68 pgs.)

1-72: Reprints Pendulum Ill. Classics series 5.00

PENGUINS OF MADAGASCAR (Based on the DreamWorks movie and TV series)
Ape Entertainment: 2010 - No. 4 ($3.95, limited series)

1-Skipper, Kowalski, Private and Rico app. 4.00

PENNY
Avon Comics: 1947 - No. 6, Sept-Oct, 1949 (Newspaper reprints)

	GD	VG	FN	VF	VF/NM	NM-
1-Photo & biography of creator	21	42	63	122	199	275
2-5	11	22	33	62	86	110
6-Perry Como photo on-c	12	24	36	67	94	120

PENNY CENTURY (See Love and Rockets)
Fantagraphics Books: Dec, 1997 - No. 7, Jul, 2000 ($2.95, B&W, mini-series)

1-7-Jaime Hernandez-s/a 3.00

PEP COMICS (See Archie Giant Series #576, 589, 601, 614, 624)
MLJ Magazines/Archie Publications No. 56 (3/46) on: Jan, 1940 - No. 411, Mar, 1987

	GD	VG	FN	VF	VF/NM	NM-
1-Intro. The Shield (1st patriotic hero) by Irving Novick; origin & 1st app. The Comet by Jack Cole, The Queen of Diamonds & Kayo Ward; The Rocket, The Press Guardian (The Falcon #1 only), Sergeant Boyle, Fu Chang, & Bentley of of Scotland Yard; Robot-c; Shield-c begin	892	1784	2676	6512	11,506	16,500
2-Origin The Rocket	271	542	813	1734	2967	4200
3	200	400	600	1280	2190	3100
4-Wizard cameo; early robot-s	161	322	483	1030	1765	2500
5-Wizard cameo in Shield story	161	322	483	1030	1765	2500
6-10: 8-Last Cole Comet; no Cole-a in #6,7	129	258	387	826	1413	2000
11-Dusty, Shield's sidekick begins (1st app.); last Press Guardian, Fu Chang	132	264	396	838	1444	2050
12-Origin & 1st app. Fireball (2/41); last Rocket & Queen of Diamonds; Danny in Wonderland begins	152	304	456	965	1658	2350
13-15	107	214	321	680	1165	1650
16-Origin Madam Satan; blood drainage-c	171	342	513	1086	1868	2650
17-Origin/1st app. The Hangman (7/41); death of The Comet; Comet is revealed as Hangman's brother	389	778	1167	2723	4762	6800
18,19,21: 21-Last Madam Satan	100	200	300	635	1093	1550
20-Classic Nazi swastika-c; last Fireball	155	310	465	992	1696	2400
22-Intro. & 1st app. Archie, Betty, & Jughead(12/41); (also see Jackpot)	4200	8400	12,600	32,000	51,000	70,000
23	331	662	993	2317	4059	5800
24,25: 24-Coach Kleats app. (unnamed until Archie #94); bondage/torture-c. 25-1st app. Archie's jalopy; 1st skinny Mr. Weatherbee prototype	258	516	774	1651	2826	4000
26-1st app. Veronica Lodge (4/42); "Remember Pearl Harbor!" cover caption	326	652	978	2282	3991	5700
27,29,30: 27-Bill of Rights-c. 29-Origin Shield retold; 30-Capt. Commando begins; bondage/torture-c; 1st Miss Grundy (definitive version); see Jackpot #4	194	388	582	1242	2121	3000
28-Classic swastika/Hangman-c	206	412	618	1318	2259	3200
31-33,35: 31-MLJ offices & artists are visited in Sgt. Boyle story; 1st app. Mr. Lodge. 32-Shield dons new costume. 33-Pre-Moose tryout (see Jughead #1)	161	322	483	1030	1765	2500
34-Bondage/Hypo-c	226	452	678	1446	2473	3500
36-1st Archie-c (2/43) w/Shield & Hangman	331	662	993	2317	4059	5800
37-40	97	194	291	621	1061	1500
41-50: 41-Archie-c begin. 47-Last Hangman issue; infinity-c. 48-Black Hood begins (5/44); ends #51,59,60	65	130	195	416	708	1000
51-60: 52-Suzie begins; 1st Mr Weatherbee-c. 56-Last Capt. Commando. 59-Black Hood not in costume; lingerie panels; Archie dresses as his aunt; Suzie ends. 60-Katy Keene begins(3/47), ends #154	39	78	117	240	395	550
61-65-Last Shield. 62-1st app. Li'l Jinx (7/47)	34	68	102	199	325	450
66-80: 66-G-Man Club becomes Archie Club (2/48); Nevada Jones by Bill Woggon. 78-1st app. Dilton	19	38	57	111	176	240
81-99	15	30	45	86	133	180
100	18	36	54	105	165	225
101-130	11	22	33	62	86	110

Pep Comics Featuring Betty and Veronica - FCBD Edition © AP

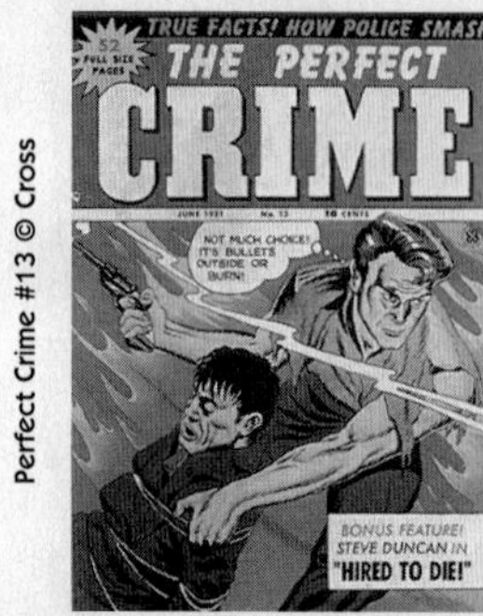

Perfect Crime #13 © Cross

Personal Love #14 © FF

GD 2.0 | VG 4.0 | FN 6.0 | VF 8.0 | VF/NM 9.0 | NM- 9.2

131(2/59)-137 6 12 18 37 59 80
138-140-Neal Adams-a (1 pg.) in each 6 12 18 41 66 90
141-149(9/61) 5 10 15 30 48 65
150-160-Super-heroes app. in each (see note). 150 (10/61?)-2nd or 3rd app. The Jaguar? 151-154,156-158-Horror/Sci/Fi-c. 157-Li'l Jinx. 159-Both 12¢ and 15¢ covers exist
6 12 18 43 69 95
161(3/63)-167,169-180: 161-3rd Josie app.; early Josie stories w/DeCarlo-a begin (see Note for others) 4 8 12 24 37 50
168,200: 168-(1/64)-Jaguar app. 200-(12/66) 4 8 12 26 41 55
181(5/65)-199: 187-Pureheart try-out story. 192-UFO-c. 198-Giantman-c(only)
3 6 9 18 27 35
201-217,219-226,228-240(4/70) 3 6 9 16 22 28
218,227-Archies Band-c only 3 6 9 17 25 32
241-270(10/72) 2 4 6 13 18 22
271-297,299 2 4 6 9 12 15
298, 300: 298-Josie and the Pussycats-c. 300(4/75) 2 4 6 13 18 22
301-340(8/78) 1 3 4 6 8 10
341-382 1 2 3 4 5 7
383(4/82),393(3/84): 383-Marvelous Maureen begins (Sci/fi). 393-Thunderbunny begins
1 2 3 5 6 8
384-392,394-399,401-410: 396-Early Cheryl Blossom-c 5.00
400(5/85),411: 400-Story featuring Archie staff (DeCarlo-a)
1 2 3 4 5 7

NOTE: **Biro** *a-2, 4, 5.* **Jack Cole** *a-1-5, 8.* **Al Fagaly** *c-55-72.* **Fuje** *a-39, 45, 47; c-34.* **Meskin** *a-2, 4, 5, 11(2).* **Montana** *c-30, 32, 33, 36, 73-87(most).* **Novick** *c-1-28, 29(w/***Schomburg***), 31i.* **Harry Sahle** *c-35, 39-50.* **Schomburg** *c-38.* **Bob Wood** *a-2, 4-6, 11. The Fly app. in 151, 154, 160. Flygirl app. in 153, 155, 156, 158. Jaguar app. in 150, 152, 157, 159, 168. Josie by* **DeCarlo** *in 161-166, 168-171, 173, 175-177, 179, 181. Katy Keene by* **Bill Woggon** *in 73-126. Bondage c-7, 12, 13, 15, 18, 21, 31, 32. Cover features: Shield #1-16; Shield/Hangman #17-27, 29-41; Hangman #28. Archie #36, 41-on.*

PEP COMICS FEATURING BETTY AND VERONICA
Archie Comic Publications: May, 2011 (Giveaway)

Free Comic Book Day Edition - Little Archie flashback 2.00

PEPE
Dell Publishing Co.: No. 1194, Apr, 1961

Four Color 1194-Movie, photo-c 4 8 12 24 37 50

PERFECT CRIME, THE
Cross Publications: Oct, 1949 - No. 33, May, 1953 (#2-14, 52 pgs.)

1-Powell-a(2) 37 74 111 222 361 500
2 (4/50) 20 40 60 117 189 260
3-10: 7-Steve Duncan begins, ends #30. 10-Flag-c 18 36 54 103 162 220
11-Used in **SOTI**, pg. 159 20 40 60 114 182 250
12-14 16 32 48 94 147 200
15- "The Most Terrible Menace" 2 pg. drug editorial (8/51)
18 36 54 105 165 225
16,17,19-25,27-29,31-33 14 28 42 80 115 150
18-Drug cover, heroin drug propaganda story, plus 2 pg. anti-drug editorial (11/51)
30 60 90 177 289 400
26-Drug-c with hypodermic needle; drug propaganda story (7/52)
29 58 87 170 278 385
30-Strangulation cover (11/52) 30 60 90 177 289 400

NOTE: **Powell** *a-No. 1, 2, 4.* **Wildey** *a-1, 5. Bondage c-11.*

PERFECT LOVE
Ziff-Davis(Approved Comics)/St. John No. 9 on: #10, 8-9/51 (cover date; 5-6/51 indicia date); #2, 10-11/51 - #10, 12/53

10(#1)(8-9/51)-Painted-c 21 42 63 126 206 285
2(10-11/51) 15 30 45 86 133 180
3,5-7: 3-Painted-c. 5-Photo-c 14 28 42 78 112 145
4,8 (Fall, 1952)-Kinstler-a; last Z-D issue 14 28 42 80 115 150
9,10 (10/53, 12/53, St. John): 9-Painted-c. 10-Photo-c
14 28 42 76 108 140

PERHAPANAUTS, THE
Dark Horse Comics: Nov, 2005 - No. 4, Feb, 2006 ($2.99, limited series)

1-4-Todd Dezago-s/Craig Rousseau-a/c 3.00
... Annual #1 (2/08, $3.50) Two covers by Rousseau and Allred 3.50
... Halloween Spooktacular1 (10/09, $3.50) Hembeck, Rousseau and others-a 3.50
,,, - Molly's Story (2/10, $3.50) Copland-a 3.50
(2nd series) (4/08 - Present, $3.50) 1-6: 1-Two covers by Art Adams and Rousseau 3.50

PERHAPANAUTS: SECOND CHANCES, THE
Dark Horse Comics: Oct, 2006 - No. 4, Jan, 2007 ($2.99, limited series)

1-4-Todd Dezago-s/Craig Rousseau-a/c 3.00

PERRI (Disney)
Dell Publishing Co.: No. 847, Jan, 1958

Four Color 847-Movie, w/2 diff-c publ. 5 10 15 35 55 75

PERRY MASON
David McKay Publications: No. 49, 1946 - No. 50, 1946

Feature Books 49, 50-Based on Gardner novels 31 62 93 186 303 420

PERRY MASON MYSTERY MAGAZINE (TV)
Dell Publishing Co.: June-Aug, 1964 - No. 2, Oct-Dec, 1964

1 6 12 18 39 62 85
2-Raymond Burr photo-c 5 10 15 32 51 70

PERSONAL LOVE (Also see Movie Love)
Famous Funnies: Jan, 1950 - No. 33, June, 1955

1-Photo-c 21 42 63 124 202 280
2-Kathryn Grayson & Mario Lanza photo-c 14 28 42 76 108 140
3-7,10: 7-Robert Walker & Joanne Dru photo-c. 10-Loretta Young & Joseph Cotton photo-c
12 24 36 69 97 125
8,9: 8-Esther Williams & Howard Keel photo-c. 9-Debra Paget & Louis Jourdan photo-c
13 26 39 72 101 130
11-Toth-a; Glenn Ford & Gene Tierney photo-c 14 28 42 81 118 155
12,16,17-One pg. Frazetta each. 17-Rock Hudson & Yvonne DeCarlo photo-c
12 24 36 69 97 125
13-15,18-23: 12-Jane Greer & William Lundigan photo-c. 14-Kirk Douglas photo-c. 15-Dale Robertson & Joanne Dru photo-c. 18-Gregory Peck & Susan Hayworth photo-c. 19-Anthony Quinn & Suzan Ball photo-c. 20-Robert Wagner & Kathleen Crowley photo-c. 21-Roberta Peters & Byron Palmer photo-c. 22-Dale Robertson photo-c. 23-Rhonda Fleming-c 11 22 33 64 90 115
24,27,28-Frazetta-a in each (8,8&6 pgs.). 27-Rhonda Fleming & Fernando Lamas photo-c. 28-Mitzi Gaynor photo-c 45 90 135 284 480 675
25-Frazetta-a (tribute to Bettie Page, 7 pg. story); Tyrone Power/Terry Moore photo-c from "King of the Khyber Rifles" 60 120 180 381 653 925
26,29,30,33: 26-Constance Smith & Byron Palmer photo-c. 29-Charlton Heston & Nicol Morey photo-c. 30-Johnny Ray & Mitzi Gaynor photo-c. 33-Dana Andrews & Piper Laurie photo-c
11 22 33 64 90 115
31-Marlon Brando & Jean Simmons photo-c; last pre-code (2/55)
14 28 42 80 115 150
32-Classic Frazetta-a (8 pgs.); Kirk Douglas & Bella Darvi photo-c
63 126 189 403 689 975

NOTE: *All have photo-c. Many feature movie stars.* **Everett** *a-5, 9, 10, 24.*

PERSONAL LOVE (Going Steady V3#3 on)
Prize Publ. (Headline): V1#1, Sept, 1957 - V3#2, Nov-Dec, 1959

V1#1 11 22 33 60 83 105
2 8 16 24 40 50 60
3-6(7-8/58) 7 14 21 35 43 50
V2#1(9-10/58)-V2#6(7-8/59) 6 12 18 29 36 42
V3#1-Wood?/Orlando-a 6 12 18 33 41 48
2 6 12 18 28 34 40

PETER CANNON - THUNDERBOLT (See Crisis on Infinite Earths)(Also see Thunderbolt)
DC Comics: Sept, 1992 - No. 12, Aug, 1993 ($1.25)

1-12 3.00

PETER COTTONTAIL
Key Publications: Jan, 1954; Feb, 1954 - No. 2, Mar, 1954 (Says 3/53 in error)

1(1/54)-Not 3-D 9 18 27 52 69 85
1(2/54)-(3-D, 25¢)-Came w/glasses; written by Bruce Hamilton
21 42 63 122 199 275
2-Reprints 3-D #1 but not in 3-D 6 12 18 31 38 45

PETER GUNN (TV)
Dell Publishing Co.: No. 1087, Apr-June, 1960

Four Color 1087-Photo-c 8 16 24 58 97 135

PETE ROSE: HIS INCREDIBLE BASEBALL CAREER
Masstar Creations Inc.: 1995

1-John Tartaglione-a 3.00

PETER PAN (Disney) (See Hook, Movie Classics & Comics, New Adventures of... & Walt Disney Showcase #36)
Dell Publishing Co.: No. 442, Dec, 1952 - No. 926, Aug, 1958

Four Color 442 (#1)-Movie 10 20 30 69 122 175
Four Color 926-Reprint of 442 4 8 12 28 44 60

PETER PAN
Disney Comics: 1991 ($5.95, graphic novel, 68 pgs.)(Celebrates video release)

Peter Panda #9 © DC

Peter Parker (2010 series) #1 © MAR

The Phantom #16 © KING

	GD 2.0	VG 4.0	FN 6.0	VF 8.0	VF/NM 9.0	NM- 9.2
nn-r/Peter Pan Treasure Chest from 1953						7.00

PETER PANDA
National Periodical Publications: Aug-Sept, 1953 - No. 31, Aug-Sept, 1958

	GD 2.0	VG 4.0	FN 6.0	VF 8.0	VF/NM 9.0	NM- 9.2
1-Grossman-c/a in all	50	100	150	315	533	750
2	26	52	78	154	252	350
3,4,6-8,10	21	42	63	126	206	285
5-Classic-c (scarce)	71	142	213	454	777	1100
9-Robot-c	30	60	90	177	289	400
11-31	15	30	45	86	133	180

PETER PAN RECORDS (See Power Records)

PETER PAN TREASURE CHEST (See Dell Giants)

PETER PARKER (See The Spectacular Spider-Man)

PETER PARKER
Marvel Comics: May, 2010 - No. 5, Sept, 2010 ($3.99/$2.99)

	GD 2.0	VG 4.0	FN 6.0	VF 8.0	VF/NM 9.0	NM- 9.2
1-($3.99) Prints material from Marvel Digital Comics; Olliffe-a; back-up w/Hembeck-s/a						4.00
2-5-($2.99): 2-4-Olliffe-a. 3-Braithwaite-c. 5-Nauck-a; Thing app.						3.00

PETER PARKER: SPIDER-MAN
Marvel Comics: Jan, 1999 - No. 57, Aug, 2003 ($2.99/$1.99/$2.25)

	GD 2.0	VG 4.0	FN 6.0	VF 8.0	VF/NM 9.0	NM- 9.2
1-Mackie-s/Romita Jr.-a; wraparound-c						4.00
1-($6.95) DF Edition w/variant-c by the Romitas	1	2	3	5	6	8
2-11,13-17-($1.99): 2-Two covers; Thor app. 3-Iceman-c/app. 4-Marrow-c/app. 5-Spider-Woman app. 7,8-Blade app. 9,10-Venom app. 11-Iron Man & Thor-c/app.						3.00
12-($2.99) Sinister Six and Venom app.						4.00
18-24,26-43: 18-Begin $2.25-c. 20-Jenkins-s/Buckingham-a start. 23-Intro Typeface. 24-Maximum Security x-over. 29-Rescue of MJ. 30-Ramos-c. 42,43-Mahfood-a						3.00
25-($2.99) Two covers; Spider-Man & Green Goblin						4.00
44-47-Humberto Ramos-c/a; Green Goblin-c/app.						3.00
48,49,51-57: 48,49-Buckingham-c/a. 51,52-Herrera-a. 56,57-Kieth-a; Sandman returns						3.00
50-($3.50) Buckingham-c/a						4.00
...'99 Annual (8/99, $3.50) Man-Thing app.						4.00
...'00 Annual ($3.50) Bounty app.; Joe Bennett-a; Black Cat back-up story						4.00
...'01 Annual ($2.99) Avery-s						4.00
...: A Day in the Life TPB (5/01, $14.95) r/#20-22,26; Webspinners #10-12						15.00
...: One Small Break TPB (2002, $16.95) r/#27,28,30-34; Andrews-c						17.00
Spider-Man: Return of the Goblin TPB (2002, $8.99) r/#44-47; Ramos-c						9.00
...Vol. 4: Trials & Tribulations TPB (2003, $11.99) r/#35,37,48-50; Cho-c						12.00

PETER PAT
United Features Syndicate: No. 8, 1939

	GD 2.0	VG 4.0	FN 6.0	VF 8.0	VF/NM 9.0	NM- 9.2
Single Series 8	36	72	108	211	343	475

PETER PAUL'S 4 IN 1 JUMBO COMIC BOOK
Capitol Stories (Charlton): No date (1953)

	GD 2.0	VG 4.0	FN 6.0	VF 8.0	VF/NM 9.0	NM- 9.2
1-Contains 4 comics bound; Space Adventures, Space Western, Crime & Justice, Racket Squad in Action	40	80	120	242	401	560

PETER PIG
Standard Comics: No. 5, May, 1953 - No. 6, Aug, 1953

	GD 2.0	VG 4.0	FN 6.0	VF 8.0	VF/NM 9.0	NM- 9.2
5,6	7	14	21	35	43	50

PETER PORKCHOPS (See Leading Comics #23) (Also see Capt. Carrot)
National Periodical Publications: 11-12/49 - No. 61, 9-11/59; No. 62, 10-12/60 (1-11: 52 pgs.)

	GD 2.0	VG 4.0	FN 6.0	VF 8.0	VF/NM 9.0	NM- 9.2
1	34	68	102	199	325	450
2	15	30	45	90	140	190
3-10: 6- "Peter Rockets to Mars!" c/story	13	26	39	74	105	135
11-30	10	20	30	56	76	95
31-62	9	18	27	47	61	75

NOTE: ***Otto Feuer** a-all. **Rube Grossman**-a most issues. **Sheldon Mayer** a-30-38, 40-44, 46-52, 61.*

PETER PORKER, THE SPECTACULAR SPIDER-HAM
Star Comics (Marvel): May, 1985 - No. 17, Sept, 1987 (Also see Marvel Tails)

	GD 2.0	VG 4.0	FN 6.0	VF 8.0	VF/NM 9.0	NM- 9.2
1-Michael Golden-c						5.00
2-17: 12-Origin/1st app. Bizarro Phil. 13-Halloween issue						4.00

NOTE: *Back-up features: 2-X-Bugs. 3-Iron Mouse. 4-Croctor Strange. 5-Thrr, Dog of Thunder.*

PETER POTAMUS (TV)
Gold Key: Jan, 1965 (Hanna-Barbera)

	GD 2.0	VG 4.0	FN 6.0	VF 8.0	VF/NM 9.0	NM- 9.2
1-1st app. Peter Potamus & So-So, Breezly & Sneezly	9	18	27	65	113	160

PETER RABBIT (See New Funnies #65 & Space Comics)
Dell Publishing Co.: No. 1, 1942

	GD 2.0	VG 4.0	FN 6.0	VF 8.0	VF/NM 9.0	NM- 9.2
Large Feature Comic 1	61	122	183	390	670	950

PETER RABBIT (Adventures of...; New Advs. of... #9 on)(Also see Funny Tunes & Space Comics)
Avon Periodicals: 1947 - No. 34, Aug-Sept, 1956

	GD 2.0	VG 4.0	FN 6.0	VF 8.0	VF/NM 9.0	NM- 9.2
1(1947)-Reprints 1943-44 Sunday strips; contains a biography & drawing of Cady	36	72	108	214	347	480
2 (4/48)	24	48	72	142	234	325
3 ('48) - 6(7/49)-Last Cady issue	21	42	63	124	202	280
7-10(1950-8/51): 9-New logo	11	22	33	62	86	110
11(11/51)-34('56)-Avon's character	9	18	27	52	69	85
...Easter Parade (1952, 25¢, 132 pgs.)	20	40	60	117	189	260
...Jumbo Book (1954-Giant Size, 25¢)-Jesse James by Kinstler (6 pgs.); space ship-c	24	48	72	140	230	320

PETER RABBIT 3-D
Eternity Comics: April, 1990 ($2.95, with glasses; sealed in plastic bag)

	GD 2.0	VG 4.0	FN 6.0	VF 8.0	VF/NM 9.0	NM- 9.2
1-By Harrison Cady (reprints)						3.00

PETER, THE LITTLE PEST (#4 titled Petey)
Marvel Comics Group: Nov, 1969 - No. 4, May, 1970

	GD 2.0	VG 4.0	FN 6.0	VF 8.0	VF/NM 9.0	NM- 9.2
1	7	14	21	47	76	105
2-4-r-Dexter the Demon & Melvin the Monster	5	10	15	32	51	70

PETE'S DRAGON (See Walt Disney Showcase #43)

PETE THE PANIC
Stanmor Publications: November, 1955

	GD 2.0	VG 4.0	FN 6.0	VF 8.0	VF/NM 9.0	NM- 9.2
nn-Code approved	6	12	18	27	33	38

PETEY (See Peter, the Little Pest)

PETTICOAT JUNCTION (TV, inspired Green Acres)
Dell Publ. Co.: Oct-Dec, 1964 - No. 5, Oct-Dec, 1965 (#1-3, 5 have photo-c)

	GD 2.0	VG 4.0	FN 6.0	VF 8.0	VF/NM 9.0	NM- 9.2
1	7	14	21	47	76	105
2-5	5	10	15	32	51	70

PETUNIA (Also see Looney Tunes and Porky Pig)
Dell Publishing Co.: No. 463, Apr, 1953

	GD 2.0	VG 4.0	FN 6.0	VF 8.0	VF/NM 9.0	NM- 9.2
Four Color 463	4	8	12	28	44	60

PHAGE (See Neil Gaiman's Teknophage & Neil Gaiman's Phage-Shadowdeath)

PHANTACEA
McPherson Publishing Co.: Sept, 1977 - No. 6, Summer, 1980 (B&W)

	GD 2.0	VG 4.0	FN 6.0	VF 8.0	VF/NM 9.0	NM- 9.2
1-Early Dave Sim-a (32 pgs.)	5	10	15	30	48	65
2-Dave Sim-a(10 pgs.)	3	6	9	14	19	24
3-6: 3-Flip-c w/Damnation Bridge. 4-Gene Day-a	2	4	6	10	14	18

PHANTASMO (See The Funnies #45)
Dell Publishing Co.: No. 18, 1941

	GD 2.0	VG 4.0	FN 6.0	VF 8.0	VF/NM 9.0	NM- 9.2
Large Feature Comic 18	38	76	114	226	368	510

PHANTOM, THE
David McKay Publishing Co.: 1939 - 1949

	GD 2.0	VG 4.0	FN 6.0	VF 8.0	VF/NM 9.0	NM- 9.2
Feature Books 20	94	188	282	597	1024	1450
Feature Books 22	66	132	198	419	722	1025
Feature Books 39	51	102	153	318	539	760
Feature Books 53,56,57	41	82	123	250	418	585

PHANTOM, THE (See Ace Comics, Defenders Of The Earth, Eat Right to Work and Win, Future Comics, Harvey Comics Hits #51,56, Harvey Hits #1, 6, 12, 15, 26, 36, 44, 48, & King Comics)

PHANTOM, THE (nn (#29)-Published overseas only) (Also see Comics Reading Libraries in the Promotional Comics section)
Gold Key(#1-17)/King(#18-28)/Charlton(#30 on): Nov, 1962 - No. 17, Jul, 1966; No. 18, Sept, 1966 - No. 28, Dec, 1967; No. 30, Feb, 1969 - No. 74, Jan, 1977

	GD 2.0	VG 4.0	FN 6.0	VF 8.0	VF/NM 9.0	NM- 9.2
1-Origin revealed on inside-c & back-c	16	32	48	114	232	350
2-King, Queen & Jack begins, ends #11	9	18	27	65	113	160
3-5	8	16	24	58	97	135
6-10	7	14	21	47	76	105
11-17: 12-Track Hunter begins	6	12	18	39	62	85
18-Flash Gordon begins; Wood-a	5	10	15	32	51	70
19-24: 20-Flash Gordon ends (both by Gil Kane). 21-Mandrake begins. 20,24-Girl Phantom app.	4	8	12	28	44	60
25-28: 25-Jeff Jones-a(4 pgs.); 1 pg. Williamson ad. 26-Brick Bradford app. 28(nn)-Brick Bradford app.	4	8	12	22	34	45
30-33: 33-Last 12¢ issue	3	6	9	17	25	32
34-40: 36,39-Ditko-a	3	6	9	16	23	30
41-66: 46-Intro. The Piranha. 62-Bolle-c	3	6	9	14	19	24
67-Origin retold; Newton-c/a	3	6	9	17	25	32
68-73-Newton-c/a	2	4	6	13	18	22
74-Classic flag-c by Newton; Newton-a;	3	6	9	16	23	30

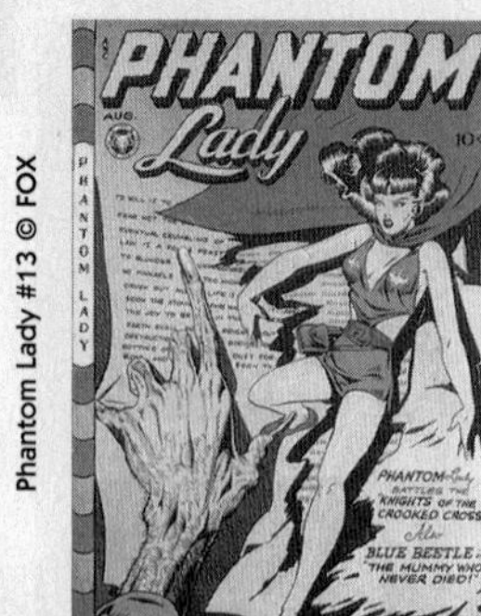

Phantom Lady #13 © FOX

Phantom Stranger #3 © DC

Phoenix (2011 series) #1 © Nemesis

	GD 2.0	VG 4.0	FN 6.0	VF 8.0	VF/NM 9.0	NM- 9.2

NOTE: *Aparo a-31-34, 36-38; c-31-38, 60, 61. Painted c-1-17.*

PHANTOM, THE
DC Comics: May, 1988 - No. 4, Aug, 1988 ($1.25, mini-series)

1-4: Orlando-c/a in all 3.00

PHANTOM, THE
DC Comics: Mar, 1989 - No. 13, Mar, 1990 ($1.50)

1-13: 1-Brief origin 3.00

PHANTOM, THE
Wolf Publishing: 1992 - No. 8, 1993 ($2.25)

1-8 3.00

PHANTOM, THE
Moonstone: 2003 - No. 26, Dec, 2008 ($3.50/$3.99)

1-26: 1-Cassaday-c/Raab-s/Quinn-a 4.00
... Annual #1 (2007, $6.50) Blevins-c; stroy and art by various incl. Nolan 6.50
... - Captain Action 1 (2010, $3.99) covers by Thibert, Sparacio, and Gilbert 4.00

PHANTOM BLOT, THE (#1 titled New Adventures of...)
Gold Key: Oct, 1964 - No. 7, Nov, 1966 (Disney)

	GD	VG	FN	VF	VF/NM	NM-
1 (Meets The Mysterious Mr. X)	6	12	18	41	66	90
2-1st Super Goof	5	10	15	34	55	75
3-7	4	8	12	22	34	45

PHANTOM EAGLE (See Mighty Midget, Marvel Super Heroes #16 & Wow #6)

PHANTOM FORCE
Image Comics/Genesis West #0, 3-7: 12/93 - #2, 1994; #0, 3/94; #3, 5/94 - #8, 10/94 ($2.50/$3.50, limited series)

0 (3/94, $2.50)-Kirby/Jim Lee-c; Kirby-p pgs. 1,5,24-29. 3.00
1 (12/93, $2.50)-Polybagged w/trading card; Kirby/Liefeld-c; Kirby plots/pencils w/inks by Liefeld, McFarlane, Jim Lee, Silvestri, Larsen, Williams, Ordway & Miki 3.00
2 ($3.50)-Kirby-a(p); Kirby/Larson-c 3.50
3-8: 3-(5/94, $2.50)-Kirby/McFarlane-c 4-(5/94)-Kirby-c(p). 5-(6/94) 3.00

PHANTOM GUARD
Image Comics (WildStorm Productions): Oct, 1997 - No. 6, Mar, 1998 ($2.50)

1-6: 1-Two covers 3.00
1-($3.50)-Voyager Pack w/Wildcore preview 3.50

PHANTOM JACK
Image Comics: Mar, 2004 - No. 5, July, 2004 ($2.95)

1-5-Mike San Giacomo-s/Mitchell Breitweiser-a. 4-Initial printings with errors exist 3.00
The Collected Edition (Speakeasy Comics, 2005, $17.99) r/series; Bendis intro 18.00

PHANTOM LADY (1st Series) (My Love Secret #24 on) (Also see All Top, Daring Adventures, Freedom Fighters, Jungle Thrills, & Wonder Boy)
Fox Features Syndicate: No. 13, Aug, 1947 - No. 23, Apr, 1949

	GD	VG	FN	VF	VF/NM	NM-
13(#1)-Phantom Lady by Matt Baker begins (see Police Comics #1 for 1st app.); Blue Beetle story	432	864	1296	3154	5577	8000
14-16: 14(#2)-Not Baker-c. 15-P.L. injected with experimental drug. 16-Negligee-c, panels; true crime stories begin	271	542	813	1734	2967	4200
17-Classic bondage cover; used in **SOTI**, illo "Sexual stimulation by combining 'headlights' with the sadist's dream of tying up a woman"	703	1406	2109	5132	9066	13,000
18,19	187	374	561	1197	2049	2900
20-22	158	316	474	1002	1726	2450
23-Bondage-c	187	374	561	1197	2049	2900

NOTE: ***Matt Baker*** *a-in all; c-13, 15-21.* ***Kamen*** *a-22, 23.*

PHANTOM LADY (2nd Series) (See Terrific Comics) (Formerly Linda)
Ajax/Farrell Publ.: V1#5, Dec-Jan, 1954/1955 - No. 4, June, 1955

	GD	VG	FN	VF	VF/NM	NM-
V1#5(#1)-By Matt Baker	123	246	369	787	1344	1900
V1#2-Last pre-code	90	180	270	576	988	1400
3,4-Red Rocket. 3-Heroin story	71	142	213	454	777	1100

PHANTOM LADY
Verotik Publications: 1994 ($9.95)

1-Reprints G. A. stories from Phantom Lady and All Top Comics; Adam Hughes-c 10.00

PHANTOM PLANET, THE
Dell Publishing Co.: No. 1234, 1961

	GD	VG	FN	VF	VF/NM	NM-
Four Color 1234-Movie	7	14	21	47	76	105

PHANTOM STRANGER, THE (1st Series)(See Saga of Swamp Thing)
National Periodical Publications: Aug-Sept, 1952 - No. 6, June-July, 1953

	GD	VG	FN	VF	VF/NM	NM-
1(Scarce)-1st app.	206	412	618	1318	2259	3200
2 (Scarce)	113	226	339	718	1234	1750
3-6 (Scarce)	97	194	291	621	1061	1500

Ashcan (8,9/52) Not distributed to newsstands, only for in house use (no known sales)

PHANTOM STRANGER, THE (2nd Series) (See Showcase #80) (See Showcase Presents for B&W reprints)
National Periodical Publs.: May-June, 1969 - No. 41, Feb-Mar, 1976; No. 42, Mar, 2010

	GD	VG	FN	VF	VF/NM	NM-
1-2nd S.A. app. P. Stranger; only 12¢ issue	12	24	36	82	154	225
2,3	7	14	21	45	73	100
4-1st new look Phantom Stranger; N. Adams-a	7	14	21	49	80	110
5-7	5	10	15	35	55	75
8-14: 14-Last 15¢ issue	4	8	12	24	37	50
15-19: All 25¢ giants (52 pgs.)	4	8	12	26	41	55
20-Dark Circle begins, ends #24.	3	6	9	17	25	32
21,22	3	6	9	14	20	25
23-Spawn of Frankenstein begins by Kaluta	4	8	12	26	41	55
24,25,27-30-Last Spawn of Frankenstein	3	6	9	20	30	40
26- Book-length story featuring Phantom Stranger, Dr. 13 & Spawn of Frankenstein	4	8	12	22	34	45
31-The Black Orchid begins (6-7/74).	3	6	9	19	29	38
32,34-38: 34-Last 20¢ issue (#35 on are 25¢)	2	4	6	13	18	22
33,39-41: 33-Deadman-c/story. 39-41-Deadman app.	3	6	9	14	20	25

42-(3/10, $2.99) Blackest Night one-shot; Syaf-a; Spectre, Deadman and Blue Devil app. 3.00

NOTE: ***N. Adams*** *a-4; c-3-19.* ***Anderson*** *a-4, 5i.* ***Aparo*** *a-7-17, 19-26; c-20-24, 33-41.* ***B. Bailey*** *a-27-30.* ***DeZuniga*** *a-12-16, 18, 19, 21, 22, 31, 34.* ***Grell*** *a-33.* ***Kaluta*** *a-23-25; c-26.* ***Meskin*** *r-15, 16, 18, 19.* ***Redondo*** *a-32, 35, 36.* ***Sparling*** *a-20.* ***Starr*** *a-17r.* ***Toth*** *a-15r. Black Orchid by* ***Carrillo***-*38-41. Dr. 13 solo in-13, 18, 19, 20, 21, 34. Frankenstein by* ***Kaluta***-*23-25; by* ***Baily***-*27-30. No Black Orchid-33, 34, 37.*

PHANTOM STRANGER (See Justice League of America #103)
DC Comics: Oct, 1987 - No. 4, Jan, 1988 (75¢, limited series)

1-4-Mignola/Russell-c/a & Eclipso app. in all. 3,4-Eclipso-c 3.00

PHANTOM STRANGER (See Vertigo Visions-The Phantom Stranger)

PHANTOM: THE GHOST WHO WALKS
Marvel Comics: Feb, 1995 - No. 3, Apr, 1995 ($2.95, limited series)

1-3 4.00

PHANTOM: THE GHOST WHO WALKS
Moonstone: 2003 ($16.95, TPB)

nn-Three new stories by Raab, Goulart, Collins, Blanco and others; Klauba painted-c 17.00

PHANTOM 2040 (TV cartoon)
Marvel Comics: May, 1995 - No. 4, Aug, 1995 ($1.50)

1-4-Based on animated series; Ditko-a(p) in all 3.00

PHANTOM WITCH DOCTOR (Also see Durango Kid #8 & Eerie #8)
Avon Periodicals: 1952

	GD	VG	FN	VF	VF/NM	NM-
1-Kinstler-c/a (7 pgs.)	48	96	144	302	514	725

PHANTOM ZONE, THE (See Adventure #283 & Superboy #100, 104)
DC Comics: January, 1982 - No. 4, April, 1982

1-4-Superman app. in all. 2-4: Batman, Green Lantern app. 3.00

NOTE: ***Colan*** *a-1-4p; c-1-4p.* ***Giordano*** *c-1-4i.*

PHAZE
Eclipse Comics: Apr, 1988 - No. 2, Oct, 1988 ($2.25)

1,2: 1-Sienkiewicz-c. 2-Gulacy painted-c 3.00

PHIL RIZZUTO (Baseball Hero)(See Sport Thrills, Accepted reprint)
Fawcett Publications: 1951 (New York Yankees)

	GD	VG	FN	VF	VF/NM	NM-
nn-Photo-c	70	140	210	445	765	1085

PHOENIX
Atlas/Seaboard Publ.: Jan, 1975 - No. 4, Oct, 1975

	GD	VG	FN	VF	VF/NM	NM-
1-Origin; Rovin-s/Amendola-a	2	4	6	8	11	14
2-4: 3-Origin & only app. The Dark Avenger. 4-New origin/costume The Protector (formerly Phoenix)	2	4	6	8	10	12

NOTE: ***Infantino*** *appears in #1, 2.* ***Austin*** *a-3i.* ***Thorne*** *c-3.*

PHOENIX
Ardden Entertainment (Atlas Comics): Mar, 2011 - Present ($2.99)

1-Krueger & Deneen-s/Zachary-a; origin re-told 3.00
... Issue Zero - NY Comicon Edition (10/10, $2.99) Dorien-a; origin prequel to #1 3.00

PHOENIX (...The Untold Story)
Marvel Comics Group: April, 1984 ($2.00, one-shot)

	GD	VG	FN	VF	VF/NM	NM-
1-Byrne/Austin-r/X-Men #137 with original unpublished ending	2	4	6	8	10	12

PHOENIX RESURRECTION, THE
Malibu Comics (Ultraverse): 1995 - 1996 ($3.95)

Pictorial Romances #4 © STJ

Picture News #8 © 299 L.S.C.

The Pilgrim #2 © Ryan & Grell

	GD 2.0	VG 4.0	FN 6.0	VF 8.0	VF/NM 9.0	NM- 9.2

Genesis #1 (12/95)-X-Men app; wraparound-c, Revelations #1 (12/95)-X-Men app; wraparound-c, Aftermath #1 (1/96)-X-Men app. 4.00
0-($1.95)-r/series 3.00
0-American Entertainment Ed. 4.00

PHOENIX WITHOUT ASHES
IDW Publishing: Aug, 2010 - No. 4, Nov, 2010 ($3.99, limited series)

1-Harlan Ellison-s/Alan Robinson-a 4.00

PICNIC PARTY (See Dell Giants)

PICTORIAL CONFESSIONS (Pictorial Romances #4 on)
St. John Publishing Co.: Sept, 1949 - No. 3, Dec, 1949

1-Baker-c/a(3) 50 100 150 315 533 750
2-Baker-a; photo-c 28 56 84 165 270 375
3-Kubert, Baker-a; part Kubert-c 29 58 87 170 278 385

PICTORIAL LOVE STORIES (Formerly Tim McCoy)
Charlton Comics: No. 22, Oct, 1949 - No. 26, July, 1950 (all photo-c)

22-26: All have "Me-Dan Cupid". 25-Fred Astaire-c 19 38 57 111 176 240

PICTORIAL LOVE STORIES
St. John Publishing Co.: October, 1952

1-Baker-c 34 68 102 204 332 460

PICTORIAL ROMANCES (Formerly Pictorial Confessions)
St. John Publ. Co.: No. 4, Jan, 1950; No. 5, Jan, 1951 - No. 24, Mar, 1954

4-Baker-a; photo-c 32 64 96 192 314 435
5,10-All Matt Baker issues. 5-Reprints all stories from #4 w/new Baker-c 30 60 90 177 289 400
6-9,12,13,15,16-Baker-c, 2-3 stories 28 56 84 165 270 375
11-Baker-c/a(3); Kubert-r/Hollywood Confessions #1 30 60 90 177 289 400
14,21-24: Baker-c/a each. 21,24-Each has signed story by Estrada 28 56 84 165 270 375
17-20(7/53, 25¢, 100 pgs.): Baker-c/a; each has two signed stories by Estrada 48 96 144 302 514 725

NOTE: ***Matt Baker** art in most issues. **Estrada** a-17-20(2), 21, 24.*

PICTURE NEWS
Lafayette Street Corp.: Jan, 1946 - No. 10, Jan-Feb, 1947

1-Milt Gross begins, ends No. 6; 4 pg. Kirby-a; A-Bomb-c/story 42 84 126 265 445 625
2-Atomic explosion panels; Frank Sinatra/Perry Como story 22 44 66 132 216 300
3-Atomic explosion panels; Frank Sinatra, June Allyson, Benny Goodman stories 20 40 60 117 189 260
4-Atomic explosion panels; "Caesar and Cleopatra" movie adapt. w/Claude Raines & Vivian Leigh; Jackie Robinson story 22 44 66 128 209 290
5-7: 5-Hank Greenberg story; Atomic explosion panel. 6-Joe Louis-c/story 17 34 51 98 154 210
8,10: 8-Monte Hale story (9-10/46; 1st?). 10-Dick Quick; A-Bomb story; Krigstein, Gross-a 18 36 54 103 162 220
9-A-Bomb story; "Crooked Mile" movie adaptation; Joe DiMaggio story. 20 40 60 114 182 250

PICTURE PARADE (Picture Progress #5 on)
Gilberton Company (Also see A Christmas Adventure): Sept, 1953 - V1#4, Dec, 1953 (28 pgs.)

V1#1-Andy's Atomic Adventures; A-bomb blast-c; (Teachers version distributed to schools exists) 20 40 60 114 182 250
2-Around the World with the United Nations 12 24 36 69 97 125
3-Adventures of the Lost One(The American Indian), 4-A Christmas Adventure (r-under same title in 1969) 12 24 36 69 97 125

PICTURE PROGRESS (Formerly Picture Parade)
Gilberton Corp.: V1#5, Jan, 1954 - V3#2, Oct, 1955 (28-36 pgs.)

V1#5-9,V2#1-9: 5-News in Review 1953. 6-The Birth of America. 7-The Four Seasons. 8-Paul Revere's Ride. 9-The Hawaiian Islands(5/54). V2#1-The Story of Flight(9/54). 2-Vote for Crazy River (The Meaning of Elections). 3-Louis Pasteur. 4-The Star Spangled Banner. 5-News in Review 1954. 6-Alaska: The Great Land. 7-Life in the Circus. 8-The Time of the Cave Man. 9-Summer Fun(5/55) 9 18 27 50 65 80
V3#1,2: 1-The Man Who Discovered America. 2-The Lewis & Clark Expedition 9 18 27 47 61 75

PICTURE SCOPE JUNGLE ADVENTURES (See Jungle Thrills)

PICTURE STORIES FROM AMERICAN HISTORY
National/All-American/E. C. Comics: 1945 - No. 4, Sum, 1947 (#1,2: 10¢, 56 pgs.; #3,4: 15¢, 52 pgs.)

1 30 60 90 177 289 400
2-4 24 48 72 140 230 320

PICTURE STORIES FROM SCIENCE
E.C. Comics: Spring, 1947 - No. 2, Fall, 1947

1-(15¢) 30 60 90 177 289 400
2-(10¢) 24 48 72 140 230 320

PICTURE STORIES FROM THE BIBLE (See Narrative Illustration, the Story of the Comics by M.C. Gaines)
National/All-American/E.C. Comics: 1942 - No. 4, Fall, 1943; 1944-46

1-4('42-Fall, '43)-Old Testament (DC) 24 48 72 142 234 325
Complete Old Testament Edition, (12/43-DC, 50¢, 232 pgs.);-1st printing; contains #1-4; 2nd - 8th (1/47) printings exist; later printings by E.C. some with 65¢-c 30 60 90 177 289 400
Complete Old Testament Edition (1945-publ. by Bible Pictures Ltd.)-232 pgs., hardbound, in color with dust jacket 30 60 90 177 289 400

NOTE: *Both Old and New Testaments published in England by Bible Pictures Ltd. in hardback, 1943, in color, 376 pgs. (2 vols.: O.T. 232 pgs. & N.T. 144 pgs.), and were also published by Scarf Press in 1979 (Old Test., $9.95) and in 1980 (New Test., $7.95)*

1-3(New Test.; 1944-46, DC)-52 pgs. ea. 20 40 60 114 182 250
The Complete Life of Christ Edition (1945, 25¢, 96 pgs.)-Contains #1&2 of the New Testament Edition 30 60 90 177 289 400
1,2(Old Testament-r in comic book form)(E.C., 1946; 52 pgs.) 20 40 60 114 182 250
1(DC),2(AA),3(EC)(New Testament-r in comic book form)(E.C., 1946; 52 pgs.) 20 40 60 114 182 250
Complete New Testament Edition (1945-E.C., 40¢, 144 pgs.)-Contains #1-3 1946 printing has 50¢-c 30 60 90 117 289 400

NOTE: *Another British series entitled **The Bible Illustrated** from 1947 has recently been discovered, with the same internal artwork. This eight edition series (5-OT, 3-NT) is of particular interest to Classics Ill. collectors because it exactly copied the C.I. logo format. The British publisher was Thorpe & Porter, who in 1951 began publishing the British Classics Ill. series. All editions of The Bible Ill. have new British painted covers. While this market is still new, and not all editions have as yet been found, current market value is about the same as the first U.S. editions of Picture Stories From The Bible.*

PICTURE STORIES FROM WORLD HISTORY
E.C. Comics: Spring, 1947 - No. 2, Summer, 1947 (52, 48 pgs.)

1-(15¢) 30 60 90 177 289 400
2-(10¢) 24 48 72 140 230 320

PILGRIM, THE
IDW Publishing: 2010 - Present ($3.99, limited series)

1,2-Mike Grell-a/c; Mark Ryan-s 4.00

PILOT SEASON...
Image Comics (Top Cow): 2008 - 2010 ($1.00/$2.99/$3.99, one-shots)

...: Asset (9/10, $3.99) Sablik-s/Marquez-a/Frison-c 4.00
...: Crosshair (10/10, $3.99) Katz-s/Jefferson-a/Silvestri-c 4.00
...: Declassified (10/09, $1.00) Preview of one-shots with covers, script and sketch pgs. 3.00
...: Demonic (1/10, $2.99) Kirkman-s/Benitez-a; two covers by Silvestri 3.00
...: Forever (10/10, $3.99) Inglesby-s/Nachlik-a/Hutomo-c 4.00
...: Murdered (11/09, $2.99) Kirkman-s/Blake-a; two covers by Silvestri 3.00
...: 7 Days From Hell (10/10, $3.99) Noto-a/Hill & Levin-s/Stelfreeze-c 4.00
...: Stellar (7/10, $2.99) Kirkman-s/Chang-a/Silvestri-c 3.00
...: 39 Minutes (9/10, $3.99) Harms-s/Lando-a/Albuquerque-c 4.00
...: Twilight Guardian (5/08, $3.99) Hickman-s 4.00

PINHEAD
Marvel Comics (Epic Comics): Dec, 1993 - No. 6, May, 1994 ($2.50)

1-($2.95)-Embossed foil-c by Kelley Jones; Intro Pinhead & Disciples (Snakeoil, Hangman, Fan Dancer & Dixie) 4.00
2-6 3.00

PINHEAD & FOODINI (TV)(Also see Foodini & Jingle Dingle Christmas...)
Fawcett Publications: July, 1951 - No. 4, Jan, 1952 (Early TV comic)

1-(52 pgs.)-Photo-c; based on TV puppet show 32 64 96 188 307 425
2,3-Photo-c 16 32 48 94 147 200
4 14 28 42 80 115 150

PINHEAD VS. MARSHALL LAW (Law in Hell)
Marvel Comics (Epic): Nov, 1993 - No. 2, Dec, 1993 ($2.95, lim. series)

1,2: 1-Embossed red foil-c. 2-Embossed silver foil-c 3.00

PINK DUST
Kitchen Sink Press: 1998 ($3.50, B&W, mature)

1-J. O'Barr-s/a 3.50

Pinky and the Brain #18 © WB

Pioneer Picture Stories #2 © S&S

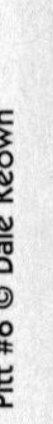
Pitt #6 © Dale Keown

PINK PANTHER, THE (TV)(See The Inspector & Kite Fun Book)
Gold Key #1-70/Whitman #71-87: April, 1971 - No. 87, Mar, 1984

	GD 2.0	VG 4.0	FN 6.0	VF 8.0	VF/NM 9.0	NM- 9.2
1-The Inspector begins	5	10	15	34	55	75
2-5	3	6	9	18	27	35
6-10	3	6	9	14	19	24
11-30: Warren Tufts-a #16-on	2	4	6	9	13	16
31-60	2	4	6	8	11	14
61-70	1	2	3	5	7	9
71-74,81-83: 81(2/82), 82(3/82), 83(4/82)	2	4	6	8	10	12
75(8/80)-77 (Whitman pre-pack) (scarce)	3	6	9	19	29	38
78(1/81)-80 (Whitman pre-pack) (not as scarce)	2	4	6	10	14	18
78 (1/81, 40¢-c) Cover price error variant	3	6	9	14	20	26
84-87(All #90266 on-c, no date or date code): 84(6/83), 85(8/83), 87(3/84)	3	6	9	14	20	26
Mini-comic No. 1(1976)(3-1/4x6-1/2")	1	3	4	6	8	10

NOTE: *Pink Panther began as a movie cartoon. (See Golden Comics Digest #38, 45 and March of Comics #376, 384, 390, 409, 418, 429, 441, 449, 461, 473, 486); #37, 72, 80-85 contain reprints.*

PINK PANTHER SUPER SPECIAL (TV)
Harvey Comics: Oct, 1993 ($2.25, 68 pgs.)

	GD 2.0	VG 4.0	FN 6.0	VF 8.0	VF/NM 9.0	NM- 9.2
V2#1-The Inspector & Wendy Witch stories also						4.00

PINK PANTHER, THE
Harvey Comics: Nov, 1993 - No. 9, July, 1994 ($1.50)

	GD 2.0	VG 4.0	FN 6.0	VF 8.0	VF/NM 9.0	NM- 9.2
V2#1-9						3.00

PINKY & THE BRAIN (See Animaniacs)
DC Comics: July, 1996 - No. 27, Nov, 1998 ($1.75/$1.95/$1.99)

	GD 2.0	VG 4.0	FN 6.0	VF 8.0	VF/NM 9.0	NM- 9.2
1-27, ...Christmas Special (1/96, $1.50)						3.00

PINKY LEE (See Adventures of...)

PINKY THE EGGHEAD
I.W./Super Comics: 1963 (Reprints from Noodnik)

	GD 2.0	VG 4.0	FN 6.0	VF 8.0	VF/NM 9.0	NM- 9.2
I.W. Reprint #1,2(nd)	2	4	6	8	11	14
Super Reprint #14-r/Noodnik Comics #4	2	4	6	8	11	14

PINOCCHIO (See 4-Color #92, 252, 545, 1203, Mickey Mouse Mag. V5#3, Movie Comics under Wonderful Advs. of..., New Advs. of..., Thrilling Comics #2, Walt Disney Showcase, Walt Disney's..., Wonderful Advs. of..., & World's Greatest Stories #2)
Dell Publishing Co.: No. 92, 1945 - No. 1203, Mar, 1962 (Disney)

	GD 2.0	VG 4.0	FN 6.0	VF 8.0	VF/NM 9.0	NM- 9.2
Four Color 92-The Wonderful Adventures of...; 16 pg. Donald Duck story ; entire book by Kelly	47	94	141	376	763	1150
Four Color 252 (10/49)-Origin, not by Kelly	10	20	30	71	128	185
Four Color 545 (3/54)-The Wonderful Advs. of...; part-r of 4-Color #92; Disney-movie	7	14	21	47	76	105
Four Color 1203 (3/62)	5	10	15	34	55	75

PINOCCHIO AND THE EMPEROR OF THE NIGHT
Marvel Comics: Mar, 1988 ($1.25, 52 pgs.)

	GD 2.0	VG 4.0	FN 6.0	VF 8.0	VF/NM 9.0	NM- 9.2
1-Adapts film						4.00

PINOCCHIO LEARNS ABOUT KITES (See Kite Fun Book)

PIN-UP PETE (Also see Great Lover Romances & Monty Hall...)
Toby Press: 1952

	GD 2.0	VG 4.0	FN 6.0	VF 8.0	VF/NM 9.0	NM- 9.2
1-Jack Sparling pin-ups	19	38	57	109	172	235

PIONEER MARSHAL (See Fawcett Movie Comics)

PIONEER PICTURE STORIES
Street & Smith Publications: Dec, 1941 - No. 9, Dec, 1943

	GD 2.0	VG 4.0	FN 6.0	VF 8.0	VF/NM 9.0	NM- 9.2
1-The Legless Air Ace begins	37	74	111	222	361	500
2 -True life story of Errol Flynn	19	38	57	109	172	235
3-9	15	30	45	88	137	185

PIONEER WEST ROMANCES (Firehair #1,2,7-11)
Fiction House Magazines: No. 3, Spring, 1950 - No. 6, Winter, 1950-51

	GD 2.0	VG 4.0	FN 6.0	VF 8.0	VF/NM 9.0	NM- 9.2
3-(52 pgs.)-Firehair continues	19	38	57	109	172	235
4-6	19	38	57	109	172	235

PIPSQUEAK (See The Adventures of...)

PIRACY
E. C. Comics: Oct-Nov, 1954 - No. 7, Oct-Nov, 1955

	GD 2.0	VG 4.0	FN 6.0	VF 8.0	VF/NM 9.0	NM- 9.2
1-Williamson/Torres-a	27	54	81	216	346	475
2-Williamson/Torres-a	17	34	51	136	218	300
3-7: 5-7-Comics Code symbol on cover	14	28	42	112	176	240

NOTE: ***Crandall** a-in all; c-2-4. **Davis** a-1, 2, 6. **Evans** a-3-7; c-7. **Ingels** a-3-7. **Krigstein** a-3-5, 7; c-5, 6. **Wood** a-1, 2; c-1.*

PIRACY
Gemstone Publishing: March, 1998 - No. 7, Sept, 1998 ($2.50)

	GD 2.0	VG 4.0	FN 6.0	VF 8.0	VF/NM 9.0	NM- 9.2
1-7: E.C. reprints						3.00
Annual 1 ($10.95) Collects #1-4						11.00
Annual 2 ($7.95) Collects #5-7						8.00

PIRANA (See The Phantom #46 & Thrill-O-Rama #2, 3)

PIRATE CORP$, THE (See Hectic Planet)
Eternity Comics/Slave Labor Graphics: 1987 - No. 4, 1988 ($1.95)

	GD 2.0	VG 4.0	FN 6.0	VF 8.0	VF/NM 9.0	NM- 9.2
1-4: 1,2-Color. 3,4-B&W						3.00
Special 1 ('89, B&W)-Slave Labor Publ.						3.00

PIRATE CORP$, THE (Volume 2)
Slave Labor Graphics: 1989 - No. 6, 1992 ($1.95)

	GD 2.0	VG 4.0	FN 6.0	VF 8.0	VF/NM 9.0	NM- 9.2
1-6-Dorkin-s/a						3.00

PIRATE OF THE GULF, THE (See Superior Stories #2)

PIRATES COMICS
Hillman Periodicals: Feb-Mar, 1950 - No. 4, Aug-Sept, 1950 (All 52 pgs.)

	GD 2.0	VG 4.0	FN 6.0	VF 8.0	VF/NM 9.0	NM- 9.2
1	24	48	72	140	230	320
2-Dave Berg-a	17	34	51	98	154	210
3,4-Berg-a	15	30	45	88	137	185

PIRATES OF CONEY ISLAND, THE
Image Comics: Oct, 2006 - No. 8 ($2.99)

	GD 2.0	VG 4.0	FN 6.0	VF 8.0	VF/NM 9.0	NM- 9.2
1-6-Rick Spears-s/Vasilis Lolos-a; two covers. 2-Cloonan var-c						3.00

PIRATES OF DARK WATER, THE (Hanna Barbera)
Marvel Comics: Nov, 1991 - No. 9, Aug, 1992 ($1.95)

	GD 2.0	VG 4.0	FN 6.0	VF 8.0	VF/NM 9.0	NM- 9.2
1-9: 9-Vess-c						3.00

P.I.'S: MICHAEL MAUSER AND MS. TREE, THE
First Comics: Jan, 1985 - No. 3, May, 1985 ($1.25, limited series)

	GD 2.0	VG 4.0	FN 6.0	VF 8.0	VF/NM 9.0	NM- 9.2
1-3: Staton-c/a(p)						3.00

PITT, THE (Also see The Draft & The War)
Marvel Comics: Mar, 1988 ($3.25, 52 pgs., one-shot)

	GD 2.0	VG 4.0	FN 6.0	VF 8.0	VF/NM 9.0	NM- 9.2
1-Ties into Starbrand, D.P.7						4.00

PITT (See Youngblood #4 & Gen 13 #3,#4)
Image Comics #1-9/Full Bleed #1/2,10-on: Jan, 1993 - No. 20 ($1.95, intended as a four part limited series)

	GD 2.0	VG 4.0	FN 6.0	VF 8.0	VF/NM 9.0	NM- 9.2
1/2-(12/95)-1st Full Bleed issue						4.00
1-Dale Keown-c/a. 1-1st app. The Pitt						4.00
2-13: All Dale Keown-c/a. 3 (Low distribution). 10 (1/96)-Indicia reads "January 1995"						3.00
14-20: 14-Begin $2.50-c, pullout poster						3.00
TPB-(1997, $9.95) r/#1/2, 1-4						10.00
TPB 2-(1999, $11.95) r/#5-9						12.00

PITT CREW
Full Bleed Studios: Aug, 1998 - No. 5, Dec, 1999 ($2.50)

	GD 2.0	VG 4.0	FN 6.0	VF 8.0	VF/NM 9.0	NM- 9.2
1-5: 1-Richard Pace-s/Ken Lashley-a. 2-4-Scott Lee-a						3.00

PITT IN THE BLOOD
Full Bleed Studios: Aug, 1996 ($2.50, one-shot)

	GD 2.0	VG 4.0	FN 6.0	VF 8.0	VF/NM 9.0	NM- 9.2
nn-Richard Pace-a/script						3.00

PIXIE & DIXIE & MR. JINKS (TV)(See Jinks, Pixie, and Dixie & Whitman Comic Books)
Dell Publishing Co./Gold Key: July-Sept, 1960 - Feb, 1963 (Hanna-Barbera)

	GD 2.0	VG 4.0	FN 6.0	VF 8.0	VF/NM 9.0	NM- 9.2
Four Color 1112	7	14	21	50	83	115
Four Color 1196,1264, 01-631-207 (Dell, 7/62)	6	12	18	37	59	80
1(2/63-Gold Key)	6	12	18	43	69	95

PIXIE PUZZLE ROCKET TO ADVENTURELAND
Avon Periodicals: Nov, 1952

	GD 2.0	VG 4.0	FN 6.0	VF 8.0	VF/NM 9.0	NM- 9.2
1	14	28	42	82	121	160

PIXIES, THE (Advs. of...)(The Mighty Atom and ...#6 on)(See A-1 Comics #16)
Magazine Enterprises: Winter, 1946 - No. 4, Fall?, 1947; No. 5, 1948

	GD 2.0	VG 4.0	FN 6.0	VF 8.0	VF/NM 9.0	NM- 9.2
1-Mighty Atom	9	18	27	52	69	85
2-5-Mighty Atom	6	12	18	29	36	42
I.W. Reprint #1(1958), 8-(Pee-Wee Pixies), 10-I.W. on cover, Super on inside	2	4	6	8	10	12

PIZZAZZ
Marvel Comics: Oct, 1977 - No. 16, Jan, 1979 (slick-color kids mag. w/puzzles, games, comics)

1-Star Wars photo-c/article; origin Tarzan; KISS photos/article; Iron-On bonus; 2 pg. pin-up

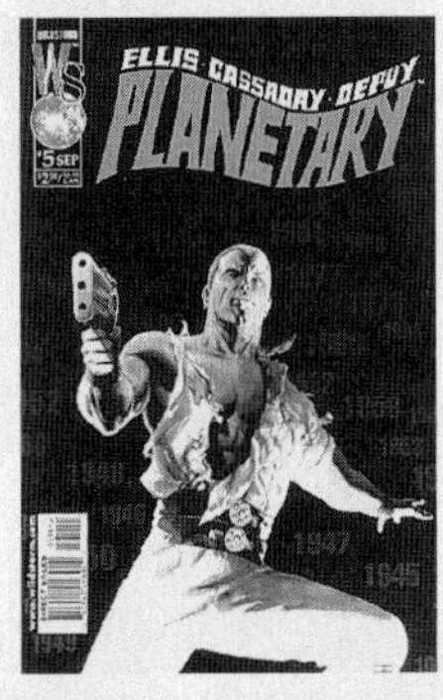

Planetary #5 © WSP

Planet Comics #59 © FH

Planet of the Apes (2011 series) #1 © 20th Century Fox

GD VG FN VF VF/NM NM-
2.0 4.0 6.0 8.0 9.0 9.2

calendars thru #8 3 6 9 20 30 40
2-Spider-Man-c; Beatles pin-up calendar 2 4 6 13 18 22
3-8: 3-Close Encounters-s; Bradbury-s. 4-Alice Cooper, Travolta; Charlie's Angels/Fonz/Hulk/ Spider-Man-c. 5-Star Trek quiz. 6-Asimov-s. 7-James Bond; Spock/Darth Vader-c.
8-TV Spider-Man photo-c/article 2 4 6 11 16 20
9-14: 9-Shaun Cassidy-c. 10-Sgt. Pepper-c/s. 12-Battlestar Galactica-s; Spider-Man app.
13-TV Hulk-c/s. 14-Meatloaf-c/s 2 4 6 10 14 18
15,16: 15-Battlestar Galactica-s. 16-Movie Superman photo-c/s, Hulk. 2 4 6 11 16 20

NOTE: ***Star Wars*** *comics in all (1-6:Chaykin-a, 7-9: DeZuniga-a, 10-13:Simonson/Janson-a. 14-16:Cockrum-a).* ***Tarzan*** *comics, 1pg.-#1-8. 1pg. "Hey Look" by Kurtzman #12-16.*

PLANETARY (See Preview in flip book Gen13 #33)
DC Comics (WildStorm Prod.): Apr, 1999 - No. 27, Dec, 2009 ($2.50/$2.95/$2.99)

1-Ellis-s/Cassaday-a/c 1 3 4 6 8 10
1-Special Edition (6/09, $1.00) r/#1 with "After Watchmen" cover frame 3.00
2-5 6.00
6-10 5.00
11-15: 12-Fourth Man revealed 4.00
16-26: 16-Begin $2.95-c. 23-Origin of The Drummer 3.00
27-($3.99) Wraparound gatefold-c 4.00
...: All Over the World and Other Stories (2000, $14.95) r/#1-6 & Preview 15.00
...: All Over the World and Other Stories-Hardcover (2000, $24.95) r/#1-6 & Preview; with dustjacket 25.00
.../Batman: Night on Earth 1 (8/03, $5.95) Ellis-s/Cassaday-a 6.00
...: Crossing Worlds (2004, $14.95) r/Batman, JLA, and The Authority x-overs 15.00
.../JLA: Terra Occulta (11/02, $5.95) Elseworlds; Ellis-s/Ordway-a 6.00
...: Leaving the 20th Century -HC (2004, $24.95) r/#13-18 25.00
...: Leaving the 20th Century -SC (2004, $14.99) r/#13-18 15.00
...: Spacetime Archaeology -HC (2010, $24.99) r/#19-27 25.00
...: Spacetime Archaeology -SC (2010, $17.99) r/#19-27 18.00
.../The Authority: Ruling the World (8/00, $5.95) Ellis-s/Phil Jimenez-a 6.00
...: The Fourth Man -Hardcover (2001, $24.95) r/#7-12 25.00
...: The Planetary Reader (8/03, $5.95) r/#13-15 6.00

PLANETARY BRIGADE (Also see Hero Squared)
Boom Studios: Feb, 2006 - No. 2, Mar, 2006 ($2.99)

1-3-Giffen & DeMatteis-s/art by various; Haley-c 3.00
... Origins 1-3 (10/06-4/07, $3.99) Giffen & DeMatteis-s/Julia Bax-a 4.00

PLANET COMICS
Fiction House Magazines: 1/40 - No. 62, 9/49; No. 63, Wint, 1949-50; No. 64, Spring, 1950; No. 65, 1951(nd); No. 66-68, 1952(nd); No. 69, Wint, 1952-53; No. 70-72, 1953(nd); No. 73, Winter, 1953-54

1-Origin Auro, Lord of Jupiter by Briefer (ends #61); Flint Baker & The Red Comet begin; Eisner/Fine-c 1275 2550 3825 9500 17,000 24,500
2-Lou Fine-c (Scarce) 443 886 1329 3234 5717 8200
3-Eisner-c 303 606 909 2121 3711 5300
4-Gale Allen and the Girl Squadron begins 290 580 870 1856 3178 4500
5,6-(Scarce): 5-Eisner/Fine-c 284 568 852 1818 3109 4400
7-12: 8-Robot-c. 12-The Star Pirate begins 213 426 639 1363 2332 3300
13,14: 13-Reff Ryan begins 155 310 465 992 1696 2400
15-(Scarce)-Mars, God of War begins (11/41); see Jumbo Comics #31 for 1st app. 303 606 909 2121 3711 5300
16-20,22 142 284 426 909 1555 2200
21-The Lost World & Hunt Bowman begin 148 296 444 947 1624 2300
23-26: 26-Space Rangers begin (9/43), end #71 129 258 387 826 1413 2000
27-30 103 206 309 659 1130 1600
31-35: 33-Origin Star Pirates Wonder Boots, reprinted in #52. 35-Mysta of the Moon begins, ends #62 90 180 270 576 988 1400
36-45: 38-1st Mysta of the Moon-c. 41-New origin of "Auro, Lord of Jupiter". 42-Last Gale Allen. 43-Futura begins 84 168 252 538 919 1300
46-60: 48-Robot-c. 53-Used in **SOTI**, pg. 32 66 132 198 419 722 1025
61-68,70: 64,70-Robot-c. 65-70-All partial-r of earlier issues. 70-r/stories from #41 49 98 147 309 522 735
69-Used in **POP**, pgs. 101,102 50 100 150 315 533 750
71-73-No series stories. 71-Space Rangers strip 40 80 120 246 411 575
I.W. Reprint 1,8,9: 1(nd)-r/#70; cover-r from Attack on Planet Mars. 8 (r/#72), 9-r/#73 8 16 24 54 90 125

NOTE: ***Anderson*** *a-33-38, 40-51 (Star Pirate).* ***Matt Baker*** *a-53-59 (Mysta of the Moon).* ***Celardo*** *c-12.* ***Bill Discount*** *a-71 (Space Rangers).* ***Elias*** *c-70.* ***Evans*** *a-46-49 (Auro, Lord of Jupiter), 50-64 (Lost World).* ***Fine*** *c-2, 5.* ***Hopper*** *a-31, 35 (Gale Allen), 41, 42, 48, 49 (Mysta of the Moon).* ***Ingels*** *a-24-31 (Lost World), 56-61 (Auro, Lord of Jupiter).* ***Lubbers*** *a-44-47 (Space Rangers); c-40, 41.* ***Moreira*** *a-43, 44 (Mysta of the Moon).* ***Renee*** *a-40-49 (Lost World); c-33, 35, 39.* ***Tuska*** *a-30 (Star Pirate).* ***M. Whitman*** *a-50-52 (Mysta of the Moon), 53-58 (Star Pirate); c-71-73.* ***Starr*** *a-59.* ***Zolnerwich*** *c-10. 13-25. Bondage c-53.*

PLANET COMICS
Pacific Comics: 1984 ($5.95)

1-Reprints Planet Comics #1(1940) 1 2 3 5 6 8

PLANET COMICS
Blackthorne Publishing: Apr, 1988 - No. 3 ($2.00, color/B&W #3)

1-New stories; Dave Stevens-c 5.00
2,3: New stories 4.00

PLANET HULK (See Incredible Hulk and Giant-Size Hulk #1 (2006))

PLANET OF THE APES (Magazine) (Also see Adventures on the... & Power Record Comics)
Marvel Comics Group: Aug, 1974 - No. 29, Feb, 1977 (B&W) (Based on movies)

1-Ploog-a 4 8 12 26 41 55
2-Ploog-a 3 6 9 17 25 32
3-10 3 6 9 14 20 26
11-20 3 6 9 16 22 28
21-28 (low distribution) 3 6 9 18 27 35
29 (low distribution) 5 10 15 35 55 75

NOTE: ***Alcala*** *a-7-11, 17-22, 24.* ***Ploog*** *a-1-4, 6, 8, 11, 13, 14, 19.* ***Sutton*** *a-11, 12, 15, 17, 19, 20, 23, 24, 29.* ***Tuska*** *a-1-6.*

PLANET OF THE APES
Adventure Comics: Apr, 1990 - No. 24, 1992 ($2.50, B&W)

1-New movie tie-in; comes w/outer-c (3 colors) 4.00
1-Limited serial numbered edition ($5.00) 5.00
1-2nd printing (no outer-c, $2.50) 3.00
2-24 3.00
Annual 1 ($3.50) 4.00
...Urchak's Folly 1-4 ($2.50, mini-series) 3.00

PLANET OF THE APES (The Human War)
Dark Horse Comics: Jun, 2001 - No. 3, Aug, 2001 ($2.99, limited series)

1-3-Follows the 2001 movie; Edginton-s 3.00

PLANET OF THE APES
Dark Horse Comics: Sept, 2001 - No. 6, Feb, 2002 ($2.99, ongoing series)

1-6: 1-3-Edginton-s. 1-Photo & Wagner covers. 2-Plunkett & photo-c 3.00

PLANET OF THE APES
BOOM! Studios: Apr, 2011 - Present ($3.99)

1-Takes place 1200 years before Taylor's arrival; Magno-a; three covers 4.00

PLANET OF VAMPIRES
Seaboard Publications (Atlas): Feb, 1975 - No. 3, July, 1975

1-Neal Adams-c(i); 1st Broderick-c/a(p); Hama-s 2 4 6 11 16 20
2,3: 2-Neal Adams-c. 3-Heath-c/a 2 4 6 8 11 14

PLANET TERRY
Marvel Comics (Star Comics)/Marvel: April, 1985 - No. 12, March, 1986 (Children's comic)

1-12 4.00
1-Variant with "Star Chase" game on last page & inside back-c 10.00

PLASM (See Warriors of Plasm)
Defiant Comics: June, 1993

0-Came bound into Diamond Previews V3#6 (6/93); price is for complete Previews with comic still attached 4.00
0-Comic only removed from Previews 2.00

PLASMER
Marvel Comics UK: Nov, 1993 - No. 4, Feb, 1994 ($1.95, limited series)

1-($2.50)-Polybagged w/4 trading cards 4.00
2-4: Capt. America & Silver Surfer app. 3.00

PLASTIC FORKS
Marvel Comis (Epic Comics): 1990 - No. 5, 1990 ($4.95, 68 pgs., limited series, mature)

Book 1-5: Squarebound 5.00

PLASTIC MAN (Also see Police Comics & Smash Comics #17)
Vital Publ. No. 1,2/Quality Comics No. 3 on: Sum, 1943 - No. 64, Nov, 1956

nn(#1)- "In The Game of Death"; Skull-c; Jack Cole-c/a begins; ends-#64? 423 846 1269 3067 5384 7700
nn(#2, 2/44)- "The Gay Nineties Nightmare" 181 362 543 1158 1979 2800
3 (Spr, '46) 118 236 354 749 1287 1825
4 (Sum, '46) 89 178 267 565 970 1375
5 (Aut, '46) 73 146 219 467 796 1125
6-10 60 120 180 381 653 925
11-15,17-20 53 106 159 334 567 800
16-Classic-c 61 122 183 390 670 950
21-30: 26-Last non-r issue? 41 82 123 256 428 600

Plastic Man #1 © DC

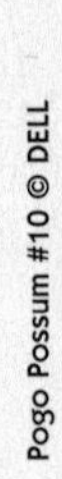

Pogo Possum #10 © DELL

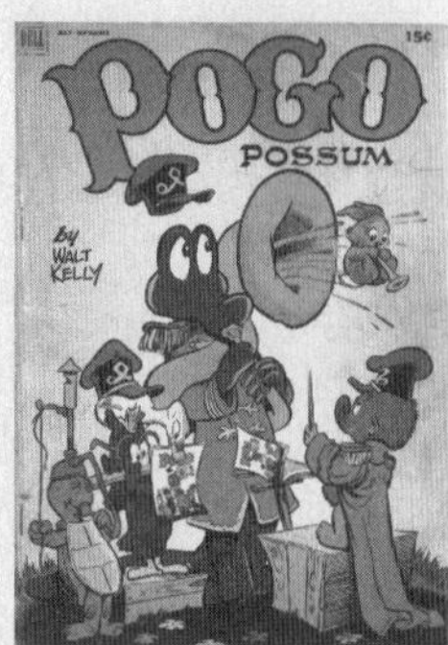

Poison Elves #69 © Drew Hayes

	GD 2.0	VG 4.0	FN 6.0	VF 8.0	VF/NM 9.0	NM- 9.2
31-40: 40-Used in POP, pg. 91	34	68	102	199	325	450
41-64: 53-Last precode issue. 54-Robot-c	26	52	78	152	249	345
Super Reprint 11,16,18: 11('63)-r/#16. 16-r/#18 & #21; Cole-a. 18('64)-Spirit-r by Eisner from Police #95	4	8	12	24	37	50

NOTE: *Cole r-44, 49, 56, 58, 59 at least. Cuidera c-32-64i.*

PLASTIC MAN (See DC Special #15 & House of Mystery #160)
National Periodical Publications/DC Comics: 11-12/66 - No. 10, 5-6/68; V4#11, 2-3/76 - No. 20, 10-11/77

	GD	VG	FN	VF	VF/NM	NM-
1-Real 1st app. Silver Age Plastic Man (House of Mystery #160 is actually tryout); Gil Kane-c/a; 12¢ issues begin	10	20	30	69	122	175
2-5: 4-Infantino-c; Mortimer-a	5	10	15	34	55	75
6-10('68): 7-G.A. Plastic Man & Woozy Winks (1st S.A. app.) app.; origin retold. 10-Sparling-a; last 12¢ issue	4	8	12	28	44	60
V4#11('76)-20: 11-20-Fradon-p. 17-Origin retold	2	4	6	8	11	14
...80-Page Giant (2003, $6.95) reprints origin and other stories in 80-Pg. Giant format						7.00
...Special 1 (8/99, $3.95)						4.00

PLASTIC MAN
DC Comics: Nov, 1988 - No. 4, Feb, 1989 ($1.00, mini-series)

	GD	VG	FN	VF	VF/NM	NM-
1-4: 1-Origin; Woozy Winks app.						3.00

PLASTIC MAN
DC Comics: Feb, 2004 - No. 20, Mar, 2006 ($2.95/$2.99)

	GD	VG	FN	VF	VF/NM	NM-
1-20-Kyle Baker-s/a in most. 1-Retells origin. 7,12-Scott Morse-s/a. 8-JLA cameo						3.00
...: On the Lam TPB (2004, $14.95) r/#1-6						15.00
...: Rubber Bandits TPB (2005, $14.99) r/#8-11,13,14						15.00

PLASTRON CAFE
Mirage Studios: Dec, 1992 - No. 4, July, 1993 ($2.25, B&W)

	GD	VG	FN	VF	VF/NM	NM-
1-4: 1-Teenage Mutant Ninja Turtles app.; Kelly Freas-c. 2-Hildebrandt painted-c. 4-Spaced & Alien Fire stories						3.00

PLAYFUL LITTLE AUDREY (TV)(Also see Little Audrey #25)
Harvey Publications: 6/57 - No. 110, 11/73; No. 111, 8/74 - No. 121, 4/76

	GD	VG	FN	VF	VF/NM	NM-
1	23	46	69	168	334	500
2	12	24	36	82	154	225
3-5	9	18	27	63	107	150
6-10	7	14	21	47	76	105
11-20	5	10	15	34	55	75
21-40	4	8	12	26	41	55
41-60	3	6	9	20	30	40
61-84: 84-Last 12¢ issue	3	6	9	16	22	28
85-99	2	4	6	11	16	20
100-52 pg. Giant	3	6	9	16	23	30
101-103: 52 pg. Giants	3	6	9	14	20	25
104-121	1	3	4	6	8	10
...In 3-D (Spring, 1988, $2.25, Blackthorne #66)						4.00

PLOP! (Also see The Best of DC #60)
National Periodical Publications: Sept-Oct, 1973 - No. 24, Nov-Dec, 1976

	GD	VG	FN	VF	VF/NM	NM-
1-Sergio Aragonés begins; Wrightson-a	4	8	12	24	37	50
2-4,6-20	3	6	9	14	20	26
5-Wrightson-a	3	6	9	16	22	28
21-24 (52 pgs.). 23-No Aragonés-a	3	6	9	16	23	30

NOTE: ***Alcala** a-1-3. **Anderson** a-5. **Aragonés** a-1-22, 24. **Ditko** a-16p. **Evans** a-1. **Mayer** a-1. **Orlando** a-21, 22; c-21. **Sekowsky** a-5, 6p. **Toth** a-11. **Wolverton** r-4, 22-24(1 pg.ea.); c-1-12, 14, 17, 18. **Wood** a-14, 16i, 18-24; c-13, 15, 16, 19.*

PLUTO (See Cheerios Premiums, Four Color #537, Mickey Mouse Magazine, Walt Disney Showcase #4, 7, 13, 20, 23, 33 & Wheaties)
Dell Publ. Co.: No. 7, 1942; No. 429, 10/52 - No. 1248, 11-1/61-62 (Disney)

	GD	VG	FN	VF	VF/NM	NM-
Large Feature Comic 7(1942)-Written by Carl Barks, Jack Hannah, & Nick George (Barks' 1st comic book work)	161	322	483	1030	1765	2500
Four Color 429 (#1)	9	18	27	65	113	160
Four Color 509	6	12	18	41	66	90
Four Color 595,654,736,853	5	10	15	32	51	70
Four Color 941,1039,1143,1248	4	8	12	28	44	60

POCKET CLASSICS
Academic Inc. Publications: 1984 (B&W, 4 1/4" x 6 3/4", 68 pages)

C1(Black Beauty. C2(The Call of the Wild). C3(Dr. Jekyll and Mr. Hyde). C4(Dracula). C5(Frankenstein). C6(Huckleberry Finn). C7(Moby Dick). C8(The Red Badge of Courage). C9(The Time Machine). C10(Tom Sawyer). C11(Treasure Island). C12(20,000 Leagues Under the Sea). C13(The Great Adventures of Sherlock Holmes). C14(Gulliver's Travels). C15(The Hunchback of Notre Dame). C16(The Invisible Man). C17(Journey to the Center of the Earth). C18(Kidnapped). C19(The Mysterious Island). C20(The Scarlet Letter). C21(The Story of My Life). C22(A Tale of Two Cities). C23(The Three Musketeers). C24(The War of the Worlds). C25(Around the World in Eighty Days). C26(Captains Courageous). C27(A Connecticut Yankee in King Arthur's Court). C28(Sherlock Holmes - The Hound of the Baskervilles). C29(The House of the Seven Gables). C30(Jane Eyre). C31(The Last of the Mohicans). C32(The Best of O. Henry). C33(The Best of Poe). C34(Two Years Before the Mast). C35(White Fang). C36(Wuthering Heights). C37(Ben Hur). C38(A Christmas Carol). C39(The Food of the Gods). C40(Ivanhoe). C41(The Man in the Iron Mask). C42(The Prince and the Pauper). C43(The Prisoner of Zenda). C44(The Return of the Native). C45(Robinson Crusoe). C46(The Scarlet Pimpernel). C47(The Sea Wolf). C48(The Swiss Family Robinson). C49(Billy Budd). C50(Crime and Punishment). C51(Don Quixote). C52(Great Expectations). C53(Heidi). C54(The Illiad). C55(Lord Jim). C56(The Mutiny on Board H.M.S. Bounty). C57(The Odyssey). C58(Oliver Twist). C59(Pride and Prejudice). C60(The Turn of the Screw) each... 8.00

Shakespeare Series:
S1(As You Like It). S2(Hamlet). S3(Julius Caesar). S4(King Lear). S5(Macbeth). S6(The Merchant of Venice). S7(A Midsummer Night's Dream). S8(Othello). S9(Romeo and Juliet). S10(The Taming of the Shrew). S11(The Tempest). S12(Twelfth Night) each... 9.00

POCKET COMICS (Also see Double Up)
Harvey Publications: Aug, 1941 - No. 4, Jan, 1942 (Pocket size; 100 pgs.) (1st Harvey comic)

	GD	VG	FN	VF	VF/NM	NM-
1-Origin & 1st app. The Black Cat, Cadet Blakey the Spirit of '76, The Red Blazer, The Phantom, Sphinx, & The Zebra; Phantom Ranger, British Agent #99, Spin Hawkins, Satan, Lord of Evil begin (1st app. of each); Simon-c/a in #1-3	107	214	321	680	1165	1650
2 (9/41)-Black Cat on-c #2-4	68	136	204	435	743	1050
3,4	53	106	159	334	567	800

POE
Cheese Comics: Sept, 1996 - No. 6, Apr, 1997 ($2.00, B&W)

	GD	VG	FN	VF	VF/NM	NM-
1-6-Jason Asala-s/a						3.00

POE
Sirius Entertainment (Dogstar Press): Oct, 1997 - No. 24 ($2.50/$2.95, B&W)

	GD	VG	FN	VF	VF/NM	NM-
1-24-Jason Asala-s/a. 20-24 ($2.95)						3.00
... Color Special (12/98, $2.95) Linsner-c						3.00

POGO PARADE (See Dell Giants)

POGO POSSUM (Also see Animal Comics & Special Delivery)
Dell Publishing Co.: No. 105, 4/46 - No. 148, 5/47; 10-12/49 - No. 16, 4-6/54

	GD	VG	FN	VF	VF/NM	NM-
Four Color 105(1946)-Kelly-c/a	48	96	144	408	829	1250
Four Color 148-Kelly-c/a	40	80	120	320	635	950
1-(10-12/49)-Kelly-c/a in all	35	70	105	273	537	800
2	24	48	72	175	350	525
3-5	16	32	48	117	239	360
6-10: 10-Infinity-c	14	28	42	102	206	310
11-16: 11-X-Mas-c	12	24	36	82	154	225

NOTE: *#1-4, 9-13: 52 pgs.; #5-8, 14-16: 36 pgs.*

POINT BLANK (See Wildcats)
DC Comics (WildStorm): Oct, 2002 - No. 5, Feb, 2003 ($2.95, limited series)

	GD	VG	FN	VF	VF/NM	NM-
1-5-Brubaker-s/Wilson-a/Bisley-c. 1-Variant-c by Wilson; Grifter and John Lynch app.						3.00
TPB (2003, $14.95), (2009, $14.99) r/#1-5; afterword by Brubaker						15.00

POISON ELVES (Formerly I, Lusiphur)
Mulehide Graphics: No. 8, 1993- No. 20, 1995 (B&W, magazine/comic size, mature readers)

	GD	VG	FN	VF	VF/NM	NM-
8-Drew Hayes-c/a/scripts.	2	4	6	8	10	12
9-11: 11-1st comic size issue	2	4	6	8	10	12
12,14,16	1	2	3	5	6	8
13,15-(low print)	2	4	6	8	11	14
15-2nd print						4.00
17-20	1	2	3	5	6	8
...Desert of the Third Sin-(1997, $14.95, TPB)-r/#13-18						15.00
...Patrons-($4.95, TPB)-r/#19,20						5.00
...Traumatic Dogs-(1996, $14.95,TPB)-Reprints I, Lusiphur #7, Poison Elves #8-12						15.00

POISON ELVES (See I, Lusiphur)
Sirius Entertainment: June, 1995 - No. 79, Sept, 2004 ; No. 80, Nov, 2007 ($2.50/$2.95, B&W, mature readers)

	GD	VG	FN	VF	VF/NM	NM-
1-Linsner-c; Drew Hayes-a/scripts in all.						5.00
1-2nd print						3.00
2-25: 12-Purple Marauder-c/app.						3.00
26-45, 47-49						3.00
46,50-79: 61-Fillbäch Brothers-s/a. 74-Art by Crilley (3 pgs.)						3.00
80-($3.50) Tribute issue to Drew Hayes; sketchbook and notebook art with commentary						3.50
... Baptism By Fire-(2003, $19.95, TPB)-r/#48-59						20.00
... Color Special #1 (12/98, $2.95)						5.00

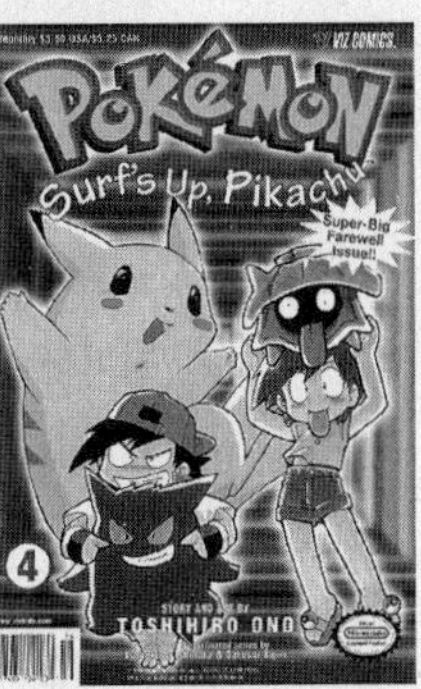

Pokemon Pt. 4 #4 © Nintendo

Police Action #3 © Seaboard

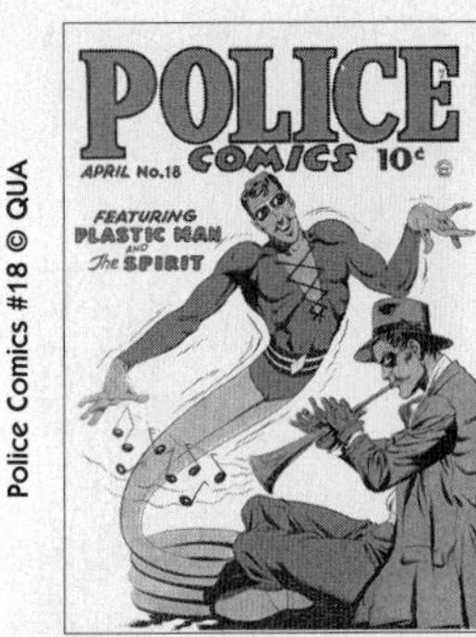

Police Comics #18 © QUA

GD 2.0 | VG 4.0 | FN 6.0 | VF 8.0 | VF/NM 9.0 | NM- 9.2

... Companion (12/02, $3.50) Back-story and character bios 3.50
... : Dark Wars TPB Vol. 1 (2005, $15.95) r/#60,62-68 16.00
... FAN Edition #1 mail-in offer; Drew Hayes-c/s/a 1 2 3 5 6 8
... Rogues-(2002, $15.95, TPB)-r/#40-47 16.00
...Salvation-(2001, $19.95, TPB)-r/#26-39 20.00
...Sanctuary-(1999, $14.95, TPB)-r/#1-12 15.00

POISON ELVES: DOMINION
Sirius Entertainment: Sept, 2005 - No. 6, Sept, 2006 ($3.50, B&W, limited series)

1-6-Keith Davidsen-s/Scott Lewis-a 3.50

POISON ELVES: HYENA
Sirius Entertainment: Sept, 2004 - No. 4, Feb, 2005 ($2.95, B&W, limited series)

1-4-Keith Davidsen-s/Scott Lewis-a 3.00
Ventures TPB Vol. 1: The Hyena Collection (2006, $14.95) r/#1-4 & 2 short stories 15.00

POISON ELVES: LOST TALES
Sirius Entertainment: Jan, 2006 - Present ($2.95, B&W, limited series)

1-11-Aaron Bordner-a; Bordner & Davidsen-s 3.00

POISON ELVES: LUSIPHUR & LIRILITH
Sirius Entertainment: 2001 - No. 4, 2001 ($2.95, B&W, limited series)

1-4-Drew Hayes-s/Jason Alexander-a 3.00
TPB (2002, $11.95) r/#1-4 12.00

POISON ELVES: PARINTACHIN
Sirius Entertainment: 2001 - No. 3, 2002 ($2.95, B&W, limited series)

1-3-Drew Hayes-c/Fillbäch Brothers-s/a 3.00
TPB (2003, $8.95) r/#1-3 9.00

POISON ELVES VENTURES
Sirius Entertainment: May, 2005 - No. 4, Apr, 2006 ($3.50, B&W, limited series)

... #1: Cassanova; ...#2: Lynn; ...#3: The Purple Marauder; #4: Jace - Bordner-a 3.50

POKÉMON (TV) (Also see Magical Pokémon Journey)
Viz Comics: Nov, 1998 - 2000 ($3.25/$3.50, B&W)

...Part 1: The Electric Tale of Pikachu
1-Toshiro Ono-s/a 1 3 4 6 8 10
1-4 (2nd through current printings) 3.50
2 6.00
3,4 4.00
TPB ($12.95) 13.00

...Part 2: Pikachu Strikes Back
1 5.00
2-4 4.00
TPB 13.00

...Part 3: Electric Pikachu Boogaloo
1 5.00
2-4 ($2.95-c) 4.00
TPB 13.00

...Part 4: Surf's Up Pikachu
1,3,4 4.00
2 ($2.95-c) 4.00
TPB 13.00

NOTE: Multiple printings exist for most issues

POKÉMON ADVENTURES
Viz Comics: Sept, 1999 - No. 4 ($5.95, B&W, magazine-size)

1-4-Includes stickers bound in 6.00

POKÉMON ADVENTURES
Viz Comics: 2000 - Present ($2.95/$4.95, B&W)

Part 2 (2/00-7/00) 1-6-Includes stickers bound in 4.00
Part 3 (8/00-2/01) 1-7 4.00
Part 4 (3/00-6/01) 1-4 5.00
Part 5 (7/01-10/01) 1-4 5.00
Part 6: 1-4, Part 7 1-5 5.00

POKÉMON: THE FIRST MOVIE
Viz Comics: 1999 ($3.95)

Mewtwo Strikes Back 1-4 4.00
Pikachu's Vacation 4.00

POKÉMON: THE MOVIE 2000
Viz Comics: 2000 ($3.95)

1-Official movie adaption 4.00
Pikachu's Rescue Adventure 4.00
...:The Power of One (mini-series) 1-3 4.00

GD 2.0 | VG 4.0 | FN 6.0 | VF 8.0 | VF/NM 9.0 | NM- 9.2

POLICE ACADEMY (TV)
Marvel Comics: Nov, 1989 - No. 6, Feb, 1990 ($1.00)

1-6: Based on TV cartoon; Post-c/a(p) in all 3.00

POLICE ACTION
Atlas News Co.: Jan, 1954 - No. 7, Nov, 1954

1-Violent-a by Robert Q. Sale 21 42 63 126 206 285
2 13 26 39 74 105 135
3-7: 7-Powell-a 12 24 36 67 94 120

NOTE: ***Ayers** a-4, 5. **Colan** a-1. **Forte** a-1, 2. **Mort Lawrence** a-5. **Maneely** a-3; c-1, 5. **Reinman** a-6, 7.*

POLICE ACTION
Atlas/Seaboard Publ.: Feb, 1975 - No. 3, June, 1975

1-3: 1-Lomax, N.Y.P.D., Luke Malone begin; McWilliams-a. 2-Origin Luke Malone, Manhunter; Ploog-a 2 4 6 8 11 14

NOTE: ***Ploog** art in all. **Sekowsky/McWilliams** a-1-3. **Thorne** c-3.*

POLICE AGAINST CRIME
Premiere Magazines: April, 1954 - No. 9, Aug, 1955

1-Disbrow-a; extreme violence (man's face slashed with knife); Hollingsworth-a 30 60 90 177 289 400
2-Hollingsworth-a 16 32 48 94 147 200
3-9 14 28 42 82 121 160

POLICE BADGE #479 (Formerly Spy Thrillers #1-4)
Atlas Comics (PrPI): No. 5, Sept, 1955

5-Maneely-c/a (6 pgs.); Heck-a 11 22 33 62 86 110

POLICE CASE BOOK (See Giant Comics Editions)

POLICE CASES (See Authentic... & Record Book of...)

POLICE COMICS
Quality Comics Group (Comic Magazines): Aug, 1941 - No. 127, Oct, 1953

1-Origin/1st app. Plastic Man by Jack Cole (r-in DC Special #15), The Human Bomb by Gustavson, & No. 711; intro. The Firebrand by Reed Crandall, The Mouthpiece by Guardineer, Phantom Lady, & The Sword; Chic Carter by Eisner app.; Firebrand-c 1-4 811 1622 2433 5920 10,460 15,000
2-Plastic Man smuggles opium 314 628 942 2198 3849 5500
3 239 478 717 1530 2615 3700
4 200 400 600 1280 2190 3100
5-Plastic Man-c begin; Plastic Man forced to smoke marijuana; Plastic Man covers begin, end #102 300 600 900 1950 3375 4800
6,7 174 348 522 1114 1907 2700
8-Manhunter begins (origin/1st app.) (3/42) 200 400 600 1280 2190 3100
9,10 139 278 417 883 1517 2150
11-The Spirit strip reprints begin by Eisner (origin-strip #1); 1st comic book app. The Spirit & 1st cover app. (9/42) 300 600 900 1950 3375 4800
12-Intro. Ebony 161 322 483 1030 1765 2500
13-Intro. Woozy Winks; last Firebrand 168 336 504 1075 1838 2600
14-19: 15-Last No. 711; Destiny begins 97 194 291 621 1061 1500
20-The Raven x-over in Phantom Lady; features Jack Cole himself 97 194 291 621 1061 1500
21,22: 21-Raven & Spider Widow x-over in Phantom Lady (cameo in #22) 81 162 243 518 884 1250
23-30: 23-Last Phantom Lady. 24-26-Flatfoot Burns by Kurtzman in all 76 152 228 486 831 1175
31-41: 37-1st app. Candy by Sahle & begins (12/44). 41-Last Spirit-r by Eisner 55 110 165 352 601 850
42,43-Spirit-r by Eisner/Fine 53 106 159 334 567 800
44-Fine Spirit-r begin, end #88,90,92 53 106 159 334 567 800
45-50: 50-(#50 on-c, #49 on inside, 1/46) 41 82 123 256 428 600
51-60: 58-Last Human Bomb 34 68 102 199 325 450
61-88,90,92: 63-(Some issues have #65 printed on cover, but #63 on inside) Kurtzman-a, 6 pgs. 90,92-Spirit by Fine 25 50 75 150 245 340
89,91,93-No Spirit stories 23 46 69 136 223 310
94-99,101,102: Spirit by Eisner in all; 101-Last Manhunter. 102-Last Spirit & Plastic Man by Jack Cole 32 64 96 192 314 435
100 39 78 117 231 378 525
103-Content change to crime; Ken Shannon & T-Man begin (1st app. of each, 12/50) 30 60 90 177 289 400
104-112,114-127: Crandall-a most issues (not in 104,105,122,125-127). 109-Atomic bomb story. 112-Crandall-a 20 40 60 114 182 250
113-Crandall-c/a(2), 9 pgs. each 21 42 63 126 206 285

NOTE: *Most Spirit stories signed by Eisner are not by him; all are reprints. **Crandall** Firebrand-1-8. Spirit by **Eisner** 1-41, 94-102; by **Eisner/Fine**-42, 43; by **Fine**-44-88, 90, 92. 103, 109. **Al Bryant** c-33, 34. **Cole** c-17-32, 35-102(most). **Crandall** c-13, 14. **Crandall/Cuidera** c-105-127. **Eisner** c-4i. **Gill Fox** c-1-3, 4p, 5-12, 15.*

Police Line-up #4 © AVON

Popeye FC #70 © KING

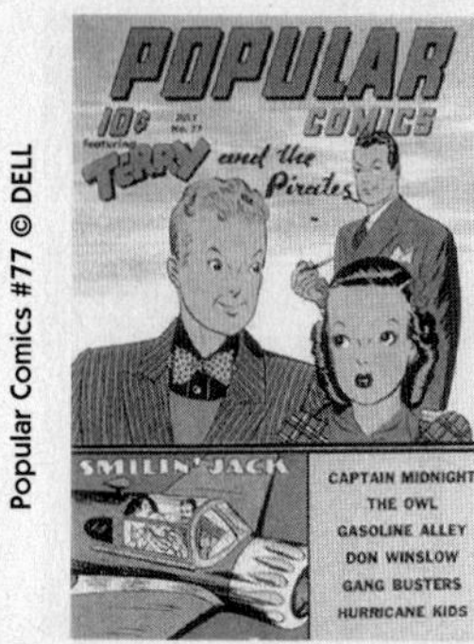

Popular Comics #77 © DELL

GD 2.0 | VG 4.0 | FN 6.0 | VF 8.0 | VF/NM 9.0 | NM- 9.2

GD 2.0 | VG 4.0 | FN 6.0 | VF 8.0 | VF/NM 9.0 | NM- 9.2

Bondage c-103, 109, 125.

POLICE LINE-UP
Avon Periodicals/Realistic Comics #3,4: Aug, 1951 - No. 4, July, 1952 (Painted-c #1-3)

1-Wood-a, 1 pg. plus part-c; spanking panel-r/Saint #5 39 78 117 240 395 550
2-Classic story "The Religious Murder Cult", drugs, perversion; r/Saint #5; c-r/Avon paperback #329 29 58 87 170 278 385
3,4: 3-Kubert-a(r?)/part-c; Kinstler-a (inside-c only) 20 40 60 118 192 265

POLICE TRAP (Public Defender In Action #7 on)
Mainline #1-4/Charlton #5,6: 8-9/54 - No. 4, 2-3/55; No. 5, 7/55 - No. 6, 9/55

1-S&K covers-all issues; Meskin-a; Kirby scripts 31 62 93 182 296 410
2-4 20 40 60 114 182 250
5,6-S&K-c/a 25 50 75 147 241 335

POLICE TRAP
Super Comics: No. 11, 1963; No. 16-18, 1964

Reprint #11,16-18: 11-r/Police Trap #3. 16-r/Justice Traps the Guilty #? 17-r/Inside Crime #3 & r/Justice Traps The Guilty #83; 18-r/Inside Crime #3 2 4 6 9 13 16

POLLY & HER PALS (See Comic Monthly #1)

POLLY & THE PIRATES
Oni Press: Sept, 2005 - No. 6, June, 2006 ($2.99, B&W, limited series)

1-6-Ted Naifeh-s/a; Polly is shanghaied by the pirate ship Titania 3.00
TPB (7/06, $11.95, digest) r/#1-6 12.00

POLLYANNA (Disney)
Dell Publishing Co.: No. 1129, Aug-Oct, 1960

Four Color 1129-Movie, Hayley Mills photo-c 7 14 21 50 83 115

POLLY PIGTAILS (Girls' Fun & Fashion Magazine #44 on)
Parents' Magazine Institute/Polly Pigtails: Jan, 1946 - V4#43, Oct-Nov, 1949

1-Infinity-c; photo-c 16 32 48 94 147 200
2-Photo-c 10 20 30 58 69 85
3-5: 3,4-Photo-c 9 18 27 52 69 85
6-10: 7-Photo-c 9 18 27 47 61 75
11-30: 22-Photo-c 8 16 24 40 50 60
31-43 7 14 21 35 43 50

PONY EXPRESS (See Tales of the...)

PONYTAIL (Teen-age)
Dell Publishing Co./Charlton No. 13 on: 7-9/62 - No. 12, 10-12/65; No. 13, 11/69 - No. 20, 1/71

12-641-209(#1) 4 8 12 24 37 50
2-12 3 6 9 18 27 35
13-20 3 6 9 14 19 24

POP COMICS
Modern Store Publ.: 1955 (36 pgs.; 5x7"; in color) (7¢)

1-Funny animal 6 12 18 28 34 40

POPEYE (See Comic Album #7, 11, 15, Comics Reading Libraries *in the Promotional Comics section,* Eat Right to Work and Win, Giant Comic Album, King Comics, Kite Fun Book, Magic Comics, March of Comics #37,52, 66, 80, 96, 117, 134, 148, 157, 169, 194, 246, 264, 274, 294, 453, 465, 477 & Wow Comics, 1st series)

POPEYE
David McKay Publications: 1937 - 1939 (All by Segar)

Feature Books nn (100 pgs.) (Very Rare) 750 1500 2250 5300 8650 12,000
Feature Books 2 (52 pgs.) 97 194 291 621 1061 1500
Feature Books 3 (100 pgs.)-r/nn issue with a new-c 87 174 261 553 952 1350
Feature Books 5,10 (76 pgs.) 77 154 231 493 847 1200
Feature Books 14 (76 pgs.) (Scarce) 84 168 252 538 919 1300

POPEYE (Strip reprints through 4-Color #70)
Dell #1-65/Gold Key #66-80/King #81-92/Charlton #94-138/Gold Key #139-155/Whitman #156 on: 1941 - 1947; #1, 2-4/48 - #65, 7-9/62; #66, 10/62 - #80, 5/66; #81, 8/66 - #92, 12/67; #94, 2/69 - #138, 1/77; #139, 5/78 - #171, 6/84 (no #93,160,161)

Large Feature Comic 24('41)-Half by Segar 71 142 213 454 777 1100
Four Color 25('41)-by Segar 86 172 258 546 936 1325
Large Feature Comic 10('43) 57 114 171 362 619 875
Four Color 17('43),26('43)-by Segar 41 82 123 324 650 975
Four Color 43('44) 28 56 84 204 415 625
Four Color 70('45)-Title: ...& Wimpy 21 42 63 150 300 450
Four Color 113('46-original strips begin),127,145('47),168 13 26 39 92 179 265
1(2-4/48)(Dell)-All new stories continue 26 52 78 190 383 575
2 13 26 39 94 185 275
3-10: 5-Popeye on moon w/rocket-c 11 22 33 75 138 200
11-20 9 18 27 63 107 150
21-40,46: 46-Origin Swee' Pee 8 16 24 52 86 120
41-45,47-50 6 12 18 43 69 95
51-60 6 12 18 37 59 80
61-65 (Last Dell issue) 5 10 15 32 51 70
66(10/62),67-Both 84 pgs. (Gold Key) 7 14 21 47 76 105
68-80 4 8 12 26 41 55
81-92,94-97 (no #93): 97-Last 12¢ issue 3 6 9 21 32 42
98,99,101-138 3 6 9 14 19 24
100 3 6 9 18 27 35
139-155: 144-50th Anniversary issue 2 4 6 8 10 12
156,157,162-167(Whitman)(no #160,161).167(3/82) 2 4 6 10 14 18
158(9/80),159(11/80)-pre-pack only 4 8 12 22 34 45
168-171:(All #90069 on-c; pre-pack) 168(6/83). 169(#168 on-c)(8/83). 170(3/84). 171(6/84) 3 6 9 16 22 28

NOTE: *Reprints-#145, 147, 149, 151, 153, 155, 157, 163-168(1/3), 170.*

POPEYE
Harvey Comics: Nov, 1993 - No. 7, Aug, 1994 ($1.50)

V2#1-7 3.00
...Summer Special V2#1-(10/93, $2.25, 68 pgs.)-Sagendorf-r & others 4.00

POPEYE SPECIAL
Ocean Comics: Summer, 1987 - No. 2, Sept, 1988 ($1.75/$2.00)

1,2: 1-Origin 4.00

POPPLES (TV, movie)
Star Comics (Marvel): Dec, 1986 - No. 4, Jun, 1987

1-4-Based on toys 4.00

POPPO OF THE POPCORN THEATRE
Fuller Publishing Co. (Publishers Weekly): 10/29/55 - No. 13, 1956 (weekly)

1 9 18 27 52 69 85
2-5 7 14 21 37 46 55
6-13 6 12 18 31 38 45

NOTE: *By* **Charles Biro.** *10¢ cover, given away by supermarkets such as IGA.*

POP-POP COMICS
R. B. Leffingwell Co.: No date (Circa 1945) (52 pgs.)

1-Funny animal 14 28 42 76 108 140

POPULAR COMICS
Dell Publishing Co.: Feb, 1936 - No. 145, July-Sept, 1948

1-Dick Tracy (1st comic book app.), Little Orphan Annie, Terry & the Pirates, Gasoline Alley, Don Winslow (1st app.), Harold Teen, Little Joe, Skippy, Moon Mullins, Mutt & Jeff, Tailspin Tommy, Smitty, Smokey Stover, Winnie Winkle & The Gumps begin (all strip-r) 771 1542 2313 5400 - -
2 257 514 771 1800 - -
3 193 386 579 1350 - -
4-6(7/36): 5-Tom Mix begins. 6-1st app. Scribbly 150 300 450 1050 - -
7-10: 8,9-Scribbly & Reglar Fellers app. 121 242 363 850 - -
11-20: 12-X-Mas-c 83 166 249 477 739 1000
21-27: 27-Last Terry & the Pirates, Little Orphan Annie, & Dick Tracy 63 126 189 362 556 750
28-37: 28-Gene Autry app. 31,32-Tim McCoy app. 35-Christmas-c; Tex Ritter app. 49 98 147 282 434 585
38-43: Tarzan in text only. 38-(4/39)-Gang Busters (Radio, 2nd app.) & Zane Grey's Tex Thorne begins? 43-The Masked Pilot app.; 1st non-funny-c? 47 94 141 270 415 560
44,45: 45-Hurricane Kid-c 36 72 108 207 321 435
46-Origin/1st app. Martan, the Marvel Man(12/39) 46 92 138 265 408 550
47-50 35 70 105 201 311 420
51-Origin The Voice (The Invisible Detective) strip begins (5/40) 37 74 111 213 327 440
52-Robot-c 42 84 126 242 371 500
53-59: 55-End of World story 33 66 99 190 295 400
60-Origin/1st app. Professor Supermind and Son (2/41) 34 68 102 196 303 410
61-71: 63-Smilin' Jack begins 26 52 78 150 230 310
72-The Owl & Terry & the Pirates begin (2/42); Smokey Stover reprints begin 42 84 126 242 371 500
73-75 29 58 87 167 259 350
76-78-Capt. Midnight in all (see The Funnies #57) 40 80 120 230 358 485
79-85-Last Owl 27 54 81 155 238 320
86-99: 98-Felix the Cat, Smokey Stover-r begin 18 36 54 104 157 210

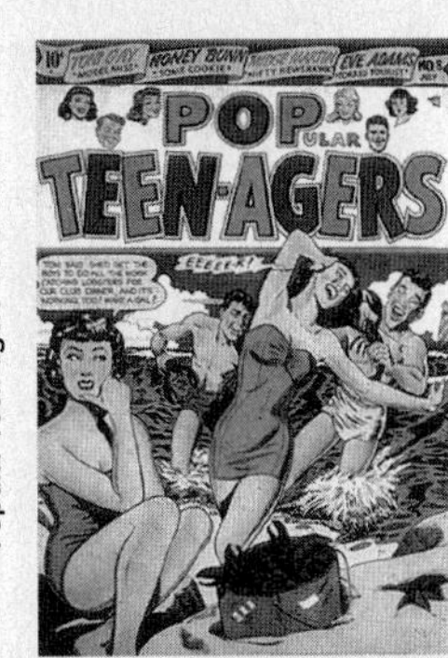

Popular Teen-agers #8 © STAR

Porky Pig #45 © WB

Power Girl #10 © DC

	GD 2.0	VG 4.0	FN 6.0	VF 8.0	VF/NM 9.0	NM- 9.2
100	20	40	60	115	175	235
101-130	10	20	30	58	89	120
131-145: 142-Last Terry & the Pirates	9	18	27	52	79	105

NOTE: *Martan, the Marvel Man c-47-49, 52, 57-59. Professor Supermind c-60-63, 64(1/2), 65, 66. The Voice c-53.*

POPULAR FAIRY TALES (See March of Comics #6, 18)

POPULAR ROMANCE
Better-Standard Publications: No. 5, Dec, 1949 - No. 29, July, 1954

	GD 2.0	VG 4.0	FN 6.0	VF 8.0	VF/NM 9.0	NM- 9.2
5	14	28	42	82	121	160
6-9: 7-Palais-a; lingerie panels	11	22	33	60	83	105
10-Wood-a (2 pgs.)	13	26	39	72	101	130
11,12,14-16,18-21,28,29	9	18	27	52	69	85
13,17-Severin/Elder-a (3&8 pgs.)	10	20	30	56	76	95
22-27-Toth-a	11	22	33	62	86	110

NOTE: *All have photo-c.* ***Tuska*** *art in most issues.*

POPULAR TEEN-AGERS (Secrets of Love) (School Day Romances #1-4)
Star Publications: No. 5, Sept, 1950 - No. 23, Nov, 1954

	GD 2.0	VG 4.0	FN 6.0	VF 8.0	VF/NM 9.0	NM- 9.2
5-Toni Gay, Midge Martin & Eve Adams continue from School Day Romances; Ginger Bunn (formerly Ginger Snapp & becomes Honey Bunn #6 on) begins; all features end #8	27	54	81	158	259	360
6-8 (7/51)-Honey Bunn begins; all have L. B. Cole-c; 6-Negligee panels	22	44	66	128	209	290
9-(...Romances; 1st romance issue, 10/51)	18	36	54	105	165	225
10-(...Secrets of Love thru #23)	17	34	51	98	154	210
11,16,18,19,22,23	15	30	45	83	124	165
12,13,17,20,21-Disbrow-a	15	30	45	88	137	185
14-Harrison/Wood-a	21	42	63	122	199	275
15-Wood?, Disbrow-a	16	32	48	94	147	200
Accepted Reprint 5,6 (nd); L.B. Cole-c	9	18	27	47	61	75

NOTE: *All have* ***L. B. Cole*** *covers.*

PORKY PIG (See Bugs Bunny &..., Kite Fun Book, Looney Tunes, March of Comics #42, 57, 71, 89, 99, 113, 130, 143, 164, 175, 192, 209, 218, 367, and Super Book #6, 18, 30)

PORKY PIG (...& Bugs Bunny #40-69)
Dell Publishing Co./Gold Key No. 1-93/Whitman No. 94 on: No. 16, 1942 - No. 81, Mar-Apr, 1962; Jan, 1965 - No. 109, June, 1984

	GD 2.0	VG 4.0	FN 6.0	VF 8.0	VF/NM 9.0	NM- 9.2
Four Color 16(#1, 1942)	81	162	243	689	1395	2100
Four Color 48(1944)-Carl Barks-a	87	174	267	740	1495	2250
Four Color 78(1945)	25	50	75	183	367	550
Four Color 112(7/46)	15	30	45	106	216	325
Four Color 156,182,191('49)	12	24	36	82	154	225
Four Color 226,241('49),260,271,277,284,295	10	20	30	69	122	175
Four Color 303,311,322,330: 322-Sci/fi-c/story	8	16	24	54	90	125
Four Color 342,351,360,370,385,399,410,426	6	12	18	43	69	95
25 (11-12/52)-30	6	12	18	37	59	80
31-40	5	10	15	32	51	70
41-60	4	8	12	26	41	55
61-81(3-4/62)	4	8	12	22	34	45
1(1/65-Gold Key)(2nd Series)	5	10	15	34	55	75
2,4,5-r/4-Color 226,284 & 271 in that order	3	6	9	20	30	40
3,6-10: 3-r/Four Color #342	3	6	9	17	25	32
11-30	3	6	9	14	19	24
31-54	2	4	6	10	14	18
55-70	2	4	6	8	11	14
71-93(Gold Key)	2	3	4	6	8	10
94-96	2	4	6	8	10	12
97(9/80),98-pre-pack only (99 known not to exist)	3	6	9	21	32	42
100	2	4	6	10	14	18
101-105: 104(2/82). 105(4/82)	2	4	6	8	11	14
106-109 (All #90140 on-c, no date or date code): 106(7/83), 107(8/83), 108(2/84), 109(6/84) low print run	3	6	9	14	20	26

NOTE: *Reprints-#1-8, 9-35(2/3); 36-46(1/4-1/2), 58, 67, 69-74, 76, 78, 102-109(1/3-1/2).*

PORKY PIG'S DUCK HUNT
Saalfield Publishing Co.: 1938 (12pgs.)(large size)(heavy linen-like paper)

	GD 2.0	VG 4.0	FN 6.0	VF 8.0	VF/NM 9.0	NM- 9.2
2178-1st app. Porky Pig & Daffy Duck by Leon Schlesinger. Illustrated text story book written in verse. 1st book ever devoted to these characters. (see Looney Tunes #1 for their 1st comic book app.)	73	146	219	467	796	1125

PORTENT, THE
Image Comics: Feb, 2006 - No. 4, Aug, 2006 ($2.99)

1-4-Peter Bergting-s/a 3.00
Vol. 1: Duende TPB (2006, 12.99) r/#1-4; pin-up art; intro. by Kaluta 13.00

PORTIA PRINZ OF THE GLAMAZONS
Eclipse Comics: Dec, 1986 - No. 6, Oct, 1987 ($2.00, B&W, Baxter paper)

1-6 3.00

POSSESSED, THE
DC Comics (Cliffhanger): Sept, 2003 - No. 6, March, 2004 ($2.95, limited series)

1-6-Johns & Grimminger-s/Sharp-a 3.00
TPB (2004, $14.95) r/#1-6; promo art and sketch pages 15.00

POST GAZETTE (See Meet the New... in the Promotional Comics section)

POWDER RIVER RUSTLERS (See Fawcett Movie Comics)

POWER & GLORY (See American Flagg! & Howard Chaykin's American Flagg!
Malibu Comics (Bravura): Feb, 1994 - No. 4, May, 1994 ($2.50, limited series, mature)

1A, 1B-By Howard Chaykin; w/Bravura stamp 3.00
1-Newsstand ed. (polybagged w/children's warning on bag), Gold ed., Silver-foil ed., Blue-foil ed.(print run of 10,000), Serigraph ed. (print run of 3,000)($2.95)-Howard Chaykin-c/a begin 4.00
2-4-Contains Bravura stamp 3.00
Holiday Special (Win '94, $2.95) 3.00

POWER COMICS
Holyoke Publ. Co./Narrative Publ.: 1944 - No. 4, 1945

	GD 2.0	VG 4.0	FN 6.0	VF 8.0	VF/NM 9.0	NM- 9.2
1-L. B. Cole-c	142	284	426	909	1555	2200
2-Hitler, Hirohito-c (scarce)	148	296	444	947	1624	2300
3-Classic L.B. Cole-c; Dr. Mephisto begins?	174	348	522	1114	1907	2700
4-L.B. Cole-c; Miss Espionage app. #3,4; Leav-a	142	284	426	909	1555	2200

POWER COMICS
Power Comics Co.: 1977 - No. 5, Dec, 1977 (B&W)

	GD 2.0	VG 4.0	FN 6.0	VF 8.0	VF/NM 9.0	NM- 9.2
1- "A Boy And His Aardvark" by Dave Sim; first Dave Sim aardvark (not Cerebus)	3	6	9	14	20	25
1-Reprint (3/77, black-c)	1	2	3	5	6	8
2-Cobalt Blue by Gustovich	1	3	4	6	8	10
3-5: 3-Nightwitch. 4-Northern Light. 5-Bluebird	1	3	4	6	8	10

POWER COMICS
Eclipse Comics (Acme Press): Mar, 1988 - No. 4, Sept, 1988 ($2.00, B&W, mini-series)

1-4: Bolland, Gibbons-r in all 3.00

POWER COMPANY, THE
DC Comics: Apr, 2002 - No. 18, Sep, 2003 ($2.50/$2.75)

1-6-Busiek-s/Grummett-a. 6-Green Arrow & Black Canary-c/app. 3.00
7-18: 7:Begin $2.75-c. 8,9-Green Arrow app. 11-Firestorm joins. 15-Batman app. 3.00
...Bork (3/02) Busiek-s/Dwyer-a; Batman & Flash (Barry Allen) app. 3.00
...Josiah Power (3/02) Busiek-s/Giffen-a; Superman app. 3.00
...Manhunter (3/02) Busiek-s/Jurgens-a; Nightwing app. 3.00
...Sapphire (3/02) Busiek-s/Bagley-a; JLA & Kobra app. 3.00
...Skyrocket (3/02) Busiek-s/Staton-a; Green Lantern (Hal Jordan) app. 3.00
...Striker Z (3/02) Busiek-s/Bachs-a; Superboy app. 3.00
...Witchfire (3/02) Busiek-s/Haley-a; Wonder Woman app. 3.00

POWER FACTOR
Wonder Color Comics #1/Pied Piper #2: May, 1987 - No. 2, 1987 ($1.95)

1,2: Super team. 2-Infantino-c 3.00

POWER FACTOR
Innovation Publishing: Oct, 1990 - No. 3, 1991 ($1.95/$2.25)

1-3: 1-R-/1st story + new-a, 2-r/2nd story + new-a. 3-Infantino-a 3.00

POWER GIRL (See All-Star #58, Infinity, Inc., JSA Classified, Showcase #97-99)
DC Comics: June, 1988 - No. 4, Sept, 1988 ($1.00, color, limited series)

1-4 3.00
TPB (2006, $14.99) r/Showcase #97-99; Secret Origins #11; JSA Classified #1-4 and pages from JSA #32,39; cover gallery 15.00

POWER GIRL
DC Comics: Jul, 2009 - Present ($2.99)

1-12: 1,2-Amanda Conner-a; covers by Conner and Hughes; Ultra-Humanite app. 3-6-Covers by Conner and March 3.00
13-22-Winick-s/Basri-a. 20,21-Crossover with Justice League: Generation Lost #18-22 3.00
...: Aliens and Apes SC (2010, $17.99) r/#7-12 18.00
...: A New Beginning SC (2010, $17.99) r/#1-6; gallery of variant covers 18.00

POWERHOUSE PEPPER COMICS (See Gay Comics, Joker Comics & Tessie the Typist)
Marvel Comics (20CC): No. 1, 1943; No. 2, May, 1948 - No. 5, Nov, 1948

	GD 2.0	VG 4.0	FN 6.0	VF 8.0	VF/NM 9.0	NM- 9.2
1-(60 pgs.)-Wolverton-a in all; c-2,3	213	426	639	1363	2332	3300
2	90	180	270	576	988	1400
3,4	84	168	252	538	919	1300

Power Man and Iron Fist #2 © MAR

Power Pack V2 #1 © MAR

Powerpuff Girls #25 © Cartoon Network

GD VG FN VF VF/NM NM-
2.0 4.0 6.0 8.0 9.0 9.2

GD VG FN VF VF/NM NM-
2.0 4.0 6.0 8.0 9.0 9.2

5-(Scarce) 95 190 285 603 1039 1475

POWERLESS
Marvel Comics: Aug, 2004 - No. 6, Jan, 2005 ($2.99, limited series)
1-6-Peter Parker, Matt Murdock and Logan without powers; Gaydos-a 3.00
TPB (2005, $14.99) r/series; sketch page by Gaydos 15.00

POWER LINE
Marvel Comics (Epic Comics): May, 1988 - No. 8, Sept, 1989 ($1.25/$1.50)
1-8: 2-Williamson-i. 3-Dr. Zero app. 4-7-Morrow-a. 8-Williamson-i 3.00

POWER LORDS
DC Comics: Dec, 1983 - No. 3, Feb, 1984 (Limited series, Mando paper)
1-3: Based on Revell toys 3.00

POWER MAN (Formerly Hero for Hire; ...& Iron Fist #50 on; see Cage & Giant-Size...)
Marvel Comics Group: No. 17, Feb, 1974 - No. 125, Sept, 1986
17-Luke Cage continues; Iron Man app. 3 6 9 16 23 30
18-20: 18-Last 20¢ issue 2 4 6 10 14 18
21-30 2 4 6 8 10 12
30-(30¢-c variant, limited distribution)(4/76) 3 6 9 17 25 32
31-46: 31-Part Neal Adams-i. 34-Last 25¢ issue. 36-r/Hero For Hire #12. 41-1st app. Thunderbolt. 45-Starlin-c. 1 3 4 6 8 10
31-34-(30¢-c variants, limited distribution)(5-8/76) 3 6 9 17 25 32
44-46-(35¢-c variants, limited distribution)(6-8/77) 4 8 12 22 34 45
47-Barry Smith-a 2 4 6 8 10 12
47-(35¢-c variant, limited distribution)(10/77) 4 8 12 26 41 55
48-50-Byrne-a(p); 48-Power Man/Iron Fist 1st meet. 50-Iron Fist joins Cage 2 4 6 10 14 18
51-56,58-65,67-77: 58-Intro El Aguila. 75-Double size. 77-Daredevil app. 6.00
57-New X-Men app. (6/79) 4 8 12 26 41 55
66-2nd app. Sabretooth (see Iron Fist #14) 5 10 15 35 55 75
78,84: 78-3rd app. Sabretooth (cameo under cloak). 84-4th app. Sabretooth 4 8 12 22 34 45
79-83,85-99,101-124: 87-Moon Knight app. 109-The Reaper app. 4.00
100,125-Double size: 100-Origin K'un L'un. 125-Death of Iron Fist 6.00
Annual 1(1976)-Punisher cameo in flashback 2 4 6 13 18 22
NOTE: *Austin c-102i. **Byrne** a-48-50; c-102, 104, 106, 107, 112-116. **Kane** c(p)-24, 25, 28, 48. **Miller** a-68, 76(2 pgs.); c-66-68, 70-74, 80i. **Mooney** a-38i, 53i, 55i. **Nebres** a-76p. **Nino** a-42i, 43i. **Perez** a-27. **B. Smith** a-47i. **Tuska** a(p)-17, 20, 24, 26, 28, 29, 36, 47. Painted c-75, 100.*

POWER MAN AND IRON FIST
Marvel Comics: Apr, 2011 - No. 5 ($2.99, limited series)
1-3-Van Lente-s/Alves-a; Victor Alvarez as Power Man 3.00

POWER OF PRIME
Malibu Comics (Ultraverse): July, 1995 - No. 4, Nov, 1995 ($2.50, lim. series)
1-4 3.00

POWER OF SHAZAM!, THE (See SHAZAM!)
DC Comics: 1994 (Painted graphic novel) (Prequel to new series)
Hardcover-($19.95)-New origin of Shazam!; Ordway painted-c/a & script 3 6 9 14 20 25
Softcover-($7.50), Softcover-($9.95)-New-c. 2 4 6 8 10 12

POWER OF SHAZAM!, THE
DC Comics: Mar, 1995 - No. 47, Mar, 1999; No. 48, Mar, 2010 ($1.50/$1.75/$1.95/$2.50)
1-Jerry Ordway scripts begin 4.00
2-20: 4-Begin $1.75-c. 6:Re-intro of Capt. Nazi. 8-Re-intro of Spy Smasher, Bulletman & Minuteman; Swan-a (7 pgs.). 11-Re-intro of Ibis, Swan-a(2 pgs.). 14-Gil Kane-a(p). 20-Superman-c/app.; "Final Night" 3.00
21-47: 21-Plastic Man-c/app. 22-Batman-c/app. 35,36-X-over w/Starman #39,40. 38-41-Mr. Mind. 43-Bulletman app. 45-JLA-c/app. 3.00
48-(3/10, $2.99) Blackest Night one-shot; Osiris rises as a Black Lantern; Kramer-a 3.00
#1,000,000 (11/98) 853rd Century x-over; Ordway-c/s/a 3.00
Annual 1 (1996, $2.95)-Legends of the Dead Earth story; Jerry Ordway-c; Mike Manley-a 4.00

POWER OF STRONGMAN, THE (Also see Strongman)
AC Comics: 1989 ($2.95)
1-Powell G.A.-r 3.00

POWER OF THE ATOM (See Secret Origins #29)
DC Comics: Aug, 1988 - No. 18, Nov, 1989 ($1.00)
1-18: 6-Chronos returns; Byrne-p. 9-JLI app. 3.00

POWER PACHYDERMS
Marvel Comics: Sept, 1989 ($1.25, one-shot)
1-Elephant super-heroes; parody of X-Men, Elektra, & 3 Stooges 3.00

POWER PACK
Marvel Comics Group: Aug, 1984 - No. 62, Feb, 1991
1-($1.00, 52 pgs.)-Origin & 1st app. Power Pack 4.00
2-18,20-26,28,30-45,47-62 3.00
19-(52 pgs.)-Cloak & Dagger, Wolverine app. 4.00
27-Mutant massacre; Wolverine & Sabretooth app. 5.00
29,46: 29-Spider-Man & Hobgoblin app. 46-Punisher app. 3.50
Graphic Novel: Power Pack & Cloak & Dagger: Shelter From the Storm ('89, SC, $7.95) Velluto/Farmer-a 10.00
...Holiday Special 1 (2/92, $2.25, 68 pgs.) 4.00
NOTE: ***Austin** scripts-53. **Mignola** c-20. **Morrow** a-51. **Spiegle** a-55i. **Williamson** a(i)-43, 50, 52.*

POWER PACK (Volume 2)
Marvel Comics: Aug, 2000 - No. 4, Nov, 2000 ($2.99, limited series)
1-4-Doran & Austin-c/a 3.00

POWER PACK
Marvel Comics: June, 2005 - No. 4, Aug, 2005 ($2.99, limited series)
1-4-Sumerak-s/Gurihiru-a; back-up Franklin Richards story. 3-Fantastic Four app. 3.00
... Digest (2006, $6.99) r/#1-4 7.00

POWER PACK: DAY ONE
Marvel Comics: May, 2008 - No. 4, Aug, 2008($2.99, limited series)
1-4-Van Lente-s/Gurihiru-a; origin retold; Coover-a back-ups. 1-Fantastic Four cameo 3.00

POWERPUFF GIRLS, THE (Also see Cartoon Network Starring... #1)
DC Comics: May, 2000 - No. 70, Mar, 2006 ($1.99/$2.25)
1 4.00
2-55,57-70: 25-Pin-ups by Allred, Byrne, Baker, Mignola, Hernandez, Warren 3.00
56-($2.95) Bonus pages; Mojo Jojo-c 4.00
...Double Whammy (12/00, $3.95) r/#1,2 & a Dexter's Lab story 4.00
...Movie: The Comic (9/02, $2.95) Movie adaptation; Phil Moy & Chris Cook-a 3.00

POWER RANGERS ZEO (TV)(Saban's...)(Also see Saban's Mighty Morphin Power Rangers)
Image Comics (Extreme Studios): Aug, 1996 ($2.50)
1-Based on TV show 3.00

POWER RECORD COMICS (Named Peter Pan Record Comics for #34-47)
Marvel Comics/Power Records: 1974 - 1978 ($1.49, 7x10" comics, 20 pgs. with 45 R.P.M. record) (Clipped corners - reduce value 20%) (Comic alone - 50%; record alone - 50%)
PR10-Spider-Man-r/from #124,125; Man-Wolf app. PR18-Planet of the Apes-r. PR19-Escape From the Planet of the Apes-r. PR20-Beneath the Planet of the Apes-r. PR21-Battle for the Planet of the Apes-r. PR24-Spider-Man II-New-a begins. PR27-Batman "Stacked Cards"; N. Adams-a(p). PR30-Batman; N. Adams-r/Det.(7 pgs.).
With record; each... 6 12 18 37 59 80
PR11-Hulk-r. PR12-Captain America-r/#168. PR13-Fantastic Four-r/#126. PR14-Frankenstein -Ploog-r/#1. PR15-Tomb of Dracula-Colan-r/#2. PR16-Man-Thing-Ploog-r/#5. PR17-Werewolf By Night-Ploog-r/Marvel Spotlight #2. PR28-Superman "Alien Creatures". PR29-Space: 1999 "Breakaway". PR31-Conan-N. Adams-a; reprinted in Conan #116. PR32-Space: 1999 "Return to the Beginning". PR33-Superman-G.A. origin, Buckler-a(p). PR34-Superman. PR35-Wonder Woman-Buckler-a(p)
With record; each... 5 10 15 32 51 70
PR11-(1981 Peter Pan records re-issue) new Abomination & Rhino-c
With record 5 10 15 35 55 75
PR25-Star Trek "Passage to Moauv". PR26-Star Trek "Crier in Emptiness." PR36-Holo-Man. PR37-Robin Hood. PR39-Huckleberry Finn. PR40-Davy Crockett. PR41-Robinson Crusoe. PR42-20,000 Leagues Under the Sea. PR45-Star Trek "Dinosaur Planet". PR46-Star Trek "The Robot Masters". PR47-Little Women
With record; each... 4 8 12 28 44 60
NOTE: *Peter Pan re-issues exist for #25-34 and are valued the same.*

POWERS
Image Comics: 2000 - No. 37, Feb, 2004 ($2.95)
1-Bendis-s/Oeming-a; murder of Retro Girl 1 3 4 6 8 10
2-6: 6-End of Retro Girl arc. 5.00
7-14: 7-Warren Ellis app. 12-14-Death of Olympia 3.50
15-37: 31-36-Origin of the Powers 3.00
Annual 1 (2001, $3.95) 4.00
...: Anarchy TPB (11/03, $14.95) r/#21-24; interviews, sketchbook, cover gallery 15.00
...Coloring/Activity Book (2001, $1.50, B&W, 8 x 10.5") Oeming-a 3.00
...: Forever TPB (2005, $19.95) r/#31-37; script for #31, sketchbook, cover gallery 20.00
...: Little Deaths TPB (2002, $19.95) r/#7,12-14, Ann. #1, Coloring/Activity Book; sketch pages, cover gallery 20.00
...: Roleplay TPB (2001, $13.95) r/#8-11; sketchbook, cover gallery 14.00
... Scriptbook (2001, $19.95) scripts for #1-11; Oeming sketches 20.00

Powers V3 #1 © Jinxworld

Preacher #19 © Ennis & Dillon

Predators (2010 series) #3 © 20th Century Fox

GD 2.0 | VG 4.0 | FN 6.0 | VF 8.0 | VF/NM 9.0 | NM- 9.2

...: Supergroup TPB (2003, $19.95) r/#15-20; sketchbook, cover gallery 20.00
...: The Definitive Collection Vol. 1 HC (2006, $29.99, dust jacket) r/#1-11 & Coloring/Activity Book, script for #1, sketch pages and covers, interviews, letter column highlights 30.00
...: The Definitive Collection Vol. 2 HC (2009, $29.99, dust jacket) r/#12-24 & Annual #1; cover gallery; 1st Bendis/Oeming Jinx story; interviews, letter column highlights 30.00
..: Who Killed Retro Girl TPB (2000, $21.95) r/#1-6; sketchbook, cover gallery, and promotional strips from Comic Shop News 22.00

POWERS
Marvel Comics (Icon): Jul, 2004 - No. 30, Sept, 2008 ($2.95/$3.95)

1-11,13-24-Bendis-s/Oeming-a. 14-Cover price error 3.00
12-($3.95, 64 pages) 2 covers; Bendis & Oeming interview 4.00
25-30-($3.95, 40 pages) 25-Two covers; Bendis interview 4.00
Annual 2008 (5/08, $4.95) Bendis-s/Oeming-a; interview with Brubaker, Simone, others 5.00
...: Legends TPB (2005, $17.95) r/#1-6; sketchbook, cover gallery 18.00
...: Psychotic TPB (1/06, $19.95) r/#7-12; Bendis & Oeming interview, cover gallery 20.00
...: Cosmic TPB (10/07, $19.95) r/#13-18; script and sketch pages 20.00
...: Secret Identity TPB (12/07, $19.95) r/#19-24; script pages 20.00

POWERS (Volume 3)
Marvel Comics (Icon): Nov, 2009 - Present ($3.95)

1-7-Bendis-s/Oeming-a 4.00

POWERS THAT BE (Becomes Star Seed No.7 on)
Broadway Comics: Nov, 1995 - No. 6, June, 1996 ($2.50)

1-6: 1-Intro of Fatale & Star Seed. 6-Begin $2.95-c. 3.00
Preview Editions 1-3 (9/95 - 11/95, B&W) 3.00

POW MAGAZINE (Bob Sproul's) (Satire Magazine)
Humor-Vision: Aug, 1966 - No. 3, Feb, 1967 (30¢)

1,2: 2-Jones-a 5 10 15 30 48 65
3-Wrightson-a 6 12 18 39 62 85

PREACHER
DC Comics (Vertigo): Apr, 1995 - No. 66, Oct, 2000 ($2.50, mature)

nn-Preview 2 4 6 11 16 20
1 ($2.95)-Ennis scripts, Dillon-a & Fabry-c in all; 1st app. Jesse, Tulip, & Cassidy 2 4 6 8 11 14
1-Special Edition (6/09, $1.00) r/#1 with "After Watchmen" cover frame 3.00
2,3: 2-1st app. Saint of Killers. 1 2 3 5 7 9
4,5 1 2 3 4 5 7
6-10 5.00
11-20: 12-Polybagged w/videogame w/Ennis text. 13-Hunters storyline begins; ends #17. 19-Saint of Killers app.; begin "Crusaders", ends #24 4.00
21-25: 21-24-Saint of Killers app. 25-Origin of Cassidy. 3.00
26-49,52-64: 52-Tulip origin 3.00
50-($3.75) Pin-ups by Jim Lee, Bradstreet, Quesada and Palmiotti 4.00
51-Includes preview of 100 Bullets; Tulip origin 4.00
65,66-($3.75) 65-Almost everyone dies. 66-Final issue 5.00
Alamo (2001, $17.95, TPB) r/#59-66; Fabry-c 18.00
All Hell's a-Coming (2000, $17.95, TPB)-r/#51-58, ...:Tall in the Saddle 18.00
... Book One HC (2009, $39.99, d.j.) r/#1-12; new Ennis intro.; pin-ups from #50,66 40.00
... Book Two HC (2010, $39.99, d.j.) r/#13-26; new Stuart Moore intro. 40.00
... Book Three HC (2010, $39.99, d.j.) r/#27-33, ...Special: Saint of Killers #1-4 & ...Special: Cassidy: Blood & Whiskey #1; new Ennis intro. 40.00
...: Dead or Alive HC (2000, $29.95) Gallery of Glenn Fabry's cover paintings for every Preacher issue; commentary by Fabry & Ennis 30.00
...: Dead or Alive SC (2003, $19.95) 20.00
Dixie Fried (1998, $14.95, TPB)-r/#27-33, Special: Cassidy 15.00
Gone To Texas (1996, $14.95, TPB)-r/#1-7; Fabry-c 15.00
Proud Americans (1997, $14.95, TPB)-r/#18-26; Fabry-c 15.00
Salvation (1999, $14.95, TPB)-r/#41-50; Fabry-c 15.00
Until the End of the World (1996, $14.95, TPB)-r/#8-17; Fabry-c 15.00
War in the Sun (1999, $14.95, TPB)-r/#34-40 15.00

PREACHER SPECIAL: CASSIDY: BLOOD & WHISKEY
DC Comics (Vertigo): 1998 ($5.95, one-shot)

1-Ennis-scripts/Fabry-c/Dillon-a 6.00

PREACHER SPECIAL: ONE MAN'S WAR
DC Comics (Vertigo): Mar, 1998 ($4.95, one-shot)

1-Ennis-scripts/Fabry-c /Snejbjerg-a 5.00

PREACHER SPECIAL: SAINT OF KILLERS
DC Comics (Vertigo): Aug, 1996 - No. 4, Nov, 1996 ($2.50, lim. series, mature)

1-4: Ennis-scripts/Fabry-c. 1,2-Pugh-a. 3,4-Ezquerra-a 3.00
1-Signed & numbered 20.00

GD 2.0 | VG 4.0 | FN 6.0 | VF 8.0 | VF/NM 9.0 | NM- 9.2

PREACHER SPECIAL: THE GOOD OLD BOYS
DC Comics (Vertigo): Aug, 1997 ($4.95, one-shot, mature)

1-Ennis-scripts/Fabry-c /Esquerra-a 5.00

PREACHER SPECIAL: THE STORY OF YOU-KNOW-WHO
DC Comics (Vertigo): Dec, 1996 ($4.95, one-shot, mature)

1-Ennis-scripts/Fabry-c/Case-a 5.00

PREACHER: TALL IN THE SADDLE
DC Comics (Vertigo): 2000 ($5.95, one-shot)

1-Ennis-scripts/Fabry-c/Dillon-a; early romance of Tulip and Jesse 6.00

PREDATOR (Also see Aliens Vs. ..., Batman vs. ..., Dark Horse Comics, & Dark Horse Presents)
Dark Horse Comics: June, 1989 - No. 4, Mar, 1990 ($2.25, limited series)

1-Based on movie; 1st app. Predator 1 2 3 4 5 7
1-2nd printing 3.00
2 5.00
3,4 4.00
Trade paperback (1990, $12.95)-r/#1-4 13.00
... Omnibus Volume 1 (8/07, $24.95, 6" x 9") r/#1-4, ... Cold War, ... Dark River, ...Bloody Sands of Time mini-series and stories from Dark Horse Comics #1,2,4-7,10-12 25.00
... Omnibus Volume 2 (2/08, $24.95, 6" x 9") r/ ... Big Game, ... Race War, ...Invaders From The, Fourth Dimension mini-series and stories from Dark Horse Comics #16-18,20,21; Dark Horse Presents #46 and A Decade of Dark Horse 25.00
... Omnibus Volume 3 (6/08, $24.95, 6" x 9") r/ ... Bad Blood, ... Kindred, ...Hell and Hot Water, ... Strange Roux mini-series and stories from Dark Horse Comics #12-14 and Dark Horse Presents #119 & 124 25.00

PREDATOR
Dark Horse Comics: June, 2009 - No. 4, Jan, 2010 ($3.50, limited series)

1-4-Arcudi-s/Saltares-a/Swanland-c; variant-c by Warner 3.50

PREDATOR: (title series) **Dark Horse Comics**

--**BAD BLOOD,** 12/93 - No. 4, 1994 ($2.50) 1-4 3.00
--**BIG GAME,** 3/91 - No. 4, 6/91 ($2.50) 1-4: 1-3-Contain 2 Dark Horse trading cards 3.00
--**BLOODY SANDS OF TIME,** 2/92 - No. 2, 2/92 ($2.50) 1,2-Dan Barry-c/a(p)/scripts 3.00
--**CAPTIVE,** 4/98 ($2.95, one-shot) 1 3.00
--**COLD WAR,** 9/91 - No. 4, 12/91 ($2.50) 1-4: All have painted-c 3.00
--**DARK RIVER,** 7/96 - No.4, 10/96 ($2.95)1-4: Miran Kim-c 3.00
--**HELL & HOT WATER,** 4/97 - No. 3, 6/97 ($2.95) 1-3 3.00
--**HELL COME A WALKIN',** 2/98 - No. 2, 3/98 ($2.95) 1,2-In the Civil War 3.00
--**HOMEWORLD,** 3/99 - No. 4, 6/99 ($2.95) 1-4 3.00
--**INVADERS FROM THE FOURTH DIMENSION,** 7/94 ($3.95, one-shot, 52 pgs.) 1 4.00
--**JUNGLE TALES.** 3/95 ($2.95t) 1-r/Dark Horse Comics 3.00
--**KINDRED,** 12/96 - No. 4, 3/97 ($2.50) 1-4 3.00
--**NEMESIS,** 12/97 - No. 2, 1/98 ($2.95) 1,2-Predator in Victorian England; Taggart-c 3.00
--**PRIMAL,** 7/97 - No. 2, 8/97 ($2.95) 1,2 3.00
--**RACE WAR** (See Dark Horse Presents #67), 2/93 - No. 4,10/93 ($2.50, color) 1-4,0: 1-4-Dorman painted-c #1-4, 0(4/93) 3.00
--**STRANGE ROUX,** 11/96 ($2.95, one-shot) 1 3.00
--**XENOGENESIS** (Also see Aliens Xenogenesis), 8/99 - No. 4, 11/99 ($2.95) 1,2-Edginton-s 3.00

PREDATORS (Based on the 2010 movie)
Dark Horse Comics: Jun, 2010 - No. 4, Jun, 2010 ($2.99, weekly limited series)

1-4-Prequel to the 2010 movie; stories by Andreyko and Lapham; Paul Lee-c 3.00
... Film Adaptation (7/10, $6.99) Tobin-s/Drujiniu-s/photo-c 7.00
...: Preserve the Game (7/10, $3.50) Sequel to the movie; Lapham-s/Jefferson-a 3.50

PREDATOR 2
Dark Horse Comics: Feb, 1991 - No. 2, June, 1991 ($2.50, limited series)

1,2: 1-Adapts movie; both w/trading cards & photo-c 3.00

PREDATOR VS. JUDGE DREDD
Dark Horse Comics: Oct, 1997 - No. 3 ($2.50, limited series)

1-3-Wagner-s/Alcatena-a/Bolland-c 3.00

PREDATOR VS. MAGNUS ROBOT FIGHTER
Dark Horse/Valiant: Oct, 1992 - No. 2, 1993 ($2.95, limited series)
(1st Dark Horse/Valiant x-over)

1,2: (Reg.)-Barry Smith-c; Lee Weeks-a. 2-w/trading cards 3.00
1 (Platinum edition, 11/92)-Barry Smith-c 10.00

Pride & Prejudice #1 © MAR

Prime #4 © MAL

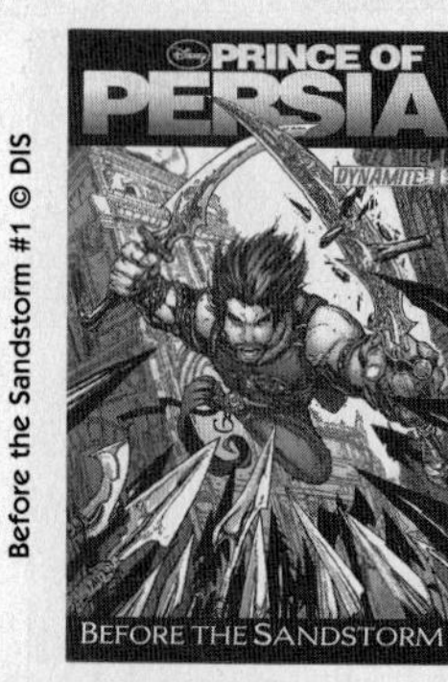

Prince of Persia: Before the Sandstorm #1 © DIS

	GD 2.0	VG 4.0	FN 6.0	VF 8.0	VF/NM 9.0	NM- 9.2

PREHISTORIC WORLD (See Classics Illustrated Special Issue)

PRELUDE TO DEADPOOL CORPS (Leads into Deadpool Corps #1)
Marvel Comics: May, 2010 - No. 5, May, 2010 ($3.99/$2.99, weekly limited series)

1-($3.99) Deadpool & Lady Deadpool vs. alternate dimension Capt. America; Liefeld-a 4.00
2-5-($2.99) Alternate reality Deadpools team-up; Dave Johnson interlocking covers 3.00

PRELUDE TO INFINITE CRISIS
DC Comics: 2005 ($5.99, squarebound)

nn-Reprints stories and panels with commentary leading into Infinite Crisis series 6.00

PREMIERE (See Charlton Premiere)

PRESIDENTIAL MATERIAL
IDW Publishing: Oct, 2008 ($3.99/$7.99)

...: Barack Obama - Biography of the candidate; Mariotte-s/Morgan-a/Campbell-c 4.00
...: John McCain - Biography of the candidate; Helfer-s/Thompson-a/Campbell-c 4.00
Flipbook ($7.99) Both issues in flipbook format 8.00

PRESTO KID, THE (See Red Mask)

PRETTY BOY FLOYD (See On the Spot)

PREZ (See Cancelled Comic Cavalcade, Sandman #54 & Supergirl #10)
National Periodical Publications: Aug-Sept, 1973 - No. 4, Feb-Mar, 1974

	GD	VG	FN	VF	VF/NM	NM-
1-Origin; Joe Simon scripts	3	6	9	18	27	35
2-4	2	4	6	13	18	22

PRICE, THE (See Eclipse Graphic Album Series)

PRIDE & JOY
DC Comics (Vertigo): July, 1997 - No. 4, Oct, 1997 ($2.50, limited series)

1-4-Ennis-s 3.00
TPB (2004, $14.95) r/#1-4 15.00

PRIDE & PREJUDICE
Marvel Comics: June, 2009 - No. 5, Oct, 2009 ($3.99, limited series)

1-5-Adaptation of the Jane Austen novel; Nancy Butler-s/Hugo Petrus-a 4.00

PRIDE AND THE PASSION, THE
Dell Publishing Co.: No. 824, Aug, 1957

	GD	VG	FN	VF	VF/NM	NM-
Four Color 824-Movie, Frank Sinatra & Cary Grant photo-c	9	18	27	63	107	150

PRIDE OF BAGHDAD
DC Comics (Vertigo): 2006 ($19.99, hardcover with dustjacket)

HC-A pride of lions escaping from the Baghdad zoo in 2003; Vaughan-s/Henrichon-a 20.00
SC-(2007, $12.99) 13.00

PRIDE OF THE YANKEES, THE (See Real Heroes & Sport Comics)
Magazine Enterprises: 1949 (The Life of Lou Gehrig)

	GD	VG	FN	VF	VF/NM	NM-
nn-Photo-c; Ogden Whitney-a	82	164	246	528	902	1275

PRIEST (Also see Asylum)
Maximum Press: Aug, 1996 - No. 2, Oct, 1996 ($2.99)

1,2 3.00

PRIMAL FORCE
DC Comics: No. 0, Oct, 1994 - No. 14, Dec, 1995 ($1.95/$2.25)

0-14: 0- Teams Red Tornado, Golem, Jack O'Lantern, Meridian & Silver Dragon. 9-begin $2.25-c 3.00

PRIMAL MAN (See The Crusaders)

PRIMAL RAGE
Sirius Entertainment: 1996 ($2.95)

1-Dark One-c; based of video game 3.00

PRIME (See Break-Thru, Flood Relief & Ultraforce)
Malibu Comics (Ultraverse): June, 1993 - No. 26, Aug, 1995 ($1.95/$2.50)

1-1st app. Prime; has coupon for Ultraverse Premiere #0 3.00
1-With coupon missing 2.00
1-Full cover holographic edition; 1st of kind w/Hardcase #1 & Strangers #1 6.00
1-Ultra 5,000 edition w/silver ink-c 4.00
2-4,6-11,14-26: 2-Polybagged w/card & coupon for U. Premiere #0. 3,4-Prototype app. 4-Direct sale w/o card.4-($2.50)-Newsstand ed. polybagged w/card. 6-Bill & Chelsea Clinton app.115-Intro Papa Verite; Pérez-c/a. 16-Intro Turbo Charge 3.00
5-($2.50, 48 pgs.)-Rune flip-c/story part B by Barry Smith; see Sludge #1 for 1st app. Rune; 3-pg. Night Man preview 4.00
12-($3.50, 68 pgs.)-Flip book w/Ultraverse Premiere #3; silver foil logo 4.00
13-($2.95, 52 pgs.)-Variant covers 4.00
...: Gross and Disgusting 1 (10/94, $3.95)-Boris-c; "Annual" on cover, published monthly in indicia 4.00
...Month "Ashcan" (8/94, 75¢)-Boris-c 3.00
... Time: A Prime Collection (1994, $9.95)-r/1-4 10.00
...Vs. The Incredible Hulk (1995)-mail away limited edition 10.00
...Vs. The Incredible Hulk Premium edition 10.00
...Vs. The Incredible Hulk Super Premium edition 15.00
NOTE: *Perez a-15; c-15, 16.*

PRIME (Also see Black September)
Malibu Comics (Ultraverse): Infinity, Sept, 1995 - V2#15, Dec, 1996 ($1.50)

Infinity, V2#1-8: Post Black September storyline. 6-8-Solitaire app. 9-Breyfogle-c/a. 10-12-Ramos-c. 15-Lord Pumpkin app. 3.00
Infinity Signed Edition (2,000 printed) 5.00

PRIME/CAPTAIN AMERICA
Malibu Comics: Mar, 1996 ($3.95, one-shot)

1-Norm Breyfogle-a 4.00

PRIME8: CREATION
Two Morrows Publishing: July, 2001 ($3.95, B&W)

1-Neal Adams-c 4.00

PRIMER (Comico...)
Comico: Oct (no month), 1982 - No. 6, Feb, 1984 (B&W)

	GD	VG	FN	VF	VF/NM	NM-
1 (52 pgs.)	2	4	6	11	16	20
2-1st app. Grendel & Argent by Wagner	9	18	27	65	113	160
3,4	2	4	6	9	12	15
5-1st Sam Kieth art in comics ('83) & 1st The Maxx	4	8	12	24	37	50
6-Intro & 1st app. Evangeline	2	4	6	13	18	22

PRIMORTALS (Leonard Nimoy's...)

PRIMUS (TV)
Charlton Comics: Feb, 1972 - No. 7, Oct, 1972

	GD	VG	FN	VF	VF/NM	NM-
1-Staton-a in all	2	4	6	11	16	20
2-7: 6-Drug propaganda story	2	4	6	8	11	14

PRINCE NAMOR, THE SUB-MARINER (Also see Namor ...)
Marvel Comics Group: Sept, 1984 - No. 4, Dec, 1984 (Limited-series)

1-4 4.00

PRINCE OF PERSIA: BEFORE THE SANDSTORM (Based on the 2010 movie)
Dynamite Entertainment: 2010 - No. 4, 2010 ($3.99, limited series)

1-4-Art by Fowler and various. 1-Chang-a. 2-Lopez-a. 3-Edwards-a 5.00

PRINCESS SALLY (Video game)
Archie Publications: Apr, 1995 - No. 3, June, 1995 ($1.50, limited series)

1-3: Spin-off from Sonic the Hedgehog 4.00

PRINCE VALIANT (See Ace Comics, Comics Reading Libraries *in the Promotional Comics section*, & King Comics #146, 147)
David McKay Publ./Dell: No. 26, 1941; No. 67, June, 1954 - No. 900, May, 1958

	GD	VG	FN	VF	VF/NM	NM-
Feature Books 26 ('41)-Harold Foster-c/a; newspaper strips reprinted, pgs. 1-28,30-63; color & 68 pgs; Foster cover is only original comic book artwork by him	103	206	309	659	1130	1600
Four Color 567 (6/54)(#1)-By Bob Fuje-Movie, photo-c	10	20	30	71	128	185
Four Color 650 (9/55), 699 (4/56), 719 (8/56),-Fuje-a	7	14	21	50	83	115
Four Color 788 (4/57), 849 (1/58), 900-Fuje-a	7	14	21	47	76	105

PRINCE VALIANT
Marvel Comics: Dec, 1994 - No. 4, Mar, 1995 ($3.95, limited series)

1-4; Kaluta-c in all. 4.00

PRINCE VANDAL
Triumphant Comics: Nov, 1993 - Apr?, 1994 ($2.50)

1-6: 1,2-Triumphant Unleashed x-over 3.00

PRIORITY: WHITE HEAT
AC Comics: 1986 - No. 2, 1986 ($1.75, mini-series)

1,2-Bill Black-a 3.00

PRISCILLA'S POP
Dell Publishing Co.: No. 569, June, 1954 - No. 799, May, 1957

	GD	VG	FN	VF	VF/NM	NM-
Four Color 569 (#1), 630 (5/55), 704 (5/56),799	4	8	12	26	41	55

PRISON BARS (See Behind...)

PRISON BREAK!
Avon Per./Realistic No. 3 on: Sept, 1951 - No. 5, Sept, 1952 (Painted c-3)

1-Wood-c & 1 pg.; has-r/Saint #7 retitled Michael Strong Private Eye

Prison Break! #3 © AVON

Prize Comics #29 © PRIZE

Professor Xavier and the X-Men #6 © MAR

	GD 2.0	VG 4.0	FN 6.0	VF 8.0	VF/NM 9.0	NM- 9.2
	41	82	123	256	428	600
2-Wood-c; Kubert-a; Kinstler inside front-c	30	60	90	177	289	400
3-Orlando, Check-a; c-/Avon paperback #179	24	48	72	140	230	320
4,5: 4-Kinstler-c & inside f/c; Lawrence, Lazarus-a. 5-Kinstler-c; Infantino-a	21	42	63	122	199	275

PRISONER, THE (TV)
DC Comics: 1988 - No. 4, 1989 ($3.50, squarebound, mini-series)

	GD 2.0	VG 4.0	FN 6.0	VF 8.0	VF/NM 9.0	NM- 9.2
1-4 (Books a-d)						4.00

PRISON RIOT
Avon Periodicals: 1952

	GD 2.0	VG 4.0	FN 6.0	VF 8.0	VF/NM 9.0	NM- 9.2
1-Marijuana Murders-1 pg. text; Kinstler-c; 2 Kubert illos on text pages	29	58	87	170	278	385

PRISON TO PRAISE
Logos International: 1974 (35¢) (Religious, Christian)

	GD 2.0	VG 4.0	FN 6.0	VF 8.0	VF/NM 9.0	NM- 9.2
nn-True Story of Merlin R. Carothers	2	4	6	11	16	20

PRIVATE BUCK
Dell Publishing Co./Rand McNally: No. 21, 1941 - No. 12, 1942 (4-1/2" x 5-1/2", 1942)

	GD 2.0	VG 4.0	FN 6.0	VF 8.0	VF/NM 9.0	NM- 9.2
Large Feature Comic 21 (#1)(1941)(Series I), 22 (1941)(Series I), 12 (1942)(Series II)	17	34	51	98	154	210
382-Rand McNally, one panel per page; small size	10	20	30	58	79	100

PRIVATE EYE (Cover title: Rocky Jorden...#6-8)
Atlas Comics (MCI): Jan, 1951 - No. 8, March, 1952

	GD 2.0	VG 4.0	FN 6.0	VF 8.0	VF/NM 9.0	NM- 9.2
1-Cover title: Crime Cases... #1-5	21	42	63	124	202	280
2,3-Tuska c/a(3)	14	28	42	76	108	140
4-8	11	22	33	60	83	105

NOTE: ***Henkel** a-6(3), 7; c-7. **Sinnott** a-6.*

PRIVATE EYE (See Mike Shayne...)

PRIVATE SECRETARY
Dell Publishing Co.: Dec-Feb, 1962-63 - No. 2, Mar-May, 1963

	GD 2.0	VG 4.0	FN 6.0	VF 8.0	VF/NM 9.0	NM- 9.2
1	3	6	9	21	32	42
2	3	6	9	17	25	32

PRIVATE STRONG (See The Double Life of...)

PRIZE COMICS (...Western #69 on) (Also see Treasure Comics)
Prize Publications: March, 1940 - No. 68, Feb-Mar, 1948

	GD 2.0	VG 4.0	FN 6.0	VF 8.0	VF/NM 9.0	NM- 9.2
1-Origin Power Nelson, The Futureman & Jupiter, Master Magician; Ted O'Neil, Secret Agent M-11, Jaxon of the Jungle, Bucky Brady & Storm Curtis begin (1st app. of each)	277	554	831	1759	3030	4300
2-The Black Owl begins (1st app.)	123	246	369	787	1344	1900
3	110	220	330	704	1202	1700
4-Classic robot-c	129	258	387	826	1413	2000
5,6: Dr. Dekkar, Master of Monsters app. in each	103	206	309	659	1130	1600
7-(Scarce)-1st app. The Green Lama (12/40); Black Owl by S&K; origin/1st app. Dr. Frost & Frankenstein; Capt. Gallant, The Great Voodini & Twist Turner begin;	232	464	696	1485	2543	3600
8,9-Black Owl & Ted O'Neil by S&K	103	206	309	659	1130	1600
10-12,14,15: 11-Origin Bulldog Denny. 14-War-c	74	148	222	470	810	1150
13-Yank & Doodle begin (8/41, origin/1st app.)	81	162	243	518	884	1250
16-20: 16-Spike Mason begins	68	136	204	435	743	1050
21,25,27,28,31-All WWII covers	55	110	165	352	601	850
22-24,26: 22-Statue of Liberty Japanese attack war-c. 23-Uncle Sam patriotic war-c. 24-Lincoln statue patriotic-c. 26-Liberty Bell-c	65	130	195	416	708	1000
29,30	43	86	129	271	461	650
32	39	78	117	240	395	550
33-Classic bondage/torture-c	55	110	165	352	601	850
34-Origin Airmale, Yank & Doodle; The Black Owl joins army, Yank & Doodle's father assumes Black Owl's role	39	78	117	231	378	525
35-36,38-39: 35-Flying Fist & Bingo begin	28	56	84	165	270	375
37-Intro. Stampy, Airmale's sidekick; Hitler-c	53	106	159	334	567	800
40-Nazi WWII-c	32	64	96	188	307	425
41-45,47-50: 45-Yank & Doodle learn Black Owl's I.D. (their father). 48-Prince Ra begins	22	44	66	132	216	300
46-Classic Zombie Horror-c/story	40	80	120	246	411	575
51-62,64,67,68: 53-Transvestism story. 55-No Frankenstein. 57-X-Mas-c. 64-Black Owl retires	17	34	51	98	154	210
63-Simon & Kirby c/a	20	40	60	117	189	260
65,66-Frankenstein-c by Briefer	18	36	54	107	169	230

NOTE: ***Briefer** a-7-on; c-65, 66. **J. Binder** a-16; c-21-29. **Guardineer** a-62. **Kiefer** c-62. **Palais** c-68. **Simon & Kirby** c-63, 75, 83.*

PRIZE COMICS WESTERN (Formerly Prize Comics #1-68)
Prize Publications (Feature): No. 69(V7#2), Apr-May, 1948 - No. 119, Nov-Dec, 1956 (No. 69-84: 52 pgs.)

	GD 2.0	VG 4.0	FN 6.0	VF 8.0	VF/NM 9.0	NM- 9.2
69(V7#2)	14	28	42	80	115	150
70-75: 74-Kurtzman-a (8 pgs.)	12	24	36	67	94	120
76-Randolph Scott photo-c; "Canadian Pacific" movie adaptation	13	26	39	72	101	130
77-Photo-c; Severin/Elder, Mart Bailey-a; "Streets of Laredo" movie adaptation	12	24	36	67	94	120
78-Photo-c; S&K-a, 10 pgs.; Severin, Mart Bailey-a; "Bullet Code", & "Roughshod" movie adaptations	15	30	45	90	140	190
79-Photo-c; Kurtzman-a, 8 pgs.; Severin/Elder, Severin, Mart Bailey-a; "Stage To Chino" movie adaptation w/George O'Brien	15	30	45	90	140	190
80-82-Photo-c; 80,81-Severin/Elder-a(2). 82-1st app. The Preacher by Mart Bailey; Severin/Elder-a(3)	13	26	39	72	101	130
83,84	10	20	30	58	79	100
85-1st app. American Eagle by John Severin & begins (V9#6, 1-2/51)	19	38	57	111	176	240
86,101-105, 109-Severin/Williamson-a	11	22	33	64	90	115
87-99,110,111-Severin/Elder-a(2-3) each	12	24	36	69	97	125
100	13	26	39	74	105	135
106-108,112	9	18	27	47	61	75
113-Williamson/Severin-a(2)/Frazetta?	12	24	36	69	97	125
114-119: Drifter series in all; by Mort Meskin #114-118	8	16	24	42	54	65

NOTE: ***Fass** a-81. **Severin & Elder** c-84-99. **Severin** a-72, 75, 77-79, 83-86, 96, 97, 100-105; c-92,100-109(most), 110-119. **Simon & Kirby** c-75, 83.*

PRIZE MYSTERY
Key Publications: May, 1955 - No. 3, Sept, 1955

	GD 2.0	VG 4.0	FN 6.0	VF 8.0	VF/NM 9.0	NM- 9.2
1	11	22	33	60	83	105
2,3	8	16	24	44	57	70

PRO, THE
Image Comics: July, 2002 ($5.95, squarebound, one-shot)

	GD 2.0	VG 4.0	FN 6.0	VF 8.0	VF/NM 9.0	NM- 9.2
1-Ennis-s/Conner & Palmiotti-a; prostitute gets super-powers						8.00
1-Second printing with different cover						6.00
Hardcover Edition (10/04, $14.95) oversized reprint plus new 8 pg. story; sketch pages						15.00

PROFESSIONAL FOOTBALL (See Charlton Sport Library)

PROFESSOR COFFIN
Charlton Comics: No. 19, Oct, 1985 - No. 21, Feb, 1986

	GD 2.0	VG 4.0	FN 6.0	VF 8.0	VF/NM 9.0	NM- 9.2
19-21: Wayne Howard-a(r); low print run	1	2	3	5	6	8

PROFESSOR OM
Innovation Publishing: May, 1990 - No. 2, 1990 ($2.50, limited series)

	GD 2.0	VG 4.0	FN 6.0	VF 8.0	VF/NM 9.0	NM- 9.2
1,2-East Meets West spin-off						3.00

PROFESSOR XAVIER AND THE X-MEN (Also see X-Men, 1st series)
Marvel Comics: Nov, 1995 - No. 18 (99¢)

	GD 2.0	VG 4.0	FN 6.0	VF 8.0	VF/NM 9.0	NM- 9.2
1-18: Stories featuring the Original X-Men. 2-vs. The Blob. 5-Vs. the Original Brotherhood of Evil Mutants. 10-Vs. The Avengers						3.00

PROGRAMME, THE
DC Comics (WildStorm): Sept, 2007 - No. 12, Aug, 2008 ($2.99, limited series)

	GD 2.0	VG 4.0	FN 6.0	VF 8.0	VF/NM 9.0	NM- 9.2
1-12: 1-Milligan-s/C.P. Smith-a; covers by Smith & Van Sciver						3.00
Book One TPB (2008, $17.99) r/#1-6; cover sketches						18.00
Book Two TPB (2008, $17.99) r/#7-12; cover sketches						18.00

PROJECT A-KO (Manga)
Malibu Comics: Mar, 1994 - No. 4, June, 1994 ($2.95)

	GD 2.0	VG 4.0	FN 6.0	VF 8.0	VF/NM 9.0	NM- 9.2
1-4-Based on anime film						3.00

PROJECT A-KO 2 (Manga)
CPM Comics: May, 1995 - No. 3, Aug, 1995 ($2.95, limited series)

	GD 2.0	VG 4.0	FN 6.0	VF 8.0	VF/NM 9.0	NM- 9.2
1-3						3.00

PROJECT A-KO VERSUS THE UNIVERSE (Manga)
CPM Comics: Oct, 1995 - No. 5, June, 1996 ($2.95, limited series, bi-monthly)

	GD 2.0	VG 4.0	FN 6.0	VF 8.0	VF/NM 9.0	NM- 9.2
1-5						3.00

PROJECT SUPERPOWERS
Dynamite Entertainment: 2008 - No. 7, 2008 ($1.00/$3.50/$2.99)

	GD 2.0	VG 4.0	FN 6.0	VF 8.0	VF/NM 9.0	NM- 9.2
0-($1.00) Two connecting covers by Alex Ross; re-intro of Golden Age heroes						3.00
0-($1.00) Variant cover by Michael Turner						5.00
1-($3.50) Covers by Ross and Turner; Jim Krueger-s/Carlos Paul-a						3.50
2-7-($2.99)						3.00
... Chapter One HC (2008, $29.99, dustjacket) r/#0-7; Ross sketch pages; layout art						30.00

Project Superpowers: Chapter 2 #5 © DE

Promethea #27 © ABC

Psycho #3 © Skywald

GD VG FN VF VF/NM NM-
2.0 4.0 6.0 8.0 9.0 9.2

GD VG FN VF VF/NM NM-
2.0 4.0 6.0 8.0 9.0 9.2

PROJECT SUPERPOWERS: CHAPTER TWO
Dynamite Entertainment: 2009 - No. 12, 2010 ($1.00/$2.99)
... Chapter Two Prelude (2008, $1.00) Ross sketch pages and mini-series previews 3.00
0-($1.00) Three connecting covers by Alex Ross; The Inheritors assemble 3.00
1-12-($2.99) 1-Krueger & Ross-s/Salazar-a; Ross sketch pages; 2 Ross covers 3.00
... X-Mas Carol (2010, $5.99) Berkenkotter-a/Ross-c 6.00

PROJECT SUPERPOWERS: MEET THE BAD GUYS
Dynamite Entertainment: 2009 - No. 4, 2009 ($2.99)
1-4: Ross & Casey-s. 1-Bloodlust. 2-The Revolutionary. 3-Dagon. 4-Supremacy 3.00

PROMETHEA
America's Best Comics: Aug, 1999 - No. 32, Apr, 2005 ($3.50/$2.95)
1-Alan Moore-s/Williams III & Gray-a; Alex Ross painted-c 3.50
1-Variant-c by Williams III & Gray 3.50
2-31-($2.95): 7-Villarrubia photo-a. 10-"Sex, Stars & Serpents". 26-28-Tom Strong app. 27-Cover swipe of Superman vs. Spider-Man treasury ed. 3.00
32-($3.95) Final issue; pages can be cut & assembled into a 2-sided poster 4.00
32-Limited edition of 1000; variant issue printed as 2-sided poster, signed by Moore and Williams; each came with a 48 page book of Promethea covers 120.00
Book 1 Hardcover ($24.95, dust jacket) r/#1-6 25.00
Book 1 TPB ($14.95) r/#1-6 15.00
Book 2 Hardcover ($24.95, dust jacket) r/#7-12 25.00
Book 2 TPB ($14.95) r/#7-12 15.00
Book 3 Hardcover ($24.95, dust jacket) r/#13-18 25.00
Book 3 TPB ($14.95) r/#13-18 15.00
Book 4 Hardcover ($24.95, dust jacket) r/#19-25 25.00
Book 4 TPB ($14.99) r/#19-25 15.00
Book 5 Hardcover ($24.95, d.j.) r/#26-32; includes 2-sided poster image from #32 25.00
Book 5 TPB ($14.99) r/#26-32; includes 2-sided poster image from #32 15.00

PROMETHEUS (VILLAINS) (Leads into JLA #16,17)
DC Comics: Feb, 1998 ($1.95, one-shot)
1-Origin & 1st app.; Morrison-s/Pearson-c 3.00

PROPELLERMAN
Dark Horse Comics: Jan, 1993 - No. 8, Mar, 1994 ($2.95, limited series)
1-8: 2,4,8-Contain 2 trading cards 3.00

PROPHET (See Youngblood #2)
Image Comics (Extreme Studios): Oct, 1993 - No. 10, 1995 ($1.95)
1-($2.50)-Liefeld/Panosian-c/a; 1st app. Mary McCormick; Liefeld scripts in 1-4; #1-3 contain coupons for Prophet #0 3.00
1-Gold foil embossed-c edition rationed to dealers 4.00
2-10: 2-Liefeld-c(p). 3-1st app. Judas. 4-1st app. Omen; Black and White Pt. 3 by Thibert. 4-Alternate-c by Stephen Platt. 5,6-Platt-c/a. 7-(9/94, $2.50)-Platt-c/a. 8-Bloodstrike app. 10-Polybagged w/trading card; Platt-c. 3.00
0-(7/94, $2.50)-San Diego Comic Con ed. (2200 copies) 3.00

PROPHET
Image Comics (Extreme Studios): V2#1, Aug, 1995 - No. 8 ($3.50)
V2#1-8: Dixon scripts in all. 1-4-Platt-a. 1-Boris-c; F. Miller variant-c. 4-Newmen app. 5,6-Wraparound-c 3.50
Annual 1 (9/95, $2.50)-Bagged w/Youngblood gaming card; Quesada-c 3.00
Babewatch Special 1 (12/95, $2.50)-Babewatch tie-in 3.00
1995 San Diego Edition-B&W preview of V2#1. 3.00
TPB-(1996, $12.95) r/#1-7 13.00

PROPHET (Volume 3)
Awesome Comics: Mar, 2000 ($2.99)
1-Flip-c by Jim Lee and Liefeld 3.00

PROPHET/CABLE
Image Comics (Extreme): Jan, 1997 - No. 2, Mar, 1997 ($3.50, limited series)
1,2-Liefeld-c/a: 2-#1 listed on cover 3.50

PROPHET/CHAPEL: SUPER SOLDIERS
Image Comics (Extreme): May, 1996 - No. 2, June, 1996 ($2.50, limited series)
1,2: 1-Two covers exist 3.00
1-San Diego Edition; B&W-c 3.00

PROPOSITION PLAYER
DC Comics (Vertigo): Dec, 1999 - No. 6, May, 2000 ($2.50, limited series)
1-6-Willingham-s/Guinan-a/Bolton-c 3.00
TPB (2003, $14.95) r/#1-6; intro. by James McManus 15.00

PROTECTORS (Also see The Ferret)
Malibu Comics: Sept, 1992 - No. 20, May, 1994 ($1.95-$2.95)
1-20 ($2.50, direct sale)-With poster & diff-c: 1-Origin; has 3/4 outer-c. 3-Polybagged w/Skycap 3.50
1-12 ($1.95, newsstand)-Without poster 3.00

PROTOTYPE (Also see Flood Relief & Ultraforce)
Malibu Comics (Ultraverse): Aug, 1993 - No. 18, Feb, 1995 ($1.95/$2.50)
1-Holo-c 6.00
1-Ultra Limited silver foil-c 4.00
1,2,4-12,14-18: 4-Intro Wrath. 5-Break-Thru & Strangers x-over. 6-Arena cameo. 7,8-Arena-c/story. 12-(7/94). 14 (10/94) 3.00
3-($2.50, 48 pgs.)-Rune flip-c/story by B. Smith (3 pgs.) 4.00
13 (8/94, $3.50)-Flip book (Ultraverse Premiere #6) 4.00
#0-(8/94, $2.50, 44 pgs.) 4.00
Giant Size 1 (10/94, $2.50, 44 pgs.) 4.00

PROTOTYPE (Based on the Activision video game)
DC Comics (WildStorm): Jun, 2009 - No. 6, Nov, 2009 ($3.99, limited series)
1-6-Darick Robertson-c/a 4.00
TPB (2010, $19.99) r/#1-6 20.00

PRUDENCE & CAUTION (Also see Dogs of War & Warriors of Plasm)
Defiant: May, 1994 - No. 2, June, 1994 ($3.50/$2.50)(Spanish versions exist)
1-($3.50, 52 pgs.)-Chris Claremont scripts in all 4.00
2-($2.50) 3.00

PRYDE AND WISDOM (Also see Excalibur)
Marvel Comics: Sept, 1996 - No. 3, Nov, 1996 ($1.95, limited series)
1-3: Warren Ellis scripts; Terry Dodson & Karl Story-c/a 3.00

PSI-FORCE
Marvel Comics Group: Nov, 1986 - No. 32, June, 1989 (75¢/$1.50)
1-25: 11-13-Williamson-i 3.00
26-32 3.00
Annual 1 (10/87) 4.00
... Classic Vol. 1 TPB (2008, $24.99) r/#1-9 25.00

PSI-JUDGE ANDERSON
Fleetway Publications (Quality): 1989 - No. 15, 1990 ($1.95, B&W)
1-15 3.00

PSI-LORDS
Valiant: Sept, 1994 - No. 10, June, 1995 ($2.25)
1-($3.50)-Chromium wraparound-c 4.00
1-Gold 5.00
2-10: 3-Chaos Effect Epsilon Pt. 2 3.00

PSYBA-RATS (Also see Showcase '94 #3,4)
DC Comics: Apr, 1995-No. 3, June, 1995 ($2.50, limited series)
1-3 3.00

PSYCHO (Magazine) (Also see Nightmare)
Skywald Publ. Corp.: Jan, 1971 - No. 24, Mar, 1975 (68 pgs.; B&W)
1-All reprints 9 18 27 60 100 140
2-Origin & 1st app. The Heap, series begins 6 12 18 41 66 90
3-Frankenstein series by Adkins begins 6 12 18 39 62 85
4,7,9,10: 4-7-Squarebound. 4-1st Out of Chaos/Satan-c/s 5 10 15 34 55 75
8-(Squarebound)1st app. Edward & Mina Sartyros, the Human Gargoyles 6 12 18 39 62 85
11-18: 13-Cannabalism; 3 pgs of Christopher Lee as Dracula photos. 18-Injury to eye-c. 4 8 12 26 41 55
19-Origin Dracula. 4 8 12 28 44 60
20-Severed Head-c 5 10 15 34 55 75
21-24: 22-1974 Fall Special; Reese, Wildey-a(r). 24-1975 Winter Special; Dave Sim scripts (1st pro work) 5 10 15 30 48 65
Annual 1 (1972)(68 pgs.) Dracula & the Heap app. 5 10 15 30 48 65
Yearbook (1974-nn)-Everett, Reese-a 4 8 12 26 41 55

NOTE: ***Boris** c-3, 5. **Buckler** a-2, 4, 5. **Gene Day** a-21, 23, 24. **Everett** a-3-6. **B. Jones** a-4. **Jeff Jones** a-6, 7, 9; c-12. **Kaluta** a-13. **Katz/Buckler** a-3. **Kim** a-24. **Morrow** a-1. **Reese** a-5. **Dave Sim** s-24. **Sutton** a-3. **Wildey** a-5.*

PSYCHO, THE
DC Comics: 1991 - No. 3, 1991 ($4.95, squarebound, limited series)
1-3-Hudnall-s/Brereton painted-a/c 5.00
TPB (Image Comics, 2006, $17.99) r/series; Brereton sketch pages; Hudnall afterword 18.00

PSYCHOANALYSIS
E. C. Comics: Mar-Apr, 1955 - No. 4, Sept-Oct, 1955

The Pulse #1 © MAR

Punch Comics #21 © CHES

The Punisher #21 © MAR

GD 2.0 | VG 4.0 | FN 6.0 | VF 8.0 | VF/NM 9.0 | NM- 9.2

1-All Kamen-c/a; not approved by code 21 42 63 168 267 365
2-4-Kamen-c/a in all 14 28 42 112 181 250

PSYCHOANALYSIS
Gemstone Publishing: Oct, 1999 - No. 4, Jan, 2000 ($2.50)

1-4-Reprints E.C. series 3.00
Annual 1 (2000, $10.95) r/#1-4 11.00

PSYCHOBLAST
First Comics: Nov, 1987 - No. 9, July, 1988 ($1.75)

1-9 3.00

PSYCHONAUTS
Marvel Comics (Epic Comics): Oct, 1993 - No. 4, Jan, 1994 ($4.95, lim. series)

1-4: American/Japanese co-produced comic 5.00

PSYLOCKE
Marvel Comics: Jan, 2010 - No. 4, Apr, 2010 ($3.99, limited series)

1-4-Finch-c/Yost-s/Tolibao-a. 3,4-Wolverine app. 4.00

PSYLOCKE & ARCHANGEL CRIMSON DAWN
Marvel Comics: Aug, 1997 - No. 4, Nov, 1997 ($2.50, limited series)

1-4-Raab-s/Larroca-a(p) 3.00

PTOLUS: CITY BY THE SPIRE
Dabel Brothers Productions/Marvel Comics (Dabel Brothers) #2 on: June, 2006 - No. 6, Mar, 2007 ($2.99)

1-(1st printing, Dabel) Adaptation of the Monte Cook novel; Cook-s 3.00
1-(2nd printing, Marvel), 2-6 3.00
Monte Cooke's Ptolus: City By the Spire TPB (2007, $14.99) r/#1-6 15.00

P.T. 109 (See Movie Comics)

PUBLIC DEFENDER IN ACTION (Formerly Police Trap)
Charlton Comics: No. 7, Mar, 1956 - No. 12, Oct, 1957

7 10 20 30 58 79 100
8-12 8 16 24 40 50 60

PUBLIC ENEMIES
D. S. Publishing Co.: 1948 - No. 9, June-July, 1949

1-True Crime Stories 27 54 81 158 259 360
2-Used in **SOTI**, pg. 95 22 44 66 132 216 300
3-5: 5-Arrival date of 10/1/48 15 30 45 88 137 185
6,8,9 15 30 45 85 130 175
7-McWilliams-a; injury to eye panel 15 30 45 88 137 185

PUBO
Dark Horse Comics: Dec, 2002 - No. 3, Mar, 2003 ($3.50, B&W, limited series)

1-3-Leland Purvis-s/a 3.50

PUDGY PIG
Charlton Comics: Sept, 1958 - No. 2, Nov, 1958

1,2 3 6 9 17 25 32

PUFFED
Image Comics: Jul, 2003 - No. 3, Sept, 2003 ($2.95, B&W)

1-3-Layman-s/Crosland-a. 1-Two covers by Crosland & Quitely 3.00

PULP FANTASTIC (Vertigo V2K)
DC Comics (Vertigo): Feb, 2000 - No. 3, Apr, 2000 ($2.50, limited series)

1-3-Chaykin & Tischman-s/Burchett-a 3.00

PULP FICTION LIBRARY: MYSTERY IN SPACE
DC Comics: 1999 ($19.95, TPB)

nn-Reprints classic sci-fi stories from Mystery in Space, Strange Adventures, Real Fact Comics and My Greatest Adventure 20.00

PULSE, THE (Also see Alias and Deadline)
Marvel Comics: Apr, 2004 - No. 14, May, 2006 ($2.99)

1-14: 1-5-Bendis-s/Bagley-a; Jessica Jones, Ben Urich, Kat Farrell app. 3-5-Green Goblin app. 6,7-Brent Anderson-a 9-Wolverine app. 10-House of M. 11-14-Gaydos-a 3.00
...: House of M Special (9/05, 50¢) tabloid newspaper format; Mayhew- "photos" 3.00
Vol. 1: Thin Air (2004, $13.99) r/#1-5, gallery of cover layouts and sketches 14.00
Vol. 2: Secret War (2005, $11.99) r/#6-9 12.00
Vol. 3: Fear (2006, $14.99) r/#11-14 and New Avengers Annual #1 15.00

PUMA BLUES
Aardvark One International/Mirage Studios #21 on: 1986 - No. 26, 1990 ($1.70-$1.75, B&W)

1-19, 21-26: 1-1st & 2nd printings. 25,26-$1.75-c 3.00
20 ($2.25)-By Alan Moore, Miller, Grell, others 5.00

GD 2.0 | VG 4.0 | FN 6.0 | VF 8.0 | VF/NM 9.0 | NM- 9.2

Trade Paperback (12/88, $14.95) 15.00

PUMPKINHEAD: THE RITES OF EXORCISM (Movie)
Dark Horse Comics: 1993 - No. 2, 1993 ($2.50, limited series)

1,2: Based on movie; painted-c by McManus 3.00

PUNCH & JUDY COMICS
Hillman Per.: 1944; No. 2, Fall, 1944 - V3#2, 12/47; V3#3, 6/51 - V3#9, 12/51

V1#1-(60 pgs.) 23 46 69 136 223 310
2 14 28 42 80 115 150
3-12(7/46) 11 22 33 64 90 115
V2#1(8/49),3-9 9 18 27 50 65 80
V2#2,10-12, V3#1-Kirby-a(2) each 21 42 63 122 199 275
V3#2-Kirby-a 19 38 57 112 179 245
3-9 9 18 27 47 61 75

PUNCH COMICS
Harry 'A' Chesler: 12/41; #2, 2/42; #9, 7/44 - #19, 10/46; #20, 7/47 - #23, 1/48

1-Mr. E, The Sky Chief, Hale the Magician, Kitty Kelly begin
152 304 456 965 1658 2350
2-Captain Glory app. 94 188 282 597 1024 1450
9-Rocketman & Rocket Girl & The Master Key begin; classic-c
97 194 291 621 1061 1500
10-Sky Chief app.; J. Cole-a; Master Key-r/Scoop #3
64 128 192 406 696 985
11-Origin Master Key-r/Scoop #1; Sky Chief, Little Nemo app.; Jack Cole-a; Fine-*ish* art by Sultan 58 116 174 371 636 900
12-Rocket Boy & Capt. Glory app; classic Skull-c 290 580 870 1856 3178 4500
13-Cover has list of 4 Chesler artists' names on tombstone
68 136 204 435 743 1050
14,15,19,21: 21-Hypo needle story 55 110 165 352 601 850
16,17-Gag-c 39 78 117 240 395 550
18-Bondage-c; hypodermic panels 68 136 204 435 743 1050
20-Unique cover with bare-breasted women. Rocket Girl-c
116 232 348 742 1271 1800
22,23-Little Nemo-not by McCay. 22-Intro Baxter (teenage)(68 pgs.)
24 48 72 140 230 320

PUNCHY AND THE BLACK CROW
Charlton Comics: No. 10, Oct, 1985 - No. 12, Feb, 1986

10-12: Al Fago funny animal-r; low print run 6.00

PUNISHER (See Amazing Spider-Man #129, Blood and Glory, Born, Captain America #241, Classic Punisher, Daredevil #182-184, 257, Daredevil and the..., Ghost Rider V2#5, 6, Marc Spector #8 & 9, Marvel Preview #2, Marvel Super Action, Marvel Tales, Power Pack #46, Spectacular Spider-Man #81-83, 140, 141, 143 & new Strange Tales #13 & 14)

PUNISHER (The...)
Marvel Comics Group: Jan, 1986 - No. 5, May, 1986 (Limited series)

1-Double size 3 6 9 14 20 25
2-5 2 4 6 8 11 14
Trade Paperback (1988)-r/#1-5 11.00
Circle of Blood TPB (8/01, $15.95) Zeck-c 16.00
Circle of Blood HC (2008, $19.99) two covers 20.00
NOTE: ***Zeck** a-1-4; c-1-5.*

PUNISHER (The...) (Volume 2)
Marvel Comics: July, 1987 - No. 104, July, 1995

1 1 3 4 6 8 10
2-9: 8-Portacio/Williams-c/a begins, ends #18. 9-Scarcer, low dist. 6.00
10-Daredevil app; ties in w/Daredevil #257 1 3 4 6 8 10
11-25,50: 13-18-Kingpin app. 19-Stroman-c/a. 20-Portacio-c(p). 24-1st app. Shadowmasters. 25,50:($1.50,52 pgs.). 25-Shadowmasters app. 4.00
26-49,51-74,76-85,87-89: 57-Photo-c; came w/outer-c (newsstand ed. w/o outer-c). 59-Punisher is severely cut & has skin grafts (has black skin). 60-62-Luke Cage app. 62-Punisher back to white skin. 68-Tarantula-c/story. 85-Prequel to Suicide Run Pt. 0. 87,88-Suicide Run Pt. 6 & 9 3.00
75-($2.75, 52 pgs.)-Embossed silver foil-c 4.00
86-($2.95, 52 pgs.)-Embossed & foil stamped-c; Suicide Run part 3 4.00
90-99: 90-bound-in cards. 99-Cringe app. 3.00
100,104: 100-($2.95, 68 pgs.). 104-Last issue 4.00
100-($3.95, 68 pgs.)-Foil cover 5.00
101-103: 102-Bullseye 3.50
"Ashcan" edition (75¢)-Joe Kubert-c 3.00
Annual 1-7 ('88-'94, 68 pgs.) 1-Evolutionary War x-over. 2-Atlantis Attacks x-over; Jim Lee-a(p) (back-up story, 6 pgs.); Moon Knight app. 4-Golden-c(p). 6-Bagged w/card. 4.00
...: A Man Named Frank (1994, $6.95, TPB) 7.00
...and Wolverine in African Saga nn (1989, $5.95, 52 pgs.)-Reprints Punisher War Journal

The Punisher V3 #4 © MAR

The Punisher (2009 series) #5 © MAR

PunisherMAX #1 © MAR

GD 2.0 | VG 4.0 | FN 6.0 | VF 8.0 | VF/NM 9.0 | NM- 9.2

#6 & 7; Jim Lee-c/a(r) 6.00
... Assassin Guild ('88, $6.95, graphic novel) 10.00
Back to School Special 1-3 (11/92-10/94, $2.95, 68 pgs.) 4.00
.../Batman: Deadly Knights (10/94, $4.95) 5.00
.../Black Widow: Spinning Doomsday's Web (1992, $9.95, graphic novel) 12.00
...Bloodlines nn (1991, $5.95, 68 pgs.) 6.00
...: Die Hard in the Big Easy nn ('92, $4.95, 52 pgs.) 5.00
...: Empty Quarter nn ('94, $6.95) 7.00
...G-Force nn (1992, $4.95, 52 pgs.)-Painted-c 5.00
...Holiday Special 1-3 (1/93-1/95,, 52 pgs.,68pgs.)-1-Foil-c 4.00
...Intruder Graphic Novel (1989, $14.95, hardcover) 20.00
...Intruder Graphic Novel (1991, $9.95, softcover) 12.00
...Invades the 'Nam: Final Invasion nn (2/94, $6.95)-J. Kubert-c & chapter break art; reprints The 'Nam #84 & unpublished #85,86 7.00
...Kingdom Gone Graphic Novel (1990, $16.95, hardcover) 20.00
...Meets Archie (8/94, $3.95, 52 pgs.)-Die cut-c; no ads; same contents as Archie Meets The Punisher 5.00
...Movie Special 1 (6/90, $5.95, squarebound, 68 pgs.) painted-c; Brent Anderson-a; contents intended for a 3 issue series which was advertised but not published 6.00
...: No Escape nn (1990, $4.95, 52 pgs.)-New-a 5.00
...Return to Big Nothing Graphic Novel (Epic, 1989, $16.95, hardcover) 25.00
...Return to Big Nothing Graphic Novel (Marvel, 1989, $12.95, softcover) 15.00
...The Prize nn (1990, $4.95, 68 pgs.)-New-a 5.00
Summer Special 1-4(8/91-7/94, 52 pgs.):1-No ads. 2-Bisley-c; Austin-a(i). 3-No ads 4.00

NOTE: ***Austin*** *c(i)-47, 48.* ***Cowan*** *c-39.* ***Golden*** *c-50, 85, 86, 100.* ***Heath*** *a-26, 27, 89, 90, 91; c-26, 27.* ***Quesada*** *c-56p, 62p.* ***Sienkiewicz*** *c-Back to School 1.****Stroman*** *a-76p(9 pgs.).* ***Williamson*** *a(i)-25, 60-62i, 64-70, 74, Annual 5; c(i)-62, 65-68.*

PUNISHER (Also see Double Edge)
Marvel Comics: Nov, 1995 - No. 18, Apr, 1997 ($2.95/$1.95/$1.50)

1 ($2.95)-Ostrander scripts begin; foil-c. 4.00
2-18: 7-Vs. S.H.I.E.L.D. 11-"Onslaught." 12-17-X-Cutioner-c/app. 17-Daredevil, Spider-Man-c/app. 3.00

PUNISHER (Marvel Knights)
Marvel Comics: Nov, 1998 - No. 4, Feb, 1999 ($2.99, limited series)

1-4: 1-Wrightson-a; Wrightson & Jusko-c 3.00
1-($6.95) DF Edition; Jae Lee variant-c 7.00

PUNISHER (Marvel Knights) (Volume 3)
Marvel Comics: Apr, 2000 - No. 12, Mar, 2001 ($2.99, limited series)

1-Ennis-s/Dillon & Palmiotti-a/Bradstreet-c 5.00
1-Bradstreet white variant-c 10.00
1-($6.95) DF Edition; Jurgens & Ordway variant-c 7.00
2-Two covers by Bradstreet & Dillon 3.00
3-($3.99) Bagged with Marvel Knights Genesis Edition; Daredevil app. 4.00
4-12: 9-11-The Russian app. 3.00
HC (6/02, $34.95) r/#1-12, Punisher Kills the Marvel Universe, and Marvel Knights Double Shot #1 35.00
... By Garth Ennis Omnibus (2008, $99.99) oversized r/#1-12, #1-7 & #13-37 of 2001 series, Punisher Kills the Marvel Universe, and Marvel Knights Double Shot #1; extras 100.00
.../Painkiller Jane (1/01, $3.50) Jusko-c; Ennis-s/Jusko and Dave Ross-a(p) 3.50
...: Welcome Back Frank TPB (4/01, $19.95) r/#1-12 20.00

PUNISHER (Marvel Knights) (Volume 4)
Marvel Comics: Aug, 2001 - No. 37, Feb, 2004 ($2.99)

1-Ennis-s/Dillon & Palmiotti-a/Bradstreet-c; The Russian app. 4.00
2-Two covers (Dillon & Bradstreet) Spider-Man-c/app. 3.00
3-37: 3-7-Ennis-s/Dillon-a. 9-12-Peyer-s/Gutierrez-a. 13,14-Ennis-s/Dilllon-a. 16,17-Wolverine app.; Robertson-a. 18-23,32-Dillon-a. 24-27-Mandrake-a. 27-Elektra app. 33-37-Spider-Man, Daredevil, & Wolverine app. 36,37-Hulk app. 3.00
...Army of One TPB (2/02, $15.95) r/#1-7; Bradstreet-c 16.00
Vol. 2 HC (2003, $29.95) r/#1-7,13-18; intro. by Mike Millar 30.00
Vol. 3 HC (2004, $29.95) r/#19-27; script pages for #19 30.00
Vol. 3: Business as Usual TPB (2003, $14.99) r/#13-18; Bradstreet-c 15.00
Vol. 4: Full Auto TPB (2003, $17.99) r/#20-26; Bradstreet-c 18.00
Vol. 5: Streets of Laredo TPB (2003, $17.99) r/#19,27-32 18.00
Vol. 6: Confederacy of Dunces TPB (2004, $13.99) r/#33-37 14.00

PUNISHER (Marvel MAX)(Title becomes "Punisher: Frank Castle MAX" with #66)
Marvel Comics: Mar, 2004 - No. 75, Dec, 2009 ($2.99/$3.99)

1-49,51-60: 1-Ennis-s/LaRosa-a/Bradstreet-c; flashback to his family's murder; Micro app. 6-Micro killed. 7-12,19-25-Fernandez-a. 13-18-Braithwaite-a. 31-36-Barracuda. 43-49-Medina-a. 51-54-Barracuda app. 60-Last Ennis-s/Bradstreet-c 3.00
50-($3.99) Barracuda returns; Chaykin-a 4.00
61-65-Gregg Hurwitz-s/Dave Johnson-c/Laurence Campbell-a 3.00
66-73-($3.99) 66-70-Six Hours to Kill; Swierczynski-s. 71-73-Parlov-a 4.00
74,75-($4.99) 74-Parlov-a. 75-Short stories; art by Lashley, Coker, Parlov & others 5.00
Annual (11/07, $3.99) Mike Benson-s/Laurence Campbell-a 4.00
...: Bloody Valentine (4/06, $3.99) Palmiotti & Gray-s/Gulacy & Palmiotti-a; Gulacy-c 4.00
...: Force of Nature (4/08, $3.99) Swierczynski-s/Lacombe-a/Deodato-c 4.00
...: MAX MGC #1 (5/10, $1.00) reprints #1 with "Marvel's Greatest Comics" cover logo 1.00
...: MAX: Naked Kill (8/09, $3.99) Campbell-a/Bradstreet-c 4.00
...: MAX Special: Little Black Book (8/08, $3.99) Gischler-s/Palo-a/Johnson-c 4.00
...: MAX X-Mas Special (2/09, $3.99) Aaron-s/Boschi-a/Bachalo-c 4.00
...: Red X-Mas (2/05, $3.99) Palmiotti & Gray-s/Texeira & Palmiotti-a; Texeira-c 4.00
...: Silent Night (2/06, $3.99) Diggle-s/Hotz-a/Deodato-c 4.00
...: The Cell (7/05, $4.99) Ennis-s/LaRosa-a/Bradstreet-c 5.00
...: The Tyger (2/06, $4.99) Ennis-s/Severin-a/Bradstreet-c: Castle's childhood 5.00
...: Very Special Holidays TPB ('06, $12.99) r/Red X-Mas, Bloody Valentine and Silent Night 13.00
...: X-Mas Special (1/07, $3.99) Stuart Moore-s/CP Smith-a 4.00
... MAX: From First to Last HC (2006, $19.99) r/The Tyger, The Cell and The End 1-shots 20.00
... MAX Vol. 1 (2005, $29.99) oversized r/#1-12; gallery of Fernandez art from #7 shown from layout to colored pages 30.00
... MAX Vol. 2 (2006, $29.99) oversized r/#13-24; gallery of Fernandez pencil art 30.00
... MAX Vol. 3 (2007, $29.99) oversized r/#25-36; gallery of Fernandez & Parlov art 30.00
... MAX Vol. 4 (2008, $29.99) oversized r/#37-49; gallery of Fernandez & Medina art 30.00
Vol. 1: In the Beginning TPB (2004, $14.99) r/#1-6 15.00
Vol. 2: Kitchen Irish TPB (2004, $14.99) r/#7-12 15.00
Vol. 3: Mother Russia TPB (2005, $14.99) r/#13-18 15.00
Vol. 4: Up is Down and Black is White TPB (2005, $14.99) r/#19-24 15.00
Vol. 5: The Slavers TPB (2006, $15.99) r/#25-30; Fernandez pencil pages 16.00
Vol. 6: Barracuda TPB (2006, $15.99) r/#31-36; Parlov sketch page 16.00
Vol. 7: Man of Stone TPB (2007, $15.99) r/#37-42 16.00
Vol. 8: Widowmaker TPB (2007, $17.99) r/#43-49 18.00
Vol. 9: Long Cold Dark TPB (2008, $15.99) r/#50-54 16.00

PUNISHER (Frank Castle in the Marvel Universe after Secret Invasion)
(Title changes to Franken-Castle for #17-21)
Marvel Comics: Mar, 2009 - No. 21, Nov, 2010 ($3.99/$2.99)

1-($3.99) Dark Reign; Sentry app.; Remender-s/Opena-a; character history; 2 covers 4.00
2-5,710($2.99) 2-7-The Hood app. 4-Microchip returns. 5-Daredevil #183 cover swipe 3.00
6-($3.99) Huat-a/McKone-c; profile pages of resurrected villains 4.00
11-Follows Dark Reign: The List - Punisher; Franken-Castle begins; Tony Moore-a 4.00
12-16-Franken-Castle continues; Legion of Monsters app. 14-Brereton & Moore-a 3.00
Franken-Castle 17-20: 19, 20-Wolverine & Daken app. 3.00
Franken-Castle 21-($3.99) Brereton-a/c; Legion of Monsters app.; Frank gets body back 4.00
Annual 1 (11/09, $3.99) Pearson-a/c; Spider-Man app. 4.00
...: Franken-Castle - The Birth of the Monster 1 (7/10, $4.99) r/#11 & Dark Reign: The List 5.00

PUNISHER AND WOLVERINE: DAMAGING EVIDENCE (See Wolverine and...)

PUNISHER ARMORY, THE
Marvel Comics: 7/90 ($1.50); No. 2, 6/91; No. 3, 4/92 - 10/94($1.75/$2.00)

1-10: 1-r/weapons pgs. from War Journal. 1,2-Jim Lee-c. 3-10- All new material. 3-Jusko painted-c 3.00

PUNISHER: IN THE BLOOD (Marvel Universe Frank Castle)
Marvel Comics: Jan, 2011 - No. 5, May, 2011 ($3.99, limited series)

1-5-Remender-s/Boschi-a; Jigsaw & Microchip app. 4.00

PUNISHER KILLS THE MARVEL UNIVERSE
Marvel Comics: Nov, 1995 ($5.95, one-shot)

1-Garth Ennis script/Doug Braithwaite-a 7.00
1-2nd printing (3/00) Steve Dillon-c 6.00
1-3rd printing (2008, $4.99) original 1995 cover 5.00

PUNISHER MAGAZINE, THE
Marvel Comics: Oct, 1989 - No. 16, Nov, 1990 ($2.25, B&W, Magazine, 52 pgs.)

1-16: 1-r/Punisher #1('86). 2,3-r/Punisher 2-5. 4-16: 4-7-r/Punisher V2#1-8. 4-Chiodo-c. 8-r/Punisher #10 & Daredevil #257; Portacio & Lee-r. 14-r/Punisher War Journal #1,2 w/new Lee-c. 16-r/Punisher W. J. #3,8 3.00

NOTE: ***Chiodo*** *painted c-4, 7, 16.* ***Jusko*** *painted c-6, 8.* ***Jim Lee*** *r-8, 14-16; c-14.* ***Portacio/Williams*** *r-7-12.*

PUNISHERMAX
Marvel Comics (MAX): Jan, 2010 - Present ($3.99)

1-12-Aaron-s/Dillon-a/Johnson-c. 1-5-Rise of the Kingpin. 6-11-Bullseye 4.00
...: Butterfly (5/10, $4.99) Valerie D'Orazio-s/Laurence Campbell-a/c 5.00
...: Get Castle (3/10, $4.99) Rob Williams-s/Laurence Campbell-a/Bradstreet-c 5.00
...: Happy Ending (10/10, $3.99) Milligan-s/Ryp-a/c 4.00
...: Hot Rods of Death (11/10, $4.99) Huston-s/Martinbrough-a/Bradstreet-c 5.00
...: Tiny Ugly World (12/10, $4.99) Lapham-s/Talajic-a/Bradstreet-c 5.00

PUNISHER NOIR

Punisher: The End #1 © MAR

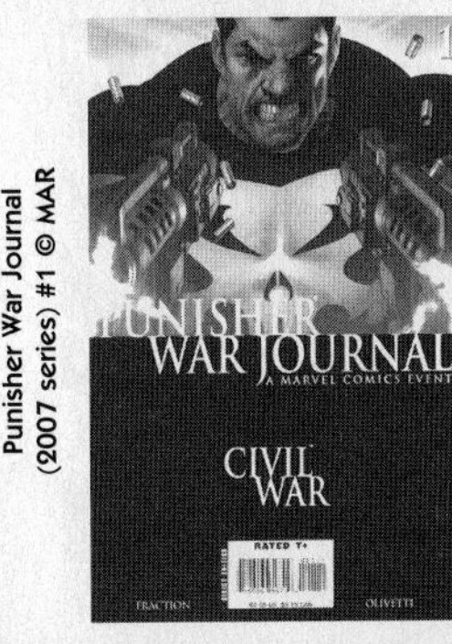
Punisher War Journal (2007 series) #1 © MAR

Purgatori #3 © Chaos!

	GD	VG	FN	VF	VF/NM	NM-
	2.0	4.0	6.0	8.0	9.0	9.2

Marvel Comics: Oct, 2009 - No. 4, Jan, 2010 ($3.99, limited series)

1-4-Pulp-style set in 1935; Tieri-s/Azaceta-a 4.00

PUNISHER: OFFICIAL MOVIE ADAPTATION
Marvel Comics: May, 2004 - No. 3, May, 2004 ($2.99, limited series)

1-3-Photo-c of Thomas Jane; Milligan-s/Olliffe-a 3.00

PUNISHER: ORIGIN OF MICRO CHIP, THE
Marvel Comics: July, 1993 - No. 2, Aug, 1993 ($1.75, limited series)

1,2 3.00

PUNISHER: P.O.V.
Marvel Comics: 1991 - No. 4, 1991 ($4.95, painted, limited series, 52 pgs.)

1-4: Starlin scripts & Wrightson painted-c/a in all. 2-Nick Fury app. 5.00

PUNISHER PRESENTS: BARRACUDA MAX
Marvel Comics (MAX): Apr, 2007 - No. 5, Aug, 2007 ($3.99, limited series)

1-5-Ennis-s/Parlov-a/c 4.00
SC (2007, $17.99) r/series; sketch pages 18.00

PUNISHER: THE END
Marvel Comics: June, 2004 ($4.50, one-shot)

1-Ennis-s/Corben-a/c 4.50

PUNISHER: THE GHOSTS OF INNOCENTS
Marvel Comics: Jan, 1993 - No. 2, Jan, 1993 ($5.95, 52 pgs.)

1,2-Starlin scripts 6.00

PUNISHER: THE MOVIE
Marvel Comics: 2004 ($12.99,TPB)

nn-Reprints Amazing Spider-Man #129; Official Movie Adaptation and Punisher V3 #1 13.00

PUNISHER 2099 (See Punisher War Journal #50)
Marvel Comics: Feb, 1993 - No. 34, Nov, 1995 ($1.25/$1.50/$1.95)

1-24,26-34: 1-Foil stamped-c. 1-Second printing. 13-Spider-Man 2099 x-over; Ron Lim-c(p). 16-bound-in card sheet 3.00
25 ($2.95, 52 pgs.)-Deluxe edition; embossed foil-cover 4.00
25 ($2.25, 52 pgs.) 4.00
(Marvel Knights) #1 (11/04, $2.99) Kirkman-s/Mhan-a/Pat Lee-c 3.00

PUNISHER VS. BULLSEYE
Marvel Comics: Jan, 2006 - No. 5, May, 2006 ($2.99, limited series)

1-5-Daniel Way-s/Steve Dillon-a 3.00
TPB (2006, $13.99) r/#1-5; cover sketch pages 14.00

PUNISHER VS. DAREDEVIL
Marvel Comics: Jun, 2000 ($3.50, one-shot)

1-Reprints Daredevil #183,#184 & #257 3.50

PUNISHER WAR JOURNAL, THE
Marvel Comics: Nov, 1988 - No. 80, July, 1995 ($1.50/$1.75/$1.95)

1-Origin The Punisher; Matt Murdock cameo; Jim Lee inks begin 5.00
2-7: 2,3-Daredevil x-over; Jim Lee-c(i). 4-Jim Lee c/a begins. 6-Two part Wolverine story begins. 7-Wolverine-c, story ends 4.00
8-49,51-60,62,63,65: 13-16,20-22: No Jim Lee-a. 13-Lee-c only. 13-15-Heath-i. 14,15-Spider-Man x-over. 19-Last Jim Lee-c/a.29,30-Ghost Rider app. 31-Andy & Joe Kubert art. 36-Photo-c. 47,48-Nomad/Daredevil-c/stories; see Nomad. 57,58-Daredevil & Ghost Rider-c/stories. 62,63-Suicide Run Pt. 4 & 7 3.00
50,61,64($2.95, 52 pgs.): 50-Preview of Punisher 2099 (1st app.); embossed-c. 61-Embossed foil cover; Suicide Run Pt. 1. 64-Die-cut-c; Suicide Run Pt. 10 4.00
64-($2.25, 52 pgs.)-Regular cover edition 4.00
66-74,76-80: 66-Bound-in card sheet 3.00
75 ($2.50, 52 pgs.) 4.00
NOTE: ***Golden*** *c-25-30, 40, 61, 62.* ***Jusko*** *painted c-31, 32.* ***Jim Lee*** *a-1i-3i, 4p-13p, 17p-19p; c-2i, 3i, 4p-15p, 17p, 18p, 19p. Painted c-40.*

PUNISHER WAR JOURNAL (Frank Castle back in the regular Marvel Universe)
Marvel Comics: Jan, 2007 - No. 26, Feb, 2009 ($2.99)

1-Civil War tie-in; Spider-Man app; Fraction-s/Olivetti-a 5.00
1-B&W edition (11/06) 5.00
2-5: 2,3-Civil War tie-in. 4-Deodato-a 4.00
6-11,13-24,26: 6-10-Punisher dons Captain America-*esque* outfit. 7-Two covers. 11-Winter Soldier app. 16-23-Chaykin-a. 18-23-Jigsaw app. 24-Secret Invasion 3.00
12,25-($3.99) 12-World War Hulk x-over; Fraction-s/Olivetti-a. 25-Secret Invasion 4.00
... Annual 1 (1/09, $3.99) Spurrier-s/Dell'edera-a 4.00
... Vol. 1: Civil War HC (2007, $19.99) r/#1-4 and #1 B&W edition; Olivetti sketch pages 20.00
... Vol. 1: Civil War SC (2007, $14.99) r/#1-4 and #1 B&W edition; Olivetti sketch pages 15.00
... Vol. 2: Goin' Out West HC (2007, $24.99) r/#5-11; Olivetti sketch page 25.00

	GD	VG	FN	VF	VF/NM	NM-
	2.0	4.0	6.0	8.0	9.0	9.2

... Vol. 2: Goin' Out West SC (2008, $17.99) r/#5-11; Olivetti sketch page 18.00
... Vol. 3: Hunter Hunted HC (2008, $19.99) r/#12-17 20.00

PUNISHER: WAR ZONE, THE
Marvel Comics: Mar, 1992 - No. 41, July, 1995 ($1.75/$1.95)

1-($2.25, 40 pgs.)-Die cut-c; Romita, Jr.-c/a begins 4.00
2-22,24,26,27-41: 8-Last Romita, Jr.-c/a. 19-Wolverine app. 24-Suicide Run Pt. 5. 27-Bound-in card sheet. 31-36-Joe Kubert-a 3.00
23-($2.95, 52 pgs.)-Embossed foil-c; Suicide Run part 2; Buscema-a(part) 4.00
25-($2.25, 52 pgs.)-Suicide Run part 8; painted-c 4.00
Annual 1,2 ('93, 94, $2.95, 68 pgs.)-1-Bagged w/card; John Buscema-a 4.00
...: River Of Blood TPB (2006, $15.99) r/#31-36; Joe Kubert-a 16.00
NOTE: ***Golden*** *c-23.* ***Romita, Jr.*** *c/a-1-8.*

PUNISHER: WAR ZONE
Marvel Comics: Feb, 2009 - No. 6, Mar, 2009 ($3.99, weekly limited series)

1-6-Ennis-s/Dillon-a/c; return of Ma Gnucci 4.00
1-Variant cover by John Romita, Jr. 6.00

PUNISHER: YEAR ONE
Marvel Comics: Dec, 1994 - No. 4, Apr, 1995 ($2.50, limited series)

1-4 3.00

PUNX
Acclaim (Valiant): Nov, 1995 - No. 3, Jan, 1996 ($2.50, unfinished lim. series)

1-3: Giffen story & art in all. 2-Satirizes Scott McCloud's Understanding Comics 3.00
(Manga) Special 1 (3/96, $2.50)-Giffen scripts 3.00

PUPPET COMICS
George W. Dougherty Co.: Spring, 1946 - No. 2, Summer, 1946

	GD	VG	FN	VF	VF/NM	NM-
1-Funny animal in both	15	30	45	83	124	165
2	11	22	33	62	86	110

PUPPETOONS (See George Pal's...)

PUREHEART (See Archie as...)

PURGATORI
Chaos! Comics: Prelude #-1, 5/96 ($1.50, 16 pgs.); 1996 - No. 3 Dec, 1996 ($3.50/$2.95, limited series)

Prelude #-1-Pulido story; Balent-c/a; contains sketches & interviews 3.00
0-(2/01, $2.99) Prelude to "Love Bites"; Rio-c/a 3.00
1/2 (12/00, $2.95) Al Rio-c/a 3.00
1-($3.50)-Wraparound cover; red foil embossed-c; Jim Balent-a 5.00
1-($19.95)-Premium Edition (1000 print run) 20.00
2-($3.00)-Wraparound-c 3.00
2-Variant-c 5.00
...: Heartbreaker 1 (3/02, $2.99) Jolley-s 3.00
...: Love Bites 1 (3/01, $2.99) Turnbull-a/Kaminski-s 3.00
...: Mischief Night 1 (11/01, $2.99) 3.00
...: Re-Imagined 1 (7/02, $2.99) Jolley-s/Neves-a 3.00
...The Dracula Gambit-($2.95) 3.00
...The Dracula Gambit Sketchbook-($2.95) 3.00
...The Vampire's Myth 1-($19.95) Premium Ed. (10,000) 20.00
...Vs. Chastity (7/00, $2.95) Two versions (Alpha and Omega) with different endings; Rio-a 3.00
...Vs. Lady Death (1/01, $2.95) Kaminski-s 3.00
...Vs. Vampirella (4/00, $2.95) Zanier-a; Chastity app. 3.00

PURGATORI
Chaos! Comics: Oct, 1998 - No. 7, Apr, 1999 ($2.95)

1-7-Quinn-s/Rio-c/a. 2-Lady Death-c 3.00

PURGATORI: DARKEST HOUR
Chaos! Comics: Sept, 2001 - No. 2, Oct, 2001 ($2.99, limited series)

1,2 3.00

PURGATORI: EMPIRE
Chaos! Comics: May, 2000 - No. 3, July, 2000 ($2.95, limited series)

1-3-Cleavenger-c 3.00

PURGATORI: GODDESS RISING
Chaos! Comics: July, 1999 - No. 4, Oct, 1999 ($2.95, limited series)

1-4-Deodato-c/a 3.00

PURGATORI: GOD HUNTER
Chaos! Comics: Apr, 2002 - No. 2, May, 2002 ($2.99, limited series)

1,2-Molenaar-a/Jolley-s 3.00

PURGATORI: GOD KILLER
Chaos! Comics: Jun, 2002 - No. 2, July, 2002 ($2.99, limited series)

Purple Claw #1 © Minoan

PvP #30 © Scott Kurtz

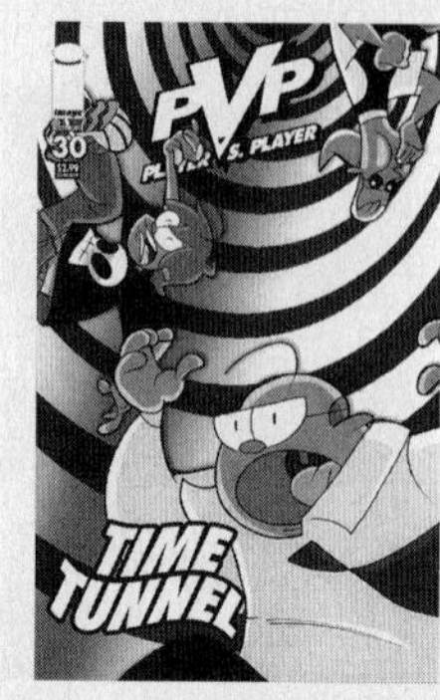

Queen and Country #14 © Greg Rucka

	GD 2.0	VG 4.0	FN 6.0	VF 8.0	VF/NM 9.0	NM- 9.2

1,2-Molenaar-a/Jolley-s 3.00

PURGATORI: THE HUNTED
Chaos! Comics: Jun, 2001 - No. 2, Aug, 2001 ($2.99, limited series)

1,2 3.00

PURPLE CLAW, THE (Also see Tales of Horror)
Minoan Publishing Co./Toby Press: Jan, 1953 - No. 3, May, 1953

	GD	VG	FN	VF	VF/NM	NM-
1-Origin; horror/weird stories in all	32	64	96	192	314	435
2,3: 1-3 r-in Tales of Horror #9-11	24	48	72	140	230	320
I.W. Reprint #8-Reprints #1	3	6	9	16	23	30

PUSH (Based on the 2009 movie)
DC Comics (WildStorm): Early Jan, 2009 - No. 6, Apr, 2009 ($3.50, limited series)

1-6-Movie prequel; Bruno Redondo-a. 1-Jock-c 3.50
TPB (2009, $19.99) r/#1-6 20.00

PUSSYCAT (Magazine)
Marvel Comics Group: Oct, 1968 (B&W reprints from Men's magazines)

	GD	VG	FN	VF	VF/NM	NM-
1-(Scarce)-Ward, Everett, Wood-a; Everett-c	17	34	51	122	249	375

PUZZLE FUN COMICS (Also see Jingle Jangle)
George W. Dougherty Co.: Spring, 1946 - No. 2, Summer, 1946 (52 pgs.)

	GD	VG	FN	VF	VF/NM	NM-
1-Gustavson-a	24	48	72	142	234	325
2	15	30	45	90	140	190

NOTE: *#1 & 2('46) each contain a* ***George Carlson*** *cover plus a 6 pg. story "Alec in Fumbleland"; also many puzzles in each.*

PvP (Player vs. Player)
Image Comics: Mar, 2003 - No. 45, Mar, 2010 ($2.95/$2.99/$3.50, B&W, reads sideways)

1-34,36-Scott Kurtz-s/a in all. 1,16-Frank Cho-c. 11-Savage Dragon-c/app. 14-Invincible app. 19-Jonathan Luna-c. 25-Cho-a (2 pgs.) 3.00
35,37-45 ($3.50): 45-Brandy from Liberty Meadows app. 3.50
#0 (7/05, 50¢) Secret Origin of Skull 3.00
...: At Large TPB (7/04, $11.95) r/#1-6 12.00
... Vol. 2: Reloaded TPB (12/04, $11.95) r/#7-12 12.00
... Vol. 3: Rides Again TPB (2005, $11.99) r/#13-18 12.00
... Vol. 4: PVP Goes Bananas TPB (2007, $12.99) r/#19-24 13.00
... Vol. 5: PVP Treks On TPB (2008, $14.99) r/#25-31 15.00
...: The Dork Ages TPB (2/04, $11.95) r/#1-6 from Dork Storm Press 12.00

QUACK!
Star Reach Productions: July, 1976 - No. 6, 1977? ($1.25, B&W)

	GD	VG	FN	VF	VF/NM	NM-
1-Brunner-c/a on Duckaneer (Howard the Duck clone); Dave Stevens, Gilbert, Shaw-a	2	4	6	10	14	18
1-2nd printing (10/76)						5.00
2-6: 2-Newton the Rabbit Wonder by Aragonés/Leialoha; Gilbert, Shaw-a; Leialoha-c. 3-The Beavers by Dave Sim begin, end #5; Gilbert, Shaw-a; Sim/Leialoha-c. 6-Brunner-a (Duckeneer); Gilbert-a	2	4	6	8	10	12

QUADRANT
Quadrant Publications: 1983 - No. 8, 1986 (B&W, nudity, adults)

	GD	VG	FN	VF	VF/NM	NM-
1-Peter Hsu-c/a in all	2	4	6	10	14	18
2-8	2	3	4	6	8	10

QUANTUM & WOODY
Acclaim Comics: June, 1997 - No. 17, No. 32 (9/99), No. 18 - No. 21, Feb, 2000 ($2.50)

1-17: 1-1st app.; two covers. 6-Copycat-c. 9-Troublemakers app. 3.00
32-(9/99); 18-(10/99),19-21 3.00
The Director's Cut TPB ('97, $7.95) r/#1-4 plus extra pages 8.00

QUANTUM LEAP (TV) (See A Nightmare on Elm Street)
Innovation Publishing: Sept, 1991 - No. 12, Jun, 1993 ($2.50, painted-c)

1-12: Based on TV show; all have painted-c. 8-Has photo gallery 4.00
Special Edition 1 (10/92)-r/#1 w/8 extra pgs. of photos & articles 4.00
Time and Space Special 1 (#13) ($2.95)-Foil logo 4.00

QUANTUM TUNNELER, THE
Revolution Studio: Oct, 2001 (no cover price, one-shot)

1-Prequel to "The One" movie; Clayton Henry-a 3.00

QUASAR (See Avengers #302, Captain America #217, Incredible Hulk #234, Marvel Team-Up #113 & Marvel Two-in-One #53)
Marvel Comics: Oct, 1989 - No. 60, Jul, 1994 ($1.00/$1.25, Direct sales #17 on)

1-Origin; formerly Marvel Boy/Marvel Man 4.00
2-15,17-24,26-49,51-60: 3-Human Torch app. 6-Venom cameo (2 pgs.). 7-Cosmic Spidey. 11-Excalibur x-over. 14-McFarlane-c. 17-Flash parody (Buried Alien). 20-Fantastic Four app. 23-Ghost Rider x-over. 26-Infinity Gauntlet x-over; Thanos-c/story. 27-Infinity Gauntlet x-over. 30-Thanos cameo in flashback; last $1.00-c. 31-Begin $1.25-c; D.P. 7 guest stars. 38-40-Infinity War x-overs. 38-Battles Warlock. 39-Thanos-c & cameo. 40-Thanos app. 42-Punisher-c/story. 53-Warlock & Moondragon app. 58-w/bound-in card sheet 3.00
16,25,50: 16-($1.50, 52 pgs.). 25-($1.50, 52 pgs.)-New costume Quasar. 50-($2.95, 52 pgs.)-Holo-grafx foil-c; Silver Surfer, Man-Thing, Ren & Stimpy app. 4.00
Special #1-3 ($1.25, newsstand)-Same as #32-34 3.00

QUEEN & COUNTRY (See Whiteout)
Oni Press: Mar, 2001 - No. 32, Aug, 2007 ($2.95/$2.99, B&W)

	GD	VG	FN	VF	VF/NM	NM-
1-Rucka-s in all. Rolston-a/Sale-c	1	2	3	4	5	7

2-5: 2-4-Rolston-a/Sale-c. 5-Snyder-c/Hurtt-a 4.00
6-24,26-32: 6,7-Snyder-c/Hurtt-a. 13-15-Alexander-a. 16-20-McNeil-a. 21-24-Hawthorne-a 26-28-Norton-a 3.00
25-($5.99) Rolston-a 6.00
Free Comic Book Day giveaway (5/02) r/#1 with "Free Comic Book Day" banner on-c 3.00
Operation: Blackwall (10/03, $8.95, TPB) r/#13-15; John Rogers intro. 9.00
Operation: Broken Ground (2002, $11.95, TPB) r/#1-4; Ellis intro. 12.00
Operation: Crystal Ball (1/03, $14.95, TPB) r/#8-12; Judd Winick intro. 15.00
Operation: Dandelion HC (8/04, $25.00) r/#21-24; Jamie S. Rich intro. 25.00
Operation: Dandelion (8/04, $11.95, TPB) r/#21-24; Jamie S. Rich intro. 12.00
Operation: Morningstar (9/02, $8.95, TPB) r/#5-7; Stuart Moore intro. 9.00
Operation: Storm Front (3/04, $14.95, TPB) r/#16-20; Geoff Johns intro. 15.00

QUEEN & COUNTRY: DECLASSIFIED
Oni Press: Nov, 2002 - No. 3, Jan, 2003 ($2.95, B&W, limited series)

1-3-Rucka-s/Hurtt-a/Morse-c 3.00
TPB (7/03, $8.95) r/#1-3; intro. by Micah Wright 9.00

QUEEN & COUNTRY: DECLASSIFIED (Volume 2)
Oni Press: Jan, 2005 - No. 3, Feb, 2006 ($2.95/$2.99, B&W, limited series)

1-3-Rucka-s/Burchett-a/c 3.00
TPB (3/06, $8.95) r/#1-3 9.00

QUEEN & COUNTRY: DECLASSIFIED (Volume 3)
Oni Press: Jun, 2005 - No. 3, Aug, 2005 ($2.95, B&W, limited series)

1-3- "Sons & Daughters;" Johnston-s/Mitten-a/c 3.00
TPB (3/06, $8.95) r/#1-3 9.00

QUEEN OF THE WEST, DALE EVANS (TV)(See Dale Evans Comics, Roy Rogers & Western Roundup under Dell Giants)
Dell Publ. Co.: No. 479, 7/53 - No. 22, 1-3/59 (All photo-c; photo back c-4-8,15)

	GD	VG	FN	VF	VF/NM	NM-
Four Color 479(#1, '53)	17	34	51	118	242	365
Four Color 528(#2, '54)	10	20	30	69	122	175
3,4: 3(4-6/54)-Toth-a. 4-Toth, Manning-a	8	16	24	54	90	125
5-10-Manning-a. 5-Marsh-a	7	14	21	47	76	105
11,19,21-No Manning 21-Tufts-a	5	10	15	34	55	75
12-18,20,22-Manning-a	6	12	18	39	62	85

QUEEN SONJA (See Red Sonja)
Dynamite Entertainment: 2009 - Present ($2.99/$3.99)

1-10: 1-Rubi-a/Ortega-s; 3 covers; back-up r/Marvel Feature #1 3.00
11-15-($3.99) 4.00

QUENTIN DURWARD
Dell Publishing Co.: No. 672, Jan, 1956

	GD	VG	FN	VF	VF/NM	NM-
Four Color 672-Movie, photo-c	7	14	21	45	73	100

QUESTAR ILLUSTRATED SCIENCE FICTION CLASSICS
Golden Press: 1977 (224 pgs.) ($1.95)

	GD	VG	FN	VF	VF/NM	NM-
11197-Stories by Asimov, Sturgeon, Silverberg & Niven; Starstream-r	3	6	9	20	30	40

QUEST FOR CAMELOT
DC Comics: July, 1998 ($4.95)

1-Movie adaption 5.00

QUEST FOR DREAMS LOST (Also see Word Warriors)
Literacy Volunteers of Chicago: July 4, 1987 ($2.00, B&W, 52 pgs.)(Proceeds donated to help fight illiteracy)

1-Teenage Mutant Ninja Turtles by Eastman/Laird, Trollords, Silent Invasion, The Realm, Wordsmith, Reacto Man, Eb'nn, Aniverse 4.00

QUESTION, THE (See Americomics, Blue Beetle (1967), Charlton Bullseye & Mysterious Suspense)

QUESTION, THE (Also see Showcase '95 #3)
DC Comics: Feb, 1987 - No. 36, Mar, 1990; No. 37, Mar, 2010 ($1.50)

1-36: Denny O'Neil scripts in all 3.00
37-(3/10, $2.99) Blackest Night one-shot; Victor Sage rises; Shiva app.; Cowan-a 3.00
Annual 1 (1988, $2.50) 4.00
Annual 2 (1989, $3.50) 4.00

Quick-Trigger Western #13 © MAR

Racket Squad in Action #15 © CC

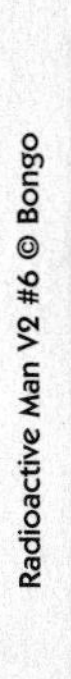

Radioactive Man V2 #6 © Bongo

	GD 2.0	VG 4.0	FN 6.0	VF 8.0	VF/NM 9.0	NM- 9.2
...: Epitaph For a Hero TPB (2008, $19.99) r/#13-18						20.00
...: Peacemaker TPB (2010, $19.99) r/#31-36						20.00
...: Pipeline TPB (2011, $14.99) r/stories from Detective Comics #854-865; sketch-a						15.00
...: Poisoned Ground TPB (2008, $19.99) r/#7-12						20.00
...: Riddles TPB (2009, $19.99) r/#25-30						20.00
...: Welcome to Oz TPB (2009, $19.99) r/#19-24						20.00
...: Zen and Violence TPB (2007, $19.99) r/#1-6						20.00

QUESTION, THE (Also see Crime Bible and 52)
DC Comics: Jan, 2005 - No. 6, Jun, 2005 ($2.95, limited series)

1-6-Rick Veitch-s/Tommy Lee Edwards-a. 4,6-Superman app. 3.00

QUESTION QUARTERLY, THE
DC Comics: Summer, 1990 - No. 5, Spring, 1992 ($2.50, 52pgs.)

1-5 4.00

NOTE: ***Cowan*** *a-1, 2, 4, 5; c-1-3, 5.* ***Mignola*** *a-5i.* ***Quesada*** *a-3-5.*

QUESTION RETURNS, THE
DC Comics: Feb, 1997 ($3.50, one-shot)

1-Brereton-c 4.00

QUESTPROBE
Marvel Comics: 8/84; No. 2, 1/85; No. 3, 11/85 (lim. series)

1-3: 1-The Hulk app. by Romita. 2-Spider-Man; Mooney-a(i). 3-Human Torch & Thing 3.00

QUICK DRAW McGRAW (TV) (Hanna-Barbera)(See Whitman Comic Books)
Dell Publishing Co./Gold Key No. 12 on: No. 1040, 12-2/59-60 - No. 11, 7-9/62; No. 12, 11/62; No. 13, 2/63; No. 14, 4/63; No. 15, 6/69 (1st show aired 9/29/59)

	GD 2.0	VG 4.0	FN 6.0	VF 8.0	VF/NM 9.0	NM- 9.2
Four Color 1040(#1) 1st app. Quick Draw & Baba Looey, Augie Doggie & Doggie Daddy and Snooper & Blabber	12	24	36	87	164	240
2(4-6/60)-4,6: 2-Augie Doggie & Snooper & Blabber stories (8 pgs. each); pre-dates both of their #1 issues. 4-Augie Doggie & Snooper & Blabber stories.	6	12	18	41	66	90
5-1st Snagglepuss app.; last 10¢ issue	7	14	21	45	73	100
7-11	5	10	15	32	51	70
12,13-Title change to ...Fun-Type Roundup (84pgs.)	7	14	21	45	73	100
14,15: 15-Reprints	4	8	12	28	44	60

QUICK DRAW McGRAW (TV)(See Spotlight #2)
Charlton Comics: Nov, 1970 - No. 8, Jan, 1972 (Hanna-Barbera)

	GD 2.0	VG 4.0	FN 6.0	VF 8.0	VF/NM 9.0	NM- 9.2
1	5	10	15	32	51	70
2-8	3	6	9	19	29	38

QUICKSILVER (See Avengers)
Marvel Comics: Nov, 1997 - No. 13, Nov, 1998 ($2.99/$1.99)

1-($2.99)-Peyer-s/Casey Jones-a; wraparound-c 4.00
2-11: 2-Two covers-variant by Golden. 4-6-Inhumans app. 3.00
12-($2.99) Siege of Wundagore pt. 4 4.00
13-Magneto-c/app.; last issue 3.00

QUICK-TRIGGER WESTERN (...Action #12; Cowboy Action #5-11)
Atlas Comics (ACI #12/WPI #13-19): No. 12, May, 1956 - No. 19, Sept, 1957

	GD 2.0	VG 4.0	FN 6.0	VF 8.0	VF/NM 9.0	NM- 9.2
12-Baker-a	15	30	45	90	140	190
13-Williamson-a, 5 pgs.	15	30	45	84	127	170
14-Everett, Crandall, Torres-a; Heath-c	14	28	42	81	118	155
15,16: 15-Torres, Crandall-a. 16-Orlando, Kirby-a	12	24	36	69	97	125
17,18: 18-Baker-a	12	24	36	67	94	120
19	10	20	30	54	72	90

NOTE: ***Ayers*** *a-17.* ***Colan*** *a-16.* ***Maneely*** *a-15, 17; c-15, 18.* ***Morrow*** *a-18.* ***Powell*** *a-14.* ***Severin*** *a-19; c-12, 13, 16, 17, 19.* ***Shores*** *a-16.* ***Tuska*** *a-17.*

QUINCY (See Comics Reading Libraries in the Promotional Comics section)

QUITTER, THE
DC Comics (Vertigo): 2005 ($19.99, B&W graphic novel)

HC ($19.99) Autobiography of Harvey Pekar; Pekar-s/Daen Haspiel-a 20.00
SC (2006, $12.99) 13.00

RACCOON KIDS, THE (Formerly Movietown Animal Antics)
National Periodical Publications (Arleigh No. 63,64): No. 52, Sept-Oct, 1954 - No. 62, Oct-Nov, 1956; No. 63, Sept, 1957; No. 64, Nov, 1957

	GD 2.0	VG 4.0	FN 6.0	VF 8.0	VF/NM 9.0	NM- 9.2
52-Doodles Duck by Mayer	15	30	45	83	124	165
53-64: 53-62-Doodles Duck by Mayer	11	22	33	62	86	110

NOTE: ***Otto Feuer****-a most issues.* ***Rube Grossman****-a most issues.*

RACE FOR THE MOON
Harvey Publications: Mar, 1958 - No. 3, Nov, 1958

	GD 2.0	VG 4.0	FN 6.0	VF 8.0	VF/NM 9.0	NM- 9.2
1-Powell-a(5); 1/2-pg. S&K-a; cover redrawn from Galaxy Science Fiction pulp (5/53)	18	36	54	103	162	220
2-Kirby/Williamson-c(r)/a(3); Kirby-p 7 more stys	26	52	78	154	252	350
3-Kirby/Williamson-c/a(4); Kirby-p 6 more stys	28	56	84	165	270	375

RACER-X
Now Comics: 8/88 - No. 11, 8/89; V2#1, 9/89 - V2#10, 1990 ($1.75)

0-Deluxe ($3.50) 4.00
1 (9/88) - 11, V2#1-10 3.00

RACER X (See Speed Racer)
DC Comics (WildStorm): Oct, 2000 - No. 3, Dec, 2000 ($2.95, limited series)

1-3: 1-Tommy Yune-s/Jo Chen-a; 2 covers by Yune. 2,3-Kabala app. 3.50

RACING PETTYS
STP Corp.: 1980 ($2.50, 68 pgs., 10 1/8" x 13 1/4")

1-Bob Kane-a. Kane bio on inside back-c. 10.00

RACK & PAIN
Dark Horse Comics: Mar, 1994 - No. 4, June, 1994 ($2.50, limited series)

1-4: Brian Pulido scripts in all. 1-Greg Capullo-c 3.00

RACK & PAIN: KILLERS
Chaos! Comics: Sept, 1996 - No. 4, Jan, 1997 ($2.95, limited series)

1-4: Reprints Dark Horse series; Jae Lee-c 3.00

RACKET SQUAD IN ACTION
Capitol Stories/Charlton Comics: May-June, 1952 - No. 29, Mar, 1958

	GD 2.0	VG 4.0	FN 6.0	VF 8.0	VF/NM 9.0	NM- 9.2
1	29	58	87	170	278	385
2-4,6: 3,4,6-Dr. Neff, Ghost Breaker app.	15	30	45	86	133	180
5-Dr. Neff, Ghost Breaker app; headlights-c	21	42	63	126	206	285
7-10: 10-Explosion-c	14	28	42	81	118	155
11-Ditko-c/a	31	62	93	182	296	410
12-Ditko explosion-c (classic); Shuster-a(2)	52	104	156	328	557	785
13-Shuster-c(p)/a.	13	26	39	72	101	130
14-Marijuana story "Shakedown"; Giordano-c	15	30	45	88	137	185
15-28: 15,20,22,23-Giordano-c	11	22	33	62	86	110
29-(15¢, 68 pgs.)	14	28	42	80	115	150

RADIANT LOVE (Formerly Daring Love #1)
Gilmor Magazines: No. 2, Dec, 1953 - No. 6, Aug, 1954

	GD 2.0	VG 4.0	FN 6.0	VF 8.0	VF/NM 9.0	NM- 9.2
2	14	28	42	76	108	140
3-6	9	18	27	52	69	85

RADICAL DREAMER
Blackball Comics: No. 0, May, 1994 - No. 4, Nov, 1994 ($1.99, bi-monthly) (1st poster format comic)

0-4: 0-2-($1.99, poster format): 0-1st app. Max Wrighter. 3,4-($2.50-c) 3.00

RADICAL DREAMER
Mark's Giant Economy Size Comics: V2#1, June, 1995 - V2#6, Feb, 1996 ($2.95, B&W, limited series)

V2#1-6 3.00
Prime (5/96, $2.95) 3.00
Dreams Cannot Die!-(1996, $20.00, softcover)-Collects V1#0-4 & V2#1-6; intro by Kurt Busiek; afterward by Mark Waid 20.00
Dreams Cannot Die!-(1996, $60.00, hardcover)-Signed & limited edition; collects V1#0-4 & V2#1-6; intro by Kurt Busiek; afterward by Mark Waid 60.00

RADIOACTIVE MAN (Simpsons TV show)
Bongo Comics: 1993 - No. 6, 1994 ($1.95/$2.25, limited series)

1-($2.95)-Glow-in-the-dark-c; bound-in jumbo poster; origin Radioactive Man; (cover dated Nov. 1952) 5.00
2-6: 2-Says #88 on-c & inside & dated May 1962; cover parody of Atlas Kirby monster-c; Superior Squad app.; origin Fallout Boy. 3-($1.95)-Cover "dated" Aug 1972 #216. 4-($2.25)-Cover "dated" Oct 1980 #412; w/trading card. 5-Cover "dated" Jan 1986 #679; w/trading card. 6-(Jan 1995 #1000) 4.00
Colossal #1-($4.95) 7.00
#4 (2001, $2.50) Faux 1953 issue; Murphy Anderson-i (6 pgs.) 3.00
#100 (2000, $2.50) Comic Book Guy-c/app.; faux 1963 issue inside 3.00
#136 (2001, $2.50) Dan DeCarlo-c/a 3.00
#222 (2001, $2.50) Batton Lash-s; Radioactive Man in 1972-style 3.00
#575 (2002, $2.50) Chaykin-c; Radioactive Man in 1984-style 3.00
1963-106 (2002, $2.50) Radioactive Man in 1960s Gold Key-style; Groening-c 3.00
#7 Bongo Super Heroes Starring... (2003, $2.50) Marvel Silver Age-style Superior Squad 3.00
#8 Official Movie Adaptation (2004, $2.99) starring Rainier Wolfcastle and Milhouse 3.00
#9 (#197 on-c) (2004, $2.50) Kirby-esque New Gods spoof; Golden Age Radio Man app. 3.00

RADIO FUNNIES
DC Comics: Mar. 1939; undated variant

Ragman: Suit of Souls #1 © DC

Raise the Dead 2 #1 © Classic Monsters

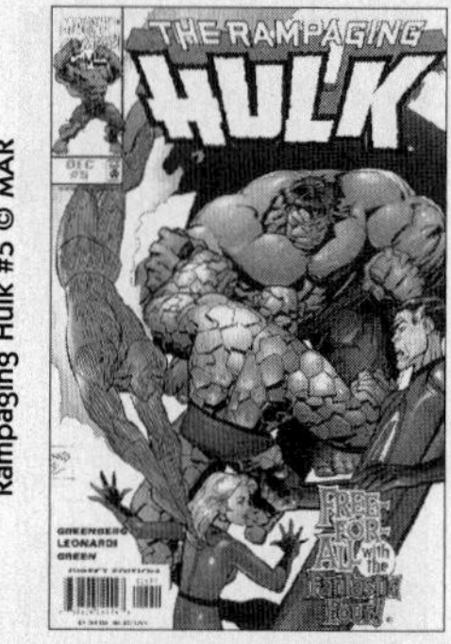

Rampaging Hulk #5 © MAR

	GD 2.0	VG 4.0	FN 6.0	VF 8.0	VF/NM 9.0	NM- 9.2

nn-(3/39) Ashcan comic, not distributed to newsstands, only for in-house use. Cover art is Adventure Comics #39 with interior being Detective Comics #19 (no known sales)
nn - Ashcan comic. No date. Cover art is Detective #26 with interior from Detective #17; one copy, graded at GD/VG, sold at auction for $4481.25 in Nov, 2009. Another copy graded at GD/VG sold at auction for $3346 in Feb, 2010.

RAGAMUFFINS
Eclipse Comics: Jan, 1985 ($1.75, one shot)

1-Eclipse Magazine-r, w/color; Colan-a 3.00

RAGGEDY ANN AND ANDY (See Dell Giants, March of Comics #23 & New Funnies)
Dell Publishing Co.: No. 5, 1942 - No. 533, 2/54; 10-12/64 - No. 4, 3/66

	GD	VG	FN	VF	VF/NM	NM-
Four Color 5(1942)	44	88	132	352	714	1075
Four Color 23(1943)	33	66	99	254	502	750
Four Color 45(1943)	27	54	81	197	399	600
Four Color 72(1945)	22	44	66	162	324	485
1(6/46)-Billy & Bonnie Bee by Frank Thomas	31	62	93	239	470	700
2,3: 3-Egbert Elephant by Dan Noonan begins	16	32	48	111	226	340
4-Kelly-a, 16 pgs.	16	32	48	117	239	360
5,6,8-10	13	26	39	92	179	265
7-Little Black Sambo, Black Mumbo & Black Jumbo only app; Christmas-c	15	30	45	104	212	320
11-20	11	22	33	75	138	200
21-Alice In Wonderland cover/story	13	26	39	92	179	265
22-27,29-39(8/49), Four Color 262 (1/50): 34-"...In Candyland"	10	20	30	67	116	165
28-Kelly-c	10	20	30	69	122	175
Four Color 306,354,380,452,533	7	14	21	50	83	115
1(10-12/64-Dell)	4	8	12	24	37	50
2,3(10-12/65), 4(3/66)	3	6	9	16	23	30

NOTE: ***Kelly** art ("Animal Mother Goose")-#1-34, 36, 37; c-28. Peterkin Pottle by **John Stanley** in 32-38.*

RAGGEDY ANN AND ANDY
Gold Key: Dec, 1971 - No. 6, Sept, 1973

	GD	VG	FN	VF	VF/NM	NM-
1	3	6	9	19	29	38
2-6	3	6	9	15	21	26

RAGGEDY ANN & THE CAMEL WITH THE WRINKLED KNEES (See Dell Jr. Treasury #8)

RAGMAN (See Batman Family #20, The Brave & The Bold #196 & Cancelled Comic Cavalcade)
National Per. Publ./DC Comics No. 5: Aug-Sept, 1976 - No. 5, Jun-Jul, 1977

	GD	VG	FN	VF	VF/NM	NM-
1-Origin & 1st app.	2	4	6	11	16	20
2-5: 2-Origin ends; Kubert-c. 4-Drug use story	2	4	6	8	10	12

NOTE: ***Kubert** a-4, 5; c-1-5. **Redondo** studios a-1-4.*

RAGMAN (2nd Series)
DC Comics: Oct, 1991 - No. 8, May, 1992 ($1.50, limited series)

1-8: 1-Giffen plots/breakdowns. 3-Origin. 8-Batman-c/story 3.00

RAGMAN: CRY OF THE DEAD
DC Comics: Aug, 1993 - No. 6, Jan, 1994 ($1.75, limited series)

1-6: Joe Kubert-c 3.00

RAGMAN: SUIT OF SOULS
DC Comics: Dec, 2010 ($3.99, one-shot)

1-Gage-s/Segovia-a/Saiz-c; origin retold 4.00

RAGS RABBIT (Formerly Babe Ruth Sports #10 or Little Max #10?; also see Harvey Hits #2, Harvey Wiseguys & Tastee Freez)
Harvey Publications: No. 11, June, 1951 - No. 18, March, 1954 (Written & drawn for little folks)

	GD	VG	FN	VF	VF/NM	NM-
11-(See Nutty Comics #5 for 1st app.)	6	12	18	31	38	45
12-18	5	10	15	24	30	35

RAI (Rai and the Future Force #9-23) (See Magnus #5-8)
Valiant: Mar, 1992 - No. 0, Oct, 1992; No. 9, May, 1993 - No. 33, Jun, 1995 ($1.95/$2.25)

	GD	VG	FN	VF	VF/NM	NM-
1-Valiant's 1st original character	2	4	6	9	13	16
2-4,0: 4-Low print run. 0-(11/92)-Origin/1st app. new Rai (Rising Spirit) & 1st full app. & partial origin Bloodshot; also see Eternal Warrior #4; tells future of all characters	2	4	6	8	10	12
5-10: 6,7-Unity x-overs. 7-Death of Rai. 9-($2.50)-Gatefold-c; story cont'd from Magnus #24; Magnus, Eternal Warrior & X-O app.						5.00
11-33: 15-Manowar Armor app. 17-19-Magnus x-over. 21-1st app. The Starwatchers (cameo); trading card. 22-Death of Rai. 26-Chaos Effect Epsilon Pt. 3						3.00

NOTE: ***Layton** c-2i, 9i. **Miller** c-6. **Simonson** c-7.*

RAIDERS OF THE LOST ARK (Movie)
Marvel Comics Group: Sept, 1981 - No. 3, Nov, 1981 (Movie adaptation)

1-3: 1-r/Marvel Comics Super Special #18 3.00

	GD 2.0	VG 4.0	FN 6.0	VF 8.0	VF/NM 9.0	NM- 9.2

NOTE: ***Buscema** a(p)-1-3; c(p)-1. **Simonson** a-3i; scripts-1-3.*

RAINBOW BRITE AND THE STAR STEALER
DC Comics: 1985

	GD	VG	FN	VF	VF/NM	NM-
nn-Movie adaptation	2	4	6	8	10	12

RAISE THE DEAD
Dynamite Entertainment: 2007 - No. 4, Aug, 2007 ($3.50)

1-4-Arthur Suydam-c/Leah Moore & John Reppion-s/Petrus-a; Phillips var-c on all 3.50
... Vol. 1 HC (2007, $19.99) r/#1-4; script, interview & sketch pages; cover gallery 20.00

RAISE THE DEAD 2
Dynamite Entertainment: 2010 - No. 4, 2011 ($3.99)

1-4-Leah Moore & John Reppion-s/Vilanova-a 4.00

RALPH KINER, HOME RUN KING
Fawcett Publications: 1950 (Pittsburgh Pirates)

	GD	VG	FN	VF	VF/NM	NM-
nn-Photo-c; life story	60	120	180	381	653	925

RALPH SNART ADVENTURES
Now Comics: June, 1986 - V2#9, 1987; V3#1 - #26, Feb, 1991; V4#1, 1992 - #4, 1992

	GD	VG	FN	VF	VF/NM	NM-
1-3, V2#1-7,V3#1-23,25,26:1-($1.00, B&W)-1(B&W),V2#1(11/86), B&W), 8,9-color. V3#1(9/88)-Color begins						3.00
V3#24-($2.50)-3-D issue, V4#1-3-Direct sale versions w/cards						3.00
V4#1-3-Newsstand versions w/random cards						3.00
Book 1	1	2	3	5	6	8
3-D Special (11/92, $3.50)-Complete 12-card set w/3-D glasses						4.00

RAMAR OF THE JUNGLE (TV)
Toby Press No. 1/Charlton No. 2 on: 1954 (no month); No. 2, Sept, 1955 - No. 5, Sept, 1956

	GD	VG	FN	VF	VF/NM	NM-
1-Jon Hall photo-c; last pre-code issue	21	42	63	122	199	275
2-5: 2-Jon Hall photo-c	15	30	45	85	130	175

RAMAYAN 3392 A.D.
Virgin Comics: Sept, 2006 - No. 8, Aug, 2008 ($2.99)

1-8: 1-Alex Ross-c; re-imagining of the Indian myth of Ramayana; poster of cover inside 3.00
... Reloaded (8/07 - No. 7, 7/08, $2.99) 1-7: 1-Two covers by Kang and Oeming 3.00
... Reloaded Guidebook (4/08, $2.99) Profiles of characters and weapons 3.00

RAMM
Megaton Comics: May, 1987 - No. 2, Sept, 1987 ($1.50, B&W)

1,2-Both have 1 pg. Youngblood ad by Liefeld 3.00

RAMPAGING HULK (The Hulk #10 on; also see Marvel Treasury Edition)
Marvel Comics Group: Jan, 1977 - No. 9, June, 1978 ($1.00, B&W magazine)

	GD	VG	FN	VF	VF/NM	NM-
1-Bloodstone story w/Buscema & Nebres-a. Origin re-cap w/Simonson-a; Gargoyle, UFO story; Ken Barr-c	3	6	9	19	29	38
2-Old X-Men app; origin old w/Simonson-a & new X-Men in text w/Cockrum illos; Bloodstone story w/Brown & Nebres-a	3	6	9	16	22	28
3-9: 3-Iron Man app.; Norem-c. 4-Gallery of villains w/Giffen-a. 5,6-Hulk vs. Sub-Mariner. 7-Man-Thing story. 8-Original Avengers app. 9-Thor vs. Hulk battle; Shanna the She-Devil story w/DeZuniga-a	2	4	6	13	18	22

NOTE: ***Alcala** a-1-3i, 5i, 8i. **Buscema** a-1. **Giffen** a-4. **Nino** a-4i. **Simonson** a-1-3p. **Starlin** a-4(w/**Nino**), 7; c-4, 5, 7.*

RAMPAGING HULK
Marvel Comics: Aug, 1998 - No. 6, Jan, 1999 ($2.99/$1.99)

1-($2.99) Flashback stories of Savage Hulk; Leonardi-a 4.00
2-6-($1.99): 2-Two covers 3.00

RAMPAGING WOLVERINE
Marvel Comics: June, 2009 ($3.99, B&W, one-shot)

1-Short stories by Fialkov, Luque, Ted McKeever, Yost, Santolouco, Firth, Nelson 4.00

RANDOLPH SCOTT (Movie star)(See Crack Western #67, Prize Comics Western #76, Western Hearts #8, Western Love #1 & Western Winners #7)

RANGE BUSTERS
Fox Features Syndicate: Sept, 1950 (One shot)

	GD	VG	FN	VF	VF/NM	NM-
1 (Exist?)	19	38	57	112	179	245

RANGE BUSTERS (Formerly Cowboy Love?; Wyatt Earp, Frontier Marshall #11 on)
Charlton Comics: No. 8, May, 1955 - No. 10, Sept, 1955

	GD	VG	FN	VF	VF/NM	NM-
8	8	16	24	42	54	65
9,10	6	12	18	28	34	40

RANGELAND LOVE
Atlas Comics (CDS): Dec, 1949 - No. 2, Mar, 1950 (52 pgs.)

	GD	VG	FN	VF	VF/NM	NM-
1-Robert Taylor & Arlene Dahl photo-c	17	34	51	98	154	210
2-Photo-c	14	28	42	80	115	150

Rangers Comics #41 © FH

RASL #5 © Jeff Smith

Rawhide Kid #45 © MAR

GD VG FN VF VF/NM NM-
2.0 4.0 6.0 8.0 9.0 9.2

RANGER, THE (See Zane Grey, Four Color #255)

RANGE RIDER, THE (TV)(See Flying A's...)

RANGE ROMANCES
Comic Magazines (Quality Comics): Dec, 1949 - No. 5, Aug, 1950 (#5: 52 pg)

1-Gustavson-c/a 26 52 78 152 244 335
2-Crandall-c/a 26 52 78 152 244 335
3-Crandall, Gustavson-a; photo-c 22 44 66 127 204 280
4-Crandall-a; photo-c 19 38 57 112 176 240
5-Gustavson-a; Crandall-a(p); photo-c 19 38 57 112 176 240

RANGERS COMICS (...of Freedom #1-7)
Fiction House Magazines: 10/41 - No. 67, 10/52; No. 68, Fall, 1952; No. 69, Winter, 1952-53 (Flying stories)

1-Intro. Ranger Girl & The Rangers of Freedom; ends #7, cover app. only #5
331 662 993 2317 4059 5800
2 97 194 291 621 1061 1500
3 71 142 213 454 777 1100
4,5 64 128 192 406 696 985
6-10: 8-U.S. Rangers begin 52 104 156 328 552 775
11,12-Commando Rangers app. 48 96 144 302 514 725
13-Commando Ranger begins-not same as Commando Rangers
47 94 141 296 498 700
14-20 41 82 123 256 428 600
21-Intro/origin Firehair (begins, 2/45) 42 84 126 265 445 625
22-30: 23-Kazanda begins, ends #28. 28-Tiger Man begins (origin/1st app., 4/46), ends #46.
30-Crusoe Island begins, ends #40 32 64 96 192 314 435
31-40: 33-Hypodermic panels 28 56 84 165 270 375
41-46: 41-Last Werewolf Hunter 22 44 66 132 216 300
47-56- "Eisnerish" Dr. Drew by Grandenetti. 48-Last Glory Forbes. 53-Last 52 pg. issue.
55-Last Sky Rangers 22 44 66 128 209 290
57-60-Straight run of Dr. Drew by Grandenetti 17 34 51 98 154 210
61-69: 64-Suicide Smith begins. 63-Used in **POP**, pgs. 85, 99. 67-Space Rangers begin,
end #69 15 30 45 85 130 175

NOTE: *Bondage, discipline covers, lingerie panels are common. Crusoe Island by* ***Larsen****-#30-36. Firehair by* ***Lubbers****-#30-49. Glory Forbes by* ***Baker****-#36-45, 47; by* ***Whitman****-#34, 35. I Confess in #41-53. Jan of the Jungle in #42-58. King of the Congo in #49-53. Tiger Man by* ***Celardo****-#30-39.* ***M. Anderson*** *a-30?* ***Baker*** *a-36-38, 42, 44.* ***John Celardo*** *a-34, 36-39.* ***Lee Elias*** *a-21-28.* ***Evans*** *a-19, 38-46, 48-52.* ***Hopper*** *a-25, 26.* ***Ingels*** *a-13-16.* ***Larsen*** *a-34.* ***Bob Lubbers*** *a-30-38, 40-44; c-40-45.* ***Moreira*** *a-41-47.* ***Tuska*** *a-16, 17, 19, 22.* ***M. Whitman*** *c-61-66.* ***Zolnerwich*** *c-1-17.*

RANGO (TV)
Dell Publishing Co.: Aug, 1967

1-Photo-c of comedian Tim Conway 4 8 12 24 37 50

RANN-THANAGAR HOLY WAR (Also see Hawkman Special #1)
DC Comics: July, 2008 - No. 8, Feb, 2009 ($3.50, limited series)

1-8-Adam Strange & Hawkman app.; Starlin-s/Lim-a. 1-Two covers by Starlin & Lim 3.50
Volume One TPB (2009, $19.99) r/#1-4 & Hawkman Special #1 20.00
Volume Two TPB (2009, $19.99) r/#5-8 & Adam Strange Special #1 20.00

RANN-THANAGAR WAR (See Adam Strange 2004 mini-series)(Prelude to Infinite Crisis)
DC Comics: July, 2005 - No. 6, Dec, 2005 ($2.50, limited series)

1-6-Adam Strange, Hawkman and Green Lantern (Kyle Rayner) app.; Gibbons-s/Reis-a 3.00
...: Infinite Crisis Special (4/06, $4.99) Kyle Rayner becomes Ion again; Jade dies 5.00
TPB (2005, $12.99) r/#1-6; cover gallery; new Bolland-c 13.00

RAPHAEL (See Teenage Mutant Ninja Turtles)
Mirage Studios: 1985 ($1.50, 7-1/2x11", B&W w/2 color cover, one-shot)

1-1st Turtles one-shot spin-off; contains 1st drawing of the Turtles as a group from 1983 8.00
1-2nd printing (11/87); new-c & 8 pgs. art 4.00

RAPHAEL BAD MOON RISING (See Teenage Mutant Ninja Turtles)
Mirage Publishing: July, 2007 - No. 4, Oct, 2007 ($3.25, B&W, limited series)

1-4-Continued from Tales of the TMNT #7; Lawson-a 3.25

RAPTURE
Dark Horse Comics: May, 2009 - No. 6, Jan, 2010 ($2.99, limited series)

1-6-Taki Soma & Michael Avon Oeming-s/a/c. 1-Maleev var-c. 2-Mack var-c 3.00

RASCALS IN PARADISE
Dark Horse Comics: Aug, 1994 - No. 3, Dec, 1994 ($3.95, magazine size)

1-3-Jim Silke-a/story 4.00
Trade paperback-($16.95)-r/#1-3 17.00

RASL
Cartoon Books: Mar, 2008 - Present ($3.50, B&W)

1-9-Jeff Smith-s/a/c 3.50

GD VG FN VF VF/NM NM-
2.0 4.0 6.0 8.0 9.0 9.2

RATCHET & CLANK (Based on the Sony videogame)
DC Comics (WildStorm thru #4): Nov, 2010 - No. 6, Apr, 2011 ($3.99/$2.99, limited series)

1-4-Fixman-s/Archer-a 4.00
5,6-($2.99) 3.00

RATFINK (See Frantic, Zany, & Ed "Big Daddy" Roth's Ratfink Comix)
Canrom, Inc.: Oct, 1964

1-Woodbridge-a 8 16 24 52 86 120

RAT PATROL, THE (TV) (Also see Wild!)
Dell Publishing Co.: Mar, 1967 - No. 5, Nov, 1967; No. 6, Oct, 1969

1-Christopher George photo-c 7 14 21 47 76 105
2-6: 3-6-Photo-c 4 8 12 28 44 60

RAVAGE 2099 (See Marvel Comics Presents #117)
Marvel Comics: Dec, 1992 - No. 33, Aug, 1995($1.25/$1.50)

1-($1.75)-Gold foil stamped-c; Stan Lee scripts 4.00
1-($1.75)-2nd printing 3.00
2-24,26-33: 5-Last Ryan-c. 6-Last Ryan-a. 14-Punisher 2099 x-over. 15-Ron Lim-c(p).
18-Bound-in card sheet 3.00
25 ($2.25, 52 pgs.) 4.00
25 ($2.95, 52 pgs.)-Silver foil embossed-c 4.50

RAVEN (See DC Special: Raven and Teen Titans titles)

RAVEN, THE (See Movie Classics)

RAVEN CHRONICLES
Caliber (New Worlds): 1995 - No. 16 ($2.95, B&W)

1-16: 10-Flip book w/Wordsmith #6. 15-Flip book w/High Caliber #4 3.00

RAVENS AND RAINBOWS
Pacific Comics: Dec, 1983 (Baxter paper)(Reprints fanzine work in color)

1-Jeff Jones-c/a(r); nudity scenes 3.00

RAWHIDE (TV)
Dell Publishing Co./Gold Key: Sept-Nov, 1959 - June-Aug, 1962; July, 1963 - No. 2, Jan, 1964

Four Color 1028 (#1) 21 42 63 150 300 450
Four Color 1097,1160,1202,1261,1269 13 26 39 93 182 270
01-684-208 (8/62, Dell) 12 24 36 82 154 225
1(10071-307) (7/63, Gold Key) 12 24 36 82 154 225
2-(12¢) 11 22 33 75 138 200

NOTE: *All have Clint Eastwood photo-c.* ***Tufts*** *a-1028.*

RAWHIDE KID
Atlas/Marvel Comics (CnPC No. 1-16/AMI No. 17-30): Mar, 1955 - No. 16, Sept, 1957; No. 17, Aug, 1960 - No. 151, May, 1979

1-Rawhide Kid, his horse Apache & sidekick Randy begin; Wyatt Earp app.;
#1 was not code approved; Maneely splash pg. 97 194 291 621 1061 1500
2 40 80 120 246 411 575
3-5 31 62 93 186 303 420
6-10: 7-Williamson-a (4 pgs.) 24 48 72 142 234 325
11-16: 16-Torres-a 20 40 60 114 182 250
17-Origin by Jack Kirby; Kirby-a begins 43 86 129 271 461 650
18-21,24-30 11 22 33 80 150 220
22-Monster-c/story by Kirby/Ayers 14 28 42 96 191 285
23-Origin retold by Jack Kirby 16 32 48 114 232 350
31-35,40: 31,32-Kirby-a. 33-35-Davis-a. 34-Kirby-a. 35-Intro & death of The Raven.
40-Two-Gun Kid x-over. 10 20 30 71 128 185
36,37,39,41,42-No Kirby. 42-1st Larry Lieber issue 9 18 27 64 110 155
38-Red Raven-c/story; Kirby-c (2/64); Colan-a 11 22 33 77 144 210
43-Kirby-a (beware: pin-up often missing) 11 22 33 77 144 210
44,46: 46-Toth-a. 46-Doc Holliday-c/s 9 18 27 61 103 145
45-Origin retold, 17 pgs. 10 20 30 71 128 185
47-49,51-60 6 12 18 39 62 90
50-Kid Colt x-over; vs. Rawhide Kid 7 14 21 45 73 100
61-70: 64-Kid Colt story. 66-Two-Gun Kid story. 67-Kid Colt story. 70-Last 12¢ issue
5 10 15 32 51 70
71-78,80-83,85 3 6 9 18 27 38
79,84,86,95: 79-Williamson-a(r). 84,86: Kirby-a. 86-Origin-r; Williamson-r/Ringo Kid #13
(4 pgs.) 3 6 9 20 30 40
87-91: 90-Kid Colt app. 91-Last 15¢ issue 3 6 9 17 25 32
92,93 (52 pg.Giants). 92-Kirby-a 4 8 12 23 36 48
94,96-99 3 6 9 16 22 28
100 (6/72)-Origin retold & expanded 3 6 9 20 30 40
101-120: 115-Last new story 2 4 6 13 18 22
121-151 2 4 6 9 13 16
133,134-(30¢-c variants, limited distribution)(5,7/76) 4 8 12 26 41 55

Rawhide Kid (2010 series) #4 © MAR

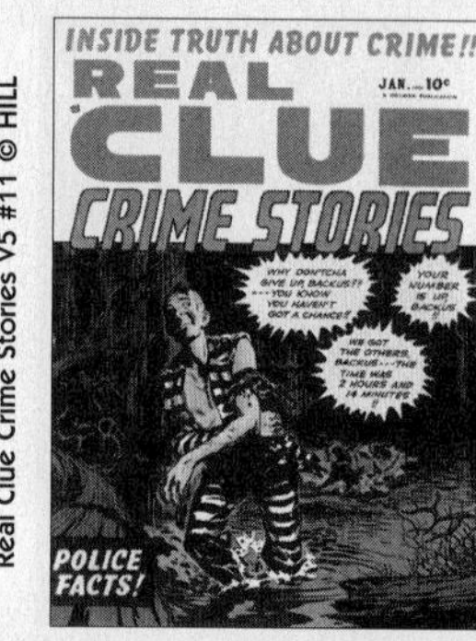

Real Clue Crime Stories V5 #11 © HILL

Real Life Comics #13 © Nedor

GD VG FN VF VF/NM NM-
2.0 4.0 6.0 8.0 9.0 9.2

GD VG FN VF VF/NM NM-
2.0 4.0 6.0 8.0 9.0 9.2

140,141-(35¢-c variants, limited distribution)(7,9/77) 6 12 18 39 62 85
Special 1(9/71, 25¢, 68 pgs.)-All Kirby/Ayers-r 5 10 15 30 48 65
NOTE: *Ayers a-13, 14, 16, 29, 37-39, 61. Colan a-5, 35, 37, 38; c-145p, 148p, 149p. Davis a-125r. Everett a-54i, 65, 66, 88, 96i, 148i(r). Gulacy c-147. Heath c-4. G. Kane c-101, 144. Keller a-5, 39, 41, 144r. Kirby a-17-32, 34, 42, 43, 84, 86, 92, 109r, 112r, 116r, 117r, 137r, Spec. 1; c-17-35, 37, 38, 40, 41, 43-47, 137r. Maneely c-1, 2, 5, 6, 14. Morisi a-13. Morrow/Williamson r-111. Roussos r-146i, 147i, 149-151i. Severin a-16; c-8, 13. Sutton a-61, 93. Torres a-99r. Tuska a-14. Wildey r-146-151(Outlaw Kid). Williamson r-79, 86, 95.*

RAWHIDE KID
Marvel Comics Group: Aug, 1985 - No. 4, Nov, 1985 (Mini-series)
1-4 5.00

RAWHIDE KID
Marvel Comics (MAX): Apr, 2003 - No. 5, June, 2003 ($2.99, limited series)
1-John Severin-a/Ron Zimmerman-s; Dave Johnson-c 3.00
2-5: 3-Dodson-c. 4-Darwyn Cooke-c. 5-J. Scott Campbell-c 3.00
Vol. 1: Slap Leather TPB (2003, $12.99) r/#1-5 13.00

RAWHIDE KID (The Sensational Seven)
Marvel Comics: Aug, 2010 - No. 4, Nov, 2010 ($3.99, limited series)
1-4-Chaykin-a/Zimmerman-s. 1-Cassaday-c. 2-Dave Johnson-c. 4-Suydam-c 4.00

RAY, THE (See Freedom Fighters & Smash Comics #14)
DC Comics: Feb, 1992 - No. 6, July, 1992 ($1.00, mini-series)
1-Sienkiewicz-c; Joe Quesada-a(p) in 1-5 5.00
2-6: 3-6-Quesada-c(p). 6-Quesada layouts only 3.00
...In a Blaze of Power (1994, $12.95)-r/#1-6 w/new Quesada-c 13.00

RAY, THE
DC Comics: May, 1994 - No. 28, Oct, 1996 ($1.75/$1.95/$2.25)
1-Quesada-c(p); Superboy app. 3.00
1-($2.95)-Collectors Edition w/diff. Quesada-c; embossed foil-c 4.00
2-5,0,6-24,26-28: 2-Quesada-c(p); Superboy app. 5-(9/94). 0-(10/94) 3.00
25-($3.50)-Future Flash (Bart Allen)-c/app; double size 4.00
Annual 1 ($3.95, 68 pgs.)-Superman app. 4.00

RAY BRADBURY COMICS
Topps Comics: Feb, 1993 - V4#1, June, 1994 ($2.95)
1-5-Polybagged w/3 trading cards each. 1-All dinosaur issue; Corben-a; Williamson/Torres/Krenkel-r/Weird Science-Fantasy #25. 3-All dinosaur issue; Steacy painted-c; Stout-a 3.00
Special Edition 1 (1994, $2.95)-The Illustrated Man 3.00
...Special: Tales of Horror #1 ($2.50), ...Trilogy of Terror V3#1 (5/94, $2.50), ...Martian Chronicles V4#1 (6/94, $2.50)-Steranko-c 3.00
NOTE: *Kelley Jones a-Trilogy of Terror V3#1. Kaluta a-Martian Chronicles V4#1. Kurtzman/Matt Wagner c-2. McKean c-4. Mignola a-4. Wood a-Trilogy of Terror V3#1r.*

RAZORLINE
Marvel Comics: Sept, 1993 (75¢, one-shot)
1-Clive Barker super-heroes: Ectokid, Hokum & Hex, Hyperkind & Saint Sinner 3.00

RAZOR'S EDGE, THE
DC Comics (WildStorm): Dec, 2004 - No. 5, Apr, 2005 ($2.95)
1-5-Warblade; Bisley-c/a; Ridley-s 3.00

REAL ADVENTURE COMICS (Action Adventure #2 on)
Gillmor Magazines: Apr, 1955
1 9 18 27 47 61 75

REAL ADVENTURES OF JONNY QUEST, THE
Dark Horse Comics: Sept, 1996 - No. 12, Sept, 1997 ($2.95)
1-12 3.00

REAL CLUE CRIME STORIES (Formerly Clue Comics)
Hillman Periodicals: V2#4, June, 1947 - V8#3, May, 1953
V2#4(#1)-S&K c/a(3); Dan Barry-a 49 98 147 309 522 735
5-7-S&K c/a(3-4). 7-Iron Lady app. 39 78 117 240 395 550
8-12 14 28 42 81 118 155
V3#1-8,10-12, V4#1-3,5-8,11,12 13 26 39 72 101 130
V3#9-Used in **SOTI**, pg. 102 15 30 45 83 124 165
V4#4-S&K-a 15 30 45 84 127 170
V4#9,10-Krigstein-a 13 26 39 74 105 135
V5#1-5,7,8,10,12 10 20 30 56 76 95
6,9,11(1/54)-Krigstein-a 11 22 33 60 83 105
V6#1-5,8,9,11 9 18 27 52 69 85
6,7,10,12-Krigstein-a. 10-Bondage-c 11 22 33 60 83 105
V7#1-3,5-11, V8#1-3: V7#6-1 pg. Frazetta ad "Prayer" - 1st app.? 10 20 30 56 76 95
4,12-Krigstein-a 11 22 33 60 83 105
NOTE: *Barry a-9, 10; c-V2#8. Briefer a-V6#6. Fuje a- V2#7(2), 8, 11. Infantino a-V2#8; c-V2#11. Lawrence a-V3#8, V5#7. Powell a-V4#11, 12. V5#4, 5, 7 are 68 pgs.*

REAL EXPERIENCES (Formerly Tiny Tessie)
Atlas Comics (20CC): No. 25, Jan, 1950
25-Virginia Mayo photo-c from movie "Red Light" 11 22 33 62 86 110

REAL FACT COMICS
National Periodical Publications: Mar-Apr, 1946 - No. 21, July-Aug, 1949
1-S&K-c/a; Harry Houdini story; Just Imagine begins (not by Finlay); Fred Ray-a 47 94 141 296 498 700
2-S&K-a; Rin-Tin-Tin & P. T. Barnum stories 28 56 84 165 270 375
3-H.G. Wells, Lon Chaney stories; early DC letter column (New Fun Comics #3 from 1935 may be the 1st) 26 52 78 154 252 350
4-Virgil Finlay-a on 'Just Imagine' begins, ends #12 (2 pgs. each); Jimmy Stewart & Jack London stories; Joe DiMaggio 1 pg. biography 29 58 87 172 281 390
5-Batman/Robin-c taken from cover of Batman #9; 5 pg. story about creation of Batman & Robin; Tom Mix story 155 310 465 992 1696 2400
6-Origin & 1st app. Tommy Tomorrow by Weisinger and Sherman (1-2/47); Flag-c; 1st writing by Harlan Ellison (letter column, non-professional); "First Man to Reach Mars" epic-c/story 84 168 252 538 919 1300
7-(No. 6 on inside)-Roussos-a; D. Fairbanks sty. 15 30 45 94 147 200
8-2nd app. Tommy Tomorrow by Finlay (5-6/47) 48 96 144 302 514 725
9-S&K-a; Glenn Miller, Indianapolis 500 stories 21 42 63 122 199 275
10-Vigilante by Meskin (based on movie serial); 4 pg. Finlay s/f story 20 40 60 118 192 265
11,12: 11-Annie Oakley, G-Men stories; Kinstler-a 14 28 42 82 121 160
13-Dale Evans and Tommy Tomorrow-c/stories 37 74 111 222 361 500
14,17,18: 14-Will Rogers story 14 28 42 80 115 150
15-Nuclear explosion part-c ("Last War on Earth" story); Clyde Beatty story 15 30 45 94 147 200
16-Tommy Tomorrow app.; 1st Planeteers? 36 72 108 211 343 475
19-Sir Arthur Conan Doyle story 15 30 45 83 124 165
20-Kubert-a, 4 pgs; Daniel Boone story 15 30 45 88 137 185
21-Kubert-a, 2 pgs; Kit Carson story 14 28 42 80 115 150
Ashcan (2/46) nn-Not distributed to newsstands, only for in house use. Covers were produced, but not the rest of the book. A copy sold in 2008 for $500.
NOTE: *Barry c-16. Virgil Finlay c-6, 8. Meskin c-10. Roussos a-1-4, 6.*

REAL FUNNIES
Nedor Publishing Co.: Jan, 1943 - No. 3, June, 1943
1-Funny animal, humor; Black Terrier app. (clone of The Black Terror) 32 64 96 188 307 425
2,3 15 30 45 94 147 200

REAL GHOSTBUSTERS, THE (Also see Slimer)
Now Comics: Aug, 1988 - No. 32, 1991 ($1.75/$1.95)
1-32: 1-Based on Ghostbusters movie. #29-32 exist? 3.00

REAL HEROES COMICS
Parents' Magazine Institute: Sept, 1941 - No. 16, Oct, 1946
1-Roosevelt-c/story 32 64 96 188 307 425
2-J. Edgar Hoover-c/story 15 30 45 83 124 165
3-5,7-10: 4-Churchill, Roosevelt stories 14 28 42 76 108 140
6-Lou Gehrig-c/story 19 38 57 112 179 245
11-16: 13-Kiefer-a 10 20 30 54 72 90

REALISTIC ROMANCES
Realistic Comics/Avon Periodicals: July-Aug, 1951 - No. 17, Aug-Sept, 1954 (No #9-14)
1-Kinstler-a; c-/Avon paperback #211 30 60 90 177 289 400
2 15 30 45 88 137 185
3,4 15 30 45 85 130 175
5,8-Kinstler-a 15 30 45 86 133 180
6-c-/Diversey Prize Novels #6; Kinstler-a 15 30 45 88 137 185
7-Evans-a?; c-/Avon paperback #360 15 30 45 88 137 185
15,17: 17-Kinstler-c 15 30 45 83 124 165
16-Kinstler marijuana story-r/Romantic Love #6 15 30 45 86 133 180
I.W. Reprint #1,8,9: #1-r/Realistic Romances #4; Astarita-a. 9-r/Women To Love #1 2 4 6 11 16 20
NOTE: *Astarita a-2-4, 7, 8, 17. Photo c-1, 2. Painted c-3, 4.*

REAL LIFE COMICS
Nedor/Better/Standard Publ./Pictorial Magazine No. 13: Sept, 1941 - No. 59, Sept, 1952
1-Uncle Sam-c/story; Daniel Boone story 61 122 183 390 670 950
2 31 62 93 182 296 410
3-Hitler cover 181 362 543 1158 1979 2800
4,5: 4-Story of American flag "Old Glory" 20 40 60 115 185 255
6-10: 6-Wild Bill Hickok story 19 38 57 112 179 245

Real Love #59 © ACE

Realm of Kings: Inhumans #3 © MAR

R.E.B.E.L.S. #16 © DC

GD VG FN VF VF/NM NM-
2.0 4.0 6.0 8.0 9.0 9.2

11-14,16-20: 17-Albert Einstein story 18 36 54 103 162 220
15-Japanese WWII-c by Schomburg 18 36 54 107 169 230
21-23,25,26,28-30: 29-A-Bomb story 15 30 45 90 140 190
24-Story of Baseball (Babe Ruth) 22 44 66 128 209 290
27-Schomburg A-Bomb-c; story of A-Bomb 21 42 63 122 199 275
31-33,35,36,42-44,48,49: 49-Baseball issue 15 30 45 84 127 170
34,37-41,45-47: 34-Jimmy Stewart story. 37-Story of motion pictures; Bing Crosby story. 38-Jane Froman story. 39- "1,000,000 A.D." story. 40-Bob Feller. 41-Jimmie Foxx story ("Jimmy" on-c); "Home Run" Baker story. 45-Story of Olympic games; Burl Ives & Kit Carson story. 46-Douglas Fairbanks Jr. & Sr. story. 47-George Gershwin story
15 30 45 88 137 185
50-Frazetta-a (5 pgs.) 30 60 90 177 289 400
51-Jules Verne "Journey to the Moon" by Evans; Severin/Elder-a
21 42 63 122 199 275
52-Frazetta-a (4 pgs.); Severin/Elder-a(2); Evans-a 33 66 99 194 317 440
53-57-Severin/Elder-a. 54-Bat Masterson-c/story 16 32 48 96 151 205
58-Severin/Elder-a(2) 17 34 51 98 154 210
59-1 pg. Frazetta; Severin/Elder-a 17 34 51 98 154 210
NOTE: ***Guardineer** a-40(2), 44. **Meskin** a-52. **Roussos** a-50. **Schomburg** c-1, 2, 4, 5, 7, 11, 13-21, 23, 24, 26, 28, 30-32, 34-40, 42, 44-47, 55. **Tuska** a-53. Photo-c 5, 6.*

REAL LIFE SECRETS (Real Secrets #2 on)
Ace Periodicals: Sept, 1949 (one-shot)
1-Painted-c 14 28 42 82 121 160

REAL LIFE STORY OF FESS PARKER (Magazine)
Dell Publishing Co.: 1955
1 9 18 27 61 103 145

REAL LIFE TALES OF SUSPENSE (See Suspense)

REAL LOVE (Formerly Hap Hazard)
Ace Periodicals (A. A. Wyn): No. 25, April, 1949 - No. 76, Nov, 1956
25 14 28 42 82 121 160
26 11 22 33 60 83 105
27-L. B. Cole-a 12 24 36 69 97 125
28-35 10 20 30 54 72 90
36-66: 66-Last pre-code (2/55) 9 18 27 50 65 80
67-76 8 16 24 42 54 65
NOTE: *Photo c-50-76. Painted c-46.*

REALM, THE
Arrow Comics/WeeBee Comics #13/Caliber Press #14 on: Feb, 1986 - No. 21, 1991 (B&W)
1-3,5-21 3.00
4-1st app. Deadworld (9/86) 4.00
Book 1 ($4.95, B&W) 5.00

REAL McCOYS, THE (TV)
Dell Publ. Co.: No. 1071, 1-3/60 - 5-7/1962 (All have Walter Brennan photo-c)
Four Color 1071,1134-Toth-a in both 9 18 27 60 100 140
Four Color 1193,1265 8 16 24 56 93 130
01-689-207 (5-7/62) 7 14 21 50 83 115

REALM OF KINGS (Also see Guardians of the Galaxy and Nova)
Marvel Comics: Jan, 2010 ($3.99, one-shot)
1-Abnett & Lanning-s/Manco & Asrar-a; Guardians of the Galaxy app. 4.00

REALM OF KINGS: IMPERIAL GUARD
Marvel Comics: Jan, 2010 - No. 5, May, 2010 ($3.99, limited series)
1-5-Abnett & Lanning-s/Walker-a; Starjammers app. 4.00

REALM OF KINGS: INHUMANS
Marvel Comics: Jan, 2010 - No. 5, May, 2010 ($3.99, limited series)
1-5-Abnett & Lanning-s/Raimondi-a; Mighty Avengers app. 4.00

REALM OF KINGS: SON OF HULK
Marvel Comics: Apr, 2010 - No. 4, July, 2010 ($3.99, limited series)
1-4-Reed-s/Munera-a; leads into Incredible Hulk #609 4.00

REALM OF THE CLAW (Also see Mutant Earth as part of a flipbook)
Image Comics: Oct, 2003 - No. 2 ($2.95)
0-(7/03, $5.95) Convention Special; cover has gold-foil title logo 6.00
1,2-Two covers by Yardin 3.00
Vol. 1 TPB (2006, $16.99) r/series; concept art & sketch pages 17.00

REAL SCREEN COMICS (#1 titled Real Screen Funnies; TV Screen Cartoons #129-138)
National Periodical Publications: Spring, 1945 - No. 128, May-June, 1959 (#1-40: 52 pgs.)
1-The Fox & the Crow, Flippity & Flop, Tito & His Burrito begin
100 200 300 635 1093 1550
2 47 94 141 296 498 700
3-5 32 64 96 188 307 425
6-10 (2-3/47) 21 42 63 122 199 275
11-20 (10-11/48): 13-The Crow x-over in Flippity & Flop
16 32 48 94 147 200
21-30 (6-7/50) 14 28 42 76 108 140
31-50 11 22 33 60 83 105
51-99 10 20 30 54 72 90
100 10 20 30 56 76 95
101-128 8 16 24 44 57 70

REAL SCREEN FUNNIES
DC Comics: Spring 1945
1-Ashcan comic, not distributed to newsstands, only for in-house use. Cover art is Real Screen Funnies #1 with interior being Detective Comics #92. Only ashcan cover to be produced using the regular production first issue art and only using the color yellow. A copy sold in 2008 for $3,000.

REAL SECRETS (Formerly Real Life Secrets)
Ace Periodicals: No. 2, Nov, 1950 - No. 5, May, 1950
2-Painted-c 11 22 33 60 83 105
3-5: 3-Photo-c 9 18 27 47 61 75

REAL SPORTS COMICS (All Sports Comics #2 on)
Hillman Periodicals: Oct-Nov, 1948 (52 pgs.)
1-Powell-a (12 pgs.) 39 78 117 240 395 550

REAL WAR STORIES
Eclipse Comics: July, 1987; No. 2, Jan, 1991 ($2.00, 52 pgs.)
1-Bolland-a(p), Bissette-a, Totleben-a(i); Alan Moore scripts (2nd printing exists, 2/88) 4.00
2-($4.95) 5.00

REAL WESTERN HERO (Formerly Wow #1-69; Western Hero #76 on)
Fawcett Publications: No. 70, Sept, 1948 - No. 75, Feb, 1949 (All 52 pgs.)
70(#1)-Tom Mix, Monte Hale, Hopalong Cassidy, Young Falcon begin
22 44 66 132 216 300
71-75: 71-Gabby Hayes begins. 71,72-Captain Tootsie by Beck. 75-Big Bow and Little Arrow app. 15 30 45 85 130 175
NOTE: *Painted/photo c-70-73; painted c-74, 75.*

REAL WEST ROMANCES
Crestwood Publishing Co./Prize Publ.: 4-5/49 - V1#6, 3/50; V2#1, Apr-May, 1950 (All 52 pgs. & photo-c)
V1#1-S&K-a(p) 26 52 78 154 252 350
2-Gail Davis and Rocky Shahan photo-c 14 28 42 80 115 150
3-Kirby-a(p) only 14 28 42 82 121 160
4-S&K-a; Whip Wilson, Reno Browne photo-c 19 38 57 111 176 240
5-Audie Murphy, Gale Storm photo-c; S&K-a 17 34 51 98 154 210
6-Produced by S&K, no S&K-a; Robert Preston & Cathy Downs photo-c
13 26 39 74 105 135
V2#1-Kirby-a(p) 13 26 39 74 105 135
NOTE: ***Meskin** a-V1#5, 6. **Severin/Elder** a-V1#3-6, V2#1. **Meskin** a-V1#6. **Leonard Starr** a-1-3. Photo-c V1#1-6, V2#1.*

REALWORLDS :...
DC Comics: 2000 ($5.95, one-shots, prestige format)
Batman - Marshall Rogers-a/Golden & Sniegoski-s; Justice League of America -Dematteis-s/ Barr-painted art; Superman - Vance-s/García-López & Rubenstein-a; Wonder Woman - Hanson & Neuwirth-s/Sam-a 6.00

RE-ANIMATOR IN FULL COLOR
Adventure Comics: Oct, 1991 - No. 3, 1992 ($2.95, mini-series)
1-3: Adapts horror movie. 1-Dorman painted-c 3.00

REAP THE WILD WIND (See Cinema Comics Herald)

REBEL, THE (TV)
Dell Publishing Co.: No. 1076, Feb-Apr, 1960 - No. 1262, Dec-Feb, 1961-62
Four Color 1076 (#1)-Sekowsky-a, photo-c 9 18 27 65 113 160
Four Color 1138 (9-11/60), 1207 (9-11/61), 1262-Photo-c
8 16 24 56 93 130

R.E.B.E.L.S.
DC Comics: Apr, 2009 - Present ($2.99)
1-9,12-26: 1-Bedard-s/Clarke-a; Vril Dox returns; Supergirl app.; 2 covers. 15-Starfire app. 19-26-Lobo app. 3.00
10,11-($3.99) Blackest Night x-over; Vril Dox joins the Sinestro Corps 4.00
Annual 1 (12/09, $4.99) Origin on Starro the Conqueror; Despero app. 5.00
...: Sons of Brainiac TPB (2011, $14.99) r/#15-20 15.00

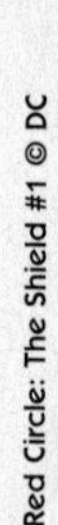

Red #1 © Ellis & Hamner

Red Circle: The Shield #1 © DC

Red Hood: Lost Days #1 © DC

	GD 2.0	VG 4.0	FN 6.0	VF 8.0	VF/NM 9.0	NM- 9.2
...: Strange Companions TPB (2010, $14.99) r/#7-9 & Annual #1						15.00
...: The Coming of Starro TPB (2010, $17.99) r/#1-6						18.00
...: The Son and the Stars TPB (2010, $17.99) r/#10-14						18.00

R.E.B.E.L.S. '94 (Becomes R.E.B.E.L.S. '95 & R.E.B.E.L.S. '96)
DC Comics: No. 0, Oct, 1994 - No. 17, Mar, 1996 ($1.95/$2.25)

	GD 2.0	VG 4.0	FN 6.0	VF 8.0	VF/NM 9.0	NM- 9.2
0-17: 8-$2.25-c begins. 15-R.E.B.E.L.S '96 begins.						3.00

RECORD BOOK OF FAMOUS POLICE CASES
St. John Publishing Co.: 1949 (25¢, 132 pgs.)

	GD 2.0	VG 4.0	FN 6.0	VF 8.0	VF/NM 9.0	NM- 9.2
nn-Kubert-a(3); r/Son of Sinbad; Baker-c	41	82	123	256	428	600

RED (Inspired the 2010 Bruce Willis movie)
DC Comics (Homage): Sept, 2003 - No. 3, Feb, 2004 ($2.95, limited series)

	GD 2.0	VG 4.0	FN 6.0	VF 8.0	VF/NM 9.0	NM- 9.2
1-3-Warren Ellis-s/Cully Hamner-a/c						5.00
Red/Tokyo Storm Warning TPB (2004, $14.95) Flip book r/both series						15.00
Red: Eyes Only (2/11, $4.99) comic prequel; Hamner-s/a/c						5.00
Red: Frank (11/10, $3.99) movie prequel; Noveck-s/Masters-a/Hamner & photo-c						4.00
Red: Joe (11/10, $3.99) movie prequel; Wagner-s/Redondo-a/Hamner & photo-c						4.00
Red: Marvin (11/10, $3.99) movie prequel; Hoeber-s/Olmos-a/Hamner & photo-c						4.00
Red: Victoria (11/10, $3.99) movie prequel; Hoeber-s/Hahn-a/Hamner & photo-c						4.00

RED ARROW
P. L. Publishing Co.: May-June, 1951 - No. 3, Oct, 1951

	GD 2.0	VG 4.0	FN 6.0	VF 8.0	VF/NM 9.0	NM- 9.2
1	11	22	33	60	83	105
2,3	9	18	27	47	61	75

RED BAND COMICS
Enwil Associates: Nov, 1944, No. 2, Jan, 1945 - No. 4, May, 1945

	GD 2.0	VG 4.0	FN 6.0	VF 8.0	VF/NM 9.0	NM- 9.2
1-Bogeyman-c/intro. (The Spirit swipe)	40	80	120	246	411	575
2-Origin Bogeyman & Santanas; c-reprint/#1	29	58	87	170	278	385
3,4-Captain Wizard app. in both (1st app.); each has identical contents/cover	27	54	81	158	259	360

REDBLADE
Dark Horse Comics: Apr, 1993 - No. 3, July, 1993 ($2.50, mini-series)

	GD 2.0	VG 4.0	FN 6.0	VF 8.0	VF/NM 9.0	NM- 9.2
1-3: 1-Double gatefold-c						3.00

RED CIRCLE, THE (Re-introduction of characters from MLJ/Archie publications)
DC Comics: Oct, 2009 ($2.99, series of one-shots)

	GD 2.0	VG 4.0	FN 6.0	VF 8.0	VF/NM 9.0	NM- 9.2
...Inferno 1 - Hangman app.; Straczynski-s/Greg Scott-a						3.00
...The Hangman 1 - Origin retold; Straczynski-s/Derenick & Sienkiewicz-a						3.00
...The Shield 1 - Origin retold; Straczynski-s/McDaniel-a						3.00
...The Web 1 - Straczynski-s/Robinson-a						3.00

RED CIRCLE COMICS (Also see Blazing Comics & Blue Circle Comics)
Rural Home Publications (Enwil): Jan, 1945 - No. 4, April, 1945

	GD 2.0	VG 4.0	FN 6.0	VF 8.0	VF/NM 9.0	NM- 9.2
1-The Prankster & Red Riot begin	43	86	129	271	461	650
2-Starr-a; The Judge (costumed hero) app.	30	60	90	177	289	400
3,4-Starr-c/a. 3-The Prankster not in costume	24	48	72	142	234	325
4-(Dated 4/45)-Leftover covers to #4 were later restapled over early 1950s coverless comics; variations in the coverless comics used are endless; Woman Outlaws, Dorothy Lamour, Crime Does Not Pay, Sabu, Diary Loves, Love Confessions & Young Love V3#3 known	18	36	54	105	165	225

RED CIRCLE SORCERY (Chilling Adventures in Sorcery #1-5)
Red Circle Prod. (Archie): No. 6, Apr, 1974 - No. 11, Feb, 1975 (All 25¢ iss.)

	GD 2.0	VG 4.0	FN 6.0	VF 8.0	VF/NM 9.0	NM- 9.2
6,8,9,11: 6-Early Chaykin-a. 7-Pino-a. 8-Only app. The Cobra	2	4	6	9	13	16
7-Bruce Jones-a with Wrightson, Kaluta, Jeff Jones	3	6	9	14	19	24
10-Wood-a(i)	2	4	6	10	14	18

NOTE: ***Chaykin*** *a-6, 10.* ***McWilliams*** *a-10(2 & 3 pgs.).* ***Mooney*** *a-11p.* ***Morrow*** *a-6-8, 9(text illos), 10, 11i; c-6-11.* ***Thorne*** *a-8, 10.* ***Toth*** *a-8, 9.*

RED DOG (See Night Music #7)

RED DRAGON
Comico: June, 1996 ($2.95)

	GD 2.0	VG 4.0	FN 6.0	VF 8.0	VF/NM 9.0	NM- 9.2
1-Bisley-c						3.00

RED DRAGON COMICS (1st Series) (Formerly Trail Blazers; see Super Magician V5#7, 8)
Street & Smith Publications: No. 5, Jan, 1943 - No. 9, Jan, 1944

	GD 2.0	VG 4.0	FN 6.0	VF 8.0	VF/NM 9.0	NM- 9.2
5-Origin Red Rover, the Crimson Crimebuster; Rex King, Man of Adventure, Captain Jack Commando, & The Minute Man begin; text origin Red Dragon; Binder-c	100	200	300	635	1093	1550
6-Origin The Black Crusader & Red Dragon (3/43); 1st story app. Red Dragon & 1st cover (classic-c)	258	516	774	1651	2826	4000
7-Classic WWII-c	219	438	657	1402	2401	3400
8-The Red Knight app.	77	154	231	493	847	1200
9-Origin Chuck Magnon, Immortal Man	77	154	231	493	847	1200

RED DRAGON COMICS (2nd Series)(See Super Magician V2#8)
Street & Smith Publications: Nov, 1947 - No. 6, Jan, 1949; No. 7, July, 1949

	GD 2.0	VG 4.0	FN 6.0	VF 8.0	VF/NM 9.0	NM- 9.2
1-Red Dragon begins; Elliman, Nigel app.; Edd Cartier-c/a	97	194	291	621	1061	1500
2-Cartier-c	66	132	198	419	722	1025
3-1st app. Dr. Neff Ghost Breaker by Powell; Elliman, Nigel app.	55	110	165	352	601	850
4-Cartier c/a	77	154	231	493	847	1200
5-7	41	82	123	249	417	585

NOTE: ***Maneely*** *a-5, 7.* ***Powell*** *a-2-7; c-3, 5, 7.*

RED EAGLE
David McKay Publications: No. 16, Aug, 1938

	GD 2.0	VG 4.0	FN 6.0	VF 8.0	VF/NM 9.0	NM- 9.2
Feature Books 16	27	54	81	158	259	360

REDEYE (See Comics Reading Libraries in the Promotional Comics section)

RED FOX (Formerly Manhunt! #1-14; also see Extra Comics)
Magazine Enterprises: No. 15, 1954

	GD 2.0	VG 4.0	FN 6.0	VF 8.0	VF/NM 9.0	NM- 9.2
15(A-1 #108)-Undercover Girl story; L.B. Cole-c/a (Red Fox); r-from Manhunt; Powell-a	19	38	57	109	172	235

RED GOOSE COMIC SELECTIONS (See Comic Selections)

RED HAWK (See A-1 Comics, Bobby Benson's ..#14-16 & Straight Arrow #2)
Magazine Enterprises: No. 90, 1953

	GD 2.0	VG 4.0	FN 6.0	VF 8.0	VF/NM 9.0	NM- 9.2
11-(A-1 Comics #90)-Powell-c/a	13	26	39	72	101	130

RED HERRING
DC Comics (WildStorm): Oct, 2009 - No. 6, Mar, 2010 ($2.99, limited series)

	GD 2.0	VG 4.0	FN 6.0	VF 8.0	VF/NM 9.0	NM- 9.2
1-6-Tischman-s/Bond-a						3.00

RED HOOD: THE LOST DAYS
DC Comics: Aug, 2010 - No. 6, Jan, 2011 ($2.99, limited series)

	GD 2.0	VG 4.0	FN 6.0	VF 8.0	VF/NM 9.0	NM- 9.2
1-6-The Return of Jason Todd; Winick-s/Raimondi-a/Tucci-c. 6-Joker & Hush app.						3.00

RED MASK (Formerly Tim Holt; see Best Comics, Blazing Six-Guns)
Magazine Enterprises No. 42-53/Sussex No. 54 (M.E. on-c): No. 42, June-July, 1954 - No. 53, May, 1956; No. 54, Sept, 1957

	GD 2.0	VG 4.0	FN 6.0	VF 8.0	VF/NM 9.0	NM- 9.2
42-Ghost Rider by Ayers continues, ends #50; Black Phantom continues; 3-D effect c/stories begin	21	42	63	122	199	275
43- 3-D effect-c/stories	19	38	57	109	172	235
44-52: 3-D effect stories only. 47-Last pre-code issue. 50-Last Ghost Rider. 51-The Presto Kid begins by Ayers (1st app.); Presto Kid-c begins; last 3-D effect story. 52-Origin The Presto Kid	17	34	51	98	154	210
53,54-Last Black Phantom; last Presto Kid-c	15	30	45	83	124	165
I.W. Reprint #1 (r-/#52). 2 (nd, r/#51 w/diff.-c). 3, 8 (nd; Kinstler-c); 8-r/Red Mask #52	3	6	9	16	22	28

NOTE: ***Ayers*** *art on Ghost Rider & Presto Kid.* ***Bolle*** *art in all (Red Mask); c-43, 44, 49.* ***Guardineer*** *a-52. Black Phantom in #42-44, 47-50, 53, 54.*

REDMASK OF THE RIO GRANDE
AC Comics: 1990 ($2.50, 28pgs.)(Has photos of movie posters)

	GD 2.0	VG 4.0	FN 6.0	VF 8.0	VF/NM 9.0	NM- 9.2
1-Bolle-c/a(r); photo inside-c						3.00

RED MENACE
DC Comics (WildStorm): Jan, 2007 - No. 6, Jun, 2007 ($2.99, limited series)

	GD 2.0	VG 4.0	FN 6.0	VF 8.0	VF/NM 9.0	NM- 9.2
1-6-Ordway-a/c; Bilson, DeMeo & Brody-s						3.00
TPB (2007, $17.99) r/series, sketch pages & variant covers						18.00

RED MOUNTAIN FEATURING QUANTRELL'S RAIDERS (Movie)(Also see Jesse James #28)
Avon Periodicals: 1952

	GD 2.0	VG 4.0	FN 6.0	VF 8.0	VF/NM 9.0	NM- 9.2
nn-Alan Ladd; Kinstler-c	28	56	84	165	270	375

RED PROPHET: THE TALES OF ALVIN MAKER
Dabel Brothers Prods./Marvel Comics (Dabel Brothers): Mar, 2006 - No. 12, Mar, 2008 ($2.99)

	GD 2.0	VG 4.0	FN 6.0	VF 8.0	VF/NM 9.0	NM- 9.2
1-12-Adaptation of Orson Scott Card novel. 1-Miguel Montenegro-a						3.00
... Vol. 1 HC (2007, $19.99, dustjacket) r/#1-6						20.00
... Vol. 1 SC (2007, $15.99) r/#1-6						16.00
... Vol. 2 HC (2008, $19.99, dustjacket) r/#7-12						20.00

"RED" RABBIT COMICS
Dearfield Comic/J. Charles Laue Publ. Co.: Jan, 1947 - No. 22, Aug-Sep, 1951

	GD 2.0	VG 4.0	FN 6.0	VF 8.0	VF/NM 9.0	NM- 9.2
1	14	28	42	76	108	140
2	8	16	24	44	57	70
3-10	7	14	21	37	46	55
11-17,19-22	7	14	21	35	43	50
18-Flying Saucer-c (1/51)	8	16	24	44	57	70

Red Robin #11 © DC

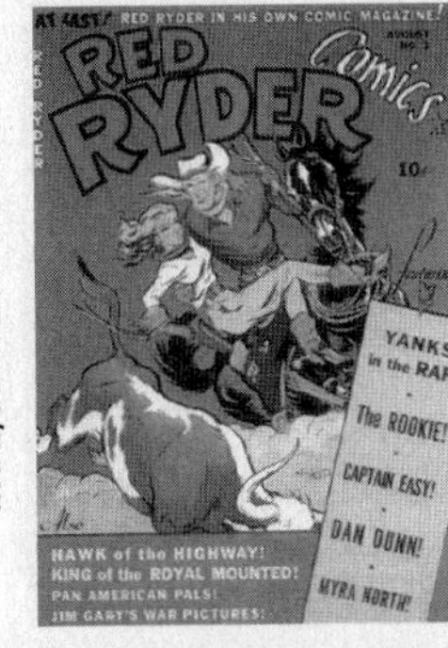

Red Ryder Comics #3 © DELL

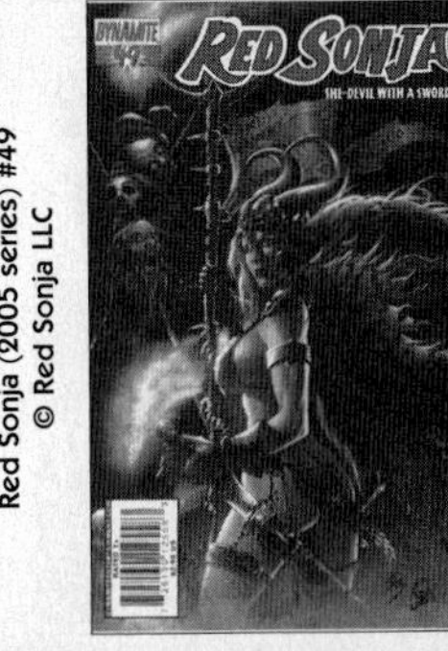

Red Sonja (2005 series) #49 © Red Sonja LLC

GD 2.0 | VG 4.0 | FN 6.0 | VF 8.0 | VF/NM 9.0 | NM- 9.2

RED RAVEN COMICS (Human Torch #2 on)(Also see X-Men #44 & Sub-Mariner #26, 2nd series)
Timely Comics: August, 1940

1-Origin & 1st app. Red Raven; Comet Pierce & Mercury by Kirby, The Human Top & The Eternal Brain; intro. Magar, the Mystic & only app.; Kirby-c (his 1st signed work) 1250 2500 3750 9400 16,700 24,000

RED ROBIN (Batman: Reborn)
DC Comics: Aug, 2009 - Present ($2.99)

1-21-Tim (Drake) Wayne in the Kingdom Come costume; Bachs-a. 1-Two covers 3.00
...: Collision SC (2010, $19.99) r/#6-12 and Batgirl (2009 series) #8 20.00
...: The Grail SC (2010, $17.99) r/#1-5 18.00

RED ROCKET 7
Dark Horse Comics: Aug, 1997 - No. 7, June, 1998 ($3.95, square format, limited series)

1-7-Mike Allred-c/s/a 4.00

RED RYDER COMICS (Hi Spot #2)(Movies, radio)(See Crackajack Funnies & Super Book of Comics)
Hawley Publ. No. 1/Dell Publishing Co.(K.K.) No. 3 on: 9/40; No. 3, 8/41 - No. 5, 12/41; No. 6, 4/42 - No. 151, 4-6/57

1-Red Ryder, his horse Thunder, Little Beaver & his horse Papoose strip reprints begin by Fred Harman; 1st meeting of Red & Little Beaver; Harman line-drawn-c #1-85 245 490 735 1568 2684 3800
3-(Scarce)-Alley Oop, Capt. Easy, Dan Dunn, Freckles & His Friends, King of the Royal Mtd., Myra North strip-r begin 54 118 162 459 930 1400
4-6: 6-1st Dell issue (4/42) 27 54 81 197 399 600
7-10 23 46 69 168 334 500
11-20 16 32 48 114 232 350
21-32-Last Alley Oop, Dan Dunn, Capt. Easy, Freckles 12 24 36 82 154 225
33-40 (52 pgs.): 40-Photo back-c begin, end #57 10 20 30 68 119 170
41 (52 pgs.)-Rocky Lane photo back-c 10 20 30 70 125 180
42-46 (52 pgs.): 46-Last Red Ryder strip-r 8 16 24 58 97 135
47-53 (52 pgs.): 47-New stories on Red Ryder begin. 49,52-Harmon photo back-c 7 14 21 49 80 110
54-92: 54-73 (36 pgs.). 59-Harmon photo back-c. 73-Last King of the Royal Mtd; strip-r by Jim Gary. 74-85 (52 pgs.)-Harman line-drawn-c. 86-92 (52 pgs.)-Harman painted-c 6 12 18 43 69 95
93-99,101-106: 94-96 (36 pgs.)-Harman painted-c. 97,98,(36 pgs.)-Harman line-drawn-c. 99,101-106 (36 pgs.)-Jim Bannon Photo-c 6 12 18 37 59 80
100 (36 pgs.)-Bannon photo-c 6 12 18 39 62 85
107-118 (52 pgs.)-Harman line-drawn-c 5 10 15 34 55 75
119-129 (52 pgs.): 119-Painted-c begin, not by Harman, end #151 5 10 15 32 51 70
130-151 (36 pgs.): 145-Title change to Red Ryder Ranch Magazine
149-Title change to Red Ryder Ranch Comics 5 10 15 30 48 65
Four Color 916 (7/58) 5 10 15 30 48 65

NOTE: *Fred Harman a-1-99; c-1-98, 107-118. Don Red Barry, Allan Rocky Lane, Wild Bill Elliott & Jim Bannon starred as Red Ryder in the movies. Robert Blake starred as Little Beaver.*

RED RYDER PAINT BOOK
Whitman Publishing Co.: 1941 (8-1/2x11-1/2", 148 pgs.)

nn-Reprints 1940 daily strips 76 152 228 479 810 1140

RED SEAL COMICS (Formerly Carnival Comics, and/or Spotlight Comics?)
Harry 'A' Chesler/Superior Publ. No. 19 on: No. 14, 10/45 - No. 18, 10/46; No. 19, 6/47 - No. 22, 12/47

14-The Black Dwarf begins (continued from Spotlight?); Little Nemo app; bondage/hypo-c; Tuska-a 81 162 243 518 884 1250
15-Torture story; funny-c 41 82 123 256 428 600
16-Used in **SOTI**, pg. 181, illo "Outside the forbidden pages of de Sade, you find draining a girl's blood only in children's comics;" drug club story r-later in Crime Reporter #1; Veiled Avenger & Barry Kuda app; Tuska-a; funny-c 63 126 189 403 689 975
17,18,20: Lady Satan, Yankee Girl & Sky Chief app; 17-Tuska-a 51 102 153 318 539 760
19-No Black Dwarf (on-c only); Zor, El Tigre app. 45 90 135 284 480 675
21-Lady Satan & Black Dwarf app. 32 64 96 192 314 435
22-Zor, Rocketman app. (68 pgs.) 32 64 96 192 314 435

REDSKIN (Thrilling Indian Stories)(Famous Western Badmen #13 on)
Youthful Magazines: Sept, 1950 - No. 12, Oct, 1952

1-Walter Johnson-a (7 pgs.) 17 34 51 98 154 210
2 11 22 33 62 86 110
3-12: 3-Daniel Boone story. 6-Geronimo story 10 20 30 54 72 90

NOTE: ***Walter Johnson** c-3, 4. **Palais** a-11. **Wildey** a-5, 11. Bondage c-6, 12.*

RED SONJA (Also see Conan #23, Kull & The Barbarians, Marvel Feature & Savage Sword Of Conan #1)
Marvel Comics Group: 1/77 - No. 15, 5/79; V1#1, 2/83 - V2#2, 3/83; V3#1, 8/83 - V3#4, 2/84; V3#5, 1/85 - V3#13, 5/86

1-Created by Robert E. Howard 2 4 6 11 16 20
2-10: 5-Last 30¢ issue 1 3 4 6 8 10
4,5-(35¢-c variants, limited distribution)(7,9/77) 3 6 9 20 30 40
11-15, V1#1,V2#2: 14-Last 35¢ issue 1 2 3 5 6 8
V3#1-13: #1-4 ($1.00, 52 pgs.) 4.00

NOTE: ***Brunner** c-12-14. **J. Buscema** a(p)-12, 13, 15; c-V#1. **Nebres** a-V3#3i(part). **N. Redondo** a-8i, V3#2i, 3i. **Simonson** a-V3#1. **Thorne** c/a-1-11.*

RED SONJA (Continues in Queen Sonja) (Also see Classic Red Sonja)
Dynamite Entertainment: No. 0, Apr, 2005 - Present (25¢/$2.99)

0-(4/05, 25¢) Greg Land-c/Mel Rubi-a/Oeming & Carey-s 3.00
1-(6/05, $2.99) Five covers by Ross, Linsner, Cassaday, Turner, Rivera; Rubi-a 3.00
2-46-Multiple covers on all. 29-Sonja dies. 34-Sonja reborn 3.00
5-RRP Edition with Red Foil logo and Isonove-a 10.00
50-('10, $4.99) new stories and reprints; Marcos, Chin, Desjardins-a; 4 covers 5.00
51-55-($3.99)-Geovani-a; multiple covers on each 4.00
Annual #1 (2007, $3.50) Oeming-s/Sadowski-a; Red Sonja Comics Chronology 4.00
Annual #2 (2009, $3.99) Gage-s/Marcos-a; wraparound Prado-c & Marcos-c 4.00
Annual #3 (2010, $5.99) Brereton-s/c/a; Batista-a 6.00
... Break the Skin (2011, $4.99) Winslade-c/Van Meter-s/Salazar-a 5.00
... Cover Showcase Vol. 1 (2007, $5.99) gallery of variant covers; Cho sketches 6.00
... Deluge (2011, $4.99) Breretonnnn-s/c; Bolson-a/var-c; reprint from Conan #48 ('74) 5.00
Giant Size Red Sonja #1 (2007, $4.99) Chaykin-c; new story and reprints and pin-ups 5.00
Giant Size Red Sonja #2 (2008, $4.99) Segovia-c; new story and reprints and pin-ups 5.00
... Goes East ($4.99) three covers; Joe Ng-a 5.00
...: Monster Isle ($4.99) two covers; Pablo Marcos-a/Roy Thomas-s 5.00
... One More Day ($4.99) two covers; Liam Sharp-a 5.00
...: Revenge of the Gods 1,2 (2011 - Present, $3.99) Sampare-a/Lieberman-s 4.00
... Vacant Shell ($4.99) two covers; Remender-s/Renaud-a 5.00
...: Wrath of the Gods 1-5 (2010 - No. 5, 2010, $3.99) Geovani-a 4.00
The Adventures of Red Sonja TPB (2005, $19.99) r/Marvel Feature #1-7 20.00
The Adventures of Red Sonja Vol. 2 TPB (2007, $19.99) r/#1-7 of '77 Marvel series 20.00
... Vol. 1 TPB (2006, $19.99) r/#0-6; gallery of covers and variants; creators interview 20.00
... Vol. 2 Arrowsmith TPB (2007, $19.99) r/#7-12; gallery of covers and variants 20.00
... Vol. 3 The Rise of Gath TPB (2007, $19.99) r/#13-18; gallery of covers and variants 20.00
... Vol. 4 Animals & More TPB (2007, $24.99) r/#19-24; gallery of covers and variants 25.00

RED SONJA/CLAW: THE DEVIL'S HANDS (See Claw the Unconquered)
DC Comics (WildStorm)/Dynamite Ent.: May, 2006 - No. 4, Aug, 2006 ($2.99, limited series)

1-4-Covers by Jim Lee & Dell'Otto.; Andy Smith-a 1-Alex Ross var-c. 2-Dell'Otto var-c. 3-Bermejo var-c. 4-Andy Smith var-c 3.00
TPB (2007, $12.99) r/#1-4; cover gallery 13.00

RED SONJA: SCAVENGER HUNT
Marvel Comics: Dec, 1995 ($2.95, one-shot)

1 3.00

RED SONJA: THE MOVIE
Marvel Comics Group: Nov, 1985 - No. 2, Dec, 1985 (Limited series)

1,2-Movie adapt-r/Marvel Super Spec. #38 3.00

RED SONJA VS. THULSA DOOM
Dynamite Entertainment: 2005 - No. 4, 2006 ($3.50)

1-4-Conrad-a; Conrad & Dell'Otto covers 3.50
..., Volume 1 TPB (2006, $14.99) r/series; cover gallery 15.00

RED STAR, THE
Image Comics/Archangel Studios: June, 2000 - No. 9, June, 2002 ($2.95)

1-Christian Gossett-s/a(p) 4.00
2-9: 9-Beck-c 3.00
#(7.5) Reprints Wizard #1/2 story with new pages 3.00
Annual 1 (Archangel Studios, 11/02, $3.50) "Run Makita Run" 4.00
TPB (4/01, $24.95, 9x12") oversized r/#1-4; intro. by Bendis 25.00
Nokgorka TPB (8/02, $24.95, 9x12") oversized r/#6-9; w/sketch pages 25.00
Wizard 1/2 (mail order) 10.00

RED STAR, THE (Volume 2)
CrossGen #1,2/Archangel Studios #3 on: Feb, 2003 - No. 5, July, 2004 ($2.95/$2.99)

1-5-Christian Gossett-s/a(p) 3.00
Prison of Souls TPB (8/04, $24.95, 9x12") oversized r/#1-5; w/sketch pages 25.00

RED STAR, THE: SWORD OF LIES
Archangel Studios: Aug, 2006 ($4.50)

Red Warrior #1 © MAR

Reload #1 © Ellis, Gulacy & Palmiotti

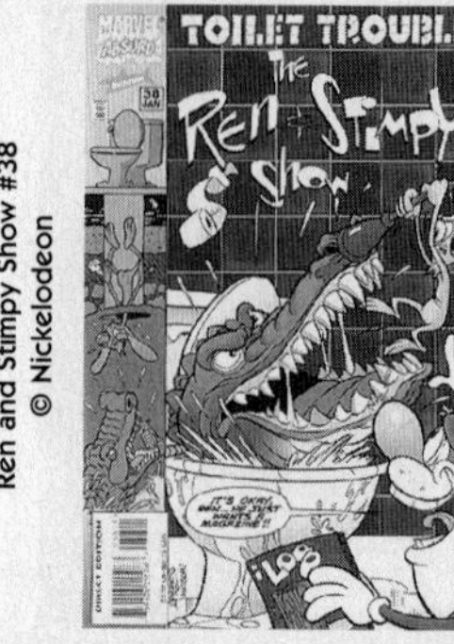

Ren and Stimpy Show #38 © Nickelodeon

	GD	VG	FN	VF	VF/NM	NM-
	2.0	4.0	6.0	8.0	9.0	9.2

1-Christian Gossett-s/a(p); origin of the Red Star team 4.50

RED TORNADO (See All-American #20 & Justice League of America #64)
DC Comics: July, 1985 - No. 4, Oct, 1985 (Limited series)

1-4: Kurt Busiek scripts in all. 1-3-Superman & Batman cameos 3.00

RED TORNADO
DC Comics: Nov, 2009 - No. 6, Apr, 2010 ($2.99, limited series)

1-6: 1-3-Benes-c. 5,6-Vixen app. 3.00
...: Family Reunion TPB (2010, $17.99) r/#1-6 18.00

RED WARRIOR
Marvel/Atlas Comics (TCI): Jan, 1951 - No. 6, Dec, 1951

	GD	VG	FN	VF	VF/NM	NM-
1-Red Warrior & his horse White Wing; Tuska-a	16	32	48	92	144	195
2-Tuska-c	10	20	30	56	76	95
3-6: 4-Origin White Wing. 6-Maneely-c	9	18	27	47	61	75

RED, WHITE & BLUE COMICS
DC Comics: 1941

nn - Ashcan comic, not distributed to newsstands, only for in-house use. Cover art is All-American Comics #20 with interior being Flash Comics #17 (no known sales)

RED WOLF (See Avengers #80 & Marvel Spotlight #1)
Marvel Comics Group: May, 1972 - No. 9, Sept, 1973

	GD	VG	FN	VF	VF/NM	NM-
1-(Western hero); Gil Kane/Severin-c; Shores-a	3	6	9	18	27	35
2-9: 2-Kane-c; Shores-a. 6-Tuska-r in back-up. 7-Red Wolf as super hero begins. 9-Origin sidekick, Lobo (wolf)	2	4	6	13	18	22

REESE'S PIECES
Eclipse Comics: Oct, 1985 - No.2, Oct, 1985 ($1.75, Baxter paper)

1,2-B&W-r in color 3.00

REFORM SCHOOL GIRL!
Realistic Comics: 1951

	GD	VG	FN	VF	VF/NM	NM-
nn-Used in **SOTI**, pg. 358, & cover ill. with caption "Comic books are supposed to be like fairy tales"; classic photo-c	459	918	1377	3350	5925	8500

(Prices vary widely on this book)

NOTE: *The cover and title originated from a digest-sized book published by Diversey Publishing Co. of Chicago in 1948. The original book "House of Fury", Doubleday, came out in 1941. The girl's real name which appears on the cover of the digest and comic is Marty Collins, Canadian model and ice skating star who posed for this special color photograph for the Diversey novel.*

REGENTS ILLUSTRATED CLASSICS
Prentice Hall Regents, Englewood Cliffs, NJ 07632: 1981 (Plus more recent reprintings) (48 pgs., B&W-a with 14 pgs. of teaching helps)

NOTE: *This series contains Classics Ill. art, and was produced from the same illegal source as* ***Cassette Books.*** *But when Twin Circle sued to stop the sale of the Cassette Books, they decided to permit this series to continue. This series was produced as a teaching aid. The 20 title series is divided into four levels based upon number of basic words used therein. There is also a teacher's manual for each level. All of the titles are still available from the publisher for about $5 each retail. The number to call for mail order purchases is (201)767-5937. Almost all of the issues have new covers taken from some interior art panel. Here is a list of the series by Regents ident. no. and the Classics Ill. counterpart.*

16770(CI#24-A2)18333(CI#3-A2)21668(CI#13-A2)32224(CI#21)33051(CI#26)35788(CI#84)37153(CI#16)44460(CI#19-A2)44808(CI#18-A2)52395(CI#4-A2)58627(CI#5-A2)60067(CI#30)68405(CI#23A1)70302(CI#29)78192(CI#7-A2)78193(CI#10-A2)79679(CI#85)92046(CI#1-A2)93062(CI#64)93512(CI#25)

RE: GEX
Awesome-Hyperwerks: Jul, 1998 - No. 0, Dec, 1998; ($2.50)

Preview (7/98) Wizard Con Edition 3.00
0-(12/98) Loeb-s/Liefeld-a/Pat Lee-c, 1-(9/98) Loeb-s/Liefeld-a/c 3.00

REGGIE (Formerly Archie's Rival...; Reggie & Me #19 on)
Archie Publications: No. 15, Sept, 1963 - No. 18, Nov, 1965

	GD	VG	FN	VF	VF/NM	NM-
15(9/63), 16(10/64), 17(8/65), 18(11/65)	5	10	15	32	51	70

NOTE: *Cover title No. 15 & 16 is Archie's Rival Reggie.*

REGGIE AND ME (Formerly Reggie)
Archie Publ.: No. 19, Aug, 1966 - No. 126, Sept, 1980 (No. 50-68: 52 pgs.)

	GD	VG	FN	VF	VF/NM	NM-
19-Evilheart app.	4	8	12	24	37	50
20-23-Evilheart app.; with Pureheart #22	3	6	9	20	30	40
24-40(3/70)	3	6	9	14	20	26
41-49(7/71)	2	4	6	11	16	20
50(9/71)-68 (1/74, 52 pgs.)	3	6	9	14	19	24
69-99	2	4	6	8	10	12
100(10/77)	2	4	6	9	12	15
101-126	1	2	3	5	7	9

REGGIE'S JOKES (See Reggie's Wise Guy Jokes)

REGGIE'S REVENGE!
Archie Comic Publications, Inc.: Spring, 1994 - No. 3 ($2.00, 52 pgs.) (Published semi-annually)

1-Bound-in pull-out poster 5.00
2,3 4.00

REGGIE'S WISE GUY JOKES
Archie Publications: Aug, 1968 - No. 55, 1980 (#5-28 are Giants)

	GD	VG	FN	VF	VF/NM	NM-
1	4	8	12	28	44	60
2-4	3	6	9	14	20	26
5-16 (1/71)(68 pg. Giants)	3	6	9	17	25	32
17-28 (52 pg. Giants)	2	4	6	13	18	22
29-40(1/77)	1	3	4	6	8	10
41-55	1	2	3	5	6	8

REGISTERED NURSE
Charlton Comics: Summer, 1963

	GD	VG	FN	VF	VF/NM	NM-
1-r/Nurse Betsy Crane & Cynthia Doyle	3	6	9	17	25	32

REG'LAR FELLERS
Visual Editions (Standard): No. 5, Nov, 1947 - No. 6, Mar, 1948

	GD	VG	FN	VF	VF/NM	NM-
5,6	9	18	27	47	61	75

REG'LAR FELLERS HEROIC (See Heroic Comics)

REID FLEMING, WORLD'S TOUGHEST MILKMAN
Eclipse Comics/ Deep Sea Comics: 1980; 8/86; V2#1, 12/86 - V2#3, 12/88; V2#4, 11/89; V2#5, 11/90 (B&W)

1-(1980, self-published) David Boswell-s/a 5.00
1-2nd, 4th & 5th printings ($2.50); (3rd print, large size, 8/86, $2.50) 3.00
V2#1 (10/86, regular size, $2.00), 1-2nd print, 3rd print ($2.00, 2/89) 3.00
2-8 , V2#2-2nd & 3rd printings, V2#4-2nd printing, V2#5 ($2.00) 3.00

REIGN IN HELL
DC Comics: Sept, 2008 - No. 8, Apr, 2009 ($3.50, limited series)

1-8-Neron, Shadowpact app.; Giffen-s; Dr. Occult back-up w/Segovia-a. 1-Two covers 3.50
TPB (2009, $19.99) r/#1-8 20.00

REIGN OF THE ZODIAC
DC Comics: Oct, 2003 - No. 8, May, 2004 ($2.75)

1-8: 1-6,8-Giffen-s/Doran-a/Harris-c. 7-Byrd-a 3.00

RELATIVE HEROES
DC Comics: Mar, 2000 - No. 6, Aug, 2000 ($2.50, limited series)

1-6-Grayson-s/Guichet & Sowd-a. 6-Superman-c/app. 3.00

RELOAD
DC Comics (Homage): May, 2003 - No. 3, Sept, 2003 ($2.95, limited series)

1-3-Warren Ellis-s/Paul Gulacy & Jimmy Palmiotti-a 3.00
.../Mek TPB (2004, $14.95, flip book) r/Reload #1-3 & Mek #1-3 15.00

RELUCTANT DRAGON, THE (Walt Disney's...)
Dell Publishing Co.: No. 13, 1940

	GD	VG	FN	VF	VF/NM	NM-
Four Color 13-Contains 2 pgs. of photos from film; 2 pg. foreword to Fantasia by Leopold Stokowski; Donald Duck, Goofy, Baby Weems & Mickey Mouse (as the Sorcerer's Apprentice) app.	219	438	657	1402	2401	3400

REMAINS
IDW Publishing: May, 2004 - No. 5, Sept, 2004 ($3.99)

1-5-Steve Niles-s/Kieron Dwyer-a 4.00

REMARKABLE WORLDS OF PROFESSOR PHINEAS B. FUDDLE, THE
DC Comics (Paradox Press): 2000 - No. 4, 2000 ($5.95, limited series)

1-4-Boaz Yakin-s/Erez Yakin-a 6.00
TPB (2001, $19.95) r/series 20.00

REMEMBER PEARL HARBOR
Street & Smith Publications: 1942 (68 pgs.) (Illustrated story of the battle)

	GD	VG	FN	VF	VF/NM	NM-
nn-Uncle Sam-c; Jack Binder-a	50	100	150	315	533	750

REN & STIMPY SHOW, THE (TV) (Nickolodeon cartoon characters)
Marvel Comics: Dec, 1992 - No. 44, July, 1996 ($1.75/$1.95)

	GD	VG	FN	VF	VF/NM	NM-
1-($2.25)-Polybagged w/scratch & sniff Ren or Stimpy air fowler (equal numbers of each were made)	1	2	3	5	6	8

1-2nd & 3rd printing; different dialogue on-c 3.00
2-6: 4-Muddy Mudskipper back-up. 5-Bill Wray painted-c. 6-Spider-Man vs. Powdered Toast Man 4.00
7-17: 12-1st solo back-up story w/Tank & Brenner 3.00
18-44: 18-Powered Toast Man app. 3.00
25 ($2.95) Deluxe edition w/die cut cover 4.00
...Don't Try This at Home (3/94, $12.95, TPB)-r/#9-12 13.00

Rescue #1 © MAR

Resurrection Man #16 © DC

Return of the Gremlins #2 © DIS

GD VG FN VF VF/NM NM-
2.0 4.0 6.0 8.0 9.0 9.2

...Eenteractive Special ('95, $2.95) 4.00
...Holiday Special 1994 (2/95, $2.95, 52 pgs.) 4.00
...Mini Comic (1995) 5.00
...Pick of the Litter nn (1993, $12.95, TPB)-r/#1-4 13.00
...Radio Daze (11/95, $1.95) 3.00
...Running Joke nn (1993, $12.95, TPB)-r/#1-4 plus new-a 13.00
...Seeck Little Monkeys (1/95, $12.95)-r/#17-20 13.00
...Special 2 (7/94, $2.95, 52 pgs.), ...Special 3 (10/94, $2.95, 52 pgs.)-Choose adventure, ...Special: Around the World in a Daze ($2.95), ...Special: Four Swerks (1/95, $2.95, 52 pgs.)-FF #1 cover swipe; cover reads "Four Swerks w/5 pg. coloring book.", ...Special: Powdered Toast Man 1 (4/94, $2.95, 52 pgs.), ...Special: Powdered Toast Man's Cereal Serial (4/95, $2.95), ...Special: Sports (10/95, $2.95) 4.00
...Tastes Like Chicken nn (11/93,$12.95,TPB)-r/#5-8 13.00
...Your Pals (1994, $12.95, TPB)-r/#13-16 13.00

RENFIELD
Caliber Press:1994 - No. 3, 1995 ($2.95, B&W, limited series)

1-3 3.00

RENO BROWNE, HOLLYWOOD'S GREATEST COWGIRL (Formerly Margie Comics; Apache Kid #53 on; also see Western Hearts, Western Life Romances & Western Love)
Marvel Comics (MPC): No. 50, April, 1950 - No. 52, Sept, 1950 (52 pgs.)

50-Reno Browne photo-c on all 29 58 87 170 278 385
51,52 24 48 72 142 234 325

REPLACEMENT GOD
Amaze Ink: June, 1995 - No. 8 ($2.95, B&W)

1-8-Zander Cannon-s/a 3.00

REPLACEMENT GOD
Image Comics: May, 1997 - No. 5 ($2.95, B&W)

1-5: 1-Flip book w/"Knute's Escapes", r/original series. 2-Flip book w/"Harris Thermidor". 3-5: 3-Flip book w/"Myth and Legend" 3.00

REPTILICUS (Becomes Reptisaurus #3 on)
Charlton Comics: Aug, 1961 - No. 2, Oct, 1961

1 (Movie) 20 40 60 140 283 425
2 11 22 33 75 138 200

REPTISAURUS (Reptilicus #1,2)
Charlton Comics: V2#3, Jan, 1962 - No. 8, Dec, 1962; Summer, 1963

V2#3-8: 3-Flying saucer-c/s. 8-Montes/Bache-c/a 6 12 18 41 66 90
Special Edition 1 (Summer, 1963) 6 12 18 39 62 85

REQUIEM FOR DRACULA
Marvel Comics: Feb, 1993 ($2.00, 52 pgs.)

nn-r/Tomb of Dracula #69,70 by Gene Colan 4.00

RESCUE (Pepper Potts in Iron Man armor)
Marvel Comics: July, 2010 ($3.99, one-shot)

1-DeConnick-s/Mutti-a/Foreman-c 4.00

RESCUERS, THE (See Walt Disney Showcase #40)

RESIDENT EVIL (Based on video game)
Image Comics (WildStorm): Mar, 1998 - No. 5 ($4.95, quarterly magazine)

1 7.00
2-5 5.00
...Code: Veronica 1-4 (2002, $14.95) English reprint of Japanese comics 15.00
...Collection One ('99, $14.95, TPB) r/#1-4 15.00

RESIDENT EVIL (Volume 2)
DC Comics (WildStorm): May, 2009 - No. 6, Feb, 2011 ($3.99)

1-6: 1,2-Liam Sharpe-a. 1-Two covers 4.00

RESIDENT EVIL: FIRE AND ICE
DC Comics (WildStorm): Dec, 2000 - No. 4, May, 2001 ($2.50, limited series)

1-4-Bermejo-c 3.00
TPB (2009, $24.99) r/#1-4 plus short stories from Resident Evil magazine 25.00

RESISTANCE (Based on the video game)
DC Comics (WildStorm): Early Mar, 2009 - No. 6, Jul, 2009 ($3.99, limited series)

1-6-Ramón Pérez-a/C.P. Smith-c 4.00
TPB (2010, $19.99) r/#1-6 20.00

RESISTANCE, THE
DC Comics (WildStorm): Nov, 2002 - No. 8, June, 2003 ($2.95)

1-8-Palmiotti & Gray-s/Santacruz-a 3.00

REST (Milo Ventimiglia Presents...)

GD VG FN VF VF/NM NM-
2.0 4.0 6.0 8.0 9.0 9.2

Devil's Due Publ.: No. 0, Aug, 2008 - Present (99¢/$3.50)

0-(99¢) Prelude to series; Powers-s/McManus-a 3.00
1,2-($3.50) 1-Two covers (Tim Sale art & Milo Ventimiglia photo) 3.50

RESTAURANT AT THE END OF THE UNIVERSE, THE (See Hitchhiker's Guide to the Galaxy & Life, the Universe & Everything)
DC Comics: 1994 - No. 3, 1994 ($6.95, limited series)

1-3 7.00

RESTLESS GUN (TV)
Dell Publishing Co.: No. 934, Sept, 1958 - No. 1146, Nov-Jan, 1960-61

Four Color 934 (#1)-Photo-c 10 20 30 70 125 180
Four Color 986 (5/59), 1045 (11-1/60), 1089 (3/60), 1146-Wildey-a; all photo-c 8 16 24 52 86 120

RESURRECTION MAN
DC Comics: May, 1997 - No. 27, Aug, 1999 ($2.50)

1-Lenticular disc on cover 5.00
2-5: 2-JLA app. 4.00
6-10: 6-Genesis-x-over. 7-Batman app. 10-Hitman-c/app. 3.00
11-27: 16,17-Supergirl x-over. 18-Deadman & Phantom Stranger-c/app. 21-JLA-c/app. 3.00
#1,000,000 (11/98) 853rd Century x-over 3.00

RETIEF (Keith Laumer's)
Adventure Comics (Malibu): Dec, 1989 - Vol. 2, No.6, ($2.25, B&W)

1-6,Vol. 2, #1-6,Vol. 3 (...of The CDT) #1-6 3.00
...and The Warlords #1-6, ...: Diplomatic Immunity #1 (4/91), ...: Giant Killer #1 (9/91), ...: Crime & Punishment #1 (11/91) 3.00

RETURN FROM WITCH MOUNTAIN (See Walt Disney Showcase #44)

RETURN OF ALISON DARE: LITTLE MISS ADVENTURES, THE (Also see Alison Dare: Little Miss Adventures)
Oni Press: Apr, 2001 - No. 3, Sept, 2001 ($2.95, B&W, limited series)

1-3-J. Torres-s/J.Bone-c/a 3.00

RETURN OF GORGO, THE (Formerly Gorgo's Revenge)
Charlton Comics: No. 2, Aug, 1963; No. 3, Fall, 1964 (12¢)

2,3-Ditko-c/a; based on M.G.M. movie 8 16 24 58 97 135

RETURN OF KONGA, THE (Konga's Revenge #2 on)
Charlton Comics: 1962

nn 8 16 24 58 97 135

RETURN OF MEGATON MAN
Kitchen Sink Press: July, 1988 - No. 3, 1988 ($2.00, limited series)

1-3: Simpson-c/a 3.00

RETURN OF THE GREMLINS (The Roald Dahl characters)
Dark Horse Comics: Mar, 2008 - No. 3, May, 2008 ($2.99, limited series)

1-3-Richardson-s/Yeagle-a. 1-Back-up reprint of intro. from 1943. 2-Back-up reprints of three Gremlin Gus 2-pagers from 1943. 3-Back-up reprints 3.00

RETURN OF THE OUTLAW
Toby Press (Minoan): Feb, 1953 - No. 11, 1955

1-Billy the Kid 10 20 30 54 72 90
2 7 14 21 35 43 50
3-11 6 12 18 31 38 45

RETURN TO JURASSIC PARK
Topps Comics: Apr, 1995 - No. 9, Feb, 1996 ($2.50/$2.95)

1-9: 3-Begin $2.95-c. 9-Artist's Jam issue 3.00

RETURN TO THE AMALGAM AGE OF COMICS: THE MARVEL COMICS COLLECTION
Marvel Comics: 1997 ($12.95, TPB)

nn-Reprints Amalgam one-shots: Challengers of the Fantastic #1, The Exciting X-Patrol #1, Iron Lantern #1, The Magnetic Men Featuring Magneto #1, Spider-Boy Team-Up #1 & Thorion of the New Asgods #1 13.00

REVEAL
Dark Horse Comics: Nov, 2002 ($6.95, squarebound)

1-Short stories of Dark Horse characters by various; Lone Wolf 2100, Buffy, Spyboy app. 7.00

REVEALING LOVE STORIES (See Fox Giants)

REVEALING ROMANCES
Ace Magazines: Sept, 1949 - No. 6, Aug, 1950

1 15 30 45 84 127 170
2 9 18 27 52 69 85
3-6 9 18 27 47 61 75

Rex Allen Comics #10 © DELL

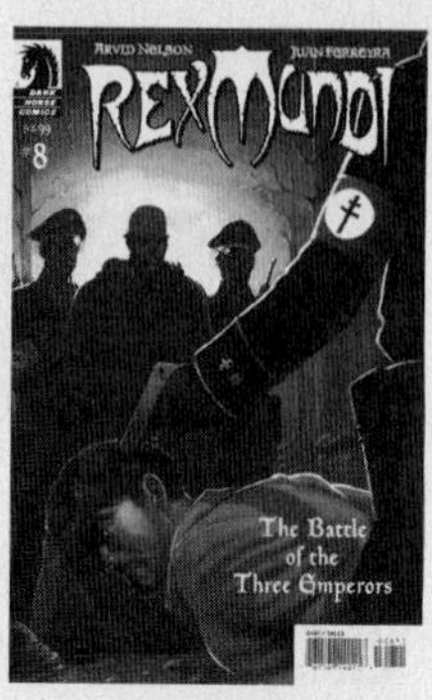

Rex Mundi V2 #8 © Arvid Nelson

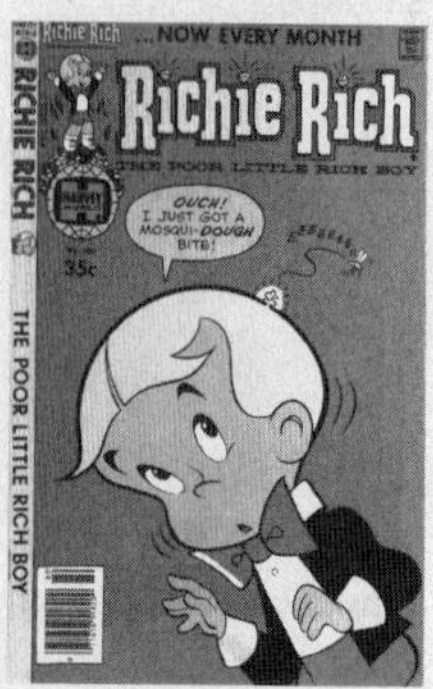

Richie Rich #180 © HARV

	GD 2.0	VG 4.0	FN 6.0	VF 8.0	VF/NM 9.0	NM- 9.2

REVELATIONS
Dark Horse Comics: Aug, 2005 - No. 6, Jan, 2006 ($2.99, limited series)

1-6-Paul Jenkins-s/Humberto Ramos-a/c 3.00

REVENGE OF THE PROWLER (Also see The Prowler)
Eclipse Comics: Feb, 1988 - No. 4, June, 1988 ($1.75/$1.95)

1,3,4: 1-$1.75. 3,4-$1.95-c; Snyder III-a(p) 3.00
2 ($2.50)-Contains flexi-disc 4.00

REVOLUTION ON THE PLANET OF THE APES
Mr. Comics: Dec, 2005 - No. 6, Aug, 2006 ($3.95)

1-6: 1,2-Salgood Sam-a 4.00

REX ALLEN COMICS (Movie star)(Also see Four Color #877 & Western Roundup under Dell Giants)
Dell Publ. Co.: No. 316, Feb, 1951 - No. 31, Dec-Feb, 1958-59 (All-photo-c)

	GD	VG	FN	VF	VF/NM	NM-
Four Color 316(#1)(52 pgs.)-Rex Allen & his horse Koko begin; Marsh-a	13	26	39	92	179	265
2 (9-11/51, 36 pgs.)	9	18	27	63	107	150
3-10	7	14	21	45	73	100
11-20	6	12	18	39	62	85
21-23,25-31	5	10	15	35	55	75
24-Toth-a	6	12	18	39	62	85

NOTE: ***Manning** a-20, 27-30. Photo back-c F.C. #316, 2-12, 20, 21.*

REX DEXTER OF MARS (See Mystery Men Comics)
Fox Features Syndicate: Fall, 1940 (68 pgs.)

	GD	VG	FN	VF	VF/NM	NM-
1-Rex Dexter, Patty O'Day, & Zanzibar (Tuska-a) app.; Briefer-c/a	200	400	600	1280	2190	3100

REX HART (Formerly Blaze Carson; Whip Wilson #9 on)
Timely/Marvel Comics (USA): No. 6, Aug, 1949 - No. 8, Feb, 1950 (All photo-c)

	GD	VG	FN	VF	VF/NM	NM-
6-Rex Hart & his horse Warrior begin; Black Rider app; Captain Tootsie by Beck	26	52	78	152	249	345
7,8: 18 pg. Thriller in each. 8-Blaze the Wonder Collie app. in text	18	36	54	103	162	220

REX MORGAN, M.D. (Also see Harvey Comics Library)
Argo Publ.: Dec, 1955 - No. 3, Apr?, 1956

	GD	VG	FN	VF	VF/NM	NM-
1-r/Rex Morgan daily newspaper strips & daily panel-r of "These Women" by D'Alessio & "Timeout" by Jeff Keate	14	28	42	76	108	140
2,3	10	20	30	54	72	90

REX MUNDI (Latin for "King of the World")
Image Comics: No. 0, Aug, 2002 - No. 18, Apr, 2006 ($2.95/$2.99)

0-18-Arvid Nelson-s. 0-13-Eric Johnson-a. 14,15-Jim DiBartolo-a. 18-Ramos-c 3.00
Vol. 1: The Guardian of the Temple TPB (1/04, $14.95) r/#0-5 15.00
Book 1: The Guardian of the Temple TPB (Dark Horse, 11/06, $16.95) r/#0-5 & Brother Matthew web comic; Dysart intro. 17.00
Vol. 2: The River Underground TPB (4/05, $14.95) r/#6-11 15.00
Book 2: The River Underground (Dark Horse, 2006, $16.95) r/#6-11 17.00
Vol. 3: The Lost Kings TPB (Dark Horse, 9/06, $16.95) r/#12-17 17.00
Book Four: Crowd and Sword TPB (Dark Horse, 12/07, $16.95) r/#18 plus V2 #1-5 and story from Dark Horse Book of Monsters 17.00

REX MUNDI (Volume 2)
Dark Horse Comics: July, 2006 - No. 19, Aug, 2009 ($2.99)

1-19-Arvid Nelson-s. 1-JH Williams-c. 16-Chen-c. 18-Linsner-c 3.00
Book Five: The Valley at the End of the World TPB (11/08, $17.95) r/#6-12 18.00

REX THE WONDER DOG (See The Adventures of...)

RHUBARB, THE MILLIONAIRE CAT
Dell Publishing Co.: No. 423, Sept-Oct, 1952 - No. 563, June, 1954

	GD	VG	FN	VF	VF/NM	NM-
Four Color 423 (#1)	6	12	18	39	62	85
Four Color 466(5/53),563	5	10	15	34	55	75

RIB
Dilemma Productions: Oct, 1995 - April, 1996 ($1.95, B&W)

Ashcan, 1 3.00

RIB
Bookmark Productions: 1996 ($2.95, B&W)

1-Sakai-c; Andrew Ford-s/a 3.00

RIB
Caliber Comics: May, 1997 - No. 5, 1998 ($2.95, B&W)

1-5: 1-"Beginnings" pts. 1 & 2 3.00

RIBIT! (Red Sonja imitation)
Comico: Jan, 1989 - No. 4, April?, 1989 ($1.95, limited series)

1-4: Frank Thorne-c/a/scripts 3.00

RIBTICKLER (Also see Fox Giants)
Fox Feature Synd./Green Publ. (1957)/Norlen (1959): 1945, No. 2, 1946, No. 3, Jul-Aug, 1946 - No. 9, Jul-Aug, 1947; 1957; 1959

	GD	VG	FN	VF	VF/NM	NM-
1-Funny animal	15	30	45	90	140	190
2-(1946)	10	20	30	54	72	90
3-9: 3,5,7-Cosmo Cat app.	9	18	27	47	61	75
3,7,8 (Green Publ.-1957), 3,7,8 (Norlen Mag.-1959)	3	6	9	16	23	30

RICHARD DRAGON
DC Comics: July, 2004 - No. 12, Jun, 2005 ($2.50)

1-12: 1-Dixon-s/McDaniel-a/c; Ben Turner app. 2,3-Nightwing app. 4-6,11,12-Lady Shiva 2.50

RICHARD DRAGON, KUNG-FU FIGHTER (See The Batman Chronicles #5, Brave & the Bold, & The Question)
National Periodical Publ./DC Comics: Apr-May, 1975 - No. 18, Nov-Dec, 1977

	GD	VG	FN	VF	VF/NM	NM-
1-Intro Richard Dragon, Ben Stanley & O-Sensei; 1st app. Barney Ling; adaptation of Jim Dennis novel "Dragon's Fists" begins, ends #4	3	6	9	14	20	26
2,3: 2-Intro Carolyn Woosan; Starlin/Weiss-c/a; bondage-c. 3-Kirby-a(p); Giordano bondage-c	2	4	6	9	12	15
4-8-Wood inks. 4-Carolyn Woosan dies. 5-1st app. Lady Shiva	2	4	6	8	10	12
9-13,15-18: 9-Ben Stanley becomes Ben Turner; intro Preying Mantis. 16-1st app. Prof Ojo. 18-1st app. Ben Turner as The Bronze Tiger	1	3	4	6	8	10
14-"Spirit of Bruce Lee"	3	6	9	14	20	26

NOTE: ***Buckler** a-14. c-15, 18. **Chua** c-13. **Estrada** a-9, 13-18. **Estrada/Abel** a-10-12. **Estrada/Wood** a-4-8. **Giordano** c-1, 3-11. **Weiss** a-2(partial) c-2i.*

RICHARD THE LION-HEARTED (See Ideal a Classical Comic)

RICHIE RICH (See Harvey Collectors Comics, Harvey Hits, Little Dot, Little Lotta, Little Sad Sack, Million Dollar Digest, Mutt & Jeff, Super Richie & 3-D Dolly; also Tastee-Freez Comics in the Promotional Comics section)

RICHIE RICH (...the Poor Little Rich Boy) (See Harvey Hits #3, 9)
Harvey Publ.: Nov, 1960 - #218, Oct, 1982; #219, Oct, 1986 - #254, Jan, 1991

	GD	VG	FN	VF	VF/NM	NM-
1-(See Little Dot #1 for 1st app.)	241	482	723	2109	4305	6500
2	71	142	213	604	1227	1850
3-5	45	90	135	360	730	1100
6-10: 8-Christmas-c	27	54	81	197	399	600
11-20	17	34	51	122	249	375
21-30	12	24	36	87	164	240
31-40	10	20	30	70	125	180
41-50: 42(2/66)-X-mas-c	8	16	24	58	97	135
51-55,57-60: 59-Buck, prototype of Dollar the Dog	6	12	18	41	66	90
56-1st app. Super Richie	7	14	21	49	80	110
61-64,66-80: 71-Nixon & Robert Kennedy caricatures; outer space-c	5	10	15	30	48	65
65-Buck the Dog (Dollar prototype) on cover	6	12	18	43	69	95
81-99	4	8	12	22	34	45
100(12/70)-1st app. Irona the robot maid	4	8	12	26	41	55
101-111,117-120	3	6	9	14	20	26
112-116: All 52 pg. Giants	3	6	9	17	25	32
121-140: 137-1st app. Mr. Cheepers and Professor Keenbean	2	4	6	9	13	16
141-160: 145-Infinity-c. 155-3rd app. The Money Monster	2	4	6	8	10	12
161-180	1	3	4	6	8	10
181-199	1	2	3	5	6	8
200	1	3	4	6	8	10
201-218: 210-Stone-Age Riches app	1	2	3	4	5	7
219-254: 237-Last original material						6.00

Harvey Comics Classics Vol. 2 TPB (Dark Horse Books, 10/07, $19.95) Reprints Richie Rich's early appearances in this title, Little Dot and Richie Rich Success Stories, mostly B&W with some color stories; history and interview with Ernie Colón 20.00

RICHIE RICH
Harvey Comics: Mar, 1991 - No. 28, Nov, 1994 ($1.00, bi-monthly)

1-28: Reprints best of Richie Rich 3.00
Giant Size 1-4 (10/91-10/93, $2.25, 68 pgs.) 4.00

RICHIE RICH ADVENTURE DIGEST MAGAZINE
Harvey Comics: 1992 - No. 7, Sept, 1994 ($1.25, quarterly, digest-size)

1-7 4.00

RICHIE RICH AND...
Harvey Comics: Oct, 1987 - No. 11, May, 1990 ($1.00)

Richie Rich and Cadbury #24 © HARV

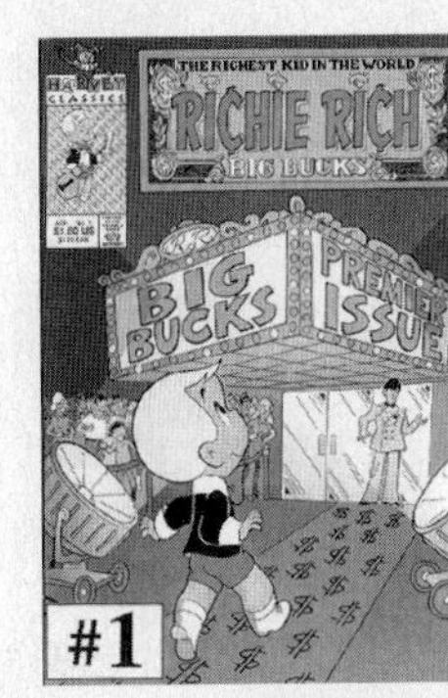

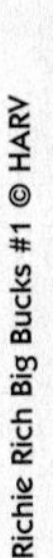

Richie Rich Big Bucks #1 © HARV

Richie Rich Dollars and Cents #5 © HARV

	GD 2.0	VG 4.0	FN 6.0	VF 8.0	VF/NM 9.0	NM- 9.2
1-Professor Keenbean						4.00
2-11: 2-Casper. 3-Dollar the Dog. 4-Cadbury. 5 Mayda Munny. 6-Irona. 7-Little Dot. 8-Professor Keenbean. 9-Little Audrey. 10-Mayda Munny. 11-Cadbury						3.00

RICHIE RICH AND BILLY BELLHOPS
Harvey Publications: Oct, 1977 (52 pgs., one-shot)

	GD 2.0	VG 4.0	FN 6.0	VF 8.0	VF/NM 9.0	NM- 9.2
1	2	4	6	11	16	20

RICHIE RICH AND CADBURY
Harvey Publ.: 10/77; #2, 9/78 - #23, 7/82; #24, 7/90 - #29, 1/91 (1-10: 52pgs.)

	GD 2.0	VG 4.0	FN 6.0	VF 8.0	VF/NM 9.0	NM- 9.2
1-(52 pg. Giant)	2	4	6	11	16	20
2-10-(52 pg. Giant)	2	4	6	8	10	12
11-23						6.00
24-29: 24-Begin $1.00-c						4.00

RICHIE RICH AND CASPER
Harvey Publications: Aug, 1974 - No. 45, Sept, 1982

	GD 2.0	VG 4.0	FN 6.0	VF 8.0	VF/NM 9.0	NM- 9.2
1	3	6	9	20	30	40
2-5	2	4	6	13	18	22
6-10: 10-Xmas-c	2	4	6	9	13	16
11-20	1	3	4	6	8	10
21-45: 22-Xmas-c						6.00

RICHIE RICH AND DOLLAR THE DOG (See Richie Rich #65)
Harvey Publications: Sept, 1977 - No. 24, Aug, 1982 (#1-10: 52 pgs.)

	GD 2.0	VG 4.0	FN 6.0	VF 8.0	VF/NM 9.0	NM- 9.2
1-(52 pg. Giant)	2	4	6	11	16	20
2-10-(52 pg. Giant)	2	4	6	8	10	12
11-24						6.00

RICHIE RICH AND DOT
Harvey Publications: Oct, 1974 (one-shot)

	GD 2.0	VG 4.0	FN 6.0	VF 8.0	VF/NM 9.0	NM- 9.2
1	3	6	9	16	22	28

RICHIE RICH AND GLORIA
Harvey Publications: Sept, 1977 - No. 25, Sept, 1982 (#1-11: 52 pgs.)

	GD 2.0	VG 4.0	FN 6.0	VF 8.0	VF/NM 9.0	NM- 9.2
1-(52 pg. Giant)	2	4	6	11	16	20
2-11-(52 pg. Giant)	2	4	6	8	10	12
12-25						6.00

RICHIE RICH AND HIS GIRLFRIENDS
Harvey Publications: April, 1979 - No. 16, Dec, 1982

	GD 2.0	VG 4.0	FN 6.0	VF 8.0	VF/NM 9.0	NM- 9.2
1-(52 pg. Giant)	2	4	6	9	13	16
2-(52 pg. Giant)	1	3	4	6	8	10
3-10	1	2	3	5	6	8
11-16						6.00

RICHIE RICH AND HIS MEAN COUSIN REGGIE
Harvey Publications: April, 1979 - No. 3, 1980 (50¢) (#1,2: 52 pgs.)

	GD 2.0	VG 4.0	FN 6.0	VF 8.0	VF/NM 9.0	NM- 9.2
1	2	4	6	9	13	16
2-3:	1	3	4	6	8	10

NOTE: *No. 4 was advertised, but never released.*

RICHIE RICH AND JACKIE JOKERS (Also see Jackie Jokers)
Harvey Publications: Nov, 1973 - No. 48, Dec, 1982

	GD 2.0	VG 4.0	FN 6.0	VF 8.0	VF/NM 9.0	NM- 9.2
1: 52 pg. Giant; contains material from unpublished Jackie Jokers #5	4	8	12	24	37	50
2,3-(52 pg. Giants). 2-R.R. & Jackie 1st meet	3	6	9	16	22	28
4,5	2	4	6	13	18	22
6-10	2	4	6	9	13	16
11-20,26: 11-1st app. Kool Katz. 26-Star Wars parody	1	3	4	6	8	10
21-25,27-40	1	2	3	4	5	7
41-48						6.00

RICHIE RICH AND PROFESSOR KEENBEAN
Harvey Comics: Sept, 1990 - No. 2, Nov, 1990 ($1.00)

	GD 2.0	VG 4.0	FN 6.0	VF 8.0	VF/NM 9.0	NM- 9.2
1,2						3.00

RICHIE RICH AND THE NEW KIDS ON THE BLOCK
Harvey Publications: Feb, 1991 - No. 3, June, 1991 ($1.25, bi-monthly)

	GD 2.0	VG 4.0	FN 6.0	VF 8.0	VF/NM 9.0	NM- 9.2
1-3: 1,2-New Richie Rich stories						3.00

RICHIE RICH AND TIMMY TIME
Harvey Publications: Sept, 1977 (50¢, 52 pgs, one-shot)

	GD 2.0	VG 4.0	FN 6.0	VF 8.0	VF/NM 9.0	NM- 9.2
1	2	4	6	11	16	20

RICHIE RICH BANK BOOK
Harvey Publications: Oct, 1972 - No. 59, Sept, 1982

	GD 2.0	VG 4.0	FN 6.0	VF 8.0	VF/NM 9.0	NM- 9.2
1	5	10	15	30	48	65
2-5: 2-2nd app. The Money Monster	3	6	9	16	23	30
6-10	2	4	6	11	16	20
11-20: 18-Super Richie app.	2	4	6	8	10	12
21-30	1	2	3	5	7	9
31-40	1	2	3	4	5	7
41-59						6.00

RICHIE RICH BEST OF THE YEARS
Harvey Publications: Oct, 1977 - No. 6, June, 1980 (128 pgs., digest-size)

	GD 2.0	VG 4.0	FN 6.0	VF 8.0	VF/NM 9.0	NM- 9.2
1(10/77)-Reprints	2	4	6	9	12	15
2-6(11/79-6/80, 95¢). #2(10/78)-Rep.. #3(6/79, 75¢)	1	2	3	5	7	9

RICHIE RICH BIG BOOK
Harvey Publications: Nov, 1992 - No. 2, May, 1993 ($1.50, 52 pgs.)

	GD 2.0	VG 4.0	FN 6.0	VF 8.0	VF/NM 9.0	NM- 9.2
1,2						4.00

RICHIE RICH BIG BUCKS
Harvey Publications: Apr, 1991 - No. 8, July, 1992 ($1.00, bi-monthly)

	GD 2.0	VG 4.0	FN 6.0	VF 8.0	VF/NM 9.0	NM- 9.2
1-8						3.00

RICHIE RICH BILLIONS
Harvey Publications: Oct, 1974 - No. 48, Oct, 1982 (#1-33: 52 pgs.)

	GD 2.0	VG 4.0	FN 6.0	VF 8.0	VF/NM 9.0	NM- 9.2
1	4	8	12	22	34	45
2-5: 2-Christmas issue	3	6	9	14	20	25
6-10	2	4	6	10	14	18
11-20	2	4	6	8	10	12
21-33	1	2	3	5	6	8
34-48: 35-Onion app.						6.00

RICHIE RICH CASH
Harvey Publications: Sept, 1974 - No. 47, Aug, 1982

	GD 2.0	VG 4.0	FN 6.0	VF 8.0	VF/NM 9.0	NM- 9.2
1-1st app. Dr. N-R-Gee	3	6	9	20	30	40
2-5	2	4	6	13	18	22
6-10	2	4	6	9	13	16
11-20	1	3	4	6	8	10
21-30	1	2	3	4	5	7
31-47: 33-Dr. Blemish app.						6.00

RICHIE RICH CASH MONEY
Harvey Comics: May, 1992 - No. 2, Aug, 1992 ($1.25)

	GD 2.0	VG 4.0	FN 6.0	VF 8.0	VF/NM 9.0	NM- 9.2
1,2						3.00

RICHIE RICH, CASPER AND WENDY - NATIONAL LEAGUE
Harvey Comics: June, 1976 (50¢)

	GD 2.0	VG 4.0	FN 6.0	VF 8.0	VF/NM 9.0	NM- 9.2
1-Newsstand version of the baseball giveaway	2	4	6	13	18	22

RICHIE RICH COLLECTORS COMICS (See Harvey Collectors Comics)

RICHIE RICH DIAMONDS
Harvey Publications: Aug, 1972 - No. 59, Aug, 1982 (#1, 23-45: 52 pgs.)

	GD 2.0	VG 4.0	FN 6.0	VF 8.0	VF/NM 9.0	NM- 9.2
1-(52 pg. Giant)	5	10	15	32	51	70
2-5	3	6	9	16	23	30
6-10	2	4	6	11	16	20
11-22	2	4	6	8	10	12
23-30-(52 pg. Giants)	2	4	6	8	11	14
31-45: 39-r/Origin Little Dot	1	2	3	5	7	9
46-50	1	2	3	4	5	7
51-59						6.00

RICHIE RICH DIGEST
Harvey Publications: Oct, 1986 - No. 42, Oct, 1994 ($1.25/$1.75, digest-size)

	GD 2.0	VG 4.0	FN 6.0	VF 8.0	VF/NM 9.0	NM- 9.2
1	1	2	3	5	6	8
2-10						5.00
11-20						4.00
21-42						4.00

RICHIE RICH DIGEST STORIES (...Magazine #?-on)
Harvey Publications: Oct, 1977 - No., 17, Oct, 1982 (75¢/95¢, digest-size)

	GD 2.0	VG 4.0	FN 6.0	VF 8.0	VF/NM 9.0	NM- 9.2
1-Reprints	2	4	6	9	12	15
2-10: Reprints	1	2	3	5	7	9
11-17: Reprints						6.00

RICHIE RICH DIGEST WINNERS
Harvey Publications: Dec, 1977 - No. 16, Sept, 1982 (75¢/95¢, 132 pgs., digest-size)

	GD 2.0	VG 4.0	FN 6.0	VF 8.0	VF/NM 9.0	NM- 9.2
1	2	4	6	9	12	15
2-5	1	2	3	5	7	9
6-16						6.00

RICHIE RICH DOLLARS & CENTS
Harvey Publications: Aug, 1963 - No. 109, Aug, 1982 (#1-43: 68 pgs.; 44-60, 71-94: 52 pgs.)

Richie Rich Fortunes #26 © HARV

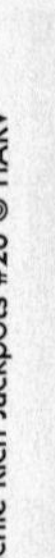
Richie Rich Jackpots #20 © HARV

Richie Rich Success Stories #66 © HARV

	GD 2.0	VG 4.0	FN 6.0	VF 8.0	VF/NM 9.0	NM- 9.2
1: (#1-64 are all reprint issues)	17	34	51	118	242	365
2	10	20	30	70	125	180
3-5: 5-r/1st app. of R.R. from Little Dot #1	9	18	27	63	107	150
6-10	7	14	21	47	76	105
11-20	5	10	15	30	48	65
21-30: 25-r/1st app. Nurse Jenny (Little Lotta #62)	4	8	12	22	34	45
31-43: 43-Last 68 pg. issue	3	6	9	18	27	35
44-60: All 52 pgs.	3	6	9	14	19	25
61-71	1	3	4	6	8	10
72-94: All 52 pgs.	2	4	6	8	10	12
95-99,101-109						6.00
100-Anniversary issue	1	2	3	5	7	9
RICHIE RICH FORTUNES						
Harvey Publications: Sept, 1971 - No. 63, July, 1982 (#1-15: 52 pgs.)						
1	6	12	18	39	62	85
2-5	3	6	9	20	30	40
6-10	2	4	6	13	18	22
11-15: 11-r/1st app. The Onion	2	4	6	9	12	15
16-30	1	2	3	5	7	9
31-40	1	2	3	4	5	7
41-63: 62-Onion app.						6.00
RICHIE RICH GEMS						
Harvey Publications: Sept, 1974 - No. 43, Sept, 1982						
1	3	6	9	20	30	40
2-5	2	4	6	13	18	22
6-10	2	4	6	9	13	16
11-20	1	3	4	6	8	10
21-30	1	2	3	4	5	7
31-43: 36-Dr. Blemish, Onion app. 38-1st app. Stone-Age Riches						6.00
RICHIE RICH GOLD AND SILVER						
Harvey Publications: Sept, 1975 - No. 42, Oct, 1982 (#1-27: 52 pgs.)						
1	3	6	9	18	27	35
2-5	2	4	6	11	16	20
6-10	2	4	6	8	11	14
11-27	1	2	3	5	7	9
28-42: 34-Stone-Age Riches app.						6.00
RICHIE RICH GOLD NUGGETS DIGEST						
Harvey Publications: Dec., 1990 - No. 4, June, 1991 ($1.75, digest-size)						
1-4						3.00
RICHIE RICH HOLIDAY DIGEST MAGAZINE (...Digest #4)						
Harvey Publications: Jan, 1980 - #3, Jan, 1982; #4, 3/88; #5, 2/89 (annual)						
1-X-Mas-c	1	3	4	6	8	10
2-5: 2,3: All X-Mas-c. 4-(3/88, $1.25), 5-(2/89, $1.75)	1	2	3	4	5	7
RICHIE RICH INVENTIONS						
Harvey Publications: Oct, 1977 - No. 26, Oct, 1982 (#1-11: 52 pgs.)						
1	2	4	6	11	16	20
2-5	2	4	6	8	10	12
6-11	1	2	3	5	6	8
12-26						6.00
RICHIE RICH JACKPOTS						
Harvey Publications: Oct, 1972 - No. 58, Aug, 1982 (#41-43: 52 pgs.)						
1-Debut of Cousin Jackpots	5	10	15	30	48	65
2-5	3	6	9	16	23	30
6-10	2	4	6	11	16	20
11-15,17-20	2	4	6	8	10	12
16-Super Richie app.	2	4	6	9	12	15
21-30	1	2	3	5	7	9
31-40,44-50: 37-Caricatures of Frank Sinatra, Dean Martin, Sammy Davis, Jr. 45-Dr. Blemish app.	1	2	3	4	5	7
41-43 (52 pgs.)	1	3	4	6	8	10
51-58						6.00
RICHIE RICH MILLION DOLLAR DIGEST (...Magazine #?-on)(See Million Dollar Digest)						
Harvey Publications: Oct, 1980 - No. 10, Oct, 1982 ($1.50)						
1	1	3	4	6	8	10
2-10						6.00
RICHIE RICH MILLIONS						
Harvey Publ.: 9/61; #2, 9/62 - #113, 10/82 (#1-48: 68 pgs.; 49-64, 85-97: 52 pgs.)						
1: (#1-3 are all reprint issues)	20	40	60	140	283	425

	GD 2.0	VG 4.0	FN 6.0	VF 8.0	VF/NM 9.0	NM- 9.2
2	11	22	33	75	138	200
3-5: All other giants are new & reprints. 5-1st 15 pg. Richie Rich story	9	18	27	65	113	160
6-10	8	16	24	58	97	135
11-20	6	12	18	41	66	90
21-30	4	8	12	28	44	60
31-48: 31-1st app. The Onion. 48-Last 68 pg. Giant	3	6	9	20	30	40
49-64: 52 pg. Giants	3	6	9	14	20	25
65-67,69-73,75-84	2	4	6	8	10	12
68-1st Super Richie-c (11/74)	2	4	6	13	18	22
74-1st app. Mr. Woody; Super Richie app.	2	4	6	8	11	14
85-97: 52 pg. Giants	2	4	6	8	11	14
98,99	1	2	3	4	5	7
100	1	2	3	5	7	9
101-113						6.00
RICHIE RICH MONEY WORLD						
Harvey Publications: Sept, 1972 - No. 59, Sept, 1982						
1-(52 pg. Giant)-1st app. Mayda Munny	6	12	18	37	59	80
2-Super Richie app.	3	6	9	18	27	35
3-5	3	6	9	16	23	30
6-10: 9,10-Richie Rich mistakenly named Little Lotta on covers	2	4	6	11	16	20
11-20: 16,20-Dr. N-R-Gee	2	4	6	8	10	12
21-30	1	2	3	5	7	9
31-50	1	2	3	4	5	7
51-59						6.00
Digest 1 (2/91, $1.75)						5.00
2-8 (12/93, $1.75)						3.00
RICHIE RICH PROFITS						
Harvey Publications: Oct, 1974 - No. 47, Sept, 1982						
1	3	6	9	20	30	40
2-5	2	4	6	13	18	22
6-10: 10-Origin of Dr. N-R-Gee	2	4	6	9	13	16
11-20: 15-Christmas-c	1	3	4	6	8	10
21-30	1	2	3	4	5	7
31-47						6.00
RICHIE RICH RELICS						
Harvey Comics: Jan, 1988 - No.4, Feb, 1989 (75¢/$1.00, reprints)						
1-4						3.00
RICHIE RICH RICHES						
Harvey Publications: July, 1972 - No. 59, Aug, 1982 (#1, 2, 41-45: 52 pgs.)						
1-(52 pg. Giant)-1st app. The Money Monster	6	12	18	37	59	80
2-(52 pg. Giant)	3	6	9	20	30	40
3-5	3	6	9	16	23	30
6-10: 7-1st app. Aunt Novo	2	4	6	11	16	20
11-20: 17-Super Richie app. (3/75)	2	4	6	8	10	12
21-40	1	2	3	5	6	8
41-45: 52 pg. Giants	1	3	4	6	8	10
46-59: 56-Dr. Blemish app.						6.00
RICHIE RICH SUCCESS STORIES						
Harvey Publications: Nov, 1964 - No. 105, Sept, 1982 (#1-38: 68 pgs., 39-55, 67-90: 52 pgs.)						
1	16	32	48	111	226	340
2	10	20	30	67	116	165
3-5	9	18	27	60	100	140
6-10	6	12	18	41	66	90
11-20	5	10	15	34	55	75
21-30: 27-1st Penny Van Dough (8/69)	4	8	12	24	37	50
31-38: 38-Last 68 pg. Giant	3	6	9	20	30	40
39-55-(52 pgs.): 44-Super Richie app.	3	6	9	14	20	25
56-66	2	4	6	8	10	12
67-90: 52 pgs.	2	4	6	8	11	14
91-99,101-105: 91-Onion app. 101-Dr. Blemish app.						6.00
100	1	2	3	5	7	9
RICHIE RICH SUMMER BONANZA						
Harvey Comics: Oct, 1991 ($1.95, one-shot, 68 pgs.)						
1-Richie Rich, Little Dot, Little Lotta						4.00
RICHIE RICH TREASURE CHEST DIGEST (...Magazine #3)						
Harvey Publications: Apr, 1982 - No. 3, Aug, 1982 (95¢, Digest Mag.) (#4 advertised but not publ.)						
1	1	2	3	5	7	9

Richie Rich Zillionz #1 © HARV

Riftwar #3 © Raymond E. Feist

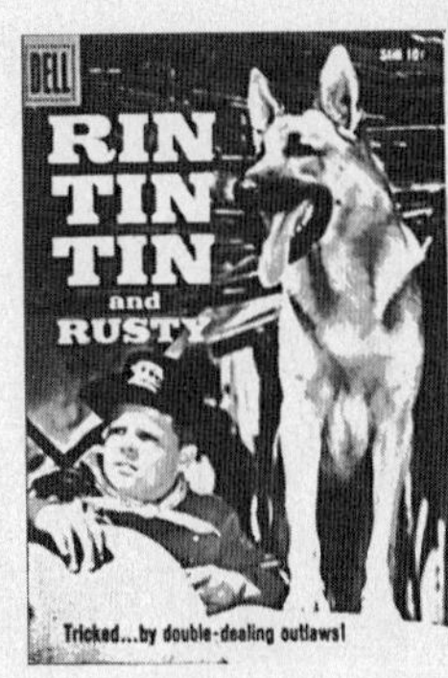

Rin Tin Tin and Rusty #28 © DELL

	GD 2.0	VG 4.0	FN 6.0	VF 8.0	VF/NM 9.0	NM- 9.2
2,3	1	2	3	4	5	7

RICHIE RICH VACATION DIGEST
Harvey Comics: Oct, 1991; Oct, 1992; Oct, 1993 ($1.75, digest-size)

	GD 2.0	VG 4.0	FN 6.0	VF 8.0	VF/NM 9.0	NM- 9.2
1-(10/91), 1-(10/92), 1-(10/93)						4.00

RICHIE RICH VACATIONS DIGEST
Harvey Publ.: 11/77; No. 2, 10/78 - No. 7, 10/81; No. 8, 8/82; No. 9, 10/82 (Digest, 132 pgs.)

	GD 2.0	VG 4.0	FN 6.0	VF 8.0	VF/NM 9.0	NM- 9.2
1-Reprints	2	4	6	9	12	15
2-6	1	2	3	5	7	9
7-9						6.00

RICHIE RICH VAULT OF MYSTERY
Harvey Publications: Nov, 1974 - No. 47, Sept, 1982

	GD 2.0	VG 4.0	FN 6.0	VF 8.0	VF/NM 9.0	NM- 9.2
1	3	6	9	20	30	40
2-5: 5-The Condor app.	2	4	6	13	18	22
6-10	2	4	6	9	13	16
11-20	1	3	4	6	8	10
21-30	1	2	3	4	5	7
31-47						6.00

RICHIE RICH ZILLIONZ
Harvey Publ.: Oct, 1976 - No. 33, Sept, 1982 (#1-4: 68 pgs.; #5-18: 52 pgs.)

	GD 2.0	VG 4.0	FN 6.0	VF 8.0	VF/NM 9.0	NM- 9.2
1	3	6	9	18	27	35
2-4: 4-Last 68 pg. Giant	2	4	6	11	16	20
5-10	2	4	6	8	10	12
11-18: 18-Last 52 pg. Giant	1	2	3	5	6	8
19-33						6.00

RICKY
Standard Comics (Visual Editions): No. 5, Sept, 1953

	GD 2.0	VG 4.0	FN 6.0	VF 8.0	VF/NM 9.0	NM- 9.2
5-Teenage humor	6	12	18	28	34	40

RICKY NELSON (TV)(See Sweethearts V2#42)
Dell Publishing Co.: No. 956, Dec, 1958 - No. 1192, June, 1961 (All photo-c)

	GD 2.0	VG 4.0	FN 6.0	VF 8.0	VF/NM 9.0	NM- 9.2
Four Color 956,998	16	32	48	111	226	340
Four Color 1115,1192: 1192-Manning-a	13	26	39	92	179	265

RIDE, THE (Also see Gun Candy flip-book)
Image Comics: June, 2004 - No. 2, July, 2004 ($2.95, B&W, anthology)

	GD 2.0	VG 4.0	FN 6.0	VF 8.0	VF/NM 9.0	NM- 9.2
1,2: Hughes-c/Wagner-s. 1-Hamner & Stelfreeze-a. 2-Jeanty & Pearson-a						3.00
... Die Valkyrie 1-3 (6/07 - No. 3, 2/08, $2.99) Stelfreeze-a/Wagner-s/Pearson-c						3.00
... Foreign Parts 1 (1/05, $2.95) Dixon-s/Haynes-a; Marz-s/Brunner-a; Pearson-c						3.00
... Halloween Special: The Key to Survival (10/07, $3.50) Tomm Coker-s/a						3.50
... Savannah 1 (4/07, $4.99) s/a by students of Savannah College of Art						5.00
... 2 For the Road 1 (10/04, $2.95) Dixon-s/Hamner & Gregory-a/Johnson-c						3.00
Vol. 1 TPB (2005, $9.99) r/#1,2, Foreign Parts, 2 For the Road; Chaykin intro.						10.00
Vol. 2 TPB (2005, $15.99) r/Gun Candy #1,2 & Die Valkyrie #1-3; sketch pages						16.00

RIDER, THE (Frontier Trail #6; also see Blazing Sixguns I.W. Reprint #10, 11)
Ajax/Farrell Publ. (Four Star Comic Corp.): Mar, 1957 - No. 5, 1958

	GD 2.0	VG 4.0	FN 6.0	VF 8.0	VF/NM 9.0	NM- 9.2
1-Swift Arrow, Lone Rider begin	13	26	39	72	101	130
2-5	8	16	24	42	54	65

RIDERS OF THE PURPLE SAGE (See Zane Grey & Four Color #372)

RIFLEMAN, THE (TV)
Dell Publ. Co./Gold Key No. 13 on: No. 1009, 7-9/59 - No. 12, 7-9/62; No. 13, 11/62 - No. 20, 10/64

	GD 2.0	VG 4.0	FN 6.0	VF 8.0	VF/NM 9.0	NM- 9.2
Four Color 1009 (#1)	20	40	60	140	283	425
2 (1-3/60)	11	22	33	75	138	200
3-Toth-a (4 pgs.); variant edition has back-c with "Something Special" comic strip	11	22	33	75	138	200
4-10: 6-Toth-a (4 pgs.)	10	20	30	69	122	175
11-20	8	16	24	54	90	125

NOTE: *Warren Tufts a-2-9. All have Chuck Connors & Johnny Crawford photo-c. Photo back c-13-15.*

RIFTWAR
Marvel Comics: July, 2009 - No. 5, Dec, 2009 ($3.99, limited series)

	GD 2.0	VG 4.0	FN 6.0	VF 8.0	VF/NM 9.0	NM- 9.2
1-5-Adaptation of Raymond E. Feist novel; Glass-s/Stegman-a						4.00

RIMA, THE JUNGLE GIRL
National Periodical Publications: Apr-May, 1974 - No. 7, Apr-May, 1975

	GD 2.0	VG 4.0	FN 6.0	VF 8.0	VF/NM 9.0	NM- 9.2
1-Origin, part 1 (#1-5: 20¢; 6,7: 25¢)	2	4	6	13	18	22
2-7: 2-4-Origin, parts 2-4. 7-Origin & only app. Space Marshal	2	3	4	6	8	10

NOTE: ***Kubert** c-1-7. **Nino** a-1-7. **Redondo** a-1-7.*

RING OF BRIGHT WATER (See Movie Classics)

RING OF THE NIBELUNG, THE
DC Comics: 1989 - No. 4, 1990 ($4.95, squarebound, 52 pgs., mature readers)

	GD 2.0	VG 4.0	FN 6.0	VF 8.0	VF/NM 9.0	NM- 9.2
1-4: Adapts Wagner cycle of operas, Gil Kane-c/a						5.00

RING OF THE NIBELUNG, THE
Dark Horse Comics: Feb, 2000 - Sept, 2001 ($2.95/$2.99/$5.99, limited series)

	GD 2.0	VG 4.0	FN 6.0	VF 8.0	VF/NM 9.0	NM- 9.2
Vol. 1 (The Rhinegold) 1-4: Adapts Wagner; P. Craig Russell-s/a						3.00
Vol. 2,3: Vol. 2 (The Valkyrie) 1-3: 1-(8/00). Vol. 3 (Siegfried) 1-3: 1-(12/00)						3.00
Vol. 4 (The Twilight of the Gods) 1-3: 1-(6/01)						3.00
4-(9/01, $5.99, 64 pgs.) Conclusion with sketch pages						6.00

RINGO KID, THE (2nd Series)
Marvel Comics Group: Jan, 1970 - No. 23, Nov, 1973; No. 24, Nov, 1975 - No. 30, Nov, 1976

	GD 2.0	VG 4.0	FN 6.0	VF 8.0	VF/NM 9.0	NM- 9.2
1-Williamson-a r-from #10, 1956.	3	6	9	18	27	35
2-11: 2-Severin-c. 11-Last 15¢ issue	2	4	6	11	16	20
12 (52 pg. Giant)	3	6	9	16	22	28
13-20: 13-Wildey-r. 20-Williamson-r/#1	2	4	6	9	13	16
21-30	2	4	6	8	10	12
27,28-(30¢-c variant, limited distribution)(5,7/76)	3	6	9	20	30	40

RINGO KID WESTERN, THE (1st Series) (See Wild Western & Western Trails)
Atlas Comics (HPC)/Marvel Comics: Aug, 1954 - No. 21, Sept, 1957

	GD 2.0	VG 4.0	FN 6.0	VF 8.0	VF/NM 9.0	NM- 9.2
1-Origin; The Ringo Kid begins	30	60	90	177	289	400
2-Black Rider app.; origin/1st app. Ringo's Horse Arab	15	30	45	90	140	190
3-5	12	24	36	69	97	125
6-8-Severin-a(3) each	13	26	39	74	105	135
9,11,12,14-21: 12-Orlando-a (4 pgs.)	10	20	30	56	76	95
10,13-Williamson-a (4 pgs.)	11	22	33	60	83	105

NOTE: ***Berg** a-8. **Maneely** a-1-5, 15, 16(text illos only), 17(4), 18, 20, 21; c-1-6, 8, 13, 15-18, 20. **J. Severin** c-10, 11. **Sinnott** a-1. **Wildey** a-16-18.*

RIN TIN TIN (See March of Comics #163,180,195)

RIN TIN TIN (TV) (...& Rusty #21 on; see Western Roundup under Dell Giants)
Dell Publishing Co./Gold Key: Nov, 1952 - No. 38, May-July, 1961; Nov, 1963 (All Photo-c)

	GD 2.0	VG 4.0	FN 6.0	VF 8.0	VF/NM 9.0	NM- 9.2
Four Color 434 (#1)	13	26	39	94	185	275
Four Color 476,523	8	16	24	56	93	130
4(3-5/54)-10	7	14	21	45	73	100
11-17,19,20	6	12	18	43	69	95
18-(4-5/57) 1st app. of Rusty and the Cavalry of Fort Apache; photo-c	8	16	24	54	90	125
21-38: 36-Toth-a (4 pgs.)	5	10	15	34	55	75
... & Rusty 1 (11/63-Gold Key)	6	12	18	37	59	80

RIO (Also see Eclipse Monthly)
Comico: June, 1987 ($8.95, 64 pgs.)

	GD 2.0	VG 4.0	FN 6.0	VF 8.0	VF/NM 9.0	NM- 9.2
1-Wildey-c/a						9.00

RIO AT BAY
Dark Horse Comics: July, 1992 - No. 2, Aug, 1992 ($2.95, limited series)

	GD 2.0	VG 4.0	FN 6.0	VF 8.0	VF/NM 9.0	NM- 9.2
1,2-Wildey-c/a						3.00

RIO BRAVO (Movie) (See 4-Color #1018)
Dell Publishing Co.: June, 1959

	GD 2.0	VG 4.0	FN 6.0	VF 8.0	VF/NM 9.0	NM- 9.2
Four Color 1018-Toth-a; John Wayne, Dean Martin, & Ricky Nelson photo-c.	21	42	63	150	300	450

RIO CONCHOS (See Movie Comics)

RIOT (Satire)
Atlas Comics (ACI No. 1-5/WPI No. 6): Apr, 1954 - No. 3, Aug, 1954; No. 4, Feb, 1956 - No. 6, June, 1956

	GD 2.0	VG 4.0	FN 6.0	VF 8.0	VF/NM 9.0	NM- 9.2
1-Russ Heath-a	34	68	102	199	325	450
2-Li'l Abner satire by Post	24	48	72	140	230	320
3-Last precode (8/54)	21	42	63	124	202	280
4-Infinity-c; Marilyn Monroe "7 Year Itch" movie satire; Mad Rip-off ads	27	54	81	158	259	360
5-Marilyn Monroe, John Wayne parody; part photo-c	27	54	81	160	263	365
6-Lorna of the Jungle satire by Everett; Dennis the Menace satire-c/story; part photo-c	21	42	63	124	202	280

NOTE: ***Berg** a-3. **Burgos** c-1, 2. **Colan** a-1. **Everett** a-4, 6. **Heath** a-1. **Maneely** a-1, 2, 4-6; c-3, 4, 6. **Post** a-1-4. **Reinman** a-2. **Severin** a-4-6.*

RIOT GEAR
Triumphant Comics: Sept, 1993 - No. 11, July, 1994 ($2.50, serially numbered)

	GD 2.0	VG 4.0	FN 6.0	VF 8.0	VF/NM 9.0	NM- 9.2
1-11: 1-2nd app. Riot Gear. 2-1st app. Rabin. 3,4-Triumphant Unleashed x-over. 3-1st app. Surzar. 4-Death of Captain Tich						3.00

Rip Hunter Time Master #8 © DC

Rising Stars Bright #1 © JMS & TCOW

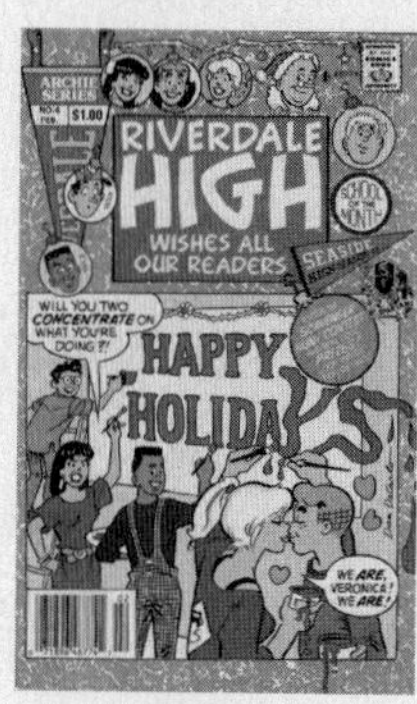

Riverdale High #4 © AP

GD VG FN VF VF/NM NM-
2.0 4.0 6.0 8.0 9.0 9.2

Violent Past 1,2: 1-(2/94, $2.50) 3.00

R.I.P.
TSR, Inc.:1990 - No. 8, 1991 ($2.95, 44 pgs.)
1-8-Based on TSR game 4.00

RIPCLAW (See Cyberforce)
Image Comics (Top Cow Prod.): Apr, 1995 - No. 3, June, 1995 (Limited series)
1/2-Gold, 1/2-San Diego ed., 1/2-Chicago ed. 1 3 4 6 8 10
1-3: Brandon Peterson-a(p) 3.00
Special 1 (10/95, $2.50) 3.00

RIPCLAW
Image Comics (Top Cow Prod.): V2#1, Dec, 1995 - No. 6, June, 1996 ($2.50)
V2#1-6: 5-Medieval Spawn/Witchblade Preview 3.00
...: Pilot Season 1 (2007, $2.99) Jason Aaron-s/Jorge Lucas-a/Tony Moore-c 3.00

RIPCORD (TV)
Dell Publishing Co.: Mar-May, 1962
Four Color 1294 7 14 21 47 76 105

R.I.P.D.
Dark Horse Comics: Oct, 1999 - No. 4, Jan, 2000 ($2.95, limited series)
1-4 3.00
TPB (2003, $12.95) r/#1-4 13.00

RIP HUNTER TIME MASTER (See Showcase #20, 21, 25, 26 & Time Masters)
National Periodical Publications: Mar-Apr, 1961 - No. 29, Nov-Dec, 1965
1-(3-4/61) 50 100 150 425 863 1300
2 25 50 75 183 367 550
3-5: 5-Last 10¢ issue 15 30 45 110 223 335
6,7-Toth-a in each 11 22 33 77 144 210
8-15 9 18 27 63 107 150
16-20: 20-Hitler c/s 7 14 21 49 80 110
21-29: 29-Gil Kane-c 6 12 18 43 69 95

RIP IN TIME (Also see Teenage Mutant Ninja Turtles #5-7)
Fantagor Press: Aug, 1986 - No.5, 1987 ($1.50, B&W)
1-5: Corben-c/a in all 3.00

RIP KIRBY (Also see Harvey Comics Hits #57, & Street Comix)
David McKay Publications: 1948
Feature Books 51,54: Raymond-c; 51-Origin 36 72 108 211 343 475

RIPLEY'S BELIEVE IT OR NOT! (See Ace Comics, All-American Comics, Mystery Comics Digest #1, 4, 7, 10, 13, 16, 19, 22, 25)

RIPLEY'S BELIEVE IT OR NOT!
Harvey Publications: Sept, 1953 - No. 4, March, 1954
1-Powell-a 14 28 42 76 108 140
2-4 10 20 30 54 72 90

RIPLEY'S BELIEVE IT OR NOT! (Continuation of Ripleys'...True Ghost Stories & Ripley's...True War Stories)
Gold Key: No. 4, April, 1967 - No. 94, Feb, 1980
4-Shrunken head photo-c; McWilliams-a 4 8 12 24 37 50
5-Subtitled "True War Stories"; Evans-a; 1st Jeff Jones-a in comics? (2 pgs.) 4 8 12 24 37 50
6-10: 6-McWilliams-a. 10-Evans-a(2) 3 6 9 20 30 40
11-20: 15-Evans-a 3 6 9 16 23 30
21-30 2 4 6 13 18 22
31-38,40-60 2 4 6 9 13 16
39-Crandall-a 2 4 6 10 14 18
61-73 1 3 4 6 8 10
74,77-83-(52 pgs.) 2 4 6 9 13 16
75,76,84-94 1 2 3 5 6 8
Story Digest Mag. 1(6/70)-4-3/4x6-1/2", 148pp. 5 10 15 34 55 75
NOTE: ***Evanish** art by **Luiz Dominguez** #22-25, 27, 30, 31, 40. **Jeff Jones** a-5(2 pgs.). **McWilliams** a-65, 66, 70, 89. **Orlando** a-8. **Sparling** c-68. Reprints-74, 77-84, 87 (part); 91, 93 (all). **Williamson, Wood** a-80r/#1.*

RIPLEY'S BELIEVE IT OR NOT!
Dark Horse Comics: May, 2002 - No. 4 ($2.99, B&W, limited series)
1-3-Nord-c/a. 1-Stories of Amelia Earhart & D.B. Cooper 3.00

RIPLEY'S BELIEVE IT OR NOT! TRUE GHOST STORIES (Along with Ripley's...True War Stories, the three issues together precede the 1967 series that starts its numbering with #4) (Also see Dan Curtis)
Gold Key: June, 1965 - No. 2, Oct, 1966
1-Williamson, Wood & Evans-a; photo-c 8 16 24 52 86 120
2-Orlando, McWilliams-a; photo-c 4 8 12 28 44 60
Mini-Comic 1(1976-3-1/4x6-1/2") 2 4 6 8 11 14
11186(1977)-Golden Press; ($1.95, 224 pgs.)-All-r 4 8 12 24 37 50
11401(3/79)-Golden Press; ($1.00, 96 pgs.)-All-r 3 6 9 15 21 26

RIPLEY'S BELIEVE IT OR NOT! TRUE WAR STORIES (Along with Ripley's...True Ghost Stories, the three issues together precede the 1967 series that starts its numbering with #4)
Gold Key: Nov, 1965 (Aug, 1965 in indicia)
1-No Williamson-a 4 8 12 28 44 60

RIPLEY'S BELIEVE IT OR NOT! TRUE WEIRD
Ripley Enterprises: June, 1966 - No. 2, Aug, 1966 (B&W Magazine)
1,2-Comic stories & text 3 6 9 18 27 35

RISE OF APOCALYPSE
Marvel Comics: Oct, 1996 - No. 4, Jan, 1997 ($1.95, limited series)
1-4: Adam Pollina-c/a 3.00

RISING STARS
Image Comics (Top Cow): Mar, 1999 - No. 24, Mar, 2005 ($2.50/$2.99)
Preview-(3/99, $5.00) Straczynski-s 6.00
0-(6/00, $2.50) Gary Frank-a/c 3.00
1/2-(8/01, $2.95) Anderson-c; art & sketch pages by Zanier 3.00
1-Four covers; Keu Cha-c/a 1 2 3 5 7 9
1-($10.00) Gold Editions-four covers 10.00
1-($50.00) Holofoil-c 50.00
2-7: 5-7-Zanier & Lashley-a(p) 1 2 3 5 7 9
8-23: 8-13-Zanier & Lashley-a(p). 14-Immonen-a. 15-Flip book B&W preview of Universe. 15-23-Brent Anderson-a 3.00
24-($3.99) Series finale; Anderson-a/c 4.00
Born In Fire TPB (11/00, $19.95) r/#1-8; foreword by Neil Gaiman 20.00
Power TPB (2002, $19.95) r/#9-16 20.00
Prelude-(10/00, $2.95) Cha-a/Lashley-c 3.00
...: Visitations (2002, $8.99) r/#0, 1/2, Preview; new Anderson-c; cover gallery 9.00
Vol. 3: Fire and Ash TPB (2005, $19.99) r/#17-24; design pages & cover gallery 20.00
Vol. 4 TPB (2006, $19.99) r/Rising Stars Bright #1-3 and Voices of the Dead #1-6 20.00
Vol. 5 TPB (2007, $16.99) r/Rising Stars: Untouchable #1-5 and ...: Visitations 17.00
Wizard #0-(3/99) Wizard supplement; Straczynski-s 3.00
Wizard #1/2 10.00

RISING STARS BRIGHT
Image Comics (Top Cow): Mar, 2003 - No. 3, May, 2003 ($2.99, limited series)
1-3-Avery-s/Jurgens & Gorder-a/Beck-c 3.00

RISING STARS: UNTOUCHABLE
Image Comics (Top Cow): Mar, 2006 - No. 5, July, 2006 ($2.99, limited series)
1-5-Avery-s/Anderson-a 3.00

RISING STARS: VOICES OF THE DEAD
Image Comics (Top Cow): June, 2005 - No. 6, Dec, 2005 ($2.99, limited series)
1-6-Avery-s/Staz Johnson-a 3.00

RIVERDALE HIGH (Archie's... #7,8)
Archie Comics: Aug, 1990 - No. 8, Oct, 1991 ($1.00, bi-monthly)
1 4.00
2-8 3.00

RIVER FEUD (See Zane Grey & Four Color #484)

RIVETS
Dell Publishing Co.: No. 518, Nov, 1953
Four Color 518 4 8 12 24 37 50

RIVETS (A dog)
Argo Publ.: Jan, 1956 - No. 3, May, 1956
1-Reprints Sunday & daily newspaper strips 6 12 18 31 38 45
2,3 5 10 15 22 26 30

ROACHMILL
Blackthorne Publ.: Dec, 1986 - No. 6, Oct, 1987 ($1.75, B&W)
1-6 3.00

ROACHMILL
Dark Horse Comics: May, 1988 - No. 10, Dec, 1990 ($1.75, B&W)
1-10: 10-Contains trading cards 3.00

ROAD RUNNER (See Beep Beep, the...)

ROAD TO PERDITION (Inspired the 2002 Tom Hanks/Paul Newman movie) (Also see On the Road to Perdition)

Robin #21 © DC

Robin #183 © DC

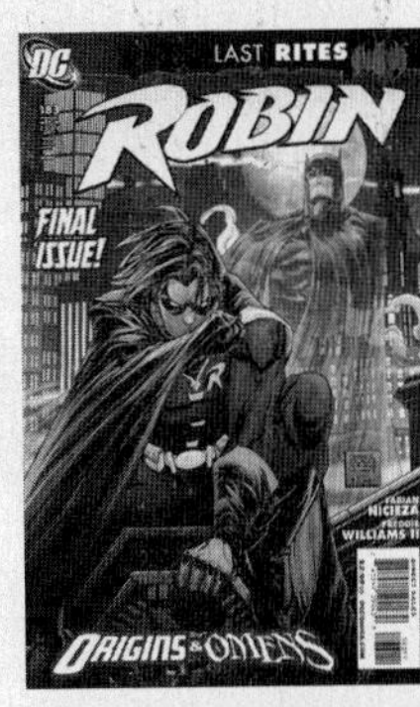

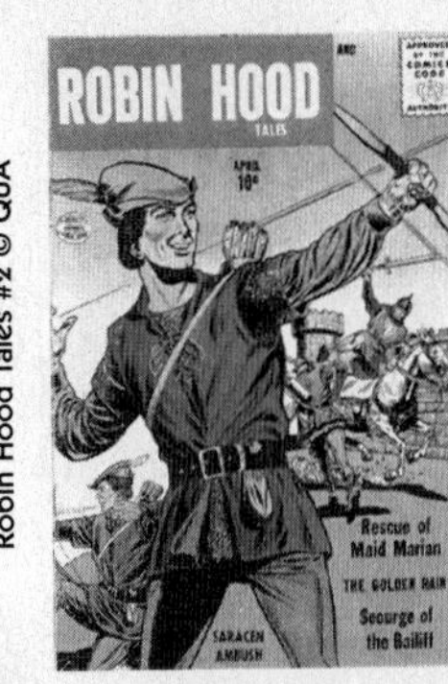

Robin Hood Tales #2 © QUA

GD 2.0 | VG 4.0 | FN 6.0 | VF 8.0 | VF/NM 9.0 | NM- 9.2

DC Comics/Paradox Press: 1998, 2002 ($13.95, B&W paperback graphic novel)

nn-(1st printing) Max Allan Collins-s/Richard Piers Rayner-a 30.00
2nd & 3rd printings (2002, $13.95) 14.00
Movie photo cover edition (2002) 14.00

ROADTRIP
Oni Press: Aug, 2000 ($2.95, B&W, one-shot)

1-Reprints Judd Winick's back-up stories from Oni Double Feature #9,10 3.00

ROADWAYS
Cult Press: May, 1994 ($2.75, B&W, limited series)

1 3.00

ROARIN' RICK'S RARE BIT FIENDS
King Hell Press: July, 1994 - No. 21, Aug, 1996 ($2.95, B&W, mature)

1-21: Rick Veitch-c/a/scripts in all. 20-(5/96). 21-(8/96)-Reads Subtleman #1 on cover 3.00
Rabid Eye: The Dream Art of Rick Veitch ($14.95, B&W, TPB)-r/#1-8 & the appendix from #12 15.00
Pocket Universe (6/96, $14.95, B&W, TPB)-Reprints 15.00

ROBERT E. HOWARD'S CONAN THE BARBARIAN
Marvel Comics: 1983 ($2.50, 68 pgs., Baxter paper)

1-r/Savage Tales #2,3 by Smith, c-r/Conan #21 by Smith. 4.00

ROBERT LOUIS STEVENSON'S KIDNAPPED (See Kidnapped)

ROBIN (See Aurora, Birds of Prey, Detective Comics #38, New Teen Titans, Robin II, Robin III, Robin 3000, Star Spangled Comics #65, Teen Titans & Young Justice)

ROBIN (See Batman #457)
DC Comics: Jan, 1991 - No. 5, May, 1991 ($1.00, limited series)

1-Free poster by N. Adams; Bolland-c on all 5.00
1-2nd & 3rd printings (without poster) 3.00
2-5 4.00
2-2nd printing 3.00
Annual 1,2 (1992-93, $2.50, 68 pgs.): 1-Grant/Wagner scripts; Sam Kieth-c. 2-Intro Razorsharp; Jim Balent-c(p) 4.00

ROBIN (See Detective #668) (Also see Red Robin)
DC Comics: Nov, 1993 - No. 183, Apr, 2009 ($1.50/$1.95/$1.99/$2.25/$2.50/$2.99)

1-($2.95)-Collector's edition w/foil embossed-c; 1st app. Robin's car, The Redbird; Azrael as Batman app. 5.00
1-Newsstand ed. 3.00
0,2-49,51-66-Regular editions: 3-5-The Spoiler app. 6-The Huntress-c/story cont'd from Showcase '94 #5. 7-Knightquest: The Conclusion w/new Batman (Azrael) vs. Bruce Wayne. 8-KnightsEnd Pt. 5. 9-KnightsEnd Aftermath; Batman-c & app. 10-(9/94)-Zero Hour. 0-(10/94). 11-(11/94). 25-Green Arrow-c/app. 26-Batman app. 27-Contagion Pt. 3; Catwoman-c/app; Penguin & Azrael app. 28-Contagion Pt. 11. 29-Penguin app. 31-Wildcat-c/app. 32-Legacy Pt. 3. 33-Legacy Pt. 7. 35-Final Night. 46-Genesis. 52,53-Cataclysm pt. 7, conclusion. 55-Green Arrow app. 62-64-Flash-c/app. 3.50
14 ($2.50)-Embossed-c; Troika Pt. 4 4.00
50-($2.95)-Lady Shiva & King Snake app. 4.00
67-74,76-78: 67-72-No Man's Land 3.00
75-($2.95) 4.00
79-97: 79-Begin $2.25-c; Green Arrow app. 86-Pander Bros.-a 3.00
98,99-Bruce Wayne: Murderer x-over pt. 6, 11 3.00
100-($3.50) Last Dixon-s 4.00
101-147: 101-Young Justice x-over. 106-Kevin Lau-c. 121,122-Willingham-s/Mays-a. 125-Tim Drake quits. 126-Spoiler becomes the new Robin. 129-131-War Games. 132-Robin moves to Bludhaven, Batgirl app. 138-Begin $2.50-c. 139-McDaniel-a begins. 146-147-Teen Titans app. 3.00
148-174: 148-One Year Later; new costume. 150-Begin $2.99-c. 152,153-Boomerang app. 168,169-Resurrection of Ra's al Ghul x-over. 174 Spoiler unmasked 3.00
175-183: 175,176-Batman R.I.P. x-over. 180-Robin vs. Red Robin 3.00
#1,000,000 (11/98) 853rd Century x-over 3.00
Annual 3-5: 3-(1994, $2.95)-Elseworlds story. 4-(1995, $2.95)-Year One story. 5-(1996, $2.95)-Legends of the Dead Earth story 4.00
Annual 6 (1997, $3.95)-Pulp Heroes story. 4.00
Annual 7 (12/07, $3.99)-Pearson-c/a; prelude to Resurrection of Ra's al Ghul x-over 4.00
.../Argent 1 (2/98, $1.95) Argent (Teen Titans) app. 3.00
.../Batgirl: Fresh Blood TPB (2005, $12.99) r/#132,133 & Batgirl #58,59 13.00
...: Days of Fire and Madness (2006, $12.99, TPB) r/#140-145 13.00
...Eighty-Page Giant 1 (9/00, $5.95) Chuck Dixon-s/Diego Barreto-a 6.00
...: Flying Solo (2000, $12.95, TPB) r/#1-6, Showcase '94 #5,6 13.00
...Plus 1 (12/96, $2.95) Impulse-c/app.; Waid-s 3.00
...Plus 2 (12/97, $2.95) Fang (Scare Tactics) app. 3.00
...: Search For a Hero (2009, $19.99, TPB) r/#175-183; cover gallery 20.00

GD 2.0 | VG 4.0 | FN 6.0 | VF 8.0 | VF/NM 9.0 | NM- 9.2

.../Spoiler Special 1 (8/08, $3.99) Follows Spoiler's return in Robin #174; Dixon-s 4.00
...: Teenage Wasteland (2007, $17.99, TPB) r/#154-162 18.00
...: The Big Leagues (2008, $12.99, TPB) r/#163-167 13.00
...: Unmasked (2004, $12.95, TPB) r/#121-125; Pearson-c 13.00
...: Violent Tendencies (2008, $17.99, TPB) r/#170-174 & Robin/Spoiler Special 1 18.00
...: Wanted (2007, $12.99, TPB) r/#148-153 13.00

ROBIN: A HERO REBORN
DC Comics: 1991 ($4.95, squarebound, trade paperback)

nn-r/Batman #455-457 & Robin #1-5; Bolland-c 5.00

ROBIN HOOD (See The Advs. of..., Brave and the Bold, Four Color #413, 669, King Classics, Movie Comics & Power Record Comics)

ROBIN HOOD (...& His Merry Men, The Illustrated Story of...) (See Classic Comics #7 & Classics Giveaways, 12/44)

ROBIN HOOD (Disney)
Dell Publishing Co.: No. 413, Aug, 1952; No. 669, Dec, 1955

	GD 2.0	VG 4.0	FN 6.0	VF 8.0	VF/NM 9.0	NM- 9.2
Four Color 413-(1st Disney movie Four Color book)(8/52)-Photo-c	9	18	27	65	113	160
Four Color 669 (12/55)-Reprints #413 plus photo-c	6	12	18	37	59	80

ROBIN HOOD (Adventures of... #7, 8)
Magazine Enterprises (Sussex Pub. Co.): No. 52, Nov, 1955 - No. 6, Jun, 1957

	GD 2.0	VG 4.0	FN 6.0	VF 8.0	VF/NM 9.0	NM- 9.2
52 (#1)-Origin Robin Hood & Sir Gallant of the Round Table	15	30	45	85	130	175
53 (#2), 3-6: 6-Richard Greene photo-c (TV)	12	24	36	67	94	120
I.W. Reprint #1,2,9: 1-r/#3. 2-r/#4. 9-r/#52 (1963)	2	4	6	9	13	16
Super Reprint #10,15: 10-r/#53. 15-r/#5	2	4	6	9	13	16

NOTE: *Bolle a-in all; c-52.* ***Powell*** *a-6.*

ROBIN HOOD (Not Disney)
Dell Publishing Co.: May-July, 1963 (one-shot)

	GD 2.0	VG 4.0	FN 6.0	VF 8.0	VF/NM 9.0	NM- 9.2
1	3	6	9	16	23	30

ROBIN HOOD (Disney) (Also see Best of Walt Disney)
Western Publishing Co.: 1973 ($1.50, 8-1/2x11", 52 pgs., cardboard-c)

	GD 2.0	VG 4.0	FN 6.0	VF 8.0	VF/NM 9.0	NM- 9.2
96151- "Robin Hood", based on movie, 96152- "The Mystery of Sherwood Forest", 96153- "In King Richard's Service", 96154- "The Wizard's Ring" each....	3	6	9	16	22	28

ROBIN HOOD
Eclipse Comics: July, 1991 - No. 3, Dec, 1991 ($2.50, limited series)

1-3: Timothy Truman layouts 3.00

ROBIN HOOD AND HIS MERRY MEN (Formerly Danger & Adventure)
Charlton Comics: No. 28, Apr, 1956 - No. 38, Aug, 1958

	GD 2.0	VG 4.0	FN 6.0	VF 8.0	VF/NM 9.0	NM- 9.2
28	10	20	30	54	72	90
29-37	8	16	24	42	54	65
38-Ditko-a (5 pgs.); Rocke-c	14	28	42	76	108	140

ROBIN HOOD TALES (Published by National Periodical #7 on)
Quality Comics Group (Comic Magazines): Feb, 1956 - No. 6, Nov-Dec, 1956

	GD 2.0	VG 4.0	FN 6.0	VF 8.0	VF/NM 9.0	NM- 9.2
1-All have Baker/Cuidera-c	32	64	96	188	307	425
2-6-Matt Baker-a	30	60	90	177	289	400

ROBIN HOOD TALES (Cont'd from Quality series)(See Brave & the Bold #5)
National Periodical Publ.: No. 7, Jan-Feb, 1957 - No. 14, Mar-Apr, 1958

	GD 2.0	VG 4.0	FN 6.0	VF 8.0	VF/NM 9.0	NM- 9.2
7-All have Andru/Esposito-c	36	72	108	211	343	475
8-14	30	60	90	177	289	400

ROBINSON CRUSOE (See King Classics & Power Record Comics)
Dell Publishing Co.: Nov-Jan, 1963-64

	GD 2.0	VG 4.0	FN 6.0	VF 8.0	VF/NM 9.0	NM- 9.2
1	3	6	9	15	21	26

ROBIN II (The Joker's Wild)
DC Comics: Oct, 1991 - No. 4, Dec, 1991 ($1.50, mini-series)

1-(Direct sales, $1.50)-With 4 diff.-c; same hologram on each 4.00
1-(Newsstand, $1.00)-No hologram; 1 version 3.00
1-Collector's set ($10.00)-Contains all 5 versions bagged with hologram trading card inside 15.00
2-(Direct sales, $1.50)-With 3 different-c 3.50
2-4-(Newsstand, $1.00)-1 version of each 3.00
2-Collector's set ($8.00)-Contains all 4 versions bagged with hologram trading card inside 10.00
3-(Direct sale, $1.50)-With 2 different-c 3.50
3-Collector's set ($6.00)-Contains all 3 versions bagged with hologram trading card inside 8.00
4-(Direct sales, $1.50)-Only one version 3.50

Robocop (2010 series) #4 © Orion Picts.

Robo Dojo #6 © WSP

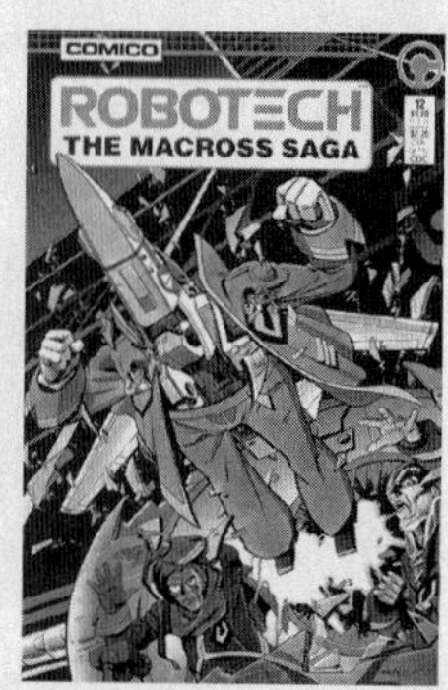

Robotech: The Macross Saga #12 © Comico

GD VG FN VF VF/NM NM-
2.0 4.0 6.0 8.0 9.0 9.2

4-Collector's set ($4.00)-Contains both versions bagged with Bat-Signal hologram trading card 6.00
Multi-pack (All four issues w/hologram sticker) 12.00
Deluxe Complete Set ($30.00)-Contains all 14 versions of #1-4 plus a new hologram trading card; numbered & limited to 25,000; comes with slipcase & 2 acid free backing boards 40.00

ROBIN III: CRY OF THE HUNTRESS
DC Comics: Dec, 1992 - No. 6, Mar, 1993 (Limited series)
1-6 ($2.50, collector's ed.)-Polybagged w/movement enhanced-c plus mini-poster of newsstand-c by Zeck 4.00
1-6 ($1.25, newsstand ed.): All have Zeck-c 3.00

ROBIN 3000
DC Comics (Elseworlds): 1992 - No. 2, 1992 ($4.95, mini-series, 52 pgs.)
1,2-Foil logo; Russell-c/a 5.00

ROBIN: YEAR ONE
DC Comics: 2000 - No. 4, 2001 ($4.95, square-bound, limited series)
1-4: Earliest days of Robin's career; Javier Pulido-c/a. 2,4-Two-Face app. 5.00
TPB (2002, 2008, $14.95/$14.99, 2 printings) r/#1-4 15.00

ROBOCOP
Marvel Comics: Oct, 1987 ($2.00, B&W, magazine, one-shot)
1-Movie adaptation 5.00

ROBOCOP (Also see Dark Horse Comics)
Marvel Comics: Mar, 1990 - No. 23, Jan, 1992 ($1.50)
1-Based on movie 4.00
2-23 3.00
nn (7/90, $4.95, 52 pgs.)-r/B&W magazine in color; adapts 1st movie 5.00

ROBOCOP
Dynamite Entertainment: 2010 - No. 6, 2010 ($3.50, limited series)
1-6-Follows the events of the first film; Neves-a 3.50

ROBOCOP (FRANK MILLER'S...)
Avatar Press: July, 2003 - No. 9, Jan, 2006 ($3.50/$3.99, limited series)
1-9-Frank Miller-s/Juan Ryp-a. 1-Three covers by Miller, Ryp, and Barrows. 2-Two covers 4.00
Free Comic Book Day Edition (4/03) Previews Robocop & Stargate SG•1; Busch-c 2.50

ROBOCOP: MORTAL COILS
Dark Horse Comics: Sept, 1993 - No. 4, Dec, 1993 ($2.50, limited series)
1-4: 1,2-Cago painted-c 3.00

ROBOCOP: PRIME SUSPECT
Dark Horse Comics: Oct, 1992 - No. 4, Jan, 1993 ($2.50, limited series)
1-4: 1,3-Nelson painted-c. 2,4-Bolton painted-c 3.00

ROBOCOP: ROULETTE
Dark Horse Comics: Dec, 1993 - No. 4, 1994 ($2.50, limited series)
1-4: 1,3-Nelson painted-c. 2,4-Bolton painted-c 3.00

ROBOCOP 2
Marvel Comics: Aug, 1990 ($2.25, B&W, magazine, 68 pgs.)
1-Adapts movie sequel 4.00

ROBOCOP 2
Marvel Comics: Aug, 1990; Late Aug, 1990 - #3, Late Sept, 1990 ($1.00, limited series)
nn-(8/90, $4.95, 68 pgs., color)-Same contents as B&W magazine 5.00
1: #1-3 reprint no number issue 3.00
2,3: 2-Guice-c(i) 3.00

ROBOCOP 3
Dark Horse Comics: July, 1993 - No. 3, Nov, 1993 ($2.50, limited series)
1-3: Nelson painted-c; Nguyen-a(p) 3.00

ROBOCOP VERSUS THE TERMINATOR
Dark Horse Comics: Sept, 1992 - No. 4, 1992 (Dec.) ($2.50, limited series)
1-4: Miller scripts & Simonson-c/a in all 3.00
1-Platinum Edition 6.00
NOTE: *All contain a different Robocop cardboard cut-out stand-up.*

ROBO DOJO
DC Comics (WildStorm): Apr, 2002 - No. 6, Sept, 2002 ($2.95, limited series)
1-6-Wolfman-s 3.00

ROBO-HUNTER (Also see Sam Slade...)
Eagle Comics: Apr, 1984 - No. 5, 1984 ($1.00)
1-5-2000 A.D. 3.00

GD VG FN VF VF/NM NM-
2.0 4.0 6.0 8.0 9.0 9.2

R.O.B.O.T. BATTALION 2050
Eclipse Comics: Mar, 1988 ($2.00, B&W, one-shot)
1 3.00

ROBOT COMICS
Renegade Press: No. 0, June, 1987 ($2.00, B&W, one-shot)
0-Bob Burden story & art 3.00

ROBOTECH
Antarctic Press: Mar, 1997 - No. 11, Nov, 1998 ($2.95)
1-11, Annual 1 (4/98, $2.95) 4.00
...Class Reunion (12/98, $3.95, B&W) 4.00
...Escape (5/98, $2.95, B&W), ...Final Fire (12/98, $2.95, B&W) 4.00

ROBOTECH
DC Comics (WildStorm): No. 0, Feb, 2003 - No. 6, Jul, 2003 ($2.50/$2.95, limited series)
0-Tommy Yune-s; art by Jim Lee, Garza, Bermejo and others; pin-up pages by various 3.00
1-6 ($2.95)-Long Vo-a 3.00
...: From the Stars (2003, $9.95, digest-size) r/#0-6 & Sourcebook 10.00
... Sourcebook (3/03, $2.95) pin-ups and info on characters and mecha; art by various 3.00

ROBOTECH: COVERT-OPS
Antarctic Press: Aug, 1998 - No. 2, Sept, 1998 ($2.95, B&W, limited series)
1,2-Gregory Lane-s/a 4.00

ROBOTECH DEFENDERS
DC Comics: Mar, 1985 - No. 2, Apr, 1985 (Mini-series)
1,2 3.00

ROBOTECH IN 3-D (TV)
Comico: Aug, 1987 ($2.50)
1-Steacy painted-c 4.00

ROBOTECH: INVASION
DC Comics (WildStorm): Feb, 2004 - No. 5, July, 2004 ($2.95, limited series)
1-5-Faerber & Yune-s/Miyazawa & Dogan-a 3.00

ROBOTECH: LOVE AND WAR
DC Comics (WildStorm): Aug, 2003 - No. 6, Jan, 2004 ($2.95, limited series)
1-6-Long Vo & Charles Park-a/Faerber & Yune-s. 2-Variant-c by Warren 3.00

ROBOTECH MASTERS (TV)
Comico: July, 1985 - No. 23, Apr, 1988 ($1.50)
1 6.00
2-23 4.00

ROBOTECH: PRELUDE TO THE SHADOW CHRONICLES
DC Comics (WildStorm): Dec, 2005 - No. 5, Mar, 2006 ($3.50, limited series)
1-5-Yune-s/Dogan & Udon Studios-a 3.50
TPB (2010, $17.99) r/#1-5; production art 18.00

ROBOTECH: SENTINELS - RUBICON
Antarctic Press: July, 1998 ($2.95, B&W)
1 4.00

ROBOTECH SPECIAL
Comico: May, 1988 ($2.50, one-shot, 44 pgs.)
1-Steacy wraparound-c; partial photo-c 5.00

ROBOTECH THE GRAPHIC NOVEL
Comico: Aug, 1986 ($5.95, 8-1/2x11", 52 pgs.)
1-Origin SDF-1; intro T.R. Edwards, Steacy-c/a; 2nd printing also exists (12/86) 7.00

ROBOTECH: THE MACROSS SAGA (TV)(Formerly Macross)
Comico: No. 2, Feb, 1985 - No. 36, Feb, 1989 ($1.50)
2 1 2 3 5 6 8
3-10 5.00
11-36: 12,17-Ken Steacy painted-c. 26-Begin $1.75-c. 35,36-($1.95) 4.00
Volume 1-4 TPB (WildStorm, 2003, $14.95, 5-3/4" x 8-1/4")1-Reprints #2-6 & Macross #1. 2- r/#7-12. 3-r/#13-18. 4-r/#19-24 15.00

ROBOTECH: THE NEW GENERATION
Comico: July, 1985 - No. 25, July, 1988
1 6.00
2-25 4.00

ROBOTECH: VERMILION
Antarctic Press: Mar, 1997 - No. 4, ($2.95, B&W, limited series)
1-4 4.00

Rocket Comics: Ignite #1 © DH

Rocket Kelly #3 © FOX

Rock Fantasy Comics #11 © R.F.C.

GD 2.0 | VG 4.0 | FN 6.0 | VF 8.0 | VF/NM 9.0 | NM- 9.2

ROBOTECH: WINGS OF GIBRALTAR
Antarctic Press: Aug, 1998 - No. 2, Sept, 1998 ($2.95, B&W, limited series)
1,2-Lee Duhig-s/a 4.00

ROBOTIX
Marvel Comics: Feb, 1986 (75¢, one-shot)
1-Based on toy 4.00

ROBOTMEN OF THE LOST PLANET (Also see Space Thrillers)
Avon Periodicals: 1952 (Also see Strange Worlds #19)
1-McCann-a (3 pgs.); Fawcette-a 116 232 348 742 1271 1900

ROB ROY
Dell Publishing Co.: 1954 (Disney-Movie)
Four Color 544-Manning-a, photo-c 7 14 21 50 83 115

ROCK, THE (WWF Wrestling)
Chaos! Comics: June, 2001 ($2.99, one-shot)
1-Photo-c; Grant-s/Neves-a 4.00

ROCK & ROLL HIGH SCHOOL
Roger Corman's Cosmic Comics: Oct, 1995 ($2.50)
1-Bob Fingerman scripts 3.00

ROCK AND ROLLO (Formerly TV Teens)
Charlton Comics: V2#14, Oct, 1957 - No. 19, Sept, 1958
V2#14-19 6 12 18 31 38 45

ROCK COMICS
Landgraphic Publ.: Jul/Aug, 1979 ($1.25, tabloid size, 28 pgs.)
1-N. Adams-c; Thor(not Marvel's) story by Adams 3 6 9 14 19 24

ROCKET COMICS
Hillman Periodicals: Mar, 1940 - No. 3, May, 1940
1-Rocket Riley, Red Roberts the Electro Man (origin), The Phantom Ranger, The Steel Shark, The Defender, Buzzard Barnes and his Sky Devils, Lefty Larson, & The Defender, the Man with a Thousand Faces begin (1st app. of each); all have Rocket Riley-c
265 530 795 1694 2897 4100
2,3 129 258 387 826 1413 2000

ROCKET COMICS: IGNITE
Dark Horse Comics: Apr, 2003 (Free Comic Book Day giveaway)
1-Previews Dark Horse series Syn, Lone, and Go Boy 7 2.50

ROCKETEER, THE (See Eclipse Graphic Album Series, Pacific Presents & Starslayer)

ROCKETEER ADVENTURE MAGAZINE, THE
Comico/Dark Horse Comics No. 3: July, 1988 ($2.00); No. 2, July, 1989 ($2.75); No. 3, Jan, 1995 ($2.95)
1-(7/88, $2.00)-Dave Stevens-c/a in all; Kaluta back-up-a; 1st app. Jonas (character based on The Shadow) 1 3 4 6 8 10
2-(7/89, $2.75)-Stevens/Dorman painted-c 6.00
3-(1/95, $2.95)-Includes pinups by Stevens, Gulacy, Plunkett, & Mignola 4.00
Volume 2-(9/96, $9.95, magazine size TPB)-Reprints #1-3 10.00

ROCKETEER SPECIAL EDITION, THE
Eclipse Comics: Nov, 1984 ($1.50, Baxter paper)(Chapter 5 of Rocketeer serial)
1-Stevens-c/a; Kaluta back-c; pin-ups inside 2 4 6 8 10 12
NOTE: *Originally intended to be published in Pacific Presents.*

ROCKETEER, THE: THE COMPLETE ADVENTURES
IDW Publishing: Oct, 2009 ($29.99/$75.00, hardcover)
HC-Reprints of Dave Stevens' Rocketeer stories in Starslayer #1-3, Pacific Presents #1,2, Rocketeer Special Edition and Rocketeer Adventure Magazine #1-3; all re-colored 30.00
... Deluxe Edition ($75.00, 8"x12" slipcased HC) larger size reprints of HC content plus 100 bonus pages of sketch art, layouts, design work; intro. by Thomas Jane 110.00
... Deluxe Edition 2nd printing ($75.00, oversized slipcased HC) 75.00

ROCKETEER, THE: THE OFFICIAL MOVIE ADAPTATION
W. D. Publications (Disney): 1991
nn-($5.95, 68 pgs.)-Squarebound deluxe edition 6.00
nn-($2.95, 68 pgs.)-Stapled regular edition 4.00
3-D Comic Book (1991, $7.98, 52 pgs.) 8.00

ROCKET KELLY (See The Bouncer, Green Mask #10); becomes Li'l Pan #6)
Fox Feature Syndicate: 1944; Fall, 1945 - No. 5, Oct-Nov, 1946
nn (1944), 1 (Fall, 1945) 36 72 108 214 347 480
2-The Puppeteer app. (costumed hero) 24 48 72 142 234 325
3-5: 5-(#5 on cover, #4 inside) 21 42 63 126 206 285

GD 2.0 | VG 4.0 | FN 6.0 | VF 8.0 | VF/NM 9.0 | NM- 9.2

ROCKETMAN (Strange Fantasy #2 on) (See Hello Pal & Scoop Comics)
Ajax/Farrell Publications: June, 1952 (Strange Stories of the Future)
1-Rocketman & Cosmo 40 80 120 246 411 575

ROCKET RACCOON (Also see Incredible Hulk #271)
Marvel Comics: May, 1985 - No. 4, Aug, 1985 (color, limited series)
1-4: Mignola-a 4.00

ROCKET SHIP X
Fox Features Syndicate: September, 1951; 1952
1 63 126 189 403 689 975
1952 (nn, nd, no publ.)-Edited 1951-c (exist?) 39 78 117 231 378 525

ROCKET TO ADVENTURE LAND (See Pixie Puzzle...)

ROCKET TO THE MOON
Avon Periodicals: 1951
nn-Orlando-c/a; adapts Otis Adelbert Kline's "Maza of the Moon"
123 246 369 787 1344 1900

ROCK FANTASY COMICS
Rock Fantasy Comics: Dec, 1989 - No. 16?, 1991 ($2.25/$3.00, B&W)(No cover price)
1-Pink Floyd part 1 5.00
1-2nd printing ($3.00-c) 3.00
2,3: 2-Rolling Stones #1. 3-Led Zeppelin #1 4.00
2,3: 2nd printings ($3.00-c, 1/90 & 2/90) 3.00
4-Stevie Nicks Not published
5-Monstrosities of Rock #1; photo back-c 4.00
5-2nd printing ($3.00, 3/90 indicia, 2/90-c) 3.00
6-9,11-15,17,18: 6-Guns n' Roses #1 (1st & 2nd printings, 3/90)-Begin $3.00-c. 7-Sex Pistols #1. 8-Alice Cooper; not published. 9-Van Halen #1; photo back-c. 11-Jimi Hendrix #1; wraparound-c 3.00
10-Kiss #1; photo back-c 2 4 6 8 10 12
16-($5.00, 68 pgs.)-The Great Gig in the Sky(Floyd) 5.00

ROCK HAPPENING (See Bunny and Harvey Pop Comics:...)

ROCK N' ROLL COMICS
DC Comics: Dec./Jan 1956 (ashcan)
nn-Ashcan comic, not distributed to newsstands, only for in house use (no known sales)

ROCK N' ROLL COMICS
Revolutionary Comics: Jun, 1989 - No. 65 ($1.50/$1.95/$2.50, B&W/col. #15 on)
1-Guns N' Roses 1 2 3 5 6 8
1-2nd thru 7th printings. 7th printing (full color w/new-c/a) 3.00
2-Metallica 1 3 4 6 8 10
2-2nd thru 6th printings (6th in color) 3.00
3-Bon Jovi (no reprints) 1 2 3 5 6 8
4-8,10-65: 4-Motley Crue(2nd printing only, 1st destroyed). 5-Def Leppard (2 printings). 6-Rolling Stones(4 printings). 7-The Who (3 printings). 8-Skid Row; not published. 10-Warrant/Whitesnake(2 printings; 1st has 2 diff.-c). 11-Aerosmith (2 printings?). 12-New Kids on the Block(2 printings). 12-3rd printing; rewritten & titled NKOTB Hate Book. 13-Led Zeppelin. 14-Sex Pistols. 15-Poison; 1st color issue. 16-Van Halen. 17-Madonna. 18-Alice Cooper. 19-Public Enemy/2 Live Crew. 20-Queensryche/Tesla. 21-Prince? 22-AC/DC; begin $2.50-c. 23-Living Colour. 26-Michael Jackson. 29-Ozzy. 45,46-Grateful Dead. 49-Rush. 50,51-Bob Dylan. 56-David Bowie 5.00
9-Kiss 2 4 6 8 10 12
9-2nd & 3rd printings 3.00
NOTE: *Most issues were reprinted except #3. Later reprints are in color. #8 was not released.*

ROCKO'S MODERN LIFE (TV)
Marvel Comics: June, 1994 - No. 7, Dec, 1994 ($1.95) (Nickelodeon cartoon)
1-7 3.00

ROCKY AND HIS FIENDISH FRIENDS (TV)(Bullwinkle)
Gold Key: Oct, 1962 - No. 5, Sept, 1963 (Jay Ward)
1 (25¢, 80 pgs.) 14 28 42 97 194 290
2,3 (25¢, 80 pgs.) 10 20 30 72 131 190
4,5 (Regular size, 12¢) 8 16 24 54 90 125

ROCKY AND HIS FRIENDS (See Kite Fun Book & March of Comics #216 in the Promotional Comics section)

ROCKY AND HIS FRIENDS (TV)
Dell Publishing Co.: No. 1128, 8-10/60 - No.1311,1962 (Jay Ward)
Four Color 1128 (#1) (8-10/60) 27 54 81 197 399 600
Four Color 1152 (12-2/61), 1166, 1208, 1275, 1311('62)
17 34 51 118 242 365

ROCKY HORROR PICTURE SHOW THE COMIC BOOK, THE
Caliber Press: Jul, 1990 - No. 3, Jan, 1991 ($2.95, mini-series, 52 pgs.)

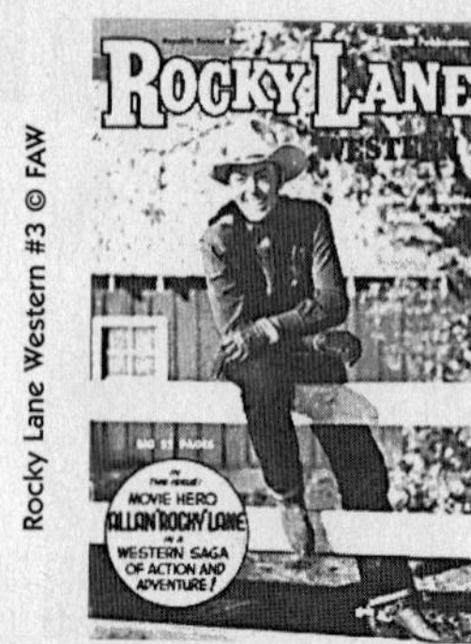

Rocky Lane Western #3 © FAW

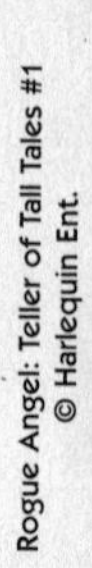

Rogue Angel: Teller of Tall Tales #1 © Harlequin Ent.

ROM #27 © Parker Brothers

GD VG FN VF VF/NM NM-
2.0 4.0 6.0 8.0 9.0 9.2

GD VG FN VF VF/NM NM-
2.0 4.0 6.0 8.0 9.0 9.2

1-3: 1-Adapts cult film plus photos, etc., 1-2nd printing 4.00
...Collection ($4.95) 5.00

ROCKY JONES SPACE RANGER (See Space Adventures #15-18)

ROCKY JORDEN PRIVATE EYE (See Private Eye)

ROCKY LANE WESTERN (Allan Rocky Lane starred in Republic movies & TV for a short time as Allan Lane, Red Ryder & Rocky Lane) (See Black Jack Fawcett Movie Comics, Motion Picture Comics & Six-Gun Heroes)
Fawcett Publications/Charlton No. 56 on: May, 1949 - No. 87, Nov, 1959

1 (36 pgs.)-Rocky, his stallion Black Jack, & Slim Pickens begin; photo-c begin, end #57; photo back-c 55 110 165 352 601 850
2 (36 pgs.)-Last photo back-c 22 44 66 132 216 300
3-5 (52 pgs.): 4-Captain Tootsie by Beck 17 34 51 98 154 210
6,10 (36 pgs.): 10-Complete western novelette "Badman's Reward" 14 28 42 76 108 140
7-9 (52 pgs.) 14 28 42 82 121 160
11-13,15-17,19,20 (52 pgs.): 15-Black Jack's Hitching Post begins, ends #25. 20-Last Slim Pickens 12 24 36 67 94 120
14,18 (36 pgs.) 10 20 30 58 79 100
21,23,24 (52 pgs.): 21-Dee Dickens begins, ends #55,57,65-68 10 20 30 58 79 100
22,25-28,30 (36 pgs. begin) 10 20 30 54 72 90
29-Classic complete novel "The Land of Missing Men" with hidden land of ancient temple ruins (r-in #65) 14 28 42 76 108 140
31-40 9 18 27 52 69 85
41-54 9 18 27 47 61 75
55-Last Fawcett issue (1/54) 9 18 27 52 69 85
56-1st Charlton issue (2/54)-Photo-c 14 28 42 82 121 160
57,60-Photo-c 10 20 30 54 72 90
58,59,61-64,66-78,80-86: 59-61-Young Falcon app. 64-Slim Pickens app. 66-68: Reprints #30,31,32 8 16 24 44 57 70
65-r/#29, "The Land of Missing Men" 9 18 27 50 65 80
79-Giant Edition (68 pgs.) 10 20 30 58 79 100
87-Last issue 9 18 27 52 69 85

NOTE: *Complete novels in #10, 14, 18, 22, 25, 30-32, 36, 38, 39, 49. Captain Tootsie in #4, 12, 20. Big Bow and Little Arrow in #11, 28, 63. Black Jack's Hitching Post in #15-25, 64, 73.*

ROCKY LANE WESTERN
AC Comics: 1989 ($2.50, B&W, one-shot?)

1-Photo-c; Giordano reprints 4.00
Annual 1 (1991, $2.95, B&W, 44 pgs.)-photo front/back & inside-c; reprints 4.00

ROD CAMERON WESTERN (Movie star)
Fawcett Publications: Feb, 1950 - No. 20, Apr, 1953

1-Rod Cameron, his horse War Paint, & Sam The Sheriff begin; photo front/back-c begin 30 60 90 177 289 400
2 15 30 45 86 133 180
3-Novel length story "The Mystery of the Seven Cities of Cibola" 14 28 42 82 121 160
4-10: 9-Last photo back-c 12 24 36 69 97 125
11-19 10 20 30 58 79 100
20-Last issue & photo-c 11 22 33 62 86 110

NOTE: *Novel length stories in No. 1-8, 12-14.*

RODEO RYAN (See A-1 Comics #8)

ROGAN GOSH
DC Comics (Vertigo): 1994 ($6.95, one-shot)

nn-Peter Milligan scripts 7.00

ROGER DODGER (Also in Exciting Comics #57 on)
Standard Comics: No. 5, Aug, 1952

5-Teen-age 6 12 18 31 38 45

ROGER RABBIT (Also see Marvel Graphic Novel)
Disney Comics: June, 1990 - No. 18, Nov, 1991 ($1.50)

1-18-All new stories 3.00
In 3-D 1 (1992, $2.50)-Sold at Wal-Mart?; w/glasses 4.00

ROGER RABBIT'S TOONTOWN
Disney Comics: Aug, 1991 - No. 5, Dec, 1991 ($1.50)

1-5 3.00

ROGER ZELAZNY'S AMBER: THE GUNS OF AVALON
DC Comics: 1996 - No. 3, 1996 ($6.95, limited series)

1-3: Based on novel 7.00

ROG 2000
Pacific Comics: June, 1982 ($2.95, 44 pgs., B&W, one-shot, magazine)

nn-Byrne-c/a (r) 2 4 6 8 10 12
2nd printing (7/82) 1 2 3 4 5 7

ROG 2000
Fantagraphics Books: 1987 - No. 2, 1987 ($2.00, limited series)

1,2-Byrne-r 3.00

ROGUE (From X-Men)
Marvel Comics: Jan, 1995 - No. 4, Apr, 1995 ($2.95, limited series)

1-4: 1-Gold foil logo 4.00
TPB-($12.95) r/#1-4 13.00

ROGUE (Volume 2)
Marvel Comics: Sept, 2001 - No. 4, Dec, 2001 ($2.50, limited series)

1-4-Julie Bell painted-c/Lopresti-a; Rogue's early days with X-Men 3.00

ROGUE (From X-Men)
Marvel Comics: Sept, 2004 - No. 12, Aug, 2005 ($2.99)

1-12: 1-Richards-a. 4-Gambit app. 11-Sunfire dies, Rogue absorbs his powers 3.00
...: Going Rogue TPB (2005, $14.99) r/#1-6 15.00
...: Forget-Me-Not TPB (2006, $14.99) r/#7-12 15.00

ROGUE ANGEL: TELLER OF TALL TALES (Based on the Alex Archer novels)
IDW Publishing: Feb, 2008 - No. 5, Jun, 2008 ($3.99)

1-5-Annja Creed adventures; Barbara-Kesel-s/Renae De Liz-a 4.00

ROGUES GALLERY
DC Comics: 1996 ($3.50, one-shot)

1-Pinups of DC villains by various artists 4.00

ROGUES, THE (VILLAINS) (See The Flash)
DC Comics: Feb, 1998 ($1.95, one-shot)

1-Augustyn-s/Pearson-c 3.00

ROKKIN
DC Comics (WildStorm): Sept, 2006 - No. 6, Feb, 2007 ($2.99, limited series)

1-6-Hartnell-s/Bradshaw-a 3.00

ROLLING STONES: VOODOO LOUNGE
Marvel Comics: 1995 ($6.95, Prestige format, one-shot)

nn-Dave McKean-script/design/art 7.00

ROLY POLY COMIC BOOK
Green Publishing Co.: 1945 - No. 15, 1946 (MLJ reprints)

1-(No number on cover or indicia, "1945 issue" on cover) Red Rube & Steel Sterling begin; Sahle-c 32 64 96 188 307 425
6-The Blue Circle & The Steel Fist app. 20 40 60 117 189 260
10-Origin Red Rube retold; Steel Sterling story (Zip #41) 28 56 84 165 270 375
11,12: The Black Hood app. in both 20 40 60 115 185 255
14-Classic decapitation-c; the Black Hood app. 58 116 174 371 636 900
15-The Blue Circle & The Steel Fist app.; cover exact swipe from Fox Blue Beetle #1 32 64 96 192 314 435

ROM (Based on the Parker Brothers toy)
Marvel Comics Group: Dec, 1979 - No. 75, Feb, 1986

1-Origin/1st app. 3 6 9 14 20 25
2-16,19-23,28-30: 5-Dr. Strange. 13-Saga of the Space Knights begins. 19-X-Men cameo. 23-Powerman & Iron Fist app. 1 2 3 5 6 8
17,18-X-Men app. 2 4 6 9 12 15
24-27: 24-F.F. cameo; Skrulls, Nova & The New Champions app. 25-Double size. 26,27-Galactus app. 1 2 3 5 7 9
31-49,51-60: 31,32-Brotherhood of Evil Mutants app. 32-X-Men cameo. 34,35-Sub-Mariner app. 41,42-Dr. Strange app. 56,57-Alpha Flight app. 58,59-Ant-Man app. 6.00
50-Skrulls app. (52 pgs.) Pin-ups by Konkle, Austin 1 2 3 4 5 7
61-74: 65-West Coast Avengers & Beta Ray Bill app. 65,66-X-Men app. 6.00
75-Last issue 2 4 6 9 12 15
Annual 1-4: (1982-85, 52 pgs.) 6.00

NOTE: ***Austin** c-3i, 18i, 61i. **Byrne** a-74i; c-56, 57, 74. **Ditko** a-59-75p, Annual 4. **Golden** c-7-12, 19. **Guice** a-61i; c-55, 58, 60p, 70p. **Layton** a-59i, 72i; c-15, 59i, 69. **Miller** c-2p?, 3p, 17p, 18p. **Russell** a(i)-64, 65, 67, 69, 71, 75; c-64, 65i, 66, 71i, 75. **Severin** c-41p. **Sienkiewicz** a-53i; c-46, 47, 52-54, 68, 71p, Annual 2. **Simonson** c-18. **P. Smith** c-59p. **Starlin** c-67. **Zeck** c-50.*

ROMANCE (See True Stories of...)

ROMANCE AND CONFESSION STORIES (See Giant Comics Edition)
St. John Publishing Co.: No date (1949) (25¢, 100 pgs.)

1-Baker-c/a; remaindered St. John love comics 50 100 150 315 533 750

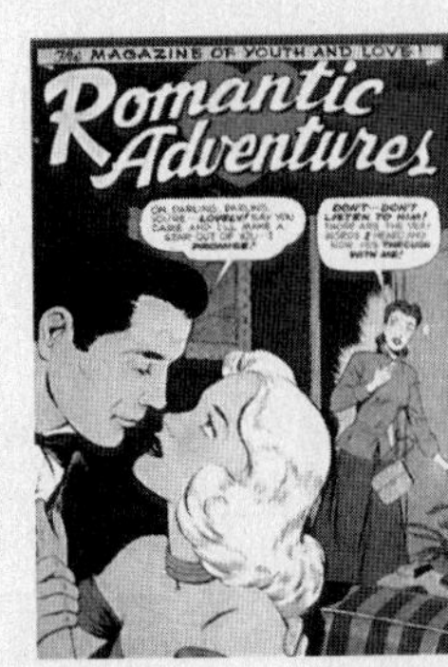

Romantic Adventures #1 © ACG

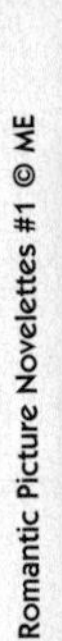

Romantic Picture Novelettes #1 © ME

Romantic Story #16 © FAW

ROMANCE DIARY
Marvel Comics (CDS)(CLDS): Dec, 1949 - No. 2, Mar, 1950

	GD 2.0	VG 4.0	FN 6.0	VF 8.0	VF/NM 9.0	NM- 9.2
1,2	15	30	45	88	137	185

ROMANCE OF FLYING, THE
David McKay Publications: 1942

	GD 2.0	VG 4.0	FN 6.0	VF 8.0	VF/NM 9.0	NM- 9.2
Feature Books 33 (nn)-WW II photos	15	30	45	86	133	180

ROMANCES OF MOLLY MANTON (See Molly Manton)

ROMANCES OF NURSE HELEN GRANT, THE
Atlas Comics (VPI): Aug, 1957

	GD 2.0	VG 4.0	FN 6.0	VF 8.0	VF/NM 9.0	NM- 9.2
1	9	18	27	50	65	80

ROMANCES OF THE WEST (Becomes Romantic Affairs #3?)
Marvel Comics (SPC): Nov, 1949 - No. 2, Mar, 1950 (52 pgs.)

	GD 2.0	VG 4.0	FN 6.0	VF 8.0	VF/NM 9.0	NM- 9.2
1-Movie photo-c of Yvonne DeCarlo & Howard Duff (Calamity Jane & Sam Bass)	23	46	69	136	223	310
2-Photo-c	15	30	45	85	130	175

ROMANCE STORIES OF TRUE LOVE (Formerly True Love Problems & Advice Illustrated)
Harvey Publications: No. 45, 5/57 - No. 50, 3/58; No. 51, 9/58 - No. 52, 11/58

	GD 2.0	VG 4.0	FN 6.0	VF 8.0	VF/NM 9.0	NM- 9.2
45-51: 45,46,48-50-Powell-a	6	12	18	31	38	45
52-Matt Baker-a	9	18	27	47	61	75

ROMANCE TALES (Formerly Western Winners #6?)
Marvel Comics (CDS): No. 7, Oct, 1949 - No. 9, April, 1950 (7-9: photo-c)

	GD 2.0	VG 4.0	FN 6.0	VF 8.0	VF/NM 9.0	NM- 9.2
7	15	30	45	84	127	170
8,9: 8-Everett-a	10	20	30	58	79	100

ROMANCE TRAIL
National Periodical Publications: July-Aug, 1949 - No. 6, May-June, 1950
(All photo-c & 52 pgs.)

	GD 2.0	VG 4.0	FN 6.0	VF 8.0	VF/NM 9.0	NM- 9.2
1-Kinstler, Toth-a; Jimmy Wakely photo-c	55	110	165	352	601	850
2-Kinstler-a; Jim Bannon photo-c	31	62	93	182	296	410
3-Tex Williams photo-c; Kinstler, Toth-a	32	64	96	192	314	435
4-Jim Bannon as Red Ryder photo-c; Toth-a	24	48	72	140	230	320
5,6: Photo-c on both. 5-Kinstler-a	22	44	66	128	209	290

ROMAN HOLIDAYS, THE (TV)
Gold Key: Feb, 1973 - No. 4, Nov, 1973 (Hanna-Barbera)

	GD 2.0	VG 4.0	FN 6.0	VF 8.0	VF/NM 9.0	NM- 9.2
1	4	8	12	28	44	60
2-4	3	6	9	18	27	35

ROMANTIC ADVENTURES (My... #49-67, covers only)
American Comics Group (B&I Publ. Co.): Mar-Apr, 1949 - No. 67, July, 1956 (Becomes My... #68 on)

	GD 2.0	VG 4.0	FN 6.0	VF 8.0	VF/NM 9.0	NM- 9.2
1	19	38	57	111	176	240
2	12	24	36	67	94	120
3-10	10	20	30	54	72	90
11-20 (4/52)	9	18	27	47	61	75
21-45,51,52: 52-Last Pre-code (2/55)	8	16	24	42	54	65
46-49-3-D effect-c/stories (TrueVision)	14	28	42	76	108	140
50-Classic cover/story "Love of A Lunatic"	12	24	36	69	97	125
53-67	7	14	21	37	46	55

NOTE: *#1-23, 52 pgs.* ***Shelly*** *a-40. Whitney c/art in many issues.*

ROMANTIC AFFAIRS (Formerly Molly Manton's Romances #2 and/or Romances of the West #2 and/or Our Love #2?)
Marvel Comics (SPC): No. 3, Mar, 1950

	GD 2.0	VG 4.0	FN 6.0	VF 8.0	VF/NM 9.0	NM- 9.2
3-Photo-c from Molly Manton's Romances #2	10	20	30	58	79	100

ROMANTIC CONFESSIONS
Hillman Periodicals: Oct, 1949 - V3#1, Apr-May, 1953

	GD 2.0	VG 4.0	FN 6.0	VF 8.0	VF/NM 9.0	NM- 9.2
V1#1-McWilliams-a	18	36	54	103	162	220
2-Briefer-a; negligee panels	11	22	33	62	86	110
3-12	10	20	30	54	72	90
V2#1,2,4-8,10-12: 2-McWilliams-a	9	18	27	50	65	80
3-Krigstein-a	10	20	30	56	76	95
9-One pg. Frazetta ad	9	18	27	50	65	80
V3#1	9	18	27	47	61	75

ROMANTIC HEARTS
Story Comics/Master/Merit Pubs.: Mar, 1951 - No. 10, Oct, 1952; July, 1953 - No. 12, July, 1955

	GD 2.0	VG 4.0	FN 6.0	VF 8.0	VF/NM 9.0	NM- 9.2
1(3/51) (1st Series)	15	30	45	84	127	170
2	9	18	27	52	69	85
3-10: Cameron-a	9	18	27	47	61	75
1(7/53) (2nd Series)-Some say #11 on-c	10	20	30	58	79	100
2	8	16	24	44	57	70
3-12	8	16	24	40	50	60

ROMANTIC LOVE
Avon Periodicals/Realistic (No #14-19): 9-10/49 - #3, 1-2/50; #4, 2-3/51 - #13, 10/52; #20, 3-4/54 - #23, 9-10/54

	GD 2.0	VG 4.0	FN 6.0	VF 8.0	VF/NM 9.0	NM- 9.2
1-c-/Avon paperback #252	32	64	96	188	307	425
2-5: 3-c-/paperback Novel Library #12. 4-c-/paperback Diversey Prize Novel #5. 5-c-/paperback Novel Library #34	20	40	60	114	182	250
6- "Thrill Crazy" marijuana story; c-/Avon paperback #207; Kinstler-a	27	54	81	160	263	365
7,8: 8-Astarita-a(2)	19	38	57	111	176	240
9-12: 9-c-/paperback Novel Library #41; Kinstler-a. 10-c-/Avon paperback #212. 11-c-/paperback Novel Library #17; Kinstler-a. 12-c-/paperback Novel Library #13	20	40	60	117	189	260
13,21-23: 22,23-Kinstler-c	19	38	57	109	172	235
20-Kinstler-c/a	20	40	60	114	182	250
nn(1-3/53)(Realistic-r)	13	26	39	74	105	135

NOTE: ***Astarita*** *a-7, 10, 11, 21. Painted c-1-3, 5, 7-11, 13. Photo c-4, 6.*

ROMANTIC LOVE
Quality Comics Group: 1963-1964

	GD 2.0	VG 4.0	FN 6.0	VF 8.0	VF/NM 9.0	NM- 9.2
I.W. Reprint #2,3,8,11: 2-r/Romantic Love #2	2	4	6	10	14	18

ROMANTIC MARRIAGE (Cinderella Love #25 on)
Ziff-Davis/St. John No. 18 on (#1-8: 52 pgs.): #1-3 (1950, no months); #4, 5-6/51 - #17, 9/52; #18, 9/53 - #24, 9/54

	GD 2.0	VG 4.0	FN 6.0	VF 8.0	VF/NM 9.0	NM- 9.2
1-Photo-c; Cary Grant/Betsy Drake photo back-c.	22	44	66	128	209	290
2-Painted-c; Anderson-a (also #15)	15	30	45	85	130	175
3-9: 3,4,8,9-Painted-c; 5-7-Photo-c	14	28	42	81	118	155
10-Unusual format; front-c is a painted-c; back-c is a photo-c complete with logo, price, etc.	21	42	63	122	199	275
11-17 13-Photo-c. 15-Signed story by Anderson. 17-(9/52)-Last Z-D issue	14	28	42	76	108	140
18-22,24: 20-Photo-c	14	28	42	76	108	140
23-Baker-c; all stories are reprinted from #15	15	30	45	84	127	170

ROMANTIC PICTURE NOVELETTES
Magazine Enterprises: 1946

	GD 2.0	VG 4.0	FN 6.0	VF 8.0	VF/NM 9.0	NM- 9.2
1-Mary Worth-r; Creig Flessel-c	16	32	48	94	147	200

ROMANTIC SECRETS (Becomes Time For Love)
Fawcett/Charlton Comics No. 5 (10/55) on: Sept, 1949 - No. 39, 4/53; No. 5, 10/55 - No. 52, 11/64 (#1-39: photo-c)

	GD 2.0	VG 4.0	FN 6.0	VF 8.0	VF/NM 9.0	NM- 9.2
1-(52 pg. issues begin, end #?)	18	36	54	103	162	220
2,3	11	22	33	62	86	110
4,9-Evans-a	12	24	36	67	94	120
5-8,10(9/50)	9	18	27	52	69	85
11-23	9	18	27	47	61	75
24-Evans-a	9	18	27	52	69	85
25-39('53)	8	16	24	44	57	70
5 (Charlton, 2nd Series)(10/55, formerly Negro Romances #4)	10	20	30	58	79	100
6-10	8	16	24	44	57	70
11-20	4	8	12	23	36	48
21-35	3	6	9	20	30	40
36-52('64)	3	6	9	16	23	30

NOTE: ***Bailey*** *a-20.* ***Powell*** *a(1st series)-5, 7, 10, 12, 16, 17, 20, 26, 29, 33, 34, 36, 37.* ***Sekowsky*** *a-26.* ***Swayze*** *a(1st series)-16, 18, 19, 23, 26-28, 31, 32, 39.*

ROMANTIC STORY (Cowboy Love #28 on)
Fawcett/Charlton Comics No. 23 on: 11/49 - #22, Sum, 1953; #23, 5/54 - #27, 12/54; #28, 8/55 - #130, 11/73

	GD 2.0	VG 4.0	FN 6.0	VF 8.0	VF/NM 9.0	NM- 9.2
1-Photo-c begin, end #24; 52 pgs. begins	18	36	54	103	162	220
2	11	22	33	62	86	110
3-5	10	20	30	54	72	90
6-14	9	18	27	50	65	80
15-Evans-a	10	20	30	54	72	90
16-22(Sum, '53; last Fawcett issue). 21-Toth-a?	8	16	24	42	54	65
23-39: 26,29-Wood swipes	7	14	21	37	46	55
40-(100 pgs.)	11	22	33	64	90	115
41-50	3	6	9	21	32	42
51-80: 57-Hypo needle story	3	6	9	16	23	30
81-99	2	4	6	10	14	18
100	2	4	6	13	28	22
101-130: 120-Bobby Sherman pin-up	2	4	6	9	12	15

Rose and Thorn #1 © DC

Route #666 © CRO

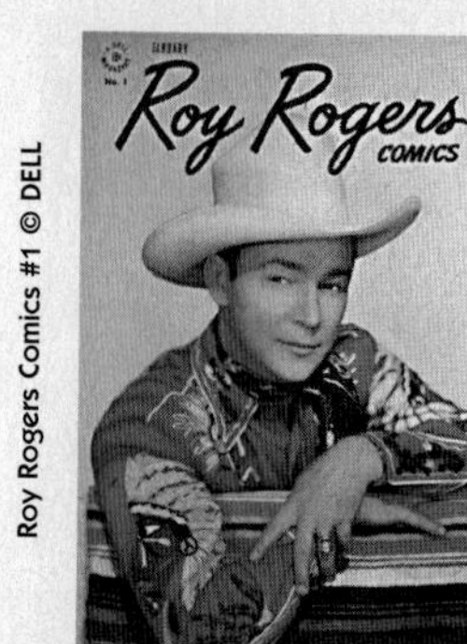

Roy Rogers Comics #1 © DELL

	GD 2.0	VG 4.0	FN 6.0	VF 8.0	VF/NM 9.0	NM- 9.2

NOTE: *Jim Aparo a-94.* ***Powell*** *a-7, 8, 16, 20, 30.* ***Marcus Swayze*** *a-2, 12, 20, 32.*

ROMANTIC THRILLS (See Fox Giants)

ROMANTIC WESTERN
Fawcett Publications: Winter, 1949 - No. 3, June, 1950 (All Photo-c)

	GD	VG	FN	VF	VF/NM	NM-
1	22	44	66	128	209	290
2-(Spr/50)-Williamson, McWilliams-a	20	40	60	114	182	250
3	15	30	45	85	130	175

ROMEO TUBBS (...That Lovable Teenager; formerly My Secret Life)
Fox Feature Syndicate/Green Publ. Co. No. 27: No. 26, 5/50 - No. 28, 7/50; No. 1, 1950; No. 27, 12/52

	GD	VG	FN	VF	VF/NM	NM-
26-Teen-age	11	22	33	64	90	115
28 (7/50)	10	20	30	58	79	100
27 (12/52)-Contains Pedro on inside; Wood-a (exist?)	15	30	45	84	127	170

RONALD McDONALD (TV)
Charlton Press (King Features Synd.): Sept, 1970 - No. 4, March, 1971

	GD	VG	FN	VF	VF/NM	NM-
1	8	16	24	56	93	130
2-4	5	10	15	32	51	70
V2#1,3-Special reprint for McDonald systems; "Not for resale" on cover	6	12	18	39	62	85

RONIN
DC Comics: July, 1983 - No. 6, Aug, 1984 ($2.50, limited series, 52 pgs.)

	GD	VG	FN	VF	VF/NM	NM-
1-5-Frank Miller-c/a/scripts in all	2	3	4	6	8	10
6-Scarcer; has fold-out poster.	2	4	6	8	10	12
Trade paperback (1987, $12.95)-Reprints #1-6						13.00

RONNA
Knight Press: Apr, 1997 ($2.95, B&W, one-shot)

	GD	VG	FN	VF	VF/NM	NM-
1-Beau Smith-s						3.00

ROOK (See Eerie Magazine & Warren Presents: The Rook)
Warren Publications: Oct, 1979 - No. 14, April, 1982 (B&W magazine)

	GD	VG	FN	VF	VF/NM	NM-
1-Nino-a/Corben-c; with 8 pg. color insert	3	6	9	16	23	30
2-4,6,7: 2-Voltar by Alcala begins. 3,4-Toth-a	2	4	6	9	13	16
5,8-14: 11-Zorro-s. 12-14-Eagle by Severin	2	4	6	9	13	16

ROOK
Harris Comics: No. 0, Jun, 1995 - No. 4, 1995 ($2.95)

	GD	VG	FN	VF	VF/NM	NM-
0-4: 0-short stories (3) w/preview. 4-Brereton-c.						3.00

ROOKIE COP (Formerly Crime and Justice?)
Charlton Comics: No. 27, Nov, 1955 - No. 33, Aug, 1957

	GD	VG	FN	VF	VF/NM	NM-
27	9	18	27	47	61	75
28-33	6	12	18	31	38	45

ROOM 222 (TV)
Dell Publishing Co.: Jan, 1970; No. 2, May, 1970 - No. 4, Jan, 1971

	GD	VG	FN	VF	VF/NM	NM-
1	5	10	15	34	55	75
2-4: 2,4-Photo-c. 3-Marijuana story. 4 r/#1	4	8	12	22	34	45

ROOTIE KAZOOTIE (TV)(See 3-D-ell)
Dell Publishing Co.: No. 415, Aug, 1952 - No. 6, Oct-Dec, 1954

	GD	VG	FN	VF	VF/NM	NM-
Four Color 415 (#1)	9	18	27	65	113	160
Four Color 459,502(#2,3), 4(4-6/54)-6	7	14	21	47	76	105

ROOTS OF THE SWAMP THING
DC Comics: July, 1986 - No.5, Nov, 1986 ($2.00, Baxter paper, 52 pgs.)

	GD	VG	FN	VF	VF/NM	NM-
1-5: r/Swamp Thing #1-10 by Wrightson & House of Mystery-r. 1-new Wrightson-c (2-5 reprinted covers).						4.00

ROSE (See Bone)
Cartoon Books: Nov, 2000 - No. 3, Feb, 2002 ($5.95, lim. series, square-bound)

	GD	VG	FN	VF	VF/NM	NM-
1-3-Prequel to Bone; Jeff Smith-s/Charles Vess painted-a/c						6.00
HC (2001, $29.95) r/#1-3; new Vess cover painting						30.00
SC (2002, $19.95) r/#1-3; new Vess cover painting						20.00
1-($6.00)-Blood & Glory Edition						6.00

ROSE AND THORN
DC Comics: Feb, 2004 - No. 6, July, 2004 ($2.95, limited series)

	GD	VG	FN	VF	VF/NM	NM-
1-6-Simone-sMelo-a/Hughes-c						3.00

ROSWELL: LITTLE GREEN MAN (See Simpsons Comics #19-22)
Bongo Comics: 1996 - No. 6 ($2.95, quarterly)

	GD	VG	FN	VF	VF/NM	NM-
1-6						4.00
...Walks Among Us ('97, $12.95, TPB) r/ #1-3 & Simpsons flip books						13.00

	GD 2.0	VG 4.0	FN 6.0	VF 8.0	VF/NM 9.0	NM- 9.2

ROUND TABLE OF AMERICA: PERSONALITY CRISIS (See Big Bang Comics)
Image Comics: Aug, 2005 ($3.50, one-shot)

	GD	VG	FN	VF	VF/NM	NM-
1-Carlos Rodriguez-a/Pedro Angosto-s						3.50

ROUNDUP (...Western Crime Stories)
D. S. Publishing Co.: July-Aug, 1948 - No. 5, Mar-Apr, 1949 (All 52 pgs.)

	GD	VG	FN	VF	VF/NM	NM-
1-Kiefer-a	18	36	54	107	169	230
2-5: 2-Marijuana drug mention story	14	28	42	82	121	160

ROUTE 666
CrossGeneration Comics: July, 2002 - No. 22, Jun, 2004 ($2.95)

	GD	VG	FN	VF	VF/NM	NM-
1-22-Bedard-s/Moline-a in most. 5-Richards-a. 15-McCrea-a						3.00
...: Highway to Horror (4/03, $15.95, TPB) r/#1-6						16.00
Vol. 2: Three-Ring Circus (2003, $15.95) r/#7-12						16.00

ROYAL ROY
Marvel Comics (Star Comics): May, 1985 - No.6, Mar, 1986 (Children's book)

	GD	VG	FN	VF	VF/NM	NM-
1-6						4.00

ROY CAMPANELLA, BASEBALL HERO
Fawcett Publications: 1950 (Brooklyn Dodgers)

	GD	VG	FN	VF	VF/NM	NM-
nn-Photo-c; life story	60	120	180	381	653	925

ROY ROGERS (See March of Comics #17, 35, 47, 62, 68, 73, 77, 86, 91, 100, 105, 116, 121, 131, 136, 146, 151, 161, 167, 176, 191, 206, 221, 236, 250)

ROY ROGERS AND TRIGGER
Gold Key: Apr, 1967

	GD	VG	FN	VF	VF/NM	NM-
1-Photo-c; reprints	4	8	12	28	44	60

ROY ROGERS ANNUAL
Wilson Publ. Co., Toronto/Dell: 1947 ("Giant Edition" on-c)(132 pgs., 50¢)

nn-Less than 5 known copies. Front and back cover art are from Roy Rogers #2. Stories reprinted from Roy Rogers #2, Four Color #137 and Four Color #153. (A copy in VG/FN was sold in 1986 for $400, in 1996 for $1200 & in 2000 for $1500; a FN+ sold for $1,650; a GD sold for $448 in 2008 and a FN sold for $717 in 2009.)

ROY ROGERS COMICS (See Western Roundup under Dell Giants)
Dell Publishing Co.: No. 38, 4/44 - No. 177, 12/47 (#38-166: 52 pgs.)

	GD	VG	FN	VF	VF/NM	NM-
Four Color 38 (1944)-49 pg. story; photo front/back-c on all 4-Color issues (1st western comic with photo-c)	148	296	444	1295	2648	4000
Four Color 63 (1945)-Color photos on all four-c	37	74	111	286	568	850
Four Color 86,95 (1945)	27	54	81	197	391	585
Four Color 109 (1946)	20	40	60	146	293	440
Four Color 117,124,137,144	16	32	48	114	232	350
Four Color 153,160,166: 166-48 pg. story	15	30	45	103	209	315
Four Color 177 (36 pgs.)-32 pg. story	14	28	42	99	200	300
HC (Dark Horse Books, 8/08, $49.95) r/Four Color #38,63,86,95,109; Roy Rogers Jr intro.						50.00

ROY ROGERS COMICS (...& Trigger #92(8/55)-on)(Roy starred in Republic movies, radio & TV) (Singing cowboy) (Also see Dale Evans, It Really Happened #8, Queen of the West Dale Evans, & Roy Rogers' Trigger)
Dell Publishing Co.: Jan, 1948 - No. 145, Sept-Oct, 1961 (#1-19: 36 pgs.)

	GD	VG	FN	VF	VF/NM	NM-
1-Roy, his horse Trigger, & Chuck Wagon Charley's Tales begin; photo-c begin, end #145	60	120	180	510	1030	1550
2	22	44	66	155	310	465
3-5	15	30	45	106	216	325
6-10	13	26	39	92	179	265
11-19: 19-Chuck Wagon Charley's Tales ends	11	22	33	80	150	220
20 (52 pgs.)-Trigger feature begins, ends #46	12	24	36	82	154	225
21-30 (52 pgs.)	10	20	30	70	125	180
31-46 (52 pgs.): 37-X-Mas-c	9	18	27	60	100	140
47-56 (36 pgs.): 47-Chuck Wagon Charley's Tales returns, ends #133. 49-X-mas-c. 55-Last photo back-c	7	14	21	47	76	105
57 (52 pgs.)-Heroin drug propaganda story	7	14	21	49	80	110
58-70 (52 pgs.): 58-Heroin drug use/dealing story. 61-X-Mas-c	7	14	21	47	76	105
71-80 (52 pgs.): 73-X-Mas-c	6	12	18	41	66	90
81-91 (36 pgs. #81-on): 85-X-Mas-c	6	12	18	39	62	85
92-99,101-110,112-118: 92-Title changed to Roy Rogers and Trigger (8/55)	6	12	18	37	59	80
100-Trigger feature returns, ends #131	6	12	18	43	69	95
111,119-124-Toth-a	7	14	21	45	73	100
125-131: 125-Toth-a (1 pg.)	5	10	15	35	55	75
132-144-Manning-a. 132-1st Dale Evans-sty by Russ Manning. 138,144-Dale Evans featured	6	12	18	39	62	85
145-Last issue	7	14	21	47	76	105

NOTE: ***Buscema*** *a-74-108(2 stories each).* ***Manning*** *a-123, 124, 132-144.* ***Marsh*** *a-110.*

Rugged Action #4 © MAR

Runaways V3 #1 © MAR

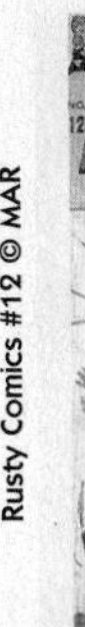
Rusty Comics #12 © MAR

	GD 2.0	VG 4.0	FN 6.0	VF 8.0	VF/NM 9.0	NM- 9.2

Photo back-c No. 1-9, 11-35, 38-55.

ROY ROGERS' TRIGGER
Dell Publishing Co.: No. 329, May, 1951 - No. 17, June-Aug, 1955

	GD	VG	FN	VF	VF/NM	NM-
Four Color 329 (#1)-Painted-c	13	26	39	92	179	265
2 (9-11/51)-Photo-c	10	20	30	73	134	195
3-5: 3-Painted-c begin, end #17, most by S. Savitt	6	12	18	43	69	95
6-17: Title merges with Roy Rogers after #17	5	10	15	35	55	75

ROY ROGERS WESTERN CLASSICS
AC Comics: 1989 -No. 4 ($2.95/$3.95, 44pgs.) (24 pgs. color, 16 pgs. B&W)

1-4: 1-Dale Evans-r by Manning, Trigger-r by Buscema; photo covers & interior photos by Roy & Dale. 2-Buscema-r (3); photo-c & B&W photos inside. 3-Dale Evans-r by Manning; Trigger-r by Buscema plus other Buscema-r; photo-c 4.00

RUDOLPH, THE RED-NOSED REINDEER
National Per. Publ.: 1950 - No. 13, Winter, 1962-63 (Issues are not numbered)

	GD	VG	FN	VF	VF/NM	NM-
1950 issue (#1); Grossman-c/a in all	22	44	66	128	209	290
1951-53 issues (3 total)	14	28	42	78	112	145
1954/55, 55/56, 56/57	12	24	36	69	97	125
1957/58, 58/59, 59/60, 60/61, 61/62	7	14	21	49	80	110
1962/63 (rare)(84 pgs.)(shows "Annual" in indicia)	11	22	33	75	138	200

NOTE: *13 total issues published. Has games & puzzles also.*

RUDOLPH, THE RED-NOSED REINDEER (Also see Limited Collectors' Edition C-20, C-24, C-33, C-42, C-50; and All-New Collectors' Edition C-53 & C-60)
National Per. Publ.: Christmas 1972 (Treasury-size)

	GD	VG	FN	VF	VF/NM	NM-
nn-Precursor to Limited Collectors' Edition title (scarce) (implied to be Lim. Coll .Ed. C-20)	20	40	60	142	276	410

RUFF AND REDDY (TV)
Dell Publ. Co.: No. 937, 9/58 - No. 12, 1-3/62 (Hanna-Barbera)(#9 on: 15¢)

	GD	VG	FN	VF	VF/NM	NM-
Four Color 937(#1)(1st Hanna-Barbera comic book)	11	22	33	79	147	215
Four Color 981,1038	8	16	24	52	86	120
4(1-3/60)-12: 8-Last 10¢ issue	7	14	21	45	73	100

RUGGED ACTION (Strange Stories of Suspense #5 on)
Atlas Comics (CSI): Dec, 1954 - No. 4, June, 1955

	GD	VG	FN	VF	VF/NM	NM-
1-Brodsky-c	14	28	42	76	108	140
2-4: 2-Last precode (2/55)	10	20	30	54	72	90

NOTE: ***Ayers** a-2, 3. **Maneely** c-2, 3. **Severin** a-2.*

RUINS
Marvel Comics (Alterniverse): July, 1995 - No. 2, Sept, 1995 ($5.00, painted, limited series)

1,2: Phil Sheldon from Marvels; Warren Ellis scripts; acetate-c 5.00
Reprint (2009, $4.99) r/#1,2; cover gallery 5.00

RULAH JUNGLE GODDESS (Formerly Zoot; I Loved #28 on) (Also see All Top Comics & Terrors of the Jungle)
Fox Features Syndicate: No. 17, Aug, 1948 - No. 27, June, 1949

	GD	VG	FN	VF	VF/NM	NM-
17	110	220	330	704	1202	1700
18-Classic girl-fight interior splash	74	148	222	470	810	1150
19,20	69	138	207	442	759	1075
21-Used in **SOTI**, pg. 388,389	73	146	219	467	796	1125
22-Used in **SOTI**, pg. 22,23	73	146	219	467	796	1125
23-27	54	108	162	343	574	825

NOTE: ***Kamen** c-17-19, 21, 22.*

RUNAWAY, THE (See Movie Classics)

RUNAWAYS
Marvel Comics: July, 2003 - No. 18, Nov, 2004 ($2.95/$2.25/$2.99)

1-($2.95) Vaughan-s/Alphona-a/Jo Chen-c 4.00
2-9-($2.50) 3.00
10-18-($2.99) 11,12-Miyazawa-a; Cloak and Dagger app. 16-The mole revealed 3.00
Hardcover (2005, $34.99) oversized r/#1-18; proposal & sketch pages; Vaughan intro. 35.00
Marvel Age Runaways Vol. 1: Pride and Joy (2004, $7.99, digest size) r/#1-6 8.00
...Vol. 2: Teenage Wasteland (2004, $7.99, digest size) r/#7-12 8.00
...Vol. 3: The Good Die Young (2004, $7.99, digest size) r/#13-18 8.00

RUNAWAYS (Also see X-Men/Runaways 2006 FCBD Edition in the Promotional Section)
Marvel Comics: Apr, 2005 - No. 30, Aug, 2008 ($2.99)

1-24: 1-6-Vaughan-s/Alphona-a/Jo Chen-c. 7,8-Miyazawa-a/Bachalo-c. 11-Spider-Man app. 12-New Avengers app. 18-Gert killed 3.00
25-30-Joss Whedon-s/Michael Ryan-a. 25-Punisher app. 3.00
...: Dead End Kids HC (2008, $19.99) r/#25-30 20.00
... Saga (2007, $3.99) re-caps the 2 series thru #24; 4 new pages w/Ramos-a; Ramos-c 4.00
Hardcover (2006, $24.99) oversized r/#1-12 & X-Men/Runaways; script & sketch pages 25.00
Hardcover Vol. 3 (2007, $24.99) oversized r/#13-24; sketch pages 25.00
...Vol. 4: True Believers (2006, $7.99, digest size) r/#1-6 8.00
...Vol. 5: Escape To New York (2006, $7.99, digest size) r/#7-12 8.00
...Vol. 6: Parental Guidance (2006, $7.99, digest size) r/#13-18 8.00

RUNAWAYS (3rd series)
Marvel Comics: Oct, 2008 - No. 14, Nov, 2009 ($2.99/$3.99)

1-9,11-14: 1-6-Terry Moore-s/Humberto Ramos-a/c. 7-9-Miyazawa-a 3.00
10-($3.99) Wolverine & the X-Men app.; Yost & Asmus-s; Pichelli & Rios-a; Lafuente-c 4.00

RUN BABY RUN
Logos International: 1974 (39¢, Christian religious)

	GD	VG	FN	VF	VF/NM	NM-
nn-By Tony Tallarico from Nicky Cruz's book	2	4	6	10	14	18

RUN, BUDDY, RUN (TV)
Gold Key: June, 1967 (Photo-c)

	GD	VG	FN	VF	VF/NM	NM-
1 (10204-706)	3	6	9	18	27	35

RUNE (See Curse of Rune, Sludge & all other Ultraverse titles for previews)
Malibu Comics (Ultraverse): 1994 - No. 9, Apr, 1995 ($1.95)

	GD	VG	FN	VF	VF/NM	NM-
0-Obtained by sending coupons from 11 comics; came w/Solution #0, poster, temporary tattoo, card	1	2	3	5	6	8

1,2,4-9: 1-Barry Windsor-Smith-c/a/stories begin, ends #6. 5-1st app. of Gemini. 6-Prime & Mantra app. 3.00
1-(1/94)-"Ashcan" edition flip book w/Wrath #1 3.00
1-Ultra 5000 Limited silver foil edition 4.00
3-(3/94, $3.50, 68 pgs.)-Flip book w/Ultraverse Premiere #1 4.00
Giant Size 1 ($2.50, 44 pgs.)-B.Smith story & art. 4.00

RUNE (2nd Series)(Formerly Curse of Rune)(See Ultraverse Unlimited #1)
Malibu Comics (Ultraverse): Infinity, Sept, 1995 - V2#7, Apr, 1996 ($1.50)

Infinity, V2#1-7: Infinity-Black September tie-in; black-c & painted-c exist. 1,3-7-Marvel's Adam Warlock app; regular & painted-c exist. 2-Flip book w/ "Phoenix Resurrection" Pt. 6 3.00
...Vs. Venom 1 (12/95, $3.95) 4.00

RUNE: HEARTS OF DARKNESS
Malibu Comics (Ultraverse): Sept, 1996 - No. 3, Nov, 1996 ($1.50, lim. series)

1-3: Moench scripts & Kyle Hotz-c/a; flip books w/6 pg. Rune story by the Pander Bros. 3.00

RUNE/SILVER SURFER
Marvel Comics/Malibu Comics (Ultraverse): Apr, 1995 ($5.95/$2.95, one-shot)

1 ($5.95, direct market)-BWS-c 6.00
1 ($2.95, newstand)-BWS-c 3.00
1-Collector's limited edition 6.00

RUSE (Also see Archard's Agents)
CrossGeneration Comics: Nov, 2001 - No. 26, Jan, 2004 ($2.95)

1-Waid-s/Guice & Perkins-a 5.00
2-26: 6-Jeff Johnson-a. 11,15-Paul Ryan-a. 12-Last Waid-s 3.00
Enter the Detective Vol. 1 TPB (2002, $15.95) r/#1-6; Guice-c 16.00
...: The Silent Partner Vol. 2 (3/03, $15.95, TPB) r/#7-12 16.00
...: Criminal Intent Vol. 3 ('03, $15.95, TPB) r/#13-18 16.00
Traveler 1,2 ($9.95): Digest-size editions of the TPBs 10.00

RUSE
Marvel Comics: May, 2011 - Present ($2.99)

1-Waid-s/Pierfederici-a/Guice-c 3.00

RUSH CITY
DC Comics: Sept, 2006 - No. 6, May, 2007 ($2.99, limited series)

1-6: 1-Dixon-s/Green-a/Jock-c. 2,3-Black Canary app. 3.00

RUSTLERS, THE (See Zane Grey Four Color 532)

RUSTY, BOY DETECTIVE
Good Comics/Lev Gleason: Mar-April, 1955 - No. 5, Nov, 1955

	GD	VG	FN	VF	VF/NM	NM-
1-Bob Wood, Carl Hubbell-a begins	9	18	27	47	61	75
2-5	6	12	18	31	38	45

RUSTY COMICS (Formerly Kid Movie Comics; Rusty and Her Family #21, 22; The Kelleys #23 on; see Millie The Model)
Marvel Comics (HPC): No. 12, Apr, 1947 - No. 22, Sept, 1949

	GD	VG	FN	VF	VF/NM	NM-
12-Mitzi app.	22	44	66	128	209	290
13	14	28	42	80	115	150
14-Wolverton's Powerhouse Pepper (4 pgs.) plus Kurtzman's "Hey Look"	22	44	66	132	216	300
15-17-Kurtzman's "Hey Look"	16	32	48	94	147	200
18,19	13	26	39	74	105	135
20-Kurtzman-a (5 pgs.)	17	34	51	98	154	210
21,22-Kurtzman-a (17 & 22 pgs.)	21	42	63	126	206	285

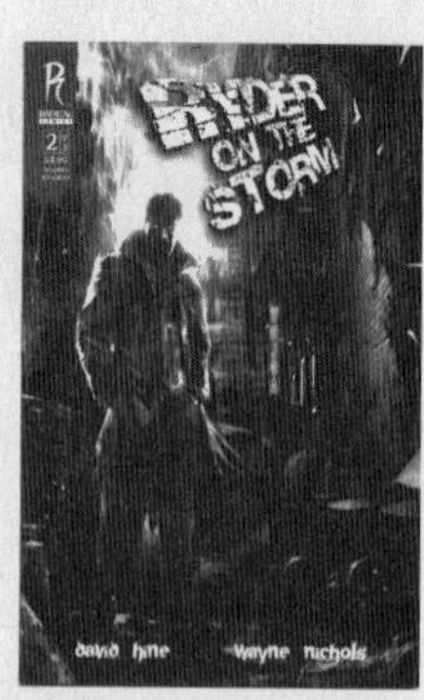

Ryder on the Storm #2 © Radical

Sabrina #32 © AP

Saddle Justice #7 © WMG

RUSTY DUGAN (See Holyoke One-Shot #2)

RUSTY RILEY
Dell Publishing Co.: No. 418, Aug, 1952 - No. 554, April, 1954 (Frank Godwin strip reprints)

	GD 2.0	VG 4.0	FN 6.0	VF 8.0	VF/NM 9.0	NM- 9.2
Four Color 418 (...a Boy, a Horse, and a Dog #1)	5	10	15	32	51	70
Four Color 451(2/53), 486 ('53), 554	4	8	12	26	41	50

RUULE
Beckett Comics: Dec, 2003 - No. 5, Apr, 2004 ($2.99)

	GD 2.0	VG 4.0	FN 6.0	VF 8.0	VF/NM 9.0	NM- 9.2
1-5-David Mack-c/Mike Hawthorne-a						3.00

RUULE: KISS & TELL
Beckett Comics: Jun, 2004 - No. 8 ($1.99)

	GD 2.0	VG 4.0	FN 6.0	VF 8.0	VF/NM 9.0	NM- 9.2
1-8: 1-Amano-s/c; Rousseau-a. 4-Maleev-c						3.00
TPB (2005, $19.99) r/#1-8						20.00

RYDER OF THE STORM
Radical Comics: Oct, 2010 - No. 3, Apr, 2011 ($4.99, limited series)

	GD 2.0	VG 4.0	FN 6.0	VF 8.0	VF/NM 9.0	NM- 9.2
1-3-David Hine-s/Wayne Nichols-a						5.00

SAARI ("The Jungle Goddess")
P. L. Publishing Co.: November, 1951

	GD 2.0	VG 4.0	FN 6.0	VF 8.0	VF/NM 9.0	NM- 9.2
1	46	92	138	290	488	685

SABAN POWERHOUSE (TV)
Acclaim Books: 1997 ($4.50, digest size)

	GD 2.0	VG 4.0	FN 6.0	VF 8.0	VF/NM 9.0	NM- 9.2
1,2-Power Rangers, BeetleBorgs, and others						4.50

SABAN PRESENTS POWER RANGERS TURBO VS. BEETLEBORGS METALLIX (TV)
Acclaim Books: 1997 ($4.50, digest size, one-shot)

	GD 2.0	VG 4.0	FN 6.0	VF 8.0	VF/NM 9.0	NM- 9.2
nn						4.50

SABAN'S MIGHTY MORPHIN POWER RANGERS
Hamilton Comics: Dec, 1994 - No. 6, May, 1995 ($1.95, limited series)

	GD 2.0	VG 4.0	FN 6.0	VF 8.0	VF/NM 9.0	NM- 9.2
1-6: 1-w/bound-in Power Ranger Barcode Card						3.00

SABAN'S MIGHTY MORPHIN POWER RANGERS (TV)
Marvel Comics: 1995 - No. 8, 1996 ($1.75)

	GD 2.0	VG 4.0	FN 6.0	VF 8.0	VF/NM 9.0	NM- 9.2
1-8						3.00

SABLE (Formerly Jon Sable, Freelance; also see Mike Grell's...)
First Comics: Mar, 1988 - No. 27, May, 1990 ($1.75/$1.95)

	GD 2.0	VG 4.0	FN 6.0	VF 8.0	VF/NM 9.0	NM- 9.2
1-27: 10-Begin $1.95-c						3.00

SABLE & FORTUNE (Also see Silver Sable and the Wild Pack)
Marvel Comics: Mar, 2006 - No. 4, June, 2006 ($2.99, limited series)

	GD 2.0	VG 4.0	FN 6.0	VF 8.0	VF/NM 9.0	NM- 9.2
1-4-John Burns-a/Brendan Cahill-s						3.00

SABRE (See Eclipse Graphic Album Series)
Eclipse Comics: Aug, 1982 - No. 14, Aug, 1985 (Baxter paper #4 on)

	GD 2.0	VG 4.0	FN 6.0	VF 8.0	VF/NM 9.0	NM- 9.2
1-14: 1-Sabre & Morrigan Tales begin. 4-6-Incredible Seven origin						3.00

SABRETOOTH (See Iron Fist, Power Man, X-Factor #10 & X-Men)
Marvel Comics: Aug, 1993 - No. 4, Nov, 1993 ($2.95, lim. series, coated paper)

	GD 2.0	VG 4.0	FN 6.0	VF 8.0	VF/NM 9.0	NM- 9.2
1-4: 1-Die-cut-c. 3-Wolverine app.						4.00
...Special 1 "In the Red Zone" (1995, $4.95) Chromium wraparound-c						6.00
V2 #1 (1/98, $5.95, one-shot) Wildchild app.						6.00
Trade paperback (12/94, $12.95) r/#1-4						13.00

SABRETOOTH
Marvel Comics: Dec, 2004 - No. 4, Feb, 2005 ($2.99, limited series)

	GD 2.0	VG 4.0	FN 6.0	VF 8.0	VF/NM 9.0	NM- 9.2
1-4-Sears-a. 3,4-Wendigo app.						3.00
...: Open Season TPB (2005, $9.99) r/#1-4						10.00

SABRETOOTH AND MYSTIQUE (See Mystique and Sabretooth)

SABRETOOTH CLASSIC
Marvel Comics: May, 1994 - No. 15, July, 1995 ($1.50)

	GD 2.0	VG 4.0	FN 6.0	VF 8.0	VF/NM 9.0	NM- 9.2
1-15: 1-3-r/Power Man & Iron Fist #66,78,84. 4-r/Spec. S-M #116. 9-Uncanny X-Men #212, 10-r/Uncanny X-Men #213. 11-r/ Daredevil #238. 12-r/Classic X-Men #10						3.00

SABRETOOTH: MARY SHELLEY OVERDRIVE
Marvel Comics: Aug, 2002 - No. 4, Nov, 2002 ($2.99, limited series)

	GD 2.0	VG 4.0	FN 6.0	VF 8.0	VF/NM 9.0	NM- 9.2
1-4-Jolley-s; Harris-c						3.00

SABRINA (Volume 2) (Based on animated series)
Archie Publications: Jan, 2000 - No. 104, Sept, 2009 ($1.79/$1.99/$2.19/$2.25/$2.50)

	GD 2.0	VG 4.0	FN 6.0	VF 8.0	VF/NM 9.0	NM- 9.2
1-Teen-age Witch magically reverted to 12 years old						4.00
2-10: 4-Begin $1.99-c						3.00
11-104: 38-Sabrina aged back to 16 years old. 39-Begin $2.19-c. 58-Manga-style begins; Tania Del Rio-a. 67-Josie and the Pussycats app. 101-Young Salem; begin $2.50-c						3.00

SABRINA'S CHRISTMAS MAGIC (See Archie Giant Series Magazine #196, 207, 220, 231, 243, 455, 467, 479, 491, 503, 515)

SABRINA'S HALLOWEEN SPOOOKTACULAR
Archie Publications: 1993 - 1995 ($2.00, 52 pgs.)

	GD 2.0	VG 4.0	FN 6.0	VF 8.0	VF/NM 9.0	NM- 9.2
1-Neon orange ink-c; bound-in poster	1	2	3	5	6	8
2,3-Titled "Sabrina's Holiday Spectacular"						5.00

SABRINA, THE TEEN-AGE WITCH (TV)(See Archie Giant Series, Archie's Madhouse 22, Archie's TV..., Chilling Advs. In Sorcery, Little Archie #59)
Archie Publications: April, 1971 - No. 77, Jan, 1983 (52 pg.Giants No. 1-17)

	GD 2.0	VG 4.0	FN 6.0	VF 8.0	VF/NM 9.0	NM- 9.2
1-52 pgs. begin, end #17	14	28	42	96	191	285
2-Archie's group x-over	9	18	27	60	100	140
3-5: 3,4-Archie's Group x-over	6	12	18	41	66	90
6-10	5	10	15	34	55	75
11-17(2/74)	4	8	12	26	41	55
18-30	3	6	9	19	29	38
31-40(8/77)	3	6	9	14	20	26
41-60(6/80)	2	4	6	10	14	18
61-70	2	4	6	8	11	14
71-76-low print run	2	4	6	11	16	20
77-Last issue; low print run	3	6	9	14	20	26

SABRINA, THE TEEN-AGE WITCH
Archie Publications: 1996 ($1.50, 32 pgs., one-shot)

	GD 2.0	VG 4.0	FN 6.0	VF 8.0	VF/NM 9.0	NM- 9.2
1-Updated origin						6.00

SABRINA, THE TEEN-AGE WITCH (Continues in Sabrina, Vol. 2)
Archie Publications: May, 1997 - No. 32, Dec, 1999 ($1.50/$1.75/$1.79)

	GD 2.0	VG 4.0	FN 6.0	VF 8.0	VF/NM 9.0	NM- 9.2
1-Photo-c with Melissa Joan Hart	1	3	4	6	8	10
2-10: 9-Begin $1.75-c						6.00
11-20						5.00
21-32: 24-Begin $1.79-c. 28-Sonic the Hedgehog-c/app.						4.00

SABU, "ELEPHANT BOY" (Movie; formerly My Secret Story)
Fox Features Syndicate: No. 30, June, 1950 - No. 2, Aug, 1950

	GD 2.0	VG 4.0	FN 6.0	VF 8.0	VF/NM 9.0	NM- 9.2
30(#1)-Wood-a; photo-c from movie	26	52	78	154	252	350
2-Photo-c from movie; Kamen-a	19	38	57	111	176	240

SACHS & VIOLENS
Marvel Comics (Epic Comics): Nov, 1993 - No. 4, July, 1994 ($2.25, limited series, mature)

	GD 2.0	VG 4.0	FN 6.0	VF 8.0	VF/NM 9.0	NM- 9.2
1-($2.75)-Embossed-c w/bound-in trading card						3.00
1-($3.50)-Platinum edition (1 for each 10 ordered)						4.00
2-4: Perez-c/a; bound-in trading card: 2-(5/94)						3.00
TPB (DC, 2006, $14.99) r/series; intro. by Peter David; creator bios.						15.00

SACRAMENTS, THE
Catechetical Guild Educational Society: Oct, 1955 (35¢)

	GD 2.0	VG 4.0	FN 6.0	VF 8.0	VF/NM 9.0	NM- 9.2
30304	6	12	18	31	38	45

SACRED AND THE PROFANE, THE (See Eclipse Graphic Album Series #9 & Epic Illustrated #20)

SADDLE JUSTICE (Happy Houlihans #1,2) (Saddle Romances #9 on)
E. C. Comics: No. 3, Spring, 1948 - No. 8, Sept-Oct, 1949

	GD 2.0	VG 4.0	FN 6.0	VF 8.0	VF/NM 9.0	NM- 9.2
3-The 1st E.C. by Bill Gaines to break away from M. C. Gaines' old Educational Comics format. Craig, Feldstein, H. C. Kiefer, & Stan Asch-a; mentioned in Love and Death	53	106	159	334	567	800
4-1st Graham Ingels-a for E.C.	46	92	138	290	488	685
5-8-Ingels-a in all	41	82	123	256	428	600

NOTE: *Craig* and *Feldstein* art in most issues. Canadian reprints known; see Table of Contents. *Craig* c-3, 4. *Ingels* c-5-8. #4 contains a biography of *Craig*.

SADDLE ROMANCES (Saddle Justice #3-8; Weird Science #12 on)
E. C. Comics: No. 9, Nov-Dec, 1949 - No. 11, Mar-Apr, 1950

	GD 2.0	VG 4.0	FN 6.0	VF 8.0	VF/NM 9.0	NM- 9.2
9,11: 9-Ingels-c/a. 11-Ingels-a; Feldstein-c	46	92	138	290	488	685
10-Wally Wood's 1st work at E. C.; Ingels-a; Feldstein-c	47	94	141	296	498	700

NOTE: *Canadian reprints known; see Table of Contents.* ***Wood/Harrison*** *a-10, 11.*

SADHU
Virgin Comics: July, 2006 - No. 8, June, 2007 ($2.99)

	GD 2.0	VG 4.0	FN 6.0	VF 8.0	VF/NM 9.0	NM- 9.2
1-8: 1,2-Gotham Chopra-s/Jeevan Kang-a						3.00
...: The Silent Ones (8/07 - No. 5, 2/08, $2.99) 1-5						3.00
...: Wheel of Destiny (4/08 - No. 5, $2.99) 1,2						3.00

SADIE SACK (See Harvey Hits #93)

SAD SACK AND THE SARGE
Harvey Publications: Sept, 1957 - No. 155, June, 1982

	GD 2.0	VG 4.0	FN 6.0	VF 8.0	VF/NM 9.0	NM- 9.2
1	13	26	39	89	170	250

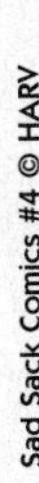
Sad Sack Comics #4 © HARV

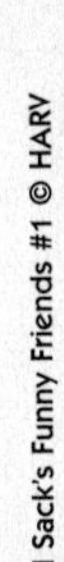
Sad Sack's Funny Friends #1 © HARV

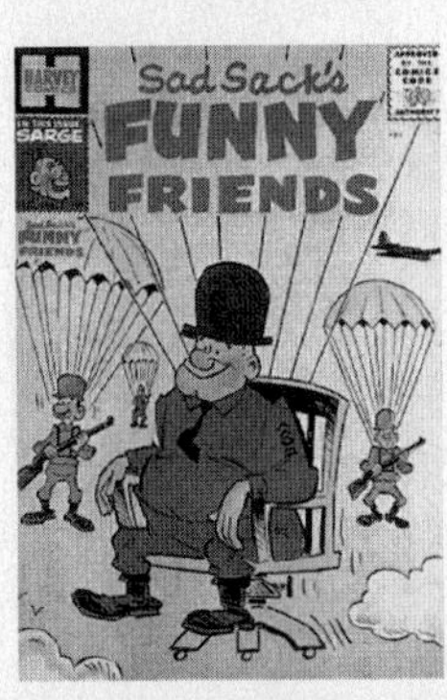

Saga of Ra's al Ghul #1 © DC

	GD 2.0	VG 4.0	FN 6.0	VF 8.0	VF/NM 9.0	NM- 9.2
2	8	16	24	52	86	120
3-10	6	12	18	41	66	90
11-20	5	10	15	32	51	70
21-30	3	6	9	20	30	40
31-50	3	6	9	14	20	25
51-70	2	4	6	9	13	16
71-90,97-99	1	3	4	6	8	10
91-96: All 52 pg. Giants	2	4	6	9	13	16
100	2	4	6	8	10	12
101-120	1	2	3	4	5	7
121-155						5.00

SAD SACK COMICS (See Harvey Collector's Comics #16, Little Sad Sack, Tastee Freez Comics #4 & True Comics #55)
Harvey Publications/Lorne-Harvey Publications (Recollections) #288 On: Sept, 1949 - No. 287, Oct, 1982; No. 288, 1992 - No. 291, 1993

	GD 2.0	VG 4.0	FN 6.0	VF 8.0	VF/NM 9.0	NM- 9.2
1-Infinity-c; Little Dot begins (1st app.); civilian issues begin, end #21; based on comic strip	77	154	231	655	1328	2000
2-Flying Fool by Powell	28	56	84	204	415	625
3	17	34	51	122	249	375
4-10	13	26	39	89	170	250
11-21	9	18	27	63	107	150
22-("Back In The Army Again" on covers #22-36); "The Specialist" story about Sad Sack's return to Army	10	20	30	69	122	175
23-30	6	12	18	39	62	85
31-50	5	10	15	30	48	65
51-80,100: 62-"The Specialist" reprinted	4	8	12	22	34	45
81-99	3	6	9	16	23	30
101-140	3	6	9	14	19	24
141-170,200	2	4	6	11	16	20
171-199	2	4	6	9	13	16
201-207: 207-Last 12¢ issue	2	4	6	8	11	14
208-222	1	3	4	6	8	10
223-228 (25¢ Giants, 52 pgs.)	2	4	6	8	11	14
229-250	1	3	4	6	8	10
251-285						6.00
286,287-Limited distribution	1	2	3	5	7	9
288,289 ($2.75, 1992): 289-50th anniversary issue						6.00
290,291 ($1.00, 1993, B&W)						3.00
3-D 1 (1/54, 25¢)-Came with 2 pairs of glasses; titled "Harvey 3-D Hits"	15	30	45	103	209	315
...At Home for the Holidays 1 (1993, no-c price)-Publ. by Lorne-Harvey' X-Mas issue						4.00

NOTE: *The Sad Sack Comics comic book was a spin-off from a Sunday Newspaper strip launched through John Wheeler's Bell Syndicate. The previous Sunday page and the first 21 comics depicted the Sad Sack in civvies. Unpopularity caused the Sunday page to be discontinued in the early '50s. Meanwhile Sad Sack returned to the Army, by popular demand, in issue No. 22, remaining there ever since. Incidentally, relatively few of the first 21 issues were ever collected and remain scarce due to this.*

SAD SACK FUN AROUND THE WORLD
Harvey Publications: 1974 (no month)

	GD 2.0	VG 4.0	FN 6.0	VF 8.0	VF/NM 9.0	NM- 9.2
1-About Great Britain	2	4	6	11	16	20

SAD SACK GOES HOME
Harvey Publications: 1951 (16 pgs. in color, no cover price)

	GD 2.0	VG 4.0	FN 6.0	VF 8.0	VF/NM 9.0	NM- 9.2
nn-By George Baker	5	10	15	34	55	75

SAD SACK LAUGH SPECIAL
Harvey Publications: Winter, 1958-59 - No. 93, Feb, 1977 (#1-9: 84 pgs.; #10-60: 68 pgs.; #61-76: 52 pgs.)

	GD 2.0	VG 4.0	FN 6.0	VF 8.0	VF/NM 9.0	NM- 9.2
1-Giant 25¢ issues begin	10	20	30	70	125	180
2	6	12	18	41	66	90
3-10	5	10	15	32	51	70
11-30	4	8	12	26	41	55
31-60: 31-Hi-Fi Tweeter app. 60-Last 68 pg. Giant	3	6	9	16	23	30
61-76-(All 52 pg. issues)	2	4	6	10	14	18
77-93	1	2	3	5	6	8

SAD SACK NAVY, GOBS 'N' GALS
Harvey Publications: Aug, 1972 - No. 8, Oct, 1973

	GD 2.0	VG 4.0	FN 6.0	VF 8.0	VF/NM 9.0	NM- 9.2
1: 52 pg. Giant	3	6	9	16	23	30
2-8	2	4	6	9	12	15

SAD SACK'S ARMY LIFE (See Harvey Hits #8, 17, 22, 28, 32, 39, 43, 47, 51, 55, 58, 61, 64, 67, 70)

SAD SACK'S ARMY LIFE (...Parade #1-57, ...Today #58 on)
Harvey Publications: Oct, 1963 - No. 60, Nov, 1975; No. 61, May, 1976

	GD 2.0	VG 4.0	FN 6.0	VF 8.0	VF/NM 9.0	NM- 9.2
1-(68 pg. issues begin)	8	16	24	52	86	120
2-10	4	8	12	28	44	60
11-20	3	6	9	20	30	40
21-34: Last 68 pg. issue	3	6	9	16	23	30
35-51: All 52 pgs.	2	4	6	10	14	18
52-61	1	3	4	6	8	10

SAD SACK'S FUNNY FRIENDS (See Harvey Hits #75)
Harvey Publications: Dec, 1955 - No. 75, Oct, 1969

	GD 2.0	VG 4.0	FN 6.0	VF 8.0	VF/NM 9.0	NM- 9.2
1	10	20	30	70	125	180
2-10	6	12	18	41	66	90
11-20	4	8	12	24	37	50
21-30	3	6	9	18	27	35
31-50	3	6	9	14	20	25
51-75	2	4	6	9	13	16

SAD SACK'S MUTTSY (See Harvey Hits #74, 77, 80, 82, 84, 87, 89, 92, 96, 99, 102, 105, 108, 111, 113, 115, 117, 119, 121)

SAD SACK USA (...Vacation #8)
Harvey Publications: Nov, 1972 - No. 7, Nov, 1973; No. 8, Oct, 1974

	GD 2.0	VG 4.0	FN 6.0	VF 8.0	VF/NM 9.0	NM- 9.2
1	3	6	9	14	20	25
2-8	2	4	6	8	10	12

SAD SACK WITH SARGE & SADIE
Harvey Publications: Sept, 1972 - No. 8, Nov, 1973

	GD 2.0	VG 4.0	FN 6.0	VF 8.0	VF/NM 9.0	NM- 9.2
1-(52 pg. Giant)	3	6	9	14	20	25
2-8	2	4	6	8	10	12

SAD SAD SACK WORLD
Harvey Publ.: Oct, 1964 - No. 46, Dec, 1973 (#1-31: 68 pgs.; #32-38: 52 pgs.)

	GD 2.0	VG 4.0	FN 6.0	VF 8.0	VF/NM 9.0	NM- 9.2
1	7	14	21	49	80	110
2-10	4	8	12	26	41	55
11-20	3	6	9	20	30	40
21-31: 31-Last 68 pg. issue	3	6	9	16	23	30
32-39-(All 52 pgs)	2	4	6	10	14	18
40-46	1	3	4	6	8	10

SAFEST PLACE IN THE WORLD, THE
Dark Horse Comics: 1993 ($2.50, one-shot)

1-Steve Ditko-c/a/scripts — 3.00

SAFETY-BELT MAN
Sirius Entertainment: June, 1994 - No. 6, 1995 ($2.50, B&W)

1-6: 1-Horan-s/Dark One-a/Sprouse-c. 2,3-Warren-c. 4-Linsner back-up story. 5,6-Crilley-a — 3.00

SAFETY-BELT MAN ALL HELL
Sirius Entertainment: June, 1996 - No. 6, Mar, 1997 ($2.95, color)

1-6-Horan-s/Fillbach Bros.-a — 3.00

SAGA OF BIG RED, THE
Omaha World-Herald: Sept, 1976 ($1.25) (In color)

nn-by Win Mumma; story of the Nebraska Cornhuskers (sports) — 6.00

SAGA OF CRYSTAR, CRYSTAL WARRIOR, THE
Marvel Comics: May, 1983 - No. 11, Feb, 1985 (Remco toy tie-in)

1,6: 1-(Baxter paper). 6-Nightcrawler app; Golden-c — 4.00
2-5,7-11: 3-Dr. Strange app. 3-11-Golden-c (painted-4,5). 11-Alpha Flight app. — 3.00

SAGA OF RA'S AL GHUL, THE
DC Comics: Jan, 1988 - No. 4, Apr, 1988 ($2.50, limited series)

1-4-r/N. Adams Batman — 6.00

SAGA OF SABAN'S MIGHTY MORPHIN POWER RANGERS (Also see Saban's Mighty Morphin Power Rangers)
Hamilton Comics: 1995 - No. 4, 1995 ($1.95, limited series)

1-4 — 3.00

SAGA OF SEVEN SUNS, THE : VEILED ALLIANCES
DC Comics (WildStorm): 2004 ($24.95, hardcover graphic novel with dustjacket)

HC-Kevin J. Anderson-s/Robert Teranishi-a — 25.00
SC-(2004, $17.95) — 18.00

SAGA OF THE ORIGINAL HUMAN TORCH
Marvel Comics: Apr, 1990 - No. 4, July, 1990 ($1.50, limited series)

1-4: 1-Origin; Buckler-c/a(p). 3-Hitler-c — 3.00

SAGA OF THE SUB-MARINER, THE
Marvel Comics: Nov, 1988 - No. 12, Oct, 1989 ($1.25/$1.50 #5 on, maxi-series)

1-12: 9-Original X-Men app. — 3.00

The Saint #4 © AVON

Sam and Twitch: The Writer #2 © TMP

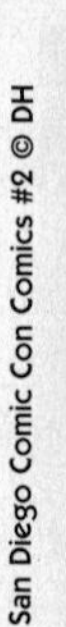
San Diego Comic Con Comics #2 © DH

GD VG FN VF VF/NM NM-
2.0 4.0 6.0 8.0 9.0 9.2

GD VG FN VF VF/NM NM-
2.0 4.0 6.0 8.0 9.0 9.2

SAGA OF THE SWAMP THING, THE (See Swamp Thing)

SAILOR MOON (Manga)
Mixx Entertainment Inc.: 1998 - Present ($2.95)

1 2 4 6 11 16 20
1-(San Diego edition) 3 6 9 14 20 25
2-5 2 4 6 8 11 14
6-10 1 2 3 5 7 8
11-25 6.00
26-35 4.00
... Rini's Moon Stick 1 15.00

SAILOR ON THE SEA OF FATE (See First Comics Graphic Novel #11)

SAILOR SWEENEY (Navy Action #1-11, 15 on)
Atlas Comics (CDS): No. 12, July, 1956 - No. 14, Nov, 1956

12-14: 12-Shores-a. 13,14-Severin-c 9 18 27 52 69 85

SAINT, THE (Also see Movie Comics(DC) #2 & Silver Streak #18)
Avon Periodicals: Aug, 1947 - No. 12, Mar, 1952

1-Kamen bondage-c/a 87 174 261 553 952 1350
2 41 82 123 256 428 600
3-5: 4-Lingerie panels 39 78 117 231 378 525
6-Miss Fury app. by Tarpe Mills (14 pgs.) 52 104 156 322 549 775
7-c-/Avon paperback #118 30 60 90 177 289 400
8,9(12/50): Saint strip-r in #8-12; 9-Kinstler-c 27 54 81 158 259 360
10-Wood-a, 1 pg; c-/Avon paperback #289 27 54 81 158 259 360
11 20 40 60 120 195 270
12-c-/Avon paperback #123 22 44 66 132 216 300

NOTE: *Lucky Dale, Girl Detective in #1,2,4,6.* **Hollingsworth** *a-4, 6. Painted-c 7, 8, 10-12.*

SAINT ANGEL
Image Comics: Mar, 2000 - No. 4, Mar, 2001 ($2.95/$3.95)

0-Altstaetter & Napton-s/Altstaetter-a 3.00
1-4-($3.95) Flip book w/Deity. 1-(6/00). 2-(10/00) 4.00

ST. GEORGE
Marvel Comics (Epic Comics): June, 1988 - No.8, Oct, 1989 ($1.25,/$1.50)

1-8: Sienkiewicz-c. 3-begin $1.50-c 3.00

SAINT GERMAINE
Caliber Comics: 1997 - No. 8, 1998 ($2.95)

1-8: 1,5-Alternate covers 3.00

ST. SWITHIN'S DAY
Trident Comics: Apr, 1990 ($2.50, one-shot)

1-Grant Morrison scripts 3.00

ST. SWITHIN'S DAY
Oni Press: Mar, 1998 ($2.95, B&W, one-shot)

1-Grant Morrison-s/Paul Grist-a 3.00

SALOMÉ (See Night Music #6)

SALVATION RUN
DC Comics: Jan, 2008 - No. 7, Jul, 2008 ($2.99, limited series)

1-7-DC villains banished to an alien planet; Willingham-s/Chen-a/c. 1-Var-c by Corroney 3.00

SAM AND MAX, FREELANCE POLICE SPECIAL
Fishwrap Prod./Comico: 1987 ($1.75, B&W); Jan, 1989 ($2.75, 44 pgs.)

1 ($1.75, B&W, Fishwrap) 4.00
2 ($2.75, color, Comico) 4.00

SAM AND TWITCH (See Spawn and Case Files:...)
Image Comics (Todd McFarlane Prod.): Aug, 1999 - No. 26, Feb, 2004 ($2.50)

1-26: 1-19-Bendis-s. 1-14-Medina-a. 15-19-Maleev-a. 20-24-McFarlane-s/Maleev-a 3.00
Book One: Udaku (2000, $21.95, TPB) B&W reprint of #1-8 22.00
...: The Brian Michael Bendis Collection Vol. 1 (2/06, $24.95) r/#1-9 in color; sketch pages 25.00
...: The Brian Michael Bendis Collection Vol. 2 (6/07, $24.95) r/#10-19; cover gallery 25.00

SAM AND TWITCH: THE WRITER
Image Comics (Todd McFarlane Prod.): May, 2010 - No. 4, Jun, 2010 ($2.99)

1-4-Blengino-s/Erbetta-a/c 3.00

SAM HILL PRIVATE EYE
Close-Up (Archie): 1950 - No. 7, 1951

1 16 32 48 92 144 195
2 10 20 30 56 76 95
3-7 10 20 30 54 72 90

SAMSON (1st Series) (Captain Aero #7 on; see Big 3 Comics)
Fox Features Syndicate: Fall, 1940 - No. 6, Sept, 1941 (See Fantastic Comics)

1-Samson begins, ends #6; Powell-a, signed 'Rensie;' Wing Turner by Tuska app; Fine-c?
194 388 582 1242 2121 3000
2-Dr. Fung by Powell; Fine-c? 80 160 240 508 874 1240
3-Navy Jones app.; Joe Simon-c 60 120 180 381 653 925
4-Yarko the Great, Master Magician begins 53 106 159 334 567 800
5,6: 6-Origin The Topper 43 86 129 271 461 650

SAMSON (2nd Series) (Formerly Fantastic Comics #10, 11)
Ajax/Farrell Publications (Four Star): No. 12, April, 1955 - No. 14, Aug, 1955

12-Wonder Boy 30 60 90 177 289 400
13,14: 13-Wonder Boy, Rocket Man 26 52 78 154 252 350

SAMSON (See Mighty Samson)

SAMSON & DELILAH (See A Spectacular Feature Magazine)

SAMUEL BRONSTON'S CIRCUS WORLD (See Circus World under Movie Classics)

SAMURAI (Also see Eclipse Graphic Album Series #14)
Aircel Publications: 1985 - No. 23, 1987 ($1.70, B&W)

1, 14-16-Dale Keown-a 4.00
1-(reprinted),2-12,17-23: 2 (reprinted issue exists) 3.00
13-Dale Keown's 1st published artwork (1987) 6.00

SAMURAI
Warp Graphics: May, 1997 ($2.95, B&W)

1 3.00

SAMURAI CAT
Marvel Comics (Epic Comics): June, 1991 - No. 3, Sept, 1991 ($2.25, limited series)

1-3: 3-Darth Vader-c/story parody 3.00

SAMURAI: HEAVEN & EARTH
Dark Horse Comics: Dec, 2004 - No. 5, Dec, 2005 ($2.99)

1-5-Luke Ross-a/Ron Marz-s 3.00
TPB (4/06, $14.95) r/#1-5; sketch pages and cover and pin-up gallery 15.00

SAMURAI: HEAVEN & EARTH (Volume 2)
Dark Horse Comics: Nov, 2006 - No. 5, June, 2007 ($2.99)

1-5-Luke Ross-a/Ron Marz-s 3.00
TPB (10/07, $14.95) r/#1-5; sketch pages and cover and pin-up gallery 15.00

SAMURAI JACK SPECIAL (TV)
DC Comics: Sept, 2002 ($3.95, one-shot)

1-Adaptation of pilot episode with origin story; Tartakovsky-s 4.00

SAMURAI: LEGEND
Marvel Comics (Soleil): 2008 - No. 4, 2009 ($5.99)

1-4-Genet-a/DiGiorgio-s; English version of French comic; preview of other titles 6.00

SAMUREE
Continuity Comics: May, 1987 - No. 9, Jan, 1991

1-9 3.00

SAMUREE
Continuity Comics: V2#1, May, 1993 - V2#4, Jan,1994 ($2.50)

V2#1-4-Embossed-c: 2,4-Adams plot, Nebres-i. 3-Nino-c(i) 3.00

SAMUREE
Acclaim Comics (Windjammer): Oct, 1995 - No. 2, Nov,1995 ($2.50, lim. series)

1,2 3.00

SAN DIEGO COMIC CON COMICS
Dark Horse Comics: 1992 - No.4, 1995 (B&W, promo comic for the San Diego Comic Con)

1-(1992)-Includes various characters published from Dark Horse including Concrete, The Mask, RoboCop and others; 1st app. of Sprint from John Byrne's Next Men; art by Quesada, Byrne, Rude, Burden, Moebius & others; pin-ups by Rude, Dorkin, Allred & others; Chadwick-c 1 3 4 6 8 10
2-(1993)-Intro of Legend imprint; 1st app. of John Byrne's Danger Unlimited, Mike Mignola's Hellboy, Art Adams' Monkeyman & O'Brien; contains stories featuring Concrete, Sin City, Martha Washington & others; Grendel, Madman, & Big Guy pin-ups; Don Martin-c. 2 4 6 9 12 15
3-(1994)-Contains stories featuring Barb Wire, The Mask, The Dirty Pair, & Grendel by Matt Wagner; contains pin-ups of Ghost, Predator & Rascals In Paradise; The Mask-c 1 2 3 5 6 8
4-(1995)-Contains Sin City story by Miller (3pg.), Star Wars, The Mask, Tarzan, Foot Soldiers; Sin City & Star Wars flip-c 1 2 3 5 6 8

SANDMAN, THE (1st Series) (Also see Adventure Comics #40, New York World's Fair & World's Finest #3)

Sandman #23 © DC

Sandman Mystery Theater #3 © DC

Sandman Presents: Lucifer #1 © DC

	GD 2.0	VG 4.0	FN 6.0	VF 8.0	VF/NM 9.0	NM- 9.2

National Periodical Publ.: Winter, 1974; No. 2, Apr-May, 1975 - No. 6, Dec-Jan, 1975-76

1-1st app. Bronze Age Sandman by Simon & Kirby (last S&K collaboration) 7 14 21 49 80 110
2-6: 6-Kirby/Wood-c/a 4 8 12 22 34 45
The Sandman By Joe Simon & Jack Kirby HC (2009, $39.99, d.j.) r/Sandman app. from World's Finest #6,7, Adventure Comics #72-102 and Sandman #1; Morrow intro. 40.00
NOTE: *Kirby a-1p, 4-6p; c-1-5, 6p.*

SANDMAN (2nd Series) (See Books of Magic, Vertigo Jam & Vertigo Preview)
DC Comics (Vertigo imprint #47 on): Jan, 1989 - No. 75, Mar, 1996 ($1.50-$2.50, mature)

1 ($2.00, 52 pgs.)-1st app. Modern Age Sandman (Morpheus); Neil Gaiman scripts begin; Sam Kieth-a(p) in #1-5; Wesley Dodds (G.A. Sandman) cameo. 4 8 12 24 37 50
2-Cain & Abel app. (from HOM & HOS) 3 6 9 14 19 24
3-5: 3-John Constantine app. 2 4 6 10 14 18
6,7 2 4 6 8 11 14
8-Death-c/story (1st app.)-Regular ed. has Jeanette Kahn publishorial & American Cancer Society ad w/no indicia on inside front-c 3 6 9 16 22 28
8-Limited ed. (600+ copies?); has Karen Berger editorial and next issue teaser on inside covers (has indicia) 5 10 15 34 55 75
9-14: 10-Has explaination about #8 mixup; has bound-in Shocker movie poster. 14-(52 pgs.)-Bound-in Nightbreed fold-out 2 4 6 8 10 12
15-20: 16-Photo-c. 17,18-Kelley Jones-a. 19-Vess-a 1 2 3 5 6 8
18-Error version w/1st 3 panels on pg. 1 in blue ink 3 6 9 20 30 40
19-Error version w/pages 18 & 20 facing each other 3 6 9 18 27 35
21,23-27: Seasons of Mist storyline. 22-World Without End preview. 24-Kelley Jones/Russell-a 6.00
22-1st Daniel (Later becomes new Sandman) 2 4 6 8 10 12
28-30 5.00
31-49,51-74: 36-(52 pgs.). 41,44-48-Metallic ink on-c. 48-Cerebus appears as a doll. 54-Re-intro Prez; Death app.; Belushi, Nixon & Wildcat cameos. 57-Metallic ink on c. 65-w/bound-in trading card. 69-Death of Sandman. 70-73-Zulli-a. 74-Jon J. Muth-a. 4.00
50-($2.95, 52 pgs.)-Black-c w/metallic ink by McKean; Russell-a; McFarlane pin-up 5.00
50-($2.95)-Signed & limited (5,000) Treasury Edition with sketch of Neil Gaiman 1 2 3 5 6 8
50-Platinum 20.00
75-($3.95)-Vess-a. 5.00
Special 1 (1991, $3.50, 68 pgs.)-Glow-in-the-dark-c 5.00
Absolute Sandman Special Edition #1 (2006, 50¢) sampling from HC; recolored r/#1 3.00
Absolute Sandman Volume One (2006, $99.00, slipcased hardcover) recolored r/#1-20; Gaiman's original proposal; script and pencils from #19; character sketch gallery 100.00
Absolute Sandman Volume Two (2007, $99.00, slipcased hardcover) recolored r/#21-39; r/A Gallery of Dreams one-shot; bonus stories, scripts and pencil art 100.00
Absolute Sandman Volume Three (2008, $99.00, slipcased hardcover) recolored r/#40-56; & Special #1; bonus galleries, scripts and pencil art; Jill Thompson intro. 100.00
Absolute Sandman Volume Four (2008, $99.00, slipcased hardcover) recolored r/#57-75; scripts & sketch pages for #57 & 75; gallery of Dreaming memorabilia; Berger intro. 100.00
...: A Gallery of Dreams ($2.95)-Intro by N. Gaiman 3.00
...: Preludes & Nocturnes ($29.95, HC)-r/#1-8. 30.00
...: The Doll's House (1990, $29.95, HC)-r/#8-16. 30.00
...: Dream Country ($29.95, HC)-r/#17-20. 30.00
...: Season of Mists ($29.95, Leatherbound HC)-r/#21-28. 50.00
...: A Game of You ($29.95, HC)-r/32-37, ...: Fables and Reflections ($29.95, HC)-r/Vertigo Preview #1, Sandman Special #1, #29-31, #38-40 & #50. ...: Brief Lives ($29.95, HC)-r/#41-49. ...: World's End ($29.95, HC)-r/#51-56 30.00
...: The Kindly Ones (1996, $34.95, HC)-r/#57-69 & Vertigo Jam #1 35.00
...: The Wake ($29.95, HC)-r/#70-75. 30.00
NOTE: *A new set of hardcover printings with new covers was introduced in 1998-99. Multiple printings exist of softcover collections. Recolored (from the Absolute HC) softcover editions were released in 2010.* ***Bachalo*** *a-12;* ***Kelley Jones*** *a-17, 18, 22, 23, 26, 27.* ***Vess*** *a-19, 75.*

SANDMAN: ENDLESS NIGHTS
DC Comics (Vertigo): 2003 ($24.95, hardcover, with dust jacket)

HC-Neil Gaiman stories of Morpheus and the Endless illustrated by Fabry, Manara, Prado, Quitely, Russell, Sienkiewicz, and Storey; McKean-c 25.00
...Special (11/03, $2.95) Previews hardcover; Dream story w/Prado-a; McKean-c 3.00
SC (2004, $17.95) 18.00

SANDMAN MIDNIGHT THEATRE
DC Comics (Vertigo): Sept, 1995 ($6.95, squarebound, one-shot)

nn-Modern Age Sandman (Morpheus) meets G.A. Sandman; Gaiman & Wagner story; McKean-c; Kristiansen-a 7.00

SANDMAN MYSTERY THEATRE (Also see Sandman (2nd Series) #1)
DC Comics (Vertigo): Apr, 1993 - No. 70, Feb, 1999 ($1.95/$2.25/$2.50)

1-G.A. Sandman advs. begin; Matt Wagner scripts begin 5.00
2-49: 5-Neon ink logo. 29-32-Hourman app. 38-Ted Knight (G.A. Starman) app. 42-Jim Corrigan (Spectre) app. 45-48-Blackhawk app. 3.00
50-($3.50, 48 pgs.) w/bonus story of S.A. Sandman, Torres-a 4.00
51-70 3.00
Annual 1 (10/94, $3.95, 68 pgs.)-Alex Ross, Bolton & others-a 5.00
...: Dr. Death and the Night of the Butcher (2007, $19.99) r/#21-28 20.00
...: The Blackhawk and The Return of the Scarlet Ghost (2010, $19.99) r/#45-52 20.00
...: The Face and the Brute (2004, $19.95) r/#5-12 20.00
...: The Hourman and The Python (2008, $19.99) r/#29-36 20.00
...: The Mist and The Phantom of the Fair (2009, $19.99) r/#37-44 20.00
...: The Scorpion (2006, $12.99) r/#17-20 13.00
...: The Tarantula (1995, $14.95) r/#1-4 15.00
...: The Vamp (2005, $12.99) r/#13-16 13.00

SANDMAN MYSTERY THEATRE (2nd Series)
DC Comics (Vertigo): Feb, 2007 - No. 5, Jun, 2007 ($2.99, limited series)

1-5-Wesley Dodds and Dian in 1997; Rieber-s/Nguyen-a 3.00

SANDMAN PRESENTS...
DC Comics (Vertigo)

Taller Tales TPB (2003, $19.95) r/S.P: The Thessaliad #1-4; Merv Pumpkinhead, Agent...; The Dreaming #55; S.P. Everything You Always...; new McKean-c; intro by Willingham 20.00

SANDMAN PRESENTS: BAST
DC Comics (Vertigo): Mar, 2003 - No. 3, May, 2003 ($2.95, limited series)

1-3-Kiernan-s/Bennett-a/McKean-c 3.00

SANDMAN PRESENTS: DEADBOY DETECTIVES (See Sandman #21-28)
DC Comics (Vertigo): Aug, 2001 - No. 4, Nov, 2001 ($2.50, limited series)

1-4:Talbot-a/McKean-c/Brubaker-s 3.00
TPB (2008, $12.99) r/#1-4 13.00

SANDMAN PRESENTS: EVERYTHING YOU ALWAYS WANTED TO KNOW ABOUT DREAMS...BUT WERE AFRAID TO ASK
DC Comics (Vertigo): Jul, 2001 ($3.95, one-shot)

1-Short stories by Willingham; art by various; McKean-c 4.00

SANDMAN PRESENTS: LOVE STREET
DC Comics (Vertigo): Jul, 1999 - No. 3, Sept, 1999 ($2.95, limited series)

1-3: Teenage Hellblazer in 1968 London; Zulli-a 3.00

SANDMAN PRESENTS: LUCIFER
DC Comics (Vertigo): Mar, 1999 - No. 3, May, 1999 ($2.95, limited series)

1-3: Scott Hampton painted-c/a 3.00

SANDMAN PRESENTS: PETREFAX
DC Comics (Vertigo): Mar, 2000 - No. 4, Jun, 2000 ($2.95, limited series)

1-4-Carey-s/Leialoha-a 3.00

SANDMAN PRESENTS: THE CORINTHIAN
DC Comics (Vertigo): Dec, 2001 - No. 3, Feb, 2002 ($2.95, limited series)

1-3-Macan-s/Zezelj-a/McKean-c 3.00

SANDMAN PRESENTS, THE: THE FURIES
DC Comics (Vertigo): 2002 ($24.95, one-shot)

Hardcover-Mike Carey-s/John Bolton-painted art; Lyta Hall's reunion with Daniel 30.00
Softcover-(2003, $17.95) 18.00

SANDMAN PRESENTS, THE: THESSALY: WITCH FOR HIRE
DC Comics (Vertigo): Apr, 2004 - No. 4, July, 2004 ($2.95, limited series)

1-4-Willingham-s/McManus-a/McPherson-c 3.00
TPB-(2005, $12.99) r/#1-4 13.00

SANDMAN PRESENTS, THE: THE THESSALIAD
DC Comics (Vertigo): Mar, 2002 - No. 4, Jun, 2002 ($2.95, limited series)

1-4-Willingham-s/McManus-a/McKean-c 3.00

SANDMAN, THE: THE DREAM HUNTERS
DC Comics (Vertigo): Oct, 1999 ($29.95/$19.95, one-shot graphic novel)

Hardcover-Neil Gaiman-s/Yoshitaka Amano-painted art 30.00
Softcover-(2000, $19.95) new Amano-c 20.00

SANDMAN, THE: THE DREAM HUNTERS
DC Comics (Vertigo): Jan, 2009 - No. 4, Apr, 2009 ($2.99, limited series)

1-4-Adaptation of the Gaiman/Amano GN by P. Craig Russell-s/a; 2 covers on each 3.00
HC (2009, $24.99) afterwords by Gaiman, Russell, Berger; cover gallery & sketch art 25.00
SC (2010, $19.99) afterwords by Gaiman, Russell, Berger; cover gallery & sketch art 20.00

SANDS OF THE SOUTH PACIFIC

Santa Claus Funnies nn (#1) © DELL

Saurians: Unnatural Selection #1 © CRO

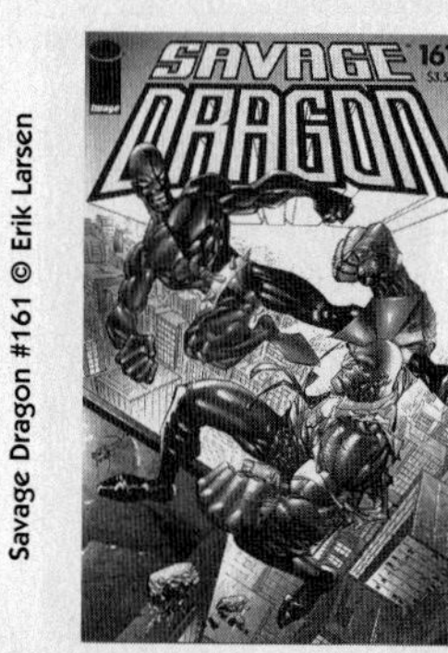

Savage Dragon #161 © Erik Larsen

	GD 2.0	VG 4.0	FN 6.0	VF 8.0	VF/NM 9.0	NM- 9.2

Toby Press: Jan, 1953

1	20	40	60	115	185	255

SANTA AND HIS REINDEER (See March of Comics #166)

SANTA AND THE ANGEL (See Dell Junior Treasury #7)
Dell Publishing Co.: Dec, 1949 (Combined w/Santa at the Zoo) (Gollub-a condensed from FC#128)

Four Color 259	5	10	15	34	55	75

SANTA AT THE ZOO (See Santa And The Angel)

SANTA CLAUS AROUND THE WORLD (See March of Comics #241 in Promotional Comics section)

SANTA CLAUS CONQUERS THE MARTIANS (See Movie Classics)

SANTA CLAUS FUNNIES (Also see Dell Giants)
Dell Publishing Co.: Dec?, 1942 - No. 1274, Dec, 1961

nn(#1)(1942)-Kelly-a	33	66	99	257	509	760
2(12/43)-Kelly-a	22	44	66	159	317	475
Four Color 61(1944)-Kelly-a	22	44	66	155	310	465
Four Color 91(1945)-Kelly-a	16	32	48	111	226	340
Four Color 128('46),175('47)-Kelly-a	13	26	39	94	185	275
Four Color 205,254-Kelly-a	12	24	36	87	164	240
Four Color 302,361,525,607,666,756,867	7	14	21	45	73	100
Four Color 958,1063,1154,1274	6	12	18	41	66	90

NOTE: *Most issues contain only one Kelly story.*

SANTA CLAUS PARADE
Ziff-Davis (Approved Comics)/St. John Publishing Co.: 1951; No. 2, Dec, 1952; No. 3, Jan, 1955 (25¢)

nn(1951-Ziff-Davis)-116 pgs. (Xmas Special 1,2)	30	60	90	177	289	400
2(12/52-Ziff-Davis)-100 pgs.; Dave Berg-a	22	44	66	132	216	300
V1#3(1/55-St. John)-100 pgs.; reprints-c/#1	19	38	57	111	176	240

SANTA CLAUS' WORKSHOP (See March of Comics #50,168 in Promotional Comics section)

SANTA IS COMING (See March of Comics #197 in Promotional Comics section)

SANTA IS HERE (See March of Comics #49 in Promotional Comics section)

SANTA'S BUSY CORNER (See March of Comics #31 in Promotional Comics section)

SANTA'S CANDY KITCHEN (See March of Comics #14 in Promotional Comics section)

SANTA'S CHRISTMAS BOOK (See March of Comics #123 in Promotional Comics section)

SANTA'S CHRISTMAS COMICS
Standard Comics (Best Books): Dec, 1952 (100 pgs.)

nn-Supermouse, Dizzy Duck, Happy Rabbit, etc.	18	36	54	107	169	230

SANTA'S CHRISTMAS LIST (See March of Comics #255 in Promotional Comics section)

SANTA'S HELPERS (See March of Comics #64, 106, 198 in Promotional Comics section)

SANTA'S LITTLE HELPERS (See March of Comics #270 in Promotional Comics section)

SANTA'S SHOW (See March of Comics #311 in Promotional Comics section)

SANTA'S SLEIGH (See March of Comics #298 in Promotional Comics section)

SANTA'S SURPRISE (See March of Comics #13 in Promotional Comics section)

SANTA'S TINKER TOTS
Charlton Comics: 1958

1-Based on "The Tinker Tots Keep Christmas"	4	8	12	24	37	50

SANTA'S TOYLAND (See March of Comics #242 in Promotional Comics section)

SANTA'S TOYS (See March of Comics #12 in Promotional Comics section)

SANTA'S VISIT (See March of Comics #283 in Promotional Comics section)

SANTA THE BARBARIAN
Maximum Press: Dec, 1996 ($2.99, one-shot)

1-Fraga/Mhan-s/a 3.00

SANTIAGO (Movie)
Dell Publishing Co.: Sept, 1956 (Alan Ladd photo-c)

Four Color 723-Kinstler-a	9	18	27	63	107	150

SARGE SNORKEL (Beetle Bailey)
Charlton Comics: Oct, 1973 - No. 17, Dec, 1976

1	2	4	6	11	16	20
2-10	2	4	6	8	10	12
11-17	1	2	3	5	7	9

SARGE STEEL (Becomes Secret Agent #9 on; also see Judomaster)
Charlton Comics: Dec, 1964 - No. 8, Mar-Apr, 1966 (All 12¢ issues)

1-Origin & 1st app.	4	8	12	24	37	50
2-5,7,8	3	6	9	16	23	30
6-2nd app. Judomaster	3	6	9	20	30	40

SATAN'S SIX
Topps Comics (Kirbyverse): Apr, 1993 - No. 4, July, 1993 ($2.95, lim. series)

1-4: 1-Polybagged w/Kirbychrome trading card; Kirby/McFarlane-c plus 8 pgs. Kirby-a(p); has coupon for Kirbychrome ed. of Secret City Saga #0. 2-4-Polybagged w/3 cards. 4-Teenagents preview 3.00

NOTE: ***Ditko** a-1. **Miller** a-1.*

SATAN'S SIX: HELLSPAWN
Topps Comics (Kirbyverse): June, 1994 - No. 3, July, 1994 ($2.50, limited series)

1-3: 1-(6/94)-Indicia incorrectly shows "Vol 1 #2". 2-(6/94) 2.50

SAURIANS: UNNATURAL SELECTION (See Sigil)
CrossGeneration Comics: Feb, 2002 - No. 2, Mar, 2002 ($2.95, limited series)

1,2-Waid-s/DiVito-a 3.00

SAVAGE
Image Comics (Shadowline): Oct, 2008 - No. 4, Jan, 2009 ($3.50, limited series)

1-4-Mayhew-c/a; Niles and Frank-s 3.50

SAVAGE AXE OF ARES
Marvel Comics: June, 2010 ($3.99, B&W, one-shot)

1-B&W short stories by Hurwitz, Palo, McKeever, Swierczynski, Manco and others 4.00

SAVAGE COMBAT TALES
Atlas/Seaboard Publ.: Feb, 1975 - No. 3, July, 1975

1,3: 1-Sgt. Stryker's Death Squad begins (origin); Goodwin-s	2	4	6	8	10	12
2-Toth-a; only app. War Hawk; Goodwin-s	2	4	6	8	11	14

NOTE: ***Buckler** c-3. **McWilliams** a-1-3; c-1. **Sparling** a-1, 3.*

SAVAGE DRAGON, THE (See Megaton #3 & 4)
Image Comics (Highbrow Entertainment): July, 1992 - No. 3, Dec, 1992 ($1.95, lim. series)

1-Erik Larsen-c/a/scripts & bound-in poster in all; 4 cover color variations w/4 different posters; 1st Highbrow Entertainment title 5.00
2-Intro SuperPatriot-c/story (10/92) 4.00
3-Contains coupon for Image Comics #0 4.00
3-With coupon missing 2.00
...Vs. Savage Megaton Man 1 (3/93, $1.95)-Larsen & Simpson-c/a. 4.00
TPB-('93, $9.95) r/#1-3 10.00

SAVAGE DRAGON, THE
Image Comics (Highbrow Entertainment): June, 1993 - Present ($1.95/$2.50/$2.99/$3.50)

1-Erik Larsen-c/a/scripts 5.00
2-30: 2-(Wondercon Exclusive): 2-($2.95, 52 pgs.)-Teenage Mutant Ninja Turtles-c/story; flip book features Vanguard #0 (See Megaton for 1st app.). 3-7: Erik Larsen-c/a/scripts. 3-Mighty Man back-up story w/Austin-a(i). 4-Flip book w/Ricochet. 5-Mighty Man flip-c & back-up plus poster. 6-Jae Lee poster. 7-Vanguard poster. 8-Deadly Duo poster by Larsen. 13A (10/94)-Jim Lee-c/a; 1st app. Max Cash (Condition Red). 13B (6/95)-Larsen story. 15-Dragon poster by Larsen. 22-TMNT-c/a; Bisley pin-up. 27-"Wondercon Exclusive" new-c. 28-Maxx-c/app. 29-Wildstar-c/app. 30-Spawn app. 3.50
25 ($3.95)-variant-c exists. 4.00
31-49,51-71: 31-God vs. The Devil; alternate version exists w/o expletives (has "God Is Good" inside Image logo) 33-Birth of Dragon/Rapture's baby. 34,35-Hellboy-c/app. 51-Origin of She-Dragon. 70-Ann Stevens killed 3.50
50-($5.95, 100 pgs.) Kaboom and Mighty Man app.; Matsuda back-c; pin-ups by McFarlane, Simonson, Capullo and others 6.00
72-74: 72-Begin $2.95-c 3.50
75-($5.95) 6.00
76-99,101-106,108-114,116-124,126-127,129-131,133-136,138: 76-New direction starts. 83,84-Madman-c/app. 84-Atomics app. 97-Dragon returns home; Mighty Man app. 134-Bomb Queen app. 3.50
100-($8.95) Larsen-s/a; inked by various incl. Sienkiewicz, Timm, Austin, Simonson, Royer; plus pin-ups by Timm, Silvestri, Miller, Cho, Art Adams, Pacheco 9.00
107-($3.95) Firebreather, Invincible, Major Damage-c/app.; flip book w/Major Damage 4.00
115-($7.95, 100 pgs.) Wraparound-c; Freak Force app.; Larsen & Englert-a 8.00
125-($4.99, 64 pgs.) new story, The Fly, & various Mr. Glum reprints 5.00
128-Wesley and the villains from Wanted app.; J.G. Jones-c 4.00
132-($6.99, 80 pgs.) new story with Larsen-a; back-up story with Fosco-a 7.00
137-(8/08) Madman and Amazing Joy Buzzards-c/app. 4.00
137-(8/08) Variant cover with Barack Obama endorsed by Savage Dragon; yellow bkgrd 10.00
137-(8/08) 2nd printing of variant cover with Barack Obama and red background 3.50
137-3rd & 4th printings: 3rd-Blue background. 4th-Purple background 3.50
139-149,151-170: 139-Start $3.50-c; Invincible app. 140,141-Witchblade & Spawn app. 145-Obama-c/app. 148-Also a FCBD edition.155-160-Dragon War. 160-163-Flip book 3.50

Savage She-Hulk #23 © MAR

Savage Sword of Conan #192 © CPI

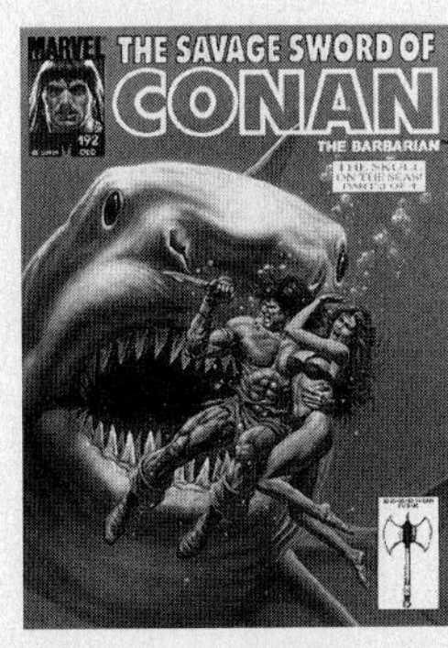

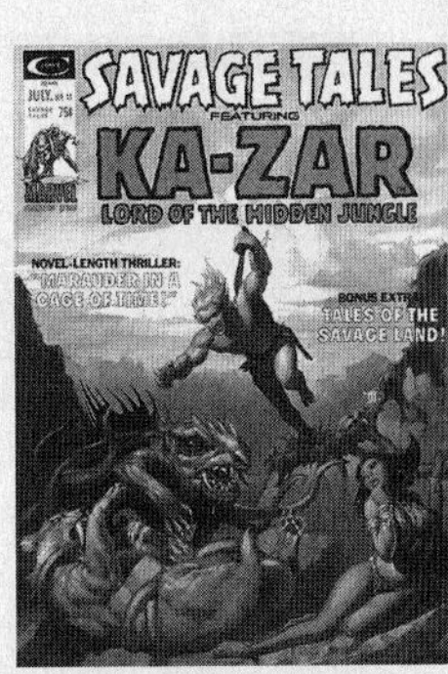

Savage Tales #11 © MAR

GD VG FN VF VF/NM NM-
2.0 4.0 6.0 8.0 9.0 9.2

150-($5.99, 100 pgs.) back up r/Daredevil's origin from Daredevil #18 (1943) 6.00
#0-(7/06, $1.95) reprints origin story from 2005 Image Comics Hardcover 3.50
...Archives Vol. 1 (12/06, $19.99) B&W rep. 1st mini-series #1-3 & #1-21 20.00
...Archives Vol. 2 (2007, $19.99) B&W rep. #22-50; roster pages of Dragon's fellow cops 20.00
...Companion (7/02, $2.95) guide to issues #1-100, character backgrounds 3.50
...Endgame (2/04, $15.95, TPB) r/#47-52 16.00
The Fallen (11/97, $12.95, TPB) r/#7-11, ...Possessed (9/98, $12.95, TPB) r/#12-16,
...Revenge (1998, $12.95, TPB) r/#17-21 13.00
...Gang War (4/00, $16.95, TPB) r/#22-26 17.00
.../Hellboy (10/02, $5.95) r/#34 & #35; Mignola-c 6.00
Image Firsts: Savage Dragon #1 (4/10, $1.00) reprints #1 1.00
...Team-Ups (10/98, $19.95, TPB) r/team-ups 20.00
...: Terminated HC (2/03, $28.95) r/#34-40 & #1/2 29.00
...: This Savage World HC (2002, $24.95) r/#76-81; intro. by Larsen 25.00
...: This Savage World SC (2003, $15.95) r/#76-81; intro. by Larsen 16.00
...: Worlds at War SC (2004, $16.95) r/#41-46; intro. by Larsen; sketch pages 17.00

SAVAGE DRAGON ARCHIVES (Also see Dragon Archives, The)

SAVAGE DRAGONBERT: FULL FRONTAL NERDITY
Image Comics: Oct, 2002 ($5.95, B&W, one-shot)
1-Reprints of the Savage Dragon/Dilbert spoof strips 6.00

SAVAGE DRAGON/DESTROYER DUCK, THE
Image Comics/ Highbrow Entertainment: Nov, 1996 ($3.95, one-shot)
1 4.00

SAVAGE DRAGON: GOD WAR
Image Comics: July, 2004 - No. 4, Oct, 2005 ($2.95, limited series)
1-4-Kirkman-s/Englert-a 3.50

SAVAGE DRAGON/MARSHALL LAW
Image Comics: July, 1997 - No. 2, Aug, 1997 ($2.95, B&W, limited series)
1,2-Pat Mills-s, Kevin O'Neill-a 3.50

SAVAGE DRAGON: SEX & VIOLENCE
Image Comics: Aug, 1997 - No. 2, Sept, 1997 ($2.50, limited series)
1,2-T&M Bierbaum-s, Mays, Lupka, Adam Hughes-a 3.50

SAVAGE DRAGON/TEENAGE MUTANT NINJA TURTLES CROSSOVER
Mirage Studios: Sept, 1993 ($2.75, one-shot)
1-Erik Larsen-c(i) only 4.00

SAVAGE DRAGON: THE RED HORIZON
Image Comics/ Highbrow Entertainment: Feb, 1997 - No. 3 ($2.50, lim. series)
1-3 3.50

SAVAGE FISTS OF KUNG FU
Marvel Comics Group: 1975 (Marvel Treasury)
1-Iron Fist, Shang Chi, Sons of Tiger; Adams, Starlin-a
3 6 9 18 27 35

SAVAGE HULK, THE (Also see Incredible Hulk)
Marvel Comics: Jan, 1996 ($6.95, one-shot)
1-Bisley-c; David, Lobdell, Wagner, Loeb, Gibbons, Messner-Loebs scripts; McKone, Kieth, Ramos & Sale-a. 7.00

SAVAGE RAIDS OF GERONIMO (See Geronimo #4)

SAVAGE RANGE (See Luke Short, Four Color 807)

SAVAGE RED SONJA: QUEEN OF THE FROZEN WASTES
Dynamite Entertainment: 2006 - No. 4, 2006 ($3.50, limited series)
1-4: 1-Three covers by Cho, Texeira & Homs; Cho & Murray-s/Homs-a 3.50
TPB (2007, $14.99) r/series; cover gallery and sketch pages 15.00

SAVAGE RETURN OF DRACULA
Marvel Comics: 1992 ($2.00, 52 pgs.)
1-r/Tomb of Dracula #1,2 by Gene Colan 4.00

SAVAGE SHE-HULK, THE (See The Avengers, Marvel Graphic Novel #18 & The Sensational She-Hulk)
Marvel Comics Group: Feb, 1980 - No. 25, Feb, 1982
1-Origin & 1st app. She-Hulk 2 4 6 9 12 15
2-5,25: 25-(52 pgs.) 6.00
6-24: 6-She-Hulk vs. Iron Man. 8-Vs. Man-Thing 5.00
NOTE: ***Austin*** *a-25i; c-23i-25i.* ***J. Buscema*** *a-1p; c-1, 2p.* ***Golden*** *c-8-11.*

SAVAGE SHE-HULK (Titled All New Savage She Hulk for #3,4)
Marvel Comics: Jun, 2009 - No. 4, Sept, 2009 ($3.99, limited series)
1-4-Lyra, daughter of the Hulk; She-Hulk & Dark Avengers app. 2-Campbell-c 4.00

GD VG FN VF VF/NM NM-
2.0 4.0 6.0 8.0 9.0 9.2

SAVAGE SWORD (ROBERT E. HOWARD'S...)
Dark Horse Comics: Dec, 2010 - Present ($7.99, squarebound)
1-Short stories by various incl. Roy Thomas, Barry-Windsor-Smith; Conan app. 8.00

SAVAGE SWORD OF CONAN (The... #41 on; ...The Barbarian #175 on)
Marvel Comics Group: Aug, 1974 - No. 235, July, 1995 ($1.00/$1.25/$2.25, B&W magazine, mature)
1-Smith-r; J. Buscema/N. Adams/Krenkel-a; origin Blackmark by Gil Kane (part 1, ends #3); Blackmark's 1st app. in magazine form-r/from paperback) & Red Sonja (3rd app.)
10 20 30 72 131 190
2-Neal Adams-c; Chaykin/N. Adams-a 6 12 18 39 62 85
3-Severin/B. Smith-a; N. Adams-a 4 8 12 28 44 60
4-Neal Adams/Kane-a(r) 4 8 12 22 34 45
5-10: 5-Jeff Jones frontispiece (r) 3 6 9 18 27 35
11-20 2 4 6 13 18 22
21-30 2 4 6 10 14 18
31-50: 34-3 pg. preview of Conan newspaper strip. 35-Cover similar to Savage Tales #1. 45-Red Sonja returns; begin $1.25-c 2 4 6 8 11 14
51-99: 63-Toth frontispiece. 65-Kane-a w/Chaykin/Miller/Simonson/Sherman finishes. 70-Article on movie. 83-Red Sonja-r by Neal Adams from #1
1 2 3 5 7 9
100 1 3 4 6 8 10
101-176: 163-Begin $2.25-c. 169-King Kull story. 171-Soloman Kane by Williamson (i). 172-Red Sonja story 6.00
177-199: 179,187,192-Red Sonja app. 190-193-4 part King Kull story. 196-King Kull story 5.00
200-220: 200-New Buscema-a; Robert E. Howard app. with Conan in story. 202-King Kull story. 204-60th anniversary (1932-92). 211-Rafael Kayanan's 1st Conan-a. 214-Sequel to Red Nails by Howard 6.00
221-230 1 2 3 5 7 9
231-234 2 4 6 9 12 15
235-Last issue 3 6 9 16 22 28
Special 1(1975, B&W)-B. Smith-r/Conan #10,13 3 6 9 17 25 32
Volume 1 TPB (Dark Horse Books, 12/07, $17.95, B&W) r/#1-10 and selected stories from Savage Tales #1-5 with covers 18.00
Volume 2 TPB (Dark Horse Books, 3/08, $17.95, B&W) r/#11-24 18.00
Volume 3 TPB (Dark Horse Books, 5/08, $19.95, B&W) r/#25-36 and selected pin-ups 20.00
Volume 4 TPB (Dark Horse Books, 9/08, $19.95, B&W) r/#37-48 and selected pin-ups 20.00
Volume 5 TPB (Dark Horse Books, 2/09, $19.95, B&W) r/#49-60 and selected pin-ups 20.00
NOTE: ***N. Adams*** *a-14p, 60, 83p(r).* ***Alcala*** *a-2 ,4, 7, 12, 15-20, 23, 24, 28, 59, 67, 69, 75, 76i, 80i, 82i, 83i, 89, 180i, 184i, 187i, 189i, 216p.* ***Austin*** *a-78i.* ***Boris*** *painted c-1, 4, 5, 7, 9, 10, 12, 15.* ***Brunner*** *a-30; c-8, 30.* ***Buscema*** *a-1-5, 7, 10-12, 15-24, 26-28, 31, 32, 36-43, 45, 47-58p, 60-67p, 70, 71-74p, 76-81p, 87-96p, 98, 99-101p, 190-204p; painted c-40.* ***Chaykin*** *c-31.* ***Chiodo*** *painted c-71, 76, 79, 81, 84, 85, 178.* ***Conrad*** *c-215, 217.* ***Corben*** *a-4, 16, 29.* ***Finlay*** *a-16.* ***Golden*** *a-98, 101; c-98, 101, 105, 106, 117, 124, 150.* ***Kaluta*** *a-11, 18; c-3, 91, 93.* ***Gil Kane*** *a-2, 3, 8, 13r, 29, 47, 64, 65, 67, 85p, 86p.* ***Rafael Kayanan*** *a-211-213, 215, 217.* ***Krenkel*** *a-9, 11, 14, 16, 24.* ***Morrow*** *a-7.* ***Nebres*** *a-93i, 101i, 107, 114.* ***Newton*** *a-6.* ***Nino*** *c/a-6.* ***Redondo*** *painted c-48-50, 52, 56, 57, 85i, 90, 96i.* ***Marie & John Severin*** *a-Special 1.* ***Simonson*** *a-7, 8, 12, 15-17.* ***Barry Smith*** *a-7, 16, 24, 82r, Special 1r.* ***Starlin*** *c-26.* ***Toth*** *a-64.* ***Williamson*** *a(i)-162, 171, 186. No. 8 , 10 & 16 contain a Robert E. Howard Conan adaptation.*

SAVAGE TALES (...Featuring Conan #4 on)(Magazine)
Marvel Comics Group: May, 1971; No. 2, 10/73; No. 3, 2/74 - No. 12, Summer, 1975 (B&W)
1-Origin/1st app. The Man-Thing by Morrow; Conan the Barbarian by Barry Smith (1st Conan x-over outside his own title); Femizons by Romita-r/in #3; Ka-Zar story by Buscema
16 32 48 114 232 350
2-B. Smith, Brunner, Morrow, Williamson-a; Wrightson King Kull reprint/ Creatures on the Loose #10 6 12 18 41 66 90
3-B. Smith, Brunner, Steranko, Williamson-a 5 10 15 32 51 70
4,5-N. Adams-c; last Conan (Smith-r/#4) plus Kane/N. Adams-a. 5-Brak the Barbarian begins, ends #8 4 8 12 28 44 60
6-Ka-Zar begins; Williamson-r; N. Adams-c 3 6 9 20 30 40
7-N. Adams-i 3 6 9 16 22 28
8,9,11: 8-Shanna, the She-Devil app. thru #10; Williamson-r
3 6 9 14 20 26
10-Neal Adams-a(i), Williamson-r 3 6 9 16 22 28
...Featuring Ka-Zar Annual 1 (Summer, '75, B&W)(#12 on inside)-Ka-Zar origin by Gil Kane; B. Smith-r/Astonishing Tales 3 6 9 17 25 32
NOTE: ***Boris*** *c-7, 10.* ***Buscema*** *a-5r, 6p, 8p; c-2.* ***Colan*** *a-1p.* ***Fabian*** *c-8.* ***Golden*** *a-1, 4; c-1.* ***Heath*** *a-10p, 11p.* ***Kaluta*** *c-9.* ***Maneely*** *r-2, 4(The Crusader in both).* ***Morrow*** *a-1, 2, Annual 1.* ***Reese*** *a-2.* ***Severin*** *a-1-7.* ***Starlin*** *a-5. Robert E. Howard adaptations-1-4.*

SAVAGE TALES
Marvel Comics Group: Nov, 1985 - No. 8, Dec, 1986 ($1.50, B&W, magazine, mature)
1-1st app. The Nam; Golden, Morrow-a 6.00
2-8: 2,7-Morrow-a. 4-2nd Nam story; Golden-a 4.00

SAVAGE TALES
Dynamite Entertainment: 2007 - Present ($4.99)

Scalped #36 © Aaron & Milosevic

Scarlet #1 © Jinxworld

Science Comics #6 © FOX

1-10: 1-Anthology; Red Sonja app.; three covers 5.00

SAVANT GARDE (Also see WildC.A.T.S...)
Image Comics/WildStorm Productions: Mar, 1997 - No. 7, Sept, 1997 ($2.50)

1-7 3.00

SAVED BY THE BELL (TV)
Harvey Comics: Mar, 1992 - No. 5, May, 1993 ($1.25, limited series)

1-5, Holiday Special (3/92), Special 1 (9/92, $1.50)-photo-c, Summer Break 1 (10/92) 3.00

SAW: REBIRTH (Based on 2004 movie Saw)
IDW Publ.: Oct, 2005 ($3.99, one-shot)

1-Guedes-a 4.00

SCALPED
DC Comics (Vertigo): Mar, 2007 - Present ($2.99, limited series)

1-46: 1-Aaron-s/Guera-a/Jock-c. 12-Leon-a 3.00
1-Special Edition (7/10, $1.00) r/#1 with "What's Next?" cover frame 1.00
...: Casino Blood TPB (2008, $14.99) r/#6-11; intro. by Garth Ennis 15.00
...: Dead Mothers TPB (2008, $17.99) r/#12-18 18.00
...: High Lonesome TPB (2009, $14.99) r/#25-29; intro. by Jason Starr 15.00
...: Indian Country TPB (2007, $9.99) r/#1-5; intro. by Brian K. Vaughan 10.00
...: Rez Blues (2011, $17.99) r/#35-42 18.00
...: The Gnawing (2010, $14.99) r/#30-34; intro. by Matt Fraction 15.00
...: The Gravel in Your Guts (2009, $14.99) r/#19-24; intro. by Ed Brubaker 15.00

SCAMP (Walt Disney)(See Walt Disney's Comics & Stories #204)
Dell Publ. Co./Gold Key: No. 703, 5/56 - No. 1204, 8-10/61; 11/67 - No. 45, 1/79

	GD 2.0	VG 4.0	FN 6.0	VF 8.0	VF/NM 9.0	NM- 9.2
Four Color 703(#1)	8	16	24	58	97	135
Four Color 777,806('57),833	6	12	18	43	69	95
5(3-5/58)-10(6-8/59)	5	10	15	34	55	75
11-16(12-2/60-61), Four Color 1204(1961)	4	8	12	28	44	60
1(12/67-Gold Key)-Reprints begin	4	8	12	26	41	55
2(3/69)-10	2	4	6	13	18	22
11-20	2	4	6	8	11	14
21-45	1	2	3	4	5	7

NOTE: *New stories-#20(in part), 22-25, 27, 29-31, 34, 36-40, 42-45. New covers-#11, 12, 14, 15, 17-25, 27, 29-31, 34, 36-38.*

SCARAB
DC Comics (Vertigo): Nov, 1993 - No. 8, June, 1994 ($1.95, limited series)

1-8-Glenn Fabry painted-c: 1-Silver ink-c. 2-Phantom Stranger app. 3.00

SCARECROW OF ROMNEY MARSH, THE (See W. Disney Showcase #53)
Gold Key: April, 1964 - No. 3, Oct, 1965 (Disney TV Show)

	GD 2.0	VG 4.0	FN 6.0	VF 8.0	VF/NM 9.0	NM- 9.2
10112-404 (#1)	5	10	15	32	51	70
2,3	4	8	12	22	34	45

SCARECROW (VILLAINS) (See Batman)
DC Comics: Feb, 1998 ($1.95, one-shot)

1-Fegredo-a/Milligan-s/Pearson-c 3.00

SCARE TACTICS
DC Comics: Dec, 1996 - No. 12, Mar, 1998 ($2.25)

1-12: 1-1st app. 3.00

SCAR FACE (See The Crusaders)

SCARFACE: SCARRED FOR LIFE (Based on the 1983 movie)
IDW Publishing: Dec, 2006 - No. 5, Apr, 2007 ($3.99, limited series)

1-5-Tony Montana survives his shooting; Layman-s/Crosland-a 4.00
Scarface: Devil in Disguise (7/07 - No. 4, 10/07, $3.99) Alberto Dose-a 4.00

SCARLET
Marvel Comics (ICON): July, 2010 - Present ($3.95)

1-5-Bendis-s/Maleev-a. 1-Second printing exists 4.00
1,2-Variant covers. 1-Deodato & Lafuente. 2-Oeming & Mack. 3,4-Oeming. 5-Bendis 6.00

SCARLET O'NEIL (See Harvey Comics Hits #59 & Invisible...)

SCARLET SPIDER
Marvel Comics: Nov, 1995 - No. 2, Jan, 1996 ($1.95, limited series)

1,2: Replaces Spider-Man title 3.00

SCARLET SPIDER UNLIMITED
Marvel Comics: Nov, 1995 ($3.95, one-shot)

1-Replaces Spider-Man Unlimited title 4.00

SCARLET WITCH (See Avengers #16, Vision &... & X-Men #4)
Marvel Comics: Jan, 1994 - No. 4, Apr, 1994 ($1.75, limited series)

1-4 3.00

SCARY GODMOTHER (Hardcover story books)
Sirius: 1997 - Present ($19.95, HC with dust jackets, one-shots)

Volume 1 (9/97) Jill Thompson-s/a; first app. of Scary Godmother 20.00
Vol. 2 - The Revenge of Jimmy (9/98, $19.95) 20.00
Vol. 3 - The Mystery Date (10/99, $19.95) 20.00
Vol. 4 - The Boo Flu (9/02, $19.95) 20.00

SCARY GODMOTHER
Sirius: 2001 - No. 6, 2002 ($2.95, B&W, limited series)

1-6-Jill Thompson-s/a 3.00
...: Activity Book (12/00, $2.95, B&W) Jill Thompson-s/a 3.00
...: Bloody Valentine Special (2/98, $3.95, B&W) Jill Thompson-s/a; pin-ups by Ross, Mignola, Russell 4.00
...: Ghoul's Out For Summer (2002,$14.95, B&W) r/#1-6 15.00
...: Holiday Spooktakular (11/98, $2.95, B&W) Jill Thompson-s/a; pin-ups by Brereton, LaBan, Dorkin, Fingerman 3.00

SCARY GODMOTHER: WILD ABOUT HARRY
Sirius: 2000 - No. 3 ($2.95, B&W, limited series)

1-3-Jill Thompson-s/a 3.00
TPB (2001, $9.95) r/series 10.00

SCARY TALES
Charlton Comics: 8/75 - #9, 1/77; #10, 9/77 - #20, 6/79; #21, 8/80 - #46, 10/84

	GD 2.0	VG 4.0	FN 6.0	VF 8.0	VF/NM 9.0	NM- 9.2
1-Origin/1st app. Countess Von Bludd, not in #2	3	6	9	19	29	38
2,4,6,9,10: 4,9-Sutton-c/a. 4-Man-Thing copy	2	4	6	9	13	16
3-Sutton painted-c; Ditko-a	2	4	6	11	16	20
5,11-Ditko-c/a.	3	6	9	14	19	24
7,8-Ditko-a	2	4	6	10	14	18
12,15,16,19,21,39-Ditko-a	2	4	6	9	13	16
13,17,20	2	4	6	8	10	12
14,18,30,32-Ditko-c/a	2	4	6	11	16	20
22-29,33-37,39,40: 37,38,40-New-a. 39-All Ditko reprints and cover	1	3	4	6	8	10
31,38: 31-Newton-c/a. 38-Mr. Jigsaw app.	1	3	4	6	8	10
41-45-New-a. 41-Ditko-a(3). 42-45-(Low print)	2	4	6	8	10	12
46-Reprints (Low print)	2	4	6	10	14	18
1(Modern Comics reprint, 1977)						6.00

NOTE: ***Adkins** a-31i; c-31i. **Ditko** a-3, 5, 7, 8(2), 11, 12, 14-16r, 18(3)r, 19r, 21r, 30r, 32, 39r, 41(3); c-5, 11, 14, 18, 30, 32. **Newton** a-31p; c-31p. **Powell** a-18r. **Staton** a-1(2 pgs.), 4, 20r; c-1, 20. **Sutton** a-4, 9; c-4, 9. **Zeck** a-9.*

SCATTERBRAIN
Dark Horse Comics: Jun, 1998 - No. 4, Sept, 1998 ($2.95, limited series)

1-4-Humor anthology by Aragonés, Dorkin, Stevens and others 3.00

SCAVENGERS
Quality Comics: Feb, 1988 - No. 14, 1989 ($1.25/$1.50)

1-14: 9-13-Guice-c 3.00

SCAVENGERS
Triumphant Comics: 1993(nd, July) - No. 11, May, 1994 ($2.50, serially numbered)

1-9,0,10,11: 5,6-Triumphant Unleashed x-over. 9-(3/94). 0-Retail ed. (3/94, $2.50, 36 pgs.). 0-Giveaway edition (3/94, 20 pgs.). 0-Coupon redemption edition. 10-(4/94) 3.00

SCENE OF THE CRIME (Also see Vertigo: Winter's Edge #2)
DC Comics (Vertigo): May, 1999 - No. 4, Aug, 1999 ($2.50, limited series)

1-4-Brubaker-s/Lark-a 3.00
...: A Little Piece of Goodnight TPB ('00, $12.95) r/#1-4; Winter's Edge #2 13.00

SCHOOL DAY ROMANCES (...of Teen-Agers #4; Popular Teen-Agers #5 on)
Star Publications: Nov-Dec, 1949 - No. 4, May-June, 1950 (Teenage)

	GD 2.0	VG 4.0	FN 6.0	VF 8.0	VF/NM 9.0	NM- 9.2
1-Toni Gayle (later Toni Gay), Ginger Snapp, Midge Martin & Eve Adams begin	27	54	81	158	259	360
2,3: 3-Jane Powell photo on-c & true life story	20	40	60	115	185	255
4-Ronald Reagan photo on-c; L.B. Cole-c	30	60	90	177	289	400

NOTE: *All have **L. B. Cole** covers.*

SCHWINN BICYCLE BOOK (...Bike Thrills, 1959)
Schwinn Bicycle Co.: 1949; 1952; 1959 (10¢)

	GD 2.0	VG 4.0	FN 6.0	VF 8.0	VF/NM 9.0	NM- 9.2
1949	6	12	18	28	34	40
1952-Believe It or Not facts; comic format; 36 pgs.	5	10	14	20	24	28
1959	3	6	8	11	13	15

SCIENCE COMICS (1st Series)
Fox Features Syndicate: Feb, 1940 - No. 8, Sept, 1940

1-Origin Dynamo (1st app., called Electro in #1), The Eagle (1st app.), & Navy Jones; Marga, The Panther Woman (1st app.), Cosmic Carson & Perisphere Payne, Dr. Doom

Scion #22 © CRO

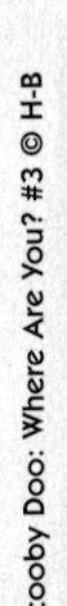
Scooby Doo: Where Are You? #3 © H-B

Scott Pilgrim... Vol. 1 © Bryan Lee O'Malley

	GD 2.0	VG 4.0	FN 6.0	VF 8.0	VF/NM 9.0	NM- 9.2
begin; bondage/hypo-c; Electro-c	432	864	1296	3154	5577	8000
2-Classic Lou Fine Dynamo-c	236	472	708	1499	2575	3650
3-Classic Lou Fine Dynamo-c	190	380	570	1207	2079	2950
4-Kirby-a; Cosmic Carson-c by Joe Simon	171	342	513	1086	1868	2650
5-8: 5,8-Eagle-c. 6,7-Dynamo-c	102	204	306	648	1112	1575

NOTE: *Cosmic Carson by* ***Tuska****-#1-3; by* ***Kirby****-#4.* ***Lou Fine*** *c-1-3 only.*

SCIENCE COMICS (2nd Series)
Humor Publications (Ace Magazines?): Jan, 1946 - No. 5, 1946

1-Palais-c/a in #1-3; A-Bomb-c	19	38	57	111	176	240
2	11	22	33	64	90	115
3-Feldstein-a (6 pgs.)	16	32	48	92	144	195
4,5: 4-Palais-c	9	18	27	52	69	85

SCIENCE COMICS
Ziff-Davis Publ. Co.: May, 1947 (8 pgs. in color)

nn-Could be ordered by mail for 10¢; like the nn Amazing Adventures (1950) & Boy Cowboy (1950); used to test the market 40 80 120 246 411 575

SCIENCE COMICS (True Science Illustrated)
Export Publication Ent., Toronto, Canada: Mar, 1951 (Distr. in U.S. by Kable News Co.)

1-Science Adventure stories plus some true science features; man on moon story 13 26 39 74 105 135

SCIENCE DOG SPECIAL (Also see Invincible)
Image Comics: Aug, 2010 ($3.50, one-shot)

1-Kirkman-s/Walker-a/c; leads into Invincible #75 3.50

SCIENCE FICTION SPACE ADVENTURES (See Space Adventures)

SCION (Also see CrossGen Chronicles)
CrossGeneration Comics: July, 2000 - No. 43, Apr, 2004 ($2.95)

1-43: 1-Marz-s/Cheung-a 3.00
...: Conflict of Conscience Vol. 1 TPB (5/01, $19.95) r/#1-7; Adam Hughes-c 20.00
...: Blood For Blood Vol. 2 TPB (2002, $19.95) r/#8-14 & CrossGen Chronicles #2 20.00
...: Divided Loyalties Vol. 3 TPB (2002, $15.95) r/#15-21 16.00
...: Sanctuary Vol. 4 TPB (2003, $15.95) r/#22-27 16.00
Vol. 5: The Far Kingdom (2003, $15.95) r/#28-33 16.00
Vol. 6: The Royal Wedding (2004, $15.95) r/#34-39 16.00
Traveler Vol. 1-3 ($9.95) Digest-sized reprints of TPBs 10.00

SCI-SPY
DC Comics (Vertigo): Apr, 2002 - No. 6, Sept, 2002 ($2.50, limited series)

1-6-Moench-s/Gulacy-c/a 3.00

SCI-TECH
DC Comics (WildStorm): Sept, 1999 - No. 4, Dec, 1999 ($2.50, limited series)

1-4-Benes-a/Choi & Peterson-s 3.00

SCOOBY DOO (TV)(...Where are you? #1-16,26; ...Mystery Comics #17-25, 27 on)
(See March Of Comics #356, 368, 382, 391 in the Promotional Comics section)
Gold Key: Mar, 1970 - No. 30, Feb, 1975 (Hanna-Barbera)

1	13	26	39	92	179	265
2-5	8	16	24	54	90	125
6-10	7	14	21	45	73	100
11-20: 11-Tufts-a	6	12	18	37	59	80
21-30	4	8	12	28	44	60

SCOOBY DOO (TV)
Charlton Comics: Apr, 1975 - No. 11, Dec, 1976 (Hanna-Barbera)

1	6	12	18	41	66	90
2-5	4	8	12	26	41	55
6-11	4	8	12	22	34	45
nn-(1976, digest, 68 pgs., B&W)	4	8	12	24	37	50

SCOOBY-DOO (TV)(Newsstand sales only) (See Dynamutt & Laff-A-Lympics)
Marvel Comics Group: Oct, 1977 - No. 9, Feb, 1979 (Hanna-Barbera)

1,6-9: 1-Dyno-Mutt begins	3	6	9	18	27	35
1-(35¢-c variant, limited distribution)(10/77)	8	16	24	54	90	125
2-5	3	6	9	16	22	28

SCOOBY-DOO (TV)
Harvey Comics: Sept, 1992 - No. 3, May, 1993 ($1.25)

V2#1,2	1	2	3	4	5	7
Big Book 1,2 (11/92, 4/93, $1.95, 52 pgs.)	1	2	3	5	7	9
Giant Size 1,2 (10/92, 3/93, $2.25, 68 pgs.)	1	2	3	5	7	9

SCOOBY DOO (TV)
Archie Comics: Oct, 1995 -No. 21, June, 1997 ($1.50)

1	1	2	3	5	6	8

2-21: 12-Cover by Scooby Doo creative designer Iwao Takamoto 5.00

SCOOBY DOO (TV)
DC Comics: Aug, 1997 - No. 159, Oct, 2010 ($1.75/$1.95/$1.99/$2.25/$2.50/$2.99)

1 6.00
2-10: 5-Begin-$1.95-c 4.00
11-45: 14-Begin $1.99-c 3.00
46-89,91-157: 63-Begin $2.25-c. 75-With 2 Garbage Pail Kids stickers. 100-Wray-c 3.00
90,158,159: 90-($2.95) Bonus stories. 158,159-($2.99-c) 4.00
...Spooky Spectacular 1 (10/99, $3.95) Comic Convention story 4.00
...Spooky Spectacular 2000 (10/00, $3.95) 4.00
...Spooky Summer Special 2001 (8/01, $3.95) Staton-a 4.00
...Super Scarefest (8/02, $3.95) r/#20,25,30-32 4.00
Vol. 1: You Meddling Kids (2003, $6.95, digest-size) r/#1-5 7.00
Vol. 2: Ruh-Roh! (2003, $6.95, digest-size) r/#6-10 7.00
Vol. 3: All Wrapped Up! (2005, $6.95, digest-size) r/#11-15 7.00
Vol. 4: The Big Squeeze! (2005, $6.95, digest-size) r/#16-20 7.00
Vol. 5: Surf's Up! (2006, $6.99, digest-size) r/#21-25 7.00
Vol. 5: Space Fright! (2006, $6.99, digest-size) r/#26-30 7.00

SCOOBY DOO: WHERE ARE YOU? (TV)
DC Comics: Nov, 2010 - Present ($2.99)

1-6 3.00

SCOOP COMICS (Becomes Yankee Comics #4-7, a digest sized cartoon book; then after #8 it becomes Snap #9)
Harry 'A' Chesler (Holyoke): November, 1941 - No. 3, Mar, 1943; No. 8, 1944

1-Intro. Rocketman & Rocketgirl & begins; origin The Master Key & begins; Dan Hastings begins; Charles Sultan-c/a	155	310	465	992	1696	2400
2-Rocket Boy begins; injury to eye story (reprinted in Spotlight #3); classic-c	174	348	522	1114	1907	2700
3-Injury to eye story-r from #2; Rocket Boy	74	128	222	470	810	1150
8-Formerly Yankee Comics; becomes Snap	47	94	141	296	498	700

SCOOTER (See Swing With...)

SCOOTER COMICS
Rucker Publ. Ltd. (Canadian): Apr, 1946

1-Teen-age/funny animal	11	22	33	60	83	105

SCOOTER GIRL
Oni Press: May, 2003 - No. 6, Feb, 2004 ($2.99, B&W, limited series)

1-6-Chynna Clugston-Major-s/a 3.00
TPB (5/04, $14.95, digest size) r/series; sketch pages 15.00

SCORPION
Atlas/Seaboard Publ.: Feb, 1975 - No. 3, July, 1975

1-Intro.; bondage-c by Chaykin	2	4	6	11	16	20
2-Chaykin-a w/Wrightson, Kaluta, Simonson assists(p)	2	4	6	11	16	20
3-Jim Craig-c/a	2	4	6	9	13	16

NOTE: ***Chaykin*** *a-1, 2; c-1.* ***Colon*** *c-2.* ***Craig*** *c/a-3.*

SCORPION KING, THE (Movie)
Dark Horse Comics: March, 2002 - No. 2, Apr, 2002 ($2.99, limited series)

1,2-Photo-c of the Rock; Richards-a 3.00

SCORPIO ROSE
Eclipse Comics: Jan, 1983 - No. 2, Oct, 1983 ($1.25, Baxter paper)

1,2: Dr. Orient back-up story begins. 2-origin. 4.00

SCOTLAND YARD (Inspector Farnsworth of)(Texas Rangers in Action #5 on?)
Charlton Comics Group: June, 1955 - No. 4, Mar, 1956

1-Tothish-a	14	28	42	80	115	150
2-4: 2-Tothish-a	10	20	30	54	72	90

SCOTT PILGRIM, ... (Inspired the 2010 movie)
Oni Press: Jul, 2004 - Vol. 6, Jul, 2010 ($11.99, B&W, 7-1/2" x 5", multiple printings exist)

Scott Pilgrim's Precious Little Life (Vol. 1) Bryan Lee O'Malley-s/a in all 12.00
Scott Pilgrim Vs. The World (Vol. 2), S.P. & The Infinite Sadness (Vol. 3), S.P. Gets it Together (Vol. 4), S.P. Vs. The Universe (Vol. 5), Scott Pilgrim's Finest Hour (Vol. 6) each 12.00
Free Scott Pilgrim #1 (Free Comic Book Day Edition, 2006) 15.00
Full-Colour Odds & Ends 2008 8.00

SCOURGE, THE
Aspen MLT: No. 0, Aug, 2010 - No. 3, Feb, 2011 ($2.50/$2.99)

0-($2.50) Lobdell-s/Battle-a; multiple covers 2.50
1-3-($2.99) Lobdell-s/Battle-a; multiple covers 3.00

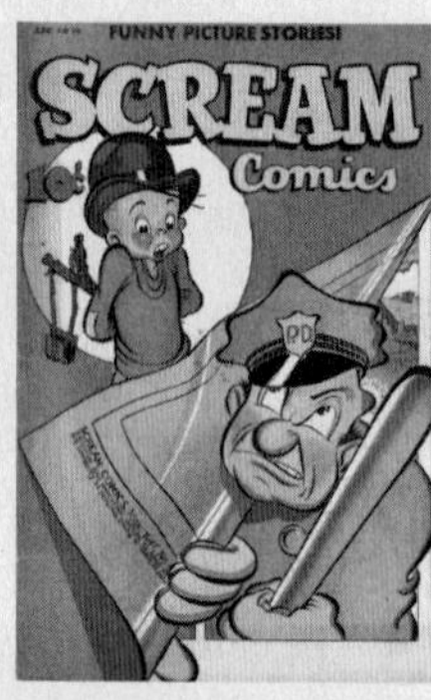

Scream Comics #14 © ACE

Sea Devils #5 © DC

Sea Hound #4 © AVON

	GD 2.0	VG 4.0	FN 6.0	VF 8.0	VF/NM 9.0	NM- 9.2

SCOURGE OF THE GODS
Marvel Comics (Soleil): 2009 - No. 3, 2009 ($5.99, limited series)
1-3-Mangin-s/Gajic-a; English version of French comic 6.00
...: The Fall 1-3 (2009 - No. 3, 2009) 6.00

SCOUT (See Eclipse Graphic Album #16, New America & Swords of Texas)
(Becomes Scout: War Shaman)
Eclipse Comics: Dec, 1985 - No. 24, Oct, 1987($1.75/$1.25, Baxter paper)
1-15,17,18,20-24: 19-Airboy preview. 10-Bissette-a. 11-Monday, the Eliminator begins. 15-Swords of Texas 3.00
16,19: 16-Scout 3-D Special ($2.50), 16-Scout 2-D Limited Edition, 19-contains flexidisk ($2.50) 4.00
...Handbook 1 (8/87, $1.75, B&W) 3.00
Mount Fire (1989, $14.95, TPB) r/#8-14 15.00

SCOUT: WAR SHAMAN (Formerly Scout)
Eclipse Comics: Mar, 1988 - No. 16, Dec, 1989 ($1.95)
1-16 3.00

SCRATCH
DC Comics: Aug, 2004 - No. 5, Dec, 2004 ($2.50, limited series)
1-5-Sam Kieth-s/a/c; Batman app. 3.00

SCREAM (...Comics) (Andy Comics #20 on)
Humor Publications/Current Books(Ace Magazines): Autumn, 1944 - No. 19, Apr, 1948

	GD	VG	FN	VF	VF/NM	NM-
1-Teenage humor	16	32	48	92	144	195
2	10	20	30	56	76	95
3-16: 11-Racist humor (Indians). 16-Intro. Lily-Belle	9	18	27	47	61	75
17,19	8	16	24	42	54	65
18-Hypo needle story	9	18	27	47	61	75

SCREAM (Magazine)
Skywald Publ. Corp.: Aug, 1973 - No. 11, Feb, 1975 (68 pgs., B&W) (Painted-c on all)

	GD	VG	FN	VF	VF/NM	NM-
1-Nosferatu-c/1st app. (series thru #11); Morrow-a. Cthulhu/Necronomicon-s	7	14	21	49	80	110
2,3: 2-(10/73) Lady Satan 1st app. & series begins; Edgar Allan Poe adaptations begin (thru #11); Phantom of the Opera-s. 3-(12/73) Origin Lady Satan	5	10	15	32	51	70
4-1st Cannibal Werewolf and 1st Lunatic Mummy	4	8	12	28	44	60
5,7,8: 5,7-Frankenstein app. 8-Buckler-a; Werewolf-s; Slither-Slime Man-s	4	8	12	28	44	60
6, 9,10: 6-(6/74) Saga of The Victims/ I Am Horror, classic GGA Hewetson series begins (thru #11); Frankenstein 2073-s. 9-Severed head-c; Marcos-a. 9,10-Werewolf-s. 10-Dracula-c/s	5	10	15	30	48	65
11- (1975 Winter Special) "Mr. Poe and the Raven" story	5	10	15	32	51	70

NOTE: ***Buckler** a-8. **Hewetson** s-1-11. **Marcos** a-9. **Miralles** c-2. **Morrow** a-1. **Poe** s-2-11. **Segrelles** a-7; c-1.*

SCREEN CARTOONS
DC Comics: Dec, 1944 (cover only ashcan)
nn-Ashcan comic, not distributed to newsstands, only for in house use. Covers were produced, but not the rest of the book. A copy sold in 2006 for $400 and in 2008 for $500.

SCREEN COMICS
DC Comics: Dec, 1944 (cover only ashcan)
nn-Ashcan comic, not distributed to newsstands, only for in house use. Covers were produced, but not the rest of the book. A copy sold in 2006 for $400 and in 2008 for $500.

SCREEN FABLES
DC Comics: Dec, 1944 (cover only ashcan)
nn-Ashcan comic, not distributed to newsstands, only for in house use. Covers were produced, but not the rest of the book. A copy sold in 2006 for $400 and in 2008 for $500.

SCREEN FUNNIES
DC Comics: Dec, 1944 (cover only ashcan)
nn-Ashcan comic, not distributed to newsstands, only for in house use. Covers were produced, but not the rest of the book. A copy sold in 2006 for $400 and in 2008 for $500.

SCREEN GEMS
DC Comics: Dec, 1944 (cover only ashcan)
nn-Ashcan comic, not distributed to newsstands, only for in house use. Covers were produced, but not the rest of the book. A copy sold in 2008 for $500 and in 2010 for $891.

SCREWBALL SQUIRREL
Dark Horse Comics: July, 1995 - No. 3, Sept, 1995 ($2.50, limited series)
1-3: Characters created by Tex Avery 3.00

SCRIBBLY (See All-American Comics, Buzzy, The Funnies, Leave It To Binky & Popular Comics)
National Periodical Publ.: 8-9/48 - No. 13, 8-9/50; No. 14, 10-11/51 - No. 15, 12-1/51-52

	GD	VG	FN	VF	VF/NM	NM-
1-Sheldon Mayer-c/a in all; 52 pgs. begin	87	174	261	553	952	1350
2	55	110	165	352	601	850
3-5	45	90	135	284	480	675
6-10	36	72	108	216	351	485
11-15: 13-Last 52 pgs.	31	62	93	184	300	415

SCUD: TALES FROM THE VENDING MACHINE
Fireman Press: 1998 - No. 5 ($2.50, B&W)
1-5: 1-Kaniuga-a. 2-Ruben Martinez-a 3.00

SCUD: THE DISPOSABLE ASSASSIN
Fireman Press: Feb, 1994 - No. 20, 1997 ($2.95, B&W)
Image Comics: No. 21, Feb, 2008 - No. 24, May, 2008 ($3.50, B&W)
1 6.00
1-2nd printing in color 3.00
2,3 4.00
4-20 3.00
21-24: 21-(2/08, $3.50) Ashley Wood-c. 22-Mahfood-c 3.50
Heavy 3PO ($12.95, TPB) r/#1-4 13.00
Programmed For Damage ($14.95, TPB) r/#5-9 15.00
Solid Gold Bomb ($17.95, TPB) r/#10-15 18.00

SEA DEVILS (See Limited Collectors' Edition #39,45, & Showcase #27-29)
National Periodical Publications: Sept-Oct, 1961 - No. 35, May-June, 1967

	GD	VG	FN	VF	VF/NM	NM-
1-(9-10/61)	56	112	168	476	963	1450
2-Last 10¢ issue	28	56	84	215	433	650
3-Begin 12¢ issues thru #35	19	38	57	134	272	410
4,5: 4-Grey-tone-c	16	32	48	117	239	360
6-10	12	24	36	82	154	225
11,12,14-20: 12-Grey-tone-c	9	18	27	63	107	150
13-Kubert, Colan-a; Joe Kubert app. in story	9	18	27	64	110	155
21-35: 22-Intro. International Sea Devils; origin & 1st app. Capt. X & Man Fish. 33,35-Grey-tone-c	7	14	21	47	76	105

NOTE: ***Heath** a-Showcase 27-29, 1-10; c-Showcase 27-29, 1-10, 14-16. **Moldoff** a-16i.*

SEA DEVILS (See Tangent Comics/ Sea Devils)

SEADRAGON (Also see the Epilion Wave)
Elite Comics: May, 1986 - No. 8, 1987 ($1.75)
1-8: 1-1st & 2nd printings exist 3.00

SEAGUY
DC Comics (Vertigo): July, 2004 - No. 3, Sept, 2004 ($2.95, limited series)
1-3-Grant Morrison-s/Cameron Stewart-a/c 3.00
TPB (2005, $9.95) r/#1-3 10.00

SEAGUY: THE SLAVES OF MICKEY EYE
DC Comics (Vertigo): Jun, 2009 - No. 3, Aug, 2009 ($3.99, limited series)
1-3-Grant Morrison-s/Cameron Stewart-a/c 4.00

SEA HOUND, THE (Captain Silver's Log Of The...)
Avon Periodicals: 1945 (no month) - No. 2, Sept-Oct, 1945

	GD	VG	FN	VF	VF/NM	NM-
nn (#1)-29 pg. novel length sty-"The Esmeralda's Treasure"	18	36	54	105	165	225
2	13	26	39	74	105	135

SEA HOUND, THE (Radio)
Capt. Silver Syndicate: No. 3, July, 1949 - No. 4, Sept, 1949

	GD	VG	FN	VF	VF/NM	NM-
3,4	10	20	30	54	72	90

SEA HUNT (TV)
Dell Publishing Co.: No. 928, 8/58 - No. 1041, 10-12/59; No. 4, 1-3/60 - No. 13, 4-6/62 (All have Lloyd Bridges photo-c)

	GD	VG	FN	VF	VF/NM	NM-
Four Color 928(#1)	11	22	33	75	138	200
Four Color 994(#2), 4-13: Manning-a #4-6,8-11,13	8	16	24	54	90	125
Four Color 1041(#3)-Toth-a	8	16	24	54	90	125

SEA OF RED
Image Comics: Mar, 2005 - No. 13, Nov, 2006 ($2.95/$2.99/$3.50)
1-12-Vampirates at sea; Remender & Dwyer-s/Dwyer & Sam-a 3.00
13-($3.50) 3.50
Vol. 1: No Grave But The Sea (9/05, $8.95) r/#1-4 9.00
Vol. 2: No Quarter (2006, $11.99) r/#5-8 12.00
Vol. 3: The Deadlights (2006, $14.99) r/#9-13 15.00

SEAQUEST (TV)
Nemesis Comics: Mar, 1994 ($2.25)

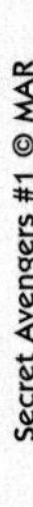
Secret Avengers #1 © MAR

Secret Hearts #5 © DC

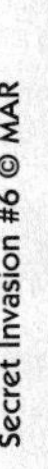
Secret Invasion #6 © MAR

GD 2.0 | VG 4.0 | FN 6.0 | VF 8.0 | VF/NM 9.0 | NM- 9.2

1-Has 2 diff-c stocks (slick & cardboard); Alcala-i 3.00

SEARCH FOR LOVE
American Comics Group: Feb-Mar, 1950 - No. 2, Apr-May, 1950 (52 pgs.)

1 12 24 36 69 97 125
2 9 18 27 47 61 75

SEARCHERS, THE (Movie)
Dell Publishing Co.: No. 709, 1956

Four Color 709-John Wayne photo-c 21 42 63 150 300 450

SEARCHERS, THE
Caliber Comics: 1996 - No. 4, 1996 ($2.95, B&W)

1-4 3.00

SEARCHERS, THE : APOSTLE OF MERCY
Caliber Comics: 1997 - No. 2, 1997 ($2.95/$3.95, B&W)

1-($2.95) 3.00
2-($3.95) 4.00

SEARS (See Merry Christmas From...)

SEASON'S GREETINGS
Hallmark (King Features): 1935 (6-1/4x5-1/4", 24 pgs. in color)

nn-Cover features Mickey Mouse, Popeye, Jiggs & Skippy. "The Night Before Christmas" told one panel per page, each panel by a famous artist featuring their character. Art by Alex Raymond, Gottfredson, Swinnerton, Segar, Chic Young, Milt Gross, Sullivan (Messmer), Herriman, McManus, Percy Crosby & others (22 artists in all)
Estimated value... 950.00

SEBASTIAN O
DC Comics (Vertigo): May, 1993 - No. 3, July, 1993 ($1.95, limited series)

1-3-Grant Morrison scripts; Steve Yeowell-a 3.00
TPB (2004, $9.95) r/#1-3; intro. chronology by Morrison 10.00

SECOND LIFE OF DOCTOR MIRAGE, THE (See Shadowman #16)
Valiant: Nov, 1993 - No. 18, May, 1995 ($2.50)

1-18: 1-With bound-in poster. 5-Shadowman x-over. 7-Bound-in trading card 3.00
1-Gold ink logo edition; no price on-c 4.00

SECRET AGENT (Formerly Sarge Steel)
Charlton Comics: V2#9, Oct, 1966; V2#10, Oct, 1967

V2#9-Sarge Steel part-r begins 3 6 9 17 25 32
10-Tiffany Sinn, CIA app. (from Career Girl Romances #39); Aparo-a
3 6 9 14 19 24

SECRET AGENT (TV) (See Four Color #1231)
Gold Key: Nov, 1966; No. 2, Jan, 1968

1-Photo-c 8 16 24 58 97 135
2-Photo-c 6 12 18 41 66 90

SECRET AGENT X-9 (See Flash Gordon #4 by King)
David McKay Publ.: 1934 (Book 1: 84 pgs.; Book 2: 124 pgs.) (8x7-1/2")

Book 1-Contains reprints of the first 13 weeks of the strip by Alex Raymond; complete except for 2 dailies 43 86 129 271 461 650
Book 2-Contains reprints immediately following contents of Book 1, for 20 weeks by Alex Raymond; complete except for two dailies. Note: Raymond mis-dated the last five strips from 6/34, and while the dating sequence is confusing, the continuity is correct
39 78 117 234 385 535

SECRET AGENT X-9 (See Magic Comics)
Dell Publishing Co.: Dec, 1937 (Not by Raymond)

Feature Books 8 47 94 141 296 498 700

SECRET AGENT Z-2 (See Holyoke One-Shot No. 7)

SECRET AVENGERS (The Heroic Age)
Marvel Comics: Jul, 2010 - Present ($3.99, limited series)

1-Bendis-s/Deodato-a/Djurdjevic-c; Steve Rogers assembles covert squad 4.00
1-Variant-c by Yardin 6.00
2-11: 2-Two covers. 2-4-Deodato-a. 5-Nick Fury app.; Aja-a 4.00

SECRET CITY SAGA (See Jack Kirby's Secret City Saga)

SECRET DEFENDERS (Also see The Defenders & Fantastic Four #374)
Marvel Comics: Mar, 1993 - No. 25, Mar, 1995 ($1.75/$1.95)

1-($2.50)-Red foil stamped-c; Dr. Strange, Nomad, Wolverine, Spider Woman & Darkhawk begin 4.00
2-11,13-24: 9-New team w/Silver Surfer, Thunderstrike, Dr. Strange & War Machine. 13-Thanos replaces Dr. Strange as leader; leads into Cosmic Powers limited series; 14-Dr. Druid. 15-Bound in card sheet. 18-Giant Man & Iron Fist app. 3.00

12,25: 12-($2.50)-Prismatic foil-c. 25 ($2.50, 52 pgs.) 4.00

SECRET DIARY OF EERIE ADVENTURES
Avon Periodicals: 1953 (25¢ giant, 100 pgs., one-shot)

nn-(Rare)-Kubert-a; Hollingsworth-c; Sid Check back-c
213 426 639 1363 2332 3300

SECRET FILES & ORIGINS GUIDE TO THE DC UNIVERSE
DC Comics: Mar, 2000; Feb, 2002 ($6.95/$4.95)

2000 (3/00, $6.95)-Overview of DC characters; profile pages by various 7.00
2001-2002 (2/02, $4.95) Olivetti-c 5.00

SECRET FILES PRESIDENT LUTHOR
DC Comics: Mar, 2001 ($4.95, one-shot)

1-Short stories & profile pages by various; Harris-c 5.00

SECRET HEARTS
National Periodical Publications (Beverly)(Arleigh No. 50-113):
9-10/49 - No. 6, 7-8/50; No. 7, 12-1/51-52 - No. 153, 7/71

1-Kinstler-a; photo-c begin, end #6 57 114 171 362 619 875
2-Toth-a (1 pg.); Kinstler-a 31 62 93 182 296 410
3,6 (1950) 27 54 81 158 259 360
4,5-Toth-a 27 54 81 160 263 365
7(12-1/51-52) (Rare) 41 82 123 249 417 585
8-10 (1952) 20 40 60 117 189 260
11-20 15 30 45 90 140 190
21-26: 26-Last precode (2-3/55) 14 28 42 81 118 155
27-40 7 14 21 49 80 110
41-50 6 12 18 37 59 80
51-60 5 10 15 32 51 70
61-75,100: 75-Last 10¢ issue 5 10 15 30 48 65
76-99,101-109 4 8 12 23 36 48
110- "Reach for Happiness" serial begins, ends #138 4 8 12 26 41 55
111-119,121-126 3 6 9 18 27 35
120,134-Neal Adams-c 4 8 12 26 41 55
127 (4/68)-Beatles cameo 4 8 12 26 41 55
128-133,135-142: 141,142- "20 Miles to Heartbreak", Chapter 2 & 3 (see Young Love for Chapters 1 & 4); Toth, Colletta-a 3 6 9 17 25 32
143-148,150-152: 144-Morrow-a 3 6 9 14 20 26
149,153: 149-Toth-a. 153-Kirby-i 3 6 9 16 22 28

SECRET HISTORY OF THE AUTHORITY: HAWKSMOOR
DC Comics (WildStorm): May, 2008 - No. 6, Oct, 2008 ($2.99, limited series)

1-6-Costa-s/Staples-a/Hamner-c 3.00
TPB (2009, $19.99) r/#1-6 20.00

SECRET INVASION (Also see Mighty Avengers, New Avengers, and Skrulls!)
Marvel Comics: June, 2008 - No. 8, Jan, 2009 ($3.99, limited series)

1-Skrull invasion; Bendis-s/Yu-a/Dell'Otto-c 4.00
1-Variant cover with blank area for sketches 4.00
1-McNiven variant-c 12.00
1-Yu variant-c 30.00
1-2nd printing with old Avengers variant-c by Yu 4.00
1 Director's Cut (2008, $4.99) r/#1 with script; concept and promo art; cover gallery 5.00
2-8-Dell'Otto-c. 8-Wasp killed 4.00
2-4-McNiven variant-c. 2-Avengers. 3-Nick Fury. 4-Tony Stark, Spider-Woman, Black Widow 6.00
2-8-Yu variant-c. 2-Hawkeye & Mockingbird. 3-Spider-Woman. 4-Nick Fury 10.00
5-Rubi variant-c 5.00
6-Cho Spider-Woman variant-c 8.00
...:Aftermath: Beta Ray Bill - The Green of Eden (6/09, $3.99) Brereton-a 4.00
...: Chronicles 1,2 (4/09,6/09, $5.99) reprints from New Avengers & Illuminati issues 6.00
... Dark Reign (2/09, $3.99) villain meeting after #8; previews new series; Maleev-a/c 4.00
... Dark Reign (2/09, $3.99) Variant Green Goblin cover by Bryan Hitch 8.00
... Requiem (2009, $3.99) Hank Pym becomes The Wasp; r/TTA #44 & Avengers #215 4.00
... Saga (2008, giveaway) history of the Skrulls told through reprint panels and text 3.00
...: The Infiltration TPB (2008, $19.99) r/FF #2; New Avengers #31,32,38,39; New Avengers: Illuminati #1,5; Mighty Avengers #7; and Avengers: The Initiative Annual #1 20.00
...: War of Kings (2/09, $3.99) Black Bolt and the Inhumans; Pelletier & Dazo-a 4.00
...: Who Do You Trust? (8/08, $3.99) short tie-in stories by various; Jimenez-c 4.00

SECRET INVASION: AMAZING SPIDER-MAN
Marvel Comics: Oct, 2008 - No. 3, Dec, 2008 ($2.99, limited series)

1-3-Jackpot battles a Super-Skrull; Santucci-a. 2-Menace app. 3.00

SECRET INVASION: FANTASTIC FOUR
Marvel Comics: July, 2008 - No. 3, Sept, 2008 ($2.99, limited series)

Secret Missions #1 © STJ

Secret Origins (3rd series) #4 © DC

Secret Romance #32 © CC

GD VG FN VF VF/NM NM-
2.0 4.0 6.0 8.0 9.0 9.2

1-3-Skrulls and Lyja invade; Kitson-a/Davis-c 3.00
1-Variant Skrull cover by McKone 5.00

SECRET INVASION: FRONT LINE
Marvel Comics: Sept, 2008 - No. 5, Jan, 2009 ($2.99, limited series)

1-5-Ben Urich covering the Skrull invasion; Reed-s/Castiello-a 3.00

SECRET INVASION: INHUMANS
Marvel Comics: Oct, 2008 - No. 4, Jan, 2009 ($2.99, limited series)

1-4-Raney-a/Sejic-c/Pokasky-s; search for Black Bolt 3.00

SECRET INVASION: RUNAWAYS/YOUNG AVENGERS (Follows Runaways #30)
Marvel Comics: Aug, 2008 - No. 3, Nov, 2008 ($2.99, limited series)

1-3-Miyazawa-a/Ryan-c 3.00

SECRET INVASION: THOR
Marvel Comics: Oct, 2008 - No. 3, Dec, 2008 ($2.99, limited series)

1-3-Fraction-s/Braithwaite-a; Skrulls invade Asgard; Beta Ray Bill app. 3.00
1-2nd printing with Beta Ray Bill cover 3.00

SECRET INVASION: X-MEN
Marvel Comics: Oct, 2008 - No. 4, Jan, 2009 ($2.99, limited series)

1-4-Carey-s/Nord-a/Dodson-c; Skrulls invade San Francisco 3.00
1-2nd printing with variant Nord-c 3.00

SECRET ISLAND OF OZ, THE (See First Comics Graphic Novel)

SECRET LOVE (See Fox Giants & Sinister House of...)

SECRET LOVE
Ajax-Farrell/Four Star Comic Corp. No. 2 on: 12/55 - No. 3, 8/56; 4/57 - No. 5, 2/58; No. 6, 6/58

1(12/55-Ajax, 1st series) 10 20 30 56 76 95
2,3 7 14 21 37 46 55
1(4/57-Ajax, 2nd series) 9 18 27 47 61 75
2-6: 5-Bakerish-a 7 14 21 35 43 50

SECRET LOVES
Comic Magazines/Quality Comics Group: Nov, 1949 - No. 6, Sept, 1950

1-Ward-c 25 50 75 150 245 340
2-Ward-c 21 42 63 124 202 280
3-Crandall-a 15 30 45 83 124 165
4,6 12 24 36 69 97 125
5-Suggestive art "Boom Town Babe"; photo-c 15 30 45 84 127 170

SECRET LOVE STORIES (See Fox Giants)

SECRET MISSIONS (Admiral Zacharia's...)
St. John Publishing Co.: February, 1950

1-Joe Kubert-c; stories of U.S. foreign agents 20 40 60 114 182 250

SECRET MYSTERIES (Formerly Crime Mysteries & Crime Smashers)
Ribage/Merit Publications No. 17 on: No. 16, Nov, 1954 - No. 19, July, 1955

16-Horror, Palais-a; Myron Fass-c 30 60 90 177 289 400
17-19-Horror. 17-Fass-c; mis-dated 3/54? 21 42 63 126 206 285

SECRET ORIGINS (1st Series) (See 80 Page Giant #8)
National Periodical Publications: Aug-Oct, 1961 (Annual) (Reprints)

1-Origin Adam Strange (Showcase #17), Green Lantern (Green Lantern #1), Challengers (partial-r/Showcase #6, 6 pgs. Kirby-a), J'onn J'onzz (Det. #225), The Flash (Showcase #4), Green Arrow (1 pg. text), Superman-Batman team (World's Finest #94), Wonder Woman (Wonder Woman #105) 44 88 132 352 714 1075
Replica Edition (1998, $4.95) r/entire book and house ads 5.00
Even More Secret Origins (2003, $6.95) reprints origins of Hawkman, Eclipso, Kid Flash, Blackhawks, Green Lantern's oath, and Jimmy Olsen-Robin team in 80 pg. Giant style 7.00

SECRET ORIGINS (2nd Series)
National Periodical Publications: Feb-Mar, 1973 - No. 6, Jan-Feb, 1974; No. 7, Oct-Nov, 1974 (All 20¢ issues) (All origin reprints)

1-Superman(r/1 pg. origin/Action #1, 1st time since G.A.), Batman(Detective #33), Ghost(Flash #88), The Flash(Showcase #4) 5 10 15 30 48 65
2-7: 2-Green Lantern & The Atom(Showcase #22 & 34), Supergirl(Action #252). 3-Wonder Woman (W.W. #1), Wildcat (Sensation #1). 4-Vigilante (Action #42) by Meskin, Kid Eternity(Hit #25). 5-The Spectre by Baily (More Fun #52,53). 6-Blackhawk(Military #1) & Legion of Super-Heroes(Superboy #147). 7-Robin (Detective #38), Aquaman (More Fun #73) 3 6 9 18 27 35
NOTE: *Infantino a-1. Kane a-2. Kubert a-1.*

SECRET ORIGINS (3rd Series)
DC Comics: 4/86 - No. 50, 8/90 (All origins)(52 pgs. #6 on)(#27 on: $1.50)

GD VG FN VF VF/NM NM-
2.0 4.0 6.0 8.0 9.0 9.2

1-Origin Superman 1 2 3 5 6 8
2-6: 2-Blue Beetle. 3-Shazam. 4-Firestorm. 5-Crimson Avenger. 6-Halo/G.A. Batman 4.00
7-9,11,12,14-20,22-26: 7-Green Lantern (Guy Gardner)/G.A. Sandman. 8-Shadow Lass/Doll Man. 9-G.A. Flash/Skyman.11-G.A. Hawkman/Power Girl. 12-Challengers of Unknown/G.A. Fury (2nd modern app.). 14-Suicide Squad; Legends spin-off. 15-Spectre/Deadman. 16-G.A. Hourman/Warlord. 17-Adam Strange story by Carmine Infantino; Dr. Occult. 18-G.A. Gr. Lantern/The Creeper. 19-Uncle Sam/The Guardian. 20-Batgirl/G.A. Dr. Mid-Nite. 22-Manhunters. 23-Floronic Man/Guardians of the Universe. 24-Blue Devil/Dr. Fate. 25-LSH/Atom. 26-Black Lightning/Miss America 4.00
10-Phantom Stranger w/Alan Moore scripts; Legends spin-off 4.00
13-Origin Nightwing; Johnny Thunder app. 4.00
21-Jonah Hex/Black Condor 4.00
27-30,36-38,40-49: 27-Zatara/Zatanna. 28-Midnight/Nightshade. 29-Power of the Atom/Mr. America; new 3 pg. Red Tornado story by Mayer (last app. of Scribbly, 8/88). 30-Plastic Man/Elongated Man. 36-Poison Ivy by Neil Gaiman & Mark Buckingham/Green Lantern. 37-Legion Of Substitute Heroes/Doctor Light. 38-Green Arrow/Speedy; Grell scripts. 40-All Ape issue. 41-Rogues Gallery of Flash. 42-Phantom Girl/GrimGhost. 43-Original Hawk & Dove/Cave Carson/Chris KL-99. 44-Batman app.; story based on Det. #40. 45-Blackhawk/El Diablo. 46-JLA/LSH/New Titans. 47-LSH. 48-Ambush Bug/Stanley & His Monster/Rex the Wonder Dog/Trigger Twins. 49-Newsboy Legion/Silent Knight/Bouncing Boy 3.00
31-35,39: 31-JSA. 32-JLA. 33-35-JLI. 39-Animal Man-c/story continued in Animal Man #10; Grant Morrison scripts; Batman app. 3.00
50-($3.95, 100 pgs.)-Batman & Robin in text, Flash of Two Worlds, Johnny Thunder, Dolphin, Black Canary & Space Museum 5.00
Annual 1 (8/87)-Capt. Comet/Doom Patrol 4.00
Annual 2 ('88, $2.00)-Origin Flash II & Flash III 4.00
Annual 3 ('89, $2.95, 84 pgs.)-Teen Titans; 1st app. new Flamebird who replaces original Bat-Girl 4.00
Special 1 (10/89, $2.00)-Batman villains: Penguin, Riddler, & Two-Face; Bolland-c; Sam Kieth-a; Neil Gaiman scripts(2) 5.00
NOTE: ***Art Adams** a-33i(part). **M. Anderson** 8, 19, 21, 25i; c-19(part). **Aparo** c/a-10. **Bissette** c-23. **Bolland** c-7. **Byrne** c/a-Annual 1. **Colan** c/a-5p. **Forte** a-37. **Giffen** a-18p, 44p, 48. **Infantino** a-17, 50p. **Kaluta** c-39. **Gil Kane** a-2, 28; c-2p. **Kirby** c-19(part). **Erik Larsen** a-13. **Mayer** a-29. **Morrow** a-21. **Orlando** a-10. **Perez** a-50i, Annual 3i; c- Annual 3. **Rogers** a-6p. **Russell** a-27i. **Simonson** c-22. **Staton** a-36, 50p. **Steacy** a-35. **Tuska** a-4p, 9p.*

SECRET ORIGINS 80 PAGE GIANT (Young Justice)
DC Comics: Dec, 1998 ($4.95, one-shot)

1-Origin-s of Young Justice members; Ramos-a (Impulse) 5.00

SECRET ORIGINS FEATURING THE JLA
DC Comics: 1999 ($14.95, TPB)

1-Reprints recent origin-s of JLA members; Cassaday-c 15.00

SECRET ORIGINS OF SUPER-HEROES (See DC Special Series #10, 19)

SECRET ORIGINS OF SUPER-VILLAINS 80 PAGE GIANT
DC Comics: Dec, 1999 ($4.95, one-shot)

1-Origin-s of Sinestro, Amazo and others; Gibbons-c 5.00

SECRET ORIGINS OF THE WORLD'S GREATEST SUPER-HEROES
DC Comics: 1989 ($4.95, 148 pgs.)

nn-Reprints Superman, JLA origins; new Batman origin-s; Bolland-c 1 2 3 4 5 7

SECRET ROMANCE
Charlton Comics: Oct, 1968 - No. 41, Nov, 1976; No. 42, Mar, 1979 - No. 48, Feb, 1980

1-Begin 12¢ issues, ends #? 3 6 9 18 27 35
2-10: 9-Reese-a 2 4 6 11 16 20
11-16,18,19,21-30 2 4 6 9 13 16
17,20: 17-Susan Dey poster. 20-David Cassidy pin-up 2 4 6 11 16 20
31-48 2 4 6 8 10 12
NOTE: *Beyond the Stars app.-No. 9, 11, 12, 14.*

SECRET ROMANCES (Exciting Love Stories)
Superior Publications Ltd.: Apr, 1951 - No. 27, July, 1955

1 16 32 48 92 144 195
2 11 22 33 64 90 115
3-10 9 18 27 52 69 85
11-13,15-18,20-27 8 16 24 44 57 70
14,19-Lingerie panels 9 18 27 47 61 75

SECRET SERVICE (See Kent Blake of the...)

SECRET SIX (See Action Comics Weekly)
National Periodical Publications: Apr-May, 1968 - No. 7, Apr-May, 1969 (12¢)

1-Origin/1st app. 6 12 18 41 66 90
2-7 4 8 12 22 34 45

SECRET SIX (See Tangent Comics/ Secret Six)

Secret Six (2008 series) #13 © DC

Secret Society of Super-Villains #7 © DC

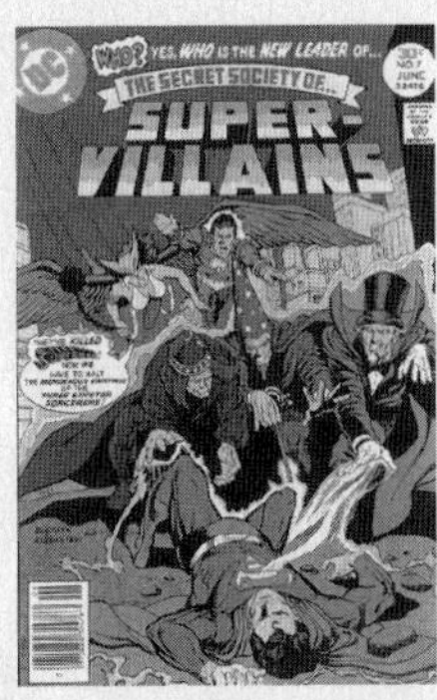

Secret Warriors #25 © MAR

	GD 2.0	VG 4.0	FN 6.0	VF 8.0	VF/NM 9.0	NM- 9.2

SECRET SIX (See Villains United)
DC Comics: Jul, 2006 - No. 6, Jan, 2007 ($2.99, limited series)

1-6-Gail Simone-s/Brad Walker-a. 4-Doom Patrol app. 3.00
...: Six Degrees of Devastation TPB (2007, $14.99) r/#1-6 15.00

SECRET SIX
DC Comics: Nov, 2008 - Present ($2.99)

1-31: 1-Gail Simone-s/Nicola Scott-a. 2-Batman app. 8-Rodriguez-a. 11-13-Wonder Woman & Artemis app. 16-Black Alice app. 17,18-Blackest Night 3.00
...: Cats in the Cradle TPB (2011, $14.99) r/#19-24 15.00
...: Danse Macabre TPB (2010, $14.99) r/#15-18 & Suicide Squad #67 (Blackest Night) 15.00
...: Depths TPB (2010, $14.99) r/#8-14 15.00
...: Unhinged TPB (2009, $14.99) r/#1-7; intro. by Paul Cornell 15.00

SECRET SKULL
IDW Publ.: Aug, 2004 - No. 4, Nov, 2004 ($3.99)

1-4-Steve Niles-s/Chuck BB-a 4.00

SECRET SOCIETY OF SUPER-VILLAINS
National Per. Publ./DC Comics: May-June, 1976 - No. 15, June-July, 1978

	GD	VG	FN	VF	VF/NM	NM-
1-Origin; JLA cameo & Capt. Cold app.	3	6	9	14	19	24
2-5,15: 2-Re-intro/origin Capt. Comet; Green Lantern x-over. 5-Green Lantern, Hawkman x-over; Darkseid app. 15-G.A. Atom, Dr. Midnite, & JSA app.	2	4	6	8	11	14
6-14: 9,10-Creeper x-over. 11-Capt. Comet; Orlando-i	2	3	4	6	8	10

SECRET SOCIETY OF SUPER-VILLAINS SPECIAL (See DC Special Series #6)

SECRETS OF HAUNTED HOUSE
National Periodical Publications/DC Comics: 4-5/75 - #5, 12-1/75-76; #6, 6-7/77 - #14, 10-11/78; #15, 8/79 - #46, 3/82

	GD	VG	FN	VF	VF/NM	NM-
1	6	12	18	37	59	80
2-4	3	6	9	20	30	40
5-Wrightson-c	4	8	12	24	37	50
6-14	2	4	6	11	16	20
15-30	2	4	6	8	11	14
31,44: 31-(12/80) Mr. E series begins (1st app.), ends #41. 44-Wrightson-c	2	4	6	9	13	16
32-(1/81) Origin of Mr. E	2	4	6	8	11	14
33-43,45,46: 34,35-Frankenstein Monster app.	1	3	4	6	8	10

NOTE: *Aparo c-7.* ***Aragones*** *a-1.* ***B. Bailey*** *a-8.* ***Bissette*** *a-46.* ***Buckler*** *c-32-40p.* ***Ditko*** *a-9, 12, 41, 45.* ***Golden*** *a-10.* ***Howard*** *a-13i.* ***Kaluta*** *c-8, 10, 11, 14, 16, 29.* ***Kubert*** *c-41, 42.* ***Sheldon Mayer*** *a-43p.* ***McWilliams*** *a-35.* ***Nasser*** *a-24.* ***Newton*** *a-30p.* ***Nino*** *a-1, 13, 19.* ***Orlando*** *c-13, 30, 43, 45i.* ***N. Redondo*** *a-4, 5, 29.* ***Rogers*** *c-26.* ***Spiegle*** *a-31-41.* ***Wrightson*** *c-5, 44.*

SECRETS OF HAUNTED HOUSE SPECIAL (See DC Special Series #12)

SECRETS OF LIFE (Movie)
Dell Publishing Co.: 1956 (Disney)

	GD	VG	FN	VF	VF/NM	NM-
Four Color 749-Photo-c	5	10	15	32	51	70

SECRETS OF LOVE (See Popular Teen-Agers...)

SECRETS OF LOVE AND MARRIAGE
Charlton Comics: V2#1, Aug, 1956 - V2#25, June, 1961

	GD	VG	FN	VF	VF/NM	NM-
V2#1-Matt Baker-c?	4	8	12	28	44	60
V2#2-6	3	6	9	19	29	38
V2#7-9-(All 68 pgs.)	5	10	15	30	48	65
10-25	3	6	9	16	23	30

SECRETS OF MAGIC (See Wisco)

SECRETS OF SINISTER HOUSE (Sinister House of Secret Love #1-4)
National Periodical Publ.: No. 5, June-July, 1972 - No. 18, June-July, 1974

	GD	VG	FN	VF	VF/NM	NM-
5-(52 pgs.).	6	12	18	41	66	90
6-9: 7-Redondo-a	4	8	12	24	37	50
10-Neal Adams-a(i)	4	8	12	26	41	55
11-18: 15-Redondo-a. 17-Barry-a; early Chaykin 1 pg. strip	3	6	9	16	23	30

NOTE: ***Alcala*** *a-6, 13, 14.* ***Glanzman*** *a-7.* ***Kaluta*** *c-6, 7.* ***Nino*** *a-8, 11-13. Ambrose Bierce adapt.-#14.*

SECRETS OF THE LEGION OF SUPER-HEROES
DC Comics: Jan, 1981 - No. 3, Mar, 1981 (Limited series)

1-3: 1-Origin of the Legion. 2-Retells origins of Brainiac 5, Shrinking Violet, Sun-Boy, Bouncing Boy, Ultra-Boy, Matter-Eater Lad, Mon-El, Karate Kid & Dream Girl 5.00

SECRETS OF TRUE LOVE
St. John Publishing Co.: Feb, 1958

	GD	VG	FN	VF	VF/NM	NM-
1	8	16	24	40	50	60

SECRETS OF YOUNG BRIDES
Charlton Comics: No. 5, Sept, 1957 - No. 44, Oct, 1964; July, 1975 - No. 9, Nov, 1976

	GD	VG	FN	VF	VF/NM	NM-
5	5	10	15	30	48	65
6-10: 8-Negligee panel	3	6	9	21	32	42
11-20	3	6	9	19	29	38
21-30: Last 10¢ issue?	3	6	9	17	25	32
31-44(10/64)	2	4	6	13	18	22
1-(2nd series) (7/75)	3	6	9	14	19	24
2-9	2	4	6	8	11	14

SECRET SQUIRREL (TV)(See Kite Fun Book)
Gold Key: Oct, 1966 (12¢) (Hanna-Barbera)

	GD	VG	FN	VF	VF/NM	NM-
1-1st Secret Squirrel and Morocco Mole, Squiddly Diddly, Winsome Witch	10	20	30	71	128	185

SECRET STORY ROMANCES (Becomes True Tales of Love)
Atlas Comics (TCI): Nov, 1953 - No. 21, Mar, 1956

	GD	VG	FN	VF	VF/NM	NM-
1-Everett-a; Jay Scott Pike-c	16	32	48	94	147	200
2	10	20	30	58	79	100
3-11: 11-Last pre-code (2/55)	9	18	27	52	69	85
12-21	9	18	27	47	61	75

NOTE: ***Colletta*** *a-10, 14, 15, 17, 21; c-10, 14, 17.*

SECRET VOICE, THE (See Great American Comics Presents...)

SECRET WAR
Marvel Comics: Apr, 2004 - No. 5, Dec, 2005 ($3.99, limited series)

1-Bendis-s/Dell'Otto painted-a/c; 5.00
1-2nd printing with gold logo on white cover and full-color Spider-Man 4.00
1-3rd printing with white cover and B&W sketched Spider-Man 4.00
2-5: 2-Wolverine-c. 3-Capt. America-c. 4-Black Widow-c. 5-Daredevil-c 4.00
2-2nd printing with white cover and B&W sketched Wolverine 4.00
... : From the Files of Nick Fury (2005, $3.99) Fury's journal entries; profiles of characters 4.00
HC (2005, $29.99, dust jacket) r/#1-5 & ...From the Files of Nick Fury; additional art 30.00
SC (2006, $24.99) r/#1-5 & ...From the Files of Nick Fury; additional art 25.00

SECRET WARRIORS (Also see 2009 Dark Reign titles)
Marvel Comics: Apr, 2009 - Present ($3.99)

1-Bendis & Hickman-s/Caselli-a/Cheung-c; Nick Fury app.; Hydra dossier; sketch pages 4.00
2-24,26-($2.99) 8-Dark Avengers app. 17-19-Howling Commandos return 3.00
25-($3.99) Baron Strucker app.; Vitti-a 4.00

SECRET WARS II (Also see Marvel Super Heroes...)
Marvel Comics Group: July, 1985 - No. 9, Mar, 1986 (Maxi-series)

1,9: 9-(52 pgs.) X-Men app., Spider-Man app. 5.00
2-8: 2,8-X-Men app. 5-1st app. Boom Boom. 5,8-Spider-Man app. 4.00

SECRET WEAPONS
Valiant: Sept, 1993 - No. 21, May, 1995 ($2.25)

1-10,12-21: 3-Reese-a(i). 5-Ninjak app. 9-Bound-in trading card. 12-Bloodshot app. 3.00
11-(Sept. on envelope, Aug on-c, $2.50)-Enclosed in manilla envelope; Bloodshot app; intro new team. 3.00

SECTAURS
Marvel Comics: June, 1985 - No. 8, Sept, 1986 (75¢) (Based on Coleco Toys)

1-8, 1-Giveaway; same-c with "Coleco 1985 Toy Fair Collectors' Edition" 3.00

SECTION ZERO
Image Comics (Gorilla): June, 2000 - No. 3, Sept, 2000 ($2.50)

1-3-Kesel-s/Grummett-a 3.00

SEDUCTION OF THE INNOCENT (Also see New York State Joint Legislative Committee to Study...)
Rinehart & Co., Inc., N. Y.: 1953, 1954 (400 pgs.) (Hardback, $4.00)(Written by Fredric Wertham, M.D.)(Also printed in Canada by Clarke, Irwin & Co. Ltd.)

	GD	VG	FN	VF	VF/NM	NM-
(1st Version)-with bibliographical note intact (pages 399 & 400)(several copies got out before the comic publishers forced the removal of this page)	154	308	462	662	794	925
Dust jacket only	36	72	108	216	351	485
(1st Version)-without bibliographical note	81	162	243	348	417	485
Dust jacket only	19	38	57	109	172	235
(2nd Version)-Published in England by Rinehart, 1954, 399 pgs. has bibliographical page; "Second print" listed on inside flap of the dust jacket; publication page has no "R" colophon; unlike 1st version	15	30	45	84	127	170
1972 r-/of 2nd version; 400 pgs. w/bibliography page; Kennikat Press	4	8	12	28	44	60

NOTE: *Material from this book appeared in the November, 1953 (Vol.70, pp50-53,214) issue of the* ***Ladies' Home Journal*** *under the title "What Parents Don't Know About Comic Books". With the release of this book, Dr. Wertham reveals seven years of research attempting to link juvenile delinquency to comic books. Many illustrations showing*

Seeker 3000 #1 © MAR

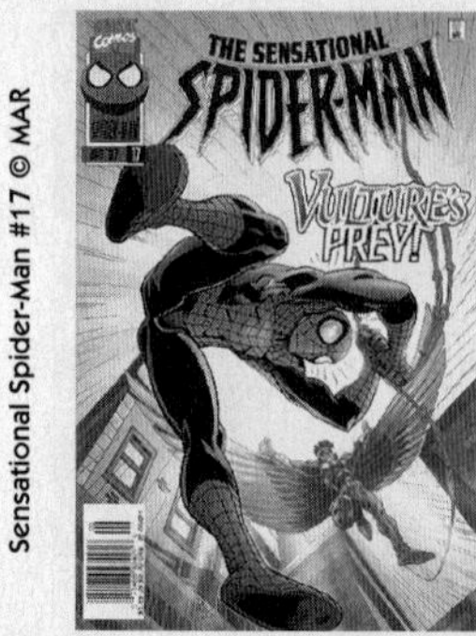

Sensational Spider-Man #17 © MAR

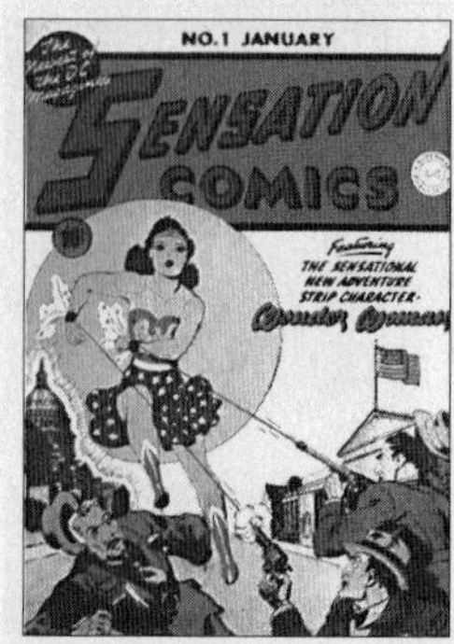

Sensation Comics #1 © DC

GD VG FN VF VF/NM NM-
2.0 4.0 6.0 8.0 9.0 9.2

excessive violence, sex, sadism, and torture are shown. This book was used at the Kefauver Senate hearings which led to the Comics Code Authority. Because of the influence this book had on the comic industry and the collector's interest in it, we feel this listing is justified. Modern printings exist in limited editions. Also see ***Parade of Pleasure.***

SEDUCTION OF THE INNOCENT! (Also see Halloween Horror)
Eclipse Comics: Nov, 1985 - 3-D#2, Apr, 1986 ($1.75)

1-6: Double listed under cover title from #7 on 4.00
3-D 1 (10/85, $2.25, 36 pgs.)-contains unpublished Advs. Into Darkness #15 (pre-code); Dave Stevens-c 5.00
2-D 1 (100 copy limited signed & #ed edition)(B&W) 1 3 4 6 8 10
3-D 2 (4/86)-Baker, Toth, Wrightson-c 5.00
2-D 2 (100 copy limited signed & #ed edition)(B&W) 1 3 4 6 8 10
NOTE: ***Anderson*** *r-2, 3.* ***Crandall*** *c/a(r)-1.* ***Meskin*** *c/a(r)-3, 3-D 1.* ***Moreira*** *r-2.* ***Toth*** *a-1-6r; c-4r.* ***Tuska*** *r-6.*

SEEKER
Sky Comics: Apr, 1994 ($2.50, one-shot)

1 3.00

SEEKERS INTO THE MYSTERY
DC Comics (Vertigo): Jan, 1996 - No. 15, Apr, 1997 ($2.50)

1-14: J.M. DeMatteis scripts in all. 1-4-Glenn Barr-a. 5,10-Muth-c/a. 6-9-Zulli-c/a. 11-14-Bolton-c; Jill Thompson-a 3.00
15-($2.95)-Muth-c/a 3.00

SEEKER 3000 (See Marvel Premiere #41)
Marvel Comics: Jun, 1998 - No. 4, Sept, 1998 ($2.99/$2.50, limited series)

1-($2.99)-Set 25 years after 1st app.; wraparound-c 4.00
2-4-($2.50) 3.00
...Premiere 1 (6/98, $1.50) Reprints 1st app. from Marvel Premiere #41; wraparound-c 3.00

SELECT DETECTIVE (Exciting New Mystery Cases)
D. S. Publishing Co.: Aug-Sept, 1948 - No. 3, Dec-Jan, 1948-49

1-Matt Baker-a 29 58 87 172 281 390
2-Baker, McWilliams-a 20 40 60 114 182 250
3 15 30 45 90 140 190

SEMPER FI (Tales of the Marine Corp)
Marvel Comics: Dec, 1988- No.9, Aug, 1989 (75¢)

1-9: Severin-c/a 3.00

SENSATIONAL POLICE CASES (Becomes Captain Steve Savage, 2nd Series)
Avon Periodicals: 1952; No. 2, 1954 - No. 4, July-Aug, 1954

nn-(1952, 25¢, 100 pgs.)-Kubert-a?; Check, Larsen, Lawrence & McCann-a; Kinstler-c 41 82 123 256 428 600
2-4: 2-Kirbyish-a (3-4/54). 4-Reprint/Saint #5 15 30 45 90 140 190
I.W. Reprint #5-(1963?, nd)-Reprints Prison Break #5(1952-Realistic); Infantino-a 3 6 9 16 23 30

SENSATIONAL SHE-HULK, THE (She-Hulk #21-23) (See Savage She-Hulk)
Marvel Comics: V2#1, 5/89 - No. 60, Feb, 1994 ($1.50/$1.75, deluxe format)

V2#1-Byrne-c/a(p)/scripts begin, end #8 4.00
2,3,5-8: 3-Spider-Man app. 3.00
4,14-17,21-23: 4-Reintro G.A. Blonde Phantom. 14-17-Howard the Duck app. 21-23-Return of the Blonde Phantom. 22-All Winners Squad app. 3.00
9-13,18-20,24-49,51-60: 25-Thor app. 26-Excalibur app.; Guice-c. 29-Wolverine app. (3 pgs.). 30-Hobgoblin-c & cameo. 31-Byrne-c/a/scripts begin again. 35-Last $1.50-c. 37-Wolverine/Punisher/Spidey-c, but no app. 39-Thing app. 56-War Zone app.; Hulk cameo. 57-Vs. Hulk-c/story. 58-Electro-c/story. 59-Jack O'Lantern app. 3.00
50-($2.95, 52 pgs.)-Embossed green foil-c; Byrne app.; last Byrne-c/a; Austin, Chaykin, Simonson-a; Miller-a(2 pgs.) 4.00
NOTE: ***Dale Keown*** *a(p)-13, 15-22.*

SENSATIONAL SHE-HULK IN CEREMONY, THE
Marvel Comics: 1989 - No. 2, 1989 ($3.95, squarebound, 52 pgs.)

nn-Part 1, nn-Part 2 4.00

SENSATIONAL SPIDER-MAN
Marvel Comics: Apr, 1989 ($5.95, squarebound, 80 pgs.)

1-r/Amazing Spider-Man Annual #14,15 by Miller & Annual #8 by Kirby & Ditko 6.00

SENSATIONAL SPIDER-MAN, THE
Marvel Comics: Jan, 1996 - No. 33, Nov, 1998 ($1.95/$1.99)

0 ($4.95)-Lenticular-c; Jurgens-a/scripts 5.00
1 5.00
1-($2.95) variant-c; polybagged w/cassette 1 2 3 5 6 8
2-5: 2-Kaine & Rhino app. 3-Giant-Man app. 4.00
6-18: 9-Onslaught tie-in; revealed that Peter & Mary Jane's unborn baby is a girl. 11-Revelations. 13-15-Ka-Zar app. 14,15-Hulk app. 3.00
19-24: Living Pharoah app. 22,23-Dr. Strange app. 3.00
25-($2.99) Spiderhunt pt. 1; Normie Osborne kidnapped 4.00
25-Variant-c 1 2 3 5 6 8
26-33: 26-Nauck-a. 27-Double-c with "The Sensational Hornet #1"; Vulture app. 28-Hornet vs. Vulture. 29,30-Black Cat-c/app. 33-Last issue; Gathering of Five concludes 3.00
#(-1) Flashback(7/97) Dezago-s/Wieringo-a 3.00
'96 Annual ($2.95) 4.00

SENSATIONAL SPIDER-MAN, THE (Previously Marvel Knights Spider-Man #1-22)
Marvel Comics: No. 23, Apr, 2006 - No. 41, Dec, 2007 ($2.99)

23-40: 23-25-Aguirre-Sacasa-s/Medina-a. 23-Wraparound-c. 24,34,37-Black Cat app. 26-New costume. 28-Unmasked; Dr. Octopus app.; Crain-a. 35-Black costume resumes 3.00
41-($3.99) One More Day pt. 3; Straczynski-s/Quesada-a/c 4.00
... Annual 1 (2007, $3.99) Flashbacks of Peter & MJ's relationship; Larroca-a/Fraction-s 4.00
... Feral HC (2006, $19.99, dustjacket) r/#23-27; sketch pages 20.00
Civil War: Peter Parker, Spider-Man TPB (2007, $17.99) r/#28-34; Crain cover concepts 18.00

SENSATION COMICS (Sensation Mystery #110 on)
National Per. Publ./All-American: Jan, 1942 - No. 109, May-June, 1952

1-Origin Mr. Terrific(1st app.), Wildcat(1st app.), The Gay Ghost, & Little Boy Blue; Wonder Woman (cont'd from All Star #8), The Black Pirate begin; intro. Justice & Fair Play Club 2950 5900 8850 22,000 42,000 62,000
1-Reprint, Oversize 13-1/2x10". WARNING: This comic is an exact duplicate reprint of the original except for its size. DC published it in 1974 with a second cover titling it as a Famous First Edition. There have been many reported cases of the outer cover being removed and the interior sold as the original edition. The reprint with the new outer cover removed is practically worthless. See Famous First Edition for value.
2-Etta Candy begins 476 952 1428 3475 6138 8800
3-W. Woman gets secretary's job 300 600 900 1920 3310 4700
4-1st app. Stretch Skinner in Wildcat 206 412 618 1318 2259 3200
5-Intro. Justin, Black Pirate's son 165 330 495 1048 1799 2550
6-Origin/1st app. Wonder Woman's magic lasso 168 336 504 1075 1838 2600
7-10 119 238 357 762 1306 1850
11,12,14-20 100 200 300 635 1093 1550
13-Hitler, Tojo, Mussolini-c (as bowling pins) 161 322 483 1030 1765 2500
21-30 81 162 243 518 884 1250
31-33 61 122 183 390 670 950
34-Sargon, the Sorcerer begins (10/44), ends #36; begins again #52 65 130 195 416 708 1000
35-40: 38-X-Mas-c 58 116 174 371 636 900
41-50: 43-The Whip app. 55 110 165 352 601 850
51-60: 51-Last Black Pirate. 56,57-Sargon by Kubert 54 108 162 343 574 825
61-67,69-80: 63-Last Mr. Terrific. 66-Wildcat by Kubert 48 96 144 302 514 725
68-Origin & 1st app. Huntress (8/47) 54 108 162 343 574 825
81-Used in **SOTI**, pg. 33,34; Krigstein-a 53 106 159 334 567 800
82-93: 83-Last Sargon. 86-The Atom app. 90-Last Wildcat. 91-Streak begins by Alex Toth. 92-Toth-a (2 pgs.) 48 96 144 302 514 725
94-1st all girl issue 71 142 213 454 777 1100
95-99,101-106: 95-Unmasking of Wonder Woman-c/story. 99-1st app. Astra, Girl of the Future, ends #106. 103-Robot-c. 105-Last 52 pgs. 106-Wonder Woman ends 63 126 189 403 689 975
100-(11-12/50) 73 146 219 467 796 1125
107-(Scarce, 1-2/52)-1st mystery issue; Johnny Peril by Toth(p), 8 pgs. & begins; continues from Danger Trail #5 (3-4/51)(see Comic Cavalcade #15 for 1st app.) 74 148 222 470 810 1150
108-(Scarce)-Johnny Peril by Toth(p) 64 128 192 406 696 985
109-(Scarce)-Johnny Peril by Toth(p) 74 148 222 470 810 1150
NOTE: ***Krigstein*** *a-(Wildcat)-81, 83, 84.* ***Moldoff*** *Black Pirate-1-25; Black Pirate not in 34-36, 43-48.* ***Oskner*** *c(i)-89-91, 94-106. Wonder Woman by* ***H. G. Peter****, all issues except #8, 17-19, 21; c-4-7, 9-18, 20-88, 92, 93.* ***Toth*** *a-91, 98; c-107. Wonder Woman c-1-106.*

SENSATION COMICS (Also see All Star Comics 1999 crossover titles)
DC Comics: May, 1999 ($1.99, one-shot)

1-Golden Age Wonder Woman and Hawkgirl; Robinson-s 3.00

SENSATION MYSTERY (Formerly Sensation Comics #1-109)
National Periodical Publ.: No. 110, July-Aug, 1952 - No. 116, July-Aug, 1953

110-Johnny Peril continues 48 96 144 302 514 725
111-116-Johnny Peril in all. 116-M. Anderson-a 48 96 144 302 514 725
NOTE: ***M. Anderson*** *c-110.* ***Colan*** *a-114p.* ***Giunta*** *a-112.* ***G. Kane*** *c(p)-108, 109, 111-115.*

SENSE & SENSABILITY
Marvel Comics: July, 2010 - No. 5, Nov, 2010 ($3.99, limited series)

1-5-Adaptation of the Jane Austen novel; Nancy Butler-s/Sonny Liew-a/c 4.00

SENSUOUS STREAKER
Marvel Publ.: 1974 (B&W magazine, 68pgs.)

Sentinel #4 © MAR

Serenity Better Days #3 © Universal

Sgt. Fury #153 © MAR

	GD 2.0	VG 4.0	FN 6.0	VF 8.0	VF/NM 9.0	NM- 9.2
1	4	8	12	26	41	55
SENTENCES: THE LIFE OF M.F. GRIMM						
DC Comics (Vertigo): 2007 ($19.99, B&W graphic novel)						
HC-Autobiography of Percy Carey (M.F. Grimm); Ronald Wimberly-a						20.00
SC (2008, $14.99)						15.00
SENTINEL						
Marvel Comics: June, 2003 - No. 12, April, 2004 ($2.99/$2.50)						
1-Sean McKeever-s/Udon Studios-a						3.00
2-12						3.00
Marvel Age Sentinel Vol. 1: Salvage (2004, $7.99, digest size) r/#1-6						8.00
Vol. 2: No Hero (2004, $7.99, digest size) r/#7-12; sketch pages						8.00
SENTINEL (2nd series)						
Marvel Comics: Jan, 2006 - No. 5, May, 2006 ($2.99, limited series)						
1-5-Sean McKeever-s/Joe Vriens-a						3.00
Vol. 3: Past Imperfect (2006, $7.99, digest size) r/#1-5						8.00
SENTINELS OF JUSTICE, THE (See Americomics & Captain Paragon &...)						
SENTINEL SQUAD O*N*E						
Marvel Comics: Mar, 2006 - No. 5, July, 2006 ($2.99, limited series)						
1-5-Lopresti-a/Layman-s						3.00
Decimation: Sentinel Squad O*N*E (2006, $13.99, TPB) r/series; sketch pg. by Caliafore						14.00
SENTRY (Also see New Avengers and Siege)						
Marvel Comics: Sept, 2000 - No. 5, Jan, 2001 ($2.99, limited series)						
1-5-Paul Jenkins-s/Jae Lee-a. 3-Spider-Man-c/app. 4-X-Men, FF app.						3.00
.../Fantastic Four (2/01, $2.99) Continues story from #5; Winslade-a						3.00
.../Hulk (2/01, $2.99) Sienkiewicz-c/a						3.00
.../Spider-Man (2/01, $2.99) back story of the Sentry; Leonardi-a						3.00
.../The Void (2/01, $2.99) Conclusion of story; Jae Lee-a						3.00
.../X-Men (2/01, $2.99) Sentry and Archangel; Texeira-a						3.00
TPB (10/01, $24.95) r/#1-5 & all one-shots; Stan Lee interview						25.00
TPB (2nd edition, 2005, $24.99)						25.00
SENTRY (Follows return in New Avengers #10)						
Marvel Comics: Nov, 2005 - No. 8, Jun, 2006 ($2.99, limited series)						
1-8-Paul Jenkins-s/John Romita Jr.-a. 1-New Avengers app. 3-Hulk app.						3.00
1-(Rough Cut) (12/05, $3.99) Romita sketch art and Jenkins script; cover sketches						4.00
...: Fallen Sun (7/10, $3.99) Siege epilogue; Jenkins-s/Raney-a/Yu-c						4.00
...: Reborn TPB (2006, $21.99) r/#1-8						22.00
SENTRY SPECIAL						
Innovation Publishing: 1991 ($2.75, one-shot)(Hero Alliance spin-off)						
1-Lost in Space preview (3 pgs.)						3.00
SERAPHIM						
Innovation Publishing: May, 1990 ($2.50, mature readers)						
1						3.00
SERENITY (Based on 2005 movie Serenity and 2003 TV series Firefly)						
Dark Horse Comics: July, 2005 - No. 3, Sept, 2005 ($2.99, limited series)						
1-3: Whedon & Matthews-s/Conrad-a. Three covers for each issue by various						4.00
...: Float Out (6/10, $3.50) Story of Wash; Patton Oswalt-s; covers by Jo Chen & Stockton						3.50
...: One For One (9/10, $1.00) reprints #1, Cassaday-c with red cover frame						1.00
...: Those Left Behind HC (11/07, $19.95, dustjacket) r/series; intro. by Nathan Fillion; pre-production art for the movie; Hughes-c						20.00
...: Those Left Behind TPB (1/06, $9.95) r/series; intro. by Nathan Fillion; Hughes-c						10.00
SERENITY BETTER DAYS (Firefly)						
Dark Horse Comics: Mar, 2008 - No. 3, May, 2008 ($2.99, limited series)						
1-3: Whedon & Matthews-s/Conrad-a; Adam Hughes-c						3.00
SERGEANT BARNEY BARKER (Becomes G. I. Tales #4 on)						
Atlas Comics (MCI): Aug, 1956 - No. 3, Dec, 1956						
1-Severin-c/a(4)	18	36	54	105	165	225
2,3: 2-Severin-c/a(4). 3-Severin-c/a(5)	14	28	42	76	108	140
SERGEANT BILKO (Phil Silvers Starring as...) (TV)						
National Periodical Publications: May-June, 1957 - No. 18, Mar-Apr, 1960						
1-All have Bob Oskner-c	58	116	174	371	636	900
2	31	62	93	186	303	420
3-5	26	52	78	154	252	350
6-18: 11,12,15,17-Photo-c	21	42	63	124	202	280
SGT. BILKO'S PVT. DOBERMAN (TV)						
National Periodical Publications: June-July, 1958 - No. 11, Feb-Mar, 1960						
1-Bob Oskner c-1-4,7,11	23	46	69	168	334	500
2	13	26	39	91	176	260
3-5: 5-Photo-c	10	20	30	70	125	180
6-11: 6,9-Photo-c	8	16	24	52	86	120
SGT. DICK CARTER OF THE U.S. BORDER PATROL (See Holyoke One-Shot)						
SGT. FURY (& His Howling Commandos)(See Fury & Special Marvel Edition)						
Marvel Comics Group (BPC earlier issues): May, 1963 - No. 167, Dec, 1981						
1-1st app. Sgt. Nick Fury (becomes agent of Shield in Strange Tales #135); Kirby/Ayers-c/a; 1st Dum-Dum Dugan & the Howlers	222	444	666	1943	3972	6000
2-Kirby-a	50	100	150	425	863	1300
3-5: 3-Reed Richards x-over. 4-Death of Junior Juniper. 5-1st Baron Strucker app.; Kirby-a	27	54	81	197	399	600
6-10: 8-Baron Zemo, 1st Percival Pinkerton app. 9-Hitler-c & app. 10-1st app. Capt. Savage (the Skipper)(9/64)	14	28	42	99	200	300
11,12,14-20: 14-1st Blitz Squad. 18-Death of Pamela Hawley	9	18	27	65	113	160
13-Captain America & Bucky app.(12/64); 2nd solo Capt. America x-over outside The Avengers; Kirby-a	38	76	114	304	602	900
13-2nd printing (1994)	2	4	6	8	10	12
21-24,26,28-30	6	12	18	43	69	95
25,27: 25-Red Skull app. 27-1st app. Eric Koenig; origin Fury's eye patch	7	14	21	45	73	100
31-33,35-50: 35-Eric Koenig joins Howlers. 43-Bob Hope, Glen Miller app. 44-Flashback on Howlers' 1st mission	4	8	12	26	41	55
34-Origin Howling Commandos	4	8	12	28	44	60
51-60	4	8	12	22	34	45
61-67: 64-Capt. Savage & Raiders x-over; peace symbol-c. 67-Last 12¢ issue; flag-c	3	6	9	18	27	35
68-80: 76-Fury's Father app. in WWI story	3	6	9	16	23	30
81-91: 91-Last 15¢ issue	3	6	9	14	19	24
92-(52 pgs.)	3	6	9	16	23	30
93-99: 98-Deadly Dozen x-over	2	4	6	13	18	22
100-Capt. America, Fantastic 4 cameos; Stan Lee, Martin Goodman & others app.	3	6	9	16	23	30
101-120: 101-Origin retold	2	4	6	10	14	18
121-130: 121-123-r/#19-21	2	4	6	8	11	14
131-167: 167-Reprints (from 1963)	2	4	6	8	10	12
133,134-(30¢-c variants, limited dist.)(5,7/76)	3	6	9	16	22	28
141,142-(35¢-c variants, limited dist.)(7,9/77)	4	8	12	22	34	45
Annual 1(1965, 25¢, 72 pgs.)-r/#4,5 & new-a	14	28	42	96	191	285
Special 2(1966)	7	14	21	45	73	100
Special 3(1967) All new material	5	10	15	30	48	65
Special 4(1968)	3	6	9	21	32	42
Special 5-7(1969-11/71)	3	6	9	17	25	32

NOTE: **Ayers** a-8, Annual 1. **Ditko** a-15i. **Gil Kane** c-37, 96. **Kirby** a-1-7, 13p, 167p(r). Special 5; c-1-8, 10-20, 25, 167p. **Severin** a-44-46, 48, 162, 164; inks-49-79, Special 4, 6; c-4i, 5, 6, 44, 46, 110, 149i, 155i, 162-166. **Sutton** a-57p. Reprints in #80, 82, 85, 87, 89, 91, 93, 95, 99, 101, 103, 105, 107, 109, 111, 121-123, 145-155, 167.

	GD 2.0	VG 4.0	FN 6.0	VF 8.0	VF/NM 9.0	NM- 9.2
SGT. FURY AND HIS HOWLING COMMANDOS						
Marvel Comics: July, 2009 ($3.99, one-shot)						
1-John Paul Leon-a/c; WWII tale set in 1942; Baron Strucker app.						4.00
SGT. FURY AND HIS HOWLING DEFENDERS (See The Defenders #147)						
SERGEANT PRESTON OF THE YUKON (TV)						
Dell Publishing Co.: No. 344, Aug, 1951 - No. 29, Nov-Jan, 1958-59						
Four Color 344(#1)-Sergeant Preston & his dog Yukon King begin; painted-c begin, end #18	11	22	33	77	144	210
Four Color 373,397,419('52)	8	16	24	52	86	120
5(11-1/52-53)-10(2-4/54): 6-Bondage-c.	6	12	18	41	66	90
11,12,14-17	6	12	18	37	59	80
13-Origin Sgt. Preston	6	12	18	41	66	90
18-Origin Yukon King; last painted-c	6	12	18	41	66	90
19-29: All photo-c	7	14	21	49	80	110
SGT. ROCK (Formerly Our Army at War; see Brave & the Bold #52 & Showcase #45)						
National Periodical Publications/DC Comics: No. 302, Mar, 1977 - No. 422, July, 1988						
302	4	8	12	28	44	60
303-310	3	6	9	16	22	28
311-320: 318-Reprints	2	4	6	10	16	20
321-350	2	4	6	8	11	14
329-Whitman variant	3	6	9	14	19	24
351-399,401-421: 412-Mlle Marie & Haunted Tank	1	2	3	5	7	9
400-(6/85) Anniversary issue	2	4	6	8	11	14
422-1st Joe, Adam, Andy Kubert-a team; last issue	2	4	6	10	14	18

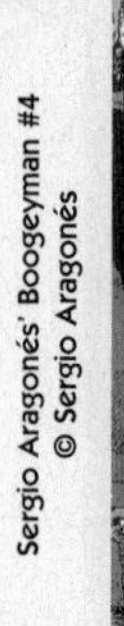

Sgt. Rock: The Lost Battalion #5 © DC

Sergio Aragonés' Boogeyman #4 © Sergio Aragonés

Seven Seas Comics #3 © UPF

	GD 2.0	VG 4.0	FN 6.0	VF 8.0	VF/NM 9.0	NM- 9.2

Annual 2-4: 2(1982)-Formerly Sgt. Rock's Prize Battle Tales #1. 3(1983). 4(1984) 2 4 6 8 10 12

NOTE: ***Estrada** a-322, 327, 331, 336, 337, 341, 342i. **Glanzman** a-384, 421. **Kubert** a-302, 303, 305r, 306, 328, 351, 356, 368, 373, 422; c-317, 318r, 319-323, 325-333-on, Annual 2, 3. **Severin** a-347. **Spiegle** a-382, Annual 2, 3. **Thorne** a-384. **Toth** a-385r. **Wildey** a-307, 311, 313, 314.*

SGT. ROCK: BETWEEN HELL AND A HARD PLACE
DC Comics (Vertigo): 2003 ($24.95, hardcover one-shot)

HC-Joe Kubert-a/c; Brian Azzarello-s 25.00
SC (2004, $17.95) 18.00

SGT. ROCK'S COMBAT TALES
DC Comics: 2005 ($9.99, digest)

Vol. 1-Reprints early app. in Our Army at War, G.I. Combat, Star Spangled War Stories 10.00

SGT. ROCK SPECIAL (Sgt. Rock #14 on; see DC Special Series #3)
DC Comics: Oct, 1988 - No. 21, Feb, 1992; No. 1, 1992; No. 2, 1994 ($2.00, quarterly/monthly, 52 pgs)

1-Reprint begin 2 4 6 8 11 14
2-21: All-r; 5-r/early Sgt. Rock/Our Army at War #81. 7-Tomahawk-r by Thorne. 9-Enemy Ace-r by Kubert. 10-All Rock issue. 11-r/1st Haunted Tank story. 12-All Kubert issue; begins monthly. 13-Dinosaur story by Heath(r). 14-Enemy Ace-r (22 pgs.) by Adams/Kubert. 15-Enemy Ace (22 pgs.) by Kubert. 16-Iron Major-c/story. 16,17-Enemy Ace-r. 19-r/Batman/Sgt. Rock team-up/B&B #108 by Aparo 1 2 3 5 6 8
1 (1992, $2.95, 68 pgs.)-Simonson-c; unpubbed Kubert-a; Glanzman, Russell, Pratt, & Wagner-a 6.00
2 (1994, $2.95) Brereton painted-c 4.00

NOTE: ***Neal Adams** r-1, 8, 14p. **Chaykin** a-2; r-3, 9(2pgs.); c-3. **Drucker** r-6. **Glanzman** r-20. **Golden** a-1. **Heath** a-2; r-5, 9-13, 16, 19, 21. **Krigstein** r-4, 8. **Kubert** r-1-17, 20, 21; c-1p, 2, 8, 14-21. **Miller** r-6p. **Severin** r-3, 6, 10. **Simonson** r-2, 4; c-4. **Thorne** r-7. **Toth** r-2, 8, 11. **Wood** r-4.*

SGT. ROCK SPECTACULAR (See DC Special Series #13)

SGT. ROCK'S PRIZE BATTLE TALES (Becomes Sgt. Rock Annual #2 on; see DC Special Series #18 & 80 Page Giant #7)
National Periodical Publications: Winter, 1964 (Giant - 80 pgs., one-shot)

1-Kubert, Heath-r; new Kubert-c 33 66 99 254 502 750
... Replica Edition (2000, $5.95) Reprints entire issue 6.00

SGT. ROCK: THE LOST BATTALION
DC Comics: Jan, 2009 - No. 6, Jun, 2009 ($2.99, limited series)

1-6-Billy Tucci-s/a. 1-Tucci & Sparacio-c 3.00
HC (2009, $24.99, d.j.) r/#1-6; production art; cover art gallery 25.00
SC (2010, $17.99) r/#1-6; production art; cover art gallery 18.00

SGT. ROCK: THE PROPHECY
DC Comics: Mar, 2006 - No. 6, Aug, 2006 ($2.99, limited series)

1-6-Joe Kubert-s/a/c. 1-Variant covers by Andy and Adam Kubert 3.00
TPB (2007, $17.99) r/#1-6 18.00

SGT. STRYKER'S DEATH SQUAD (See Savage Combat Tales)

SERGIO ARAGONÉS' ACTIONS SPEAK
Dark Horse Comics: Jan, 2001 - No. 6, Jun, 2001 ($2.99, B&W, limited series)

1-6-Aragonés-c/a; wordless one-page cartoons 3.00

SERGIO ARAGONÉS' BLAIR WHICH?
Dark Horse Comics: Dec, 1999 ($2.95, B&W, one-shot)

nn-Aragonés-c/a; Evanier-s. Parody of "Blair Witch Project" movie 3.00

SERGIO ARAGONÉS' BOOGEYMAN
Dark Horse Comics: June, 1998 - No. 4, Sept, 1998 ($2.95, B&W, lim. series)

1-4-Aragonés-c/a 3.00

SERGIO ARAGONÉS DESTROYS DC
DC Comics: June, 1996 ($3.50, one-shot)

1-DC Superhero parody book; Aragonés-c/a; Evanier scripts 3.50

SERGIO ARAGONÉS' DIA DE LOS MUERTOS
Dark Horse Comics: Oct, 1998 ($2.95, one-shot)

1-Aragonés-c/a; Evanier scripts 3.00

SERGIO ARAGONÉS' GROO & RUFFERTO
Dark Horse Comics: Dec, 1998 - No. 4, Mar, 1999 ($2.95, lim. series)

1-3-Aragonés-c/a 3.00

SERGIO ARAGONÉS' GROO: DEATH AND TAXES
Dark Horse Comics: Dec, 2001 - No. 4, Apr, 2002 ($2.99, lim. series)

1-4-Aragonés-c/a; Evanier-s 3.00

SERGIO ARAGONÉS' GROO: HELL ON EARTH
Dark Horse Comics: Nov, 2007 - No. 4, Apr, 2008 ($2.99, lim. series)

1-4-Aragonés-c/a; Evanier-s 3.00

SERGIO ARAGONÉS' GROO: MIGHTIER THAN THE SWORD
Dark Horse Comics: Jan, 2000 - No. 4, Apr, 2000 ($2.95, lim. series)

1-4-Aragonés-c/a; Evanier-s 3.00

SERGIO ARAGONÉS' GROO: THE HOGS OF HORDER
Dark Horse Comics: Oct, 2009 - No. 4, Mar, 2010 ($3.99, lim. series)

1-4-Aragonés-c/a; Evanier-s 4.00

SERGIO ARAGONÉS' GROO THE WANDERER (See Groo...)

SERGIO ARAGONÉS' GROO: 25TH ANNIVERSARY SPECIAL
Dark Horse Comics: Aug, 2007 ($5.99, one-shot)

nn-Aragonés-c/a; Evanier scripts; wraparound cover 6.00

SERGIO ARAGONÉS' LOUDER THAN WORDS
Dark Horse Comics: July, 1997 - No. 6, Dec, 1997 ($2.95, B&W, limited series)

1-6-Aragonés-c/a 3.00

SERGIO ARAGONÉS MASSACRES MARVEL
Marvel Comics: June, 1996 ($3.50, one-shot)

1-Marvel Superhero parody book; Aragonés-c/a; Evanier scripts 3.50

SERGIO ARAGONÉS STOMPS STAR WARS
Marvel Comics: Jan, 2000 ($2.95, one-shot)

1-Star Wars parody; Aragonés-c/a; Evanier scripts 3.00

SEVEN
Intrinsic Comics: July, 2007 ($3.00)

1-Jim Shooter-s/Paul Creddick-a 3.00

SEVEN BLOCK
Marvel Comics (Epic Comics): 1990 ($4.50, one-shot, 52 pgs.)

1-Dixon-s/Zaffino-a 6.00
nn-(IDW Publ., 2004, $5.99) reprints #1 6.00

SEVEN BROTHERS (John Woo's...)
Virgin Comics: Oct, 2006 - No. 5, Feb, 2007 ($2.99)

1-5-Garth Ennis-s/Jeevan Kang-a. 1-Two covers by Amano & Horn. 2-Kang var-c 3.00
TPB (6/07, $14.99) r/#1-5; cover gallery, deleted scenes and concept art 15.00
Volume 2 (9/07 - No. 5, 2/08) 1-Edison George-a. 4,5-David Mack-c 3.00

SEVEN DEAD MEN (See Complete Mystery #1)

SEVEN DWARFS (Also see Snow White)
Dell Publishing Co.: No. 227, 1949 (Disney-Movie)

Four Color 227 9 18 27 65 113 160

SEVEN MILES A SECOND
DC Comics (Vertigo Verité): 1996 ($7.95, one-shot)

nn-Wojnarowicz-s/Romberg-a 8.00

SEVEN SAMUROID, THE (See Image Graphic Novel)

SEVEN SEAS COMICS
Universal Phoenix Features/Leader No. 6: Apr, 1946 - No. 6, 1947(no month)

1-South Sea Girl by Matt Baker, Capt. Cutlass begin; Tugboat Tessie by Baker app. 90 180 270 576 988 1400
2-Swashbuckler-c 68 136 204 432 746 1060
3,5,6: 3-Six pg. Feldstein-a 69 138 207 442 759 1075
4-Classic Baker-c 90 180 270 576 988 1400

NOTE: ***Baker** a-1-6; c-3-6.*

SEVEN SOLDIERS OF VICTORY (Book-ends for seven related mini-series)
DC Comics: No. 0, Apr, 2005; No. 1; Dec, 2006 ($2.95/$3.99)

0-Grant Morrison-s/J.H. Williams-a 3.00
1-($3.99) Series conclusion; Grant Morrison-s/J.H. Williams-a 4.00
... Volume One (2006, $14.99) r/#0, Shining Knight #1,2; Zatanna #1,2; Guardian #1,2; and Klarion the Witch Boy #1; intro. by Morrison; character design sketches 15.00
... Volume Two (2006, $14.99) r/Shining Knight #3,4; Zatanna #3; Guardian #3,4; and Klarion the Witch Boy #2,3 15.00
... Volume Three ('06, $14.99) r/Zatanna #4; Mister Miracle #1,2; Bulleteer #1,2; Frankenstein #1 and Klarion the Witch Boy #4; 15.00
... Volume Four ('07, $14.99) r/Mister Miracle #3,4; Bulleteer #3,4; Frankenstein #2-4 and Seven Soldiers of Victory #1; script pages 15.00

SEVEN SOLDIERS: BULLETEER
DC Comics: Jan, 2006 - No. 4, May, 2006 ($2.99, limited series)

1-4-Grant Morrison-s/Yanick Paquette-a/c 3.00

Seven Soldiers: Shining Knight #1 © DC

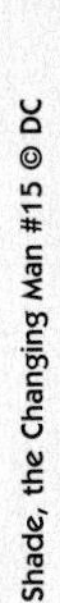

Shade, the Changing Man #15 © DC

Shadow Comics #1 © CN

GD 2.0 | VG 4.0 | FN 6.0 | VF 8.0 | VF/NM 9.0 | NM- 9.2

SEVEN SOLDIERS: FRANKENSTEIN
DC Comics: Jan, 2006 - No. 4, May, 2006 ($2.99, limited series)
1-4-Grant Morrison-s/Doug Mahnke-a/c 3.00

SEVEN SOLDIERS: GUARDIAN
DC Comics: May, 2005 - No. 4, Nov, 2005 ($2.99, limited series)
1-4-Grant Morrison-s/Cameron Stewart-a; Newsboy Army app. 3.00

SEVEN SOLDIERS: KLARION THE WITCH BOY
DC Comics: June, 2005 - No. 4, Dec, 2005 ($2.99, limited series)
1-4-Grant Morrison-s/Frazer Irving-a 3.00

SEVEN SOLDIERS: MISTER MIRACLE
DC Comics: Nov, 2005 - No. 4, May, 2006 ($2.99, limited series)
1-4: 1-Grant Morrison-s/Pasqual Ferry-a/c. 3,4-Freddie Williams II-a/c 3.00

SEVEN SOLDIERS: SHINING KNIGHT
DC Comics: May, 2005 - No. 4, Oct, 2005 ($2.99, limited series)
1-4-Grant Morrison-s/Simone Bianchi-a 3.00

SEVEN SOLDIERS: ZATANNA
DC Comics: June, 2005 - No. 4, Dec, 2005 ($2.99, limited series)
1-4-Grant Morrison-s/Ryan Sook-a 3.00

1776 (See Charlton Classic Library)

7TH VOYAGE OF SINBAD, THE (Movie)
Dell Publishing Co.: Sept, 1958 (photo-c)
Four Color 944-Buscema-a 12 24 36 82 154 225

77 SUNSET STRIP (TV)
Dell Publ. Co./Gold Key: No. 1066, Jan-Mar, 1960 - No. 2, Feb, 1963 (All photo-c)
Four Color 1066-Toth-a 10 20 30 70 125 180
Four Color 1106,1159-Toth-a 8 16 24 58 97 135
Four Color 1211,1263,1291, 01-742-209(7-9/62)-Manning-a in all 8 16 24 54 90 125
1,2: Manning-a. 1(11/62-G.K.) 8 16 24 54 90 125

77TH BENGAL LANCERS, THE (TV)
Dell Publishing Co.: May, 1957
Four Color 791-Photo-c 7 14 21 47 76 105

SEYMOUR, MY SON (See More Seymour)
Archie Publications (Radio Comics): Sept, 1963
1-DeCarlo-a? 3 6 9 20 30 40

SHADE, THE (See Starman)
DC Comics: Apr, 1997 - No. 4, July, 1997 ($2.25, limited series)
1-4-Robinson-s/Harris-c: 1-Gene Ha-a. 2-Williams/Gray-a 3-Blevins-a. 4-Zulli-a 3.00

SHADE, THE CHANGING MAN (See Cancelled Comic Cavalcade)
National Per. Publ./DC Comics: June-July, 1977 - No. 8, Aug-Sept, 1978
1-1st app. Shade; Ditko-c/a in all 2 4 6 11 16 20
2-8 2 3 4 6 8 10

SHADE, THE CHANGING MAN (2nd series) (Also see Suicide Squad #16)
DC Comics (Vertigo imprint #33 on): July, 1990 - No. 70, Apr, 1996 ($1.50-$2.25, mature)
1-($2.50, 52 pgs.)-Peter Milligan scripts in all 4.00
2-41,45-49,51-59: 6-Preview of World Without End. 17-Begin $1.75-c. 33-Metallic ink on-c. 41-Begin $1.95-c 3.00
42-44-John Constantine app. 3.50
50-($2.95, 52 pgs.) 4.00
60-70: 60-begin $2.25-c 3.00
...: Edge of Vision TPB (2009, $19.99) r/#7-13 20.00
...: Scream Time TPB (2010, $19.99) r/#14-19 20.00
...: The American Scream TPB (2003, 2009, $17.95/$17.99) r/#1-6 18.00
NOTE: *Bachalo a-1-9, 11-13, 15-21, 23-26, 33-39, 42-45, 47, 49, 50; c-30, 33-41.*

SHADO: SONG OF THE DRAGON (See Green Arrow #63-66)
DC Comics: 1992 - No. 4, 1992 ($4.95, limited series, 52 pgs.)
Book One - Four: Grell scripts; Morrow-a(i) 5.00

SHADOW, THE (See Batman #253, 259 & Marvel Graphic Novel #35)

SHADOW, THE (Pulp, radio)
Archie Comics (Radio Comics): Aug, 1964 - No. 8, Sept, 1965 (All 12¢)
1-Jerrry Siegel scripts in all; Shadow-c. 9 18 27 60 100 140
2-8: 2-App. in super-hero costume on-c only; Reinman-a(backup). 3-Superhero begins; Reinman-a (book-length novel). 3,4,6,7-The Fly 1 pg. strips. 4-8-Reinman-a. 5-8-Siegel scripts. 7-Shield app. 5 10 15 35 55 75

SHADOW, THE
National Periodical Publications: Oct-Nov, 1973 - No. 12, Aug-Sept, 1975
1-Kaluta-a begins 6 12 18 43 69 95
2 4 8 12 22 34 45
3-Kaluta/Wrightson-a 4 8 12 24 37 50
4,6-Kaluta-a ends. 4-Chaykin, Wrightson part-i 3 6 9 19 29 38
5,7-12: 11-The Avenger (pulp character) x-over 2 4 6 13 18 22
NOTE: ***Craig** a-10. **Cruz** a-10-12. **Kaluta** a-1, 2, 3p, 4, 6; c-1-4, 6, 10-12. **Kubert** c-9. **Robbins** a-5, 7-9; c-5, 7, 8.*

SHADOW, THE
DC Comics: May, 1986 - No. 4, Aug, 1986 (limited series)
1-4: Howard Chaykin art in all 3.00
Blood & Judgement ($12.95)-r/1-4 13.00

SHADOW, THE
DC Comics: Aug, 1987 - No. 19, Jan, 1989 ($1.50)
1-19: Andrew Helfer scripts in all. 3.00
Annual 1,2 (12/87, '88,)-2-The Shadow dies; origin retold (story inspired by the movie "Citizen Kane"). 4.00
NOTE: ***Kyle Baker** a-7i, 8-19, Annual 2. **Chaykin** c-Annual 1. **Helfer** scripts in all. **Orlando** a-Annual 1. **Rogers** c/a-7. **Sienkiewicz** c/a-1-6.*

SHADOW, THE (Movie)
Dark Horse Comics: June, 1994 - No. 2, July, 1994 ($2.50, limited series)
1,2-Adaptation from Universal Pictures film 3.00
NOTE: ***Kaluta** c/a-1, 2.*

SHADOW AND DOC SAVAGE, THE
Dark Horse Comics: July, 1995 - No. 2, Aug, 1995 ($2.95, limited series)
1,2 3.50

SHADOW AND THE MYSTERIOUS 3, THE
Dark Horse Comics: Sept, 1994 ($2.95, one-shot)
1-Kaluta co-scripts. 3.00
NOTE: ***Stevens** c-1.*

SHADOW CABINET (See Heroes)
DC Comics (Milestone): No. 0, Jan, 1994 - No. 17, Oct, 1995 ($1.75/$2.50)
0-(1/94, $2.50, 52 pgs.)-Silver ink-c; Simonson-c 4.00
1-17: 1-(6/94) Byrne-c 3.00

SHADOW COMICS (Pulp, radio)
Street & Smith Publications: Mar, 1940 - V9#5, Aug-Sept, 1949
NOTE: *The Shadow first appeared on radio in 1929 and was featured in pulps beginning in April, 1931, written by Walter Gibson. The early covers of this series were reprinted from the pulp covers.*
V1#1-Shadow, Doc Savage, Bill Barnes, Nick Carter (radio), Frank Merriwell, Iron Munro, the Astonishing Man begin 476 952 1428 3475 6138 8800
2-The Avenger begins, ends #6; Capt. Fury only app. 213 426 639 1363 2332 3300
3(nn-5/40)-Norgil the Magician app.; cover is exact swipe of Shadow pulp from 1/33 152 304 456 965 1658 2350
4,5: 4-The Three Musketeers begins, ends #8. 5-Doc Savage ends 113 226 339 718 1234 1750
6,8,9: 9-Norgil the Magician app. 95 190 285 603 1039 1475
7-Origin/1st app. The Hooded Wasp & Wasplet (11/40); series ends V3#8; Hooded Wasp/Wasplet app. on-c thru #9 100 200 300 635 1093 1550
10-Origin The Iron Ghost, ends #11; The Dead End Kids begins, ends #14 95 190 285 603 1039 1475
11-Origin Hooded Wasp & Wasplet retold 95 190 285 603 1039 1475
12-Dead End Kids app. 89 178 267 565 970 1375
V2#1(11/41, Vol.II#2 in indicia) Dead End Kids -s 86 172 258 546 936 1325
2-(Rare, Vol.II#3 in indicia) Giant ant-c 165 330 495 1048 1799 2550
3-Origin & 1st app. Supersnipe (3/42); series begins; Little Nemo story (Vol.II#4 in indicia) 139 278 417 883 1517 2150
4,5: 4,8-Little Nemo story 74 148 222 470 810 1150
6-9: 6-Blackstone the Magician story 71 142 213 454 777 1100
10,12: 10-Supersnipe app.' Skull-c 69 138 207 442 759 1075
11-Classic Devil Kyoti World War 2 sunburst-c 82 164 246 528 902 1275
V3#1,2,5,7-12: 10-Doc Savage begins, not in V5#5, V6#10-12, V8#4 68 136 204 435 743 1050
3-1st Monstrodamus-c/sty 77 154 231 493 847 1200
4-2nd Monstrodamus; classic-c of giant salamander getting shot in the head 84 168 252 538 919 1300
6-Classic underwater-c 90 180 270 576 988 1400
V4#1-12 48 96 144 302 514 725
V5#1-12 42 84 126 267 451 635

Shadowhawk V3 #5 © Jim Valentino

Shadowland #1 © MAR

Shadowman V2 #13 © Acclaim

	GD 2.0	VG 4.0	FN 6.0	VF 8.0	VF/NM 9.0	NM- 9.2
V6#1-11: 9-Intro. Shadow, Jr. (12/46)	40	80	120	242	401	560
12-Powell-c/a; atom bomb panels	42	84	126	267	451	635
V7#1,2,5,7-9,12: 2,5-Shadow, Jr. app.; Powell-a	40	80	120	242	401	560
3,6,11-Powell-c/a	44	88	132	277	469	660
4-Powell-c/a; Atom bomb panels	46	92	138	290	488	685
10(1/48)-Flying Saucer-c/story (2nd of this theme; see The Spirit 9/28/47); Powell-c/a	58	116	174	371	636	900
V8#1-12-Powell-a. 3-Powell Spider-c/a	44	88	132	277	469	660
V9#1,5-Powell-a	42	84	126	267	451	635
2-4-Powell-c/a	44	88	132	277	469	660

NOTE: ***Binder** c-V3#1. **Powell** art in most issues beginning V6#12. Painted c-1-6.*

SHADOWDRAGON
DC Comics: 1995 ($3.50, annual)

Annual 1-Year One story 4.00

SHADOW EMPIRES: FAITH CONQUERS
Dark Horse Comics: Aug, 1994 - No. 4, Nov, 1994 ($2.95, limited series)

1-4 3.00

SHADOWHAWK (See Images of Shadowhawk, New Shadowhawk, Shadowhawk II, Shadowhawk III & Youngblood #2)
Image Comics (Shadowline Ink): Aug, 1992 - No. 4, Mar, 1993; No. 12, Aug, 1994 - No. 18, May, 1995 ($1.95/$2.50)

1-($2.50)-Embossed silver foil stamped-c; Valentino/Liefeld-c; Valentino-c/a/ scripts in all; has coupon for Image #0; 1st Shadowline Ink title 5.00
1-With coupon missing 2.00
1-($1.95)-Newsstand version w/o foil stamp 3.00
2-13,0,1418: 2-Shadowhawk poster w/McFarlane-i; brief Spawn app.; wraparound-c w/silver ink highlights. 3-($2.50)-Glow-in-the-dark-c. 4-Savage Dragon-c/story; Valentino/Larsen-c. 5-11-(See Shadowhawk II and III). 12-Cont'd from Shadowhawk III; pull-out poster by Texeira.13-w/ShadowBone poster; WildC.A.T.s app. 0 (10/94)-Liefeld c/a/story; ShadowBart poster. 14-(10/94, $2.50)-The Others app. 16-Supreme app. 17-Spawn app.; story cont'd from Badrock & Co. #6. 18-Shadowhawk dies; Savage Dragon & Brigade app. 3.00
Special 1(12/94, $3.50, 52 pgs.)-Silver Age Shadowhawk flip book 4.00
Gallery (4/94, $1.95) 3.00
Out of the Shadows ($19.95)-r/Youngblood #2, Shadowhawk #1-4, Image Zero #0, Operation: Urban Storm (Never published) 20.00
.../Vampirella (2/95, $4.95)-Pt.2 of x-over (See Vampirella/Shadowhawk for Pt. 1) 5.00
NOTE: *Shadowhawk was originally a four issue limited series. The story continued in Shadowhawk II, Shadowhawk III & then became Shadowhawk again with issue #12.*

SHADOWHAWK II (Follows Shadowhawk #4)
Image Comics (Shadowline Ink): V2#1, May, 1993 - V2#3, Aug, 1993 ($3.50/$1.95/$2.95, limited series)

V2#1 ($3.50)-Cont'd from Shadowhawk #4; die-cut mirricard-c 4.00
2 ($1.95)-Foil embossed logo; reveals identity; gold-c variant exists 3.00
3 ($2.95)-Pop-up-c w/Pact ashcan insert 4.00

SHADOWHAWK III (Follows Shadowhawk II #3)
Image Comics (Shadowline Ink): V3#1, Nov, 1993 - V3#4, Mar, 1994 ($1.95, limited series);

V3#1-4: 1-Cont'd from Shadowhawk II; intro Valentine; gold foil & red foil stamped-c variations. 2-(52 pgs.)-Shadowhawk contracts HIV virus; U.S. Male by M. Anderson (p) in free 16 pg.insert. 4-Continues in Shadowhawk #12 3.00

SHADOWHAWK (Volume 2) (Also see New Man #4)
Image Comics: May, 2005 - No. 15, Sept, 2006 ($2.99/$3.50)

1-4-Eddie Collins as Shadowhawk; Rodríguez-a; Valentino-co-plotter 3.50
5-15-($3.50) 5-Cover swipe of Superman Vs. Spider-Man treasury edition 3.50
...One Shot #1 (7/06, $1.99) r/Return of Shadowhawk 3.00
Return of Shadowhawk (12/04, $2.99) Valentino-s/a/c; Eddie Collins origin retold 3.00

SHADOWHAWK (Volume 3)
Image Comics: May, 2010 - No. 5, Dec, 2010 ($3.50)

1-5-Rodríguez-a. 1-Back-up with Valentino-a/Niles-s 3.50

SHADOWHAWKS OF LEGEND
Image Comics (Shadowline Ink): Nov, 1995 ($4.95, one-shot)

nn-Stories of past Shadowhawks by Kurt Busiek, Beau Smith & Alan Moore 5.00

SHADOW, THE: HELL'S HEAT WAVE (Movie, pulp, radio)
Dark Horse Comics: Apr, 1995 - No. 3, June, 1995 ($2.95, limited series)

1-3: Kaluta story 3.00

SHADOW HUNTER (Jenna Jameson's...)
Virgin Comics: No. 0, Dec, 2007 - No. 3 ($2.99)

0-Preview issue; creator interviews; gallery of covers for upcoming issues; Greg Horn-c 3.00
1-3: 1-Two covers by Horn & Land; Jameson & Christina Z-s/Singh-a. 2-Three covers 3.00

SHADOWHUNT SPECIAL
Image Comics (Extreme Studios): Apr, 1996 ($2.50)

1-Retells origin of past Shadowhawks; Valentino script; Chapel app. 3.00

SHADOW, THE: IN THE COILS OF THE LEVIATHAN (Movie, pulp, radio)
Dark Horse Comics: Oct, 1993 - No. 4, Apr, 1994 ($2.95, limited series)

1-4-Kaluta-c & co-scripter 3.00
Trade paperback (10/94, $13.95)-r/1-4 14.00

SHADOWLAND (Also see Daredevil #508-512 & Black Panther: The Man Without Fear #513)
Marvel Comics: Sept, 2010 - No. 5, Jan, 2011 ($3.99, limited series)

1-5: 1-Diggle-s/Tan-a; Bullseye killed; Cassaday-c. 2-Ghost Rider app. 4.00
1-Variant-c by Tan 6.00
...: After the Fall 1 (2/11, $3.99) Finch-c; Black Panther app. 4.00
...: Bullseye 1 (10/10, $3.99) Chen-a; Bullseye's funeral 4.00
...: Elektra 1 (11/10, $3.99) Wells-s/Rios-a/Takeda-c 4.00
...: Ghost Rider 1 (11/10, $3.99) Williams-s/Crain-a/c 4.00
...: Spider-Man 1 (12/10, $3.99) Shang-Chi & Mr. Negative app.; Siqueira-a 4.00

SHADOWLAND: BLOOD IN THE STREETS (Leads into Heroes For Hire)
Marvel Comics: Oct, 2010 - No. 4, Jan, 2011 ($3.99, limited series)

1-4-Johnston-s/Alves-a; Misty Knight, Silver Sable, Paladin, Shroud app. 4.00

SHADOWLAND: DAUGHTERS OF THE SHADOW
Marvel Comics: Oct, 2010 - No. 3, Dec, 2010 ($3.99, limited series)

1-3-Henderson-s/Rodriguez-a; Colleen Wing app. 3-Preview of Black Panther #513 4.00

SHADOWLAND: MOON KNIGHT
Marvel Comics: Oct, 2010 - No. 3, Dec, 2010 ($3.99, limited series)

1-3-Hurwitz-s/Dazo-a 4.00

SHADOWLAND: POWER MAN
Marvel Comics: Oct, 2010 - No. 4, Jan, 2011 ($3.99, limited series)

1-4-Van Lente-s/Asrar-a. 1-New Power Man debut; Iron Fist app. 4.00

SHADOWLINE SAGA: CRITICAL MASS, A
Marvel Comics (Epic): Jan, 1990 - No. 7, July, 1990 ($4.95, lim. series, 68 pgs)

1-6: Dr. Zero, Powerline, St. George 5.00
7 ($5.95, 84 pgs.)-Morrow-a, Williamson-c(i) 6.00

SHADOWMAN (See X-O Manowar #4)
Valiant/Acclaim Comics (Valiant): May, 1992 - No. 43, Dec, 1995 ($2.50)

1-Partial origin 5.00
2-5: 3-1st app. Sousa the Soul Eater 4.00
6-43: 8-1st app. Master Darque. 16-1st app. Dr. Mirage (8/93). 15-Minor Turok app. 17,18-Archer & Armstrong x-over. 19-Aerosmith-c/story. 23-Dr. Mirage x-over. 24-(4/94). 25-Bound-in trading card. 29-Chaos Effect. 43-Shadowman jumps to his death 3.00
0-($2.50, 4/94)-Regular edition 3.00
0-($3.50)-Wraparound chromium-c edition 4.00
0-Gold 15.00
Yearbook 1 (12/94, $3.95) 4.00

SHADOWMAN (Volume 2)
Acclaim Comics (Valiant Heroes): Mar, 1997 - No. 20 ($2.50, mature)

1-20: 1-1st app. Zero; Garth Ennis scripts begin, end #4. 2-Zero becomes new Shadowman. 4-Origin; Jack Boniface (original Shadowman) rises from the grave. 5-Jamie Delano scripts begin. 9-Copycat-c 3.00
1-Variant painted cover 3.00
#0 Gold 5.00

SHADOWMAN (Volume 3)
Acclaim Comics: July, 1999 - No. 5, Nov, 1999 ($3.95/$2.50)

1-($3.95)-Abnett & Lanning-s/Broome & Benjamin-a 4.00
2-5-($2.50): 3,4-Flip book with Unity 2000 3.00

SHADOWMASTERS
Marvel Comics: Oct, 1989 - No.4, Jan, 1990 ($3.95, squarebound, 52 pgs.)

1-4: Heath-a(i). 1-Jim Lee-c; story cont'd from Punisher 4.00

SHADOW OF THE BATMAN
DC Comics: Dec, 1985 - No. 5, Apr, 1986 ($1.75, limited series)

	GD 2.0	VG 4.0	FN 6.0	VF 8.0	VF/NM 9.0	NM- 9.2
1-Detective-r (all have wraparound-c)	1	2	3	5	6	8
2,3,5: 3-Penguin-c & cameo. 5-Clayface app.						6.00
4-Joker-c/story	1	2	3	4	5	7

NOTE: ***Austin** a(new)-2i, 3i; r-2-4i. **Rogers** a(new)-1, 2p, 3p, 4, 5; r-1-5p; c-1-5. **Simonson** a-1r.*

SHADOW OF THE TORTURER, THE
Innovation: July, 1991 - No. 3, 1992 ($2.50, limited series)

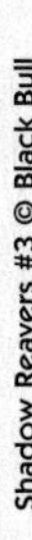
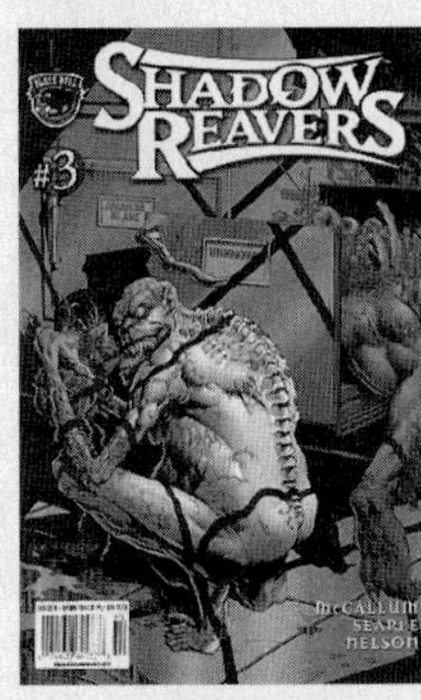

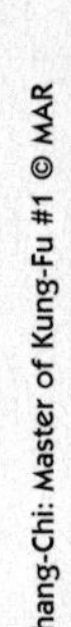

Shanna the She-Devil #2 © MAR

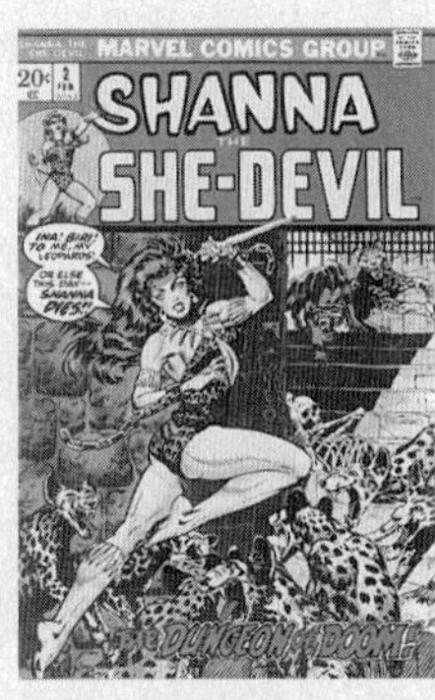

GD VG FN VF VF/NM NM-
2.0 4.0 6.0 8.0 9.0 9.2

GD VG FN VF VF/NM NM-
2.0 4.0 6.0 8.0 9.0 9.2

1-3: Based on Pocket Books novel 3.00

SHADOW ON THE TRAIL (See Zane Grey & Four Color #604)

SHADOWPACT (See Day of Vengeance)
DC Comics: Jul, 2006 - No. 25, Jul, 2008 ($2.99)

1-25: 1-Bill Willingham-s; Detective Chimp, Ragman, Blue Devil, Nightshade, Enchantress and Nightmaster app. 1-Superman app. 13-Zauriel app.; S. Hampton-a 3.00
...: Cursed TPB (2007, $14.99) r/#4,9-13 15.00
...: Darkness and Light TPB (2008, $14.99) r/#14-19 15.00
...: The Burning Age TPB (2008, $17.99) r/#20-25 18.00
...: The Pentacle Plot TPB (2007, $14.99) r/#1-3,5-8 15.00

SHADOW PLAY (Tales of the Supernatural)
Whitman Publications: June, 1982

1-Painted-c 1 2 3 5 6 8

SHADOWPLAY
IDW Publ.: Sept, 2005 - No. 4, Dec, 2005 ($3.99)

1-4-Benson-s/Templesmith-a; Christina Z-s/Wood-a; 2 covers by Templesmith & Wood 4.00
TPB (3/06, $17.99) r/series; flip book format 18.00

SHADOW REAVERS
Black Bull Ent.: Oct, 2001 - No. 5, Mar, 2002 ($2.99)

1-5-Nelson-a; two covers for each issue 3.00
Limited Preview Edition (5/01, no cover price) 3.00

SHADOW RIDERS
Marvel Comics UK, Ltd.: June, 1993 - No. 4, Sept, 1993 ($1.75, limited series)

1-($2.50)-Embossed-c; Cable-c/story 4.00
2-4-Cable app. 2-Ghost Rider app. 3.00

SHADOWS
Image Comics: Feb, 2003 - No. 4, Nov, 2003 ($2.95)

1-4-Jade Dodge-s/Matt Camp-a/c 3.00

SHADOWS & LIGHT
Marvel Comics: Feb, 1998 - No. 3, July, 1998 ($2.99, B&W, quarterly)

1-3: 1-B&W anthology of Marvel characters; Black Widow art by Gene Ha, Hulk by Wrightson, Iron Man by Ditko & Daredevil by Stelfreeze; Stelfreeze painted-c. 2-Weeks, Sharp, Starlin, Thompson-a. 3-Buscema, Grindberg, Giffen, Layton-a 3.00

SHADOW'S FALL
DC Comics (Vertigo): Nov, 1994 - No. 6, Apr, 1995 ($2.95, limited series)

1-6: Van Fleet-c/a in all. 3.00

SHADOWS FROM BEYOND (Formerly Unusual Tales)
Charlton Comics: V2#50, October, 1966

V2#50-Ditko-c 4 8 12 22 34 45

SHADOW STATE
Broadway Comics: Dec, 1995 - No. 5, Apr, 1996 ($2.50)

1-5: 1,2-Fatale back-up story; Cockrum-a(p) 3.00
Preview Edition 1,2 (10-11/95, $2.50, B&W) 3.00

SHADOW STRIKES!, THE (Pulp, radio)
DC Comics: Sept, 1989 - No.31, May, 1992 ($1.75)

1-4,7-31: 31-Mignola-c 3.00
5,6-Doc Savage x-over 4.00
Annual 1 (1989, $3.50, 68 pgs.)-Spiegle a; Kaluta-c 4.00

SHADOW WAR OF HAWKMAN
DC Comics: May, 1985 - No. 4, Aug, 1985 (limited series)

1-4 3.00

SHAGGY DOG & THE ABSENT-MINDED PROFESSOR (See Four Color #1199, Movie Comics & Walt Disney Showcase #46)(Disney-Movie)
Dell Publ. Co.: No. 985, May, 1959

Four Color 985 7 14 21 50 83 115

SHALOMAN (Jewish-themed stories and history)
Al Wiesner/ Mark 1 Comics: 1988 - Present (B&W)

V1#1-Al Wiesner-s/a in all 5.00
2-9 3.00
V2 #1(The New Adventures)-4,6-10, V3 (The Legend of...) #1-12 3.00
V2 #5 (Color)-Shows Vol 2, No. 4 in indicia 3.00
V4 (The Saga of ...) #1(2004), 2-8: 8-Chanukah & The Holocaust 3.00
...: The Sequel (11/09) 3.00
...: The Sequel 2 (2011) Genesis #2 Jews in Space 3.00
The Saga of Shaloman (20th Anniversary Edition) TPB (10/08, $15.99) r/V4 #1-8 16.00

SHAMAN'S TEARS (Also see Maggie the Cat)
Image Comics (Creative Fire Studio): 5/93 - No. 2, 8/93; No. 3, 11/94 - No. 0, 1/96 ($2.50/$1.95)

0-2: 0-(DEC-c, 1/96)-Last Issue. 1-(5/93)-Embossed red foil-c; Grell-c/a & scripts in all. 2-Cover unfolds into poster (8/93-c, 7/93 inside) 3.00
3-12: 3-Begin $1.95-c. 5-Re-intro Jon Sable. 12-Re-intro Maggie the Cat (1 pg.) 3.00

SHANG-CHI: MASTER OF KUNG-FU ("Master of Kung Fu" on cover for #1&2)
Marvel Comics: Nov, 2002 - No. 6, Apr, 2003 ($2.99, limited series)

1-6-Moench-s/Gulacy-c/a 3.00
...One-Shot 1 (11/09, $3.99, B&W) Deadpool app. 4.00
... Vol. 1: The Hellfire Apocalypse TPB (2003, $14.99) r/#1-6 15.00

SHANGRI-LA
Image Comics: Jan, 2004 ($7.95, B&W, square-bound graphic novel)

1-Marc Bryant-s/Shepherd Hendrix-a 8.00

SHANNA, THE SHE-DEVIL (See Savage Tales #8)
Marvel Comics Group: Dec, 1972 - No. 5, Aug, 1973 (All are 20¢ issues)

1-1st app. Shanna; Steranko-c; Tuska-a(p) 4 8 12 24 37 50
2-Steranko-c; heroin drug story 3 6 9 20 30 40
3-5 2 4 6 13 18 22

SHANNA, THE SHE-DEVIL
Marvel Comics: Apr, 2005 - No. 7, Oct, 2005 ($3.50, limited series)

1-7-Reintro of Shanna; Frank Cho-s/a/c in all 3.50
HC (2005, $24.99, dust jacket) r/#1-7 25.00
SC (2006, $16.99) r/#1-7 17.00

SHANNA, THE SHE-DEVIL: SURVIVAL OF THE FITTEST
Marvel Comics: Oct, 2007 - No. 4, Jan, 2008 ($2.99, limited series)

1-4-Khari Evans-a/c; Gray & Palmiotti-s 3.00
SC (2008, $10.99) r/#1-4 11.00

SHAOLIN COWBOY
Burlyman Entertainment: Dec, 2004 - Present ($3.50)

1-7-Geof Darrow-s/a. 3-Moebius-c 3.50

SHARK FIGHTERS, THE (Movie)
Dell Publishing Co.: Jan, 1957

Four Color 762-Buscema-a; photo-c 7 14 21 50 83 115

SHARK-MAN
Thrill House/Image Comics: Jul, 2006; Jul, 2007; Jan, 2008 - No. 3, Jun, 2008 ($3.99/$3.50)

1,2: 1-(Thrill House, 7/06, $3.99)-Steve Pugh-s/a. 2-(Image Comics, 7/07) 4.00
1-3: 1-(Image, 1/08, $3.50) reprints Thrill House #1 3.50

SHARKY
Image Comics: Feb, 1998 - No. 4, 1998 ($2.50, bi-monthly)

1-4: 1-Mask app.; Elliot-s/a. Horley painted-c. 3-Three covers by Horley, Bisley, & Horley/Elliot. 4-Two covers (swipe of Avengers #4 and wraparound) 3.00
1-($2.95) "$1,000,000" variant 3.00
2-($2.50) Savage Dragon variant-c 3.00

SHARP COMICS (Slightly large size)
H. C. Blackerby: Winter, 1945-46 - V1#2, Spring, 1946 (52 pgs.)

V1#1-Origin Dick Royce Planetarian 40 80 120 246 411 575
2-Origin The Pioneer; Michael Morgan, Dick Royce, Sir Gallagher, Planetarian, Steve Hagen, Weeny and Pop app. 36 72 108 211 343 475

SHARPY FOX (See Comic Capers & Funny Frolics)
I. W. Enterprises/Super Comics: 1958; 1963

1,2-I.W. Reprint (1958): 2-r/Kiddie Kapers #1 2 4 6 8 10 12
14-Super Reprint (1963) 2 4 6 8 10 12

SHATTER (See Jon Sable #25-30)
First Comics: June, 1985; Dec, 1985 - No. 14, Apr, 1988. ($1.75, Baxter paper/deluxe paper)

1 (6/85)-1st computer generated-a in a comic book (1st printing) 4.00
1-(2nd print.); 1(12/85)-14: computer generated-a & lettering in all 3.00
Special 1 (1988) 3.00

SHATTERED IMAGE
Image Comics (WildStorm Productions): Aug, 1996 - No. 4, Dec, 1996 ($2.50, lim. series)

1-4: 1st Image company-wide x-over; Kurt Busiek scripts in all. 1-Tony Daniel-c/a(p). 2-Alex Ross-c/swipe (Kingdom Come) by Ryan Benjamin & Travis Charest 3.00

SHAUN OF THE DEAD (Movie)
IDW Publishing: June, 2005 - No. 4, Sept, 2005 ($3.99, limited series)

1-4-Adaptation of 2004 movie; Zach Howard-a 4.00

Shazam! #19 © DC

Sheena, Queen of the Jungle #8 © FH

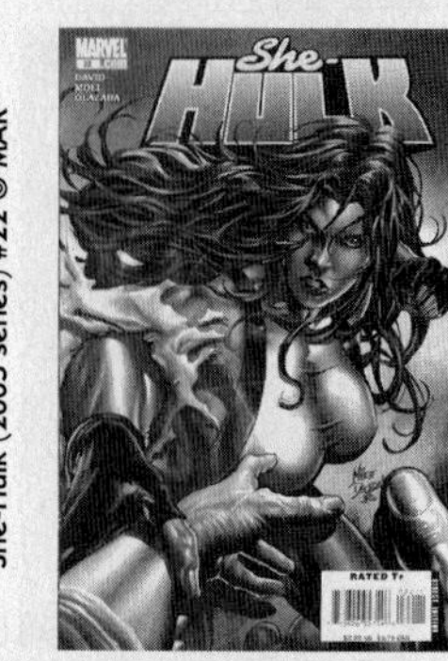

She-Hulk (2005 series) #22 © MAR

GD VG FN VF VF/NM NM-
2.0 4.0 6.0 8.0 9.0 9.2

TPB (12/05, $17.99) r/series; sketch pages and cover gallery 18.00

SHAZAM (See Billy Batson and the Magic of Shazam!, Giant Comics to Color, Limited Collectors' Edition, Power Of Shazam! and Trials of Shazam!)

SHAZAM! (TV)(See World's Finest #253 for story from unpublished #36)
National Periodical Publ./DC Comics: Feb, 1973 - No. 35, May-June, 1978

1-1st revival of original Captain Marvel since G.A. (origin retold), by C.C. Beck; Mary Marvel & Captain Marvel Jr. app.; Superman-c 6 12 18 43 69 95
2-5: 2-Infinity photo-c.; re-intro Mr. Mind & Tawny. 3-Capt. Marvel-r. (10/46). 4-Origin retold; Capt. Marvel-r. (1949). 5-Capt. Marvel Jr. origin retold; Capt. Marvel-r. (1948, 7 pgs.) 3 6 9 18 27 35
6,7,9-11: 6-photo-c; Capt. Marvel-r (1950, 6 pgs.). 9-Mr. Mind app. 10-Last C.C. Beck issue. 11-Schaffenberger-a begins. 3 6 9 14 20 26
8 (100 pgs.) 8-r/Capt. Marvel Jr. by Raboy; origin/C.M. #80; origin Mary Marvel/C.M.A. #18; origin Mr. Tawny/C.M.A. #79 6 12 18 41 66 90
12-17-(All 100 pgs.). 15-vs. Lex Luthor & Mr. Mind 5 10 15 32 51 70
18-24,26-30: 21-24-All reprints. 26-Sivana app. (10/76). 27-Kid Eternity teams up w/Capt. Marvel. 28-1st S.A. app. of Black Adam. 30-1st DC app. 3 Lt. Marvels 2 4 6 11 16 20
25-1st app. Isis 3 6 9 14 19 24
31-35: 31-1st DC app. Minuteman. 34-Origin Capt. Nazi & Capt. Marvel Jr. retold 3 6 9 14 19 24
...: The Greatest Stories Ever Told TPB (2008, $24.99) reprints; Alex Ross-c 25.00

NOTE: *Reprints in #1-8, 10, 12-17, 21-24.* ***Beck*** *a-1-10, 12-17r, 21-24r; c-1, 3-9.* ***Nasser*** *c-35p.* ***Newton*** *a-35p.* ***Raboy*** *a-5r, 8r, 17r.* ***Schaffenberger*** *a-11, 14-20, 25, 26, 27p, 28, 29-31p, 33i, 35i; c-20, 22, 23, 25, 26i, 27i, 28-33.*

SHAZAM!
DC Comics: March, 2011 ($2.99, one-shot)

1-Richards-a/Chiang-c; Blaze app.; story continues in Titans #32 3.00

SHAZAM! AND THE SHAZAM FAMILY! ANNUAL
DC Comics: 2002 ($5.95, squarebound, one-shot)

1-Reprints Golden Age stories including 1st Mary Marvel and 1st Black Adam 6.00

SHAZAM!: POWER OF HOPE
DC Comics: Nov, 2000 ($9.95, treasury size, one-shot)

nn-Painted art by Alex Ross; story by Alex Ross and Paul Dini 10.00

SHAZAM!: THE MONSTER SOCIETY OF EVIL
DC Comics: 2007 - No. 4, 2007 ($5.99, square-bound, limited series)

1-4: Jeff Smith-s/a/c in all. 1-Retelling of origin. 2-Mary Marvel & Dr. Sivana app. 6.00
HC (2007, $29.99, over-sized with dust jacket that unfolds to a poster) r/#1-4; Alex Ross intro.; Smith afterword; sketch pages, script pages and production notes 30.00
SC (2009, $19.99) r/#1-4; Alex Ross intro. 20.00

SHAZAM: THE NEW BEGINNING
DC Comics: Apr, 1987 - No. 4, July, 1987 (Legends spin-off) (Limited series)

1-4: 1-New origin & 1st modern app. Captain Marvel; Marvel Family cameo. 2-4-Sivana & Black Adam app. 4.00

SHEA THEATRE COMICS
Shea Theatre: No date (1940's) (32 pgs.)

nn-Contains Rocket Comics; MLJ cover in one color 11 22 33 60 83 105

SHE-BAT (See Murcielaga, She-Bat & Valeria the She-Bat)

SHE-DRAGON (See Savage Dragon #117)
Image Comics: July, 2006 ($5.99, one-shot)

nn- She-Dragon in Dimension-X; origin retold; Franchesco-a/Larsen-s; sketch pages 6.00

SHEENA (Movie)
Marvel Comics: Dec, 1984 - No. 2, Feb, 1985 (limited series)

1,2-r/Marvel Comics Super Special #34; Tanya Roberts movie 4.00

SHEENA, QUEEN OF THE JUNGLE (See Jerry Iger's Classic..., Jumbo Comics, & 3-D Sheena)
Fiction House Magazines: Spr, 1942; No. 2, Wint, 1942-43; No. 3, Spr, 1943; No. 4, Fall, 1948; No. 5, Sum, 1949; No. 6, Spr, 1950; No. 7-10, 1950(nd); No. 11, Spr, 1951 - No. 18, Wint, 1952-53 (#1-3: 68 pgs.; #4-7: 52 pgs.)

1-Sheena begins 277 554 831 1756 3028 4300
2 (Winter, 1942-43) 119 238 357 762 1306 1850
3 (Spring, 1943) 86 172 258 546 936 1325
4,5 (Fall, 1948, Sum, 1949): 4-New logo; cover swipe from Jumbo #20 53 106 159 334 567 800
6,7 (Spring, 1950, 1950) 45 90 135 284 480 675
8-10(1950 - Win/50, 36 pgs.) 41 82 123 256 428 600
11-17: 15-Cover swipe from Jumbo #43 37 74 111 222 361 500
18-Used in **POP**, pg. 98 39 78 117 231 378 525
I.W. Reprint #9-r/#18; c-r/White Princess #3 4 8 12 28 44 60

NOTE: ***Baker*** *c-5-10?* ***Whitman*** *c-11-18(most).*

SHEENA, QUEEN OF THE JUNGLE
Devil's Due Publishing: Mar, 2007 - Present (99¢/$3.50)

1-5: 1-Rodi-s/Merhoff-a; 5 covers 3.50
... 99¢ Special (3/07) Revival of the character; Rodi-s/Cummings-a; sketch pages; history 2.25
...: Dark Rising (10/08 - Present) 1-3 3.50
... Trail of the Mapinguari (4/08, $5.50) Two covers 5.50

SHEENA 3-D SPECIAL (Also see Blackthorne 3-D Series #1)
Eclipse Comics: Jan, 1985 ($2.00)

1-Dave Stevens-c 5.00

SHE-HULK (Also see The Savage She-Hulk & The Sensational She-Hulk)
Marvel Comics: May, 2004 - No. 12, Apr, 2005 ($2.99)

1-4-Bobillo-a/Slott-s/Granov-c. 1-Avengers app. 4-Spider-Man-c/app. 3.00
5-12: Mayhew-c. 9-12-Pelletier-a. 10-Origin of Titania 3.00
Vol. 1: Single Green Female TPB (2004, $14.99) r/#1-6 15.00
Vol. 2: Superhuman Law TPB (2005, $14.99) r/#7-12 15.00

SHE-HULK (2nd series)
Marvel Comics: Dec, 2005 - No. 38, Apr, 2009 ($2.99)

1,2,4-7,9-24: 1-Bobillo-a/Slott-s/Horn-c. 1-New Avengers app. 2-Hawkeye-c/app. 9-Jen marries John Jameson. 12-Thanos app. 16-Wolverine app. 3.00
3-($3.99) 100th She-Hulk issue; new story w/art by various incl. Bobillo, Conner, Mayhew & Powell; r/Savage She-Hulk #1 and r/Sensational She-Hulk #1 4.00
8-Civil War 15.00
8-2nd printing with variant Bobillo-c 3.00
25-($3.99) Intro. the Behemoth; Juggernaut cameo; Handbook bio pages of She-Hulk 4.00
26-37: 27-Iron Man app. 30-Hercules app. 31-X-Factor app. 32,33-Secret Invasion 3.00
38-($3.99) Thundra, Valkyrie and Invisible Woman app. 4.00
...: Cosmic Collision 1 (2/09, $3.99) Lady Liberators app.; David-s/Asrar-a/Sejic-c 4.00
... Sensational 1 (5/10, $4.99) 30th Anniversary celebration; Stan Lee app.; Frank-c 5.00
Vol. 3: Time Trials (2006, $14.99) r/#1-5; Bobillo sketch page 15.00
Vol. 4: Laws of Attraction (2007, $19.99) r/#6-12; Paul Smith sketch page 20.00
Vol. 5: Planet Without a Hulk (2007, $19.99) r/#14-21; Slott's original series pitch 20.00
...: Jaded HC (2008, $19.99) r/#22-27; cover gallery 20.00

SHE-HULKS
Marvel Comics: Jan, 2011 - No. 4, Apr, 2011 ($3.99/$2.99, limited series)

1-($3.99) She-Hulk & Lyra team-up; Stegman-a/McGuinness-c; character profile pages 4.00
2-4-($2.99) McGuinness-c 3.00

SHERIFF BOB DIXON'S CHUCK WAGON (TV) (See Wild Bill Hickok #22)
Avon Periodicals: Nov, 1950

1-Kinstler-c/a(3) 14 28 42 76 108 140

SHERIFF OF TOMBSTONE
Charlton Comics: Nov, 1958 - No. 17, Sept, 1961

V1#1-Giordano-c; Severin-a 6 12 18 41 66 90
2 4 8 12 22 34 45
3-10 3 6 9 17 25 32
11-17 3 6 9 14 20 25

SHERLOCK HOLMES (See Marvel Preview, New Adventures of..., & Spectacular Stories)

SHERLOCK HOLMES (All New Baffling Adventures of...)(Young Eagle #3 on?)
Charlton Comics: Oct, 1955 - No. 2, Mar, 1956

1-Dr. Neff, Ghost Breaker app. 40 80 120 243 402 560
2 35 70 105 208 339 470

SHERLOCK HOLMES (Also see The Joker)
National Periodical Publications: Sept-Oct, 1975

1-Cruz-a; Simonson-c 3 6 9 16 23 30

SHERLOCK HOLMES
Dynamite Entertainment: 2009 - No. 5, 2009 ($3.50, limited series)

1-5-Cassaday-c/Moore & Reppion-s/Aaron Campbell-a 3.50

SHERLOCK HOLMES: YEAR ONE
Dynamite Entertainment: 2011 - Present ($3.99, limited series)

1-Beatty-s; multiple covers on each 4.00

SHERRY THE SHOWGIRL (Showgirls #4)
Atlas Comics: July, 1956 - No. 3, Dec, 1956; No. 5, Apr, 1957 - No. 7, Aug, 1957

1-Dan DeCarlo-c/a in all 19 38 57 111 176 240
2 14 28 42 76 108 140

Shi: Black, White and Red #2 © Billy Tucci

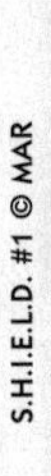
S.H.I.E.L.D. #1 © MAR

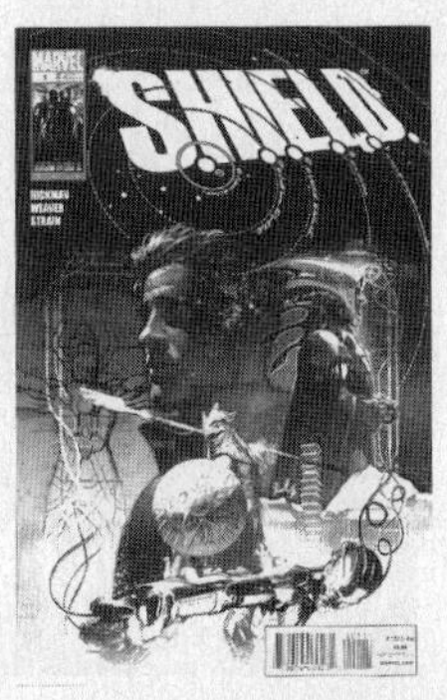

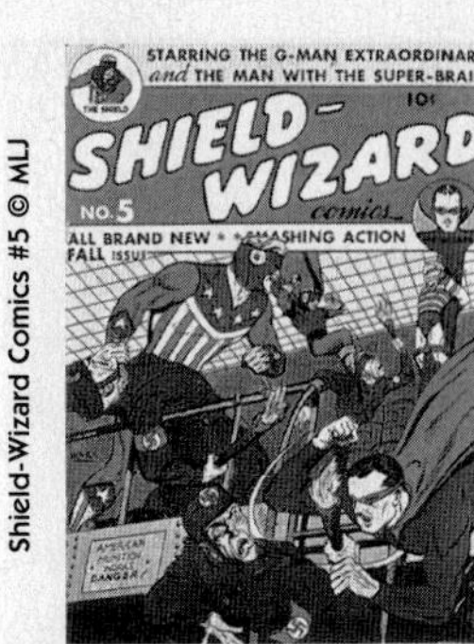

Shield-Wizard Comics #5 © MLJ

	GD 2.0	VG 4.0	FN 6.0	VF 8.0	VF/NM 9.0	NM- 9.2

3,5-7 — 12 24 36 67 94 120

SHE'S JOSIE (See Josie)

SHEVA'S WAR
DC Comics (Helix): Oct, 1998 - No. 5, Feb, 1999 ($2.95, mini-series)

1-5-Christopher Moeller-s/painted-a/c — 3.00

SHI (one-shots and TPBs)
Crusade Comics

...: Akai (2001, $2.99)-Intro. Victoria Cross; Tucci-a/c; J.C. Vaughn-s — 3.00
...: Akai Victoria Cross Ed. ($5.95, edition of 2000) variant Tucci-c — 6.00
...: C.G.I. (2001, $4.99) preview of unpublished series — 5.00
.../ Cyblade: The Battle for the Independents (9/95, $2.95) Tucci-c; Hellboy, Bone app. — 3.00
.../ Cyblade: The Battle for the Independents (9/95, $2.95) Silvestri variant-c — 3.00
.../ Daredevil: Honor Thy Mother (1/97, $2.95) Flip book — 3.00
...: Judgment Night (200, $3.99) Wolverine app.; Battlebook card and pages; Tucci-a — 4.00
...: Kaidan (10/96, $2.95) Two covers; Tucci-c; Jae Lee wraparound-c — 3.00
...: Masquerade (3/98, $3.50) Painted art by Lago, Texeira, and others — 3.50
...: Nightstalkers (9/97, $3.50) Painted art by Val Mayerik — 3.50
...: Rekishi (1/97, $2.95) Character bios and story summaries of Shi: The Way of the Warrior told in Detective Joe Labianca's point of view; Christopher Golden script; Tucci-c; J.G. Jones-a; flip book w/Shi: East Wind Rain preview — 3.00
...: The Art of War Tourbook (1998, $4.95) Blank cover for sketches; early Tucci-a inside — 5.00
.../ Vampirella (10/97, $2.95) Ellis-s/Lau-a — 3.00
... Vs. Tomoe (8/96, $3.95) Tucci-a/scripts; wraparound foil-c — 4.00
... Vs. Tomoe (6/96, $5.00. B&W)-Preview Ed.; sold at San Diego Comic Con — 5.00
The Definitive Shi Vol. 1 (2006-2007, $24.99, TPB) B&W r/Way of the Warrior, Tomoe, Rekishi, and Senryaku series; cover gallery with sketches; Tucci & Sparacio-c — 25.00

SHI: BLACK, WHITE AND RED
Crusade Comics: Mar, 1998 - No. 2, May, 1998 ($2.95, B&W&Red, mini-series)

1,2-J.G. Jones-painted art — 3.00
...- Year of the Dragon Collected Edition (2000, $5.95) r/#1&2 — 6.00

SHIDIMA
Image Comics: Jan, 2001 - No. 7, Nov, 2002 ($2.95, limited series)

1-7-Prequel to Warlands — 3.00
#0-(10/01, $2.25) Short story and sketch pages — 3.00

SHI: EAST WIND RAIN
Crusade Comics: Nov, 1997 - No. 2, Feb, 1998 ($3.50, limited series)

1,2-Shi at WW2 Pearl Harbor — 3.50

S.H.I.E.L.D. (Nick Fury & His Agents of...) (Also see Nick Fury)
Marvel Comics Group: Feb, 1973 - No. 5, Oct, 1973 (All 20¢ issues)

1-All contain reprint stories from Strange Tales #146-155; new Steranko-c — 3 6 9 14 19 24
2-New Steranko flag-c — 2 4 6 10 14 18
3-5: 3-Kirby/Steranko-c(r). 4-Steranko-c(r) — 2 4 6 8 10 12

NOTE: *Buscema a-3p(r). Kirby layouts 1-5; c-3 (w/Steranko). Steranko a-3r, 4r(2).*

S.H.I.E.L.D.
Marvel Comics: Jun, 2010 - Present ($3.99/$2.99)

1-($3.99) Leonardo DaVinci app.; Weaver-a/Hickman-s/Parel-c; 4 printings — 4.00
1-Variant-c by Weaver — 6.00
1-Director's Cut (9/10, $4.99) r/#1 with character sketch-a and bios; design-a — 5.00
2-6-($2.99) 2-Three printings. 3-Galactus app. — 3.00
Infinity (6/11, $4.99) DaVinci, Nostradamus, Newton & Tesla app.; Parel-c — 5.00

SHIELD, THE (Becomes Shield-Steel Sterling #3; #1 titled Lancelot Strong; also see Advs. of the Fly, Double Life of Private Strong, Fly Man, Mighty Comics, The Mighty Crusaders, The Original... & Pep Comics #1)
Archie Enterprises, Inc.: June, 1983 - No. 2, Aug, 1983

1,2: Steel Sterling app. 2-Kanigher-s — 4.00
America's 1st Patriotic Comic Book Hero, The Shield (2002, $12.95, TPB) r/Pep Comics #1-5, Shield-Wizard Comics #1; foreward by Robert M. Overstreet — 13.00

SHIELD, THE (Archie Ent. character) (Continued from The Red Circle)
DC Comics: Nov, 2009 - No. 10, Aug, 2010 ($3.99)

1-10: 1-Magog app.; Inferno back-up feature thru #6; Green Arrow app. 2,3-Grodd app. 7-10-The Fox back-up feature; Oeming-a — 4.00
...: Kicking Down the Door TPB ('10, $19.99) r/#1-6, Red Circle: The Web & RC: The Shield — 20.00

SHIELD, THE: SPOTLIGHT (TV)
IDW Publishing: Jan, 2004 - No. 5, May, 2004 ($3.99)

1-5-Jeff Marriote-s/Jean Diaz-a/Tommy Lee Edwards-c — 4.00
TPB (7/04, $19.99) r/#1-5; Michael Chiklis photo-c — 20.00

SHIELD-STEEL STERLING (Formerly The Shield)
Archie Enterprises, Inc.: No. 3, Dec, 1983 (Becomes Steel Sterling No. 4)

3-Nino-a; Steel Sterling by Kanigher & Barreto — 3.00

SHIELD WIZARD COMICS (Also see Pep Comics & Top-Notch Comics)
MLJ Magazines: Summer, 1940 - No. 13, Spring, 1944

1-(V1#5 on inside)-Origin The Shield by Irving Novick & The Wizard by Ed Ashe, Jr; Flag-c — 514 1028 1542 3750 6625 9500
2-(Winter/40)-Origin The Shield retold; Wizard's sidekick, Roy the Super Boy begins (see Top-Notch #8 for 1st app.) — 271 542 813 1734 2967 4200
3,4 — 171 342 513 1086 1868 2650
5-Dusty, the Boy Detective begins; Nazi bondage-c — 148 296 444 947 1624 2300
6,7: 6-Roy the Super Boy app. 7-Shield dons new costume (Summer, 1942); S & K-c? — 142 284 426 909 1555 2200
8-Nazi bondage-c; Hitler photo on-c — 155 310 465 992 1696 2400
9-Japanese WWII bondage-c — 107 214 321 680 1165 1650
10-Nazi swastica-c — 110 220 330 704 1202 1700
11,12 — 100 200 300 635 1093 1550
13-Japanese WWII bondage/torture-c (scarce) — 116 232 348 742 1271 1800

NOTE: *Bob Montana c-13. Novick c-1,3-6,8-11. Harry Sahle c-12.*

SHI: FAN EDITIONS
Crusade Comics: 1997

1-3-Two covers polybagged in FAN #19-21 — 3.00
1-3-Gold editions — 4.00

SHI: HEAVEN AND EARTH
Crusade Comics: June, 1997 - No. 4, Apr, 1998 ($2.95)

1-4 — 3.00
4-($4.95) Pencil-c variant — 5.00
Rising Sun Edition-signed by Tucci in FanClub Starter Pack — 4.00
"Tora No Shi" variant-c — 3.00

SHI: JU-NEN
Dark Horse Comics: July, 2004 - No. 4, May, 2005 ($2.99, mini-series)

1-4-Tucci-a/Tucci & Vaughn-s; origin retold — 3.00
TPB (2/06, $12.95) r/#1-4; Tucci and Sparacio-c — 13.00

SHINING KNIGHT (See Adventure Comics #66)

SHINOBI (Based on Sega video game)
Dark Horse Comics: Aug, 2002 ($2.99, one-shot)

1-Medina-a/c — 3.00

SHIP AHOY
Spotlight Publishers: Nov, 1944 (52 pgs.)

1-L. B. Cole-c — 19 38 57 109 172 235

SHIP OF FOOLS
Image Comics: Aug, 1997 - No. 3 ($2.95, B&W)

0-3-Glass-s/Oeming-a — 3.00

SHI: POISONED PARADISE
Avatar Press: July, 2002 - No. 2, Aug, 2002 ($3.50, limited series)

1,2-Vaughn and Tucci-s/Waller-a; 1-Four covers — 3.50

SHIPWRECKED! (Disney-Movie)
Disney Comics: 1990 ($5.95, graphic novel, 68 pgs.)

nn-adaptation; Spiegle-a — 6.00

SHI: SEMPO
Avatar Press: Aug, 2003 - No. 2, ($3.50, B&W, limited series)

1,2-Vaughn and Tucci-s/Alves-a; 1-Four covers — 3.50

SHI: SENRYAKU
Crusade Comics: Aug, 1995 - No. 3, Nov, 1995 ($2.95, limited series)

1-3: 1-Tucci-c; Quesada, Darrow, Sim, Lee, Smith-a. 2-Tucci-c; Silvestri, Balent, Perez, Mack-a. 3-Jusko-c; Hughes, Ramos, Bell, Moore-a — 3.00
1-variant-c (no logo) — 4.00
Hardcover ($24.95)-r/#1-3; Frazetta-c. — 25.00
Trade Paperback ($13.95)-r/#1-3; Frazetta-c. — 14.00

SHI: THE ILLUSTRATED WARRIOR
Crusade Comics: 2002 - No. 7, 2003 ($2.99, B&W)

1-7-Story text with Tucci full page art — 3.00

SHI: THE SERIES
Crusade Comics: Aug, 1997 - No. 13 ($2.95, color #1-10, B&W #11)

1-10 — 3.00

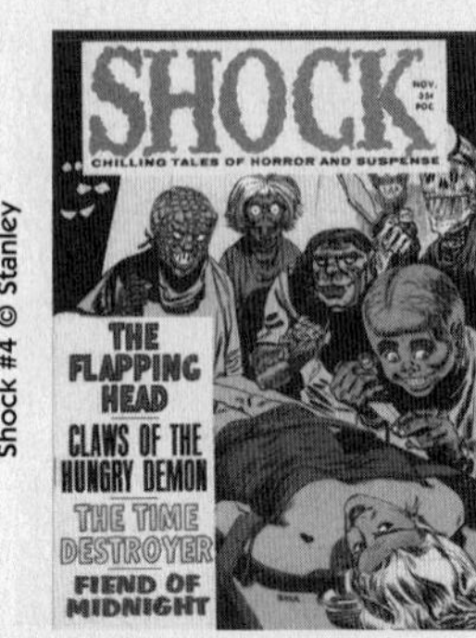

Shock #4 © Stanley

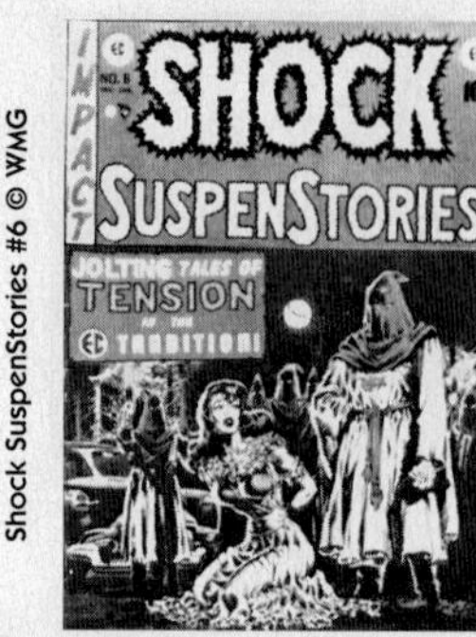

Shock SuspenStories #6 © WMG

Showcase #6 © DC

	GD 2.0	VG 4.0	FN 6.0	VF 8.0	VF/NM 9.0	NM- 9.2
11-13: 11-B&W. 12-Color; Lau-a						3.00
#0 Convention Edition						5.00

SHI: THE WAY OF THE WARRIOR
Crusade Comics: Mar, 1994 - No. 12, Apr, 1997 ($2.50/$2.95)

	GD	VG	FN	VF	VF/NM	NM-
1/2						4.00
1	2	4	6	8	10	12
1-Commemorative ed., B&W, new-c; given out at 1994 San Diego Comic Con	2	4	6	10	14	18
1-Fan appreciation edition -r/#1						3.00
1-Fan appreciation edition (variant)						6.00
1- 10th Anniversary Edition (2004, $2.99)						3.00
2						5.00
2-Commemorative edition (3,000)	2	4	6	9	13	16
2-Fan appreciation edition -r/#2						3.00
3						4.00
4-7: 4-Silvestri poster. 7-Tomoe app.						3.00
5,6: 5-Silvestri variant-c. 6-Tomoe #1 variant-c						3.50
5-Gold edition						12.00
6,8-12: 6-Fan appreciation edition						3.00
8-Combo Gold edition						6.00
8-Signed Edition-(5000)						3.00
Trade paperback (1995, $12.95)-r/#1-4						13.00
Trade paperback (1995, $14.95)-r/#1-4 revised; Julie Bell-c						15.00

SHI: YEAR OF THE DRAGON
Crusade Comics: 2000 - No. 3, 2000 ($2.99, limited series)

	GD	VG	FN	VF	VF/NM	NM-
1-3: 1-Two covers; Tucci-a/c; flashback to teen-aged Ana						3.00

SHMOO (See Al Capp's... & Washable Jones &...)

SHOCK (Magazine)
Stanley Publ.: May, 1969 - V3#4, Sept, 1971 (B&W reprints from horror comics, including some pre-code) (No V2#1,3)

	GD	VG	FN	VF	VF/NM	NM-
V1#1-Cover-r/Weird Tales of the Future #7 by Bernard Baily; r/Weird Chills #1	7	14	21	49	80	110
2-Wolverton-r/Weird Mysteries 5; r-Weird Mysteries #7 used in **SOTI**; cover reprints cover to Weird Chills #1	6	12	18	37	59	80
3,5,6	4	8	12	26	41	55
4-Harrison/Williamson-r/Forbid. Worlds #6	4	8	12	28	44	60
V2#2(5/70), V1#8(7/70), V2#4(9/70)-6(1/71), V3#1-4: V2#4-Cover swipe from Weird Mysteries #6	4	8	12	24	37	50

NOTE: ***Disbrow** r-V2#4; Bondage c-V1#4, V2#6, V3#1.*

SHOCK DETECTIVE CASES (Formerly Crime Fighting Detective) (Becomes Spook Detective Cases No. 22)
Star Publications: No. 20, Sept, 1952 - No. 21, Nov, 1952

	GD	VG	FN	VF	VF/NM	NM-
20,21-L.B. Cole-c; based on true crime cases	23	46	69	136	223	310

NOTE: ***Palais** a-20. No. 21-Fox-r.*

SHOCK ILLUSTRATED (...Adult Crime Stories; Magazine format)
E. C. Comics: Sept-Oct, 1955 - No. 3, Spring, 1956 (Adult Entertainment on-c #1,2)(All 25¢)

	GD	VG	FN	VF	VF/NM	NM-
1-All by Kamen; drugs, prostitution, wife swapping	18	36	54	105	165	225
2-Williamson-a redrawn from Crime SuspenStories #13 plus Ingels, Crandall, Evans & part Torres-i; painted-c	19	38	57	109	172	235
3-Only 100 known copies bound & given away at E.C. office; Crandall, Evans-a; painted-c; shows May, 1956 on-c	116	232	348	742	1271	1800

SHOCKING MYSTERY CASES (Formerly Thrilling Crime Cases)
Star Publications: No. 50, Sept, 1952 - No. 60, Oct, 1954 (All crime reprints?)

	GD	VG	FN	VF	VF/NM	NM-
50-Disbrow "Frankenstein" story	42	84	126	265	445	625
51-Disbrow-a	27	54	81	158	259	360
52-60: 56-Drug use story	25	50	75	147	241	335

NOTE: ***L. B. Cole** covers on all; a-60(2 pgs.). **Hollingsworth** a-52. **Morisi** a-55.*

SHOCKING TALES DIGEST MAGAZINE
Harvey Publications: Oct, 1981 (95¢)

	GD	VG	FN	VF	VF/NM	NM-
1-1957-58-r; Powell, Kirby, Nostrand-a	2	4	6	9	13	16

SHOCK ROCKETS
Image Comics (Gorilla): Apr, 2000 - No. 6, Oct, 2000 ($2.50)

	GD	VG	FN	VF	VF/NM	NM-
1-6-Busiek-s/Immonen & Grawbadger-a. 6-Flip book w/Superstar preview						3.00
...: We Have Ignition TPB (Dark Horse, 8/04, $14.95, 6" x 9") r/#1-6						15.00

SHOCK SUSPENSTORIES (Also see EC Archives • Shock SuspenStories)
E. C. Comics: Feb-Mar, 1952 - No. 18, Dec-Jan, 1954-55

	GD	VG	FN	VF	VF/NM	NM-
1-Classic Feldstein electrocution-c	89	178	267	712	1131	1550
2	47	94	141	376	601	825
3,4: 4-Used in **SOTI**, pg. 387,388	36	72	108	288	457	625
5-Hanging-c	43	86	129	344	547	750
6-Classic hooded vigilante bondage-c	60	120	180	480	765	1050
7-Classic face melting-c	56	112	168	448	712	975
8-Williamson-a	34	68	102	272	436	600
9-11: 9-Injury to eye panel. 10-Junkie story	30	60	90	240	383	525
12- "The Monkey" classic junkie cover/story; anti-drug propaganda issue	39	78	117	312	494	675
13-Frazetta's only solo story for E.C., 7 pgs.	41	82	123	328	527	725
14-Used in Senate Investigation hearings	25	50	75	200	318	435
15-Used in 1954 Reader's Digest article, "For the Kiddies to Read"	22	44	66	176	281	385
16-18: 16- "Red Dupe" editorial; rape story	21	42	63	168	264	360

NOTE: ***Ray Bradbury** adaptations-1, 7, 9. **Craig** a-11; c-11. **Crandall** a-9-13, 15-18. **Davis** a-1-5. **Evans** a-7, 8, 14-18; c-16-18. **Feldstein** c-1, 7-9, 12. **Ingels** a-1, 2, 6. **Kamen** a-in all; c-10, 13, 15. **Krigstein** a-14, 18. **Orlando** a-1, 3-7, 9, 10, 12, 16, 17. **Wood** a-2-15; c-2-6, 14.*

SHOCK SUSPENSTORIES (Also see EC Archives • Shock SuspenStories)
Russ Cochran/Gemstone Publishing: Sept, 1992 - No. 18, Dec, 1996 ($1.50/$2.00/$2.50, quarterly)

	GD	VG	FN	VF	VF/NM	NM-
1-18: 1-3: Reprints with original-c. 17-r/HOF #17						3.00

SHOGUN WARRIORS
Marvel Comics Group: Feb, 1979 - No. 20, Sept, 1980 (Based on Mattel toys of the classic Japanese animation characters) (1-3: 35¢; 4-19: 40¢; 20: 50¢)

	GD	VG	FN	VF	VF/NM	NM-
1-Raydeen, Combatra, & Dangard Ace begin; Trimpe-a	2	4	6	9	12	15
2-20: 2-Lord Maurkon & Elementals of Evil app.; Rok-Korr app. 6-Shogun vs. Shogun. 7,8-Cerberus. 9-Starchild. 11-Austin-c. 12-Simonson-c. 14-16-Doctor Demonicus. 17-Juggernaut. 19,20-FF x-over	2	3	4	6	8	10

SHOOK UP (Magazine) (Satire)
Dodsworth Publ. Co.: Nov, 1958

	GD	VG	FN	VF	VF/NM	NM-
V1#1	4	8	12	28	44	60

SHORT RIBS
Dell Publishing Co.: No. 1333, Apr - June, 1962

	GD	VG	FN	VF	VF/NM	NM-
Four Color 1333	5	10	15	34	55	75

SHORTSTOP SQUAD (Baseball)
Ultimate Sports Ent. Inc.: 1999 ($3.95, one-shot)

	GD	VG	FN	VF	VF/NM	NM-
1-Ripken Jr., Larkin, Jeter, Rodriguez app.; Edwards-c/a						4.00

SHORT STORY COMICS (See Hello Pal,...)

SHORTY SHINER (The Five-Foot Fighter in the Ten Gallon Hat)
Dandy Magazine (Charles Biro): June, 1956 - No. 3, Oct, 1956

	GD	VG	FN	VF	VF/NM	NM-
1	7	14	21	37	46	55
2,3	5	10	15	24	30	35

SHOTGUN SLADE (TV)
Dell Publishing Co.: No. 1111, July-Sept, 1960

	GD	VG	FN	VF	VF/NM	NM-
Four Color 1111-Photo-c	6	12	18	41	66	90

SHOWCASE (See Cancelled Comic Cavalcade & New Talent...)
National Per. Publ./DC Comics: 3-4/56 - No. 93, 9/70; No. 94, 8-9/77 - No. 104, 9/78

	GD	VG	FN	VF	VF/NM	NM-
1-Fire Fighters; w/Fireman Farrell	278	556	834	2433	4967	7500
2-Kings of the Wild; Kubert-a (animal stories)	85	170	255	723	1462	2200
3-The Frogmen by Russ Heath; Heath greytone-c (early DC example, 7-8/56)	89	178	267	757	1529	2300
4-Origin/1st app. The Flash (1st DC Silver Age hero, Sept-Oct, 1956); Kanigher-s; Infantino & Kubert-c/a; 1st app. Iris West and The Turtle; r/in Secret Origins #1 ('61 & '73); Flash shown reading G.A. Flash Comics #13; back-up story w/Broome-s/Infantino & Kubert-a	1650	3300	4950	17,500	36,750	56,000
5-Manhunters; Meskin-a	83	166	249	706	1428	2150
6-Origin/1st app. Challengers of the Unknown by Kirby, partly r/in Secret Origins #1 & Challengers #64,65 (1st S.A. hero team & 1st original concept S.A. series)(1-2/57)	304	608	912	2736	5618	8500
7-Challengers of the Unknown by Kirby (2nd app.) reprinted in Challengers of the Unknown #75	152	304	456	1330	2715	4100
8-The Flash (5-6/57, 2nd app.); origin & 1st app. Captain Cold	840	1680	2520	7600	13,050	18,500
9-Lois Lane (Pre-#1, 7-8/57) (1st Showcase character to win own series) Superman app. on-c	660	1320	1980	5280	9640	14,000
10-Lois Lane; Jor-El cameo; Superman app. on-c	237	474	711	2074	4237	6400
11-Challengers of the Unknown by Kirby (3rd)	144	288	432	1224	2487	3750
12-Challengers of the Unknown by Kirby (4th)	144	288	432	1224	2487	3750
13-The Flash (3rd app.); origin Mr. Element	307	614	921	2763	5682	8600

Showcase #34 © DC

Showcase #75 © DC

Showcase #96 © DC

	GD 2.0	VG 4.0	FN 6.0	VF 8.0	VF/NM 9.0	NM- 9.2
14-The Flash (4th app.); origin Dr. Alchemy, former Mr. Element (rare in NM)	329	658	987	2961	6081	9200
15-Space Ranger (7-8/58, 1st app., also see My Greatest Aventure #22)	156	312	468	1365	2783	4200
16-Space Ranger (9-10/58, 2nd app.)	77	154	231	655	1328	2000
17-(11-12/58)-Adventures on Other Worlds; origin/1st app. Adam Strange by Gardner Fox & Mike Sekowsky	193	386	579	1689	3445	5200
18-Adventures on Other Worlds (2nd A. Strange)	96	192	288	816	1658	2500
19-Adam Strange; 1st Adam Strange logo	104	208	312	884	1792	2700
20-Rip Hunter; origin & 1st app. (5-6/59); Moreira-a	85	170	255	723	1462	2200
21-Rip Hunter (7-8/59, 2nd app.); Sekowsky-c/a	45	90	135	360	730	1100
22-Origin & 1st app. Silver Age Green Lantern by Gil Kane and John Broome (9-10/59); reprinted in Secret Origins #2	633	1266	1900	5600	10,800	16,000
23-Green Lantern (11-12/59, 2nd app.); nuclear explosion-c	156	312	468	1365	2783	4200
24-Green Lantern (1-2/60, 3rd app.)	156	312	468	1365	2783	4200
25,26-Rip Hunter by Kubert. 25-Grey tone-c	38	76	114	304	602	900
27-Sea Devils (7-8/60, 1st app.); Heath-c/a	77	154	231	655	1328	2000
28-Sea Devils (9-10/60, 2nd app.); Heath-c/a	40	80	120	320	635	950
29-Sea Devils; Heath-c/a; grey tone c-27-29	43	86	129	344	697	1050
30-Origin Silver Age Aquaman (1-2/61) (see Adventure #260 for 1st S.A. origin)	77	154	231	655	1328	2000
31,32-Aquaman	40	80	120	320	635	950
33-Aquaman	40	80	120	320	635	950
34-Origin & 1st app. Silver Age Atom by Gil Kane & Murphy Anderson (9-10/61); reprinted in Secret Origins #2	115	230	345	978	1989	3000
35-The Atom by Gil Kane (2nd); last 10¢ issue	54	108	162	459	930	1400
36-The Atom by Gil Kane (1-2/62, 3rd app.)	43	86	129	344	697	1050
37-Metal Men (3-4/62, 1st app.)	58	116	174	493	997	1500
38-Metal Men (5-6/62, 2nd app.)	33	66	99	258	509	760
39-Metal Men (7-8/62, 3rd app.)	26	52	78	186	373	560
40-Metal Men (9-10/62, 4th app.)	23	46	69	168	334	500
41,42-Tommy Tomorrow (parts 1 & 2). 42-Origin	14	28	42	102	206	310
43-Dr. No (James Bond); Nodel-a; originally published as British Classics Illustrated #158A & as #6 in a European Detective series, all with diff. painted-c. This Showcase #43 version is actually censored, deleting all racial skin color and dialogue thought to be racially demeaning (1st DC S.A. movie adaptation)(based on Ian Fleming novel & movie)	45	90	135	360	730	1100
44-Tommy Tomorrow	11	22	33	77	144	210
45-Sgt. Rock (7-8/63); pre-dates B&B #52; origin retold; Heath-c	36	72	108	280	553	825
46,47-Tommy Tomorrow	10	20	30	71	128	185
48,49-Cave Carson (3rd tryout series; see B&B)	9	18	27	63	107	150
50,51-I Spy (Danger Trail-r by Infantino), King Farady story (#50 has new 4 pg. story)	8	16	24	56	93	130
52-Cave Carson	8	16	24	58	97	135
53,54-G.I. Joe (11-12/64, 1-2/65); Heath-a	11	22	33	77	144	210
55-Dr. Fate & Hourman (3-4/65); origin of each in text; 1st solo app. G.A. Green Lantern in Silver Age (pre-dates Gr. Lantern #40); 1st S.A. app. Solomon Grundy	23	46	69	168	334	500
56-Dr. Fate & Hourman	14	28	42	96	191	285
57-Enemy Ace by Kubert (7-8/65, 4th app. after Our Army at War #155)	21	42	63	150	300	450
58-Enemy Ace by Kubert (5th app.)	17	34	51	118	242	365
59-Teen Titans (11-12/65, 3rd app.)	16	32	48	111	226	340
60-1st S. A. app. The Spectre; Anderson-a (1-2/66); origin in text	26	52	78	190	383	575
61-The Spectre by Anderson (2nd app.)	13	26	39	94	185	275
62-Origin & 1st app. Inferior Five (5-6/66)	9	18	27	65	113	160
63,65-Inferior Five. 63-Hulk parody. 65-X-Men parody (11-12/66)	6	12	18	43	69	95
64-The Spectre by Anderson (5th app.)	13	26	39	92	179	265
66,67-B'wana Beast	6	12	18	39	62	85
68-Maniaks (1st app., spoof of The Monkees)	6	12	18	41	66	90
69,71-Maniaks. 71-Woody Allen-c/app.	6	12	18	39	62	85
70-Binky (9-10/67)-Tryout issue; 1950's Leave It To Binky reprints with art changes	6	12	18	43	69	95
72-Top Gun (Johnny Thunder-r)-Toth-a	5	10	15	34	55	75
73-Origin/1st app. Creeper; Ditko-c/a (3-4/68)	12	24	36	82	154	225
74-Intro/1st app. Anthro; Post-c/a (5/68)	8	16	24	58	97	135
75-Origin/1st app. Hawk & the Dove; Ditko-c/a	11	22	33	75	138	200
76-1st app. Bat Lash (8/68)	8	16	24	58	97	135
77-1st app. Angel & The Ape (9/68)	7	14	21	49	80	110
78-1st app. Jonny Double (11/68)	5	10	15	32	51	70
79-1st app. Dolphin (12/68); Aqualad origin-r	6	12	18	43	69	95
80-1st S.A. app. Phantom Stranger (1/69); Neal Adams-c	10	20	30	71	128	185
81-Windy & Willy; r/Many Loves of Dobie Gillis #26 with art changes	6	12	18	39	62	85
82-1st app. Nightmaster (5/69) by Grandenetti & Giordano; Kubert-c	7	14	21	49	80	110
83,84-Nightmaster by Wrightson w/Jones/Kaluta ink assist in each; Kubert-c. 83-Last 12¢ issue 84-Origin retold; begin 15¢	7	14	21	49	80	110
85-87-Firehair; Kubert-a	3	6	9	16	23	30
88-90-Jason's Quest: 90-Manhunter 2070 app.	3	6	9	14	20	25
91-93-Manhunter 2070: 92-Origin. 93-(9/70) Last 15¢ issue	3	6	9	14	20	25
94-Intro/origin new Doom Patrol & Robotman(8-9/77)	2	4	6	11	16	20
95,96-The Doom Patrol. 95-Origin Celsius	2	3	4	6	8	10
97-99-Power Girl; origin-97,98; JSA cameos	2	4	6	8	10	12
100-(52 pgs.)-Most Showcase characters featured	2	4	6	11	16	20
101-103-Hawkman; Adam Strange x-over	2	3	4	6	8	10
104-(52 pgs.)-O.S.S. Spies at War	2	3	4	6	8	10

NOTE: ***Anderson*** *a-22-24i, 34-36i, 55, 56, 60, 61, 64, 101-103i; c-50i, 51i, 55, 56, 60, 61, 64.* ***Aparo*** *c-94-96.* ***Boring*** *c-10.* ***Estrada*** *a-104.* ***Fraden*** *c(p)-30, 31, 33.* ***Heath*** *c-3, 27-29.* ***Infantino*** *c/a(p)-4, 8, 13, 14; c-50p, 51p.* ***Gil Kane*** *a-22-24p, 34-36p; c-17-19, 22-24p(w/****Giella****), 31.* ***Kane/Anderson*** *c-34-36.* ***Kirby*** *c-11, 12.* ***Kirby/Stein*** *c-6, 7.* ***Kubert*** *a-2, 4i, 25, 26, 45, 53, 54, 72; c-25, 26, 53, 54, 57, 58, 82-87, 101-104; c-2, 4i.* ***Moreira*** *c-5.* ***Orlando*** *a-62p, 63p, 97i; c-62, 63, 97i.* ***Sekowsky*** *a-65p.* ***Sparling*** *a-78.* ***Staton*** *a-94, 95-99p, 100; c-97-100p.*

SHOWCASE '93
DC Comics: Jan, 1993 - No. 12, Dec, 1993 ($1.95, limited series, 52 pgs.)

1-12: 1-Begin 4 part Catwoman story & 6 part Blue Devil story; begin Cyborg story; Art Adams/Austin-c. 3-Flash by Charest (p). 6-Azrael in Bat-costume (2 pgs.). 7,8-Knightfall parts 13 & 14. 6-10-Deathstroke app. (6,10-cameo). 9,10-Austin-i. 10-Azrael as Batman in new costume app.; Gulacy-c. 11-Perez-c. 12-Creeper app.; Alan Grant scripts 4.00

NOTE: ***Chaykin*** *c-9.* ***Fabry*** *c-8.* ***Giffen*** *a-12.* ***Golden*** *c-3.* ***Zeck*** *c-6.*

SHOWCASE '94
DC Comics: Jan, 1994 - No. 12, Dec, 1994 ($1.95, limited series, 52 pgs.)

1-12: 1,2-Joker & Gunfire stories. 1-New Gods. 4-Riddler story. 5-Huntress-c/story w/app. new Batman. 6-Huntress-c/story w/app. Robin; Atom story. 7-Penguin story by Peter David, P. Craig Russell, & Michael T. Gilbert; Penguin-c by Jae Lee. 8,9-Scarface origin story by Alan Grant, John Wagner,& Teddy Kristiansen; Prelude to Zero Hour. 10-Zero Hour tie-in story. 11-Man-Bat. 4.00

NOTE: ***Alan Grant*** *scripts-3, 4.* ***Kelley Jones*** *c-12.* ***Mignola*** *c-3.* ***Nebres*** *a(i)-2.* ***Quesada*** *c-10.* ***Russell*** *a-7p.* ***Simonson*** *c-5.*

SHOWCASE '95
DC Comics: Jan, 1995 - No. 12, Dec, 1995 ($2.50/$2.95, limited series)

1-4-Supergirl story. 3-Eradicator-c.; The Question story. 4-Thorn c/story 4.00
5-12: 5-Thorn-c/story; begin $2.95-c. 8-Spectre story. 12-The Shade story by James Robinson & Wade Von Grawbadger; Maitresse story by Claremont & Alan Davis 4.00

SHOWCASE '96
DC Comics: Jan, 1996 - No. 12, Dec, 1996 ($2.95, limited series)

1-12: 1-Steve Geppi cameo. 3-Black Canary & Lois Lane-c/story; Deadman story by Jamie Delano & Wade Von Grawbadger, Gary Frank-c. 4-Firebrand & Guardian-c/story; The Shade & Dr. Fate "Times Past" story by James Robinson & Matt Smith begins, ends #5. 6-Superboy-c/app.; Atom app.; Capt. Marvel (Mary Marvel)-c/app. 8-Supergirl by David & Dodson. 11-Scare Tactics app. 11,12-Legion of Super-Heroes vs. Brainiac. 12-Jesse Quick app. 4.00

SHOWCASE PRESENTS... (B&W archive reprints of DC Silver Age stories)
DC Comics: 2005 - Present ($9.99/$16.99/$17.99/$19.99, B&W, over 500 pgs., squarebound)

Adam Strange Vol. 1 (2007, $16.99) r/Showcase #17-19 & Mystery in Space #53-84 17.00
Ambush Bug (2009, $16.99) r/first app. in DC Comics Presents #52 other early app. 17.00
Aquaman Vol. 1 (2007, $16.99) r/Aquaman #1-6 & other early app. 17.00
Aquaman Vol. 2 (2008, $16.99) r/Aquaman #7-23 & other early app. 17.00
Aquaman Vol. 3 (2009, $16.99) r/Aquaman #24-39 & other early app. 17.00
The Atom Vol. 1 (2007, $16.99) r/Showcase #34-36 & The Atom #1-17 17.00
The Atom Vol. 2 (2008, $16.99) r/The Atom #18-38 17.00
Batgirl Vol. 1 (2007, $16.99) r/early apps. from Detective #359 (1967) thru 1975 17.00
Bat Lash Vol. 1 (2009, $9.99) r/#1-7, Showcase #76, DC Special Series #16, and Jonah Hex #49,51,52 10.00
Batman Vol. 1 (2006, $16.99) r/"new look" from Detective #327-342, Batman #164-174 17.00
Batman Vol. 2 (2007, $16.99) r/"new look" from Detective #343-358, Batman #175-188 17.00
Batman Vol. 3 (2008, $16.99) r/"new look" from Detective #359-375, Batman #189, 190-192,194-197,199-202 17.00
Batman and the Outsiders Vol. 1 (2007, $16.99) r/#1-19, Annual #1; Brave and the Bold #200; and New Teen Titans #37 17.00
Blackhawk Vol. 1 (2008, $16.99) r/#108-127 17.00

Showcase Presents Dial H For Hero © DC

Showcase Presents Superman Family Vol. 3 © DC

Shrek (2010 series) #2 © DreamWorks

GD VG FN VF VF/NM NM-
2.0 4.0 6.0 8.0 9.0 9.2

GD VG FN VF VF/NM NM-
2.0 4.0 6.0 8.0 9.0 9.2

Booster Gold Vol. 1 (2008, $16.99) r/#1-25 & Action Comics #594 17.00
The Brave and the Bold Batman Team-ups Vol. 1 (2007, $16.99) r/#59,64,67-71,74-87 17.00
The Brave and the Bold Batman Team-ups Vol. 2 (2007, $16.99) r/#88-108 17.00
The Brave and the Bold Batman Team-ups Vol. 3 (2008, $16.99) r/#109-134 17.00
Challengers of the Unknown Vol. 1 (2006, $16.99) r/#1-17 & Showcase #6,7,11,12 17.00
Challengers of the Unknown Vol. 2 (2008, $16.99) r/#18-37 17.00
DC Comics Presents: The Superman Team-ups Vol. 1 (2009, $17.99) r/#1-26 18.00
Dial H For Hero ('10, $9.99) r/early apps. in House of Mystery #156-173 10.00
The Doom Patrol Vol. 1 (2009, $16.99) r/#86-101 and My Greatest Adventure #80-85 17.00
The Doom Patrol Vol. 2 (2010, $19.99) r/#102-121 20.00
The Elongated Man Vol. 1 ('06, $16.99) r/early apps. in Flash & Detective ('60-'68) 17.00
Eclipso Vol. 1 (2009, $9.99) r/stories from House of Secrets #61-80 10.00
Enemy Ace Vol. 1 (2008, $16.99) r/Our Army at War #151 & other early app. 17.00
The Flash Vol. 1 (2007, $16.99) r/Flash Comics #104 (last G.A. issue), Showcase #4,8,13,14 & The Flash #105-119 17.00
The Flash Vol. 2 (2008, $16.99) r/The Flash #120-140 17.00
The Flash Vol. 3 (2009, $16.99) r/The Flash #141-161 17.00
The Great Disaster Featuring The Atomic Knights and Hercules Vol. 1 (2007, $16.99) 17.00
Green Arrow Vol. 1 (2006, $16.99) r/Adventure #250-269, Brave and the Bold #50,71,85; Justice League of America #4; World's Finest #95-134,136,138,140 17.00
Green Lantern Vol. 1 (2005, $9.99) r/Showcase #22-24 & Green Lantern #1-17 10.00
Green Lantern Vol. 1 (2010, $19.99) r/Showcase #22-24 & Green Lantern #1-17 20.00
Green Lantern Vol. 2 (2007, $16.99) r/Green Lantern #18-38 17.00
Green Lantern Vol. 3 (2008, $16.99) r/Green Lantern #39-59 17.00
Green Lantern Vol. 4 (2009, $16.99) r/Green Lantern #60-75 17.00
Green Lantern Vol. 5 (2011, $19.99) r/Green Lantern #76-87,89 and back up stories from Flash #217-246 20.00
Haunted Tank Vol. 1 ('06, $16.99) r/G.I. Combat #87-119, Brave & The Bold #52 and Our Army at War #155; Russ Heath-c 17.00
Haunted Tank Vol. 2 ('08, $16.99) r/G.I. Combat #120-156 17.00
Hawkman Vol. 1 ('07, $16.99) r/Brave & The Bold #34-36,42-44, Mystery in Space #87-90, Hawkman #1-11, and The Atom #7 17.00
Hawkman Vol. 2 ('08, $16.99) r/Brave & The Bold #70, Hawkman #12-27, The Atom #31, & The Atom and Hawkman #39-45 17.00
The House of Mystery Vol. 1 ('06, $16.99) r/House of Mystery #174-194 ('68-'71) 17.00
The House of Mystery Vol. 2 ('07, $16.99) r/House of Mystery #195-211 ('71-'73) 17.00
The House of Mystery Vol. 3 ('09, $16.99) r/House of Mystery #212-226 ('73-'74) 17.00
The House of Secrets Vol. 1 ('08, $16.99) r/House of Secrets #81-98 ('69-'72) 17.00
The House of Secrets Vol. 2 ('09, $17.99) r/House of Secrets #99-119 ('72-'74) 18.00
Jonah Hex Vol. 1 (2005, $16.99) r/All Star Western #10-12, Weird Western Tales #13,14, 16-33; plus the complete adventures of Outlaw from All Star Western #2-8 17.00
Justice League of America Vol. 1 ('05, $16.99) r/Brave & the Bold #28-30, J.L. of A. #1-16 and Mystery in Space #75 17.00
Justice League of America Vol. 2 ('07, $16.99) r/Justice League of America #17-36 17.00
Justice League of America Vol. 3 ('07, $16.99) r/Justice League of America #37-60 17.00
Justice League of America Vol. 4 ('09, $16.99) r/Justice League of America #61-83 17.00
Justice League of America Vol. 5 ('11, $19.99) r/Justice League of America #84-106 20.00
Legion of Super-Heroes Vol. 1 ('07, $16.99) r/Adventure #247 & early app. thru 1964 17.00
Legion of Super-Heroes Vol. 2 ('08, $16.99) r/app. in Adventure & Superboy 1964-66 17.00
Legion of Super-Heroes Vol. 3 ('09, $16.99) r/Adventure #349-368 & S.P. Jimmy Olsen #106 17.00
Legion of Super-Heroes Vol. 4 ('10, $19.99) r/app. in Adv., Action & Superboy 1968-72 20.00
Martian Manhunter Vol. 1 (2007, $16.99) r/Detective #225-304 & Batman #78 (prototype) 17.00
Martian Manhunter Vol. 2 ('09, $16.99) r/Detective #305-326 & House of Myst. #143-173 17.00
Metal Men Vol. 1 (2007, $16.99) r/#1-16; Brave & Bold #55, Showcase #37-40 17.00
Metamorpho Vol. 1 ('05, $16.99) r/Brave&Bold #57,58,66,68; Metamorpho #1-17;JLA #42 17.00
Our Army at War Vol. 1 ('10, $19.99) r/#1-20 20.00
Phantom Stranger Vol. 1 (2006, $16.99) r/#1-21 (2nd series) & Showcase #80 17.00
Phantom Stranger Vol. 2 (2008, $16.99) r/#22-41 and various 1970-1978 appearances 17.00
Robin The Boy Wonder Vol. 1 (2007, $16.99) r/back-ups from Batman, Detective, WF 17.00
Secrets of Sinister House ('10, $17.99) r/#5-18 and Sinister House of Secret Love #1-4 18.00
Sgt. Rock Vol. 1 ('07, $16.99) r/G.I. Combat #68, Our Army at War #81-117 17.00
Sgt. Rock Vol. 2 ('08, $16.99) r/Our Army at War #118-148 17.00
Sgt. Rock Vol. 3 ('10, $19.99) r/Our Army at War #149-163,165-172,174-176,178-180 20.00
Shazam! Vol. 1 ('06, $16.99) r/#1-33 17.00
Strange Adventures Vol. 1 ('08, $16.99) r/#54-73 17.00
Supergirl Vol. 1 ('07, $16.99) r/prototype from Superman #123 (8/58); 1st app. Action #252 (5/59) and early appearances thru Nov. 1961 17.00
Supergirl Vol. 2 ('08, $16.99) r/appearances in Action Comics #283-321 (1961-1965) 17.00
Superman Vol. 1 ('05, $9.99) r/Action #241-257 & Superman #122-134 (1958-59) 10.00
Superman Vol. 1 ('10, $19.99) r/Action #241-257 & Superman #122-134 (1958-59) 20.00
Superman Vol. 2 ('06, $16.99) r/Action #258-275 & Superman #134-145 (1959-61) 17.00
Superman Vol. 3 ('07, $16.99) r/Action #279-292 & Superman #146-156 & Annual #3,4 17.00
Superman Vol. 4 ('08, $16.99) r/Action #293-309 & Superman #157-166 (1962-64) 17.00
Superman Family Vol. 1 ('06, $16.99) Superman's Pal, Jimmy Olsen #1-22; Showcase #9 and Superman #22 17.00
Superman Family Vol. 2 ('08, $16.99) Superman's Pal, Jimmy Olsen #23-34; Showcase #10 and Superman's Girl Friend, Lois Lane #1-7 17.00
Superman Family Vol. 3 ('09, $16.99) Superman's Pal, Jimmy Olsen #35-44 and Superman's Girl Friend, Lois Lane #8-16 17.00
Teen Titans Vol. 1 ('06, $16.99) r/#1-18; Brave & the Bold #54,60; Showcase #59 17.00
Teen Titans Vol. 2 ('07, $16.99) r/#19-37, World's Finest #205 and Brave & Bold #83,94 17.00
The Unknown Soldier Vol. 1 ('06, $16.99) r/Star Spangled War Stories #158-188 17.00
The War That Time Forgot Vol. 1 ('07, $16.99) r/S.S.W.S. #90,92,94-125,127,128 17.00
Warlord Vol. 1 ('09, $16.99) r/#1-28 and debut in 1st Issue Special #1 17.00
The Witching Hour Vol. 1 ('11, $19.99) r/#1-19 17.00
Wonder Woman Vol. 1 ('07, $16.99) r/#98-117 17.00
Wonder Woman Vol. 2 ('08, $16.99) r/#118-137 17.00
World's Finest Vol. 1 ('07, $16.99) r/#71-111 & Superman #76 17.00
World's Finest Vol. 2 ('08, $16.99) r/#112-145 17.00
World's Finest Vol. 3 ('10, $17.99) r/#146-160,162-169,171-173 ('64-'68) 18.00

SHOWGIRLS (Formerly Sherry the Showgirl #3)
Atlas Comics (MPC No. 2): No. 4, 2/57; June, 1957 - No. 2, Aug, 1957

4-(2/57) Dan DeCarlo-c/a begins 12 24 36 67 94 120
1-(6/57) Millie, Sherry, Chili, Pearl & Hazel begin 14 28 42 80 115 150
2 11 22 33 62 86 110

SHREK (Movie)
Dark Horse Comics: Sept, 2003 - No. 3, Dec, 2003 ($2.99, limited series)

1-3-Takes place after 1st movie; Evanier-s/Bachs-a; CGI cover 3.00

SHREK (Movie)
Ape Entertainment: 2010 - No. 4, 2011 ($3.95, limited series)

1-3-Short stories by various 4.00

SHROUD, THE (See Super-Villain Team-Up #5)
Marvel Comics: Mar, 1994 - No. 4, June, 1994 ($1.75, mini-series)

1-4: 1,2,4-Spider-Man & Scorpion app. 3.00

SHROUD OF MYSTERY
Whitman Publications: June, 1982

1 1 2 3 4 5 7

SHRUGGED
Aspen MLT, Inc.: No. 0, June, 2006 - No. 8, Feb, 2009 ($2.50/$2.99)

0-($2.50) Turner & Mastromauro-s/Gunnell-a; intro. story and character profiles 3.00
1-8-($2.99) 1-Six covers. 2-Three covers 3.00
... : Beginnings (5/06, $1.99) Prequel intro. to Ange and Dev; Gunnell-a; development art 3.00

SHUT UP AND DIE
Image Comics/Halloween: 1998 - No. 3, 1998 ($2.95,B&W, bi-monthly)

1-3: Hudnall-s 3.00

SICK (Sick Special #131) (Magazine) (Satire)
Feature Publ./Headline Publ./Crestwood Publ. Co./Hewfred Publ./ Pyramid Comm./Charlton Publ. No. 109 (4/76) on: Aug, 1960 - No. 134, Fall, 1980

V1#1-Jack Paar photo on-c; Torres-a; Untouchables-s; Ben Hur movie photo-s 15 30 45 103 209 315
2-Torres-a; Elvis app.; Lenny Bruce app. 10 20 30 70 125 180
3-5-Torres-a in all. 3-Khruschev-c; Hitler-s. 4-Newhart-s; Castro-s; John Wayne. 5-JFK/Castro-c; Elvis pin-up; Hitler. 9 18 27 63 107 150
6-Photo-s of Ricky Nelson & Marilyn Monroe; JFK 9 18 27 65 113 160

V2#1,2,4-8 (#7,8,10-14): 1-(#7) Hitler-s; Brando photo-s. 2-(#8) Dick Clark-s. 4-(#10) Untouchables-c; Candid Camera-s. 5-(#11) Nixon-c; Lone Ranger-s; JFK-s. 6-(#12) Beatnik-c/s. 8-(#14) Liz Taylor pin-up, JFK-s; Dobie Gillis-s; Sinatra & Dean Martin photo-s 8 16 24 58 97 135
3-(#9) Marilyn Monroe/JFK-c; Kingston Trio-s 9 18 27 63 107 150

V3#1-7(#15-21): 1-(#15) JFK app.; Liz Tayor/Richard Burton-s. 2-(#16) Ben Casey/ Frankenstein-c/s; Hitler photo-s. 5-(#19) Nixon back-c/s; Sinatra photo-s. 6-(#20) 1st Huckleberry Fink-c 5 10 15 34 55 75
8-(#22) Cassius Clay vs. Liston-s; 1st Civil War Blackouts-/Pvt. Bo Reargard w/ Jack Davis-a 6 12 18 39 62 85

V4#1-5 (#23-27): Civil War Blackouts-/Pvt. Bo Reargard w/ Jack Davis-a in all. 1-(#23) Smokey Bear-c; Tarzan-s. 2-(#24) Goldwater & Paar-s; Castro-s. 3-(#25) Frankenstein-c; Cleopatra/Liz Taylor-s; Steve Reeves photo-s. 4-(#26) James Bond-s; Hitler-s. 5-(#27) Taylor/Burton pin-up; Sinatra, Martin, Andress, Ekberg photo-s 4 8 12 28 44 60

28,31,36,39: 31-Pink Panther movie photo-s; Burke's Law-s. 39-Westerns; Elizabeth Montgomery photo-s; Beat mag-s 4 8 12 24 37 50
29,34,37,38: 29-Beatles-c by Jack Davis. 34-Two pg. Beatles-s & photo pin-up. 37-Playboy

Sick #32 © Feature

Sif #1 © MAR

Silent Hill: Dying Inside #1 © Konami

GD VG FN VF VF/NM NM-
2.0 4.0 6.0 8.0 9.0 9.2

parody issue. 38-Addams Family-s 4 8 12 28 44 60
30,32,35,40: 30-Beatles photo pin-up; James Bond photo-s. 32-Ian Fleming-s; LBJ-s; Tarzan-s. 35-Beatles cameo; Three Stooges parody. 40-Tarzan-s; Crosby/Hope-s; Beatles parody 5 10 15 30 48 65
33-Ringo Starr photo-c & spoof on "A Hard Day's Night"; inside-c has Beatles photos 6 12 18 41 66 90
41,50,51,53,54,60: 41-Sports Illustrated parody-c/s. 50-Mod issue; flip-c w/1967 calendar w/Bob Taylor-a. 51-Get Smart-s. 53-Beatles cameo; nudity panels. 54-Monkees-c. 60-TV Daniel Boone-s 3 6 9 20 30 40
42-Fighting American-c revised from Simon/Kirby-c; "Good girl" art by Sparling; profile on Bob Powell; superhero parodies 6 12 18 37 59 80
43-49,52,55-59: 43-Sneaker set begins by Sparling. 45-Has #44 on-c & #45 on inside; TV Westerns-s; Beatles cameo. 46-Hell's Angels-s; NY Mets-s. 47-UFO/Space-c. 49-Men's Adventure mag. parody issue; nudity. 52-LBJ-s. 55-Underground culture special. 56-Alfred E. Neuman-c; inventors issue. 58-Hippie issue-c/s. 59-Hippie-s 3 6 9 17 25 32
61-64,66-69,71,73,75-80: 63-Tiny Tim-c & poster; Monkees-s. 64-Flip-c. 66-Flip-c; Mod Squad-s. 69-Beatles cameo; Peter Sellers photo-s. 71-Flip-c; Clint Eastwood-s. 76-Nixon-s; Marcus Welby-s. 78-Ma Barker-s; Courtship of Eddie's Father-s; Abbie Hoffman-s 3 6 9 16 22 28
65,70,74: 65-Cassius Clay/Brando/J. Wayne-c; Johnny Carson-s. 70-(9/69) John & Yoko-c, 1/2 pg. story. 74-Clay, Agnew, Namath & others as superheroes-c/s; Easy Rider-s; Ghost and Mrs. Muir-s 3 6 9 17 25 32
72-(84 pgs.) Xmas issue w/2 pg. slick color poster; Tarzan-s; 2 pg. Superman & superheroes-s 4 8 12 22 34 45
81-85,87-95,98,99: 81-(2/71) Woody Allen photo-s. 85 Monster Mag. parody-s; Nixon-s w/Ringo & John cameo. 88-Klute photo-s; Nixon paper dolls page. 92-Lily Tomlin; Archie Bunker pin-up. 93-Woody Allen 2 4 6 13 18 22
86,96,97,100: 86-John & Yoko, Tiny Tim-c; Love Story movie photo-s. 96-Kung Fu-c; Mummy-s, Dracula & Frankenstein app. 97-Superman-s; 1974 Calendar; Charlie Brown & Snoopy pin-up. 100-Serpico-s; Cosell-s; Jacques Cousteau-s 3 6 9 14 19 24
101-103,105-114,116,119,120: 101-Three Musketeers-s; Dick Tracy-s. 102-Young Frankenstein-s. 103-Kojak-s; Evel Knievel-s. 105-Towering Inferno-s; Peanuts/Snoopy-s. 106-Cher-c/s. 10 7-Jaws-c/s. 108-Pink Panther-c/s; Archie-s. 109-Adam & Eve-s(nudity). 110-Welcome Back Kotter-s. 111-Sonny & Cher-s. 112-King Kong-c/s. 120-Star Trek-s 2 4 6 9 13 16
104,115,117,118: 104-Muhammad Ali-c/s. 115-Charlie's Angels-s. 117-Bionic Woman & Six Million $ Man-c/s; Cher D'Flower begins by Sparling (nudity). 118-Star Wars-s; Popeye-s 2 4 6 11 16 20
121-125,128-130: 122-Darth Vader-s. 123-Jaws II-s. 128-Superman-c/movie parody. 130-Alien movie-s 2 4 6 10 14 18
126,127: 126-(68 pgs.) Battlestar Galactica-c/s; Star Wars-s; Wonder Woman-s. 127-Mork & Mindy-s; Lord of the Rings-s 2 4 6 13 18 22
131-(1980 Special) Star Wars/Star Trek/Flash Gordon wraparound-c/s; Superman parody; Battlestar Galactica-s 3 6 9 14 19 24
132,133: 132-1980 Election-c/s; Apocalypse Now-s. 133-Star Trek-s; Chips-s; Superheroes page 2 4 6 13 18 22
134 (scarce)(68 pg. Giant)-Star Wars-c; Alien-s; WKRP-s; Mork & Mindy-s; Taxi-s; MASH-s 4 8 12 21 30 40
Annual 1- Birthday Annual (1966)-3 pg. Huckleberry Fink fold out 4 8 12 23 34 50
Annual 2- 7th Annual Yearbook (1967)-Davis-c, 2 pg. glossy poster insert 4 8 12 23 34 50
Annual 3 (1968) "Big Sick Laff-in" on-c (84 pgs.)-w/psychedelic posters; Frankenstein poster 3 6 9 18 27 35
Annual 1969 "Great Big Fat Annual Sick", 1969 "9th Year Annual Sick", 1970, 1971 3 6 9 17 25 32
Annual 12,13-(1972,1973, 84 pgs.) 13-Monster-c 3 6 9 17 25 32
Annual 14,15-(1974,1975, 84 pgs.) 14-Hitler photo-s 3 6 9 17 25 32
Annual 2-4 (1980) 2 4 6 9 13 16
Special 1 (1980) Buck Rogers-c/s; MASH-s 3 6 9 14 19 24
Special 2 (1980) Wraparound Star Wars:Empire Strikes Back-c; Charlie's Angels/Farrah-s; Rocky-s; plus reprints 3 6 9 14 19 24
Yearbook 15(1975, 84 pgs.) Paul Revere-c 3 6 9 16 23 30

NOTE: *Davis a-42, 87; c-22, 23, 25, 29, 31, 32.* **Powell** *a-7, 31, 57.* **Simon** *a-1-3, 10, 41, 42, 87, 99; c-1, 47, 57, 59, 69, 91, 95-97, 99, 100, 102, 107, 112.* **Torres** *a-1-3, 29, 31, 47, 49.* **Tuska** *a-14, 41-43. Civil War Blackouts-23, 24. #42 has biography of Bob Powell.*

SIDEKICK (Paul Jenkins'...)
Image Comics (Desperado): June, 2006 - No. 5, May, 2007 ($3.50, limited series)

1-5-Paul Jenkins-s/Chris Moreno-a 3.50
... Super Summer Sidekick Spectacular 1 (7/07, $2.99) 3.00
... Super Summer Sidekick Spectacular 2 (9/07, $3.50) 3.50

SIDEKICKS

GD VG FN VF VF/NM NM-
2.0 4.0 6.0 8.0 9.0 9.2

Fanboy Ent., Inc.: Jun, 2000 - No. 3, Apr, 2001 ($2.75, B&W, lim. series)

1-3-J.Torres-s/Takesi Miyazawa-a. 3-Variant-c by Wieringo 3.00
...: Super Fun Summer Special (Oni Press, 7/03, $2.99) art by various incl. Wieringo 3.00
...: The Substitute (Oni Press, 7/02, $2.95) 3.00
...: The Transfer Student TPB (Oni Press, 6/02, $8.95, 9" x 6") r/#1-3 9.00
...: The Transfer Student TPB 2nd Ed. (10/03, $11.95, 9" x 6") r/#1-3; The Substitute 12.00

SIDESHOW
Avon Periodicals: 1949 (one-shot)

1-(Rare)-Similar to Bachelor's Diary 50 100 150 315 533 750

SIEGE
Marvel Comics: Mar, 2010 - No. 4, Jun, 2010 ($3.99, limited series)

1-4-Asgard is invaded; Bendis-s/Coipel-a. 4-End of The Sentry 4.00
1-4-Variant covers by Dell'Otto 8.00
...: Captain America (6/10, $2.99) Gage-s/Dallocchio-a/Djurdjevic-c; both Caps app. 4.00
...: Loki (6/10, $2.99) Gillen-s/McKelvie-a/Djurdjevic-c; Hela & Mephisto app. 4.00
...: Secret Warriors (6/10, $2.99) Hickman-s/Vitti-a/Djurdjevic-c; Phobos attacks 4.00
...: Spider-Man (6/10, $2.99) Reed-s/Santucci-a/Djurdjevic-c; Venom & Ms. Marvel app. 4.00
...: Storming Asgard - Heroes & Villains (3/10, $3.99) Dossiers on participants; Land-c 4.00
...: The Cabal (2/10, $3.99) series prelude; Bendis-s/Lark-a; covers by Finch & Davis 4.00
...: Young Avengers (6/10, $2.99) McKeever-s/Asrar-a/Djurdjevic-c; Wrecking Crew app. 4.00

SIEGE: EMBEDDED
Marvel Comics: Mar, 2010 - No. 4, Jul, 2010 ($3.99, limited series)

1-4-Reed-s/Samnee-a/Granov-c; Ben Urich & Volstagg cover the invasion 4.00

SIEGEL AND SHUSTER: DATELINE 1930s
Eclipse Comics: Nov, 1984 - No. 2, Sept, 1985 ($1.50/$1.75, Baxter paper #1)

1,2: 1-Unpublished samples of strips from the '30s; includes 'Interplanetary Police'; Shuster-c. 2 ($1.75, B&W)-unpublished strips; Shuster-c 3.00

SIF (See Thor titles)
Marvel Comics: Jun, 2010 ($3.99, one shot)

1-Deconnick-s/Stegman-a/Foreman-c; Beta Ray Bill app. 4.00

SIGIL (Also see CrossGen Chronicles)
CrossGeneration Comics: Jul, 2000 - No. 43, Jan, 2004 ($2.95)

1-43: 1-Barbara Kesel-s/Ben & Ray Lai-a. 12-Waid-s begin. 21-Chuck Dixon-s begin 3.00
...: Mark of Power TPB (5/01, $19.95) r/#1-7; Moeller painted-c 20.00
...: The Marked Man Vol. 2 TPB (2002, $19.95) r/#8-14 20.00
...: The Lizard God Vol. 3 TPB (2002, $15.95) r/#15-20 16.00
Vol. 4: Hostage Planet (4/03, $15.95) r/#21-26 16.00
Vol. 5: Death Match (2003, $15.95) r/#27-32 16.00

SIGIL
Marvel Comics: May, 2011 - Present ($2.99)

1,2-Carey-s/Kirk-a 3.00
1-Variant-c by McGuinness 5.00

SIGMA
Image Comics (WildStorm): March, 1996 - No. 3, June, 1996 ($2.50, limited series)

1-3: 1-"Fire From Heaven" prelude #2; Coker-a. 2-"Fire From Heaven" pt. 6. 3-"Fire From Heaven" pt. 14. 3.00

SILENT DRAGON
DC Comics (WildStorm): Sept, 2005 - No. 6, Feb, 2006 ($2.99, limited series)

1-6-Tokyo 2066 A.D.; Leinil Yu-a/c; Andy Diggle-s 3.00
TPB (2006, $19.99) r/series; sketch page 20.00

SILENT HILL: DEAD/ALIVE
IDW Publishing: Dec, 2005 - No. 5, Apr, 2006 ($3.99, limited series)

1-5-Stakal-a/Ciencin-s. 1-Four covers. 2-5-Two covers 4.00

SILENT HILL: DYING INSIDE
IDW Publishing: Feb, 2004 - No. 5, June, 2004 ($3.99, limited series)

1-5-Based on the Konami computer game. 1-Templesmith-a; Ashley Wood-c 4.00
...: Paint It Black (2/05, $7.49) Ciencin-s/Thomas-a 7.50
...: The Grinning Man 5/05, $7.49) Ciencin-s/Stakal-a 7.50
TPB (8/04, $19.99) r/#1-5; Ashley Wood-c 20.00

SILENT HILL: PAST LIFE
IDW Publishing: Oct, 2010 - No. 4, Jan, 2011 ($3.99, limited series)

1-4-Waltz-s; two covers on each 4.00

SILENT HILL: SINNER'S REWARD
IDW Publishing: Feb, 2008 - No. 4, Apr, 2008 ($3.99, limited series)

1-4-Waltz-s/Stamb-a 4.00

Silver Age #1 © DC

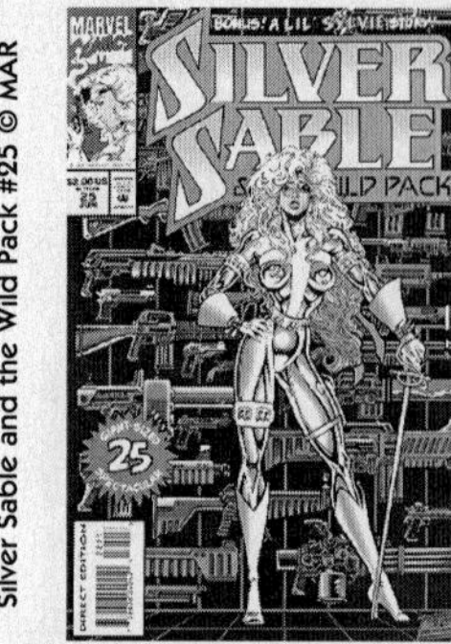

Silver Sable and the Wild Pack #25 © MAR

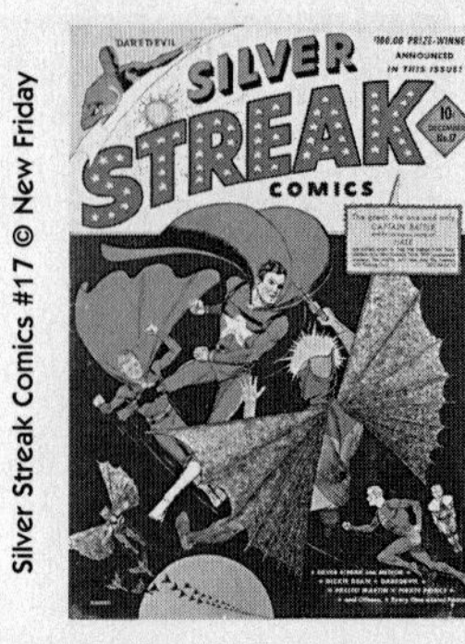

Silver Streak Comics #17 © New Friday

GD VG FN VF VF/NM NM-
2.0 4.0 6.0 8.0 9.0 9.2

SILENT INVASION, THE
Rengade Press: Apr, 1986 - No.12, Mar, 1988 ($1.70/$2.00, B&W)
1-12-UFO sightings of the '50's 3.00
Book 1- reprints ($7.95) 8.00

SILENT MOBIUS
Viz Select Comics: 1991 - No. 5, 1992 ($4.95, color, squarebound, 44 pgs.)
1-5: Japanese stories translated to English 5.00

SILENT SCREAMERS (Based on the Aztech Toys figures)
Image Comics: Oct, 2000 ($4.95)
Nosferatu Issue - Alex Ross front & back-c 5.00

SILENT WAR
Marvel Comics: Mar, 2007 - No. 6, Aug, 2007 ($2.99, limited series)
1-6-Inhumans, Black Bolt and Fantastic Four app.; Hine-s/Irving-a/Watson-c 3.00
TPB (2007, $14.99) r/series 15.00

SILKE
Dark Horse Comics: Jan, 2001 - No. 4, Sept, 2001 ($2.95)
1-4-Tony Daniel-s/a 3.00

SILKEN GHOST
CrossGen Comics: June, 2003 - No. 5, Oct, 2003 ($2.95, limited series)
1-5-Dixon-s/Rosado-a 3.00
Traveler Vol. 1 (2003, $9.95) digest-sized reprint #1-5 10.00

SILLY PILLY (See Frank Luther's...)

SILLY SYMPHONIES (See Dell Giants)

SILLY TUNES
Timely Comics: Fall, 1945 - No. 7, June, 1947
1-Silly Seal, Ziggy Pig begin 22 44 66 132 216 300
2-(2/46) 14 28 42 80 115 150
3-7: 6-New logo 12 24 36 67 94 120

SILVER (See Lone Ranger's Famous Horse...)

SILVER AGE
DC Comics: July, 2000 ($3.95, limited series)
1-Waid-s/Dodson-a; "Silver Age" style x-over; JLA & villains switch bodies 4.00
...: Challengers of the Unknown ($2.50) Joe Kubert-c; vs. Chronos 3.00
...: Dial H For Hero ($2.50) Jim Mooney-c; vs. Martian Manhunter 3.00
...: Doom Patrol ($2.50) Ramona Fradon-c/Peyer-s 3.00
...: Flash ($2.50) Carmine Infantino-c; Kid Flash and Elongated Man app. 3.00
...: Green Lantern ($2.50) Gil Kane-c/Busiek-s/Anderson-a; vs. Sinestro 3.00
...: Justice League of America ($2.50) Ty Templeton-c 3.00
...: Showcase ($2.50) Dick Giordano-c/a; Batgirl, Adam Strange app. 3.00
... Secret Files ($4.95) Intro. Agamemno; short stories & profile pages 5.00
...: Teen Titans ($2.50) Nick Cardy-c; vs. Penguin, Mr. Element, Black Manta 3.00
...: The Brave and the Bold ($2.50) Jim Aparo-c; Batman & Metal Men 3.00
... 80-Page Giant ($5.95) Conclusion of x-over; "lost" Silver Age stories 6.00

SILVERBACK
Comico: 1989 - No. 3, 1990 ($2.50, color, limited series, mature readers)
1-3: Character from Grendel: Matt Wagner-a 3.00

SILVERBLADE
DC Comics: Sept, 1987 - No. 12, Sept, 1988
1-12: Colan-c/a in all 3.00

SILVERHAWKS
Star Comics/Marvel Comics #6: Aug, 1987 - No. 6, June, 1988 ($1.00)
1-6 3.00

SILVERHEELS
Pacific Comics: Dec, 1983 - No. 3, May, 1984 ($1.50)
1-3 3.00

SILVER KID WESTERN
Key/Stanmor Publications: Oct, 1954 - No. 5, July, 1955
1 10 20 30 54 72 90
2 6 12 18 31 38 45
3-5 6 12 18 28 34 40
I.W. Reprint #1,2-Severin-c: 1-r/#? 2-r/#1 2 4 6 8 11 14

SILVER SABLE AND THE WILD PACK (See Amazing Spider-Man #265 and Sable & Fortune)
Marvel Comics: June, 1992 - No. 35, Apr, 1995 ($1.25/$1.50
1-($2.00)-Embossed & foil stamped-c; Spider-Man app. 4.00
2-24,26-35: 4,5-Dr. Doom-c/story. 6,7-Deathlok-c/story. 9-Origin Silver Sable. 10-Punisher-c/s. 15-Capt. America-c/s. 16,17-Intruders app. 18,19-Venom-c/s. 19-Siege of Darkness x-over. 23-Daredevil (in new costume) & Deadpool app. 24-Bound-in card sheet. Li'l Sylvie backup story 3.00
25-($2.00, 52 pgs.)-Li'l Sylvie backup story 4.00

SILVER STAR (Also see Jack Kirby's...)
Pacific Comics: Feb, 1983 - No. 6, Jan, 1984 ($1.00)
1-6: 1-1st app. Last of the Viking Heroes. 1-5-Kirby-c/a. 2-Ditko-a 5.00
...: Graphite Edition TPB (TwoMorrows Publ., 3/06, $19.95) r/series in B&W including Kirby's original pencils; sketch pages; original screenplay 20.00
Jack Kirby's Silver Star, Volume 1 HC (Image Comics, 2007, $34.99) r/series in color; sketch pages; original screenplay 35.00

SILVER STREAK COMICS (Crime Does Not Pay #22 on)
Your Guide Publs. No. 1-7/New Friday Publs. No. 8-17/Comic House Publ./ Newsbook Publ.: Dec, 1939 - No. 21, May, 1942; No. 23, 1946; No # 22 (Silver logo-#1-5)
1-(Scarce)-Intro the Claw by Cole (r-in Daredevil #21), Red Reeves Boy Magician (ends #2), Captain Fearless (ends #2), The Wasp (ends #2), Mister Midnight (ends #2) begin; Spirit Man only app. Calling The Duke begins (ends #2). Barry Lane only app. Silver Metallic-c begin, end #5; Claw-c 1,2,6-8 1000 2000 3000 7400 13,200 19,000
2-The Claw ends (by Cole); makes pact w/Hitler; Simon-c/a (The Claw); ad for Marvel Mystery Comics #2 (12/39). Lance Hale begins (receives super powers). Solar Patrol app. 389 778 1167 2723 4762 6800
3-1st app. & origin Silver Streak (2nd with Lightning speed); Dickie Dean the Boy Inventor, Lance Hale, Ace Powers (ends #6), Bill Wayne The Texas Terror (ends #6) & The Planet Patrol (ends #6) begin. Detective Snoop, Sergeant Drake only app. 331 662 993 2317 4059 5800
4-Sky Wolf begins (ends #6); Silver Streak by Jack Cole (new costume); 1st app. Jackie, Lance Hale's sidekick. Lance Hale gains immortality 168 336 504 1075 1838 2600
5-Cole c/a(2); back-c ad for Claw app. in #6 194 388 582 1242 2121 3000
6-(Scarce, 9/40)-Origin & 1st app. Daredevil (blue & yellow costume) by Jack Binder; The Claw returns as the Green Claw; classic Cole Claw-c 1367 2734 4100 10,250 18,375 26,500
7-Claw vs. Daredevil serial begins c/sty, ends #11. Daredevil new costume-blue & red by Jack Cole & 3 other Cole stories (38 pgs.). Origin Whiz, S. S.'s Falcon 2nd app. Daredevil & 1st Daredevil-c (by Cole). Cloud Curtis, Presto Martin begins. Dynamo Hill & Zongar The Miracleman only app. 757 1514 2271 5526 9763 14,000
8-Claw vs. Daredevil by Cole c/sty; last Cole Silver streak. Dan Dearborn begins (ends) #12. Secret Agent X-101 begins, ends #9 354 708 1062 2478 4339 6200
9-Claw vs. Daredevil by Cole. Silver Streak-c by Bob Wood 213 426 639 1363 2332 3300
10-Origin & 1st app. Captain Battle (5/41) by Binder; Claw vs. Daredevil by Cole; Silver Streak/robot-c by Bob Wood 177 354 531 1124 1937 2750
11-Intro. Mercury by Bob Wood, Silver Streak's sidekick; conclusion Claw vs. Daredevil by Rico; in 'Presto Martin,' 2nd pg., newspaper says 'Roussos does it again' 123 246 369 787 1344 1900
12-Daredevil-c by Rico; Lance Hale finds lost valley w/cave men, battles dinosaurs, sabre-toothed cats; his last app. 94 188 282 597 1024 1450
13-15: 13-Origin Thun-Dohr. Bingham Boys app. 86 172 258 546 936 1325
16-Hitler-c 103 206 309 659 1130 1600
17-Last Daredevil issue. 84 168 252 538 919 1300
18-The Saint begins (2/42, 1st app.) by Leslie Charteris (see Movie Comics #2 by DC); The Saint-c 68 136 204 435 743 1050
19-21 (1942): 19,20-Ned of the Navy app.; Wolverton's Scoop Scuttle in 20,21. 20-Last Captain Battle, Dickie Dean & Cloud Curtis; Red Reed, Alonzo Appleseed only app. 21-Hitler app. in strip on cover 50 100 150 315 533 750
23(1946(An Atomic Comic)-Reprints; bondage-c 54 108 162 343 574 825
nn(11/46)(Newsbook Publ.)-R-/S.S. story from #4-7 plus 2 Captain Fearless stories, all in color; bondage/torture-c (scarce) 61 122 183 390 670 950

NOTE: ***Jack Binder*** *a-8-12, 15; c-3, 4, 13-15, 17.* ***Dick Briefer*** *a-9-20.* ***Jack Cole*** *a-(Claw)-#2, 3, 6-10. (Daredevil)-#6-10, (Dickie Dean)-#3-10, (Pirate Prince)-#7, (Silver Streak)-#4-8, nn; c-5 (Silver Streak), 6 (Claw), 7, 8 (Daredevil).* ***Bill Everett*** *Red Reed begins #20.* ***Fred Guardineer*** *a-#8-12.* ***Don Rico*** *a-11-17 (Daredevil), 15, 19 (Silver Streak); c-11, 12, 16.* ***Joe Simon*** *a-2 (Solar Patrol), 3 (Silver Streak); c-2.* ***Basil Wolverton*** *a-20.* ***Bob Wood*** *a-8-15 (Presto Martin), 9 (Silver Streak); c-9, 10. Captain Battle c-11, 13-15, 17. Claw c-#1, 2, 6-8. Daredevil c-7, 8, 12. Dickie Dean c-19. Ned of the Navy c-20 (war). The Saint c-18. Silver Streak c-5, 10, 16, 23.*

SILVER STREAK COMICS (Homage with Golden Age size and Golden Age art styles)
Image Comics: No. 24, Dec, 2009 ($3.99, one-shot)
24-New Daredevil, Claw, Silver Streak & Captain Battle stories; Larsen, Grist, Gilbert-a 4.00

SILVER SURFER (See Fantastic Four, Fantasy Masterpieces V2#1, Fireside Book Series, Marvel Graphic Novel, Marvel Presents #8, Marvel's Greatest Comics & Tales To Astonish #92)

SILVER SURFER, THE (Also see Essential Silver Surfer)
Marvel Comics Group: Aug, 1968 - No. 18, Sept, 1970; June, 1982

Silver Surfer #12 © MAR

Silver Surfer (2011 series) #1 © MAR

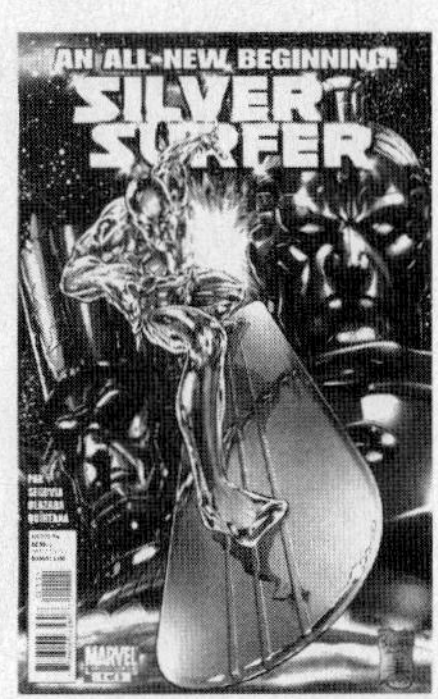

Simpsons Comics #128 © Bongo

GD 2.0 | VG 4.0 | FN 6.0 | VF 8.0 | VF/NM 9.0 | NM- 9.2

1-More detailed origin by John Buscema (p); The Watcher back-up stories begin (origin), end #7; (No. 1-7: 25¢, 68 pgs.) 48 96 144 408 829 1250
2 21 42 63 150 300 450
3-1st app. Mephisto 18 36 54 131 266 400
4-Lower distribution; Thor & Loki app. 41 82 123 328 664 1000
5-7-Last giant size. 5-The Stranger app.; Fantastic Four app. 6-Brunner inks. 7-(8/69)-Early cameo Frankenstein's monster (see X-Men #40) 13 26 39 94 185 275
8-10: 8-18-(15¢ issues) 11 22 33 75 138 200
11-13,15-18: 15-Silver Surfer vs. Human Torch; Fantastic Four app. 17-Nick Fury app. 18-Vs. The Inhumans; Kirby-c/a 10 20 30 70 125 180
14-Spider-Man x-over 14 28 42 99 200 300
... Omnibus Vol. 1 Hardcover (2007, $74.99, dustjacket) r/#1-18 re-colored with original letter pages, Fantastic Four Annual #5 & Not Brand Echh #13; Lee and Buscema bios 75.00
V2#1 (6/82, 52 pgs.)-Byrne-c/a 2 4 6 8 10 12
NOTE: ***Adkins** a-8-15i. **Brunner** a-6i. **J. Buscema** a-1-17p. **Colan** a-1-3p. **Reinman** a-1-4i. #1-14 were reprinted in Fantasy Masterpieces V2#1-14.*

SILVER SURFER (Volume 3) (See Marvel Graphic Novel #38)
Marvel Comics Group: V3#1, July, 1987 - No. 146, Nov, 1998

1-Double size ($1.25) 1 3 4 6 8 10
2-17: 15-Ron Lim-c/a begins (9/88) 5.00
18-33,39-43: 25,31 ($1.50, 52 pgs.). 25-Skrulls app. 32,39-No Ron Lim-c/a. 39-Alan Grant scripts 4.00
34-Thanos returns (cameo); Starlin scripts begin 5.00
35-38: 35-1st full Thanos app. in Silver Surfer (3/90); reintro Drax the Destroyer on last pg. (cameo). 36-Recaps history of Thanos; Capt. Marvel & Warlock app. in recap. 37-1st full app. Drax the Destroyer; Drax-c. 38-Silver Surfer battles Thanos 6.00
44,45,49-Thanos stories (c-44,45) 5.00
46-48: 46-Return of Adam Warlock (2/91); re-intro Gamora & Pip the Troll. 47-Warlock battles Drax. 48-Last Starlin scripts (also #50) 5.00
50-($1.50, 52 pgs.)-Embossed & silver foil-c; Silver Surfer has brief battle w/Thanos; story cont'd in Infinity Gauntlet #1 1 2 3 5 6 8
50-2nd & 3rd printings 4.00
51-59: 51-53: Infinity Gauntlet x-over . 54-57: Infinity Gauntlet x-overs. 54-Rhino app. 55,56-Thanos-c & app. 57-Thanos-c & cameo. 58,59-Infinity Gauntlet x-overs; 58-Lim-c only. 59-Thanos battles Silver Surfer-c/story; Thanos joins 4.00
60-74,76-99,101-124,126-139: 63-Capt. Marvel app. 67-69-Infinity War x-overs. 76-78-Jack of Hearts-c/s. 83-85-Infinity Crusade x-over; 83,84-Thanos cameo. 85-Storm, Wonder Man x-over. 86-Thor-c/s. 87-Dr. Strange & Warlock app. 88-Thanos-c/s. 95-FF app. 96-Hulk & FF app. 97-Terrax & Nova app. 101-Bound in card sheet. 106-Doc Doom app. 121-Quasar & Beta Ray Bill app. 123-w/card insert; begin Garney-a. 126-Dr. Strange-c/app. 128-Spider-Man & Daredevil-c/app. 138-Thing-c 3.00
75,82: 75-($2.50, 52 pgs.)-Embossed foil-c; Lim-c/a. 82-(52 pgs.) 4.00
100 ($2.25, 52 pgs.)-Wraparound-c 3.00
100 ($3.95, 52 pgs.)-Enhanced-c 5.00
125 ($2.95)-Wraparound-c; Vs. Hulk-c/app. 4.00
140-146: 140-142,144,145-Muth-c/a. 143,146-Cowan-a. 146-Last issue 3.00
#(-1) Flashback (7/97) 3.00
Annual 1 (1988, $1.75)-Evolutionary War app.; 1st Ron Lim-a on Silver Surfer (20 pg. back-up story & pin-ups) 5.00
Annual 2-7 ('89-'94, 68 pgs.): 2-Atlantis Attacks. 4-3 pg. origin story; Silver Surfer battles Guardians of the Galaxy. 5-Return of the Defenders, part 3; Lim-c/a (3 pgs. of pin-ups only). 6-Polybagged w/trading card; 1st app. Legacy; card is by Lim/Austin 4.00
Annual '97 ($2.99), .../Thor Annual '98 ($2.99) 4.00
Ashcan (1995, 75¢) reprints part of V1#3; Lim-c 3.00
...Dangerous Artifacts-(1996, $3.95)-Ron Marz scripts; Galactus-c/app. 4.00
Graphic Novel (1988, HC, $14.95) Judgment Day; Lee-s/Buscema-a 15.00
The Enslavers Graphic Novel (1990, $16.95) 17.00
Homecoming Graphic Novel (1991, $12.95, softcover) Starlin-s 15.00
Inner Demons TPB (4/98, $3.50)r/#123,125,126 4.00
...: Rebirth of Thanos TPB (2006, $24.99) r/#34-38, Thanos Quest #1,2; Logan's Run #6 25.00
...: The First Coming of Galactus nn (11/92, $5.95, 68 pgs.)-Reprints Fantastic Four #48-50 with new Lim-c 6.00
Wizard 1/2 2 4 6 9 12 15
NOTE: ***Austin** c(i)-7, 8, 71, 73, 74, 76, 79. **Cowan** a-143,146. **Cully Hamner** a-83p. **Ron Lim** a(p)-15-31, 33-38, 40-55, (56, 57-part-p), 60-65, 73-82, Annual 2, 4; c(p)-15-31, 32-38, 40-84, 86-92, Annual 2, 4-6. **Muth** c/a-140-142,144,145. **M. Rogers** a-1-10, 12, 19, 21; c-1-9, 11, 12, 21.*

SILVER SURFER (Volume 4)
Marvel Comics: Sept, 2003 - No. 14, Dec, 2004 ($2.25/$2.99)

1-6: 1-Milx-a; Jusko-c. 2-Jae Lee-c 3.00
7-14-($2.99) 3.00
...Vol. 1: Communion (2004, $14.99) r/#1-6 15.00

SILVER SURFER (Volume 5)
Marvel Comics: Apr, 2011 - No. 5 ($2.99, limited series)

1-3-Pagulayan-c. 1-Segovia-a 3.00

SILVER SURFER, THE
Marvel Comics (Epic): Dec, 1988 - No. 2, Jan, 1989 ($1.00, lim. series)

1,2: By Stan Lee scripts & Moebius-c/a 5.00
HC (1988, $19.95, dust jacket) r/#1,2; "Making Of" text section and sketch pages 30.00
...: Parable ('98, $5.99) r/#1&2 6.00

SILVER SURFER: IN THY NAME
Marvel Comics: Jan, 2008 - No. 4, Apr, 2008 ($2.99, limited series)

1-4-Spurrier-s/Huat-a. 1-Turner-c. 2-Dell'Otto-c. 3-Paul Pope-c. 4-Galactus app. 3.00

SILVER SURFER: LOFTIER THAN MORTALS
Marvel Comics: Oct, 1999 - No. 2, Oct, 1999 ($2.50, limited series)

1,2-Remix of Fantastic Four #57-60; Velluto-a 3.00

SILVER SURFER: REQUIEM
Marvel Comics: July, 2007 - No. 4, Oct, 2007 ($3.99, limited series)

1-4-Straczynski-s/Ribic-a. 1-Origin retold; Fantastic Four app. 4.00
HC (2007, $19.99) r/#1-4, Ribic cover sketches 20.00

SILVER SURFER/SUPERMAN
Marvel Comics: 1996 ($5.95,one-shot)

1-Perez-s/Lim-c/a(p) 6.00

SILVER SURFER VS. DRACULA
Marvel Comics: Feb, 1994 ($1.75, one-shot)

1-r/Tomb of Dracula #50; Everett Vampire-r/Venus #19; Howard the Duck back-up by Brunner; Lim-c(p) 4.00

SILVER SURFER/WARLOCK: RESURRECTION
Marvel Comics: Mar, 1993 - No. 4, June, 1993 ($2.50, limited series)

1-4: Starlin-c/a & scripts 3.00

SILVER SURFER/WEAPON ZERO
Marvel Comics: Apr, 1997 ($2.95, one-shot)

1-"Devil's Reign" pt. 8 3.00

SILVERTIP (Max Brand)
Dell Publishing Co.: No. 491, Aug, 1953 - No. 898, May, 1958

Four Color 491 (#1); all painted-c 8 16 24 52 86 120
Four Color 572,608,637,667,731,789,898-Kinstler-a 5 10 15 30 48 65
Four Color 835 5 10 15 30 48 65

SIMON DARK
DC Comics: Dec, 2007 - No. 18, May, 2009 ($2.99)

1-Intro. Simon Dark; Steve Niles-s/Scott Hampton-a/c 4.00
1-Second printing with full face variant cover 3.00
2-18 3.00
...: Ashes TPB (2009, $17.99) r/#7-12 18.00
...: The Game of Life TPB (2009, $17.99) r/#13-18 18.00
...: What Simon Does TPB (2008, $14.99) r/#1-6 15.00

SIMPSONS COMICS (See Bartman, Futurama, Itchy & Scratchy & Radioactive Man)
Bongo Comics Group: 1993 - Present ($1.95/$2.50/$2.99)

1-($2.25)-FF#1-c swipe; pull-out poster; flip book 1 3 4 6 8 10
2-5: 2-Patty & Selma flip-c/sty. 3-Krusty, Agent of K.L.O.W.N. flip-c/story. 4-Infinity-c; flip-c of Busman #1; w/trading card. 5-Wraparound-c w/trading card 6.00
6-40: All Flip books. 6-w/Chief Wiggum's "Crime Comics". 7-w/"McBain Comics". 8-w/"Edna, Queen of the Congo". 9-w/"Barney Gumble". 10-w/"Apu". 11-w/"Homer". 12-w/"White Knuckled War Stories". 13-w/"Jimbo Jones' Wedgie Comics". 14-w/"Grampa". 15-w/"Itchy & Scratchy". 16-w/"Bongo Grab Bag". 17-w/"Headlight Comics". 18-w/"Milhouse". 19,20-w/"Roswell." 21,22-w/"Roswell". 23-w/"Hellfire Comics". 24-w/"Lil' Homey". 36-39-Flip book w/Radioactive Man 5.00
41-49,51-99: 43-Flip book w/Poochie. 52-Dini-s. 77-Dixon-s. 85-Begin $2.99-c 4.00
50-($5.95) Wraparound-c; 80 pgs.; square-bound 1 2 3 5 6 8
100-($6.99) 100 pgs.; square-bound; clip issue of past highlights 1 2 3 5 6 8
101-177: 102-Barks Ducks homage. 117-Hank Scorpio app. 122-Archie spoof. 132-Movie poster enclosed. 132-133-Two-parter. 144-Flying Hellfish flashback. 150-w/Poster. 163-Aragonés-s/a 3.00
... A Go-Go (1999, $11.95)-r/#32-35; ...Big Bonanza (1998, $11.95)-r/#28-31, ...Extravaganza (1994, $10.00)-r/#1-4; infinity-c, ...On Parade (1998, $11.95)-r/#24-27, ...Simpsorama (1996, $10.95)-r/#11-14 12.00
Simpsons Classics 1-28 (2004-Present, $3.99, magazine-size, quarterly) reprints 4.00
Simpsons Comics Barn Burner ('04, $14.95) r/#57-61,63 15.00
Simpsons Comics Beach Blanket Bongo ('07, $14.95) r/#71-75,77 15.00
Simpsons Comics Belly Buster ('04, $14.95) r/#49,51,53-56 15.00

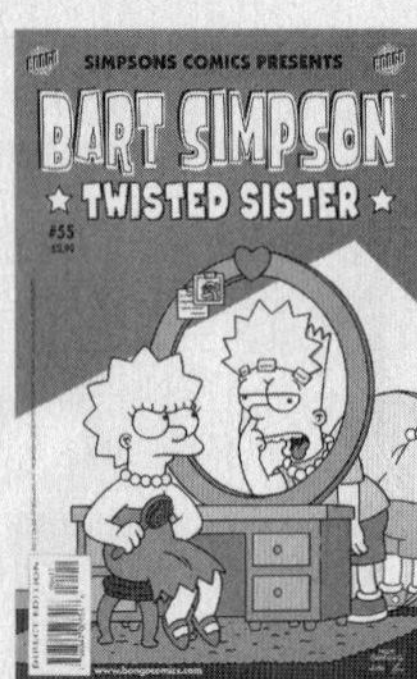

Simpsons Comics Presents Bart Simpson #55 © Bongo

Sin City: A Dame to Kill For #1 © Frank Miller

Sins of Youth: JLA Jr. #1 © DC

	GD 2.0	VG 4.0	FN 6.0	VF 8.0	VF/NM 9.0	NM- 9.2

Simpsons Comics Hit the Road! ('08, $15.95) r/#85,86,88,89,90 — 16.00
Simpsons Comics Jam-Packed Jamboree ('06, $14.95) r/#64-69 — 15.00
Simpsons Comics Madness ('03, $14.95) r/#43-48 — 15.00
Simpsons Comics Royale ('01, $14.95) r/various Bongo issues — 15.00
Simpsons Comics Treasure Trove 1-4 ('08-'09, $3.99, 6" x 8") r/various Bongo issues — 4.00
Simpsons Summer Shindig ('07-'10, $4.99) 1-4-Anthology. 1-Batman/Ripken insert — 5.00
Simpsons Winter Wing Ding ('06-'10, $4.99) 1-5-Holiday anthology. 1-Dini-s — 5.00

SIMPSONS COMICS AND STORIES
Welsh Publishing Group: 1993 ($2.95, one-shot)

1-(Direct Sale)-Polybagged w/Bartman poster — 1 2 3 5 6 8
1-(Newsstand Edition)-Without poster — 5.00

SIMPSONS COMICS PRESENTS BART SIMPSON
Bongo Comics Group: 2000 - Present ($2.50/$2.99, quarterly)

1-58: 7-9-Dan DeCarlo-layouts. 13-Begin $2.99-c. 17,37-Bartman app. 50-Aragonés-s/a — 3.00
The Big Book of Bart Simpson TPB (2002, $12.95) r/#1-4 — 13.00
The Big Bad Book of Bart Simpson TPB (2003, $12.95) r/#5-8 — 13.00
The Big Bratty Book of Bart Simpson TPB (2004, $12.95) r/#9-12 — 13.00
The Big Beefy Book of Bart Simpson TPB (2005, $13.95) r/#13-16 — 14.00
The Big Bouncy Book of Bart Simpson TPB (2006, $13.95) r/#17-20 — 14.00
The Big Beastly Book of Bart Simpson TPB (2007, $14.95) r/#21-24 — 15.00
The Big Brilliant Book of Bart Simpson TPB (2008, $14.95) r/#25-28 — 15.00

SIMPSONS FUTURAMA CROSSOVER CRISIS II (TV) (Also see Futurama/Simpsons Infinitely Secret Crossover Crisis)
Bongo Comics: 2005 - No. 2, 2005 ($3.00, limited series)

1,2-The Professor brings the Simpsons' Springfield crew to the 31st century — 3.00

SIMPSONS SUPER SPECTACULAR (TV)
Bongo Comics: 2006 - Present ($2.99)

1-12: 2-Bartman, Stretch Dude and The Cupcake Kid team up; back-up story Brereton-a. 5-Ramona Fradon-a on Metamorpho spoof. 8-Spirit spoof. 9,10-Radioactive Man app. — 3.00

SINBAD, JR (TV Cartoon)
Dell Publishing Co.: Sept-Nov, 1965 - No. 3, May, 1966

1 — 4 8 12 24 37 50
2,3 — 3 6 9 18 27 35

SIN CITY (See Dark Horse Presents, A Decade of Dark Horse, & San Diego Comic Con Comics #2,4)
Dark Horse Comics (Legend)
TPB ($15.00) Reprints early DHP stories — 15.00
Booze, Broads & Bullets TPB ($15.00) — 15.00
Frank Miller's Sin City: One For One (8/10, $1.00) reprints debut story from DHP #51 — 1.00

SIN CITY (FRANK MILLER'S...) (Reissued TPBs to coincide with the April 2005 movie)
Dark Horse Books: Feb, 2005 ($17.00/$19.00, 6" x 9" format with new Miller covers)

Volume 1: The Hard Goodbye ($17.00) reprints stories from Dark Horse Presents #51-62 and DHP Fifth Anniv. Special; covers and publicity pieces — 17.00
Volume 2: A Dame to Kill For ($17.00) r/Sin City: A Dame to Kill For #1-6 — 17.00
Volume 3: The Big Fat Kill ($17.00) r/Sin City: The Big Fat Kill #1-5; pin-up gallery — 17.00
Volume 4: That Yellow Bastard ($19.00) r/Sin City: That Yellow Bastard #1-6; pin-up gallery by Mike Allred, Kyle Baker, Jeff Smith and Bruce Timm; cover gallery — 19.00
Volume 5: Family Values ($12.00) r/Sin City: Family Values GN — 12.00
Volume 6: Booze, Broads & Bullets ($15.00) r/Sin City: The Babe Wore Red and Other Stories; Silent Night; story from A Decade of Dark Horse; Lost Lonely & Lethal; Sex & Violence; and Just Another Saturday Night — 15.00
Volume 7: Hell and Back ($28.00) r/Sin City: Hell and Back #1-9; pin-up gallery — 28.00

SIN CITY: A DAME TO KILL FOR
Dark Horse Comics (Legend): Nov, 1993 - No. 6, May, 1994 ($2.95, B&W, limited series)

1-6: Frank Miller-c/a & story in all. 1-1st app. Dwight. — 6.00
Limited Edition Hardcover — 85.00
Hardcover — 25.00
TPB ($15.00) — 15.00

SIN CITY: FAMILY VALUES
Dark Horse Comics (Legend): Oct, 1997 ($10.00, B&W, squarebound, one-shot)

nn-Miller-c/a & story — 10.00
Limited Edition Hardcover — 75.00

SIN CITY: HELL AND BACK
Dark Horse (Maverick): Jul, 1999 - No. 9 ($2.95/$4.95, B&W, limited series)

1-8-Miller-c/a & story. 7-Color — 4.00
9-($4.95) — 6.00

SIN CITY: JUST ANOTHER SATURDAY NIGHT
Dark Horse Comics (Legend): Aug, 1997 (Wizard 1/2 offer, B&W, one-shot)

1/2-Miller-c/a & story — 1 2 3 5 6 8
nn (10/98, $2.50) r/#1/2 — 3.00

SIN CITY: LOST, LONELY & LETHAL
Dark Horse Comics (Legend): Dec, 1996 ($2.95, B&W and blue, one-shot)

nn-Miller-c/s/a; w/pin-ups — 5.00

SIN CITY: SEX AND VIOLENCE
Dark Horse Comics (Legend): Mar, 1997 ($2.95, B&W and blue, one-shot)

nn-Miller-c/a & story — 5.00

SIN CITY: SILENT NIGHT
Dark Horse Comics (Legend): Dec, 1995 ($2.95, B&W, one-shot)

1-Miller-c/a & story; Marv app. — 5.00

SIN CITY: THAT YELLOW BASTARD (Second Ed. TPB listed under Sin City (Frank Miller's...)
Dark Horse Comics (Legend): Feb, 1996 - No. 6, July, 1996 ($2.95/$3.50, B&W and yellow, limited series)

1-5: Miller-c/a & story in all. 1-1st app. Hartigan. — 5.00
6-($3.50) Error & corrected — 5.00
Limited Edition Hardcover — 25.00
TPB ($15.00) — 15.00

SIN CITY: THE BABE WORE RED AND OTHER STORIES
Dark Horse Comics (Legend): Nov, 1994 ($2.95, B&W and red, one-shot)

1-r/serial run in Previews as well as other stories; Miller-c/a & scripts; Dwight app. — 4.00

SIN CITY: THE BIG FAT KILL (Second Edition TPB listed under Sin City (Frank Miller's...)
Dark Horse Comics (Legend): Nov, 1994 - No. 5, Mar, 1995 ($2.95, B&W, limited series)

1-5-Miller story & art in all; Dwight app. — 5.00
Hardcover — 25.00
TPB ($15.00) — 15.00

SIN CITY: THE FRANK MILLER LIBRARY
Dark Horse Books: Set 1, Nov, 2005; Set 2, Mar, 2006 ($150, slipcased hardcover, 8" x 12")

Set 1 - Individual hardcovers for Volume 1: The Hard Goodbye, Volume 2: A Dame to Kill For, Volume 3: The Big Fat Kill, Volume 4: That Yellow Bastard; new red foil stamped covers; slipcase box is black with red foil graphics — 150.00
Set 2 - Individual hardcovers for Volume 5: Family Values, Volume 6: Booze, Broads & Bullets, Volume 7: Hell and Back, new red foil stamped covers; The Art of Sin City red hardcover; slipcase box is black with red foil graphics — 150.00

SINDBAD (See Capt. Sindbad under Movie Comics, and Fantastic Voyages of Sindbad)

SINGING GUNS (See Fawcett Movie Comics)

SINGLE SERIES (Comics on Parade #30 on)(Also see John Hix...)
United Features Syndicate: 1938 - No. 28, 1942 (All 68 pgs.)

Note: See Individual Alphabetical Listings for prices

1-Captain and the Kids (#1)
2-Broncho Bill (1939) (#1)
3-Ella Cinders (1939)
4-Li'l Abner (1939) (#1)
5-Fritzi Ritz (#1)
6-Jim Hardy by Dick Moores (#1)
7-Frankie Doodle
8-Peter Pat (On sale 7/14/39)
9-Strange As It Seems
10-Little Mary Mixup
11-Mr. and Mrs. Beans
12-Joe Jinks
13-Looy Dot Dope
14-Billy Make Believe
15-How It Began (1939)
16-Illustrated Gags (1940)-Has ad for Captain and the Kids #1 reprint listed below
17-Danny Dingle
18-Li'l Abner (#2 on-c)
19-Broncho Bill (#2 on-c)
20-Tarzan by Hal Foster
21-Ella Cinders (#2 on-c; on sale 3/19/40)
22-Iron Vic
23-Tailspin Tommy by Hal Forrest (#1)
24-Alice in Wonderland (#1)
25-Abbie and Slats
26-Little Mary Mixup (#2 on-c, 1940)
27-Jim Hardy by Dick Moores (1942)
28-Ella Cinders & Abbie and Slats (1942)
1-Captain and the Kids (1939 reprint)-2nd Edition
1-Fritzi Ritz (1939 reprint)-2nd ed.

NOTE: *Some issues given away at the 1939-40 New York World's Fair (#6).*

SINGULARITY 7
IDW Publ.: July, 2004 - No. 4, Oct, 2004 ($3.99, limited series)

1-4-Templesmith-s/a — 4.00

SINISTER HOUSE OF SECRET LOVE, THE (Becomes Secrets of Sinister House No. 5 on)
National Periodical Publ.: Oct-Nov, 1971 - No. 4, Apr-May, 1972

1 (all 52 pgs.) — 17 34 51 122 249 375
2,4: 2-Jeff Jones-c — 10 20 30 67 116 165
3-Toth-a; greytone-c — 10 20 30 69 122 175

SINS OF YOUTH... (Also see Young Justice: Sins of Youth)

Six-Gun Heroes #5 © FAW

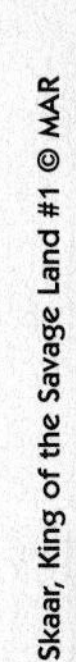
Skaar, King of the Savage Land #1 © MAR

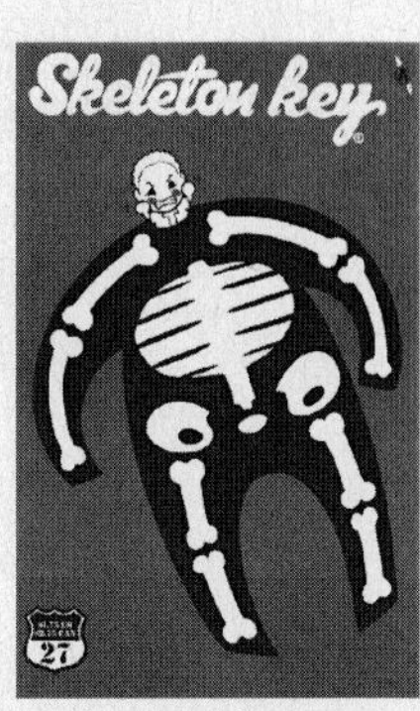

Skeleton Key #27 © Amaze Ink

GD 2.0 VG 4.0 FN 6.0 VF 8.0 VF/NM 9.0 NM- 9.2

DC Comics: May 2000 ($4.95/$2.50, limited crossover series)

Secret Files 1 ($4.95) Short stories and profile pages; Nauck-c 5.00
...Aquaboy/Lagoon Man; Batboy and Robin; JLA Jr.; Kid Flash/Impulse; Starwoman and the JSA, Superman, Jr./Superboy, Sr.; The Secret/ Deadboy, Wonder Girls ($2.50-c) Old and young heroes switch ages 3.00

SIR APROPOS OF NOTHING
IDW Publishing: Nov, 2009 - Present ($3.99)

1-3-Peter David-s/Robin Riggs-a; two covers on each. 2-Kaluta-c 4.00

SIR CHARLES BARKLEY AND THE REFEREE MURDERS
Hamilton Comics: 1993 ($9.95, 8-1/2" x 11", 52 pgs.)

nn-Photo-c; Sports fantasy comic book fiction (uses real names of NBA superstars). Script by Alan Dean Foster, art by Joe Staton. Comes with bound-in sheet of 35 gummed "Moods of Charles Barkley" stamps. Photo/story on Barkley 2 4 6 8 10 12
Special Edition of 100 copies for charity signed on an affixed book plate by Barkley, Foster & Staton 150.00
Ashcan edition given away to dealers, distributors & promoters (low distribution). Four pages in color, balance of story in b&w 2 4 6 8 10 12

SIR EDWARD GREY, WITCHFINDER: IN THE SERVICE OF ANGELS (From Hellboy)
Dark Horse Comics: July, 2009 - No. 5, Nov, 2009 ($2.99, limited series)

1-5-Mignola-s/c; Stenbeck-a 3.00

SIREN (Also see Eliminator & Ultraforce)
Malibu Comics (Ultraverse): Sept, 1995 - No. 3, Dec, 1995 ($1.50)

Infinity, 1-3: Infinity-Black-c & painted-c exists. 1-Regular-c & painted-c; War Machine app. 2-Flip book w/Phoenix Resurrection Pt. 3 3.00
Special 1-(2/96, $1.95, 28 pgs.)-Origin Siren; Marvel Comic's Juggernaut-c/app. 3.00

SIREN: SHAPES
Image Comics: May, 1998 - No. 3, Nov, 1998 ($2.95, B&W, limited series)

1-3-J. Torres -s 3.00

SIR LANCELOT (TV)
Dell Publishing Co.: No. 606, Dec, 1954 - No. 775, Mar, 1957

Four Color 606 (not TV) 7 14 21 49 80 110
Four Color 775(...and Brian)-Buscema-a; photo-c 9 18 27 65 113 160

SIR WALTER RALEIGH (Movie)
Dell Publishing Co.: May, 1955 (Based on movie "The Virgin Queen")

Four Color 644-Photo-c 7 14 21 45 73 100

SISTERHOOD OF STEEL (See Eclipse Graphic Adventure Novel #13)
Marvel Comics (Epic Comics): Dec, 1984 -No. 8, Feb, 1986 ($1.50, Baxter paper, mature)

1-8 3.00

SIX
Image Comics: Aug, 2004 ($5.95, B&W)

1-Oeming-s/c; Beavers-a 6.00

6 BLACK HORSES (See Movie Classics)

SIX FROM SIRIUS
Marvel Comics (Epic Comics): July, 1984 - No. 4, Oct, 1984 ($1.50, limited series, mature)

1-4: Moench scripts; Gulacy-c/a in all 3.00

SIX FROM SIRIUS II
Marvel Comics (Epic Comics): Feb, 1986 - No. 4, May, 1986 ($1.50, limited series, mature)

1-4: Moench scripts; Gulacy-c/a in all 3.00

SIX-GUN HEROES
Fawcett Publications: March, 1950 - No. 23, Nov, 1953 (Photo-c #1-23)

1-Rocky Lane, Hopalong Cassidy, Smiley Burnette begin (same date as Smiley Burnette #1) 31 62 93 186 303 420
2 16 32 48 94 147 200
3-5: 5-Lash LaRue begins 14 28 42 76 108 140
6-15 11 22 33 62 86 110
16-22: 17-Last Smiley Burnette. 18-Monte Hale begins 10 20 30 54 72 90
23-Last Fawcett issue 10 20 30 58 79 100

NOTE: *Hopalong Cassidy photo c-1-3. Monte Hale photo c-18. Rocky Lane photo c-4, 5, 7, 9, 11, 13, 15, 17, 20, 21, 23. Lash LaRue photo c-6, 8, 10, 12, 14, 16, 19, 22.*

SIX-GUN HEROES (Cont'd from Fawcett; Gunmasters #84 on) (See Blue Bird)
Charlton Comics: No. 24, Jan, 1954 - No. 83, Mar-Apr, 1965 (All Vol. 4)

24-Lash LaRue, Hopalong Cassidy, Rocky Lane & Tex Ritter begin; photo-c 14 28 42 80 115 150
25 10 20 30 54 72 90
26-30: 26-Rod Cameron story. 28-Tom Mix begins? 9 18 27 47 61 75
31-40: 38-40-Jingles & Wild Bill Hickok (TV) 8 16 24 42 54 65
41-46,48,50: 41-43-Wild Bill Hickok (TV) 8 16 24 40 50 60
47-Williamson-a, 2 pgs; Torres-a 8 16 24 42 54 65
49-Williamson-a (5 pgs.) 9 18 27 50 65 80
51-56,58-60: 58-Gunmaster app. 3 6 9 20 30 40
57-Origin & 1st app. Gunmaster 4 8 12 26 41 55
61,63-70 3 6 9 16 23 30
62-Origin Gunmaster 3 6 9 20 30 40
71-75,77,78,80-83 2 4 6 13 18 22
76,79: 76-Gunmaster begins. 79-1st app. & origin of Bullet, the Gun-Boy 3 6 9 14 19 24

SIXGUN RANCH (See Luke Short & Four Color #580)

SIX-GUN WESTERN
Atlas Comics (CDS): Jan, 1957 - No. 4, July, 1957

1-Crandall-a; two Williamson text illos 18 36 54 105 165 225
2,3-Williamson-a in both 14 28 42 80 115 150
4-Woodbridge-a 10 20 30 58 79 100

NOTE: *Ayers a-2, 3.* ***Maneely*** *a-1; c-2, 3.* ***Orlando*** *a-2.* ***Pakula*** *a-2.* ***Powell*** *a-3.* ***Romita*** *a-1, 4.* ***Severin*** *c-1, 4.* ***Shores*** *a-2.*

SIX MILLION DOLLAR MAN, THE (TV)
Charlton Comics: 6/76 - No. 4, 12/76; No. 5, 10/77; No. 6, 2/78 - No. 9, 6/78

1-Staton-c/a; Lee Majors photo on-c 3 6 9 17 25 32
2-Neal Adams-c; Staton-a 2 4 6 13 18 22
3-9 2 4 6 11 16 20

SIX MILLION DOLLAR MAN, THE (TV)(Magazine)
Charlton Comics: July, 1976 - No. 7, Nov, 1977 (B&W)

1-Neal Adams-c/a 4 8 12 22 34 45
2-Neal Adams-c 3 6 9 16 23 30
3-N. Adams part inks; Chaykin-a 3 6 9 14 19 24
4-7 2 4 6 11 16 20

SIX STRING SAMURAI
Awesome-Hyperwerks: Sept, 1998 ($2.95)

1-Stinsman & Fraga-a 3.00

67 SECONDS
Marvel Comics (Epic Comics): 1992 ($15.95, 54 pgs., graphic novel)

nn-James Robinson scripts; Steve Yeowell-c/a 2 4 6 11 14 18

SKAAR: KING OF THE SAVAGE LAND
Marvel Comics: Jun, 2011 - No. 5 ($2.99, limited series)

1,2-Shanna & Ka-Zar app.; Ching-a. 1-Komarck-c. 2-McGuinness-c 3.00

SKAAR: SON OF HULK (Title continues in Son of Hulk #13)(Also see World War Hulk x-over)
Marvel Comics: Aug, 2008 - No. 12, Aug, 2009 ($2.99)

1-Garney-a/Pak-s; 2 covers by Pagulayan and Julie Bell; origin 4.00
1-Second printing - 2 covers by Garney and Hulk movie image 3.00
1-Third printing - Garney sketch variant-c 3.00
2-12: 2-6-Back-up story with Guice-a. 7-12-Silver Surfer app. 3.00
Planet Skaar Prologue 1 (7/09, $3.99) Panosian-a; Fantastic Four & She-Hulk app. 4.00
... Presents - Savage World of Sakaar (11/08, $3.99) Pak-s/art by various; Garney-c 4.00

SKATEMAN
Pacific Comics: Nov, 1983 (Baxter paper, one-shot)

1-Adams-c/a 4.00

SKELETON HAND (...In Secrets of the Supernatural)
American Comics Gr. (B&M Dist. Co.): Sept-Oct, 1952 - No. 6, Jul-Aug, 1953

1 46 92 138 290 488 685
2 34 68 102 199 325 450
3-6 26 52 78 154 252 350

SKELETON KEY
Amaze Ink: July, 1995 - No. 30, Jan, 1998 ($1.25/$1.50/$1.75, B&W)

1-30 3.00
Special #1 (2/98, $4.95) Unpublished short stories 5.00
Sugar Kat Special (10/98, $2.95) Halloween stories 3.00
Beyond The Threshold TPB (6/96. $11.95)-r/#1-6 12.00
Cats and Dogs TPB ($12.95)-r/#25-30 13.00
The Celestial Calendar TPB ($19.95)-r/#7-18 20.00
Telling Tales TPB ($12.95)-r/#19-24 13.00

SKELETON KEY (Volume 2)
Amaze Ink: 1999 - No. 4, 1999 ($2.95, B&W)

Skullkickers #4 © Jim Zubkavich

Skyman #4 © CCG

Slam-Bang Comics #3 © FAW

1-4-Andrew Watson-s/a 3.00

SKELETON WARRIORS
Marvel Comics: Apr, 1995 - No. 4, July, 1995 ($1.50)
1-4: Based on animated series. 3.00

SKIN GRAFT: THE ADVENTURES OF A TATTOOED MAN
DC Comics (Vertigo): July, 1993 - No. 4, Oct, 1993 ($2.50, lim. series, mature)
1-4 3.00

SKINWALKER
Oni Press: May, 2002 - No. 4, Sept, 2002 ($2.95, limited series)
1-4-Hurtt & Dela Cruz-a; Talon-c 3.00
1-(5/05) Free Comic Book Day Edition 3.00

SKI PARTY (See Movie Classics)

SKREEMER
DC Comics: May, 1989 - No. 6, Oct, 1989 ($2.00, limited series, mature)
1-6: Contains graphic violence; Milligan-s 3.00
TPB (2002, $19.95) r/#1-6 20.00

SKRULL KILL KREW
Marvel Comics: Sept, 1995 - No. 5, Dec, 1995 ($2.95, limited series)
1-5: Grant Morrison & Mark Millar scripts; Steve Yeowell-a. 2,3-Cap America app. 3.00
TPB (2006, $16.99) r/#1-5 17.00

SKRULL KILL KREW
Marvel Comics: Jun, 2009 - No. 5, Dec, 2009 ($3.99, limited series)
1-5-Felber-s/Robinson-a 4.00

SKRULLS! (Tie-in to Secret Invasion crossover)
Marvel Comics: 2008 ($4.99, one-shot)
1-Skrull history, profiles of Skrulls, their allies & foes; checklist of appearances; Horn-c 5.00

SKRULLS VS. POWER PACK (Tie-in to Secret Invasion crossover)
Marvel Comics: Sept, 2008 - No. 4 ($2.99, limited series)
1-4-Van Lente-s/Hamscher-a; Franklin Richards app. 3.00

SKUL, THE
Virtual Comics (Byron Preiss Multimedia): Oct, 1996 - No. 3, Dec, 1996 ($2.50, lim. series)
1-3: Ron Lim & Jimmy Palmiotti-a 3.00

SKULL & BONES
DC Comics: 1992 - No. 3, 1992 ($4.95, limited series, 52 pgs.)
Book 1-3: 1-1st app. 5.00

SKULLKICKERS
Image Comics: Sept, 2010 - Present ($2.99)
1-Jim Zubkavich-s/Edwin Huang-a; two covers 4.00
1-(2nd & 3rd printings), 2-6 3.00

SKULL, THE SLAYER
Marvel Comics Group: Aug, 1975 - No. 8, Nov, 1976 (20¢/25¢)

	GD	VG	FN	VF	VF/NM	NM-
1-Origin & 1st app.; Gil Kane-c	2	4	6	10	14	18
2-8: 2-Gil Kane-c. 5,6-(Regular 25¢-c). 8-Kirby-c	2	3	4	6	8	10
5,6-(30¢-c variants, limited distribution)(5,7/76)	3	6	9	18	27	35

SKY BLAZERS (CBS Radio)
Hawley Publications: Sept, 1940 - No. 2, Nov, 1940

	GD	VG	FN	VF	VF/NM	NM-
1-Sky Pirates, Ace Archer, Flying Aces begin	60	120	180	381	653	925
2	39	78	117	231	378	525

SKY DOLL
Marvel Comics (Soleil): 2008 - No. 3, 2008 ($5.99, mature)
1-3-Barbucci & Canepa-s/a; English version of French comic; preview of other titles 6.00
...: Doll's Factory 1,2 (2009 - No. 2, 2009, $5.99) Barbucci & Canepa-s/a 6.00
...: Lacrima Christi 1,2 (9/10 - No. 2, 10/10, $5.99) Barbucci & Canepa and others-s/a 6.00
...: Space Ship 1,2 (7/10 - No. 2, 8/10, $5.99) Barbucci & Canepa and others-s/a 6.00

SKYE RUNNER
DC Comics (WildStorm): June, 2006 - No. 6, Mar, 2007 ($2.99)
1-6: 1-Three covers; Warner-s/Garza-a. 2-Three covers, incl. Campbell 3.00

SKYMAN (See Big Shot Comics & Sparky Watts)
Columbia Comics Gr.: Fall?, 1941 - No. 2, Fall?, 1942; No. 3, 1948 - No. 4, 1948

	GD	VG	FN	VF	VF/NM	NM-
1-Origin Skyman, The Face, Sparky Watts app.; Whitney-c/a; 3rd story-r from Big Shot #1; Whitney c-1-4	126	252	378	806	1378	1950
2 (1942)-Yankee Doodle	60	120	180	381	653	925
3,4 (1948)	39	78	117	240	395	550

SKYPILOT
Ziff-Davis Publ. Co.: No. 10, 1950(nd) - No. 11, Apr-May, 1951

	GD	VG	FN	VF	VF/NM	NM-
10,11-Frank Borth-a; Saunders painted-c	15	30	45	84	127	170

SKY RANGER (See Johnny Law...)

SKYROCKET
Harry 'A' Chesler: 1944

	GD	VG	FN	VF	VF/NM	NM-
nn-Alias the Dragon, Dr. Vampire, Skyrocket & The Desperado app.; WWII Japan zero-c	34	68	102	199	325	450

SKY SHERIFF (Breeze Lawson...) (Also see Exposed & Outlaws)
D. S. Publishing Co.: Summer, 1948

	GD	VG	FN	VF	VF/NM	NM-
1-Edmond Good-c/a	14	28	42	76	108	140

SKY WOLF (Also see Airboy)
Eclipse Comics: Mar, 1988 - No. 3, Oct, 1988 ($1.25/$1.50/$1.95, lim. series)
1-3 3.00

SLAINE, THE BERSERKER (Slaine the King #21 on)
Quality: July, 1987 - No. 28, 1989 ($1.25/$1.50)
1-28 3.00

SLAINE, THE HORNED GOD
Fleetway: 1998 - No. 3 ($6.99)
1-3-Reprints series from 2000 A.D.; Bisley-a 7.00

SLAM BANG COMICS (Western Desperado #8)
Fawcett Publications: Mar, 1940 - No. 7, Sept, 1940 (Combined with Master Comics #7)

	GD	VG	FN	VF	VF/NM	NM-
1-Diamond Jack, Mark Swift & The Time Retarder, Lee Granger, Jungle King begin & continue in Master	213	426	639	1363	2332	3300
2	87	174	261	553	952	1350
3-Classic-c	174	348	522	1114	1907	2700
4-7: 6-Intro Zoro, the Mystery Man (also in #7)	65	130	195	416	708	1000

Ashcan (1940) Not distributed to newsstands, only for in house use. A copy sold in 2006 for $4,500.

SLAPSTICK
Marvel Comics: Nov, 1992 - No. 4, Feb, 1993 ($1.25, limited series)
1-4: Fry/Austin-c/a. 4-Ghost Rider, D.D., F.F. app. 3.00

SLAPSTICK COMICS
Comic Magazines Distributors: nd (1946?) (36 pgs.)

	GD	VG	FN	VF	VF/NM	NM-
nn-Firetop feature; Post-a(2)	25	50	75	147	241	335

SLASH-D DOUBLECROSS
St. John Publishing Co.: 1950 (Pocket-size, 132 pgs.)

	GD	VG	FN	VF	VF/NM	NM-
nn-Western comics	21	42	63	122	199	275

SLAUGHTERMAN
Comico: Feb, 1983 - No. 2, 1983 ($1.50, B&W)
1,2 3.00

SLAVE GIRL COMICS (See Malu... & White Princess of the Jungle #2)
Avon Periodicals/Eternity Comics (1989): Feb, 1949 - No. 2, Apr, 1949 (52 pgs.); Mar, 1989 (B&W, 44 pgs)

	GD	VG	FN	VF	VF/NM	NM-
1-Larsen-c/a	103	206	309	659	1130	1600
2-Larsen-a	73	146	219	467	796	1125

1-(3/89, $2.25, B&W, 44 pgs.)-r/#1 4.00

SLAVE LABOR STORIES
SLG Publishing: May, 2003 (Giveaway, B&W)
1-Free Comic Book Day Edition; short stories by various; Dorkin Milk & Cheese-c 2.50

SLEDGE HAMMER (TV)
Marvel Comics: Feb, 1988 - No. 2, Mar,1988 ($1.00, limited series)
1,2 3.00

SLEEPER
DC Comics (WildStorm): Mar, 2003 - No. 12, Mar, 2004 ($2.95)
1-12-Brubaker-s/Phillips-c/a. 3-Back-up preview of The Authority: High Stakes pt. 2 3.00
...: All False Moves TPB (2004, $17.95) r/#7-12 18.00
...: Out in the Cold TPB (2004, $17.95) r/#1-6 18.00

SLEEPER: SEASON TWO
DC Comics (WildStorm): Aug, 2004 - No. 12, July, 2005 ($2.95/$2.99)
1-12-Brubaker-s/Phillips-c/a. 3.00
TPB (2009, $24.99) r/#1-12 25.00
...: A Crooked Line TPB (2005, $17.99) r/#1-6 18.00
...: The Long Way Home TPB (2005, $14.99) r/#7-12 15.00

Sleepwalker #28 © MAR

Smallville #10 © DC

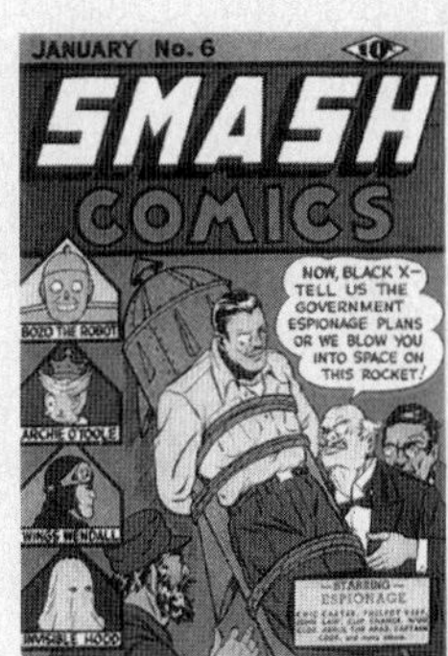

Smash Comics #6 © QUA

GD 2.0 | VG 4.0 | FN 6.0 | VF 8.0 | VF/NM 9.0 | NM- 9.2

GD 2.0 | VG 4.0 | FN 6.0 | VF 8.0 | VF/NM 9.0 | NM- 9.2

SLEEPING BEAUTY (See Dell Giants & Movie Comics)
Dell Publishing Co.: No. 973, May, 1959 - No. 984, June, 1959 (Disney)

Four Color 973 (...and the Prince) 10 20 30 72 131 190
Four Color 984 (...Fairy Godmother's) 9 18 27 61 103 145

SLEEPWALKER
Marvel Comics: June, 1991 - No. 33, Feb, 1994 ($1.00/$1.25)

1-1st app. Sleepwalker 3.50
2-33: 4-Williamson-i. 5-Spider-Man-c/stor. 7-Infinity Gauntlet x-over. 8-Vs. Deathlok-c/story. 11-Ghost Rider-c/story. 12-Quesada-c/a(p) 14-Intro Spectra. 15-F.F.-c/story. 17-Darkhawk & Spider-Man x-over. 18-Infinity War x-over; Quesada/Williamson-c. 21,22-Hobgoblin app. 19-($2.00)-Die-cut Sleepwalker mask-c 3.00
25-($2.95, 52 pgs.)-Holo-grafx foil-c; origin 4.00
Holiday Special 1 (1/93, $2.00, 52 pgs.)-Quesada-c(p) 4.00

SLEEPWALKING
Hall of Heroes: Jan, 1996 ($2.50, B&W)

1-Kelley Jones-c 3.00

SLEEPY HOLLOW (Movie Adaption)
DC Comics (Vertigo): 2000 ($7.95, one-shot)

1-Kelley Jones-a/Seagle-s 8.00

SLEEZE BROTHERS, THE
Marvel Comics (Epic Comics): Aug, 1989 - No. 6, Jan, 1990 ($1.75, mature)

1-6: 4-6 (9/89 - 11/89 indicia dates) 3.00
nn-(1991, $3.95, 52 pgs.) 4.00

SLICK CHICK COMICS
Leader Enterprises: 1947(nd) - No. 3, 1947(nd)

1-Teenage humor 14 28 42 76 108 140
2,3 10 20 30 54 72 90

SLIDERS (TV)
Acclaim Comics (Armada): June, 1996 - No. 2, July, 1996 ($2.50, lim. series)

1,2: D.G. Chichester scripts; Dick Giordano-a. 3.00

SLIDERS: DARKEST HOUR (TV)
Acclaim Comics (Armada): Oct, 1996 - No. 3, Dec, 1996 ($2.50, limited series)

1-3 3.00

SLIDERS SPECIAL
Acclaim Comics (Armada): Nov, 1996 - No 3, Mar, 1997 ($3.95, limited series)

1-3: 1-Narcotica-Jerry O'Connell-s. 2-Blood and Splendor. 3-Deadly Secrets 4.00

SLIDERS: ULTIMATUM (TV)
Acclaim Comics (Armada): Sept, 1996 - No. 2, Sept, 1996 ($2.50, lim. series)

1,2 3.00

SLIMER! (TV cartoon) (Also see the Real Ghostbusters)
Now Comics: 1989 - No. 19, Feb?, 1991 ($1.75)

1-19: Based on animated cartoon 3.00

SLIM MORGAN (See Wisco)

SLINGERS (See Spider-Man: Identity Crisis issues)
Marvel Comics: Dec, 1998 - No. 12, Nov, 1999 ($2.99/$1.99)

0-(Wizard #88 supplement) Prelude story 3.00
1-($2.99) Four editions w/different covers for each hero, 16 pages common to all, the other pages from each hero's perspective 4.00
2-12: 2-Two-c. 12-Saltares-a 3.00

SLITHISS ATTACKS! (Also see Very Weird Tales)
Oceanspray Comics Group: Dec, 2001 – No. 4, Aug, 2004 ($3.00/$4.00)

1-($3.00) Origin and 1st app. of the monster Slithiss; 1st app. Overconfident Man 15.00
2-($4.00) 2nd app. Overconfident Man; "Chris Lamo" Newport, OR murder parody 12.00
3-($3.00) Rutland Vermont Halloween x-over; 3rd app. Overconfident Man 12.00
4-($3.00) 4th app. Overconfident Man 10.00
Special Edition 1($20.00) reprints #1-2 without letter column 20.00
Special Edition 1($20.00) second printing 20.00
NOTE: *Created in prevention classes taught by Jon McClure at the Oceanspray Family Center in Newport, OR and paid for by the Housing Authority of Lincoln County, all books are b&w with color covers. Bob Overstreet and other comics' professionals wrote letters of encouragement that were published in issues #2-4. Issues #1-2 penciled and inked by various artists; #3-4 penciled by James Gilmer. All comics feature characters created by students, signed and numbered by Jon McClure. Issue #1 had a 200 issue print run, while issues #2-4 have print runs of 100 each. Special Edition #1 had a print run of 26 issues, while the second printing had a 10 issue print run. Ties in with live action movie Face Eater released in 2007 and card game FaceEater released in 2010.*

SLUDGE
Malibu Comics (Ultraverse): Oct, 1993 - No. 12, Dec, 1994 ($2.50/$1.95)

1-($2.50, 48 pgs.)-Intro/1st app. Sludge; Rune flip-c/story Pt. 1 (1st app., 3 pgs.) by Barry Smith; The Night Man app. (3 pg. preview); The Mighty Magnor 1 pg strip begins by Aragonés (cont. in other titles) 4.00
1-Ultra 5000 Limited silver foil 5.00
2-11: 3-Break-Thru x-over. 4-2 pg. Mantra origin. 8-Bloodstorm app. 3.00
12 ($3.50)-Ultraverse Premiere #8 flip book; Alex Ross poster 4.00
...:Red Xmas (12/94, $2.50, 44 pgs.) 4.00

SLUGGER (Little Wise Guys Starring...)(Also see Daredevil Comics)
Lev Gleason Publications: April, 1956

1-Biro-c 7 14 21 37 46 55

SMALL GODS
Image Comics: Jun, 2004 - No. 12, Nov, 2005 ($2.95/$2.99, B&W)

1-12-Rand-s/Ferreyna-a 3.00
... Special #1 (6/05, $2.95) flip cover 3.00
Vol. 1: Killing Grin (1/05, $9.95, TPB) r/#1-4; sketch pages, cover gallery & script page 10.00

SMALLVILLE (Based on TV series)
DC Comics: May, 2003 - No. 11 ($3.50/$3.95, bi-monthly)

1-6-Photo-c. 1-Plunkett-a; interviews with cast; season 1 episode guide begins 3.50
7-11-($3.95) 7-Chloe Chronicles begin; season 2 episode guide begins 4.00
Vol. 1 TPB (2004, $9.95) r/#1-4 & Smallville: The Comic; photo-c 10.00

SMALLVILLE: THE COMIC (Based on TV series)
DC Comics: Nov, 2002 ($3.95, 64 pages, one-shot)

1-Photo-c; art by Martinez and Leon; interviews with cast; season 2 preview 4.00

SMASH COMICS (Becomes Lady Luck #86 on)
Quality Comics Group: Aug, 1939 - No. 85, Oct, 1949

1-Origin Hugh Hazard & His Iron Man, Bozo the Robot, Espionage, Starring Black X by Eisner, & Hooded Justice (Invisible Justice #2 on); Chic Carter & Wings Wendall begin; 1st Robot on the cover of a comic book (Bozo) 326 652 978 2282 3991 5700
2-The Lone Star Rider app; Invisible Hood gains power of invisibility; bondage/torture-c 135 270 405 864 1482 2100
3-Captain Cook & Eisner's John Law begin 69 138 207 442 759 1075
4,5: 4-Flash Fulton begins 66 132 198 419 722 1025
6-12: 12-One pg. Fine-a 61 122 183 390 670 950
13-Magno begins (8/40); last Eisner issue; The Ray app. in full page ad; The Purple Trio begins 62 124 186 394 677 960
14-Intro. The Ray (9/40) by Lou Fine & others 300 600 900 2010 3505 5000
15,16: 16-The Scarlet Seal begins 124 248 372 787 1356 1925
17-Wun Cloo becomes plastic super-hero by Jack Cole (9-months before Plastic Man) 129 258 387 826 1413 2000
18-Midnight by Jack Cole begins (origin & 1st app., 1/41) 165 330 495 1048 1799 2550
19-22: Last Ray by Fine; The Jester begins-#22 87 174 261 553 952 1350
23,24: 24-The Sword app.; last Chic Carter; Wings Wendall dons new costume #24,25 67 134 201 426 731 1035
25-Origin/1st app. Wildfire; Rookie Rankin begins 75 150 225 476 821 1165
26-30: 28-Midnight-c begin, end #85 64 128 192 406 696 985
31,32,34: The Ray by Rudy Palais; also #33 54 108 162 346 591 835
33-Origin The Marksman 62 124 186 394 680 965
35-37 49 98 147 309 522 735
38-The Yankee Eagle begins; last Midnight by Jack Cole; classic-c by Cole 98 196 294 622 1074 1525
39,40-Last Ray issue 50 100 150 315 533 750
41,44-50 40 80 120 246 411 575
42-Lady Luck begins by Klaus Nordling 135 270 405 864 1482 2100
43-Lady Luck-c (1st & only in Smash) 74 148 222 470 810 1150
51-60 30 60 90 177 289 400
61-70 23 46 69 136 223 310
71-85: 79-Midnight battles the Men from Mars-c/s 21 42 63 122 199 275
NOTE: ***Al Bryant** c-54, 63-68. **Cole** a-17-38, 68, 69, 72, 73, 78, 80, 83, 85; c-38, 60-62, 69-84. **Crandall** a-(Ray)-23-29, 35-38; c-36, 39, 40, 42-44, 46. **Fine** a(Ray)-14, 15, 16(w/**Tuska**), 17-22. **Fox** c-24-35. **Fuje** Ray-30. **Gil Fox** a-6-7, 9, 11-13. **Guardineer** a-(The Marksman)-39-?, 49, 52. **Gustavson** a-4-7, 9, 11-13 (The Jester)-22-46; (Magno)-13-21; (Midnight)-39(Cole inks), 49, 52, 63-65. **Kotzky** a-(Espionage)-33-38; c-45, 47-53. **Nordling** a-49, 52, 63-65. **Powell** a-11, 12, (Abdul the Arab)-13-24.Black X c-2, 6, 9, 11, 13, 16. Bozo the Robot c-1, 3, 5, 8, 10, 12, 14, 18, 20, 22, 24, 26. Midnight c-28-85. The Ray c-15, 17, 19, 21, 23, 25, 27. Wings Wendall c-4, 7.*

SMASH COMICS (Also see All Star Comics 1999 crossover titles)
DC Comics: May, 1999 ($1.99, one-shot)

1-Golden Age Doctor Mid-nite and Hourman 3.00

SMASH HIT SPORTS COMICS
Essankay Publications: V2#1, Jan, 1949

V2#1-L.B. Cole-c/a 28 56 84 165 270 375

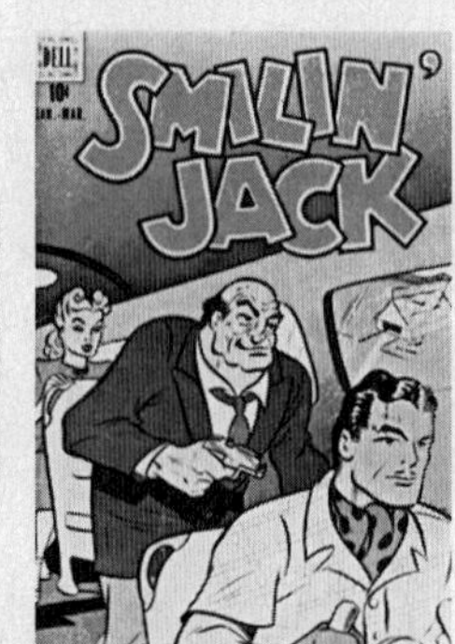

Smilin' Jack #2 © DELL

Smurfs #1 © MAR

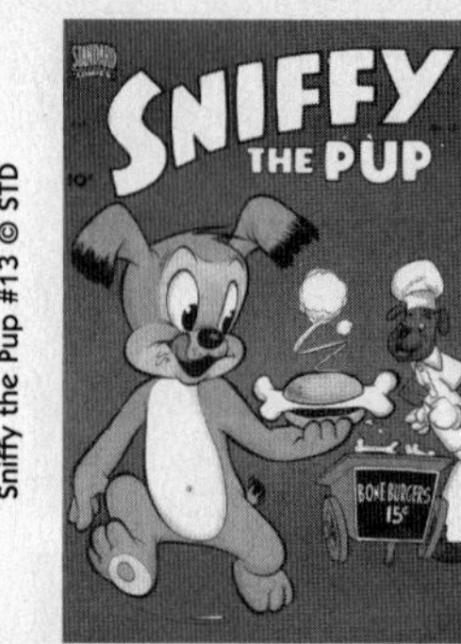

Sniffy the Pup #13 © STD

SMAX (Also see Top Ten)
America's Best Comics: Oct, 2003 - No. 5, May, 2004 ($2.95, limited series)

	GD 2.0	VG 4.0	FN 6.0	VF 8.0	VF/NM 9.0	NM- 9.2
1-5-Alan Moore-s/Zander Cannon-a						3.00
... Collected Edition (2004, $19.95, HC with dustjacket) r/#1-5						20.00
... Collected Edition SC (2005, $12.99) r/#1-5						13.00

SMILE COMICS (Also see Gay Comics, Tickle, & Whee)
Modern Store Publ.: 1955 (52 pgs.; 5x7-1/4") (7¢)

	GD 2.0	VG 4.0	FN 6.0	VF 8.0	VF/NM 9.0	NM- 9.2
1	6	12	18	31	38	45

SMILEY BURNETTE WESTERN (Also see Patches #8 & Six-Gun Heroes)
Fawcett Publ.: March, 1950 - No. 4, Oct, 1950 (All photo front & back-c)

	GD 2.0	VG 4.0	FN 6.0	VF 8.0	VF/NM 9.0	NM- 9.2
1-Red Eagle begins	25	50	75	150	245	340
2-4	16	32	48	94	147	200

SMILEY (THE PSYCHOTIC BUTTON) (See Evil Ernie)
Chaos! Comics: July, 1998 - Present ($2.95, one-shots)

	GD 2.0	VG 4.0	FN 6.0	VF 8.0	VF/NM 9.0	NM- 9.2
1-Ivan Reis-a						3.00
... Holiday Special (1/99), ...'s Spring Break (4/99), ...Wrestling Special (5/99)						3.00

SMILIN' JACK (See Famous Feature Stories and Popular Comics) (Also see Super Book of Comics #1&2 and Super-Book of Comics #7&19 in the Promotional Comics section)
Dell Publishing Co.: No. 5, 1940 - No. 8, Oct-Dec, 1949

	GD 2.0	VG 4.0	FN 6.0	VF 8.0	VF/NM 9.0	NM- 9.2
Four Color 5	71	142	213	454	777	1100
Four Color 10 (1940)	61	122	183	387	664	940
Large Feature Comic 12,14,25 (1941)	58	116	174	371	636	900
Four Color 4 (1942)	36	72	108	281	553	825
Four Color 14 (1943)	28	56	84	204	415	625
Four Color 36,58 (1943-44)	21	42	63	148	297	445
Four Color 80 (1945)	13	26	39	94	185	275
Four Color 149 (1947)	10	20	30	69	122	175
1 (1-3/48)	10	20	30	70	125	180
2	6	12	18	41	66	90
3-8 (10-12/49)	5	10	15	32	51	70

SMILING SPOOK SPUNKY (See Spunky)

SMITTY (See Popular Comics, Super Book #2, 4 & Super Comics)
Dell Publishing Co.: No. 11, 1940 - No. 7, Aug-Oct, 1949; No. 909, Apr, 1958

	GD 2.0	VG 4.0	FN 6.0	VF 8.0	VF/NM 9.0	NM- 9.2
Four Color 11 (1940)	45	90	135	284	480	675
Large Feature Comic 26 (1941)	36	72	108	216	351	485
Four Color 6 (1942)	20	40	60	142	286	430
Four Color 32 (1943)	14	28	42	97	194	290
Four Color 65 (1945)	12	24	36	84	157	230
Four Color 99 (1946)	10	20	30	71	128	185
Four Color 138 (1947)	9	18	27	64	110	155
1 (2-4/48)	9	18	27	63	107	150
2-(5-7/48)	5	10	15	32	51	70
3,4: 3-(8-10/48), 4-(11-1/48-49)	4	8	12	28	44	60
5-7, Four Color 909 (4/58)	4	8	12	24	37	50

SMOKEY BEAR (TV) (See March Of Comics #234, 362, 372, 383, 407)
Gold Key: Feb, 1970 - No. 13, Mar, 1973

	GD 2.0	VG 4.0	FN 6.0	VF 8.0	VF/NM 9.0	NM- 9.2
1	3	6	9	19	29	38
2-5	2	4	6	10	14	18
6-13	2	4	6	8	10	12

SMOKEY STOVER (See Popular Comics, Super Book #5,17,29 & Super Comics)
Dell Publishing Co.: No. 7, 1942 - No. 827, Aug, 1957

	GD 2.0	VG 4.0	FN 6.0	VF 8.0	VF/NM 9.0	NM- 9.2
Four Color 7 (1942)-Reprints	26	52	78	186	373	560
Four Color 35 (1943)	15	30	45	104	212	320
Four Color 64 (1944)	12	24	36	87	164	240
Four Color 229 (1949)	6	12	18	41	66	90
Four Color 730,827	5	10	15	32	51	70

SMOKEY THE BEAR (See Forest Fire for 1st app.)
Dell Publ. Co.: No. 653, 10/55 - No. 1214, 8/61 (See March of Comics #234)

	GD 2.0	VG 4.0	FN 6.0	VF 8.0	VF/NM 9.0	NM- 9.2
Four Color 653 (#1)	10	20	30	70	125	180
Four Color 708,754,818,932	6	12	18	41	66	90
Four Color 1016,1119,1214	4	8	12	28	44	60

SMOKY (See Movie Classics)

SMURFS (TV)
Marvel Comics: 1982 (Dec) - No. 3, 1983

	GD 2.0	VG 4.0	FN 6.0	VF 8.0	VF/NM 9.0	NM- 9.2
1-3	2	4	6	10	14	18
...Treasury Edition 1 (64 pgs.)-r/#1-3	3	6	9	18	27	35

SNAFU (Magazine)
Atlas Comics (RCM): Nov, 1955 - V2#2, Mar, 1956 (B&W)

	GD 2.0	VG 4.0	FN 6.0	VF 8.0	VF/NM 9.0	NM- 9.2
V1#1-Heath/Severin-a; Everett, Maneely-a	15	30	45	84	127	170
V2#1,2-Severin-a	11	22	33	62	86	110

SNAGGLEPUSS (TV)(See Hanna-Barbera Band Wagon, Quick Draw McGraw #5 & Spotlight #4)
Gold Key: Oct, 1962 - No. 4, Sept, 1963 (Hanna-Barbera)

	GD 2.0	VG 4.0	FN 6.0	VF 8.0	VF/NM 9.0	NM- 9.2
1	8	16	24	58	97	135
2-4	6	12	18	43	69	95

SNAKE EYES (G.I. Joe)
Devil's Due Publ.: Aug, 2005 - No. 6, Jan, 2006 ($2.95)

	GD 2.0	VG 4.0	FN 6.0	VF 8.0	VF/NM 9.0	NM- 9.2
1-6-Santalucia-a						3.00
...: Declassified TPB (4/06, $18.95) r/series; source guide						19.00

SNAKE PLISSKEN CHRONICLES, (John Carpenter's...)
Hurricane Entertainment: June, 2003 - No. 4 ($2.99)

	GD 2.0	VG 4.0	FN 6.0	VF 8.0	VF/NM 9.0	NM- 9.2
Preview Issue (8/02, no cover price) B&W preview; John Carpenter interview						3.00
1-4: 1-Three covers; Rodriguez-a						3.00

SNAKES AND LADDERS
Eddie Campbell Comics: 2001 ($5.95, B&W, one-shot)

	GD 2.0	VG 4.0	FN 6.0	VF 8.0	VF/NM 9.0	NM- 9.2
nn-Alan Moore-s/Eddie Campbell-a						6.00

SNAKES ON A PLANE (Adaptation of the 2006 movie)
Virgin Comics: Oct, 2006 - No. 2, Nov, 2006 ($2.99, limited series)

	GD 2.0	VG 4.0	FN 6.0	VF 8.0	VF/NM 9.0	NM- 9.2
1,2: 1-Dixon-s/Purcell-a. JG Jones and photo-c. 2-Klebs, Jr.-a; Moore & photo-c						3.00

SNAKE WOMAN (Shekhar Kapur's...)
Virgin Comics: July, 2006 - No. 10, Apr, 2007 ($2.99)

	GD 2.0	VG 4.0	FN 6.0	VF 8.0	VF/NM 9.0	NM- 9.2
1-10: 1-6-Michael Gaydos-a/Zeb Wells-s. 1-Two covers by Gaydos & Singh						3.00
#0 (5/07, 99¢) origin of the Snake Goddess; background info; Gaydos-a/c						3.00
... Curse of the 68 (3/08 - No. 4, 5/08, $2.99) 1-4: 1-Ingale-a. 2-Manu-a						3.00
... Tale of the Snake Charmer 1-6 (6/07-12/07, $2.99) Vivek Shinde-a						3.00
... Vol. 1 TPB (6/07, $14.99) r/#1-5; Gaydos sketch pages; creator commentary						15.00
... Vol. 2 TPB (9/07, $14.99) r/#6-10; Cebulski intro.						15.00

SNAP (Formerly Scoop #8; becomes Jest #10,11 & Komik Pages #10)
Harry 'A' Chesler: No. 9, 1944

	GD 2.0	VG 4.0	FN 6.0	VF 8.0	VF/NM 9.0	NM- 9.2
9-Manhunter, The Voice; WWII gag-c	29	58	87	170	278	385

SNAPPY COMICS
Cima Publ. Co. (Prize Publ.): 1945

	GD 2.0	VG 4.0	FN 6.0	VF 8.0	VF/NM 9.0	NM- 9.2
1-Airmale app.; 9 pg. Sorcerer's Apprentice adapt; Kiefer-a	33	66	99	194	317	440

SNARKY PARKER (See Life With...)

SNIFFY THE PUP
Standard Publ. (Animated Cartoons): No. 5, Nov, 1949 - No. 18, Sept, 1953

	GD 2.0	VG 4.0	FN 6.0	VF 8.0	VF/NM 9.0	NM- 9.2
5-Two Frazetta text illos	10	20	30	58	79	100
6-10	7	14	21	35	43	50
11-18	6	12	18	28	34	40

SNOOPER AND BLABBER DETECTIVES (TV) (See Whitman Comic Books)
Gold Key: Nov, 1962 - No. 3, May, 1963 (Hanna-Barbera)

	GD 2.0	VG 4.0	FN 6.0	VF 8.0	VF/NM 9.0	NM- 9.2
1	7	14	21	49	80	110
2,3	6	12	18	37	59	80

SNOW WHITE (See Christmas With... (in Promotional Comics section), Mickey Mouse Magazine, Movie Comics & Seven Dwarfs)
Dell Publishing Co.: No. 49, July, 1944 - No. 382, Mar, 1952 (Disney-Movie)

	GD 2.0	VG 4.0	FN 6.0	VF 8.0	VF/NM 9.0	NM- 9.2
Four Color 49 (...& the Seven Dwarfs)	47	94	141	376	763	1150
Four Color 382 (1952)-origin; partial reprint of Four Color 49	9	18	27	65	113	160

SNOW WHITE
Marvel Comics: Jan, 1995 ($1.95, one-shot)

	GD 2.0	VG 4.0	FN 6.0	VF 8.0	VF/NM 9.0	NM- 9.2
1-r/1937 Sunday newspaper pages						3.00

SNOW WHITE AND THE SEVEN DWARFS
Whitman Publications: April, 1982 (60¢)

	GD 2.0	VG 4.0	FN 6.0	VF 8.0	VF/NM 9.0	NM- 9.2
nn-r/Four Color 49	1	2	3	5	6	8

SNOW WHITE AND THE SEVEN DWARFS GOLDEN ANNIVERSARY
Gladstone: Fall, 1987 ($2.95, magazine size, 52 pgs.)

	GD 2.0	VG 4.0	FN 6.0	VF 8.0	VF/NM 9.0	NM- 9.2
1-Contains poster	2	4	6	8	11	14

SOAP OPERA LOVE
Charlton Comics: Feb, 1983 - No. 3, June, 1983

Sojourn #22 © CRO

Soldier Zero #1 © BOOM! Ent.

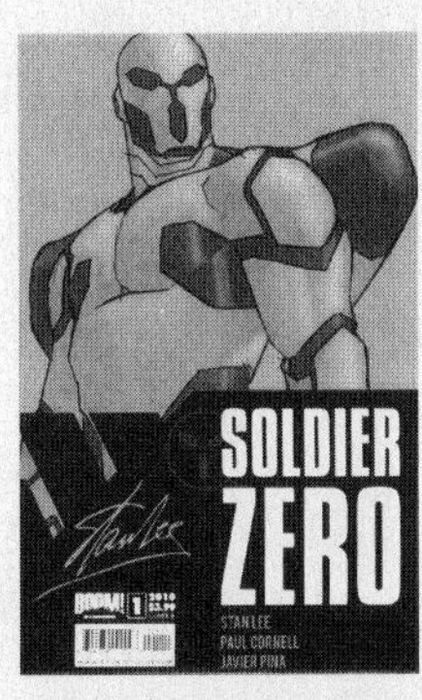

Solo #3 © MAR

	GD 2.0	VG 4.0	FN 6.0	VF 8.0	VF/NM 9.0	NM- 9.2
1-3-Low print run	3	6	9	18	27	35

SOAP OPERA ROMANCES
Charlton Comics: July, 1982 - No. 5, March, 1983

1-5-Nurse Betsy Crane-r; low print run	3	6	9	18	27	35

SOCK MONKEY
Dark Horse Comics: Sept, 1998 - No. 2, Oct, 1998 ($2.95/$2.99, B&W)

1,2-Tony Millionaire-s/a 4.00

Vol. 2 -(Tony Millionaire's Sock Monkey) July, 1999 - No. 2, Aug, 1999

1,2 3.00

Vol. 3 -(Tony Millionaire's Sock Monkey) Nov, 2000 - No. 2, Dec, 2000

1,2 3.00

Vol. 4 -(Tony Millionaire's Sock Monkey) May, 2003 - No. 2, Aug, 2003

1,2 3.00

...The Inches Incident (Sept, 2006 - No. 4, Apr, 2007) 1-4-Tony Millionaire-s/a 3.00

SOJOURN
White Cliffs Publ. Co.: Sept, 1977 - No. 2, 1978 ($1.50, B&W & color, tabloid size)

1,2: 1-Tor by Kubert, Eagle by Severin, E. V. Race, Private Investigator by Doug Wildey, T. C. Mars by Aragonés begin plus other strips 2 4 6 8 10 12

NOTE: Most copies came folded. Unfolded copies are worth 50% more.

SOJOURN
CrossGeneration Comics: July, 2001 - No. 34, May, 2004 ($2.95)

Prequel -Ron Marz-s/Greg Land-c/a; preview pages 3.00
1-Ron Marz-s/Greg Land-c/a in most 6.00
2,3 5.00
4-24: 7-Immonen-a. 12-Brigman-a. 17-Lopresti-a. 21-Luke Ross-a 3.00
25-34: 25-$1.00-c. 34-Cariello-a 3.00
...: From the Ashes TPB (2001, $19.95) r/#1-6; Land painted-c 20.00
...: The Dragon's Tale TPB (2002, $15.95) r/#7-12; Jusko painted-c 16.00
...: The Warrior's Tale TPB (2003, $15.95) r/#13-18 16.00
Vol. 4: The Thief's Tale (2003, $15.95) r/#19-24 16.00
Vol. 5: The Sorcerer's Tale (Checker Book Publ.,2007, $17.95) r/#25-30 18.00
Vol. 6: The Berzerker's Tale (Checker Book Publ.,2007, $17.95) r/#31-34, Prequel 18.00
Traveler Vol.1,2 ($9.95) digest-sized reprints of TPBs 10.00

SOLAR (...Man of the Atom) (Also see Doctor Solar)
Valiant/Acclaim Comics (Valiant): Sept, 1991 - No. 60, Apr, 1996 ($1.75-$2.50, 44 pgs.)

1-Layton-a(i) on Solar; Barry Windsor-Smith-c/a 2 4 6 8 10 12
2-9: 2-Layton-a(i) on Solar, B. Smith-a. 3-1st app. Harada (11/91). 7-vs. X-O Armor 6.00
10-(6/92, $3.95)-1st app. Eternal Warrior (6 pgs.); black embossed-c; origin & 1st app. Geoff McHenry (Geomancer) 2 4 6 9 12 15
10-($3.95)-2nd printing 4.00
11-15: 11-1st full app. Eternal Warrior. 12,13-Unity x-overs. 14-1st app. Fred Bender (becomes Dr. Eclipse). 15-2nd Dr. Eclipse 4.00
16-60: 17-X-O Manowar app. 23-Solar splits. 29-1st Valiant Vision book. 33-Valiant Vision; bound-in trading card. 38-Chaos Effect Epsilon Pt.1. 46-52-Dan Jurgens-a(p)/scripts w/Giordano-i. 53,54-Jurgens scripts only. 60-Giffen scripts; Jeff Johnson-a(p) 3.00
0-($9.95, trade paperback)-r/Alpha and Omega origin story; polybagged w/poster 10.00
...:Second Death (1994, $9.95)-r/issues #1-4. 10.00

NOTE: *#1-10 all have free 8 pg. insert "Alpha and Omega" which is a 10 chapter Solar origin story. All 10 centerfolds can pieced together to show climax of story.* ***Ditko*** *a-11p, 14p.* ***Giordano*** *a-46, 47, 48, 49, 50, 51, 52i.* ***Johnson*** *a-60p.* ***Jurgens*** *a-46, 47, 48, 49, 50 , 51, 52p.* ***Layton*** *a-1-3i; c-2i, 11i, 17i, 25i.* ***Miller*** *c-12.* ***Quesada*** *c-17p, 20-23p, 29p.* ***Simonson*** *c-13.* ***B. Smith*** *a-1-10; c-1, 3, 5, 7, 19i.* ***Thibert*** *c-22i, 23i.*

SOLAR LORD
Image Comics: Mar, 1999 - No. 7, Sept, 1999 ($2.50)

1-7-Khoo Fuk Lung-s/a 3.00

SOLARMAN (See Pendulum Ill. Originals)
Marvel Comics: Jan, 1989 - No. 2, May, 1990 ($1.00, limited series)

1,2 3.00

SOLAR, MAN OF THE ATOM (Man of the Atom on cover)
Acclaim Comics (Valiant Heroes): Vol. 2, May, 1997 ($3.95, one-shot, 46 pgs) (1st Valiant Heroes Special Event)

Vol. 2-Reintro Solar; Ninjak cameo; Warren Ellis scripts; Darick Robertson-a 4.00

SOLAR, MAN OF THE ATOM: HELL ON EARTH
Acclaim Comics (Valiant Heroes): Jan, 1998 - No. 4 ($2.50, limited series)

1-4-Priest-s/ Zircher-a(p) 3.00

SOLAR, MAN OF THE ATOM: REVELATIONS
Acclaim Comics (Valiant Heroes): Nov, 1997 ($3.95, one-shot, 46 pgs.)

1-Krueger-s/ Zircher-a(p) 4.00

SOLDIER & MARINE COMICS (Fightin' Army #16 on)
Charlton Comics (Toby Press of Conn. V1#11): No. 11, Dec, 1954 - No. 15, Aug, 1955; V2#9, Dec, 1956

	GD 2.0	VG 4.0	FN 6.0	VF 8.0	VF/NM 9.0	NM- 9.2
V1#11 (12/54)-Bob Powell-a	9	18	27	52	69	85
V1#12(2/55)-15: 12-Photo-c. 14-Photo-c; Colan-a	7	14	21	35	43	50
V2#9(Formerly Never Again; Jerry Drummer V2#10 on)	6	12	18	31	38	45

SOLDIER COMICS
Fawcett Publications: Jan, 1952 - No. 11, Sept, 1953

1	14	28	42	76	108	140
2	8	16	24	44	57	70
3-5	8	16	24	42	54	65
6-11: 8-Illo. in **POP**	8	16	24	40	50	60

SOLDIERS OF FORTUNE
American Comics Group (Creston Publ. Corp.): Mar-Apr, 1951 - No. 13, Feb-Mar, 1953

1-Capt. Crossbones by Shelly, Ace Carter, Lance Larson begin	23	46	69	136	223	310
2	14	28	42	81	118	155
3-10: 6-Bondage-c	12	24	36	69	97	125
11-13 (War format)	9	18	27	47	61	75

NOTE: ***Shelly*** *a-1-3, 5.* ***Whitney*** *a-6, 8-11, 13; c-1-3, 5, 6.*

SOLDIERS OF FREEDOM
Americomics: 1987 - No. 2, 1987 ($1.75)

1,2 3.00

SOLDIER X (Continued from Cable)
Marvel Comics: Sept, 2002 - No. 12, Aug, 2003 ($2.99/$2.25)

1,10,11,12-($2.99) 1-Kordey-a/Macan-s. 10-Bollers-s/Ranson-a 3.00
2-9-($2.25) 3.00

SOLDIER ZERO (From Stan Lee)
BOOM! Studios: Oct, 2010 - Present ($3.99)

1-7: 1-4-Cornell-s/Pina-a 4.00

SOLITAIRE (Also See Prime V2#6-8)
Malibu Comics (Ultraverse): Nov, 1993 - No. 12, Dec, 1994 ($1.95)

1-($2.50)-Collector's edition bagged w/playing card 4.00
1-12: 1-Regular edition w/o playing card. 2,4-Break-Thru x-over. 3-2 pg. origin The Night Man. 4-Gatefold-c. 5-Two pg. origin the Strangers 3.00

SOLO
Marvel Comics: Sept, 1994 - No. 4, Dec, 1994 ($1.75, limited series)

1-4: Spider-Man app. 3.00

SOLO (Movie)
Dark Horse Comics: July, 1996 - No. 2, Aug, 1996 ($2.50, limited series)

1,2: Adaptation of film; photo-c 3.00

SOLO (Anthology showcasing individual artists)
DC Comics: Dec, 2004 - No. 12, Oct, 2006 ($4.95/$4.99)

1-11: 1-Tim Sale-a; stories by Sale and various. 2-Richard Corben-a; stories by Corben and Arcudi. 3-Paul Pope. 4-Howard Chaykin. 5-Darwyn Cooke. 6-Jordi Bernet. 7-Michael Allred; Teen Titans & Doom Patrol app. 8-Teddy Kristiansen. 9-Scott Hampton. 10-Damion Scott. 11-Sergio Aragonés. 12-Brendan McCarthy 5.00

SOLO AVENGERS (Becomes Avenger Spotlight #21 on)
Marvel Comics: Dec, 1987 - No. 20, July, 1989 (75¢/$1.00)

1-Jim Lee-a on back-up story 4.00
2-20: 11-Intro Bobcat 3.00

SOLOMON AND SHEBA (Movie)
Dell Publishing Co.: No. 1070, Jan-Mar, 1960

Four Color 1070-Sekowsky-a; photo-c	8	16	24	58	97	135

SOLOMON GRUNDY
DC Comics: May, 2009 - No. 7, Nov, 2009 ($2.99)

1-7-Scott Kolins-s/a. 2-Bizarro app. 7-Blackest Night prelude 3.00
TPB (2010, $19.99) r/#1-7 20.00

SOLOMON KANE (Based on the Robert E. Howard character. Also see Blackthorne 3-D Series #60 & Marvel Premiere)
Marvel Comics: Sept, 1985 - No. 6, July, 1986 (Limited series)

1-Double size 4.00
2-6: 3-6-Williamson-a(i) 3.00

SOLOMON KANE
Dark Horse Comics: Sept, 2008 - No. 5, Feb, 2009 ($2.99)

The Solution #14 © MAR

The Son of Satan #5 © MAR

Soulfire V2 #3 © Aspen MLT

	GD 2.0	VG 4.0	FN 6.0	VF 8.0	VF/NM 9.0	NM- 9.2
1-5: 1-Two covers by Cassaday and Joe Kubert; Guevara-a						3.00
...: Death's Black Riders 1-4 (1/10 - No. 4, 6/10, $3.50) Robertson-c						3.50

SOLUS
CG Entertainment, Inc.: Apr, 2003 - No. 8, Jan, 2004 ($2.95)

	GD	VG	FN	VF	VF/NM	NM-
1-8: 1-4,6,7-George Pérez-a/c; Barbara Kesel-s. 5-Ryan-a. 8-Kirk-a						3.00
Vol. 1: Genesis (1/04, $15.95) r/#1-6						16.00

SOLUTION, THE
Malibu Comics (Ultraverse): Sept, 1993 - No. 17, Feb, 1995 ($1.95)

	GD	VG	FN	VF	VF/NM	NM-
1,3-15: 1-Intro Meathook, Deathdance, Black Tiger, Tech. 4-Break-Thru x-over; gatefold-c. 5-2 pg. origin The Strangers. 11-Brereton-c						3.00
1-($2.50)-Newsstand ed. polybagged w/trading card						4.00
1-Ultra 5000 Limited silver foil						5.00
0-Obtained w/Rune #0 by sending coupons from 11 comics						4.00
2-($2.50, 48 pgs.)-Rune flip-c/story by B. Smith; The Mighty Magnor 1 pg. strip by Aragonés						4.00
16 ($3.50)-Flip-c Ultraverse Premiere #10						4.00
17 ($2.50)						3.00

SOMERSET HOLMES (See Eclipse Graphic Novel Series)
Pacific Comics/ Eclipse Comics No. 5, 6: Sept, 1983 - No. 6, Dec, 1984 ($1.50, Baxter paper)

	GD	VG	FN	VF	VF/NM	NM-
1-6: 1-Brent Anderson-c/a. Cliff Hanger by Williamson in all						3.00

SONG OF THE SOUTH (See Brer Rabbit)

SONIC & KNUCKLES
Archie Comics: Aug, 1995 ($2.00)

	GD	VG	FN	VF	VF/NM	NM-
1	1	2	3	5	7	9

SONIC DISRUPTORS
DC Comics: Dec, 1987 - No. 7, July, 1988 ($1.75, unfinished limited series)

	GD	VG	FN	VF	VF/NM	NM-
1-7						3.00

SONIC'S FRIENDLY NEMESIS KNUCKLES
Archie Publications: July, 1996 - No. 3, Sept, 1996 ($1.50, limited series)

	GD	VG	FN	VF	VF/NM	NM-
1-3						5.00

SONIC SUPER SPECIAL
Archie Publications: 1997 - Present ($2.00/$2.25/$2.29, 48 pgs)

	GD	VG	FN	VF	VF/NM	NM-
1-3						4.00
4-6,8-15: 10-Sabrina-c/app. 15-Sin City spoof						3.00
7-(w/Image) Spawn, Maxx, Savage Dragon-c/app.; Valentino-a						3.00

SONIC THE HEDGEHOG (TV, video game)
Archie Comics: No. 0, Feb, 1993 - No. 3, May, 1993 ($1.25, mini-series)

	GD	VG	FN	VF	VF/NM	NM-
0(2/93),1: Shaw-a(p) & covers on all	3	6	9	20	30	40
2,3	3	6	9	16	23	30
Beginnings TPB (2003, $10.95) r/#0-3						11.00
...: The Beginning TPB (2006, $10.95) r/#0-3						11.00

SONIC THE HEDGEHOG (TV, video game)
Archie Comics: July, 1993 - Present ($1.25-$2.99)

	GD	VG	FN	VF	VF/NM	NM-
1	4	8	12	22	34	45
2,3	3	6	9	16	23	30
4-10: 8-Neon ink-c.	2	4	6	11	16	20
11-20	2	4	6	9	13	16
21-30 ($1.50): 25-Silver ink-c	2	4	6	8	10	12
31-50	1	2	3	5	6	8
51-93						4.00
94-212: 117-Begin $2.19-c. 152-Begin $2.25-c. 157-Shadow app. 198-Begin $2.50						3.00
213-225: 213-Begin $2.99-c						3.00
Free Comic Book Day Edition 1 (2007)- Leads into Sonic the Hedgehog #175						2.25
Free Comic Book Day Edition 2009 - Reprints Sonic the Hedgehog #1 from July 1993						2.25
Free Comic Book Day Edition 2010 - New story						2.25
Triple Trouble Special (10/95, $2.00, 48 pgs.)	1	2	3	5	6	8

SONIC UNIVERSE (Sonic the Hedgehog)
Archie Publications: Apr, 2009 - Present ($2.50/$2.99)

	GD	VG	FN	VF	VF/NM	NM-
1-15						3.00
16-28: 16-Begin $2.99-c						3.00

SONIC VS. KNUCKLES "BATTLE ROYAL" SPECIAL
Archie Publications: 1997 ($2.00, one-shot)

	GD	VG	FN	VF	VF/NM	NM-
1						6.00

SONIC X (Sonic the Hedgehog)
Archie Publications: Nov, 2005 - No. 40, Feb, 2009 ($2.25)

	GD	VG	FN	VF	VF/NM	NM-
1-Sam Speed app.						4.00
2-40						3.00

SON OF AMBUSH BUG (See Ambush Bug)
DC Comics: July, 1986 - No. 6, Dec, 1986 (75¢)

	GD	VG	FN	VF	VF/NM	NM-
1-6: Giffen-c/a in all. 5-Bissette-a.						3.00

SON OF BLACK BEAUTY (Also see Black Beauty)
Dell Publishing Co.: No. 510, Oct, 1953 - No. 566, June, 1954

	GD	VG	FN	VF	VF/NM	NM-
Four Color 510, 566	4	8	12	26	41	55

SON OF FLUBBER (See Movie Comics)

SON OF HULK (Continues from Skaar: Son of Hulk #12) (See Realm of Kings)
Marvel Comics: No. 13, Sept, 2009 - No. 17, Jan, 2010 ($2.99)

	GD	VG	FN	VF	VF/NM	NM-
13-17: 13,15-17-Galactus app.						3.00

SON OF M (Also see House of M series)
Marvel Comics: Feb, 2006 - No. 6, July, 2006 ($2.99, limited series)

	GD	VG	FN	VF	VF/NM	NM-
1-6: 1-Powerless Quicksilver; Martinez-a. 2-Quicksilver regains powers; Inhumans app.						3.00
Decimation: Son of M (2006, $13.99, TPB) r/series; Martinez sketch pages						14.00

SON OF MUTANT WORLD
Fantagor Press: 1990 - No. 5, 1990? ($2.00, bi-monthly)

	GD	VG	FN	VF	VF/NM	NM-
1-5: 1-3: Corben-c/a. 4,5 ($1.75, B&W)						3.00

SON OF ORIGINS OF MARVEL COMICS (See Fireside Book Series)

SON OF SATAN (Also see Ghost Rider #1 & Marvel Spotlight #12)
Marvel Comics Group: Dec, 1975 - No. 8, Feb, 1977 (25¢)

	GD	VG	FN	VF	VF/NM	NM-
1-Mooney-a; Kane-c(p), Starlin splash(p)	3	6	9	18	27	40
2,6-8: 2-Origin The Possessor. 8-Heath-a	2	4	6	10	14	18
3-5-(Regular 25¢ editions)(4-8/76): 5-Russell-p	2	4	6	10	14	18
3-5-(30¢-c variants, limited distribution)	4	8	12	20	30	40

SON OF SINBAD (Also see Abbott & Costello & Daring Adventures)
St. John Publishing Co.: Feb, 1950

	GD	VG	FN	VF	VF/NM	NM-
1-Kubert-c/a	45	90	135	284	480	675

SON OF SUPERMAN (Elseworlds)
DC Comics: 1999 ($14.95, prestige format, one-shot)

	GD	VG	FN	VF	VF/NM	NM-
nn-Chaykin & Tischman-s/Williams III & Gray-a						15.00

SON OF TOMAHAWK (See Tomahawk)

SON OF VULCAN (Formerly Mysteries of Unexplored Worlds #1-48; Thunderbolt V3#51 on)
Charlton Comics: V2#49, Nov, 1965 - V2#50, Jan, 1966

	GD	VG	FN	VF	VF/NM	NM-
V2#49,50: 50-Roy Thomas scripts (1st pro work)	3	6	9	17	25	32

SONS OF KATIE ELDER (See Movie Classics)

SORCERY (See Chilling Adventures in... & Red Circle...)

SORORITY SECRETS
Toby Press: July, 1954

	GD	VG	FN	VF	VF/NM	NM-
1	10	20	30	58	79	100

SOULFIRE (MICHAEL TURNER PRESENTS:...)
Aspen MLT, Inc.: No. 0, 2004 - No. 10, Jul, 2009 ($2.50/$2.99)

	GD	VG	FN	VF	VF/NM	NM-
0-($2.50) Turner-a/c; Loeb-s; intro. to characters & development sketches						2.50
1-($2.99) Two covers						3.00
1-Diamond Previews Exclusive						5.00
2-9: 2,3-Two covers. 4-Four covers						3.00
10-($3.99) Benitez-a						4.00
...: The Collected Edition Vol. 1 (5/05, $6.99) r/#1,2; cover gallery						7.00
Hardcover Volume 1 (12/05, $24.99) r/#0-5 & preview from Wizard Mag.; Johns intro.						25.00

SOULFIRE (MICHAEL TURNER PRESENTS:...) (Volume 2)
Aspen MLT, Inc.: No. 0, Oct, 2009 - No. 9, Jan, 2011 ($2.50/$2.99)

	GD	VG	FN	VF	VF/NM	NM-
0-($2.50) Marcus To-a						3.00
1-9-($2.99) 1-Five covers. 9-Covers by To and Linsner						3.00

SOULFIRE: CHAOS REIGN
Aspen MLT, Inc.: No. 0, June, 2006 - No. 3, Jan, 2007 ($2.50/$2.99)

	GD	VG	FN	VF	VF/NM	NM-
0-($2.50) Three covers; Marcus To-a; J.T. Krul-s						3.00
1-3-($2.99) 1-Three covers						3.00
...: Beginnings (7/06, $1.99) Marcus To-a; J.T. Krul-s						3.00
...: Beginnings 1 (7/07, $1.99) Francisco Herrera-a; J.T. Krul-s						3.00

SOULFIRE: DYING OF THE LIGHT
Aspen MLT, Inc.: No. 0, 2004 - No. 5, Feb, 2006 ($2.50/$2.99)

	GD	VG	FN	VF	VF/NM	NM-
0-($2.50) Three covers; Gunnell-a; Krul-s; back-story to the Soulfire universe						3.00

Sovereign Seven #18 © Chris Claremont

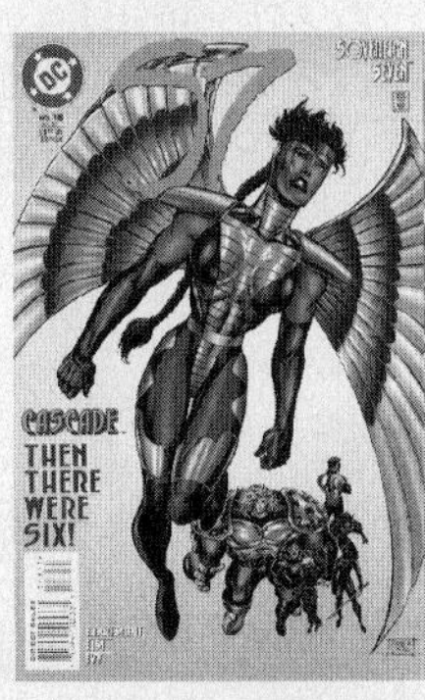

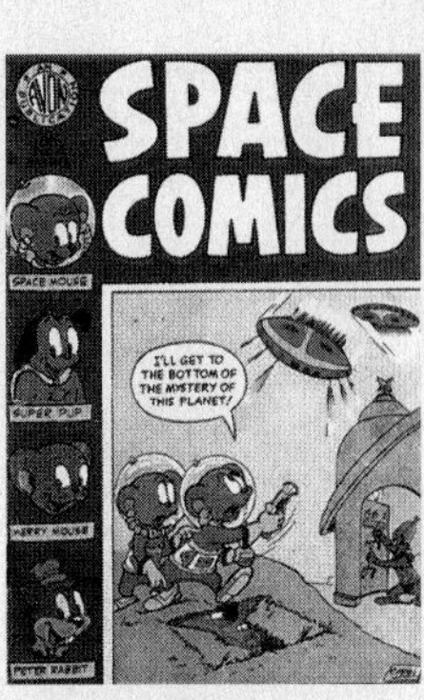

	GD 2.0	VG 4.0	FN 6.0	VF 8.0	VF/NM 9.0	NM- 9.2
1-5-($2.99) 1-Five covers						3.00
... Vol. 1 TPB (2007, $14.99) r/#0-5; Gunnell sketch pages, cover gallery						15.00
SOULFIRE: NEW WORLD ORDER						
Aspen MLT, Inc.: No. 0, Jul, 2007; May, 2009 - No. 5, Dec, 2009 ($2.50/$2.99)						
0 (7/07, $2.50) Two covers; Herrera-a/Krul-s						3.00
1-5-($2.99) 1-Four covers						3.00
SOULFIRE: SHADOW MAGIC						
Aspen MLT, Inc.: No. 0, Nov, 2008 - No. 5, May, 2009 ($2.50/$2.99)						
0-($2.50) Two covers; Sana Takeda-a						3.00
1-5-($2.99) 1-Two covers						3.00
SOUL SAGA						
Image Comics (Top Cow): Feb, 2000 - No. 5, Apr, 2001 ($2.50)						
1-5: 1-Madureira-c; Platt & Batt-a						3.00
SOULSEARCHERS AND COMPANY						
Claypool Comics: June, 1995 - No. 82, Jan, 2007 ($2.50, B&W)						
1-10: Peter David scripts						5.00
11-25						3.00
26-82						3.00
SOULWIND						
Image Comics: Mar, 1997 - No. 8 ($2.95, B&W, limited series)						
1-8: 5-"The Day I Tried To Live" pt. 1						3.00
Book Five; The August Ones (Oni Press, 3/01, $8.50)						8.50
...The Kid From Planet Earth (1997, $9.95, TPB)						10.00
...The Kid From Planet Earth (Oni Press, 1/00, $8.50, TPB)						8.50
...The Day I Tried to Live (Oni Press, 4/00, $8.50, TPB)						8.50
The Complete Soulwind TPB ($29.95, 11/03, 8" x 5 1/2") r/Oni Books #1-5						30.00
SOUPY SALES COMIC BOOK (TV)(The Official...)						
Archie Publications: 1965						
1	9	18	27	60	100	140
SOUTHERN KNIGHTS, THE (See Crusaders #1)						
Guild Publ/Fictioneer Books: No. 2, 1983 - No. 41, 1993 (B&W)						
2-Magazine size	1	2	3	5	6	8
3-35, 37-41						3.00
36-($3.50-c)						4.00
Dread Halloween Special 1, Primer Special 1 (Spring, 1989, $2.25)						3.00
Graphic Novels #1-4						4.00
SOVEREIGN SEVEN (Also see Showcase '95 #12)						
DC Comics: July, 1995 - No. 36, July, 1998 ($1.95) (1st creator-owned mainstream DC comic)						
1-1st app. Sovereign Seven (Reflex, Indigo, Cascade, Finale, Cruiser, Network & Rampart); 1st app. Maitresse; Darkseid app.; Chris Claremont-s & Dwayne Turner-c/a begins						4.00
1-Gold						8.00
1-Platinum						40.00
2-25: 2-Wolverine cameo. 4-Neil Gaiman cameo. 5,8-Batman app. 7-Ramirez cameo (from the movie Highlander). 9-Humphrey Bogart cameo from Casablanca. 10-Impulse app; Manoli Wetherell & Neal Conan cameo from Uncanny X-Men #226. 11-Robin app. 16-Final Night. 24-Superman app. 25-Power Girl app.						3.00
26-36: 26-Begin $2.25-c. 28-Impulse-c/app.						3.00
Annual 1 (1995, $3.95)-Year One story; Big Barda & Lobo app.; Jeff Johnson-c/a						4.00
Annual 2 (1996, $2.95)-Legends of the Dead Earth; Leonardi-c/a						4.00
...Plus 1(2/97, $2.95)-Legion-c/app.						4.00
TPB-($12.95) r/#1-5, Annual #1 & Showcase '95 #12						13.00
SPACE: ABOVE AND BEYOND (TV)						
Topps Comics: Jan, 1996 - No. 3, Mar, 1996 ($2.95, limited series)						
1-3: Adaptation of pilot episode; Steacy-c.						3.00
SPACE: ABOVE AND BEYOND--THE GAUNTLET (TV)						
Topps Comics: May, 1996 -No. 2, June, 1996 ($2.95, limited series)						
1,2						3.00
SPACE ACE (Also see Manhunt!)						
Magazine Enterprises: No. 5, 1952						
5(A-1 #61)-Guardineer-a	55	110	165	352	601	850
SPACE ACE: DEFENDER OF THE UNIVERSE (Based on the Don Bluth video game)						
CrossGen Comics: Oct, 2003 - No. 6 ($2.95, limited series)						
1,2-Kirkman-s/Borges-a						3.00
SPACE ACTION						
Ace Magazines (Junior Books): June, 1952 - No. 3, Oct, 1952						
1-Cameron-a in all (1 story)	77	154	231	493	847	1200
2,3	54	108	162	343	574	825
SPACE ADVENTURES (War At Sea #22 on)						
Capitol Stories/Charlton Comics: 7/52 - No. 21, 8/56; No. 23, 5/58 - No. 59, 11/64; V3#60, 10/67; V1#2, 7/68 - V1#8, 7/69; No. 9, 5/78 - No. 13, 3/79						
1	54	108	162	343	574	825
2	28	56	84	165	270	375
3-5: 4,6-Flying saucer-c/stories	22	44	66	132	216	300
6-9: 7-Sex change story "Transformation". 8-Robot-c. 9-A-Bomb panel	20	40	60	120	195	270
10,11-Ditko-c/a. 10-Robot-c. 11-Two Ditko stories	53	106	159	334	567	800
12-Ditko-c (classic)	77	154	231	493	847	1200
13-(Fox-r, 10-11/54); Blue Beetle-c/story	16	32	48	94	147	200
14,15,17,18: 14-Blue Beetle-c/story; Fox-r (12-1/54-55, last pre-code). 15,17,18-Rocky Jones-c/s.(TV); 15-Part photo-c	20	40	60	118	192	265
16-Krigstein-a; Rocky Jones-c/story (TV)	22	44	66	128	209	290
19	15	30	45	88	137	185
20-Reprints Fawcett's "Destination Moon"	22	44	66	132	216	300
21-(8/56) (no #22)(Becomes War At Sea)	15	30	45	88	137	185
23-(5/58; formerly Nyoka, The Jungle Girl)-Reprints Fawcett's "Destination Moon"	20	40	60	118	192	265
24,25,31,32-Ditko-a. 24-Severin-a(signed "LePoer")	20	40	60	118	192	265
26,27-Ditko-a(4) each. 26,28-Flying saucer-c	21	42	63	126	206	285
28-30	11	22	33	64	90	115
33-Origin/1st app. Capt. Atom by Ditko (3/60)	50	100	150	315	533	750
34-40,42-All Captain Atom by Ditko	21	42	63	124	202	280
41,43,45-59: 45-Mercury Man app.	5	10	15	32	51	70
44-1st app. Mercury Man	5	10	15	34	55	75
V3#60(#1, 10/67)-Origin & 1st app. Paul Mann & The Saucers From the Future	5	10	15	32	51	70
2,5,6,8 (1968-69)-Ditko-a: 2-Aparo-c/a	3	6	9	20	30	40
3,4,7: 4-Aparo-c/a	3	6	9	16	23	30
9-13(1978-79)-Capt. Atom-r/Space Adventures by Ditko; 9-Reprints origin/1st app. Capt. Atom from #33						6.00
NOTE: ***Aparo** a-V3#60. c-V3#8. **Ditko** c-12, 31-42. **Giordano** c-3, 4, 7-9, 18p. **Krigstein** c-15. **Shuster** a-11. Issues 13 & 14 have Blue Beetle logos; #15-18 have Rocky Jones logos.*						
SPACE ARK						
Americomics (AC Comics)/ Apple Comics #3 on: June, 1985 - No. 5, Sept, 1987 ($1.75)						
1-5: Funny animal (#1,2-color; #3-5-B&W)						3.00
SPACE BUSTERS						
Ziff-Davis Publ. Co.: Spring, 1952 - No. 2, Fall, 1952						
1-Krigstein-a(3); Painted-c by Norman Saunders	81	162	243	518	884	1250
2-Kinstler-a(2 pgs.); Saunders painted-c	61	122	183	390	670	950
NOTE: ***Anderson** a-2. Bondage c-2.*						
SPACE CADET (See Tom Corbett,...)						
SPACE CIRCUS						
Dark Horse Comics: July, 2000 - No. 4, Oct, 2000 ($2.95, limited series)						
1-4-Aragonés-a/Evanier-s						3.00
SPACE COMICS (Formerly Funny Tunes)						
Avon Periodicals: No. 4, Mar-Apr, 1954 - No. 5, May-June, 1954						
4,5-Space Mouse, Peter Rabbit, Super Pup (formerly Spotty the Pup), & Merry Mouse continue from Funny Tunes	8	16	24	40	50	60
I.W. Reprint #8 (nd)-Space Mouse-r	2	4	6	8	10	12
SPACED						
Anthony Smith Publ. #1,2/Unbridled Ambition/Eclipse Comics #10 on: 1982 - No. 13, 1988 ($1.25/$1.50, B&W, quarterly)						
1-($1.25-c)						4.00
2-13, Special Edition (1983, Mimeo)						3.00
SPACE DETECTIVE						
Avon Periodicals: July, 1951 - No. 4, July, 1952						
1-Rod Hathway, Space Detective begins, ends #4; Wood-c/a(3)-23 pgs.; "Opium Smugglers of Venus" drug story; Lucky Dale-r/Saint #4	116	232	348	742	1271	1800
2-Tales from the Shadow Squad story; Wood/Orlando-c; Wood inside layouts; "Slave Ship of Saturn" story	90	180	270	576	988	1400
3,4: 3-Kinstler-c. 4-Kinstlerish-a by McCann	43	86	129	271	461	650
I.W. Reprint #1(Reprints #2), 8(Reprints cover #1 & part Famous Funnies #191)	4	8	12	22	34	45
SPACE EXPLORER (See March of Comics #202)						
SPACE FAMILY ROBINSON (TV)(...Lost in Space #15-37, ...Lost in Space On Space Station One #38 on)(See Gold Key Champion)						

Space Ghost (2005 series) #1 © H-B

Spaceman #4 © MAR

Space Western #41 © CC

Gold Key: Dec, 1962 - No. 36, Oct, 1969; No. 37, 10/73 - No. 54, 11/78; No. 55, 3/81 - No. 59, 5/82 (All painted covers)

	GD 2.0	VG 4.0	FN 6.0	VF 8.0	VF/NM 9.0	NM- 9.2
1-(Low distribution); Spiegle-a in all	20	40	60	140	283	425
2(3/63)-Family becomes lost in space	11	22	33	77	144	210
3-5	8	16	24	54	90	125
6-10: 6-Captain Venture back-up stories begin	6	12	18	43	69	95
11-20: 14-(10/65). 15-Title change (1/66)	5	10	15	30	48	65
21-36: 28-Last 12¢ issue. 36-Captain Venture ends	4	8	12	23	36	45
37-48: 37-Origin retold	2	4	6	10	14	18
49-59: Reprints #49,50,55-59	2	4	6	8	10	12

NOTE: *The TV show first aired on 9/15/65. Title changed after TV show debuted.*

SPACE FAMILY ROBINSON (See March of Comics #320, 328, 352, 404, 414)

SPACE GHOST (TV) (Also see Golden Comics Digest #2 & Hanna-Barbera Super TV Heroes #3-7)
Gold Key: March, 1967 (Hanna-Barbera) (TV debut was 9/10/66)

	GD 2.0	VG 4.0	FN 6.0	VF 8.0	VF/NM 9.0	NM- 9.2
1 (10199-703)-Spiegle-a	27	54	81	197	399	600

SPACE GHOST (TV cartoon)
Comico: Mar, 1987 ($3.50, deluxe format, one-shot) (Hanna-Barbera)

	GD 2.0	VG 4.0	FN 6.0	VF 8.0	VF/NM 9.0	NM- 9.2
1-Steve Rude-c/a	1	2	3	5	6	8

SPACE GHOST (TV cartoon)
DC Comics: Jan, 2005 - No. 6, June, 2005 ($2.95/$2.99, limited series)

	GD 2.0	VG 4.0	FN 6.0	VF 8.0	VF/NM 9.0	NM- 9.2
1-6-Alex Ross-c/Ariel Olivetti-a/Joe Kelly-s; origin of Space Ghost						3.00
TPB (2005, $14.99) r/series; cover gallery						15.00

SPACE GIANTS, THE (TV cartoon)
FBN Publications: 1979 ($1.00, B&W, one-shots)

	GD 2.0	VG 4.0	FN 6.0	VF 8.0	VF/NM 9.0	NM- 9.2
1-Based on Japanese TV series	2	4	6	9	12	15

SPACEHAWK
Dark Horse Comics: 1989 - No. 3, 1990 ($2.00, B&W)

	GD 2.0	VG 4.0	FN 6.0	VF 8.0	VF/NM 9.0	NM- 9.2
1-3-Wolverton-c/a(r) plus new stories by others.						4.00

SPACE JAM
DC Comics: 1996 ($5.95, one-shot, movie adaption)

	GD 2.0	VG 4.0	FN 6.0	VF 8.0	VF/NM 9.0	NM- 9.2
1-Wraparound photo cover of Michael Jordan	1	2	3	5	6	8

SPACE KAT-ETS (...in 3-D)
Power Publishing Co.: Dec, 1953 (25¢, came w/glasses)

	GD 2.0	VG 4.0	FN 6.0	VF 8.0	VF/NM 9.0	NM- 9.2
1	30	60	90	177	289	400

SPACEKNIGHTS
Marvel Comics: Oct, 2000 - No. 5, Feb, 2001 ($2.99, limited series)

	GD 2.0	VG 4.0	FN 6.0	VF 8.0	VF/NM 9.0	NM- 9.2
1-5-Starlin-s/Batista-a						3.00

SPACEMAN (Speed Carter...)
Atlas Comics (CnPC): Sept, 1953 - No. 6, July, 1954

	GD 2.0	VG 4.0	FN 6.0	VF 8.0	VF/NM 9.0	NM- 9.2
1-Grey tone-c	71	142	213	454	777	1100
2	44	88	132	277	469	660
3-6: 4-A-Bomb explosion-c	40	80	120	242	401	560

NOTE: *Everett c-1, 3.* ***Heath*** *a-1.* ***Maneely*** *a-1(3), 2(4), 3(3), 4-6; c-5, 6.* ***Romita*** *a-1.* ***Sekowsky*** *c-4.* ***Sekowsky/Abel*** *a-4(3).* ***Tuska*** *a-5(3).*

SPACE MAN
Dell Publ. Co.: No. 1253, 1-3/62 - No. 8, 3-5/64; No. 9, 7/72 - No. 10, 10/72

	GD 2.0	VG 4.0	FN 6.0	VF 8.0	VF/NM 9.0	NM- 9.2
Four Color 1253 (#1)(1-3/62)(15¢-c)	7	14	21	49	80	110
2,3: 2-(15¢-c). 3-(12¢-c)	4	8	12	28	44	60
4-8-(12¢-c)	4	8	12	22	34	45
9,10-(15¢-c): 9-Reprints #1253. 10-Reprints #2	2	4	6	9	12	15

SPACEMAN (From the Atomics)
Oni Press: July, 2002 ($2.95, one-shot)

	GD 2.0	VG 4.0	FN 6.0	VF 8.0	VF/NM 9.0	NM- 9.2
1-Mike Allred-s/a; Lawrence Marvit additional art						3.00

SPACE MOUSE (Also see Funny Tunes & Space Comics)
Avon Periodicals: April, 1953 - No. 5, Apr-May, 1954

	GD 2.0	VG 4.0	FN 6.0	VF 8.0	VF/NM 9.0	NM- 9.2
1	10	20	30	58	79	100
2	7	14	21	37	46	55
3-5	6	12	18	31	38	45

SPACE MOUSE (Walter Lantz...#1; see Comic Album #17)
Dell Publishing Co./Gold Key: No. 1132, Aug-Oct, 1960 - No. 5, Nov, 1963 (Walter Lantz)

	GD 2.0	VG 4.0	FN 6.0	VF 8.0	VF/NM 9.0	NM- 9.2
Four Color 1132,1244, 1(11/62)(G.K.)	4	8	12	28	44	60
2-5	4	8	12	24	37	50

SPACE MYSTERIES
I.W. Enterprises: 1964 (Reprints)

	GD 2.0	VG 4.0	FN 6.0	VF 8.0	VF/NM 9.0	NM- 9.2
1-r/Journey Into Unknown Worlds #4 w/new-c	3	6	9	16	22	28
8,9: 9-r/Planet Comics #73	3	6	9	16	22	28

SPACE: 1999 (TV) (Also see Power Record Comics)
Charlton Comics: Nov, 1975 - No. 7, Nov, 1976

	GD 2.0	VG 4.0	FN 6.0	VF 8.0	VF/NM 9.0	NM- 9.2
1-Origin Moonbase Alpha; Staton-c/a	3	6	9	16	23	30
2,7: 2-Staton-a	2	4	6	13	18	22
3-6: All Byrne-a; c-3,5,6	3	6	9	16	23	30
nn (Charlton Press, digest, 100 pgs., B&W, no cover price) new stories & art	4	8	12	28	44	60

SPACE: 1999 (TV)(Magazine)
Charlton Comics: Nov, 1975 - No. 8, Nov, 1976 (B&W) (#7 shows #6 inside)

	GD 2.0	VG 4.0	FN 6.0	VF 8.0	VF/NM 9.0	NM- 9.2
1-Origin Moonbase Alpha; Morrow-c/a	3	6	9	16	22	28
2-8: 2,3-Morrow-c/a. 4-6-Morrow-c. 5,8-Morrow-a	2	4	6	11	16	20

SPACE PATROL (TV)
Ziff-Davis Publishing Co. (Approved Comics): Summer, 1952 - No. 2, Oct-Nov, 1952 (Painted-c by Norman Saunders)

	GD 2.0	VG 4.0	FN 6.0	VF 8.0	VF/NM 9.0	NM- 9.2
1-Krigstein-a	94	188	282	597	1024	1450
2-Krigstein-a(3)	66	132	198	419	722	1025

SPACE PIRATES (See Archie Giant Series #533)

SPACE RANGER (See Mystery in Space #92, Showcase #15 & Tales of the Unexpected)

SPACE SQUADRON (In the Days of the Rockets)(Becomes Space Worlds #6)
Marvel/Atlas Comics (ACI): June, 1951 - No. 5, Feb, 1952

	GD 2.0	VG 4.0	FN 6.0	VF 8.0	VF/NM 9.0	NM- 9.2
1-Space team; Brodsky c-1,5	71	142	213	454	777	1100
2: Tuska c-2-4	55	110	165	352	601	850
3-5: 3-Capt. Jet Dixon by Tuska(3). 4-Weird advs. begin	48	96	144	302	514	725

SPACE THRILLERS
Avon Periodicals: 1954 (25¢ Giant)

	GD 2.0	VG 4.0	FN 6.0	VF 8.0	VF/NM 9.0	NM- 9.2
nn-(Scarce)-Robotmen of the Lost Planet; contains 3 rebound comics of The Saint & Strange Worlds. Contents could vary	126	252	378	806	1378	1950

SPACE TRIP TO THE MOON (See Space Adventures #23)

SPACE USAGI
Mirage Studios: June, 1992 - No. 3, 1992 ($2.00, B&W, mini-series)
V2#1, Nov, 1993 - V2#3, Jan, 1994 ($2.75)

	GD 2.0	VG 4.0	FN 6.0	VF 8.0	VF/NM 9.0	NM- 9.2
1-3: Stan Sakai-c/a/scripts, V2#1-3						3.00

SPACE USAGI
Dark Horse Comics: Jan, 1996 - No. 3, Mar, 1996 ($2.95, B&W, limited series)

	GD 2.0	VG 4.0	FN 6.0	VF 8.0	VF/NM 9.0	NM- 9.2
1-3: Stan Sakai-c/a/scripts						3.00

SPACE WAR (Fightin' Five #28 on)
Charlton Comics: Oct, 1959 - No. 27, Mar, 1964; No. 28, Mar, 1978 - No. 34, 3/79

	GD 2.0	VG 4.0	FN 6.0	VF 8.0	VF/NM 9.0	NM- 9.2
V1#1-Giordano-c begin, end #3	13	26	39	89	170	250
2,3	8	16	24	54	90	125
4-6,8,10-Ditko-c/a	13	26	39	89	170	250
7,9,11-15 (3/62): Last 10¢ issue	6	12	18	41	66	90
16 (6/52)-27 (3/64): 18,19-Robot-c	5	10	15	35	55	75
28 (3/78),29-31,33,34-Ditko-c/a(r): 30-Staton, Sutton/Wood-a. 31-Ditko-c/a(3); same-c as Strange Suspense Stories #2 (1968); atom blast-c	1	3	4	6	8	10
32-r/Charlton Premiere V2#2; Sutton-a						5.00

SPACE WESTERN (Formerly Cowboy Western Comics; becomes Cowboy Western Comics #46 on)
Charlton Comics (Capitol Stories): No. 40, Oct, 1952 - No. 45, Aug, 1953

	GD 2.0	VG 4.0	FN 6.0	VF 8.0	VF/NM 9.0	NM- 9.2
40-Intro Spurs Jackson & His Space Vigilantes; flying saucer story	55	110	165	352	601	850
41,43-45: 41-Flying saucer-c. 45-Hitler app.	41	82	123	256	428	600
42-Atom bomb explosion-c	43	86	129	271	456	640

SPACE WORLDS (Formerly Space Squadron #1-5)
Atlas Comics (Male): No. 6, April, 1952

	GD 2.0	VG 4.0	FN 6.0	VF 8.0	VF/NM 9.0	NM- 9.2
6-Sol Brodsky-c	45	90	135	284	480	675

SPANKY & ALFALFA & THE LITTLE RASCALS (See The Little Rascals)

SPANNER'S GALAXY
DC Comics: Dec, 1984 - No. 6, May, 1985 (limited series)

	GD 2.0	VG 4.0	FN 6.0	VF 8.0	VF/NM 9.0	NM- 9.2
1-6: Mandrake-c/a in all.						3.00

SPARKIE, RADIO PIXIE (Radio)(Becomes Big Jon & Sparkie #4)
Ziff-Davis Publ. Co.: Winter, 1951 - No. 3, July-Aug, 1952 (Painted-c)(Sparkie #2,3; #1?)

Sparkle Comics #2 © UFS

Sparta USA #1 © Lapham & Timmons

Spawn #200 © TMP

	GD 2.0	VG 4.0	FN 6.0	VF 8.0	VF/NM 9.0	NM- 9.2
1-Based on children's radio program	27	54	81	158	259	360
2,3: 3-Big Jon and Sparkie on-c only	18	36	54	105	165	225

SPARKLE COMICS
United Features Synd.: Oct-Nov, 1948 - No. 33, Dec-Jan, 1953-54

	GD	VG	FN	VF	VF/NM	NM-
1-Li'l Abner, Nancy, Captain & the Kids, Ella Cinders (#1-3: 52 pgs.)	15	30	45	83	124	165
2	9	18	27	50	65	80
3-10	8	16	24	40	50	60
11-20	7	14	21	35	43	50
21-32	6	12	18	28	34	40
33-(2-3/54) 2 pgs. early Peanuts by Schulz	10	20	30	54	72	90

SPARKLE PLENTY (See Harvey Comics Library #2 & Dick Tracy)

SPARKLER COMICS (1st series)
United Feature Comic Group: July, 1940 - No. 2, 1940

	GD	VG	FN	VF	VF/NM	NM-
1-Jim Hardy	39	78	117	231	378	525
2-Frankie Doodle	28	56	84	165	270	375

SPARKLER COMICS (2nd series)(Nancy & Sluggo #121 on)(Cover title becomes Nancy and Sluggo #101? on)
United Features Syndicate: July, 1941 - No. 120, Jan, 1955

	GD	VG	FN	VF	VF/NM	NM-
1-Origin 1st app. Sparkman; Tarzan (by Hogarth in all issues), Captain & the Kids, Ella Cinders, Danny Dingle, Dynamite Dunn, Nancy, Abbie & Slats, Broncho Bill, Frankie Doodle, begin; Spark Man c-1-9,11,12; Hap Hopper c-10,13	230	460	690	1449	2450	3450
2	76	152	228	479	807	1135
3,4	57	114	171	359	610	860
5-9: 9-Spark Man's new costume	54	108	162	338	562	785
10-Spark Man's secret ID revealed	54	108	162	338	562	785
11,12-Spark Man war-c. 12-Spark Man's new costume (color change)	41	82	123	256	428	600
13-Hap Hopper war-c	39	78	117	240	395	550
14-Tarzan-c by Hogarth	50	100	150	315	533	750
15,17: 15-Capt & Kids-c. 17-Nancy & Sluggo-c	34	68	102	199	325	450
16,18-Spark Man war-c	40	80	120	246	411	575
19-1st Race Riley and the Commandos-c/s	39	78	117	240	395	550
20-Nancy war-c	34	68	102	199	325	450
21,25,28,31,34,37,39-Tarzan-c by Hogarth	42	84	126	267	451	635
22-24,26,27,29,30: 22-Race Riley & the Commandos strips begin, ends #44	29	58	87	170	278	385
32,33,35,36,38,40	18	36	54	105	165	225
41,43,45,46,48,49	14	28	42	80	115	150
42,44,47,50-Tarzan-c (42,47,50 by Hogarth)	26	52	78	156	256	355
51,52,54-70: 57-Li'l Abner begins (not in #58); Fearless Fosdick app. in #58	14	28	42	76	108	140
53-Tarzan-c by Hogarth	22	44	66	132	216	300
71-80	10	20	30	54	72	90
81,82,84-86: 86 Last Tarzan; lingerie panels	9	18	27	47	61	75
83-Tarzan-c; Li'l Abner ends	13	26	39	74	105	135
87-96,98-99	8	16	24	44	57	70
97-Origin Casey Ruggles by Warren Tufts	9	18	27	50	65	80
100	9	18	27	50	65	80
101-107,109-112,114-119	7	14	21	37	46	55
108,113-Toth-a	8	16	24	42	54	65
120-(10-11/54) 2 pgs. early Peanuts by Schulz	10	20	30	54	72	90

SPARKLING LOVE
Avon Periodicals/Realistic (1953): June, 1950; 1953

	GD	VG	FN	VF	VF/NM	NM-
1(Avon)-Kubert-a; photo-c	25	50	75	150	245	340
nn(1953)-Reprint; Kubert-a	11	22	33	62	86	110

SPARKLING STARS
Holyoke Publishing Co.: June, 1944 - No. 33, March, 1948

	GD	VG	FN	VF	VF/NM	NM-
1-Hell's Angels, FBI, Boxie Weaver, Petey & Pop, & Ali Baba begin	20	40	60	114	182	250
2-Speed Spaulding story	12	24	36	69	97	125
3-Actual FBI case photos & war photos	10	20	30	54	72	90
4-10: 7-X-Mas-c	9	18	27	50	65	80
11-19: 13-Origin/1st app. Jungo the Man-Beast-c/s	8	16	24	44	57	70
20-Intro Fangs the Wolf Boy	9	18	27	50	65	80
21-33: 29-Bondage-c. 31-Sid Greene-a	8	16	24	42	54	65

SPARK MAN (See Sparkler Comics)
Frances M. McQueeny: 1945 (36 pgs., one-shot)

	GD	VG	FN	VF	VF/NM	NM-
1-Origin Spark Man r/Sparkler #1-3; female torture story; cover redrawn from Sparkler #1	31	62	93	182	296	410

SPARKS (William Katt Presents...)
Catastrophic Comics: June, 2008 - Present ($2.99)

1,2: 1-Folino-s/Ringuet-a; origin of Sparks 3.00

SPARKY WATTS (Also see Big Shot Comics & Columbia Comics)
Columbia Comic Corp.: Nov?, 1942 - No. 10, 1949

	GD	VG	FN	VF	VF/NM	NM-
1(1942)-Skyman & The Face app; Hitler-c	81	162	243	518	884	1250
2(1943)	30	60	90	177	289	400
3(1944)	21	42	63	122	199	275
4(1944)-Origin	18	36	54	105	165	225
5(1947)-Skyman app.; Boody Rogers-c/a	15	30	45	88	137	185
6,7,9,10: 6(1947),10(1949)	11	22	33	60	83	105
8(1948)-Surrealistic-c	14	28	42	76	108	140

NOTE: ***Boody Rogers** c-1-8.*

SPARTACUS (Movie)
Dell Publishing Co.: No. 1139, Nov, 1960 (Kirk Douglas photo-c)

	GD	VG	FN	VF	VF/NM	NM-
Four Color 1139-Buscema-a	12	24	36	82	154	225

SPARTACUS (Television series)
Devil's Due Publishing: Oct, 2009 - No. 2 ($3.99)

1,2: 1-DeKnight-s. 2-Palmiotti-s 4.00

SPARTAN: WARRIOR SPIRIT (Also see WildC.A.T.S: Covert Action Teams)
Image Comics (WildStorm Productions): July, 1995 - No. 4, Nov, 1995 ($2.50, lim. series)

1-4: Kurt Busiek scripts; Mike McKone-c/a 3.00

SPARTA: USA
DC Comics (WildStorm): May, 2010 - No. 6, Oct, 2010 ($2.99, limited series)

1-6: 1-Lapham-s/Timmons-a; covers by Timmons and Lapham 3.00

SPAWN (Also see Curse of the Spawn and Sam & Twitch)
Image Comics (Todd McFarlane Prods.): May, 1992 - Present ($1.95/$2.50/$2.99)

	GD	VG	FN	VF	VF/NM	NM-
1-1st app. Spawn; McFarlane-c/a begins; McFarlane/Steacy-c; 1st Todd McFarlane Productions title.	2	4	6	8	10	12
1-Black & white edition	2	4	6	13	18	22
2,3: 2-1st app. Violator; McFarlane/Steacy-c	1	3	4	6	8	10
4-Contains coupon for Image Comics #0	1	3	4	6	8	10
4-With coupon missing						3.00
4-Newsstand edition w/o poster or coupon						3.00
5-Cerebus cameo (1 pg.) as stuffed animal; Spawn mobile poster #1	1	2	3	5	7	8
6-8,10: 7-Spawn Mobile poster #2. 8-Alan Moore scripts; Miller poster. 10-Cerebus app.; Dave Sim scripts; 1 pg. cameo app. by Superman						5.00
9-Neil Gaiman scripts; Jim Lee poster; 1st Angela.	1	2	3	4	5	7
11-17,19,20,22-30: 11-Miller script; Darrow poster. 12-Bloodwulf poster by Liefeld. 14,15-Violator app. 16,17-Grant Morrison scripts; Capullo-c/a(p). 23,24-McFarlane-a/stories. 25-(10/94). 19-(10/94). 20-(11/94)						4.00
18-Grant Morrison script, Capullo-c/a(p); low distr.	1	2	3	5	7	9
21-low distribution	1	2	3	5	7	9
31-49: 31-1st app. The Redeemer; new costume (brief). 32-1st full app. new costume. 38-40,42,44,46,48-Tony Daniel-c/a(p). 38-1st app. Cy-Gor. 40,41-Cy-Gor & Curse app.						4.00
50-($3.95, 48 pgs.)						5.00
51-66: 52-Savage Dragon app. 56-w/ Darkchylde preview. 57-Cy-Gor-c/app. 64-Polybagged w/McFarlane Toys catalog. 65-Photo-c of movie Spawn and McFarlane						4.00
67-97: 81-Billy Kincaid returns. 97-Angela-c/app.						3.00
98,99,101-149-($2.50): 98,99-Angela app.						3.00
100-($4.95) Angela dies; 6 covers by McFarlane, Ross, Miller, Capullo, Wood, Mignola						5.00
150-($4.95) 4 covers by McFarlane, Capullo, Tan, Jim Lee						5.00
151-184: 151-($2.95) Wraparound-c by Tan. 167-Clown app. 179-Mayhew-a						3.00
185-199,201-206: 185-McFarlane & Holguin-s/Portacio-a begins. 193-Sam & Twitch app.						3.00
200-(1/11, $3.99) 7 covers by McFarlane, Capullo, Finch, Jim Lee, Liefeld, Silvestri, Wood						4.00
Annual 1-Blood & Shadows ('99, $4.95) Ashley Wood-c/a; Jenkins-s						5.00
...: Architects of Fear (2/11, $6.99, squarebound GN) Briclot-a						7.00
...: Armegeddon Complete Collection TPB ('07, $29.95) r/#150-163						30.00
...: Armegeddon, Part 1 TPB (10/06, $14.99) r/#150-155						15.00
...: Armegeddon, Part 2 TPB (2/07, $15.95) r/#156-164						16.00
...Bible-(8/96, $1.95)-Character bios						4.00
Book 1 TPB($9.95) r/#1-5; Book 2-r/#6-9,11; Book 3 -r/#12-15, Book 4- r/#16-20; Book 5-r/#21-25; Book 6- r/#26-30; Book 7-r/#31-34; Book 8-r/#35-38; Book 9-r/#39-42; Book 10-r/#43-47						11.00
Book 11 TPB ($10.95) r/#48-50; Book 12-r/#51-54						11.00
... Collection Vol. 1 (10/05, $19.95) r/#1-8,11,12; intro. by Frank Miller						20.00
... Collection Vol. 2 HC (7/07, $49.95) r/#13-33						50.00
... Collection Vol. 2 SC (9/06, $29.95) r/#13-33						30.00

Special Agent #4 © PMI

Special Marvel Edition #1 © MAR

Spectacular Spider-Man (magazine) #2 © MAR

GD VG FN VF VF/NM NM-
2.0 4.0 6.0 8.0 9.0 9.2

... Collection Vol. 3 (3/07, $29.95) r/#34-54 30.00
... Collection Vol. 4 (9/07, $29.95) r/#55-75 30.00
... Collection Vol. 5 ('08, $29.95) r/#76-95 30.00
... Collection Vol. 6 (8/08, $29.95) r/#96-116; cover gallery 30.00
Image Firsts: Spawn #1 (4/10, $1.00) reprints #1
... Godslayer Vol. 1 (9/06, $6.99) Anacleto-c/a; Holguin-s; sketch pages 7.00
...: Neonoir TPB (11/08, $14.95) r/#170-175 15.00
...: New Flesh TPB ('07, $14.95) r/#166-169 15.00
...Simony (5/04, $7.95) English translation of French Spawn story; Briclot-a 8.00

NOTE: *Capullo a-16p-18p; c-16p-18p. Daniel a-38-40, 42, 44, 46. McFarlane a-1-15; c-1-15p. Thibert a-16i(part). Posters come with issues 1, 4, 7-9, 11, 12. #25 was released before #19 & 20.*

SPAWN-BATMAN (Also see Batman/Spawn: War Devil under Batman: One-Shots)
Image Comics (Todd McFarlane Productions): 1994 ($3.95, one-shot)
1-Miller scripts; McFarlane-c/a 6.00

SPAWN: BLOOD FEUD
Image Comics (Todd McFarlane Prods.): June, 1995 - No. 4, Sept, 1995 ($2.25, lim. series)
1-4-Alan Moore scripts, Tony Daniel-a 4.00

SPAWN FAN EDITION
Image Comics (Todd McFarlane Productions): Aug, 1996 - No. 3, Oct, 1996 (Giveaway, 12 pgs.) (Polybagged w/Overstreet's FAN)
1-3: Beau Smith scripts; Brad Gorby-a(p). 1-1st app. Nordik, the Norse Hellspawn. 2-1st app. McFallon. 3-1st app. Mercy 1 2 3 5 6 8
1-3-(Gold): All retailer incentives 16.00
1-3-Variant-c 1 2 3 5 6 8
2-(Platinum)-Retailer incentive 25.00

SPAWN GODSLAYER
Image Comics (Todd McFarlane Prods.): May, 2007 - No. 8, Apr, 2008 ($2.99)
1-8: 1-Holguin-s/Tan-a/Anacleto-c 3.00

SPAWN: THE DARK AGES
Image Comics (Todd McFarlane Productions): Mar, 1999 - No. 28, Oct, 2001 ($2.50)
1-Fabry-c; Holguin-s/Sharp-a; variant-c by McFarlane 3.00
2-28 3.00

SPAWN THE IMPALER
Image Comics (Todd McFarlane Prods.): Oct, 1996 - No. 3, Dec, 1996 ($2.95, limited series)
1-3-Mike Grell scripts, painted-a 3.00

SPAWN: THE UNDEAD
Image Comics (Todd McFarlane Prod.): Jun, 1999 - No. 9, Feb, 2000 ($1.95/$2.25)
1-9-Dwayne Turner-c/a; Jenkins-s. 7-9-($2.25-c) 3.00
TPB (6/08, $24.99) r/#1-9 25.00

SPAWN/WILDC.A.T.S
Image Comics (WildStorm): Jan, 1996 - No. 4, Apr, 1996 ($2.50, lim. series)
1-4: Alan Moore scripts in all. 3.00

SPEAKER OF THE DEAD (ORSON SCOTT CARD'S...) (Ender's Game)
Marvel Comics: Mar, 2011 - No. 5 ($3.99, limited series)
1-3-Johnston-s/Mhan-a/Camuncoli-c 4.00

SPECIAL AGENT (Steve Saunders...)(Also see True Comics #68)
Parents' Magazine Institute (Commended Comics No. 2): Dec, 1947 - No. 8, Sept, 1949 (Based on true FBI cases)
1-J. Edgar Hoover photo on-c 12 24 36 67 94 120
2 8 16 24 40 50 60
3-8 7 14 21 35 43 50

SPECIAL COLLECTORS' EDITION (See Savage Fists of Kung-Fu)

SPECIAL COMICS (Becomes Hangman #2 on)
MLJ Magazines: Winter, 1941-42
1-Origin The Boy Buddies (Shield & Wizard x-over); death of The Comet retold (see Pep #17); origin The Hangman retold; Hangman-c 320 640 960 2240 3920 5600

SPECIAL EDITION (See Gorgo and Reptisaurus)

SPECIAL EDITION COMICS
Fawcett Publications: 1940 (August) (68 pgs., one-shot)
1-1st book devoted entirely to Captain Marvel; C.C. Beck-c/a; only app. of Captain Marvel with belt buckle; Capt. Marvel appears with button-down flap; 1st story (came out before Captain Marvel #1) 784 1568 2352 5723 10,112 14,500

NOTE: *Prices vary widely on this book. Since this book is all Captain Marvel stories, it is actually a pre-Captain Marvel #1. There is speculation that this book almost became* ***Captain Marvel #1****. After* ***Special Edition*** *was published, there was an editor change at Fawcett. The new editor commissioned Kirby to do a nn* ***Captain Marvel*** *book early in 1941. This book was followed by a 2nd book several months later. This 2nd book was advertised as a #3 (making Special Edition the #1, & the nn issue the #2). However, the 2nd book did come out as a #2.*

GD VG FN VF VF/NM NM-
2.0 4.0 6.0 8.0 9.0 9.2

SPECIAL EDITION: SPIDER-MAN VS. THE HULK (See listing under The Amazing Spider-Man)

SPECIAL EDITION X-MEN
Marvel Comics Group: Feb, 1983 ($2.00, one-shot, Baxter paper)
1-r/Giant-Size X-Men #1 plus one new story 2 4 6 8 10 12

SPECIAL FORCES
Image Comics: Oct, 2007 - No. 4, Mar, 2009 ($2.99)
1-4-Iraq war combat; Kyle Baker-s/a/c 3.00

SPECIAL MARVEL EDITION (Master of Kung Fu #17 on)
Marvel Comics Group: Jan, 1971 - No. 16, Feb, 1974 (#1-3: 25¢, 68 pgs.; #4: 52 pgs.; #5-16: 20¢, regular ed.)
1-Thor-r by Kirby; 68 pgs. 4 8 12 22 34 45
2-4: Thor-r by Kirby; 2,3-68 pg. Giant. 4-(52 pgs.) 3 6 9 14 20 25
5-14: Sgt. Fury-r; 11-r/Sgt. Fury #13 (Capt. America) 2 4 6 8 11 14
15-Master of Kung Fu (Shang-Chi) begins (1st app., 12/73); Starlin-a; origin/1st app. Nayland Smith & Dr. Petrie 13 26 39 94 185 275
16-1st app. Midnight; Starlin-a (2nd Shang-Chi) 7 14 21 49 80 110

NOTE: *Kirby c-10-14.*

SPECIAL MISSIONS (See G.I. Joe...)

SPECIAL WAR SERIES (Attack V4#3 on?)
Charlton Comics: Aug, 1965 - No. 4, Nov, 1965
V4#1-D-Day (also see D-Day listing) 4 8 12 24 37 50
2-Attack! 3 6 9 16 22 28
3-War & Attack (also see War & Attack) 2 4 6 13 18 22
4-Judomaster (intro/1st app.; see Sarge Steel) 8 16 24 52 86 120

SPECIES (Movie)
Dark Horse Comics: June, 1995 - No. 4, Sept, 1995 ($2.50, limited series)
1-4: Adaptation of film 3.00

SPECIES: HUMAN RACE (Movie)
Dark Horse Comics: Nov, 1996 - No. 4, Feb, 1997 ($2.95, limited series)
1-4 3.00

SPECTACULAR ADVENTURES (See Adventures)

SPECTACULAR FEATURE MAGAZINE, A (Formerly My Confessions) (Spectacular Features Magazine #12)
Fox Feature Syndicate: No. 11, April, 1950
11 (#1)-Samson and Delilah 27 54 81 160 263 365

SPECTACULAR FEATURES MAGAZINE (Formerly A Spectacular Feature Magazine)
Fox Feature Syndicate: No. 12, June, 1950 - No. 3, Aug, 1950
12 (#2)-Iwo Jima; photo flag-c 27 54 81 158 259 360
3-True Crime Cases From Police Files 22 44 66 128 209 290

SPECTACULAR SCARLET SPIDER
Marvel Comics: Nov, 1995 - No. 2, Dec, 1995 ($1.95, limited series)
1,2: Replaces Spectacular Spider-Man 3.00

SPECTACULAR SPIDER-GIRL
Marvel Comics: Jul, 2010 - No. 4, Oct, 2010 ($3.99, limited series)
1-4-Frenz-a; Frank Castle and the Hobgoblin app. 4.00

SPECTACULAR SPIDER-MAN, THE (See Marvel Special Edition and Marvel Treasury Edition)

SPECTACULAR SPIDER-MAN, THE (Magazine)
Marvel Comics Group: July, 1968 - No. 2, Nov, 1968 (35¢)
1-(B&W)-Romita/Mooney 52 pg. story plus updated origin story with Everett-a(i) 11 22 33 80 150 220
1-Variation w/single c-price of 40¢ 11 22 33 80 150 220
2-(Color)-Green Goblin-c & 58 pg. story; Romita painted-c (story reprinted in King Size Spider-Man #9); Romita/Mooney-a 10 20 30 70 125 180

SPECTACULAR SPIDER-MAN, THE (Peter Parker...#54-132, 134)
Marvel Comics Group: Dec, 1976 - No. 263, Nov, 1998
1-Origin recap in text; return of Tarantula 6 12 18 41 66 90
2-Kraven the Hunter app. 3 6 9 18 27 35
3-5: 3-Intro Lightmaster. 4-Vulture app. 3 6 9 14 20 25
6-8-Morbius app.; 6-r/Marvel Team-Up #3 w/Morbius 3 6 9 16 22 28
7,8-(35¢-c variants, limited distribution)(6,7/77) 5 10 15 35 55 75
9-20: 9,10-White Tiger app. 11-Last 30¢-c. 17,18-Angel & Iceman app. (from Champions); Ghost Rider cameo. 18-Gil Kane-c 2 4 6 8 11 14
9-11-(35¢-c variants, limited distribution)(8-10/77) 3 6 9 20 30 40
21,24-26: 21-Scorpion app. 26-Daredevil app. 2 3 4 6 8 10

Spectacular Spider-Man #183 © MAR

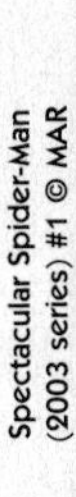
Spectacular Spider-Man (2003 series) #1 © MAR

The Spectre (4th series) #1 © DC

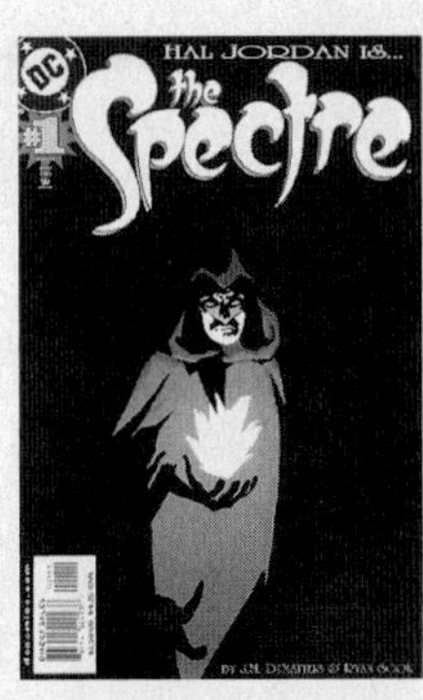

GD VG FN VF VF/NM NM-
2.0 4.0 6.0 8.0 9.0 9.2

22,23-Moon Knight app. 2 4 6 8 10 12
27-Miller's 1st art on Daredevil (2/79); also see Captain America #235
5 10 15 35 55 75
28-Miller Daredevil (p) 4 8 12 26 41 55
29-55,57,59: 33-Origin Iguana. 38-Morbius app. 1 2 3 4 5 7
56-2nd app. Jack O'Lantern (Macendale) & 1st Spidey/Jack O'Lantern battle (7/81)
1 2 3 5 6 8
58-Byrne-a(p) 1 2 3 5 6 8
60-Double size; origin retold with new facts revealed 1 2 3 5 6 8
61-63,65-68,71-74: 65-Kraven the Hunter app. 6.00
64-1st app. Cloak & Dagger (3/82) 2 4 6 10 14 18
69,70-Cloak & Dagger app. 1 2 3 5 7 9
75-Double size 1 2 3 4 5 7
76-80: 78,79-Punisher cameo 6.00
81,82-Punisher, Cloak & Dagger app. 1 2 3 5 6 8
83-Origin Punisher retold (10/83) 2 4 6 8 10 12
84,86-89,91-99: 94-96-Cloak & Dagger app. 98-Intro The Spot 6.00
85-Hobgoblin (Ned Leeds) app. (12/83); gains powers of original Green Goblin
(see Amazing Spider-Man #238) 2 4 6 8 10 12
90-Spider-Man's new black costume, last panel (ties w/Amazing Spider-Man #252 &
Marvel Team-Up #141 for 1st app.) 2 3 4 6 8 10
100-(3/85)-Double size 1 2 3 4 5 7
101-115,117,118,120-129: 107-110-Death of Jean DeWolff. 111-Secret Wars II tie-in.
128-Black Cat new costume 5.00
116,119-Sabretooth-c/story 2 3 4 6 8 10
130-132: 130-Hobgoblin app. 131-Six part Kraven tie-in. 132-Kraven tie-in
2 3 4 6 8 10
133-140: 138-1st full app. Tombstone (origin #139). 140-Punisher cameo 5.00
141-143-Punisher app. 1 2 3 4 5 7
144-146,148-157: 151-Tombstone returns 4.00
147-1st brief app. new Hobgoblin (Macendale), 1 page; continued in Web of Spider-Man #48
2 4 6 8 11 14
158-Spider-Man gets new powers (1st Cosmic Spidey, cont'd in Web of Spider-Man #59)
1 2 3 5 6 8
159-Cosmic Spider-Man app. 1 2 3 4 5 7
160-170: 161-163-Hobgoblin app. 168-170-Avengers x-over. 169-1st app. The Outlaws 3.00
171-188,190-199: 180,181,183,184-Green Goblin app. 197-199-Original X-Men-c/story 3.00
189-($2.95, 52 pgs.)-Silver hologram on-c; battles Green Goblin; origin Spidey retold;
Vess poster w/Spidey & Hobgoblin 5.00
189-(2nd printing)-Gold hologram on-c 3.00
195-(Deluxe ed.)-Polybagged w/"Dirt" magazine #2 & Beastie Boys/Smithereens
music cassette 4.00
200-($2.95)-Holo-grafx foil-c; Green Goblin-c/story 4.00
201-219,221,222,224,226-228,230-247: 212-w/card sheet. 203-Maximum Carnage x-over.
204-Begin 4 part death of Tombstone story. 207,208-The Shroud-c/story. 208-Siege of
Darkness x-over (#207 is a tie-in). 209-Black Cat back-up. 215,216-Scorpion app.
217-Power & Responsibility Pt. 4. 231-Return of Kaine; Spider-Man corpse discovered.
232-New Doc Octopus app. 233-Carnage-c/app. 235-Dragon Man cameo.
236-Dragon Man-c/app; Lizard app.; Peter Parker regains powers. 238,239-Lizard app.
239-w/card insert. 240-Revelations storyline begins. 241-Flashback 3.00
213-Collectors ed. polybagged w/16 pg. preview & animation cel; foil-c; 1st meeting
Spidey & Typhoid Mary 4.00
213-Version polybagged w/Gamepro #7; no-c date, price 3.00
217,219 ($2.95)-Deluxe edition foil-c: flip book 4.00
220 ($2.25, 52 pgs.)-Flip book, Mary Jane reveals pregnancy 4.00
223,229: ($2.50) 229-Spidey quits 3.00
223,225: ($2.95)-223-Die Cut-c. 225-Newsstand ed. 3.00
225,229: ($3.95) 225-Direct Market Holodisk-c (Green Goblin). 229-Acetate-c,
Spidey quits 4.00
240-Variant-c 4.00
248,249,251-254,256: 249-Return of Norman Osborn 256-1st app. Prodigy 3.00
250-($3.25) Double gatefold-c 4.00
255-($2.99) Spiderhunt pt. 4 4.00
257-262: 257-Double cover with "Spectacular Prodigy #1"; battles Jack O'Lantern.
258-Spidey is cleared. 259,260-Green Goblin & Hobgoblin app. 262-Byrne-s 3.00
263-Final issue; Byrne-c; Aunt May returns 5.00
#(-1) Flashback (7/97) 3.00
Annual 1 (1979)-Doc Octopus-c & 46 pg. story 2 4 6 8 11 14
Annual 2 (1980)-Origin/1st app. Rapier 1 2 3 5 6 8
Annual 3-5: ('81-'83) 3-Last Man-Wolf 5.00
Annual 6-14: 8 ('88,$ 1.75)-Evolutionary War x-over; Daydreamer returns Gwen Stacy "clone"
back to real self (not Gwen Stacy). 9 ('89, $2.00, 68 pgs.)-Atlantis Attacks. 10 ('90, $2.00,
68 pgs.)-McFarlane-a. 11 ('91, $2.00, 68 pgs.)-Iron Man app. 12 ('92, $2.25, 68 pgs.)-
Venom solo story cont'd from Amazing Spider-Man Annual #26. 13 ('93, $2.95, 68 pgs.)-

GD VG FN VF VF/NM NM-
2.0 4.0 6.0 8.0 9.0 9.2

Polybagged w/trading card; John Romita, Sr. back-up-a 4.00
Special 1 (1995, $3.95)-Flip book 4.00
NOTE: ***Austin** c-21i, Annual 11i. **Buckler** a-103, 107-111, 116, 117, 119, 122, Annual 1, Annual 10; c-103, 107-111, 113, 116-119, 122, Annual 1. **Buscema** a-121. **Byrne** c(p)-17, 43, 58, 101, 102. **Giffen** a-120p. **Hembeck** c/a-86p. **Larsen** c-Annual 11p. **Miller** c-46p, 48p, 50, 51p, 52p, 54p, 55, 56p, 57, 60. **Mooney** a-7i, 11i, 21p, 23p, 25p, 26p, 29-34p, 36p, 37p, 39i, 41, 42i, 49p, 50i, 51i, 53p. 54-57i, 59-66i, 68i, 71i, 73-79i, 81-83i, 85i, 87-99i, 102i, 125p, Annual 1i, 2p. **Nasser** c-37p. **Perez** c-10. **Simonson** c-54i. **Zeck** a-22, 118, 131, 132; c-131, 132.*

SPECTACULAR SPIDER-MAN (2nd series)
Marvel Comics: Sept, 2003 - No. 27, June, 2005 ($2.25/$2.99)

1-Jenkins-s/Ramos-a/c; Venom-c/app. 4.00
2-26: 2-5-Venom app. 6-9-Dr. Octopus app. 11-13-The Lizard app. 14-Rivera painted-a.
15,16-Capt. America app. 17,18-Ramos-a. 20-Spider-Man gets organic webshooters
21,22-Caldwell-a. 23-26-Sarah & Gabriel app.; Land-c 3.00
27-($2.99) Last issue; Uncle Ben app. in flashback; Buckingham-a 4.00
... Vol. 1: The Hunger TPB (2003, $11.99) r/#1-5 12.00
... Vol. 2: Countdown TPB (2004, $11.99) r/#6-10 12.00
... Vol. 3: Here There Be Monsters TPB (2004, $9.99) r/#11-14 10.00
... Vol. 4: Disassembled TPB (2004, $14.99) r/#15-20 15.00
... Vol. 5: Sins Remembered (2005, $9.99) r/#23-26 10.00
... Vol. 6: The Final Curtain (2005, $14.99) r/#21,22,27 & Peter Parker: Spider-Man #39-41 15.00

SPECTACULAR STORIES MAGAZINE (Formerly A Star Presentation)
Fox Feature Syndicate (Hero Books): No. 4, July, 1950; No. 3, Sept, 1950

4-Sherlock Holmes (true crime stories) 36 72 108 214 347 480
3-The St. Valentine's Day Massacre (true crime) 24 48 72 140 230 320

SPECTRE, THE (1st Series) (See Adventure Comics #431-440, More Fun & Showcase)
National Periodical Publ.: Nov-Dec, 1967 - No. 10, May-June, 1969 (All 12¢)

1-(11-12/67)-Anderson-c/a 14 28 42 96 191 285
2-5-Neal Adams-c/a; 3-Wildcat x-over 10 20 30 67 116 165
6-8,10: 6-8-Anderson inks. 7-Hourman app. 7 14 21 49 80 110
9-Wrightson-a 8 16 24 52 86 120

SPECTRE, THE (2nd Series) (See Saga of the Swamp Thing #58, Showcase '95 #8 &
Wrath of the...)
DC Comics: Apr, 1987 - No. 31, Oct, 1989 ($1.00, new format)

1-Colan-a begins 5.00
2-32: 9-Nudity panels. 10-Batman cameo. 10,11-Millennium tie-ins 3.00
Annual 1 (1988, $2.00)-Deadman app. 4.00
NOTE: ***Art Adams** c-Annual 1. **Colan** a-1-6. **Kaluta** c-1-3. **Mignola** c-7-9. **Morrow** a-9-15. **Sears** c/a-22. **Vess** c-13-15.*

SPECTRE, THE (3rd Series) (Also see Brave and the Bold #72, 75, 116, 180, 199 &
Showcase '95 #8)
DC Comics: Dec, 1992 - No. 62, Feb, 1998 ($1.75/$1.95/$2.25/$2.50)

1-($1.95)-Glow-in-the-dark-c; Mandrake-a begins 5.00
2,3 4.00
4-7,9-12,14-20: 10-Kaluta-c. 11-Hildebrandt painted-c. 16-Aparo/K. Jones-a.
19-Snyder III-c. 20-Sienkiewicz-c 3.00
8,13-($2.50)-Glow-in-the-dark-c 4.00
21-62: 22-(9/94)-Superman-c & app. 23-(11/94). 43-Kent Williams-c. 44-Kaluta-c.
47-Final Night x-over. 49-Begin Bolton-c. 51-Batman-c/app. 52-Gianni-c. 54-Corben-c.
60-Harris-c 3.00
#0 (10/94) Released between #22 & #23 3.00
Annual 1 (1995, $3.95)-Year One story 4.00
NOTE: ***Bisley** c-27. **Fabry** c-2. **Kelley Jones** c-31. **Vess** c-5.*

SPECTRE, THE (4th Series) (Hal Jordan; also see Day of Judgment #5 and
Legends of the DC Universe #33-36)
DC Comics: Mar, 2001 - No. 27, May, 2003 ($2.50/$2.75)

1-DeMatteis-s/Ryan Sook-c/a 4.00
2-27: 3,4-Superman & Batman-c/app. 5-Two-Face-c/app. 20-Begin $2.75-c. 21-Sinestro
returns. 24-JLA app. 3.00

SPECTRE, THE (See Crisis Aftermath: The Spectre)

SPEEDBALL (See Amazing Spider-Man Annual #12, Marvel Super-Heroes &
The New Warriors)
Marvel Comics: Sept, 1988(10/88-inside) - No. 11, July, 1989 (75¢)

1-11: Ditko/Guice-a-1-4, c-1; Ditko a-1-10; c-1-11p 4.00

SPEED BUGGY (TV)(Also see Fun-In #12, 15)
Charlton Comics: July, 1975 - No. 9, Nov, 1976 (Hanna-Barbera)

1 3 6 9 16 22 28
2-9 2 4 6 10 14 18

SPEED CARTER SPACEMAN (See Spaceman)

SPEED COMICS (New Speed)(Also see Double Up)

Speed Comics #3 © HARV

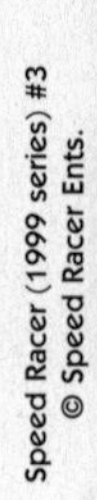

Speed Racer (1999 series) #3 © Speed Racer Ents.

Spider-Girl #27 © MAR

Brookwood Publ./Speed Publ./Harvey Publications No. 14 on: 10/39 - #11, 8/40; #12, 3/41 - #44, 1-2/47 (#14-16: pocket size, 100 pgs.)

	GD 2.0	VG 4.0	FN 6.0	VF 8.0	VF/NM 9.0	NM- 9.2
1-Origin & 1st app. Shock Gibson; Ted Parrish, the Man with 1000 Faces begins; Powell-a; becomes Champion #2 on?; has earliest? full page panel in comics	354	708	1062	2478	4339	6200
2-Powell-a	119	238	357	762	1306	1850
3	68	136	204	435	743	1050
4,5: 4-Powell-a? 5-Dinosaur-c	55	110	165	352	601	850
6-11: 7-Mars Mason begins, ends #11	50	100	150	315	533	750
12 (3/41; shows #11 in indicia)-The Wasp begins; Major Colt app. (Capt. Colt #12)	53	106	159	334	567	800
13-Intro. Captain Freedom & Young Defenders; Girl Commandos, Pat Parker (costumed heroine), War Nurse begins; Major Colt app.	61	122	183	390	670	950
14-16 (100 pg. pocket size, 1941): 14-2nd Harvey comic (See Pocket); Shock Gibson dons new costume. 15-Pat Parker dons costume, last in costume #23; no Girl Commandos	90	180	270	576	988	1400
17-Black Cat begins (4/42, early app.; see Pocket #1); origin Black Cat-r/Pocket #1; not in #40,41; S&K-c	84	168	252	538	919	1300
18-20-S&K-c	71	142	213	454	777	1100
21-Hitler, Tojo-c; Kirby-c	100	200	300	635	1093	1550
22-Kirby-c	71	142	213	454	777	1100
23-Origin Girl Commandos; Kirby-c	71	142	213	454	777	1100
24-Pat Parker team-up with Girl Commandos; Hitler, Tojo, & Mussolini-c	90	180	270	576	988	1400
25,27-30	54	108	162	343	574	825
26-Flag-c	58	116	174	371	636	900
31-Schomburg Hitler & Tojo-c	103	206	309	659	1130	1600
32-36-Schomburg-c	57	114	171	362	619	875
37,39-42, 44	41	82	123	256	428	600
38-Iwo-Jima Flag-c	43	86	129	271	461	650
43-Robot-c	45	90	135	284	480	675

NOTE: ***Al Avison*** *c-14-16, 30, 43.* ***Briefer*** *a-6, 7.* ***Jon Henri*** *(Kirbyesque) c-17-20.* ***Kubert*** *a-37, 38, 42-44.* ***Kirby/Caseneuve*** *c-21-23.* ***Cecelia Munson*** *a-7-11(Mars Mason).* ***Palais*** *c-37, 39-42.* ***Powell*** *a-1, 2, 4-7, 28, 31, 44.* ***Schomburg*** *c-31-36.* ***Tuska*** *a-3, 6, 7. Bondage c-18, 35. Captain Freedom c-16-24, 25(part), 26-44(w/Black Cat #27, 29, 31, 32-40). Shock Gibson c-1-15.*

SPEED DEMON (Also see Marvel Versus DC #3 & DC Versus Marvel #4)
Marvel Comics (Amalgam): Apr, 1996 ($1.95, one-shot)

	GD 2.0	VG 4.0	FN 6.0	VF 8.0	VF/NM 9.0	NM- 9.2
1						3.00

SPEED DEMONS (Formerly Frank Merriwell at Yale #1-4?; Submarine Attack #11 on)
Charlton Comics: No. 5, Feb, 1957 - No. 10, 1958

	GD 2.0	VG 4.0	FN 6.0	VF 8.0	VF/NM 9.0	NM- 9.2
5-10	7	14	21	35	43	50

SPEED FORCE (See The Flash 2nd Series #143-Cobalt Blue)
DC Comics: Nov, 1997 ($3.95, one-shot)

	GD 2.0	VG 4.0	FN 6.0	VF 8.0	VF/NM 9.0	NM- 9.2
1-Flash & Kid Flash vs. Cobalt Blue; Waid-s/Aparo & Sienkiewicz-a; Flash family stories and pin-ups by various						4.00

SPEED RACER (Also see The New Adventures of...)
Now Comics: July, 1987 - No. 38, Nov, 1990 ($1.75)

	GD 2.0	VG 4.0	FN 6.0	VF 8.0	VF/NM 9.0	NM- 9.2
1						4.00
2-38, 1-2nd printing						3.00
Special 1 (1988, $2.00)						3.00
Special 2 (1988, $3.50)						4.00

SPEED RACER (Also see Racer X)
DC Comics (WildStorm): Oct, 1999 - No. 3, Dec, 1999 ($2.50, limited series)

	GD 2.0	VG 4.0	FN 6.0	VF 8.0	VF/NM 9.0	NM- 9.2
1-3-Tommy Yune-s/a; origin of Racer X; debut of the Mach 5						3.00
...: Born To Race (2000, $9.95, TPB) r/series & conceptual art						10.00
...: The Original Manga Vol. 1 ('00, $9.95, TPB) r/1950s B&W manga						10.00

SPEED RACER: CHRONICLES OF THE RACER
IDW Publishing: 2007 - No. 4, Apr, 2008 ($3.99)

	GD 2.0	VG 4.0	FN 6.0	VF 8.0	VF/NM 9.0	NM- 9.2
1-4-Multiple covers for each						4.00

SPEED RACER FEATURING NINJA HIGH SCHOOL
Now Comics: Aug, 1993 - No. 2, 1993 ($2.50, mini-series)

	GD 2.0	VG 4.0	FN 6.0	VF 8.0	VF/NM 9.0	NM- 9.2
1,2: 1-Polybagged w/card. 2-Exists?						3.00

SPEED RACER: RETURN OF THE GRX
Now Comics: Mar, 1994 - No. 2, Apr, 1994 ($1.95, limited series)

	GD 2.0	VG 4.0	FN 6.0	VF 8.0	VF/NM 9.0	NM- 9.2
1,2						3.00

SPEED SMITH-THE HOT ROD KING (Also see Hot Rod King)
Ziff-Davis Publishing Co.: Spring, 1952

	GD 2.0	VG 4.0	FN 6.0	VF 8.0	VF/NM 9.0	NM- 9.2
1-Saunders painted-c	23	46	69	136	223	310

SPEEDY GONZALES
Dell Publishing Co.: No. 1084, Mar, 1960

	GD 2.0	VG 4.0	FN 6.0	VF 8.0	VF/NM 9.0	NM- 9.2
Four Color 1084	5	10	15	34	55	75

SPEEDY RABBIT (See Television Puppet Show)
Realistic/I. W. Enterprises/Super Comics: nd (1953); 1963

	GD 2.0	VG 4.0	FN 6.0	VF 8.0	VF/NM 9.0	NM- 9.2
nn (1953)-Realistic Reprint?	2	4	6	10	14	18
I.W. Reprint #1 (2 versions w/diff. c/stories exist)-Peter Cottontail #? Super Reprint #14(1963)	2	4	6	8	10	12

SPELLBINDERS
Quality: Dec, 1986 - No. 12, Jan, 1988 ($1.25)

	GD 2.0	VG 4.0	FN 6.0	VF 8.0	VF/NM 9.0	NM- 9.2
1-12: Nemesis the Warlock, Amadeus Wolf						3.00

SPELLBINDERS
Marvel Comics: May, 2005 - No. 6, Oct, 2005 ($2.99, limited series)

	GD 2.0	VG 4.0	FN 6.0	VF 8.0	VF/NM 9.0	NM- 9.2
1-6-Carey-s/Perkins-a						3.00
...: Signs and Wonders TPB (2006, $7.99, digest) r/#1-6						8.00

SPELLBOUND (See The Crusaders)

SPELLBOUND (Tales to Hold You... #1, Stories to Hold You...)
Atlas Comics (ACI 1-15/Male 16-23/BPC 24-34): Mar, 1952 - #23, June, 1954; #24, Oct, 1955 - #34, June, 1957

	GD 2.0	VG 4.0	FN 6.0	VF 8.0	VF/NM 9.0	NM- 9.2
1-Horror/weird stories in all	74	148	222	470	810	1150
2-Edgar A. Poe app.	40	80	120	246	411	575
3-5: 3-Whitney-a; cannibalism story	36	72	108	216	351	485
6-Krigstein-a	36	72	108	216	351	485
7-10: 8-Ayers-a	31	62	93	182	296	410
11-16,18-20: 14-Ed Win-a	26	52	78	154	252	350
17-Krigstein-a	26	52	78	156	256	355
21-23: 23-Last precode (6/54)	21	42	63	126	206	285
24-28,30,31,34: 25-Orlando-a	20	40	60	117	189	260
29-Ditko-a (4 pgs.)	21	42	63	126	206	285
32,33-Torres-a	20	40	60	117	189	260

NOTE: ***Brodsky*** *a-5; c-1, 5-7, 10, 11, 13, 15, 25-27, 32.* ***Colan*** *a-17.* ***Everett*** *a-2, 5, 7, 10, 16, 28, 31; c-2, 8, 9, 14, 17-19, 28, 30.* ***Forgione/Abel*** *a-29.* ***Forte/Fox*** *a-16.* ***Al Hartley*** *a-2.* ***Heath*** *a-2, 4, 8, 9, 12, 14, 16; c-3, 4, 12, 16, 20, 21.* ***Infantino*** *a-15.* ***Keller*** *a-5.* ***Kida*** *a-2, 14.* ***Maneely*** *a-7, 14, 27; c-24, 29, 31.* ***Mooney*** *a-5, 13, 18.* ***Mac Pakula*** *a-22, 32.* ***Post*** *a-8.* ***Powell*** *a-19, 20, 32.* ***Robinson*** *a-1.* ***Romita*** *a-24, 26, 27.* ***R.Q. Sale*** *a-29.* ***Sekowsky*** *a-5.* ***Severin*** *c-29.* ***Sinnott*** *a-8, 16, 17.*

SPELLBOUND
Marvel Comics: Jan, 1988 - Apr, 1988 ($1.50, bi-weekly, Baxter paper)

	GD 2.0	VG 4.0	FN 6.0	VF 8.0	VF/NM 9.0	NM- 9.2
1-5						3.00
6 ($2.25, 52 pgs.)						4.00

SPELLJAMMER (Also see TSR Worlds Comics Annual)
DC Comics: Sept, 1990 - No. 15, Nov, 1991 ($1.75)

	GD 2.0	VG 4.0	FN 6.0	VF 8.0	VF/NM 9.0	NM- 9.2
1-15: Based on TSR game. 11-Heck-a.						3.00

SPENCER SPOOK (Formerly Giggle Comics)
American Comics Group: No. 100, Mar-Apr, 1955 - No. 101, May-June, 1955

	GD 2.0	VG 4.0	FN 6.0	VF 8.0	VF/NM 9.0	NM- 9.2
100,101	7	14	21	37	46	55

SPIDER, THE
Eclipse Books: 1991 - Book 3, 1991 ($4.95, 52 pgs., limited series)

	GD 2.0	VG 4.0	FN 6.0	VF 8.0	VF/NM 9.0	NM- 9.2
Book 1-3-Truman-c/a						5.00

SPIDER-BOY (Also see Marvel Versus DC #3)
Marvel Comics (Amalgam): Apr, 1996 ($1.95)

	GD 2.0	VG 4.0	FN 6.0	VF 8.0	VF/NM 9.0	NM- 9.2
1-Mike Wieringo-c/a; Karl Kesel story; 1st app. of Bizarnage, Insect Queen, Challengers of the Fantastic, Sue Storm: Agent of S.H.I.E.L. D., & King Lizard						3.00

SPIDER-BOY TEAM-UP
Marvel Comics (Amalgam): June, 1997 ($1.95, one-shot)

	GD 2.0	VG 4.0	FN 6.0	VF 8.0	VF/NM 9.0	NM- 9.2
1-Karl Kesel & Roger Stern-s/Jo Ladronn-a(p)						3.00

SPIDER-GIRL (See What If... #105)
Marvel Comics: Oct, 1998 - No. 100, Sept, 2006 ($1.99/$2.25/$2.99)

	GD 2.0	VG 4.0	FN 6.0	VF 8.0	VF/NM 9.0	NM- 9.2
0-($2.99)-r/1st app. Peter Parker's daughter from What If #105; previews regular series, Avengers-Next and J2	1	2	3	4	5	7
1-DeFalco-s/Olliffe & Williamson-s	1	2	3	4	5	7
2-Two covers						4.00
3-16,18-20: 3-Fantastic Five-c/app. 10,11-Spider-Girl time-travels to meet teenaged Spider-Man						3.00
17-($2.99) Peter Parker suits up						4.00
21-24,26-49,51-59: 21-Begin $2.25-c. 31-Avengers app.						3.00
25-($2.99) Spider-Girl vs. the Savage Six						4.00
50-($3.50)						4.00

Spider-Girl (2011 series) #1 © MAR

Spider-Man #44 © MAR

Spider-Man: The Offical Movie Adaptation © MAR

GD	VG	FN	VF	VF/NM	NM-
2.0	4.0	6.0	8.0	9.0	9.2

59-99-($2.99) 59-Avengers app.; Ben Parker born. 75-May in Black costume. 82-84-Venom bonds with Normie Osborn. 93-Venom-c. 95-Tony Stark app. 3.00
100-($3.99) Last issue; story plus Rogues Gallery, profile pages; r/#27,53 4.00
1999 Annual ($3.99) 4.00
...: The End! (10/10, $3.99) Frenz & Buscema-a; Mayhem app. 4.00
Wizard #1/2 (1999) 3.00
... A Fresh Start (1/99,$5.99, TPB) r/#1&2 6.00
... Presents The Buzz and Darkdevil (2007, $7.99, digest) r/mini-series 8.00
TPB (10/01, $19.95) r/#0-8; new Olliffe-c 20.00
Marvel Age Spider-Girl Vol. 1: Legacy (2004, $7.99, digest size) r/#0-5 8.00
Marvel Age Spider-Girl Vol. 2: Like Father, Like Daughter (2004, $7.99, digest) r/#6-11 8.00
Spider-Girl Vol. 3: Avenging Allies (2005, $7.99, digest) r/#12-16 & 1999 Annual 8.00
Spider-Girl Vol. 4: Turning Point (2005, $7.99, digest) r/#17-21 & #1/2 8.00
Spider-Girl Vol. 5: Endgame (2006, $7.99, digest) r/#22-27 8.00
Spider-Girl Vol. 6: Too Many Spiders! (2006, $7.99, digest) r/#28-33 8.00
Spider-Girl Vol. 7: Betrayed (2006, $7.99, digest) r/#34-38 & #51 8.00
Spider-Girl Vol. 8: Duty Calls (2007, $7.99, digest) r/#39-44 8.00
Spider-Girl Vol. 9: Secret Lives (2007, $7.99, digest) r/#45-50 8.00

SPIDER-GIRL (Araña Corazon from Arana Heart of the Spider)
Marvel Comics: Jan, 2011 - Present ($3.99/$2.99)

1-($3.99) Tobin-s/Henry-a/Kitson-c; back-up w/Haspiel-a; Fantastic Four app. 4.00
1-Variant-c by Del Mundo 5.00
2-5-($2.99) 2,3-Red Hulk app. 4,5-Ana Kravenoff app. 3.00

SPIDER-HAM 25TH ANNIVERSARY SPECIAL
Marvel Comics: Aug, 2010 ($3.99, one-shot)

1-Jusko-c/DeFalco-s/Chabot-a; Peter Porker vs. the Swinester Six 4.00

SPIDER-MAN (See Amazing..., Friendly Neighborhood..., Giant-Size..., Marvel Age..., Marvel Knights..., Marvel Tales, Marvel Team-Up, Spectacular..., Spidey Super Stories, Ultimate Marvel Team-Up, Ultimate..., Venom, & Web Of...)

SPIDER-MAN (Peter Parker Spider-Man on cover but not indicia #75-on)
Marvel Comics: Aug, 1990 - No. 98, Nov, 1998 ($1.75/$1.95/ $1.99)

1-Silver edition, direct sale only (unbagged) 1 2 3 5 6 8
1-Silver bagged edition; direct sale, no price on comic, but $2.00 on plastic bag (125,000 print run) 20.00
1-Regular edition w/Spidey face in UPC area (unbagged); green-c 6.00
1-Regular bagged edition w/Spidey face in UPC area; green cover (125,000) 12.00
1-Newsstand bagged w/UPC code 8.00
1-Gold edition, 2nd printing (unbagged) with Spider-Man in box (400,000-450,000) 5.00
1-Gold 2nd printing w/UPC code; (less than 10,000 print run) intended for Wal-Mart; much scarcer than originally believed 120.00
1-Platinum ed. mailed to retailers only (10,000 print run); has new McFarlane-a & editorial material instead of ads; stiff-c, no cover price 130.00
2-26: 2-McFarlane-c/a/scripts continue. 6,7-Ghost Rider & Hobgoblin app. 8-Wolverine cameo; Wolverine storyline begins. 12-Wolverine storyline ends. 13-Spidey's black costume returns; Morbius app. 14-Morbius app. 15-Erik Larsen-c/a; Beast c/s. 16-X-Force-c/story w/Liefeld assists; continues in X-Force #4; reads sideways; last McFarlane issue. 17-Thanos-c/story; Leonardi/Williamson-c/a. 13,14-Spidey in black costume. 18-Ghost Rider-c/story. 18-23-Sinister Six storyline w/Erik Larsen-c/a/scripts. 19-Hulk & Hobgoblin-c & app. 20-22-Deathlok app. 22,23-Ghost Rider, Hulk, Hobgoblin app. 23-Wrap-around gatefold-c. 24-Infinity War x-over w/Demogoblin & Hobgoblin-c/story. 24-Demogoblin dons new costume & battles Hobgoblin-c/story. 26-($3.50, 52 pgs.)-Silver hologram on-c w/gatefold poster by Ron Lim; Spidey retells his origin. 4.00
26-2nd printing; gold hologram on-c 3.50
27-45: 32-34-Punisher-c/story. 37-Maximum Carnage x-over. 39,40-Electro-c/s (cameo #38). 41-43-Iron Fist-c/stories w/Jae Lee-c/a. 42-Intro Platoon. 44-Hobgoblin app. 3.50
46-49,51-53, 55, 56,58-74,76-81: 46-Begin $1.95-c; bound-in card sheet. 51-Power & Responsibility Pt. 3. 52,53-Venom app. 60-Kaine revealed. 61-Origin Kaine. 65-Mysterio app. 66-Kaine-c/app.; Peter Parker app. 67-Carnage-c/app. 68,69-Hobgoblin-c/app. 72-Onslaught x-over; Spidey vs. Sentinels. 74-Daredevil-c/app. 77-80-Morbius-c/app. 3.00
46-($2.95)-Polybagged; silver ink-c w/16 pg. preview of cartoon series & animation style print; bound-in trading card sheet 4.00
50-($2.50)-Newsstand edition 3.00
50-($3.95)-Collectors edition w/holographic-c 4.00
51-($2.95)-Deluxe edition foil-c; flip book 4.00
54-($2.75, 52 pgs.)-Flip book 4.00
57-($2.50) 3.00
57-($2.95)-Die cut-c 4.00
65-($2.95)-Variant-c; polybagged w/cassette 4.00
75-($2.95)-Wraparound-c; Green Goblin returns; death of Ben Reilly (who was the clone) 4.00
82-97: 84-Juggernaut app. 91-Double cover with "Dusk #1"; battles the Shocker. 93-Ghost Rider app. 3.00
98-Double cover; final issue 4.00

GD	VG	FN	VF	VF/NM	NM-
2.0	4.0	6.0	8.0	9.0	9.2

#(-1) Flashback (7/97) 3.00
Annual '97 ($2.99), '98 ($2.99)-Devil Dinosaur-c/app. 4.00
NOTE: *Erik Larsen c/a-15, 18-23. M. Rogers/Keith Williams c/a-27, 28.*

SPIDER-MAN (one-shots, hardcovers and TPBs)
...& Arana Special: The Hunter Revealed (5/06, $3.99) Del Rio-s; art by Del Rio & various 4.00
...and Batman ('95, $5.95) DeMatteis-s; Joker, Carnage app. 6.00
...and Daredevil ('84, $2.00) 1-r/Spectacular Spider-Man #26-28 by Miller 4.00
...and The Human Torch in...Bahia de Los Muertos! 1 (5/09, $3.99) Beland-s/Juan Doe-a; Diablo app.; printed in two versions (English and Spanish language) 4.00
...: Back in Black HC (2007, $34.99, dustjacket) oversized r/Amaz. S-M #539-543, Friendly Neighborhood S-M #17-23 & Annual #1; cover pencils and sketch pages 35.00
...: Back in Black SC (2008, $24.99) same contents as HC 25.00
...: Back in Black Handbook (2007, $3.99) Official Handbook format; Lopresti-c 4.00
...: Back in Quack (11/10, $3.99) Howard the Duck, Beverly and Man-Thing app. 4.00
...: Birth of Venom TPB (2007, $29.99) r/Secret Wars #8, AS-M #252-259,298-300,315-317, AS-M Annual #25, Fantastic Four #274 and Web of Spider-Man #1 30.00
...: Brand New Day HC (2008, $24.99, dustjacket) r/Amaz. S-M #546-551, Spider-Man: Swing Shift and story from Venom Super-Special 25.00
...: Carnage nn (6/93, $6.95, TPB)-r/Amazing S-M #344,345,359-363; spot varnish-c 7.00
.../Daredevil (10/02, $2.99) Vatche Mavlian-c/a; Brett Matthews-s 3.00
...: Dead Man's Hand 1 (4/97, $2.99) 3.00
...: Death of the Stacys HC (2007, $19.99, dustjacket) r/Amazing Spider-Man #88-92 and #121,122; intro. by Gerry Conway; afterword by Romita; cover gallery incl. reprints 20.00
.../Dr. Strange: "The Way to Dusty Death" nn (1992, $6.95, 68 pgs.) 7.00
...: Election Day HC (2009, $29.99) r/#584-588; includes Barack Obama app from #583 30.00
.../Elektra '98-($2.99) vs. The Silencer 3.00
... Family (2005, $4.99, 100 pgs.) new story and reprints; Spider-Ham app. 5.00
... Fear Itself (3/09, $3.99) Spider-Man and Man-Thing; Stuart Moore-s/Joe Suitor-a 4.00
... Fear Itself Graphic Novel (2/92, $12.95) 18.00
Giant-Sized Spider-Man (12/98, $3.99) r/team-ups 4.00
...: Grim Hunt - The Kraven Saga (5/10, free) prelude to Grim Hunt arc; Kraven history 2.00
Holiday Special 1995 ($2.95) 4.00
...: Hot Shots nn (1/96, $2.95) fold out posters by various, inc. Vess and Ross 4.00
Identity Crisis (9/98, $19.95, TPB) 20.00
...: Kraven's Last Hunt HC (2006, $19.99) r/Amaz. S-M #293,294; Web of S-M #31,32 and Spect. S-M #131-132; intro. by DeMatteis; Zeck-a; cover pencils and interior pencils 20.00
...: Legacy of Evil 1 (6/96, $3.95) Kurt Busiek script & Mark Texeira-c/a 4.00
...Legends Vol. 1: Todd McFarlane ('03, $19.95, TPB)-r/Amaz. S-M #298-305 20.00
...Legends Vol. 2: Todd McFarlane ('03, $19.99, TPB)-r/Amaz. S-M #306-314, & Spec. Spider-Man Annual #10 20.00
...Legends Vol. 3: Todd McFarlane ('04, $24.99, TPB)-r/Amaz. S-M #315-323,325,328 25.00
...Legends Vol. 4: Spider-Man & Wolverine ('03, $13.95, TPB) r/Spider-Man & Wolverine #1-4 and Spider-Man/Daredevil #1 14.00
.../Marrow (2/01, $2.99) Garza-a 3.00
.../Mary Jane: ... You Just Hit the Jackpot TPB (2009, $24.99) early apps. & key stories 25.00
...: One More Day HC (2008, $24.99, dustjacket) r/Amaz. S-M #544-545, Friendly N.S-M #24, Sensational S-M #41 and Marvel Spotlight: Spider-Man-One More Day 25.00
...: Origin of the Hunter (6/10, $3.99) r/Kraven apps. in ASM #15 & 34; new Mayhew-a 4.00
..., Peter Parker: Back in Black HC (2007, $34.99) oversized r/Sensational Spider-Man #35-40 & Annual #1, Spider-Man Family #1,2; Marvel Spotlight: Spider-Man and Spider-Man Back in Black Handbook; cover sketches 35.00
..., Punisher, Sabretooth: Designer Genes (1993, $8.95) 9.00
...Return of the Goblin TPB (See Peter Parker: Spider-Man)
...Revelations ('97, $14.99, TPB) r/end of Clone Saga plus 14 new pages by Romita Jr. 15.00
...: Saga of the Sandman TPB (2007, $19.99) r/1st app. Amazing S-M #4 and other app. 20.00
...: Son of the Goblin (2004, $15.99, TPB) r/AS-M#136-137,312 & Spec. S-M #189,200 16.00
... Special: Black and Blue and Read All Over 1 (11/06, $3.99) new story and r/ASM #12 4.00
Special Edition 1 (12/92-c, 11/92 inside)-The Trial of Venom; ordered thru mail with $5.00 donation or more to UNICEF; embossed metallic ink; came bagged w/bound-in poster; Daredevil app. 1 3 4 6 8 10
Super Special (7/95, $3.95)-Planet of the Symbiotes 4.00
The Best of Spider-Man Vol. 2 (2003, $29.99, HC with dust jacket) r/AS-M V2 #37-45, Peter Parker: S-M #44-47, and S-M's Tangled Web #10,11; Pearson-c 30.00
The Best of Spider-Man Vol. 3 (2004, $29.99, HC with d.j.) r/AS-M V2 #46-58, 500 30.00
The Best of Spider-Man Vol. 4 (2005, $29.99, HC with d.j.) r/#501-514; sketch pages 30.00
The Best of Spider-Man Vol. 5 (2006, $29.99, HC with d.j.) r/#515-524; sketch pages 30.00
The Complete Frank Miller Spider-Man (2002, $29.95, HC) r/Miller-s/a 30.00
The Death of Captain Stacy ($3.50) r/AS-M#88-90 4.00
The Death of Gwen Stacy ($14.95) r/AS-M#96-98,121,122 15.00
...: The Movie ($12.95) adaptation by Stan Lee-s/Alan Davis-a; plus r/Ultimate Spider-Man #8, Peter Parker #35, Tangled Web #10; photo-c 13.00
...: The Official Movie Adaptation ($5.95) Stan Lee-s/Alan Davis-a 6.00
...: The Other HC (2006, $29.99, dust jacket) r/Amazing S-M #525-528, Friendly Neighborhood S-M #1-4 and Marvel Knights S-M #19-22; gallery of variant covers 30.00

Spider-Man Adventures #6 © MAR

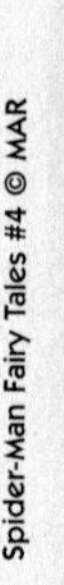
Spider-Man Fairy Tales #4 © MAR

Spider-Man/Gen 13 © MAR & WSP

GD 2.0 | VG 4.0 | FN 6.0 | VF 8.0 | VF/NM 9.0 | NM- 9.2

...: The Other SC (2006, $24.99) r/crossover; gallery of variant covers 25.00
...: The Other Sketchbook (2005, $2.99) sketch page preview of 2005-6 x-over 3.00
Torment TPB (5/01$15.95) r/#1-5, Spec. S-M #10 16.00
... Vs. Doctor Octopus ($17.95) reprints early battles; Sean Chen-c 18.00
... Vs. Punisher (7/00, $2.99) Michael Lopez-c/a 3.00
...Vs. Silver Sable (2006, $15.99, TPB)-r/Amazing Spider-Man #265,279-281 & Peter Parker, The Spectacular Spider-Man #128,129 16.00
...Vs. The Black Cat (2005, $14.99, TPB)-r/Amaz. S-M #194,195,204,205,226,227 15.00
...Vs. Vampires (12/10, $3.99) Blade app.; Castro-a/Grevioux-s 4.00
...Vs. Venom (1990, $8.95, TPB)-r/Amaz. S-M #300,315-317 w/new McFarlane-c 9.00
...Visionaries (10/01, $19.95, TPB)-r/Amaz. S-M #298-305; McFarlane-a 20.00
...Visionaries: John Romita (8/01, $19.95, TPB)-r/Amaz. S-M #39-42, 50,68,69,108,109; new Romita-c 20.00
...Visionaries: Kurt Busiek (2006, $19.99, TPB)-r/Untold Tales of Spider-Man #1-8 20.00
...Visionaries: Roger Stern (2007, $24.99, TPB)-r/Amazing Spider-Man #206 & Spectacular Spider-Man #43-52,54; Stern interview 25.00
...With Great Power Comes Great Responsibility (6/11, $3.99) r/Ultimate Spider-Man #33,97, and Ultimate Comics Spider-Man #1 4.00
Wizard 1/2 ($10.00) Leonardi-a; Green Goblin app. 10.00

SPIDER-MAN ADVENTURES
Marvel Comics: Dec, 1994 - No. 15, Mar, 1996 ($1.50)
1-15 ($1.50)-Based on animated series 3.00
1-($2.95)-Foil embossed-c 4.00

SPIDER-MAN AND HIS AMAZING FRIENDS (See Marvel Action Universe)
Marvel Comics Group: Dec, 1981 (one-shot)
1-Adapted from NBC TV cartoon show; Green Goblin-c/story; 1st Spidey, Firestar, Iceman team-up; Spiegle-p 5.00

SPIDER-MAN AND POWER PACK
Marvel Comics: Jan, 2007 - No. 4, Apr, 2007 ($2.99, limited series)
1-4-Sumerak-s/Gurihiru-a; Sandman app. 3,4-Venom app. 3.00
...: Big City Heroes (2007, $6.99, digest) r/#1-4 7.00

SPIDER-MAN AND THE FANTASTIC FOUR
Marvel Comics: Jun, 2007 - No. 4, Sept, 2007 ($2.99, limited series)
1-4-Mike Wieringo-a/c; Jeff Parker-s. 1,4-Impossible Man app. 3.00
...: Silver Rage TPB (2007, $10.99) r/#1-4; series outline and cover sketches 11.00

SPIDER-MAN AND THE SECRET WARS
Marvel Comics: Feb, 2010 - No. 4, May, 2010 ($2.99, limited series)
1-4-Tobin-s/Scherberger-a. 3-Black costume app. 3.00

SPIDER-MAN AND THE INCREDIBLE HULK (See listing under Amazing...)

SPIDER-MAN AND THE UNCANNY X-MEN
Marvel Comics: Mar, 1996 ($16.95, trade paperback)
nn-r/Uncanny X-Men #27, Uncanny X-men #35, Amazing Spider-Man #92, Marvel Team-Up Annual #1, Marvel Team-Up #150, & Spectacular Spider-Man #197-199 17.00

SPIDER-MAN & WOLVERINE (See Spider-Man Legends Vol. 4 for TPB reprint)
Marvel Comics: Aug, 2003 - No. 4, Nov, 2003 ($2.99, limited series)
1-4-Matthews-s/Mavlian-a 3.00

SPIDER-MAN AND X-FACTOR
Marvel Comics: May, 1994 - No. 3, July, 1994 ($1.95, limited series)
1-3 3.00

SPIDER-MAN /BADROCK
Maximum Press: Mar, 1997 ($2.99, mini-series)
1A, 1B(#2)-Jurgens-s 3.00

SPIDER-MAN/BLACK CAT: THE EVIL THAT MEN DO (Also see Marvel Must Haves)
Marvel Comics: Aug, 2002 - No. 6, Mar, 2006 ($2.99, limited series)
1-6-Kevin Smith-s/Terry Dodson-c/a 3.00
HC (2006, $19.99, dust jacket) r/#1-6; script to #6 with sketches 20.00

SPIDER-MAN: BLUE
Marvel Comics: July, 2002 - No. 6, Apr, 2003 ($3.50, limited series)
1-6: Jeph Loeb-s/Tim Sale-a/c; flashback to early MJ and Gwen Stacy 3.50
HC (2003, $21.99, with dust jacket) over-sized r/#1-6; intro. by John Romita 22.00
SC (2004, $14.99) r/#1-6; cover gallery 15.00

SPIDER-MAN: BRAND NEW DAY (See Amazing Spider-Man Vol. 2)

SPIDER-MAN: BREAKOUT (See New Avengers #1)
Marvel Comics: June, 2005 - No. 5, Oct, 2005 ($2.99, limited series)
1-5-Bedard-s/Garcia-a. 1-U-Foes app. 5-New Avengers app. 3.00
TPB (2006, $13.99) r/#1-5 14.00

SPIDER-MAN: CHAPTER ONE
Marvel Comics: Dec, 1998 - No. 12, Oct, 1999 ($2.50, limited series)
1-Retelling/updating of origin; John Byrne-s/c/a 3.00
1-($6.95) DF Edition w/variant-c by Jae Lee 7.00
2-11: 2-Two covers (one is swipe of ASM #1); Fantastic Four app. 9-Daredevil. 11-Giant-Man-c/app. 3.00
12-($3.50) Battles the Sandman 4.00
0-(5/99) Origins of Vulture, Lizard and Sandman 3.00

SPIDER-MAN CLASSICS
Marvel Comics: Apr, 1993 - No. 16, July, 1994 ($1.25)
1-14,16: 1-r/Amaz. Fantasy #15 & Strange Tales #115. 2-16-r/Amaz. Spider-Man #1-15. 6-Austin-c(i) 3.00
15-($2.95)-Polybagged w/16 pg. insert & animation style print; r/Amazing Spider-Man #14 (1st Green Goblin) 4.00

SPIDER-MAN COLLECTOR'S PREVIEW
Marvel Comics: Dec, 1994 ($1.50, 100 pgs., one-shot)
1-wraparound-c; no comics 4.00

SPIDER-MAN COMICS MAGAZINE
Marvel Comics Group: Jan, 1987 - No. 13, 1988 ($1.50, digest-size)
1-13-Reprints 6.00

SPIDER-MAN: DEATH AND DESTINY
Marvel Comics: Aug, 2000 - No. 3, Oct, 2000 ($2.99, limited series)
1-3-Aftermath of the death of Capt. Stacy 3.00

SPIDER-MAN/ DOCTOR OCTOPUS: OUT OF REACH
Marvel Comics: Jan, 2004 - No. 5, May, 2004 ($2.99, limited series)
1-5: 1-Keron Grant-a/Colin Mitchell-s 3.00
Marvel Age... TPB (2004, $5.99, digest size) r/#1-5 6.00

SPIDER-MAN/ DOCTOR OCTOPUS: YEAR ONE
Marvel Comics: Aug, 2004 - No. 5, Dec, 2004 ($2.99, limited series)
1-5-Kaare Andrews-a/Zeb Wells-s 3.00

SPIDER-MAN FAIRY TALES
Marvel Comics: July, 2007 - No. 4, Oct, 2007 ($2.99, limited series)
1-4: 1-Cebulski-s/Tercio-a. 2-Henrichon-a. 3-Kobayashi-a. 4-Dragotta-p/Allred-i 3.00
TPB (2007, $10.99) r/#1-4 11.00

SPIDER-MAN FAMILY (Also see Amazing Spider-Man Family)
Marvel Comics: Apr, 2007 - No. 9, Aug, 2008 ($4.99, anthology)
1-9-New tales and reprints. 1-Black costume, Sandman, Black Cat app. 4-Agents of Atlas app., Kirk-a; Puppet Master by Eliopoulos. 8-Iron Man app. 9-Hulk app. 5.00
... Featuring Spider-Clan 1 (1/07, $4.99) new Spider-Clan story; reprints w/Spider-Man 2099 and Amazing Spider-Man #252 (black costume) 5.00
... Featuring Spider-Man's Amazing Friends 1 (10/06, $4.99) new story with Iceman and Firestar; Mini Marvels w/Giarrusso-a; reprints w/Spider-Man 2099 5.00
...: Back In Black (2007, $7.99, digest) r/new content from #1-3 8.00
...: Untold Team-Ups (2008, $9.99, digest) r/new content from #4-6 10.00

SPIDER-MAN/FANTASTIC FOUR (Spider-Man and the Fantastic Four on cover)
Marvel Comics: Sept, 2010 - No. 4, Dec, 2010 ($3.99, limited series)
1-4-Gage-s/Alberti-a; Dr. Doom app. 4.00

SPIDER-MAN: FEVER
Marvel Comics: Jun, 2010 - No. 3, Aug, 2010 ($3.99, limited series)
1-3-Brendan McCarthy-s/a; Dr. Strange app. 4.00

SPIDER-MAN: FRIENDS AND ENEMIES
Marvel Comics: Jan, 1995 - No. 4, Apr, 1995 ($1.95, limited series)
1-4-Darkhawk, Nova & Speedball app. 3.00

SPIDER-MAN: FUNERAL FOR AN OCTOPUS
Marvel Comics: Mar, 1995 - No. 3, May, 1995 ($1.50, limited series)
1-3 3.00

SPIDER-MAN/ GEN 13
Marvel Comics: Nov, 1996 ($4.95, one-shot)
nn-Peter David-s/Stuart Immonen-a 5.00

SPIDER-MAN: GET KRAVEN
Marvel Comics: Aug, 2002 - No. 6, Jan, 2003 ($2.99/$2.25, limited series)
1-($2.99) McCrea-a/Quesada-c; back-up story w/Rio-a 4.00
2-6-($2.25) 2-Sub-Mariner app. 3.00

SPIDER-MAN: HOBGOBLIN LIVES

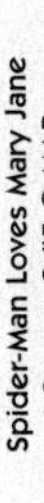

Spider-Man Loves Mary Jane Season 2 #5 © MAR

Spider-Man Noir #1 © MAR

Spider-Man Team-Up #6 © MAR

	GD 2.0	VG 4.0	FN 6.0	VF 8.0	VF/NM 9.0	NM- 9.2

Marvel Comics: Jan, 1997 - No. 3, Mar, 1997 ($2.50, limited series)

1-3-Wraparound-c 3.00
TPB (1/98, $14.99) r/#1-3 plus timeline 15.00

SPIDER-MAN: HOUSE OF M (Also see House of M and related x-overs)
Marvel Comics: Aug, 2005 - No. 5, Dec, 2005 ($2.99, limited series)

1-5-Waid & Peyer-s/Larroca-a; rich and famous Peter Parker in mutant-ruled world 3.00
House of M: Spider-Man TPB (2006, $13.99) r/series 14.00

SPIDER-MAN/ HUMAN TORCH
Marvel Comics: Mar, 2005 - No. 5, July, 2005 ($2.99, limited series)

1-5-Ty Templeton-a/Dan Slott-s; team-ups from early days to the present 3.00
...: I'm With Stupid (2006, $7.99, digest) r/#1-5 8.00

SPIDER-MAN: INDIA
Marvel Comics: Jan, 2005 - No. 4, Apr, 2005 ($2.99, limited series)

1-4-Pavitr Prabhakar gains spider powers; Kang-a/Seetharaman-s 3.00

SPIDER-MAN: LEGEND OF THE SPIDER-CLAN (See Marvel Mangaverse for TPB)
Marvel Comics: Dec, 2002 - No. 5, Apr, 2003 ($2.25, limited series)

1-5-Marvel Mangaverse Spider-Man; Kaare Andrews-s/Skottie Young-c/a 3.00

SPIDER-MAN: LIFELINE
Marvel Comics: Apr, 2001 - No. 3, June, 2001 ($2.99, limited series)

1-3-Nicieza-s/Rude-c/a; The Lizard app. 3.00

SPIDER-MAN LOVES MARY JANE (Also see Mary Jane limited series)
Marvel Comics: Feb, 2006 - No. 20, Sept, 2007 ($2.99)

1-20-Mary Jane & Peter in high school; McKeever-s/Miyazawa-a/c. 5-Gwen Stacy app. 16-18,20-Firestar app. 17-Felecia Hardy app. 3.00
... Vol. 1: Super Crush (2006, $7.99, digest) r/#1-5; cover concepts page 8.00
... Vol. 2: The New Girl (2006, $7.99, digest) r/#6-10; sketch pages 8.00
... Vol. 3: My Secret Life (2007, $7.99, digest) r/#11-15; sketch pages 8.00
... Vol. 4: Still Friends (2007, $7.99, digest) r/#16-20 8.00
Hardcover Vol. 1 (2007, $24.99) oversized reprints of #1-5, Mary Jane #1-4 and Mary Jane: Homecoming #1-4; series proposals, sketch pages and covers; coloring process 25.00
Hardcover Vol. 2 (2008, $39.99) oversized reprints of #6-20, sketch & layout pages 40.00

SPIDER-MAN LOVES MARY JANE SEASON 2
Marvel Comics: Oct, 2008 - No. 5, Feb, 2009 ($2.99, limited series)

1-5-Terry Moore-s/c; Craig Rousseau-a 3.00
1-Variant-c by Alphona 8.00

SPIDER-MAN: MADE MEN
Marvel Comics: Aug, 1998 ($5.99, one-shot)

1-Spider-Man & Daredevil vs. Kingpin 6.00

SPIDER-MAN MAGAZINE
Marvel Comics: 1994 - No. 3, 1994 ($1.95, magazine)

1-3: 1-Contains 4 S-M promo cards & 4 X-Men Ultra Fleer cards; Spider-Man story by Romita, Sr.; X-Men story; puzzles & games. 2-Doc Octopus & X-Men stories 4.00

SPIDER-MAN: MAXIMUM CLONAGE
Marvel Comics: 1995 ($4.95)

Alpha #1-Acetate-c, Omega #1-Chromium-c. 5.00

SPIDER-MAN MEGAZINE
Marvel Comics: Oct, 1994 - No. 6, Mar, 1995 ($2.95, 100 pgs.)

1-6: 1-r/ASM #16,224,225, Marvel Team-Up #1 4.00

SPIDER-MAN NOIR
Marvel Comics: Dec, 2008 - No. 4, May, 2009 ($3.99, limited series)

1-4-Pulp-style Spider-Man in 1933; DiGiandomenico-a; covers by Zircher & Calero 4.00
...: Eyes Without a Face 1-4 (2/10 - No. 4, 5/10) DiGiandomenico-a; Zircher & Calero-c 4.00

SPIDER-MAN: POWER OF TERROR
Marvel Comics: Jan, 1995 - No. 4, Apr, 1995 ($1.95, limited series)

1-4-Silvermane & Deathlok app. 3.00

SPIDER-MAN/PUNISHER: FAMILY PLOT
Marvel Comics: Feb, 1996 - No. 2, Mar, 1996 ($2.95, limited series)

1,2 3.00

SPIDER-MAN: QUALITY OF LIFE
Marvel Comics: Jul, 2002 - No. 4, Oct, 2002 ($2.99, limited series)

1-4-All CGI art by Scott Sava; Rucka-s; Lizard app. 3.00
TPB (2002, $12.99) r/#1-4; a "Making of..." section detailing the CGI process 13.00

SPIDER-MAN: REDEMPTION
Marvel Comics: Sept, 1996 - No. 4, Dec, 1996 ($1.50, limited series)

1-4: DeMatteis scripts; Zeck-a 3.00

SPIDER-MAN/ RED SONJA
Marvel Comics: Oct, 2007 - No. 5, Feb, 2008 ($2.99, limited series)

1-5-Rubi-a/Oeming-s/Turner-c; Venom & Kulan Gath app. 3.00
HC (2008, $19.99, dustjacket) r/#1-5 and Marvel Team-Up #79; sketch pages 20.00

SPIDER-MAN: REIGN
Marvel Comics: Feb, 2007 - No. 4, May, 2007 ($3.99, limited series)

1-Kaare Andrews-s/a; red costume on cover 4.00
1-Variant cover with black costume 10.00
2-4 4.00
HC (2007, $19.99, dustjacket) r/#1-4; sketch pages and cover variant gallery 20.00
HC 2nd printing (2007, $19.99, dustjacket) with variant black cover 20.00
SC (2008, $14.99) r/#1-4; sketch pages and cover variant gallery 15.00

SPIDER-MAN: REVENGE OF THE GREEN GOBLIN
Marvel Comics: Oct, 2000 - No. 3, Dec, 2000 ($2.99, limited series)

1-3-Frenz & Olliffe-a; continues in AS-M #25 & PP:S-M #25 3.00

SPIDER-MAN SAGA
Marvel Comics: Nov, 1991 - No. 4, Feb, 1992 ($2.95, limited series)

1-4: Gives history of Spider-Man: text & illustrations 3.00

SPIDER-MAN 1602
Marvel Comics: Dec, 2009 - No. 5, Apr, 2010 ($3.99, limited series)

1-5- Peter Parquagh from Marvel 1602; Parker-s/Rosanas-a 4.00

SPIDER-MAN: SWEET CHARITY
Marvel Comics: Aug, 2002 ($4.95, one-shot)

1-The Scorpion-c/app.; Campbell-c/Zimmerman-s/Robertson-a 5.00

SPIDER-MAN'S TANGLED WEB (Titled **"Tangled Web"** in indicia for #1-4)
Marvel Comics: Jun, 2001 - No. 22, Mar, 2003 ($2.99)

1-3: "The Thousand" on-c; Ennis-s/McCrea-a/Fabry-c 4.00
4-"Severance Package" on-c; Rucka-s/Risso-a; Kingpin-c/app. 5.00
5,6-Flowers for Rhino; Milligan-s/Fegredo-a 3.00
7-10,12,15-20,22: 7-9-Gentlemen's Agreement; Bruce Jones-s/Lee Weeks-a. 10-Andrews-s/a. 12-Fegredo-a. 15-Paul Pope-s/a. 18-Ted McKeever-s/a. 19-Mahfood-a. 20-Haspiel-a 3.00
11,13,21-($3.50) 11-Darwyn Cooke-s/a. 13-Phillips-a. 21-Christmas-s by Cooke & Bone 4.00
14-Azzarello & Scott Levy (WWE's Raven)-s about Crusher Hogan 4.00
TPB (10/01, $15.95) r/#1-6 16.00
Volume 2 TPB (4/02, $14.95) r/#7-11 15.00
Volume 3 TPB (2002, $15.99) r/#12-17; Jason Pearson-c 16.00
Volume 4 TPB (2003, $15.99) r/#18-22; Frank Cho-c 16.00

SPIDER-MAN TEAM-UP
Marvel Comics: Dec, 1995 - No. 7, June, 1996 ($2.95)

1-7: 1-w/ X-Men. 2-w/Silver Surfer. 3-w/Fantastic Four. 4-w/Avengers. 5-Gambit & Howard the Duck-c/app. 7-Thunderbolts-c/app. 4.00
... Special 1 (5/05, $2.99) Fantastic Four app.; Todd Dezago-s/Shane Davis-a 4.00

SPIDER-MAN: THE ARACHNIS PROJECT
Marvel Comics: Aug, 1994 - No. 6, Jan, 1995 ($1.75, limited series)

1-6-Venom, Styx, Stone & Jury app. 3.00

SPIDER-MAN: THE CLONE JOURNAL
Marvel Comics: Mar, 1995 ($2.95, one-shot)

1 4.00

SPIDER-MAN: THE CLONE SAGA
Marvel Comics: Nov, 2009 - No. 6, Apr, 2010 ($3.99, limited series)

1-6-Retelling of the saga with different ending; DeFalco & Mackie-s/Nauck-a 4.00

SPIDER-MAN: THE FINAL ADVENTURE
Marvel Comics: Nov, 1995 - No. 4, Feb, 1996 ($2.95, limited series)

1-4: 1-Nicieza scripts; foil-c 3.00

SPIDER-MAN: THE JACKAL FILES
Marvel Comics: Aug, 1995 ($1.95, one-shot)

1 3.00

SPIDER-MAN: THE LOST YEARS
Marvel Comics: Aug, 1995-No. 3, Oct, 1995; No. 0, 1996 ($2.95/$3.95,lim. series)

0-(1/96, $3.95)-Reprints. 4.00
1-3-DeMatteis scripts, Romita, Jr.-c/a 3.00
NOTE: ***Romita** c-0i. **Romita, Jr.** a-0r, 1-3p. c-0-3p. **Sharp** a-0r.*

SPIDER-MAN: THE MANGA
Marvel Comics: Dec, 1997 - No. 31, June, 1999 ($3.99/$2.99, B&W, bi-weekly)

Spider-Man Unlimited (3rd series) #1 © MAR

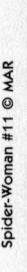

Spider-Woman #11 © MAR

Spidey Super-Stories #43 © MAR

GD 2.0 | VG 4.0 | FN 6.0 | VF 8.0 | VF/NM 9.0 | NM- 9.2

1-($3.99)-English translation of Japanese Spider-Man 4.00
2-31-($2.99) 3.00

SPIDER-MAN: THE MUTANT AGENDA
Marvel Comics: No. 0, Feb, 1994; No. 1, Mar, 1994 - No. 3, May, 1994 ($1.75, limited series)

0-(2/94, $1.25, 52 pgs.)-Crosses over w/newspaper strip; has empty pages to paste in newspaper strips; gives origin of Spidey 3.00
1-3: Beast & Hobgoblin app. 1-X-Men app. 3.00

SPIDER-MAN: THE MYSTERIO MANIFESTO (Listed as "Spider-Man and Mysterio" in indicia)
Marvel Comics: Jan, 2001 - No. 3, Mar, 2001 ($2.99, limited series)

1-3-Daredevil-c/app.; Weeks & McLeod-a 3.00

SPIDER-MAN: THE PARKER YEARS
Marvel Comics: Nov, 1995 ($2.50, one-shot)

1 3.00

SPIDER-MAN 2: THE MOVIE
Marvel Comics: Aug, 2004 ($3.50/$12.99, one-shot)

1-($3.50) Movie adaptation; Johnson, Lim & Olliffe-a 3.50
TPB-($12.99) Movie adaptation; r/Amazing Spider-Man #50, Ultimate Spider-Man #14,15 13.00

SPIDER-MAN 2099 (See Amazing Spider-Man #365)
Marvel Comics: Nov, 1992 - No. 46, Aug, 1996 ($1.25/$1.50/$1.95)

1-(stiff-c)-Red foil stamped-c; begins origin of Miguel O'Hara (Spider-Man 2099); Leonardi/Williamson-c/a begins 4.00
1-2nd printing, 2-12,14-24,26-40: 2-Origin continued, ends #3. 4-Doom 2099 app. 19-Bound-in trading cards. 35-Variant-c. 36-Two-c; Jae Lee-a. 37,38-Two-c 3.00
13-Extra 16 pg. insert on Midnight Sons 4.00
25-($2.25, 52 pgs.)-Newsstand edition 4.00
25-($2.95, 52 pgs.)-Deluxe edition w/embossed foil-c 4.50
41-46: 46-The Vulture app; Mike McKone-a(p) 3.00
Annual 1 (1994, $2.95, 68 pgs.) 4.00
Special 1 (1995, $3.95) 4.00
NOTE: *Chaykin c-37.* ***Ron Lim*** *a(p)-18; c(p)-13, 16, 18.* ***Kelley Jones*** *c/a-9.* ***Leonardi/Williamson*** *a-1-8, 10-13, 15-17, 19, 20, 22-25; c-1-13, 15, 17-19, 20, 22-25, 35.*

SPIDER-MAN 2099 MEETS SPIDER-MAN
Marvel Comics: 1995 ($5.95, one-shot)

nn-Peter David script; Leonardi/Williamson-c/a. 6.00

SPIDER-MAN UNIVERSE
Marvel Comics: Mar, 2000 - No. 7, Oct, 2000 ($4.95/$3.99, reprints)

1-5-Reprints recent issues from the various Spider-Man titles 5.00
6,7-($3.99) 4.00

SPIDER-MAN UNLIMITED
Marvel Comics: May, 1993 - No. 22, Nov, 1998 ($3.95, #1-12 were quarterly, 68 pgs.)

1-Begin Maximum Carnage storyline, ends; Carnage-c/story 5.00
2-12: 2-Venom & Carnage-c/story; Lim-c/a(p) in #2-6. 10-Vulture app. 4.00
13-22: 13-Begin $2.99-c; Scorpion-c/app. 15-Daniel-c; Puma-c/app. 19-Lizard-c/app. 20-Hannibal King and Lilith app. 21,22-Deodato-a 3.00

SPIDER-MAN UNLIMITED (Based on the TV animated series)
Marvel Comics: Dec, 1999 - No. 5, Apr, 2000 ($2.99/$1.99)

1-($2.99) Venom and Carnage app. 4.00
2-5: 2-($1.99) Green Goblin app. 3.00

SPIDER-MAN UNLIMITED (3rd series)
Marvel Comics: Mar, 2004 - No. 15, July, 2006 ($2.99)

1-16: 1-Short stories by various incl. Miyazawa & Chen-a. 2-Mays-a. 6-Allred-c. 14-Finch-c/a; Black Cat app. 3.00

SPIDER-MAN UNMASKED
Marvel Comics: Nov, 1996 ($5.95, one-shot)

nn-Art w/text 6.00

SPIDER-MAN: VENOM AGENDA
Marvel Comics: Jan, 1998 ($2.99, one-shot)

1-Hama-s/Lyle-c/a 3.00

SPIDER-MAN VS. DRACULA
Marvel Comics: Jan, 1994 ($1.75, 52 pgs., one-shot)

1-r/Giant-Size Spider-Man #1 plus new Matt Fox-a 4.00

SPIDER-MAN VS. WOLVERINE
Marvel Comics Group: Feb, 1987; V2#1, 1990 (68 pgs.)

1-Williamson-c/a(i); intro Charlemagne; death of Ned Leeds (old Hobgoblin) 2 4 6 12 16 20

GD 2.0 | VG 4.0 | FN 6.0 | VF 8.0 | VF/NM 9.0 | NM- 9.2

V2#1 (1990, $4.95)-Reprints #1 (2/87) 5.00

SPIDER-MAN: WEB OF DOOM
Marvel Comics: Aug, 1994 - No. 3, Oct, 1994 ($1.75, limited series)

1-3 3.00

SPIDER-MAN: WITH GREAT POWER...
Marvel Comics: Mar, 2008 - No. 5, Sept, 2008 ($3.99, limited series)

1-5-Origin and early days re-told; Lapham-s/Harris-a/c 4.00

SPIDER-MAN: YEAR IN REVIEW
Marvel Comics: Feb, 2000 ($2.99)

1-Text recaps of 1999 issues 3.00

SPIDER REIGN OF THE VAMPIRE KING, THE (Also see The Spider)
Eclipse Books: 1992 - No. 3, 1992 ($4.95, limited series, coated stock, 52 pgs.)

Book One - Three: Truman scripts & painted-c 5.00

SPIDER'S WEB, THE (See G-8 and His Battle Aces)

SPIDER-WOMAN (Also see The Avengers #240, Marvel Spotlight #32, Marvel Super Heroes Secret Wars #7, Marvel Two-In-One #29 and New Avengers)
Marvel Comics Group: April, 1978 - No. 50, June, 1983 (New logo #47 on)

1-New complete origin & mask added 2 4 6 11 16 20
2-5,7-18: 2-Excalibur app. 3,11,12-Brother Grimm app. 13,15-The Shroud-c/s. 16-Sienkiewicz-c 1 2 3 4 5 7
6,19,20,28,29,32: 6-Morgan LeFay app. 6,19,32-Werewolf by Night-c/s. 20,28,29-Spider-Man app. 32-Universal Monsters photo/Miller-c 1 2 3 5 6 8
21-27,30,31,33-36 6.00
37,38-X-Men x-over: 37-1st app. Siryn of X-Force; origin retold 2 4 6 8 10 12
39-49: 46-Kingpin app. 49-Tigra-c/story 5.00
50-(52 pgs.)-Death of Spider-Woman; photo-c 2 4 6 9 13 16
NOTE: ***Austin*** *a-37i.* ***Byrne*** *c-26p.* ***Infantino*** *a-1-19.* ***Layton*** *c-19.* ***Miller*** *c-32p.*

SPIDER-WOMAN
Marvel Comics: Nov, 1993 - No. 4, Feb, 1994 ($1.75, mini-series)

V2#1-4: 1,2-Origin; U.S. Agent app. 3.00

SPIDER-WOMAN
Marvel Comics: July, 1999 - No. 18, Dec, 2000 ($2.99/$1.99/$2.25)

1-($2.99) Byrne-s/Sears-a 4.00
2-18: 2-11-($1.99). 2-Two covers. 12-Begin $2.25-c. 15-Capt. America-c/app. 3.00

SPIDER-WOMAN (Printed version of the motion comic for computers)
Marvel Comics: Nov, 2009 - No. 7, May, 2010 ($3.99/$2.99)

1-($3.99) Bendis-s/Maleev-a; covers by Maleev & Alex Ross; Jessica joins S.W.O.R.D. 4.00
2-6-($2.99) 2-4-Madame Hydra app. 6-Thunderbolts app. 3.00
7-($3.99) New Avengers app. 4.00

SPIDER-WOMAN: ORIGIN (Also see New Avengers)
Marvel Comics: Feb, 2006 - No. 5, June, 2006 ($2.99, limited series)

1-5-Bendis & Reed-s/Jonathan & Joshua Luna-a/c 3.00
1-Variant cover by Olivier Coipel 3.00
HC (2006, $19.99) r/series 20.00
SC (2007, $13.99) r/series 14.00

SPIDEY SUPER STORIES (Spider-Man) (Also see Fireside Books)
Marvel/Children's TV Workshop: Oct, 1974 - No. 57, Mar, 1982 (35¢, no ads)

1-Origin (stories simplified for younger readers) 5 10 15 30 48 65
2-Kraven 3 6 9 18 27 35
3-10,15: 6-Iceman. 15-Storm-c/sty 3 6 9 14 20 26
11-14,16-20: 19,20-Kirby-c 3 6 9 14 19 24
21-30: 24-Kirby-c 2 4 6 13 18 22
31-53: 31-Moondragon-c/app.; Dr. Doom app. 33-Hulk. 34-Sub-Mariner. 38-F.F. 39-Thanos-c/story. 44-Vision. 45-Silver Surfer & Dr. Doom app. 2 4 6 11 16 20
54-57: 56-Battles Jack O'Lantern-c/sty (exactly one year after 1st app. in Machine Man #19) 3 6 9 14 20 26

SPIKE AND TYKE (See M.G.M.'s...)

SPIKE... (Also see Buffy the Vampire Slayer and related titles)
IDW Publ.: Aug, 2005; Jan, 2006; Apr, 2006 ($7.49, squarebound, one-shots)

...: Lost & Found (4/06, $7.49) Scott Tipton-s/Fernando Goni-a 8.00
...: Old Times (8/05, $7.49) Peter David-s/Fernando Goni-a; Cecily/Halfrek app. 8.00
...: Old Wounds (1/06, $7.49) Tipton-s/Goni-a; flashback to Black Dahlia murder case 8.00
TPB (7/06, $19.99) r/one-shots 20.00

SPIKE (Buffy the Vampire Slayer)

Spike #5 © 20th Century Fox

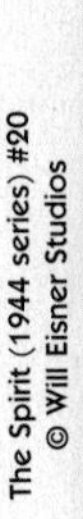
The Spirit (1944 series) #20 © Will Eisner Studios

The Spirit (2007 series) #28 © Will Eisner Studios

	GD 2.0	VG 4.0	FN 6.0	VF 8.0	VF/NM 9.0	NM- 9.2

IDW Publ.: Oct, 2010 - No. 8 ($3.99, limited series)

1-5-Lynch-s; multiple covers on each. 1,2-Urru-a. 5-Willow app. 4.00

SPIKE: AFTER THE FALL (Also see Angel: After the Fall) (Follows the last Angel TV episode)
IDW Publ.: July, 2008 - No. 4, Oct, 2008 ($3.99, limited series)

1-4-Lynch-s/Urru-a; multiple covers on each 4.00

SPIKE: ASYLUM (Buffy the Vampire Slayer)
IDW Publ.: Sept, 2006 - No. 5, Jan, 2007 ($3.99, limited series)

1-5-Lynch-s/Urru-a; multiple covers on each 4.00

SPIKE: SHADOW PUPPETS (Buffy the Vampire Slayer)
IDW Publ.: June, 2007 - No. 4, Sept, 2007 ($3.99, limited series)

1-4-Lynch-s/Urru-a; multiple covers on each 4.00

SPIKE: THE DEVIL YOU KNOW (Buffy the Vampire Slayer)
IDW Publ.: Jun, 2010 - No. 4, Sept, 2010 ($3.99, limited series)

1-4-Bill Williams-s/Chris Cross-a/Urru-c 4.00

SPIKE VS. DRACULA (Buffy the Vampire Slayer)
IDW Publ.: Feb, 2006 - No. 5, Mar, 2006 ($3.99, limited series)

1-5: 1-Peter David-s/Joe Corroney-a; Dru and Bela Lugosi app. 4.00

SPIN & MARTY (TV) (Walt Disney's)(See Walt Disney Showcase #32)
Dell Publishing Co. (Mickey Mouse Club): No. 714, June, 1956 - No. 1082, Mar-May, 1960 (All photo-c)

	GD	VG	FN	VF	VF/NM	NM-
Four Color 714 (#1)	12	24	36	82	154	225
Four Color 767,808 (#2,3)	9	18	27	63	107	150
Four Color 826 (#4)-Annette Funicello photo-c	20	40	60	140	283	425
5(3-5/58) - 9(6-8/59)	8	16	24	52	86	120
Four Color 1026,1082	8	16	24	52	86	120

SPIN ANGELS
Marvel Comics (Soleil): 2009 - No. 4, 2009 ($5.99)

1-4-English version of French comics; Jean-Luc Sala-s/Pierre-Mony Chan-a 6.00

SPINE-TINGLING TALES (Doctor Spektor Presents...)
Gold Key: May, 1975 - No. 4, Jan, 1976 (All 25¢ issues)

	GD	VG	FN	VF	VF/NM	NM-
1-1st Tragg-r/Mystery Comics Digest #3	2	4	6	9	13	16
2-4: 2-Origin Ra-Ka-Tep-r/Mystery Comics Digest #1; Dr. Spektor #12. 3-All Durak-r issue; 4-Baron Tibor's 1st app.-r/Mystery Comics Digest #4; painted-c	1	2	3	5	7	9

SPINWORLD
Amaze Ink (Slave Labor Graphics): July, 1997 - No. 4, Jan, 1998 ($2.95/$3.95, B&W, mini-series)

1-3-Brent Anderson-a(p) 3.00
4-($3.95) 4.00

SPIRAL PATH, THE
Eclipse Comics: July, 1986 - No. 2 ($1.75, Baxter paper, limited series)

1,2 3.00

SPIRAL ZONE
DC Comics: Feb, 1988 - No. 4, May, 1988 ($1.00, mini-series)

1-4-Based on Tonka toys 3.00

SPIRIT, THE (Newspaper comics - see Promotional Comics section)

SPIRIT, THE (1st Series)(Also see Police Comics #11 and The Best of the Spirit TPB)
Quality Comics Group (Vital): 1944 - No. 22, Aug, 1950

	GD	VG	FN	VF	VF/NM	NM-
nn(#1)- "Wanted Dead or Alive"	113	226	339	718	1234	1750
nn(#2)- "Crime Doesn't Pay"	50	100	150	315	533	750
nn(#3)- "Murder Runs Wild"	42	84	126	265	445	625
4,5: 4-Flatfoot Burns begins, ends #22. 5-Wertham app.	36	72	108	216	351	485
6-10	31	62	93	182	296	410
11-Crandall-c	29	58	87	170	278	385
12-17-Eisner-c. 19-Honeybun app.	39	78	117	236	388	540
18-21-Strip-r by Eisner; Eisner-c	47	94	141	296	498	700
22-Used by N.Y. Legis. Comm; classic Eisner-c	113	226	339	718	1234	1750
Super Reprint #11-r/Quality Spirit #19 by Eisner	3	6	9	18	27	35
Super Reprint #12-r/Spirit #17 by Fine; Sol Brodsky-c	3	6	9	18	27	35

SPIRIT, THE (2nd Series)
Fiction House Magazines: Spring, 1952 - No. 5, 1954

	GD	VG	FN	VF	VF/NM	NM-
1-Not Eisner	43	86	129	267	454	640
2-Eisner-c/a(2)	42	84	126	265	445	625
3-Eisner/Grandenetti-c	39	78	117	231	378	525
4-Eisner/Grandenetti-c; Eisner-a	39	78	117	236	388	540
5-Eisner-c/a(4)	41	82	123	256	428	600

SPIRIT, THE
Harvey Publications: Oct, 1966 - No. 2, Mar, 1967 (Giant Size, 25¢, 68 pgs.)

	GD	VG	FN	VF	VF/NM	NM-
1-Eisner-r plus 9 new pgs.(origin Denny Colt, Take 3, plus 2 filler pgs.) (#3 was advertised, but never published)	9	18	27	63	107	150
2-Eisner-r plus 9 new pgs.(origin of the Octopus)	8	16	24	52	86	120

SPIRIT, THE (Underground)
Kitchen Sink Enterprises (Krupp Comics): Jan, 1973 - No. 2, Sept, 1973 (Black & White)

	GD	VG	FN	VF	VF/NM	NM-
1-New Eisner-c & 4 pgs. new Eisner-a plus-r (titled Crime Convention)	4	8	12	24	37	50
2-New Eisner-c & 4 pgs. new Eisner-a plus-r (titled Meets P'Gell)	4	8	12	26	41	55

SPIRIT, THE (Magazine)
Warren Publ. Co./Krupp Comic Works No. 17 on: 4/74 - No. 16, 10/76; No. 17, Winter, 1977 - No. 41, 6/83 (B&W w/color) (#6-14,16 are squarebound)

	GD	VG	FN	VF	VF/NM	NM-
1-Eisner-r begin; 8 pg. color insert	7	14	21	49	80	110
2-5: 2-Powder Pouf-s; UFO-s. 4-Silk Satin-s	4	8	12	28	44	60
6-9,11-15: 7-All Ebony issue. 8-Female Foes issue. 8,12-Sand Seref-s. 9-P'Gell & Octopus-s. 12-X-Mas issue	4	8	12	26	41	55
10-Giant Summer Special ($1.50)-Origin	4	8	12	28	44	60
16-Giant Summer Special ($1.50)-Olga Bustle-c/s	4	8	12	26	41	55
17,18(8/78): 17-Lady Luck-r	3	6	9	18	27	35
19-21-New Eisner-a. 20,21-Wood-r (#21-r/A DP on the Moon by Wood). 20-Outer Space-r	3	6	9	18	27	35
22-41: 22,23-Wood-r (#22-r/Mission the Moon by Wood). 28-r/last story (10/5/52). 30-(7/81)-Special Spirit Jam issue w/Caniff, Corben, Bolland, Byrne, Miller, Kurtzman, Rogers, Sienkiewicz-a & 40 others. 36-Begin Spirit Section-r; r/1st story (6/2/40) in color; new Eisner-c/a(18 pgs.)($2.95). 37-r/2nd story in color plus 18 pgs. new Eisner-a. 38-41: r/3rd - 6th stories in color. 41-Lady Luck Mr. Mystic in color	3	6	9	16	22	28
Special 1(1975)-All Eisner-a (mail only, 1500 printed, full color)	14	28	42	99	200	300

NOTE: *Covers pencilled/inked by* ***Eisner*** *only #1-9,12-16; painted by Eisner & Ken Kelly #10 & 11; painted by Eisner #17-up; one color story reprinted in #1-10.* ***Austin*** *a-30i.* ***Byrne*** *a-30p.* ***Miller*** *a-30p.*

SPIRIT, THE
Kitchen Sink Enterprises: Oct, 1983 - No. 87, Jan, 1992 ($2.00, Baxter paper)

1-60: 1-Origin-r/12/23/45 Spirit Section. 2-r/ 1/20/46-2/10/46. 3-r/2/17/46-3/10/46. 4-r/3/17/46-4/7/46. 11-Last color issue. 54-r/section 2/19/50 4.00
61-87: 85-87-Reprint the Outer Space Spirit stories by Wood. 86-r/A DP on the Moon by Wood from 1952 4.00

SPIRIT, THE (Also see Batman/The Spirit in Batman one-shots)
DC Comics: Feb, 2007 - No. 32, Oct, 2009 ($2.99)

1-32: 1-6,8-12-Darwyn Cooke-s/a/c. 2-P'Gell app. 3-Origin re-told. 7-Short stories by Baker, Bernet, Palmiotti, Simonson & Sprouse; Cooke-c. 13-Short stories by various 3.00
... Book One HC (2007, $24.99, die-cut dust jacket) r/#1-6 and Batman/The Spirit 25.00
... Book One SC (2007, $19.99) r/#1-6 and Batman/The Spirit 20.00
... Book Two HC (2008, $24.99, die-cut dust jacket) r/#7-13 25.00
... Book Two SC (2009, $19.99) r/#7-13 20.00
... Book Three SC (2009, $19.99) r/#14-20 20.00
... Book Four SC (2009, $19.99) r/#21-25 20.00
... Book Five SC (2009, $19.99) r/#26-32 20.00
... Femme Fatales TPB (2008, $19.99) r/1940s stories focusing on the Spirit's female adversaries like Silk Satin, P'gell, Powder Pouf and Silken Floss; Michael Uslan intro. 20.00
... Special 1 (2008, $2.99) r/stories from '47, '49, '50 newspaper strips; the Octopus app. 3.00

SPIRIT, THE (First Wave)
DC Comics: Jun, 2010 - Present ($3.99/$2.99)(B&W back-up stories by various)

1-10: 1-Schultz-s/Moritat-a; covers by Ladronn and Schultz; back-up by O'Neil & Sienkiewicz. 2-Back-up by Ellison & Baker. 7-Corben-a back-up. 8-Ploog-a back-up 4.00
11,12-($2.99) Hine-s/Moritat-a; no back-up story 3.00

SPIRIT JAM
Kitchen Sink Press: Aug, 1998 ($5.95, B&W, oversized, square-bound)

nn-Reprints Spirit (Magazine) #30 by Eisner & 50 others; and "Cerebus Vs. The Spirit" from Cerebus Jam #1 6.00

SPIRIT, THE: THE NEW ADVENTURES
Kitchen Sink Press: 1997 - No. 8, Nov, 1998 ($3.50, anthology)

1-Moore-s/Gibbons-c/a 4.00
2-8: 2-Gaiman-s/Eisner-c. 3-Moore-s/Bolland-c/Moebius back-c. 4-Allred-s/a; Busiek-s/Anderson-a. 5-Chadwick-s/c/a(p); Nyberg-i. 6-S.Hampton & Mandrake-a 3.50

Spitfire #1 © MAR

Spongebob Comics #1 © United Plankton Pictures

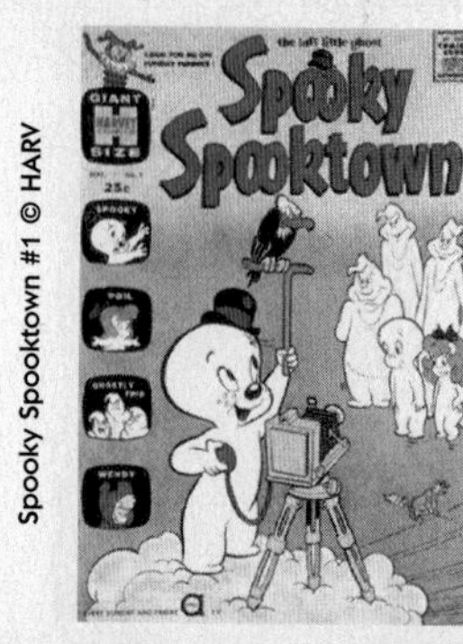

Spooky Spooktown #1 © HARV

GD VG FN VF VF/NM NM-
2.0 4.0 6.0 8.0 9.0 9.2

Will Eisner's The Spirit Archives Volume 27 (Dark Horse, 2009, $49.95) r/#1-8 50.00

SPIRIT: THE ORIGIN YEARS
Kitchen Sink Press: May, 1992 - No. 10, Dec, 1993 ($2.95, B&W)

1-10: 1-r/sections 6/2/40(origin)-6/23/40 (all 1940s) 3.00

SPIRITMAN (Also see Three Comics)
No publisher listed: No date (1944) (10¢)
(Triangle Sales Co. ad on back cover)

1-Three 16pg. Spirit sections bound together, (1944, 10¢, 52 pgs.)
21 42 63 126 206 285
2-Two Spirit sections (3/26/44, 4/2/44) bound together; by Lou Fine
20 40 60 114 182 250

SPIRIT OF THE BORDER (See Zane Grey & Four Color #197)

SPIRIT OF THE TAO
Image Comics (Top Cow): Jun, 1998 - No. 15, May, 2000 ($2.50)

Preview 5.00
1-14: 1-D-Tron-s/Tan & D-Tron-a 3.00
15-($4.95) 5.00

SPIRIT WORLD (Magazine)
National Periodical Publications: Fall, 1971 (B&W)

1-New Kirby-a; Neal Adams-c; poster inside 7 14 21 47 76 105
(1/2 price without poster)

SPITFIRE (Female undercover agent)
Malverne Herald (Elliot)(J. R. Mahon): No. 132, 1944 (Aug) - No. 133, 1945

132,133: Both have Classics Gift Box ads on b/c with checklist to #20. 132-British spitfire WWII-c. 133-Female agent/Nazi WWII-c 25 50 75 147 241 335

SPITFIRE (WW2 speedster from MI:13)
Marvel Comics: Oct, 2010 ($3.99, one-shot)

1-Cornell-s/Casagrande-a; Blade app. 4.00

SPITFIRE AND THE TROUBLESHOOTERS
Marvel Comics: Oct, 1986 - No. 9, June, 1987 (Codename: Spitfire #10 on)

1-3,5-9 3.00
4-McFarlane-a 4.00

SPITFIRE COMICS (Also see Double Up)
Harvey Publications: Aug, 1941 - No. 2, Oct, 1941 (Pocket size; 100 pgs.)

1-Origin The Clown, The Fly-Man, The Spitfire & The Magician From Bagdad; British spitfire, Nazi bomber WWII-c 76 152 228 486 831 1175
2-(Rare) Fly-Man-c 69 138 207 442 759 1075

SPLITTING IMAGE
Image Comics: Mar, 1993 - No. 2, 1993 ($1.95)

1,2-Simpson-c/a; parody comic 3.00

SPONGEBOB COMICS (TV's Spongebob Squarepants)
United Plankton Pictures: 2011 - Present ($2.99)

1,2-Short stories by various. 1-Kochalka back-c 3.00

SPOOF
Marvel Comics Group: Oct, 1970; No. 2, Nov, 1972 - No. 5, May, 1973

1-Infinity-c; Dark Shadows-c & parody 4 8 12 24 37 50
2-5: 2-All in the Family. 3-Beatles, Osmond's, Jackson 5, David Cassidy, Nixon & Agnew-c. 5-Rod Serling, Woody Allen, Ted Kennedy-c 3 6 9 17 25 32

SPOOK (Formerly Shock Detective Cases)
Star Publications: No. 22, Jan, 1953 - No. 30, Oct, 1954

22-Sgt. Spook-r; acid in face story; hanging-c 39 78 117 240 395 550
23,25,27: 25-Jungle Lil-r. 27-Two Sgt. Spook-r 28 56 84 168 274 380
24-Used in **SOTI**, pgs. 182,183-r/Inside Crime #2; Transvestism story
29 58 87 172 281 390
26,28-30: 26-Disbrow-a. 28,29-Rulah app. 29-Jo-Jo app. 30-Disbrow-c/a(2); only Star-c 28 56 84 168 274 380

NOTE: *L. B. Cole covers-all issues except #30; a-28(1 pg.). Disbrow a-26(2), 28, 29(2), 30(2); No. 30 r/Blue Bolt Weird Tales #114.*

SPOOK COMICS
Baily Publications/Star: 1946

1-Mr. Lucifer story 31 62 93 186 303 420

SPOOKY (The Tuff Little Ghost; see Casper The Friendly Ghost)
Harvey Publications: 11/55 - 139, 11/73; No. 140, 7/74 - No. 155, 3/77; No. 156, 12/77 - No. 158, 4/78; No. 159, 9/78; No. 160, 10/79; No. 161, 9/80

1-Nightmare begins (see Casper #19) 43 86 129 344 697 1050

GD VG FN VF VF/NM NM-
2.0 4.0 6.0 8.0 9.0 9.2

2 20 40 60 144 290 435
3-10(1956-57) 12 24 36 82 154 225
11-20(1957-58) 8 16 24 52 86 120
21-40(1958-59) 6 12 18 37 59 80
41-60 4 8 12 28 44 60
61-80,100 3 6 9 20 30 40
81-99 3 6 9 17 25 32
101-120 2 4 6 11 16 20
121-126,133-140 2 4 6 8 11 14
127-132: All 52 pg. Giants 2 4 6 11 16 20
141-161 1 2 3 5 7 9

SPOOKY
Harvey Comics: Nov, 1991 - No. 4, Sept, 1992 ($1.00/$1.25)

1 4.00
2-4: 3-Begin $1.25-c 3.00
...Digest 1-3 (10/92, 6/93, 10/93, $1.75, 100 pgs.)-Casper, Wendy, etc. 4.00

SPOOKY HAUNTED HOUSE
Harvey Publications: Oct, 1972 - No. 15, Feb, 1975

1 3 6 9 18 27 35
2-5 2 4 6 10 14 18
6-10 2 4 6 8 10 12
11-15 1 2 3 5 7 9

SPOOKY MYSTERIES
Your Guide Publ. Co.: No date (1946) (10¢)

1-Mr. Spooky, Super Snooper, Pinky, Girl Detective app.
20 40 60 114 182 250

SPOOKY SPOOKTOWN
Harvey Publ.: 9/61; No. 2, 9/62 - No. 52, 12/73; No. 53, 10/74 - No. 66, 12/76

1-Casper, Spooky; 68 pgs. begin 15 30 45 103 209 315
2 9 18 27 63 107 150
3-5 7 14 21 45 73 100
6-10 5 10 15 34 55 75
11-20 4 8 12 24 37 50
21-39: 39-Last 68 pg. issue 3 6 9 20 30 40
40-45: All 52 pgs. 2 4 6 11 16 20
46-66: 61-Hot Stuff/Spooky team-up story 1 2 3 5 7 9

SPORT COMICS (Becomes True Sport Picture Stories #5 on)
Street & Smith Publications: Oct, 1940 (No mo.) - No. 4, Nov, 1941

1-Life story of Lou Gehrig 54 108 162 346 591 835
2 31 62 93 182 296 410
3,4 26 52 78 154 252 350

SPORT LIBRARY (See Charlton Sport Library)

SPORTS ACTION (Formerly Sport Stars)
Marvel/Atlas Comics (ACI No. 2,3/SAI No. 4-14): No. 2, Feb, 1950 - No. 14, Sept, 1952

2-Powell painted-c; George Gipp life story 43 86 129 269 455 640
1-(nd,no price, no publ., 52pgs, #1 on-c; has same-c as #2; blank inside-c (giveaway?) 22 44 66 132 216 300
3-Everett-a 24 48 72 142 234 325
4-11,14: Weiss-a 22 44 66 128 209 290
12,13: 12-Everett-c. 13-Krigstein-a 23 46 69 136 223 310

NOTE: *Title may have changed after No. 3, to Crime Must Lose No. 4 on, due to publisher change. Sol Brodsky c-4-7, 13, 14. Maneely c-3, 8-11.*

SPORT STARS
Parents' Magazine Institute (Sport Stars): Feb-Mar, 1946 - No. 4, Aug-Sept, 1946 (Half comic, half photo magazine)

1- "How Tarzan Got That Way" story of Johnny Weissmuller
40 80 120 243 402 560
2-Baseball greats 26 52 78 154 252 350
3,4 23 46 69 136 223 310

SPORT STARS (Becomes Sports Action #2 on)
Marvel Comics (ACI): Nov, 1949 (52 pgs.)

1-Knute Rockne; painted-c 45 90 135 284 480 675

SPORT THRILLS (Formerly Dick Cole; becomes Jungle Thrills #16)
Star Publications: No. 11, Nov, 1950 - No. 15, Nov, 1951

11-Dick Cole begins; Ted Williams & Ty Cobb life stories
27 54 81 160 263 365
12-Joe DiMaggio, Phil Rizzuto stories & photos on-c; L.B. Cole-c/a
22 44 66 130 213 295

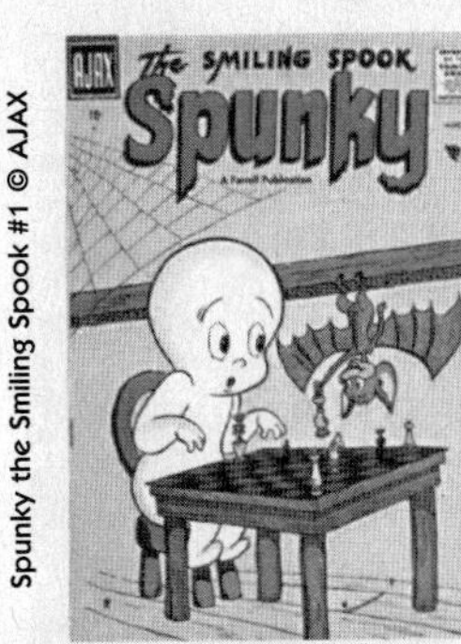

Spunky the Smiling Spook #1 © AJAX

Spyboy/Young Justice #1 © DH & DC

Squadron Supreme TPB © MAR

GD 2.0 | VG 4.0 | FN 6.0 | VF 8.0 | VF/NM 9.0 | NM- 9.2

13-15-All L. B. Cole-c. 13-Jackie Robinson, Pee Wee Reese stories & photo on-c.
14-Johnny Weissmuler life story 22 44 66 130 213 295
Accepted Reprint #11 (#15 on-c, nd); L.B. Cole-c 10 20 30 54 72 90
Accepted Reprint #12 (nd); L.B. Cole-c; Joe DiMaggio & Phil Rizzuto life stories-r/#12
10 20 30 54 72 90

SPOTLIGHT (TV) (newsstand sales only)
Marvel Comics Group: Sept, 1978 - No. 4, Mar, 1979 (Hanna-Barbera)
1-Huckleberry Hound, Yogi Bear; Shaw-a 3 6 9 20 30 40
2,4: 2-Quick Draw McGraw, Augie Doggie, Snooper & Blabber. 4-Magilla Gorilla, Snagglepuss 3 6 9 18 23 30
3-The Jetsons; Yakky Doodle 3 6 9 20 30 40

SPOTLIGHT COMICS
Country Press Inc.: Sept, 1940
nn-Ashcan, not distributed to newsstands, only for in house use. A NM copy sold in 2009 for $1015.

SPOTLIGHT COMICS (Becomes Red Seal Comics #14 on?)
Harry 'A' Chesler (Our Army, Inc.): Nov, 1944, No. 2, Jan, 1945 - No. 3, 1945
1-The Black Dwarf (cont'd in Red Seal?), The Veiled Avenger, & Barry Kuda begin; Tuska-c 94 188 282 597 1024 1450
2 57 114 171 362 619 875
3-Injury to eye story (reprinted from Scoop #3) 60 120 180 381 653 925

SPOTTY THE PUP (Becomes Super Pup #4, see Television Puppet Show)
Avon Periodicals/Realistic Comics: No. 2, Oct-Nov, 1953 - No. 3, Dec-Jan, 1953-54 (Also see Funny Tunes)
2,3 7 14 21 35 43 50
nn (1953, Realistic-r) 4 8 12 18 22 25

SPUNKY (...Junior Cowboy)(...Comics #2 on)
Standard Comics: April, 1949 - No. 7, Nov, 1951
1-Text illos by Frazetta 11 22 33 62 86 110
2-Text illos by Frazetta 9 18 27 47 61 75
3-7 6 12 18 31 38 45

SPUNKY THE SMILING SPOOK
Ajax/Farrell (World Famous Comics/Four Star Comic Corp.): Aug, 1957 - No. 4, May, 1958
1-Reprints from Frisky Fables 10 20 30 54 72 90
2-4 6 12 18 31 38 45

SPY AND COUNTERSPY (Becomes Spy Hunters #3 on)
American Comics Group: Aug-Sept, 1949 - No. 2, Oct-Nov, 1949 (52 pgs.)
1-Origin, 1st app. Jonathan Kent, Counterspy 27 54 81 158 259 360
2 17 34 51 98 154 210

SPYBOY
Dark Horse Comics: Oct, 1999 - No. 17, May, 2001 ($2.50/$2.95/$2.99)
1-17: 1-6-Peter David-s/Pop Mhan-a. 7,8-Meglia-a. 9-17-Mhan-a 3.00
13.1-13.3 (4/03-8/03, $2.99), 13.2,13.3-Mhan-a 3.00
... Special (5/02, $4.99) David-s/Mhan-a 5.00

SPYBOY: FINAL EXAM
Dark Horse Comics: May, 2004 - No. 4, Aug, 2004 ($2.99, limited series)
1-4-Peter David-s/Pop Mhan-a/c 3.00
TPB (2005, $12.95) r/series 13.00

SPYBOY/ YOUNG JUSTICE
Dark Horse Comics: Feb, 2002 - No. 3, Apr, 2002 ($2.99, limited series)
1-3: 1-Peter David-s/Todd Nauck-a/Pop Mhan-c. 2-Mhan-a 3.00

SPY CASES (Formerly The Kellys)
Marvel/Atlas Comics (Hercules Publ.): No. 26, Sept, 1950 - No. 19, Oct, 1953
26 (#1) 24 48 72 140 230 320
27(#2),28(#3, 2/51): 27-Everett-a; bondage-c 14 28 42 82 121 160
4(4/51) - 7,9,10 13 26 39 74 105 135
8-A-Bomb-c/story 14 28 42 82 121 160
11-19: 10-14-War format 11 22 33 60 83 105
NOTE: *Sol Brodsky c-1-5, 8, 9, 11-14, 17, 18. **Maneely** a-8; c-7, 10. **Tuska** a-7.*

SPY FIGHTERS
Marvel/Atlas Comics (CSI): March, 1951 - No. 15, July, 1953
(Cases from official records)
1-Clark Mason begins; Tuska-a; Brodsky-c 25 50 75 147 241 335
2-Tuska-a 14 28 42 81 118 155
3-13: 3-5-Brodsky-c. 7-Heath-c 14 28 42 76 108 140
14,15-Pakula-a(3), Ed Win-a. 15-Brodsky-c 14 28 42 78 112 145

SPY-HUNTERS (Formerly Spy & Counterspy)
American Comics Group: No. 3, Dec-Jan, 1949-50 - No. 24, June-July, 1953 (#3-14: 52 pgs.)
3-Jonathan Kent continues, ends #10 23 46 69 136 223 310
4-10: 4,8,10-Starr-a 14 28 42 80 115 150
11-15,17-22,24: 18-War-c begin. 21-War-c/stories begin
10 20 30 56 76 95
16-Williamson-a (9 pgs.) 15 30 45 88 137 185
23-Graphic torture, injury to eye panel 20 40 60 114 182 250
NOTE: ***Drucker** a-12. **Whitney** a-many issues; c-7, 8, 10-12, 15, 16.*

SPYMAN (Top Secret Adventures on cover)
Harvey Publications (Illustrated Humor): Sept, 1966 - No. 3, Feb, 1967 (12¢)
1-Origin and 1st app. of Spyman. Steranko-a(p)-1st pro work; 1 pg. Neal Adams ad; Tuska-c/a, Crandall-a(i) 7 14 21 45 73 100
2-Simon-c; Steranko-a(p) 4 8 12 28 44 60
3-Simon-c 4 8 12 26 41 55

SPY SMASHER (See Mighty Midget, Whiz & Xmas Comics) (Also see Crime Smasher)
Fawcett Publications: Fall, 1941 - No. 11, Feb, 1943
1-Spy Smasher begins; silver metallic-c 331 662 993 2317 4059 5800
2-Raboy-c 152 304 456 965 1658 2350
3,4: 3-Bondage-c. 4-Irvin Steinberg-c 102 204 306 648 1112 1575
5-7: Raboy-a; 6-Raboy-c/a. 7-Part photo-c (movie) 87 174 261 553 952 1350
8,11: War-c 73 146 219 467 796 1125
9-Hitler, Tojo, Mussolini-c. 110 220 330 704 1202 1700
10-Hitler-c 100 200 300 635 1093 1550

SPY THRILLERS (Police Badge No. 479 #5)
Atlas Comics (PrPl): Nov, 1954 - No. 4, May, 1955
1-Brodsky c-1,2 21 42 63 122 199 275
2-Last precode (1/55) 14 28 42 78 112 145
3,4 11 22 33 62 86 110

SQUADRON SUPREME (Also see Marvel Graphic Novel - ...: Death of a Universe)
Marvel Comics Group: Aug, 1985 - No. 12, Aug, 1986 (Maxi-series)
1-Double size 4.00
2-12 3.00
TPB ($24.99) r/#1-12; Alex Ross painted-c; printing inks contain some of the cremated remains of late writer Mark Gruenwald 50.00
TPB-2nd printing ($24.99): Inks contain no ashes 25.00
...Death of a Universe TPB (2006, $24.99) r/Marvel Graphic Novel, Thor #280, Avengers #5,6; Avengers/Squadron Supreme Annual and Squadron Supreme: New World Order 25.00

SQUADRON SUPREME (Also see Supreme Power)
Marvel Comics: May, 2006 - No. 7, Nov, 2006 ($2.99)
1-7-Straczynski-s/Frank-a/c 3.00
Saga of Squadron Supreme (2006, $3.99) summary of Supreme Power #1-18; plus Hyperion and Nighthawk limited series; wraparound-c; preview of Squadron Supreme #1 4.00
... Vol. 1: The Pre-War Years (2006, $20.99, dustjacket) r/#1-5 & Saga of S.S. 21.00

SQUADRON SUPREME
Marvel Comics: Sept, 2008 - No. 12, Aug, 2009 ($2.99)
1-12: 1-Set 5 years after Ultimate Power; Nick Fury app.; Chaykin-s/Turini-a/Land-c 3.00

SQUADRON SUPREME: HYPERION VS. NIGHTHAWK
Marvel Comics: Mar, 2007 - No. 4, June, 2007 ($2.99, limited series)
1-4-Hyperion and Nighthawk in Darfur; Gulacy-a/c; Guggenheim-s 3.00
TPB (2007, $10.99) r/#1-4 11.00

SQUADRON SUPREME: NEW WORLD ORDER
Marvel Comics: Sept, 1998 ($5.99, one-shot)
1-Wraparound-c; Kaminski-s 6.00

SQUALOR
First Comics: Dec, 1989 - Aug, 1990 ($2.75, limited series)
1-4: Sutton-a 3.00

SQUEE (Also see JohnnyThe Homicidal Maniac)
Slave Labor Graphics: Apr, 1997 - No. 4, May, 1998 ($2.95, B&W)
1-4: Jhonen Vasquez-s/a in all 3.00

SQUEEKS (Also see Boy Comics)
Lev Gleason Publications: Oct, 1953 - No. 5, June, 1954
1-Funny animal; Biro-c; Crimebuster's pet monkey "Squeeks" begins
10 20 30 54 72 90
2-Biro-c 6 12 18 31 38 45
3-5: 3-Biro-c 6 12 18 28 34 40

Stanley and His Monster (1993 series) #3 © DC

Starborn #1 © Boom Studios & POW Ent.

Star Comics V2 #2 © CEN

	GD 2.0	VG 4.0	FN 6.0	VF 8.0	VF/NM 9.0	NM- 9.2

S.R. BISSETTE'S SPIDERBABY COMIX
SpiderBaby Grafix: Aug, 1996 - No. 2 ($3.95, B&W, magazine size)

Preview-(8/96, $3.95)-Graphic violence & nudity; Laurel & Hardy app. 4.00
1,2 4.00

S.R. BISSETTE'S TYRANT
SpiderBaby Grafix: Sept, 1994 - No. 4 ($2.95, B&W)

1-4 4.00

STALKER (Also see All Star Comics 1999 and crossover issues)
National Periodical Publications: June-July, 1975 - No. 4, Dec-Jan, 1975-76

	GD	VG	FN	VF	VF/NM	NM-
1-Origin & 1st app; Ditko/Wood-c/a	2	4	6	10	14	18
2-4-Ditko/Wood-c/a	2	3	4	6	8	10

STALKERS
Marvel Comics (Epic Comics): Apr, 1990 - No. 12, Mar, 1991 ($1.50)

1-12: 1-Chadwick-c 3.00

STAMP COMICS (Stamps... on-c; Thrilling Adventures In...#8)
Youthful Magazines/Stamp Comics, Inc.: Oct, 1951 - No. 7, Oct, 1952

	GD	VG	FN	VF	VF/NM	NM-
1-(15¢) ('Stamps' on indicia No. 1-3,5,7)	26	52	78	152	249	345
2	15	30	45	86	133	180
3-6: 3,4-Kiefer, Wildey-a	14	28	42	81	118	155
7-Roy Krenkel (4 pgs.)	17	34	51	98	154	210

NOTE: *Promotes stamp collecting; gives stories behind various commemorative stamps. No. 2, 10¢ printed over 15¢ c-price.* ***Kiefer*** *a-1-7.* ***Kirkel*** *a-1-6.* ***Napoli*** *a-2-7.* ***Palais*** *a-2-4, 7.*

STAND, THE ... (Based on the Stephen King novel)
Marvel Comics: 2008 - Present ($3.99, limited series)

...: American Nightmares 1-5 (5/09 - No. 5, 10/09, $3.99) Aguirre-Sacasa-s/Perkins-a 4.00
...: Captain Trips 1-5 (12/08 - No. 5, 3/09, $3.99) Aguirre-Sacasa-s/Perkins-a 4.00
...: Hardcases 1-5 (8/10 - No. 5, 1/11, $3.99) Aguirre-Sacasa-s/Perkins-a 4.00
...: No Man's Land 1-3 (4/11 - No. 5, $3.99) Aguirre-Sacasa-s/Perkins-a 4.00
...: Soul Survivors 1-5 (12/09 - No. 5, 5/10, $3.99) Aguirre-Sacasa-s/Perkins-a 4.00

STAN LEE MEETS...
Marvel Comics: Nov, 2006 - Jan, 2007 ($3.99, series of one-shots)

Doctor Doom 1 (12/06) Lee-s/Larroca-a/c; Loeb-s/McGuinness-a; r/Fantastic Four #87 4.00
Doctor Strange 1 (11/06) Lee-s/Davis-a/c; Bendis-s/Bagley-a; r/Marvel Premiere #3 4.00
Silver Surfer 1 (1/07) Lee-s/Wieringo-a/c; Jenkins-s/Buckingham-a; r/S.S. #14 4.00
Spider-Man 1 (11/06) Lee-s/Coipel-a/c; Whedon-s/Gaydos-a; Hembeck-s/a; r/AS-M #87 4.00
The Thing 1 (12/06) Lee-s/Weeks-a/c; Thomas-s/Kolins-a; r/FF #79; FF #51 cover swipe 4.00
HC (2007, $24.99, dustjacket) r/one-shots; interviews and features 25.00

STANLEY & HIS MONSTER (Formerly The Fox & the Crow)
National Periodical Publ.: No. 109, Apr-May, 1968 - No. 112, Oct-Nov, 1968

	GD	VG	FN	VF	VF/NM	NM-
109-112	4	8	12	22	34	45

STANLEY & HIS MONSTER
DC Comics: Feb, 1993 - No. 4, May, 1993 ($1.50, limited series)

1-4 3.00

STAN SHAW'S BEAUTY & THE BEAST
Dark Horse Comics: Nov, 1993 ($4.95, one-shot)

1 5.00

STAR
Image Comics (Highbrow Entertainment): June, 1995 - No. 4, Oct, 1995 ($2.50, lim. series)

1-4 3.00

STARBLAST
Marvel Comics: Jan, 1994 - No. 4, Apr, 1994 ($1.75, limited series)

1-($2.00, 52 pgs.)-Nova, Quasar, Black Bolt; painted-c 4.00
2-4 3.00

STAR BLAZERS
Comico: Apr, 1987 - No. 4, July, 1987 ($1.75, limited series)

1-4 3.00

STAR BLAZERS
Comico: 1989 ($1.95/$2.50, limited series)

1-5- Steacy wraparound painted-c on all 3.00

STAR BLAZERS (The Magazine of Space Battleship Yamato)
Argo Press: No. 0, Aug, 1995 - No. 3, Dec, 1995 ($2.95)

0-3 3.00

STARBORN (From Stan Lee)
BOOM! Studios: Dec, 2010 - Present ($3.99)

1-5-Roberson-s/Randolph-a; three covers on each 4.00

STAR BRAND
Marvel Comics (New Universe): Oct, 1986 - No. 19, May, 1989 (75¢/$1.25)

1-15: 14-begin $1.25-c 3.00
16-19-Byrne story & art; low print run 5.00
Annual 1 (10/87) 3.00
... Classic Vol. 1 TPB (2006, $19.99) r/#1-7 20.00

STARCHILD
Tailspin Press: 1992 - No. 12 ($2.25/$2.50, B&W)

1,2-('92),0(4/93),3-12: 0-Illos by Chadwick, Eisner, Sim, M. Wagner. 3-(7/93). 4-(11/93). 6-(2/94) 3.00

STARCHILD: MYTHOPOLIS
Image Comics: No. 0, July, 1997 - No. 4, Apr, 1998 ($2.95, B&W, limited series)

0-4-James Owen-s/a 3.00

STAR COMICS
Ultem Publ. (Harry 'A' Chesler)/Centaur Publications: Feb, 1937 - V2#7 (No. 23), Aug, 1939 (#1-6: large size)

	GD	VG	FN	VF	VF/NM	NM-
V1#1-Dan Hastings (s/f) begins	232	464	696	1485	2543	3600
2	103	206	309	659	1130	1600
3-Classic Black Americana cover (rare)	219	438	657	1402	2401	3400
4-6 (#6, 9/37): 4,5-Little Nemo-c/stories	87	174	261	553	952	1350
7-9: 8-Severed head centerspread; Impy & Little Nemo by Winsor McCay Jr, Popeye app. by Bob Wood; Mickey Mouse & Popeye app. as toys in Santa's bag on-c; X-Mas-c	77	154	231	493	847	1200
10 (1st Centaur; 3/38)-Impy by Winsor McCay Jr; Don Marlow by Guardineer begins	97	194	291	621	1061	1500
11-1st Jack Cole comic-a, 1 pg. (4/38)	73	146	219	467	796	1125
12-15: 12-Riders of the Golden West begins; Little Nemo app. 15-Speed Silvers by Gustavson & The Last Pirate by Burgos begins	58	116	174	371	636	900
16 (12/38)-The Phantom Rider & his horse Thunder begins, ends V2#6	60	120	180	381	658	935
V2#1(#17, 2/39)-Phantom Rider-c (only non-funny-c)	65	130	195	416	708	1000
2-7(#18-23): 2-Diana Deane by Tarpe Mills app. 3-Drama of Hollywood by Mills begins. 7-Jungle Queen app.	52	104	156	322	549	775

NOTE: ***Biro*** *c-6, 9, 10.* ***Burgos*** *a-15, 16, V2#1-7.* ***Ken Ernst*** *a-10, 12, 14.* ***Filchock*** *c-15, 18, 22.* ***Gill Fox*** *c-14, 19.* ***Guardineer*** *a-6, 8-14.* ***Gustavson*** *a-13-16, V2#1-7.* ***Winsor McCay*** *c-4, 5.* ***Tarpe Mills*** *a-15, V2#1-7.* ***Schwab*** *c-20, 23.* ***Bob Wood*** *a-10, 12, 13; c-7, 8.*

STAR COMICS MAGAZINE
Marvel Comics (Star Comics): Dec, 1986 - No. 13, 1988 ($1.50, digest-size)

	GD	VG	FN	VF	VF/NM	NM-
1,9-Spider-Man-c/s	2	4	6	8	11	14
2-8-Heathcliff, Ewoks, Top Dog, Madballs-r in #1-13	1	2	3	5	7	9
10-13	2	4	6	8	10	12

S.T.A.R. CORPS
DC Comics: Nov, 1993 - No. 6, Apr, 1994 ($1.50, limited series)

1-6: 1,2-Austin-c(i). 1-Superman app. 3.00

STARCRAFT (Based on the video game)
DC Comics (WildStorm): July, 2009 - No. 7, Jan, 2010 ($2.99)

1-7-Furman-s; two covers on each 3.00
HC (2010, $19.99, dustjacket) r/#1-7 20.00

STAR CROSSED
DC Comics (Helix): June, 1997 - No. 3, Aug, 1997 ($2.50, limited series)

1-3-Matt Howarth-s/a 3.00

STARDUST (See Neil Gaiman and Charles Vess' Stardust)

STARDUST KID, THE
Image Comics/Boom! Studios #4-on: May, 2005 - No. 4 ($3.50)

1-4-J.M. DeMatteis-s/Mike Ploog-a 3.50

STAR FEATURE COMICS
I. W. Enterprises: 1963

	GD	VG	FN	VF	VF/NM	NM-
Reprint #9-Stunt-Man Stetson-r/Feat. Comics #141	2	4	6	10	13	16

STARFIRE (Not the Teen Titans character)
National Periodical Publ./DC Comics: Aug-Sept, 1976 - No. 8, Oct-Nov, 1977

	GD	VG	FN	VF	VF/NM	NM-
1-Origin (CCA stamp fell off cover art; so it was approved by code)	2	4	6	8	11	14
2-8	1	2	3	5	6	8

STARGATE

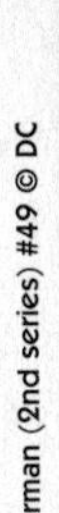
Starjammers (2004 series) #1 © MAR

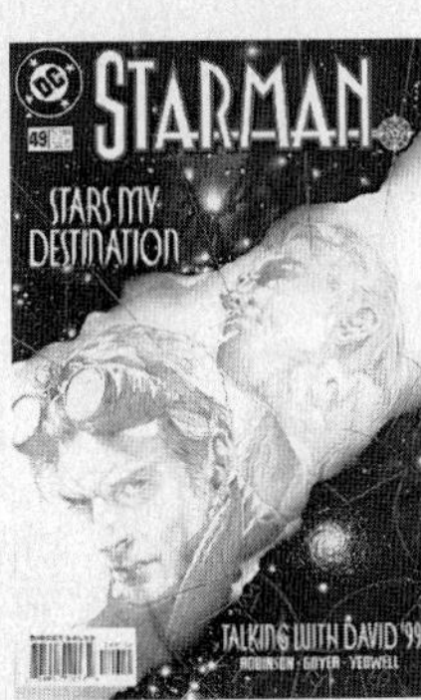

Starman (2nd series) #49 © DC

Star Ranger V2 #10 © CEN

GD VG FN VF VF/NM NM-
2.0 4.0 6.0 8.0 9.0 9.2

Dynamite Entertainment
...: Daniel Jackson 1-4 (2010 - No. 4, 2010, $3.99) Watson-a/Murray-s 4.00
...: Vala Mal Doran 1-5 (2010 - No. 5, 2010, $3.99) Razek-a/Jerwa-s 4.00

STAR HUNTERS (See DC Super Stars #16)
National Periodical Publ./DC Comics: Oct-Nov, 1977 - No. 7, Oct-Nov, 1978
1,7: 1-Newton-a(p). 7-44 pgs. 2 4 6 8 10 12
2-6 1 2 3 4 5 7
NOTE: ***Buckler** a-4-7p; c-1-7p. **Layton** a-1-5i; c-1-6i. **Nasser** a-3p. **Sutton** a-6i.*

STARJAMMERS (See X-Men Spotlight on Starjammers)

STARJAMMERS (Also see Uncanny X-Men)
Marvel Comics: Oct, 1995 - No. 4, Jan, 1996 ($2.95, limited series)
1-4: Foil-c; Ellis scripts 3.00

STARJAMMERS
Marvel Comics: Sept, 2004 - No. 6, Jan, 2005 ($2.99, limited series)
1-6-Kevin J. Anderson-s. 1-Garza-a. 2-6-Lucas-a 3.00

STARK TERROR
Stanley Publications: Dec, 1970 - No. 5, Aug, 1971 (B&W, magazine, 52 pgs.)
(1950s Horror reprints, including pre-code)
1-Bondage, torture-c 7 14 21 47 76 105
2-4 (Gillmor/Aragon-r) 4 8 12 26 41 55
5 (ACG-r) 4 8 12 22 34 45

STARLET O'HARA IN HOLLYWOOD (Teen-age) (Also see Cookie)
Standard Comics: Dec, 1948 - No. 4, Sept, 1949
1-Owen Fitzgerald-a in all 26 52 78 154 252 350
2 15 30 45 85 130 175
3,4 14 28 42 76 108 140

STAR-LORD THE SPECIAL EDITION (Also see Marvel Comics Super Special #10, Marvel Premiere & Preview & Marvel Spotlight V2#6,7)
Marvel Comics Group: Feb, 1982 (one-shot, direct sales) (1st Baxter paper comic)
1-Byrne/Austin-a; Austin-c; 8 pgs. of new-a by Golden (p); Dr. Who story by Dave Gibbons; 1st deluxe format comic 6.00

STARLORD
Marvel Comics: Dec, 1996 - No. 3, Feb, 1997 ($2.50, limited series)
1-3-Timothy Zahn-s 3.00

STARLORD MEGAZINE
Marvel Comics: Nov, 1996 ($2.95, one-shot)
1-Reprints w/preview of new series 3.00

STARMAN (1st Series) (Also see Justice League & War of the Gods)
DC Comics: Oct, 1988 - No. 45, Apr, 1992 ($1.00)
1-Origin 4.00
2-25,29-45: 4-Intro The Power Elite. 9,10,34-Batman app. 14-Superman app. 17-Power Girl app. 38-War of the Gods x-over. 42-45-Eclipso-c/stories 3.00
26-1st app. David Knight (G.A.Starman's son). 5.00
27,28: 27-Starman (David Knight) app. 28-Starman disguised as Superman; leads into Superman #50 4.00

STARMAN (2nd Series) (Also see The Golden Age, Showcase 95 #12, Showcase 96 #4,5)
DC Comics: No. 0, Oct, 1994 - No. 80, Aug, 2001; No. 81, Mar, 2010 ($1.95/$2.25/$2.50)
0,1: 0-James Robinson scripts, Tony Harris-c/a(p) & Wade Von Grawbadger-a(i) begins; Sins of the Father storyline begins, ends #3; 1st app. new Starman (Jack Knight); reintro of the G.A. Mist & G.A. Shade; 1st app. Nash; David Knight dies 1 2 3 4 5 7
2-7: 2-Reintro Charity from Forbidden Tales of Dark Mansion. 3-Reintro/2nd app. "Blue" Starman (1st app. in 1st Issue Special #12); Will Payton app. (both cameos). 5-David Knight app. 6-The Shade "Times Past" story; Kristiansen-a. 7-The Black Pirate cameo 5.00
8-17: 8-Begin $2.25-c. 10-1st app. new Mist (Nash). 11-JSA "Times Past" story; Matt Smith-a. 12-16-Sins of the Child. 17-The Black Pirate app. 4.00
18-37: 18-G.A. Starman "Times Past" story; Watkiss-a. 19-David Knight app. 20-23-G.A. Sandman app. 24-26-Demon Quest; all 3 covers make-up triptych. 33-36-Batman-c/app. 37-David Knight and deceased JSA members app. 3.00
38-49,51-56: 38-Nash vs. Justice League Europe. 39,40-Crossover w/ Power of Shazam! #35,36; Bulletman app. 42-Demon-c/app. 43-JLA-c/app. 44-Phantom Lady-c/app. 46-Gene Ha-a. 51-Jor-El app. 52,53-Adam Strange-c/app. 3.00
50-($3.95) Gold foil logo on-c; Star Boy (LSH) app. 4.00
57-79: 57-62-Painted covers by Harris and Alex Ross. 72-Death of Ted Knight 3.00
80-($3.95) Final issue; cover by Harris & Robinson 4.00
81-(3/10, $2.99) Blackest Night one-shot; The Shade vs. David Knight; Harris-c 3.00
#1,000,000 (11/98) 853rd Century x-over; Snejbjerg-a 3.00
Annual 1 (1996, $3.50)-Legends of the Dead Earth story; Prince Gavyn & G.A. Starman stories; J.H. Williams III, Bret Blevins, Craig Hamilton-c/a(p) 4.00
Annual 2 (1997, $3.95)-Pulp Heroes story; 4.00
...80 Page Giant (1/99, $4.95) Harris-c 5.00
...Secret Files 1 (4/98, $4.95)-Origin stories and profile pages 5.00
...The Mist (6/98, $1.95) Girlfrenzy; Mary Marvel app. 3.00
A Starry Knight-($17.95, TPB) r/#47-53 18.00
Grand Guignol-(2004, $19.95, TPB)-r/#61-73 20.00
Infernal Devices-($17.95, TPB) r/#29-35,37,38 18.00
Night and Day-($14.95, TPB)-r/#7-10,12-16 15.00
Sins of the Father-($12.95, TPB)-r/#0-5 13.00
Sons of the Father-($14.99, TPB)-r/#75-80 15.00
Stars My Destination-(2003, $14.95, TPB)-r/#55-60 15.00
Times Past-($17.95, TPB)-r/stories of other Starmen 18.00
The Starman Omnibus Vol. One (2008, $49.99, HC with dj) r/#0,1-16; Robinson intro. 50.00
The Starman Omnibus Vol. Two (2009, $49.99, HC with dj) r/#17-29, Annual #1, Showcase '95 #12, Showcase '96 #4,5; Harris intro.; merchandise gallery 50.00
The Starman Omnibus Vol. Three (2009, $49.99, HC with dj) r/#30-38, Annual #2, Starman Secret Files #1 and The Shade #1-4 50.00
The Starman Omnibus Vol. Four (2010, $49.99, HC with dj) r/#39-46, 80 Page Giant #1, Power of Shazam! #35,36; Starman: The Mist #1 and Batman/Hellboy/Starman #1,2 50.00
The Starman Omnibus Vol. Five (2010, $49.99, HC with dj) r/#47-60, #1,000,000; Stars and S.T.R.I.P.E. #0; All Star Comics 80 Page Giant #1; JSA: All Stars #4 50.00
The Starman Omnibus Vol. Six (2011, $49.99, HC with dj) r/#61-81, Johns intro. 50.00

STARMAN/CONGORILLA (See Justice League: Cry For Justice)
DC Comics: Mar, 2011 ($2.99, one-shot)
1-Animal Man and Rex the Wonder Dog app.; Robinson-s/Booth-a/Ha-c 3.00

STARMASTERS
Marvel Comics: Dec, 1995 - No. 3, Feb, 1996 ($1.95, limited series)
1-3-Continues in Cosmic Powers Unlimited #4 3.00

STAR PRESENTATION, A (Formerly My Secret Romance #1,2; Spectacular Stories #4 on) (Also see This Is Suspense)
Fox Features Syndicate (Hero Books): No. 3, May, 1950
3-Dr. Jekyll & Mr. Hyde by Wood & Harrison (reprinted in Startling Terror Tales #10); "The Repulsing Dwarf" by Wood; Wood-c 58 116 174 371 636 900

STAR QUEST COMIX (Warren Presents... on cover)
Warren Publications: Oct, 1978 ($1.50, B&W magazine, 84 pgs., square-bound)
1-Corben, Maroto, Neary-a; Ken Kelly-c; Star Wars 2 4 6 9 12 15

STAR RAIDERS (See DC Graphic Novel #1)

STAR RANGER (Cowboy Comics #13 on)
Chesler Publ./Centaur Publ.: Feb, 1937 - No. 12, May, 1938 (Large size: No. 1-6)
1-(1st Western comic)-Ace & Deuce, Air Plunder; Creig Flessel-a 226 452 678 1446 2473 3500
2 97 194 291 621 1061 1500
3-6 84 168 252 538 919 1300
7-9: 8(12/37)-Christmas-c; Air Patrol, Gold coast app.; Guardineer centerfold 61 122 183 390 670 950
V2#10 (1st Centaur; 3/38) 90 180 270 576 988 1400
11,12 66 132 198 419 722 1025
NOTE: ***J. Cole** a-10, 12; c-12. **Ken Ernst** a-11. **Gill Fox** a-8(illo), 9, 10. **Guardineer** a-1, 3, 6, 7, 8(illos), 9, 10, 12. **Gustavson** a-8-10, 12. **Fred Schwab** c-2-11. **Bob Wood** a-8-10.*

STAR RANGER FUNNIES (Formerly Cowboy Comics)
Centaur Publications: V1#15, Oct, 1938 - V2#5, Oct, 1939
V1#15-Lyin Lou, Ermine, Wild West Junior, The Law of Caribou County by Eisner, Cowboy Jake, The Plugged Dummy, Spurs by Gustavson, Red Coat, Two Buckaroos & Trouble Hunters begin 97 194 291 621 1061 1500
V2#1 (1/39) 73 146 219 467 796 1125
2-5: 2-Night Hawk by Gustavson. 4-Kit Carson app. 60 120 180 381 653 925
NOTE: ***Jack Cole** a-V2#1, 3; c-V2#1. **Filchock** c-V2#2, 3. **Guardineer** a-V2#3. **Gustavson** a-V2#2. **Pinajian** c/a-V2#5.*

STAR REACH (Mature content)
Star Reach Publ.: Apr, 1974 - No. 18, Oct, 1979 (B&W, #12-15 w/color)
1-(75¢, 52 pgs.) Art by Starlin, Simonson. Chaykin-c/a; origin Death. Cody Starbuck-sty 3 6 9 18 27 35
1-2nd, 3th, and 4th printings ($1.00-$1.50-c) 6.00
2-11: 2-Adams, Giordano-a; 1st Stephanie Starr-c/s. 3-1st Linda Lovecraft. 4-1st Sherlock Duck. 5-1st Gideon Faust by Chaykin. 6-Elric-c. 7-BWS-c. 9-14-Sacred & Profane-c/s by Steacy. 11-Samurai 2 4 6 8 11 14
2-2nd printing 4.00

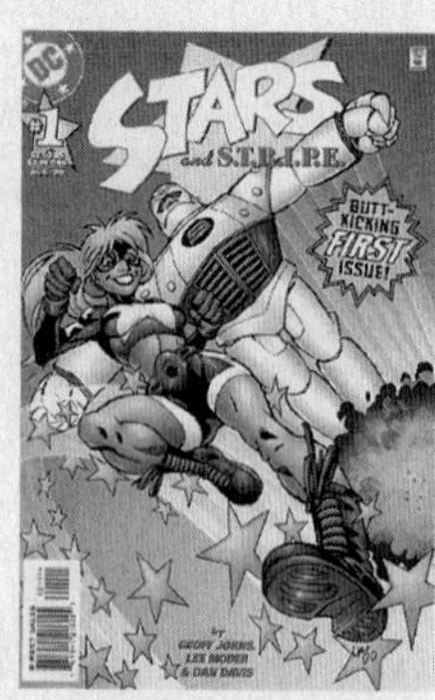

Stars and S.T.R.I.P.E. #1 © DC

Starslayer #18 © FC

Star Spangled Comics #125 © DC

GD 2.0 | VG 4.0 | FN 6.0 | VF 8.0 | VF/NM 9.0 | NM- 9.2

12-15 (44 pgs.): 12-Zelazny-s. Nasser-a, Brunner-c 2 4 6 9 13 16
16-18-Magazine size: 17-Poe's Raven-c/s 2 4 6 9 13 16
NOTE: **Adams** *c-2.* **Bonivert** *a-17.* **Brunner** *a-3,5; c-3,10,12.* **Chaykin** *a-1,4,5; c-1(1st ed),4,5; back-c-1(2nd,3rd,4th ed).* **Gene Day** *a-6,8,9,11,15.* **Friedrich** *s-2,3,8,10.* **Gasbarri** *a-7.* **Gilbert** *a-9,12.* **Giordano** *a-2.* **Gould** *a-6.* **Hirota/Mukaide** *s/a-7.* **Jones** *c-6.* **Konz** *a-17.* **Leialoha** *a-3,4,6-i, 13,15; c-13,15.* **Lyda** *a-6,12-15.* **Marrs** *a-2-5,7,10,14,15,16,18; c-18; back-c-2.* **Mukaide** *a-18.* **Nasser** *a-12.* **Nino** *a-6;* **Russell** *a-8,10; c-8.* **Dave Sim** *s-7; lettering-9.* **Simonson** *a-1.* **Skeates** *a-1,2.* **Starlin** *a-1(x2), 2(x2); back-c-1(1st ed); c-1(2nd,3rd,4th ed).* **Barry Smith** *c-7.* **Staton** *a-5,6,7.* **Steacy** *a-8-14; c-9,11,14,16.* **Vosburg** *a-2-5,7,10.* **Workman** *a-2-5,8.* *Nudity panels in most. Wraparound-c: 3-5,7-11,13-16,18.*

STAR REACH CLASSICS
Eclipse Comics: Mar, 1984 - No. 6, Aug, 1984 ($1.50, Baxter paper)
1-6: 1-Neal Adams-r/Star Reach #1; Sim & Starlin-a 3.00

STARR FLAGG, UNDERCOVER GIRL (See Undercover...)

STARRIORS
Marvel Comics: Aug, 1984 - Feb, 1985 (Limited series) (Based on Tomy toys)
1-4 3.00

STARR THE SLAYER
Marvel Comics (MAX): Nov, 2009 - No. 4, Feb, 2010 ($3.99, limited series)
1-4- Richard Corben-c/a; Daniel Way-s 4.00

STARS AND S.T.R.I.P.E. (Also see JSA)
DC Comics: July, 1999 - No. 14, Sept, 2000 ($2.95/$2.50)
0-($2.95) Moder and Weston-a; Starman app. 3.00
1-Johns and Robinson-s/Moder-a; origin new Star Spangled Kid 3.00
2-14: 4-Marvel Family app. 9-Seven Soldiers of Victory-c/app. 3.00
JSA Presents: Stars and S.T.R.I.P.E. Vol. 1 TPB (2007, $17.99) r/#1-8; Johns intro. 18.00
JSA Presents: Stars and S.T.R.I.P.E. Vol. 2 TPB (2008, $17.99) r/#0,9-14 18.00

STARS AND STRIPES COMICS
Centaur Publications: No. 2, May, 1941 - No. 6, Dec, 1941
2(#1)-The Shark, The Iron Skull, A-Man, The Amazing Man, Mighty Man, Minimidget begin; The Voice & Dash Dartwell, the Human Meteor, Reef Kinkaid app.; Gustavson Flag-c 226 452 678 1446 2473 3500
3-Origin Dr. Synthe; The Black Panther app. 123 246 369 787 1344 1900
4-Origin/1st app. The Stars and Stripes; injury to eye-c 103 206 309 659 1130 1600
5(#5 on cover & inside) 71 142 213 454 777 1100
5(#6)-(#5 on cover, #6 on inside) 71 142 213 454 777 1100
NOTE: **Gustavson** *c/a-3.* **Myron Strauss** *c-4, 5(#5), 5(#6).*

STAR SEED (Formerly Powers That Be)
Broadway Comics: No. 7, 1996 - No. 9 ($2.95)
7-9 3.00

STARSHIP TROOPERS
Dark Horse Comics: 1997 - No. 2, 1997 ($2.95, limited series)
1,2-Movie adaption 3.00

STARSHIP TROOPERS: BRUTE CREATIONS
Dark Horse Comics: 1997 ($2.95, one-shot)
1 3.00

STARSHIP TROOPERS: DOMINANT SPECIES
Dark Horse Comics: Aug, 1998 - No. 4, Nov, 1998 ($2.95, limited series)
1-4-Strnad-s/Bolton-c 3.00

STARSHIP TROOPERS: INSECT TOUCH
Dark Horse Comics: 1997 - No. 3, 1997 ($2.95, limited series)
1-3 3.00

STAR SLAMMERS (See Marvel Graphic Novel #6)
Malibu Comics (Bravura): May, 1994 - No. 4, Aug, 1994 ($2.50, unfinished limited series)
1-4: W. Simonson-a/stories; contain Bravura stamps 3.00

STAR SLAMMERS SPECIAL
Dark Horse Comics (Legend): June, 1996 ($2.95, one-shot)
nn-Simonson-c/a/scripts; concludes Bravura limited series. 3.00

STARSLAYER
Pacific Comics/First Comics No. 7 on: Feb, 1982 - No. 6, Apr, 1983; No. 7, Aug, 1983 - No. 34, Nov, 1985
1-Origin & 1st app.; 1 pg. Rocketeer brief app. which continues in #2 6.00
2-Origin/1st full app. the Rocketeer (4/82) by Dave Stevens (Chapter 1 of Rocketeer saga; see Pacific Presents #1,2) 2 4 6 9 12 15
3-Chapter 2 of Rocketeer saga by Stevens 1 3 4 6 8 10
4,6,7: 7-Grell-a ends 4.00
5-2nd app. Groo the Wanderer by Aragones 1 2 3 5 6 8

GD 2.0 | VG 4.0 | FN 6.0 | VF 8.0 | VF/NM 9.0 | NM- 9.2

8-34: 10-1st app. Grimjack (11/83, ends #17). 18-Starslayer meets Grimjack. 20-The Black Flame begins (9/84, 1st app.), ends #33. 27-Book length Black Flame story 3.00
NOTE: **Grell** *a-1-7; c-1-8.* **Stevens** *back c-2, 3.* **Sutton** *a-17p, 20-22p, 24-27p, 29-33p.*

STARSLAYER (The Director's Cut)
Acclaim Comics (Windjammer): June, 1994 - No. 8, Dec, 1995 ($2.50)
1-8: Mike Grell-c/a/scripts 3.00

STAR SPANGLED COMICS (Star Spangled War Stories #131 on)
National Periodical Publications: Oct, 1941 - No. 130, July, 1952
1-Origin/1st app. Tarantula; Captain X of the R.A.F., Star Spangled Kid (see Action #40), Armstrong of the Army begin; Robot-c 503 1006 1509 3672 6486 9300
2 165 330 495 1048 1799 2550
3-5 103 206 309 659 1130 1600
6-Last Armstrong/Army; Penniless Palmer begins 63 126 189 403 689 975
7-(4/42)-Origin/1st app. The Guardian by S&K, & Robotman (by Paul Cassidy & created by Siegel);The Newsboy Legion (1st app.), Robotman & TNT begin; last Captain X 703 1406 2109 5132 9066 13,000
8-Origin TNT & Dan the Dyna-Mite 239 478 717 1530 2615 3700
9,10 168 336 504 1075 1838 2600
11-17 123 246 369 787 1344 1900
18-Origin Star Spangled Kid 152 304 456 965 1658 2350
19-Last Tarantula 123 246 369 787 1344 1900
20-Liberty Belle begins (5/43) 139 278 417 883 1517 2150
21-29-Last S&K issue; 23-Last TNT. 25-Robotman by Jimmy Thompson begins. 29-Intro Robbie the Robotdog 103 206 309 659 1130 1600
30-40: 31-S&K-c 61 122 183 390 670 950
41-51: 41,49-Kirby-c. 51-Robot-c by Kirby 55 110 165 352 601 850
52-64: 53 by S&K. 64-Last Newsboy Legion & The Guardian 50 100 150 315 533 750
65-Robin begins with c/app. (2/47); Batman cameo in 1 panel; Robin-c begins, end #95 177 354 531 1124 1937 2750
66-Batman cameo in Robin story 84 168 252 538 919 1300
67,68,70-80: 68-Last Liberty Belle? 72-Burnley Robin-c 68 136 204 435 743 1050
69-Origin/1st app. Tomahawk by F. Ray; atom bomb story & splash (6/47); black-c (rare in high grade) 155 310 465 992 1696 2400
81-Origin Merry, Girl of 1000 Gimmicks in Star Spangled Kid story 57 114 171 362 624 885
82,85: 82-Last Robotman? 85-Last Star Spangled Kid? 52 104 156 325 555 785
83-Tomahawk enters the lost valley, a land of dinosaurs; Capt. Compass begins, ends #130 53 106 159 334 567 800
84,87 (Rare): 87-Batman cameo in Robin 86 172 258 546 936 1325
86-Batman cameo in Robin story 60 120 180 381 653 925
88(1/49)-94: Batman-c/stories in all. 91-Federal Men begin, end #93. 94-Manhunters Around the World begin, end #121 61 122 183 390 670 950
95-Batman story; last Robin-c 54 108 162 343 574 825
96,98-Batman cameo in Robin stories. 96-1st Tomahawk-c (also #97-121) 40 80 120 242 401 560
97,99 35 70 105 208 339 470
100 (1/50)-Pre-Bat-Hound tryout in Robin story (pre-dates Batman #92). 41 82 123 249 417 585
101-109,118,119,121: 121-Last Tomahawk-c 32 64 96 190 310 430
110,111,120-Batman cameo in Robin stories. 120-Last 52 pg. issue 34 68 102 199 325 450
112-Batman & Robin story 36 72 108 214 347 480
113-Frazetta-a (10 pgs.) 41 82 123 256 428 600
114-Retells Robin's origin (3/51); Batman & Robin story 43 86 129 271 461 650
115,117-Batman app. in Robin stories 35 70 105 208 339 470
116-Flag-c 35 70 105 208 339 470
122-(11/51)-Ghost Breaker-c/stories begin (origin/1st app.), ends #130 (Ghost Breaker covers #122-130) 45 90 135 284 480 675
123-126,128,129 31 62 93 186 303 420
127-Batman app. 34 68 102 199 325 450
130-Batman cameo in Robin story 36 72 108 214 347 480
NOTE: *Most all issues after #29 signed by Simon & Kirby are not by them.* **Bill Ely** *c-122-130.* **Mortimer** *c-65-74(most), 76-95(most).* **Fred Ray** *c-96-106, 109, 110, 112, 113, 115-120.* **S&K** *c-7-31, 33, 34, 36, 37, 39, 40, 48, 49, 50-54, 56-58.* **Hal Sherman** *c-1-6.* **Dick Sprang** *c-75.*

STAR SPANGLED COMICS (Also see All Star Comics 1999 crossover titles)
DC Comics: May, 1999 ($1.99, one-shot)
1-Golden Age Sandman and the Star Spangled Kid 3.00

STAR SPANGLED KID (See Action #40, Leading Comics & Star Spangled Comics)

Star Spangled War Stories #40 © DC

Starstruck #12 © Lee & Kaluta

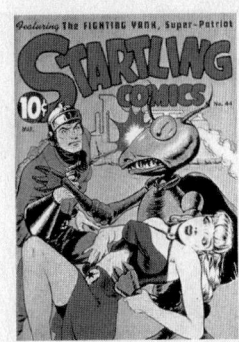

Startling Comics #44 © Nedor

	GD 2.0	VG 4.0	FN 6.0	VF 8.0	VF/NM 9.0	NM- 9.2

STAR SPANGLED WAR STORIES
DC Comics: Aug/Sept 1952

nn - Ashcan comic, not distributed to newsstands, only for in-house use. Cover art is Western Comics #28 with interior being Western Comics #13 (no known sales)

STAR SPANGLED WAR STORIES (Formerly Star Spangled Comics #1-130; Becomes The Unknown Soldier #205 on) (See Showcase)
National Periodical Publications: No. 131, 8/52 - No. 133, 10/52; No. 3, 11/52 - No. 204, 2-3/77

Issue	GD	VG	FN	VF	VF/NM	NM-
131(#1)	148	296	444	947	1624	2300
132	87	174	261	553	952	1350
133-Used in **POP**, pg. 94	74	148	222	470	810	1150
3-6: 4-Devil Dog Dugan app. 6-Evans-a	54	108	162	343	574	825
7-10	28	56	84	215	433	650
11-20	25	50	75	183	367	550
21-30: 30-Last precode (2/55)	21	42	63	153	307	460
31-33,35-40	16	32	48	117	239	360
34-Krigstein-a	17	34	51	120	245	370
41-44,46-50: 50-1st S.A. issue	15	30	45	106	216	325
45-1st DC grey tone war-c (5/56)	37	74	111	286	568	850
51,52,54-63,65,66, 68-83	13	26	39	94	185	275
53-"Rock Sergeant," 3rd Sgt. Rock prototype; inspired "P.I. & The Sand Fleas" in G.I. Combat #56 (1/57)	23	46	69	168	334	500
64-Pre-Sgt. Rock Easy Co. story (12/57)	16	32	48	117	239	360
67-Two Easy Co. stories without Sgt. Rock	17	34	51	120	245	370
84-Origin Mlle. Marie	23	46	69	168	334	500
85-89-Mlle. Marie in all	15	30	45	106	216	325
90-1st app. "War That Time Forgot" series; dinosaur issue-c/story (4-5/60) (also see Weird War Tales #94 & #99)	48	96	144	408	829	1250
91,93-No dinosaur stories	15	30	45	106	216	325
92-2nd dinosaur-c/s	23	46	69	168	334	500
94 (12/60)- "Ghost Ace" story; Baron Von Richter as The Enemy Ace (predates Our Army at War #151)	27	54	81	197	399	600
95-99: Dinosaur-c/s	18	36	54	131	266	400
100-Dinosaur-c/story.	21	42	63	150	300	450
101-115: All dinosaur issues	15	30	45	106	216	325
116-125,127-133,135-137: 120-1st app. Caveboy and Dino. 137-Last dinosaur story; Heath Birdman-#129,131	13	26	39	94	185	275
126-No dinosaur story	12	24	36	82	154	225
134-Dinosaur story; Neal Adams-a	15	30	45	106	216	325
138-New Enemy Ace-c/stories begin by Joe Kubert (4-5/68), end #150 (also see Our Army at War #151 and Showcase #57)	16	32	48	111	226	340
139-Origin Enemy Ace (7/68)	12	24	36	82	154	225
140-143,145: 145-Last 12¢ issue (6-7/69)	9	18	27	63	107	150
144-Neal Adams/Kubert-a	10	20	30	68	119	170
146-Enemy Ace-c/app.	7	14	21	49	80	110
147,148-New Enemy Ace stories	8	16	24	56	93	130
149,150-Last new Enemy Ace by Kubert. Viking Prince by Kubert	8	16	24	52	86	120
151-1st solo app. Unknown Soldier (6-7/70); Enemy Ace-r begin (from Our Army at War, Showcase & SSWS); end #161	18	36	54	131	266	400
152-Reprints 2nd Enemy Ace app.	7	14	21	45	73	100
153,155-Enemy Ace reprints; early Unknown Soldier stories	6	12	18	39	62	85
154-Origin Unknown Soldier	13	26	39	94	185	275
156-1st Battle Album; Unknown Soldier story; Kubert-c/a	5	10	15	35	55	75
157-Sgt. Rock x-over in Unknown Soldier story.	5	10	15	30	48	65
158-163-(52 pgs.): New Unknown Soldier stories; Kubert-c/a. 161-Last Enemy Ace-r	4	8	12	26	41	55
164-183,200: 181-183-Enemy Ace vs. Balloon Buster serial app; Frank Thorne-a. 200-Enemy Ace back-up	3	6	9	16	22	28
184-199,201-204	2	4	6	13	18	22

NOTE: ***Anderson** a-28. **Chaykin** a-167. **Drucker** a-59, 61, 64, 66, 67, 73-84. **Estrada** a-149. **John Giunta** a-72. **Glanzman** a-167, 171, 172, 174. **Heath** a-42,122, 132, 133; c-67, 122, 132-134. **Kaluta** a-197i; c-167. **G. Kane** a-169. **Kubert** a-6-163(most later issues), 200. **Maurer** a-160, 165. **Severin** a-65, 162. **S&K** c-7-31, 33, 34, 37, 40. **Simonson** a-170, 172, 174, 180. **Sutton** a-168. **Thorne** a-183. **Toth** a-164. **Wildey** a-161. Suicide Squad in 110, 116-118, 120, 121, 127.*

STAR SPANGLED WAR STORIES (Featuring Mademoiselle Marie)
DC Comics: Nov, 2010 ($3.99, one-shot)

Issue	GD	VG	FN	VF	VF/NM	NM-
1-Mademoiselle Marie in 1944 France; Tucci-s/Justiniano-a/Bolland-c						4.00

STARSTREAM (Adventures in Science Fiction)(See Questar illustrated)
Whitman/Western Publishing Co.: 1976 (79¢, 68 pgs, cardboard-c)

Issue	GD	VG	FN	VF	VF/NM	NM-
1-4: 1-Bolle-a. 2-4-McWilliams & Bolle-a	2	4	6	10	14	18

STARSTRUCK
Marvel Comics (Epic Comics): Feb, 1985 - No. 6, Feb, 1986 ($1.50, mature)

Issue	GD	VG	FN	VF	VF/NM	NM-
1-6: Kaluta-a						4.00

STARSTRUCK
Dark Horse Comics: Aug, 1990 - No. 4, Nov?, 1990 ($2.95, B&W, 52pgs.)

Issue	GD	VG	FN	VF	VF/NM	NM-
1-3: Kaluta-r/Epic series plus new-c/a in all						4.00
4 (68 pgs.)-contains 2 trading cards						5.00
Reprint 1-13 (IDW, 8/09 - No. 13, Sept, 2010, $3.99) newly colored; Galactic Girl Guides						4.00

STAR STUDDED
Cambridge House/Superior Publishers: 1945 (25¢, 132 pgs.); 1945 (196 pgs.)

Issue	GD	VG	FN	VF	VF/NM	NM-
nn-Captain Combat by Giunta, Ghost Woman, Commandette, & Red Rogue app.; Infantino-a	36	72	108	211	343	475
nn-The Cadet, Edison Bell, Hoot Gibson, Jungle Lil (196 pgs.); copies vary; Blue Beetle in some	34	68	102	199	325	450

STARTLING COMICS
Better Publications (Nedor): June, 1940 - No. 53, Sept, 1948

Issue	GD	VG	FN	VF	VF/NM	NM-
1-Origin Captain Future-Man Of Tomorrow, Mystico (By Sansone), The Wonder Man; The Masked Rider & his horse Pinto begins; Masked Rider formerly in pulps; drug use story	290	580	870	1856	3178	4500
2 -Don Davis, Espionage Ace begins	103	206	309	659	1130	1600
3	84	168	252	538	919	1300
4	61	122	183	390	670	950
5-9	53	106	159	334	567	800
10-The Fighting Yank begins (9/41, origin/1st app.)	417	834	1251	2919	5110	7300
11-2nd app. Fighting Yank	129	258	387	826	1413	2000
12-Hitler, Hirohito, Mussolini-c	142	284	426	909	1555	2200
13-15	66	132	198	419	722	1025
16-Origin The Four Comrades; not in #32,35	68	136	204	435	743	1050
17-Last Masked Rider & Mystico	52	104	156	322	549	775
18-Pyroman begins (12/42, origin)(also see America's Best Comics #3 for 1st app., 11/42)	103	206	309	659	1130	1600
19	54	108	162	343	574	825
20,21: 20-The Oracle begins (3/43); not in issues 26,28,33,34. 21-Origin The Ape, Oracle's enemy	56	112	168	356	608	860
22-34: 34-Origin The Scarab & only app.	54	108	162	346	591	835
35-Hypodermic syringe attacks Fighting Yank in drug story	56	112	168	356	608	860
36-43: 36-Last Four Comrades. 38-Bondage/torture-c. 40-Last Capt. Future & Oracle. 41-Front Page Peggy begins; A-Bomb-c. 43-Last Pyroman	47	94	141	296	498	700
44,45: 44-Lance Lewis, Space Detective begins; Ingels-c; sci/fi-c begin. 45-Tygra begins (intro/origin, 5/47); Ingels-c/a (splash pg. & inside f/c B&W ad)	77	154	231	493	847	1200
46-Classic Ingels-c; Ingels-a	119	238	357	762	1306	1850
47,48,50-53: 50,51-Sea-Eagle app.	71	142	213	454	777	1100
49-Classic Schomburg Robot-c; last Fighting Yank	486	972	1458	3550	6275	9000

NOTE: ***Ingels** a-44, 45; c-44, 45, 46(wash). **Schomburg (Xela)** c-21-43; 47-53 (airbrush). **Tuska** c-45? Bondage c-16, 21, 37, 46-49. Captain Future c-1-9, 13, 14. Fighting Yank c-10-12, 15-17, 21, 22, 24, 26, 28, 30, 32, 34, 36, 38, 40, 42. Pyroman c-18-20, 23, 25, 27, 29, 31, 33, 35, 37, 39, 41, 43.*

STARTLING STORIES: BANNER
Marvel Comics: July, 2001 - No. 4, Oct, 2001 ($2.99, limited series)

Issue	GD	VG	FN	VF	VF/NM	NM-
1-4-Hulk story by Azzarello; Corben-c/a						3.00
TPB (11/01, $12.95) r/1-4						13.00

STARTLING STORIES: FANTASTIC FOUR - UNSTABLE MOLECULES (See Fantastic Four - ...)

STARTLING STORIES: THE MEGALOMANIACAL SPIDER-MAN
Marvel Comics: Jun, 2002 ($2.99, one-shot)

Issue	GD	VG	FN	VF	VF/NM	NM-
1-Spider-Man spoof; Peter Bagge-s/a						3.00

STARTLING STORIES: THE THING
Marvel Comics: 2003 ($3.50, one-shot)

Issue	GD	VG	FN	VF	VF/NM	NM-
1-Zimmerman-s/Kramer-a; Inhumans and the Hulk app.						3.50

STARTLING STORIES: THE THING - NIGHT FALLS ON YANCY STREET
Marvel Comics: Jun, 2003 - No. 4, Sept, 2003 ($3.50, limited series)

Issue	GD	VG	FN	VF	VF/NM	NM-
1-4-Dorkin-s/Haspiel-a. 2,3-Frightful Four app.						3.50

STARTLING TERROR TALES
Star Publications: No. 10, May, 1952 - No. 14, Feb, 1953; No. 4, Apr, 1953 - No. 11, 1954

Issue	GD	VG	FN	VF	VF/NM	NM-
10-(1st Series)-Wood/Harrison-a (r/A Star Presentation #3) Disbrow/Cole-c; becomes 4 different titles after #10; becomes Confessions of Love #11 on, The Horrors #11 on, Terrifying Tales #11 on, Terrors of the Jungle #11 on & continues w/Startling Terror #11	77	154	231	489	837	1185

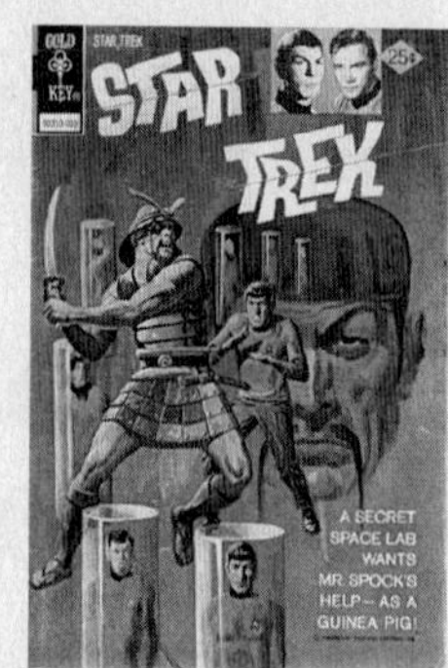

Star Trek #26 © Paramount

Star Trek (1984 DC series) #51 © Paramount

Star Trek: Captain's Log: Pike © Paramount

	GD 2.0	VG 4.0	FN 6.0	VF 8.0	VF/NM 9.0	NM- 9.2
11-(8/52)-L. B. Cole Spider-c; r-Fox's "A Feature Presentation" #5 (blue-c)	174	348	522	1114	1907	2700
11-Black-c (variant; believed to be a pressrun change) (Unique)	181	362	543	1158	1979	2800
12,14	33	66	99	194	317	440
13-Jo-Jo-r; Disbrow-a	34	68	102	204	332	460
4-9,11(1953-54) (2nd Series): 11-New logo	29	58	87	172	281	390
10-Disbrow-a	35	70	105	208	339	470

NOTE: *L. B. Cole covers-all issues. Palais a-V2#8r, V2#11r.*

STAR TREK (TV) (See Dan Curtis Giveaways, Dynabrite Comics & Power Record Comics)
Gold Key: 7/67; No. 2, 6/68; No. 3, 12/68; No. 4, 6/69 - No. 61, 3/79

	GD 2.0	VG 4.0	FN 6.0	VF 8.0	VF/NM 9.0	NM- 9.2
1-Photo-c begin, end #9; photo back-c is on all copies, no variant exists with an ad on the back-c	50	100	150	425	863	1300
2-Regular version has an ad on back-c	22	44	66	159	317	475
2 (rare variation w/photo back-c)	33	66	99	254	502	750
3-5-All have back-c ads	14	28	42	99	200	300
3 (rare variation w/photo back-c)	24	48	72	175	350	525
6-9	11	22	33	77	144	210
10-20	6	12	18	43	69	95
21-30	6	12	18	37	59	80
31-40	4	8	12	28	44	60
41-61: 52-Drug propaganda story	4	8	12	22	34	45
...the Enterprise Logs nn (8/76)-Golden Press, ($1.95, 224 pgs.)-r/#1-8 plus 7 pgs. by McWilliams (#11185)-Photo-c	6	12	18	39	62	85
...the Enterprise Logs Vol. 2 ('76)-r/#9-17 (#11187)-Photo-c	5	10	15	34	55	75
...the Enterprise Logs Vol. 3 ('77)-r/#18-26 (#11188); McWilliams-a (4 pgs.)-Photo-c	5	10	15	34	55	75
Star Trek Vol. 4 (Winter '77)-Reprints #27,28,30-34,36,38 (#11189) plus 3 pgs. new art	5	10	15	34	55	75
... : The Key Collection (Checker Book Publ. Group, 2004, $22.95) r/#1-8						23.00
... : The Key Collection Volume 2 (Checker, 2004, $22.95) r/#9-16						23.00
... : The Key Collection Volume 3 (Checker, 2005, $22.95) r/#17-24						23.00
... : The Key Collection Volume 4 (Checker, 2005, $22.95) r/#25-33						23.00
... : The Key Collection Volume 5 (Checker, 2006, $22.95) r/#34,36,38,39,40-43						23.00

NOTE: *McWilliams a-38, 40-44, 46-61. #29 reprints #1; #35 reprints #4; #37 reprints #5; #45 reprints #7. The tabloids all have photo covers and blank inside covers. Painted covers #10-44, 46-59.*

STAR TREK
Marvel Comics Group: April, 1980 - No. 18, Feb, 1982

	GD 2.0	VG 4.0	FN 6.0	VF 8.0	VF/NM 9.0	NM- 9.2
1: 1-3-r/Marvel Super Special; movie adapt.	2	4	6	10	14	18
2-16: 5-Miller-c	1	3	4	6	8	10
17-Low print run	2	4	6	8	11	14
18-Last issue; low print run	2	4	6	11	16	20

NOTE: *Austin c-18i. Buscema a-13. Gil Kane a-15. Nasser c/a-7. Simonson c-17.*

STAR TREK (Also see Who's Who In Star Trek)
DC Comics: Feb, 1984 - No. 56, Nov, 1988 (75¢, Mando paper)

	GD 2.0	VG 4.0	FN 6.0	VF 8.0	VF/NM 9.0	NM- 9.2
1-Sutton-a(p) begins	1	3	4	6	8	10
2-5						6.00
6-10: 7-Origin Saavik						5.00
11-20: 19-Walter Koenig story						4.00
21-32						3.50
33-($1.25, 52 pgs.)-20th anniversary issue						4.00
34-49: 37-Painted-c						3.00
50-($1.50, 52 pgs.)						4.00
51-56						3.00
Annual 1-3: 1(1985). 2(1986). 3(1988, $1.50)						4.00
...: To Boldly Go TPB (Titan Books, 7/05, $19.95) r/#1-6; Koenig foreward; cast interviews						20.00
...: The Trial of James T. Kirk TPB (Titan Books, 6/06, $19.95) r/#7-12; cast interviews						20.00
...: The Return of the Worthy TPB (Titan Books, 12/06, $19.95) r/#13-18; cast interviews						20.00

NOTE: *Morrow a-28, 35, 36, 56. Orlando c-8i. Perez c-1-3. Spiegle a-19. Starlin c-24, 25. Sutton a-1-6p, 8-18p, 20-27p, 29p, 31-34p, 39-52p, 55p; c-4-6p, 8-22p, 46p.*

STAR TREK
DC Comics: Oct, 1989 - No. 80, Jan, 1996 ($1.50/$1.75/$1.95/$2.50)

	GD 2.0	VG 4.0	FN 6.0	VF 8.0	VF/NM 9.0	NM- 9.2
1-Capt. Kirk and crew						6.00
2,3						4.00
4-23,25-30: 10-12-The Trial of James T. Kirk. 21-Begin $1.75-c						3.00
24-($2.95, 68 pgs.)-40 pg. epic w/pin-ups						4.00
31-49,51-60						3.00
50-($3.50, 68 pgs.)-Painted-c						4.00
61-74,76-80						3.00
75 ($3.95)						4.00
Annual 1-6('90-'95, 68 pgs.): 1-Morrow-a. 3-Painted-c						4.00
Special 1-3 ('9-'95, 68 pgs.)-1-Sutton-a.						4.00
...: The Ashes of Eden (1995, $14.95, 100 pgs.)-Shatner story						15.00
...Generations (1994, $3.95, 68 pgs.)-Movie adaptation						4.00
...Generations (1994, $5.95, 68 pgs.)-Squarebound						6.00

STAR TREK...(TV)
DC Comics (WildStorm): one-shots

	GD 2.0	VG 4.0	FN 6.0	VF 8.0	VF/NM 9.0	NM- 9.2
All of Me (4/00, $5.95, prestige format) Lopresti-a						6.00
Enemy Unseen TPB (2001, $17.95) r/Perchance to Dream, Embrace the Wolf, The Killing Shadows; Struzan-c						18.00
Enter the Wolves (2001, $5.95) Crispin & Weinstein-s; Mota-a/c						6.00
New Frontier - Double Time (11/00, $5.95)-Captain Calhoun's USS Excalibur; Peter David-s; Stelfreeze-c						6.00
Other Realities TPB (2001, $14.95) r/All of Me, New Frontier - Double Time, and DS9-N-Vector; Van Fleet-c						15.00
Special (2001, $6.95) Stories from all 4 series by various; Van Fleet-c						7.00

STAR TREK: ALIEN SPOTLIGHT
IDW Publishing: Sept, 2007 - Feb, 2008 ($3.99, series of one-shots)

	GD 2.0	VG 4.0	FN 6.0	VF 8.0	VF/NM 9.0	NM- 9.2
... Andorians (11/07) Storrie-s/O'Grady-a; Counselor Troi app.; two art & one photo-c						4.00
... Borg (1/08) Harris-s/Murphy-a; Janeway & Next Gen crew app.; two art & one photo-c						4.00
... Cardassians (12/09) Padilla-a; Garak & Kira app.						4.00
... The Gorn (9/07) Messina-a; Chekov app.; two art & one photo-c						4.00
... Orions (12/07) Casagrande-a; Capt. Pike app.; two art & one photo-c						4.00
... Q (8/09) Casagrande-a; takes place after Star Trek 8 movie; two art & one photo-c						4.00
... Romulans (2/08) John Byrne-s/a; Kirk era; two art & one photo-c						4.00
... Romulans (5/09) Wagner Reis-a; David Williams-c						4.00
... Tribbles (3/09) Hawthorne-a; first encounter with Klingons; one art & one photo-c						4.00
... Vulcans (10/07) Spock's early Enterprise days with Capt. Pike; two art & one photo-c						4.00

STAR TREK: ASSIGNMENT EARTH
IDW Publishing: May, 2008 - No. 5, Sept, 2008 ($3.99, limited series)

	GD 2.0	VG 4.0	FN 6.0	VF 8.0	VF/NM 9.0	NM- 9.2
1-5-Further adventures of Gary Seven and Roberta; John Byrne-s/a/c. 5-Nixon app.						4.00

STAR TREK: BURDEN OF KNOWLEDGE
IDW Publishing: Jun, 2010 - No. 4, Sept, 2010 ($3.99, limited series)

	GD 2.0	VG 4.0	FN 6.0	VF 8.0	VF/NM 9.0	NM- 9.2
1-4-Original series Kirk and crew; Manfredi-a						4.00

STAR TREK: CAPTAIN'S LOG
IDW Publishing: one-shots

	GD 2.0	VG 4.0	FN 6.0	VF 8.0	VF/NM 9.0	NM- 9.2
...: Harriman (4/10, $3.99) Captain of the Enterprise-B following Kirk's "demise"; Currie-a						4.00
...: Jellico (10/10, $3.99) Woodward-a						4.00
...: Pike (9/10, $3.99) Events that put Pike in the chair; Woodward-a						4.00
...: Sulu (1/10, $3.99) Manfredi-a						4.00

STAR TREK: COUNTDOWN (Prequel to the 2009 movie)
IDW Publishing: Jan, 2009 - No. 4, Apr, 2009 ($3.99, limited series)

	GD 2.0	VG 4.0	FN 6.0	VF 8.0	VF/NM 9.0	NM- 9.2
1-4: 1-Ambassador Spock on Romulus; intro. Nero; Messina-a						4.00

STAR TREK: CREW
IDW Publishing: Mar, 2009 - No. 5, Jul, 2009 ($3.99, limited series)

	GD 2.0	VG 4.0	FN 6.0	VF 8.0	VF/NM 9.0	NM- 9.2
1-5: John Byrne-s/a; Captain Pike era						4.00

STAR TREK: DEBT OF HONOR
DC Comics: 1992 ($24.95/$14.95, graphic novel)

	GD 2.0	VG 4.0	FN 6.0	VF 8.0	VF/NM 9.0	NM- 9.2
Hardcover ($24.95) Claremont-s/Hughes-a(p)						25.00
Softcover ($14.95)						15.00

STAR TREK: DEEP SPACE NINE (TV)
Malibu Comics: Aug, 1993 - No. 32, Jan, 1996 ($2.50)

	GD 2.0	VG 4.0	FN 6.0	VF 8.0	VF/NM 9.0	NM- 9.2
1-Direct Sale Edition w/line drawn-c						4.00
1-Newsstand Edition with photo-c						3.00
0-(1/95, $2.95)-Terok Nor						3.00
2-30: 2-Polybagged w/trading card. 9-4 pg. prelude to Hearts & Minds						3.00
31-($3.95)						4.00
32-($3.50)						4.00
Annual 1 (1/95, $3.95, 68 pgs.)						4.00
Special 1 (1995, $3.50)						4.00
Ultimate Annual 1 (12/95, $5.95)						6.00
...:Lightstorm (12/94, $3.50)						4.00

STAR TREK: DEEP SPACE NINE (TV)
Marvel Comics (Paramount Comics): Nov, 1996 - No. 15, Mar, 1998 ($1.95/$1.99)

	GD 2.0	VG 4.0	FN 6.0	VF 8.0	VF/NM 9.0	NM- 9.2
1-15: 12,13-"Telepathy War" pt. 2,3						3.00

STAR TREK: DEEP SPACE NINE: FOOL'S GOLD
IDW Publishing: Dec, 2009 - No. 4, Mar, 2010 ($3.99)

	GD 2.0	VG 4.0	FN 6.0	VF 8.0	VF/NM 9.0	NM- 9.2
1-4-Mantovani-a						4.00

STAR TREK: DEEP SPACE NINE -- N-VECTOR (TV)

Star Trek: Infestation #1 © CBS

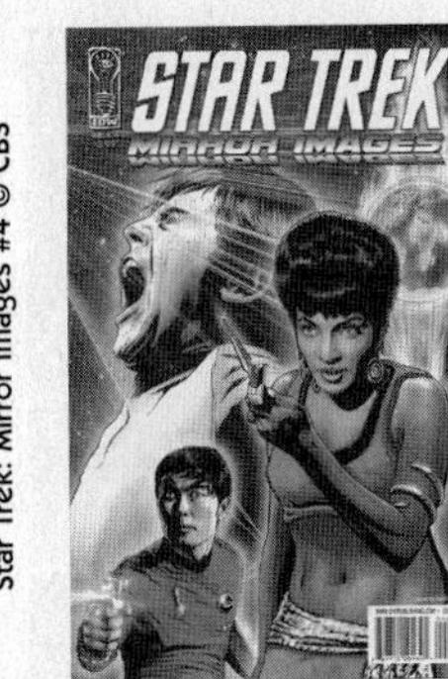

Star Trek: Mirror Images #4 © CBS

Star Trek: The Next Generation #5 © Paramount

GD 2.0 | VG 4.0 | FN 6.0 | VF 8.0 | VF/NM 9.0 | NM- 9.2

DC Comics (WildStorm): Aug, 2000 - No. 4, Nov, 2000 ($2.50, limited series)

1-4-Cypress-a 3.00

STAR TREK DEEP SPACE NINE-THE CELEBRITY SERIES
Malibu Comics: May, 1995 ($2.95)

1-Blood and Honor; Mark Lenard script 3.00
1-Rules of Diplomacy; Aron Eisenberg script 3.00

STAR TREK: DEEP SPACE NINE HEARTS AND MINDS
Malibu Comics: June, 1994 - No. 4, Sept, 1994 ($2.50, limited series)

1-4 3.00
1-Holographic-c 4.00

STAR TREK: DEEP SPACE NINE, THE MAQUIS
Malibu Comics: Feb, 1995 - No. 3, Apr, 1995 ($2.50, limited series)

1-3-Newsstand-c, 1-Photo-c 3.00

STAR TREK: DEEP SPACE NINE/THE NEXT GENERATION
Malibu Comics: Oct, 1994 - No. 2, Nov, 1994 ($2.50, limited series)

1,2: Parts 2 & 4 of x-over with Star Trek: TNG/DS9 from DC Comics 3.00

STAR TREK: DEEP SPACE NINE WORF SPECIAL
Malibu Comics: Dec, 1995 ($3.95, one-shot)

1-Includes pinups 4.00

STAR TREK: DIVIDED WE FALL
DC Comics (WildStorm): July, 2001 - No. 4, Oct, 2001 ($2.95, limited series)

1-4: Ordover & Mack-s; Lenara Kahn, Verad and Odan app. 3.00

STAR TREK EARLY VOYAGES (TV)
Marvel Comics (Paramount Comics): Feb, 1997 - No. 17, Jun, 1998 ($2.95/$1.95/$1.99)

1-($2.95) 4.00
2-17 3.00

STAR TREK: ENTERPRISE EXPERIMENT
IDW Publishing: Apr, 2008 - No. 5, Aug, 2008 ($3.99, limited series)

1-5-Year Four story; D.C. Fontana & Derek Chester-s; Purcell-a 4.00

STAR TREK: FIRST CONTACT (Movie)
Marvel Comics (Paramount Comics): Nov, 1996 ($5.95, one-shot)

nn-Movie adaption 6.00

STAR TREK: INFESTATION (Crossover with G.I. Joe, Transformers & Ghostbusters)
IDW Publishing: Feb, 2011 - No. 2, Feb, 2011 ($3.99, limited series)

1,2-Zombies in the Kirk era; Maloney & Erskine-a; two covers on each 4.00

STAR TREK: KHAN RULING IN HELL
IDW Publishing: Oct, 2010 - No. 4, Jan, 2011 ($3.99, limited series)

1-4-Khan and the Botany Bay crew after banishment on Ceti Alpha V; Mantovani-a 4.00

STAR TREK: KLINGONS: BLOOD WILL TELL
IDW Publishing: Apr, 2007 - No. 5 ($3.99, limited series)

1-5-Star Trek TOS episodes from the Klingon viewpoint; Messina-a. 2-Tribbles 4.00
1-($4.99) Klingon Language Variant; comic with Kliingon text; English script 5.00

STAR TREK: LEONARD McCOY, FRONTIER DOCTOR
IDW Publishing: Apr, 2010 - No. 4, Jul, 2010 ($3.99, limited series)

1-4-Dr. McCoy right before Star Trek: TMP; John Byrne-s/a 4.00

STAR TREK: MIRROR IMAGES
IDW Publishing: June, 2008 - No. 5, Nov, 2008 ($3.99, limited series)

1-5-Further adventures in the Mirror Universe. 3-Mirror-Picard app. 4.00

STAR TREK: MIRROR MIRROR
Marvel Comics (Paramount Comics): Feb, 1997 ($3.95, one-shot)

1-DeFalco-s 4.00

STAR TREK: MISSION'S END
IDW Publishing: Mar, 2009 - No. 5, July, 2009 ($3.99, limited series)

1-5-Kirk, Spock, Bones crew, their last mission on the pre-movie Enterprise 4.00

STAR TREK MOVIE ADAPTATION
IDW Publishing: Feb, 2010 - No. 6, Aug, 2010 ($3.99, limited series)

1-6-Adaptation of 2009 movie; Messina-a; regular & photo-c on each 4.00

STAR TREK MOVIE SPECIAL
DC Comics: 1984 (June) - No. 2, 1987 ($1.50); No. 1, 1989 ($2.00, 52 pgs)

nn-(#1)-Adapts Star Trek III; Sutton-p (68 pgs.) 4.00
2-Adapts Star Trek IV; Sutton-a; Chaykin-c. (68 pgs.) 4.00
1 (1989)-Adapts Star Trek V; painted-c 4.00

STAR TREK: NERO
IDW Publishing: Aug, 2009 - No. 4, Nov, 2009 ($3.99, limited series)

1-4-Nero's ship after the attack on the Kelvin to the arrival of Spock 4.00

STAR TREK: NEW FRONTIER
IDW Publishing: Mar, 2008 - No. 5, July, 2008 ($3.99, limited series)

1-5-Capt. Calhoun & Adm. Shelby app.; Peter David-s 4.00

STAR TREK: OPERATION ASSIMILATION
Marvel Comics (Paramount Comics): Dec, 1996 ($2.95, one-shot)

1 4.00

STAR TREK: ROMULANS SCHISMS
IDW Publishing: Sept, 2009 - No. 3, Nov, 2009 ($3.99, limited series)

1-3-John Byrne-s/a/c 4.00

STAR TREK: ROMULANS THE HOLLOW CROWN
IDW Publishing: Sept, 2008 - No. 2, Oct, 2008 ($3.99, limited series)

1,2-John Byrne-s/a/c 4.00

STAR TREK VI: THE UNDISCOVERED COUNTRY (Movie)
DC Comics: 1992

1-($2.95, regular edition, 68 pgs.)-Adaptation of film 4.00
nn-($5.95, prestige edition)-Has photos of movie not included in regular edition; painted-c by Palmer; photo back-c 6.00

STAR TREK: SPOCK: REFLECTIONS
IDW Publishing: July, 2009 - No. 4, Oct, 2009 ($3.99, limited series)

1-4-Flashbacks of Spock's childhood and career; Messina & Manfredi-a 4.00

STAR TREK: STARFLEET ACADEMY
Marvel Comics (Paramount Comics): Dec, 1996 - No. 19, Jun, 1998 ($1.95/$1.99)

1-19: Begin new series. 12-"Telepathy War" pt. 1. 18-English & Klingon editions 3.00

STAR TREK: TELEPATHY WAR
Marvel Comics (Paramount Comics): Nov, 1997 ($2.99, 48 pgs., one-shot)

1-"Telepathy War" x-over pt. 6 4.00

STAR TREK - THE MODALA IMPERATIVE
DC Comics: Late July, 1991 - No. 4, Late Sept, 1991 ($1.75, limited series)

1-4 3.00
TPB ($19.95) r/series and ST:TNG - The Modala Imperative 20.00

STAR TREK: THE NEXT GENERATION (TV)
DC Comics: Feb, 1988 - No. 6, July, 1988 (limited series)

1 ($1.50, 52 pgs.)-Sienkiewicz painted-c 6.00
2-6 ($1.00) 4.00

STAR TREK: THE NEXT GENERATION (TV)
DC Comics: Oct, 1989 -No. 80, 1995 ($1.50/$1.75/$1.95)

1-Capt. Picard and crew from TV show 1 2 3 5 7 9
2,3 5.00
4-10 4.00
11-23,25-49,51-60 3.00
24,50: 24-($2.50, 52 pgs.). 50-($3.50, 68 pgs.)-Painted-c 5.00
61-74,76-80 3.00
75-($3.95, 50 pgs.) 4.00
Annual 1-6 ('90-'95, 68 pgs.) 4.00
Special 1 -3('93-'95, 68 pgs.)-1-Contains 3 stories 4.00
...-The Series Finale (1994, $3.95, 68 pgs.) 4.00

STAR TREK: THE NEXT GENERATION (TV)
DC Comics (WildStorm): one-shots

Embrace the Wolf (6/00, $5.95, prestige format) Golden & Sniegoski-s 6.00
Forgiveness (2001, $24.95, HC) David Brin-s/Scott Hampton painted-a; dust jacket-c 30.00
Forgiveness (2002, $17.95, SC) 18.00
The Gorn Crisis (1/01, $29.95, HC) Kordey painted-a/dust jacket-c 30.00
The Gorn Crisis (1/01, $17.95, SC) Kordey painted-a 18.00

STAR TREK: THE NEXT GENERATION/DEEP SPACE NINE (TV)
DC Comics: Dec, 1994 - No. 2, Jan, 1995 ($2.50, limited series)

1,2-Parts 1 & 3 of x-over with Star Trek: DS9/TNG from Malibu Comics 3.00

STAR TREK: THE NEXT GENERATION: GHOSTS
IDW Publishing: Nov, 2009 - No. 5, Mar, 2010 ($3.99)

1-5-Cannon-s/Aranda-a 4.00

STAR TREK: THE NEXT GENERATION - ILL WIND
DC Comics: Nov, 1995 - No. 4, Feb, 1996 ($2.50, limited series)

Star Trek: The Next Generation: The Space Between #6 © Paramount

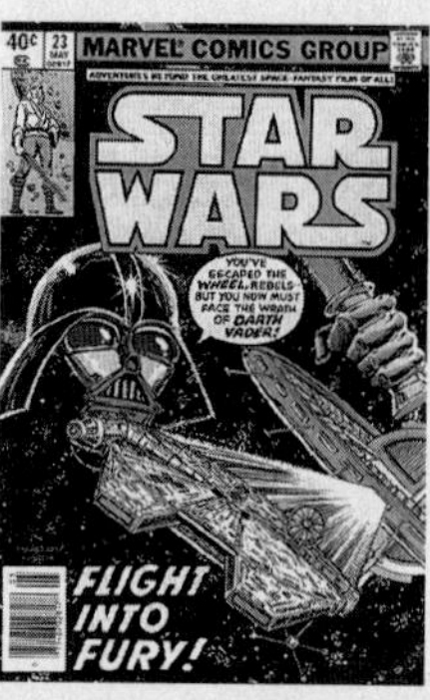

Star Wars #23 © LucasFilm

Star Wars #44 © LucasFilm

GD VG FN VF VF/NM NM-
2.0 4.0 6.0 8.0 9.0 9.2

1-4: Hugh Fleming painted-c on all 3.00

STAR TREK: THE NEXT GENERATION: INTELLIGENCE GATHERING
IDW Publishing: Jan, 2008 - No. 5, May, 2008 ($3.99)
1-5-Messina-a/Scott & David Tipton-s; two covers on each 4.00

STAR TREK: THE NEXT GENERATION - PERCHANCE TO DREAM
DC Comics/WildStorm: Feb, 2000 - No. 4, May, 2000 ($2.50, limited series)
1-4-Bradstreet-c 3.00

STAR TREK: THE NEXT GENERATION - RIKER
Marvel Comics (Paramount Comics): July, 1998 ($3.50, one-shot)
1-Riker joins the Maquis 4.00

STAR TREK: THE NEXT GENERATION - SHADOWHEART
DC Comics: Dec, 1994 - No. 4, Mar, 1995 ($1.95, limited series)
1-4 3.00

STAR TREK: THE NEXT GENERATION - THE KILLING SHADOWS
DC Comics/WildStorm: Nov, 2000 - No. 4, Feb, 2001 ($2.50, limited series)
1-4-Scott Ciencin-s; Sela app. 3.00

STAR TREK: THE NEXT GENERATION: THE LAST GENERATION
IDW Publishing: Nov, 2008 - No. 5, Mar, 2009 ($3.99, limited series)
1-5-Purcell-a; alternate timeline with Klingon war; Sulu app. 4.00

STAR TREK: THE NEXT GENERATION - THE MODALA IMPERATIVE
DC Comics: Early Sept, 1991 - No. 4, Late Oct, 1991 ($1.75, limited series)
1-4 3.00

STAR TREK: THE NEXT GENERATION: THE SPACE BETWEEN
IDW Publishing: Jan, 2007 - No. 6, June, 2007 ($3.99)
1-6-Single issue stories from various seasons; photo & art covers 4.00

STAR TREK: THE WRATH OF KHAN
IDW Publishing: Jun, 2009 - No. 3, Jul, 2009 ($3.99, limited series)
1-3-Movie adaptation; Chee Yang Ong-a 4.00

STAR TREK UNLIMITED
Marvel Comics (Paramount Comics): Nov, 1996 - No. 10, July, 1998 ($2.95/$2.99)
1,2-Stories from original series and Next Generation 5.00
3-10: 3-Begin $2.99-c. 6-"Telepathy War" pt. 4. 7-Q & Trelane swap Kirk & Picard 4.00

STAR TREK UNTOLD VOYAGES
Marvel Comics (Paramount Comics): May, 1998 - No. 5, July, 1998 ($2.50)
1-5-Kirk's crew after the 1st movie 3.00

STAR TREK: VOYAGER
Marvel Comics (Paramount Comics): Nov, 1996 - No. 15, Mar, 1998 ($1.95/$1.99)
1-15: 13-"Telepathy War" pt. 5. 14-Seven of Nine joins crew 3.00

STAR TREK: VOYAGER
DC Comics/WildStorm: one-shots and trade paperbacks
- Elite Force (7/00, $5.95) The Borg app.; Abnett & Lanning-s 6.00
... Encounters With the Unknown TPB (2001, $19.95) reprints 20.00
- False Colors (1/00, $5.95) Photo-c and Jim Lee-c; Jeff Moy-a 6.00

STAR TREK: VOYAGER-- THE PLANET KILLER
DC Comics/WildStorm: Mar, 2001 - No. 3, May, 2001 ($2.95, limited series)
1-3-Voyager vs. the Planet Killer from the ST:TOS episode; Teranishi-a 3.00

STAR TREK: VOYAGER SPLASHDOWN
Marvel Comics (Paramount Comics): Apr, 1998 - No. 4, July, 1998 ($2.50, limited series)
1-4-Voyager crashes on a water planet 3.00

STAR TREK/ X-MEN
Marvel Comics (Paramount Comics): Dec, 1996 ($4.99, one-shot)
1-Kirk's crew & X-Men; art by Silvestri, Tan, Winn & Finch; Lobdell-s 5.00

STAR TREK/ X-MEN: 2ND CONTACT
Marvel Comics (Paramount Comics): May, 1998 ($4.99, 64 pgs., one-shot)
1-Next Gen. crew & X-Men battle Kang, Sentinels & Borg following First Contact movie 5.00
1-Painted wraparound variant cover 5.00

STAR TREK: YEAR FOUR (Also see Star Trek: Enterprise Experiment)
IDW Publishing: July, 2007 - No. 5, Nov, 2007 ($3.99, limited series)
1-5: 1-Original series crew; Tischman-s/Conley-a; three covers on each 4.00

STAR WARS (Movie) (See Classic..., Contemporary Motivators, Dark Horse Comics, The Droids, The Ewoks, Marvel Movie Showcase, Marvel Special Ed.)
Marvel Comics Group: July, 1977 - No. 107, Sept, 1986

GD VG FN VF VF/NM NM-
2.0 4.0 6.0 8.0 9.0 9.2

1-(Regular 30¢ edition)-Price in square w/UPC code; #1-6 adapt first movie;
first issue on sale before movie debuted 7 14 21 47 76 105
1-(35¢-c; limited distribution - 1500 copies?)- Price in square w/UPC code
(Prices vary widely on this book. In 2005 a CGC certified 9.4 sold for $6,500, a CGC certified 9.2 sold for $3,403, and a CGC certified 6.0 sold for $610)
115 230 345 978 1989 3000

NOTE: *The rare 35¢ edition has the cover price in a square box, and the UPC box in the lower left hand corner has the UPC code lines running through it.*

2-4-(30¢ issues). 4-Battle with Darth Vader 4 8 12 24 37 50
2-4-(35¢ with UPC code; not reprints) 10 20 30 69 122 175
5,6: 5-Begin 35¢-c on all editions. 6-Stevens-a(i).
3 6 9 16 22 28
7-20 2 4 6 9 13 16
21-70: 39-44-The Empire Strikes Back-r by Al Williamson in all. 50-Giant.
68-Reintro Boba Fett. 2 4 6 8 10 12
71-80 2 4 6 8 11 14
81-90: 81-Boba Fett app. 2 4 6 9 13 16
91,93-99: 98-Williamson-a. 2 4 6 11 16 20
92,100-106: 92,100-($1.00, 52 pgs.). 3 6 9 14 20 26
107(low dist.); Portacio-a(i) 6 12 18 39 62 85
1-9: Reprints; has "reprint" in upper lefthand corner of cover or on inside or price and number inside a diamond with no date or UPC on cover; 30¢ and 35¢ issues published 4.00
Annual 1 (12/79, 52 pgs.)-Simonson-c 2 4 6 8 11 14
Annual 2 (11/82, 52 pgs.), 3(12/83, 52 pgs.) 2 4 6 8 10 12
... A Long Time Ago...Vol. 1 TPB (Dark Horse Comics, 6/02, $29.95) r/#1-14 30.00
... A Long Time Ago...Vol. 2 TPB (Dark Horse Comics, 7/02, $29.95) r/#15-28 30.00
... A Long Time Ago...Vol. 3 TPB (Dark Horse Comics, 11/02, $29.95) r/#39-53 30.00
... A Long Time Ago...Vol. 4 TPB (Dark Horse Comics, 1/03, $29.95) r/#54-67 & Ann. 2 30.00
... A Long Time Ago...Vol. 5 TPB (Dark Horse Comics, 3/03, $29.95) r/#68-81 & Ann. 3 30.00
... A Long Time Ago...Vol. 6 TPB (Dark Horse Comics, 5/03, $29.95) r/#82-93 30.00
... A Long Time Ago...Vol. 7 TPB (Dark Horse Comics, 6/03, $29.95) r/#96-107 30.00

***Austin** a-11-15i, 21i, 38; c-12-15i, 21i. **Byrne** c-13p. **Chaykin** a-1-10p; c-1. **Golden** c/a-38. **Miller** c-47p; pin-up-43. **Nebres** c/a-Annual 2i. **Portacio** a-107i. **Sienkiewicz** c-92i, 98. **Simonson** a-16p, 49p, 51-63p, 65p, 66p; c-16, 49-51, 52p, 53-62, Annual 1. **Steacy** painted a-105i, 106i; c-105. **Williamson** a-39-44p, 50p, 98; c-39, 40, 41-44p. Painted c-81, 87, 92, 95, 98, 100, 105.*

STAR WARS (Monthly series) (Becomes Star Wars Republic #46-on)
Dark Horse Comics: Dec, 1998 - No. 45, Aug, 2005 ($2.50/$2.95/$2.99)
1-45: 1-6-Prelude To Rebellion; Strnad-s. 4-Brereton-c. 7-12-Outlander. 13,17-18-($2.95). 13-18-Emissaries to Malastare; Truman-s. 14-16-($2.50) Schultz-c. 19-22-Twilight; Duursema-a. 23-26-Infinity's End. 42-45-Rite of Passage 3.00
5,6 (Holochrome-c variants) 6.00
#0 Another Universe.com Ed.($10.00) r/serialized pages from Pizzazz Magazine; new Dorman painted-c 10.00
... A Valentine Story (2/03, $3.50) Leia & Han Solo on Hoth; Winick-s/Chadwick-a/c 3.50
...: Rite of Passage (2004, $12.95) r/#42-45 13.00
...: The Stark Hyperspace War (903, $12.95) r/#36-39 13.00

STAR WARS
Dark Horse Comics (Free Comic Book Day giveaways)
...: Clone Wars #0 (5/09) flip book with short stories of Usagi Yojimbo, Emily the Strange 2.50
...: Clone Wars Adventures (7/04) based on Cartoon Network series; Fillbach Bros. -a 2.50
...: FCBD 2005 Special (5/05) Anakin & Obi-Wan during Clone Wars 2.50
...: FCBD 2006 Special (5/06) Clone Wars story; flip book with Conan FCBD Special 2.50
...: Tales - A Jedi's Weapon (5/02, 16 pgs.) Anakin Skywalker Episode 2 photo-c 2.50
Free Comic Book Day and Star Wars: The Clone Wars (5/11) flip book with Avatar: The Last Airbender 2.00

STAR WARS: A NEW HOPE - THE SPECIAL EDITION
Dark Horse Comics: Jan, 1997 - No. 4, Apr, 1997 ($2.95, limited series)
1-4-Dorman-c 4.00

STAR WARS: BLOOD TIES: JANGO AND BOBA FETT
Dark Horse Comics: Aug, 2010 - No. 4, Nov, 2010 ($3.50, limited series)
1-4-Scalf painted-a/c 3.50

STAR WARS: BOBA FETT
Dark Horse Comics: Dec, 1995 - No. 3, Aug, 1997 ($3.95) (Originally intended as a one-shot)
1-Kennedy-c/a 6.00
2,3 5.00
Death, Lies, & Treachery TPB (1/98, $12.95) r/#1-3 13.00
... - Agent of Doom (11/00, $2.99) Ostrander-s/Cam Kennedy-a 3.00
... - Overkill (3/06, $2.99) Hughes-c/Andrews-s/Velasco-a 3.00
Twin Engines of Destruction (1/97, $2.95) 3.00

STAR WARS: BOBA FETT: ENEMY OF THE EMPIRE
Dark Horse Comics: Jan, 1999 - No. 4, Apr, 1999 ($2.95, limited series)

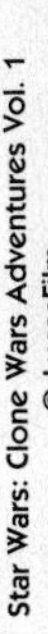
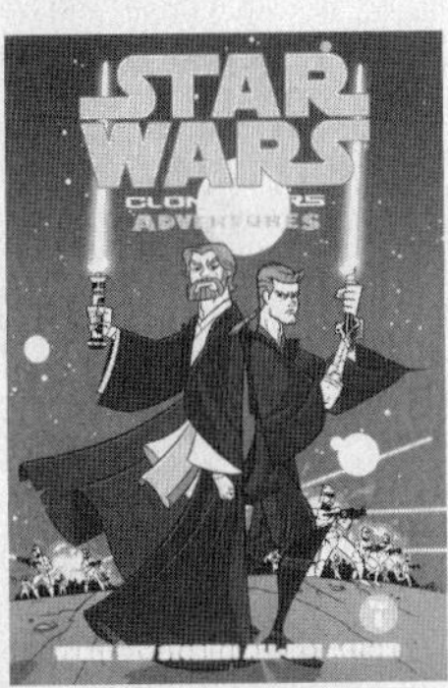
Star Wars: Clone Wars Adventures Vol. 1 © LucasFilm

Star Wars: Empire #7 © LucasFilm

Star Wars: Infinities - The Empire Strikes Back #4 © LucasFilm

GD VG FN VF VF/NM NM-
2.0 4.0 6.0 8.0 9.0 9.2

GD VG FN VF VF/NM NM-
2.0 4.0 6.0 8.0 9.0 9.2

1-4-Recalls 1st meeting of Fett and Vader 3.00

STAR WARS: CHEWBACCA
Dark Horse Comics: Jan, 2000 - No. 4, Apr, 2000 ($2.95, limited series)
1-4-Macan-s/art by various incl. Anderson, Kordey, Gibbons; Phillips-c 3.00

STAR WARS: CLONE WARS ADVENTURES
Dark Horse Comics: 2004 - Present ($6.95, digest-sized)
1-9-Short stories inspired by Clone Wars animated series 7.00

STAR WARS: CRIMSON EMPIRE
Dark Horse Comics: Dec, 1997 - No. 6, May, 1998 ($2.95, limited series)
1-Richardson-s/Gulacy-a 1 2 3 4 5 7
2-6 5.00

STAR WARS: CRIMSON EMPIRE II: COUNCIL OF BLOOD
Dark Horse Comics: Nov, 1998 - No. 6, Apr, 1999 ($2.95, limited series)
1-6-Richardson & Stradley-s/Gulacy-a 3.00

STAR WARS: DARK EMPIRE
Dark Horse Comics: Dec, 1991 - No. 6, Oct, 1992 ($2.95, limited series)
Preview-(99¢) 3.00
1-All have Dorman painted-c 1 2 3 5 7 9
1-3-2nd printing 4.00
2-Low print run 2 4 6 8 10 12
3 6.00
4-6 4.00
Gold Embossed Set (#1-6)-With gold embossed foil logo (price is for set) 90.00
Platinum Embossed Set (#1-6) 120.00
Trade paperback (4/93, 16.95) 17.00
Dark Empire 1 - TPB 3rd printing (2003, $16.95) 17.00
Ltd. Ed. Hardcover ($99.95) Signed & numbered 100.00

STAR WARS: DARK EMPIRE II
Dark Horse Comics: Dec, 1994 - No. 6, May, 1995 ($2.95, limited series)
1-Dave Dorman painted-c 5.00
2-6: Dorman-c in all. 4.00
Platinum Embossed Set (#1-6) 35.00
Trade paperback ($17.95) 18.00
TPB Second Edition (9/06, $19.95) r/#1-6 and Star Wars: Empire's End #1,2 20.00

STAR WARS: DARK FORCE RISING
Dark Horse Comics: May, 1997 - No. 6, Oct, 1997 ($2.95, limited series)
1-6 4.00
TPB (2/98, $17.95) r/#1-6 18.00

STAR WARS: DARK TIMES (Continued from Star Wars Republic #84)(Continues in Star Wars: Rebellion #15)
Dark Horse Comics: Oct, 2006 - No. 17, Jun, 2010 ($2.99)
1-17-Nineteen years before Episode IV; Doug Wheatley-a. 11-Celeste Morne awakens 13-17-Blue Harvest 3.00
#0-(7/09, $2.99) Prologue to Blue Harvest 3.00
... Volume 1: The Path To Nowhere (1/08, $17.95, TPB) r/#1-5 18.00

STAR WARS: DARTH MAUL
Dark Horse Comics: Sept, 2000 - No. 4, Dec, 2000 ($2.95, limited series)
1-4-Photo-c and Struzan painted-c; takes place 6 months before Ep. 1 3.00

STAR WARS: DROIDS (See Dark Horse Comics #17-19)
Dark Horse Comics: Apr, 1994 - #6, Sept, 1994; V2#1, Apr, 1995 - V2#8, Dec, 1995 ($2.50, limited series)
1-($2.95)-Embossed-c 4.00
2-6 , Special 1 (1/95, $2.50), V2#1-8 3.00
Star Wars Omnibus: Droids One TPB (6/08, $24.95) r/#1-6, Special 1, V2#1-8, Star Wars: The Protocol Offensive and "Artoo's Day Out" story from Star Wars Galaxy Magazine #1 25.00

STAR WARS: EMPIRE
Dark Horse Comics: Sept, 2002 - No. 40, Feb, 2006 ($2.99)
1-40: 1-Benjamin-a; takes place weeks before SW: A New Hope. 7,28-Boba Fett-c. 14-Vader after the destruction of the Death Star. 15-Death of Biggs; Wheatley-a 3.00
... Volume 1 (2003, $12.95, TPB) r/#1-4 13.00
... Volume 2 (2004, $17.95, TPB) r/#8-12,15 18.00
... Volume 3: The Imperial Perspective (2004, $17.95, TPB) r/#13,14,16-19 18.00
... Volume 4: The Heart of the Rebellion (2005, $17.95, TPB) r/#5,6,20-22 & Star Wars: A Valentine Story 18.00
... Volume 5 (2006, $14.95, TPB) r/#23-27 18.00
... Volume 6: In the Shadows of Their Fathers (10/06, $17.95, TPB) r/#29-34 18.00
... Volume 7: The Wrong Side of the War (1/07, $17.95, TPB) r/#34-40 18.00

STAR WARS: EMPIRE'S END
Dark Horse Comics: Oct, 1995 - No. 2, Nov, 1995 ($2.95, limited series)
1,2-Dorman-c 3.00

STAR WARS: EPISODE 1 THE PHANTOM MENACE
Dark Horse Comics: May, 1999 - No. 4 ($2.95, movie adaptation)
1-4-Regular and photo-c; Damaggio & Williamson-a 3.00
TPB ($12.95) r/#1-4 13.00
...Anakin Skywalker-Photo-c & Bradstreet-c, ...Obi-Wan Kenobi-Photo-c & Egeland-c, ...Queen Amidala-Photo-c & Bradstreet-c, ...Qui-Gon Jinn-Photo-c & Bradstreet-c 3.00
Gold foil covers; Wizard 1/2 10.00

STAR WARS: EPISODE II - ATTACK OF THE CLONES
Dark Horse Comics: Apr, 2002 - No. 4, May, 2002 ($3.99, movie adaptation)
1-4-Regular and photo-c; Duursema-a 4.00
TPB ($17.95) r/#1-4; Struzan-c 18.00

STAR WARS: EPISODE III - REVENGE OF THE SITH
Dark Horse Comics: May, 2005 - No. 4, May, 2005 ($2.99, movie adaptation)
1-4-Wheatley-a/Dorman-c 3.00
TPB ($12.95) r/#1-4; Dorman-c 13.00

STAR WARS: GENERAL GRIEVOUS
Dark Horse Comics: Mar, 2005 - No. 4, June, 2005 ($2.99, limited series)
1-4-Leonardi-a/Dixon-s 3.00
TPB (2005, $12.95) r/#1-4 13.00

STAR WARS HANDBOOK
Dark Horse Comics: July, 1998 - Present ($2.95, one-shots)
...X-Wing Rogue Squadron (7/98)-Guidebook to characters and spacecraft 3.00
...Crimson Empire (7/99) Dorman-c 3.00
...Dark Empire (3/00) Dorman-c 3.00

STAR WARS: HEIR TO THE EMPIRE
Dark Horse Comics: Oct, 1995 - No.6, Apr, 1996 ($2.95, limited series)
1-6: Adaptation of Zahn novel 3.00

STAR WARS: INFINITIES - A NEW HOPE
Dark Horse Comics: May, 2001 - No. 4, Oct, 2001 ($2.99, limited series)
1-4: "What If..." the Death Star wasn't destroyed in Episode 4 3.00
TPB (2002, $12.95) r/ #1-4 13.00

STAR WARS: INFINITIES - THE EMPIRE STRIKES BACK
Dark Horse Comics: July, 2002 - No. 4, Oct, 2002 ($2.99, limited series)
1-4: "What If..." Luke died on the ice planet Hoth; Bachalo-c 3.00
TPB (2/03, $12.95) r/ #1-4 13.00

STAR WARS: INFINITIES - RETURN OF THE JEDI
Dark Horse Comics: Nov, 2003 - No. 4, Mar, 2004 ($2.99, limited series)
1-4:"What If..." ; Benjamin-a 3.00

STAR WARS: INVASION
Dark Horse Comics: July, 2009 - Present ($2.99)
1-5-Jo Chen-c 3.00
#0-(10/09, $3.50) Dorman-c; Han Solo and Chewbacca app. 3.50
...-Rescues 1-6 (5/10 - No. 6, 12/10) Chen-c 3.00

STAR WARS: JABBA THE HUTT
Dark Horse Comics: Apr, 1995 ($2.50, one-shots)
nn, ...The Betrayal, ...The Dynasty Trap, ...The Hunger of Princess Nampi 3.00

STAR WARS: JANGO FETT - OPEN SEASONS
Dark Horse Comics: Apr, 2002 - No. 4, July, 2002 ($2.99, limited series)
1-4: 1-Bachs & Fernandez-a 3.00

STAR WARS: JEDI
Dark Horse Comics: Feb, 2003 - Jun, 2004 ($4.99, one-shots)
... - Aayla Secura (8/03) Ostrander-s/Duursema-a 5.00
... - Count Dooku (11/03) Duursema-a 5.00
... - Mace Windu (2/03) Duursema-a 5.00
... - Shaak Ti (5/03) Ostrander-s/Duursema-a 5.00
... - Yoda (6/04) Barlow-s/Hoon-a 5.00

STAR WARS: JEDI ACADEMY - LEVIATHAN
Dark Horse Comics: Oct, 1998 - No. 4, Jan, 1999 ($2.95, limited series)
1-4: 1-Lago-c. 2-4-Chadwick-c 3.00

STAR WARS: JEDI COUNCIL: ACTS OF WAR
Dark Horse Comics: Jun, 2000 - No. 4, Sept, 2000 ($2.95, limited series)

Star Wars: Knight Errant #1 © LucasFilm

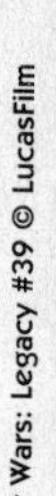

Star Wars: Legacy #39 © LucasFilm

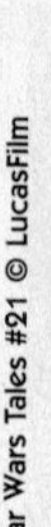

Star Wars Tales #21 © LucasFilm

	GD 2.0	VG 4.0	FN 6.0	VF 8.0	VF/NM 9.0	NM- 9.2
1-4-Stradley-s; set one year before Episode 1						3.00

STAR WARS: JEDI QUEST
Dark Horse Comics: Sept, 2001 - No. 4, Dec, 2001 ($2.99, limited series)

1-4-Anakin's Jedi training; Windham-s/Mhan-a 3.00

STAR WARS: JEDI VS. SITH
Dark Horse Comics: Apr, 2001 - No. 6, Sept, 2001 ($2.99, limited series)

1-6: Macan-s/Bachs-a/Robinson-c 3.00

STAR WARS: KNIGHT ERRANT
Dark Horse Comics: Oct, 2010 - Present ($2.99)

1-4-John Jackson Miller-s/Federico Dallocchio-a 3.00

STAR WARS: KNIGHTS OF THE OLD REPUBLIC
Dark Horse Comics: Jan, 2006 - No. 50, Feb. 2010 ($2.99)

1-50-Takes place 3,964 years before Episode IV. 1-6-Brian Ching-a/Travis Charest-c 3.00
... Handbook (11/07, $2.99) profiles of characters, ships, locales 3.00
.../Rebellion #0 (3/06, 25¢) flip book preview of both series 3.00
... Vol. 1 Commencement TPB (11/06, $18.95) r/#0-6 19.00
... Vol. 2 Flashpoint TPB (5/07, $18.95) r/#17-12 19.00
... Vol. 3 Days of Fear, Nights of Anger TPB (1/08, $18.95) r/#13-18 19.00

STAR WARS: LEGACY
Dark Horse Comics: No. 0, June, 2006 - No. 50, Aug, 2010 ($2.99)

0-(25¢) Dossier of characters, settings, ships and weapons; Duursema-c 3.00
0 1/2-(1/08, $2.99) Updated dossier of characters, settings, ships, and history 3.00
1-50: 1-Takes place 130 years after Episode IV; Hughes-c/Duursema-a. 4-Duursema-c 7,39-Luke Skywalker on-c. 16-Obi-Wan Kenobi app. 50-Wraparound-c 3.00
...: Broken Vol. 1 TPB (4/07, $17.95) r/#1-3,5,6 18.00
...: One for One (9/10, $1.00) reprints #1 with red cover frame 1.00
... War (12/10, $3.50) Ostrander-s/Duursema-a; Darth Krayt app. 3.50

STAR WARS: MARA JADE
Dark Horse Comics: Aug, 1998 - No. 6, Jan, 1999 ($2.95, limited series)

1-6-Ezquerra-a 3.00

STAR WARS: OBSESSION (Clone Wars)
Dark Horse Comics: Nov, 2004 - No. 5, Apr, 2005 ($2.99, limited series)

1-5-Blackman-s/Ching-a/c; Anakin & Obi-Wan 5 months before Episode III 3.00
...: Clone Wars Vol. 7 (2005, $17.95) r/#1-5 and 2005 Free Comic Book Day edition 18.00

STAR WARS: PURGE
Dark Horse Comics: Dec, 2005 ($2.99, one-shot)

nn-Vader vs. remaining Jedi one month after Episode III; Hughes-c/Wheatley-a 5.00
... - Seconds To Die (11/09, $3.50) Vader app.; Charest-c/Ostrander-s 3.50
... - The Hidden Blade (4/10, $3.50) Vader app.; Scalf-c/a; Blackman-s 3.50

STAR WARS: QUI-GON & OBI-WAN - LAST STAND ON ORD MANTELL
Dark Horse Comics: Dec, 2000 - No. 3, Mar, 2001 ($2.99, limited series)

1-3: 1-Three covers (photo, Tony Daniel, Bachs) Windham-s 3.00

STAR WARS: QUI-GON & OBI-WAN - THE AURORIENT EXPRESS
Dark Horse Comics: Feb, 2002 - No. 2, Mar, 2002 ($2.99, limited series)

1,2-Six years prior to Phantom Menace; Marangon-a 3.00

STAR WARS: REBELLION (Also see Star Wars: Knights of the Old Republic flip book)
Dark Horse Comics: Apr, 2006 - Present ($2.99)

1-16-Takes place 9 months after Episode IV; Luke Skywalker app. 1-Badeaux-a/c 3.00
Vol. 1 TPB (2/07, $14.95) r/#0 (flip book) & #1-5 15.00

STAR WARS: REPUBLIC (Formerly Star Wars monthly series)
Dark Horse Comics: No. 46, Sept, 2002 - No. 83, Feb, 2006 ($2.99)

46-83-Events of the Clone Wars 3.00
...: Clone Wars Vol. 1 (2003, $14.95) r/#46-50 15.00
...: Clone Wars Vol. 2 (2003, $14.95) r/#51-53 & Star Wars: Jedi - Shaak Ti 15.00
...: Clone Wars Vol. 3 (2004, $14.95) r/#55-59 15.00
...: Clone Wars Vol. 4 (2004, $16.95) r/#54, 63 & Star Wars: Jedi - Aayla Secura & Dooku 17.00
...: Clone Wars Vol. 5 (2004, $17.95) r/#60-62, 64 & Star Wars: Jedi - Yoda 18.00
...: Clone Wars Vol. 6 (2005, $17.95) r/#65-71 18.00
(Clone Wars Vol. 7 - see Star Wars: Obsession)
...: Clone Wars Vol. 8 (2006, $17.95) r/#72-78 18.00
...: Clone Wars Vol. 9 (2006, $17.95) r/#79-83 & Star Wars: Purge 18.00
...: Honor and Duty TPB (5/06, $12.95) r/#46-48,78 13.00

STAR WARS: RETURN OF THE JEDI (Movie)
Marvel Comics Group: Oct, 1983 - No. 4, Jan, 1984 (limited series)

	GD 2.0	VG 4.0	FN 6.0	VF 8.0	VF/NM 9.0	NM- 9.2
1-4-Williamson-p in all; r/Marvel Super Special #27	1	3	4	6	8	10
Oversized issue (1983, $2.95, 10-3/4x8-1/4", 68 pgs., cardboard-c)-r/#1-4	2	4	6	10	13	16

STAR WARS: RIVER OF CHAOS
Dark Horse Comics: June, 1995 - No. 4, Sept, 1995 ($2.95, limited series)

1-4: Louise Simonson scripts 3.00

STAR WARS: SHADOWS OF THE EMPIRE
Dark Horse Comics: May, 1996 - No. 6, Oct, 1996 ($2.95, limited series)

1-6: Story details events between The Empire Strikes Back & Return of the Jedi; Russell-a(i). 3.00

STAR WARS: SHADOWS OF THE EMPIRE - EVOLUTION
Dark Horse Comics: Feb, 1998 - No. 5, June, 1998 ($2.95, limited series)

1-5: Perry-s/Fegredo-c. 3.00

STAR WARS: SHADOW STALKER
Dark Horse Comics: Sept, 1997 ($2.95, one-shot)

nn-Windham-a. 3.00

STAR WARS: SPLINTER OF THE MIND'S EYE
Dark Horse Comics: Dec, 1995 - No. 4, June, 1996 ($2.50, limited series)

1-4: Adaption of Alan Dean Foster novel 3.00

STAR WARS: STARFIGHTER
Dark Horse Comics: Jan, 2002 - No. 3, March, 2002 ($2.99, limited series)

1-3-Williams & Gray-c 3.00

STAR WARS: TAG & BINK ARE DEAD
Dark Horse Comics: Oct, 2001 - No. 2, Nov, 2001($2.99, limited series)

1,2-Rubio-s 3.00
Star Wars: Tag & Bink Were Here TPB (11/06, $14.95) r/both SW: Tag & Bink series 15.00

STAR WARS: TAG & BINK II
Dark Horse Comics: Mar, 2006 - No. 2, Apr, 2006($2.99, limited series)

1-Tag & Bink invade Return of the Jedi; Rubio-s. 2-T&B as Jedi younglings during Ep II 3.00

STAR WARS TALES
Dark Horse Comics: Sept, 1999 - No. 24, Jun, 2005 ($4.95/$5.95/$5.99, anthology)

1-4-Short stories by various 5.00
5-24 ($5.95/$5.99-c) Art and photo-c on each 6.00
Volume 1-6 ($19.95) 1-(1/02) r/#1-4. 2-('02) r/#5-8. 3-(1/03) r/#9-12. 4-(1/04) r/#13-16 5-(1/05) r/#17-20; introduction pages from #1-20. 6-(1/06) r/#21-24 20.00

STAR WARS: TALES - A JEDI'S WEAPON (See Promotional Comics section)

STAR WARS: TALES FROM MOS EISLEY
Dark Horse Comics: Mar, 1996 ($2.95, one-shot)

nn-Bret Blevins-a. 3.00

STAR WARS: TALES OF THE JEDI (See Dark Horse Comics #7)
Dark Horse Comics: Oct, 1993 - No. 5, Feb, 1994 ($2.50, limited series)

1-5: All have Dave Dorman painted-c. 3-r/Dark Horse Comics #7-9 w/new coloring & some panels redrawn 4.00
1-5-Gold foil embossed logo; limited # printed-7500 (set) 50.00
Star Wars Omnibus: Tales of the Jedi Volume One TPB (11/07, $24.95) r/#1-5, ... - The Golden Age of the Sith #0-5 and ... - The Fall of the Sith Empire #1-5 25.00

STAR WARS: TALES OF THE JEDI-DARK LORDS OF THE SITH
Dark Horse Comics: Oct, 1994 - No. 6, Mar, 1995 ($2.50, limited series)

1-6: 1-Polybagged w/trading card 3.00

STAR WARS: TALES OF THE JEDI-REDEMPTION
Dark Horse Comics: July, 1998 - No. 5, Nov, 1998 ($2.95, limited series)

1-5: 1-Kevin J. Anderson-s/Kordey-c 3.00

STAR WARS: TALES OF THE JEDI-THE FALL OF THE SITH EMPIRE
Dark Horse Comics: June, 1997 - No. 5, Oct, 1997 ($2.95, limited series)

1-5 3.00

STAR WARS: TALES OF THE JEDI-THE FREEDON NADD UPRISING
Dark Horse Comics: Aug, 1994 - No. 2, Nov, 1994 ($2.50, limited series)

1,2 3.00

STAR WARS: TALES OF THE JEDI-THE GOLDEN AGE OF THE SITH
Dark Horse Comics: July, 1996 - No. 5, Feb, 1997 (99¢/$2.95, limited series)

0-(99¢)-Anderson-s 3.00
1-5-Anderson-s 3.00

STAR WARS: TALES OF THE JEDI-THE SITH WAR
Dark Horse Comics: Aug, 1995 - No. 6, Jan, 1996 ($2.50, limited series)

1-6: Anderson scripts 3.00

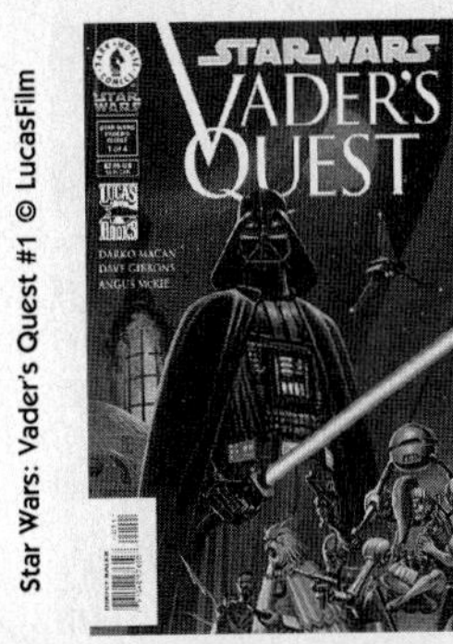

Star Wars: Vader's Quest #1 © LucasFilm

Steampunk #8 © Kelly & Bachalo

Stephen King's N. #1 © Stephen King

GD VG FN VF VF/NM NM-
2.0 4.0 6.0 8.0 9.0 9.2

GD VG FN VF VF/NM NM-
2.0 4.0 6.0 8.0 9.0 9.2

STAR WARS: THE BOUNTY HUNTERS
Dark Horse Comics: July, 1999 - Oct, 1999 ($2.95, one-shots)
...Aurra Sing (7/99), ...Kenix Kil (10/99), ...Scoundrel's Wages (8/99) Lando Calrissian app. 3.00

STAR WARS: THE CLONE WARS (Based on the Cartoon Network series)
Dark Horse Comics: Sept, 2008 - No. 12, Jan, 2010 ($2.99)
1-12: 1-6-Gilroy-s/Hepburn-a/Filoni-c 3.00

STAR WARS: THE FORCE UNLEASHED (Based on the LucasArts video game)
Dark Horse Comics: Aug, 2008 ($15.95, one-shot graphic novel)
GN-Intro. Starkiller, Vader's apprentice; takes place 2 years before Battle of Yavin 16.00

STAR WARS: THE JABBA TAPE
Dark Horse Comics: Dec, 1998 ($2.95, one-shot)
nn-Wagner-s/Plunkett-a 3.00

STAR WARS: THE LAST COMMAND
Dark Horse Comics: Nov, 1997 - No. 6, July, 1998 ($2.95, limited series)
1-6: Based on the Timothy Zaun novel 4.00

STAR WARS: THE OLD REPUBLIC (Based on the video game)
Dark Horse Comics: July, 2010 - No. 6, Dec, 2010 ($2.99, limited series)
1-3 (Threat of Peace)-Chestny-s/Sanchez-a. 1-Two covers 3.00
4-6 (Blood of the Empire)-Freed-s/Dave Ross-a 3.00

STAR WARS: THE PROTOCOL OFFENSIVE
Dark Horse Comics: Sept, 1997 ($4.95, one-shot)
nn-Anthony Daniels & Ryder Windham-s 5.00

STAR WARS: UNDERWORLD - THE YAVIN VASSILIKA
Dark Horse Comics: Dec, 2000 - No. 5, June, 2001 ($2.99, limited series)
1-5-(Photo and Robinson covers) 3.00

STAR WARS: UNION
Dark Horse Comics: Nov, 1999 - No. 4, Feb, 2000 ($2.95, limited series)
1-4-Wedding of Luke and Mara Jade; Teranishi-a/Stackpole-s 3.00

STAR WARS: VADER'S QUEST
Dark Horse Comics: Feb, 1999 - No. 4, May, 1999 ($2.95, limited series)
1-4-Follows destruction of 1st Death Star; Gibbons-a 3.00

STAR WARS: VISIONARIES
Dark Horse Comics: Apr, 2005 ($17.95, TPB)
nn-Short stories from the concept artists for Revenge of the Sith movie 18.00

STAR WARS: X-WING ROGUE SQUADRON (Star Wars: X-Wing Rogue Squadron-The Phantom Affair #5-8 appears on cover only)
Dark Horse Comics: July, 1995 - No. 35, Nov, 1998 ($2.95)
1/2 8.00
1-24,26-35: 1-4-Baron scripts. 5-20-Stackpole scripts 3.00
25-($3.95) 4.00
The Phantom Affair TPB ($12.95) r/#5-8 13.00

STAR WARS: X-WING ROGUE SQUADRON: ROGUE LEADER
Dark Horse Comics: Sept, 2005 - No. 3, Nov, 2005 ($2.99)
1-3-Takes place one week after the Batttle of Endor 3.00

S.T.A.T.
Majestic Entertainment: Dec, 1993 ($2.25)
1 3.00

STATIC (See Charlton Action: Featuring "Static")

STATIC (See Heroes)
DC Comics (Milestone): June, 1993 - No. 45, Mar, 1997 ($1.50/$1.75/$2.50)
1-($2.95)-Collector's Edition; polybagged w/poster & trading card & backing board (direct sales only) 4.00
1-Platinum Edition with red background cover 5.00
1-13,15-24,26-45: 2-Origin. 8-Shadow War; Simonson silver ink-c. 27-Kent Williams-c 3.00
14-($2.50, 52 pgs.)-Worlds Collide Pt. 14 4.00
25 ($3.95) 4.00
...: Trial by Fire (2000, $9.95) r/#1-4; Leon-c 10.00

STATIC SHOCK!: REBIRTH OF THE COOL (TV)
DC Comics: Jan, 2001 - No. 4, Sept, 2001 ($2.50, limited series)
1-4: McDuffie-s/Leon-c/a 3.00

STATIC-X
Chaos! Comics: Aug, 2002 ($5.99)
1-Polybagged with music CD; metal band as super-heroes; Pulido-s 6.00

STEALTH (Pilot Season: ...)
Image Comics (Top Cow): May, 2010 ($2.99)
1-Kirkman-s/Mitchell-a/Silvestri-c 3.00

STEAMPUNK
DC/WildStorm (Cliffhanger): Apr, 2000 - No. 12, Aug, 2002 ($2.50/$3.50)
Catechism (1/00) Prologue -Kelly-s/Bachalo-a 3.00
1-4,6-11: 4-Four covers by Bachalo, Madureira, Ramos, Campbell 3.00
5,12-($3.50) 4.00
...: Drama Obscura ('03, $14.95) r/#6-12 15.00
...: Manimatron ('01, $14.95) r/#1-5, Catechism, Idiosincratica 15.00

STEED AND MRS. PEEL (TV)(Also see The Avengers)
Eclipse Books/ ACME Press: 1990 - No. 3, 1991 ($4.95, limited series)
Books One - Three: Grant Morrison scripts 5.00

STEEL (Also see JLA)
DC Comics: Feb, 1994 - No. 52, July, 1998 ($1.50/$1.95/$2.50)
1-8,0,9-52: 1-From Reign of the Supermen storyline. 6,7-Worlds Collide Pt. 5 &12. 8-(9/94). 0-(10/94). 9-(11/94). 46-Superboy-c/app. 50-Millennium Giants x-over 3.00
1-(3/11, $2.99, one-shot) Benes-a/Garner-c; Reign of Doomsday x-over 4.00
Annual 1 (1994, $2.95)-Elseworlds story 3.00
Annual 2 (1995, $3.95)-Year One story 4.00
...Forging of a Hero TPB (1997, $19.95) reprints early app. 20.00

STEEL: THE OFFICIAL COMIC ADAPTION OF THE WARNER BROS. MOTION PICTURE
DC Comics: 1997 ($4.95, Prestige format, one-shot)
nn-Movie adaption; Bogdanove & Giordano-a 5.00

STEELGRIP STARKEY
Marvel Comics (Epic): June, 1986 - No. 6, July, 1987 ($1.50, lim. series, Baxter paper)
1-6 3.00

STEEL STERLING (Formerly Shield-Steel Sterling; see Blue Ribbon, Jackpot, Mighty Comics, Mighty Crusaders, Roly Poly & Zip Comics)
Archie Enterprises, Inc.: No. 4, Jan, 1984 - No. 7, July, 1984
4-7: 4-6-Kanigher-s; Barreto-a. 5,6-Infantino-a. 6-McWilliams-a 4.00

STEEL, THE INDESTRUCTIBLE MAN (See All-Star Squadron #8 and J.L. of A. Annual #2)
DC Comics: Mar, 1978 - No. 5, Oct-Nov, 1978

	GD 2.0	VG 4.0	FN 6.0	VF 8.0	VF/NM 9.0	NM- 9.2
1	2	4	6	8	11	14
2-5: 5-44 pgs.	1	2	3	4	6	8

STEELTOWN ROCKERS
Marvel Comics: Apr, 1987 - No. 6, Sept, 1990 ($1.00, limited series)
1-6: Small town teens form rock band 3.00

STEPHEN COLBERT'S TEK JANSEN (From the animated shorts on The Colbert Report)
Oni Press: July, 2007 - No. 5, Jan, 2009 ($3.99, limited series)
1-Chantier-a/Layman & Peyer-s; back-up story by Massey-s/Rodriguez-a; Chantier-c 4.00
1-Variant-c by John Cassaday 6.00
1-Second printing with flip book of Cassaday & Chantier covers 4.00
2-5: 2-(6/08) Flip book with covers by Rodriguez & Wagner. 3-Flip-c by Darwyn Cooke 4.00

STEPHEN KING'S N. THE COMIC SERIES
Marvel Comics: May, 2010 - No. 4, Aug, 2010 ($3.99, limited series)
1-4-Guggenheim-s/Maleev-a/c 4.00

STEVE AUSTIN (See Stone Cold Steve Austin)

STEVE CANYON (See Harvey Comics Hits #52)
Dell Publishing Co.: No. 519, 11/53 - No. No. 1033, 9/59 (All Milton Caniff-a except #519, 939, 1033)

	GD 2.0	VG 4.0	FN 6.0	VF 8.0	VF/NM 9.0	NM- 9.2
Four Color 519 (1, '53)	8	16	24	56	93	130
Four Color 578 (8/54), 641 (7/55), 737 (10/56), 804 (5/57), 939 (10/58), 1033 (9/59) (photo-c)	5	10	15	34	55	75

STEVE CANYON
Grosset & Dunlap: 1959 (6-3/4x9", 96 pgs., B&W, no text, hardcover)

	GD 2.0	VG 4.0	FN 6.0	VF 8.0	VF/NM 9.0	NM- 9.2
100100-Reprints 2 stories from strip (1953, 1957)	6	12	18	31	38	45
100100 (softcover edition)	5	10	15	24	30	35

STEVE CANYON COMICS
Harvey Publ.: Feb, 1948 - No. 6, Dec, 1948 (Strip reprints, No. 4,5: 52pgs.)

	GD 2.0	VG 4.0	FN 6.0	VF 8.0	VF/NM 9.0	NM- 9.2
1-Origin; has biography of Milton Caniff; Powell-a, 2 pgs.; Caniff-a	20	40	60	115	185	255
2-Caniff, Powell-a in #2-6	14	28	42	80	115	150
3-6: 6-Intro Madame Lynx-c/story	14	28	42	76	108	140

Steve Rogers: Super-Soldier #1 © MAR

Stone V2 #1 © Haberlin & Portacio

StormWatch #11 © WSP

GD 2.0 | VG 4.0 | FN 6.0 | VF 8.0 | VF/NM 9.0 | NM- 9.2

STEVE CANYON IN 3-D
Kitchen Sink Press: June, 1986 ($2.25, one-shot)

1-Contains unpublished story from 1954 5.00

STEVE DITKO'S STRANGE AVENGING TALES
Fantagraphics Books: Feb, 1997 ($2.95, B&W)

1-Ditko-c/s/a 3.00

STEVE DONOVAN, WESTERN MARSHAL (TV)
Dell Publishing Co.: No. 675, Feb, 1956 - No. 880, Feb, 1958 (All photo-c)

Four Color 675-Kinstler-a 8 16 24 52 86 120
Four Color 768-Kinstler-a 6 12 18 43 69 95
Four Color 880 5 10 15 30 48 65

STEVE ROGERS: SUPER-SOLDIER (Captain America - The Heroic Age)
Marvel Comics: Sept, 2010 - No. 4, Dec, 2010 ($3.99, limited series)

1-4-Brubaker-s/Eaglesham-a/Pacheco-c. 1-Back-up rep. of origin from CA #1 ('41) 4.00
Annual 1 (6/11, $3.99) Continued from Uncanny X-Men Annual #3; Roberson-a 4.00

STEVE ROPER
Famous Funnies: Apr, 1948 - No. 5, Dec, 1948

1-Contains 1944 daily newspaper-r 12 24 36 69 97 125
2 9 18 27 47 61 75
3-5 8 16 24 40 50 60

STEVE SAUNDERS SPECIAL AGENT (See Special Agent)

STEVE SAVAGE (See Captain...)

STEVE ZODIAC & THE FIRE BALL XL-5 (TV)
Gold Key: Jan, 1964

10108-401 (#1) 8 16 24 52 86 120

STEVIE (Mazie's boy friend)(Also see Flat-Top, Mazie & Mortie)
Mazie (Magazine Publ.): Nov, 1952 - No. 6, Apr, 1954

1-Teenage humor; Stevie, Mortie & Mazie begin 9 18 27 47 61 75
2-6 6 12 18 31 38 45

STEVIE MAZIE'S BOY FRIEND (See Harvey Hits #5)

STEWART THE RAT (See Eclipse Graphic Album Series)

ST. GEORGE (See listing under Saint...)

STIG'S INFERNO
Vortex/Eclipse: 1985 - No. 7, Mar, 1987 ($1.95, B&W)

1-7 ($1.95) 3.00
Graphic Album (1988, $6.95, B&W, 100 pgs.) 7.00

STING OF THE GREEN HORNET (See The Green Hornet)
Now Comics: June, 1992 - No. 4, 1992 ($2.50, limited series)

1-4: Butler-c/a 3.00
1-4 ($2.75)-Collectors Ed.; polybagged w/poster 4.00

STOKER'S DRACULA (Reprints unfinished Dracula story from 1974-75 with new ending)
Marvel Comics: 2004 - No. 4, May, 2005 ($3.99, B&W)

1-4: 1-Reprints from Dracula Lives! #5-8; Roy Thomas-s/Dick Giordano-a. 2-R/#10,11 & Legion of Monsters #1. 3,4-New story/artwork to finish story. 4-Giordano afterword 4.00
HC (2005, $24.99) r/#1-4; foreward by Thomas; Giordano afterword; bonus art & covers 25.00

STONE
Avalon Studios: Aug, 1998 - No. 4, Apr, 1999 ($2.50, limited series)

1-4-Portacio-a/Haberlin-s 3.00
1-Alternate-c 5.00
2-($14.95) DF Stonechrome Edition 15.00

STONE (Volume 2)
Avalon Studios: Aug, 1999 - No. 4, May, 2000 ($2.50)

1-4-Portacio-a/Haberlin-s 3.00
1-Chrome-c 5.00

STONE COLD STEVE AUSTIN (WWF Wrestling)
Chaos! Comics: Oct, 1999 - No. 4, Feb, 2000 ($2.95)

1-4-Reg. & photo-c; Steven Grant-s 3.00
1-Premium Ed. ($10.00) 10.00
Preview ($5.00) 5.00

STONE PROTECTORS
Harvey Pubications: May, 1994 - No. 3, Sept, 1994

nn (1993, giveaway)(limited distribution, scarce) 6.00
1-3-Ace Novelty action figures 4.00

GD 2.0 | VG 4.0 | FN 6.0 | VF 8.0 | VF/NM 9.0 | NM- 9.2

STONEY BURKE (TV)
Dell Publishing Co.: June-Aug, 1963 - No. 2, Sept-Nov, 1963

1,2-Jack Lord photo-c on both 3 6 9 17 25 32

STONY CRAIG
Pentagon Publishing Co.: 1946 (No #)

nn-Reprints Bell Syndicate's "Sgt. Stony Craig" newspaper strips 8 16 24 40 50 60

STORIES BY FAMOUS AUTHORS ILLUSTRATED (Fast Fiction #1-5)
Seaboard Publ./Famous Authors Ill.: No. 6, Aug, 1950 - No. 13, Mar, 1951

1-Scarlet Pimpernel-Baroness Orczy 27 54 81 160 263 365
2-Capt. Blood-Raphael Sabatini 26 52 78 154 252 350
3-She, by Haggard 30 60 90 177 289 400
4-The 39 Steps-John Buchan 18 36 54 107 169 230
5-Beau Geste-P. C. Wren 18 36 54 107 169 230

NOTE: *The above five issues are exact reprints of Fast Fiction #1-5 except for the title change and new Kiefer covers on #1 and 2. Kiefer c(r)-3-5. The above 5 issues were released before Famous Authors #6.*

6-Macbeth, by Shakespeare; Kiefer art (8/50); used in **SOTI**, pg. 22,143; Kiefer-c; 36 pgs. 24 48 72 142 234 325
7-The Window; Kiefer-c/a; 52 pgs. 18 36 54 107 169 230
8-Hamlet, by Shakespeare; Kiefer-c/a; 36 pgs. 21 42 63 126 206 285
9,10: 9-Nicholas Nickleby, by Dickens; G. Schrotter-a; 52 pgs. 10-Romeo & Juliet, by Shakespeare; Kiefer-c/a; 36 pgs. 18 36 54 107 169 230
11-13: 11-Ben-Hur; Schrotter-a; 52 pgs. 12-La Svengali; Schrotter-a; 36 pgs. 13-Scaramouche; Kiefer-c/a; 36 pgs. 18 36 54 103 162 220

NOTE: *Artwork was prepared/advertised for #14, The Red Badge Of Courage. Gilberton bought out Famous Authors, Ltd. and used that story as C.I. #98. Famous Authors, Ltd. then published the Classics Junior series. The Famous Authors titles were published as part of the regular Classics Ill. Series in Brazil starting in 1952.*

STORIES FROM THE TWILIGHT ZONE
Skylark Pub: Mar, 1979, 68 pgs. (B&W comic digest, 5-1/4x7-5/8")

15405-2: Pfevfer-a, 56 pgs, new comics 3 6 9 18 27 35

STORIES OF ROMANCE (Formerly Meet Miss Bliss)
Atlas Comics (LMC): No. 5, Mar, 1956 - No. 13, Aug, 1957

5-Baker-a? 11 22 33 62 86 110
6-10,12,13 8 16 24 42 54 65
11-Baker, Romita-a; Colletta-c/a 10 20 30 58 79 100

NOTE: *Ann Brewster a-13.* ***Colletta*** *a-9(2), 11; c-5, 11.*

STORM
Marvel Comics: Feb, 1996 - No. 4, May, 1996 ($2.95, limited series)

1-4-Foil-c; Dodson-a(p); Ellis-s: 2-4-Callisto app. 4.00

STORM
Marvel Comics: Apr, 2006 - No. 6, Sept, 2006 ($2.99, limited series)

1-6: Ororo and T'Challa meet as teens; Eric Jerome Dickey-s 3.00
HC (2007, $19.99, dustjacket) r/#1-6 20.00
SC (2008, $14.99) r/#1-6 15.00

STORMBREAKER: THE SAGA OF BETA RAY BILL (Also see Thor)
Marvel Comics: Mar, 2005 - No. 6, Aug, 2005 ($2.99, limited series)

1-6-Oeming & Berman-s/DiVito-a; Galactus app. 6-Spider-Man app. 3.00
TPB (2006, $16.99) r/#1-6 17.00

STORMING PARADISE
DC Comics (WildStorm): Sept, 2008 - No. 6, Aug, 2009 ($2.99, limited series)

1-6-WWII invasion of Japan; Dixon-s/Guice-a/c 3.00
TPB (2009, $19.99) r/#1-6 20.00

STORM SHADOW (G.I. Joe character)
Devil's Due Publishing: May, 2007 - No. 7, Nov, 2007 ($3.50)

1-7-Larry Hama-s 3.50

STORMWATCH (Also see The Authority)
Image Comics (WildStorm Prod.): May, 1993 - No. 50, Jul, 1997 ($1.95/$2.50)

1-8,0,9-36: 1-Intro StormWatch (Battalion, Diva, Winter, Fuji, & Hellstrike); 1st app. Weatherman; Jim Lee-c & part scripts; Lee plots in all. 1-Gold edition.1-3-Includes coupon for limited edition StormWatch trading card #00 by Lee. 3-1st brief app. Backlash. 0-($2.50)-Polybagged w/card; 1st full app. Backlash. 9-(4/94, $2.50)-Intro Defile. 10-(6/94),11,12-Both (8/94). 13,14-(9/94). 15-(10/94). 21-Reads #1 on-c. 22-Direct Market; Wildstorm Rising Pt. 9, bound-in card. 23-Spartan joins team. 25-(6/94, June 1995 on-c, $2.50). 35-Fire From Heaven Pt. 5. 36-Fire From Heaven Pt. 12 3.00
10-Alternate Portacio-c, see Deathblow #5 3.00
22-($1.95)-Newsstand, Wildstorm Rising Pt. 9 3.00
37-(7/96, $3.50, 38 pgs.)-Weatherman forms new team; 1st app. Jenny Sparks, Jack Hawksmoor & Rose Tattoo; Warren Ellis scripts begin; Justice League #1-c/swipe 4.00

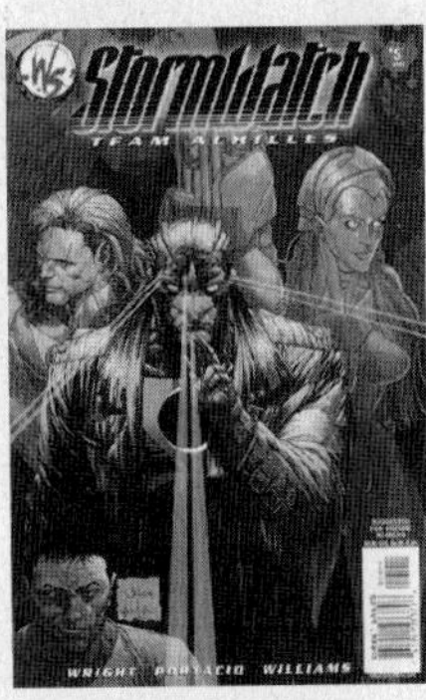

StormWatch: Team Achilles #5 © WSP

Straight Arrow #4 © ME

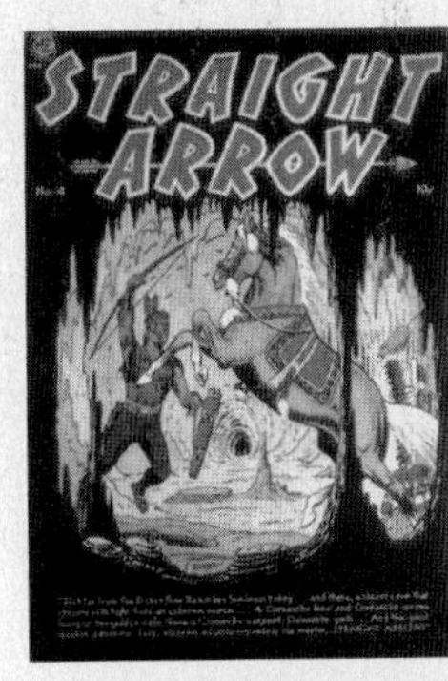

Strange Adventures #19 © DC

38-49: 44-Three covers. 3.00
50-($4.50) 4.50
Special 1 ,2(1/94, 5/95, $3.50, 52 pgs.) 4.00
Sourcebook 1 (1/94, $2.50) 3.00
Forces of Nature ('99, $14.95, TPB) r/V1 #37-42 15.00
Lightning Strikes ('00, $14.95, TPB) r/V1 #43-47 15.00

STORMWATCH (Also see The Authority)
Image Comics (WildStorm): Oct, 1997 - No. 11, Sept, 1998 ($2.50)

1-Ellis-s/Jimenez-a(p); two covers by Bennett 3.00
1-($3.50)-Voyager Pack bagged w/Gen 13 preview 4.00
2-4: 4-1st app. Midnighter and Apollo 3.00
5-11: 7,8-Freefall app. 9-Gen13 & DV8 app. 3.00
A Finer World ('99, $14.95, TPB) r/V2 #4-9 15.00
Change or Die ('99, $14.95, TPB) r/V1 #48-50 & V2 #1-3 15.00
Final Orbit ('01, $9.95, TPB) r/V2 #10,11 & WildC.A.T.S./Aliens; Hitch-c 10.00

STORMWATCHER
Eclipse Comics (Acme Press): Apr, 1989 - No. 4, Dec, 1989 ($2.00, B&W)

1-4 3.00

STORMWATCH: P.H.D. (Post Human Division)
DC Comics (WildStorm): Jan, 2007 - No. 24, Jan, 2010 ($2.99)

1-24: 1-Two covers by Mahnke & Hairsine; Gage-s/Mahnke-a. 2-Var-c by Dell'Otto 3.00
...: Armageddon 1 (2/08, $2.99) Gage-s/Fernández-a/McKone-c 3.00
TPB (2007, $17.99) r/#1-4,6,7 & story from Worldstorm #1 18.00
... Book Two TPB (2008, $17.99) r/#5,8-12; sketch pages and concept art 18.00
... Book Three TPB (2009, $17.99) r/#13-19 18.00

STORMWATCH: TEAM ACHILLES
DC Comics (WildStorm): Sept, 2002 - No. 23, Aug, 2004 ($2.95)

1-8: 1-Two covers by Portacio; Portacio-a/Wright-s. 5,6-The Authority app. 3.00
9-23: 9-Back-up preview of The Authority: High Stakes pt. 1 3.00
TPB (2003, $14.95) r/Wizard Preview and #1-6; Portacio art pages 15.00
Book 2 (2004, $14.95) r/#7-11 & short story from Eye of the Storm Annual 15.00

STORMY (Disney) (Movie)
Dell Publishing Co.: No. 537, Feb, 1954

Four Color 537 (...the Thoroughbred)-on top 2/3 of each page; Pluto story on bottom 1/3
5 10 15 30 48 65

STORY OF JESUS (See Classics Illustrated Special Issue)

STORY OF MANKIND, THE (Movie)
Dell Publishing Co.: No. 851, Jan, 1958

Four Color 851-Vincent Price/Hedy Lamarr photo-c 7 14 21 47 76 105

STORY OF MARTHA WAYNE, THE
Argo Publ.: April, 1956

1-Newspaper strip-r 6 12 18 29 36 42

STORY OF RUTH, THE
Dell Publishing Co.: No. 1144, Nov-Jan, 1961 (Movie)

Four Color 1144-Photo-c 8 16 24 58 97 135

STORY OF THE COMMANDOS, THE (Combined Operations)
Long Island Independent: 1943 (15¢, B&W, 68 pgs.) (Distr. by Gilberton)

nn-All text (no comics); photos & illustrations; ad for Classic Comics on back cover (Rare)
32 64 96 192 314 435

STORY OF THE GLOOMY BUNNY, THE (See March of Comics #9)

STRAIGHT ARROW (Radio)(See Best of the West & Great Western)
Magazine Enterprises: Feb-Mar, 1950 - No. 55, Mar, 1956 (All 36 pgs.)

1-Straight Arrow (alias Steve Adams) & his palomino Fury begin; 1st mention of Sundown Valley & the Secret Cave 46 92 138 290 488 685
2-Red Hawk begins (1st app?) by Powell (origin), ends #55
23 46 69 136 223 310
3-Frazetta-c 31 62 93 182 296 410
4,5: 4-Secret Cave-c 21 42 63 122 199 275
6-10 17 34 51 100 158 215
11-Classic story "The Valley of Time", with an ancient civilization made of gold
22 44 66 128 209 290
12-19 14 28 42 82 121 160
20-Origin Straight Arrow's Shield 16 32 48 92 144 195
21-Origin Fury 19 38 57 109 172 235
22-Frazetta-c 25 50 75 147 241 335
23,25-30: 25-Secret Cave-c. 28-Red Hawk meets The Vikings
11 22 33 62 86 110
24-Classic story "The Dragons of Doom!" with prehistoric pteradactyls
14 28 42 82 121 160
31-38: 36-Red Hawk drug story by Powell 10 20 30 54 72 90
39-Classic story "The Canyon Beast", with a dinosaur egg hatching a Tyranosaurus Rex
14 28 42 76 108 140
40-Classic story "Secret of The Spanish Specters", with Conquistadors' lost treasure
11 22 33 64 90 115
41,42,44-54: 45-Secret Cave-c 9 18 27 50 65 80
43-Intro & 1st app. Blaze, S. Arrow's Warrior dog 10 20 30 58 79 100
55-Last issue 11 22 33 62 86 110

NOTE: ***Fred Meagher** a 1-55; c-1, 2, 4-21, 23-55. **Powell** a 2-55. **Whitney** a-1. Many issues advertise the radio premiums associated with Straight Arrow.*

STRAIGHT ARROW'S FURY (Also see A-1 Comics)
Magazine Enterprises: No. 119, 1954 (one-shot)

A-1 119-Origin; Fred Meagher-c/a 15 30 45 85 130 175

STRANDED
Virgin Comics: Dec, 2007 - No. 5, June, 2008 ($2.99)

1-5-Carey-s/Kotian-a. 1-Silvestri-c. 2-5-Moeller-c 3.00

STRANGE (Tales You'll Never Forget)
Ajax-Farrell Publ. (Four Star Comic Corp.): March, 1957 - No. 6, May, 1958

1 21 42 63 126 206 285
2-Censored r/Haunted Thrills 14 28 42 76 108 140
3-6 10 20 30 58 79 100

STRANGE (Dr. Strange)
Marvel Comics (Marvel Knghts): Nov, 2004 - No. 6, July, 2005 ($3.50)

1-6-Straczynski & Barnes-s/Peterson-a; Dr. Strange's origin retold 3.50
...: Beginnings and Endings TPB (2006, $17.99) r/#1-6 18.00

STRANGE (Dr. Strange)
Marvel Comics: Jan, 2010 - No. 4, Apr, 2010 ($3.99, limited series)

1-4-Waid-s/Rios-a/Coker-c 4.00

STRANGE ADVENTURES
DC Comics: July/Aug 1950

nn - Ashcan comic, not distributed to newsstands, only for in-house use. Cover art is All Star Comics #47 with interior being Detective Comics #140. A second example has the interior of Detective Comics #146. A third example has an unidentified issue of Detective Comics as the interior. This is the only ashcan with multiple interiors. A FN+ copy sold for $1,000 in 2007.

STRANGE ADVENTURES
National Periodical Publ.: Aug-Sept, 1950 - No. 244, Oct-Nov, 1973 (No. 1-12: 52 pgs.)

1-Adaptation of "Destination Moon"; preview of movie w/photo-c from movie (also see Fawcett Movie Comic #2); adapt. of Edmond Hamilton's "Chris KL-99" in #1-3; Darwin Jones begins 219 438 657 1916 3908 5900
2 98 196 294 833 1692 2550
3,4 68 136 204 578 1177 1775
5-8,10: 7-Origin Kris KL-99 59 118 177 502 1014 1525
9-(6/51)-Origin/1st app. Captain Comet (c/story) 137 274 411 1165 2358 3550
11-20: 12,13,17,18-Toth-a. 14-Robot-c 39 78 117 312 619 925
21-30: 28-Atomic explosion panel. 30-Robot-c 33 66 99 254 502 750
31,34-38 30 60 90 231 458 685
32,33-Krigstein-a 31 62 93 239 470 700
39-Ill. in **SOTI** "Treating police contemptuously" (top right)
34 68 102 267 526 785
40-49-Last Capt. Comet; not in 45,47,48 29 58 87 218 439 660
50-53-Last precode issue (2/55) 22 44 66 159 317 475
54-70 17 34 51 118 242 365
71-99 13 26 39 94 185 275
100 14 28 42 99 200 300
101-110: 104-Space Museum begins by Sekowsky 11 22 33 77 144 210
111-116,118,119: 114-Star Hawkins begins, ends #185; Heath-a in Wood E.C. style
11 22 33 75 138 200
117-(6/60)-Origin/1st app. Atomic Knights. 45 90 135 360 730 1100
120-2nd app. Atomic Knights 21 42 63 150 300 450
121,122,125,127,128,130,131,133,134: 134-Last 10¢ issue
10 20 30 69 122 175
123,126-3rd & 4th app. Atomic Knights 13 26 39 89 170 250
124-Intro/origin Faceless Creature 10 20 30 73 134 195
129,132,135,138,141,147-Atomic Knights app. 10 20 30 73 134 195
136,137,139,140,143,145,146,148,149,151,152,154,155,157-159: 136-Robot cover. 159-Star Rovers app.; Gil Kane/Anderson-a. 8 16 24 54 90 125
142-2nd app. Faceless Creature 9 18 27 63 107 150
144-Only Atomic Knights-c (by M. Anderson) 11 22 33 77 144 210

Strange Adventures #231 © DC

Strange Confessions #2 © Z-D

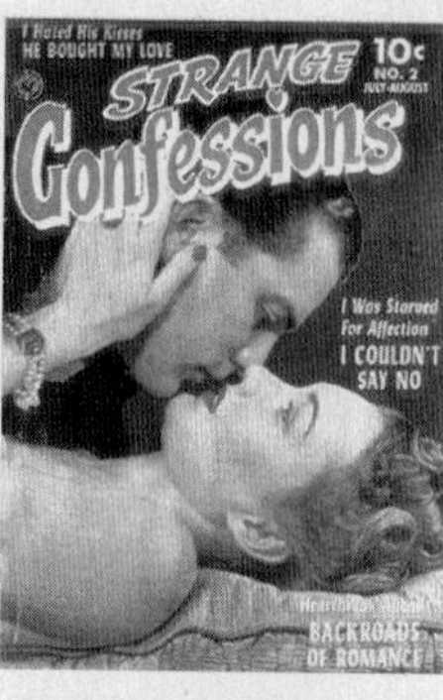

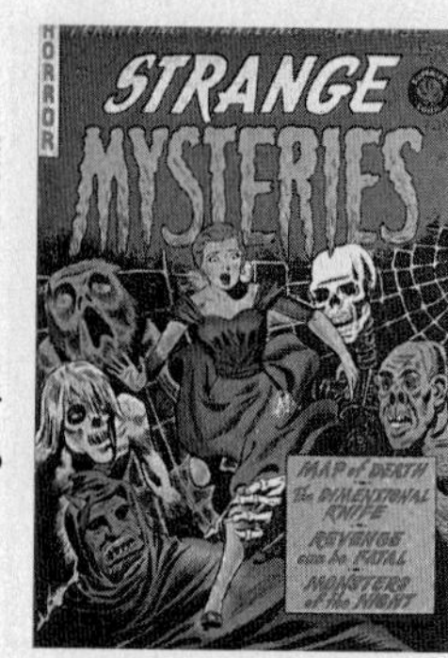

Strange Mysteries #10 © SUPR

GD VG FN VF VF/NM NM-
2.0 4.0 6.0 8.0 9.0 9.2

150,153,156,160: Atomic Knights in each. 150-Greytone-c. 153-(6/63)-3rd app. Faceless Creature; atomic explosion-c. 160-Last Atomic Knights
9 18 27 60 100 140
161-179: 161-Last Space Museum. 163-Star Rovers app. 170-Infinity-c. 177-Intro/origin Immortal Man 7 14 21 45 73 100
180-Origin/1st app. Animal Man 15 30 45 104 212 320
181-183,185-189: 187-Intro/origin The Enchantress 6 12 18 39 62 85
184-2nd app. Animal Man by Gil Kane 10 20 30 71 128 185
190-1st app. Animal Man in costume 12 24 36 87 164 240
191-194,196-200,202-204 5 10 15 35 55 75
195-1st full app. Animal Man 7 14 21 50 83 115
201-Last Animal Man; 2nd full app. 6 12 18 41 66 90
205-(10/67)-Intro/origin Deadman by Infantino & begin series, ends #216
13 26 39 94 185 275
206-Neal Adams-a begins 11 22 33 75 138 200
207-210 10 20 30 68 119 170
211-216: 211-Space Museum-r. 216-(1-2/69)-Deadman story finally concludes in Brave & the Bold #86 (10-11/69); secret message panel by Neal Adams (pg. 13); tribute to Steranko
9 18 27 61 103 145
217-r/origin & 1st app. Adam Strange from Showcase #17, begin-r; Atomic Knights-r begin
3 6 9 16 23 30
218-221,223-225: 218-Last 12¢ issue. 225-Last 15¢ issue
3 6 9 14 20 26
222-New Adam Strange story; Kane/Anderson-a 3 6 9 21 32 42
226,227,230-236-(68-52 pgs.): 226, 227-New Adam Strange text story w/illos by Anderson (8,6 pgs.) 231-Last Atomic Knights-r. 235-JLA-c/s 3 6 9 14 20 26
228,229 (68 pgs.) 3 6 9 17 25 32
237-243 2 4 6 10 14 18
244-Last issue 2 4 6 11 16 20

NOTE: ***Neal Adams*** *a-206-216; c-207-218, 228, 235.* ***Anderson*** *a-8-52, 94, 96, 99, 115, 117, 119-163, 217r, 218r, 222, 223-225r, 226, 229r, 242i(r); c-18, 19, 21, 23, 24, 27, 30, 32-44(most); c/r-157i, 190i, 217-224, 228-231, 233, 235-239, 241-243.* ***Ditko*** *a-188, 189.* ***Drucker*** *a-42, 43, 45.* ***Elias*** *a-212.* ***Finlay*** *a-2, 3, 6, 7, 210r, 229r.* ***Giunta*** *a-237r.* ***Heath*** *a-116.* ***Infantino*** *a-10-101, 106-151, 154, 157-163, 180, 190, 218-221r, 223-244p(r); c-50; c(r)-190p, 197, 199-211, 218-221, 223-244.* ***Kaluta*** *c-238, 240.* ***Gil Kane*** *a-8-116, 124, 125, 130, 138, 146-157, 173-186, 204r, 222r, 227-231r; c(p)-11-17, 25, 154, 157.* ***Kubert*** *a-55(2 pgs.), 226; c-219, 220, 225-227, 232, 234.* ***Moreira*** *c-26, 28, 29, 71.* ***Morrow*** *c-230.* ***Mortimer*** *c-8.* ***Powell*** *a-4.* ***Sekowsky*** *a-71p, 97-162p, 217p(r), 218p(r); c-206, 217-219r.* ***Simon & Kirby*** *a-2r (2 pgs)* ***Sparling*** *a-201.* ***Toth*** *a-8, 12, 13, 17-19.* ***Wood*** *a-154i. Atomic Knights in #117, 120, 123, 126, 129, 132, 135, 138, 141, 144, 147, 150, 153, 156, 160. Atomic Knights reprints by* ***Anderson*** *in 217-221, 223-231. Chris KL99 in 1-3, 5, 7, 9, 11, 15. Capt. Comet covers-9-14, 17-19, 24, 26, 27, 32-44.*

STRANGE ADVENTURES
DC Comics (Vertigo): Nov, 1999 - No. 4, Feb, 2000 ($2.50, limited series)
1-4: 1-Bolland-c; art by Bolland, Gibbons, Quitely 3.00

STRANGE ADVENTURES
DC Comics: May, 2009 - No. 8, Dec, 2009 ($3.99, limited series)
1-8: 1-Starlin-s in all; Adam Strange, Capt. Comet, Bizarro & Prince Gavyn app. 4.00
TPB (2010, $19.99) r/#1-8; cover gallery 20.00

STRANGE AS IT SEEMS (See Famous Funnies-A Carnival of Comics, Feature Funnies #1, The John Hix Scrap Book & Peanuts)

STRANGE AS IT SEEMS
United Features Syndicate: 1939
Single Series 9, 1, 2 34 68 102 199 325 450

STRANGE ATTRACTORS
RetroGraphix: 1993 - No. 15, Feb, 1997 ($2.50, B&W)
1-15: 1-(5/93), 2-(8/93), 3-(11/93), 4-(2/94) 3.00
Volume One-($14.95, trade paperback)-r/#1-7 15.00

STRANGE ATTRACTORS: MOON FEVER
Caliber Comics: Feb, 1997 - No. 3, June, 1997 ($2.95, B&W, mini-series)
1-3 3.00

STRANGE COMBAT TALES
Marvel Comics (Epic Comics): Oct, 1993 - No. 4, Jan, 1994 ($2.50, limited series)
1-4 3.00

STRANGE CONFESSIONS
Ziff-Davis Publ. Co.: Jan-Mar (Spring on-c), 1952 - No. 4, Fall, 1952 (All have photo-c)
1(Scarce)-Kinstler-a 54 108 162 343 574 825
2(Scarce, 7-8/52) 39 78 117 234 385 535
3(Scarce, 9-10/52)-#3 on-c, #2 on inside; Reformatory girl story; photo-c
39 78 117 231 378 525
4(Scarce) 37 74 111 222 361 500

STRANGE DAYS
Eclipse Comics: Oct, 1984 - No. 3, Apr, 1985 ($1.75, Baxter paper)
1-3: Freakwave, Johnny Nemo, & Paradax from Vanguard Illustrated; nudity, violence & strong language 3.00

STRANGE DAYS (Movie)
Marvel Comics: Dec, 1995 ($5.95, squarebound, one-shot)
1-Adaptation of film 6.00

STRANGE FANTASY (Eerie Tales of Suspense!)(Formerly Rocketman #1)
Ajax-Farrell: Aug, 1952 - No. 14, Oct-Nov, 1954
2(#1, 8/52)-Jungle Princess story; Kamenish-a; reprinted from Ellery Queen #1
48 96 144 302 514 725
2(10/52)-No Black Cat or Rulah; Bakerish, Kamenish-a; hypo/meathook-c
43 86 129 271 461 650
3-Rulah story, called Pulah 40 80 120 242 401 560
4-Rocket Man app. (2/53) 39 78 117 231 378 525
5,6,8,10,12,14 29 58 87 170 278 385
7-Madam Satan/Slave story 39 78 117 231 378 525
9(w/Black Cat), 9(w/Boy's Ranch; S&K-a), 9(w/War)(A rebinding of Harvey interiors; not publ. by Ajax) 34 68 102 206 336 465
9-Regular issue; Steve Ditko's 3rd published work (tied with Captain 3D)
47 94 141 296 498 700
11-Jungle story 36 72 108 216 351 485
13-Bondage-c; Rulah (Kolah) story 36 72 108 216 351 485

STRANGE GALAXY
Eerie Publications: V1#8, Feb, 1971 - No. 11, Aug, 1971 (B&W, magazine)
V1#8-Reprints-c/Fantastic V19#3 (2/70) (a pulp) 4 8 12 22 34 45
9-11 3 6 9 18 27 35

STRANGE GIRL
Image Comics: June, 2005 - No. 18, Sept, 2007 ($2.95/$2.99/$3.50)
1-12: 1-Rick Remender-s/Eric Nguyen-a 3.00
13-18-($3.50) 3.50
... Vol. 1: Girl Afraid TPB (2005, $12.99) r/#1-4; sketch pages and pin-ups 13.00

STRANGE JOURNEY
America's Best (Steinway Publ.) (Ajax/Farrell): Sept, 1957 - No. 4, Jun, 1958 (Farrell reprints)
1 20 40 60 114 182 250
2-4: 2-Flying saucer-c. 3-Titanic-c 15 30 45 83 124 165

STRANGE LOVE (See Fox Giants)

STRANGE MYSTERIES
Superior/Dynamic Publications: Sept, 1951 - No. 21, Jan, 1955
1-Kamenish-a & horror stories begin 68 136 204 435 743 1050
2 39 78 117 231 378 525
3-5 36 72 108 216 351 485
6-8 32 64 96 188 307 425
9-Bondage 3-D effect-c 39 78 117 231 378 525
10-Used in **SOTI**, pg. 181 30 60 90 177 289 400
11-18 24 48 72 142 234 325
19-r/Journey Into Fear #1; cover is a splash from one story; Baker-r(2)
25 50 75 150 245 340
20,21-Reprints; 20-r/#1 with new-c 19 38 57 111 176 240

STRANGE MYSTERIES
I. W. Enterprises/Super Comics: 1963 - 1964
I.W. Reprint #9; Rulah-r/Spook #28; Disbrow-a 3 6 9 20 30 40
Super Reprint #10-12,15-17(1963-64): 10,11-r/Strange #2,1. 12-r/Tales of Horror #5 (3/53) less-c. 15-r/Dark Mysteries #23. 16-r/The Dead Who Walk. 17-r/Dark Mysteries #22
3 6 9 20 30 40
Super Reprint #18-r/Witchcraft #1; Kubert-a 3 6 9 20 30 40

STRANGE PLANETS
I. W. Enterprises/Super Comics: 1958; 1963-64
I.W. Reprint #1(nd)-Reprints E. C. Incredible S/F #30 plus-c/Strange Worlds #3
6 12 18 39 62 85
I.W. Reprint #9-Orlando/Wood-r/Strange Worlds #4; cover-r from Flying Saucers #1
7 14 21 49 80 110
Super Reprint #10-Wood-r (22 pg.) from Space Detective #1; cover-r/Attack on Planet Mars
7 14 21 49 80 110
Super Reprint #11-Wood-r (25 pg.) from An Earthman on Venus
8 16 24 54 90 125
Super Reprint #12-Orlando-r/Rocket to the Moon 7 14 21 49 80 110
Super Reprint #15-Reprints Journey Into Unknown Worlds #8; Heath, Colan-r
4 8 12 28 44 60
Super Reprint #16-Reprints Avon's Strange Worlds #6; Kinstler, Check-a

Strangers #8 © MAL

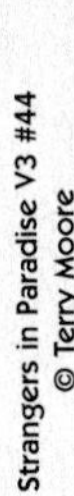
Strangers in Paradise V3 #44 © Terry Moore

Strange Suspense Stories #3 © FAW

GD VG FN VF VF/NM NM-
2.0 4.0 6.0 8.0 9.0 9.2

5 10 15 30 48 65
Super Reprint #18-r/Great Exploits #1 (Daring Adventures #6); Space Busters, Explorer Joe, The Son of Robin Hood; Krigstein-a 4 8 12 24 37 50

STRANGERS
Image Comics: Mar, 2003 - No. 6, Sept, 2003 ($2.95)
1-6-Randy & Jean-Marc Lofficier-s; two covers. 2-Nexus back-up story 3.00

STRANGERS, THE
Malibu Comics (Ultraverse): June, 1993 - No. 24, May, 1995 ($1.95/$2.50)
1-4,6-12,14-20: 1-1st app. The Strangers; has coupon for Ultraverse Premiere #0; 1st app. the Night Man (not in costume). 2-Polybagged w/trading card. 7-Break-Thru x-over. 8-2 pg. origin Solution. 12-Silver foil logo; wraparound-c. 17-Rafferty app. 3.00
1-With coupon missing 2.00
1-Full cover holographic edition, 1st of kind w/Hardcase #1 & Prime #1 6.00
1-Ultra 5000 limited silver foil 4.00
4-($2.50)-Newsstand edition bagged w/card 4.00
5-($2.50, 52 pgs.)-Rune flip-c/story by B. Smith (3 pgs.); The Mighty Magnor 1 pg. strip by Aragones; 3-pg. Night Man preview 4.00
13-($3.50, 68 pgs.)-Mantra app.; flip book w/Ultraverse Premiere #4 4.00
21-24 ($2.50) 3.00
...:The Pilgrim Conundrum Saga (1/95, $3.95, 68pgs.) 4.00

STRANGERS IN PARADISE
Antarctic Press: Nov, 1993 - No. 3, Feb, 1994 ($2.75, B&W, limited series)
1 5 10 15 30 48 65
1-2nd/3rd prints 1 2 3 5 6 8
2 (2300 printed) 4 8 12 22 34 45
3 3 6 9 16 23 30
Trade paperback (Antarctic Press, $6.95)-Red -c (5000 print run) 10.00
Trade paperback (Abstract Studios, $6.95)-Red-c (2000 print run) 15.00
Trade paperback (Abstract Studios, $6.95, 1st-4th printing)-Blue- 7.00
Hardcover ('98, $29.95) includes first draft pages 30.00
Gold Reprint Series ($2.75) 1-3-r/#1-3 3.00

STRANGERS IN PARADISE
Abstract Studios: Sept, 1994 - No. 14, July, 1996 ($2.75, B&W)
1 2 4 6 9 13 16
1,3- 2nd printings 4.00
2,3: 2-Color dream sequence 1 2 3 5 6 8
4-10 4.00
4-6-2nd printings 3.00
11-14: 14-The Letters of Molly & Poo 4.00
Gold Reprint Series ($2.75) 1-13-r/#1-13 3.00
I Dream Of You ($16.95, TPB) r/#1-9 17.00
It's a Good Life ($8.95, TPB) r/#10-13 9.00

STRANGERS IN PARADISE (Volume Three)
Homage Comics #1-8/Abstract Studios #9-on: Oct, 1996 - No. 90, May, 2007 ($2.75-$2.99, color #1-5, B&W #6-on)
1-Terry Moore-c/s/a in all; dream seq. by Jim Lee-a 5.00
1-Jim Lee variant-c 1 2 3 6 7 8
2-5 4.00
6-16: 6-Return to B&W. 13-15-High school flashback. 16-Xena Warrior Princess parody; two covers 3.00
17-89: 33-Color issue. 46-Molly Lane. 49-Molly & Poo. 86-David dies 3.00
90-Last issue; 3 covers of Katchoo, Francine and David forming a triptych 3.00
...Lyrics and Poems (2/99) 3.00
...Source Book (2003, $2.95) Background on characters & story arcs, checklists 3.00
Brave New World ('02, $8.95, TPB) r/#44,45,47,48 9.00
Child of Rage ($15.95, TPB) r/#31-38 16.00
David's Story (6/04, $8.95, TPB) r/#61-63 9.00
Ever After ('07, $15.95, TPB) r/#83-90 16.00
Flower to Flame ('03, $15.95, TPB) r/#55-60 16.00
Heart in Hand ('03, $12.95, TPB) r/#50-54 13.00
High School ('98, $8.95, TPB) r/#13-16 9.00
Immortal Enemies ('98, $14.95, TPB) r/#6-12 15.00
Love & Lies (2006, $14.95, TPB)r/#77-82 15.00
Love Me Tender ($12.95, TPB) r/#1-5 in B&W w/ color Lee seq. 13.00
Molly & Poo (2005, $8.95, TPB)r/#46,49,73 9.00
My Other Life ($14.95, TPB) r/#25-30 15.00
Pocket Book 1-5 ($17.95, 5 1/2" x 8", TPB) 1-r/Vol.1 & 2. 2-r/#1-17 in B&W. 3-r/#18-24,26-32,34-38. 4-r/#41-45,47,48,50-60. 5-r/#46,49,61-76 18.00
Sanctuary ($15.95, TPB) r/#17-24 16.00
Tattoo ($14.95, TPB) r/#70-76; sketch pages and fan tattoo photos 15.00
Tomorrow Now (11/04, $14.95, TPB) r/#64-69 15.00

GD VG FN VF VF/NM NM-
2.0 4.0 6.0 8.0 9.0 9.2

Tropic of Desire ($12.95, TPB) r/#39-43 13.00
The Complete... : Volume 3 Part 1 HC ($49.95) r/#1-12 50.00
The Complete... : Volume 3 Part 2 HC ($49.95) r/#13-15,17-25 50.00
The Complete... : Volume 3 Part 3 HC ('01, $49.95) r/#26-38 50.00
The Complete... : Volume 3 Part 4 HC ('02, $39.95) r/#39-46,49 40.00
The Complete... : Volume 3 Part 5 HC ('03, $49.95) r/#47,48,50-57 50.00
The Complete... : Volume 3 Part 6 HC ('04, $49.95) r/#58-69 50.00
The Complete... : Volume 3 Part 7 HC ('06, $49.95) r/#70-80 50.00

STRANGE SPORTS STORIES (See Brave & the Bold #45-49, DC Special, and DC Super Stars #10)
National Periodical Publications: Sept-Oct, 1973 - No. 6, July-Aug, 1974
1 3 6 9 16 23 30
2-6: 2-Swan/Anderson-a 2 4 6 9 13 16

STRANGE STORIES FROM ANOTHER WORLD (Unknown World #1)
Fawcett Publications: No. 2, Aug, 1952 - No. 5, Feb, 1953
2-Saunders painted-c 50 100 150 315 533 750
3-5-Saunders painted-c 39 78 117 240 395 550

STRANGE STORIES OF SUSPENSE (Rugged Action #1-4)
Atlas Comics (CSI): No. 5, Oct, 1955 - No. 16, Aug, 1957
5(#1) 41 82 123 250 418 585
6,9 26 52 78 154 252 350
7-E. C. swipe cover/Vault of Horror #32 27 54 81 158 259 360
8-Morrow/Williamson-a; Pakula-a 28 56 84 165 270 375
10-Crandall, Torres, Meskin-a 27 54 81 158 259 360
11-13: 12-Torres, Pakula-a. 13-E.C. art swipes 22 44 66 132 216 300
14-16: 14-Williamson/Mayo-a. 15-Krigstein-a. 16-Fox, Powell-a
24 48 72 142 234 325
NOTE: ***Everett** a-6, 7, 13; c-8, 9, 11-14. **Forte** a-12, 16. **Heath** a-5. **Maneely** c-5. **Morisi** a-11. **Morrow** a-13. **Powell** a-8. **Sale** a-11. **Severin** c-7. **Wildey** a-14.*

STRANGE STORY (Also see Front Page)
Harvey Publications: June-July, 1946 (52 pgs.)
1-The Man in Black Called Fate by Powell 32 64 96 192 314 435

STRANGE SUSPENSE STORIES (Lawbreakers Suspense Stories #10-15; This Is Suspense #23-26; Captain Atom V1#78 on)
Fawcett Publications/Charlton Comics No. 16 on: 6/52 - No. 5, 2/53; No. 16, 1/54 - No. 22, 11/54; No. 27, 10/55 - No. 77, 10/65; V3#1, 10/67 - V1#9, 9/69
1-(Fawcett)-Powell, Sekowsky-a 84 168 252 538 919 1300
2-George Evans horror story 49 98 147 309 522 735
3-5 (2/53)-George Evans horror stories 41 82 123 250 418 585
16(1-2/54)-Formerly Lawbreakers S.S. 30 60 90 177 289 400
17,21: 21-Shuster-a 24 48 72 140 230 320
18-E.C. swipe/HOF 7; Ditko-c/a(2) 40 80 120 242 401 560
19-Ditko electric chair-c; Ditko-a 54 108 162 343 574 825
20-Ditko-c/a(2) 40 80 120 242 401 560
22(11/54)-Ditko-c, Shuster-a; last pre-code issue; becomes This Is Suspense
36 72 108 216 351 485
27(10/55)-(Formerly This Is Suspense #26) 15 30 45 86 133 180
28-30,38 12 24 36 69 97 125
31-33,35,37,40-Ditko-c/a(2-3 each) 21 42 63 126 206 285
34-Story of ruthless business man, Wm. B. Gaines; Ditko-c/a
47 94 141 296 498 700
36-(15¢, 68 pgs.); Ditko-a(4) 26 52 78 154 252 350
39,41,52,53-Ditko-a 19 38 57 111 176 240
42-44,46,49,54-60 6 12 18 39 62 85
45,47,48,50,51-Ditko-c/a 13 26 39 92 179 265
61-74 5 10 15 30 48 65
75(6/65)-Reprints origin/1st app. Captain Atom by Ditko from Space Advs. #33; r/Severin-a/Space Advs. #24 (75-77: 12¢ issues) 11 22 33 77 144 210
76,77-Captain Atom-r by Ditko/Space Advs. 6 12 18 43 69 95
V3#1(10/67): 12¢ issues begin 3 6 9 20 30 40
V1#2-Ditko-c/a; atom bomb-c 3 6 9 20 30 40
V1#3-9: 3-8-All 12¢ issues. 9-15¢ issue 2 4 6 13 18 22
NOTE: ***Alascia** a-19. **Aparo** a-60, V3#1, 2, 4; c-V1#4, 8, 9. **Baily** a-1-3; c-2, 5. **Evans** c-3, 4. **Giordano** c-16, 17p, 24p, 25p. **Montes/Bache** c-66. **Powell** a-4. **Shuster** a-19, 21. **Marcus Swayze** a-27.*

STRANGE TALES (...Featuring Warlock #178-181; Doctor Strange #169 on)
Atlas (CCPC #1-67/ZPC #68-79/VPI #80-85)/Marvel #86(7/61) on:
June, 1951 - No. 168, May, 1968; No. 169, Sept, 1973 - No. 188, Nov, 1976
1-Horror/weird stories begin 314 628 942 2198 3849 5500
2 110 220 330 704 1202 1700
3,5: 3-Atom bomb panels 84 168 252 538 919 1300
4-Cosmic eyeball story "The Evil Eye" 87 174 261 553 952 1350

Strange Tales #28 © MAR

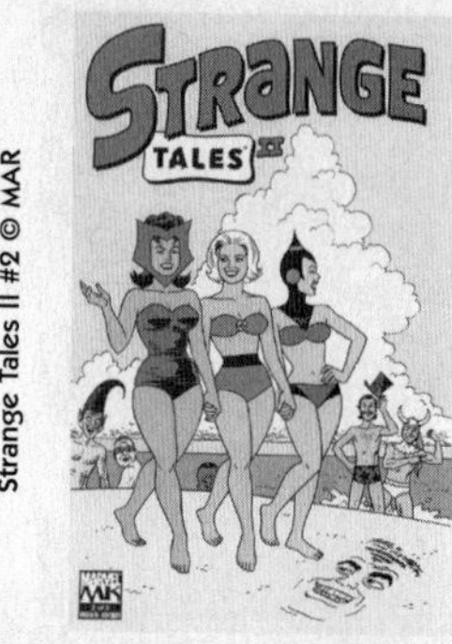

Strange Tales II #2 © MAR

Strange Terrors #3 © STJ

GD VG FN VF VF/NM NM-
2.0 4.0 6.0 8.0 9.0 9.2

6-9: 6-Heath-c/a. 7-Colan-a 60 120 180 381 653 925
10-Krigstein-a 61 122 183 390 670 950
11-14,16-20 43 86 129 271 461 650
15-Krigstein-a 44 88 132 277 469 660
21,23-27,29-34: 27-Atom bomb panels. 33-Davis-a. 34-Last pre-code issue (2/55) 39 78 117 231 378 525
22-Krigstein, Forte/Fox-a 39 78 117 234 385 535
28-Jack Katz story used in Senate Investigation report, pgs. 7 & 169 39 78 117 240 395 550
35-41,43,44: 37-Vampire story by Colan 21 42 63 150 300 450
42,45,59,61-Krigstein-a; #61 (2/58) 21 42 63 153 307 460
46-57,60: 51-(10/56) 1st S.A. issue. 53,56-Crandall-a. 60-(8/57) 20 40 60 140 283 425
58,64-Williamson-a in each, with Mayo-#58 20 40 60 144 290 435
62,63,65,66: 62-Torres-a. 66-Crandall-a 19 38 57 139 280 420
67-Prototype ish. (Quicksilver) 22 44 66 159 317 475
68,71,72,74,77,80: Ditko/Kirby-a in #67-80 21 42 63 150 300 450
69,70,73,75,76,78,79: 69-Prototype ish. (Prof. X). 70-Prototype ish. (Giant Man). 73-Prototype ish. (Ant-Man). 75-Prototype ish. (Iron Man). 76-Prototype ish. (Human Torch). 78-Prototype ish. (Ant-Man). 79-Prototype ish. (Dr. Strange) (12/60) 24 48 72 175 350 525
81-83,85-88,90,91-Ditko/Kirby-a in all: 86-Robot-c. 90-(11/61)-Atom bomb blast panel 20 40 60 140 283 425
84-Prototype ish. (Magneto)(5/61); has powers like Magneto of X-Men, but two years earlier; Ditko/Kirby-a 23 46 69 168 334 500
89-1st app. Fin Fang Foom (10/61) by Kirby 48 96 144 392 796 1200
92-Prototype ish. (Ancient One & Ant-Man); last 10¢ issue 21 42 63 150 300 450
93,95,96,98-100: Kirby-a 18 36 54 131 266 400
94-Creature similar to The Thing; Kirby-a 21 42 63 150 300 450
97-1st app. Aunt May & Uncle Ben by Ditko (6/62), before Amazing Fantasy #15; (see Tales Of Suspense #7); Kirby-a 37 74 111 295 585 875
101-Human Torch begins by Kirby (10/62); origin recap Fantastic Four & Human Torch; Human Torch-c begin 115 230 345 978 1989 3000
102-1st app. Wizard; robot-c 41 82 123 324 650 975
103-105: 104-1st app. Trapster. 105-2nd Wizard 35 70 105 273 537 800
106,108,109: 106-Fantastic Four guests (3/63) 27 54 81 197 399 600
107-(4/63)-Human Torch/Sub-Mariner battle; 4th S.A. Sub-Mariner app. & 1st x-over outside of Fantastic Four 37 74 111 294 585 875
110-(7/63)-Intro Doctor Strange, Ancient One & Wong by Ditko 146 292 438 1241 2521 3800
111-2nd Dr. Strange 37 74 111 294 585 875
112,113 18 36 54 131 266 400
114-Acrobat disguised as Captain America, 1st app. since the G.A.; intro. & 1st app. Victoria Bentley; 3rd Dr. Strange app. & begin series (11/63) 40 80 120 320 635 950
115-Origin Dr. Strange; Human Torch vs. Sandman (Spidey villain; 2nd app. & brief origin); early Spider-Man x-over, 12/63 47 94 141 376 763 1150
116-(1/64)-Human Torch battles The Thing; 1st Thing x-over 16 32 48 114 232 350
117,118,120: 120-1st Iceman x-over (from X-Men) 13 26 39 94 185 275
119-Spider-Man x-over (2 panel cameo) 14 28 42 102 206 310
121,122,124,126-134: Thing/Torch team-up in 121-134. 126-Intro Clea. 128-Quicksilver & Scarlet Witch app. (1/65). 130-The Beatles cameo. 134-Last Human Torch; The Watcher-c/story; Wood-a(i) 11 22 33 77 144 210
123-1st app. The Beetle (see Amazing Spider-Man #21 for next app.); 1st Thor x-over (8/64); Loki app. 13 26 39 89 170 250
125-Torch & Thing battle Sub-Mariner (10/64) 13 26 39 92 179 265
135-Col. (formerly Sgt.) Nick Fury becomes Nick Fury Agent of Shield (origin/1st app.) by Kirby (8/65); series begins 21 42 63 150 300 450
136-140: 138-Intro Eternity 8 16 24 58 97 135
141-147,149: 145-Begins alternating-c features w/Nick Fury (odd #'s) & Dr. Strange (even #'s). 146-Last Ditko Dr. Strange who is in consecutive stories since #113; only full Ditko Dr. Strange-c this title. 147-Dr. Strange (by Everett #147-152) continues thru #168, then Dr. Strange #169 7 14 21 45 73 100
148-Origin Ancient One 8 16 24 58 97 135
150(11/66)-John Buscema's 1st work at Marvel 7 14 21 49 80 110
151-Kirby/Steranko-c/a; 1st Marvel work by Steranko 10 20 30 68 119 170
152,153-Kirby/Steranko-a 8 16 24 52 86 120
154-158-Steranko-a/script 8 16 24 52 86 120
159-Origin Nick Fury retold; Intro Val; Captain America-c/story; Steranko-a 9 18 27 30 100 140
160-162-Steranko-a/scripts; Capt. America app. 8 16 24 52 86 120
163-166,168-Steranko-a(p). 168-Last Nick Fury (gets own book next month) & last Dr. Strange who also gets own book 7 14 21 50 83 115

GD VG FN VF VF/NM NM-
2.0 4.0 6.0 8.0 9.0 9.2

167-Steranko pen/script; classic flag-c 9 18 27 60 100 140
169-1st app. Brother Voodoo(origin in #169,170) & begin series, ends #173. 3 6 9 18 27 35
170-174: 174-Origin Golem 2 4 6 13 18 22
175-177: 177-Brunner-c 2 4 6 11 16 20
178-(2/75)-Warlock by Starlin begins; origin Warlock & Him retold; 1st app. Magus; Starlin-c/a/scripts in #178-181 (all before Warlock #9) 3 6 9 21 32 42
179-181-All Warlock. 179-Intro/1st app. Pip the Troll. 180-Intro Gamora. 181-(8/75)-Warlock story continued in Warlock #9 3 6 9 17 25 32
182-188: 185,186-(Regular 25¢ editions) 1 3 4 6 8 10
185,186-(30¢-c variants, limited distribution)(5,7/76) 2 4 6 11 16 20
Annual 1(1962)-Reprints from Strange Tales #73,76,78, Tales of Suspense #7,9, Tales to Astonish #1,6,7, & Journey Into Mystery #53,55,59; (1st Marvel annual?) 50 100 150 425 863 1300
Annual 2(7/63)-Reprints from Strange Tales #67, Strange Worlds (Atlas) #1-3, World of Fantasy #16; new Human Torch vs. Spider-Man story by Kirby/Ditko (1st Spidey x-over; 4th app.); Kirby-c 81 162 243 689 1395 2100

NOTE: ***Briefer** a-17. **Burgos** a-123p. **J. Buscema** a-174p. **Colan** a-7, 11, 20, 37, 53, 169-173p, 188p. **Davis** c-71. **Ditko** a-46, 50, 67-122, 123-125p, 126-146, 175r, 182-188r; c-51, 93, 115, 121, 146. **Everett** a-4, 21, 40-42, 73, 147-152, 164i; c-8, 10, 11, 13, 15, 24, 45, 49-54, 56, 58, 60, 61, 63, 148, 150, 152, 158i. **Forte** a-27, 43, 50, 53, 54, 60. **Heath** a-2, 6; c-6, 18-20. **Kamen** a-45. **G. Kane** c-170-173, 182p. **Kirby** Human Torch-101-105, 108, 109, 114, 120; Nick Fury-135p, 141-143p; (Layouts)-135-153; other **Kirby** a-67-100p; c-68-70, 72-74, 76-92, 94, 95, 101-114, 116-123, 125-130, 132-135, 136p, 138-145, 147, 149, 151p. **Kirby/Ayers** c-101-106, 108-110. **Kirby/Ditko** a-80, 88, 121; c-75, 93, 97, 100, 139. **Lawrence** a-29. **Leiber/ Fox** a-110-113. **Maneely** a-3, 7, 37, 42; c-33, 40. **Moldoff** a-20. **Mooney** a-174i. **Morisi** a-53, 56. **Morrow** a-54. **Orlando** a-41, 44, 46, 49, 52. **Powell** a-42, 44, 49, 54, 130-134p; c-131p. **Reinman** a-11, 50, 74, 88, 91, 95, 104, 106, 112i, 124-127i. **Robinson** a-17. **Romita** c-169. **Roussos** c-201i. **R.Q. Sale** a-56; c-16. **Sekowski** a-3, 11. **Severin** a(i)-136-138; c-137. **Starlin** a-178, 179, 180p, 181p; c-178-180, 181p. **Steranko** a-151-161, 162-168p; c-151i, 153, 155, 157, 159, 161, 163, 165, 167. **Torres** a-53, 62. **Tuska** a-14, 166p. **Whitney** a-149. **Wildey** a-42, 56. **Woodbridge** a-59. Fantastic Four cameos #101-134. Jack Katz app.-26.*

STRANGE TALES
Marvel Comics Group: Apr, 1987 - No. 19, Oct, 1988

V2#1-19 3.00

STRANGE TALES
Marvel Comics: Nov, 1994 ($6.95, one-shot)

V3#1-acetate-c 7.00

STRANGE TALES (Anthology; continues stories from Man-Thing #8 and Werewolf By Night #6)
Marvel Comics: Sept, 1998 - No. 2, Oct, 1998 ($4.99)

1,2: 1-Silver Surfer app. 2-Two covers 5.00

STRANGE TALES (Humor anthology)
Marvel Comics: Nov, 2009 - No. 3, Jan, 2010 ($4.99, limited series)

1-3: 1-Paul Pope, Kochalka, Bagge and others-s/a. 2-Bagge-c/a. 3-Sakai-c/a 5.00

STRANGE TALES II (Humor anthology)
Marvel Comics: Dec, 2010 - No. 3, Feb, 2011 ($4.99, limited series)

1-3: 2-Jaime Hernandez-c. 3-Terry Moore-s/a; Pekar-s/Templeton-a 5.00

STRANGE TALES: DARK CORNERS
Marvel Comics: May, 1998 ($3.99, one-shot)

1-Anthology; stories by Baron & Maleev, McGregor & Dringenberg, DeMatteis & Badger; Estes painted-c 4.00

STRANGE TALES OF THE UNUSUAL
Atlas Comics (ACI No. 1-4/WPI No. 5-11): Dec, 1955 - No. 11, Aug, 1957

1-Powell-a 45 90 135 284 480 675
2 29 58 87 170 278 385
3-Williamson-a (4 pgs.) 30 60 90 177 289 400
4,6,8,11 21 42 63 126 206 285
5-Crandall, Ditko-a 26 52 78 152 249 345
7,9: 7-Kirby, Orlando-a. 9-Krigstein-a 23 46 69 136 223 310
10-Torres, Morrow-a 21 42 63 126 206 285

NOTE: ***Baily** a-6. **Brodsky** c-2-4. **Everett** a-2, 6; c-6, 9, 11. **Heck** a-1. **Maneely** c-1. **Orlando** a-7. **Pakula** a-10. **Romita** a-1. **R.Q. Sale** a-3. **Wildey** a-3.*

STRANGE TERRORS
St. John Publishing Co.: June, 1952 - No. 7, Mar, 1953

1-Bondage-c; Zombies spelled Zoombies on-c; Fine-*esque* -a 61 122 183 390 670 950
2 37 74 111 222 361 500
3-Kubert-a; painted-c 42 84 126 265 445 625
4-Kubert-a (reprinted in Mystery Tales #18); Ekgren painted-c; Fine-*esque* -a; Jerry Iger caricature 55 110 165 352 601 850
5-Kubert-a; painted-c 42 84 126 265 445 625

Strange Worlds #7 © AVON

Stray Bullets #1 © David Lapham

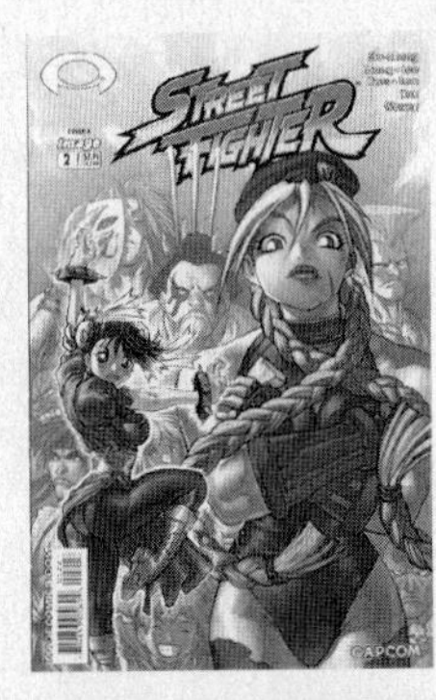

Street Fighter #2 © Capcom

	GD 2.0	VG 4.0	FN 6.0	VF 8.0	VF/NM 9.0	NM- 9.2
6-Giant (25¢, 100 pgs.)(1/53); bondage-c	54	108	162	343	574	825
7-Giant (25¢, 100 pgs.); Kubert-c/a	56	112	168	356	608	860

NOTE: *Cameron a-6, 7. Morisi a-6.*

STRANGE WORLD OF YOUR DREAMS
Prize Publications: Aug, 1952 - No. 4, Jan-Feb, 1953

	GD	VG	FN	VF	VF/NM	NM-
1-Simon & Kirby-a	64	128	192	406	696	985
2,3-Simon & Kirby-c/a. 2-Meskin-a	50	100	150	315	533	750
4-S&K-c; Meskin-a	41	82	123	256	428	600

STRANGE WORLDS (#18 continued from Avon's Eerie #1-17)
Avon Periodicals: 11/50 - No. 9, 11/52; No. 18, 10-11/54 - No. 22, 9-10/55 (No #11-17)

	GD	VG	FN	VF	VF/NM	NM-
1-Kenton of the Star Patrol by Kubert (r/Eerie #1 from 1947); Crom the Barbarian by John Giunta	148	296	444	947	1624	2300
2-Wood-a; Crom the Barbarian by Giunta; Dara of the Vikings app.; used in **SOTI**, pg. 112; injury to eye panel	129	258	387	826	1413	2000
3-Wood/Orlando-a (Kenton), Wood/Williamson/Frazetta/Krenkel/Orlando-a (7 pgs.); Malu Slave Girl Princess app.; Kinstler-c	245	490	735	1568	2684	3800
4-Wood-c/a (Kenton); Orlando-a; origin The Enchanted Daggar; Sultan-a; classic cover	145	290	435	921	1586	2250
5-Orlando/Wood-a (Kenton); Wood-c	77	154	231	493	847	1200
6-Kinstler-a(2); Orlando/Wood-c; Check-a	48	96	144	302	514	725
7-Fawcette & Becker/Alascia-a	41	82	123	256	428	600
8-Kubert, Kinstler, Hollingsworth & Lazarus-a; Lazarus Robot-c	41	82	123	256	428	600
9-Kinstler, Fawcette, Alascia-a	39	78	117	240	395	550
18-(Formerly Eerie #17)-Reprints "Attack on Planet Mars" by Kubert	32	64	96	192	314	435
19-r/Avon's "Robotmen of the Lost Planet"; last pre-code issue; Robot-c	32	64	96	192	314	435
20-War-c/story; Wood-c(r)/U.S. Paratroops #1	11	22	33	60	83	105
21,22-War-c/stories. 22-New logo	9	18	27	52	69	85
I.W. Reprint #5-Kinstler-a(r)/Avon's #9	4	8	12	24	37	50

STRANGE WORLDS
Marvel Comics (MPI No. 1,2/Male No. 3,5): Dec, 1958 - No. 5, Aug, 1959

	GD	VG	FN	VF	VF/NM	NM-
1-Kirby & Ditko-a; flying saucer issue	90	180	270	576	988	1400
2-Ditko-c/a	52	104	156	322	549	775
3-Kirby-a(2)	42	84	126	265	445	625
4-Williamson-a	41	82	123	256	428	600
5-Ditko-a	37	74	111	222	361	500

NOTE: *Buscema a-3, 4. Ditko a-1-5; c-2.. Heck a-2. Kirby a-1, 3. Kirby/Brodsky c-1, 3-5.*

STRAWBERRY SHORTCAKE
Marvel Comics (Star Comics): Jun, 1985 - No. 6, Feb, 1986 (Children's comic)

	GD	VG	FN	VF	VF/NM	NM-
1-6: Howie Post-a	2	3	4	6	8	10

STRAY
DC Comics (Homage Comics): 2001 ($5.95, prestige format, one-shot)

	GD	VG	FN	VF	VF/NM	NM-
1-Pollina-c/a; Lobdell & Palmiotti-s						6.00

STRAY BULLETS
El Capitan Books: 1995 - Present ($2.95/$3.50, B&W, mature readers)

	GD	VG	FN	VF	VF/NM	NM-
1-David Lapham-c/a/scripts	2	4	6	8	10	12
2,3						6.00
4-8						4.00
9-21,31,32-($2.95)						3.50
22-30,33-40-($3.50) 22-Includes preview to Murder Me Dead						3.50
Free Comic Book Day giveaway (5/02) Reprints #2 with "Free Comic Book Day" banner on-c; flip book with The Matrix (printing of internet comic)						2.50
Innocence of Nihilism Volume 1 HC ($29.95, hardcover) r/#1-7						30.00
Somewhere Out West Volume 2 HC ($34.95, hardcover) r/#8-14						35.00
Other People Volume 3 HC ($34.95, hardcover) r/#15-22						35.00
Volume 1-3 TPB ($11.95, softcover) 1-r/#1-4. 2-r/#5-8. 3-r/ #9-12						12.00
Volume 4-7 TPB ($14.95) 4- r/#13-16. 5- r/#17-20. 6- r/#21-24. 7-r/#25-28						15.00

NOTE: *Multiple printings of most issues exist & are worth cover price.*

STRAY TOASTERS
Marvel Comics (Epic Comics): Jan, 1988 - No. 4, April, 1989 ($3.50, squarebound, limited series)

	GD	VG	FN	VF	VF/NM	NM-
1-4: Sienkiewicz-c/a/scripts						4.00

STREET COMIX
Street Enterprises/King Features: 1973 (50¢, B&W, 36 pgs.)(20,000 print run)

	GD	VG	FN	VF	VF/NM	NM-
1-Rip Kirby	2	4	6	8	11	14
2-Flash Gordon	2	4	6	10	14	18

STREETFIGHTER
Ocean Comics: Aug, 1986 - No. 4, Spr, 1987 ($1.75, limited series)

	GD 2.0	VG 4.0	FN 6.0	VF 8.0	VF/NM 9.0	NM- 9.2
1-4: 2-Origin begins						3.00

STREET FIGHTER
Malibu Comics: Sept, 1993 - No. 3, Nov, 1993 ($2.95)

	GD	VG	FN	VF	VF/NM	NM-
1-3: 3-Includes poster; Ferret x-over						3.00

STREET FIGHTER
Image Comics: Sept, 2003 - No. 14, Feb, 2005 ($2.95)

	GD	VG	FN	VF	VF/NM	NM-
1-Back-up story w/Madureira-a; covers by Madureira and Tsang						3.00
2-6,8-14: 2-Two covers by Campbell and Warren; back-up story w/Warren-a						3.00
7-($4.50) Larocca-c						4.50
... Vol. 1 (3/04, $9.99, digest-size) r/main stories from #1-6						10.00

STREET FIGHTER: THE BATTLE FOR SHADALOO
DC Comics/CAP Co. Ltd.: 1995 ($3.95, one-shot)

	GD	VG	FN	VF	VF/NM	NM-
1-Polybagged w/trading card & Tattoo						4.00

STREET FIGHTER II
Tokuma Comics (Viz): Apr, 1994 - No. 8, Nov, 1994 ($2.95, limited series)

	GD	VG	FN	VF	VF/NM	NM-
1-8						3.00

STREET FIGHTER II
UDON Comics: No. 0, Oct, 2005 - No. 6, Nov, 2006 ($1.99/$3.95/$2.95)

	GD	VG	FN	VF	VF/NM	NM-
0-(10/05, $1.99) prelude to series; Alvin Lee-a						3.00
1-($3.95) Two covers by Alvin Lee & Ed McGuinness						4.00
2-6-($2.95)						3.00

STREET FIGHTER LEGENDS
UDON Comics: Aug, 2006 ($3.95)

	GD	VG	FN	VF	VF/NM	NM-
1-Spotlight on Sakura; two covers						4.00

STREETS
DC Comics: 1993 - No. 3, 1993 ($4.95, limited series, 52 pgs.)

	GD	VG	FN	VF	VF/NM	NM-
Book 1-3-Estes painted-c						5.00

STREET SHARKS
Archie Publications: Jan, 1996 - No. 3, Mar, 1996 ($1.50, limited series)

	GD	VG	FN	VF	VF/NM	NM-
1-3						3.00

STREET SHARKS
Archie Publications: May, 1996 - No. 6 ($1.50, published 8 times a year)

	GD	VG	FN	VF	VF/NM	NM-
1-6						3.00

STRICTLY PRIVATE (You're in the Army Now)
Eastern Color Printing Co.: July, 1942 (#1 on sale 6/15/42)

	GD	VG	FN	VF	VF/NM	NM-
1,2: Private Peter Plink. 2-Says 128 pgs. on-c	24	48	72	142	234	325

STRIKE!
Eclipse Comics: Aug, 1987 - No. 6, Jan, 1988 ($1.75)

	GD	VG	FN	VF	VF/NM	NM-
1-6, ...Vs. Sgt. Strike Special 1 (5/88, $1.95)						3.00

STRIKEBACK! (The Hunt For Nikita)
Malibu Comics (Bravura): Oct, 1994 - No. 3, Jan, 1995 ($2.95, unfinished limited series)

	GD	VG	FN	VF	VF/NM	NM-
1-3: Jonathon Peterson script, Kevin Maguire-c/a						3.00
1-Gold foil embossed-c						5.00

STRIKEBACK!
Image Comics (WildStorm Productions): Jan, 1996 - No. 5, May, 1996 ($2.50, lim. series)

	GD	VG	FN	VF	VF/NM	NM-
1-5: Reprints original Bravura series w/additional story & art by Kevin Maguire & Jonathon Peterson; new Maguire-c in all. 4,5-New story & art						3.00

STRIKEFORCE: AMERICA
Comico: Dec, 1995 ($2.95)

	GD	VG	FN	VF	VF/NM	NM-
V2#1-Polybagged w/gaming card; S. Clark-a(p)						3.00

STRIKEFORCE: MORITURI
Marvel Comics Group: Dec, 1986 - No. 31, July, 1989

	GD	VG	FN	VF	VF/NM	NM-
1,13: 13-Double size						4.00
2-12,14-31: 14-Williamson-i. 25-Heath-c						3.00

STRIKEFORCE MORITURI: ELECTRIC UNDERTOW
Marvel Comics: Dec, 1989 - No. 5, Mar, 1990 ($3.95, 52 pgs., limited series)

	GD	VG	FN	VF	VF/NM	NM-
1-5 Squarebound						4.00

STRONG GUY REBORN (See X-Factor)
Marvel Comics: Sept, 1997 ($2.99, one-shot)

	GD	VG	FN	VF	VF/NM	NM-
1-Dezago-s/Andy Smith, Art Thibert-a						3.00

Stryke Force V2 #1 © TCOW

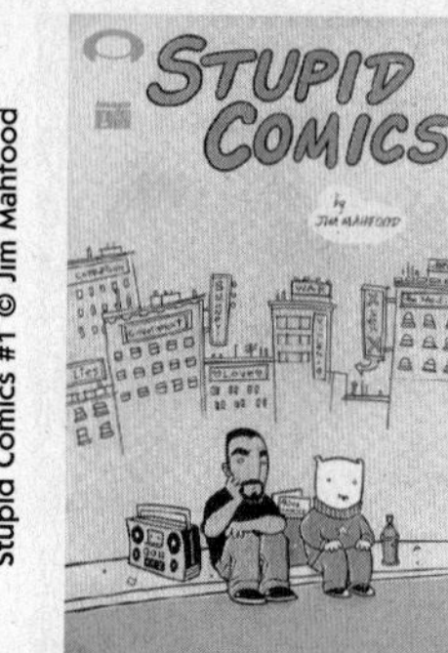

Stupid Comics #1 © Jim Mahfood

Sub-Mariner Comics #1 © MAR

	GD 2.0	VG 4.0	FN 6.0	VF 8.0	VF/NM 9.0	NM- 9.2

STRONG MAN (Also see Complimentary Comics & Power of...)
Magazine Enterprises: Mar-Apr, 1955 - No. 4, Sept-Oct, 1955

1(A-1 #130)-Powell-c/a 23 46 69 136 223 310
2-4: (A-1 #132,134,139)-Powell-a. 2-Powell-c 18 36 54 105 165 225

STRONTIUM DOG
Eagle Comics: Dec, 1985 - No. 4, Mar, 1986 ($1.25, limited series)

1-4, Special 1: 4-Moore script. Special 1 (1986)-Moore script 3.00

STRYFE'S STRIKE FILE
Marvel Comics: Jan, 1993 ($1.75, one-shot, no ads)

1-Stroman, Capullo, Andy Kubert, Brandon Peterson-a; silver metallic ink-c; X-Men tie-in to X-Cutioner's Song 4.00
1-Gold metallic ink 2nd printing 3.00

STRYKEFORCE
Image Comics (Top Cow): May, 2004 - No. 5, Oct, 2004 ($2.99)

1-5-Faerber-s/Kirkham-a. 4,5-Preview of HumanKind 3.00
Vol. 1 TPB (2005, $16.99) r/#1-5 & Codename: Strykeforce #0-3; sketch pages 17.00

STUMBO THE GIANT (See Harvey Hits #49,54,57,60,63,66,69,72,78,88 & Hot Stuff #2)

STUMBO TINYTOWN
Harvey Publications: Oct, 1963 - No. 13, Nov, 1966 (All 25¢ giants)

1-Stumbo, Hot Stuff & others begin 14 28 42 97 194 290
2 9 18 27 61 103 145
3-5 7 14 21 45 73 100
6-13 6 12 18 37 59 80

STUNT DAWGS
Harvey Comics: Mar, 1993 ($1.25, one-shot)

1 3.00

STUNTMAN COMICS (Also see Thrills Of Tomorrow)
Harvey Publ.: Apr-May, 1946 - No. 2, June-July, 1946; No. 3, Oct-Nov, 1946

1-Origin Stuntman by S&K reprinted in Black Cat #9; S&K-c
116 232 348 742 1271 1800
2-S&K-c/a; The Duke of Broadway story 68 136 204 435 743 1050
3-Small size (5-1/2x8-1/2"; B&W; 32 pgs.); distributed to mail subscribers only; S&K-a; Kid Adonis by S&K reprinted in Green Hornet #37
103 206 309 659 1130 1600
(Also see All-New #15, Boy Explorers #2, Flash Gordon #5 & Thrills of Tomorrow)

STUPID COMICS (Also see 40 oz. Collected)
Oni Press/Image Comics: July, 2000; Sept, 2002 - Present ($2.95, B&W)

1-(Oni Press, 7/00) Jim Mahfood 1 page satire strips reprinted from JAVA magazine 3.00
1-3-(Image Comics, 9/02; 10/03) Jim Mahfood 1 page and 2 page satire strips 3.00
TPB (4/06, $12.99) r/#1(Oni) and #1-3(Image); Phoenix New Times strips 13.00

STUPID HEROES
Mirage Studios: Sept, 1993 - No. 3, Dec, 1994 ($2.75, unfinished limited series)

1-3-Laird-c/a & scripts; 2 trading cards bound in 3.00

STUPID, STUPID RAT TAILS (See Bone)
Cartoon Books: Dec, 1999 - No. 3, Feb, 2000 ($2.95, limited series)

1-3-Jeff Smith-a/Tom Sniegoski-s 3.00

SUBHUMAN
Dark Horse Comics: Nov, 1998 - No. 4, Feb, 1999 ($2.95, limited series)

1-4-Mark Schultz-c 3.00

SUBMARINE ATTACK (Formerly Speed Demons)
Charlton Comics: No. 11, May, 1958 - No. 54, Feb-Mar, 1966

11 4 8 12 26 41 55
12-20 3 6 9 19 29 38
21-30 3 6 9 17 25 32
31-54 3 6 9 14 20 26
NOTE: *Glanzman c/a-25. Montes/Bache a-38, 40, 41.*

SUB-MARINER (See All-Select, All-Winners, Blonde Phantom, Daring, The Defenders, Fantastic Four #4, Human Torch, The Invaders, Iron Man &..., Marvel Mystery, Marvel Spotlight #27, Men's Adventures, Motion Picture Funnies Weekly, Namora, Namor, The..., Prince Namor, The Sub-Mariner, Saga Of The..., Tales to Astonish #70 & 2nd series, USA & Young Men)

SUB-MARINER, THE (2nd Series)(Sub-Mariner #31 on)
Marvel Comics Group: May, 1968 - No. 72, Sept, 1974 (No. 43: 52 pgs.)

1-Origin Sub-Mariner; story continued from Iron Man & Sub-Mariner #1
21 42 63 150 300 450
2-Triton app. 10 20 30 69 122 175
3-5: 5-1st Tiger Shark (9/68) 8 16 24 52 86 120
6,7,9,10: 6-Tiger Shark-c & 2nd app., cont'd from #5. 7-Photo-c. (1968).
9-1st app. Serpent Crown (origin in #10 & 12) 6 12 18 37 59 80
8-Sub-Mariner vs. Thing 10 20 30 68 119 170
8-2nd printing (1994) 2 4 6 8 10 12
11-13,15: 15-Last 12¢ issue 5 10 15 30 48 65
14-Sub-Mariner vs. G.A. Human Torch; death of Toro (1st modern app. & only app. Toro, 6/69)
6 12 18 43 69 95
16-20: 19-1st Sting Ray (11/69); Stan Lee, Romita, Heck, Thomas, Everett & Kirby cameos. 20-Dr. Doom app. 4 8 12 22 34 45
21,23-33,37-39,41,42: 25-Origin Atlantis. 30-Capt. Marvel x-over. 37-Death of Lady Dorma. 38-Origin retold. 42-Last 15¢ issue. 3 6 9 17 25 32
22,40: 22-Dr. Strange x-over. 40-Spider-Man x-over 3 6 9 18 27 35
34-Prelude (w/#35) to 1st Defenders story; Hulk & Silver Surfer x-over
9 18 27 60 100 140
35-Namor/Hulk/Silver Surfer team-up to battle The Avengers-c/story (3/71); hints at teaming up again 7 14 21 47 76 105
36-Wrightson-a(i) 3 6 9 20 30 40
43-King Size Special (52 pgs.) 3 6 9 21 32 42
44,45-Sub-Mariner vs. Human Torch 3 6 9 19 29 38
46-49,56,62,64-72: 47,48-Dr. Doom app. 49-Cosmic Cube story. 62-1st Tales of Atlantis, ends #66. 64-Hitler cameo. 67-New costume; F.F. x-over. 69-Spider-Man x-over (6 panels)
2 4 6 9 13 16
50-1st app. Nita, Namor's niece (later Namorita in New Warriors)
2 4 6 11 16 20
51-55,57,58,60,61,63-Everett issues: 61-Last artwork by Everett; 1st 4 pgs. completed by Mortimer; pgs. 5-20 by Mooney 2 4 6 10 14 18
59-1st battle with Thor; Everett-a 3 6 9 21 32 42
Special 1 (1/71)-r/Tales to Astonish #70-73 3 6 9 21 32 42
Special 2 (1/72)-(52 pgs.)-r/T.T.A. #74-76; Everett-a 3 6 9 17 25 32
NOTE: *Bolle a-67i. Buscema a(p)-1-8, 20, 24. Colan a(p)-10, 11, 40, 43, 46-49, Special 1, 2; c(p)-10, 11, 40. Craig a-17i, 19-23i. Everett a-45r, 50-55, 57, 58, 59-61(plot), 63(plot); c-47, 48i, 55, 57-59i, 61, Spec. 2. G. Kane c(p)-42-52, 58, 66, 70, 71. Mooney a-24i, 25i, 32-35i, 39i, 42i, 44i, 45i, 60i, 61i, 65p, 66p, 68i. Severin c/a-38i. Starlin c-59p. Tuska a-41p, 42p, 69-71p. Wrightson a-36i. #53, 54-r/stories Sub-Mariner Comics #41 & 39.*

SUB-MARINER (The Initiative, follows Civil War series)
Marvel Comics: Aug, 2007 - No. 6, Jan, 2008 ($2.99, limited series)

1-6: 1-Turner-c/Briones-a/Cherniss & Johnson-s; Iron Man app. 3-Yu-c; Venom app. 3.00
...: Revolution TPB (208, $14.99) r/#1-6 15.00

SUB-MARINER COMICS (1st Series) (The Sub-Mariner #1, 2, 33-42)(Official True Crime Cases #24 on; Amazing Mysteries #32 on; Best Love #33 on)
Timely/Marvel Comics (TCI 1-7/SePI 8/MPI 9-32/Atlas Comics (CCC 33-42)): Spring, 1941 - No. 23, Sum, 1947; No. 24, Wint, 1947 - No. 31, 4/49; No. 32, 7/49; No. 33, 4/54 - No. 42, 10/55

1-The Sub-Mariner by Everett & The Angel begin
3050 6100 9150 23,000 44,000 65,000
2-Everett-a 595 1190 1785 4350 7675 11,000
3-Churchill assassination-c; 40 pg. S-M story 541 1082 1623 3950 6975 10,000
4-Everett-a, 40 pgs.; 1 pg. Wolverton-a 400 800 1200 2800 4900 7000
5-Gabrielle/Klein-c 314 628 942 2198 3849 5500
6-10: 9-Wolverton-a, 3 pgs.; flag-c 300 600 900 2010 3505 5000
11-Classic Schomburg-c 300 600 900 2070 3635 5200
12-15 226 452 678 1446 2473 3500
16-20 181 362 543 1158 1979 2800
21-Last Angel; Everett-a 132 264 396 838 1444 2050
22-Young Allies app. 132 264 396 838 1444 2050
23-The Human Torch, Namora x-over (Sum/47); 2nd app. Namora after Marvel Mystery #82 155 310 465 992 1696 2400
24-Namora x-over (3rd app.) 134 268 402 851 1463 2075
25-The Blonde Phantom begins (Spr/48), ends No. 31; Kurtzman-a; Namora x-over; last quarterly issue 148 296 444 947 1624 2300
26-28: 28-Namora cover; Everett-a 132 264 396 838 1444 2050
29-31 (4/49): 29-The Human Torch app. 31-Capt. America app.
132 264 396 838 1444 2050
32 (7/49, Scarce)-Origin Sub-Mariner 245 490 735 1568 2684 3800
33 (4/54)-Origin Sub-Mariner; The Human Torch app.; Namora x-over in Sub-Mariner #33-42
113 226 339 718 1234 1750
34,35-Human Torch in each 92 184 276 584 1005 1425
36,37,39-41: 36,39-41-Namora app. 90 180 270 576 988 1400
38-Origin Sub-Mariner's wings; Namora app.; last pre-code (2/55)
95 190 285 603 1039 1475
42-Last issue 100 200 300 635 1093 1550
NOTE: *Angel by Gustavson-#1, 8. Brodsky c-34-36, 42. Everett a-1-4, 22-24, 26-42; c-32, 33, 40. Maneely a-38; c-37, 39-41. Rico c-27-31. Schomburg c-1-4, 6, 8-18, 20. Sekowsky c-24. 25, 26(w/Rico). Shores c-21-23, 38. Bondage c-13, 22, 24, 25, 34.*

SUB-MARINER COMICS 70th ANNIVERARY SPECIAL

Sugar & Spike #7 © DC

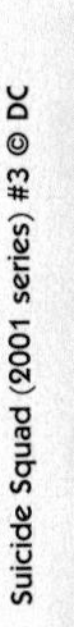

Suicide Squad (2001 series) #3 © DC

Sun Girl #2 © MAR

	GD 2.0	VG 4.0	FN 6.0	VF 8.0	VF/NM 9.0	NM- 9.2

Marvel Comics: June, 2009 ($3.99, one-shot)

1-New WWII story, Breitweiser-a; Williamson-a; r/debut app. from Marvel Comics #1						4.00

SUB-MARINER: THE DEPTHS
Marvel Comics: Nov, 2008 - No. 5, May, 2009 ($3.99, limited series)

1-5-Peter Milligan-s/Esad Ribic-a/c						4.00

SUBSPECIES
Eternity Comics: May, 1991 - No. 4, Aug, 1991 ($2.50, limited series)

1-4: New stories based on horror movie						3.00

SUBTLE VIOLENTS
CFD Productions: 1991 ($2.50, B&W, mature)

1-Linsner-c & story	1	3	4	8	10	12
San Diego Limited Edition	4	8	12	24	37	50

SUE & SALLY SMITH (Formerly My Secret Life)
Charlton Comics: V2#48, Nov, 1962 - No. 54, Nov, 1963 (Flying Nurses)

V2#48	3	6	9	17	25	32
49-54	2	4	6	13	18	22

SUGAR & SPIKE (Also see The Best of DC & DC Silver Age Classics)
National Periodical Publications: Apr-May, 1956 - No. 98, Oct-Nov, 1971

1 (Scarce)	320	640	960	2240	3920	5600
2	123	246	369	787	1344	1900
3-5: 3-Letter column begins	76	152	228	486	831	1175
6-10	46	92	138	290	488	685
11-20	37	74	111	222	361	500
21-29: 26-Christmas-c	26	52	78	154	252	350
30-Scribbly & Scribbly, Jr. x-over	27	54	81	158	259	360
31-40	20	40	60	117	189	260
41-60	9	18	27	63	107	150
61-80: 69-1st app. Tornado-Tot-c/story. 72-Origin & 1st app. Bernie the Brain	7	14	21	50	83	115
81-84,86-95: 84-Bernie the Brain apps. as Superman in 1 panel (9/69)	6	12	18	39	62	85
85 (68 pgs.)-r/#72	6	12	18	43	69	95
96 (68 pgs.)	7	14	21	47	76	105
97,98 (52 pgs.)	6	12	18	43	69	95
No. 1 Replica Edition (2002, $2.95) reprint of #1						4.00

NOTE: *All written and drawn by* **Sheldon Mayer.** *Issues with Paper Doll pages cut or missing are common.*

SUGAR BOWL COMICS (Teen-age)
Famous Funnies: May, 1948 - No. 5, Jan, 1949

1-Toth-c/a	15	30	45	83	124	165
2,4,5	9	18	27	50	65	80
3-Toth-a	10	20	30	56	76	95

SUGARFOOT (TV)
Dell Publishing Co.: No. 907, May, 1958 - No. 1209, Oct-Dec, 1961

Four Color 907 (#1)-Toth-a, photo-c	11	22	33	79	147	215
Four Color 992 (5-7/59), Toth-a, photo-c	10	20	30	73	134	195
Four Color 1059 (11-1/60), 1098 (5-7/60), 1147 (11-1/61), 1209-all photo-c. 1059,1098,1147-all have variant edition, back-c comic strip	8	16	24	58	97	135

SUGARSHOCK (Also see MySpace Dark Horse Presents)
Dark Horse Comics: Oct, 2009 ($3.50, one-shot)

1-Joss Whedon-s/Fabio Moon-a/c; story from online comic; Moon sketch pgs.						3.50

SUICIDE SQUAD (See Brave & the Bold, Doom Patrol & Suicide Squad Spec., Legends #3 & note under Star Spangled War stories)
DC Comics: May, 1987 - No. 66, June, 1992; No. 67, Mar, 2010 (Direct sales only #32 on)

1-Chaykin-c						4.00
2-66: 9-Millennium x-over. 10-Batman-c/story. 13-JLI app. (Batman). 16-Re-intro Shade The Changing Man. 23-1st Oracle. 27-34,36,37-Snyder-a. 40-43-"The Phoenix Gambit" Batman storyline. 40-Free Batman/Suicide Squad poster						3.00
67-(3/10, $2.99) Blackest Night one-shot; Fiddler rises as a Black Lantern; Califiore-a						3.00
Annual 1 (1988, $1.50)-Manhunter x-over						4.00
...: Trial By Fire TPB (2011, $19.99) r/#1-8 & Secret Origins #14						20.00

SUICIDE SQUAD (2nd series)
DC Comics: Nov, 2001 - No. 12, Oct, 2002 ($2.50)

1-12-Giffen-s/Medina-a; Sgt. Rock app. 4-Heath-a. 10-J. Severin-a. 12-JSA app.						3.00

SUICIDE SQUAD (3rd series)
DC Comics: Nov, 2007 - No. 8, Jun, 2008 ($2.99, limited series)

1-8-Ostrander-s/Pina-a/Snyder III-c						3.00
...: From the Ashes TPB (2008, $19.99) r/#1-8						20.00

SUMMER FUN (See Dell Giants)

SUMMER FUN (Formerly Li'l Genius; Holiday Surprise #55)
Charlton Comics: No. 54, Oct, 1966 (Giant)

54	4	8	12	22	34	45

SUMMER FUN (Walt Disney's...)
Disney Comics: Summer, 1991 ($2.95, annual, 68 pgs.)

1-D. Duck, M. Mouse, Brer Rabbit, Chip 'n' Dale & Pluto, Li'l Bad Wolf, Super Goof, Scamp stories						4.00

SUMMER LOVE (Formerly Brides in Love?)
Charlton Comics: V2#46, Oct, 1965; V2#47, Oct, 1966; V2#48, Nov, 1968

V2#46-Beatles-c & 8 pg. story	13	26	39	89	170	250
47-(68 pgs.) Beatles-c & 12 pg. story	10	20	30	71	128	185
48	3	6	9	16	22	28

SUMMER MAGIC (See Movie Comics)

SUNDANCE (See Hotel Deparee...)

SUNDANCE KID (Also see Blazing Six-Guns)
Skywald Publications: June, 1971 - No. 3, Sept, 1971 (52 pgs.)(Pre-code reprints & new-s)

1-Durango Kid; Two Kirby Bullseye-r	3	6	9	16	22	28
2,3: 2-Swift Arrow, Durango Kid, Bullseye by S&K; Meskin plus 1 pg. origin. 3-Durango Kid, Billy the Kid, Red Hawk-r	2	4	6	11	16	20

SUNDAY PIX (Christian religious)
David C. Cook Pub/USA Weekly Newsprint Color Comics: V1#1, Mar,1949 - V16#26, July 19, 1964 (7x10", 12 pgs., mail subscription only)

V1#1	8	16	24	42	54	65
V1#2-up	6	12	18	27	33	38
V2#1-52 (1950)	5	10	15	23	28	32
V3-V6 (1951-1953)	4	9	13	18	22	26
V7-V11#1-7,23-52 (1954-1959)	2	4	6	13	18	22
V11#8-22 (2/22-5/31/59) H.G. Wells First Men in the Moon serial	3	6	9	14	19	24
V12#1-19,21-52; V13-V15#1,2,9-52; V16#1-26(7/19/64)	2	4	6	10	14	18
V12#20 (5/15/60) 2 page interview with Peanuts' Charles Schulz	4	8	12	24	37	50
V15#3-8 (2/24/63) John Glenn, Christian astronaut	3	6	9	16	23	30

SUN DEVILS
DC Comics: July, 1984 - No. 12, June, 1985 ($1.25, maxi series)

1-12: 6-Death of Sun Devil						3.00

SUNDIATA: A LEGEND OF AFRICA
NBM Publishing Inc.: 2002 ($15.95, hardcover with dustjacket)

nn-Will Eisner-s/a; adaptation of an African folk tale						16.00

SUN FUN KOMIKS
Sun Publications: 1939 (15¢, B&W & red)

1-Satire on comics (rare)	181	362	543	1158	1979	2800

NOTE: *Hitler, Stalin and Mussolini featured gag in 1-page story written in Hebrew and English. Nazi swastika and Nazi flag app. in a different 1-page "Gussie the Gob" story. First Hitler app. in comics?*

SUNFIRE & BIG HERO SIX (See Alpha Flight)
Marvel Comics: Sept, 1998 - No. 3, Nov, 1998 ($2.50, limited series)

1-3-Lobdell-s						3.00

SUN GIRL (See The Human Torch & Marvel Mystery Comics #88)
Marvel Comics (CCC): Aug, 1948 - No. 3, Dec, 1948

1-Sun Girl begins; Miss America app.	181	362	543	1158	1979	2800
2,3: 2-The Blonde Phantom begins	123	246	369	787	1344	1900

SUNNY, AMERICA'S SWEETHEART (Formerly Cosmo Cat #1-10)
Fox Features Syndicate: No. 11, Dec, 1947 - No. 14, June, 1948

11-Feldstein-c/a	126	252	378	806	1378	1950
12-14-Feldstein-c/a; 13,14-Lingerie panels. 13-L.B. Cole-a	90	180	270	576	988	1400
I.W. Reprint #8-Feldstein-a; r/Fox issue	10	20	30	73	129	185

SUN-RUNNERS (Also see Tales of the...)
Pacific Comics/Eclipse Comics/Amazing Comics: 2/84 - No. 3, 5/84; No. 4, 11/84 - No. 7, 1986 (Baxter paper)

1-7: P. Smith-a in #2-4						3.00
Christmas Special 1 (1987, $1.95)-By Amazing						3.00

SUNSET CARSON (Also see Cowboy Western)
Charlton Comics: Feb, 1951 - No. 4, 1951 (No month) (Photo-c on each)

Superboy #107 © DC

Superboy (3rd series) #62 © DC

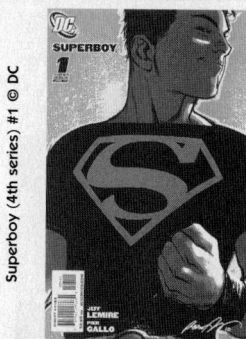

Superboy (4th series) #1 © DC

	GD 2.0	VG 4.0	FN 6.0	VF 8.0	VF/NM 9.0	NM- 9.2

1-Photo/retouched-c (Scarce, all issues) 58 116 174 371 636 900
2-Kit Carson story; adapts "Kansas Raiders" w/Brian Donlevy, Audie Murphy & Margaret Chapman 41 82 123 256 428 600
3,4 34 68 102 199 325 450

SUNSET PASS (See Zane Grey & 4-Color #230)

SUPER ANIMALS PRESENTS PIDGY & THE MAGIC GLASSES
Star Publications: Dec, 1953 (25¢, came w/glasses)

1-(3-D Comics)-L. B. Cole-c 40 80 120 246 411 575

SUPER BAD JAMES DYNOMITE
5-D Comics: Dec, 2005 - No. 5, Feb, 2007 ($3.99)

1-5-Created by the Wayans brothers 4.00

SUPERBOY
DC Comics: Jan, 1942

nn-Ashcan comic, not distributed to newsstands, only for in house use. Covers were produced, but not the rest of the book. A CGC certified 9.2 copy sold in 2003 for $6,600.

SUPERBOY (See Adventure, Aurora, DC Comics Presents, DC 100 Page Super Spectacular #15, DC Super Stars, 80 Page Giant #10, More Fun Comics, The New Advs. of... & Superman Family #191, Young Justice)

SUPERBOY (1st Series)(...& the Legion of Super-Heroes with #231)
(Becomes The Legion of Super-Heroes No. 259 on)
National Periodical Publ./DC Comics: Mar-Apr, 1949 - No. 258, Dec, 1979 (#1-16: 52 pgs.)

1-Superman cover; intro in More Fun #101 (1-2/45) 865 1730 2595 6315 11,158 16,000
2-Used in **SOTI**, pg. 35-36,226 242 484 726 1537 2644 3750
3 187 374 561 1197 2049 2900
4,5: 5-1st pre-Supergirl tryout (c/story, 11-12/49) 129 258 387 826 1413 2000
6-9: 8-1st Superbaby 113 226 339 718 1234 1750
10-1st app. Lana Lang 123 246 369 787 1344 1900
11-15: 11-2nd Lana Lang app.; 1st Lana cover 82 164 246 528 902 1275
16-20: 20-2nd Jor-El cover 57 114 171 362 619 875
21-26,28-30: 21-Lana Lang app. 47 94 141 296 498 700
27-Low distribution 48 96 144 302 514 725
31-38: 38-Last pre-code issue (1/55) 40 80 120 246 411 575
39-48,50 (7/56) 37 74 111 222 361 500
49 (6/56)-1st app. Metallo (Jor-El's robot) 39 78 117 240 395 550
51-60: 52-1st S.A. issue. 56-Krypto-c 29 58 87 170 278 385
61-67 24 48 72 140 230 320
68-Origin/1st app. original Bizarro (10-11/58) 66 132 198 419 722 1025
69-77,79: 76-1st Supermonkey 20 40 60 118 192 265
78-Origin Mr. Mxyzptlk & Superboy's costume 27 54 81 160 263 365
80-1st meeting Superboy/Supergirl (4/60) 25 50 75 150 245 340
81,83-85,87,88: 83-Origin/1st app. Kryptonite Kid 12 24 36 87 164 240
82-1st Bizarro Krypto 13 26 39 89 170 250
86-(1/61)-4th Legion app; Intro Pete Ross 19 38 57 139 280 420
89-(6/61)-1st app. Mon -El; 2nd Phantom Zone 26 52 78 190 383 575
90-92: 90-Pete Ross learns Superboy's I.D. 92-Last 10¢ issue 12 24 36 84 157 230
93-10th Legion app.(12/61); Chameleon Boy app. 12 24 36 87 164 240
94-97,99: 94-1st app. Superboy Revenge Squad 11 22 33 75 138 200
98-(7/62) Legion app; origin & 1st app. Ultra Boy; Pete Ross joins Legion 13 26 39 91 176 260
100-(10/62)-Ultra Boy app; 1st app. Phantom Zone villains, Dr. Xadu & Erndine. 2 pg. map of Krypton; origin Superboy retold; r-cover of Superman #1 18 36 54 131 266 400
101-120: 104-Origin Phantom Zone. 115-Atomic bomb-c. 117-Legion app. 9 18 27 65 113 160
121-128: 124-(10/65)-1st app. Insect Queen (Lana Lang). 125-Legion cameo. 126-Origin Krypto the Super Dog retold with new facts 8 16 24 58 97 135
129-(80-pg. Giant G-22)-Reprints origin Mon-El 10 20 30 67 116 165
130-137,139,140: 131-Legion statues cameo in Dog Legionnaires story. 132-1st app. Supremo. 133-Superboy meets Robin 7 14 21 49 80 110
138 (80-pg. Giant G-35) 8 16 24 54 90 125
141-146,148-155,157: 145-Superboy's parents regain their youth. 148-Legion app. 157-Last 12¢ issue 6 12 18 41 66 90
147(6/68)-Giant G-47; 1st origin of L.S.H. (Saturn Girl, Lightning Lad, Cosmic Boy); origin Legion of Super-Pets-r/Adv. #293 7 14 21 49 80 110
147 Replica Edition (2003, $6.95) reprints entire issue; cover recreation by Ordway 7.00
156-(Giant G-59) 7 14 21 45 73 100
158-164,166-171,175: 171-1st app. Aquaboy 3 6 9 19 29 38
165,174 (Giant G-71,G-83): 165-r/1st app. Krypto the Superdog from Adventure Comics #210 6 12 18 39 62 85
172,173,176-Legion app.: 172-1st app. & origin Yango (The Super Ape). 176-Partial photo-c; last 15¢ issue 3 6 9 20 30 40

	GD 2.0	VG 4.0	FN 6.0	VF 8.0	VF/NM 9.0	NM- 9.2

177-184,186,187 (All 52 pgs.): 182-All new origin of the classic World's Finest team (Superman & Batman) as teenagers (2/72, 22pgs). 184-Origin Dial H for Hero-r 3 6 9 21 32 42
185-Also listed as DC 100 Pg. Super Spectacular #12; Legion-c/story; Teen Titans, Kid Eternity(r/Hit #46), Star Spangled Kid-r(S.S. #55) 8 16 24 54 90 125
188-190,192,194,196: 188-Origin Karkan. 196-Last Superboy solo story 3 6 9 14 19 24
191,193,195: 191-Origin Sunboy retold; Legion app. 193-Chameleon Boy & Shrinking Violet get new costumes. 195-1st app. Erg-1/Wildfire; Phantom Girl gets new costume 3 6 9 14 20 26
197-Legion series begins; Lightning Lad's new costume 3 6 9 20 30 40
198,199: 198-Element Lad & Princess Projectra get new costumes 3 6 9 14 20 26
200-Bouncing Boy & Duo Damsel marry; J'onn J'onzz cameo 3 6 9 16 23 30
201,204,206,207,209: 201-Re-intro Erg-1 as Wildfire. 204-Supergirl resigns from Legion. 206-Ferro Lad & Invisible Kid app. 209-Karate Kid gets new costume 2 4 6 11 16 20
202,205-(100 pgs.): 202-Light Lass gets new costume; Mike Grell's 1st comic work-i (5-6/74) 5 10 15 30 48 65
203-Invisible Kid killed by Validus 3 6 9 16 22 28
208,210: 208-(68 pgs.). 208-Legion of Super-Villains app. 210-Origin Karate Kid 3 6 9 14 20 26
211-220: 212-Matter-Eater Lad resigns. 216-1st app. Tyroc, who joins the Legion in #218 2 4 6 9 13 16
221-230,246-249: 226-Intro. Dawnstar. 228-Death of Chemical King 2 4 6 8 10 12
231-245: (Giants). 240-Origin Dawnstar. 242-(52 pgs.). 243-Legion of Substitute Heroes app. 243-245-(44 pgs.). 2 4 6 9 13 16
244,245-(Whitman variants; low print run, no issue# shown on cover) 3 6 9 14 20 26
246-248-(Whitman variants; low ...) 2 4 6 11 16 20
250-258: 253-Intro Blok. 257-Return of Bouncing Boy & Duo Damsel by Ditko 2 3 4 6 8 10
251-258-(Whitman variants; low print run) 2 4 6 10 14 18
Annual 1 (Sum/64, 84 pgs.)-Origin Krypto-r 16 32 48 111 226 340
Spectacular 1 (1980, Giant)-1st comic distributed only through comic stores; mostly-r 2 4 6 8 10 12
...: The Greatest Team-Up Stories Ever Told TPB (2010, $19.99) r/team-ups with Robin, Supergirl, young versions of Aquaman, Green Arrow, Bruce Wayne; Davis-c 20.00

NOTE: ***Neal Adams*** *c-143, 145, 146, 148-155, 157-161, 163, 164, 166-168, 172, 173, 175, 176, 178.* ***M. Anderson*** *a-178,179, 245i.* ***Ditko*** *a-257p.* ***Grell*** *a-202i, 203-219, 220-224p, 235p; c-207-232, 235, 236p, 237, 239p, 240p, 243p, 246, 258.* ***Nasser*** *a(p)-222, 225, 226, 230, 231, 233, 236.* ***Simonson*** *a-237p.* ***Starlin*** *a(p)-239, 250, 251; c-238.* ***Staton*** *a-227p, 243-249p, 252-258p; c-247-251p.* ***Swan/Moldoff*** *c-109.* ***Tuska*** *a-172, 173, 176, 183, 235p.* ***Wood*** *inks-153-155, 157-161. Legion app.-172, 173, 176, 177, 183, 184, 188, 190, 191, 193, 195, 197-258.*

SUPERBOY (TV)(2nd Series)(The Adventures of...#19 on)
DC Comics: Feb, 1990 - No. 22, Dec, 1991 ($1.00/$1.25)

1-Photo-c from TV show; Mooney-a(p) 4.00
2-22: Mooney-a in 2-8,18-20; 8-Bizarro-c/story; Arthur Adams-a(i). 9-12,14-17-Swan-a 3.00
...Special 1 (1992, $1.75) Swan-a 4.00

SUPERBOY (3rd Series)
DC Comics: Feb, 1994 - No. 100, Jul, 2002 ($1.50/$1.95/$1.99/$2.25)

1-Metropolis Kid from Reign of the Supermen 4.00
2-8,0,9-24,26-76: 6,7-Worlds Collide Pts. 3 & 8. 8-(9/94)-Zero Hour x-over. 0-(10/94). 9-(11/94)-King Shark app. 21-Legion app. 28-Supergirl-c/app. 33-Final Night. 38-41-"Meltdown". 45-Legion-c/app. 47-Green Lantern-c/app. 50-Last Boy on Earth begins. 60-Crosses Hypertime. 68-Demon-c/app. 3.00
25-($2.95)-New Gods & Female Furies app.; w/pin-ups 4.00
77-99: 77-Begin $2.25-c. 79-Superboy's powers return. 80,81-Titans app. 83-New costume. 85-Batgirl app. 90,91-Our Worlds at War x-over 3.00
100-($3.50) Sienkiewicz-c; Grummett & McCrea-a; Superman cameo 4.00
#1,000,000 (11/98) 853rd Century x-over 3.00
Annual 1 (1994, $2.95, 68 pgs.)-Elseworlds story, Pt. 2 of The Super Seven (see Adventures Of Superman Annual #6) 4.00
Annual 2 (1995, $3.95)-Year One story 4.00
Annual 3 (1996, $2.95)-Legends of the Dead Earth 4.00
Annual 4 (1997, $3.95)-Pulp Heroes story 4.00
...Plus 1 (Jan, 1997, $2.95) w/Capt. Marvel Jr. 4.00
...Plus 2 (Fall, 1997, $2.95) w/Slither (Scare Tactics) 4.00
.../Risk Double-Shot 1 (Feb, 1998, $1.95) w/Risk (Teen Titans) 3.00

Super Comics #10 © DELL

Super Dinosaur #1 © Kirkman & Howard

Super Duck Comics #20 © MLJ

	GD 2.0	VG 4.0	FN 6.0	VF 8.0	VF/NM 9.0	NM- 9.2

SUPERBOY (4th Series)
DC Comics: Jan, 2011 - Present ($2.99)

	GD	VG	FN	VF	VF/NM	NM-
1-5: 1-Lemire-s/Gallo-a/Albuquerque-c; Parasite & Poison Ivy app. 2,3-Noto-c						3.00
1-5: 1-Variant-c by Cassaday. 2-March-var-c. 3-Nguyen var-c. 4-Lau var-c. 5-Manapul						4.00

SUPERBOY & THE RAVERS
DC Comics: Sept, 1996 - No. 19, March, 1998 ($1.95)

	GD	VG	FN	VF	VF/NM	NM-
1-19: 4-Adam Strange app. 7-Impulse-c/app. 9-Superman-c/app.						3.00

SUPERBOY COMICS
DC Comics: Jan. 1942

nn - Ashcan comic, not distributed to newsstands, only for in-house use. Cover art is Detective Comics #57 with interior being Action Comics #38. A CGC certified 9.2 copy sold for $6,600 in 2003 and for $15,750 in 2008.

SUPERBOY/ROBIN: WORLD'S FINEST THREE
DC Comics: 1996 - No. 2, 1996 ($4.95, squarebound, limited series)

	GD	VG	FN	VF	VF/NM	NM-
1,2: Superboy & Robin vs. Metallo & Poison Ivy; Karl Kesel & Chuck Dixon scripts; Tom Grummett-c(p)/a(p)						5.00

SUPERBOY'S LEGION (Elseworlds)
DC Comics: 2001 - No. 2, 2001 ($5.95, squarebound, limited series)

	GD	VG	FN	VF	VF/NM	NM-
1,2-31st century Superboy forms Legion; Farmer-s/i; Davis-a(p)/c						6.00

SUPERBOY: THE BOY OF STEEL
DC Comics: 2010 ($19.99, hardcover with dustjacket)

	GD	VG	FN	VF	VF/NM	NM-
HC-Reprints stories from Adventure Comics #0-3,5,6 & Superman Secret Files 2009						20.00

SUPER BRAT (Li'l Genius #5 on)
Toby Press: Jan, 1954 - No. 4, July, 1954

	GD	VG	FN	VF	VF/NM	NM-
1	8	16	24	44	57	70
2-4: 4-Li'l Teevy by Mel Lazarus	6	12	18	27	33	38
I.W. Reprint #1,2,3,7,8('58): 1-r/#1	2	4	6	8	10	12
I.W. (Super) Reprint #10('63)	2	4	6	8	10	12

SUPERCAR (TV)
Gold Key: Nov, 1962 - No. 4, Aug, 1963 (All painted-c)

	GD	VG	FN	VF	VF/NM	NM-
1	12	24	36	82	154	225
2,3	7	14	21	49	80	110
4-Last issue	8	16	24	54	90	125

SUPER CAT (Formerly Frisky Animals; also see Animal Crackers)
Star Publications #56-58/Ajax/Farrell Publ. (Four Star Comic Corp.): No. 56, Nov, 1953 - No. 58, May, 1954; Aug, 1957 - No. 4, May, 1958

	GD	VG	FN	VF	VF/NM	NM-
56-58-L.B. Cole-c on all	19	38	57	112	179	245
1(1957-Ajax)- "The Adventures of..." c-only	10	20	30	54	72	90
2-4	7	14	21	35	43	50

SUPER CIRCUS (TV)
Cross Publishing Co.: Jan, 1951 - No. 5, Sept, 1951 (Mary Hartline)

	GD	VG	FN	VF	VF/NM	NM-
1-(52 pgs.)-Cast photos on-c	15	30	45	85	130	175
2-Cast photos on-c	10	20	30	58	79	100
3-5	9	18	27	50	65	80

SUPER CIRCUS (TV)
Dell Publ. Co.: No. 542, Mar, 1954 - No. 694, Mar, 1956 (Mary Hartline)

	GD	VG	FN	VF	VF/NM	NM-
Four Color 542: Mary Hartline photo-c	7	14	21	47	76	105
Four Color 592,694: Mary Hartline photo-c	6	12	18	43	69	95

SUPER COMICS
Dell Publishing Co.: May, 1938 - No. 121, Feb-Mar, 1949

	GD	VG	FN	VF	VF/NM	NM-
1-Terry & The Pirates, The Gumps, Dick Tracy, Little Orphan Annie, Little Joe, Gasoline Alley, Smilin' Jack, Smokey Stover, Smitty, Tiny Tim, Moon Mullins, Harold Teen, Winnie Winkle begin	226	452	678	1446	2473	3500
2	82	164	246	528	902	1275
3	73	146	219	467	796	1125
4,5: 4-Dick Tracy-c; also #8-10,17,26(part),31	57	114	171	362	619	875
6-10	47	94	141	296	498	700
11-20: 20-Smilin' Jack-c (also #29,32)	39	78	117	240	395	550
21-29: 21-Magic Morro begins (origin & 1st app., 2/40). 22,27-Ken Ernst-c (also #25?); Magic Morro c-22,25,27,34	34	68	102	199	325	450
30- "Sea Hawk" movie adaptation-c/story with Errol Flynn	35	70	105	208	339	470
31-40: 34-Ken Ernst-c	28	56	84	165	270	375
41-50: 41-Intro Lightning Jim. 43-Terry & The Pirates ends	23	46	69	138	227	315
51-60	19	38	57	109	172	235
61-70: 62-Flag-c. 65-Brenda Starr-r begin? 67-X-Mas-c	17	34	51	98	154	210
71-80	14	28	42	80	115	150
81-99	13	26	39	74	105	135
100	14	28	42	78	112	145
101-115-Last Dick Tracy (moves to own title)	10	20	30	56	76	95
116-121: 116,118-All Smokey Stover. 117-All Gasoline Alley. 119-121-Terry & The Pirates app. in all	9	18	27	50	65	80

SUPER COPS, THE
Red Circle Productions (Archie): July, 1974 (one-shot)

	GD	VG	FN	VF	VF/NM	NM-
1-Morrow-c/a; art by Pino, Hack, Thorne	2	4	6	8	11	14

SUPER COPS
Now Comics: Sept, 1990 - No. 4, Dec?, 1990 ($1.75)

	GD	VG	FN	VF	VF/NM	NM-
1-($2.75, 52 pgs.)-Dave Dorman painted-c (both printings)						4.00
2-4						3.00

SUPER CRACKED (See Cracked)

SUPER DC GIANT (25-50¢, all 68-52 pg. Giants)
National Per. Publ.: No. 13, 9-10/70 - No. 26, 7-8/71; V3#27, Summer, 1976 (No #1-12)

	GD	VG	FN	VF	VF/NM	NM-
S-13-Binky	11	22	33	75	138	200
S-14-Top Guns of the West; Kubert-c; Trigger Twins, Johnny Thunder, Wyoming Kid-r; Moreira-r (9-10/70)	6	12	18	37	59	80
S-15-Western Comics; Kubert-c; Pow Wow Smith, Vigilante, Buffalo Bill-r; new Gil Kane-a (9-10/70)	6	12	18	37	59	80
S-16-Best of the Brave & the Bold; Batman-r & Metamorpho origin-r from Brave & the Bold; Spectre pin-up.	4	8	12	28	44	60
S-17-Love 1970 (scarce)	25	50	75	183	367	550
S-18-Three Mouseketeers; Dizzy Dog, Doodles Duck, Bo Bunny-r; Sheldon Mayer-a	10	20	30	37	116	165
S-19-Jerry Lewis; Neal Adams pin-up	10	20	30	69	122	175
S-20-House of Mystery; N. Adams-c; Kirby-r(3)	8	16	24	52	86	120
S-21-Love 1971 (scarce)	29	58	87	223	449	675
S-22-Top Guns of the West; Kubert-c	4	8	12	26	41	55
S-23-The Unexpected	5	10	15	30	48	65
S-24-Supergirl	4	8	12	26	41	55
S-25-Challengers of the Unknown; all Kirby/Wood-r	4	8	12	23	36	48
S-26-Aquaman (1971)-r/S.A. Aquaman origin story from Showcase #30	4	8	12	23	36	48
27-Strange Flying Saucers Adventures (Sum, 1976)	3	6	9	19	29	38

NOTE: ***Sid Greene** r-27p(2), **Heath** r-27. **G. Kane** a-14r(2), 15, 27r(p). **Kubert** r-16.*

SUPER DINOSAUR
Image Comics: Apr, 2011 - Present ($2.99)

	GD	VG	FN	VF	VF/NM	NM-
1-Robert Kirkman-s/Jason Howard-a						3.00
... Origin Special #1 FCBD Edition (5/11, giveaway) origin story and character profiles						2.00

SUPER-DOOPER COMICS
Able Mfg. Co./Harvey: 1946 - No. 7, May, 1946; No. 8, 1946 (10¢, 32 pgs., paper-c)

	GD	VG	FN	VF	VF/NM	NM-
1-The Clock, Gangbuster app.	24	48	72	142	234	325
2	14	28	42	82	121	160
3,4,6	14	28	42	76	108	140
5-Capt. Freedom app?	14	28	42	82	121	160
7,8-Shock Gibson. 7-Where's Theres A Will by Ed Wheelan, Steve Case Crime Rover, Penny & Ullysses Jr. 8-Sam Hill app.	14	28	42	82	121	160

SUPER DUCK COMICS (The Cockeyed Wonder) (See Jolly Jingles)
MLJ Mag. No. 1-4(9/45)/Close-Up No. 5 on (Archie): Fall, 1944 - No. 94, Dec, 1960 (Also see Laugh #24)(#1-5 are quarterly)

	GD	VG	FN	VF	VF/NM	NM-
1-Origin; Hitler & Hirohito-c	84	168	252	538	919	1300
2-Bill Vigoda-c	29	58	87	170	278	385
3-5: 4-20-Al Fagaly-c (most)	20	40	60	114	182	250
6-10	15	30	45	83	124	165
11-20(6/48)	11	22	33	62	86	110
21,23-40 (10/51)	10	20	30	54	72	90
22-Used in **SOTI**, pg. 35,307,308	11	22	33	62	86	110
41-60 (2/55)	8	16	24	44	57	70
61-94	7	14	21	35	43	50

SUPER DUPER (Formerly Pocket Comics #1-4?)
Harvey Publications: No. 5, 1941 - No. 11, 1941

	GD	VG	FN	VF	VF/NM	NM-
5-Captain Freedom & Shock Gibson app.	32	64	96	188	307	425
8,11	20	40	60	114	182	250

SUPER DUPER COMICS (Formerly Latest Comics?)
F. E. Howard Publ.: No. 3, May-June, 1947

	GD	VG	FN	VF	VF/NM	NM-
3-1st app. Mr. Monster	21	42	63	122	199	275

Super Friends (2008 series) #27 © DC

Supergirl #8 © DC

Supergirl (2005 series) #58 © DC

GD VG FN VF VF/NM NM-
2.0 4.0 6.0 8.0 9.0 9.2

GD VG FN VF VF/NM NM-
2.0 4.0 6.0 8.0 9.0 9.2

SUPER FRIENDS (TV) (Also see Best of DC & Limited Collectors' Edition)
National Periodical Publications/DC Comics: Nov, 1976 - No. 47, Aug, 1981 (#14 is 44 pgs.)

1-Superman, Batman, Robin, Wonder Woman, Aquaman, Atom, Wendy, Marvin & Wonder Dog begin (1st Super Friends) 5 10 15 32 51 70
2-Penquin-c/sty 3 6 9 16 23 30
3-5 3 6 9 14 20 26
6-10,14: 7-1st app. Wonder Twins & The Seraph. 8-1st app. Jack O'Lantern. 9-1st app. Icemaiden. 14-Origin Wonder Twins 2 4 6 13 18 22
11-13,15-30: 13-1st app. Dr. Mist. 25-1st app. Fire as Green Fury. 28-Bizarro app. 2 4 6 9 13 16
13-16,20-23,25,32-(Whitman variants; low print run, no issue# on cover) 2 4 6 11 16 20
31,47: 31-Black Orchid app. 47-Origin Fire & Green Fury 2 4 6 10 14 18
32-46: 36,43-Plastic Man app. 2 4 6 8 11 14
TBP (2001, $14.95) r/#1,6-9,14,21,27 & Limited Collectors' Edition C-41; Alex Ross-c 15.00
...: Truth, Justice and Peace TPB (2003, $14.95) r/#10,12,13,25,28,29,31,36,37 15.00
NOTE: *Estrada a-1p, 2p. Orlando a-1p. Staton a-43, 45.*

SUPER FRIENDS (All ages stories with puzzles and games)(Based on Mattel toy line)
DC Comics: May, 2008 - No. 29, Sept, 2010 ($2.25/$2.99)

1-29-Superman, Batman, Wonder Woman, Aquaman, Flash & Green Lantern. 29-Begin $2.99-c; Bat-Mite & Mr. Mxyzptlk app. 3.00
...: Calling All Super Friends TPB (2009, $12.99) r/#8-14; puzzles and games 13.00
...: For Justice TPB (2009, $12.99) r/#1-7; puzzles and games 13.00
...: Head of the Class TPB (2010, $12.99) r/#15-21; puzzles and games 13.00
...: Mystery in Space TPB (2011, $12.99) r/#22-28; puzzles and games 13.00

SUPER FUN
Gillmor Magazines: Jan, 1956 (By A.W. Nugent)

1-Comics, puzzles, cut-outs by A.W. Nugent 7 14 21 35 43 50

SUPER FUNNIES (...Western Funnies #3,4)
Superior Comics Publishers Ltd. (Canada): Dec, 1953 - No. 4, Sept, 1954

1-(3-D, 10¢)-...Presents Dopey Duck; make your own 3-D glasses cut-out inside front-c; did not come w/glasses 36 72 108 214 347 480
2-Horror & crime satire 15 30 45 83 124 165
3-Phantom Ranger-c/s; Geronimo, Billy the Kid app. 10 20 30 54 72 90
4-Phantom Ranger-c/story 10 20 30 54 72 90

SUPERGIRL
DC Comics: Feb. 1944

nn - Ashcan comic, not distributed to newsstands, only for in-house use. Cover art is Boy Commandos #1 with interior being Action Comics #80. A copy sold for $15,750 in 2008.

SUPERGIRL (See Action, Adventure #281, Brave & the Bold, Crisis on Infinite Earths #7, Daring New Advs. of..., Super DC Giant, Superman Family, & Super-Team Family)

SUPERGIRL
National Periodical Publ.: Nov, 1972 - No. 9, Dec-Jan, 1973-74; No. 10, Sept-Oct, 1974 (1st solo title)(20¢)

1-Zatanna back-up stories begin, end #5 7 14 21 49 80 110
2-4,6,7,9 4 8 12 24 37 50
5,8,10: 5-Zatanna origin-r. 8-JLA x-over; Batman cameo. 10-Prez 4 8 12 26 41 55
NOTE: *Zatanna in #1-5, 7(Guest); Prez app. in #10. #1-10 are 20¢ issues.*

SUPERGIRL (Formerly Daring New Adventures of...)
DC Comics: No. 14, Dec, 1983 - No. 23, Sept, 1984

14-23: 16-Ambush Bug app. 20-JLA & New Teen Titans app. 4.00
...Movie Special (1985)-Adapts movie; Morrow-a; photo back-c 4.00

SUPERGIRL
DC Comics: Feb, 1994 - No. 4, May, 1994 ($1.50, limited series)

1-4: Guice-a(i) 3.00

SUPERGIRL (See Showcase '96 #8)
DC Comics: Sept, 1996 - No. 80, May, 2003 ($1.95/$1.99/$2.25/$2.50)

1-Peter David scripts & Gary Frank-c/a 1 2 3 5 6 8
1-2nd printing 3.00
2,4-9: 4-Gorilla Grodd-c/app. 6-Superman-c/app. 9-Last Frank-a 4.00
3-Final Night, Gorilla Grodd app. 5.00
10-19: 14-Genesis x-over. 16-Power Girl app. 3.50
20-35: 20-Millennium Giants x-over; Superman app. 23-Steel-c/app. 24-Resurrection Man x-over. 25-Comet ID revealed; begin $1.99-c 3.00
36-46: 36,37-Young Justice x-over 3.00
47-49,51-74: 47-Begin $2.25-c. 51-Adopts costume from animated series. 54-Green Lantern app. 59-61-Our Worlds at War x-over. 62-Two-Face-c/app. 66,67-Demon-c/app. 68-74-Mary Marvel app. 70-Nauck-a. 73-Begin $2.50-c 3.00
50-($3.95) Supergirl's final battle with the Carnivore 4.00
75-80: 75-Re-intro. Kara Zor-El; cover swipe of Action Comics #252 by Haynes; Benes-a. 78-Spectre app. 80-Last issue; Romita-c 3.00
#1,000,000 (11/98) 853rd Century x-over 3.00
Annual 1 (1996, $2.95)-Legends of the Dead Earth 4.00
Annual 2 (1997, $3.95)-Pulp Heroes; LSH app.; Chiodo-c 4.00
...: Many Happy Returns TPB (2003, $14.95) r/#75-80; intro. by Peter David 15.00
...Plus (2/97, $2.95) Capt.(Mary) Marvel-c/app.; David-s/Frank-a 4.00
.../Prysm Double-Shot 1 (Feb, 1998, $1.95) w/Prysm (Teen Titans) 3.00
...: Wings (2001, $5.95) Elseworlds; DeMatteis-s/Tolagson-a 6.00
TPB-('98, $14.95) r/Showcase '96 #8 & Supergirl #1-9 15.00

SUPERGIRL (See Superman/Batman #8 & #19)
DC Comics: No. 0, Oct, 2005 - Present ($2.99)

0-Reprints Superman/Batman #19 with white variant of that cover 3.00
1-Loeb-s/Churchill-a; two covers by Churchill & Turner; Power Girl app. 5.00
1-2nd printing with B&W sketch variant of Turner-c 3.00
1-3rd printing with variant-c homage to Action Comics #252 by Churchill 3.00
2-4: 2-Teen Titans app. 3-Outsiders app.; covers by Turner & Churchill 3.00
5-($3.99) Supergirl vs. Supergirl; Churchill & Turner-c 4.00
6-49: 6-9-One Year Later; Power Girl app. 11-Intro. Powerboy. 12-Terra debut; Conner-a 20-Amazons Attack x-over. 21,22-Karate Kid app. 28-31-Resurrection Man app. 35,36-New Krypton x-over; Argo City story re-told; Superwoman app. 35-Ross-c. 36-Zor-El dies 3.00
50-($4.99) Lana Lang Insect Queen app.; Superwoman returns; back-up story co-written by Helen Slater with Chiang-a; Turner-c 5.00
50-Variant cover by Middleton 6.00
51-62: 51-52-New Krypton. 52-Brainiac 5 app. 53-57-Bizarro-Girl app. 55-61-Reeder-c 3.00
58-DC 75th Anniversary variant cover by Conner 6.00
Annual 1 (11/09, $3.99) Origin of Superwoman 4.00
Annual 2 (12/10, $4.99) Silver Age Legion of Super-Heroes app.; Reeder-c 5.00
...: Beyond Good and Evil TPB (2008, $17.99) r/#23-27 and Action Comics #850 18.00
...: Candor TPB (2007, $14.99) r/#6-9; and pages from JSA Classified #2, Superman #223, Superman/Batman #27 and JLA #122,123 15.00
...: Death & The Family TPB (2010, $17.99) r/#48-50 & Annual #1 18.00
...: Friends & Fugitives TPB (2010, $17.99) r/#43,45-47; Action Comics #881,882 18.00
...: Identity TPB (2007, $19.99) r/#10-16 and story from DCU Infinite Holiday Special 20.00
...: Power TPB (2006, $14.99) r/#1-5 and Superman/Batman #19; variant-c gallery 15.00
...: Way of the World TPB (2009, $17.99) r/#28-33 18.00
...: Who is Superwoman TPB (2009, $17.99) r/#34,37-42 18.00

SUPERGIRL AND THE LEGION OF SUPER-HEROES (Continues from Legion of Super-Heroes #15, Apr, 2006)(Continues as Legion of Super-Heroes #37)
DC Comics: No. 16, May, 2006 - No. 36, Jan, 2008 ($2.99)

16-Supergirl appears in the 31st century 4.00
16-2nd printing 3.00
17-36: 23-Mon-El cameo. 24,25-Mon-El returns 3.00
...: Adult Education TPB (2007, $14.99) r/#20-25 & LSH #6,9,13-15 15.00
...: Dominator War TPB (2007, $14.99) r/#26-30 15.00
...: Strange Visitor From Another Century TPB (2006, $14.99) r/#16-19 & LSH #11,12,15 15.00
...: The Quest For Cosmic Boy TPB (2008, $14.99) r/#31-36 15.00

SUPERGIRL: COSMIC ADVENTURES IN THE 8TH GRADE (Cartoony all-ages title)
DC Comics: Feb, 2008 - No. 6, Jul, 2009 ($2.50, limited series)

1-6: 1-Supergirl lands on Earth; Eric Jones-a. 5,6-Comet & Streaky app. 3.00
TPB (2009, $12.99) r/#1-6; sketch art 13.00

SUPERGIRL/LEX LUTHOR SPECIAL (Supergirl and Team Luthor on-c)
DC Comics: 1993 ($2.50, 68 pgs., one-shot)

1-Pin-ups by Byrne & Thibert 4.00

SUPER GOOF (Walt Disney) (See Dynabrite & The Phantom Blot)
Gold Key No. 1-57/Whitman No. 58 on: Oct, 1965 - No. 74, July, 1984

1 4 8 12 28 44 60
2-5 3 6 9 16 23 30
6-10 3 6 9 14 19 24
11-20 2 4 6 8 11 14
21-30 1 3 4 6 8 10
31-50 1 2 3 4 5 7
51-57 6.00
58,59 (Whitman) 1 2 3 5 6 8
60(8/80), 62(11/80) 3-pack only (scarce) 4 8 12 24 37 50
61(9-10/80) 3-pack only (rare) 4 8 12 26 41 55
63-66('81) 1 2 3 5 6 8
63 (1/81, 40¢-c) Cover price error variant (scarce) 2 4 6 10 14 18
67-69: 67(2/82), 68(2-3/82), 69(3/82) 6.00

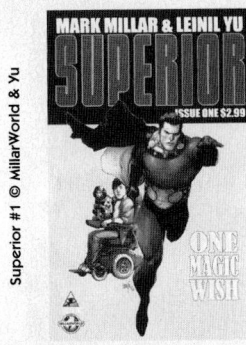

Superior #1 © MillarWorld & Yu

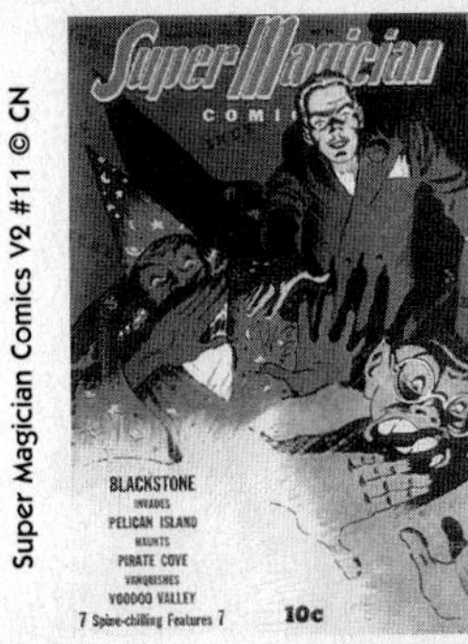

Super Magician Comics V2 #11 © CN

Superman #14 © DC

	GD 2.0	VG 4.0	FN 6.0	VF 8.0	VF/NM 9.0	NM- 9.2

70-74 (#90180 on-c; pre-pack, nd, nd code): 70(5/83), 71(8/83), 72(5/84), 73(6/84), 74(7/84) 3 6 9 16 22 28

NOTE: *Reprints in #16, 24, 28, 29, 37, 38, 43, 45, 46, 54(1/2), 56-58, 65(1/2), 72(r-#2).*

SUPER GREEN BERET (Tod Holton...)
Lightning Comics (Milson Publ. Co.): Apr, 1967 - No. 2, Jun, 1967

1-(25¢, 68 pgs) 5 10 15 32 51 70
2-(25¢, 68 pgs) 4 8 12 22 34 45

SUPER HEROES (See Giant-Size... & Marvel...)

SUPER HEROES
Dell Publishing Co.: Jan, 1967 - No. 4, June, 1967

1-Origin & 1st app. Fab 4 4 8 12 24 37 50
2-4 3 6 9 17 25 32

SUPER-HEROES BATTLE SUPER-GORILLAS (See DC Special #16)
National Periodical Publications: Winter, 1976 (52 pgs., all reprints, one-shot)

1-Superman, Batman, Flash stories; Infantino-a(p) 2 4 6 11 16 20

SUPER HEROES VERSUS SUPER VILLAINS
Archie Publications (Radio Comics): July, 1966 (no month given)(68 pgs.)

1-Flyman, Black Hood, Web, Shield-r; Reinman-a 6 12 18 43 69 95

SUPER HERO SQUAD (See Marvel Super Hero Squad)

SUPERHERO WOMEN, THE - FEATURING THE FABULOUS FEMALES OF MARVEL COMICS (See Fireside Book Series)

SUPERICHIE (Formerly Super Richie)
Harvey Publications: No. 5, Oct, 1976 - No. 18, Jan, 1979 (52 pgs. giants)

5-Origin/1st app. new costumes for Rippy & Crashman 2 4 6 9 13 16
6-18 2 4 6 8 10 12

SUPERIOR
Marvel Comics (ICON): Dec, 2010 - Present ($2.99)

1-4-Mark Millar-s/Leinil Yu-a. 1-1st & 2nd printings 3.00

SUPERIOR STORIES
Nesbit Publishers, Inc.: May-June, 1955 - No. 4, Nov-Dec, 1955

1-The Invisible Man by H.G. Wells 23 46 69 136 223 310
2-4: 2-The Pirate of the Gulf by J.H. Ingrahams. 3-Wreck of the Grosvenor by William Clark Russell. 4-The Texas Rangers by O'Henry 11 22 33 62 86 110

NOTE: ***Morisi** c/a in all. Kiwanis stories in #3 & 4. #4 has photo of Gene Autry on-c.*

SUPER MAGIC (Super Magician Comics #2 on)
Street & Smith Publications: May, 1941

V1#1-Blackstone the Magician-c/story; origin/1st app. Rex King (Black Fury); Charles Sultan-c; Blackstone-c begin 174 348 522 1114 1907 2700

SUPER MAGICIAN COMICS (Super Magic #1)
Street & Smith Publications: No. 2, Sept, 1941 - V5#8, Feb-Mar, 1947

V1#2-Blackstone the Magician continues; Rex King, Man of Adventure app. 66 132 198 419 722 1025
3-Tao-Anwar, Boy Magician begins 41 82 123 256 428 600
4-7,9-12: 4-Origin Transo. 11-Supersnipe app. 39 78 117 240 395 550
8-Abbott & Costello story (1st app?, 11/42) 40 80 120 246 411 575
V2#1-The Shadow app. 41 82 123 250 418 585
2-12: 5-Origin Tigerman. 8-Red Dragon begins 21 42 63 126 206 285
V3#1-12: 5-Origin Mr. Twilight 21 42 63 126 206 285
V4#1-12: 5-KKK-c/sty. 11-Nigel Elliman Ace of Magic begins (3/46) 18 36 54 103 162 220
V5#1-6 18 36 54 103 162 220
7,8-Red Dragon by Edd Cartier-c/a 39 78 117 236 388 540

NOTE: ***Jack Binder** c-1-14(most). Red Dragon c-V5#7, 8.*

SUPERMAN (See Action Comics, Advs. of..., All-New Coll. Ed., All-Star Comics, Best of DC, Brave & the Bold, Cosmic Odyssey, DC Comics Presents, Heroes Against Hunger, JLA, The Kents, Krypton Chronicles, Limited Coll. Ed., Man of Steel, Phantom Zone, Power Record Comics, Special Edition, Steel, Super Friends, Superman: The Man of Steel, Superman: The Man of Tomorrow, Taylor's Christmas Tabloid, Three-Dimension Advs., World Of Krypton, World Of Metropolis, World Of Smallville & World's Finest)

SUPERMAN (Becomes Adventures of...#424 on)
National Periodical Publ./DC Comics: Summer, 1939 - No. 423, Sept, 1986
(#1-5 are quarterly)

1(nn)-1st four Action stories reprinted; origin Superman by Siegel & Shuster; has a new 2 pg. origin plus 4 pgs. omitted in Action story; see The Comics Magazine #1 & More Fun #14-17 for Superman prototype app.; cover r/splash page from Action #10; 1st pin-up Superman on back-c - 1st pin-up in comics 33,333 66,667 100,000 240,000 400,000 560,000

1-Reprint, Oversize 13-1/2x10". **WARNING:** This comic is an exact duplicate reprint of the original except for its size. DC published it in 1978 with a second cover titling it as a Famous First Edition. There have been many reported cases of the outer cover being removed and the interior sold as the original edition. The reprint with the new outer cover removed is practically worthless. See Famous First Edition for value.

2-All daily strip-r; full pg. ad for N.Y. World's Fair 2133 4266 6400 16,000 27,000 38,000
3-2nd story-r from Action #5; 3rd story-r from Action #6 1200 2400 3600 9000 15,500 22,000
4-2nd mention of Daily Planet (Spr/40); also see Action #23; 2nd & 3rd app. Luthor (red-headed; also see Action #23) 730 1460 2190 5329 9414 13,500
5-4th Luthor app. (grey hair) 595 1190 1785 4350 7675 11,000
6,7: 6-1st splash pg. in a Superman comic. 7-1st Perry White? (11-12/40) 411 822 1233 2877 5039 7200
8-10: 10-5th app. Luthor (1st bald Luthor, 5-6/41) 371 742 1113 2600 4550 6500
11-13,15: 13-Jimmy Olsen & Luthor app. 300 600 900 1950 3375 4800
14-Patriotic Shield-c classic by Fred Ray 503 1006 1509 3672 6486 9300
16,18-20: 16-1st Lois Lane-c this title (5-6/42); 2nd Lois-c after Action #29 258 516 774 1651 2826 4000
17-Hitler, Hirohito-c 371 742 1113 2600 4550 6500
21,22,25: 25-Clark Kent's only military service; Fred Ray's only super-hero story 168 336 504 1075 1838 2600
23-Classic periscope-c 206 412 618 1318 2259 3200
24-Classic Jack Burnley flag-c 300 600 900 1950 3375 4800
26-Classic war-c 271 542 813 1734 2967 4200
27-29: 27,29-Lois Lane-c. 28-Lois Lane Girl Reporter series begins, ends #40,42 145 290 435 921 1586 2250
28-Overseas edition for Armed Forces; same as reg. #28 145 290 435 921 1586 2250
30-Origin & 1st app. Mr. Mxyztplk (9-10/44)(pronounced "Mix-it-plk") in comic books; name later became Mxyzptlk ("Mix-yez-pit-l-ick"); the character was inspired by a combination of the name of Al Capp's Joe Blyfstyk (the little man with the black cloud over his head) & the devilish antics of Bugs Bunny; he first app. in newspapers 3/7/44; Superman flies for the first time 277 554 831 1759 3030 4300
31-40: 33-(3-4/45)-3rd app. Mxyztplk. 35,36-Lois Lane-c. 38-Atomic bomb story (1-2/46); delayed because of gov't censorship; Superman shown reading Batman #32 on cover. 40-Mxyztplk-c 123 246 369 787 1344 1900
41-50: 42-Lois Lane-c. 45-Lois Lane as Superwoman (see Action #60 for 1st app.). 46-(5-6/47)-1st app. Superboy this title? 48-1st time Superman travels thru time 100 200 300 635 1093 1550
51,52: 51-Lois Lane-c 89 178 267 565 970 1375
53-Third telling of Superman origin; 10th anniversary issue ('48); classic origin-c by Boring 300 600 900 2070 3635 5200
54,56-60: 57-Lois Lane as Superwoman-c. 58-Intro Tiny Trix 89 178 267 565 970 1375
55-Used in **SOTI**, pg. 33 90 180 270 576 988 1400
61-Origin Superman retold; origin Green Kryptonite (1st Kryptonite story); Superman returns to Krypton for 1st time & sees his parents for 1st time since infancy, discovers he's not an Earth man 158 316 474 1003 1727 2450
62-70: 62-Orson Welles-c/story. 65-1st Krypton Foes: Mala, Kizo, & U-Ban. 66-2nd Superbaby story. 67-Perry Como-c/story. 68-1st Luthor-c this title (see Action Comics) 87 174 261 553 952 1350
71-75: 74-2nd Luthor-c this title. 75-Some have #74 on-c 84 168 252 538 919 1300
76-Batman x-over; Superman & Batman learn each other's I.D. for the 1st time (5-6/52) (also see World's Finest #71) 239 478 717 1530 2615 3700
77-81: 78-Last 52 pg. issue. 81-Used in **POP**, pg. 88 74 148 222 470 810 1150
82-87,89,90: 89-1st Curt Swan-c in title 68 136 204 435 743 1050
88-Prankster, Toyman & Luthor team-up 73 146 219 467 796 1125
91-95: 95-Last precode issue (2/55) 60 120 180 381 653 925
96-99: 96-Mr. Mxyztplk-c/story 54 108 162 343 574 825
100 (9-10/55)-Shows cover to #1 on-c 232 464 696 1485 2543 3600
101-105,107-110: 109-1st S.A. issue 52 104 156 328 552 775
106 (7/56)-Retells origin 53 106 159 334 567 800
111-120 47 94 141 296 498 700
121,122,124-127,129: 127-Origin/1st app. Titano. 129-Intro/origin Lori Lemaris, The Mermaid 41 82 123 256 428 600
123-Pre-Supergirl tryout-c/story (8/58). 58 116 174 371 636 900
128-(4/59)-Red Kryptonite used. Bruce Wayne x-over who protects Superman's i.d. (3rd story) 42 84 126 265 445 625
130-(7/59)-2nd app, Krypto, the Superdog with Superman (see Sup.'s Pal Jimmy Olsen #29) (all other previous app. w/Superboy) 43 86 129 271 461 650
131-139: 135-2nd Lori Lemaris app. 139-Lori Lemaris app.; 34 68 102 199 325 450
140-1st Blue Kryptonite & Bizarro Supergirl; origin Bizarro Jr. #1 34 68 102 206 336 465
141-145,148: 142-2nd Batman x-over 29 58 87 170 278 385
146-(7/61)-Superman's life story; back-up hints at Earth II. Classic-c

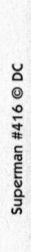

Superman #147 © DC

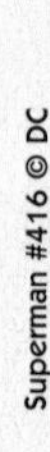

Superman #416 © DC

Superman (2nd series) #132 © DC

GD 2.0 | VG 4.0 | FN 6.0 | VF 8.0 | VF/NM 9.0 | NM- 9.2

39 78 117 235 385 535
147(8/61)-7th Legion app; 1st app. Legion of Super-Villains; 1st app. Adult Legion; swipes-c to Adv. #247 36 72 108 216 351 485
149(11/61)-8th Legion app. (cameo); "The Death of Superman" imaginary story; last 10¢ issue 34 68 102 199 325 450
150,151,153,154,157,159,160: 157-Gold Kryptonite used (see Adv. #299); Mon -El app.; Lightning Lad cameo (11/62) 13 26 39 89 170 250
152,155,156,158,162: 152(4/62)-15th Legion app. 155-(8/62)-Legion app; Lightning Man & Cosmic Man, & Adult Legion app. 156,162-Legion app. 158-1st app. Flamebird & Nightwing & Nor-Kan of Kandor (12/62) 13 26 39 91 176 260
161-1st told death of Ma and Pa Kent 13 26 39 91 176 260
161-2nd printing (1987, $1.25)-New DC logo; sold thru So Much Fun Toy Stores (cover title: Superman Classic) 4.00
163-166,168-180: 166-XMas-c. 168-All Luthor issue; JFK tribute/memorial. 169-Bizarro Invasion of Earth-c/story; last Sally Selwyn. 170-Pres. Kennedy story is finally published after delay from #168 due to assassination. 172,173-Legion cameos. 174-Super-Mxyzptlk; Bizarro app. 11 22 33 75 138 200
167-New origin Brainiac, text reference of Brainiac 5 descending from adopted human son Brainiac II; intro Tharla (later Luthor's wife) 13 26 39 89 170 250
181,182,184-186,188-192,194-196,198,200: 181-1st 2465 story/series. 182-1st S.A. app. of The Toyman (1/66). 189-Origin/destruction of Krypton II. 9 18 27 63 107 150
183 (Giant G-18) 11 22 33 77 144 210
187,193,197 (Giants G-23,G-31,G-36) 10 20 30 67 116 165
199-1st Superman/Flash race (8/67): also see Flash #175 & World's Finest #198,199 (r-in Limited Coll. Ed. C-48) 28 56 84 204 415 625
201,203-206,208-211,213-216: 213-Brainiac-5 app. 216-Last 12¢ issue 6 12 18 41 66 90
202 (80-pg. Giant G-42)-All Bizarro issue 7 14 21 47 76 105
207,212,217 (Giants G-48,G-54,G-60): 207-30th anniversary Superman (6/68) 7 14 21 47 76 105
218-221,223-226,228-231 5 10 15 35 55 75
222,239(Giants, G-66,G-84) 6 12 18 43 69 95
227,232(Giants, G-72,G-78)-All Krypton issues 6 12 18 43 69 95
233-2nd app. Morgan Edge; Clark Kent switches from newspaper reporter to TV newscaster; all Kryptonite on earth destroyed; classic Neal Adams-c 9 18 27 65 113 160
234-238 5 10 15 35 55 75
240-Kaluta-a; last 15¢ issue 4 8 12 28 44 60
241-244 (All 52 pgs.): 241-New Wonder Woman app. 243-G.A.-r/#38 5 10 15 30 48 65
245-Also listed as DC 100 Pg. Super Spectacular #7; Air Wave, Kid Eternity, Hawkman-r; Atom-r/Atom #3 10 20 30 68 119 170
246-248,250,251,253 (All 52 pgs.): 246-G.A.-r/#40. 248-World of Krypton story. 251-G.A.-r/#45. 253-Finlay-a, 2 pgs., G.A.-r/#1 5 10 15 30 48 65
249,254-Neal Adams-a. 249-(52 pgs.); 1st app. Terra-Man (Swan-a) & origin-s by Dick Dillin (p) & Neal Adams (inks) 6 12 18 41 66 90
252-Also listed as DC 100 Pg. Super Spectacular #13; Ray(r/Smash #17), Black Condor, (r/Crack #18), Hawkman(r/Flash #24); Starman-r/Adv. #67; Dr. Fate & Spectre-r/More Fun #57; N. Adams-c 11 22 33 77 144 210
255-271,273-277,279-283: 263-Photo-c. 264-1st app. Steve Lombard. 276-Intro Capt. Thunder. 279-Batman, Batgirl app. 282-Luthor battlesuit 3 6 9 14 19 24
272,278,284-All 100 pgs. G.A.-r in all. 272-r/2nd app. Mr. Mxyztplk from Action #80 5 10 15 32 51 70
285-299: 289-Partial photo-c. 292-Origin Lex Luthor retold 2 4 6 9 13 16
300-(6/76) Superman in the year 2001 3 6 9 20 30 40
301-350: 301,320-Solomon Grundy app. 323-Intro. Atomic Skull. 327-329-(44 pgs.). 327-Kobra app. 330-More facts revealed about I.D. 331,332-1st/2nd app. Master Jailer. 335-Mxyzptlk marries Ms. Bgbznz. 336-Rose & Thorn app. 338-(8/79) 40th Anniv. issue; the bottled city of Kandor enlarged. 344-Frankenstein & Dracula app. 1 3 4 6 8 10
321-323,325-327,329-332,335-345,348,350 (Whitman variants; low print run; no issue # on cover) 2 4 6 9 13 16
351-399: 353-Brief origin. 354,355,357-Superman 2020 stories (354-Debut of Superman III). 356-World of Krypton story (also #360,367,375). 366-Fan letter by Todd McFarlane. 369-Christmas-c. 372-Superman 2021 story. 376-Free 16 pg. preview Daring New Advs. of Supergirl. 377-Free 16 pg. preview Masters of the Universe 1 2 3 4 5 7
400 (10/84, $1.50, 68 pgs.)-Many top artists featured; Chaykin painted cover, Miller back-c; Steranko-s/a (10 pages) 1 3 4 6 8 10
401-422: 405-Super-Batman story. 408-Nuclear Holocaust-c/story. 411-Special Julius Schwartz tribute issue. 414,415-Crisis x-over. 422-Horror-c 6.00
409-(7/85) Variant-c with Superman/Superhombre logo (no reported sales)
423-Alan Moore scripts; Curt Swan-a/George Pérez-a(i); "Whatever Happened to the Man of Tomorrow?" story, cont'd in Action #583 2 4 6 8 10 12
Annual 1(10/60, 84 pgs.)-Reprints 1st Supergirl story/Action #252; r/Lois Lane #1; Krypto-r (1st Silver Age DC annual) 81 162 243 689 1395 2100
Annual 2(Win, 1960-61)-Super-villain issue; Brainiac, Titano, Metallo, Bizarro origin-r 37 74 111 284 562 840
Annual 3(Sum, 1961)-Strange Lives of Superman 24 48 72 175 350 525
Annual 4(Win, 1961-62)-11th Legion app; 1st Legion origins (text & pictures); advs. in time, space & on alien worlds 20 40 60 146 293 440
Annual 5(Sum, 1962)-All Krypton issue 16 32 48 117 239 360
Annual 6(Win, 1962-63)-Legion-r/Adv. #247 15 30 45 103 209 315
Annual 7(Sum, 1963)-Silver Anniversary Issue; origin-r/Superman-Batman team/Adv. #275; cover gallery of famous issues 12 24 36 86 161 235
Annual 8(Win, 1963-64)-All origins issue 11 22 33 77 144 210
Annual 9(8/64)-Was advertised but came out as 80 Page Giant #1 instead
Annual 9(1983)-Toth/Austin-a 1 2 3 4 5 7
Annuals 10-12: 10(1984, $1.25)-M. Anderson-i. 11(1985)-Moore-s. 12(1986)-Bolland-c 6.00
Special 1-3('83-'85): 1-G. Kane-c/a; contains German-r 6.00
The Amazing World of Superman "Official Metropolis Edition" (1973, $2.00, treasury-size)-Origin retold; Wood-r(i) from Superboy #153,161; poster incl. (half price if poster missing) 4 8 12 28 44 60
11195 (2/79, $1.95, 224 pgs.)-Golden Press 4 8 12 24 37 50

NOTE: **N. Adams** *a-249i, 254p; c-204-206, 210, 212-215, 219, 231i, 233-237, 240-243, 249-252, 254, 263, 307, 308, 313, 314, 317.* **Adkins** *a-323i.* **Austin** *c-368i.* **Wayne Boring** *art-late 1940's to early 1960's.* **Buckler** *a(p)-352, 363, 364, 369; c(p)-324-327, 356, 363, 368, 369, 373, 376, 378.* **Burnley** *a-252r; c-19-25, 30, 33, 34, 35p, 38p, 39p, 45p.* **Fine** *a-252r.* **Kaluta** *a-400.* **Gil Kane** *a-272r, 367, 372, 375, Special 2; c-374p, 375p, 377, 381, 382, 384-390, 392, Annual 9, Special 2.* **Joe Kubert** *c-216.* **Morrow** *a-238.* **Mortimer** *a-250r.* **Perez** *c-364p.* **Fred Ray** *a-25; c-6, 8-18.* **Starlin** *c-355.* **Staton** *a-354i, 355i.* **Swan/Moldoff** *c-149.* **Williamson** *a(i)-408-410, 412-416; c-408i, 409i.* **Wrightson** *a-400, 416.*

SUPERMAN (2nd Series) (Title continues numbering from Adventures of Superman #649)
DC Comics: Jan, 1987 - No. 226, Apr, 2006; No. 650, May, 2006 - Present (75¢-$2.99)

0-(10/94) Zero Hour; released between #93 & #94 3.00
1-Byrne-c/a begins; intro new Metallo 6.00
2-8,10: 3-Legends x-over; Darkseid-c & app. 7-Origin/1st app. Rampage. 8-Legion app. 4.00
9-Joker-c 5.00
11-15,17-20,22-49,51,52,54-56,58-67: 11-1st new Mr. Mxyzptlk. 12-Lori Lemaris revived. 13-1st app. new Toyman. 13,14-Millennium x-over. 20-Doom Patrol app.; Supergirl cameo. 31-Mr. Mxyzptlk app. 37-Newsboy Legion app. 41-Lobo app. 44-Batman storyline, part 1. 45-Free extra 8 pgs. 54-Newsboy Legion story. 63-Aquaman x-over. 67-Last $1.00-c 3.00
16,21: 16-1st app. new Supergirl (4/88). 21-Supergirl-c/story; 1st app. Matrix who becomes new Supergirl 4.00
50-($1.50, 52 pgs.)-Clark Kent proposes to Lois 5.00
50-2nd printing 3.00
53-Clark reveals i.d. to Lois (Cont'd from Action #662) 4.00
53-2nd printing 3.00
57-($1.75, 52 pgs.) 4.00
68-72: 65,66,68-Deathstroke-c/stories. 70-Superman & Robin team-up 3.00
73-Doomsday cameo 5.00
74-Doomsday Pt. 2 (Cont'd from Justice League #69); Superman battles Doomsday 6.00
73,74-2nd printings 3.00
75-($2.50)-Collector's Ed.; Doomsday Pt. 6; Superman dies; polybagged w/poster of funeral, obituary from Daily Planet, postage stamp & armband premiums (direct sales only) 2 4 6 11 16 20
75-Direct sales copy (no upc code, 1st print) 1 3 4 6 8 10
75-Direct sales copy (no upc code, 2nd-4th prints) 3.00
75-Newsstand copy w/upc code 1 3 4 6 8 10
75-Platinum Edition; given away to retailers 4 8 12 28 44 60
76,77-Funeral For a Friend parts 4 & 8 4.00
78-($1.95)-Collector's Edition with die-cut outer-c & mini poster; Doomsday cameo 4.00
78-($1.50)-Newsstand Edition w/poster and different-c; Doomsday-c & cameo 3.00
79-81,83-89: 83-Funeral for a Friend epilogue; new Batman (Azrael) cameo. 87,88-Bizarro-c/story 3.00
82-($3.50)-Collector's Edition w/all chromium-c; real Superman revealed; Green Lantern x-over from G.L. #46; no ads 6.00
82-($2.00, 44 pgs.)-Regular Edition w/different-c 4.00
90-99: 93-(9/94)-Zero Hour. 94-(11/94). 95-Atom app. 96-Brainiac returns 3.00
100-Death of Clark Kent foil-c 4.00
100-Newsstand 3.00
101-122: 101-Begin $1.95-c; Black Adam app. 105-Green Lantern app. 110-Plastic Man-c/app. 114-Brainiac app; Dwyer-c. 115-Lois leaves Metropolis. 116-(10/96)-1st app. Teen Titans by Jurgens & Perez in 8 pg. preview. 117-Final Night. 118-Wonder Woman app. 119-Legion app. 122-New powers 3.00
123-Collector's Edition w/glow in the dark-c, new costume 6.00
123-Standard ed., new costume 4.00
124-149: 128-Cyborg-c/app. 131-Birth of Lena Luthor. 132-Superman Red/Superman Blue.

Superman (2nd series) #167 © DC

Superman #700 © DC

Superman Earth One HC © DC

GD 2.0 VG 4.0 FN 6.0 VF 8.0 VF/NM 9.0 NM- 9.2

134-Millennium Giants. 136,137-Superman 2999. 139-Starlin-a. 140-Grindberg-a 3.00
150-($2.95) Standard Ed.; Brainiac 2.0 app.; Jurgens-s 3.00
150-($3.95) Collector's Ed. w/holo-foil enhanced variant-c 4.00
151-158: 151-Loeb-s begins; Daily Planet reopens 3.00
159-174: 159-$2.25-c begin. 161-Joker-c/app. 162-Aquaman-c/app. 163-Young Justice app. 165-JLA app.; Ramos; Madureira, Liefeld, A. Adams, Wieringo, Churchill-a. 166-Collector's and reg. editions. 167-Return to Krypton. 168-Batman-c/app.(cont'd in Detective #756). 171-173-Our Worlds at War. 173-Sienkiewicz-a (2 pgs.). 174-Adopts black & red "S" logo 3.00
175-($3.50) Joker: Last Laugh x-over; Doomsday-c/app. 4.00
176-189,191-199: 176,180-Churchill-a. 180-Dracula app. 181-Bizarro-c/app. 184-Return to Krypton II. 189-Van Fleet-c. 192,193,195,197-199-New Supergirl app. 3.00
190-($2.25) Regular edition 3.00
190-($3.95) Double-Feature Issue; included reprint of Superman: The 10¢ Adventure 4.00
200-($3.50) Gene Ha-c/art by various; preview art by Yu & Bermejo 4.00
201-Mr Majestic-c/app.; cover swipe of Action #1 3.00
202,203-Godfall parts 3,6; Turner-c; Caldwell-a(p). 203-Jim Lee sketch pages 3.00
204-Jim Lee-c/a begins; Azzarello-s 3.00
204-Diamond Retailer Summit edition with sketch-c 8 16 24 54 90 125
205-214: 205-Two covers by Jim Lee and Michael Turner. 208-JLA app. 211-Battles Wonder Woman 3.00
215-($2.99) Conclusion to Azzarello/Lee arc 4.00
216-218,220-226: 216-Captain Marvel app. 221-Bizarro & Zoom app. 226-Earth-2 Superman story; Chaykin,Sale, Benes, Ordway-a 3.00
219-Omac/Sacrifice pt. 1; JLA app. 4.00
219-2nd printing with red background variant-c 3.00
(Title continues numbering from Adventures of Superman #649)
650-(5/06) One Year Later; Clark powerless after Infinite Crisis 4.00
651-665,667-669,671-674.676-680: 652-Begin $2.99-c. 654-658,662-664,667-Pacheco-a. 665-Origin of Jimmy Olsen. 671-673-Insect Queen. 676-680-Ross-c 3.00
666, 670,675-($3.99) 666-Simonson-a. 670-The Third Kryptonian. 675-Ross-c 4.00
681-699: 681-683-New Krypton x-over; Ross-c. 685-Mon-El freed from Phantom Zone. 694-Mon-El new costume. 698,699-Last Stand of New Krypton x-over 3.00
700-(8/10, $4.99) Cover by Gary Frank; Robinson-s; Straczynski-s begin 5.00
700-Variant-c by Risso 8.00
701-709: 701-"Grounded" begins; Straczynski-s/Cassaday-c. 704,706-Wilson-s 3.00
701-DC 75th Variant-c by Cassaday (Superman #1 swipe) 8.00
#1,000,000 (11/98) 853rd Century x-over; Gene Ha-c 3.00
Annual 1,2: 1 (1987)-No Byrne-a. 2 (1988)-Byrne-a; Newsboy Legion; Guardian returns 4.00
Annual 3-6 ('91-'94 68 pgs.): 1-Armageddon 2001 x-over; Batman app.; Austin-c(i) & part inks. 4-Eclipso app. 6-Elseworlds sty 4.00
Annual 3-2nd & 3rd printings; 3rd has silver ink 4.00
Annual 7 (1995, $3.95, 69 pgs.)-Year One story 4.00
Annual 8 (1996, $2.95)-Legends of the Dead Earth story 4.00
Annual 9 (1997, $3.95)-Pulp Heroes story 4.00
Annual 10 (1998, $2.95)-Ghosts; Wrightson-c 4.00
Annual 11 (1999, $2.95)-JLApe; Art Adams-c 4.00
Annual 12 (2000, $3.50)-Planet DC 4.00
Annual 13 (1/08, $3.99) Finale of Camelot Falls 4.00
Annual 14 (10/09, $3.99) Origin of Mon-El re-told; Pina-a/Guedes-c 4.00
...: 80 Page Giant (2/99, $4.95) Jurgens-c 5.00
...: 80 Page Giant 1 (5/10, $5.99) Lopresti-c; short stories by various 6.00
...: 80 Page Giant 2 (6/99, $4.95) Harris-c 5.00
...: 80 Page Giant 3 (11/00, $5.95) Nowlan-c; art by various 6.00
...: 80 Page Giant 2011 (4/11, $5.99) Nguyen-c; art by various; Bizarros app. 6.00
Special 1 (1992, $3.50, 68 pgs.)-Simonson-c/a 5.00

SUPERMAN (Hardcovers and Trade Paperbacks)
... and the Legion of Super-Heroes HC (2008, $24.99) r/Action Comics #858-863, covers and variants; intro. by Giffen; Gary Frank design sketch pages 25.00
... and the Legion of Super-Heroes SC (2009, $14.99) same contents as HC 15.00
...: Back in Action TPB (2007, $14.99) r/Action Comics #841-843 and DC Comics Presents #4,17,24; commentary by Busiek 15.00
.../Batman: Saga of the Super Sons TPB (2007, $19.99) r/Super Sons stories from '70s World's Finest #215,216,221,222,224,228,230,231,233,242,263 & Elseworlds 80-Page Giant 20.00
...: Brainiac HC (2009, $19.99, dustjacket) r/Action Comics #866-870 & Superman: New Krypton Special #1 20.00
...: Brainiac SC (2010, $12.99) r/Action #866-870 & Superman: New Krypton Spec. #1 13.00
...: Camelot Falls HC (2007, $19.99, dustjacket) r/Superman #654-658 20.00
...: Camelot Falls SC (2008, $12.99) r/Superman #654-658 13.00
...: Camelot Falls Vol. 2 HC (2008, $19.99, dj) r/Superman #662-664,667 & Ann. #13 20.00
...: Camelot Falls Vol. 2 The Weight of the World SC (2008, $12.99) r/Superman #662-664,667 & Ann. #13 13.00
...: Chronicles Vol. 1 ('06, $14.99, TPB) r/early Superman app. in Action Comics #1-13, New York World's Fair 1939 and Superman #1 15.00
...: Chronicles Vol. 2 ('07, $14.99, TPB) r/early Superman app. in Action Comics #14-20 and Superman #2,3 15.00
...: Chronicles Vol. 3 ('07, $14.99, TPB) r/early Superman app. in Action Comics #21-25, Superman #3,4 and New York World's Fair 1940 15.00
...: Chronicles Vol. 4 ('08, $14.99, TPB) r/early Superman app. in Action Comics #26-31, Superman #6,7 15.00
...: Chronicles Vol. 5 ('08, $14.99, TPB) r/early Superman app. in Action Comics #32-36, Superman #8,9 and World's Best Comics #1 15.00
...: Chronicles Vol. 6 ('09, $14.99, TPB) r/early Superman app. in Action Comics #37-40, Superman #10,11 and World's Finest Comics #2,3 15.00
...: Chronicles Vol. 7 ('09, $14.99, TPB) r/early Superman app. in Action Comics #41-43, Superman #12,13 and World's Finest Comics #4 15.00
...: Chronicles Vol. 8 ('10, $14.99, TPB) r/early Superman app. in Action Comics #44-47, and Superman #14,15 15.00
...: Codename: Patriot HC ('10, $24.99, d.j.) r/partial New Krypton storyline 25.00
...: Critical Condition ('03, $14.95, TPB) r/2000 Kryptonite poisoning storyline 15.00
.../ Doomsday: The Collection Edition (2006, $19.99) r/Superman/Doomsday: Hunter/Prey #1-3, Doomsday Ann. #1, Superman: The Doomsday Wars #1-3, Advs. of Superman #594 and Superman #175; intro. by Dan Jurgens 20.00
...: Daily Planet (2006, $19.99, TPB)-Reprints stories of Daily Planet staff 20.00
... Earth One HC (2010, $19.99)-Updated re-imagining of Superman's debut in Metropolis; Straczynski-s/Shane Davis-a; sketch pages b;y Davis 20.00
...: Emperor Joker TPB (2007, $14.99) reprints 2000 x-over from Superman titles 15.00
...: Endgame (2000, $14.95, TPB)-Reprints Y2K and Brainiac story line 15.00
...: Ending Battle (2009, $14.99, TPB) r/crossover of Superman titles from 2002 15.00
...: Eradication! The Origin of the Eradicator (1996, $12.95, TPB) 13.00
...: Escape From Bizarro World HC (2008, $24.99, dustjacket) r/Action #855-857; early apps. in Superman #140, DC Comics Presents #71 and Man of Steel #5; Vaughan intro. 25.00
...: Escape From Bizarro World SC (2009, $14.99) same contents as hardcover 15.00
...: Exile (1998, $14.95, TPB)-Reprints space exile following execution of Kryptonian criminals; 1st Eradicator 15.00
...: For Tomorrow Volume 1 HC (2005, $24.99, dustjacket) r/#204-209; intro by Azzarello; new cover and sketch section by Lee 25.00
...: For Tomorrow Volume 1 SC (2005, $14.99) r/#204-209; foil-stamped S emblem-c 15.00
...: For Tomorrow Volume 2 HC (2005, $24.99, dustjacket) r/#210-215; afterword and sketch section by Lee; new Lee-c with foil-stamped S emblem 25.00
...: For Tomorrow Volume 2 SC (2005, $14.99) r/#210-215; foil-stamped S emblem-c 15.00
...: Godfall HC (2004, $19.95, dustjacket) r/Action #812-813, Advs. of Superman #625-626, Superman #202-203; Caldwell sketch pages; Turner cover gallery; new Turner-c 20.00
...: Godfall SC (2004, $9.99) r/Action #812-813, Advs. of Superman #625-626, Superman #202-203; Caldwell sketch pages; Turner cover gallery; new Turner-c 10.00
...: Infinite Crisis TPB (2006, $12.99) r/Infinite Crisis #5, I.C. Secret Files and Origins 2006, Action Comics #836, Superman #226 and Advs. of Superman #649 13.00
... In the Forties ('05, $19.99, TPB) Intro. by Bob Hughes 20.00
... In the Fifties ('02, $19.95, TPB) Intro. by Mark Waid 20.00
... In the Sixties ('01, $19.95, TPB) Intro. by Mark Waid 20.00
... In the Seventies ('00, $19.95, TPB) Intro. by Christopher Reeve 20.00
... In the Eighties ('06, $19.99, TPB) Intro. by Jerry Ordway 20.00
... In the Name of Gog ('05, $17.99, TPB) r/Action Comics #820-825 18.00
... Kryptonite HC ('08, $24.99) r/Superman Confidential #1-5,11; Darwyn Cooke intro. 25.00
...: Last Son HC (2008, $19.99) r/Action Comics #844-846,851 and Annual #11; sketch pages and variant covers; Marc McClure intro. 20.00
... Mon-El HC ('10, $24.99) r/Superman #684-690, Action #874 & Annual #1, Superman: Secret Files 2009 #1 25.00
... Mon-El SC ('11, $17.99) r/Superman #684-690, Action #874 & Annual #1, Superman: Secret Files 2009 #1 18.00
... Mon-El - Man of Valor HC ('10, $24.99) r/Superman #692-697 & Annual #14, Adventure #11, Superman: Secret Files 2009 #1 25.00
... : New Krypton Vol. 1 HC ('09, $24.99, d.j.) r/Superman #681, Action #871 & one-shots 25.00
... : New Krypton Vol. 1 SC ('10, $17.99) r/Superman #681, Action #871 & one-shots 18.00
... : New Krypton Vol. 2 HC ('09, $24.99, d.j.) r/Superman #682,683, Action #872,873 & Supergirl #35,36; gallery of covers and variants 25.00
... : New Krypton Vol. 2 SC ('10, $17.99) same contents as HC 18.00
... : New Krypton Vol. 3 HC ('10, $24.99, d.j.) r/Superman: World of New Krypton #1-5 & Action Comics Annual #10; gallery of covers and variants 25.00
... : New Krypton Vol. 3 SC ('11, $17.99) same contents as HC 18.00
... : New Krypton Vol. 4 HC ('10, $24.99, d.j.) r/Superman: World of New Krypton #6-12; gallery of covers and variants; sketch and design art 25.00
... : Nightwing and Flamebird HC ('10, $24.99, d.j.) r/Action #875-879 & Annual #12 25.00
... : Nightwing and Flamebird SC ('10, $17.99) r/Action #875-879 & Annual #12 18.00
... : Nightwing and Flamebird Vol. 2 HC ('10, $24.99, d.j.) r/Action #883-889, Superman #696 & Adventure Comics #8-10 25.00
... No Limits ('00, $14.95, TPB) Reprints early 2000 stories 15.00
...: Our Worlds at War Book 1 ('02, $19.95, TPB) r/1st half of x-over 20.00

Superman: The Third Kryptonian SC © DC

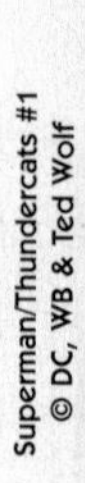

Superman/Thundercats #1 © DC, WB & Ted Wolf

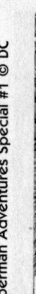

Superman Adventures Special #1 © DC

GD VG FN VF VF/NM NM-
2.0 4.0 6.0 8.0 9.0 9.2

...: Our Worlds at War Book 2 ('02, $19.95, TPB) r/2nd half of x-over 20.00
...: Our Worlds at War - The Complete Collection ('06, $24.99, TPB) r/entire x-over 25.00
...: Past and Future (2008, $19.99, TPB) r/time travel stories 1947-1983 20.00
...: President Lex TPB (2003, $17.95) r/Luthor's run for the White House; Harris-c 18.00
...: Redemption TPB (2007, $12.99) r/Superman #659,666 & Action Comics #848,849 13.00
...: Return to Krypton (2004, $17.95, TPB) r/2001-2002 x-over 18.00
...: Sacrifice (2005, $14.99, TPB) prelude x-over to Infinite Crisis; r/Superman #218-220, Advs. of Superman #642,643; Action #829, Wonder Woman #219,220 15.00
...: Shadows Linger (2008, $14.99, TPB) r/Superman #671-675 15.00
... : Strange Attractors (2006, $14.99, TPB) r/Action Comics #827,828,830-835 15.00
... : Tales From the Phantom Zone ('09, $19.99, TPB) r/Phantom Zone stories 1961-68 20.00
...: That Healing Touch TPB (2005, $14.99) r/Advs. of Superman #633-638 & Superman Secret Files 2004 15.00
...: The Adventures of Nightwing and Flamebird TPB (2009, $19.99)-reprints appearances in Superman Family #173,183-194 20.00
The Bottle City of Kandor TPB (2007, $14.99)-Reprints 1st app. in Action #242 and other stories; Nightwing and Flamebird app. 15.00
The Coming of Atlas HC (2009, $19.99, dustjacket)-r/Superman #677-680 & Atlas' debut from First Issue Special #1 (1975); intro by James Robinson 20.00
The Coming of Atlas SC (2010, $14.99) same contents as HC 15.00
The Death of Clark Kent (1997, $19.95, TPB)-Reprints Man of Steel #43 (1 page), Superman #99 (1 page),#100-102, Action #709 (1 page), #710,711, Advs. of Superman #523-525, Superman:The Man of Tomorrow #1 20.00
The Death of Superman (1993, $4.95, TPB)-Reprints Man of Steel #17-19, Superman #73-75, Advs. of Superman #496,497, Action #683,684, & Justice League #69

1 2 3 5 6 8

The Death of Superman, 2nd & 3rd printings 5.00
The Death of Superman Platinum Edition 15.00
...: The Greatest Stories Ever Told ('04, $19.95, TPB) Ross-c, Uslan intro. 20.00
...: The Greatest Stories Ever Told Vol. 2 ('06, $19.99, TPB) Ross-c, Greenberger intro. 20.00
...: The Journey ('06, $14.99, TPB) r/Action Comics #831 & Superman #217,221-225 15.00
...: The Man of Steel Vol. 2 ('03, $19.95, TPB) r/Superman #1-3, Action #584-586, Advs. of Superman #424-426 & Who's Who Update '87 20.00
...: The Man of Steel Vol. 3 ('04, $19.95, TPB) r/Superman #4-6, Action #587-589, Advs. of Superman #427-429; intro. by Ordway; new Ordway-c 20.00
...: The Man of Steel Vol. 4 ('05, $19.99, TPB) r/Superman #7,8; Action #590,591; Advs. of Superman #430,431; Legion of Super-Heroes #37,38; new Ordway-c 20.00
...: The Man of Steel Vol. 5 ('06, $19.99, TPB) r/Superman #9-11, Action #592-593, Advs. of Superman #432-435; intro. by Mike Carlin; new Ordway-c 20.00
...: The Man of Steel Vol. 6 ('08, $19.99, TPB) r/Superman #12 & Ann. #1, Action #594-595 & Ann. #1, Advs. of Superman Ann.#1; Booster Gold #23; new Ordway-c 20.00
The Third Kryptonian ('08, $14.99, TPB) r/Action #847, Superman #668-670 & Ann. #13 15.00
The Trial of Superman ('97, $14.95, TPB) reprints story arc 15.00
The World of Krypton ('08, $14.99, TPB) r/World of Krypton Vol. 2 #1-4 and various tales of Krypton and its history; Kupperberg intro. 15.00
The Wrath of Gog ('05, $14.99, TPB) reprints Action Comics #812-819 15.00
...: They Saved Luthor's Brain ('00, $14.95) r/ "death" and return of Luthor 15.00
...: 3-2-1 Action! ('08, $14.99) Jimmy Olsen super-powered stories; Steve Rude-c 15.00
...: 'Til Death Do Us Part ('01, $17.95) reprints; Mahnke-c 18.00
...: Time and Time Again (1994, $7.50, TPB)-Reprints 8.00
...: Transformed ('98, $12.95, TPB) r/post Final Night powerless Superman to Electric Superman 13.00
...: Unconventional Warfare (2005, $14.95, TPB) r/Adventures of Superman #625-632 and pages from Superman Secret Files 2004 15.00
...: Up, Up and Away! (2006, $14.99, TPB) r/Superman #650-653 and Action #837-840 15.00
... Vs. Brainiac (2008, $19.99, TPB) reprints 1st meeting in Action #242 and other duels 20.00
... Vs. Lex Luthor (2006, $19.99, TPB) reprints 1st meeting in Action #23 and 11 other classic duels 1940-2001 20.00
... Vs. The Flash (2005, $19.99, TPB) reprints their races from Superman #199, Flash #175, World's Finest #198, DC Comics Presents #1&2, Advs. of Superman #463 & DC First: Flash/Superman; new Alex Ross-c 20.00
... Vs. The Revenge Squad (1999, $12.95, TPB) 13.00
...: Whatever Happened to the Man of Tomorrow? TPB (1/97, $5.99) r/Superman #423 & Action Comics #583, intro. by Paul Kupperberg 6.00
...: Whatever Happened to the Man of Tomorrow? Deluxe Edition HC (2009, $24.99, d.j.) r/Superman #423, Action #583, DC Comics Presents #85, Superman Ann #11 25.00
...: Whatever Happened to the Man of Tomorrow? SC (2010, $14.99) r/same as HC 15.00

NOTE: ***Austin*** *a(i)-1-3.* ***Byrne*** *a-1-16p, 17, 19-21p, 22; c-1-17, 20-22; scripts-1-22.* ***Guice*** *c/a-64.* ***Kirby*** *c-37p.* ***Joe Quesada*** *c-Annual 4.* ***Russell*** *c/a-23i.* ***Simonson*** *c-69i. #19-21 2nd printings sold in multi-packs.*

SUPERMAN (one-shots)

Daily News Magazine Presents DC Comics' Superman nn-(1987, 8 pgs.)-Supplement to New York Daily News; Perez-c/a 5.00
...: A Nation Divided (1999, $4.95)-Elseworlds Civil War story 5.00
... & Savage Dragon: Chicago (2002, $5.95) Larsen-a; Ross-c 6.00
... & Savage Dragon: Metropolis (11/99, $4.95) Bogdanove-a 5.00
...: At Earth's End (1995, $4.95)-Elseworlds story 5.00
...: Blood of My Ancestors (2003, $6.95)-Gil Kane & John Buscema-a 7.00
...: Distant Fires (1998, $5.95)-Elseworlds; Chaykin-s 6.00
...: Emperor Joker (10/00, $3.50)-Follows Action #769 4.00
...: End of the Century (2/00, $24.95, HC)-Immonen-s/a 25.00
...: End of the Century (2003, $17.95, SC)-Immonen-s/a 18.00
... For Earth (1991, $4.95, 52 pgs, printed on recycled paper)-Ordway wraparound-c 5.00
...IV Movie Special (1987, $2.00)-Movie adaptation; Heck-a 4.00
...Gallery, The 1 (1993, $2.95)-Poster-a 3.00
..., Inc. (1999, $6.95)-Elseworlds Clark as a sports hero; Garcia-Lopez-a 7.00
...: Infinite City HC (2005, $24.99, dustjacket) Mike Kennedy-s/Carlos Meglia-a 25.00
...: Infinite City SC (2006, $17.99) Mike Kennedy-s/Carlos Meglia-a 18.00
...: Kal (1995, $5.95)-Elseworlds story 6.00
...: Lex 2000 (1/01, $3.50)-Election night for the Luthor Presidency 4.00
...: Monster (1999, $5.95)-Elseworlds story; Anthony Williams-a 6.00
... Movie Special-(9/83)-Adaptation of Superman III; other versions exist with store logos on bottom 1/3 of-c 4.00
...: New Krypton Special 1-(12/08, $3.99) Funeral of Pa Kent; newly enlarged Kandor 4.00
...: Our Worlds at War Secret Files 1-(8/01, $5.95)-Stories & profile pages 6.00
... Plus 1(2/97, $2.95)-Legion of Super-Heroes-c/app. 4.00
...'s Metropolis-(1996, $5.95, prestige format)-Elseworlds; McKeever-c/a 6.00
...: Speeding Bullets-(1993, $4.95, 52 pgs.)-Elseworlds 5.00
.../Spider-Man-(1995, $3.95)-r/DC and Marvel Presents... 4.00
... 10-Cent Adventure 1 (3/02, 10¢) McDaniel-a; intro. Cir-El Supergirl 3.0
...: The Earth Stealers 1-(1988, $2.95, 52 pgs, prestige format) Byrne script; painted-c 4.00
...: The Earth Stealers 1-2nd printing 3.00
...: The Legacy of Superman #1 (3/93, $2.50, 68 pgs.)-Art Adams-c; Simonson-a 4.00
...: The Last God of Krypton ('99,$4.95) Hildebrandt Bros.-a/Simonson-s 5.00
...: The Odyssey ('99, $4.95) Clark Kent's post-Smallville journey 5.00
...: 3-D (12/98, $3.95)-with glasses 4.00
.../Thundercats (1/04, $5.95) Winick-s/Garza-a; two covers by Garza & McGuinness 6.00
.../Through the Ages (2006, $3.99) r/Action #1, Superman ('87) #7; origins and pin-ups 4.00
.../Toyman-(1996, $1.95) 3.00
...: True Brit (2004, $24.95, HC w/dust jacket) Elseworlds; Kal-El's rocket lands in England; co-written by John Cleese and Kim Howard Johnson; John Byrne-a 25.00
...: True Brit (2005, $17.99, TPB) Elseworlds; Kal-El's rocket lands in England 18.00
...: Under A Yellow Sun (1994, $5.95, 68 pgs.)-A Novel by Clark Kent; embossed-c 6.00
... Vs. Darkseid: Apokolips Now! 1 (3/03, $2.95) McKone-a; Kara (Supergirl #75) app. 3.00
...: War of the Worlds (1999, $5.95)-Battles Martians 6.00
...: Where is thy Sting? (2001, $6.95)-McCormack-Sharp-c/a 7.00
...: Y2K (2/00, $4.95)-1st Brainiac 13 app.; Guice-c/a 5.00

SUPERMAN ADVENTURES, THE (Based on animated series)
DC Comics: Oct, 1996 - No. 66, Apr, 2002 ($1.75/$1.95/$1.99)

1-Rick Burchett-c/a begins; Paul Dini script; Lex Luthor app.; silver ink, wraparound-c 4.00
2-20,22: 2-McCloud scripts begin; Metallo-c/app. 3-Brainiac-c/app. 6-Mxyzptlk-c/app. 3.00
21-($3.95) 1st animated Supergirl 5.00
23-66: 23-Begin $1.99-c; Livewire app. 25-Batgirl-c/app. 28-Manley-a. 54-Retells Superman #233 "Kryptonite Nevermore" 58-Ross-c 3.00
Annual 1 (1997, $3.95)-Zatanna and Bruce Wayne app. 4.00
Special 1 (2/98, $2.95) Superman vs. Lobo 4.00
TPB (1998, $7.95) r/#1-6 8.00
... Vol 1: Up, Up and Away (2004, $6.95, digest) r/#16,19,22-24; Amancio-a 7.00
... Vol 2: The Never-Ending Battle (2004, $6.95) r/#25-29 7.00
... Vol 3: Last Son of Krypton (2006, $6.99) r/#30-34 7.00
... Vol 4: The Man of Steel (2006, $6.99) r/#35-39 7.00

SUPERMAN ALIENS 2: GOD WAR (Also see Superman Vs. Aliens)
DC Comics/Dark Horse Comics: May, 2002 - No. 4, Nov, 2002 ($2.99, limited series)

1-4-Bogdanove & Nowlan-a; Darkseid & New Gods app. 3.00
TPB (6/03, $12.95) r/#1-4 13.00

SUPERMAN & BATMAN: GENERATIONS (Elseworlds)
DC Comics: 1999 - No. 4, 1999 ($4.95, limited series)

1-4-Superman & Batman team-up from 1939 to the future; Byrne-c/s/a 5.00
TPB (2000, $14.95) r/series 15.00

SUPERMAN & BATMAN: GENERATIONS II (Elseworlds)
DC Comics: 2001 - No. 4, 2001 ($5.95, limited series)

1-4-Superman, Batman & others team-up from 1942-future; Byrne-c/s/a 6.00
TPB (2003, $19.95) r/series 20.00

SUPERMAN & BATMAN: GENERATIONS III (Elseworlds)
DC Comics: Mar, 2003 - No. 12, Feb, 2004 ($2.95, limited series)

1-12-Superman & Batman through the centuries; Byrne-c/s/a 3.00

Superman & Bugs Bunny #2 © DC & WB

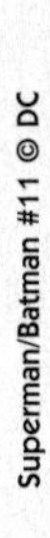
Superman/Batman #11 © DC

Superman Family #195 © DC

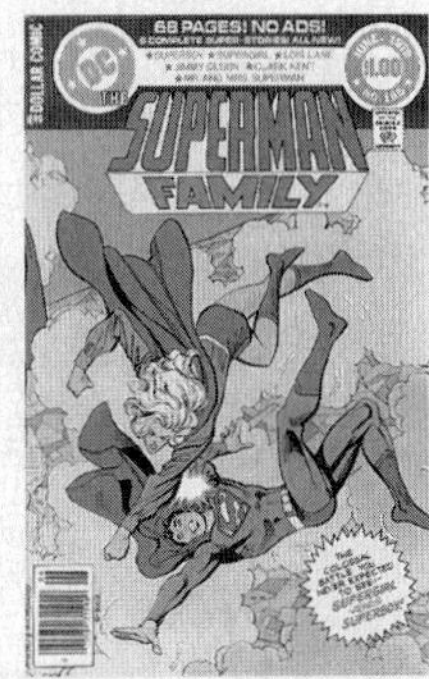

	GD	VG	FN	VF	VF/NM	NM-
	2.0	4.0	6.0	8.0	9.0	9.2

GD VG FN VF VF/NM NM-
2.0 4.0 6.0 8.0 9.0 9.2

SUPERMAN & BATMAN VS. ALIENS AND PREDATOR
DC Comics: 2007 - No. 2, 2007 ($5.99, squarebound, limited series)

1,2-Schultz-s/Olivetti-a 6.00
TPB (2007, $12.99) r/#1,2; pencil breakdown pages 13.00

SUPERMAN AND BATMAN VS. VAMPIRES AND WEREWOLVES
DC Comics: Early Dec, 2008 - No. 6, Late Feb, 2009 ($2.99, limited series)

1-6-Van Hook-s/Mandrake-a/c. 1-Wonder Woman app. 5-Demon-c/app. 3.00
TPB (2009, $14.99) r/#1-6; intro. by John Landis 15.00

SUPERMAN & BATMAN: WORLD'S FUNNEST (Elseworlds)
DC Comics: 2000 ($6.95, square-bound, one-shot)

nn-Mr. Mxyzptlk and Bat-Mite destroy each DC Universe; Dorkin-s; art by various incl. Ross, Timm, Miller, Allred, Moldoff, Gibbons, Cho, Jimenez 7.00

SUPERMAN & BUGS BUNNY
DC Comics: Jul, 2000 - No. 4, Oct, 2000 ($2.50, limited series)

1-4-JLA & Looney Tunes characters meet 3.00

SUPERMAN/BATMAN
DC Comics: Oct, 2003 - Present ($2.95/$2.99)

1-Two covers (Superman or Batman in foreground) Loeb-s/McGuinness-a; Metallo app. 5.00
1-2nd printing (Batman cover) 3.00
1-3rd printing; new McGuinness cover 3.00
1-Diamond/Alliance Retailer Summit Edition-variant 7 14 21 45 73 100
1-(6/06, Free Comic Book Day giveaway) reprints #1 2.50
2-6: 2,5-Future Superman app. 6-Luthor in battlesuit 3.00
7-Pat Lee-c/a; Superboy & Robin app. 3.00
8-Michael Turner-c/a; intro. new Kara Zor-El 5.00
8-Second printing with sketch cover 3.00
8-Third printing with new Turner cover 3.00
9-13-Michael Turner-c/a; Wonder Woman app. 10,13-Variant-c by Jim Lee 3.00
14-25: 14-18-Pacheco-a; Lightning Lord, Saturn Queen & Cosmic King app. 19-Supergirl app.; leads into Supergirl #1. 21-25-Bizarro app. 25-Superman & Batman covers; 2nd printing with white bkgrd cover 3.00
26-($3.99) Sam Loeb tribute issue; 2 covers by Turner; story & art by 26 various; back-up by Loeb & Sale 5.00
27-49: 27-Flashback to Earth-2 Power Girl & Huntress; Maguire-a. 34-36-Metal Men app. 3.00
50-($3.99) Thomas Wayne meets Jor-El; Justice League app. 4.00
51-74: 51,52-Mr. Mxyzptlk app. 66,67-Blackest Night; Man-Bat and Bizarro app. 3.00
75-($4.99) Quitely-c; Legion of Super-Heroes app.; Ordway-a; 2-pg. features by various 5.00
76-82: 76-Aftermath of Batman's "death". 77-Supergirl/Damian team-up 3.00
Annual #1 (12/06, $3.99) Re-imaging of 1st meeting from World's Finest #71 4.00
Annual #2 (5/08, $3.99) Kolins-a; re-imaging of Superman as Supernova story 4.00
Annual #3 (3/09, $3.99) Composite Superman-c by Wrightson; Batista-a 4.00
Annual #4 (8/10, $4.99) Batman Beyond; Levitz-s/Guedes-a/Lau-c 8.00
...Absolute Power HC (2005, $19.99) r/#14-18 20.00
...Absolute Power SC (2006, $12.99) r/#14-18 13.00
...Big Noise SC (2010, $14.99) r/#64,68-71 15.00
...Enemies Among Us SC (2009, $12.99) r/#28-33 13.00
...Finest Worlds SC (2010, $14.99) r/#50-56 15.00
...Night and Day HC (2010, $19.99) r/#60-63,65-67 20.00
...Public Enemies HC (2004, $19.95) r/#1-6 & Secret Files 2003; sketch art pages 20.00
...Public Enemies SC (2005, $12.99) r/#1-6 & Secret Files 2003; sketch art pages 13.00
...Public Enemies SC (2009, $14.99) r/#1-6 & Secret Files 2003; sketch art pages 15.00
...Secret Files 2003 (11/03, $4.95) Reis-a; pin-ups by various; Loeb/Sale short-s 5.00
... : Supergirl HC (2004, $19.95) r/#8-13; intro by Loeb, cover gallery, sketch pages 20.00
... : Supergirl SC (2005, $12.99) r/#8-13; intro by Loeb, cover gallery, sketch pages 13.00
... : The Search For Kryptonite HC (2008, $19.99) r/#44-49; Davis sketch pages 20.00
... : The Search For Kryptonite SC (2009, $12.99) r/#44-49; Davis sketch pages 13.00
... : Torment HC (2008, $19.99) r/#37-42; cover gallery, Nguyen sketch pages 20.00
... : Vengeance HC (2006, $19.99) r/#20-25; sketch pages 20.00
... : Vengeance SC (2008, $12.99) r/#20-25; sketch pages 13.00

SUPERMAN/BATMAN: ALTERNATE HISTORIES
DC Comics: 1996 ($14.95, trade paperback)

nn-Reprints Detective Comics Annual #7, Action Comics Annual #6, Steel Annual #1, Legends of the Dark Knight Annual #4 15.00

SUPERMAN: BIRTHRIGHT
DC Comics: Sept, 2003 - No. 12, Sept, 2004 ($2.95, limited series)

1-12-Waid-s/Leinil Yu-a; retelling of origin and early Superman years 3.00
HC (2004, $29.95, dustjacket) r/series; cover gallery; Waid proposal with Yu concept art 30.00
SC (2005, $19.99) r/series; cover gallery; Waid proposal with Yu concept art 20.00

SUPERMAN COMICS
DC Comics: 1939

nn - Ashcan comic, not distributed to newsstands, only for in-house use. Cover art is Action Comics #7 with interior being Action Comics #8. A CGC certified 9.0 copy sold for $37,375 in 2005 and for $90,000 in 2007.

SUPERMAN CONFIDENTIAL (See Superman Hardcovers and TPBs listings for reprint)
DC Comics: Jan, 2007 - No. 14, Jun, 2008 ($2.99)

1-14: 1-5,9-Darwyn Cooke-s/Tim Sale-a/c; origin of Kryptonite re-told. 8-10-New Gods and Darkside app. 3.00
...: Kryptonite TPB (2009, $14.99) r/#1-5,11; intro. by Darwyn Cooke; Tim Sale sketch-a 15.00

SUPERMAN: DAY OF DOOM
DC Comics: Jan, 2003 - No. 4, Feb, 2003 ($2.95, weekly limited series)

1-4-Jurgens-s/Jurgens & Sienkiewicz-a 3.00
TPB (2003, $9.95) r/#1-4 10.00

SUPERMAN/DOOMSDAY: HUNTER/PREY
DC Comics: 1994 - No. 3, 1994 ($4.95, limited series, 52 pgs.)

1-3 5.00

SUPERMAN FAMILY, THE (Formerly Superman's Pal Jimmy Olsen)
National Per. Publ./DC Comics: No. 164, Apr-May, 1974 - No. 222, Sept, 1982

	GD	VG	FN	VF	VF/NM	NM-
164-(100 pgs.) Jimmy Olsen, Supergirl, Lois Lane begin	5	10	15	30	48	65
165-169 (100 pgs.)	3	6	9	19	29	38
170-176 (68 pgs.)	3	6	9	14	19	24
177-190 (52 pgs.): 177-181-52 pgs. 182-Marshall Rogers-a; $1.00 issues begin; Krypto begins, ends #192. 183-Nightwing-Flamebird begins, ends #194. 189-Brainiac 5, Mon -El app.	2	4	6	9	13	16
191-193,195-199: 191-Superboy begins, ends #198	2	3	4	6	8	10
194,200: 194-Rogers-a. 200-Book length sty	2	4	6	8	10	12
201-210,212-222	1	2	3	5	6	8
211-Earth II Batman & Catwoman marry	2	4	6	8	11	14

NOTE: ***N. Adams** c-182-185. **Anderson** a-186i. **Buckler** c(p)-190, 191, 209, 210, 215, 217, 220. **Jones** a-191-193. **Gil Kane** c(p)-221, 222. **Mortimer** a(p)-191-193, 199, 201-222. **Orlando** a(i)-186, 187. **Rogers** a-182, 194. **Staton** a-191-194, 196p. **Tuska** a(p)-203, 207-209.*

SUPERMAN/FANTASTIC FOUR
DC Comics/Marvel Comics: 1999 ($9.95, tabloid size, one-shot)

1-Battle Galactus and the Cyborg; wraparound-c by Alex Ross and Dan Jurgens; Jurgens-s/a; Thibert-a 10.00

SUPERMAN FOR ALL SEASONS
DC Comics: 1998 - No, 4, 1998 ($4.95, limited series, prestige format)

1-Loeb-s/Sale-a/c; Superman's first year in Metropolis 6.00
2-4 5.00
Hardcover (1999, $24.95) r/#1-4 25.00

SUPERMAN FOR EARTH (See Superman one-shots)

SUPERMAN FOREVER
DC Comics: Jun, 1998 ($5.95, one-shot)

1-($5.95)-Collector's Edition with a 7-image lenticular-c by Alex Ross; Superman returns to normal; s/a by various 7.00
1-($4.95) Standard Edition with single image Ross-c 5.00

SUPERMAN/GEN13
DC Comics (WildStorm): Jun, 2000 - No. 3, Aug, 2000 ($2.50, limited series)

1-3-Hughes-s/ Bermejo-a; Campbell variant-c for each 3.00
TPB (2001, $9.95) new Bermejo-c; cover gallery 10.00

SUPERMAN: KING OF THE WORLD
DC Comics: June, 1999 ($3.95/$4.95, one-shot)

1-($3.95) Regular Ed. 4.00
1-($4.95) Collectors' Ed. with gold foil enhanced-c 5.00

SUPERMAN: LAST SON OF EARTH
DC Comics: 2000 - No. 2, 2000 ($5.95, limited series, prestige format)

1,2-Elseworlds; baby Clark rockets to Krypton; Gerber-s/Wheatley-a 6.00

SUPERMAN: LAST STAND OF NEW KRYPTON
DC Comics: May, 2010 - No. 3, Late June, 2010 ($3.99, limited series)

1-3-Robinson & Gates-s/Woods-a. 2-Pérez-c. 3-Sook-c 4.00
HC (2010, $24.99, DJ) r/#1,2, Adventure Comics #8,9, Supergirl #51 & Superman #698 25.00
Vol. 2 HC (2010, $19.99, DJ) r/#3, Adventure #10,11, Supergirl #52 & Superman #699 20.00

SUPERMAN: LAST STAND ON KRYPTON
DC Comics: 2003 ($6.95, one-shot, prestige format)

1-Sequel to Superman: Last Son of Earth; Gerber-s/Wheatley-a 7.00

SUPERMAN: LOIS LANE (Girlfrenzy)

Superman Secret Files & Origins 2004 © DC

Superman: Secret Origin #4 © DC

Superman's Girlfriend Lois Lane #104 © DC

GD VG FN VF VF/NM NM-
2.0 4.0 6.0 8.0 9.0 9.2

DC Comics: Jun, 1998 ($1.95, one shot)
1-Connor & Palmiotti-a 3.00

SUPERMAN/MADMAN HULLABALOO!
Dark Horse Comics: June, 1997 - No. 3, Aug, 1997 ($2.95, limited series)
1-3-Mike Allred-c/s/a 3.00
TPB (1997, $8.95) 9.00

SUPERMAN: METROPOLIS
DC Comics: Apr, 2003 - No. 12, Mar, 2004 ($2.95, limited series)
1-12-Focus on Jimmy Olsen; Austen-s. 1-6-Zezelj-a. 7-12-Kristiansen-a. 8,9-Creeper app. 3.00

SUPERMAN METROPOLIS SECRET FILES
DC Comics: Jun, 2000 ($4.95, one shot)
1-Short stories, pin-ups and profile pages; Hitch and Neary-c 5.00

SUPERMAN: PEACE ON EARTH
DC Comics: Jan, 1999 ($9.95, Treasury-sized, one-shot)
1-Alex Ross painted-c/a; Paul Dini-s 12.00

SUPERMAN: RED SON
DC Comics: 2003 - No. 3, 2003 ($5.95, limited series, prestige format)
1-Elseworlds; Superman's rocket lands in Russia; Mark Millar-s/Dave Johnson-c/a 10.00
2,3 6.00
TPB (2004, $17.95) r/#1-3; intro. by Tom DeSanto; sketch pages 18.00
... - The Deluxe Edition HC (2009, $24.99, d.j.) r/#1-3; sketch art by various 25.00

SUPERMAN RED/ SUPERMAN BLUE
DC Comics: Feb, 1998 ($4.95, one shot)
1-Polybagged w/3-D glasses and reprint of Superman 3-D (1955); Jurgens-plot/3-D cover; script and art by various 5.00
1-($3.95)-Standard Ed.; comic only, non 3-D cover 4.00

SUPERMAN RETURNS... (2006 movie)
DC Comics: Aug, 2006 ($3.99, movie tie-in stories by Singer, Dougherty and Harris)
Prequel 1 - Krypton to Earth; Olivetti-a/Hughes-c; retells Jor-El's story 6.00
Prequel 2 - Ma Kent; Kerschl-a/Hughes-c; Ma Kent during Clark childhood and absence 4.00
Prequel 3 - Lex Luthor; Leonardi-a/Hughes-c; Luthor's 5 years in prison 4.00
Prequel 4 - Lois Lane; Dias-a/Hughes-c; Lois during Superman's absence 4.00
The Movie and Other Tales of the Man of Steel (2006, $12.99, TPB) adaptation; origin from Amazing World of Superman; Action #810, Superman #185; Advs. of Superman #575 13.00
The Official Movie Adaptation (2006, $6.99) Pasko-s/Haley-a; photo-c 7.00
...: The Prequels TPB (2006, $12.99) r/the 4 prequels 13.00

SUPERMAN: SAVE THE PLANET
DC Comics: Oct, 1998 ($2.95, one-shot)
1-($2.95) Regular Ed.; Luthor buys the Daily Planet 3.00
1-($3.95) Collector's Ed. with acetate cover 4.00

SUPERMAN SCRAPBOOK (Has blank pages; contains no comics)

SUPERMAN: SECRET FILES
DC Comics: Jan, 1998; May 1999 ($4.95)
1,2: 1-Retold origin story, "lost" pages & pin-ups 5.00
... & Origins 2004 (8/04) pin-ups by Lee, Turner and others 5.00
... & Origins 2005 (1/06) short stories and pin-ups by various 5.00
... 2009 (10/09, $4.99) short stories and pin-ups about New Krypton x-over 5.00

SUPERMAN: SECRET IDENTITY
DC Comics: 2004 - No. 4, 2004 ($5.95, squarebound, limited series)
1-4-Busiek-s/Immonen-a/c 6.00

SUPERMAN: SECRET ORIGIN
DC Comics: Nov, 2009 - No. 6, Oct, 2010 ($3.99, limited series)
1-6-Geoff Johns-s/Gary Frank-a/c; origin mythos re-told. 2-Legion app. 5-Metallo app. 4.00
1-6-Variant covers by Frank 6.00
HC (2011, $29.99) r/#1-6; intro. by David Goyer; variant covers 30.00

SUPERMAN'S GIRLFRIEND LOIS LANE (See Action Comics #1, 80 Page Giant #3, 14, Lois Lane, Showcase #9, 10, Superman #28 & Superman Family)

SUPERMAN'S GIRLFRIEND LOIS LANE (See Showcase #9,10)
National Periodical Publ.: Mar-Apr, 1958 - No. 136, Jan-Feb, 1974; No. 137, Sept-Oct, 1974
1-(3-4/58) 329 658 987 2961 6081 9200
2 85 170 255 723 1462 2200
3 54 108 162 459 930 1400
4,5 43 86 129 344 697 1050
6,7 35 70 105 273 537 800
8-10: 9-Pat Boone-c/story 29 58 87 218 439 660
11-13,15-19: 12-(10/59)-Aquaman app. 17-(5/60) 2nd app. Brainiac.
18 36 54 131 266 400
14-Supergirl x-over; Batman app. on-c only 19 38 57 139 280 420
20-Supergirl-c/sty 19 38 57 134 272 410
21-28: 23-1st app. Lena Thorul, Lex Luthor's sister; 1st Lois as Elastic Lass. 27-Bizarro-c/story 14 28 42 99 200 300
29-Aquaman, Batman, Green Arrow cover app. and cameo; last 10¢ issue
15 30 45 104 212 320
30-32,34-46,48,49 10 20 30 67 116 165
33(5/62)-Mon -El app. 10 20 30 69 122 175
47-Legion app. 10 20 30 69 122 175
50(7/64)-Triplicate Girl, Phantom Girl & Shrinking Violet app.
10 20 30 69 122 175
51-55,57-67,69: 59-Jor -El app.; Batman back-up sty 7 14 21 50 83 115
56-Saturn Girl app. 8 16 24 52 86 120
68-(Giant G-26) 9 18 27 61 103 145
70-Penguin & Catwoman app. (1st S.A. Catwoman, 11/66; also see Detective #369 for 3rd app.); Batman & Robin cameo 23 46 69 168 334 500
71-Batman & Robin cameo (3 panels); Catwoman story cont'd from #70 (2nd app.); see Detective #369 for 3rd app 14 28 42 95 188 280
72,73,75,76,78 6 12 18 39 62 85
74-1st Bizarro Flash (5/67); JLA cameo 6 12 18 41 66 90
77-(Giant G-39) 7 14 21 50 83 115
79-Neal Adams-c or c(i) begin, end #95,108 6 12 18 41 66 90
80-85,87,88,90-92: 92-Last 12¢ issue 5 10 15 30 48 65
86,95 (Giants G-51,G-63)-Both have Neal Adams-c 6 12 18 43 69 95
89,93: 89-Batman x-over; all N. Adams-c. 93-Wonder Woman-c/story
5 10 15 32 51 70
94,96-99,101-103,107-110 4 8 12 24 37 50
100 4 8 12 26 41 55
104-(Giant G-75) 6 12 18 39 62 85
105-Origin/1st app. The Rose & the Thorn. 6 12 18 39 62 85
106-"Black Like Me" story; Lois changes her skin color to black
8 16 24 54 90 125
111-Justice League-c/s; Morrow-a; last 15¢ issue 4 8 12 26 41 55
112,114-123 (52 pgs.): 122-G.A. Lois Lane-r/Superman #30. 123-G.A. Batman-r/Batman #35 (w/Catwoman) 4 8 12 24 37 50
113-(Giant G-87) Kubert-a (previously unpublished G.A. story)(scarce in NM)
6 12 18 43 69 95
124-135: 130-Last Rose & the Thorn. 132-New Zatanna story
3 6 9 16 23 30
136,137: 136-Wonder Woman x-over 3 6 9 18 27 35
Annual 1(Sum, 1962)-r/L. Lane #12; Aquaman app. 19 38 57 139 280 420
Annual 2(Sum, 1963) 14 28 42 95 188 280
NOTE: *Buckler a-117-121p. Curt Swan or Kurt Schaffenberger a-1-81(most); c(p)-1-15.*

SUPERMAN/SHAZAM: FIRST THUNDER
DC Comics: Nov, 2005 - No. 4, Feb, 2006 ($3.50, limited series)
1-4-Retells first meeting; Winick-s/Middleton-a. Dr. Sivana app. 3.50

SUPERMAN: SILVER BANSHEE
DC Comics: Dec, 1998 - No. 2, Jan, 1999 ($2.25, mini-series)
1,2-Brereton-s/c; Chin-a 3.00

SUPERMAN'S NEMESIS: LEX LUTHOR
DC Comics: Mar, 1999 - No. 4, Jun, 1999 ($2.50, mini-series)
1-4-Semeiks-a 3.00

SUPERMAN'S PAL JIMMY OLSEN (Superman Family #164 on)
(See Action Comics #6 for 1st app. & 80 Page Giant)
National Periodical Publ.: Sept-Oct, 1954 - No. 163, Feb-Mar, 1974 (Fourth World #133-148)
1 540 1080 1620 4860 9180 13,500
2 142 284 426 1207 2454 3700
3-Last pre-code issue 83 166 249 706 1428 2150
4,5 53 106 159 451 913 1375
6-10 39 78 117 312 619 925
11-20: 15-1st S.A. issue 27 54 81 197 399 600
21-28,30 17 34 51 122 249 375
29-(6/58) 1st app. Krypto with Superman 18 36 54 131 266 400
31-Origin & 1st app. Elastic Lad (Jimmy Olsen) 15 30 45 110 223 335
32-40: 33-One pg. biography of Jack Larson (TV Jimmy Olsen). 36-Intro Lucy Lane. 37-2nd app. Elastic Lad & 1st cover app. 13 26 39 89 170 250
41-50: 41-1st J.O. Robot. 48-Intro/origin Superman Emergency Squad
10 20 30 72 131 190
51-56: 56-Last 10¢ issue 9 18 27 61 103 145
57-62,64-70: 57-Olsen marries Supergirl. 62-Mon-El & Elastic Lad app. but not as

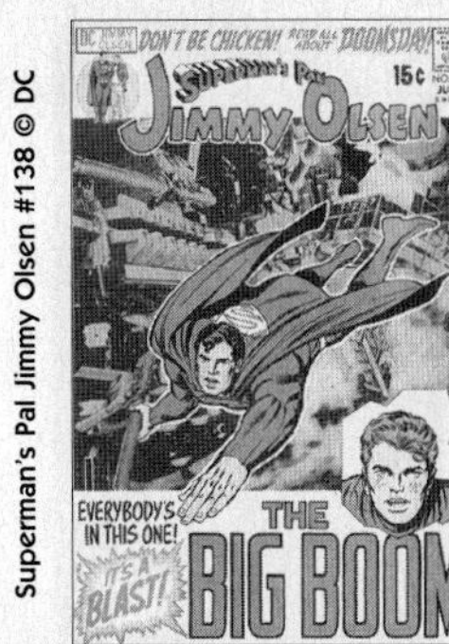

Superman's Pal Jimmy Olsen #138 © DC

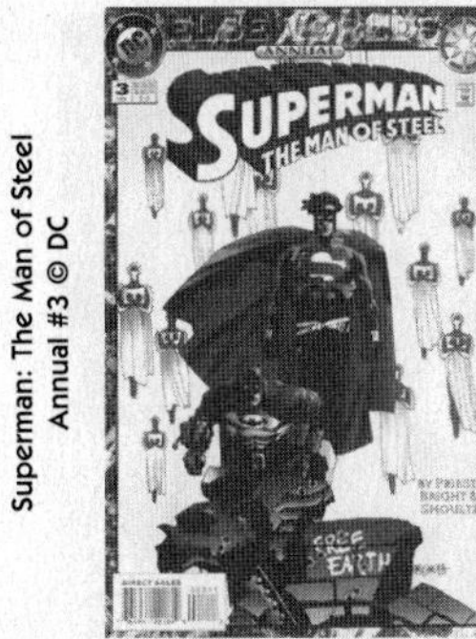

Superman: The Man of Steel Annual #3 © DC

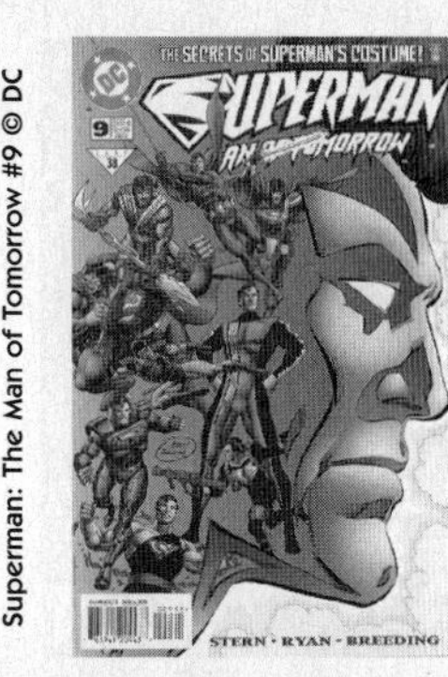

Superman: The Man of Tomorrow #9 © DC

GD VG FN VF VF/NM NM-
2.0 4.0 6.0 8.0 9.0 9.2

Legionnaires. 70-Element Boy (Lad) app. 7 14 21 45 73 100
63(9/62)-Legion of Super-Villains app. 7 14 21 47 76 105
71,74,75,78,80-84,86,89,90: 86-Jimmy Olsen Robot becomes Congorilla 6 12 18 37 59 80
72,73,76,77,79,85,87,88: 72(10/63)-Legion app; Elastic Lad (Olsen) joins. 73-Ultra Boy app. 76,85-Legion app. 76-Legion app. 77-Olsen with Colossal Boy's powers & costume; origin Titano retold. 79-(9/64)-Titled The Red-headed Beatle of 1000 B.C. 85-Legion app. 87-Legion of Super-Villains app. 88-Star Boy app. 6 12 18 39 62 85
91-94,96-98 5 10 15 30 48 65
95 (Giant G-25) 7 14 21 47 76 105
99-Olsen w/powers & costumes of Lightning Lad, Sun Boy & Element Lad 5 10 15 32 51 70
100-Legion cameo 5 10 15 34 55 75
101-103,105-112,114-120: 106-Legion app. 110-Infinity-c. 117-Batman & Legion cameo. 120-Last 12¢ issue 4 8 12 24 37 50
104 (Giant G-38) 6 12 18 39 62 85
113,122,131,140 (Giants G-50,G-62,G-74,G-86) 5 10 15 34 55 75
121,123-130,132 4 8 12 22 34 45
133-(10/70)-Jack Kirby story & art begins; re-intro Newsboy Legion; 1st app. Morgan Edge 6 12 18 41 66 90
134-1st app. Darkseid (1 panel, 12/70) 7 14 21 47 76 105
135-2nd app. Darkseid (1 pg. cameo; see New Gods & Forever People); G.A. Guardian app. 5 10 15 30 48 65
136-139: 136-Origin new Guardian. 138-Partial photo-c. 139-Last 15¢ issue 4 8 12 24 37 50
141-150: (25¢,52 pgs.). 141-Photo-c; Newsboy Legion-r by S&K begin; full pg. self-portrait of Jack Kirby; Don Rickles cameo. 149,150-G.A. Plastic Man-r in both; 150-Newsboy Legion app. 4 8 12 22 34 45
151-163 3 6 9 16 23 30
... Special 1 (12/08, $4.99) New Krypton tie-in; The Guardian and Dubbilex app. 5.00
... Special 2 (10/09, $4.99) New Krypton tie-in; Mon-El app.; Chang-a 5.00
Superman: The Amazing Transformations of Jimmy Olsen TPB (2007, $14.99) reprints Olsen's transformations into Wolf-Man, Elastic Lad, Turtle Boy and others; new Bolland-c 15.00
NOTE: *Issues #141-148 contain **Simon & Kirby** Newsboy Legion reprints from Star Spangled #7, 8, 9, 10, 11, 12, 13, 14 in that order. **N. Adams** c-109-112, 115, 117, 118, 120, 121, 132, 134-136, 147, 148. **Kirby** a-133-139p, 141-148p; c-133, 137, 139, 142, 145p. **Kirby/N. Adams** c-137, 138, 141-144, 146. **Curt Swan** c-1-14(most)., 140.*

SUPERMAN SPECTACULAR (Also see DC Special Series #5)
DC Comics: 1982 (Magazine size, 52 pgs., square binding)
1-Saga of Superman Red/ Superman Blue; Luthor and Terra-Man app.; Gonzales & Colletta-a 1 3 4 6 8 10

SUPERMAN: STRENGTH
DC Comics: 2005 - No. 3, 2005 ($5.95, limited series)
1-3: Alex Ross-c/Scott McCloud-s/Aluir Amancio-a 6.00

SUPERMAN / SUPERGIRL: MAELSTROM
DC Comics: Early Jan, 2009 - No. 5, Mar, 2009 ($2.99, limited series)
1-5: Palmiotti & Gray-s/Noto-c/a; Darkseid app. 3.00
TPB (2009, $12.99) r/#1-5 13.00

SUPERMAN / SUPERHOMBRE
DC Comics: Apr, 1945
nn - Ashcan comic, not distributed to newsstands, only for in-house use (no known sales)

SUPERMAN / TARZAN: SONS OF THE JUNGLE
Dark Horse Comics: Oct, 2001 - No. 3, May, 2002 ($2.99, limited series)
1-3-Elseworlds; Kal-El lands in the jungle; Dixon-s/Meglia-a/Ramos-c 3.00

SUPERMAN: THE DARK SIDE
DC Comics: 1998 - No. 3, 1998 ($4.95, squarebound, mini-series)
1-3: Elseworlds; Kal-El lands on Apokolips 5.00

SUPERMAN: THE DOOMSDAY WARS
DC Comics: 1998 - No. 3, 1999 ($4.95, squarebound, mini-series)
1-3: Superman & JLA vs. Doomsday; Jurgens-s/a(p) 5.00

SUPERMAN: THE KANSAS SIGHTING
DC Comics: 2003 - No. 2, 2003 ($6.95, squarebound, mini-series)
1,2-DeMatteis-s/Tolagson-a 7.00

SUPERMAN: THE LAST FAMILY OF KRYPTON
DC Comics: Oct, 2010 - No. 3, Dec, 2010 ($4.99, limited series)
1-3-Elseworlds; the El family lands on Earth; Bates-s/Arlem-a/Massafera-c 5.00

SUPERMAN: THE MAN OF STEEL (Also see Man of Steel, The)
DC Comics: July, 1991 - No. 134, Mar, 2003 ($1.00/$1.25/$1.50/$1.95/$2.25)
0-(10/94) Zero Hour; released between #37 & #38 3.00
1-($1.75, 52 pgs.)-Painted-c 5.00
2-16: 3-War of the Gods x-over. 5-Reads sideways. 10-Last $1.00-c. 14-Superman & Robin team-up 3.00
17-1st brief app. Doomsday 1 2 3 4 5 7
17,18: 17-2nd printing. 18-2nd & 3rd printings 3.00
18-1st full app. Doomsday 1 2 3 5 7 9
19-Doomsday battle issue (c/story) 6.00
20-22: 20,21-Funeral for a Friend. 22-($1.95)-Collector's Edition w/die-cut outer-c & bound-in poster; Steel-c/story 4.00
22-($1.50)-Newsstand Ed. w/poster & different-c 3.00
23-49,51-99: 30-Regular edition. 32-Bizarro-c/story. 35,36-Worlds Collide Pt. 1 & 10. 37-(9/94)-Zero Hour x-over. 38-(11/94). 48-Aquaman app. 54-Spectre-c/app; Lex Luthor app. 56-Mxyzptlk-c/app. 57-G.A. Flash app. 58-Supergirl app. 59-Parasite-c/app.; Steel app. 60-Reintro Bottled City of Kandor. 62-Final Night. 64-New Gods app. 67-New powers. 75-"Death" of Mxyzptlk. 78,79-Millennium Giants. 80-Golden Age style. 92-JLA app. 98-Metal Men app. 3.00
30-($2.50)-Collector's Edition; polybagged with Superman & Lobo vinyl clings that stick to wraparound-c; Lobo-c/story 4.00
50 ($2.95)-The Trial of Superman 4.00
100-($2.99) New Fortress of Solitude revealed 3.00
100-($3.99) Special edition with fold out cardboard-c 4.00
101,102-101-Batman app. 3.00
103-133: 103-Begin $2.25. 105-Batman-c/app. 111-Return to Krypton. 115-117-Our Worlds at War. 117-Maxima killed. 121-Royal Flush Gang app. 128-Return to Krypton II. 3.00
134-($2.75) Last issue; Steel app.; Bogdanove-c 3.00
#1,000,000 (11/98) 853rd Century x-over; Gene Ha-c 3.00
Annual 1-5 ('92-'96,68 pgs.): 1-Eclipso app.; Joe Quesada-c(p). 2-Intro Edge. 3 -Elseworlds; Mignola-c; Batman app. 4-Year One story. 5-Legends of the Dead Earth story 4.00
Annual 6 (1997, $3.95)-Pulp Heroes story 4.00
...Gallery (1995, $3.50) Pin-ups by various 4.00

SUPERMAN: THE MAN OF TOMORROW
DC Comics: 1995 - No. 15, Fall, 1999 ($1.95, quarterly)
1-15: 1-Lex Luthor app. 3-Lex Luthor-c/app; Joker app. 4-Shazam! app. 5-Wedding of Lex Luthor. 10-Maxima-c/app. 13-JLA-c/app. 3.00
#1,000,000 (11/98) 853rd Century x-over; Gene Ha-c 3.00

SUPERMAN: THE SECRET YEARS
DC Comics: Feb, 1985 - No. 4, May, 1985 (limited series)
1-4-Miller-c on all 4.00

SUPERMAN: THE WEDDING ALBUM
DC Comics: Dec, 1996 ($4.95, 96 pgs, one-shot)
1-Standard Edition-Story & art by past and present Superman creators; gatefold back-c. Byrne-c 5.00
1-Collector's Edition-Embossed cardstock variant-c w/ metallic silver ink and matte and gloss varnishes 5.00
Retailer Rep. Program Edition (#'d to 250, signed by Bob Rozakis on back-c) 50.00
TPB ('97, $14.95) r/Wedding and honeymoon stories 15.00

SUPERMAN 3-D (See Three-Dimension Adventures)

SUPERMAN-TIM (See Promotional Comics section)

SUPERMAN VILLAINS SECRET FILES
DC Comics: Jun, 1998 ($4.95, one shot)
1-Origin stories, "lost" pages & pin-ups 5.00

SUPERMAN VS. ALIENS (Also see Superman Aliens 2: God War)
DC Comics/Dark Horse Comics: July, 1995 - No. 3, Sept, 1995 ($4.95, limited series)
1-3: Jurgens/Nowlan-a 5.00

SUPERMAN VS. MUHAMMAD ALI (See All-New Collectors' Edition C-56 for original 1978 printing)
DC Comics: 2010
... Deluxe Edition (2010, $19.99, HC w/dustjacket) recolored reprint in comic size; new intro. by Neal Adams; afterword by Jenette Kahn; sketch pages, key to cover celebs 20.00
... Facsimile Edition (2010, $39.99, HC no dustjacket) recolored reprint in original Treasury size; new intro. by Neal Adams; key to cover celebs 40.00

SUPERMAN VS. PREDATOR
DC Comics/Dark Horse Comics: 2000 - No. 3, 2000 ($4.95, limited series)
1-3-Micheline-s/Maleev-a 5.00
TPB (2001, $14.95) r/series 15.00

SUPERMAN VS. THE AMAZING SPIDER-MAN (Also see Marvel Treasury Edition No. 28)
National Periodical Publications/Marvel Comics Group: 1976
($2.00, Treasury sized, 100 pgs.)

Superman: War of the Supermen #4 © DC

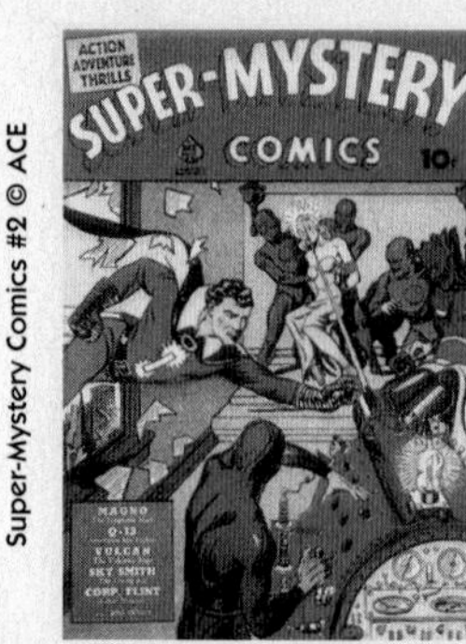

Super-Mystery Comics #2 © ACE

Supernatural: Beginning's End #4 © WB

	GD 2.0	VG 4.0	FN 6.0	VF 8.0	VF/NM 9.0	NM- 9.2
1-Superman and Spider-Man battle Lex Luthor and Dr. Octopus; Andru/Giordano-a; 1st Marvel/DC x-over.	8	16	24	54	90	125
1-2nd printing; 5000 numbered copies signed by Stan Lee & Carmine Infantino on front cover & sold through mail	13	26	39	91	176	260
nn-(1995, $5.95)-r/#1						6.00

SUPERMAN VS. THE TERMINATOR: DEATH TO THE FUTURE
Dark Horse/DC Comics: Dec, 1999 - No. 4, Mar, 2000 ($2.95, limited series)

1-4-Grant-s/Pugh-a/c: Steel and Supergirl app. 3.00

SUPERMAN: WAR OF THE SUPERMEN
DC Comics: No. 0, Jun, 2010 - No. 4, Jul, 2010 ($2.99, limited series)

0-Free Comic Book Day issue; Barrows-c 1.00
1-4: 1-New Krypton destroyed 3.00
HC (2011, $19.99) r/#0-4 & Superman #700 20.00

SUPERMAN/WONDER WOMAN: WHOM GODS DESTROY
DC Comics: 1997 ($4.95, prestige format, limited series)

1-4-Elseworlds; Claremont-s 5.00

SUPERMAN WORKBOOK
National Periodical Publ./Juvenile Group Foundation: 1945 (B&W, reprints, 68 pgs)

	GD	VG	FN	VF	VF/NM	NM-
nn-Cover-r/Superman #14	181	362	543	1158	1979	2800

SUPERMAN: WORLD OF NEW KRYPTON
DC Comics: May, 2009 - No. 12,Apr, 2010 ($2.99, limited series)

1-12: Robinson & Rucka-s/Woods-a; Frank-c and variant for each. 4-Green Lantern app. 3.00

SUPER MARIO BROS. (Also see Adventures of the..., Blip, Gameboy, and Nintendo Comics System)
Valiant Comics: 1990 - No. 5?, 1991 ($1.95, slick-c) V2#1, 1991 - No. 5, 1991

	GD	VG	FN	VF	VF/NM	NM-
1-Wildman-a	1	3	4	6	8	10
2-5, V2#1-5-($1.50)						6.00
Special Edition 1 (1990, $1.95)-Wildman-a						6.00

SUPER MARKET COMICS
Fawcett Publications: No date (1950s)

nn - Ashcan comic, not distributed to newsstands, only for in-house use (no known sales)

SUPER MARKET VARIETIES
Fawcett Publications: No date (1950s)

nn - Ashcan comic, not distributed to newsstands, only for in-house use (no known sales)

SUPERMEN OF AMERICA
DC Comics: Mar, 1999 ($3.95/$4.95, one-shot)

1-($3.95) Regular Ed.; Immonen-s/art by various 4.00
1-($4.95) Collectors' Ed. with membership kit 5.00

SUPERMEN OF AMERICA (Mini-series)
DC Comics: Mar, 2000 - No. 6, Aug, 2000 ($2.50)

1-6-Nicieza-s/Braithwaite-a 3.00

SUPERMOUSE (...the Big Cheese; see Coo Coo Comics)
Standard Comics/Pines No. 35 on (Literary Ent.): Dec, 1948 - No. 34, Sept, 1955; No. 35, Apr, 1956 - No. 45, Fall, 1958

	GD	VG	FN	VF	VF/NM	NM-
1-Frazetta text illos (3)	28	56	84	165	270	375
2-Frazetta text illos	15	30	45	84	127	170
3,5,6-Text illos by Frazetta in all	13	26	39	74	105	135
4-Two pg. text illos by Frazetta	14	28	42	78	112	145
7-10	9	18	27	47	61	75
11-20: 13-Racist humor (Indians)	7	14	21	37	46	55
21-45	6	12	18	31	38	45
1-Summer Holiday issue (Summer, 1957, 25¢, 100 pgs.)-Pines	14	28	42	80	115	150
2-Giant Summer issue (Summer, 1958, 25¢, 100 pgs.)-Pines; has games, puzzles & stories	10	20	30	58	79	100

SUPER-MYSTERY COMICS
Ace Magazines (Periodical House): July, 1940 - V8#6, July, 1949

	GD	VG	FN	VF	VF/NM	NM-
V1#1-Magno, the Magnetic Man & Vulcan begins (1st app.); Q-13, Corp. Flint, & Sky Smith begin	314	628	942	2198	3849	5500
2	103	206	309	659	1130	1600
3-The Black Spider begins (1st app.)	82	164	246	528	902	1275
4-Origin Davy	58	116	174	371	636	900
5-Intro. The Clown & begin series (12/40)	62	124	186	394	677	960
6(2/41)	52	104	156	328	557	785
V2#1(4/41)-Origin Buckskin	51	102	153	321	541	760
2-6(2/42): 6-Vulcan begins again	48	96	144	302	514	725
V3#1(4/42),2: 1-Black Ace begins	42	84	126	267	451	635
3-Intro. The Lancer; Dr. Nemesis & The Sword begin; Kurtzman-c/a(2) (Mr. Risk & Paul Revere Jr.); Robot-c	53	106	159	334	567	800
4-Kurtzman-c/a; classic-c	90	180	270	576	988	1400
5-Kurtzman-a(2); L.B. Cole-a; Mr. Risk app.	52	104	156	328	552	775
6(10/43)-Mr. Risk app.; Kurtzman's Paul Revere Jr.; L.B. Cole-a	52	104	156	328	552	775
V4#1(1/44)-L.B. Cole-a	45	90	135	284	480	675
2-6(4/45): 2,5,6-Mr. Risk app.	32	64	96	192	314	435
V5#1(7/45)-6	32	64	96	192	314	435
V6#1,2,4,5,6: 4-Last Magno. Mr. Risk app. in #2,4-6. 6-New logo	27	54	81	158	259	360
3-Torture c-story	36	72	108	216	351	485
V7#1-6, V8#1-4,6	25	50	75	147	241	335
V8#5-Meskin, Tuska, Sid Greene-a	25	50	75	150	245	340

NOTE: ***Sid Greene** a-V7#4. **Mooney** c-V1#5, 6, V2#1-6. **Palais** a-V5#3, 4; c-V4#6-V5#4, V6#2, V8#4. Bondage c-V2#5, 6, V3#2, 5. Magno c-V1#1-V3#6, V4#2-V5#5, V6#2. The Sword c-V4#1, 6(w/Magno).*

SUPERNATURAL: BEGINNING'S END (Based on the CW television series)
DC Comics (WildStorm): Mar, 2010 - No. 6, Aug, 2010 ($2.99, limited series)

1-6-Prequel to the series; Dabb & Loflin-s/Olmos-a. 1-Olmos and photo-c 3.00
TPB (2010, $14.99) r/#1-6; character sketch pages 15.00

SUPERNATURAL FREAK MACHINE: A CAL MCDONALD MYSTERY
IDW Publishing: Mar, 2005 - No. 3 ($3.99)

1-3-Steve Niles-s/Kelley Jones-a 4.00

SUPERNATURAL LAW (Formerly Wolff & Byrd, Counselors of the Macabre)
Exhibit A Press: No. 24, Oct, 1999 - Present ($2.50/$2.95/$3.50, B&W)

24-35-Batton Lash-s/a. 29-Marie Severin-c. 33-Cerebus spoof 3.00
36-40-($2.95). 37-Frank Cho pin-up and story panels 3.00
(#41) ...First Amendment Issue (2005, $3.50) anti-censorship story; CBLDF info 3.50
(#42) With a Silver Bullet (2006, $3.50) new stories and pin-ups 3.50
(#43) At the Box Office (2006, $3.50) new stories and pin-ups 3.50
(#44) Wolff & Byrd: The Movie (2007, $3.50) new stories and pin-ups 3.50
45-($3.50) Toxic Avenger and Lloyd Kaufman app. 3.50
#1 (2005, $2.95) r/Wolff & Byrd with redrawn and re-toned art; relettered 3.00

SUPERNATURAL LAW SECRETARY MAVIS
Exhibit A Press: 2001 - Present ($2.95/$3.50, B&W)

1-3: 3-DeCarlo-c 3.00
4,5-($3.50) Jaime Hernandez-c 3.50

SUPERNATURAL: ORIGINS (Based on the CW television series)
DC Comics (WildStorm): July, 2007 - No. 6, Dec, 2007 ($2.99, limited series)

1-6: 1-Bradstreet-c; Johnson-s/Smith-a; back-up w/Johns-s/Hester-a 3.00
TPB (2008, $14.99) r/#1-6; sketch pages 15.00

SUPERNATURAL: RISING SON (Based on the CW television series)
DC Comics (WildStorm): Jun, 2008 - No. 6, Nov, 2008 ($2.99, limited series)

1-6-Johnson & Dessertine-s/Olmos-a. 1-Oliver-c 3.00
1-Variant-c by Nguyen 6.00
TPB (2009, $14.99) r/#1-6 15.00

SUPERNATURALS
Marvel Comics: Dec, 1998 - No. 4, Dec, 1998 ($3.99, weekly limited series)

1-4-Pulido-s/Balent-c; bound-in Halloween masks 4.00
1-4-With bound-in Ghost Rider mask (1 in 10) 4.00

SUPERNATURAL THRILLERS
Marvel Comics Group: Dec, 1972 - No. 6, Nov, 1973; No. 7, Jun, 1974 - No. 15, Oct, 1975

	GD	VG	FN	VF	VF/NM	NM-
1-It!; Sturgeon adap. (see Astonishing Tales #21)	4	8	12	22	34	45
2-4,6: 2-The Invisible Man; H.G. Wells adapt. 3-The Valley of the Worm; R.E. Howard adapt. 4-Dr. Jekyll & Mr. Hyde; R.L. Stevenson adapt.. 6-The Headless Horseman; last 20¢ issue	3	6	9	14	20	25
5-1st app. The Living Mummy	7	14	21	47	76	105
7-15: 7-The Living Mummy begins	3	6	9	18	27	35

NOTE: ***Brunner** c-11. **Buckler** a-5p. **Ditko** a-8r, 9r. **G. Kane** a-3p; c-3, 9p, 15p. **Mayerik** a-2p, 7, 8, 9p, 10p, 11. **McWilliams** a-14i. **Mortimer** a-4. **Steranko** c-1, 2. **Sutton** a-15. **Tuska** a-6p.*

SUPERPATRIOT (Also see Freak Force & Savage Dragon #2)
Image Comics (Highbrow Entertainment): July, 1993 - No. 4, Dec, 1993 ($1.95, lim. series)

1-4: Dave Johnson-c/a; Larsen scripts; Giffen plots 3.00

SUPERPATRIOT: AMERICA'S FIGHTING FORCE
Image Comics: July, 2002 - No. 4, Oct, 2002 ($2.95, limited series)

1-4-Cory Walker-a/c; Savage Dragon app. 3.00

SUPERPATRIOT: LIBERTY & JUSTICE

Supersnipe Comics #15 © S&S

Super-Villain Team-Up/ MODOK's 11 #1 © MAR

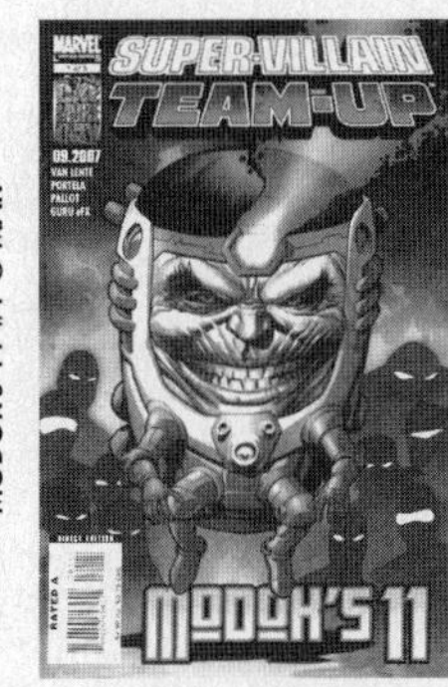

Superworld Comics #2 © Hugo Gernsback

GD 2.0 | VG 4.0 | FN 6.0 | VF 8.0 | VF/NM 9.0 | NM- 9.2

Image Comics (Highbrow Entertainment): July, 1995 - No. 4, Oct, 1995 ($2.50, lim. series)

1-4: Dave Johnson-c/a. 1-1st app. Liberty & Justice 3.00
TPB (2002, $12.95) r/#1-4; new cover by Dave Johnson; sketch pages 13.00

SUPERPATRIOT: WAR ON TERROR
Image Comics: July, 2004 - No. 4, May, 2007 ($2.95/$2.99, limited series)

1-4-Kirkman-s/Su-a 3.00

SUPER POWERS (1st Series)
DC Comics: July, 1984 - No. 5, Nov, 1984

1-5: 1-Joker/Penguin-c/story; Batman app.; all Kirby-c. 5-Kirby c/a 5.00

SUPER POWERS (2nd Series)
DC Comics: Sept, 1985 - No. 6, Feb, 1986

1-6: Kirby-c/a; Capt. Marvel & Firestorm join; Batman cameo; Darkseid storyline in all. 4-Batman cameo. 5,6-Batman app. 5.00

SUPER POWERS (3rd Series)
DC Comics: Sept, 1986 - No. 4, Dec, 1986

1-4: 1-Cyborg joins; 1st app. Samurai from Super Friends TV show. 1-4-Batman cameos; Darkseid storyline in #1-4 4.00

SUPER PUP (Formerly Spotty The Pup) (See Space Comics)
Avon Periodicals: No. 4, Mar-Apr, 1954 - No. 5, 1954

4,5: 4-Atom bomb-c. 5-Robot-c 7 14 21 35 43 50

SUPER RABBIT (See All Surprise, Animated Movie Tunes, Comedy Comics, Comic Capers, Ideal Comics, It's A Duck's Life, Movie Tunes & Wisco)
Timely Comics (CmPI): Fall, 1944 - No. 14, Nov, 1948

1-Hitler & Hirohito-c; war effort paper recycling PSA by S&K; Ziggy Pig & Silly Seal begin
135 270 405 864 1482 2100
2 40 80 120 246 411 575
3-5 27 54 81 158 259 360
6-Origin 29 58 87 170 278 385
7-10: 9-Infinity-c 18 36 54 105 165 225
11-Kurtzman's "Hey Look" 19 38 57 109 172 235
12-14 18 36 54 105 165 225
I.W. Reprint #1,2('58),7,10('63): 1-r/#13. 2-r/#10. 2 4 6 10 14 18

SUPER RICHIE (Superichie #5 on) (See Richie Rich Millions #68)
Harvey Publications: Sept, 1975 - No. 4, Mar, 1976 (All 52 pg. Giants)

1 3 6 9 16 23 30
2-4 2 4 6 11 16 20

SUPER SLUGGERS (Baseball)
Ultimate Sports Ent. Inc.: 1999 ($3.95, one-shot)

1-Bonds, Piazza, Caminiti, Griffey Jr. app.; Martinbrough-c/a 4.00

SUPERSNIPE COMICS (Formerly Army & Navy #1-5)
Street & Smith Publications: V1#6, Oct, 1942 - V5#1, Aug-Sept, 1949
(See Shadow Comics V2#3)

V1#6-Rex King - Man of Adventure (costumed hero, see Super Magic/Magician) by Jack Binder begins; Supersnipe by George Marcoux continues from Army & Navy #5; Bill Ward-a 90 180 270 576 988 1400
7,10-12: 10,11-Little Nemo app. 50 100 150 315 533 750
8-Hitler, Tojo, Mussolini in Hell with Devil-c 116 232 348 742 1271 1800
9-Doc Savage x-over in Supersnipe; Hitler-c 119 238 357 762 1306 1850
V2 #1: Both V2#1(2/44) & V2#2(4/44) have V2#1 on outside-c; Huck Finn by Clare Dwiggins begins, ends V3#5 (rare) 74 148 222 470 810 1150
V2#2 (4/44) has V2#1 on outside-c; classic shark-c 43 86 129 271 461 650
3-12 30 60 90 177 289 400
V3#1-12: 8-Bobby Crusoe by Dwiggins begins, ends V3#12. 9-X-Mas-c
22 44 66 132 216 300
V4#1-12, V5#1: V4#10-X-Mas-c 18 36 54 105 165 225
NOTE: *George Marcoux c-V1#6-V3#4. Doc Savage app. in some issues.*

SUPER SOLDIER (See Marvel Versus DC #3)
DC Comics (Amalgam): Apr, 1996 ($1.95, one-shot)

1-Mark Waid script & Dave Gibbons-c/a. 3.00

SUPER SOLDIER: MAN OF WAR
DC Comics (Amalgam): June, 1997 ($1.95, one-shot)

1-Waid & Gibbons-s/Gibbons & Palmiotti-c/a. 3.00

SUPER SOLDIERS
Marvel Comics UK: Apr, 1993 - No. 8, Nov, 1993 ($1.75)

1-($2.50)-Embossed silver foil logo 4.00
2-8: 5-Capt. America app. 6-Origin; Nick Fury app.; neon ink-c 3.00

SUPERSPOOK (Formerly Frisky Animals on Parade)
Ajax/Farrell Publications: No. 4, June, 1958

4 8 16 24 44 57 70

SUPER SPY (See Wham Comics)
Centaur Publications: Oct, 1940 - No. 2, Nov, 1940 (Reprints)

1-Origin The Sparkler 84 168 252 538 919 1300
2-The Inner Circle, Dean Denton, Tim Blain, The Drew Ghost, The Night Hawk by Gustavson, & S.S. Swanson by Glanz app. 52 104 156 328 557 785

SUPERSTAR: AS SEEN ON TV
Image Comics (Gorilla): 2001 ($5.95)

1-Busiek-s/Immonen-a 6.00

SUPER STAR HOLIDAY SPECIAL (See DC Special Series #21)

SUPER-TEAM FAMILY
National Periodical Publ./DC Comics: Oct-Nov, 1975 - No. 15, Mar-Apr, 1978

1-Reprints by Neal Adams & Kane/Wood; 68 pgs. begin, ends #4. New Gods app.
3 6 9 16 23 30
2,3: New stories 3 6 9 14 20 25
4-7: Reprints. 4-G.A. JSA-r & Superman/Batman/Robin-r from World's Finest. 5-52 pgs. begin 2 4 6 10 14 18
8-14: 8-10-New Challengers of the Unknown stories. 9-Kirby-a. 11-14: New stories
3 6 9 14 19 24
15-New Gods app. New stories 3 6 9 14 20 26
NOTE: *Neal Adams r-1-3. Brunner c-3. Buckler c-8p. Tuska a-7r. Wood a-1i(r), 3.*

SUPER TV HEROES (See Hanna-Barbera...)

SUPER-VILLAIN CLASSICS
Marvel Comics Group: May, 1983

1-Galactus -The Origin; Kirby-a 6.00

SUPER-VILLAIN TEAM-UP (See Fantastic Four #6 & Giant-Size...)
Marvel Comics Group: 8/75 - No. 14, 10/77; No. 15, 11/78; No. 16, 5/79; No. 17, 6/80

1-Giant-Size Super-Villain Team-Up #2; Sub-Mariner & Dr. Doom begin, end #10
5 10 15 30 48 65
2-5: 5-1st app. The Shroud 3 6 9 14 19 24
5-(30¢-c variant, limited distribution)(4/76) 4 8 12 23 36 48
6,7-(25¢ editions) 6-(6/76)-F.F., Shroud app. 7-Origin Shroud
2 4 6 8 11 14
6,7-(30¢-c, limited distribution)(6,8/76) 3 6 9 20 30 40
8-17: 9-Avengers app. 11-15-Dr. Doom & Red Skull app.
2 4 6 8 11 14
12-14-(35¢-c variants, limited distribution)(6,8,10/77) 4 8 12 24 37 50
NOTE: *Buckler c-4p, 5p, 7p. Buscema c-1. Byrne/Austin c-14. Evans a-1p, 3p. Everett a-1p. Giffen a-8p, 13p; c-13p. Kane c-2p, 9p. Mooney a-4i. Starlin c-6. Tuska r-1p, 15p. Wood r-15p.*

SUPER-VILLAIN TEAM-UP/ MODOK'S 11
Marvel Comics: Sept, 2007 - No. 5, Jan, 2008 ($2.99, limited series)

1-5: 1-MODOK's origin re-told; Portela-a/Powell-c; Purple Man & Mentallo app. 3.00
... TPB (2008, $13.99) r/#1-5 14.00

SUPER WESTERN COMICS (Also see Buffalo Bill)
Youthful Magazines: Aug, 1950 (One shot)

1-Buffalo Bill begins; Wyatt Earp, Calamity Jane & Sam Slade app; Powell-c/a
14 28 42 82 121 160

SUPER WESTERN FUNNIES (See Super Funnies)

SUPERWOMAN
DC Comics: Jan 1942

nn - Ashcan comic, not distributed to newsstands, only for in-house use. Cover art is More Fun Comics #73 with interior being Action Comics #38 (no known sales)

SUPERWORLD COMICS
Hugo Gernsback (Komos Publ.): Apr, 1940 - No. 3, Aug, 1940 (68 pgs.)

1-Origin & 1st app. Hip Knox, Super Hypnotist; Mitey Powers & Buzz Allen, the Invisible Avenger, Little Nemo begin; cover by Frank R. Paul (all have sci/fi-c) (Scarce) 811 1622 2433 5920 10,460 15,000
2-Marvo 1-2 Go+, the Super Boy of the Year 2680 (1st app.); Paul-c (Scarce)
432 864 1296 3154 5577 8000
3 (Scarce) 354 708 1062 2478 4339 6200

SUPER ZOMBIES
Dynamite Entertainment: 2009 - No. 5, 2009 ($3.50)

1-5- Mel Rubi-a; Guggenheim & Gonzales-s; two covers for each by Rubi & Neves 3.50

SUPREME (Becomes ...The New Adventures #43-48)(See Youngblood #3)

Supreme #7 © Rob Liefeld

Sure-Fire Comics #1 © ACE

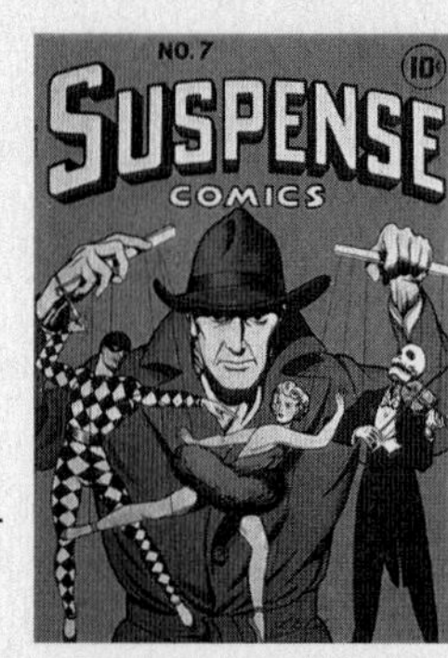

Suspense Comics #7 © Continental

GD VG FN VF VF/NM NM-
2.0 4.0 6.0 8.0 9.0 9.2

(Also see Bloodwulf Special, Legend of Supreme, & Trencher #3)
Image Comics (Extreme Studios)/ Awesome Entertainment #49 on:
V2#1, Nov, 1992 - V2#42, Sept, 1996; V3#49 - No. 56, Feb, 1998

V2#1-Liefeld-a(i) & scripts; embossed foil logo 4.00
1-Gold Edition 6.00
2-(3/93)-Liefeld co-plots & inks; 1st app. Grizlock 3.00
3-42: 3-Intro Bloodstrike; 1st app. Khrome. 5-1st app. Thor. 6-1st brief app. The Starguard. 7-1st full app. The Starguard. 10-Black and White Pt 1 (1st app.) by Art Thibert (2 pgs. ea. installment). 25-(5/94)-Platt-c. 11-Coupon #4 for Extreme Prejudice #0; Black and White Pt. 7 by Thibert. 12-(4/94)-Platt-c. 13,14-(6/94). 15 (7/94). 16 (7/94)-Stormwatch app. 18-Kid Supreme Sneak Preview; Pitt app.19,20-Polybagged w/trading card. 20-1st app. Woden & Loki (as a dog); Overtkill app. 21-1st app. Loki (in true form). 21-23-Poly-bagged trading card. 32-Lady Supreme cameo. 33-Origin & 1st full app. of Lady Supreme (Probe from the Starguard); Babewatch! tie-in. 37-Intro Loki; Fraga-c. 40-Retells Supreme's past advs. 41-Alan Moore scripts begin; Supreme revised; intro The Supremacy; Jerry Ordway-c (Joe Bennett variant-c exists). 42-New origin w/Rick Veitch-a; intro Radar, The Hound Supreme & The League of Infinity 3.00
28-Variant-c by Quesada & Palmiotti 3.00
(#43-48-**See Supreme: The New Adventures**)
V3#49,51: 49-Begin $2.99-c 3.00
50-($3.95)-Double sized, 2 covers, pin-up gallery 4.00
52a,52b-($3.50) 4.00
53-56: 53-Sprouse-a begins. 56-McGuinness-c 3.00
Annual 1-(1995, $2.95) 4.00
...: Supreme Sacrifice (3/06, $3.99) Flip book with Suprema; Kirkman-s/Malin-a 4.00
...: The Return TPB (Checker Book Publ., 2003, $24.95) r/#53-56 & Supreme; The Return #1-6; Ross-c; additional sketch pages by Ross 25.00
...: The Story of the Year TPB (Checker Book Publ., 2002, $26.95) r/#41-52; Ross-c 27.00
NOTE: ***Rob Liefeld** a(i)-1, 2; co-plots-2-4; scripts-1, 5, 6. **Ordway** c-41. **Platt** c-12, 25. **Thibert** c(i)-7-9.*

SUPREME: GLORY DAYS
Image Comics (Extreme Studios): Oct, 1994 - No. 2, Dec, 1994 ($2.95/$2.50, limited series)
1,2: 2-Diehard, Roman, Superpatriot, & Glory app. 3.00

SUPREME POWER (Also see Squadron Supreme 2006 series)
Marvel Comics (MAX): Oct, 2003 - No. 18, Oct, 2005 ($2.99)
1-($2.99) Straczynski-s/Frank-a; Frank-c 3.00
1-($4.99) Special Edition with variant Quesada-c; includes r/early Squadron Supreme apps. 5.00
2-18: 4-Intro. Nighthawk. 6-The Blur debuts. 10-Princess Zarda returns. 17-Hyperion revealed as alien. 18-Continues in mini-series 3.00
Vol. 1: Contact TPB (2004, $14.99) r/#1-6 15.00
Vol. 2: Powers & Principalities TPB (2004, $14.99) r/#7-12 15.00
Vol. 3: High Command TPB (2005, $14.99) r/#13-18 15.00
Vol. 1 HC (2005, $29.99, 7 1/2" x 11" with dustjacket) r/#1-12; Avengers #85 & 86, Straczynski intro., Frank cover sketches and character design pages 30.00
Vol. 2 HC (2006, $29.99, 7 1/2" x 11" with dustjacket) r/#13-18; ...: Hyperion #1-5; character design pages 30.00

SUPREME POWER: HYPERION
Marvel Comics (MAX): Nov, 2005 - No. 5, Mar, 2006 ($2.99, limited series)
1-5: 1-Straczynski-s/Jurgens-a/Dodson-c 3.00
TPB (2006, $14.99) r/#1-5 15.00

SUPREME POWER: NIGHTHAWK
Marvel Comics (MAX): Nov, 2005 - No. 6, Apr, 2006 ($2.99, limited series)
1-6-Daniel Way-s/Steve Dillon-a; origin of Whiteface 3.00
TPB (2006, $16.99) r/#1-6; cover concept art 17.00

SUPREME: THE NEW ADVENTURES (Formerly Supreme)
Maximum Press: V3#43, Oct, 1996 - V3#48, May, 1997 ($2.50)
V3#43-48: 43-Alan Moore scripts begin; Joe Bennett-a; Rick Veitch-a (8 pgs.); Dan Jurgens-a (1 pg.); intro Citadel Supreme & Suprematons; 1st Allied Supermen of America 3.00

SUPREME: THE RETURN
Awesome Entertainment: May, 1999 - No. 6, June, 2000 ($2.99)
1-6: Alan Moore-s. 1,2-Sprouse & Gordon-a/c. 2,4-Liefeld-c. 6-Kirby app. 3.00

SURE-FIRE COMICS (Lightning Comics #4 on)
Ace Magazines: June, 1940 - No. 4, Oct, 1940 (Two No. 3's)
V1#1-Origin Flash Lightning & begins; X-The Phantom Fed, Ace McCoy, Buck Steele, Marvo the Magician, The Raven, Whiz Wilson (Time Traveler) begin (all 1st app.); Flash Lightning c-1-4 181 362 543 1158 1979 2800
2 82 164 246 528 902 1275
3(9/40), 3(#4)(10/40)-nn on-c, #3 on inside 60 120 180 381 653 925

SURF 'N' WHEELS
Charlton Comics: Nov, 1969 - No. 6, Sept, 1970

GD VG FN VF VF/NM NM-
2.0 4.0 6.0 8.0 9.0 9.2

1 3 6 9 20 30 40
2-6 3 6 9 14 19 24

SURGE
Eclipse Comics: July, 1984 - No. 4, Jan, 1985 ($1.50, lim. series, Baxter paper)
1-4 Ties into DNAgents series 3.00

SURPRISE ADVENTURES (Formerly Tormented)
Sterling Comic Group: No. 3, Mar, 1955 - No. 5, July, 1955
3-5: 3,5-Sekowsky-a 9 18 27 50 65 80

SUSIE Q. SMITH
Dell Publishing Co.: No. 323, Mar, 1951 - No. 553, Apr, 1954
Four Color 323 (#1) 5 10 15 32 51 70
Four Color 377, 453 (2/53), 553 4 8 12 26 41 55

SUSPENSE (Radio/TV issues #1-11; Real Life Tales of... #1-4) (Amazing Detective Cases #3 on?)
Marvel/Atlas Comics (CnPC No. 1-10/BFP No. 11-29): Dec, 1949 - No. 29, Apr, 1953 (#1-8, 17-23: 52 pgs.)
1-Powell-a; Peter Lorre, Sidney Greenstreet photo-c from Hammett's "The Verdict" 60 120 180 381 653 925
2-Crime stories; Dennis O'Keefe & Gale Storm photo-c from Universal movie "Abandoned" 36 72 108 211 343 475
3-Change to horror 41 82 123 256 428 600
4,7-10: 7-Dracula-sty 32 64 96 192 314 435
5-Krigstein, Tuska, Everett-a 34 68 102 204 332 460
6-Tuska, Everett, Morisi-a 34 68 102 199 325 450
11-13,15-17,19,20 26 52 78 154 252 350
14-Clasic Heath Hypo-c; A-Bomb panels 39 78 117 231 378 525
18,22-Krigstein-a 27 54 81 158 259 360
21,23,24,26-29: 24-Tuska-a 23 46 69 136 223 310
25-Electric chair-c/story 32 64 96 192 314 435
NOTE: ***Ayers** a-20. **Briefer** a-5, 7, 27. **Brodsky** c-4, 6-9, 11, 16, 17, 25. **Colan** a-8(2), 9. **Everett** a-5, 6(2), 19, 23, 28; c-21-23, 26. **Fuje** a-29. **Heath** a-5, 6, 8, 10, 12, 14; c-14, 19, 24. **Maneely** a-12, 23, 24, 28, 29; c-5, 6p, 10, 13, 15, 18. **Mooney** a-24, 28. **Morisi** a-6, 12. **Palais** a-10. **Rico** a-7-9. **Robinson** a-29. **Romita** a-20(2), 25. **Sekowsky** a-11, 13, 14. **Sinnott** a-23, 25. **Tuska** a-5, 6(2), 12; c-12. **Whitney** a-15, 16, 22. **Ed Win** a-27.*

SUSPENSE COMICS
Continental Magazines: Dec, 1943 - No. 12, Sept, 1946
1-The Grey Mask begins; bondage/torture-c; L. B. Cole-a (7 pgs.) 423 846 1269 3067 5384 7700
2-Intro. The Mask; Rico, Giunta, L. B. Cole-a (7 pgs.) 271 542 813 1734 2967 4200
3-L.B. Cole-a; classic Schomburg-c (Scarce) 5000 10,000 15,000 30,000 40,000 50,000
4-6: 4-L. B. Cole-c begin 210 420 630 1334 2292 3250
7,9,10,12: 9-L.B. Cole eyeball-c 161 322 483 1030 1765 2500
8-Classic L. B. Cole spider-c 420 840 1260 2940 5170 7400
11-Classic Devil-c 314 628 942 2198 3849 5500
NOTE: ***L. B. Cole** c-4-12. **Fuje** a-8. **Larsen** a-11. **Palais** a-10, 11. Bondage c-1, 3, 4.*

SUSPENSE DETECTIVE
Fawcett Publications: June, 1952 - No. 5, Mar, 1953
1-Evans-a (11 pgs); Baily-c/a 45 90 135 284 480 675
2-Evans-a (10 pgs.) 27 54 81 160 263 365
3-5 23 46 69 136 223 310
NOTE: ***Baily** a-4, 5; c-1-3. **Sekowsky** a-2, 4, 5; c-5.*

SUSPENSE STORIES (See Strange Suspense Stories)

SUSSEX VAMPIRE, THE (Sherlock Holmes)
Caliber Comics: 1996 ($2.95, 32 pgs., B&W, one-shot)
nn-Adapts Sir Arthur Conan Doyle's story; Warren Ellis scripts 3.00

SUZIE COMICS (Formerly Laugh Comix; see Laugh Comics, Liberty Comics #10, Pep Comics & Top-Notch Comics #28)
Close-Up No. 49,50/MLJ Mag./Archie No. 51 on: No. 49, Spring, 1945 - No. 100, Aug, 1954
49-Ginger begins 26 52 78 154 252 350
50-55: 54-Transvestism story. 55-Woggon-a 16 32 48 94 147 200
56-Katy Keene begins by Woggon 17 34 51 98 154 210
57-65 14 28 42 76 108 140
66-80 12 24 36 69 97 125
81-87,89-99 11 22 33 60 83 105
88,100: 88-Used in **POP**, pgs. 76,77; Bill Woggon draws himself in story. 100-Last Katy Keene 12 24 36 69 97 125
NOTE: ***Al Fagaly** c-49-67. Katy Keene app. in 53-82, 85-100.*

SWAMP FOX, THE (TV, Disney)(See Walt Disney Presents #2)
Dell Publishing Co.: No. 1179, Dec, 1960
Four Color 1179-Leslie Nielsen photo-c 8 16 24 56 93 130

Swamp Thing #16 © DC

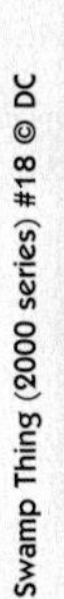

Swamp Thing (2000 series) #18 © DC

Sweeney #5 © STD

	GD 2.0	VG 4.0	FN 6.0	VF 8.0	VF/NM 9.0	NM- 9.2

SWAMP THING (See Brave & the Bold, Challengers of the Unknown #82, DC Comics Presents #8 & 85, DC Special Series #2, 14, 17, 20, House of Secrets #92, Limited Collectors' Edition C-59, & Roots of the...)

SWAMP THING
National Per. Publ./DC Comics: Oct-Nov, 1972 - No. 24, Aug-Sept, 1976

	GD	VG	FN	VF	VF/NM	NM-
1-Wrightson-c/a begins; origin	16	32	48	114	232	350
2-1st brief app. Patchwork Man (1 panel)	9	18	27	60	100	140
3-1st full app. Patchwork Man (see House of Secrets #140)	7	14	21	47	76	105
4-6,	6	12	18	39	62	85
7-Batman-c/story	6	12	18	43	69	95
8-10: 10-Last Wrightson issue	5	10	15	35	55	75
11-20: 11-19-Redondo-a. 13-Origin retold (1 pg.)	3	6	9	19	29	38
21-24: 23,24-Swamp Thing reverts back to Dr. Holland. 23-New logo	3	6	9	19	29	38
Secret of the Swamp Thing (2005, $9.99, digest) r/#1-10						10.00

NOTE: ***J. Jones** a-9i(assist). **Kaluta** a-9i. **Redondo** c-12-19, 21. **Wrightson** issues (#1-10) reprinted in DC Special Series #2, 14, 17, 20 & Roots of the Swamp Thing.*

SWAMP THING (Saga Of The... #1-38,42-45) (See Essential Vertigo:...)
DC Comics (Vertigo imprint #129 on): May, 1982 - No. 171, Oct, 1996 (Direct sales #65 on)

	GD	VG	FN	VF	VF/NM	NM-
1-Origin retold; Phantom Stranger series begins; ends #13; Yeates-c/a begins						6.00
2-15: 2-Photo-c from movie. 13-Last Yeates-a						4.00
16-19: Bissette-a.						5.00
20-1st Alan Moore issue	3	6	9	14	20	26
21-New origin	2	4	6	13	18	22
21 Special Editon (5/09, $1.00) reprint with "After Watchmen" cover frame						3.00
22,23,25: 25-John Constantine 1-panel cameo	2	4	6	9	12	15
24-JLA x-over; Last Yeates-c.	2	4	6	9	13	16
26-30	1	2	3	5	6	8
31-33,35,36: 33-r/1st app. from House of Secrets #92						6.00
34	1	2	3	5	7	9
37-1st app. John Constantine (Hellblazer) (6/85)	2	4	6	9	13	16
38-40: John Constantine app.	1	2	3	5	7	9
41-52,54-64: 44-Batman cameo. 44-51-John Constantine app. 46-Crisis x-over; Batman cameo. 49-Spectre app. 50-($1.25, 52 pgs.)-Deadman, Dr. Fate, Demon. 52-Arkham Asylum-c/story; Joker-c/cameo. 58-Spectre preview. 64-Last Moore issue						4.00
53-($1.25, 52 pgs.)-Arkham Asylum; Batman-c/story						5.00
65-83,85-99,101-124,126-149,151-153: 65-Direct sales only begins. 66-Batman & Arkham Asylum story. 70,76-John Constantine x-over; 76-X-over w/Hellblazer #9. 79-Superman-c/story. 85-Jonah Hex app. 102-Preview of World Without End. 116-Photo-c. 129-Metallic ink on-c. 140-Millar scripts begin, end #171						3.00
84-Sandman (Morpheus) cameo.						4.00
100,125,150: 100 ($2.50, 52 pgs.). 125-($2.95, 52 pgs.)-20th anniversary issue. 150 (52 pgs.)-Anniversary issue						4.00
154-171: 154-$2.25-c begins. 165-Curt Swan-a(p). 166,169,171-John Constantine & Phantom Stranger app. 168-Arcane returns						3.00
Annual 1,3-6('82-91): 1-Movie Adaptation; painted-c. 3-New format; Bolland-c. 4-Batman-c/story. 5-Batman cameo; re-intro Brother Power (Geek),1st app. since 1968						4.00
Annual 2 (1985)-Moore scripts; Bissette-a(p); Deadman, Spectre app.						7.00
Annual 7(1993, $3.95)-Children's Crusade						4.00
...A Murder of Crows (2001, $19.95)-r/#43-50; Moore-s						20.00
...: Earth To Earth (2002, $17.95)-r/#51-56; Batman app.						18.00
...: Infernal Triangles (2006, $19.99, TPB) r/#77-81 & Annual #3; cover gallery						20.00
...Love and Death (1990, $17.95)-r/#28-34 & Annual #2; Totleben painted-c						18.00
...: Regenesis (2004, $17.95, TPB) r/#65-70; Veitch-s						18.00
...: Reunion (2003, $19.95, TPB) r/#57-64; Moore-s						20.00
...: Roots (1998, $7.95) Jon J Muth-s/painted-a/c						8.00
Saga of the Swamp Thing ('87, '89)-r/#21-27 (1st & 2nd print)						13.00
...: Spontaneous Generation (2005, $19.99) r/#71-76						20.00
...: The Curse (2000, $19.95, TPB) r/#35-42; Bisley-c						20.00

NOTE: ***Bissette** a(p)-16-19, 21-27, 29, 30, 34-36, 39-42, 44, 46, 50, 64; c-17i, 24-32p, 35-37p, 40p, 44p, 46-50p, 51-58, 61, 62, 63p. **Kaluta** c/a-74. **Spiegle** a-1-3, 6. **Sutton** a-98p. **Totleben** a(i)-10, 16-27, 29, 31, 34-40, 42, 44, 46, 48, 50, 53, 55i; c-25-32i, 33, 35-40i, 42i, 44i, 46-50i, 53, 55i, 59p, 64, 65, 68, 73, 76, 80, 82, 84, 89, 91-100, Annual 4, 5. **Vess** painted c-121, 129-139, Annual 7. **Williamson** 86i. **Wrightson** a-18i(r), 33r. John Constantine appears in #37-40, 44-51, 65-67, 70-77, 80-90, 99, 114, 115, 130, 134-138.*

SWAMP THING
DC Comics (Vertigo): May, 2000 - No. 20, Dec, 2001 ($2.50)

	GD	VG	FN	VF	VF/NM	NM-
1-3-Tefé Holland's return; Vaughan-s/Petersen-a; Hale painted-c.						3.50
4-20: 7-9-Bisley-c. 10-John Constantine-c/app. 10-12-Fabry-c. 13-15-Mack-c 18-Swamp Thing app.						3.00
Preview-16 pg. flip book w/Lucifer Preview						3.00

SWAMP THING
DC Comics (Vertigo): May, 2004 - No. 29, Sept, 2006 ($2.95/$2.99)

	GD	VG	FN	VF	VF/NM	NM-
1-29: 1-Diggle-s/Breccia-a; Constantine app. 2-6-Sargon app. 7,8,20-Corben-c/a. 21-29-Eric Powell-c						3.00
...: Bad Seed (2004, $9.95) r/#1-6						10.00
...: Healing the Breach (2006, $17.99) r/#15-20						18.00
...: Love in Vain (2005, $14.99) r/#9-14						15.00

SWAT MALONE (America's Home Run King)
Swat Malone Enterprises: Sept, 1955

	GD	VG	FN	VF	VF/NM	NM-
V1#1-Hy Fleishman-a	11	22	33	62	86	110

SWEATSHOP
DC Comics: Jun, 2003 - No. 6, Nov, 2003 ($2.95)

	GD	VG	FN	VF	VF/NM	NM-
1-6-Peter Bagge-s/a; Destefano-a						3.00

SWEENEY (Formerly Buz Sawyer)
Standard Comics: No. 4, June, 1949 - No. 5, Sept, 1949

	GD	VG	FN	VF	VF/NM	NM-
4,5: 5-Crane-a	9	18	27	47	61	75

SWEE'PEA (Also see Popeye #46)
Dell Publishing Co.: No. 219, Mar, 1949

	GD	VG	FN	VF	VF/NM	NM-
Four Color 219	8	16	24	56	93	130

SWEET CHILDE
Advantage Graphics Press: 1995 - No. 2, 1995 ($2.95, B&W, mature)

	GD	VG	FN	VF	VF/NM	NM-
1,2						3.00

SWEETHEART DIARY (Cynthia Doyle #66-on)
Fawcett Publications/Charlton Comics No. 32 on: Wint, 1949; #2, Spr, 1950; #3, 6/50 - #5, 10/50; #6, 1951(nd); #7, 9/51 - #14, 1/53; #32, 10/55; #33, 4/56 - #65, 8/62 (#1-14: photo-c)

	GD	VG	FN	VF	VF/NM	NM-
1	20	40	60	114	182	250
2	12	24	36	69	97	125
3,4-Wood-a	15	30	45	86	133	180
5-10: 8-Bailey-a	10	20	30	56	76	95
11-14: 13-Swayze-a. 14-Last Fawcett issue	9	18	27	47	61	75
32 (10/55; 1st Charlton issue)(Formerly Cowboy Love #31)	9	18	27	52	69	85
33-40: 34-Swayze-a	7	14	21	35	43	50
41-(68 pgs.)	8	16	24	40	50	60
42-60	3	6	9	20	30	40
61-65	3	6	9	18	27	35

SWEETHEARTS (Formerly Captain Midnight)
Fawcett Publications/Charlton No. 122 on: #68, 10/48 - #121, 5/53; #122, 3/54; V2#23, 5/54 - #137, 12/73

	GD	VG	FN	VF	VF/NM	NM-
68-Photo-c begin	18	36	54	103	162	220
69,70	11	22	33	62	86	110
71-80	9	18	27	52	69	85
81-84,86-93,95-99,105	9	18	27	47	61	75
85,94,103,110,117-George Evans-a	10	20	30	54	72	90
100	9	18	27	52	69	85
101,107-Powell-a	9	18	27	50	65	80
102,104,106,108,109,112-116,118	8	16	24	44	57	70
111-1 pg. Ronald Reagan biography	10	20	30	56	76	95
119-Marilyn Monroe & Richard Widmark photo-c (1/54?); also appears in story; part Wood-a	63	126	189	403	689	975
120-Atom Bomb story	12	24	36	67	94	120
121-Liz Taylor/Fernanado Lamas photo-c	32	64	96	188	307	425
122-(1st Charlton? 3/54)-Marijuana story	13	26	39	72	101	130
V2#23 (5/54)-28: 28-Last precode issue (2/55)	8	16	24	42	54	65
29-39,41,43-45,47-50	4	8	12	26	41	55
40-Photo-c; Tommy Sands story	4	8	12	28	44	60
42-Ricky Nelson photo-c/story	8	16	24	58	97	135
46-Jimmy Rodgers photo-c/story	4	8	12	28	44	60
51-60	4	8	12	22	34	45
61-80,100	3	6	9	19	29	38
81-99	3	6	9	17	25	32
101-110	2	4	6	13	18	22
111-120,122-124,126-137	2	4	6	10	14	18
121,125-David Cassidy pin-ups	2	4	6	13	18	22

NOTE: *Photo c-68-121(Fawcett), 40, 42, 46(Charlton). **Swayze** a(Fawcett)-70-118(most).*

SWEETHEART SCANDALS (See Fox Giants)

SWEETIE PIE
Dell Publishing Co.: No. 1185, May-July, 1961 - No. 1241, Nov-Jan, 1961/62

	GD	VG	FN	VF	VF/NM	NM-
Four Color 1185 (#1)	5	10	15	30	48	65
Four Color 1241	4	8	12	24	37	50

Sweet Tooth #10 © Jeff Lemire

Swing With Scooter #9 © DC

The Sword #9 © Luna Bros.

SWEETIE PIE
Ajax-Farrell/Pines (Literary Ent.): Dec, 1955 - No. 15, Fall, 1957

	GD 2.0	VG 4.0	FN 6.0	VF 8.0	VF/NM 9.0	NM- 9.2
1-By Nadine Seltzer	10	20	30	54	72	90
2 (5/56; last Ajax?)	7	14	21	35	43	50
3-15	6	12	18	28	34	40

SWEET LOVE
Home Comics (Harvey): Sept, 1949 - No. 5, May, 1950 (All photo-c)

	GD 2.0	VG 4.0	FN 6.0	VF 8.0	VF/NM 9.0	NM- 9.2
1	10	20	30	58	79	100
2	7	14	21	37	46	55
3,4: 3-Powell-a	6	12	18	31	38	45
5-Kamen, Powell-a	9	18	27	47	61	75

SWEET ROMANCE
Charlton Comics: Oct, 1968

	GD 2.0	VG 4.0	FN 6.0	VF 8.0	VF/NM 9.0	NM- 9.2
1	3	6	9	14	20	25

SWEET SIXTEEN (...Comics and Stories for Girls)
Parents' Magazine Institute: Aug-Sept, 1946 - No. 13, Jan, 1948 (All have movie stars photos on covers)

	GD 2.0	VG 4.0	FN 6.0	VF 8.0	VF/NM 9.0	NM- 9.2
1-Van Johnson's life story; Dorothy Dare, Queen of Hollywood Stunt Artists begins (in all issues); part photo-c	22	44	66	132	216	300
2-Jane Powell, Roddy McDowall "Holiday in Mexico" photo on-c; Alan Ladd story	15	30	45	88	137	185
3,5,6,8-11: 5-Ann Francis photo on-c; Gregory Peck story. 6-Dick Haymes story. 8-Shirley Jones photo on-c. 10-Jean Simmons photo on-c; James Stewart story	13	26	39	72	101	130
4-Elizabeth Taylor photo on-c	28	56	84	165	270	375
7-Ronald Reagan's life story	22	44	66	132	216	300
12-Bob Cummings, Vic Damone story	14	28	42	76	108	140
13-Robert Mitchum's life story	14	28	42	78	112	145

SWEET XVI
Marvel Comics: May, 1991 - No. 5, Sept, 1991 ($1.00)

	GD 2.0	VG 4.0	FN 6.0	VF 8.0	VF/NM 9.0	NM- 9.2
1-5: Barbara Slate story & art						3.00

SWEET TOOTH
DC Comics (Vertigo): Nov, 2009 - Present ($1.00/$2.99)

	GD 2.0	VG 4.0	FN 6.0	VF 8.0	VF/NM 9.0	NM- 9.2
1-($1.00) Jeff Lemire-s/a						3.00
2-19-($2.99) 18-Printed sideways						3.00
...: In Captivity TPB (2010, $12.99) r/#6-11						13.00
...: Out of the Deep Woods TPB (2010, $9.99) r/#1-5						10.00

SWIFT ARROW (Also see Lone Rider & The Rider)
Ajax/Farrell Publications: Feb-Mar, 1954 - No. 5, Oct-Nov, 1954; Apr, 1957 - No. 3, Sept, 1957

	GD 2.0	VG 4.0	FN 6.0	VF 8.0	VF/NM 9.0	NM- 9.2
1(1954) (1st Series)	16	32	48	92	144	195
2	10	20	30	56	76	95
3-5: 5-Lone Rider story	9	18	27	50	65	80
1 (2nd Series) (Swift Arrow's Gunfighters #4)	9	18	27	50	65	80
2,3: 2-Lone Rider begins	8	16	24	40	50	60

SWIFT ARROW'S GUNFIGHTERS (Formerly Swift Arrow)
Ajax/Farrell Publ. (Four Star Comic Corp.): No. 4, Nov, 1957

	GD 2.0	VG 4.0	FN 6.0	VF 8.0	VF/NM 9.0	NM- 9.2
4	8	16	24	40	50	60

SWING WITH SCOOTER
National Periodical Publ.: June-July, 1966 - No. 35, Aug-Sept, 1971; No. 36, Oct-Nov, 1972

	GD 2.0	VG 4.0	FN 6.0	VF 8.0	VF/NM 9.0	NM- 9.2
1	9	18	27	63	107	150
2,6-10: 9-Alfred E. Newman swipe in last panel	5	10	15	35	55	75
3-5: 3-Batman cameo on-c. 4-Batman cameo inside. 5-JLA cameo	6	12	18	37	59	80
11-13,15-19: 18-Wildcat of JSA 1pg. text. 19-Last 12¢-c	3	6	9	21	32	42
14-Alfred E. Neuman cameo	4	8	12	22	34	45
20 (68 pgs.)	5	10	15	32	51	70
21-23,25-31	3	6	9	18	27	35
24-Frankenstein-c.	4	8	12	22	34	45
32-34 (68 pgs.). 32-Batman cameo. 33-Interview with David Cassidy. 34-Interview with Rick Ely (The Rebels)	5	10	15	30	48	65
35-(52 pgs.). 1 pg. app. Clark Kent and 4 full pgs. of Superman	7	14	21	50	83	115
36-Bat-signal refererence to Batman	4	8	12	22	34	45

NOTE: ***Aragonés*** a-13 (1pg.), 18(1pg.), 30(2pgs.) ***Orlando*** *a-1-11; c-1-11, 13. #20, 33, 34: 68 pgs.; #35: 52 pgs.*

SWISS FAMILY ROBINSON (Walt Disney's...; see King Classics & Movie Comics)
Dell Publishing Co.: No. 1156, Dec, 1960

	GD 2.0	VG 4.0	FN 6.0	VF 8.0	VF/NM 9.0	NM- 9.2
Four Color 1156-Movie-photo-c	7	14	21	49	80	110

S.W.O.R.D. (Sentient World Observation and Response Department)
Marvel Comics: Jan, 2010 - No. 5, May, 2010 ($3.99/$2.99)

	GD 2.0	VG 4.0	FN 6.0	VF 8.0	VF/NM 9.0	NM- 9.2
1-($3.99) Cassaday-c/Gillen-s/Sanders-a; Commander Brand & Henry Gyrich app.						4.00
2-5-($2.99): 2,3-Cassaday-c. 4,5-Del Mundo-c						3.00

SWORD, THE
Image Comics: Oct, 2007 - No. 24, May, 2010 ($2.99/$4.99)

	GD 2.0	VG 4.0	FN 6.0	VF 8.0	VF/NM 9.0	NM- 9.2
1-Luna Brothers-s/a						4.00
1-(2nd printing)						3.00
2-23: 12-Zakros killed						3.00
24-($4.99) Final issue						5.00
..., Vol. 1: Fire (TPB, 2008, $14.99) r/#1-6						15.00
..., Vol. 2: Water (TPB, 2008, $14.99) r/#7-12						15.00
..., Vol. 3: Earth (TPB, 2009, $14.99) r/#13-18						15.00
..., Vol. 4: Water (TPB, 2010, $14.99) r/#19-24						15.00

SWORD & THE DRAGON, THE
Dell Publishing Co.: No. 1118, June, 1960

	GD 2.0	VG 4.0	FN 6.0	VF 8.0	VF/NM 9.0	NM- 9.2
Four Color 1118-Movie, photo-c	7	14	21	50	83	115

SWORD & THE ROSE, THE (Disney)
Dell Publishing Co.: No. 505, Oct, 1953 - No. 682, Feb, 1956

	GD 2.0	VG 4.0	FN 6.0	VF 8.0	VF/NM 9.0	NM- 9.2
Four Color 505-Movie, photo-c	8	16	24	56	93	130
Four Color 682-When Knighthood Was in Flower-Movie, reprint of #505; Renamed the Sword & the Rose for the novel; photo-c	7	14	21	47	76	105

SWORD IN THE STONE, THE (See March of Comics #258 & Movie Comics & Wart and the Wizard)

SWORD OF DAMOCLES
Image Comics (WildStorm Productions): Mar, 1996 - No. 2, Apr, 1996 ($2.50, limited series)

	GD 2.0	VG 4.0	FN 6.0	VF 8.0	VF/NM 9.0	NM- 9.2
1,2: Warren Ellis scripts. 1-Prelude to "Fire From Heaven" x-over; 1st app. Sword						3.00

SWORD OF DRACULA
Image Comics: Oct, 2003 - No. 6, Sept, 2004 ($2.95, B&W, limited series)

	GD 2.0	VG 4.0	FN 6.0	VF 8.0	VF/NM 9.0	NM- 9.2
1-6-Tony Harris-c. 1,2-Greg Scott-a						3.00
TPB (IDW, 2/05, $14.99) r/series						15.00

SWORD OF RED SONJA: DOOM OF THE GODS
Dynamite Entertainment: 2007 - No. 4, 2007 ($3.50, limited series)

	GD 2.0	VG 4.0	FN 6.0	VF 8.0	VF/NM 9.0	NM- 9.2
1-4-Lui Antonio-a; multiple covers on each						3.50

SWORD OF SORCERY
National Periodical Publications: Feb-Mar, 1973 - No. 5, Nov-Dec, 1973 (20¢)

	GD 2.0	VG 4.0	FN 6.0	VF 8.0	VF/NM 9.0	NM- 9.2
1-Leiber Fafhrd & The Grey Mouser; Chaykin/Neal Adams (Crusty Bunkers) art; Kaluta-c	3	6	9	16	23	30
2,3: 2-Wrightson-c(i); Adams-a(i). 3-Wrightson-i(5 pgs.)	2	4	6	9	13	16
4,5: 5-Starlin-a(p); Conan cameo	2	4	6	8	10	12

NOTE: ***Chaykin*** *a-1-4p; c-2p, 3-5.* ***Kaluta*** *a-3i.* ***Simonson*** *a-3i, 4i, 5p; c-5.*

SWORD OF THE ATOM
DC Comics: Sept, 1983 - No. 4, Dec, 1983 (Limited series)

	GD 2.0	VG 4.0	FN 6.0	VF 8.0	VF/NM 9.0	NM- 9.2
1-4: Gil Kane-c/a in all						4.00
Special 1-3('84, '85, '88): 1,2-Kane-c/a each						4.00
TPB (2007, $19.99) r/#1-4 and Special #1-3						20.00

SWORDS OF TEXAS (See Scout #15)
Eclipse Comics: Oct, 1987 - No. 4, Jan, 1988 ($1.75, color, Baxter paper)

	GD 2.0	VG 4.0	FN 6.0	VF 8.0	VF/NM 9.0	NM- 9.2
1-4: Scout app.						3.00

SWORDS OF THE SWASHBUCKLERS (See Marvel Graphic Novel)
Marvel Comics (Epic Comics): May, 1985 - No. 12, Jun, 1987 ($1.50; mature)

	GD 2.0	VG 4.0	FN 6.0	VF 8.0	VF/NM 9.0	NM- 9.2
1-12-Butch Guice-c/a (Cont'd from Marvel G.N.)						3.00

SWORN TO PROTECT
Marvel Comics: Sept, 1995 ($1.95) (Based on card game)

	GD 2.0	VG 4.0	FN 6.0	VF 8.0	VF/NM 9.0	NM- 9.2
nn-Overpower Game Guide; Jubilee story						3.00

SYN
Dark Horse Comics: Aug, 2003 - No. 5, Feb, 2004 ($2.99, limited series)

	GD 2.0	VG 4.0	FN 6.0	VF 8.0	VF/NM 9.0	NM- 9.2
1-5-Giffen-s/Titus-a						3.00

SYPHONS
Now Comics: V2#1, May, 1994 - V2#3, 1994 ($2.50, limited series)

	GD 2.0	VG 4.0	FN 6.0	VF 8.0	VF/NM 9.0	NM- 9.2
V2#1-3: 1-Stardancer, Knightfire, Raze & Brigade begin						3.00
TPB (9/04, $15.95) B&W reprints #1-3; intro. by Tony Caputo						16.00

SYSTEM, THE
DC Comics (Vertigo Verite): May, 1996 - No. 3, July, 1996 ($2.95, lim. series)

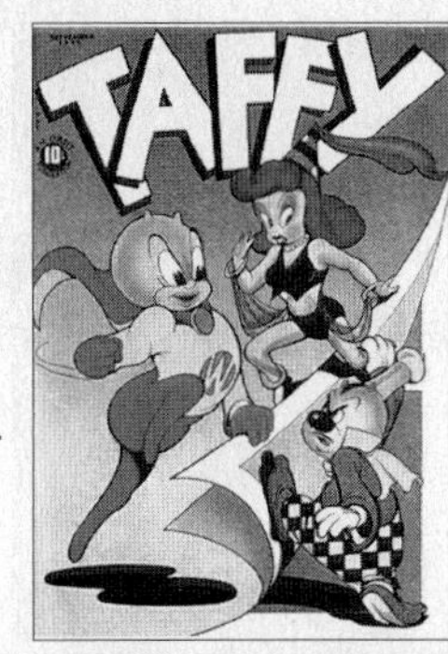

Taffy Comics #4 © Orbit

Tails #1 © Sega

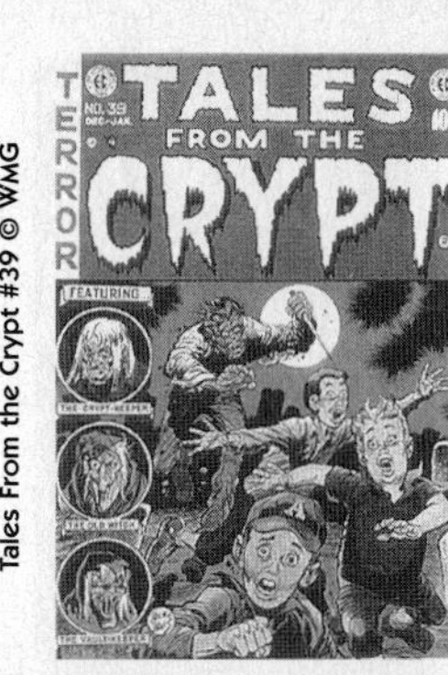

Tales From the Crypt #39 © WMG

GD 2.0 | VG 4.0 | FN 6.0 | VF 8.0 | VF/NM 9.0 | NM- 9.2

1-3: Kuper-c/a 3.00
TPB (1997, $12.95) r/#1-3 13.00

TAFFY COMICS (Also see Dotty Dripple)
Rural Home/Orbit Publ.: Mar-Apr, 1945 - No. 12, 1948

1-L.B. Cole-c; origin & 1st app. of Wiggles The Wonderworm plus 7 chapter WWII funny animal adventures 60 120 180 381 653 925
2-L.B. Cole-c with funny animal Hitler; Wiggles-c/stories in #1-4 39 78 117 231 378 525
3,4,6-12: 6-Perry Como-c/story. 7-Duke Ellington, 2 pgs. 8-Glenn Ford-c/story. 9-Lon McCallister part photo-c & story. 10-Mort Leav-c. 11-Mickey Rooney-c/story 15 30 45 83 124 165
5-L.B. Cole-c; Van Johnson-c/story 21 42 63 124 202 280

TAILGUNNER JO
DC Comics: Sept, 1988 - No. 6, Jan, 1989 ($1.25)

1-6 3.00

TAILS
Archie Publications: Dec, 1995 - No. 3, Feb, 1996 ($1.50, limited series)

1-3: Based on Sonic, the Hedgehog video game 6.00

TAILS OF THE PET AVENGERS (Also see Lockjaw and the Pet Avengers)
Marvel Comics: Apr, 2010 ($3.99, one-shot)

1-Lockjaw, Frog Thor, Zabu, Lockheed and Redwing in short solo stories by various 4.00
...: The Dogs of Summer (9/10, $3.99) Eliopolous-s; see Avengers vs. the Pet Avengers 4.00

TAILSPIN
Spotlight Publishers: November, 1944

nn-Firebird app.; L.B. Cole-c 28 56 84 165 270 375

TAILSPIN TOMMY (Also see Popular Comics)
United Features Syndicate/Service Publ. Co.: 1940; 1946

Single Series 23(1940) 39 78 117 240 395 550
Best Seller (nd, 1946)-Service Publ. Co. 15 30 45 86 133 180

TAKE A CHANCE (C.E. Murphy's...)
Dabel Brothers Prods.: Dec, 2008 - No. 5, Apr, 2009 ($3.99)

1-4-C.E. Murphy-s/Ardian Syaf-a/c 4.00

TAKIO
Marvel Comics (Icon): 2011 ($9.95, HC graphic novel)

HC-Bendis-s/Oeming-a/c; Oeming sketch pages 10.00

TAKION
DC Comics: June, 1996 - No. 7, Dec, 1996 ($1.75)

1-7: Lopresti-c/a(p). 1-Origin; Green Lantern app. 6-Final Night x-over 3.00

TALENT SHOWCASE (See New Talent Showcase)

TALE OF ONE BAD RAT, THE
Dark Horse Comics: Oct, 1994 - No. 4, Jan, 1995 ($2.95, limited series)

1-4: Bryan Talbot-c/a/scripts 3.00
HC ($69.95, signed and numbered) R/#1-4 70.00

TALES CALCULATED TO DRIVE YOU BATS
Archie Publications: Nov, 1961 - No. 7, Nov, 1962; 1966 (Satire)

1-Only 10¢ issue; has cut-out Werewolf mask (price includes mask) 13 26 39 89 170 250
2-Begin 12¢ issues 8 16 24 54 90 125
3-6: 3-UFO cover 6 12 18 43 69 95
7-Storyline change 6 12 18 41 66 90
1(1966, 25¢, 44 pg. Giant)-r/#1; UFO cover 6 12 18 39 62 85

TALES CALCULATED TO DRIVE YOU MAD
E.C. Publications: Summer, 1997 - No. 8, Winter, 1999 ($3.99/$4.99, satire)

1-6-Full color reprints of Mad: 1-(#1-3), 2-(#4-6), 3-(#7-9), 4-(#10-12) 5-(#13-15), 6-(#16-18) 5.00
7,8-($4.99-c): 7-(#19-21), 8-(#22,23) 5.00

TALES FROM RIVERDALE DIGEST
Archie Publ.: June, 2005 - No. 39, Oct, 2010 ($2.39/$2.49/$2.69, digest-size)

1-39: 1-Sabrina and Josie & the Pussycats app. 11-Begin $2.49-c. 34-Begin $2.69 3.00

TALES FROM THE AGE OF APOCALYPSE
Marvel Comics: 1996 ($5.95, prestige format, one-shots)

1, ...: Sinister Bloodlines (1997, $5.95) 6.00

TALES FROM THE BOG
Aberration Press: Nov, 1995 - No. 7, Nov, 1997 ($2.95/$3.95, B&W)

1-7 4.00
Alternate #1 (Director's Cut) (1998, $2.95) 3.00

TALES FROM THE BULLY PULPIT
Image Comics: Aug, 2004 ($6.95, square-bound)

1-Teddy Roosevelt and Edison's ghost with a time machine; Cereno-s/MacDonald-a 7.00

TALES FROM THE CLERKS (See Jay and Silent Bob, Clerks and Oni Double Feature)
Graphitti Designs, Inc.: 2006 ($29.95, TPB)

nn-Reprints all the Kevin Smith Clerks and Jay and Silent Bob stories; new Clerks II story with Mahfood-a; cover gallery, sketch pages, Mallrats credits covers; Smith intro. 30.00

TALES FROM THE CRYPT (Formerly The Crypt Of Terror; see Three Dimensional...) (Also see EC Archives • Tales From the Crypt)
E.C. Comics: No. 20, Oct-Nov, 1950 - No. 46, Feb-Mar, 1955

20-See Crime Patrol #15 for 1st Crypt Keeper 119 238 357 952 1514 2075
21-Kurtzman-r/Haunt of Fear #15(#1) 100 200 300 800 1275 1750
22-Moon Girl costume at costume party, one panel 77 154 231 616 983 1350
23-25: 24-E. A. Poe adaptation 63 126 189 504 802 1100
26-30: 26-Wood's 2nd EC-c 50 100 150 400 638 875
31-Williamson-a(1st at E.C.); B&W and color illos. in **POP**; Kamen draws himself, Gaines & Feldstein; Ingels, Craig & Davis draw themselves in his story 51 102 153 408 654 900
32,35-39: 38-Censored-c 43 86 129 344 547 750
33-Origin The Crypt Keeper 65 130 195 520 830 1140
34-Used in **POP**, pg. 83; lingerie panels 44 88 132 352 564 775
40-Used in Senate hearings & in Hartford Cournat anti-comics editorials-1954 44 88 132 352 559 765
41-45: 45-2 pgs. showing E.C. staff 42 84 126 336 536 735
46-Low distribution; pre-advertised cover for unpublished 4th horror title "Crypt of Terror" used on this book 49 98 147 392 629 865

NOTE: ***Ray Bradbury*** *adaptations-34, 36.* ***Craig*** *a-20, 22-24; c-20.* ***Crandall*** *a-38, 44.* ***Davis*** *a-24-46; c-29-46.* ***Elder*** *a-37, 38.* ***Evans*** *a-32-34, 36, 40, 41, 43, 46.* ***Feldstein*** *a-20-23; c-21-25, 28. Ingels a-in all.* ***Kamen*** *a-20, 22, 25, 27-31, 33-36, 39, 41-45.* ***Krigstein*** *a-40, 42, 45.* ***Kurtzman*** *a-21.* ***Orlando*** *a-27-30, 35, 37, 39, 41-45.* ***Wood*** *a-21, 24, 25; c-26, 27. Canadian reprints known; see Table of Contents.*

TALES FROM THE CRYPT (Magazine)
Eerie Publications: No. 10, July, 1968 (35¢, B&W)

10-Contains Farrell reprints from 1950s 5 10 15 35 55 75

TALES FROM THE CRYPT
Gladstone Publishing: July, 1990 - No. 6, May, 1991 ($1.95/$2.00, 68 pgs.)

1-r/TFTC #33 & Crime S.S. #17; Davis-c(r) 4.00
2-6: 2,3,5,6-Davis-c(r). 4-Begin $2.00-c; Craig-c(r) 4.00

TALES FROM THE CRYPT
Extra-Large Comics (Russ Cochran)/Gemstone Publishing: Jul, 1991 - No. 6 ($3.95, 10 1/4 x13 1/4", 68 pgs.)

1-Davis-c(r); Craig back-c(r); E.C. reprints 4.00
2-6 ($2.00, comic sized) 4.00

TALES FROM THE CRYPT
Russ Cochran: Sept, 1991 - No. 7, July, 1992 ($2.00, 64 pgs.)

1-7 4.00

TALES FROM THE CRYPT (Also see EC Archives • Tales From the Crypt)
Russ Cochran/Gemstone: Sept, 1992 - No. 30, Dec, 1999 ($1.50, quarterly)

1-4-r/Crypt of Terror #17-19, TFTC #20 w/original-c 3.00
5-30: 5-15 ($2.00)-r/TFTC #21-23 w/original-c. 16-30 ($2.50) 3.00
Annual 1-6('93-'99) 1-r/#1-5. 2- r/#6-10. 3- r/#11-15. 4- r/#16-20. 5-r/#21-25. 6- r/#26-30 14.00

TALES FROM THE CRYPT
Papercutz: July, 2007 - Present ($3.95)

1-6: 1-New stories in the same vein as the originals; Cryptkeeper app. Kyle Baker-c 4.00

TALES FROM THE GREAT BOOK
Famous Funnies: Feb, 1955 - No. 4, Jan, 1956 (Religious themes)

1-Story of Samson; John Lehti-a in all 9 18 27 50 65 80
2-4: 2-Joshua. 3-Joash the Boy King. 4-David 7 14 21 35 43 50

TALES FROM THE HEART OF AFRICA (The Temporary Natives)
Marvel Comics (Epic Comics): Aug, 1990 ($3.95, 52 pgs.)

1 4.00

TALES FROM THE TOMB (Also see Dell Giants)
Dell Publishing Co.: Oct, 1962 (25¢ giant)

1(02-810-210)-All stories written by John Stanley 14 28 42 97 194 290

TALES FROM THE TOMB (Magazine)
Eerie Publications: V1#6, July, 1969 - V7#3, 1975 (52 pgs.)

Tales of Horror #11 © Minoan

Tales of Suspense #4 © MAR

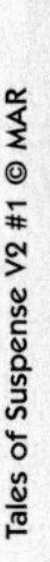
Tales of Suspense V2 #1 © MAR

	GD 2.0	VG 4.0	FN 6.0	VF 8.0	VF/NM 9.0	NM- 9.2
V1#6	7	14	21	49	80	110
V1#7,8	6	12	18	39	62	85
V2#1-6: 4-LSD story-r/Weird V3#5. 6-Rulah-r	5	10	15	32	51	70
V3#1-Rulah-r	5	10	15	32	51	70
2-6('71),V4#1-5('72),V5#1-6('73),V6#1-6('74),V7#1-3('75)	4	8	12	28	44	60

TALES OF ASGARD
Marvel Comics Group: Oct, 1968 (25¢, 68 pgs.); Feb, 1984 ($1.25, 52 pgs.)

	GD	VG	FN	VF	VF/NM	NM-
1-Reprints Tales of Asgard (Thor) back-up stories from Journey into Mystery #97-106; new Kirby-c; Kirby-a	5	10	15	34	55	75
V2#1 (2/84)-Thor-r; Simonson-c						5.00

TALES OF ARMY OF DARKNESS
Dynamite Entertainment: 2006 ($5.95, one-shot)

	GD	VG	FN	VF	VF/NM	NM-
1-Short stories by Kuhoric, Kirkman, Bradshaw, Sablik, Ottley, Acs, O'Hare and others						6.00

TALES OF EVIL
Atlas/Seaboard Publ.: Feb, 1975 - No. 3, July, 1975 (All 25¢ issues)

	GD	VG	FN	VF	VF/NM	NM-
1-3: 1-Werewolf w/Sekowsky-a. 2-Intro. The Bog Beast; Sparling-a. 3-Origin The Man-Monster; Buckler-a(p)	2	4	6	9	12	15

NOTE: ***Grandenetti** a-1, 2. **Lieber** c-1. **Sekowsky** a-1. **Sutton** a-2. **Thorne** c-2.*

TALES OF GHOST CASTLE
National Periodical Publications: May-June, 1975 - No. 3, Sept-Oct, 1975 (All 25¢ issues)

	GD	VG	FN	VF	VF/NM	NM-
1-Redondo-a; 1st app. Lucien the Librarian from Sandman (1989 series)	3	6	9	18	27	35
2,3: 2-Nino-a. 3-Redondo-a.	2	4	6	10	14	18

TALES OF G.I. JOE
Marvel Comics: Jan, 1988 - No. 15, Mar, 1989

	GD	VG	FN	VF	VF/NM	NM-
1 ($2.25, 52 pgs.)						4.00
2-15 ($1.50): 1-15-r/G.I. Joe #1-15						3.00

TALES OF HORROR
Toby Press/Minoan Publ. Corp.: June, 1952 - No. 13, Oct, 1954

	GD	VG	FN	VF	VF/NM	NM-
1	41	82	123	249	417	585
2-Torture scenes	32	64	96	192	314	435
3-11,13: 9-11-Reprints Purple Claw #1-3	22	44	66	132	216	300
12-Myron Fass-c/a; torture scenes	24	48	72	140	230	320

NOTE: ***Andru** a-5. **Baily** a-5. **Myron Fass** a-2, 3, 12; c-1-3, 12. **Hollingsworth** a-2. **Sparling** a-6, 9; c-9.*

TALES OF JUSTICE
Atlas Comics(MjMC No. 53-66/Male No. 67): No. 53, May, 1955 - No. 67, Aug, 1957

	GD	VG	FN	VF	VF/NM	NM-
53	15	30	45	83	124	165
54-57: 54-Powell-a	11	22	33	60	83	105
58,59-Krigstein-a	12	24	36	67	94	120
60-63,65: 60-Powell-a	10	20	30	54	72	90
64,66,67: 64,67-Crandall-a. 66-Torres, Orlando-a	10	20	30	56	76	95

NOTE: ***Everett** a-53, 60. **Orlando** a-65, 66. **Severin** a-64; c-58, 60, 65. **Wildey** a-64, 67.*

TALES OF LEONARDO BLIND SIGHT (See Tales of the TMNT Vol. 2 #5)
Mirage Publishing: June, 2006 - No. 4, Sept, 2006 ($3.25, B&W, limited series)

	GD	VG	FN	VF	VF/NM	NM-
1-4-Jim Lawson-s/a						3.25

TALES OF SUSPENSE (Becomes Captain America #100 on)
Atlas (WPI No. 1,2/Male No. 3-12/VPI No. 13-18)/Marvel No. 19 on:
Jan, 1959 - No. 99, Mar, 1968

	GD	VG	FN	VF	VF/NM	NM-
1-Williamson-a (5 pgs.); Heck-c; #1-4 have sci/fi-c	156	312	468	1365	2783	4200
2,3: 2-Robot-c. 3-Flying saucer-c/story	54	108	162	459	930	1400
4-Williamson-a (4 pgs.); Kirby/Everett-c/a	43	86	129	344	697	1050
5-Kirby monster-c begin	39	78	117	312	619	925
6,8,10	35	70	105	273	537	800
7-Prototype ish. (Lava Man); 1 panel app. Aunt May (see Str. Tales #97)	37	74	111	294	585	875
9-Prototype ish. (Iron Man)	38	76	114	304	602	900
11,12,15,17-19: 12-Crandall-a.	28	56	84	208	422	635
13-Elektro-c/story	28	56	84	215	433	650
14-Intro/1st app. Colossus-c/sty	38	76	114	304	602	900
16-1st Metallo-c/story (4/61, Iron Man prototype)	34	68	102	262	519	775
20-Colossus-c/story (2nd app.)	29	58	87	223	449	675
21-25: 25-Last 10¢ issue	25	50	75	183	367	550
26,27,29,30,33,34,36-38: 33-(9/62)-Hulk 1st x-over cameo (picture on wall)	24	48	72	175	350	525
28-Prototype ish. (Stone Men)	24	48	72	178	357	535
31-Prototype ish. (Dr. Doom)	26	52	78	190	383	575
32-Prototype ish. (Dr. Strange)(8/62)-Sazzik The Sorcerer app.; "The Man and the Beehive" story, 1 month before TTA #35 (2nd Antman), came out after "The Man in the Ant Hill" in TTA #27 (1/62) (1st Antman)-Characters from both stories were tested to see which got best fan response	35	70	105	273	537	800
35-Prototype issue (The Watcher)	26	52	78	190	383	575
39 (3/63)-Origin/1st app. Iron Man & begin series; 1st Iron Man story has Kirby layouts	900	1800	2700	8100	16,550	25,000
40-2nd app. Iron Man (in new armor)	178	356	534	1558	3179	4800
41-3rd app. Iron Man; Dr. Strange (villain) app.	108	216	324	918	1859	2800
42-45: 45-Intro. & 1st app. Happy & Pepper	69	138	207	587	1194	1800
46,47: 46-1st app. Crimson Dynamo	52	104	156	442	896	1350
48-New Iron Man armor by Ditko	60	120	180	510	1030	1550
49-1st X-Men x-over (same date as X-Men #3, 1/64); also 1st Avengers x-over (w/o Captain America); 1st Tales of the Watcher back-up story & begins (2nd app. Watcher; see F.F. #13)	77	154	231	655	1328	2000
50-1st app. Mandarin	38	76	114	304	602	900
51-1st Scarecrow	28	56	84	204	415	625
52-1st app. The Black Widow (4/64)	41	82	123	328	664	1000
53-Origin The Watcher; 2nd Black Widow app.	28	56	84	204	415	625
54,55	21	42	63	150	300	450
56-1st app. Unicorn	23	46	69	168	334	500
57-Origin/1st app. Hawkeye (9/64)	41	82	123	324	650	975
58-Captain America battles Iron Man (10/64)-Classic-c; 2nd Kraven app. (Cap's 1st app. in this title)	41	82	123	328	664	1000
59-Iron Man plus Captain America double feature begins (11/64); 1st S.A. Captain America solo story; intro Jarvis, Avenger's butler; classic-c	41	82	123	328	664	1000
60-2nd app. Hawkeye (#64 is 3rd app.)	24	48	72	175	350	525
61,62,64: 62-Origin Mandarin (2/65)	14	28	42	99	200	300
63-1st Silver Age origin Captain America (3/65)	29	58	87	223	449	675
65-G.A. Red Skull in WWII stories(also in #66);-1st Silver-Age Red Skull (5/65).	23	46	69	168	334	500
66-Origin Red Skull	17	34	51	122	249	375
67-70: 69-1st app. Titanium Man. 70-Begin alternating-c features w/Capt. America (even #'s) & Iron Man (odd #'s)	10	20	30	69	122	175
71-78: 75-1st app. Agent 13 later named Sharon Carter; intro Batroc. 78-Col. Nick Fury app.	8	16	24	52	86	120
79-Begin 3 part Iron Man Sub-Mariner battle story; Sub-Mariner-c & cameo; 1st app. Cosmic Cube; 1st modern Red Skull	9	18	27	63	107	150
80-Iron Man battles Sub-Mariner story cont'd in Tales to Astonish #82; classic Red Skull-c	9	18	27	63	107	150
81-96,98: 82-Intro the Adaptoid by Kirby (also in #83,84). 88-Mole Man app. in Iron Man story. 92-1st Nick Fury x-over (cameo, as Agent of S.H.I.E.L.D., 8/67). 94-Intro Modok. 95-Capt. America's i.d. revealed. 98-1st brief app. new Zemo (son?); #99 is 1st full app.	7	14	21	47	76	105
97-1st Whiplash	9	18	27	60	100	140
99-Captain America story cont'd in Captain America #100; Iron Man story cont'd in Iron Man & Sub-Mariner #1	8	16	24	58	97	135

Onmibus (See Iron Man Omnibus for reprints of #39-83)

NOTE: ***Abel** a-73-81i(as Gary Michaels), **J. Buscema** a-1; c-3. **Colan** a-39, 73-99p; c(p)-73, 75, 77, 79, 81, 83, 85-87, 89, 91, 93, 95, 97, 99. **Crandall** a-12. **Davis** a-38. **Ditko** a-1-15, 17-44, 46, 47-49p; c-2, 10i, 13i, 23i. **Kirby/Ditko** a-7; c-10, 13, 22, 28, 34. **Everett** a-8. **Forte** a-5, 9. **Giacoia** a-82. **Heath** a-2, 10. **Gil Kane** a-88p, 89-91; c-88, 89-91p. **Kirby** a(p)-2-4, 6-35, 40, 41, 43, 59-75, 77-86, 92-99; layouts-69-75, 77; c(p)4-28(most), 29-56, 58-72, 74, 76, 78, 80, 82, 84, 86, 92, 94, 96, 98. **Leiber/Fox** a-42, 43, 45, 51. **Reinman** a-26, 44i, 49i, 52i, 53i. **Tuska** a-58, 70-74. **Wood** c/a-71i.*

TALES OF SUSPENSE
Marvel Comics: V2#1, Jan, 1995 ($6.95, one-shot)

	GD	VG	FN	VF	VF/NM	NM-
V2#1-James Robinson script; acetate-c.						7.00

TALES OF SUSPENSE: CAPTAIN AMERICA & IRON MAN #1 COMMEMORATIVE EDITION
Marvel Comics: 2004 ($3.99, one-shot)

	GD	VG	FN	VF	VF/NM	NM-
nn-Reprints Captain America (2004) #1 and Iron Man (2004) #1						4.00

TALES OF SWORD & SORCERY (See Dagar)

TALES OF TELLOS (See Tellos)
Image Comics: Oct, 2004 - No. 3, ($3.50, anthology)

	GD	VG	FN	VF	VF/NM	NM-
1-3: 1-Dezago-s; art by Yates & Rousseau; Wieringo-c. 3-Porter-a						3.50

TALES OF TERROR
Toby Press Publications: 1952 (no month)

	GD	VG	FN	VF	VF/NM	NM-
1-Fawcette-c; Ravielli-a	27	54	81	158	259	360

NOTE: *This title was cancelled due to similarity to the E.C. title.*

TALES OF TERROR (See Movie Classics)

TALES OF TERROR (Magazine)
Eerie Publications: Summer, 1964

	GD	VG	FN	VF	VF/NM	NM-
1	6	12	18	41	66	90

TALES OF TERROR

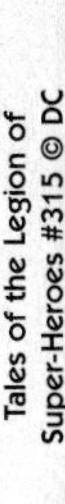

Tales of the Legion of Super-Heroes #315 © DC

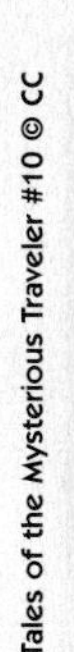

Tales of the Mysterious Traveler #10 © CC

Tales of the Teen Titans #52 © DC

Eclipse Comics: July, 1985 - No. 13, July, 1987 ($2.00, Baxter paper, mature)

1-13: 5-1st Lee Weeks-a. 7-Sam Kieth-a. 10-Snyder-a. 12-Vampire story 3.00

TALES OF TERROR (IDW's...)
IDW Publishing: Sept, 2004 ($16.99, hardcover)

1-Anthology of short graphic stories and text stories; incl. 30 Days of Night 17.00

TALES OF TERROR ANNUAL
E.C. Comics: 1951 - No. 3, 1953 (25¢, 132 pgs., 16 stories each)

	GD 2.0	VG 4.0	FN 6.0	VF 8.0	VF/NM 9.0	NM- 9.2
nn(1951)(Scarce)-Feldstein infinity-c	825	1650	2475	6600	-	-
2(1952)-Feldstein-c	265	530	795	1694	2897	4100
3(1953)-Feldstein bondage/torture-c	213	426	639	1363	2332	3300

NOTE: *No. 1 contains three horror and one science fiction comic which came out in 1950. No. 2 contains a horror, crime, and science fiction book which generally had cover dates in 1951, and No. 3 had horror, crime, and shock books that generally appeared in 1952. All E.C. annuals contain four complete books that did not sell on the stands which were rebound in the annual format, minus the covers, and sold from the E.C. office and on the stands in key cities. The contents of each annual may vary in the same year. Crypt Keeper, Vault Keeper, Old Witch app. on all-c.*

TALES OF TERROR ILLUSTRATED (See Terror Illustrated)

TALES OF TEXAS JOHN SLAUGHTER (See Walt Disney Presents, 4-Color #997)

TALES OF THE BEANWORLD
Beanworld Press/Eclipse Comics: Feb, 1985 - No. 19, 1991; No. 20, 1993 - No. 21, 1993 ($1.50/$2.00, B&W)

1-21 3.00

TALES OF THE BIZARRO WORLD
DC Comics: 2000 ($14.95, TPB)

nn-Reprints early Bizarro stories; new Jaime Hernandez-c 15.00

TALES OF THE DARKNESS
Image Comics (Top Cow): Apr, 1998 - No. 4, Dec, 1998 ($2.95)

1-4: 1,2-Portacio-c/a(p). 3,4-Lansing & Nocon-a(p) 3.00
1-American Entertainment Ed. 3.00
#1/2 (1/01, $2.95) 3.00

TALES OF THE DRAGON GUARD (English version of French comic title)
Marvel Comics (Soleil): Apr, 2010 - No. 3, Jun, 2010 ($5.99, limited series)

1-3: 1-Ange-s/Varanda-a. 2-Briones-a. 3-Guinebaud-a 6.00
...: Into the Veil 1-3 (11/10 - No. 3, 1/11) 1-Briones-a. 2-Paty-a. 3-Sieurac-a 6.00

TALES OF THE GREEN BERET
Dell Publishing Co.: Jan, 1967 - No. 5, Oct, 1969

	GD 2.0	VG 4.0	FN 6.0	VF 8.0	VF/NM 9.0	NM- 9.2
1-Glanzman-a in 1-4 & 5r	4	8	12	20	30	40
2-5: 5-Reprints #1	3	6	9	16	23	30

TALES OF THE GREEN HORNET
Now Comics: Sept, 1990 - No. 2, 1990; V2#1, Jan, 1992 - No.4, Apr, 1992; V3#1, Sept, 1992 - No. 3, Nov, 1992

1,2 3.00
V2#1-4 ($1.95) 3.00
V3#1 ($2.75)-Polybagged w/hologram trading card 4.00
V3#2,3 ($2.50) 3.00

TALES OF THE GREEN LANTERN CORPS (See Green Lantern #107)
DC Comics: May, 1981 - No. 3, July, 1981 (Limited series)

1-3: 1-Origin of G.L. & the Guardians, Annual 1 (1/85)-Gil Kane-c/a 5.00
TPB (2009, $19.99) r/#1-3 & stories from G.L. #148-151-154,161,162,164-167 ('82-'83) 20.00
Volume 2 TPB (2010, $19.99) r/Annual #1 and stories from G.L. ('83-'85) 20.00
Volume 3 TPB (2010, $19.99) r/Green Lantern #201-206 ('86) 20.00

TALES OF THE INVISIBLE SCARLET O'NEIL (See Harvey Comics Hits #59)

TALES OF THE KILLERS (Magazine)
World Famous Periodicals: V1#10, Dec, 1970 - V1#11, Feb, 1971 (B&W, 52 pg)

	GD 2.0	VG 4.0	FN 6.0	VF 8.0	VF/NM 9.0	NM- 9.2
V1#10-One pg. Frazetta; r/Crime Does Not Pay	5	10	15	30	48	65
11-similar-c to Crime Does Not Pay #47; contains r/Crime Does Not Pay	4	8	12	26	41	55

TALES OF THE LEGION (Formerly Legion of Super-Heroes)
DC Comics: No. 314, Aug, 1984 - No. 354, Dec, 1987

314-354: 326-r-begin 3.00
Annual 4,5 (1986, 1987)-Formerly LSH Annual 4.00

TALES OF THE MARINES (Formerly Devil-Dog Dugan #1-3)
Atlas Comics (OPI): No. 4, Feb, 1957 (Marines At War #5 on)

	GD 2.0	VG 4.0	FN 6.0	VF 8.0	VF/NM 9.0	NM- 9.2
4-Powell-a; Severin-c	10	20	30	56	76	105

TALES OF THE MARVELS
Marvel Comics: 1995/1996 (all acetate, painted-c)

...Blockbuster 1 (1995, $5.95, one-shot), ...Inner Demons 1 (1996, $5.95, one shot), ...Wonder Years 1,2 (1995, $4.95, limited series) 6.00

TALES OF THE MARVEL UNIVERSE
Marvel Comics: Feb, 1997 ($2.95, one-shot)

1-Anthology; wraparound-c; Thunderbolts, Ka-Zar app. 4.00

TALES OF THE MYSTERIOUS TRAVELER (See Mysterious...)
Charlton Comics: Aug, 1956 - No. 13, June, 1959; V2#14, Oct, 1985 - No. 15, Dec, 1985

	GD 2.0	VG 4.0	FN 6.0	VF 8.0	VF/NM 9.0	NM- 9.2
1-No Ditko-a; Giordano/Alascia-c	50	100	150	315	533	750
2-Ditko-a(1)	41	82	123	256	428	600
3-Ditko-c/a(1)	42	84	126	265	445	625
4-7-Ditko-c/a(3-4 stories each)	48	96	144	302	514	725
8,9-Ditko-a(1-3 each). 8-Rocke-c	41	82	123	250	418	585
10,11-Ditko-c/a(3-4 each)	44	88	132	277	469	660
12	18	36	54	105	165	225
13-Baker-a (r?)	19	38	57	111	176	240
V2#14,15 (1985)-Ditko-c/a-low print run	2	3	4	6	8	10

TALES OF THE NEW GODS
DC Comics: 2008 ($19.99, TPB)

SC-Reprints from Jack Kirby's Fourth World, Orion and Mister Miracle Special 20.00

TALES OF THE NEW TEEN TITANS
DC Comics: June, 1982 - No. 4, Sept, 1982 (Limited series)

1-4 5.00

TALES OF THE PONY EXPRESS (TV)
Dell Publishing Co.: No. 829, Aug, 1957 - No. 942, Oct, 1958

	GD 2.0	VG 4.0	FN 6.0	VF 8.0	VF/NM 9.0	NM- 9.2
Four Color 829 (#1) -Painted-c	5	10	15	30	48	65
Four Color 942-Title -Pony Express	5	10	15	30	48	65

TALES OF THE REALM
CrossGen Comics/MVCreations #4-on: Oct, 2003 - No. 5, May, 2004 ($2.95, limited series)

1-5-Robert Kirkman-s/Matt Tyree-a 3.00
Volume 1 HC (8/04, $39.95, dust jacket) r/#1-5; sketch pages and concept art 40.00

TALES OF THE SINESTRO CORPS (See Green Lantern and Green Lantern Corps x-over)
DC Comics: Nov, 2007 - Jan, 2008 ($2.99/$3.99, one-shots)

...: Cyborg-Superman (12/07, $2.99) Burnett-s/Blaine-a/VanSciver-c; JLA app. 3.00
...: Ion (1/08, $2.99) Marz-s/Lacombe-a/Benes-c; Sodam Yat app. 3.00
...: Parallax (11/07, $2.99) Marz-s/Melo-a; Kyle Rayner vs. Parallax 3.00
...: Superman-Prime (12/07, $3.99) Johns-s/VanSciver-c; origin re-told w/Ordway-a 4.00

TALES OF THE TEENAGE MUTANT NINJA TURTLES (See Teenage Mutant...)
Mirage Studios: May, 1987 - No. 7, Aug (Apr-c), 1989 (B&W, $1.50)

1-7: 2-Title merges w/Teenage Mutant Ninja... 4.00

TALES OF THE TEEN TITANS (Formerly The New Teen Titans)
DC Comics: No. 41, Apr, 1984 - No. 91, July, 1988 (75¢)

41,45-49: 46-Aqualad & Aquagirl join 4.00
42-44: The Judas Contract part 1-3 with Deathstroke the Terminator in all; concludes in Annual #3. 44-Dick Grayson becomes Nightwing (3rd to be Nightwing) & joins Titans; Jericho (Deathstroke's son) joins; origin Deathstroke 5.00
50-Double size; app. Betty Kane (Bat-Girl) out of costume 5.00
51,52,56-91: 52-1st brief app. Azrael (not same as newer character). 56-Intro Jinx. 57-Neutron app. 59-r/DC Comics Presents #26. 60-91-r/New Teen Titans Baxter series. 68-B. Smith-c. 70-Origin Kole 3.00
53-55: 53-1st full app. Azrael; Deathstroke cameo. 54,55-Deathstroke-c/stories 4.00
Annual 3(1984, $1.25)-Part 4 of The Judas Contract; Deathstroke-c/story; Death of Terra; indicia says Teen Titans Annual; previous annuals listed as New Teen Titans Annual #1,2 5.00
Annual 4-(1986, $1.25) 4.00

TALES OF THE TEXAS RANGERS (See Jace Pearson...)

TALES OF THE THING (Fantastic Four)
Marvel Comics: May, 2005 - No. 3, July, 2005 ($2.50, limited series)

1-3-Dr. Strange app; Randy Green-c 3.00

TALES OF THE TMNT (Also see Teenage Mutant Ninja Turtles)
Mirage Studios: Jan, 2004 - Present ($2.95/$3.25, B&W)

1-7: 1-Brizuela-a 3.25
8-70: 8-Begin $3.25-c. 47-Origin of the Super Turtles 3.25

TALES OF THE UNEXPECTED (Becomes The Unexpected #105 on)(See Adventure #75, Super DC Giant)
National Periodical Publications: Feb-Mar, 1956 - No. 104, Dec-Jan, 1967-68

	GD 2.0	VG 4.0	FN 6.0	VF 8.0	VF/NM 9.0	NM- 9.2
1	104	208	312	884	1792	2700

Tales of the Unexpected #43 © DC

Tales of the Vampires #2 © 20th Century Fox

Tales to Astonish #93 © MAR

	GD 2.0	VG 4.0	FN 6.0	VF 8.0	VF/NM 9.0	NM- 9.2
2	43	86	129	344	697	1050
3-5	32	64	96	248	492	735
6-10: 6-1st Silver Age issue	26	52	78	190	383	575
11,14,19,20	18	36	54	131	266	400
12,13,16,18,21-24: All have Kirby-a. 16-Characters named 'Thor' (with a magic hammer) and Loki by Kirby (8/57, characters do not look like Marvel's Thor & Loki)	22	44	66	159	317	475
15,17-Grey tone-c; Kirby-a	24	48	72	177	356	535
25-30	16	32	48	111	226	340
31-39	14	28	42	96	191	285
40-Space Ranger begins (8/59, 3rd ap.), ends #82	104	208	312	884	1792	2700
41,42-Space Ranger stories	38	76	114	304	602	900
43-1st Space Ranger-c this title; grey tone-c	67	134	201	570	1160	1750
44-46	28	56	84	215	433	650
47-50	24	48	72	175	350	525
51-60: 54-Dinosaur-c/story	20	40	60	140	283	425
61-67: 67-Last 10¢ issue	16	32	48	114	232	350
68-82: 82-Last Space Ranger	11	22	33	77	144	210
83-90,92-99	7	14	21	47	76	105
91,100: 91-1st Automan (also in #94,97)	7	14	21	49	80	110
101-104	6	12	18	43	69	95

NOTE: ***Neal Adams*** *c-104.* ***Anderson*** *a-50.* ***Brown*** *a-50-82(Space Ranger); c-19, 40, & many Space Ranger-c.* ***Cameron*** *a-24, 27, 29; c-24.* ***Heath*** *a-49.* ***Bob Kane*** *a-24, 48.* ***Kirby*** *a-12, 13, 15-18, 21-24; c-13, 18, 22.* ***Meskin*** *a-15, 18, 26, 27, 35, 66.* ***Moreira*** *a-16, 20, 29, 38, 44, 62, 71; c-38.* ***Roussos*** *c-10.* ***Wildey*** *a-31.*

TALES OF THE UNEXPECTED (See Crisis Aftermath: The Spectre)
DC Comics: Dec, 2006 - No. 8, Jul, 2007 ($3.99, limited series)

	GD 2.0	VG 4.0	FN 6.0	VF 8.0	VF/NM 9.0	NM- 9.2
1-8-The Spectre, Lapham-s/Battle-a; Dr. 13, Azzarello-s/Chiang-a. 4-Wrightson-c						4.00
1-Variant Spectre cover by Neal Adams						5.00
The Spectre: Tales of the Unexpected TPB (2007, $14.99) r/#4-8						15.00

TALES OF THE VAMPIRES (Also see Buffy the Vampire Slayer and related titles)
Dark Horse Comics: 2003 - No. 5, Apr, 2004 ($2.99, limited series)

	GD 2.0	VG 4.0	FN 6.0	VF 8.0	VF/NM 9.0	NM- 9.2
1-Short stories by Joss Whedon and others. 1-Totleben-c. 3-Powell-c. 4-Edlund-c						3.00
TPB (11/04, $15.95) r/#1-5; afterword by Marv Wolfman						16.00

TALES OF THE WEST (See 3-D...)

TALES OF THE WITCHBLADE
Image Comics (Top Cow Productions): Nov, 1996 - No. 9 ($2.95)

	GD 2.0	VG 4.0	FN 6.0	VF 8.0	VF/NM 9.0	NM- 9.2
1/2	1	2	3	5	7	9
1/2 Gold	2	4	6	9	12	15
1-Daniel-c/a(p)	1	3	4	6	8	10
1-Variant-c by Turner	2	4	6	9	12	15
1-Platinum Edition	3	6	9	16	23	30
2,3						6.00
4-6: 6-Green-c						5.00
7-9: 9-Lara Croft-c						3.00
7-Variant-c by Turner	1	2	3	5	6	8
Witchblade: Distinctions (4/01, $14.95, TPB) r/#1-6; Green-c						15.00

TALES OF THE WITCHBLADE COLLECTED EDITION
Image Comics (Top Cow): May, 1998 - No. 2 ($4.95/$5.95, square-bound)

	GD 2.0	VG 4.0	FN 6.0	VF 8.0	VF/NM 9.0	NM- 9.2
1,2: 1-r/#1,2. 2-($5.95) r/#3,4						6.00

TALES OF THE WIZARD OF OZ (See Wizard of OZ, 4-Color #1308)

TALES OF THE ZOMBIE (Magazine)
Marvel Comics Group: Aug, 1973 - No. 10, Mar, 1975 (75¢, B&W)

	GD 2.0	VG 4.0	FN 6.0	VF 8.0	VF/NM 9.0	NM- 9.2
V1#1-Reprint/Menace #5; origin	5	10	15	32	51	70
2,3: 2-Everett biog. & memorial	4	8	12	26	41	55
V2#1(#4)-Photos & text of James Bond movie "Live & Let Die"	3	6	9	21	32	42
5-10: 8-Kaluta-a	3	6	9	19	29	38
Annual 1(Summer,'75)(#11)-B&W; Everett, Buscema-a	3	6	9	21	32	42

NOTE: Brother Voodoo app. 2, 5, 6, 10. ***Alcala*** *a-7-9.* ***Boris*** *c-1-4.* ***Colan*** *a-2r, 6.* ***Heath*** *a-5r.* ***Reese*** *a-2.* ***Tuska*** *a-2r.*

TALES OF THUNDER
Deluxe Comics: Mar, 1985

	GD 2.0	VG 4.0	FN 6.0	VF 8.0	VF/NM 9.0	NM- 9.2
1-Dynamo, Iron Maiden, Menthor app.; Giffen-a						4.00

TALES OF VOODOO
Eerie Publications: V1#11, Nov, 1968 - V7#6, Nov, 1974 (Magazine)

	GD 2.0	VG 4.0	FN 6.0	VF 8.0	VF/NM 9.0	NM- 9.2
V1#11	7	14	21	45	73	100
V2#1(3/69)-V2#4(9/69)	5	10	15	30	48	65
V3#1-6('70): 4- "Claws of the Cat" redrawn from Climax #1	4	8	12	24	37	50
V4#1-6('71), V5#1-7('72), V6#1-6('73), V7#1-6('74)	4	8	12	24	37	50
Annual 1	4	8	12	26	41	55

NOTE: *Bondage-c-V1#10, V2#4, V3#4.*

TALES OF WELLS FARGO (TV)(See Western Roundup under Dell Giants)
Dell Publishing Co.: No. 876, Feb, 1958 - No. 1215, Oct-Dec, 1961

	GD 2.0	VG 4.0	FN 6.0	VF 8.0	VF/NM 9.0	NM- 9.2
Four Color 876 (#1)-Photo-c	9	18	27	60	100	140
Four Color 968 (2/59), 1023, 1075 (3/60), 1113 (7-9/60)-All photo-c. 1075,1113-Both have variant edition, back-c comic strip	8	16	24	56	93	130
Four Color 1167 (3-5/61), 1215-Photo-c	8	16	24	52	86	120

TALESPIN (Also see Cartoon Tales & Disney's Talespin Limited Series)
Disney Comics: June, 1991 - No. 7, Dec, 1991 ($1.50)

	GD 2.0	VG 4.0	FN 6.0	VF 8.0	VF/NM 9.0	NM- 9.2
1-7						3.00

TALES TO ASTONISH (Becomes The Incredible Hulk #102 on)
Atlas (MAP No. 1/ZPC No. 2-14/VPI No. 15-21/Marvel No. 22 on: Jan, 1959 - No. 101, Mar, 1968

	GD 2.0	VG 4.0	FN 6.0	VF 8.0	VF/NM 9.0	NM- 9.2
1-Jack Davis-a; monster-c.	156	312	468	1365	2783	4200
2-Ditko flying saucer-c (Martians); #2-4 have sci/fi-c.	62	124	186	527	1064	1600
3,4	44	88	132	352	714	1075
5-Prototype issue (Stone Men); Williamson-a (4 pgs.); Kirby monster-c begin	46	92	138	368	747	1125
6-Prototype issue (Stone Men)	37	74	111	286	568	850
7-Prototype issue (Toad Men)	37	74	111	286	568	850
8-10	34	68	102	267	526	785
11-14,17-20: 13-Swipes story from Menace #8	28	56	84	209	422	635
15-Prototype issue (Electro)	33	66	99	257	509	760
16-Prototype issue (Stone Men)	29	58	87	223	449	675
21-(7/61)-Hulk prototype	29	58	87	223	449	675
22-26,28-31,33,34	24	48	72	175	350	525
27-1st Ant-Man app. (1/62); last 10¢ issue (see Strange Tales #73,78 & Tales of Suspense #32)	533	1066	1600	4800	9900	15,000
32-Sandman prototype	25	50	75	183	367	550
35-(9/62)-2nd app. Ant-Man, 1st in costume; begin series & Ant-Man-c	185	370	555	1619	3310	5000
36-3rd app. Ant-Man	81	162	243	689	1395	2100
37,39,40	47	94	141	376	763	1150
38-1st app. Egghead	48	96	144	392	796	1200
41-43	38	76	114	304	602	900
44-Origin & 1st app. The Wasp (6/63)	50	100	150	425	863	1300
45-47	26	52	78	190	383	575
48-Origin & 1st app. The Porcupine	27	54	81	197	399	600
49-Ant-Man becomes Giant Man (11/63)	31	62	93	239	470	700
50,51,53-56,58: 50-Origin/1st app. Human Top (alias Whirlwind). 58-Origin Colossus	17	34	51	122	249	375
52-Origin/1st app. Black Knight (2/64)	22	44	66	159	317	475
57-Early Spider-Man app. (7/64)	38	76	114	304	602	900
59-Giant Man vs. Hulk feature story (9/64); Hulk's 1st app. this title	33	66	99	254	502	750
60-Giant Man & Hulk double feature begins	24	48	72	175	350	525
61,64-69: 61-All Ditko issue; 1st mailbag. 65-New Giant Man costume. 68-New Human Top costume. 69-Last Giant Man	13	26	39	89	170	250
62-1st app./origin The Leader; new Wasp costume; Hulk pin-up page missing from many copies	14	28	42	99	200	300
63-Origin Leader continues	13	26	39	94	185	275
70-Sub-Mariner & Incredible Hulk begins (8/65)	14	28	42	99	200	300
71-81: 72-Begin alternating-c features w/Sub-Mariner (even #'s) & Hulk (odd #'s). 79-Hulk vs. Hercules-c/story. 81-1st app. Boomerang	7	14	21	49	80	110
82-Iron Man battles Sub-Mariner (1st Iron Man x-over outside The Avengers & TOS); story cont'd from Tales of Suspense #80	8	16	24	58	97	135
83-89,94-99: 97-X-Men cameo (brief)	6	12	18	43	69	95
90-1st app. The Abomination	8	16	24	52	86	120
90-The Abomination debut continues & 1st cover	8	16	24	52	86	120
92-1st Silver Surfer x-over (outside of Fantastic Four, 6/67); 1 panel cameo only	8	16	24	52	86	120
93-Hulk battles Silver Surfer-c/story (1st full x-over)	16	32	48	117	239	360
100-Hulk battles Sub-Mariner full-length story	8	16	24	54	90	125
101-Hulk story cont'd in Incredible Hulk #102; Sub-Mariner story continued in Iron Man & Sub-Mariner #1	8	16	24	58	97	135

NOTE: ***Ayers*** *c(i)-9-12, 16, 18, 19.* ***Berg*** *a-1.* ***Burgos*** *a-62-64p.* ***Buscema*** *a-85-87p.* ***Colan*** *a(p)-70-76, 78-82, 84, 85, 101; c(p)-71-76, 78, 80, 82, 84, 86, 88, 90.* ***Ditko*** *a-1, 3-48, 50i, 60-67p; c-2, 7i, 8i, 14i, 17i.* ***Everett*** *a-78, 79i, 80-84, 85-90i, 94i, 95, 96; c(i)-79-81, 83, 86, 88.* ***Forte*** *a-6.* ***Kane*** *a-76, 88-91; c-89, 91.* ***Kirby*** *a(p)-1, 5-34-40, 44, 49-51, 68-70, 82, 83; layouts-71-84; c(p)-1, 3-48, 50-70, 72, 73, 75, 77, 78, 79, 81, 85, 90.* ***Kirby/Ditko*** *a-7, 8, 12, 13, 50; c-7, 8, 10, 13.* ***Leiber/Fox*** *a-47, 48, 50, 51.* ***Powell*** *a-65-69p, 73, 74.* ***Reinman*** *a-6, 36, 45, 46,*

Taleweaver #2 © Agimat, LLC

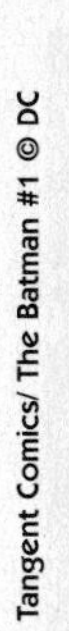
Tangent Comics/ The Batman #1 © DC

Tank Girl 2 #4 © Deadline

GD 2.0 | VG 4.0 | FN 6.0 | VF 8.0 | VF/NM 9.0 | NM- 9.2

54i, 56-60i.

TALES TO ASTONISH (2nd Series)
Marvel Comics Group: Dec, 1979 - No. 14, Jan, 1981
V1#1-Reprints Sub-Mariner #1 by Buscema 2 4 6 8 10 12
2-14: Reprints Sub-Mariner #2-14 1 2 3 4 5 7

TALES TO ASTONISH
Marvel Comics: V3#1, Oct, 1994 ($6.95, one-shot)
V3#1-Peter David scripts; acetate, painted-c 7.00

TALES TO HOLD YOU SPELLBOUND (See Spellbound)

TALES TO OFFEND
Dark Horse Comics: July, 1997 ($2.95, one-shot)
1-Frank Miller-s/a, EC-style cover 3.50

TALES TOO TERRIBLE TO TELL (Becomes Terrology #10, 11)
New England Comics: Wint, 1989-90 - No. 11, Nov-Dec.1993 ($2.95/$3.50, B&W with card-stock covers)
1-($2.95) Reprints of non-EC pre-code horror; EC-style cover by Bissette 4.00
1-($3.50, 5-6/93) Second printing with alternate cover not by Bissette 4.00
2-8-($3.50) Story reprints, history of the pre-code titles and creators; cover galleries (B&W) inside & on back-c (color) 4.00
9-11-($2.95) 10,11-"Terrology" on cover 4.00

TALEWEAVER
DC Comics (WildStorm): Nov, 2001 - No. 6, Apr, 2002 ($3.50, limited series)
1-6-Philip Tan-a/Leonard Banaag-s. 2-Variant-c by Anacleto 3.50

TALKING KOMICS
Belda Record & Publ. Co.: 1947 (20 pgs, slick-c)
Each comic contained a record that followed the story - much like the Golden Record sets. Known titles: Chirpy Cricket, Lonesome Octopus, Sleepy Santa, Grumpy Shark, Flying Turtle, Happy Grasshopper
with records... 3 6 9 18 27 35

TALLY-HO COMICS
Swappers Quarterly (Baily Publ. Co.): Dec, 1944
nn-Frazetta's 1st work as Giunta's assistant; Man in Black horror story; violence; Giunta-c 48 96 144 302 514 725

TALULLAH (See Comic Books Series I)

TAMMY, TELL ME TRUE
Dell Publishing Co.: No. 1233, 1961
Four Color 1233-Movie 6 12 18 43 69 95

TANGENT COMICS
.../ THE ATOM, DC Comics: Dec, 1997 ($2.95, one-shot)
1-Dan Jurgens-s/Jurgens & Paul Ryan-a 3.00
.../ THE BATMAN, DC Comics: Sept, 1998 ($1.95, one-shot)
1-Dan Jurgens-s/Klaus Janson-a 3.00
.../ DOOM PATROL, DC Comics: Dec, 1997 ($2.95, one-shot)
1- Dan Jurgens-s/Sean Chen & Kevin Conrad-a 3.00
.../ THE FLASH, DC Comics: Dec, 1997 ($2.95, one-shot)
1-Todd Dezago-s/Gary Frank & Cam Smith-a 3.00
.../ GREEN LANTERN, DC Comics: Dec, '97 ($2.95, one-shot)
1-James Robinson-s/J.H. Williams III & Mick Gray-a 3.00
.../ JLA, DC Comics: Sept, 1998 ($1.95, one-shot)
1-Dan Jurgens-s/Banks & Rapmund-a 3.00
.../ THE JOKER, DC Comics: Dec, 1997 ($2.95, one-shot)
1-Karl Kesel-s/Matt Haley & Tom Simmons-a 3.00
.../ THE JOKER'S WILD, DC Comics: Sept, 1998 ($1.95, one-shot)
1-Kesel & Simmons-s/Phillips & Rodriguez-a 3.00
.../ METAL MEN, DC Comics: Dec, 1997 ($2.95, one-shot)
1-Ron Marz-s/Mike McKone & Mark McKenna-a 3.00
.../ NIGHTWING, DC Comics: Dec, 1997 ($2.95, one-shot)
1-John Ostrander-s/Jan Duursema-a 3.00
.../ NIGHTWING: NIGHTFORCE, DC Comics: Sept, 1998 ($1.95, one-shot)
1-John Ostrander-s/Jan Duursema-a 3.00
.../ POWERGIRL, DC Comics: Sept, 1998 ($1.95, one-shot)
1-Marz-s/Abell & Vines-a 3.00
.../ SEA DEVILS, DC Comics: Dec, 1997 ($2.95, one-shot)
1-Kurt Busiek-s/Vince Giarrano & Tom Palmer-a 3.00
.../ SECRET SIX, DC Comics: Dec, 1997 ($2.95, one-shot)
1-Chuck Dixon-s/Tom Grummett & Lary Stucker-a 3.00
.../ THE SUPERMAN, DC Comics: Sept, 1998 ($1.95, one-shot)
1-Millar-s/Guice-a 3.00
.../ TALES OF THE GREEN LANTERN, DC Comics: Sept, 1998 ($1.95, one-shot)
1-Story & art by various 3.00
.../ THE TRIALS OF THE FLASH, DC Comics: Sept, 1998 ($1.95, one-shot)
1-Dezago-s/Pelletier & Lanning-a 3.00
.../ WONDER WOMAN DC Comics: Sept, 1998 ($1.95, one-shot),
1-Peter David-s/Unzueta & Mendoza-a 3.00
... Volume One TPB (2007, $19.99) r/The Atom, Metal Men, Green Lantern, The Flash, Sea Devils one-shots; intro and new cover by Jurgens 20.00
... Volume Two TPB (2008, $19.99) r/Batman, Doom Patrol, Joker, Nightwing and Secret Six one-shots; new cover by Jurgens 20.00
... Volume Three TPB (2008, $19.99) r/The Superman, Wonder Woman, Nightwing: Nightforce, The Joker's Wild, The Trials of the Flash, Tales of the Green Lantern, Powergirl, and JLA one-shots; new cover by Jurgens 20.00

TANGENT: SUPERMAN'S REIGN
DC Comics: May, 2008 - No. 12, Apr, 2009 ($2.99, limited series)
1-12-Jurgens-s; Flash & Green Lantern app.; back-up histories of Tangent heroes 3.00
Volume 1 TPB (2009, $19.99) r/#1-6 & Justice League of America #16 20.00
Volume 2 TPB (2009, $19.99) r/#7-12 20.00

TANGLED WEB (See Spider-Man's Tangled Web)

TANK GIRL
Dark Horse Comics: May, 1991 - No. 4, Aug, 1991 ($2.25, B&W, mini-series)
1-Contains Dark Horse trading cards 6.00
2-4 4.00
...: Dark Nuggets (Image Comics, 12/09, $3.99) Martin-s/Dayglo-a 4.00
...: Dirty Helmets (Image Comics, 4/10, $3.99) Martin-s/Dayglo-a 4.00
...: Hairy Heroes (Image Comics, 8/10, $3.99) Martin-s/Dayglo-a 4.00

TANK GIRL: APOCALYPSE
DC Comics: Nov, 1995 - No. 4, Feb, 1996 ($2.25, limited series)
1-4 3.00

TANK GIRL: MOVIE ADAPTATION
DC Comics: 1995 ($5.95, 68 pgs., one-shot)
nn-Peter Milligan scripts 6.00

TANK GIRL: THE GIFTING
IDW Publishing: May, 2007 - No. 4, Aug, 2007 ($3.99, limited series)
1-4: 1-Ashley Wood-a/c; Alan Martin-s; 3 covers 4.00

TANK GIRL: THE ODYSSEY
DC Comics: May, 1995 - No.4, Oct, 1995 ($2.25, limited series)
1-4: Peter Milligan scripts; Hewlett-a 3.00

TANK GIRL: THE ROYAL ESCAPE
IDW Publishing: Mar, 2010 - No. 4, Jun, 2010 ($3.99, limited series)
1-4: Alan Martin-s/Rufus Dayglo-a/c 4.00

TANK GIRL 2
Dark Horse Comics: June, 1993 - No. 4, Sept, 1993 ($2.50, lim. series, mature)
1-4: Jamie Hewlett & Alan Martin-s/a 3.00
TPB (2/95, $17.95) r/#1-4 18.00

TAPPAN'S BURRO (See Zane Grey & 4-Color #449)

TAPPING THE VEIN (Clive Barker's...)
Eclipse Comics: 1989 - No. 5, 1992 ($6.95, squarebound, mature, 68 pgs.)
Book 1-5: 1-Russell-a, Bolton-c. 2-Bolton-a. 4-Die-cut-c 7.00
TPB (2002, $24.95, Checker Book Publ. Group) r/#1-5 25.00

TARANTULA (See Weird Suspense)

TARGET: AIRBOY
Eclipse Comics: Mar, 1988 ($1.95)
1 3.00

TARGET COMICS (...Western Romances #106 on)
Funnies, Inc./Novelty Publications/Star Publ.: Feb, 1940 - V10#3 (#105), Aug-Sept, 1949
V1#1-Origin & 1st app. Manowar, The White Streak by Burgos, & Bulls-Eye Bill by Everett; City Editor (ends #5), High Grass Twins by Jack Cole (ends #4), T-Men by Joe Simon (ends #9), Rip Rory (ends #4), Fantastic Feature Films by Tarpe Mills (ends #39), & Calling 2-R (ends #14) begin; marijuana use story
459 918 1377 3350 5925 8500

Target Comics #11 © NOVP

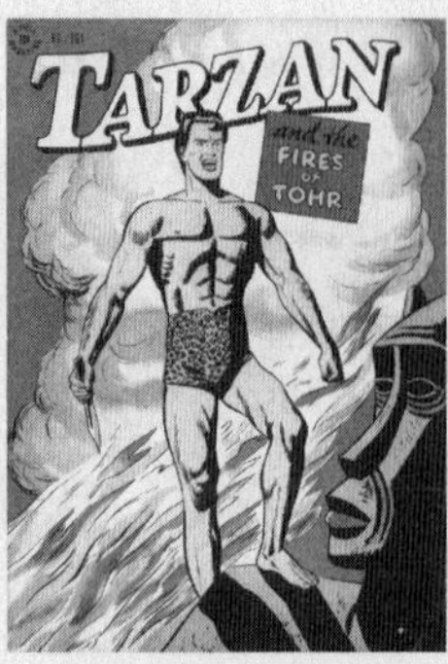

Tarzan Four Color #161 © ERB

Tarzan (1977 series) #2 © ERB

	GD 2.0	VG 4.0	FN 6.0	VF 8.0	VF/NM 9.0	NM- 9.2
2-Everett-c/a	232	464	696	1485	2543	3600
3,4-Everett, Jack Cole-a	135	270	405	864	1482	2100
5-Origin The White Streak in text; Space Hawk by Wolverton begins (6/40) (see Blue Bolt & Circus)	432	864	1296	3154	5577	8000
6-The Chameleon by Everett begins (7/40, 1st app.); White Streak origin cont'd. in text; early mention of comic collecting in letter column; 1st letter column in comics? (7/40)	219	438	657	1402	2401	3400
7-Wolverton Spacehawk-c/story (Scarce)	865	1730	2595	6315	11,158	16,000
8-Classic sci-fi cover	213	426	639	1363	2332	3300
9,12: 12-(1/41)	142	284	426	909	1555	2200
10-Intro/1st app. The Target (11/40); Simon-c; Spacehawk-s; text piece by Wolverton	258	516	774	1651	2826	4000
11-Origin The Target & The Targeteers	181	362	543	1158	1979	2800
V2#1-Target by Bob Wood; Uncle Sam flag-c	90	180	270	576	988	1400
2-Ten part Treasure Island serial begins; Harold Delay-a; reprinted in Catholic Comics V3#1-10 (see Key Comics #5)	68	136	204	435	743	1050
3-5: 4-Kit Carter, The Cadet begins	61	122	183	390	670	950
6-9: Red Seal with White Streak in #6-10	58	116	174	371	636	900
10-Classic-c	103	206	309	659	1130	1600
11,12: 12-10-part Last of the Mohicans serial begins; Delay-a	57	114	171	362	619	875
V3#1-3,5-7,9,10: 10-Last Wolverton issue	47	94	141	296	498	700
4-V for Victory-c	60	120	180	381	653	925
8-Hitler, Tojo, Flag-c; 6-part Gulliver Travels serial begins; Delay-a.	81	162	243	518	884	1250
11,12	18	36	54	105	165	225
V4#1-4,7-12: 8-X-Mas-c	14	28	42	76	108	140
5-Classic Statue of Liberty-c	15	30	45	88	137	185
6-Targetoons by Wolverton	15	30	45	85	137	185
V5#1-8	12	24	36	67	94	120
V6#1-4,6-10	11	22	33	64	90	115
5-Tojo-c	18	36	54	105	165	225
V7#1-12	10	20	30	58	79	100
V8#1,3-5,8,9,11,12	10	20	30	56	76	95
2,6,7-Krigstein-a	11	22	33	62	86	110
10-L.B. Cole-c	25	50	75	150	245	340
V9#1,4,6,8,10-L.B. Cole-c	25	50	75	150	245	340
2,3,5,7,9,11, V10#1	10	20	30	56	76	95
12-Classic L.B. Cole-c	37	74	111	222	361	500
V10#2,3-L.B. Cole-c	25	50	75	150	245	340

NOTE: ***Certa** c-V8#9, 11, 12, V9#5, 9, 11, V10#1. **Jack Cole** a-1-8. **Everett** a-1-9; c(signed Blake)-1, 2. **Al Fago** c-V6#8. **Sid Greene** c-V2#9, 12, V3#3. **Walter Johnson** c-V5#6, V6#4. **Tarpe Mills** a-1-4, 6, 8, 11, V3#1. **Rico** a-V7#4, 10, V8#5, 6, V9#3; c-V7#6, 8, 10, V8#2, 4, 6, 7. **Simon** a-1, 2. **Bob Wood** c-V2#2, 3, 5, 6.*

TARGET: THE CORRUPTORS (TV)
Dell Publishing Co.: No. 1306, Mar-May, 1962 - No. 3, Oct-Dec, 1962
(All have photo-c)

	GD 2.0	VG 4.0	FN 6.0	VF 8.0	VF/NM 9.0	NM- 9.2
Four Color 1306(#1), #2,3	6	12	18	37	59	80

TARGET WESTERN ROMANCES (Formerly Target Comics; becomes Flaming Western Romances #3)
Star Publications: No. 106, Oct-Nov, 1949 - No. 107, Dec-Jan, 1949-50

	GD 2.0	VG 4.0	FN 6.0	VF 8.0	VF/NM 9.0	NM- 9.2
106(#1)-Silhouette nudity panel; L.B. Cole-c	25	50	75	150	245	340
107(#2)-L.B. Cole-c; lingerie panels	22	44	66	132	216	300

TARGITT
Atlas/Seaboard Publ.: March, 1975 - No. 3, July, 1975

	GD 2.0	VG 4.0	FN 6.0	VF 8.0	VF/NM 9.0	NM- 9.2
1-3: 1-Origin; Nostrand-a in all. 2-1st in costume. 3-Becomes Man-Stalker	2	4	6	8	10	12

TARZAN (See Aurora, Comics on Parade, Crackajack, DC 100-Page Super Spec., Edgar Rice Burroughs'..., Famous Feature Stories #1, Golden Comics Digest #4, 9, Jeep Comics #1-29, Jungle Tales of..., Limited Collectors' Edition, Popular, Sparkler, Sport Stars #1, Tip Top & Top Comics)

TARZAN
Dell Publishing Co./United Features Synd.: No. 5, 1939 - No. 161, Aug, 1947

	GD 2.0	VG 4.0	FN 6.0	VF 8.0	VF/NM 9.0	NM- 9.2
Large Feature Comic 5('39)-(Scarce)-By Hal Foster; reprints 1st dailies from 1929	187	374	561	1197	2049	2900
Single Series 20('40)-By Hal Foster	123	246	369	787	1344	1900
Four Color 134(2/47)-Marsh-c/a	52	104	156	442	896	1350
Four Color 161(8/47)-Marsh-c/a	45	90	135	360	730	1100

TARZAN (...of the Apes #138 on)
Dell Publishing Co./Gold Key No. 132 on: 1-2/48 - No. 131, 7-8/62; No. 132, 11/62 - No. 206, 2/72

	GD 2.0	VG 4.0	FN 6.0	VF 8.0	VF/NM 9.0	NM- 9.2
1-Jesse Marsh-a begins	96	192	288	816	1658	2500
2	41	82	123	328	664	1000
3-5	30	60	90	231	458	685
6-10: 6-1st Tantor the Elephant. 7-1st Valley of the Monsters	25	50	75	183	367	550
11-15: 11-Two Against the Jungle begins, ends #24. 13-Lex Barker photo-c begin	20	40	60	146	293	440
16-20	16	32	48	117	239	360
21-24,26-30	14	28	42	97	194	290
25-1st "Brothers of the Spear" episode; series ends #156,160,161,196-206	15	30	45	106	216	325
31-40	11	22	33	77	144	210
41-54: Last Barker photo-c	9	18	27	65	113	160
55-60: 56-Eight pg. Boy story	8	16	24	58	97	135
61,62,64-70	7	14	21	49	80	110
63-Two Tarzan stories, 1 by Manning	7	14	21	50	83	115
71-79	6	12	18	43	69	95
80-99: 80-Gordon Scott photo-c begin	6	12	18	39	62	85
100	6	12	18	43	69	95
101-109	6	12	18	37	59	80
110 (Scarce)-Last photo-c	6	12	18	43	69	95
111-120	5	10	15	34	55	75
121-131: Last Dell issue	5	10	15	32	51	70
132-1st Gold Key issue	5	10	15	34	55	75
133-138,140-154	4	8	12	26	41	55
139-(12/63)-1st app. Korak (Boy); leaves Tarzan & gets own book (1/64)	7	14	21	45	73	100
155-Origin Tarzan; text article on Tarzana, CA	5	10	15	32	51	70
156-161: 157-Banlu, Dog of the Arande begins, ends #159, 195. 169-Leopard Girl app.	4	8	12	22	34	45
162,165,168,171 (TV)-Ron Ely photo covers	4	8	12	23	36	48
163,164,166,167,169,170: 169-Leopard Girl app.	3	6	9	21	32	42
172-199,201-206: 178-Tarzan origin-r/#155; Leopard Girl app., also in #179, 190-193	3	6	9	19	29	38
200	4	8	12	22	34	45
Story Digest 1-(6/70, G.K., 148pp.)(scarce)	7	14	21	49	80	110

NOTE: *#162, 165, 168, 171 are TV issues. #1-153 all have **Marsh** art on Tarzan. #154-161, 163, 164, 166, 167, 172-177 all have **Manning** art on Tarzan. #178, 202 have **Manning** Tarzan reprints. No "Brothers of the Spear" in #1-24, 157-159, 162-195. #39-126, 128-156 all have **Russ Manning** art on "Brothers of the Spear". #196-201, 203-205 all have **Manning** B.O.T.S. reprints; #25-38, 127 all have Jesse **Marsh** art on B.O.T.S. #206 has a Marsh B.O.T.S. reprint. **Gollub** c-8-12. **Marsh** c-1-7. **Doug Wildey** a-162, 179-187. Many issues have front and back photo covers.*

TARZAN (Continuation of Gold Key series)
National Periodical Publications: No. 207, Apr, 1972 - No. 258, Feb, 1977

	GD 2.0	VG 4.0	FN 6.0	VF 8.0	VF/NM 9.0	NM- 9.2
207-Origin Tarzan by Joe Kubert, part 1; John Carter begins (origin); 52 pg. issues thru #209	6	12	18	39	62	85
208,209-(52 pgs.): 208-210-Parts 2-4 of origin. 209-Last John Carter	3	6	9	21	32	42
210-220: 210-Kubert-a. 211-Hogarth, Kubert-a. 212-214: Adaptations from "Jungle Tales of Tarzan". 213-Beyond the Farthest Star begins, ends #218. 215-218,224,225-All by Kubert. 215-part Foster-r. 219-223: Adapts "The Return of Tarzan" by Kubert	3	6	9	14	19	24
221-229: 221-223-Continues adaptation of "The Return of Tarzan". 226-Manning-a	2	4	6	10	14	18
230-DC 100 Page Super Spectacular; Kubert, Kaluta-a(p); Korak begins, ends #234; Carson of Venus app.	4	8	12	26	41	55
231-235-New Kubert-a.: 231-234-(All 100 pgs.)-Adapts "Tarzan and the Lion Man"; Rex, the Wonder Dog r-#232, 233. 235-(100 pgs.)-Last Kubert issue.	4	8	12	24	37	50
236,237,239-258: 240-243 adapts "Tarzan & the Castaways". 250-256 adapts "Tarzan the Untamed." 252,253-r/#213	2	4	6	8	10	12
238-(68 pgs.)	2	4	6	13	18	22
Digest 1-(Fall, 1972, 50¢, 164 pgs.)(DC)-Digest size; Kubert-c; Manning-a	4	8	12	26	41	55
Edgar Rice Burroughs' Tarzan The Joe Kubert Years - Volume One HC (Dark Horse Books, 10/05, $49.95, dust jacket) recolored r/#207-214; intro. by Joe Kubert						50.00
Edgar Rice Burroughs' Tarzan The Joe Kubert Years - Volume Two HC (Dark Horse Books, 2/06, $49.95, dust jacket) recolored r/#215-224; intro. by Joe Kubert						50.00
Edgar Rice Burroughs' Tarzan The Joe Kubert Years - Volume Three HC (Dark Horse Books, 6/06, $49.95, dust jacket) recolored r/#225,227-235; Kubert intro. and sketch pages						50.00

NOTE: ***Anderson** a-207, 209, 217, 218. **Chaykin** a-216. **Finlay** a(r)-212. **Foster** strip-r #207-209, 211, 212, 221. **Heath** a-230i. **G. Kane** a(r)-232p, 233p. **Kubert** a-207-225, 227-235, 257r, 258r; c-207-249, 253. **Lopez** a-250-255p; c-250p, 251, 252, 254. **Manning** strip-r 230-235, 238. **Morrow** a-208. **Nino** a-231-234. **Sparling** a-230, 231. **Starr** a-233r.*

TARZAN (Lord of the Jungle)
Marvel Comics Group: June, 1977 - No. 29, Oct, 1979

	GD 2.0	VG 4.0	FN 6.0	VF 8.0	VF/NM 9.0	NM- 9.2
1-New adaptions of Burroughs stories; Buscema-a	2	4	6	8	11	14

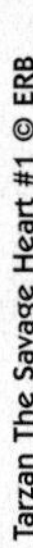
Tarzan The Savage Heart #1 © ERB

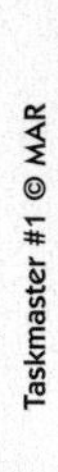
Taskmaster #1 © MAR

Team America #8 © MAR

	GD	VG	FN	VF	VF/NM	NM-
	2.0	4.0	6.0	8.0	9.0	9.2

1-(35¢-c variant, limited distribution)(6/77) 4 8 12 24 37 50
2-29: 2-Origin by John Buscema. 9-Young Tarzan. 12-14-Jungle Tales of Tarzan.
25-29-New stories 1 2 3 4 5 7
2-5-(35¢-c variants, limited distribution)(7-10/77) 3 6 9 16 23 30
Annual 1-3: 1-(1977). 2-(1978). 3-(1979) 1 2 3 5 6 8
NOTE: *N. Adams c-11i, 12i. Alcala a-9i, 10i; c-8i, 9i. Buckler c-25-27p, Annual 3p. John Buscema a-1-3, 4-18p, Annual 1; c-1-7, 8p, 9p, 10, 11p, 12p, 13, 14-19p, 21p, 22, 23p, 24p, 28p, Annual 1. Mooney a-22i. Nebres a-22i. Russell a-29i.*

TARZAN
Dark Horse Comics: July, 1996 - No. 20, Mar, 1998 ($2.95)
1-20: 1-6-Suydam-c 3.00

TARZAN / CARSON OF VENUS
Dark Horse Comics: May, 1998 - No. 4, Aug, 1998 ($2.95, limited series)
1-4-Darko Macan-s/Igor Korday-a 3.00

TARZAN FAMILY, THE (Formerly Korak, Son of Tarzan)
National Periodical Publications: No. 60, Nov-Dec, 1975 - No. 66, Nov-Dec, 1976
60-62-(68 pgs.): 60-Korak begins; Kaluta-r 2 4 6 11 16 20
63-66 (52 pgs.) 2 4 6 9 12 15
NOTE: *Carson of Venus-r 60-65. New John Carter-62-64, 65r, 66r. New Korak-60-66. Pellucidar feature-66. Foster strip r-60(9/4/32-10/16/32), 62(6/29/32-7/31/32), 63(10/11/31-12/13/31). Kaluta Carson of Venus-60-65. Kubert a-61, 64; c-60-64. Manning strip-r 60-62, 64. Morrow a-66r.*

TARZAN/JOHN CARTER: WARLORDS OF MARS
Dark Horse Comics: Jan, 1996 - No. 4, June, 1996 ($2.50, limited series)
1-4: Bruce Jones scripts in all. 1,2,4-Bret Blevins-c/a. 2-(4/96)-Indicia reads #3 3.00

TARZAN KING OF THE JUNGLE (See Dell Giant #37, 51)

TARZAN, LORD OF THE JUNGLE
Gold Key: Sept, 1965 (Giant) (25¢, soft paper-c)
1-Marsh-r 8 16 24 56 93 130

TARZAN: LOVE, LIES AND THE LOST CITY (See Tarzan the Warrior)
Malibu Comics: Aug. 10, 1992 - No. 3, Sept, 1992 ($2.50, limited series)
1-($3.95, 68 pgs.)-Flip book format; Simonson & Wagner scripts 4.00
2,3-No Simonson or Wagner scripts 3.00

TARZAN MARCH OF COMICS (See March of Comics #82, 98, 114, 125, 144, 155, 172, 185, 204, 223, 240, 252, 262, 272, 286, 300, 332, 342, 354, 366)

TARZAN OF THE APES
Metropolitan Newspaper Service: 1934? (Hardcover, 4x12", 68 pgs.)
1-Strip reprints 25 50 75 147 241 335

TARZAN OF THE APES
Marvel Comics Group: July, 1984 - No. 2, Aug, 1984 (Movie adaptation)
1,2: Origin-r/Marvel Super Spec. 4.00

TARZAN'S JUNGLE ANNUAL (See Dell Giants)

TARZAN'S JUNGLE WORLD (See Dell Giant #25)

TARZAN: THE BECKONING
Malibu Comics: 1992 - No. 7, 1993 ($2.50, limited series)
1-7 3.00

TARZAN: THE LOST ADVENTURE (See Edgar Rice Burroughs' ...)

TARZAN-THE RIVERS OF BLOOD
Dark Horse Comics: Nov, 1999 - No. 8 ($2.95, limited series)
1-4: Korday-c/a 3.00

TARZAN THE SAVAGE HEART
Dark Horse Comics: Apr, 1999 - No. 4, July, 1999 ($2.95, limited series)
1-4: Grell-c/a 3.00

TARZAN THE WARRIOR (Also see Tarzan: Love, Lies and the Lost City)
Malibu Comics: Mar, 19, 1992 - No. 5, 1992 ($2.50, limited series)
1-5: 1-Bisley painted pack-c (flip book format-c) 3.00
1-2nd printing w/o flip-c by Bisley 3.00

TARZAN VS. PREDATOR AT THE EARTH'S CORE
Dark Horse Comics: Jan, 1996 - No. 4, June, 1996 ($2.50, limited series)
1-4: Lee Weeks-c/a; Walt Simonson scripts 3.00

TASKMASTER
Marvel Comics: Apr, 2002 - No. 4, July, 2002 ($2.99, limited series)
1-4-Udon Studio-s/a. 1-Iron Man app. 3.00

TASKMASTER
Marvel Comics: Nov, 2010 - No. 4, ($3.99, limited series)

	GD	VG	FN	VF	VF/NM	NM-
	2.0	4.0	6.0	8.0	9.0	9.2

1-4-Van Lente-s/Palo-a; Hydra & A.I.M. app. 4.00

TASMANIAN DEVIL & HIS TASTY FRIENDS
Gold Key: Nov, 1962 (12¢)
1-Bugs Bunny, Elmer Fudd, Sylvester, Yosemite Sam, Road Runner & Wile E. Coyote x-over 13 26 39 94 185 275

TATTERED BANNERS
DC Comics (Vertigo): Nov, 1998 - No. 4, Feb, 1999 ($2.95, limited series)
1-4-Grant & Giffen-s/McMahon-a 3.00

TEAM AMERICA (See Captain America #269)
Marvel Comics Group: June, 1982 - No. 12, May, 1983
1,12: 1-Origin; Ideal Toy motorcycle characters. 12-Double size 4.00
2-11: 9-Iron Man app. 11-Ghost Rider app. 3.00
NOTE: *There are 16 pg. variants known for most issues, possibly all. The only ad is on the inside front cover.*

TEAM HELIX
Marvel Comics: Jan, 1993 - No. 4, Apr, 1993 ($1.75, limited series)
1-4: Teen Super Group. 1,2-Wolverine app. 3.00

TEAM ONE: STORMWATCH (Also see StormWatch)
Image Comics (WildStorm Productions): June, 1995 - No. 2, Aug, 1995 ($2.50, lim. series)
1,2: Steven T. Seagle scripts 3.00

TEAM ONE: WILDC.A.T.S (Also see WildC.A.T.S)
Image Comics (WildStorm Productions): July, 1995 - No. 2, Aug, 1995 ($2.50, lim. series)
1,2: James Robinson scripts 3.00

TEAM 7
Image Comics (WildStorm): Oct, 1994 - No.4, Feb, 1995 ($2.50, limited series)
1-4: Dixon scripts in all, 1-Portacio variant-c 3.00

TEAM 7-DEAD RECKONING
Image Comics (WildStorm): Jan, 1996 - No. 4, Apr, 1996 ($2.50, limited series)
1-4: Dixon scripts in all 3.00

TEAM 7-OBJECTIVE HELL
Image Comics (WildStorm): May, 1995 - No. 3, July, 1995 ($1.95/$2.50, limited series)
1-($1.95)-Newstand; Dixon scripts in all; Barry Smith-c 3.00
1-3: 1-($2.50)-Direct Market; Barry Smith-c, bound-in card 3.00

TEAM SUPERMAN
DC Comics: July, 1999 ($2.95, one-shot)
1-Jeanty-a/Stelfreeze-c 3.00
...Secret Files 1 (5/98, $4.95)Origin-s and pin-ups of Superboy, Supergirl and Steel 5.00

TEAM TITANS (See Deathstroke & New Titans Annual #7)
DC Comics: Sept, 1992 - No. 24, Sept, 1994 ($1.75/$1.95)
1-Five different #1s exist w/origins in 1st half & the same 2nd story in each: Kilowat, Mirage, Nightrider w/Netzer/Pérez-a, Redwing, & Terra w/part Pérez-p; Total Chaos Pt. 3 4.00
2-24: 2-Total Chaos Pt 6. 11-Metallik app. 24-Zero Hour x-over 3.00
Annual 1,2 ('93, '94, $3.50, 68 pgs.): 2-Elseworlds tory 4.00

TEAM X/TEAM 7
Marvel Comics: Nov, 1996 ($4.95, one-shot)
1 5.00

TEAM X 2000
Marvel Comics: Feb, 1999 ($3.50, one-shot)
1-Kevin Lau-a; Bishop vs. Shi'ar Empire 4.00

TEAM YANKEE
First Comics: Jan, 1989 - No. 6, Feb, 1989 ($1.95, weekly limited series)
1-6 3.00

TEAM YOUNGBLOOD (Also see Youngblood)
Image Comics (Extreme Studios): Sept, 1993 - No. 22, Sept, 1995 ($1.95/$2.50)
1-22: 1-9-Liefeld scripts in all: 1,2,4-6,8-Thibert-c(i). 1-1st app. Dutch & Masada. 3-Spawn cameo. 5-1st app. Lynx. 7,8-Coupons 1 & 4 for Extreme Prejudice #0; Black and White Pt. 4 & 8 by Thibert. 8-Coupon #4 for E. P. #0. 9-Liefeld wraparound-c &(p)/a(p) on Pt. I. 16,17-Bagged w/trading card. 21-Angela & Glory-app. 3.00

TEAM ZERO
DC Comics (WildStorm Productions): Feb, 2006 - No. 6, Jul, 2006 ($2.99, limited series)
1-6-Dixon-s/Mahnke-a 3.00
TPB (2008, $17.99) r/#1-6 18.00

TECH JACKET
Image Comics: Nov, 2002 - No. 6, Apr, 2003 ($2.95)

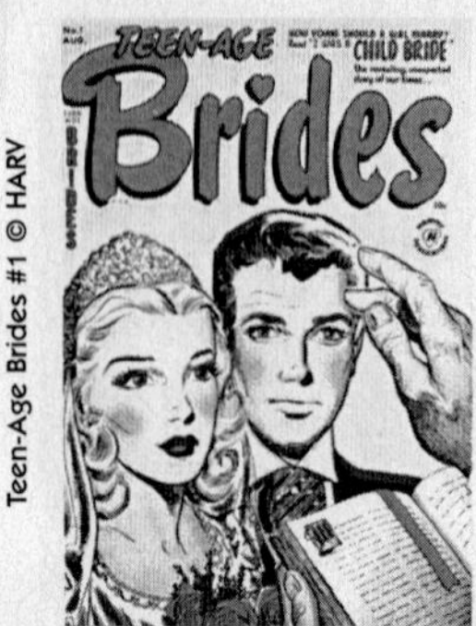

Teen-Age Brides #1 © HARV

Teenage Hotrodders #20 © CC

Teenage Mutant Ninja Turtles #22 © MS

GD 2.0 | VG 4.0 | FN 6.0 | VF 8.0 | VF/NM 9.0 | NM- 9.2

1-6-Kirkman-s/Su-a 3.00
Vol. 1: Lost and Found TPB (7/03, $12.95, 7-3/4" x 5-1/4") B&W r/#1-6; Valentino intro. 13.00

TEDDY ROOSEVELT & HIS ROUGH RIDERS (See Real Heroes #1)
Avon Periodicals: 1950

1-Kinstler-c; Palais-a; Flag-c 18 36 54 105 165 225

TEDDY ROOSEVELT ROUGH RIDER (See Battlefield #22 & Classics Illustrated Special Issue)

TED MCKEEVER'S METROPOL (See Transit)
Marvel Comics (Epic Comics): Mar, 1991 - No. 12, Mar, 1992 ($2.95, limited series)

V1#1-12: Ted McKeever-c/a/scripts 4.00

TED MCKEEVER'S METROPOL A.D.
Marvel Comics (Epic Comics): Oct, 1992 - No. 3, Dec, 1992 ($3.50, limited series)

V2#1-3: Ted McKeever-c/a/scripts 4.00

TEENA
Magazine Enterprises/Standard Comics No. 20 on: No. 11, 1948 - No. 15, 1948; No. 20, Aug, 1949 - No. 22, Oct, 1950

A-1 #11-Teen-age; Ogden Whitney-c 10 20 30 54 72 90
A-1 #12, 15 9 18 27 47 61 75
20-22 (Standard) 7 14 21 35 43 50

TEEN-AGE BRIDES (True Bride's Experiences #8 on)
Harvey/Home Comics: Aug, 1953 - No. 7, Aug, 1954

1-Powell-a 11 22 33 62 86 110
2-Powell-a 8 16 24 44 57 70
3-7: 3,6-Powell-a 8 16 24 40 50 60

TEEN-AGE CONFESSIONS (See Teen Confessions)

TEEN-AGE CONFIDENTIAL CONFESSIONS
Charlton Comics: July, 1960 - No. 22, 1964

1 4 8 12 24 37 50
2-10 3 6 9 16 23 30
11-22 2 4 6 13 18 22

TEEN-AGE DIARY SECRETS (Formerly Blue Ribbon Comics; becomes Diary Secrets #10 on)
St. John Publishing Co.: No. 4, 9/49; nn (#5), 9/49 - No. 7, 11/49; No. 8, 2/50; No. 9, 8/50

4(9/49)-Oversized; part mag., part comic 39 78 117 240 395 550
nn(#5)(no indicia)-Oversized, all comics; contains sty "I Gave Boys the Green Light." 39 78 117 231 378 525
6,8: (Reg. size) -Photo-c; Baker-a(2-3) in each 39 78 117 240 395 550
7,9-Digest size (Pocket Comics); Baker-a(5); both have same contents; diff.-c 50 100 150 315 533 750

TEEN-AGE DOPE SLAVES (See Harvey Comics Library #1)

TEENAGE HOTRODDERS (Top Eliminator #25 on; see Blue Bird)
Charlton Comics: Apr, 1963 - No. 24, July, 1967

1 6 12 18 37 59 80
2-10 3 6 9 20 30 40
11-24 3 6 9 17 25 32

TEEN-AGE LOVE (See Fox Giants)

TEEN-AGE LOVE (Formerly Intimate)
Charlton Comics: V2#4, July, 1958 - No. 96, Dec, 1973

V2#4 4 8 12 28 44 60
5-9 3 6 9 20 30 40
10(9/59)-20 3 6 9 17 25 32
21-35 3 6 9 16 22 28
36-70 2 4 6 13 18 22
71-79,81,82,85-87,90-96: 61&62-Jonnie Love begins (origin) 2 4 6 10 14 18
80,84,88-David Cassidy pin-ups 3 6 9 14 19 24
83,89: 83-Bobby Sherman pin-up. 89-Danny Bonaduce pin-up 2 4 6 13 18 22

TEENAGE MUTANT NINJA TURTLES (Also see Anything Goes, Donatello, First Comics Graphic Novel, Gobbledygook, Grimjack #26, Leonardo, Michaelangelo, Raphael & Tales Of The...)
Mirage Studios: 1984 - No. 62, Aug, 1993 ($1.50/$1.75, B&W; all 44-52 pgs.)

1-1st printing (3000 copies)-Origin and 1st app. of the Turtles and Splinter. Only printing to have ad for Gobbledygook #1 & 2; Shredder app. (#1-4: 7-1/2x11") (Prices vary widely on this book. In 2005 a CGC certified 9.4 sold for $8,300, a CGC certified 9.2 sold for $2,850, and a CGC certified 6.0 sold for $1,300. In 2009, a CGC 9.6 sold for $11,500. In Feb. 2011, a CGC 9.2 copy sold for $3,107.)
1-2nd printing (6/84)(15,000 copies) 3 6 9 16 23 30
1-3rd printing (2/85)(36,000 copies) 2 4 6 9 13 16
1-4th printing, new-c (50,000 copies) 6.00
1-5th printing, new-c (8/88-c, 11/88 inside) 5.00
1-Counterfeit. **Note**: Most counterfeit copies have a half inch wide white streak or scratch marks across the center of back cover. Black part of cover is a bluish black instead of a deep black. Inside paper is very white & inside cover is bright white (no value)
2-1st printing (1984; 15,000 copies) 12 24 36 82 154 225
2-2nd printing 2 4 6 9 12 15
2-3rd printing; new Corben-c/a (2/85) 2 4 6 9 12 15
2-Counterfeit with glossy cover stock (no value).
3-1st printing (1985, 44 pgs.) 9 18 27 63 107 150
3-Variant, 500 copies, given away in NYC. Has 'Laird's Photo' in white rather than light blue 12 24 36 82 154 225
3-2nd printing; contains new back-up story 1 3 4 6 8 10
4-1st printing (1985, 44 pgs.) 6 12 18 41 66 90
4,5-2nd printing (5/87, 11/87) 5.00
5-Fugitoid begins, ends #7; 1st full color-c (1985) 4 8 12 24 37 50
6-1st printing (1986) 3 6 9 16 23 30
6-2nd printing (4/88-c, 5/88 inside) 4.00
7-4 pg. Eastman/Corben color insert; 1st color TMNT (1986, $1.75-c); Bade Biker back-up story 2 4 6 11 16 20
7-2nd printing (1/89) w/o color insert 4.00
8-Cerebus-c/story with Dave Sim-a (1986) 2 4 6 9 12 15
9,10: 9 (9/86)-Rip In Time by Corben 1 3 4 6 8 10
11-15 6.00
16-18: 18-Mark Bode'-a 5.00
18-2nd printing ($2.25, color, 44 pgs.)-New-c 4.00
19-34: 19-Begin $1.75-c. 24-26-Veitch-c/a. 5.00
32-2nd printing ($2.75, 52 pgs., full color) 4.00
35-49,51: 35-Begin $2.00-c. 5.00
50-Features pin-ups by Larsen, McFarlane, Simonson, etc. 6.00
52-62: 52-Begin $2.25-c 5.00
nn (1990, $5.95, B&W)-Movie adaptation 6.00
Book 1,2($1.50, B&W): 2-Corben-c 5.00
...Christmas Special 1 (12/90, $1.75, B&W, 52 pgs.)-Cover title: Michaelangelo Christmas Special; r/Michaelangelo one-shot plus new Raphael story 5.00
... Color Special (11/09, $3.25) full color reprint of #1 4.00
...Special (The Maltese Turtle) nn (1/93, $2.95, color, 44 pgs.) 5.00
...Special: "Times" Pipeline nn (9/92, $2.95, color, 44 pgs.)-Mark Bode-c/a 5.00
Hardcover ($100)-r/#1-10 plus one-shots w/dust jackets - limited to 1000 w/letter of authenticity 100.00
Softcover ($40)-r/#1-10 40.00

TEENAGE MUTANT NINJA TURTLES
Mirage Studios: V2#1, Oct, 1993 - V2#13, Oct, 1995 ($2.75)

V2#1-13: 1-Wraparound-c 4.00

TEENAGE MUTANT NINJA TURTLES
Image Comics (Highbrow Ent.): June, 1996 - No. 23, Oct, 1999 ($1.95-$2.95)

1-23: 1-8: Eric Larsen-c(i) on all. 10-Savage Dragon-c/app. 3.00

TEENAGE MUTANT NINJA TURTLES
Mirage Publishing: V4#1, Dec, 2001 - No. 28 ($2.95, B&W)

V4#1-9,11-28-Laird-s/a(i)/Lawson-a(p). 3.00
10-($3.95) Splinter dies 4.00

TEENAGE MUTANT NINJA TURTLES
Dreamwave Productions: June 2003 - No. 7 ($2.95, color)

1-7-Animated style; Peter David-s/Lesean-a 3.00
Vol. 1 TPB (2003, $9.95) r/#1-4; cover gallery and sketch pages 10.00

TEENAGE MUTANT NINJA TURTLES (Adventures)
Archie Publications: Jan, 1996 - No. 3, Mar, 1996 ($1.50, limited series)

1-3 4.00

TEENAGE MUTANT NINJA TURTLES ADVENTURES (TV)
Archie Comics: 8/88 - No. 3, 12/88; 3/89 - No. 72, Oct, 1995 ($1.00/$1.25/$1.50/$1.75)

1-Adapts TV cartoon; not by Eastman/Laird 5.00
2,3 (Mini-series) 4.00
1 (2nd on-going series) 5.00
1-2nd printing 3.00
2-18,20-30: 5-Begins original stories not based on TV. 14-Simpson-a(p). 22-Colan-c/a 4.00
2-11: 2nd printings 3.00
19,20,51-54: 19-1st Mighty Mutanimals (also in #20, 51-54 2 4 6 9 12 15
31-49 5.00

Teen-Age Romances #45 © STJ

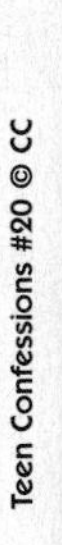
Teen Confessions #20 © CC

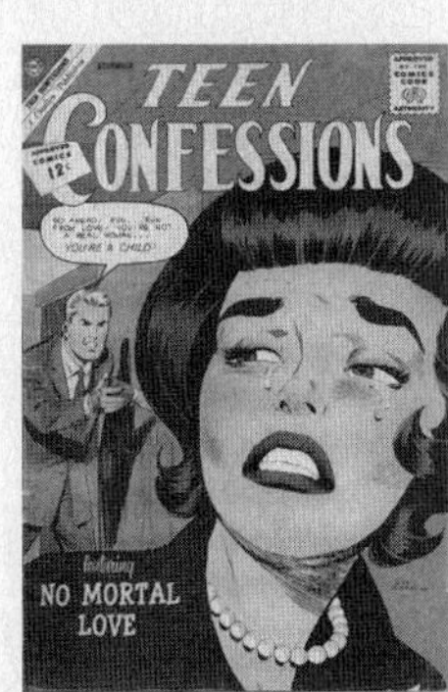

Teen Titans #9 © DC

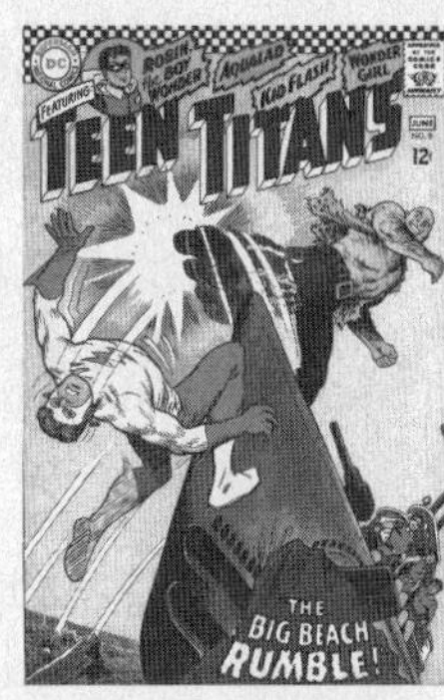

	GD 2.0	VG 4.0	FN 6.0	VF 8.0	VF/NM 9.0	NM- 9.2
50-Poster by Eastman/Laird	1	2	3	5	7	9
55-60	1	2	3	4	5	7
61-70: 62-w/poster	2	3	4	6	8	10
71	2	4	6	8	10	12
72- Last issue	2	4	6	9	13	16
nn (1990, $2.50)-Movie adaptation						4.00
nn (Spring, 1991, $2.50, 68 pgs.)-(Meet Archie)						5.00
nn (Sum, 1991, $2.50, 68 pgs.)-(Movie II)-Adapts movie sequel						4.00
...Meet the Conservation Corps 1 (1992, $2.50, 68 pgs.)						4.00
...III The Movie: The Turtles are Back...In Time (1993, $2.50, 68 pgs.)						4.00
Special 1,4,5 (Sum/92, Spr/93, Sum/93, 68 pgs.)-1-Bill Wray-c						4.00
Giant Size Special 6 (Fall/93, $1.95, 52 pgs.)						4.00
Special 7-10 (Win/93-Fall//94, 52 pgs.): 9-Jeff Smith-c						4.00

NOTE: *There are 2nd printings of #1-11 w/B&W inside covers. Originals are color.*

TEENAGE MUTANT NINJA TURTLES CLASSICS DIGEST (TV)
Archie Comics: Aug, 1993 - No. 8, Mar, 1995? ($1.75)

	GD	VG	FN	VF	VF/NM	NM-
1-8: Reprints TMNT Advs.						4.00

TEENAGE MUTANT NINJA TURTLES/FLAMING CARROT CROSSOVER
Mirage Publishing: Nov, 1993 - No. 4, Feb, 1994 ($2.75, limited series)

	GD	VG	FN	VF	VF/NM	NM-
1-4: Bob Burden story						4.00

TEENAGE MUTANT NINJA TURTLES PRESENTS: APRIL O'NEIL
Archie Comics: Mar, 1993 - No. 3, June, 1993 ($1.25, limited series)

	GD	VG	FN	VF	VF/NM	NM-
1-3						4.00

TEENAGE MUTANT NINJA TURTLES PRESENTS: DONATELLO AND LEATHERHEAD
Archie Comics: July, 1993 - No. 3, Sept, 1993 ($1.25, limited series)

	GD	VG	FN	VF	VF/NM	NM-
1-3						4.00

TEENAGE MUTANT NINJA TURTLES PRESENTS: MERDUDE
Archie Comics: Oct, 1993 - No. 3, Dec, 1993 ($1.25, limited series)

	GD	VG	FN	VF	VF/NM	NM-
1-3-See Mighty Mutanimals #7 for 1st app. Merdude						4.00

TEENAGE MUTANT NINJA TURTLES/SAVAGE DRAGON CROSSOVER
Mirage Studios: Aug, 1995 ($2.75, one-shot)

	GD	VG	FN	VF	VF/NM	NM-
1						4.00

TEEN-AGE ROMANCE (Formerly My Own Romance)
Marvel Comics (ZPC): No. 77, Sept, 1960 - No. 86, Mar, 1962

	GD	VG	FN	VF	VF/NM	NM-
77-83	5	10	15	30	48	65
84-86-Kirby-c. 84-Kirby-a(2 pgs.). 85,86-(3 pgs.)	6	12	18	37	59	80

TEEN-AGE ROMANCES
St. John Publ. Co. (Approved Comics): Jan, 1949 - No. 45, Dec, 1955 (#3,7,10-18,21 are 1/2 inch taller than other issues)

	GD	VG	FN	VF	VF/NM	NM-
1-Baker-c/a(1)	61	122	183	390	670	950
2,3: 2-Baker-c/a. 3-Baker-c/a(3)	39	78	117	240	395	550
4,5,7,8-Photo-c; Baker-a(2-3) each	30	60	90	177	289	400
6-Photo-c; part magazine; Baker-a (10/49)	32	64	96	188	307	425
9-Baker-c/a; Kubert-a	39	78	117	231	378	525
10-12,20-Baker-c/a(2-3) each	34	68	102	199	325	450
13-19,21,22-Complete issues by Baker	39	78	117	235	385	535
23-25-Baker-c/a(2-3) each	32	64	96	192	314	435
26,27,33,34,36-40,42: Baker-c/a. 33,40-Signed story by Estrada. 38-Suggestive-c. 42-r/Cinderella Love #9; Last pre-code (3/55)	22	44	66	132	216	300
28-30-No Baker-a	13	26	39	74	105	135
31,32-Baker-c. 31-Estrada-s	20	40	60	114	182	250
35-Baker-c/a (16 pgs.)	23	46	69	136	223	310
41-Baker-c; Infantino-a(r); all stories are Ziff-Davis-r	20	40	60	114	182	250
43-45-Baker-c/a	22	44	66	132	216	300

TEEN-AGE TALK
I.W. Enterprises: 1964

	GD	VG	FN	VF	VF/NM	NM-
Reprint #1	2	4	6	10	14	18
Reprint #5,8,9: 5-r/Hector #? 9-Punch Comics #?; L.B. Cole-c reprint from School Day Romances #1	2	4	6	9	13	16

TEEN-AGE TEMPTATIONS (Going Steady #10 on)(See True Love Pictorial)
St. John Publishing Co.: Oct, 1952 - No. 9, Aug, 1954

	GD	VG	FN	VF	VF/NM	NM-
1-Baker-c/a; has story "Reform School Girl" by Estrada	71	142	213	454	777	1100
2,4-Baker-c	32	64	96	188	307	425
3,5-7,9-Baker-c/a	39	78	117	231	378	525
8-Teenagers smoke reefer; Baker-c/a	41	82	123	256	428	600

NOTE: ***Estrada** a-1, 3-5.*

TEEN BEAM (Formerly Teen Beat #1)
National Periodical Publications: No. 2, Jan-Feb, 1968

	GD	VG	FN	VF	VF/NM	NM-
2-Superman cameo; Herman's Hermits, Yardbirds, Simon & Garfunkel, Lovin Spoonful, Young Rascals app.; Orlando, Drucker-a(r); Monkees photo-c;	15	30	45	106	216	325

TEEN BEAT (Becomes Teen Beam #2)
National Periodical Publications: Nov-Dec, 1967

	GD	VG	FN	VF	VF/NM	NM-
1-Photos & text only; Monkees photo-c; Beatles, Herman's Hermits, Animals, Supremes, Byrds app.	16	32	48	114	232	350

TEEN COMICS (Formerly All Teen; Journey Into Unknown Worlds #36 on)
Marvel Comics (WFP): No. 21, Apr, 1947 - No. 35, May, 1950

	GD	VG	FN	VF	VF/NM	NM-
21-Kurtzman's "Hey Look"; Patsy Walker, Cindy (1st app.?), Georgie, Margie app.; Syd Shores-a begins, end #23	18	36	54	105	165	225
22,23,25,27,29,31-35: 22-(6/47)-Becomes Hedy Devine #22 (8/47) on?	15	30	45	83	124	165
24,26,28,30-Kurtzman's "Hey Look"	15	30	45	85	130	175

TEEN CONFESSIONS
Charlton Comics: Aug, 1959 - No. 97, Nov, 1976

	GD	VG	FN	VF	VF/NM	NM-
1	8	16	24	52	86	120
2	4	8	12	28	44	60
3-10	4	8	12	22	34	45
11-30	3	6	9	18	27	35
31-Beatles-c	11	22	33	77	144	210
32-36,38-55	3	6	9	15	21	26
37 (1/66)-Beatles Fan Club story; Beatles-c	11	22	33	77	144	210
56-58,60-76,78-97: 89,90-Newton-c	2	4	6	10	14	18
59-Kaluta's 1st pro work? (12/69)	3	6	9	20	30	40
77-Partridge Family poster	3	6	9	14	20	24

TEENIE WEENIES, THE (America's Favorite Kiddie Comic)
Ziff-Davis Publishing Co.: No. 10, 1950 - No. 11, Apr-May, 1951 (Newspaper reprints)

	GD	VG	FN	VF	VF/NM	NM-
10,11-Painted-c	20	40	60	114	182	250

TEEN-IN (Tippy Teen)
Tower Comics: Summer, 1968 - No. 4, Fall, 1969

	GD	VG	FN	VF	VF/NM	NM-
nn(#1, Summer, 1968)(25¢) Has 3 full pg. B&W photos of Sonny & Cher, Donovan and Herman's Hermits; interviews and photos of Eric Clapton, Jim Morrison and others	10	20	30	70	125	180
nn(#2, Spring, 1969),3,4	6	12	18	43	69	95

TEEN LIFE (Formerly Young Life)
New Age/Quality Comics Group: No. 3, Winter, 1945 - No. 5, Fall, 1945 (Teenage magazine)

	GD	VG	FN	VF	VF/NM	NM-
3-June Allyson photo on-c & story	14	28	42	76	108	140
4-Duke Ellington photo on-c & story	11	22	33	64	90	115
5-Van Johnson, Woody Herman & Jackie Robinson articles; Van Johnson & Woody Herman photos on-c	14	28	42	78	112	145

TEEN LOVE STORIES (Magazine)
Warren Publ. Co.: Sept, 1969 - No. 3, Jan, 1970 (68 pgs., photo covers, B&W)

	GD	VG	FN	VF	VF/NM	NM-
1-Photos & articles plus 36-42 pgs. new comic stories in all; Frazetta-a	8	16	24	52	86	120
2,3: 2-Anti-marijuana story	5	10	15	35	55	75

TEEN ROMANCES
Super Comics: 1964

	GD	VG	FN	VF	VF/NM	NM-
10,11,15-17-Reprints	2	4	6	8	11	14

TEEN SECRET DIARY (Nurse Betsy Crane #12 on)
Charlton Comics: Oct, 1959 - No. 11, June, 1961; No. 1, 1972

	GD	VG	FN	VF	VF/NM	NM-
1	5	10	15	32	51	70
2	3	6	9	21	32	42
3-11	3	6	9	18	27	35
1 (1972)(exist?)	3	6	9	15	21	26

TEEN TALK (See Teen)

TEEN TITANS (See Brave & the Bold #54,60, DC Super-Stars #1, Marvel & DC Present, New Teen Titans, New Titans, Official...Index and Showcase #59)
National Periodical Publications/DC Comics: 1-2/66 - No. 43, 1-2/73; No. 44, 11/76 - No. 53, 2/78

	GD	VG	FN	VF	VF/NM	NM-
1-(1-2/66)-Titans join Peace Corps; Batman, Flash, Aquaman, Wonder Woman cameos	33	66	99	254	502	750
2	15	30	45	104	212	320
3-5: 4-Speedy app.	10	20	30	71	128	185
6-10: 6-Doom Patrol app.; Beast Boy x-over; readers polled on him joining Titans	8	16	24	58	97	135

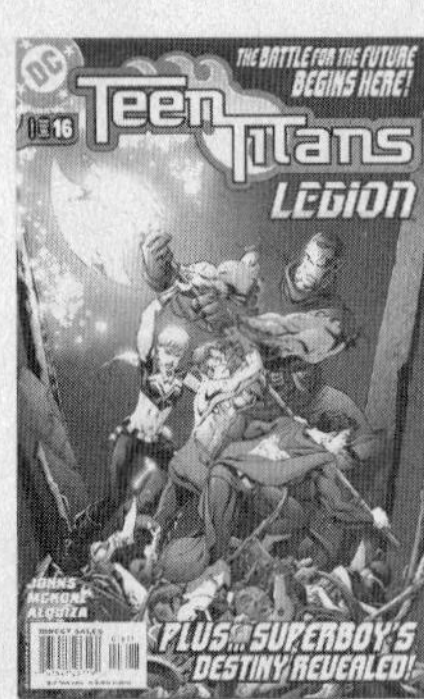

Teen Titans (2003 series) #16 © DC

Teen Titans Go! #47 © DC

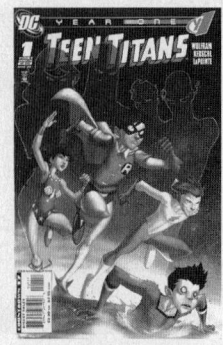

Teen Titans Year One #1 © DC

GD VG FN VF VF/NM NM-
2.0 4.0 6.0 8.0 9.0 9.2

GD VG FN VF VF/NM NM-
2.0 4.0 6.0 8.0 9.0 9.2

11-18: 11-Speedy app. 13-X-Mas-c 7 14 21 47 76 105
19-Wood-i; Speedy begins as regular 7 14 21 49 80 110
20-22: All Neal Adams-a. 21-Hawk & Dove app.; last 12¢ issue. 22-Origin Wonder Girl
9 18 27 63 107 150
23-Wonder Girl dons new costume 6 12 18 37 59 80
24-31: 25-Flash, Aquaman, Batman, Green Arrow, Green Lantern, Superman, & Hawk & Dove guests; 1st app. Lilith who joins T.T. West in #50. 29-Hawk & Dove & Ocean Master app. 30-Aquagirl app. 31-Hawk & Dove app.; last 15¢ issue
5 10 15 32 51 70
32-34,40-43 3 6 9 20 30 40
35-39-(52 pgs.): 36,37-Superboy-r. 38-Green Arrow/Speedy-r; Aquaman/Aqualad story. 39-Hawk & Dove-r. 4 8 12 23 36 48
44-(11/76) Dr. Light app.; Mal becomes the Guardian 3 6 9 14 20 26
45,47,49,51,52 3 6 9 14 19 24
46,48: 46-Joker's daughter begins (see Batman Family). 48-Intro Bumblebee; Joker's daughter becomes Harlequin 3 6 9 17 25 32
50-1st revival original Bat-Girl; intro. Teen Titans West
3 6 9 18 27 35
53-Origin retold 3 6 9 16 22 28
... Lost Annual 1 (3/08, $4.99) Sixties-era story by Bob Haney; Jay Stephens & Mike Allred-a; President Kennedy app.; Nick Cardy-c and sketch pages 5.00

NOTE: *Aparo a-36.* ***Buckler*** *c-46-53.* ***Cardy*** *c-1-16.* ***Kane*** *a(p)-19, 22-24, 39r.* ***Tuska*** *a(p)-31, 36, 38, 39. DC Super-Stars #1 (3/76) was released before #44.*

TEEN TITANS (Also see Titans Beat in the Promotional Comics section)
DC Comics: Oct, 1996 - No. 24, Sept, 1998 ($1.95)

1-Dan Jurgens-c/a(p)/scripts & George Pérez-c/a(i) begin; Atom forms new team (Risk, Argent, Prysm, & Joto); 1st app. Loren Jupiter & Omen; no indicia. 1-3-Origin. 4.00
2-24: 4,5-Robin, Nightwing, Supergirl, Capt. Marvel Jr. app. 12-"Then and Now" begins w/original Teen Titans-c/app. 15-Death of Joto. 17-Capt. Marvel Jr. and Fringe join. 19-Millennium Giants x-over. 23,24-Superman app. 3.00
Annual 1 (1997, $3.95)-Pulp Heroes story 4.00

TEEN TITANS (Also see Titans/Young Justice: Graduation Day)
DC Comics: Sept, 2003 - Present ($2.50/$2.99/$3.99)

1-McKone-c/a;Johns-s 5.00
1-Variant-c by Michael Turner 6.00
1-2nd and 3rd printings 3.00
2-Deathstroke app. 5.00
2-2nd printing 3.00
3-15: 4-Impulse becomes Kid Flash. 5-Raven returns. 6-JLA app. 4.00
16-33: 16-Titans go to 31st Century; Legion and Fatal Five app. 17-19-Future Titans app. 21-23-Dr. Light. 24,25-Outsiders #24,25 x-over. 27,28-Liefeld-a. 32,33-Infinite Crisis 3.00
34-49,51-71: 34-One Year Later begins; two covers by Daniel and Benes. 36-Begin $2.99-c. 40-Jericho returns. 42-Kid Devil origin; Snejbjerg-a. 43-Titans East. 48,49-Amazons Attack x-over; Supergirl app. 51-54-Future Titans app. 3.00
50-($3.99) Art by Pérez (4 pgs.), McKone (6 pgs.), Nauck and Green; future Titans app. 4.00
72-88: 72-Begin $3.99-c; Ravager back-up features. 77,78-Blackest Night. 83-87-Coven of Three back-up; Naifeh-a. 88-Nicola Scott-a begins 4.00
89-92-($2.99) 89-Robin (Damian) joins 3.00
Annual 1 (4/06, $4.99) Infinite Crisis x-over; Benes-c 5.00
Annual 2009 (6/09, $4.99) Deathtrap x-over prelude; McKeever-s 5.00
... And Outsiders Secret Files and Origins 2005 (10/05, $4.99) Daniel-c 5.00
...: Cold Case (2/11, $4.99) Captain Cold and the Rogues app.; Sean Murphy-a 6.00
.../Legion Special (11/04, $3.50) (cont'd from #16) Reis-a; leads into 2005 Legion of Super-Heroes series; LSH preview by Waid & Kitson 4.00
#1/2 (Wizard mail offer) origin of Ravager; Reis-a 8.00
.../Outsiders Secret Files 2003 (12/03, $5.95) Reis & Jimenez-a; pin-ups by various 6.00
...: A Kid's Game TPB (2004, $9.95) r/#1-7; Turner-c from #1; McKone sketch pages 10.00
...: Beast Boys and Girls TPB (2005, $9.99) r/#13-15 and Beast Boy #1-4 10.00
...: Changing of the Guard TPB (2009, $14.99) r/#62-69 15.00
...: Child's Play TPB (2010, $14.99) r/#71-78 15.00
...: Deathtrap TPB (2009, $14.99) r/#70, Annual #1, Titans #12,13, Vigilante #4-6 15.00
...: Family Lost TPB (2004, $9.95) r/#8-12 & #1/2 10.00
...: Life and Death TPB (2006, $14.99) r/#29-33 and pages from Infinite Crisis x-over 15.00
...: On the Clock TPB (2008, $14.99) r/#55-61 15.00
.../ Outsiders: The Death and Return of Donna Troy (2006, $14.99) r/Titans/Young Justice: Graduation Day #1-3, Teen Titans/Outsiders Secret Files 2003 and DC Special: The Return of Donna Troy #1-4; cover gallery 15.00
.../ Outsiders: The Insiders (2006, $14.99) r/Teen Titans/ #24-26 & Outsiders #24,25,28 15.00
...: Ravager - Fresh Hell TPB (2010, $14.99) r/#71-76,79-82 & Faces of Evil: Deathstroke 15.00
... Spotlight: Cyborg TPB (2009, $19.99) r/DC Special: Cyborg #1-6 20.00
... Spotlight: Raven TPB (2008, $14.99) r/DC Special: Raven #1-5 15.00
...: The Future is Now (2005, $9.99) r/#15-23 & Teen Titans/Legion Special 10.00
...: The Hunt For Raven (2011, $17.99) r/#79-87 18.00
...: Titans Around the World TPB (2007, $14.99) r/#34-41 15.00
...: Titans of Tomorrow TPB (2008, $14.99) r/#50-54 15.00

TEEN TITANS GO! (Based on Cartoon Network series)
DC Comics: Jan, 2004 - No. 55, Jul, 2008 ($2.25)

1-12,14-55: 1,2-Nauck-a/Bullock-c/J. Torres-s. 8-Mad Mod app. 14-Speedy-c. 28-Doom Patrol app. 31-Nightwing app. 36-Wonder Girl. 38-Mad Mod app.; Clugston-a 3.00
1-(9/04, Free Comic Book Day giveaway) r/#1; 2 bound-in Wacky Packages stickers 4.00
13-($2.95) Bonus pages with Shazam! reprint 4.00
Jam Packed Action (2005, $7.99, digest) adaptations of two TV episodes 8.00
... Vol 1: Truth, Justice, Pizza! (2004, $6.95, digest-size) r/#1-5 7.00
... Vol 2: Heroes on Patrol (2005, $6.99, digest-size) r/#6-10 7.00
... Vol 3: Bring It On! (2005, $6.99, digest-size) r/#11-15 7.00
... Vol 4: Ready For Action! (2006, $6.99, digest-size) r/#16-20 7.00
... Vol 5: On The Move! (2006, $6.99, digest-size) r/#21-25 7.00
... Titans Together TPB (2007, $12.99) r/#26-32 13.00

TEEN TITANS SPOTLIGHT
DC Comics: Aug, 1986 - No. 21, Apr, 1988

1-21: 7-Guice's 1st work at DC. 14-Nightwing; Batman app. 15-Austin-c(i). 18,19-Millennium x-over. 21-($1.00-c)-Original Teen Titans; Spiegle-a 3.00

Note: ***Guice*** *a-7p, 8p; c-7,8.* ***Orlando*** *c/a-11p.* ***Perez*** *c-1, 17i, 19.* ***Sienkiewicz*** *c-10*

TEEN TITANS YEAR ONE
DC Comics: Mar, 2008 - No. 6, Aug, 2008 ($2.99, limited series)

1-6-The original five form a team; Wolfram-s/Kerschl-a 3.00
TPB (2008, $14.99) r/#1-6; bonus pin-up 15.00

TEEPEE TIM (...Heap Funny Indian Boy)(Formerly Ha Ha Comics)
American Comics Group: No. 100, Feb-Mar, 1955 - No. 102, June-July, 1955

100-102 6 12 18 31 38 45

TEGRA JUNGLE EMPRESS (Zegra Jungle Empress #2 on)
Fox Features Syndicate: August, 1948

1-Blue Beetle, Rocket Kelly app.; used in **SOTI**, pg. 31
68 136 204 435 743 1050

TEK JANSEN (See Stephen Colbert's...)

TEKNO COMIX HANDBOOK
Tekno Comix: May, 1996 ($3.95, one-shot)

1-Guide to the Tekno Universe 4.00

TEKNOPHAGE (See Neil Gaiman's...)

TEKNOPHAGE VERSUS ZEERUS
BIG Entertainment: July, 1996 ($3.25, one-shot)

1-Paul Jenkins script 3.25

TEKWORLD (William Shatner's... on-c only)
Epic Comics (Marvel): Sept, 1992 - Aug, 1994 ($1.75)

1-Based on Shatner's novel, TekWar, set in L.A. in the year 2120 4.00
2-24 3.00

TELARA CHRONICLES (Based on the videogame Rift: Planes of Telara)
DC Comics (WildStorm): Jan, 2010; Nov, 2010 - No. 4, Feb, 2011 ($3.99, limited series)

0-(1/10, free) Preview of series 1.00
1-4-Pop Mhan-a/Drew Johnson-c 4.00
TPB (2011, $17.99) r/#0-4; background info on Telara 18.00

TELEVISION (See TV)

TELEVISION COMICS (Early TV comic)
Standard Comics (Animated Cartoons): No. 5, Feb, 1950 - No. 8, Nov, 1950

5-1st app. Willy Nilly 10 20 30 54 72 90
6-8: #6 on inside has #2 on cover 8 16 24 42 54 65

TELEVISION PUPPET SHOW (Early TV comic) (See Spotty the Pup)
Avon Periodicals: 1950 - No. 2, Nov, 1950

1-1st app. Speedy Rabbit, Spotty The Pup 20 40 60 114 182 250
2 14 28 42 82 121 160

TELEVISION TEENS MOPSY (See TV Teens)

TELL IT TO THE MARINES
Toby Press Publications: Mar, 1952 - No. 15, July, 1955

1-Lover O'Leary and His Liberty Belles (with pin-ups), ends #6; Spike & Bat begin, end #6 19 38 57 111 176 240
2-Madame Cobra-c/story 12 24 36 67 94 120
3-5 10 20 30 54 72 90
6-12,14,15: 7-9,14,15-Photo-c 8 16 24 42 54 65

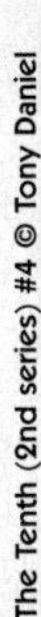
The Tenth (2nd series) #4 © Tony Daniel

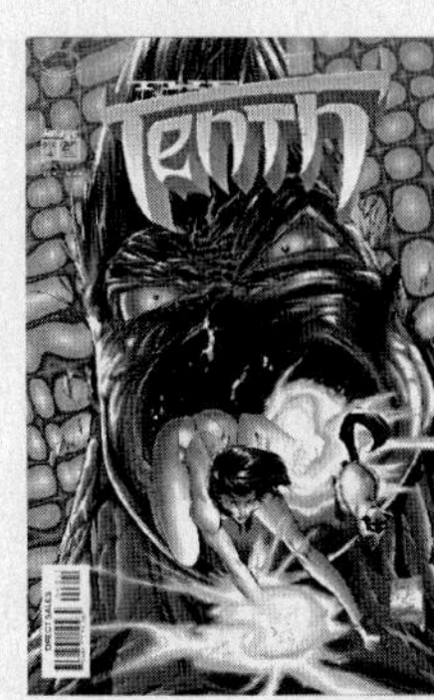

Terminal City #4 © Dean Motter

Terminator: 1984 #3 © Studio Canal

	GD 2.0	VG 4.0	FN 6.0	VF 8.0	VF/NM 9.0	NM- 9.2
13-John Wayne photo-c	15	30	45	83	124	165
I.W. Reprint #9-r/#1 above	2	4	6	8	10	12
Super Reprint #16(1964)-r/#4 above	2	4	6	8	10	12

TELLOS
Image Comics: May, 1999 - No. 10, Nov, 2000 ($2.50)

1-Dezago-s/Wieringo-a 3.00
1-Variant-c ($7.95) 8.00
2-10: 4-Four covers 3.00
...: Maiden Voyage (3/01, $5.95) Didier Crispeels-a/c 6.00
...: Sons & Moons (2002, $5.95) Nick Cardy-c 6.00
...: The Last Heist (2001, $5.95) Rousseau-a/c 6.00
Prelude ($5.00, AnotherUniverse.com) 5.00
Prologue ($3.95, Dynamic Forces) 4.00
...Collected Edition 1 (12/99, $8.95) r/#1-3 9.00
... Colossal, Vol. 1 TPB (2008, $17.99) r/#1-10, Prelude, Prologue, Scatterjack-s from Section Zero #1, cover gallery, Wieringo sketch pages; Dezago afterword 18.00
...: Kindred Spirits (2/01, $17.95) r/#6-10, Section Zero #1 (Scatterjack-s) 18.00
...: Reluctant Heroes (2/01, $17.95) r/#1-5, Prelude, Prologue; sketchbook 18.00

TEMPEST (See Aquaman, 3rd Series)
DC Comics: Nov, 1996 - No. 4, Feb, 1997 ($1.75, limited series)

1-4: Formerly Aqualad; Phil Jimenez-c/a/scripts in all 3.00

TEMPUS FUGITIVE
DC Comics: 1990 - No. 4, 1991 ($4.95, squarebound, 52 pgs.)

Book 1,2: Ken Steacy painted-c/a & scripts 6.00
Book 3,4-($5.95-c) 6.00
TPB (Dark Horse Comics, 1/97, $17.95) 18.00

TEN COMMANDMENTS (See Moses & the... and Classics Illustrated Special)

TENDER LOVE STORIES
Skywald Publ. Corp.: Feb, 1971 - No. 4, July, 1971 (Pre-code reprints and new stories)

	GD	VG	FN	VF	VF/NM	NM-
1 (All 25¢, 52 pgs.)	4	8	12	28	44	60
2-4	4	8	12	22	34	45

TENDER ROMANCE (Ideal Romance #3 on)
Key Publications (Gilmour Magazines): Dec, 1953 - No. 2, Feb, 1954

	GD	VG	FN	VF	VF/NM	NM-
1-Headlight & lingerie panels; B. Baily-c	19	38	57	111	176	240
2-Bernard Baily-c	12	24	36	67	94	120

TENSE SUSPENSE
Fago Publications: Dec, 1958 - No. 2, Feb, 1959

	GD	VG	FN	VF	VF/NM	NM-
1	10	20	30	54	72	90
2	8	16	24	40	50	60

TEN STORY LOVE (Formerly a pulp magazine with same title)
Ace Periodicals: V29#3, June-July, 1951 - V36#5(#209), Sept, 1956 (#3-6: 52 pgs.)

	GD	VG	FN	VF	VF/NM	NM-
V29#3(#177)-Part comic, part text; painted-c	15	30	45	86	133	180
4-6(1/52)	10	20	30	56	76	95
V30#1(3/52)-6(1/53)	10	20	30	54	72	90
V31#1(2/53),V32#2(4/53)-6(12/53)	9	18	27	52	69	85
V33#1(1/54)-3(5#54, #195), V34#4(7/54, #196)-6(10/54, #198)	9	18	27	50	65	80
V35#1(12/54, #199)-3(4/55, #201)-Last precode	9	18	27	47	61	75
V35#4-6(9/55, #201-204), V36#1(11/55, #205)-3, 5(9/56, #209)	8	16	24	44	57	70
V36#4-L.B. Cole-a	10	20	30	56	76	95

TENTH, THE
Image Comics: Jan, 1997 - No. 4, June, 1997 ($2.50, limited series)

1-4-Tony Daniel-c/a, Beau Smith-s 5.00
Abuse of Humanity TPB ($10.95) r/#1-4 11.00
Abuse of Humanity TPB (10/98, $11.95) r/#1-4 & 0(8/97) 12.00

TENTH, THE
Image Comics: Sept, 1997 - No. 14, Jan, 1999 ($2.50)

0-(8/97, $5.00) American Ent. Ed. 6.00
1-Tony Daniel-c/a, Beau Smith-s 6.00
2-9: 3,7-Variant-c 4.00
10-14 3.00
...Configuration (8/98) Re-cap and pin-ups 3.00
...Collected Edition 1 ('98, $4.95, square-bound) r/#1,2 5.00
...Special (4/00, $2.95) r/#0 and Wizard #1/2 3.00
Wizard #1/2-Daniel-s/Steve Scott-a 10.00

TENTH, THE (Volume 3) (The Black Embrace)
Image Comics: Mar, 1999 - No. 4, June, 1999 ($2.95)

1-4-Daniel-c/a 3.00
TPB (1/00, $12.95) r/#1-4 13.00

TENTH, THE (Volume 4) (Evil's Child)
Image Comics: Sept, 1999 - No. 4, Mar, 2000 ($2.95, limited series)

1-4-Daniel-c/a 3.00

TENTH, THE (Darkk Dawn)
Image Comics: July, 2005 ($4.99, one-shot)

1-Kirkham-a/Bonny-s 5.00

TENTH, THE : RESURRECTED
Dark Horse Comics: July, 2001 - No. 4, Feb, 2002 ($2.99, limited series)

1-4: 1-Two covers; Daniel-s/c; Romano-a 3.00

10th MUSE
Image Comics (TidalWave Studios): Nov, 2000 - No. 9, Jan, 2002 ($2.95)

1-Character based on wrestling's Rena Mero; regular & photo covers 3.00
2-9: 2-Photo and 2 Lashley covers; flip book Dollz preview. 5-Savage Dragon app.; 2 covers by Lashley and Larsen. 6-Tellos x-over 3.00

TEN WHO DARED (Disney)
Dell Publishing Co.: No. 1178, Dec, 1960

	GD	VG	FN	VF	VF/NM	NM-
Four Color 1178-Movie, painted-c; cast member photo on back-c	7	14	21	49	80	110

TERMINAL CITY
DC Comics (Vertigo): July, 1996 - No. 9, Mar, 1997 ($2.50, limited series)

1-9: Dean Motter scripts, 7,8-Matt Wagner-c 3.00
TPB ('97, $19.95) r/series 20.00

TERMINAL CITY: AERIAL GRAFFITI
DC Comics (Vertigo): Nov, 1997 - No. 5, Mar, 1998 ($2.50, limited series)

1-5: Dean Motter-s/Lark-a/Chiarello-c 3.00

TERMINATOR, THE (See Robocop vs. ... & Rust #12 for 1st app.)
Now Comics: Sept, 1988 - No. 17, 1989 ($1.75, Baxter paper)

	GD	VG	FN	VF	VF/NM	NM-
1-Based on movie	1	3	4	6	8	10

2-5 6.00
6-11,13-17 4.00
12-($2.95, 52 pgs.)-Intro. John Connor 5.00
Trade paperback (1989, $9.95) 10.00

TERMINATOR, THE
Dark Horse Comics: Aug, 1990 - No. 4, Nov, 1990 ($2.50, limited series)

1-Set 39 years later than the movie 4.00
2-4 3.00

TERMINATOR, THE
Dark Horse Comics: 1998 - No. 4, Dec, 1998 ($2.95, limited series)

1-4-Alan Grant-s/Steve Pugh-a/c 3.00
...Special (1998, $2.95) Darrow-c/Grant-s 3.00

TERMINATOR, THE: ALL MY FUTURES PAST
Now Comics: V3#1, Aug, 1990 - V3#2, Sept, 1990 ($1.75, limited series)

V3#1,2 3.00

TERMINATOR, THE: ENDGAME
Dark Horse Comics: Sept, 1992 - No. 3, Nov, 1992 ($2.50, limited series)

1-3: Guice-a(p); painted-c 3.00

TERMINATOR, THE: HUNTERS AND KILLERS
Dark Horse Comics: Mar, 1992 - No. 3, May, 1992 ($2.50, limited series)

1-3 3.00

TERMINATOR, THE: 1984
Dark Horse Comics: Sept, 2010 - No. 3, Nov, 2010 ($3.50, limited series)

1-3: Takes place during and after the 1st movie; Zack Whedon-s/Andy MacDonald-a 3.50

TERMINATOR, THE: ONE SHOT
Dark Horse Comics: July, 1991 ($5.95, 56 pgs.)

nn-Matt Wagner-a; contains stiff pop-up inside 6.00

TERMINATOR: REVOLUTION (Follows Terminator 2: Infinity series)
Dynamite Entertainment: 2008 - No. 5, 2009 ($3.50, limited series)

1-5-Furman-s/Antonio-a. 1-3-Two covers 3.50

TERMINATOR: SALVATION MOVIE PREQUEL
IDW Publishing: Jan, 2009 - No. 4, Apr, 2009 ($3.99, limited series)

1-4: Alan Robinson-a/Dara Naraghi-s 4.00

Terra Obscura #1 © ABC

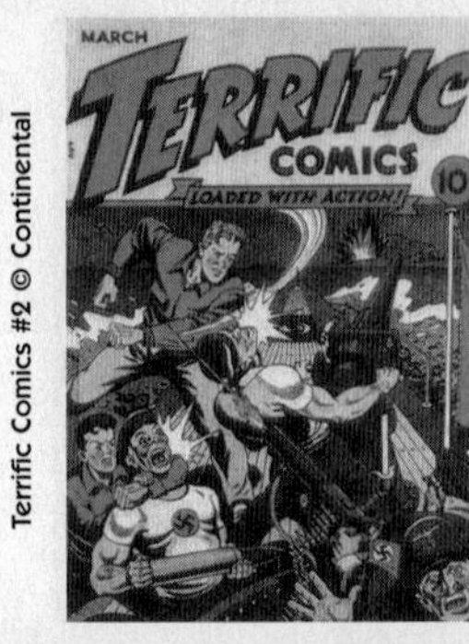

Terrific Comics #2 © Continental

Terrors of the Jungle #21 © STAR

	GD	VG	FN	VF	VF/NM	NM-
	2.0	4.0	6.0	8.0	9.0	9.2

0-Salvation Movie Preview (4/09) Mariotte-s/Figueroa-a 4.00

TERMINATOR, THE: SECONDARY OBJECTIVES
Dark Horse Comics: July, 1991 - No. 4, Oct, 1991 ($2.50, limited series)
1-4: Gulacy-c/a(p) in all 3.00

TERMINATOR, THE: THE BURNING EARTH
Now Comics: V2#1, Mar, 1990 - V2#5, July, 1990 ($1.75, limited series)
V2#1: Alex Ross painted art (1st published work) 2 4 6 9 12 15
2-5: Ross-c/a in all 1 3 4 6 8 10
Trade paperback (1990, $9.95)-Reprints V2#1-5 12.00
Trade paperback (ibooks, 2003, $17.95)-Digitally remastered reprint 18.00

TERMINATOR, THE: THE DARK YEARS
Dark Horse Comics: Aug, 1999 - No. 4, Dec, 1999 ($2.95, limited series)
1-4-Alan Grant-s/Mel Rubi-a; Jae Lee-c 3.00

TERMINATOR, THE: THE ENEMY FROM WITHIN
Dark Horse Comics: Nov, 1991 - No. 4, Feb, 1992 ($2.50, limited series)
1-4: All have Simon Bisley painted-c 3.00

TERMINATOR, THE: 2029
Dark Horse Comics: Mar, 2010 - No. 3, May, 2010 ($3.50, limited series)
1-3: Kyle Reese before his time-jump to 1984; Zack Whedon-s/Andy MacDonald-a 3.50

TERMINATOR 2: CYBERNETIC DAWN
Malibu: Nov, 1995 - No.4, Feb, 1996; No. 0. Apr, 1996 ($2.50, lim. series)
0 (4/96, $2.95)-Erskine-c/a; flip book w/Terminator 2: Nuclear Twilight 3.00
1-4: Continuation of film. 3.00

TERMINATOR 2: INFINITY
Dynamite Entertainment: 2007 - No. 7 ($3.50)
1-7: 1-Furman-s/Raynor-a; 3 covers. 6,7-Painkiller Jane x-over 3.50

TERMINATOR 2: JUDGEMENT DAY
Marvel Comics: Early Sept, 1991 - No. 3, Early Oct, 1991 ($1.00, lim. series)
1-3: Based on movie sequel; 1-3-Same as nn issues 3.00
nn (1991, $4.95, squarebound, 68 pgs.)-Photo-c 5.00
nn (1991, $2.25, B&W, magazine, 68 pgs.) 3.00

TERMINATOR 2: NUCLEAR TWILIGHT
Malibu: Nov, 1995 - No.4, Feb, 1996; No. 0, Apr, 1996 ($2.50, lim. series)
0 (4/96, $2.95)-Erskine-c/a; flip book w/Terminator 2: Cybernetic Dawn 3.00
1-4:Continuation of film. 3.00

TERMINATOR 3: RISE OF THE MACHINES (... BEFORE THE RISE on cover)
Beckett Comics: July, 2003 - No. 6, Jan, 2004 ($5.95, limited series)
1-6: 1,2-Leads into movie; 2 covers on each. 3-6-Movie adaptation 6.00

TERM LIFE
Image Comics (Shadowline): Jan, 2011 ($16.99, graphic novel)
SC-Lieberman-s/Thornborrow-a/DeStefano-l 17.00

TERRA (See Supergirl (2005 series) #12)
DC Comics: Jan, 2009 - No. 4, Feb, 2009 ($2.99, limited series)
1-4-Conner-a/c. 1,2,4-Power Girl app. 2-4-Geo-Force app. 3.00
TPB (2009, $14.99) r/#1-4 & Supergirl #12 15.00

TERRAFORMERS
Wonder Color Comics: April, 1987 - No. 2, 1987 ($1.95, limited series)
1,2-Kelley Jones-a 3.00

TERRANAUTS
Fantasy General Comics: Aug, 1986 - No. 2, 1986 ($1.75, limited series)
1,2 3.00

TERRA OBSCURA (See Tom Strong)
America's Best Comics: Aug, 2003 - No. 6, Feb, 2004 ($2.95)
1-6-Alan Moore & Peter Hogan-s/Paquette-a 3.00
TPB (2004, $14.95) r/#1-6 15.00

TERRA OBSCURA VOLUME 2 (See Tom Strong)
America's Best Comics: Oct, 2004 - No. 6, May, 2005 ($2.95)
1-6-Alan Moore & Peter Hogan-s/Paquette-a; Tom Strange app. 3.00
TPB (2005, $14.99) r/#1-6 15.00

TERRARISTS
Marvel Comics (Epic): Nov, 1993 - No. 4, Feb, 1994 ($2.50, limited series)
1-4-Bound-in trading cards in all 3.00

TERRIFIC COMICS (Also see Suspense Comics)
Continental Magazines: Jan, 1944 - No. 6, Nov, 1944
1-Kid Terrific; opium story 326 652 978 2282 3991 5700
2-1st app. The Boomerang by L.B. Cole & Ed Wheelan's "Comics" McCormick, called the world's #1 comic book fan begins 232 464 696 1485 2543 3600
3-Diana becomes Boomerang's costumed aide; L.B. Cole-c 232 464 696 1485 2543 3600
4-Classic war-c (Scarce) 423 846 1269 3000 5250 7500
5-The Reckoner begins; Boomerang & Diana by L.B. Cole; Classic Schomburg bondage & hooded vigilante-c (Scarce) 1000 2000 3000 6000 11,000 16,000
6-L.B. Cole-c/a 210 420 630 1334 2292 3250
NOTE: ***L.B. Cole** a-1, 2(2), 3-6. **Fuje** a-5, 6. **Rico** a-2; c-1. **Schomburg** c-2, 5.*

TERRIFIC COMICS (Formerly Horrific; Wonder Boy #17 on)
Mystery Publ.(Comic Media)/(Ajax/Farrell): No. 14, Dec, 1954; No. 16, Mar, 1955 (No #15)
14-Art swipe/Advs. into the Unknown #37; injury-to-eye-c; pg. 2, panel 5 swiped from Phantom Stranger #4; surrealistic Palais-a; Human Cross story; classic-c 77 154 231 493 847 1200
16-Wonder Boy-c/story (last pre-code) 28 56 84 165 270 375

TERRIFYING TALES (Formerly Startling Terror Tales #10)
Star Publications: No. 11, Jan, 1953 - No. 15, Apr, 1954
11-Used in **POP**, pgs. 99,100; all Jo-Jo-r 49 98 147 309 522 735
12-Reprints Jo-Jo #19 entirely; L.B. Cole splash 47 94 141 296 503 710
13-All Rulah-r; classic devil-c 53 106 159 334 567 800
14-All Rulah reprints 44 88 132 277 469 660
15-Rulah, Zago-r; used in **SOTI**-r/Rulah #22 44 88 132 277 469 660
NOTE: *All issues have **L.B. Cole** covers; bondage covers-No. 12-14.*

TERROR ILLUSTRATED (Adult Tales of...)
E.C. Comics: Nov-Dec, 1955 - No. 2, Spring (April on-c), 1956 (Magazine, 25¢)
1-Adult Entertainment on-c 21 42 63 122 199 275
2-Charles Sultan-a 15 30 45 88 137 185
NOTE: ***Craig, Evans, Ingels, Orlando** art in each. **Crandall** c-1, 2.*

TERROR INC. (See A Shadowline Saga #3)
Marvel Comics: July, 1992 - No. 13, July, 1993 ($1.75)
1-8,11-13: 6,7-Punisher-c/story. 13-Ghost Rider app. 3.00
9,10-Wolverine-c/story 4.00

TERROR INC.
Marvel Comics (MAX): Oct, 2007 - No. 5, Apr, 2008 ($3.99, limited series)
1-5: 1-Lapham-s/Zircher-a; origin of Mr. Terror retold 4.00

TERROR INC. - APOCALYPSE SOON
Marvel Comics (MAX): July, 2009 - No. 4, Sept, 2009 ($3.99, limited series)
1-4: 1-Lapham-s/Turnbull-a 4.00

TERRORS OF DRACULA (Magazine)
Modern Day Periodical/Eerie Publ.: Vol. 1 #3, May, 1979 - Vol. 3 #2, Sept, 1981 (B&W)
Vol. 1 #3 (5/79, 1st issue) 4 8 12 26 41 55
#4(8/79), #5(11/79) 3 6 9 20 30 40
Vol. 2 #1-3: 1-(2/80). 2-(5/80). 3-(8/80) 3 6 9 17 25 32
Vol. 3 #1 (5/81), #2 (9/81) 3 6 9 19 29 38

TERRORS OF THE JUNGLE (Formerly Jungle Thrills)
Star Publications: No. 17, 5/52 - No. 21, 2/53; No. 4, 4/53 - No. 10, 9/54
17-Reprints Rulah #21, used in **SOTI**; L.B. Cole bondage-c 48 96 144 302 514 725
18-Jo-Jo-r 37 74 111 222 361 500
19,20(1952)-Jo-Jo-r; Disbrow-a 36 72 108 211 343 475
21-Jungle Jo, Tangi-r; used in **POP**, pg. 100 & color illos. 39 78 117 231 378 525
4-10: All Disbrow-a. 5-Jo-Jo-r. 8-Rulah, Jo-Jo-r. 9-Jo-Jo-r; Disbrow-a; Tangi by Orlando10-Rulah-r 39 78 117 231 378 525
NOTE: ***L.B. Cole** c-all; bondage c-17, 19, 21, 5, 7.*

TERROR TALES (See Beware Terror Tales)

TERROR TALES (Magazine)
Eerie Publications: V1#7, 1969 - V6#6, Dec, 1974; V7#1, Apr, 1976 - V10, 1979? (V1-V6: 52 pgs.; V7 on: 68 pgs.)
V1#7 7 14 21 47 76 105
V1#8-11('69): 9-Bondage-c 5 10 15 30 48 65
V2#1-6('70), V3#1-6('71), V4#1-7('72), V5#1-6('73), V6#1-6('74), V7#1,4('76) (no V7#2), V8#1-3('77) 4 8 12 26 41 55
V7#3-(7/76) LSD story-r/Weird V3#5 4 8 12 26 41 55
V9#2-4, V10#1(1/79) 4 8 12 28 44 60

TERROR TITANS

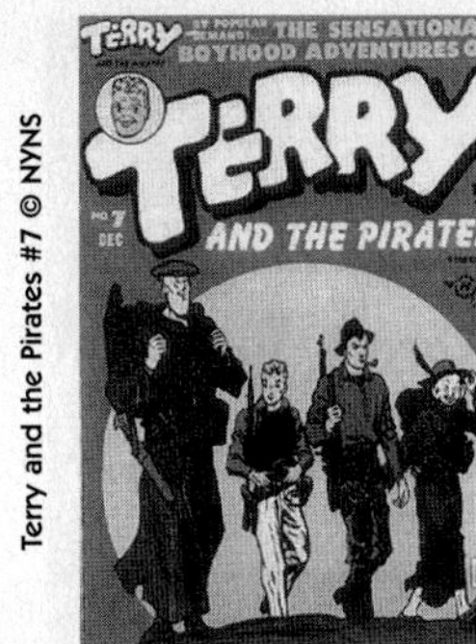

Terry and the Pirates #7 © NYNS

Tessie the Typist #11 © MAR

The Texan #4 © STJ

	GD 2.0	VG 4.0	FN 6.0	VF 8.0	VF/NM 9.0	NM- 9.2

DC Comics: Dec, 2008 - No. 6, May, 2009 ($2.99, limited series)

1-6: 1-Ravager and Clock King at the Dark Side Club; Bennett-a. 3-Static app. 3.00
TPB (2009, $17.99) r/#1-6 18.00

TERRY AND THE PIRATES (See Famous Feature Stories, Merry Christmas From Sears Toyland, Popular Comics, Super Book #3,5,9,16,28, & Super Comics)

TERRY AND THE PIRATES
Dell Publishing Co.: 1939 - 1953 (By Milton Caniff)

	GD	VG	FN	VF	VF/NM	NM-
Large Feature Comic 2(1939)	87	174	261	553	952	1350
Large Feature Comic 6(1938)-r/1936 dailies	71	142	213	454	777	1100
Four Color 9(1940)	67	134	201	426	731	1035
Large Feature Comic 27('41), 6('42)	57	114	171	362	624	885
Four Color 44('43)	32	64	96	250	495	740
Four Color 101('45)	20	40	60	144	290	435
Family Album(1942)	20	40	60	114	182	250

TERRY AND THE PIRATES (Formerly Boy Explorers; Long John Silver & the Pirates #30 on) (Daily strip-r) (Two #26's)
Harvey Publications/Charlton No. 26-28: No. 3, 4/47 - No. 26, 4/51; No. 26, 6/55 - No. 28, 10/55

	GD	VG	FN	VF	VF/NM	NM-
3(#1)-Boy Explorers by S&K; Terry & the Pirates begin by Caniff; 1st app. The Dragon Lady	39	78	117	231	378	525
4-S&K Boy Explorers	22	44	66	132	216	300
5-11: 11-Man in Black app. by Powell	13	26	39	72	101	130
12-20: 16-Girl threatened with red hot poker	10	20	30	56	76	95
21-26(4/51)-Last Caniff issue & last pre-code issue	10	20	30	54	72	90
26-28('55)(Formerly This Is Suspense)-No Caniff-a	9	18	27	47	61	75

NOTE: *Powell a (Tommy Tween)-5-10, 12, 14; 15-17(1/2 to 2 pgs. each).*

TERRY BEARS COMICS (TerryToons, The... #4)
St. John Publishing Co.: June, 1952 - No. 3, Mar, 1953

	GD	VG	FN	VF	VF/NM	NM-
1-By Paul Terry	10	20	30	54	72	90
2,3	7	14	21	35	43	50

TERRY-TOONS ALBUM (See Giant Comics Edition)

TERRY-TOONS COMICS (1st Series) (Becomes Paul Terry's Comics #85 on; later issues titled "Paul Terry's...")
Timely/Marvel No. 1-59 (8/47)(Becomes Best Western No. 58 on?, Marvel)/ St. John No. 60 (9/47) on: Oct, 1942 - No. 86, May, 1951

	GD	VG	FN	VF	VF/NM	NM-
1 (Scarce)-Features characters that 1st app. on movie screen; Gandy Goose & Sourpuss begin; war-c; Gandy Goose c-1-37	213	426	639	1363	2332	3300
2	71	142	213	454	777	1100
3-5	50	100	150	315	533	750
6,8-10: 9,10-World War II gag-c	39	78	117	231	378	525
7-Hitler, Hirohito, Mussolini-c	77	154	231	493	847	1200
11-20	26	52	78	154	252	350
21-37	19	38	57	109	172	235
38-Mighty Mouse begins (1st app., 11/45); Mighty Mouse-c begin, end #86; Gandy, Sourpuss welcome Mighty Mouse on-c	181	362	543	1158	1979	2800
39-2nd app. Mighty Mouse	55	110	165	352	601	850
40-49: 43-Infinity-c	30	60	90	177	289	400
50-1st app. Heckle & Jeckle (11/46)	47	94	141	296	498	700
51-60: 55-Infinity-c. 60-(9/47)-Atomic explosion panel; 1st St. John issue	17	34	51	98	154	210
61-86: 85,86-Same book as Paul Terry's Comics #85,86 with only a title change; published at same time?	15	30	45	83	124	165

TERRY-TOONS COMICS (2nd Series)
St. John Publishing Co./Pines: June, 1952 - No. 9, Nov, 1953; 1957; 1958

	GD	VG	FN	VF	VF/NM	NM-
1-Gandy Goose & Sourpuss begin by Paul Terry	18	36	54	105	165	225
2	10	20	30	56	76	95
3-9	9	18	27	52	69	85
Giant Summer Fun Book 101,102-(Sum, 1957, Sum, 1958, 25¢, Pines)(TV) CBS Television Presents...; Tom Terrific, Mighty Mouse, Heckle & Jeckle Gandy Goose app.	14	28	42	80	115	150

TERRYTOONS, THE TERRY BEARS (Formerly Terry Bears Comics)
Pines Comics: No. 4, Summer, 1958 (CBS Television Presents...)

	GD	VG	FN	VF	VF/NM	NM-
4	7	14	21	35	43	50

TESSIE THE TYPIST (Tiny Tessie #24; see Comedy Comics, Gay Comics & Joker Comics)
Timely/Marvel Comics (20CC): Summer, 1944 - No. 23, Aug, 1949

	GD	VG	FN	VF	VF/NM	NM-
1-Doc Rockblock & others by Wolverton	90	180	270	576	988	1400
2-Wolverton's Powerhouse Pepper	42	84	126	265	445	625
3-(3/45)-No Wolverton	21	42	63	122	199	275
4,5,7,8-Wolverton-a. 4-(Fall/45)	34	68	102	199	325	450
6-Kurtzman's "Hey Look", 2 pgs. Wolverton-a	34	68	102	199	325	450
9-Wolverton's Powerhouse Pepper (8 pgs.) & 1 pg. Kurtzman's "Hey Look"	36	72	108	216	351	485
10-Wolverton's Powerhouse Pepper (4 pgs.)	34	68	102	199	325	450
11-Wolverton's Powerhouse Pepper (8 pgs.)	36	72	108	216	351	485
12-Wolverton's Powerhouse Pepper (4 pgs.) & 1 pg. Kurtzman's "Hey Look"	34	68	102	199	325	450
13-Wolverton's Powerhouse Pepper (4 pgs.)	34	68	102	199	325	450
14,15: 14-Wolverton's Dr. Whackyhack (1 pg.); 1-1/2 pgs. Kurtzman's "Hey Look". 15-Kurtzman's "Hey Look" (3 pgs.) & 3 pgs. Giggles 'n' Grins	24	48	72	142	234	325
16-18-Kurtzman's "Hey Look" (?, 2 & 1 pg.)	19	38	57	109	172	235
19-Annie Oakley story (8 pgs.)	14	28	42	82	121	160
20-23: 20-Anti-Wertham editorial (2/49)	14	28	42	80	115	150

NOTE: *Lana app.-21. Millie The Model app.-13, 15, 17, 21. Rusty app.-10, 11, 13, 15, 17.*

TESTAMENT
DC Comics (Vertigo): Feb, 2006 - No. 22, Mar, 2008 ($2.99)

1-22: 1-5-Rushkoff-s/Sharp-a. 6,7-Gross & Erskine-a 3.00
...: Akedah TPB (2006, $9.99) r/#1-5; Rushkoff intro. 10.00
...: Babel TPB (2007, $12.99) r/#11-16 13.00
...: Exodus TPB (2008, $14.99) r/#17-22 15.00
...: West of Eden TPB (2007, $12.99) r/#6-10; Rushkoff commentary 13.00

TEXAN, THE (Fightin' Marines #15 on; Fightin' Texan #16 on)
St. John Publishing Co.: Aug, 1948 - No. 15, Oct, 1951

	GD	VG	FN	VF	VF/NM	NM-
1-Buckskin Belle	16	32	48	94	147	200
2	10	20	30	58	79	100
3,10: 10-Oversized issue	10	20	30	58	79	100
4,5,7,15-Baker-c/a	21	42	63	126	206	285
6,9-Baker-c	16	32	48	94	147	200
8,11,13,14-Baker-c/a(2-3) each	24	48	72	142	234	325
12-All Matt Baker-c/a; Peyote story	30	60	90	177	289	400

NOTE: ***Matt Baker** c-4-9, 11-15. **Larsen** a-4-6, 8-10, 15. **Tuska** a-1, 2, 7-9.*

TEXAN, THE (TV)
Dell Publishing Co.: No. 1027, Sept-Nov, 1959 - No. 1096, May-July, 1960

	GD	VG	FN	VF	VF/NM	NM-
Four Color 1027 (#1)-Photo-c	8	16	24	56	93	130
Four Color 1096-Rory Calhoun photo-c	8	16	24	52	86	120

TEXAS CHAINSAW MASSACRE
DC Comics (WildStorm): Jan, 2007 - No. 6, Jun, 2007 ($2.99, limited series)

1-6: 1-Two covers by Bermejo & Bradstreet; Abnett & Lanning-s 3.00
...: About a Boy #1 (9/07, $2.99) Abnett & Lanning-s/Gomez-a/Robertson-c 3.00
...: Book Two TPB (2009, $14.99) r/one shots & New Line Cinema's Tales of Horror story 15.00
...: By Himself #1 (10/07, $2.99) Abnett & Lanning-s/Craig-a/Robertson-c 3.00
...: Cut! #1 (8/07, $2.99) Pfeiffer-s/Raffaele-a/Robertson-c 3.00
...: Raising Cain 1-3 (7/08 - No. 3, 9/08, $3.50) Bruce Jones-s/Chris Gugliotti-a 3.50

TEXAS JOHN SLAUGHTER (See Walt Disney Presents, 4-Color #997, 1181 & #2)

TEXAS KID (See Two-Gun Western, Wild Western)
Marvel/Atlas Comics (LMC): Jan, 1951 - No. 10, July, 1952

	GD	VG	FN	VF	VF/NM	NM-
1-Origin; Texas Kid (alias Lance Temple) & his horse Thunder begin; Tuska-a	23	46	69	136	223	310
2	13	26	39	74	105	135
3-10	10	20	30	56	76	95

NOTE: ***Maneely** a-1-4; c-1, 3, 5-10.*

TEXAS RANGERS, THE (See Jace Pearson of... and Superior Stories #4)

TEXAS RANGERS IN ACTION (Formerly Captain Gallant or Scotland Yard?)
Charlton Comics: No. 5, Jul, 1956 - No. 79, Aug, 1970 (See Blue Bird Comics)

	GD	VG	FN	VF	VF/NM	NM-
5	8	16	24	44	57	70
6,7,9,10	6	12	18	28	34	40
8-Ditko-a (signed)	10	20	30	54	72	90
11-(68 pg. Giant) Williamson-a (5&8 pgs.); Torres/Williamson-a (5 pgs.)	10	20	30	54	72	90
12,14-20: 12-(68 pg. Giant, 6/58)	5	10	15	23	28	32
13-Williamson-a (5 pgs); Torres, Morisi-a	8	16	24	42	54	65
21-30	3	6	9	16	22	28
31-59: 32-Both 10¢-c & 15¢-c exist	2	4	6	13	18	22
60-Riley's Rangers begin	3	6	9	14	19	24
61-65,68-70	2	4	6	8	11	14
66,67: 66-1st app. The Man Called Loco. 67-Origin	2	4	6	9	13	16
71-79: 77-(4/70) Ditko-c & a (8 pgs.)	1	3	4	6	8	10
76 (Modern Comics-r, 1977)						4.00

TEXAS SLIM (See A-1 Comics)

Tex Ritter Western #1 © FAW

Thanos Imperative #3 © MAR

The Thing! #12 © CC

GD VG FN VF VF/NM NM-
2.0 4.0 6.0 8.0 9.0 9.2

TEX DAWSON, GUN-SLINGER (Gunslinger #2 on)
Marvel Comics Group: Jan, 1973 (20¢)(Also see Western Kid, 1st series)
1-Steranko-c; Williamson-r (4 pgs.); Tex Dawson-r by Romita(3) from 1955; Tuska-r 3 6 9 18 27 35

TEX FARNUM (See Wisco)

TEX FARRELL (...Pride of the Wild West)
D. S. Publishing Co.: Mar-Apr, 1948
1-Tex Farrell & his horse Lightning; Shelly-c 15 30 45 88 137 185

TEX GRANGER (Formerly Calling All Boys; see True Comics)
Parents' Magazine Inst./Commended: No. 18, Jun, 1948 - No. 24, Sept, 1949
18-Tex Granger & his horse Bullet begin 12 24 36 67 94 120
19 10 20 30 54 72 90
20-24: 22-Wild Bill Hickok story. 23-Vs. Billy the Kid; Tim Holt app. 8 16 24 44 57 70

TEX MORGAN (See Blaze Carson and Wild Western)
Marvel Comics (CCC): Aug, 1948 - No. 9, Feb, 1950
1-Tex Morgan, his horse Lightning & sidekick Lobo begin 28 56 84 165 270 375
2 18 36 54 105 165 225
3-6: 3,4-Arizona Annie app. 14 28 42 76 108 140
7-9: All photo-c. 7-Captain Tootsie by Beck. 8-18 pg. story "The Terror of Rimrock Valley"; Diablo app. 18 36 54 105 165 225
NOTE: *Tex Taylor app.-6, 7, 9.* ***Brodsky*** *c-6.* ***Syd Shores*** *c-2, 5.*

TEX RITTER WESTERN (Movie star; singing cowboy; see Six-Gun Heroes and Western Hero)
Fawcett No. 1-20 (1/54)/Charlton No. 21 on: Oct, 1950 - No. 46, May, 1959 (Photo-c: 1-21)
1-Tex Ritter, his stallion White Flash & dog Fury begin; photo front/back-c begin 43 86 129 271 461 650
2 21 42 63 124 202 280
3-5: 5-Last photo back-c 16 32 48 94 147 200
6-10 14 28 42 80 115 150
11-19 10 20 30 58 79 100
20-Last Fawcett issue (1/54) 11 22 33 62 86 110
21-1st Charlton issue; photo-c (3/54) 14 28 42 80 115 150
22-B&W photo back-c begin, end #32 9 18 27 52 69 85
23-30: 23-25-Young Falcon app. 9 18 27 47 61 75
31-38,40-45 8 16 24 42 54 65
39-Williamson-a; Whitman-c (1/58) 9 18 27 47 61 75
46-Last issue 8 16 24 44 57 70

TEX TAYLOR (...The Fighting Cowboy on-c #1, 2)(See Blaze Carson, Kid Colt, Tex Morgan, Wild West, Wild Western, & Wisco)
Marvel Comics (HPC): Sept, 1948 - No. 9, March, 1950
1-Tex Taylor & his horse Fury begin 29 58 87 170 278 385
2 15 30 45 88 137 185
3 14 28 42 82 121 160
4-6: All photo-c. 4-Anti-Wertham editorial. 5,6-Blaze Carson app. 15 30 45 92 144 195
7-9: 7-Photo-c;18 pg. Movie-Length Thriller "Trapped in Time's Lost Land!" with sabretoothed tigers, dinosaurs; Diablo app. 8-Photo-c; 18 pg. Movie-Length Thriller "The Mystery of Devil-Tree Plateau!" with dwarf horses, dwarf people & a lost miniature Inca type village; Diablo app. 9-Photo-c; 18 pg. Movie-Length Thriller "Guns Along the Border!" Captain Tootsie by Schreiber; Nimo the Mountain Lion app. 19 38 57 109 172 235
NOTE: ***Syd Shores*** *c-1-3.*

THANE OF BAGARTH (Also see Hercules, 1967 series)
Charlton Comics: No. 24, Oct, 1985 - No. 25, Dec, 1985
24,25-Low print run 6.00

THANOS
Marvel Comics: Dec, 2003 - No. 12, Sept, 2004 ($2.99)
1-12: 1-6-Starlin-s/a(p)/Milgrom-i; Galactus app. 7-12-Giffen-s/Lim-a 3.00
Vol. 4: Epiphany TPB (2004, $14.99) r/#1-6 15.00
Vol. 5: Samaritan TPB (2004, $14.99) r/#7-12 15.00

THANOS IMPERATIVE, THE
Marvel Comics: Aug, 2010 - No. 6, Jan, 2011 ($3.99, limited series)
1-6-Abnett & Lanning-s/Sepulveda-a; Vision and Silver Surfer app. 4.00
...: Devastation (3/11, $3.99) Sepulveda-a; leads into The Annihilators #1 4.00
...: Ignition (7/10, $3.99) Walker-a; prequel to series 4.00
Thanos Sourcebook (8/10, $3.99) profiles/history of Thanos and Nova Corps members 4.00

THANOS QUEST, THE (See Capt. Marvel #25, Infinity Gauntlet, Iron Man #55, Logan's Run, Marvel Feature #12, Marvel Universe: The End, Silver Surfer #34 & Warlock #9)
Marvel Comics: 1990 - No. 2, 1990 ($4.95, squarebound, 52 pgs.)
1,2-Both have Starlin scripts & covers (both printings) 1 2 3 4 5 7
1-(3/2000, $3.99) r/material from #1&2 4.00

THAT DARN CAT (See Movie Comics & Walt Disney Showcase #19)

THAT'S MY POP! GOES NUTS FOR FAIR
Bystander Press: 1939 (76 pgs., B&W)
nn-by Milt Gross 32 64 96 188 307 425

THAT WILKIN BOY (Meet Bingo...)
Archie Publications: Jan, 1969 - No. 52, Oct, 1982
1-1st app. Bingo's Band, Samantha & Tough Teddy 4 8 12 28 44 60
2-5 3 6 9 16 23 30
6-11 2 4 6 13 18 22
12-26-Giants. 12-No # on-c 3 6 9 14 20 26
27-40(1/77) 2 4 6 8 10 12
41-49 1 2 3 4 5 7
50-52 (low print) 2 4 6 8 10 12

THB
Horse Press: Oct, 1994 - Present ($5.50/$2.50/$2.95, B&W)
1 ($5.50) Paul Pope-s/a in all 1 2 3 5 6 8
1 (2nd Printing)-r/#1 w/new material 3.00
2 ($2.50) 5.00
3-5 4.00
69 (1995, no price, low distribution, 12 pgs.)-story reprinted in #1 (2nd Printing) 3.00
Giant THB-($4.95) 5.00
Giant THB 1 V2-(2003, $6.95) 7.00
...M3/THB: Mars' Mightiest Mek #1 (2000, $3.95) 4.00
...6A: Mek-Power #1, 6B: Mek-Power #2, 6C: Mek-Power #3 (2000, $3.95) 4.00
... 6D: Mek-Power #4 (2002, $4.95) 5.00

T.H.E. CAT (TV)
Dell Publishing Co.: Mar, 1967 - No. 4, Oct, 1967 (All have photo-c)
1 4 8 12 22 34 45
2-4 3 6 9 17 25 32

THERE'S A NEW WORLD COMING
Spire Christian Comics/Fleming H. Revell Co.: 1973 (35/49¢)
nn 2 4 6 9 13 16

THEY ALL KISSED THE BRIDE (See Cinema Comics Herald)

THIEF OF BAGHDAD
Dell Publishing Co.: No. 1229, Oct-Dec, 1961 (one-shot)
Four Color 1229-Movie, Crandall/Evans-a, photo-c 7 14 21 45 73 100

THIMK (Magazine) (Satire)
Counterpoint: May, 1958 - No. 6, May, 1959
1 10 20 30 58 79 100
2-6 8 16 24 40 50 60

THING!, THE (Blue Beetle #18 on)
Song Hits No. 1,2/Capitol Stories/Charlton: Feb, 1952 - No. 17, Nov, 1954
1-Weird/horror stories in all; shrunken head-c 94 188 282 597 1024 1450
2,3 60 120 180 381 653 925
4-6,8,10: 5-Severed head-c; headlights 54 108 162 343 574 825
7-Injury to eye-c & inside panel 73 146 219 467 796 1125
9-Used in **SOTI**, pg. 388 & illo "Stomping on the face is a form of brutality which modern children learn early" 84 168 252 538 919 1300
11-Necronomicon story; Hansel & Gretel parody; Injury-to-eye panel; Check-a 66 132 198 419 722 1025
12-1st published Ditko-c; "Cinderella" parody; lingerie panels. Ditko-a 94 188 282 597 1024 1450
13,15-Ditko-c/a(3 & 5) 92 184 276 584 1005 1425
14-Extreme violence/torture; Rumpelstiltskin story; Ditko-c/a(4) 94 188 282 597 1024 1450
16-Injury to eye panel 34 68 102 206 336 465
17-Ditko-c; classic parody "Through the Looking Glass"; Powell-r/Beware Terror Tales #1 & recolored 82 164 246 528 902 1275
NOTE: *Excessive violence, severed heads, injury to eye are common No. 5 on.* ***Al Fago*** *c-4.* ***Forgione*** *c-1i, 2, 6, 8, 9. All* ***Ditko*** *issues #14, 15.* ***Giordano*** *a-6.*

THING, THE (See Fantastic Four, Marvel Fanfare, Marvel Feature #11,12, Marvel Two-In-One and Startling Stories:...- Night Falls on Yancy Street)
Marvel Comics Group: July, 1983 - No. 36, June, 1986
1-Life story of Ben Grimm; Byrne scripts begin 5.00

The Thing #1 © MAR

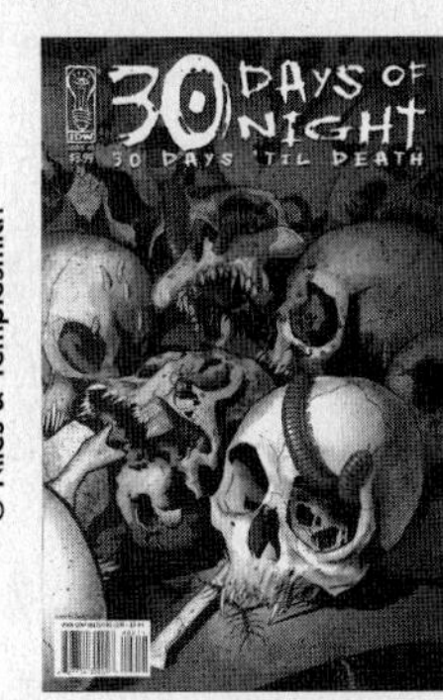
30 Days of Night: 30 Days 'Til Death #2 © Niles & Templesmith

This Magazine is Haunted #10 © FAW

GD 2.0 VG 4.0 FN 6.0 VF 8.0 VF/NM 9.0 NM- 9.2

2-36: 5-Spider-Man, She-Hulk app. 4.00
NOTE: *Byrne a-2i, 7; c-1, 7, 36i; scripts-1-13, 19-22. Sienkiewicz c-13i.*

THING, THE (Fantastic Four)
Marvel Comics: Jan, 2006 - No. 8 ($2.99)

1-8: 1-DiVito-a/Slott-s. 4-Lockjaw app. 6-Spider-Man app. 8-Super-Hero poker game 3.00
...: Idol of Millions TPB (2006, $20.99) r/#1-8; Divito sketch page 21.00

THING & SHE-HULK: THE LONG NIGHT (Fantastic Four)
Marvel Comics: May, 2002 ($2.99, one-shot)

1-Hitch-c/a(pg. 1-25); Reis-a(pg. 26-39); Dezago-s 3.00

THING, THE (From Another World)
Dark Horse Comics: 1991 - No. 2, 1992 ($2.95, mini-series, stiff-c)

1,2-Based on Universal movie; painted-c/a 3.00

THING, THE: FREAKSHOW (Fantastic Four)
Marvel Comics: Aug, 2002 - No. 4, Nov, 2002 ($2.99, limited series)

1-4-Geoff Johns-s/Scott Kolins-a 3.00
TPB (2005, $17.99) r/#1-4 & Thing & She-Hulk: The Long Night one-shot 18.00

THING FROM ANOTHER WORLD: CLIMATE OF FEAR, THE
Dark Horse Comics: July, 1992 - No. 4, Dec, 1992 ($2.50, mini-series)

1-4: Painted-c 3.00

THING FROM ANOTHER WORLD: ETERNAL VOWS
Dark Horse Comics: Dec, 1993 - No. 4, 1994 ($2.50, mini-series)

1-4-Gulacy-c/a 3.00

THIRD WORLD WAR
Fleetway Publ. (Quality): 1990 - No. 6, 1991 ($2.50, thick-c, mature)

1-6 3.00

THIRTEEN (...Going on 18)
Dell Publishing Co.: 11-1/61-62 - No. 25, 12/67; No. 26, 7/69 - No. 29, 1/71

	GD	VG	FN	VF	VF/NM	NM-
1	6	12	18	41	66	90
2-10	5	10	15	30	48	65
11-25	4	8	12	24	37	50
26-29-r	3	6	9	18	27	35

NOTE: *John Stanley script-No. 3-29; art?*

13: ASSASSIN
TSR, Inc.: 1990 - No. 8, 1991 ($2.95, 44 pgs.)

1-8: Agent 13; Alcala-a(i); Springer back-up-a 4.00

13th SON, THE
Dark Horse Comics: Nov, 2005 - No. 4, Feb, 2006 ($2.99, limited series)

1-4-Kelley Jones-s/a/c 3.00

30 DAYS OF NIGHT
Idea + Design Works: June, 2002 - No. 3, Oct, 2002 ($3.99, limited series)

1-Vampires in Alaska; Steve Niles-s/Ben Templesmith-a/Ashley Wood-c 30.00
1-2nd printing 10.00
2 12.00
3 10.00
Annual 2004 (1/04, $4.99) Niles-s/art by Templesmith and others 5.00
Annual 2005 (12/05, $7.49) Niles-s/art by Nat Jones 7.50
... 5th Anniversary (10/07 - No. 3, $2.99) reprints original series 3.00
... Sourcebook (10/07, $7.49) Illustrated guide to the 30 Days world 7.50
... Three Tales TPB (7/06, $19.99) r/Annual 2005, ...: Dead Space #1-3, and short story from Tales of Terror (IDW's...) 20.00
TPB (2003, $17.99) r/#1-3, foreword by Clive Barker; script for #1 18.00
The Complete 30 Days of Night (2004, $75.00, oversized hardcover with slipcase) r/#1-3; prequel; script pages for #1-3; original cover and promotional materials 75.00

30 DAYS OF NIGHT
IDW Publishing: July, 2004 (Free Comic Book Day edition)

Previews CSI: Bad Rap; The Shield: Spotlight; 24: One Shot; and 30 Days of Night 2.50

30 DAYS OF NIGHT: BEYOND BARROW
IDW Publishing: Sept, 2007 - No. 3, Dec, 2007 ($3.99, limited series)

1-3-Niles-s/Sienkiewicz-a/c 4.00

30 DAYS OF NIGHT: BLOODSUCKER TALES
IDW Publishing: Oct, 2004 - No. 8, May, 2005 ($3.99, limited series)

1-8-Niles-s/Chamberlain-a; Fraction-s/Templesmith-a/c 4.00
HC (8/05, $49.99) r/#1-8; cover gallery 50.00
SC (8/05, $24.99) r/#1-8; cover gallery 25.00

30 DAYS OF NIGHT: DEAD SPACE
IDW Publishing: Jan, 2006 - No. 3, Mar, 2006 ($3.99, limited series)

1-3-Niles and Wickline-s/Milx-a/c 4.00

30 DAYS OF NIGHT: EBEN & STELLA
IDW Publishing: May, 2007 - No. 3, July, 2007 ($3.99, limited series)

1-3-Niles and DeConnick-s/Randall-a/c 4.00

30 DAYS OF NIGHT: RED SNOW
IDW Publishing: Aug, 2007 - No. 3, Oct, 2007 ($3.99, limited series)

1-3-Ben Templesmith-s/a/c 4.00

30 DAYS OF NIGHT: RETURN TO BARROW
IDW Publishing: Mar, 2004 - No. 6, Aug, 2004 ($3.99, limited series)

1-6-Steve Niles-s/Ben Templesmith-a/c 4.00
TPB (2004, $19.99) r/#1-6; cover gallery 20.00

30 DAYS OF NIGHT: SPREADING THE DISEASE
IDW Publishing: Dec, 2006 - No. 5, Apr, 2007 ($3.99, limited series)

1-5: 1-Wickline-s/Sanchez-a. 3-5-Sandoval-a 4.00

30 DAYS OF NIGHT: 30 DAYS 'TIL DEATH
IDW Publishing: Dec, 2008 - No. 4, Mar, 2009 ($3.99, limited series)

1-4-David Lapham-s/a; covers by Lapham and Templesmith 4.00

THIRTY SECONDS OVER TOKYO (See American Library)

THIS IS SUSPENSE! (Formerly Strange Suspense Stories; Strange Suspense Stories #27 on)
Charlton Comics: No. 23, Feb, 1955 - No. 26, Aug, 1955

	GD	VG	FN	VF	VF/NM	NM-
23-Wood-a(r)/A Star Presentation #3 "Dr. Jekyll & Mr. Hyde"; last pre-code issue	24	48	72	140	230	320
24-Censored Fawcett-r; Evans-a (r/Suspense Detective #1)	14	28	42	80	115	150
25,26: 26-Marcus Swayze-a	10	20	30	56	76	95

THIS IS THE PAYOFF (See Pay-Off)

THIS IS WAR
Standard Comics: No. 5, July, 1952 - No. 9, May, 1953

	GD	VG	FN	VF	VF/NM	NM-
5-Toth-a	14	28	42	80	115	150
6,9-Toth-a	11	22	33	62	86	110
7,8: 8-Ross Andru-c	9	18	27	47	61	75

THIS IS YOUR LIFE, DONALD DUCK (See Donald Duck..., Four Color #1109)

THIS MAGAZINE IS CRAZY (Crazy #? on)
Charlton Publ. (Humor Magazines): V3#2, July, 1957 - V4#8, Feb, 1959 (25¢, magazine, 68 pgs.)

	GD	VG	FN	VF	VF/NM	NM-
V3#2-V4#7: V4#5-Russian Sputnik-c parody	10	20	30	56	76	95
V4#8-Davis-a (8 pgs.)	11	22	33	60	83	105

THIS MAGAZINE IS HAUNTED (Danger and Adventure #22 on)
Fawcett Publications/Charlton No. 15(2/54) on: Oct, 1951 - No. 14, 12/53; No. 15, 2/54 - V3#21, Nov, 1954

	GD	VG	FN	VF	VF/NM	NM-
1-Evans-a; Dr. Death as host begins	68	136	204	435	743	1050
2,5-Evans-a	45	90	135	284	480	675
3,4: 3-Vampire-c/story	36	72	108	216	351	485
6-9,11,12,14	27	54	81	160	263	365
10-Severed head-c	47	94	141	296	498	700
13-Severed head-c/story	45	90	135	284	480	675
15,20: 15-Dick Giordano-c. 20-Cover is swiped from panel in The Thing #16	22	44	66	132	216	300
16,19-Ditko-c. 19-Injury-to-eye panel; story-r/#1	41	82	123	249	417	585
17-Ditko-c/a(4); blood drainage story	48	96	144	302	514	725
18-Ditko-c/a(1 story); E.C. swipe/Haunt of Fear #5; injury-to-eye panel; reprints "Caretaker of the Dead" from Beware Terror Tales & recolored	42	84	126	265	445	625
21-Ditko-c, Evans-r/This Magazine Is Haunted #1	38	76	114	224	367	510

NOTE: *Baily a-1, 3, 4, 21r/#1. Moldoff c/a-1-13. Powell a-3-5, 11, 12, 17. Shuster a-18-20. Issues 19-21 have reprints which have been recolored from This Magazine is Haunted #1.*

THIS MAGAZINE IS HAUNTED (2nd Series) (Formerly Zaza the Mystic; Outer Space #17 on)
Charlton Comics: V2#12, July, 1957 - V2#16, May, 1958

	GD	VG	FN	VF	VF/NM	NM-
V2#12-14-Ditko-c/a in all	40	80	120	246	411	575
15-No Ditko-c/a	14	28	42	80	115	150
16-Ditko-a(4).	28	56	84	165	270	375

THIS MAGAZINE IS WILD (See Wild)

THIS WAS YOUR LIFE (Religious)
Jack T. Chick Publ.: 1964 (3 1/2 x 5 1/2", 40 pgs., B&W and red)

	GD	VG	FN	VF	VF/NM	NM-
nn, Another version (5x2 3/4", 26 pgs.)	2	4	6	10	14	18

Thor #160 © MAR

Thor #366 © MAR

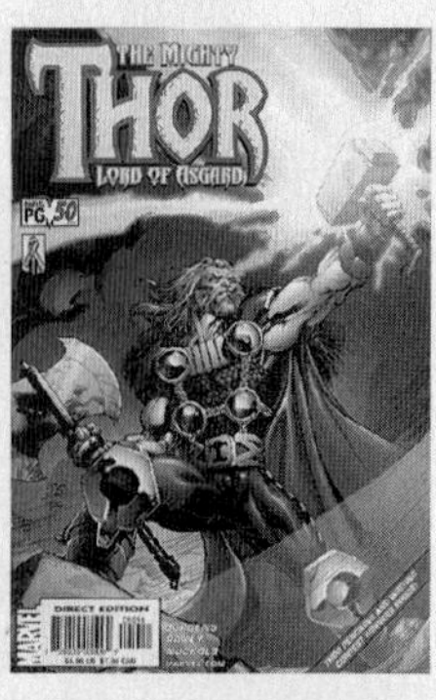

Thor V2 #50 © MAR

THOR (See Avengers #1, Giant-Size..., Marvel Collectors Item Classics, Marvel Graphic Novel #33, Marvel Preview, Marvel Spectacular, Marvel Treasury Edition, Special Marvel Edition & Tales of Asgard)

THOR (Journey Into Mystery #1-125, 503-on)(The Mighty Thor #413-490)
Marvel Comics Group: No. 126, Mar, 1966 - No. 502, Sept, 1996

	GD 2.0	VG 4.0	FN 6.0	VF 8.0	VF/NM 9.0	NM- 9.2
126-Thor continues (#125-130 Thor vs. Hercules)	24	48	72	175	350	525
127-130: 127-1st app. Pluto	11	22	33	75	138	200
131-133,135-140: 132-1st app. Ego. 136- Intro. Sif	9	18	27	65	113	160
134-Intro High Evolutionary	10	20	30	69	122	175
141-150: 146-Inhumans begin (early app.), end #151 (see Fantastic Four #45 for 1st app.). 146,147-Origin The Inhumans. 148-1st app. Wrecker. 148,149-Origin Black Bolt in each. 149-Origin Medusa, Crystal, Maximus, Gorgon, Karnak	8	16	24	56	93	130
151-157,159,160: 159-Origin Dr. Blake (Thor) concl.	7	14	21	49	80	110
158-Origin-r/#83; origin Dr. Blake	9	18	27	65	113	160
161,167,170-179: 179-Last Kirby issue	6	12	18	37	59	80
162,168,169-Origin Galactus; Kirby-a	7	14	21	45	73	100
163,164-2nd & 3th brief app. Warlock (Him)	6	12	18	37	59	80
165-1st full app. Warlock (Him) (6/69, see Fantastic Four #67); last 12¢ issue; Kirby-a	8	16	24	54	90	125
166-2nd full app. Warlock (Him); battles Thor	7	14	21	47	76	105
180,181-Neal Adams-a	6	12	18	41	66	90
182-192: 192-Last 15¢ issue	4	8	12	26	41	55
193-(25¢, 52 pgs.); Silver Surfer x-over	11	22	33	75	138	200
194-199	4	8	12	22	34	45
200	4	8	12	28	44	60
201-206,208-224	3	6	9	14	20	25
207-Rutland, Vermont Halloween x-over	3	6	9	16	22	28
225-Intro. Firelord	3	6	9	18	27	35
226-245: 226-Galactus app.	2	4	6	10	14	18
246-250-(Regular 25¢ editions)(4-8/76)	2	4	6	10	14	18
246-250-(30¢-c variants, limited distribution)	4	8	12	22	34	45
251-280: 271-Iron Man x-over. 274-Death of Balder the Brave	1	3	4	6	8	10
260-264-(35¢-c variants, limited distribution)(6-10/77)	4	8	12	22	34	45
281-299: 294-Origin Asgard & Odin	1	2	3	5	6	8
300-(12/80)-End of Asgard; origin of Odin & The Destroyer	2	4	6	8	10	12
301-336: 316-Iron Man x-over. 332,333-Dracula app.						5.00
337-Simonson-c/a begins, ends #382; Beta Ray Bill becomes new Thor	2	4	6	9	12	15
338-340: Beta Ray Bill app. 340-Donald Blake returns as Thor						6.00
341-373,375-381,383: 341-Clark Kent & Lois Lane cameo. 373-X-Factor tie-in						4.00
374-Mutant Massacre; X-Factor app.						5.00
382-($1.25)-Anniversary issue; last Simonson-a						6.00
384-Intro. new Thor						6.00
385-399,401-410,413-428: 385-Hulk x-over. 391-Spider-Man x-over; 1st Eric Masterson. 395-Intro Earth Force. 408-Eric Masterson becomes Thor. 427,428-Excalibur x-over						4.00
400,411: 400-($1.75, 68 pgs.)-Origin Loki. 411-Intro New Warriors (appears in costume in last panel); Juggernaut-c/story						6.00
412-1st full app. New Warriors (Marvel Boy, Kid Nova, Namorita, Night Thrasher, Firestar & Speedball)	1	2	3	4	5	7
429-431,434-443: 429,430-Ghost Rider x-over. 434-Capt. America x-over. 437-Thor vs. Quasar; Hercules app.;Tales of Asgard back-up stories begin. 443-Dr. Strange & Silver Surfer x-over; last $1.00-c						3.00
432,433: 432-(52 pgs.)-Thor's 350th issue (vs. Loki); reprints origin & 1st app. from Journey into Mystery #83. 433-Intro new Thor						4.00
444-449,451-473: 448-Spider-Man-c/story. 455,456-Dr. Strange back-up. 457-Old Thor returns (3 pgs.). 459-Intro Thunderstrike. 460-Starlin scripts begin. 465-Super Skrull app. 466-Drax app. 469,470-Infinity Watch x-over. 472-Intro the Godlings						3.00
450-($2.50, 68 pgs.)-Flip-book format; r/story JIM #85 (1st Loki) plus-c plus a gallery of past-c; gatefold-c						4.00
474,476-481,483-499: 474-Begin $1.50-c; bound-in trading cards. 490-The Absorbing Man app. 491-Warren Ellis scripts begins, ends #494; Deodato-c/a begins. 492-Reintro The Enchantress; Beta Ray Bill dies. 495-Wm. Messner-Loebs scripts begin; Isherwood-c/a.						3.00
475 ($2.00, 52 pgs.)-Regular edition						4.00
475 ($2.50, 52 pgs.)-Collectors edition w/foil embossed-c						5.00
482 ($2.95, 84 pgs.)-400th Thor issue						5.00
500 ($2.50)-Double-size; wraparound-c; Deodato-c/a; Dr. Strange app.						5.00
501-Reintro Red Norvell						4.00
502-Onslaught tie-in; Red Norvell, Jane Foster & Hela app.						5.00
600-up (See Thor 2007 series)						
Special 2(9/66)-(See Journey Into Mystery for 1st annual)	10	20	30	67	116	165
Special 2 (2nd printing, 1994)	2	4	6	8	10	12
King Size Special 3(1/71)	4	8	12	24	37	50
Special 4(12/71)-r/Thor #131,132 & JIM #113	3	6	9	20	30	40
Annual 5,6: 5(11/76). 6(10/77)-Guardians of the Galaxy app.	2	4	6	11	16	20
Annual 7,8: 7(1978). 8(1979)-Thor vs. Zeus-c/story	2	4	6	8	10	12
Annual 9-12: 9('81). 10('82). 11('83). 12('84)						6.00
Annual 13-19('85-'94, 68 pgs.):14-Atlantis Attacks. 16-3 pg. origin; Guardians of the Galaxy x-over.18-Polybagged w/card						4.00
...Alone Against the Celestials nn (6/92, $5.95)-r/Thor #387-389						6.00
...Legends Vol. 2: Walter Simonson Book 2 TPB (2003, $24.99) r/#349-355,357-359						25.00
...Legends Vol. 3: Walter Simonson Book 3 TPB (2004, $24.99) r/#360-369						25.00
...: The Eternals Saga TPB (2006, $24.99) r/#283-291 & Annual #7; profile pages						25.00
...: The Eternals Saga Vol. 2 TPB ('07, $24.99) r/#292-301; Thomas & Gruenwald essays						25.00
... Visionaries: Mike Deodato Jr. TPB (2004, $19.99) r/#491-494,498-500						20.00
... Visionaries: Walter Simonson (Vol. 1) TPB (5/01, $24.95) r/#337-348						25.00
... Visionaries: Walter Simonson Vol. 4 TPB (2007, $24.99) r/#371-373 & Balder the Brave #1-4						25.00
... Visionaries: Walter Simonson Vol. 5 TPB (2008, $24.95) r/#375-382						25.00
...: Worldengine (8/96, $9.95)-r/#491-494; Deodato-c/a; story & new intermission by Warren Ellis						10.00

NOTE: ***Neal Adams*** *a-180,181; c-179-181.* ***Austin*** *a-342i, 346i; c-312i.* ***Buscema*** *a(p)-178, 182-213, 215-226, 231-238, 241-253, 254r, 256-259, 272-278, 283-285, 370, Annual 6, 8, 11i; c(p)-175, 182-196, 198-200, 202-204, 206, 211, 212, 215, 219, 221, 226, 256, 259, 261, 262, 272-278, 283, 289, 370, Annual 6.* ***Everett*** *a(i)-143, 170-175; c(i)-171, 172, 174, 176, 241.* ***Gil Kane*** *a-318p; c(p)-201, 205, 207-210, 216, 220, 222, 223, 231, 233-240, 242, 243, 318.* ***Kirby*** *a(p)-126-177, 179, 194r, 254r; c(p)-126-169, 171-174, 176-178, 249-253, 255, 257, 258, Annual 5, Special 2-4.* ***Mooney*** *a(i)-201, 204, 214-216, 218, 322i, 324i, 325i, 327i.* ***Sienkiewicz*** *c-332, 333, 335.* ***Simonson*** *a-260-271p, 337-354, 357-367, 380, Annual 7p; c-260, 263-271, 337-355, 357-369, 371, 373-382, Annual 7.* ***Starlin*** *c-213.*

THOR (Volume 2)
Marvel Comics: July, 1998 - No. 85, Dec, 2004 ($2.99/$1.99/$2.25)

	GD 2.0	VG 4.0	FN 6.0	VF 8.0	VF/NM 9.0	NM- 9.2
1-($2.99)-Follows Heroes Return; Jurgens-s/Romita Jr. & Janson-a; wraparound-c; battles the Destroyer						6.00
1-Variant-c	1	2	3	5	6	8
1-Rough Cut-($2.99) Features original script and pencil pages						3.00
1-Sketch cover						20.00
2-($1.99) Two covers; Avengers app.						4.00
3-11,13-23: 3-Assumes Jake Olson ID. 4-Namor-c/app. 8-Spider-Man-c/app. 14-Iron Man c/app. 17-Juggernaut-c						3.00
12-($2.99) Wraparound-c; Hercules appears						4.00
12-($10.00) Variant-c by Jusko						10.00
24,26-31,33,34: 24-Begin $2.25-c. 26-Mignola-c/Larsen-a. 29-Andy Kubert-a. 30-Maximum Security x-over; Beta Ray Bill-c/app. 33-Intro. Thor Girl						3.00
25-($2.99) Regular edition						4.00
25-($3.99) Gold foil enhanced cover						5.00
32-($3.50, 100 pgs.) new story plus reprints w/Kirby-a; Simonson-a						5.00
35-($2.99) Thor battles The Gladiator; Andy Kubert-a						4.00
36-49,51-61: 37-Starlin-a. 38,39-BWS-c. 38-42-Immonen-a. 40-Odin killed. 41-Orbik-c. 44-'Nuff Said silent issue. 51-Spider-Man app. 57-Art by various. 58-Davis-a; x-over with Iron Man #64. 60-Brereton-c						3.00
50-($4.95) Raney-c/a; back-ups w/Nuckols-a & Armenta-s/Bennett-a						5.00
62-84: 62-Begin $2.99-c. 64-Loki-c/app. 80-Oeming-s begins; Avengers app.						3.00
85-Last issue; Thor dies; Oeming-s/DiVito-a/Epting-c						3.00
...1999 Annual ($3.50) Jurgens-s/a(p)						4.00
...2000 Annual ($3.50) Jurgens-s/Ordway-a(p); back-up stories						4.00
...2001 Annual ($3.50) Jurgens-s/Grummett-a(p); Lightle-c						4.00
...Across All Worlds (9/01, $19.95, TPB) r/#28-35						20.00
Avengers Disassembled: Thor TPB (2004, $16.99) r/#80-85; afterword by Oeming						17.00
...Resurrection ($5.99, TPB) r/#1,2						6.00
...: The Dark Gods (7/00, $15.95, TPB) r/#9-13						16.00
...Vol. 1: The Death of Odin (7/02, $12.99, TPB) r/#39-44						13.00
...Vol. 2: Lord of Asgard (9/02, $15.99, TPB) r/#45-50						16.00
...Vol. 3: Gods on Earth (2003, $21.99, TPB) r/#51-58, Avengers #63, Iron Man #64, Marvel Double-Shot #1; Beck-c						22.00
...Vol. 4: Spiral (2003, $19.99, TPB) r/#59-67; Brereton-c						20.00
...Vol. 5: The Reigning (2004, $17.99, TPB) r/#68-74						18.00
...Vol. 6: Gods and Men (2004, $13.99, TPB) r/#75-79						14.00

THOR (Also see Fantastic Four #538)(Resumes original numbering with #600)
Marvel Comics: Sept, 2007 - No. 12, Mar, 2009; No. 600, Apr, 2009 - No. 621, May, 2011 ($2.99/$3.99) (Continues numbering as Journey Into Mystery #622) (Also see Mighty Thor #1)

	GD 2.0	VG 4.0	FN 6.0	VF 8.0	VF/NM 9.0	NM- 9.2
1-Straczynski-s/Coipel-a/c						4.00
1-Variant-c by Michael Turner						5.00
1-Zombie variant-c by Suydam						5.00
1-Non-zombie variant-c by Suydam						5.00

Thor #620 © MAR

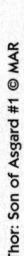

Thor: Son of Asgard #1 © MAR

Thor The Mighty Avenger #1 © MAR

GD VG FN VF VF/NM NM-
2.0 4.0 6.0 8.0 9.0 9.2

1-"Marvel's Geatest Comics" edition (5/10, $1.00) r/#1 1.00
2-12: 2-Two covers by Dell'Otto and Coipel. 3-Iron Man app.; McGuinness var-c. 4-Bermejo var-c. 5-Campbell var-c. 6-Art Adams var-c. 7,8-Djurdjevic-a/c; Coipel var-c 3.00
2-Second printing with wraparound-c 3.00

(After #12 [Mar, 2009] numbering reverted back to original Journey Into Mystery/Thor numbering with #600, Apr, 2009)

600 (4/09, $4.99) Two wraparound-c by Coipel & Djurdjevic; Coipel, Djurdjevic & Aja-a; r/Tales of Asgard from Journey Into Mystery #106,107,112,113,115; Kirby-a 5.00
601-603,611-621-($3.99) 601-603-Djurdjevic-a. 602-Sif returns. 617-Loki returns 4.00
604-610-($2.99) Tan-a. 607-609-Siege x-over. 610-Braithwaite-a; Ragnarok app. 3.00
620.1 (5/11, $2.99) Brooks-a; Grey Gargoyle app. 3.00
Annual 1 (11/09, $3.99) Suayan, Grindberg, Gaudiano-a; Djurdjevic-c 4.00
...: Ages of Thunder (6/08, $3.99) Fraction-s/Zircher-a/Djurdjevic-c 4.00
... & Hercules: Encyclopædia Mythologica (2009, $4.99) profile pages of the Pantheons 5.00
... Giant-Size Finale 1 (1/01, $3.99) Dr. Doom app.; r/origin from JIM #83 4.00
... God-Size Special (2/09, $3.99) story of Skurge the Executioner re-told; art by Brereton, Braithwaite, Allred and Sepulveda; plus reprint of Thor #362 (1985) 4.00
...: Man of War (1/09, $3.99) Fraction-s/Mann & Zircher-a/Djurdjevic-c 4.00
...: Reign of Blood (8/08, $3.99) Fraction-s/Evans & Zircher-a/Djurdjevic-c 4.00
...: Spotlight (5/11, $3.99) movie photo-c; movie preview; creator interviews 4.00
...: The Rage of Thor (10/10, $3.99) Milligan-s/Suayan-c/a 4.00
...: The Trial of Thor (8/09, $3.99) Milligan-s/Nord-c/a 4.00
...: Truth of History (12/08, $3.99) Thor and crew in ancient Egypt; Alan Davis-s/a/c 4.00
...: Whosoever Wields This Hammer 1 (6/11, $4.99) recolored r/J.I.M. #83,84,88 5.00
...: Wolves of the North (2/11, $3.99) Carey-s/Perkins-a 4.00
... By J. Michael Straczynski Vol. 1 HC (2008, $19.99) r/#1-6; variant cover gallery 20.00

THOR AND THE WARRIORS FOUR
Marvel Comics: Jun, 2010 - No. 4, Sept, 2010 ($2.99, limited series)
1-4-Thor and Power Pack team-up; Gurihiru-a; back-up with Coover-s/a 3.00

THOR: BLOOD OATH
Marvel Comics: Nov, 2005 - No. 6, Feb, 2006 ($2.99, limited series)
1-6-Oeming-s/Kolins-a/c 3.00
HC (2006, $19.99, dust jacket) r/series; afterword by Oeming 20.00
SC (2006, $14.99) r/series; afterword by Oeming 15.00

THOR CORPS
Marvel Comics: Sept, 1993 - No. 4, Jan, 1994 ($1.75, limited series)
1-4: 1-Invaders cameo. 2-Invaders app. 3-Spider-Man 2099, Rawhide Kid, Two-Gun Kid & Kid Colt app. 4-Painted-c 3.00

THOR: FIRST THUNDER
Marvel Comics: Nov, 2010 - No. 5, Mar, 2011 ($3.99, limited series)
1-5: 1-Huat-a; new retelling of origin; reprint of debut in JIM #83 4.00

THOR: FOR ASGARD
Marvel Comics: Nov, 2010 - No. 6, Apr, 2011 ($3.99, limited series)
1-6-Bianchi-a/c. 1-Frost Giants app. 4.00

THOR: GODSTORM
Marvel Comics: Nov, 2001 - No. 3, Jan, 2002 ($3.50, limited series)
1-3-Steve Rude-c/a; Busiek-s; Avengers app. 4.00

THORION OF THE NEW ASGODS
Marvel Comics (Amalgam): June, 1997 ($1.95, one-shot)
1-Keith Giffen-s/John Romita Jr.-c/a 3.00

THOR: SON OF ASGARD
Marvel Comics: May, 2004 - No. 12, Mar, 2005 ($2.99, limited series)
1-12: Teenaged Thor, Sif, and Balder; Tocchini-a. 1-6-Granov-c. 7-12-Jo Chen-c 3.00
... Vol. 1: The Warriors Teen (2004, $7.99, digest) r/#1-6 8.00
... Vol. 2: Worthy (2005, $7.99, digest) r/#7-12 8.00

THOR: TALES OF ASGARD BY STAN LEE & JACK KIRBY
Marvel Comics: 2009 - No. 6, 2009 ($3.99, limited series)
1-6-Reprints back-up stories from Journey Into Mystery #97-120; new covers by Coipel 4.00

THOR: THE LEGEND
Marvel Comics: Sept, 1996 ($3.95, one-shot)
nn-Tribute issue 4.00

THOR THE MIGHTY AVENGER
Marvel Comics: Sept, 2010 - No. 8, Mar, 2011 ($2.99, limited series)
1-8-Re-imagining of Thor's origin; Langridge-s/Samnee-a. 1-Mr. Hyde app. 3.00
Free Comic Book Day 2011 (giveaway) Captain America app. 2.50

THOR: VIKINGS

GD VG FN VF VF/NM NM-
2.0 4.0 6.0 8.0 9.0 9.2

Marvel Comics (MAX): Sept, 2003 - No. 5, Jan, 2004 ($3.50, limited series)
1-5-Garth Ennis-s/Glenn Fabry-a/c 3.50
TPB (2004, $13.99) r/series 14.00

THOSE MAGNIFICENT MEN IN THEIR FLYING MACHINES (See Movie Comics)

THRAX
Event Comics: Nov, 1996 ($2.95, one-shot)
1 3.00

THREE CABALLEROS (Walt Disney's...)
Dell Publishing Co.: No. 71, 1945
Four Color 71-by Walt Kelly, c/a 60 120 180 510 1030 1550

THREE CHIPMUNKS, THE (TV) (Also see Alvin)
Dell Publishing Co.: No. 1042, Oct-Dec, 1959
Four Color 1042 (#1)-(Alvin, Simon & Theodore) 8 16 24 56 93 130

THREE COMICS (Also see Spiritman)
The Penny King Co.: 1944 (10¢, 52 pgs.) (2 different covers exist)
1,3,4-Lady Luck, Mr. Mystic, The Spirit app. (3 Spirit sections bound together); Lou Fine-a 26 52 78 154 252 350
NOTE: *No. 1 contains Spirit Sections 4/9/44 - 4/23/44, and No. 4 is also from 4/44.*

3-D (NOTE: The prices of all the 3-D comics listed include glasses. Deduct 40-50 percent if glasses are missing, and reduce slightly if glasses are loose.)

3-D ACTION
Atlas Comics (ACI): Jan, 1954 (Oversized, 15¢)(2 pairs of glasses included)
1-Battle Brady; Sol Brodsky-c 39 78 117 236 388 540

3-D ADVENTURE COMICS
Stats, Etc.: Aug, 1986 (one shot)
1-Promo material 4.00

3-D ALIEN TERROR
Eclipse Comics: June, 1986 ($2.50)
1-Old Witch, Crypt-Keeper, Vault Keeper cameo; Morrow, John Pound-a, Yeates-c 6.00
...in 2-D: 100 copies signed, numbered(B&W) 1 3 4 8 10 12

3-D ANIMAL FUN (See Animal Fun)

THREE DAYS IN EUROPE
Oni Press: Nov, 2002 - No. 5, Apr, 2003 ($2.95, B&W, limited series)
1-5-Johnston-s/Hawthorne-a 3.00
TPB (11/03, $14.95, digest-sized) r/#1-5 15.00

3-D BATMAN (Also see Batman 3-D)
National Periodical Publications: 1953 (Reprinted in 1966)
1953-(25¢)-Reprints Batman #42 & 48 (Penguin-c/story); Tommy Tomorrow story; came with pair of 3-D Bat glasses 103 206 309 659 1130 1600
1966-Reprints 1953 issue; new cover by Infantino/Anderson; has inside-c photos of Batman & Robin from TV show (50¢) 21 42 63 150 300 450

3-D CIRCUS
Fiction House Magazines (Real Adventures Publ.): 1953 (25¢, w/glasses)
1 28 56 84 165 270 375

3-D COMICS (See Mighty Mouse, Tor and Western Fighters)

3-D DOLLY
Harvey Publications: December, 1953 (25¢, came with 2 pairs of glasses)
1-Richie Rich story redrawn from his 1st app. in Little Dot #1; shows cover in 3-D on inside 47 94 141 296 498 700

3-D-ELL
Dell Publishing Co.: No. 1, 1953; No. 3, 1953 (3-D comics) (25¢, came w/glasses)
1-Rootie Kazootie (#2 does not exist) 30 60 90 177 289 400
3-Flukey Luke 28 56 84 165 270 375

3-D EXOTIC BEAUTIES
The 3-D Zone: Nov, 1990 ($2.95, 28 pgs.)
1-L.B. Cole-c 1 2 3 5 7 9

3-D FEATURES PRESENTS JET PUP
Dimensions Publications: Oct-Dec (Winter on-c), 1953 (25¢, came w/glasses)
1-Irving Spector-a(2) 30 60 90 177 289 400

3-D FUNNY MOVIES
Comic Media: 1953 (25¢, came w/glasses)
1-Bugsey Bear & Paddy Pelican 34 68 102 199 325 450

THREE-DIMENSION ADVENTURES (Superman)

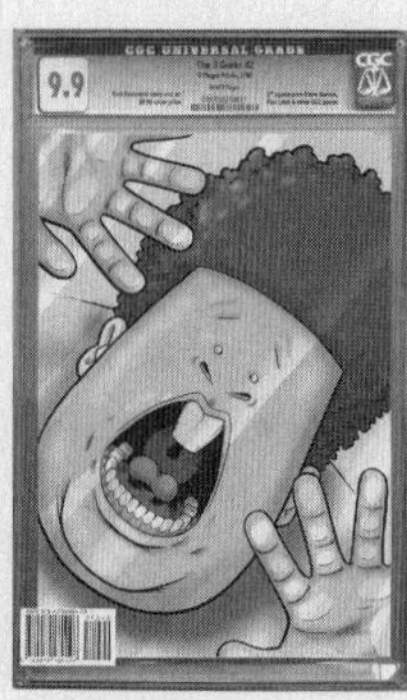

Three Geeks: Slab Madness! #2 © Rich Koslowski

Three Mouseketeers #21 © DC

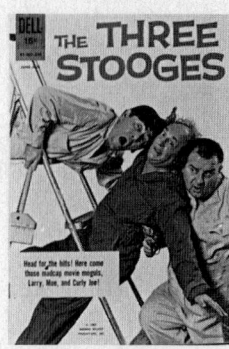

Three Stooges #39 © DELL

	GD 2.0	VG 4.0	FN 6.0	VF 8.0	VF/NM 9.0	NM- 9.2

National Periodical Publications: 1953 (25¢, large size, came w/glasses)
nn-Origin Superman (new art) 103 206 309 659 1130 1600

THREE DIMENSIONAL ALIEN WORLDS (See Alien Worlds)
Pacific Comics: July, 1984 (1st Ray Zone 3-D book)(one-shot)
1-Bolton-a(p); Stevens-a(i); Art Adams 1st published-a(p) 6.00

THREE DIMENSIONAL DNAGENTS (See New DNAgents)

THREE DIMENSIONAL E. C. CLASSICS (Three Dimensional Tales From the Crypt No. 2)
E. C. Comics: Spring, 1954 (Prices include glasses; came with 2 pair)
1-Stories by Wood (Mad #3), Krigstein (W.S. #7), Evans (F.C. #13), & Ingels (CSS #5); Kurtzman-c (rare in high grade due to unstable paper) 95 190 285 603 1039 1475
NOTE: *Stories redrawn to 3-D format. Original stories not necessarily by artists listed. CSS: Crime SuspenStories; F.C.: Frontline Combat; W.S.: Weird Science.*

THREE DIMENSIONAL TALES FROM THE CRYPT (Formerly Three Dimensional E. C. Classics)(Cover title: ...From the Crypt of Terror)
E. C. Comics: No. 2, Spring, 1954 (Prices include glasses; came with 2 pair)
2-Davis (TFTC #25), Elder (VOH #14), Craig (TFTC #24), & Orlando (TFTC #22) stories; Feldstein-c (rare in high grade) 94 188 282 597 1024 1450
NOTE: *Stories redrawn to 3-D format. Original stories not necessarily by artists listed. TFTC: Tales From the Crypt; VOH: Vault of Horror.*

3-D LOVE
Steriographic Publ. (Mikeross Publ.): Dec, 1953 (25¢, came w/glasses)
1 34 68 102 199 325 450

3-D NOODNICK (See Noodnick)

3-D ROMANCE
Steriographic Publ. (Mikeross Publ.): Jan, 1954 (25¢, came w/glasses)
1 34 68 102 199 325 450

3-D SHEENA, JUNGLE QUEEN (Also see Sheena 3-D)
Fiction House Magazines: 1953 (25¢, came w/glasses)
1-Maurice Whitman-c 68 136 204 432 746 1060

3-D SUBSTANCE
The 3-D Zone: July, 1990 ($2.95, 28 pgs.)
1-Ditko-c/a(r) 5.00

3-D TALES OF THE WEST
Atlas Comics (CPS): Jan, 1954 (Oversized) (15¢, came with 2 pair of glasses)
1 (3-D)-Sol Brodsky-c 39 78 117 231 378 525

3-D THREE STOOGES (Also see Three Stooges)
Eclipse Comics: Sept, 1986 - No. 2, Nov, 1986; No. 3, Oct, 1987; No. 4, 1989 ($2.50)
1-4: 3-Maurer-r. 4-r-/"Three Missing Links" 5.00
1-3 (2-D) 5.00

3-D WHACK (See Whack)

3-D ZONE, THE
The 3-D Zone (Renegade Press)/Ray Zone: Feb, 1987 - No. 20, 1989 ($2.50)
1,3,4,7-9,11,12,14,15,17,19,20: 1-r/A Star Presentation. 3-Picture Scope Jungle Advs. 4-Electric Fear. 7-Hollywood 3-D Jayne Mansfield photo-c. 8-High Seas 3-D, 9-Redmask-r. 11-Danse Macabre; Matt Fox c/a(r). 12-3-D Presidents. 14-Tyranostar. 15-3-Dementia Comics; Kurtzman-c, Kubert, Maurer-a. 17-Thrilling Love. 19-Cracked Classics. 20-Commander Battle and His Atomic Submarine 1 2 3 5 6 8
2,5,6,10,13,16,18: 2-Wolverton-r. 5-Krazy Kat-r. 6-Ratfink. 10-Jet 3-D; Powell & Williamson-r. 13-Flash Gordon. 16-Space Vixens; Dave Stevens-c/a. 18-Spacehawk; Wolverton-r 1 2 3 5 7 9
NOTE: ***Davis** r-19. **Ditko** r-19. **Elder** r-19. **Everett** r-19. **Feldstein** r-17. **Frazetta** r-17. **Heath** r-19. **Kamen** r-17. **Severin** r-19. **Ward** r-17,19. **Wolverton** r-2,18,19. **Wood** r-1,17. Photo c-12*

3 GEEKS, THE (Also see Geeksville)
3 Finger Prints: 1996 - No. 11, Jun, 1999 (B&W)
1,2 -Rich Koslowski-s/a in all 1 2 3 5 6 8
1-(2nd printing) 3.00
3-7, 9-11 3.00
8-(48 pgs.) 4.00
10-Variant-c 3.50
...48 Page Super-Sized Summer Spectacular (7/04, $4.95) 5.00
...Full Circle (7/03, $4.95) Origin story of the 3 Geeks; "Buck Rodinski" app. 5.00
How to Pick Up Girls If You're a Comic Book Geek (color)(7/97) 4.00
When the Hammer Fallls TPB (2001, $14.95) r/#8-11 15.00

3 GEEKS: SLAB MADNESS!
3 Finger Prints: Sept, 2008 - No. 3, Mar, 2009 ($2.99, B&W, limited series)
1-3-Rich Koslowski-s/a; intro. The Cee-Gee-Cee 3.00

300 (Adapted for 2007 movie)
Dark Horse Comics: May, 1998 - No. 5, Sept, 1998 ($2.95/$3.95, limited series)
1-Frank Miller-s/c/a; Spartans vs. Persians war 15.00
1-Second printing 5.00
2-4 8.00
5-($3.95-c) 12.00
HC ($30.00) -oversized reprint of series 30.00

3 LITTLE KITTENS
BroadSword Comics: Aug, 2002 - No. 3, Dec, 2002 ($2.95, limited series)
1-3-Jim Balent-s/a; two covers 3.00

3 LITTLE PIGS (Disney)(...and the Wonderful Magic Lamp)
Dell Publishing Co.: No. 218, Mar, 1949
Four Color 218 (#1) 10 20 30 70 125 180

3 LITTLE PIGS, THE (See Walt Disney Showcase #15 & 21)
Gold Key: May, 1964; No. 2, Sept, 1968 (Walt Disney)
1-Reprints Four Color #218 3 6 9 20 30 40
2 3 6 9 15 21 26

THREE MOUSEKETEERS, THE (1st Series)(See Funny Stuff #1)
National Per. Publ.: 3-4/56 - No. 24, 9-10/59; No. 25, 8-9/60 - No. 26, 10-12/60
1 18 36 54 131 266 400
2 10 20 30 70 125 180
3-5,7,9,10 8 16 24 52 86 120
6,8-Grey tone-c 9 18 27 65 113 160
11-26: 24-Cover says 11/59, inside says 9-10/59 7 14 21 47 76 105
NOTE: ***Rube Grossman** a-1-26. **Sheldon Mayer** a-1-8; c-1-7.*

THREE MOUSEKETEERS, THE (2nd Series) (See Super DC Giant)
National Periodical Publications: May-June, 1970 - No. 7, May-June, 1971 (#5-7: 68 pgs.)
1-Mayer-r in all 6 12 18 39 62 85
2-4: 4-Doodles Duck begins (1st app.) 4 8 12 24 37 50
5-7:(68 pgs.). 5-Dodo & the Frog, Bo Bunny begin 5 10 15 35 55 75

THREE MUSKETEERS, THE (Also see Disney's The Three Musketeers)
Gemstone Publishing: 2004 ($3.95, squarebound, one-shot)
nn-Adaptation of the 2004 DVD movie; Petrossi-c/a 4.00

THREE NURSES (Confidential Diary #12-17; Career Girl Romances #24 on)
Charlton Comics: V3#18, May, 1963 - V3#23, Mar, 1964
V3#18-23 3 6 9 18 27 35

THREE RASCALS
I. W. Enterprises: 1958; 1963
I.W. Reprint #1,2,10: 1-(Says Super Comics on inside)-(M.E.'s Clubhouse Rascals) DeCarlo-a. #2-(1958). 10-(1963)-r/#1 2 4 6 8 10 12

THREE RING COMICS
Spotlight Publishers: March, 1945
1-Funny animal 16 32 48 92 144 195

THREE RING COMICS (Also see Captain Wizard & Meteor Comics)
Century Publications: April, 1946
1-Prankster-c; Captain Wizard, Impossible Man, Race Wilkins, King O'Leary, & Dr. Mercy app. 35 70 105 208 339 470

THREE ROCKETEERS (See Blast-Off)

THREE STOOGES (See Comic Album #18, Top Comics, The Little Stooges, March of Comics #232, 248, 268, 280, 292, 304, 316, 336, 373, Movie Classics & Comics & 3-D Three Stooges)

THREE STOOGES
Jubilee No. 1/St. John No. 1 (9/53) on: Feb, 1949 - No. 2, May, 1949; Sept, 1953 - No. 7, Oct, 1954
1-(Scarce, 1949)-Kubert-a; infinity-c 116 232 348 742 1271 1800
2-(Scarce)-Kubert, Maurer-a 81 162 243 518 884 1250
1(9/53)-Hollywood Stunt Girl by Kubert (7 pgs.) 68 136 204 432 746 1060
2(3-D, 10/53, 25¢)-Came w/glasses; Stunt Girl story by Kubert 41 82 123 256 428 600
3(3-D, 10/53, 25¢)-Came w/glasses; has 3-D-c 39 78 117 240 395 550
4(3/54)-7(10/54): 4-1st app. Li'l Stooge? 39 78 117 240 395 550
NOTE: *All issues have **Kubert-Maurer** art & **Maurer** covers. 6, 7-Partial photo-c.*

THREE STOOGES
Dell Publishing Co./Gold Key No. 10 (10/62) on: No. 1043, Oct-Dec, 1959 - No. 55, June, 1972

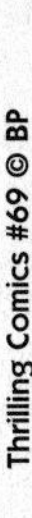
Thrilling Comics #69 © BP

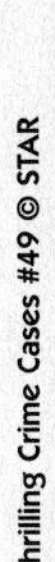
Thrilling Crime Cases #49 © STAR

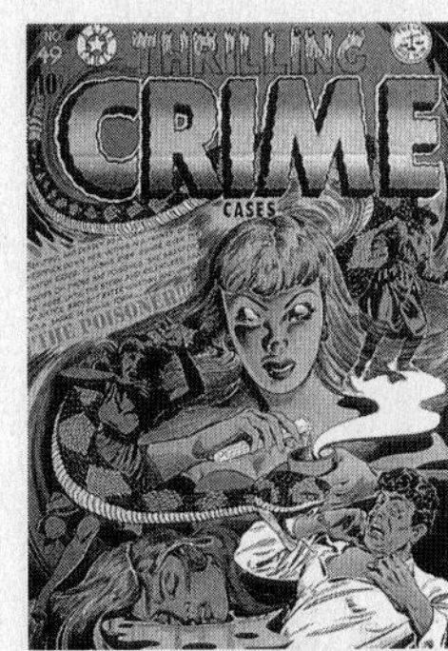

Thrillkiller '62 © DC

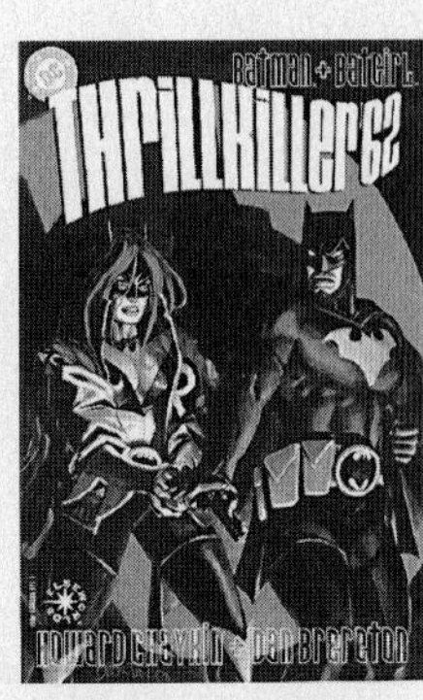

GD VG FN VF VF/NM NM-
2.0 4.0 6.0 8.0 9.0 9.2

Four Color 1043 (#1) 22 44 66 161 321 480
Four Color 1078,1127,1170,1187 12 24 36 84 157 230
6(9-11/61) - 10: 6-Professor Putter begins; ends #16
10 20 30 68 119 170
11-14,16,18-20 8 16 24 56 93 130
15-Go Around the World in a Daze (movie scenes) 9 18 27 60 100 140
17-The Little Monsters begin (5/64)(1st app.?) 9 18 27 60 100 140
21,23-30 7 14 21 45 73 100
22-Movie scenes from "The Outlaws Is Coming" 7 14 21 49 80 110
31-55 5 10 15 34 55 75
NOTE: *All Four Colors, 6-50, 52-55 have photo-c.*

THREE STOOGES IN 3-D, THE
Eternity Comics: 1991 ($3.95, high quality paper, w/glasses)
1-Reprints Three Stooges by Gold Key; photo-c 5.00

THREE STRIKES
Oni Press: Apr, 2003 - No. 5, Oct, 2003 ($2.99, B&W, limited series)
1-5-Brian Hurtt-a/DeFilippis & Weir-s 3.00
TPB (3/04, $14.95, digest-size) r/#1-5; Ed Brubaker intro. 15.00

3 WORLDS OF GULLIVER
Dell Publishing Co.: No. 1158, July, 1961 (2 issues exist with diff. covers)
Four Color 1158-Movie, photo-c 7 14 21 45 73 100

THRILL COMICS (See Flash Comics, Fawcett)

THRILLER
DC Comics: Nov, 1983 - No. 12, Nov, 1984 ($1.25, Baxter paper)
1-12: 1-Intro Seven Seconds; Von Eeden-c/a begins. 2-Origin. 5,6-Elvis satire 3.00

THRILLING ADVENTURES IN STAMPS COMICS (Formerly Stamp Comics)
Stamp Comics, Inc. (Very Rare): V1#8, Jan, 1953 (25¢, 100 pgs.)
V1#8-Harrison, Wildey, Kiefer, Napoli-a 75 150 225 476 818 1160

THRILLING ADVENTURE STORIES (See Tigerman)
Atlas/Seaboard Publ.: Feb, 1975 - No. 2, Aug, 1975 (B&W, 68 pgs.)
1-Tigerman, Kromag the Killer begin; Heath, Thorne-a; Doc Savage movie photos
of Ron Ely 3 6 9 16 23 30
2-Heath, Toth, Severin, Simonson-a; Adams-c 4 8 12 22 34 45

THRILLING COMICS
Better Publ./Nedor/Standard Comics: Feb, 1940 - No. 80, April, 1951
1-Origin & 1st app. Dr. Strange (37 pgs.), ends #?; Nickie Norton of the Secret Service
begins 300 600 900 2070 3635 5200
2-The Rio Kid, The Woman in Red, Pinocchio begins
134 268 402 851 1463 2075
3-The Ghost & Lone Eagle begin 87 174 261 553 952 1350
4-6,8-10 (11/40): 5-Dr. Strange changed to Doc Strange. 10-1st WWII-c (Nazi)
68 136 204 435 743 1050
7-Classic-c 94 188 282 597 1024 1450
11-18,20 60 120 180 381 653 925
19-Origin & 1st app. The American Crusader (8/41), ends #39,41
68 136 204 435 743 1050
21-30: 24-Intro. Mike, Doc Strange's sidekick (1/42). 27-Robot-c.
29-Last Rio Kid 53 106 159 334 567 800
31-40: 36-Commando Cubs begin (7/43, 1st app.) 50 100 150 315 533 750
41-Classic Hitler & Mussolini WWII-c 181 362 543 1158 1979 2800
42,43,46-51: 51(12/45)-Last WWII-c (Japanese) 43 86 129 271 461 650
44-Hitler WWII-c by Schomburg 142 284 426 909 1555 2200
45-Hitler pict. on-c 65 130 195 416 708 1000
52-Classic Schomburg hooded bondage-c; the Ghost ends
63 126 189 403 689 975
53,54: 53-The Phantom Detective begins. The Cavalier app. in both; no Commando Cubs
in either 40 80 120 246 411 575
55-The Lone Eagle ends 38 76 114 228 369 510
56 (10/46)-Princess Pantha begins (not on-c), 1st app.
48 96 144 302 514 725
57-Doc Strange-c; 2nd Princess Pantha 42 84 126 265 445 625
58-66: All Princess Pantha jungle-c, w/Doc Strange #59, his last-c. 61-Ingels-a; The Lone
Eagle app. 65-Last Phantom Detective & Commando Cubs. 66-Frazetta text illo
41 82 123 250 418 585
67,70,71-Last jungle-c; Frazetta-a(5-7 pgs.) in each 47 94 141 296 498 700
68,69-Frazetta-a(2), 8 & 6 pgs.; 9 & 7 pgs. 50 100 150 315 533 750
72,73: 72-Buck Ranger, Cowboy Detective c/stys begin (western theme), end #80;
Frazetta-a(5-7 ps.) in each 39 78 117 240 395 550
74-Last Princess Pantha; Tara app. 27 54 81 160 263 365
75-78: 75-All western format begins 14 28 42 81 118 155
79-Krigstein-a 15 30 45 83 124 165
80-Severin & Elder, Celardo, Moreira-a 15 30 45 83 124 165
NOTE: *Bondage c-5, 9, 13, 20, 22, 27-30, 38, 41, 52, 54, 70.* ***Kinstler*** *a-45.* ***Leo Morey*** *a-7.* ***Schomburg*** *(sometimes signed as* ***Xela****) c-7, 9-19, 36-80 (airbrush 62-71).* ***Tuska*** *a-62, 63. Woman in Red not in #19, 23, 31-33, 39-45. No. 45 exists as a Canadian reprint but numbered #48. No. 72 exists as a Canadian reprint with no* ***Frazetta*** *story. American Crusader c-20-24. Buck Ranger c-72-80. Commando Cubs c-37, 39, 41, 43, 45, 47, 49, 51. Doc Strange c-1-19, 25-36, 38, 40, 42, 44, 46, 48, 50, 52-57, 59. Princess Pantha c-58, 60-71.*

THRILLING COMICS (Also see All Star Comics 1999 crossover titles)
DC Comics: May, 1999 ($1.99, one-shot)
1-Golden Age Hawkman and Wildcat; Russ Heath-a 3.00

THRILLING CRIME CASES (Formerly 4Most; becomes Shocking Mystery Cases #50 on)
Star Publications: No. 41, June-July, 1950 - No. 49, July, 1952
41 28 56 84 165 270 375
42-45: 42-L. B. Cole-c/a (1); Chameleon story (Fox-r)
25 50 75 147 241 335
46-48: 47-Used in **POP**, pg. 84 24 48 72 142 234 325
49-(7/52)-Classic L. B. Cole-c 45 90 135 284 480 675
NOTE: ***L. B. Cole*** *c-all; a-43p, 45p, 46p, 49(2 pgs.).* ***Disbrow*** *a-48.* ***Hollingsworth*** *a-48.*

THRILLING ROMANCES
Standard Comics: No. 5, Dec, 1949 - No. 26, June, 1954
5 15 30 45 88 137 185
6,8 11 22 33 60 83 105
7-Severin/Elder-a (7 pgs.) 13 26 39 72 101 130
9,10-Severin/Elder-a; photo-c 12 24 36 67 94 120
11,14-21,26: 14-Gene Tierney & Danny Kaye photo-c from movie "On the Riviera".
15-Tony Martin/Janet Leigh photo-c 10 20 30 56 76 95
12-Wood-a (2 pgs.); Tyrone Power/ Susan Hayward photo-c
13 26 39 74 105 135
13-Severin-a 11 22 33 60 83 105
22-25-Toth-a 12 24 36 67 94 120
NOTE: *All photo-c.* ***Celardo*** *a-9, 16.* ***Colletta*** *a-23, 24(2).* ***Toth*** *text illos-19.* ***Tuska*** *a-9.*

THRILLING SCIENCE TALES
AC Comics: 1989 - No. 2 ($3.50, 2/3 color, 52 pgs.)
1,2: 1-r/Bob Colt #6(saucer); Frazetta, Guardineer (Space Ace), Wood, Krenkel, Orlando, WIlliamson-r; Kaluta-c. 2-Capt. Video-r by Evans, Capt. Science-r by Wood, Star Pirate-r by Whitman & Mysta of the Moon-r by Moreira 4.00

THRILLING TRUE STORY OF THE BASEBALL...
Fawcett Publications: 1952 (Photo-c, each)
...Giants-photo-c; has Willie Mays rookie photo-biography; Willie Mays, Eddie Stanky &
others photos on-c 68 136 204 432 746 1060
...Yankees-photo-c; Yogi Berra, Joe DiMaggio, Mickey Mantle & others photos on-c
66 132 198 419 722 1025

THRILLING WONDER TALES
AC Comics : 1991 ($2.95, B&W)
1-Includes a Bob Powell Thun'da story 3.00

THRILLKILLER
DC Comics : Jan, 1997 - No. 3, Mar, 1997($2.50, limited series)
1-3-Elseworlds Robin & Batgirl; Chaykin-s/Brereton-c/a 3.00
...'62 ('98, $4.95, one-shot) Sequel; Chaykin-s/Brereton-c/a 5.00
TPB-(See Batman: Thrillkiller)

THRILLOGY
Pacific Comics: Jan, 1984 (One-shot, color)
1-Conrad-c/a 3.00

THRILL-O-RAMA
Harvey Publications (Fun Films): Oct, 1965 - No. 3, Dec, 1966
1-Fate (Man in Black) by Powell app.; Doug Wildey-a(2); Simon-c
5 10 15 34 55 75
2-Pirana begins (see Phantom #46); Williamson 2 pgs.; Fate (Man in Black)
app.; Tuska/Simon-c 4 8 12 22 34 45
3-Fate (Man in Black) app.; Sparling-c 3 6 9 19 29 38

THRILLS OF TOMORROW (Formerly Tomb of Terror)
Harvey Publications: No. 17, Oct, 1954 - No. 20, April, 1955
17-Powell-a (horror); r/Witches Tales #7 15 30 45 88 137 185
18-Powell-a (horror); r/Tomb of Terror #1 14 28 42 82 121 160
19,20-Stuntman-c/stories by S&K (r/from Stuntman #1 & 2); 19 has origin &
is last pre-code (2/55) 31 62 93 182 296 410
NOTE: ***Kirby*** *c-19, 20.* ***Palais*** *a-17.* ***Simon*** *c-18?*

THROBBING LOVE (See Fox Giants)

T.H.U.N.D.E.R. Agents #1 © Radiant Assets

Thunderbolts #148 © MAR

Thundercats: The Return #1
© WB & Ted Wolf

GD 2.0 VG 4.0 FN 6.0 VF 8.0 VF/NM 9.0 NM- 9.2

THROUGH GATES OF SPLENDOR
Spire Christian Comics (Flemming H. Revell Co.): 1973, 1974 (36 pages) (39-49 cents)
nn-1973 Edition 2 4 6 10 14 18
nn-1974 Edition 2 4 6 8 10 12

THULSA DOOM (Robert E. Howard character)
Dynamite Entertainment: 2009 - No. 4, 2009 ($3.50, limited series)
1-4-Alex Ross-c/Lui Antonio-a 3.50

THUMPER (Disney)
Dell Publishing Co.: No, 19, 1942 - No. 243, Sept, 1949
Four Color 19-Walt Disney's...Meets the Seven Dwarfs; reprinted in Silly Symphonies
43 86 129 344 697 1050
Four Color 243-...Follows His Nose 11 22 33 75 138 200

THUN'DA (...King of the Congo)
Magazine Enterprises: 1952 - No. 6, 1953
1(A-1 #47)-Origin; Frazetta c/a; only comic done entirely by Frazetta; all Thun'da stories, no Cave Girl 161 322 483 1030 1765 2500
2(A-1 #56)-Powell-c/a begins, ends #6; Intro/1st app. Cave Girl in filler strip (also app. in 3-6)
24 48 72 142 234 325
3(A-1 #73), 4(A-1 #78) 18 36 54 105 165 225
5(A-1 #83), 6(A-1 #86) 17 34 51 98 154 210

THUN'DA TALES (See Frank Frazetta's...)

THUNDER AGENTS (See Dynamo, Noman & Tales Of Thunder)
Tower Comics: 11/65 - No. 17, 12/67; No. 18, 9/68, No. 19, 11/68, No. 20, 11/69 (No. 1-16: 68 pgs.; No. 17 on: 52 pgs.)(All are 25¢)
1-Origin & 1st app. Dynamo, Noman, Menthor, & The Thunder Squad; 1st app. The Iron Maiden 18 36 54 131 266 400
2-Death of Egghead; A-bomb blast panel 10 20 30 71 128 185
3-5: 4-Guy Gilbert becomes Lightning who joins Thunder Squad; Iron Maiden app.
8 16 24 58 97 135
6-10: 7-Death of Menthor. 8-Origin & 1st app. The Raven
7 14 21 45 73 100
11-15: 13-Undersea Agent app.; no Raven story 6 12 18 41 66 90
16-19 6 12 18 39 62 85
20-Special Collectors Edition; all reprints 4 8 12 28 44 60
...Archives Vol. 1 (DC Comics, 2003, $49.95, HC) r/#1-4, restored and recolored 50.00
...Archives Vol. 2 (DC Comics, 2003, $49.95, HC) r/#5-7, Dynamo #1 50.00
...Archives Vol. 3 (DC Comics, 2003, $49.95, HC) r/#8-10, Dynamo #2 50.00
...Archives Vol. 4 (DC Comics, 2004, $49.95, HC) r/#11, Noman #1,2 & Dynamo #3 50.00
NOTE: ***Crandall*** *a-1, 4p, 5p, 18, 20r; c-18.* ***Ditko*** *a-6, 7p, 12p, 13?, 14p, 16, 18.* ***Giunta*** *a-6.* ***Kane*** *a-1, 5p, 6p?, 14, 16p; c-14, 15.* ***Reinman*** *a-13.* ***Sekowsky*** *a-6.* ***Tuska*** *a-1p, 7, 8, 10, 13-17, 19.* ***Whitney*** *a-9p, 10, 13, 15, 17, 18; c-17.* ***Wood*** *a-1-11, 15(w/****Ditko****-12, 18), (inks-#9, 13, 14, 16, 17), 19i, 20r; c-1-8, 9i, 10-13(#10 w/****Williamson****(p)), 16.*

T.H.U.N.D.E.R. AGENTS (See Blue Ribbon Comics, Hall of Fame Featuring the..., JCP Features & Wally Wood's...)
JC Comics (Archie Publications): May, 1983 - No. 2, Jan, 1984
1,2: 1-New Manna/Blyberg-c/a. 2-Blyberg-c 6.00

T.H.U.N.D.E.R. AGENTS
DC Comics: Jan, 2011 - Present ($3.99/$2.99)
1-3-($3.99): 1-Spencer-s/Cafu-a/Quitely-c. 3-Chaykin-a (5 pgs.) 4.00
4,5-($2.99) 4-Pérez-a (5 pgs.) 3.00
1-Variant-c by Darwyn Cooke 8.00

THUNDER BIRDS (See Cinema Comics Herald)

THUNDERBOLT (See The Atomic...)

THUNDERBOLT (Peter Cannon...; see Crisis on Infinite Earths & Peter...)
Charlton Comics: Jan, 1966; No. 51, Mar-Apr, 1966 - No. 60, Nov, 1967
1-Origin & 1st app. Thunderbolt 4 8 12 28 44 60
51-(Formerly Son of Vulcan #50) 3 6 9 20 30 40
52-59: 54-Sentinels begin. 59-Last Thunderbolt & Sentinels (back-up story)
3 6 9 14 19 24
60-Prankster app. 3 6 9 15 21 26
57,58 ('77)-Modern Comics-r 6.00
NOTE: ***Aparo*** *a-60.* ***Morisi*** *a-1, 51-56, 58; c-1, 51-56, 58, 59.*

THUNDERBOLT JAXON (Revival of 1940s British comics character)
DC Comics (WildStorm): Apr, 2006 - No. 5, Sept, 2006 ($2.99, limited series)
1-5-Dave Gibbons-s/John Higgins-a 3.00
TPB (2007, $19.99) r/#1-5; intro. by Gibbons; cover gallery 20.00

THUNDERBOLTS (Also see New Thunderbolts and Incredible Hulk #449)
Marvel Comics: Apr, 1997 - No. 81, Sept, 2003; No. 100, May, 2006 - Present ($1.95-$2.99)

GD 2.0 VG 4.0 FN 6.0 VF 8.0 VF/NM 9.0 NM- 9.2

1-($2.99)-Busiek-s/Bagley-c/a 1 2 3 5 7 9
1-2nd printing; new cover colors 3.00
2-4: 2-Two covers. 4-Intro. Jolt 6.00
5-11: 9-Avengers app. 3.50
12-($2.99)-Avengers and Fantastic Four-c/app. 4.00
13-24: 14-Thunderbolts return to Earth. 21-Hawkeye app. 3.00
25-($2.99) Wraparound-c 4.00
26-38: 26-Manco-a 3.00
39-($2.99) 100 Page Monster; Iron Man reprints 4.00
40-49: 40-Begin $2.25-c; Sandman-c/app. 44-Avengers app. 47-Captain Marvel app. 49-Zircher-a 3.00
50-($2.99) Last Bagley-a; Captain America becomes leader 4.00
51-74,76,77,80,81: 51,52-Zircher-a; Dr. Doom app. 80,81-Spider-Man app. 3.00
75-($3.50) Hawkeye leaves the team; Garcia-a 4.00
78,79-($2.99-c) Velasco-a begins 3.00
(See New Thunderbolts for #82-99)
100 (5/06, $3.99) resumes from New Thunderbolts #18; back-up origin stories 4.00
101-109: 103-105-Civil War x-over 3.00
110-New team begins including Bullseye, Venom and Norman Osborn; Ellis-s/Deodato-a 5.00
111-136,138-149: 111-121-Ellis-s/Deodato-a. 112-Stan Lee cameo. 123-125-Secret Invasion x-over. 128-Dark Reign begins. 130,131-X-over with Deadpool #8,9. 141-143-Siege 3.00
137-(12/09, $3.99) Iron Fist and Luke Cage app. 4.00
150-(1/11, $4.99) Thunderbolts vs. Avengers; r/#1; storyline synopses of #1-150 5.00
151-156-($2.99) 151-153-Land-c. 155-Satana joins 3.00
Annual '97 ($2.99)-Wraparound-c 4.00
Annual 2000 ($3.50) Breyfogle-a 4.00
...: Breaking Point (1/08, $2.99, one-shot) Gage-s/Denham-a/Djurdjevic-c 3.00
... By Warren Ellis Vol. 1 HC (2007, $24.99, dustjacket) r/#150-154, ...: Desperate Measures and stories from Civil War: Choosing Sides and The Initiative 25.00
... By Warren Ellis Vol. 1: Faith in Monsters SC (2008, $19.99) same contents as HC 20.00
Civil War: Thunderbolts TPB (2007, $13.99) r/#101-105 14.00
...: Desperate Measures (9/07, $2.99, one-shot) Jenkins-s/Steve Lieber-a 3.00
...: Distant Rumblings (#-1) (7/97, $1.95) Busiek-s 5.00
First Strikes (1997, $4.99,TPB) r/#1,2 5.00
...: From the Marvel Vault (6/11, $3.99) Jack Monroe app.; Nicieza-s/Aucoin-a 4.00
...: Guardian Protocols (2007, $10.99) r/#106-109 11.00
...: International Incident (4/08, $2.99, one-shot) Gage-s/Oliver-a/Djurdjevic-c 3.00
...: Life Sentences (7/01, $3.50) Adlard-a 4.00
...: Marvel's Most Wanted TPB ('98, $16.99) r/origin stories of original Masters of Evil 17.00
...: Reason in Madness (7/08, $2.99, one-shot) Gage-s/Oliver-a/Djurdjevic-c 3.00
Wizard #0 (bagged with Wizard #89) 3.00

THUNDERBOLTS PRESENTS: ZEMO - BORN BETTER
Marvel Comics: Apr, 2007 - No. 4, July, 2007 ($2.99, limited series)
1-4-History of Baron Zemo; Nicieza-s/Grummett-a/c 3.00
TPB (2007, $10.99) r/#1-4 11.00

THUNDERBUNNY (See Blue Ribbon Comics #13, Charlton Bullseye & Pep Comics #393)
Red Circle Comics: Jan, 1984 (Direct sale only)
WaRP Graphics: Second series No. 1, 1985 - No. 6, 1985
Apple Comics: No. 7, 1986 - No. 12, 1987
1-Humor/parody; origin Thunderbunny; 2 page pin-up by Anderson 5.00
(2nd series) 1,2-Magazine size 3.00
3-12-Comic size 3.00

THUNDERCATS (TV)
Marvel Comics (Star Comics)/Marvel #22 on: Dec, 1985 - No. 24, June, 1988 (75¢)
1-Mooney-c/a begins 2 4 6 8 11 14
2-20: 2-(65¢ & 75¢ cover exists). 12-Begin $1.00-c. 18-20-Williamson-i
1 2 3 5 7 9
21-24: 23-Williamson-c(i) 1 3 4 6 8 10

THUNDERCATS (TV)
DC Comics (WildStorm): No. 0, Oct, 2002 - No. 5, Feb, 2003 ($2.50/$2.95, limited series)
0-($2.50) J. Scott Campbell-c/a 3.00
1-5-($2.95) 1-McGuinness-a/c; variant cover by Art Adams; rebirth of Mumm-Ra 3.00
.../ Battle of the Planets (7/03, $4.95) Kaare Andrews-s/a; 2 covers by Campbell & Ross 5.00
...: Origins-Heroes & Villains (2/04, $3.50) short stories by various 3.50
...Reclaiming Thundera TPB (2003, $12.95) r/#0-5 13.00
... Sourcebook (1/03, $2.95) pin-ups and info on characters; art by various; A. Adams-c 3.00

THUNDERCATS: DOGS OF WAR
DC Comics (WildStorm): Aug, 2003 - No. 5, Dec, 2003 ($2.95, limited series)
1-5: 1-Two covers by Booth & Pearson; Booth-a/Layman-s. 2-4-Two covers 3.00
TPB (2004, $14.95) r/#1-5 15.00

THUNDERCATS: ENEMY'S PRIDE

Thunderstrike (2011 series) #2 © MAR

The Tick Color #5 © Ben Edlund

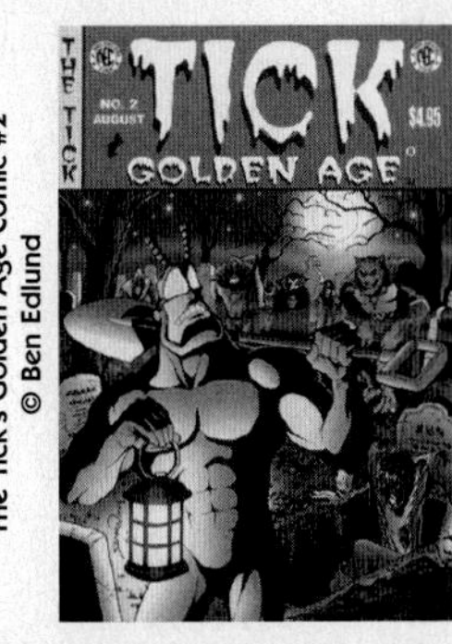

The Tick's Golden Age Comic #2 © Ben Edlund

GD VG FN VF VF/NM NM-
2.0 4.0 6.0 8.0 9.0 9.2

DC Comics (WildStorm): Aug, 2004 - No. 5 ($2.95, limited series)
1-5-Vriens-a/Layman-s 3.00
TPB (2005, $14.99) r/#1-5 15.00

THUNDERCATS: HAMMERHAND'S REVENGE
DC Comics (WildStorm): Dec, 2003 - No. 5, Apr, 2004 ($2.95, limited series)
1-5-Avery-s/D'Anda-a. 2-Variant-c by Warren 3.00
TPB (2004, $14.95) r/#1-5 15.00

THUNDERCATS: THE RETURN
DC Comics (WildStorm): Apr, 2003 - No. 5, Aug, 2003 ($2.95, limited series)
1-5: 1-Two covers by Benes & Cassaday; Gilmore-s 3.00
TPB (2004, $12.95) r/series 13.00

THUNDER MOUNTAIN (See Zane Grey, Four Color #246)

THUNDERSTRIKE (See Thor #459)
Marvel Comics: June, 1993 - No. 24, July, 1995 ($1.25)
1-($2.95, 52 pgs.)-Holo-grafx lightning patterned foil-c; Bloodaxe returns 4.00
2-24: 2-Juggernaut-c/s. 4-Capt. America app. 4-6-Spider-Man app. 8-bound-in trading card sheet. 18-Bloodaxe app. 24-Death of Thunderstrike 3.00
Marvel Double Feature...Thunderstrike/Code Blue #13 ($2.50)-Same as Thunderstrike #13 w/Code Blue flip book 4.00

THUNDERSTRIKE
Marvel Comics: Jan, 2011 - No. 5 ($3.99, limited series)
1-4-DeFalco-s/Frenz-a. 1-Back-up origin retold; Nauck-a 4.00

TICK, THE (Also see The Chroma-Tick)
New England Comics Press: Jun, 1988 - No. 12, May, 1993 ($1.75/$1.95/$2.25; B&W, over-sized)
Special Edition 1-1st comic book app. serially numbered & limited to 5,000 copies 5 10 15 34 55 75
Special Edition 1-(5/96, $5.95)-Double-c; foil-c; serially numbered (5,001 thru 14,000) & limited to 9,000 copies 1 2 3 5 6 8
Special Edition 2-Serially numbered and limited to 3000 copies 5 10 15 30 48 65
Special Edition 2-(8/96, $5.95)-Double-c; foil-c; serially numbered (5,001 thru 14,000) & limited to 9,000 copies 1 2 3 5 6 8
1-Regular Edition 1st printing; reprints Special Ed. 1 w/minor changes 4 8 12 24 37 50
1-2nd printing 6.00
1-3rd-5th printing 3.00
2-Reprints Special Ed. 2 w/minor changes 2 4 6 13 18 22
2-8-All reprints 3.00
3-5 ($1.95): 4-1st app. Paul the Samurai 1 3 4 6 8 10
6,8 ($2.25) 5.00
7-1st app. Man-Eating Cow 6.00
8-Variant with no logo, price, issue number or company logos. 2 4 6 10 14 18
9-12 ($2.75) 4.00
12-Special Edition; card-stock, virgin foil-c; numbered edition 2 4 6 13 18 22
Pseudo-Tick #13 (11/00, $3.50) Continues story from #12 (1993) 4.00
Promo Sampler-(1990)-Tick-c/story 1 2 3 5 6 8

TICK, THE (One shots)
... Big Back to School Special 1-(10/98, $3.50, B&W) Tick & Arthur undercover in H.S. 3.50
... Big Cruise Ship Vacation Special 1-(9/00, $3.50, B&W) 3.50
... Big Father's Day Special 1-(6/00, $3.50, B&W) 3.50
... Big Halloween Special 1-(10/99, $3.50, B&W) 3.50
... Big Halloween Special 2000 (10/00, $3.50) 3.50
... Big Halloween Special 2001 (9/01, $3.95) 4.00
... Big Mother's Day Special 1-(4/00, $3.50, B&W) 3.50
... Big Red-N-Green Christmas Spectacle 1-(12/01, $3.95) 4.00
... Big Romantic Adventure 1-(2/98, $2.95, B&W) Candy box-c with candy map on back 3.50
... Big Summer Annual 1-(7/99, $3.50, B&W) Chainsaw Vigilante vs. Barry 3.50
... Big Summer Fun Special 1-(8/98, $3.50, B&W) Tick and Arthur at summer camp 3.50
... Big Tax Time Terror 1-(4/00, $3.50, B&W) 3.50
... Big Year 2000 Spectacle 1-(3/00, $3.50, B&W) 3.50
... Incredible Internet Comic 1-(7/01, $3.95, color) r/New England Comics website story 4.00
FCBD Special Edition (5/10) - reprints debut from 1988; Ben Edlund-s/a 2.00
Introducing the Tick 1-(4/02, $3.95, color) summary of Tick's life and adventures 4.00
The Tick's Back #0 -(8/97, $2.95, B&W) 3.50
The Tick's Comic Con Extravaganza -(6/07, $3.95, color) Wang-c 4.00
The Tick's 20th Anniversary Special Edition #1 (5/07, $5.95) short stories by various; history of the character; creator profiles; 2 covers by Suydam & Bisley 6.00

GD VG FN VF VF/NM NM-
2.0 4.0 6.0 8.0 9.0 9.2

--MASSIVE SUMMER DOUBLE SPECTACLE
1,2-(7,8/00, $3.50, B&W) 3.50

TICK & ARTIE
1-(6/02, $3.50, color) prints strips from Internet comic 4.00
2-(10/02, $3.95) 4.00

TICK AND ARTHUR, THE
New England Comics: Feb, 1999 - No. 6 ($3.50, B&W)
1-6-Sean Wang-s/a 3.50

TICK BIG BLUE DESTINY, THE
New England Comics: Oct, 1997 - No. 9 ($2.95)
1-4: 1-"Keen" Ed. 2-Two covers 3.50
1-($4.95) "Wicked Keen" Ed. w/die cut-c 5.00
5-($3.50) 3.50
6-Luny Bin Trilogy Preview #0 (7/98, $1.50) 3.50
7-9: 7-Luny Bin Trilogy begins 3.50

TICK BIG BLUE YULE LOG SPECIAL, THE
New England Comics: Dec, 1997; 1999 ($2.95, B&W)
1-"Jolly" and "Traditional" covers; flip book w/"Arthur Teaches the Tick About Hanukkah" 3.50
...1999 ($3.50) 3.50
Tick Big Yule Log Special 2001-(12/00, $3.50, B&W) 3.50

TICK, THE : CIRCUS MAXIMUS
New England Comics: Mar, 2000 - No. 4, Jun, 2000 ($3.50, B&W)
1-4-Encyclopedia of characters from Tick comics 3.50
Giant No. 1 (8/03, $14.95) r/#1-4, Redux 15.00
Redux No. 1 (4/01, $3.50) 3.50

TICK, THE - COLOR
New England Comics: Jan, 2001 - Present ($3.95)
1-6: 1-Marc Sandroni-a 4.00

TICK, THE : DAYS OF DRAMA
New England Comics: July, 2005 - No. 6, June, 2006 ($4.95/$3.95, limited series)
1-($4.95) Dave Garcia-a; has a mini-comic attached to cover 5.00
2-6-($3.95) 4.00

TICK, THE - HEROES OF THE CITY
New England Comics: Feb, 1999 - Present ($3.50, B&W)
1-6-Short stories by various 3.50

TICK KARMA TORNADO (The...)
New England Comics Press: Oct, 1993 - No. 9, Mar, 1995 ($2.75, B&W)
1-($3.25) 4.00
2-9: 2-$2.75-c begins 3.50

TICK NEW SERIES (The...)
New England Comics: Dec, 2009 - Present ($4.95)
1-8 5.00

TICK'S BIG XMAS TRILOGY, THE
New England Comics: Dec, 2002 - No. 3, Dec, 2002 ($3.95, limited series)
1-3 4.00

TICK'S GOLDEN AGE COMIC, THE
New England Comics: May, 2002 - No. 3, Feb, 2003 ($4.95, Golden Age size)
1-3-Facsimile 1940s-style Tick issue; 2 covers 5.00
Giant Edition TPB (9/03, $12.95) r/#1-3 13.00

TICK'S GIANT CIRCUS OF THE MIGHTY, THE
New England Comics: Summer, 1992 - No. 3, Fall, 1993 ($2.75, B&W, magazine size)
1-(A-O). 2-(P-Z). 3-1993 Update 4.00

TICKLE COMICS (Also see Gay, Smile, & Whee Comics)
Modern Store Publ.: 1955 (7¢, 5x7-1/4", 52 pgs)
1 6 12 18 28 34 40

TICK TOCK TALES
Magazine Enterprises: Jan, 1946 - V3#33, Jan-Feb, 1951
1-Koko & Kola begin 16 32 48 94 147 200
2 10 20 30 58 79 100
3-10 10 20 30 54 72 90
11-33: 19-Flag-c. 23-Muggsy Mouse, The Pixies & Tom-Tom the Jungle Boy app. 24-X-mas-c. 25-The Pixies & Tom-Tom app. 9 18 27 47 61 75

TIGER (Also see Comics Reading Libraries in the Promotional Comics section)
Charlton Press (King Features): Mar, 1970 - No. 6, Jan, 1971 (15¢)

Tigra #1 © MAR

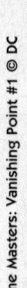

Time Masters: Vanishing Point #1 © DC

Tim Holt #21 © ME

	GD 2.0	VG 4.0	FN 6.0	VF 8.0	VF/NM 9.0	NM- 9.2
1	3	6	9	14	19	24
2-6	2	4	6	8	11	14

TIGER BOY (See Unearthly Spectaculars)

TIGER GIRL
Gold Key: Sept, 1968 (15¢)

	GD 2.0	VG 4.0	FN 6.0	VF 8.0	VF/NM 9.0	NM- 9.2
1(10227-809)-Sparling-c/a; Jerry Siegel scripts; advertising on back-c	4	8	12	26	41	55
1-Variant edition with pin-up on back cover	5	10	15	34	55	75

TIGERMAN (Also see Thrilling Adventure Stories)
Seaboard Periodicals (Atlas): Apr, 1975 - No. 3, Sept, 1975 (All 25¢ issues)

	GD 2.0	VG 4.0	FN 6.0	VF 8.0	VF/NM 9.0	NM- 9.2
1-3: 1-Origin; Colan-c. 2,3-Ditko-p in each	2	4	6	9	13	16

TIGER WALKS, A (See Movie Comics)

TIGRA (The Avengers)
Marvel Comics: May, 2002 - No. 4, Aug, 2002 ($2.99, limited series)

1-4-Christina Z-s/Deodato-c/a — 3.00

TIGRESS, THE
Hero Graphics: Aug, 1992 - No. 6?, June, 1993 ($3.95/$2.95/$3.95, B&W)

1,6: 1-Tigress vs. Flare. 6-44 pgs. — 4.00
2-5: 2-$2.95-c begins — 3.00

TILLIE THE TOILER (See Comic Monthly)
Dell Publishing Co.: No. 15, 1941 - No. 237, July, 1949

	GD 2.0	VG 4.0	FN 6.0	VF 8.0	VF/NM 9.0	NM- 9.2
Four Color 15(1941)	45	90	135	284	480	675
Large Feature Comic 30(1941)	34	68	102	199	325	450
Four Color 8(1942)	22	44	66	155	310	465
Four Color 22(1943)	16	32	48	111	226	340
Four Color 55(1944), 89(1945)	12	24	36	88	167	245
Four Color 106('45),132('46): 132-New stories begin	10	20	30	68	119	170
Four Color 150,176,184	9	18	27	63	107	150
Four Color 195,213,237	7	14	21	50	83	115

TIMBER WOLF (See Action Comics #372, & Legion of Super-Heroes)
DC Comics: Nov, 1992 - No. 5, Mar, 1993 ($1.25, limited series)

1-5 — 3.00

TIME BANDITS
Marvel Comics Group: Feb, 1982 (one-shot, Giant)

1-Movie adaptation — 4.00

TIME BEAVERS (See First Comics Graphic Novel #2)

TIME BOMB
Radical Comics: Jul, 2010 - No. 3, Dec, 2010 ($4.99, limited series)

1-3-Palmiotti & Gray-s/Gulacy-a/c — 5.00

TIME BREAKERS
DC Comics (Helix): Jan, 1997 - No. 5, May, 1997 ($2.25, limited series)

1-5-Pollack-s — 3.00

TIMECOP (Movie)
Dark Horse Comics: Sept, 1994 - No. 2, Nov, 1994 ($2.50, limited series)

1,2-Adaptation of film — 3.00

TIME FOR LOVE (Formerly Romantic Secrets)
Charlton Comics: V2#53, Oct, 1966; Oct, 1967 - No. 47, May, 1976

	GD 2.0	VG 4.0	FN 6.0	VF 8.0	VF/NM 9.0	NM- 9.2
V2#53(10/66) Herman-s Hermits app.	3	6	9	20	30	40
1-(10/67)	4	8	12	22	34	45
2-(12/67) -10	3	6	9	15	21	26
11,12,14-20	2	4	6	11	16	20
13-(11/69) Ditko-a (7 pgs.)	3	6	9	16	23	30
21-27	2	4	6	9	13	16
28,29,31: 28-Shirley Jones poster. 29-Bobby Sherman pin-up. 31-Bobby Sherman pin-up	2	4	6	11	16	20
30-(10/72)-David Cassidy full page poster	3	6	9	17	25	32
32-47	2	4	6	8	11	14

TIMELESS TOPIX (See Topix)

TIMELY PRESENTS: ALL WINNERS
Marvel Comics: Dec, 1999 ($3.99)

1-Reprints All Winners Comics #19 (Fall 1946); new Lago-c — 4.00

TIMELY PRESENTS: HUMAN TORCH
Marvel Comics: Feb, 1999 ($3.99)

1-Reprints Human Torch Comics #5 (Fall 1941); new Lago-c — 4.00

TIME MACHINE, THE
Dell Publishing Co.: No. 1085, Mar, 1960 (H.G. Wells)

	GD 2.0	VG 4.0	FN 6.0	VF 8.0	VF/NM 9.0	NM- 9.2
Four Color 1085-Movie, Alex Toth-a; Rod Taylor photo-c	13	26	39	92	179	265

TIME MASTERS
DC Comics: Feb, 1990 - No. 8, Sept, 1990 ($1.75, mini-series)

1-8: New Rip Hunter series. 5-Cave Carson, Viking Prince app. 6-Dr. Fate app. — 3.00
TPB (2008, $19.99) r/#1-8 and Secret Origins #43; intro. by Geoff Johns — 20.00

TIME MASTERS: VANISHING POINT (Tie-in to Batman: The Return of Bruce Wayne)
DC Comics: Sept, 2010 - No. 6, Feb, 2011 ($3.99, limited series)

1-6-Jurgens-s/a/c; Rip Hunter, Superman, Green Lantern & Booster Gold app. — 4.00

TIMESLIP COLLECTION
Marvel Comics: Nov, 1998 ($2.99, one-shot)

1-Pin-ups reprinted from Marvel Vision magazine — 3.00

TIMESLIP SPECIAL (The Coming of the Avengers)
Marvel Comics: Oct, 1998 ($5.99, one-shot)

1-Alternate world Avengers vs. Odin — 6.00

TIMESTORM 2009/2099
Marvel Comics: June, 2009 - No. 4, Oct, 2009 ($3.99, limited series)

1-4-Punisher 2099 transports Spider-Man to 2099; Wolverine app.; Battle-a — 4.00
...: Spider-Man One Shot (8/09, $3.99) Reed-s/Craig-a/Renaud-c — 4.00
...: X-Men One Shot (8/09, $3.99) Reed-s/Irving-a/Renaud-c — 4.00

TIME TO RUN (Based on 1973 Billy Graham movie)
Spire Christian Comics (Fleming H. Revell Co.): 1975 (39¢)

	GD 2.0	VG 4.0	FN 6.0	VF 8.0	VF/NM 9.0	NM- 9.2
nn-By Al Hartley	2	4	6	9	13	16

TIME TUNNEL, THE (TV)
Gold Key: Feb, 1967 - No. 2, July, 1967 (12¢)

	GD 2.0	VG 4.0	FN 6.0	VF 8.0	VF/NM 9.0	NM- 9.2
1-Photo back-c on both issues	7	14	21	47	76	105
2	5	10	15	34	55	75

TIME TWISTERS
Quality Comics: Sept, 1987 - No. 21, 1989 ($1.25/$1.50)

1-21: Alan Moore scripts in 1-4, 6-9, 14 (2 pg.). 14-Bolland-a (2 pg.). 15,16-Guice-c — 3.00

TIME 2: THE EPIPHANY (See First Comics Graphic Novel #9)

TIMEWALKER (Also see Archer & Armstrong)
Valiant: Jan, 1994 - No. 15, Oct, 1995 ($2.50)

1-15,0(3/96): 2-"JAN" on-c, February, 1995 in indicia. — 3.00
Yearbook 1 (5/95, $2.95) — 3.00

TIME WARP (See The Unexpected #210)
DC Comics, Inc.: Oct-Nov, 1979 - No. 5, June-July, 1980 ($1.00, 68 pgs.)

	GD 2.0	VG 4.0	FN 6.0	VF 8.0	VF/NM 9.0	NM- 9.2
1	2	4	6	11	16	20
2-5	2	4	6	8	11	14

NOTE: *Aparo a-1.* ***Buckler*** *a-1p.* ***Chaykin*** *a-2.* ***Ditko*** *a-1-4.* ***Kaluta*** *c-1-5.* ***G. Kane*** *a-2.* ***Nasser*** *a-4.* ***Newton*** *a-1-5p.* ***Orlando*** *a-2.* ***Sutton*** *a-1-3.*

TIME WARRIORS: THE BEGINNING
Fantasy General Comics: 1986 (Aug) - No. 2, 1986? ($1.50)

1,2-Alpha Track/Skellon Empire — 3.00

TIM HOLT (Movie star) (Becomes Red Mask #42 on; also see Crack Western #72, & Great Western)
Magazine Enterprises: 1948 - No. 41, April-May, 1954 (All 36 pgs.)

	GD 2.0	VG 4.0	FN 6.0	VF 8.0	VF/NM 9.0	NM- 9.2
1-(A-1 #14)-Line drawn-c w/Tim Holt photo on-c; Tim Holt, His horse Lightning & sidekick Chito begin	50	100	150	315	533	750
2-(A-1 #17)(9-10/48)-Photo-c begin, end #18	26	52	78	154	252	350
3-(A-1 #19)-Photo back-c	20	40	60	117	189	260
4(1-2/49),5: 5-Photo front/back-c	15	30	45	85	130	175
6-(5/49)-1st app. The Calico Kid (alias Rex Fury), his horse Ebony & Sidekick Sing-Song (begin series); photo back-c	22	44	66	132	216	300
7-10: 7-Calico Kid by Ayers. 8-Calico Kid by Guardineer (r-in/Great Western #10). 9-Map of Tim's Home Range	14	28	42	82	121	160
11-The Calico Kid becomes The Ghost Rider (origin & 1st app.) by Dick Ayers (r-in/Great Western I.W. #8); his horse Spectre & sidekick Sing-Song begin series	45	90	135	284	480	675
12-16,18-Last photo-c	13	26	39	74	105	135
17-Frazetta Ghost Rider-c	40	80	120	246	411	575
19,22,24: 19-Last Tim Holt-c; Bolle line-drawn-c begin; Tim Holt photo on covers #19-28, 30-41. 22-interior photo-c	11	22	33	62	86	110

20-Tim Holt becomes Redmask (origin); begin series; Redmask-c #20-on

Tim Tyler Cowboy #15 © KING

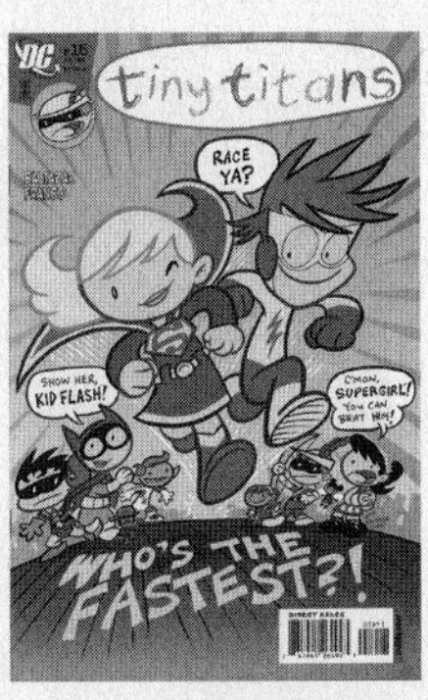

Tiny Titans #16 © DC

Tip Top Comics #24 © UFS

	GD 2.0	VG 4.0	FN 6.0	VF 8.0	VF/NM 9.0	NM- 9.2
	15	30	45	86	133	180
21-Frazetta Ghost Rider/Redmask-c	36	72	108	216	351	485
23-Frazetta Redmask-c	28	56	84	165	270	375
25-1st app. Black Phantom	18	36	54	105	165	225
26-30: 28-Wild Bill Hickok, Bat Masterson team up with Redmask. 29-B&W photo-c	10	20	30	58	79	100
31-33-Ghost Rider ends	10	20	30	54	72	90
34-Tales of the Ghost Rider begins (horror)-Classic "The Flower Women" & "Hard Boiled Harry!"	14	28	42	82	121	160
35-Last Tales of the Ghost Rider	11	22	33	62	86	110
36-The Ghost Rider returns, ends #41; liquid hallucinogenic drug story	13	26	39	74	105	135
37-Ghost Rider classic "To Touch Is to Die!", about Inca treasure	13	26	39	74	105	135
38-The Black Phantom begins (not in #39); classic Ghost Rider "The Phantom Guns of Feather Gap!"	13	26	39	74	105	135
39-41: All 3-D effect c/stories	14	28	42	81	118	155

NOTE: ***Dick Ayers** a-7, 9-41. **Bolle** a-1-41; c-19, 20, 22, 24-28, 30-41.*

TIM McCOY (Formerly Zoo Funnies; Pictorial Love Stories #22 on)
Charlton Comics: No. 16, Oct, 1948 - No. 21, Aug, 1949 (Western Movie Stories)

	GD	VG	FN	VF	VF/NM	NM-
16-John Wayne, Montgomery Clift app. in "Red River"; photo back-c	34	68	102	199	325	450
17-21: 17-Allan "Rocky" Lane guest stars. 18-Rod Cameron guest stars. 19-Whip Wilson, Andy Clyde guest star; Jesse James story. 20-Jimmy Wakely guest stars. 21-Johnny Mack Brown guest stars	24	48	72	142	234	325

TIMMY
Dell Publishing Co.: No. 715, Aug, 1956 - No. 1022, Aug-Oct, 1959

	GD	VG	FN	VF	VF/NM	NM-
Four Color 715 (#1)	5	10	15	30	48	65
Four Color 823 (8/57), 923 (8/58), 1022	4	8	12	26	41	55

TIMMY THE TIMID GHOST (Formerly Win-A-Prize?; see Blue Bird)
Charlton Comics: No. 3, 2/56 - No. 44, 10/64; No. 45, 9/66; 10/67 - No. 23, 7/71; V4#24, 9/85 - No. 26, 1/86

	GD	VG	FN	VF	VF/NM	NM-
3(1956) (1st Series)	12	24	36	69	97	125
4,5	8	16	24	42	54	65
6-10	3	6	9	20	30	40
11,12(4/58,10/58)-(100 pgs.)	6	12	18	43	69	95
13-20	3	6	9	18	27	35
21-45(1966)	3	6	9	14	19	24
1(10/67, 2nd series)	3	6	9	16	22	28
2-10	2	4	6	10	14	18
11-23: 23 (7/71)	1	3	4	8	10	12
24-26 (1985-86): Fago-r (low print run)						6.00

TIM TYLER (See Harvey Comics Hits #54)

TIM TYLER (Also see Comics Reading Libraries in the Promotional Comics section)
Better Publications: 1942

	GD	VG	FN	VF	VF/NM	NM-
1	15	30	45	85	130	175

TIM TYLER COWBOY
Standard Comics (King Features Synd.): No. 11, Nov, 1948 - No. 18, 1950

	GD	VG	FN	VF	VF/NM	NM-
11-By Lyman Young	9	18	27	50	65	80
12-18: 13-15-Full length western adventures	7	14	21	35	43	50

TINKER BELL (Disney, TV)(See Walt Disney Showcase #37)
Dell Publishing Co.: No. 896, Mar, 1958 - No. 982, Apr-June, 1959

	GD	VG	FN	VF	VF/NM	NM-
Four Color 896 (#1)-The Adventures of...	8	16	24	56	93	130
Four Color 982-The New Advs. of...	8	16	24	52	86	120

TINY FOLKS FUNNIES
Dell Publishing Co.: No. 60, 1944

	GD	VG	FN	VF	VF/NM	NM-
Four Color 60	14	28	42	97	194	290

TINY TESSIE (Tessie #1-23; Real Experiences #25)
Marvel Comics (20CC): No. 24, Oct, 1949 (52 pgs.)

	GD	VG	FN	VF	VF/NM	NM-
24	14	28	42	76	108	140

TINY TIM (Also see Super Comics)
Dell Publishing Co.: No. 4, 1941 - No. 235, July, 1949

	GD	VG	FN	VF	VF/NM	NM-
Large Feature Comic 4('41)	40	80	120	246	411	575
Four Color 20(1941)	37	74	111	218	354	490
Four Color 42(1943)	15	30	45	103	209	315
Four Color 235	6	12	18	37	59	80

TINY TITANS (Teen Titans)
DC Comics: Apr, 2008 - Present ($2.25/$2.50/$2.99)

	GD	VG	FN	VF	VF/NM	NM-
1-29-All ages stories of Teen Titans in Elementary school; Baltazar & Franco-s/a						3.00
1-(6/08, Free Comic Book Day giveaway) r/#1; Baltazar & Franco-s/a						2.25
30-38: 30-Begin $2.99-c. 37-Marvel Family app.						3.00
...: Adventures in Awesomeness TPB (2009, $12.99) r/#7-12; pin-ups						13.00
...: The First Rule of Pet Club... TPB (2010, $12.99) r/#19-25; pin-ups						13.00
...: Welcome To The Treehouse TPB (2009, $12.99) r/#1-6; pin-ups						13.00
...: Sidekickin' It TPB (2010, $12.99) r/#13-18; pin-ups						13.00

TINY TITANS / LITTLE ARCHIE (Teen Titans) (Digest-size reprint in World of Archie Double Digest Magazine #5)
DC Comics: Dec, 2010 - No. 3, Feb, 2011 ($2.99)

	GD	VG	FN	VF	VF/NM	NM-
1-3-Character crossover; Baltazar & Franco-s/a. 2-Josie and the Pussycats app.						3.00

TINY TOT COMICS
E. C. Comics: Mar, 1946 - No. 10, Nov-Dec, 1947 (For younger readers)

	GD	VG	FN	VF	VF/NM	NM-
1(nn)-52 pg. issues begin, end #4	39	78	117	240	395	550
2 (5/46)	22	44	66	130	213	295
3-10: 10-Christmas-c	20	40	60	120	195	270

TINY TOT FUNNIES (Formerly Family Funnies; becomes Junior Funnies)
Harvey Publ. (King Features Synd.): No. 9, June, 1951

	GD	VG	FN	VF	VF/NM	NM-
9-Flash Gordon, Mandrake, Dagwood, Daisy, etc.	8	16	24	42	54	65

TINY TOTS COMICS
Dell Publishing Co.: 1943 (Not reprints)

	GD	VG	FN	VF	VF/NM	NM-
1-Kelly-a(2); fairy tales	39	78	117	240	395	550

TIPPY & CAP STUBBS (See Popular Comics)
Dell Publishing Co.: No. 210, Jan, 1949 - No. 242, Aug, 1949

	GD	VG	FN	VF	VF/NM	NM-
Four Color 210 (#1)	5	10	15	32	51	70
Four Color 242	4	8	12	26	41	55

TIPPY'S FRIENDS GO-GO & ANIMAL
Tower Comics: July, 1966 - No. 15, Oct, 1969 (25¢)

	GD	VG	FN	VF	VF/NM	NM-
1	10	20	30	68	119	170
2-5,7,9-15: 12-15 titled "Tippy's Friend Go-Go"	6	12	18	39	62	85
6-The Monkees photo-c	9	18	27	61	103	145
8-Beatles app. on front/back-c	11	22	33	75	138	200

TIPPY TEEN (See Vicki)
Tower Comics: Nov, 1965 - No. 25, Oct, 1969 (25¢)

	GD	VG	FN	VF	VF/NM	NM-
1	11	22	33	75	138	200
2-4,6-10	7	14	21	45	73	100
5-1 pg. Beatles pin-up	7	14	21	50	83	115
11-20: 16-Twiggy photo-c	6	12	18	43	69	95
21-25	6	12	18	39	62	85
Special Collectors' Editions nn-(1969, 25¢)	6	12	18	43	69	95

TIPPY TERRY
Super/I. W. Enterprises: 1963

	GD	VG	FN	VF	VF/NM	NM-
Super Reprint #14('63)-r/Little Groucho #1	2	4	6	8	10	12
I.W. Reprint #1 (nd)-r/Little Groucho #1	2	4	6	8	10	12

TIP TOP COMICS
United Features #1-188/St. John #189-210/Dell Publishing Co. #211 on:
4/36 - No. 210, 1957; No. 211, 11-1/57-58 - No. 225, 5-7/61

	GD	VG	FN	VF	VF/NM	NM-
1-Tarzan by Hal Foster, Li'l Abner, Broncho Bill, Fritzi Ritz, Ella Cinders, Capt. & The Kids begin; strip-r (1st comic book app. of each)	800	1600	2400	4800	8250	11,700
2	181	362	543	1158	1979	2800
3-Tarzan-c	161	322	483	1030	1765	2500
4	94	188	282	597	1024	1450
5-8,10: 7-Photo & biography of Edgar Rice Burroughs. 8-Christmas-c	66	132	198	419	722	1025
9-Tarzan-c	84	168	252	538	919	1300
11,13,16,18-Tarzan-c: 11-Has Tarzan pin-up	63	126	189	403	689	975
12,14,15,17,19,20: 20-Christmas-c	49	98	147	309	522	735
21,24,27,30-(10/38)-Tarzan-c	52	104	156	328	552	775
22,23,25,26,28,29	39	78	117	229	375	520
31,35,38,40	36	72	108	211	343	475
32,36-Tarzan-c: 32-1st published Jack Davis-a (cartoon). 36-Kurtzman panel (1st published comic work)	53	106	159	334	567	800
33,34,37,39-Tarzan-c	48	96	144	302	514	725
41-Reprints 1st Tarzan Sunday; Tarzan-c	53	106	159	334	567	800
42,44,46,48,49	30	60	90	177	289	400
43,45,47,50,52-Tarzan-c. 43-Mort Walker panel	39	78	117	236	388	540
51,53	29	58	87	170	278	385

54-Origin Mirror Man & Triple Terror, also featured on cover

Tip Topper Comics #1 © UFS

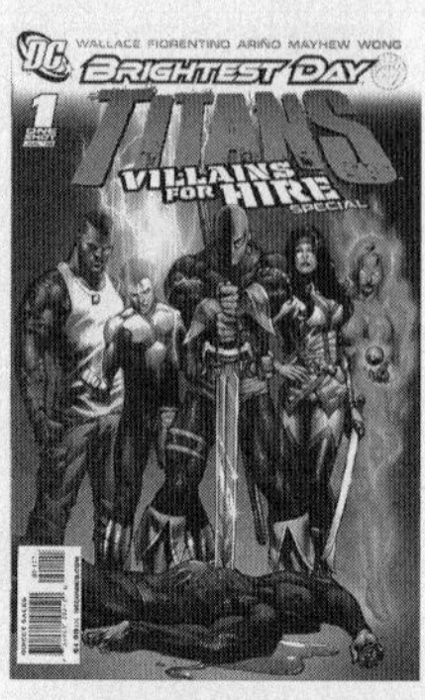

Titans: Villains For Hire Special #1 © DC

Tomahawk #9 © DC

	GD 2.0	VG 4.0	FN 6.0	VF 8.0	VF/NM 9.0	NM- 9.2
	37	74	111	218	354	490
55,56,58: Last Tarzan by Foster	24	48	72	142	234	325
57,59-62-Tarzan by Hogarth	31	62	93	182	296	410
63-80: 65,67-70,72-74,77,78-No Tarzan	15	30	45	88	137	185
81-90	14	28	42	80	115	150
91-99	13	26	39	72	101	130
100	14	28	42	76	108	140
101-140: 110-Gordo story. 111-Li'l Abner app. 118, 132-No Tarzan. 137-Sadie Hawkins Day story	10	20	30	54	72	90
141-170: 145,151-Gordo stories. 157-Last Li'l Abner; lingerie panels	8	16	24	44	57	70
171,172,174-183: 171-Tarzan reprints by B. Lubbers begin; end #188	9	18	27	47	61	75
173-Peanuts by Schulz	14	28	42	80	115	150
184-225-Peanuts apps.(4 pg. to 8 pg stories) in most						
Issues with Peanuts	10	20	30	54	72	90
Issues without Peanuts	8	16	24	40	50	60
Bound Volumes (Very Rare) sold at 1939 World's Fair; bound by publisher in pictorial comic boards (also see Comics on Parade)						
Bound issues 1-12	326	652	978	2282	3991	5700
Bound issues 13-24	177	354	531	1124	1937	2750
Bound issues 25-36	155	310	465	992	1696	2400

NOTE: *Tarzan by* **Foster**-*#1-40, 44-50; by* **Rex Maxon**-*#41-43; by* **Burne Hogarth**-*#57, 59, 62.*

TIP TOPPER COMICS
United Features Syndicate: Oct-Nov, 1949 - No. 28, 1954

	GD	VG	FN	VF	VF/NM	NM-
1-Li'l Abner, Abbie & Slats	12	24	36	67	94	120
2	8	16	24	44	57	70
3-5: 5-Fearless Fosdick app.	8	16	24	40	50	60
6-10: 6-Fearless Fosdick app.	7	14	21	37	46	55
11-16	6	12	18	31	38	45
17(6-7/52) (2nd app. of Peanuts by Schulz in comics?) (see United Comics #22 for 5-6/52 app.)	16	32	48	94	147	200
18-26: 18-24,26-Early Peanuts (2 pgs.). 25-Early Peanuts (3 pgs.) 26-Twin Earths	13	26	39	74	105	135
27,28-Twin Earths	8	16	24	40	50	60

NOTE: *Many lingerie panels in Fritzi Ritz stories.*

TITAN A.E.
Dark Horse Comics: May, 2000 - No. 3, July, 2000 ($2.95, limited series)

	NM-
1-3-Movie prequel; Al Rio-a	3.00

TITANS (Also see Teen Titans, New Teen Titans and New Titans)
DC Comics: Mar, 1999 - No. 50, Apr, 2003 ($2.50/$2.75)

	NM-
1-Titans re-form; Grayson-s; 2 covers	4.00
2-11,13-24,26-50: 2-Superman-c/app. 9,10,21,22-Deathstroke app. 24-Titans from "Kingdom Come" app. 32-36-Asamiya-c. 44-Begin $2.75-c	3.00
12-($3.50, 48 pages)	4.00
25-($3.95) Titans from "Kingdom Come" app.; Wolfman & Faerber-s; art by Pérez, Cardy, Grummett, Jimenez, Dodson, Pelletier	4.00
Annual 1 ('00, $3.50) Planet DC; intro Bushido	4.00
... East Special 1 (1/08, $3.99) Winick-s/Churchill-a; continues in Titans #1 (2008)	4.00
...Secret Files 1,2 (3/99, 10/00; $4.95) Profile pages & short stories	5.00

TITANS (Also see Teen Titans)
DC Comics: Jun, 2008 - Present ($3.50/$2.99)

	NM-
1-($3.50) Titans re-form again; Winick-s/Churchill-a; covers by Churchill & Van Sciver	3.50
2-33: 2-4-Trigon returns. 6-10-Jericho app. 24-Deathstroke & Luthor app.	3.00
...: Villains For Hire Special 1 (7/10, $4.99) Deathstroke's team; Atom (Ryan Choi) killed	5.00
...: Fractured TPB (2010, $17.99) r/#14,16-22	18.00
...: Lockdown TPB (2009, $14.99) r/#7-11	15.00
...: Old Friends HC (2008, $24.99) r/#1-6 & Titans East Special	25.00
...: Villains For Hire TPB (2011, $14.99) r/#24-27 & Villains For Hire Special 1	15.00

TITANS/ LEGION OF SUPER-HEROES: UNIVERSE ABLAZE
DC Comics: 2000 - No. 4, 2000 ($4.95, prestige format, limited series)

	NM-
1-4-Jurgens-s/a; P. Jimenez-a; teams battle Universo	5.00

TITAN SPECIAL
Dark Horse Comics: June, 1994 ($3.95, one-shot)

	NM-
1-($3.95, 52 pgs.)	4.00

TITANS: SCISSORS, PAPER, STONE
DC Comics: 1997 ($4.95, one-shot)

	NM-
1-Manga style Elseworlds; Adam Warren-s/a(p)	5.00

TITANS SELL-OUT SPECIAL
DC Comics: Nov, 1992 ($3.50, 52 pgs., one-shot)

	NM-
1-Fold-out Nightwing poster; 1st Teeny Titans	4.00

TITANS/ YOUNG JUSTICE: GRADUATION DAY
DC Comics: Early July, 2003 - No. 3, Aug, 2003 ($2.50, limited series)

	NM-
1,2-Winick-s/Garza-a; leads into Teen Titans and The Outsiders series. 2-Lilith dies	3.00
3-Death of Donna Troy (Wonder Girl)	3.00
TPB (2003, $6.95) r/#1-3; plus previews of Teen Titans and The Outsiders series	7.00

T-MAN (Also see Police Comics #103)
Quality Comics Group: Sept, 1951 - No. 38, Dec, 1956

	GD	VG	FN	VF	VF/NM	NM-
1-Pete Trask, T-Man begins; Jack Cole-a	41	82	123	256	428	600
2-Crandall-c	22	44	66	132	216	300
3,7,8: All Crandall-c	21	42	63	122	199	275
4,5-Crandall-c/a each	22	44	66	128	209	290
6-"The Man Who Could Be Hitler" c/story; Crandall-c.	26	52	78	154	252	350
9,10-Crandall-c	19	38	57	109	172	235
11-Used in **POP**, pg. 95 & color illo.	15	30	45	86	133	180
12,13,15-19,22-26: 23-H-Bomb panel. 24-Last pre-code issue (4/55). 25-Not Crandall-a	14	28	42	78	112	145
14-Hitler-c	20	40	60	114	182	250
20-H-Bomb explosion-c/story	17	34	51	98	154	210
21- "The Return of Mussolini" c/story	15	30	45	85	130	175
27-33,35-38	13	26	39	74	105	135
34-Hitler-c	17	34	51	98	154	210

NOTE: *Anti-communist stories common.* **Crandall** *c-2-10p.* **Cuidera** *c(i)-1-38. Bondage c-15.*

TMNT... (Also see Teenage Mutant Ninja Turtles and related titles)
Mirage Publishing: March 2007 ($3.25/$4.95, B&W, one-shots)

	NM-
...: Raphael Movie Prequel 1; ...: Michelangelo Movie Prequel 2; ...: Donatello Movie Prequel 3; ...: April Movie Prequel 4; ...: Leonardo Movie Prequel 5; back-story for movie	3.25
...: The Official Movie Adaptation ($4.95) adapts 2007 movie; Munroe-c	5.00

TMNT MUTANT UNIVERSE SOURCEBOOK
Archie Comics: 1992 - No. 3, 1992? ($1.95, 52 pgs.)(Lists characters from A-Z)

	NM-
1-3: 3-New characters; fold-out poster	4.00

TNT COMICS
Charles Publishing Co.: Feb, 1946 (36 pgs.)

	GD	VG	FN	VF	VF/NM	NM-
1-Yellowjacket app.	31	62	93	186	303	420

TOBY TYLER (Disney, see Movie Comics)
Dell Publishing Co.: No. 1092, Apr-June, 1960

	GD	VG	FN	VF	VF/NM	NM-
Four Color 1092-Movie, photo-c	6	12	18	43	69	95

TODAY'S BRIDES
Ajax/Farrell Publishing Co.: Nov, 1955; No. 2, Feb, 1956; No. 3, Sept, 1956; No. 4, Nov, 1956

	GD	VG	FN	VF	VF/NM	NM-
1	9	18	27	50	65	80
2-4	7	14	21	35	43	50

TODAY'S ROMANCE
Standard Comics: No. 5, March, 1952 - No. 8, Sept, 1952 (All photo-c?)

	GD	VG	FN	VF	VF/NM	NM-
5-Photo-c	11	22	33	60	83	105
6-Photo-c; Toth-a	11	22	33	62	86	110
7,8	9	18	27	50	65	80

TOE TAGS FEATURING GEORGE A. ROMARO
DC Comics: Dec, 2004 - No. 6, May, 2005 ($2.95/$2.99)

	NM-
1-6-Zombie story by George Romaro; Wrightson-c/Castillo-a	3.00

TOKA (Jungle King)
Dell Publishing Co.: Aug-Oct, 1964 - No. 10, Jan, 1967 (Painted-c #1,2)

	GD	VG	FN	VF	VF/NM	NM-
1	5	10	15	30	48	65
2	3	6	9	18	27	35
3-10	3	6	9	16	22	28

TOKYO STORM WARNING (See Red/Tokyo Storm Warning for TPB)
DC Comics (Cliffhanger): Aug, 2003 - No. 3, Dec, 2003 ($2.95, limited series)

	NM-
1-3-Warren Ellis-s/James Raiz-a	3.00

TOMAHAWK (Son of... on-c of #131-140; see Star Spangled Comics #69 & World's Finest Comics #65)
National Periodical Publications: Sept-Oct, 1950 - No. 140, May-June, 1972

	GD	VG	FN	VF	VF/NM	NM-
1-Tomahawk & boy sidekick Dan Hunter begin by Fred Ray	181	362	543	1158	1979	2800
2-Frazetta/Williamson-a (4 pgs.)	66	132	198	419	722	1025
3-5	41	82	123	256	428	600
6-10: 7-Last 52 pg. issue	36	72	108	211	343	475

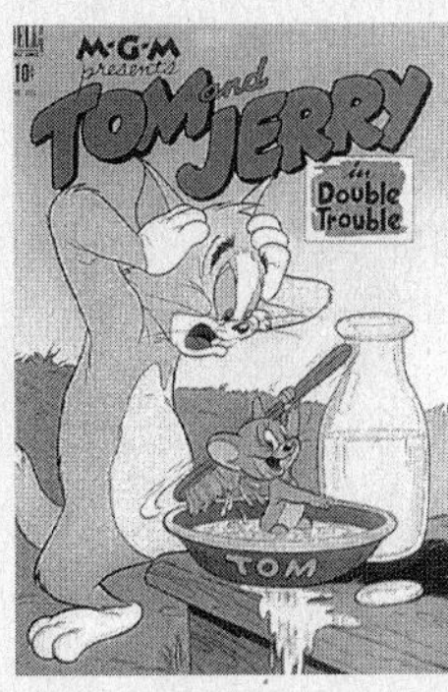

Tom and Jerry Four Color #163 © Loew's Inc.

Tomb of Dracula #7 © MAR

Tomb of Terror #9 © HARV

	GD 2.0	VG 4.0	FN 6.0	VF 8.0	VF/NM 9.0	NM- 9.2
11-20	24	48	72	142	234	325
21-27,30: 30-Last precode (2/55)	21	42	63	126	206	285
28-1st app. Lord Shilling (arch-foe)	22	44	66	132	216	300
29-Frazetta-r/Jimmy Wakely #3 (3 pgs.)	26	52	78	154	252	350
31-40	18	36	54	107	169	230
41-50	10	20	30	71	128	185
51-56,58-60	9	18	27	64	110	155
57-Frazetta-r/Jimmy Wakely #6 (3 pgs.)	10	20	30	71	128	185
61-77: 77-Last 10¢ issue	9	18	27	60	100	140
78-85: 81-1st app. Miss Liberty. 83-Origin Tomahawk's Rangers	7	14	21	50	83	115
86-99: 96-Origin/1st app. The Hood, alias Lady Shilling	6	12	18	39	62	85
100	6	12	18	41	66	90
101-110: 107-Origin/1st app. Thunder-Man	5	10	15	30	48	65
111-115,120,122: 122-Last 12¢ issue	4	8	12	28	44	60
116-1st Neal Adams cover	7	14	21	45	73	100
117-119,121,123-130-Neal Adams-c	5	10	15	32	51	70
131-Frazetta-r/Jimmy Wakely #7 (3 pgs.); origin Firehair retold	4	8	12	22	34	45
132-135: 135-Last 15¢ issue	3	6	9	17	25	32
136-138,140 (52 pg. Giants)	3	6	9	20	30	40
139-Frazetta-r/Star Spangled #113	4	8	12	22	34	45

NOTE: ***Fred Ray*** *c-1, 2, 8, 11, 30, 34, 35, 40-43, 45, 46, 82. Firehair by* ***Kubert****-131-134, 136.* ***Maurer*** *a-138.* ***Severin*** *a-135.* ***Starr*** *a-5.* ***Thorne*** *a-137, 140.*

TOM AND JERRY (See Comic Album #4, 8, 12, Dell Giant #21, Dell Giants, Golden Comics Digest #1, 5, 8, 13, 15, 18, 22, 25, 28, 35, Kite fun Book & March of Comics #21, 46, 61, 70, 88, 103, 119, 128, 145, 154, 173, 190, 207, 224, 281, 295, 305, 321,333, 345, 361, 365, 388, 400, 444, 451, 463, 480)

TOM AND JERRY (...Comics, early issues) (M.G.M.)
(Formerly Our Gang No. 1-59) (See Dell Giants for annuals)
Dell Publishing Co./Gold Key No. 213-327/Whitman No. 328 on: No. 193, 6/48; No. 60, 7/49 - No. 212, 7-9/62; No. 213, 11/62 - No. 291, 2/75; No. 292, 3/77 - No. 342, 5/82 - No. 344, 6/84

	GD 2.0	VG 4.0	FN 6.0	VF 8.0	VF/NM 9.0	NM- 9.2
Four Color 193 (#1)-Titled "M.G.M. Presents..."	22	44	66	159	317	475
60-Barney Bear, Benny Burro cont. from Our Gang; Droopy begins	12	24	36	82	154	225
61	10	20	30	67	116	165
62-70: 66-X-Mas-c	8	16	24	56	93	130
71-80: 77,90-X-Mas-c. 79-Spike & Tyke begin	7	14	21	45	73	100
81-99	6	12	18	41	66	90
100	6	12	18	43	69	95
101-120	5	10	15	34	55	75
121-140: 126-X-Mas-c	5	10	15	30	48	65
141-160	4	8	12	26	41	55
161-200	4	8	12	24	37	50
201-212(7-9/62)(Last Dell issue)	4	8	12	22	34	45
213,214-(84 pgs.)-Titled "...Funhouse"	6	12	18	41	66	90
215-240: 215-Titled "...Funhouse"	3	6	9	17	25	32
241-270	2	4	6	11	16	20
271-300: 286- "Tom & Jerry"	2	4	6	8	11	14
301-327 (Gold Key)	1	3	4	6	8	10
328,329 (Whitman)	2	4	6	8	11	14
330(8/80),331(10/80), 332-(3-pack only)	3	6	9	20	30	40
333-341: 339(2/82), 340(2-3/82), 341(4/82)	2	4	6	8	10	12
342-344 (All #90058, no date, date code, 3-pack): 342(6/83), 343(8/83), 344(6/84)	3	6	9	14	19	24
Mouse From T.R.A.P. 1(7/66)-Giant, G. K.	5	10	15	30	48	65
Summer Fun 1(7/67, 68 pgs.)(Gold Key)-Reprints Barks' Droopy from Summer Fun #1	5	10	15	30	48	65

NOTE: *#60-87, 98-121, 268, 277, 289, 302 are 52 pgs.. Reprints-#225, 241, 245, 247, 252, 254, 266, 268, 270, 292-327, 329-342, 344.*

TOM & JERRY
Harvey Comics: Sept, 1991 - No. 18, Aug, 1994 ($1.25)

	GD 2.0	VG 4.0	FN 6.0	VF 8.0	VF/NM 9.0	NM- 9.2
1-18: 1-Tom & Jerry, Barney Bear-r by Carl Barks						3.00
50th Anniversary Special 1 (10/91, $2.50, 68 pgs.)-Benny the Lonesome Burro-r by Barks (story/a)/Our Gang #9						4.00

TOMB OF DARKNESS (Formerly Beware)
Marvel Comics Group: No. 9, July, 1974 - No. 23, Nov, 1976

	GD 2.0	VG 4.0	FN 6.0	VF 8.0	VF/NM 9.0	NM- 9.2
9	3	6	9	18	27	35
10-23: 11,16,18-21-Kirby-a. 15,19-Ditko-r. 17-Woodbridge-r/Astonishing #62; Powell-r. 20-Everett Venus-r/Venus #19. 22-r/Tales To Astonish #27; 1st Hank Pym. 23-Everett-r	2	4	6	13	18	22
20,21-(30¢-c variants, limited distribution)(5,7/76)	4	8	12	24	37	50

TOMB OF DRACULA (See Giant-Size Dracula, Dracula Lives, Nightstalkers, Power Record Comics & Requiem for Dracula)
Marvel Comics Group: Apr, 1972 - No. 70, Aug, 1979

	GD 2.0	VG 4.0	FN 6.0	VF 8.0	VF/NM 9.0	NM- 9.2
1-1st app. Dracula & Frank Drake; Colan-p in all; Neal Adams-c	16	32	48	114	232	350
2	9	18	27	60	100	140
3-6: 3-Intro. Dr. Rachel Van Helsing & Inspector Chelm. 6-Neal Adams-c	7	14	21	47	76	105
7-9	6	12	18	41	66	90
10-1st app. Blade the Vampire Slayer (who app. in 1998 and 2002 movies)	21	42	63	150	300	450
11,14-16,20:	5	10	15	32	51	70
12-2nd app. Blade; Brunner-c(p)	9	18	27	63	107	150
13-Origin Blade	10	20	30	71	128	185
17,19: 17-Blade bitten by Dracula. 19-Blade discovers he is immune to vampire's bite. 1st mention of Blade having vampire blood in him	7	14	21	45	73	100
18-Two-part x-over cont'd in Werewolf by Night #15	6	12	18	41	66	90
21,24-Blade app.	5	10	15	32	51	70
22,23,26,27,29	3	6	9	20	30	40
25-1st app. & origin Hannibal King	4	8	12	28	44	60
25-2nd printing (1994)	2	4	6	8	10	12
28-Blade app. on-c & inside as an illusion	4	8	12	28	44	60
30,41-45-Blade app. 45-Intro. Deacon Frost, the vampire who bit Blade's mother	4	8	12	26	41	55
31-40	3	6	9	18	27	35
43-45-(30¢-c variants, limited distribution)	7	14	21	49	80	110
46,47-(Regular 25¢ editions)(4-8/76)	3	6	9	14	20	25
46,47-(30¢-c variants, limited distribution)	4	8	12	24	37	50
48,49,51-57,59,60: 57,59,60-(30¢-c)	3	6	9	14	20	25
50-Silver Surfer app.	4	8	12	24	37	50
57,59,60-(35¢-c variants)(6-9/77)	4	8	12	24	37	50
58-All Blade issue (Regular 30¢ edition)	5	10	15	30	48	65
58-(35¢-c variant)(7/77)	8	16	24	56	93	130
61-69	3	6	9	14	20	25
70-Double size	4	8	12	24	37	50

NOTE: ***N. Adams*** *c-1, 6.* ***Colan*** *a-1-70p; c(p)-8, 38-42, 44-56, 58-70.* ***Wrightson*** *c-43.*

TOMB OF DRACULA, THE (Magazine)
Marvel Comics Group: Oct, 1979 - No. 6, Aug, 1980 (B&W)

	GD 2.0	VG 4.0	FN 6.0	VF 8.0	VF/NM 9.0	NM- 9.2
1,3: 1-Colan-a; features on movies "Dracula" and "Love at First Bite" w/photos. 3-Good girl cover-a; Miller-a (2 pg. sketch)	2	4	6	11	16	20
2,6: 2-Ditko-a (36 pgs.); Nosferatu movie feature. 6-Lilith story w/Sienkiewicz-a	2	4	6	8	11	14
4,5: Stephen King interview	2	4	6	13	18	22

NOTE: ***Buscema*** *a-4p, 5p.* ***Chaykin*** *c-5, 6.* ***Colan*** *a(p)-1, 3-6.* ***Miller*** *a-3.* ***Romita*** *a-2p.*

TOMB OF DRACULA
Marvel Comics (Epic Comics): 1991 - No. 4, 1992 ($4.95, 52 pgs., squarebound, mini-series)

	GD 2.0	VG 4.0	FN 6.0	VF 8.0	VF/NM 9.0	NM- 9.2
Book 1-4: Colan/Williamson-a; Colan painted-c						5.00

TOMB OF DRACULA
Marvel Comics: Dec, 2004 - No. 4, Mar, 2005 ($2.99, limited series)

	GD 2.0	VG 4.0	FN 6.0	VF 8.0	VF/NM 9.0	NM- 9.2
1-4-Blade app.; Tolagson-a/Sienkiewicz-c						3.00

TOMB OF LEGEIA (See Movie Classics)

TOMB OF TERROR (Thrills of Tomorrow #17 on)
Harvey Publications: June, 1952 - No. 16, July, 1954

	GD 2.0	VG 4.0	FN 6.0	VF 8.0	VF/NM 9.0	NM- 9.2
1	46	92	138	290	488	685
2	30	60	90	177	289	400
3-Bondage-c; atomic disaster story	31	62	93	182	296	410
4-12: 4-Heart ripped out. 8-12-Nostrand-a	29	58	87	170	278	385
13-Special S/F issue	39	78	117	235	385	535
14-Classic S/F-c; Check-a	57	114	171	362	619	875
15-S/F issue; c-shows face exploding	119	238	357	762	1306	1850
16-Special S/F issue; Nostrand-a	36	72	108	216	351	485

NOTE: ***Edd Cartier*** *a-13?* ***Elias*** *c-2, 5-16.* ***Kremer*** *a-1, 7; c-1.* ***Nostrand*** *a-8-12, 15r 16.* ***Palais*** *a-2, 3, 5-7.* ***Powell*** *a-1, 3, 5, 9-16.* ***Sparling*** *a-12, 13, 15.*

TOMB OF TERROR
Marvel Comics: Dec, 2010 ($3.99, B&W, one-shot)

	GD 2.0	VG 4.0	FN 6.0	VF 8.0	VF/NM 9.0	NM- 9.2
1-Short stories of Man-Thing, Son of Satan, Werewolf By Night & The Living Mummy						4.00

TOMB RAIDER (one-shots)
Image Comics (Top Cow Prod.)

	GD 2.0	VG 4.0	FN 6.0	VF 8.0	VF/NM 9.0	NM- 9.2
...: Arabian Nights (8/04, $5.99) Avery-s/Tan-a/c						6.00
... Cover Gallery 2006 (4/06, $2.99) artist galleries and series gallery; pin-ups						3.00

Tomb Raider: The Series #22 © Eidos

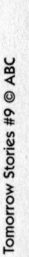

Tom Mix Western #8 © FAW

Tomorrow Stories #9 © ABC

	GD 2.0	VG 4.0	FN 6.0	VF 8.0	VF/NM 9.0	NM- 9.2
.../The Darkness Special 1 (2001, TopCowStore.com)-Wohl-s/Tan-a						3.00
Epiphany 1 (8/03, $4.99)-Jurgens-s/Banks-a/Haley-c; preview of Witchblade Animated						5.00
Takeover 1 (1/04, $2.99)-Benefiel-a/Daniel-c						3.00
... Vs. The Wolf-Men: Monster War 2005 (7/05, $2.99) 2nd part of Monster War x-over						3.00
.../Witchblade/Magdalena/Vampirella #1 (8/05, $2.99, B&W) three covers; Chin-a						3.00

TOMB RAIDER: JOURNEYS
Image Comics (Top Cow Prod.): Jan, 2002 - No. 12, May, 2003 ($2.50/$2.99)

	GD	VG	FN	VF	VF/NM	NM-
1-12: 1-Avery-s/Drew Johnson-a. 1-Two covers by Johnson & Hughes						3.00

TOMB RAIDER: THE GREATEST TREASURE OF ALL
Image Comics (Top Cow Prod.): 2002; Oct, 2005 ($6.99)

	GD	VG	FN	VF	VF/NM	NM-
Prelude (2002, 16 pgs., no cover price) Jusko-c/a						3.00
1-(10/05, $6.99) Jusko-a/Jurgens-s; sketch pages, reference photos, art in progress						7.00

TOMB RAIDER: THE SERIES (Also see Witchblade/Tomb Raider)
Image Comics (Top Cow Prod.): Dec, 1999 - No. 50, Mar, 2005 ($2.50/$2.99)

	GD	VG	FN	VF	VF/NM	NM-
1-Jurgens-s/Park-a; 3 covers by Park, Finch, Turner						5.00
2-24,26-29,31-50: 21-Black-c w/foil. 31-Mhan-a. 37-Flip book preview of Stryke Force						3.00
25-Michael Turner-c/a; Witchblade app.; Endgame x-over with Witchblade #60 & Evo #1						4.00
30-($4.99) Tony Daniel-a						5.00
#0 (6/01, $2.50) Avery-s/Ching-a/c						3.00
#1/2 (10/01, $2.95) Early days of Lara Croft; Jurgens-s/Lopez-a						3.00
...: Chasing Shangri-La (2002, $12.95, TPB) r/#11-15						13.00
Free Comic Book Day giveaway - (5/02) r/#1 with "Free Comic Book Day" banner on-c						2.50
... Gallery (12/00, $2.95) Pin-ups & previous covers by various						3.00
... Magazine (6/01, $4.95) Hughes-c; r/#1,2; Jurgens interview						5.00
...: Mystic Artifacts (2001, $14.95, TPB) r/#5-10						15.00
...: Saga of the Medusa Mask (9/00, $9.95, TPB) r/#1-4; new Park-c						10.00
... Vol. 1 Compendium (11/06, $59.99) r/#1-50; variant covers and pin-up art						60.00

TOMB RAIDER/WITCHBLADE SPECIAL (Also see Witchblade/Tomb Raider)
Top Cow Prod.: Dec, 1997 (mail-in offer, one-shot)

	GD	VG	FN	VF	VF/NM	NM-
1-Turner-s/a(p); green background cover	1	3	4	6	8	10
1-Variant-c with orange sun background	1	3	4	6	8	10
1-Variant-c with black sides	1	3	4	6	8	10
1-Revisited (12/98, $2.95) reprints #1, Turner-c						3.00
...: Trouble Seekers TPB (2002, $7.95) rep. T.R./W & W/T.R. & W/T.R. 1/2; new Turner-c						8.00

TOMBSTONE TERRITORY
Dell Publishing Co.: No. 1123, Aug, 1960

	GD	VG	FN	VF	VF/NM	NM-
Four Color 1123	8	16	24	56	93	130

TOM CAT (Formerly Bo; Atom The Cat #9 on)
Charlton Comics: No. 4, Apr, 1956 - No. 8, July, 1957

	GD	VG	FN	VF	VF/NM	NM-
4-Al Fago-c/a	8	16	24	44	57	70
5-8	6	12	18	31	38	45

TOM CORBETT, SPACE CADET (TV)
Dell Publishing Co.: No. 378, Jan-Feb, 1952 - No. 11, Sept-Nov, 1954 (All painted covers)

	GD	VG	FN	VF	VF/NM	NM-
Four Color 378 (#1)-McWilliams-a	15	30	45	106	216	325
Four Color 400,421-McWilliams-a	10	20	30	69	122	175
4(11-1/53) - 11	8	16	24	54	90	125

TOM CORBETT SPACE CADET (See March of Comics #102)

TOM CORBETT SPACE CADET (TV)
Prize Publications: V2#1, May-June, 1955 - V2#3, Sept-Oct, 1955

	GD	VG	FN	VF	VF/NM	NM-
V2#1-Robot-c	32	64	96	192	314	435
2,3-Meskin-c	24	48	72	142	234	325

TOM, DICK & HARRIET (See Gold Key Spotlight)

TOM LANDRY AND THE DALLAS COWBOYS
Spire Christian Comics/Fleming H. Revell Co.: 1973 (35/49¢)

	GD	VG	FN	VF	VF/NM	NM-
nn-35¢ edition	3	6	9	14	19	24
nn-49¢ edition	2	4	6	9	13	16

TOM MIX WESTERN (Movie, radio star) (Also see The Comics, Crackajack Funnies, Master Comics, 100 Pages Of Comics, Popular Comics, Real Western Hero, Six Gun Heroes, Western Hero & XMas Comics)
Fawcett Publications: Jan, 1948 - No. 61, May, 1953 (1-17: 52 pgs.)

	GD	VG	FN	VF	VF/NM	NM-
1 (Photo-c, 52 pgs.)-Tom Mix & his horse Tony begin; Tumbleweed Jr. begins, ends #52,54,55	53	106	159	334	567	800
2 (Photo-c)	25	50	75	150	245	340
3-5 (Painted/photo-c): 5-Billy the Kid & Oscar app.	19	38	57	111	176	240
6-8: 6,7 (Painted/photo-c). 8-Kinstler tempera-c	16	32	48	94	147	200
9,10 (Paint/photo-c) 9-Used in **SOTI**, pgs. 323-325	15	30	45	90	140	190
11-Kinstler oil-c	14	28	42	82	121	160
12 (Painted/photo-c)	14	28	42	78	112	145
13-17 (Painted-c, 52 pgs.)	14	28	42	78	112	145
18,22 (Painted-c, 36 pgs.)	12	24	36	69	97	125
19 (Photo-c, 52 pgs.)	13	26	39	74	105	135
20,21,23 (Painted-c, 52 pgs.)	12	24	36	69	97	125
24,25,27-29 (52 pgs.): 24-Photo-c begin, end #61. 29-Slim Pickens app.	11	22	33	60	83	105
26,30 (36 pgs.)	10	20	30	56	76	95
31-33,35-37,39,40,42 (52 pgs.): 39-Red Eagle app.	10	20	30	56	76	95
34,38 (36 pgs. begin)	9	18	27	52	69	85
41,43-60: 57-(9/52)-Dope smuggling story	8	16	24	40	50	60
61-Last issue	9	18	27	47	61	75

NOTE: *Photo-c from 1930s Tom Mix movies (he died in 1940). Many issues contain ads for Tom Mix, Rocky Lane, Space Patrol and other premiums. Captain Tootsie by* **C.C. Beck** *in #6-11, 20.*

TOM MIX WESTERN
AC Comics: 1988 - No. 2, 1989? ($2.95, B&W w/16 pgs. color, 44 pgs.)

	GD	VG	FN	VF	VF/NM	NM-
1-Tom Mix-r/Master #124,128,131,102 plus Billy the Kid-r by Severin; photo front/back/inside-c						4.00
2-($2.50, B&W)-Gabby Hayes-r; photo covers						4.00
...Holiday Album 1 (1990, $3.50, B&W, one-shot, 44 pgs.)-Contains photos & 1950s Tom Mix-r; photo inside-c						4.00

TOMMY OF THE BIG TOP (Thrilling Circus Adventures)
King Features Synd./Standard Comics: No. 10, Sep, 1948 - No. 12, Mar, 1949

	GD	VG	FN	VF	VF/NM	NM-
10-By John Lehti	9	18	27	52	69	85
11,12	7	14	21	35	43	50

TOMMYSAURUS REX
Image Comics: Aug, 2004 ($11.95, B&W, graphic novel)

	GD	VG	FN	VF	VF/NM	NM-
Vol. 1 - Doug TenNapel-s/a						12.00

TOMMY TOMORROW (See Action Comics #127, Real Fact #6, Showcase #41,42,44,46,47 & World's Finest #102)

TOMOE (Also see Shi: The Way Of the Warrior #6)
Crusade Comics: July, 1995 - No. 3, June, 1996($2.95)

	GD	VG	FN	VF	VF/NM	NM-
0-3: 2-B&W Dogs o' War preview. 3-B&W Demon Gun preview						3.00
0 (3/96, $2.95)-variant-c.						3.00
0-Commemorative edition (5,000)	2	4	6	8	10	12
1-Commemorative edition (5,000)	2	4	6	9	12	15
1-($2.95)-FAN Appreciation edition						3.00
TPB (1997, $14.95) r/#0-3						15.00

TOMOE: UNFORGETTABLE FIRE
Crusade Comics: June, 1997 ($2.95, one-shot)

	GD	VG	FN	VF	VF/NM	NM-
1-Prequel to Shi: The Series						3.00

TOMOE-WITCHBLADE/FIRE SERMON
Crusade Comics: Sept, 1996 ($3.95, one-shot)

	GD	VG	FN	VF	VF/NM	NM-
1-Tucci-c						5.00
1-($9.95)-Avalon Ed. w/gold foil-c						10.00

TOMOE-WITCHBLADE/MANGA SHI PREVIEW EDITION
Crusade Comics: July, 1996 ($5.00, B&W)

	GD	VG	FN	VF	VF/NM	NM-
nn-San Diego Preview Edition						5.00

TOMORROW KNIGHTS
Marvel Comics (Epic Comics): June, 1990 - No. 6, Mar, 1991 ($1.50)

	GD	VG	FN	VF	VF/NM	NM-
1-6: 1-($1.95, 52 pgs.)						3.00

TOMORROW STORIES
America's Best Comics: Oct, 1999 - No. 12, Aug, 2002 ($3.50/$2.95)

	GD	VG	FN	VF	VF/NM	NM-
1-Two covers by Ross and Nowlan; Moore-s						3.50
2-12-($2.95)						3.00
... Special (1/06, $6.99) Nowlan-c; Moore-s; Greyshirt tribute to Will Eisner						7.00
... Special 2 (5/06, $6.99) Gene Ha-c; Moore-s; Promethea app.						7.00
Book 1 Hardcover (2002, $24.95) r/#1-6						25.00
Book 1 TPB (2003, $17.95) r/#1-6						18.00
Book 2 Hardcover (2004, $24.95) r/#7-12						25.00
Book 2 TPB (2005, $17.99) r/#7-12						18.00

TOM SAWYER (See Adventures of... & Famous Stories)

TOM SKINNER-UP FROM HARLEM (See Up From Harlem)

TOM STRONG (Also see Many Worlds of Tesla Strong)
America's Best Comics: June, 1999 - No. 36, May, 2006 ($3.50/$2.95/$2.99)

	GD	VG	FN	VF	VF/NM	NM-
1-Two covers by Ross and Sprouse; Moore-s/Sprouse-a						4.00
1-Special Edition (9/09, $1.00) reprint with "After Watchmen" cover frame						3.00

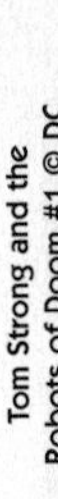
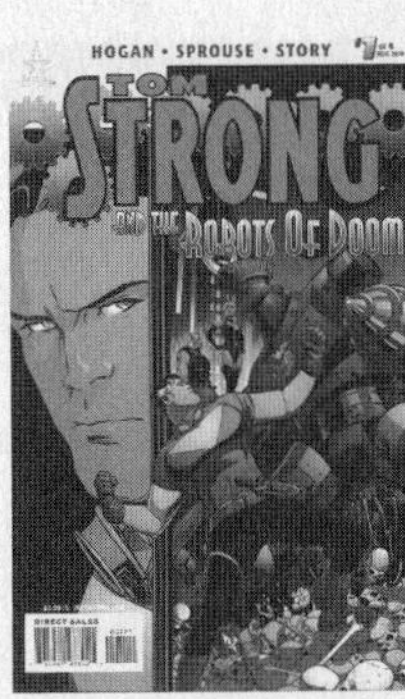

Tom Strong and the Robots of Doom #1 © DC

The Toodles #10 © Z-D

Top Cat (2nd series) #19 © H-B

GD 2.0 | VG 4.0 | FN 6.0 | VF 8.0 | VF/NM 9.0 | NM- 9.2

2-36: 4-Art Adams-a (8 pgs.) 13-Fawcett homage w/art by Sprouse, Baker, Heath
 20-Origin of Tom Stone. 22-Ordway-a. 31,32-Moorcock-s 3.00
...: Book One HC ('00, $24.95) r/#1-7, cover gallery and sketchbook 25.00
...: Book One TPB ('01, $14.95) r/#1-7, cover gallery and sketchbook 15.00
...: Book Two HC ('02, $24.95) r/#8-14, sketchbook 25.00
...: Book Two TPB ('03, $14.95) r/#8-14, sketchbook 15.00
...: Book Three HC ('04, $24.95) r/#15-19, sketchbook 25.00
...: Book Three TPB ('04, $17.95) r/#15-19, sketchbook 18.00
...: Book Four HC ('04, $24.95) r/#20-25, sketch pages 25.00
...: Book Four TPB ('05, $17.99) r/#20-25, sketch pages 18.00
...: Book Five HC ('05, $24.99) r/#26-30, sketch pages 25.00
...: Book Five TPB ('06, $17.99) r/#26-30, sketch pages 18.00
...: Book Six HC ('06, $24.99) r/#31-36 25.00
...: Book Six TPB ('08, $17.99) r/#31-36 18.00
...: The Deluxe Edition Book One (2009, $39.99, d.j.) r/#1-12; Moore intro.; sketch-a 40.00
...: The Deluxe Edition Book Two (2010, $39.99, d.j.) r/#13-24; sketch-a 40.00

TOM STRONG AND THE ROBOTS OF DOOM
DC Comics (WildStorm): Aug, 2010 - No. 6, Jan, 2011 ($3.99, limited series)
1-6-Hogan-s/Sprouse-a. 1-Covers by Sprouse & Williams 4.00

TOM STRONG'S TERRIFIC TALES
America's Best Comics: Jan, 2002 - No. 12 ($3.50/$2.95)
1-Short stories; Moore-s; art by Adams, Rivoche, Hernandez, Weiss 3.50
2-12-($2.95) 2-Adams, Ordway, Weiss-a; Adams-c. 4-Rivoche-a. 5-Pearson, Aragonés-a
 11-Timm-a 3.00
...: Book One HC ('04, $24.95) r/#1-6, cover gallery and sketch pages 25.00
...: Book One SC ('05, $17.99) r/#1-6, cover gallery and sketch pages 18.00
...: Book Two HC ('05, $24.95) r/#7-12, covers 25.00

TOM TERRIFIC! (TV)(See Mighty Mouse Fun Club Magazine #1)
Pines Comics (Paul Terry): Summer, 1957 - No. 6, Fall, 1958
(See Terry Toons Giant Summer Fun Book)
1-1st app.?; CBS Television Presents... 21 42 63 126 206 285
2-6-(scarce) 16 32 48 94 147 200

TOM THUMB
Dell Publishing Co.: No. 972, Jan, 1959
Four Color 972-Movie, George Pal 8 16 24 58 97 135

TOM-TOM, THE JUNGLE BOY (See A-1 Comics & Tick Tock Tales)
Magazine Enterprises: 1947 - No. 3, 1947; Nov, 1957 - No. 3, Mar, 1958
1-Funny animal 12 24 36 67 94 120
2,3(1947): 3-Christmas issue 9 18 27 50 65 80
Tom-Tom & Itchi the Monk 1(11/57) - 3(3/58) 5 10 15 24 30 35
I.W. Reprint No. 1,2,8,10: 1,2,8-r/Koko & Kola #? 2 4 6 8 10 12

TONGUE LASH
Dark Horse Comics: Aug, 1996 - No. 2, Sept, 1996 ($2.95, lim. series, mature)
1,2: Taylor-c/a 3.00

TONGUE LASH II
Dark Horse Comics: Feb, 1999 - No. 2, Mar, 1999 ($2.95, lim. series, mature)
1,2: Taylor-c/a 3.00

TONKA (Disney)
Dell Publishing Co.: No. 966, Jan, 1959
Four Color 966-Movie (Starring Sal Mineo)-photo-c 8 16 24 58 97 135

TONTO (See The Lone Ranger's Companion...)

TONY TRENT (The Face #1,2)
Big Shot/Columbia Comics Group: No. 3, 1948 - No. 4, 1949
3,4: 3-The Face app. by Mart Bailey 18 36 54 105 165 225

TOODLES, THE (The Toodle Twins with #1)
Ziff-Davis (Approved Comics)/Argo: No. 10, July-Aug, 1951; Mar, 1956 (Newspaper-r)
10-Painted-c, some newspaper-r by The Baers 12 24 36 69 97 125
...Twins 1(Argo, 3/56)-Reprints by The Baers 8 16 24 42 54 65

TOO MUCH COFFEE MAN
Adhesive Comics: July, 1993 - No. 10, Dec, 2000 ($2.50, B&W)
1-Shannon Wheeler story & art 2 4 6 9 12 15
2,3 1 2 3 5 7 9
4,5 6.00
6-10 4.00
Full Color Special-nn($2.95),2-(7/97, $3.95) 4.00

TOO MUCH COFFEE MAN SPECIAL
Dark Horse Comics: July, 1997 ($2.95, B&W)
nn-Reprints Dark Horse Presents #92-95 4.00

TOO MUCH HOPELESS SAVAGES
Oni Press: June, 2003 - No. 4, Apr, 2004 ($2.99, B&W, limited series)
1-4-Van Meter-s/Norrie-a 3.00
TPB (8/04, $11.95, digest-size) r/series 12.00

TOOTS AND CASPER
Dell Publishing Co.: No. 5, 1942
Large Feature Comic 5 20 40 60 114 182 250

TOP ADVENTURE COMICS
I. W. Enterprises: 1964 (Reprints)
1-r/High Adv. (Explorer Joe #2); Krigstein-r 2 4 6 11 16 20
2-Black Dwarf-r/Red Seal #22; Kinstler-c 2 4 6 13 18 22

TOP CAT (TV) (Hanna-Barbera)(See Kite Fun Book)
Dell Publishing Co./Gold Key No. 4 on: 12-2/61-62 - No. 3, 6-8/62; No. 4, 10/62 - No. 31, 9/70
1 (TV show debuted 9/27/61) 13 26 39 94 185 275
2-Augie Doggie back-ups in #1-4 8 16 24 54 90 125
3-5: 3-Last 15¢ issue. 4-Begin 12¢ issues; Yakky Doodle app. in 1 pg. strip.
 5-Touché Turtle app. 6 12 18 43 69 95
6-10 5 10 15 32 51 70
11-20 4 8 12 24 37 50
21-31-Reprints 3 6 9 19 29 38

TOP CAT (TV) (Hanna-Barbera)(See TV Stars #4)
Charlton Comics: Nov, 1970 - No. 20, Nov, 1973
1 6 12 18 37 59 80
2-10 3 6 9 20 30 40
11-20 3 6 9 17 25 32
NOTE: *#8 (1/72) went on sale late in 1972 between #14 and #15 with the 1/73 issues.*

TOP COMICS
K. K. Publications/Gold Key: July, 1967 (All reprints)
nn-The Gnome-Mobile (Disney-movie) 2 4 6 13 18 22
1-Beagle Boys (#7), Beep Beep the Road Runner (#5), Bugs Bunny, Chip 'n' Dale, Daffy Duck (#50), Flipper, Huey, Dewey & Louie, Junior Woodchucks, Lassie, The Little Monsters (#71), Moby Duck, Porky Pig (has Gold Key label - says Top Comics on inside), Scamp, Super Goof, Tom & Jerry, Top Cat (#21), Tweety & Sylvester (#7), Walt Disney C&S (#322), Woody Woodpecker known issues; each character given own book
 2 4 6 9 13 16
1-Donald Duck (not Barks), Mickey Mouse 2 4 6 13 18 22
1-Flintstones 4 8 12 22 34 45
1-Huckleberry Hound, Yogi Bear (#30) 3 6 9 14 19 24
1-The Jetsons 5 10 15 30 48 65
1-Tarzan of the Apes (#169) 3 6 9 16 22 28
1-Three Stooges (#35) 3 6 9 18 27 35
1-Uncle Scrooge (#70) 3 6 9 16 23 30
1-Zorro (r/G.K. Zorro #7 w/Toth-a; says 2nd printing) 3 6 9 14 19 24
2-Bugs Bunny, Daffy Duck, Mickey Mouse (#114), Porky Pig, Super Goof,
 Tom & Jerry, Tweety & Sylvester, Walt Disney's C&S (r/#325), Woody Woodpecker
 2 4 6 9 12 15
2-Donald Duck (not Barks), Three Stooges, Uncle Scrooge (#71)-Barks-c, Yogi Bear (#30),
 Zorro (r/#8; Toth-a) 2 4 6 11 16 20
2-Snow White & 7 Dwarfs(6/67)(1944-r) 2 4 6 10 14 18
3-Donald Duck 2 4 6 11 16 20
3-Uncle Scrooge (#72) 2 4 6 13 18 22
3,4-The Flintstones 4 8 12 22 34 45
3,4: 3-Mickey Mouse (r/#115), Tom & Jerry, Woody Woodpecker, Yogi Bear.
 4-Mickey Mouse, Woody Woodpecker 2 4 6 9 12 15
NOTE: *Each book in this series is identical to its counterpart except for cover, and came out at same time. The number in parentheses is the original issue it contains.*

TOP COW (Company one-shots)
Image Comics (Top Cow Productions)
... Book of Revelations (7/03, $3.99)-Pin-ups and info; art by various; Gossett-c 4.00
... Convention Sketchbook 2004 (4/04, $3.00, B&W) art by various 3.00
... Holiday Special Vol. 1 (12/10, $12.99) Flip book with Jingle Belle 13.00
... Preview Book 2005 (3/05, 99¢) Preview pages of Tomb Raider, Darkness, Rising Stars 3.00
... Productions, Inc./Ballistic Studios Swimsuit Special (5/95, $2.95) 3.00
...'s Best of: Dave Finch Vol. 1 TPB (8/06, $19.99) r/issues of Cyberforce, Aphrodite IX,
 Ascension and The Darkness; art & cover gallery 20.00
...'s Best of: Michael Turner Vol. 1 TPB (12/05, $24.99) r/Witchblade #1,10,12,18,19,25 &
 Witchblade/Tomb Raider chapters 1&3; Tomb Raider #25; art & cover gallery 25.00

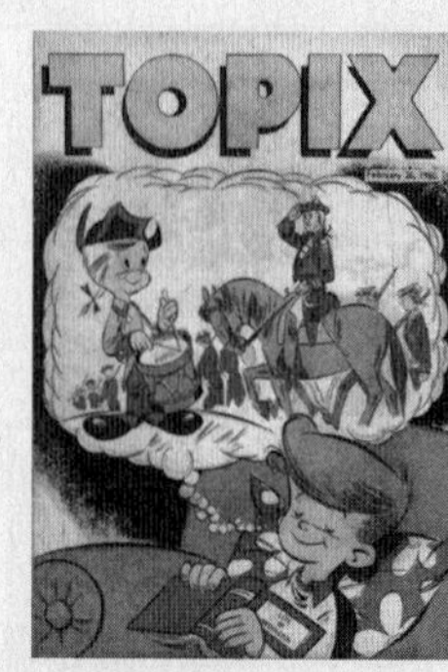

Topix V8 #19 © CG

Top Love Stories #15 © STAR

Top-Notch Comics #5 © AP

GD 2.0 VG 4.0 FN 6.0 VF 8.0 VF/NM 9.0 NM- 9.2

...: Secrets: Special Winter Lingerie Edition 1 (1/96, $2.95) Pin-ups 3.00
... 2001 Preview (no cover price) Preview pages of Tomb Raider; Jusko-a; flip cover & pages of Inferno 3.00

TOP COW CLASSICS IN BLACK AND WHITE
Image Comics (Top Cow): Feb, 2000 - Present ($2.95, B&W reprints)

...: Aphrodite IX #1(9/00) B&W reprint 3.00
...: Ascension #1(4/00) B&W reprint plus time-line of series 3.00
...: Battle of the Planets #1(1/03) B&W reprint plus script and cover gallery 3.00
...: Darkness #1(3/00) B&W reprint plus time-line of series 3.00
...: Fathom #1(5/00) B&W reprint 3.00
...: Magdalena #1(10/02) B&W reprint plus time-line of series 3.00
...: Midnight Nation #1(9/00) B&W preview 3.00
...: Rising Stars #1(7/00) B&W reprint plus cover gallery 3.00
...: Tomb Raider #1(12/00) B&W reprint plus back-story 3.00
...: Witchblade #1(2/00) B&W reprint plus back-story 3.00
...: Witchblade #25(5/01) B&W reprint plus interview with Wohl & Haberlin 3.00

TOP DETECTIVE COMICS
I. W. Enterprises: 1964 (Reprints)

9-r/Young King Cole #14; Dr. Drew (not Grandenetti) 2 4 6 10 14 18

TOP DOG (See Star Comics Magazine, 75¢)
Star Comics (Marvel): Apr, 1985 - No. 14, June, 1987 (Children's book)

1-14: 10-Peter Parker & J. Jonah Jameson cameo 4.00

TOP ELIMINATOR (Teenage Hotrodders #1-24; Drag 'n' Wheels #30 on)
Charlton Comics: No. 25, Sept, 1967 - No. 29, July, 1968

25-29 3 6 9 16 22 28

TOP FLIGHT COMICS: Four Star Publ.: 1947 (Advertised, not published)

TOP FLIGHT COMICS
St. John Publishing Co.: July, 1949

1(7/49, St. John)-Hector the Inspector; funny animal 10 20 30 54 72 90

TOP GUN (See Luke Short, 4-Color #927 & Showcase #72)

TOP GUNS OF THE WEST (See Super DC Giant)

TOPIX (...Comics) (Timeless Topix-early issues) (Also see Men of Battle, Men of Courage & Treasure Chest)(V1-V5#1,V7 on-paper-c)
Catechetical Guild Educational Society: 11/42 - V10#15, 1/28/52 (Weekly - later issues)

V1#1(8 pgs.,8x11") 24 48 72 140 230 320
2,3(8 pgs.,8x11") 14 28 42 80 115 150
4-8(16 pgs.,8x11") 11 22 33 64 90 115
V2#1-10(16 pgs.,8x11"): V2#8-Pope Pius XII 10 20 30 56 76 95
V3#1-10(16 pgs.,8x11"): V3#1-(9/44) 10 20 30 54 72 90
V4#1-10: V4#1-(9/45) 9 18 27 47 61 75
V5#1(10/46,52 pgs.,2(11/46),no #3),4(1/47)-9(6/47),10(7/47), no #13,4(10/47), 14(11/47),15(12/47) 8 16 24 40 50 60
11(8/47),12(9/47)-Life of Christ editions 10 20 30 54 72 90
V6#4(1/48),5(2/48),7(3/48),8(4/48),9(5/48),10(6/48),11(7/48)-14 (no #1-3,6) 7 14 21 35 43 50
V7#1(9/1/48)-20(6/15/49), 36 pgs. 6 12 18 29 36 42
V8#1(9/19/49)-3,5-11,13-30(5/15/50) 6 12 18 28 34 40
4-Dagwood Splits the Atom(10/10/49)-Magazine format 8 16 24 42 54 65
12-Ingels-a 10 20 30 54 72 90
V9#1(9/25/50)-11,13-30(5/14/51) 6 12 18 27 33 38
12-Special 36 pg. Xmas issue, text illos format 6 12 18 28 34 40
V10#1(10/1/51)-15: 14-Hollingsworth-a 6 12 18 27 33 38

TOP JUNGLE COMICS
I. W. Enterprises: 1964 (Reprint)

1(nd)-Reprints White Princess of the Jungle #3, minus cover; Kintsler-a 3 6 9 16 23 30

TOP LOVE STORIES (Formerly Gasoline Alley #2)
Star Publications: No. 3, 5/51 - No. 19, 3/54

3(#1) 21 42 63 126 206 285
4,5,7-9: 8-Wood story 18 36 54 105 165 225
6-Wood-a 22 44 66 132 216 300
10-16,18,19-Disbrow-a 18 36 54 105 165 225
17-Wood art (Fox-r) 19 38 57 112 176 240

NOTE: *All have* **L. B. Cole** *covers.*

TOP-NOTCH COMICS (...Laugh #28-45; Laugh Comix #46 on)
MLJ Magazines: Dec, 1939 - No. 45, June, 1944

1-Origin/1st app. The Wizard; Kardak the Mystic Magician, Swift of the Secret Service (ends #3), Air Patrol, The Westpointer, Manhunters (by J. Cole), Mystic (ends #2) & Scott Rand (ends #3) begin; Wizard covers begin, end #8 524 1048 1572 3825 6763 9700
2-(1/40)-Dick Storm (ends #8), Stacy Knight M.D. (ends #4) begin; Jack Cole-a; 1st app. Nazis swastika on-c 245 490 735 1568 2684 3800
3-Bob Phantom, Scott Rand on Mars begin; J. Cole-a 171 342 513 1086 1868 2650
4-Origin/1st app. Streak Chandler on Mars; Moore of the Mounted only app.; J. Cole-a 152 304 456 965 1658 2350
5-Flag-c; origin/1st app. Galahad; Shanghai Sheridan begins (ends #8); Shield cameo; Novick-a; classic-c 171 342 513 1086 1868 2650
6-Meskin-a 113 226 339 718 1234 1750
7-The Shield x-over in Wizard; The Wizard dons new costume 148 296 444 947 1624 2300
8-Origin/1st app. The Firefly & Roy, the Super Boy (9/40, 2nd costumed boy hero after Robin?; also see Toro in Human Torch #1 (Fall/40) 155 310 465 992 1696 2400
9-Origin & 1st app. The Black Hood; 1st Black Hood-c & logo (10/40); Fran Frazier begins (Scarce) 649 1298 1947 4738 8369 12,000
10-2nd app. Black Hood 213 426 639 1363 2332 3300
11-3rd Black Hood 135 270 405 864 1482 2100
12-15 111 222 333 705 1215 1725
16-18,20 97 194 291 621 1061 1500
19-Classic bondage-c 107 214 321 680 1165 1650
21-30: 23-26-Roy app. 24-No Wizard. 25-Last Bob Phantom. 27-Last Firefly. 28-Suzie, Pokey Oakey begin. 29-Last Kardak 67 134 201 426 731 1035
31-44: 33-Dotty & Ditto by Woggon begins (2/43, 1st app.). 44-Black Hood series ends 42 84 126 265 445 625
45-Last issue 46 92 138 290 488 685

NOTE: **J. Binder** *a-1-3.* **Meskin** *a-2, 3, 6, 15.* **Bob Montana** *a-30; c-28-31.* **Harry Sahle** *c-42-45.* **Woggon** *a-33-40, 42. Bondage c-17, 19. Black Hood also appeared on radio in 1944.Black Hood app. on c-9-34, 41-44. Roy the Super Boy app. on c-8, 9, 11-27. The Wizard app. on c-1-8, 11-13, 15-22, 24, 25, 27. Pokey Oakey app. on c-28-43. Suzie app. on c-44-on.*

TOPPER & NEIL (TV)
Dell Publishing Co.: No. 859, Nov, 1957

Four Color 859 5 10 15 30 48 65

TOPPS COMICS: Four Star Publications: 1947 (Advertised, not published)

TOPS
July, 1949 - No. 2, Sept, 1949 (25¢, 10-1/4x13-1/4", 68 pgs.)
Tops Magazine, Inc. (Lev Gleason): (Large size-magazine format; for the adult reader)

1 (Rare)-Story by Dashiell Hammett; Crandall/Lubbers, Tuska, Dan Barry, Fuje-a; Biro painted-c 155 310 465 992 1696 2400
2 (Rare)-Crandall/Lubbers, Biro, Kida, Fuje, Guardineer-a 142 284 426 909 1555 2200

TOPS COMICS
Consolidated Book Publishers: 1944 (10¢, 132 pgs.)

2000-(Color-c, inside in red shade & some in full color)-Ace Kelly by Rick Yager, Black Orchid, Don on the Farm, Dinky Dinkerton (Rare) 27 54 81 158 259 360

NOTE: *This book is printed in such a way that when the staple is removed, the strips on the left side of the book correspond with the same strips on the right side. Therefore, if strips are removed from the book, each strip can be folded into a complete comic section of its own.*

TOPS COMICS (See Tops in Humor)
Consolidated Book (Lev Gleason): 1944 (7-1/4x5", 32 pgs.)

2001-The Jack of Spades (costumed hero) 17 34 51 98 154 210
2002-Rip Raider 10 20 30 58 79 100
2003-Red Birch (gag cartoons) 6 12 18 28 34 40
2004-Gag cartoons 16 32 48 92 144 195

TOP SECRET
Hillman Publ.: Jan, 1952

1 20 40 60 114 182 250

TOP SECRET ADVENTURES (See Spyman)

TOP SECRETS (...of the F.B.I.)
Street & Smith Publications: Nov, 1947 - No. 10, July-Aug, 1949

1-Powell-c/a 36 72 108 211 343 475
2-Powell-c/a 25 50 75 147 241 335
3-6,8,10-Powell-a 22 44 66 132 216 300
9-Powell-c/a 23 46 69 136 223 310
7-Used in SOTI, pg. 90 & illo. "How to hurt people"; used by N.Y. Legis. Comm.; Powell-c/a 34 68 102 206 336 465

NOTE: **Powell** *c-1-3, 5-10.*

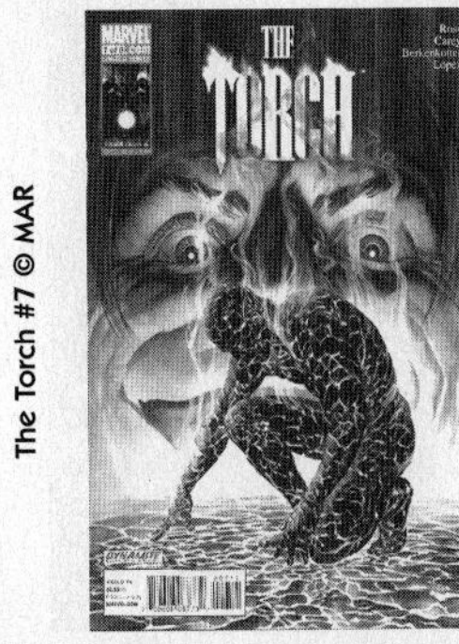

The Torch #7 © MAR

Torchwood #1 © BBC

Total Justice #3 © DC

	GD 2.0	VG 4.0	FN 6.0	VF 8.0	VF/NM 9.0	NM- 9.2

TOPS IN ADVENTURE
Ziff-Davis Publishing Co.: Fall, 1952 (25¢, 132 pgs.)
1-Crusader from Mars, The Hawk, Football Thrills, He-Man; Powell-a; painted-c 47 94 141 296 498 700

TOPS IN HUMOR (See Tops Comics?)
Consolidated Book Publ. (Lev Gleason)/Wise Publs.: 1944 (7-1/4x5", #2 digest size)
2001(#1)-Origin The Jack of Spades, Ace Kelly by Rick Yager, Black Orchid (female crime fighter) app. 17 34 51 98 154 210
2-Wise Publs.; WWII serviceman humor 12 24 36 67 94 120

TOP SPOT COMICS
Top Spot Publ. Co.: 1945
1-The Menace, Duke of Darkness app. 36 72 108 214 347 480

TOPSY-TURVY (Teenage)
R. B. Leffingwell Publ.: Apr, 1945
1-1st app. Cookie 16 32 48 94 147 200

TOP TEN
America's Best Comics: Sept, 1999 - No. 12, Oct, 2001 ($3.50/$2.95)
1-Two covers by Ross and Ha/Cannon; Alan Moore-s/Gene Ha-a 3.50
2-11-($2.95) 3.00
12-($3.50) 3.50
Hardcover ('00, $24.95) Dust jacket with Gene Ha-a; r/#1-7 25.00
Softcover ('00, $14.95) new Gene Ha-c; r/#1-7 15.00
Book 2 HC ('02, $24.95) Dust jacket with Gene Ha-a; r/#8-12 25.00
Book 2 SC ('03, $14.95) new Gene Ha-c; r/#8-12 15.00
...: The Forty-Niners HC (2005, $24.99, dust jacket) prequel set in 1949; Moore-s/Ha-a 25.00

TOP TEN: BEYOND THE FARTHEST PRECINCT
America's Best Comics: Oct, 2005 - No. 5, Feb, 2006 ($2.99, limited series)
1-5-Jerry Ordway-a/Paul DiFilippo-s 3.00
TPB (2006, $14.99) r/series; cover sketch pages 15.00

TOP TEN SEASON TWO
America's Best Comics: Dec, 2008 - No. 4, Mar, 2009 ($2.99, limited series)
1-4-Cannon-s/Ha-a 3.00
... Special (5/09, $2.99) Cannon-s/Daxiong-a/Ha-c 3.00

TOR (Prehistoric Life on Earth) (Formerly One Million Years Ago)
St. John Publ. Co.: No. 2, Oct, 1953; No. 3, May, 1954 - No. 5, Oct, 1954
3-D 2(10/53)-Kubert-c/a 14 28 42 76 108 140
3-D 2(10/53)-Oversized, otherwise same contents 12 24 36 67 94 120
3-D 2(11/53)-Kubert-c/a; has 3-D cover 12 24 36 67 94 120
3-5-Kubert-c/a: 3-Danny Dreams by Toth; Kubert 1 pg. story (w/self portrait) 14 28 42 76 108 140
NOTE: *The two October 3-D's have same contents and* **Powell** *art; the October & November issues are titled 3-D Comics. All 3-D issues are 25¢ and came with 3-D glasses.*

TOR (See Sojourn)
National Periodical Publications: May-June, 1975 - No. 6, Mar-Apr, 1976
1-New origin by Kubert 2 4 6 9 13 16
2-6: 2-Origin-r/St. John #1 1 2 3 5 6 8
NOTE: ***Kubert*** *a-1, 2-6r; c-1-6.* ***Toth*** *a(p)-3r.*

TOR (3-D)
Eclipse Comics: July, 1986 - No. 2, Aug, 1987 ($2.50)
1,2: 1-r/One Million Years Ago. 2-r/Tor 3-D #2 5.00
...2-D: 1,2-Limited signed & numbered editions 1 2 3 4 5 7

TOR
Marvel Comics (Epic Comics/Heavy Hitters): June, 1993 - No. 4, 1993 ($5.95, lim. series)
1-4: Joe Kubert-c/a/scripts 6.00

TOR (Joe Kubert's...)
DC Comics: Jul, 2008 - No. 6, Dec, 2008 ($2.99, limited series)
1-6-New story; Joe Kubert-c/a/scripts 3.00
...: A Prehistoric Odyssey HC (2009, $24.99, DJ) r/#1-6; Roy Thomas intro.; sketch-a 25.00
...: A Prehistoric Odyssey SC (2010, $14.99) r/#1-6; Roy Thomas intro.; sketch-a 15.00

TOR BY JOE KUBERT
DC Comics: 2001 - 2003 ($49.95, hardcovers with dust jacket)
Volume 1 (2001) r/One Million Years Ago #1 & 3-D Comics #1&2 in flat color; script pages, sketch pages, proposals for TV and newspapers strips; intro. by Roy Thomas 50.00
Volume 2 (2002) r/Tor (St. John) #3-5; Danny Dreams; portfolio section 50.00
Volume 3 (2003) r/Tor (DC '75) #1; (Marvel '93) #1-4; portfolio section 50.00

TORCH, THE
Marvel Comics (with Dynamite Ent.): Nov, 2009 - No. 8, Jul, 2010 ($3.99, limited series)
1-8-Thinker resurrects the Golden Age Human Torch; Toro app; Alex Ross-c on all; Berkenkotter-a. 3-5-Namor app. 4.00

TORCH OF LIBERTY SPECIAL
Dark Horse Comics (Legend): Jan, 1995 ($2.50, one-shot)
1-Byrne scripts 3.00

TORCHWOOD (Based on the BBC TV series)
Titan Comics: Sept, 2010 - Present ($3.99)
1-6: 1-Barrowman-s/Edwards-a; Churchill & photo-c. 2-Art by Yeowell & Grist 4.00

TORCHY (...Blonde Bombshell) (See Dollman, Military, & Modern)
Quality Comics Group: Nov, 1949 - No. 6, Sept, 1950
1-Bill Ward-c, Gil Fox-a 168 336 504 1075 1838 2600
2,3-Fox-c/a 71 142 213 454 777 1100
4-Fox-c/a(3), Ward-a (9 pgs.) 87 174 261 553 952 1350
5,6-Ward-c/a, 9 pgs; Fox-a(3) each 102 204 306 648 1112 1575
Super Reprint #16(1964)-r/#4 with new-c 10 20 30 60 93 125

TO RIVERDALE AND BACK AGAIN (Archie Comics Presents...)
Archie Comics: 1990 ($2.50, 68 pgs.)
nn-Byrne-c, Colan-a(p); adapts NBC TV movie 5.00

TORMENTED, THE (Becomes Surprise Adventures #3 on)
Sterling Comics: July, 1954 - No. 2, Sept, 1954
1,2: Weird/Horror stories 27 54 81 160 263 365

TORNADO TOM (See Mighty Midget Comics)

TORSO (See Jinx: Torso)

TOTAL ECLIPSE
Eclipse Comics: May, 1988 - No. 5, Apr, 1989 ($3.95, 52 pgs., deluxe size)
Book 1-5: 3-Intro/1st app. new Black Terror. 4-Many copies have upside down pages and are mis-cut 4.00

TOTAL ECLIPSE
Image Comics: July, 1998 (one-shot)
1-McFarlane-c; Eclipse Comics character pin-ups by Image artists 2.50

TOTAL ECLIPSE: THE SERAPHIM OBJECTIVE
Eclipse Comics: Nov, 1988 ($1.95, one-shot, Baxter paper)
1-Airboy, Valkyrie, The Heap app. 3.00

TOTAL JUSTICE
DC Comics: Oct, 1996 - No. 3, Nov, 1996 ($2.25, bi-weekly limited series) (Based on toyline)
1-3 3.00

TOTAL RECALL (Movie)
DC Comics: 1990 ($2.95, 68 pgs., movie adaptation, one-shot)
1-Arnold Schwarzenegger photo-c 4.00

TOTAL WAR (M.A.R.S. Patrol #3 on)
Gold Key: July, 1965 - No. 2, Oct, 1965 (Painted-c)
1-Wood-a in both issues 7 14 21 45 73 100
2 5 10 15 34 55 75

TOTEMS (Vertigo V2K)
DC Comics (Vertigo): Feb, 2000 ($5.95, one-shot)
1-Swamp Thing, Animal Man, Zatanna, Shade app.; Fegredo-c 6.00

TO THE HEART OF THE STORM
Kitchen Sink Press: 1991 (B&W, graphic novel)
Softcover-Will Eisner-s/a/c 15.00
Hardcover ($24.95) 25.00
TPB-(DC Comics, 9/00, $14.95) reprints 1991 edition 15.00

TO THE LAST MAN (See Zane Grey Four Color #616)

TOUCH OF SILVER, A
Image Comics: Jan, 1997 - No. 6, Nov, 1997 ($2.95, B&W, bi-monthly)
1-6-Valentino-s/a; photo-c: 5-color pgs. w/Round Table 3.00
TPB ($12.95) r/#1-6 13.00

TOUGH KID SQUAD COMICS
Timely Comics (TCI): Mar, 1942
1-(Scarce)-Origin & 1st app.The Human Top & The Tough Kid Squad; The Flying Flame app. 892 1784 2676 6512 11,506 16,500

TOWER OF SHADOWS (Creatures on the Loose #10 on)
Marvel Comics Group: Sept, 1969 - No. 9, Jan, 1971

Toy Story #4 © DIS & Pixar

Trail Blazers #3 © CN

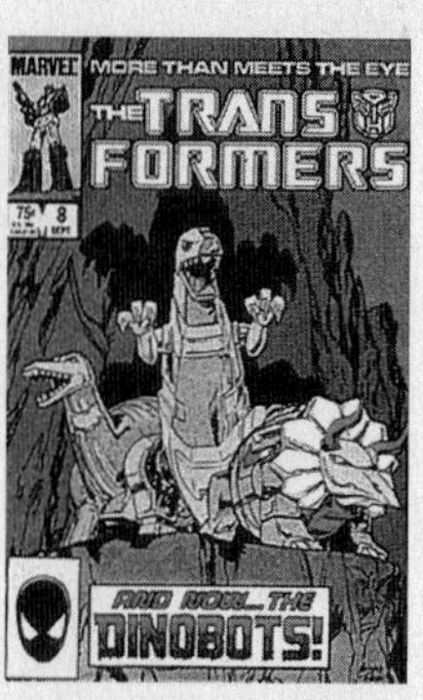

Transformers #8 © Hasbro

GD 2.0 VG 4.0 FN 6.0 VF 8.0 VF/NM 9.0 NM- 9.2

GD 2.0 VG 4.0 FN 6.0 VF 8.0 VF/NM 9.0 NM- 9.2

1-Romita-c, classic Steranko-a; Craig-a(p) 9 18 27 60 100 140
2,3: 2-Neal Adams-a. 3-Barry Smith, Tuska-a 5 10 15 32 51 70
4,6: 4-Marie Severin-c. 6-Wood-a 4 8 12 28 44 60
5-B. Smith-a(p), Wood-a; Wood draws himself (1st pg., 1st panel)
5 10 15 30 48 65
7-9: 7-B. Smith-a(p), Wood-a. 8-Wood-a; Wrightson-c. 9-Wrightson-c;
Roy Thomas app. 5 10 15 32 51 70
Special 1(12/71, 52 pgs.)-Neal Adams-a; Romita-c 4 8 12 28 44 60
NOTE: *J. Buscema a-1p, 2p, Special 1r. Colan a-3p, 6p, Special 1. J. Craig a(r)-1p. Ditko a-6, 8, 9r, Special 1. Everett a-9(i)r; c-5i. Kirby a-9(p)r. Severin c-5p, 6. Steranko a-1p. Tuska a-3. Wood a-5-8. Issues 1-9 contain new stories with some pre-Marvel age reprints in 6-9. H. P. Lovecraft adaptation-9.*

TOXIC AVENGER (Movie)
Marvel Comics: Apr, 1991 - No. 11, Feb, 1992 ($1.50)

1-11: Based on movie character. 3,10-Photo-c 3.00

TOXIC CRUSADERS (TV)
Marvel Comics: May, 1992 - No. 8, Dec, 1992 ($1.25)

1-8: 1-3,8-Sam Kieth-c; based on USA Network cartoon 3.00

TOXIC GUMBO
DC Comics (Vertigo): 1998 ($5.95, one-shot, mature)

1-McKeever-a/Lydia Lunch-s 6.00

TOXIN (Son of Carnage)
Marvel Comics: June, 2005 - No. 6, Nov, 2005 ($2.99, limited series)

1-6-Milligan-s/Robertson-a; Spider-Man app. 3.00
...: The Devil You Know TPB (2006, $17.99) r/#1-6 18.00

TOYBOY
Continuity Comics: Oct, 1986 - No. 7, Mar, 1989 ($2.00, Baxter paper)

1-7 3.00
NOTE: *N. Adams a-1; c-1, 2,5. Golden a-7p; c-6,7. Nebres a(i)-1,2.*

TOYLAND COMICS
Fiction House Magazines: Jan, 1947 - No. 2, Mar, 1947; No. 3, July, 1947

1-Wizard of the Moon begins 30 60 90 177 289 400
2,3-Bob Lubbers-c. 3-Tuska-a 17 34 51 100 158 215
NOTE: *All above contain strips by Al Walker.*

TOY STORY (Disney/Pixar movies)
BOOM! Entertainment (BOOM! KIDS): No. 0, Nov, 2009 - No. 7, Sept, 2010 ($2.99)

0-7: 0,1-Three covers. 2-7-Two covers 3.00
Free Comic Book Day Edition (5/10, giveaway) r/#0 The Return of Buzz Lightyear 2.00
...: The Return of Buzz Lightyear (10/10, Halloween giveaway, 8-1/2" x 5-1/4") 2.00

TOY STORY: MYSTERIOUS STRANGER (Disney/Pixar movies)
BOOM! Entertainment (BOOM! KIDS): May, 2009 - No. 4, July, 2009 ($2.99)

1-4-Jolley-s/Moreno-a. 1-Three covers. 2-4-Two covers 3.00

TOY STORY: TALES FROM THE TOY CHEST (Disney/Pixar movies)
BOOM! Entertainment (BOOM! KIDS): July, 2010 - No. 4, Oct, 2010 ($2.99)

1-4-Snider-s/Luthi-a. 1-Two covers. 2-4-One cover 3.00

TOY TOWN COMICS
Toytown/Orbit Publ./B. Antin/Swapper Quarterly: 1945 - No. 7, May, 1947

1-Mertie Mouse; L. B. Cole-c/a; funny animal 39 78 117 240 395 550
2-L. B. Cole-a 22 44 66 132 216 300
3-7-L. B. Cole-a. 5-Wiggles the Wonderworm-c 20 40 60 114 182 250

TRACKER
Image Comics (Top Cow): Nov, 2009 - No. 5, Sept, 2010 ($2.99/$3.99)

1,2-Lincoln-s/Tsai-a. 1-Two covers 3.00
3-5-($3.99) 4.00

TRAGG AND THE SKY GODS (See Gold Key Spotlight, Mystery Comics Digest #3,9 & Spine Tingling Tales)
Gold Key/Whitman No. 9: June, 1975 - No. 8, Feb, 1977; No. 9, May, 1982 (Painted-c #3-8)

1-Origin 3 6 9 14 19 24
2-8: 4-Sabre-Fang app. 8-Ostellon app. 2 4 6 8 11 14
9-(Whitman, 5/82) r/#1 1 2 3 5 7 9
NOTE: *Santos a-1, 2, 9r; c-3-7. Spiegel a-3-8.*

TRAIL BLAZERS (Red Dragon #5 on)
Street & Smith Publications: 1941; No. 2, Apr, 1942 - No. 4, Oct, 1942
(True stories of American heroes)

1-Life story of Jack Dempsey & Wright Brothers 35 70 105 208 339 470
2-Brooklyn Dodgers-c/story; Ben Franklin story 22 44 66 128 209 290
3,4: 3-Fred Allen, Red Barber, Yankees stories 20 40 60 115 183 250

TRAIL COLT (Also see Extra Comics, Manhunt! & Undercover Girl)
Magazine Enterprises: 1949 - No. 2, 1949

nn(A-1 #24)-7 pg. Frazetta-a r-in Manhunt #13; Undercover Girl app.; The Red Fox by
L. B. Cole; Ingels-c; Whitney-a (Scarce) 39 78 117 240 395 550
2(A-1 #26)-Undercover Girl; Ingels-c; L. B. Cole-a (6 pgs.)
31 62 93 182 296 410

TRANSFORMERS, THE (TV)(See G.I. Joe and...)
Marvel Comics Group: Sept, 1984 - No. 80, July, 1991 (75¢/$1.00)

1-Based on Hasbro Toys 3 6 9 18 27 35
2-5: 2-Golden-c. 3-(1/85) Spider-Man (black costume)-c/app. 4-Texeira-c; brief app. of
Dinobots 2 4 6 11 16 20
2-10: 2nd & 3rd prints 4.00
6-10: 6-1st Josie Beller. 8-Dinobots 1st full app. 9-Circuit Breaker 1st full app. 10-Intro
Constructicons 2 4 6 8 11 14
11-49: 11-1st app. Jetfire. 14-Jetfire becomes an Autobot; 1st app. of Grapple, Hoist, Smokescreen, Skids, and Tracks. 17-1st app. of Blaster, Powerglide, Cosmos, Seaspray, Warpath, Beachcomber, Preceptor, Straxus, Kickback, Bombshell, Shrapnel, Dirge, and Ramjet. 19-1st Omega Supreme. 21-1st app. of Aerialbots; 1st Slingshot; Circuit Breaker app. 22-Retells origin of Circuit Breaker, 1st Stunticons. 23-Battle at Statue of Liberty. 24-1st app. Protectobots, Combaticons; Optimus Prime killed. 25-1st Predacons. 26-Intro The Mechanic, Prime's Funeral. 27-1st Trypticon app.; Grimlock named new Autobot leader. 28-The Mechanic app. 29-Intro Scraplets, 1st app. of Triple Changers
1 2 3 5 6 8
50-60: 53-Jim Lee-c. 54-Intro Micromasters. 60-Brief 1st app. of Primus
2 4 6 8 10 12
61-70: 61-Origin of Cybertron and the Transformers, Unicron app.; app. of Primus, creator of the Transformers. 62-66 Matrix Quest 5-part series. 67-Jim Lee-c
2 4 6 10 14 18
71-77: 75-($1.50, 52 pgs.) (Low print run) 3 6 9 18 27 35
78,79 (Low print run) 4 8 12 24 37 50
80-Last issue 5 10 15 30 48 65
NOTE: *Second and third printings of most early issues (1-9?) exist and are worth less than originals. Was originally planned as a four issue mini-series. Wrightson a-64i(4 pgs.).*

TRANSFORMERS
IDW Publishing: No. 0, Oct, 2005 (99¢, one-shot)

0-Prelude to Transformers: Infiltration series; Furman-s/Su-a; 4 covers 3.00

TRANSFORMERS
IDW Publishing: Nov, 2009 - Present ($3.99)

1-17: Multple covers on each 4.00
...: Continuum (11/09, $3.99) Plot synopses of recent Transformers storylines 4.00

TRANSFORMERS (Free Comic Book Day Editions)
Dreamwave Productions/IDW Publishing

... Animated (IDW, 5/08) Free Comic Book Day Edition; from the Cartoon Network series 2.00
... Armada (Dreamwave Prods., 5/03) Free Comic Book Day Edition 3.00
.../Beast Wars Special (IDW, 2006) Free Comic Book Day Edition; flip book 3.00
.../G.I. Joe (IDW, 2009) Free Comic Book Day Edition; flip book 2.00
... Movie Prequel (IDW, 5/07) Free Comic Book Day Edition; Figueroa-c 3.00

TRANSFORMERS: ALL HAIL MEGATRON
IDW Publishing: Jul, 2008 - No. 16, Oct, 2009 ($3.99, limited series)

1-16: 1-8,10-12-McCarthy-s/Guidi-a; 2 covers 4.00

TRANSFORMERS: ALLIANCE (Prequel to 2009 Transformers 2 movie)
IDW Publishing: Dec, 2008 - No. 4, Mar, 2009 ($3.99, limited series)

1-4-Milne-a; 2 covers 4.00

TRANSFORMERS ANIMATED: THE ARRIVAL
IDW Publishing: Sept, 2008 - No. 5, Dec, 2008 ($3.99, limited series)

1-5-Brizuela-a; 2 covers 4.00

TRANSFORMERS ARMADA (Continues as Transformers Energon with #19)
(Also see Promotional Comics section for FCBD Ed.)
Dreamwave Productions: July, 2002 - No. 18, Dec, 2003 ($2.95)

1-Sarracini-s/Raiz-a; wraparound gatefold-c 4.00
2-18 4.00
Vol. 1 TPB (2003, $13.95) r/#1-5 14.00
Vol. 2 TPB (2003, $15.95) r/#6-11 16.00

TRANSFORMERS ARMADA: MORE THAN MEETS THE EYE
Dreamwave Productions: Mar, 2004 - No. 3, May, 2004 ($4.95, limited series)

1-3-Pin-ups with tech info; art by Pat Lee & various 5.00

TRANSFORMERS, BEAST WARS: THE ASCENDING
IDW Publishing: Aug, 2007 - No. 4, Nov, 2007 ($3.99, limited series)

Transformers (2009 series) #5 © Hasbro

Transformers/ G.I. Joe #3 © Hasbro

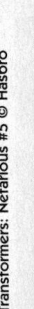

Transformers: Nefarious #5 © Hasbro

	GD 2.0	VG 4.0	FN 6.0	VF 8.0	VF/NM 9.0	NM- 9.2

1-4-Furman-s/Figueroa-a; multiple covers on all 4.00

TRANSFORMERS, BEAST WARS: THE GATHERING
IDW Publishing: Feb, 2006 - No. 4, May, 2006 ($2.99, limited series)

1-4-Furman-s/Figueroa-a; multiple covers on all 3.00
TPB (8/06, $17.99) r/series; sketch pages & gallery of covers and variants 18.00

TRANSFORMERS: BUMBLEBEE
IDW Publishing: Dec, 2009 - No. 4, Mar, 2010 ($3.99, limited series)

1-4: Zander Cannon-s; multiple covers on all 4.00

TRANSFORMERS COMICS MAGAZINE (Digest)
Marvel Comics: Jan, 1987 - No. 10, July, 1988

	GD	VG	FN	VF	VF/NM	NM-
1,2-Spider-Man-c/s	2	4	6	9	12	15
3-10	2	4	6	8	10	12

TRANSFORMERS: DEFIANCE (Prequel to 2009 Transformers 2 movie)
IDW Publishing: Jan, 2009 - No. 4, Apr, 2009 ($3.99, limited series)

1-4-Mowry-s; 2 covers 4.00

TRANSFORMERS: DEVASTATION
IDW Publishing: Sept, 2007 - No. 6, Feb, 2008 ($3.99, limited series)

1-6-Furman-s/Su-a; multiple covers on all 4.00

TRANSFORMERS: DRIFT
IDW Publishing: Sept, 2010 - No. 4, Oct, 2010 ($3.99, limited series)

1-4-McCarthy-s/Milne-a; multiple covers on all 4.00

TRANSFORMERS ENERGON (Continued from Transformers Armada #18)
Dreamwave Productions: No. 19, Jan, 2004 - No. 30, Dec, 2004 ($2.95)

19-30-Furman-s 3.00

TRANSFORMERS: ESCALATION
IDW Publishing: Nov, 2006 - No. 6, Apr, 2007 ($3.99, limited series)

1-6-Furman-s/Su-a; multiple covers 4.00

TRANSFORMERS: EVOLUTIONS - HEARTS OF STEEL
IDW Publishing: June, 2006 - No. 4, Sept, 2006 ($2.99, limited series)

1-4-Bumblebee meets John Henry in 1880s railroad times 3.00

TRANSFORMERS: GENERATION 1
Dreamwave Productions: Apr, 2002 - No. 6, Oct, 2002 ($2.95)

Preview- 6 pg. story; robot sketch pages; Pat Lee-a 3.00
1-Pat Lee-a; 2 wraparound covers by Lee 5.00
2-6: 2-Optimus Prime reactivated; 2 covers by Pat Lee 4.00
...Vol. 1 HC (2003, $49.95) r/#1-6; black hardcover with red foil lettering and art 50.00
...Vol. 1 TPB (2002, $17.95) r/#1-6 plus six page preview; 8 pg. preview of future issues 18.00

TRANSFORMERS: GENERATION 1 (Volume 2)
Dreamwave Productions: Apr, 2003 - No. 6, Sept, 2003 ($2.95)

1-6: 1-Pat Lee-a; 2 wraparound gatefold covers by Lee 4.00
1-($5.95) Chrome wraparound variant-c 6.00
...Vol. 2 TPB (IDW Publ., 3/06, $19.99) r/#1-6 plus cover gallery 20.00

TRANSFORMERS: GENERATION 1 (Volume 3)
Dreamwave Productions: No. 0, Dec, 2003 - Present ($2.95)

0-10: 0-Pat Lee-a. 1-Figueroa-a; wrapaound-c 3.00

TRANSFORMERS: GENERATION 2
Marvel Comics: Nov, 1993 - No. 12, Oct, 1994 ($1.75)

	GD	VG	FN	VF	VF/NM	NM-
1-($2.95, 68 pgs.)-Collector's ed. w/bi-fold metallic-c	1	3	4	6	8	10
1-11: 1-Newsstand edition (68 pgs.). 2-G.I. Joe app., Snake-Eyes, Scarlett, Cobra Commander app. 5-Red Alert killed, Optimus Prime gives Grimlock leadership of Autobots. 6-G.I. Joe app.	1	2	3	4	5	7
12-($2.25, 52 pgs.)	1	3	4	6	8	10

TRANSFORMERS: GENERATIONS
IDW Publishing: Mar, 2006 - No. 12, Mar, 2007 ($1.99/$2.49/$3.99)

1,2: 1-R/Transformers #7 (1985); preview of Transformers, Beast Wars. 2-R/#13 3.00
3-10-($2.49) 3-R/Transformers #14 (1986). 4-6-Reprint #16-18. 7-R/#24 3.00
11,12-($3.99) 4.00
Volume 1 (12/06, $19.99) r/#1-6; cover gallery 20.00

TRANSFORMERS/G.I. JOE
Dreamwave Productions: Aug, 2003 - No. 6, Mar, 2004 ($2.95/$5.25)

1-Art & gatefold wraparound-c by Jae Lee; Ney Rieber-s; variant-c by Pat Lee 4.00
1-($5.95) Holofoil wraparound-c by Norton 6.00
2-6-Jae Lee-a/c 3.00
TPB (8/04, $17.95) r/#1-6; cover gallery and sketch pages 18.00

TRANSFORMERS/G.I. JOE: DIVIDED FRONT
Dreamwave Productions: Oct, 2004 ($2.95)

1-Art & gatefold wraparound-c by Pat Lee 3.00

TRANSFORMERS: HEADMASTERS
Marvel Comics Group: July, 1987 - No. 4, Jan, 1988 ($1.00, limited series)

1-Springer, Akin, Garvey-a 6.00
2-4-Springer-c on all 5.00

TRANSFORMERS: INFESTATION (Crossover with Star Trek, Ghostbusters & G.I. Joe)
IDW Publishing: Feb, 2011 - No. 2, Feb, 2011 ($3.99, limited series)

1,2-Abnett & Lanning-s/Roche-a; covers by Roche & Snyder III 4.00

TRANSFORMERS: INFILTRATION
IDW Publishing: Jan, 2006 - No. 6, June, 2006 ($2.99, limited series)

1-6-Furman-s/Su-a; multiple covers on all 3.00
... Cover Gallery (8/06, $5.99) 6.00

TRANSFORMERS: IRONHIDE
IDW Publishing: May, 2010 - No. 4, Aug, 2010 ($3.99, limited series)

1-4: Mike Costa-s; multiple covers on all 4.00

TRANSFORMERS: LAST STAND OF THE WRECKERS
IDW Publishing: Jan, 2010 - No. 5, May, 2010 ($3.99, limited series)

1-5-Nick Roche-s/a; two covers 4.00

TRANSFORMERS: MAXIMUM DINOBOTS
IDW Publishing: Dec, 2008 - No. 5, Apr, 2009 ($3.99, limited series)

1-5-Furman-s/Roche-a; 2 covers for each 4.00

TRANSFORMERS: MEGATRON ORIGIN
IDW Publishing: May, 2007 - No. 4, Sept, 2008 ($3.99, limited series)

1-4-Alex Milne-a; 2 covers 4.00

TRANSFORMERS: MICROMASTERS
Dreamwave Productions: June, 2004 - No. 4 ($2.95, limited series)

1-4-Ruffolo-a; Pat Lee-c 3.00

TRANSFORMERS: MORE THAN MEETS THE EYE
Dreamwave Productions: Apr, 2003 - No. 8, Nov, 2003 ($5.25)

1-8-Pin-ups with tech info on Autobots and Decepticons; art by Pat Lee & various 5.25
Vol. 1,2 (2004, $24.95, TPB) 1-r/#1-4. 2-r/#5-8 25.00

TRANSFORMERS: MOVIE ADAPTATION (For the 2007 live action movie)
IDW Publishing: June, 2007 - No. 4, June, 2007 ($3.99, weekly limited series)

1-4: Wraparound covers on each; Milne-a 4.00

TRANSFORMERS: MOVIE PREQUEL (For the 2007 live action movie)
IDW Publishing: Feb, 2007 - No. 4, May, 2007 ($3.99, limited series)

1-4: 1-Origin of the Transformers on Cybertron; multiple covers on each 4.00
Special (6/08, $3.99) 2 covers 4.00
TPB (6/07, $19.99) r/series; gallery of covers and variants 20.00

TRANSFORMERS: NEFARIOUS (Sequel to Transformers: Revenge of the Fallen movie)
IDW Publishing: Mar, 2010 - No. 6, Aug, 2010 ($3.99, limited series)

1-6: Furman-s; multiple covers on all 4.00

TRANSFORMERS: PRIME
IDW Publishing: Jan, 2011 - No. 4, Jan, 2011 ($3.99, weekly limited series)

1-4: 1-Mike Johnson-s/E.J. Su-a 4.00

TRANSFORMERS: REVENGE OF THE FALLEN OFFICIAL MOVIE ADAPTATION
(For the 2009 live action movie sequel)
IDW Publishing: May, 2009 - No. 4, June, 2009 ($3.99, weekly limited series)

1-4: Furman-s; 2 covers on each 4.00

TRANSFORMERS: SAGA OF THE ALLSPARK (From the 2007 live action movie)
IDW Publishing: Jul, 2008 - No. 4, Oct, 2008 ($3.99, limited series)

1-4-Launch of the Allspark into outer space; Furman-s/Roche-c 4.00

TRANSFORMERS: SECTOR 7 (From the 2007 live action movie)
IDW Publishing: Sept, 2010 - No. 5, Jan, 2011 ($3.99, limited series)

1-5-Barber-s 4.00

TRANSFORMERS: SPOTLIGHT
IDW Publishing: Sept, 2006 - Present ($3.99, multiple covers on each)

... Arcee (2/08); ... Blaster (1/08); ... Blurr (11/08); ... Cliffjumper (6/09); ... Cyclonus (6/08); ...Doubledealer (8/08); ...Drift (4/09); ...Grimlock (3/08); ...Hardhead (7/08); Hot Rod (11/06); ... Jazz (3/09); ... Kup (4/07); ... Metroplex (7/09); ... Mirage (3/08); ... Nightbeat (10/06); ... Prowl (4/10);... Ramjet (11/07); ... Shockwave (9/06); ... Sideswipe (9/08);

Transformers: Sector 7 #1 © Hasbro

Transmetropolitan #14 © Ellis & Robertson

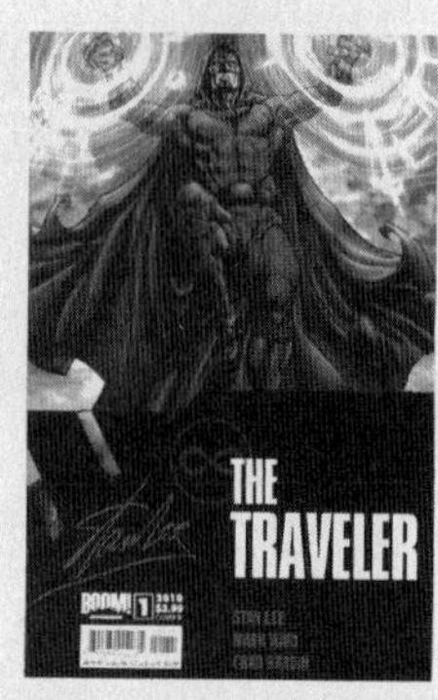
The Traveler #1 © BOOM & POW

GD VG FN VF VF/NM NM-
2.0 4.0 6.0 8.0 9.0 9.2

... Sixshot (12/06); ... Soundwave (3/07); ... Ultra Magnus (1/07) 4.00
... Optimus Prime: 3-D (11/08, $5.99, with glasses) Furman-s/Figueroa-a 6.00

TRANSFORMERS: STORMBRINGER
IDW Publishing: Jul, 2006 - No. 4, Oct, 2006 ($2.99, limited series)
1-4-Furman-s/Figueroa-a; multiple covers on all 3.00
TPB (2/07, $17.99) r/series; cover gallery and sketch pages 18.00

TRANSFORMERS SUMMER SPECIAL
Dreamwave Productions: May, 2004 ($4.95)
1-Pat Lee-a; Figueroa-a 5.00

TRANSFORMERS: TALES OF THE FALLEN
IDW Publishing: Aug, 2009 - Present ($3.99, limited series)
1-4: 2,4-Furman-s mulitple covers on all 4.00

TRANSFORMERS: TARGET 2006
IDW Publishing: Apr, 2007 - No. 5, Aug, 2007 ($3.99, limited series)
1-5-Reprints from 1980s series; multiple covers on all 4.00

TRANSFORMERS: THE ANIMATED MOVIE
IDW Publishing: Oct, 2006 - No. 4, Jan, 2007 ($3.99, limited series)
1-4-Adapts animated movie; Don Figueroa-a 4.00

TRANSFORMERS, THE MOVIE
Marvel Comics Group: Dec, 1986 - No. 3, Feb, 1987 (75¢, limited series)
1-3-Adapts animated movie 5.00

TRANSFORMERS: THE REIGN OF STARSCREAM
IDW Publishing: Apr, 2008 - No. 5, Aug, 2008 ($3.99, limited series)
1-5-Continuation of the 2007 movie; Milne-a; multiple covers 4.00

TRANSFORMERS: THE WAR WITHIN
Dreamwave Productions: Oct, 2002 - No. 6, Mar, 2003 ($2.95)
1-6-Furman-s/Figueroa-a. 1-Wraparound gatefold-c 3.00
TPB (2003, $15.95) r/#1-6; plus cover gallery 16.00

TRANSFORMERS UNIVERSE
Marvel Comics Group: Dec, 1986 - No. 4, Mar, 1987 ($1.25, limited series)
1-4-A guide to all characters 6.00
TPB-r/#1-4 15.00

TRANSFORMERS WAR WITHIN: THE AGE OF WRATH
Dreamwave Productions: Sept, 2004 - No. 6 ($2.95, limited series)
1-3-Furman-s/Ng-a 3.00

TRANSFORMERS WAR WITHIN: THE DARK AGES
Dreamwave Productions: Oct, 2003 - No. 6 ($2.95)
1-6: 1-Furman-s/Wildman-a; two covers by Pat Lee & Figueroa 3.00
TPB (2004, $17.95) r/#1-6; plus cover gallery and design sketches 18.00

TRANSIT
Vortex Publ.: March, 1987 - No. 5, Nov, 1987 (B&W)
1-5-Ted McKeever-s/a 1 2 3 5 6 8

TRANSMETROPOLITAN
DC Comics (Helix/Vertigo): Sept, 1997 - No. 60, Nov, 2002 ($2.50)
1-Warren Ellis-s/Darick Robertson-a(p) 2 4 6 8 10 12
1-Special Edition (5/09, $1.00) r/#1 with "After Watchmen" cover frame 3.00
2,3 1 2 3 4 5 7
4-8 4.00
9-60: 15-Jae Lee-c. 25-27-Jim Lee-c. 37-39-Bradstreet-c 3.00
Back on the Street ('97, $7.95) r/#1-3 8.00
Back on the Street ('09, $14.99) r/#1-6; intro. by Garth Ennis 15.00
Dirge ('03/'10, $14.95/$14.95) r/#43-48 15.00
Filth of the City ('01, $5.95) Spider's columns with pin-up art by various 6.00
Gouge Away ('02/'09, $14.95/$14.99) r/#31-36 15.00
I Hate It Here ('00, $5.95) Spider's columns with pin-up art by various 6.00
Lonely City ('01/'09, $14.95/$14.99) r/#25-30; intro. by Patrick Stewart 15.00
Lust For Life ('98, $14.95) r/#4-12 15.00
Lust For Life ('09, $14.99) r/#7-12 15.00
One More Time ('04, $14.95) r/#55-60 15.00
Spider's Thrash ('02/'10, $14.95/$14.99) r/#37-42; intro. by Darren Aronofsky 15.00
Tales of Human Waste ('04, $9.95) r/Filth of the City, I Hate It Here & story from Vertigo Winter's Edge 2 10.00
The Cure ('03/'11, $14.95/$14.99) r/#49-54 15.00
The New Scum ('00, $12.95) r/#19-24 & Vertigo: Winter's Edge #3 13.00
The New Scum ('09, $14.99) r/#19-24 & Vertigo: Winter's Edge #3 15.00
Year of the Bastard ('99, $12.95)('09, $12.99) r/#13-18 13.00

GD VG FN VF VF/NM NM-
2.0 4.0 6.0 8.0 9.0 9.2

TRANSMUTATION OF IKE GARUDA, THE
Marvel Comics (Epic Comics): July, 1991 - No. 2, 1991 ($3.95, 52 pgs.)
1,2 4.00

TRAPPED!
Periodical House Magazines (Ace): Oct, 1954 - No. 4, April, 1955
1 (All reprints) 10 20 30 54 72 90
2-4: 4-r/Men Against Crime #4 in its entirety 7 14 21 35 43 50
NOTE: *Colan a-1, 4. Sekowsky a-1.*

TRASH
Trash Publ. Co.: Mar, 1978 - No. 4, Oct, 1978 (B&W, magazine, 52 pgs.)
1,2: 1-Star Wars parody. 2-UFO-c 2 4 6 10 14 18
3-Parodies of KISS, the Beatles, and monsters 3 6 9 14 19 24
4-(84 pgs.)-Parodies of Happy Days, Rocky movies 3 6 9 14 20 26

TRAVELER, THE (Developed by Stan Lee)
BOOM! Studios: Nov, 2010 - Present ($3.99)
1-5-Waid-s/Hardin-a; three covers on each 4.00

TRAVELS OF JAIMIE McPHEETERS, THE (TV)
Gold Key: Dec, 1963
1-Kurt Russell photo on-c plus photo back-c 4 8 12 26 41 55

TREASURE CHEST (Catholic Guild; also see Topix)
George A. Pflaum: 3/12/46 - V27#8, July, 1972 (Educational comics)
(Not published during Summer)
V1#1 28 56 84 165 270 375
2-6 (5/21/46): 5-Dr. Styx app. by Baily 14 28 42 80 115 150
V2#1-20 (9/3/46-5/27/47) 11 22 33 60 83 105
V3#1-5,7-20 (1st slick cover) 10 20 30 54 72 90
V3#6-Jules Verne's "Voyage to the Moon" 11 22 33 64 90 115
V4#1-20 (9/9/48-5/31/49) 9 18 27 47 61 75
V5#1-20 (9/6/49-5/31/50) 8 16 24 44 57 70
V6#1-20 (9/14/50-5/31/51) 8 16 24 42 54 65
V7#1-20 (9/13/51-6/5/52) 8 16 24 40 50 60
V8#1-20 (9/11/52-6/4/53) 7 14 21 37 46 55
V9#1-20 ('53-'54), V10#1-20 ('54-'55) 7 14 21 35 43 50
V11('55-'56), V12('56-'57) 6 12 18 29 36 42
V13#1,3-5,7,9-V17#1 ('57-'63) 6 12 18 27 33 38
V13#2,6,8-Ingels-a 6 12 18 41 66 90
V17#2- "This Godless Communism" series begins(not in odd #'d issues); cover shows hammer & sickle over Statue of Liberty; 8 pg. Crandall-a of family life under communism 18 36 54 125 255 385
V17#3,5,7,9,11,13,15,17,19 3 6 9 17 25 32
V17#4,6,14- "This Godless Communism" stories 14 28 42 96 191 285
V17#8-Shows red octopus encompassing Earth, firing squad; 8 pgs. Crandall-a 16 32 48 111 226 340
V17#10- "This Godless Communism" - how Stalin came to power, part I; Crandall-a 14 28 42 102 206 310
V17#12-Stalin in WWII, forced labor, death by exhaustion; Crandall-a 14 28 42 102 206 310
V17#16-Kruschev takes over; de-Stalinization 14 28 42 102 206 310
V17#18-Kruschev's control; murder of revolters, brainwash, space race by Crandall 14 28 42 102 206 310
V17#20-End of series; Kruschev-people are puppets, firing squads hammer & sickle over Statue of Liberty, snake around communist manifesto by Crandall 17 34 51 118 242 365
V18#1-20, V19#11-20, V20#1-20(1964-65) 3 6 9 16 23 30
V18#2-Kruschev on-c 5 10 15 24 30 35
V18#5- "What About Red China?" - describes how communists took over China 9 18 27 60 100 140
V18#11-Crandall draws himself & 13 other artists on cover 3 6 9 18 27 35
V19#1-10- "Red Victim" anti-communist series in all 9 18 27 60 100 140
V21-V25(1965-70)-(two V24#5's 11/7/68 & 11/21/68) (no V24#6): V22#17-Flying saucer wraparound-c 3 6 9 14 19 24
V26, V27#1-8 (V26,27-68 pgs.) 3 6 9 16 22 28
Summer Edition V1#1-6('66), V2#1-6('67) 3 6 9 16 23 30
NOTE: ***Anderson** a-V18#13. **Borth** a-V7#10-19 (serial), V8#8-17 (serial), V9#1-10 (serial), V13#2, 6, 11, V14-V25 (except V22#1-3, 11-13), Summer Ed. V1#3-6. **Crandall** a-V16#7, 9, 12, 14, 16-18, 20; V17#1, 2, 4-6, 10, 12, 14, 16-18, 20; V18#1, 2, 3(2 pg.), 7, 9-20; V19#4, 11, 13, 16, 19, 20; V20#1, 2, 4, 6, 8-10, 12, 14-16, 18, 20; V21#1-5, 8-11, 13, 16-18; V22#3, 7, 9-11, 14; V23#3, 6, 9, 16, 18; V24#7, 8, 10, 13, 16; V25#8, 16; V27#1-7r, 8r(2 pg.), Summer Ed. V1#3-5, V2#3; c-V16#7, V18#2(part), 7, 11, V19#4, 19, 20, V20#15, V21#5, 9, V22#3, 7, 9, 11, V23#9, 16, V24#13, 16, V25#8, Summer Ed. V1#2 (back c-V1#2-5). **Powell** a-V10#11. V19#11, 15, V10#13, V13#6, 8 all have wraparound covers.*

TREASURE CHEST OF THE WORLD'S BEST COMICS

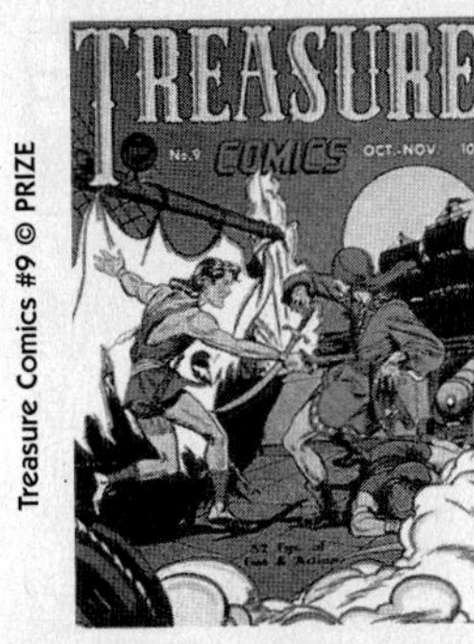

Treasure Comics #9 © PRIZE

Treehouse of Horror #16 © Bongo

Trinity #39 © DC

GD 2.0 | VG 4.0 | FN 6.0 | VF 8.0 | VF/NM 9.0 | NM- 9.2

Superior, Toronto, Canada: 1945 (500 pgs., hard-c)

Contains Blue Beetle, Captain Combat, John Wayne, Dynamic Man, Nemo, Li'l Abner; contents can vary - represents random binding of extra books; Captain America on-c 97 194 291 621 1061 1500

TREASURE COMICS
Prize Publications? (no publisher listed): No date (1943) (50¢, 324 pgs., cardboard-c)

1-(Rare)-Contains rebound Prize Comics #7-11 from 1942 (blank inside-c) 271 542 813 1734 2967 4200

TREASURE COMICS
Prize Publ. (American Boys' Comics): June-July, 1945 - No. 12, Fall, 1947

1-Paul Bunyan & Marco Polo begin; Highwayman & Carrot Topp only app.; Kiefer-a 50 100 150 315 533 750
2-Arabian Knight, Gorilla King, Dr. Styx begin 30 60 90 177 289 400
3,4,9,12: 9-Kiefer-a 24 48 72 140 230 320
5-Marco Polo-c; Krigstein-a 31 62 93 182 296 410
6,11-Krigstein-a; 11-Krigstein-c 30 60 90 177 289 400
7,8-Frazetta-a (5 pgs. each). 7-Capt. Kidd Jr. app. 41 82 123 256 428 600
10-Simon & Kirby-c/a 37 74 111 222 361 500
NOTE: *Barry a-9-11; c-12. Kiefer a-3, 5, 7; c-2, 6, 7. Roussos a-11.*

TREASURE ISLAND (See Classics Illustrated #64, Doc Savage Comics #1, King Classics, Movie Classics & Movie Comics)
Dell Publishing Co.: No. 624, Apr, 1955 (Disney)

Four Color 624-Movie, photo-c 8 16 24 54 90 125

TREASURY OF COMICS
St. John Publishing Co.: 1947; No. 2, July, 1947 - No. 4, Sept, 1947; No. 5, Jan, 1948

nn(#1)-Abbie an' Slats (nn on-c, #1 on inside) 14 28 42 80 115 150
2-Jim Hardy Comics; featuring Windy & Paddles 11 22 33 62 86 110
3-Bill Bumlin 10 20 30 54 72 90
4-Abbie an' Slats 11 22 33 62 86 110
5-Jim Hardy Comics #1 11 22 33 62 86 110

TREASURY OF COMICS
St. John Publishing Co.: Mar, 1948 - No. 5, 1948 (Reg. size); 1948-1950 (Over 500 pgs., $1.00)

1 19 38 57 111 176 240
2(#2 on-c, #1 on inside) 12 24 36 67 94 120
3-5 10 20 30 56 76 95
1-(1948, 500 pgs., hard-c)-Abbie & Slats, Abbott & Costello, Casper, Little Annie Rooney, Little Audrey, Jim Hardy, Ella Cinders (16 books bound together) (Rare) 142 284 426 909 1555 2200
1(1949, 500 pgs.)-Same format as above 113 232 348 742 1271 1800
1(1950, 500 pgs.)-Same format as above; different-c; (also see Little Audrey Yearbook) (Rare) 113 232 348 742 1271 1800

TREASURY OF DOGS, A (See Dell Giants)

TREASURY OF HORSES, A (See Dell Giants)

TREEHOUSE OF HORROR (Bart Simpson's...)
Bongo Comics: 1995 - Present ($2.95/$2.50/$3.50/$4.50/$4.99, annual)

1-(1995, $2.95)-Groening-c; Allred, Robinson & Smith stories 5.00
2-(1996, $2.50)-Stories by Dini & Bagge; infinity-c by Groening 5.00
3-(1997, $2.50)-Dorkin-s/Groening-c 5.00
4-(1998, $2.50)-Lash & Dixon-s/Groening-c 5.00
5-(1999, $3.50)-Thompson-s; Shaw & Aragonés-s/a; TenNapel-s/a 5.00
6-(2000, $4.50)-Mahfood-s/a; DeCarlo-a; Morse-s/a; Kuper-s/a 5.00
7-(2001, $4.50)-Hamill-s/Morrison-a; Ennis-s/McCrea-a; Sakai-s/a; Nixey-s/a; Brereton back-c 5.00
8-(2002, $3.50)-Templeton, Shaw, Barta, Simone, Thompson-s/a 5.00
9-(2003, $4.99)-Lord of the Rings-Brereton-a; Dini, Naifeh, Millidge, Boothby, Noto-s/a 5.00
10-(2004, $4.99)-Monsters of Rock w/Alice Cooper, Gene Simmons, Rob Zombie and Pat Boone; art by Rodriguez, Morrison, Morse, Templeton 5.00
11-(2005, $4.99)-EC style w/art by John Severin, Angelo Torres & Al Williamson and flip book with Dracula by Wolfman/Colan and Squish Thing by Wein/Wrightson 5.00
12-(2006, $4.99)-Terry Moore, Kyle Baker, Eric Powell-s/a 5.00
13-(2007, $4.99)-Oswalt, Posehn, Lennon-s; Guerra, Austin, Barta, Rodriguez-a 5.00
14-(2008, $4.99)-s/a by Niles & Fabry; Boothby & Matsumoto; Gilbert Hernandez 5.00
15-(2009, $4.99)-s/a by Jeffrey Brown, Tim Hensley, Ben Jones and others 5.00
16-(2010, $4.99)-s/a by Kelley Jones, Evan Dorkin and others; Mars Attacks homage 5.00

TREKKER (See Dark Horse Presents #6)
Dark Horse Comics: May, 1987 - No. 6, Mar,1988 ($1.50, B&W)

1-6: Sci/Fi stories 3.00
Color Special 1 (1989, $2.95, 52 pgs.) 4.00
Collection ($5.95, B&W) 6.00
Special 1 (6/99, $2.95, color) 3.00

TRENCHCOAT BRIGADE, THE
DC Comics (Vertigo): Mar, 1999 - No. 4, Jun, 1999 ($2.50, limited series)

1-4: Hellblazer, Phantom Stranger, Mister E, Dr. Occult app. 3.00

TRENCHER (See Blackball Comics)
Image Comics: May, 1993 - No. 4, Oct, 1993 ($1.95, unfinished limited series)

1-4: Keith Giffen-c/a/scripts. 3-Supreme-c/story 3.00

TRIALS OF SHAZAM!
DC Comics: Oct, 2006 - No. 12, May, 2008 ($2.99)

1-12: 1-8-Winick-s/Porter-a. 9-11-Cascioli-a. 10-Shadowpact app. 12-JLA app. 3.00
... Volume 1 TPB (2007, $14.99) r/#1-6 and story from DCU Brave New World #1 15.00
... Volume 2 TPB (2008, $14.99) r/#7-12 15.00

TRIB COMIC BOOK, THE
Winnipeg Tribune: Sept. 24, 1977 - Vol. 4, #36, 1980 (8-1/2"x11", 24 pgs., weekly) (155 total issues)

V1# 1-Color pages (Sunday strips)-Spiderman, Asterix, Disney's Scamp, Wizard of Id, Doonesbury, Inside Woody Allen, Mary Worth, & others (similar to Spirit sections) 2 4 6 10 14 18
V1#2-15, V2#1-52, V3#1-52, V4#1-33 1 3 4 6 8 10
V4#34-36 (not distributed) 2 4 6 11 16 20
NOTE: *All issues have Spider-Man. Later issues contain Star Trek and Star Wars. 20 strips in ea. The first newspaper to put Sunday pages into a comic book format.*

TRIBE (See WildC.A.T.S #4)
Image Comics/Axis Comics No. 2 on: Apr, 1993; No. 2, Sept, 1993 - No. 3, 1994 ($2.50/$1.95)

1-By Johnson & Stroman; gold foil & embossed on black-c 4.00
1-($2.50)-Ivory Edition; gold foil & embossed on white-c; available only through the creators 4.00
2,3: 2-1st Axis Comics issue. 3-Savage Dragon app. 3.00

TRIBUTE TO STEVEN HUGHES, A
Chaos! Comics: Sept, 2000 ($6.95)

1-Lady Death & Evil Ernie pin-ups by various artists; testimonials 7.00

TRICK 'R TREAT
DC Comics (WildStorm): 2009 ($19.95,SC)

nn-Short Halloween-themed story anthology; Andreyko-s; art by Huddleston & others 20.00

TRIGGER (See Roy Rogers'...)

TRIGGER
DC Comics (Vertigo): Feb, 2005 - No. 8, Sept, 2005 ($2.95/$2.99)

1-8-Jason Hall-s/John Watkiss-a/c 3.00

TRIGGER TWINS
National Periodical Publications: Mar-Apr, 1973 (20¢, one-shot)

1-Trigger Twins & Pow Wow Smith-r/All-Star Western #94,103 & Western Comics #81; Infantino-r(p) 2 4 6 13 18 22

TRINITY (See DC Universe: Trinity)

TRINITY
DC Comics: Aug, 2008 - No. 52, July, 2009 ($2.99, weekly series)

1-52-Superman, Batman & Wonder Woman star; Busiek-s/Bagley-a. 52-Wraparound-c 3.00
Vol. 1 TPB (2009, $29.99) r/#1-17 30.00
Vol. 2 TPB (2009, $29.99) r/#18-35 30.00
Vol. 3 TPB (2009, $29.99) r/#36-52 30.00

TRINITY ANGELS
Acclaim Comics (Valiant Heroes): July, 1997 - No. 12, June, 1998 ($2.50)

1-12-Maguire-s/a(p):4-Copycat-c 3.00

TRINITY: BLOOD ON THE SANDS
Image Comics (Top Cow): July, 2009 ($2.99, one-shot)

1-Witchblade, The Darkness and Angelus in the 14th century Arabian desert 3.00

TRIPLE GIANT COMICS (See Archie All-Star Specials under Archie Comics)

TRIPLE THREAT
Special Action/Holyoke/Gerona Publ.: Winter, 1945

1-Duke of Darkness, King O'Leary 32 64 96 192 314 435

TRIPLE-X
Dark Horse Comics: Dec, 1994 - No. 7, June, 1995 ($3.95, B&W, limited series)

1-7 4.00

Trouble #5 © MAR

True Blood #1 © HBO

True Comics #15 © PMI

GD VG FN VF VF/NM NM-
2.0 4.0 6.0 8.0 9.0 9.2

GD VG FN VF VF/NM NM-
2.0 4.0 6.0 8.0 9.0 9.2

TRIUMPH (Also see JLA #28-30, Justice League Task Force & Zero Hour)
DC Comics: June, 1995 - No. 4, Sept, 1995 ($1.75, limited series)
1-4: 3-Hourman, JLA app. 3.00

TRIUMPHANT UNLEASHED
Triumphant Comics: No. 0, Nov, 1993 - No. 1, Nov, 1993 ($2.50, lim. series)
0-Serially numbered, 0-Red logo, 0-White logo (no cover price; giveaway),
1-Cover is negative & reverse of #0-c 3.00

TROJAN WAR (Adaptation of Trojan war histories from ancient Greek and Roman sources)
Marvel Comics: July, 2009 - No. 5, Nov, 2009 ($3.99, limited series)
1-5-Roy Thomas-s/Miguel Sepulveda-a/Dennis Calero-c 4.00

TROLL (Also see Brigade)
Image Comics (Extreme Studios): Dec, 1993 ($2.50, one-shot, 44 pgs.)
1-1st app. Troll; Liefeld scripts; Matsuda-c/a(p) 4.00
Halloween Special (1994, $2.95)-Maxx app. 4.00
...Once A Hero (8/94, $2.50) 3.00

TROLLORDS
Tru Studios/Comico V2#1 on: 2/86 - No. 15, 1988; V2#1, 11/88 - V2#4, 1989 (1-15: $1.50, B&W)
1-First printing 5.00
1-Second printing, 2-15: 6-Christmas issue; silver logo 3.00
V2#1-4 ($1.75, color, Comico) 3.00
Special 1 ($1.75, 2/87, color)-Jerry's Big Fun Bk. 3.00

TROLLORDS
Apple Comics: July, 1989 - No. 6, 1990 ($2.25, B&W, limited series)
1-6: 1-"The Big Batman Movie Parody" 3.00

TROLL PATROL
Harvey Comics: Jan, 1993 ($1.95, 52 pgs.)
1 4.00

TROLL II (Also see Brigade)
Image Comics (Extreme Studios): July, 1994 ($3.95, one-shot)
1 4.00

TRON (Based on the video game and film)
Slave Labor Graphics: Apr, 2006 - No. 6 ($3.50/$3.95)
1-4: 1-DeMartinis-a/Walker & Jones-s 4.00
5,6-($3.95) 4.00

TRON: BETRAYAL
Marvel Comics: Nov, 2010 - No. 2, Dec, 2010 ($3.99, limited series)
1,2-Prequel to Tron Legacy movie; Larroca-c 4.00

TRON: ORIGINAL MOVIE ADAPTATION
Marvel Comics: Jan, 2011 - No. 2, Feb, 2011 ($3.99, limited series)
1,2-Peter David-s/Mirco Pierfederici-a/Greg Land-c 4.00

TROUBLE
Marvel Comics (Epic): Sept, 2003 - No. 5, Jan, 2004 ($2.99, limited series)
1-5-Photo-c; Richard and Ben meet Mary and May; Millar-s/Dodson-a 3.00
1-2nd printing with variant Frank Cho-c 5.00

TROUBLED SOULS
Fleetway: 1990 ($9.95, trade paperback)
nn-Garth Ennis scripts & John McCrea painted-c/a. 10.00

TROUBLEMAKERS
Acclaim Comics (Valiant Heroes): Apr, 1997 - No. 19, June, 1998 ($2.50)
1-19: Fabian Nicieza scripts in all. 1-1st app. XL, Rebound & Blur; 2 covers. 8-Copycat-c.
12-Shooting of Parker 3.00

TROUBLE SHOOTERS, THE (TV)
Dell Publishing Co.: No. 1108, Jun-Aug, 1960

	GD	VG	FN	VF	VF/NM	NM-
Four Color 1108-Keenan Wynn photo-c	5	10	15	34	55	75

TROUBLE WITH GIRLS, THE
Malibu Comics (Eternity Comics) #7-14/Comico V2#1-4/Eternity V2#5 on: 8/87 - #14, 1988; V2#1, 2/89 - V2#23, 1991? ($1.95, B&W/color)
1-14 ($1.95, B&W, Eternity)-Gerard Jones scripts & Tim Hamilton-c/a in all. 3.00
V2#1-23-Jones scripts, Hamilton-c/a. 3.00
Annual 1 (1988, $2.95) 4.00
Christmas Special 1 (12/91, $2.95, B&W, Eternity)-Jones scripts, Hamilton-c/a 4.00
Graphic Novel 1,2 (7/88, B&W)-r/#1-3 & #4-6 8.00

TROUBLE WITH GIRLS, THE: NIGHT OF THE LIZARD
Marvel Comics (Epic Comics/Heavy Hitters): 1993 - No. 4, 1993 ($2.50/$1.95, lim. series)
1-Embossed-c; Gerard Jones scripts & Bret Blevins-c/a in all 3.00
2-4: 2-Begin $1.95-c. 3.00

TROUT
Oni Press: Oct, 2001 - No. 2, Feb, 2002 ($2.95, B&W, limited series)
1,2-Troy Nixey-s/a 3.00

TRUE ADVENTURES (Formerly True Western)(Men's Adventures #4 on)
Marvel Comics (CCC): No. 3, May, 1950 (52 pgs.)

	GD	VG	FN	VF	VF/NM	NM-
3-Powell, Sekowsky-a; Brodsky-c	17	34	51	98	154	210

TRUE ANIMAL PICTURE STORIES
True Comics Press: Winter, 1947 - No. 2, Spring-Summer, 1947

	GD	VG	FN	VF	VF/NM	NM-
1,2	10	20	30	56	76	95

TRUE AVIATION PICTURE STORIES (Becomes Aviation Adventures & Model Building #16 on)
Parents' Mag. Institute: 1942; No. 2, Jan-Feb, 1943 - No. 15, Sept-Oct, 1946

	GD	VG	FN	VF	VF/NM	NM-
1-(#1 & 2 titled ...Aviation Comics Digest)(not digest size)	15	30	45	85	130	175
2	10	20	30	56	76	95
3-14: 3-10-Plane photos on-c. 11,13-Photo-c	9	18	27	50	65	80
15-(Titled "True Aviation Adventures & Model Building")	9	18	27	47	61	75

TRUE BELIEVERS
Marvel Comics: Sept, 2008 - No. 5, Jan, 2009 ($2.99, limited series)
1-5-Cary Bates-s/Paul Gulacy-a. 1,2-Reed Richards app. 3-Luke Cage app. 3.00

TRUE BLOOD (Based on the HBO vampire series)
IDW Publishing: Aug, 2010 - No. 6, Dec, 2010 ($3.99)
1-Messina-a; 4 covers by Messina, Campbell, Currie and Corroney 4.00
2-6-Multiple covers on each 4.00
...: Legacy Edition (1/11, $4.99) r/#1, cover gallery; full script 5.00

TRUE BLOOD: TAINTED LOVE (Based on the HBO vampire series)
IDW Publishing: Feb, 2011 - Present ($3.99)
1-Corroney-a; multiple covers 4.00

TRUE BLOOD: THE GREAT REVELATION (Prequel to the 2008 HBO vampire series)
HBO/Top Cow: July, 2008 (no cover price, one shot continued on HBO website)
1-David Wohl-s/Jason Badower-a/c 4.00

TRUE BRIDE'S EXPERIENCES (Formerly Teen-Age Brides)
(True Bride-To-Be Romances No. 17 on)
True Love (Harvey Publications): No. 8, Oct, 1954 - No. 16, Feb, 1956

	GD	VG	FN	VF	VF/NM	NM-
8-"I Married a Farmer"	9	18	27	50	65	80
9,10: 10-Last pre-code (2/55)	7	14	21	37	46	55
11-15	6	12	18	31	38	45
16-Last issue	7	14	21	37	46	55

NOTE: *Powell a-8-10, 12, 13.*

TRUE BRIDE-TO-BE ROMANCES (Formerly True Bride's Experiences)
Home Comics/True Love (Harvey): No. 17, Apr, 1956 - No. 30, Nov, 1958

	GD	VG	FN	VF	VF/NM	NM-
17-S&K-c, Powell-a	10	20	30	56	76	95
18-20,22,25-28,30	6	12	18	31	38	45
21,23,24,29-Powell-a. 29-Baker-a (1 pg.)	7	14	21	35	43	50

TRUE COMICS (Also see Outstanding American War Heroes)
True Comics/Parents' Magazine Press: April, 1941 - No. 84, Aug, 1950

	GD	VG	FN	VF	VF/NM	NM-
1-Marathon run story; life story Winston Churchill	31	62	93	182	296	410
2-Red Cross story; Everett-a	15	30	45	85	130	175
3-Baseball Hall of Fame story; Chiang Kai-Shek-c/s	17	34	51	100	158	215
4,5: 4-Story of American flag "Old Glory". 5-Life story of Joe Louis	14	28	42	80	115	150
6-Baseball World Series story	15	30	45	90	140	190
7-10: 7-Buffalo Bill story. 10,11-Teddy Roosevelt	11	22	33	62	86	110
11-14,16,18-20: 11-Thomas Edison, Douglas MacArthur stories. 13-Harry Houdini story. 14-Charlie McCarthy story. 18-Story of America begins, ends #26. 19-Eisenhower-c/s	10	20	30	54	72	90
15-Flag-c; Bob Feller story	10	20	30	58	79	100
17-Brooklyn Dodgers story	11	22	33	64	90	115
21-30: 24-Marco Polo story. 28-Origin of Uncle Sam. 29-Beethoven story. 30-Cooper Brothers baseball story	9	18	27	47	61	75
31-Red Grange "Galloping Ghost" story	8	16	24	40	50	60

32-46: 33-Origin/1st app. Steve Saunders, Special Agent of the FBI, series begins.
35-Mark Twain story. 38-General Bradley-c/s. 39-FDR story. 44-Truman story.

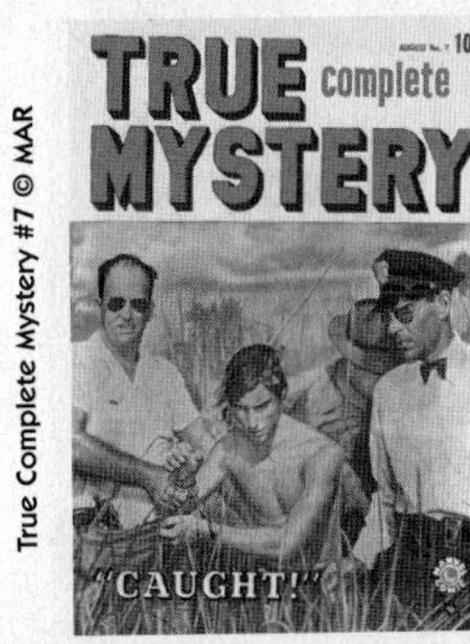

True Complete Mystery #7 © MAR

True Love Pictorial #4 © STJ

True Sport Picture Stories V2 #7 © S&S

	GD 2.0	VG 4.0	FN 6.0	VF 8.0	VF/NM 9.0	NM- 9.2
46-George Gershwin story	7	14	21	37	46	55
47-Atomic bomb issue (c/story, 3/46)	10	20	30	56	76	95
48-54,56-65: 49-1st app. Secret Warriors. 53-Bobby Riggs story. 58-Jim Jeffries (boxer) story; Harry Houdini story. 59-Bob Hope story; pirates-c/s. 60-Speedway Speed Demon-c/story.	7	14	21	35	43	50
55-(12/46)-1st app. Sad Sack by Baker (1/2 pg.)	9	18	27	47	61	75
66-Will Rogers-c/story	7	14	21	37	46	55
67-1st oversized issue (12/47); Steve Saunders, Special Agent begins	8	16	24	42	54	65
68-70,74-77,79: 68-70,74-77-Features Steve Sanders True FBI advs. 68-Oversized; Admiral Byrd-c/s. 69-Jack Benny story. 74-Amos 'n' Andy story	6	12	18	31	38	45
71-Joe DiMaggio-c/story.	9	18	27	47	61	75
72-Jackie Robinson story; True FBI advs.	8	16	24	40	50	60
73-Walt Disney's life story	9	18	27	47	61	75
78-Stan Musial-c/story; True FBI advs.	8	16	24	40	50	60
80-84 (Scarce)-All distr. to subscribers through mail only; paper-c. 80-Rocket trip to the moon story. 81-Red Grange story. 84-Wyatt Earp app. (1st app. in comics?); Rube Marquard story	18	36	54	103	162	220

(Prices vary widely on issues 80-84)

NOTE: *Bob Kane a-7. Palais a-80. Powell c/a-80. #80-84 have soft covers and combined with Tex Granger, Jack Armstrong, and Calling All Kids. #68-78 featured true FBI adventures.*

TRUE COMICS AND ADVENTURE STORIES
Parents' Magazine Institute: 1965 (Giant) (25¢)

	GD	VG	FN	VF	VF/NM	NM-
1,2: 1-Fighting Hero of Viet Nam; LBJ on-c	3	6	9	18	27	35

TRUE COMPLETE MYSTERY (Formerly Complete Mystery)
Marvel Comics (PrPI): No. 5, Apr, 1949 - No. 8, Oct, 1949

	GD	VG	FN	VF	VF/NM	NM-
5	26	52	78	154	252	350
6-8: 6-8-Photo-c	20	40	60	114	182	250

TRUE CONFIDENCES
Fawcett Publications: 1949 (Fall) - No. 4, June, 1950 (All photo-c)

	GD	VG	FN	VF	VF/NM	NM-
1-Has ad for Fawcett Love Adventures #1, but publ. as Love Memoirs #1 as Marvel published the title first; Swayze-a	18	36	54	105	165	225
2-4: 3-Swayze-a. 4-Powell-a	12	24	36	67	94	120

TRUE CRIME CASES (...From Official Police Files)
St. John Publishing Co.: 1944 (25¢, 100 pg. Giant)

	GD	VG	FN	VF	VF/NM	NM-
nn-Matt Baker-c	48	96	144	302	514	725

TRUE CRIME COMICS (Also see Complete Book of...)
Magazine Village: No. 2, May, 1947; No. 3, July-Aug, 1948 - No. 6, June-July, 1949; V2#1, Aug-Sept, 1949 (52 pgs.)

	GD	VG	FN	VF	VF/NM	NM-
2-Jack Cole-c/a; used in **SOTI**, pgs. 81,82 plus illo. "A sample of the injury-to-eye motif" & illo. "Dragging living people to death"; used in **POP**, pg. 105; "Murder, Morphine and Me" classic drug propaganda story used by N.Y. Legis. Comm.	181	362	543	1158	1979	2800
3-Classic Cole-c/a; drug story with hypo, opium den & with drawing addict	123	246	369	787	1344	1900
4-Jack Cole-c/a; c-taken from a story panel in #3 (r-(2) **SOTI** & **POP** stories/#2?)	100	200	300	635	1093	1550
5-Jack Cole-c, Marijuana racket story (Canadian ed. w/cover similar to #3 exists w/out drug story)	69	138	207	442	759	1075
6-Not a reprint, original story (Canadian ed. reprints #4 w/different coloring on-c)	55	110	165	352	601	850
V2#1-Used in **SOTI**, pgs. 81,82 & illo. "Dragging living people to death"; Toth, Wood (3 pgs.), Roussos-a; Cole-r from #2	90	180	270	576	988	1400

NOTE: *V2#1 was reprinted in Canada as V2#9 (12/49); same-c & contents minus Wood-a.*

TRUE FAITH
Fleetway: 1990 ($9.95, graphic novel)

	GD	VG	FN	VF	VF/NM	NM-
nn-Garth Ennis scripts	2	4	6	12	16	20
Reprinted by DC/Vertigo ('97, $12.95)						13.00

TRUE GHOST STORIES (See Ripley's...)

TRUE LIFE ROMANCES (...Romance on cover)
Ajax/Farrell Publications: Dec, 1955 - No. 3, Aug, 1956

	GD	VG	FN	VF	VF/NM	NM-
1	10	20	30	58	79	100
2	8	16	24	40	50	60
3-Disbrow-a	8	16	24	44	57	70

TRUE LIFE SECRETS
Romantic Love Stories/Charlton: Mar-April, 1951 - No. 28, Sept, 1955; No. 29, Jan, 1956

	GD	VG	FN	VF	VF/NM	NM-
1-Photo-c begin, end #3?	15	30	45	84	127	170
2	9	18	27	52	69	85
3-11,13-19:	8	16	24	44	57	70
12-"I Was An Escort Girl" story	10	20	30	54	72	90
20-29: 25-Last precode (3/55)	8	16	24	40	50	60

TRUE LIFE TALES (Formerly Mitzi's Romances #8?)
Marvel Comics (CCC): No. 8, Oct, 1949 - No. 2, Jan, 1950 (52 pgs.)

	GD	VG	FN	VF	VF/NM	NM-
8(#1, 10/49), 2-Both have photo-c	12	24	36	69	97	125

TRUE LOVE
Eclipse Comics: Jan, 1986 - No. 2, Jan, 1986 ($2.00, Baxter paper)

	GD	VG	FN	VF	VF/NM	NM-
1,2-Love stories reprinted from pre-code Standard Comics; Toth-a(p) in both; 1-Dave Stevens-c. 2-Mayo-a						4.00

TRUE LOVE CONFESSIONS
Premier Magazines: May, 1954 - No. 11, Jan, 1956

	GD	VG	FN	VF	VF/NM	NM-
1-Marijuana story	14	28	42	82	121	160
2	9	18	27	50	65	80
3-11	8	16	24	44	57	70

TRUE LOVE PICTORIAL
St. John Publishing Co.: Dec, 1952 - No. 11, Aug, 1954

	GD	VG	FN	VF	VF/NM	NM-
1-Only photo-c	21	42	63	122	199	275
2-Baker-c/a	30	60	90	177	289	400
3-5(All 25¢, 100 pgs.): 4-Signed story by Estrada. 5-(4/53)-Formerly Teen-Age Temptations; Kubert-a in #3; Baker-c/a in #3-5	47	94	141	296	498	700
6,7: Baker-c/a; signed stories by Estrada	28	56	84	165	270	375
8,10,11-Baker-c/a	28	56	84	165	270	375
9-Baker-c	22	44	66	132	216	300

TRUE LOVE PROBLEMS AND ADVICE ILLUSTRATED (Becomes Romance Stories of True Love No. 45 on)
McCombs/Harvey Publ./Home Comics: June, 1949 - No. 6, Apr, 1950; No. 7, Jan, 1951 - No. 44, Mar, 1957

	GD	VG	FN	VF	VF/NM	NM-
V1#1	15	30	45	86	133	180
2-Elias-c	10	20	30	54	72	90
3-10: 3,4,7-9-Elias-c	8	16	24	42	54	65
11-13,15-23,25-31: 31-Last pre-code (1/55)	7	14	21	35	43	50
14,24-Rape scene	7	14	21	37	46	55
32-37,39-44	6	12	18	29	36	42
38-S&K-c	9	18	27	52	69	85

NOTE: *Powell a-1, 2, 7-14, 17-25, 28, 29, 33, 40, 41. #3 has True Love... on inside.*

TRUE MOVIE AND TELEVISION (Part teenage magazine)
Toby Press: Aug, 1950 - No. 3, Nov, 1950; No. 4, Mar, 1951 (52 pgs.)(1-3: 10¢)

	GD	VG	FN	VF	VF/NM	NM-
1-Elizabeth Taylor photo-c; Gene Autry, Shirley Temple app.	58	116	174	371	636	900
2-(9/50)-Janet Leigh/Liz Taylor/Ava Gardner & others photo-c; Frazetta John Wayne illo from J.Wayne Adv. Comics #2 (4/50)	42	84	126	265	445	625
3-June Allyson photo-c; Montgomery Cliff, Esther Williams, Andrews Sisters app; Li'l Abner featured; Sadie Hawkins' Day	31	62	93	182	296	410
4-Jane Powell photo-c (15¢)	20	40	60	114	182	250

NOTE: *16 pgs. in color, rest movie material in black & white.*

TRUE SECRETS (Formerly Our Love?)
Marvel (IPS)/Atlas Comics (MPI) #4 on: No. 3, Mar, 1950; No. 4, Feb, 1951 - No. 40, Sept, 1956

	GD	VG	FN	VF	VF/NM	NM-
3 (52 pgs.)(IPS one-shot)`	15	30	45	86	133	180
4,5,7-10	10	20	30	58	79	100
6,22-Everett-a	12	24	36	69	97	125
11-20	10	20	30	54	72	90
21,23-28: 24-Colletta-c. 28-Last pre-code (2/55)	9	18	27	50	65	80
29-40: 34,36-Colletta-a	8	16	24	44	57	70

TRUE SPORT PICTURE STORIES (Formerly Sport Comics)
Street & Smith Publications: V1#5, Feb, 1942 - V5#2, July-Aug, 1949

	GD	VG	FN	VF	VF/NM	NM-
V1#5-Joe DiMaggio-c/story	37	74	111	218	354	490
6-12 (1942-43): 12-Jack Dempsey story	21	42	63	122	199	275
V2#1-12 (1943-45): 7-Stan Musial-c/story; photo story of the New York Yankees	20	40	60	115	185	255
V3#1-12 (1946-47): 7-Joe DiMaggio, Stan Musial, Bob Feller & others back from the armed service story. 8-Billy Conn vs. Joe Louis-c/story	19	38	57	111	176	240
V4#1-12 (1947-49), V5#1,2	18	36	54	105	165	225

NOTE: *Powell a-V3#10, V4#1-4, 6-8, 10-12; V5#1, 2; c-V3#10-12, V4#2-7, 9-12. Ravielli c-V5#2.*

TRUE STORIES OF ROMANCE
Fawcett Publications: Jan, 1950 - No. 3, May, 1950 (All photo-c)

	GD	VG	FN	VF	VF/NM	NM-
1	15	30	45	83	124	165

True War Romances #2 © QUA

Tug & Buster #7 © Marc Hempel

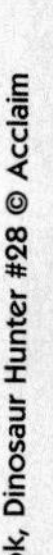
Turok, Dinosaur Hunter #28 © Acclaim

	GD 2.0	VG 4.0	FN 6.0	VF 8.0	VF/NM 9.0	NM- 9.2
2,3: 3-Marcus Swayze-a	11	22	33	62	86	110

TRUE STORY OF JESSE JAMES, THE (See Jesse James, Four Color 757)

TRUE SWEETHEART SECRETS
Fawcett Publs.: 5/50; No. 2, 7/50; No. 3, 1951(nd); No. 4, 9/51 - No. 11, 1/53 (All photo-c)

	GD 2.0	VG 4.0	FN 6.0	VF 8.0	VF/NM 9.0	NM- 9.2
1-Photo-c; Debbie Reynolds?	15	30	45	90	140	190
2-Wood-a (11 pgs.)	18	36	54	107	169	230
3-11: 4,5-Powell-a. 8-Marcus Swayze-a. 11-Evans-a	12	24	36	67	94	120

TRUE TALES OF LOVE (Formerly Secret Story Romances)
Atlas Comics (TCI): No. 22, April, 1956 - No. 31, Sept, 1957

	GD 2.0	VG 4.0	FN 6.0	VF 8.0	VF/NM 9.0	NM- 9.2
22	10	20	30	58	79	100
23-24,26-31-Colletta-a in most:	8	16	24	44	57	70
25-Everett-a; Colletta-a	9	18	27	50	65	80

TRUE TALES OF ROMANCE
Fawcett Publications: No. 4, June, 1950

	GD 2.0	VG 4.0	FN 6.0	VF 8.0	VF/NM 9.0	NM- 9.2
4-Photo-c	10	20	30	58	79	100

TRUE 3-D
Harvey Publications: Dec, 1953 - No. 2, Feb, 1954 (25¢)(Both came with 2 pair of glasses)

	GD 2.0	VG 4.0	FN 6.0	VF 8.0	VF/NM 9.0	NM- 9.2
1-Nostrand, Powell-a	5	10	15	35	55	75
2-Powell-a	6	12	18	37	59	80

NOTE: *Many copies of #1 surfaced in 1984.*

TRUE-TO-LIFE ROMANCES (Formerly Guns Against Gangsters)
Star Publ.: #8, 11-12/49; #9, 1-2/50; #3, 4/50 - #5, 9/50; #6, 1/51 - #23, 10/54

	GD 2.0	VG 4.0	FN 6.0	VF 8.0	VF/NM 9.0	NM- 9.2
8(#1, 1949)	24	48	72	140	230	320
9(#2),4-10	17	34	51	100	158	215
3-Janet Leigh/Glenn Ford photo on-c plus true life story of each	19	38	57	109	172	235
11,22,23	15	30	45	86	133	180
12-14,17-21-Disbrow-a	16	32	48	94	147	200
15,16-Wood & Disbrow-a in each	19	38	57	109	172	235

NOTE: ***Kamen** a-13. **Kamen/Feldstein** a-14. All have **L.B. Cole** covers.*

TRUE WAR EXPERIENCES
Harvey Publications: Aug, 1952 - No. 4, Dec, 1952

	GD 2.0	VG 4.0	FN 6.0	VF 8.0	VF/NM 9.0	NM- 9.2
1	8	16	24	56	93	130
2-4	5	10	15	32	51	70

TRUE WAR ROMANCES (Becomes Exotic Romances #22 on)
Quality Comics Group: Sept, 1952 - No. 21, June, 1955

	GD 2.0	VG 4.0	FN 6.0	VF 8.0	VF/NM 9.0	NM- 9.2
1-Photo-c	14	28	42	82	121	160
2-(10/52)	9	18	27	50	65	80
3-10: 3-(12/52). 9-Whitney-a	8	16	24	44	57	70
11-21: 20-Last precode (4/55). 14-Whitney-a	8	16	24	40	50	60

TRUE WAR STORIES (See Ripley's...)

TRUE WESTERN (True Adventures #3)
Marvel Comics (MMC): Dec, 1949 - No. 2, March, 1950

	GD 2.0	VG 4.0	FN 6.0	VF 8.0	VF/NM 9.0	NM- 9.2
1-Photo-c; Billy The Kid story	16	32	48	94	147	200
2-Alan Ladd photo-c	19	38	57	112	179	245

TRUMP
HMH Publishing Co.: Jan, 1957 - No. 2, Mar, 1957 (50¢, magazine)

	GD 2.0	VG 4.0	FN 6.0	VF 8.0	VF/NM 9.0	NM- 9.2
1-Harvey Kurtzman satire	25	50	75	150	245	340
2-Harvey Kurtzman satire	20	40	60	117	189	260

NOTE: ***Davis, Elder, Heath, Jaffee** art-#1,2; **Wood** a-1. Article by Mel Brooks in #2.*

TRUMPETS WEST (See Luke Short, Four Color #875)

TRUTH ABOUT CRIME (See Fox Giants)

TRUTH ABOUT MOTHER GOOSE (See Mother Goose, Four Color #862)

TRUTH BEHIND THE TRIAL OF CARDINAL MINDSZENTY, THE (See Cardinal Mindszenty in the Promotional Comics section))

TRUTHFUL LOVE (Formerly Youthful Love)
Youthful Magazines: No. 2, July, 1950

	GD 2.0	VG 4.0	FN 6.0	VF 8.0	VF/NM 9.0	NM- 9.2
2-Ingrid Bergman's true life story	12	24	36	69	97	125

TRUTH RED, WHITE & BLACK
Marvel Comics: Jan, 2003 - No. 6 ($3.50, limited series)

	GD 2.0	VG 4.0	FN 6.0	VF 8.0	VF/NM 9.0	NM- 9.2
1-Kyle Baker-a/Robert Morales-s; the testing of Captain America's super-soldier serum						3.50
2-7: 3-Isaiah Bradley 1st dons the Captain America costume						3.50
TPB (2004, $17.99) r/series						18.00

TRY-OUT WINNER BOOK
Marvel Comics: Mar, 1988

	GD 2.0	VG 4.0	FN 6.0	VF 8.0	VF/NM 9.0	NM- 9.2
1-Spider-Man vs. Doc Octopus						5.00

TSR WORLD (...Annual on cover only)
DC Comics: 1990 ($3.95, 84 pgs.)

	GD 2.0	VG 4.0	FN 6.0	VF 8.0	VF/NM 9.0	NM- 9.2
1-Advanced D&D, ForgottenRealms, Dragonlance & 1st app. Spelljammer						4.00

TSUNAMI GIRL
Image Comics: 1999 - No. 3, 1999 ($2.95)

	GD 2.0	VG 4.0	FN 6.0	VF 8.0	VF/NM 9.0	NM- 9.2
1-3-Sorayama-c/Paniccia-s/a						3.00

TUBBY (See Marge's...)

TUFF GHOSTS STARRING SPOOKY
Harvey Publications: July, 1962 - No. 39, Nov, 1970; No. 40, Sept, 1971 - No. 43, Oct, 1972

	GD 2.0	VG 4.0	FN 6.0	VF 8.0	VF/NM 9.0	NM- 9.2
1-12¢ issues begin	11	22	33	77	144	210
2-5	7	14	21	45	73	100
6-10	5	10	15	32	51	70
11-20	4	8	12	24	37	50
21-30: 29-Hot Stuff/Spooky team-up story	3	6	9	16	23	30
31-39,43	2	4	6	13	18	22
40-42: 52 pg. Giants	3	6	9	14	20	25

TUFFY
Standard Comics: No. 5, July, 1949 - No. 9, Oct, 1950

	GD 2.0	VG 4.0	FN 6.0	VF 8.0	VF/NM 9.0	NM- 9.2
5-All by Sid Hoff	7	14	21	37	46	55
6-9	5	10	15	24	30	35

TUFFY TURTLE
I. W. Enterprises: No date

	GD 2.0	VG 4.0	FN 6.0	VF 8.0	VF/NM 9.0	NM- 9.2
1-Reprint	2	4	6	8	11	14

TUG & BUSTER
Art & Soul Comics: Nov, 1995 - No. 7, Feb, 1998 ($2.95, B&W, bi-monthly)

	GD 2.0	VG 4.0	FN 6.0	VF 8.0	VF/NM 9.0	NM- 9.2
1-7: Marc Hempel-c/a/scripts						3.00
1-(Image Comics, 8/98, $2.95, B&W)						3.00

TURF
Image Comics: Apr, 2010 - No. 5 ($2.99, limited series)

	GD 2.0	VG 4.0	FN 6.0	VF 8.0	VF/NM 9.0	NM- 9.2
1-2-Jonathan Ross-s/Tommy Lee Edwards-a						3.00

TUROK
Acclaim Comics: Mar, 1998 - No. 4, Jun, 1998 ($2.50)

	GD 2.0	VG 4.0	FN 6.0	VF 8.0	VF/NM 9.0	NM- 9.2
1-4-Nicieza-s/Kayanan-a						3.00
..., Child of Blood 1 (1/98, $3.95) Nicieza-s/Kayanan-a						4.00
... Evolution 1 (8/02, $2.50) Nicieza-s/Kayanan-a						3.00
..., Redpath 1 (10/97, $3.95) Nicieza-s/Kayanan-a						4.00
... / Shadowman 1 (2/99, $3.95) Priest-s/Broome & Jimenez-a						4.00
...: Spring Break in the Lost Land 1 (7/97, $3.95) Nicieza-s/Kayanan-a						4.00
...: Tales of the Lost Land 1 (4/98, $3.95)						4.00
...: The Empty Souls 1 (4/97, $3.95) Nicieza-s/Kayanan-a; variant-c						4.00

TUROK, DINOSAUR HUNTER (See Magnus Robot Fighter #12 & Archer & Armstrong #2)
Valiant/Acclaim Comics: June, 1993 - No. 47, Aug, 1996 ($2.50)

	GD 2.0	VG 4.0	FN 6.0	VF 8.0	VF/NM 9.0	NM- 9.2
1-($3.50)-Chromium & foil-c						4.00
1-Gold foil-c variant						5.00
0, 2-47: 4-Andar app. 5-Death of Andar. 7-9-Truman/Glanzman-a. 11-Bound-in trading card. 16-Chaos Effect						3.00
Yearbook 1 (1994, $3.95, 52 pgs.)						4.00

TUROK, SON OF STONE (See Dan Curtis, Golden Comics Digest #31 & March of Comics #378, 399, 408)
Dell Publ. Co. #1-29(9/62)/Gold Key #30(12/62)-85(7/73)/Gold Key or Whitman #86(9/73)-125(1/80)/Whitman #126(3/81) on: No. 596, 12/54 - No. 29, 9/62; No. 30, 12/62 - No. 91, 7/74; No. 92, 9/74 - No. 125, 1/80; No. 126, 3/81 - No. 130, 4/82

	GD 2.0	VG 4.0	FN 6.0	VF 8.0	VF/NM 9.0	NM- 9.2
Four Color 596 (12/54)(#1)-1st app./origin Turok & Andar; dinosaur-c. Created by Matthew H. Murphy; written by Alberto Giolitti	52	104	156	442	896	1350
Four Color 656 (10/55)(#2)-1st mention of Lanok	29	58	87	223	449	675
3(3-5/56)-5: 3-Cave men	21	42	63	150	300	450
6-10: 8-Dinosaur of the deep; Turok enters Lost Valley; series begins. 9-Paul S. Newman-s (most issues thru end)	14	28	42	102	206	310
11-20: 17-Prehistoric Pygmies	12	24	36	86	161	235
21-29	9	18	27	65	113	160
30-1st Gold Key. 30-33-Painted back-c.	10	20	30	67	116	165
31-Drug use story	9	18	27	65	113	160
32-40	8	16	24	52	86	120
41-50	6	12	18	41	66	90

Turok, Son of Stone #1 © RH

Tweety and Sylvester Four Color #406 © WB

21 #3 © TCOW

	GD 2.0	VG 4.0	FN 6.0	VF 8.0	VF/NM 9.0	NM- 9.2
51-57,59,60	6	12	18	37	59	80
58-Flying Saucer c/story	6	12	18	39	62	85
61-70: 62-12¢ & 15¢ covers. 63,68-Line drawn-c	5	10	15	30	48	65
71-84: 84-Origin & 1st app. Hutec	4	8	12	26	41	55
85-99: 93-r-c/#19 w/changes. 94-r-c/#28 w/changes. 97-r-c/#31 w/changes. 98-r/#58 w/o spaceship & spacemen on-c. 99-r-c/#52 w/changes.	3	6	9	21	32	42
100	4	8	12	26	41	55
101-129: 114,115-(52 pgs.). 129(2/82)	4	8	12	22	34	45
130(4/82)-Last issue	6	12	18	37	59	80
Giant 1(30031-611) (11/66)-Slick-c; r/#10-12 & 16 plus cover to #11	10	20	30	72	131	190
Giant 1-Same as above but with paper-c	11	22	33	77	144	210

NOTE: *Most painted-c; line-drawn #63 & 130.* ***Alberto Gioletti*** *a-24-27, 30-119, 123; painted-c No. 30-129.* ***Sparling*** *a-117, 120-130. Reprints-#36, 54, 57, 75, 112, 114(1/3), 115(1/3), 118, 121, 125, 127(1/3), 128, 129(1/3), 130(1/3), Giant 1. Cover r-93, 94, 97-99, 126(all different from original covers.*

TUROK, SON OF STONE
Dark Horse Comics: Oct, 2010 - Present ($3.50)

	GD 2.0	VG 4.0	FN 6.0	VF 8.0	VF/NM 9.0	NM- 9.2
1-Shooter-s/Francisco-a/Swanland-c; back-up reprint of debut in Four Color 596						3.50
1-Variant-c by Francisco						5.00

TUROK THE HUNTED
Valiant/Acclaim Comics: Mar, 1995 - No. 2, Apr, 1995 ($2.50, limited series)

	GD 2.0	VG 4.0	FN 6.0	VF 8.0	VF/NM 9.0	NM- 9.2
1,2-Mike Deodato-a(p); price omitted on #1						3.00

TUROK THE HUNTED
Acclaim Comics (Valiant): Feb, 1996 - No. 2, Mar, 1996 ($2.50, limited series)

	GD 2.0	VG 4.0	FN 6.0	VF 8.0	VF/NM 9.0	NM- 9.2
1,2-Mike Grell story						3.00

TUROK, TIMEWALKER
Acclaim Comics (Valiant): Aug, 1997 - No. 2, Sept, 1997 ($2.50, limited series)

	GD 2.0	VG 4.0	FN 6.0	VF 8.0	VF/NM 9.0	NM- 9.2
1,2-Nicieza story						3.00

TUROK 2 (Magazine)
Acclaim Comics: Oct, 1998 ($4.99, magazine size)

	GD 2.0	VG 4.0	FN 6.0	VF 8.0	VF/NM 9.0	NM- 9.2
...Seeds of Evil-Nicieza-s/Broome & Benjamin-a; origin back-up story						5.00
#2 Adon's Curse -Mack painted-c/Broome & Benjamin-a; origin pt. 2						5.00

TUROK 3: SHADOW OF OBLIVION
Acclaim Comics: Sept, 2000 ($4.95, one-shot)

	GD 2.0	VG 4.0	FN 6.0	VF 8.0	VF/NM 9.0	NM- 9.2
1-Includes pin-up gallery						5.00

TURTLE SOUP
Mirage Studios: Sept, 1987 ($2.00, 76 pgs., B&W, one-shot)

	GD 2.0	VG 4.0	FN 6.0	VF 8.0	VF/NM 9.0	NM- 9.2
1-Featuring Teenage Mutant Ninja Turtles	1	2	3	5	6	8

TURTLE SOUP
Mirage Studios: Nov, 1991 - No. 4, 1992 ($2.50, limited series, coated paper)

	GD 2.0	VG 4.0	FN 6.0	VF 8.0	VF/NM 9.0	NM- 9.2
1-4: Features the Teenage Mutant Ninja Turtles						4.00

TV CASPER & COMPANY
Harvey Publications: Aug, 1963 - No. 46, April, 1974 (25¢ Giants)

	GD 2.0	VG 4.0	FN 6.0	VF 8.0	VF/NM 9.0	NM- 9.2
1- 68 pg. Giants begin; Casper, Little Audrey, Baby Huey, Herman & Catnip, Buzzy the Crow begin	11	22	33	77	144	210
2-5	6	12	18	43	69	95
6-10	5	10	15	30	48	65
11-20	4	8	12	24	37	50
21-31: 31-Last 68 pg. issue	3	6	9	18	27	35
32-46: All 52 pgs.	3	6	9	16	23	30

NOTE: *Many issues contain reprints.*

TV FUNDAY FUNNIES (See Famous TV...)

TV FUNNIES (See New Funnies)

TV FUNTIME (See Little Audrey)

TV LAUGHOUT (See Archie's...)

TV SCREEN CARTOONS (Formerly Real Screen)
National Periodical Publ.: No. 129, July-Aug, 1959 - No. 138, Jan-Feb, 1961

	GD 2.0	VG 4.0	FN 6.0	VF 8.0	VF/NM 9.0	NM- 9.2
129-138 (Scarce)	6	12	18	43	69	95

TV STARS (TV) (Newsstand sales only)
Marvel Comics Group: Aug, 1978 - No. 4, Feb, 1979 (Hanna-Barbera)

	GD 2.0	VG 4.0	FN 6.0	VF 8.0	VF/NM 9.0	NM- 9.2
1-Great Grape Ape app.	3	6	9	18	27	35
2,4: 4-Top Cat app.	3	6	9	16	22	28
3-Toth-c/a; Dave Stevens inks	3	6	9	17	25	32

TV TEENS (Formerly Ozzie & Babs; Rock and Rollo #14 on)
Charlton Comics: V1#14, Feb, 1954 - V2#13, July, 1956

	GD 2.0	VG 4.0	FN 6.0	VF 8.0	VF/NM 9.0	NM- 9.2
V1#14 (#1)-Ozzie & Babs	10	20	30	54	72	90
15 (#2)	6	12	18	33	41	48
V2#3(6/54) - 6-Don Winslow	6	12	18	31	38	45
7-13-Mopsy. 8(7/55). 9-Paper dolls	6	12	18	29	36	42

TWEETY AND SYLVESTER (1st Series) (TV) (Also see Looney Tunes and Merrie Melodies)
Dell Publishing Co.: No. 406, June, 1952 - No. 37, June-Aug, 1962

	GD 2.0	VG 4.0	FN 6.0	VF 8.0	VF/NM 9.0	NM- 9.2
Four Color 406 (#1)	10	20	30	72	131	190
Four Color 489,524	6	12	18	43	69	95
4 (3-5/54) - 20	5	10	15	35	55	75
21-37	4	8	12	28	44	60

(See March of Comics #421, 433, 445, 457, 469, 481)

TWEETY AND SYLVESTER (2nd Series)(See Kite Fun Book)
Gold Key No. 1-102/Whitman No. 103 on: Nov, 1963; No. 2, Nov, 1965 - No. 121, Jun, 1984

	GD 2.0	VG 4.0	FN 6.0	VF 8.0	VF/NM 9.0	NM- 9.2
1	5	10	15	30	48	65
2-10	3	6	9	18	27	35
11-30	2	4	6	13	18	22
31-50	2	4	6	9	12	15
51-70	1	3	4	6	8	10
71-102	1	2	3	5	6	8
103,104 (Whitman)	1	3	4	6	8	10
105(9/80),106(10/80),107(12/80) 3-pack only	3	6	9	20	30	40
108-116: 113(2/82),114(2-3/82),115(3/82),116(4/82)	2	4	6	8	10	12
117-121 (All # 90094 on-c; nd, nd code): 117(6/83). 118(7/83). 119(2/84)-r(1/3). 120(5/84). 121(6/84)	3	6	9	14	19	24
Digest nn (Charlton/Xerox Pub., 1974) (low print run)	3	6	9	16	23	30
Mini Comic No. 1(1976, 3-1/4x6-1/2")	1	3	4	6	8	10

TWELVE, THE (Golden Age Timely heroes)
Marvel Comics: No. 0; 2008; No. 1, Mar, 2008 - No. 12, ($2.99, limited series)

	GD 2.0	VG 4.0	FN 6.0	VF 8.0	VF/NM 9.0	NM- 9.2
0-Rockman, Laughing Mask & Phantom Reporter intro. stories (1940s); series preview						3.00
1/2 (2008, $3.99) r/early app. of Fiery Mask, Mister E and Rockman; Weston-c						4.00
1-8-Straczynski-s/Weston-a; Timely heroes re-surface in the present						3.00
...: Spearhead 1 (5/10, $3.99) Weston-s/a; Phantom Reporter in WW2; Invaders app.						4.00

12 O'CLOCK HIGH (TV)
Dell Publishing Co.: Jan-Mar, 1965 - No. 2, Apr-June, 1965 (Photo-c)

	GD 2.0	VG 4.0	FN 6.0	VF 8.0	VF/NM 9.0	NM- 9.2
1- Sinnott-a	6	12	18	39	62	85
2	5	10	15	30	48	65

2099 A.D.
Marvel Comics: May, 1995 ($3.95, one-shot)

	GD 2.0	VG 4.0	FN 6.0	VF 8.0	VF/NM 9.0	NM- 9.2
1-Acetate-c by Quesada & Palmiotti						4.00

2099 APOCALYPSE
Marvel Comics: Dec, 1995 ($4.95, one-shot)

	GD 2.0	VG 4.0	FN 6.0	VF 8.0	VF/NM 9.0	NM- 9.2
1-Chromium wraparound-c; Ellis script						5.00

2099 GENESIS
Marvel Comics: Jan, 1996 ($4.95, one-shot)

	GD 2.0	VG 4.0	FN 6.0	VF 8.0	VF/NM 9.0	NM- 9.2
1-Chromium wraparound-c; Ellis script						5.00

2099 MANIFEST DESTINY
Marvel Comics: Mar, 1998 ($5.99, one-shot)

	GD 2.0	VG 4.0	FN 6.0	VF 8.0	VF/NM 9.0	NM- 9.2
1-Origin of Fantastic Four 2099; intro Moon Knight 2099						6.00

2099 UNLIMITED
Marvel Comics: Sept, 1993 - No. 10, 1996 ($3.95, 68 pgs.)

	GD 2.0	VG 4.0	FN 6.0	VF 8.0	VF/NM 9.0	NM- 9.2
1-10: 1-1st app. Hulk 2099 & begins. 1-3-Spider-Man 2099 app. 9-Joe Kubert-c; Len Wein & Nancy Collins scripts						4.00

2099 WORLD OF DOOM SPECIAL
Marvel Comics: May, 1995 ($2.25, one-shot)

	GD 2.0	VG 4.0	FN 6.0	VF 8.0	VF/NM 9.0	NM- 9.2
1-Doom's "Contract w/America"						3.00

2099 WORLD OF TOMORROW
Marvel Comics: Sept, 1996 - No. 8, Apr, 1997 ($2.50) (Replaces 2099 titles)

	GD 2.0	VG 4.0	FN 6.0	VF 8.0	VF/NM 9.0	NM- 9.2
1-8: 1-Wraparound-c. 2-w/bound-in card. 4,5-Phalanx						3.00

21
Image Comics (Top Cow Productions): Feb, 1996 - No. 3, Apr, 1996 ($2.50)

	GD 2.0	VG 4.0	FN 6.0	VF 8.0	VF/NM 9.0	NM- 9.2
1-3: Len Wein scripts						3.00
1-Variant-c						3.00

21 DOWN
DC Comics (WildStorm): Nov, 2002 - No. 12, Nov, 2003 ($2.95)

	GD 2.0	VG 4.0	FN 6.0	VF 8.0	VF/NM 9.0	NM- 9.2
1-12: 1-Palmiotti & Gray-s/Saiz-a/Jusko-c						3.00
...: The Conduit (2003, $19.95, TPB) r/#1-7; intro. by Garth Ennis						20.00

24: Nightfall #5 © 20th Century Fox

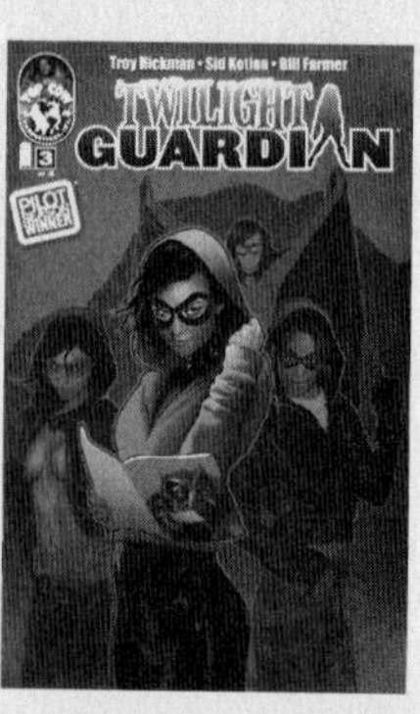

Twilight Guardian #3 © TCOW

Two-Fisted Tales #27 © WMG

GD 2.0 | VG 4.0 | FN 6.0 | VF 8.0 | VF/NM 9.0 | NM- 9.2

GD 2.0 | VG 4.0 | FN 6.0 | VF 8.0 | VF/NM 9.0 | NM- 9.2

24 (Based on TV series)
IDW Publishing: July, 2004 - July, 2005 ($6.99/$7.49, square-bound, one-shots)

...: Midnight Sun (7/05, $7.49) J.C. Vaughn & Mark Haynes-s; Renato Guedes-a 7.50
...: One Shot (7/04, $6.99)-Jack Bauer's first day on the job at CTU; Vaughn & Haynes-s; Guedes-a 7.50
...: Stories (1/05, $7.49) Manny Clark-a; Vaughn & Haynes-s 7.50

24: NIGHTFALL (Based on TV series)
IDW Publishing: Nov, 2006 - No. 6 ($3.99, limited series)

1-5-Two years before Season One; Vaughn & Haynes-s; Diaz-a; two covers 4.00

28 DAYS LATER (Based on the 2002 movie)
Boom! Studios: July, 2009 - Present ($3.99)

1-22: 1-Covers by Bradstreet and Phillips 4.00

2020 VISIONS
DC Comics (Vertigo): May, 1997 - No. 12, Apr, 1998 ($2.25, limited series)

1-12-Delano-s: 1-3-Quitely-a. 4-"la tormenta"-Pleece-a 3.00

20,000 LEAGUES UNDER THE SEA (Movie)(See King Classics, Movie Comics & Power Record Comics)
Dell Publishing Co.: No. 614, Feb, 1955 (Disney)

Four Color 614-Movie, painted-c 8 16 24 58 97 135

TWICE TOLD TALES (See Movie Classics)

TWILIGHT
DC Comics: 1990 - No. 3, 1991 ($4.95, 52 pgs, lim. series, squarebound, mature)

1-3: Tommy Tomorrow app; Chaykin scripts, Garcia-Lopez-c/a 5.00

TWILIGHT EXPERIMENT
DC Comics (WildStorm): Apr, 2004 - No. 6, Sept, 2005 ($2.95, limited series)

1-6-Gray & Palmiotti-s/Santacruz-a 3.00

TWILIGHT GUARDIAN (Also see Pilot Season: Twilight Guardian)
Image Comics (Top Cow): Jan, 2011 - No. 4, Apr, 2011 ($3.99, limited series)

1-4-Hickman-s/Kotean-a 4.00

TWILIGHT MAN
First Publishing: June, 1989 - No. 4, Sept, 1989 ($2.75, limited series)

1-4 3.00

TWILIGHT ZONE, THE (TV) (See Dan Curtis & Stories From...)
Dell Publishing Co./Gold Key/Whitman No. 92: No. 1173, 3-5/61 - No. 91, 4/79; No. 92, 5/82

Four Color 1173 (#1)-Crandall-c/a 20 40 60 144 290 435
Four Color 1288-Crandall/Evans-c/a 12 24 36 82 154 225
01-860-207 (5-7/62-Dell, 15¢) 9 18 27 63 107 150
12-860-210 on-c; 01-860-210 on inside(8-10/62-Dell)-Evans-c/a (3 stories) 9 18 27 63 107 150
1(11/62-Gold Key)-Crandall/Frazetta-a (10 & 11 pgs.); Evans-a 13 26 39 91 176 260
2 8 16 24 58 97 135
3-11: 3(11 pgs.),4(10 pgs.),9-Toth-a 6 12 18 43 69 95
12-15: 12-Williamson-a. 13,15-Crandall-a. 14-Orlando/Crandall/Torres-a 5 10 15 35 55 75
16-20 4 8 12 26 41 55
21-25: 21-Crandall-a(r). 25-Evans/Crandall-a(r); Toth-r/#4; last 12¢ issue 3 6 9 20 30 40
26,27: 26-Flying Saucer-c/story; Crandall, Evans-a(r). 27-Evans-r(2) 3 6 9 19 29 38
28-32: 32-Evans-a(r) 3 6 9 17 25 32
33-51: 43-Celardo-a. 51-Williamson-a 2 4 6 13 18 22
52-70 2 4 6 10 14 18
71-82,86-91: 71-Reprint 2 4 6 8 11 14
83-(52 pgs.) 3 6 9 14 20 25
84-(52 pgs.) Frank Miller's 1st comic book work 5 10 15 35 55 75
85-Frank Miller-a (2nd) 3 6 9 18 27 35
92-(Whitman, 5/82) Last issue; r/#1. 2 4 6 9 13 16
Mini Comic #1(1976, 3-1/4x6-1/2") 2 4 6 8 10 12

NOTE: ***Bolle** a-13(w/**McWilliams**), 50, 55, 57, 59, 77, 78, 80, 83, 84. **McWilliams** a-59, 78, 80, 82, 84. **Miller** a-84, 85. **Orlando** a-15, 19, 20, 22, 23. **Sekowsky** a-3. **Simonson** a-50, 54, 55, 83r. **Weiss** a-39, 79r(#39). (See Mystery Comics Digest 3, 6, 9, 12, 15, 18, 21, 24). Reprints-26(1/3), 71, 73, 79, 83, 84, 86, 92. Painted c-1-91.*

TWILIGHT ZONE, THE (TV)
Now Comics: Nov, 1990 ($2.95); Oct, 1991; V2#1, Nov, 1991 - No. 11, Oct, 1992 ($1.95); V3#1, 1993 - No. 4, 1993 ($2.50)

1-(11/90, $2.95, 52 pgs.)-Direct sale edition; Neal Adams-a, Sienkiewicz-c; Harlan Ellison scripts 5.00
1-(11/90, $1.75)-Newsstand ed. w/N. Adams-c 4.00
1-Prestige Format (10/91, $4.95)-Reprints above with extra Harlan Ellison short story 5.00
1-Collector's Edition (10/91, $2.50)-Non-code approved and polybagged; reprints 11/90 issue; gold logo, 1-Reprint ($2.50)-r/direct sale 11/90 version, 1-Reprint ($2.50)-r/newsstand 11/90 version each... 4.00
V2#1-Direct sale & newsstand ed. w/different-c 3.00
V2#2-8,10-11 3.00
V2#9-($2.95)-3-D Special; polybagged w/glasses & hologram on-c 4.00
V2#9-($4.95)-Prestige Edition; contains 2 extra stories & a different hologram on-c; polybagged w/glasses 5.00
V3#1-4, Anniversary Special 1 (1992, $2.50) 3.00
Annual 1 (4/93, $2.50)-No ads 3.00
...Science Fiction Special (3/93, $3.50) 4.00

TWINKLE COMICS
Spotlight Publishers: May, 1945

1 24 48 72 142 234 325

TWIST, THE
Dell Publishing Co.: July-Sept, 1962

01-864-209-Painted-c 4 8 12 24 37 50

TWISTED TALES (See Eclipse Graphic Album Series #15)
Pacific Comics/Independent Comics Group (Eclipse) #9,10: 11/82 - No. 8, 5/84; No. 9, 11/84; No. 10, 12/84 (Baxter paper)

1-9: 1-B. Jones/Corben-c; Alcala-a; nudity/violence in al. 2-Wrightson-c; Ploog-a 5.00
10-Wrightson painted art; Morrow-a 1 2 3 4 5 7

NOTE: ***Bolton** painted c-4, 6, 7; a-7. **Conrad** a-1, 3, 5; c-1i, 3, 5. **Guice** a-8. **Wildey** a-3.*

TWO BIT THE WACKY WOODPECKER (See Wacky...)
Toby Press: 1951 - No. 3, May, 1953

1 10 20 30 54 72 90
2,3 6 12 18 31 38 45

TWO FACE: YEAR ONE
DC Comics: 2008 - No. 2, 2008 ($5.99, squarebound, limited series)

1,2-Origin re-told; Sable-s/Saiz & Haun-a 6.00

TWO-FISTED TALES (Formerly Haunt of Fear #15-17)
(Also see EC Archives • Two-Fisted Tales)
E. C. Comics: No. 18, Nov-Dec, 1950 - No. 41, Feb-Mar, 1955

18(#1)-Kurtzman-c 94 188 282 752 1201 1650
19-Kurtzman-c 68 136 204 544 865 1185
20-Kurtzman-c 44 88 132 352 564 775
21,22-Kurtzman-c 37 74 111 296 473 650
23-25-Kurtzman-c 29 58 87 232 366 500
26-29,31-Kurtzman-c. 31-Civil War issue 21 42 63 168 267 365
30-Classic Davis-c 23 46 69 184 292 400
32-35: 33- "Atom Bomb" by Wood. 35-Civil War issue 21 42 63 168 267 365
36-41 16 32 48 128 207 285
Two-Fisted Annual (1952, 25¢, 132 pgs.) 107 214 321 803 1227 1650
Two-Fisted Annual (1953, 25¢, 132 pgs.) 79 158 237 593 909 1225

NOTE: ***Berg** a-29. **Colan** a-30,39p. **Craig** a-18, 19, 32. **Crandall** a-35, 36. **Davis** a-20-36, 40; c-30, 34, 35, 41, Annual 2. **Estrada** a-30. **Evans** a-34, 40, 41; c-40. **Feldstein** a-18. **Krigstein** a-41. **Kubert** a-32, 33. **Kurtzman** a-18-25; c-18-29, 31, Annual 1. **Severin** a-26, 28, 29, 31, 34-41 (No. 37-39 are all-**Severin** issues); c-36-39. **Severin/Elder** a-19-29, 31, 33, 36. **Wood** a-18-28, 30-35, 41; c-32, 33. Special issues: #26 (ChanJin Reservoir), 31 (Civil War), 35 (Civil War). Canadian reprints known; see Table of Contents. #25-Davis biog. #27-Wood biog. #28-Kurtzman biog.*

TWO-FISTED TALES
Russ Cochran/Gemstone Publishing: Oct, 1992 - No. 24, May, 1998 ($1.50/$2.00/$2.50)

1-24: 1-4r/Two-Fisted Tales #18-21 w/original-c 3.00

TWO-GUN KID (Also see All Western Winners, Best Western, Black Rider, Blaze Carson, Kid Colt, Western Winners, Wild West, & Wild Western)
Marvel/Atlas (MCI No. 1-10/HPC No. 11-59/Marvel No. 60 on): 3/48(No mo.) - No. 10, 11/49; No. 11, 12/53 - No. 59, 4/61; No. 60, 11/62 - No. 92, 3/68; No. 93, 7/70 - No. 136, 4/77

1-Two-Gun Kid & his horse Cyclone begin; The Sheriff begins 116 232 348 742 1271 1800
2 47 94 141 296 498 700
3,4: 3-Annie Oakley app. 37 74 111 222 361 500
5-Pre-Black Rider app. (Wint. 48/49); Anti-Wertham editorial (1st?) 39 78 117 235 385 535
6-10(11/49): 8-Blaze Carson app. 9-Black Rider app. 29 58 87 170 278 385
11(12/53)-Black Rider app.; 1st to have Atlas globe on-c; explains how Kid Colt

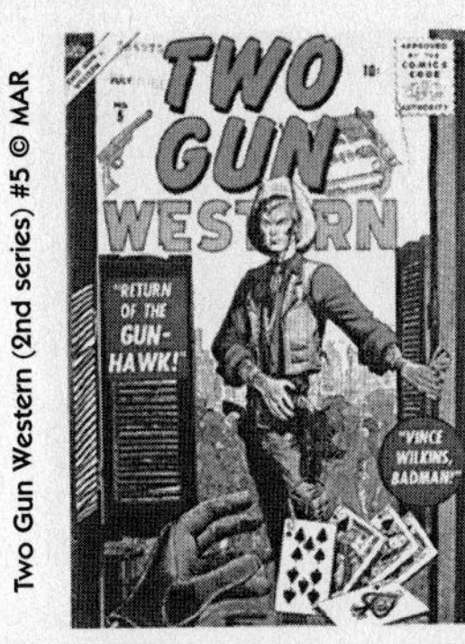

Two Gun Western (2nd series) #5 © MAR

2001: A Space Odyssey #10 © MGM

Ultimate Armor Wars #1 © MAR

GD VG FN VF VF/NM NM-
2.0 4.0 6.0 8.0 9.0 9.2

became an outlaw 23 46 69 136 223 310
12-Black Rider app. 21 42 63 124 202 280
13-20: 14-Opium story 17 34 51 98 154 210
21-24,26-29 15 30 45 90 140 190
25,30: 25-Williamson-a (5 pgs.). 30-Williamson/Torres-a (4 pgs.)
15 30 45 94 147 200
31-33,35,37-40 9 18 27 61 103 145
34-Crandall-a 9 18 27 63 107 150
36,41,42,48-Origin in all 9 18 27 63 107 150
43,44,47 7 14 21 50 83 115
45,46-Davis-a 8 16 24 54 90 125
49,50,52,53-Severin-a(2/3) in each 7 14 21 47 76 105
51-Williamson-a (5 pgs.) 8 16 24 54 90 125
54,55,57,59-Severin-a(3) in each. 59-Kirby-a; last 10¢ issue (4/61)
7 14 21 47 76 105
56 6 12 18 43 69 95
58,60-New origin. 58-Kirby/Ayers-c/a "The Monster of Hidden Valley" cover/story
(Kirby monster-c) 8 16 24 54 90 125
60-Edition w/handwritten issue number on cover 9 18 27 63 107 150
61,62-Kirby-a 6 12 18 43 69 95
63-74: 64-Intro. Boom-Boom 5 10 15 32 51 70
75-77-Kirby-a (reprint) 6 12 18 37 59 80
78-89 4 8 12 24 37 50
90,95-Kirby-a 4 8 12 26 41 55
91,92: 92-Last new story; last 12¢ issue 4 8 12 22 34 45
93,94,96-99 3 6 9 14 20 26
100-Last 15¢-c 3 6 9 16 22 28
101-Origin retold/#58; Kirby-a 3 6 9 16 22 28
102-120-reprints 2 4 6 9 13 16
121-136-reprints. 129-131-(Regular 25¢ editions) 2 4 6 9 13 16
129-131-(30¢-c variants, limited distribution)(4-8/76) 4 8 12 26 41 55

NOTE: ***Ayers** a-13, 24, 26, 27. **Davis** c-45-47. **Drucker** a-23. **Everett** a-82, 91. **Fuje** a-13. **Heath** a-3(2), 4(3), 5(2), 7; c-13, 21, 23, 53. **Keller** a-16, 19, 28, 42. **Kirby** a-54, 55, 57-62, 75-77, 90, 95, 101, 119, 120, 129; c-10, 52, 54-65, 67-72, 74-76, 116. **Maneely** a-20; c-11, 12, 16, 19, 20, 24-28, 30, 35, 41, 42, 49. **Powell** a-38, 102, 104. **Severin** a-9, 29, 51, 55, 57, 99r(3); c-9, 39, 51. **Shores** c-1-8, 11. **Trimpe** c-99. **Tuska** a-11, 12. **Whitney** a-87, 89-92, 98-113, 124, 129; c-87, 89, 91, 113. **Wildey** a-21. **Williamson** a-110r. Kid Colt in #13, 14, 16-21.*

TWO GUN KID: SUNSET RIDERS
Marvel Comics: Nov, 1995 - No. 2, Dec, 1995 ($6.95, squarebound, lim. series)

1,2: Fabian Nicieza scripts in all. 1-Painted-c. 7.00

TWO GUN WESTERN (1st Series) (Formerly Casey Crime Photographer #1-4? or My Love #1-4?)
Marvel/Atlas Comics (MPC): No. 5, Nov, 1950 - No. 14, June, 1952

5-The Apache Kid (Intro & origin) & his horse Nightwind begin by Buscema
26 52 78 152 249 345
6-10: 8-Kid Colt, The Texas Kid & his horse Thunder begin?
19 38 57 111 176 240
11-14: 13-Black Rider app. 14 28 42 80 115 150

NOTE: ***Maneely** a-6, 7, 9; c-6, 11-13. **Morrow** a-9. **Romita** a-8. **Wildey** a-8.*

2-GUN WESTERN (2nd Series) (Formerly Billy Buckskin #1-3; Two-Gun Western #5 on)
Atlas Comics (MgPC): No. 4, May, 1956

4-Colan, Ditko, Severin, Sinnott-a; Maneely-c 15 30 45 88 137 185

TWO-GUN WESTERN (Formerly 2-Gun Western)
Atlas Comics (MgPC): No. 5, July, 1956 - No. 12, Sept, 1957

5-Return of the Gun-Hawk-c/story; Black Rider app. 15 30 45 85 130 175
6,7 12 24 36 67 94 120
8,10,12-Crandall-a 13 26 39 72 101 130
9,11-Williamson-a in both (5 pgs. each) 14 28 42 76 108 140

NOTE: ***Ayers** a-9. **Colan** a-5. **Everett** c-12. **Forgione** a-5, 6. **Kirby** a-12. **Maneely** a-6, 8, 12; c-5, 6, 8, 11. **Morrow** a-9, 10. **Powell** a-7, 11. **Severin** c-10. **Sinnott** a-5. **Wildey** a-9.*

TWO MINUTE WARNING
Ultimate Sports Ent.: 2000 - No. 2 ($3.95, cardstock covers)

1,2-NFL players & Teddy Roosevelt battle evil 4.00

TWO MOUSEKETEERS, THE (See 4-Color #475, 603, 642 under M.G.M.'s...;

TWO ON A GUILLOTINE (See Movie Classics)

TWO-STEP
DC Comics (Cliffhanger): Dec, 2003 - No. 3, Jul, 2004 ($2.95, limited series)

1-3-Warren Ellis-s/Amanda Conner-a 3.00
TPB (2010, $19.99) r/#1-3; sketch pages; script for #1 with B&W art 20.00

2000 A.D. MONTHLY/PRESENTS (Showcase #25 on)
Eagle Comics/Quality Comics No. 5 on: 4/85 - #6, 9/85; 4/86 - #54, 1991 ($1.25-$1.50, Mando paper)

GD VG FN VF VF/NM NM-
2.0 4.0 6.0 8.0 9.0 9.2

1-6,1-25:1-4 r/British series featuring Judge Dredd; Alan Moore scripts begin.
1-25 ($1.25)-Reprints from British 2000 AD 3.00
26,27/28, 29/30, 31-54: 27/28, 29/30,31-Guice-c 3.00

2001, A SPACE ODYSSEY (Movie) (See adaptation in Treasury edition)
Marvel Comics Group: Dec, 1976 - No. 10, Sept, 1977 (30¢)

1-Kirby-c/a in all 3 6 9 16 22 28
2-7,9,10 2 4 6 8 11 14
7,9,10-(35¢-c variants, limited distribution)(6-9/77) 3 6 9 16 23 30
8-Origin/1st app. Machine Man (called Mr. Machine) 3 6 9 16 22 28
8-(35¢-c variant, limited distribution)(6,8/77) 4 8 12 28 44 60
...Treasury 1 ('76, 84 pgs.)-All new Kirby-a 3 6 9 16 23 30

2001 NIGHTS
Viz Premiere Comics: 1990 - No. 10, 1991 ($3.75, B&W, lim. series, mature readers, 84 pgs.)

1-10: Japanese sci-fi. 1-Wraparound-c 5.00

2010 (Movie)
Marvel Comics Group: Apr, 1985 - No. 2, May, 1985

1,2-r/Marvel Super Special movie adaptation. 3.00

TYPHOID (Also see Daredevil)
Marvel Comics: Nov, 1995 - No. 4, Feb, 1996 ($3.95, squarebound, lim. series)

1-4: Van Fleet-c/a 4.00

UFO & ALIEN COMIX
Warren Publishing Co.: Jan, 1978 (B&W magazine, 84 pgs., one-shot)

nn-Toth-a, J. Severin-a(r); Pie-s 2 4 6 10 14 18

UFO & OUTER SPACE (Formerly UFO Flying Saucers)
Gold Key: No. 14, June, 1978 - No. 25, Feb, 1980 (All painted covers)

14-Reprints UFO Flying Saucers #3 1 3 4 6 8 10
15,16-Reprints 1 3 4 6 8 10
17-25: 17-20-New material. 23-McWilliams-a. 24-(3 pg.-r). 25-Reprints UFO Flying Saucers #2 w/cover 1 3 4 6 8 10

UFO ENCOUNTERS
Western Publishing Co.: May, 1978 ($1.95, 228 pgs.)

11192-Reprints UFO Flying Saucers 4 8 12 26 41 55
11404-Vol.1 (128 pgs.)-See UFO Mysteries for Vol. 2 4 8 12 22 34 45

UFO FLYING SAUCERS (UFO & Outer Space #14 on)
Gold Key: Oct, 1968 - No. 13, Jan, 1977 (No. 2 on, 36 pgs.)

1(30035-810) (68 pgs.) 5 10 15 32 51 70
2(11/70), 3(11/72), 4(11/74) 3 6 9 16 23 30
5(2/75)-13: Bolle-a #4 on 2 4 6 11 16 20

UFO MYSTERIES
Western Publishing Co.: 1978 ($1.00, reprints, 96 pgs.)

11400-(Vol.2)-Cont'd from UFO Encounters, pgs. 129-224
4 8 12 22 34 45

ULTIMAN GIANT ANNUAL (See Big Bang Comics)
Image Comics: Nov, 2001 ($4.95, B&W, one-shot)

1-Homage to DC 1960's annuals 5.00

ULTIMATE... (Collects 4-issue alternate titles from X-Men Age of Apocalypse crossovers)
Marvel Comics: May, 1995 ($8.95, trade paperbacks, gold foil covers)

Amazing X-Men, Astonishing X-Men, Factor-X, Gambit & the X-Ternals, Generation Next, X-Calibre, X-Man 9.00
Weapon X 10.00

ULTIMATE ADVENTURES
Marvel Comics: Nov, 2002 - No. 6, Dec, 2003 ($2.25)

1-6: 1-Intro. Hawk-Owl; Zimmerman-s/Fegredo-a. 3-Ultimates app. 3.00
One Tin Soldier TPB (2005, $12.99) r/#1-6 13.00

ULTIMATE ANNUALS
Marvel Comics: 2006; 2007 ($13.99, SC)

Vol. 1 (2006, $13.99) r/Ult. FF Ann. #1, Ult. X-Men Ann. #1, Ult S-M #1, Ultimates Ann #1 14.00
Vol. 2 (2007, $13.99) r/Ult. FF Ann. #2, Ult. X-Men Ann. #2, Ult S-M #2, Ultimates Ann #2 14.00

ULTIMATE ARMOR WARS (Follows Ultimatum x-over)
Marvel Comics: Nov, 2009 - No. 4, Apr, 2010 ($3.99, limited series)

1-4-Warren Ellis-s/Steve Kurth-a/Brandon Peterson-c. 1-Variant-c by Kurth 4.00

ULTIMATE AVENGERS (Follows Ultimatum x-over)
Marvel Comics: Oct, 2009 - Present ($3.99)

1-6-Mark Millar-s/Carlos Pacheco-a/c; Red Skull app. 4.00

Ultimate Captain America #1 © MAR

Ultimate Fantastic Four #41 © MAR

Ultimate Origins #5 © MAR

GD	VG	FN	VF	VF/NM	NM-
2.0	4.0	6.0	8.0	9.0	9.2

1-Variant Red Skull-c by Leinil Yu 8.00
7-12-(Ultimate Avengers 2 #1-6 on cover) Yu-a; Punisher joins. 10-Origin Ghost Rider 4.00
7-Variant Ghost Rider-c by Silvestri 8.00
13-18-(Ultimate Avengers 3 #1-6 on cover) Dillon-a; Blade and a new Daredevil app. 4.00

ULTIMATE AVENGERS VS. NEW ULTIMATES (Death of Spider-Man tie-in)
Marvel Comics: Apr, 2011 - No. 6 ($3.99, limited series)

1-3: 1-Millar-s/Yu-a/c; variant covers by Cho & Hitch. 3-Punisher app. 4.00

ULTIMATE CAPTAIN AMERICA
Marvel Comics: Mar, 2011 - No. 4, Jun, 2011 ($3.99)

1-4: 1-Aaron-s/Garney-a; 2 covers by Garney & McGuinness 4.00
Annual 1 (12/08, $3.99, one-shot) Origin of the Black Panther; Djurdjevic-a 4.00

ULTIMATE CIVIL WAR: SPIDER-HAM (See Civil War and related titles)
Marvel Comics: March, 2007 ($2.99, one-shot)

1-Spoof of Civil War series featuring Spider-Ham; art by various incl. Olivetti, Severin 3.00

ULTIMATE DAREDEVIL AND ELEKTRA
Marvel Comics: Jan, 2003 - No. 4, Mar, 2003 ($2.25, limited series)

1-4-Rucka-s/Larroca-c/a; 1st meeting of Elektra and Matt Murdock 3.00
... Vol.1 TPB (2003, $11.99) r/#1-4, Daredevil Vol. 2 #9; Larroca sketch pages 12.00

ULTIMATE DOOM (Follows Ultimate Mystery mini-series)
Marvel Comics: Feb, 2011 - No. 4, May, 2011 ($3.99, limited series)

1-4-Bendis-s/Sandoval-a; Fantastic Four, Spider-Man, Jessica Drew & Nick Fury app. 4.00

ULTIMATE ELEKTRA
Marvel Comics: Oct, 2004 - No. 5, Feb, 2005 ($2.25, limited series)

1-5-Carey-s/Larroca-c/a. 2-Bullseye app. 3.00
... : Devil's Due TPB (2005, $11.99) r/#1-5 12.00

ULTIMATE ENEMY (Follows Ultimatum x-over)(Leads into Ultimate Mystery)
Marvel Comics: Mar, 2010 - No. 4, July, 2010 ($3.99, limited series)

1-4-Bendis-s/Sandoval-a 1-Covers by McGuinness and Pearson 4.00

ULTIMATE EXTINCTION (See Ultimate Nightmare and Ultimate Secret limited series)
Marvel Comics: Mar, 2006 - No. 5, July, 2006 ($2.99, limited series)

1-5-The coming of Gah Lak Tus; Ellis-s/Peterson-a 3.00
TPB (2006, $12.99) r/#1-5 13.00

ULTIMATE FANTASTIC FOUR (Continues in Ultimatum mini-series)
Marvel Comics: Feb, 2004 - No. 60, Apr, 2009 ($2.25/$2.50/$2.99)

1-Bendis & Millar-s/Adam Kubert-a/Hitch-c 5.00
2-20: 2-Adam Kubert-a/c; intro. Moleman 7-Ellis-s/Immonen-a begin; Dr. Doom app. 13-18-Kubert-a. 19,20-Jae Lee-a. 20-Begin $2.50-c 3.50
21-Marvel Zombies; begin Greg Land-c/a; Mark Millar-s; variant-c by Land 5.00
22-29,33-59: 24-26-Namor app. 28-President Thor. 33-38-Ferry-a. 42-46-Silver Surfer 3.00
30-32-Marvel Zombies; Millar-s/Land-a; Dr. Doom app. 5.00
30-32-Zombie variant-c by Suydam 6.00
50-White variant-c by Kirkham 5.00
60-($3.99) Ultimatum crossover; Kirkham-a 4.00
Annual 1 (10/05, $3.99) The Inhumans app.; Jae Lee-a/Mark Millar-s/Greg Land-c 4.00
Annual 2 (10/06, $3.99) Mole Man app.; Immonen & Irving-a/Carey-s 4.00
.../Ult. X-Men Annual 1 (11/08, $3.99) Continued from Ult. X-Men/Ult. F.F. Annual #1 4.00
.../X-Men 1 (3/06, $2.99) Carey-s/Ferry-a; continued from Ult. X-Men/Fantastic Four #1 3.00
... Vol. 1: The Fantastic (2004, $12.99, TPB) r/#1-6; cover gallery 13.00
... Vol. 2: Doom (2004, $12.99, TPB) r/#7-12 13.00
... Vol. 3: N-Zone (2005, $12.99, TPB) r/#13-18 13.00
... Vol. 4: Inhuman (2005, $12.99, TPB) r/#19,20 & Annual #1 13.00
... Vol. 5: Crossover (2006, $12.99, TPB) r/#21-26 13.00
... Vol. 6: Frightful (2006, $14.99, TPB) r/#27-32; gallery of cover sketches & variants 15.00
... Vol. 7: God War (2007, $16.99, TPB) r/#33-38 17.00
... Vol. 8: Devils (2007, $12.99, TPB) r/#39-41 & Annual #2 13.00
... Vol. 9: Silver Surfer (2007, $13.99, TPB) r/#42-46 14.00
Volume 1 HC (2005, $29.99, 7x11", dust jacket) r/#1-12; introduction, proposals and scripts by Millar and Bendis; character design pages by Hitch 30.00
Volume 2 HC (2006, $29.99, 7x11", dust jacket) r/#13-20; Jae Lee sketch page 30.00
Volume 3 HC (2007, $29.99, 7x11", dust jacket) r/#21-32; Greg Land sketch pages 30.00
Volume 4 HC (2007, $29.99, 7x11", dust jacket) r/#33-41, Annual #2, Ultimate FF/X-Men and Ultimate X-Men/FF; character design pages 30.00
Volume 5 HC (2008, $34.99, 7x11", dust jacket) r/#42-53 35.00

ULTIMATE GALACTUS TRILOGY
Marvel Comics: 2007 ($34.99, hardcover, dustjacket)

HC-Oversized reprint of Ultimate Nightmare #1-5, Ultimate Secret #1-4, Ultimate Vision #0, and Ultimate Extinction #1-5; sketch pages and cover galery 35.00

GD	VG	FN	VF	VF/NM	NM-
2.0	4.0	6.0	8.0	9.0	9.2

ULTIMATE HULK
Marvel Comics: Dec, 2008 ($3.99, one-shot)

Annual 1 (12/08, $3.99) Zarda battles Hulk; McGuinness & Djurdjevic-a/Loeb-s 4.00

ULTIMATE HUMAN
Marvel Comics: Mar, 2008 - No. 4, Jun, 2008 ($2.99, limited series)

1-4-Iron Man vs. The Hulk; The Leader app.; Ellis-s/Nord-a 3.00
HC (2008, $19.99) r/#1-4 20.00

ULTIMATE IRON MAN
Marvel Comics: May, 2005 - No. 5, Feb, 2006 ($2.99, limited series)

1-Origin of Iron Man; Orson Scott Card-s/Andy Kubert-a; two covers 4.00
1-2nd & 3rd printings; each with B&W variant-c 3.00
2-5-Kubert-c 3.00
Volume 1 HC (2006, $19.99, dust jacket) r/#1-5; rough cut of script for #1, cover sketches 20.00
Volume 1 SC (2006, $14.99) r/#1-5; rough cut of script for #1, cover sketches 15.00

ULTIMATE IRON MAN II
Marvel Comics: Feb, 2008 - No. 5, July, 2008 ($2.99, limited series)

1-5-Early days of the Iron Man prototype; Orson Scott Card-s/Pasqual Ferry-a/c 3.00

ULTIMATE MARVEL FLIP MAGAZINE
Marvel Comics: July, 2005 - No. 26, Aug, 2007 ($3.99/$4.99)

1-11-Reprints Ultimate Fantastic Four and Ultimate X-Men in flip format 4.00
12-26-($4.99) 5.00

ULTIMATE MARVEL MAGAZINE
Marvel Comics: Feb, 2001 - No. 11, 2002 ($3.99, magazine size)

1-11: Reprints of recent stories from the Ultimate titles plus Marvel news and features. 1-Reprints Ultimate Spider-Man #1&2. 11-Lord of the Rings-c 4.00

ULTIMATE MARVEL SAMPLER
Marvel Comics: 2007 (no cover price, limited series)

1-Previews of 2008 Ultimate Marvel story arcs; Finch-c 3.00

ULTIMATE MARVEL TEAM-UP (Spider-Man Team-up)
Marvel Comics: Apr, 2001 - No. 16, July, 2002 ($2.99/$2.25)

1-Spider-Man & Wolverine; Bendis-s in all; Matt Wagner-a/c 5.00
2,3-Hulk; Hester-a 3.50
4,5,9-16: 4,5-Iron Man; Allred-a. 9-Fantastic Four; Mahfood-a. 10-Man-Thing; Totleben-a. 11-X-Men; Clugston-Major-a. 12,13-Dr. Strange; McKeever-a.14-Black Widow; Terry Moore-a. 15,16-Shang-Chi; Mays-a 3.00
6-8-Punisher; Sienkiewicz-a. 7,8-Daredevil app. 4.00
TPB (11/01, $14.95) r/#1-5 15.00
... Ultimate Collection TPB ('06, $29.99) r/#1-16 & Ult. Spider-Man Spec.; sketch pages 30.00
HC (8/02, $39.99) r/#1-16 & Ult. Spider-Man Special; Bendis afterword 40.00
...: Vol. 2 TPB (2003, $11.99) r/#9-13; Mahfood-c 12.00
...: Vol. 3 TPB (2003, $12.99) r/#14-16 & Ultimate Spider-Man Super Special; Moore-c 13.00

ULTIMATE MYSTERY (Follows Ultimate Enemy)(Leads into Ultimate Doom)
Marvel Comics: Sept, 2010 - No. 4, Dec, 2010 ($3.99, limited series)

1-4-Bendis-s/Sandoval-a; Rick Jones returns; Captain Marvel app. 1-3-Campbell-c 4.00

ULTIMATE NEW ULTIMATES (Follows Ultimatum x-over)
Marvel Comics: May, 2010 - No. 5, Mar, 2011 ($3.99)

1-5: 1-Jeph Loeb-s/Frank Cho-a; 6-page wraparound-c by Cho; Defenders app. 4.00
1-Villains variant-c by Yu 8.00

ULTIMATE NIGHTMARE (Leads into Ultimate Secret limited series)
Marvel Comics: Oct, 2004 - No. 5, Feb, 2005 ($2.25, limited series)

1-5: Ellis-s; Ultimates, X-Men, Nick Fury app. 1,2,4,5-Hairsine-a/c. 3-Epting-a 3.00
Ultimate Galactus Book 1: Nightmare TPB (2005, $12.99) r/Ultimate Nightmare #1-5 13.00

ULTIMATE ORIGINS
Marvel Comics: Aug, 2008 - No. 5, Dec, 2008 ($2.99, limited series)

1-5-Bendis-s/Guice-a. 1-Nick Fury origin in the 1940s. 2-Capt. America origin 3.00

ULTIMATE POWER
Marvel Comics: Dec, 2006 - No. 9, Feb, 2008 ($2.99, limited series)

1-9: 1-Ultimate FF meets the Squadron Supreme; Bendis-s; Land-a/c. 2-Spider-Man, X-Men and the Ultimates app. 6-Doom app. 3.00
1-Variant sketch-c 5.00
1-Director's Cut (2007, $3.99) r/#1 and B&W pencil and ink pages; covers to #2,3 4.00
HC (2008, $34.99) oversized r/series; profile pages; B&W sketch art 35.00

ULTIMATES, THE (Avengers of the Ultimate line)
Marvel Comics: Mar, 2002 - No. 13, Apr, 2004 ($2.25)

1-Intro. Capt. America; Millar-s/Hitch-a & wraparound-c 6.00

The Ultimates #12 © MAR

Ultimate Spider-Man #156 © MAR

Ultimate Thor #1 © MAR

GD 2.0 | VG 4.0 | FN 6.0 | VF 8.0 | VF/NM 9.0 | NM- 9.2

2-Intro. Giant-Man and the Wasp 4.00
3-12: 3-1st Capt. America in new costume. 4-Intro. Thor. 5-Ultimates vs. The Hulk. 8-Intro. Hawkeye 3.00
13-($3.50) 4.00
... MGC #1 (5/11, $1.00) r/#1 with "Marvel's Greatest Comics" logo on cover 1.00
... Saga (2007, $3.99) Re-caps 1st 2 Ultimates series; new framing art by Charest; prelude to Ultimates 3 series; Brooks-c 4.00
... Volume 1 HC (2004, $29.99) oversized r/series; commentary pages with Millar & Hitch; cover gallery and character design pages; intro. by Joss Whedon 30.00
... Volume 1: Super-Human TPB (8/02, $12.99) r/#1-6 13.00
... Volume 2: Homeland Security TPB (2004, $17.99) r/#7-13 18.00

ULTIMATES 2
Marvel Comics: Feb, 2005 - No. 13, Feb, 2007 ($2.99/$3.99)

1-Millar-s/Hitch-a; Giant-Man becomes Ant-Man 4.00
2-11: 6-Intro. The Defenders. 7-Hawkeye shot. 8-Intro The Liberators 3.00
12,13-($3.99) Wraparound-c; X-Men, Fantastic Four, Spider-Man app. 4.00
13-Variant white cover featuring The Wasp 40.00
Annual 1 (10/05, $3.99) Millar-s/Dillon-a/Hitch-c; Defenders app. 4.00
Annual 2 (10/06, $3.99) Deodato-a; flashback to WWII with Sook-a; Falcon app. 4.00
HC (2007, $34.99) oversized r/series; commentary pages with Millar & Hitch; cover gallery, sketch and script pages; intro. by Jonathan Ross 35.00
... Volume 1: Gods & Monsters TPB (2005, $15.99) r/#1-6 16.00
... Volume 2: Grand Theft America TPB (2007, $19.99) r/#7-13; cover gallery w/sketches 20.00

ULTIMATES 3
Marvel Comics: Feb, 2008 - No. 5, Nov, 2008 ($2.99)

1-Loeb-s/Madureira-a; two gatefold wraparound covers by Madureira; Scarlet Witch shot 4.00
1,2-Second printings: 1-Wraparound cover by Madureira. 2-Madureira-c 3.00
2-5: 2-Spider-Man app. 3-Wolverine app. 5-Two gatefold wraparound-c (Heroes & Ultron) 3.00
2-Variant Thor cover by Turner 8.00
3-Variant Scarlet Witch cover by Cho 8.00
4-Variant Valkyrie cover by Finch 4.00

ULTIMATE SECRET (See Ultimate Nightmare limited series)
Marvel Comics: May, 2005 - No. 4, Dec, 2005 ($2.99, limited series)

1-4-Ellis-s; Captain Marvel app. 1,2-McNiven-a. 2,3-Ultimates & FF app. 3.00
Ultimate Galactus Book 2: Secret TPB (2006, $12.99) r/#1-4 13.00

ULTIMATE SECRETS
Marvel Comics: 2008 ($3.99, one-shot)

1-Handbook-styled profiles of secondary teams and characters from Ultimate universe 4.00

ULTIMATE SIX (Reprinted in Ultimate Spider-Man Vol. 5 hardcover)
Marvel Comics: Nov, 2003 - No. 7, June, 2004 ($2.25) (See Ultimate Spider-Man for TPB)

1-The Ultimates & Spider-Man team-up; Bendis-s/Quesada & Hairsine-a; Cassaday-c 5.00
2-7-Hairsine-a; Cassaday-c 3.00

ULTIMATE SPIDER-MAN
Marvel Comics: Oct, 2000 - No. 133, June, 2009 ($2.99/$2.25/$2.99/$3.99)

	GD	VG	FN	VF	VF/NM	NM-
1-Bendis-s/Bagley & Thibert-a; cardstock-c; introduces revised origin and cast separate from regular Spider-continuity	6	12	18	41	66	90
1-Variant white-c (Retailer incentive)	9	18	27	60	100	140
1-DF Edition	4	8	12	28	44	60
1-Kay Bee Toys variant edition	2	4	6	9	12	15
2-Cover with Spider-Man on car	3	6	9	18	27	35
2-Cover with Spider-Man swinging past building	3	6	9	18	27	35
3,4: 4-Uncle Ben killed	3	6	9	16	23	30
5-7: 6,7-Green Goblin app.	3	6	9	18	27	35
8-13: 13-Reveals secret to MJ	1	3	4	6	8	10

14-21: 14-Intro. Gwen Stacy & Dr. Octopus 5.00
22-($3.50) Green Goblin returns 6.00
23-32 4.00
33-1st Ultimate Venom-c; intro. Eddie Brock 5.00
34-38-Ultimate Venom 4.00
39-49,51-59: 39-Nick Fury app. 43,44-X-Men app. 46-Prelude to Ultimate Six; Sandman app. 51-53-Elektra app. 54-59-Doctor Octopus app. 3.00
50-($2.99) Intro. Black Cat 4.00
60-Intro. Ultimate Carnage on cover 4.00
61-Intro Ben Reilly; Punisher app. 3.00
62-Gwen Stacy killed by Carnage 4.00
63-92: 63,64-Carnage app. 66,67-Wolverine app. 68,69-Johnny Storm app. 78-Begin $2.50-c. 79-Debut Moon Knight. 81-85-Black Cat app. 90-Vulture app. 91-94-Deadpool 3.00
93-99: 93-Begin $2.99-c. 95-Morbius & Blade app. 97-99-Clone Saga 3.00
100-($3.99) Wraparound-c; Clone Saga; re-cap of previous issues 4.00
101-103-Clone Saga continues; Fantastic Four app. 102-Spider-Woman origin 3.00
104-($3.99) Clone Saga concludes; Fantastic Four and Dr. Octopus app. 4.00
105-132: 106-110-Daredevil app. 111-Last Bagley art; Immonen-a (6 pgs.) 112-Immonen-a; Norman Osborn app. 118-Liz Allen ignites. 123,128-Venom app. 129-132-Ultimatum 3.00
133-($3.99) Ultimatum crossover; Spider-Woman app. 4.00
(Issues #150-up, see second series)
Annual 1 (10/05, $3.99) Kitty Pryde app.; Bendis-s/Brooks-a/Bagley-c 4.00
Annual 2 (10/06, $3.99) Punisher, Moon Knight and Daredevil app.; Bendis-s/Brooks-a 4.00
Annual 3 (12/08, $3.99) Mysterio app.; Bendis-s/Lafuente-a 4.00
Collected Edition (1/01, $3.99) r/#1-3 4.00
Free Comic Book Day giveaway (5/02) - r/#1 with "Free Comic Book Day" banner on-c 2.50
...Special (7/02, $3.50) art by Bagley and various incl. Romita,Sr., Brereton, Cho, Mack, Sienkiewicz, Phillips, Pearson, Oeming, Mahfood, Russell 4.00
Ultimate Spider-Man 100 Project (2007, $10.00, SC, charity book for the HERO Initiative) collection of 100 variant covers by Romita Sr. & Jr., Cho, Bagley, Quesada and more 10.00
...: Venom HC (2007, $19.99) r/#33-39 20.00
...(Vol. 1): Power and Responsibility TPB (4/01, $14.95) r/#1-7 15.00
...(Vol. 2): Learning Curve TPB (12/01, $14.95) r/#8-13 15.00
...(Vol. 3): Double Trouble TPB (6/02, $17.95) r/#14-21 18.00
Vol. 4: Legacy TPB (2002, $14.99) r/#22-27 15.00
Vol. 5: Public Scrutiny TPB (2003, $11.99) r/#28-32 12.00
Vol. 6: Venom TPB (2003, $15.99) r/#33-39 16.00
Vol. 7: Irresponsible TPB (2003, $12.99) r/#40-45 13.00
Vol. 8: Cats & Kings TPB (2004, $17.99) r/#47-53 18.00
Vol. 9: Ultimate Six TPB (2004, $17.99) r/#46 & Ultimate Six #1-7 18.00
Vol. 10: Hollywood TPB (2004, $12.99) r/#54-59 13.00
Vol. 11: Carnage TPB (2004, $12.99) r/#60-65 13.00
Vol. 12: Superstars TPB (2005, $12.99) r/#66-71 13.00
Vol. 13: Hobgoblin TPB (2005, $15.99) r/#72-78 16.00
Vol. 14: Warriors TPB (2005, $17.99) r/#79-85 18.00
Vol. 15: Silver Sable TPB (2006, $15.99) r/#86-90 & Annual #1 16.00
Vol. 16: Deadpool TPB (2006, $19.99) r/#91-96 & Annual #2 20.00
Vol. 17: Clone Saga TPB (2007, $24.99) r/#97-105 25.00
Vol. 18: Ultimate Knights TPB (2007, $13.99) r/#106-111 14.00
Vol. 19: Death of a Goblin TPB (2008, $14.99) r/#112-117 15.00
Hardcover (3/02, $34.95, 7x11", dust jacket) r/#1-13 & Amazing Fantasy #15; sketch pages and Bill Jemas' initial plot and character outlines 35.00
Volume 2 HC (2003, $29.99, 7x11", dust jacket) r/#14-27; pin-ups & sketch pages 30.00
Volume 3 HC (2003, $29.99, 7x11", dust jacket) r/#28-39 & #1/2; script pages 30.00
Volume 4 HC (2004, $29.99, 7x11", dust jacket) r/#40-45, 47-53; sketch pages 30.00
Volume 5 HC (2004, $29.99, 7x11", dust jacket) r/#46,54-59, Ultimate Six #1-7 30.00
Volume 6 HC (2005, $29.99, 7x11", dust jacket) r/#60-71; sketch page 30.00
Volume 7 HC (2006, $29.99, 7x11", dust jacket) r/#72-85; sketch & profile pages 30.00
Volume 8 HC (2007, $29.99, 7x11", dust jacket) r/#86-96 & Annual #1&2; sketch page 30.00
Volume 9 HC (2008, $39.99, 7x11", dust jacket) r/#97-111; sketch pages 40.00
Volume 10 HC (2009, $39.99, 7x11", dust jacket) r/#112-122; sketch pages 40.00

	GD	VG	FN	VF	VF/NM	NM-
Wizard #1/2	1	3	4	6	8	10

ULTIMATE SPIDER-MAN (2nd series)(Follows Ultimatum x-over)
Marvel Comics: Oct, 2009 - No. 15, Dec, 2010; No. 150, Jan, 2011 - Present ($3.99)

1-15: 1-Bendis-s/Lafuente-a/c; new Mysterio. 1-Variant-c by Djurdjevic. 7,8-Miyazawa-a. 9-Spider-Woman app. 4.00
150-(1/11, $5.99) Resumes original numbering; wraparound-c by Lafuente; Bendis-s with art by Lafuente, Pichelli, Joëlle Jones, McKelvie & Young; r/Ult. S-M Special #1 6.00
150-Variant wraparound-c by Bagley 10.00
151-157: 151-154-Black Cat & Mysterio app. 157-Spider-Man shot by Punisher 4.00

ULTIMATE TALES FLIP MAGAZINE
Marvel Comics: July, 2005 - No. 26, Aug, 2007 ($3.99/$4.99)

1-11-Each reprints 2 issues of Ultimate Spider-Man in flip format 4.00
12-26-($4.99) 5.00

ULTIMATE THOR
Marvel Comics: Dec, 2010 - No. 4, Apr, 2011 ($3.99, limited series)

1-4: 1-Hickman-s/Pacheco-a; two covers by Pacheco & Choi; origin story 4.00

ULTIMATE VISION
Marvel Comics: No. 0, Jan, 2007 - No. 5, Jan, 2008 ($2.99, limited series)

0-Reprints back-up serial from Ultimate Extinction and related series; pin-ups 3.00
1-5: 1-(2/07) Carey-s/Peterson-a/c 3.00
TPB (2007, $14.99) r/#0-5; design pages and cover gallery 15.00

ULTIMATE WAR
Marvel Comics: Feb, 2003 - No. 4, Apr, 2003 ($2.25, limited series)

1-4-Millar-s/Bachalo-c/a; The Ultimates vs. Ultimate X-Men 3.00
Ultimate X-Men Vol. 5: Ultimate War TPB (2003, $10.99) r/#1-4 11.00

ULTIMATE WOLVERINE VS. HULK

Ultimate X #1 © MAR

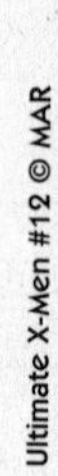

Ultimate X-Men #12 © MAR

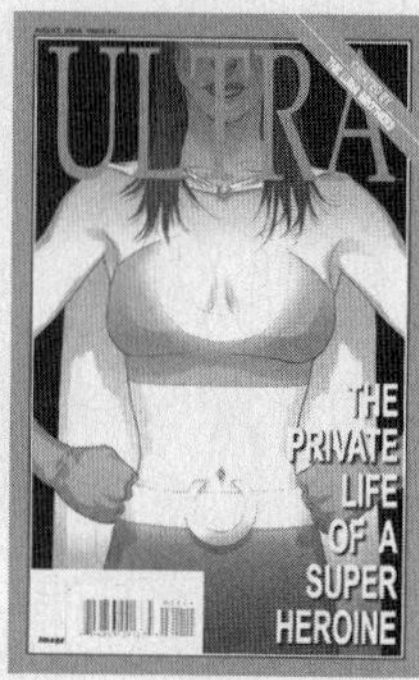

Ultra #1 © Luna Bros. Prods.

GD VG FN VF VF/NM NM-
2.0 4.0 6.0 8.0 9.0 9.2

GD VG FN VF VF/NM NM-
2.0 4.0 6.0 8.0 9.0 9.2

Marvel Comics: Feb, 2006 - No. 6, July, 2009 ($2.99, limited series)

1,2-Leinil Yu-a/c; Damon Lindelof-s. 2-(4/06) 3.00
1,2-(2009) New printings 3.00
3-6: 3-(5/09) Intro. She-Hulk. 4-Origin She-Hulk 3.00

ULTIMATE X (Follows Ultimatum x-over)
Marvel Comics: Apr, 2010 - Present ($3.99)

1-4: 1-Jeph Loeb-s/Art Adams-a; two covers by Adams 4.00

ULTIMATE X-MEN
Marvel Comics: Feb, 2001 - No. 100, Apr, 2009 ($2.99/$2.25/$2.50)

1-Millar-s/Adam Kubert & Thibert-a; cardstock-c; introduces revised origin and cast separate from regular X-Men continuity 3 6 9 14 20 25
1-DF Edition 3 6 9 16 23 30
1-DF Sketch Cover Edition 4 8 12 22 34 45
1-Free Comic Book Day Edition (7/03) r/#1 with "Free Comic Book Day" banner on-c 2.50
2 2 4 6 11 16 20
3-6 2 4 6 8 11 14
7-10 6.00
11-24,26-33: 13-Intro. Gambit. 18,19-Bachalo-a. 23,24-Andrews-a 4.00
25-($3.50) leads into the Ultimate War mini-series; Kubert-a 5.00
34-Spider-Man-c/app.; Bendis-s begin; Finch-a 5.00
35-74: 35-Spider-Man app. 36,37-Daredevil-c/app. 40-Intro. Angel. 42-Intro. Dazzler. 44-Beast dies. 46-Intro. Mr. Sinister. 50-53-Kubert-a; Gambit app. 54-57,59-63-Immonen-a. 60-Begin $2.50-c. 61-Variant Coipel-c. 66-Kirkman-s begin. 69-Begin $2.99-c 3.00
61-Retailer Edition with variant Coipel B&W sketch-c 10.00
75-($3.99) Turner-c; intro. Cable; back-up story with Emma Frost's students 4.00
76-99: 76-Intro. Bishop. 91-Fantastic Four app. 92-96-Phoenix app. 96-Spider-Man app. 99-Ultimatum x-over 3.00
100-($3.99) Ultimatum x-over; Brooks-a 4.00
Annual 1 (10/05, $3.99) Vaughan-s/Raney-a; Gambit & Rogue in Vegas 4.00
Annual 2 (10/06, $3.99) Kirkman-s/Larroca-a; Nightcrawler & Dazzler 4.00
.../Fantastic Four 1 (2/06, $2.99) Carey-s/Ferry-a; concluded in Ult. Fantastic Four/X-Men 3.00
.../Ult. Fantastic Four Ann. 1 (11/08, $3.99) Continues in Ult. F.F./Ult. X-Men Annual #1 4.00
.../Fantastic Four TPB (2006, $12.99) reprints Ult X-Men/Ult. FF x-over and Official Handbook of the Ultimate Marvel Universe #1-2 13.00
... Ultimate Collection Vol. 1 (2006, $24.99) r/#1-12 & #1/2; unused Bendis script for #1 25.00
... Ultimate Collection Vol. 2 (2007, $24.99) r/#13-25; Kubert cover sketch pages 25.00
...: (Vol. 1) The Tomorrow People TPB (7/01, $14.95) r/#1-6 15.00
...: (Vol. 2) Return to Weapon X TPB (4/02, $14.95) r/#7-12 15.00
Vol. 3: World Tour TPB (2002, $17.99) r/#13-20 18.00
Vol. 4: Hellfire and Brimstone TPB (2003, $12.99) r/#21-25 13.00
Vol. 5 (See Ultimate War)
Vol. 6: Return of the King TPB (2003, $16.99) r/#26-33 17.00
Vol. 7: Blockbuster TPB (2004, $12.99) r/#34-39 13.00
Vol. 8: New Mutants TPB (2004, $12.99) r/#40-45 13.00
Vol. 9: The Tempest TPB (2004, $10.99) r/#46-49 11.00
Vol. 10: Cry Wolf TPB (2005, $8.99) r/#50-53 9.00
Vol. 11: The Most Dangerous Game TPB (2005, $9.99) r/#54-57 10.00
Vol. 12: Hard Lessons TPB (2005, $12.99) r/#58-60 & Annual #1 13.00
Vol. 13: Magnetic North TPB (2006, $12.99) r/#61-65 13.00
Vol. 14: Phoenix? TPB (2006, $14.99) r/#66-71 15.00
Vol. 15: Magical TPB (2007, $11.99) r/#72-74 & Annual #2 12.00
Vol. 16: Cable TPB (2007, $14.99) r/#75-80; sketch pages 15.00
Vol. 17: Sentinels TPB (2008, $17.99) r/#81-88 18.00
Volume 1 HC (8/02, $34.99, 7x11", dust jacket) r/#1-12 & Giant-Size X-Men #1; sketch pages and Millar and Bendis' initial plot and character outlines 35.00
Volume 2 HC (2003, $29.99, 7x11", dust jacket) r/#13-25; script for #20 30.00
Volume 3 HC (2003, $29.99, 7x11", dust jacket) r/#26-33 & Ultimate War #1-4 30.00
Volume 4 HC (2005, $29.99, 7x11", dust jacket) r/#34-45 30.00
Volume 5 HC (2006, $29.99, 7x11", dust jacket) r/#46-57; Vaughan intro.; sketch pages 30.00
Volume 6 HC (2006, $29.99, 7x11", dust jacket) r/#58-65, Annual #1 & Wizard #1/2 30.00
Volume 7 HC (2007, $29.99, 7x11", dust jacket) r/#66-74, Annual #2 30.00
Wizard #1/2 2 4 6 9 12 15

ULTIMATUM
Marvel Comics: Jan, 2009 - No. 5, July, 2009 ($3.99, limited series)

1-5-Loeb-s/Finch-a; cover by Finch & ; Ultimate heroes vs. Magneto 4.00
1-5-Variant covers by McGuinness 8.00
5-Double gatefold variant-c by Finch 4.00
March on Ultimatum Saga ('08, giveaway) text and art panel history of Ultimate universe 3.00
...: Fantastic Four Requiem 1 (9/09,$3.99) Pokaski-s/Atkins-a; Dr. Strange app. 4.00
...: Spider-Man Requiem 1,2 (8/09, 9/09,$3.99) Bendis-s/Bagley & Immonen-a 4.00
...: X-Men Requiem 1 (9/09,$3.99) Coleite-s/Oliver-a/Brooks-c 4.00
NOTE: *Numerous variant covers and 2nd & 3rd printings exist.*

ULTRA
Image Comics: Aug, 2004 - No. 8, Mar, 2005 ($2.95, limited series)

1-8: 1-Intro. Ultra/Pearl Penalosa; Luna Brothers-s/a 3.00
Vol. 1: Seven Days TPB (4/05, $17.95) r/#1-8; sketch pages 18.00

ULTRAFORCE (1st Series) (Also see Avengers/Ultraforce #1)
Malibu Comics (Ultraverse): Aug, 1994 - No. 10, Aug, 1995 ($1.95/$2.50)

0 (9/94, $2.50)-Perez-c/a. 4.00
1-($2.50, 44 pgs.)-Bound-in trading card; team consisting of Prime, Prototype, Hardcase, Pixx, Ghoul, Contrary & Topaz; Gerard Jones scripts begin, ends #6; Pérez-c/a begins 4.00
1-Ultra 5000 Limited Silver Foil Edition 5.00
1-Holographic-c, no price 1 2 3 4 5 7
2-5: Perez-c/a in all. 2 (10/94, $1.95)-Prime quits, Strangers cameo. 3-Origin of Topaz; Prime rejoins. 5-Pixx dies. 3.00
2 ($2.50)-Florescent logo; limited edition stamp on-c 4.00
6-10: 6-Begin $2.50-c, Perez-c/a. 7-Ghoul story, Steve Erwin-a. 8-Marvel's Black Knight enters the Ultraverse (last seen in Avengers #375); Perez-c/a. 9,10-Black Knight app.; Perez-c. 10-Leads into Ultraforce/Avengers Prelude 3.00
Malibu "Ashcan ": Ultraforce #0A (6/94) 3.00
.../Avengers Prelude 1 (8/95, $2.50)-Perez-c. 3.00
.../Avengers 1 (8/95, $3.95)-Warren Ellis script; Perez-c/a; foil-c 4.00

ULTRAFORCE (2nd Series)(Also see Black September)
Malibu Comics (Ultraverse): Infinity, Sept, 1995 - V2#15, Dec, 1996 ($1.50)

Infinity, V2#1-15: Infinity-Team consists of Marvel's Black Knight, Ghoul, Topaz, Prime & redesigned Prototype; Warren Ellis scripts begin, ends #3; variant-c exists. 1-1st app.Cromwell, Lament & Wreckage. 2-Contains free encore presentation of Ultraforce #1; flip book "Phoenix Resurrection" Pt. 7. 7-Darick Robertson, Jeff Johnson & others-a. 8,9-Intro. Future Ultraforce (Prime, Hellblade, Angel of Destruction, Painkiller & Whipslash); Gary Erskine-c/a. 9-Foxfire app. 10-Len Wein scripts & Deodato Studios-c/a begin. 10-Lament back-up story. 11-Ghoul back-up story by Pander Bros. 12-Ultraforce vs. Maxis (cont'd in Ultraverse Unlimited #2); Exiles & Iron Clad app. 13-Prime leaves; Hardcase returns 3.00
Infinity (2000 signed) 4.00
.../Spider-Man ($3.95)-Marv Wolfman script; Green Goblin app; 2 covers exist. 4.00

ULTRAGIRL
Marvel Comics: Nov, 1996 - No. 3 Mar, 1997($1.50, limited series)

1-3: 1-1st app. 3.00

ULTRA KLUTZ
Onward Comics: 1981; 6/86 - #27, 1/89, #28, 4/90 - #31, 1990? ($1.50/$1.75/$2.00, B&W)

1 (1981)-Re-released after 2nd #1 3.00
1-30: 1-(6/86). 27-Photo back-c 3.00
31-($2.95, 52 pgs.) 4.00

ULTRAMAN
Nemesis Comics: Mar, 1994 - No. 4, Sept, 1994 ($1.75/$1.95)

1-($2.25)-Collector's edition; foil-c; special 3/4 wraparound-c 4.00
1-($1.75)-Newsstand edition 3.00
2-4: 3-$1.95-c begins 3.00
#(-1) (3/93) 3.00

ULTRAMAN TIGA
Dark Horse Comics: Aug, 2003 - No. 10, June, 2004 ($3.99)

1-10-Khoo Fuk Lung-a/Tony Wong-s 4.00

ULTRAVERSE DOUBLE FEATURE
Malibu Comics (Ultraverse): Jan, 1995 ($3.95, one-shot, 68 pgs.)

1-Flip-c featuring Prime & Solitaire. 4.00

ULTRAVERSE ORIGINS
Malibu Comics (Ultraverse): Jan, 1994 (99¢, one-shot)

1-Gatefold-c; 2 pg. origins all characters 3.00
1-Newsstand edition; different-c, no gatefold 3.00

ULTRAVERSE PREMIERE
Malibu Comics (Ultraverse): 1994 (one-shot)

0-Ordered thru mail w/coupons 5.00

ULTRAVERSE UNLIMITED
Malibu Comics (Ultraverse): June, 1996; No. 2, Sept, 1996 ($2.50)

1,2: 1-Adam Warlock returns to the Marvel Universe; Rune-c/app. 2-Black Knight, Reaper & Sierra Blaze return to the Marvel Universe 3.00

ULTRAVERSE YEAR ONE
Malibu Comics (Ultraverse): 1994 ($4.95, one-shot)

nn-In-depth synopsis of the first year's titles & stories. 5.00

Umbrella Academy: Apocalypse Suite #5 © Gerald Way

Uncanny X-Force #1 © MAR

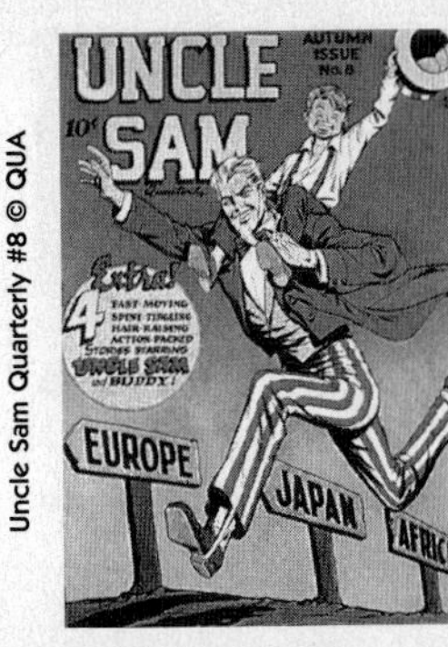

Uncle Sam Quarterly #8 © QUA

GD VG FN VF VF/NM NM-
2.0 4.0 6.0 8.0 9.0 9.2

ULTRAVERSE YEAR TWO
Malibu Comics (Ultraverse): Aug, 1995 ($4.95, one-shot)
nn-In-depth synopsis of second year's titles & stories 5.00

ULTRAVERSE YEAR ZERO: THE DEATH OF THE SQUAD
Malibu Comics (Ultraverse): Apr, 1995 - No. 4, July, 1995 ($2.95, lim. series)
1-4: 3-Codename: Firearm back-up story. 3.00

UMBRELLA ACADEMY (Zero Killer & Pantheon City on back-c)
Dark Horse Comics: Apr, 2007
1-Free Comic Book Day Edition - previews of the upcoming series; James Jean-c 10.00

UMBRELLA ACADEMY: APOCALYPSE SUITE
Dark Horse Comics: Sept, 2007 - No. 6, Feb, 2008 ($2.99, limited series)
1-Origin of the Umbrella Aademy; Gerald Way-s/Gabriel Bá-a/James Jean-c 5.00
1-White variant-c by Bá 15.00
1-Variant-c by Gerald Way 10.00
1-2nd printing with variant-c by Bá 3.00
2-6 3.00
...: One for One (9/10, $1.00) r/#1 with red cover frame 1.00
Vol.1: Apocalypse Suite TPB (7/08, $17.95) r/#1-6, FCBD story and web shorts; design art; Grant Morrison intro.; cover gallery 18.00

UMBRELLA ACADEMY: DALLAS
Dark Horse Comics: Nov, 2008 - No. 6, May, 2009 ($2.99, limited series)
1-6-Gerald Way-s/Gabriel Bá-a/c 3.00
1-Wraparound variant-c by Jim Lee 5.00

UNBIRTHDAY PARTY WITH ALICE IN WONDERLAND (See Alice In Wonderland, Four Color #341)

UNBOUND
Image Comics (Desperado): Jan, 1998 ($2.95, B&W)
1-Pruett-s/Peters-a 3.00

UNCANNY ORIGINS
Marvel Comics: Sept, 1996 - No. 14, Oct, 1997 (99¢)
1-14: 1-Cyclops. 2-Quicksilver. 3-Archangel. 4-Firelord. 5-Hulk. 6-Beast. 7-Venom. 8-Nightcrawler. 9-Storm. 10-Black Cat. 11-Black Knight. 12-Dr. Strange. 13-Daredevil. 14-Iron Fist 3.00

UNCANNY TALES
Atlas Comics (PrPI/PPI): June, 1952 - No. 56, Sept, 1957
1-Heath-a; horror/weird stories begin 94 188 282 597 1024 1450
2 50 100 150 315 533 750
3-5 43 86 129 271 461 650
6-Wolvertonish-a by Matt Fox 45 90 135 284 480 675
7-10: 8-Atom bomb story; Tothish-a (by Sekowsky?). 9-Crandall-a 39 78 117 236 388 540
11-20: 17-Atom bomb panels; anti-communist story; Hitler story. 19-Krenkel-a. 20-Robert Q. Sale-c 30 60 90 177 289 400
21-25,27: 25-Nostrand-a? 26 52 78 154 252 350
26-Spider-Man prototype c/story 37 74 111 222 361 500
28-Last precode issue (1/55); Kubert-a; #1-28 contain 2-3 sci/fi stories each 27 54 81 158 259 360
29-41,43-49,51 19 38 57 112 179 245
42,54,56-Krigstein-a 20 40 60 115 185 255
50,53,55-Torres-a 19 38 57 112 179 245
52-Oldest Iron Man prototype (2/57) 30 60 90 177 289 400
NOTE: ***Andru*** *a-15, 27.* ***Ayers*** *a-14, 22, 28, 37.* ***Bailey*** *a-51.* ***Briefer*** *a-19, 20.* ***Brodsky*** *c-1, 3, 4, 6, 8, 12-16, 19.* ***Brodsky/Everett*** *c-9.* ***Cameron*** *a-47.* ***Colan*** *a-11, 16, 17, 49, 52.* ***Drucker*** *a-37, 42, 45.* ***Everett*** *a-2, 9, 12, 32, 36, 39, 48; c-7, 11, 17, 39, 41, 50, 52, 53.* ***Fass*** *a-9, 10, 15, 24.* ***Forte*** *a-18, 27, 33-35, 52, 53.* ***Heath*** *a-13, 14; c-5, 10, 18.* ***Keller*** *a-3.* ***Lawrence*** *a-14, 17, 19, 23, 27, 28, 35.* ***Maneely*** *a-4, 8, 10, 16, 29, 35; c-2, 22, 26, 33, 38.* ***Moldoff*** *a-23.* ***Morisi*** *a-48, 52.* ***Morrow*** *a-46, 51.* ***Orlando*** *a-49, 50, 53.* ***Powell*** *a-12, 18, 34, 36, 38, 43, 50, 56.* ***Robinson*** *a-3, 13.* ***Reinman*** *a-12, 36.* ***Romita*** *a-10.* ***Roussos*** *a-8.* ***Sale*** *a-34, 47, 53; c-20.* ***Sekowsky*** *a-25.* ***Sinnott*** *a-14, 15, 38, 52.* ***Torres*** *a-53.* ***Tothish****-a by* ***Andru****-27.* ***Wildey*** *a-22, 48.*

UNCANNY TALES
Marvel Comics Group: Dec, 1973 - No. 12, Oct, 1975
1-Crandall-r/Uncanny Tales #9('50s) 3 6 9 20 30 40
2-12: 7,12-Kirby-a 3 6 9 14 19 24
NOTE: ***Ditko*** *reprints-#4, 6-8, 10-12.*

UNCANNY X-FORCE
Marvel Comics: Dec, 2010 - Present ($3.99)
1-7: 1-Wolverine, Psylocke, Archangel, Fantomex & Deadpool team; Opeña-a; Ribic-c 4.00
1-Variant-c by Clayton Crain 10.00
5.1 (5/11, $2.99) Albuquerque-a/Bianchi-c; Lady Deathstrike app. 3.00
...: The Apocalypse Solution 1 (5/11, $4.99) r/#1-3 5.00

UNCANNY X-MEN, THE (See **X-Men, The**, 1st series, #142-on)

UNCANNY X-MEN AND THE NEW TEEN TITANS (See Marvel and DC Present...)

UNCANNY X-MEN: FIRST CLASS
Marvel Comics: Sept, 2009 - No. 8, Apr, 2010 ($2.99)
1-8: 1-The X-Men #94 (1975) team; Cruz-a; Inhumans app. 3.00
... Giant-Size Special (8/09, $3.99) short stories by various; Scottie Young-c 4.00

UNCENSORED MOUSE, THE
Eternity Comics: Apr, 1989 - No. 2, Apr, 1989 ($1.95, B&W)(Came sealed in plastic bag) (Both contain racial stereotyping & violence)
1,2-Early Gottfredson strip-r in each 2 4 6 11 16 20
NOTE: *Both issues contain unauthorized reprints. Series was cancelled.* ***Win Smith*** *r-1, 2.*

UNCLE CHARLIE'S FABLES (Also see Adventures in Wonderland)
Lev Gleason Publ.: Jan, 1952 - No. 5, Sept, 1952 (All have Biro painted-c)
1-Peter Pester by Hy Mankin begins, ends #5. Michael the Misfit by Kida, Janice & the Lazy Giant by Maurer, Lawrence the Fortune Teller app.; has photo of Biro 15 30 45 88 137 185
2-Fuje-a; Biro photo 10 20 30 54 72 90
3-5: 5-Two Who Built a Dream, The Blacksmith & The Gypsies by Maurer, The Sleepy King by Hubbel; has photo of Biro 9 18 27 47 61 75
NOTE: ***Kida*** *a-1. Hubbell a- 5.* ***Hy Mankin*** *a-1-5.* ***Norman Maurer*** *a-1, 5.* ***Dick Rockwell*** *a-5.*

UNCLE DONALD & HIS NEPHEWS DUDE RANCH (See Dell Giant #52)

UNCLE DONALD & HIS NEPHEWS FAMILY FUN (See Dell Giant #38)

UNCLE JOE'S FUNNIES
Centaur Publications: 1938 (B&W)
1-Games, puzzles & magic tricks, some interior art; Bill Everett-c 65 130 195 416 708 1000

UNCLE MILTY (TV)
Victoria Publications/True Cross: Dec, 1950 - No. 4, July, 1951 (52 pgs.)(Early TV comic)
1-Milton Berle photo on-c of #1,2 54 108 162 343 574 825
2 35 70 105 208 339 470
3,4 29 58 87 172 281 390

UNCLE REMUS & HIS TALES OF BRER RABBIT (See Brer Rabbit, 4-Color #129, 208, 693)

UNCLE SAM
DC Comics (Vertigo): 1997 - No. 2, 1997 ($4.95, limited series)
1,2-Alex Ross painted c/a. Story by Ross and Steve Darnell 5.00
Hardcover (1998, $17.95) 18.00
Softcover (2000, $9.95) 10.00

UNCLE SAM AND THE FREEDOM FIGHTERS
DC Comics: Sept, 2006 - No. 8, Apr, 2007 ($2.99, limited series)
1-8-Acuña-a/c; Gray & Palmiotti-s. 3-Intro. Black Condor 3.00
TPB (2007, $14.99) r/#1-8 and story from DCU Brave New World #1 15.00

UNCLE SAM AND THE FREEDOM FIGHTERS
DC Comics: Nov, 2007 - No. 8, Jun, 2008 ($2.99, limited series)
1-8-Gray & Palmiotti-s/Arlem-a/Johnson-c 3.00
...: Brave New World TPB (2008, $14.99) r/#1-8 15.00

UNCLE SAM QUARTERLY (Blackhawk #9 on)(See Freedom Fighters)
Quality Comics Group: Autumn, 1941 - No. 8, Fall, 1943 (see National Comics)
1-Origin Uncle Sam; Fine/Eisner-c, chapter headings, 2 pgs. by Eisner; (2 versions: dark cover, no price; light cover with price sticker); Jack Cole-a 377 754 1131 2639 4620 6600
2-Cameos by The Ray, Black Condor, Quicksilver, The Red Bee, Alias the Spider, Hercules & Neon the Unknown; Eisner, Fine-c/a 132 264 396 838 1444 2050
3-Tuska-c/a; Eisner-a(2) 97 194 291 621 1061 1500
4 87 174 261 553 952 1350
5,7-Hitler, Mussolini & Tojo-c 116 232 348 742 1271 1800
6,8 67 134 201 426 731 1035
NOTE: ***Kotzky*** *(or* ***Tuska****) a-3-8.*

UNCLE SCROOGE (Disney) (Becomes Walt Disney's... #210 on) (See Cartoon Tales, Dell Giants #33, 55, Disney Comic Album, Donald and Scrooge, Dynabrite, Four Color #178, Gladstone Comic Album, Walt Disney's Comics & Stories #98, Walt Disney's ...)
Dell #1-39/Gold Key #40-173/Whitman #174-209: No. 386, 3/52 - No. 39, 8-10/62; No. 40, 12/62 - No. 209, 7/84
Four Color 386(#1)-in "Only a Poor Old Man" by Carl Barks; r-in Uncle Scrooge & Donald Duck #1('65) & The Best of Walt Disney Comics ('74). The 2nd cover app. of Uncle Scrooge (see Dell Giant Vacation Parade #2 (7/51) for 1st-c) 185 370 555 1619 3310 5000
1-(1986)-Reprints F.C. #386; given away with lithograph "Dam Disaster at Money Lake"

Uncle Scrooge #391 © DIS

Uncle Wiggily Four Color #349 © DELL

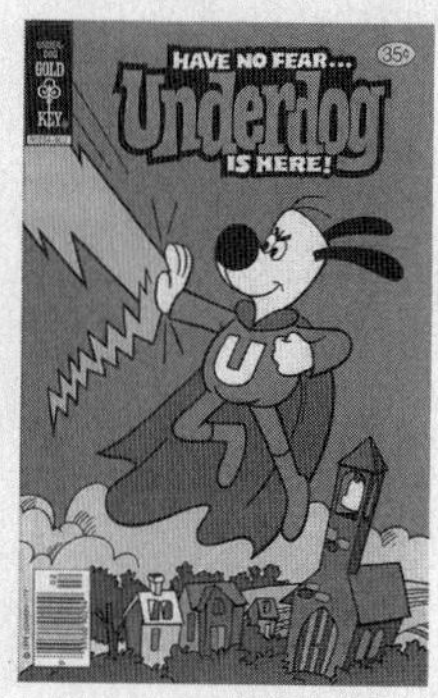

Underdog #23 © Leonardo TTV

	GD 2.0	VG 4.0	FN 6.0	VF 8.0	VF/NM 9.0	NM- 9.2
& as a subscription offer giveaway to Gladstone subscribers	3	6	9	15	20	24
Four Color 456(#2)-in "Back to the Klondike" by Carl Barks; r-in Best of U.S. & D.D. #1('66) & Gladstone C.A. #4	92	184	276	782	1591	2400
Four Color 495(#3)-r-in #105	62	124	186	527	1064	1600
4(12-2/53-54)-r-in Gladstone Comic Album #11	45	90	135	360	730	1100
5-r-in Gladstone Special #2 & Walt Disney Digest #1	38	76	114	304	602	900
6-r-in U.S. #106,165,233 & Best of U.S. & D.D. #1('66)	33	66	99	254	502	750
7-The Seven Cities of Cibola by Barks; r-in #217 & Best of D.D. & U.S. #2 ('67)	29	58	87	223	449	675
8-10: 8-r-in #111,222. 9-r-in #104,214. 10-r-in #67	26	52	78	190	383	575
11-20: 11-r-in #237. 17-r-in #215. 19-r-in Gladstone C.A. #1. 20-r-in #213	22	44	66	159	317	475
21-30: 24-X-Mas-c. 26-r-in #211	17	34	51	122	249	375
31-35,37-40: 34-r-in #228. 40-X-Mas-c	14	28	42	99	200	300
36-1st app. Magica De Spell; Number one dime 1st identified by name	16	32	48	111	226	340
41-60: 48-Magica De Spell-c/story (3/64). 49-Sci/fi-c. 51-Beagle Boys-c/story (8/64)	12	24	36	87	164	240
61-63,65,66,68-71:71-Last Barks issue w/original story (#71-he only storyboarded the script)	11	22	33	77	144	210
64-(7/66) Barks Vietnam War story "Treasure of Marco Polo" banned for reprints by Disney from 1977-1989 because of its Third World revolutionary war theme. It later appeared in the hardcover Carl Barks Library set (4/89) and Walt Disney's Uncle Scrooge Adventures #42 (1/97)	16	32	48	111	226	340
67,72,73: 67,72,73-Barks-r	10	20	30	70	125	180
74-84: 74-Barks-r(1pg.). 75-81,83-Not by Barks. 82,84-Barks-r begin	8	16	24	52	86	120
85-100	7	14	21	45	73	100
101-110	6	12	18	37	59	80
111-120	4	8	12	28	44	60
121-141,143-152,154-157	4	8	12	22	34	45
142-Reprints Four Color #456 with-c	4	8	12	23	36	48
153,158,162-164,166,168-170,178,180: No Barks	3	6	9	16	22	28
159-160,165,167	3	6	9	16	23	30
161(r/#14), 171(r/#11), 177(r/#16),183(r/#6)-Barks-r	3	6	9	16	23	30
172(1/80),173(2/80)-Gold Key. Barks-a	3	6	9	18	27	35
174(3/80),175(4/80),176(5/80)-Whitman. Barks-a	4	8	12	23	36	48
177(6/80),178(7/80)	4	8	12	24	37	50
179(9/80)(r/#9)-(Very low distribution)	36	72	108	281	553	825
180(11/80),181(12/80, r/4-Color #495), pre-pack?	8	16	24	52	86	120
182-195: 182-(50¢-c). 184,185,187,188-Barks-a. 182,186,191-194-No Barks. 189(r/#5), 190(r/#4), 195(r/4-Color #386)	3	6	9	16	23	30
182(1/81, 40¢-c) Cover price error variant	4	8	12	23	36	48
196(4/82),197(5/82): 196(r/#13)	3	6	9	18	27	35
198-209 (All #90038 on-c; pre-pack; no date or date code): 198(4/83), 199(5/83), 200(6/83), 201(6/83), 202(7/83), 203(7/83), 204(8/83), 205(8/83), 206(4/84), 207(5/83), 208(6/84), 209(7/84). 198-202,204-206: No Barks. 203(r/#12), 207(r/#93,92), 208(r/U.S. #18), 209(r/U.S. #21)-Barks-r	3	6	9	20	30	40
Uncle Scrooge & Money(G.K.)-Barks-r/from WDC&S #130 (3/67)	5	10	15	34	55	75
Mini Comic #1(1976)(3-1/4x6-1/2")-r/U.S. #115; Barks-c	2	4	6	8	10	12

NOTE: *Barks c-Four Color 386, 456, 495, #4-37, 39, 40, 43-71.*

UNCLE SCROOGE (See Walt Disney's Uncle Scrooge for previous issues)
Boom Entertainment (BOOM! Kids): No. 384, Oct, 2009 - Present ($2.99/$3.99)

384-399: 384-Magica de Spell app.; 2 covers. 392-399-Duck Tales						3.00
400-(2/11, $3.99) "Carl Barks" apps. as Scrooge story-teller; Rosa wraparound-c						4.00
400-$6.99) Deluxe Edition with Barks painted cover of Four Color #386 cover image						7.00
401,402: 401-($3.99)-Rosa-s/a						4.00

UNCLE SCROOGE & DONALD DUCK
Gold Key: June, 1965 (25¢, paper cover)

1-Reprint of Four Color #386(#1) & lead story from Four Color #29	8	16	24	54	90	125

UNCLE SCROOGE COMICS DIGEST
Gladstone Publishing: Dec, 1986 - No. 5, Aug, 1987 ($1.25, Digest-size)

1,3	1	2	3	5	6	8
2,4						6.00
5 (low print run)	1	2	3	5	7	9

UNCLE SCROOGE GOES TO DISNEYLAND (See Dell Giants)
Gladstone Publishing Ltd.: Aug, 1985 ($2.50)

1-Reprints Dell Giant w/new-c by Mel Crawford, based on old cover	2	4	6	8	10	12
...Comics Digest 1 ($1.50, digest size)	2	4	6	8	11	14

UNCLE SCROOGE IN COLOR
Gladstone Publishing: 1987 ($29.95, Hardcover, 9-1/4"X12-1/4", 96 pgs.)

nn-Reprints "Christmas on Bear Mountain" from Four Color 178 by Barks; Uncle Scrooge's Christmas Carol (published as Donald Duck & the Christmas Carol, A Little Golden Book), reproduced from the original art as adapted by Norman McGary from pencils by Barks; and Uncle Scrooge the Lemonade King, reproduced from the original art, plus Barks' original pencils	4	8	12	24	37	50
nn-Slipcase edition of 750, signed by Barks, issued at $79.95						300.00

UNCLE SCROOGE THE LEMONADE KING
Whitman Publishing Co.: 1960 (A Top Top Tales Book, 6-3/8"x7-5/8", 32 pgs.)

2465-Storybook pencilled by Carl Barks, finished art adapted by Norman McGary	34	68	102	262	524	785

UNCLE WIGGILY (See March of Comics #19) (Also see Animal Comics)
Dell Publishing Co.: No. 179, Dec, 1947 - No. 543, Mar, 1954

Four Color 179 (#1)-Walt Kelly-c	14	28	42	97	194	290
Four Color 221 (3/49)-Part Kelly-c	9	18	27	63	107	150
Four Color 276 (5/50), 320 (#1, 3/51)	8	16	24	52	86	120
Four Color 349 (9-10/51), 391 (4-5/52)	6	12	18	43	69	95
Four Color 428 (10/52), 503 (10/53), 543	5	10	15	34	55	75

UNDEAD, THE
Chaos! Comics (Black Label): Feb, 2002 ($4.99, B&W)

1-Pulido-s/Denham-a						5.00

UNDERCOVER GIRL (Starr Flagg) (See Extra Comics, Manhunt! & Trail Colt)
Magazine Enterprises: No. 5, 1952 - No. 7, 1954

5(#1)(A-1 #62)-Fallon of the F.B.I. in all	28	56	84	165	270	375
6(A-1 #98), 7(A-1 #118)-All have Starr Flagg	26	52	78	154	252	350

NOTE: *Powell c-6, 7. Whitney a-5-7.*

UNDERDOG (TV)(See Kite Fun Book, March of Comics #426, 438, 467, 479)
Charlton Comics/Gold Key: July, 1970 - No. 10, Jan, 1972; Mar, 1975 - No. 23, Feb, 1979

1 (1st series, Charlton)-1st app. Underdog	9	18	27	65	113	160
2-10	6	12	18	37	59	80
1 (2nd series, Gold Key)	7	14	21	45	73	100
2-10	4	8	12	24	37	50
11-20: 13-1st app. Shack of Solitude	3	6	9	19	29	38
21-23	3	6	9	20	30	40

UNDERDOG
Spotlight Comics: 1987 - No. 3?, 1987 ($1.50)

1-3						4.00

UNDERDOG (Volume 2)
Harvey Comics: Nov, 1993 - No. 5, July, 1994 ($2.25)

1-5						4.00
Summer Special (10/93, $2.25, 68 pgs.)						4.00

UNDERSEA AGENT
Tower Comics: Jan, 1966 - No. 6, Mar, 1967 (25¢, 68 pgs.)

1-Davy Jones, Undersea Agent begins	9	18	27	60	100	140
2-6: 2-Jones gains magnetic powers. 5-Origin & 1st app. of Merman. 6-Kane/Wood-c(r)	6	12	18	39	62	85

NOTE: *Gil Kane a-3-6; c-4, 5. Moldoff a-2i.*

UNDERSEA FIGHTING COMMANDOS (See Fighting Undersea...)
I.W. Enterprises: 1964

I.W. Reprint #1,2('64): 1-r/#? 2-r/#1; Severin-c	2	4	6	9	13	16

UNDERTAKER (World Wrestling Federation)(Also see WWE Undertaker)
Chaos! Comics: Feb, 1999 - No. 10, Jan, 2000 ($2.50/$2.95)

Preview (2/99)						3.00
1-10: Reg. and photo covers for each. 1-(4/99)						3.00
1-($6.95) DF Ed.; Brereton painted-c						7.00
...Halloween Special (10/99, $2.95) Reg. & photo-c						3.00
Wizard #0						3.00

UNDERWATER CITY, THE
Dell Publishing Co.: No. 1328, 1961

Four Color 1328-Movie, Evans-a	7	14	21	47	76	105

UNDERWORLD (...True Crime Stories)

Underworld Crime #3 © FAW

The Unexpected #122 © DC

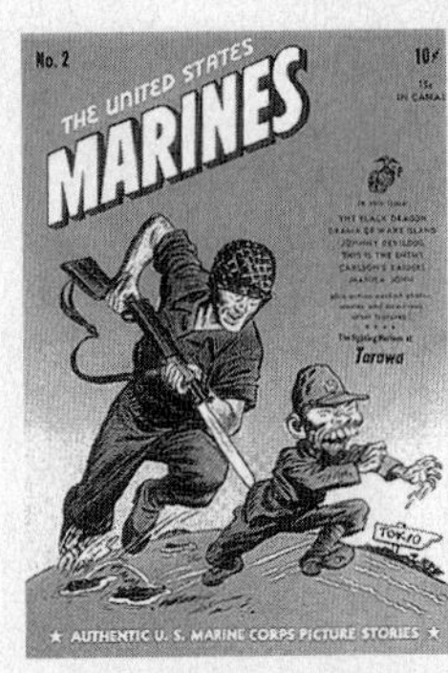

United States Marines #2 © WHW

GD 2.0 | VG 4.0 | FN 6.0 | VF 8.0 | VF/NM 9.0 | NM- 9.2

D. S. Publishing Co.: Feb-Mar, 1948 - No. 9, June-July, 1949 (52 pgs.)
1-Moldoff (Shelly)-c; excessive violence 47 94 141 296 498 700
2-Moldoff (Shelly)-c; Ma Barker story used in **SOTI**, pg. 95; female electrocution panel; lingerie art 43 86 129 271 456 640
3-McWilliams-c/a; extreme violence, mutilation 40 80 120 242 404 565
4-Used in Love and Death by Legman; Ingels-a 36 72 108 211 343 475
5-Ingels-a 24 48 72 142 234 325
6-9: 8-Ravielli-a. 9-R.Q. Sale-a 20 40 60 114 182 250

UNDERWORLD
DC Comics: Dec, 1987 - No. 4, Mar, 1988 ($1.00, limited series, mature)
1-4 3.00

UNDERWORLD (Movie)
IDW Publishing: Sept, 2003; Dec, 2005 ($6.99)
1-Movie adaptation; photo-c 7.00
... Evolution (12/05, $7.49) adaptation of movie sequel; Vazquez-a 7.50
TPB (7/04, $19.99) r/#1 and Underworld:Red in Tooth and Claw #1-3 20.00

UNDERWORLD
Marvel Comics: Apr, 2006 - No. 5, Aug, 2006 ($2.99, limited series)
1-5: Staz Johnson-a. 2-Spider-Man app. 3,4-Punisher app. 3.00

UNDERWORLD CRIME
Fawcett Publications: June, 1952 - No. 9, Oct, 1953
1 34 68 102 199 325 450
2 21 42 63 122 199 275
3-6,8,9 (8,9-exist?) 19 38 57 112 179 245
7-(6/53)-Red hot poker/bondage/torture-c 50 100 150 315 533 750

UNDERWORLD: RED IN TOOTH AND CLAW (Movie)
IDW Publishing: Feb, 2004 - No. 3, Apr, 2004 ($3.99, limited series)
1-3-The early days of the Vampire and Lycan war; Postic & Marinkovich-a 4.00

UNDERWORLD: RISE OF THE LYCANS (Movie)
IDW Publishing: Nov, 2008 - No. 2, Nov, 2008 ($3.99, limited series)
1,2-Grevioux-s/Huerta-a 4.00

UNDERWORLD STORY, THE (Movie)
Avon Periodicals: 1950
nn-(Scarce)-Ravielli-c 29 58 87 172 281 390

UNDERWORLD UNLEASHED
DC Comics: Nov, 1995 - No. 3, Jan, 1996 ($2.95, limited series)
1-3: Mark Waid scripts & Howard Porter-c/a(p) 3.50
...: Abyss: Hell's Sentinel 1-($2.95)-Alan Scott, Phantom Stranger, Zatanna app. 3.00
...: Apokolips-Dark Uprising 1 ($1.95) 3.00
...: Batman-Devil's Asylum 1-($2.95)-Batman app. 3.00
...: Patterns of Fear-($2.95) 3.00
TPB (1998, $17.95) r/#1-3 & Abyss-Hell's Sentinel 18.00

UNEARTHLY SPECTACULARS
Harvey Publications: Oct, 1965 - No. 3, Mar, 1967
1-(12¢)-Tiger Boy; Simon-c 4 8 12 26 41 55
2-(25¢ giants)-Jack Q. Frost, Tiger Boy & Three Rocketeers app.; Williamson, Wood, Kane-a; r-1 story/Thrill-O-Rama #2 5 10 15 30 48 65
3-(25¢ giants)-Jack Q. Frost app.; Williamson/Crandall-a; r-from Alarming Advs. #1,1962 5 10 15 30 48 65
NOTE: *Crandall a-3r. G. Kane a-2. Orlando a-3. Simon, Sparling, Wood c-2. Simon/Kirby a-3r. Torres a-1?. Wildey a-1(3). Williamson a-2, 3r. Wood a-2(2).*

UNEXPECTED, THE (Formerly Tales of the...)
National Per. Publ./DC Comics: No. 105, Feb-Mar, 1968 - No. 222, May, 1982
105-Begin 12¢ cover price 7 14 21 47 76 105
106-113: 113-Last 12¢ issue (6-7/69) 5 10 15 32 51 70
114,115,117,118,120-125 4 8 12 23 36 48
116 (36 pgs.)-Wrightson-a 4 8 12 24 37 50
119-Wrightson-a, 8pgs.(36 pgs.) 5 10 15 35 55 75
126,127,129-136-(52 pgs.) 4 8 12 23 36 48
128(52 pgs.)-Wrightson-a 5 10 15 35 55 75
137-156 3 6 9 16 22 28
157-162-(100 pgs.) 5 10 15 30 48 65
163-188: 187,188-(44 pgs.) 2 4 6 11 16 20
189,190,192-195 ($1.00, 68 pgs.): 189 on are combined with House of Secrets & The Witching Hour 2 4 6 13 18 22
191-Rogers-a(p) ($1.00, 68 pgs.) 3 6 9 14 19 24
196-222: 200-Return of Johnny Peril by Tuska. 205-213-Johnny Peril app. 210-Time Warp story. 222-Giffen-a 2 4 6 8 10 12
NOTE: *Neal Adams c-110, 112-115, 118, 121, 124. J. Craig a-195. Ditko a-189, 221p, 222p; c-222. Drucker a-107r, 132r. Giffen a-219, 222. Kaluta c-203, 212. Kirby a-127r, 162. Kubert c-204, 214-216, 219-221. Mayer a-217p, 220, 221p. Moldoff a-136r. Moreira a-133. Mortimer a-212p. Newton a-204p. Orlando a-202; c-191. Perez a-217p. Redondo a-155, 166, 195. Reese a-145. Sparling a-107, 205-209p, 212p. Spiegle a-217. Starlin c-198. Toth a-126r, 127r. Tuska a-127, 132, 134, 136, 139, 152, 180, 200p. Wildey a-128r, 193. Wood a-122i, 133i, 137i, 138i. Wrightson a-161r(2 pgs.). Johnny Peril in #106-114, 116, 117, 200, 205-213.*

UNEXPECTED ANNUAL, THE (See DC Special Series #4)

UNHOLY UNION
Image Comics (Top Cow): July, 2007 ($3.99, one-shot)
1-Witchblade & The Darkness meet Hulk, Ghost Rider & Doctor Strange; Silvestri-c 4.00

UNIDENTIFIED FLYING ODDBALL (See Walt Disney Showcase #52)

UNION
Image Comics (WildStorm Productions): June, 1993 - No. 0, July, 1994 ($1.95, lim. series)
0-(7/94, $2.50) 3.00
0-Alternate Portacio-c (See Deathblow #5) 5.00
1-($2.50)-Embossed foil-c; Texeira-c/a in all 4.00
1-($1.95)-Newsstand edition w/o foil-c 3.00
2-4: 4-(7/94) 3.00

UNION
Image Comics (WildStorm Prod.): Feb, 1995 - No. 9, Dec, 1995 ($2.50)
1-3,5-9: 3-Savage Dragon app. 6-Fairchild from Gen 13 app. 3.00
4-($1.95, Newsstand)-WildStorm Rising Pt. 3 3.00
4-($2.50, Direct Market)-WildStorm Rising Pt. 3, bound-in card 3.00

UNION: FINAL VENGEANCE
Image Comics (WildStorm Productions): Oct, 1997 ($2.50)
1-Golden-c/Heisler-s 3.00

UNION JACK
Marvel Comics: Dec, 1998 - No. 3, Feb, 1999 ($2.99, limited series)
1-3-Raab-s/Cassaday-s/a 3.00

UNION JACK
Marvel Comics: Nov, 2006 - No. 4, Feb, 2007 ($2.99, limited series)
1-4-Gage-s/Perkins-c/a 3.00
...: London Falling TPB (2007, $10.99) r/#1-4; Perkins sketch page 11.00

UNITED COMICS (Formerly Fritzi Ritz #7; has Fritzi Ritz logo)
United Features Syndicate: Aug, 1940; No. 8, 1950 - No. 26, Jan-Feb, 1953
1(68 pgs.)-Fritzi Ritz & Phil Fumble 23 46 69 136 223 310
8-Fritzi Ritz, Abbie & Slats 8 16 24 44 57 70
9-21: 20-Strange As It Seems; Russell Patterson Cheesecake-a 8 16 24 40 50 60
22-(5-6/52) 2 pgs. early Peanuts by Schulz (1st in comics?) 20 40 60 114 182 250
23-26: 23-(7-8/52). 24-(9-10/52). 25-(11-12/52). 26-(1-2/53). All have 2 pgs. early Peanuts by Schulz 14 28 42 80 115 150
NOTE: *Abbie & Slats reprinted from Tip Top.*

UNITED NATIONS, THE (See Classics Illustrated Special Issue)

UNITED STATES AIR FORCE PRESENTS: THE HIDDEN CREW
U.S. Air Force: 1964 (36 pgs.)
nn-Schaffenberger-a 2 4 6 10 14 18

UNITED STATES FIGHTING AIR FORCE (Also see U.S. Fighting Air Force)
Superior Comics Ltd.: Sept, 1952 - No. 29, Oct, 1956
1 13 26 39 72 101 130
2 8 16 24 42 54 65
3-10 7 14 21 37 46 55
11-29 7 14 21 35 43 50

UNITED STATES MARINES
William H. Wise/Life's Romances Publ. Co./Magazine Ent. #5-8/Toby Press #7-11: 1943 - No. 4, 1944; No. 5, 1952 - No. 8, 1952; No. 7 - No. 11, 1953
nn-Mart Bailey-c/a; Marines in the Pacific theater 21 42 63 122 199 275
2-Bailey-a; Tojo classic-c 58 116 174 371 636 900
3-Tojo-c 53 106 159 334 567 800
4-WWII photos; Tony DiPreta-a 14 28 42 82 121 160
5(A-1 #55)-Bailey-a, 6(A-1 #60), 7(A-1 #68), 8(A-1 #72) 10 20 30 58 79 100
7-11 (Toby) 9 18 27 52 69 85
NOTE: *Powell a-5-7.*

UNITY
Valiant: No. 0, Aug, 1992 - No. 1, 1992 (Free comics w/limited dist., 20 pgs.)

The Unknown #1 © BOOM! Studios

Unknown Soldier (2008 series) #19 © DC

The Un-Men #6 © DC

GD VG FN VF VF/NM NM-
2.0 4.0 6.0 8.0 9.0 9.2

0 (Blue)-Prequel to Unity x-overs in all Valiant titles; B. Smith-c/a. (Free to everyone that bought all 8 titles that month.) 3.00
0 (Red)-Same as above, but w/red logo (5,000). 3.00
1-Epilogue to Unity x-overs; B. Smith-c/a. (1 copy available for every 8 Valiant books ordered by dealers.) 3.00
1 (Gold), 1-(Platinum)-Promotional copy. 6.00
...: The Lost Chapter 1 (Yearbook) (2/95, $3.95)-"1994" in indicia 4.00

UNITY 2000 (See preludes in Shadowman #3,4 flipbooks)
Acclaim Comics: Nov, 1999 - No. 3, Jan, 2000 ($2.50, unfinished limited series planned for 6 issues)
Preview -B&W plot preview and cover art; paper cover 3.00
1-3-Starlin-a/Shooter-s 3.00

UNIVERSAL MONSTERS
Dark Horse Comics: 1993 ($4.95/$5.95, 52 pgs.)(All adapt original movies)
Creature From the Black Lagoon nn-($4.95)-Art Adams/Austin-c/a, Dracula nn-($4.95), Frankenstein nn-($3.95)-Painted-c/a, The Mummy nn-($4.95)-Painted-c
1 2 3 4 5 7
...: Cavalcade of Horror TPB (1/06, $19.95) r/one-shots; Eric Powell intro. & cover 20.00

UNIVERSAL PRESENTS DRACULA-THE MUMMY& OTHER STORIES
Dell Publishing Co.: Sept-Nov, 1963 (one-shot, 84 pgs.) (Also see Dell Giants)
02-530-311-r/Dracula 12-231-212, The Mummy 12-437-211 & part of Ghost Stories No. 1
16 32 48 111 226 340

UNIVERSAL SOLDIER (Movie)
Now Comics: Sept, 1992 - No. 3, Nov, 1992 (Limited series, polybagged, mature)
1-3 ($2.50, Direct Sales) 1-Movie adapatation; hologram on-c (all direct sales editions have painted-c) 4.00
1-3 ($1.95, Newsstand)-Rewritten & redrawn code approved version; all newsstand editions have photo-c 3.00

UNIVERSAL WAR ONE
Marvel Comics (Soleil): 2008 - No. 3, 2008 ($5.99, limited series)
1-3-Denis Bajram-s/a; English version of French comic. 1-Bajram interview 6.00
...: Revelations 1-3 (2009 - No. 3, 2009, $5.99) Bajram-s/a 6.00

UNIVERSE
Image Comics (Top Cow): Sept, 2001 - No. 8, July, 2002 ($2.50)
1-7-Jenkins-s 3.00
8-($4.95) extra short-s by Jenkins; pin-up pages 5.00

UNIVERSE X (See Earth X)
Marvel Comics: Sept, 2000 - No. 12, Sept, 2001 ($3.99/$3.50, limited series)
0-Ross-c/Braithwaite-a/Ross & Krueger-s 4.00
1-12: 5-Funeral of Captain America 4.00
... Beasts (6/00, $3.99) Yeates-a/Ross-c 4.00
... Cap (Capt. America) (2/01, $3.99) Yeates & Totleben-a/Ross-c; Cap dies 4.00
... 4 (Fantastic 4) (10/00, $3.99) Brent Anderson-a/Ross-c 4.00
... Iron Men (9/01, $3.99) Anderson-a/Ross-c; leads into #12 4.00
... Omnibus (6/01, $3.99) Ross B&W sketchbook and character bios 4.00
Sketchbook- Wizard supplement; B&W character sketches and bios 3.00
...Spidey (1/01, $3.99) Romita Sr. flashback-a/Guice-a/Ross-c 4.00
...X (11/01, $3.99) Series conclusion; Braithwaith-a/Ross wraparound-c 4.00
Volume 1 TPB (1/02, $24.95) r/#0-7 & Spidey, 4, & Cap; new Ross-c 25.00
Volume 2 TPB (6/02, $24.95) r/#8-12 &X, Beasts, Iron Men and Omnibus 25.00

UNKNOWN, THE
BOOM! Studios: May, 2009 - No. 4, Aug, 2009 ($3.99)
1-4-Mark Waid-s/Minck Oosterveer-a; two covers on each 4.00
...: The Devil Made Flesh 1-4 (9/09 - No. 4, 12/09, $3.99) Waid-s/Oosterveer-a 4.00

UNKNOWN MAN, THE (Movie)
Avon Periodicals: 1951
nn-Kinstler-c 28 56 84 165 270 375

UNKNOWN SOLDIER (Formerly Star-Spangled War Stories)
National Periodical Publications/DC Comics: No. 205, Apr-May, 1977 - No. 268, Oct, 1982 (See Our Army at War #168 for 1st app.)
205 3 6 9 18 27 35
206-210,220,221,251: 220,221 (44pgs.). 251-Enemy Ace begins
3 6 9 14 19 24
211-218,222-247,250,252-264 2 4 6 11 16 20
219-Miller-a (44 pgs.) 3 6 9 16 23 30
248,249,265-267: 248,249-Origin. 265-267-Enemy Ace vs. Balloon Buster.
2 4 6 11 16 20
268-Death of Unknown Soldier 3 6 9 20 30 40

GD VG FN VF VF/NM NM-
2.0 4.0 6.0 8.0 9.0 9.2

NOTE: *Chaykin a-234. Evans a-265-267; c-235. Kubert c-Most. Miller a-219p. Severin a-251-253, 260, 261, 265-267. Simonson a-254-256. Spiegle a-258, 259, 262-264.*

UNKNOWN SOLDIER, THE (Also see Brave &the Bold #146)
DC Comics: Winter, 1988-'89 - No. 12, Dec, 1989 ($1.50, maxi-series, mature)
1-12: 8-Begin $1.75-c 5.00

UNKNOWN SOLDIER
DC Comics (Vertigo): Apr, 1997 - No 4, July, 1997 ($2.50, mini-series)
1-Ennis-s/Plunkett-a/Bradstreet-c in all 6.00
2-4 4.00
TPB (1998, $12.95) r/#1-4 13.00

UNKNOWN SOLDIER
DC Comics (Vertigo): Dec, 2008 - No. 25, Dec, 2010 ($2.99)
1-25: 1-Dysart-s/Ponticelli-a; intro. Lwanga Moses; two covers by Kordey and Corben. 2-20,22-25-Ponticelli-a. 21-Veitch-a 3.00
...: Dry Season TPB (2010, $14.99) r/#15-20; war history 15.00
...: Easy Kill TPB (2010, $17.99) r/#7-14; war history 18.00
...: Haunted House TPB (2009, $9.99) r/#1-6; glossary 10.00

UNKNOWN WORLD (Strange Stories From Another World #2 on)
Fawcett Publications: June, 1952
1-Norman Saunders painted-c 46 92 138 290 488 685

UNKNOWN WORLDS (See Journey Into...)

UNKNOWN WORLDS
American Comics Group/Best Synd. Features: Aug, 1960 - No. 57, Aug, 1967
1-Schaffenberger-c 18 36 54 125 255 385
2-Dinosaur-c/story 11 22 33 75 138 200
3-5 9 18 27 65 113 160
6-11: 9-Dinosaur-c/story. 11-Last 10¢ issue 8 16 24 54 90 125
12-19: 12-Begin 12¢ issues?; ends #57 6 12 18 43 69 95
20-Herbie cameo (12-1/62-63) 7 14 21 45 73 100
21-35: 31-Herbie one pagers thru #39 5 10 15 32 51 70
36- "The People vs. Hendricks" by Craig; most popular ACG story ever
5 10 15 34 55 75
37-46 4 8 12 28 44 60
47-Williamson-a r-from Adventures Into the Unknown #96, 3 pgs.; Craig-a
5 10 15 30 48 65
48-57: 53-Frankenstein app. 4 8 12 26 41 55
NOTE: *Ditko a-49, 50p, 54. Forte a-3, 6, 11. Landau a-56(2). Reinman a-3, 9, 13, 20, 22, 23, 36, 38, 54. Whitney c/a-most issues. John Force, Magic Agent app.-35, 36, 48, 50, 52, 54, 56.*

UNKNOWN WORLDS OF FRANK BRUNNER
Eclipse Comics: Aug, 1985 - No. 2, Aug, 1985 ($1.75)
1,2-B&W-r in color 3.50

UNKNOWN WORLDS OF SCIENCE FICTION
Marvel Comics: Jan, 1975 - No. 6, Nov, 1975; 1976 ($1.00, B&W Magazine)
1-Williamson/Krenkel/Torres/Frazetta-r/Witzend #1, Neal Adams-r/Phase 1; Brunner & Kaluta-r; Freas/Romita-c 3 6 9 16 23 30
2-6: 5-Kaluta text illos 3 6 9 14 19 24
Special 1(1976,100 pgs.)-Newton painted-c 3 6 9 16 22 28
NOTE: *Brunner a-2; c-4, 6. Buscema a-Special 1p. Chaykin a-5. Colan a(p)-1, 3, 5, 6. Corben a-4. Kaluta a-2, Special 1(ext illos); c-2. Morrow a-3, 5. Nino a-3, 6, Special 1. Perez a-2, 3. Ray Bradbury interview in #1.*

UNLIMITED ACCESS (Also see Marvel Vs. DC)
Marvel Comics: Dec, 1997 - No. 4, Mar, 1998 ($2.99/$1.99, limited series)
1-Spider-Man, Wonder Woman, Green Lantern & Hulk app. 4.00
2,3-($1.99): 2-X-Men, Legion of Super-Heroes app. 3-Original Avengers vs. original Justice League 3.00
4-($2.99) Amalgam Legion vs. Darkseid & Magneto 3.00

UN-MEN, THE
DC Comics (Vertigo): Oct, 2007 - No. 13, Oct, 2008 ($2.99)
1-13-Whalen-s/Hawthorne-a/Hanuka-c 3.00
...: Children of Paradox TPB (2008, $19.99) r/#6-13 20.00
...: Get Your Freak On! TPB (2008, $9.99) r/#1-5; cover gallery 10.00

UNSANE (Formerly Mighty Bear #13, 14? or The Outlaws #10-14?)(Satire)
Star Publications: No. 15, June, 1954
15-Disbrow-a(2); L. B. Cole-c 34 68 102 199 325 450

UNSEEN, THE
Visual Editions/Standard Comics: No. 5, 1952 - No. 15, July, 1954
5-Horror stories in all; Toth-a 42 84 126 265 450 635
6,7,9,10-Jack Katz-a 32 64 96 188 307 425
8,11,13,14 25 50 75 150 245 340

Untamed Love #1 © QUA

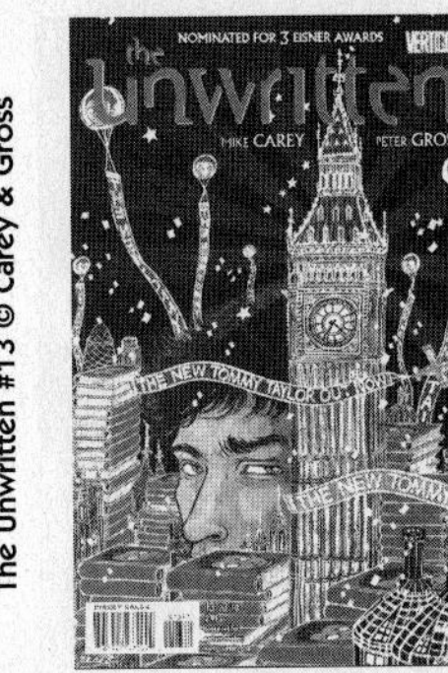

The Unwritten #13 © Carey & Gross

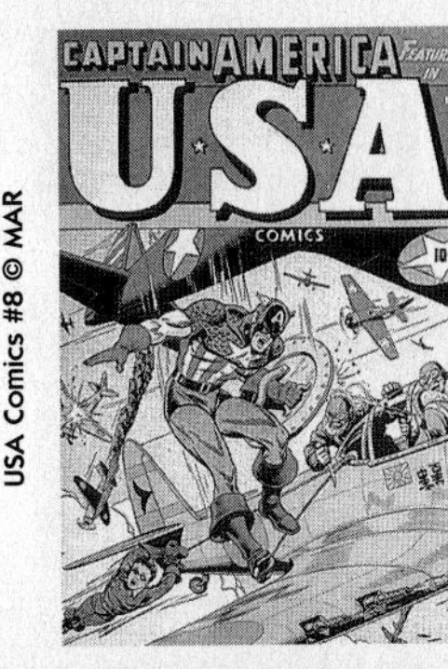

USA Comics #8 © MAR

GD VG FN VF VF/NM NM-
2.0 4.0 6.0 8.0 9.0 9.2

12,15-Toth-a. 12-Tuska-a 32 64 96 188 307 425
NOTE: ***Nick Cardy** c-12. **Fawcette** a-13, 14. **Sekowsky** a-7, 8(2), 10, 13, 15.*

UNTAMED
Marvel Comics (Epic Comics/Heavy Hitters): June, 1993 - No. 3, Aug, 1993 ($1.95, lim. series)
1-($2.50)-Embossed-c 3.50
2,3 3.00

UNTAMED LOVE (Also see Frank Frazetta's Untamed Love)
Quality Comics Group (Comic Magazines): Jan, 1950 - No. 5, Sept, 1950
1-Ward-c, Gustavson-a 26 52 78 154 252 350
2,4: 2-5-Photo-c 16 32 48 94 147 200
3,5-Gustavson-a 17 34 51 100 158 215

UNTOLD LEGEND OF CAPTAIN MARVEL, THE
Marvel Comics: Apr, 1997 - No. 3, June, 1997 ($2.50, limited series)
1-3 3.00

UNTOLD LEGEND OF THE BATMAN, THE (Also see Promotional section)
DC Comics: July, 1980 - No. 3, Sept, 1980 (Limited series)
1-Origin; Joker-c; Byrne's 1st work at DC 1 2 3 5 6 8
2,3 5.00
NOTE: ***Aparo** a-1i, 2, 3. **Byrne** a-1p.*

UNTOLD ORIGIN OF THE FEMFORCE, THE (Also see Femforce)
AC Comics: 1989 ($4.95, 68 pgs.)
1-Origin Femforce; Bill Black-a(i) & scripts 6.00

UNTOLD TALES OF BLACKEST NIGHT (Also see Blackest Night crossover titles)
DC Comics: Dec, 2010 ($4.99, one-shot)
1-Short stories by various incl. Johns, Benes, Booth; 2 covers by Kirkham & Van Sciver 5.00

UNTOLD TALES OF CHASTITY
Chaos! Comics: Nov, 2000 ($2.95, one-shot)
1-Origin; Steven Grant-s/Peter Vale-c/a 3.00
1-Premium Edition with glow in the dark cover 13.00

UNTOLD TALES OF LADY DEATH
Chaos! Comics: Nov, 2000 ($2.95, one-shot)
1-Origin of Lady Death; Cremator app.; Kaminski-s 3.00
1-Premium Edition with glow in the dark cover by Steven Hughes 13.00

UNTOLD TALES OF PURGATORI
Chaos! Comics: Nov, 2000 ($2.95, one-shot)
1-Purgatori in 57 B.C.; Rio-a/Grant-s 3.00
1-Premium Edition with glow in the dark cover 13.00

UNTOLD TALES OF SPIDER-MAN (Also see Amazing Fantasy #16-18)
Marvel Comics: Sept, 1995 - No. 25, Sept, 1997 (99¢)
1-Kurt Busiek scripts begin; Pat Olliffe-c/a in all (except #9). 4.00
2-22, -1(7/97), 23-25: 2-1st app. Batwing. 4-1st app. The Spacemen (Gantry, Orbit, Satellite & Vacuum). 8-1st app. The Headsman; The Enforcers (The Big Man, Montana, The Ox & Fancy Dan) app. 9-Ron Frenz-a. 10-1st app. Commanda. 16-Reintro Mary Jane Watson. 21-X-Men-c/app. 25-Green Goblin 3.00
...'96-(1996, $1.95, 46 pgs.)-Kurt Busiek scripts; Mike Allred-c/a; Kurt Busiek & Pat Olliffe app. in back-up story; contains pin-ups 4.00
...'97-(1997, $1.95)-Wraparound-c 4.00
...: Strange Encounters ('98, $5.99) Dr. Strange app. 6.00

UNTOLD TALES OF THE NEW UNIVERSE (Based on Marvel's 1986 New Universe titles)
Marvel Comics: May, 2006 ($2.99, series of one-shots)
...: D. P. 7 - Takes place between issues #4 & 5 of D. P. 7 series; Bright-a/Cebulski-s 3.00
...: Justice - Peter David-s/Carmine Di Giandomenico-a 3.00
...: Nightmask - Takes place between issues #4 & 5 of Nightmask series; The Gnome app. 3.00
...: Psi-Force - Tony Bedard-s/Russ Braun-a 3.00
...: Star Brand - Romita & Romita Jr.-c/Pulido-a 3.00
TPB (2006, $15.99) r/one-shots & stories from Amaz. Fantasy #18,19 & New Avengers #16 16.00

UNTOUCHABLES, THE (TV)
Dell Publishing Co.: No. 1237, 10-12/61 - No. 4, 8-10/62 (All have Robert Stack photo-c)
Four Color 1237(#1) 18 36 54 127 259 390
Four Color 1286 13 26 39 92 179 265
01-879-207, 12-879-210(01879-210 on inside) 9 18 27 63 107 150

UNTOUCHABLES
Caliber Comics: Aug, 1997 - No. 4 ($2.95, B&W)
1-4: 1-Pruett-s; variant covers by Kaluta & Showman 3.00

UNUSUAL TALES (Blue Beetle & Shadows From Beyond #50 on)
Charlton Comics: Nov, 1955 - No. 49, Mar-Apr, 1965
1 32 64 96 188 307 425
2 16 35 48 94 147 200
3-5 14 28 42 80 115 150
6-Ditko-c only 18 36 54 105 165 225
7,8-Ditko-c/a. 8-Robot-c 29 58 87 170 278 385
9-Ditko-c/a (20 pgs.) 31 62 93 186 303 420
10-Ditko-c/a(4) 32 64 96 192 314 435
11-(3/58, 68 pgs.)-Ditko-a(4) 31 62 93 186 303 420
12,14-Ditko-a 19 38 57 111 176 240
13,16-20 7 14 21 47 76 105
15-Ditko-c/a 24 48 72 142 234 325
21,24,28 6 12 18 39 62 85
22,23,25-27,29-Ditko-a 10 20 30 68 119 170
30-49 5 10 15 30 48 65
NOTE: ***Colan** a-11. **Ditko** c-22, 23, 25-27, 31(part).*

UNWRITTEN, THE
DC Comics (Vertigo): July, 2009 - Present ($1.00/$2.99)
1-($1.00) Intro. Tommy Taylor; Mike Carey-s/Peter Gross-a; two covers (white & black) 3.00
2-16,18-23-($2.99) 3.00
17-($3.99) Story printed sideways; Pick-a-Story format 4.00
...: Dead Man's Knock TPB (2011, $14.99) r/#13-18; intro. by novelist Steven Hall 15.00
...: Inside Man TPB (2010, $12.99) r/#6-12; intro. by Paul Cornell 13.00
...: Tommy Taylor and the Bogus Identity TPB (2010, $9.99) r/#1-5; sketch art; prose 10.00

UP FROM HARLEM (Tom Skinner...)
Spire Christian Comics (Fleming H. Revell Co.): 1973 (35/49¢)
nn-(35¢ cover) 2 4 6 10 14 18
nn-(49¢ cover) 2 4 6 8 11 14

UP-TO-DATE COMICS
King Features Syndicate: No date (1938) (36 pgs.; B&W cover) (10¢)
nn-Popeye & Henry cover; The Phantom, Jungle Jim & Flash Gordon by Raymond, The Katzenjammer Kids, Curley Harper & others. Note: Variations in content exist. 25 50 75 147 241 335

UP YOUR NOSE AND OUT YOUR EAR (Satire)
Klevart Enterprises: Apr, 1972 - No. 2, June, 1972 (52 pgs., magazine)
V1#1,2 2 4 6 11 16 20

URTH 4 (Also see Earth 4)
Continuity Comics: May, 1989 - No. 4, Dec, 1990 ($2.00, deluxe format)
1-4: Ms. Mystic characters. 2-Neal Adams-c(i) 3.00

URZA-MISHRA WAR ON THE WORLD OF MAGIC THE GATHERING
Acclaim Comics (Armada): 1996 - No. 2, 1996 ($5.95, limited series)
1,2 6.00

U.S. (See Uncle Sam)

USA COMICS
Timely Comics (USA): Aug, 1941 - No. 17, Fall, 1945
1-Origin Major Liberty (called Mr. Liberty #1), Rockman by Wolverton; 1st app. The Whizzer by Avison; The Defender with sidekick Rusty & Jack Frost begin; The Young Avenger only app.; S&K-c plus 1 pg. art 1100 2200 3300 8250 14,125 20,000
2-Origin Captain Terror & The Vagabond; last Wolverton Rockman; Hitler-c 411 822 1233 2877 5039 7200
3-No Whizzer 303 606 909 2121 3711 5300
4-Last Rockman, Major Liberty, Defender, Jack Frost, & Capt. Terror; Corporal Dix app. 300 600 900 1920 3310 4700
5-Origin American Avenger & Roko the Amazing; The Blue Blade, The Black Widow & Victory Boys, Gypo the Gypsy Giant & Hills of Horror only app.; Sergeant Dix begins; no Whizzer; Hitler, Mussolini & Tojo-c 300 600 900 1920 3310 4700
6-Captain America (ends #17), The Destroyer, Jap Buster Johnson, Jeep Jones begin; Terror Squad only app. 400 800 1200 2800 4900 7000
7-Captain Daring, Disk-Eyes the Detective by Wolverton app.; origin & only app. Marvel Boy (3/43); Secret Stamp begins; no Whizzer, Sergeant Dix; classic Schomburg-c 732 864 1296 3154 5577 8000
8,10: 10-The Thunderbird only app. 309 618 927 2163 3782 5400
9-Last Secret Stamp; Hitler-c; classic-c 331 662 993 2317 4059 5800
11,12: 11-No Jeep Jones 226 452 678 1446 2473 3500
13-17: 13-No Whizzer; Jeep Jones ends. 15-No Destroyer; Jap Buster Johnson ends 148 296 444 947 1624 2300
NOTE: ***Brodsky** c-14. **Gabrielle** c-4. **Schomburg** c-6, 7, 10, 12, 13, 15-17. **Shores** a-1, 4; c-9, 11. **Ed Win** a-4. Cover features: 1-The Defender; 2, 3-Captain Terror; 4-Major Liberty; 5-Victory Boys; 6-17-Captain America & Bucky.*

USA COMICS 70TH ANNIVERSARY SPECIAL
Marvel Comics: Sept, 2009 ($3.99, one-shot)

Usagi Yojimbo #112 © Stan Sakai

U.S. 1 #4 © MAR

U.S. Tank Commandos #3 © AVON

	GD 2.0	VG 4.0	FN 6.0	VF 8.0	VF/NM 9.0	NM- 9.2
1-New story of The Destroyer; Arcudi-s/Ellis-a; r/All Winners #3; two covers						4.00

U.S. AGENT (See Jeff Jordan...)

U.S. AGENT (See Captain America #354)
Marvel Comics: June, 1993 - No. 4, Sept, 1993 ($1.75, limited series)

1-4 — 3.00

U.S. AGENT
Marvel Comics: Aug, 2001 - No. 3, Oct, 2001 ($2.99, limited series)

1-3: Ordway-s/a(p)/c. 2,3-Captain America app. — 3.00

USAGI YOJIMBO (See Albedo, Doomsday Squad #3 & Space Usagi)
Fantagraphics Books: July, 1987 - No. 38 ($2.00/$2.25, B&W)

	GD	VG	FN	VF	VF/NM	NM-
1	1	2	3	5	7	9
1,8,10-2nd printings						3.00
2-9						4.00
10,11: 10-Leonardo app. (TMNT). 11-Aragonés-a						6.00
12-29						3.00
30-38: 30-Begin $2.25-c						3.00
Color Special 1 (11/89, $2.95, 68 pgs.)-new & r						4.00
Color Special 2 (10/91, $3.50)						4.00
Color Special #3 (10/92, $3.50)-Jeff Smith's Bone promo on inside-c						4.00
Summer Special 1 (1986, B&W, $2.75)-r/early Albedo issues						4.00

USAGI YOJIMBO
Mirage Studios: V2#1, Mar, 1993 - No. 16, 1994 ($2.75)

V2#1-16: 1-Teenage Mutant Ninja Turtles app. — 3.00

USAGI YOJIMBO
Dark Horse Comics: V3#1, Apr, 1996 - Present ($2.95/$2.99/$3.50, B&W)

	NM-
V3#1-99,101-116: Stan Sakai-c/a	3.00
100-(1/07, $3.50) Stan Sakai roast by various incl. Aragonés, Wagner, Miller, Geary	3.50
117-134-($3.50)	3.50
...: One For One (8/10, $1.00) Reprints #1	1.00
Color Special #4 (7/97, $2.95) "Green Persimmon"	3.00
Daisho TPB ('98, $14.95) r/Mirage series #7-14	15.00
Demon Mask TPB ('01, $15.95)	16.00
Glimpses of Death TPB (7/06, $15.95) r/#76-82	16.00
Grasscutter TPB ('99, $16.95) r/#13-22	17.00
Gray Shadows TPB ('00, $14.95) r/#23-30	15.00
Seasons TPB ('99, $14.95) r/#7-12	15.00
Shades of Death TPB ('97, $14.95) r/Mirage series #1-6	15.00
The Brink of Life and Death TPB ('98, $14.95) r/Mirage series #13,15,16 & Dark Horse series #1-6	15.00
The Shrouded Moon TPB (1/03, $15.95) r/#46-52	16.00

U.S. AIR FORCE COMICS (Army Attack #38 on)
Charlton Comics: Oct, 1958 - No. 37, Mar-Apr, 1965

	GD	VG	FN	VF	VF/NM	NM-
1	6	12	18	43	69	95
2	4	8	12	23	36	48
3-10	3	6	9	20	30	40
11-20	3	6	9	18	27	35
21-37	3	6	9	16	22	28

NOTE: *Glanzman c/a-9, 10, 12. Montes/Bache a-33.*

USA IS READY
Dell Publishing Co.: 1941 (68 pgs., one-shot)

	GD	VG	FN	VF	VF/NM	NM-
1-War propaganda	41	82	123	249	417	585

U.S. BORDER PATROL COMICS (Sgt. Dick Carter of the...) (See Holyoke One Shot)

USER
DC Comics (Vertigo): 2001 - No. 3, 2001 ($5.95, limited series)

1-3-Devin Grayson-s; Sean Phillips & John Bolton-a — 6.00

U.S. FIGHTING AIR FORCE (Also see United States Fighting Air Force)
I. W. Enterprises: No date (1960s?)

	GD	VG	FN	VF	VF/NM	NM-
1,9(nd): 1-r/United States Fighting...#?. 9-r/#1	2	4	6	8	11	14

U.S. FIGHTING MEN
Super Comics: 1963 - 1964 (Reprints)

	GD	VG	FN	VF	VF/NM	NM-
10-r/With the U.S. Paratroops #4(Avon)	2	4	6	9	13	16
11,12,15-18: 11-r/Monty Hall #10. 12,16,17,18-r/U.S. Fighting Air Force #10,3,?&? 15-r/Man Comics #11	2	4	6	9	13	16

U.S. JONES (Also see Wonderworld Comics #28)
Fox Features Syndicate: Nov, 1941 - No. 2, Jan, 1942

	GD	VG	FN	VF	VF/NM	NM-
1-U.S. Jones & The Topper begin; Nazi-c	129	258	387	826	1413	2000
2-Nazi-c	86	172	258	546	936	1325

U.S. MARINES
Charlton Comics: Fall, 1964 (12¢, one-shot)

	GD	VG	FN	VF	VF/NM	NM-
1-1st app. Capt. Dude; Glanzman-a	4	8	12	22	34	45

U.S. MARINES IN ACTION
Avon Periodicals: Aug, 1952 - No. 3, Dec, 1952

	GD	VG	FN	VF	VF/NM	NM-
1-Louis Ravielli-c/a	10	20	30	56	76	95
2,3: 3-Kinstler-c	8	16	24	42	54	65

U.S. 1
Marvel Comics Group: May, 1983 - No. 12, Oct, 1984 (7,8: painted-c)

1-12: 2-Sienkiewicz-c. 3-12-Michael Golden-c — 3.00

U.S. PARATROOPS (See With the...)

U.S. PARATROOPS
I. W. Enterprises: 1964?

	GD	VG	FN	VF	VF/NM	NM-
1,8: 1-r/With the U.S. Paratroops #1; Wood-c. 8-r/With the U.S. Paratroops #6; Kinstler-c	2	4	6	9	13	16

U.S. TANK COMMANDOS
Avon Periodicals: June, 1952 - No. 4, Mar, 1953

	GD	VG	FN	VF	VF/NM	NM-
1-Kinstler-c	11	22	33	60	83	105
2-4: Kinstler-c	8	16	24	44	57	70
I.W. Reprint #1,8: 1-r/#1. 8-r/#3	2	4	6	9	13	16

NOTE: *Kinstler a-I.W. #1; c-1-4, I.W. #1, 8.*

U.S. WAR MACHINE (Also see Iron Man and War Machine)
Marvel Comics (MAX): Nov, 2001 - No. 12, Jan, 2002 ($1.50, B&W, weekly limited series)

	NM-
1-12-Chuck Austen-s/a/c	3.00
TPB (12/01, $14.95) r/#1-12	15.00

U.S. WAR MACHINE 2.0
Marvel Comics (MAX): Sept, 2003 - No. 3, Sept, 2003 ($2.99, weekly, limited series)

1-3-Austen-s/Christian Moore-CGI art — 3.00

"V" (TV)
DC Comics: Feb, 1985 - No. 18, July, 1986

	NM-
1-Based on TV movie & series (Sci/Fi)	5.00
2-18: 17,18-Denys Cowan-c/a	4.00

VACATION COMICS (Also see A-1 Comics)
Magazine Enterprises: No. 16, 1948 (one-shot)

	GD	VG	FN	VF	VF/NM	NM-
A-1 16-The Pixies, Tom Tom, Flying Fredd & Koko & Kola	6	12	18	31	38	45

VACATION DIGEST
Harvey Comics: Sept, 1987 ($1.25, digest size)

	GD	VG	FN	VF	VF/NM	NM-
1	1	2	3	5	6	8

VACATION IN DISNEYLAND (Also see Dell Giants)
Dell Publishing Co./Gold Key (1965): Aug-Oct, 1959; May, 1965 (Walt Disney)

	GD	VG	FN	VF	VF/NM	NM-
Four Color 1025-Barks-a	15	30	45	103	209	315
1(30024-508)(G.K., 5/65, 25¢)-r/Dell Giant #30 & cover to #1 ('58); celebrates Disneyland's 10th anniversary	5	10	15	35	55	75

VACATION PARADE (See Dell Giants)

VALERIA THE SHE BAT
Continuity Comics: May, 1993 - No. 5, Nov, 1993

	GD	VG	FN	VF	VF/NM	NM-
1-Premium; acetate-c; N. Adams-a/scripts; given as gift to retailers	1	2	3	5	6	8
5 (11/93)-Embossed-c; N. Adams-a/scripts						3.00

NOTE: *Due to lack of continuity, #2-4 do not exist.*

VALERIA THE SHE BAT
Acclaim Comics (Windjammer): Sept, 1995 - No.2, Oct, 1995 ($2.50, limited series)

1,2 — 3.00

VALKYRIE (See Airboy)
Eclipse Comics: May,1987 - No. 3, July, 1987 ($1.75, limited series)

1-3: 2-Holly becomes new Black Angel — 3.00

VALKYRIE
Marvel Comics: Jan, 1997; Nov, 2010 ($2.95/$3.99, one-shots)

	NM-
1-(1/97, $2.95) w/pin-ups	3.00
1-(11/10, $3.99) Origin re-told; Winslade-a/Glass-s; Anacleto-c	4.00

VALKYRIE!
Eclipse Comics: July, 1988 - No. 3, Sept, 1988 ($1.95, limited series)

Valkyrie (2010) #1 © MAR

Vampirella #7 © WP

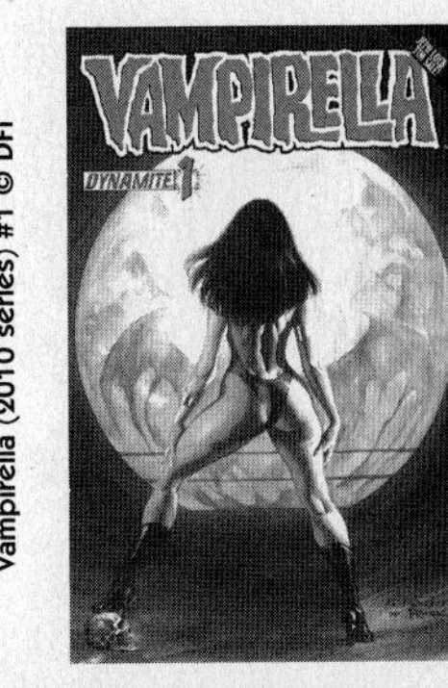

Vampirella (2010 series) #1 © DFI

GD 2.0 VG 4.0 FN 6.0 VF 8.0 VF/NM 9.0 NM- 9.2

1-3 3.00

VALLEY OF THE DINOSAURS (TV)
Charlton Comics: Apr, 1975 - No. 11, Dec, 1976 (Hanna-Barbara)

1-W. Howard-i 3 6 9 14 19 24
2,4-11: 2-W. Howard-i 2 4 6 8 11 14
3-Byrne text illos (early work, 7/75) 2 4 6 10 14 18

VALLEY OF THE DINOSAURS (Volume 2)
Harvey Comics: Oct, 1993 ($1.50, giant-sized)

1-Reprints 5.00

VALLEY OF GWANGI (See Movie Classics)

VALOR
E. C. Comics: Mar-Apr, 1955 - No. 5, Nov-Dec, 1955

1-Williamson/Torres-a; Wood-c/a 28 56 84 224 355 485
2-Williamson-c/a; Wood-a 21 42 63 168 272 375
3,4: 3-Williamson, Crandall-a. 4-Wood-c 16 32 48 128 207 285
5-Wood-c/a; Williamson/Evans-a 15 30 45 120 190 260

NOTE: *Crandall a-3, 4.* ***Ingels*** *a-1, 2, 4, 5.* ***Krigstein*** *a-1-5.* ***Orlando*** *a-3, 4; c-3.* ***Wood*** *a-1, 2, 5; c-1, 4, 5.*

VALOR
Gemstone Publishing: Oct, 1998 - No. 5, Feb, 1999 ($2.50)

1-5-Reprints 3.00

VALOR (Also see Legion of Super-Heroes & Legionnaires)
DC Comics: Nov, 1992 - No. 23, Sept, 1994 ($1.25/$1.50)

1-22: 1-Eclipso The Darkness Within aftermath. 2-Vs. Supergirl. 4-Vs. Lobo. 12-Lobo cameo. 14-Legionnaires, JLA app. 17-Austin-c(i); death of Valor. 18-22-Build-up to Zero Hour 3.00
23-Zero Hour tie-in 3.00

VALOR THUNDERSTAR AND HIS FIREFLIES
Now Comics: Dec, 1986 ($1.50)

1-Ordway-c(p) 3.00

VAMPI (Vampirella's...)
Harris Publications (Anarchy Studios): Aug, 2000 - No. 25, Feb, 2003 ($2.95/$2.99)

Limited Edition Preview Book (5/00) Preview pages & sketchbook 3.00
1-(8/00, $2.95) Lau-a(p)/Conway-s 4.00
1-Platinum Edition 20.00
2-25: 17-Barberi-a 3.00
2-25-Deluxe Edition variants ($9.95): 4-Finch-c. 5-Wieringo-c. 6-Cha-c 10.00
...Digital 1 (11/01, $2.95) CGI art; Haberlin-s 3.00
...Digital Preview (Anarchy Studios, 7/01, $2.95) preview of CGI art 3.00
Switchblade Kiss HC (2001, $24.95) r/#1-6 25.00
Vicious Preview Ed. (Apr, 2003, $1.99) Flip book w/ Xin: Journey of the Monkey King Preview Ed. 3.00
Wizard #1/2 (mail order, $9.95) includes sketch pages 10.00

VAMPIRE BITES
Brainstorm Comics: May, 1995 - No. 2, Sept, 1996 ($2.95, B&W)

1,2:1-Color pin-up 3.00

VAMPIRE LESTAT, THE
Innovation Publishing: Jan, 1990 - No. 12, 1991 ($2.50, painted limited series)

1-Adapts novel; Bolton painted-c on all 2 4 6 10 14 18
1-2nd printing (has UPC code, 1st prints don't) 3.00
1-3rd & 4th printings 3.00
2-1st printing 1 2 3 5 6 8
2-2nd & 3rd printings 3.00
3-5 5.00
3-6,9-2nd printings 3.00
6-12 4.00

VAMPIRELLA (Magazine)(See Warren Presents)
Warren Publishing Co./Harris Publications #113: Sept, 1969 - No. 112, Feb, 1983; No. 113, Jan, 1988? (B&W)

1-Intro. Vampirella in original costume & wings; Frazetta-c/intro. page; Adams-a; Crandall-a 45 90 135 360 730 1100
2-1st app. Vampirella's cousin Evily-c/s; 1st/only app. Draculina, Vampirella's blonde twin sister 15 30 45 106 216 325
3 (Low distribution) 38 76 114 304 602 900
4,6 12 24 36 82 154 225
5,7,9: 5,7-Frazetta-c. 9-Barry Smith-a; Boris/Wood-c 12 24 36 87 164 240
8-Vampirella begins by Tom Sutton as serious strip (early issues-gag line) 13 26 39 89 170 250
10-No Vampi story; Brunner, Adams, Wood-a 8 16 24 56 93 130
11-Origin & 1st app. Pendragon; Frazetta-c 9 18 27 63 107 150
12-Vampi by Gonzales begins 9 18 27 63 107 150
13-15: 14-1st Maroto-a; Ploog-a 9 18 27 60 100 140
16,22,25: 16-1st full Dracula-c/app. 22-Color insert preview of Maroto's Dracula. 25-Vampi on cocaine-s 8 16 24 58 97 135
17,18,20,21,23,24: 17-Tomb of the Gods begins by Maroto, ends #22. 18-22-Dracula-s 8 16 24 54 90 125
19 (1973 Annual) Creation of Vampi text bio 9 18 27 64 110 155
26,28,34,35,39,40: All have 8 pg. color inserts. 28-Board game inside covers. 34,35-1st Fleur the Witch Woman. 39,40-Color Dracula-s. 40-Wrightson bio 6 12 18 41 66 90
27 (1974 Annual) New color Vampi-s; mostly-r 7 14 21 47 76 105
29,38,45: 38-2nd Vampi as Cleopatra/Blood Red Queen of Hearts; 1st Mayo-a. 6 12 18 39 62 85
30-32: 30-Intro. Pantha; Corben-a(color). 31-Origin Luana, the Beast Girl. 32-Jones-a 6 12 18 41 66 90
33-Wrightson-a; Pantha ends 6 12 18 41 66 90
36,37: 36-1st Vampi as Cleopatra/Blood Red Queen of Hearts; issue has 8 pg. color insert. 37-(1975 Annual) 6 12 18 43 69 95
41-44,47,48: 41-Dracula-s 5 10 15 35 55 75
46-(10/75) Origin-r from Annual 1 6 12 18 37 59 80
49-1st Blind Priestess; The Blood Red Queen of Hearts storyline begins; Poe-s 5 10 15 35 55 75
50-Spirit cameo by Eisner; 40 pg. Vampi-s; Pantha & Fleur app.; Jones-a 5 10 15 35 55 75
51-53,56,57,59-62,65,66,68,75,79,80,82-86,88,89: 60-62,65,66-The Blood Red Queen of Hearts app. 60-1st Blind Priestess-c 4 8 12 26 41 55
54,55,63,81,87: 54-Vampi-s (42 pgs.); 8 pg. color Corben-a. 55-All Gonzales-a(r). 63-10 pgs. Wrightson-a 4 8 12 26 41 55
58,70,72: 58-(92 pgs.) 70-Rook app. 5 10 15 30 48 65
64,73: 64-(100 pg. Giant) All Mayo-a; 70 pg. Vampi-s. 73-69 pg. Vampi-s; Mayo-a 5 10 15 32 51 70
67,69,71,74,76-78-All Barbara Leigh photo-c 5 10 15 30 48 65
90-99: 90-Toth-a. 91-All-r; Gonzales-a. 93-Cassandra St. Knight begins, ends #103; new Pantha series begins, ends #108 4 8 12 26 41 55
100 (96 pg. r-special)-Origin reprinted from Ann. 1; mostly reprints; Vampirella appears topless in new 21 pg. story 8 16 24 58 97 135
101-104,106,107: All lower print run. 101,102-The Blood Red Queen of Hearts app. 107-All Maroto reprint-a issue 6 12 18 43 69 95
105,108-110: 108-Torpedo series by Toth begins; Vampi nudity splash page. 110-(100 pg. Summer Spectacular) 6 12 18 43 69 95
111,112: Low print run. 111-Giant Collector's Edition ($2.50) 112-(84 pgs.) last Warren issue 8 16 24 54 90 125
113 (1988)-1st Harris Issue; very low print run 25 50 75 183 367 550
Annual 1(1972)-New definitive origin of Vampirella by Gonzales; reprints by Neal Adams (from #1), Wood (from #9) 25 50 75 183 367 550
Special 1 (1977) Softcover (color, large-square bound)-Only available thru mail order 15 30 45 104 212 320
Special 1 (1977) Hardcover (color, large-square bound)-Only available through mail order (scarce)(500 produced, signed & #'d) 32 64 96 249 495 740
#1 1969 Commemorative Edition (2001, $4.95) reprints entire #1 5.00
...Crimson Chronicles Vol. 1 (2004, $19.95, TPB) reprints stories from #1-10 20.00
...Crimson Chronicles Vol. 2 (2005, $19.95, TPB) reprints stories from #11-18 20.00
...Crimson Chronicles Vol. 3 (2005, $19.95, TPB) reprints stories from #19-28 20.00
...Crimson Chronicles Vol. 4 (2006, $19.95, TPB) reprints stories from #29-41 20.00

NOTE: ***Ackerman*** *s-1-3.* ***Neal Adams*** *a-1, 10p, 19p(r/#10), 44(1 pg.), Annual 1.* ***Alcala*** *a-78, 90, 93i.* ***Bodé/Todd*** *c-3.* ***Bodé/Jones*** *c-4.* ***Boris/Wood*** *c-9.* ***Brunner*** *a-10, 12(1 pg.).* ***Corben*** *a-30, 31, 33, 36, 54; c-30, 31, 33, 54.* ***Crandall*** *a-1, 19(r/#1).* ***Frazetta*** *c-1, 5, 7, 11, 31.* ***Heath*** *a-58, 61, 67, 76-78, 83.* ***Infantino*** *a-57-62.* ***Jones*** *a-5, 9, 12, 27, 32 (color), 33(2 pg.), 34, 50i, 83r.* ***Ken Kelly*** *c-6, 38, 39, 40(back-c), 46, 70, 95.* ***Nebres*** *a-84, 88-90, 92-96.* ***Nino*** *a-59i, 61i, 67, 76, 85, 90.* ***Ploog*** *a-14.* ***Barry Smith*** *a-9.* ***Starlin*** *a-78.* ***Sutton*** *a-1-5, 7-11, Annual 1.* ***Toth*** *a-90i, 108, 110.* ***Wood*** *a-9, 10, 12, 19(r/#12), 27r, Annual 1; c-9(partial).* ***Wrightson*** *a-33(w/****Jones****), 40(Bio cameo) 63r. All reprint issues-19, 74, 83, 91, 105, 107, 109, 111. Annuals from 1973 on are included in regular numbering. Later annuals are same format as regular issues. Color inserts (8 pgs.) in 22, 25-28, 30-35, 39, 40, 45, 46, 49, 54, 55, 67, 72. 16 pg color insert in #36.*

VAMPIRELLA (Also see Cain/... & Vengeance of...)
Harris Publications: Nov, 1992 - No. 5, Nov, 1993 ($2.95)

0-Bagged 5.00
0-Gold 3 6 9 16 23 30
1-Jim Balent inks in #1-3; Adam Hughes c-1-3 2 4 6 11 16 20
1-2nd printing 5.00
1-(11/97) Commemorative Edition 4.00
2 2 4 6 9 12 15
3-5: 4-Snyder III-c. 5-Brereton painted-c 1 2 3 5 6 8
Trade paperback nn (10/93, $5.95)-r/#1-4; Jusko-c 1 2 3 4 5 7

NOTE: *Issues 1-5 contain certificates for free* ***Dave Stevens*** *Vampirella poster.*

Vampirella (The New Monthly) #9 © Harris

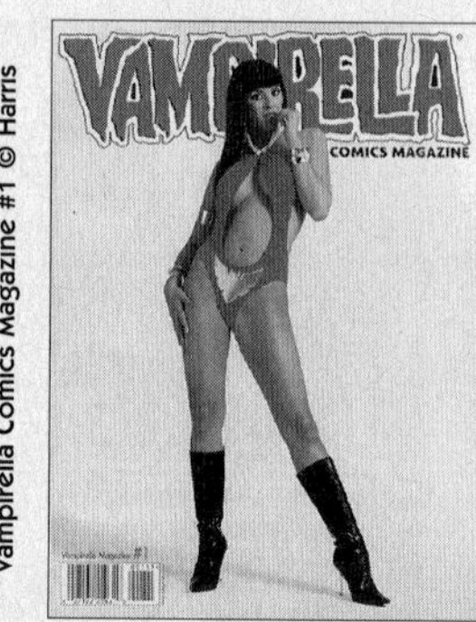

Vampirella Comics Magazine #1 © Harris

Vampirella/Painkiller Jane #1 © Harris

GD 2.0 | VG 4.0 | FN 6.0 | VF 8.0 | VF/NM 9.0 | NM- 9.2

VAMPIRELLA (THE NEW MONTHLY)
Harris Publications: Nov, 1997 - No. 26, Apr, 2000 ($2.95)

1-3-"Ascending Evil" -Morrison & Millar-s/Conner & Palmiotti-a. 1-Three covers by Quesada/Palmiotti, Conner, and Conner/Palmiotti 4.00
1-3-($9.95) Jae Lee variant covers 10.00
1-($24.95) Platinum Ed.w/Quesada-c 25.00
4-6-"Holy War"-Small & Stull-a, 4-Linsner variant-c 4.00
7-9-"Queen's Gambit"-Shi app. 7-Two covers. 8-Pantha-c/app. 4.00
7-($9.95) Conner variant-c 10.00
10-12-"Hell on Earth"; Small-a/Coney-s. 12-New costume 4.00
10-Jae Lee variant-c 1 3 4 6 8 10
13-15-"World's End" Zircher-p; Pantha back-up, Texeira-a 4.00
16,17: 16-Pantha-c;Texeira-a; Vampi back-up story. 17-(Pantha #2) 4.00
18-20-"Rebirth": Jae Lee-c on all. 18-Loeb-s/Sale-a. 19-Alan Davis-a. 20-Bruce Timm-a 4.00
18-20-($9.95) Variant covers: 18-Sale. 19-Davis. 20-Timm 12.00
21-26: 21,22-Dangerous Games; Small-a. 23-Lady Death-c/app.; Cleavenger-a. 24,25-Lau-a. 26-Lady Death & Pantha-c/app.; Cleavenger-a. 4.00
0-(1/99) also variant-c with Pantha #0; same contents 4.00
TPB ($7.50) r/#1-3 "Ascending Evil" 8.00
Ascending Evil Ashcan (8/97, $1.00) 3.00
...: Grant Morrison/Mark Millar Collection TPB (2006, $24.95) r/#1-6; interviews 25.00
Hell on Earth Ashcan (7/98, $1.00) 3.00
... Presents: Tales of Pantha TPB (2006, $19.95) r/stories from #13-17 & one-shots 20.00
The End Ashcan (3/00, $6.00) 6.00
...30th Anniversary Celebration Preview (7/99) B&W preview of #18-20 10.00

VAMPIRELLA
Harris Publications: June, 2001 - No. 22, Aug, 2003 ($2.95/$2.99)

1-Four covers (Mayhew w/foil logo, Campbell, Anacleto, Jae Lee) Mayhew-a; Mark Millar-s 4.00
2-22: 2-Two covers (Mayhew & Chiodo). 3-Timm var-c. 4-Horn var-c. 7-10-Dawn Brown-a; Pantha back-up w/Texeira-a. 15-22-Conner-c 3.00
Giant-Size Ashcan (5/01, $5.95) B&W preview art and Mayhew interview 6.00
...: Halloween Trick & Treat (10/04, $4.95) stories & art by various; three covers 5.00
... : Nowheresville Preview Edition (3/01, $2.95)- previews Mayhew art and photo models 3.00
...Nowheresville TPB (1/02, $12.95) r/#1-3 with cover gallery 13.00
... Summer Special #1 (2005, $5.95) Batman Begins photo-c and 2 variant-c 6.00
...: 2006 Halloween Special (2006, $2.95) Conner-c; Hester-s/Segovia-a; 4 covers 3.00

VAMPIRELLA
Dynamite Entertainment: 2010 - Present ($3.99)

1-Four covers (Campbell, Madureira, J. Djurdjevic, Alex Ross swipe of Frazetta's #1) 4.00
1-Variant-c of blood-soaked Vampirella by Alex Ross 8.00
2-4-Trautmann-s/Wagner Reis-a; four covers 4.00

VAMPIRELLA & PANTHA SHOWCASE
Harris Publications: Jan, 1997 ($1.50, one-shot)

1-Millar-s/Texeira-c/a; flip book w/"Blood Lust"; Robinson-s/Jusko-c/a 4.00

VAMPIRELLA & THE BLOOD RED QUEEN OF HEARTS
Harris Publications: Sept, 1996 ($9.95, 96 pgs., B&W, squarebound, one-shot)

nn-r/Vampirella #49,60-62,65,66,101,102; John Bolton-c; Michael Bair back-c 1 3 4 6 8 10

VAMPIRELLA: BLOODLUST
Harris Publications: July, 1997 - No. 2, Aug, 1997 ($4.95, limited series)

1,2-Robinson-s/Jusko-painted c/a 5.00

VAMPIRELLA CLASSIC
Harris Publications: Feb, 1995 - No. 5, Nov, 1995 ($2.95, limited series)

1-5: Reprints Archie Goodwin stories. 4.00

VAMPIRELLA COMICS MAGAZINE
Harris Publications: Oct, 2003 - No. 9 ($3.95/$9.95, magazine-sized)

1-9-($3.95) 1-Texiera-c; b&w and color stories, Alan Moore interview; reviews. 2-KISS interview. 4-Chiodo-c. 6-Brereton-c 4.00
1-9-($9.95) 1-Three covers (Model Photo cover, Palmiotti-c, Wheatley Frankenstein-c) 10.00

VAMPIRELLA: CROSSOVER GALLERY
Harris Publications: Sept, 1997 ($2.95, one-shot)

1-Wraparound-c by Campbell, pinups by Jae Lee, Mack, Allred, Art Adams, Quesada & Palmiotti and others 4.00

VAMPIRELLA: DEATH & DESTRUCTION
Harris Publications: July, 1996 - No. 3, Sept, 1996 ($2.95, limited series)

1-3: Amanda Conner-a(p) in all. 1-Tucci-c. 2-Hughes-c. 3-Jusko-c 4.00
1-($9.95)-Limited Edition; Beachum-c 10.00

GD 2.0 | VG 4.0 | FN 6.0 | VF 8.0 | VF/NM 9.0 | NM- 9.2

VAMPIRELLA/DRACULA & PANTHA SHOWCASE
Harris Publications: Aug, 1997 ($1.50, one-shot)

1-Ellis, Robinson, and Moore-s; flip book w/"Pantha" 4.00

VAMPIRELLA/DRACULA: THE CENTENNIAL
Harris Publications: Oct, 1997 ($5.95, one-shot)

1-Ellis, Robinson, and Moore-s; Beachum, Frank/Smith, and Mack/Mays-a Bolton-painted-c 6.00

VAMPIRELLA: INTIMATE VISIONS
Harris Publications: 2006 ($3.95, one-shots)

..., Amanda Conner 1 - r/Vampirella Monthly #1 with commentary; interview; 2 covers 4.00
..., Joe Jusko 1 - r/Vampirella; Blood Lust #1 with commentary; interview; 2 covers 4.00

VAMPIRELLA: JULIE STRAIN SPECIAL
Harris Publications: Sept, 2000 ($3.95, one-shot)

1-Photo-c w/yellow background; interview and photo gallery 4.00
1-Limited Edition ($9.95); cover photo w/black background 10.00

VAMPIRELLA/LADY DEATH (Also see Lady Death/Vampirella)
Harris Publications: Feb, 1999 ($3.50, one-shot)

1-Small-a/Nelson painted-c 4.00
1-Valentine Edition ($9.95); pencil-c by Small 10.00

VAMPIRELLA: LEGENDARY TALES
Harris Publications: May, 2000 - No. 2, June, 2000 ($2.95, B&W)

1,2-Reprints from magazine; Cleavenger painted-c 3.00
1,2-($9.95) Variant painted-c by Mike Mayhew 10.00

VAMPIRELLA LIVES
Harris Publications: Dec, 1996 - No. 3, Feb, 1997 ($3.50/$2.95, limited series)

1-Die cut-c; Quesada & Palmiotti-c, Ellis-s/Conner-a 4.00
1-Deluxe Ed.-photo-c 4.00
2,3-($2.95)-Two editions (1 photo-c): 3-J. Scott Campbell-c 4.00

VAMPIRELLA: MORNING IN AMERICA
Harris Publications/Dark Horse Comics: 1991 - No. 4, 1992 ($3.95, B&W, lim. series, 52 pgs.)

1,2-All have Kaluta painted-c 1 2 3 5 6 8
3,4 1 3 4 6 8 10

VAMPIRELLA OF DRAKULON
Harris Publications: Jan, 1996 - No. 5, Sept, 1996 ($2.95)

0-5: All reprints. 0-Jim Silke-c. 3-Polybagged w/card. 4-Texeira-c 4.00

VAMPIRELLA/PAINKILLER JANE
Harris Publications: May, 1998 ($3.50, one-shot)

1-Waid & Augustyn-s/Leonardi & Palmiotti-a 4.00
1-($9.95) Variant-c 10.00

VAMPIRELLA PIN-UP SPECIAL
Harris Publications: Oct, 1995 ($2.95, one-shot)

1-Hughes-c, pin-ups by various 5.00
1-Variant-c 5.00

VAMPIRELLA QUARTERLY
Harris Publications: Spring, 2007 - Summer, 2008 ($4.95/$4.99, quarterly)

Spring, 2007 - Summer, 2008-New stories and re-colored reprints; five or six covers 5.00

VAMPIRELLA: RETRO
Harris Publications: Mar, 1998 - No. 3, May, 1998 ($2.50, B&W, limited series)

1-3: Reprints; Silke painted covers 4.00

VAMPIRELLA: REVELATIONS
Harris Publications: No. 0, Oct, 2005 - No. 3, Feb, 2006 ($2.99, limited series)

0-3-Vampirella's origin retold, Lilith app.; Carey-s/Lilly-a; two covers on each 4.00
... Book 1 TPB (2006, $12.95) r/series; Carey interview, script for #1, Lilly sketch pages 13.00

VAMPIRELLA: SAD WINGS OF DESTINY
Harris Publications: Sept, 1996 ($3.95, one-shot)

1-Jusko-c 5.00

VAMPIRELLA: SECOND COMING
Harris Publications: 2009 - No. 4 ($1.99, limited series)

1-4: 1-Hester-s/Sampere-a; multiple covers on each. 3,4-Rio-a 3.00

VAMPIRELLA/SHADOWHAWK: CREATURES OF THE NIGHT (Also see Shadowhawk)
Harris Publications: 1995 ($4.95, one-shot)

1 5.00

VAMPIRELLA/SHI (See Shi/Vampirella)

Vampire, PA #1 © Vaughn & Solof

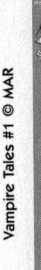

Vampire Tales #1 © MAR

Vault of Evil #2 © MAR

	GD 2.0	VG 4.0	FN 6.0	VF 8.0	VF/NM 9.0	NM- 9.2

Harris Publications: Oct, 1997 ($2.95, one-shot)

1-Ellis-s 4.00
1-Chromium-c 6.00

VAMPIRELLA: SILVER ANNIVERSARY COLLECTION
Harris Publications: Jan, 1997 - No. 4 Apr, 1997 ($2.50, limited series)

1-4: Two editions: Bad Girl by Beachum, Good Girl by Silke 4.00

VAMPIRELLA'S SUMMER NIGHTS
Harris Publications: 1992 (one-shot)

	GD	VG	FN	VF	VF/NM	NM-
1-Art Adams infinity cover; centerfold by Stelfreeze	3	7	10	19	27	35

VAMPIRELLA STRIKES
Harris Publications: Sept, 1995 - No. 8, Dec, 1996 ($2.95, limited series)

1-8: 1-Photo-c. 2-Deodato-c; polybagged w/card. 5-Eudaemon-c/app; wraparound-c; alternate-c exists. 6-(6/96)-Mark Millar script; Texeira-c; alternate-c exists. 7-Flip book 4.00
1-Newsstand Edition; diff. photo-c., 1-Limited Ed.; diff. photo-c 4.00
Annual 1-(12/96, $2.95) Delano-s; two covers 4.00

VAMPIRELLA: 25TH ANNIVERSARY SPECIAL
Harris Publications: Oct, 1996 ($5.95, squarebound, one-shot)

nn-Reintro The Blood Red Queen of Hearts; James Robinson, Grant Morrison & Warren Ellis scripts; Mark Texeira, Michael Bair & Amanda Conner-a(p); Frank Frazetta-c 7.00
nn-($6.95)-Silver Edition 8.00

VAMPIRELLA VS. HEMORRHAGE
Harris Publications: Apr, 1997($3.50)

1 4.00

VAMPIRELLA VS. PANTHA
Harris Publications: Mar, 1997 ($3.50)

1-Two covers; Millar-s/Texeira-c/a 4.00

VAMPIRELLA/WETWORKS (See Wetworks/Vampirella)
Harris Publications: June, 1997 ($2.95, one-shot)

1 3.00
1-($9.95) Alternate Edition; cardstock-c 10.00

VAMPIRELLA/WITCHBLADE
Harris Publications: 2003; Oct, 2004; Oct, 2005 ($2.99, one-shots)

1-Brian Wood-s/Steve Pugh-a; 3 covers by Texeira, Conner and Pugh 3.00
...: The Feast (10/05, $2.99) Joyce Chin-a; covers by Chin, Conner, Rodriguez 3.00
...: Union of the Damned (10/04, $2.99, one-shot) Sharp-a; three covers 3.00
Trilogy TPB (2006, $12.95) r/one-shots; art gallery and gallery of multiple covers 13.00

VAMPIRE, PA
Moonstone: 2010 - No. 3, Oct, 2010 ($3.99)

1-3: 1-Intro. Vampire Hunter Dean; J.C. Vaughn-s/Brendon & Brian Fraim-a; three covers. 3-Zombie Proof back-up; Spencer-a 4.00

VAMPIRE'S CHRISTMAS, THE (Also see Dark Ivory)
Image Comics: Oct, 2003 ($5.95, over-sized graphic novel)

nn-Linsner-s/a; Dubisch-painted-a 6.00

VAMPIRE TALES
Marvel Comics Group: Aug, 1973 - No. 11, June, 1975 (75¢, B&W, magazine)

	GD	VG	FN	VF	VF/NM	NM-
1-Morbius, the Living Vampire begins by Pablo Marcos (1st solo Morbius series & 5th Morbius app.)	7	14	21	49	80	110
2-Intro. Satana; Steranko-r	5	10	15	32	57	70
3,5,6: 3-Satana app. 5-Origin Morbius. 6-1st Lilith app. in this title (see Giant-Size Chillers #1 for debut)	4	8	12	28	44	60
4,7	4	8	12	22	34	45
8-1st solo Blade story (see Tomb of Dracula)	5	10	15	32	51	70
9-Blade app.	4	8	12	28	44	60
10,11	4	8	12	22	34	45
Annual 1(10/75)-Heath-r/#9	4	8	12	22	34	45

NOTE: ***Alcala** a-6, 8, 9i. **Boris** c-4, 6. **Chaykin** a-7. **Everett** a-1r. **Gulacy** a-7p. **Heath** a-9. **Infantino** a-3r. **Gil Kane** a-4, 5r.*

VAMPIRE VERSES, THE
CFD Productions: Aug, 1995 - No. 4, 1995 ($2.95, B&W, mature)

1-4 3.00

VAMPI VICIOUS
Harris Publications (Anarchy Studios): Aug, 2003 - No. 3, Nov, 2003 ($2.99)

1-3: 1-McKeever-s/Dogan-a; 3 covers by Dogan, Lau & Noto. 3-Kau-a 3.00

VAMPI VICIOUS CIRCLE
Harris Publications (Anarchy Studios): Jun, 2004 - No. 3, Sept, 2004 ($2.99/$9.95)

1-3: B. Clay Moore-s 3.00
1-3-($9.95) Limited Edition w/variant-c. 1-Noto-c. 2-Norton-c. 3-Lucas-c 10.00

VAMPI VICIOUS RAMPAGE
Harris Publications (Anarchy Studios): Feb, 2005 - No. 2, Apr, 2005 ($2.99)

1,2: Raab-s/Lau-a; two covers on each 3.00

VAMPI VS. XIN
Harris Publications (Anarchy Studios): Oct, 2004 - No. 2, Jan, 2005 ($2.99)

1,2-Faerber-s/Lau-a; two covers 3.00

VAMPS
DC Comics (Vertigo): Aug, 1994 - No. 6, Jan, 1995 ($1.95, lim. series, mature)

1-6-Bolland-c 3.00
Trade paperback ($9.95)-r/#1-6 10.00

VAMPS: HOLLYWOOD & VEIN
DC Comics (Vertigo): Feb, 1996 - No. 6, July, 1996 ($2.25, lim. series, mature)

1-6: Winslade-c 3.00

VAMPS: PUMPKIN TIME
DC Comics (Vertigo): Dec, 1998 - No. 3, Feb, 1999 ($2.50, lim. series, mature)

1-3: Quitely-c 3.00

VANGUARD (...Outpost: Earth) (See Megaton)
Megaton Comics: 1987 ($1.50)

1-Erik Larsen-c(p) 4.00

VANGUARD (See Savage Dragon #2)
Image Comics (Highbrow Entertainment): Oct, 1993 - No. 6, 1994 ($1.95)

1-6: 1-Wraparound gatefold-c; Erik Larsen back-up-a; Supreme x-over. 3-(12/93)-Indicia says December 1994. 4-Berzerker back-up. 5-Angel Medina-a(p) 3.00

VANGUARD (See Savage Dragon #2)
Image Comics: Aug, 1996 - No. 4, Feb, 1997 ($2.95, B&W, limited series)

1-4 3.00

VANGUARD: ETHEREAL WARRIORS
Image Comics: Aug, 2000 ($5.95, B&W)

1-Fosco & Larsen-a 6.00

VANGUARD ILLUSTRATED
Pacific Comics: Nov, 1983 - No. 11, Oct, 1984 (Baxter paper)(Direct sales only)

1,3-6,8-11: 1-Nudity scenes 3.00
2-1st app. Stargrazers (see Legends of the Stargrazers; Dave Stevens-c 5.00
7-1st app. Mr. Monster (r-in Mr. Monster #1); nudity scenes 5.00

NOTE: ***Evans** a-7. **Kaluta** c-5, 7p. **Perez** a-6; c-6. **Rude** a-1-4; c-4. **Williamson** c-3.*

VANGUARD: STRANGE VISITORS
Image Comics: Oct, 1996 - No.4, Feb, 1997 ($2.95, B&W, limited series)

1-4: 3-Supreme-c/app. 3.00

VAN HELSING: FROM BENEATH THE RUE MORGUE (Based on the 2004 movie)
Dark Horse Comics: Apr, 2004 ($2.99, one-shot)

1-Hugh Jackman photo-c; Dysart-s/Alexander-a 3.00

VANITY (See Pacific Presents #3)
Pacific Comics: Jun, 1984 - No. 2, Aug, 1984 ($1.50, direct sales)

1,2: Origin 2.50

VARIETY COMICS (The Spice of Comics)
Rural Home Publ./Croyden Publ. Co.: 1944 - No. 2, 1945; No. 3, 1946

	GD	VG	FN	VF	VF/NM	NM-
1-Origin Captain Valiant	21	42	63	122	199	275
2-Captain Valiant	14	28	42	80	115	150
3(1946-Croyden)-Captain Valiant	12	24	36	69	97	125

VARIETY COMICS (See Fox Giants)

VARSITY
Parents' Magazine Institute: 1945

	GD	VG	FN	VF	VF/NM	NM-
1	8	16	24	44	57	70

VAULT OF EVIL
Marvel Comics Group: Feb, 1973 - No. 23, Nov, 1975

	GD	VG	FN	VF	VF/NM	NM-
1 (1950s reprints begin)	3	6	9	18	27	35
2-23: 3,4-Brunner-c. 11-Kirby-a	2	4	6	13	18	22

NOTE: ***Ditko** a-14r, 15r, 20-22r. **Drucker** a-10r(Mystic #52), 13r(Uncanny Tales #42). **Everett** a-11r(Menace #2), 13r(Menace #4); c-10. **Heath** a-5r. **Gil Kane** c-1, 6. **Kirby** a-11. **Krigstein** a-20r(Uncanny Tales #54). **Reinman** r-1. **Tuska** a-6r.*

VAULT OF HORROR (Formerly War Against Crime #1-11) (Also see EC Archives)
E. C. Comics: No. 12, Apr-May, 1950 - No. 40, Dec-Jan, 1954-55

The Vault of Horror #15 © WMG

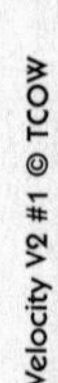

Velocity V2 #1 © TCOW

Venom (2011 series) #1 © MAR

GD 2.0 | VG 4.0 | FN 6.0 | VF 8.0 | VF/NM 9.0 | NM- 9.2

12 (Scarce)-ties w/Crypt Of Terror as 1st horror comic 497 994 1491 3976 6338 8700
13-Morphine story 101 202 303 808 1292 1775
14 89 178 267 712 1131 1550
15- "Terror in the Swamp" is same story w/minor changes as "The Thing in the Swamp" from Haunt of Fear #15 77 154 231 616 983 1350
16 59 118 177 472 749 1025
17-Classic werewolf-c 69 138 207 552 876 1200
18,19 47 94 141 376 601 825
20-25: 22-Frankenstein-c & adaptation. 23-Used in **POP**, pg. 84; Davis-a(2); Ingels bio. 24-Craig bio. 40 80 120 320 510 700
26-B&W & color illos in **POP** 40 80 120 320 510 700
27-36: 30-Dismemberment-c. 31-Ray Bradbury biog. 32-Censored-c. 35-X-Mas-c. 36- "Pipe Dream" classic opium addict story by Krigstein; "Twin Bill" cited in articles by T.E. Murphy, Wertham 33 66 99 264 425 585
37-1st app. Drusilla, a Vampirella look alike; Williamson-a 34 68 102 272 436 600
38-39: 39-Bondage-c 33 66 99 264 425 575
40-Low distribution 40 80 120 320 510 700

NOTE: ***Craig*** *art in all but No. 13 & 33; c-12-40.* ***Crandall*** *a-33, 34, 39.* ***Davis*** *a-17-38.* ***Evans*** *a-27, 28, 30, 32, 33.* ***Feldstein*** *a-12-16.* ***Ingels*** *a-13-20, 22-40.* ***Kamen*** *a-15-22, 25, 29, 35.* ***Krigstein*** *a-36, 38-40.* ***Kurtzman*** *a-12, 13.* ***Orlando*** *a-24, 31, 40.* ***Wood*** *a-12-14. #22, 29 & 31 have Ray Bradbury adaptations. #16 & 17 have H. P. Lovecraft adaptations.*

VAULT OF HORROR, THE
Gladstone Publ.: Aug, 1990 - No. 6, June, 1991 ($1.95, 68 pgs.)(#4 on: $2.00)
1-Craig-c(r); all contain EC reprints 4.00
2-6: 2,4-6-Craig-c(r). 3-Ingels-c(r) 4.00

VAULT OF HORROR
Russ Cochran/Gemstone Publishing: Sept, 1991 - No. 5, May, 1992 ($2.00); Oct, 1992 - No. 29, Oct, 1999 ($1.50/$2.00/$2.50)
1-29: E.C reprints. 1-4r/VOH #12-15 w/original-c 4.00

V...-COMICS (Morse code for "V" - 3 dots, 1 dash)
Fox Features Syndicate: Jan, 1942 - No. 2, Mar-Apr, 1942
1-Origin V-Man & the Boys; The Banshee & The Black Fury, The Queen of Evil, & V-Agents begin; Nazi-c 129 258 387 826 1413 2000
2-Nazi bondage/torture-c 90 180 270 576 988 1400

VECTOR
Now Comics: 1986 - No. 4, 1986? ($1.50, 1st color comic by Now Comics)
1-4: Computer-generated art 3.00

VEILS
DC Comics (Vertigo): 1999 ($24.95, one-shot)
Hardcover-($24.95) Painted art and photography; McGreal-s 25.00
Softcover ($14.95) 15.00

VELOCITY (Also see Cyberforce)
Image Comics (Top Cow Productions): Nov, 1995 - No. 3, Jan, 1996 ($2.50, limited series)
1-3: Kurt Busiek scripts in all. 2-Savage Dragon-c/app. 3.00
...: Pilot Season 1 (10/07, $2.99) Casey-s/Maguire-a 3.00
Vol. 2 #1-3 (6/10 - No. 4, $3.99) Rocafort-a/Marz-s; multiple covers 4.00

VENGEANCE OF THE MOON KNIGHT
Marvel Comics: Nov, 2009 - Present ($3.99/$2.99)
1,9: 1-($3.99) Hurwitz-s/Opeña-a; covers by Yu, Ross & Finch; back-up r/Moon Knight #1 ('80) 9-Spider-Man & Sandman app.; Campbell-c 4.00
2-8,10: 2-Sentry app. 5-Spider-Man app. 7,8-Deadpool app. 10-Secret Avengers app. 3.00

VENGEANCE OF VAMPIRELLA (Becomes Vampirella: Death & Destruction)
Harris Comics: Apr, 1994 - No. 25, Apr, 1996 ($2.95)
1-($3.50)-Quesada/Palmiotti "bloodfoil" wraparound-c 1 2 3 5 6 8
1-2nd printing; blue foil-c 4.00
1-Gold 20.00
2-8: 8-Polybagged w/trading card 5.00
9-25: 10-w/coupon for Hyde -25 poster. 11,19-Polybagged w/ trading card. 25-Quesada & Palmiotti red foil-c 4.00
...: Bloodshed (1995, $6.95) 7.00

VENGEANCE OF VAMPIRELLA: THE MYSTERY WALK
Harris Comics: Nov, 1995 ($2.95, one-shot)
0 3.00

VENGEANCE SQUAD
Charlton Comics: July, 1975 - No. 6, May, 1976 (#1-3 are 25¢ issues)
1-Mike Mauser, Private Eye begins by Staton 2 4 6 8 11 14
2-6: Morisi-a in all 1 2 3 5 6 8
5,6 (Modern Comics-r, 1977) 4.00

VENOM
Marvel Comics: June, 2003 - No. 18, Nov, 2004 ($2.25)
1-7-Herrera-a/Way-s. 6,7-Wolverine app. 3.00
8-18-($2.99): 8-10-Wolverine-c/app.; Kieth-c. 11-Fantastic Four app. 3.00
... Vol. 1: Shiver (2004, $13.99, TPB) r/#1-5 14.00
... Vol. 2: Run (2004, $19.99, TPB) r/#6-13 20.00
... Vol. 3: Twist (2004, $13.99, TPB) r/#14-18 14.00

VENOM (See Amazing Spider-Man #654 & 654.1)
Marvel Comics: May, 2011 - Present ($3.99)
1-Flash Thompson with the symbiote; Remender-s/Tony Moore-a/Quesada-c 4.00

VENOM: Marvel Comics (Also see Amazing Spider-Man #298-300)
... ALONG CAME A SPIDER, 1/96 - No. 4, 4/96 ($2.95)-Spider-Man & Carnage app. 3.00
... CARNAGE UNLEASHED, 4/95 - No. 4, 7/95 ($2.95) 3.00
... DARK ORIGIN, 10/08 - No. 5, 2/09 ($2.99) 1-5-Medina-a 3.00
... /DEADPOOL: WHAT IF?, 4/11 ($2.99) Remender-s/Moll-a/Young-c; Galactus app. 3.00
... DEATHTRAP: THE VAULT, 3/93 ($6.95) r/Avengers: Deathtrap: The Vault 7.00
... FUNERAL PYRE, 8/93- No. 3, 10/93 ($2.95)-#1-Holo-grafx foil-c; Punisher app. in all 3.00

VENOM: LETHAL PROTECTOR
Marvel Comics: Feb, 1993 - No. 6, July, 1993 ($2.95, limited series)
1-Red holo-grafx foil-c; Bagley-c/a in all 5.00
1-Gold variant sold to retailers 15.00
1-Black-c (at least 58 copies have been authenticated by CGC since 2000) 9 18 27 63 107 150
NOTE: Counterfeit copies of the black-c exist and are valueless
2-6: Spider-Man app. in all 3.00
... LICENSE TO KILL,6/97 - No. 3, 8/97 ($1.95) 3.00
... NIGHTS OF VENGEANCE, 8/94 - No. 4, 11/94 ($2.95), #1-Red foil-c 3.00
... ON TRIAL, 3/97 - No. 3, 5/97 ($1.95) 3.00
... SEED OF DARKNESS, 7/97 ($1.95) #(-1) Flashback 3.00
... SEPARATION ANXIETY,12/94- No. 4, 3/95 ($2.95) #1-Embossed-c 3.00
... SIGN OF THE BOSS,3/97 - No. 2, 10/97 ($1.99) 3.00
... SINNER TAKES ALL, 8/95 - No. 5, 10/95 ($2.95) 3.00
... SUPER SPECIAL, 8/95($3.95) #1-Flip book 4.00
... THE ENEMY WITHIN, 2/94 - No. 3, 4/94 ($2.95)-Demogoblin & Morbius app. 1-Glow-in-the-dark-c 3.00
... THE FINALE, 11/97 - No. 3, 1/98 ($1.99) 3.00
... THE HUNGER, 8/96- No. 4, 11/96 ($1.95) 3.00
... THE HUNTED, 5/96-No. 3, 7/96 ($2.95) 3.00
... THE MACE, 5/94 - No. 3, 7/94 ($2.95)-#1-Embossed-c 3.00
... THE MADNESS, 11/93- No. 3, 1/94 ($2.95)-Kelley Jones-c/a(p). 1-Embossed-c; Juggernaut app. 3.00
... TOOTH AND CLAW, 12/96 - No. 3, 2/97 ($1.95)-Wolverine-c/app. 3.00
... VS. CARNAGE, 9/04 - No. 4, 12/04 ($2.99)-Milligan-s/Crain-a; Spider-Man app. 3.00
TPB (2004, $9.99) r/#1-4 10.00

VENTURE
AC Comics (Americomics): Aug, 1986 - No. 3, 1986? ($1.75)
1-3: 1-3-Bolt. 1-Astron. 2-Femforce. 3-Fazers 3.00

VENTURE
Image Comics: Jan, 2003 - No. 4, Sept, 2003 ($2.95)
1-4-Faerber-s/Igle-a 3.00

VENUS (See Agents of Atlas, Marvel Spotlight #2 & Weird Wonder Tales)
Marvel/Atlas Comics (CMC 1-9/LCC 10-19): Aug, 1948 - No. 19, Apr, 1952 (Also see Marvel Mystery #91)
1-Venus & Hedy Devine begin; 1st app. Venus; Kurtzman's "Hey Look" 161 322 483 1030 1765 2500
2 87 174 261 553 952 1350
3,5 61 122 183 390 670 950
4-Kurtzman's "Hey Look" 62 124 186 394 677 960
6-9: 6-Loki app. 7,8-Painted-c. 9-Begin 52 pgs.; book-length feature "Whom the Gods Destroy!" 53 106 159 334 567 800
10-S/F-horror issues begin (7/50) 81 162 243 518 884 1250

Veronica #202 © AP

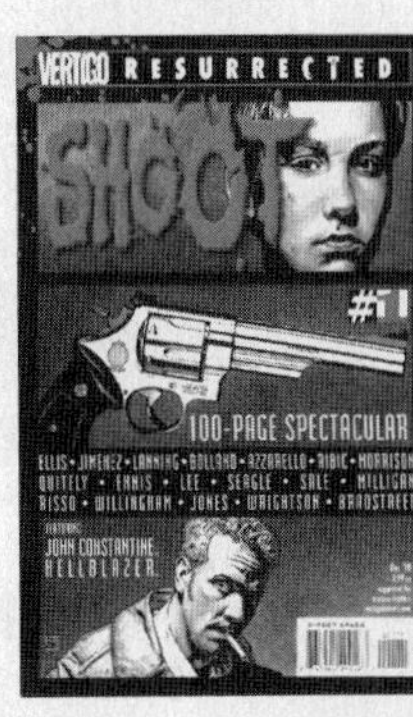

Vertigo Resurrected: Shoot #1 © DC

Vertigo Winter's Edge #1 © DC

GD 2.0 | VG 4.0 | FN 6.0 | VF 8.0 | VF/NM 9.0 | NM- 9.2

11-S/F end of the world (11/50) 90 180 270 576 988 1400
12-Colan-a 50 100 150 315 533 750
13-16-Venus by Everett, 2-3 stories each; covers-#13,15,16; 14-Everett part cover (Venus).
90 180 270 576 988 1400
17-19-Classic Everett horror & skull covers; Venus app. 17-Bondage-c (scarce)
181 362 543 1158 1979 2800

NOTE: ***Berg*** *s/f story-13.* ***Everett*** *c-13, 14(part; Venus only), 15-19.* ***Heath*** *s/f story-11.* ***Maneely*** *s/f story 10(3pg.), 16.* ***Morisi*** *a-19.* ***Syd Shores*** *c-6.*

VERI BEST SURE FIRE COMICS
Holyoke Publishing Co.: No date (circa 1945) (Reprints Holyoke one-shots)

1-Captain Aero, Alias X, Miss Victory, Commandos of the Devil Dogs, Red Cross, Hammerhead Hawley, Capt. Aero's Sky Scouts, Flagman app.; same-c as Veri Best Sure Shot #1 39 78 117 240 395 550

VERI BEST SURE SHOT COMICS
Holyoke Publishing Co.: No date (circa 1945) (Reprints Holyoke one-shots)

1-Capt. Aero, Miss Victory by Quinlan, Alias X, The Red Cross, Flagman, Commandos of the Devil Dogs, Hammerhead Hawley, Capt. Aero's Sky Scouts; same-c as Veri Best Sure Fire #1 39 78 117 240 395 550

VERMILLION
DC Comics (Helix): Oct, 1996 - No. 12, Sept, 1997 ($2.25/$2.50)

1-12: 1-4: Lucius Shepard scripts. 4,12-Kaluta-c 3.00

VERONICA (Also see Archie's Girls, Betty &...)
Archie Comics: Apr, 1989 - Present

1-(75¢-c) 7.00
2-10: 2-(75¢-c) 4.50
11-38 3.50
39-Love Showdown pt. 4, Cheryl Blossom 5.50
40-70: 34-Neon ink-c 3.00
71-201,203-206: 134-Begin $2.19-c. 152,155-Cheryl Blossom app. 163-Begin $2.25-c 3.00
202-Intro. Kevin Keller; cover has blue backgound 8.00
202-Second printing; cover has black backgound 5.00

VERONICA'S PASSPORT DIGEST MAGAZINE (Becomes Veronica's Digest Magazine #3 on)
Archie Comics: Nov, 1992 - No. 6 ($1.50/$1.79, digest size)

1 5.00
2-6 3.00

VERONICA'S SUMMER SPECIAL (See Archie Giant Series Magazine #615, 625)

VERTICAL
DC Comics (Vertigo): 2003 ($4.95, 3-1/4" wide pages, one-shot)

1-Seagle-s/Allred & Bond-a; odd format 1/2 width pages with some 20" long spreads 5.00

VERTIGO DOUBLE SHOT
DC Comics (Vertigo): 2008 ($2.99)

1-Reprints House of Mystery (2008) #1 and Young Liars #1 in flip-book format 3.00

VERTIGO: FIRST CUT
DC Comics (Vertigo): 2008 ($4.99, TPB)

TPB-Reprints first issues of DMZ, Army@Love, Jack of Fables, Exterminators, Scalped, Crossing Midnight, and Loveless; preview of Air 5.00

VERTIGO: FIRST OFFENSES
DC Comics (Vertigo): 2005 ($4.99, TPB)

TPB-Reprints first issues of The Invisibles, Preacher, Fables, Sandman Mystery Theater, and Lucifer 5.00

VERTIGO: FIRST TASTE
DC Comics (Vertigo): 2005 ($4.99, TPB)

TPB-Reprints first issues of Y: The Last Man, 100 Bullets, Transmetropolitan, Books of Magick: Life During Wartime, Death: The High Cost of Living, and Saga of the Swamp Thing #21 (Alan Moore's first story on that title) 5.00

VERTIGO GALLERY, THE: DREAMS AND NIGHTMARES
DC Comics (Vertigo): 1995 ($3.50, one-shot)

1-Pin-ups of Vertigo characters by Sienkiewicz, Toth, Van Fleet & others; McKean-c 4.00

VERTIGO JAM
DC Comics (Vertigo): Aug, 1993 ($3.95, one-shot, 68 pgs.)(Painted-c by Fabry)

1-Sandman by Neil Gaiman, Hellblazer, Animal Man, Doom Patrol, Swamp Thing, Kid Eternity & Shade the Changing Man 5.00

VERTIGO POP! BANGKOK
DC Comics (Vertigo): July, 2003 - No. 4, Oct, 2003 ($2.95, limited series)

1-4-Camuncoli-c/a; Jonathan Vankin-s 3.00

GD 2.0 | VG 4.0 | FN 6.0 | VF 8.0 | VF/NM 9.0 | NM- 9.2

VERTIGO POP! LONDON
DC Comics (Vertigo): Jan, 2003 - No. 4, Apr, 2003 ($2.95, limited series)

1-4-Philip Bond-c/a; Peter Milligan-s 3.00

VERTIGO POP! TOKYO
DC Comics (Vertigo): Sept, 2002 - No. 4, Dec, 2002 ($2.95, limited series)

1-4-Seth Fisher-c/a; Jonathan Vankin-s 3.00
Tokyo Days, Bangkok Nights TPB (2009, $19.99) r/#1-4 & Vertogo Pop! Bangkok #1-4 20.00

VERTIGO PREVIEW
DC Comics (Vertigo): 1992 (75¢, one-shot, 36 pgs.)

1-Vertigo previews; Sandman story by Neil Gaiman 3.00

VERTIGO RAVE
DC Comics (Vertigo): Fall, 1994 (99¢, one-shot)

1-Vertigo previews 3.00

VERTIGO RESURRECTED: ...
DC Comics (Vertigo): Dec, 2010 - Present ($7.99, squarebound, reprints)

The Extremist 1 (1/11) r/The Extremist #1-4 8.00
Finals 1 (5/11) r/Finals #1-4; Jill Thompson-a 8.00
Hellblazer 1 (2/11) r/Hellblazer #57,58,245,246 8.00
Shoot 1 (12/10) r/short stories by various incl. Quitely, Sale, Bolland, Risso, Jim Lee 8.00
Winter's Edge 1 (2/11) r/Vertigo's Winter Edge #1-3; Bermejo-c 8.00

VERTIGO SECRET FILES
DC Comics (Vertigo): Aug, 2000 ($4.95)

...: Hellblazer 1 (8/00, $4.95) Background info and story summaries 5.00
...: Swamp Thing 1 (11/00, $4.95) Backstories and origins; Hale-c 5.00

VERTIGO VERITE: THE UNSEEN HAND
DC Comics (Vertigo): Sept, 1996 - No. 4, Dec, 1996 ($2.50, limited series)

1-4: Terry LaBan scripts in all 3.00

VERTIGO VISIONS
DC Comics (Vertigo): June, 1993 - Present (one-shots)

Dr. Occult 1 (7/94, $3.95) 4.00
Dr. Thirteen 1 (9/98, $5.95) Howarth-s 6.00
Prez 1 (7/95, $3.95) 4.00
The Geek 1 (6/93, $3.95) 4.00
The Eaters ($4.95, 1995)-Milligan story. 5.00
The Phantom Stranger 1 (10/93, $3.50) 4.00
Tomahawk 1 (7/98, $4.95) Pollack-s 5.00

VERTIGO WINTER'S EDGE
DC Comics (Vertigo): 1998, 1999 ($7.95/$6.95, square-bound, annual)

1-Winter stories by Vertigo creators; Desire story by Gaiman/Bolton; Bolland wraparound-c 8.00
2,3-($6.95)-Winter stories: 2-Allred-c. 3-Bond-c; Desire by Gaiman/Zulli 7.00

VERTIGO X ANNIVERSARY PREVIEW
DC Comics (Vertigo): 2003 (99¢, one-shot, 48 pgs.)

1-Previews of upcoming titles and interviews; Endless Nights, Shade, The Originals 3.00

VERY BEST OF DENNIS THE MENACE, THE
Fawcett Publ.: July, 1979 - No. 2, Apr, 1980 (95¢/$1.00, digest-size, 132 pgs.)

1,2-Reprints 2 4 6 8 10 12

VERY BEST OF DENNIS THE MENACE, THE
Marvel Comics Group: Apr, 1982 - No. 3, Aug, 1982 ($1.25, digest-size)

1-3: Reprints 2 3 4 6 8 10
1,2-Mistakenly printed with DC logo on cover 2 4 6 9 12 15

NOTE: ***Hank Ketcham*** *c-all. A few thousand of #1 & 2 were printed with DC emblem.*

VERY VICKY
Meet Danny Ocean: 1993? - No. 8, 1995 ($2.50, B&W)

1-8, ...: Calling All Hillbillies (1995, $2.50) 3.00

VERY WEIRD TALES (Also see Slithiss Attacks!)
Oceanspray Comics Group: Aug, 2002 - No. 2, Oct, 2002 ($4.00)

1-Mutant revenge, methamphetamine, corporate greed horror stories
1 3 4 6 8 10
2-Weird fantasy and horror stories 1 2 3 5 6 8

NOTE: *Created in prevention classes taught by Jon McClure at the Oceanspray Family Center in Newport, Oregon, and paid for by the Housing Authority of Lincoln County. All books are b&w with color covers. Issues #1-2 penciled and inked by various artists. All comics feature characters created by students and are signed and numbered by Jon McClure. Issues #1-2 have print runs of 100 each.*

VEXT
DC Comics: Mar, 1999 - No. 6, Aug, 1999 ($2.50, limited series)

Vic Verity Magazine #1 © Vic Verity Pubs.

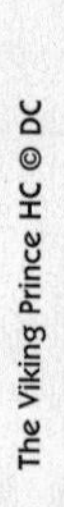

The Viking Prince HC © DC

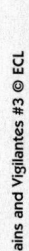

Villains and Vigilantes #3 © ECL

	GD 2.0	VG 4.0	FN 6.0	VF 8.0	VF/NM 9.0	NM- 9.2

GD VG FN VF VF/NM NM- 2.0 4.0 6.0 8.0 9.0 9.2

1-6-Giffen-s. 1-Superman app. 3.00

V FOR VENDETTA
DC Comics: Sept, 1988 - No. 10, May, 1989 ($2.00, maxi-series)

1-Alan Moore scripts in all; David Lloyd-a 1 2 3 4 5 7
2-10 5.00
HC (1990) Limited edition 60.00
HC (2005, $29.99, dustjacket) r/series; foreward by Lloyd; promo art and sketches 30.00
Trade paperback (1990, $14.95) 15.00

VIC BRIDGES FAZERS SKETCHBOOK AND FACT FILE
AC Comics: Nov, 1986 ($1.75)

1 3.00

VICE
Image Comics (Top Cow): Nov, 2005 - No. 5 ($2.99)

1-5-Coleite-s/Kirkham-a. 1-Three covers 3.00
1-Code Red Edition; variant Benitez-c 3.00

VIC FLINT(Crime Buster...)(See Authentic Police Cases #10-14 & Fugitives From Justice #2)
St. John Publ. Co.: Aug, 1948 - No. 5, Apr, 1949 (Newspaper reprints; NEA Service)

1 14 28 42 78 112 145
2 10 20 30 54 72 90
3-5 9 18 27 47 61 75

VIC FLINT (Crime Buster...)
Argo Publ.: Feb, 1956 - No. 2, May, 1956 (Newspaper reprints)

1,2 9 18 27 47 61 75

VIC JORDAN (Also see Big Shot Comics #32)
Civil Service Publ.: April, 1945

1-1944 daily newspaper-r 14 28 42 76 108 140

VICKI (Humor)
Atlas/Seaboard Publ.: Feb, 1975 - No. 4, Aug, 1975 (No. 1,2: 68 pgs.)

1,2-(68 pgs.)-Reprints Tippy Teen; Good Girl art 4 8 12 28 44 60
3,4 (Low print) 5 10 15 30 48 65

VICKI VALENTINE (...Summer Special #1)
Renegade Press: July, 1985 - No. 4, July, 1986 ($1.70, B&W)

1-4: Woggon, Rausch-a; all have paper dolls. 2-Christmas issue 3.00

VICKY
Ace Magazine: Oct, 1948 - No. 5, June, 1949

nn(10/48)-Teenage humor 8 16 24 42 54 65
4(12/48), nn(2/49), 4(4/49), 5(6/49): 5-Dotty app. 7 14 21 37 46 55

VICTORIAN UNDEAD
DC Comics (WildStorm): Jan, 2010 - No. 6, Jun, 2010 ($2.99)

1-6-Sherlock Holmes vs. Zombies; Edginton-s/Fabbri-a. 1-Two covers (Moore, Coleby) 3.00
...: Sherlock Holmes vs. Jekyll and Hyde (12/10, $4.99) Domingues-a/Van Sciver-c 5.00
...: Sherlock Holmes vs. Zombies TPB (2010, $17.99) r/#1-6; character design sketch art 18.00
... Volume 2 (1/11 - No. 5, 5/11) 1-3-($3.99) "Sherlock Holmes vs. Dracula" on-c; Fabbri-a 4.00
... Volume 2 - 4,5-($2.99) "Sherlock Holmes vs. Dracula" on-c; Fabbri-a 3.00

VIC TORRY & HIS FLYING SAUCER (Also see Mr. Monster's...#5)
Fawcett Publications: 1950 (one-shot)

nn-Book-length saucer story by Powell; photo/painted-c
69 138 207 442 759 1075

VICTORY
Topps Comics: June, 1994 ($2.50, unfinished limited series)

1-Kurt Busiek script; Giffen-c/a; Rob Liefeld variant-c exists 3.00

VICTORY
Image Comics: May, 2003 - No. 4, Feb, 2004 ($2.95, limited series)

1-4: 1-Two covers; Francisco-a. 4-Two covers 3.00

VICTORY (Volume 2)
Image Comics: Aug, 2004 - No. 4, Jan, 2005 ($2.95, limited series)

1-4: 1-Three covers; Francisco-a 3.00

VICTORY COMICS
Hillman Periodicals: Aug, 1941 - No. 4, Dec, 1941 (#1 by Funnies, Inc.)

1-The Conqueror by Bill Everett, The Crusader, & Bomber Burns begin; Conqueror's origin in text; Everett-c 300 600 900 2010 3505 5000
2-Everett-c/a 132 264 396 838 1444 2050
3,4 86 172 258 470 898 1325

VIC VERITY MAGAZINE
Vic Verity Publ: 1945; No. 2, Jan?, 1947 - No. 7, Sept, 1946 (A comic book)

1-C. C. Beck-c/a 25 50 75 150 245 340
2-Beck-c 15 30 45 88 137 185
3-7: 6-Beck-a. 7-Beck-c 14 28 42 82 121 160

VIDEO JACK
Marvel Comics (Epic Comics): Nov, 1987 - No. 6, Nov, 1988 ($1.25)

1-5 3.00
6-Neal Adams, Keith Giffen, Wrightson, others-a 5.00

VIETNAM JOURNAL
Apple Comics: Nov, 1987 - No. 16, Apr, 1991 ($1.75/$1.95, B&W)

1-16: Don Lomax-c/a/scripts in all, 1-2nd print 4.00
...: Indian Country Vol. 1 (1990, $12.95)-r/#1-4 plus one new story 13.00

VIETNAM JOURNAL: VALLEY OF DEATH
Apple Comics: June, 1994 - No. 2, Aug, 1994 ($2.75, B&W, limited series)

1,2: By Don Lomax 4.00

VIGILANTE, THE (Also see New Teen Titans #23 & Annual V2#2)
DC Comics: Oct, 1983 - No. 50, Feb, 1988 ($1.25, Baxter paper)

1-Origin 4.00
2-16,19-49: 3-Cyborg app. 4-1st app. The Exterminator; Newton-a(p). 6,7-Origin. 20,21-Nightwing app. 35-Origin Mad Bomber. 47-Batman-c/s 3.00
17,18-Alan Moore scripts 4.00
50-Ken Steacy painted-c 3.00
Annual nn, 2 ('85, '86) 4.00

VIGILANTE
DC Comics: Nov, 2005 - No. 6, Apr, 2006 ($2.99, limited series)

1-6-Bruce Jones-s. 1,2,4-6-Ben Oliver-a 3.00

VIGILANTE
DC Comics: Feb, 2009 - No. 12, Jan, 2010 ($2.99)

1-12: 1-Wolfman-s/Leonardi-a. 3-Nightwing app. 5-X-over with Titans and Teen Titans 3.00

VIGILANTE: CITY LIGHTS, PRAIRIE JUSTICE (Also see Action Comics #42, Justice League of America #78, Leading Comics & World's Finest #244)
DC Comics: Nov, 1995 - No. 4, Feb, 1996 ($2.50, limited series)

1-4: James Robinson scripts/Tony Salmons-a/Mark Chiarello-c 3.00
TPB (2009, $19.99) r/#1-4 20.00

VIGILANTES, THE
Dell Publishing Co.: No. 839, Sept, 1957

Four Color 839-Movie 7 14 21 47 76 105

VIGILANTE 8: SECOND OFFENSE
Chaos! Comics: Dec, 1999 ($2.95, one-shot)

1-Based on video game 3.00

VIKING
Image Comics: Apr, 2009 - Present ($2.99)

1-4-Ivan Brandon-s/Nic Klein-a 3.00

VIKING PRINCE, THE
DC Comics: 2010 ($39.99, hardcover with dustjacket)

HC-Recolored reprints of apps. in Brave and the Bold #1-5, 7-24 & team-up with Sgt. Rock in Our Army at War #162,163; new intro. by Joe Kubert 40.00

VIKINGS, THE (Movie)
Dell Publishing Co.: No. 910, May, 1958

Four Color 910-Buscema-a, Kirk Douglas photo-c 8 16 24 54 90 125

VILLAINS AND VIGILANTES
Eclipse Comics: Dec, 1986 - No. 4, May, 1987 ($1.50/$1.75, limited series, Baxter paper)

1-4: Based on role-playing game. 2-4 ($1.75-c) 3.00

VILLAINS UNITED (Leads into Infinite Crisis)
DC Comics: July, 2005 - No. 6, Dec, 2005 ($2.95/$2.50, limited series)

1-6-Simone-s/JG Jones-c. 1-The Secret Six and the "Society" form 3.00
...: Infinite Crisis Special 1 (6/06, $4.99) Simone-s/Eaglesham-a 5.00
TPB (2005, $12.99) r/#1-6; background info on villains 13.00

VILLAINY OF DOCTOR DOOM, THE
Marvel Comics: 1999 ($17.95, TPB)

nn-Reprints early battle with the Fantastic Four 18.00

VIMANARAMA
DC Comics (Vertigo): Apr, 2005 - No. 3, June, 2005 ($2.95, limited series)

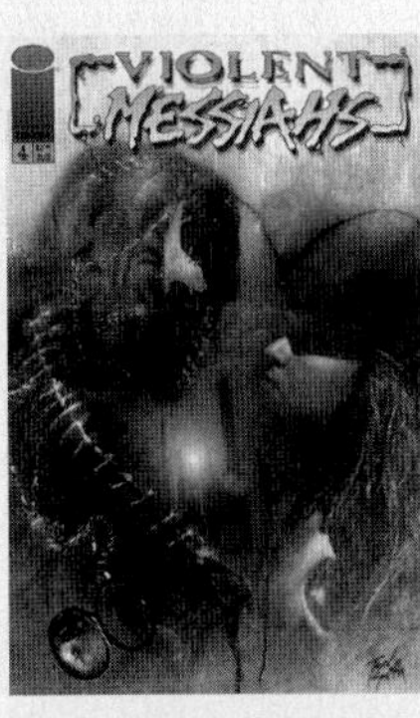

Violent Messiahs #4 © Hurricane

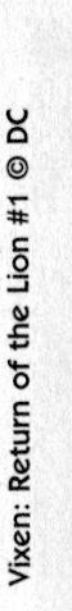
Vixen: Return of the Lion #1 © DC

Voodoo #17 © AJAX

	GD 2.0	VG 4.0	FN 6.0	VF 8.0	VF/NM 9.0	NM- 9.2

1-3-Grant Morrison-s/Philip Bond-a 3.00
TPB (2005, $12.99) r/#1-3 13.00

VINTAGE MAGNUS (...Robot Fighter)
Valiant: Jan, 1992 - No. 4, Apr, 1992 ($2.25, limited series)

1-4: 1-Layton-c; r/origin from Magnus R.F. #22 3.00

VINYL UNDERGROUND
DC Comics (Vertigo): Dec, 2007 - No. 12, Nov, 2008 ($2.99)

1-12: 1-Spencer-s/Gane & Stewart-a/Phillips-c 3.00
...: Pretty Dead Things TPB ('08, $17.99) r/#6-12 18.00
...: Watching the Detectives TPB ('08, $9.99) r/#1-5; David Laphan intro. 10.00

VIOLATOR (Also see Spawn #2)
Image Comics (Todd McFarlane Prods.): May, 1994 - No. 3, Aug, 1994 ($1.95, lim. series)

1-Alan Moore scripts in all 5.00
2,3: Bart Sears-c(p)/a(p) 4.00

VIOLATOR VS. BADROCK
Image Comics (Extreme Studios): May, 1995 - No. 4, Aug, 1995 ($2.50, limited series)

1-4: Alan Moore scripts in all. 1-1st app Celestine; variant-c (3?) 3.00

VIOLENT MESSIAHS (...: Lamenting Pain on cover for #9-12, numbered as #1-4)
Image Comics: June, 2000 - No. 12 ($2.95)

1-Two covers by Travis Smith and Medina 4.00
1-Tower Records variant edition 5.00
2-8: 5-Flip book sketchbook 3.00
9-12-Lamenting Pain; 2 covers on each 3.00
...: Genesis (12/01, $5.95) r/'97 B&W issue, Wizard 1/2 prologue 6.00
...: The Book of Job TPB (7/02, $24.95) r/#1-8; Foreward by Gossett 25.00

VIP (TV)
TV Comics: 2000 ($2.95, unfinished series)

1-Based on the Pamela Lee (Anderson) TV show; photo-c 3.00

VIPER (TV)
DC Comics: Aug, 1994 - No. 4, Nov, 1994 ($1.95, limited series)

1-4-Adaptation of television show 3.00

VIRGINIAN, THE (TV)
Gold Key: June, 1963

1(10060-306)-Part photo-c of James Drury plus photo back-c
4 8 12 28 44 60

VIRTUA FIGHTER (Video Game)
Marvel Comics: Aug, 1995 (2.95, one-shot)

1-Sega Saturn game 3.00

VIRUS
Dark Horse Comics: 1993 - No. 4, 1993 ($2.50, limited series)

1-4: Ploog-c 3.00

VISION, THE
Marvel Comics: Nov, 1994 - No. 4, Feb, 1995 ($1.75, limited series)

1-4 3.00

VISION, THE (AVENGERS ICONS: ...)
Marvel Comics: Oct, 2002 - No. 4, Jan, 2003 ($2.99, limited series)

1-4-Geoff Johns-s/Ivan Reis-a 3.00
...: Yesterday and Tomorrow TPB (2005, $14.99) r/#1-4 & Avengers #57 (1st app.) 15.00

VISION AND THE SCARLET WITCH, THE (See Marvel Fanfare)
Marvel Comics Group: Nov, 1982 - No. 4, Feb, 1983 (Limited series)

1-4: 2-Nuklo & Future Man app. 4.00

VISION AND THE SCARLET WITCH, THE
Marvel Comics Group: Oct, 1985 - No. 12, Sept, 1986 (Maxi-series)

V2#1-12: 1-Origin; 1st app. in Avengers #57. 2-West Coast Avengers x-over 4.00

VISIONS
Vision Publications: 1979 - No. 5, 1983 (B&W, fanzine)

1-Flaming Carrot begins(1st app?); N. Adams-c 5 10 15 35 55 75
2-N. Adams, Rogers-a; Gulacy back-c; signed & numbered to 2000
5 10 15 30 48 65
3-Williamson-c(p); Steranko back-c 4 8 12 22 34 45
4-Flaming Carrot-c & info. 4 8 12 22 34 45
5-1 pg. Flaming Carrot 3 6 9 16 23 30

NOTE: ***Eisner** a-4. **Miller** a-4. **Starlin** a-3. **Williamson** a-5. After #4, Visions became an annual publication of The Atlanta Fantasy Fair.*

VISITOR, THE
Valiant/Acclaim Comics (Valiant): Apr, 1995 - No. 13, Nov, 1995 ($2.50)

1-13: 8-Harbinger revealed. 13-Visitor revealed to be Sting from Harbinger 3.00

VISITOR VS. THE VALIANT UNIVERSE, THE
Valiant: Feb, 1995 - No. 2, Mar, 1995 ($2.95, limited series)

1,2 3.00

VIX
Image Comics: Jun, 2008 ($3.50)

1-Hosely-s/Humphreys-a 3.50

VIXEN: RETURN OF THE LION (From Justice League of America)
DC Comics: Dec, 2008 - No. 5, Apr, 2009 ($2.99, limited series)

1-5-G. Willow Wilson-s/Cafu-a; Justice League app. 3.00
TPB (2009, $17.99) r/#1-5 18.00

VOGUE (Also see Youngblood)
Image Comics (Extreme Studios): Oct, 1995 - No.3, Jan, 1996 ($2.50, limited series)

1-3: 1-Liefeld-c, 1-Variant-c 3.00

VOID INDIGO (Also see Marvel Graphic Novel)
Marvel Comics (Epic Comics): 11/84 - No. 2, 3/85 ($1.50, direct sales, unfinished series, mature)

1,2: Cont'd from Marvel G.N.; graphic sex & violence 3.00

VOLCANIC REVOLVER
Oni Press: Dec, 1998 - No. 3, Mar, 1999 ($2.95, B&W, limited series)

1-3: Scott Morse-s/a 3.00
TPB (12/99, $9.95, digest size) r/#1-3 and Oni Double Feature #7 prologue 10.00

VOLTRON (TV)
Modern Publishing: 1985 - No. 3, 1985 (75¢, limited series)

1-3: Ayers-a in all 6.00

VOLTRON: A LEGEND FORGED (TV)
Devils Due Publishing: Jul, 2008 - No. 5, Apr, 2009 ($3.50)

1-5-Blaylock-s/Bear-a; 4 covers 3.50

VOLTRON: DEFENDER OF THE UNIVERSE (TV)
Image Comics: No. 0, May, 2003 - No. 5, Sept, 2003 ($2.50)

0-Jolley-s/Brooks-a; character pin-ups with background info 3.00
1-5-($2.95) 1-Three covers by Norton, Brooks and Andrews; Norton-a 3.00
...: Revelations TPB (2004, $11.95, digest-sized) r/#1-5; cover gallery 12.00

VOLTRON: DEFENDER OF THE UNIVERSE (TV)
Image Comics: Jan, 2004 - No. 11, Dec, 2004 ($2.95)

1-11: 1-Jolley-s; wraparound-c 3.00

VOODA (Jungle Princess) (Formerly Voodoo) (See Crown Comics)
Ajax-Farrell (Four Star Publications): No. 20, April, 1955 - No. 22, Aug, 1955

20-Baker-c/a (r/Seven Seas #6) 39 78 117 240 395 550
21,22-Baker-a plus Kamen/Baker story, Kimbo Boy of Jungle, & Baker-c(p) in all.
22-Censored Jo-Jo-r (name Powaa) 36 72 108 211 343 475

NOTE: *#20-22 each contain one heavily censored-r of South Sea Girl by **Baker** from Seven Seas Comics with name changed to Vooda. #20-r/Seven Seas #6; #21-r/#4; #22-r/#3.*

VOODOO (Weird Fantastic Tales) (Vooda #20 on)
Ajax-Farrell (Four Star Publ.): May, 1952 - No. 19, Jan-Feb, 1955

1-South Sea Girl-r by Baker 61 122 183 390 670 950
2-Rulah story-r plus South Sea Girl from Seven Seas #2 by Baker (name changed from Alani to El'nee) 50 100 150 315 533 750
3-Bakerish-a; man stabbed in face 41 82 123 249 417 585
4,8-Baker-r. 8-Severed head panels 41 82 123 249 417 585
5-Nazi death camp story (flaying alive) 39 78 117 231 378 525
6,7,9,10: 6-Severed head panels 36 72 108 216 351 485
11-18: 14-Zombies take over America. 15-Opium drug story-r/Ellery Queen #3. 16-Post nuclear world story.17-Electric chair panels
31 62 93 186 303 420
19-Bondage-c; Baker-r(2)/Seven Seas #5 w/minor changes & #1, heavily modified; last pre-code; contents & covers change to jungle theme
39 78 117 234 385 535
Annual 1(1952, 25¢, 100 pgs.)-Baker-a (scarce) 135 270 405 864 1482 2100

VOODOO
Image Comics (WildStorm): Nov, 1997 - No. 4, Mar, 1998 ($2.50, lim. series)

1-4:Alan Moore-s in all; Hughes-c. 2-4-Rio-a 3.00
1-Platinum Ed 10.00
Dancing on the Dark TPB ('99, $9.95) r/#1-4 10.00

Vortex #15 © Vortex Publ.

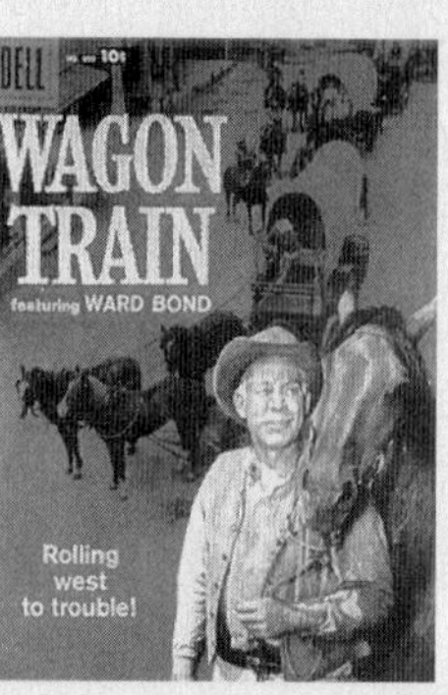

Wagon Train Four Color #895 © Revere

The Walking Dead #75 © Robert Kirkman

	GD 2.0	VG 4.0	FN 6.0	VF 8.0	VF/NM 9.0	NM- 9.2
...-Zealot: Skin Trade (8/95, $4.95)						5.00

VOODOO (See Tales of...)

VOODOO CHILD (Weston Cage & Nicolas Cage's...)
Virgin Comics: July, 2007 - No. 6, Dec, 2007 ($2.99)

	GD	VG	FN	VF	VF/NM	NM-
1-6: 1-Mike Carey-s/Dean Hyrapiet-a; covers by Hyrapiet & Templesmith						3.00
Vol. 1 TPB (1/08, $14.99) r/#1-6; variant covers; intro by Weston Cage & Nicolas Cage						15.00

VOODOOM
Oni Press: June, 2000 ($4.95, B&W)

	GD	VG	FN	VF	VF/NM	NM-
1-Scott Morse-s/Jim Mahfood-a						5.00

VORTEX
Vortex Publs.: Nov, 1982 - No. 15, 1988 (No month) ($1.50/$1.75, B&W)

	GD	VG	FN	VF	VF/NM	NM-
1 ($1.95)-Peter Hsu-a; Ken Steacy-c; nudity	1	2	3	5	7	9
2,12: 2-1st app. Mister X (on-c only). 12-Sam Kieth-a						6.00
3-11,13-15						3.00

VORTEX
Comico: 1991 - No. 2? ($2.50, limited series)

	GD	VG	FN	VF	VF/NM	NM-
1,2: Heroes from The Elementals						3.00

VOYAGE TO THE BOTTOM OF THE SEA (Movie, TV)
Dell Publishing Co./Gold Key: No. 1230, Sept-Nov, 1961; Dec, 1964 - #16, Apr, 1970 (Painted-c)

	GD	VG	FN	VF	VF/NM	NM-
Four Color 1230 (1961)	10	20	30	70	125	180
10133-412(#1, 12/64)(Gold Key)	8	16	24	52	86	120
2(7/65) - 5: Photo back-c, 1-5	5	10	15	34	55	75
6-14	4	8	12	28	44	60
15,16-Reprints	3	6	9	18	27	35

VOYAGE TO THE DEEP
Dell Publishing Co.: Sept-Nov, 1962 - No. 4, Nov-Jan, 1964 (Painted-c)

	GD	VG	FN	VF	VF/NM	NM-
1	5	10	15	34	55	75
2-4	4	8	12	24	37	50

WACKO
Ideal Publ. Corp.: Sept, 1980 - No. 3, Oct, 1981 (84 pgs., B&W, magazine)

	GD	VG	FN	VF	VF/NM	NM-
1-3	2	4	6	8	11	14

WACKY ADVENTURES OF CRACKY (Also see Gold Key Spotlight)
Gold Key: Dec, 1972 - No. 12, Sept, 1975

	GD	VG	FN	VF	VF/NM	NM-
1	3	6	9	14	20	26
2	2	4	6	10	14	18
3-12	2	4	6	8	10	12

(See March of Comics #405, 424, 436, 448)

WACKY DUCK (...Comics #3-6; formerly Dopey Duck; Justice Comics #7 on) (See Film Funnies)
Marvel Comics (NPP): No. 3, Fall, 1946 - No. 6, Summer, 1947; Aug, 1948 - No. 2, Oct, 1948

	GD	VG	FN	VF	VF/NM	NM-
3	24	48	72	140	230	320
4-Infinity-c	21	42	63	122	199	275
5,6(1947)-Becomes Justice comics	18	36	54	107	169	230
1(1948)	18	36	54	105	165	225
2(1948)	14	28	42	82	121	160
I.W. Reprint #1,2,7('58): 1-r/Wacky Duck #6	2	4	6	9	13	16
Super Reprint #10(I.W. on-c, Super-inside)	2	4	6	9	13	16

WACKY QUACKY (See Wisco)

WACKY RACES (TV)
Gold Key: Aug, 1969 - No. 7, Apr, 1972 (Hanna-Barbera)

	GD	VG	FN	VF	VF/NM	NM-
1	5	10	15	34	55	75
2-7	4	8	12	22	34	45

WACKY SQUIRREL (Also see Dark Horse Presents)
Dark Horse Comics: Oct, 1987 - No. 4, 1988 ($1.75, B&W)

	GD	VG	FN	VF	VF/NM	NM-
1-4: 4-Superman parody						3.00
Halloween Adventure Special 1 (1987, $2.00)						3.00
Summer Fun Special 1 (1988, $2.00)						3.00

WACKY WITCH (Also see Gold Key Spotlight)
Gold Key: March, 1971 - No. 21, Dec, 1975

	GD	VG	FN	VF	VF/NM	NM-
1	4	8	12	24	37	50
2	3	6	9	14	20	26
3-10	2	4	6	10	14	18
11-21	2	4	6	8	10	12

(See March of Comics #374, 398, 410, 422, 434, 446, 458, 470, 482)

WACKY WOODPECKER (See Two Bit the...)
I. W. Enterprises/Super Comics: 1958; 1963

	GD	VG	FN	VF	VF/NM	NM-
I.W. Reprint #1,2,7 (nd-reprints Two Bit...): 7-r/Two-Bit, the Wacky Woodpecker #1.	2	4	6	8	11	14
Super Reprint #10('63): 10-r/Two-Bit, The Wacky Woodpecker #?	2	4	6	8	11	14

WAGON TRAIN (1st Series) (TV) (See Western Roundup under Dell Giants)
Dell Publishing Co.: No. 895, Mar, 1958 - No. 13, Apr-June, 1962 (All photo-c)

	GD	VG	FN	VF	VF/NM	NM-
Four Color 895 (#1)	10	20	30	70	125	180
Four Color 971(#2),1019(#3)	7	14	21	45	73	100
4(1-3/60),6-13	6	12	18	39	62	85
5-Toth-a	6	12	18	43	69	95

WAGON TRAIN (2nd Series)(TV)
Gold Key: Jan, 1964 - No. 4, Oct, 1964 (All front & back photo-c)

	GD	VG	FN	VF	VF/NM	NM-
1-Tufts-a in all	5	10	15	32	51	70
2-4	4	8	12	24	37	50

WAITING PLACE, THE
Slave Labor Graphics: Apr, 1997 - No. 6, Sept, 1997 ($2.95)

	GD	VG	FN	VF	VF/NM	NM-
1-6-Sean McKeever-s						3.00
Vol. 2 - 1(11/99), 2-11						3.00
12-($4.95)						5.00

WAITING ROOM WILLIE (See Sad Case of...)

WAKE THE DEAD
IDW Publ.: Sept, 2003 - No. 5, Mar, 2004 ($3.99, limited series)

	GD	VG	FN	VF	VF/NM	NM-
1-5-Steve Niles-s/Chee-a						4.00
TPB (6/04, $19.99) r/series; intro. by Michael Dougherty; embossed die cut cover						20.00

WALK IN (Dave Stewart's ...)
Virgin Comics: Dec, 2006 - No. 6, May, 2007 ($2.99)

	GD	VG	FN	VF	VF/NM	NM-
1-6: 1-5-Parker-s/Padlekar-a. 6-Parker-a						3.00

WALKING DEAD, THE (Inspired the 2010 AMC television series)
Image Comics: Oct, 2003 - Present ($2.95/$2.99, B&W)

	GD	VG	FN	VF	VF/NM	NM-
1-Robert Kirkman-s in all/Tony Moore-a	7	14	21	45	73	100
1 Special Edition (5/08, $3.99) r/#1; Kirkman afterword; original script and proposal						5.00
2-Tony Moore-a	3	6	9	20	30	40
3-6-Tony Moore-a	2	4	6	9	12	15
7-10: 7-Charlie Adlard-a begins	1	2	3	5	6	8
11-20						5.00
21-40						4.00
41-60,62-74,76-83						3.00
61-Preview of Chew						6.00
75-(7/10, $3.99) Orange background-c; back-up alien/sci-fi "fantasy" in color; TV series preview with cast photos						4.00
75-Variant-c homage to issue #1						10.00
Image Firsts: The Walking Dead #1 (3/10, $1.00) reprints #1						1.00
... Book 1 HC (2006, $29.99) r/#1-12; sketch pages, cover gallery; Kirkman afterword						30.00
... Book 2 HC (2006, $29.99) r/#13-24; sketch pages, cover gallery						30.00
... Book 3 HC (2007, $29.99) r/#25-36; sketch pages, cover gallery						30.00
... Book 4 HC (2008, $29.99) r/#37-48; sketch pages, cover gallery						30.00
... Book 5 HC (2010, $29.99) r/#49-60; sketch pages, cover gallery						30.00
...Vol. 1: Days Gone Bye (5/04, $9.95, TPB) r/#1-4						10.00
...Vol. 2: Miles Behind Us (10/04, $12.95, TPB) r/#7-12						13.00
...Vol. 3: Safety Behind Bars (2005, $12.95, TPB) r/#13-18						13.00
...Vol. 4: The Heart's Desire (2005, $12.99, TPB) r/#19-24						13.00
...Vol. 5: The Best Defense (2006, $12.99, TPB) r/#25-30						13.00
...Vol. 6: This Sorrowful Life (2007, $12.99, TPB) r/#31-36						13.00
...Vol. 7: The Calm Before (2007, $12.99, TPB) r/#37-42						13.00
...Vol. 8: Made to Suffer (2008, $14.99, TPB) r/#43-48						15.00
...Vol. 9: Here We Remain (2009, $14.99, TPB) r/#49-54						15.00
...Vol. 10: The Road Ahead (2009, $14.99, TPB) r/#55-60						15.00
...Vol. 11: Fear the Hunters (2010, $14.99, TPB) r/#61-66						15.00
...Vol. 12: Life Among Them (2010, $14.99, TPB) r/#67-72						15.00
...Vol. 13: Too Far Gone (2010, $14.99, TPB) r/#73-78						15.00

WALKING DEAD SURVIVORS' GUIDE, THE
Image Comics: Apr, 2011 - No. 4 ($2.99, B&W)

	GD	VG	FN	VF	VF/NM	NM-
1-Alphabetical listings of character profiles, first (and last) apps. and current status						3.00

WALKING DEAD WEEKLY, THE (Reprints)
Image Comics: Jan, 2011 - Present ($2.99, B&W, weekly)

	GD	VG	FN	VF	VF/NM	NM-
1-4-Reprints issues with original letter columns. 1-New Kirkman afterword						3.00

Wall•E #4 © DIS & Pixar

Walt Disney's Christmas Parade #2 © DIS

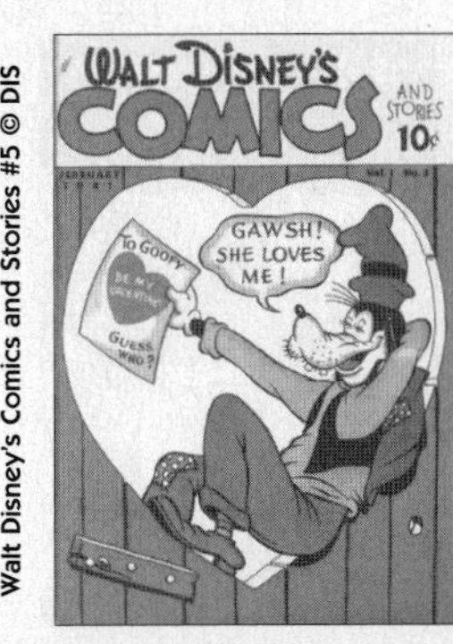

Walt Disney's Comics and Stories #5 © DIS

GD 2.0 | VG 4.0 | FN 6.0 | VF 8.0 | VF/NM 9.0 | NM- 9.2

WALL·E (Based on the Disney/Pixar movie)
BOOM! Studios: No. 0, Nov, 2009 - No. 7, Jun, 2010 ($2.99)

0-7: 0-Prequel; J. Torres-s 3.00

WALLY (Teen-age)
Gold Key: Dec, 1962 - No. 4, Sept, 1963

1 3 6 9 21 32 42
2-4 3 6 9 17 25 32

WALLY THE WIZARD
Marvel Comics (Star Comics): Apr, 1985 - No. 12, Mar, 1986 (Children's comic)

1-12: Bob Bolling a-1,3; c-1,9,11,12 5.00
1-Variant with "Star Chase" game on last page and inside back-c 9.00

WALLY WOOD'S T.H.U.N.D.E.R. AGENTS (See Thunder Agents)
Deluxe Comics: Nov, 1984 - No. 5, Oct, 1986 ($2.00, 52 pgs.)

1-5: 5-Jerry Ordway-c/a in Wood style 6.00
NOTE: ***Anderson** a-2i, 3i. **Buckler** a-4. **Ditko** a-3, 4. **Giffen** a-1p-4p. **Perez** a-1p, 2, 4; c-1-4.*

WALT DISNEY CHRISTMAS PARADE (Also see Christmas Parade)
Whitman Publ. Co. (Golden Press): Wint, 1977 ($1.95, cardboard-c, 224 pgs.)

11191-Barks-r/Christmas in Disneyland #1, Dell Christmas Parade #9 & Dell Giant #53
4 8 12 26 41 55

WALT DISNEY COMICS DIGEST
Gold Key: June, 1968 - No. 57, Feb, 1976 (50¢, digest size)

1-Reprints Uncle Scrooge #5; 192 pgs. 7 14 21 50 83 115
2-4-Barks-r 5 10 15 34 55 75
5-Daisy Duck by Barks (8 pgs.); last published story by Barks (art only)
plus 21 pg. Scrooge-r by Barks 8 16 24 52 86 120
6-13-All Barks-r 4 8 12 22 34 45
14,15 3 6 9 16 23 30
16-Reprints Donald Duck #26 by Barks 3 6 9 21 32 42
17-20-Barks-r 3 6 9 18 27 35
21-31,33,35-37-Barks-r; 24-Toth Zorro 3 6 9 16 23 30
32,41,45,47-49 2 4 6 11 16 20
34,38,39: 34-Reprints 4-Color #318. 38-Reprints Christmas in Disneyland #1.
39-Two Barks-r/WDC&S #272, 4-Color #1073 plus Toth Zorro-r
3 6 9 16 23 30
40-Mickey Mouse-r by Gottfredson 2 4 6 13 18 22
42,43-Barks-r 2 4 6 13 18 22
44-(Has Gold Key emblem, 50¢)-Reprints 1st story of 4-Color #29,256,275,282
5 10 15 32 51 70
44-Republished in 1976 by Whitman; not identical to original; a bit smaller, blank back-c, 69¢
3 6 9 16 23 30
46,50,52-Barks-r. 52-Barks-r/WDC&S #161,132 2 4 6 11 16 20
51-Reprints 4-Color #71 3 6 9 16 23 30
53-55: 53-Reprints Dell Giant #30. 54-Reprints Donald Duck Beach Party #2.
55-Reprints Dell Giant #49 2 4 6 10 14 18
56-r/Uncle Scrooge #32 (Barks) 2 4 6 13 18 22
57-r/Mickey Mouse Almanac('57) & two Barks stories 2 4 6 11 16 20
NOTE: ***Toth** a-52r. #1-10, 196 pgs.; #11-41, 164 pgs.; #42 on, 132 pgs. Old issues were being reprinted & distributed by Whitman in 1976.*

WALT DISNEY GIANT (Disney)
Bruce Hamilton Co. (Gladstone): Sept, 1995 - No. 7, Sept, 1996 ($2.25, bi-monthly, 48 pgs.)

1-7: 1-Scrooge McDuck in the Yukon; Rosa-c/a/scripts plus r/F.C. #218. 2-Uncle Scrooge-r by Barks plus 17 pg. text story. 3-Donald the Mighty Duck; Rosa-c; Barks & Rosa-r. 4-Mickey and Goofy; new-a (story actually stars Goofy. Mickey Mouse by Caesar Ferioli; Donald Duck by Giorgio Cavazzano (1st in U.S.). 6-Uncle Scrooge & the Jr. Woodchucks; new-a and Barks-r. 7-Uncle Scrooge-r by Barks plus new-a 4.00
NOTE: *Series was initially solicited as Uncle Walt's Collectory. Issue #8 was advertised, but later cancelled.*

WALT DISNEY PAINT BOOK SERIES
Whitman Publ. Co.: No dates; circa 1975 (Beware! Has 1930s copyright dates) (79¢-c, 52 pgs. B&W, treasury-sized) (Coloring books, text stories & comics-r)

#2052 (Whitman #886-r) Mickey Mouse & Donald Duck Gag Book
3 6 9 21 32 42
#2053 (Whitman #677-r) 3 6 9 21 32 42
#2054 (Whitman #670-r) Donald-c 4 8 12 23 36 48
#2055 (Whitman #627-r) Mickey-c 3 6 9 21 32 42
#2056 (Whitman #660-r) Buckey Bug-c 3 6 9 19 29 38
#2057 (Whitman #887-r) Mickey & Donald-c 3 6 9 21 32 42

WALT DISNEY PRESENTS (TV)(Disney)
Dell Publishing Co.: No. 997, 6-8/59 - No. 6, 12-2/1960-61; No. 1181, 4-5/61 (All photo-c)

Four Color 997 (#1) 7 14 21 49 80 110
2(12-2/60)-The Swamp Fox(origin), Elfego Baca, Texas John Slaughter (Disney TV show)
begin 5 10 15 32 51 70
3-6: 5-Swamp Fox by Warren Tufts 5 10 15 30 48 65
Four Color 1181-Texas John Slaughter 6 12 18 39 62 85

WALT DISNEY'S CHRISTMAS PARADE (Also see Christmas Parade)
Gladstone: Winter, 1988; No. 2, Winter, 1989 ($2.95, 100 pgs.)

1-Barks-r/painted-c 2 4 6 8 10 12
2-Barks-r 1 2 3 5 7 9

WALT DISNEY'S CHRISTMAS PARADE
Gemstone Publishing: Dec, 2003; 2004, 2005, 2006,2008 ($8.95/$9.50, prestige format)

1-4: 1-Reprints and 3 new European holiday stories. 2-All reprints. 3-Reprints and 2 new stories, 4-Reprints and 5 new stories 9.00
5-($9.50) R/Uncle Scrooge #47 and European stories 9.50

WALT DISNEY'S COMICS AND STORIES (Cont. of Mickey Mouse Magazine)
(#1-30 contain Donald Duck newspaper reprints) (Titled "Comics And Stories" #264 to #?; titled "Walt Disney's Comics And Stories" #511 on)
Dell Publishing Co./Gold Key #264-473/Whitman #474-510/Gladstone #511-547/ Disney Comics #548-585/Gladstone #586-633/Gemstone Publishing #634-698/ Boom! Kids #699-on: 10/40 - #263, 8/62; #264, 10/62 - #510, 7/84; #511, 10/86 - #633, 2/99; #634, 7/03 - #698, 11/08; #699, 10/09 - Present

NOTE: The whole number can always be found at the bottom of the title page in the lower left-hand or right hand panel.

1(V1#1-c; V2#1-indicia)-Donald Duck strip-r by Al Taliaferro & Gottfredson's
Mickey Mouse begin 2250 4500 6750 15,750 28,875 42,000
2 892 1784 2676 6512 11,506 16,500
3 389 778 1167 2723 4762 6800
4-X-Mas-c; 1st Huey, Dewey & Louie-c this title (See Mickey Mouse Magazine
V4#2 for 1st-c ever) 300 600 900 1920 3310 4700
4-Special promotional, complimentary issue; cover same except one corner was blanked out & boxed in to identify the giveaway (not a paste-over). This special pressing was probably sent out to former subscribers to Mickey Mouse Mag. whose subscriptions had expired.
(Very rare-5 known copies) 423 846 1269 3000 5250 7500
5-Goofy-c 245 490 735 1568 2684 3800
6-10: 8-Only Clarabelle Cow-c. 9-Taliaferro-c (1st) 206 412 618 1318 2259 3200
11-14: 11-Huey, Dewey & Louie-c/app. 155 310 465 992 1696 2400
15-17: 15-The 3 Little Kittens (17 pgs.). 16-The 3 Little Pigs (29 pgs.); X-Mas-c.
17-The Ugly Duckling (4 pgs.) 135 270 405 864 1482 2100
18-21 119 238 357 762 1306 1850
22-30: 22-Flag-c. 24-The Flying Gauchito (1st original comic book story done for WDC&S).
27-Jose Carioca by Carl Buettner (2nd original story in WDC&S)
100 200 300 635 1093 1550
31-New Donald Duck stories by Carl Barks begin (See F.C. #9 for 1st Barks Donald Duck)
400 800 1200 2800 4900 7000
32-Barks-a 232 464 696 1485 2543 3600
33-Barks-a; infinity-c 161 322 483 1030 1765 2500
34-Gremlins by Walt Kelly begin, end #41; Barks-a 129 258 387 826 1413 2000
35,36-Barks-a 123 246 369 787 1344 1900
37-Donald Duck by Jack Hannah 71 142 213 454 777 1100
38-40-Barks-a. 39-X-Mas-c. 40,41-Gremlins by Kelly
81 162 243 518 884 1250
41-50-Barks-a. 43-Seven Dwarfs-c app. (4/44). 45-50-Nazis in Gottfredson's Mickey Mouse
Stories 68 136 204 435 743 1050
51-60-Barks-a. 51-X-Mas-c. 52-Li'l Bad Wolf begins, ends #203 (not in #55). 58-Kelly flag-c
33 66 99 254 502 750
61-70: Barks-a. 61-Dumbo story. 63,64-Pinocchio stories. 63-Cover swipe from New Funnies #94. 64-X-Mas-c. 65-Pluto story. 66-Infinity-c. 67,68-Mickey Mouse Sunday-r by
Bill Wright 28 56 84 215 433 650
71-80: Barks-a. 75-77-Brer Rabbit stories, no Mickey Mouse. 76-X-Mas-c
24 48 72 175 350 525
81-87,89,90: Barks-a. 82-Goofy-c. 82-84-Bongo stories. 86-90-Goofy & Agnes app.
89-Chip 'n' Dale story 20 40 60 144 290 435
88-1st app. Gladstone Gander by Barks (1/48) 24 48 72 177 356 535
91-97,99: Barks-a. 95-1st WDC&S Barks-c. 96-No Mickey Mouse; Little Toot begins,
ends #97. 99-X-Mas-c 18 36 54 131 266 400
98-1st Uncle Scrooge app. in WDC&S (11/48) 31 62 93 239 470 700
100-(1/49)-Barks-a 22 44 66 155 310 465
101-110-Barks-a. 107-Taliaferro-c; Donald acquires super powers
16 32 48 111 226 340
111,114,117-All Barks-a 14 28 42 96 191 285
112-Drug (ether) issue (Donald Duck) 13 26 39 94 185 275
113,115,116,118-123: No Barks. 116-Dumbo x-over. 121-Grandma Duck begins, ends #168;
not in #135,142,146,155 10 20 30 72 131 190

Walt Disney's Comics and Stories #120 © DIS

Walt Disney's Comics and Stories #714 © DIS

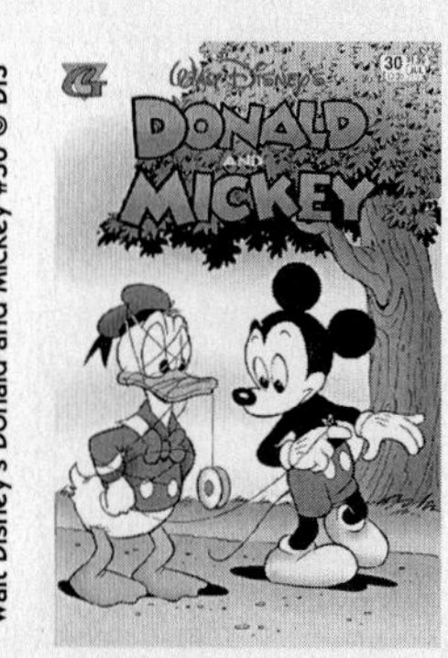

Walt Disney's Donald and Mickey #30 © DIS

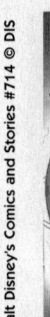

	GD 2.0	VG 4.0	FN 6.0	VF 8.0	VF/NM 9.0	NM- 9.2
124,126-130-All Barks-a. 124-X-Mas-c	12	24	36	84	157	230
125-1st app. Junior Woodchucks (2/51); Barks-a	16	32	48	111	226	340
131,133,135-137,139-All Barks-a	11	22	33	79	147	215
132-Barks-a(2) (D. Duck & Grandma Duck)	12	24	36	82	154	225
134-Intro. & 1st app. The Beagle Boys (11/51)	18	36	54	131	266	400
138-Classic Scrooge money story	15	30	45	106	216	325
140-(5/52)-1st app. Gyro Gearloose by Barks; 2nd Barks Uncle Scrooge-c; 3rd Uncle Scrooge cover app.	18	36	54	131	266	400
141-150-All Barks-a. 143-Little Hiawatha begins, ends #151,159	10	20	30	68	119	170
151-170-All Barks-a	9	18	27	60	100	140
171-199-All Barks-a	8	16	24	54	90	125
200	8	16	24	58	97	135
201-240: All Barks-a. 204-Chip 'n' Dale & Scamp begin	7	14	21	47	76	105
241-283: Barks-a. 241-Dumbo x-over. 247-Gyro Gearloose begins, ends #274. 256-Ludwig Von Drake begins, ends #274	6	12	18	41	66	90
284,285,287,290,295,296,309-311-Not by Barks	3	6	9	20	30	40
286,288,291-294,297,298,308-All Barks stories; 293-Grandma Duck's Farm Friends. 297-Gyro Gearloose. 298-Daisy Duck's Diary-r	4	8	12	24	37	50
289-Annette-c & back-c & story; Barks-s	4	8	12	28	44	60
299-307-All contain early Barks-r (#43-117). 305-Gyro Gearloose	4	8	12	26	41	55
312-Last Barks issue with original story	4	8	12	26	41	55
313-315,317-327,329-334,336-341	3	6	9	16	22	28
316-Last issue published during life of Walt Disney	3	6	9	16	22	28
328,335,342-350-Barks-r	3	6	9	16	22	28
351-360-With posters inside; Barks reprints (2 versions of each with & without posters)	4	8	12	26	41	55
351-360-Without posters...	3	6	9	14	19	24
361-400-Barks-r	3	6	9	14	20	26
401-429-Barks-r	3	6	9	14	19	24
430,433,437,438,441,444,445,466-No Barks	2	4	6	8	11	14
431,432,434-436,439,440,442,443-Barks-r	2	4	6	10	14	18
446-465,467-473-Barks-r	2	4	6	9	13	16
474(3/80),475-478 (Whitman)	3	6	9	14	19	24
479(8/80),481(10/80)-484(1/81) pre-pack only	5	10	15	32	51	70
480 (8-12/80)-(Very low distribution)	10	20	30	71	128	185
484 (1/81, 40¢-c) Cover price error variant (scarce)	6	12	18	39	62	85
485-499: 494-r/WDC&S #98	2	4	6	11	16	20
500-510 (All #90011 on-c; pre-packs): 500(4/83), 501(5/83), 502&503(7/83), 504-506(all 8/83), 507(4/84), 508(5/84), 509(6/84), 510(7/84). 506-No Barks	2	4	6	13	18	22
511-Donald Duck by Daan Jippes (1st in U.S.; in all through #518); Gyro Gearloose Barks-r begins (in most through #547); Wuzzles by Disney Studio (1st by Gladstone)	3	6	9	17	25	32
512,513	2	4	6	10	14	18
514-516,520	2	4	6	8	10	12
517-519,521,522,525,527,529,530,532-546: 518-Infinity-c. 522-r/1st app. Huey, Dewey & Louie from D. Duck Sunday. 535-546-Barks-r. 537-1st Donald Duck by William Van Horn in WDC&S. 541-545-52 pgs. 546,547-68 pgs. 546-Kelly-r. 547-Rosa-a						6.00
523,524,526,528,531,547: Rosa-s/a in all. 523-1st Rosa 10 pager	2	4	6	9	12	15
548-($1.50, 6/90)-1st Disney issue; new-a; no M. Mouse	1	2	3	4	5	7
549,551-570,572,573,577-579,581,584 ($1.50): 549-Barks-r begin, ends #585, not in #555, 556, & 564. 551-r/1 story from F.C. #29. 556,578-r/Mickey Mouse Cheerios Premium by Dick Moores. 562,563,568-570, 572, 581-Gottfredson strip-r. 570-Valentine issue; has Mickey/Minnie centerfold. 584-Taliaferro strip-r						4.00
550 ($2.25, 52 pgs.)-Donald Duck by Barks; previously printed only in The Netherlands (1st time in U.S.); r/Chip 'n Dale & Scamp from #204						5.00
571-($2.95, 68 pgs)-r/Donald Duck's Atom Bomb by Barks from 1947 Cheerios premium						6.00
574-576,580,582,583 ($2.95, 68 pgs.): 574-r/1st Pinocchio Sunday strip (1939-40). 575-Gottfredson-r, Pinocchio-r/WDC&S #64. 580-r/Donald Duck's 1st app. from Silly Symphony strip 12/16/34 by Taliaferro; Gottfredson strip-r begin; not in #584 & 600. 582,583-r/Mickey Mouse on Sky Island from WDC&S #1,2						5.00
585 ($2.50, 52 pgs.)-r/#140; Barks-r/WDC&S #140						5.00
586,587: 586-Gladstone issues begin again; begin $1.50-c; Gottfredson-r begins (not in #600). 587-Donald Duck by William Van Horn begins						4.00
588-597: 588,591-599-Donald Duck by William Van Horn						3.00
598,599 ($1.95, 36 pgs.): 598-r/1st drawings of Mickey Mouse by Ub Iwerks						3.00
600 ($2.95, 48 pgs.)-L.B. Cole-c(r)/WDC&S #1; Barks-r/WDC&S #32 plus Rosa, Jippes, Van Horn-r and new Rosa centerspread						4.00
601-611 ($5.95, 64 pgs., squarebound, bi-monthly): 601-Barks-c, r/Mickey Mouse V1#1, Rosa-a/scripts. 602-Rosa-c. 604-Taliaferro strip-r/1st Silly Symphony Sundays from 1932. 604,605-Jippes-a. 605-Walt Kelly-c; Gottfredson "Mickey Mouse Outwits the Phantom Blot" r/F.C. #16						6.00
612-633 ($6.95): 633-(2/99) Last Gladstone issue						7.00
634-675: 634-(7/03) First Gemstone issue; William Van Horn-c. 666-Mickey's Inferno						7.00
676-681: 676-Begin $7.50-c. 677-Bucky Bug's 75th Anniversary						7.50
682-698-($7.99)						8.00
699-714: 699-(9/09, $2.99) First BOOM! Kids issue. 700-Back-up story w/Van Horn-a						3.00
715-717: 715-(1/11, $3.99) 70th Anniverary issue; cover swipe of #1 by Van Horn; Jippes, Rosa-a. 716-Barks reprints						4.00

NOTE: *(#1-38, 68 pgs.; #39-42, 60 pgs.; #43-57, 61-134, 143-168, 446, 447, 52 pgs.; #58-60, 135-142, 169-540, 36 pgs.)*

NOTE: ***Barks*** *art in all issues #31 on, except where noted; c-95, 96, 104, 108, 109, 130-172, 174-178, 183, 198-200, 204, 206-209, 212-216, 218, 220, 226, 228-233, 235-238, 240-243, 247, 250, 253, 256, 260, 261, 276-283, 288-292, 295-298, 301, 303, 304, 306, 307, 309, 310, 313-316, 319, 321, 322, 324, 326, 328, 329, 331, 332, 334, 341, 342, 350, 351, 527r, 530r, 540(never before published), 546r, 557-586r(most), 596p, 601p.* ***Kelly*** *a-24p, 34-41, 43; r-522-524, 546, 547, 582, 583; covers(most)-34-118, 531r, 537r, 541r-543r, 562r, 571r, 605r. Walt Disney's Comics & Stories featured Mickey Mouse serials which were in practically every issue from #1 through #394 and #511 to date. The titles of the serials, along with the issues they are in, are listed in previous editions of this price guide.* ***Floyd Gottfredson*** *Mickey Mouse serials in issues #1-14, 18-66, 69-74, 78-100, 128, 562, 563, 568-572, 582, 583, 586-599 , 601-603 , 605-present , plus "Service with a Smile" in #13; "Mickey Mouse in a Warplant" (3 pgs.), and "Pluto Catches a Nazi Spy" (4 pgs.) in #62; "Mystery Next Door", #93; "Sunken Treasure", #94; "Aunt Marissa", #95 (r in #575); "Gangland", #98 (r in #562); "Thanksgiving Dinner", #99 (r in #567); and "The Talking Dog", #100 (r in #563); "Morty's Escapade," #128. "The Brave Little Tailor", #580; "Introducing Mickey Mouse Movies ", #581; Circus Roustabout, #585; "Rumplewatt the Giant", #604. Mickey Mouse by* ***Paul Murry*** *#152-547 except 155-57 (**Dick Moore**), 327-29 (**Tony Strobl**), 348-50 (**Jack Manning**), 533 (**Bill Wright**).* ***Don Rosa*** *story/a-523, 524, 526, 528, 531, 547, 601-present.* ***Al Taliaferro*** *Silly Symphonies in #5-"Three Little Pigs"; #13-"Birds of a Feather"; #14-"The Boarding School Mystery"; #15-"Cookieland" and "Three Little Kittens"; #16-"The Practical Pig"; #17-"The Ugly Duckling"; "The Wise Little Hen" in #580; and "Ambrose the Robber Kitten"; #19-"Penguin Isle"; and "Bucky Bug" in #20-23, 25, 26, 28 (one continuous story from 1932-34; first 2 pgs. not Taliaferro).* ***Gottfredson*** *strip r-562, 563, 568-572, 581, 585, 586, 590.* ***Taliaferro*** *strip r-584, 580.* ***Van Horn*** *a-537, 545, 561, 574, 587, 588, 591-present.*

WALT DISNEY'S COMICS DIGEST
Gladstone: Dec, 1986 - No. 7, Sept, 1987

	GD 2.0	VG 4.0	FN 6.0	VF 8.0	VF/NM 9.0	NM- 9.2
1	1	2	3	5	6	8
2-7						6.00

WALT DISNEY'S COMICS PENNY PINCHER
Gladstone: May, 1997 - No. 4, Aug, 1997 (99¢, limited series)

	GD 2.0	VG 4.0	FN 6.0	VF 8.0	VF/NM 9.0	NM- 9.2
1-4						3.00

WALT DISNEY'S DONALD AND MICKEY (Formerly Walt Disney's Mickey and Donald)
Gladstone (Bruce Hamilton Co.): No. 19, Sept, 1993 - No. 30, 1995 ($1.50, 36 & 68 pgs.)

	GD 2.0	VG 4.0	FN 6.0	VF 8.0	VF/NM 9.0	NM- 9.2
19,21-24,26-30: New & reprints. 19,21,23,24-Barks-r. 19,26-Murry-r. 22-Barks "Omelet" story r/WDC&S #146. 27-Mickey Mouse story by Caesar Ferioli (1st U.S work). 29-Rosa-c; Mickey Mouse story actually starring Goofy (does not include Mickey except on title page.)						4.00
20,25-($2.95, 68 pgs.): 20-Barks, Gottfredson-r						5.00

NOTE: *Donald Duck stories were all reprints.*

WALT DISNEY'S DONALD DUCK
Gemstone Publishing: 2006

	GD 2.0	VG 4.0	FN 6.0	VF 8.0	VF/NM 9.0	NM- 9.2
... Free Comic Book Day (5/06) r/WDC&S #531; Rosa-s/a; P&S. Block-s/a; Van Horn-s/a						2.50

WALT DISNEY'S DONALD DUCK ADVENTURES (D.D. Adv. #1-3)
Gladstone: 11/87-No. 20, 4/90 (1st Series); No. 21,8/93-No. 48, 2/98(3rd Series)

	GD 2.0	VG 4.0	FN 6.0	VF 8.0	VF/NM 9.0	NM- 9.2
1	1	2	3	5	6	8
2-r/F.C. #308						4.00
3,4,6,7,9-11,13,15-18: 3-r/F.C. #223. 4-r/F.C. #62. 9-r/F.C. #159, "Ghost of the Grotto". 11-r/F.C. #159, "Adventure Down Under." 16-r/F.C. #291; Rosa-c. 18-r/FC #318; Rosa-c						3.00
5,8: 5-Don Rosa-c/a. 8-Rosa-a						5.00
12($1.50, 52pgs)-Rosa-c/a w/Barks poster						6.00
14-r/F.C. #29, "Mummy's Ring"						4.00
19($1.95, 68 pgs.)-Barks-r/F.C. #199 (1 pg.)						4.00
20($1.95, 68 pgs.)-Barks-r/F.C. #189 & cover-r; William Van Horn-a						4.00
21,22: 21-r/D.D. #46. 22-r/F.C. #282						3.00
23-25,27,29,31,32-($1.50, 36 pgs.): 21,23,29-Rosa-c. 23-Intro/1st app. Andold Wild Duck by Marco Rota. 24-Van Horn-a. 27-1st Pat Block-a, "Mystery of Widow's Gap." 31,32-Block-c						3.00
26,28($2.95, 68 pgs.): 26-Barks-r/F.C. #108, "Terror of the River". 28-Barks-r/F.C. #199, "Sheriff of Bullet Valley"						4.00
30($2.95, 68 pgs.)-r/F.C. #367, Barks' "Christmas for Shacktown"						4.00
33($1.95, 68 pgs.)-r/F.C. #408, Barks' "The Golden Helmet;"Van Horn-c						4.00
34-43: 34-Resume $1.50-c. 34,35,37-Block-a/scripts. 38-Van Horn-c/a						3.00
44-48-($1.95-c)						3.00

NOTE: ***Barks*** *a-1-22r, 26r, 28r, 33r, 36r; c-3r, 8r, 10r, 14r, 20r.* ***Block*** *a-27, 30, 34, 35, 37; c-27, 30-32, 34, 35, 37; c-27, 30, 31, 32, 34, 35, 37.* ***Rosa*** *a-5, 8, 12, 43; c-13, 16, 18, 21, 23, 43.*

WALT DISNEY'S DONALD DUCK ADVENTURES (2nd Series)

Walt Disney's Donald Duck Adventures #18 © DIS

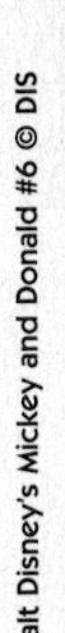

Walt Disney's Mickey and Donald #6 © DIS

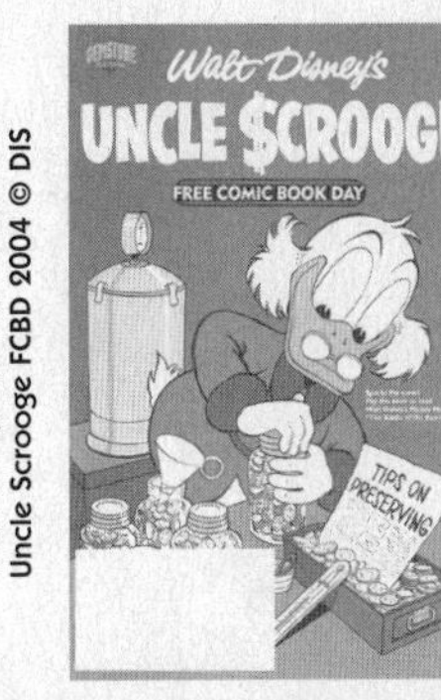

Walt Disney's Mickey Mouse and Uncle Scrooge FCBD 2004 © DIS

GD 2.0 VG 4.0 FN 6.0 VF 8.0 VF/NM 9.0 NM- 9.2

Disney Comics: June, 1990 - No. 38, July, 1993 ($1.50)

1-Rosa-a & scripts 5.00
2-21,23,25,27-33,35,36,38: 2-Barks-r/WDC&S #35; William Van Horn-a begins, ends #20. 9-Barks-r/F.C. #178. 9,11,14,17-No Van Horn-a. 11-Mad #1 cover parody. 14-Barks-r. 17-Barks-r. 21-r/FC #203 by Barks. 29-r/MOC #20 by Barks 3.00
22,24,26,34,37: 22-Rosa-a (10 pgs.) & scripts. 24-Rosa-a & scripts. 26-r/March of Comics #41 by Barks. 34-Rosa-c/a. 37-Rosa-a; Barks-r 4.00
NOTE: *Barks r-2, 4, 9(F.C. #178), 14(D.D. #45), 17, 21, 26, 27, 29 , 35, 36(D.D #60)-38. Taliaferro a-34r, 36r.*

WALT DISNEY'S DONALD DUCK ADVENTURES
Gemstone Publishing: May, 2003 (giveaway promoting 2003 return of Disney Comics)

...Free Comic Book Day Edition - cover logo on red background; reprints "Maharajah Donald" & "The Peaceful Hills" from March of Comics #4; Barks-s/a; Kelly original-c on back-c 2.50
...San Diego Comic-Con 2003 Edition - cover logo on gold background 2.50
...ANA World's Fair of Money Baltimore Edition - cover logo on green background 2.50
...WizardWorld Chicago 2003 Edition - cover logo on blue background 2.50

WALT DISNEY'S DONALD DUCK ADVENTURES (Take-Along Comic)
Gemstone Publishing: July, 2003 - No. 21, Nov, 2006 ($7.95, 5" x 7-1/2")

1-21-Mickey Mouse & Uncle Scrooge app. 9-Christmas-c 8.00
... , The Barks/Rosa Collection Vol. 2 (3/08, $8.99) reprints Donald Duck's Atom Bomb, Super Snooper & The Trouble With Dimes by Barks; The Duck Who Fell to Earth, Super Snooper Strikes Again & The Money Pit by Rosa 9.00
... , The Barks/Rosa Collection Vol. 3 (9/08, $8.99) r/FC #408 "The Golden Helmet" by Barks & DDA #43 "The Lost Charts of Columbus" by Rosa; cover gallery and bonus art 9.00

WALT DISNEY'S DONALD DUCK AND FRIENDS (Continues as Donald Duck and Friends)
Gemstone Publishing: No. 308, Oct, 2003 - No. 346, Dec, 2006 ($2.95)

308-346: 308-Numbering resumes from Gladstone Donald Duck series; Halloween-c. 332-Halloween-c; r/#26 by Carl Barks 3.00

WALT DISNEY'S DONALD DUCK AND MICKEY MOUSE (Formerly Walt Disney's Donald and Mickey)
Gladstone (Bruce Hamilton Company): Sept, 1995 - No. 7, Sept, 1996 ($1.50, 32 pgs.)

1-7: 1-Barks-r and new Mickey Mouse stories in all. 5,6-Mickey Mouse stories by Caesar Ferioli. 7-New Donald Duck and Mickey Mouse x-over story; Barks-r/WDC&S #51 3.00
NOTE: *Issue #8 was advertised, but cancelled.*

WALT DISNEY'S DONALD DUCK AND UNCLE SCROOGE
Gemstone Publishing: Nov, 2005 ($6.95, square-bound one-shot)

nn-New story by John Lustig and Pat Block and r/Uncle Scrooge #59 7.00

WALT DISNEY'S DONALD DUCK FAMILY
Gemstone Publishing: Jun, 2008 ($8.99, square-bound)

... The Daan Jippes Collection Vol. 1 - R/Barks-s re-drawn by Jippes for Dutch comics 9.00

WALT DISNEY'S DONALD DUCK IN THE CASE OF THE MISSING MUMMY
Gemstone Publishing: Oct, 2007 ($8.99, square-bound one-shot)

nn-New story by Shelley and Pat Block and r/Donald Duck FC #29 9.00

WALT DISNEY'S GYRO GEARLOOSE
Gemstone Publishing: May, 2008

... Free Comic Book Day (5/08) short stories by Barks, Rosa, Van Horn, Gerstein 2.50

WALT DISNEY SHOWCASE
Gold Key: Oct, 1970 - No. 54, Jan, 1980 (No. 44-48: 68pgs., 49-54: 52pgs.)

1-Boatniks (Movie)-Photo-c 3 6 9 18 27 35
2-Moby Duck 3 6 9 14 19 24
3,4,7: 3-Bongo & Lumpjaw-r. 4,7-Pluto-r 2 4 6 10 14 18
5-$1,000,000 Duck (Movie)-Photo-c 3 6 9 16 22 28
6-Bedknobs & Broomsticks (Movie) 3 6 9 16 22 28
8-Daisy & Donald 2 4 6 11 16 20
9- 101 Dalmatians (cartoon feat.); r/F.C. #1183 3 6 9 17 25 32
10-Napoleon & Samantha (Movie)-Photo-c 3 6 9 17 22 28
11-Moby Duck-r 2 4 6 10 14 18
12-Dumbo-r/Four Color #668 2 4 6 11 16 20
13-Pluto-r 2 4 6 10 14 18
14-World's Greatest Athlete (Movie)-Photo-c 3 6 9 16 22 28
15- 3 Little Pigs-r 2 4 6 11 16 20
16-Aristocats (cartoon feature); r/Aristocats #1 3 6 9 16 22 28
17-Mary Poppins; r/M.P. #10136-501-Photo-c 3 6 9 16 22 28
18-Gyro Gearloose; Barks-r/F.C. #1047,1184 3 6 9 18 27 35
19-That Darn Cat; r/That Darn Cat #10171-602-Hayley Mills photo-c 3 6 9 16 22 28
20,23-Pluto-r 2 4 6 11 16 20
21-Li'l Bad Wolf & The Three Little Pigs 2 4 6 10 14 18
22-Unbirthday Party with Alice in Wonderland; r/Four Color #341 3 6 9 14 19 24
24-26: 24-Herbie Rides Again (Movie); sequel to "The Love Bug"; photo-c. 25-Old Yeller (Movie); r/F.C. #869; Photo-c. 26-Lt. Robin Crusoe USN (Movie); r/Lt. Robin Crusoe USN #10191-601; photo-c 2 4 6 11 16 20
27-Island at the Top of the World (Movie)-Photo-c 3 6 9 14 19 24
28-Brer Rabbit, Bucky Bug-r/WDC&S #58 2 4 6 11 16 20
29-Escape to Witch Mountain (Movie)-Photo-c 3 6 9 14 19 24
30-Magica De Spell; Barks-r/Uncle Scrooge #36 & WDC&S #258 3 6 9 21 32 42
31-Bambi (cartoon feature); r/Four Color #186 2 4 6 13 18 22
32-Spin & Marty-r/F.C. #1026; Mickey Mouse Club (TV)-Photo-c 3 6 9 14 19 24
33-40: 33-Pluto-r/F.C. #1143. 34-Paul Revere's Ride with Johnny Tremain (TV); r/F.C. #822. 35-Goofy-r/F.C. #952. 36-Peter Pan-r/F.C. #442. 37-Tinker Bell & Jiminy Cricket-r/F.C. #982,989. 38,39-Mickey & the Sleuth, Parts 1 & 2. 40-The Rescuers (cartoon feature) 2 4 6 9 13 16
41-Herbie Goes to Monte Carlo (Movie); sequel to "Herbie Rides Again"; photo-c 2 4 6 10 14 18
42-Mickey & the Sleuth 2 4 6 9 13 16
43-Pete's Dragon (Movie)-Photo-c 2 4 6 13 18 22
44-Return From Witch Mountain (new) & In Search of the Castaways-r (Movies)-Photo-c; 68 pg. giants begin 3 6 9 14 19 24
45-The Jungle Book (Movie); r/#30033-803 3 6 9 17 25 32
46-48: 46-The Cat From Outer Space (Movie)(new), & The Shaggy Dog (Movie)-r/F.C. #985; photo-c. 47-Mickey Mouse Surprise Party-r. 48-The Wonderful Advs. of Pinocchio-r/F.C. #1203; last 68 pg. issue 2 4 6 10 14 18
49-54: 49-North Avenue Irregulars (Movie); Zorro-r/Zorro #11; 52 pgs. begin; photo-c. 50-Bedknobs & Broomsticks-r/#6; Mooncussers-r/World of Adv. #1; photo-c. 51-101 Dalmatians-r. 52-Unidentified Flying Oddball (Movie); r/Picnic Party #8; photo-c. 53-The Scarecrow-r (TV). 54-The Black Hole (Movie)-Photo-c (predates Black Hole #1) 2 4 6 9 13 16

WALT DISNEY'S MAGAZINE (TV)(Formerly Walt Disney's Mickey Mouse Club Magazine) (50¢, bi-monthly)
Western Publishing Co.: V2#4, June, 1957 - V4#6, Oct, 1959

V2#4-Stories & articles on the Mouseketeers, Zorro, & Goofy and other Disney characters & people 7 14 21 45 73 100
V2#5, V2#6(10/57) 6 12 18 41 66 90
V3#1(12/57), V3#3-5 6 12 18 37 59 80
V3#2-Annette Funicello photo-c 10 20 30 73 134 195
V3#6(10/58)-TV Zorro photo-c 8 16 24 52 86 120
V4#1(12/58) - V4#2-4,6(10/59) 6 12 18 37 59 80
V4#5-Annette Funicello photo-c, w/ 2-photo articles 10 20 30 73 134 195
NOTE: *V2#4-V3#6 were 11-1/2x8-1/2", 48 pgs.; V4#1 on were 10x8", 52 pgs. (Peak circulation of 400,000).*

WALT DISNEY'S MERRY CHRISTMAS (See Dell Giant #39)

WALT DISNEY'S MICKEY AND DONALD (M & D #1,2)(Becomes Walt Disney's Donald & Mickey #19 on)
Gladstone: Mar, 1988 - No. 18, May, 1990 (95¢)

1-Don Rosa-a; r/1949 Firestone giveaway 6.00
2-8: 3-Infinity-c. 4-8-Barks-r 3.00
9-15: 9-r/1948 Firestone giveaway; X-Mas-c 3.00
16($1.50, 52 pgs.)-r/FC #157 5.00
17-(68 pgs.) Barks M.M.-r/FC #79 plus Barks D.D.-r; Rosa-a; x-mas-c 6.00
18($1.95, 68 pgs.)-Gottfredson-r/WDC&S #13,72-74; Kelly-c(r); Barks-r 5.00
NOTE: *Barks reprints in 1-15, 17, 18. Kelly c-13r, 14 (r/Walt Disney's C&S #58), 18r.*

WALT DISNEY'S MICKEY MOUSE
Gemstone Publishing: May, 2007

... Free Comic Book Day (5/07) Floyd Gottfredson-s/a 2.50

WALT DISNEY'S MICKEY MOUSE ADVENTURES (Take-Along Comic)
Gemstone Publishing: Aug, 2004 - No. 12 ($7.95, 5" x 7-1/2")

1-12-Goofy, Donald Duck & Uncle Scrooge app. 8.00

WALT DISNEY'S MICKEY MOUSE AND BLOTMAN IN BLOTMAN RETURNS
Gemstone Publishing: Dec, 2006 ($5.99, squarebound, one-shot)

nn-Wraparound-c by Noel Van Horn; Super Goof back-up story 6.00

WALT DISNEY'S MICKEY MOUSE AND FRIENDS (See Mickey Mouse and Friends for #296)
Gemstone Publishing: No. 257, Oct, 2003 - No. 295, Dec, 2006 ($2.95)

257-295: 257-Numbering resumes from Gladstone Mickey Mouse series; Halloween-c. 285-Return of the Phantom Blot 3.00

WALT DISNEY'S MICKEY MOUSE AND UNCLE SCROOGE
Gemstone Publishing: June, 2004 (Free Comic Book Day giveaway)

nn-Flip book with r/Uncle Scrooge #15 and r/Mickey Mouse Four Color #79 (only Barks drawn

Walt Disney's Uncle Scrooge #379 © DIS

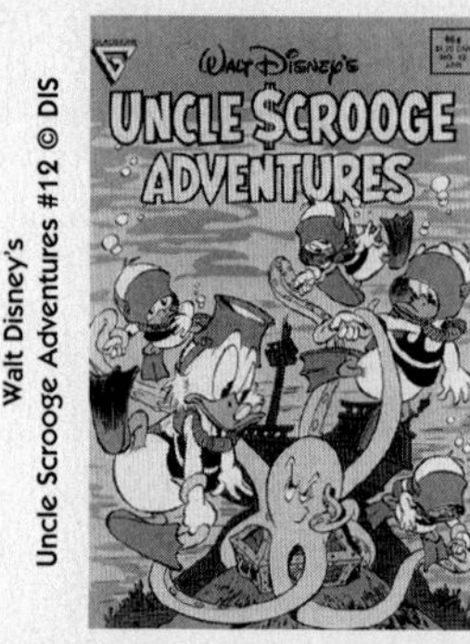

Walt Disney's Uncle Scrooge Adventures #12 © DIS

Wambi, Jungle Boy #10 © FH

	GD 2.0	VG 4.0	FN 6.0	VF 8.0	VF/NM 9.0	NM- 9.2

Mickey Mouse story) 2.50

WALT DISNEY'S MICKEY MOUSE CLUB MAGAZINE (TV)(Becomes Walt Disney's Magazine)
Western Publishing Co.: Winter, 1956 - V2#3, Apr, 1957 (11-1/2x8-1/2", quarterly, 48 pgs.)

V1#1 13 26 39 93 182 270
2-4 8 16 24 58 97 135
V2#1,2 7 14 21 47 76 105
3-Annette photo-c 12 24 36 87 164 240
Annual(1956)-Two different issues; ($1.50-Whitman); 120 pgs., cardboard covers, 11-3/4x8-3/4"; reprints 13 26 39 93 182 270
Annual(1957)-Same as above 11 22 33 80 150 220

WALT DISNEY'S MICKEY MOUSE MEETS BLOTMAN
Gemstone Publishing: Aug, 2005 ($5.99, squarebound, one-shot)

nn-Wraparound-c by Noel Van Horn; Super Goof back-up story 6.00

WALT DISNEY'S PINOCCHIO SPECIAL
Gladstone: Spring, 1990 ($1.00)

1-50th anniversary edition; Kelly-r/F.C. #92 3.00

WALT DISNEY'S SPRING FEVER
Gemstone Publishing: Apr, 2007; Apr, 2008 ($9.50, squarebound)

1,2: 1-New stories and reprints incl. "Mystery of the Swamp" by Carl Barks 9.50

WALT DISNEY'S THE ADVENTUROUS UNCLE SCROOGE MCDUCK
Gladstone: Jan, 1998 - No. 2, Mar, 1998 ($1.95)

1,2: 1-Barks-a(r). 2-Rosa-a(r) 3.00

WALT DISNEY'S THE JUNGLE BOOK
W.D. Publications (Disney Comics): 1990 ($5.95, graphic novel, 68 pgs.)

nn-Movie adaptation; movie rereleased in 1990 6.00
nn-($2.95, 68 pgs.)-Comic edition; wraparound-c 4.00

WALT DISNEY'S UNCLE SCROOGE (Formerly Uncle Scrooge #1-209)
Gladstone #210-242/Disney Comics #243-280/Gladstone #281-318/Gemstone #319 on: No. 210, 10/86 - No. 242, 4/90; No. 243, 6/90 - No. 318, 2/99; No. 319, 7/03 - No. 383, 11/08

210-1st Gladstone issue; r/WDC&S #134 (1st Beagle Boys) 2 4 6 9 13 16
211-218: 216-New story ("Go Slowly Sands of Time") plotted and partly scripted by Barks. 217-r/U.S. #7, "Seven Cities of Cibola" 2 4 6 9 12 15
219-"Son Of The Sun" by Rosa (his 1st pro work) 3 6 9 14 20 25
220-Don Rosa-a/scripts 1 2 3 5 6 8
221-223,225,228-234,236-240 4.00
224,226,227,235: 224-Rosa-c/a. 226,227-Rosa-a. 235-Rosa-a/scripts 5.00
241-($1.95, 68 pgs.)-Rosa finishes over Barks-r 6.00
242-($1.95, 68 pgs.)-Barks-r; Rosa-a(1 pg.) 6.00
243-249,251-260,264-275,277-280,282-284-($1.50): 243-1st by Disney Comics. 274-All Barks issue. 275-Contains centerspread by Rosa. 279-All Barks issue; Rosa-c. 283-r/WDC&S #98 3.00
250-($2.25, 52 pgs.)-Barks-r; wraparound-c 4.00
261-263,276-Don Rosa-c/a 5.00
281-Gladstone issues start again; Rosa-c 6.00
285-The Life and Times of Scrooge McDuck Pt. 1; Rosa-c/a/scripts 1 3 4 6 8 10
286-293: The Life and Times of Scrooge McDuck Pt. 2-8; Rosa-c/a/scripts. 293-($1.95, 36 pgs.)-The Life and Times of Scrooge McDuck Pt. 9 6.00
294-299, 301-308-($1.50, 32 pgs.): 294-296-The Life and Times of Scrooge McDuck Pt. 10-12. 296-Christmas-c. 297-The Life and Times of Uncle Scrooge Pt. 0; Rosa-c/a/scripts 3.00
300-($2.25, 48 pgs.)-Rosa-c; Barks-r/WDC&S #104 and U.S. #216; r/U.S. #220; includes new centerfold. 4.00
309-($6.95) Low print run 2 4 6 11 16 20
310-($6.95) Low print run 3 6 9 20 30 40
311-320-($6.95) 318-(2/99) Last Gladstone issue. 319-(7/03) First Gemstone issue; The Dutchman's Secret by Don Rosa 2 4 6 8 10 12
321-360 7.00
361-366: 361-Begin $7.50-c 7.50
367-383-($7.99) 8.00
... Adventures, The Barks/Rosa Collection Vol. 1 (Gemstone, 7/07, $8.50) reprints Pygmy Indians appearances in U.S. #18 by Barks and WDC&S #633 by Rosa 8.50
Walt Disney's The Life and Times of Scrooge McDuck by Don Rosa TPB (Gemstone, 2005, $16.99) Reprints #285-296, with foreword, commentaries & sketch pages by Rosa 17.00
Walt Disney's The Life and Times of Scrooge McDuck Companion by Don Rosa TPB (Gemstone, 2006, $16.99) additional chapters, with foreword & commentaries 17.00

NOTE: ***Barks** r-210-218, 220-223, 224(2pg.), 225-234, 236-242, 245, 246, 250-253, 255, 256, 258, 261(2 pg.), 265, 267, 268, 270(2), 272-284, 299-present; c(r)-210, 212, 221, 228, 229, 232, 233, 284. scripts-287, 293. **Rosa** a-219, 220, 224, 226, 227, 235, 261-263, 268, 275-277, 285-297; c-219, 224, 231, 261-263, 276, 278-281, 285-296; scripts-219, 220, 224, 235, 261-263, 268, 276, 285-296.*

WALT DISNEY'S UNCLE SCROOGE
Gemstone Publishing

nn-(5/05, FCBD) Reprints Uncle Scrooge's debut in Four Color Comics #386; Barks-s/a 2.50

WALT DISNEY'S UNCLE SCROOGE ADVENTURES (U. Scrooge Advs. #1-3)
Gladstone Publishing: Nov, 1987 - No. 21, May, 1990; No. 22, Sept, 1993 - No. 54, Feb, 1998

1-Barks-r begin, ends #26 1 2 3 5 6 8
2-4 4.00
5,9,14: 5-Rosa-c/a; no Barks-r. 9,14-Rosa-a 5.00
6-8,10-13,15-19: 10-r/U.S. #18(all Barks) 3.00
20,21 ($1.95, 68 pgs.) 20-Rosa-c/a. 21-Rosa-a 5.00
22 ($1.50)-Rosa-c; r/U.S. #26 5.00
23-($2.95, 68 pgs.)-Vs. The Phantom Blot-r/P.B. #3; Barks-r 4.00
24-26,29,31,32,34-36: 24,25,29,31,32-Rosa-c. 25-r/U.S. #21 3.00
27-Guardians of the Lost Library - Rosa-c/a/story; origin of Junior Woodchuck Guidebook 3.00
28-($2.95, 68 pgs.)-r/U.S. #13 w/restored missing panels 4.00
30-($2.95, 68 pgs.)-r/U.S. #12; Rosa-c 4.00
33-($2.95, 64 pgs.)-New Barks story 4.00
37-54 3.00

NOTE: ***Barks** r-1-4, 6-8, 10-13, 15-21, 23, 22, 24; c(r)-15, 16, 17, 21. **Rosa** a-5, 9, 14, 20, 21, 27, 51; c-5, 13, 14, 17(finishes), 20, 22, 24, 25, 27, 28, 51; scripts-5, 9, 14, 27.*

WALT DISNEY'S UNCLE SCROOGE AND DONALD DUCK
Gladstone: Jan, 1998 - No. 2, Mar, 1998 ($1.95)

1,2: 1-Rosa-a(r) 3.00

WALT DISNEY'S UNCLE SCROOGE ADVENTURES IN COLOR
Gladstone Publ.: Dec, 1995 - Present ($8.95/$9.95, squarebound, 56 issue limited series) (Polybagged w/card) (Series chronologically reprints all the stories written & drawn by Carl Barks)

1-56: 1-(12/95)-r/FC #386. 15-(12/96)-r/US #15. 16-(12/96)-r/US #16. 18-(1/97)-r/US #18 10.00

WALT DISNEY'S VACATION PARADE
Gemstone Publishing: 2004 - No. 5, July, 2008 ($8.95/$9.95, squarebound, annual)

1-3: 1-Reprints stories from Dell Giant Comics Vacation Parade 1 (July 1950) 9.00
4,5-($9.95): 4-(5/07). 5-(7/08) 10.00

WALT DISNEY'S WHEATIES PREMIUMS (See Wheaties in the Promotional section)

WALT DISNEY'S WORLD OF THE DRAGONLORDS
Gemstone Publishing: 2005 ($12.99, squarebound, graphic novel)

SC-Uncle Scrooge, Donald & nephews app.; Byron Erickson-s/Giorgio Cavazzano-a 13.00

WALT DISNEY TREASURES - DISNEY COMICS: 75 YEARS OF INNOVATION
Gemstone Publishing: 2006 ($12.99, TPB)

SC-Reprints from 1930-2004, including debut of Mickey Mouse newspaper strip 13.00

WALT DISNEY TREASURES - UNCLE SCROOGE: A LITTLE SOMETHING SPECIAL
Gemstone Publishing: 2008 ($16.99, TPB)

SC-Uncle Scrooge classics from 1954-2006, including "The Seven Cities of Cibola" 17.00

WALTER LANTZ ANDY PANDA (Also see Andy Panda)
Gold Key: Aug, 1973 - No. 23, Jan, 1978 (Walter Lantz)

1-Reprints 3 6 9 14 19 24
2-10-All reprints 2 4 6 9 12 15
11-23: 15,17-19,22-Reprints 1 2 3 5 7 9

WALT KELLY'S...
Eclipse Comics: Dec, 1987; Apr, 1988 ($1.75/$2.50, Baxter paper)

...Christmas Classics 1 (12/87)-Kelly-r/Peter Wheat & Santa Claus Funnies, ...Springtime Tales 1 (4/88, $2.50)-Kelly-r 4.00

WALTONS, THE (See Kite Fun Book)

WALT SCOTT (See Little People)

WALT SCOTT'S CHRISTMAS STORIES (See Little People, 4-Color #959, 1062)

WAMBI, JUNGLE BOY (See Jungle Comics)
Fiction House Magazines: Spr, 1942; No. 2, Win, 1942-43; No. 3, Spr, 1943; No. 4, Fall, 1948; No. 5, Sum, 1949; No. 6, Spr, 1950; No. 7-10, 1950(nd); No. 11, Spr, 1951 - No. 18, Win, 1952-53 (#1-3: 68 pgs.)

1-Wambi, the Jungle Boy begins 95 190 285 603 1039 1475
2 (1942)-Kiefer-c 50 100 150 315 533 750
3 (1943)-Kiefer-c/a 39 78 117 240 395 550
4 (1948)-Origin in text 28 56 84 165 270 375
5 (Fall, 1949, 36 pgs.)-Kiefer-c/a 23 46 69 136 223 310
6-10: 7-(52 pgs.)-New logo 20 40 60 114 182 250

Wanted #1 © Millar & Jones

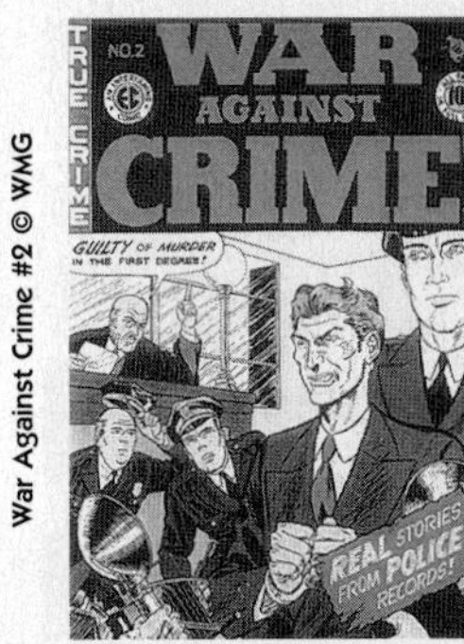

War Against Crime #2 © WMG

War Birds #3 © FH

	GD 2.0	VG 4.0	FN 6.0	VF 8.0	VF/NM 9.0	NM- 9.2
11-18	15	30	45	84	127	170
I.W. Reprint #8('64)-r/#12 with new-c	3	6	9	14	20	25

NOTE: ***Alex Blum** c-8. **Kiefer** c-1-5. **Whitman** c-11-18.*

WANDERERS (See Adventure Comics #375, 376)
DC Comics: June, 1988 - No. 13, Apr, 1989 ($1.25) (Legion of Super-Heroes spin off)

	GD	VG	FN	VF	VF/NM	NM-
1-13: 1,2-Steacy-c. 3-Legion app.						3.00

WANDERING STAR
Pen & Ink Comics/Sirius Entertainment No. 12 on: 1993 - No. 21, Mar, 1997 ($2.50/$2.75, B&W)

	GD	VG	FN	VF	VF/NM	NM-
1-1st printing; Teri Sue Wood c/a/scripts in all	1	2	3	5	6	8
1-2nd and 3rd printings						3.00
2-1st printing.						4.00
2-21: 2-2nd printing. 12-(1/96)-1st Sirius issue						3.00
Trade paperback ($11.95)-r/1-7; 1st printing of 1000, signed and #'d						18.00
Trade paperback-2nd printing, 2000 signed						15.00
TPB Volume 2,3 (11/98, 12/98, $14.95) 2-r/#8-14, 3-r/#15-21						15.00

WANTED
Image Comics (Top Cow): Dec, 2003 - No. 6, Feb, 2004 ($2.99)

	GD	VG	FN	VF	VF/NM	NM-
1-Three covers; Mark Millar-s/J.G. Jones-a; intro Wesley Gibson						3.00
1-4-Death Row Edition; r/#1-4 with extra sketch pages and deleted panels						3.00
2-6: 2-Cameos of DC villains. 6-Giordano-a in flashback scenes						3.00
...Dossier (5/04, $2.99) Pin-ups and character info; art by Jones, Romita Jr. & others						3.00
Image Firsts: Wanted #1 (9/10, $1.00) reprints #1						1.00
... Movie Edition Vol. 1 TPB (2008, $19.99) r/#1-6 & Dossier; movie photo-c; sketch pages & cover gallery; interviews with movie cast and director						20.00
HC (2005, $29.99) r/#1-6 & Dossier; intro by Vaughan, sketch pages & cover gallery						30.00

WANTED COMICS
Toytown Publications/Patches/Orbit Publ.: No. 9, Sept-Oct, 1947 - No. 53, April, 1953 (#9-33: 52 pgs.)

	GD	VG	FN	VF	VF/NM	NM-
9-True crime cases; radio's Mr. D. A. app.	26	52	78	154	252	350
10,11: 10-Giunta-a; radio's Mr. D. A. app.	16	32	48	94	147	200
12-Used in **SOTI**, pg. 277	18	36	54	105	165	225
13-Heroin drug propaganda story	16	32	48	94	147	200
14-Marijuana drug mention story (2 pgs.)	15	30	45	88	137	185
15-17,19,20	14	28	42	76	108	140
18-Marijuana story, "Satan's Cigarettes"; r-in #45 & retitled	26	52	78	154	252	350
21,22: 21-Krigstein-a. 22-Extreme violence	14	28	42	78	112	145
23,25-34,36-38,40-44,46-48,53	12	24	36	67	94	120
24-Krigstein-a; "The Dope King", marijuana mention story	15	30	45	90	140	190
35-Used in **SOTI**, pg. 160	15	30	45	84	127	170
39-Drug propaganda story "The Horror Weed"	19	38	57	111	176	240
45-Marijuana story from #18	14	28	42	76	108	140
49-Has unstable pink-c that fades easily; rare in mint condition	14	28	42	80	115	150
50-Has unstable pink-c like #49; surrealist-c by Buscema; horror stories	15	30	45	83	124	165
51- "Holiday of Horror" junkie story; drug-c	15	30	45	90	140	190
52-Classic "Cult of Killers" opium use story	15	30	45	88	137	185

NOTE: ***Buscema** c-50, 51. **Lawrence** and **Leav** c/a most issues. **Syd Shores** c/a-48; c-37. Issues 9-46 have wanted criminals with their descriptions & drawn picture on cover.*

WANTED: DEAD OR ALIVE (TV)
Dell Publishing Co.: No. 1102, May-July, 1960 - No. 1164, Mar-May, 1961

	GD	VG	FN	VF	VF/NM	NM-
Four Color 1102 (#1)-Steve McQueen photo-c	12	24	36	82	154	225
Four Color 1164-Steve McQueen photo-c	9	18	27	63	107	150

WANTED, THE WORLD'S MOST DANGEROUS VILLAINS (See DC Special)
National Periodical Publ.: July-Aug, 1972 - No. 9, Aug-Sept, 1973 (All reprints & 20¢ issues)

	GD	VG	FN	VF	VF/NM	NM-
1-Batman, Green Lantern (story r-from G.L. #1), & Green Arrow	4	8	12	22	34	45
2-Batman/Joker/Penguin-c/story r-from Batman #25; plus Flash story (r-from Flash #121)	3	6	9	17	25	32
3-9: 3-Dr. Fate(r/More Fun #65), Hawkman(r/Flash #100), & Vigilante(r/Action #69). 4-Green Lantern(r/All-American #61) & Kid Eternity(r/Kid Eternity #15). 5-Dollman/Green Lantern. 6-Burnley Starman; Wildcat/Sargon. 7-Johnny Quick(r/More Fun #76), Hawkman(r/Flash #90), Hourman by Baily(r/Adv. #72). 8-Dr. Fate/Flash(r/Flash #114). 9-S&K Sandman/Superman	3	6	9	14	20	26

NOTE: ***B. Bailey** a-7r. **Infantino** a-2r. **Kane** r-1, 5. **Kubert** r-3i, 6, 7. **Meskin** r-3, 7. **Reinman** r-4, 6.*

WAR (See Fightin' Marines #122)
Charlton Comics: Jul, 1975 - No. 9, Nov, 1976; No. 10, Sept, 1978 - No. 47, 1984

	GD	VG	FN	VF	VF/NM	NM-
1-Boyette painted-c	3	6	9	14	19	24
2-10: 3-Sutton painted-c	2	4	6	8	10	12
11-20	1	2	3	5	6	8
21-40	1	2	3	4	5	7
41,42,44-47 (lower print run): 47-Reprints	1	2	3	5	6	8
43 (2/84) (lower print run) Ditko-a (7 pgs.)	2	4	6	8	10	12
7,9 (Modern Comics-r, 1977)						6.00

WAR, THE (See The Draft & The Pitt)
Marvel Comics: 1989 - No. 4, 1990 ($3.50, squarebound, 52 pgs.)

	GD	VG	FN	VF	VF/NM	NM-
1-4: Characters from New Universe						4.00

WAR ACTION (Korean War)
Atlas Comics (CPS): April, 1952 - No. 14, June, 1953

	GD	VG	FN	VF	VF/NM	NM-
1	20	40	60	117	189	260
2-Hartley-a	13	26	39	72	101	130
3-10,14: 7-Pakula-a. 14-Colan-a	10	20	30	56	76	95
11-13-Krigstein-a. 11-Romita-a	11	22	33	60	83	105

NOTE: ***Berg** c-11. **Brodsky** a-2; c-1-4. **Heath** a-1; c-7, 14. **Keller** a-6. **Maneely** a-1; c-12. **Sale** a-7.**Tuska** a-2, 8.*

WAR ADVENTURES
Atlas Comics (HPC): Jan, 1952 - No. 13, Feb, 1953

	GD	VG	FN	VF	VF/NM	NM-
1-Tuska-a	20	40	60	114	182	250
2	12	24	36	67	94	120
3-7,9-13: 3-Pakula-a. 7-Maneely-c. 9-Romita-a	10	20	30	56	76	95
8-Krigstein-a	11	22	33	60	83	105

NOTE: ***Brodsky** c-1-3, 6, 8, 11, 12. **Heath** a-2, 5, 7, 10; c-4, 5, 9, 13. **Reinman** a-13. **Robinson** a-3; c-10.*

WAR ADVENTURES ON THE BATTLEFIELD (See Battlefield)

WAR AGAINST CRIME! (Becomes Vault of Horror #12 on)
E. C. Comics: Spring, 1948 - No. 11, Feb-Mar, 1950

	GD	VG	FN	VF	VF/NM	NM-
1-Real Stories From Police Records on-c #1-9	81	162	243	518	884	1250
2,3	47	94	141	296	498	700
4-9	42	84	126	265	445	625
10-1st Vault Keeper app. & 1st Vault of Horror	223	446	669	1784	2842	3900
11-2nd Vault Keeper app.; 1st EC horror-c	143	286	429	1144	1822	2500

NOTE: *All have **Johnny Craig** covers. **Feldstein** a-4, 7-9. **Harrison/Wood** a-11. **Ingels** a-1, 2, 8. **Palais** a-8. Changes to horror with #10.*

WAR AGAINST CRIME
Gemstone Publishing: Apr, 2000 - No. 11, Feb, 2001 ($2.50)

	GD	VG	FN	VF	VF/NM	NM-
1-11: E.C. reprints						3.00

WAR AND ATTACK (Also see Special War Series #3)
Charlton Comics: Fall, 1964; V2#54, June, 1966 - V2#63, Dec, 1967

	GD	VG	FN	VF	VF/NM	NM-
1-Wood-a (25 pgs.)	5	10	15	32	51	70
V2#54(6/66)-#63 (Formerly Fightin' Air Force)	3	6	9	16	22	28

NOTE: ***Montes/Bache** a-55, 56, 60, 63.*

WAR AT SEA (Formerly Space Adventures)
Charlton Comics: No. 22, Nov, 1957 - No. 42, June, 1961

	GD	VG	FN	VF	VF/NM	NM-
22	7	14	21	37	46	55
23-30	6	12	18	27	33	38
31-42	3	6	9	17	25	32

WAR BATTLES
Harvey Publications: Feb, 1952 - No. 9, Dec, 1953

	GD	VG	FN	VF	VF/NM	NM-
1-Powell-a; Elias-c	9	18	27	63	107	150
2-Powell-a	5	10	15	34	55	75
3,4,7-9: 3,7-Powell-a	5	10	15	32	51	70
5-Flamethrower cover	12	24	36	67	94	120
6-Nostrand-a	6	12	18	39	62	85

WAR BIRDS
Fiction House Magazines: 1952(nd) - No. 3, Winter, 1952-53

	GD	VG	FN	VF	VF/NM	NM-
1	16	32	48	94	147	200
2,3	11	22	33	62	86	110

WARBLADE: ENDANGERED SPECIES (Also see WildC.A.T.S: Covert Action Teams)
Image Comics (WildStorm Productions): Jan, 1995 - No. 4, Apr, 1995 ($2.50, limited series)

	GD	VG	FN	VF	VF/NM	NM-
1-4: 1-Gatefold wraparound-c						3.00

WAR COMBAT (Becomes Combat Casey #6 on)
Atlas Comics (LBI No. 1/SAI No. 2-5): March, 1952 - No. 5, Nov, 1952

	GD	VG	FN	VF	VF/NM	NM-
1	18	36	54	103	162	220
2	11	22	33	62	86	110
3-5	10	20	30	54	72	90

NOTE: ***Berg** a-2, 4, 5. **Brodsky** c-1, 2, 4, 5. **Henkel** a-5. **Maneely** a-1, 4; c-3. **Reinman** a-2.*

War Fury #3 © Comic Media

War Heroes #10 © DELL

Warlock (1999 series) #2 © MAR

	GD 2.0	VG 4.0	FN 6.0	VF 8.0	VF/NM 9.0	NM- 9.2

WAR COMICS (War Stories #5 on)(See Key Ring Comics)
Dell Publishing Co.: May, 1940 (No month given) - No. 4, Sept, 1941

	GD	VG	FN	VF	VF/NM	NM-
1-Sikandur the Robot Master, Sky Hawk, Scoop Mason, War Correspondent begin; McWilliams-c; 1st war comic	65	130	195	416	708	1000
2-Origin Greg Gilday (5/41)	36	72	108	211	343	475
3-Joan becomes Greg Gilday's aide	24	48	72	142	234	325
4-Origin Night Devils	25	50	75	147	241	335

WAR COMICS
Marvel/Atlas (USA No. 1-41/JPI No. 42-49): Dec, 1950 - No. 49, Sept, 1957

	GD	VG	FN	VF	VF/NM	NM-
1	27	54	81	158	259	360
2	15	30	45	86	133	180
3-10	14	28	42	76	108	140
11-Flame thrower w/burning bodies on-c	17	34	51	98	154	210
12-20: 16-Romita-a	11	22	33	64	90	115
21,23-32: 26-Valley Forge story. 32-Last pre-code issue (2/55)	10	20	30	56	76	95
22-Krigstein-a	11	22	33	60	83	105
33-37,39-42,44,45,47,48: 40-Romita-a	10	20	30	56	76	95
38-Kubert/Moskowitz-a	11	22	33	60	83	105
43,49-Torres-a. 43-Severin/Elder E.C. swipe from Two-Fisted Tales #31	11	22	33	60	83	105
46-Crandall-a	11	22	33	60	83	105

NOTE: ***Ayers** a-17.**Berg** a-13. **Colan** a-4, 36, 48, 49; c-17. **Drucker** a-37, 43, 48. **Everett** a-17. **Heath** a-6-9, 16, 19, 25, 36; c-11, 16, 19, 23, 25, 26, 29-32, 36. **G. Kane** a-19. **Lawrence** a-36. **Maneely** a-7, 9, 13, 14, 20, 23; c-6, 27, 37. **Orlando** a-42, 48. **Pakula** a-26, 40. **Ravielli** a-27. **Reinman** a-11, 16, 26. **Robinson** a-15; c-13. **Severin** a-26, 27; c-48. **Shores** a-13. **Sinnott** a-37.*

WAR DANCER (Also see Charlemagne, Doctor Chaos #2 & Warriors of Plasm)
Defiant: Feb, 1994 - No. 6, July, 1994 ($2.50)

	GD	VG	FN	VF	VF/NM	NM-
1-3,5,6: 1-Intro War Dancer; Weiss-c/a begins. 1-3-Weiss-a(p). 6-Pre-Schism issue						3.00
4-($3.25, 52 pgs.)-Charlemagne app.						4.00

WAR DOGS OF THE U.S. ARMY
Avon Periodicals: 1952

	GD	VG	FN	VF	VF/NM	NM-
1-Kinstler-c/a	15	30	45	84	127	170

WARFRONT
Harvey Publications: 9/51 - #35, 11/58; #36, 10/65; #39, 2/67

	GD	VG	FN	VF	VF/NM	NM-
1-Korean War	10	20	30	69	122	175
2	6	12	18	39	62	85
3-10	5	10	15	32	51	70
11,12,14,16-20	4	8	12	28	44	60
13,15,22-Nostrand-a	6	12	18	39	62	85
21,23-27,31-33,35	4	8	12	28	44	60
28-30,34-Kirby-c	6	12	18	41	66	90
36-(12/66)-Dynamite Joe begins, ends #39; Williamson-a	5	10	15	32	51	70
37-Wood-a (17 pgs.)	5	10	15	32	51	70
38,39-Wood-a, 2-3 pgs.; Lone Tiger app.	4	8	12	28	44	60

NOTE: ***Powell** a-1-6, 9-11, 14, 17, 20, 23, 25-28, 30, 31, 34, 36. **Powell/Nostrand** a-12, 13, 15. **Simon** c-36?, 38.*

WAR FURY
Comic Media/Harwell (Allen Hardy Assoc.): Sept, 1952 - No. 4, Mar, 1953

	GD	VG	FN	VF	VF/NM	NM-
1-Heck-c/a in all; Palais-a; bullet hole in forehead-c; all issues are very violent; soldier using flame thrower on enemy	37	74	111	222	361	500
2-4: 4-Morisi-a	20	40	60	114	182	250

WAR GODS OF THE DEEP (See Movie Classics)

WARHAWKS
TSR, Inc.: 1990 - No. 10, 1991 ($2.95, 44 pgs.)

	GD	VG	FN	VF	VF/NM	NM-
1-10-Based on TSR game, Spiegle a-1-6						4.00

WARHEADS
Marvel Comics UK: June, 1992 - No. 14, Aug, 1993 ($1.75)

	GD	VG	FN	VF	VF/NM	NM-
1-Wolverine-c/story; indicia says #2 by mistake						4.00
2-14: 2-Nick Fury app. 3-Iron Man-c/story. 4,5-X-Force. 5-Liger vs. Cable. 6,7-Death's Head II app. (#6 is cameo)						3.00

WAR HEROES (See Marine War Heroes)

WAR HEROES
Dell Publishing Co.: 7-9/42 (no month); No. 2, 10-12/42 - No. 10, 10-12/44 (Quarterly)

	GD	VG	FN	VF	VF/NM	NM-
1-General Douglas MacArthur-c	27	54	81	158	259	360
2-James Doolittle and other officers-c	15	30	45	86	133	180
3,5: 3-Pro-Russian back-c	14	28	42	76	108	140
4-Disney's Gremlins app.	18	36	54	107	169	230
6-10: 6-Tothish-a by Discount	10	20	30	56	76	95

	GD 2.0	VG 4.0	FN 6.0	VF 8.0	VF/NM 9.0	NM- 9.2

NOTE: *No. 1 was to be released in July, but was delayed. Painted c-4, 6-9.*

WAR HEROES
Ace Magazines: May, 1952 - No. 8, Apr, 1953

	GD	VG	FN	VF	VF/NM	NM-
1	12	24	36	67	94	120
2-Lou Cameron-a	8	16	24	44	57	70
3-8: 6,7-Cameron-a	8	16	24	40	50	60

WAR HEROES (Also see Blue Bird Comics)
Charlton Comics: Feb, 1963 - No. 27, Nov, 1967

	GD	VG	FN	VF	VF/NM	NM-
1,2: 2-John F. Kennedy story	4	8	12	26	41	55
3-10	3	6	9	18	27	35
11-26	3	6	9	14	20	26
27-1st Devils Brigade by Glanzman	3	6	9	18	27	35

NOTE: ***Montes/Bache** a-3-7, 21, 25, 27; c-3-7.*

WAR HEROES
Image Comics: July, 2008 - No. 6 ($2.99, limited series)

	GD	VG	FN	VF	VF/NM	NM-
1-3-Soldiers given super powers; Mark Millar-s/Tony Harris-a/c; four covers						3.00

WAR IS HELL
Marvel Comics Group: Jan, 1973 - No. 15, Oct, 1975

	GD	VG	FN	VF	VF/NM	NM-
1-Williamson-a(r), 5 pgs.; Ayers-a	3	6	9	17	25	32
2-8-Reprints. 6-(11/73). 7-(6/74). 7,8-Kirby-a	2	4	6	10	14	18
9-Intro Death	5	10	15	32	51	70
10-15-Death app.	3	6	9	17	25	32

NOTE: ***Bolle** a-3r. **Powell** a-1. **Woodbridge** a-1. Sgt. Fury reprints-7, 8.*

WAR IS HELL: THE FIRST FLIGHT OF THE PHANTOM EAGLE
Marvel Comics (MAX): May, 2008 - No. 5, Sept, 2008 ($3.99, limited series)

	GD	VG	FN	VF	VF/NM	NM-
1-5-World War I fighter pilots; Ennis-s/Chaykin-a/Cassaday-c						4.00

WARLANDS
Image Comics: Aug, 1999 - No. 12, Feb, 2001 ($2.50)

	GD	VG	FN	VF	VF/NM	NM-
1-9,11,12-Pat Lee-a(p)/Adrian Tsang-s						3.00
10-($2.95) Flip book w/Shidima preview						4.00
... Chronicles 1,2 (2/00, 7/00; $7.95) 1-r/#1-3. 2-r/#4-6						8.00
...Darklyte TPB (8/01, $14.95) r/#0,1/2,1-6 w/cover gallery; new Lee-c						15.00
...Epilogue: Three Stories (3/01, $5.95) includes r/Wizard #1/2 & AE #0						6.00
Another Universe #0						3.00
Wizard #1/2						5.00

WARLANDS: THE AGE OF ICE (Volume 2)
Image Comics: July, 2001 - No. 9, Nov, 2002 ($2.95)

	GD	VG	FN	VF	VF/NM	NM-
#0-(2/02, $2.25)						3.00
#1/2 (4/02, $2.25)						3.00
1-9: 2-Flip book preview of Banished Knights						3.00
TPB (2003, $15.95) r/#1-9						16.00

WARLANDS: DARK TIDE RISING (Volume 3)
Image Comics: Dec, 2002 - No. 6, May, 2003 ($2.95)

	GD	VG	FN	VF	VF/NM	NM-
1-6: 1-Wraparound gatefold-c						3.00

WARLOCK (The Power of...)(Also see Avengers Annual #7, Fantastic Four #66, 67, Incredible Hulk #178, Infinity Crusade, Infinity Gauntlet, Infinity War, Marvel Premiere #1, Marvel Two-In-One Annual #2, Silver Surfer V3#46, Strange Tales #178-181 & Thor #165)
Marvel Comics Group: Aug, 1972 - No. 8, Oct, 1973; No. 9, Oct, 1975 - No. 15, Nov, 1976

	GD	VG	FN	VF	VF/NM	NM-
1-Origin by Kane	8	16	24	56	93	130
2,3	4	8	12	28	44	60
4-8: 4-Death of Eddie Roberts	3	6	9	18	27	35
9-Starlin's 2nd Thanos saga begins, ends #15; new costume Warlock; Thanos cameo only; story cont'd from Strange Tales #178-181; Starlin-c/a in #9-15	4	8	12	26	41	55
10-Origin Thanos & Gamora; recaps events from Capt. Marvel #25-34. Thanos vs.The Magus-c/story	4	8	12	28	44	60
11-Thanos app.; Warlock dies	3	6	9	20	30	40
12-14: (Regular 25¢ edition) 14-Origin Star Thief; last 25¢ issue	3	6	9	17	25	32
12-14-(30¢-c, limited distribution)	5	10	15	30	48	65
15-Thanos-c/story	3	6	9	18	27	35

NOTE: ***Buscema** a-2p; c-8p. **G. Kane** a-1p, 3-5p; c-1p, 2, 3, 4p, 5p, 7p. **Starlin** a-9-14p, 15; c-9, 10, 11p, 12p, 13-15. **Sutton** a-1-8i.*

WARLOCK (...Special Edition on-c)
Marvel Comics Group: Dec, 1982 - No. 6, May, 1983 ($2.00, slick paper, 52 pgs.)

	GD	VG	FN	VF	VF/NM	NM-
1-Warlock-r/Strange Tales #178-180.						4.00
2-6: 2-r/Str. Tales #180,181 & Warlock #9. 3-r/Warlock #10-12(Thanos origin recap). 4-r/Warlock #12-15. 5-r/Warlock #15, Marvel Team-Up #55 & Avengers Ann. #7. 6-r/2nd half						

Warlord (2009 series) #14 © DC

Warlord of Mars #1 © Savage Tales

War Machine (2009 series) #7 © MAR

	GD 2.0	VG 4.0	FN 6.0	VF 8.0	VF/NM 9.0	NM- 9.2

Avengers Annual #7 & Marvel Two-in-One Annual #2 4.00
Special Edition #1(12/83) 4.00
NOTE: *Byrne a-5r. Starlin a-1-6r; c-1-6(new). Direct sale only.*

WARLOCK
Marvel Comics: V2#1, May, 1992 - No. 6, Oct, 1992 ($2.50, limited series)

V2#1-6: 1-Reprints 1982 reprint series w/Thanos 3.00

WARLOCK
Marvel Comics: Nov, 1998 - No. 4, Feb, 1999 ($2.99, limited series)

1-4-Warlock vs. Drax 3.00

WARLOCK (M-Tech)
Marvel Comics: Oct, 1999 - No. 9, June, 2000 ($1.99/$2.50)

1-5: 1-Quesada-c. 2-Two covers 3.00
6-9: 6-Begin $2.50-c. 8-Avengers app. 3.00

WARLOCK
Marvel Comics: Nov, 2004 - No. 4, Feb, 2005 ($2.99, limited series)

1-4-Adlard-a/Williams-c 3.00

WARLOCK AND THE INFINITY WATCH (Also see Infinity Gauntlet)
Marvel Comics: Feb, 1992 - No. 42, July, 1995 ($1.75) (Sequel to Infinity Gauntlet)

1-Starlin-scripts begin; brief origin recap; sequel to Infinity Gauntlet 4.00
2,3: 2-Reintro Moondragon 3.00
4-24,26: 7-Reintro The Magus; Moondragon app.; Thanos cameo on last 2 pgs. 8,9-Thanos battles Gamora-c/story. 8-Magus & Moondragon app. 10-Thanos-c/story; Magus app. 13-Hulk x-over. 21-Drax vs. Thor 3.00
25-($2.95, 52 pgs.)-Die-cut & embossed double-c; Thor & Thanos app. 4.00
28-42: 28-$1.95-c begins; bound-in card sheet 3.00
NOTE: *Austin c/a-1-4i, 7i. Leonardi a(p)-3, 4. Medina c/a(p)-1, 2, 5; 6, 9, 10, 14, 15, 20. Williams a(i)-8, 12, 13, 16-19.*

WARLOCK CHRONICLES
Marvel Comics: June, 1993 - No. 8, Feb, 1994 ($2.00, limited series)

1-($2.95)-Holo-grafx foil & embossed-c; origin retold; Starlin scripts begin; Keith Williams-a(i) in all 4.00
2-8: 3-Thanos & Mephisto-c/story. 4-Vs. Magus-c/s. 8-Contains free 16 pg. Razorline insert 3.00

WARLOCK 5
Aircel Pub.: 11/86 - No. 22, 5/89; V2#1, June, 1989 - V2#5, 1989 ($1.70, B&W)

1-5,7-11-Gordon Derry-s/Denis Beauvais-a thru #11. 5-Green Cyborg on-c. 5-Misnumbered as #6 (no #6); Blue Girl on-c. 3.00
12-22-Barry Blair-s/a. 18-$1.95-c begins 4.00
V2#1-5 ($2.00, B&W)-All issues by Barry Blair 3.00
Compilation 1,2: 1-r/#1-5 (1988, $5.95); 2-r/#6-9 6.00

WARLORD (See 1st Issue Special #8) (B&W reprints in Showcase Presents: Warlord)
National Periodical Publications/DC Comics #123 on: 1-2/76; No.2, 3-4/76; No.3, 10-11/76 - No. 133, Win, 1988-89

	GD	VG	FN	VF	VF/NM	NM-
1-Story cont'd. from 1st Issue Special #8	4	8	12	24	37	50
2-Intro. Machiste	3	6	9	14	20	25
3-5	2	4	6	9	12	15
6-10: 6-Intro Mariah. 7-Origin Machiste. 9-Dons new costume	1	3	4	6	8	10
11-20: 11-Origin-r. 12-Intro Aton. 15-Tara returns; Warlord has son						6.00
21-36,40,41: 27-New facts about origin. 28-1st app. Wizard World. 32-Intro Shakira. 40-Warlord gets new costume						5.00
22-Whitman variant edition	2	4	6	13	18	22
37-39: 37,38-Origin Omac by Starlin. 38-Intro Jennifer Morgan, Warlord's daughter. 39-Omac ends.						6.00
42-48: 42-47-Omac back-up series. 48-(52 pgs.)-1st app. Arak; contains free 14 pg. Arak Son of Thunder; Claw The Unconquered app.						5.00
49-62,64-99,101-132: 49-Claw The Unconquered app. 50-Death of Aton. 51-Reprints #1. 55-Arion Lord of Atlantis begins, ends #62. 91-Origin w/new facts. 114,115-Legends x-over. 125-Death of Tara. 131-1st DC work by Rob Liefeld (9/88)						4.00
63-The Barren Earth begins; free 16pg. Masters of the Universe preview						5.00
100-($1.25, 52 pgs.)						5.00
133-($1.50, 52 pgs.)						5.00
Annual 1-6 ('82-'87): 1-Grell-c,/a(p). 6-New Gods app.						5.00
The Savage Empire TPB (1991, $19.95) r/#1-10,12 & First Issue Special #8; Grell intro.						25.00

NOTE: *Grell a-1-15, 16-50p, 51r, 52p, 59p, Annual 1p; c-1-70, 100-104, 112, 116, 117, Annual 1, 5. Wayne Howard a-64i. Starlin a-37-39p.*

WARLORD
DC Comics: Jan, 1992 - No. 6, June, 1992 ($1.75, limited series)

1-6: Grell-c & scripts in all 3.00

WARLORD
DC Comics: Apr, 2006 - No. 10, Jan, 2007 ($2.99)

1-10: 1-Bruce Jones-s/Bart Sears-a. 10-Winslade-a 3.00

WARLORD
DC Comics: Jun, 2009 - No. 16, Sept, 2010 ($2.99)

1-16: 1-Grell-s/Prado-a/Grell-c. 7-9,11,12,15,16-Grell-s/a/c. 10-Hardin-a 3.00
...: The Saga SC (2010, $17.99) r/#1-6; cover gallery 18.00

WARLORD OF MARS
Dynamite Entertainment: 2010 - Present ($1.00/$3.99)

1-($1.00) John Carter on Earth; Sadowski-a; covers by Ross, Campbell, Jusko. Parrillo 3.00
2-5-($3.99) Four covers on each. 3-Carter arrives on Mars. 4-Dejah Thoris intro. 4.00

WARLORD OF MARS: DEJAH THORIS
Dynamite Entertainment: 2011 - Present ($3.99)

1,2: 1-Five covers; Nelson-s/Rafael-a. 2-Four covers 4.00

WARLORDS (See DC Graphic Novel #2)

WAR MACHINE (Also see Iron Man #281,282 & Marvel Comics Presents #152)
Marvel Comics: Apr, 1994 - No. 25, Apr, 1996 ($1.50)

"Ashcan" edition (nd, 75¢, B&W, 16 pgs.) 3.00
1-($2.00, 52 pgs.)-Newsstand edition; Cable app. 4.00
1-($2.95, 52 pgs.)-Collectors ed.; embossed foil-c 5.00
2-14, 16-25: 2-Bound-in trading card sheet; Cable app. 2,3-Deathlok app. 8-red logo 3.00
8-($2.95)-Polybagged w/16 pg. Marvel Action Hour preview & acetate print; yellow logo 4.00
15 ($2.50)-Flip book 4.00

WAR MACHINE (Also see Dark Reign and Secret Invasion crossovers)
Marvel Comics: Feb, 2009 - No. 12, Feb, 2010 ($2.99)

1-12: 1-5-Pak-s/Manco-a/c; cyborg Jim Rhodes. 10-12-Dark Reign 3.00
1-Variant Titanium Man cover by Deodato 6.00

WAR MAN
Marvel Comics (Epic Comics): Nov, 1993 - No. 2, Dec, 1993 ($2.50, lim. series)

1,2 3.00

WAR OF KINGS
Marvel Comics: May, 2009 - No. 6, Oct, 2009 ($3.99, limited series)

1-6-Pelletier-a/Abnett & Lanning-s; Inhumans vs. the Shi'Ar 4.00
... Saga (2009, giveaway) synopsies of stories involving Kree, Shi'Ar, Inhumans, etc. 3.00
...: Savage World of Skaar 1 (8/09, $3.99) Gorgon & Starbolt land on Sakaar 4.00
...: Who Will Rule? 1 (11/09, $3.99) Pelletier-a; profile pages 4.00

WAR OF KINGS: ASCENSION
Marvel Comics: June, 2009 - No. 4, Sept, 2009 ($3.99, limited series)

1-4-Alves-a/Abnett & Lanning-s; Darkhawk app. 4.00

WAR OF KINGS: DARKHAWK (Leads into War Of Kings: Ascension limited series)
Marvel Comics: Apr, 2009 - No. 2, May, 2009 ($3.99, limited series)

1,2-Cebulski-s/Tolibao & Dazo-a/Peterson-c; r/Darkhawk #1,2 (1991) origin 4.00

WAR OF KINGS: WARRIORS
Marvel Comics: Sept, 2009 - No. 2, Oct, 2009 ($3.99, limited series)

1,2-Prequel to x-over; Gage-s/Asrar & Magno-a 4.00

WAR OF THE GODS
DC Comics: Sept, 1991 - No. 4, Dec, 1991 ($1.75, limited series)

1-4: Perez layouts, scripts & covers. 1-Contains free mini posters (Robin, Deathstroke). 2-4-Direct sale versions include 4 pin-ups printed on cover stock plus different-c 4.00

WAR OF THE UNDEAD
IDW Publishing: Jan, 2007 - No. 3, Apr, 2007 ($3.99, limited series)

1-3-Bryan Johnson-s/Walter Flanagan-a 4.00

WAR OF THE WORLDS, THE
Caliber: 1996 - No. 5 ($2.95, B&W, 32 pgs.)(Based on H. G. Wells novel)

1-5: 1-Randy Zimmerman scripts begin 3.00

WARP
First Comics: Mar, 1983 - No. 19, Feb, 1985 ($1.00/$1.25, Mando paper)

1-Sargon-Mistress of War app.; Brunner-c/a thru #9 4.00
2-19: 2-Faceless Ones begin. 10-New Warp advs., & Outrider begin 3.00
Special 1-3: 1(7/83, 36 pgs.)-Origin Chaos-Prince of Madness; origin of Warp Universe begins, ends #3. 2(1/84)-Lord Cumulus vs. Sargon Mistress of War ($1.00). 3(6/84)-Chaos-Prince of Madness 3.00

WARPATH (Indians on the...)
Key Publications/Stanmor: Nov, 1954 - No. 3, Apr, 1955

Warriors Three #2 © MAR

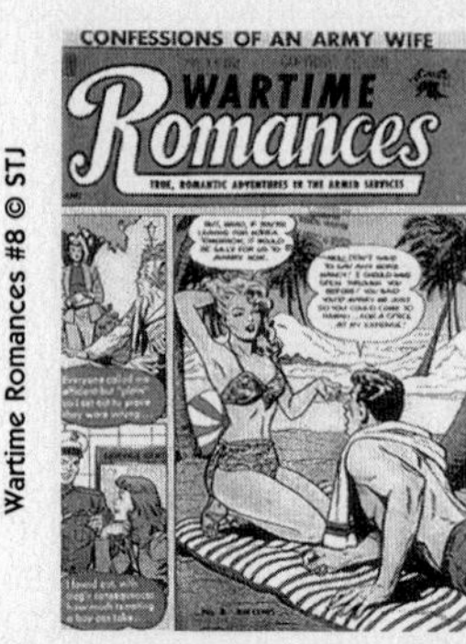

Wartime Romances #8 © STJ

War Victory Adventures #2 © HARV

	GD 2.0	VG 4.0	FN 6.0	VF 8.0	VF/NM 9.0	NM- 9.2
1	11	22	33	62	86	110
2,3	8	16	24	40	50	60

WARPED
Empire Entertainment (Solson): Jun, 1990 - No. 2, Oct-Nov, 1990 (B&W mag)

	GD 2.0	VG 4.0	FN 6.0	VF 8.0	VF/NM 9.0	NM- 9.2
1,2						3.00

WARP GRAPHICS ANNUAL
WaRP Graphics: Dec, 1985; 1988 ($2.50)

	GD 2.0	VG 4.0	FN 6.0	VF 8.0	VF/NM 9.0	NM- 9.2
1-Elfquest, Blood of the Innocent, Thunderbunny & Myth Adventures						5.00
1 (1988)						4.00

WARREN PRESENTS
Warren Publications: Jan, 1979 - No. 14, Nov, 1981(B&W magazine)

	GD 2.0	VG 4.0	FN 6.0	VF 8.0	VF/NM 9.0	NM- 9.2
1-Eerie, Creepy, & Vampirella-r; Ring of the Warlords; Merlin-s; Dax-s; Sanjulian-c	3	6	9	15	21	26
2-6(10/79): 2-The Rook. 3-Alien Invasions Comix. 4-Movie Aliens. 5-Dracula '79. 6-Strange Stories of Vampires Comix	2	4	6	9	13	16
8(10/80)-r/1st app. Pantha from Vamp. #30	2	4	6	11	16	20
9(11/80) Empire Encounters Comix	2	4	6	10	14	18
13(10/81),14(11/81):13-Sword and Sorcery Comix	3	6	9	14	19	24
(#7,10,11,12 may not exist, or may be a Special below)						
Special-Alien Collectors Edition (1979)	3	6	9	14	19	24
Special-Close Encounters of the Third Kind (1978)	2	4	6	9	13	16
Special-Lord of the Rings (6/79)	3	6	9	19	29	38
Special-Meteor (1/80)	2	4	6	9	13	16
Special-Moonraker/James Bond (10/79)	2	4	6	9	13	16
Special-Star Wars (1977)	3	6	9	19	29	38

WAR REPORT
Ajax/Farrell Publications (Excellent Publ.): Sept, 1952 - No. 5, May, 1953

	GD 2.0	VG 4.0	FN 6.0	VF 8.0	VF/NM 9.0	NM- 9.2
1	14	28	42	80	115	150
2-Flame thrower w/burning bodies on-c	15	30	45	85	130	175
3,5	9	18	27	47	61	75
4-Used in **POP**, pg. 94	9	18	27	52	69	85

WARRIOR (Wrestling star)
Ultimate Creations: May, 1996 - No. 4, 1997 ($2.95)

	GD 2.0	VG 4.0	FN 6.0	VF 8.0	VF/NM 9.0	NM- 9.2
1-4: Warrior scripts; Callahan-c/a. 3-Wraparound-c. 4-Warrior #3 in indicia; pin-ups						3.00
1-Variant-c.						5.00
X-Mas (11/96, $3.50) listed as "No. 3" in indicia; pin-ups by various; Quesada-c						4.00

WARRIOR COMICS
H.C. Blackerby: 1945 (1930s DC reprints)

	GD 2.0	VG 4.0	FN 6.0	VF 8.0	VF/NM 9.0	NM- 9.2
1-Wing Brady, The Iron Man, Mark Markon	21	42	63	126	206	285

WARRIOR OF WAVERLY STREET, THE
Dark Horse Comics: Nov, 1996 - No. 2, Dec, 1996 ($2.95, mini-series)

	GD 2.0	VG 4.0	FN 6.0	VF 8.0	VF/NM 9.0	NM- 9.2
1,2-Darrow-c						3.00

WARRIORS
CFD Productions: 1993 (B&W, one-shot)

	GD 2.0	VG 4.0	FN 6.0	VF 8.0	VF/NM 9.0	NM- 9.2
1-Linsner, Dark One-a	2	4	6	10	14	18

WARRIORS, THE: OFFICIAL MOVIE ADAPTATION (Based on the 1979 movie)
Dabel Brothers Publishing/Dynamite Ent.: Feb, 2009 - No. 5, 2010 ($3.99, limited series)

	GD 2.0	VG 4.0	FN 6.0	VF 8.0	VF/NM 9.0	NM- 9.2
1-5: 1-Three covers plus wraparound photo-c; Dibari-a. 3-Eric Powell-c						4.00
...: Jailbreak 1 (7/09, $3.99) Apon & Herman-a						4.00

WARRIORS OF PLASM (Also see Plasm)
Defiant: Aug, 1993 - No. 13, Aug, 1995 ($2.95/$2.50)

	GD 2.0	VG 4.0	FN 6.0	VF 8.0	VF/NM 9.0	NM- 9.2
1-4: Shooter-scripts; Lapham-c/a: 1-1st app. Glory. 4-Bound-in fold-out poster						4.00
5-7,10-13: 5-Begin $2.50-c. 13-Schism issue						3.00
8,9-($2.75, 44 pgs.)						4.00
The Collected Edition (2/94, $9.95)-r/Plasm #0, WOP #1-4 & Splatterball						10.00

WARRIORS THREE (Fandral, Volstagg, and Hogun from Thor)
Marvel Comics: Jan, 2011 - No. 4, Apr, 2011 ($3.99, limited series)

	GD 2.0	VG 4.0	FN 6.0	VF 8.0	VF/NM 9.0	NM- 9.2
1-4-Bill Willingham-s/Neil Edwards-a. 2,4-Conner-c						4.00

WAR ROMANCES (See True...)

WAR SHIPS
Dell Publishing Co.: 1942 (36 pgs.)(Similar to Large Feature Comics)

	GD 2.0	VG 4.0	FN 6.0	VF 8.0	VF/NM 9.0	NM- 9.2
nn-Cover by McWilliams; contains photos & drawings of U.S. war ships	18	36	54	103	162	220

WAR STORIES (Formerly War Comics)
Dell Publ. Co.: No. 5, 1942(nd); No. 6, Aug-Oct, 1942 - No. 8, Feb-Apr, 1943

	GD 2.0	VG 4.0	FN 6.0	VF 8.0	VF/NM 9.0	NM- 9.2
5-Origin The Whistler	26	52	78	152	249	345
6-8: 6-8-Night Devils app. 8-Painted-c	20	40	60	114	182	250

WAR STORIES (Korea)
Ajax/Farrell Publications (Excellent Publ.): Sept, 1952 - No. 5, May, 1953

	GD 2.0	VG 4.0	FN 6.0	VF 8.0	VF/NM 9.0	NM- 9.2
1	14	28	42	76	108	140
2	8	16	24	44	57	70
3-5	9	18	27	47	61	75

WAR STORIES (See Star Spangled...)

WAR STORY
DC Comics (Vertigo): Nov, 2001 - Present ($4.95, series of World War II one-shots)

	GD 2.0	VG 4.0	FN 6.0	VF 8.0	VF/NM 9.0	NM- 9.2
...: Archangel (4/03) Ennis-s/Erskine-a						5.00
...: Condors (3/03) Ennis-s/Ezquerra-a						5.00
...: D-Day Dodgers (12/01) Ennis-s/Higgins-a						5.00
...: J For Jenny (2/03) Ennis-s/Lloyd-a						5.00
...: Johann's Tiger (11/01) Ennis-s/Weston-a						5.00
...: Nightingale (2/02) Ennis-s/Lloyd-a						5.00
...: Screaming Eagles (1/02) Ennis-s/Gibbons-a						5.00
...: The Reivers (1/03) Ennis-s/Kennedy-a						5.00
Vol. 1 (2004, $19.95) r/Johann's Tiger, D-Day Dodgers, Screaming Eagles, Nightingale						20.00
Vol. 2 (2006, $19.99) r/J For Jenny, The Reivers, Condors, Archangel; Ennis afterword						20.00

WARSTRIKE
Malibu Comics (Ultraverse): May, 1994 - No. 7, Nov, 1995 ($1.95)

	GD 2.0	VG 4.0	FN 6.0	VF 8.0	VF/NM 9.0	NM- 9.2
1-7: 1-Simonson-c						3.00
1-Ultra 5000 Limited silver foil						4.00
Giant Size 1 (12/94, $2.50, 44pgs.)-Prelude to Godwheel						4.00

WART AND THE WIZARD (See The Sword & the Stone under Movie Comics)
Gold Key: Feb, 1964 (Walt Disney)(Characters from Sword in the Stone movie)

	GD 2.0	VG 4.0	FN 6.0	VF 8.0	VF/NM 9.0	NM- 9.2
1 (10102-402)	4	8	12	28	44	60

WAR THAT TIME FORGOT, THE
DC Comics: Jul, 2008 - No. 12, Jun, 2009 ($2.99, limited series)

	GD 2.0	VG 4.0	FN 6.0	VF 8.0	VF/NM 9.0	NM- 9.2
1-12: 1-Bruce Jones-s/Al Barrionuevo-a/Neal Adams-c; Enemy Ace app.						3.00
... Vol. 1 TPB (2009, $17.99) r/#1-6						18.00
... Vol. 2 TPB (2009, $17.99) r/#7-12						18.00

WARTIME ROMANCES
St. John Publishing Co.: July, 1951 - No. 18, Nov, 1953

	GD 2.0	VG 4.0	FN 6.0	VF 8.0	VF/NM 9.0	NM- 9.2
1-All Baker-c/a	45	90	135	284	480	675
2-All Baker-c/a	34	68	102	199	325	450
3,4-All Baker-c/a	32	64	96	188	307	425
5-8-Baker-c/a(2-3) each	30	60	90	177	289	400
9,11,12,16,18: Baker-c/a each. 9-Two signed stories by Estrada	24	48	72	142	234	325
10,13-15,17-Baker-c only	20	40	60	117	189	260

WAR VICTORY ADVENTURES (#1 titled War Victory Comics)
U.S. Treasury Dept./War Victory/Harvey Publ.: Sum, 1942 - No. 3, Wint, 1943-44 (5¢/10¢)

	GD 2.0	VG 4.0	FN 6.0	VF 8.0	VF/NM 9.0	NM- 9.2
1-(5¢)(Promotion of Savings Bonds)-Featuring America's greatest comic art by top syndicated cartoonists; Blondie, Joe Palooka, Green Hornet, Dick Tracy, Superman, Gumps, etc.; (36 pgs.); all profits were contributed to U.S.O. & Army/Navy relief funds	43	86	129	271	456	640
2-(10¢) Battle of Stalingrad story; Powell-a (8/43); flag & WWII Japanese-c	40	80	120	246	411	575
3-(10¢) Capt. Red Cross-c & text only; WWII Nazi-c; Powell-a	40	80	120	242	401	560

WAR WAGON, THE (See Movie Classics)

WAR WINGS
Charlton Comics: Oct, 1968

	GD 2.0	VG 4.0	FN 6.0	VF 8.0	VF/NM 9.0	NM- 9.2
1	3	6	9	14	20	26

WARWORLD!
Dark Horse Comics: Feb, 1989 ($1.75, B&W, one-shot)

	GD 2.0	VG 4.0	FN 6.0	VF 8.0	VF/NM 9.0	NM- 9.2
1-Gary Davis sci/fi art in Moebius style						3.00

WASHABLE JONES AND THE SHMOO (Also see Al Capp's Shmoo)
Toby Press: June, 1953

	GD 2.0	VG 4.0	FN 6.0	VF 8.0	VF/NM 9.0	NM- 9.2
1- "Super-Shmoo"	19	38	57	109	172	235

WASH TUBBS (See The Comics, Crackajack Funnies)
Dell Publishing Co.: No. 11, 1942 - No. 53, 1944

	GD 2.0	VG 4.0	FN 6.0	VF 8.0	VF/NM 9.0	NM- 9.2
Four Color 11 (#1)	25	50	75	183	367	550
Four Color 28 (1943)	17	34	51	118	242	365

Weapon X: First Class #2 © MAR

Web of Horror #1 © Major Magazines

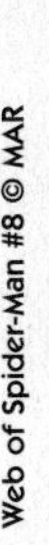
Web of Spider-Man #8 © MAR

	GD 2.0	VG 4.0	FN 6.0	VF 8.0	VF/NM 9.0	NM- 9.2
Four Color 53	13	26	39	91	176	260

WASTELAND
DC Comics: Dec, 1987 - No. 18, May, 1989 ($1.75-$2.00 #13 on, mature)

1-5(4/88), 5(5/88), 6(5/88)-18: 13,15-Orlando-a 3.00
NOTE: ***Orlando*** *a-12, 13, 15.* ***Truman*** *a-10; c-13.*

WATCHMEN
DC Comics: Sept, 1986 - No. 12, Oct, 1987 (maxi-series)

1-Alan Moore scripts & Dave Gibbons-c/a in all 2 4 6 11 16 20
1-(2009, $1.50) Second printing 3.00
2-12 2 4 6 9 12 15
Hardcover Collection-Slip-cased-r/#1-12 w/new material; produced by Graphitti Designs 100.00
HC (2008, $39.99) recolored r/#1-12; design & promotional art; Moore & Gibbons intros 40.00
Trade paperback (1987, $14.95)-r/#1-12 25.00

WATER BIRDS AND THE OLYMPIC ELK (Disney)
Dell Publishing Co.: No. 700, Apr, 1956

Four Color 700-Movie 5 10 15 34 55 75

WATERWORLD: CHILDREN OF LEVIATHAN
Acclaim Comics: Aug, 1997 - No. 4, Nov, 1997 ($2.50, mini-series)

1-4 3.00

WAY OF THE RAT
CrossGeneration Comics: Jun, 2002 - No. 24, June, 2004 ($2.95)

1-24: 1-Dixon-s/ Jeff Johnson-a. 5-Whigham-a. 9,14-Luke Ross-a 3.00
Free Comic Book Day Special (6/03) reprints #1 w/features, interviews, CrossGen info 3.00
...: The Walls of Zhumar Vol. 1 (1/03, $15.95) r/#1-6 16.00
Vol. 2: The Dragon's Wake (2003, $15.95) r/#7-12 16.00

WEAPON X
Marvel Comics: Apr, 1994 ($12.95, one-shot)

nn-r/Marvel Comics Presents #72-84 13.00

WEAPON X
Marvel Comics: Mar, 1995 - No. 4, June, 1995 ($1.95)

1-Age of Apocalypse 4.00
2-4 3.00

WEAPON X
Marvel Comics: Nov, 2002 - No. 28, Nov, 2004 ($2.25/$2.99)

1-7: 1-Sabretooth-c/app.; Tieri-s/Jeanty-a 3.00
8-28: 8-Begin $2.99-c. 14-Invaders app. 15-Chamber joins. 16-18,21-25-Wolverine app. 3.00
Vol. 1: The Draft TPB (2003, $21.99) r/#1-5, #1/2 & The Draft one-shots 22.00
Vol. 2: The Underground TPB (2003, $19.99) r/#6-13 20.00
Wizard #1/2 (2002) 5.00

WEAPON X: DAYS OF FUTURE NOW
Marvel Comics: Sept, 2005 - No. 5, Jan, 2006 ($2.99, limited series)

1-5-Tieri-s/Sears-a; Chamber, Sauron & Fantomex app. 3.00
TPB (2006, $13.99) r/#1-5 14.00

WEAPON X: FIRST CLASS
Marvel Comics: Jan, 2009 - No. 3, Mar, 2009 ($3.99, limited series)

1-3:1-Sabretooth-c/app. 2-Deadpool-c/app. 4.00

WEAPON X NOIR
Marvel Comics: May, 2010 ($3.99, one-shot)

1-Dennis Calero-s/a; C.P. Smith-c 4.00

WEAPON X: THE DRAFT (Leads into 2002 Weapon X series)
Marvel Comics: Oct, 2002 ($2.25, one-shots)

...Kane 1- JH Williams-c/Raimondi-a 3.00
...Marrow 1- JH Williams-c/Badeaux-a 3.00
...Sauron 1- JH Williams-c/Kerschl-a; Emma Frost app. 3.00
...Wild Child 1- JH Williams-c/Van Sciver-a; Aurora (Alpha Flight) app. 3.00
...Zero 1- JH Williams-c/Plunkett-a; Wolverine app. 3.00

WEAPON ZERO
Image Comics (Top Cow Productions): No. T-4(#1), June, 1995 - No. T-0(#5), Dec, 1995 ($2.50, limited series)

T-4(#1): Walt Simonson scripts in all. 5.00
T-3(#2) - T-1(#4) 4.00
T-0(#5) 3.00

WEAPON ZERO
Image Comics (Top Cow Productions): V2#1, Mar, 1996 - No. 15, Dec, 1997 ($2.50)

V2#1-Walt Simonson scripts. 4.00
2-14: 8-Begin Top Cow. 10-Devil's Reign 3.00
15-($3.50) Benitez-a 4.00

WEAPON ZERO/SILVER SURFER
Image Comics/Marvel Comics: Jan, 1997($2.95, one-shot)

1-Devil's Reign Pt. 1 3.00

WEASELGUY: ROAD TRIP
Image Comics: Sept, 1999 - No. 2 ($3.50, limited series)

1,2-Steve Buccellato-s/a 3.50
1-Variant-c by Bachalo 5.00

WEASELGUY/WITCHBLADE
Hyperwerks: July, 1998 ($2.95, one-shot)

1-Steve Buccellato-s/a; covers by Matsuda and Altstaetter 3.00

WEASEL PATROL SPECIAL, THE (Also see Fusion #17)
Eclipse Comics: Apr, 1989 ($2.00, B&W, one-shot)

1-Funny animal 3.00

WEAVEWORLD
Marvel Comics (Epic): Dec, 1991 - No. 3, 1992 ($4.95, lim. series, 68 pgs.)

1-3: Clive Barker adaptation 5.00

WEB, THE (Also see Mighty Comics & Mighty Crusaders)
DC Comics (Impact Comics): Sept, 1991 - No. 14, Oct, 1992 ($1.00)

1-14: 5-The Fly x-over 9-Trading card inside 4.00
Annual 1 (1992, $2.50, 68 pgs.)-With Trading card 4.00
NOTE: ***Gil Kane*** *c-5, 9, 10, 12-14.* ***Bill Wray*** *a(i)-1-9, 10(part).*

WEB, THE (Continued from The Red Circle)
DC Comics: Nov, 2009 - No. 10, Aug, 2010 ($3.99)

1-10: 1-Roger Robinson-a; The Hangman back-up feature. 3-Batgirl app. 5-Caldwell-a 4.00

WEB OF EVIL
Comic Magazines/Quality Comics Group: Nov, 1952 - No. 21, Dec, 1954

1-Used in **SOTI**, pg. 388. Jack Cole-a; morphine use story
61 132 183 390 670 950
2-4,6,7: 2,3-Jack Cole-a. 4,6,7-Jack Cole-c/a 42 84 126 265 445 625
5-Electrocution-c/story; Jack Cole-c/a 51 102 153 318 539 760
8-11-Jack Cole-a 40 80 120 242 401 560
12,13,15,16,19-21 26 52 78 154 252 350
14-Part Crandall-c; Old Witch swipe 27 54 81 160 263 365
17-Opium drug propaganda story 27 54 81 158 259 360
18-Acid-in-face story 27 54 81 160 263 365
NOTE: ***Jack Cole*** *a(2 each)-2, 6, 8, 9.* ***Cuidera*** *c-1-21i.* ***Ravielli*** *a-13.*

WEB OF HORROR
Major Magazines: Dec, 1969 - No. 3, Apr, 1970 (Magazine)

1-Jeff Jones painted-c; Wrightson-a, Kaluta-a 9 18 27 60 100 140
2-Jones painted-c; Wrightson-a(2), Kaluta-a 8 16 24 52 86 120
3-Wrightson-c/a (1st published-c); Brunner, Kaluta, Bruce Jones-a
9 18 27 65 113 160

WEB OF MYSTERY
Ace Magazines (A. A. Wyn): Feb, 1951 - No. 29, Sept, 1955

1 57 114 171 362 619 875
2-Bakerish-a 32 64 96 192 314 435
3-10: 4-Colan-a 29 58 87 170 278 385
11-18,20-26: 12-John Chilly's 1st cover art. 13-Surrealistic-c. 20-r/The Beyond #1
25 50 75 147 241 335
19-Reprints Challenge of the Unknown #6 used in N.Y. Legislative Committee
25 50 75 147 241 335
27-Bakerish-a(r/The Beyond #2); last pre-code ish 22 44 66 128 209 290
28,29: 28-All-r 17 34 51 100 158 215
NOTE: *This series was to appear as "Creepy Stories", but title was changed before publication.* ***Cameron*** *a-6, 8, 11-13, 17-20, 22, 24, 25, 27; c-8, 13, 17.* ***Palais*** *a-28r.* ***Sekowsky*** *a-1-3, 7, 8, 11, 14, 21, 29.* ***Tothish*** *a-by* ***Bill Discount*** *#16. 29-all-r, 19-28-partial-r.*

WEB OF SCARLET SPIDER
Marvel Comics: Oct, 1995 - No. 4, Jan, 1996 ($1.95, limited series)

1-4: Replaces "Web of Spider-Man" 3.00

WEB OF SPIDER-MAN (Replaces Marvel Team-Up)
Marvel Comics Group: Apr, 1985 - No. 129, Sept, 1995

1-Painted-c (5th app. black costume?) 2 4 6 10 14 18
2,3 6.00
4-8: 7-Hulk x-over; Wolverine splash 5.00
9-13: 10-Dominic Fortune guest stars; painted-c 4.00

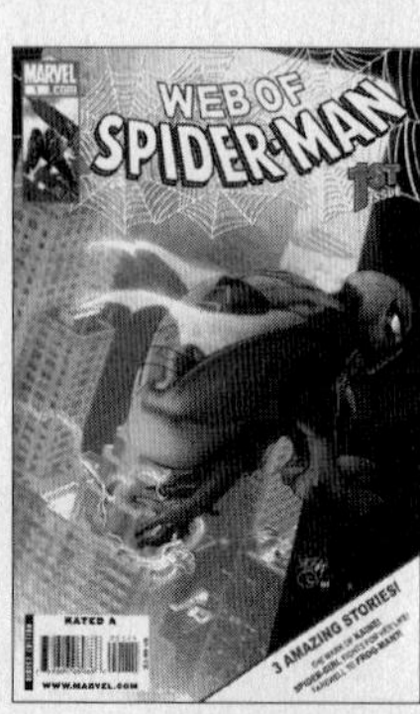

Web of Spider-Man (2009 series) #1 © MAR

Wednesday Comics #8 © DC

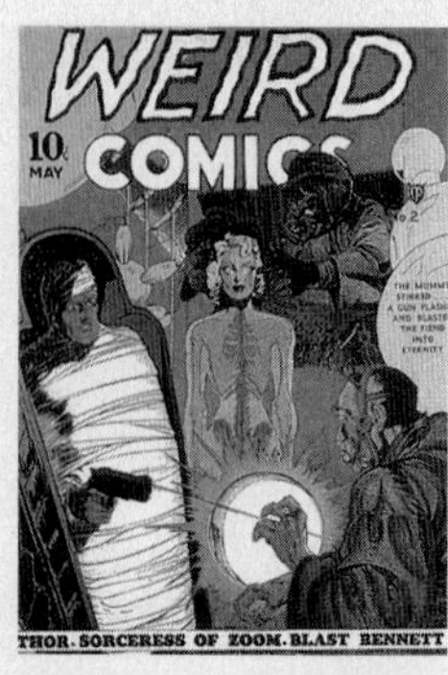

Weird Comics #2 © FOX

GD VG FN VF VF/NM NM-
2.0 4.0 6.0 8.0 9.0 9.2

14-17,19-28: 19-Intro Humbug & Solo 3.00
18-1st app. Venom (behind the scenes, 9/86) 4.00
29-Wolverine, new Hobgoblin (Macendale) app. 1 2 3 5 6 8
30-Origin recap The Rose & Hobgoblin I (entire book is flashback story); Punisher & Wolverine cameo 4.00
31,32-Six part Kraven storyline begins 1 2 3 5 6 8
33-37,39-47,49: 36-1st app. Tombstone 3.00
38-Hobgoblin app.; begin $1.00-c 4.00
48-Origin Hobgoblin II(Demogoblin) cont'd from Spectacular Spider-Man #147; Kingpin app. 1 2 3 5 7 9
50-($1.50, 52 pgs.) 4.00
51-58 3.00
59-Cosmic Spidey cont'd from Spect. Spider-Man 4.00
60-89,91-99,101-106: 66,67-Green Goblin (Norman Osborn) app. as a super-hero. 69,70-Hulk x-over. 74-76-Austin-c(i). 76-Fantastic Four x-over. 78-Cloak & Dagger app. 81-Origin/1st app. Bloodshed. 84-Begin 6 part Rose & Hobgoblin II storyline; last $1.00-c. 86-Demon leaves Hobgoblin; 1st Demogoblin. 93-Gives brief history of Hobgoblin. 93,94-Hobgoblin (Macendale) Reborn-c/story, parts 1,2; MoonKnight app. 94-Venom cameo. 95-Begin 4 part x-over w/Spirits of Venom w/Ghost Rider/Blaze/Spidey vs. Venom & Demogoblin (cont'd in Ghost Rider/Blaze #5,6). 96-Spirits of Venom part 3; painted-c. 101,103-Maximum Carnage x-over. 103-Venom & Carnage app. 104-106-Nightwatch back-up stories 3.00
90-($2.95, 52 pgs.)-Polybagged w/silver hologram-c, gatefold poster showing Spider-Man & Spider-Man 2099 (Williamson-i) 5.00
90-2nd printing; gold hologram-c 4.00
100-($2.95, 52 pgs.)-Holo-grafx foil-c; intro new Spider-Armor 4.00
107-111: 107-Intro Sandstorm; Sand & Quicksand app. 3.00
112-116, 118, 119, 121-124, 126-128: 112-Begin $1.50-c; bound-in trading card sheet. 113-Regular Ed.; Gambit & Black Cat app. 118-1st solo clone story; Venom app. 3.00
113-($2.95)-Collector's ed. polybagged w/foil-c; 16 pg. preview of Spider-Man cartoon & animation cel 4.00
117-($1.50)-Flip book; Power & Responsibility Pt.1 3.00
117-($2.95)-Collector's edition; foil-c; flip book 4.00
119-($6.45)-Direct market edition; polybagged w/ Marvel Milestone Amazing Spider-Man #150 & coupon for Amazing Spider-Man #396, Spider-Man #53, & Spectacular Spider-Man #219. 7.00
120 ($2.25)-Flip book w/ preview of the Ultimate Spider-Man 4.00
125 ($3.95)-Holodisk-c; Gwen Stacy clone 4.00
125,129: 125 ($2.95)-Newsstand. 129-Last issue 3.00
Annual 1 (1985) 5.00
Annual 2 (1986)-New Mutants; Art Adams-a 1 2 3 5 6 8
Annual 3-10 ('87-'94, 68 pgs.): 4-Evolutionary War x-over. 5-Atlantis Attacks; Captain Universe by Ditko (p) & Silver Sable stories; F.F. app. 6-Punisher back-up plus Capt. Universe by Ditko; G. Kane-a. 7-Origins of Hobgoblin I, Hobgoblin II, Green Goblin I & II & Venom; Larsen/Austin-c. 9-Bagged w/card 4.00
Super Special 1 (1995, $3.95)-flip book 4.00

NOTE: ***Art Adams*** *a-Annual 2.* ***Byrne*** *c-3-6.* ***Chaykin*** *c-10.* ***Mignola*** *a-Annual 2.* ***Vess*** *c-1, 8, Annual 1, 2.* ***Zeck*** *a-6i, 31, 32; c-31, 32.*

WEB OF SPIDER-MAN (Anthology)
Marvel Comics: Dec, 2009 - No. 12, Nov, 2010 ($3.99)

1-12: 1-Spider-Girl app. thru #7; Ben Reilly app. 2-6-Origins of villains retold. 7-Kraven origin; Paper Doll app.; Mahfood-a. 9-11-Jackpot back-up; Takeda-a. 11,12-Black Cat app. 4.00

WEBSPINNERS: TALES OF SPIDER-MAN
Marvel Comics: Jan, 1999 - No. 18, Jun, 2000 ($2.99/$2.50)

1-DeMatteis-s/Zulli-a; back-up story w/Romita Sr. art 4.00
1-($6.95) DF Edition 7.00
2,3: 2-Two covers 3.00
4-11,13-18: 4,5-Giffen-a; Silver Surfer-c/app. 7-9-Kelly-s/Sears and Smith-a. 10,11-Jenkins-s/Sean Phillips-a 3.00
12-($3.50) J.G. Jones-c/a; Jenkins-s 4.00

WEDDING BELLS
Quality Comics Group: Feb, 1954 - No. 19, Nov, 1956

	GD 2.0	VG 4.0	FN 6.0	VF 8.0	VF/NM 9.0	NM- 9.2
1-Whitney-a	16	32	48	94	147	200
2	11	22	33	60	83	105
3-9: 8-Last precode (4/55)	9	18	27	50	65	80
10-Ward-a (9 pgs.)	15	30	45	83	124	165
11-14,17	8	16	24	44	57	70
15-Baker-c	13	26	39	74	105	135
16-Baker-c/a	15	30	45	85	130	175
18,19-Baker-a each	11	22	33	64	90	115

WEDDING OF DRACULA
Marvel Comics: Jan, 1993 ($2.00, 52 pgs.)

GD VG FN VF VF/NM NM-
2.0 4.0 6.0 8.0 9.0 9.2

1-Reprints Tomb of Dracula #30,45,46 4.00

WEDNESDAY COMICS (Newspaper-style, twice folded pages on 20" x 14" newsprint)
DC Comics: Sept, 2009 - No. 12, Nov, 2009 ($3.99, weekly limited series)

1-12-Superman, Batman, Kamandi, Hawkman, Deadman, Green Lantern, Flash, Teen Titans, Metamorpho, Adam Strange, Supergirl, Metal Men, Wonder Woman, The Demon with Catwoman, Sgt. Rock; s-a/ by various incl. Ryan Sook, Joe Kubert, Gaiman, Allred, Risso, Kyle Baker, Paul Pope, Conner, Simonson, Garcia-Lopez, Stelfreeze, Bermejo 4.00

WEEKENDER, THE (Illustrated...)
Rucker Pub. Co.: V1#1, Sept, 1945? - V1#4, Nov, 1945; V2#1, Jan, 1946 - V2#3, Aug, 1946 (52 pgs.)

V1#1-4: 1-Same-c as Zip Comics #45, inside-c and back-c blank; Steel Sterling, Senor Banana, Red Rube and Ginger. 2-Capt. Victory on-c. 3-Super hero-c; Mr. E, Dan Hastings, Sky Chief and the Echo. 4-Same-c as Punch Comics #10 (9/44); r/Hale the Magician (7 pgs.) & r/Mr. E (8 pgs.-Lou Fine? or Gustavson?) plus 3 humor strips & many B&W photos & r/newspaper articles plus cheesecake photos of Hollywood stars 18 36 54 105 165 225
V2#1-Same-c as Dynamic Comics #11; 36 pgs. comics, 16 in newspaper format with photos; partial Dynamic Comics reprints; 4 pgs. of cels from the Disney film Pinocchio; Little Nemo story by Winsor McCay, Jr.; Jack Cole-a 20 40 60 117 189 260
V2#2,3: 2-Same-c as Dynamic Comics #9 by Raboy; Dan Hastings (Tuska), Rocket Boy, The Echo, Lucky Coyne. 3-Humor-c by Boddington?; Dynamic Man, Ima Slooth, Master Key, Dynamic Boy, Captain Glory 18 36 54 105 165 225

WEIRD
Eerie Publications: V1#10, 1/66 - V8#6, 12/74; V9#1, 1/75 - V14#3, Nov, 1981 (Magazine) (V1-V8: 52 pgs.; V9 on: 68 pgs.)

V1#10(#1)-Intro. Morris the Caretaker of Weird (ends V2#10); Burgos-a 8 16 24 56 93 130
11,12 6 12 18 37 59 80
V2#1-4(10/67), V3#1(1/68), V2#6(4/68)-V2#7,9,10(12/68) 6 12 18 37 59 80
V2#8-r/Ditko's 1st story/Fantastic Fears #5 6 12 18 43 69 95
V3#1(2/69)-V3#4 5 10 15 32 51 70
V3#5(12/69)-Rulah reprint; "Rulah" changed to "Pulah", LSD story reprinted in Horror Tales V4#4, Tales From the Tomb V2#4, & 20 5 10 15 32 51 70
V4#1-6('70), V5#1-6('71), V6#1-7('72), V7#1-7('73), V8#1-3, V8#4(8/74), V8#4(10/74), (V8#5 does not exist), V8#6('74), V9#1-4(1/75-'76), V10#1-3('77), V11#1-4('78), V12#1(2/79)-V14#3(11/81) 5 10 15 30 48 65

NOTE: *There are two V8#4 issues (8/74 & 10/74). V9#4 (12/76) has a cover swipe from Horror Tales V5#1 (2/73). There are two V13#3 issues (6/80 & 9/80).*

WEIRD
DC Comics (Paradox Press): Sum, 1997 - No. 4 ($2.99, B&W, magazine)

1-4: 4-Mike Tyson-c 3.00

WEIRD, THE
DC Comics: Apr, 1988 - No. 4, July, 1988 ($1.50, limited series)

1-4: Wrightson-c/a in all 5.00

WEIRD ADVENTURES
P. L. Publishing Co. (Canada): May-June, 1951 - No. 3, Sept-Oct, 1951

	GD 2.0	VG 4.0	FN 6.0	VF 8.0	VF/NM 9.0	NM- 9.2
1- "The She-Wolf Killer" by Matt Baker (6 pgs.)	61	122	183	390	670	950
2-Bondage/hypodermic panel	47	94	141	296	498	700
3-Male bondage/torture-c; severed head story	41	82	123	256	428	600

WEIRD ADVENTURES
Ziff-Davis Publishing Co.: No. 10, July-Aug, 1951

10-Painted-c 40 80 120 242 401 560

WEIRD CHILLS
Key Publications: July, 1954 - No. 3, Nov, 1954

1-Wolverton-r/Weird Mysteries No. 4; blood transfusion-c by Baily 100 200 300 635 1093 1550
2-Extremely violent injury to eye-c by Baily; Hitler story 123 246 369 787 1344 1900
3-Bondage E.C. swipe-c by Baily 50 100 150 315 533 750

WEIRD COMICS
Fox Features Syndicate: Apr, 1940 - No. 20, Jan, 1942

1-The Birdman, Thor, God of Thunder (ends #5), The Sorceress of Zoom, Blast Bennett, Typhon, Voodoo Man, & Dr. Mortal begin; George Tuska bondage-c 486 972 1458 3550 6275 9000
2-Lou Fine-c 236 472 708 1499 2575 3650
3,4: 3-Simon-c. 4-Torture-c 126 252 378 806 1378 1950
5-Intro. Dart & sidekick Ace (8/40) (ends #20); bondage/hypo-c 129 258 387 826 1413 2000

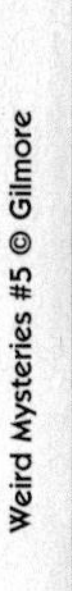
Weird Fantasy #17 © WMG

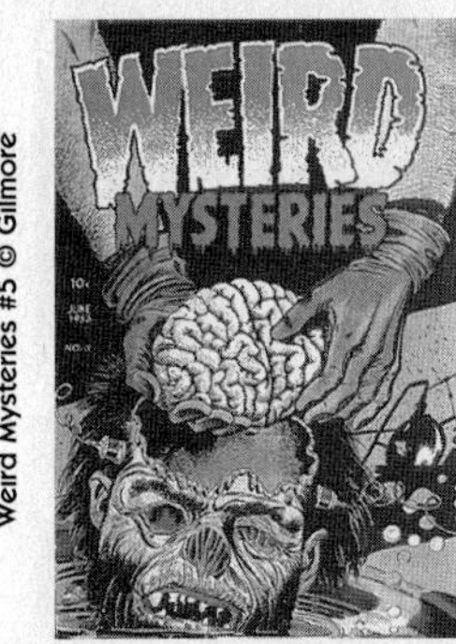

Weird Mysteries #5 © Gilmore

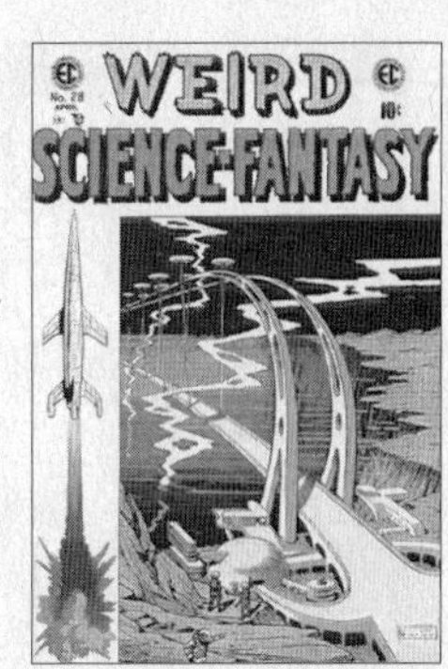

Weird Science-Fantasy #28 © WMG

	GD 2.0	VG 4.0	FN 6.0	VF 8.0	VF/NM 9.0	NM- 9.2
6,7-Dynamite Thor app. in each. 6-Super hero covers begin	94	188	282	597	1024	1450
8-Dynamo, the Eagle (11/40, early app.; see Science #1) & sidekick Buddy & Marga, the Panther Woman begin	92	184	276	584	1005	1425
9,10: 10-Navy Jones app.	74	148	222	470	810	1150
11-19: 16-Flag-c. 17-Origin The Black Rider.	55	110	165	352	601	850
20-Origin The Rapier; Swoop Curtis app; Churchill & Hitler-c	87	174	261	553	952	1350

NOTE *Cover features: Sorceress of Zoom-4; Dr. Mortal-5; Dart & Ace-6-13, 15; Eagle-14, 16-20.*

WEIRD FANTASY (Formerly A Moon, A Girl, Romance; becomes Weird Science-Fantasy #23 on)
E. C. Comics: No. 13, May-June, 1950 - No. 22, Nov-Dec, 1953

	GD 2.0	VG 4.0	FN 6.0	VF 8.0	VF/NM 9.0	NM- 9.2
13(#1) (1950)	200	400	600	1600	2550	3500
14-Necronomicon story; Cosmic Ray Bomb explosion-c/story by Feldstein; Feldstein & Gaines star	97	194	291	776	1238	1700
15,16: 16-Used in **SOTI**, pg. 144	66	132	198	528	839	1150
17 (1951)	54	108	162	432	691	950
6-10: 6-Robot-c	47	94	141	376	601	825
11-13 (1952): 11-Feldstein bio. 12-E.C. artists cameo; Orlando bio. 13-Anti-Wertham "Cosmic Correspondence"	39	78	117	312	494	675
14-Frazetta/Williamson(1st team-up at E.C.)/Krenkel-a (7 pgs.); Orlando draws E.C. staff	50	100	150	400	638	875
15-Williamson/Evans-a(3), 4,3,&7 pgs.	39	78	117	312	494	675
16-19-Williamson/Krenkel-a in all. 18-Williamson/Feldstein-c; classic anti-prejudice story "Judgment Day". 19-Williamson bio.	36	72	108	288	462	635
20-Frazetta/Williamson-a (7 pgs.)	40	80	120	320	510	700
21-Frazetta/Williamson-c & Williamson/Krenkel-a	53	106	159	424	675	925
22-Bradbury adaptation	29	58	87	232	366	500

NOTE: ***Crandall*** *a-22.* ***Elder*** *a-17.* ***Feldstein*** *a-13(#1)-8; c-13(#1)-18 (#18 w/****Williamson****), 20.* ***Harrison/Wood*** *a-13.* ***Kamen*** *a-13(#1)-16, 18-22.* ***Krigstein*** *a-22.* ***Kurtzman*** *a-13(#1)-17(#5), 6.* ***Orlando*** *a-9-22 (2 stories in #16); c-19, 22.* ***Severin/Elder*** *a-18-21.* ***Wood*** *a-13(#1)-14, 17(2 stories ea. in #10-13). Ray Bradbury adaptations in #13,17-19, 22. Canadian reprints exist; see Table of Contents.*

WEIRD FANTASY
Russ Cochran/Gemstone Publ.: Oct, 1992 - No. 22, Jan, 1998 ($1.50/$2.00/$2.50)

1-22: 1,2: 1,2-r/Weird Fantasy #13,14; Feldstein-c. 3-5-r/Weird Fantasy #15-17 — 4.00

WEIRD HORRORS (Nightmare #10 on)
St. John Publishing Co.: June, 1952 - No. 9, Oct, 1953

	GD 2.0	VG 4.0	FN 6.0	VF 8.0	VF/NM 9.0	NM- 9.2
1-Tuska-a	61	122	183	390	670	950
2,3: 3-Hashish story	39	78	117	231	378	525
4,5	34	68	102	199	325	450
6-Ekgren-c; atomic bomb story	57	114	171	362	619	875
7-Ekgren-c; Kubert, Cameron-a	57	114	171	362	619	875
8,9-Kubert-c/a	41	82	123	256	428	600

NOTE: ***Cameron*** *a-7, 9.* ***Finesque*** *a-1-5.* ***Forgione*** *a-6.* ***Morisi*** *a-3. Bondage c-8.*

WEIRD MYSTERIES
Gillmor Publications: Oct, 1952 - No. 12, Sept, 1954

	GD 2.0	VG 4.0	FN 6.0	VF 8.0	VF/NM 9.0	NM- 9.2
1-Partial Wolverton-c swiped from splash page "Flight to the Future" in Weird Tales of the Future #2; "Eternity" has an Ingels swipe	107	214	321	680	1165	1650
2- "Robot Woman" by Wolverton; Bernard Baily-c reprinted in Mister Mystery #18; acid in face panel	142	284	426	909	1555	2200
3,6: Both have decapitation-c	71	142	213	454	777	1100
4- "The Man Who Never Smiled" (3 pgs.) by Wolverton; Classic B. Baily skull-c	148	296	444	947	1624	2300
5-Wolverton story "Swamp Monster" (6 pgs.). Classic exposed brain-c	174	348	522	1114	1907	2700
7-Used in **SOTI**, illo "Indeed", illo "Sex and blood"	97	194	291	621	1061	1500
8-Wolverton-c panel-r/#5; used in a '54 Readers Digest anti-comics article by T. E. Murphy entitled "For the Kiddies to Read"	63	126	189	403	689	975
9-Excessive violence, gore & torture	60	120	180	381	653	925
10-Silhouetted nudity panel	54	108	162	343	574	825
11,12: 12-r/Mr. Mystery #8(2), Weird Mysteries #3 & Weird Tales of the Future #6	52	104	156	322	549	775

NOTE: ***Baily*** *c-2-12. Anti-Wertham column in #5. #1-12 all have 'The Ghoul Teacher' (host).*

WEIRD MYSTERIES (Magazine)
Pastime Publications: Mar-Apr, 1959 (35¢, B&W, 68 pgs.)

	GD 2.0	VG 4.0	FN 6.0	VF 8.0	VF/NM 9.0	NM- 9.2
1-Torres-a; E. C. swipe from Tales From the Crypt #46 by Tuska "The Ragman"	11	22	33	62	86	110

WEIRD MYSTERY TALES (See DC 100 Page Super Spectacular)

WEIRD MYSTERY TALES (See Cancelled Comic Cavalcade)
National Periodical Publications: July-Aug, 1972 - No. 24, Nov, 1975

	GD 2.0	VG 4.0	FN 6.0	VF 8.0	VF/NM 9.0	NM- 9.2
1-Kirby-a; Wrightson splash pg.	6	12	18	37	59	80
2-Titanic-c/s	3	6	9	21	32	42
3,21: 21-Wrightson-c	3	6	9	18	27	35
4-10	3	6	9	14	19	24
11-20,22-24	2	4	6	11	16	20

NOTE: ***Alcala*** *a-5, 10, 13, 14.* ***Aparo*** *c-4.* ***Bailey*** *a-8.* ***Bolle*** *a-8?.* ***Howard*** *a-4.* ***Kaluta*** *a-4, 24; c-1.* ***G. Kane*** *a-10.* ***Kirby*** *a-1, 2p, 3p.* ***Nino*** *a-5, 6, 9, 13, 16, 21.* ***Redondo*** *a-9, 17.* ***Sparling*** *c-6.* ***Starlin*** *a-3?, 4.* ***Wood*** *a-23.*

WEIRD ROMANCE (Seduction of the Innocent #9)
Eclipse Comics: Feb, 1988 ($2.00, B&W)

1-Pre-code horror-r; Lou Cameron-r(2) — 4.00

WEIRD SCIENCE (Formerly Saddle Romances) (Becomes Weird Science-Fantasy #23 on) (Also see EC Archives • Weird Science)
E. C. Comics: No. 12, May-June, 1950 - No. 22, Nov-Dec, 1953

	GD 2.0	VG 4.0	FN 6.0	VF 8.0	VF/NM 9.0	NM- 9.2
12(#1) (1950)-"Lost in the Microcosm" classic-c/story by Kurtzman; "Dream of Doom" stars Gaines & E.C. artists	200	400	600	1600	2550	3500
13-Flying saucers over Washington-c/story, 2 years before supposed UFO sighting	97	194	291	776	1238	1700
14-Robot, End of the World-c/story by Feldstein	91	182	273	728	1164	1600
15-War of Worlds-c/story (1950)	83	166	249	664	1057	1450
5-Atomic explosion-c	61	122	183	488	782	1075
6-8,10	53	106	159	424	675	925
9-Wood's 1st EC-c	56	112	168	448	712	975
11-14 (1952) 11-Kamen bio. 12-Wood bio	39	78	117	312	494	675
15-18-Williamson/Krenkel-a in each; 15-Williamson-a. 17-Used in **POP**, pgs. 81,82. 18-Bill Gaines doll app. in story	40	80	120	320	510	700
19,20-Williamson/Frazetta-a (7 pgs. each). 19-Used in **SOTI**, illo "A young girl on her wedding night stabs her sleeping husband to death with a hatpin..." 19-Bradbury bio.	49	98	147	392	626	860
21-Williamson/Frazetta-a (6 pgs.); Wood draws E.C. staff; Gaines & Feldstein app. in story	49	98	147	392	626	860
22-Williamson/Frazetta/Krenkel-a (8 pgs.); Wood draws himself in his story (last pg. & panel)	49	98	147	392	626	860

NOTE: ***Elder*** *a-14, 19.* ***Evans*** *a-22.* ***Feldstein*** *a-12(#1)-8; c-12(#1)-8, 11.* ***Ingels*** *a-15.* ***Kamen*** *a-12(#1)-13, 15-18, 20, 21.* ***Kurtzman*** *a-12(#1)-7.* ***Orlando*** *a-10-22.* ***Wood*** *a-12(#1), 13(#2), 5-22 (#9, 10, 12, 13 all have 2* ***Wood*** *stories); c-9, 10, 12-22. Canadian reprints exist; see Table of Contents. Ray Bradbury adaptations in #17-22.*

WEIRD SCIENCE
Gladstone Publishing: Sept, 1990 - No. 4, Mar, 1991 ($1.95/$2.00, 68 pgs.)

1-4: Wood-c(r); all reprints in each — 5.00

WEIRD SCIENCE (Also see EC Archives • Weird Science)
Russ Cochran/Gemstone Publishing: Sept, 1992 - No. 22, Dec, 1997 ($1.50/$2.00/$2.50)

1-22: 1,2: r/Weird Science #12,13 w/original-c. ,4-r/#14,15. 5-7-w/original-c — 4.00

WEIRD SCIENCE-FANTASY (Formerly Weird Science & Weird Fantasy) (Becomes Incredible Science Fiction #30)
E. C. Comics: No. 23 Mar, 1954 - No. 29, May-June, 1955 (#23,24: 15¢)

	GD 2.0	VG 4.0	FN 6.0	VF 8.0	VF/NM 9.0	NM- 9.2
23-Williamson, Wood-a; Bradbury adaptation	36	72	108	288	462	635
24-Williamson & Wood-a; Harlan Ellison's 1st professional story, "Upheaval!", later adapted into a short story as "Mealtime", and then into a TV episode of Voyage to the Bottom of the Sea as "The Price of Doom"	36	72	108	288	462	635
25-Williamson-c; Williamson/Torres/Krenkel-a plus Wood-a; Bradbury adaptation; cover price back to 10¢	40	80	120	320	510	700
26-Flying Saucer Report; Wood, Crandall-a; A-bomb panels	38	76	114	304	482	660
27-Adam Link/I Robot series begins	36	72	108	288	462	635
28-Williamson/Krenkel/Torres-a; Wood-a	37	74	111	296	473	650
29-Classic Frazetta-c; Williamson/Krenkel & Wood-a; Adam Link/I Robot series concludes; last pre-code issue; new logo	109	218	327	872	1386	1900

NOTE: ***Crandall*** *a-26, 27, 29.* ***Evans*** *a-26.* ***Feldstein*** *c-24, 26, 28.* ***Kamen*** *a-27, 28.* ***Krigstein*** *a-23-25.* ***Orlando*** *a-in all.* ***Wood*** *a-in all; c-23, 27. The cover to #29 was originally intended for Famous Funnies #217 (Buck Rogers), but was rejected for being "too violent."*

WEIRD SCIENCE-FANTASY
Russ Cochran/Gemstone Publishing: Nov, 1992 - No. 7, May , 1994 ($1.50/$2.00/$2.50)

1-7: 1,2: r/Weird Science-Fantasy #23,24. 3-7 r/#25-29 — 4.00

WEIRD SCIENCE-FANTASY ANNUAL
E. C. Comics: 1952, 1953 (Sold thru the E. C. office & on the stands in some major cities) (25¢, 132 pgs.)

	GD 2.0	VG 4.0	FN 6.0	VF 8.0	VF/NM 9.0	NM- 9.2
1952-Feldstein-c	277	554	831	2078	3189	4300
1953-Feldstein-c	168	336	504	1260	1930	2600

NOTE: *The 1952 annual contains books cover-dated in 1951 & 1952, and the 1953 annual from 1952 & 1953. Contents of each annual may vary in same year.*

WEIRD SECRET ORIGINS
DC Comics: Oct, 2004 ($5.95, square-bound, one-shot)

nn-Reprints origins of Dr. Fate, Spectre, Congorilla, Metamorpho, Animal Man & others — 6.00

Weird Tales of the Future #7 © Aragon

Weird War Tales #1 © DC

Weird Western Tales #12 © DC

	GD 2.0	VG 4.0	FN 6.0	VF 8.0	VF/NM 9.0	NM- 9.2

WEIRD SUSPENSE
Atlas/Seaboard Publ.: Feb, 1975 - No. 3, July, 1975

	GD	VG	FN	VF	VF/NM	NM-
1-3: 1-Tarantula begins. 3-Friedrich-s	2	4	6	8	11	14

NOTE: ***Boyette** a-1-3. **Buckler** c-1, 3.*

WEIRD SUSPENSE STORIES (Canadian reprints of Crime SuspenStories #1-3; see Table of Contents)

WEIRD TALES ILLUSTRATED
Millennium Publications: 1992 - No. 2, 1992 ($2.95, high quality paper)

	GD	VG	FN	VF	VF/NM	NM-
1,2-Bolton painted-c. 1-Adapts E.A. Poe & Harlan Ellison stories. 2-E.A. Poe & H.P. Lovecraft adaptations						4.00
1-($4.95, 52 pgs.)-Deluxe edition w/Tim Vigil-a not in regular #1; stiff-c; Bolton painted-c						6.00

WEIRD TALES OF THE FUTURE
S.P.M. Publ. No. 1-4/Aragon Publ. No. 5-8: Mar, 1952 - No. 8, July-Aug, 1953

	GD	VG	FN	VF	VF/NM	NM-
1-Andru-a(2); Wolverton partial-c	113	226	339	718	1234	1750
2,3-Wolverton-c/a(3) each. 2- "Jumpin Jupiter" satire by Wolverton begins, ends #5	168	336	504	1075	1838	2600
4- "Jumpin Jupiter" satire, partial Wolverton-c	142	284	426	909	1555	2200
5-Wolverton-c/a(2); "Jumpin Jupiter" satire	168	336	504	1075	1838	2600
6-Bernard Baily-c	58	116	174	371	636	900
7- "The Mind Movers" from the art to Wolverton's "Brain Bats of Venus" from Mr. Mystery #7 which was cut apart, pasted up, partially redrawn, and rewritten by Harry Kantor, the editor; Baily-c	142	284	426	909	1555	2200
8-Reprints Weird Mysteries #1(10/52) minus cover; gory cover showing heart ripped out, by B. Baily	94	188	282	597	1024	1450

WEIRD TALES OF THE MACABRE (Magazine)
Atlas/Seaboard Publ.: Jan, 1975 - No. 2, Mar, 1975 (75¢, B&W)

	GD	VG	FN	VF	VF/NM	NM-
1-Jeff Jones painted-c; Boyette-a	4	8	12	24	37	50
2-Boris Vallejo painted-c; Severin-a	4	8	12	28	44	60

WEIRD TERROR (Also see Horrific)
Allen Hardy Associates (Comic Media): Sept, 1952 - No. 13, Sept, 1954

	GD	VG	FN	VF	VF/NM	NM-
1- "Portrait of Death", adapted from Lovecraft's "Pickman's Model"; lingerie panels, Hitler story	60	120	180	381	653	925
2,3: 2-Text on Marquis DeSade, Torture, Demonology, & St. Elmo's Fire. 3-Extreme violence, whipping, torture; article on sin eating, dowsing	49	98	147	309	522	735
4-Dismemberment, decapitation, article on human flesh for sale, Devil, whipping	49	98	147	309	522	735
5-Article on body snatching, mutilation; cannibalism story	42	84	126	265	450	635
6-Dismemberment, decapitation, man hit by lightning	46	92	138	290	488	685
7-Body burning in fireplace-c	46	92	138	290	488	685
8,11: 8-Decapitation story; Ambrose Bierce adapt. 11-End of the world story w/atomic blast panels; Tothish-a by Bill Discount	42	84	126	265	450	635
9,10,13: 13-Severed head panels	39	78	117	231	378	525
12-Discount-a	39	78	117	231	378	525

NOTE: ***Don Heck** a-most issues; c-1-13. **Landau** a-6. **Morisi** a-2-5, 7, 9, 12. **Palais** a-1, 5, 6, 8(2), 10, 12. **Powell** a-10. **Ravielli** a-11.*

WEIRD THRILLERS
Ziff-Davis Publ. Co. (Approved Comics): Sept-Oct, 1951 - No. 5, Oct-Nov, 1952
(#2-5: painted-c)

	GD	VG	FN	VF	VF/NM	NM-
1-Rondo Hatton photo-c	94	188	282	597	1024	1450
2-Toth, Anderson, Colan-a	65	130	195	416	708	1000
3-Two Powell, Tuska-a; classic-c; Everett-a	92	184	276	584	1005	1425
4-Kubert, Tuska-a	61	122	183	390	670	950
5-Powell-a	57	114	171	362	619	875

NOTE: ***M. Anderson** a-2, 3. **Roussos** a-4. #2, 3 reprinted in Nightmare #10 & 13; #4, 5 reprinted in Amazing Ghost Stories #16 & #15.*

WEIRD VAMPIRE TALES (Comic magazine)
Modern Day Periodical Pub.: V3 #1, Apr, 1979 - V5 #3, Mar, 1982 (B&W)

	GD	VG	FN	VF	VF/NM	NM-
V3 #1 (4/79) First issue, no V1 or V2	4	8	12	26	41	55
V3 #2-4	3	6	9	20	30	40
V4 #2 (4/80), V4 #3 (7/80) (no V4 #1)	3	6	9	18	27	35
V5 #1 (1/81), V5 #2 (two issues, 4/81 & 8/81)	3	6	9	18	27	35
V5 #3 (3/82) Last issue; low print	4	8	12	22	34	45

WEIRD WAR TALES
National Periodical Publ./DC Comics: Sept-Oct, 1971 - No. 124, June, 1983 (#1-5: 52 pgs.)

	GD	VG	FN	VF	VF/NM	NM-
1-Kubert-a in #1-4,7; c-1-7	23	46	69	168	334	500
2,3-Drucker-a: 2-Crandall-a. 3-Heath-a	11	22	33	75	138	200
4,5: 5-Toth-a; Heath-a	9	18	27	63	107	150
6,7,9,10: 6,10-Toth-a. 7-Heath-a	6	12	18	43	69	95
8-Neal Adams-c/a(i)	7	14	21	49	80	110
11-20	4	8	12	23	36	48
21-35	3	6	9	17	25	32
36-(68 pgs.)-Crandall & Kubert-r/#2; Heath-r/#3; Kubert-c	3	6	9	19	29	38
37-50: 38,39-Kubert-c	2	4	6	10	14	18
51-63: 58-Hitler-c/app. 60-Hindenburg-c/s	2	4	6	9	13	16
64-Frank Miller-a (1st DC work)	4	8	12	28	44	60
65-67,69-89,91,92: 89-Nazi Apes-c/s.	2	4	6	8	10	12
68-Frank Miller-a (2nd DC work)	3	6	9	20	30	40
90-Hitler app.	2	4	6	8	11	14
93-Intro/origin Creature Commandos	2	4	6	8	11	14
94-Return of War that Time Forgot; dinosaur-c/s	2	4	6	10	14	18
95,96,98,102-123: 98-Sphinx-c. 102-Creature Commandos battle Hitler. 110-Origin/1st app. Medusa. 123-1st app. Captain Spaceman	2	4	6	8	10	12
97,99,100,101,124: 99-War that Time Forgot. 100-Creature Commandos in War that Time Forgot. 101-Intro/origin G.I. Robot	2	4	6	8	11	14

NOTE: ***Chaykin** a-76, 82. **Ditko** a-95, 99, 104-106. **Evans** c-73, 74, 83, 85. **Kane** c-116, 118. **Kubert** c-55, 58, 60, 62, 72, 75-81, 87, 88, 90-96, 100, 103, 104, 106, 107. **Newton** a-122. **Starlin** c-89. **Sutton** a-91, 92, 103. **Creature Commandos** -93, 97, 100, 102, 105, 108-112, 114, 116-119, 121, 124. **G.I. Robot** - 101, 108, 111, 113, 116-118, 120, 122. **War That Time Forgot** - 94, 99, 100, 103, 106, 109, 120.*

WEIRD WAR TALES
DC Comics (Vertigo): June, 1997 - No. 4, Sept, 1997 ($2.50)

	GD	VG	FN	VF	VF/NM	NM-
1-4-Anthology by various						3.00

WEIRD WAR TALES
DC Comics (Vertigo): April, 2000 ($4.95, one-shot)

	GD	VG	FN	VF	VF/NM	NM-
1-Anthology by various; last Biukovic-a						5.00

WEIRD WAR TALES
DC Comics: Nov, 2010 ($3.99, one-shot)

	GD	VG	FN	VF	VF/NM	NM-
1-Anthology by various incl. Cooke, Strnad, Pugh; Cooke-c						4.00

WEIRD WESTERN TALES (Formerly All-Star Western)
National Per. Publ./DC Comics: No. 12, June-July, 1972 - No. 70, Aug, 1980

	GD	VG	FN	VF	VF/NM	NM-
12-(52 pgs.)-3rd app. Jonah Hex; Bat Lash, Pow Wow Smith reprints; El Diablo by Neal Adams/Wrightson	13	26	39	94	185	275
13-Jonah Hex-c & 4th app.; Neal Adams-a	9	18	27	65	113	160
14-Toth-a	7	14	21	49	80	110
15-Adams-c/a; no Jonah Hex	5	10	15	30	48	65
16,17,19,20	5	10	15	30	48	65
18,29: 18-1st all Jonah Hex issue (7-8/73) & begins. 29-Origin Jonah Hex	6	12	18	43	69	95
21-28,30: Jonah Hex in all	4	8	12	24	37	50
31-38: Jonah Hex in all. 38-Last Jonah Hex	3	6	9	19	29	38
39-Origin/1st app. Scalphunter & begins	2	4	6	13	18	22
40-47,50-69: 64-Bat Lash-c/story	2	4	6	8	10	12
48,49: (44 pgs.)-1st & 2nd app. Cinnamon	2	4	6	8	11	14
70-Last issue	2	4	6	9	13	16

NOTE: ***Alcala** a-16, 17. **Evans** inks-39-48; c-39i, 40, 47. **G. Kane** a-15, 20. **Kubert** c-12, 33. **Starlin** c-44, 45. **Wildey** a-26. 48 & 49 are 44 pgs..*

WEIRD WESTERN TALES (Blackest Night crossover)
DC Comics: No. 71, March, 2010 ($2.99, one-shot)

	GD	VG	FN	VF	VF/NM	NM-
71-Jonah Hex, Scalphunter, Super-Chief, Firehair and Bat Lash rise as Black Lanterns						3.00

WEIRD WESTERN TALES
DC Comics (Vertigo): Apr, 2001 - No. 4, Jul, 2001 ($2.50, limited series)

	GD	VG	FN	VF	VF/NM	NM-
1-4-Anthology by various						3.00

WEIRD WONDER TALES
Marvel Comics Group: Dec, 1973 - No. 22, May, 1977

	GD	VG	FN	VF	VF/NM	NM-
1-Wolverton-r/Mystic #6 (Eye of Doom)	3	6	9	20	30	40
2-10	3	6	9	14	20	25
11-22: 16-18-Venus-r by Everett from Venus #19,18 & 17. 19-22-r/Dr. Droom (re-named Dr. Druid) by Kirby. 22-New art by Byrne	2	4	6	13	18	22
15-17-(30¢-c variants, limited distribution)(4-8/76)	3	6	9	20	30	40

NOTE: *All 1950s & early 1960s reprints. **Check** r-1. **Colan** r-17. **Ditko** r-4, 5, 10-13, 19-21. **Drucker** r-12, 20. **Everett** r-3(Spellbound #16), 6(Astonishing #10), 9(Adv. Into Mystery #5). **Heath** a-13r. **Heck** a-10r, 14r. **Gil Kane** c-1, 2, 10. **Kirby** r-4, 6, 10, 11, 13, 15-22; c-17, 19, 20. **Krigstein** r-19. **Kubert** r-22. **Maneely** r-8. **Mooney** r-7p. **Powell** r-3, 7. **Torres** r-7. **Wildey** r-2, 7.*

WEIRD WORLD OF JACK STAFF (See Jack Staff)
Image Comics: Feb, 2010 - Present ($3.50)

	GD	VG	FN	VF	VF/NM	NM-
1-6-Paul Grist-s/a. 2-Ian Churchill-c						3.50

WEIRD WORLDS (See Adventures Into...)

WEIRD WORLDS (Magazine)

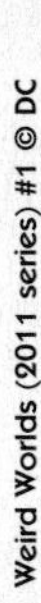

Weird Worlds (2011 series) #1 © DC

Wendy Parker #2 © MAR

West Coast Avengers Annual #4 © MAR

Eerie Publications: V1#10(12/70), V2#1(2/71) - No. 4, Aug, 1971 (52 pgs.)

	GD 2.0	VG 4.0	FN 6.0	VF 8.0	VF/NM 9.0	NM- 9.2
V1#10-Sci-fi/horror	5	10	15	30	48	65
V2#1-4	4	8	12	26	41	55

WEIRD WORLDS (Also see Ironwolf: Fires of the Revolution)
National Periodical Publications: Aug-Sept, 1972 - No. 9, Jan-Feb, 1974; No. 10, Oct-Nov, 1974 (All 20¢ issues)

	GD 2.0	VG 4.0	FN 6.0	VF 8.0	VF/NM 9.0	NM- 9.2
1-Edgar Rice Burrough's John Carter Warlord of Mars & David Innes begin (1st DC app.); Kubert-c	3	6	9	16	22	28
2-4: 2-Infantino/Orlando-c. 3-Murphy Anderson-c. 4-Kaluta-a	2	4	6	10	14	18
5-7: .5-Kaluta-c. 7-Last John Carter.	2	4	6	8	11	14
8-10: 8-Iron Wolf begins by Chaykin (1st app.)	2	4	6	8	11	14

NOTE: ***Neal Adams** a-2i, 3i. John Carter by **Andersonin** #1-3. **Chaykin** c-7, 8. **Kaluta** a-4; c-4-6, 10. **Orlando** a-4i; c-2, 3, 4i. **Wrightson** a-2i, 4i.*

WEIRD WORLDS
DC Comics: Mar, 2011 - No. 6 ($3.99, limited series)

	NM- 9.2
1-3-Short stories of Lobo, Garbage Man and Tanga; Ordway-a; Maguire-s/a; Lopresti-s/a	4.00

WELCOME BACK, KOTTER (TV) (See Limited Collectors' Edition #57 for unpublished #11)
National Periodical Publ./DC Comics: Nov, 1976 - No. 10, Mar-Apr, 1978

	GD 2.0	VG 4.0	FN 6.0	VF 8.0	VF/NM 9.0	NM- 9.2
1-Sparling-a(p)	3	6	9	16	23	30
2-10: 3-Estrada-a	2	4	6	10	14	18

WELCOME SANTA (See March of Comics #63,183)

WELCOME TO HOLSOM
Gospel Publishing House: 2005 - Present (no cover price)

	NM- 9.2
1-12-Craig Schutt-s/Steven Butler-a	3.00

WELCOME TO THE LITTLE SHOP OF HORRORS
Roger Corman's Cosmic Comics: May, 1995 -No. 3, July, 1995 ($2.50, limited series)

	NM- 9.2
1-3	3.00

WELCOME TO TRANQUILITY
DC Comics (WildStorm): Feb, 2007 - No. 12, Jan, 2008 ($2.99)

	NM- 9.2
1-12: 1-Simone-s/Googe-a; two covers by Googe and Campbell. 8-Pearson-a	3.00
...: Armageddon 1 (1/08, $2.99) Gage-s/Googe-a	3.00
...: One Foot in the Grave 1-6 (7/10 - No. 6, 2/11, $3.99) Simone-s/Domingues-a	4.00
... Book One TPB (2008, $19.99) r/#1-6 and variant cover gallery	20.00
... Book Two TPB (2008, $19.99) r/#7-12; sketch pages	20.00

WELLS FARGO (See Tales of...)

WENDY AND THE NEW KIDS ON THE BLOCK
Harvey Comics: Mar, 1991 - No. 3, July, 1991 ($1.25)

	NM- 9.2
1-3	5.00

WENDY DIGEST
Harvey Comics: Oct, 1990 - No. 5, Mar, 1992 ($1.75, digest size)

	NM- 9.2
1-5	4.00

WENDY PARKER COMICS
Atlas Comics (OMC): July, 1953 - No. 8, July, 1954

	GD 2.0	VG 4.0	FN 6.0	VF 8.0	VF/NM 9.0	NM- 9.2
1	11	22	33	60	83	105
2	8	16	24	44	57	70
3-8	8	16	24	40	50	60

WENDY, THE GOOD LITTLE WITCH (TV)
Harvey Publ.: 8/60 - #82, 11/73; #83, 8/74 - #93, 4/76; #94, 9/90 - #97, 12/90

	GD 2.0	VG 4.0	FN 6.0	VF 8.0	VF/NM 9.0	NM- 9.2
1-Wendy & Casper the Friendly Ghost begin	28	56	84	204	415	625
2	13	26	39	94	185	275
3-5	10	20	30	71	128	185
6-10	8	16	24	52	86	120
11-20	6	12	18	39	62	85
21-30	4	8	12	28	44	60
31-50	3	6	9	18	27	35
51-64,66-69	2	4	6	13	18	22
65 (2/71)-Wendy origin.	3	6	9	17	25	32
70-74: All 52 pg. Giants	3	6	9	16	23	30
75-93	2	4	6	9	13	16
94-97 (1990, $1.00-c): 94-Has #194 on-c						5.00

(See Casper the Friendly Ghost #20 & Harvey Hits #7, 16, 21, 23, 27, 30, 33)

WENDY THE GOOD LITTLE WITCH (2nd Series)
Harvey Comics: Apr, 1991 - No. 15, Aug, 1994 ($1.00/$1.25 #7-11/$1.50 #12-15)

	NM- 9.2
1-15-Reprints Wendy & Casper stories. 12-Bunny app.	3.00

WENDY WITCH WORLD
Harvey Publications: 10/61; No. 2, 9/62 - No. 52, 12/73; No. 53, 9/74

	GD 2.0	VG 4.0	FN 6.0	VF 8.0	VF/NM 9.0	NM- 9.2
1-(25¢, 68 pg. Giants begin)	13	26	39	93	182	270
2-5	8	16	24	52	86	120
6-10	6	12	18	37	59	80
11-20	4	8	12	28	44	60
21-30	4	8	12	22	34	45
31-39: 39-Last 68 pg. issue	3	6	9	17	25	32
40-45: 52 pg. issues	2	4	6	13	18	22
46-53	2	4	6	9	13	16

WEREWOLF (Super Hero) (Also see Dracula & Frankenstein)
Dell Publishing Co.: Dec, 1966 - No. 3, April, 1967

	GD 2.0	VG 4.0	FN 6.0	VF 8.0	VF/NM 9.0	NM- 9.2
1-1st app.	4	8	12	24	37	50
2,3	3	6	9	16	23	30

WEREWOLF BY NIGHT (See Giant-Size..., Marvel Spotlight #2-4 & Power Record Comics)
Marvel Comics Group: Sept, 1972 - No. 43, Mar, 1977

	GD 2.0	VG 4.0	FN 6.0	VF 8.0	VF/NM 9.0	NM- 9.2
1-Ploog-a cont'd. from Marvel Spotlight #4	13	26	39	89	170	250
2	7	14	21	47	76	105
3-5	5	10	15	35	55	75
6-10	4	8	12	26	41	55
11-14,16-20	3	6	9	19	29	38
15-New origin Werewolf; Dracula-c/story cont'd from Tomb of Dracula #18; classic Ploog-c	5	10	15	30	48	65
21-31	3	6	9	14	20	26
32-Origin & 1st app. Moon Knight (8/75)	11	22	33	75	138	200
33-2nd app. Moon Knight	6	12	18	41	66	90
34,36,38-43	3	6	9	14	19	24
35-Starlin/Wrightson-c	3	6	9	16	23	30
37-Moon Knight app; part Wrightson-c	4	8	12	22	34	45
38,39-(30¢-c variants, limited distribution)(5,7/76)	4	8	12	24	37	50

NOTE: ***Bolle** a-6i. **G. Kane** a-11p, 12p; c-21, 22, 24-30, 34p. **Mooney** a-7i. **Ploog** 1-4p, 5, 6p, 7p, 13-16p; c-5-8, 13-16. **Reinman** a-8i. **Sutton** a(i)-9, 11, 16, 35.*

WEREWOLF BY NIGHT (Vol. 2, continues in Strange Tales #1 (9/98))
Marvel Comics Group: Feb, 1998 - No. 6, July, 1998 ($2.99)

	NM- 9.2
1-6-Manco-a: 2-Two covers. 6-Ghost Rider-c/app.	3.00

WEREWOLVES & VAMPIRES (Magazine)
Charlton Comics: 1962 (One Shot)

	GD 2.0	VG 4.0	FN 6.0	VF 8.0	VF/NM 9.0	NM- 9.2
1	9	18	27	65	113	160

WEREWOLVES ON THE MOON: VERSUS VAMPIRES
Dark Horse Comics: June, 2009 - No. 3 ($3.50, limited series)

	NM- 9.2
1,2-Dave Land-s & Fillbach Brothers-s/a	3.50

WEST COAST AVENGERS
Marvel Comics Group: Sept, 1984 - No. 4, Dec, 1984 (lim. series, Mando paper)

	NM- 9.2
1-Origin & 1st app. W.C. Avengers (Hawkeye, Iron Man, Mockingbird & Tigra)	6.00
2-4	4.00

WEST COAST AVENGERS (Becomes Avengers West Coast #48 on)
Marvel Comics Group: Oct, 1985 - No. 47, Aug, 1989

	NM- 9.2
V2#1	4.00
2-41	3.00
42-47: 42-Byrne-a(p)/scripts begin. 46-Byrne-c; 1st app. Great Lakes Avengers	3.00
Annual 1-3 (1986-1988): 3-Evolutionary War app.	4.00
Annual 4 (1989, $2.00)-Atlantis Attacks; Byrne/Austin-a	4.00

WESTERN ACTION
I. W. Enterprises: No. 7, 1964

	GD 2.0	VG 4.0	FN 6.0	VF 8.0	VF/NM 9.0	NM- 9.2
7-Reprints Cow Puncher #? by Avon	2	4	6	8	11	14

WESTERN ACTION
Atlas/Seaboard Publ.: Feb, 1975

	GD 2.0	VG 4.0	FN 6.0	VF 8.0	VF/NM 9.0	NM- 9.2
1-Kid Cody by Wildey & The Comanche Kid stories; intro. The Renegade	2	4	6	8	11	14

WESTERN ACTION THRILLERS
Dell Publishers: Apr, 1937 (10¢, square binding; 100 pgs.)

	GD 2.0	VG 4.0	FN 6.0	VF 8.0	VF/NM 9.0	NM- 9.2
1-Buffalo Bill, The Texas Kid, Laramie Joe, Two-Gun Thompson, & Wild West Bill app.	84	168	252	538	919	1300

WESTERN ADVENTURES COMICS (Western Love Trails #7 on)
Ace Magazines: Oct, 1948 - No. 6, Aug, 1949

	GD 2.0	VG 4.0	FN 6.0	VF 8.0	VF/NM 9.0	NM- 9.2
nn(#1)-Sheriff Sal, The Cross-Draw Kid, Sam Bass begin	21	42	63	122	199	275
nn(#2)(12/48)	13	26	39	74	105	135

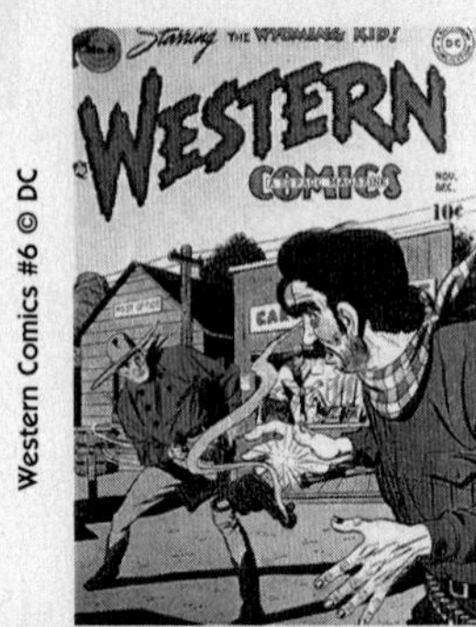

Western Comics #6 © DC

Western Gunfighters #16 © MAR

Western Hearts #2 © STD

	GD 2.0	VG 4.0	FN 6.0	VF 8.0	VF/NM 9.0	NM- 9.2
nn(#3)(2/49)-Used in **SOTI**, pgs. 30,31	14	28	42	76	108	140
4-6	11	22	33	62	86	110

WESTERN BANDITS
Avon Periodicals: 1952 (Painted-c)

	GD	VG	FN	VF	VF/NM	NM-
1-Butch Cassidy, The Daltons by Larsen; Kinstler-a; c-part-r/paperback Avon Western Novel #1	16	32	48	92	144	195

WESTERN BANDIT TRAILS (See Approved Comics)
St. John Publishing Co.: Jan, 1949 - No. 3, July, 1949

	GD	VG	FN	VF	VF/NM	NM-
1-Tuska-a; Baker-c; Blue Monk, Ventrilo app.	28	56	84	165	270	375
2-Baker-c	22	44	66	128	209	290
3-Baker-c/a; Tuska-a	26	52	78	154	252	350

WESTERN COMICS (See Super DC Giant #15)
National Per. Publ: Jan-Feb, 1948 - No. 85, Jan-Feb, 1961 (1-27: 52pgs.)

	GD	VG	FN	VF	VF/NM	NM-
1-Wyoming Kid & his horse Racer, The Vigilante in "Jesse James Rides Again" (Meskin-a), Cowboy Marshal, Rodeo Rick begin	74	148	222	470	810	1150
2	36	72	108	211	343	475
3,4-Last Vigilante	32	64	96	188	307	425
5-Nighthawk & his horse Nightwind begin (not in #6); Captain Tootsie by Beck	27	54	81	158	259	360
6,7,9,10	21	42	63	122	199	275
8-Origin Wyoming Kid; 2 pg. pin-ups of rodeo queens	34	68	102	199	325	450
11-20	18	36	54	103	162	220
21-40: 24-Starr-a. 27-Last 52 pgs. 28-Flag-c	14	28	42	82	121	160
41,42,44-49: 49-Last precode issue (2/55)	14	28	42	80	115	150
43-Pow Wow Smith begins, ends #85	14	28	42	81	118	155
50-60	12	24	36	67	94	120
61-85-Last Wyoming Kid. 77-Origin Matt Savage Trail Boss. 82-1st app. Fleetfoot, Pow Wow's girlfriend	10	20	30	56	76	95

NOTE: ***G. Kane, Infantino*** *art in most.* ***Meskin*** *a-1-4.* ***Moreira*** *a-28-39.* ***Post*** *a-3-5.*

WESTERN CRIME BUSTERS
Trojan Magazines: Sept, 1950 - No. 10, Mar-Apr, 1952

	GD	VG	FN	VF	VF/NM	NM-
1-Six-Gun Smith, Wilma West, K-Bar-Kate, & Fighting Bob Dale begin; headlight-a	36	72	108	216	351	485
2	19	38	57	111	176	240
3-5: 3-Myron Fass-c	18	36	54	105	165	225
6-Wood-a	32	64	96	188	307	425
7-Six-Gun Smith by Wood	32	64	96	188	307	425
8	18	36	54	105	165	225
9-Tex Gordon & Wilma West by Wood; Lariat Lucy app.	32	64	96	188	307	425
10-Wood-a	29	58	87	172	281	390

WESTERN CRIME CASES (Formerly Indian Warriors #7,8; becomes The Outlaws #10 on)
Star Publications: No. 9, Dec, 1951

	GD	VG	FN	VF	VF/NM	NM-
9-White Rider & Super Horse; L. B. Cole-c	21	42	63	122	199	275

WESTERNER, THE (Wild Bill Pecos)
"Wanted" Comic Group/Toytown/Patches: No. 14, June, 1948 - No. 41, Dec, 1951 (#14-31: 52 pgs.)

	GD	VG	FN	VF	VF/NM	NM-
14	15	30	45	85	130	175
15-17,19-21: 19-Meskin-a	9	18	27	52	69	85
18,22-25-Krigstein-a	11	22	33	60	83	105
26(4/50)-Origin & 1st app. Calamity Kate, series ends #32; Krigstein-a	14	28	42	78	112	145
27-Krigstein-a(2)	13	26	39	74	105	135
28-41: 33-Quest app. 37-Lobo, the Wolf Boy begins	8	16	24	40	50	60

NOTE: ***Mort Lawrence*** *a-20-27, 29, 37, 39; c-19, 22-24, 26, 27.* ***Leav*** *c-14-18, 20, 31.* ***Syd Shores*** *a-39; c-34, 35, 37-41.*

WESTERNER, THE
Super Comics: 1964

	GD	VG	FN	VF	VF/NM	NM-
Super Reprint 15-17: 15-r/Oklahoma Kid #? 16-r/Crack West. #65; Severin-c; Crandall-r. 17-r/Blazing Western #2; Severin-c	2	4	6	8	11	14

WESTERN FIGHTERS
Hillman Periodicals/Star Publ.: Apr-May, 1948 - V4#7, Mar-Apr, 1953 (#1-V3#2: 52 pgs.)

	GD	VG	FN	VF	VF/NM	NM-
V1#1-Simon & Kirby-c	36	72	108	216	351	485
2-Not Kirby-a	14	28	42	80	115	150
3-Fuje-c	12	24	36	67	94	120
4-Krigstein, Ingels, Fuje-a	13	26	39	74	105	135
5,6,8,9,12	10	20	30	54	72	90
7,10-Krigstein-a	11	22	33	62	86	110
11-Williamson/Frazetta-a	30	60	90	177	289	400
V2#1-Krigstein-a	11	22	33	62	86	110
2-12: 4-Berg-a	8	16	24	44	57	70
V3#1-11,V4#1,4-7	8	16	24	42	54	65
12,V4#2,3-Krigstein-a	11	22	33	62	86	110
3-D 1(12/53, 25¢, Star Publ.)-Came w/glasses; L. B. Cole-c	36	72	108	211	343	475

NOTE: ***Kinstlerish*** *a-V2#6, 8, 9, 12; V3#2, 5-7, 11, 12; V4#1(plus cover).* ***McWilliams*** *a-11.* ***Powell*** *a-V2#2.* ***Reinman*** *a-1-12, V4#3.* ***Rowich*** *c-5, 6i.* ***Starr*** *a-5.*

WESTERN FRONTIER
P. L. Publishers: Apr-May, 1951 - No. 7, 1952

	GD	VG	FN	VF	VF/NM	NM-
1	14	28	42	76	108	140
2	8	16	24	44	57	70
3-7	7	14	21	37	46	55

WESTERN GUNFIGHTERS (1st Series) (Apache Kid #11-19)
Atlas Comics (CPS): No. 20, June, 1956 - No. 27, Aug, 1957

	GD	VG	FN	VF	VF/NM	NM-
20	13	26	39	74	105	135
21-Crandall-a	13	26	39	74	105	135
22-Wood & Powell-a	18	36	54	103	162	220
23,24: 23-Williamson-a. 24-Toth-a	13	26	39	74	105	135
25-27	10	20	30	54	72	90

NOTE: ***Berg*** *a-20.* ***Colan*** *a-20, 26, 27.* ***Crandall*** *a-21.* ***Heath*** *a-25.* ***Maneely*** *a-24, 25; c-22, 23, 25.* ***Morisi*** *a-24.* ***Morrow*** *a-26.* ***Pakula*** *a-23.* ***Severin*** *c-20, 27.* ***Torres*** *a-26.* ***Woodbridge*** *a-27.*

WESTERN GUNFIGHTERS (2nd Series)
Marvel Comics Group: Aug, 1970 - No. 33, Nov, 1975 (#1-6: 25¢, 68 pgs.)

	GD	VG	FN	VF	VF/NM	NM-
1-Ghost Rider begins; Fort Rango, Renegades & Gunhawk app.	6	12	18	39	62	85
2,3,5,6: 2-Origin Nightwind (Apache Kid's horse)	4	8	12	22	34	45
4-Barry Smith-a	4	8	12	24	37	50
7-(52 pgs) Origin Ghost Rider retold	3	6	9	20	30	40
8-13: 10-Origin Black Rider. 12-Origin Matt Slade	3	6	9	14	20	25
14-Steranko-c	3	6	9	17	25	32
15-20	2	4	6	10	14	18
21-33	2	4	6	9	13	16

NOTE: ***Baker*** *r-2, 3.* ***Colan*** *r-2.* ***Drucker*** *r-3.* ***Everett*** *a-6i.* ***G. Kane*** *c-29, 31.* ***Kirby*** *a-1p(r), 5, 10-12; c-19, 21.* ***Kubert*** *r-2.* ***Maneely*** *r-2, 10.* ***Morrow*** *r-29.* ***Severin*** *c-10.* ***Shores*** *a-3, 4.* ***Barry Smith*** *a-4.* ***Steranko*** *c-14.* ***Sutton*** *a-1, 2i, 5, 4.* ***Torres*** *r-26('57).* ***Wildey*** *r-8, 9.* ***Williamson*** *r-2, 18.* ***Woodbridge*** *r-27('57). Renegades in #4, 5; Ghost Rider in #1-7.*

WESTERN HEARTS
Standard Comics: Dec, 1949 - No. 10, Mar, 1952 (All photo-c)

	GD	VG	FN	VF	VF/NM	NM-
1-Severin-a; Whip Wilson & Reno Browne photo-c	23	46	69	136	223	310
2-Beverly Tyler & Jerome Courtland photo-c from movie "Palomino"; Williamson/Frazetta-a (2 pgs.)	23	46	69	136	223	310
3-Rex Allen photo-c	14	28	42	80	115	150
4-7,10: 4-Severin & Elder, Al Carreno-a. 5-Ray Milland & Hedy Lamarr photo-c from movie "Copper Canyon". 6-Fred MacMurray & Irene Dunn photo-c from movie "Never a Dull Moment". 7-Jock Mahoney photo-c. 10-Bill Williams & Jane Nigh photo-c	14	28	42	78	112	145
8-Randolph Scott & Janis Carter photo-c from "Santa Fe"; Severin & Elder-a	14	28	42	80	115	150
9-Whip Wilson & Reno Browne photo-c; Severin & Elder-a	15	30	45	83	124	165

WESTERN HERO (Wow Comics #1-69; Real Western Hero #70-75)
Fawcett Publications: No. 76, Mar, 1949 - No. 112, Mar, 1952

	GD	VG	FN	VF	VF/NM	NM-
76(#1, 52 pgs.)-Tom Mix, Hopalong Cassidy, Monte Hale, Gabby Hayes, Young Falcon (ends #78,80), & Big Bow and Little Arrow (ends #102,105) begin; painted-c begin	16	32	48	94	147	200
77 (52 pgs.)	11	22	33	64	90	115
78,80-82 (52 pgs.): 81-Capt. Tootsie by Beck	11	22	33	60	83	105
79,83 (36 pgs.): 83-Last painted-c	10	20	30	54	72	90
84-86,88-90 (52 pgs.): 84-Photo-c begin, end #112. 86-Last Hopalong Cassidy	10	20	30	53	76	95
87,91,95,99 (36 pgs.): 87-Bill Boyd begins, ends #95	9	18	27	50	65	80
92-94,96-98,101 (52 pgs.): 96-Tex Ritter begins. 101-Red Eagle app.	9	18	27	52	69	85
100 (52 pgs.)	10	20	30	56	76	95
102-111: 102-Begin 36 pg. issues	9	18	27	50	65	80
112-Last issue	9	18	27	52	69	85

NOTE: *1/2 to 1 pg. Rocky Lane (Carnation) in 80-83, 86, 88, 97. Photo covers feature Hopalong Cassidy #84, 86, 89; Tom Mix #85, 87, 90, 92, 94, 97; Monte Hale #88, 91, 93, 95, 98, 100, 104, 107, 110; Tex Ritter #96, 99, 101, 105, 108, 111; Gabby Hayes #103.*

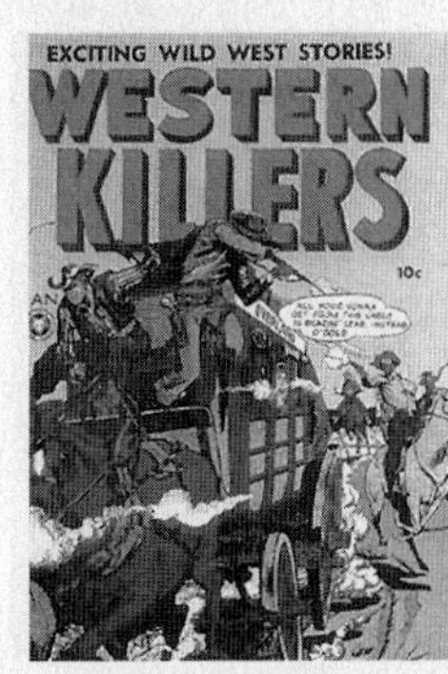

Western Killers #62 © FOX

Western Picture Stories #4 © CMC

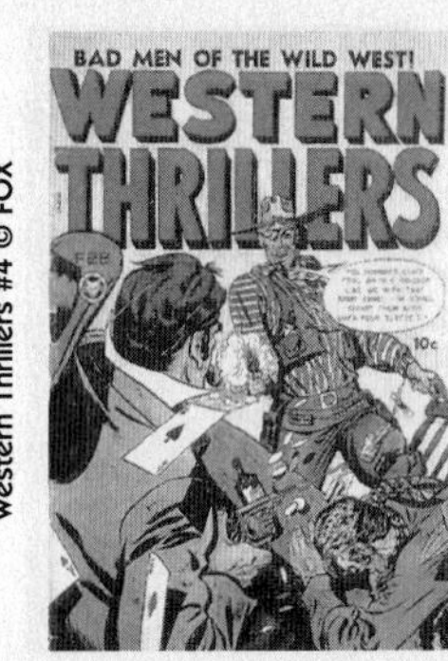

Western Thrillers #4 © FOX

WESTERN KID (1st Series)
Atlas Comics (CPC): Dec, 1954 - No. 17, Aug, 1957

	GD 2.0	VG 4.0	FN 6.0	VF 8.0	VF/NM 9.0	NM- 9.2
1-Origin; The Western Kid (Tex Dawson), his stallion Whirlwind & dog Lightning begin	18	36	54	107	169	230
2 (2/55)-Last pre-code	11	22	33	62	86	110
3-8	10	20	30	54	72	90
9,10-Williamson-a in both (4 pgs. each)	10	20	30	56	76	95
11-17	8	16	24	44	57	70

NOTE: *Ayers a-6, 7. **Maneely** c-2-7, 10, 13-15. **Romita** a-1-17; c-1, 12. **Severin** c-11, 16, 17.*

WESTERN KID, THE (2nd Series)
Marvel Comics Group: Dec, 1971 - No. 5, Aug, 1972 (All 20¢ issues)

	GD 2.0	VG 4.0	FN 6.0	VF 8.0	VF/NM 9.0	NM- 9.2
1-Reprints; Romita-c/a(3)	3	6	9	18	27	35
2,4,5: 2-Romita-a; Severin-c. 4-Everett-r	2	4	6	13	18	22
3-Williamson-a	3	6	9	14	20	26

WESTERN KILLERS
Fox Features Syndicate: nn, July?, 1948; No. 60, Sept, 1948 - No. 64, May, 1949; No. 6, July, 1949

	GD 2.0	VG 4.0	FN 6.0	VF 8.0	VF/NM 9.0	NM- 9.2
nn(#59?)(nd, F&J Trading Co.)-Range Busters; formerly Blue Beetle #57?	24	48	72	140	230	320
60 (#1, 9/48)-Extreme violence; lingerie panel	26	52	78	152	249	345
61-Jack Cole, Starr-a	21	42	63	122	199	275
62-64, 6 (#6-exist?)	19	38	57	111	176	240

WESTERN LIFE ROMANCES (My Friend Irma #3 on?)
Marvel Comics (IPP): Dec, 1949 - No. 2, Mar, 1950 (52 pgs.)

	GD 2.0	VG 4.0	FN 6.0	VF 8.0	VF/NM 9.0	NM- 9.2
1-Whip Wilson & Reno Browne photo-c	20	40	60	114	182	250
2-Audie Murphy & Gale Storm photo-c	16	32	48	94	147	200

WESTERN LOVE
Prize Publ.: July-Aug, 1949 - No. 5, Mar-Apr, 1950 (All photo-c & 52 pgs.)

	GD 2.0	VG 4.0	FN 6.0	VF 8.0	VF/NM 9.0	NM- 9.2
1-S&K-a; Randolph Scott photo-c from movie "Canadian Pacific" (see Prize Comics #76)	31	62	93	182	296	410
2,5-S&K-a: 2-Whip Wilson & Reno Browne photo-c. 5-Dale Robertson photo-c	23	46	69	136	223	310
3,4: 3-Pat Williams photo-c	15	30	45	85	130	175

NOTE: *Meskin & Severin/Elder a-2-5.*

WESTERN LOVE TRAILS (Formerly Western Adventures)
Ace Magazines (A. A. Wyn): No. 7, Nov, 1949 - No. 9, Mar, 1950

	GD 2.0	VG 4.0	FN 6.0	VF 8.0	VF/NM 9.0	NM- 9.2
7	12	24	36	67	94	120
8,9	10	20	30	54	72	90

WESTERN MARSHAL (See Steve Donovan...)
Dell Publishing Co.: No. 534, 2-4/54 - No. 640, 7/55 (Based on Ernest Haycox's "Trailtown")

	GD 2.0	VG 4.0	FN 6.0	VF 8.0	VF/NM 9.0	NM- 9.2
Four Color 534 (#1)-Kinstler-a	6	12	18	39	62	85
Four Color 591 (10/54), 613 (2/55), 640-All Kinstler-a	5	10	15	34	55	75

WESTERN OUTLAWS (Junior Comics #9-16; My Secret Life #22 on)
Fox Features Syndicate: No. 17, Sept, 1948 - No. 21, May, 1949

	GD 2.0	VG 4.0	FN 6.0	VF 8.0	VF/NM 9.0	NM- 9.2
17-Kamen-a; Iger shop-a in all; 1 pg. "Death and the Devil Pills" r-in Ghostly Weird #122	32	64	96	188	307	425
18-21	19	38	57	111	176	240

WESTERN OUTLAWS
Atlas Comics (ACI No. 1-14/WPI No. 15-21): Feb, 1954 - No. 21, Aug, 1957

	GD 2.0	VG 4.0	FN 6.0	VF 8.0	VF/NM 9.0	NM- 9.2
1-Heath, Powell-a; Maneely hanging-c	21	42	63	122	199	275
2	12	24	36	67	94	120
3-10: 7-Violent-a by R.Q. Sale	10	20	30	54	72	90
11,14-Williamson-a in both (6 pgs. each)	11	22	33	60	83	105
12,18,20,21: Severin covers	9	18	27	50	65	80
13,15: 13-Baker-a. 15-Torres-a	10	20	30	54	72	90
16-Williamson text illo	9	18	27	50	65	80
17,19-Crandall-a. 17-Williamson text illo	10	20	30	54	72	90

NOTE: ***Ayers** a-7, 10, 18, 20. **Bolle** a-21. **Colan** a-5, 10, 11, 17. **Drucker** a-11. **Everett** a-9, 10. **Heath** a-1; c-3, 4, 8, 16. **Kubert** a-9p. **Maneely** a-13, 16, 17, 19; c-1, 5, 7, 9, 10, 12, 13. **Morisi** a-18. **Powell** a-3, 16. **Romita** a-7, 13. **Severin** a-8, 16, 19; c-17, 18, 20, 21. **Tuska** a-6, 15.*

WESTERN OUTLAWS & SHERIFFS (Formerly Best Western)
Marvel/Atlas Comics (IPC): No. 60, Dec, 1949 - No. 73, June, 1952

	GD 2.0	VG 4.0	FN 6.0	VF 8.0	VF/NM 9.0	NM- 9.2
60 (52 pgs.)	21	42	63	122	199	275
61-65: 61-Photo-c	16	32	48	94	147	200
66-Story contains 5 hangings	17	34	51	98	154	210
67-Cannibalism story	17	34	51	98	154	210
68-72	14	28	42	76	108	140
73-Black Rider story; Everett-c	15	30	45	83	124	165

NOTE: ***Maneely** a-62, 67; c-62, 69-73. **Robinson** a-68. **Sinnott** a-70. **Tuska** a-69-71.*

WESTERN PICTURE STORIES (1st Western comic)
Comics Magazine Company: Feb, 1937 - No. 4, June, 1937

	GD 2.0	VG 4.0	FN 6.0	VF 8.0	VF/NM 9.0	NM- 9.2
1-Will Eisner-a	200	400	600	1280	2190	3100
2-Will Eisner-a	102	204	306	648	1112	1575
3,4: 3-Eisner-a. 4-Caveman Cowboy story	86	172	258	546	936	1325

WESTERN PICTURE STORIES (See Giant Comics Edition #6, 11)

WESTERN ROMANCES (See Target...)

WESTERN ROUGH RIDERS
Gillmor Magazines No. 1,4 (Stanmor Publ.): Nov, 1954 - No. 4, May, 1955

	GD 2.0	VG 4.0	FN 6.0	VF 8.0	VF/NM 9.0	NM- 9.2
1	9	18	27	47	61	75
2-4	7	14	21	35	43	50

WESTERN ROUNDUP (See Dell Giants & Fox Giants)

WESTERN SERENADE
DC Comics: May/June, 1949

nn - Ashcan comic, not distributed to newsstands, only for in-house use (no known sales)

WESTERN TALES (Formerly Witches...)
Harvey Publications: No. 31, Oct, 1955 - No. 33, July-Sept, 1956

	GD 2.0	VG 4.0	FN 6.0	VF 8.0	VF/NM 9.0	NM- 9.2
31,32-All S&K-a; Davy Crockett app. in each	15	30	45	86	133	180
33-S&K-a; Jim Bowie app.	15	30	45	84	127	170

NOTE: *#32 & 33 contain Boy's Ranch reprints. **Kirby** c-31.*

WESTERN TALES OF BLACK RIDER (Formerly Black Rider; Gunsmoke Western #32 on)
Atlas Comics (CPS): No. 28, May, 1955 - No. 31, Nov, 1955

	GD 2.0	VG 4.0	FN 6.0	VF 8.0	VF/NM 9.0	NM- 9.2
28 (#1): The Spider (a villain) dies	19	38	57	112	179	245
29-31	14	28	42	82	121	160

NOTE: ***Lawrence** a-30. **Maneely** c-28-30. **Severin** a-28. **Shores** c-31.*

WESTERN TEAM-UP
Marvel Comics Group: Nov, 1973 (20¢)

	GD 2.0	VG 4.0	FN 6.0	VF 8.0	VF/NM 9.0	NM- 9.2
1-Origin & 1st app. The Dakota Kid; Rawhide Kid-r; Gunsmoke Kid-r by Jack Davis	4	8	12	22	34	45

WESTERN THRILLERS (My Past Confessions #7 on)
Fox Features Syndicate/M.S. Distr. No. 52: Aug, 1948 - No. 6, June, 1949; No. 52, 1954?

	GD 2.0	VG 4.0	FN 6.0	VF 8.0	VF/NM 9.0	NM- 9.2
1- "Velvet Rose" (Kamenish-a); "Two-Gun Sal", "Striker Sisters" (all women outlaws issue); Brodsky-c	48	96	144	302	514	725
2	24	48	72	140	230	320
3-6: 4,5-Bakerish-a; 5-Butch Cassidy app.	19	38	57	111	176	240
52-(Reprint, M.S. Dist.)-1954? No date given (becomes My Love Secret #53)	9	18	27	47	61	75

WESTERN THRILLERS (Cowboy Action #5 on)
Atlas Comics (ACI): Nov, 1954 - No. 4, Feb, 1955 (All-r/Western Outlaws & Sheriffs)

	GD 2.0	VG 4.0	FN 6.0	VF 8.0	VF/NM 9.0	NM- 9.2
1	5	30	45	88	137	185
2-4	10	20	30	54	72	90

NOTE: ***Heath** c-3. **Maneely** a-1; c-2. **Powell** a-4. **Robinson** a-4. **Romita** c-4. **Tuska** a-2.*

WESTERN TRAILS (Ringo Kid Starring in...)
Atlas Comics (SAI): May, 1957 - No. 2, July, 1957

	GD 2.0	VG 4.0	FN 6.0	VF 8.0	VF/NM 9.0	NM- 9.2
1-Ringo Kid app.; Severin-c	14	28	42	76	108	140
2-Severin-c	9	18	27	50	65	80

NOTE: ***Bolle** a-1, 2. **Maneely** a-1, 2. **Severin** c-1, 2.*

WESTERN TRUE CRIME (Becomes My Confessions)
Fox Features Syndicate: No. 15, Aug, 1948 - No. 6, June, 1949

	GD 2.0	VG 4.0	FN 6.0	VF 8.0	VF/NM 9.0	NM- 9.2
15(#1)-Kamen-a; formerly Zoot #14 (5/48)?	32	64	96	188	307	425
16(#2)-Kamenish-a; headlight panels, violence	23	46	69	136	223	310
3-Kamen-a	25	50	75	147	241	335
4-6: 4-Johnny Craig-a	15	30	45	90	140	190

WESTERN WINNERS (Formerly All-Western Winners; becomes Black Rider #8 on & Romance Tales #7 on?)
Marvel Comics (CDS): No. 5, June, 1949 - No. 7, Dec, 1949

	GD 2.0	VG 4.0	FN 6.0	VF 8.0	VF/NM 9.0	NM- 9.2
5-Two-Gun Kid, Kid Colt, Black Rider; Shores-c	31	62	93	182	296	410
6-Two-Gun Kid, Black Rider, Heath Kid Colt story; Captain Tootsie by C.C. Beck	26	52	78	152	249	345
7-Randolph Scott Photo-c w/true stories about the West	26	52	78	152	249	345

WEST OF THE PECOS (See Zane Grey, 4-Color #222)

WESTWARD HO, THE WAGONS (Disney)
Dell Publishing Co.: No. 738, Sept, 1956 (Movie)

	GD 2.0	VG 4.0	FN 6.0	VF 8.0	VF/NM 9.0	NM- 9.2
Four Color 738-Fess Parker photo-c	9	18	27	63	107	150

WE3

Wetworks #42 © WSP

What If...? (2nd series) #85 © MAR

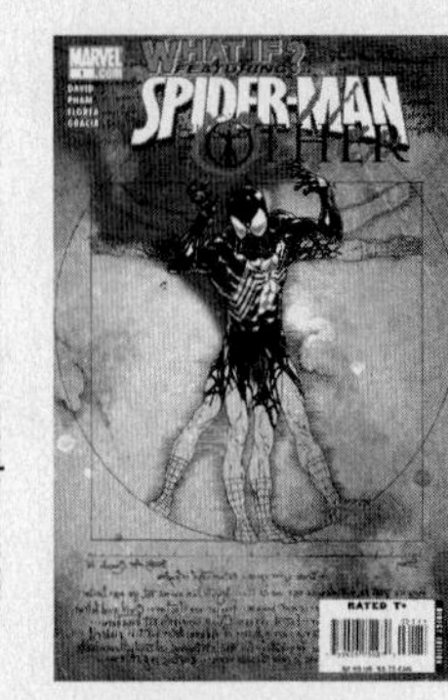

What If...? Spider-Man The Other © MAR

GD 2.0 VG 4.0 FN 6.0 VF 8.0 VF/NM 9.0 NM- 9.2

DC Comics (Vertigo): Oct, 2004 - No. 3, May, 2005 ($2.95, limited series)

1-3-Domestic animal cyborgs: Grant Morrison-s/Frank Quitely-a 3.00
TPB (2005, $12.99) r/series 13.00

WETWORKS (See WildC.A.T.S: Covert Action Teams #2)
Image Comics (WildStorm): June, 1994 - No. 43, Aug, 1998 ($1.95/$2.50)

1-"July" on-c; gatefold wraparound-c; Portacio/Williams-c/a 4.00
1-Chicago Comicon edition 6.00
1-(2/98, $4.95) "3-D Edition" w/glasses 5.00
2-4 3.00
2-Alternate Portacio-c, see Deathblow #5 6.00
5-7,9-24: 5-($2.50). 13-Portacio-c. 16,17-Fire From Heaven Pts. 4 & 11 3.00
8 ($1.95)-Newstand, Wildstorm Rising Pt. 7 3.00
8 ($2.50)-Direct Market, Wildstorm Rising Pt. 7 3.00
25-($3.95) 4.00
26-43: 32-Variant-c by Pat Lee & Charest. 39,40-Stormwatch app. 42-Gen 13 app. 3.00
Sourcebook 1 (10/94, $2.50)-Text & illustrations (no comics) 3.00
Voyager Pack (8/97, $3.50)- #32 w/Phantom Guard preview 4.00

WETWORKS
DC Comics (WildStorm): Nov, 2006 - No. 15, Jan, 2008 ($2.99)

1-15: 1-Carey-s/Portacio-a; two covers by Portacio and Van Sciver. 2-Golden var-c 3-Pearson var-c. 4-Powell var-c 3.00
...: Armageddon 1 (1/08, $2.99) Gage-s/Badeaux-a 3.00
... Book One (2007, $14.99) r/#1-5 and stories from Eye of the storm Annual and Coup D'Etat Afterword 15.00
... Book Two (2008, $14.99) r/#6-9,13-15 15.00
...: Mutations 1 (11/10, $3.99) Grevioux & Long-s/Gopez-a 4.00

WETWORKS/VAMPIRELLA (See Vampirella/Wetworks)
Image Comics (WildStorm Productions): July, 1997 ($2.95, one-shot)

1-Gil Kane-c 4.00

WHACK (Satire)
St. John Publishing Co. (Jubilee Publ.): Oct, 1953 - No. 3, May, 1954

1-(3-D, 25¢)-Kubert-a; Maurer-c; came w/glasses 24 48 72 142 234 325
2,3-Kubert-a in each. 2-Bing Crosby on-c; Mighty Mouse & Steve Canyon parodies. 3-Li'l Orphan Annie parody; Maurer-c 15 30 45 84 127 170

WHACKY (See Wacky)

WHA...HUH?
Marvel Comics: 2005 ($3.99, one-shot)

1-Humor spoofs of Marvel characters; Mahfood-a/c; Bendis, Stan Lee and others-s 4.00

WHAM COMICS (See Super Spy)
Centaur Publications: Nov, 1940 - No. 2, Dec, 1940

1-The Sparkler, The Phantom Rider, Craig Carter and his Magic Ring, Detecto, Copper Slug, Speed Silvers by Gustavson, Speed Centaur & Jon Linton (s/f) begin 161 322 483 1030 1765 2500
2-Origin Blue Fire & Solarman; The Buzzard app. 103 206 309 659 1130 1600

WHAM-O GIANT COMICS
Wham-O Mfg. Co. : April, 1967 (98¢, newspaper size, one-shot)(Six issue subscription was advertised)

1-Radian & Goody Bumpkin by Wood; 1 pg. Stanley-a; Fine, Tufts-a; flying saucer reports; wraparound-c 9 18 27 65 113 160

WHATEVER HAPPENED TO BARON VON SHOCK?
Image Comics: May, 2010 - Present ($3.99)

1-4-Rob Zombie-s/Donny Hadiwidjaja-a 4.00

WHAT IF? (1st Series) (What If? Featuring... #13 & #?-33) (Also see Hero Initiative)
Marvel Comics Group: Feb, 1977 - No. 47, Oct, 1984; June, 1988 (All 52 pgs.)

1-Brief origin Spider-Man, Fantastic Four 3 6 9 20 30 40
2-Origin The Hulk retold 2 4 6 10 14 18
3-5: 3-Avengers. 4-Invaders. 5-Capt. America 2 4 6 8 11 14
6-10,13,17: 7-Betty Brant as Spider-Girl. 8-Daredevil; Spidey parody. 9-Origins Venus, Marvel Boy, Human Robot, 3-D Man. 13-Conan app.; John Buscema-c/a(p). 17-Ghost Rider & Son of Satan app. 2 3 4 6 8 10
11,12,14-16: 11-Marvel Bullpen as F.F. 1 2 3 5 6 8
18-26,29: 18-Dr. Strange. 19-Spider-Man. 22-Origin Dr. Doom retold 1 2 3 4 5 7
27-X-Men app.; Miller-c 3 6 9 14 20 26
28-Daredevil by Miller; Ghost Rider app. 2 4 6 10 16 20
30-"What If...Spider-Man's Clone Had Lived?" 2 4 6 8 10 12
31-Begin $1.00-c; featuring Wolverine & the Hulk; X-Men app.; death of Hulk, Wolverine & Magneto 3 6 9 16 22 28

GD 2.0 VG 4.0 FN 6.0 VF 8.0 VF/NM 9.0 NM- 9.2

32-34,36-47: 32,36-Byrne-a. 34-Marvel crew each draw themselves. 37-Old X-Men & Silver Surfer app. 39-Thor battles Conan 5.00
35-What if Elektra had lived?; Miller/Austin-a. 2 4 6 8 10 12
Special 1 ($1.50, 6/88)-Iron Man, F.F., Thor app. 5.00
... Classic Vol. 1 TPB (2004, $24.99) r/#1-6; checklist 25.00
... Classic Vol. 2 TPB (2005, $24.99) r/#7-12 25.00
... Classic Vol. 3 TPB (2006, $24.99) r/#14,15,17-20 25.00
... Classic Vol. 4 TPB (2007, $24.99) r/#21-26; checklist of all What If? series/issues 25.00

NOTE: ***Austin*** *a-27p, 32i, 34, 35i; c-35i, 36i.* ***J. Buscema*** *a-13p, 15p; c-10, 13p, 23p.* ***Byrne*** *a-32i, 36; c-36p.* ***Colan*** *a-21p; c-17p, 18p, 21p.* ***Ditko*** *a-35, Special 1.* ***Golden*** *c-29, 40-42.* ***Guice*** *a-40p.* ***Gil Kane*** *a-3p, 24p; c(p)-2-4, 7, 8.* ***Kirby*** *a-11p; c-9p, 11p.* ***Layton*** *a-32i, 33i; c-30, 32p, 33i, 34.* ***Mignola*** *c-39i.* ***Miller*** *a-28p, 32i, 34(1), 35p; c-27, 28p.* ***Mooney*** *a-8i, 30i.* ***Perez*** *a-15p.* ***Robbins*** *a-4p.* ***Sienkiewicz*** *c-43-46.* ***Simonson*** *a-15p, 32i.* ***Starlin*** *a-32i.* ***Stevens*** *a-8, 16i(part).* ***Sutton*** *a-2i, 18p, 28.* ***Tuska*** *a-5p.* ***Weiss*** *a-37p.*

WHAT IF...? (2nd Series)
Marvel Comics: V2#1, July, 1989 - No. 114, Nov, 1998 ($1.25/$1.50)

V2#1-...The Avengers Had Lost the Evolutionary War 5.00
2-5: 2-Daredevil, Punisher app. 4.00
6-X-Men app. 5.00
7-Wolverine app.; Liefeld-c/a(1st on Wolvie?) 6.00
8,10,11,13-15,17-30: 10-Punisher app. 11-Fantastic Four app.; McFarlane-c(i).13-Prof. X; Jim Lee-c. 14-Capt. Marvel; Lim/Austin-c.15-F.F.; Capullo-c/a(p). 17-Spider-Man/Kraven. 18-F.F. 19-Vision. 20,21-Spider-Man. 22-Silver Surfer by Lim/Austin-c/a 23-X-Men. 24-Wolverine; Punisher app. 25-(52 pgs.)-Wolverine app. 26-Punisher app. 27-Namor/F.F. 28,29-Capt. America. 29-Swipes cover to Avengers #4. 30-(52 pgs.)-F.F. 4.00
9,12-X-Men 5.00
16-Wolverine battles Conan; Red Sonja app.; X-Men cameo 5.00
31-40,42-49: 31-Cosmic Spider-Man & Venom app.; Hobgoblin cameo. 32,33-Phoenix; X-Men app. 35-Fantastic Five (w/Spidey). 36-Avengers vs. Guardians of the Galaxy. 37-Wolverine; Thibert-c(i). 38-Thor; Rogers-p(part). 40-Storm; X-Men app. 42-Spider-Man. 43-Wolverine. 44-Venom/Punisher. 45-Ghost Rider. 46-Cable. 47-Magneto. 49-Infinity Gauntlet w/Silver Surfer & Thanos 3.00
41,50: 41-(52 pgs.)-Avengers vs. Galactus. 50-(52 pgs.)-Foil embossed-c; "What If Hulk Had Killed Wolverine" 4.00
51-(7/93) "What If the Punisher Became Captain America" (see it happen in 2007's Punisher War Journal #6-10) 6.00
52-99,101-104: 52-Dr. Doom. 54-Death's Head. 57-Punisher as Shield. 58-"What if Punisher Had Killed Spider-Man" w/cover similar to Amazing S-M #129. 59-...Wolverine led Alpha Flight. 60-X-Men Wedding Album. 61-Bound-in card sheet. 61,86,88-Spider-Man. 74,77,81,84,85-X-Men. 76-Last app. Watcher in title. 78-Bisley-c. 80-Hulk. 87-Sabretooth. 89-Fantastic Four. 90-Cyclops & Havok. 91-The Hulk. 93-Wolverine. 94-Juggernaut. 95-Ghost Rider 3.00
100-($2.99, double-sized) Gambit and Rogue, Fantastic Four 4.00
105-Spider-Girl (Peter Parker's daughter) debut; Sienkiewicz-a; (Betty Brant also app. as a Spider-Girl in What If? (1st series) #7) 2 4 6 12 16 20
106-114: 106-Gambit. 108-Avengers. 111-Wolverine. 114-Secret Wars 3.00
#(-1) Flashback (7/97) 3.00

WHAT IF...? (one-shots)
Marvel Comics: Feb, 2005 ($2.99)

... Aunt May Had Died Instead of Uncle Ben? - Brubaker-s/DiVito-a/Brase-c 3.00
... Dr. Doom Had Become The Thing? - Karl Kesel-s/Paul Smith-a/c 3.00
... General Ross Had Become The Hulk? - Peter David-s/Pat Olliffe-a/Gary Frank-c 3.00
... Jessica Jones Had Joined The Avengers? - Bendis-s/Gaydos-a/McNiven-c 3.00
... Karen Page Had Lived? - Bendis-s/Lark-a/c 3.00
... Magneto and Professor X Had Formed The X-Men Together? - Claremont-s/Raney-a 3.00
What If...: Why Not? TPB (2005, $16.99) r/one-shots 17.00

WHAT IF... (one-shots)
Marvel Comics: Feb, 2006 ($2.99)

... : Captain America - Fought in the Civil War?; Bedard-s/Di Giandomenico-a 3.00
... : Daredevil - The Devil Who Dares; Daredevil in feudal Japan; Veitch-s/Edwards-a 3.00
... : Fantastic Four - Were Cosmonauts?; Marshall Rogers-a/c; Mike Carey-s 3.00
... : Submariner - Grew Up on Land?; Pak-s/Lopez-a 3.00
... : Thor - Was the Herald of Galactus?; Kirkman-s/Oeming-a/c 3.00
... : Wolverine - In the Prohibition Era; Way-s/Proctor-a/Harris-c 3.00
What If: Mirror Mirror TPB (2006, $16.99) r/one-shots; design pages and Rogers sketches 17.00

WHAT IF ?... (one-shots altering recent Marvel "event" series)
Marvel Comics: Jan, 2007 - Feb, 2007 ($3.99)

... Avengers Disassembled; Parker-s/Lopresti-a/c 4.00
... Spider-Man The Other; Peter David-s/Khoi Pham-a; Venom app. 4.00
... Wolverine Enemy of the State; Robinson-s/DiGiandomenico-a/Alexander-c 4.00
... X-Men Age of Apocalypse; Remeder-s/Wilkins-a/Djurdjevic-c 4.00
... X-Men Deadly Genesis; Hine-s/Yardin-a/c 4.00
What If?: Event Horizon TPB (2007, $16.99) r/one-shots; design pages and cover sketches 17.00

What If...? #200 © MAR

Where Monsters Dwell #10 © MAR

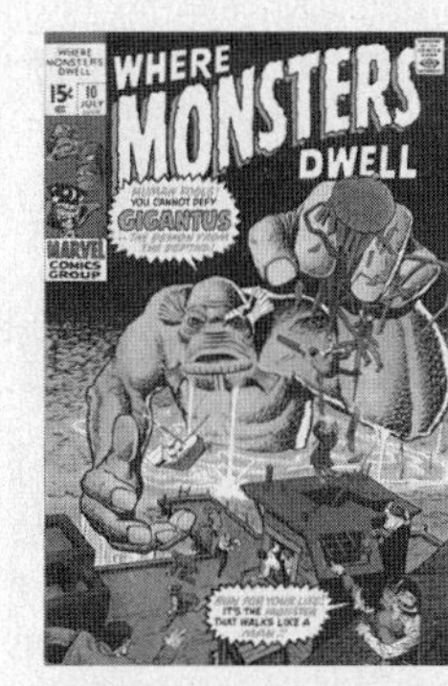

White Princess of the Jungle #1 © AVON

	GD	VG	FN	VF	VF/NM	NM-
	2.0	4.0	6.0	8.0	9.0	9.2

WHAT IF ?... (one-shots altering recent Marvel "event" series)
Marvel Comics: Dec, 2007 - Feb, 2008 ($3.99)

... Annihilation; Nova, Iron Man and Captain America app. 4.00
... Civil War; 2 covers by Silvestri & Djurdjevic 4.00
... Planet Hulk; Pagulayan-c; Kirk, Sandoval & Hembeck-a 4.00
... Spider-Man vs. Wolverine; Romita Jr.-c; Henry-a; Nick Fury app. 4.00
... X-Men - Rise and Fall of the Shi'ar Empire; Coipel-c 4.00
What If?: Civil War TPB (2008, $16.99) r/one-shots; design pages and cover sketches 17.00

WHAT IF ?... (one-shots altering recent Marvel "event" series)
Marvel Comics: Feb, 2009 ($3.99) (Serialized back-up Runaways story in each issue)

... Fallen Son; if Iron Man had died instead of Capt. America; McGuinness-c 4.00
... House of M; if the Scarlet Witch had said "No more powers" instead; Cheung-c 4.00
... Newer Fantastic Four; team of Spider-Man, Hulk, Iron Man and Wolverine 4.00
... Secret Wars; if Doctor Doom had kept the Beyonder's power; origin re-told 4.00
... Spider-Man Back in Black; if Mary Jane had been shot instead of Aunt May 4.00

WHAT IF ?... (one-shots)
Marvel Comics: Feb, 2010 ($3.99)

... Astonishing X-Men; if Ord resurrected Jean Grey; Campbell-c 4.00
... Daredevil vs. Elektra; Kayanan-a; Klaus Janson-c swipe of Daredevil #168 4.00
... Secret Invasion; if the Skrulls succeeded; Yu-c 4.00
... Spider-Man: House of M; if Gwen Stacy survived the House of M; Dodson-c 4.00
... World War Hulk; if the heroes lost the war; Romita Jr.-c 4.00

WHAT IF ?... (one-shots) (4 part Deadpool back-up story in all but #200)
Marvel Comics: Feb, 2011 ($3.99)

... #200 ($4.99) Siege on cover; if Osborn won the Siege of Asgard; Stan Lee back-up 5.00
... Dark Reign; if Norman Osborn was killed; Tanaka-a/Deodato-c 4.00
... Iron Man: Demon in an Armor; if Tony Stark became Dr. Doom; Nolan-a 4.00
... Spider-Man; if Spider-Man killed Kraven; Jimenez-c 4.00
... Wolverine: Father; if Wolverine raised Daken; Tocchini-a; Yu-a 4.00

'WHAT'S NEW? - THE COLLECTED ADVENTURES OF PHIL & DIXIE'
Palliard Press: Oct, 1991 - No. 2, 1991 ($5.95, mostly color, sq.-bound, 52 pgs.)

1,2-By Phil Foglio 6.00

WHAT THE- -?!
Marvel Comics: Aug, 1988 - No. 26, 1993 ($1.25/$1.50/$2.50, semi-annual #5 on)

1-All contain parodies 4.00
2-24: 3-X-Men parody; Todd McFarlane-a. 5-Punisher/Wolverine parody; Jim Lee-a. 6-Punisher, Wolverine, Alpha Flight. 9-Wolverine. 16-EC back-c parody. 17-Wolverine/Punisher parody. 18-Star Trek parody w/Wolverine. 19-Punisher, Wolverine, Ghost Rider. 21-Weapon X parody. 22-Punisher/Wolverine parody 3.00
25-Summer Special 1 (1993, $2.50)-X-Men parody 4.00
26-Fall Special ($2.50, 68 pgs.)-Spider-Ham 2099-c/story; origin Silver Surfer; Hulk & Doomsday parody; indica reads "Winter Special." 4.00
NOTE: ***Austin** a-6i. **Byrne** a-2, 6, 10; c-2, 6-8, 10, 12, 13. **Golden** a-22. **Dale Keown** a-8p(8 pgs.). **McFarlane** a-3. **Rogers** c-15i, 16p. **Severin** a-2. **Staton** a-21p. **Williamson** a-2i.*

WHEE COMICS (Also see Gay, Smile & Tickle Comics)
Modern Store Publications: 1955 (7¢, 5x7-1/4", 52 pgs.)

1-Funny animal 6 12 18 28 34 40

WHEEDIES (See Panic #11 -EC Comics)

WHEELIE AND THE CHOPPER BUNCH (TV)
Charlton Comics: July, 1975 - No. 7, July, 1976 (Hanna-Barbera)

1-3: 1-Byrne text illo (see Nightmare for 1st art); Staton-a. 2-Byrne-a. 2,3-Mike Zeck text illos. 3-Staton-a; Byrne-c/a 3 6 9 17 25 32
4-7-Staton-a 2 4 6 12 16 20

WHEN KNIGHTHOOD WAS IN FLOWER (See The Sword & the Rose, 4-Color #505, 682)

WHEN SCHOOL IS OUT (See Wisco in Promotional Comics section)

WHERE CREATURES ROAM
Marvel Comics Group: July, 1970 - No. 8, Sept, 1971

1-Kirby/Ayers-c/a(r) 4 8 12 26 41 55
2-8: 2-5,7,8-Kirby-c/a(r). 6-Kirby-a(r) 3 6 9 19 29 38
NOTE: ***Ditko** r-1-6, 7. **Heck** r-2, 5. All contain pre super-hero reprints.*

WHERE IN THE WORLD IS CARMEN SANDIEGO (TV)
DC Comics: June, 1996 - No. 4, Dec, 1996 ($1.75)

1-4: Adaptation of TV show 3.00

WHERE MONSTERS DWELL
Marvel Comics Group: Jan, 1970 - No. 38, Oct, 1975

1-Kirby/Ditko-r; all contain pre super-hero-r 4 8 12 28 44 60
2-10: 4-Crandall-a(r) 3 6 9 20 30 40
11,13-20: 11-Last 15¢ issue. 18,20-Starlin-c 3 6 9 17 25 32
12-Giant issue (52 pgs.) 4 8 12 22 34 45
21-Reprints 1st Fin Fang Foom app. 3 6 9 16 22 28
22-37 3 6 9 14 20 25
38-Williamson-r/World of Suspense #3 3 6 9 16 22 28
NOTE: ***Colan** r-12. **Ditko** a(r)-4, 6, 8, 10, 12, 17-19, 23-25, 37. **Kirby** r-1-3, 5-16, 18-27, 30-32, 34-36, 38; c-12? **Reinman** a-3r, 4r, 12r. **Severin** c-15.*

WHERE'S HUDDLES? (TV) (See Fun-In #9)
Gold Key: Jan, 1971 - No. 3, Dec, 1971 (Hanna-Barbera)

1 3 6 9 19 29 38
2,3: 3-r/most #1 2 4 6 11 16 20

WHIP WILSON (Movie star) (Formerly Rex Hart; Gunhawk #12 on; see Western Hearts, Western Life Romances, Western Love)
Marvel Comics: No. 9, April, 1950 - No. 11, Sept, 1950 (#9,10: 52 pgs.)

9-Photo-c; Whip Wilson & his horse Bullet begin; origin Bullet; issue #23 listed on splash page; cover changed to #9 49 98 147 309 522 735
10,11: Both have photo-c. 11-36 pgs. 28 56 84 168 274 380
I.W. Reprint #1(1964)-Kinstler-c; r-Marvel #11 3 6 9 16 22 28

WHIRLWIND COMICS (Also see Cyclone Comics)
Nita Publication: June, 1940 - No. 3, Sept, 1940

1-Origin & 1st app. Cyclone; Cyclone-c 245 490 735 1568 2684 3800
2,3: Cyclone-c 103 206 309 659 1130 1600

WHIRLYBIRDS (TV)
Dell Publishing Co.: No. 1124, Aug, 1960 - No. 1216, Oct-Dec, 1961

Four Color 1124 (#1)-Photo-c 8 16 24 56 93 130
Four Color 1216-Photo-c 8 16 24 52 86 120

WHISKEY DICKEL, INTERNATIONAL COWGIRL
Image Comics: Aug, 2003 ($12.95, softcover, B&W)

nn-Mark Ricketts-s/Mike Hawthorne-a; pin-up by various incl. Oeming, Thompson, Mack 13.00

WHISPER (Female Ninja)
Capital Comics: Dec, 1983 - No. 2, 1984 ($1.75, Baxter paper)

1,2: 1-Origin; Golden-c, Special (11/85, $2.50) 4.00

WHISPER (Vol. 2)
First Comics: Jun, 1986 - No. 37, June, 1990 ($1.25/$1.75/$1.95)

1-37 3.00

WHISPER
Boom! Studios: Nov, 2006 ($3.99)

1-Grant-s/Dzialowski-a 4.00

WHITE CHIEF OF THE PAWNEE INDIANS
Avon Periodicals: 1951

nn-Kit West app.; Kinstler-c 16 32 48 92 144 195

WHITE EAGLE INDIAN CHIEF (See Indian Chief)

WHITE FANG
Disney Comics: 1990 ($5.95, 68 pgs.)

nn-Graphic novel adapting new Disney movie 6.00

WHITE INDIAN
Magazine Enterprises: No. 11, July, 1953 - No. 15, 1954

11(A-1 94), 12(A-1 101), 13(A-1 104)-Frazetta-r(Dan Brand) in all from Durango Kid. 11-Powell-c 20 40 60 114 182 250
14(A-1 117), 15(A-1 135)-Check-a; Torres-a-#15 14 28 42 76 108 140
NOTE: *#11 contains reprints from Durango Kid #1-4; #12 from #5, 9, 10, 11; #13 from #7, 12, 13, 16. #14 & 15 contain all new stories.*

WHITEOUT (Also see Queen & Country)
Oni Press: July, 1998 - No. 4, Nov, 1998 ($2.95, B&W, limited series)

1-4: 1-Matt Wagner-c. 2-Mignola-c. 3-Gibbons-c 3.00
TPB (5/99, $10.95) r/#1-4; Miller-c 11.00

WHITEOUT: MELT
Oni Press: Sept, 1999 - No. 4, Feb, 2000 ($2.95, B&W, limited series)

1-4-Greg Rucka-s/Steve Lieber-a 3.00
Whiteout: Melt, The Definitive Edition TPB (9/07, $13.95) r/#1-4; Rucka afterword 14.00

WHITE PRINCESS OF THE JUNGLE (Also see Jungle Adventures & Top Jungle Comics)
Avon Periodicals: July, 1951 - No. 5, Nov, 1952

1-Origin of White Princess (Taanda) & Capt'n Courage (r); Kinstler-c 55 110 165 352 601 850

Whiz Comics #2 (#3) © FAW

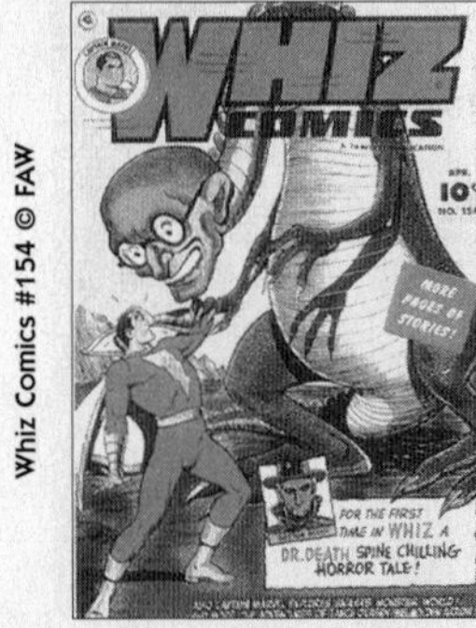

Whiz Comics #154 © FAW

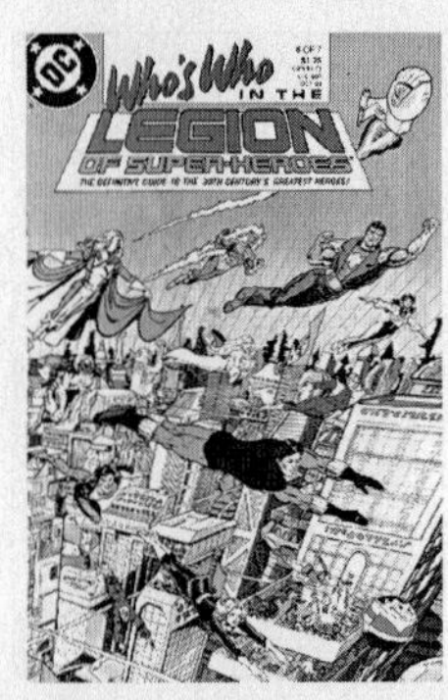

Who's Who in the LSH #6 © DC

	GD 2.0	VG 4.0	FN 6.0	VF 8.0	VF/NM 9.0	NM- 9.2
2-Reprints origin of Malu, Slave Girl Princess from Avon's Slave Girl Comics #1 w/Malu changed to Zora; Kinstler-c/a(2)	40	80	120	246	411	575
3-Origin Blue Gorilla; Kinstler-c/a	37	74	111	218	354	490
4-Jack Barnum, White Hunter app.; r/Sheena #9	32	64	96	188	307	425
5-Blue Gorilla by McCann?; Kinstler inside-c; Fawcette/Alascia-a(3)	34	68	102	199	325	450

WHITE RIDER AND SUPER HORSE (Formerly Humdinger V2#2; Indian Warriors #7 on; also see Blue Bolt #1, 4Most & Western Crime Cases)
Novelty-Star Publications/Accepted Publ.: No. 4, 9/50 - No. 6, 3/51

4-6-Adapts "The Last of the Mohicans". 4(#1)-(9/50)-Says #11 on inside	16	32	48	92	144	195
Accepted Reprint #5(r/#5),6 (nd); L.B. Cole-c	9	18	27	50	65	80

NOTE: *All have* **L. B. Cole** *covers.*

WHITE TIGER
Marvel Comics: Jan, 2007 - No. 6, Nov, 2007 ($2.99, limited series)

1-6: 1-David Mack-c; Pierce & Liebe-s/Briones-a; Spider-Man & Black Widow app. 3.00
...: A Hero's Compulsion SC (2007,$14.99) r/#1-6; re-cap art and profile page 15.00

WHITE WILDERNESS (Disney)
Dell Publishing Co.: No. 943, Oct, 1958

Four Color 943-Movie	6	12	18	43	69	95

WHITMAN COMIC BOOK, A
Whitman Publishing Co.: Sept., 1962 (136 pgs.; 7-3/4x5-3/4; hardcover) (B&W)

1-3,5,7: 1-Yogi Bear. 2-Huckleberry Hound. 3-Mr. Jinks and Pixie & Dixie. 5-Augie Doggie & Loopy de Loop. 7-Bugs Bunny-r from #47,51,53,54 & 55	7	14	21	45	73	100
4,6: 4-The Flintstones. 6-Snooper & Blabber Fearless Detectives/Quick Draw McGraw of the Wild West	7	14	21	49	80	110
8-Donald Duck-reprints most of WDC&S #209-213. Includes 5 Barks stories, 1 complete Mickey Mouse serial by Paul Murry & 1 Mickey Mouse serial missing the 1st episode	8	16	24	54	90	125

NOTE: *Hanna-Barbera #1-6(TV), reprints of British tabloid comics. Dell reprints-#7,8.*

WHIZ COMICS (Formerly Flash & Thrill Comics #1)(See 5 Cent Comics)
Fawcett Publications: No. 2, Feb, 1940 - No. 155, June, 1953

1-(nn on cover, #2 inside)-Origin & 1st newsstand app. Captain Marvel (formerly Captain Thunder) by C. C. Beck (created by Bill Parker), Spy Smasher, Golden Arrow, Ibis the Invincible, Dan Dare, Scoop Smith, Sivana, & Lance O'Casey begin	7100	14,200	21,300	42,000	71,000	100,000

(The only Mint copy sold in 1995 for $176,000 cash)

1-Reprint, oversize 13-1/2x10". **WARNING**: This comic is an exact duplicate reprint (except for dropping "Gangway for Captain Marvel" from-c) of the original except for its size. DC published it in 1974 with a second cover titling it as a Famous First Edition. There have been many reported cases of the outer cover being removed and the interior sold as the original edition. The reprint with the new outer cover removed is practically worthless. See Famous First Edition for value.

2-(3/40, nn on cover, #3 inside); cover to Flash #1 redrawn, pg. 12, panel 4; Spy Smasher reveals I.D. to Eve	486	972	1458	3550	6275	9000
3-(4/40, #3 on-c, #4 inside)-1st app. Beautia	343	686	1029	2400	4200	6000
4-(5/40, #4 on cover, #5 inside)-Brief origin Capt. Marvel retold	300	600	900	1950	3375	4800
5-Captain Marvel wears button-down flap on splash page only	258	516	774	1651	2826	4000
6-10: 7-Dr. Voodoo begins (by Raboy-#9-22)	187	374	561	1197	2049	2900
11-14: 12-Capt. Marvel does not wear cape	129	258	387	826	1413	2000
15-Origin Sivana; Dr. Voodoo by Raboy	142	284	426	909	1555	2200
16-18-Spy Smasher battles Captain Marvel	132	264	396	838	1444	2050
19-Classic shark-c	123	246	369	787	1344	1900
20	97	194	291	621	1061	1500
21-(9/41)-Origin & 1st cover app. Lt. Marvels, the 1st team in Fawcett comics. In this issue, Capt. Death similar to Ditko's later Dr. Strange	100	200	300	635	1093	1550
22-24: 23-Only Dr. Voodoo by Tuska	77	154	231	493	847	1200
25-(12/41)-Captain Nazi jumps from Master Comics #21 to take on Capt. Marvel solo after being beaten by Capt. Marvel/Bulletman team, causing the creation of Capt. Marvel Jr.; 1st app./origin of Capt. Marvel Jr. (part II of trilogy origin by CC. Beck & Mac Raboy); Captain Marvel sends Jr. back to Master #22 to aid Bulletman against Capt. Nazi; origin Old Shazam in text	595	1190	1785	4350	7675	11,000
26-30	60	120	180	381	658	935
31,32: 32-1st app. The Trolls; Hitler/Mussolini satire by Beck	53	106	159	334	567	800
33-Spy Smasher, Captain Marvel x-over on cover and inside	60	120	180	381	658	935
34,36-40: 37-The Trolls app. by Swayze	41	82	123	249	417	585
35-Captain Marvel & Spy Smasher-c	49	98	147	309	522	735
41-50: 43-Spy Smasher, Ibis, Golden Arrow x-over in Capt. Marvel. 44-Flag-c. 47-Origin recap (1 pg.)	36	72	108	216	351	485
51-60: 52-Capt. Marvel x-over in Ibis. 57-Spy Smasher, Golden Arrow, Ibis cameo	29	58	87	172	281	390
61-70	27	54	81	160	263	365
71,77-80	26	52	78	152	249	345
72-76-Two Captain Marvel stories in each; 76-Spy Smasher becomes Crime Smasher	26	52	78	154	252	350
81-85,87-99: 91-Infinity-c	26	52	78	152	249	345
86-Captain Marvel battles Sivana Family; robot-c	30	60	90	177	289	400
100-(8/48)-Anniversary issue	31	62	93	182	296	410
101-106: 102-Commando Yank app. 106-Bulletman app.	25	50	75	147	241	335
107-149: 107-Capitol Building photo-c. 108-Brooklyn Bridge photo-c. 112-Photo-c. 139-Infinity-c. 140-Flag-c. 142-Used in **POP**, pg. 89	25	50	75	147	241	335
150-152-(Low dist.)	30	60	90	177	289	400
153-155-(Scarce):154,155-1st/2nd Dr. Death stories	39	78	117	240	395	550

NOTE: **C.C. Beck** *Captain Marvel-No. 25(part).* **Krigstein** *Golden Arrow-No. 75, 78, 91, 95, 96, 98-100.* **Mac Raboy** *Dr. Voodoo-No. 9-22. Captain Marvel-No. 25(part).* **M.Swayze** *a-37, 38, 59; c-38.* **Schaffenberger** *c-138-155(most).* **Wolverton** *1/2 pg. "Culture Corner"-No. 65-67, 68(2 1/2 pgs), 70-85, 87-96, 98-100, 102-109, 112-121, 123, 125, 126, 128-131, 133, 134, 136, 142, 143, 146.*

WHIZ KIDS (Also see Big Bang Comics)
Image Comics: Apr, 2003 ($4.95, B&W, one-shot)

1-Galahad, Cyclone, Thunder Girl and Moray app.; Jeff Austin-a 5.00

WHOA, NELLIE (Also see Love & Rockets)
Fantagraphics Books: July, 1996 - No. 3, Sept, 1996 ($2.95, B&W, lim. series)

1-3: Jamie Hernandez-c/a/scripts 3.00

WHODUNIT
D.S. Publishing Co.: Aug-Sept, 1948 - No. 3, Dec-Jan, 1948-49 (#1,2: 52 pgs.)

1-Baker-a (7 pgs.)	24	48	72	140	230	320
2,3-Detective mysteries	13	26	39	74	105	135

WHODUNNIT?
Eclipse Comics: June, 1986 - No. 3, Apr, 1987 ($2.00, limited series)

1-3: Spiegle-a. 2-Gulacy-c 3.00

WHO FRAMED ROGER RABBIT (See Marvel Graphic Novel)

WHO IS NEXT?
Standard Comics: No. 5, Jan, 1953

5-Toth, Sekowsky, Andru-a; crime stories	20	40	60	114	182	250

WHO IS THE CROOKED MAN?
Crusade: Sept, 1996 ($3.50, B&W, 40 pgs.)

1-Intro The Martyr, Scarlet 7 & Garrison 4.00

WHO'S MINDING THE MINT? (See Movie Classics)

WHO'S WHO IN STAR TREK
DC Comics: Mar, 1987 - #2, Apr, 1987 ($1.50, limited series)

1,2 6.00

NOTE: **Byrne** *a-1, 2.* **Chaykin** *c-1, 2.* **Morrow** *a-1, 2.* **McFarlane** *a-2.* **Perez** *a-1, 2.* **Sutton** *a-1, 2.*

WHO'S WHO IN THE LEGION OF SUPER-HEROES
DC Comics: Apr, 1987 - No. 7, Nov, 1988 ($1.25, limited series)

1-7 4.00

WHO'S WHO: THE DEFINITIVE DIRECTORY OF THE DC UNIVERSE
DC Comics: Mar, 1985 - No. 26, Apr, 1987 (Maxi-series, no ads)

1-DC heroes from A-Z 4.00
2-26: All have 1-2 pgs-a by most DC artists 4.00

NOTE: **Art Adams** *a-4, 11, 18, 20.* **Anderson** *a-1-5, 7-12, 14, 15, 19, 21, 23-25.* **Aparo** *a-2, 3, 9, 10, 12, 13, 14, 15, 17, 18, 21, 23.* **Byrne** *a-4, 7, 14, 16, 18i, 19, 22i, 24; c-22.* **Cowan** *a-3-5, 8, 10-13, 16-18, 22-25.* **Ditko** *a-19-22.* **Evans** *a-20.* **Giffen** *a-1, 3,-6, 8, 13, 15, 17, 18, 23.* **Grell** *a-6, 9, 14, 20, 23, 25, 26.* **Infantino** *a-1-10, 12, 15, 17-22, 24, 25.* **Kaluta** *a-14, 21.* **Gil Kane** *a-1-11, 13, 14, 16, 19, 21-23, 25.* **Kirby** *a-2-6, 8-18, 20, 22, 25.* **Kubert** *a-2, 3, 7-11, 19, 20, 25.* **Erik Larsen** *a-24.* **McFarlane** *a-10-12, 17, 19, 25, 26.* **Morrow** *a-4, 7, 25, 26.* **Orlando** *a-1, 4, 10, 11, 21i.* **Perez** *a-1-5, 8-19, 22-26; c-1-4, 13-18.* **Rogers** *a-1, 2, 5-7, 11, 12, 15, 24.* **Starlin** *a-13, 14, 16.* **Stevens** *a-4, 7, 18.*

WHO'S WHO UPDATE '87
DC Comics: Aug, 1987 - No. 5, Dec, 1987 ($1.25, limited series)

1-5: Contains art by most DC artists 4.00

NOTE: **Giffen** *a-1.* **McFarlane** *a-1-4; c-4.* **Perez** *a-1-4.*

WHO'S WHO UPDATE '88
DC Comics: Aug, 1988 - No. 4, Nov, 1988 ($1.25, limited series)

1-4: Contains art by most DC artists 4.00

NOTE: **Giffen** *a-1.* **Erik Larsen** *a-1.*

Widowmaker #4 © MAR

Wilbur Comics #8 © AP

WildC.A.T.S: Covert Action Teams #16 © WSP

	GD 2.0	VG 4.0	FN 6.0	VF 8.0	VF/NM 9.0	NM- 9.2

WICKED, THE
Avalon Studios: Dec, 1999 - No. 7, Aug, 2000 ($2.95)

Preview-(7/99, $5.00, B&W)						5.00
1-7-Anacleto-c/Martinez-a						3.00
...: Medusa's Tale (11/00, $3.95, one shot) story plus pin-up gallery						4.00
...: Vol. 1: Omnibus (2003, $19.95) r/#0-8; Drew-c						20.00

WIDOWMAKER
Marvel Comics: Feb, 2011 - No. 4, Apr, 2011 ($3.99, limited series)

1-4-Black Widow, Hawkeye & Mockingbird app. 1,2-Jae Lee-c. 3,4-Noto-c 4.00

WIDOW WARRIORS
Dynamite Entertainment: 2010 - No. 4, 2010 ($3.99, limited series)

1-4-Pat Lee-a/c 4.00

WILBUR COMICS (Teen-age) (Also see Laugh Comics, Laugh Comix, Liberty Comics #10 & Zip Comics)
MLJ Magazines/Archie Publ. No. 8, Spring, 1946 on: Sum', 1944 - No. 87, 11/59; No. 88, 9/63; No. 89, 10/64; No. 90, 10/65 (No. 1-46: 52 pgs.) (#1-11 are quarterly)

1	57	114	171	362	619	875
2(Fall, 1944)	32	64	96	188	307	425
3,4(Wint, '44-45; Spr, '45)	22	44	66	132	216	300
5-1st app. Katy Keene (Sum, '45) & begin series; Wilbur story same as Archie story in Archie #1 except Wilbur replaces Archie	113	226	339	718	1234	1750
6-10: 10-(Fall, 1946)	25	50	75	147	241	335
11-20	15	30	45	90	140	190
21-30: 30-(4/50)	12	24	36	67	94	120
31-50	9	18	27	52	69	85
51-70	8	16	24	44	57	70
71-90: 88-Last 10¢ issue (9/63)	4	8	12	26	41	55

NOTE: *Katy Keene in No. 5-56, 58-61, 63-69.* ***Al Fagaly*** *c-6-9, 12-24 at least.* ***Vigoda*** *c-2.*

WILD
Atlas Comics (IPC): Feb, 1954 - No. 5, Aug, 1954

1	27	54	81	158	259	360
2	17	34	51	98	154	210
3-5	15	30	45	88	137	185

NOTE: ***Berg*** *a-5; c-4.* ***Burgos*** *c-3.* ***Colan*** *a-4.* ***Everett*** *a-1-3.* ***Heath*** *a-2, 3, 5.* ***Maneely*** *a-1-3, 5; c-1, 5.* ***Post*** *a-2, 5.* ***Ed Win*** *a-1, 3.*

WILD! (This Magazine Is...) (Satire)
Dell Publishing Co.: Jan, 1968 - No. 3, 1968 (35¢, magazine, 52 pgs.)

1-3: Hogan's Heroes, The Rat Patrol & Mission Impossible TV spoofs	3	6	9	16	22	28

WILD ANIMALS
Pacific Comics: Dec, 1982 ($1.00, one-shot, direct sales)

1-Funny animal; Sergio Aragonés-a; Shaw-c/a 4.00

WILD BILL ELLIOTT (Also see Western Roundup under Dell Giants)
Dell Publishing Co.: No. 278, 5/50 - No. 643, 7/55 (No #11,12) (All photo-c)

Four Color 278 (#1, 52pgs.)-Titled "Bill Elliott"; Bill & his horse Stormy begin; photo front/back-c begin	12	24	36	84	157	230
2 (11/50), 3 (52 pgs.)	8	16	24	52	86	120
4-10 (10-12/52)	6	12	18	41	66	90
Four Color 472 (6/53),520(12/53)-Last photo back-c	5	10	15	34	55	75
13 (4-6/54) - 17 (4-6/55)	5	10	15	32	51	70
Four Color 643 (7/55)	5	10	15	30	48	65

WILD BILL HICKOK (Also see Blazing Sixguns)
Avon Periodicals: Sept-Oct, 1949 - No. 28, May-June, 1956

1-Ingels-c	24	48	72	140	230	320
2-Painted-c; Kit West app.	14	28	42	76	108	140
3-5-Painted-c (4-Cover by Howard Winfield)	10	20	30	58	79	100
6-10,12: 8-10-Painted-c. 12-Kinsler-c?	10	20	30	56	76	95
11,13,14-Kinstler-c/a (#11-c & inside-f/c art only)	11	22	33	60	83	105
15,17,18,20: 18-Kit West story. 20-Kit West by Larsen	9	18	27	50	65	80
16-Kamen-a; r-3 stories/King of the Badmen of Deadwood	9	18	27	52	69	85
19-Meskin-a	9	18	27	50	65	80
21-Reprints 2 stories/Chief Crazy Horse	9	18	27	47	61	75
22-McCann-a?; r/Sheriff Bob Dixon's...	9	18	27	47	61	75
23-27: 23-Kinstler-c. 24-27-Kinstler-c/a(r) (24,25-r?)	9	18	27	47	61	75
28-Kinstler-c/a (new); r-/Last of the Comanches	9	18	27	50	65	80
I.W. Reprint #1-r/#2; Kinstler-c	2	4	6	9	13	16
Super Reprint #10-12: 10-r/#18. 11-r/#?. 12-r/#8	2	4	6	9	13	16

NOTE: *#23, 25 contain numerous editing deletions in both art and script due to code.* ***Kinstler*** *c-6, 7, 11-14, 17, 18, 20-22, 24-28.* ***Howard Larsen*** *a-1, 2, 4, 5, 6(3), 7-9, 11, 12, 17, 18, 20-24, 26.* ***Meskin*** *a-7.* ***Reinman*** *a-6, 17.*

WILD BILL HICKOK AND JINGLES (TV)(Formerly Cowboy Western) (Also see Blue Bird)
Charlton Comics: No. 68, Aug, 1958 - No. 75, Dec, 1959

68,69-Williamson-a (all are 10¢ issues)	11	22	33	60	83	105
70-Two pgs. Williamson-a	8	16	24	42	54	65
71-75 (#76, exist?)	6	12	18	28	34	40

WILD BILL PECOS WESTERN (Also see The Westerner)
AC Comics: 1989 ($3.50, 1/2 color/1/2 B&W, 52 pgs.)

1-Syd Shores-c/a(r)/Westerner; photo back-c 4.00

WILD BOY OF THE CONGO (Also see Approved Comics)
Ziff-Davis No. 10-12,4-8/St. John No. 9,11 on: No. 10, 2-3/51 - No. 12, 8-9/51; No. 4, 10-11/51 - No. 9, 10/53; No. 11-#15,6/55 (No #10, 1953)

10(#1)(2-3/51)-Origin; bondage-c by Saunders (painted); used in **SOTI**, pg. 189; painted-c begin thru #9 (except #7)	24	48	72	140	230	320
11(4-5/51),12(8-9/51)-Norman Saunders painted-c	14	28	42	80	115	150
4(10-11/51)-Saunders painted bondage-c	14	28	42	80	115	150
5(Winter,'51)-Saunders painted-c	13	26	39	72	101	130
6,8,9(10/53): Painted-c. 6-Saunders-c	13	26	39	72	101	130
7(8-9/52)-Kinstler-a	14	28	42	80	115	150
11-13-Baker-c. 11-r/#7 w/new Baker-c; Kinstler-a (2 pgs.)	15	30	45	85	130	175
14(4/55)-Baker-c; r-#12('51)	15	30	45	85	130	175
15(6/55)	11	22	33	60	83	105

WILDCAT (See Sensation Comics #1)

WILDC.A.T.S ADVENTURES (TV cartoon)
Image Comics (WildStorm): Sept, 1994 - No. 10, June, 1995 ($1.95/$2.50)

1-10						3.00
Sourcebook 1 (1/95, $2.95)						3.00

WILDC.A.T.S: COVERT ACTION TEAMS (Also see Alan Moore's... for TPB reprints)
Image Comics (WildStorm Productions): Aug, 1992 - No. 4, Mar, 1993; No. 5, Nov, 1993 - No. 50, June, 1998 ($1.95/$2.50)

1-1st app; Jim Lee/Williams-c/a & Lee scripts begin; contains 2 trading cards (Two diff versions of cards inside); 1st WildStorm Productions title						5.00
1-All gold foil signed edition						15.00
1-All gold foil unsigned edition						8.00
1-Newsstand edition w/o cards						3.00
1-"3-D Special"(8/97, $4.95) w/3-D glasses; variant-c by Jim Lee.						5.00
2-($2.50)-Prism foil stamped-c; contains coupon for Image Comics #0 & 4 pg. preview to Portacio's Wetworks (back-up)						5.00
2-With coupon missing						2.00
2-Direct sale misprint w/o foil-c						5.00
2-Newsstand ed., no prism or coupon						3.00
3-Lee/Liefeld-c (1/93-c, 12/92 inside)						4.00
4-($2.50)-Polybagged w/Topps trading card; 1st app. Tribe by Johnson & Stroman; Youngblood cameo						4.00
4-Variant w/red card						6.00
5-7-Jim Lee/Williams-c/a; Lee script						3.00
8-X-Men's Jean Grey & Scott Summers cameo						4.00
9-12: 10-1st app. Huntsman & Soldier; Claremont scripts begin, ends #13. 11-1st app. Savant, Tapestry & Mr. Majestic.						3.00
11-Alternate Portacio-c, see Deathblow #5						5.00
13-19,21-24: 15-James Robinson scripts begin, ends #20. 15,16-Black Razor story. 21-Alan Moore scripts begin, end #34; intro Tao & Ladytron; new WildC.A.T.S team forms (Mr. Majestic, Savant, Condition Red (Max Cash), Tao & Ladytron). 22-Maguire-a						3.00
20-($2.50)-Direct Market, WildStorm Rising Pt. 2 w/bound-in card						4.00
20-($1.95)-Newsstand, WildStorm Rising Part 2						3.00
25-($4.95)-Alan Moore script; wraparound foil-c.						5.00
26-49: 29-(5/96)-Fire From Heaven Pt 7; reads Apr on-c. 30-(6/96)-Fire From Heaven Pt. 13; Spartan revealed to have transplanted personality of John Colt (from Team One: WildC.A.T.S). 31-(9/96)-Grifter rejoins team; Ladytron dies						3.00
40-($3.50)Voyager Pack bagged w/Divine Right preview						5.00
50-($3.50) Stories by Robinson/Lee, Choi & Peterson/Benes, and Moore/Charest; Charest sketchbook; Lee wraparound-c						4.00
50-Chromium cover						6.00
Annual 1 (2/98, $2.95) Robinson-s						4.00
Compendium (1993, $9.95)-r/#1-4; bagged w/#0						10.00
Sourcebook 1 (9/93, $2.50)-Foil embossed-c						3.00
Sourcebook 1-($1.95)-Newsstand ed. w/o foil embossed-c						3.00
Sourcebook 2 (11/94, $2.50)-wraparound-c						3.00

Wildcats V5 #23 © WSP

Wildcore #7 © Aegis

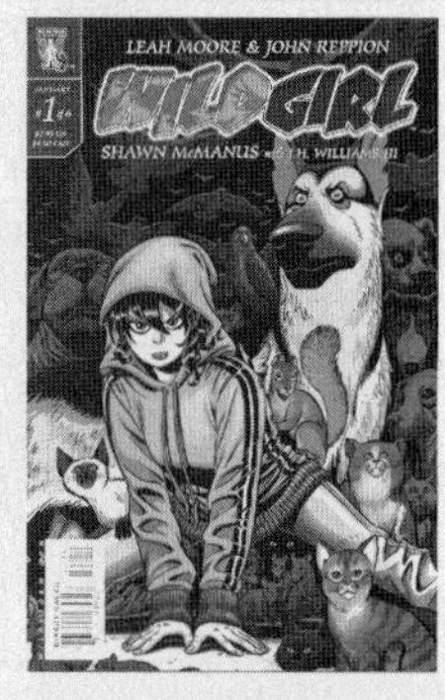

Wild Girl #1 © DC

	GD 2.0	VG 4.0	FN 6.0	VF 8.0	VF/NM 9.0	NM- 9.2

Special 1 (11/93, $3.50, 52 pgs.)-1st Travis Charest WildC.A.T.S-a 4.00
...A Gathering of Eagles (5/97, $9.95, TPB) r/#10-12 10.00
.../ Cyberforce: Killer Instinct TPB (2004, $14.95) r/#5-7 & Cyberforce V2 #1-3 15.00
...Gang War ('98, $16.95, TPB) r/#28-34 17.00
...Homecoming (8/98, $19.95, TPB) r/#21-27 20.00
James Robinson's Complete Wildc.a.t.s TPB (2009, $24.99) r/#15-20,50; Annual 1, WildStorm Rising #1, Team One Wildc.a.t.s #1,2; cover and pin-up gallery 25.00

WILDCATS
DC Comics (WildStorm): Mar, 1999 - No. 28, Dec, 2001 ($2.50)

1-Charest-a; six covers by Lee, Adams, Bisley, Campbell, Madureira and Ramos; Lobdell-s 4.00
1-($6.95) DF Edition; variant cover by Ramos 7.00
2-28: 2-Voodoo cover. 3-Bachalo variant-c. 5-Hitch-a/variant-c. 7-Meglia-a. 8-Phillips-a begins. 17-J.G. Jones-c. 18,19-Jim Lee-c. 20,21-Dillon-a 3.00
Annual 2000 (12/00, $3.50) Bermejo-a; Devil's Night x-over 4.00
...: Battery Park ('03, $17.95, TPB) r/#20-28; Phillips-c 18.00
... Ladytron (10/00, $5.95) Origin; Casey-s/Canete-a 6.00
... Mosaic (2/00, $3.95) Tuska-a (10 pg. back-up story) 4.00
...: Serial Boxes ('01, $14.95, TPB) r/#14-19; Phillips-c 15.00
...: Street Smart ('00, $24.95, HC) r/#1-6; Charest-c 25.00
...: Street Smart ('02, $14.95, SC) r/#1-6; Charest-c 15.00
...: Vicious Circles ('00, $14.95, TPB) r/#8-13; Phillips-c 15.00

WILDCATS (Volume 4)
DC Comics (WildStorm): Dec, 2006 ($2.99)

1-Grant Morrison-s/Jim Lee-a; Jim Lee-c 3.00
1-Variant-c by Todd McFarlane/Jim Lee 6.00
...: Armageddon 1 (2/08, $2.99) Gage-s/Caldwell-a 3.00

WILDCATS (Volume 5) (World's End on cover for #1,2)
DC Comics (WildStorm): Sept, 2008 - No. 30, Feb, 2011 ($2.99)

1-30: 1-Christos Gage-s/Neil Googe-a. 5-Woods-a 3.00
...: Family Secrets TPB (2010, $17.99) r/#8-12 18.00
...: World's End TPB (2009, $17.99) r/#1-7 18.00

WILDC.A.T.S/ ALIENS
Image Comics/Dark Horse: Aug, 1998 ($4.95, one-shot)

	GD	VG	FN	VF	VF/NM	NM-
1-Ellis-s/Sprouse-a/c; Aliens invade Skywatch; Stormwatch app.; death of Winter; destruction of Skywatch	1	2	3	5	6	8
1-Variant-c by Gil Kane	1	3	4	6	8	10

WILDCATS: NEMESIS
DC Comics (WildStorm): Nov, 2005 - No. 9, July, 2006 ($2.99, limited series)

1-9: 1-Robbie Morrison-s/Talent Caldwell & Horacio Domingues-a/Caldwell-c 3.00
TPB (2006, $19.99) r/#1-9; cover gallery 20.00

WILDC.A.T.S: SAVANT GARDE FAN EDITION
Image Comics/WildStorm Productions: Feb, 1997 - No. 3, Apr, 1997 (Giveaway, 8 pgs.) (Polybagged w/Overstreet's FAN)

1-3: Barbara Kesel-s/Christian Uche-a(p) 3.00
1-3-(Gold): All retailer incentives 10.00

WILDC.A.T.S TRILOGY
Image Comics (WildStorm Productions): June, 1993 - No. 3, Dec, 1993 ($1.95, lim. series)

1-($2.50)-1st app. Gen 13 (Fairchild, Burnout, Grunge, Freefall) Multi-color foil-c; Jae Lee-c/a in all 5.00
1-($1.95)-Newsstand ed. w/o foil-c 3.00
2,3-($1.95)-Jae Lee-c/a 3.00

WILDCATS VERSION 3.0
DC Comics (WildStorm): Oct, 2002 - No. 24, Oct, 2004 ($2.95)

1-24: 1-Casey-s/Nguyen-a; two covers by Nguyen and Rian Hughes and Nguyen. 8-Back-up preview of The Authority: High Stakes pt. 3 3.00
...: Brand Building TPB (2003, $14.95) r/#1-6 15.00
...: Full Disclosure TPB (2004, $14.95) r/#7-12 15.00
...: Year One TPB (2010, $24.99) r/#1-12 25.00
...: Year Two TPB (2011, $24.99) r/#13-24 25.00

WILDC.A.T.S/ X-MEN: THE GOLDEN AGE (See also X-Men/WildC.A.T.S.: The Dark Age)
Image Comics (WildStorm Productions): Feb, 1997 ($4.50, one-shot)

1-Lobdell-s/Charest-a; Two covers (Charest, Jim Lee) 5.00
1-"3-D" Edition ($6.50) w/glasses 7.00

WILDC.A.T.S/ X-MEN: THE MODERN AGE
Image Comics (WildStorm Productions): Aug, 1997 ($4.50, one-shot)

1-Robinson-s/Hughes-a; Two covers (Hughes, Paul Smith) 5.00
1-"3-D" Edition ($6.50) w/glasses 7.00

WILDC.A.T.S/ X-MEN: THE SILVER AGE
Image Comics (WildStorm Productions): June, 1997 ($4.50, one-shot)

1-Lobdell-s/Jim Lee-a; Two covers(Neal Adams, Jim Lee) 5.00
1-"3-D" Edition ($6.50) w/glasses 7.00

WILDCORE
Image Comics (WildStorm Prods.): Nov, 1997 - No. 10, Dec, 1998 ($2.50)

1-10: 1-Two covers (Booth/McWeeney, Charest) 3.00
1-($3.50)-Voyager Pack w/DV8 preview 4.00
1-Chromium-c 5.00

WILD DOG
DC Comics: Sept, 1987 - No. 4, Dec, 1987 (75¢, limited series)

1-4 3.00
Special 1 (1989, $2.50, 52 pgs.) 4.00

WILDERNESS TREK (See Zane Grey, Four Color 333)

WILDFIRE (See Zane Grey, FourColor 433)

WILDFLOWER
Sirius Entertainment/Neko Press: 1996 - Present (B&W)

1-5-('96, $2.50) Billy Martinez-s/a 3.00
... Beginnings TPB (Neko Press, 2003, $14.99) r/#1-5 15.00
... Dark Euphoria 1 (2004, $2.99) Kiethan Jones-a/c; Martinez-s 3.00
... Dark Euphoria 1,2 (2004, $3.99) w/alternate-c by Martinez 4.00
... Tribal Screams 1-4 (12/00 - 2/03, $2.99) 3.00
... Tribal Screams 1 ($4.99) w/alternate-c by Dark One 5.00
... Y2K (16 pgs, edition of 2000) each contains an original Martinez sketch 10.00

WILD FRONTIER (Cheyenne Kid #8 on)
Charlton Comics: Oct, 1955 - No. 7, Apr, 1957

	GD	VG	FN	VF	VF/NM	NM-
1-Davy Crockett	10	20	30	54	72	90
2-6-Davy Crockett in all	7	14	21	37	46	55
7-Origin & 1st app. Cheyenne Kid	9	18	27	47	61	75

WILD GIRL
DC Comics (WildStorm): Jan, 2005 - No. 6, Jun, 2005 ($2.95/$2.99)

1-6-Leah Moore & John Reppion-s/Shawn McManus-a/c 3.00

WILDGUARD: CASTING CALL
Image Comics: Sept, 2003 - No. 6, Feb, 2004 ($2.95)

1-6: 1-Nauck-s/a; two covers by Nauck and McGuinness. 2-Wieringo var-c. 6-Noto var-c 3.00
... Vol. 1: Casting Call (1/05, $17.95, TPB) r/#1-6; cover gallery; Todd Nauck bio 18.00
Wildguard: Fire Power 1 (12/04, $3.50) Nauck-a; two covers 3.50
Wildguard: Fool's Gold (7/05 - No. 2, 7/05, $3.50) 1,2-Todd Nauck-s/a 3.50
Wildguard: Insider (5/08 - No. 3, 7/08, $3.50) 1-3-Todd Nauck-s/a 3.50

WILDSIDERZ
DC Comics (WildStorm): No. 0, Aug, 2005 - No. 2, Jan, 2006 ($1.99/$3.50)

0-(8/05, $1.99) Series preview & character profiles; J. Scott Campbell-a 3.00
1,2: 1-(10/05, $3.50) J. Scott Campbell-s/a; Andy Hartnell-s 3.50

WILDSTAR (Also see The Dragon & The Savage Dragon)
Image Comics (Highbrow Entertainment): Sept, 1995 - No. 3, Jan, 1996 ($2.50, lim. series)

1-3: Al Gordon scripts; Jerry Ordway-c/a 3.00

WILDSTAR: SKY ZERO
Image Comics (Highbrow Entertainment): Mar, 1993 - No. 4, Nov, 1993 ($1.95, lim. series)

1-4: 1-($2.50)-Embossed-c w/silver ink; Ordway-c/a in all 3.00
1-($1.95)-Newsstand ed. w/silver ink-c, not embossed 3.00
1-Gold variant 6.00

WILD STARS
Collector's Edition/Little Rocket Productions: Summer, 1984 - Present (B&W)

Vol. 1 #1 (Summer 1984, $1.50) 5.00
Vol. 2 #1 (Winter 1988, $1.95) Foil-c; die-cut front & back-c 5.00
Vol. 3: #1-6-Brunner-c; Tierney-s. 1,2-Brewer-a. 3-6-Simons-a 3.00
7-($5.95) Simons-a 6.00
TPB (2004, $17.95) r/Vol. 1-3 18.00

WILDSTORM
Image Comics/DC Comics (WildStorm Publishing): 1994 - Present (one-shots, TPBs)

... After the Fall TPB (2009, $19.99) r/back-up stories from Wildcats V5 #1-11, The Authority V5 #1-11; Gen 13 V4 #21-28, and Stormwatch: PHD #13-20 20.00
...Annual 2000 (12/00, $3.50) Devil's Night x-over; Moy-a 4.00
...: Armageddon TPB (2008, $17.99) r/Armageddon one-shots in Midnighter, Welcome To Tranquility, Wetworks, Gen13, Stormwatch PHD, and Wildcats titles 18.00
...Chamber of Horrors (10/95, $3.50)-Bisley-c 4.00

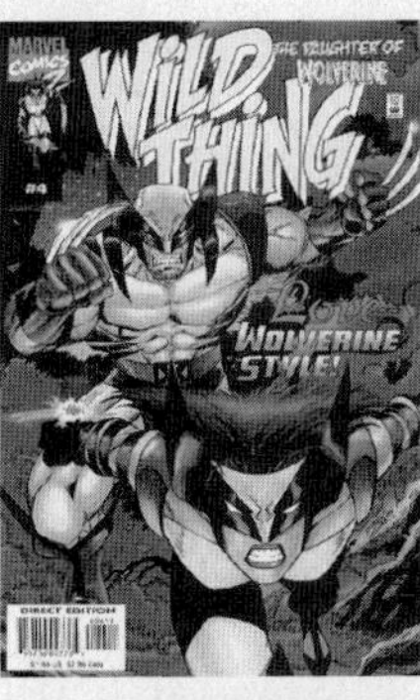

Wild Thing #4 © MAR

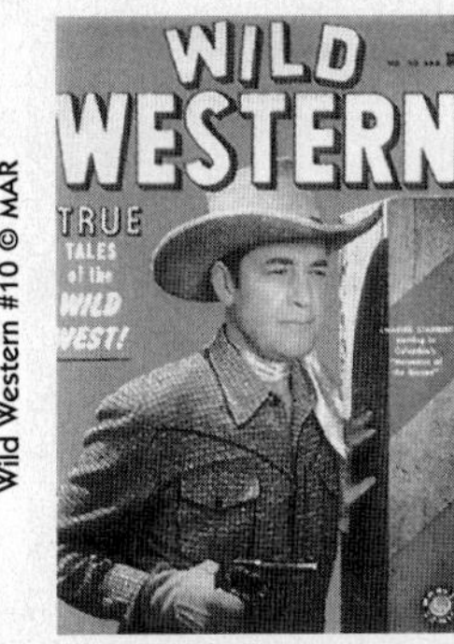

Wild Western #10 © MAR

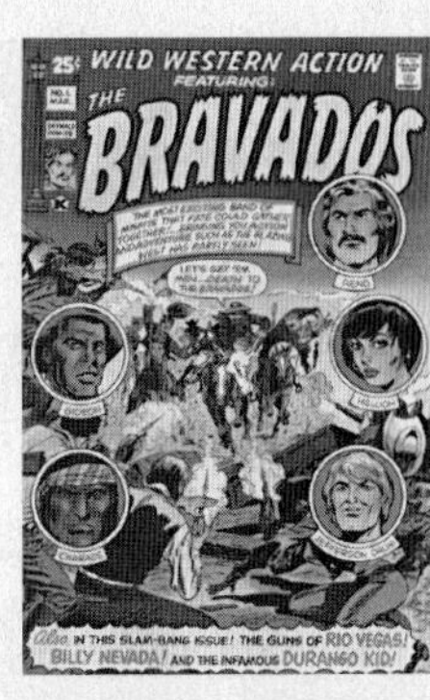

Wild Western Action #1 © Skywald

GD 2.0 | VG 4.0 | FN 6.0 | VF 8.0 | VF/NM 9.0 | NM- 9.2

...Fine Arts: Spotlight on Gen13 (2/08, $3.50) art and covers with commentary 3.50
...Fine Arts: Spotlight on Jim Lee (2/07, $3.50) art and covers by Lee with commentary 3.50
...Fine Arts: Spotlight on J. Scott Campbell (5/07, $3.50) art and covers with commentary 3.50
...Fine Arts: Spotlight on The Authority (1/08, $3.50) art and covers with commentary 3.50
...Fine Arts: Spotlight on WildCATs (3/08, $3.50) art and covers with commentary 3.50
...Fine Arts: The Gallery Collection (12/98, $19.95) Lee-c 20.00
...Halloween 1 (10/97, $2.50) Warner-c 3.00
...Rarities 1(12/94, $4.95, 52 pgs.)-r/Gen 13 1/2 & other stories 5.00
...Summer Special 1 (2001, $5.95) Short stories by various; Hughes-c 6.00
...Swimsuit Special 1 (12/94, $2.95), ...Swimsuit Special 2 (1995, $2.50) 3.00
...Swimsuit Special '97 #1 (7/97, $2.50) 3.00
...Thunderbook 1 (10/00, $6.95) Short stories by various incl. Hughes, Moy 7.00
...Ultimate Sports 1 (8/97, $2.50) 3.00
...Universe Sourcebook (5/95, $2.50) 3.00
...Universe 2008 Convention Exclusive ('08, no cover price) preview of World's End x-over 3.00

WILDSTORM!
Image Comics (WildStorm Publishing): Aug, 1995 - No. 4, Nov, 1995 ($2.50, B&W/color, anthology)

1-4: 1-Simonson-a 3.00

WILDSTORM PRESENTS: ...
DC Comics (WildStorm): Jan, 2011 - Present ($7.99, squarebound, reprints)

1-(1/11) r/short stories by various incl. Pearson, Conner, Corben, Jeanty, Mahnke 8.00
Planetary: Lost Worlds (2/11) r/Planetary/Authority & Planetary/JLA: Terra Occulta 8.00

WILDSTORM REVELATIONS
DC Comics (WildStorm): Mar, 2008 - No. 6, May, 2008 ($2.99, limited series)

1-6-Beatty & Gage-s/Craig-a. 2-The Authority app. 3.00
TPB (2008, $17.99) r/#1-6; cover sketches 18.00

WILDSTORM RISING
Image Comics (WildStorm Publishing): May, 1995 - No.2, June, 1995 ($1.95/$2.50)

1-($2.50)-Direct Market, WildStorm Rising Pt. 1 w/bound-in card 3.00
1-($1.95)-Newstand, WildStorm Rising Pt. 1 3.00
2-($2.50)-Direct Market, WildStorm Rising Pt. 10 w/bound-in card; continues in WildC.A.T.S #21. 3.00
2-($1.95)-Newstand, WildStorm Rising Pt. 10 3.00
Trade paperback (1996, $19.95)-Collects x-over; B. Smith-c 20.00

WILDSTORM SPOTLIGHT
Image Comics (WildStorm Publishing): Feb, 1997 - No. 4 ($2.50)

1-4: 1-Alan Moore-s 3.00

WILDSTORM UNIVERSE '97
Image Comics (WildStorm Publishing): Dec, 1996 - No. 3 ($2.50, limited series)

1-3: 1-Wraparound-c. 3-Gary Frank-c 3.00

WILDTHING
Marvel Comics UK: Apr, 1993 - No. 7, Oct, 1993 ($1.75)

1-($2.50)-Embossed-c; Venom & Carnage cameo 3.00
2-7: 2-Spider-Man & Venom. 6-Mysterio app. 3.00

WILD THING (Wolverine's daughter in the M2 universe)
Marvel Comics: Oct, 1999 - No. 5, Feb, 2000 ($1.99)

1-5: 1-Lim-a in all. 2-Two covers 3.00
Wizard #0 supplement; battles the Hulk 3.00
Spider-Girl Presents Wild Thing. Crash Course (2007, $7.99, digest) r/#0-5 8.00

WILDTIMES
DC Comics (WildStorm Productions): Aug, 1999 ($2.50, one-shots)

...Deathblow #1 -set in 1899; Edwards-a; Jonah Hex app., ...DV8 #1 -set in 1944; Altieri-s/p; Sgt. Rock app., ...Gen13 #1 -set in 1969; Casey-s/Johnson-a; Teen Titans app., ...Grifter #1 -set in 1923; Paul Smith-a, ...Wetworks #1 -Waid-s/Lopresti-a; Superman app. 3.00
...WildC.A.T.s #0 -Wizard supplement; Charest-c 3.00

WILD WEST (Wild Western #3 on)
Marvel Comics (WFP): Spring, 1948 - No. 2, July, 1948

1-Two-Gun Kid, Arizona Annie, & Tex Taylor begin; Shores-c 34 68 102 199 325 450
2-Captain Tootsie by Beck; Shores-c 22 44 66 132 216 300

WILD WEST (Black Fury #1-57)
Charlton Comics: V2#58, Nov, 1966

V2#58 2 4 6 11 16 20

WILD WEST C.O.W.-BOYS OF MOO MESA (TV)
Archie Comics: Dec, 1992 - No. 3, Feb, 1993 (limited series)
V2#1, Mar, 1993 - No. 3, July, 1993 ($1.25)

1-3,V2#1-3 3.00

WILD WESTERN (Formerly Wild West #1,2)
Marvel/Atlas (WFP): No. 3, 9/48 - No. 57, 9/57 (3-11: 52 pgs, 12-on: 36 pgs)

3(#1)-Tex Morgan begins; Two-Gun Kid, Tex Taylor, & Arizona Annie continue from Wild West 27 54 81 158 259 360
4-Last Arizona Annie; Captain Tootsie by Beck; Kid Colt app. 20 40 60 114 182 250
5-2nd app. Black Rider (1/49); Blaze Carson, Captain Tootsie (by Beck) app. 23 46 69 136 223 310
6-8: 6-Blaze Carson app; anti-Wertham editorial 15 30 45 88 137 185
9-Photo-c; Black Rider begins, ends #19 19 38 57 109 172 235
10-Charles Starrett photo-c 22 44 66 128 209 290
11-(Last 52 pg. issue) 15 30 45 85 130 175
12-14,16-19: All Black Rider-c/stories. 12-14-The Prairie Kid & his horse Fury app. 15 30 45 83 124 165
15-Red Larabee, Gunhawk (origin), his horse Blaze, & Apache Kid begin, end #22; Black Rider-c/story 15 30 45 84 127 170
20-30: 20-Kid Colt-c begin. 24-Has 2 Kid Colt stories. 26-1st app. The Ringo Kid? (2/53); 4 pg. story. 30-Katz-a 12 24 36 69 97 125
31-40 10 20 30 54 72 90
41-47,49-51,53,57 9 18 27 47 61 75
48-Williamson/Torres-a (4 pgs); Drucker-a 10 20 30 56 76 95
52-Crandall-a 10 20 30 56 76 95
54,55-Williamson-a in both (5 & 4 pgs.), #54 with Mayo plus 2 text illos 10 20 30 56 76 95
56-Baker-a? 9 18 27 47 61 75

NOTE: *Annie Oakley in #46, 47. Apache Kid in #15-22, 39. Arizona Kid in #21, 23. Arrowhead in #34-39. Black Rider in #5, 9-19, 33-44. Fighting Texan in #17. Kid Colt in #4-6, 9-11, 20-47, 52, 54-56. Outlaw Kid in #43. Red Hawkins in #13, 14. Ringo Kid in #26, 39, 41, 43, 44, 46, 47, 50, 52-56. Tex Morgan in #3, 4, 6, 9, 11. Tex Taylor in #3-6, 9, 11. Texas Kid in #23-25. Two-Gun Kid in #3-6, 9, 11, 12, 33-39, 41. Wyatt Earp in #47.* ***Ayers*** *a-41, 42, 53, 54.* ***Berg*** *a-26; c-24.* ***Colan*** *a-49.* ***Forte*** *a-28, 30.* ***Al Hartley*** *a-16.* ***Heath*** *a-4, 5, 8; c-34, 44.* ***Keller*** *a-24, 26(2), 29-40, 44-46, 48, 52.* ***Maneely*** *a-10, 12, 15, 16, 28, 35, 38, 40-45; c-18-22, 33, 35, 36, 38-42, 45, 53, 54, 56, 57.* ***Morisi*** *a-23, 52.* ***Pakula*** *a-42, 52.* ***Powell*** *a-51.* ***Romita*** *a-24(2).* ***Severin*** *a-46, 47; c-48.* ***Shores*** *a-3, 5, 30, 31, 33, 35, 36, 38, 41; c-3-5.* ***Sinnott*** *a-34-39.* ***Wildey*** *a-43. Bondage c-19.*

WILD WESTERN ACTION (Also see The Bravados)
Skywald Publ. Corp.: Mar, 1971 - No. 3, June, 1971 (25¢, reprints, 52 pgs.)

1-Durango Kid, Straight Arrow-r; with all references to "Straight" in story relettered to "Swift"; Bravados begin; Shores-a (new) 3 6 9 16 22 28
2,3: 2-Billy Nevada, Durango Kid. 3-Red Mask, Durango Kid 2 4 6 10 14 18

WILD WESTERN ROUNDUP
Red Top/Decker Publications/I. W. Enterprises: Oct, 1957; 1960-'61

1(1957)-Kid Cowboy-r 5 10 15 22 26 30
I.W. Reprint #1('60-61)-r/#1 by Red Top 2 4 6 8 11 14

WILD WEST RODEO
Star Publications: 1953 (15¢)

1-A comic book coloring book with regular full color cover & B&W inside 9 18 27 47 61 75

WILD WILD WEST, THE (TV)
Gold Key: June, 1966 - No. 7, Oct, 1969 (All have Robert Conrad photo-c)

1-McWilliams-a 11 22 33 79 147 215
1-Variant edition with photo back-c (scarce) 12 24 36 87 164 240
2-Robert Conrad photo-c; McWilliams-a 9 18 27 60 100 140
2-Variant edition with Conrad photo back-c (scarce) 9 18 27 65 113 160
3-7 7 14 21 50 83 115
3-Variant edition with photo back-c (scarce) 9 18 27 60 110 140

WILD, WILD WEST, THE (TV)
Millennium Publications: Oct, 1990 - No. 4, Jan?, 1991 ($2.95, limited series)

1-4-Based on TV show 3.00

WILKIN BOY (See That...)

WILL EISNER READER
Kitchen Sink Press: 1991 ($9.95, B&W, 8 1/2" x 11", TPB)

nn-Reprints stories from Will Eisner's Quarterly; Eisner-s/a/c 10.00
nn-(DC Comics, 10/00, $9.95) 10.00

WILL EISNER'S JOHN LAW: ANGELS AND ASHES, DEVILS AND DUST
IDW Publ.: Apr, 2006 - No. 4 ($3.99, B&W, limited series)

1-New stories with Will Eisner's characters; Gary Chaloner-s/a 4.00

WILLIE COMICS (Formerly Ideal #1-4; Crime Cases #24 on; Li'l Willie #20 & 21)

Will To Power #10 © DH

Wings Comics #43 © FH

Winnie The Pooh #25 © DIS

	GD 2.0	VG 4.0	FN 6.0	VF 8.0	VF/NM 9.0	NM- 9.2

(See Gay Comics, Laugh, Millie The Model & Wisco)
Marvel Comics (MgPC): #5, Fall, 1946 - #19, 4/49; #22, 1/50 - #23, 5/50 (No #20 & 21)

5(#1)-George, Margie, Nellie the Nurse & Willie begin	26	52	78	154	252	350
6,8,9	15	30	45	86	133	180
7(1),10,11-Kurtzman's "Hey Look"	15	30	45	88	137	185
12,14-18,22,23	14	28	42	82	121	160
13,19-Kurtzman's "Hey Look" (#19-last by Kurtzman?)	15	30	45	83	124	165

NOTE: *Cindy app. in #17. Jeanie app. in #17. Little Lizzie app. in #22.*

WILLIE MAYS (See The Amazing...)

WILLIE THE PENGUIN
Standard Comics: Apr, 1951 - No. 6, Apr, 1952

1-Funny animal	9	18	27	50	65	80
2-6	6	12	18	29	36	42

WILLIE THE WISE-GUY (Also see Cartoon Kids)
Atlas Comics (NPP): Sept, 1957

1-Kida, Maneely-a	9	18	27	52	69	85

WILLOW
Marvel Comics: Aug, 1988 - No. 3, Oct, 1988 ($1.00)

1-3-R/Marvel Graphic Novel #36 (movie adaptation) 3.00

WILL ROGERS WESTERN (Formerly My Great Love #1-4; see Blazing & True Comics #66)
Fox Features Syndicate: No. 5, June, 1950 - No. 2, Aug, 1950

5(#1)	31	62	93	186	303	420
2: Photo-c	26	52	78	154	252	350

WILL TO POWER (Also see Comic's Greatest World)
Dark Horse Comics: June, 1994 - No. 12, Aug, 1994 ($1.00, weekly limited series, 20 pgs.)

1-12: 12-Vortex kills Titan. 3.00
NOTE: ***Mignola** c-10-12. **Sears** c-1-3.*

WILL-YUM!
Dell Publishing Co.: No. 676, Feb, 1956 - No. 902, May, 1958

Four Color 676 (#1), 765 (1/57), 902	4	8	12	26	41	55

WIN A PRIZE COMICS (Timmy The Timid Ghost #3 on?)
Charlton Comics: Feb, 1955 - No. 2, Apr, 1955

V1#1-S&K-a; Poe adapt; E.C. War swipe	67	134	201	426	731	1035
2-S&K-a	48	96	144	302	514	725

WINDY & WILLY (Also see Showcase #81)
National Periodical Publications: May-June, 1969 - No. 4, Nov-Dec, 1969

1- r/Dobie Gillis with some art changes begin	5	10	15	32	51	70
2-4	3	6	9	20	30	40

WINGS COMICS
Fiction House Mag.: 9/40 - No. 109, 9/49; No. 110, Wint, 1949-50; No. 111, Spring, 1950; No. 112, 1950(nd); No. 113 - No. 115, 1950(nd); No. 116, 1952(nd); No. 117, Fall, 1952 - No. 122, Wint, 1953-54; No. 123 - No. 124, 1954(nd)

1-Skull Squad, Clipper Kirk, Suicide Smith, Jane Martin, War Nurse, Phantom Falcons, Greasemonkey Griffin, Parachute Patrol & Powder Burns begin	271	542	813	1734	2967	4200
2	100	200	300	635	1093	1550
3-5	68	136	204	432	746	1060
6-10: 8-Indicia shows #7 (#8 on cover)	54	108	162	343	574	825
11-15	49	98	147	309	522	735
16-Origin & 1st app. Captain Wings & begin series	53	106	159	334	567	800
17-20	42	84	126	265	445	625
21-30	40	80	120	246	411	575
31-40	37	74	111	218	354	490
41-50	30	60	90	177	289	400
51-60: 60-Last Skull Squad	28	56	84	165	270	375
61-67: 66-Ghost Patrol begins (becomes Ghost Squadron #71 on), ends #112?	25	50	75	150	245	340
68,69: 68-Clipper Kirk becomes The Phantom Falcon-origin, Part 1; part 2 in #69	25	50	75	150	245	340
70-72: 70-1st app. The Phantom Falcon in costume, origin-Part 3; Capt. Wings battles Col. Kamikaze in all	24	48	72	144	237	330
73-99: 80-Phantom Falcon by Larsen. 99-King of the Congo begins?	24	48	72	144	237	330
100-(12/48)	25	50	75	150	245	340
101-124: 111-Last Jane Martin. 112-Flying Saucer-c/story (1950). 115-Used in **POP**, pg. 89	19	38	57	111	176	240

NOTE: *Bondage covers are common. Captain Wings battles Sky Hag-#75, 76; ...Mr. Atlantis-#85-92; ...Mr. Pupin(Red Agent)-#98-103. Capt. Wings by **Elias**-#52-64, 68, 69; by **Lubbers**-#29-32, 70-111; by **Renee**-#33-46. **Evans** a-85-106, 108-111(Jane Martin); text illos-72-84. **Larsen** a-52, 59, 64, 73-77. Jane Martin by **Fran Hopper**-#68-84; Suicide Smith by **John Celardo**-#72, 74, 76, 80-104; by **Hollingsworth**-#68-70, 105-109, 111; Ghost Squadron by **Astarita**-#67-79; by **Maurice Whitman**-#80-111. King of the Congo by **Moreira**-#99, 100. Skull Squad by **M. Baker**-#52-60; Clipper Kirk by **Baker**-#60, 61; by **Colan**-#53; by **Ingels**-(some issues?). Phantom Falcon by **Larsen**-#73-84. **Elias** c-58-72. **Fawcette** c-3-12, 16, 17, 19, 22-33. **Lubbers** c-74-109. **Tuska** a-5. **Whitman** c-110-124. **Zolnerwich** c-15, 21.*

WINGS OF THE EAGLES, THE
Dell Publishing Co.: No. 790, Apr, 1957 (10¢ & 15¢ editions exist)

Four Color 790-Movie; John Wayne photo-c; Toth-a	13	26	39	90	173	255

WINKY DINK (Adventures of...)
Pines Comics: No. 75, Mar, 1957 (one-shot)

75-Marv Levy-c/a	6	12	18	31	38	45

WINKY DINK (TV)
Dell Publishing Co.: No. 663, Nov, 1955

Four Color 663 (#1)	8	16	24	52	86	120

WINNIE-THE-POOH (Also see Dynabrite Comics)
Gold Key No. 1-17/Whitman No. 18 on: January, 1977 - No. 33, July, 1984
(Walt Disney) (Winnie-The-Pooh began as Edward Bear in 1926 by Milne)

1-New art	3	6	9	17	25	32
2-5: 5-New material	2	4	6	10	14	18
6-17: 12-up-New material	2	4	6	8	11	14
18,19(Whitman)	2	4	6	10	14	18
20,21('80) pre-pack only	4	8	12	24	37	50
22('80) (scarcer) pre-pack only	5	10	15	30	48	65
23-28: 27(2/82), 28(4/82)	2	4	6	11	16	20
29-33 (#90299 on-c, no date or date code; pre-pack): 29(4/82), 30(5/83), 31(8/83), 32(4/84), 33(7/84)	3	6	9	17	25	32

WINNIE WINKLE (See Popular Comics & Super Comics)
Dell Publishing Co.: 1941 - No. 7, Sept-Nov, 1949

Large Feature Comic 2 (1941)	28	56	84	165	270	375
Four Color 94 (1945)	12	24	36	82	154	225
Four Color 174	8	16	24	58	97	135
1(3-5/48)-Contains daily & Sunday newspaper-r from 1939-1941	8	16	24	52	86	120
2 (6-8/48)	6	12	18	37	59	80
3-7	4	8	12	28	44	60

WINTER MEN, THE
DC Comics (WildStorm): Oct, 2005 - No. 5, Nov, 2006 ($2.99, limited series)

1-5-Brett Lewis-s/John Paul Leon-a 3.00
... Winter Special (2/09, $3.99) Lewis-s/Leon-a 4.00
TPB (2010, $19.99) r/#1-5 & Winter Special; original proposal, development & sketch-a 20.00

WINTER SOLDIER: WINTER KILLS (See Captain America 2005 series)
Marvel Comics: Feb, 2007 ($3.99, one-shot)

1-Flashback to Christmas Eve 1944; Toro & Sub-Mariner app.; Brubaker-s/Weeks-a 4.00

WINTERWORLD
Eclipse Comics: Sept, 1987 - No. 3, Mar, 1988 ($1.75, limited series)

1-3 3.00

WISDOM
Marvel Comics (MAX): Jan, 2007 - No. 6, July, 2007 ($3.99, limited series)

1-6: 1-Hairsine-a/c; Cornell-s. 3-6-Manuel Garcia-a 4.00
...: Rudiments of Wisdom TPB (2007, $21.99) r/#1-6; series pitch and sketch page 22.00

WISE GUYS (See Harvey...)

WISE LITTLE HEN, THE
David McKay Publ./Whitman: 1934 ,1935(48 pgs.); 1937 (Story book)

nn-(1934 edition w/dust jacket)(48 pgs. with color, 8-3/4x9-3/4") -Debut of Donald Duck (see Advs. of Mickey Mouse); Donald app. on cover with Wise Little Hen & Practical Pig; painted cover; same artist as the B&W's from Silly Symphony Cartoon, The Wise Little Hen (1934) (McKay)

Book w/dust jacket	239	478	717	1530	2615	3700
Dust jacket only	55	110	165	352	601	850
nn-(1935 edition w/dust jacket), same as 1934 ed.	139	278	417	883	1517	2150
888 (1937)(9-1/2x13", 12 pgs.)(Whitman) Donald Duck app.	34	68	102	199	325	450

WISE SON: THE WHITE WOLF
DC Comics (Milestone): Nov, 1996 - No. 4, Feb, 1997 ($2.50, limited series)

1-4: Ho Che Anderson-c/a 3.00

Witchblade #134 © TCOW

Witches #1 © MAR

Witches Tales #3 © HARV

WIT AND WISDOM OF WATERGATE (Humor magazine)
Marvel Comics: 1973, 76 pgs., squarebound

	GD 2.0	VG 4.0	FN 6.0	VF 8.0	VF/NM 9.0	NM- 9.2
1-Low print run	5	10	15	30	48	65

WITCHBLADE (Also see Cyblade/Shi, Tales Of The..., & Top Cow Classics)
Image Comics (Top Cow Productions): Nov, 1995 - Present ($2.50/$2.99)

	GD 2.0	VG 4.0	FN 6.0	VF 8.0	VF/NM 9.0	NM- 9.2
0	1	2	3	5	6	8
1/2-Mike Turner/Marc Silvestri-c.	3	6	9	20	30	40
1/2 Gold Ed., 1/2 Chromium-c	3	6	9	20	30	40
1/2-(Vol. 2, 11/02, $2.99) Wohl-s/Ching-a/c						3.00
1-Mike Turner-a(p)	4	8	12	21	30	40
1,2-American Ent. Encore Ed.	1	2	3	4	5	7
2,3	2	4	6	11	16	20
4,5	2	4	6	9	13	16
6-9: 8-Wraparound-c. 9-Tony Daniel-a(p)	1	2	3	5	7	9
9-Sunset variant-c	2	4	6	8	10	12
9-DF variant-c	2	4	6	11	16	20
10-Flip book w/Darkness #0, 1st app. the Darkness	2	4	6	8	10	12
10-Variant-c	2	4	6	9	12	15
10-Gold logo	3	6	9	16	23	30
10-($3.95) Dynamic Forces alternate-c	1	2	3	5	6	8
11-15						5.00
16-19: 18,19-"Family Ties" Darkness x-over pt. 1,4						4.00
18-Face to face variant-c, 18-American Ent. Ed., 19-AE Gold Ed.	1	2	3	5	6	8
20-25: 24-Pearson, Green-a. 25-($2.95) Turner-a(p)						4.00
25 (Prism variant)						30.00
25 (Special)						15.00
26-39: 26-Green-a begins						3.00
27 (Variant)						10.00
40-49,51-53: 40-Begin Jenkins & Veitch-s/Keu Cha-a. 47-Zulli-c/a						3.00
40-Pittsburgh Convention Preview edition; B&W preview of #40						3.00
49-Gold logo	1	2	3	5	6	8
50-($4.95) Darkness app.; Ching-a; B&W preview of Universe						5.00
54-59: 54-Black outer-c with gold foil logo; Wohl-s/Manapul-a						3.00
60-74,76-91,93-99: 60-($2.99) Endgame x-over with Tomb Raider #25 & Evo #1. 64,65-Magdalena app. 71-Kirk-a. 77,81-85-Land-c. 80-Four covers. 87-Bachalo-a						3.00
75-($4.99) Manapul-a						5.00
92-($4.99) Origin of the Witchblade; art by various incl. Bachalo, Perez, Linsner, Cooke						5.00
100-($4.99) Five covers incl. Turner, Silvestri, Linsner; art by various; Jake dies						5.00
101-124,126-143: 103-Danielle Baptiste gets the Witchblade; Linsner variant-c. 116-124, 140,141-Sejic-a. 126-128-War of the Witchblades. 134-136-Aphrodite IV app. 139-Gaydos-a. 143-Matt Dow Smith-a						3.00
125-($3.99) War of the Witchblades begins; 3 covers; Sejic-a						4.00
... and Tomb Raider (4/05, $2.99) Jae Lee-c; art by Lee and Texiera						3.00
...: Animated (8/03, $2.99) Magdalena & Darkness app.; Dini-s/Bone, Bullock, Cooke-a/c						3.00
... Annual 2009 (4/09, $3.99) Basaldua-a						4.00
... Annual #1 (12/10, $4.99) the Witchblade in Stalingrad 1942, Shasteen-a; Haley-a						5.00
...: Art of the Witchblade (7/06, $2.99) pin-ups by various incl. Turner, Land, Linsner						3.00
...: Bearers of the Blade (7/06, $2.99) pin-up/profiles of bearers of the Witchblade						3.00
...: Blood Oath (8/04, $4.99) Sara teams with Phenix & Sibilla; Roux-a						5.00
...: Blood Relations TPB (2003, $12.99) r/#54-58						13.00
... Compendium Vol. 1 (2006, $59.99) r/#1-50; gallery of variant covers and art						60.00
... Compendium Vol. 2 (2007, $59.99) r/#51-100; gallery of variant covers and art						60.00
... Cover Gallery Vol. 1 (12/05, $2.99) intro. by Stan Lee						3.00
.../Darkchylde (7/00, $2.50) Green-s/a(p)						3.00
.../Dark Minds (6/04, $9.99) new story plus r/Dark Minds/Witchblade #1						10.00
.../Darkness: Family Ties Collected Edition (10/98, $9.95) r/#18,19 and Darkness #9,10						10.00
.../Darkness Special (12/99, $3.95) Green-c/a						4.00
...: Demon 1 (2003, $6.99) Mark Millar-s/Jae Lee-c/a						7.00
.../Devi (4/08, $3.99) Basaldua-a/Land-c; continues in Devi/Witchblade						4.00
...: Distinctions (See Tales of the Witchblade)						
...: Due Process (8/10, $3.99) Alina Urusov-a/c; Phil Smith-s						4.00
.../Elektra (3/97, $2.95) Devil's Reign Pt. 6						4.00
... Gallery (11/00, $2.95) Profile pages and pin-ups by various; Turner-c						3.00
Image Firsts: Witchblade #1 (4/10, $1.00) reprints #1						1.00
Infinity (5/99, $3.50) Lobdell-s/Pollina-c/a						4.00
.../Lady Death (11/01, $4.95) Manapul-c/a						5.00
...: Prevailing TPB (2000, $14.95) r/#20-25; new Turner-c						15.00
...: Revelations TPB (2000, $24.95) r/#9-17; new Turner-c						25.00
.../The Punisher (6/07, $3.99) Marz-s/Melo-a/Linsner-c						4.00
.../Tomb Raider #1/2 (7/00, $2.95) Covers by Turner and Cha						4.00
...: Vol. 1 TPB (1/08, $4.99) r/#80-85; Marz intro.; cover gallery						5.00
...: Vol. 2 TPB (2/08, $14.99) r/#86-92; cover gallery						15.00
...: Vol. 3 TPB (3/08, $14.99) r/#93-100; Edginton intro.; cover gallery						15.00
... vs. Frankenstein: Monster War 2005 (8/05, $2.99) pt. 3 of x-over						3.00
...: Witch Hunt Vol. 1 TPB (2/06, $14.99) r/#80-85; Marz intro.; Choi afterward; cover gallery						15.00
Wizard #500						10.00
.../Wolverine (6/04, $2.99) Basaldua-c/a; Claremont-s						3.00

WITCHBLADE/ALIENS/THE DARKNESS/PREDATOR
Dark Horse Comics/Top Cow Productions: Nov, 2000 ($2.99)

	GD 2.0	VG 4.0	FN 6.0	VF 8.0	VF/NM 9.0	NM- 9.2
1-3-Mel Rubi-a						4.00

WITCHBLADE COLLECTED EDITION
Image Comics (Top Cow Productions): July, 1996 - No. 8 ($4.95/$6.95, squarebound, limited series)

	GD 2.0	VG 4.0	FN 6.0	VF 8.0	VF/NM 9.0	NM- 9.2
1-7-($4.95): Two issues reprinted in each						5.00
8-($6.95) r/#15-17						7.00
...Slipcase (10/96, $10.95)-Packaged w/ Coll. Ed. #1-4						11.00

WITCHBLADE: DESTINY'S CHILD
Image Comics (Top Cow): Jun, 2000 - No. 3, Sept, 2000 ($2.95, lim. series)

	GD 2.0	VG 4.0	FN 6.0	VF 8.0	VF/NM 9.0	NM- 9.2
1-3: 1-Boller-a/Keu Cha-c						3.00

WITCHBLADE: MANGA (Takeru Manga)
Image Comics (Top Cow): Feb, 2007 - No. 12, Mar, 2008 ($2.99/$3.99)

	GD 2.0	VG 4.0	FN 6.0	VF 8.0	VF/NM 9.0	NM- 9.2
1-4-Colored reprints of Japanese Witchblade manga. 1-Three covers. 2-Two covers						3.00
5-12-($3.99)						4.00

WITCHBLADE: OBAKEMONO
Image Comics (Top Cow Productions): 2002 ($9.95, one-shot graphic novel)

	GD 2.0	VG 4.0	FN 6.0	VF 8.0	VF/NM 9.0	NM- 9.2
1-Fiona Avery-s/Billy Tan-a; forward by Straczynski						10.00

WITCHBLADE: SHADES OF GRAY
Dynamite Ent./Top Cow: 2007 - No. 4, 2007 ($3.50, lim. series)

	GD 2.0	VG 4.0	FN 6.0	VF 8.0	VF/NM 9.0	NM- 9.2
1,2: 1-Sara Pezzini meets Dorian Gray; Segovia-a; multiple covers						3.50

WITCHBLADE/ TOMB RAIDER SPECIAL (Also see Tomb Raider/...)
Image Comics (Top Cow Productions): Dec, 1998 ($2.95)

	GD 2.0	VG 4.0	FN 6.0	VF 8.0	VF/NM 9.0	NM- 9.2
1-Based on video game character; Turner-a(p)						4.00
1-Silvestri variant-c						6.00
1-Turner bikini variant-c						10.00
1-Prism-c						12.00
Wizard 1/2 -Turner-s						10.00

WITCHCRAFT (See Strange Mysteries, Super Reprint #18)
Avon Periodicals: Mar-Apr, 1952 - No. 6, Mar, 1953

	GD 2.0	VG 4.0	FN 6.0	VF 8.0	VF/NM 9.0	NM- 9.2
1-Kubert-a; 1 pg. Check-a	74	148	222	470	810	1150
2-Kubert & Check-a; classic skull-c	53	106	159	334	567	800
3,6: 3-Lawrence-a; Kinstler inside-c	42	84	126	265	450	635
4-People cooked alive c/story	53	106	159	334	567	800
5-Kelly Freas painted-c	57	114	171	362	619	875

NOTE: ***Hollingsworth** a-4-6; c-4, 6. **McCann** a-3?*

WITCHCRAFT
DC Comics (Vertigo): June, 1994 - No. 3, Aug, 1994 ($2.95, limited series)

	GD 2.0	VG 4.0	FN 6.0	VF 8.0	VF/NM 9.0	NM- 9.2
1-3: James Robinson scripts & Kaluta-c in all						4.00
1-Platinum Edition						15.00
Trade paperback-(1996, $14.95)-r/#1-3; Kaluta-c						15.00

WITCHCRAFT: LA TERREUR
DC Comics (Vertigo): Apr, 1998 - No. 3, Jun, 1998 ($2.50, limited series)

	GD 2.0	VG 4.0	FN 6.0	VF 8.0	VF/NM 9.0	NM- 9.2
1-3: Robinson-s/Zulli & Locke-a; interlocking cover images						3.00

WITCHES
Marvel Comics: Aug, 2004 - No. 4, Sept, 2004 ($2.99, limited series)

	GD 2.0	VG 4.0	FN 6.0	VF 8.0	VF/NM 9.0	NM- 9.2
1-4: 1,2-Deodato, Jr-a; Dr. Strange app. 3,4-Conrad-a						3.00
... Vol. 1: The Gathering (2004, $9.99) r/series						10.00

WITCHES TALES (Witches Western Tales #29,30)
Witches Tales/Harvey Publications: Jan, 1951 - No. 28, Dec, 1954 (date misprinted as 4/55)

	GD 2.0	VG 4.0	FN 6.0	VF 8.0	VF/NM 9.0	NM- 9.2
1-Powell-a (1 pg.)	57	114	171	362	619	875
2-Eye injury panel	36	72	108	216	351	485
3-7,9,10	28	56	84	165	270	375
8-Eye injury panels	29	58	87	170	278	385
11-13,15,16: 12-Acid in face story	26	52	78	154	252	350
14,17-Powell/Nostrand-a. 17-Atomic disaster story	27	54	81	160	263	365
18-Nostrand-a; E.C. swipe/Shock S.S.	27	54	81	160	263	365
19-Nostrand-a; E.C. swipe/ "Glutton"; Devil-c	30	60	90	177	289	400
20-24-Nostrand-a. 21-E.C. swipe; rape story. 23-Wood E.C. swipes/Two-Fisted Tales #34	27	54	81	160	263	365

Witching Hour #30 © DC

Wizards of Mickey #8 © DIS

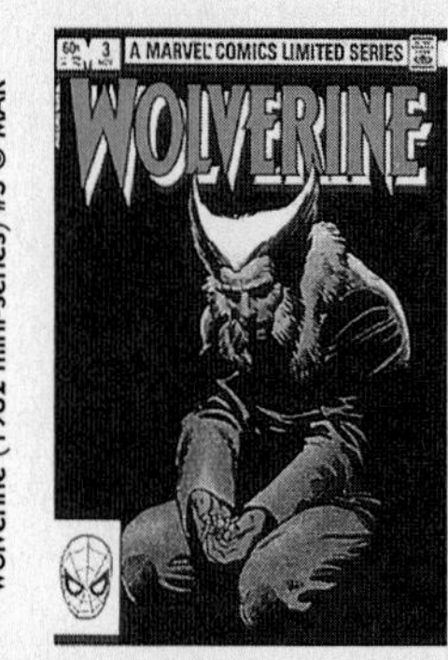

Wolverine (1982 mini-series) #3 © MAR

GD VG FN VF VF/NM NM-
2.0 4.0 6.0 8.0 9.0 9.2

25-Nostrand-a; E.C. swipe/Mad Barber; decapitation-c
47 94 141 296 498 700
26-28: 27-r/#6 with diff.-c. 28-r/#8 with diff.-c 19 38 57 111 176 240

NOTE: **Check** a-24. **Elias** c-8, 10, 16-27. **Kremer** a-18; c-25. **Nostrand** a-17-25; 14, 17(w/**Powell**). **Palais** a-1, 2, 4(2), 5(2), 7-9, 12, 14, 15, 17. **Powell** a-3-7, 10, 11, 19-27. Bondage-c 1, 3, 5, 6, 8, 9.

WITCHES TALES (Magazine)
Eerie Publications: V1#7, July, 1969 - V7#1, Feb, 1975 (B&W, 52 pgs.)

V1#7(7/69) 7 14 21 45 73 100
V1#8(9/69), 9(11/69) 6 12 18 37 59 80
V2#1-6('70), V3#1-6('71) 5 10 15 30 48 65
V4#1-6('72), V5#1-6('73), V6#1-6('74), V7#1 4 8 12 26 41 55

NOTE: *Ajax/Farrell reprints in early issues.*

WITCHES' WESTERN TALES (Formerly Witches Tales)(Western Tales #31 on)
Harvey Publications: No. 29, Feb, 1955 - No. 30, Apr, 1955

29,30-Featuring Clay Duncan & Boys' Ranch; S&K-r/from Boys' Ranch including-c.
29-Last pre-code 15 30 45 86 133 180

WITCHFINDER, THE
Image Comics (Liar): Sept, 1999 - No. 3, Jan, 2000 ($2.95)

1-3-Romano-a/Sharon & Matthew Scott-plot 3.00

WITCH HUNTER
Malibu Comics (Ultraverse): Apr, 1996 ($2.50, one-shot)

1 3.00

WITCHING, THE
DC Comics (Vertigo): Aug, 2004 - No. 10, May, 2005 ($2.95/$2.99)

1-10-Vankin-s/Gallagher-a/McPherson-c. 1,2-Lucifer app. 3.00

WITCHING HOUR ("The ..." in later issues)
National Periodical Publ./DC Comics: Feb-Mar, 1969 - No. 85, Oct, 1978

1-Toth-a, plus Neal Adams-a (2 pgs.) 13 26 39 94 185 275
2,6: 6-Toth-a 7 14 21 49 80 110
3,5-Wrightson-a; Toth-p. 3-Last 12¢ issue 8 16 24 52 86 120
4,12-Toth-a 5 10 15 35 55 75
7-11-Adams-c; Toth-a in all. 8-Adams-a 7 14 21 47 76 105
13-Neal Adams-c/a, 2pgs. 7 14 21 49 80 110
14-Williamson/Garzon, Jones-a; N. Adams-c 7 14 21 50 83 115
15 3 6 9 20 30 40
16-21-(52 pg. Giants) 4 8 12 24 37 50
22-37,39,40 3 6 9 14 19 24
38-(100 pgs.) 5 10 15 35 55 75
41-60 2 4 6 10 14 18
61-83,85 2 4 6 8 11 14
84-(44 pgs.) 2 4 6 9 13 16

NOTE: *Combined with The Unexpected with #189.* **Neal Adams** c-7-11, 13, 14. **Alcala** a-24, 27, 33, 41, 43. **Anderson** a-9, 38. **Cardy** c-4, 5. **Kaluta** a-7. **Kane** a-12p. **Morrow** a-10, 13, 15, 16. **Nino** a-31, 40, 45, 47. **Redondo** a-20, 23, 24, 34, 65; c-53. **Reese** a-23. **Sparling** a-1. **Toth** a-1, 3-12, 38r. **Tuska** a-11, 12. **Wood** a-15.

WITCHING HOUR, THE
DC Comics (Vertigo): 1999 - No. 3, 2000 ($5.95, limited series)

1-3-Bachalo & Thibert-c/a; Loeb & Bachalo-s 6.00
Hardcover (2000, $29.95) r/#1-3; embossed cover 30.00
Softcover (2003, $19.95), (2009, $19.99) r/#1-3 20.00

WITHIN OUR REACH
Star Reach Productions: 1991 ($7.95, 84 pgs.)

nn-Spider-Man, Concrete by Chadwick, Gift of the Magi by Russell; X-mas stories;
Chadwick-c; Spidey back-c 8.00

WITH THE MARINES ON THE BATTLEFRONTS OF THE WORLD
Toby Press: 1953 (no month) - No. 2, Mar, 1954 (Photo covers)

1-John Wayne story 29 58 87 172 281 390
2-Monty Hall in #1,2 10 20 30 58 79 100

WITH THE U.S. PARATROOPS BEHIND ENEMY LINES (Also see U.S. Paratroops...; #2-6 titled U.S. Paratroops...)
Avon Periodicals: 1951 - No. 6, Dec, 1952

1-Wood-c & inside f/c 17 34 51 98 154 210
2-Kinstler-c & inside f/c only 11 22 33 60 83 105
3-6: 6-Kinstler-c & inside f/c only 10 20 30 54 72 90

NOTE: **Kinstler** c-2, 4-6.

WITNESS, THE (Also see Amazing Mysteries, Captain America #71, Ideal #4, Marvel Mystery #92 & Mystic #7)
Marvel Comics (MjMe): Sept, 1948

1(Scarce)-Rico-c? 258 516 774 1651 2826 4000

GD VG FN VF VF/NM NM-
2.0 4.0 6.0 8.0 9.0 9.2

WITTY COMICS
Irwin H. Rubin Publ./Chicago Nite Life News No. 2: 1945 - No. 2, 1945

1-The Pioneer, Junior Patrol; Japanese war-c 30 60 90 177 289 400
2-The Pioneer, Junior Patrol 15 30 45 86 133 180

WIZARD OF FOURTH STREET, THE
Dark Horse Comics: Dec, 1987 - No. 2, 1988 ($1.75, B&W, limited series)

1,2: Adapts novel by S/F author Simon Hawke 3.00

WIZARD OF OZ (See Classics Illustrated Jr. 535, Dell Jr. Treasury No. 5, First Comics Graphic Novel, Marvelous..., & Marvel Treasury of Oz)
Dell Publishing Co.: No. 1308, Mar-May, 1962 (TV)

Four Color 1308 11 22 33 75 138 200

WIZARDS OF MICKEY (Mickey Mouse)
BOOM! Studios: Jan, 2010 - No. 8, Aug, 2010 ($2.99)

1-8: 1,2-Ambrosio-s; 3 covers on each. 3-8-Two covers 3.00

WIZARD'S TALE, THE
Image Comics (Homage Comics): 1997 ($19.95, squarebound, one-shot)

nn-Kurt Busiek-s/David Wenzel-painted-a/c 20.00

WOLF & RED
Dark Horse Comics: Apr, 1995 - No. 3, June, 1995 ($2.50, limited series)

1-3: Characters created by Tex Avery 3.00

WOLFF & BYRD, COUNSELORS OF THE MACABRE (Becomes Supernatural Law with issue #24)
Exhibit A Press: May, 1994 - No. 23, Aug, 1999 ($2.50, B&W)

1-23-Batton Lash-s/a 3.00

WOLF GAL (See Al Capp's...)

WOLFMAN, THE (See Movie Classics)

WOLFPACK
Marvel Comics: Feb, 1988 ($7.95); Aug, 1988 - No. 12, July, 1989 (Lim. series)

1-1st app./origin (Marvel Graphic Novel #31) 8.00
1-12 3.00

WOLVERINE (See Alpha Flight, Daredevil #196, 249, Ghost Rider; Wolverine; Punisher, Havok &..., Incredible Hulk #180, Incredible Hulk &..., Kitty Pryde And..., Marvel Comics Presents, New Avengers, Power Pack, Punisher and..., Rampaging ..., Spider-Man vs... & X-Men #94)

WOLVERINE (See Incredible Hulk #180 for 1st app.)
Marvel Comics Group: Sept, 1982 - No. 4, Dec, 1982 (limited series)

1-Frank Miller-c/a(p) in all; Claremont-s 5 10 15 34 55 75
2-4 4 8 12 26 41 55
... By Claremont & Miller HC (2006, $19.99) r/#1-4 & Uncanny X-Men #172-173 20.00
TPB 1(7/87, $4.95)-Reprints #1-4 with new Miller-c 2 4 6 10 14 18
TPB nn (2nd printing, $9.95)-r/#1-4 2 4 6 8 10 12

WOLVERINE
Marvel Comics: Nov, 1988 - No. 189, June, 2003 ($1.50/$1.75/$1.95/$1.99/$2.25)

1 4 8 12 22 34 45
2 2 4 6 13 18 22
3-5: 4-BWS back-c 2 4 6 9 13 16
6-9: 6-McFarlane back-c. 7,8-Hulk app. 1 3 4 6 8 10
10-1st battle with Sabretooth (before Wolverine had his claws)
3 6 9 16 23 30
11-16: 11-New costume 1 2 3 5 6 8
17-20: 17-Byrne-c/a(p) begins, ends #23 1 2 3 4 5 7
21-30: 24,25,27-Jim Lee-c. 26-Begin $1.75-c 5.00
31-40,44,47 4.00
41-Sabretooth claims to be Wolverine's father; Cable cameo 6.00
41-Gold 2nd printing ($1.75) 3.00
42-Sabretooth, Cable & Nick Fury app.; Sabretooth proven not to be Wolverine's father
1 2 3 5 6 8
42-Gold ink 2nd printing ($1.75) 3.00
43-Sabretooth cameo (2 panels); saga ends 5.00
45,46-Sabretooth-c/stories 5.00
48-51: 48,49-Sabretooth app. 48-Begin 3 part Weapon X sequel. 50-(64 pgs.)-Die cut-c; Wolverine back to old yellow costume; Forge, Cyclops, Jubilee, Jean Grey & Nick Fury app. 51-Sabretooth-c & app. 4.00
52-74,76-80: 54-Shatterstar (from X-Force) app. 55-Gambit, Jubilee, Sunfire-c/story. 55-57,73-Gambit app. 57-Mariko Yashida dies (Late 7/92). 58,59-Terror, Inc. x-over. 60-64-Sabretooth storyline (60,62,64-c) 4.00
75-($3.95, 68 pgs.)-Wolverine hologram on-c 5.00
81-84,86: 81-bound-in card sheet 3.00

Wolverine #132 © MAR

Wolverine V3 #75 © MAR

Wolverine V4 #1 © MAR

GD 2.0 | VG 4.0 | FN 6.0 | VF 8.0 | VF/NM 9.0 | NM- 9.2

85-($2.50)-Newsstand edition 3.00
85-($3.50)-Collectors edition 5.00
87-90 ($1.95)-Deluxe edition 3.50
87-90 ($1.50)-Regular edition 3.00
91-99,101-114: 91-Return from "Age of Apocalypse," 93-Juggernaut app. 94-Gen X app. 101-104-Elektra app. 104-Origin of Onslaught. 105-Onslaught x-over. 110-Shaman-c/app. 114-Alternate-c 3.00
100 ($3.95)-Hologram-c; Wolverine loses humanity 1 2 3 5 7 9
100 ($2.95)-Regular-c. 4.00
115-124: 115- Operation Zero Tolerance 3.00
125-($2.99) Wraparound-c; Viper secret 4.00
125-($6.95) Jae Lee variant-c 7.00
126-144: 126,127-Sabretooth-c/app. 128-Sabretooth & Shadowcat app.; Platt-a. 129-Wendigo-c/app. 131-Initial printing contained lettering error. 133-Begin Larsen-s/ Matsuda-a. 138-Galactus-c/app. 139-Cable app.; Yu-a. 142,143-Alpha Flight app. 3.00
145-($2.99) 25th Anniversary issue; Hulk and Sabretooth app. 4.00
145-($3.99) Foil enhanced cover (also see Promotional section for Nabisco mail-in ed.) 5.00
146-149: 147-Apocalypse: The Twelve; Angel-c/app. 149-Nova-c/app. 3.00
150-($2.99) Steve Skroce-s/a 4.00
151-174,176-182,184-189: 151-Begin $2.25-c. 154,155-Liefeld-s/a. 156-Churchill-a. 159-Chen-a begins. 160-Sabretooth app. 163-Texeira-a(p). 167-BWS-c. 172,173-Alpha Flight app. 176-Colossus app. 185,186-Punisher app. 3.00
175,183-($3.50) 175-Sabretooth app. 4.00
#(-1) Flashback (7/97) Logan meets Col. Fury; Nord-a 3.00
Annual nn (1990, $4.50, squarebound, 52 pgs.)-The Jungle Adventure; Simonson scripts; Mignola-c/a 5.00
Annual 2 (12/90, $4.95, squarebound, 52 pgs.)-Bloodlust 5.00
Annual nn (#3, 8/91, $5.95, 68 pgs.)-Rahne of Terror; Cable & The New Mutants app.; Andy Kubert-c/a (2nd print exists) 6.00
Annual '95 (1995, $3.95) 4.00
Annual '96 (1996, $2.95)- Wraparound-c; Silver Samurai, Yukio, and Red Ronin app. 4.00
Annual '97 ($2.99) - Wraparound-c 4.00
Annual 1999, 2000 ($3.50) : 1999-Deadpool app. 4.00
Annual 2001 ($2.99) - Tieri-s; JH Williams-c 4.00
...Battles The Incredible Hulk nn (1989, $4.95, squarebound, 52 pg.) r/Incr. Hulk #180,181 5.00
Best of Wolverine Vol. 1 HC (2004, $29.99) oversized reprints of Hulk #181, mini-series #1-4, Capt. America Ann, #8, Uncanny X-Men #205 & Marvel Comics Presents #72-84 30.00
...Black Rio (11/98, $5.99)-Casey-s/Oscar Jimenez-a 6.00
...Blood Debt TPB (7/01, $12.95)-r/#150-153; Skroce-c 13.00
...Blood Hungry nn (1993, $6.95, 68 pgs.)-Kieth-r/Marvel Comics Presents #85-92 w/ new Kieth-c 7.00
...: Bloody Choices nn (1993, $7.95, 68 pgs.)-r/Graphic Novel; Nick Fury app. 8.00
... Cable Guts and Glory (10/99, $5.99) Platt-a 6.00
... Classic Vol. 1 TPB (2005, $12.99) r/#1-5 13.00
... Classic Vol. 2 TPB (2005, $12.99) r/#6-10 13.00
... Classic Vol. 3 TPB (2006, $14.99) r/#11-16; The Gehenna Stone Affair 15.00
... Classic Vol. 4 TPB (2006, $14.99) r/#17-23 15.00
... Classic Vol. 5 TPB (2007, $14.99) r/#24-30 15.00
.../Deadpool: Weapon X TPB (7/02, $21.99)-r/#162-166 & Deadpool #57-60 22.00
... Doombringer (11/97, $5.99)-Silver Samurai-c/app. 6.00
... Evilution (9/94, $5.95) 6.00
...: Global Jeopardy 1 (12/93, $2.95, one-shot)-Embossed-c; Sub-Mariner, Zabu, Ka-Zar, Shanna & Wolverine app.; produced in cooperation with World Wildlife Fund 3.00
...:Inner Fury nn (1992, $5.95, 52 pgs.)-Sienkiewicz-c/a 6.00
...: Judgment Night (2000, $3.99) Shi app.; Battlebook 4.00
...: Killing (9/93)-Kent Williams-a 6.00
...: Knight of Terra (1995, $6.95)-Ostrander script 7.00
... Legends Vol. 2: Meltdown (2003, $19.99) r/Havok & Wolverine: Meltdown #1-4 20.00
... Legends Vol. 3 (2003, $12.99) r/#181-186 13.00
... Legends Vol. 4,5: 4-(See Wolverine: Xisle). 5-(See Wolverine: Snikt!)
... Legends Vol. 6: Marc Silvestri Book 1 (2004, $19.99) r/#31-34, 41-42, 48-50 20.00
.../ Nick Fury: The Scorpio Connection Hardcover (1989, $16.95) 25.00
.../ Nick Fury: The Scorpio Connection Softcover(1990, $12.95) 15.00
...: Not Dead Yet (12/98, $14.95, TPB)-r/#119-122 15.00
...: Save The Tiger 1 (7/92, $2.95, 84 pgs.)-Reprints Wolverine stories from Marvel Comics Presents #1-10 w/new Kieth-c 4.00
...Scorpio Rising ($5.95, prestige format, one-shot) 6.00
.../Shi: Dark Night of Judgment (Crusade Comics, 2000, $2.99) Tucci-a 34.00
...Triumphs And Tragedies-(1995, $16.95, trade paperback)-r/Uncanny X-Men #109,172,173, Wolverine limited series #4, & Wolverine #41,42,75 17.00
...Typhoid's Kiss (6/94, $6.95)-r/Wolverine stories from Marvel Comics Presents #109-116 7.00
...Vs. Spider-Man 1 (3/95, $2.50) -r/Marvel Comics Presents #48-50 4.00
.../Witchblade 1 (3/97, $2.95) Devil's Reign Pt. 5 4.00
Wizard #1/2 (1997) Joe Phillips-a(p) 10.00

GD 2.0 | VG 4.0 | FN 6.0 | VF 8.0 | VF/NM 9.0 | NM- 9.2

NOTE: ***Austin*** *c-3i.* ***Bolton*** *c(back)-5.* ***Buscema*** *a-1-16,25,27p; c-1-10.* ***Byrne*** *a-17-22p, 23; c-1(back), 17-22, 23p.* ***Colan*** *a-24.* ***Andy Kubert*** *c/a-51.* ***Jim Lee*** *c-24, 25, 27.* ***Silvestri*** *a(p)-31-43, 45, 46, 48-50, 52, 53, 55-57; c-31-42p, 43, 45p, 46p, 48, 49p, 50p, 52p, 53p, 55-57p.* ***Stroman*** *a-44p; c-60p.* ***Williamson*** *a-1i, 3-8i; c(i)-1, 3-6.*

WOLVERINE (Volume 3) (Titled Dark Wolverine from #75-90)(See Daken: Dark Wolverine)
Marvel Comics: July, 2003 - No. 90, Oct, 2010 ($2.25/$2.50/$2.99)

1-Rucka-s/Robertson-a 5.00
2-19: 6-Nightcrawler app. 13-16-Sabretooth app. 3.00
20-Millar-s/Romita, Jr.-a begin, Elektra app. 4.00
20-B&W variant-c 5.00
21-39: 21-Elektra-c/app. 23,24-Daredevil app. 26-28-Land-c. 29-Quesada-c; begin $2.50-c. 33-35-House of M. 36,37-Decimation. 36-Quesada-c. 39-Winter Soldier app. 3.00
40,43-48: 40-Begin $2.99-c; Winter Soldier app.; Texeira-a. 43-46-Civil War; Ramos-a. 45-Sub-Mariner app. 3.00
41,49-($3.99) 41-C.P. Smith-a/Stuart Moore-s 4.00
42-Civil War 5.00
50-($3.99) Sabretooth app.; Bianchi-a/c & Loeb-s begin; wraparound-c; McGuinness-a 4.00
50-($3.99) Variant Edition; uncolored art and cover; Bianchi pencil art page 4.00
51-55-(Regular and variant uncolored editions) Bianchi-a/Loeb-s; Sabretooth app. 3.00
55-EC-style variant-c by Greg Land 5.00
56-($3.99) Howard Chaykin-a/c 4.00
57-65: 57-61-Suydam Zombie-c; Chaykin-a. 62-65-Mystique app. 3.00
66-Old Man Logan begins; Millar-s/McNiven-a; McNiven wraparound-c 3.00
66-Variant-c by Michael Turner 5.00
66-Variant sketch-c by Michael Turner 20.00
66-2nd printing with McNiven variant-c of Logan and Hulk gang member 3.00
66-(5/10, $1.00) Reprint with "Marvel's Greatest Comics" on cover 1.00
67-74: 67-72-Old Man Logan (concludes in Wolverine: Old Man Logan Giant-Sized Special). 67-Intro. Ashley, Spider-Man's granddaughter.72-Red Skull app. 73,74-Andy Kubert-a 3.00
75-($3.99) Dark Reign, Daken as Wolverine on Osborn's team; Camuncoli-a 4.00
76-90: 76-86-Multiple covers for each. 76-Dark Reign; Yu-c. 82-84-Siege. 88,89-Franken-Castle x-over; Punisher app. 3.00
#900 (7/10, $4.99) Short stories by various incl. Finch, Rivera, Segovia, McGuinness 5.00
Annual 1 (12/07, $3.99) Hurwitz-s/Frusin-a 4.00
Annual 2 (11/08, $3.99) Swierczynski-s/Deodato-a/c 4.00
...: Blood & Sorrow TPB (2007, $13.99) r/#41,49, stories from Giant-Size Wolverine #1 and X-Men Unlimited #12 14.00
...: Chop Shop 1 (1/09, $2.99) Benson-s/Boschi-a/Hanuka-c 3.00
Civil War: Wolverine TPB (2007, $17.99) r/#42-48; gallery of B&W cover inks 18.00
... Dangerous Games 1 (8/08, $3.99) Spurrier-s/Oliver-a; Remender-s/Opena-a 4.00
...Enemy of the State HC Vol. 1 (2005, $19.99) r/#20-25; Ennis intro.; variant covers 20.00
...Enemy of the State HC Vol. 2 (2005, $19.99) r/#26-32 20.00
...Enemy of the State SC Vol. 1 (2005, $14.99) r/#20-25; Ennis intro.; variant covers 15.00
...Enemy of the State SC Vol. 2 (2006, $16.99) r/#26-32 17.00
...Enemy of the State - The Complete Edition (2006, $34.99) r/#20-32; Ennis intro.; sketch pages, variant covers and pin-up art 35.00
...: Evolution SC (2008, $14.99) r/#50-55 15.00
...: Flies to a Spider (2/09, $3.99) Bradstreet-c/Hurwitz-s/Opena-a 4.00
...: Killing Made Simple (10/08, $3.99) Yost-s/Turnbull-a 4.00
...: Mr. X (5/10, $3.99) Tieri-s/Diaz-a/Mattina-c 4.00
...: Old Man Logan Giant-Sized Special (11/09, $4.99) Continued from #72; cover gallery 5.00
...Origins & Endings HC (2006, $19.99) r/#36-40 20.00
...Origins & Endings SC (2006, $13.99) r/#36-40 14.00
...: Origin of an X-Man Free Comic Book Day 2009 (5/09) Gurihiru-a/McGuinness-c 2.50
...: Revolver (8/09, $3.99) Gischler-s/Pastoras-a 4.00
... Saga (2009, giveaway) history of the character in text and comic panels 3.00
...: Saudade (2008, $4.99) English adaptation of Wolverine story from French comic 5.00
...: Savage (4/10, $3.99) J. Scott Campbell-c; The Lizard app. 4.00
...Special: Firebreak (2/08, $3.99) Carey-s/Kolins-a; Lolos-a 4.00
...: Switchback 1 (3/09, $3.99) short stories; art by Pastoras & Doe 4.00
...: The Amazing Immortal Man & Other Bloody Tales (7/08, $3.99) Lapham short stories 4.00
...: The Anniversary (6/09, $3.99) Mariko flashback short stories; art by various 4.00
...: The Death of Wolverine HC (2008, $19.99) r/#56-61 20.00
...: The Road to Hell (11/10, $3.99) Previews new Wolverine titles and Generation Hope 4.00
...: Under the Boardwalk (2/10, $3.99) Coker-a 4.00
...Vol. 1: The Brotherhood (2003, $12.99) r/#1-6 13.00
...Vol. 2: Coyote Crossing (2004, $11.99) r/#7-11 12.00
... Weapon X Files (2009, $4.99) Handbook-style pages of Wolverine characters 5.00
...: Wendigo! 1 (3/10, $3.99) Gulacy-a; back-up with Thor 4.00

WOLVERINE (Volume 4)
Marvel Comics: Nov, 2010 - Present ($3.99)

1-5-Jae Lee-c/Guedes-a; Wolverine Goes to Hell. 1-Back-up with Silver Samurai 4.00
5.1-(4/11, $2.99) Aaron-s/Palo-a/Rivera-c 3.00
6-8-Jae Lee-c/Acuña-a; X-Men & Magneto app. 4.00

Wolverine and Jubilee #1 © MAR

Wolverine Origins #50 © MAR

Women of Marvel #2 © MAR

GD VG FN VF VF/NM NM-
2.0 4.0 6.0 8.0 9.0 9.2

#1000 (4/11, $4.99) Short stories by various incl. Palmiotti, Green, Luke Ross; Segovia-c 5.00

WOLVERINE AND JUBILEE
Marvel Comics: Mar, 2011 - No. 4, Jun, 2011 ($2.99, limited series)

1-4: 1-Vampire Jubilee; Kathryn Immonen-s/Phil Noto-a; Coipel-c 3.00

WOLVERINE AND POWER PACK
Marvel Comics: Jan, 2009 - No. 4, Apr, 2009 ($2.99, limited series)

1-4-Sumerak-s. 1,2-GuriHiru-a. 1-Sauron app. 3-Meet Wolverine as a child; Koblish-a 3.00

WOLVERINE AND THE PUNISHER: DAMAGING EVIDENCE
Marvel Comics: Oct, 1993 - No. 3, Dec, 1993 ($2.00, limited series)

1-3: 2,3-Indicia says "The Punisher and Wolverine..." 3.00

WOLVERINE/CAPTAIN AMERICA
Marvel Comics: Apr, 2004 - No. 4, Apr, 2004 ($2.99, limited series)

1-4-Derenick-a/c 3.00

WOLVERINE: DAYS OF FUTURE PAST
Marvel Comics: Dec, 1997 - No. 3, Feb, 1998 ($2.50, limited series)

1-3: J.F. Moore-s/Bennett-a 3.00

WOLVERINE/DOOP (Also see X-Force and X-Statix)(Reprinted in X-Statix Vol. 2)
Marvel Comics: July, 2003 - No. 2, July, 2003 ($2.99, limited series)

1,2-Peter Milligan-s/Darwyn Cooke & J. Bone-a 3.00

WOLVERINE: FIRST CLASS
Marvel Comics: May, 2008 - No. 21, Jan, 2010 ($2.99)

1-21: 1-Wolverine and Kitty Pryde's first mission; DiVito-a. 2,9-Sabretooth app. 3.00

WOLVERINE/GAMBIT: VICTIMS
Marvel Comics: Sept, 1995 - No. 4, Dec, 1995 ($2.95, limited series)

1-4: Jeph Loeb scripts & Tim Sale-a; foil-c 4.00

WOLVERINE/HERCULES: MYTHS, MONSTERS & MUTANTS
Marvel Comics: May, 2011 - No. 4 ($2.99, limited series)

1,2-Tieri-s/Santacruz-a/Jusko-c 3.00

WOLVERINE/HULK
Marvel Comics: Apr, 2002 - No. 4, July, 2002 ($3.50, limited series)

1-4-Sam Kieth-s/a/c 4.00
Wolverine Legends Vol. 1: Wolverine/Hulk (2003, $9.99, TPB) r/#1-4 10.00

WOLVERINE: MANIFEST DESTINY
Marvel Comics: Dec, 2008 - No. 4, Mar, 2009 ($2.99, limited series)

1-4-Aaron-s/Segovia-a 3.00

WOLVERINE: NETSUKE
Marvel Comics: Nov, 2002 - No. 4, Feb, 2003 ($3.99, limited series)

1-4-George Pratt-s/painted-a 4.00

WOLVERINE: NOIR (1930s Pulp-style)
Marvel Comics: Apr, 2009 - No. 4, Sept, 2009 ($3.99, limited series)

1-4-C.P. Smith-a/Stuart Moore; covers by Smith & Calero; alternate Logan as detective 4.00

WOLVERINE: ORIGINS
Marvel Comics: June, 2006 - No. 50, Sept, 2010 ($2.99)

1-15: 1-Daniel Way-s/Steve Dillon-a/Quesada-c 3.00
1-10-Variant covers. 1-Turner. 2-Quesada & Hitch. 3-Bianchi. 4-Dell'Otto. 7-Deodato 4.00
16-($3.99) Captain America WW2 app.; preview of Wolverine #56; r/X-Men #268 4.00
16-Variant-c by McGuinness 4.00
17-24: 17-20-Capt. America & Bucky app. 21-24-Deadpool app.; Bianchi-c 3.00
25-($3.99) Deadpool app.; Bianchi-c; r/Deadpool's 1st app. in New Mutants #98 4.00
26-49: 26-Origin of Dakan; Way-s/Segovia-a/Land-c. 28-Hulk & Wendigo app. 3.00
50-($3.99) Last issue; Nick Fury app. 4.00
Annual 1 (9/07, $3.99) Way-s/Andrews-a; flashback to 1932 4.00
... Vol. 1 - Born in Blood HC (2006, $19.99, dustjacket) r/#1-5; variant covers 20.00
... Vol. 1 - Born in Blood SC (2007, $13.99) r/#1-5; variant covers 14.00
... Vol. 2 - Savior HC (2007, $19.99, dustjacket) r/#6-10; variant covers 20.00
... Vol. 2 - Savior SC (2007, $13.99) r/#6-10; variant covers 14.00
... Vol. 3 - Swift & Terrible HC (2007, $19.99, dustjacket) r/#11-15 20.00
... Vol. 3 - Swift & Terrible SC (2007, $13.99) r/#11-15 14.00
... Vol. 4 - Our War HC (2008, $19.99, dustjacket) r/#16-20 & Annual #1 20.00
... Vol. 4 - Our War SC (2008, $14.99) r/#16-20 & Annual #1 15.00

WOLVERINE/PUNISHER
Marvel Comics: May, 2004 - No. 5, Sept, 2004 ($2.99, limited series)

1-5: Milligan-s/Weeks-a 3.00
... Vol. 1 TPB (2004, $13.99) r/series 14.00

WOLVERINE/PUNISHER REVELATIONS (Marvel Knights)
Marvel Comics: Jun, 1999 - No. 4, Sept, 1999 ($2.95, limited series)

1-4: Pat Lee-a(p) 4.00
...: Revelation (4/00, $14.95, TPB) r/#1-4 15.00

WOLVERINE SAGA
Marvel Comics: Sept, 1989 - No. 4, Mid-Dec, 1989 ($3.95, lim. series, 52 pgs.)

1-Gives history; Liefeld/Austin-c (front & back) 5.00
2-4: 2-Romita, Jr./Austin-c. 4-Kaluta-c 5.00

WOLVERINE: SNIKT!
Marvel Comics: July, 2003 - No. 5, Nov, 2003 ($2.99, limited series)

1-5-Manga-style; Tsutomu Nihei-s/a 3.00
Wolverine Legends Vol. 5: Snikt! TPB (2003, $13.99) r/#1-5 14.00

WOLVERINE: SOULTAKER
Marvel Comics: May, 2005 - No. 5, Aug, 2005 ($2.99, limited series)

1-5-Yoshida-s/Nagasawa-a/Terada-c; Yukio app. 3.00
TPB (2005, $13.99) r/#1-5 14.00

WOLVERINE: THE BEST THERE IS
Marvel Comics: Feb, 2011 - Present ($3.99)

1-5: 1,2-Huston-s/Ryp-a; covers by Hitch and Djurdjevic. 3-5-Hitch-c 4.00
... - Contagion 1 (6/11, $4.99) r/#1-3, cover gallery 5.00

WOLVERINE: THE END
Marvel Comics: Jan, 2004 - No. 6, Dec, 2004 ($2.99, limited series)

1-5-Jenkins-s/Castellini-a 3.00
1-Wizard World Texas variant-c 20.00
TPB (2005, $14.99) r/#1-5 15.00

WOLVERINE: THE ORIGIN
Marvel Comics: Nov, 2001 - No. 6, July, 2002 ($3.50, limited series)

1-Origin of Logan; Jenkins-s/Andy Kubert-a; Quesada-c 40.00
1-DF edition 60.00
2 15.00
3 9.00
4-6 6.00
HC (3/02, $34.95, 11" x 7-1/2") r/#1-6; dust jacket; sketch pages and treatments 35.00
HC (2006, $19.99) r/#1-6; dust jacket; sketch pages and treatments 20.00
SC (2002, $14.95) r/#1-6; afterwords by Jemas and Quesada 15.00

WOLVERINE WEAPON X
Marvel Comics: June, 2009 - No. 16, Oct, 2010 ($3.99)

1-16: 1-5,11-Aaron-s/Garney-a. 1-Four covers. 2,3-Two covers. 11-15-Deathlok app. 4.00

WOLVERINE: XISLE
Marvel Comics: June, 2003 - No. 5, June, 2003 ($2.50, weekly limited series)

1-5-Bruce Jones-s/Jorge Lucas-a 3.00
Wolverine Legends Vol. 4 TPB (2003, $13.99) r/ #1-5 14.00

WOMEN IN LOVE (A Feature Presentation #5)
Fox Features Synd./Hero Books: Aug, 1949 - No. 4, Feb, 1950

	GD 2.0	VG 4.0	FN 6.0	VF 8.0	VF/NM 9.0	NM- 9.2
1	34	68	102	199	325	450
2-Kamen/Feldstein-c	28	56	84	165	270	375
3	20	40	60	114	182	250
4-Wood-a	23	46	69	136	223	310

WOMEN IN LOVE (Thrilling Romances for Adults)
Ziff-Davis Publishing Co.: Winter, 1952 (25¢, 100 pgs.)

	GD 2.0	VG 4.0	FN 6.0	VF 8.0	VF/NM 9.0	NM- 9.2
nn-(Scarce)-Kinstler-a; painted-c	57	114	171	362	619	875

WOMEN OF MARVEL
Marvel Comics: 2006, 2007 ($24.99, TPB)

SC-Reprints 1st apps. of Dazzler, Ms. Marvel, Shanna, The Cat plus notable stories of other female Marvel characters; Mayhew-c 25.00
Vol. 2 (2007) More stories of female Marvel characters; Mayhew-c; cover process art 25.00

WOMEN OF MARVEL
Marvel Comics: Jan, 2011 - No. 2, Feb, 2011 ($3.99, limited series)

1,2-Short stories of female Marvel characters. 1-Pichelli-c. 2-Land-c 4.00

WOMEN OUTLAWS (My Love Memories #9 on)(Also see Red Circle)
Fox Features Syndicate: July, 1948 - No. 8, Sept, 1949

	GD 2.0	VG 4.0	FN 6.0	VF 8.0	VF/NM 9.0	NM- 9.2
1-Used in **SOTI**, illo "Giving children an image of American womanhood"; negligee panels	81	162	243	518	884	1250
2,3: 3-Kamenish-a	60	120	180	381	653	925
4-8	47	94	141	296	498	700

Wonder Comics #17 © BP

Wonder Girl #6 © DC

Wonder Woman #6 © DC

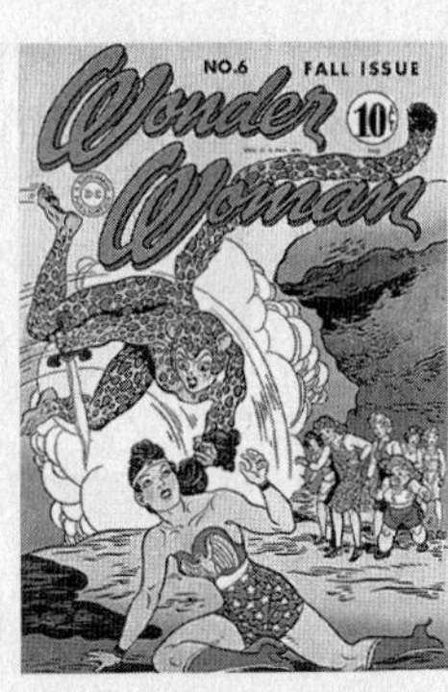

GD VG FN VF VF/NM NM-
2.0 4.0 6.0 8.0 9.0 9.2

nn(nd)-Contains Cody of the Pony Express; same cover as #7 22 44 66 132 216 300

WOMEN TO LOVE
Realistic: No date (1953)
nn-(Scarce)-Reprints Complete Romance #1; c-/Avon paperback #165 39 78 117 240 395 550

WONDER BOY (Formerly Terrific Comics) (See Blue Bolt, Bomber Comics & Samson)
Ajax/Farrell Publ.: No. 17, May, 1955 - No. 18, July, 1955 (Code approved)
17-Phantom Lady app. Bakerish-c/a 47 94 141 296 498 700
18-Phantom Lady app. 39 78 117 240 395 550
NOTE: *Phantom Lady not by Matt Baker.*

WONDER COMICS (Wonderworld #3 on)
Fox Features Syndicate: May, 1939 - No. 2, June, 1939 (68 pgs.)
1-(Scarce)-Wonder Man only app. by Will Eisner; Dr. Fung (by Powell), K-5 begins; Bob Kane-a; Eisner-c 1450 2900 4350 11,000 19,500 28,000
2-(Scarce)-Yarko the Great, Master Magician (see Samson) by Eisner begins; 'Spark' Stevens by Bob Kane, Patty O'Day, Tex Mason app. Lou Fine's 1st-c; Fine-a (2 pgs.); Yarko-c (Wonder Man-c #1) 486 972 1458 3550 6275 9000

WONDER COMICS
Great/Nedor/Better Publications: May, 1944 - No. 20, Oct, 1948
1-The Grim Reaper & Spectro, the Mind Reader begin; Hitler/Hirohito bondage-c 226 452 678 1446 2473 3500
2-Origin The Grim Reaper; Super Sleuths begin, end #8,17 81 162 243 518 884 1250
3-5: 3-Indicia reads "Vol. 1, #2" 73 146 219 467 796 1125
6-10: 6-Flag-c. 8-Last Spectro. 9-Wonderman begins 54 108 162 343 574 825
11-14: 11-Dick Devens, King of Futuria begins, ends #14. 11,12-Ingels-c & splash pg. 14-Bondage-c 68 136 204 435 743 1050
15-Tara begins (origin), ends #20 77 154 231 493 847 1200
16,18: 16-Spectro app.; last Grim Reaper. 18-The Silver Knight begins 68 136 204 435 743 1050
17-Wonderman with Frazetta panels; Jill Trent with all Frazetta inks 71 142 213 454 777 1100
19-Frazetta panels 68 136 204 435 743 1050
20-Most of Silver Knight by Frazetta 76 152 228 486 831 1175
NOTE: ***Ingels** c-11, 12. **Roussos** a-19. **Schomburg (Xela)** c-1-10; (airbrush)-13-20. Bondage c-12, 13, 15. Cover features: Grim Reaper #1-8; Wonder Man #9-15; Tara #16-20.*

WONDER DUCK (See Wisco)
Marvel Comics (CDS): Sept, 1949 - No. 3, Mar, 1950
1-Funny animal 17 34 51 98 154 210
2,3 12 24 36 69 97 125

WONDERFUL ADVENTURES OF PINOCCHIO, THE (See Movie Comics & Walt Disney Showcase #48)
Whitman Publishing Co.: April, 1982 (Walt Disney)
nn-(#3 Continuation of Movie Comics?); r/FC #92 6.00

WONDERFUL WIZARD OF OZ (Adaptation of the original 1900 L. Frank Baum book) (Also see the sequel Marvelous Land of Oz)
Marvel Comics: Feb, 2009 - No. 8, Sept, 2009 ($3.99, limited series)
1-8-Eric Shanower-a/Skottie Young-a/c 4.00
1-Variant Good Witch & Dorothy wraparound cover by J. Scott Campbell 8.00
1-Variant Scarecrow & Dorothy cover by Eric Shanower 10.00
1-(4/10, $1.00) Reprint with "Marvel's Greatest Comics" on cover 3.00
... Sketchbook (2008, giveaway) Young character design sketches; Shanower intro. 3.00
HC (2009, $29.99, dustjacket) r/#1-8; Shanower intro.; cover gallery; sketch art 30.00

WONDERFUL WORLD FOR BOYS AND GIRLS
DC Comics: May, 1964
nn - Ashcan comic, not distributed to newsstands, only for in-house use (no known sales)

WONDERFUL WORLD OF DISNEY, THE (Walt Disney)
Whitman Publishing Co.: 1978 (Digest, 116 pgs.)
1-Barks-a (reprints) 3 6 9 16 23 30
2 (no date) 2 4 6 11 16 20

WONDERFUL WORLD OF THE BROTHERS GRIMM (See Movie Comics)

WONDER GIRL (Cassandra Sandsmark from Teen Titans)
DC Comics: Nov, 2007 - No. 6, Apr, 2008 ($2.99, limited series)
1-6-Torres-s/Greene-a; Hercules app. 2-6-Female Furies app. 5,6-Wonder Woman app. 3.00
Teen Titans Spotlight: Wonder Girl TPB (2008, $17.99) r/#1-6 18.00
1-(3/11, $2.99, one-shot) Nicola Scott-c; intro. Solstice 3.00

WONDERLAND COMICS
Feature Publications/Prize: Summer, 1945 - No. 9, Feb-Mar, 1947
1-Alex in Wonderland begins; Howard Post-c 21 42 63 124 202 280
2-Howard Post-c/a(2) 14 28 42 76 108 140
3-9: 3,4-Post-c 11 22 33 60 83 105

WONDER MAN (See The Avengers #9, 151)
Marvel Comics Group: Mar, 1986 ($1.25, one-shot, 52 pgs.)
1 4.00

WONDER MAN
Marvel Comics Group: Sept, 1991 - No. 29, Jan, 1994 ($1.00)
1-29: 1-Free fold out poster by Johnson/Austin. 1-3-Johnson/Austin-c/a. 2-Avengers West Coast x-over. 4 Austin-c(i) 3.00
Annual 1 (1992, $2.25)-Immonen-a (10 pgs.) 4.00
Annual 2 (1993, $2.25)-Bagged w/trading card 4.00

WONDER MAN
Marvel Comics: Feb, 2007 - No. 5, June, 2007 ($2.99, limited series)
1-5: 1-Peter David-s/Andrew Currie-a; Beast app. 4-Nauck-a 3.00
...: My Fair Super Hero TPB (2007, $13.99) r/#1-5; Currie sketch page 14.00

WONDERS OF ALADDIN, THE
Dell Publishing Co.: No. 1255, Feb-Apr, 1962
Four Color 1255-Movie 6 12 18 43 69 95

WONDER WOMAN (See Adventure Comics #459, All-Star Comics, Brave & the Bold, DC Comics Presents, JLA, Justice League of America, Legend of..., Power Record Comics, Sensation Comics, Super Friends and World's Finest Comics #244)

WONDER WOMAN
DC Comics: Jan 1942
1-Ashcan comic, not distributed to newsstands, only for in-house use. Cover art is Sensation Comics #1 with interior being Sensation Comics #2. A CGC certified 8.5 copy sold for $17,250 in 2002.

WONDER WOMAN
National Periodical Publications/All-American Publ./DC Comics: Summer, 1942 - No. 329, Feb, 1986
1-Origin Wonder Woman retold (more detailed than All Star #8); H. G. Peter-c/a begins 2750 5500 8250 20,700 37,850 55,000
1-Reprint, Oversize 13-1/2x10". **WARNING:** This comic is an exact reprint of the original except for its size. DC published it in 1974 with a second cover titling it as a Famous First Edition. There have been many reported cases of the outer cover being removed and the interior sold as the original edition. The reprint with the new outer cover removed is practically worthless. See Famous First Edition for value.
2-Origin/1st app. Mars; Duke of Deception app. 432 864 1296 3154 5577 8000
3 271 542 813 1734 2967 4200
4,5: 5-1st Dr. Psycho app. 206 412 618 1318 2259 3200
6-9: 6-1st Cheetah app. 155 310 465 992 1696 2400
10-Invasion from Saturn classic sci-fi-c/s 161 322 483 1030 1765 2500
11-20 116 232 348 742 1271 1800
21-30: 23-Story from Wonder Woman's childhood 97 194 291 621 1061 1500
31-33,35-40: 38-Last H.G. Peter-c 77 154 231 493 847 1200
34-Robot-c 81 162 243 518 884 1250
41-44,46-48 68 136 204 435 743 1050
45-Origin retold 135 270 405 864 1482 2100
49-Used in **SOTI**, pgs. 234,236; last 52 pg. issue 69 138 207 442 759 1075
50-(44 pgs.)-Used in **POP**, pg. 97 69 138 207 442 759 1075
51-60: 60-New logo 61 122 183 390 670 950
61-72: 62-Origin of W.W. i.d. 64-Story about 3-D movies. 70-1st Angle Man app. 72-Last pre-code (2/55) 57 114 171 362 619 875
73-90: 80-Origin The Invisible Plane. 85-1st S.A. issue. 89-Flying saucer-c/story 50 100 150 315 533 750
91-94,96,97,99: 97-Last H. G. Peter-a 42 84 126 265 445 625
95-A-Bomb-c 43 86 129 271 461 650
98-New origin & new art team (Andru & Esposito) begin (5/58); origin W.W. id w/new facts 45 90 135 284 480 675
100-(8/58) 48 96 144 302 514 725
101-104,106,108-110 39 78 117 240 395 550
105-(Scarce, 4/59)-W. W.'s secret origin; W. W. appears as girl (no costume yet) (called Wonder Girl - see DC Super-Stars #1) 161 322 483 1030 1765 2500
107-1st advs. of Wonder Girl; 1st Merboy; tells how Wonder Woman won her costume 47 94 141 296 498 700
111-120 32 64 96 192 314 435
121-126: 121-1st app. Wonder Woman Family. 122-1st app. Wonder Tot. 124-Wonder Woman Family app. 126-Last 10¢ issue 27 54 81 158 259 360
127-130: 128-Origin The Invisible Plane retold. 129-3rd app. Wonder Woman Family

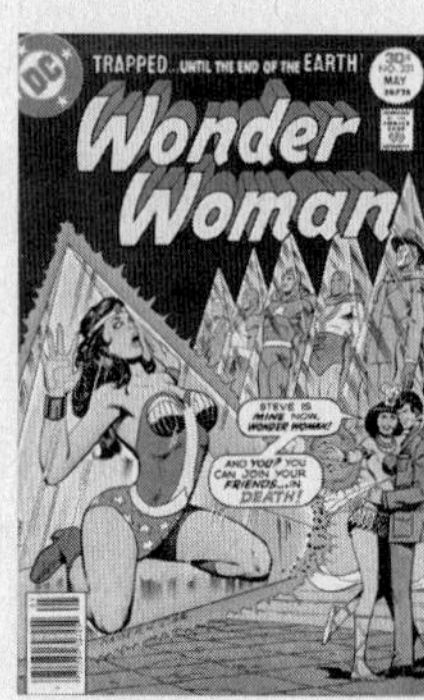

Wonder Woman #231 © DC

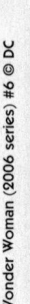

Wonder Woman (2006 series) #6 © DC

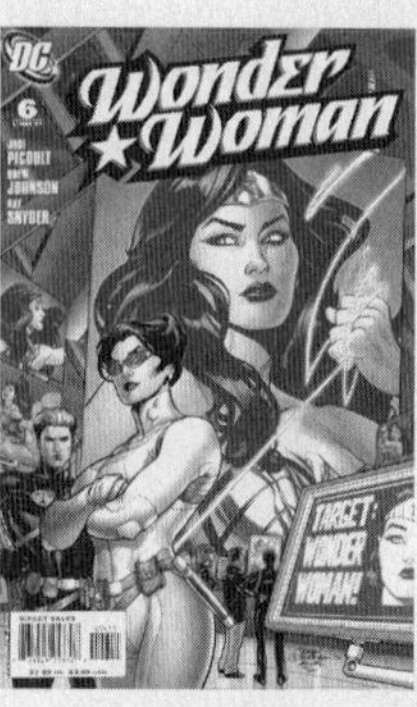

Wonder Woman #600 © DC

	GD 2.0	VG 4.0	FN 6.0	VF 8.0	VF/NM 9.0	NM- 9.2
(#133 is 4th app.)	13	26	39	94	185	275
131-150: 132-Flying saucer-c	12	24	36	82	154	225
151-155,157,158,160-170 (1967): 151-Wonder Girl solo issue	9	18	27	63	107	150
156-(8/65)-Early mention of a comic book shop & comic collecting; mentions DCs selling for $100 a copy	9	18	27	65	113	160
159-Origin retold (1/66); 1st S.A. origin?	10	20	30	72	131	190
171-176	7	14	21	49	80	110
177-W. Woman/Supergirl battle	9	18	27	63	107	150
178-1st new Wonder Woman on-c only; appears in old costume w/powers inside	9	18	27	64	110	155
179-Classic-c; wears no costume to issue #203	9	18	27	61	103	145
180-195: 180-Death of Steve Trevor. 182-Last 12¢ issue. 195-Wood inks	6	12	18	37	59	80
196 (52 pgs.)-Origin-r/All Star #8 (6 out of 9 pgs.)	6	12	18	39	62	85
197,198 (52 pgs.)-Reprints	6	12	18	39	62	85
199-Jeff Jones painted-c; 52 pgs.	8	16	24	58	97	135
200 (5-6/72)-Jeff Jones-c; 52 pgs.	9	18	27	61	103	145
201,202-Catwoman app. 202-Fafhrd & The Grey Mouser debut.	4	8	12	26	41	55
203,205-210,212: 212-The Cavalier app.	3	6	9	19	29	38
204-Return to old costume; death of I Ching.	4	8	12	26	41	55
211,214-(100 pgs.)	8	16	24	52	86	120
213,215,216,218-220: 220-N. Adams assist	3	6	9	17	25	32
217: (68 pgs.)	4	8	12	22	34	45
221,222,224-227,229,230,233-236,238-240	2	4	6	10	14	18
223,228,231,232,237,241,248: 223-Steve Trevor revived as Steve Howard & learns W.W.'s I.D. 228-Both Wonder Women team up & new World War II stories begin, end #243. 231,232: JSA app. 237-Origin retold. 240-G.A. Flash app. 241-Intro Bouncer; Spectre app. 248-Steve Trevor Howard dies (44 pgs.)	2	4	6	11	16	20
242-246,252-266,269,270: 243-Both W. Women team-up again. 269-Last Wood a(i) for DC? (7/80)	2	3	4	6	8	10
247,249-251,271: 247,249 (44 pgs.). 249-Hawkgirl app. 250-Origin/1st app. Orana, the new Wonder Woman. 251-Orana dies. 271-Huntress & 3rd Life of Steve Trevor begin	2	4	6	8	10	12
250-252,255-262,264-(Whitman variants, low print run, no issue # on cover)	2	4	6	11	16	20
267,268-Re-intro Animal Man (5/80 & 6/80)	2	4	6	8	10	12
272-280,284-286,289,290,294-299,301-325						6.00
281-283: Joker-c/stories in Huntress back-ups	2	3	4	6	8	10
287,288,291-293: 287-New Teen Titans x-over. 288-New costume & logo. 291-293-Three part epic with Super-Heroines	1	2	3	4	5	7
300-($1.50, 76 pgs.)-Anniv. issue; Giffen-a; New Teen Titans, Bronze Age Sandman, JLA & G.A. Wonder Woman app.; 1st app. Lyta Trevor who becomes Fury in All-Star Squadron #25; G.A. Wonder Woman & Steve Trevor revealed as married	1	2	3	5	7	9
326-328	1	2	3	4	5	7
329 (Double size)-S.A. W.W. & Steve Trevor wed	2	4	6	9	13	16
...: Chronicles Vol. 1 TPB (2010, $17.99) reprints debut in All Star Comics #8, apps. in Sensation Comics #1-9 and Wonder Woman #1						18.00
Diana Prince: Wonder Woman Vol. 1 TPB (2008, $19.99) r/#178-183						20.00
Diana Prince: Wonder Woman Vol. 2 TPB (2008, $19.99) r/#185-189, Brave and the Bold #87, and Superman's Girl Friend, Lois Lane #93						20.00
Diana Prince: Wonder Woman Vol. 3 TPB ('08, $19.99) r/#190-198, World's Finest #204						20.00
Diana Prince: Wonder Woman Vol. 4 TPB ('09, $19.99) r/#199-204, Brave & Bold #105						20.00
...: The Greatest Stories Ever Told TPB (2007, $19.99) intro. by Lynda Carter; Ross-c						20.00

NOTE: ***Andru/Esposito** c-66-160(most). **Buckler** a-300. **Colan** a-288-305p; c-288-290p. **Giffen** a-300p. **Grell** c-217. **Kaluta** c-297. **Gil Kane** c-294p, 303-305, 307, 312, 314. **Miller** c-298p. **Morrow** c-233. **Nasser** a-232p; c-231p, 232p. **Bob Oskner** c(i)-39-65(most). **Perez** c-283p, 284p. **Spiegle** a-312. **Staton** a(p)-241, 271-287, 289, 290, 294-299; c(p)-241, 245, 246. Huntress back-up stories 271-287, 289, 290, 294-299, 301-321.*

WONDER WOMAN

DC Comics: Feb, 1987 - No. 226, Apr, 2006 (75¢/$1.00/$1.25/$1.95/$1.99/$2.25/$2.50)

	GD 2.0	VG 4.0	FN 6.0	VF 8.0	VF/NM 9.0	NM- 9.2
0-(10/94) Zero Hour; released between #90 & #91						5.00
1-New origin; Perez-c/a begins	2	4	6	8	10	12
2-5						6.00
6-20: 9-Origin Cheetah. 12,13-Millennium x-over. 18,26-Free 16 pg. story						5.00
21-49: 24-Last Perez-a; scripts continue thru #62						4.00
50-($1.50, 52 pgs.)-New Titans, Justice League						5.00
51-62: Perez scripts. 60-Vs. Lobo; last Perez-c. 62-Last $1.00-c						4.00
63-New direction & Bolland-c begin; Deathstroke story continued from W. W. Special #1						5.00
64-84						3.00
85-1st Deodato-a; ends #100	3	5	7	10	12	14
86-88: 88-Superman-c & app.						6.00
89-97: 90-(9/94)-1st Artemis. 91-(11/94). 93-Hawkman app. 96-Joker-c						5.00
98,99						4.00
100 ($2.95, Newsstand)-Death of Artemis; Bolland-c ends.						4.00
100 ($3.95, Direct Market)-Death of Artemis; foil-c.						6.00
101-119, 121-125: 101-Begin $1.95-c; Byrne-c/a/scripts begin. 101-104-Darkseid app. 105-Phantom Stranger cameo. 106-108-Phantom Stranger & Demon app. 107,108-Arion app. 111-1st app. new Wonder Girl. 111,112-Vs. Doomsday. 112-Superman app. 113-Wonder Girl-c/app; Sugar & Spike app.						3.00
120 ($2.95)-Perez-c						4.00
126-149: 128-Hippolyta becomes new W.W. 130-133-Flash (Jay Garrick) & JSA app. 136-Diana returns to W.W. role; last Byrne issue. 137-Priest-s. 139-Luke-s/Paquette-a begin; Hughes-c thru #146						3.00
150-($2.95) Hughes-c/Clark-a; Zauriel app.						4.00
151-158-Hughes-c. 153-Superboy app.						3.00
159-163: 159-Begin $2.25-c. 160,161-Clayface app. 162,163-Aquaman app.						3.00
164-171: Phil Jimenez-s/a begin; Hughes-c; Batman app. 168,169-Pérez co-plot 169-Wraparound-c.170-Lois Lane-c/app.						3.00
172-Our Worlds at War; Hippolyta killed						4.00
173,174: 173-Our Worlds at War; Darkseid app. 174-Every DC heroine app.						3.00
175-($3.50) Joker: Last Laugh; JLA app.; Jim Lee-c						4.00
176-199: 177-Paradise Island returns. 179-Jimenez-c. 184,185-Hippolyta-c/app.; Hughes-c 186-Cheetah app. 189-Simonson-s/Ordway-a begin. 190-Diana's new look. 195-Rucka-s/Drew Johnson-a begin. 197-Flash-c/app. 198,199-Noto-c						3.00
200-($3.95) back-up stories in 1940s and 1960s styles; pin-ups by various						4.00
201-218,220-225: 203,204-Batman-c/app. 204-Matt Wagner-c. 212-JLA app. 214-Flash app. 215-Morales-a begins. 218-Begin $2.50-c. 220-Batman app.						3.00
219-Omac tie-in/Sacrifice pt. 4; Wonder Woman kills Max Lord; Superman app.						4.00
219-(2nd printing) Altered cover with red background						3.00
226-Last issue; flashbacks to meetings with Superman; Rucka-s/Richards-a						4.00
#1,000,000 (11/98) 853rd Century x-over; Deodato-c						3.00
Annual 1,2: 1 ('88, $1.50)-Art Adams-a. 2 ('89, $2.00, 68 pgs.)-All women artists issue; Perez-c(i)/a.						4.00
Annual 3 (1992, $2.50, 68 pgs.)-Quesada-c(p)						4.00
Annual 4 (1995, $3.50)-Year One						4.00
Annual 5 (1996, $2.95)-Legends of the Dead Earth story; Byrne scripts; Cockrum-a						4.00
Annual 6 (1997, $3.95)-Pulp Heroes						4.00
Annual 7,8 ('98,'99, $2.95)-7-Ghosts; Wrightson-c. 8-JLApe, A.Adams-c						4.00
...: Beauty and the Beasts TPB (2005, $19.95) r/#15-19 & Action Comics #600						20.00
...: Bitter Rivals TPB (2004, $13.95) r/#200-205; Jones-c						14.00
...: Challenge of the Gods TPB ('04, $19.95) r/#8-14; Pérez-s/a						20.00
...: Destiny Calling TPB (2006, $19.99) r/#20-24 & Annual #1; Pérez-c & pin-up gallery						20.00
...Donna Troy (6/98, $1.95) Girlfrenzy; Jimenez-a						3.00
...: Down To Earth TPB (2004, $14.95) r/#195-200; Greg Land-c						15.00
... 80-Page Giant 1 (2002, $4.95) reprints in format of 1960s' 80-Page Giants						5.00
...: Eyes of the Gorgon TPB ('05, $19.99) r/#206-213						20.00
Gallery (1996, $3.50)-Bolland-c; pin-ups by various						4.00
...: Gods and Mortals TPB ('04, $19.95) r/#1-7; Pérez-a						20.00
...: Gods of Gotham TPB ('01, $5.95) r/#164-167; Jimenez-s/a						6.00
...: Land of the Dead TPB ('06, $12.99) r/#214-217 & Flash #219						13.00
Lifelines TPB ('98, $9.95) r/#106-112; Byrne-c/a						10.00
...: Mission's End TPB ('06, $19.99) r/#218-226; cover gallery						20.00
...: Our Worlds at War (10/01, $2.95) History of the Amazons; Jae Lee-c						3.00
...: Paradise Found TPB ('03, $14.95) r/#171-177, Secret Files #3; Jimenez-s/a						15.00
...: Paradise Lost TPB ('02, $14.95) r/#164-170; Jimenez-s/a						15.00
Plus 1 (1/97, $2.95)-Jesse Quick-c/app.						4.00
Second Genesis TPB (1997, $9.95)-r/#101-105						10.00
Secret Files 1-3 (3/98, 7/99, 5/02; $4.95)						5.00
Special 1 (1992, $1.75, 52 pgs.)-Deathstroke-c/story continued in Wonder Woman #63						5.00
...: The Blue Amazon (2003, $6.95) Elseworlds; McKeever-a						7.00
The Challenge Of Artemis TPB (1996, $9.95)-r/#94-100; Deodato-c/a						10.00
...: The Once and Future Story (1998, $4.95) Trina Robbins-s/Doran & Guice-a						5.00

NOTE: ***Art Adams** a-Annual 1. **Byrne** c/a 101-107. **Bolton** a-Annual 1. **Deodato** a-85-100. **Perez** a-Annual 1; c-Annual 1(i). **Quesada** c(p)-Annual 3.*

WONDER WOMAN (Also see Amazons Attack mini-series)

DC Comics: Aug, 2006 - No. 44, Jul, 2010; No. 600, Aug, 2010 - Present ($2.99)

	GD 2.0	VG 4.0	FN 6.0	VF 8.0	VF/NM 9.0	NM- 9.2
1-Donna Troy as Wonder Woman after Infinite Crisis; Heinberg-s/Dodson-a/c						3.00
1-Variant-c by Adam Kubert						4.00
2-44: 2-4-Giganta & Hercules app. 6-Jodi Picoult-s begins. 8-Hippolyta returns. 9-12-Amazons Attack tie-in; JLA app. 14-17-Simone-s/Dodson-a/c. 20-23-Stalker app. 26-33-Rise of the Olympian. 40,41-Power Girl app.						3.00
14-DC Nation Convention giveaway edition						6.00
(Title re-numbered after #44, July 2010 to cumilative numbering of #600)						
600-(8/10, $4.99) Short stories and pin-ups by various incl. Pérez, Conner, Kramer, Jim Lee; intro. by Lynda Carter; debut of new costume; cover by Pérez						5.00
600-Variant cover by Adam Hughes						8.00

Wonderworld Comics #24 © FOX

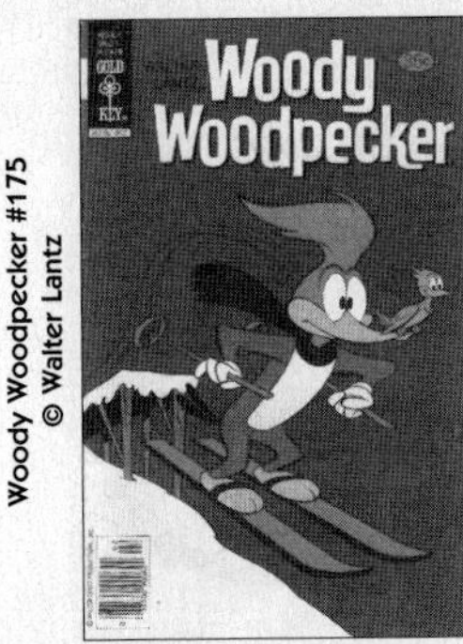

Woody Woodpecker #175 © Walter Lantz

World Around Us #1 © GIL

	GD 2.0	VG 4.0	FN 6.0	VF 8.0	VF/NM 9.0	NM- 9.2

600-2nd printing with new costume cover by Don Kramer 5.00
601-608: 601-606-Kramer-a; two covers by Kramer and Garner. 608-Borges-a 3.00
... Annual 1 (11/07, $3.99) Story cont'd from #4; Heinberg-s/Dodson-a/c; back-up Frank-a 4.00
...: Contagion SC (2010, $14.99) r/#40-44 15.00
...: Ends of the Earth HC (2009, $24.99) r/#20-25 25.00
...: Ends of the Earth SC (2010, $14.99) r/#20-25 15.00
...: Love and Murder HC (2007, $19.99) r/#6-10 20.00
...: Rise of the Olympian HC (2009, $24.99) r/#26-33 & pages from DC Universe #0 25.00
...: Rise of the Olympian SC (2009, $14.99) r/#26-33 & pages from DC Universe #0 15.00
...: The Circle HC (2008, $24.99) r/#14-19; Mercedes Lackey intro.;Dodson sketch pages 25.00
...: The Circle SC (2009, $14.99) r/#14-19; Mercedes Lackey intro.;Dodson sketch pages 15.00
...: Warkiller SC (2010, $14.99) r/#34-39 15.00
...: Who is Wonder Woman? HC (2007, $19.99) r/#1-4 & Annual #1; Vaughan intro. 20.00
...: Who is Wonder Woman? SC (2009, $14.99) r/#1-4 & Annual #1; Vaughan intro. 15.00

WONDER WOMAN: AMAZONIA
DC Comics: 1997 ($7.95, Graphic Album format, one shot)

1-Elseworlds; Messner-Loebs-s/Winslade-a 8.00

WONDER WOMAN SPECTACULAR (See DC Special Series #9)

WONDER WOMAN: SPIRIT OF TRUTH
DC Comics: Nov, 2001 ($9.95, treasury size, one-shot)

nn-Painted art by Alex Ross; story by Alex Ross and Paul Dini 10.00

WONDER WOMAN: THE HIKETEIA
DC Comics: 2002 ($24.95, hardcover, one-shot)

nn-Wonder Woman battles Batman; Greg Rucka-s/J.G. Jones-a 25.00
Softcover (2003, $17.95) 18.00

WONDERWORLD COMICS (Formerly Wonder Comics)
Fox Features Syndicate: No. 3, July, 1939 - No. 33, Jan, 1942

	GD 2.0	VG 4.0	FN 6.0	VF 8.0	VF/NM 9.0	NM- 9.2
3-Intro The Flame by Fine; Dr. Fung (Powell-a), K-51 (Powell-a?), & Yarko the Great, Master Magician (Eisner-a) continues; Eisner/Fine-c	703	1406	2109	5132	9066	13,000
4-Lou Fine-c	331	662	993	2317	4059	5800
5,6,9,10: Lou Fine-c	194	388	582	1242	2121	3000
7-Classic Lou Fine-c	326	652	978	2282	3991	5700
8-Classic Lou Fine-c	290	580	870	1856	3178	4500
11-Origin The Flame	148	296	444	947	1624	2300
12-15:13-Dr. Fung ends; last Fine-c(p)	119	238	357	762	1306	1850
16-20	87	174	261	553	952	1350
21-Origin The Black Lion & Cub	81	162	243	518	884	1250
22-27: 22,25-Dr. Fung app.	63	126	189	403	689	975
28-Origin & 1st app. U.S. Jones (8/41); Lu-Nar, the Moon Man begins	87	174	261	553	952	1350
29,31,33	52	104	156	328	552	775
30-Intro & Origin Flame Girl	92	184	276	584	1005	1425
32-Hitler-c	87	174	261	553	952	1350

NOTE: *Spies at War by **Eisner** in #13, 17. Yarko by **Eisner** in #3-11. **Eisner** text illos-3. **Lou Fine** a-3-11; c-3-13, 15(i); text illos-4. **Nordling** a-4-14. **Powell** a-3-12. **Tuska** a-5-9. Bondage-c 14, 15, 28, 31, 32. Cover features: The Flame-#3, 5-31; U.S. Jones-#32, 33.*

WONDERWORLDS
Innovation Publishing: 1992 ($3.50, squarebound, 100 pgs.)

1-Rebound super-hero comics, contents may vary; Hero Alliance, Terraformers, etc. 5.00

WOODSY OWL (See March of Comics #395)
Gold Key: Nov, 1973 - No. 10, Feb, 1976 (Some Whitman printings exist)

	GD 2.0	VG 4.0	FN 6.0	VF 8.0	VF/NM 9.0	NM- 9.2
1	2	4	6	13	18	22
2-10	2	4	6	8	10	12

WOODY WOODPECKER (Walter Lantz... #73 on?)(See Dell Giants for annuals)
(Also see The Funnies, Jolly Jingles, Kite Fun Book, New Funnies)
Dell Publishing Co./Gold Key No. 73-187/Whitman No. 188 on:
No. 169, 10/47 - No. 72, 5-7/62; No. 73, 10/62 - No. 201, 3/84 (nn 192)

	GD 2.0	VG 4.0	FN 6.0	VF 8.0	VF/NM 9.0	NM- 9.2
Four Color 169(#1)-Drug turns Woody into a Mr. Hyde	16	32	48	111	226	340
Four Color 188	11	22	33	75	138	200
Four Color 202,232,249,264,288	8	16	24	58	97	135
Four Color 305,336,350	6	12	18	41	66	90
Four Color 364,374,390,405,416,431('52)	5	10	15	34	55	75
16 (12-1/52-53) - 30('55)	4	8	12	28	44	60
31-50	4	8	12	22	34	45
51-72 (Last Dell)	3	6	9	18	27	35
73-75 (Giants, 84 pgs., Gold Key)	5	10	15	32	51	70
76-80	3	6	9	16	22	28
81-103: 103-Last 12¢ issue	3	6	9	14	19	24
104-120	2	4	6	11	16	20
121-140	2	4	6	9	12	15
141-160	1	3	4	6	8	10
161-187	1	2	3	5	7	9
188,189 (Whitman)	2	4	6	9	13	16
190(9/80),191(11/80)-pre-pack only	4	8	12	22	34	45
(No #192)						
193-197: 196(2/82), 197(4/82)	2	4	6	11	16	20
198-201 (All #90062 on-c, no date or date code, pre-pack): 198(6/83), 199(7/83), 200(8/83), 201(3/84)	3	6	9	16	22	28
Christmas Parade 1(11/68-Giant)(G.K.)	4	8	12	26	41	55
Summer Fun 1(6/66-G.K.)(84 pgs.)	5	10	15	30	48	65
nn (1971, 60¢, 100 pgs. digest) B&W one page gags	3	6	9	17	25	32

NOTE: *15¢ Canadian editions of the 12¢ issues exist. Reprints-No. 92, 102, 103, 105, 106, 124, 125, 152, 153, 157, 162, 165, 194(1/3)-200(1/3).*

WOODY WOODPECKER (See Comic Album #5,9,13, Dell Giant #24, 40, 54, Dell Giants, The Funnies, Golden Comics Digest #1, 3, 5, 8, 15, 16, 20, 24, 32, 37, 44, March of Comics #16, 34, 85, 93, 109, 124, 139, 158, 177, 184, 203, 222, 239, 249, 261, 420, 454, 466, 478, New Funnies & Super Book #12, 24)

WOODY WOODPECKER
Harvey Comics: Sept, 1991 - No. 15, Aug, 1994 ($1.25)

1-15: 1-r/W.W. #53 3.00
50th Anniversary Special 1 (10/91, $2.50, 68 pgs.) 4.00

WOODY WOODPECKER AND FRIENDS
Harvey Comics: Dec, 1991 - No. 4, 1992 ($1.25)

1-4 3.00

WORD WARRIORS (Also see Quest for Dreams Lost)
Literacy Volunteers of Chicago: 1987 ($1.50, B&W)(Proceeds donated to help literacy)

1-Jon Sable by Grell, Ms. Tree, Streetwolf; Chaykin-c 3.00

WORLD AROUND US, THE (Illustrated Story of...)
Gilberton Publishers (Classics Illustrated): Sep, 1958 -No. 36, Oct, 1961 (25¢)

	GD 2.0	VG 4.0	FN 6.0	VF 8.0	VF/NM 9.0	NM- 9.2
1-Dogs; Evans-a	9	18	27	52	69	85
2-4: 2-Indians; Check-a. 3-Horses; L. B. Cole-c. 4-Railroads; L. B. Cole-a (5 pgs.)	9	18	27	47	61	75
5-Space; Ingels-a	10	20	30	56	76	95
6-The F.B.I.; Disbrow, Evans, Ingels-a	10	20	30	56	76	95
7-Pirates; Disbrow, Ingels, Kinstler-a	9	18	27	52	69	85
8-Flight; Evans, Ingels, Crandall-a	9	18	27	52	69	85
9-Army; Disbrow, Ingels, Orlando-a	9	18	27	47	61	75
10-13: 10-Navy; Disbrow, Kinstler-a. 11-Marine Corps. 12-Coast Guard; Ingels-a (9 pgs.). 13-Air Force; L.B. Cole-c	9	18	27	47	61	75
14-French Revolution; Crandall, Evans, Kinstler-a	10	20	30	56	76	95
15-Prehistoric Animals; Al Williamson-a, 6 & 10 pgs. plus Morrow-a	10	20	30	58	79	100
16-18: 16-Crusades; Kinstler-a. 17-Festivals; Evans, Crandall-a. 18-Great Scientists; Crandall, Evans, Torres, Williamson, Morrow-a	9	18	27	52	69	85
19-Jungle; Crandall, Williamson, Morrow-a	10	20	30	58	79	100
20-Communications; Crandall, Evans, Torres-a	10	20	30	56	76	95
21-American Presidents; Crandall/Evans, Morrow-a	10	20	30	56	76	95
22-Boating; Morrow-a	8	16	24	44	57	70
23-Great Explorers; Crandall, Evans-a	9	18	27	52	69	85
24-Ghosts; Morrow, Evans-a	10	20	30	56	76	95
25-Magic; Evans, Morrow-a	10	20	30	56	76	95
26-The Civil War	11	22	33	62	86	110
27-Mountains (High Advs.); Crandall/Evans, Morrow, Torres-a	9	18	27	52	69	85
28-Whaling; Crandall, Evans, Morrow, Torres, Wildey-a; L.B. Cole-c	9	18	27	52	69	85
29-Vikings; Crandall, Evans, Torres, Morrow-a	10	20	30	58	79	100
30-Undersea Adventure; Crandall/Evans, Kirby, Morrow, Torres-a	10	20	30	56	76	95
31-Hunting; Crandall/Evans, Ingels, Kinstler, Kirby-a	9	18	27	52	69	85
32,33: 32-For Gold & Glory; Morrow, Kirby, Crandall, Evans-a. 33-Famous Teens; Torres, Crandall, Evans-a	9	18	27	52	69	85
34-36: 34-Fishing; Crandall/Evans-a. 35-Spies; Kirby, Morrow?, Evans-a. 36-Fight for Life (Medicine); Kirby-a	9	18	27	52	69	85

NOTE: See Classics Illustrated Special Edition. Another *World Around Us* issue entitled *The Sea* had been prepared in 1962 but was never published in the U.S. It was published in the British/European *World Around Us* series. Those series then continued with seven additional WAU titles not in the U.S. series.

WORLD BELOW, THE
Dark Horse Comics: Mar, 1999 - No. 4, Jun, 1999 ($2.50, limited series)

1-4-Paul Chadwick-s/c/a 3.00
TPB (1/07, $12.95) r/#1-4; intro. by Chadwick; gallery of sketches and covers 13.00

World of Mystery #6 © MAR

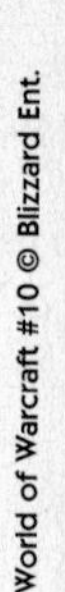

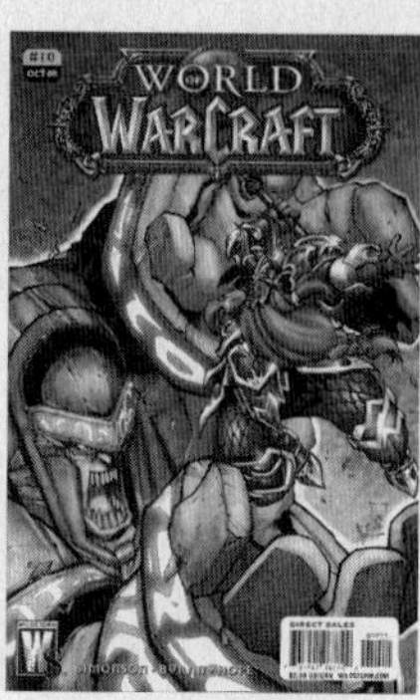

World of Warcraft #10 © Blizzard Ent.

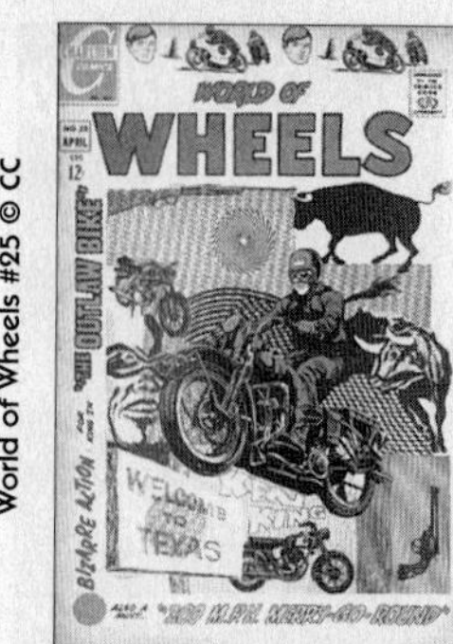

World of Wheels #25 © CC

	GD 2.0	VG 4.0	FN 6.0	VF 8.0	VF/NM 9.0	NM- 9.2

WORLD BELOW, THE: DEEPER AND STRANGER
Dark Horse Comics: Dec, 1999 - No. 4, Mar, 2000 ($2.95, B&W)

1-4-Paul Chadwick-s/c/a 3.00

WORLD FAMOUS HEROES MAGAZINE
Comic Corp. of America (Centaur): Oct, 1941 - No. 4, Apr, 1942 (comic book)

	GD	VG	FN	VF	VF/NM	NM-
1-Gustavson-c; Lubbers, Glanzman-a; Davy Crockett, Paul Revere, Lewis & Clark, John Paul Jones stories; Flag-c	110	220	330	704	1202	1700
2-Lou Gehrig life story; Lubbers-a	47	94	141	296	498	700
3,4-Lubbers-a. 4-Wild Bill Hickok story; 2 pg. Marlene Dietrich story	43	86	129	271	461	650

WORLD FAMOUS STORIES
Croyden Publishers: 1945

	GD	VG	FN	VF	VF/NM	NM-
1-Ali Baba, Hansel & Gretel, Rip Van Winkle, Mid-Summer Night's Dream	14	28	42	76	108	140

WORLD IS HIS PARISH, THE
George A. Pflaum: 1953 (15¢)

	GD	VG	FN	VF	VF/NM	NM-
nn-The story of Pope Pius XII	6	12	18	31	38	45

WORLD OF ADVENTURE (Walt Disney's...)(TV)
Gold Key: Apr, 1963 - No. 3, Oct, 1963 (12¢)

	GD	VG	FN	VF	VF/NM	NM-
1-Disney TV characters; Savage Sam, Johnny Shiloh, Capt. Nemo, The Mooncussers	3	6	9	21	32	42
2,3	3	6	9	15	21	26

WORLD OF ARCHIE, THE (See Archie Giant Series Mag. #148, 151, 156, 160, 165, 171, 177, 182, 188, 193, 200, 208, 213, 225, 232, 237, 244, 249, 456, 461, 468, 473, 480, 485, 492, 497, 504, 509, 516, 521, 532, 543, 554, 565, 574, 587, 599, 612, 627)

WORLD OF ARCHIE
Archie Comics: Aug, 1992 - No. 22 ($1.25/$1.50)

1 4.00
2-15: 9-Neon ink-c 3.00
16-22 3.00

WORLD OF ARCHIE DOUBLE DIGEST MAGAZINE
Archie Comics: Dec, 2010 - Present ($3.99)

1-7: 5-Reprints Tiny Titans/Little Archie #1-3 with sketch pages 4.00

WORLD OF FANTASY
Atlas Comics (CPC No. 1-15/ZPC No. 16-19): May, 1956 - No. 19, Aug, 1959

	GD	VG	FN	VF	VF/NM	NM-
1	48	96	144	302	514	725
2-Williamson-a (4 pgs.)	32	64	96	188	307	425
3-Sid Check, Roussos-a	28	56	84	165	270	375
4-7	22	44	66	132	216	300
8-Matt Fox, Orlando, Berg-a	24	48	72	142	234	325
9-Krigstein-a	22	44	66	132	216	300
10-15: 10-Colan-a. 11-Torres-a	20	40	60	114	182	250
16-Williamson-a (4 pgs.); Ditko, Kirby-a	28	56	84	165	270	375
17-19-Ditko, Kirby-a	28	56	84	165	270	375

NOTE: ***Ayers** a-3. **B. Baily** a-4. **Berg** a-5, 6, 8. **Brodsky** c-3. **Check** a-3. **Ditko** a-17, 19. **Everett** a-2; c-4-7, 9, 12, 13. **Forte** a-4, 8. **Infantino** a-14. **Kirby** c-15, 17-19. **Krigstein** a-9. **Maneely** c-2, 14. **Mooney** a-14. **Morrow** a-7. **Orlando** a-8, 13, 14. **Pakula** a-9. **Powell** a-4, 6. **Reinman** a-8, 10. **R.Q. Sale** a-3, 7, 9, 10. **Severin** c-1.*

WORLD OF GIANT COMICS, THE (See Archie All-Star Specials under Archie Comics)

WORLD OF GINGER FOX, THE (Also see Ginger Fox)
Comico: Nov, 1986 ($6.95, 8 1/2 x 11", 68 pgs., mature)

Graphic Novel ($6.95) 7.00
Hardcover ($27.95) 28.00

WORLD OF JUGHEAD, THE (See Archie Giant Series Mag. #9, 14, 19, 24, 30, 136, 143, 149, 152, 157, 161, 166, 172, 178, 183, 189, 194, 202, 209, 215, 227, 233, 239, 245, 251, 457, 463, 469, 475, 481, 487, 493, 499, 505, 511, 517, 523, 531, 542, 553, 564, 577, 590, 602)

WORLD OF KRYPTON, THE (World of...#3) (See Superman #248)
DC Comics, Inc.: 7/79 - No. 3, 9/79; 12/87 - No. 4, 3/88 (Both are lim. series)

1-3 (1979, 40¢; 1st comic book mini-series): 1-Jor-El marries Lara. 3-Baby Superman sent to Earth; Krypton explodes; Mon-el app. 6.00
1-4 (75¢)-Byrne scripts; Byrne/Simonson-c 4.00

WORLD OF METROPOLIS, THE
DC Comics: Aug, 1988 - No. 4, July, 1988 ($1.00, limited series)

1-4: Byrne scripts 4.00

WORLD OF MYSTERY
Atlas Comics (GPI): June, 1956 - No. 7, July, 1957

	GD	VG	FN	VF	VF/NM	NM-
1-Torres, Orlando-a; Powell-a?	47	94	141	296	498	700
2-Woodish-a	20	40	60	120	195	270
3-Torres, Davis, Ditko-a	24	48	72	140	230	320
4-Pakula, Powell-a	24	48	72	140	230	320
5,7: 5-Orlando-a	20	40	60	117	189	260
6-Williamson/Mayo-a (4 pgs.); Ditko-a; Colan-a; Crandall text illo	24	48	72	140	230	320

NOTE: ***Ayers** a-4. **Brodsky** c-2, 5, 6. **Colan** a-6, 7. **Everett** c-1, 3. **Pakula** a-4, 6. **Romita** a-2. **Severin** c-7.*

WORLD OF SMALLVILLE
DC Comics: Apr, 1988 - No. 4, July, 1988 (75¢, limited series)

1-4: Byrne scripts 4.00

WORLD OF SUSPENSE
Atlas News Co.: Apr, 1956 - No. 8, July, 1957

	GD	VG	FN	VF	VF/NM	NM-
1	41	82	123	256	428	600
2-Ditko-a (4 pgs.)	24	48	72	140	230	320
3,7-Williamson-a in both (4 pgs.); #7-with Mayo	23	46	69	136	223	310
4-6,8	20	40	60	117	189	260

NOTE: ***Berg** a-6. **Cameron** a-2. **Ditko** a-2. **Drucker** a-1. **Everett** a-1, 5; c-6. **Heck** a-5. **Maneely** a-1; c-1-3. **Orlando** a-5. **Powell** a-6. **Reinman** a-4. **Roussos** a-6. **Shores** a-1.*

WORLD OF WARCRAFT (Based on the Blizzard Entertainment video game)
DC Comics (WildStorm): Jan, 2008 - No. 25, Jan, 2010 ($2.99)

1-Walt Simonson-s/Lullabi-a; cover by Samwise Didier 8.00
1-Variant cover by Jim Lee 12.00
1,2-Second printing with Jim Lee sketch cover 5.00
2-Two covers by Jim Lee and Samwise Didier 5.00
3-24: 3-14-Two covers on each 3.00
25-($3.99) Walt & Louise Simonson-s 4.00
... Special 1 (2/10, $3.99) Costa-s/Mhan-a/c 4.00
... Book One HC (2008, $19.99, dustjacket) r/#1-7; intro. by Chris Metzen of Blizzard 20.00
... Book One SC (2009, $14.99) r/#1-7; intro. by Chris Metzen of Blizzard 15.00
... Book Two HC (2009, $19.99, dustjacket) r/#8-14 20.00
... Book Two SC (2010, $14.99) r/#8-14 15.00
... Book Three HC (2010, $19.99, dustjacket) r/#15-21 20.00

WORLD OF WARCRAFT: ASHBRINGER
DC Comics (WildStorm): Nov, 2008 - No. 4, Feb, 2009 ($3.99)

1-4-Neilson-s/Lullabi & Washington-a; 2 covers by Robinson & Lullabi 4.00
TPB (2010, $14.99) r/#1-4 15.00

WORLD OF WARCRAFT: CURSE OF THE WORGEN
DC Comics (WildStorm #1,2): Jan, 2011 - No. 5 ($3.99/$2.99)

1,2-($3.99) Neilson & Waugh-s/Lullabi & Washington-a; Polidora-c 4.00
3,4-($2.99) 3.00

WORLD OF WHEELS (Formerly Dragstrip Hotrodders)
Charlton Comics: No. 17, Oct, 1967 - No. 32, June, 1970

	GD	VG	FN	VF	VF/NM	NM-
17-20-Features Ken King	3	6	9	18	27	35
21-32-Features Ken King	3	6	9	16	22	28

Modern Comics Reprint 23(1978) 6.00

WORLD OF WOOD
Eclipse Comics: 1986 - No. 4, 1987; No. 5, 2/89 ($1.75, limited series)

1-4:1-Dave Stevens-c. 2-Wood/Stevens-c 5.00
5 ($2.00, B&W)-r/Avon's Flying Saucers 5.00

WORLD'S BEST COMICS
DC Comics: Feb 1940

nn - Ashcan comic, not distributed to newsstands, only for in-house use. Cover art is Action Comics #29 with interior being Action Comics #24. One copy sold for $21,000 in 2000.

WORLD'S BEST COMICS (World's Finest Comics #2 on)
National Per. Publications (100 pgs.): Spring, 1941 (Cardboard-c)(DC's 6th annual format comic)

	GD	VG	FN	VF	VF/NM	NM-
1-The Batman, Superman, Crimson Avenger, Johnny Thunder, The King, Young Dr. Davis, Zatara, Lando, Man of Magic, & Red, White & Blue begin; Superman, Batman & Robin covers begin (inside-c is blank); Fred Ray-c; 15¢ cover price	1475	2950	4425	10,400	17,700	25,000

WORLD'S BEST COMICS: GOLDEN AGE SAMPLER
DC Comics: 2003 (99¢, one-shot, samples from DC Archive editions)

1-Golden Age reprints from Superman #6, Batman #5, Sensation #11, Police #11 3.00

WORLD'S BEST COMICS: SILVER AGE SAMPLER
DC Comics: 2004 (99¢, one-shot, samples from DC Archive editions)

1-Silver Age reprints from Justice League #4, Adventure #247, Our Army at War #81 3.00

WORLDS BEYOND (Stories of Weird Adventure)(Worlds of Fear #2 on)
Fawcett Publications: Nov, 1951

World's Finest Comics #2 © DC

World's Finest Comics #90 © DC

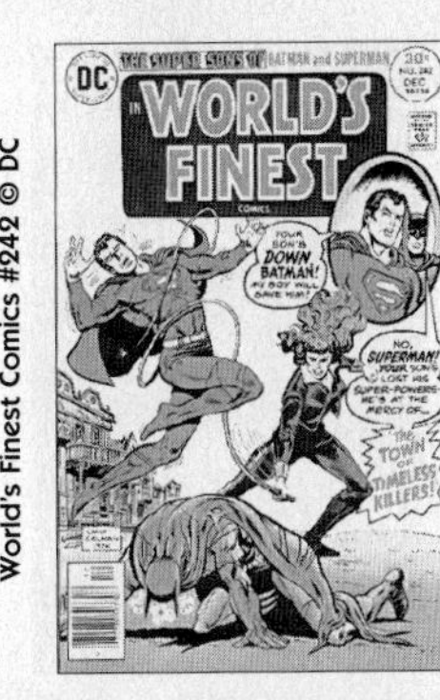

World's Finest Comics #242 © DC

GD VG FN VF VF/NM NM-
2.0 4.0 6.0 8.0 9.0 9.2

GD VG FN VF VF/NM NM-
2.0 4.0 6.0 8.0 9.0 9.2

1-Powell, Bailey-a; Moldoff-c 53 106 159 334 567 800

WORLDS COLLIDE
DC Comics: July, 1994 ($2.50, one-shot)
1-($2.50, 52 pgs.)-Milestone & Superman titles x-over 4.00
1-($3.95, 52 pgs.)-Polybagged w/vinyl clings 5.00

WORLD'S FAIR COMICS (See New York...)

WORLD'S FINEST (Also see Legends of The World's Finest)
DC Comics: 1990 - No. 3, 1990 ($3.95, squarebound, limited series, 52 pgs.)
1-3: Batman & Superman team-up against The Joker and Lex Luthor; Dave Gibbons scripts & Steve Rude-c/a. 2,3-Joker/Luthor painted-c by Steve Rude 5.00
TPB-(1992, $19.95) r/#1-3; Gibbons intro. 20.00
...: The Deluxe Edition HC (2008, $29.99) r/#1-3; Gibbons intro. from 1992; Gibbons story outline and sketches; Rude sketch pages and notes 30.00

WORLD'S FINEST
DC Comics: Dec, 2009 - No. 4, Mar, 2010 ($2.99, limited series)
1-4: Gates-s/two covers by Noto on each. 3-Supergirl/Batgirl team up. 4-Noto-a 3.00
TPB (2010, $14.99) r/#1-4, Action Comics #865 & DC Comics Presents #31 15.00

WORLD'S FINEST COMICS (Formerly World's Best Comics #1)
National Periodical Publ./DC Comics: No. 2, Sum, 1941 - No. 323, Jan, 1986 (#1-17 have cardboard covers) (#2-9 have 100 pgs.)
2 (100 pgs.)-Superman, Batman & Robin covers continue from World's Best; (cover price 15¢ #2-70) 423 846 1269 3000 5250 7500
3-The Sandman begins; last Johnny Thunder; origin & 1st app. The Scarecrow 320 640 960 2240 3920 5600
4-Hop Harrigan app.; last Young Dr. Davis 245 490 735 1568 2684 3800
5-Intro. TNT & Dan the Dyna-Mite; last King & Crimson Avenger 245 490 735 1568 2684 3800
6-Star Spangled Kid begins (Sum/42); Aquaman app.; S&K Sandman with Sandy in new costume begins, ends #7 181 362 543 1158 1979 2800
7-Green Arrow begins (Fall/42); last Lando & Red, White & Blue; S&K art 181 362 543 1158 1979 2800
8-Boy Commandos begin (by Simon(p) #12); last The King; includes "Minute Man Answers the Call" promo 171 342 513 1086 1868 2650
9-Batman cameo in Star Spangled Kid; S&K-a; last 100 pg. issue; Hitler, Mussolini, Tojo-c 210 420 630 1334 2292 3250
10-S&K-a; 76 pg. issues begin 161 322 483 1030 1765 2500
11-17: 17-Last cardboard cover issue 135 270 405 864 1482 2100
18-20: 18-Paper covers begin; last Star Spangled Kid. 19-Joker story. 20-Last quarterly issue 129 258 387 826 1413 2000
21-30: 21-Begin bi-monthly. 30-Johnny Everyman app. 89 178 267 565 970 1375
31-40: 33-35-Tomahawk app. 35-Penguin app. 82 164 246 528 902 1275
41-50: 41-Boy Commandos end. 42-The Wyoming Kid begins (9-10/49), ends #63. 43-Full Steam Foley begins, ends #48. 48-Last square binding. 49-Tom Sparks, Boy Inventor begins; robot-c 69 138 207 442 759 1075
51-60: 51-Zatara ends. 54-Last 76 pg. issue. 59-Manhunters Around the World begins (7-8/52), ends #62 66 132 198 419 722 1025
61-64: 61-Joker story. 63-Capt. Compass app. 65 130 195 416 708 1000
65-Origin Superman; Tomahawk begins (7-8/53), ends #101 94 188 282 597 1024 1450
66-70-(15¢ issues, scarce)-Last 15¢, 68pg. issue 68 136 204 435 743 1050
71-(10¢ issue, scarce)-Superman & Batman begin as team (7-8/54); were in separate stories until now; Superman & Batman exchange identities; 10¢ issues begin 148 296 444 947 1624 2300
72,73-(10¢ issue, scarce) 97 194 291 621 1061 1500
74-Last pre-code issue 68 136 204 435 743 1050
75-(1st code approved, 3-4/55) 66 132 198 419 722 1025
76-80: 77-Superman loses powers & Batman obtains them 53 106 159 334 567 800
81-90: 84-1st S.A. issue. 88-1st Joker/Luthor team-up. 89-2nd Batmen of All Nations (aka Club of Heroes). 90-Batwoman's 1st app. in World's Finest (10/57, 3rd app. anywhere) plus-c app. 27 54 81 197 399 600
91-93,95-99: 96-99-Kirby Green Arrow. 99-Robot-c 20 40 60 144 290 435
94-Origin Superman/Batman team retold 48 96 144 392 796 1200
100 (3/59) 33 66 99 254 507 760
101-110: 102-Tommy Tomorrow begins, ends #124 14 28 42 96 191 285
111-121: 111-1st app. The Clock King. 113-Intro. Miss Arrowette in Green Arrow; 1st Bat-Mite/Mr. Mxyzptlk team-up (11/60). 117-Batwoman-c. 121-Last 10¢ issue 12 24 36 82 154 225
122-128: 123-2nd Bat-Mite/Mr. Mxyzptlk team-up (2/62). 125-Aquaman begins (5/62), ends #139 (Aquaman #1 is dated 1-2/62) 10 20 30 68 119 170
129-Joker/Luthor team-up-c/story 11 22 33 77 144 210
130-142: 135-Last Dick Sprang story. 140-Last Green Arrow. 142-Origin The Composite Superman (villain); Legion app. 8 16 24 58 97 135
143-150: 143-1st Mailbag. 144-Clayface/Brainiac team-up; last Clayface until Action #443 7 14 21 49 80 110
151-153,155,157-160: 157-2nd Super Sons story; last app. Kathy Kane (Bat-Woman) until Batman Family #10; 1st Bat-Mite Jr. 6 12 18 41 66 90
154-1st Super Sons story; last Bat-Woman in costume until Batman Family #10. 7 14 21 45 73 100
156-1st Bizarro Batman; Joker-c/story 10 20 30 68 119 170
161,170 (80-Pg. Giants G-28,G-40) 7 14 21 47 76 105
162-165,167,168,171,172: 168,172-Adult Legion app. 5 10 15 35 55 75
166-Joker-c/story 6 12 18 41 66 90
169-3rd app. new Batgirl(9/67)(cover and 1 panel cameo); 3rd Bat-Mite/Mr. Mxyzptlk team-up 5 10 15 41 66 90
173-('68)-1st S.A. app. Two-Face as Batman becomes Two-Face in story 9 18 27 63 107 150
174-Adams-c 6 12 18 37 59 80
175,176-Neal Adams-c/a; both reprint J'onn J'onzz origin/Detective #225,226 6 12 18 41 66 90
177-Joker/Luthor team-up-c/story 6 12 18 41 66 90
178-(9/68) Intro. of Super Nova (revived in "52" weekly series); Adams-c 6 12 18 43 69 95
179-(80 Page Giant G-52) -Adams-c; r/#94 6 12 18 43 69 95
180,182,183,185,186: Adams-c on all. 182-Silent Knight-r/Brave & Bold #6. 185-Last 12¢ issue. 186-Johnny Quick-r 4 8 12 28 44 60
181,184,187: 187-Green Arrow origin-r by Kirby (Adv. #256) 4 8 12 24 37 50
188,197:(Giants G-64,G-76; 64 pages) 6 12 18 39 62 85
189-196: 190-193-Robin-r 3 6 9 21 32 42
198,199-3rd Superman/Flash race (see Flash #175 & Superman #199). 199-Adams-c 10 20 30 67 116 165
200-Adams-c 4 8 12 26 41 55
201-203: 203-Last 15¢ issue. 3 6 9 19 29 38
204,205-(52 pgs.) Adams-c: 204-Wonder Woman app. 205-Shining Knight-r (6 pgs.) by Frazetta/Adv. #153; Teen Titans x-over 4 8 12 22 34 45
206 (Giant G-88, 64 pgs.) 5 10 15 32 51 70
207,212-(52 pgs.) 3 6 9 21 32 42
208-211(25¢-c) Adams-c: 208-(52 pgs.) Origin Robotman-r/Det. #138. 209-211-(52 pgs.) 4 8 12 22 34 45
213,214,216-222,229: 217-Metamorpho begins, ends #220; Batman/Superman team-ups resume. 229-r/origin Superman-Batman team 2 4 6 13 18 22
215-(12/72-1/73) Intro. Batman Jr. & Superman Jr. (see Superman/Batman: Saga of the Super Sons TPB for all the Super Sons stories) 3 6 9 19 29 38
223-228-(100 pgs.). 223-N. Adams-r. 223-Deadman origin. 226-N. Adams, S&K, Toth-r; Manhunter part origin-r/Det. #225,226. 227-Deadman app. 5 10 15 32 51 70
230-(68 pgs.) 3 6 9 18 27 35
231-243: 231, 233, 238, 242-Super Sons 2 4 6 9 13 16
244-246-Adams-c: 244-$1.00, 84 pg. issues begin; Green Arrow, Black Canary, Wonder Woman, Vigilante begin; 246-Death of Stuff in Vigilante; origin Vigilante retold 3 6 9 14 20 26
247-252 (84 pgs.): 248-Last Vigilante. 249-The Creeper begins by Ditko, 84 pgs. 250-The Creeper origin retold by Ditko. 252-Last 84 pg. issue 2 4 6 13 18 22
253-257,259-265: 253-Capt. Marvel begins; 68 pgs. begin, end #265. 255-Last Creeper. 256-Hawkman begins. 257-Black Lightning begins. 263-Super Sons. 264-Clay Face app. 2 4 6 8 11 14
258-Adams-c 2 4 6 10 14 18
266-270,272-282-(52 pgs.). 267-Challengers of the Unknown app.; 3 Lt. Marvels return. 268-Capt. Marvel Jr. origin retold. 274-Zatanna begins. 279, 280-Capt. Marvel Jr. & Kid Eternity learn they are brothers 1 3 4 6 8 10
271-(52pgs.) Origin Superman/Batman team retold 2 4 6 8 10 12
283-299: 284-Legion app. 1 2 3 4 5 7
300-($1.25, 52pgs.)-Justice League of America, New Teen Titans & The Outsiders app.; Perez-a (4 pgs.) 1 2 3 5 7 9
301-322: 304-Origin Null and Void. 309,319-Free 16 pg. story in each (309-Flash Force 2000, 319-Mask preview) 5.00
323-Last issue 6.00

NOTE: ***Neal Adams** a-230ir; c-174-176, 178-180, 182, 183, 185, 186, 199-205, 208-211, 244-246, 258. **Austin** a-244-246i. **Burnley** a-8, 10; c-7-9, 11-14, 15p?, 16-18p, 20-31p. **Colan** a-274p, 297, 299. **Ditko** a-249-255. **Giffen** a-322; c-284p, 322. **G. Kane** a-38, 174r, 282, 283; c-281, 282, 289. **Kirby** a-187. **Kubert** Zatara-40-44. **Miller** c-285p. **Mooney** c-134. **Morrow** a-245-248. **Mortimer** c-16-21, 26-71. **Nasser** a(p)-244-246, 259, 260. **Newton** a-253-281p. **Orlando** a-224r. **Perez** a-300i; c-271, 276, 277p, 278p. **Fred Ray** c-1-5. **Fred Ray/Robinson** c-13-16.*

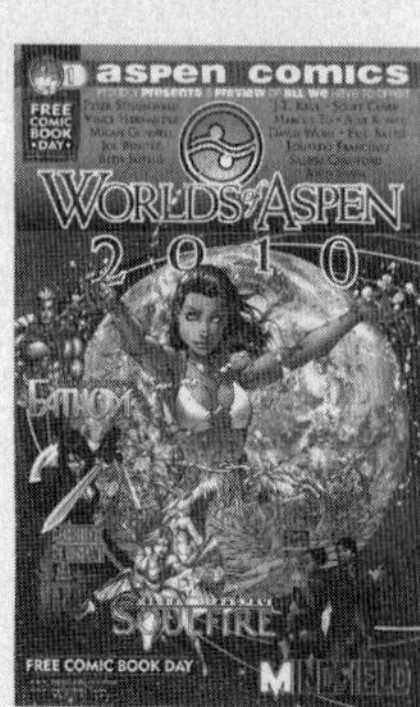

Worlds of Aspen 2010 © Aspen MLT

Worlds Unknown #5 © MAR

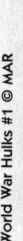

World War Hulks #1 © MAR

GD VG FN VF VF/NM NM-
2.0 4.0 6.0 8.0 9.0 9.2

*Robinson a-5, 6, 9-11, 13?, 14-16; c-6. **Rogers** a-259p. **Roussos** a-212r. **Simonson** c-291. **Spiegle** a-275-278, 284. **Staton** a-262p, 273p. **Swan/Moldoff** c-126. **Swan/Mortimer** c-79-82. **Toth** a-228r. **Tuska** a-230r, 250p, 252p, 254p, 257p, 283p, 284p, 308p. Boy Commandos by **Infantino** #39-41.*

WORLD'S FINEST COMICS DIGEST (See DC Special Series #23)

WORLD'S FINEST: OUR WORLDS AT WAR
DC Comics: Oct, 2001 ($2.95, one-shot)

1-Concludes the Our Worlds at War x-over; Jae Lee-c; art by various 3.00

WORLD'S GREATEST ATHLETE (See Walt Disney Showcase #14)

WORLD'S GREATEST SONGS
Atlas Comics (Male): Sept, 1954

1-(Scarce)-Heath & Harry Anderson-a; Eddie Fisher life story plus-c; gives lyrics to Frank Sinatra song "Young at Heart" 39 78 117 240 395 550

WORLD'S GREATEST STORIES
Jubilee Publications: Jan, 1949 - No. 2, May, 1949

1-Alice in Wonderland; Lewis Carroll adapt. 32 64 96 188 307 425
2-Pinocchio 30 60 90 177 289 400

WORLDS OF ASPEN
Aspen MLT, Inc.: 2006 - 2011 (Free Comic Book Day giveaways)

...: FCBD 2006, 2007, #3, #4 Editions; Fathom, Soulfire, Shrugged short stories; Turner-c 2.50
... 2010 (5/10) Previews Fathom, Mindfield, Soulfire, Executive Assistant: Iris and Dellec 2.50
... 2011 (5/11) Previews Fathom, Soulfire, Charismagic, Lady Mechanika & others 2.00

WORLDS OF FEAR (Stories of Weird Adventure)(Formerly Worlds Beyond #1)
Fawcett Publications: V1#2, Jan, 1952 - V2#10, June, 1953

V1#2 47 94 141 296 498 700
3-Evans-a 40 80 120 246 411 575
4-6(9/52) 38 76 114 226 368 510
V2#7-9 36 72 108 211 343 475
10-Saunders painted-c; man with no eyes surrounded by eyeballs-c plus eyes ripped out story 110 220 330 704 1202 1700

*NOTE: **Moldoff** c-2-8. **Powell** a-2, 4, 5. **Sekowsky** a-4, 5.*

WORLDSTORM
DC Comics (WildStorm): Nov, 2006 (Dec on cover) - No. 2, May, 2007 ($2.99)

1,2-Previews and pin-ups for re-launched WildStorm titles.1-Art Adams-c 3.00

WORLDS UNKNOWN
Marvel Comics Group: May, 1973 - No. 8, Aug, 1974

1-r/from Astonishing #54; Torres, Reese-a 3 6 9 16 23 30
2-8 2 4 6 11 16 20

*NOTE: **Adkins/Mooney** a-5. **Buscema** c/a-4p. **W. Howard** c/a-3i. **Kane** a(p)-1,2; c(p)-5, 6, 8. **Sutton** a-2. **Tuska** a(p)-7, 8; c-7p. No. 7, 8 has Golden Voyage of Sinbad movie adaptation.*

WORLD WAR HULK (See Incredible Hulk #106)
Marvel Comics: Aug, 2007 - No. 5, Jan, 2008 ($3.99, limited series)

1-Hulk returns to Earth; Iron Man and Avengers app.; Romita Jr.-a/Pak-s/Finch-c 4.00
1-Variant cover by Romita Jr. 6.00
2-5: 2-Hulk battles The Avengers and FF; Finch-c. 3,4-Dr. Strange app. 5-Sentry app. 4.00
2-5-Variant cover by Romita Jr. 6.00
...: Aftersmash 1 (1/08, $3.99) Sandoval-a/Land-c; Hercules, Iron Man app. 4.00
...: Gamma Files (2007, $3.99) profile pages of Hulk characters 4.00
...Prologue: World Breaker 1 (7/07, one-shot) Rio, Weeks, Phillips, Miyazawa-a 4.00
TPB (2008, $19.99) r/#1-5 20.00

WORLD WAR HULK AFTERSMASH: DAMAGE CONTROL
Marvel Comics: Mar, 2008 - No. 3, May, 2008 ($2.99, limited series)

1-3-The clean-up; McDuffie-s. 2-Romita- Jr.-c. 3-Romita Sr.-c 3.00

WORLD WAR HULK AFTERSMASH: WARBOUND
Marvel Comics: Feb, 2008 - No. 5, Jun, 2008 ($2.99, limited series)

1-5-Kirk & Sandoval-a/Cheung-c 3.00

WORLD WAR HULK: FRONT LINE (See Incredible Hulk #106)
Marvel Comics: Aug, 2007 - No. 6, Dec, 2007 ($2.99, limited series)

1-6-Ben Urich & Sally Floyd report World War Hulk; Jenkins-s/Bachs-a 3.00
TPB (2008, $16.99) r/#1-5 & WWH Prologue: World Breaker 17.00

WORLD WAR HULK: GAMMA CORPS
Marvel Comics: Sept, 2007 - No. 4, Jan, 2008 ($2.99, limited series)

1-4-Tieri-s/Ferreira-a/Roux-c 3.00
TPB (2008, $10.99) r/#1-4 11.00

WORLD WAR HULKS
Marvel Comics: Jun, 2010; Sept, 2010 ($3.99, one-shot & limited series)

1-Short stories by various; Deadpool app.; Romita Jr.-c 4.00

GD VG FN VF VF/NM NM-
2.0 4.0 6.0 8.0 9.0 9.2

...: Spider-Man vs. Thor 1,2 (9/10 - No. 2, 9/10) Gillen-s/Molina-a 4.00
...: Wolverine vs. Captain America 1,2 (9/10 - No. 2, 9/10) "Capt America vs Wolv." on-c 4.00

WORLD WAR HULK: X-MEN (See New Avengers: Illuminati and Incredible Hulk #92)
Marvel Comics: Aug, 2007 - No. 3, Oct, 2007 ($2.99, limited series)

1-3-Gage-s/DiVito-a/McGuinness-c; Hulk invades the Xavier Institute 3.00
TPB (2008, $24.99) r/#1-3, Avengers: The Initiative #4-5, Irredeemable Ant-Man #10, Iron Man #19-20, and Ghost Rider #12-13 25.00

WORLD WAR STORIES
Dell Publishing Co.: Apr-June, 1965 - No. 3, Dec, 1965

1-Glanzman-a in all 4 8 12 26 41 55
2,3 3 6 9 17 25 32

WORLD WAR II (See Classics Illustrated Special Issue)

WORLD WAR II: 1946
Antarctic Press: Oct, 1998 - No. 2 ($3.95, B&W)

1,2-Nomura-s/a 4.00

WORLD WAR III
Ace Periodicals: Mar, 1953 - No. 2, May, 1953

1-(Scarce)-Atomic bomb blast-c; Cameron-a 123 246 369 787 1344 1900
2-Used in **POP**, pg. 78 & B&W & color illos; Cameron-a 65 130 195 416 708 1000

WORLDWATCH
Wild and Wooly Press: June, 2004 - No. 3, Dec, 2004 ($2.95)

1-3-Austen-s/Derenick-a. 1-B&W. 2,3-Color 3.00

WORLD WITHOUT END
DC Comics: 1990 - No. 6, 1991 ($2.50, limited series, mature, stiff-c)

1-6: Horror/fantasy; all painted-c/a 3.00

WORLD WRESTLING FEDERATION BATTLEMANIA
Valiant: 1991 - No. 5?, 1991 ($2.50, magazine size, 68 pgs.)

1-5: 5-Includes 2 free pull-out posters 4.00

WORST FROM MAD, THE (Annual)
E. C. Comics: 1958 - No. 12, 1969 (Each annual cover is reprinted from the cover of the Mad issues being reprinted)(Value is 1/2 if bonus is missing)

nn(1958)-Bonus; record labels & travel stickers; 1st Mad annual; r/Mad #29-34 43 86 129 271 461 650
2(1959)-Bonus is small 33 1/3 rpm record entitled "Meet the Staff of Mad"; r/Mad #35-40 42 84 126 265 445 625
3(1960)-Has 20x30" campaign poster "Alfred E. Neuman for President"; r/Mad #41-46 16 32 48 114 232 350
4(1961)-Sunday comics section; r/Mad #47-54 15 30 45 108 219 330
5(1962)-Has 33-1/3 record; r/Mad #55-62 22 44 66 159 317 475
6(1963)-Has 33-1/3 record; r/Mad #63-70 22 44 66 159 317 475
7(1964)-Mad protest signs; r/Mad #71-76 10 20 30 71 128 185
8(1965)-Build a Mad Zeppelin 11 22 33 77 144 210
9(1966)-33-1/3 rpm record; Beatles on-c 15 30 45 104 212 320
10(1967)-Mad bumper sticker 7 14 21 47 76 105
11(1968)-Mad cover window stickers 6 12 18 43 69 95
12(1969)-Mad picture postcards; Orlando-a 6 12 18 43 69 95

*NOTE: Covers: **Bob Clarke**-#8. **Mingo**-#7, 9-12.*

WOTALIFE COMICS (Formerly Nutty Life #2; Phantom Lady #13 on)
Fox Features Syndicate/Norlen Mag.: No. 3, Aug-Sept, 1946 - No. 12, July, 1947; 1959

3-Cosmo Cat, Li'l Pan, others begin 12 24 36 67 94 120
4-12-Cosmo Cat, Li'l Pan in all 10 20 30 54 72 90
1(1959-Norlen)-Atomic Rabbit, Atomic Mouse; reprints cover to #6; reprints entire book? 8 16 24 40 50 60

WOTALIFE COMICS
Green Publications: 1957 - No. 5, 1957

1 7 14 21 35 43 50
2-5 5 10 15 22 26 30

WOW COMICS ("Wow, What A Magazine!" on cover of first issue)
Henle Publishing Co.: July, 1936 - No. 4, Nov, 1936 (52 pgs., magazine size)

1-Buck Jones in "The Phantom Rider" (1st app. in comics), Fu Manchu; Capt. Scott Dalton begins; Will Eisner-a (1st in comics); Baily-a(1); Briefer-c 300 600 900 2010 3505 5000
2-Ken Maynard, Fu Manchu, Popeye by Segar plus article on Popeye; Eisner-a 213 426 639 1363 2332 3300
3-Eisner-c/a(3); Popeye by Segar, Fu Manchu, Hiram Hick by Bob Kane, Space Limited app.; Jimmy Dempsey talks about Popeye's punch; Bob Ripley Believe it or Not begins; Briefer-a

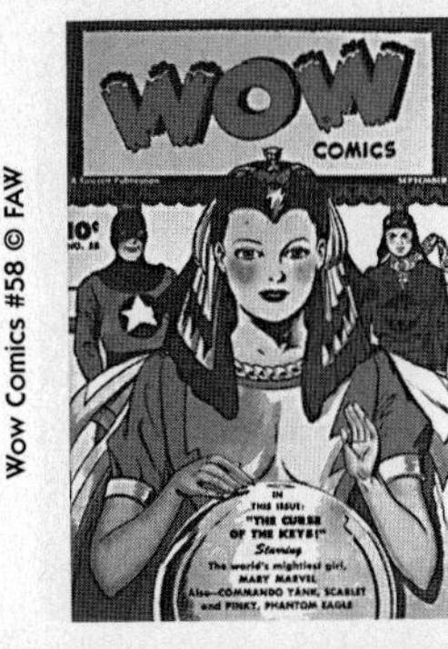

Wow Comics #58 © FAW

Wulf #1 © Nemesis Group

WWE Heroes #5 © WWE

GD VG FN VF VF/NM NM-
2.0 4.0 6.0 8.0 9.0 9.2

200 400 600 1280 2190 3100
4-Flash Gordon by Raymond, Mandrake, Popeye by Segar, Tillie The Toiler, Fu Manchu, Hiram Hick by Bob Kane; Eisner-a(3); Briefer-c/a
245 490 735 1568 2684 3800

WOW COMICS (Real Western Hero #70 on)(See XMas Comics)
Fawcett Publ.: Winter, 1940-41; No. 2, Summer, 1941 - No. 69, Fall, 1948

nn(#1)-Origin Mr. Scarlet by S&K; Atom Blake, Boy Wizard, Jim Dolan, & Rick O'Shay begin; Diamond Jack, The White Rajah, & Shipwreck Roberts, only app.; 1st mention of Gotham City in comics; the cover was printed on unstable paper stock and is rarely found in fine or mint condition; blank inside-c; bondage-c by Beck
1350 2700 4050 10,400 18,700 27,000
2 (Scarce)-The Hunchback begins 232 464 696 1485 2543 3600
3 (Fall, 1941) 103 206 309 659 1130 1600
4-Origin & 1st app. Pinky 105 210 315 667 1146 1625
5 61 122 183 390 670 950
6-Origin & 1st app. The Phantom Eagle (7/15/42); Commando Yank begins
61 122 183 390 670 950
7,8 54 108 162 343 574 825
9 (1/6/43)-Capt. Marvel, Capt. Marvel Jr., Shazam app.; Scarlet & Pinky x-over; Mary Marvel-c/stories begin (cameo #9) 174 348 522 1114 1907 2700
10-Swayze-c/a on Mary Marvel 63 126 189 403 689 975
11-17,19,20: 15-Flag-c 48 96 144 302 514 725
18-1st app. Uncle Marvel (10/43); infinity-c 50 100 150 315 533 750
21-30: 23-Robot-c. 28-Pinky x-over in Mary Marvel 32 64 96 188 307 425
31-40: 32-68-Phantom Eagle by Swayze 22 44 66 132 216 300
41-50 21 42 63 124 202 280
51-58: Last Mary Marvel 20 40 60 117 189 260
59-69: 59-Ozzie (teenage) begins. 62-Flying Saucer gag-c (1/48). 65-69-Tom Mix stories (cont'd in Real Western Hero) 19 38 57 109 172 235
NOTE: *Cover features: Mr. Scarlet-#1-5; Commando Yank-#6, 7, (w/Mr. Scarlet #8); Mary Marvel-#9-56, (w/Commando Yank-#46-50), (w/Mr. Scarlet & Commando Yank-#51), (w/Mr. Scarlet & Pinky #53), (w/Phantom Eagle #54, 56), (w/Commando Yank & Phantom Eagle #58); Ozzie-#59-69.*

WRAITHBORN
DC Comics (WildStorm): Nov, 2005 - No. 6, July, 2006 ($2.99, limited series)
1-6-Marcia Chen & Joe Benitez-s/a 3.00
TPB (2007, $19.99) r/series; sketch pages and unused cover sketches 20.00

WRATH (Also see Prototype #4)
Malibu Comics: Jan, 1994 - No. 9, Nov, 1995 ($1.95)
1-9: 2-Mantra x-over. 3-Intro/1st app. Slayer. 4,5-Freex app. 8-Mantra & Warstrike app. 9-Prime app. 3.00
1-Ultra 5000 Limited silver foil 5.00
Giant Size 1 (2.50, 44 pgs.) 4.00

WRATH OF THE SPECTRE, THE
DC Comics: May, 1988 - No. 4, Aug, 1988 ($2.50, limited series)
1-3: Aparo-r/Adventure #431-440 5.00
4-Three scripts intended for Adventure #441-on, but not drawn by Aparo until 1988
1 2 3 5 6 8
TPB (2005, $19.99) r/series; Peter Sanderson intro. 20.00

WRECK OF GROSVENOR (See Superior Stories #3)

WRETCH, THE
Caliber: 1996 ($2.95, B&W)
1-Phillip Hester-a/scripts 3.00

WRETCH, THE
Amaze Ink: 1997 - No. 4, 1998 ($2.95, B&W)
1-4-Phillip Hester-a/scripts 3.00
... Vol. 1: Everyday Doomsday (4/03, $13.95) 14.00

WRINGLE WRANGLE (Disney)
Dell Publishing Co.: No. 821, July, 1957
Four Color 821-Based on movie "Westward Ho, the Wagons"; Marsh-a; Fess Parker photo-c
8 16 24 52 86 120

WULF
Ardden Entertainment: Mar, 2011 - Present ($2.99)
1-Steve Niles-s/Nat Jones-a/c; Lomax app. 3.00

WULF THE BARBARIAN
Atlas/Seaboard Publ.: Feb, 1975 - No. 4, Sept, 1975
1,2: 1-Origin; Janson-a. 2-Intro. Berithe the Swordswoman; Janson-a w/Neal Adams, Wood, Reese-a assists 2 4 6 9 13 16
3,4: 3-Skeates-s. 4-Friedrich-s 2 4 6 8 10 12

GD VG FN VF VF/NM NM-
2.0 4.0 6.0 8.0 9.0 9.2

WWE HEROES (WWE Wrestling) (#7 titled WWE Undertaker)
Titan Comics: Apr, 2010 - Present ($3.99)
1-6: 1-Two covers by Andy Smith and Liam Sharp. 5-Covers by Smith and Mayhew 4.00
7,8-"Undertaker" on cover; Rey Mysterio app. 4.00

WYATT EARP
Atlas Comics/Marvel No. 23 on (IPC): Nov, 1955 - #29, June, 1960; #30, Oct, 1972 - #34, June, 1973
1 21 42 63 122 199 275
2-Williamson-a (4 pgs.) 14 28 42 76 108 140
3-6,8-11: 3-Black Bart app. 8-Wild Bill Hickok app. 11 22 33 60 83 105
7,12-Williamson-a, 4 pgs. ea.; #12 with Mayo 11 22 33 64 90 115
13-20: 17-1st app. Wyatt's deputy, Grizzly Grant 10 20 30 54 72 90
21-Davis-c 9 18 27 50 65 80
22-24,26-29: 22-Ringo Kid app. 23-Kid From Texas app. 29-Last 10¢ issue
8 16 24 42 54 65
25-Davis-a 8 16 24 44 57 70
30-Williamson-r (1972) 2 4 6 13 18 22
31-34-Reprints. 32-Torres-a(r) 2 4 6 9 13 16
NOTE: ***Ayers** a-8, 10(2), 17, 20(4), 26(5). **Berg** a-9. **Everett** c-6. **Kirby** c-25, 29. **Maneely** a-1; c-1-4, 8, 12, 17, 20. **Maurer** a-2(2), 3(4), 4(4), 8(4). **Severin** a-4, 9(4), 10; c-2, 9, 10, 14. **Wildey** a-5, 17, 24, 28.*

WYATT EARP (TV) (Hugh O'Brian Famous Marshal)
Dell Publishing Co.: No. 860, Nov, 1957 - No. 13, Dec-Feb, 1960-61 (Hugh O'Brian photo-c)
Four Color 860 (#1)-Manning-a 9 18 27 65 113 160
Four Color 890,921(6/58)-All Manning-a 7 14 21 49 80 110
4 (9-11/58) - 12-Manning-a. 4-Variant edition exists with back-c comic strip; Russ Manning-a. 5-Photo back-c 6 12 18 37 59 80
13-Toth-a 6 12 18 39 62 85

WYATT EARP FRONTIER MARSHAL (Formerly Range Busters) (Also see Blue Bird)
Charlton Comics: No. 12, Jan, 1956 - No. 72, Dec, 1967
12 9 18 27 47 61 75
13-19 6 12 18 31 38 45
20-(68 pgs.)-Williamson-a(4), 8,5,5,& 7 pgs. 10 20 30 54 72 90
21-(100 pgs.) Mastroserio, Maneely, Severin-a (signed LePoer)
5 10 15 32 51 70
22-30 3 6 9 16 23 30
31-50 2 4 6 12 16 20
51-72 (1967) 2 4 6 9 11 14

WYNONNA EARP
Image Comics (WildStorm Productions): Dec, 1996 - No. 5, Apr, 1997 ($2.50)
1-5-Smith-s/Chin-a 3.00

WYNONNA EARP: HOME ON THE STRANGE
IDW Publishing: Dec, 2003 - No. 3, Feb, 2004 ($3.99)
1-3-Smith-s/Ferreira-a 4.00

WYRMS
Marvel Comics (Dabel Brothers): Feb, 2007 - No. 6, Jan, 2008 ($2.99)
1-6-Orson Scott Card & Jake Black-s. 1-3-Batista-a 3.00
TPB (2008, $14.99) r/#1-6 15.00

X (Comics' Greatest World: X #1 only) (Also see Comics' Greatest World & Dark Horse Comics #8)
Dark Horse Comics: Feb, 1994 - No. 25, Apr, 1996 ($2.00/$2.50)
1-25: 3-Pit Bulls x-over. 8 -Ghost-c & app. 18-Miller-c.; Predator app. 19-22-Miller-c. 3.00
Hero Illustrated Special #1,2 (1994, $1.00, 20 pgs.) 3.00
One Shot to the Head (1994, $2.50, 36 pgs.)-Miller-c. 3.00
NOTE: ***Miller** c-18-22. **Quesada** c-6. **Russell** a-6.*

XANADU COLOR SPECIAL
Eclipse Comics: Dec, 1988 ($2.00, one-shot)
1-Continued from Thoughts & Images 3.00

XAVIER INSTITUTE ALUMNI YEARBOOK (See X-Men titles)
Marvel Comics: Dec, 1996 ($5.95, square-bound, one-shot)
1-Text w/art by various 6.00

X-BABIES
Marvel Comics: Dec, 2009 - No. 4, Mar, 2010 ($3.99, limited series)
1-4-Schigiel-s/Chabot-a; Skottie Young 4.00
...: Murderama (8/98, $2.95) J.J. Kirby-a 4.00
...: Reborn (1/00, $3.50) J.J. Kirby-a 4.00

X-CALIBRE

Xena/Army of Darkness: What... Again?! #2 © Universal & Orion

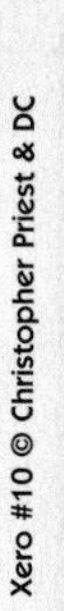

Xero #10 © Christopher Priest & DC

X-Factor V3 #38 © MAR

GD 2.0 | VG 4.0 | FN 6.0 | VF 8.0 | VF/NM 9.0 | NM- 9.2

Marvel Comics: Mar, 1995 - No. 4, July, 1995 ($1.95, limited series)
1-4-Age of Apocalypse 3.00

X-CAMPUS
Marvel Comics: July, 2010 - No. 4, Nov, 2010 ($4.99, limited series)
1-4-Alternate version of X-Men; stories by European creators; Nauck-c 5.00

XENA (TV)
Dynamite Entertainment: 2006 - 2007 ($3.50)
1-4-Three covers on each; Neves-a/Layman-s 3.50
Vol. 2 #1-4-(Dark Xena) Four covers; Salonga-a/Layman-s 3.50
Annual 1 (2007, $4.95) Three covers; Salonga-a/Champagne-s 5.00
... Vol. 2: Dark Xena TPB (2007, $14.99) r/Vol. 2 #1-4; variant cover gallery 15.00

XENA / ARMY OF DARKNESS: WHAT...AGAIN?!
Dynamite Entertainment: 2008 - No. 4, 2009 ($3.50, limited series)
1-4-Xena, Gabrielle, & Autolycus team up with Ash; Montenegro-a; two covers on each 3.50

XENA: WARRIOR PRINCESS (TV)
Topps Comics: Aug, 1997 - No. 0, Oct, 1997 ($2.95)
1-Two stories by various; J. Scott Campbell-c 1 3 4 6 8 10
1,2-Photo-c 1 3 4 6 8 10
2-Stevens-c 1 3 4 6 8 10
0-(10/97)-Lopresti-c, 0-(10/97)-Photo-c 1 2 3 5 6 8
...First Appearance Collection ('97, $9.95) r/Hercules the Legendary Journeys #3-5 and 5-page story from TV Guide 10.00

XENA: WARRIOR PRINCESS (TV)
Dark Horse Comics: Sept, 1999 - No. 14, Oct, 2000 ($2.95/$2.99)
1-14: 1-Mignola-c and photo-c. 2,3-Bradstreet-c & photo-c 3.50

XENA: WARRIOR PRINCESS AND THE ORIGINAL OLYMPICS (TV)
Topps Comics: Jun, 1998 - No. 3, Aug, 1998 ($2.95, limited series)
1-3-Regular and Photo-c; Lim-a/T&M Bierbaum-s 3.50

XENA: WARRIOR PRINCESS-BLOODLINES (TV)
Topps Comics: May, 1998 - No. 2, June, 1998 ($2.95, limited series)
1,2-Lopresti-s/c/a. 2-Reg. and photo-c 3.50
1-Bath photo-c, 1-American Ent. Ed. 4.50

XENA: WARRIOR PRINCESS / JOXER: WARRIOR PRINCE (TV)
Topps Comics: Nov, 1997 - No. 3, Jan, 1998 ($2.95, limited series)
1-3-Regular and Photo-c; Lim-a/T&M Bierbaum-s 3.50

XENA: WARRIOR PRINCESS-THE DRAGON'S TEETH (TV)
Topps Comics: Dec, 1997 - No. 3, Feb, 1998 ($2.95, limited series)
1-3-Regular and Photo-c; Teranishi-a/Thomas-s 3.50

XENA: WARRIOR PRINCESS-THE ORPHEUS TRILOGY (TV)
Topps Comics: Mar, 1998 - No. 3, May, 1998 ($2.95, limited series)
1-3-Regular and Photo-c; Teranishi-a/T&M Bierbaum-s 3.50

XENA: WARRIOR PRINCESS VS. CALLISTO (TV)
Topps Comics: Feb, 1998 - No. 3, Apr, 1998 ($2.95, limited series)
1-3-Regular and Photo-c; Morgan-a/Thomas-s 3.50

XENOBROOD
DC Comics: No. 0, Oct, 1994 - No. 6, Apr, 1995 ($1.50, limited series)
0-6: 0-Indicia says "Xenobroods" 3.00

XENON
Eclipse Comics: Dec, 1987 - No. 23, Nov. 1, 1988 ($1.50, B&W, bi-weekly)
1-23 3.00

XENOZOIC TALES (Also see Cadillacs & Dinosaurs, Death Rattle #8)
Kitchen Sink Press: Feb, 1986 - No. 14, Oct, 1996
1-Mark Schultz-s/a in all 1 3 4 6 8 10
1(2nd printing)(1/89) 3.00
2-14 5.00
Volume 1 ($14.95) r/#1-6 & Death Rattle #8 15.00
Volume 2 (5/03, $14.95, TPB) B&W r/#7-14; intro by Frank Cho 15.00

XENYA
Sanctuary Press: Apr, 1994 - No. 3 ($2.95)
1-3: 1-Hildebrandt-c; intro Xenya 3.00

XERO
DC Comics: May, 1997 - No. 12, Apr, 1998 ($1.75)
1-7 3.00
8-12 3.00

X-FACTOR (Also see The Avengers #263, Fantastic Four #286 and Mutant X)
Marvel Comics Group: Feb, 1986 - No. 149, Sept, 1998
1-($1.25, 52 pgs)-Story recaps 1st app. from Avengers #263; story cont'd from F.F. #286; return of original X-Men (now X-Factor); Guice/Layton-a; Baby Nathan app. (2nd after X-Men #201) 1 2 3 5 6 8
2-4 4.00
5-1st brief app. Apocalypse (2 pages) 5.00
6-1st full app. Apocalypse 2 4 6 8 10 12
7-10: 10-Sabretooth app. (11/86, 3 pgs.) cont'd in X-Men #212; 1st app. in an X-Men comic book 4.00
11-22: 13-Baby Nathan app. in flashback. 14-Cyclops vs. The Master Mold. 15-Intro wingless Angel 3.00
23-1st brief app. Archangel (2 pages) 1 2 3 5 6 8
24-1st full app. Archangel (now in Uncanny X-Men); Fall Of The Mutants begins; origin Apocalypse 1 3 4 6 8 10
25,26: Fall Of The Mutants; 26-New outfits 4.00
27-37,39,41-49,51-59,63-70,72-83,87-91,93-99,101: 35-Origin Cyclops. 51-53-Sabretooth app. 52-Liefeld-c(p). 54-Intro Crimson; Silvestri-c/a(p). 63-Portacio/Thibert-c/a(p) begins, ends #69. 65-68-Lee co-plots. 65-The Apocalypse Files begins, ends #68. 66,67-Baby Nathan app. 67-Inhumans app. 68-Baby Nathan is sent into future to save his life. 69,70-X-Men(w/Wolverine) x-over. 77-Cannonball (of X-Force) app. 87-Quesada-c/a(p) in monthly comic begins,ends #92. 88-1st app. Random 3.00
38,50,60-62,71,75: 38,50-(52 pgs.): 50-Liefeld/McFarlane-c. 60-X-Tinction Agenda x-over; New Mutants (w/Cable) x-over in #60-62; Wolverine in #62. 61,62-X-Tinction Agenda. 62-Jim Lee-c. 71-New team begins (Havok, Polaris, Strong Guy, Wolfsbane & Madrox); Stroman-c/a begins. 75-(52 pgs.) 4.00
40-Rob Liefield-c/a (4/89, 1st at Marvel?) 5.00
60,71-2nd printings. 60-Gold ink 2nd printing. 71-2nd printing ($1.25) 3.00
84-86 -Jae Lee a(p); 85,86-Jae Lee-c. Polybagged with trading card in each; X-Cutioner's Song x-overs. 4.00
92-($3.50, 68 pgs.)-Wraparound-c by Quesada w/Havok hologram on-c; begin X-Men 30th anniversary issues; Quesada-a. 6.00
92-2nd printing 4.00
100-($2.95, 52 pgs.)-Embossed foil-c; Multiple Man dies. 6.00
100-($1.75, 52 pgs.)-Regular edition 4.00
102-105,107: 102-bound-in card sheet 3.00
106-($2.00)-Newsstand edition 3.00
106-($2.95)-Collectors edition 4.00
108-124,126-148: 112-Return from Age of Apocalypse. 115-card insert. 119-123-Sabretooth app. 123-Hound app. 124-w/Onslaught Update. 126-Onslaught x-over; Beast vs. Dark Beast. 128-w/card insert; return of Multiple Man. 130-Assassination of Grayson Creed. 146,148-Moder-a 3.00
125-($2.95)-"Onslaught"; Post app.; return of Havok 4.00
149-Last issue 4.00
#(-1) Flashback (7/97) Matsuda-a 3.00
Annual 1-9: 1-(10/86-'94, 68 pgs.) 3-Evolutionary War x-over. 4-Atlantis Attacks; Byrne/Simonson-a;Byrne-c. 5-Fantastic Four, New Mutants x-over; Keown 2 pg. pin-up. 6-New Warriors app.; 5th app. X-Force cont'd from X-Men Annual #15. 7-1st Quesada-a(p) on X-Factor plus-c(p). 8-Bagged w/trading card. 9-Austin-a(i) 4.00
...Prisoner of Love (1990, $4.95, 52 pgs.)-Starlin scripts; Guice-a 5.00
... Visionaries: Peter David Vol. 1 TPB (2005, $15.99) r/#71-75 16.00
... Visionaries: Peter David Vol. 2 TPB (2007, $15.99) r/#76-78 & Incr. Hulk #390-392 16.00
... Visionaries: Peter David Vol. 3 TPB (2007, $15.99) r/#79-83 & Annual #7 16.00
NOTE: ***Art Adams** a-41p, 42p. **Buckler** a-50p. **Liefeld** a-40; c-40, 50i, 52p. **McFarlane** c-50i. **Mignola** c-70. **Brandon Peterson** a-78p(part). **Whilce Portacio** c/a(p)-63-69. **Quesada** a(p)-87-92, Annual 7. c(p)-78, 79, 82, Annual 7. **Simonson** c/a-10, 11, 13-15, 17-19, 21, 23-31, 33, 34, 36-39; c-12, 16. **Paul Smith** a-44-48; c-43. **Stroman** a(p)-71-75, 77, 78(part), 80, 81; c(p)-71-77, 80, 81, 84. **Zeck** c-2.*

X-FACTOR (Volume 2)
Marvel Comics: June, 2002 - No. 4, Oct, 2002 ($2.50)
1-4: Jensen-s/Ranson-a. 1-Phillips-c. 2,3-Edwards-c 3.00

X-FACTOR (Volume 3)
Marvel Comics: Jan, 2006 - Present ($2.99)
1-24: 1-Peter David-s/Ryan Sook-a. 8,9-Civil War. 21-24-Endangered Species back-up 3.00
25-49: 25-27-Messiah Complex x-over; Finch-c. 26-2nd printing with new Eaton-c 3.00
50-(12/09, $3.99) Madrox in the future; DeLandro-a/Yardin-c 4.00
200-(2/10, $4.99) Resumes original series numbering; 3 covers; Fantastic Four app. 5.00
201-218-($2.99) 201,202-Dr. Doom and the Fantastic Four app. 211,212-Thor app. 3.00
... Special: Layla Miller (10/08, $3.99) David-s/DeLandro-a 4.00
...: The Quick and the Dead (7/08, $2.99) Raimondi-a; Quicksilver regains powers 3.00
...: The Longest Night HC (2006, $19.99, dust jacket) r/#1-6; sketch pages by Sook 20.00
...: The Longest Night SC (2007, $14.99) r/#1-6; sketch pages by Sook 15.00
...: Life and Death Matters HC (2007, $19.99, dust jacket) r/#7-12 20.00

X-Factor Forever #1 © MAR

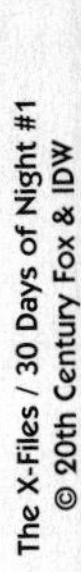

The X-Files / 30 Days of Night #1 © 20th Century Fox & IDW

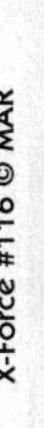

X-Force #116 © MAR

	GD 2.0	VG 4.0	FN 6.0	VF 8.0	VF/NM 9.0	NM- 9.2
...: Life and Death Matters SC (2007, $14.99) r/#7-12						15.00
...: The Many Lives of Madrox SC (2007, $14.99) r/#13-17						15.00
...: Heart of Ice HC (2007, $19.99, dust jacket) r/#18-24						20.00
...: Heart of Ice SC (2008, $17.99, dust jacket) r/#18-24						18.00

X-FACTOR (Volume 2)
Marvel Comics: June, 2002 - No. 4, Oct, 2002 ($2.50)

1-4: Jensen-s/Ranson-a. 1-Phillips-c. 2,3-Edwards-c						2.50

X-FACTOR FOREVER
Marvel Comics: May, 2010 - No. 5, Sept, 2010 ($3.99, limited series)

1-5-Louise Simonson-s/Dan Panosian-a; back-up origin of Apocalypse						4.00

X-51 (Machine Man)
Marvel Comics: Sept, 1999 - No. 12, Jul, 2000 ($1.99/$2.50)

1-7: 1-Joe Bennett-a. 2-Two covers						3.00
8-12: 8-Begin $2.50-c						3.00
Wizard #0						3.00

X-FILES, THE (TV)
Topps Comics: Jan, 1995 - No. 41, July, 1998 ($2.50)

-2(9/96)-Black-c; r/X-Files Magazine #1&2	1	3	4	6	8	10
-1(9/96)-Silver-c; r/Hero Illustrated Giveaway	1	3	4	6	8	10
0-($3.95)-Adapts pilot episode						4.00
0-"Mulder" variant-c	1	2	3	5	6	8
0-"Scully" variant-c	1	2	3	5	6	8
1/2-W/certificate	3	6	9	14	20	25
1-New stories based on the TV show; direct market & newsstand editions; Miran Kim-c on all	3	6	9	16	23	30
2	2	4	6	10	14	18
3,4	1	2	3	5	6	8
5-10						5.00
11-41: 11-Begin $2.95-c. 21-W/bound-in card. 40,41-Reg. & photo-c						4.00
Annual 1,2 ($3.95)						4.00
Afterflight TPB ($5.95) Art by Thompson, Saviuk, Kim						6.00
Collection 1 TPB ($19.95)-r/#1-6.						20.00
Collection 2 TPB ($19.95)-r/#7-12, Annual #1.						20.00
...Fight the Future ('98, $5.95) Movie adaptation						6.00
Hero Illustrated Giveaway (3/95)	2	4	6	9	12	15
Special Edition 1-5 ($4.95)-r/#1-3, 4-6, 7-9, 10-12, 13, Annual 1						5.00
Star Wars Galaxy Magazine Giveaway (B&W)	1	3	4	6	8	10
Trade paperback ($19.95)						20.00
Volume 1 TPB (Checker Books, 2005, $19.95) r/#13-17, #0, Season One: Squeeze						20.00
Volume 2 TPB (Checker Books, 2005, $19.95) r/#18-24, #1/2, Comics Digest #1						20.00
Volume 3 TPB (Checker Books, 2006, $19.95) r/#23-26, Fire, Ice, Hero Ill. Giveaway						20.00

X-FILES, THE (TV)
DC Comics (WildStorm): No. 0, Sept, 2008 - No. 6, Jun, 2009 ($3.99/$3.50)

0-($3.99) Spotnitz-s/Denham-a; photo-c						4.00
1-6-($3.50) 1-Spotnitz-s/Denham-a; 2 covers. 4-Wolfman-s						3.50
TPB (2009, $19.99) r/#0-6						20.00

X-FILES COMICS DIGEST, THE
Topps Comics: Dec, 1995 - No. 3 ($3.50, quarterly, digest-size)

1-3: 1,2: New X-Files stories w/Ray Bradbury Comics-r. 1-Reg. & photo-c						4.00

NOTE: *Adlard a-1, 2. **Jack Davis** a-2r. **Russell** a-1r.*

X-FILES, THE: GROUND ZERO (TV)
Topps Comics: Nov, 1997 - No. 4, March, 1998 ($2.95, limited series)

1-4-Adaptation of the Kevin J. Anderson novel						4.00

X-FILES, THE: SEASON ONE (TV)
Topps Comics: July, 1997 - July, 1998 ($4.95, adaptations of TV episodes)

1,2,Squeeze, Conduit, Ice, Space, Fire, Beyond the Sea, Shadows						5.00

X-FILES, THE / 30 DAYS OF NIGHT
DC Comics (WildStorm)/IDW: Sept, 2010 - No. 6, Feb, 2011 ($3.99, limited series)

1-6-Steve Niles & Adam Jones-s/Tom Mandrake-a. 1-Three covers						4.00

X-FORCE (Becomes X-Statix) (Also see The New Mutants #100)
Marvel Comics: Aug, 1991 - No. 129, Aug, 2002 ($1.00-$2.25)

1-($1.50, 52 pgs.)-Polybagged with 1 of 5 diff. Marvel Universe trading cards inside (1 each); 6th app. of X-Force; Liefeld-c/a begins						5.00
1-1st printing with Cable trading card inside						6.00
1-2nd printing; metallic ink-c (no bag or card)						3.00
2-4: 2-Deadpool-c/story. 3-New Brotherhood of Evil Mutants app. 4-Spider-Man x-over; cont'd from Spider-Man #16; reads sideways						4.00
5-10: 6-Last $1.00-c. 7,9-Weapon X back-ups. 8-Intro The Wild Pack (Cable, Kane, Domino, Hammer, G.W. Bridge, & Grizzly); Liefeld-c/a (4); Mignola-a. 10-Weapon X full-length story (part 3). 11-1st Weapon Prime; Deadpool-c/story						4.00
11-15,19-24,26-33: 15-Cable leaves X-Force						3.00
16-18-Polybagged w/trading card in each; X-Cutioner's Song x-overs						4.00
25-($3.50, 52 pgs.)-Wraparound-c w/Cable hologram on-c; Cable returns						4.00
34-37,39-45: 34-bound-in card sheet						3.00
38,40-43: 38-($2.00)-Newsstand edition. 40-43 ($1.95)-Deluxe edition						3.00
38-($2.95)-Collectors edition (prismatic)						5.00
44-49,51-67: 44-Return from Age of Apocalypse. 45-Sabretooth app. 49-Sebastian Shaw app. 52-Blob app., Onslaught cameo. 55-Vs. S.H.I.E.L.D. 56-Deadpool app. 57-Mr. Sinister & X-Man-c/app. 57,58-Onslaught x-over. 59-W/card insert; return of Longshot. 60-Dr. Strange						3.00
50 ($3.95)-Gatefold wrap-around foil-c						4.00
50 ($3.95)-Liefeld variant-c						5.00
68-74: 68-Operation Zero Tolerance						3.00
75,100-($2.99): 75-Cannonball-c/app.						4.00
76-99,101,102: 81-Pollina poster. 95-Magneto-c. 102-Ellis-s/Portacio-a						3.00
103-115: 103-Begin $2.25-c; Portacio-a thru #106. 115-Death of old team						3.00
116-New team debuts; Allred-c/a; Milligan-s; no Comics Code stamp on-c						4.00
117-129: 117-Intro. Mr. Sensitive. 120-Wolverine-c/app. 123-'Nuff Said issue. 124-Darwyn Cooke-a/c. 128-Death of U-Go Girl. 129-Fegredo-a						3.00
#(-1) Flashback (7/97) story of John Proudstar; Pollina-a						3.00
Annual 1-3 ('92-'94, 68 pgs.)-1-1st Greg Capullo-a(p) on X-Force. 2-Polybagged w/trading card; intro X-Treme & Neurtap						4.00
...And Cable '95 (12/95, $3.95)-Impossible Man app.						4.00
...And Cable '96, ...'97 ('96, 7/97) -'96-Wraparound-c						4.00
...And Spider-Man: Sabotage nn (11/92, $6.95)-Reprints X-Force #3,4 & Spider-Man #16						7.00
.../ Champions '98 ($3.50)						4.00
Annual 99 ($3.50)						4.00
...: Famous, Mutant & Mortal HC (2003, $29.99) oversized r/#116-129; foreward by Milligan; gallery of covers and pin-ups; script for #123						30.00
...New Beginnings TPB (10/01, $14.95) r/#116-120						15.00
...Rough Cut ($2.99) Pencil pages and script for #102						3.00
...Youngblood (8/96, $4.95)-Platt-c						5.00

NOTE: ***Capullo** a(p)-15-25, Annual 1; c(p)-14-27. **Rob Liefeld** a-1-7, 9p; c-1-9, 11p; plots-1-12. **Mignola** a-8p.*

X-FORCE
Marvel Comics: Oct, 2004 - No. 6, Mar, 2005 ($2.99, limited series)

1-6-Liefeld-c/a; Nicieza-s. 5,6-Wolverine & The Thing app.						3.00
X-Force & Cable Vol. 1: The Legend Returns (2005, $14.99) r/#1-6						15.00

X-FORCE (Also see Uncanny X-Force)
Marvel Comics: Apr, 2008 - No. 28, Sept, 2010 ($2.99)

1-Crain-a; Wolverine & X-23 app.; two covers (regular and bloody) by Crain on #1-5						4.00
2-21,23-28: 2,3-Bastion app. 4-6-Archangel app. 7-10-Choi-a. 9-11-Ghost Rider app. 26-28-Second Coming x-over; Granov-c. 26-Nightcrawler killed						3.00
22-($3.99) Necrosha x-over; Crain-a						4.00
...Annual 1 (2/10, $3.99) Kirkman-s/Pearson-a/c; Deadpool back-up w/Barberi-a						4.00
.../Cable: Messiah War 1 (5/09, $3.99) Choi-a; covers by Andrews and Choi						4.00
... Special: Ain't No Dog (8/08, $3.99) Huston-s/Palo-a; Dell'Edera-a; Hitch-c						4.00

X-FORCE MEGAZINE
Marvel Comics: Nov, 1996 ($3.95, one-shot)

1-Reprints						4.00

X-FORCE: SEX AND VIOLENCE
Marvel Comics: Sept, 2010 - No. 3, Nov, 2010 ($3.99, limited series)

1-3-Dell'Otto-a/Kyle & Yost-s; Domino & Wolverine vs. The Hand & The Assassins Guild						4.00

X-FORCE: SHATTERSTAR
Marvel Comics: Apr, 2005 - No. 4, July, 2005 ($2.99, limited series)

1-4-Liefeld-c/s; Michaels-a						3.00
TPB (2005, $15.99) r/#1-4 & New Mutants #99,100						16.00

X-INFERNUS
Marvel Comics: Feb, 2009 - No. 4, May, 2009 ($3.99, limited series)

1-4-Illyana Rasputin in Limbo; Cebulski-s/Camuncoli-a/Finch-c						4.00

XIN: JOURNEY OF THE MONKEY KING
Anarchy Studios: May, 2003 - No. 3, July, 2003 ($2.99)

Preview Edition (Apr, 2003, $1.99) Flip book w/ Vampi Vicious Preview Edition						3.00
1-3-Kevin Lau-a. 1-Three covers by Lau, Park and Nauck. 2-Three covers						3.00

XIN: LEGEND OF THE MONKEY KING
Anarchy Studios: Nov, 2002 - No. 3, Jan, 2003 ($2.99)

Preview Edition (Summer 2002, Diamond Dateline supplement)						3.00
1-3-Kevin Lau-a. 1-Two covers by Lau & Madureira. 2-Two covers by Lau & Oeming						3.00

X-Man #34 © MAR

X-Men #15 © MAR

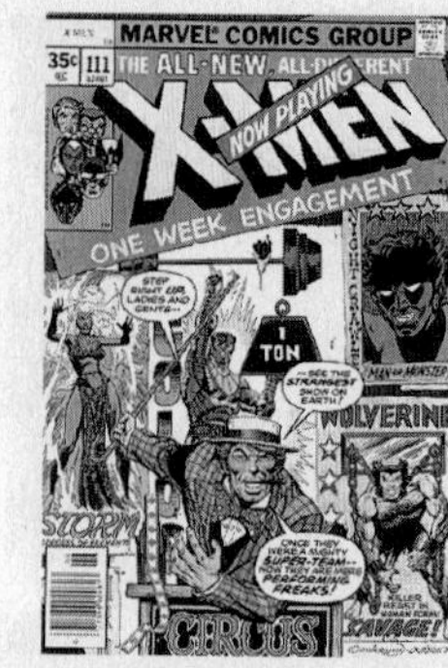

X-Men #111 © MAR

GD 2.0 | VG 4.0 | FN 6.0 | VF 8.0 | VF/NM 9.0 | NM- 9.2

TPB (10/03, $12.95) r/#1-3; cover gallery and sketch pages 13.00

X-MAN (Also see X-Men Omega & X-Men Prime)
Marvel Comics: Mar, 1995 - No. 75, May, 2001 ($1.95/$1.99/$2.25)

1-Age of Apocalypse 5.00
1-2nd print 3.00
2-4,25: 25-($2.99)-Wraparound-c 4.00
5-24, 26-28: 5-Post Age of Apocalypse stories begin. 5-7-Madelyne Pryor app. 10-Professor X app. 12-vs. Excalibur. 13-Marauders, Cable app. 14-Vs. Cable; Onslaught app. 15-17-Vs. Holocaust. 17-w/Onslaught Update. 18-Onslaught x-over; X-Force-c/app; Marauders app. 19-Onslaught x-over. 20-Abomination-c/app.; w/card insert. 23-Bishop app. 24-Spider-Man, Morbius-c/app. 27-Re-appearance of Aurora(Alpha Flight) 3.00
29-49,51-62: 29-Operation Zero Tolerance. 37,38-Spider-Man-c/app. 56-Spider-Man app. 3.00
50-($2.99) Crossover with Generation X #50 4.00
63-74: 63-Ellis & Grant-s/Olivetti-a begins. 64-Begin $2.25-c 3.00
75 ($2.99) Final issue; Alcatena-a 4.00
#(-1) Flashback (7/97) 3.00
...'96, ...'97-($2.95)-Wraparound-c; '96-Age of Apocalypse 4.00
...: All Saints' Day ('97, $5.99) Dodson-a 6.00
.../Hulk '98 ($2.99) Wraparound-c; Thanos app. 4.00

XMAS COMICS
Fawcett Publications: 12?/1941 - No. 2, 12?/1942; (50¢, 324 pgs.)
No. 7, 12?/1947 (25¢, 132 pgs.)(#3-6 do not exist)

1-Contains Whiz #21, Capt. Marvel #3, Bulletman #2, Wow #3, & Master #18; front & back-c by Raboy. Not rebound, remaindered comics; printed at same time as originals 411 822 1233 2877 5039 7200
2-Capt. Marvel, Bulletman, Spy Smasher 174 348 522 1114 1907 2700
7-Funny animals (Hoppy, Billy the Kid & Oscar) 65 130 195 416 708 1000

XMAS COMICS
Fawcett Publications: No. 4, Dec, 1949 - No. 7, Dec, 1952 (50¢, 196 pgs.)

4-Contains Whiz, Master, Tom Mix, Captain Marvel, Nyoka, Capt. Video, Bob Colt, Monte Hale, Hot Rod Comics, & Battle Stories. Not rebound, remaindered comics; printed at the same time as originals. Stocking on cover is made of green or red felt 81 162 243 518 884 1250
5-7-Same as above. 5- Red felt on-c. 7-Bill Boyd app.; stocking on cover is made of green felt (novelty cover) 61 122 183 390 670 950

X-MEN, THE (See Adventures of Cyclops and Phoenix, Amazing Adventures, Archangel, Brotherhood, Capt. America #172, Classic X-Men, Exiles, Further Adventures of Cyclops & Phoenix, Gambit, Giant-Size..., Heroes For Hope..., Kitty Pryde & Wolverine, Marvel & DC Present, Marvel Collector's Edition:..., Marvel Fanfare, Marvel Graphic Novel, Marvel Super Heroes, Marvel Team-Up, Marvel Triple Action, The Marvel X-Men Collection, New Mutants, Nightcrawler, Official Marvel Index To..., Rogue, Special Edition..., Ultimate..., Uncanny..., Wolverine, X-Factor, X-Force, X-Terminators)

X-MEN, THE (1st series)(Becomes Uncanny X-Men at #142)(The X-Men #1-93; X-Men #94-141) (The Uncanny X-Men on-c only #114-141)
Marvel Comics Group: Sept, 1963 - No. 66, Mar, 1970; No. 67, Dec, 1970 - No. 141, Jan, 1981

1-Origin/1st app. X-Men (Angel, Beast, Cyclops, Iceman & Marvel Girl); 1st app. Magneto & Professor X 850 1700 2550 8000 19,000 30,000
2-1st app. The Vanisher 156 312 468 1365 2783 4200
3-1st app. The Blob (1/64) 92 184 276 782 1591 2400
4-1st Quicksilver & Scarlet Witch & Brotherhood of the Evil Mutants (3/64); 1st app. Toad; 2nd app. Magneto 96 192 288 816 1658 2500
5-Magneto & Evil Mutants-c/story 64 128 192 544 1097 1650
6,7: 6-Sub-Mariner app. 7-Magneto app. 50 100 150 425 863 1300
8,9,11: 8-1st Unus the Untouchable. 9-Early Avengers app. (1/65); 1st Lucifer. 11-1st app. The Stranger. 42 84 126 336 681 1025
10-1st S.A. app. Ka-Zar & Zabu the sabertooth (3/65) 42 84 126 339 690 1040
12-Origin Prof. X; Origin/1st app. Juggernaut 46 92 138 368 747 1125
13-Juggernaut and Human Torch app. 32 64 96 246 486 725
14,15: 14-1st app. Sentinels. 15-Origin Beast 33 66 99 254 502 750
16-20: 19-1st app. The Mimic (4/66) 19 38 57 139 280 420
21-27,29,30: 27-Re-enter The Mimic (r-in #75); Spider-Man cameo 14 28 42 96 191 285
28-1st app. The Banshee (1/67)(r-in #76) 19 38 57 139 280 420
28-2nd printing (1994) 2 4 6 8 10 12
31-34,36,37,39: 34-Adkins-c/a. 39-New costumes 11 22 33 80 150 220
35-Spider-Man x-over (8/67)(r-in #83); 1st app. Changeling 24 48 72 175 350 525
38,40: 38-Origins of the X-Men series begins, ends #57. 40-(1/68) 1st app. Frankenstein's monster at Marvel 12 24 36 84 157 230
41-49: 42-Death of Prof. X (Changeling disguised as). 44-1st S.A. app. G.A. Red Raven. 49-Steranko-c; 1st Polaris 11 22 33 75 138 200
50,51-Steranko-c/a 11 22 33 77 144 210
52 10 20 30 70 125 180
53-Barry Smith-c/a (his 1st comic book work) 11 22 33 77 144 210
54,55-B. Smith-c. 54-1st app. Alex Summers who later becomes Havok. 55-Summers discovers he has mutant powers 11 22 33 77 144 210
56,57,59-63,65-Neal Adams-a(p). 56-Intro Havok w/o costume. 60-1st Sauron. 65-Return of Professor X. 12 24 36 82 154 225
58-1st app. Havok in costume; N. Adams-a(p) 13 26 39 94 185 275
62,63-2nd printings (1994) 2 4 6 8 10 12
64-1st app. Sunfire 11 22 33 77 144 210
66-Last new story w/original X-Men; battles Hulk 12 24 36 86 161 235
67-70: 67-Reprints begin, end #93. 67-70: (52 pgs.) 9 18 27 65 113 160
71-93: 71-Last 15¢ issue. 72: (52 pgs.). 73-86-r/#25-38 w/new-c. 83-Spider-Man-c/story. 87-93-r/#39-45 with covers 8 16 24 56 93 130
94 (8/75)-New X-Men begin (see Giant-Size X-Men for 1st app.); Colossus, Nightcrawler, Thunderbird, Storm, Wolverine, & Banshee join; Angel, Marvel Girl & Iceman resign 70 140 210 550 900 1250
95-Death of Thunderbird 16 32 48 111 226 340
96,97 10 20 30 73 134 195
98,99-(Regular 25¢ edition)(4,6/76) 10 20 30 72 131 190
98,99-(30¢-c variants, limited distribution) 17 34 51 124 252 380
100-Old vs. New X-Men; part origin Phoenix; last 25¢ issue (8/76) 12 24 36 82 154 225
100-(30¢-c variant, limited distribution) 21 42 63 150 300 450
101-Phoenix origin concludes 13 26 39 89 170 250
102-104: 102-Origin Storm. 104-1st brief app. Starjammers; Magneto-c/story 8 16 24 58 97 135
105-107-(Regular 30¢ editions). 106-(8/77)Old vs. New X-Men. 107-1st full app. Starjammers; last 30¢ issue 8 16 24 54 90 125
105-107-(35¢-c variants, limited distribution) 13 26 39 89 170 250
108-Byrne-a begins (see Marvel Team-Up #53) 8 16 24 58 97 135
109-1st app. Weapon Alpha (becomes Vindicator) 8 16 24 54 90 125
110,111: 110-Phoenix joins 7 14 21 45 73 100
112-116 7 14 21 45 73 100
117-119: 117-Origin Professor X 6 12 18 39 62 85
120-1st app. Alpha Flight, story line begins (4/79); 1st app. Vindicator (formerly Weapon Alpha); last 35¢ issue 8 16 24 54 90 125
121-1st full Alpha Flight story 7 14 21 50 83 115
122-128: 123-Spider-Man x-over. 124-Colossus becomes Proletarian 5 10 15 35 55 75
129-Intro Kitty Pryde (1/80); last Banshee; Dark Phoenix saga begins; intro. Emma Frost (White Queen) 6 12 18 41 66 90
130-1st app. The Dazzler by Byrne (2/80) 6 12 18 37 59 80
131-135: 131-Dazzler app.; 1st White Queen-c. 133-Wolverine app. 134-Phoenix becomes Dark Phoenix 5 10 15 35 55 75
136,138: 138-Dazzler app.; Cyclops leaves 5 10 15 30 48 65
137-Giant; death of Phoenix 6 12 18 41 66 90
139-Alpha Flight app.; Kitty Pryde joins; new costume for Wolverine 5 10 15 35 55 75
140-Alpha Flight app. 5 10 15 35 55 75
141-Intro Future X-Men & The New Brotherhood of Evil Mutants; 1st app. Rachel (Phoenix II); Death of Franklin Richards 6 12 18 37 59 80

X-MEN: Titled THE UNCANNY X-MEN #142, Feb, 1981 - Present

142-Rachel app.; deaths of alt. future Wolverine, Storm & Colossus 6 12 18 41 66 90
143-Last Byrne issue 5 10 15 32 51 70
144-150: 144-Man-Thing app. 145-Old X-Men app. 148-Spider-Woman, Dazzler app. 150-Double size 2 4 6 9 13 16
151-157,159-161,163,164: 161-Origin Magneto. 163-Origin Binary. 164-1st app. Binary as Carol Danvers 2 4 6 8 10 12
158-1st app. Rogue in X-Men (6/82, see Avengers Annual #10) 3 6 9 16 23 30
162-Wolverine solo story 2 4 6 10 14 18
165-Paul Smith-c/a begins, ends #175 2 4 6 8 11 14
166-170: 166-Double size; Paul Smith-a. 167-New Mutants app. (3/83); same date as New Mutants #1; 1st meeting w/X-Men; ties into N.M. #3,4; Starjammers app.; contains skin "Tattooz" decals. 168-1st brief app. Madelyne Pryor (last page) in X-Men (see Avengers Annual #10) 2 3 4 6 8 10
171-Rogue joins X-Men; Simonson-c/a 2 4 6 13 18 22
172-174: 172,173-Two part Wolverine solo story. 173-Two cover variations, blue & black. 174-Phoenix cameo 1 3 4 6 8 10
175-(52 pgs.)-Anniversary issue; Phoenix returns 2 4 6 8 10 12
176-185,187-192,194-199: 181-Sunfire app. 182-Rogue solo story. 184-1st app. Forge (8/84). 190,191-Spider-Man & Avengers x-over. 195-Power Pack x-over 1 2 3 5 7 9

Uncanny X-Men #317 © MAR

Uncanny X-Men #400 © MAR

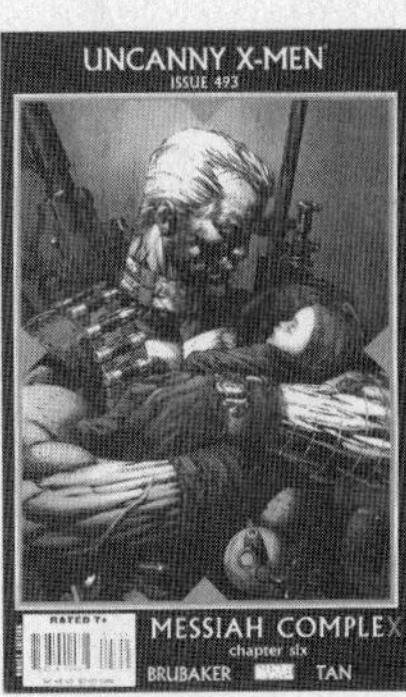

Uncanny X-Men #493 © MAR

GD VG FN VF VF/NM NM-
2.0 4.0 6.0 8.0 9.0 9.2

186,193: 186-Double-size; Barry Smith/Austin-a. 193-Double size; 100th app. New X-Men; 1st app. Warpath in costume (see New Mutants #16) 1 3 4 6 8 10
200-(12/85, $1.25, 52 pgs.) 2 4 6 8 10 12
201-(1/86)-1st app. Cable? (as baby Nathan; see X-Factor #1); 1st Whilce Portacio-c/a(i) on X-Men (guest artist) 3 6 9 16 23 30
202-204,206-209: 204-Nightcrawler solo story; 2nd Portacio-a(i) on X-Men. 207-Wolverine/Phoenix story 1 2 3 5 7 9
205-Wolverine solo story by Barry Smith 2 4 6 9 13 16
210,211-Mutant Massacre begins 3 6 9 14 19 24
212,213-Wolverine vs. Sabretooth (Mutant Mass.) 3 6 9 16 22 28
214-221,223,224: 219-Havok joins (7/87); brief app. Sabretooth. 221-1st app. Mr. Sinister 1 2 3 5 6 8
222-Wolverine battles Sabretooth-c/story 3 6 9 14 20 26
225-242: 225-227: Fall Of The Mutants. 226-Double size. 240-Sabretooth app. 242-Double size, X-Factor app., Inferno tie-in 1 2 3 5 6 8
243,245-247: 245-Rob Liefeld-a(p) 1 2 3 5 6 8
244-1st app. Jubilee 3 6 9 18 27 35
248-1st Jim Lee art on X-Men (1989) 2 4 6 13 18 22
248-2nd printing (1992, $1.25) 3.00
249-252: 252-Lee-c 1 2 3 4 5 7
253-255: 253-All new X-Men begin. 254-Lee-c 1 2 3 4 5 7
256,257-Jim Lee-c/a begins 1 2 3 5 7 9
258-Wolverine solo story; Lee-c/a 1 2 3 5 7 9
259-Silvestri-c/a; no Lee-a 1 2 3 4 5 7
260-265-No Lee-a. 260,261,264-Lee-c 1 2 3 4 5 7
266-(8/90) 1st full app. Gambit (see Annual #14)-No Lee-a 4 8 12 24 37 50
267-Jim Lee-c/a resumes; 2nd full Gambit app. 2 4 6 9 13 16
268-Capt. America, Black Widow & Wolverine team-up; Lee-a 2 4 6 10 14 18
268,270: 268-2nd printing. 270-Gold 2nd printing 3.00
269,273,274: 269-Lee-a. 273-New Mutants (Cable) & X-Factor x-over; Golden, Byrne & Lee part pencils 1 2 3 4 5 7
270-X-Tinction Agenda begins 1 2 3 5 6 8
271,272-X-Tinction Agenda 1 2 3 5 6 8
275-(52 pgs.)-Tri-fold-c by Jim Lee (p); Prof. X 1 2 3 5 6 8
275-Gold 2nd printing 4.00
276-280: 277-Last Lee-c/a. 280-X-Factor x-over 6.00
281-(10/91)-New team begins (Storm, Archangel, Colossus, Iceman & Marvel Girl); Whilce Portacio-c/a begins; Byrne scripts begin; wraparound-c (white logo) 1 2 3 4 5 7
281-2nd printing with red metallic ink logo w/o UPC box ($1.00-c); does not say 2nd printing inside 3.00
282-1st brief app. Bishop (cover & 1 page) 2 4 6 8 10 12
282-Gold ink 2nd printing ($1.00-c) 3.00
283-1st full app. Bishop (12/91) 2 4 6 8 10 12
284-299: 284-Last $1.00-c. 286,287-Lee plots. 287-Bishop joins team. 288-Lee/Portacio plots. 290-Last Portacio-c/a. 294-Peterson-a(p) begins (#292 is 1st Peterson-c). 294-296 ($1.50)-Bagged w/trading card in each; X-Cutioner's Song x-overs; Peterson/Austin-c/a on all 4.00
300-($3.95, 68 pgs.)-Holo-grafx foil-c; Magneto app. 6.00
301-303,305-309,311 3.00
297,303,307-Gold Edition 1 2 3 4 5 7
304-($3.95, 68 pgs.)-Wraparound-c with Magneto hologram on-c; 30th anniversary issue; Jae Lee-a (4 pgs.) 6.00
310-($1.95)-Bound-in trading card sheet 3.00
312-$1.50-c begins; bound-in card sheet; 1st Madureira 4.00
313-321 3.00
316,317-($2.95)-Foil enhanced editions 4.00
318-321-($1.95)-Deluxe editions 3.00
322-Onslaught 5.00
323,324,326-346: 323-Return from Age of Apocalypse. 328-Sabretooth-c. 329,330-Dr. Strange app. 331-White Queen-c/app. 334-Juggernaut app.; w/Onslaught Update. 335-Onslaught, Avengers, Apocalypse, & X-Man app. 336-Onslaught. 338-Archangel's wings return to normal. 339-Havok vs. Cyclops; Spider-Man app. 341-Gladiator-c/app. 342-Deathbird cameo; two covers. 343,344-Phalanx 3.00
325-($3.95)-Anniversary issue; gatefold-c 5.00
342-Variant-c 1 3 4 6 8 10
347-349:347-Begin $1.99-c. 349-"Operation Zero Tolerance" 3.00
350-($3.99, 48 pgs.) Prismatic etched foil gatefold wraparound-c; Trial of Gambit; Seagle-s begin 1 2 3 5 6 8
351-359: 353-Bachalo-a begins. 354-Regular-c. 355-Alpha Flight-c/app. 356-Original X-Men-c 3.00
354-Dark Phoenix variant-c 5.00
360-($2.99) 35th Anniv. issue; Pacheco-c 4.00
360-($3.99) Etched Holo-foil enhanced-c 5.00
360-($6.95) DF Edition with Jae Lee variant-c 7.00
361-374: 361-Gambit returns; Skroce-a. 362-Hunt for Xavier pt. 1; Bachelo-a. 364-Yu-a. 366-Magneto-c. 369-Juggernaut-c 3.00
375-($2.99) Autopsy of Wolverine 4.00
376-379: 376,377-Apocalypse: The Twelve 3.00
380-($2.99) Polybagged with X-Men Revolution Genesis Edition preview 4.00
381,382,384-389,391-393: 381-Begin $2.25-c; Claremont-s. 387-Maximum Security 3.00
383-($2.99) 4.00
390-Colossus dies to cure the Legacy Virus 4.00
394-New look X-Men begins; Casey-s/Churchill-c/a 3.50
395-399-Poptopia. 398-Phillips & Wood-a 3.00
400-($3.50) Art by Ashley Wood, Eddie Campbell, Hamner, Phillips, Pulido and Matt Smith; wraparound-c by Wood 4.00
401-415: 401-'Nuff Said issue; Garney-a. 404,405,407-409,413-415-Phillips-a 3.00
416-421: 416-Asamiya-a begins. 421-Garney-a 3.00
422-($3.50) Alpha Flight app.; Garney-a 4.00
423-(25¢-c) Holy War pt. 1; Garney-a/Philip Tan-c 3.00
424-449,452-454: 425,426,429,430-Tan-a. 428-Birth of Nightcrawler. 437-Larroca-a begins. 444-New team, new costumes; Claremont-s/Davis-a begins. 448,449-Coipel-a 3.00
450,451,455-459-X-23 app.; Davis-a 3.00
460-471: 460-Begin $2.50-c; Raney-a. 462-465-House of M. 464-468-Bachalo-a 3.00
472-499: 472-Begin $2.99-c; Bachalo-a. 475-Wraparound-c. 492-494-Messiah Complex 3.00
500-($3.99) X-Men new HQ in San Francisco; Magneto app.; Land & Dodson-a; wraparound covers by Alex Ross and Greg Land 5.00
500-Classic X-Men Dynamic Forces variant-c by Ross 8.00
500-X-Men variant-c by Michael Turner 30.00
500-X-Women variant-c by Dodson 15.00
501-511,515-521,523-525: 501-Brubaker & Fraction-s/Land-a. 523-525-Second Coming 3.00
512-514,522-($3.99). 513,514-Utopia x-over. 522-Kitty Pryde returns to Earth; Portacio-a 4.00
526-535-($3.99) 526-The Heroic Age; aftermath of Second Coming. 530-534-Land-a 4.00
534.1 (6/11, $2.99) Pacheco-a/c 3.00
#(-1) Flashback (7/97) Ladronn-c/Hitch & Neary-a 3.00
Special 1(12/70)-Kirby-c/a; origin The Stranger 10 20 30 69 122 175
Special 2(11/71, 52 pgs.) 8 16 24 52 86 120
Annual 3(1979, 52 pgs.)-New story; Miller/Austin-c; Wolverine still in old yellow costume 5 10 15 30 48 65
Annual 4(1980, 52 pgs.)-Dr. Strange guest stars 3 6 9 14 20 25
Annual 5(1981, 52 pgs.) 2 4 6 8 10 12
Annual 6-8('82-'84 52 pgs.)-6-Dracula app. 1 2 3 5 6 8
Annual 9,10('85, '86)-9-New Mutants x-over cont'd from New Mutants Special Ed. #1; Art Adams-a. 10-Art Adams-a 2 4 6 8 10 12
Annual 11-13:('87-'89, 68 pgs.): 12-Evolutionary War; A.Adams-a(p). 13-Atlantis Attacks 5.00
Annual 14(1990, $2.00, 68 pgs.)-1st app. Gambit (minor app., 5 pgs.); Fantastic Four, New Mutants (Cable) & X-Factor x-over; Art Adams-c/a(p) 3 6 9 16 23 30
Annual 15 (1991, $2.00, 68 pgs.)-4 pg. origin; New Mutants x-over; 4 pg. Wolverine solo back-up story; 4th app. X-Force cont'd from New Warriors Annual #1 5.00
Annual 16-18 ('92-'94, 68 pgs.)-16-Jae Lee-c/a(p). 17-Bagged w/card 4.00
Annual '95-(11/95, $3.95)-Wraparound-c 4.00
Annual '96,'97-Wraparound-c 4.00
.../Fantastic Four Annual '98 ($2.99) Casey-s 4.00
Annual '99 ($3.50) Jubilee app. 4.00
Annual 2000 ($3.50) Cable app.; Ribic-a 4.00
Annual 2001 ($3.50, printed wide-ways) Ashley Wood-c/a; Casey-s 4.00
Annual (Vol. 2) #1 (8/06, $3.99) Storm & Black Panther wedding prelude 4.00
Annual (Vol. 2) #2 (3/09, $3.99) Dark Reign; flashback to Sub-Mariner/Emma Frost 4.00
Annual (Vol. 2) #3 (5/11, $3.99) Escape From the Negative Zone; Bradshaw-a 4.00
....At The State Fair of Texas (1983, 36 pgs., one-shot); Supplement to the Dallas Times Herald 2 4 6 9 12 15
...: The Dark Phoenix Saga TPB 1st printing (1984, $12.95) 40.00
...: The Dark Phoenix Saga TPB 2nd-5th printings 25.00
...: The Dark Phoenix Saga TPB 6th-10th printings 20.00
... Days of Future Past TPB (2004, $19.99) r/#138-143 & Annual #4 20.00
... Eve of Destruction TPB (2005, $14.99) r/#391-393 & X-Men #111-113; Churchill-c 15.00
...:Dream's End (2004, $17.99)-r/Death of Colossus story arc from Uncanny X-Men #388-390, Cable #87, Bishop #16 and X-Men #108,110; debut pages from Giant-Size X-Men #1 18.00
... From The Ashes TPB (1990, $14.95) r/#168-176 15.00
... Future History - The Messiah War Sourcebook (2009, $3.99) Cable's files on X-Men 4.00
...: God Loves, Man Kills ($6.95)-r/Marvel Graphic Novel #5 7.00
...: God Loves, Man Kills - Special Edition (2003, $4.99)-reprint with new Hughes-c 5.00
...: God Loves, Man Kills HC (2007, $19.99) reprint with Claremont & Anderson interviews; original artist Neal Adams' six sketch pages and interview 20.00

X-Men (2nd series) #75 © MAR

X-Men (2nd series) #134 © MAR

X-Men (2nd series) #238 © MAR

GD VG FN VF VF/NM NM-
2.0 4.0 6.0 8.0 9.0 9.2

...: Hope (5/10, $2.99) Collects Cable and Hope back-ups; Dillon-a 3.00
House of M: Uncanny X-Men TPB (2006, $13.99) r/#462-465 and selections from Secrets Of The House of M one-shot 14.00
...In The Days of Future Past TPB (1989, $3.95, 52 pgs.) 6.00
...Old Soldiers TPB (2004, $19.99) r/#213,215 & Ann. #11; New Mutants Ann. #2&3 20.00
...Poptopia TPB (10/01, $15.95) r/#394-399 16.00
...: Rise & Fall of the Shi'Ar Empire HC (2007, $34.99, dustjacket) r/#475-486; bonus art 35.00
...: Rise & Fall of the Shi'Ar Empire SC (2008, $29.99) r/#475-486; bonus art 30.00
...: Sword of the Braddocks (5/09, $3.99) Psylocke vs. Slaymaster; Claremont-s 4.00
...: The Complete Onslaught Epic Book 1 TPB (2007, $29.99) r/X-Men #53-54, Uncanny X-Men #334-335, Fantastic Four #414-415, Avengers #400-401, Onslaught: X-Men, Cable #34 and Incredible Hulk #444 30.00
...: The Complete Onslaught Epic Book 2 TPB ('08, $29.99) r/Excalibur #100, Wolverine #104, X-Factor #125-126, Amazing Spider-Man #415, Green Goblin #12, Spider-Man #72, Punisher #11, X-Man #18 & X-Force #57 30.00
...: The Extremists TPB (2007, $13.99) r/#487-491 14.00
...: The Heroic Age (9/10, $3.99) Beast, Steve Rogers and Princess Powerful app. 4.00
Uncanny X-Men Omnibus Vol. 1 HC (2006, $99.99, dust jacket) r/Giant-Size X-Men #1, (Uncanny) X-Men #94-131 & Annual #3; cover gallery, promo and sketch art 100.00
Vignettes TPB (9/01, $17.95) r/Claremont & Bolton Classic X-Men #1-13 18.00
Vignettes Vol. 2 TPB (2005, $17.99) r/Claremont & Bolton Classic X-Men #14-25 18.00
... Vol. 1: Hope TPB (2003, $12.99) r/#410-415; Harris-c 13.00
... Vol. 2: Dominant Species TPB (2003, $11.99) r/#416-420; Asamiya-c 12.00
... Vol. 3: Holy War TPB (2003, $17.99) r/#421-427 18.00
... Vol. 4: The Draco TPB (2004, $15.99) r/#428-434 16.00
... Vol. 5: She Lies with Angels TPB (2004, $11.99) r/#437-441 12.00
... Vol. 6: Bright New Mourning TPB (2004, $14.99) r/#435,436,442,443 & (New) X-Men #155,156; Larroca sketch covers 15.00
...Vs. Apocalypse Vol. 1: The Twelve TPB (2008, $29.99) r/#376-377, Cable #73-76, X-Men #96,97 and Wolverine #145-147 30.00
... - The New Age Vol. 1: The End of History (2004, $12.99) r/#444-449 13.00
... - The New Age Vol. 2: The Cruelest Cut (2005, $11.99) r/#450-454 12.00
... - The New Age Vol. 3: On Ice (2006, $15.99) r/#455-461 16.00
... - The New Age Vol. 4: End of Greys (2006, $14.99) r/#466-471 15.00
... - The New Age Vol. 5: First Foursaken (2006, $11.99) r/#472-474 & Annual #1 12.00

NOTE: **Art Adams** *a-Annual 9, 10p, 12p, 14p; c-218p.* **Neal Adams** *a-56-63p, 65p; c-56-63.* **Adkins** *a-34, 35p; c-31, 34, 35.* **Austin** *a-108i, 109i, 111-117i, 119-143i, 186i, 204i, 228i, 294-297i, Annual 3i, 7i, 9i, 13; c-109-111i, 114-122i, 123, 124-141i, 142, 143, 196i, 204i, 228i, 294-297i, Annual 3i.* **J. Buscema** *c-42, 43, 45.* **Buscema/Tuska** *a-45.* **Byrne** *a(p)-108, 109, 111-143, 273; c(p)-113-116, 127, 129, 131-141.* **Capullo** *c-14.* **Ditko** *r-86, 89-91, 93.* **Everett** *c-73.* **Golden** *a-273, Annual 7p.* **Guice** *a-216p, 217p.* **G. Kane** *c(p)-33, 74-76, 79, 80, 94, 95.* **Kirby** *a(p)-1-17 (#12-17, 67r-layouts); c(p)-1-17, 25, 30 (18, 26-parts).* **Layton** *a-105i; c-112i, 113i.* **Jim Lee** *a(p)-248, 256-258, 267-277; c(p)-252, 254, 256-261, 264, 267, 270, 275-277, 286.* **Perez** *a-Annual 3p; c(p)-112, 128, Annual 3.* **Peterson** *a(p)-294-300, 304(part); c(p)-294-299.* **Whilce Portacio** *a(p)-281-286, 289, 290; a(i)-267; c-281-285p, 289p, 290; c(i)-267.* **Romita, Jr.** *a-300; c-300.* **Roussos** *a-84i.* **Simonson** *a-171p; c-171, 217.* **B. Smith** *a-53, 186p, 198p, 205, 214; c-53-55, 186p, 198, 205, 212, 214, 216.* **Paul Smith** *a(p)-165-170, 172-175, 278; c-165-170, 172-175, 278.* **Sparling** *a-78p.* **Steranko** *a-50p, 51p; c-49-51.* **Sutton** *a-106i.* **Art Thibert** *a(i)-281-286; c(i)-281, 282, 284, 285.* **Toth** *a-12p, 67p(r).* **Tuska** *a-40-42i, 43-46p, 88i(r); c-39-41, 77p, 78p.* **Williamson** *a-202i, 203i, 211i; c-202i, 203i, 206i.* **Wood** *c-14i.*

UNCANNY X-MEN AND THE NEW TEEN TITANS (See Marvel and DC Present...)

X-MEN (2nd Series)
Marvel Comics: Oct, 1991 - Present ($1.00-$2.99)

1 a-d (four different covers, $1.50, 52 pgs.)-Jim Lee-c/a begins, ends #11; new team begins (Cyclops, Beast, Wolverine, Gambit, Psylocke & Rogue); new Uncanny X-Men & Magneto app.; 5.00
1 e ($3.95)-Double gate-fold-c consisting of all four covers from 1a-d by Jim Lee; contains all pin-ups from #1a-d plus inside-c foldout poster; no ads; printed on coated stock 6.00
2-7: 4-Wolverine back to old yellow costume (same date as Wolverine #50); last $1.00-c. 5-Byrne scripts. 6-Sabretooth-c/story 5.00
8-10: 8-Gambit vs. Bishop-c/story; last Lee-a; Ghost Rider cameo cont'd in Ghost Rider #26. 9-Wolverine vs. Ghost Rider; cont'd/G.R. #26. 10-Return of Longshot 5.00
11-13,17-24,26-29,31: 12,13-Art Thibert-c/a. 28,29-Sabretooth app. 4.00
11-Silver ink 2nd printing; came with X-Men board game 2 4 6 9 12 15
14-16-($1.50)-Polybagged with trading card in each; X-Cutioner's Song x-overs; 14-Andy Kubert-c/a begins 5.00
25-($3.50, 52 pgs.)-Wraparound-c with Gambit hologram on-c; Professor X erases Magneto's mind 2 4 6 8 10 12
25-30th anniversary issue w/B&W-c with Magneto in color & Magneto hologram & no price on-c 2 4 6 9 12 15
25-Gold 30.00
30-($1.95)-Wedding issue w/bound-in trading card sheet 5.00
32-37: 32-Begin $1.50-c; bound-in card sheet. 33-Gambit & Sabretooth-c/story 4.00
36,37-($2.95)-Collectors editions (foil-c) 5.00
38-44,46-49,51-53, 55-65: 42,43- Paul Smith-a. 46,49,53-56-Onslaught app. 51-Waid scripts begin, end #56. 54-(Reg. edition)-Onslaught revealed as Professor X. 55,56-Onslaught x-over; Avengers, FF & Sentinels app. 56-Dr. Doom app. 57-Xavier taken into custody; Byrne-c/swipe (X-Men,1st Series #138). 59-Hercules-c/app. 61-Juggernaut-c/app. 62-Re-intro. Shang Chi; two covers. 63-Kingpin cameo. 64- Kingpin app. 4.00
45-($3.95)-Annual issue; gatefold-c 5.00
50-($2.95)-Vs. Onslaught, wraparound-c. 4.00
50-($3.95)-Vs. Onslaught, wraparound foil-c. 5.00
50-($2.95)-Variant gold-c. 3 6 9 20 30 40
50-($2.95)-Variant silver-c. 1 2 3 5 6 8
54-(Limited edition)-Embossed variant-c; Onslaught revealed as Professor X 3 6 9 16 23 30
66-69,71-74,76-79: 66-Operation Zero Tolerance. 76-Origin of Maggott 3.00
70-($2.99, 48 pgs.)-Joe Kelly-s begin, new members join 4.00
75-($2.99, 48 pgs.) vs. N'Garai; wraparound-c 4.00
80-($3.99) 35th Anniv. issue; holo-foil-c 5.00
80-($2.99) Regular-c 4.00
80-($6.95) Dynamic Forces Ed.; Quesada-c 7.00
81-93,95: 82-Hunt for Xavier pt. 2. 85-Davis-a. 86-Origin of Joseph. 87-Magneto War ends. 88-Juggernaut app. 3.00
94-($2.99) Contains preview of X-Men: Hidden Years 4.00
96-99: 96,97-Apocalypse: The Twelve 3.00
100-($2.99) Art Adams-c; begin Claremont-s/Yu-a 4.00
100-DF alternate-c 1 3 4 6 8 10
101-105,107,108,110-114: 101-Begin $2.25-c. 107-Maximum Security x-over; Bishop-c/app. 108-Moira MacTaggart dies; Senator Kelly shot. 111-Magneto-c. 112,113-Eve of Destruction 3.00
106-($2.99) X-Men battle Domina 4.00
109-($3.50, 100 pgs.) new and reprinted Christmas-themed stories 5.00
114-(7/01) Title change to "New X-Men," Morrison-s/Quitely-c/a begins 4.00
114-(8/10, $1.00) "Marvel's Greatest Comics" reprint 1.00
115-Two covers (Quitely & BWS) 3.00
116-125,127-149: 116-Emma Frost joins. 117,118-Van Sciver-a. 121,122,135-Quitely-a. 127-Leon & Sienkiewicz-a. 128-Kordey-a. 132,139-141-Jimenez-a. 136-138-Quitely-a 142-Sabretooth app.; Bachalo-c/a thru #145. 146-Magneto returns; Jimenez-a 3.00
126-($3.25) Quitely-a; defeat of Cassanova 4.00
150-($3.50) Jean Grey dies again; last Jimenez-a 4.00
151-156: 151-154-Silvestri-c/a 3.00
157-169: 157-X-Men Reload begins 3.00
170-184: 171- Begin $2.50-c. 175,176-Crossover with Black Panther #8,9. 181-184-Apocalypse returns 3.00
185-199,201-229,231-247: 185-Begin $2.99-c. 188-190,192-194,197-199-Bachalo-a. 195,196,201-203-Ramos-a. 201-204-Endangered Species back-up. 205-207-Messiah Complex x-over. 208-Romita Jr.-a. 210-Starts X-Men: Legacy. 228,229-Acuña-a. 235-237-Second Coming x-over. 238-The Heroic Age. 245-Age of X begins 3.00
200-($3.99) Two wraparound covers by Bachalo & Finch; Bachalo & Ramos-a 4.00
230-($3.99) Acuña-a; Rogue vs. Emplate 4.00
#(-1) Flashback (7/97); origin of Magneto 3.00
Annual 1-3 ('92-'94, $2.25-$2.95, 68 pgs.) 1-Lee-c & layouts; #2-Bagged w/card 4.00
Special '95 ($3.95) 4.00
... '96,...'97-Wraparound-c 4.00
.../ Dr. Doom '98 Annual ($2.99) Lopresti-a 4.00
... Annual '99 ($3.50) Adam Kubert-c 4.00
Annual 2000 ($3.50) Art Adams-c/Claremont-s/Eaton-a 4.00
...2001 Annual ($3.50) Morrison-s/Yu-a; issue printed sideways 4.00
...2007 Annual #1 (3/07, $3.99) Casey-s/Brooks-a; Cable and Mystique app. 4.00
...Legacy Annual 1 (11/09, $3.99) Acuña-a; Emplate returns 4.00
Animation Special Graphic Novel (12/90, $10.95) adapts animated series 11.00
Ashcan #1 (1994, 75¢) Introduces new team members 3.00
... Archives Sketchbook (12/00, $2.99) Early B&W character design sketches by various incl. Lee, Davis, Yu, Pacheco, BWS, Art Adams, Liefeld 3.00
...: Bizarre Love Triangle TPB (2005, $9.99)-r/X-Men #171-174 10.00
.../ Black Panther TPB (2006, $11.99)-r/X-Men #175,176 & Black Panther (2005) #8,9 12.00
...: Blinded By the Light (2007, $14.99)-r/X-Men #200-204 15.00
...: Blind Science (7/10, $3.99) Second Coming x-over; Parel-c 4.00
...: Blood of Apocalypse (2006, $17.99)-r/X-Men #182-187 18.00
...: Day of the Atom (2005, $19.99)-r/X-Men #157-165 20.00
Decimation: X-Men - The Day After TPB (2006, $15.99) r/#177-181 & Decimation: House of M - The Day After 16.00
...: Declassified (10/00, $3.50) Profile pin-ups by various; Jae Lee-c 4.00
...: Endangered Species (8/07, $3.99) prologue to 17-part back-up series in X-Men titles 4.00
...: Endangered Species HC (2008, $24.99, d.j.) over-sized r/prologue and 17-part series 25.00
...: Fatal Attractions ('94, $17.95)-r/x-Factor #92, X-Force #25, Uncanny X-Men #304, X-Men #25, Wolverine #75, & Excalibur #71 18.00
...: Golgotha (2005, $12.99)-r/X-Men #166-170 13.00
... Millennial Visions (8/00, $3.99) Various artists interpret future X-Men 4.00

X-Men (2010 series) #1 © MAR

X-Men: Age of Apocalypse One Shot © MAR

X-Men/Alpha Flight (1998) #1 © MAR

	GD	VG	FN	VF	VF/NM	NM-
	2.0	4.0	6.0	8.0	9.0	9.2

... Millennial Visions 2 (1/02, $3.50) Various artists interpret future X-Men 4.00
...: Mutant Genesis (2006, $19.99)-r/X-Men #1-7; sketch pages and extra art 20.00
New X-Men: E is for Extinction TPB (11/01, $12.95) r/#114-117 13.00
New X-Men: Imperial TPB (7/02, $19.99) r/#118-126; Quitely-c 20.00
New X-Men: New Worlds TPB (2002, $14.99) r/#127-133; Quitely-c 15.00
New X-Men: Riot at Xavier's TPB (2003, $11.99) r/#134-138; Quitely-c 12.00
New X-Men: Vol. 5: Assault on Weapon Plus TPB (2003, $14.99) r/#139-145 15.00
New X-Men: Vol. 6: Planet X TPB (2004, $12.99) r/#146-150 13.00
New X-Men: Vol. 7: Here Comes Tomorrow TPB (2004, $10.99) r/#151-154 11.00
New X-Men: Volume 1 HC (2002, $29.99) oversized r/#114-126 & 2001 Annual 30.00
New X-Men: Volume 2 HC (2003, $29.99) oversized r/#127-141; sketch & script pages 30.00
New X-Men: Volume 3 HC (2004, $29.99) oversized r/#142-154; sketch & script pages 30.00
New X-Men Omnibus HC (2006, $99.99) oversized r/#114-154 & Annual 2001; Morrison's original pitch; sketch & script pages; variant covers & promo art; Carey intro. 140.00
...: Odd Men Out (2008, $3.99) Two unpublished stories with Dave Cockrum-a 4.00
... Original Sin 1 (12/08, $3.99) Wolverine and Daken; Deodato & Eaton-a 4.00
... Origin: Colossus (7/08, $3.99) Yost-s/Hairsine-a; Piotr Rasputin before joining X-Men 4.00
... Phoenix Force Handbook (9/10, $4.99) bios of those related to the Phoenix; Raney-c 5.00
...: Pixies and Demons Director's Cut (2008, $3.99) r/FCBD 2008 story with script 4.00
... Pizza Hut Mini-comics-(See Marvel Collector's Edition: X-Men in Promotional Comics section)
... Premium Edition #1 (1993)-Cover says "Toys 'R' Us Limited Edition X-Men" 3.00
...: Rarities (1995, $5.95)-Reprints 6.00
...: Return of Magik Must Have (2008, $3.99) r/X-Men Unlimited #14, New X-Men #37 and X-Men: Divided We Stand #2; Coipel-c 4.00
...: Road Trippin' ('99, $24.95, TPB) r/X-Men road trips 25.00
...: Supernovas ('07, $34.99, oversized HC w/d.j.) r/X-Men 188-199 & Annual #1 35.00
...: Supernovas ('08, $29.99, SC) r/X-Men 188-199 & Annual #1 30.00
...: The Coming of Bishop ('95, $12.95)-r/Uncanny X-Men #282-285, 287,288 13.00
...: The Magneto War (3/99, $2.99) Davis-a 3.00
...: The Rise of Apocalypse ('98, $16.99)-r/Rise Of Apocalypse #1-4, X-Factor #5,6 17.00
... Visionaries: Chris Claremont ('98, $24.95)-r/Claremont-s; art by Byrne, BWS, Jim Lee 25.00
... Visionaries: Jim Lee ('02, $29.99)-r/Jim Lee-a from various issues between Uncanny X-Men #248 & 286; r/Classic X-Men #39 and X-Men Annual #1 30.00
... Visionaries: Joe Madureira (7/00, $17.95)-r/Uncanny X-Men #325,326,329,330,341-343; new Madureira-c 18.00
... Vs. Hulk (3/09, $3.99) Claremont-s/Raapack-a; r/X-Men #66 4.00
...: Zero Tolerance ('00, $24.95, TPB) r/crossover series 25.00
NOTE: ***Jim Lee*** *a-1-11p; c-1-6p, 7, 8, 9p, 10, 11p.* ***Art Thibert*** *a-6-9i, 12, 13; c-6i, 12, 13.*

X-MEN
Marvel Comics: Sept, 2010 - Present ($3.99)
1-9: 1-6-"Curse of the Mutants" x-over; Medina-a. 7-9-Spider-Man app.; Bachalo-a 4.00
...: Curse of the Mutants - Blade 1 (10/10, $3.99) Tim Green-a 4.00
...: Curse of the Mutants - Smoke and Blood 1 (11/10, $3.99) Crain-c 4.00
...: Curse of the Mutants Spotlight 1 (1/11, $3.99) creator profiles and interviews 4.00
...: Curse of the Mutants - Storm and Gambit 1 (11/10, $3.99) Bachalo-a; 2 covers 4.00
...: Curse of the Mutants - X-Men vs. Vampires 1,2 (11/10 - No. 2, 12/10, $3.99) Bradshaw-c 4.00

X-MEN (Free Comic Book Day giveaways)
Marvel Comics: 2006; May, 2008
FCBD 2008 Edition #1-(5/08) Features Pixie; Carey-s/Land-a/c 2.50
.../Runaways: FCBD 2006 Edition; new x-over story; Mighty Avengers preview; Chen-c 2.50

X-MEN ADVENTURES (TV)
Marvel Comics: Nov, 1992 - No. 15, Jan, 1994 ($1.25)(Based on animated series)
1-Wolverine, Cyclops, Jubilee, Rogue, Gambit 4.00
2-15: 3-Magneto-c/story. 6-Sabretooth-c/story. 7-Cable-c/story. 10-Archangel guest star. 11-Cable-c/story. 15-($1.75, 52 pgs.) 3.00

X-MEN ADVENTURES II (TV)
Marvel Comics: Feb, 1994 - No. 13, Feb, 1995 ($1.25/$1.50)(Based on 2nd TV season)
1-13: 4-Bound-in trading card sheet. 5-Alpha Flight app. 3.00
...Captive Hearts/Slave Island (TPB, $4.95)-r/X-Men Adventures #5-8 5.00
...The Irresistible Force, The Muir Island Saga (5.95, 10/94, TPB) r/X-Men Advs. #9-12 6.00

X-MEN ADVENTURES III (TV)(See Adventures of the X-Men)
Marvel Comics: Mar, 1995 - No. 13, Mar, 1996 ($1.50) (Based on 3rd TV season)
1-13 3.00

X-MEN: AGE OF APOCALYPSE
Marvel Comics: May, 2005 - No. 6, June, 2005 ($2.99, weekly limited series)
1-6-Bachalo-c/a; Yoshida-s; follows events in the "Age of Apocalypse" storyline 3.00
... One Shot (5/05, $3.99) prequel to series; Hitch wraparound-c; pin-ups by various 4.00
X-Men: The New Age of Apocalypse TPB (2005, $20.99) r/#1-6 & one-shot 21.00

X-MEN ALPHA
Marvel Comics: 1994 ($3.95, one-shot)
nn-Age of Apocalypse; wraparound chromium-c 1 2 3 5 6 8
nn ($49.95)-Gold logo 50.00

X-MEN/ALPHA FLIGHT
Marvel Comics Group: Dec, 1985 - No. 2, Dec, 1985 ($1.50, limited series)
1,2: 1-Intro The Berserkers; Paul Smith-a 5.00

X-MEN/ALPHA FLIGHT
Marvel Comics Group: May, 1998 - No. 2, June, 1998 ($2.99, limited series)
1,2-Flashback to early meeting; Raab-s/Cassaday-s/a 3.00

X-MEN AND POWER PACK
Marvel Comics: Dec, 2005 - No. 4, Mar, 2006 ($2.99, limited series)
1-4-Sumerak-s/Gurihiru-a. 1-Wolverine & Sabretooth app. 3.00
...: The Power of X (2006, $6.99, digest size) r/#1-4 7.00

X-MEN AND THE MICRONAUTS, THE
Marvel Comics Group: Jan, 1984 - No. 4, Apr, 1984 (Limited series)
1-4: Guice-c/a(p) in all 5.00

X-MEN: APOCALYPSE/DRACULA
Marvel Comics: Apr, 2006 - No. 4, July, 2006 ($2.99, limited series)
1-4-Tieri-s/Henry-a/Jae Lee-c 3.00
TPB (2006, $10.99) r/series; cover gallery 11.00

X-MEN ARCHIVES
Marvel Comics: Jan, 1995 - No. 4, Apr, 1995 ($2.25, limited series)
1-4: Reprints Legion stories from New Mutants. 4-Magneto app. 3.00

X-MEN ARCHIVES FEATURING CAPTAIN BRITAIN
Marvel Comics: July, 1995 - No. 7, 1996 ($2.95, limited series)
1-7: Reprints early Capt. Britain stories 3.00

X-MEN BLACK SUN (See Black Sun:...)

X-MEN BOOKS OF ASKANI
Marvel Comics: 1995 ($2.95, one-shot)
1-Painted pin-ups w/text 3.00

X-MEN: CHILDREN OF THE ATOM
Marvel Comics: Nov, 1999 - No. 6 ($2.99, limited series)
1-6-Casey-s; X-Men before issue #1. 1-3-Rude-c/a. 4-Paul Smith-a/Rude-c. 5,6-Essad Ribic-c/a 3.00
TPB (11/01, $16.95) r/series; sketch pages; Casey intro. 17.00

X-MEN CHRONICLES
Marvel Comics: Mar, 1995 - No. 2, June, 1995 ($3.95, limited series)
1,2: Age of Apocalypse x-over. 1-wraparound-c 5.00

X-MEN: CLANDESTINE
Marvel Comics: Oct, 1996 - No. 2, Nov, 1996 ($2.95, limited series, 48 pgs.)
1,2: Alan Davis-c(p)/a(p)/scripts & Mark Farmer-c(i)/a(i) in all; wraparound-c 4.00

X-MEN CLASSIC (Formerly Classic X-Men)
Marvel Comics: No. 46, Apr, 1990 - No. 110, Aug, 1995 ($1.25/$1.50)
46-110: Reprints from X-Men. 54-(52 pgs.). 57,60-63,65-Russell-c(i); 62-r/X-Men #158(Rogue). 66-r/#162(Wolverine). 69-Begins-r of Paul Smith issues (#165 on). 70,79,90,97(52 pgs.). 70-r/X-Men #166. 90-r/#186. 100-($1.50). 104-r/X-Men #200 4.00

X-MEN CLASSICS
Marvel Comics Group: Dec, 1983 - No. 3, Feb, 1984 ($2.00, Baxter paper)
1-3: X-Men-r by Neal Adams 6.00
NOTE: ***Zeck*** *c-1-3.*

X-MEN: COLOSSUS BLOODLIINE
Marvel Comics: Nov, 2005 - No. 5, Mar, 2006 ($2.99, limited series)
1-5-Colossus returns to Russia; David Hine-s/Jorge Lucas-a; Bachalo-c 3.00
TPB (2006, $13.99) r/#1-5 14.00

X-MEN: DEADLY GENESIS (See Uncanny X-Men #475)
Marvel Comics: Jan, 2006 - No. 6, July, 2006 ($3.99/$3.50, limited series)
1-($3.99) Silvestri-c swipe of Giant-Size X-Men #1; Hairsine-a/Brubaker-s 4.00
2-6-($3.50) 2-Silvestri-c; Banshee killed. 4-Intro Kid Vulcan 3.50
HC (2006, $24.99, dust jacket) r/#1-6 25.00
SC (2006, $19.99) r/#1-6 20.00

X-MEN: DIE BY THE SWORD
Marvel Comics: Dec, 2007 - No. 5, Feb, 2008 ($2.99, limited series)
1-5-Excalibur and The Exiles app.; Claremont-s/Santacruz-a 3.00
TPB (2008, $13.99) r/#1-5; handbook pages of Merlyn, Roma and Saturne 14.00

X-Men: Evolution #4 © MAR

X-Men: Hidden Years #2 © MAR

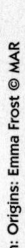

X-Men: Origins: Emma Frost © MAR

GD 2.0 | VG 4.0 | FN 6.0 | VF 8.0 | VF/NM 9.0 | NM- 9.2

GD 2.0 | VG 4.0 | FN 6.0 | VF 8.0 | VF/NM 9.0 | NM- 9.2

X-MEN: DIVIDED WE STAND
Marvel Comics: June, 2008 - No. 2, July, 2008 ($3.99, limited series)
1,2-Short stories by various; Peterson-c 4.00

X-MEN: EARTHFALL
Marvel Comics: Sept, 1996 ($2.95, one-shot)
1-r/Uncanny X-Men #232-234; wraparound-c 4.00

X-MEN: EMPEROR VULCAN
Marvel Comics: Nov, 2007 - No. 5, Mar, 2008 ($2.99, limited series)
1-5: 1-Starjammers app.; Yost-s/Diaz-a/Tan-c 3.00
TPB (2008, $13.99) r/#1-5 14.00

X-MEN: EVOLUTION (Based on the animated series)
Marvel Comics: Feb, 2002 - No. 9, Sept, 2002 ($2.25)
1-9: 1-8-Grayson-s/Udon-a. 9-Farber-s/J.J.Kirby-a 3.00
TPB (7/02, $8.99) r/#1-4 9.00
Vol. 2 TPB (2003, $11.99) r/#5-9; Asamiya-c 12.00

X-MEN FAIRY TALES
Marvel Comics: July, 2006 - No. 4, Oct, 2006 ($2.99, limited series)
1-4-Re-imagining of classic stories; Cebulski-s. 2-Baker-a. 3-Sienkiewicz-a. 4-Kobayashi-a 3.00
TPB (2006, $10.99) r/#1-4 11.00

X-MEN/ FANTASTIC FOUR
Marvel Comics: Feb, 2005 - No. 5, June, 2005 ($3.50, limited series)
1-5-Pat Lee-a/c; Yoshida-s; the Brood app. 3.50
HC (2005, $19.99, 7 1/2" x 11", dustjacket) oversized r/#1-5; cover gallery 20.00

X-MEN FIRST CLASS
Marvel Comics: Nov, 2006 - No. 8, Jun, 2007 ($2.99, limited series)
1-8-Xavier's first class of X-Men; Cruz-a/Parker-s. 5-Thor app. 7-Scarlet Witch app. 3.00
... Special 1 (7/07, $3.99) Nowlan-c; Nowlan, Paul Smith, Coover, Dragotta & Allred-a 4.00
... - Tomorrow's Brightest HC (2007, $24.99, d.j) r/#1-8; cover & character design art 25.00
... - Tomorrow's Brightest SC (2007, $19.99) r/#1-8; cover & character design art 20.00

X-MEN FIRST CLASS (2nd series)
Marvel Comics: Aug, 2007 - No. 16, Nov, 2008 ($2.99)
1-16: 1-Cruz-a/Parker-s; Fantastic Four app. 8-Man-Thing app. 10-Romita Jr.-c 3.00
... Giant-Size Special 1 (12/08, $3.99) 5 new short stories; Haspiel-a; r/X-Men #40 4.00
... - Mutant Mayhem TPB (2008, $13.99) r/#1-5 & X-Men First Class Special 14.00

X-MEN FIRST CLASS FINALS
Marvel Comics: Apr, 2009 - No. 4, July, 2009 ($3.99, limited series)
1-4-Cruz-a/Parker-s. 1-3-Coover-a 4.00

X-MEN FIRSTS
Marvel Comics: Feb, 1996 ($4.95, one-shot)
1-r/Avengers Annual #10, Uncanny X-Men #266, #221; Incredible Hulk #181 5.00

X-MEN FOREVER
Marvel Comics: Jan, 2001 - No. 6, June, 2001 ($3.50, limited series)
1-6-Jean Grey, Iceman, Mystique, Toad, Juggernaut app.; Maguire-a 3.50

X-MEN FOREVER
Marvel Comics: Aug, 2009 - No. 24, July, 2010 ($3.99)
1-24: 1-Claremont-s/Grummett-a/c. 7-Nick Fury app. 4.00
... Alpha 1 (2009, $4.99) r/X-Men (1991) #1-3; 8 page preview of X-Men Forever #1 5.00
... Annual 1 (6/10, $4.99) Wolverine & Jean Grey romance; Sana Takeda-a/c 5.00
... Giant-Size 1 (7/10, $3.99) Grell-a/c; Lilandra & Gladiator app.; r/(Uncanny)X-Men #108 4.00

X-MEN FOREVER 2
Marvel Comics: Aug, 2010 - Present ($3.99)
1-16: 1-Claremont-s/Grummett-a/c. 2,3-Spider-Man app. 9,10-Grell-a 4.00

X-MEN: HELLBOUND
Marvel Comics: July, 2010 - No. 3, Sept, 2010 ($3.99, limited series)
1-3-Second Coming x-over; Tolibao-a/Djurdjevic-c; Majik rescued from Limbo 4.00

X-MEN: HELLFIRE CLUB
Marvel Comics: Jan, 2000 - No. 4, Apr, 2000 ($2.50, limited series)
1-4-Origin of the Hellfire Club 3.00

X-MEN: HIDDEN YEARS
Marvel Comics: Dec, 1999 - No. 22, Sept. 2001 ($3.50/$2.50)
1-New adventures from pre-#94 era; Byrne-s/a(p) 4.00
2-4,6-11,13-22-($2.50): 2-Two covers. 3-Ka-Zar app. 8,9-FF-c/app. 3.00
5-($2.75) 3.00
12-($3.50) Magneto-c/app. 4.00

X-MEN: KING BREAKER
Marvel Comics: Feb, 2009 - No. 4, May, 2009 ($3.99, limited series)
1-4-Emperor Vulcan and a Shi'ar invasion; Havok, Rachel Grey and Polaris app. 4.00

X-MEN: KITTY PRYDE - SHADOW & FLAME
Marvel Comics: Aug, 2005 - No. 5, Dec, 2005 ($2.99, limited series)
1-5-Akira Yoshida-s/Paul Smith-a/c; Kitty & Lockheed go to Japan 3.00
TPB (2006, $14.99) r/#1-5 15.00

X-MEN LEGACY (See X-Men 2nd series)

X-MEN: LIBERATORS
Marvel Comics: Nov, 1998 - No. 4, Feb, 1999 ($2.99, limited series)
1-4-Wolverine, Nightcrawler & Colossus; P. Jimenez 3.00

X-MEN LOST TALES
Marvel Comics: 1997 ($2.99)
1,2-r/Classic X-Men back-up stories 3.00

X-MEN: MAGNETO TESTAMENT
Marvel Comics: Nov, 2008 - No. 5, Mar, 2009 ($3.99, limited series)
1-5-Max Eisenhardt in 1930s Nazi-occupied Poland; Pak-s/DiGiandomenico-a. 5-Back-up story of artist Dina Babbitt with Neal Adams-a 4.00

X-MEN: MANIFEST DESTINY
Marvel Comics: Nov, 2008 - No. 5, Mar, 2009 ($3.99, limited series)
1-5-Short stories of X-Men re-location to San Francisco; s/a by various 4.00
... Nightcrawler 1 (5/09, $3.99) Molina & Syaf-a; Mephisto app. 4.00

X-MEN: MESSIAH COMPLEX
Marvel Comics: Dec, 2007 ($3.99)
1-Part 1 of x-over with X-Men, Uncanny X-Men, X-Factor and New X-Men; 2 covers 4.00
... - Mutant Files (2007, $3.99) Handbook pages of x-over participants; Kolins-c 4.00
HC (2008, $39.99, oversized) r/#1, Uncanny X-Men #492-494, X-Men #205-207, New X-Men #44-46 and X-Factor #25-27 40.00

X-MEN NOIR
Marvel Comics: Nov, 2008 - No. 4, May, 2009 ($3.99, limited series)
1-4-Pulp-style story set in 1930s NY; Van Lente-s/Calero-a 4.00
...: Mark of Cain (2/10 - No. 4, 5/10, $3.99) an Lente-s/Calero-a 4.00

X-MEN OMEGA
Marvel Comics: June, 1995 ($3.95, one-shot)
nn-Age of Apocalypse finale 1 3 4 6 8 10
nn-($49.95)-Gold edition 50.00

X-MEN: ORIGINS
Marvel Comics: Oct, 2008 - Present ($3.99, series of one-shots)
...: Beast (11/08) High school years; Carey-s; painted-a/c by Woodward 4.00
...: Cyclops (3/10) Magneto app.; Delperdang-a/Granov-c 4.00
...: Deadpool (9/10) Fernandez-a/Swierczynski-s 4.00
...: Emma Frost (7/10) Moline-a; r/excerpt from 1st app. in Uncanny X-Men #129 4.00
...: Gambit (8/09) Mr. Sinister, Sabretooth and the Marauders app.; Yardin-a 4.00
...: Iceman (1/10) Noto-a 4.00
...: Jean Grey (10/08) Childhood & early X-days; McKeever-s; Mayhew painted-a/c 4.00
...: Nightcrawler (5/10) Cary Nord-a; r/excerpt from 1st app. in Giant-Size X-Men #1 4.00
...: Sabretooth (4/09) Childhood and early meetings with Wolverine; Panosian-a/c 4.00
...: Wolverine (6/09) Pre-X-Men days and first meeting with Xavier; Texeira-a/c 4.00

X-MEN: PHOENIX
Marvel Comics: Dec, 1999 - No. 3, Mar, 2000 ($2.50, limited series)
1-3: 1-Apocalypse app. 3.00

X-MEN: PHOENIX - ENDSONG
Marvel Comics: Mar, 2005 - No. 5, June, 2005 ($2.99, limited series)
1-5-The Phoenix Force returns to Earth; Greg Land-c/a; Greg Pak-s 3.00
HC (2005, $19.99, dust jacket) r/#1-5; Land sketch pages 20.00
SC (2006, $14.99) 15.00

X-MEN: PHOENIX - LEGACY OF FIRE
Marvel Comics: July, 2003 - No. 3, Sep, 2003 ($2.99, limited series)
1-3-Manga-style; Ryan Kinnard-s/a/c; intro page art by Adam Warren 3.00

X-MEN: PHOENIX - WARSONG
Marvel Comics: Nov, 2006 - No. 5, Mar, 2007 ($2.99, limited series)
1-5-Tyler Kirkham-a/Greg Pak-s/Marc Silvestri-c 3.00
HC (2007, $19.99, dustjacket) r/#1-5; variant cover gallery and Handbook pages 20.00
SC (2007, $14.99) r/#1-5; variant cover gallery and Handbook pages 15.00

X-MEN: PIXIE STRIKES BACK

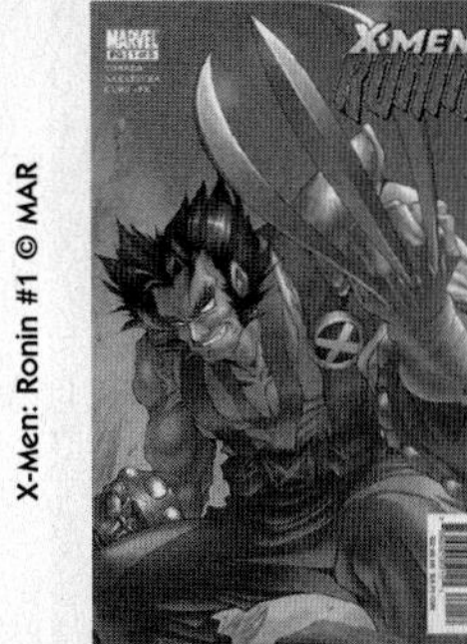

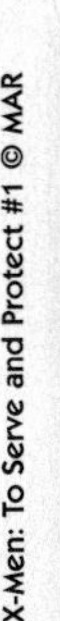
X-Men: Ronin #1 © MAR

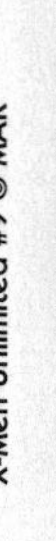
X-Men: To Serve and Protect #1 © MAR

X-Men Unlimited #9 © MAR

	GD	VG	FN	VF	VF/NM	NM-
	2.0	4.0	6.0	8.0	9.0	9.2

Marvel Comics: Apr, 2010 - No. 4, July, 2010 ($3.99, limited series)

1-4-Kathryn Immonen-s/Sara Pichelli-a/Stuart Immonen-c 4.00

X-MEN PRIME
Marvel Comics: July, 1995 ($4.95, one-shot)

nn-Post Age of Apocalyse begins 1 3 4 6 8 10

X-MEN RARITIES
Marvel Comics: 1995 ($5.95, one-shot)

nn-Reprints hard-to-find stories 6.00

X-MEN ROAD TO ONSLAUGHT
Marvel Comics: Oct, 1996 ($2.50, one-shot)

nn-Retells Onslaught Saga 3.00

X-MEN: RONIN
Marvel Comics: May, 2003 - No. 5, July, 2003 ($2.99, limited series)

1-5-Manga-style X-Men; Torres-s/Nakatsuka-a 3.00

X-MEN: SEARCH FOR CYCLOPS
Marvel Comics: Oct, 2000 - No. 4, Mar, 2001 ($2.99, limited series)

1-4-Two covers (Raney, Pollina); Raney-a 3.00

X-MEN: SECOND COMING
Marvel Comics: May, 2010 - No. 2, Sept, 2010 ($3.99)

1-Cable & Hope return to the present; Bastion app.; Finch-a; covers by Granov & Finch 4.00
2-Conclusion to x-over; covers by Granov & Finch 4.00
...: Prepare (4/10, free) previews x-over; short story w/Immonen-a; cover sketch art 3.00

X-MEN / SPIDER-MAN ("X-Men and Spider-Man" on cover)
Marvel Comics: Jan, 2009 - No. 4, Apr, 2009 ($3.99, limited series)

1-4: 1-Team-up from pre-blue Beast days; Kraven app.; Gage-s/Alberti-a 4.00

X-MEN SPOTLIGHT ON... STARJAMMERS (Also see X-Men #104)
Marvel Comics: 1990 - No. 2, 1990 ($4.50, 52 pgs.)

1,2: Features Starjammers 5.00

X-MEN SURVIVAL GUIDE TO THE MANSION
Marvel Comics: Aug, 1993 ($6.95, spiralbound)

1 7.00

X-MEN: THE COMPLETE AGE OF APOCALYPSE EPIC
Marvel Comics: 2005 - Vol. 4, 2006 ($29.99, TPB)

Book 1-4: Chronological reprintings of the crossover 30.00

X-MEN: THE EARLY YEARS
Marvel Comics: May, 1994 - No. 17, Sept, 1995 ($1.50/$2.50)

1-16: r/X-Men #1-8 w/new-c 3.00
17-$2.50-c; r/X-Men #17,18 4.00

X-MEN: THE END
Marvel Comics: Oct, 2004 - No. 6, Feb, 2005 ($2.99, limited series)

1-6-Claremont-s/Chen-a/Land-c 3.00
... Book One: Dreamers and Demons TPB (2005, $14.99) r/#1-6 15.00

X-MEN: THE END - HEROES AND MARTYRS (Volume 2)
Marvel Comics: May, 2005 - No. 6, Oct, 2005 ($2.99, limited series)

1-6-Claremont-s/Chen-a/Land-c; continued from X-Men: The End 3.00
... Vol. 2 TPB (2006, $14.99) r/#1-6 15.00

X-MEN: THE END (MEN & X-MEN) (Volume 3)
Marvel Comics: Mar, 2006 - No. 6, Aug, 2006 ($2.99, limited series)

1-6-Claremont-s/Chen-a. 1-Land-c. 2-6-Gene Ha-c 3.00
... Vol. 3 TPB (2006, $14.99) r/#1-6 15.00

X-MEN: THE MANGA
Marvel Comics: Mar, 1998 - No. 26, June, 1999 ($2.99, B&W)

1-26-English version of Japanese X-Men comics: 23,24-Randy Green-c 3.00

X-MEN: THE MOVIE
Marvel Comics: Aug, 2000; Sept, 2000

Adaptation (9/00, $5.95) Macchio-s/Williams & Lanning-a 6.00
Adaptation TPB (9/00, $14.95) Movie adaptation and key reprints of main characters; four photo covers (movie X, Magneto, Rogue, Wolverine) 15.00
Prequel: Magneto (8/00, $5.95) Texeira & Palmiotti-a; art & photo covers 6.00
Prequel: Rogue (8/00, $5.95) Evans & Nikolakakis-a; art & photo covers 6.00
Prequel: Wolverine (8/00, $5.95) Waller & McKenna-a; art & photo covers 6.00
TPB X-Men: Beginnings (8/00, $14.95) reprints 3 prequels w/photo-c 15.00

X-MEN 2: THE MOVIE
Marvel Comics: 2003

Adaptation (6/03, $3.50) Movie adaptation; photo-c; Austen-s/Zircher-a 4.00
Adaptation TPB (2003, $12.99) Movie adaptation & r/Prequels Nightcrawler & Wolverine 13.00
Prequel: Nightcrawler (5/03, $3.50) Kerschl-a; photo cover 4.00
Prequel: Wolverine (5/03, $3.50) Mandrake-a; photo cover; Sabretooth app. 4.00

X-MEN: THE 198 (See House of M)
Marvel Comics: Mar, 2006 - No. 5, July, 2006 ($2.99, limited series)

1-5-Hine-s/Muniz-a 3.00
... Files (2006, $3.99) profiles of the 198 mutants who kept their powers after House of M 4.00
Decimation: The 198 (2006, $15.99, TPB) r/#1-5 & X-Men: The 198 Files 16.00

X-MEN: THE TIMES AND LIFE OF LUCAS BISHOP
Marvel Comics: Apr, 2009 - No. 3, June, 2009 ($3.99, limited series)

1-3-Swierczynski-s/Stroman-a. 1-Bishop's birth and childhood 4.00

X-MEN: THE ULTRA COLLECTION
Marvel Comics: Dec, 1994 - No. 5, Apr, 1995 ($2.95, limited series)

1-5: Pin-ups; no scripts 3.00

X-MEN: THE WEDDING ALBUM
Marvel Comics: 1994 ($2.95, magazine size, one-shot)

1-Wedding of Scott Summers & Jean Grey 3.00

X-MEN: TO SERVE AND PROTECT
Marvel Comics: Jan, 2011 - No. 4, Apr, 2011 ($3.99, limited series)

1-4-Short story anthology by various.1-Bradshaw-c. 2-Camuncoli-c 4.00

X-MEN TRUE FRIENDS
Marvel Comics: Sept, 1999 - No. 3, Nov, 1999 ($2.99, limited series)

1-3-Claremont-s/Leonardi-a 3.00

X-MEN 2099 (Also see 2099: World of Tomorrow)
Marvel Comics: Oct, 1993 - No. 35, Aug, 1996 ($1.25/$1.50/$1.95)

1-($1.75)-Foil-c; Ron Lim/Adam Kubert-a begins 4.00
1-2nd printing ($1.75) 3.00
1-Gold edition (15,000 made); sold thru Diamond for $19.40 20.00
2-24,26-35: 3-Death of Tina; Lim-c/a(p) in #1-8. 8-Bound-in trading card sheet. 35-Nostromo (from X-Nation) app; storyline cont'd in 2099: World of Tomorrow 3.00
25-($2.50)-Double sized 4.00
Special 1 ($3.95) 4.00
...: Oasis ($5.95, one-shot) -Hildebrandt Bros.-c/a 6.00

X-MEN ULTRA III PREVIEW
Marvel Comics: 1995 ($2.95)

nn-Kubert-a 3.00

X-MEN UNIVERSE
Marvel Comics: Dec, 1999 - No. 15, Feb, 2001 ($4.99/$3.99)

1-8-Reprints stories from recent X-Men titles 5.00
9-15-($3.99) 4.00

X-MEN UNIVERSE: PAST, PRESENT AND FUTURE
Marvel Comics: Feb, 1999 ($2.99, one-shot)

1-Previews 1999 X-Men events; background info 3.00

X-MEN UNLIMITED
Marvel Comics: 1993 - No. 50, Sept, 2003 ($3.95/$2.99, 68 pgs.)

1-Chris Bachalo-c/a; Quesada-a. 6.00
2-11: 2-Origin of Magneto script. 3-Sabretooth-c/story. 10-Dark Beast vs. Beast; Mark Waid script. 11-Magneto & Rogue 5.00
12-33: 12-Begin $2.99-c; Onslaught x-over; Juggernaut-c/app. 19-Caliafore-a. 20-Generation X app. 27-Origin Thunderbird. 29-Maximum Security x-over; Bishop-c/app. 30-Mahfood-a. 31-Stelfreeze-c/a. 32-Dazzler; Thompson-c/a 33-Kaluta-c 4.00
34-37,39,40-42-($3.50) 34-Von Eeden-a. 35-Finch, Conner, Maguire-a. 36-Chiodo-c/a; Larroca, Totleben-a. 39-Bachalo-c; Pearson-a. 41-Bachalo-c; X-Statix app. 4.00
38-($2.25) Kitty Pryde; Robertson-a 3.00
43-50-($2.50) 43-Sienkiewicz-c/a; Paul Smith-a. 45-Noto-c. 46-Bisley-a. 47-Warren-s/Mays-a. 48-Wolverine story w/Isanove painted-a 3.00
X-Men Legends Vol. 4: Hated and Feared TPB (2003, $19.99) r/stories by various 20.00
NOTE: ***Bachalo*** *c/a-1.* ***Quesada*** *a-1.* ***Waid*** *scripts-10*

X-MEN UNLIMITED
Marvel Comics: Apr, 2004 - No. 14, Jun, 2006 ($2.99)

1-14: 1-6-Pat Lee-c; short stories by various. 2-District X preview; Granov-a 3.00

X-MEN VS. AGENTS OF ATLAS
Marvel Comics: Dec, 2009 - No. 2, Jan, 2010 ($3.99, limited series)

X-O Manowar #57 © Acclaim

Xombi (2011 series) #1 © Milestone Media

X-Treme X-Men #25 © MAR

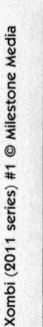

GD	VG	FN	VF	VF/NM	NM-
2.0	4.0	6.0	8.0	9.0	9.2

1,2-Pagulayan-a. 1-McGuinness-c. 2-Granov-c 4.00

X-MEN VS. DRACULA
Marvel Comics: Dec, 1993 ($1.75)

1-r/X-Men Annual #6; Austin-c(i) 4.00

X-MEN VS. THE AVENGERS, THE
Marvel Comics Group: Apr, 1987 - No. 4, July, 1987 ($1.50, limited series, Baxter paper)

1 5.00
2-4 4.00

X-MEN VS. THE BROOD, THE
Marvel Comics Group: Sept, 1996 - No. 2, Oct, 1996 ($2.95, limited series)

1,2-Wraparound-c; Ostrander-s/Hitch-a(p) 3.00
TPB('97, $16.99) reprints X-Men/Brood: Day of Wrath #1,2 & Uncanny X-Men #232-234 17.00

X-MEN VISIONARIES
Marvel Comics: 1995,1996,2000 (trade paperbacks)

nn-($8.95) Reprints X-Men stories; Adam & Andy Kubert-a 9.00
...2: The Neal Adams Collection (1996) r/X-Men #56-63,65 30.00
...2: The Neal Adams Col. (2nd printing, 2000, $24.95) new Adams-c 25.00

X-MEN/WILDC.A.T.S.: THE DARK AGE (See also WildC.A.T.S./X-Men...)
Marvel Comics: 1998 ($4.50, one-shot)

1-Two covers (Broome & Golden); Ellis-s 5.00

X-MEN: WORLDS APART
Marvel Comics: Dec, 2008 - No. 4, Mar, 2009 ($3.99, limited series)

1-4-Storm and the Black Panther vs. the Shadow King. 1-Campbell-c 4.00

X-NATION 2099
Marvel Comics: Mar, 1996 - No. 6, Aug, 1996 ($1.95)

1-($3.95)-Humberto Ramos-a(p); wraparound, foil-c 4.00
2-6: 2,3-Ramos-a. 4-Exodus-c/app. 6-Reed Richards app 3.00

X NECROSIA
Marvel Comics: Dec, 2009 ($3.99)

1-Beginning of X-Force/X-Men/New Mutants x-over; Crain-a; Selene returns 4.00
...: The Gathering (2/10, $3.99) Wither, Blink, Senyaka. Mortis & Eliphas short stories 4.00

X-O MANOWAR (1st Series)
Valiant/Acclaim Comics (Valiant) No. 43 on: Feb, 1992 - No. 68, Sept, 1996 ($1.95/$2.25/$2.50, high quality)

0-(8/93, $3.50)-Wraparound embossed chromium-c by Quesada; Solar app.; origin Aric (X-O Manowar) 4.00
0-Gold variant 5.00
1-Intro/1st app. & partial origin of Aric (X-O Manowar); Barry Smith/Layton-a
1 2 3 5 6 8
2-4: 2-B. Smith/Layton-c. 3-Layton-c(i). 4-1st app. Shadowman 6.00
5-15: 5-B. Smith-c. 6-Begin $2.25-c; Ditko-a(p). 7,8-Unity x-overs. 7-Miller-c. 8-Simonson-c. 12-1st app. Randy Calder. 14,15-Turok-c/stories 3.00
15-Hot pink logo variant; came with Ultra Pro Rigid Comic Sleeves box; no price on cover 4.00
16-24,26-43: 20-Serial number contest insert. 27-29-Turok x-over. 28-Bound-in trading card. 30-1st app. new "good skin"; Solar app. 33-Chaos Effect Delta Pt. 3. 42-Shadowman app.; includes X-O Manowar Birthquake! Prequel 3.00
25-($3.50)-Has 16 pg. Armorines #0 bound-in w/origin 4.00
44-68: 44-Begin $2.50-c. 50-X, 50-O, 51, 52, 63-Bart Sears-c/a/scripts. 68-Revealed that Aric's past stories were premonitions of his future 3.00
...: Birth HC (2008, $24.95) recolored reprints #0-6; script and breakdowns for #0; cover gallery; new "The Rise of Lydia" story by Layton and Leeke 25.00
Trade paperback nn (1993, $9.95)-Polybagged with copy of X-O Database #1 inside 10.00
Yearbook 1 (4/95, $2.95) 3.00
NOTE: ***Layton** a-1i, 2i(part); c-1, 2i, 3i, 6i, 21i. **Reese** a-4i(part); c-26i.*

X-O MANOWAR (2nd Series)(Also see Iron Man/X-O Manowar: Heavy Metal)
Acclaim Comics (Valiant Heroes): V2#1, Oct, 1996 - No. 21, Jun, 1998 ($2.50)

V2#1-21: 1-Mark Waid & Brian Augustyn scripts begin; 1st app. Donavon Wylie; Rand Banion dies; painted variant-c exists. 2-Donavon Wylie becomes new X-O Manowar. 7-9-Augustyn-s. 10-Copycat-c 3.00

X-O MANOWAR FAN EDITION
Acclaim Comics (Valiant Heroes): Feb, 1997 (Overstreet's FAN giveaway)

1-Reintro the Armorines & the Hard Corps; 1st app. Citadel; Augustyn scripts; McKone-c/a 4.00

X-O MANOWAR/IRON MAN: IN HEAVY METAL (See Iron Man/X-O Manowar: Heavy Metal)
Acclaim Comics (Valiant Heroes): Sept, 1996 ($2.50, one-shot)
(1st Marvel/Valiant x-over)

1-Pt 1 of X-O Manowar/Iron Man x-over; Arnim Zola app.; Nicieza scripts; Andy Smith-a 2.50

XOMBI
DC Comics (Milestone): Jan, 1994 - No. 21, Feb, 1996 ($1.75/$2.50)

0-($1.95)-Shadow War x-over; Simonson silver ink varnish-c 3.00
1-21: 1-John Byrne-c 3.00
1-Platinum 8.00

XOMBI
DC Comics: May, 2011 - Present ($2.99)

1-Rozum-s/Irving-a/c 3.00

X-PATROL
Marvel Comics (Amalgam): Apr, 1996 ($1.95, one-shot)

1-Cruz-a(p) 3.00

XSE
Marvel Comics: Nov, 1996 - No. 4, Feb, 1997 ($1.95, limited series)

1-4: 1-Bishop & Shard app. 3.00
1-Variant-c 4.00

X-STATIX
Marvel Comics: Sept, 2002 - No. 26, Oct, 2004 ($2.99/$2.25)

1-($2.99)Allred-a/c; intro. Venus Dee Milo; back-up w/Cooke-a 4.00
2-9-($2.25) 4-Quitely-c. 5-Pope-c/a 3.00
10-26: 10-Begin $2.99-c; Bond-a; U-Go Girl flashback. 13,14-Spider-Man app. 21-25-Avengers app. 26-Team dies 3.00
... Vol. 1: Good Omens TPB (2003, $11.99) r/#1-5 12.00
... Vol. 2: Good Guys & Bad Guys TPB (2003, $15.99) r/#6-10 & Wolverine/Doop #1&2 16.00
... Vol. 3: Back From the Dead TPB (2004, $19.99) r/#11-18 20.00
... Vol. 4: X-Statix Vs. the Avengers TPB (2004, $19.99) r/#19-26; pin-ups 20.00

X-STATIX PRESENTS: DEAD GIRL
Marvel Comics: Mar, 2006 - No. 5, July, 2006 ($2.99, limited series)

1-5-Dr. Strange, Dead Girl, Miss America, Tike app. Milligan-s/Dragotta & Allred-a 3.00
TPB (2006, $13.99) r/series 14.00

X-TERMINATORS
Marvel Comics: Oct, 1988 - No. 4, Jan, 1989 ($1.00, limited series)

1-1st app.; X-Men/X-Factor tie-in; Williamson-i 4.00
2-4 3.00

X, THE MAN WITH THE X-RAY EYES (See Movie Comics)

X-TREME X-MEN (Also see Mekanix)
Marvel Comics: July, 2001 - No. 46, Jun, 2004 ($2.99/$3.50)

1-Claremont-s/Larroca-c/a 4.00
2-24: 2-Two covers (Larroca & Pacheco); Psylocke killed 3.00
25-35, 40-46: 25-30-God Loves, Man Kills II; Stryker app.; Kordey-a 3.00
36-39-($3.50) 3.50
Annual 2001 ($4.95) issue opens longways 5.00
... Vol. 1: Destiny TPB (2002, $19.95) r/#1-9 20.00
... Vol. 2: Invasion TPB (2003, $19.99) r/#10-18 20.00
... Vol. 3: Schism TPB (2003, $16.99) r/#19-23; X-Treme X-Posé #1&2 17.00
... Vol. 4: Mekanix TPB (2003, $16.99) r/Mekanix #1-6 17.00
... Vol. 5: God Loves Man Kills TPB (2003, $19.99) r/#25-30 20.00
... Vol. 6: Intifada TPB (2004, $16.99) r/#24,31-35 17.00
... Vol. 7: Storm the Arena TPB (2004, $16.99) r/#36-39 17.00
... Vol. 8: Prisoner of Fire TPB (2004, $19.99) r/#40-46 and Annual 2001 20.00

X-TREME X-MEN: SAVAGE LAND
Marvel Comics: Nov, 2001 - No. 4, Feb, 2002 ($2.99, limited series)

1-4-Claremont-s/Sharpe-c/a; Beast app. 3.00

X-TREME X-POSE
Marvel Comics: Jan, 2003 - No. 2, Feb, 2003 ($2.99, limited series)

1,2-Claremont-s/Ranson-a/Migliari-c 3.00

X-23 (See debut in NYX #3)(See NYX X-23 HC for reprint)
Marvel Comics: Mar, 2005 - No. 6, July, 2005 ($2.99, limited series)

1-Origin of the Wolverine clone girl; Tan-a 4.00
1-Variant Billy Tan-c with red background 5.00
2-6-Origin continues 3.00
2-Variant B&W sketch-c 5.00
One shot 1 (5/10, $3.99) Urasov-c/Lui-s; Wolverine & Jubilee app. 4.00
...: Innocence Lost MGC 1 (5/11, $1.00) r/#1 with "Marvel's Greatest Comics" cover logo 1.00
...: Innocence Lost TPB (2006, $15.99) r/#1-6 16.00

X-23

X-23 (2010 series) #3 © MAR

Yankee Comics #3 © CHES

Year One: Batman Scarecrow #1 © DC

	GD 2.0	VG 4.0	FN 6.0	VF 8.0	VF/NM 9.0	NM- 9.2

Marvel Comics: Nov, 2010 - Present ($3.99)

Issue	GD	VG	FN	VF	VF/NM	NM-
1-Marjorie Liu-s/Will Conrad-a; three covers by Luo, Djurdjevic & Dell'Otto; origin retold						4.00
2-8-($2.99) 2-Covers by Luo and Mayhew. 3-Takeda-a. 4-8-Gambit app. 8-Daken app.						3.00

X-23: TARGET X
Marvel Comics: Feb, 2007 - No. 6, July, 2007 ($2.99, limited series)

Issue	GD	VG	FN	VF	VF/NM	NM-
1-6-Kyle & Yost-s/Choi & Oback-a. 6-Gallery of variant covers and sketches						3.00
TPB (2007, $15.99) r/#1-6; gallery of variant covers and sketches						16.00

X-UNIVERSE
Marvel Comics: May, 1995 - No. 2, June, 1995 ($3.50, limited series)

Issue	GD	VG	FN	VF	VF/NM	NM-
1,2: Age of Apocalypse						5.00

X-VENTURE (Super Heroes)
Victory Magazines Corp.: July, 1947 - No. 2, Nov, 1947

Issue	GD	VG	FN	VF	VF/NM	NM-
1-Atom Wizard, Mystery Shadow, Lester Trumble begin	110	220	330	704	1202	1700
2	54	108	162	346	591	835

X-WOMEN
Marvel Comics: 2010 ($4.99, one-shot)

Issue	GD	VG	FN	VF	VF/NM	NM-
1-Milo Manara-a/Chris Claremont-s; a female X-Men adventure; Quesada afterword						5.00

XYR (See Eclipse Graphic Album Series #21)

YAK YAK
Dell Publishing Co.: No. 1186, May-July, 1961 - No. 1348, Apr-June, 1962

Issue	GD	VG	FN	VF	VF/NM	NM-
Four Color 1186 (#1)- Jack Davis-c/a; 2 versions, one minus 3 pgs.	8	16	24	58	97	135
Four Color 1348 (#2)-Davis c/a	8	16	24	52	86	120

YAKKY DOODLE & CHOPPER (TV) (See Dell Giant #44)
Gold Key: Dec, 1962 (Hanna-Barbera)

Issue	GD	VG	FN	VF	VF/NM	NM-
1	7	14	21	50	83	115

YANG (See House of Yang)
Charlton Comics: Nov, 1973 - No. 13, May, 1976; V14#15, Sept, 1985 - No. 17, Jan, 1986 (No V14#14, series resumes with #15)

Issue	GD	VG	FN	VF	VF/NM	NM-
1-Origin; Sattler-a begins; slavery-s	2	4	6	11	16	20
2-13(1976)	1	2	3	6	9	10
15-17(1986): 15-Reprints #1 (Low print run)						6.00
3,10,11(Modern Comics-r, 1977)						6.00

YANKEE COMICS
Harry 'A' Chesler: Sept, 1941 - No. 7, 1942?

Issue	GD	VG	FN	VF	VF/NM	NM-
1-Origin The Echo, The Enchanted Dagger, Yankee Doodle Jones, The Firebrand, & The Scarlet Sentry; Black Satan app.; Yankee Doodle Jones app. on all covers	194	388	582	1242	2121	3000
2-Origin Johnny Rebel; Major Victory app.; Barry Kuda begins	82	164	246	528	902	1275
3,4: 4-(3/42)	60	120	180	381	653	925
4 (nd, 1940s; 7-1/4x5", 68 pgs, distr. to the service)-Foxy Grandpa, Tom, Dick & Harry, Impy, Ace & Deuce, Dot & Dash, Ima Slooth by Jack Cole (Remington Morse publ.)	15	30	45	85	130	175
5-7 (nd; 10¢, 7-1/4x5", 68 pgs.)(Remington Morse publ.)-urges readers to send their copies to servicemen.	14	28	42	76	108	140

YANKEE DOODLE THE SPIRIT OF LIBERTY
Spire Publications: 1984 (no price, 36 pgs)

Issue	GD	VG	FN	VF	VF/NM	NM-
nn-Al Hartley-s/c/a	2	4	6	9	13	16

YANKS IN BATTLE
Quality Comics Group: Sept, 1956 - No. 4, Dec, 1956; 1963

Issue	GD	VG	FN	VF	VF/NM	NM-
1-Cuidera-c(i)	11	22	33	60	83	105
2-4: Cuidera-c(i)	8	16	24	40	50	60
I.W. Reprint #3(1963)-r/#?; exist?	2	4	6	9	12	15

YARDBIRDS, THE (G. I. Joe's Sidekicks)
Ziff-Davis Publishing Co.: Summer, 1952

Issue	GD	VG	FN	VF	VF/NM	NM-
1-By Bob Oskner	10	20	30	58	79	100

YARN MAN (See Megaton Man)
Kitchen Sink : Oct, 1989 ($2.00, B&W, one-shot)

Issue	GD	VG	FN	VF	VF/NM	NM-
1-Donald Simpson-c/a/scripts						3.00

YARNS OF YELLOWSTONE
World Color Press: 1972 (50¢, 36 pgs.)

Issue	GD	VG	FN	VF	VF/NM	NM-
nn-Illustrated by Bill Chapman	2	4	6	9	12	15

YEAH!
DC Comics (Homage): Oct, 1999 - No. 9, Jun, 2000 ($2.95)

Issue	GD	VG	FN	VF	VF/NM	NM-
1-Bagge-s/Hernandez-a						3.00
2-9: 2-Editorial page contains adult language						3.00

YELLOW CLAW (Also see Giant Size Master of Kung Fu)
Atlas Comics (MjMC): Oct, 1956 - No. 4, Apr, 1957

Issue	GD	VG	FN	VF	VF/NM	NM-
1-Origin by Joe Maneely	107	214	321	680	1165	1650
2-Kirby-a	86	172	258	546	936	1325
3,4-Kirby-a; 4-Kirby/Severin-a	82	164	246	528	902	1275

NOTE: *Everett c-3. Maneely c-1. Reinman a-2i, 3. Severin c-2, 4.*

YELLOWJACKET COMICS (Jack in the Box #11 on)(See TNT Comics)
E. Levy/Frank Comunale/Charlton: Sept, 1944 - No. 10, June, 1946

Issue	GD	VG	FN	VF	VF/NM	NM-
1-Intro & origin Yellowjacket; Diana, the Huntress begins; E.A. Poe's "The Black Cat" adaptation	66	132	198	419	722	1025
2-Yellowjacket-c begin, end #10	41	82	123	256	428	600
3,5	40	80	120	246	411	575
4-E.A. Poe's "Fall of the House Of Usher" adaptation; Palais-a	41	82	123	256	428	600
6	48	96	144	302	514	725
7-Classic skull-c; Toth-a (1 pg. gag feature)	97	194	291	621	1061	1500
8-10: 1,3,4,6-10-Have stories narrated by old witch in "Tales of Terror" (1st horror series?)	47	94	141	296	503	710

YELLOWSTONE KELLY (Movie)
Dell Publishing Co.: No. 1056, Nov-Jan, 1959/60

Issue	GD	VG	FN	VF	VF/NM	NM-
Four Color 1056-Clint Walker photo-c	6	12	18	37	59	80

YELLOW SUBMARINE (See Movie Comics)

YEAR ONE: BATMAN/RA'S AL GHUL
DC Comics: 2005 - No. 2, 2005 ($5.99, squarebound, limited series)

Issue	GD	VG	FN	VF	VF/NM	NM-
1-Devin Grayson-s/Paul Gulacy-a						6.00
TPB (2006, $9.99) r/#1,2						10.00

YEAR ONE: BATMAN SCARECROW
DC Comics: 2005 - No. 2, 2005 ($5.99, squarebound, limited series)

Issue	GD	VG	FN	VF	VF/NM	NM-
1-Scarecrow's origin; Bruce Jones-s/Sean Murphy-a						6.00

YIN FEI THE CHINESE NINJA
Leung's Publications: 1988 - No. 8, 1990 ($1.80/$2.00, 52 pgs.)

Issue	GD	VG	FN	VF	VF/NM	NM-
1-8						4.00

YOGI BEAR (See Dell Giant #41, Golden Comics Digest, Kite Fun Book, March of Comics #253, 265, 279, 291, 309, 319, 337, 344, Movie Comics under "Hey There It's..." & Whitman Comic Books)

YOGI BEAR (TV) (Hanna-Barbera) (See Four Color #990)
Dell Publishing Co./Gold Key No. 10 on: No. 1067, 12-2/59-60 - No. 9, 7-9/62; No. 10, 10/62 - No. 42, 10/70

Issue	GD	VG	FN	VF	VF/NM	NM-
Four Color 1067 (#1)-TV show debuted 1/30/61	11	22	33	75	138	200
Four Color 1104,1162 (5-7/61)	7	14	21	49	80	110
4(8-9/61) - 6(12-1/61-62)	6	12	18	37	59	80
Four Color 1271(11/61)	6	12	18	37	59	80
Four Color 1349(1/62)-Photo-c	8	16	24	58	97	135
7(2-3/62) - 9(7-9/62)-Last Dell	6	12	18	37	59	80
10(10/62-G.K.), 11(1/63)-titled "Yogi Bear Jellystone Jollies" (80 pgs.); 11-X-Mas-c	7	14	21	49	80	110
12(4/63), 14-20	5	10	15	30	48	65
13(7/63, 68 pgs.)-Surprise Party	7	14	21	47	76	105
21-30	3	6	9	20	30	40
31-42	3	6	9	17	25	32

YOGI BEAR (TV)
Charlton Comics: Nov, 1970 - No. 35, Jan, 1976 (Hanna-Barbera)

Issue	GD	VG	FN	VF	VF/NM	NM-
1	5	10	15	30	48	65
2-6,8-10	3	6	9	17	25	32
7-Summer Fun (Giant, 52 pgs.)	4	8	12	28	44	60
11-20	3	6	9	16	22	28
21-35: 28-31-partial-r	2	4	6	11	16	20
Digest (nn, 1972, 75¢-c, B&W, 100 pgs.) (scarce)	3	6	9	19	29	38

YOGI BEAR (TV)(See The Flintstones, 3rd series & Spotlight #1)
Marvel Comics Group: Nov, 1977 - No. 9, Mar, 1979 (Hanna-Barbera)

Issue	GD	VG	FN	VF	VF/NM	NM-
1,7-9: 1-Flintstones begin (Newsstand sales only)	3	6	9	16	23	30
2-6	2	4	6	11	16	20

YOGI BEAR (TV)
Harvey Comics: Sept, 1992 - No. 6, Mar, 1994 ($1.25/$1.50) (Hanna-Barbera)

Issue	GD	VG	FN	VF	VF/NM	NM-
V2#1-6						3.00

Young Allies #1 © MAR

Young Allies Comics #13 © MAR

Youngblood V4 #1 © Rob Liefeld

	GD 2.0	VG 4.0	FN 6.0	VF 8.0	VF/NM 9.0	NM- 9.2

...Big Book V2#1,2 ($1.95, 52 pgs): 1-(11/92). 2-(3/93) 4.00
...Giant Size V2#1,2 ($2.25, 68 pgs.): 1-(10/92). 2-(4/93) 3.00

YOGI BEAR (TV)
Archie Publ.: May, 1997

1 3.00

YOGI BEAR'S EASTER PARADE (See The Funtastic World of Hanna-Barbera #2)

YOGI BERRA (Baseball hero)
Fawcett Publications: 1951 (Yankee catcher)

	GD	VG	FN	VF	VF/NM	NM-
nn-Photo-c (scarce)	73	146	219	467	796	1125

YOSEMITE SAM (...& Bugs Bunny) (TV)
Gold Key/Whitman: Dec, 1970 - No. 81, Feb, 1984

	GD	VG	FN	VF	VF/NM	NM-
1	5	10	15	30	48	65
2-10	3	6	9	16	23	30
11-20	2	4	6	11	16	20
21-30	2	4	6	9	13	16
31-50	2	4	6	8	10	12
51-65 (Gold Key)	1	2	3	5	7	9
66,67 (Whitman)	2	4	6	8	10	12
68(9/80), 69(10/80), 70(12/80) 3-pack only	3	6	9	19	29	38
71-78: 76(2/82), 77(3/82), 78(4/82)	2	4	6	9	13	16
79-81 (All #90263 on-c, no date or date code; 3-pack): 79(7/83). 80(8/83). 81(2/84)-(1/3-r)	3	6	9	14	19	24

(See March of Comics #363, 380, 392)

YOUNG ALLIES
Marvel Comics: Aug, 2010 - No. 6, Jan, 2011 ($3.99/$2.99)

1-($3.99) Wraparound-c; Nomad, Araña, Firestar, Gravity, Toro team-up; origin pages 4.00
2-6-($2.99) 2-Lafuente-c/McKeever-s/Baldeon-a. 6-Miyazawa-c; Emma Frost app. 3.00

YOUNG ALLIES COMICS (All-Winners #21; see Kid Komics #2)
Timely Comics (USA 1-7/NPI 8,9/YAI 10-20): Sum, 1941 - No. 20, Oct, 1946

	GD	VG	FN	VF	VF/NM	NM-
1-Origin/1st app. The Young Allies (Bucky, Toro, others); 1st meeting of Captain America & Human Torch; Red Skull-c & app.; S&K-c/splash; Hitler-c; Note: the cover was altered after its preview in Human Torch #5. Stalin was shown with Hitler but was removed due to Russia becoming an ally	1350	2700	4050	10,200	18,100	26,000
2-(Winter, 1941)-Captain America & Human Torch app.; Simon & Kirby-c	400	800	1200	2800	4900	7000
3-Remember Pearl Harbor issue (Spring, 1942); Stan Lee scripts; Vs. Japanese-c/full-length story; Captain America & Human Torch app.; Father Time story by Alderman	314	628	942	2198	3849	5500
4-The Vagabond & Red Skull, Capt. America, Human Torch app. Classic Red Skull-c	459	918	1377	3350	5925	8500
5-Captain America & Human Torch app.	226	452	678	1446	2473	3500
6,7	158	316	474	1003	1727	2450
8-Classic Schomburg WW2 bondage-c	174	348	522	1114	1907	2700
9-Hitler, Tojo, Mussolini-c.	226	452	678	1446	2473	3500
10-Classic Schomburg Hooded Villain bondage-c; origin Tommy Tyme & Clock of Ages; ends #19	174	348	522	1114	1907	2700
11-16: 12-Classic decapitation story. 16-Last Schomburg WWII-c	129	258	387	826	1413	2000
17-20	103	206	309	659	1130	1600

NOTE: ***Brodsky** c-15. **Ferstadt** a-3. **Gabriele** a-3; c-3, 4. **S&K** c-1, 2. **Schomburg** c-5-13, 16-19. **Shores** c-20.*

YOUNG ALLIES 70TH ANNIVERSARY SPECIAL
Marvel Comics: Aug, 2009 ($3.99, one-shot)

1-Bucky & Young Allies app.; Stern-s/Rivera-a; Terry Vance rep. from Marvel Myst. #14 4.00

YOUNG ALL-STARS
DC Comics: June, 1987 - No. 31, Nov, 1989 ($1.00, deluxe format)

1-31: 1-1st app. Iron Munro & The Flying Fox. 8,9-Millennium tie-ins 3.00
Annual 1 (1988, $2.00) 4.00

YOUNG AVENGERS
Marvel Comics: Apr, 2005 - No. 12, Aug, 2006 ($2.99)

1-Intro. Iron Lad, Patriot, Hulkling, Asgardian; Heinberg-s/Cheung-a 5.00
1-Director's Cut (2005, $3.99) r/#1 plus character sketches; original script 4.00
2-12: 3-6-Kang app. 7-DiVito-a. 9-Skrulls app. 3.00
... Special 1 (2/06, $3.99) origins of the heroes; art by various incl. Neal Adams, Jae Lee, Bill Sienkiewicz, Gene Ha, Michael Gaydos and Pasqual Ferry 4.00
... Vol. 1: Sidekicks HC (2005, $19.99, dustjacket) r/#1-6; character design sketches 20.00
... Vol. 1: Sidekicks TPB (2006, $14.99) r/#1-6; character design sketches 15.00
... Vol. 2: Family Matters HC (2006, $22.99, dustjacket) r/#7-12 & YA Special #1 23.00
... Vol. 2: Family Matters SC (2007, $17.99) r/#7-12 & YA Special #1 18.00
HC (2008, $29.99, d.j.) oversized reprint of #1-12 and Special #1; script & sketch pages 30.00

YOUNG AVENGERS PRESENTS
Marvel Comics: Mar, 2008 - No. 6, Aug, 2008 ($2.99, limited series)

1-4: 1-Patriot; Bucky app. 2-Hulkling; Captain Marvel app. 3-Wiccan & Speed. 4-Vision. 5-Stature. 6-Hawkeye; Clint Barton app.; Alan Davis-a 3.00

YOUNGBLOOD (See Brigade #4, Megaton Explosion & Team Youngblood)
Image Comics (Extreme Studios): Apr, 1992 - No. 4, Feb, 1993 ($2.50, lim. series); No. 6, June, 1994 (No #5) - No. 10, Dec, 1994 ($1.95/$2.50)

1-Liefeld-c/a/scripts in all; flip book format with 2 trading cards; 1st Image/Extreme Studios title. 5.00
1,2-2nd printing 3.00
2-(JUN-c, July 1992 indicia)-1st app. Shadowhawk in solo back-up story; 2 trading cards inside; flip book format; 1st app. Prophet, Kirby, Berzerkers, Darkthorn 3.00
3,0,4,5: 3-(OCT-c, August 1992 indicia)-Contains 2 trading cards inside (flip book); 1st app. Supreme in back-up story; 1st app. Showdown. 0-(12/92, $1.95)-Contains 2 trading cards; 2 cover variations exist, green or beige logo; w/Image #0 coupon. 4-(2/93)-Glow-in-the-dark cover w/2 trading cards; 2nd app. Dale Keown's The Pitt; Bloodstrike app. 5-Flip book w/Brigade #4 3.00
6-($3.50, 52 pgs.)-Wraparound-c 4.00
7-10: 7, 8-Liefeld-c(p)/a(p)/story. 8,9-(9/94) 9-Valentino story & art 3.00
Battlezone 1 (May-c, 4/93 inside, $1.95)-Arsenal book; Liefeld-c(p) 3.00
Battlezone 2 (7/94, $2.95)-Wraparound-c 4.00
Image Firsts: Youngblood #1 (3/10, $1.00) reprints #1 3.00
...Super Special (Winter '97, $2.99) Sprouse -a 4.00
Yearbook 1 (7/93, $2.50)-Fold out panel; 1st app. Tyrax & Kanan 3.00
Vol. 1 HC (2008, $34.99) oversized r/#1-5, recolored and remastered; sketch art and cover gallery; Mark Millar intro. 35.00
TPB (1996, $16.95)-r/Team Youngblood #8-10 & Youngblood #6-8,10 17.00

YOUNGBLOOD
Image Comics (Extreme Studios)/Maximum Press No. 14: V2#1, Sept, 1995 - No. 14, Dec, 1996 ($2.50)

V2#1-10,14: Roger Cruz-a in all. 4-Extreme Destroyer Pt. 4 w/gaming card. 5-Variant-c exists. 6-Angela & Glory. 7-Shadowhunt Pt. 3; Shadowhawk app. 8,10-Thor (from Supreme) app. 10-(7/96). 14-(12/96)-1st Maximum Press issue 3.00

YOUNGBLOOD (Volume 3)
Awesome/ Awesome-Hyperwerks #2: Feb, 1998 - No. 2, Aug, 1998 ($2.50)

1-Alan Moore-s/Skroce & Stucker-a; 12 diff. covers 3.00
2-(8/98) Skroce & Liefeld covers 3.00
...Imperial 1 (Arcade Comics, 6/04, $2.99) Kirkman-sMychaels-a 3.00

YOUNGBLOOD (Volume 4)
Image Comics: Jan, 2008 - Present ($2.99/$3.99)

1-7-Casey-s/Donovan-a; two covers by Donovan & Liefeld on each 3.00
8-Obama flip cover by Liefeld; Obama app. in story 3.00
9-($3.99) Obama flip cover by Liefeld; Free Agent rejoins; Obama app. in story 4.00

YOUNGBLOOD: STRIKEFILE
Image Comics (Extreme Studios): Apr, 1993 - No. 11, Feb, 1995 ($1.95/$2.50/$2.95)

1-10: 1-($1.95)-Flip book w/Jae Lee-c/a & Liefeld-c/a in #1-3; 1st app. The Allies,Giger, & Glory. 3-Thibert-i asisst. 4-Liefeld-c(p); no Lee-a. 5-Liefeld-c(p). 8-Platt-c 3.00
NOTE: *Youngblood: Strikefile began as a four issue limited series.*

YOUNGBLOOD/X-FORCE
Image Comics (Extreme Studios): July, 1996 ($4.95, one-shot)

1-Cruz-a(p); two covers exist 5.00

YOUNG BRIDES (True Love Secrets)
Feature/Prize Publ.: Sept-Oct, 1952 - No. 30, Nov-Dec, 1956 (Photo-c: 1-4)

	GD	VG	FN	VF	VF/NM	NM-
V1#1-Simon & Kirby-a	39	78	117	231	378	525
2-S&K-a	21	42	63	122	199	275
3-6-S&K-a	19	38	57	111	176	240
V2#1-7,10-12 (#7-18)-S&K-a	18	36	54	105	165	225
8,9-No S&K-a	10	20	30	56	76	95
V3#1-3(#19-21)-Last precode (3-4/55)	10	20	30	54	72	90
4,6(#22,24), V4#1,3(#25,27)	9	18	27	50	65	80
V3#5(#23)-Meskin-c	9	18	27	52	69	85
V4#2(#26)-All S&K issue	18	36	54	103	162	220
V4#4(#28)-S&K-a	15	30	45	83	124	165
V4#5,6(#29,30)	10	20	30	54	72	90

YOUNG DR. MASTERS (See The Adventures of Young Dr. Masters)

YOUNG DOCTORS, THE
Charlton Comics: Jan, 1963 - No. 6, Nov, 1963

	GD	VG	FN	VF	VF/NM	NM-
V1#1	3	6	9	21	32	42

Young Hearts #2 © MAR

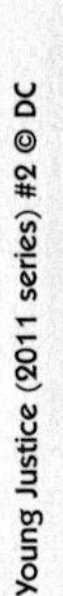

Young Justice (2011 series) #2 © DC

Young Liars #17 © David Lapham

	GD 2.0	VG 4.0	FN 6.0	VF 8.0	VF/NM 9.0	NM- 9.2
2-6	3	6	9	14	19	24

YOUNG EAGLE
Fawcett Publications/Charlton: 12/50 - No. 10, 6/52; No. 3, 7/56 - No. 5, 4/57 (Photo-c: 1-10)

	GD	VG	FN	VF	VF/NM	NM-
1-Intro Young Eagle	18	36	54	103	162	220
2-Complete picture novelette "The Mystery of Thunder Canyon"	10	20	30	58	79	100
3-9	9	18	27	50	65	80
10-Origin Thunder, Young Eagle's Horse	8	16	24	44	57	70
3-5(Charlton)-Formerly Sherlock Holmes?	7	14	21	35	43	50

YOUNG GUNS SKETCHBOOK
Marvel Comics: Feb, 2005 ($3.99, one-shot)

1-Sketch pages from 2005 Marvel projects by Coipel, Granov, McNiven, Land & others 4.00

YOUNG HEARTS
Marvel Comics (SPC): Nov, 1949 - No. 2, Feb, 1950

	GD	VG	FN	VF	VF/NM	NM-
1-Photo-c	15	30	45	88	137	185
2-Colleen Townsend photo-c from movie	11	22	33	62	86	110

YOUNG HEARTS IN LOVE
Super Comics: 1964

	GD	VG	FN	VF	VF/NM	NM-
17,18: 17-r/Young Love V5#6 (4-5/62)	2	4	6	9	13	16

YOUNG HEROES (Formerly Forbidden Worlds #34)
American Comics Group (Titan): No. 35, Feb-Mar, 1955 - No. 37, Jun-Jul, 1955

	GD	VG	FN	VF	VF/NM	NM-
35-37-Frontier Scout	10	20	30	54	72	90

YOUNG HEROES IN LOVE
DC Comics: June, 1997 - No. 17; #1,000,000, Nov, 1998 ($1.75/$1.95/$2.50)

1-1st app. Young Heroes; Madan-a 4.00
2-17: 3-Superman-c/app. 7-Begin $1.95-c 3.00
#1,000,000 (11/98, $2.50) 853 Century x-over 3.00

YOUNG INDIANA JONES CHRONICLES, THE
Dark Horse Comics: Feb, 1992 - No. 12, Feb, 1993 ($2.50)

1-12: Dan Barry scripts in all 3.00
NOTE: ***Dan Barry** a(p)-1, 2, 5, 6, 10; c-1-10. **Morrow** a-3, 4, 5p, 6p. **Springer** a-1i, 2i.*

YOUNG INDIANA JONES CHRONICLES, THE
Hollywood Comics (Disney): 1992 ($3.95, squarebound, 68 pgs.)

1-3: 1-r/YIJC #1,2 by D. Horse. 2-r/#3,4. 3-r/#5,6 4.00

YOUNG JUSTICE (Also see Teen Titans, Titans/Young Justice and DC Comics Presents: ...)
DC Comics: Sept, 1998 - No. 55, May, 2003 ($2.50/$2.75)

1-Robin, Superboy & Impulse team-up; David-s/Nauck-a 4.00
2,3: 3-Mxyzptlk app. 3.00
4-20: 4-Wonder Girl, Arrowette and the Secret join. 6-JLA app. 13-Supergirl x-over. 20-Sins of Youth aftermath 3.00
21-49: 25-Empress ID revealed. 28,29-Forever People app. 32-Empress origin. 35,36-Our Worlds at War x-over. 38-Joker: Last Laugh. 41-The Ray joins. 42-Spectre-c/app. 44,45-World Without YJ x-over pt. 1,5; Ramos-c. 48-Begin $2.75-c 3.00
50-($3.95) Wonder Twins, CM3 and other various DC teen heroes app. 4.00
51-55: 53,54-Darkseid app. 55-Last issue; leads into Titans/Young Justice mini-series 3.00
#1,000,000 (11/98) 853 Century x-over 3.00
...: A League of Their Own (2000, $14.95, TPB) r/#1-7, Secret Files #1 15.00
...: 80-Page Giant (5/99, $4.95) Ramos-c; stories and art by various 5.00
...: In No Man's Land (7/99, $3.95) McDaniel-c 4.00
...: Our Worlds at War (8/01, $2.95) Jae Lee-c; Linear Men app. 3.00
...: Secret Files (1/99, $4.95) Origin-s & pin-ups 5.00
...: The Secret (6/98, $1.95) Girlfrenzy; Nauck-a 3.00

YOUNG JUSTICE (Based on the 2011 Cartoon Network series)
DC Comics: No. 0, Mar, 2011 - Present ($2.99)

0-2-Mike Norton-a. 1-Miss Martian joins; Joker app. 2-Joker-c/app. 3.00
FCBD 2011 Young Justice Batman BB Super Sampler (7/11) Flash app. 2.00

YOUNG JUSTICE: SINS OF YOUTH (Also see Sins of Youth x-over issues and Sins of Youth: Secret Files)
DC Comics: May, 2000 - No. 2, May, 2000 ($3.95, limited series)

1,2-Young Justice, JLA & JSA swap ages; David-s/Nauck-a 4.00
TPB (2000, $19.95) r/#1,2 & all x-over issues) 20.00

YOUNG KING COLE (...Detective Tales)(Becomes Criminals on the Run)
Premium Group/Novelty Press: Fall, 1945 - V3#12, July, 1948

	GD	VG	FN	VF	VF/NM	NM-
V1#1-Toni Gayle begins	32	64	96	188	307	425
2	15	30	45	90	140	190
3-4	15	30	45	84	127	170
V2#1-7(8-9/46-7/47): 6,7-Certa-c	12	24	36	67	94	120
V3#1,3-6,8,9,12: 3-Certa-c. 5-McWilliams-c/a. 8,9-Harmon-c	11	22	33	64	90	115
2-L.B. Cole-a; Certa-c	15	30	45	90	140	190
7-L.B. Cole-c/a	20	40	60	120	195	270
10,11-L.B. Cole-c	18	36	54	105	165	225

YOUNG LAWYERS, THE (TV)
Dell Publishing Co.: Jan, 1971 - No. 2, Apr, 1971

	GD	VG	FN	VF	VF/NM	NM-
1	3	6	9	16	23	30
2	2	4	6	11	16	20

YOUNG LIARS (David Lapham's...)(See Vertigo Double Shot for reprint of #1)
DC Comics (Vertigo): May, 2008 - No. 18, Oct, 2009 ($2.99)

1-18: 1-Intro. Sadie Dawkins; David Lapham-s/a/c in all 3.00
...: Daydream Believer TPB (2008, $9.99) r/#1-6; Gerald Way intro. 10.00
...: Maestro TPB (2009, $14.99) r/#7-12; Peter Milligan intro. 15.00
...: Rock Life TPB (2010, $14.99) r/#13-18; Brian Azzarello intro. 15.00

YOUNG LIFE (Teen Life #3 on)
New Age Publ./Quality Comics Group: Summer, 1945 - No. 2, Fall, 1945

	GD	VG	FN	VF	VF/NM	NM-
1-Skip Homeier, Louis Prima stories	16	32	48	94	147	200
2-Frank Sinatra photo on-c plus story	18	36	54	107	169	230

YOUNG LOVE (Sister title to Young Romance)
Prize(Feature)Publ.(Crestwood): 2-3/49 - No. 73, 12-1/56-57; V3#5, 2-3/60 - V7#1, 6-7/63

	GD	VG	FN	VF	VF/NM	NM-
V1#1-S&K-c/a(2)	55	110	165	352	601	850
2-Photo-c begin; S&K-a	30	60	90	177	289	400
3-S&K-a	21	42	63	122	199	275
4-6-Minor S&K-a	15	30	45	88	137	185
V2#1(#7)-S&K-a(2)	21	42	63	122	199	275
2-5(#8-11)-Minor S&K-a	14	28	42	82	121	160
6,8(#12,14)-S&K-c only. 14-S&K 1 pg. art	16	32	48	94	147	200
7,9-12(#13,15-18)-S&K-c/a	21	42	63	122	199	275
V3#1-4(#19-22)-S&K-c/a	20	40	60	114	182	250
5-7,9-12(#23-25,27-30)-Photo-c resume; S&K-a	16	32	48	94	147	200
8(#26)-No S&K-a	10	20	30	56	76	95
V4#1,6(#31,36)-S&K-a	15	30	45	86	133	180
2-5,7-12(#32-35,37-42)-Minor S&K-a	14	28	42	76	108	140
V5#1-12(#43-54), V6#3,7,9(#57,61,63)-Last precode	9	18	27	52	69	85
V6#1,2,4-6,8(#55,56,58-60,62) S&K-a	11	22	33	60	83	105
V6#10-12(#64-66)	5	10	15	32	51	70
V7#1-7(#67-73)	4	8	12	28	44	60
V3#5(2-3/60),6(4-5/60)(Formerly All For Love)	4	8	12	24	37	50
V4#1(6-7/60)-6(4-5/61)	4	8	12	23	36	48
V5#1(6-7/61)-6(4-5/62)	4	8	12	23	36	48
V6#1(6-7/62)-6(4-5/63), V7#1	4	8	12	22	34	45

NOTE: ***Meskin** a-14(2), 27, 42. **Powell** a-V4#6. **Severin/Elder** a-V1#3. S&K art not in #53, 57, 61, 63-65. Photo-c most V3#5-V5#11.*

YOUNG LOVE
National Periodical Publ.(Arleigh Publ. Corp #49-61)/DC Comics:
#39, 9-10/63 - #120, Wint./75-76; #121, 10/76 - #126, 7/77

	GD	VG	FN	VF	VF/NM	NM-
39	6	12	18	39	62	85
40-50	4	8	12	28	44	60
51-68,70	4	8	12	26	41	55
69-(68 pg. Giant)(8-9/68)	7	14	21	45	73	100
71,72,74-77,80	3	6	9	21	32	42
73,78,79-Toth-a	4	8	12	22	34	45
81-99: 88-96-(52 pg. Giants)	3	6	9	20	30	40
100	3	6	9	21	32	42
101-106,115-120	3	6	9	17	25	32
107 (100 pgs.)	8	16	24	58	97	135
108-114 (100 pgs.)	8	16	24	52	86	120
121-126 (52 pgs.)	4	8	12	26	41	55

NOTE: ***Bolle** a-117. **Colan** a-107r. **Nasser** a-123, 124. **Orlando** a-122. **Simonson** c-125. **Toth** a-73, 78, 79, 122-125r. **Wood** a-109r(4 pgs.).*

YOUNG LOVER ROMANCES (Formerly & becomes Great Lover...)
Toby Press: No. 4, June, 1952 - No. 5, Aug, 1952

	GD	VG	FN	VF	VF/NM	NM-
4,5-Photo-c	10	20	30	54	72	90

YOUNG LOVERS (My Secret Life #19 on)(Formerly Brenda Starr?)
Charlton Comics: No. 16, July, 1956 - No. 18, May, 1957

	GD	VG	FN	VF	VF/NM	NM-
16,17('56): 16-Marcus Swayze-a	10	20	30	58	79	100
18-Elvis Presley picture-c, text story (biography)(Scarce)	66	132	198	419	722	1025

Young Men #28 © MAR

Youthful Romances #6 © Ribage

Y: The Last Man #60 © Vaughan & Guerra

	GD 2.0	VG 4.0	FN 6.0	VF 8.0	VF/NM 9.0	NM- 9.2

YOUNG MARRIAGE
Fawcett Publications: June, 1950

1-Powell-a; photo-c	14	28	42	76	108	140

YOUNG MEN (Formerly Cowboy Romances)(...on the Battlefield #12-20(4/53); ...In Action #21)
Marvel/Atlas Comics (IPC): No. 4, 6/50 - No. 11, 10/51; No. 12, 12/51 - No. 28, 6/54

4-(52 pgs.)	20	40	60	114	182	250
5-11	14	28	42	80	115	150
12-23: 12-20-War format. 21-23-Hot Rod issues starring Flash Foster	14	28	42	76	108	140
24-(12/53)-Origin Captain America, Human Torch, & Sub-Mariner which are revived thru #28; Red Skull app.	300	600	900	2070	3635	5200
25-28: 25-Romita-c/a (see Men's Advs.). 27-Death of Golden Age Red Skull	135	270	405	864	1482	2100
25-2nd printing (1994)	2	4	6	8	10	12

NOTE: ***Berg*** *a-7, 14, 17, 18, 20; c-17?* ***Brodsky*** *c-4-9, 13, 14, 16, 17, 21-25.* ***Burgos*** *c-26-28.* ***Colan*** *a-14, 15, 20.* ***Everett*** *a-18-20.* ***Heath*** *a-13, 14.* ***Maneely*** *c-10-12, 15.* ***Pakula*** *a-14, 15.* ***Robinson*** *c-18. Captain America by* ***Romita***-*#24?, 25, 26?, 27, 28. Human Torch by* ***Burgos***-*#25, 27, 28. Sub-Mariner by* ***Everett***-*#24-28.*

YOUNG REBELS, THE (TV)
Dell Publishing Co.: Jan, 1971

1-Photo-c	3	6	9	14	19	24

YOUNG ROMANCE COMICS (The 1st romance comic)
Prize/Headline (Feature Publ.) (Crestwood): Sept-Oct, 1947 - V16#4, June-July, 1963 (#1-33: 52 pgs.)

V1#1-S&K-c/a(2)	68	136	204	435	743	1050
2-S&K-c/a(2-3)	39	78	117	231	378	525
3-6-S&K-c/a(2-3) each	34	68	102	199	325	450
V2#1-6(#7-12)-S&K-c/a(2-3) each	30	60	90	177	289	400
V3#1-3(#13-15): V3#1-Photo-c begin; S&K-a	20	40	60	114	182	250
4-12(#16-24)-Photo-c; S&K-a	20	40	60	114	182	250
V4#1-11(#25-35)-S&K-a	19	38	57	109	172	235
12(#36)-S&K, Toth-a	20	40	60	114	182	250
V5#1-12(#37-48), V6#4-12(#52-60)-S&K-a	19	38	57	109	172	235
V6#1-3(#49-51)-No S&K-a	11	22	33	60	83	105
V7#1-11(#61-71)-S&K-a in most	15	30	45	85	130	175
V7#12(#72), V8#1-3(#73-75)-Last precode (12-1/54-55)-No S&K-a	10	20	30	54	72	90
V8#4(#76, 4-5/55), 5(#77)-No S&K-a	9	18	27	50	65	80
V8#6-8(#78-80, 12-1/55-56)-S&K-a	14	28	42	76	108	140
V9#3,5,6(#81, 2-3/56, 83,84)-S&K-a	14	28	42	76	108	140
4, V10#1(#82,85)-All S&K-a	14	28	42	81	118	155
V10#2-6(#86-90, 10-11/57)-S&K-a	9	18	27	60	100	140
V11#1,2,5,6(#91,92,95,96)-S&K-a	9	18	27	60	100	140
3,4(#93,94), V12#2,4,5(#98,100,101)-No S&K	5	10	15	32	51	70
V12#1,3,6(#97,99,102)-S&K-a	9	18	27	60	100	140
V13#1(#103)-Powell-a; S&K's last-a for Crestwood	9	18	27	60	100	140
2,4-6(#104-108)	4	8	12	28	44	60
V13#3(#105, 4-5/60)-Elvis Presley-c app. only	8	16	24	58	97	135
V14#1-6, V15#1-6, V16#1-4(#109-124)	4	8	12	26	41	55

NOTE: ***Meskin*** *a-16, 24(2), 33, 47, 50.* ***Robinson/Meskin*** *a-6.* ***Leonard Starr*** *a-11. Photo c-13-32, 34-65. Issues 1-3 say "Designed for the More* ***Adult*** *Readers of* ***Comics****" on cover.*

YOUNG ROMANCE COMICS (Continued from Prize series)
National Periodical Publ.(Arleigh Publ. Corp. No. 127): No. 125, Aug-Sept, 1963 - No. 208, Nov-Dec, 1975

125	8	16	24	52	86	120
126-140	5	10	15	32	51	70
141-153,156-162,165-169	4	8	12	24	37	50
154-Neal Adams-c	5	10	15	35	55	75
155-1st publ. Aragonés-s (no art)	5	10	15	32	51	70
163,164-Toth-a	4	8	12	28	44	60
170-172 (68 pg. Giants): 170-Michell from Young Love ends; Lily Martin, the Swinger begins	5	10	15	32	51	70
173-183 (52 pgs.)	4	8	12	24	37	50
184-196	3	6	9	18	27	35
197-204-(100 pgs.)	8	16	24	52	86	120
205-208	3	6	9	17	25	32

YOUNG X-MEN
Marvel Comics: May, 2008 - No. 12, May, 2009 ($2.99)

1-12: 1-Cyclops forms new team; Guggenheim-s/Paquette-a/Dodson-c. 11,12-Acuña-a 3.00

YOUR DREAMS (See Strange World of...)

YOUR UNITED STATES
Lloyd Jacquet Studios: 1946

	GD 2.0	VG 4.0	FN 6.0	VF 8.0	VF/NM 9.0	NM- 9.2

nn-Used in **SOTI**, pg. 309,310; Sid Greene-a	24	48	72	140	230	320

YOUTHFUL HEARTS (Daring Confessions #4 on)
Youthful Magazines: May, 1952 - No. 3, Sept, 1952

1- "Monkey on Her Back" swipes E.C. drug story/Shock SuspenStories #12; Frankie Laine photo on-c; Doug Wildey-a in al	32	64	96	188	307	425
2,3: 2-Vic Damone photo on-c. 3-Johnny Raye photo on-c	20	40	60	114	182	250

YOUTHFUL LOVE (Truthful Love #2)
Youthful Magazines: May, 1950

1	15	30	45	84	127	170

YOUTHFUL ROMANCES
Pix-Parade #1-14/Ribage #15 on: 8-9/49 - No. 5, 4/50; No. 6, 2/51; No. 7, 5/51 - #14, 10/52; #15, 1/53 - #18, 7/53; No. 5, 9/53 - No. 9, 8/54

1-(1st series)-Titled Youthful Love-Romances	27	54	81	158	259	360
2-Walter Johnson c-1-4	17	34	51	98	154	210
3-5	15	30	45	84	127	170
6,7,9-14(10/52, Pix-Parade; becomes Daring Love #15). 10(1/52)-Mel Torme photo-c/story. 12-Tony Bennett photo-c, 8pg. story & text bio.13-Richard Hayes (singer) photo-c/story; Bob & Ray photo/text story.	14	28	42	80	115	150
8-Frank Sinatra photo/text story; Wood-c/a	20	40	60	117	189	260
15-18 (Ribage)-All have photos on-c. 15-Spike Jones photo-c/story. 16-Tony Bavaar photo-c	14	28	42	76	108	140
5(9/53, Ribage)-Les Paul & Mary Ford photo-c/story; Charlton Heston photo/text story	13	26	39	72	101	130
6-9: 6-Bobby Wayne (singer) photo-c/story; Debbie Reynolds photo/text story. 7(2/54)-Tony Martin photo-c/story; Cyd Charise photo/text story. 8(5/54)-Gordon McCrae photo-c/story. (8/54)-Ralph Flanagan (band leader) photo-c/story; Audrey Hepburn photo/text story	12	24	36	67	94	120

YTHAQ: NO ESCAPE
Marvel Comics (Soleil): 2009 - No. 3, 2009 ($5.99, limited series)

1-3-English language version of French comic; Arleston-s/Floch-a 6.00

YTHAQ: THE FORSAKEN WORLD
Marvel Comics (Soleil): 2008 - No. 3, 2009 ($5.99, limited series)

1-3-English language version of French comic; Arleston-s/Floch-a 6.00

Y: THE LAST MAN
DC Comics (Vertigo): Sept, 2002 - No. 60, Mar, 2008 ($2.95/$2.99)

1-Intro. Yorick Brown; Vaughan-s/Guerra-a/J.G. Jones-c	2	4	6	8	10	12
2	1	2	3	5	6	8

3-5 6.00
6-59: 16,17-Chadwick-a. 21,22-Parlov-a. 32,39-41,48,53,54-Sudzuka-a. 3.00
60-($4.99) Final issue; sixty years in the future 5.00
... Double Feature Edition (2002, $5.95) r/#1,2 6.00
... Special Edition (2009, $1.00) r/#1, "After Watchmen" trade dress on cover 3.00
... - Cycles TPB (2003, $12.95) r/#6-10; sketch pages by Guerra 13.00
... - Girl on Girl TPB (2005, $12.99) r/#32-36 13.00
... - Kimono Dragons TPB (2006, $14.99) r/#43-48 15.00
... - Motherland TPB (2007, $14.99) r/#49-54 15.00
... - One Small Step TPB (2004, $12.95) r/#11-17 13.00
... - Paper Dolls TPB (2006, $14.99) r/#37-42 15.00
... - Ring of Truth TPB (2005, $14.99) r/#24-31 15.00
... - Safeword TPB (2004, $12.95) r/#18-23 13.00
... - Unmanned TPB (2002, $12.95) r/#1-5 13.00
... - Whys and Wherefores TPB (2008, $14.99) r/#55-60 15.00
... - The Deluxe Edition Book One HC (2008, $29.99, dustjacket) oversized r/#1-10; Guerra sketch pages 30.00
... - The Deluxe Edition Book Two HC (2009, $29.99, dustjacket) oversized r/#11-23; full script to #18 30.00
... - The Deluxe Edition Book Three HC (2010, $29.99, dustjacket) oversized r/#24-36; full script to #36 30.00
... - The Deluxe Edition Book Four HC (2010, $29.99, dustjacket) oversized r/#37-48; full script to #42 30.00
... - The Deluxe Edition Book Five HC (2011, $29.99, dustjacket) oversized r/#49-60; full script to #60 30.00

Y2K: THE COMIC
New England Comics Press: Oct, 1999 ($3.95, one-shot)

1-Y2K scenarios and survival tips 4.00

YUPPIES FROM HELL (Also see Son of...)
Marvel Comics: 1989 ($2.95, B&W, one-shot, direct sales, 52 pgs.)

Zatanna (2010 series) #7 © DC

Zen Intergalactic Ninja #6 © S&C

Ziggy Pig - Silly Seal Comics #5 © MAR

	GD 2.0	VG 4.0	FN 6.0	VF 8.0	VF/NM 9.0	NM- 9.2
1-Satire						3.00

ZAGO, JUNGLE PRINCE (My Story #5 on)
Fox Features Syndicate: Sept, 1948 - No. 4, Mar, 1949

	GD 2.0	VG 4.0	FN 6.0	VF 8.0	VF/NM 9.0	NM- 9.2
1-Blue Beetle app.; partial-r/Atomic #4 (Toni Luck)	65	130	195	416	708	1000
2,3-Kamen-a	53	106	159	334	567	800
4-Baker-c	45	90	135	284	480	675

ZANE GREY'S STORIES OF THE WEST
Dell Publishing Co./Gold Key 11/64: No. 197, 9/48 - No. 996, 5-7/59; 11/64 (All painted-c)

	GD 2.0	VG 4.0	FN 6.0	VF 8.0	VF/NM 9.0	NM- 9.2
Four Color 197(#1)(9/48)	11	22	33	75	138	200
Four Color 222,230,236('49)	7	14	21	47	76	105
Four Color 246,255,270,301,314,333,346	5	10	15	32	51	70
Four Color 357,372,395,412,433,449,467,484	4	8	12	28	44	60
Four Color 511-Kinstler-a; Kubert-a	5	10	15	32	51	70
Four Color 532,555,583,604,616,632(5/55)	4	8	12	28	44	60
27(9-11/55) - 39(9-11/58)	4	8	12	28	44	60
Four Color 996(5-7/59)	4	8	12	28	44	60
10131-411-(11/64-G.K.)-Nevada; r/4-Color #996	3	6	9	20	30	40

ZANY (Magazine)(Satire)(See Frantic & Ratfink)
Candor Publ. Co.: Sept, 1958 - No. 4, May, 1959

	GD 2.0	VG 4.0	FN 6.0	VF 8.0	VF/NM 9.0	NM- 9.2
1-Bill Everett-c	12	24	36	69	97	125
2-4: 4-Everett-c	9	18	27	47	61	75

ZATANNA (See Adv. Comics #413, JLA #161, Supergirl #1, World's Finest Comics #274)
DC Comics: July, 1993 - No. 4, Oct, 1993 ($1.95, limited series)

	NM- 9.2
1-4	3.00
...: Everyday Magic (2003, $5.95, one-shot) Dini-s/Mays-a/Bolland-c; Constantine app.	6.00
Special 1(1987, $2.00)-Gray Morrow-c/a	4.00

ZATANNA
DC Comics: Jul, 2010 - Present ($2.99)

	NM- 9.2
1-10: 1-Dini-s/Roux-a/c. 4,5,7-Hardin-a. 7-Beechen-s. 8-Chang-a	3.00
1-6-Variant-c by Bolland	6.00
...: The Mistress of Magic TPB (2011, $17.99) r/#1-6; variant cover gallery	18.00

ZAZA, THE MYSTIC (Formerly Charlie Chan; This Magazine Is Haunted V2#12 on)
Charlton Comics: No. 10, Apr, 1956 - No. 11, Sept, 1956

	GD 2.0	VG 4.0	FN 6.0	VF 8.0	VF/NM 9.0	NM- 9.2
10,11	12	24	36	69	97	125

ZEALOT (Also see WildC.A.T.S: Covert Action Teams)
Image Comics: Aug, 1995 - No. 3, Nov, 1995 ($2.50, limited series)

	NM- 9.2
1-3	3.00

ZEGRA JUNGLE EMPRESS (Formerly Tegra)(My Love Life #6 on)
Fox Features Syndicate: No. 2, Oct, 1948 - No. 5, April, 1949

	GD 2.0	VG 4.0	FN 6.0	VF 8.0	VF/NM 9.0	NM- 9.2
2	65	130	195	416	708	1000
3-5	52	104	156	322	549	775

ZEN (Intergalactic Ninja)
Zen Comics Publishing: No. 0, Apr, 2003 - No. 4, Aug, 2003 ($2.95)

	NM- 9.2
0-4-Bill Maus-a/Steve Stern-s. 0-Wraparound-c	3.00

ZEN INTERGALACTIC NINJA
No Publisher: 1987 -1993 ($1.75/$2.00, B&W)

	GD 2.0	VG 4.0	FN 6.0	VF 8.0	VF/NM 9.0	NM- 9.2
1	2	4	6	10	14	18
2-6: Copyright-Stern & Cote	1	3	4	6	8	10
V2#1-4-($2.00)						3.00
V3#1-5-($2.95)						3.00
... :Christmas Special 1 (1992, $2.95)						3.00
... :Earth Day Special 1 (1993, $2.95)						3.00

ZEN, INTERGALACTIC NINJA (mini-series)
Zen Comics/Archie Comics: Sept, 1992 - No. 3, 1992 ($1.25)(Formerly a B&W comic by Zen Comics)

	NM- 9.2
1-3: 1-Origin Zen; contains mini-poster	3.00

ZEN INTERGALACTIC NINJA
Entity Comics: No. 0, June-July, 1993 - No. 3, 1994 ($2.95, B&W, limited series)

	NM- 9.2
0-Gold foil stamped-c; photo-c of Zen model	3.00
1-3: Gold foil stamped-c; Bill Maus-c/a	3.00
0-(1993, $3.50, color)-Chromium-c by Jae Lee	4.00
...Sourcebook 1-(1993, $3.50)	4.00
...Sourcebook '94-(1994, $3.50)	4.00

ZEN INTERGALACTIC NINJA: APRIL FOOL'S SPECIAL
Parody Press: 1994 ($2.50, B&W)

	NM- 9.2
1-w/flip story of Renn Intergalactic Chihuahua	3.00

ZEN INTERGALACTIC NINJA COLOR
Entity Comics: 1994 - No. 7, 1995 ($2.25)

	NM- 9.2
1-($3.95)-Chromium die cut-c	4.00
1, 0-($2.25)-Newsstand; Jae Lee-c; r/...All New Color Special #0	3.00
2-($2.50)-Flip book	3.00
2-($3.50)-Flip book, polybagged w/chromium trading card	4.00
3-7	3.00
Summer Special (1994, $2.95)	3.00
Yearbook: Hazardous Duty 1 (1995)	3.00
Zen-isms 1 (1995, 2.95)	3.00
Ashcan-Tour of the Universe-(no price) w/flip cover	3.00

ZEN INTERGALACTIC NINJA COMMEMORATIVE EDITION
Zen Comics Publishing: 1997 ($5.95, color)

	NM- 9.2
1-Stern-s/Cote-a	6.00

ZEN INTERGALACTIC NINJA MILESTONE
Entity Comics: 1994 - No. 3, 1994 ($2.95, limited series)

	NM- 9.2
1-3: Gold foil logo; r/Defend the Earth	3.00

ZEN INTERGALATIC NINJA SPRING SPECTACULAR
Entity Comics: 1994 ($2.95, B&W, one-shot)

	NM- 9.2
1-Gold foil logo	3.00

ZEN INTERGALACTIC NINJA STARQUEST
Entity Comics: 1994 - No. 6, 1995 ($2.95, B&W)

	NM- 9.2
1-6: Gold foil logo	3.00

ZEN, INTERGALACTIC NINJA: THE HUNTED
Entity Comics: 1993 - No. 3, 1994 ($2.95, B&W, limited series)

	NM- 9.2
1-3: Newsstand Edition; foil logo	3.00
1-($3.50)-Polybagged w/chromium card by Kieth; foil logo	4.00

ZERO GIRL
DC Comics (Homage): Feb, 2001 - No. 5, Jun, 2001 ($2.95, limited series)

	NM- 9.2
1-5-Sam Kieth-s/a	3.00
TPB (2001, $14.95) r/#1-5; intro. by Alan Moore	15.00

ZERO GIRL: FULL CIRCLE
DC Comics (Homage): Jan, 2003 - No. 5, May, 2003 ($2.95, limited series)

	NM- 9.2
1-5-Sam Kieth-s/a	3.00
TPB (2003, $17.95) r/#1-5	18.00

ZERO HOUR: CRISIS IN TIME (Also see Showcase '94 #8-10)
DC Comics: No. 4(#1), Sept, 1994 - No. 0(#5), Oct, 1994 ($1.50, limited series)

	NM- 9.2
4(#1)-0(#5)	4.00
"Ashcan"-(1994, free, B&W, 8 pgs.) several versions exist	3.00
TPB ('94, $9.95)	10.00

ZERO KILLER
Dark Horse Comics: Jul, 2007 - No.6, Oct, 2009 ($2.99)

	NM- 9.2
1-6-Arvid Nelson-s/Matt Camp-a	3.00

ZERO PATROL, THE
Continuity Comics: Nov, 1984 - No. 2 ($1.50); 1987 - No. 5, May, 1989 ($2.00)

	NM- 9.2
1,2: Neal Adams-c/a; Megalith begins	4.00
1-5 (#1,2-reprints above, 1987)	3.00

ZERO TOLERANCE
First Comics: Oct, 1990 - No. 4, Jan, 1991 ($2.25, limited series)

	NM- 9.2
1-4: Tim Vigil-c/a(p) (his 1st color limited series)	3.00

ZERO ZERO
Fantagraphics: Mar, 1995 -No. 27 ($3.95/$4.95, B&W, anthology, mature)

	NM- 9.2
1-7,9-15,17-25	5.00
8,16	6.00
26-($4.95) Bagge-c	5.00

ZIGGY PIG-SILLY SEAL COMICS (See Animal Fun, Animated Movie-Tunes, Comic Capers, Krazy Komics, Silly Tunes & Super Rabbit)
Timely Comics (CmPL): Fall, 1944 - No. 4, Summer, 1945; No. 5, Summer, 1946; No. 6, Sept, 1946

	GD 2.0	VG 4.0	FN 6.0	VF 8.0	VF/NM 9.0	NM- 9.2
1-Vs. the Japanese	30	60	90	177	289	400
2-(Spring, 1945)	15	30	45	88	137	185
3-5	15	30	45	83	124	165
6-Infinity-c	15	30	45	90	140	190
I.W. Reprint #1(1958)-r/Krazy Komics	2	4	6	10	14	18
I.W. Reprint #2,7,8	2	4	6	10	14	18

Zip Comics #18 © MLJ

Zombies vs. Robots #1 © IDW

Zoo Funnies #4 © CC

ZIP COMICS
MLJ Magazines: Feb, 1940 - No. 47, Summer, 1944 (#1-7?: 68 pgs.)

	GD 2.0	VG 4.0	FN 6.0	VF 8.0	VF/NM 9.0	NM- 9.2
1-Origin Kalathar the Giant Man, The Scarlet Avenger, & Steel Sterling; Mr. Satan (by Edd Ashe), Nevada Jones (masked hero) & Zambini, the Miracle Man, War Eagle, Captain Valor begins	459	918	1377	3350	5925	8500
2-Nevada Jones adds mask & horse Blaze	258	516	774	1651	2826	4000
3-Biro robot-c	226	452	678	1446	2473	3500
4,5-Biro WWII-c	168	336	504	1075	1838	2600
6-8-Biro-c	148	296	444	947	1624	2300
9-Last Kalathar & Mr. Satan; classic-c	174	348	522	1114	1907	2700
10-Inferno, the Flame Breather begins, ends #13	161	322	483	1030	1765	2500
11-Inferno without costume	116	232	348	742	1271	1800
12-Biro bondage/torture-c with dwarf ghouls	123	246	369	787	1344	1900
13-Electrocution-c	142	284	426	909	1555	2200
14-Biro bondage/torture guillotine-c	116	232	348	742	1271	1800
15-Classic spider-c	145	290	435	921	1586	2250
16-Female hanging execution-c by Biro	116	232	348	742	1271	1800
17-Last Scarlet Avenger; women in bondage being cooked alive-c by Biro	148	296	444	947	1624	2300
18-Wilbur begins (9/41, 1st app.); sci-fi-c	142	284	426	909	1555	2200
19	113	226	339	718	1234	1750
20-Origin & 1st app. Black Jack (11/41); Hitler-c	200	400	600	1280	2190	3100
21,23-Nazi WWII-c	103	206	309	659	1130	1600
22-Classic Nazi Grim Reaper w/sickle, V for Victory-c	226	452	678	1446	2473	3500
24,25: 25-Last Nevada Jones	97	194	291	621	1061	1500
26-Black Witch begins; last Captain Valor; "Remember Pearl Harbor!" cover caption	110	220	330	704	1202	1700
27-Intro. Web (7/42) plus-c app.; Japanese WWII-c	206	412	618	1318	2259	3200
28-Origin Web; classic Baron Gastapo Nazi WWII-c	174	348	522	1114	1907	2700
29-The Hyena app. (scarce); Nazi WWII-c	116	232	348	742	1271	1800
30-WWII-c	71	142	213	454	777	1100
31,33-35: All WWII-c. 34-1st Applejack app. 35-Last Zambini, Black Jack	58	116	174	371	636	900
32-Classic skeleton Nazi WWII-c	103	206	309	659	1130	1600
36-38: 38-Last Web issue	53	106	159	334	567	800
39-Red Rube begins (origin, 8/43)	54	108	162	343	574	825
40-43	47	94	141	296	498	700
44-46: WWII covers. 45-Wilbur ends	50	100	150	315	533	750
47-Last issue; scarce	53	106	159	334	567	800

NOTE: *Biro a-5, 9, 17; c-3-17. **Meskin** a-1-3, 5-7, 9, 10, 12, 13, 15, 16 at least. **Montana** c-29, 30, 32-35. **Novick** c-18-28, 31. **Sahle** c-37, 38, 40-46. Bondage c-8, 9, 33, 34. Cover features: Steel Sterling-1-43, 47; (w/Blackjack-20-27 & Web-27-35), 28-39; (w/Red Rube-40-43); Red Rube-44-47.*

ZIP-JET (Hero)
St. John Publishing Co.: Feb, 1953 - No. 2, Apr-May, 1953

	GD 2.0	VG 4.0	FN 6.0	VF 8.0	VF/NM 9.0	NM- 9.2
1-Rocketman-r from Punch Comics; #1-c from splash in Punch #10	81	162	243	518	884	1250
2	50	100	150	315	533	750

ZIPPY THE CHIMP (CBS TV Presents...)
Pines (Literary Ent.): No. 50, March, 1957; No. 51, Aug, 1957

	GD 2.0	VG 4.0	FN 6.0	VF 8.0	VF/NM 9.0	NM- 9.2
50,51	8	16	24	40	50	60

ZODY, THE MOD ROB
Gold Key: July, 1970

	GD 2.0	VG 4.0	FN 6.0	VF 8.0	VF/NM 9.0	NM- 9.2
1	3	6	9	16	23	30

ZOMBIE
Marvel Comics: Nov, 2006 - No. 4, Feb, 2007 ($3.99, limited series)

1-4-Kyle Hotz-a/c; Mike Raicht-s 4.00
TPB (2007, $13.99) r/#1-4 14.00
...: Simon Garth (1/08 - No. 4, 4/08) Hotz-s/a/c 4.00

ZOMBIE KING
Image Comics: No. 0, June, 2005 ($2.95, B&W, one-shot)

0-Frank Cho-s/a 5.00

ZOMBIE PROOF
Moonstone: 2007 - Present ($3.50)

1-3: 1-J.C. Vaughn-s/Vincent Spencer-a; two covers by Spencer and Neil Vokes 3.50
1-Baltimore Comic-Con 2007 variant-c by Vokes (ltd. ed. of 500) 5.00
2-Big Apple 2008 Convention Edition; Tucci-c (ltd. ed. of 250) 5.00
3-Convention Edition; Beck-c (ltd. ed. of 100) 5.00

ZOMBIES!: ECLIPSE OF THE UNDEAD
IDW Publ.: Nov, 2006 - No. 4, Feb, 2007 ($3.99, limited series)

1-4-Torres-s/Herrera-a; two covers 4.00

ZOMBIES!: FEAST
IDW Publ.: May, 2006 - No. 5, Oct, 2006 ($3.99, limited series)

1-5: 1-Chris Bolton-a/Shane McCarthy-s. 3-Lorenzana-a 4.00

ZOMBIES!: HUNTERS
IDW Publ.: May, 2008 ($3.99)

1-Don Figueroa-a/c; Dara Naraghi-s 4.00

ZOMBIES VS. ROBOTS
IDW Publ.: Oct, 2006 - No. 2, Dec, 2006 ($3.99, limited series)

1-Chris Ryall-s/Ashley Wood-a; two covers by Wood 15.00
2 10.00

ZOMBIES VS. ROBOTS AVENTURE
IDW Publ.: Feb, 2010 - No. 4, May, 2010 ($3.99, limited series)

1-4-Short stories; Ryall-s; art by Matthews III, McCaffrey, & Hernandez; Wood-c 4.00

ZOMBIES VS. ROBOTS VS. AMAZONS
IDW Publ.: Sept, 2007 - No. 3, Feb, 2008 ($3.99, limited series)

1-3-Chris Ryall-s/Ashley Wood-a; two covers by Wood on each 5.00

ZOMBIE TALES THE SERIES
BOOM! Studios: Apr, 2008 - No. 12, Mar, 2009 ($3.99)

1-Niles-s; Lansdale-s/Barreto-a; two covers on each 4.00

ZOMBIE WORLD (one-shots)
Dark Horse Comics

... :Eat Your Heart Out (4/98, $2.95) Kelley Jones-c/s/a 3.00
... :Home For The Holidays (12/97, $2.95) 3.00

ZOMBIE WORLD: CHAMPION OF THE WORMS
Dark Horse Comics: Sept, 1997 - No. 3, Nov, 1997 ($2.95, limited series)

1-3-Mignola & McEown-c/s/a 3.00

ZOMBIE WORLD: DEAD END
Dark Horse Comics: Jan, 1998 - No. 2, Feb, 1998 ($2.95, limited series)

1,2-Stephen Blue-c/s/a 3.00

ZOMBIE WORLD: TREE OF DEATH
Dark Horse Comics: Jun, 1999 - No. 4, Oct, 1999 ($2.95, limited series)

1-4-Mills-s/Deadstock-a 3.00

ZOMBIE WORLD: WINTER'S DREGS
Dark Horse Comics: May, 1998 - No. 4, Aug, 1998 ($2.95, limited series)

1-4-Fingerman-s/Edwards-a 3.00

ZONE (Also see Dark Horse Presents)
Dark Horse Comics: 1990 ($1.95, B&W)

1-Character from Dark Horse Presents 2.50

ZONE CONTINUUM, THE
Caliber Press: 1994 ($2.95, B&W)

1 3.00

ZOO ANIMALS
Star Publications: No. 8, 1954 (15¢, 36 pgs.)

	GD 2.0	VG 4.0	FN 6.0	VF 8.0	VF/NM 9.0	NM- 9.2
8-(B&W for coloring)	8	16	24	42	54	65

ZOO FUNNIES (Tim McCoy #16 on)
Charlton Comics/Children Comics Publ.: Nov, 1945 - No. 15, 1947

	GD 2.0	VG 4.0	FN 6.0	VF 8.0	VF/NM 9.0	NM- 9.2
101(#1)(11/45, 1st Charlton comic book)-Funny animal; Al Fago-c	21	42	63	122	199	275
2(12/45, 52 pgs.) Classic-c	15	30	45	83	124	165
3-5	11	22	33	62	86	110
6-15: 8-Diana the Huntress app.	9	18	27	52	69	85

ZOO FUNNIES (Becomes Nyoka, The Jungle Girl #14 on?)
Capitol Stories/Charlton Comics: July, 1953 - No. 13, Sept, 1955; Dec, 1984

	GD 2.0	VG 4.0	FN 6.0	VF 8.0	VF/NM 9.0	NM- 9.2
1-1st app.? Timothy The Ghost; Fago-c/a	11	22	33	64	90	115
2	8	16	24	42	54	65
3-7	7	14	21	37	46	55
8-13-Nyoka app.	9	18	27	52	69	85
1(1984) (Low print run)	1	2	3	4	5	7

ZOONIVERSE
Eclipse Comics: 8/86 - No. 6, 6/87 ($1.25/$1.75, limited series, Mando paper)

1-6 3.00

Zoot Comics #13 © FOX

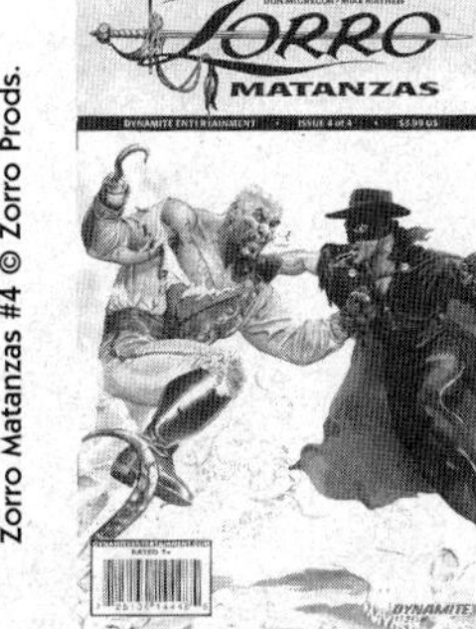
Zorro Matanzas #4 © Zorro Prods.

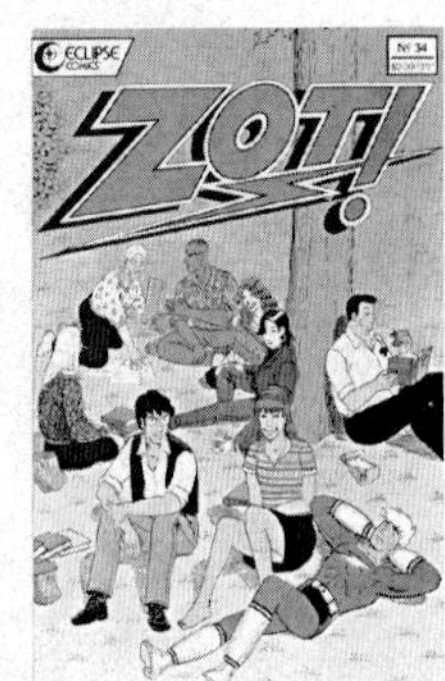
Zot! #34 © Scott McCloud

ZOO PARADE (TV)
Dell Publishing Co.: #662, 1955 (Marlin Perkins)

	GD 2.0	VG 4.0	FN 6.0	VF 8.0	VF/NM 9.0	NM- 9.2
Four Color 662	5	10	15	32	51	70

ZOOM COMICS
Carlton Publishing Co.: Dec, 1945 (one-shot)

	GD 2.0	VG 4.0	FN 6.0	VF 8.0	VF/NM 9.0	NM- 9.2
nn-Dr. Mercy, Satannas, from Red Band Comics; Capt. Milksop origin retold	39	78	117	240	395	550

ZOOT (Rulah Jungle Goddess #17 on)
Fox Features Syndicate: nd (1946) - No. 16, July, 1948 (Two #13s & 14s)

	GD 2.0	VG 4.0	FN 6.0	VF 8.0	VF/NM 9.0	NM- 9.2
nn-Funny animal only	21	42	63	126	206	285
2-The Jaguar app.	19	38	57	111	176	240
3(Fall, 1946) - 6-Funny animals & teen-age	13	26	39	72	101	130
7-(6/47)-Rulah, Jungle Goddess (origin/1st app.)	110	220	330	704	1202	1700
8-10	73	146	219	467	796	1125
11-Kamen bondage-c	76	152	228	486	831	1175
12-Injury-to-eye panels, torture scene	55	110	165	352	601	850
13(2/48)	54	108	162	343	574	825
14(3/48)-Used in **SOTI**, pg. 104, "One picture showing a girl nailed by her wrists to trees with blood flowing from the wounds, might be taken straight from an ill. ed. of the Marquis deSade"	71	142	213	454	777	1100
13(4/48),14(5/48)-Western True Crime #15 on?	54	108	162	343	574	825
15,16	54	108	162	343	574	825

ZORRO (Walt Disney with #882)(TV)(See Eclipse Graphic Album)
Dell Publishing Co.: May, 1949 - No. 15, Sept-Nov, 1961 (Photo-c 882 on)
(Zorro first appeared in a pulp story Aug 19, 1919)

	GD 2.0	VG 4.0	FN 6.0	VF 8.0	VF/NM 9.0	NM- 9.2
Four Color 228 (#1)	18	36	54	131	266	400
Four Color 425,617,732	11	22	33	77	144	210
Four Color 497,538,574-Kinstler-a	12	24	36	82	154	225
Four Color 882-Photo-c begin;1st TV Disney; Toth-a	14	28	42	96	191	285
Four Color 920,933,960,976-Toth-a in all	11	22	33	76	141	205
Four Color 1003('59)-Toth-a	11	22	33	76	141	205
Four Color 1037-Annette Funicello photo-c	13	26	39	92	179	265
8(12-2/59-60)	8	16	24	56	93	130
9-Toth-a	9	18	27	60	100	140
10,11,13-15-Last photo-c	8	16	24	54	90	125
12-Toth-a; last 10¢ issue	9	18	27	60	100	140

NOTE: ***Warren Tufts** a-4-Color 1037, 8, 9, 10, 13.*

ZORRO (Walt Disney)(TV)
Gold Key: Jan, 1966 - No. 9, Mar, 1968 (All photo-c)

	GD 2.0	VG 4.0	FN 6.0	VF 8.0	VF/NM 9.0	NM- 9.2
1-Toth-a	8	16	24	52	86	120
2,4,5,7-9-Toth-a. 5-r/F.C. #1003 by Toth	5	10	15	30	48	65
3,6-Tufts-a	4	8	12	28	44	60

NOTE: *#1-9 are reprinted from Dell issues.* **Tufts** *a-3, 4. #1-r/F.C. #882. #2-r/F.C. #960. #3-r/#12-c & #8 inside. #4-r/#9-c & insides. #6-r/#11(all); #7-r/#14-c. #8-r/F.C. #933 inside & back-c & #976-c. #9-r/F.C. #920.*

ZORRO (TV)
Marvel Comics: Dec, 1990 - No. 12, Nov, 1991 ($1.00)

	GD 2.0	VG 4.0	FN 6.0	VF 8.0	VF/NM 9.0	NM- 9.2
1-12: Based on TV show. 12-Toth-c						3.00

ZORRO (Also see Mask of Zorro)
Topps Comics: Nov, 1993 - No. 11, Nov, 1994 ($2.50/$2.95)

	GD 2.0	VG 4.0	FN 6.0	VF 8.0	VF/NM 9.0	NM- 9.2
0-(11/93, $1.00, 20 pgs.)-Painted-c; collector's ed.						3.00
1,4,6-9,11: 1-Miller-c. 4-Mike Grell-c. 6-Mignola-c. 7-Lady Rawhide-c by Gulacy. 8-Perez-c. 10-Julie Bell-c. 11-Lady Rawhide-c						3.00
2-Lady Rawhide-app. (not in costume)						5.00
3-1st app. Lady Rawhide in costume, 3-Lady Rawhide-c by Adam Hughes	1	2	3	5	6	8
5-Lady Rawhide app.						4.00
10-($2.95)-Lady Rawhide-c/app.						4.00
The Lady Wears Red (12/98, $12.95, TPB) r/#1-3						13.00
Zorro's Renegades (2/99, $14.95, TPB) r/#4-8						15.00

ZORRO
Dynamite Entertainment: 2008 - Present ($3.50)

	GD 2.0	VG 4.0	FN 6.0	VF 8.0	VF/NM 9.0	NM- 9.2
1-20: 1-Origin retold; Wagner-s; three covers. 2-20-Two covers on all						3.50

ZORRO MATANZAS
Dynamite Entertainment: 2010 - No. 4, 2010 ($3.99)

	GD 2.0	VG 4.0	FN 6.0	VF 8.0	VF/NM 9.0	NM- 9.2
1-4-Mayhew-a/McGregor-s						4.00

ZOT!
Eclipse Comics: 4/84 - No. 10, 7/85; No. 11, 1/87 - No. 36 7/91 ($1.50, Baxter-p)

	GD 2.0	VG 4.0	FN 6.0	VF 8.0	VF/NM 9.0	NM- 9.2
1						5.00
2,3						4.00
4-10: 4-Origin. 10-Last color issue						3.00
10 1/2 (6/86, 25¢, Not Available Comics) Ashcan; art by Feazell & Scott McCloud						4.00
11-14,15-35-($2.00-c) B&W issues						3.00
14 1/2 (Adventures of Zot! in Dimension 10 1/2)(7/87) Antisocialman app.						3.00
36-($2.95-c) B&W						5.00
... The Complete Black and White Collection TPB (2008, $24.95) r/#11-36 with commentary, interviews and bonus artwork						25.00

Z-2 COMICS (Secret Agent...)(See Holyoke One-Shot #7)

ZULU (See Movie Classics)

MISTER LAZARUS
DISPENSES WISE ADVICE

OOOOOH! MISS GUISEWITE IS SIMPLY HORRIBLE!
WHY ARE YOU UPSET, DARLING?

THE NERVE! SHE WON'T LET ME BORROW HER COPY OF HOGAN'S ALLEY!
WHY DO YOU NEED TO BORROW A COPY? WHERE'S OUR COPY?

THE NEWSSTAND SOLD HER THEIR LAST COPY!
WELL, IF THAT DOESN'T BEAT ALL! IT'S MY FAVORITE COMICS MAGAZINE!

MAYBE KINDLY MR. LAZARUS CAN HELP US!
MR. LAZARUS, DO YOU KNOW WHERE WE CAN BUY A COPY OF HOGAN'S ALLEY?
AH, YOU YOUNG FOLKS NEVER LEARN...

I SUBSCRIBE SO I NEVER MISS AN ISSUE! PLUS I SAVE MONEY!
OF COURSE! IT ALL MAKES SENSE NOW!

I'M GUARANTEED TO GET THE INTERVIEWS, ESSAYS, REPRINTS, REVIEWS AND MORE THAT EVERY ISSUE CONTAINS!
NO OTHER MAGAZINE COMES CLOSE TO ITS SCOPE!

ANY PASSIONATE COMICS FAN SHOULD SUBSCRIBE TO HOGAN'S ALLEY! NEWSSTAND DISTRIBUTION IS SIMPLY TOO UNRELIABLE!
INDEED!

WE OWE IT TO OURSELVES— AND OUR FAMILY— TO SUBSCRIBE TO HOGAN'S ALLEY!
WE'LL DO IT FOR THE CHILDREN!
YOU'RE RAISING THE NEXT GENERATION OF COMICS FANS!
NCS Members only

BUSINESS CARD ADS

THE OVERSTREET COMIC BOOK PRICE GUIDE BUSINESS CARD ADS are a great way to advertise in the Guide! Simply send us your business card and we'll reduce it and run it as is. Have your ad seen by thousands of serious comic book collectors for an entire year! If you are a comic book or collectible dealer, retail establishment, mail-order house, etc., you can reach potential customers throughout the United States and around the world in our **BUSINESS CARDS ADS**!

For more information, contact our Advertising Dept.
Gemstone Publishing, Inc., 1966 Greenspring Dr., Timonium, MD 21093
or e-mail **feedback@gemstonepub.com**.

BUSINESS CARD ADS

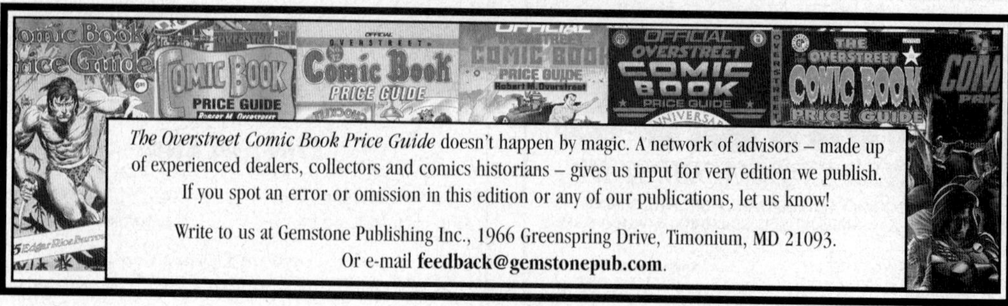

The Overstreet Comic Book Price Guide doesn't happen by magic. A network of advisors – made up of experienced dealers, collectors and comics historians – gives us input for very edition we publish. If you spot an error or omission in this edition or any of our publications, let us know!

Write to us at Gemstone Publishing Inc., 1966 Greenspring Drive, Timonium, MD 21093.
Or e-mail **feedback@gemstonepub.com**.

DIRECTORY LISTINGS

(PAID ADVERTISING - STORE LISTINGS)

You can have your store listed here for very reasonable rates. Send for details for next year's Guide. The following list of stores have paid to be included in this list. We cannot assume any responsibility in your dealings with these shops. This list is provided for your information only. When planning trips, it would be advisable to make appointments in advance. Remember, to get your shop included in the next edition, contact us for rates.

Gemstone Publishing, Inc., 1966 Greenspring Drive, Timonium, MD 21093.
TOLL FREE: 800-45-COMIC ext. 467
FAX: 410-252-6148
E-MAIL: feedback@gemstonepub.com

Items stocked by these shops are noted at the end of each listing and are coded as follows:

(a) Golden Age Comics
(b) Silver Age Comics
(c) Bronze Age Comics
(d) New Comics & Magazines
(e) Back Issue magazines
(f) Comic Supplies
(g) Collectible Card Games
(h) Role Playing Games
(i) Gaming Supplies
(j) Manga
(k) Anime
(l) Underground Comics
(m) Original Comic Art
(n) Pulps
(o) Big Little Books
(p) Books - Used
(q) Books - New
(r) Comic Related Posters
(s) Movie Posters
(t) Trading Cards
(u) Statues/Mini-busts, etc.
(v) Premiums (Rings, Decoders, etc.)
(w) Action Figures
(x) Other Toys
(y) Records/CDs
(z) DVDs/VHS
(1) Doctor Who Items
(2) Simpsons Items
(3) Star Trek Items
(4) Star Wars Items
(5) HeroClix

Wonderland Comics
112 Main Street #15
Putnam, CT 06260
PH: (800) 696-2510
FAX: (860) 935-0000
WonderlandComics@aol.com
www.WonderlandComics.com
(a-j,l,r-x,1-5)

FLORIDA

Emerald City Comics and Collectibles, Inc.
2475 North McMullin Booth Rd.
Suite I
Clearwater, FL 33759
PH: (727) 797-0664
E-Mail: CowardlyLion
@emeraldcitycomics.com
www.emeraldcitycomics.com
(a-j,m,r,t-x,z,1-5)

Samuel Frazer
11005 Lakeland Circle
Fort Myers, FL 33913
PH/FAX: (239) 768-0649
sfrazer457@aol.com
(a,b,o)

Paul Dyroff
P.O. Box 953972
Lake Mary, FL 32795
PH: (407) 688-2768
PH: (321) 368-3993
pdyroff@cfl.rr.com
www.paulscollectibles.com
(a-c,e,l-p,r,s,t,v,x,y)

Phil's Comic Shoppe
6512 West Atlantic Blvd.
Margate, FL 33063
PH: (954) 977-6947
philscomix@att.net
(b-d,f,l,m,t,u,w)

CGC
P.O. Box 4738
Sarasota, FL 34230
PH: (877) NM-COMIC
FAX: (941) 360-2558
www.CGCcomics.com

Emerald City Comics and Collectibles, Inc.
9249 Seminole Boulevard
Seminole, FL 33772
PH: (727) 398-BOOK (2665)
E-Mail: CowardlyLion
@emeraldcitycomics.com
www.emeraldcitycomics.com
(a-k,m,r-x,z,1-5)

David T. Alexander Collectibles
P.O. Box 273086
Tampa, FL 33618
PH: (813) 968-1805
dtacollectibles@gmail.com
www.dtacollectibles.com
(a-c,e,l-o,r-t,v,x,3,4)

Pedigree Comics, Inc.
12541 Equine Lane
Wellington, FL 33414
PH/FAX: (561) 422-1120
CELL: (561) 596-9111
E-Mail: DougSchmell
@pedigreecomics.com
www.pedigreecomics.com

GEORGIA

Odin's Comics
937 Killian Hill Rd.
Lilburn, GA 30047
PH: (770) 923-0123
www.odinscomics.com
(a-i,r,t,u,w,x,5)

ILLINOIS

Yesterday
1143 W. Addison St.
Chicago, IL 60613
PH: (773) 248-8087
(a-c,e,f,l,n-p,r-t,v,x-z,1,3,4)

The Paper Escape
205 West First Street
Dixon, IL 61021
PH: (815) 284-7567
E-Mail:paperescape@
paperescape.com
www.paperescape.com
(b-d,f-j,p-r,t,u,w,x,z,1,3-5)

Dreamland Comics
105 W. Rockland Rd.
Libertyville, IL 60048
PH: (847) 680-0727
FAX: (847) 680-4495
info@dreamland-comics.com
www.dreamland-comics.com
(a-j,r,t,u,w,3-5)

INDIANA

Comics Ina Flash
P.O. Box 3611
Evansville, IN 47735-3611
PH/FAX: (812) 401-6127
comicflash@aol.com
www.comicsinaflash.com

Books Comics and Things
2212 Maplecrest Rd.
Fort Wayne, IN 46815
PH: (260) 493-6116
bct@bctcomics.com
www.bctcomics.com
www.SuperHeroGameLand.com
(a-j,r,u,w,4,5)

Books Comics and Things
5936 W. Jefferson Blvd.
Fort Wayne, IN 46804
PH: (260) 755-2425
jscott@bctcomics.com
www.bctcomics.com
(b-j,r,t,u,w,x,1,5)

IOWA

Daydreams Comics
21 S. Dubuque St.
Iowa City, IA 52240
PH: (319) 354-6632
E-Mail: daydreamscomics
@yahoo.com
www.daydreamscomics.com
(a-d,f,j,t)

KANSAS

B•Bop Comics South
A Friendly Frank's Company
5336 W. 95th Street
Prairie Village, KS 66207
PH: (913) 383-1777
(a-g,i,j,l-u,w,x,1-5)

KENTUCKY

Comic Book World, Inc.
7130 Turfway Rd.
Florence, KY 41042
PH: (859) 371-9562
FAX: (859) 371-6925
comicbw@one.net
www.comicbookworld.com
(a-j,l,n-p,r,t,u,w,1-5)

Comic Book World, Inc.
6905 Shepherdsville Rd.
Louisville, KY 40219
PH: (502) 964-5500
FAX: (502) 964-5500
cbwdoug@bellsouth.net
www.comicbookworld.com
(a-j,l,n-p,r,t,u,w,x,1-5)

Leroy Harper
P.O. Box 212
West Paducah, KY 42086
PH: (270) 748-9364
LHCOMICS@hotmail.com

LOUISIANA

BT & SJ Giles
P.O. Box 271
Keithville, LA 71047
PH: (318) 925-6654
billygiles@comcast.net
(a,b,d,e,n-q,z)

MAINE

Top Shelf Comics
25 Central St.
Bangor, ME 04401
PH: (207) 947-4939
FAX: (207) 947-1758
TopShelf@tcomics.com
www.tcomics.com
(a-f)

MARYLAND

E. Gerber
1720 Belmont Ave.; Suite C
Baltimore, MD 21244

Esquire Comics.com
Mark S. Zaid, ESQ.
P.O. Box 3422492
Bethesda, MD 20827
PH: (202) 498-0011
esquirecomics@aol.com
www.esquirecomics.com
(b-k,r,u,w,4,5)

Alternate Worlds
Yorktowne Plaza Center
72 Cranbrook Road
Cockeysville, MD 21030
PH: (410) 666-3290
AltWorldStore@comcast.net
Alternateworlds.biz
(b-i,q,r,u,w,1,3-5)

Comics To Astonish Inc.
9400 Snowden River Pkwy.
Suite 112
Columbia, MD 21045
PH: (410) 381-2732
comics2u@aol.com
www.ComicsToAstonish.com
(a-k,m,r,t,u,w,z,2,3,5)

Greg Reece's Rare Comics
11028 Graymarsh Pl.
Ijamsville, MD 21754
PH: (240) 575-8600
greg@gregreececomics.com
www.gregreececomics.com
(a,b,c,e,f)

Diamond Comic Distributors
1966 Greenspring Drive
Timonium, MD 21093
PH: (800) 45-COMIC

Diamond Comic Distributors
1966 Greenspring Drive
Timonium, MD 21093
PH: (800) 45-COMIC

Diamond International Galleries
1966 Greenspring Drive
Timonium, MD 21093
PH: (888) 355-9800
PH: (410) 427-9422
GalleryQuestions@
DiamondGalleries.com
www.DiamondGalleries.com

MASSACHUSETTS

Gary Dolgoff Comics
116 Pleasant St.
Easthampton, MA 01027
PH: (413) 529-0326
FAX: (413) 529-9824
gary@gdcomics.com
www.gdcomics.com

That's Entertainment II
56 John Fitch Highway
Fitchburg, MA 01420
PH: (978) 342-8607
fitch@thatse.com
www.ThatsE.com
(a-z,1-5)

Superworld Comics, Inc.
456 Main St., Suite F
Holden, MA 01520
PH: (508) 829-2259
Ted@Superworldcomics.com
www.Superworldcomics.com
(a-c,e)

Bill Cole Enterprises Inc.
P.O. Box 60
Randolph, MA 02368-0060
PH: (781) 986-2653
FAX: (781) 986-2656
sales@bcemylar.com
www.bcemylar.com

The Time Capsule
1732 Fall River Ave.
Seekonk, MA 02771
PH: (508) 336-4790
thetimecapsule@mail.com
www.thetimecapsule.com
(a-g,j,k,r,t,u,w-z,2-5)

The Outer Limits
437 Moody St.
Waltham, MA 02453
PH: (781) 891-0444
askOuterLimits@aol.com
www.eouterlimits.com
(a-j,l-x,z,1-5)

That's Entertainment
244 Park Avenue (Rt. 9)
Worcester, MA 01609
PH: (508) 755-4207
ken@thatse.com
www.ThatsE.com
(a-z,1-5)

MICHIGAN

Motor City Comics
33228 W. 12 Mile Rd.
PMB 286
Farmington Hills, MI 48334
PH: (248) 426-8059
FAX: (248) 426-8064
michaelg@motorcitycomics.com
www.motorcitycomics.com
(a-c,l-o,r,v,w,x)

The Amazing Book-Store
3718 Richfield Rd.
Flint, MI 48506
PH: (810) 736-3025
amazingbookstore@comcast.net
amazebookstore.com
(a-g,i,l,r,t-w,5)

Fanfare Sports & Entertainment, Inc.
4415 S. Westnedge Ave.
Kalamazoo, MI 49008
PH: (269) 349-8866
www.fanfare-se.com
(a-k,m,r,t,u,w-z,1-5)

Harley Yee Comics
P.O. Box 51758
Livonia, MI 48151-5758
PH: (800) 731-1029
FAX: (734) 421-7928
HarleyComx@aol.com
www.HarleyYeeComics.com

MINNESOTA

Source Comics & Games
1601 West Larpenteur Ave.
Falcon Heights, MN 55113
PH: (651) 645-0386
FAX: (651) 644-0922
BobSource@aol.com
www.SourceComicsandGames.com

Midway Book & Comic
1579 University Ave.
St. Paul, MN 55104
PH: (651) 644-7605
FAX: (651) 644-8786
(a-f,n-p)

Uncle Sven's Comic Shoppe
1838 St. Clair Ave.
St. Paul, MN 55105
PH: (651) 699-3409
svenscomics@aol.com
(d,f-i,l,n,t,u,w,x,1-5)

MISSOURI

B•Bop Comics & Games North
A Friendly Frank's Company
6320 N.W. Barry Rd.
Kansas City, MO 64154
PH: (816) 746-4569
(a-m,p-r,t,u,w,x,z,2-5)

NEBRASKA

Robert Beerbohm Comic Art
P.O. Box 507
Fremont, NE 68026
PH: (402) 727-4071
Robert@BLBComics.com
www.BLBComics
(a,b,c,e,l-o,r)

Krypton Comics Inc.
2819 S. 125th Ave.
Suite 261
Omaha, NE 68144
PH: (402) 391-4131
E-Mail:Dean@
KryptonComicsOmaha.com
www.KryptonComicsOmaha.com
(a-j,r,u,w,x,1-5)

NEVADA

Redbeard's Book Den
P.O. Box 217
Crystal Bay, NV 89402
PH: (775) 831-4848
FAX: (775) 831-4483
www.redbeardsbookden.com
(a,b,c,l,o,p)

Cosmic Comics!
3830 E. Flamingo Suite F-2
Las Vegas, NV 89121
PH: (702) 451-6611
fudge-man@cox.net
CosmicComicsLasVegas.com
(a-d,f,i-k,n,o,r,u,v,w,4,5)

NEW HAMPSHIRE

Rare Books & Comics
James F. Payette
P.O. Box 750
Bethlehem, NH 03574
PH: (603) 869-2097
FAX: (603) 869-3475
JimPayette@msn.com
www.JamesPayetteComics.com
(a,b,c,e,n,o,p)

NEW JERSEY

A Time Lost...and Found
325 E. Atlantic Avenue
Audubon, NJ 08106
PH: (856) 547-7900
famarcus@aol.com
(b-f,j,l,r-u,w,x,1,3)

Nationwide Comics
Buying All 10¢ & 12¢
original priced comics
Derek Woywood
Clementon, NJ 08021
PH: (856) 217-5737 or
Hotline: (800) 938-0325
FAX: (714) 288-8992
dwoywood@yahoo.com
www.philadelphiacomic-con.com
(a,b,d-h,m,n,q)

ZAPP Comics
700 Tennent Road
Superfoodtown Center
Manalapan, NJ 07726
PH: (732) 617-1333
FAX: (732) 617-1334
ZAPPcomics@aol.com
www.zappcomics.com

Neat Stuff Collectibles
Brian Schutzer
704 76th Street
North Bergen, NJ 07047
PH: 1-800-903-7246
E-Mail: neatstuffcollectibles
@yahoo.com
www.NeatStuffCollectibles.com

J&S Comics
168 W. Sylvania Ave.
Neptune, NJ 07753
PH: (732) 988-5717
jandscomics@aol.com
www.jscomics.com

Fat Jack's Comicrypt
521 White Horse Pike
Oaklyn, NJ 08107
PH: (856) 858-3877
FAX: (215) 963-9361
fatjacks@comcast.net
(b-g,r,u,w,5)

J&S Comics
Jim Walsh
98 Madison Avenue
Red Bank, NJ 07701
PH: (732) 988-5717
jandscomics@aol.com
www.jscomics.com

All-Star Auctions
Nadia Mannarino
122 West End Avenue
Ridgewood, NJ 07450
PH: (201) 652-1305
FAX: (501) 325-6504
nadia@allstarauctions.net
www.allstarauctions.net

ZAPP Comics
574 Valley Road
A&P Center
Wayne, NJ 07470
PH: (973) 628-4500
FAX: (732) 525-0071
ben@zappcomics.com
www.zappcomics.com
(a-g,i,j,l,o,t,u,w,x,2-5)

JHV Associates
(By Appointment Only)
P. O. Box 317
Woodbury Heights, NJ 08097
PH: (856) 845-4010
FAX: (856) 845-3977
JHVassoc@hotmail.com
(a,b,n,s)

NEW MEXICO

Astro-Zombies
3100 Central Ave. SE
Albuquerque, NM 87106
PH: (505) 232-7800
info@astrozombies.com
astrozombies.com
(a-g,i,l,m,r,t-x,y,2,4,5)

NEW YORK

Excellent Adventures Comics
110 Milton Ave. (Rt. #50)
Ballston Spa, NY 12020
PH: (518) 884-9498
jbelskis37@aol.com
www.myspace.com/EAComics
(a-f,l-p,r-x,1-4)

Pinocchio Collectibles
1814 McDonald Ave.
(off Ave. P)
Brooklyn, NY 11223
PH: (718) 645-2573
a19gaba@aol.com
(b-d,f,i,w,x)

HighGradeComics.com
17 Bethany Drive
Commack, NY 11725
PH: (631) 543-1917
FAX: (631) 864-1921
BobStorms@
HighGradeComics.com
www.HighGradeComics.com
(a,b,c,e)

Comicollectors.net
Marnin Rosenberg
P.O. Box 2047
Great Neck, NY 11022
PH: (516) 466-8147
www.comiccollectors.net
www.collectorsassemble.com

Mahopac Cards & Comics
50 Miller Road
P.O. Box 444
Mahopac, NY 10541
PH: (845) 621-2699
FAX: (845) 621-6719
mahopaccards@aol.com
www.mahopaccards.com
(d,f,g,i,j,k,t,u,w,4,5)

Best Comics International
1300 Jericho Turnpike
New Hyde Park, NY 11040
PH: (516) 328-1900
TommyBest@aol.com
www.bestcomics.com
(a-d,f,r-t,w,3-5)

ComicConnect.com
873 Broadway
Suite 201
New York, NY 10003
PH: (212) 895-3999
FAX: (212) 260-4304
support@comicconnect.com
www.comicconnect.com
(a,b,c,m,n,s,v)

Metropolis Collectibles
873 Broadway
Suite 201
New York, NY 10003
PH: (800) 229-6387
FAX: (212) 260-4304
E-Mail: buying@
metropoliscomics.com
www.metropoliscomics.com

Midtown Comics
64 Fulton Street
New York, NY 10038
PH: (800) 411-3341
PH: (212) 302-8192
FAX: (646) 421-2033
info@midtowncomics.com
www.midtowncomics.com

Midtown Comics
459 Lexington Ave.
(Corner of 45th Street)
New York, NY 10017
PH: (800) 411-3341
PH: (212) 302-8192
FAX: (646) 421-2033
info@midtowncomics.com
www.midtowncomics.com

Midtown Comics
200 West 40th Street
New York, NY 10018
PH: (800) 411-3341
FAX: (646) 421-2033
info@midtowncomics.com
www.midtowncomics.com

Amazing Comics
12 Gillette Avenue
Sayville, NY 11782
PH: (631) 567-8069
info@amazingco.com
www.amazingco.com

Four Color Comics
Rob Rogovin
P.O. Box 1399
Scarsdale, NY 10583
PH: (914) 722-4696
FAX: (914) 722-7657
keybooks@aol.com
www.fourcolorcomics.com

Fourth World Comics
33 Route 111
Smithtown, NY 11787
PH: (631) 366-4440
fourgle@aol.com
fourthworldcomics.com
(a-k,q,r,t-x,z,1-5)

NORTH DAKOTA

Barry's Collectors Corner
1826 S. Washington St.
Grand Cities Mall
Grand Forks, ND 58201
PH: (701) 795-1386
UNDBKB@aol.com
(a-z,1-5)

OHIO

Up Up & Away!
4016 Harrison Avenue
Cincinnati, OH 45211
PH: (513) 661-6300
kendall@upupandawaycomics.com
www.upupandawaycomics.com
(a-j,m,u,w,z,2-5)

Bookery Fantasy
16 W. Main St.
Fairborn, OH 45324
PH: (937) 879-1408
BookeryFan@aol.com
www.BookeryFantasy.com
(a-j,l,n-p,s,u,w,1-5)

Comics and Friends
7850 Mentor Ave.
Mentor, OH 44060
PH: (440) 255-4242
joe@comicsandfriends.com
www.comicsandfriends.com
(a-f,j,l,m,r,u,w,x,1-5)

Parker's Records & Comics
1222 Suite C Rt. 28
Milford, OH 45150
PH/FAX: (513) 575-3665
dkparker39@fuse.net
(a-i,y)

OKLAHOMA

All Star Comics
6900 N. May Ave. #10
Oklahoma City, OK 73116
PH/FAX: (405) 842-7800
WGreenewood@cox.net
(a-f,n,o,r,s,u,w,1-4)

Comic Empire of Tulsa
3122 S. Mingo
Tulsa, OK 74146
PH: (918) 664-5808
(a-f,l)

Want List Comics
(Appointment Only)
P.O. Box 701932
Tulsa, OK 74170
PH: (918) 299-0440
E-Mail: wlc777@cox.net
(a,b,c,m,n,o,s,t,x,3)

OREGON

Emerald City Comics
770 E. 13th Ave.
Eugene, OR 97401
PH: (541) 345-2568
(c-k,r,x,z,5)

Nostalgia Collectibles
527 Willamette Street
Eugene, OR 97401
PH: (541) 484-9202
darrell7g@comcast.net
nostalgiacollectibleseugene.com
(a-g,i,l,n-r,t,u,w,x,1-5)

Future Dreams
1847 East Burnside St.
Suite 116
Portland, OR 97214-1587
PH: (503) 231-8311
fdb@hevanet.com
www.futuredreamsbooks.com
(a-g,i,j,l-n,p-u,w,x,3,4)

PENNSYLVANIA

New Dimension Comics
Clearview Mall
101 Clearview Circle
Butler, PA 16001
PH: (724) 282-5283
butler@ndcomics.com
www.ndcomics.com
(a-l,n,o,r,t,u,w,x,1-5)

New Dimension Comics
Piazza Plaza
20550 Route 19 (Perry Hwy.)
Cranberry Township, PA
16066
PH: (724) 776-0433
cranberry@ndcomics.com
www.ndcomics.com
(a-l,n,o,r,t,u,w,x,1-5)

New Dimension Comics Megastore
516 Lawrence Ave.
Ellwood City, PA 16117
PH: (724) 758-2324
ec@ndcomics.com
www.ndcomics.com
(a-l,n,o,r,t,u,w,x,1-5)

Comic Collection
931 Bustleton Pike
At Street Road
Feasterville, PA 19053
PH: (215) 357-3322
comicdeity@aol.com
ComicCollectionStore.com
TheComicCollection.net
(a-m,o,q-z,1-5)

Comic Universe
446 MacDade Blvd.
Folsom, PA 19033
PH: (610) 461-7960
chessflink@yahoo.com
www.ComicUniverse.net
(a-g,j-r,t,u,w,x,z,1-5)

The Comic Store
28 McGovern Ave.
Lancaster, PA 17602
PH: (717) 397-8737
FAX: (717) 397-8903
comicstore@juno.com
www.comicstorepa.com

Fat Jack's Comicrypt
2006 Sansom St.
Philadelphia, PA 19103
PH: (215) 963-0788
FAX: (215) 963-9361
fatjacks@comcast.net
(a-j,l,r,u,w,5)

Eide's Entertainment
1121 Penn Ave.
Pittsburgh, PA 15222
PH: (412) 261-0900
FAX: (412) 261-3102
eides@eides.com
www.eides.com
(a-g,i-z,1-5)

New Dimension Comics
Pittsburgh Century III Mall
3075 Clairton Rd. #940
West Mifflin, PA 15213
PH: (412) 655-8661
century3@ndcomics.com
www.ndcomics.com
(a-l,n,o,r,t,u,w,x,1-5)

Hake's Americana
P.O. Box 12001
York, PA 17402
PH: (866) 404-9800
www.hakes.com

RHODE ISLAND

The Time Capsule
537 Pontiac Ave.
Cranston, RI 02910
PH: (401) 781-5017
thetimecapsule@mail.com
www.thetimecapsule.com
(a-h,l-o,s-z,2-4)

TENNESSEE

Comics Universe
1869 Hwy 45 Bypass
Jackson, TN 38305
PH/FAX: (731) 664-9131
(a-d,f,m,p-r,w)

Dewayne's World - Comics & Games
459 E. Sullivan Street
Kingsport, TN 37660
PH/FAX: (423) 247-8997
dewayne@
dewaynes-world.com
www.dewaynes-world.com
(a-d,f-i,r,u,w,3-5)

TEXAS

Lone Star Comics
511 E. Abram St.
Arlington, TX 76010
PH: (817) 860-7827
FAX: (817) 860-2769
customerservice@
lonestarcomics.com
www.mycomicshop.com/
overstreet
(a-f,j,n,p,u,1-4)

Comic Heaven
P.O. Box 900
Big Sandy, TX 75755
PH: (903) 636-5555
www.comicheaven.net

Classics Incorporated
Matt Nelson
1440 Halsey Way
Suite #114
Carrollton, TX 75007
PH: (972) 980-8040
www.classicsincorporated.com
Spectre52@aol.com

Worldwide Comics
1440 Halsey Way
Suite #110
Carrollton, TX 75007
PH: (972) 345-2505
www.wwcomics.com
Spectre52@aol.com

Heritage Auction Galleries
3500 Maple Avenue
17th Floor
Dallas, TX 75219-3941
PH: (800) 872-6467
www.HA.com

Titan Comics
3701 W. Northwest Hwy Suite
#125
Dallas, TX 75220
PH: (214) 350-4420
info@titancomics.com
www.titancomics.com
(a-d,f,l,m,r,u)

William Hughes' Vintage Collectables
P.O. Box 270244
Flower Mound, TX 75027
PH: (972) 539-9190
FAX: (972) 691-8837
Whughes199@yahoo.com
www.VintageCollectables.net

Bedrock City Comic Co.
6517 Westheimer
Houston, TX 77057
PH: (713) 780-0675
www.bedrockcity.com
(a-g,j-o,r-x,z,1-5)

Bedrock City Comic Co.
4683 FM1960 West
Houston, TX 77069
PH: (281) 444-9763
www.bedrockcity.com
(a-g,j-o,r-x,z,1-5)

Bedrock City Comic Co.
106 W. Bay Area Blvd.
Webster, TX 77598
PH: (281) 557-2748
www.bedrockcity.com
(a-g,j-o,r-x,z,1-5)

VIRGINIA

Trilogy Shop #2
700 E. Little Creek Rd.
Norfolk, VA 23518
PH: (757) 587-2540
trilogy2@TrilogyComics.net
www.TrilogyComics.net
(d-j,5)

B & D Comic Shop
802 Elm Avenue SW
Roanoke, VA 24016
PH: (540) 342-6642
FAX: (540) 342-6694
bdcomics1@verizon.net
www.banddcomics.com
(c-f,r,w)

Trilogy Comics #1
5773 Princess Anne Rd.
Virginia Beach, VA 23462
PH: (757) 490-2205
trilogy1@TrilogyComics.net
www.TrilogyComics.net
(a-j,n-p,s-u,w,5)

WASHINGTON

DreamStrands Comics & Such
115 N. 85th St.
Seattle, WA 98103
PH: (206) 297-3737
delanor@dreamstrands.com
www.dreamstrands.com
(b-d,f,g,i,j,r,u,w,x,3-5)

Golden Age Collectables
1501 Pike Place Market
#401 Lower Level
Seattle, WA 98101
PH: (206) 622-9799
FAX: (206) 622-9595
GACollect@Gmail.com
www.GoldenAgeCollectables.com
(a-x,1-5)

WEST VIRGINIA

Comic World
1204 - 4th Avenue
Huntington, WV 25701
PH: (304) 522-3923
(a-d,f,l,t,u,w,5)

WISCONSIN

Nationwide Comics
Buying All 10¢ & 12¢
original priced comics
Bart Mitchell
Janesville, WI 53545
PH: (608) 752-8128 or
Hotline: (800) 938-0325
FAX: (714) 288-8992
Bart@nationwidecomics.net
www.nationwidecomics.net
(a,b,d-h,m,n,q)

Capital City Comics
1910 Monroe St.
Madison, WI 53711
PH: (608) 251-8445
(a-f,j,l-o,r,u,w,y,z)

Jef Hinds Comics
PO Box 44803
Madison, WI 53744-4803
PH: (608) 277-8750
jhcomics@jhcomics.com
www.jhcomics.com
(a-c,e,m-o,s,w)

CANADA

ALBERTA

Another Dimension
424B - 10 St. NW
Calgary, Alberta T2N 1V9
PH: (403) 283-7078
FAX: (403) 283-7080
comics@another-dimension.com
www.another-dimension.com

MANITOBA

Doug Sulipa's Comic World
Box 21986
Steinbach, MB., R5G 1B5
PH: (204) 346-3674
FAX: (204) 346-1632
dsulipa@gmail.com
www.dougcomicworld.com
(a-e,h,l,n-t,y,z,3,4)

Comics America
552 Academy Road
Winnipeg, MB, R3N 03E
PH: (204) 489-0580
FAX: (204) 489-0589
comics_america@mts.net
www.comicsamerica.com

ONTARIO

Big B Comics
1045 Upper James St.
Hamilton, ONT. L9C 3A6
PH: (905) 318-9636
FAX: (905) 318-9055
mailbox@bigbcomics.com
www.bigbcomics.com
(a-g,i,j,l,m,q,u,w,x,1-5)

Imperial Coin & Stamp Co.
227 King St. East
Hamilton, ONT. L8N 1B6
PH: (905) 528-8313
FAX: (905) 528-8673
(a-c,e,f,n,o)

Vintage Comics
PO Box 25055
Kitchener, ONT. N2A 4A5
Toll Free: (888) 551-8155
info@vintagecomics.com
www.vintagecomics.com

B.A's COMICS
426 Hamilton Road
London, ONT. N5Z 1R9
PH: (519) 439-9636
ba.lm@rogers.com
(a-f,l-o,t)

Pendragon Comics
3759 Lakeshore Boulevard West
Toronto, ONT M8W 1R1
PH: (416) 253-6974
pendragoncomics@rogers.com
pendragoncomics.com
(a-g,l,p)

QUEBEC

Heroes Comics
1116 Cure LaBelle
Laval, QC H7V 2V5
PH: (450) 686-9155
FAX: (450) 686-2097
heroescomics@videotron.ca
(a-d,f-i,m,r,t-x,2-5)

FRANCE

Editions Déesse
8, Rue Cochin
Paris, France 75005
PH: +33 1 46 34 18 31
eds@editions-deesse.com
www.editions-deesse.com
(a-f,l,m,n,r,u)

INTERNET

ComicLink Auctions & Exchange
PH: (718) 246-0300
buysell@ComicLink.com
www.ComicLink.com

Slab-Pro
PH: (631) 630-1859
info@slab-pro.com
www.slab-pro.com

(PAID ADVERTISING - STORE LISTINGS)

You can have your store listed here for very reasonable rates. Send for details for next year's Guide. The preceding list of stores have paid to be included in this list. We cannot assume any responsibility in your dealings with these shops. This list is provided for your information only. When planning trips, it would be advisable to make appointments in advance. Remember, to get your shop included in the next edition, contact us for rates.

Gemstone Publishing, Inc., 1966 Greenspring Drive, Timonium, MD 21093.
TOLL FREE: 800-45-COMIC ext. 467
FAX: 410-252-6148
E-MAIL: feedback@gemstonepub.com

Items stocked by these shops are noted at the end of each listing and are coded as follows:

(a) Golden Age Comics
(b) Silver Age Comics
(c) Bronze Age Comics
(d) New Comics & Magazines
(e) Back Issue magazines
(f) Comic Supplies
(g) Collectible Card Games
(h) Role Playing Games
(i) Gaming Supplies
(j) Manga
(k) Anime
(l) Underground Comics
(m) Original Comic Art
(n) Pulps
(o) Big Little Books
(p) Books - Used
(q) Books - New
(r) Comic Related Posters
(s) Movie Posters
(t) Trading Cards
(u) Statues/Mini-busts, etc.
(v) Premiums (Rings, Decoders, etc.)
(w) Action Figures
(x) Other Toys
(y) Records/CDs
(z) DVDs/VHS
(1) Doctor Who Items
(2) Simpsons Items
(3) Star Trek Items
(4) Star Wars Items
(5) HeroClix

GLOSSARY

a - Story art; a(i) - Story art inks; a(p) - Story art pencils;
a(r) - Story art reprint.

ADULT MATERIAL - Contains story and/or art for "mature" readers. Re: sex, violence, strong language.

ADZINE - A magazine primarily devoted to the advertising of comic books and collectibles as its first publishing priority as opposed to written articles.

ALLENTOWN COLLECTION - A collection discovered in 1987-88 just outside Allentown, Pennsylvania. The Allentown collection consisted of 135 Golden Age comics, characterized by high grade and superior paper quality.

ANNUAL - (1) A book that is published yearly; (2) Can also refer to some square bound comics.

ARRIVAL DATE - The date written (often in pencil) or stamped on the cover of comics by either the local wholesaler, newsstand owner, or distributor. The date precedes the cover date by approximately 15 to 75 days, and may vary considerably from one locale to another or from one year to another.

ASHCAN - A publisher's in-house facsimile of a proposed new title. Most ashcans have black and white covers stapled to an existing coverless comic on the inside; other ashcans are totally black and white. In modern parlance, it can also refer to promotional or sold comics, often smaller than standard comic size and usually in black and white, released by publishers to advertise the forthcoming arrival of a new title or story.

ATOM AGE - Comics published from 1946-1956.

B&W - Black and white art.

BACK-UP FEATURE - A story or character that usually appears after the main feature in a comic book; often not featured on the cover.

BAD GIRL ART - A term popularized in the early '90s to describe an attitude as well as a style of art that portrays women in a sexual and often action-oriented way.

BAXTER PAPER - A high quality, heavy, white paper used in the printing of some comics.

BC - Abbreviation for Back Cover.

BI-MONTHLY - Published every two months.

BI-WEEKLY - Published every two weeks.

BONDAGE COVER - Usually denotes a female in bondage.

BOUND COPY - A comic that has been bound into a book. The process requires that the spine be trimmed and sometimes sewn into a book-like binding.

BRITISH ISSUE - A comic printed for distribution in Great Britain; these copies sometimes have the price listed in pence or pounds instead of cents or dollars.

BRITTLENESS - A severe condition of paper deterioration where paper loses its flexibility and thus chips and/or flakes easily.

BRONZE AGE - Comics published from 1970 to 1984.

BROWNING - (1) The aging of paper characterized by the ever-increasing level of oxidation characterized by darkening; (2) The level of paper deterioration one step more severe than tanning and one step before brittleness.

c - Cover art; c(i) - Cover inks; c(p) - Cover pencils; c(r) - Cover reprint.

CAMEO - The brief appearance of one character in the strip of another.

CANADIAN ISSUE - A comic printed for distribution in Canada; these copies sometimes have no advertising.

CCA - Abbreviation for **Comics Code Authority**.

CCA SEAL - An emblem that was placed on the cover of all CCA approved comics beginning in April-May, 1955.

CENTER CREASE - See **Subscription Copy**.

CENTERFOLD or CENTER SPREAD - The two folded pages in the center of a comic book at the terminal end of the staples.

CERTIFIED GRADING - A process provided by a professional grading service that certifies a given grade for a comic and seals the book in a protective **Slab.**

CF - Abbreviation for **Centerfold**.

CFO - Abbreviation for Centerfold Out.

CGC - Abbreviation for the certified comic book grading company, Comics Guaranty, LLC.

CIRCULATION COPY - See **Subscription Copy**.

CIRCULATION FOLD - See **Subscription Fold**.

CLASSIC COVER - A cover considered by collectors to be highly desirable because of its subject matter, artwork, historical importance, etc.

CLEANING - A process in which dirt and dust is removed.

COLOR TOUCH - A restoration process by which colored ink is used to hide color flecks, color flakes, and larger areas of missing color. Short for Color Touch-Up.

COLORIST - An artist who paints the color guides for comics. Many modern colorists use computer technology.

COMIC BOOK DEALER - (1) A seller of comic books; (2) One who makes a living buying and selling comic books.

COMIC BOOK REPAIR - When a tear, loose staple or centerfold has been mended without changing or adding to the original finish of the book. Repair may involve tape, glue or nylon gossamer, and is easily detected; it is considered a defect.

COMICS CODE AUTHORITY - A voluntary organization comprised of comic book publishers formed in 1954 to review (and possibly censor) comic books before they were printed and distributed. The emblem of the CCA is a white stamp in the upper right hand corner of comics dated after February 1955. The term "post-Code" refers to the time after this practice started, or approximately 1955 to the present.

COMPLETE RUN - All issues of a given title.

CON - A convention or public gathering of fans.

CONDITION - The state of preservation of a comic book, often inaccurately used interchangeably with **Grade**.

CONSERVATION - The European Confederation of Conservator-Restorers' Organizations (ECCO) in its professional guidelines, defines conservation as follows: "Conservation consists mainly of direct action carried out on cultural heritage with the aim of stabilizing condition and retarding further deterioration."

COPPER AGE - Comics published from 1984 to 1992.

COSMIC AEROPLANE COLLECTION - A collection from Salt Lake City, Utah discovered by Cosmic Aeroplane Books, characterized by the moderate to high grade copies of 1930s-40s comics with pencil check marks in the margins of inside pages. It is thought that these comics were kept by a commercial illustration school and the check marks were placed beside panels that instructors wanted students to draw.

COSTUMED HERO - A costumed crime fighter with "developed" human powers instead of super powers.

COUPON CUT or COUPON MISSING - A coupon has been neatly removed with scissors or razor blade from the interior or exterior of the comic as opposed to having been ripped out.

COVER GLOSS - The reflective quality of the cover inks.

COVER TRIMMED - Cover has been reduced in size by neatly cutting away rough or damaged edges.

COVERLESS - A comic with no cover attached. There is a niche demand for coverless comics, particularly in the case of hard-to-find key books otherwise impossible to locate intact.

C/P - Abbreviation for **Cleaned and Pressed**. See **Cleaning**.

CREASE - A fold which causes ink removal, usually resulting in a white line. See **Reading Crease**.

CROSSOVER - A story where one character appears prominently in the story of another character. See **X-Over**.

CVR - Abbreviation for Cover.

DEALER - See **Comic Book Dealer**.

DEACIDIFICATION - Several different processes that reduce acidity in paper.

DEBUT - The first time that a character appears anywhere.

DEFECT - Any fault or flaw that detracts from perfection.

DENVER COLLECTION - A collection consisting primarily of early 1940s high grade number one issues bought at auction in Pennsylvania by a Denver, Colorado dealer.

DIE-CUT COVER - A comic book cover with areas or edges precut by a printer to a special shape or to create a desired effect.

DISTRIBUTOR STRIPES - Color brushed or sprayed on the edges of comic book stacks by the distributor/wholesaler to code them for expedient exchange at the sales racks. Typical colors are red, orange, yellow, green, blue, and purple. Distributor stripes are not a defect.

DOUBLE - A duplicate copy of the same comic book.

DOUBLE COVER - When two covers are stapled to the comic interior instead of the usual one; the exterior cover often protects the interior cover from wear and damage. This is considered a desirable situation by some collectors and may increase collector value; this is not considered a defect.

DRUG PROPAGANDA STORY - A comic that makes an editorial stand about drug use.

DRUG USE STORY - A comic that shows the actual use of drugs: needle use, tripping, harmful effects, etc.

DRY CLEANING - A process in which dirt and dust is removed.

DUOTONE - Printed with black and one other color of ink. This process was common in comics printed in the 1930s.

DUST SHADOW - Darker, usually linear area at the edge of some comics stored in stacks. Some portion of the cover was not covered by the comic immediately above it and it was exposed to settling dust particles. Also see **Oxidation Shadow** and **Sun Shadow**.

EDGAR CHURCH COLLECTION - See **Mile High Collection**.

EMBOSSED COVER - A comic book cover with a pattern, shape or image pressed into the cover from the inside, creating a raised area.

ENCAPSULATION - Refers to the process of sealing certified comics in a protective plastic enclosure. Also see **Slabbing.**

EYE APPEAL - A term which refers

to the overall look of a comic book when held at approximately arm's length. A comic may have nice eye appeal yet still possess defects which reduce grade.

FANZINE - An amateur fan publication.

FC - Abbreviation for Front Cover.

FILE COPY - A high grade comic originating from the publisher's file; contrary to what some might believe, not all file copies are in Gem Mint condition. An arrival date on the cover of a comic does not indicate that it is a file copy, though a copyright date may.

FIRST APPEARANCE - See **Debut**.

FLASHBACK - When a previous story is recalled.

FOIL COVER - A comic book cover that has had a thin metallic foil hot stamped on it. Many of these "gimmick" covers date from the early '90s, and might include chromium, prism and hologram covers as well.

FOUR COLOR - Series of comics produced by Dell, characterized by hundreds of different features; named after the four color process of printing. See **One Shot**.

FOUR COLOR PROCESS - The process of printing with the three primary colors (red, yellow, and blue) plus black.

FUMETTI - Illustration system in which individual frames of a film are colored and used for individual panels to make a comic book story. The most famous example is DC's *Movie Comics* #1-6 from 1939.

GATEFOLD COVER - A double-width fold-out cover.

GENRE - Categories of comic book subject matter; e.g. Science Fiction, Super-Hero, Romance, Funny Animal, Teenage Humor, Crime, War, Western, Mystery, Horror, etc.

GIVEAWAY - Type of comic book intended to be given away as a premium or promotional device instead of being sold.

GLASSES ATTACHED - In 3-D comics, the special blue and red cellophane and cardboard glasses are still attached to the comic.

GLASSES DETACHED - In 3-D comics, the special blue and red cellophane and cardboard glasses are not still attached to the comic; obviously less desirable than **Glasses Attached**.

GOLDEN AGE - Comics published from 1938 (*Action Comics* #1) to 1945.

GOOD GIRL ART - Refers to a style of art, usually from the 1930s-50s, that portrays women in a sexually implicit way.

GREY-TONE COVER - A cover art style in which pencil or charcoal underlies the normal line drawing, used to enhance the effects of light and shadow, thus producing a richer quality. These covers, prized by most collectors, are sometimes referred to as **Painted Covers** but are not actually painted.

HC - Abbreviation for Hardcover.

HEADLIGHTS - Forward illumation devices installed on all automobiles and many other vehicles... OK, OK, it's a euphemism for a comic book cover prominently featuring a woman's breasts in a provocative way. Also see **Bondage Cover** for another collecting euphemism that has long since outlived its appropriateness in these politically correct times.

HOT STAMPING - The process of pressing foil, prism paper and/or inks on cover stock.

HRN - Abbreviation for Highest Reorder Number. This refers to a method used by collectors of Gilberton's *Classic Comics* and *Classics Illustrated* series to distinguish first editions from later printings.

ILLO - Abbreviation for Illustration.

IMPAINT - Another term for **Color Touch**.

INDICIA - Publishing and title information usually located at the bottom of the first page or the bottom of the inside front cover. In some pre-1938 comics and many modern comics, it is located on internal pages.

INFINITY COVER - Shows a scene that repeats itself to infinity.

INKER - Artist that does the inking.

INTRO - Same as **Debut**.

INVESTMENT GRADE COPY - (1) Comic of sufficiently high grade and demand to be viewed by collectors as instantly liquid should the need arise to sell; (2) A comic in VF or better condition; (3) A comic purchased primarily to realize a profit.

ISSUE NUMBER - The actual edition number of a given title.

ISH - Short for Issue.

JLA - Abbreviation for Justice League of America.

JSA -Abbreviation for Justice Society of America.

KEY, KEY BOOK or KEY ISSUE - An issue that contains a first appearance, origin, or other historically or artistically important feature considered especially desirable by collectors.

LAMONT LARSON - Pedigreed collection of high grade 1940s comics with the initials or name of its original owner, Lamont Larson.

LENTICULAR COVERS or "FLICKER" COVERS - A comic book cover overlayed with a ridged plastic sheet such that the special artwork underneath appears to move when the cover is tilted at different angles perpendicular to the ridges.

LETTER COL or LETTER COLUMN - A feature in a comic book that prints and sometimes responds to letters written by its readers.

LINE DRAWN COVER - A cover

published in the traditional way where pencil sketches are over-drawn with india ink and then colored. See also **Grey-Tone Cover**, **Photo Cover**, and **Painted Cover**.

LOGO - The title of a strip or comic book as it appears on the cover or title page.

LSH - Abbreviation for Legion of Super-Heroes.

MAGIC LIGHTNING COLLECTION - A collection of high grade 1950s comics from the San Francisco area.

MARVEL CHIPPING - A bindery (trimming/cutting) defect that results in a series of chips and tears at the top, bottom, and right edges of the cover, caused when the cutting blade of an industrial paper trimmer becomes dull. It was dubbed Marvel Chipping because it can be found quite often on Marvel comics from the late '50s and early '60s but can also occur with any company's comic books from the late 1940s through the middle 1960s.

MILE HIGH COLLECTION - High grade collection of over 22,000 comics discovered in Denver, Colorado in 1977, originally owned by Mr. Edgar Church. Comics from this collection are now famous for extremely white pages, fresh smell, and beautiful cover ink reflectivity.

MODERN AGE - A catch-all term applied to comics published since 1992.

MYLAR™ - An inert, very hard, space-age plastic used to make high quality protective bags and sleeves for comic book storage. "Mylar" is a trademark of the DuPont Co.

ND - Abbreviation for **No Date**.

NN - Abbreviation for **No Number**.

NO DATE - When there is no date given on the cover or indicia page.

NO NUMBER - No issue number is given on the cover or indicia page; these are usually first issues or one-shots.

N.Y. LEGIS. COMM. - New York Legislative Committee to Study the Publication of Comics (1951).

ONE-SHOT - When only one issue is published of a title, or when a series is published where each issue is a different title (e.g. Dell's *Four Color Comics*).

ORIGIN - When the story of a character's creation is given.

OVER GUIDE - When a comic book is priced at a value over *Guide* list.

OXIDATION SHADOW - Darker, usually linear area at the edge of some comics stored in stacks. Some portion of the cover was not covered by the comic immediately above it, and it was exposed to the air. Also see **Dust Shadow** and **Sun Shadow**.

p - Art pencils.

PAINTED COVER - (1) Cover taken from an actual painting instead of a line drawing; (2) Inaccurate name for a grey-toned cover.

PANELOLOGIST - One who researches comic books and/or comic strips.

PANNAPICTAGRAPHIST - One possible term for someone who collects comic books; can you figure out why it hasn't exactly taken off in common parlance?

PAPER COVER - Comic book cover made from the same newsprint as the interior pages. These books are extremely rare in high grade.

PARADE OF PLEASURE - A book about the censorship of comics.

PB - Abbreviation for Paperback.

PEDIGREE - A book from a famous and usually high grade collection - e.g. Allentown, Lamont Larson, Edgar Church/Mile High, Denver, San Francisco, Cosmic Aeroplane, etc. Beware of non-pedigree collections being promoted as pedigree books; only outstanding high grade collections similar to those listed qualify.

PENCILER - Artist that does the pencils...you're figuring out some of these definitions without us by now, aren't you?

PERFECT BINDING - Pages are glued to the cover as opposed to being stapled to the cover, resulting in a flat binded side. Also known as **Square Back or Square Bound**.

PG - Abbreviation for Page.

PHOTO COVER - Comic book cover featuring a photographic image instead of a line drawing or painting.

PIECE REPLACEMENT - A process by which pieces are added to replace areas of missing paper.

PIONEER AGE - Comics published from the 1500s to 1828.

PLATINUM AGE - Comics published from 1883 to 1938.

POLYPROPALENE - A type of plastic used in the manufacture of comic book bags; now considered harmful to paper and not recommended for long term storage of comics.

POP - Abbreviation for the anti-comic book volume, *Parade of Pleasure*.

POST-CODE - Describes comics published after February 1955 and usually displaying the CCA stamp in the upper right-hand corner.

POUGHKEEPSIE - Refers to a large collection of Dell Comics file copies believed to have originated from the warehouse of Western Publishing in Poughkeepsie, NY.

PP - Abbreviation for Pages.

PRE-CODE - Describes comics published before the **Comics Code Authority** seal began appearing on covers in 1955.

PRE-HERO DC - A term used to describe *More Fun* #1-51 (pre-Spectre), *Adventure* #1-39 (pre-

Sandman), and *Detective* #1-26 (pre-Batman). The term is actually inaccurate because technically there were "heroes" in the above books.

PRE-HERO MARVEL - A term used to describe *Strange Tales* #1-100 (pre-Human Torch), *Journey Into Mystery* #1-82 (pre-Thor), *Tales To Astonish* #1-35 (pre-Ant Man), and *Tales Of Suspense* #1-38 (pre-Iron Man).

PRESERVATION - Another term for **Conservation**.

PRESSING - A term used to describe a variety of processes or procedures, professional and amateur, under which an issue is pressed to eliminate wrinkles, bends, dimples and/or other perceived defects and thus improve its appearance. Some types of pressing involve disassembling the book and performing other work on it prior to its pressing and reassembly. Some methods are generally easily discerned by professionals and amateurs. Other types of pressing, however, can pose difficulty for even experienced professionals to detect. In all cases, readers are cautioned that unintended damage can occur in some instances. Related defects will diminish an issue's grade correspondingly rather than improve it.

PROVENANCE - When the owner of a book is known and is stated for the purpose of authenticating and documenting the history of the book. Example: A book from the Stan Lee or Forrest Ackerman collection would be an example of a value-adding provenance.

PULP - Cheaply produced magazine made from low grade newsprint. The term comes from the wood pulp that was used in the paper manufacturing process.

QUARTERLY - Published every three months (four times a year).

R - Abbreviation for Reprint.

RARE - 10-20 copies estimated to exist.

RAT CHEW - Damage caused by the gnawing of rats and mice.

RBCC - Abbreviation for Rockets Blast Comic Collector, one of the first and most prominent adzines instrumental in developing the early comic book market.

READING COPY - A comic that is in FAIR to GOOD condition and is often used for research; the condition has been sufficiently reduced to the point where general handling will not degrade it further.

READING CREASE - Book-length, vertical front cover crease at staples, caused by bending the cover over the staples. Square-bounds receive these creases just by opening the cover too far to the left.

REILLY, TOM - A large high grade collection of 1939-1945 comics with 5000+ books.

REINFORCEMENT - A process by which a weak or split page or cover is reinforced with adhesive and reinforcement paper.

REPRINT COMICS - In earlier decades, comic books that contained newspaper strip reprints; modern reprint comics usually contain stories originally featured in older comic books.

RESTORATION - Any attempt, whether professional or amateur, to enhance the appearance of an aging or damaged comic book using additive procedures. These procedures may include any or all of the following techniques: recoloring, adding missing paper, trimming, re-glossing, reinforcement, glue, etc. Amateur work can lower the value of a book, and even professional restoration has now gained a negative aura in the modern marketplace from some quarters. In all cases a restored book can never be worth the same as an unrestored book in the same condition. There is no consensus on the inclusion of pressing, non-aqueous cleaning, tape removal and in some cases staple replacement in this definition. Until such time as there is consensus, we encourage continued debate and interaction among all interested parties and reflection upon the standards in other hobbies and art forms.

REVIVAL - An issue that begins republishing a comic book character after a period of dormancy.

ROCKFORD - A high grade collection of 1940s comics with 2000+ books from Rockford, IL.

ROLLED SPINE - A condition where the left edge of a comic book curves toward the front or back; a defect caused by folding back each page as the comic was read.

ROUND BOUND - Standard saddle stitch binding typical of most comics.

RUN - A group of comics of one title where most or all of the issues are present. See **Complete Run**.

S&K - Abbreviation for the legendary creative team of Joe Simon and Jack Kirby, creators of Marvel Comics' Captain America.

SADDLE STITCH - The staple binding of magazines and comic books.

SAN FRANCISCO COLLECTION - (see **Reilly, Tom**)

SCARCE - 20-100 copies estimated to exist.

SEDUCTION OF THE INNOCENT - An inflammatory book written by Dr. Frederic Wertham and published in 1953; Wertham asserted that comics were responsible for rampant juvenile deliquency in American youth.

SET - (1) A complete run of a given title; (2) A grouping of comics for sale.

SEMI-MONTHLY - Published twice a month, but not necessarily **Bi-Weekly**.

SEWN SPINE - A comic with many spine perforations where binders' thread held it into a bound volume. This is considered a defect.
SF - Abbreviation for Science Fiction (the other commonly used term, "sci-fi," is often considered derogatory or indicative of more "low-brow" rather than "literary" science fiction, i.e. "sci-fi television."
SILVER AGE - Comics published from 1956 to 1970.
SILVER PROOF - A black and white actual size print on thick glossy paper hand-painted by an artist to indicate colors to the engraver.
SLAB - Colloquial term for the plastic enclosure used by grading certification companies to seal in certified comics.
SLABBING - Colloquial term for the process of encapsulating certified comics in a plastic enclosure.
SOTI - Abbreviation for **Seduction of the Innocent**.
SPINE - The left-hand edge of the comic that has been folded and stapled.
SPINE ROLL - A condition where the left edge of the comic book curves toward the front or back, caused by folding back each page as the comic was read.
SPINE SPLIT SEALED - A process by which a spine split is sealed using an adhesive.
SPLASH PAGE - A **Splash Panel** that takes up the entire page.
SPLASH PANEL - (1) The first panel of a comic book story, usually larger than other panels and usually containing the title and credits of the story; (2) An oversized interior panel.
SQUARE BACK or SQUARE BOUND - See **Perfect Binding**.
STORE STAMP - Store name (and sometimes address and telephone number) stamped in ink via rubber stamp and stamp pad.
SUBSCRIPTION COPY - A comic sent through the mail directly from the publisher or publisher's agent. Most are folded in half, causing a subscription crease or fold running down the center of the comic from top to bottom; this is considered a defect.
SUBSCRIPTION CREASE - See **Subscription Copy**.
SUBSCRIPTION FOLD - See **Subscription Copy**. Differs from a **Subscription Crease** in that no ink is missing as a result of the fold.
SUN SHADOW - Darker, usually linear area at the edge of some comics stored in stacks. Some portion of the cover was not covered by the comic immediately above it, and it suffered prolonged exposure to light. A serious defect, unlike a **Dust Shadow**, which can sometimes be removed. Also see **Oxidation Shadow**.
SUPER-HERO - A costumed crime fighter with powers beyond those of mortal man.
SUPER-VILLAIN - A costumed criminal with powers beyond those of mortal man; the antithesis of **Super-Hero**.
SWIPE - A panel, sequence, or story obviously borrowed from previously published material.
TEAR SEALS - A process by which a tear is sealed using an adhesive.
TEXT ILLO. - A drawing or small panel in a text story that almost never has a dialogue balloon.
TEXT PAGE - A page with no panels or drawings.
TEXT STORY - A story with few if any illustrations commonly used as filler material during the first three decades of comics.
3-D COMIC - Comic art that is drawn and printed in two color layers, producing a 3-D effect when viewed through special glasses.
3-D EFFECT COMIC - Comic art that is drawn to appear as if in 3-D but isn't.
TITLE - The name of the comic book.
TITLE PAGE - First page of a story showing the title of the story and possibly the creative credits and indicia.
TRIMMED - (1) A bindery process which separates top, right, and bottom of pages and cuts comic books to the proper size; (2) A repair process in which defects along the edges of a comic book are removed with the use of scissors, razor blades, and/or paper cutters. Comic books which have been repaired in this fashion are considered defectives.
TTA - Abbreviation for *Tales to Astonish*.
UK - Abbreviation for British edition (United Kingdom).
UNDER GUIDE - When a comic book is priced at a value less than *Guide* list.
UPGRADE - To obtain another copy of the same comic book in a higher grade.
VARIANT COVER - A different cover image used on the same issue.
VERY RARE - 1 to 10 copies estimated to exist.
VICTORIAN AGE - Comics published from 1828 to 1883.
WANT LIST - A listing of comics needed by a collector, or a list of comics that a collector is interested in purchasing.
WAREHOUSE COPY - Originating from a publisher's warehouse; similar to file copy.
WHITE MOUNTAIN COLLECTION - A collection of high grade 1950s and 1960s comics which originated in New England.
X-OVER - Short for **Crossover**.
ZINE - Short for **Fanzine**.

FEATURE ARTICLE INDEX

Over the years, *The Overstreet Comic Book Price Guide* has grown into much more than a simple catalog of values. Almost since the very beginning, Bob has worked hard to make sure that the book reflects the latest information about the hobby, and this has resulted in some fascinating in-depth articles about aspects of the industry and the rich history of comics. Sadly, many of you may never have read a lot of these articles, or even knew they existed.

These two pages contain a comprehensive index to every feature article ever published in *The Overstreet Comic Book Price Guide*. From interviews with legendary creators to exhaustively researched retrospectives, it's all here. Enjoy this look back at the Overstreet legacy, and remember, many of these editions are still available through Gemstone and your local comic book dealer.

Note: The first three editions of *The Guide* had no feature articles, but from #4 on, a tradition was born that has carried through to the very volume. This index begins with the 4th edition and lists all articles published up to and including last year's 40th edition of *The Guide*.

AUTHOR (S)	TITLE	EDITION	PGS.
Borock, Steve (cont.)	A CGC Primer: How Professional Comic Book Certification Works	#38 (2008)	1052-1055
Braden, Scott	Strange Adventures - A Conversation with Murphy Anderson	#27 (1997)	A-30-32
	Built to Last (with J.C. Vaughn)	#28 (1998)	89-102
Calhoun, Pat S.	Living on Borrowed Time! A Nostalgic Look at the Early Years of DC's Challengers of the Unknown (with Gary M. Carter)	#24 (1994)	A-157-164
	100 Years - A Century of Comics	#25 (1995)	A-107-123
Carter, Gary M.	DC Before Superman (written with Ken Lane Carter)	#13 (1983)	A-72-86
	The Silver Age...The Beginning: A Comparative Chronology of the First Sliver Age Comic Books	#20 (1990)	A-94-107
	Journey into the Unknown World of Atlas Fantasy (written with Pat S. Calhoun)	#22 (1992)	A-87-103
	Silver Sagas of the Scarlet Speedster: Whirlwind Adventures of the Fastest Man Alive! 1956-1960	#23 (1993)	A-80-86
CGC Grading Team	A CGC Primer: How Professional Comic Book Certification Works	#39 (2009)	1029-1032
	CGC Turns 10: A Decade of Comic Book Certification Innovation	#40 (2010)	1007-1009
Chesney, Landon	The Archives of the Comic Book Price Guide	#06 (1976)	44-45
Colabuono, Gary	Golden Age Ashcans - Comics' First Editions (with Mark Zaid)	#38 (2008)	1040-1045
DeFuccio, Jerry	An Interview with Will Eisner, Creator of the Spirit	#06 (1976)	31-37
	Norman Mingo and Alfred: The World's Greatest Facelift	#12 (1982)	A-45-57
	Charles Clarence Beck: The World's Second Mightiest Mortal	#15 (1985)	A-78-88
Dempsey, "Little" Jimmy	Great Old Radio Premiums	#13 (1983)	A-62-63
DeStefano, Brandon	Comics at the Movies: A Brief History of Comic Characters on the Big Screen	#39 (2009)	1033-1039
Disbrow, Jay	Confessions of a Former Comic Book Artist	#08 (1978)	A-31-38
Estrada, Jackie	Friends of Lulu Sound Off on Comics	#28 (1998)	79-81
Fulop, Scott D.	Archie Comics Publications: The Mirth of a Legend	#21 (1991)	A-77-78
Hamilton, Bruce	The Mystery of the 12 Missing EC's	#25 (1995)	A-99-106
	Special Feature: Grading - The Next Revolution for Comic Books	#29 (1999)	17-21
Hancer, Kevin B.	Edgar Rice Burroughs and the Comics	#05 (1975)	33-38
Hessee, Tim	The Pop Hollinger Story: The First Comic Book Collector/Dealer	#12 (1982)	A-58-66
Huesman, Mark	Legiondary Adventures	#29 (1999)	101-106
Hughes, Rob	When the Bat Flew Alone!	#39 (2009)	1041-1054
Irons, Christopher	The Man Behind the Cover - L. B. Cole	#18 (1988)	A-77
Kronenberg, Michael	Indelible Shadows: The Spectacular Rise of Artist Jim Lee	#36 (2006)	1052-1055
	Patriot Act!!! (Captain America profile)	#37 (2007)	1024-1029
Leavitt, Craig	Katy Keene - The Overstreet Connection	#14 (1984)	A-67-78
Lee, Stan	Twenty-Five Years? I Don't Believe It!	#16 (1986)	A-82-84
Marek, Carl, et al.	Good Girl Art - An Introduction: Why it Was and What it Was (produced by the American Comic Book Co.)	#06 (1976)	38-43
	Esoteric Comics: The Ultimate Collection (produced by the American Comic Book Co. in Consultation with Scott Shaw)	#07 (1977)	A-30-35
	Women in Comics (in collaboration with Art Amsie)	#08 (1978)	A-54-75
	For Those Who Know How to Look	#09 (1979)	A-35-42
McClure, Jon Martin	A History of Publisher Experimentation and Variant Comic Books	#40 (2010)	1010-1038
Miller, John Jackson	From "A Long Time Ago" To Today's Galaxy	#38 (2008)	1046-1051
Moore, Dale	Comic Book Charites: Lifelines of the Industry	#34 (2004)	964-966
Murray, Will	Marvel's Hammer: The Mighty Thor	#36 (2006)	1028-1039
	The Untold Origin of Daredevil	#37 (2007)	1030-1035
Novinskie, Charles S.	Sixty Years of Wonder Woman	#31 (2001)	26-29
	Conan #1: When Marvel Went Barbarian	#40 (2010)	1042-1043
	1970: Television, Animation, & Adaptations	#40 (2010)	1044-1045

AUTHOR (S)	TITLE	EDITION	PGS.
Olson, Richard D. Ph.D.	The American Comic Book: 1897-1932	#26 (1996)	1-2
	The American Comic Book: 1933-Present The Modern Comic Book	#26 (1996)	10-11
	The Golden Age and Beyond: The Modern Comic Book (Revised)	#27 (1997)	23-24
	The Golden Age and Beyond: The Modern Comic Book (Revised)	#28 (1998)	211-211
	My Friend, Leonard Brown	#40 (2010)	1050-1051
Olshevsky, George	The Origin of Marvel Comics	#10 (1980)	A-46-73
Overstreet, Robert M.	Bob's Bizarre Tales	#30 (2000)	42-63
	And When The Vault Was Opened... (with Gary M. Carter)	#38 (2008)	1036-1039
Overstreet Staff	The Man Behind the Cover - Ron Dias	#17 (1987)	A-84
Rausch, Barbara A.	Katy WHO?...Never Heard of it...	#14 (1984)	A-52-56
Ray, Benn	A Brief History of Super-Teams: Top Ten Greatest Super-Teams	#29 (1999)	108-112
Robbins, Trina	Tarpe Mills - An Appreication	#08 (1978)	A-76
Saffel, Steve	Spider-Man: An Amazing Success Story	#22 (1992)	A-77-86
Schiff, Jack	Reminiscience of a Comic Book Editor (with Gene Reed)	#13 (1983)	A-64-70
Seals, John	Standing on the Shoulders of Giants: The HERO Initiative	#39 (2009)	1025-1027
Shooter, Jim	Marvel and Me	#16 (1986)	A-85-96
Taylor, Terry	Walt Disney's Snow White and the Seven Dwarfs - Fifty Years of Collectibles	#17 (1987)	A-101-111
Thomas, Harry B.	1941: Comic Books Go To War: Those fabulous comics of World War II (with Gary M. Carter)	#21 (1991)	A-79-98
Townsend, John Ph.D.	Three Uncanny Decades of X-Men	#24 (1994)	A-146-156
Vaughn, J.C.	Built to Last (with Scott Braden)	#28 (1998)	89-102
	The American Comic Book: 1897 - 1932 In the Beginning: The Platinum Age	#28 (1998)	201-203
	Avenues of Collecting: A Walk Through the Comic Book Neighborhood	#29 (1999)	91-94
	Just Another Justice League?	#29 (1999)	95-100
	EC, MAD and Beyond: Al Feldstein	#30 (2000)	24-28
	Flights to EC and Beyond with Al Williamson	#30 (2000)	36-39
	Extraordinary! (John K. Snyder III profile)	#31 (2001)	42-44
	Bendis! (Brian Michael Bendis profile)	#31 (2001)	46-48
	Archie at 60	#32 (2002)	47-49
	A Brief History of the Justice Society	#33 (2003)	850-852
	Variant Watch: Ultimate Spider-Man #1	#33 (2003)	862-863
	Comic Book Ages: Start the Discussion (with Arnold T. Blumberg)	#33 (2003)	866-867
	Comic Book Ages: Defining Eras (with Arnold T. Blumberg)	#34 (2004)	948-951
	70 Years and Still Quacking	#34 (2004)	952-955
	(Joe) Simon Says	#34 (2004)	960-963
	Enduring Duo: Wolfman & Perez (Teen Titans at 25, Crisis at 20)	#35 (2005)	993-995
	Little Lulu at 70 (and 60)	#35 (2005)	996-997
	Iron Man: Heavy Metal	#35 (2005)	998-1000
	Publisher Spotlight: Dark Horse Comics	#35 (2005)	1012-1013
	Wonder Woman: Revisited and Renewed	#36 (2006)	1041-1043
	The Semi-Secret Origins of The Overstreet Comic Book Price Guide (Bob Overstreet interview)	#37 (2007)	1016-1023
	Perspective on History: Stephen Fishler	#40 (2010)	1052-1053
Ward, Bill	The Man Behind Torchy	#08 (1978)	A-40-53
Weist, Jerry	The Golden Age and Beyond: A Short History of Comic Book Fandom & Comic Book Collecting in America	#26 (1996)	652-667
Zaid, Mark	Golden Age Ashcans - Comics' First Editions (with Gary Colabuono)	#38 (2008)	1040-1045
Zone, Ray	Anaglyphs - A Survey of 3-D Comic Books	#11 (1981)	A-44-53

THE CGC STORY

How the Company Was Created and Our Grading Process

By the CGC Grading Team

CGC-certified comics are pictured throughout the *Guide*, at cons, and offered in all types of auctions. Expert third-party certification provides buyers confidence that a comic is accurately represented, and sellers know they are getting fair value for their comics. Certification has proven to be a popular practice: CGC has graded over 1,000,000 comics! Most collectors that see value in certification have no idea how their books come to be graded. They may not know and perhaps wonder where the grading scale came from or what happens to their books once they enter the world of CGC. Read on for a firsthand look at the process of professional comic book certification at CGC.

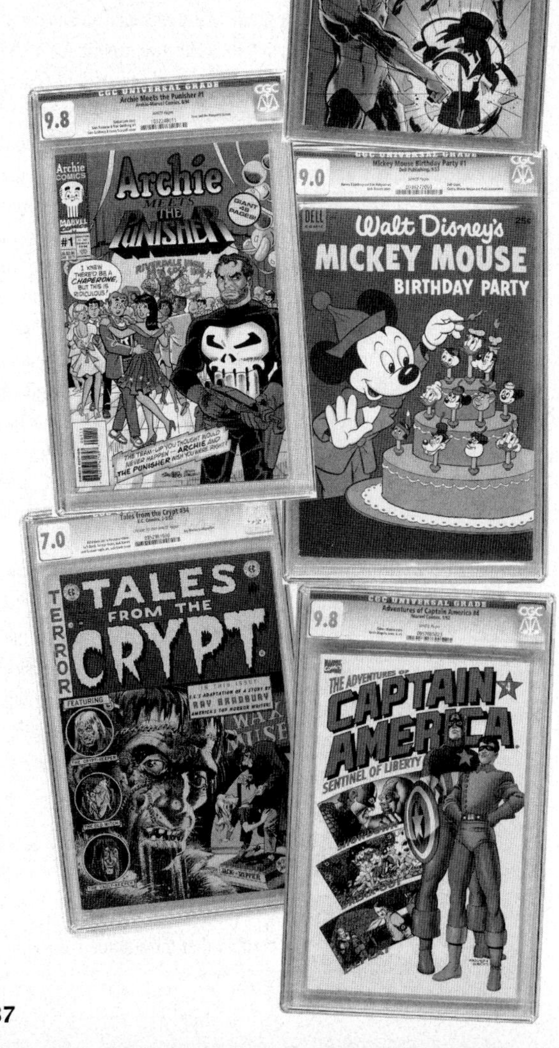

Bringing the Company Together

In January of 2000 CGC was launched under the umbrella of the Certified Collectibles Group, which also includes Numismatic Guaranty Corporation (NGC), the largest third-party coin grading company in the world, Numismatic Conservation Services (NCS), the leading authority in numismatic conservation and Paper Money Guaranty (PMG), the world's leading currency certification company. The Collectibles Group sought out talented and ethical individuals to grade comic books. Experts needed a history of necessary skills to verify a comic book's authenticity and to detect restoration that can affect its value. To identify these individuals, many of the most respected individuals in the hobby were consulted, and, based on their recommendations a core grading team was selected.

The members of the CGC grading team come from diverse backgrounds, and many were comic book dealers at some time in their careers. Experience in the commercial sector can be an essential ingredient in becoming familiar with market standards. Upon joining CGC, all graders immediately cease all commercial trading. All CGC employees are prohibited from commercially buying and selling comic books to ensure they remain completely impartial, having no vested interest other than a dedication to serving clients through accurate and consistent grading.

When it was time to develop a uniform grading standard, the hobby's leaders were once again called upon. Everyone seemed to agree that *The Overstreet Comic Book Price Guide* was the foundation of this standard, but there were a number of subjective interpretations of its published definitions. It was critical to understand how these guidelines were being applied to the everyday buying and selling of comics. To accomplish this, approximately 50 of the hobby's top experts took part in an extensive grading test. Their grades were averaged and an accurate grading standard reflecting the collective experience of the hobby's most prominent figures was thus developed. CGC now had the best standard and the best team to apply it.

With the graders in place and the grading scale established, the next step was to develop a tamper-evident holder for the long-term storage and display of certified comics. This proved to be a technical challenge. Exhaustive material tests were conducted to determine that the holders were archival safe. To create a true first line of defense, it was determined that the comic book should be sealed in a soft inner well, then sealed again inside a tamper evident hard plastic case with interlocking ridges to enable compact storage. The CGC certified grade appears on a label sealed inside the holder for an additional level of security.

The Grading Journey

Step 1 – Submitting your Books

There are two ways comic books can be submitted for certification - they may be submitted by authorized dealers or by Collectors Society members. The Collectors Society is an online community with direct access to certification service from CGC, and submissions can be prepared online. Both dealers and Collectors Society members typically send their comics to CGC's offices by registered mail or through an insured express company. Submissions are also accepted at many of the Comic Cons that occur around the country.

Step 2 – Comic Book Reception

Every day, CGC's Receiving Department opens newly arrived packages and immediately verifies that the number of books in each package matches the number shown on the submitted invoice. Once this is done, a more detailed comparison is made to ensure that their invoice descriptions correspond to the actual comics. This information is entered into a computer, and from this time forth, the comics will be traceable at all stages of the grading process by their invoice number and their line number within that invoice. Each book is checked to see that it is properly prepared for grading in an appropriately sized comic bag with backing board and then is labeled with a numbered barcode containing the pertinent data of invoice number and line item information for quick reading by the computer. Before any grading is performed, each book is examined by a CGC Restoration Detection Expert. If any form of restoration work is detected, this information is entered into the computer, making it available to the grading team.

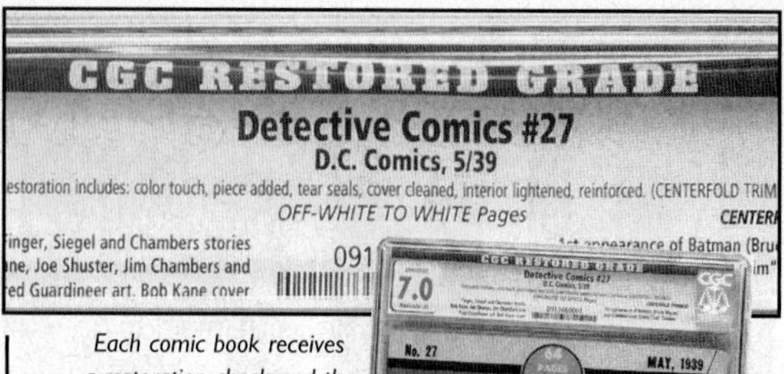

Each comic book receives a restoration check and the results appear on the label.

Step 3 – the Grading Begins

After being examined by a Restoration Detection Expert, a book then passes to a pre-grader. At this stage the comics are properly sleeved and barcoded for grading and have been separated from their original invoice. This step is taken to ensure that graders do not know whose books they are grading, as a further guarantee of impartiality. The pre-grader begins the grading process by counting the book's pages and entering into the computer any peculiarities or flaws that may affect a book's grade. Some examples of this would be "a tear on third page," "a corner crease – does not break color," "a ¼" inch spine split," and so forth. He then enters this information, if not readily noticeable, into the "Graders Notes" field and assigns his grading opinion.

When the next grader examines the comic, he is not able to see the first person's assigned grade, so as to not influence his own evaluation. After determining his own grade for the comic, he can then view the Graders Notes entered by the previous grader, and he may add to this commentary if he believes more remarks are in order. This same process is repeated as the comic passes to the Grading Finalizer. He makes a final restoration check before determining his own grade, at which time he then reviews the grades and notes entered by the previous graders. If all grades are in agreement or are very close, he will then assign the book's final grade. It then is forwarded to the Encapsulation Department for sealing. If there is disagreement among the graders, a discussion will ensue until a final determination is made and the book forwarded.

Step 4 – Encapsulating the Comics

After each comic has been graded and the necessary numbers and text entered into their respective data fields, all the comics on a particular invoice are taken from the Grading Department into the Encapsulation Department. Here, appropriately color-coded labels are printed bearing the proper descriptive text, including each book's grade and identification number. This is critical, as it serves to make each certified comic unique and is also a significant deterrent to counterfeiting CGC's valued product. All of the above information is duplicated in a barcode, which appears underneath the written text on the comic's label.

The newly-printed labels are stacked in the same sequence as the comics to be encapsulated with them, ensuring that each book and its label match one another. The comic is now ready to be fitted inside an archival-quality interior well, which is then sealed within a transparent capsule, along with the book's color-coded label. This is accomplished through a combination of compression and ultrasonic vibration.

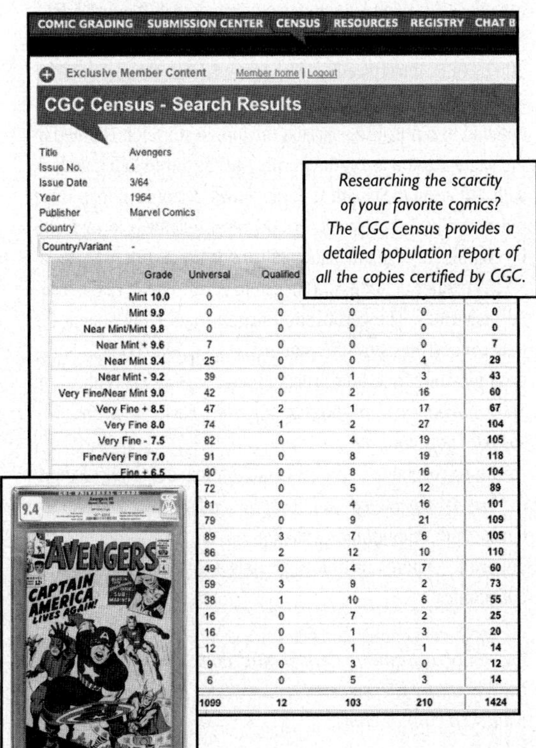

CGC Census - Search Results

Title	Avengers
Issue No.	4
Issue Date	3/64
Year	1964
Publisher	Marvel Comics
Country	
Country/Variant	-

Grade	Universal	Qualified			
Mint 10.0	0	0			
Mint 9.9	0	0	0	0	0
Near Mint/Mint 9.8	0	0	0	0	0
Near Mint + 9.6	7	0	0	0	7
Near Mint 9.4	25	0	0	4	29
Near Mint - 9.2	39	0	1	3	43
Very Fine/Near Mint 9.0	42	0	2	16	60
Very Fine + 8.5	47	2	1	17	67
Very Fine 8.0	74	1	2	27	104
Very Fine - 7.5	82	0	4	19	105
Fine/Very Fine 7.0	91	0	8	19	118
Fine + 6.5	80	0	8	16	104
	72	0	5	12	89
	81	0	4	16	101
	79	0	9	21	109
	89	3	7	6	105
	86	2	12	10	110
	49	0	4	7	60
	59	3	9	2	73
	38	1	10	6	55
	16	0	7	2	25
	16	0	1	3	20
	12	0	1	1	14
	9	0	3	0	12
	6	0	5	3	14
	1099	12	103	210	1424

Researching the scarcity of your favorite comics? The CGC Census provides a detailed population report of all the copies certified by CGC.

Step 5 – The Comics are Shipped

After encapsulation, all comics are returned briefly to the Grading Department for a quality control inspection. Here, they are examined to make certain that their labels are correct for both the grade and its accompanying descriptive information. Quality control also inspects each book for any flaws in its holder, such as scuffs or nicks. While these are quite rare, CGC is careful to make certain that the comics it certifies are not only accurately graded, but attractively presented as well. When all the comics have been inspected, they're delivered to our Shipping Department for packaging. The comics are counted and their labels checked against the original invoice to make certain that no mistakes have occurred. A Shipping Department employee then verifies the method of transport as selected by the submitter on the invoice and prepares the comics for delivery or they are held in CGC's vault for in-person pick-up by the submitter.

No matter whether the US Postal Service or some private carrier is used, the method of packaging is essentially the same. The encapsulated comics are placed vertically inside sturdy cardboard boxes. In 2005, CGC developed a custom shipping box to enable the highest level of stability during shipping. A copy of the submitter's invoice is included before the box is sealed and heavy tape is used to prevent accidental or unauthorized opening of the box while it's in transit.

The barcode of every comic book is scanned before it is placed into its shipping box. The status of the book is changed to "shipped" in our tracking system, and we retain a record of what books were shipped in which box. This is the final crucial step of our detailed internal tracking system.

The CGC Label

Comic books certified by CGC bear color-coded labels that have different meanings. Whenever purchasing a CGC-certified comic, be certain to note not only the book's grade but also its label category. A Universal label is denoted by the color blue and indicates that a book was not found to have any qualifying defects or signs of restoration. There is one exception to this policy: At CGC's discretion, comics having a very minor amount of glue and/or color touch-up may still qualify for a Universal label provided that they were produced approximately 1950 or earlier and that such restoration is noted underneath the assigned grade.

As its name implies, the Restored label, identified by its purple color, is used for books found to have restoration work performed on them. The grade assigned is based on the book's appearance, with the restoration noted. A distinction is made between Amateur and Professional restoration, this judgment being based on the materials used. Since the degree of work performed is also significant with restored books, there are a total of seven possible descriptions under the Restored label. Each description is prefaced with the word

Apparent, followed by Slight, Moderate or Extensive in combination with the final descriptors Amateur or Professional. Examples of Restored labels might read Apparent Moderate Professional or Apparent Slight Amateur, both descriptions then being followed by the book's grade. Finally, comics which have had no restoration other than a trimming of their covers or edges are labeled as simply Apparent, followed by their grade.

The Qualified label is green, and this indicates that one qualifying defect is present on a book. An example of such a qualifying feature would be a missing Marvel Value Stamp that does not affect the story. While such a book technically may grade 1.5, it may appear to grade 9.6. In such instances, assigning a grade of just 1.5 does not fully represent the value of the comic to a collector. Through use of the green Qualified label, a comic buyer is able to make an informed decision as to what he is purchasing in terms of its overall desirability. Because of the complexity involved, green labels are assigned quite seldom and then only when considered absolutely necessary. In addition, comic books that have an unwitnessed signature, and therefore are not eligible for the Signature Series label (see below), get the Qualified label. This is the most common use for the Qualified label. This shows what the grade of the book would have been if the signature was not present.

CGC encapsulation is not limited to standard size comics. Magazines and small promotional comics are included as well.

CGC's Signature Series label is yellow, and this is used when a comic book has been signed or been sketched on by a creator in the presence of a CGC representative, assuring the signature's or sketch's authenticity. Only books that meet CGC's strict criteria for authenticity are eligible for the Signature Series label. In addition to the certified grade, the yellow label includes who signed it and when it was signed. If appropriate, a Signature Series label may state where a book was signed. In 2007, CGC introduced a Signature Series Restored label. Similar to the CGC Signature Series label in color, it is differentiated by a purple bar across the top. Restoration is noted in the same fashion as on the purple CGC Restored label, and, as with the regular Signature Series label, restored books must be signed in the presence of CGC representatives in order to be eligible for signature authentication.

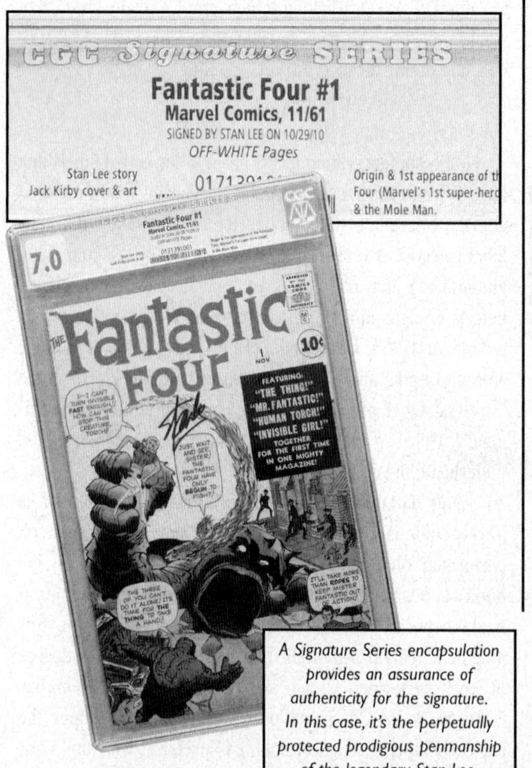

A Signature Series encapsulation provides an assurance of authenticity for the signature. In this case, it's the perpetually protected prodigious penmanship of the legendary Stan Lee.

In October of 2003, CGC began to certify comic book related magazines. The certification process and label system for magazines is exactly the same as for comic books. Some examples of comic book related magazines CGC certifies are *MAD Magazine, Vampirella, Creepy, Eerie* and *Famous Monsters of Filmland*.

More recently CGC introduced grading and encapsulation for *Sports Illustrated* and *Playboy* magazines, Movie Lobby Cards and Photographs making us the first independent, impartial, expert third-party grading service for all types of collectibles.

For more information on comic book certification and CGC's many services, please visit their website at www.CGCcomics.com

GEPPI'S ENTERTAINMENT MUSEUM PRESENTS

The OVERSTREET HALL OF FAME

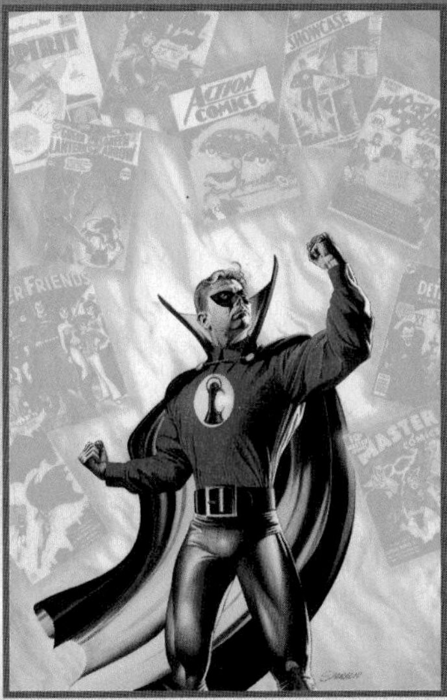

The Overstreet Hall of Fame was conceived to single out individuals who have made great contributions to the comic book arts. This includes writers, artists, editors, publishers and others who have plied their craft in insightful and meaningful ways.

While such evaluations are inherently subjective, they also serve to aid in reflecting upon those who shaped the experience of reading comic books over the years. This year's class of inductees begins on this next page.

THE PREVIOUS INDUCTEES

Class of 2006
Murphy Anderson
Jim Aparo
Jim Lee
Mac Raboy

Class of 2007
Dave Cockrum
Steve Ditko
Bruce Hamilton
Martin Nodell
George Pérez
Jim Shooter
Dave Stevens
Alex Toth
Michael Turner

Class of 2008
Carl Barks
Will Eisner
Al Feldstein
Harvey Kurtzman
Stan Lee
Marshall Rogers
John Romita, Sr.
John Romita, Jr.
Julius Schwartz
Mike Wieringo

Class of 2009
Neal Adams
Matt Baker
Chris Claremont
Palmer Cox
Bill Everett
Frank Frazetta
Neil Gaiman
William M. Gaines
Carmine Infantino
Jack Kirby
Joe Kubert
Paul Levitz
Russ Manning
Todd McFarlane
Don Rosa
John Severin
Joe Simon
Al Williamson

Class of 2010
Sergio Aragonés
M.C. Gaines
Archie Goodwin
Winsor McCay
Mike Mignola
Frank Miller
Robert M. Overstreet
Mike Richardson
Jerry Robinson
Joe Shuster
Jerry Siegel
Jim Steranko
Wally Wood

CREEPY #1
1964. © WARREN

The general public might recognize his style from his covers for *TV Guide* and *Time* or his movie poster and promotional work for such films as *It's a Mad, Mad, Mad, Mad World*, *Viva Max!* and *Kelly's Heroes*, but comic book fans have long known the distinctive art of Jack Davis in a variety of genres. At EC Comics, his horror stories included appearances in *Tales from the Crypt*, *The Haunt of Fear*, *The Vault of Horror*, *Crime SuspenStories*, and *Shock SuspenStories* and later the "Picto-Fiction" series *Terror Illustrated*. His action-adventure work appeared in *Frontline Combat*, *Two-Fisted Tales* and *Piracy*, and his material was also seen in *Incredible Science-Fiction*. As much as he won fans for all of his work (including Westerns for Atlas such as *Rawhide Kid*), though, it was in humor where he defined himself. His work appeared in almost all the early issues of *MAD* (and many later ones, too), all 12 issues of *Panic*, as well as *Trump*, *Humbug*, *Help!* and even *Cracked*.

HOWARD THE DUCK MAGAZINE #3
February 1980. © MAR

INCREDIBLE SCIENCE FICTION #30
July-August 1955. © WMG

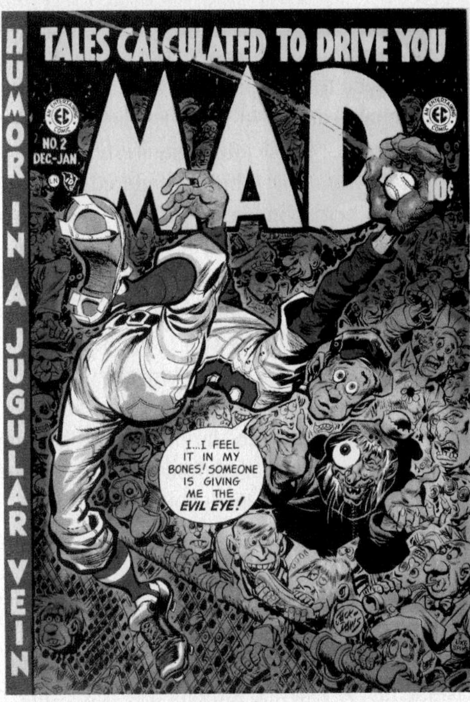

MAD #2
December 1952-January 1953. © WMG

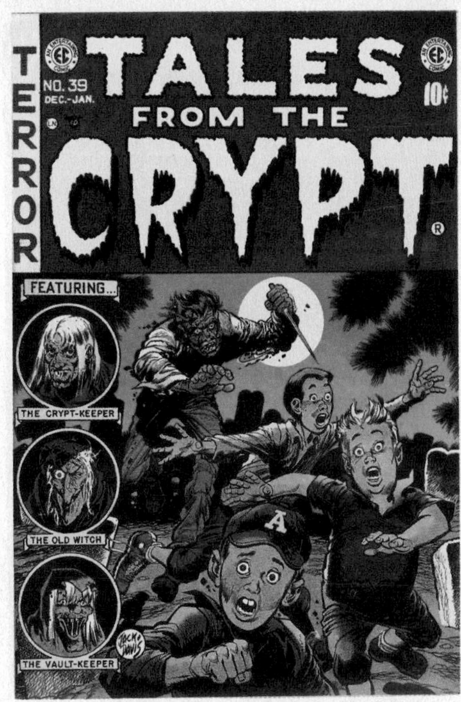

TALES FROM THE CRYPT #39
December 1953-January 1954. © WMG

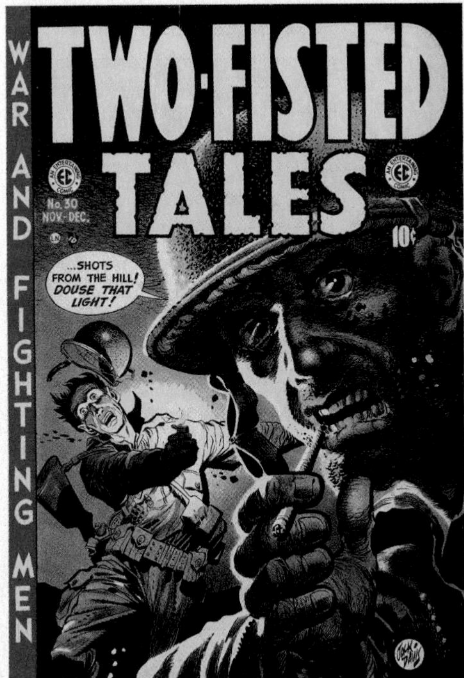

TWO-FISTED TALES #30
November-December 1952. © WMG

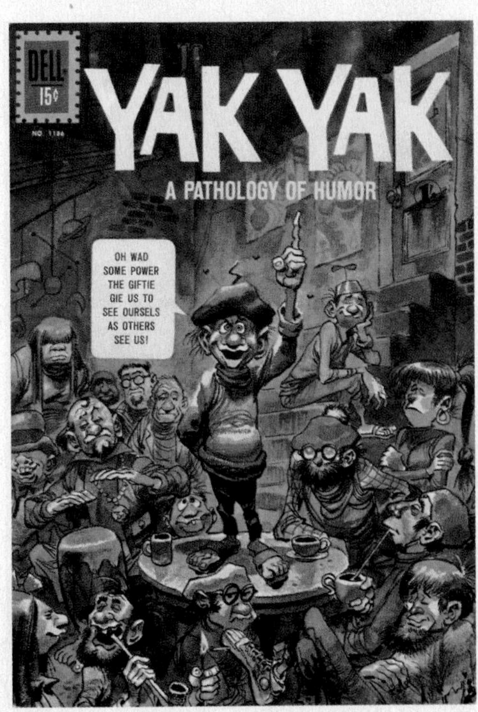

YAK YAK FOUR COLOR #1186
May-July 1961. © DELL

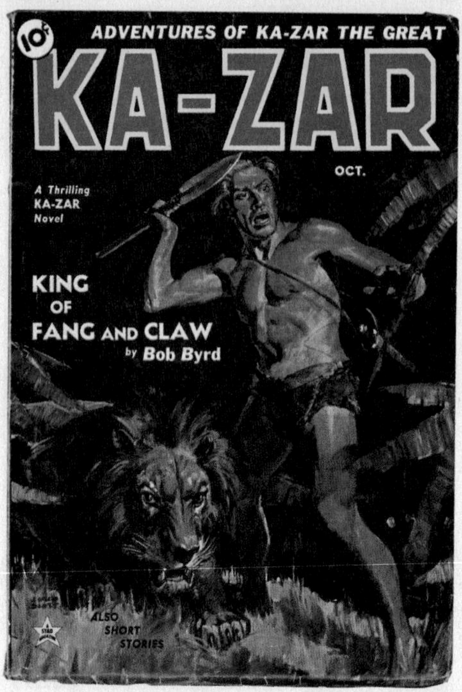

KA-ZAR #1
Pulp magazine. October 1936. © MAR

In 1931 Martin Goodman joined with future MLJ Magazines (Archie) co-founders Louis Silberkleit and Maurice Coyne to start pulp magazine publisher Columbia Publications. In 1932 he started his own business. His first publication was *Western Supernovel Magazine*, which premiered in May 1933, and he began building a variety of publishing companies from there. Under his umbrella came *Mystery Tales*, *Real Sports*, *Star Detective*, *Marvel Science Stories, Ka-Zar* and others.

In 1939, he contracted with Lloyd Jacquet's Funnies, Inc. to provide the content for what became *Marvel Comics* #1, which featured the Human Torch and the Sub-Mariner. With that comic as a hit, he hired his own staff, starting with writer-artist-editor Joe Simon. Timely Comics was born. A few years later, he hired his nephew by marriage, Stan Lee, as editor.

Eventually Timely Comics became Atlas Comics, and Atlas Comics became Marvel Comics. After selling Marvel in the late 1960s, he started a new Atlas line in 1974. While it didn't last at the time, it has recently been revived by his grandson, Jason Goodman.

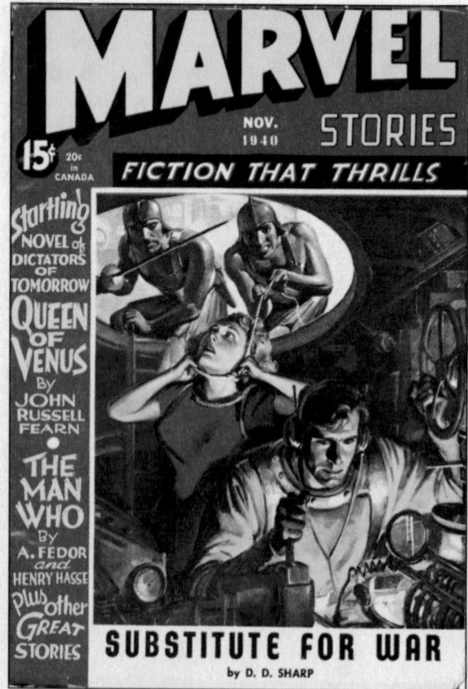

MARVEL STORIES nn
Pulp magazine. November 1940. © MAR

MARVEL TALES nn
Pulp magazine. May 1940. © MAR

MARVEL COMICS #1
November 1939. © MAR

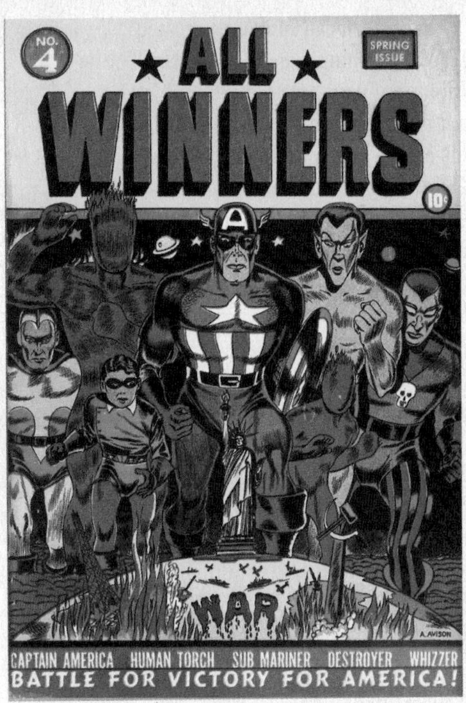

ALL WINNERS COMICS #4
Spring 1942. © MAR

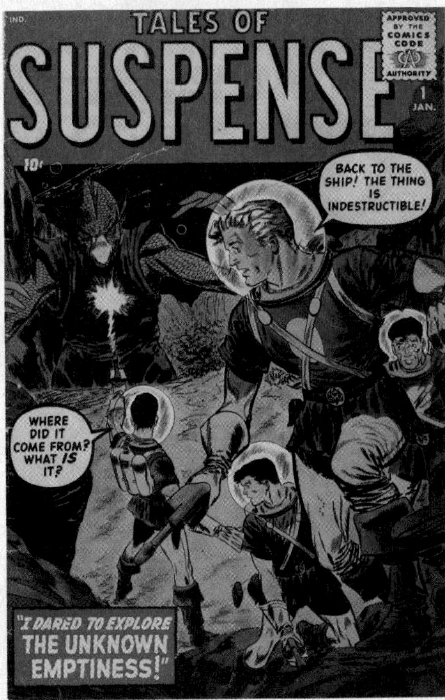

TALES OF SUSPENSE #1
January 1959. © MAR

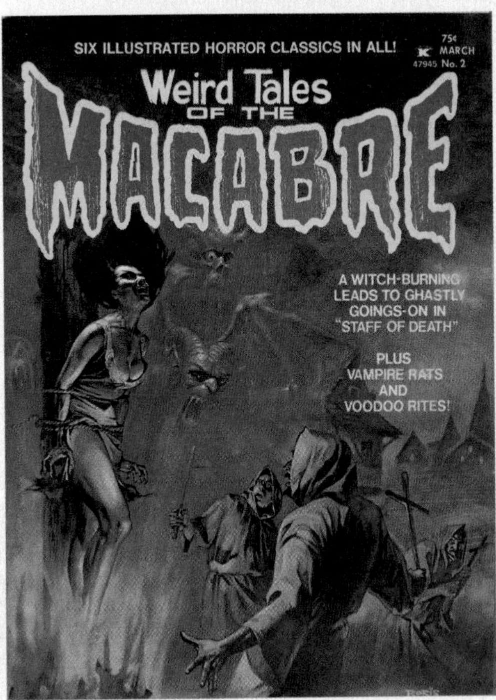

WEIRD TALES OF THE MACABRE #2
March 1975. © Atlas-Seaboard

In 2007, Dean Mullaney created IDW Publishing's archival imprint The Library of American Comics, which he edits and designs. Almost immediately his efforts began to usher in a new Golden Age of classic comic strip reprint collections, significant in both the material itself and the manner in which it is presented. In its first four years, LoAC has been nominated for nine Eisner awards and other accolades, and it has been called "the gold standard for archival comic strip reprints."

Under his guidance, Milton Caniff's *Terry and the Pirates*, Alex Raymond's *Rip Kirby*, Chester Gould's *Dick Tracy*, Harold Gray's *Little Orphan Annie*, Archie Goodwin and Al Williamson's *Secret Agent Corrigan*, Chic Young's *Blondie* and other strips have been showcased for seasoned fans and new readers alike.

In 1978, he launched Eclipse Comics when he published Don McGregor's *Sabre*, the first graphic novel created for the comics specialty market. Eclipse championed creator ownership and the first line of Japanese manga in English translation, and had the first digitally-colored comic book.

BRINGING UP FATHER: FROM SEA TO SHINING SEA
December 2009. © King Features Syndicate

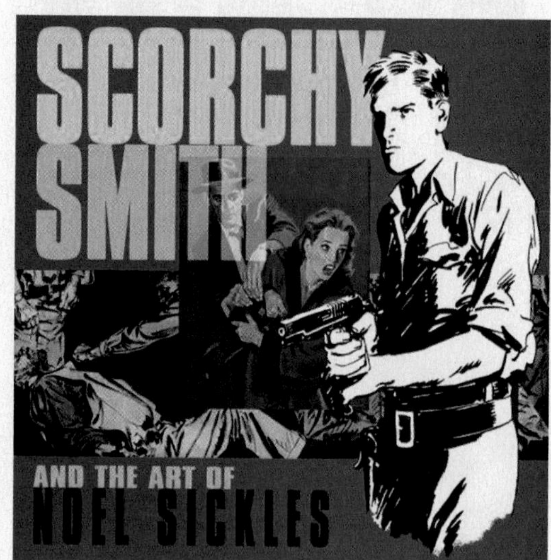

SCORCHY SMITH AND THE ART OF NOEL SICKLES
July 2008. © AP Newsfeatures

THE COMPLETE TERRY AND THE PIRATES VOLUME ONE: 1934-1936
September 2007. © Tribune Media Services

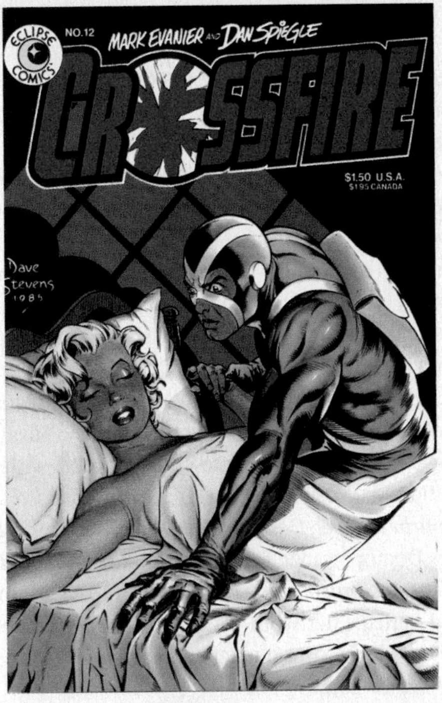

CROSSFIRE #12
June 1985. Dave Stevens cover. © Mark Evanier

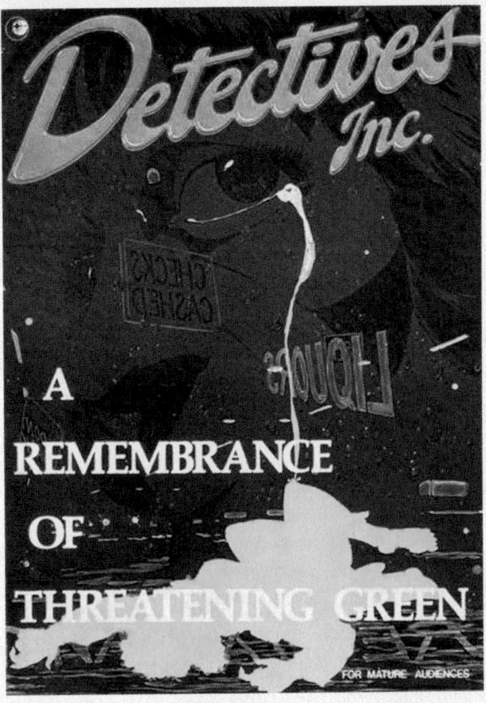

DETECTIVES, INC.
May 1980. © Don McGregor

ECLIPSE GRAPHIC ALBUM SERIES #1
October 1978. The 1st direct sale GN.
© Don McGregor

ECLIPSE MAGAZINE #6
July 1982. © ECL

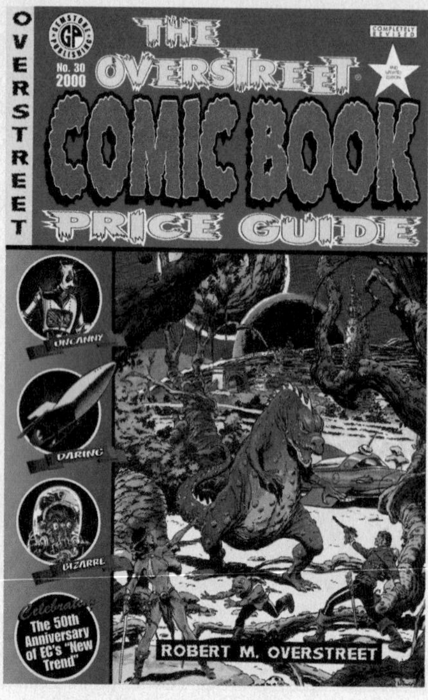

OVERSTREET C.B.P.G #30
2000. Coloring over Al Williamson art. © Gemstone

Beginning with coloring *A Moon, a Girl... Romance* #9 (October 1949), Marie Severin became a highly regarded contributor to EC Comics. There she labored on the company's whole line, including the horror, action-adventure, science fiction and humor titles ranging from *Crime SuspenStories* to *MAD*, often working closely with her brother, artist John Severin, and writer-artist-editor Harvey Kurtzman. While noted as a colorist, she became highly capable in most artistic roles, including penciling, inking and lettering. When EC closed down, she worked at pre-Marvel Atlas before the industry took a downturn and she left. She reentered the business shortly before Atlas became Marvel and was there for the Silver Age growth. While continuing to color and deal with production issues, she illustrated *Captain America*, *Captain Marvel*, *Daredevil*, *Strange Tales* (taking over Doctor Strange from Steve Ditko), *Sub-Mariner*, *Tales to Astonish*, and *X-Men*. Her EC background (and perhaps her work with Kurtzman) influenced her wonderful stint on Marvel's self-parody series *Not Brand Ecch!*

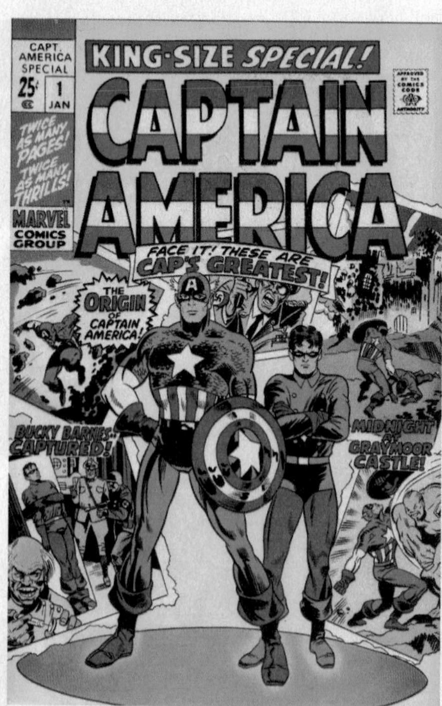

CAPTAIN AMERICA ANNUAL #1
January 1971. © MAR

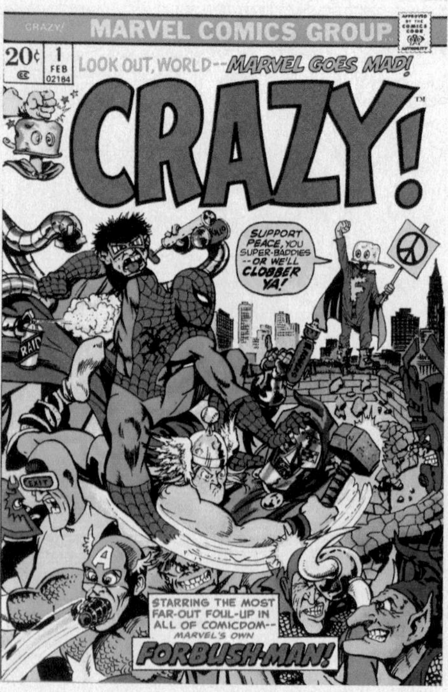

CRAZY #1
February 1973. © MAR

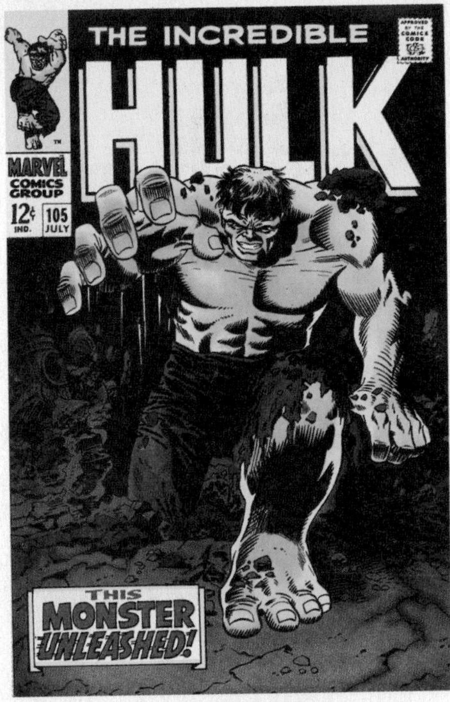

INCREDIBLE HULK #105
July 1968. © MAR

IRON MAN #25
May 1970. © MAR

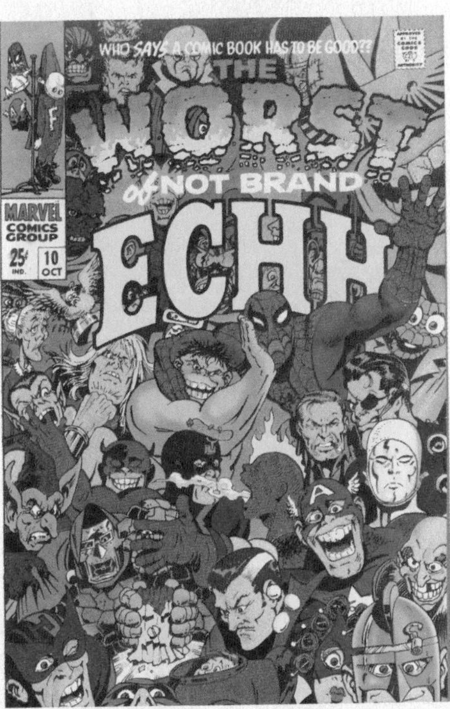

NOT BRAND ECHH #10
October 1968. © MAR

THOR #175
April 1970. © MAR

While attending the Rhode Island School of Design, writer-artist Walt Simonson created *Star Slammers*, a different version of which years later would become *Marvel Graphic Novel* #6 and later a *Star Slammers* series from Malibu's Bravura imprint. Between those two periods he established himself as a creative force, chiefly with the award-winning Manhunter back-up feature in *Detective Comics*, on which he collaborated with writer Archie Goodwin. Following work on DC's *Metal Men* and *Hercules Unbound* and Heavy Metal's *Alien* adaptation (again with Goodwin), he made his way to Marvel. Beginning with *Thor* #337, Simonson wrote and illustrated a definitive run on the title, eventually ending with Thor #382. Over the years, his other Marvel work included *Battlestar Galactica*, *Star Wars*, *Fantastic Four*, *The Avengers*, *X-Factor* (with wife Louise Simonson) and others. At DC, among other work, provided covers for *Jack Kirby's Fourth World*, wrote and illustrated 25 issues of *Orion*, illustrated *Elric: The Making of a Sorcerer*, and wrote the Catwoman and The Demon strip in *Wednesday Comics*.

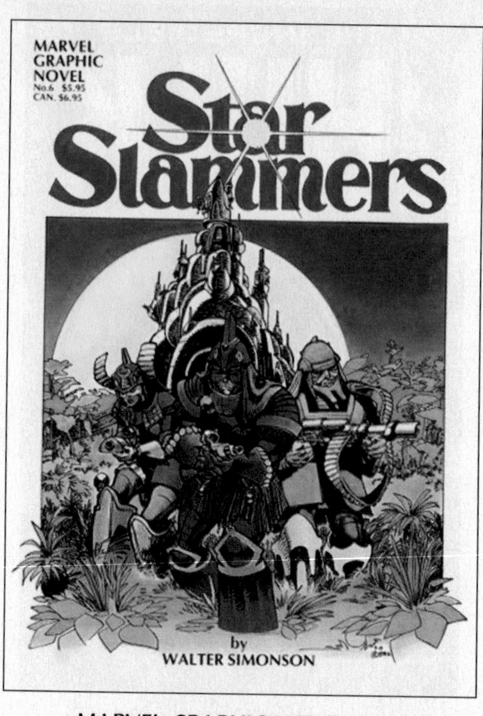

MARVEL GRAPHIC NOVEL #6
1983. © Walt Simonson

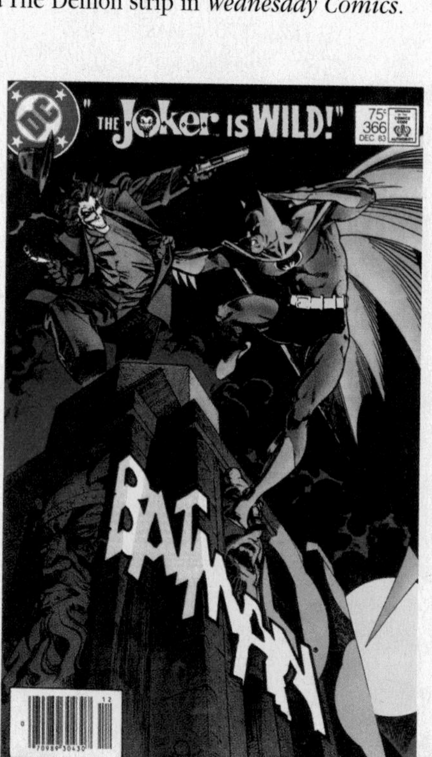

BATMAN #366
December 1983. © DC

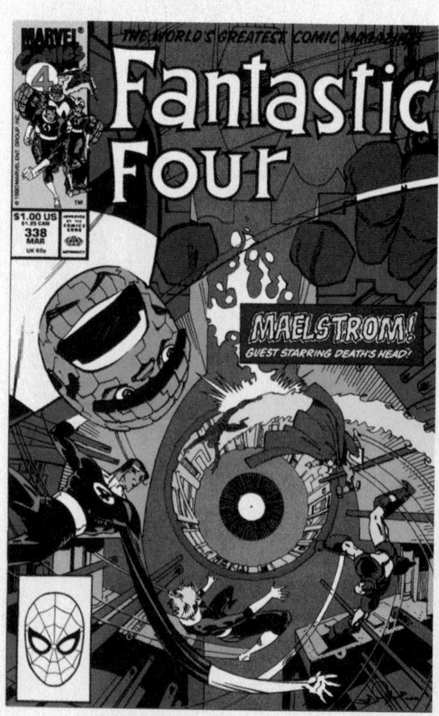

FANTASTIC FOUR #338
March 1990. © MAR

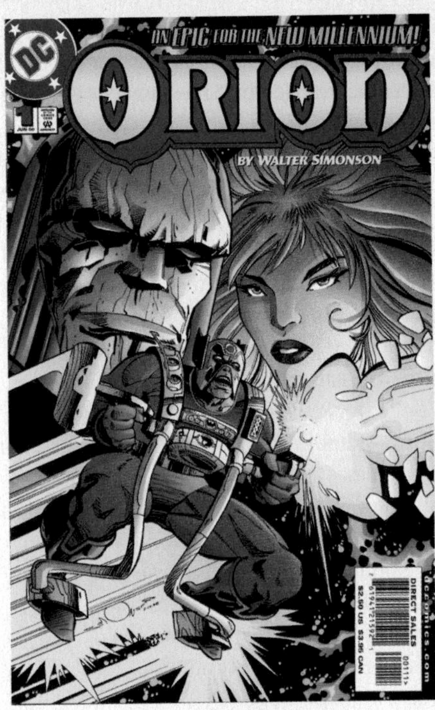

ORION #1
June 2000. © DC

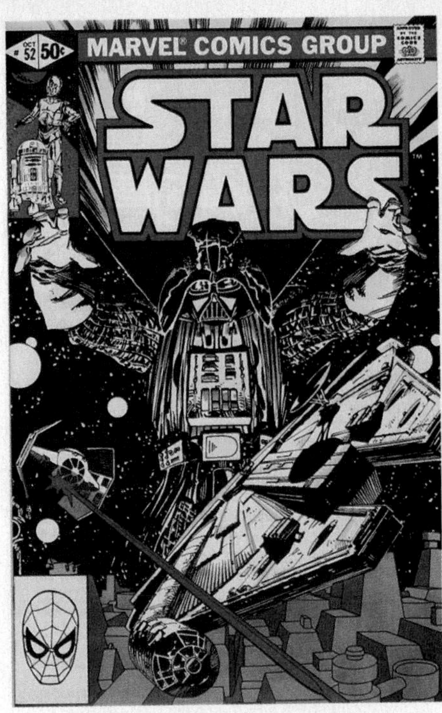

STAR WARS #52
October 1981. © LucasFilm

THOR #337
November 1983. © MAR

X-FACTOR #13
February 1987. © MAR

NEW FUN COMICS #1
February 1935. The start of DC Comics. © DC

Honored in 2008 with a posthumous Eisner Award for his contributions to the comic book industry, Major Malcolm Wheeler-Nicholson might have become the forgotten titan of comic book history, except for the efforts of comics historians. The former soldier, adventurer and inventor was also a successful and prolific author and in the 1920s he made a solid living from writing novels and short stories, often for the pulp magazines. When the Great Depression forced him and his family to move back to New York from Europe, he turned his attention to a new enterprise.

Comic books had, of course, been around in one form or another, for more than 90 years, but they had almost exclusively been collections of reprinted newspaper comic strips and priced for adults. Wheeler-Nicholson not only wrote and commissioned original content, he priced them at 10¢. In 1934, he launched *New Fun Comics*. DC Comics - and with it a new form of the comics business - was born.

NEW FUN COMICS #3
April 1935. © DC

NEW COMICS #1
December 1935. © DC

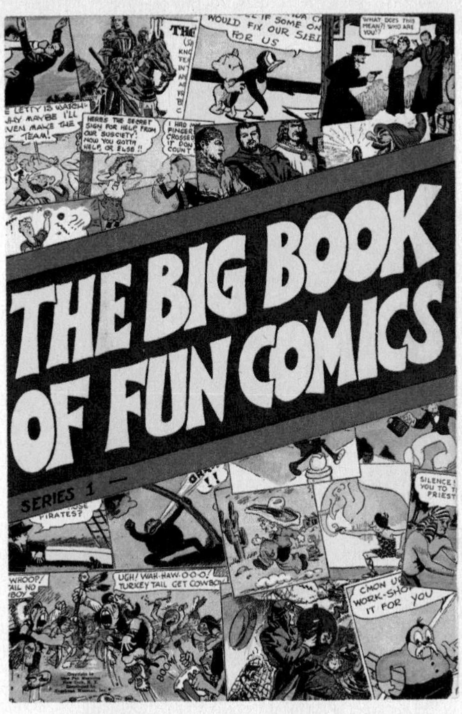

THE BIG BOOK OF FUN COMICS #1
March 1936. © DC

MORE FUN COMICS #12
August 1936. © DC

NEW ADVENTURE COMICS #19
September 1937. © DC

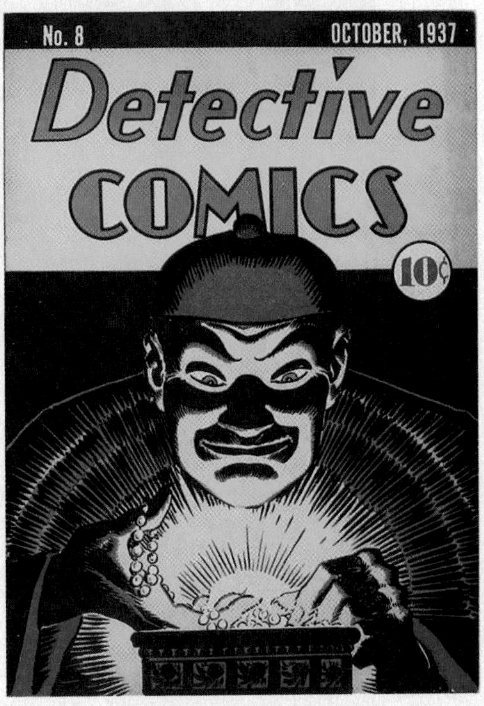

DETECTIVE COMICS #8
October 1937. © DC

RECORD SETTERS

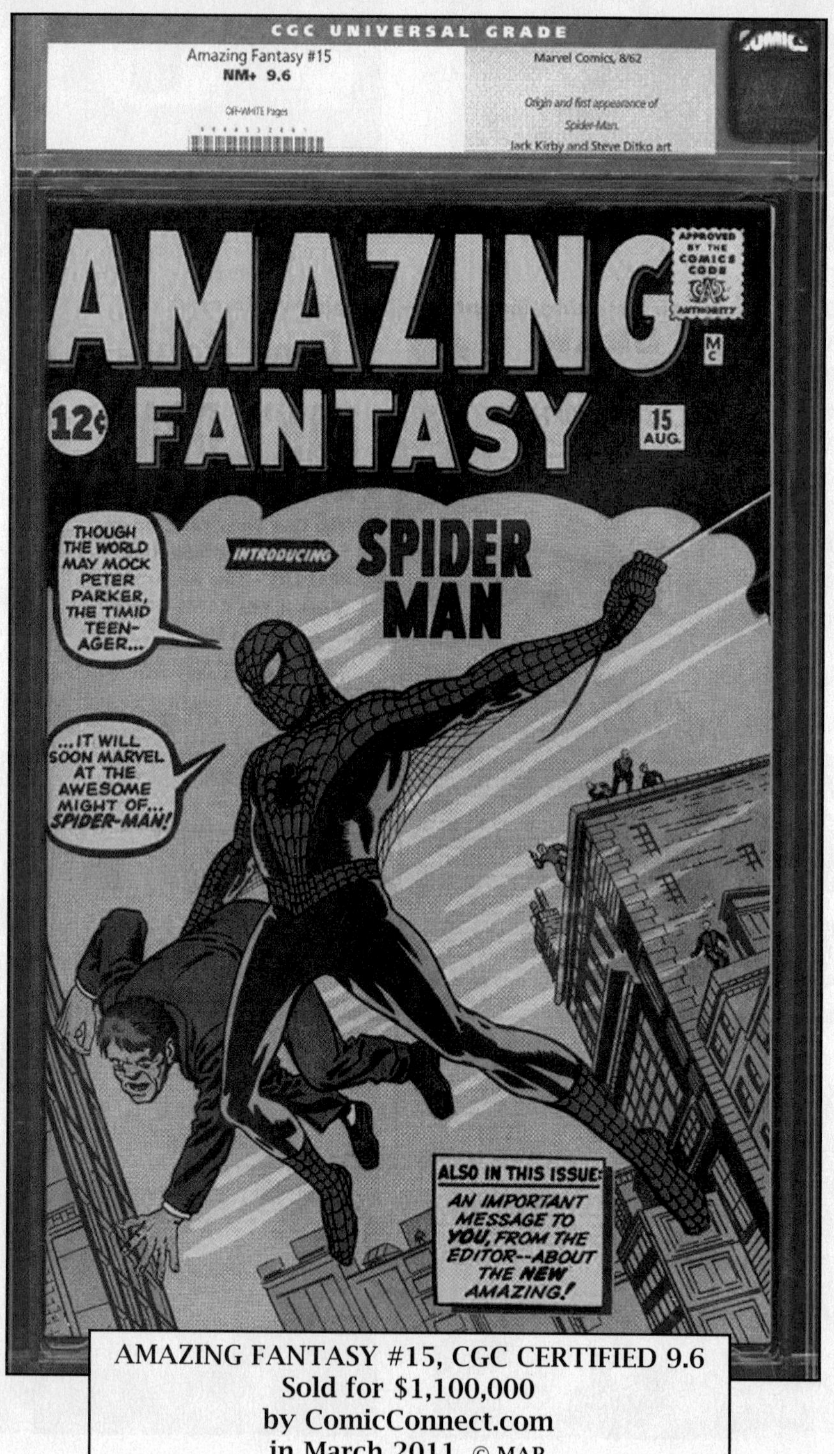

AMAZING FANTASY #15, CGC CERTIFIED 9.6
Sold for $1,100,000
by ComicConnect.com
in March 2011. © MAR

RECORD SETTERS

TALES OF SUSPENSE #39, CGC 9.4
Sold for $147,500
by Pedigree Comics
in March 2011. © MAR

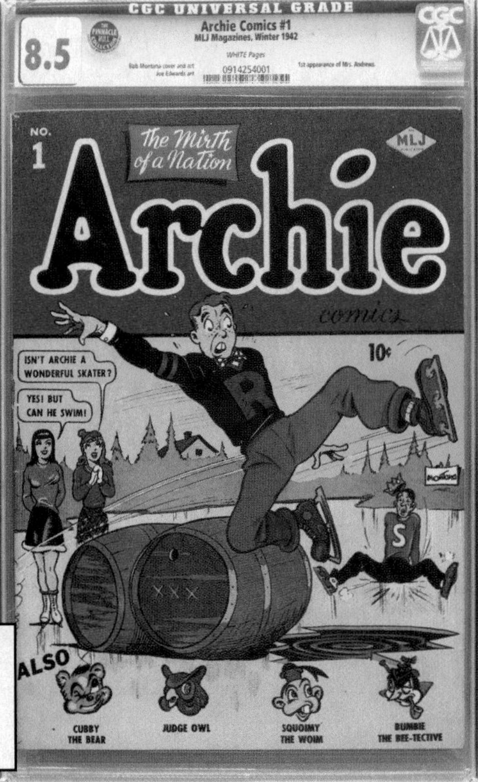

ARCHIE COMICS #1, CGC 8.5
Sold for $167,300
by Heritage Auctions
in February 2011. © AP

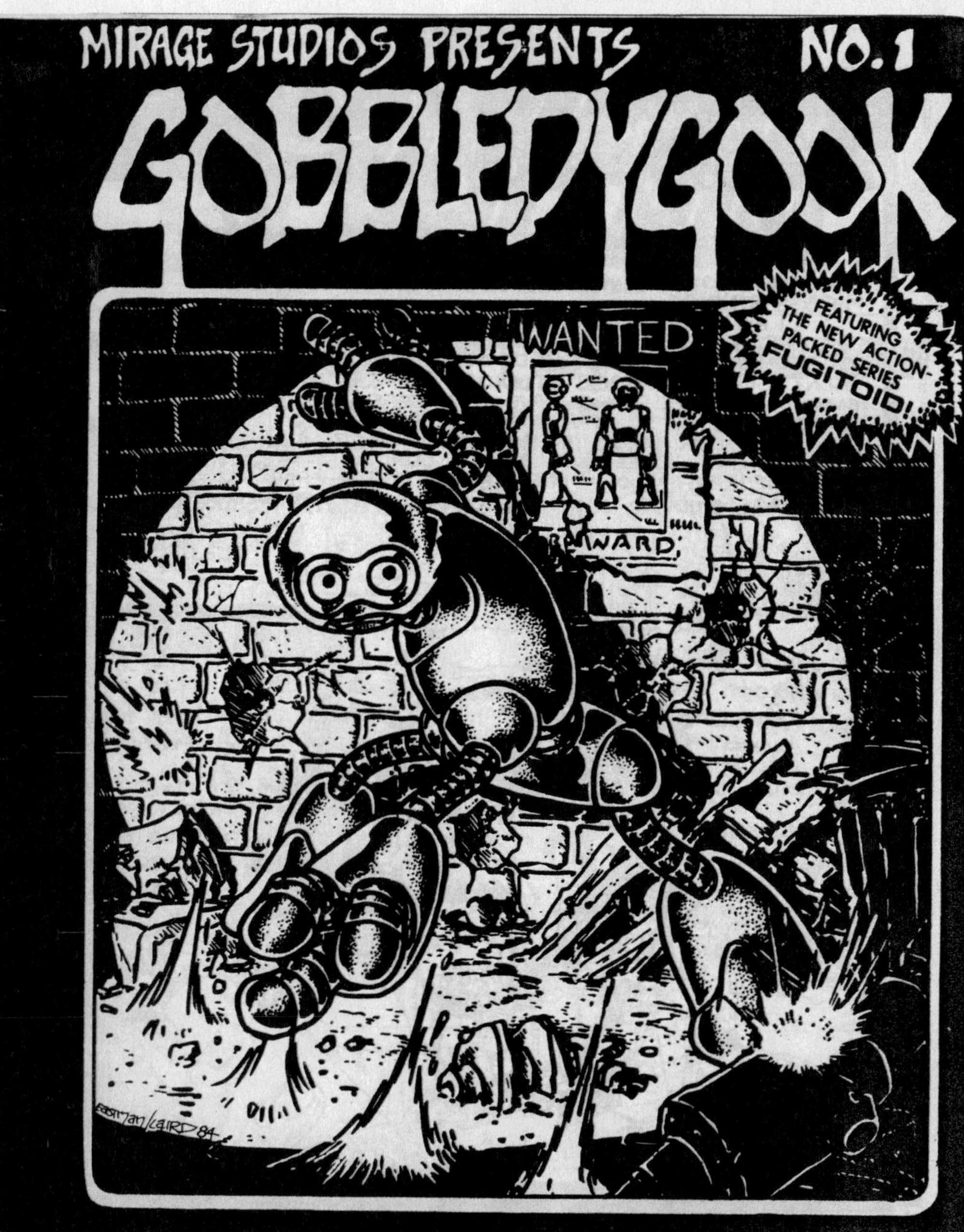

GOBBLEDYGOOK #1, in VF+ condition
Sold for $11,352.50
by Heritage Auctions
in February 2011. © MIRAGE

RECORD SETTERS

GREEN LANTERN #76, CGC 9.8
Sold for $37,343.75
by Heritage Auctions
in November 2010. © DC

FANTASTIC FOUR #1, CGC 9.4
Sold for $300,000
by Metropolis Collectibles
in May 2011. © MAR

Kizoic

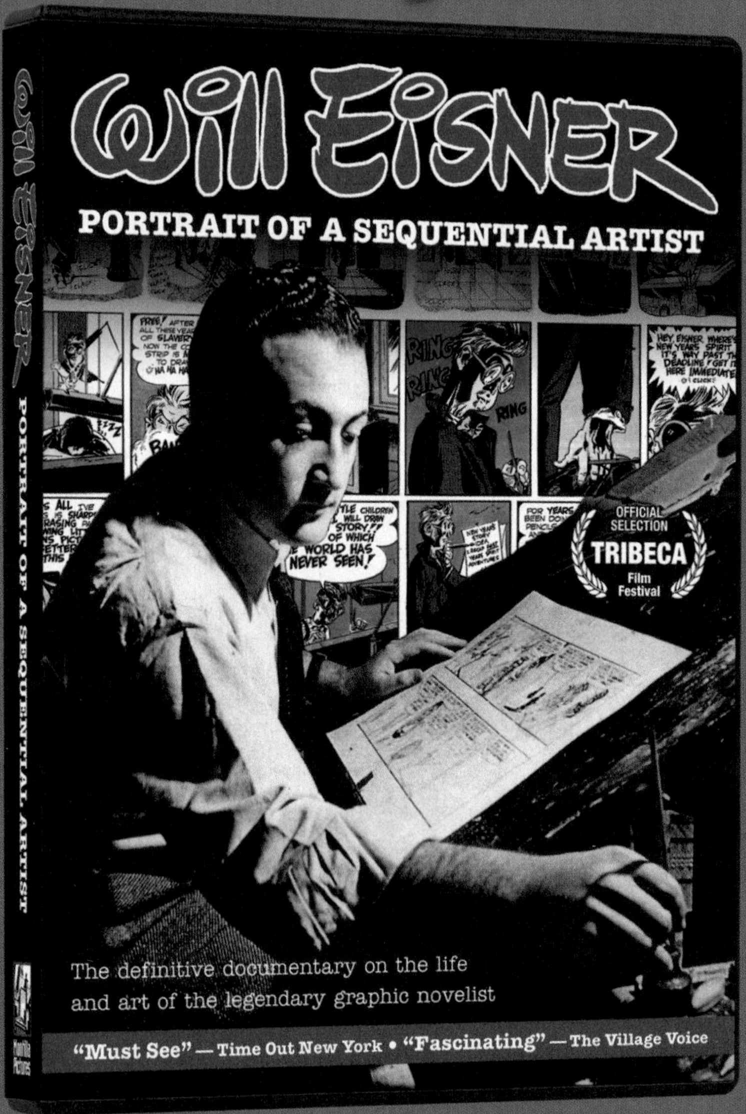

If you love comics of the '70s & '80s, get a BACK ISSUE!

Edited by former DC and Dark Horse editor **MICHAEL EURY, BACK ISSUE** magazine celebrates comic books of the 1970s, 1980s, and today through recurring (and rotating) departments such as "Pro2Pro" (a dialogue between two professionals), "Greatest Stories Never Told" (spotlighting unrealized comics series or stories), and more!

(84-page magazine with COLOR)
SINGLE ISSUES: $7.95 US
DIGITAL EDITIONS: $2.95

8-ISSUE SUBSCRIPTIONS:
$60 Standard US, $80 First Class
(Canada: $85, Elsewhere: $107 Surface, $155 Airmail).

Call or write for a FREE CATALOG, or go online for an ULTIMATE BUNDLE, with all the issues at HALF-PRICE!

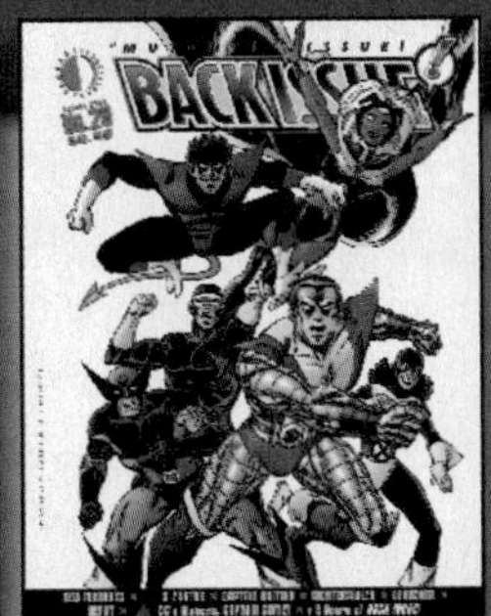

TwoMorrows. Celebrating The Art & History Of Comics.

TwoMorrows Publishing • 10407 Bedfordtown Drive • Raleigh, NC 27614 USA • 919-449-0344
E-mail: twomorrow@aol.com • www.twomorrows.com

The Avenger of Blood

By Rob Hughes

"By the fear of the Lord men depart from evil", and there are many sides of the Almighty.
Many manifestations in which He has revealed Himself to mankind.
To the chosen elect, He is the Everlasting Father, faithful protector of great compassion and everlasting mercy. For others, He is the mysterious and greatly feared Lord of Hosts known only from ancient tales of awe inspiring miracles, magnificent deliverances and epic battles.
But woe to the evil and them that work iniquity.
To these He is a God of inescapable vengeance whose anger kindles hot as he pours out his blazing fury in the terrible visage men know as

The Spectre

THE
SPECTRE
BY JERRY SIEGEL and BERNARD BAILY
NO ONE KNOWS THAT JIM CORRIGAN, HARD-FISTED DETECTIVE, IS IN REALITY THE EARTHBOUND SPECTRE, WHOSE MISSION IS TO RID THIS WORLD OF CRIME.....

Famous Spectre splash panel (used in **More Fun Comics** *#57–#65) revealing the hero's secret identity and his divine purpose. This particular splash is from issue #60 (Oct., 1940) and represents one of the most memorable of all Golden Age images. Artwork by Bernard Baily.*

The first of all supernatural superheroes materialized into existence at the dawn of the Golden Age of comic books. Writer Jerry Siegel (who had previously, along with artist Joe Shuster created the greatest of all superheroes: Superman in *Action Comics* #1, June, 1938) teamed up with a relatively unknown artist named Bernard Baily (who would also create the Hourman for *Adventure Comics* #48 in March, 1940) to bring forth the most awesome and ultra-powerful character this side of the Almighty Himself.

Drawing from the various ghost stories appearing in the classic pulp title *Weird Tales*, Siegel brought to life a dark and forboding hero that was, in so many ways, just as original a concept as Superman. He certainly was more powerful. In fact, his powers seemed almost limitless. An eerie being who had been directly empowered by, and granted divine authority over life and death from the Lord. In a private and rarely granted interview, Siegel explained that he wrote the "mysterious, heavenly voice", (that first appeared in the two-part origin story) as God's own, personal voice. Thus, making the Spectre a very special creation. His sacred mission: To utterly destroy all forms of evil and corruption and wipe clean criminal activities from the face of the Earth. Judgement Day had arrived. A reckoning was due.

The Genesis occurred in *More Fun Comics #51* (January, 1940). Readers took their very first glimpse of the Spectre in a small, one panel teaser advertisement at the end of the Buccaneer story announcing, " 'The Spectre!' Who is he?? What is he?" Who and what indeed. For here in this small panel appeared an odd looking character

"Who is He? What is He?"

Soon we would know! Two Spectre teaser ads which appeared in print one month before (left) and just prior (right), respectively, to the superhero's first appearance in **More Fun Comics** *#52. From* **More Fun Comics** *#51 (January, 1940) and* **Action Comics** *#21 (February, 1940).*

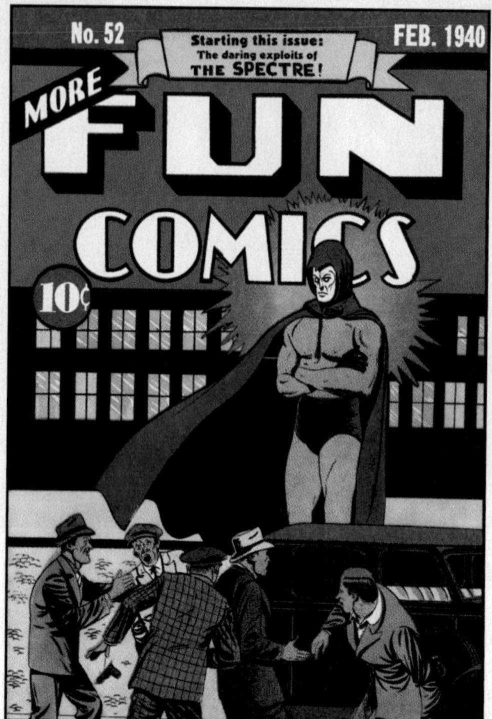

No. 52
Starting this issue: The daring exploits of THE SPECTRE!
FEB. 1940
MORE FUN COMICS
10¢

More Fun Comics #52 (February, 1940)
First appearance and origin (Part 1) of the Spectre, written by Jerry Siegel and drawn by Bernard Baily. With the publication of this issue, the Spectre became the first and greatest of all supernatural superheroes. First Spectre cover by Baily.

with a lime-green face, royal blue chest and adorned in a purple hood and cloak. A diamond in the rough. A few color alterations and the final polishing needed to be made before the power could be unleashed.

1940. The golden year of the Golden Age. The Spectre appeared full blown and stoically intimidating as he confronted a group of frightened thugs on the cover of *More Fun Comics #52* (February, 1940) This landmark issue would mark the only time in which the Spectre utilized a blue hooded cloak and trunks. Forest green became his trademark color for the duration of his career hereafter. The splash panel of this debut issue introduced him (in costume) as "The 'Spectre', a supernatural being whose mission on Earth is to stamp out crime and to enforce justice with the aid of such weird powers as becoming invisible, walking through walls and delivering death with a glance..." His origin is perhaps the most tragic and darkly ironic in all comic history.

The two-part Golden Age classic opens with the "hard boiled", tough as nails detective Jim Corrigan sharing a private moment with close friend Wayne Grant as he prepares to attend an engagement party with his wife-to-be Clarice Winston; "A beautiful and wealthy young socialite." One of Corrigan's informants named "Stodie" tips him off to a fur heist that will go down that very night at the Westmore Warehouse. Corrigan arrives on the scene and single handedly takes out a quad of thieves with a combination of right hooks and left uppercuts. Infuriated that this young and fearless detective has interfered and once again spoiled his plans, "Gat" Benson, a mobster gang leader, kidnaps Corrigan and Clarice and takes the couple to an abandoned warehouse on the waterfront. One of "Gat's" men cold clocks Jim from behind and places him in a hollow barrel, fills it to the rim with water and cement, and heaves the wooden tomb into the cold river below. Jim Corrigan dies. "Up toward the streaming light ahead streaks Jim's figure at infinite speed..." At the gates of Eternity, Jim's spirit hovers before the Lord (represented in a large commanding voice) who speaks to the detective from a brightly lit cloud; "Listen Jim Corrigan and you will learn... Your mission on Earth is unfinished... You shall remain Earthbound battling crime on your

More Fun Comics #53 (March, 1940)
The Spectre's second appearance and part 2 of his origin as the story continues from issue #52. Slain in the line of duty, Jim Corrigan dons the famed forest-green cloak for the first time. Cover art by Baily.

I SHALL NOT BE SATISFIED UNTIL CRIMINAL ACTIVITIES UPON THIS EARTH ARE A THING OF THE PAST !!
IT LOOKS BAD FOR ORGANIZED CRIME! TO FOLLOW THE ADVENTURES OF THIS ASTOUNDING CHARACTER, BE SURE TO SECURE THE NEXT AND EVERY FORTH-COMING ISSUE OF :
MORE FUN COMICS!
SUPERMAN every month in ACTION COMICS!

After avenging his own murder and saving Clarice, the Spectre accepts his divine mission and vows to war on all criminal activities until they are completely eradicated. From More Fun Comics #53.

world with supernatural powers, until all vestiges of it are gone!" Corrigan's protests go unanswered as his spiritual essence hurls back down across the cosmos to the bottom of the river. Shocked at the sight of a lifeless hand protruding out from a barrel of cement, Jim realizes he is looking at his own slain physical body. He vows vengeance on "Gat" Benson and quickly discovers his ability to fly, suspend in midair, turn invisible, and perform any feat he wishes. Part one closes with Corrigan rushing to save his beloved Clarice from the clutches of Benson and his murderous gang.

More Fun Comics #53 (March, 1940) begins with Corrigan gliding through the warehouse wall to confront his slayers. As one of the gangsters turns to shoot Clarice, Jim fixes his eyes upon the criminal and inaugurates his famous Death Stare which would become The Spectre's grim, unmistakable calling card in the years to follow. The gangster collapses to the floor dead. A second thug named Ricky advances to finish off Clarice (who has fainted) but Corrigan stands in the gap and wills the would-be killer to age at a furiously rapid rate until only a skeleton remains. Jim states, "You've robbed, you've killed and this is your reward. Die!".

Benson flees in utter terror but Corrigan heads off the gang leader. In desperation, "Gat" reels and fires at Clarice. The bullet finds its mark as Jim rushes forward to touch Benson, sending him into unconsciousness. Jim discovers he has gained even more amazing abilities for as soon as he touches his fiancée, "No wound! As soon as I touched it - it Healed Instantly." Realizing that he could never again lead any sort of normal life, Corrigan breaks off the engagement with Clarice and returns home in painful solidarity.

Within the lone confines of his room, "Jim busies himself constructing a strange costume" stating, "I'll continue to be Jim Corrigan, detective - but when I battle crime as The Spectre, I'll cloak my identity in this costume!" And thus, as a lone, tortured figure gazes up into the twilight pondering his colossal mission, his skin transforms into a murky gray, the pupils of his eyes disappear, and with the donning of a kelly-green hooded cloak, gloves, trunks, and low-cut boots the Spectre vows, "I shall not be satisfied until criminal activities on this Earth are a thing of the past!! And since that day, a lonely man has walked the Earth...A man both more and less than mortal. For the day Jim Corrigan died...The Spectre was born!"

Soon after this phantom's arrival upon this mortal planet, a warning spread like wildfire throughout the underworld: "If the Spectre was after you, say your prayers because you were as good as dead." Doomed evil doers began fleeing in every direction like frightened rats. During the next five years, they began to realize that their lives, yea,

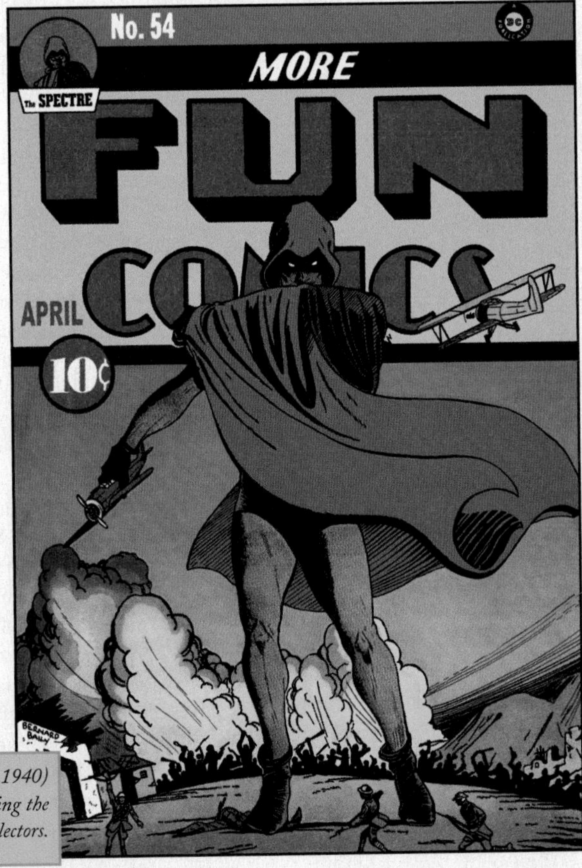

More Fun Comics #54 (April, 1940)
The most spectacular of all the Spectre covers during the Golden-Age by Baily. A favorite among comic collectors.

rather their immortal souls hung in a delicate balance with this terrifying ghost lurking about. In his informative book *Over 50 Years of American Comic Books*, Ron Goulart describes the Astral Avenger as "the most intimidating of all superheroes. As much a figure of horror as a good guy...A grim uniquely talented chap, the Spectre didn't just collar crooks - he enjoyed himself by destroying them." And exterminate these criminal roaches he did, since it was the only way of attaining the salvation of eternal rest his soul so earnestly longed for.

In Peter Sanderson's commentary, *The Dark Justice of...The Spectre*, Michael Fleisher, (who would eventually script the most prolific and controversial series ever published on the character) writes; "In general, I very much liked the kind of raw, rough-edged quality that a lot of comic book characters had in their earliest appearances. The Spectre was for me sort of a vengeful Old Testament God-like character, wreaking vengeance from beyond the grave."

More Fun Comics #57 (July, 1940)
Towering Spectre, looming over twilight, moon-lit rooftops to engage two doomed thugs. Classic Spectre splash panel used for the first time in this issue with cover and story art by Baily.

"In the original Spectre series, Jim Corrigan is engaged to Clarice Winston and he gets killed by gangsters. But God allows him to walk the Earth as a Spectre, though Clarice doesn't know he's dead. Corrigan walks up to her and breaks their engagement. He's decided that he's separated from the realm of mortals and has to sever his links with them."

The Spectre demands a full confession with the terrible threat of a walk through the Valley of Death.
From More Fun Comics #55.

"[Corrigan] was now committed to a life in which all he expressed was his anger. His mission was to exterminate evil, but he didn't have a real life. He didn't have real loves and real friendships. He didn't have recreation and relaxation and the joy of real living. He only has that he was some sort of divinely appointed executioner."

More Fun Comics #54 (April, 1940) displays the most outstanding and definitive Spectre cover. A dark and moody illustration by the talented Bernard Baily that ranks up with the all-time greatest Golden Age covers. The ultimately powerful and ominous Spectre looming over an entire world torn apart by war and violence. The Avenger of Blood has come down from Heaven and the sins of mankind were about to be weighed in the balances...and found wanting.

Detective Corrigan began his new existence by opposing a spiritualist named Rhani-Set who was deceiving and extorting money from Clarice's mother. After exposing the swami as a fraud, Corrigan tells him; "why don't you try and earn an honest living?" Humiliated and enraged, Rhani-Set kidnaps Clarice and demands a ransom of $100,000 for her safe return. Realizing that this greedy dog will stop at nothing to achieve his

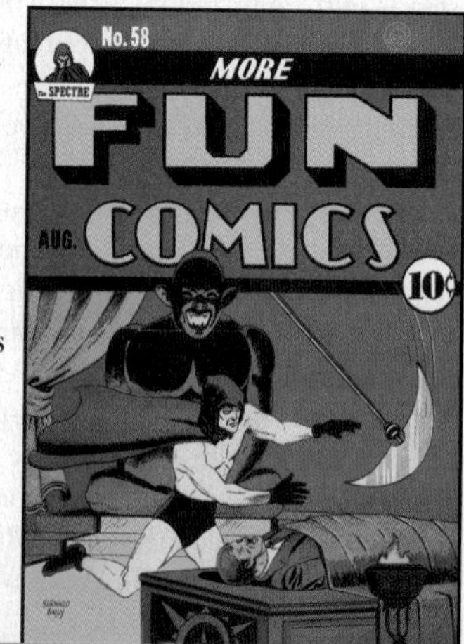

More Fun Comics #58 (August, 1940)
Superb human sacrifice and pagan idol cover as the Spectre rushes to the rescue of a helpless, would-be victim. Art by Baily.

goals, Corrigan transforms into his wrathful identity and confronts the evil swami. Rhani-Set fires his pistol and the deadly bullet speeds toward the helpless girl. At that very instant, time itself is halted as the Lord raises his servant up to stand before Him revealing, "Jim Corrigan - once again judgement is to be passed upon you! We have relented - your mission is too gigantic for one individual - you shall be permitted to pass on to eternal rest!" Corrigan pleads, "But I can't pass onto another world now, as much as I'd care to! Clarice is in danger. She needs my help!" The Lord answers, "The decision is yours! Eternal rest or eternally Earth-bound! What is your answer?" And thus, "For Clarice's sake, Jim dooms his soul to the bitter fate of forever haunting Earth!" by stating, "I choose to remain Earth-bound!" The Lord concludes "So shall it be!" and sends the Spectre back to Earth to save his beloved from certain death. He does. Rhani-Set and one of his henchmen turn and shriek in horror as "The Spectre permits them to glimpse death in his eyes, and die of fright." A final caption summed it up; "Now doomed to haunt crime and the world forever, The Spectre begins his lone battle against the underworld in earnest."

The Spectre's gray complexion paled to a pasty white with the release of *More Fun Comics #55* (May, 1940). Even more amazing abilities would come forth as Detective Corrigan reads the guilty thoughts of Simmons, the 1st National Bank bookkeeper who had been embezzling money from his employer. Corrigan transforms and commands Simmons to confess his crime or walk into the Valley of Death with his grim alter-ego. The bookkeeper quickly agrees and turns himself over to the authorities. This issue also introduced the Spectre's first supernatural nemesis; Zor - a spirit confined to Earth to spread evil. With the Lord's intervention, the Spectre captures Zor in his own "Paralysis-Ray", leaving the wicked spirit in stationary isolation for all eternity. Returning Clarice to her home, Corrigan would once again have to subdue his emotions and compassion for his lost love by saying, "As Jim Corrigan I loved you Clarice deeply! But now I am the Spectre! My work is to destroy evil and to that end I dedicate myself."

THE SPECTRE'S EYES SEEM GROW TO COLOSSAL SIZE...
THOSE EYES ARE BORING INTO MY SOUL!

The Spectre uses the dreaded "Death-Stare", as his huge eyes pierce into the black soul of a helpless thug. From More Fun Comics #59.

The most famous and recognizable depiction of the Spectre appeared for the first time in *More Fun Comics #57* (July, 1940). This gloomy and alluring splash panel (used until issue #65) would become a true Golden Age classic and prepared any unsuspecting or faint of heart readers for this solemn hero and the dark tale that followed.

The Grim Avenger continued to mete out hot

XNON'S SPELL LIFTING! I'M FREE! THANK YOU! THANK YOU!

Calling upon the Almighty for dire help, the Spectre is given the "Ring of Life and Death" to do battle with the tyrannical Xnon. From More Fun Comics #60.

fiery indignation and smite wrongdoers in the most horrifying means. A lasting impression was graphically etched into the minds of these wicked murderers. In *More Fun Comics #58* (August, 1940) an arsonist named Pete received this lesson in spades as he planned to burn a warehouse to cinders with the owner tied to a beam inside. With no more effort than a slight wave of the Spectre's hand, the flame freezes into a harmless icicle. In disbelief, Pete looks upon the face of death reflected in the ice and straight forward melts into a formless mound of goo, "consumed by the villainy within him." Another mobster, after being cornered at every turn asks this relentless hunter "What manner of creature are you?" The Spectre replies, "I'm your sins, Morris and I've finally caught up with you!" With desperate, escape minded law-breakers speeding away, the dark wraith enlarges to immense stature in front of their on-rushing automobile to easily reach down and hurl them into interstellar space. Crime and pollution eliminated with one throw. Soon afterward, when he offered an award by Bob Brant whom this guardian angel had saved from an untimely death on several occasions, the Spectre explains, "I seek no reward! My only desire is to see justice done! Good Bye!"

Introducing himself in *More Fun Comics #59* (September, 1940) as "A ghost who has a strong dislike for thieves and murderers," to a small-time hood named Mulligan, the Spectre explains, "you represent the type of vermin I've sworn to stamp out of this world." Stamp right out of existence in fact. He tread down these fugitives like mire in the streets. This dreaded phantom came to devour and purify the very essence of evil. There was no hiding. No escape. Issue #60 introduced the power-mad Xnon. A scheming kidnapper who wielded a power-rod that enslaved and almost forced the Spectre to perform a hideous crime of mass murder. The Almighty intercedes at the last crucial moment and grants his ambassador to Earth "The Ring of Life and of Death! No man made mechanism is capable of resisting it!" After a full hearted thanks to his Creator, the Spectre rushes through the cosmos to do battle once again with Xnon. Imprisoning the would-be-conqueror at the center of a meteor, the victorious hero concludes, "and so ends Xnon and his mad ambitions."

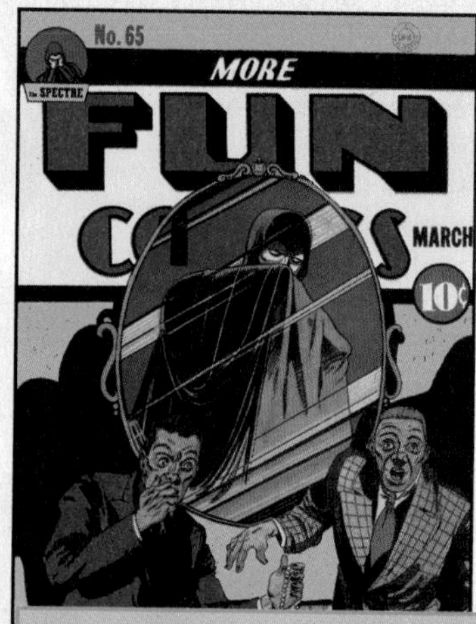

More Fun Comics #65 (March, 1941)
Famous mirror cover as the Spectre confronts two terrified jewel thieves.
Baily cover art.

The Spectre would soon adapt the uncanny ability to sense the presence of evil as if it were a tangible entity calling to him for punishment. The timely spook thwarts an assassination attempt on the President of the United States in *More Fun Comics #62* (December, 1940), "as the thug fires, the face of the Spectre appears between the Chief Executive and the bullet! The 'Man of Darkness' opens his mouth and swallows the bullet!"

As a keen weapon of God's wrath, the Spectre was continually called upon to oppose evil spirits and various other super-powered beings, banishing them from Earth forever. In *More Fun Comics #63* (January, 1941), he pursued a revenge-seeking soul named "Trigger", ultimately forcing him to recess into nothingness due to the bright and brilliant glow of "the Ring of Life." *More Fun Comics #64* (February, 1941) reveals a rare glimpse of the Spectre's compassionate side as he heals his close friend of a life threatening fever. Wayne states,

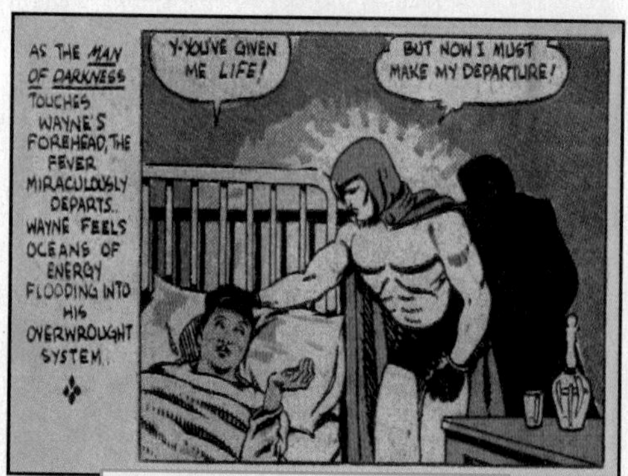

The Spectre as divine healer.
Neutralizing a potentially fatal fever.
From More Fun Comics #64.

The Blue Flame begins his short-lived career as a master jewel thief.
From More Fun Comics #65.

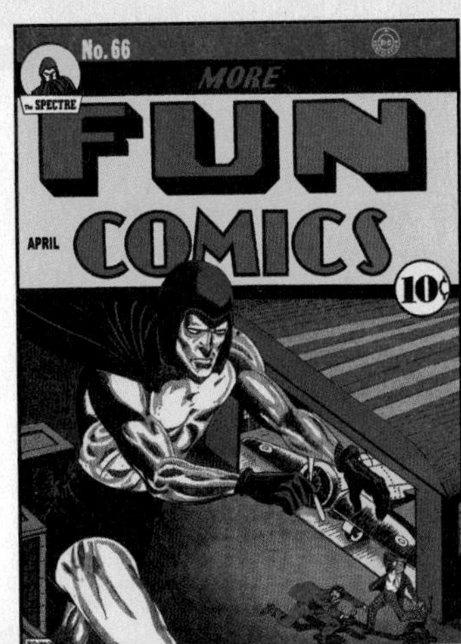

More Fun Comics #66 (April, 1941)
The Spectre battles the Black Doom in this issue. Second to last Spectre cover by Baily.

"You've given me life!" as the fever miraculously departs. The Ghostly Guardian's strange and unique ability to look back across the sands of time, to the very past itself, manifested in *More Fun Comics #65* (March, 1941). He used this power to bring a jewel thief calling himself "the Blue Flame" to justice (giving his alter-ego Jim Corrigan full credit for the capture). It would also be in this particular issue that the twilight superhero would be referred to as "the Dark Knight". A recognizable title that was later attributed to one particular manhunter who patrolled Gotham City by night.

More Fun Comics #66 (April, 1941) brought forth a hateful villain with world domination as his agenda; the Black Doom. The tale opens with gargantuan werewolf-like monsters rampaging through the street of Cliffland. Havoc, destruction and utter chaos following in their wake. As the Spectre soars to intercept these wild marauding beasts, a weird drum beat seems to summon them to return from whence they came. Discovering another dimension existing inside a prehistoric painting hanging in the downtown museum, the Spectre dives into the picture and beholds a strange leader of dark intent; "What a Man! A face as evil as Satan. Fiery eyes as foreboding as a flaming pit. A conglomeration of all the qualities that make up a repulsive, unclean thing; the Black Doom!" This demonic dictator strikes out at our hero, encircling him in a black cloud of dense vapor. Nevertheless, this avenging ghost is completely relentless and undaunted in his quest to crush and stamp out evil and, "with astounding swiftness, the forces of darkness shrink to reveal the Spectre surrounded by a protective glow of pure light." The God-like hero from Heaven speaks to his adversary, "You forget that good is more powerful than evil." Reducing the army of maddened monsters to harmless oily fluid, the Spectre leaps out from the ancient painting and straightway destroys the art work in a burst of flame summing, "Thus perishes the gate to reality! And thus also ends the menace to mankind."

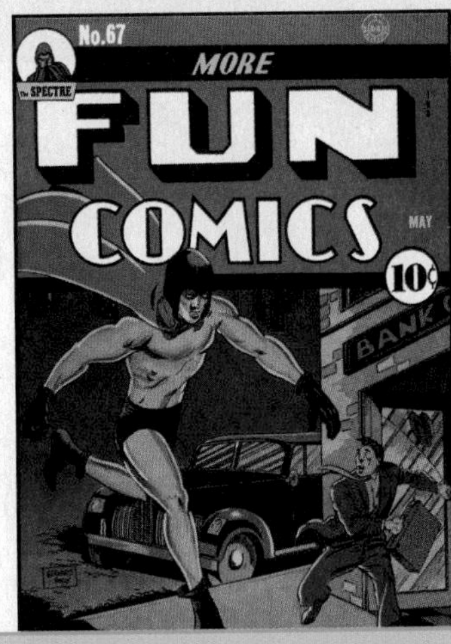

More Fun Comics #67 (May, 1941)
Classic and last Spectre cover for this title. The hero's dark and mysterious appeal was fast becoming a byword, and soon he would be a back-up feature. Cover art by Baily.

More Fun Comics #67 (May, 1941) marked the very last time the Spectre would adorn the cover of this title. By issue #101 he was gone altogether. The dreadful spirit of wrath who had once invoked trembling terror for any law-breaker unfortunate enough to cross his path, had lost his unique appeal. He had, like several other Golden Age superheroes, fallen away from his dark roots, mysterious inception and gloomy surroundings to be thrust into the spotlight of recognition and familiarity. The enigmatic primal power vanished. This killed The Grim Avenger and bound him to a death from which he would not be resurrected in his full glory for nearly 30 years.

Acknowledgements:
Jack K. Der: *For his fantastic graphic design, professionalism, and yet another huge "favor."*
Dr. John Townsend: *For taking the time to make all of those color Xeroxes, providing me with the interior story information.*
Ralph D. Hughes: *For his stunning artwork. His interpretation of the Spectre is my most favorite.*
Frank Brunner: *Superb splash painting, capturing the grim mood and true direction of the article.*
Jerry Siegel and Bernard Baily: *Two Golden Age legends that created one of the most popular and enduring superheroes of all time. May the Lord rest you both.*
And to the collectors, dealers and individuals that helped me in acquiring and presenting this material: Stephen Geppi, Daniel Greenhalgh, Bill Hughes, Sharon Hughes, Monika Hughes, Maggie Hughes, Matt "Stinklin" Nelson, Bill Ponseti, Stephen Fishler, Jason LaMarr and Harley Yee.
God Bless you all.

AN ORIGINAL

Major Malcolm Wheeler-Nicholson

A DC PUBLICATION

By Nicky Wheeler-Nicholson Brown

Major Malcolm Wheeler-Nicholson was honored with a posthumous Eisner Award in 2008 for his contributions to the comic book industry. His background was a mystery to many comic book fans and historians. So who is this guy—the Major—and what did he do that was so important?

It's not easy to squeeze a life full of adventure and accomplishments into a couple of paragraphs, so...a few highlights: Malcolm Wheeler-Nicholson was born near Greeneville, Tennessee on January 7, 1890 and spent his childhood there and in the Pacific Northwest. He had quite a career in the Army, all of it verifiable in military records.

MWN served under General Pershing on the Mexican border chasing bandits and revolutionaries, among them probably Pancho Villa, while commanding Troop K of the historic African-American Buffalo Soldiers. By 1915 he was in the Philippines breaking world records for machine gun readiness and in his off-duty moments winning polo cups.

During WWI he was in Military Intelligence and in 1917 was in Siberia attached to the Japanese Embassy. He saw first hand the cruelty of the Cossacks towards the local peasantry as well as the nuances of the constantly changing alliances between the Chinese and Japanese, the Cossack chiefs and Bolshevik Revolutionaries. These real life experiences would later appear in adventure stories and in his non-fiction articles and books.

Enter the roaring twenties and the Major is posted to Paris. There he met Elsa Karolina Bjorkbom, a Swedish woman of aristocratic background. After a fairytale proposal in the Eiffel Tower, they were married in the Kaiser's Chapel in Koblentz, Germany. MWN became concerned that poor leadership as a result of Army promotion practices was a direct cause of great loss of life during WWI. With the hubris

© Wheeler-Nicholson Family

of youth he brought this to the attention of Army leadership. Somebody in the top brass wasn't too keen about this and he was recalled to Fort Dix in 1921. There was a dramatic assassination attempt in the dark of night and miraculously he survived. A court martial ensued. He was acquitted of all charges except that of publishing an open letter to President Harding, and he discharged from the Army in the very last days of 1922.

That's a lot of adventure for anyone's life but that was just the beginning. MWN began writing adventure stories and published a work of non-fiction in 1922. Over his lifetime he wrote at least 117 short stories, novels and serials, not including reprints and appearances in foreign editions. In addition there are several novels in hardback and paperback

The Major and his wife Elsa.

and works under two known pseudonyms. But wait there's more—comic scripts and non-fiction.

The Major's first venture as a writer of comic scripts and a publisher was in 1925 working with colleagues like screenwriter N. Brewster Morse and artist Oscar Hitt. Robert Louis Stevenson scholars note MWN as the first person to publish RLS in comic strip form and comic book format. Classic Comics and graphic novels anyone? Like a lot of creative people MWN wasn't all that great with the details of business and by the end of 1926 the venture was at an end.

MWN was a popular writer and in 1928 he was able to move the family to France so that Elsa could be closer to her family. He continued writing for the pulps while living in Paris and an ancient chateau in Vic sur Aisnes. Unfortunately the Great Depression caught up with the Wheeler-Nicholsons and they were forced to return to New York in May of 1930. It was harder and harder to make money writing for the pulps and support a family of seven so what did the Major decide to do in the midst of the Depression? Why—start a comic book publishing company with the unique idea of using all original art and scripts instead of reprints from newspapers.

Surprisingly it turned out to be a very good idea but somebody else ended up making the money. Sound familiar? Even worse, others have been credited with his ideas and hard work and MWN's contributions have often been denigrated. In fact, Major Malcolm Wheeler-Nicholson began the company that is still with us some 75 years later as DC Comics. MWN's original comic book *New Fun Comics* arrived on the newsstands in 1934. Based on his writing for the pulps it was his idea that these original scripts should be full of adventure and action and he wrote many of those scripts. In 1937 he entered into a new venture with Harry Donenfeld's financial backing and Jack Liebowitz as his partner. The new venture? *Detective Comics* or *DC Comics* with *Action Comics* already in the works.

MWN had the foresight to recognize

and nurture talent so after sending him the first drawings of Superman he promptly hired Siegel and Shuster. In 1935 they appeared in *New Fun*. Jerry Siegel said they never would have made it into print without the Major's help. Bob Kane (Batman) was also one of the early artists that the Major hired and there are many others—artists, writers and editors who went on to make their marks in comic book history. Donenfeld may have been the consummate salesman and Liebowitz the financial whiz, but without the Major's creative vision they'd be known today as the publishers of *Spicy Detective*.

What happened after that auspicious beginning is a tangled tale. The upshot was that against his will the Major was forced out of the company he founded. Although it was a crushing blow, being a disciplined soldier, he picked himself up and returned to writing. During WWII the Major wrote three books of non-fiction that were well received beginning with *Battle Shield of the Republic* as well as numerous articles in *Look* and *Harpers Magazine* among others.

Before his death in 1965 there was still one more chapter to be written of his extraordinary life. In 1948 on a trip to Sweden he discovered formulas for an unusual type of paint that he realized would have tremendous military and industrial applications. Teaching himself basic chemistry, he developed these in the family kitchen. The formulas proved successful and patents were created of these and several other futuristic ideas, most of which have been implemented.

Major Malcolm Wheeler-Nicholson deserves recognition for his prolific creative output and for the tremendous contribution he made to the founding of the modern comic book industry. It's important to the history of this distinctive American art form that the Major's story is added to those of other pioneers. There's obviously much more to this great adventure tale so here's to "More Fun" in the future with comic book history.

DC Comics was launched with **New Fun Comics #1** in February 1935

The COMIC BOOK LEGAL DEFENSE FUND

CBLDF COMIC BOOK LEGAL DEFENSE FUND

BY BRADY BONNEY

The Comic Book Legal Defense Fund serves the comics community by defending the First Amendment rights of retailers, creators, and readers when those rights are threatened.

The CBLDF is a grassroots organization that exists because of the generous support of the comics community. The donations of individuals and small businesses add up to make CBLDF the first responder to First Amendment emergencies when they arise.

The CBLDF was founded in 1986 by artist and publisher Denis Kitchen to help store manager Michael Correa of Friendly Frank's, a shop in Lansing, Illinois. Correa was found guilty of distributing obscene material, fined, and sentenced to one year of court supervision after local law enforcement purchased 15 comics from him.The comics included titles now regarded as classic, including *Elektra: Assassin, Love & Rockets, Elfquest, Heavy Metal,* and *Omaha the Cat Dancer*.

As the publisher of *Omaha*, Kitchen felt a responsibility to help Correa. He said, "*Omaha* contained adult content, without question. But *Omaha* was also an artistic and literary success, having received high critical praise internationally. I also knew that the other titles seized could not qualify as pornographic. More importantly, Michael Correa was not charged with selling any of the titles to a minor. The police arrested the manager simply for having 'obscene' books on display."

Kitchen took action by rallying artists including Will Eisner, Robert Crumb, and Frank Miller to create a portfolio of prints to raise money towards an appeal. The appeal was successfully argued by pioneering First Amendment lawyer Burton Joseph, and Correa was a free man. Afterwards, Kitchen had several thousand dollars remaining. Feeling that this would not be an isolated incident, he used it to establish the CBLDF as a permanent institution.

Over the years, the CBLDF has led the charge in dozens of defense cases on behalf of many, including: Paul Mavrides, artist of the *Fabulous Furry Freak Brothers* against the State of California's Board of Equalization; cartoonist Kieron Dwyer against Starbucks; publisher Top Shelf Productions against U.S. Customs; and DC Comics creators Joe Lansdale, Timothy Truman and Sam Glanzman against the Winter Brothers. The Fund also squelches dozens of small incidents in retail stores and libraries every year by helping defuse situations before they can become a case. Full

Frank Miller provided this chilling image used on promotional materials.

details on all of these cases can be read at cbldf.org.

Most recently, CBLDF claimed a victory in a case that cost over $100,000 defending Gordon Lee, owner of Rome, Georgia store Legends, against baseless and inflated charges that took three years to resolve. Were it not for the CBLDF, Lee says he almost surely wouldn't still be in business today.

Lee participated in a local Halloween event where he handed out comics left over from Free Comic Book Day instead of candy. One of the comics in his overstock was *Alternative Comics* #2, a Free Comic Book Day title that included an eight page selection of Nick Bertozzi's graphic novel *The Salon*, a biographical work about the life of Pablo Picasso, where, for a short scene, Picasso appeared painting in the nude. Even though nudity was present in the book, it was not sexual in nature. A copy of *Alternative Comics* #2 was allegedly given to a minor at the Halloween function, but instead of being confronted with the accusation and given the opportunity to apologize, Lee was arrested under two felony charges, and five misdemeanor charges.

The Fund hired Begner & Begner, the best obscenity firm in Georgia, to manage the case. Over the course of three years, the firm fought for Lee, first knocking out the felony charges. On the eve of trial, 18 months into the case, prosecutors dropped all charges and then refiled the next day, because they claimed they had named the wrong victim. That morning, CBLDF litigator Alan Begner said, "I have never—as a criminal trial lawyer for thirty years—seen a complete changing of the facts like this. The dismissal of the charges ... reflects the prosecution's admission that everything that was presented as evidence before was untrue." In November 2007, after three years, prosecutors were still unable to prove their accusations against Lee, and created a mistrial during opening statements. District Attorney Leigh Patterson eventually agreed to drop all charges against Lee. Were it not for the CBLDF, Lee would have had to plead guilty to a crime he didn't commit or risk bankruptcy defending himself.

Many of the CBLDF's retail members express that they see their membership as an insurance policy, which they hope never to need. The CBLDF assures that whenever there is a First Amendment emergency, they'll be the first to respond. To learn more about any of the CBLDF's cases, or to make a contribution to the cause, visit CBLDF.org.

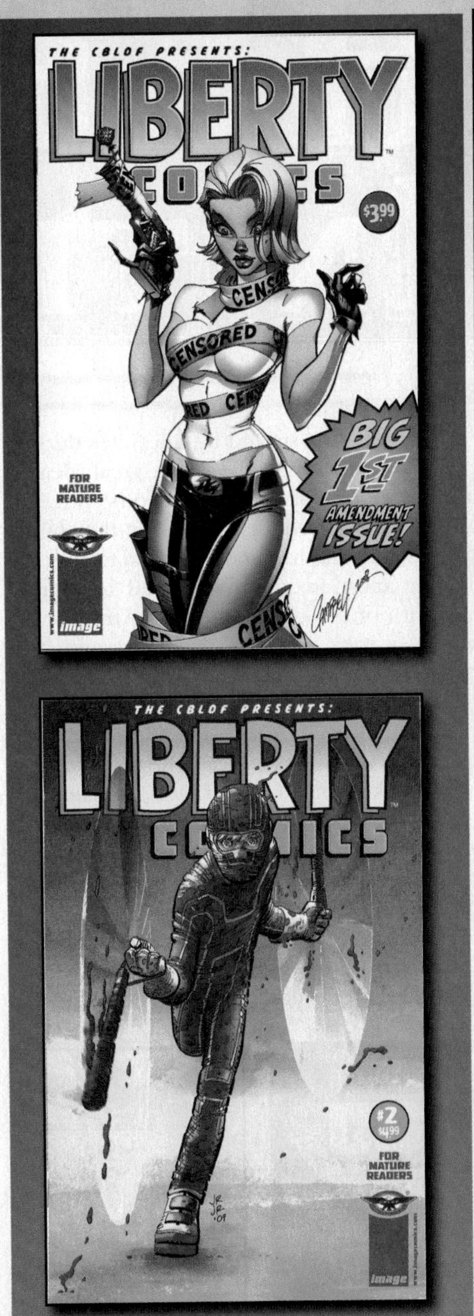

*The first and second issues of **Liberty Comics**, an anthology of short stories by top creators, about the protection of free speech rights.*

The Hero Initiative

THE HERO INITIATIVE
HERO
HELPING COMIC BOOK CREATORS IN NEED

By Charles S. Novinskie

Microsoft was started by Bill Gates during a recession, proof positive that a great idea is truly recession-proof. Comparisons can be made to the late 20th century when the comic book industry was in something akin to a recession, but most frequently referred to as the near death of the comic book industry. Comic companies were closing their doors and creators were left without steady employment.

Enter comic journalist Jim McLauchlin and the then-owner of Crossgen Comics, Mark Alessi. Like many great ideas, this one started with two like-minded folks sharing a vision, in this case the desire to help comic creators that have toiled at their trade for decades with no pension, no benefits, no way to support themselves later in life.

Helping creators in need became the focus of the Hero Initiative as they shouted to one and all, "Everyone deserves a Golden Age!", a reference to the organizations original desire to help creators that worked during the Golden Age of Comics, a period from the 1930s through the late 1950s.

A Commitment to Our Roots (ACTOR, as Hero was first known) was born in October of 2000, becoming the first-ever, federally chartered not-for-profit corporation dedicated strictly to helping comic book creators in need.

In reality, anyone that meets the criteria of ever having worked in the comic book industry as a freelance writer, penciller, inker, colorist or letterer for a minimum of 10 years is eligible. Over the past ten years, as the economy worsened, more and more creators needed assistance to stay afloat. The reality was so bad that ACTOR had to change their name in July of 2006 because out of work Hollywood actors were applying for assistance based on the ACTOR acronym (true story). To date, The Hero

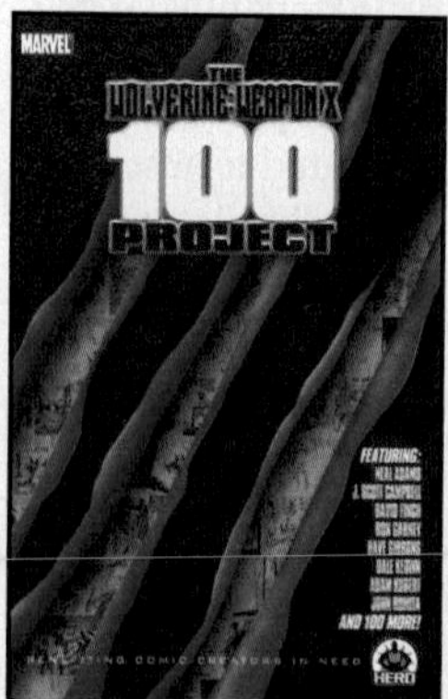

Creators donate their talents in various ways to help.

Initiative has provided grants of over $400,000 to numerous comic book creators in need. Hero has also provided short-term, non-interest loans to creators that were between assignments.

While Hero respects the privacy of creators and keeps disbursements confidential, some creators have allowed us to share their stories to help promote the cause: Bill Messner-Loebs was provided assistance when he needed a place to live, Lea Hernandez was helped out after a devastating house fire, and Jim Sanders was provided assistance when all other sources of help were exhausted.

To date over 40 creators have been aided through everything from rough patches to costly, life-saving operations. Some have intimated that without Hero's intervention, suicide might have been their next step without intervention.

A John Romita Sr. New Avengers sketch cover.

The real beauty is that with the exception of one full-time and one part-time paid employee, the entire organization is run by volunteers. Donations to Hero come from fans, creators, retailers, publishers, distributors and printers. While the need is great, the organization continues to grow and expand in the form of auctions, benefit books and the overall kindness and generosity of people that have a true love for this industry and want to give back and help any way they can.

Governed by a Fund Raising Committee and a Disbursement Committee, The Hero Initiative has board members from the comics industry: the Disbursement Committee (comprised of Walt Simonson, Denny O'Neil, John Romita Sr., Jim Valentino, George Pérez, Howard Chaykin, Roy Thomas, Jim McLauchlin and Charlie Novinskie) votes on disbursing funds and evaluates each creator's situation on a case-by-case basis. The Fund Raising Committee (Jim McLauchlin, Steve Borock, Mike Malve, Brian Pulido, Joe Quesada, Beth Widera, and Mark Waid) finds revenue streams that keep positive cash flow coming in so that Hero can provide for the needs of the ever growing list of creators in need. Many creators and retailers have donated their services, time, and talents for the cause. Poker matches, softball games, creator lunches and even green "Excelsior" wrist bands endorsed by Stan Lee have all contributed to promoting The Hero Initiative cause.

If you'd like to donate or volunteer your time, or know a creator in need, please don't hesitate to contact The Hero Initiative at www.heroinitiative.org.

Charlie Novinskie, an Overstreet Advisor, has been with The Hero Initiative since the early years.

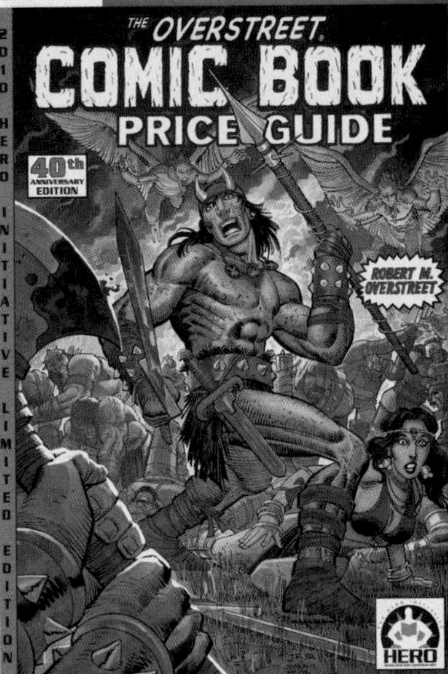

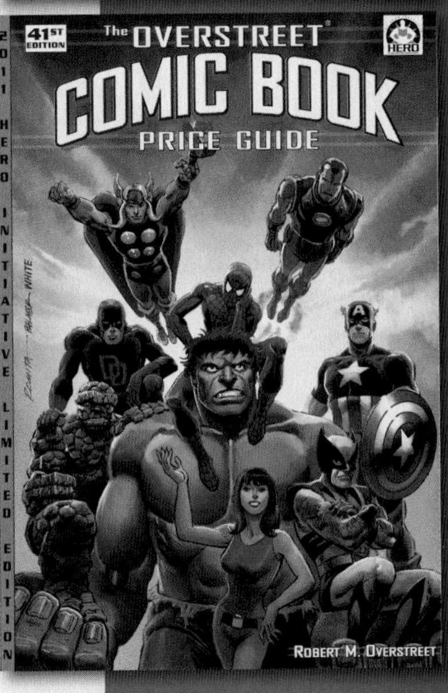

The 40th and 41st editions of **The Overstreet Comic Book Price Guide** sported these variant covers by the talented Romitas.

BLOOD IS THE HARVEST
1950. © CG

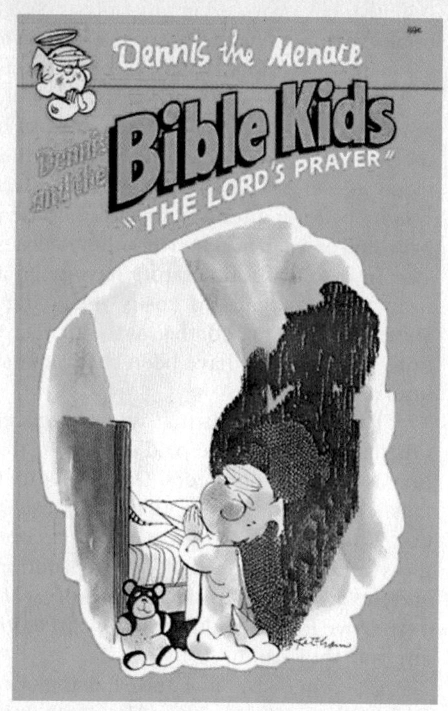

DENNIS THE MENACE AND THE BIBLE KIDS #7
1977. © Word Press

THE FIRST CHRISTMAS
1953. © Real Adventures

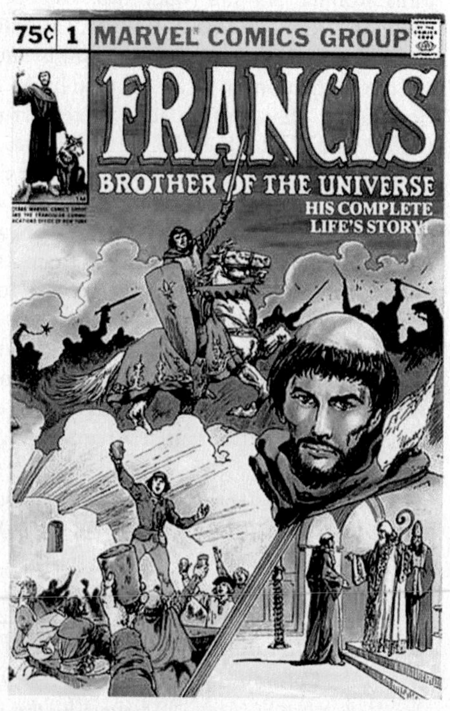

FRANCIS, BROTHER OF THE UNIVERSE #1
1980. © MAR

THE LIFE OF POPE JOHN PAUL II #1
1982. © MAR

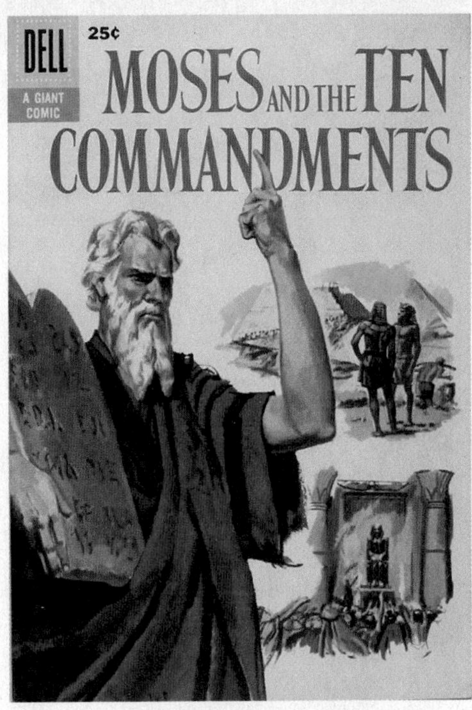

MOSES AND THE TEN COMMANDMENTS
August 1957. © DELL

MOTHER TERESA OF CALCUTTA #1
1984. © MAR

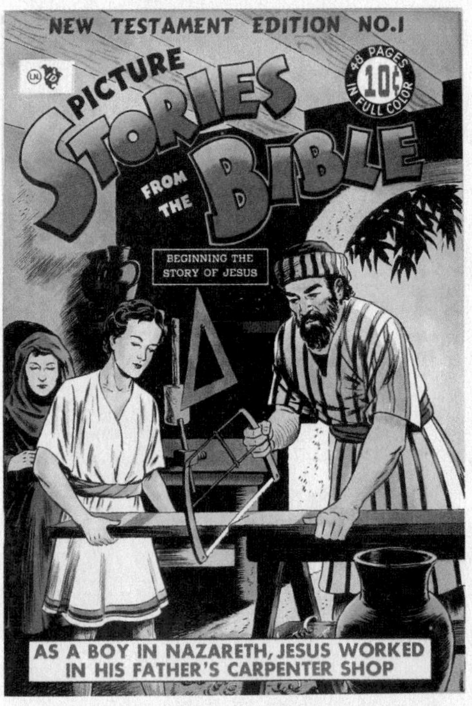

PICTURE STORIES FROM THE BIBLE
NEW TESTAMENT EDITION #1. 1946. © WMG

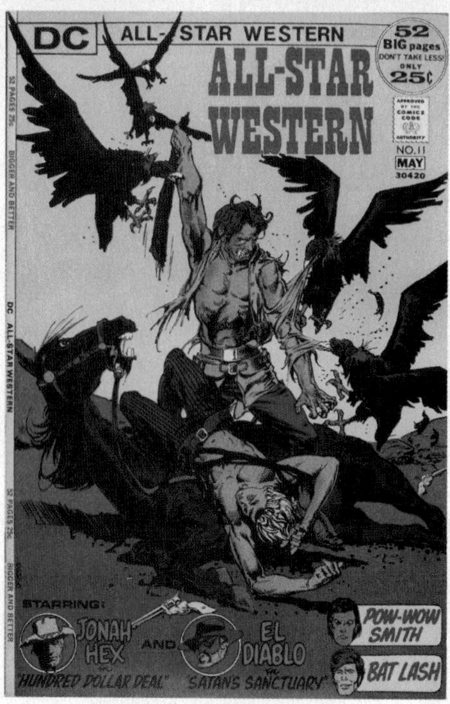

ALL STAR WESTERN #11
April-May 1972. © DC

GENE AUTRY COMICS #9
July 1943. © FAW

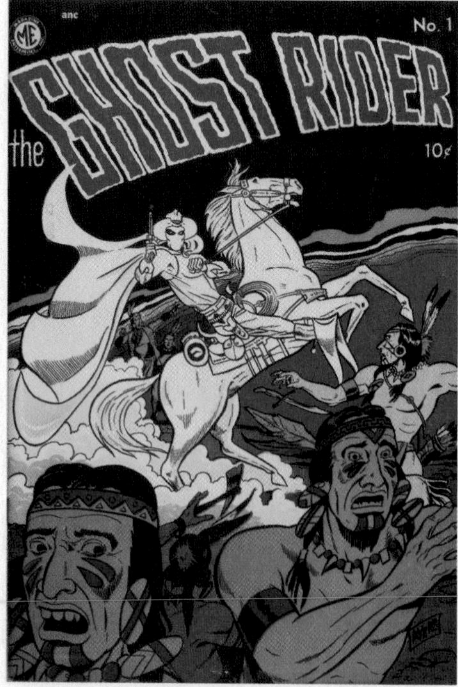

GHOST RIDER #1 (A-1 #27)
1959. © ME

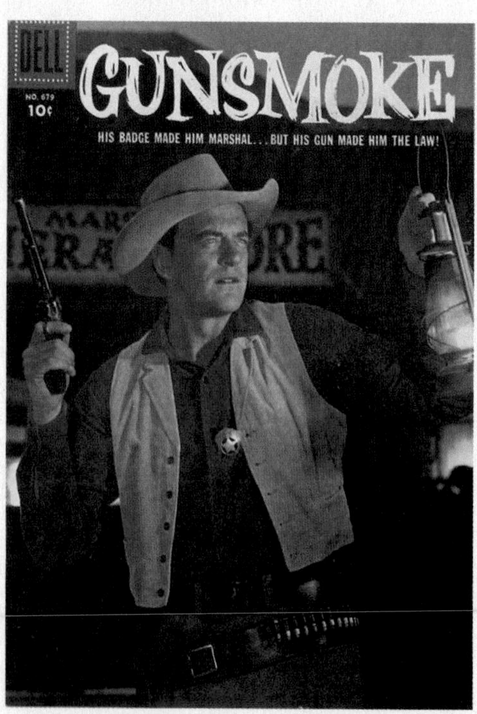

GUNSMOKE FOUR COLOR #679
February 1956. © CBS

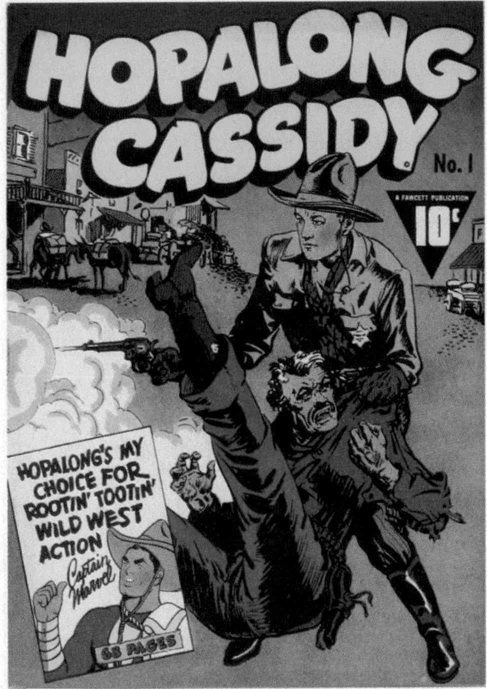

HOPALONG CASSIDY #1
February 1943. © FAW

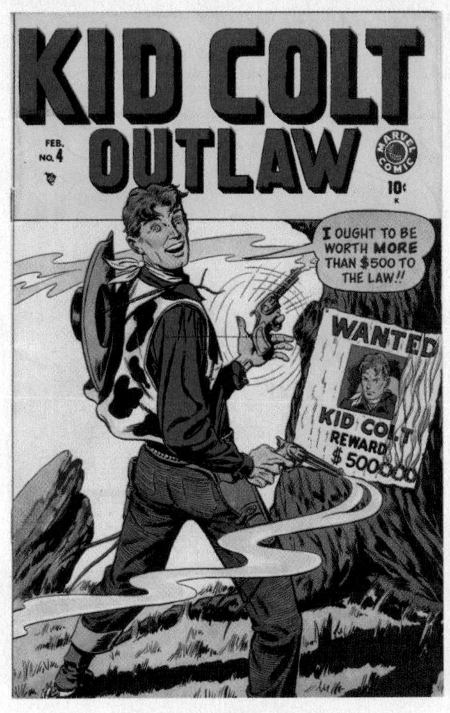

KID COLT OUTLAW #4
February 1949. © MAR

LONE RANGER #92
February 1956. © Lone Ranger Inc.

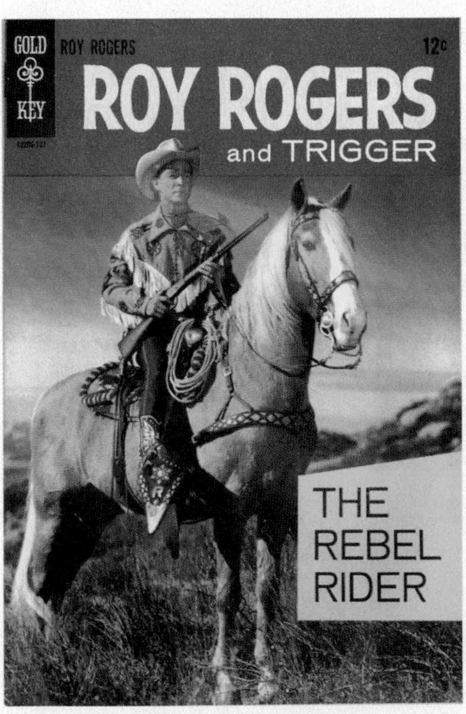

ROY ROGERS AND TRIGGER #1
July 1967. © GK

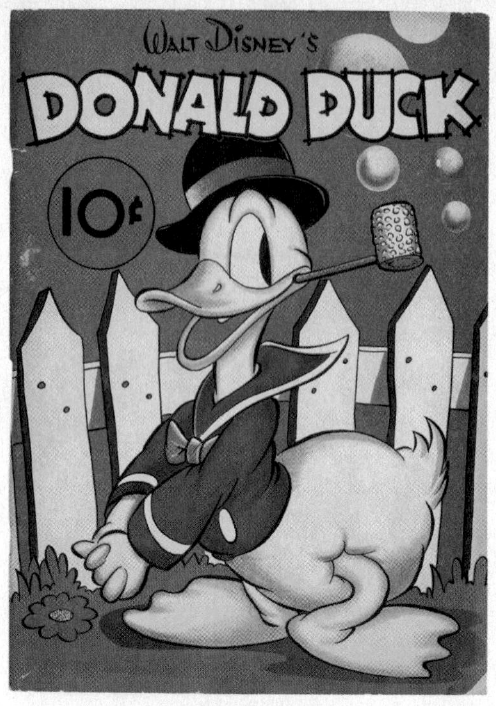

DONALD DUCK nn
1938. 1st Disney comic book. © DIS

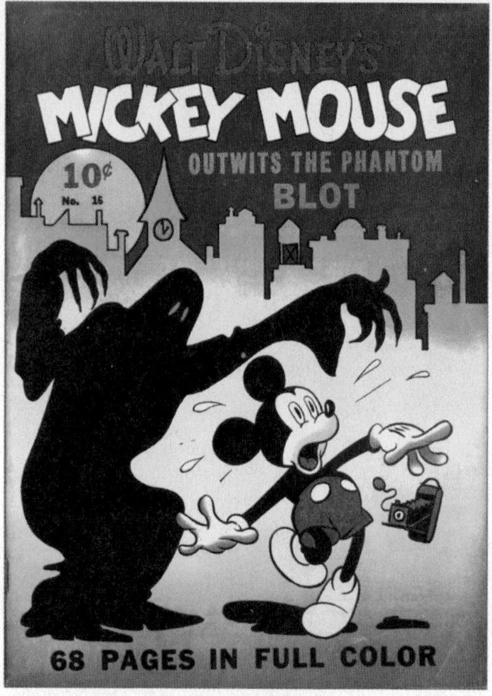

FOUR COLOR (SERIES 1) #16
1941. 1st Mickey Mouse comic book. © DIS

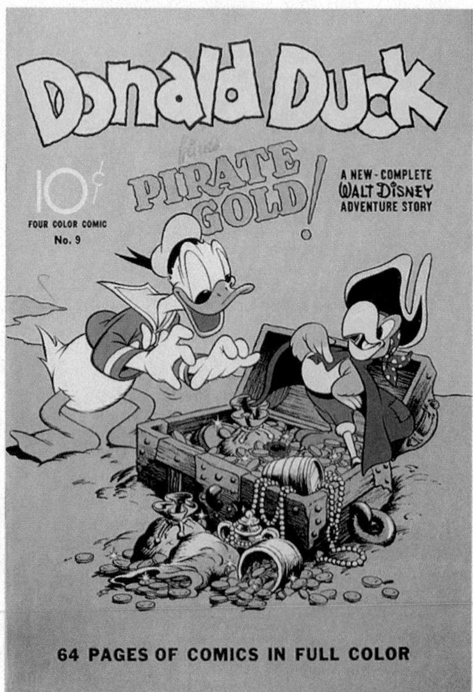

FOUR COLOR (SERIES 2) #9
August 1942. 1st Donald Duck art by Carl Barks. © DIS

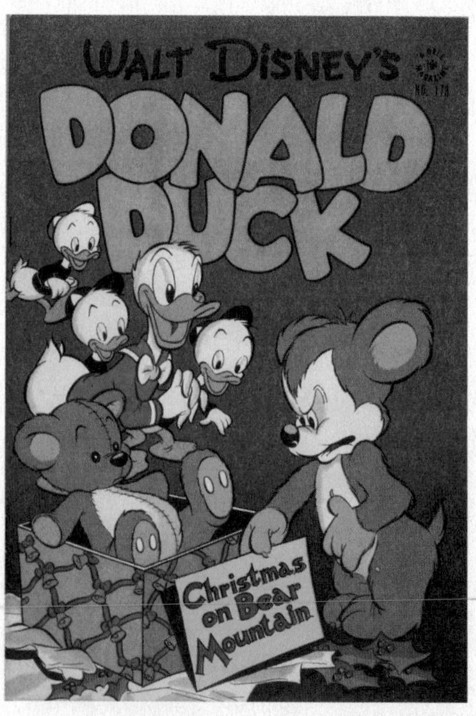

FOUR COLOR #178
December 1947. 1st app. Uncle Scrooge. © DIS

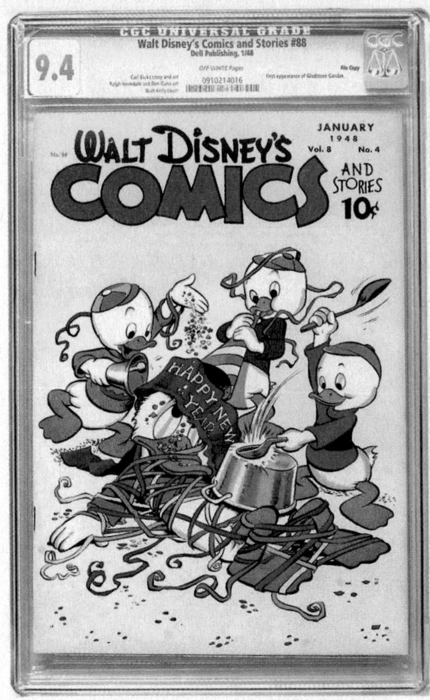

WALT DISNEY'S COMICS AND STORIES #88
January 1948. 1st app. Gladstone Gander. © DIS

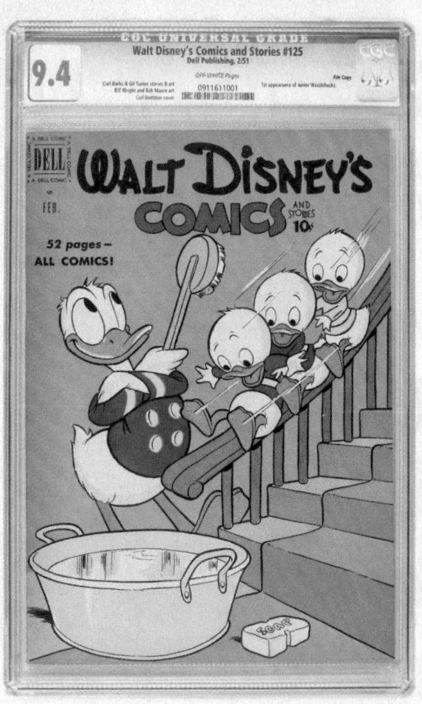

WALT DISNEY'S COMICS AND STORIES #125
February 1951. 1st app. Junior Woodchucks. © DIS

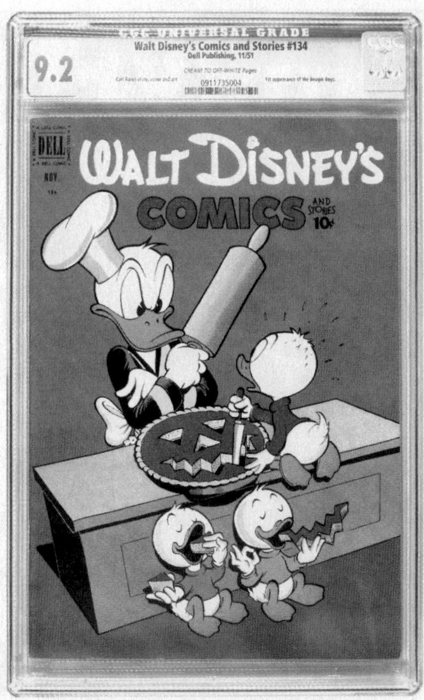

WALT DISNEY'S COMICS AND STORIES #134
November 1951. 1st app. Beagle Boys. © DIS

WALT DISNEY'S COMICS AND STORIES #140
May 1952. 1st app. Gyro Gearloose. © DIS

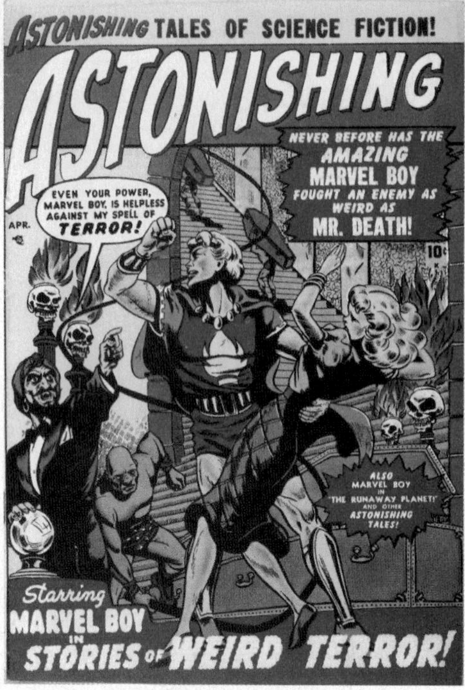

ASTONISHING #3
April 1951. © MAR

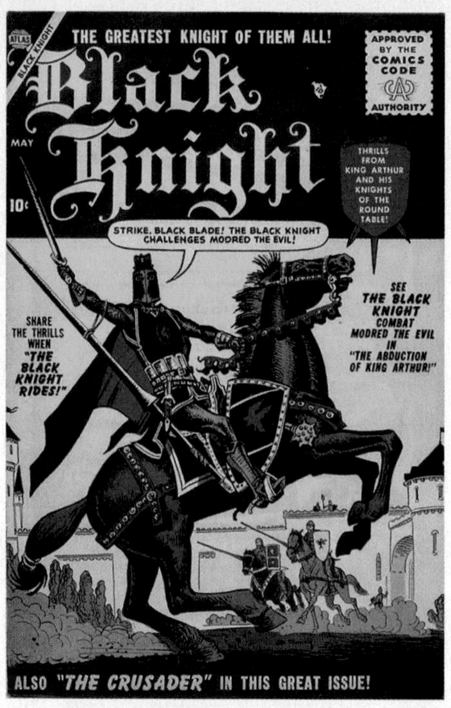

BLACK KNIGHT #1
May 1955. © MAR

JANN OF THE JUNGLE #10
March 1956. © MAR

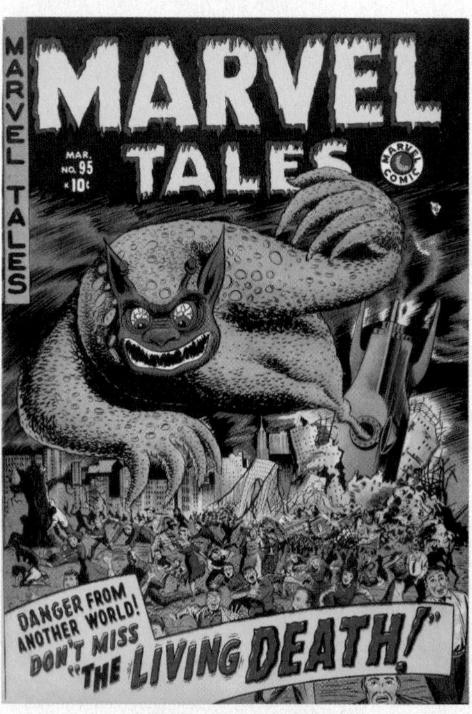

MARVEL TALES #95
March 1950. © MAR

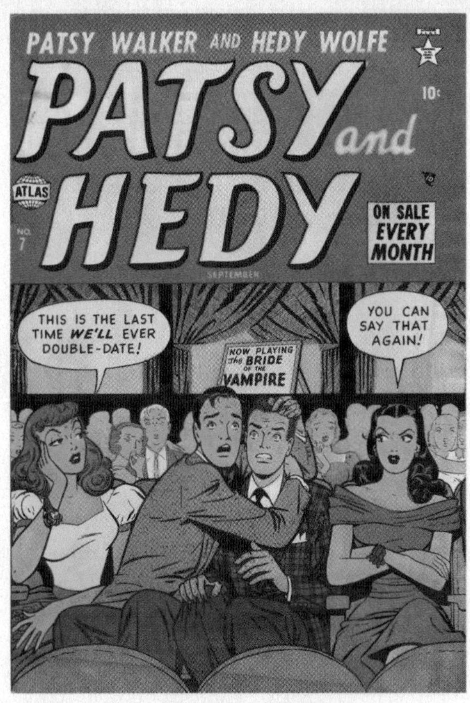

PATSY AND HEDY #7
September 1952. © MAR

UNCANNY TALES #1
June 1952. © MAR

VENUS #10
July 1950. © MAR

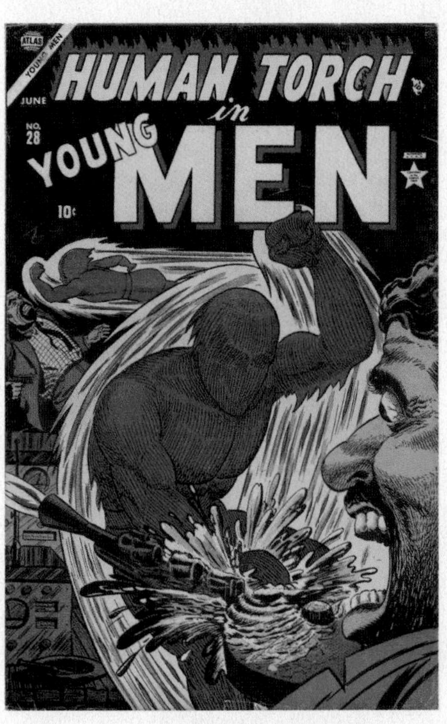

YOUNG MEN #28
June 1954. © MAR

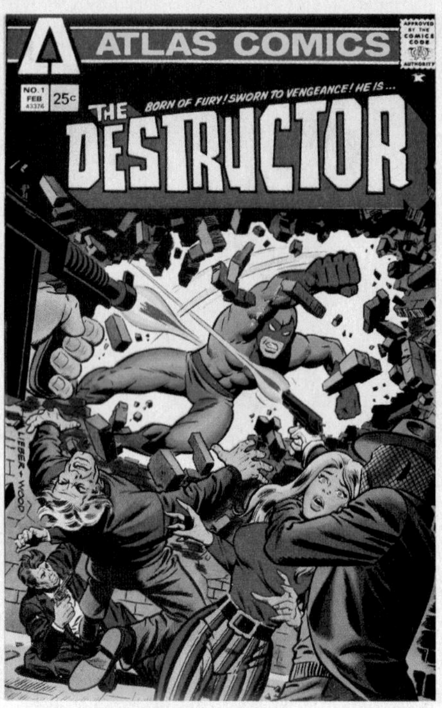

THE DESTRUCTOR #1
February 1975. © A-S

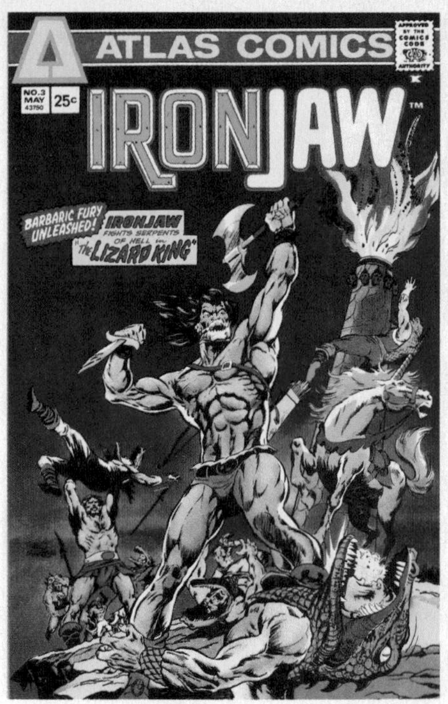

IRONJAW #3
May 1975. © A-S

PLANET OF VAMPIRES #1
February 1975. © A-S

THE SCORPION #1
February 1975. © A-S

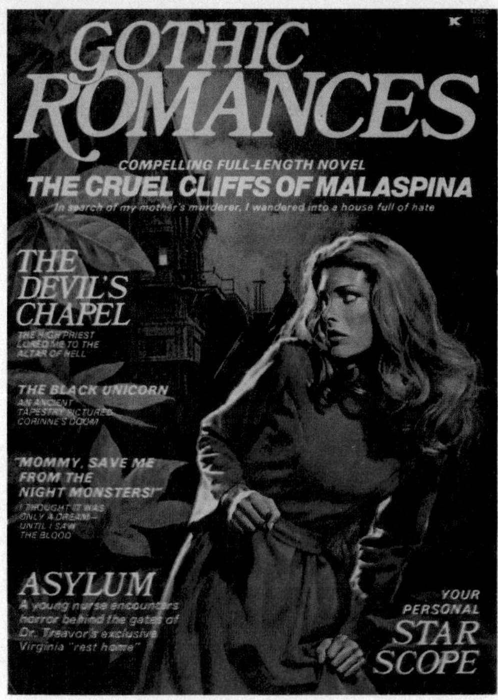

GOTHIC ROMANCES #1
December 1974. © A-S

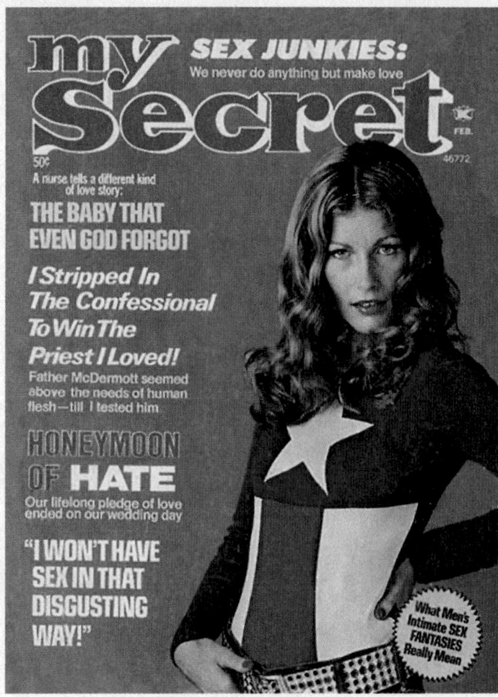

MY SECRETS #1
February 1975. © A-S

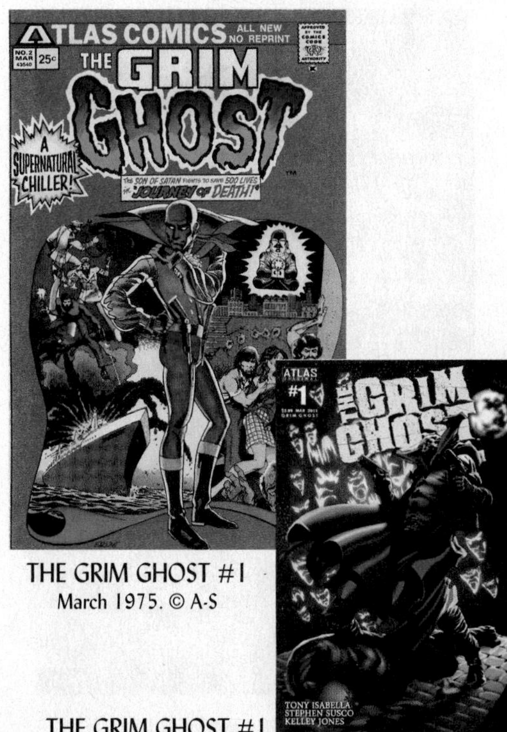

THE GRIM GHOST #1
March 1975. © A-S

THE GRIM GHOST #1
March 2011. © Nemesis, Ltd.

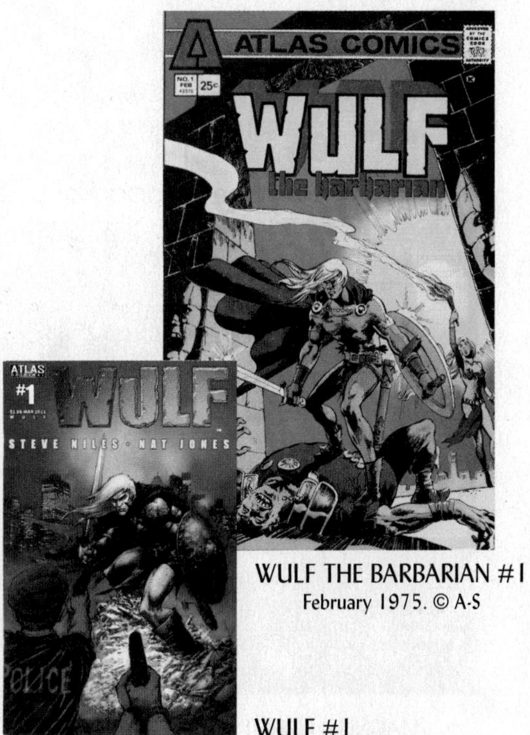

WULF THE BARBARIAN #1
February 1975. © A-S

WULF #1
March 2011. © Nemesis, Ltd.

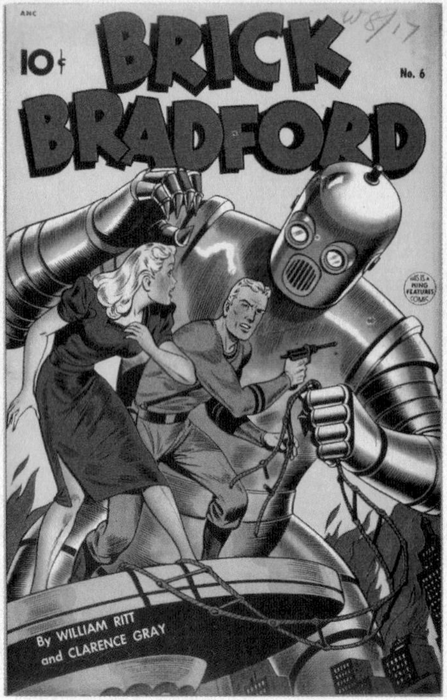

BRICK BRADFORD #6
October 1948. © STD

DESTINATION MOON
1950. © FAW

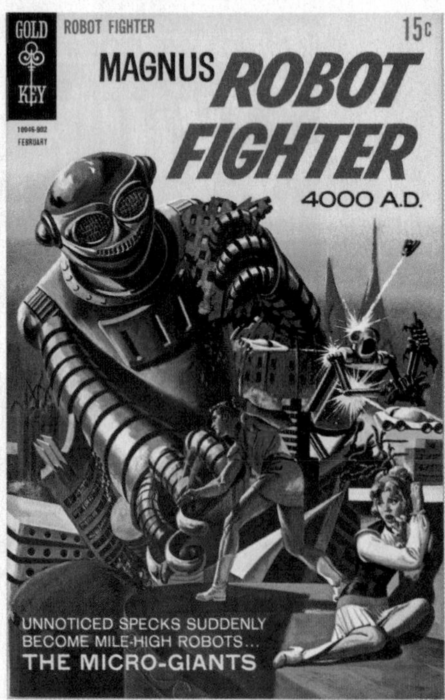

MAGNUS, ROBOT FIGHTER #25
February 1962. © RH

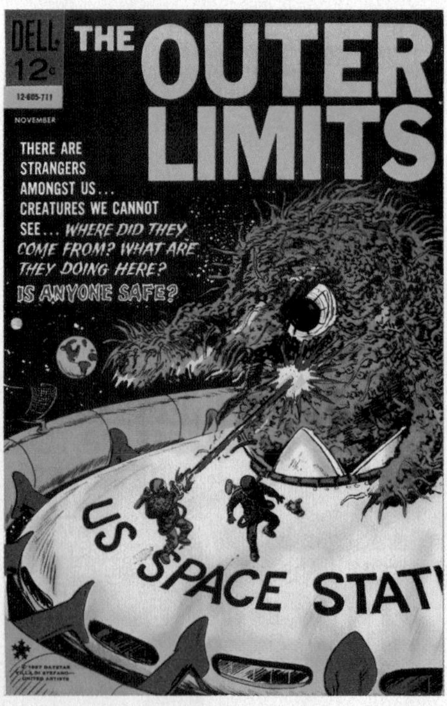

THE OUTER LIMITS #16
November 1967. © DELL

GALLERY

PLANET COMICS #36
May 1945. © FH

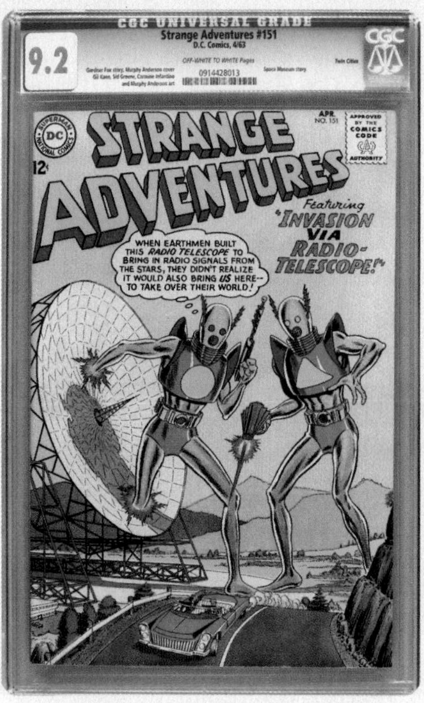

STRANGE ADVENTURES #151
May 1963. © DC

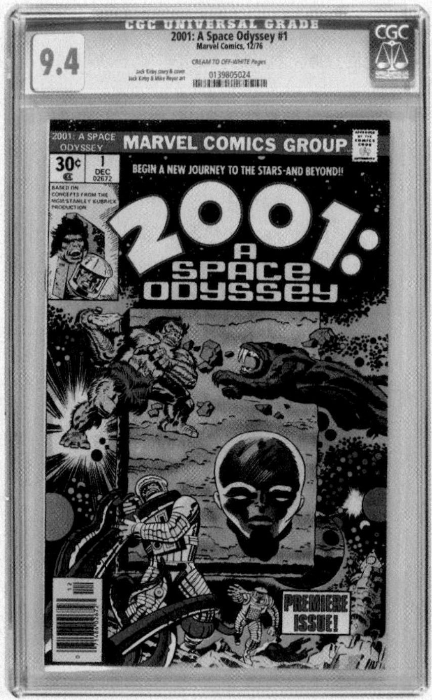

2001: A SPACE ODYSSEY #1
December 1976. © MGM

WEIRD SCIENCE #5
January-February 1951. © WMG

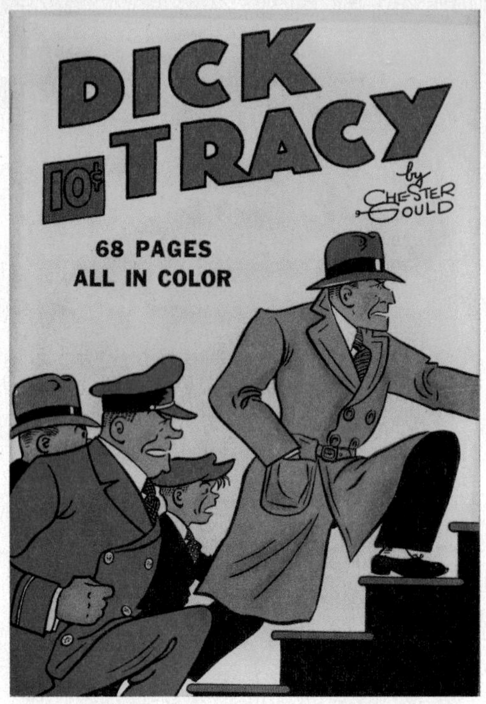

FOUR COLOR COMICS SERIES 1 #1
1939. © NYNS

FOUR COLOR COMICS #67
April 1945. © DIS

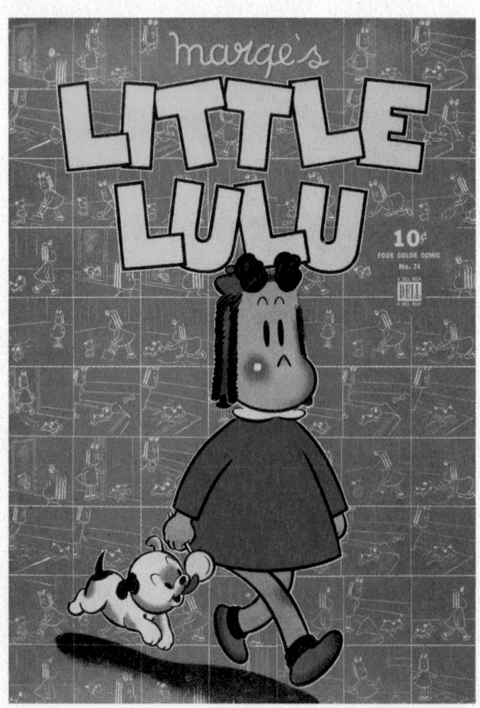

FOUR COLOR COMICS #74
June 1945. © M. Buell

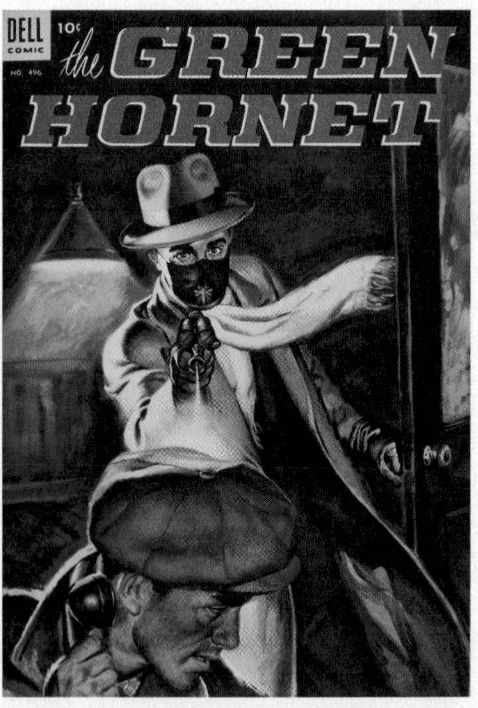

FOUR COLOR COMICS #496
September 1953. © DELL

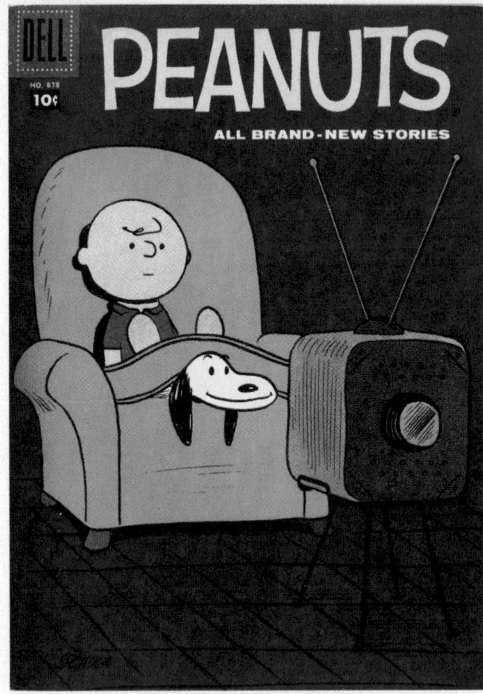

FOUR COLOR COMICS #878
February 1958. © UFS

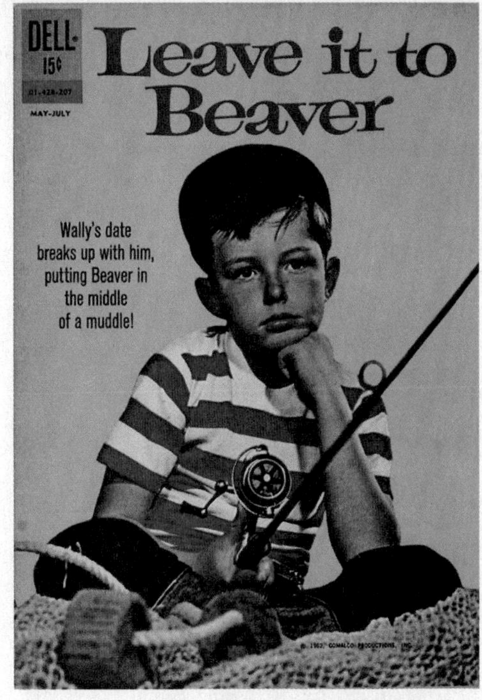

FOUR COLOR COMICS #912
June 1958. © Gomalco

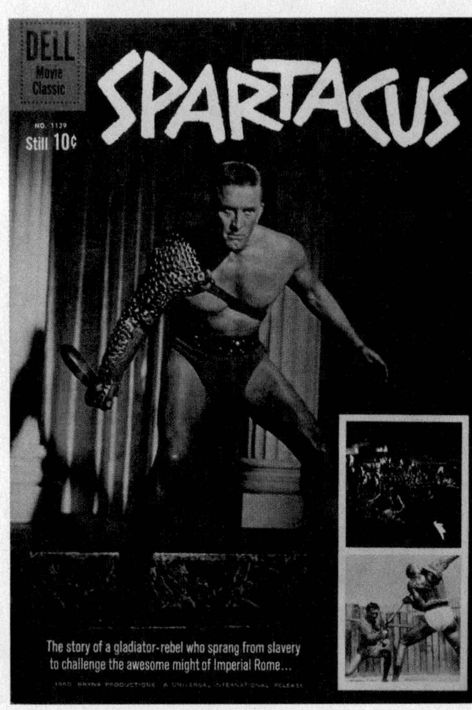

FOUR COLOR COMICS #1139
November 1960. © Brynn Prods.

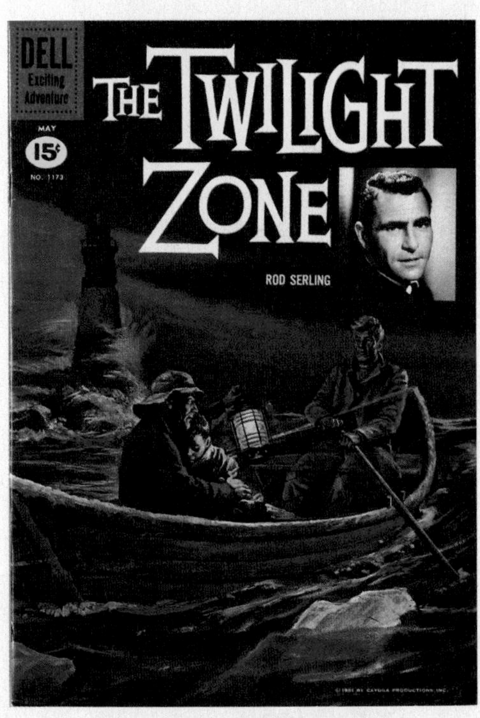

FOUR COLOR COMICS #1173
March-May 1961. © Cayuga Prods.

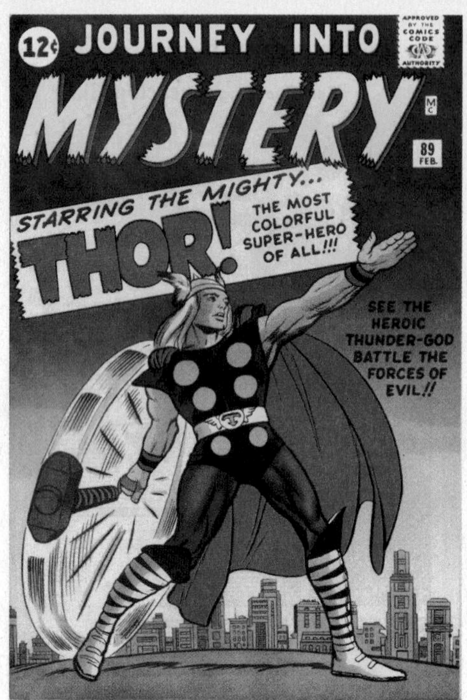

JOURNEY INTO MYSTERY #89
February 1963. © MAR

THOR #160
January 1969. © MAR

THOR ANNUAL #3
January 1971. © MAR

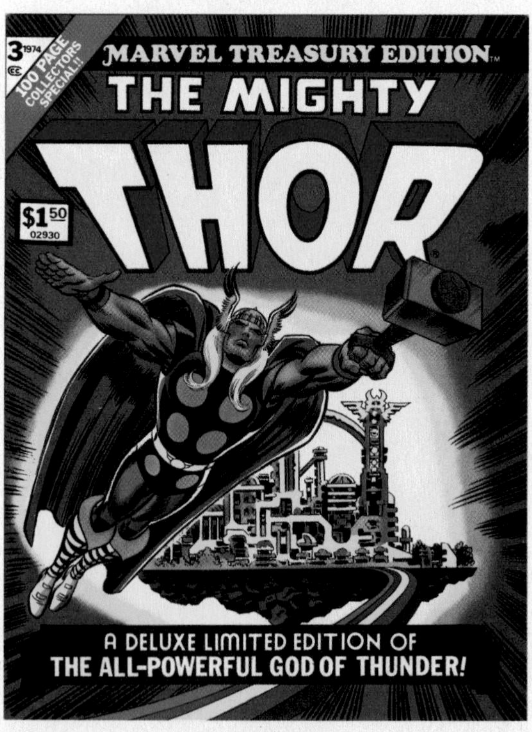

MARVEL TREASURY EDITION #3
1974. © MAR

THOR #264
October 1977. © MAR

THOR #390
April 1988. © MAR

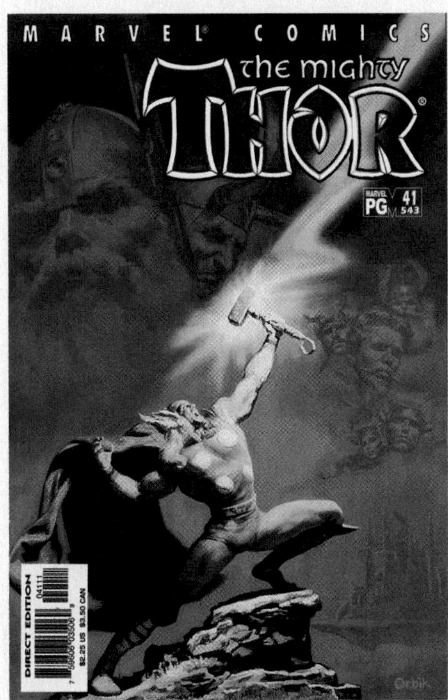

THOR Vol. 2 #41
November 2001. © MAR

THOR Vol. 3 #8
June 2008. © MAR

SHOWCASE #22
September-October 1959. © DC

GREEN LANTERN #18
January 1963. © DC

GREEN LANTERN #40
October 1965. © DC

GREEN LANTERN #77
June 1970. © DC

DC SPECIAL #17
Summer 1975. © DC

GREEN LANTERN #110
November 1978. © DC

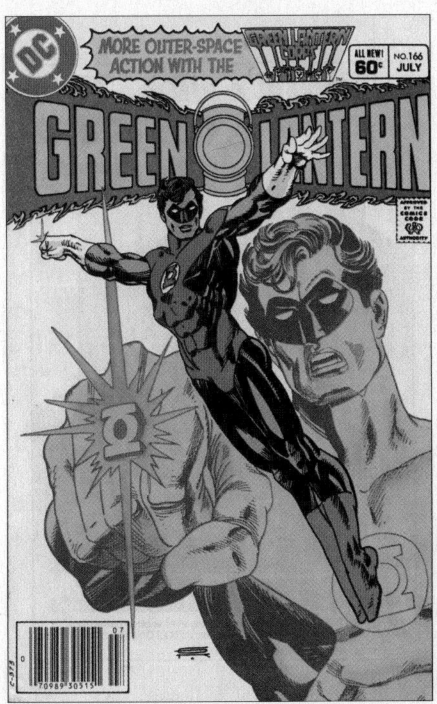

GREEN LANTERN #116
July 1983. © DC

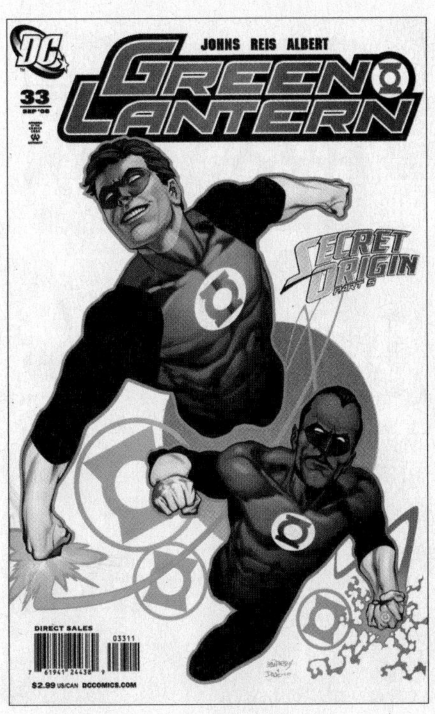

GREEN LANTERN #33
Fourth series. September 2008. © DC

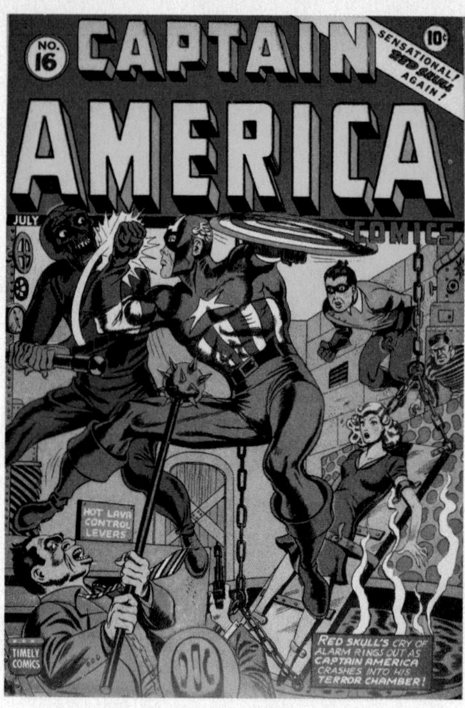

CAPTAIN AMERICA COMICS #16
July 1942. © MAR

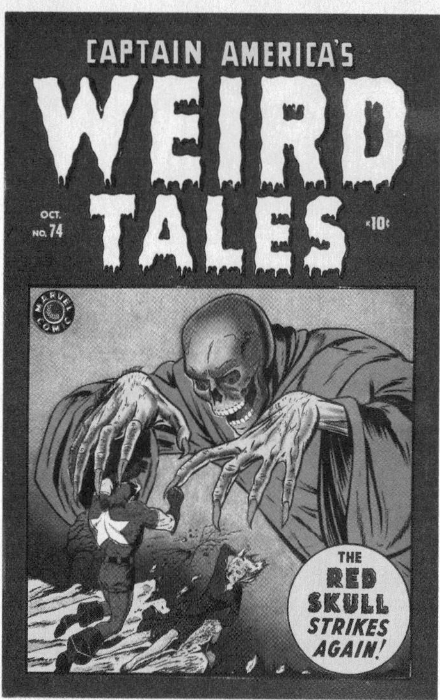

CAPTAIN AMERICA COMICS #74
October 1949. © MAR

TALES OF SUSPENSE #80
August 1966. © MAR

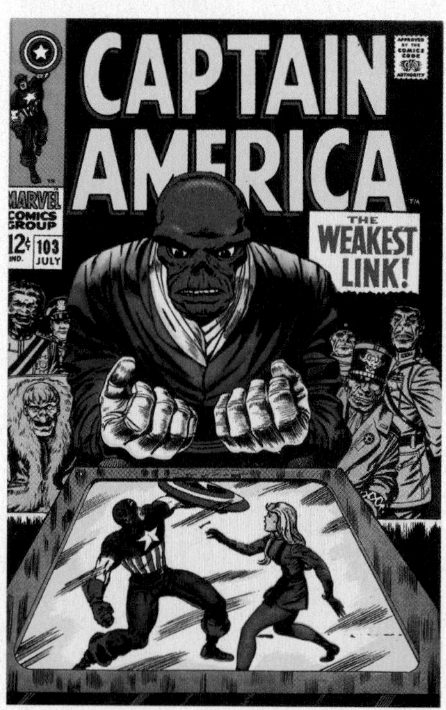

CAPTAIN AMERICA #103
July 1968. © MAR

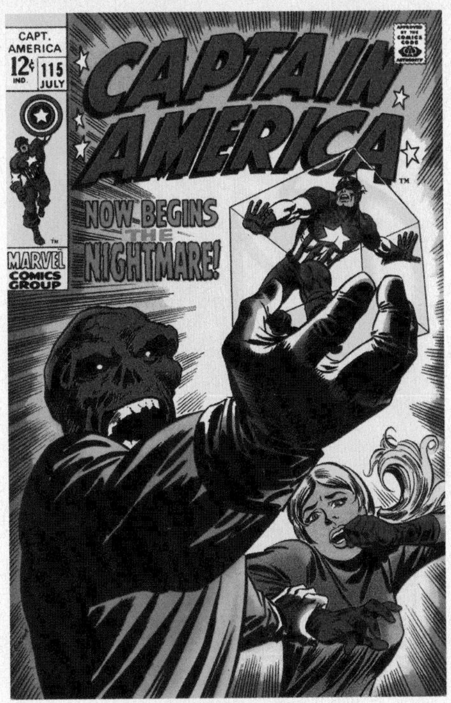

CAPTAIN AMERICA #115
July 1969. © MAR

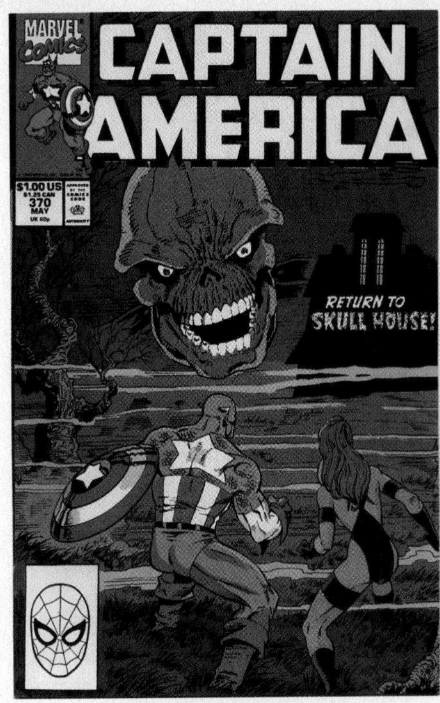

CAPTAIN AMERICA #370
May 1990. © MAR

CAPTAIN AMERICA #446
December 1995. © MAR

CAPTAIN AMERICA Vol. 5 #38
July 2008. © MAR

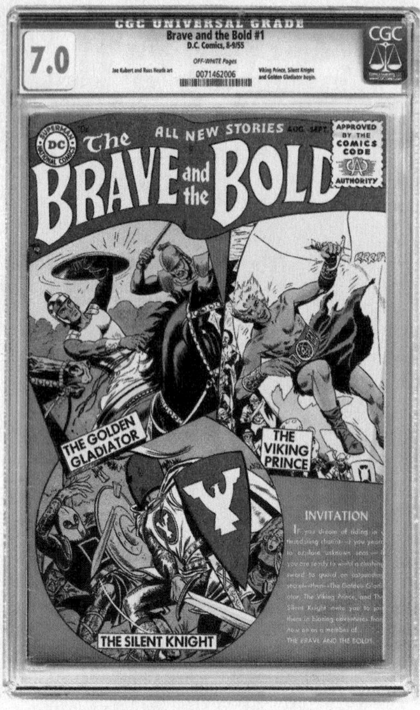

THE BRAVE AND THE BOLD #1
August-September 1955. © DC

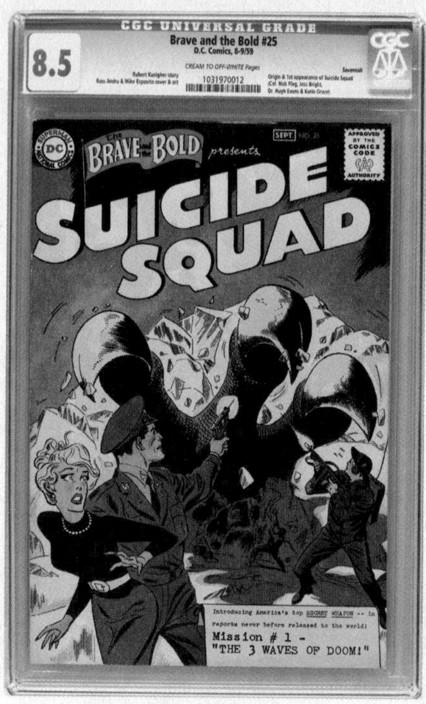

THE BRAVE AND THE BOLD #25
August-September 1959. © DC

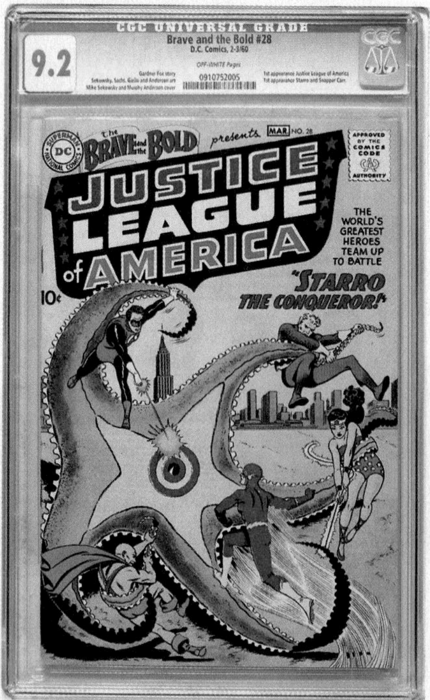

THE BRAVE AND THE BOLD #28
February-March 1960. © DC

THE BRAVE AND THE BOLD #54
June-July 1964. © DC

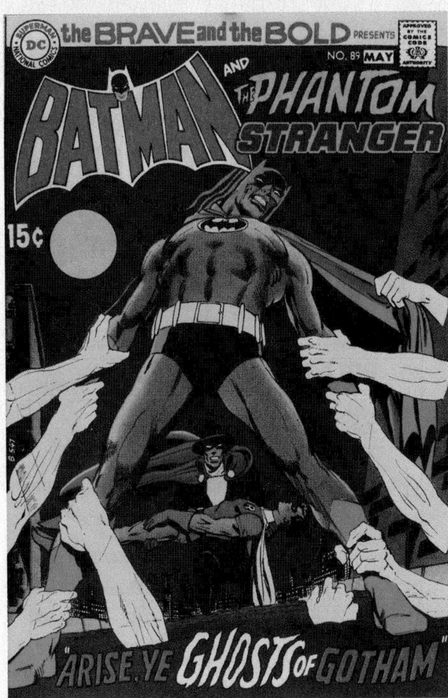

THE BRAVE AND THE BOLD #89
April-May 1970. © DC

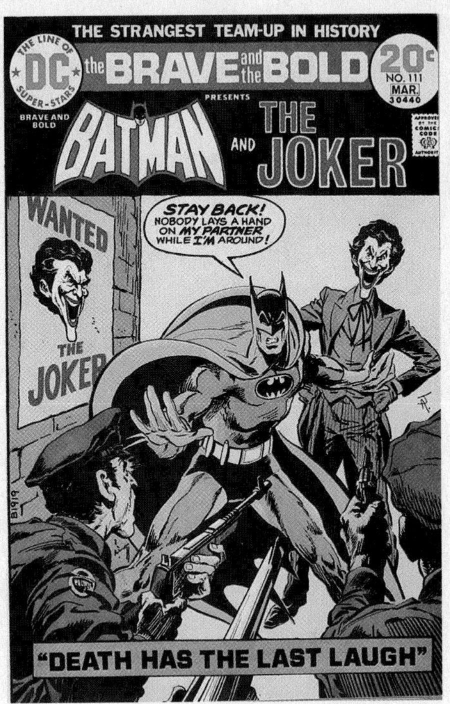

THE BRAVE AND THE BOLD #111
February-March 1974. © DC

THE BRAVE AND THE BOLD #162
May 1980. © DC

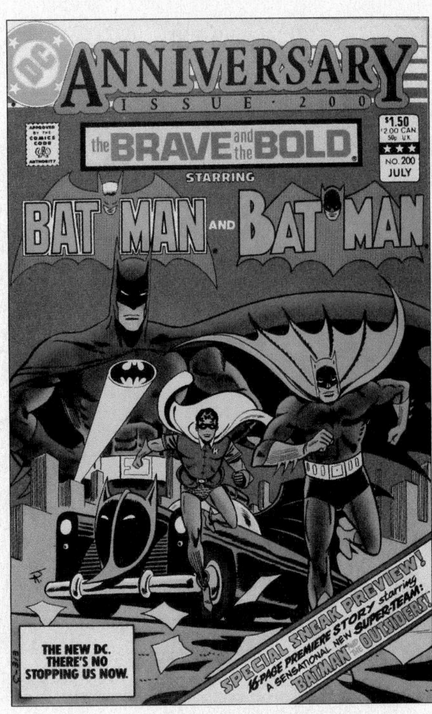

THE BRAVE AND THE BOLD #200
July 1983. © DC

SHOWCASE #17
November-December 1958. © DC

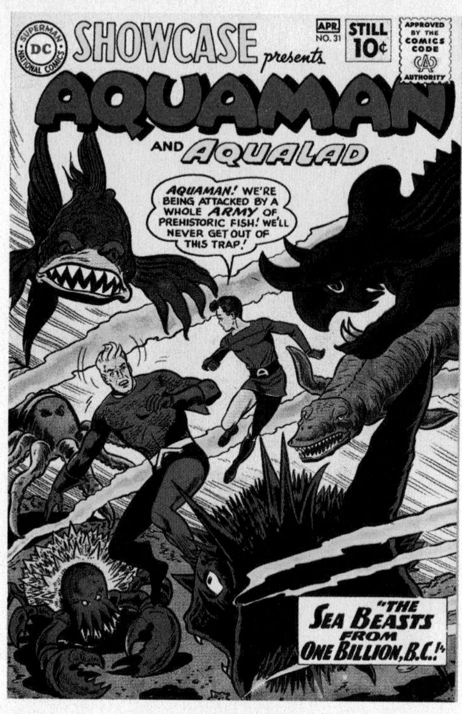

SHOWCASE #31
March-April 1961. © DC

SHOWCASE #36
January-February 1962. © DC

SHOWCASE #50
May-June 1964. © DC

SHOWCASE #62
May-June 1966. © DC

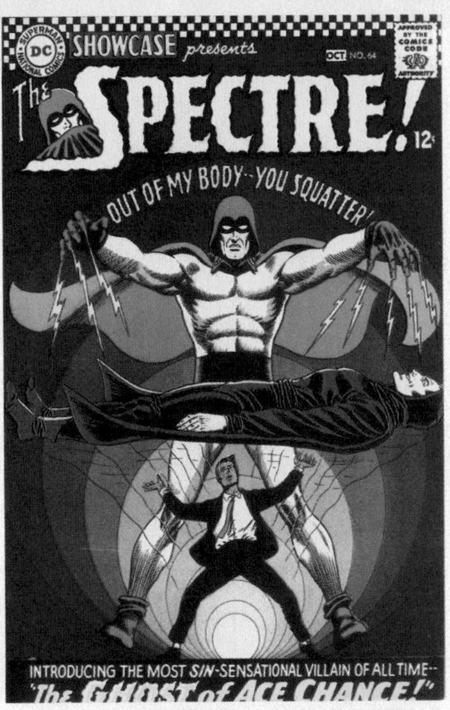

SHOWCASE #64
Setember-October 1966. © DC

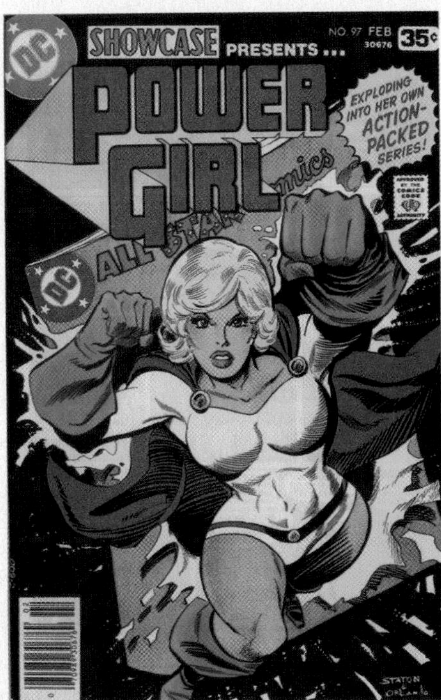

SHOWCASE #97
February 1978. © DC

SHOWCASE #100
May 1978. © DC

OVERSTREET ADVISORS

WELDON ADAMS
Comics Historian
Fort Worth, TX

GRANT ADEY
Fats Comics
Brisbane, QLD,
Australia

DAVID T. ALEXANDER
David Alexander Comics
Tampa, FL

TYLER ALEXANDER
David Alexander Comics
Tampa, FL

LON ALLEN
Heritage Comics Auctions
Dallas, TX

DAVE ANDERSON
Want List Comics
Tulsa, OK

STEPHEN BARRINGTON
Flea Market Comics
Chickasaw, AL

LAUREN BECKER
Warp 9 Comics
Clawson, MI

ROBERT BEERBOHM
Robert Beerbohm
Comic Art
Fremont, NE

JON BERK
Collector
Hartford, CT

JIM BERRY
Collector
Portland, OR

JON BEVANS
Diamond Int. Galleries
Timonium, MD

PETER BILELIS, ESQ.
Collector
South Windsor, CT

BRIAN BLOCK
WB Auction Services
Adamstown, PA

DR. ARNOLD T. BLUMBERG
Collector
Baltimore, MD

STEVE BOROCK
Heritage Comics Auctions
Dallas, TX

KEVIN BOYD
CGC Signature Series Director
Toronto, ONT Canada

MICHAEL BROWNING
Collector
Danville, WV

MICHAEL CARBONARO
Neatstuffcollectibles.com
Englewood, NJ

BRETT CARRERAS
Brett's Comic Pile
Richmond, VA

GARY CARTER
Collector
Coronado, CA

FRANK CWIKLIK
Metropolis Comics
New York, NY

JOHN CHRUSCINSKI
Tropic Comics
Lyndora, PA

GARY COLABUONO
Dealer/Collector
Arlington Heights, IL

BILL COLE
Bill Cole Enterprises, Inc.
Randolph, MA

TIM COLLINS
RTS Unlimited, Inc.
Lakewood, CO

ANDREW COOKE
Writer/Director
New York City, NY

JON B. COOKE
Editor - Comic Book
Artist Magazine
West Kingston, RI

JACK COPLEY
Coliseum of Comics
Florida

DAN CUSIMANO
Flying Donut Trading Co.
Reston, VA

OVERSTREET ADVISORS

GARY DOLGOFF
Gary Dolgoff Comics
Easthampton, MA

WALTER DURAJLIJA
Big B Comics
Hamilton, ONT
Canada

KEN DYBER
Collector
Portland, OR

BRUCE ELLSWORTH
Fats Comics
Brisbane, QLD, Australia

PETER DIXON
Paradise Comics
Toronto, ONT
Canada

CONRAD ESCHENBERG
Collector/Dealer
Cold Spring, NY

MICHAEL EURY
Author
Lake Oswego, OR

RICHARD EVANS
Bedrock City Comics
Houston, TX

D'ARCY FARRELL
Pendragon Comics
Toronto, ONT Canada

STEPHEN FISHLER
Metropolis Collectibles, Inc.
New York, NY

DAN FOGEL
Hippy Comix, Inc.
El Sobrante, CA

STEPHEN H. GENTNER
Golden Age Specialist
Portland, OR

STEVE GEPPI
Diamond Int. Galleries
Timonium, MD

MICHAEL GOLDMAN
Motor City Comics
Farmington Hills, MI

TOM GORDON III
ComicsPriceGuide.com
Hampstead, MD

JAMIE GRAHAM
Graham Crackers
Chicago, IL

DANIEL GREENHALGH
Showcase New England
Northford, CT

ERIC J. GROVES
Dealer/Collector
Oklahoma City, OK

JOHN HAINES
Dealer/Collector
Kirtland, OH

JIM HALPERIN
Heritage Comics
Auctions
Dallas, TX

JASON HAMLIN
Brett's Comic Pile
Richmond, VA

MARK HASPEL
Primary Grader
Certified Guaranty Co.,
LLC

JOHN HAUSER
Dealer/Collector
New Berlin, WI

JEF HINDS
Jef Hinds Comics
Madison, WI

GREG HOLLAND
Collector
Alexander, AR

JOHN HONE
Collector
Silver Spring, MD

BILL HUGHES
Dealer/Collector
Flower Mound, TX

ROB HUGHES
Arch Angels
Pacific Beach, CA

ED JASTER
Heritage Comics Auctions
Dallas, TX

BRIAN KETTERER
Collector
Philadelphia, PA

OVERSTREET ADVISORS

DENNIS KEUM
Fantasy Comics
Goldens Bridge, NY

PHIL LEVINE
Paperpeddler
Rare and Esoteric Comics and Collectibles
Three Bridges, NJ

PAUL LITCH
Modern Age Specialist
Certified Guaranty Co., LLC

TOMMY MALETTA
Best Comics International
New Hyde Park, NY

JOE MANNARINO
All Star Auctions
Ridgewood, NJ

NADIA MANNARINO
All Star Auctions
Ridgewood, NJ

HARRY MATETSKY
Collector
Middletown, NJ

DAVE MATTEINI
Collector
New York, NY

JON McCLURE
Comics Historian, Writer
Portland, OR

TODD MCDEVITT
New Dimension Comics
Cranberry Township, PA

MIKE McKENZIE
Alternate Worlds
Cockeysville, MD

FRED McSURLEY
Dealer/Collector
Holland, Ohio

PETER MEROLO
Collector
Sedona, AZ

JOHN JACKSON MILLER
Comics Historian, Writer
Waupaca, WI

BRENT MOESHLIN
Quality Comix
Montgomery, AL

STEVE MORTENSEN
Miracle Comics
Santa Clara, CA

MICHAEL NAIMAN
Silver Age Specialist
Chapel Hill, NC

MARC NATHAN
Cards, Comics & Collectibles
Reisterstown, MD

JOSHUA NATHANSON
ComicLink
Brooklyn, NY

MATT NELSON
Classics Incorporated
Carrolltown, TX

JAMIE NEWBOLD
Southern California Comics
San Diego, CA

CHARLIE NOVINSKIE
Silver Age Specialist
Lake Havasu City, AZ

RICHARD OLSON
Collector/Academician
Poplarville, MS

TERRY O'NEILL
Terry's Comics
Orange, CA

JIM PAYETTE
Golden Age Specialist
Bethlehem, NH

JOHN PETTY
Collector/Historian
Coram, NY

JIM PITTS
Avalon Collectibles
Mountain View, CA

BILL PONSETI
Collector
Philadelphia, PA

RON PUSSELL
Redbeard's Book Den
Crystal Bay, NV

JEFF RADER
Paperpeddler
Rare and Esoteric Comics and Collectibles
Lake Havasu, AZ

GREG REECE
Greg Reece's Rare Comics
Ijamsville, MD

OVERSTREET ADVISORS

STEPHEN RITTER
Collector
Beavercreek, OH

DAVE ROBIE
Big Little Books
Specialist
Lancaster, PA

ROBERT ROGOVIN
Four Color Comics
Scarsdale, NY

MARNIN ROSENBERG
Collectors Assemble
Great Neck, NY

CHUCK ROZANSKI
Mile High Comics
Denver, CO

BARRY SANDOVAL
Heritage Comics Auctions
Dallas, TX

BUDDY SAUNDERS
Lone Star Comics
Arlington, TX

CONAN SAUNDERS
Lone Star Comics
Arlington, TX

MATT SCHIFFMAN
Bronze Age Specialist
Bend, OR

DOUG SCHMELL
Pedigree Comics, Inc.
Wellington, FL

DOUG SIMPSON
Paradise Comics
Toronto, ONT Canada

BEN SMITH
ComicConnect
New York, NY

MARK SQUIREK
Collector
Timonium, MD

TONY STARKS
Silver Age Specialist
Evansville, IN

AL STOLTZ
Basement Comics
Havre de Grace, MD

KEN STRIBLING
Action Island
Jackson, MS

DOUG SULIPA
"Everything 1960-1996"
Manitoba, Canada

CHRIS SWARTZ
Collector
San Diego, CA

MAGGIE THOMPSON
Comics Buyer's Guide
Iola, WI

MICHAEL TIERNEY
The Comic Book Store
Little Rock, AR

TED VAN LIEW
Superworld Comics
Worcester, MA

JOE VERENEAULT
JHV Associates
Woodbury Heights, NJ

BOB WAYNE
DC Comics
New York City, NY

LON WEBB
Dark Adventure Comics
Norcross, GA

RICK WHITELOCK
New Force Comics
Lynn Haven, FL

MIKE WILBUR
Diamond Int. Galleries
Timonium, MD

MARK WILSON
PGC Mint
Castle Rock, WA

ALEX WINTER
Hake's Americana
York, PA

HARLEY YEE
Dealer/Collector
Detroit, MI

MARK ZAID
EsquireComics.com
Bethesda, MD

VINCENT ZURZOLO, JR.
Metropolis Collectibles, Inc.
New York, NY

OVERSTREET PRICE GUIDE BACK ISSUES

The Overstreet® Comic Book Price Guide has held the record for being the longest running annual comic book publication. We are now celebrating our 41st anniversary, and the demand for the Overstreet® price guides is very strong. Collectors have created a legitimate market for them, and they continue to bring record prices each year. Collectors also have a record of comic book prices going back further than any other source in comic fandom. The prices listed below are for NM condition only, with GD-25% and FN-50% of the NM value. Canadian editions exist for a couple of the early issues. Abbreviations: SC-softcover, HC-hardcover, L-leather bound.

1970

#1 White SC
$1825.00

1970

#1 Blue SC
(2nd Printing)
$1550.00

1972

#2 SC $650.00
#2 HC $1100.00

1973

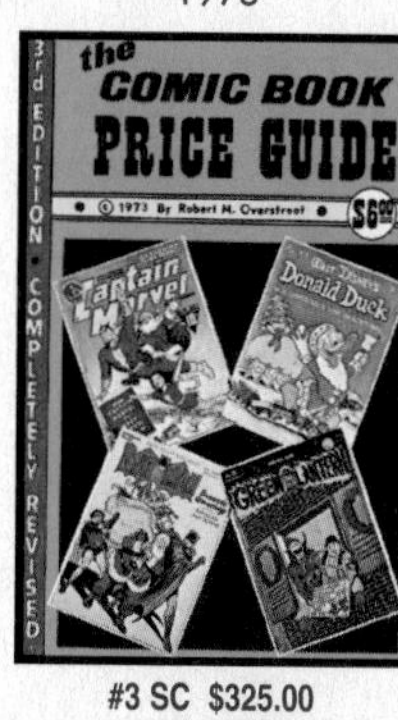

#3 SC $325.00
#3 HC $950.00

1974

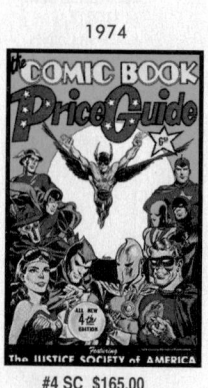

#4 SC $165.00
#4 HC $475.00

1975

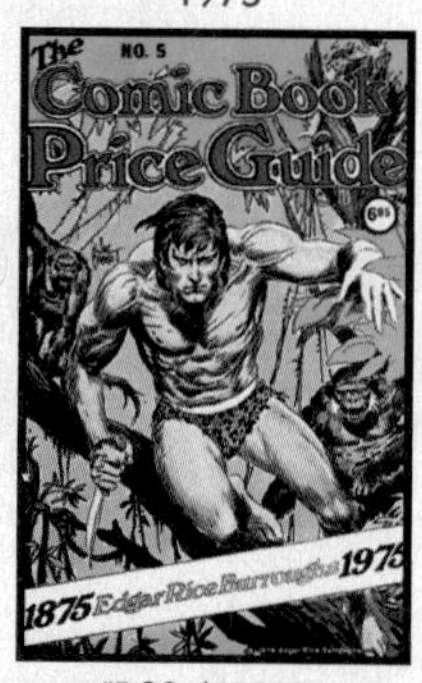

#5 SC $155.00
#5 HC $260.00

1976

#6 SC $105.00
#6 HC $155.00

1977

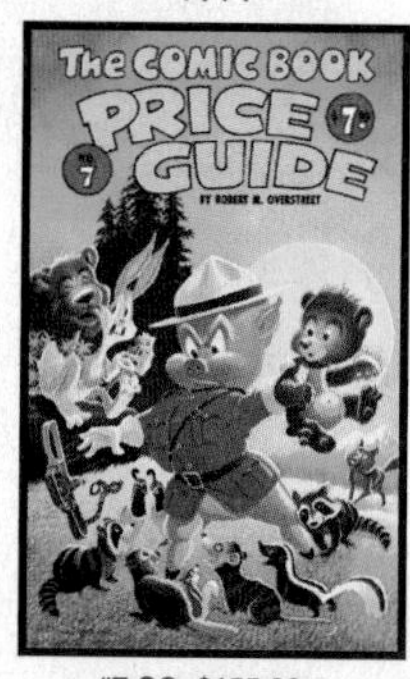

#7 SC $155.00
#7 HC $230.00

1978

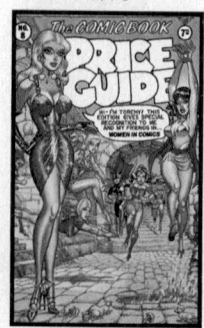

#8 SC $130.00
#8 HC $180.00

1979

#9 SC $130.00
#9 HC $180.00

1980

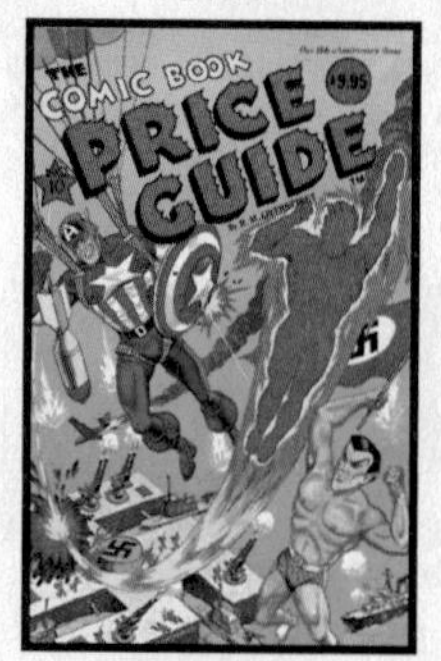

#10 SC $140.00
#10 HC $190.00

1981

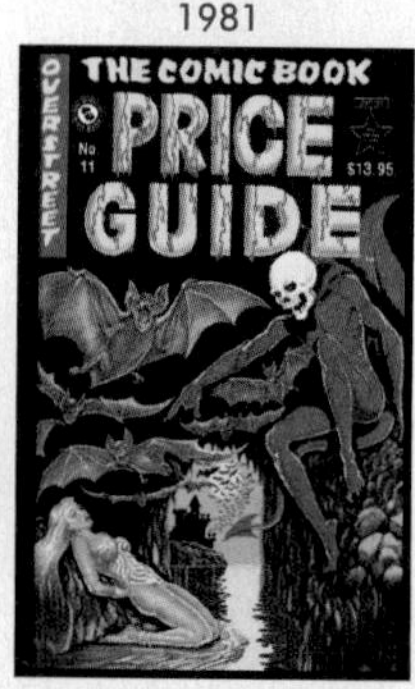

#11 SC $85.00
#11 HC $115.00

1982

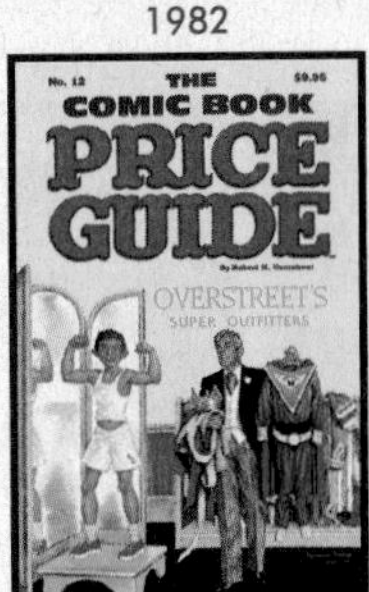

#12 SC $85.00
#12 HC $115.00

1983

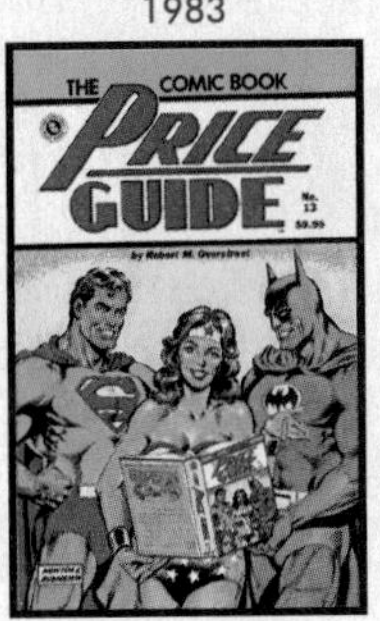

#13 SC $85.00
#13 HC $115.00

1984

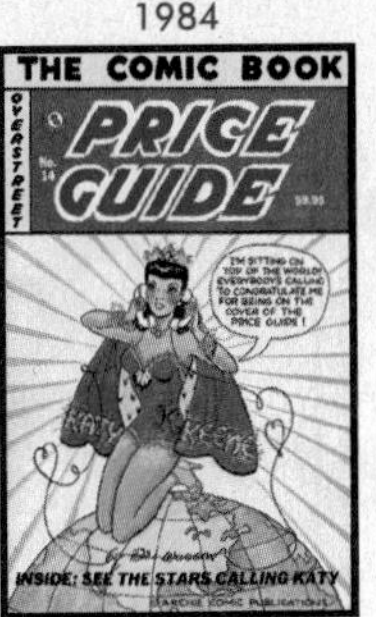

#14 SC $55.00
#14 HC $110.00
#14 L $170.00

1985

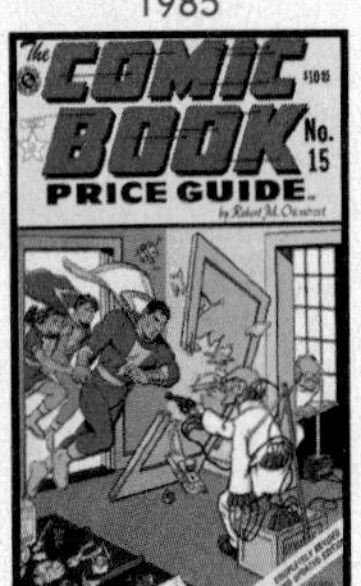

#15 SC $55.00
#15 HC $80.00
#15 L $160.00

1986

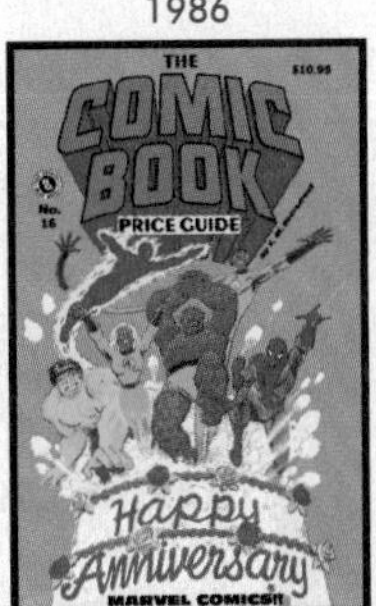

#16 SC $60.00
#16 HC $85.00
#16 L $170.00

1987

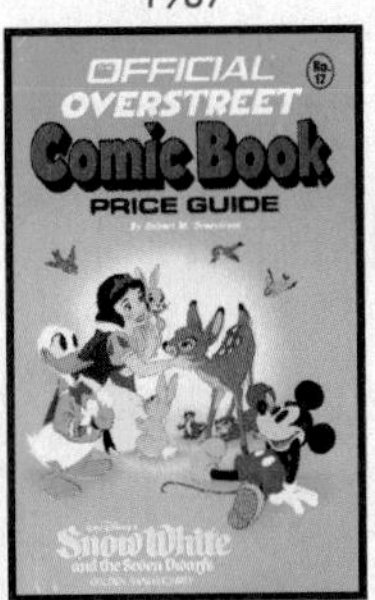

#17 SC $55.00
#17 HC $110.00
#17 L $160.00

1988

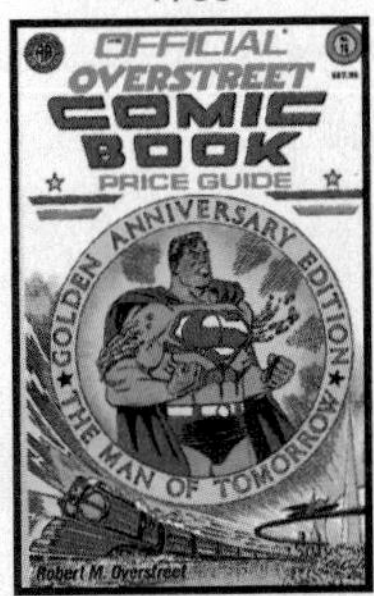

#18 SC $45.00
#18 HC $65.00
#18 L $160.00

1989

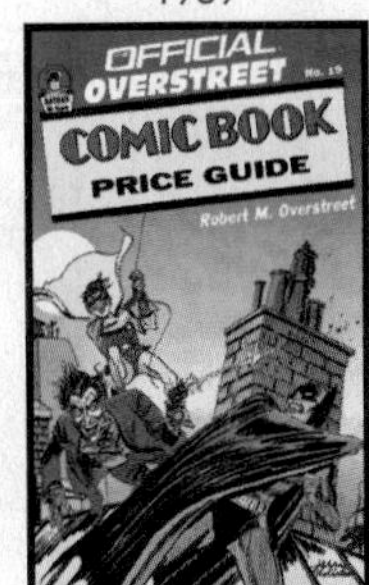

#19 SC $50.00
#19 HC $60.00
#19 L $170.00

1990

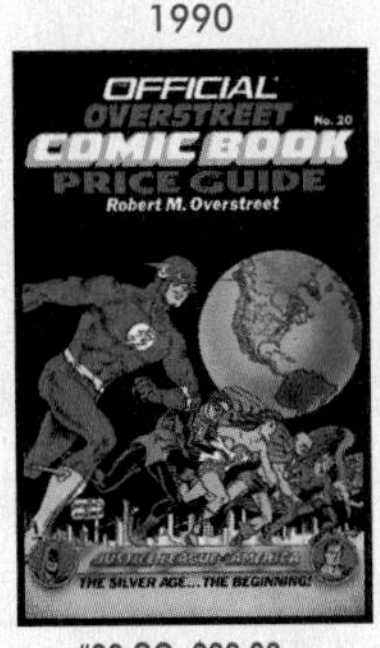

#20 SC $32.00
#20 HC $50.00
#20 L $135.00

1991

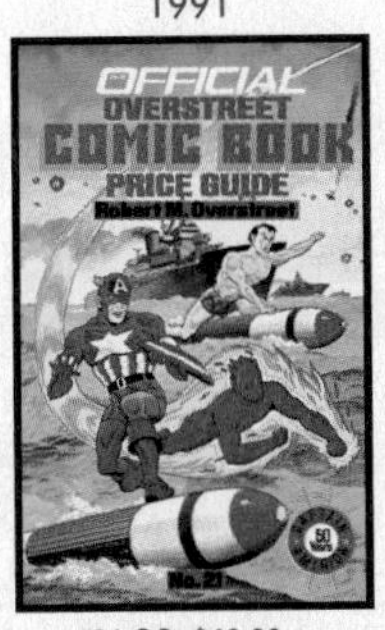

#21 SC $40.00
#21 HC $60.00
#21 L $145.00

1992

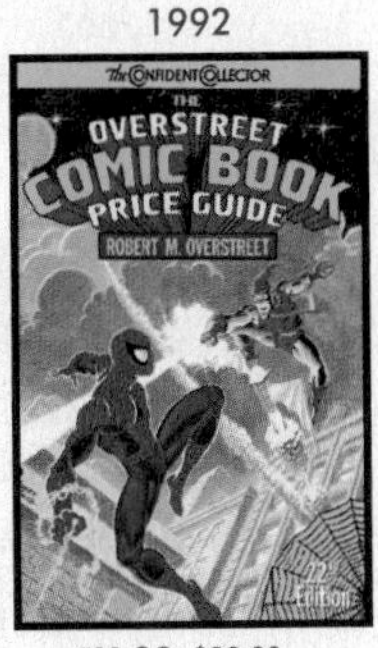

#22 SC $32.00
#22 HC $50.00

1993

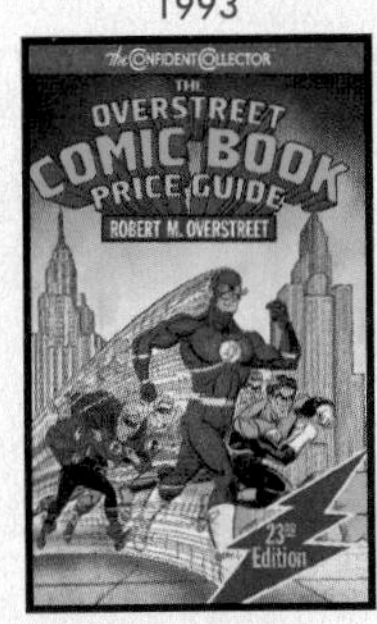

#23 SC $32.00
#23 HC $50.00

1994

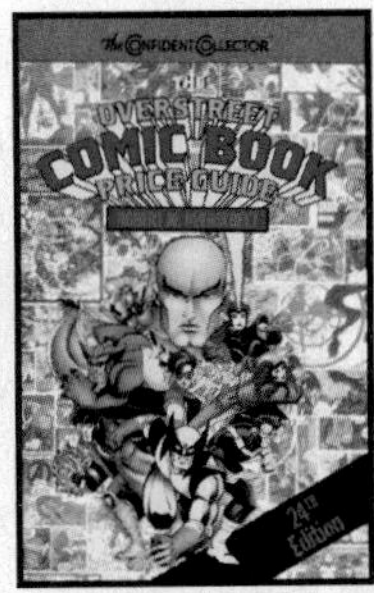

#24 SC $26.00
#24 HC $36.00

1995

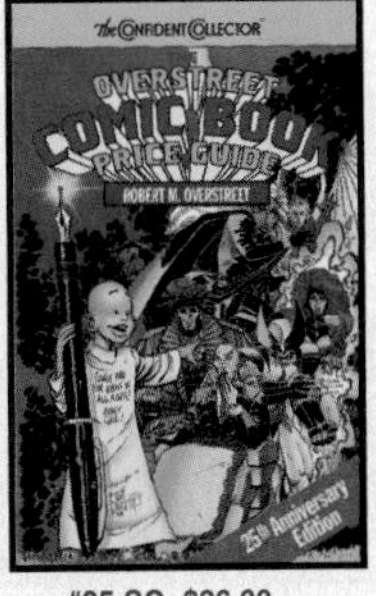

#25 SC $26.00
#25 HC $36.00
#25 L $110.00

1996

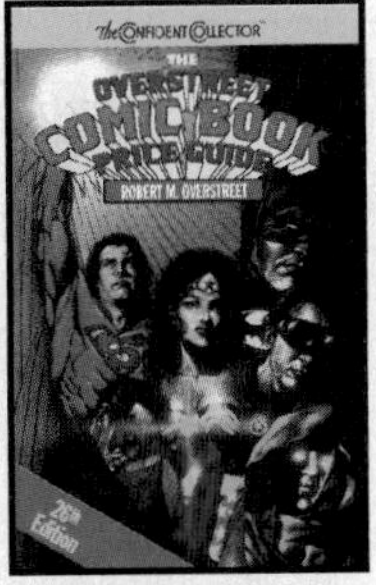

#26 SC $20.00
#26 HC $30.00
#26 L $100.00

1997

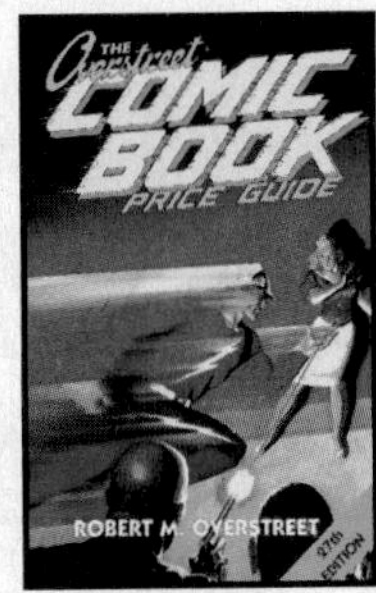

#27 SC $22.00
#27 HC $38.00
#27 L $125.00

1997

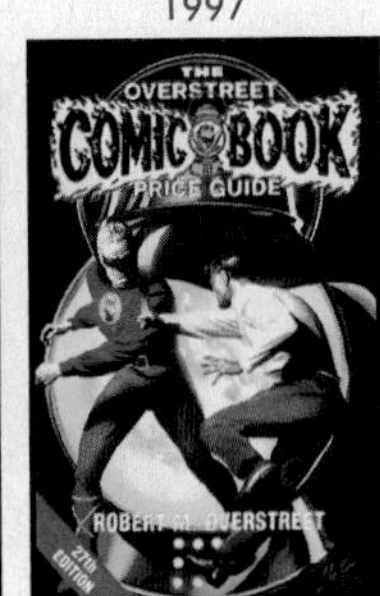

#27 SC $22.00
#27 HC $38.00
#27 L $125.00

1998

#28 SC $20.00
#28 HC $35.00

1998

#28 SC $20.00
#28 HC $35.00

1999

#29 SC $25.00
#29 HC $40.00

1999

#29 SC $20.00
#29 HC $37.00

2000

#30 SC $22.00
#30 HC $32.00

2000

#30 SC $22.00
#30 HC $32.00

2001

#31 SC $22.00
#31 HC $32.00

2001

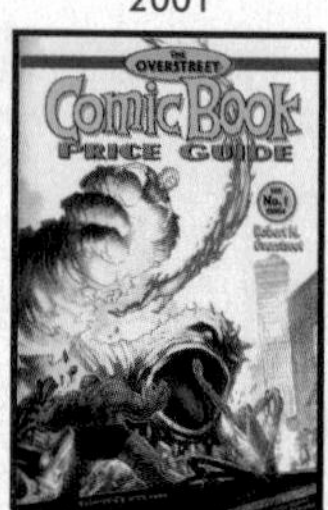

#31 SC $22.00
#31 HC $32.00

2001

#31 Bookstore Ed.
SC only $22.00

2002

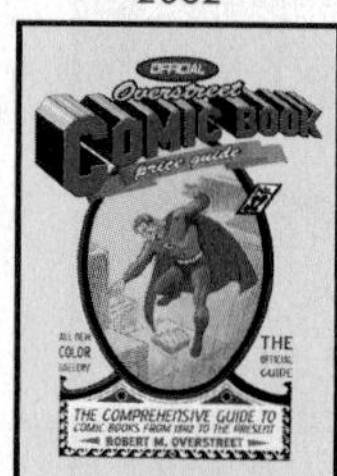

#32 SC $22.00
#32 HC $32.00

2002

#32 SC $22.00
#32 HC $32.00

2002

#32 Bookstore Ed.
SC only $22.00

2003

#33 SC $25.00
#33 HC $32.00

2003

#33 SC $25.00
#33 HC $32.00

2003

#33 Bookstore Ed.
SC only $25.00

2004

#34 SC $25.00
#34 HC $32.00

2004

#34 SC $25.00
#34 HC $32.00

2004

#34 Bookstore Ed.
SC only $25.00

2005

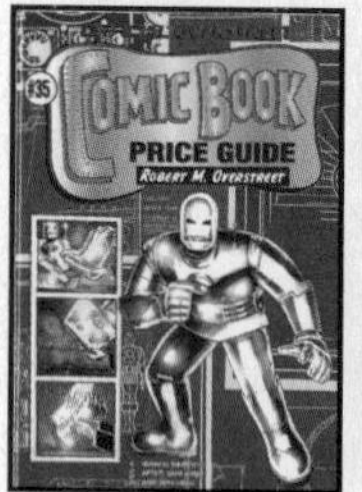

#35 SC $25.00
#35 HC $32.00

2005

Comic Book PRICE GUIDE

#35 SC $25.00
#35 HC $55.00

2005

#35 Bookstore Ed.
SC only $25.00

2006

#36 SC $25.00
#36 HC $32.00

2006

#36 SC $25.00
#36 HC $32.00

2006

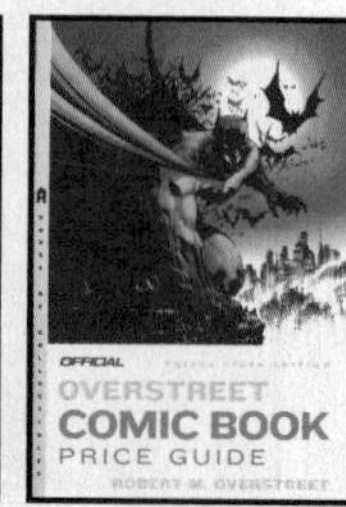

#36 Bookstore Ed.
SC only $25.00

2007

#37 SC $30.00
#37 HC $35.00

2007

#37 SC $30.00
#37 HC $35.00

2007

#37 Bookstore Ed.
SC only $30.00

2008

#38 SC $30.00
#38 HC $35.00

2008

#38 SC $30.00
#38 HC $35.00

2008

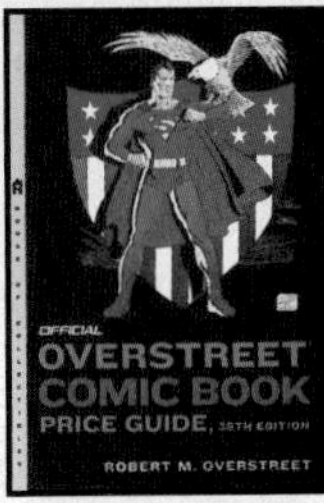

#38 Bookstore Ed.
SC only $30.00

2009

#39 SC $30.00
#39 HC $35.00

2009

#39 SC $30.00
#39 HC $35.00

2009

#39 Bookstore Ed.
SC only $30.00

2010

#40 SC $30.00
#40 HC $35.00

2010

#40 SC $30.00
#40 HC $35.00

2010

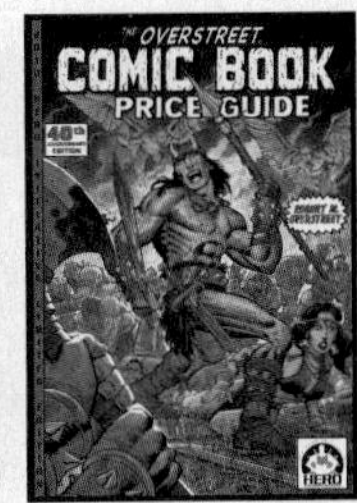

#40 HERO Initiative Ed.
HC only $35.00

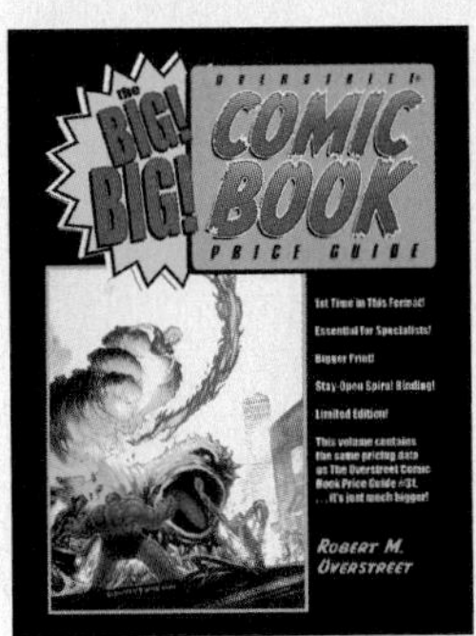

#31 Workbook - 2001
$35.00

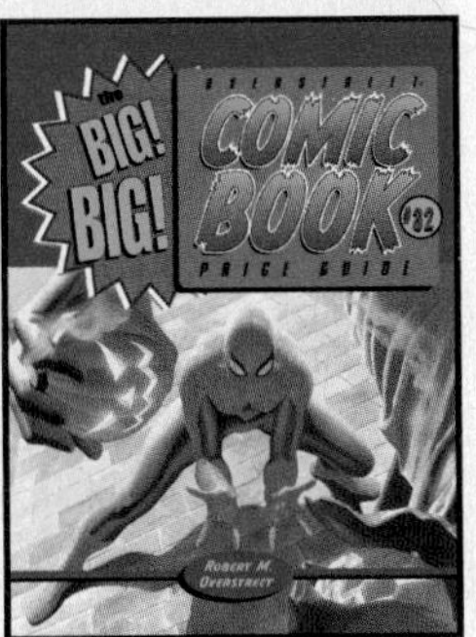

#32 Workbook - 2002
$35.00

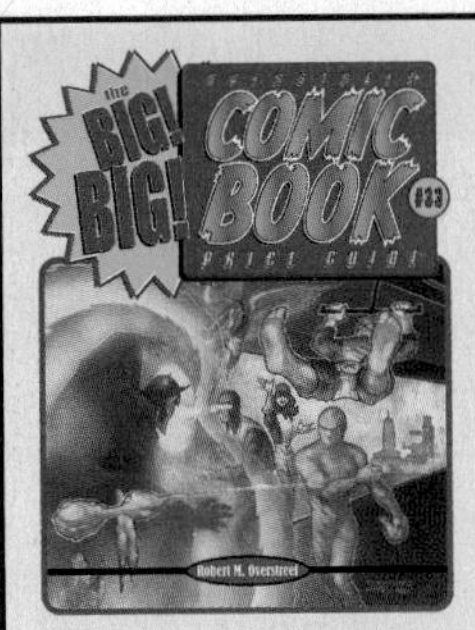

#33 Workbook - 2003
$37.00

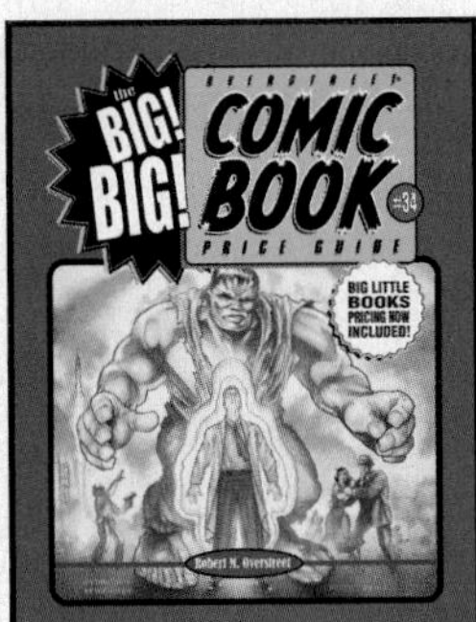

#34 Workbook - 2004
$37.00

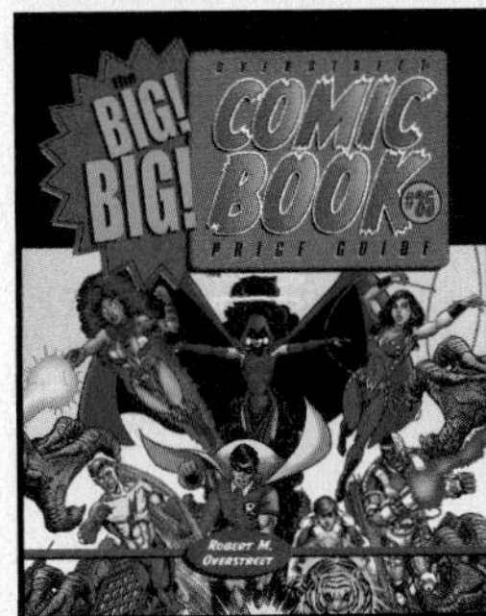

#35 Workbook - 2005
$37.00

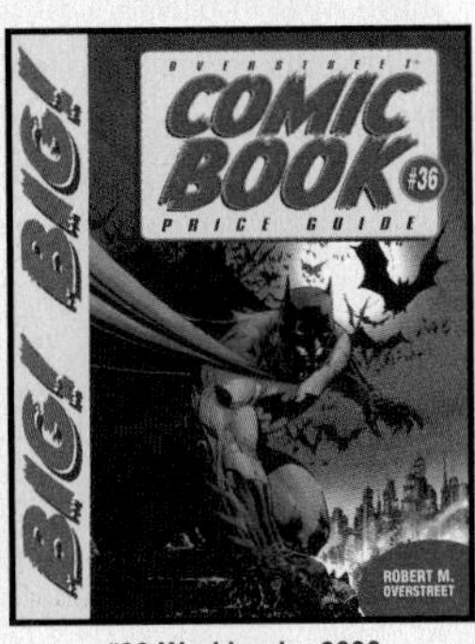

#36 Workbook - 2006
$37.00

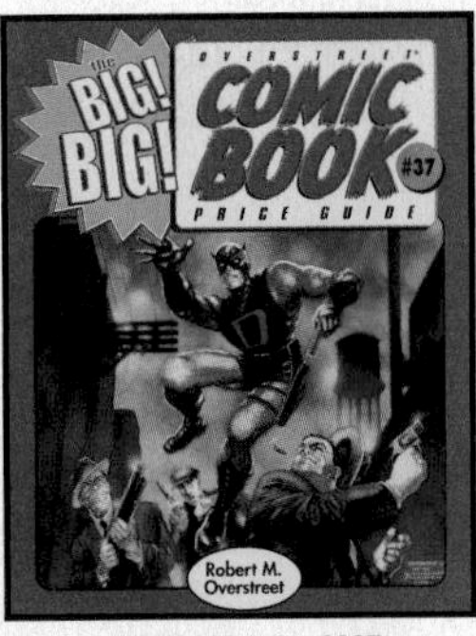

#37 Workbook - 2007
$37.00

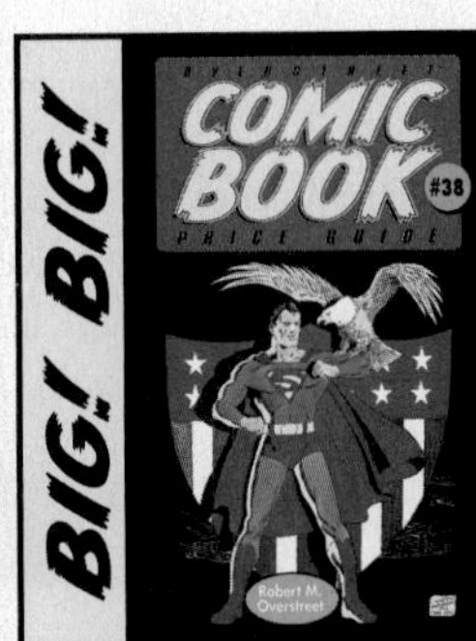

#38 Workbook - 2008
$37.00

ADVERTISERS' INDEX

A

B

C

D

E

F

G

H

I

J

L

M

N

P

Q

R

S

T

V

W

Y

Z

LOOKING FOR A
COMIC SHOP NEAR YOU?

COMIC SHOP LOCATOR SERVICE
COMICS
comicshoplocator.com
888-COMIC-BOOK